Revised Edition
with supplement

CHAMBERS BIOGRAPHICAL DICTIONARY

Editors
J O Thorne MA
T C Collocott MA

W & R Chambers

W & R Chambers
Edinburgh EH2 1DG

Revised Edition
© 1974 W & R Chambers Ltd

Reprinted 1982, 1983

ISBN 0 550 16001 9
      0 550 18013 3

Printed in Great Britain by
Butler & Tanner Ltd,
Frome and London

Preface

LYTTON STRACHEY, arch-priest of the reaction against the dusty biographical techniques of the 19th century, aimed at 'a brevity which excludes everything which is redundant and nothing that is significant'. For him this was a self-imposed discipline; for the compilers of a biographical dictionary it is a stark necessity imposed by the limits of available space, confronting them with a formidable exercise in eclecticism which is rendered more difficult as each year brings its new crop of celebrities. The high reputation which *Chambers Biographical Dictionary* has built up over more than half a century testifies to the success with which past editors have faced this problem, and in preparing this new revised version we are very conscious of the debt which we owe to our predecessors and of our responsibility to maintain the standards which they have set.

It may be appropriate here to examine some features of the new edition. Considerably larger than its precursor, it contains 1440 pages in place of 1006 and accommodates well over 15,000 biographies as against something under 11,000 previously. Every existing entry has been examined with a view to revision, and although a large number of articles of proved excellence have needed little attention, many have been rewritten or amplified, while some outdated entries possessing no ostensible interest for modern readers have been removed. Fame and public esteem are constantly subject to the vagaries of fashion, and critical assessments are changed by modern research. Thus Monteverdi, whose great importance in the history of music is today more fully recognized, now receives 59 lines in place of 5, T. S. Eliot has 144 instead of 6, and the meagre allowance formerly given to the great Impressionist painters has been increased to match their current status. Conversely, Lord Lytton has less than half the space previously given to him, and the Victorian sentimental subject painters, whose treatment in the old edition has for some time appeared over-generous by modern standards, have been pared down. Other articles, adequate in length and admirable in their time, have been refashioned because modern criticism and scholarship have modified the traditional image. Many of the standard figures of literature, philosophy and history fall into this category—Shakespeare and Trollope, Hume and Hegel, Charles II and Wolsey, to quote a few examples.

It is in the choice of new names that we are faced with the most onerous part of our task. The hard core of established notabilities provides an uncontroversial nucleus, but the vast array of lesser luminaries presents a problem to which there can be no completely satisfactory solution. It is all too easy to set up worthiness and the more orthodox forms of prestige as the criterion and to end by producing a kind of Debrett of the Establishment and the 'meritocracy" this at least we hope to have avoided, but that we should please everybody is manifestly out of the question. Our method has been to ask ourselves the question 'Is he (or she) likely to be looked up?', and to answer it as honestly as possible. Thus alongside the more traditional figures we find not only Kurosawa the film-director and Ellington the jazz musician, but Van Meegeren the art forger, Joyce the traitor, Streicher the war-criminal, Christie the murderer—in fact anybody considered sufficiently interesting whatever his calling. The past few decades have added new categories to the range of human skills and failings, such as astronauts, radio-astronomers, nuclear scientists and film stars, to say nothing of genocides, action painters and Angry Young Men, who now take their place within the pages of the dictionary as well as formerly omitted characters from earlier times like Hölderlin, Kilvert, Stubbs and Telemann, whose reputations were either unestablished or temporarily eclipsed when the earlier edition was published. When all this is done we are still left with an extensive card-index of those who have just failed to get in, and to those readers whose favourite characters may be languishing in its drawers we offer our apologies.

The unique position which *Chambers Biographical Dictionary* holds among works of its kind owes much to the policy of clothing the bare facts with human interest and critical observation, and in the new edition we have taken care to preserve this tradition. We have not been as extravagant as Curll, whose biographies were said by Arbuthnot to have 'added a new terror to death', nor have we sought to emulate the pious eulogies which prompted Carlyle to write 'How delicate, how decent is English biography, bless its mealy mouth', but we have endeavoured to produce something more than a catalogue of facts, that is to say a book which may be read as well as looked up.

Several improvements may be noticed in the layout and design of the work. A modern type-face of larger size places less strain on the eyes, and the resultant small loss in lines per page has been recouped by increasing the type area. The headwords in bold capitals stand out more clearly, and a system of numbering has been introduced so that persons of the same surname may be readily distinguished and their relationship, if any, immediately established. A standard sequence of essential basic information—surname (bold capitals), christian names and titles (small bold), pronunciation (where given), dates, designation, birthplace (where known)—now commences each entry in place of the somewhat haphazard arrangement hitherto adopted. The pronunciation of difficult names is indicated, using the simplified phonetic system detailed on p. vii. Bibliographical notes giving useful suggestions for further reading appear at the end of most articles. The supplementary index, now extended from 10 to 35 pages, will be an invaluable aid for devotees of quiz games and crosswords, for settling arguments, or for the idle pursuit of general knowledge.

Finally we wish to express our grateful thanks to all who have assisted in the compilation of this work, among them acknowledged experts in many fields, who have contributed articles or supplied information, members of university staffs, librarians, colleagues on the editorial staff of W. & R. Chambers Ltd and others. We have spent much time in checking the accuracy of our information, but among so many thousands of facts a few mistakes must lurk undetected. We shall therefore be glad (if at the same time sorry) to have any errors reported to us for correction in future editions.

J O Thorne   1961

Note on this edition

Here, as in all editions subsequent to 1961, every effort has been made to continue the process of addition and revision. Many of the original entries have been updated by the inclusion of new biographical material, new works of reference or, sadly, death dates. The addition of a supplement has allowed us to increase our range of notable figures. These, like those in the text, have been selected from a wide range of fields and nationalities.

1974

Key to Pronunciation

Vowel Sounds

ay	=	a in fate		*oo*	=	oo in moon
a	=	a in lad		*u*	=	u in but
ah	=	a in father		*ü*	=	Ger. ü, Fr. u, etc. (nearly *ee*)
e	=	e in led		*œ*	=	Ger. ö, Fr. œu, etc. (nearly as *u* in fur)
ee	=	e in we				
ė	=	e in other		Diphthongs		
i	=	i in lid		*yoo*	=	u in tube
ī	=	i in mine		*aw*	=	aw in saw
o	=	o in lot		*ow*	=	ow in cow
ō	=	o in vote		*oy*	=	oy in boy

The *tilde* sign (˜) over a vowel denotes that it is nasalized, i.e., pronounced partly through the nose. The nasalized -ai and e after i is represented by *ī*, e.g., Pétain, Bastien-Lepage (*pay-tī, bas-tyī-lė-pazh*).

Consonant Sounds

The consonants b, d, f, h, j, k, l, m, n, p, r, t, v, w, y (not used as vowel), z, have in English unambiguous values, and are used for these values.

g	=	g in get		*y'*	=	final y sound as in Fr. Ligne (*leen'y'*)
s	=	s in set				or y sound after palatalized con-
ch	=	ch in church				sonants, as in Russ. Lifar (*li-far'y'*)
sh	=	sh in shore		*r'*	=	unvoiced consonant as in Fr. Del-
zh	=	z in azure				ambre (*dė-lã'br'*)
th	=	th in thin				
TH	=	th in this				
KH	=	ch in Scots loch				

Accentuation

The sign ′ is used to denote that the preceding syllable is stressed. Stress is not generally indicated in French names, where the correct effect is better obtained by slightly raising the pitch of the voice on the final syllable.

SUPPLEMENT

ADRIAN, Edgar Douglas, 1st Baron Adrian. Died 1977.

AGNEW, Spiro Theodore (1918–) American Republican vice-president, born in Baltimore, son of a Greek immigrant, after service in World War II graduated in law from Baltimore University (1947). In 1966 he was elected governor of Maryland on a liberal platform, introducing anti-racial-discrimination legislation that year. By 1968, however, his attitude to such problems as race rioting and civil disorders had become much more conservative. As a compromise figure acceptable to most shades of Republican opinion, he was Nixon's running mate in the 1968 election, and took office as vice-president in 1969. He resigned in 1973.

ALLENDE (GOSSENS), Salvador (1908–73), Chilean politician, was born at Valparaiso. He took an interest in politics from an early age and was often in trouble with the authorities for his radical activism. During his medical studies he was arrested several times and was suspended from the university for a time. He was a founder member in 1933 of the Chilean Socialist Party, a marxist alternative for those not satisfied with the Soviet-orientated official Communist Party. He was elected to the chamber of deputies in 1937, was minister of Health (1939–42), and in 1945 was elected to the senate (its president 1965–69). He contested unsuccessfully the presidential elections of 1952, 1958 and 1964, but won by a hairbreadth in 1970 with the promise to establish a socialist society, while maintaining a liberal parliamentary form of government. He went on to implement his policies but met with extensive opposition. In 1972 he increased his majority slightly, but he was killed during a military coup d'état in September 1973.

ANDRIĆ, Ivo. Died 1975.

ANSERMET, Ernest Alexandre (1883–1969), Swiss conductor, was born at Vevey. While reading physics and mathematics at Lausanne University, he continued privately his music studies. He gave up teaching mathematics in 1910 to devote his time to music. He was conductor of the Montreux Kursaal in 1912 and then travelled in France and Germany before taking up the post of conductor of Diaghilev's Russian Ballet (1915–23). In 1918 he founded the Orchestre de la Suisse Romande, whose conductor he remained till 1967. He was known for his interpretations of modern French and Russian composers. His compositions include a symphonic poem *Feuilles de printemps*, piano pieces and songs.

ANTONIONI, Michelangelo (1912–), Italian film director, born at Ferrara, educated at Bologna University, began as a film critic before becoming an assistant director in 1942. He made several documentaries (1945–50) before turning to feature films, often scripted by himself, notable for their preoccupation with character study rather than plot. They include *Cronaco di un Amore* (1950), *Le Amiche* (1955) and *Il Grido* (1957). He gained an international reputation, however, with *L'Avventura* (1959), a long, slow-moving study of its two main characters, followed by other outstanding works, such as *La Notte* (1961), *L'Eclisse* (1962), *Blow-up* (1967), *Zabriskie Point* (1970). See study by Cameron and Wood (1969).

ARMSTRONG, (4) John. Died 1973.

ARMSTRONG, Neil (1930–), American astronaut, born at Wapakoneta, Ohio, educated there and at Purdue University. A fighter pilot in Korea and later a civilian test pilot, in 1962 he was chosen as an astronaut and in 1966 he commanded Gemini 8. In 1969 with **Edwin (Buzz) Aldrin** (born 1930 at Montclair, N.J., educated there, at West Point and at Massachusetts Institute of Technology; set up space-walking record in 1966 during flight of Gemini 12) and **Michael Collins** (born 1930 at Rome, educated at Washington and at West Point, one of the astronauts in Gemini 10) he set out in Apollo 11 on a successful moon-landing expedition. Armstrong and Aldrin became in that order the first men to set foot on the moon, Collins remaining in the command module.

AUDEN, Wystan Hugh. Died 1973.

AYRTON, (1) Michael. Died 1975.

BARNARD, Christiaan Neethling (1922–), South African surgeon, born at Beaufort West, graduated from Cape Town medical school. After a period of research in America he returned to Cape Town in 1958 to work on open-heart surgery and organ transplantation. In December 1967 at Groote Schuur Hospital he performed the first successful human heart transplant. The recipient, Louis Washkansky, died of pneumonia, drugs given to prevent tissue rejection having heightened the risk of infection. A second patient, Philip Blaiberg, operated on in January 1968, was able to leave hospital, but died in Aug. 1969. See his autobiography (1970).

BATES, Herbert Ernest. Died 1974.

BEN-GURION, David. Died 1973.

BEST, Charles Herbert. Died 1978.

BLACKETT, Baron Patrick Maynard Stuart. Died 1974.

BLISS, Sir Arthur. Died 1975.

BLUNDEN, Edmund Charles. Died 1974.

BÖLL, Heinrich (1917–), German writer, was born at Cologne. His first novel, *Der Zug war Pünktlich* (*The Train was on Time*) was published in 1949. A trilogy, *Und Sagte kein Einziges Worte* (*And Never Said a Solitary Word*, 1953), *Haus ohne Hüter* (*The Unguarded House*, 1954), and *Das Brot der Frühen Jahre* (*The Bread of our Early Years*, 1955) depicting life in Germany during and after the Nazi régime, gained him a world-wide reputation. Recent novels, characteristically satirising modern German society, include *Gruppenbild mit Dame*. He was awarded the 1972 Nobel prize for literature. See study by Macpherson (1972).

BONHOEFFER, Dietrich (1906–45), German Lutheran pastor and theologian, born at Breslau, son of an eminent psychiatrist, and educated at Tübingen and at Berlin, where he was influenced by Karl Barth. He left Germany in 1933 in protest against the Nazi enforcement of anti-Jewish legislation, and worked in German parishes in London until 1935 when he returned to Germany, to become head of a pastoral seminary until its closure by the Nazis in 1937. He became deeply involved in the German resistance movement and in 1943 was arrested and imprisoned until 1945 when he was hanged at Flossenbürg. His controversial writings, of increasing importance in modern theology, include *Sanctorum Communio* (1927, trans. 1963) and *Act and Being* (1931, trans. 1962), on the nature of the Church, and the best-known and most-interpreted, *Ethics* (1949, trans. 1955) and *Widerstand und Ergeburg* (1951, trans. as *Letters and Papers from Prison* in 1953), on the place of Christian belief and the concept of Christ in the modern world. See *Lives* by Bosanquet (1968) and Bethge (1970), and studies by Godsey (1960) and Marlé (1968).

BORGES, Jorge Luis (*bor'häs*) (1899–), Argentinian writer, born in Buenos Aires, educated there and at Geneva and Cambridge. From 1918 he was in Spain, where he was acquainted with an avant-garde literary group, returning to Argentina in 1921. His first book of poems, *Fervor de Buenos Aires*, was published in 1923. He continued publishing poems and essays, and in 1941 appeared the first collection of the short stories for which he is famous. Later collections include *Ficciónes* (1945, trans. 1962), *El Aleph* (1949), *La Muerta y la Brújula* (*Death and the Compass*, 1951) and *El Hacedor* (*Dreamtigers*, 1960). Some stories from *El Aleph* appear in the collection of translations, *Labyrinths* (1962). See *Conversations with Jorge Luis Borges* by R. Burgin (1973).

BOULANGER, Nadia (1887–), French musician, was born in Paris of a musical family, and studied at the Conservatoire (1879–1904), where she won several prizes. She went on to write many vocal and instrumental works, winning second prize at the Grand Prix de Rome in 1908 for her cantata, *La Sirène*. After 1918 she devoted herself to teaching, first at home and later at the Conservatoire and the École Normale de Musique. She is also a noted organist and conductor.

BOULEZ, Pierre (1925–), French conductor and composer, was born at Montbrison and studied at the Paris Conservatoire (1943–45) after a year as an engineering student at Lyons. In 1948 he became musical director of Barrault's Théâtre Marigny and from then he established his reputation as an interpreter of contemporary music. He left France in 1959 and settled at Baden-Baden in Germany. His early work, notably the *Sonatine* for flute and piano (1946) and two piano sonatas (1946 and 1948), rebelled against what he saw as the conservatism of such composers as Stravinsky and Schoenberg. In later compositions he has developed the very individual view of music already apparent in the *Sonatine*, namely that whereas tonal music of the past can be seen as a straight-forward progression from a point of departure, contemporary music describes a fluid and infinite universe out of which it is the

composer's task to make a coherent work of art. Of his later works, *Le Marteau sans maître* (1955) gained him a worldwide reputation, confirmed by *Pli selon pli* and the third piano sonata. See his *Penser la musique aujourd'hui* (trans. 1970).

BRANDT, Willy (1913–), West German politician, born Karl Herbert Frahm at Lübeck, educated there, joined the Social Democrats at seventeen, and, as a fervent anti-Nazi, fled in 1933 to Norway, where he changed his name, took Norwegian citizenship, attended Oslo Univ., and worked as a journalist. On the occupation of Norway in 1940, he went to Sweden, continuing as a journalist in support of the German and Norwegian resistance movements. In 1945 he returned to Germany, in 1948 regained German citizenship, and from 1949 to 1957 was a member of the *Bundestag*, being president of the *Bundesrat* (1955–57). Notably a pro-Western, anti-Communist leader, he became mayor of West Berlin (1957–66) and chairman of the S.P.D. in 1964. In 1966 he led his party into a coalition government with the Christian Democrats under Kiesinger's chancellorship. In 1969 he was elected chancellor in a coalition government with the Free Democrats. He was awarded the 1971 Nobel peace prize. He resigned as chancellor in 1974.

BRITTEN, (Edward) Benjamin. Created Baron of Aldeburgh in 1976. Died 1976.

BULGAKOV, Mikhail Afanasievich (1891–1940), Russian writer, was born in Kiev where he studied medicine, graduating in 1916. In 1920 he gave up his medical practice and went to Moscow, where he worked for some years as a reporter. His first published work was a collection of short stories, *Diavoliada* (1925). He had considerable success as a playwright in Russia and in the West, the most famous of his plays being *The White Guard* (1926), but with increasingly strict censorship they were taken out of production. He was till 1936 literary adviser and assistant producer at the Moscow Arts Theatre under Stanislavsky (q.v.). His experiences there are described in his unfinished novel *Black Snow* (1965, trans. 1968). From 1936 until he went blind in 1939, he worked at the Bolshoi Theatre. Like his plays, his novels were considered too outspoken when they were written and are only now being published in Russia. In them he satirizes contemporary life in Russia. In addition to *Black Snow* he wrote *The Heart of a Dog* (trans. 1968) and *The Master and Margarita* (trans. 1967).

BUÑUEL, Luis (1900–), Spanish film director, born in Calanda, educated at Madrid University, with Salvador Dali achieved a *succès de scandale* with their surrealistic, macabre, poetic *Un Chien Andalou* (1928) and *L'Age d'or* (1930). His first solo venture, *Las Hurdes* (1932), a documentary on Spanish poverty, was banned in Spain, and Buñuel eventually settled in Mexico (1947), his career in eclipse. *Los Olvidados* (1950), a realistic study of juvenile delinquency, re-established him, and later films, such as *Nazarin* (1958), *Viridiana* (1961), *Belle de Jour* (1966), and *La*

Voie Lactée (1969), illustrate his poetic, often erotic, use of imagery, his black humour, and his hatred of Catholicism, often expressed in blasphemy. See study by Durgnat (1967).

BURGESS, Guy Francis de Moncy (1910-63), British traitor (see also MACLEAN, DONALD, and PHILBY), son of a naval officer, educated at Eton, Royal Naval College, Dartmouth, and at Trinity College, Cambridge, where he became a Communist. Recruited as a Soviet agent in the 1930s, he worked with the B.B.C. (1936-39), wrote war propaganda (1939-41), and, ostensibly again with the B.B.C. (1941-44), served with MI5, during the war. Thereafter, he was a member of the Foreign Office, and finally second secretary under Philby in Washington in 1950. Recalled in 1951 for 'serious misconduct', he, together with Maclean, disappeared in the Soviet Union in 1951 (although the Russians denied the fact until 1956), and died there. See book by Purdy and Sutherland (1963).

BURRA, Edward. Died 1976.

BUTOR, Michel Marie François (1926–), French writer, was born at Lille. He is one of the more popular writers of the *nouveau roman*, his novels including *L'Emploi du temps* (1959, trans. 1961), *Degrés* (1960), *Mobile* (1962) and *Réseau Aérien* (1963).

CALLAGHAN, James. In 1976 he became Prime Minister when Harold Wilson resigned.

CALLAS, Maria Meneghini. Died 1977.

CARTER, James Earl, (Jimmy) (1924–), 39th President of the U.S.A., born in Plains, Georgia, graduated from the U.S. Naval Academy in 1946 and served in the U.S. Navy until 1953 when he took over the family peanut business and other business enterprises. As Governor of Georgia (1970-74) he expressed an enlightened policy towards the rights of coloured people and women. In 1976 he won the Democratic presidential nomination over several much more prominent figures and went on to win a narrow victory over Gerald Ford for the presidency. Throughout his campaign he presented an air of informality, honesty, morality and religious fervour which appealed to an American electorate who were tired of the scandal and intrigue of the Nixon administration. On his election he promised to institute a populist form of government giving the people a greater say in the administration. He also promised to set up effective energy and health programmes, to concern himself with civil and human rights issues and to try to restrict the making of nuclear weapons.

CASALS, Pau (Pablo). Died 1973.

CASEY, Richard Gardiner, Baron Casey. Died 1976.

CASSIN, René (1887-1976), French jurist, was born at Bayonne and educated at Aix and Paris universities. He was professor of International Law at Lille (1920-29) and at Paris (1929-60), combining this with membership of the French delegation to the League of Nations (1924-38). During World War II he joined General de Gaulle in London. He was principal legal adviser in negotiations with the British government and, in the later years of the war, held important posts in the French government in

exile in London and Algiers, and subsequently in the Council of State (of which he was president, 1944-60) in liberated France. Since the war he has been increasingly concerned with the safeguarding of human rights. He was the principal author of the Universal Declaration of the Rights of Man (1948) and played a leading part in the establishment of UNESCO. He has been a member of the European Court of Human Rights since 1959 and its president (1965-68). In 1968 he was awarded the Nobel prize for peace.

CASTLE, Barbara Anne, née Betts (1911–), British Labour politician, educated at Bradford Girls' Grammar School and at St Hugh's College, Oxford, married in 1944 **Edward Cyril Castle** (b. 1907), a journalist, worked in local government before World War II, entered parliament in 1945 as M.P. for Blackburn. During the 1950s she was a convinced 'Bevanite', outspoken in her defence of radical causes. Chairman of the Labour party (1958-59), after Labour came into power in 1964 she attained cabinet rank as minister of overseas development (1964-1965). She was a controversial minister of transport (1965-68), introducing a 70 m.p.h. speed limit and the 'breathalyzer' test for drunken drivers, in an effort to cut down road accidents. She took over the newly-created post of secretary of state for employment and productivity (1968-70) to deal with the government's difficult prices and incomes policy. In 1974 she became minister of health and social security. In 1976 when James Callaghan became Prime Minister she returned to the back benches.

CHADWICK, Sir James. Died 1974.

CHANDLER, Raymond (1888-1959), American writer, born in Chicago, brought up in England from the age of seven, educated at Dulwich College and in France and Germany, worked as a freelance writer in London. In 1912 he went to California, and served in the Canadian army in France and in the R.A.F. during World War I. After a variety of jobs, during the Depression he began to write short stories and novelettes for the detective-story pulp magazines of the day. On such stories he based his subsequent full-length 'private eye' novels, *The Big Sleep* (1939), *Farewell, My Lovely* (1940), *The High Window* (1942) and *The Lady in the Lake* (1943), all of which were successfully filmed. Chandler himself went to Hollywood in 1943 and worked on film scripts. He did much to establish the conventions of his genre, particularly with his cynical but honest anti-hero, Philip Marlowe, who also appeared in such later works as *The Little Sister* (1949), *The Long Goodbye* (1953) and *Playback* (1958). See *Raymond Chandler Speaking* (ed. by Gardiner and Walker, 1962) and study by Durham (1963).

CHAPLIN, (1) Sir Charles Spencer. Knighted in 1975. Died 1977.

CHIANG KAI-SHEK. Died 1975.

CHICHESTER, Sir Francis (1901-72), British yachtsman, born at Barnstaple, Devonshire, educated at Marlborough. He emigrated to New Zealand in 1919, where he eventually made a fortune as a land agent. He became interested in flying, returned to Britain in

1929 for a course of instruction, and between that year and 1936 made several pioneer flights, the first being a solo one to Australia in a Gipsy Moth plane. One of these flights (in 1931) ended when he was badly injured by a crash in Japan. He spent the war years in Britain as an air navigation instructor, afterwards starting a map-publishing business. In 1953 he took up yacht racing. He was found in 1957 to have lung cancer, but recovered and in 1960 won the first solo transatlantic yacht race, with his boat 'Gipsy Moth III', sailing from Plymouth to New York in 40 days. He made a successful solo circumnavigation of the world (1966–67) in 'Gipsy Moth IV', sailing from Plymouth to Sydney in 107 days and from there back to Plymouth, via Cape Horn, in 119 days. He later went on to Greenwich, where he was knighted with Sir Francis Drake's sword. See his auto-biography, *The Lonely Sea and the Sky* (1964), and *Gipsy Moth Circles the World* (1967).

CHOU EN-LAI. Died 1976.

CHRISTIE, (2) Dame Agatha Mary Clarissa. Died 1976.

CONNOLLY, Cyril. Died 1974.

COSTELLO, (1) John Aloysius. Died 1976.

CROSBY, Harry, 'Bing'. Died 1977.

DALLAPICCOLA, Luigi. Died 1975.

DAM, Carl Peter Henrik. Died 1976.

DE VALERA, Eamon. Died 1975.

DUBČEK, Alexander (1921–), Czecho-slovakian statesman, born in Uhrovek, Slovakia, lived from 1925 to 1938 in the Soviet Union, where his father was a member of a Czechoslovakian industrial cooperative. He joined the Communist party in 1939, fought as a Slovak patriot against the Nazis (1944–45), and gradually rose in the party hierarchy until in January 1968 he became first secretary. He introduced a series of far-reaching economic and political reforms, including abolition of censorship, increased freedom of speech, and suspension of ex-president Novotny and other former 'Stalinist' party leaders. Despite his avowed declaration of democracy within a Communist framework, his policy of liberali-zation led in August 1968 to the occupation of Czechoslovakia by Soviet forces. In 1969, however, after having been unable to break down the policy of passive disobedience and peaceful demonstration by the people, the Russians exerted strong pressure on the Czechoslovak government, and Dubček was replaced as first secretary by Husak. He was elected president of the Federal Assembly by the two houses of parliament, but expelled from the Presidium in September and de-prived of party membership in 1970.

EDEN, (1) Sir (Robert) Anthony, 1st Earl of Avon. Died 1977.

ELLINGTON, Edward, 'Duke'. Died 1974.

ERHARD, Ludwig. Died 1977.

ERNST, Max. Died 1976.

EVANS, (3) Dame Edith. Died 1976.

FORD, Gerald Rudolph, (1913–), 38th President of the U.S.A., born in Omaha, Nebraska, studied law at Yale, and served in the U.S. Navy during World War II. From 1948 until 1973 he was a Republican Member of the House of Representatives. On the resignation of Spiro Agnew in 1973 he was appointed Vice-President, becoming President in 1974 when President Nixon resigned be-cause of the Watergate scandal. He became unpopular because of his right-wing attitude and conflicts with Congress. Always intensely loyal to President Nixon he granted him a full pardon in September 1974. He was defeated in the 1976 Presidential election by Jimmy Carter.

FORSSMAN, Werner. Died 1976.

FRANCO (BAHAMONDE), Francisco. Died 1975. Succeeded as Spanish leader by King Juan Carlos I.

FULBRIGHT, J(ames) William (1905–), American Democrat politician and lawyer, born in Sumner, Mo., educated in Arkansas, at Oxford, and at George Washington University law school, was elected to the House of Representatives in 1942, where he introduced a resolution in 1943 advocating the creation of, and U.S. participation in, the United Nations. In 1944 he entered the Senate and was responsible for the famous act of 1946 establishing an exchange scholar-ship system for students and teachers between the U.S. and other countries. He distinguished himself in 1954 by his opposition to Joseph McCarthy. He advocated a more liberal U.S. foreign policy, particularly in relation to Communist China and Cuba, and criticised the escalation of the war in Vietnam. He wrote *Old Myths and New Realities* (1965) and *The Arrogance of Power* (1967). See study by Johnson and Gwertzman (1969).

GALBRAITH, John Kenneth. Died 1976.

GLOUCESTER, Prince Henry, Duke of. Died 1974.

GOLDWYN, Samuel. Died 1974.

GREENWOOD, Walter. Died 1974.

GRIVAS, George Theodorou. Died 1974.

HAILE SELASSIE. Deposed 1974; died 1975.

HARRISSON, Tom. Died 1976.

HEATH, Edward Richard George. Became leader of the opposition in 1974 but was succeeded by Margaret Thatcher in 1975.

HEIDEGGER, Martin. Died 1976.

HEINEMANN, Gustav (1899–), West German statesman was born at Schwelm, in the Ruhr district, and educated at Marburg and Münster. He practised as an advocate from 1926 and lectured on law at Cologne (1933–39). After the war he was a founder of the Christian Democratic Union, and was minister of the Interior in Adenauer's govern-ment (1949–50), resigning over a fundamental difference of opinion on defence policy. He later joined the Social Democratic Party, was elected to the *Bundestag* (1957) and was minister of Justice in Kiesinger's government from 1966. In 1969 he was elected president but resigned in 1974.

HEISENBERG, Werner Karl. Died 1976.

HEPWORTH, Dame Barbara. Died 1975.

HERTZ, (1) Gustav. Died 1975.

HILL, (2) Archibald Vivian. Died 1977.

HONECKER, Erich (1912–), German political leader, born at Wichelskirchen, in the Saar district of Western Germany, joined in Communist party activities from an early age. He was arrested by the Nazis in 1935 and sentenced to 10 years penal servitude.

He became a full member of the Politburo in 1958. In 1971 he succeeded Ulbricht as the East German party leader.

HOWARD, Bernard Marmaduke, 16th Duke of Norfolk. Died 1975.

HUMPHREY, Hubert Horatio. Died 1978.

HUXLEY, Sir Julian Sorell. Died 1975.

IBN FAISAL, Abdul Aziz. Died 1975.

IVES, Charles Edward (1874–1954), American composer, was born at Danbury, Conn., studied music at Yale and worked in insurance till 1930, when he retired. His music is firmly based in the American tradition, but at the same time he experimented with dissonances, polytonal harmonies, conflicting rhythms, &c., anticipating modern European trends. He composed five symphonies, chamber music (including the well known 2nd piano sonata, the *Concord Sonata*), and many songs. In 1947 he was awarded the Pulitzer prize for his 3rd symphony (composed 1911). See his *Memos* (ed. Kirkpatrick 1973).

JACOBSEN, Arne (1902–71), Danish architect, born in Copenhagen, educated at the Royal Danish Academy. In 1929 in conjunction with F. Lassen he won a House of the Future competition and thereafter designed many private houses including those for Bellevue seaside resort near Copenhagen. In 1943 he escaped to Sweden from Nazi rule. In 1956 he was appointed professor of Architecture at the Royal Danish Academy. He has designed many fine buildings which are elegant and without gimmick, including St Catherine's College, Oxford, and the Central Bank of Denmark.

JARRY, Alfred (1873–1907), French writer, born at Laval (Mayenne) and educated at Rennes. His play, *Ubu-Roi*, was first written when he was 15; later rewritten, it was produced in 1896. Ubu, the hero, symbolises the crassness of the bourgeoisie pushed to absurd lengths by power-lust. He wrote short stories and poems and other plays in the rather surrealist style of *Ubu-Roi*. He also invented a logic of the absurd, which he called *pataphysique*. He became an alcoholic and died in Paris.

KAWABATA, Yasunari (1899–1972), Japanese writer, was born at Osaka and educated at Tokyo University (1920–24), reading English and then Japanese literature. In 1922 he published some short stories, *Tales to hold in the Palm of your Hand*. His first novel, *Dancer of Izu Province*, was published in 1925. He experimented with various Western novel forms, but by the mid-1930s returned to traditional Japanese ones. Later novels include *Red Group of Asakusa* (1930), *Snow Country* (1947, trans. 1957), *Thousand Cranes* (1949, trans. 1959), *Kyoto* (1962) and *The Sound of the Mountain* (trans. 1971). He won the 1968 Nobel prize for literature.

KEATON, Joseph Francis, 'Buster' (1895–1966), American film comedian, born in Pickway, Kan., son of vaudeville artists of Scots and Irish descent, joined their act at the age of three as 'The Three Keatons', developing great acrobatic skill, until 1917 when he went to Hollywood and made his film début in *The Butcher Boy* (1917). Renowned for his 'deadpan' expression under any circumstances, he starred in and directed such classics as *Our Hospitality* (1923), *The Navigator* (1924) and *The General* (1926). His reputation went into eclipse with the advent of talking films until in the 1950s and 1960s many of his silent masterpieces were re-released, and he himself began to appear in character rôles in current films. He received a special Academy Award in 1959 for his 'unique talents'. See his Autobiography (with C. Samuels, 1967) and studies by J. Lebel (1967), R. Blesh (1967) and D. Robinson (1969).

KHAN, (Mohammed) Ayub. Died 1974.[1]

KIEPURA, Jan (1902–66), Polish tenor, born at Sosnowiec, graduated at Warsaw University in 1924, made his first appearance concert in 1923 and his operatic début in 1925 at Warsaw as *Faust*. In 1926–28 he sang with the Vienna State Opera, appearing subsequently at all the leading European opera houses and the N.Y. Metropolitan.

KIESINGER, Kurt Georg (1904–), West German politician, born at Ebingen, practised as a lawyer (1935–40), and, having joined the Nazi party in 1933, although not an active member in the following years, served during World War II at the Foreign Office on radio propaganda. Interned after the war until 1947, he was released by the Allies as a 'fellow traveller' and completely exonerated by a German court in 1948. The next year he became a member of the *Bundestag* until 1958, when he became a minister-president of Baden-Württemberg until 1966. He was president of the *Bundesrat* (1962–63), and in 1966 succeeded Erhard as chancellor after economic crisis had forced the latter's resignation. Long a convinced supporter of Adenauer's plans for European unity, he formed with Willy Brandt a government combining the Christian Democratic Union and the Social Democrats, until in 1969 he was succeeded as chancellor by Brandt.

KING, Cecil (Harmsworth) (1901–), British newspaper proprietor, nephew of the Harmsworth brothers (q.v.), joined the *Daily Mirror* in 1926. Appointed a director in 1929, he was chairman of Daily Mirror Newspapers Ltd and Sunday Pictorial Newspapers Ltd (1951–63) and chairman of the International Publishing Corporation (1963–68).

KISSINGER, Henry Alfred (1923–), American politician, born at Fürth, Germany, settled in America 1938. He was professor of Government at Harvard (1962-71) and in 1968 he became Nixon's adviser on national security affairs. He was awarded the 1973 Nobel Peace Prize with the Vietnamese Le Duc Tho and became Secretary of State. He played a major rôle in the peace negotiations between the Arabs and Israelis but ceased to be Secretary of State in 1977 when Jimmy Carter became President.

KRISHNA MENON, Vengalil Krishnan. Died 1974.

LANE, Sir Allen Lane Williams (1902–70), British publisher and pioneer of paperback books, born and educated at Bristol, apprenticed in 1919 to The Bodley Head under its founder and his relative John Lane (1854–1925), resigned as managing director in 1936 in order to form Penguin Books Ltd, a revolutionary step in the publishing trade.

He began by reprinting novels in paper covers at 6d each, expanding to other series, such as non-fictional Pelicans and children's Puffins, establishing a highly successful publishing concern. He was knighted in 1952 and created C.H. in 1969.

LEAVIS, Frank Raymond. Died 1978.

LEESE, Sir Oliver William Hargreaves, Bart. Died 1978.

LINDBERGH, Charles Augustus. Died 1974.

LINKLATER, Eric. Died 1974.

LIN YUTANG. Died 1976.

LIPPMANN, Walter. Died 1974.

LOWRY, (Laurence) Stephen. Died 1976.

LÜBKE, Heinrich (1894–1972), West German politician, born in Westphalia. In 1959 he succeeded Theodor Heuss as president of the German Federal Republic, being himself succeeded in 1969 by Gustav Heinemann.

MACLEAN, Donald Duart (1913–), British traitor (see also BURGESS and PHILBY), son of Liberal cabinet minister, Sir Donald Maclean (d. 1932), educated at Gresham's School and Trinity College, Cambridge, at the same time as Burgess and Philby and similarly influenced by Communism. He joined the Diplomatic Service in 1935, serving in Paris, Washington (1944–48) and Cairo (1948–50), and from 1944 acted as a Russian agent. After a 'nervous breakdown' in 1950, he became head of the American Department of the Foreign Office, but by 1951 was a suspected traitor, and in May of that year, after Philby's warning, disappeared with Burgess to Russia. He was joined in 1953 by his wife, Melinda (b. America 1916) and children, but she left him to marry Philby in 1966.

McGOVERN, George Stanley (1922-), American Democrat politician, born the son of a Methodist minister at Avon, S. Dakota. Following distinguished service in the U.S.A.A.F. in World War II, he became a university professor of history and government at Dakota Wesleyan University, member of the House of Representatives (1956-61) and Senator for South Dakota (from 1963). In July 1972, following a campaign expounding his new radicalism, he was chosen as Democratic candidate to oppose Nixon in the presidential election but was defeated.

McLUHAN, (Herbert) Marshall (1911-), Canadian writer, born in Edmonton, studied English Literature at the universities of Manitoba and Cambridge. In 1946 he became professor at St Michael's College, Toronto. In 1963, having directed two surveys into culture and communication media, he was appointed director of the Univ. of Toronto's Centre for Culture and Technology. He holds controversial views on the effect of the communication media on the development of civilization, claiming that it is the media *per se*, not the information and ideas which they disseminate, that influence society. He sees the invention of printing, with its emphasis on the eye rather than the ear, as the destroyer of a cohesive, interdependent society, since it encouraged man to be more introspective, individualistic and self-centred. His publications include *The Mechanical Bride* (1951), *The Gutenberg Galaxy* (1962), *Understanding Media* (1964),

The Medium is the Massage (with Q. Fiore, 1967), and *Counter-Blast* (1970).

McNAMARA, Robert Strange (1916-), American Democrat politician and businessman, born in San Francisco. After service in the U.S.A.A.F. (1943–46) he worked his way up in Ford Motor Company to president by 1960, and in 1961 joined the Kennedy administration as secretary of defence, in which post he was particularly concerned with the cost of continuation and escalation of the war in Vietnam. In 1968 he resigned to become president of the World Bank.

MAGRITTE, René (1898–1967), Belgian surrealist painter, born at Lessines, Hainaut, educated at secondary school in Charleroi and at the Académie Royale des Beaux-Arts (1916–18) in Brussels, where he lived thereafter. In 1924 he became a leading member of the newly-formed Belgian surrealist group, similar to the already-established French group. After his first, badly-received, one-man show in Brussels in 1927, he lived in Paris until 1930, and there associated with André Breton and others. Apart from a brief Impressionist phase in the 1940s, Magritte remained constant to Surrealism, producing works of dreamlike incongruity, such as *Rape*, in which he substitutes a torso for a face. His major paintings include *The Wind and the Song* (1928–29) and *The Human Condition* (1, 1934; 2, 1935). He was acclaimed in the U.S., although himself denying it, as an early innovator of the 'pop art' of the 1960s. He died in Brussels.

MAILER, Norman (1923-), American writer, born in Long Branch, N.J., educated at Harvard, served as an infantryman (1944–1946), and in 1948 published *The Naked and the Dead*, a panoramic World War II novel, acclaimed as a definitive study of men at war. Later novels, including *The Deer Park* (1955) and *An American Dream* (1964), had a more mixed reception. Identified with many of the current liberal protest movements in modern America, Mailer has also written political studies, such as *The Presidential Papers* (1963), attacking U.S. politics, and *The Armies of the Night* (1968, Pulitzer prize in 1969), an autobiographical report, part novel, part documentary, of the 1967 Vietnam protest march to Washington.

MAKARIOS III. Overthrown by a military coup in Aug. 1974 but was reinstated in 1975. Died 1977.

MALRAUX, André. Died 1976.

MAO TSE-TUNG. Died 1976.

MARCUSE, Herbert (1898-), U.S. philosopher and writer, born in Berlin, educated at the Augusta Gymnasium in Berlin and at the universities of Berlin and Freiburg. He helped to establish the Frankfurt Institute of Social Research but on its closure by the Nazis in 1933 he fled to Geneva and then to America. Having worked in intelligence in World War II he was afterwards appointed chief of the Office of Intelligence Research, becoming an expert on Russian affairs. In 1951 he was appointed research fellow at the Columbian Russian Institute, in 1952 lecturer at Harvard's Russian Research Centre, in 1954 professor of Politics and Philosophy at Brandeis University, Waltham,

Mass. and in 1965 professor of Philosophy at the University of California. His world view is based on Marx and Freud but qualified to a great extent by Libertarianism. He feels that the full possibilities of technological advances have not been explored or their benefits passed on to the workers because the ruling classes are afraid of innovations which would render the old social code inapplicable. Fearing that modern workers are unlikely to revolt against this system, he looks to youth to express in word and deed the unspoken, and even unrecognized, desires of the workers. It is his belief that the oppressed have the right to use violence to communicate their views to a tyrannical establishment if all non-violent protests are fruitless. His publications include *Eros and Civilization* (1955), *Soviet Marxism* (1958), *One-dimensional Man* (1964) and *Repressive Tolerance* (1965). See study by MacIntyre (1970).

MARX, Julius (Groucho). Died 1977.

MEIR, Golda (*née* **Mabovich**) (1898–   ), Israeli politician, was born at Kiev, her family emigrating to Milwaukee, U.S.A., when she was eight years old. She married in 1917 and settled in Palestine in 1921, where she took up social work and became a leading figure in the Labour movement. She was Israeli ambassador to the Soviet Union (1948–49), minister of labour (1949–1956), and foreign minister (1956–66). She was elected prime minister in 1969 and resigned in 1974.

MOLLET, Guy Alcide. Died 1975.

MONOD, (3) Jacques. Died 1976.

MONTGOMERY, (1) Bernard Law, 1st Viscount Montgomery of Alamein. Died 1976.

MORAND, Paul. Died 1977.

MORAVIA, Alberto, pseudonym of **Alberto Pincherle** (1907–   ), Italian novelist and short-story writer, born in Rome of middleclass parents, spent some years in a sanatorium as a result of a tubercular infection. Before the outbreak of World War II he travelled extensively and lived for a time in the U.S.A. when out of favour with the Fascist government. His first novel, *Gli indifferenti* (1929; *The Time of Indifference*), which achieved popular success, contains many of the ingredients of his later novels and short stories. He analyses without compassion but without explicit moral judgement the members of decadent bourgeois society in Rome, portraying in a fatalistic way their preoccupation with sex and money, their apathy, their lack of communication, the total incapability of action of even the intellectuals who acknowledge the corruption but cannot break away from it. In *La Romana* (1947; *Woman of Rome*) many of these themes remain but his canvas has broadened to include the corruption and socio-economic problems of the working-class. In *Raconti romani* (1954; *Roman Tales*), he turns his critical eye to the corruption of the lower-middle class. Apart from the aforementioned titles, his works include *Agostino* (1957), *L'amore conjugale* (1949; *Conjugal Love*), *La ciociara* (1957; *Two Women*). See study by Dego (1966).

MUIRHEAD, (2) (Litellus) Russell. Died 1976.

NABOKOV, Vladimir. Died 1977.

NERUDA, Pablo (Neftalí Reyes) (1904–73), Chilean poet, was born at Parral, in southern Chile, and educated at Santiago. He made his name with *Viente poemas de amor y una canción desesperada* (*Twenty Love Poems and a Song of Despair*, 1924). From 1927 he held diplomatic posts in various Eastern Asian and European countries (in Spain during the civil war) and in Mexico from 1940. It was on his way back to Chile from Mexico in 1943 that he visited the Inca city of Macchu Picchu, which was the inspiration of one of his greatest poems. Once settled in Chile again he joined the Communist party and was elected to the senate in 1945. When the party was outlawed in 1948 he left to travel in Russia and China, returning in 1952. He was awarded the Stalin prize in 1953. He was the Chilean ambassador in Paris (1970–72). His works include *Residencia en la Tierra* I, II and III (1933, 1935, 1947), *Alturas de Macchu Picchu* (1945), which later became part of *Canto General* (published in Mexico, 1950), and *Odas elementales* (1954). In 1971 he was awarded the Nobel prize for literature.

OISTRAKH, David Feodorovitch (1908–1974), Russian violinist, was born at Odessa, where he studied at the Conservatoire, graduating in 1926. He went to Moscow in 1928 and began to teach at the Conservatoire there in 1934, being appointed professor in 1939. He has made concert tours in Europe and America, and was awarded the Stalin prize in 1945 and the Lenin prize in 1960. His son **Igor Davidovitch** (1931–   ), born at Odessa, is also a noted violinist.

ONASSIS, Aristotle Socrates. Died 1975.

PASOLINI, Pier Paulo (1922–75), Italian film director, was born at Bologna. He became a committed marxist in the years after the war. He moved to Rome and out of his experience of life in the poor districts came his novels *Ragazzi di vita* (1957) and *Una vita violente* (1959). In the 1950s he also worked as a film scriptwriter and actor. He made his début as director with *Accatone* (1961), a bare and uncompromising enquiry into slum life, made with a largely non-professional cast. Later films also show up the decadence and inequality of society from a marxist viewpoint. But his *Gospel According to St Matthew* (1964) is considered to be the finest cinematic treatment of the subject. Other films include *Theorem* (1968), *Pigsty* (1969), *The Decameron* (1972) and *The Canterbury Tales* (1973). See study by Stack (1969).

PERÓN, Juan Domingo. Died 1974.

PHILBY, Harold Adrian Russell, 'Kim' (1911–   ), British 'double agent', born in Ambala, India, son of **Harry St John Philby** (1885–1960), Arabist and adviser to King Ibn Saud, educated at Westminster and Trinity College, Cambridge, where, like Burgess and Maclean (qq.v.), he became a Communist. Already recruited as a Soviet agent, he was employed by the British Secret Intelligence Service (MI6), from 1944–46 as head of the anti-Communist counter-espionage. He was first secretary of the British embassy in Washington, working in liaison with the

C.I.A., from 1949 until 1951 when he was asked to resign because of his earlier Communist sympathies. From 1956 he worked in Beirut as foreign correspondent for the *Observer* and the *Economist*, obtaining the posts with the help of the British Foreign Office, until 1963, when he admitted the truth and disappeared to Russia, where he was granted citizenship. See his *My Silent War* (1968) and studies by B. Page *et al.*, E. H. Cookridge, H. Trevor-Roper (all 1968). His third wife, **Eleanor** (born in U.S., died 1968), joined him in Russia (1963) but returned to the West (1965). See her *Kim Philby: The Spy I Loved* (1968).

PILE, Sir Frederick Alfred, 2nd Bart. Died 1976.

PISTON, Walter. Died 1976.

PLOMER, William Charles Franklin. Died 1973.

POLANYI, Michael. Died 1976.

POMPIDOU, Georges Jean Raymond (1911–1974), French statesman, was born at Montboudif in the Auvergne and trained as an administrator. In 1944 he joined de Gaulle's staff, their continued association being based on a similarity of opinion, though he has more moderate views. He held various government posts from 1946, culminating in his appointment as prime minister in 1962 (he was elected to the National Assembly in 1967). He resigned the premiership in 1968, and was elected president in 1969.

POWELL, (John) Enoch (1912–), British Conservative politician and scholar, born at Stechford, Birmingham, educated at King Edward's there and at Trinity College, Cambridge, becoming professor of Greek at Sydney University (1937–39). He enlisted in World War II as a private in 1939, was commissioned in 1940 and rose to the rank of brigadier. In 1946 he joined the Conservative party, in 1950 entering parliament as M.P. for Wolverhampton, and held office as parliamentary secretary, ministry of housing (1955–57), as financial secretary to the treasury from 1957, resigning with Thorneycroft (q.v.) in 1958, and as minister of health from 1960, again resigning over the appointment of Sir Alec Douglas-Home as prime minister in 1963. His austere brand of intellectualism, his adherence to the principles of high Toryism in economic planning, and his radical views on defence and foreign commitments made him a significant figure within his party. He has created more general controversy by his outspoken attitude on the problems of coloured immigration and racial integration. Because of his opposition to the common market he did not stand for election in Feb. 1974 but was returned to parliament as an Ulster Unionist in Oct. 1974. See *Life* (1970) by A. Roth.

RADCLIFFE, (2) Cyril John, Viscount. Died 1978.

RATTIGAN, Terence Mervyn. Died 1977.

REAGAN, Ronald W. (1911–), American Republican politician and former film and TV actor, born in Tampico, Ill., educated at Eureka College, Ill., made his film début in *Love Is On the Air* (1937). Although originally a Democrat and supporter of liberal causes, Reagan became increasingly anti-Communist and in 1962 joined the Republican party as an extreme rightwinger. He stood for the governorship of California in 1966 and won a comfortable victory in that predominantly Democrat state. He stood unsuccessfully for the Republican presidential nomination in 1968.

REED, (1) Sir Carol. Died 1976.

RIDEAL, Sir Eric Keightley. Died 1974.

ROBERTSON, (1) Brian Hubert, 1st Baron of Oakridge. Died 1974.

ROBESON, Paul Le Roy. Died 1976.

ROBINSON, Sir Robert. Died 1975.

ROGERS, William Pierce (1913–), U.S. Republican politician, born in Norfolk, New York, educated at the University of Colgate and Cornell University law school. He was assistant district attorney in New York under Dewey (q.v.). In 1957 he became attorney general in the Eisenhower government. In this capacity he played a leading rôle in drafting the Civil Rights Act of 1957. In 1967 he was a delegate to the United Nations. He was secretary of state in the Nixon administration from 1969 until 1973.

RYLE, (1) Gilbert. Died 1976.

SAINT-JOHN PERSE. Died 1975.

SARRAUTE, Nathalie (*née* Tcherniak) (1920–), French writer, was born at Ivanovo in Russia, her parents settling in France when she was a child. She was educated at the Lycée Fénelon and the Sorbonne, graduating in arts and law. She spent a year at Oxford (1922–23) doing graduate studies before establishing a law practice in France. In *Tropismes* (1939, trans. 1964) she rejected traditional plot development and characterization to describe a world between the real and the imaginary. She has developed her theories further in her later novels: *Portrait d'un Inconnu* (1948, trans. 1958), *Martereau* (1953, trans. 1959), *Le Planétarium* (1959, trans. 1960), *Les Fruits d'or* (1963, trans. 1964) and *Entre la vie et la mort* (1968). She has also written a play, *Le Silence, Le Mensonge* (1967). See her *L'Ère du Soupçon* (1956).

SCHUSCHNIGG, Kurt von. Died 1977.

SHERRIFF, Robert Cedric. Died 1976.

SHIPTON, (1) Eric Earle. Died 1977.

SHOSTAKOVICH, Dmitri. Died 1975.

SMITH, Sydney Goodsir. Died 1975.

SOLZHENITSYN, Aleksandr Isayevich (1918–), Russian writer, was born at Kislovodsk and brought up at Rostov where he graduated in mathematics and physics in 1941. He was imprisoned (1945–53) for unfavourable comment on Stalin's conduct of the war. His first novel, *One Day in the Life of Ivan Denisovich* (1962, trans. 1963), set in a prison camp, was acclaimed both in Khrushchev's Russia and the West, but his denunciation in 1967 of the strict censorship obtaining in Russia led to the banning of his later novels, *The Cancer Ward* (2 vols., trans. 1968, 1969) and *The First Circle* (trans. 1968). They are semi-autobiographical (he has suffered from cancer) and show up corruptions in Russian society while defending socialism. He was expelled from the Soviet Writers' Union in 1969, and was awarded the Nobel Prize for literature in 1970. After some trouble with the authorities, he accepted it. His novel, *August, 1914*, the first part of a projected trilogy on the theme of the emergence of modern from Tsarist Russia, was published in the West in 1971 (trans. 1972), and *The Gulag Archipelago*, a factual account of the Stalinist terror, in 1973. In 1974 he left Russia to live in Switzerland.

SPEAIGHT, Robert William. Died 1976.

SPENCE, (1) Sir Basil Unwin. Died 1976.

SPENDER, (4) Stephen. Died 1977.

SPOCK, Dr Benjamin McLane (1903–), American child-care expert, was born at New Haven, Conn., and studied at Yale and Columbia Univs. He practised pediatrics from 1933 and in 1946 wrote his *Common Sense Book of Baby and Child Care*. In 1968 he appealed successfully against a conviction under the anti-conscription law.

STOKOWSKI, Leopold. Died 1977.

SZELL, George (1897–1970), American conductor and pianist, was born in Budapest and educated at the Vienna State Academy. He made his début as a conductor in Berlin (1914) and later conducted many of the world's major orchestras. He settled in the U.S. in 1939 and in 1946 he began his long tenure of office as musical director and conductor of the Cleveland Symphony Orchestra.

THANT, U. Died 1974.

THOMSON, (4) Sir George Paget. Died 1975.

THOMSON, (11) Roy Herbert, 1st Baron of Fleet. Died 1976.

THORNDIKE, (2) Dame Sybil. Died 1976.

TOYNBEE, (2) Arnold Joseph. Died 1975.

TRILLING, Lionel. Died 1975.

TRUDEAU, Pierre Elliott (1919–), Canadian politician, born in Montreal, was called to the Quebec bar in 1943. One of the founders in 1950 of *Cité Libre*, a magazine opposed to the policies of Maurice Duplessis, then premier of Quebec, he began to practise law in Montreal in 1951. He urged the reform of the educational and electoral systems and the separation of church and state in Quebec and in 1956 was active in the short-lived *Rassemblement*, a group of left-wing opponents of Duplessis. From 1961–65 he was associate professor of Law at the University of Montreal and in 1965, having rejected the New Democratic party for the Liberal party, was elected to the House of Commons. In 1966 he was appointed parliamentary secretary to the prime minister and in 1967, as minister of justice and attorney general, he opposed the separation of Quebec from the rest of Canada. In April 1968 he succeeded Lester Pearson as federal leader of the Liberal party and prime minister. He then called a general election at which his party secured an overall majority.

UPDIKE, John Hoyer (1932–), American writer, born at Shillington, Pa., educated at Harvard, studied for a year at Ruskin School of Drawing and Fine Art, Oxford. His novels, which include *The Poorhouse Fair* (1959), *Rabbit, Run* (1960), *The Centaur* (1963), *Of the Farm* (1966) and *Couples* (1968), explore in depth the interaction of human relationships, particularly between son and parents or husband and wife, often contrasting American small-town life of the past with an emptier, more rootless present. His short stories, such as *The Same Door* (1959), *Pigeon Feathers* (1962) and *The Music School* (1966), evoke similar themes.

VAUGHAN, (5) Keith. Died 1977.

VISCONTI, Count Luchino (1906–), Italian stage and film director, was born in Milan. An early interest in music and the theatre led him to stage designing and the production of opera (notably his stagings at La Scala for Maria Callas), and ballet. A short spell as assistant to Renoir turned his attention to the cinema. His first film as director, *Ossessione* (1942), took Italy by storm, in spite of trouble from the censors. In that film, and in *La Terra Trema* (1947), he showed already the strict realism, formal beauty and the concern with social problems which are the hallmarks of all his films. These include *Il Gattopardo* (*The Leopard*, 1963), *The Damned* (1969) and *Death in Venice* (1971). See study by Nowell-Smith (1967).

VORSTER, Balthazar Johannes (1915–), South African politician, was born at Jamestown and graduated in Law at Stellenbosch University in 1938. He had developed an interest in politics as a student and joined an extreme Afrikaner nationalist movement. He contested the Brakpan seat for the Afrikaner party in 1948, being narrowly defeated, but was later accepted in the National party, becoming M.P. for Nigel in 1953. In Dr Verwoerd's government he was from 1961 minister of justice, being responsible for several controversial measures. After the assassination of Dr Verwoerd in September 1966 he was elected prime minister. Under him *apartheid* has remained the official policy.

WALDHEIM, Kurt (1918–), Austrian statesman, born near Vienna, educated at Vienna. He entered the Austrian foreign service in 1945, worked at the Paris embassy (1948–51) and was head of the personnel department at the foreign ministry (1951–55). He was minister and subsequently ambassador to Canada (1955–60) and director-general of political affairs at the ministry (1960–64). From that year he was permanent representative at the U.N., with a break (1968–70) to take the post of foreign minister. In 1971 he fought unsuccessfully the Austrian presidential election, and in 1972 succeeded U Thant as secretary-general of the U.N.

WHEELER, (2) Sir Robert Eric Mortimer. Died 1976

WILDER, Thornton Niven. Died 1976.

WILSON, (James) Harold. Became prime minister in 1974 but resigned in 1976 and was succeeded by James Callaghan. He was knighted in 1976.

WODEHOUSE, Pelham Grenville. Died 1975.

ZHUKOV, Georgi Konstantinovich. Died 1974.

ZUCKMAYER, Carl. Died 1977.

A

AAGESEN, Svend, *aw'ge-sen,* 12th century author of the earliest Danish history, covering the period 300–1185.

AAKJAER, Jeppe, *awk'ayr* (1866–1930), Danish novelist and poet. A regionalist and a leader of the 'Jutland movement' in Danish literature, he wrote much in the Jutland dialect, into which he translated some of Burns's poems. See his novel *Vredens Børn* (Children of Wrath, 1904), and poems *Rugens Sange* (Songs of the Rye, 1906). For English translations of some of the poems see R. P. Keigwin, *The Jutland Wind* (1944).

AALTO, Alvar, *ahl'tō* (1899–   ), Finnish architect, born at Kuortane, designer of modern public and industrial buildings in Finland, and also of contemporary furniture. In 1950 he went to the U.S.A. and taught architecture at Yale University and at the Massachusetts Institute of Technology. See study by Neunschwander (1954).

AALTONEN, Wäinö (Valdemar), *ahl'ton-en* (1894–1966), Finnish sculptor, born at St Mårtens, studied at Helsinki. One of the leading Finnish sculptors, he was the most versatile, and worked in many styles. His best-known works are the bust of *Sibelius* (in the Gothenburg Museum) and the statue of the Olympic runner *Paavo Nurmi* (commissioned by the Finnish Government in 1924).

AANRUD, Hans, *on'roo* (1863–1953), Norwegian writer of short stories dealing with life in his native valley of Gausdal, and of comedies satirizing the artificialities of urban culture. His delightful children's books, *Sidsel Longskirt* (1903) and *Solve Suntrap* (1910), deserve their place among the classics. See *Collected Stories* (5 vols. 1933).

AARESTRUP, Emil, *aw'res-droob* (1800–56), Danish poet, whose first collection, *Poems,* appeared in 1838, followed by *Posthumous Poems* (1863).

AASEN, Ivar, *aw'sen* (1813–96), Norwegian philologist, prose writer, and poet, born at Sunnmore, founder of the Landsmaal (country language) or nynorsk (new Norse), a standard of the chiefly western dialects with reference to Old Norse; see his *Dictionary of the Norwegian Popular Language* (1850). He died at Oslo.

ABANCOURT, Charles Xavier Joseph d', *a-bã-koor* (1758–92), minister to Louis XVI, and a nephew of Calonne, was murdered by the mob at Versailles.

ABA-NOVÁK, Vilmos (1894–1941), Hungarian painter, born and died in Budapest, celebrated for church murals at Szeged, Budapest (destroyed in World War II), and elsewhere.

ABARBANEL, Isaac Ben Jehudah (1437–1508), a Jewish writer, was born at Lisbon and died at Venice. His works comprise commentaries on the Bible and philosophical treatises. His eldest son, **Juda Leon (Leo Hebraeus),** *c.* 1460–1535, a doctor and philosopher, wrote *Dialoghi di Amore* (1535).

ABATI. See ABBATE.

ABAUZIT, Firmin, *a-bō-zeet* (1679–1767), born of Protestant parentage at Uzès in Languedoc, on the revocation of the Edict of Nantes (1685) was sent to Geneva, where he became widely learned. He travelled in Holland and England in 1698, and died at Geneva, having published many theological and archaeological treatises (2 vols. Amst. 1773).

ABB, St. See EBBA.

ABBADIE, Antoine Thompson d', *a-ba-dee* (1810–97), and **Michel Arnaud d'** (1815–93), born in Dublin of French family, were educated in France, and both travelled in Abyssinia during 1837–48.

ABBAS (566–652), the uncle of Mohammed, at first hostile to him, but ultimately the chief promoter of his religion. He was the founder of the Abbasides, who ruled as khalifs of Baghdad from 750 till the Mongol conquest in 946.

ABBAS EFFENDI. See ABD-UL-BAHA.

ABBAS HILMI (1874–1944), was educated at Vienna, succeeded his father, Tewfik, as khedive of Egypt (1892), and was deposed (1914).

ABBAS-MIRZA (*c.* 1783–1833), the favourite son of Shah Feth-Ali, led the Persian armies with great bravery, but with little success, in the wars with Russia (1811–13 and 1826–28).

ABBAS PASHA (1813–54), viceroy of Egypt, in 1841 took an active part in the Syrian war of his grandfather, Mehemet Ali. The death of his uncle, Ibrahim Pasha, in 1848, called him to the throne; bigoted and sensual, he did much to undo the progress made under Mehemet Ali.

ABBAS THE GREAT (1557–1628), shah of Persia (1585–1628), won back lost territory from the Uzbegs, Turks, and the Great Mogul.

ABBATE, Niccolo dell', *ab-bah'tay* (1512–71), a fresco painter of Modena, who died in Paris, having executed frescoes for the palace of Fontainebleau. Few of his frescoes are extant, but the Louvre has a collection of his drawings.

ABBE, *ab'-bè,* (1) **Cleveland** (1838–1916), American meteorologist, born in New York. He wrote on the atmosphere and on climate, and was responsible for the introduction of the system of Standard Time.

(2) **Ernst** (1840–1905), German physicist, born at Eisenach, died at Jena. He became professor at the university of Jena in 1870, and in 1878 director of the astronomical and meteorological observatories. He was a partner in the optical works of Carl Zeiss, on whose death he became owner in 1888. Famous for his researches in optics, he was inventor of the arrangement known as Abbe's homogeneous immersion.

ABBEY, Edwin Austin (1852–1911), A.R.A. (1896), R.A. (1898), painter, was born at

Philadelphia, U.S., but settled in England in 1878. He is known for his illustrations of the works of Shakespeare and Herrick, for his panels of the *Quest of the Holy Grail* in Boston public library, and for his picture of Edward VII's coronation. See *Life* by E. V. Lucas (1921).

ABBOT, (1) Charles. See COLCHESTER, LORD.

(2) **Charles Greely** (1872–   ), American astrophysicist, born at Wilton, N.H., noted for his work on solar physics.

(3) **Ezra** (1819–84), American scholar and biblical critic.

(4) **George** (1562–1633), English prelate, son of a Guildford cloth worker. He entered Balliol College, Oxford, where he obtained a fellowship (1583); and through Lord Buckhurst's influence he rose to be master of University College (1597), dean of Winchester (1600), and thrice vice-chancellor of Oxford University (1600–05). To a new patron, the Earl of Dunbar, with whom he visited Scotland (1608), he owed his promotion to the sees of Lichfield (1609), London (1610), and finally Canterbury (1611). A sincere but narrow-minded Calvinist, he was equally opposed to Catholics and to heretics. He died at Croydon and was buried at Guildford, where in 1619 he had founded a hospital. His brother, **Robert** (1560–1617), from 1615 Bishop of Salisbury, was a learned theologian.

ABBOTT, (1) Charles. See TENTERDEN.

(2) **Edwin Abbott** (1838–1926), Broadchurch theologian and Shakespearian scholar, born in London, author of *Shakespearian Grammar* (1870) and other works.

(3) **Jacob** (1803–79), American clergyman, author of *The Young Christian* and innumerable other works, was born at Hallowell, Me. His son, **Lyman, D.D.** (1835–1922), born at Roxbury, Mass., in 1887 succeeded Henry Ward Beecher at Plymouth Church, Brooklyn, edited *The Outlook*, and wrote *Reminiscences* (1915), *Silhouettes of my Contemporaries* (1922), and other books.

(4) **Sir James** (1807–96), born at Blackheath, at sixteen joined the Bengal Artillery; in 1839–40 rode from Herat to Khiva—the first Englishman there—and the Caspian; served splendidly in Hazara 1846–53; came home a major-general in 1867; and was made a K.C.B. in 1894.

ABD-AL-LATIF. See ABD-UL-LATIF.

ABD-AL-RAHMAN. See ABD-ER-RAHMAN.

ABD-EL-KADER, *kah'dèr* (1807–83), Algerian hero, born at Mascara. After the French conquest of Algiers the Arab tribes of Oran elected him as their emir; and with great perseverance and skill he waged his long struggle with the French 1832–47. In 1834 he forced Gen. Desmichels to a treaty; and in June 1835 he severely defeated a large French army at Makta. Eventually crushed by overpowering force, he took refuge in Morocco and began a crusade against the enemies of Islam, but was defeated at Isly in 1844. He surrendered in 1847 and was sent to France, and afterwards lived in Brusa and Damascus, where he died.

ABD-EL-KRIM (1880–1963), Moroccan chief, led revolts in 1921 and 1924 against Spain and France, but surrendered before their combined forces in 1926 and was exiled to Réun-

ion. Amnestied in 1947 to live in France, he went to Egypt and there formed the North African Liberation Committee. See W. B. Harris's *France, Spain and the Rif* (1927).

ABDERHALDEN, Emil (1877–1950), a Swiss chemist and physiologist born at Oberuzwil, whose early researches on proteins helped to clarify a subject which, at that time, was little understood. In 1911 he was appointed professor of Physiology at Halle and subsequently worked mainly on the structure of proteins, the synthesis of polypeptides, and the mechanism of alcoholic fermentation.

ABD-ER-RAHMAN. The name of five emirs of Cordoba of which the following are noteworthy:

Abd-er-Rahman I (731–788), first Ommiad khalif of Cordoba (755–788), survived the Abbasid massacre of 750. His army is supposed to have fought the famous action against Charlemagne's rearguard at Roncesvalles in 778.

Abd-er-Rahman II (788–852), ruled from 822, was a patron of the arts and of architecture.

Abd-er-Rahman III (891–961), ruled from 912; under him the khalifate reached the peak of its power, extending its boundaries in successful campaigns against the Fatimids and against the kings of Leon and Navarre. He was a patron of the arts and made Cordoba a cultural centre.

ABD-ER-RAHMAN (d. 732), Saracen leader, defeated and killed by Charles Martel at the battle of Tours.

ABD-ER-RAHMAN (1778–1859), Sultan of Fez and Morocco, succeeded his uncle in 1822, and was involved in Abd-el-Kader's war against the French in Algeria. His subjects' piracy brought risk of war with more than one European state.

ABD-ER-RAHMAN (1830–1901), Emir of Afghanistan, elevated to power through British influence in 1880 after having been for ten years a pensioner of Russia. He was a grandson of Dost Mohammed.

ABD-UL-AZIZ (1830–76), Sultan of Turkey, succeeded his brother, Abd-ul-Medjid (q.v.), in 1861. At first he showed himself liberal-minded and open to western ideas; but his misgovernment led in 1875 to risings in Bosnia, Herzegovina, and Bulgaria. At last a conspiracy forced him to abdicate; and five days later he was found dead. See also IBN SAUD.

ABD-UL-BAHA, or **Abbas Effendi** (1844–1921), son and successor of Baha-Ullah (q.v.).

ABD-UL-HAMID II (1842–1918), Sultan of Turkey, second son of Sultan Abd-ul-Medjid, succeeded in 1876, on the deposition of his brother Murad V. His reign was notable for wars with Russia (1877–78) and Greece (1897), the Armenian atrocities of 1894–96, and domestic troubles which culminated in deposition and exile in 1909. See *Life* by Pears (1917), and J. Haslip, *The Sultan* (1958).

ABDULLAH IBN HUSSEIN, *hoos-sayn* (1882–1951), 1st King of Jordan (1946–51), the second son of Hussein ibn Ali (q.v.) and grandfather of King Hussein (q.v.), was made ruler of the British mandated territory of Transjordania in 1921 and became king when the mandate ended in 1946. He was assassinated in 1951.

ABD-UL-LATIF (1162–1231), an Arabian writer, who was born and died at Baghdad, but taught medicine and philosophy at Cairo and Damascus. His best-known book is a work on Egypt.

ABD-UL-MEDJID (1823–61), Sultan of Turkey, succeeded his father, Mahmud II, in 1839. He continued the reforms of the previous reign; was saved from Egyptian aggression by the Christian powers; in 1850 refused chivalrously to give up Kossuth; and played a difficult part well during the Crimean War (1854–56); but thereafter allowed affairs to drift into financial ruin.

ABD-UR-RAHMAN. See ABD-ER-RAHMAN.

À BECKET, Thomas. See BECKET.

À BECKETT, Gilbert Abbott (1811–56), English humorist, born in London and educated at Westminster, in 1841 was called to the bar, in 1849 became a metropolitan police magistrate, and died at Boulogne. Besides writing for *Punch*, *The Times*, &c., he was author of *Quizziology of the British Drama*, *The Comic Blackstone*, and Comic Histories of England and Rome, the second illustrated by Cruikshank, the last two by Leech. One son, **Gilbert** (1837–91), was a playwright; another **Arthur William** (1844–1909), journalist, playwright, and barrister, wrote *The À Becketts of Punch* (1903).

ABEGG, Richard (1869–1910), German chemist, born at Danzig, became professor of Chemistry at Breslau, 1899. He was one of the first chemists to perceive the chemical significance of the newly-discovered (1897) electron, and his ' rule of eight ' (1904) concerning the electronic basis of linkages between atoms was an important stage in the development of modern valency theory. His early death was the result of a balloon accident.

ABEL, *ay'bl*, (1) **Sir Frederick Augustus** (1826–1902), English chemist, was born in London, and devoted himself to the science of explosives, expounding his discoveries in *Gun-cotton* (1866), *Electricity Applied to Explosive Purposes* (1884), &c. He was chemist to the War Department and Ordnance Committees, and was made C.B. in 1877, K.C.B. and D.C.L. 1883, and a baronet 1893. He became secretary to the Imperial Institute in 1887, and was president of the British Association in 1890.

(2) **Karl Friedrich**, *ah'bel* (1725–87), German musician, born at Köthen, famous as a player on the viola-da-gamba and composer. In 1758 he came to England, where he was appointed chamber musician to Queen Charlotte. With Johann Christian Bach he promoted a celebrated series of concerts in London.

(3) **Niels Henrik** (1802–29), Norwegian mathematician, born at Findöe, occupied mainly with the theory of elliptical functions. See Life by Bjerknes (Fr. trans. 1885).

ABELARD, or **Abailard, Peter** (1079–1142), the keenest thinker and boldest theologian of the 12th century, was born at Le Pallet, 10 miles SE. of Nantes, the eldest son of a noble Breton house. He studied under Roscellin, in 1115 became a lecturer in the cathedral school of Notre-Dame, and for a few years he enjoyed extraordinary repute and influence. Among his pupils were Peter Lombard Bérenger and Arnold of Brescia. But within the precincts of Notre-Dame lived the beautiful Héloïse, niece of the canon Fulbert, then seventeen years of age; and with her Abelard, thirty-eight years of age and acting as her tutor, fell passionately in love. The lovers fled together to Brittany, where Héloïse bore a son, and was privately married to Abelard. When shortly after Héloïse, denying the marriage (lest it should stand in Abelard's way), left her uncle's house for the convent of Argenteuil, Fulbert caused Abelard to be mutilated so as to be incapable of ecclesiastical preferment. Abelard entered the abbey of St Denis as monk; Héloïse took the veil at Argenteuil. Soon a synod at Soissons (1121) condemned his teaching on the Trinity as heretical. In the hermit's hut at Nogent-sur-Seine to which he retired, Abelard was soon again besieged by importunate disciples; the hermitage became a monastic school known as Paraclete, which, when Abelard was invited to become abbot of St Gildas-de-Rhuys in Brittany, was given to Héloïse and a sisterhood. In his abbey Abelard maintained for ten years a struggle with disorderly and unfriendly monks, and at last fled to Cluny, where he lived a model of ascetism and theological labour, and recanted some of the doctrines that had given most offence. Again, however, his adversaries, headed by Bernard of Clairvaux (q.v.), accused him of numerous heresies, of which he was found guilty by a council at Sens and by the pope. On his way to Rome to defend himself he died at the priory of St Marcel, near Chalon, April 21, 1142. His remains were buried by Héloïse at Paraclete, where hers were afterwards laid beside them; and thence the ashes of both were taken to Paris in 1800, and in 1817 were buried in one sepulchre at Père Lachaise, where still they lie. Abelard was a conceptualist rather than a nominalist, and in theology was held to be rationalist. His ethical system he set down in the work *Nosce Teipsum*. *Sic et Non* is a curious collection of contradictions from the works of the Fathers. His *Historia Calamitatum Mearum* forms the subject of a remarkable drama by Rémusat; and the still extant correspondence between Abelard and Héloïse suggested to Pope his *Epistle of Eloisa to Abelard*. The best edition of Abelard's works is by Cousin (2 vols. 1849–59). His work on the Trinity, long lost, was published by Stölzle in 1891. See monographs by Rémusat (Paris 1845), Wilkens (Göttingen 1855), Carriere (Giessen 1853), Deutsch (Leip. 1883), Compayré (Eng. trans. 1893), McCabe (1901), Sikes (1932), Gilson (1938).

ABENCERRAGES, *a-ben-ser-ah'jes* (from the Arabic for ' saddler's son '), a noble Moorish family which came to Spain in the 8th century, and is said to have been massacred in the Alhambra under Abu Hassan (1466–84). It figures in Spanish historical romances of the 15th and 16th centuries, e.g., Perez de Hita's *Guerras Civiles de Granada;* the theme of the massacre was used by Chateaubriand in a play and by Cherubini in an opera.

ABEN-EZRA (1093–1167), mediaeval scholar, born at Toledo, was one of the most learned Jews of his time, distinguished in philosophy, mathematics, astronomy, and medicine. He visited France, Egypt, and England, and passed his later years in Rome.

ABERCORN. See HAMILTON.

ABERCROMBIE, (1) **John** (1780–1844), Scottish physician, born at Aberdeen, took his M.D. in Edinburgh (1803), and, establishing a practice there, after Dr Gregory's death (1821), was recognized as the first consulting physician in Scotland.

(2) **Lascelles** (1881–1938), English poet, born at Ashton-on-Mersey, professor of English at Leeds (1922) and London (1929), reader at Oxford (1935), was an expert in both the theory and the practice of the art of poetry. In addition to his poetry, his works include *The Idea of Great Poetry* (1925), and *Romanticism* (1926).

(3) **Sir (Leslie) Patrick** (1879–1957), British architect, was professor of Town Planning at University College, London (1935–46). His great work was the *Greater London Plan* (1944), and he was consultant for the replanning of a number of other cities, including Plymouth, Hull, and Bath. He was knighted in 1945.

ABERCROMBY, (1) **James, 1st Baron Dunfermline** (1776–1858), third son of (3), entered parliament in 1807, held the office of Speaker (1835–39), and was then raised to the peerage. He wrote a memoir of his father (1861).

(2) **Sir John** (1772–1817), British general, second son of (3), served on his father's staff, was interned (1803–09) by Napoleon, became a divisional commander in India, and in November 1810 captured Mauritius.

(3) **Sir Ralph** (1734–1801), Scottish general, was born at Menstrie, Clackmannanshire, studied law at Edinburgh and Leipzig, but joined the Dragoons in 1756 and served in the Seven Years' War. He was M.P. for Clackmannanshire, 1774–80; in 1793 he accompanied the Duke of York to Holland, where he won the admiration of the army. The West Indies campaign he conducted with distinguished success. In 1797 he was sent to command the forces in Ireland, but his remonstrances against the policy of the government led to his removal to the Scottish command. In 1801 he received the command of the expedition to the Mediteranean, and effected a successful landing at Aboukir bay, but was mortally wounded in the ensuing battle. The peerage conferred on his widow was afterwards enjoyed by his eldest son, with the title of Baron Abercromby.

ABERDARE, Henry Austin Bruce, 1st Baron (1815–95), British statesman, born at Duffryn, Glamorganshire, was called to the bar in 1837, and in 1852 was returned by Merthyr-Tydvil as a Liberal. Home secretary under Gladstone in 1868, he was raised to the peerage in 1873, and was lord president of the Council in 1873–74.

ABERDEEN, Earls of, (1) **George Hamilton Gordon, 4th Earl** (1784-1860), born at Edinburgh, January 28, was educated at Harrow; in 1801 succeeded to the earldom; made a tour through Greece; and took his M.A. from

St John's College, Cambridge (1804). In 1806 he was elected a Scottish representative peer; in 1813–14 was ambassador to Vienna; and in 1828 became foreign secretary in the new Wellington ministry. The general principle which guided his policy was that of nonintervention, which, joined to his well-known sympathy with Metternich, exposed him to the suspicion of hostility to popular liberty. His gradual abandonment of high Tory principles was evinced by his support of the repeal of the Test and Corporation Acts, and of the Catholic Emancipation Act. In 1841 he again became foreign secretary, his chief services as such being the conclusion of the Chinese war, the Ashburton Treaty, and the Oregon Treaty. His Nonintrusion Act (1843) could not heal the Disruption of the Scottish Church, and was virtually repealed by the Act for the Abolition of Patronage, 1874. Like Peel, he was honestly converted to free trade principles, and with Peel he resigned in 1846, immediately after the repeal of the Corn Laws. In 1852, on Lord Derby's resignation, he was selected as the fittest man to head a coalition ministry, which for some time was extremely popular. The vacillating policy displayed in the conduct of the Crimean war undermined its stability, and the gross mismanagement of the commissariat in the winter of 1854 filled up the measure of the popular discontent. Roebuck's motion, calling for inquiry, was carried by a strong majority; and on February 1, 1855, Lord Aberdeen resigned office. He died in London, December 13, 1860. See Lives by his son (1893), Lady F. Balfour (1922).

(2) **John Campbell Hamilton Gordon, 7th Earl and 1st Marquis** (1847–1934), was viceroy of Ireland in 1886 and 1905–15, in 1893–98 was governor of Canada, and in 1915 was made a marquis. In 1877 he married Ishbel-Maria Marjoribanks (1857–1939), youngest daughter of the first Lord Tweedmouth. She was interested in women questions and the Irish peasantry, and wrote on Canada (1894) and tuberculosis (1908). See their *Reminiscences* (1925).

ABERHART, William (1878–1943), Canadian politician, born in Huron County, Ontario, educated at Queen's University, became in 1915 principal of Crescent Heights School, Calgary, where he remained till 1935, when he became a member of the Alberta Legislature, forming his own Social Credit Party and becoming premier in the same year. In 1937 he admitted that he could not carry out his pledge of giving each Albertan a 'dividend' of £5 monthly on the province's natural resources, but he was returned to power in 1940.

ABERNETHY, John (1764–1831), British surgeon, was born in London, April 3, the grandson of the Rev. John Abernethy (1680–1740), an Irish Presbyterian clergyman and controversialist. In 1779 he was apprenticed to the assistant surgeon at St Bartholomew's Hospital and in 1787 was himself elected assistant surgeon, and soon after began to lecture. After initial diffidence, his power soon developed itself; and his lectures at last attracted crowds. In 1813 he was appointed surgeon to Christ's Hospital, in 1814 professor of Anatomy and Surgery to the College of Surgeons, and in 1815 full surgeon to St Bartholomew's, a post which he resigned in 1829. His practice increased with his celebrity, which the eccentricity and rudeness of his manners helped to heighten. He died at Enfield, April 28, 1831. Of his Works (4 vols. 1830) the most important is his *Constitutional Origin and Treatment of Local Diseases* (1809). See Life by George Macilwain (3rd ed. 2 vols. 1857).

ABERSHAW, Jerry (1773–95), English highwayman who, from his base at the Bald-faced Stag Inn, near Kingston, haunted Wimbledon Common, and was hanged at last for shooting a constable.

ABINGER, Baron. See SCARLETT.

ABINGTON, (1). See HABINGTON.

(2) **Frances,** *née* **Barton** (1737–1815), English actress, was flower girl, street singer, milliner, and kitchenmaid before making her first appearance on the stage at the Haymarket in 1755. She rose to fame in Dublin after 1759 and subsequently returned to Drury Lane under Garrick. Extremely versatile, she excelled not only in the parts of Shakespeare's heroines but also in a great variety of comedy roles (Lady Teazle, Polly Peachum, Lucy Lockit, &c.). Reynolds painted her portrait as Miss Prue in *Love for Love*.

ABNEY, Sir William de Wiveleslie (1844–1920), English chemist, born at Derby, became assistant secretary in 1899, and adviser, in 1903, to the Board of Education. He was knighted in 1900. Known for his researches in photographic chemistry and colour photography, he did important pioneer work in photographing the solar spectrum.

ABOUT, Edmond François Valentin, *a-boo* (1828–85), French author, was born at Dieuze, in Lorraine. After a schooling in Paris, he studied archaeology at Athens; and then returning to Paris, devoted himself to a literary career. He received the Cross of the Legion of Honour in 1868, and was elected to the Academy in 1884 but died just before his formal reception in the following January. His works include *Le Roi des montagnes* (1856; Eng. trans. 1897), *Madelon* (1863), *Alsace* (1872), which cost him a week's imprisonment at the hands of the Germans, and *Le Roman d'un brave homme* (1880).

ABOYNE. See GORDON Family (4).

ABRAHAM, the father of the Hebrew people, came from the Chaldean town of Ur, near the Persian Gulf, into Canaan at a date variously estimated at from 2866 B.C. to 1700 B.C. See Gen. xi-xxv. See study by C. L. Woolley (1936).

ABRAHAM-A-SANTA-CLARA, real name **Ulrich Megerle** (1644–1709), German monk, a very eccentric but popular Augustinian who was born at Kreenheinstetten, and died court preacher in Vienna. See study by K. Bertsche (1922).

ABRAVANEL. See ABARBANEL.

ABRUZZI, Luigi Amedeo, Duke of the, *a-broot'see* (1873–1933), cousin of Victor Emmanuel III, noted for his Alaskan, Himalayan, and African climbs, and his expedition to 86° 33′ N., commanded the Italian navy 1914–17.

ABSALON. See AXEL.

ABT, Franz (1819–85), German composer of over 400 popular songs, including 'When the Swallows Homeward Fly', was born at Eilenburg, and died at Wiesbaden.

ABU-BEKR (573–634), the father of Mohammed's wife, Ayesha, was born at Mecca, became the Prophet's most trusted follower, and in 632 succeeded him as the first khalif. He died at Medina and was buried near Mohammed.

ABULFARAJ, or **Bar-Hebraeus** (1226–86), Syrian historian, was born in Armenia of a Jewish father. A master of Syriac, Arabic, and Greek, he was equally learned in philosophy, theology, and medicine. At the age of twenty, he was made a bishop, and as Bishop of Aleppo rose to the second highest dignity among the Jacobite Christians. Of his numerous writings, the best known is a Syriac universal history (ed. and trans. Budge, 1932). He died in Persia.

ABU'L FARAJ AL-ISFAHANI (897–967), Arabic literary historian. His greatest work *Al-Aghani* is a treasury of Arabic song and poetry.

ABULFEDA, Ismail-ibn-Ali (1273–1331), a Moslem prince and historian, born at Damascus, ruled from 1310 over Hamat in Syria. A generous patron of literature and science, in his Arabic *Annals* he has left one of our most valuable sources of Saracen history. It has been edited and translated into Latin (5 vols. 1789–94) by Reiske; the earlier part, *Historia Anteislamica,* by Fleischer (1831). His other great work is his *Geography.*

ABUL-WAFA. See ALBUZJANI.

ABU TAMMAM, Habib ibn Aus (807–c. 850), Arabian poet, was born near Lake Tiberias, the son of a Christian. He rose to favour under the Caliphs Mahmun and Mutasim, travelled extensively and late in life, held up by a snowstorm on one of his journeys, discovered a private library of desert poetry at Hamadhan. This led to his anthology, the *Hamasu,* in his selections for which he was said to be a better poet than in his own compositions. He ended his life at Mosul as director of the horse post.

ACCUM, Friedrich (1769–1838), German chemist, born at Buckeburg, came in 1793 to London, where he lived for nearly thirty years. He pioneered the introduction of gaslighting, and his *Treatise on Adulteration of Food and Culinary Poisons* (1820) did much to arouse public opinion against unclean food and dishonest trading.

ACHAEMENIDES, *ak-e-men'i-deez,* a dynasty in ancient Persia, founded by the 7th century ruler Achaemenes. Cyrus the Great (q.v.) and Darius I-III (qq.v.) belonged to it.

ACHARD, Franz Karl, *ah-shahr* (1753–1821), Swiss chemist, born at Berlin, took up Andreas Marggraf's discovery of sugar in beet and perfected a process for its extraction on a commercial scale, after which he opened (1801) the first beet sugar factory, in Silesia.

ACHENBACH, Andreas, *akh'en-ba*KH (1815–1910), German landscape and marine painter, born at Cassel. He studied at St Petersburg and travelled extensively in Holland, Scandinavia and Italy, where he produced many watercolours. His paintings of the North Sea coasts of Europe had considerable influence in Germany, and he was regarded as the father of 19th century German landscape painting. His brother and pupil **Oswald** (1827–1905) was also a landscape painter.

ACHESON, *aych'é-sén,* (1) **Dean Gooderham** (1893–1971), U.S. lawyer and politician, born at Middletown, Conn., educated at Yale and Harvard, was under-secretary (1945–47) and under-secretary of state from 1949 till January 1953 in the Truman administration. He helped to shape U.N.R.R.A. in 1945 and took a major share in establishing the idea behind the Marshall Plan of help to Europe in 1947. See his *A Citizen Looks at Congress* (1957), *Present at the Creation* (1969).

(2) **Edward Goodrich** (1856–1931), American chemist and inventor, born at Washington, Pa., worked under Edison, helped to develop the electric furnace, and did noteworthy research on graphite and lubricants.

ACHMET. See AHMED.

ACKERMANN, Rudolph (1764–1834), a native of Saxony, in 1795 opened a print shop in London and published a well-known set of coloured engravings of London. He is said to have introduced lithography as a fine art into England, and originated the ' Annuals ' with his *Forget-me-not* (1825).

ACLAND, (1) **Sir Arthur Herbert Dyke** (1847–1926), English politician, second son of (5), educated at Rugby and Christ Church, in 1886–99 was Liberal M.P. for Rotherham, and in 1892–95 held the cabinet office of vice-president of the Committee of Council on Education. He succeeded to the baronetcy in 1919.

(2) **Sir Henry Wentworth** (1815–1900), English physician, born at Exeter, brother of (5), educated at Harrow and Christ Church, Oxford, became Lee's reader in Anatomy at Christ Church in 1845, and was regius professor of Medicine (1857–90). He greatly improved the status of the university medical school, and fought for the establishment of natural science as a subject in the curriculum. He was made K.C.B. (1884), baronet (1890).

(3) **John Dyke** (1746–78), English soldier and politician, was elected M.P. in 1774. A supporter of Lord North's belligerent attitude towards the American colonies, he accompanied Burgoyne's expedition and was captured in battle.

(4) **Sir Richard Thomas Dyke** (1906–), English politician, grandson of (1), educated at Rugby and Balliol College, Oxford, entered parliament (1931), resigned from the Liberals to found, with J. B. Priestley, the Common Wealth Party (1942) and, consistent with its advocacy of public ownership on moral grounds, gave away his Devon family estate to the National Trust. His party eclipsed, he became Labour M.P. in 1945, but resigned in 1955 in protest against Labour support for Britain's nuclear defence policy. His books include *Unser Kampf* (1940), *What it will be Like* (1943), *Nothing Left to Believe* (1949) and *Waging Peace* (1958). He succeeded as 15th baronet in 1939.

(5) **Sir Thomas Dyke** (1809–98), English politician, brother of (2) born at Exeter

educated at Harrow and Christ Church, entered parliament in 1837 as a Conservative, but by 1865 had turned a decisive Liberal; he sat until 1886. In 1871 he succeeded as 11th baronet.

ACONZIO, Jacopo, or **Jacobus Acontius** (*c.* 1500–66), Italian writer, was a native of Trent, who came in 1557 to Basel, and in 1559 to England. His antidogmatic *Stratagemata Satanae* (1565) offers a very early advocacy of toleration; he was also a lawyer, courtier, and engineer.

ACOSTA, Gabriel, or **Uriel d'** (*c.* 1591–1640), a Portuguese Jew, born at Oporto, was bred a Catholic, but early adopted the faith of his fathers, and fled to Amsterdam, only to find there how little modern Judaism accorded with the Mosaic Law. For his *Examination of Pharisaic Traditions* (in Spanish, 1624), a charge of atheism was brought against him by the Jews before a Christian magistracy; and having lost all his property, twice suffered excommunication, and submitted to humiliating penance, he at last shot himself. See his autobiographical *Exemplar Humanae Vitae* (Gouda 1647, 1893).

ACTON, (1) **John Emerich Edward Dalberg, 1st Baron Acton of Aldenham** (1834–1902), English historian, grandson of (2), was born at Naples, January 10, and succeeded his father as baronet in 1837. He was educated at Oscott under Wiseman, and at Munich by Döllinger, opposed the dogma of papal infallibility, and as leader of the Liberal Catholics in England edited a review and a paper in their interest. He sat for five years in parliament, and Gladstone made him Baron Acton. He had written on Wolsey, the Vatican decrees, German history, &c., when in 1895 he became professor of History at Cambridge. He planned the *Cambridge Modern History*, but died June 19, 1902. See Bibliography by W. A. Shaw (1903), and Cardinal Gasquet, *Lord Acton and his Circle* (1906), and L. Kochan (1954).

(2) **Sir John Francis Edward** (1736–1811), minister of Ferdinand IV of Naples, was born at Besançon, an English doctor's son. Passing in 1779 from the naval service of Tuscany to that of Naples, he became successively admiral and generalissimo, and soon managed the entire administration. His measures, able but arbitrary, ultimately caused a reaction in favour of the French party; and he fell from power in 1806, and died at Palermo, August 12, 1811, having twenty years before succeeded to a Shropshire baronetcy.

ACUÑA, Hernando de, *a-koo'nya* (*c.* 1520–*c.* 1580), Spanish soldier, diplomat, and poet, was of Portuguese extraction, but wrote in Spanish. He put into verse under the title *El caballero determinado* a translation by Charles V of a French romance by Olivier de la Marche. Other poems, Italian in style, were published in 1591 by his widow.

ADALBERT, St, (1) (939–997), the apostle of the Prussians, was chosen Bishop of Prague, his birthplace, in 982, but the hostility of the corrupt clergy whom he tried to reform obliged him to withdraw to Rome. He then went off to carry the gospel to the Hungarians, to the Poles, and then to the Prussians, by whom he was murdered. His feast day is April 23.

(2) (d. 981), German Benedictine missionary, sent by the emperor Otho at the request of princess Olga to convert the Russians. He became first Bishop of Magdeburg in 968, and died near Merseburg.

(3) (*c.* 1000–72), Archbishop of Bremen and Hamburg, and papal legate to the north, extended his spiritual sway over Scandinavia, and carried Christianity to the Wends. In 1063 he became tutor to the young Henry IV, and soon, in spite of the opposition of the nobles, ruled over the whole kingdom.

ADAM, Fr. *a-dā',* Engl. *ad'ém,* (1) **Adolphe Charles** (1803–56), French composer, son of the pianist **Louis Adam** (1758–1848), wrote some successful operas, as *Le Postillon de Longjumeau* (1835), long popular, and *Si j'étais Roi* (1852), but is chiefly remembered for the ballet *Giselle* (1841), from a story by Gautier. He was born and died in Paris.

(2) **Alexander** (1741–1809), Scottish author of *Roman Antiquities* (1791), was born near Forres. The son of a small farmer, in 1757 he came to Edinburgh University, in 1761 he obtained the headmastership of Watson's Hospital, and in 1768 the rectorship of the High School.

(3) **James** (1730–94), Scottish architect, younger brother and partner of (8) and son of William Adam of Maryburgh (1689–1748), also an architect of renown. He studied in Rome and joined the family partnership in 1763. In 1769 he succeeded his brother as architect of the king's works. He designed a few buildings independently, notably the Glasgow Infirmary (1792).

(4) **Jean** (1710–65), Scottish poetess, was born near Greenock and died in the Glasgow poorhouse after a joyless life, first as schoolmistress, then as hawker. Her *Poems* (1734), religious effusions in the Tate and Brady style, by no means support the claim advanced for her authorship of ' There's nae luck aboot the hoose', which, with much more likelihood, is ascribed to Mickle (q.v.). See a long article in *Athenaeum* for January 27, 1877.

(5) **Juliette,** *née* **Lamber** (1836–1936), French writer born at Verberie, Oise, wife of the senator Edmond Adam (1816–77), assembled round her during the Empire a salon of wits, artists, and advanced politicians, produced stories and books on social and political questions, and in 1879 founded the *Nouvelle Revue.* In 1895–1905 she published her *Mémoires.* See Life by A. Elliott (1922).

(6) **Louis.** See ADAM, ADOLPHE.

(7) **Paul Auguste Marie** (1862–1920), French novelist and essayist, born in Paris. Among his numerous novels are *Chair molle* (1885), *Le Mystère des foules* (1895), *Lettres de malaisie* (1879), and *La Force* (1899). He was cofounder of *Symboliste* and other French literary periodicals.

(8) **Robert** (1728–92), Scottish architect, born at Kirkcaldy, brother of (3). He studied at Edinburgh and in Italy (1754). From 1761–69 he was architect of the king's works, jointly with Sir William Chambers. He established a practice in London in 1758 and during the next forty years he and his brother James succeeded in transforming

the prevailing Palladian fashion in architecture by a series of romantically elegant variations on diverse classical originals. Their style of interior decoration was based on ancient Greek and Roman characterized by the use of the oval, and lines of decoration in hard plaster, enlivened by painted panels in low relief. One of their greatest projects was the Adelphi (demolished 1936), off the Strand in London, a residential block built as a speculative venture, which brought the brothers' finances into very low water, and was eventually disposed of by a lottery. Home House, Portland Square, and Lansdowne House are good surviving examples of their work, which is illustrated in *The Works in Architecture of Robert and James Adam* (1773, 1779, and 1822). They also designed furniture and fittings to suit the houses they planned. See also the *Architecture of Robert and James Adam* by A. T. Bolton (1922), and *Robert Adam and his Brothers* by J. Swarbrick (1915).

ADAM DE LA HALE. See HALLE.

ADAM OF BREMEN (d. *c.* 1075), German historian, author of *Gesta Hammaburgensis Ecclesiae Pontificum,* the most important source for northern European history between the 8th and 11th centuries.

ADAMIC, Louis (1899–1951), American writer, born in Blato, Dalmatia. The son of Slovene peasants, he emigrated to the United States in 1913, served with the American army, became naturalized in 1918 and began writing short stories in the early 'twenties, thereafter utilizing his experiences and personal observations in his books—for example, as an immigrant in *Laughing in the Jungle* (1932). Other works include *Dynamite: the Story of Class Violence in America* (1931); an autobiographical survey, *My America, 1928–38* (1938); *From Many Lands* (1940); *Dinner at the White House* (1946), and *The Eagle and the Root* (1950).

ADAMNAN, St (*c.* 625–704), Irish monk, Columba's biographer, born and educated in Donegal, in his 28th year joined the Columban brotherhood of Iona, of which, in 679, he was chosen abbot. In 686 he paid a visit to his friend and pupil, Aldfrid, king of Northumbria, to procure the release of some Irish captives; and was converted to the Roman views as to the holding of Easter and the shape of the tonsure. Those views he endeavoured to inculcate in Iona, and also in Ireland, but he failed, at least in Iona, and it is said that mortification at the failure caused his death. He left a treatise *De Locis Sanctis,* one of our earliest descriptions of Palestine. *Adamnan's Vision,* a professed account of his visit to heaven and hell, is a work of the 10th or 11th century; but certainly his is the *Vita Sancti Columbae,* which reveals a great deal concerning the remarkable community of Iona. There are editions by Reeves (1857, from an 8th century codex discovered at Schaffhausen in 1845) and Fowler (Oxf. 1895, 1920).

ADAMS, (1) **Bertha Leith.** See LAFFAN.

(2) **Charles Francis** (1807–86), American diplomat, the son of (7) and father of (3), was born in Boston, studied at Harvard, and was admitted to the bar in 1828. He served five

years in the legislature of Massachusetts, and in 1858–61 was a congressman for Massachusetts. In 1861–68 he was minister to England, in 1871–72 an 'Alabama' arbitrator. He published his grandfather's *Life and Works*. See the Life (1900) by his son **Charles Francis** (1835–1915).

(3) **Henry Brooks** (1838–1918), American historian, son of (2), born at Boston, educated at Harvard, acted as his father's secretary in England (1861–68), was a journalist in Washington (1868–70), and taught mediaeval and American history at Harvard (1870–77). He wrote several important historical works, but his *magnum opus* was *History of the United States during the Administrations of Jefferson and Madison* (9 vols., 1889–91). See his autobiographical *The Education of Henry Adams* (1907), and J. T. Adams, *The Adams Family* (1933).

(4) **John** (1735–1826), second president of the United States, was born in Braintree, (now Quincy) Mass., October 31, the son of a farmer, and distinguished himself at Harvard. Admitted to the bar in 1758, he settled at Boston in 1768. Of strongly colonial sympathies, he declined the post of advocate-general in the Court of Admiralty, and in 1765 led the protest against the Stamp Act. His health failing, he withdrew in 1771 to Braintree, but in 1774 was sent as a delegate from Massachusetts to the first Continental Congress. He proposed the election of Washington as commander-in-chief, and was the 'colossus of the debate' on the 'Declaration of Independence'. President of the Board of War, and a member of over ninety committees, of twenty-five of which he was chairman, he worked incessantly; but retired from congress in 1777, only to be sent to France and to Holland as commissioner from the new republic. He was one of the commissioners who in 1783 signed the treaty of peace, and in 1785–88 was minister to England. While in London, he published his *Defence of the Constitution of the United States* (3 vols. 1787). In 1789 he became vice-president of the United States under Washington. They were re-elected in 1792; and in 1796 Adams was chosen president by the Federalists. His administration was noted for fierce dissensions among the leaders of that party, especially between Adams and Alexander Hamilton. Defeated on seeking re-election in 1800, Adams retired in chagrin to his home at Quincy, where he died. See his *Life and Works* (ed. by C. F. Adams, 10 vols. 1850–56), the Life by J. Q. and C. F. Adams (2 vols. 1871), that by Morse (1885), J. T. Adams, *The Adams Family* (1930) and *Diary and Autobiography* (ed. Butterfield, etc., 4 vols., 1961).

(5) **John**, or **Alexander Smith** (*c.* 1760–1829), a ringleader in the mutiny of the *Bounty* (1789; see BLIGH), and the only survivor when the island was next visited in 1809, most of the remainder having been murdered in 1794 by the Tahitians who had accompanied them.

(6) **John Couch** (1819–92), English astronomer, was born at Laneast, near Launceston, graduated as senior wrangler at St John's College, Cambridge, in 1843, became fellow and mathematical tutor, and in 1858 Lowndean professor of Astronomy. Soon after taking his degree, he undertook to find out the cause of the irregularities in the motion of Uranus. In a paper of June 1, 1846, Leverrier assigned to an unknown planet almost the same place as Adams had done in a paper left with the astronomer royal at Greenwich in October 1845 and Galle working on these results at Berlin actually observed Neptune in 1846. The Astronomical Society awarded equal honours to both in 1848. Adams also made important researches as to the secular acceleration of the moon's mean motion, and on the November meteors. See Sir H. S. Jones, *John Couch Adams and the Discovery of Neptune* (1907).

(7) **John Quincy** (1767–1848), sixth president of the United States, son of (4) was born at Quincy, July 11, and at fourteen became private secretary to the American envoy at St Petersburg. He was secretary to the commission for peace between the colonies and the mother country; but in 1785 began to study at Harvard, and was admitted to the bar in 1790. Successively minister to the Hague, London, Lisbon, and Berlin, in 1803 he was elected to the U.S. senate from Massachusetts, and in 1806, boldly denouncing the right of searching ships claimed by the British government, he lost favour with the Federal party and his seat. In 1809 he was minister to St Petersburg; in 1814, a member of a commission to negotiate peace between Great Britain and the United States; in 1815–17 minister at the court of St James's. As secretary of state under President Monroe, he negotiated with Spain the treaty for the acquisition of Florida, and was alleged to be the real author of the 'Monroe Doctrine'. In 1825 Adams was elected president by the House of Representatives—no election having been made by the people. Failing to be re-elected, he retired to his home at Quincy, depressed and impoverished. In 1830 he was elected to the lower house of congress, where he became noted as a promoter of anti-slavery views; and he was returned to each successive congress until his death in the Speaker's room, February 23, 1848. See his Diary (ed. Nevins, 1928). Lives by Morse (1882) and Stoddart (1887), his *Writings* (ed. Ford, 1913 *et seq.*), J. T. Adams, *The Adams Family* (1930).

(8) **Samuel** (1722–1803), American statesman, born at Boston, was lieutenant-governor of Massachusetts 1789–94, and then governor till 1797. His ignorance of military matters led him to think Washington's conduct of the war weak and dilatory. In 1776 he anticipated Napoleon by applying the term, 'a nation of shopkeepers', to the English. See Life by Wells (3 vols. 1865) and Morse (1884), and his Works edited by H. A. Cushing (1897).

(9) **Walter Sydney** (1876–1956), American astronomer, born at Antioch, was director of Mount Wilson observatory from 1923. His work on stellar spectra led to the discovery of a spectroscopic method of measuring the distance of stars.

(10) **William** (1564–1620), English sailor, born at Gillingham, Kent, took service with the Dutch as a navigator. As pilot of the

Dutch vessel *de Liefde* he reached the Japanese port of Bungo in April 1600. At the instigation of jealous Portuguese traders he was cast into prison as a pirate, but was freed after building two fine ships for the Emperor Iyéyasu; receiving a pension, the rank of samurai, and ' living like unto a lordship in England '. He also served as the agent of the Dutch East India Company. See his letters in Vol. I of *Purchas*, and his Log (ed. Purnell, 1916).

ADANSON, Michel, *a-dã-sõ* (1727–1806), French botanist, having spent 1748–53 in Senegal, published *Histoire naturelle du Sénégal* (1757) and *Familles naturelles des plantes* (1763), and left an unfinished encyclopaedia. The baobab genus *Adansonia* is named after him.

ADDAMS, Jane (1860–1935), American social reformer, was born at Cedarville, Illinois. After visiting Toynbee Hall, London, England, she founded Hull House in Chicago. She worked to secure social justice in housing, factory inspection, the treatment of immigrants and Negroes, and for women and children. She worked for female suffrage and the cause of pacifism and in 1931 was awarded the Nobel peace prize. In 1910 she became the first woman president of the National Conference of Social Work. She was also president of the Women's International League for Peace and Freedom. She published several works on social conditions and social work, among them *Democracy and Social Ethics* (1902). See Adams and Foster, *Heroines of Modern Progress* (1922) and Life by M. Tims (1961).

ADDINGTON. See SIDMOUTH.

ADDISON, (1) **Christopher, 1st Viscount** (1869–1951), British Labour politician, born at Hogsthorpe, Lincs., educated at Trinity College School, Harrogate, qualified at St Bartholomew's Hospital, London, and became professor of Anatomy at Sheffield University. In 1910 he was elected Liberal M.P. for Hoxton, representing the constituency till 1922. He became parliamentary secretary to the Board of Education in 1914, minister of Munitions in 1916, and Britain's first minister of Health in 1919. Difficulties with Lloyd George led to his resignation in 1921 and to his joining the Labour Party. Elected M.P. for Swindon, he became minister of Agriculture in 1929. Created a baron in 1937, he assumed leadership of the Labour Peers in 1940. In 1945 he became leader of the House of Lords and Dominions secretary. A quiet, almost ingratiating tactician, he had a sure ascendancy over the House of Lords in an historic period. An able administrator, he was the ' father ' of the ' panel ' system, of housing subsidies, of agricultural marketing legislation. Publications: *Politics From Within, 1911–18* (1925), and *Four And a Half Years* (1934). See Life by R. J. Minney (1958).

(2) **Joseph** (1672–1719), English essayist, born May 1, was the eldest son of Lancelot Addison (1632–1703), then rector of Milston, in Wiltshire, and from 1683 dean of Lichfield, and was educated at Amesbury, Lichfield, the Charterhouse, and Queen's College and Magdalen, Oxford. In 1693 he began his literary career with a poetical address to Dryden. Next year appeared his *Account of the Greatest English Poets*, and a translation of the fourth book of the *Georgics*. Through Charles Montague, Earl of Halifax, he obtained in 1699 a pension of £300, and spent four years in France, Italy, Austria, Germany, and Holland, during which he wrote his *Letter to Lord Halifax*, and made notes for his *Remarks on Italy*, and his *Dialogue on Medals*. *The Campaign*, a commissioned poem celebrating the victory of Blenheim (1704), secured for him a commissionership of Excise. While secretary to the Earl of Sunderland, he produced his opera *Rosamond* (1706); in 1707 he attended Lord Halifax to Hanover. In 1708–11 he was secretary to Lord Wharton, lord-lieutenant of Ireland, and here he formed a warm friendship with Swift. Elected to parliament for Malmesbury, he kept the seat for life. He contributed largely to the *Tatler*, started by his friend Steele in 1709; 41 papers being wholly by Addison, and 34 by him and Steele conjointly. In March 1711 was founded the *Spectator*, 274 numbers of which (those signed with one of the letters C L I O), were the work of Addison. His fortune was now so much augmented, that in 1711 he was able to purchase for £10,000 the estate of Bilton, near Rugby. His tragedy *Cato* (1713) aroused such vehement party enthusiasm that it kept the stage for thirty-five nights. In the Whig interest, he attacked the Treaty of Utrecht in *The Late Trial and Conviction of Count Tariff*. After the accession of George I, he became once more, for about a year, secretary to the Earl of Sunderland as lord-lieutenant of Ireland. In 1715, a suspicion that he was the author of Tickell's translation of the first book of the *Iliad*, brought him into collision with Pope, who afterwards satirized him in the famous character of Atticus. He also wrote his comedy of *The Drummer*, which was acted without success at Drury Lane; and, in the Hanoverian cause, issued (1715–16) the *Freeholder*. He was made a commissioner for trade and the colonies, and in 1716 married Charlotte, Countess of Warwick. In 1717 he was appointed secretary of state, but resigned his post, owing to his failing health, in March 1718. Almost his last literary undertaking was unfortunately a paper war, on the Peerage Bill of 1719, with his old friend Steele. A sufferer from asthma, and then from dropsy, he died at Holland House, June 17, 1719. As a light essayist, he has no equal in English literature. In the *Spectator* may be traced the foundations of all that is sound and healthy in modern English thought. Addison's criticism does not aim at being profound, but is distinguished for its sobriety and good sense. His prose style reflects the grace and subtlety of his humour. *Cato*, written with great elegance and correctness, is wanting in dramatic spirit. See the Life, by Lucy Aikin (1843), and Macaulay's review of it; also Courthopes *Addison* (1884), and Life by Smithers (1954).

(3) **Thomas** (1793–1860), English physician, was born near Newcastle, and graduated in medicine at Edinburgh in 1815. He settled in London, and in 1837 became physician to Guy's Hospital. His chief researches were on

pneumonia, tuberculosis and especially on the disease of the suprarenal capsules, known as 'Addison's Disease'.

ADELA (1062?–1137), youngest daughter of William the Conqueror, in 1080 married Stephen, Count of Blois, by whom she had nine children. Her third son, Stephen (q.v.), became King of England in her lifetime. She had a flair for administration and was cultured and pious. See Alice Green's *Lives of the Princesses of England*.

ADELAER ('Eagle'), honorific title of Cort Sivertsen (1622–75), Danish naval commander, born at Brevig, in Norway, who fought splendidly for Venice against the Turks, and in 1663 was recalled to the service of Denmark.

ADELAIDE, Ger. Adelheid, St (931?–999). A daughter of Rudolf II of Burgundy, she married Lothair, son of Hugh of Italy, in 947. On his death in 950 she was imprisoned by his successor Berengar II, but escaped and married Otto I of Germany, by whom she had a son, Otto II (955–983) over whom she exercised considerable influence when he came to rule, though they quarrelled over her extravagant charities. On the accession of Otto III in 996, she retired to a convent and spent the rest of her life in 'pious exercises and the foundation of churches'.

ADELAIDE, Queen (1792–1849), daughter of the Duke of Saxe-Coburg Meiningen, in 1818 married the Duke of Clarence, who in 1830 succeeded to the English throne as William IV. She was much more worthy than popular. See Memoir by Doran (1861) and by M. F. Sandars (1915).

ADELUNG, (1) Friedrich von (1768–1843), German philologist, nephew of (2), born at Stettin, carried out research on Indian dialects and also studied Russian history. He died at St Petersburg.

(2) **Johann Christoph** (1732–1806), German linguist and lexicographer, was born at Spantekow, and died at Dresden, where, since 1787, he had held the office of chief librarian.

ADENAUER, Konrad, *ah'dĕn-ow-ĕr* (1876–1967), German statesman, born at Cologne. He studied at Freiburg, Munich, and Bonn univs. before practising law in his native city, of which he became Lord Mayor in 1917. A member of the Centre Party under the Weimar Republic, Adenauer was a member of the Provincial Diet and of the Prussian State Council, of which he was president (1920–33). The Nazis, in 1933, first suspended and then dismissed him from all his offices, and imprisoned him in 1934 and 1944. In 1945, under Allied occupation, he became Lord Mayor again, and founded the Christian Democratic Union. He was chancellor from 1949 (re-elected in 1953 and 1957), and was his own foreign minister from 1951–55. In 1955 he visited Moscow and diplomatic relations were established with the Russians. In the 1957 elections he gained an absolute majority of 43, a tribute to his policy of the rebuilding of Western Germany on a basis of partnership with other European nations through N.A.T.O. and the European customs union, with the ultimate aim of bargaining from strength for the reunification of Germany. He engaged in a public con-

troversy over his succession with Erhard (q.v.) in 1959, consolidated the new Franco-German friendship and modified the German desire for reunification. His restraint during the Berlin crisis (1961–62) as well as his great age (85) caused a fall in the fortunes of his parties at the polls (1961), necessitating a coalition with the Free Democrats, who pressed him for an early retirement. He complied in October 1963. See *Life* by Paul Weymar (1957).

ADICKES, Erich (1866–1928), German philosopher and academic, was born at Lesum near Bremen. This Kantian scholar is famous for a special study of the status of the 'Thing-in-itself', which is to be found in *Kant und das Ding an Sich* (Berlin, 1924). He held that the principle of contradiction has an unlimited validity which extends to things-in-themselves. See G. Martin, *Kant's Metaphysics and Theory of Science* (1955).

ADLER, (1) Alfred (1870–1937), pioneer Austrian psychiatrist, born in Vienna. He first practised as an ophthalmologist but later turned to mental disease and became a prominent member of the psychoanalytical group that formed around Freud. In 1911 he seceded from the psychoanalysts and developed his own 'Individual Psychology'—i.e., that department of psychology which investigates the psychology of the individual considered as different from others—a theory developed in Adler's *Practice and Theory of Individual Psychology*. His main contributions to psychology include the 'inferiority complex', and his special treatment of neurosis as the 'exploitation of shock'. See *Individual Psychology of A. Adler* (ed. Ansbacher, H. L. and R. R., 1958).

(2) **Nathan Marcus** (1803–90), Jewish Rabbi, was born at Hanover and educated at Göttingen, Erlangen, and Würzburg. He became chief rabbi of Oldenburg in 1829, of Hanover in 1830, and of the united congregations of the British Empire in 1845. His son and successor, **Hermann** (1839–1911), born in Hanover, graduated B.A. at London (1859), and Ph.D. at Leipzig (1861). A staunch defender of his coreligionists, he published *The Jews in England; Ibn Gabirol*, &c.

ADOLPHUS, (1) John (1768–1845), British lawyer and historian, born in London of German ancestry, was called to the bar in 1807, and became a successful Old Bailey practitioner. His works fill over 20 volumes, the chief a *History of George III's Reign* (1802; new ed. 1840–43). See *Life* (1871).

(2) **John Leycester** (1795–1862), British barrister, son of (1), *inter alia* published *Letters to Richard Heber* (1821), showing Scott to have written the Waverley novels.

ADRIAN IV (pope 1154–59), the only Englishman to become pope. Nicolas Breakspear by name, he was born at Langley, near St Albans, became first a lay brother in the monastery of St Rufus, near Avignon, and in 1137 was elected its abbot. His zeal for strict discipline raised a combination to defame his character, and he had to appear before Eugenius III at Rome. Here he not only cleared himself, but acquired the esteem of the pope, who appointed him cardinal-bishop of Albano in 1146. In 1154 he was raised to the papal see, one of his early acts being to grant Ireland to Henry II. Adrian was at first on friendly terms with the Emperor Frederick I; but his high notions of the papal supremacy led to that long contest between popes and Hohenstaufens which ended in the destruction of the dynasty. See Life by Alfred Tarleton (1896).

ADRIAN, Edgar Douglas, 1st Baron Adrian (1889–), English scientist, born in London, professor of Physiology at Cambridge 1937– 1951, was made O.M. 1942, P.R.S. 1950, master of Trinity, Cambridge, 1951 and a baron in 1955. He carried out important research on the nervous system, and on 'brain waves'. He shared the 1932 Nobel prize for medicine for work on the function of neurons.

ADSHEAD. See BONE (3).

ADY, Endre, *aw'di* (1877–1919), Hungarian lyrical poet, born at Ermindszent, went to Paris in 1903 and absorbed French literary influences,which he later infused into Hungarian poetry, enriching it with new ideas and forms. See study by J. Reményi (Slav. Rev. 1944).

Æ. See RUSSELL (5).

AELFRIC, *el'frik* (*c.* 955–1020), called **Grammaticus,** English writer, was a pupil of Bishop Ethelwold of Winchester, most likely at the Benedictine monastery of Abingdon; and, after ruling the new monastery at Cerne Abbas, became abbot of Eynsham. He has been confused by Wright, Dean Hook, and Freeman with Aelfric, Archbishop of Canterbury (995–1005); and by Wharton and Thorpe with Aelfric, Archbishop of York (1032–1051). His Latin and English grammar and glossary, and his *Colloquium,* are less important than his eighty *Homilies,* edited by Thorpe for the Aelfric Society (1844–46).

AELIANUS, Claudius, *ee-li-ah'nus,* called the **Sophist,** Latin writer, a native of Praeneste, who taught rhetoric in Rome *c.* 220. We have his *Varia Historia* and *De Natura Animalium.*

AELRED. See AILRED.

AEMILIUS PAULUS (d. 216 B.C.), Roman consul who fell at Cannae. His son, Lucius Aemilius Paulus (or Paullus) Macedonicus, in 168 B.C. was re-elected consul and defeated Perseus, king of Macedon, at Pydna. His son, adopted by Scipio, was known as **Scipio Aemilianus.**

AENEAS SILVIUS. See PIUS II.

AESCHINES, *ees'kin-ees* (389 B.C.–314 B.C.), Athenian orator, second only to Demosthenes. Demosthenes advocated strenuous opposition to Philip of Macedon, then pursuing his designs for the subjugation of the several Greek states; while Aeschines, as head of the peace party, was a member of more than one embassy sent by the Athenians to Philip. The result justified the sagacious fears of Demosthenes. But when it was proposed to reward him with a golden crown, Aeschines indicted the proposer, Ctesiphon, for bringing forward an illegal proposition. Demosthenes replied in perhaps the greatest of his speeches; and Aeschines, defeated, had to leave Athens. He established a school of eloquence in Rhodes, and died at Samos, 314 B.C. Only his oration against Ctesiphon and two others survive. See Jebb's *Attic Orators.*

AESCHYLUS, *ees'kil-us* (525 B.C.–456 B.C.) the father of Greek tragedy, was born at Eleusis, the town of the Mysteries, near Athens. The first attempts at tragedy had been made by Thespis; and there were older contemporaries of Aeschylus, with whom he contended successfully. He fought for Athens in the great Persian wars, and was wounded at Marathon. His first victory as a poet was gained in 485 B.C.; and, having won thirteen first prizes in tragic competitions, he was exceedingly hurt at being defeated by Sophocles in 468 B.C. This may have induced him to leave Athens and go to Sicily, where he produced a new edition of his extant *Persae.* His trial before the Areopagus on the charge of divulging the Mysteries is also stated as a cause of his departure. His last great victory was won in 458 B.C., with the trilogy which we still possess. He died at Gela in Sicily. Out of some sixty plays ascribed to him, we have only seven extant, the *Suppliants,* the *Persae,* the *Seven against Thebes,* the *Prometheus Bound* (in some ways the perfection of its author's art), and the trilogy of the *Oresteia,* three plays on the fate of Orestes, comprising the *Agamemnon* (perhaps the greatest Greek play that has survived), *Choephori,* and *Eumenides.* The genius of Aeschylus is quite peculiar in Greek literature, and he has no equal. What distinguishes him most from great contemporaries like Pindar, or great successors like Sophocles, is the grandeur of his conceptions in theology, in the providential ruling of the world, the inheritance of sin, and the conflict of rude with purer religion. See G. Murray's text (*Oxford Classical Texts,* 1937), his translations (1920–39), and study (1940); also books by Copleston (1871), Finley (1955).

AESOP, *ee'sop,* Greek fabulist, who lived in the later half of the 6th cent. B.C. He is supposed to have been a native of Phrygia and a slave, but to have been afterwards made free. He then visited the court of Croesus, and, gaining his confidence, was sent on several missions, in one of which, to Delphi, he was thrown over a precipice by the priests, infuriated at his witty blasphemies. The traditions of his ugliness and his buffoonery may be dismissed. We know from Aristophanes that fables bearing the name of Aesop were popular at his time; but the only Greek version of them preserved to us is that of Babrius (q.v.). See J. Jacobs' *Fables of Aesop* (2 vols. 1889).

AËTIUS, *ah-ee'shi-us* (*c.* 390–454), Roman general, born in Moesia, in 433 became patrician, consul, and general-in-chief; and as such maintained the empire against the barbarians for twenty years, defeating West Goths, Burgundians, rebellious Gauls, and Franks. His crowning victory was that at Châlons over Attila (q.v.) in 451; three years later the Emperor Valentinian III, jealous of his greatness, stabbed him to death.

AFANASIEV, Alexander Nikolaievitch, *af-a-nas'yef* (1826–71), Russian folklorist, held a post in a government office at Moscow. His works are on Slavonic mythology and Russian folk tales.

AFFONSO. See ALFONSO.

AFFRE, Denis Auguste (1793–1848), French

prelate, from 1840 Archbishop of Paris, was shot in the June insurrection, while bearing a green branch on a barricade. See *Life* by Cruice (Paris 1849).

AFRICANUS, Sextus Julius (*c.* 160–*c.* 240), traveller and historian born in Libya, wrote a history of the world from the creation to A.D. 221. His chronology, which antedates Christ's birth by 3 years, was accepted by Byzantine churches.

AFZELIUS, Adam, *af-zee'li-us* (1750–1836), Swedish botanist, was born at Larf, Vester-götland, and after years of botanical research on the Guinea coast became professor of Materia Medica at Uppsala. He founded the Linnaean Institute there, and edited and published Linnaeus's autobiography. A brother **Johan** (1753–1837) was professor of Chemistry at Uppsala, another brother **Per Af** (1760–1843) was professor of Medicine at the same university and director of the Finnish Army health services, and another relative **Arvid August** (1785–1871), the parish priest of Enkoeping, is famous for his collections of Swedish and Icelandic folk songs and stories.

AGA KHAN. Title of the hereditary head of the Ismailian sect of Muslims, of which the following are noteworthy:

(1) **Aga Khan III** (1877–1957), in full **Aga Sultan Sir Mohammed Shah,** born at Karachi, succeeded to the title in 1885. In 1910 he founded the Aligarh University. He worked for the British cause in both World Wars, and in 1937 was president of the League of Nations. He owned several Derby winners.

(2) **Aga Khan IV** (1936–   ), **Karim,** grandson of (1), son of Aly Khan, succeeded as 49th Imam. He was educated at Le Rosey in Switzerland, and later read oriental history at Harvard.

AGARDH, Karl Adolf (1785–1859), a Swedish bishop and botanist, his specialty algae. His son, **Jakob Georg** (1813–1901), succeeded him in the chair of Botany (1854–79) at Lund.

AGAR-ELLIS. See ELLIS.

AGASSIZ, *a-ga-see,* (1) **Alexander** (1835–1910), Swiss oceanographer and marine zoologist, son of (2), born at Neuchâtel, became connected with the Harvard Museum in 1859, amassed a fortune in the copper-mines of Lake Superior, and was curator of the museum in 1873–85. He founded the zoological station at Newport, Rhode Island; and made improvements in the technique of deep sea research.

(2) **Jean Louis Rodolphe** (1807–73), Swiss naturalist, born at Motier, graduated in medicine in 1830, his Latin description of the *Fishes of Brazil* having the year before elicited a warm encomium from Cuvier. In 1831–32 he worked in Paris, and in 1832 accepted a professorship at Neuchâtel. In 1833 he commenced the publication of his *Researches on the Fossil Fishes,* after studying the glacial phenomena of the Alps wrote *Études sur les glaciers* (1840) and *Système glaciaire* (1847). In 1839 he published a *Natural History of the Freshwater Fishes of Central Europe.* In 1846–48 he lectured in the U.S., and in 1848 was elected to the chair of Natural History at Harvard. In 1855–63 he and his daughters conducted a young ladies' school at Cambridge, Mass.; he declined chairs at

Zürich and Paris, and received the Order of the Legion of Honour. Of his *Contributions to the Natural History of the United States,* he lived to issue only four vols. To a Museum of Comparative Zoology, established at Harvard in 1858, Agassiz gave all his collections; and four years of incessant work here so undermined his health that he decided upon a trip to Brazil, ultimately transformed into an important scientific expedition, described in *A Journey in Brazil.* See *Life and Correspondence,* ed. by Mrs Agassiz (1886), monograph by Holder (1892), and *Life, Letters, and Works,* by Marcou (1896).

AGATE, James Evershed, *ay'* (1877–1947), English critic and essayist, born in Manchester, wrote dramatic criticism for several papers and for the B.B.C., before becoming dramatic critic of the *Sunday Times* from 1923. He wrote also on literature and films, and was author of essays and diaries.

AGATHA, St, a beautiful Sicilian who rejected the love of the Prefect Quintilianus, and suffered a cruel martyrdom in 251. Her feast day is Feb. 5; she is the patron saint of Catania, and is invoked against fire and lightning.

AGATHARCOS, *ag-a-thar'kos,* Athenian artist of the time of Pericles, named by Vitruvius as the founder of scene painting.

AGATHOCLES, *a-gath'o-kleez* (361–289 B.C.), Tyrant of Syracuse from 317, fought the Carthaginians, and in 304 took the title of King of Sicily. A poisoned toothpick (perhaps really cancer of the jaw) is said to have caused his death.

AGESILAUS, *-lay'us* (444–360 B.C.), King of Sparta from 399, was one of the most brilliant soldiers of antiquity. Called on by the Ionians to assist them against Artaxerxes, he commenced a splendid campaign in Asia; but the Corinthian war recalled him to Greece. At Coronea (394) he defeated the allied forces, and peace was concluded in favour of Sparta (387). Afterwards, in the Theban war, though hard pressed by Pelopidas and Epaminondas, and defeated at Mantinea (362), he bravely defended his country.

AGGREY, James Emman Kwegyir (1875–1927), African missionary and teacher, was born at Anamabu, in the Gold Coast (now Ghana). After attending a Methodist missionary school in Cape Coast, he trained as a missionary at Livingstone College, North Carolina, U.S.A. (B.A. with honours, 1902), and after further university and church work in America, returned to Africa and joined the staff of Achimota College. He particularly stressed, to black and white people alike, the Christian outlook on the colour question. See biography by E. W. Smith (1929).

AGIS IV. King of Sparta, succeeded in 244 B.C., and, having proposed a redistribution of property, was strangled, 241 B.C.

AGNES, St, a Roman Christian who was martyred in her thirteenth year. Her symbol is a lamb and her feast day Jan. 21. See Keyes: *Three Ways of Love* (1964).

AGNES, St, of Assisi (1197–1253), daughter of Count Favorino Scifi, born at Assisi. In 1211, against violent parental opposition, she joined her sister (see ST CLARE) who had shortly before entered a monastery to embrace the Franciscan way of life. The sisters became cofounders of the Order of the Poor Ladies of San Damiano, and in 1219 Agnes became Abbess of a newly established community of the order at Monticelli.

AGNESI, Maria Gaetana, *an-yay'zee* (1718–1799), Italian scholar. A native of Milan, remarkable alike as linguist, philosopher, mathematician, and theologian, who, when her father was disabled, took his place as professor of Mathematics at Bologna.

AGNON, Shmuel Yosef (Shmuel Czaczkes) (1888–1970), Israeli writer, born in Buczacz, Galicia (now Poland), went to Palestine in 1907, studied in Berlin from 1913 to 1924, when he settled permanently in Jerusalem and changed his surname to Agnon. He wrote an epic trilogy of novels on Eastern European Jewry in the early 20th century, *Bridal Canopy* (1931, trans. 1937), *A Guest for the Night* (1939) and *Days Gone By* (1945), as well as several volumes of short stories, a novella, *In the Heart of the Seas* (1933, trans. 1947), *Two Tales* (trans. 1966), etc. He became the first Israeli to win the Nobel prize for Literature in 1966 (jointly with Sachs (q.v.)).

AGOULT, Marie de Flavigny, Comtesse d', pseud. **Daniel Stern,** *ah-goo* (1805–76), French author, was born at Frankfort, and educated at a convent in Paris. She married the Comte d'Agoult in 1827, but soon left him for Liszt, to whom she bore three daughters, the eldest of whom married Émile Ollivier, and the third, Hans von Bülow, and later Wagner. Her best work is *Esquisses morales* (1849). See her *Mémoires* (1927).

AGRICOLA, (1) Georg, real surname **Bauer** (1494–1555), German mineralogist, was born at Glauchau. From 1518–22 he was rector of the school at Zwickau. In 1527 he was practising medicine in Joachimstal, but after moving to Chemnitz in 1531 he devoted himself to the study of mining. Agricola was Germany's first systematic mineralogist.

(2) **Gnaeus Julius** (37–93), Roman statesman and soldier, was born at Forum Julii (now Fréjus in Provence). Having served with distinction in Britain, Asia, and Aquitania, he was in A.D. 77 elected consul, and proceeded as governor to Britain. He was the first Roman general who effectually subdued the island, and the only one who displayed as much genius in civilizing as in conquering the inhabitants. In his last campaign (*c.* A.D. 86), his decisive victory over the Caledonians under Galgacus, in the battle of Mons Graupius, established the Roman dominion to some distance north of the Forth. After this campaign, his fleet circumnavigated the coast, for the first time discovering Britain to be an island. The news of Agricola's successes inflamed the jealousy of Domitian, and in A.D. 87 he was recalled. Thenceforth he lived in retirement. The jealousy of the emperor is supposed to have hastened his death. His Life by his son-in-law Tacitus is one of the best classical biographies.

(3) **Johann,** real name **Schneider** or **Schnitter,** also called **Magister Islebius** (1492–1566), German reformer, born at Eisleben, was one of the most zealous founders of Protestantism. Having studied at Wittenberg

and Leipzig, he was sent in 1525 by Luther to Frankfurt, to institute the Protestant worship there; then preached at Eisleben until in 1536 appointed to a chair at Wittenberg, which, however, he had to resign in 1540 for his opposition to Luther in the great Antinomian controversy. He died court preacher at Berlin. He wrote many theological books, but his collection of German proverbs (1528–1529) is more lasting. See Life by Kawerau (1881).

(4) **Martin** (1486–1556), German musical theorist, born in Schwiebus; his real name was **Sohr** or **Sore.** Appointed to be teacher and cantor at the first Protestant school in Magdeburg in 1524, posts he held for the rest of his life, he claimed to be a self-taught musician and wrote extensively, with considerable literary power, of all branches of music. His writings in support of modern methods of notation were of special importance.

(5) **Rudolphus,** real name **Roelof Huysmann** (1443–85), Dutch humanist, the foremost scholar of the ' New Learning ' in Germany, was born near Groningen, in Friesland, August 23. From Groningen he passed to Louvain, Paris, and Italy, where, during 1473–80, he attended the lectures of the most celebrated men of his age. In 1483 he established himself in the Palatinate, where he sojourned alternately at Heidelberg and Worms, dividing his time between private studies and public lectures, and enjoying high popularity. He distinguished himself also as a musician and painter. He revisited Italy (1484), and died at Heidelberg, October 28. Most of his works were collected by Alard of Amsterdam (2 vols. Cologne, 1539). See Tresling's *Vita Agricolae* (Gron. 1830), and Bezold's German monograph (Mun. 1884).

AGRIPPA I and **II.** See HEROD.

AGRIPPA, Marcus Vipsanius (63–12 B.C.), a Roman general who commanded Octavian's fleet at Actium (31 B.C.), and did good service in Gaul, Spain, Syria, and Pannonia.

AGRIPPA VON NETTESHEIM, Heinrich Cornelius (1486–1535), German cabalistic philosopher, born at Cologne. He was sent by Maximilian I on a secret mission to Paris (1506), and in 1509 he was invited to teach theology at Dôle. His lectures on Reuchlin's *De Verbo Mirifico* drew on him the bitter hatred of the monks, and he was obliged to resume a diplomatic career. He was sent, in 1510, by Maximilian to London, where he was Colet's guest. In 1511 he was with the army in Italy; in 1515 he lectured at Pavia, and was made doctor both of law and medicine. In 1518 he became town orator at Metz; but in 1520 he was back in Cologne, having roused the hostility of the Inquisition by his defence of a witch. Dominicans and ecclesiastical authorities persecuted him, so that he went to Fribourg in Switzerland, where he started a medical practice. In 1524 he removed to Lyons, as physician to the queen mother of France; but here his character of occult philosopher, of semi-Lutheran even, soon furnished pretexts for neglect. He could get no salary; and at last, in 1528, he departed to Antwerp, where he was appointed historiographer to Charles V. He then began to publish his works. *De Occulta Philosophia* (1531–33), procured him the title of magician, while *De Incertitudine et Vanitate Scientiarum* (1530) displeased both emperor and monks. Once more he could get no salary, and was thrown into gaol for debt. Then he retired to Mechlin, and married a third wife, who proved unfaithful; and then, again forced to flee, he set out on the way to Lyons. He had hardly crossed the French border when he was cast into prison for slandering the queen mother; and though he was soon released, he reached Grenoble only to die (February 18). His complete works appeared at Lyons (2 vols. 1550). See his Life by Henry Morley (2 vols. 1856).

AGRIPPINA. (1) The daughter of M. Vipsanius Agrippa and Julia, daughter of Augustus, married Germanicus, and on his sudden and suspicious death in Asia, carried his ashes with dutiful affection to Rome. The esteem in which she was held by the people made her hateful to Tiberius, and in A.D. 30 he banished her to the island of Pandataria, where she died by voluntary starvation three years later.

(2) Daughter of (1), called **Colonia Agrippina** after her birthplace, Cologne, first married Cnaeus Domitius Ahenobarbus, by whom she had a son, afterwards the Emperor Nero. Her third husband was the Emperor Claudius, though her own uncle. She soon persuaded him to adopt as his successor Nero, to the exclusion of Britannicus, his own son by his former wife, Messalina. She then proceeded to poison all his rivals and enemies, and finally the emperor himself. Her ascendancy proving intolerable, Nero put her to death in A.D. 59.

AGUADO, Alejandro María, *a-gwah'THŌ* (1784–1842), Jewish financier, born in Seville, from 1815 a banker in Paris, who left a fortune of above 60 million francs.

AGUESSEAU, Henri François d', *a-ges-sō* (1668–1751), French jurist, pronounced by Voltaire the most learned magistrate that France ever possessed, was born at Limoges. A steady defender of the rights of the people and of the Gallican Church, he was three times chancellor of France, in 1717–18, 1720–1722, and 1737–50. His works fill 13 vols. 1759–89 (2 vols. 1865). See Lives by Boullée (1849) and Monnier (1864).

AGUILAR, Grace, *a-gee-lahr'*, angl. *a-gwil'ar* (1816–1847), English authoress, was born of Jewish parentage at Hackney, and from 1828 lived mostly in Devonshire. She wrote *The Spirit of Judaism* (1841), and other graceful religious fictions.

AGUILÓ I FUSTER, Marian, *a-gee'lō ee foos-ter'* (1825–97), Spanish writer and philologist, was born in Valencia, and worked as librarian there and at Barcelona. He was a powerful influence in the renaissance of the Catalan language and the poetic tradition of Catalonia. He published *Romancer popular de la terra catalana* (1893), and a dictionary of Catalan was published posthumously.

AGUINALDO, Emilio (1870–1964), Filipino revolutionary, led the rising against Spain in the Philippines (1896–98), and against the United States (1899–1901), but after capture in 1901 took the oath of allegiance to America.

AHAB, son of Omri, king of Israel from about 876 to 853 B.C., married Jezebel, a Sidonian princess, and introduced Phoenician elements into Hebrew life and religion. He conducted a campaign against the Assyrians and fought Benhadad of Damascus with whom he disputed the territory east of Jordan. He was killed in battle *c.* 853 B.C.

AHASUERUS. See XERXES.

AHMED, the name of three sultans of Turkey:

Ahmed I (1589–1617), son of Mohammed III, succeeded in 1603. He waged a losing war with Persia (1602–12).

Ahmed II (1642–95), son of Ibrahim, succeeded in 1691. Disastrous defeat at Slankamen (1691) by the Austrians lost him Hungary.

Ahmed III (1673–1736), son of Mohammed IV, succeeded in 1703, sheltered Charles XII of Sweden after Poltava (1709) thus falling foul of Peter the Great with whom he waged a successful war terminated by the Peace of the Pruth (1711). He successfully fought the Venetians (1715), but soon after was defeated by the Austrians, losing his territories around the Danube. He was deposed by the Janissaries and died in prison.

AHMED ARABI, or Arabi Pasha, *a-rah'bee* (*c.* 1840–1911), Egyptian rebel leader, was defeated at Tel-el-Kebir (1882), taken prisoner, and condemned to death, but instead was banished to Ceylon and pardoned in 1901.

AHMED SHAH (*c.* 1724–73), the first monarch of Afghanistan, served in the bodyguard of Nadir Shah (q.v.), and on his assassination, retired to Afghanistan, whose tribes he induced to revolt and to choose him sovereign. His wealth and military talents made him popular, and he extended his conquests from Khorasan to Sirhind, and from the Oxus to the Indian Sea. See Life by Ganda Singh (1959).

AHO JUHANI, pseud. of **Juhani Brofeldt** (1861–1921), Finnish writer, was born at Lapinlahti and studied at Helsinki University. He lived for some time in Paris, and was greatly influenced by Daudet and de Maupassant. His first writings were in verse, but his greatest achievements were short stories of country life, such as *When Father Bought a Lamp,* and *The Railway.* His novels include *The Parson's Daughter* (1885), *The Parson's Wife* (1893), *Conscience* (1914), *Do You Remember?* (1920). He also wrote a historical novel, *Panu,* in 1898.

AIDAN, St (d. 651), the founder of the Northumbrian Church, was sent from Iona in 635, in answer to King Oswald's summons to become Bishop of Northumbria. He established himself on Lindisfarne, and making missionary journeys to the mainland, achieved a great work, in spite of the ravages of Penda, the heathen ruler of Mercia. He died at Bamburgh.

AÏDÉ, Hamilton, *ah-ee-day* (1830–1906), English poet and novelist, was born at Paris, the son of an Armenian and of a daughter of Admiral Sir George Collier. He studied at Bonn, served in the British army (1845–52), and then settling down in the New Forest, devoted himself to literature. His poems include *Eleonore* (1856), and *Songs without Music* (1882); his novels, *Rita* (1859), *The*

Marstons (1868), and *Passages in the Life of a Lady* (1887).

AIKEN, Conrad Potter (1889–1973), American poet, born at Savannah, made his name with *Earth Triumphant* (1914), *Punch, the Immortal Liar* (1921), and *Senlin* (1925). His *Selected Poems* won the 1930 Pulitzer prize. He has also written short stories and novels. See his autobiographical *Ushant* (1952).

AIKIN, (1) **John** (1747–1822), English author and biographer, father of (2), born at Kibworth. After studying at Edinburgh, London, and Leyden he practised as a physician. A voluminous author, he wrote Lives of Howard, Selden, and Usher; the *General Biography* (10 vols. 1799–1815); and the well-known *Evenings at Home* (6 vols. 1792–1795), written in conjunction with his sister, Anna Letitia Barbauld (q.v.).

(2) **Lucy** (1781–1864), daughter of (1), also a writer, was born at Warrington and died at Hampstead. She wrote *Epistles on Women* (1810); *Memoir of John Aikin, M.D.* (1823); *Memoirs of the Courts of Elizabeth, James I, and Charles I* (6 vols. 1818–33); *Life of Addison* (1843). See her *Memoirs* (1864).

AILLY, Pierre d', or **Petrus de Alliaco,** *ah-yee* (1350–1420), French theologian and Nominalist philosopher, born at Compiègne, became chancellor of the university of Paris, Bishop of Compiègne, cardinal (1411), and papal legate in Germany. At the Council of Constance he headed the reform party, but agreed to the sentence on Huss and Jerome of Prague.

AILRED, or **Ethelred of Rievaulx** (1109–66), English chronicler, born at Hexham, was page to Prince Henry of Scotland, became a monk at Rievaulx abbey, went to convert the Picts, wrote sermons, historical works, and biographies of St Edward and St Ninian.

AIMARD, Gustave, pseud. of Olivier Gloux (1818–83), French novelist, called the French Fenimore Cooper, was born in Paris, and shipping as a cabin boy to America, spent ten years of adventure in Arkansas and Mexico. He travelled also in Spain, Turkey, and the Caucasus; in Paris, served as an officer of the Garde Mobile (1848); organized the Francs-tireurs de la Presse (1870–71). His adventure stories include *La Grande Flibuste* (1860) and *Forêt vierge* (1873).

AINGER, Alfred (1837–1904), English biographer, born in London, master of the Temple from 1894, is best known as the biographer and editor of Lamb and Hood; he wrote also on Crabbe. See *Life and Letters* by E. Sichel (1906).

AINLEY, Henry Hinchliffe (1879–1945), English actor born in Leeds and remembered for his ability, his good looks, his charm, and his mellifluous voice. He started life as a bank clerk, but his appearance as Paolo in *Paolo and Francesca* (1902) placed him at one bound in the forefront of his profession. His wide range of parts included the title role in *Hassan* (1923), and James Fraser in *The First Mrs Fraser* (1929). The latter part of his career was chequered by attacks of illness which ultimately caused his retiral from the stage in 1932.

AINMILLER, or **Ainmüller, Max Emanuel** (1807–70), a Munich stained-glass artist, executed windows for many European cathedrals, including Cologne, Basel, Glasgow, and St Paul's in London.

AINSLIE, Hew (1792–1878), Scottish poet, born in Ayrshire, in 1822 emigrated to America, where he managed breweries. He wrote three or four very fair lyrics, more than a hundred very indifferent ones, and a *Pilgrimage to the Land of Burns* (1822; new ed. 1892).

AINSWORTH, (1) **Robert** (1660–1743), English lexicographer, was born at Woodvale, near Manchester, and died in London. His Latin-English and English-Latin Dictionary was published in 1736.

(2) **William Harrison** (1805–82), English author, was born in Manchester, February 4, and educated at the grammar school. A solicitor's son, in his seventeenth year he was articled to a solicitor; and on his father's death in 1824, went up to London to complete his legal studies. Two years later, however, he married a publisher's daughter, and himself turned publisher for eighteen months. He had contributed some articles to magazines prior to 1822, so that his first-born was not *Sir John Chiverton* (1826), an anonymous novel, praised by Scott, but partly, it seems now, the work of a Mr Aston. His earliest success was *Rookwood* (1834), with its vivid description of Dick Turpin's ride to York. By 1881 he had published no fewer than thirty-nine novels. Several of these appeared originally in *Bentley's Miscellany, Ainsworth's Magazine* (1842–54), and the *New Monthly,* of which he was successively editor; and seven of them were illustrated by Cruikshank—viz., *Rookwood, Jack Sheppard* (1839), *Tower of London* (1840), *Guy Fawkes* (1841), *Miser's Daughter* (1842), *Windsor Castle* (1843), and *St James's* (1844). To these may be added his *Crichton* (1837), *Old St Paul's* (1841), and *Lancashire Witches* (1848), as possessing some intrinsic claim to literary merit. He died at Reigate, January 3, 1882. See Life by Ellis (1910).

AIRD, Thomas (1802–76), minor poet, born at Bowden, Roxburghshire. 'The Devil's Dream' is the best known of his *Poems,* to the fifth edition (1878) of which a Life by J. Wallace is prefixed.

AIRY, Sir George Biddell (1801–92), astronomer royal from 1836 till his retirement in 1881, born at Alnwick, became a fellow of Trinity College, Cambridge (1824), having been senior wrangler the previous year. In 1826 he was appointed Lucasian professor of Mathematics, in 1828 professor of Astronomy. He discovered an inequality in the motions of the Earth and Venus, and determined the mass of the earth, using pendulum readings taken at the top and bottom of a deep mine-shaft. See his Autobiography (1896).

AITKEN, *ay'ken,* (1) **John** (1839–1919), Scottish physicist, was born and died at Falkirk. He is known for his researches on atmospheric dust, dew, cyclones, &c. His *Collected Scientific Papers* were edited by Knott (1923).

(2) **Robert Grant** (1864–1951), American astronomer, born at Jackson, California. He joined Lick Observatory in 1895, and was director 1930–35. His discovery of more than

3000 double stars gained him the gold medal of the Royal Astronomical Society in 1932. He published *Binary Stars* (1918; 2nd ed. 1935), and *New General Catalogue of Double Stars* (1932).

(3) **Robert Ingersoll** (1878–1949), American sculptor, born in San Francisco. He studied in San Francisco, and was well known for his busts of Jefferson, Franklin and others.

AKAHITO, Yamabe no, *ah-ka-hee-tō* (early 8th cent.), Japanese major poet. A minor official at the Imperial Court, Akahito seems to have kept his position largely through his mastery of the *uta*. His impression of snow-capped Mt Fuji is a famous example. He is one of 'the twin stars '—Hitomaro is the other—of the great anthology of classical Japanese poetry known as the *Manyoshu (Collection of a Myriad Leaves)*, translated by J. L. Pierson (1929–49), and Keene's *Anthology of Japanese Literature* (1955).

AKBAR, i.e., 'the great,' properly **Jelal-ed-din-Mohammed** (1542–1605), Mogul emperor of India, was born November 23 at Amarkot during the flight of his father, Humayun, to Persia. Humayun recovered the throne of Delhi in 1555, but died within a year. The young prince at first committed the administration to a regent, Beiram, but in 1560 took the power into his own hands. At this time only a few of the many provinces once subdued by the Mongol invaders were actually subject to the throne of Delhi; in ten or twelve years, Akbar's empire embraced the whole of India north of the Vindhya Mountains. His wisdom, vigour, and humanity are unexampled in the East. He promoted commerce by constructing roads, establishing a uniform system of weights and measures, organizing a vigorous police, and adjusting taxation. For a born Mohammedan, his tolerance was wonderful; and Portuguese missionaries from Goa were sent at his request to give him an account of the Christian faith. He even attempted to promulgate a new religion of his own, an eclectic kind of deism or natural religion. Literature received great encouragement. Abul-Fazl, the able minister of Akbar, has left a valuable history of his reign, entitled *Akbar-nameh*. Akbar died October 13, at Agra, and was buried in a noble mausoleum at Sikandra. See works by Malleson (1890), Noer (trans. 1890), Vincent Smith (1920), Binyon (1932).

À KEMPIS, Thomas. See KEMPIS.

AKENSIDE, Mark, *ay'ken-sīd* (1721–70), English poet and physician, was born at Newcastle, the son of a butcher. He studied theology, but abandoned it for medicine, and practised at Northampton, and later in London. His success as a practitioner was never very great, owing to his haughty and pedantic manner, which Smollett sketches to the life in *Peregrine Pickle* ; but while studying at Leyden he had formed an intimacy with Jeremiah Dyson, and this rich and generous friend allowed him £300 a year. He died in London, having nine years earlier been appointed one of the physicians to the queen. He contributed verses to the *Gentleman's Magazine*, and in 1744, appeared his famous *Pleasures of the Imagination*, a didactic poem begun in his eighteenth year.

AKERS, Benjamin Paul (1825–61), an American sculptor, born near Portland, died at Philadelphia, remembered especially for his *Pearl Diver*.

AKHMATOVA, Anna, *akh-mah'tō-va*, pseud. of **Anna Andreyevna Gorenko** (1888–1966), Russian poet, born in Odessa. The daughter of a naval officer, she married in 1910 **Nicholas Gumilev** (q.v.), himself a writer, who at first considerably influenced her style. Later she developed an impressionist technique. She remained as far as possible neutral to the revolution; but, after a period of silence from the early 'twenties until 1940, her verse (previously acceptable) was banned in 1946 as being ' too remote from socialist reconstruction '. She was ' rehabilitated ' in the 'fifties, and received official tributes on her death. Her works include *Evening* (1912), *The Willow* (1940) and the banned *Requiem* (Munich, 1963), a moving cycle of poems on the Stalin purges, during which her only son was arrested. See *Works* (vol. 1, Munich, 1966).

AKHNATON, or **Amenhotep (Amenophis) IV** (14th cent. B.C.), a king of Egypt of the 18th dynasty, who renounced the old gods and introduced a purified and universalized solar cult.

AKIBA BEN JOSEPH (*c.* 50–135), a very influential Jewish rabbi, who studied under Rabbi Eliezer, and had a great share in redacting the oral law or Mishna. He entered heartily into the revolt of Bar Cochba (q.v.), and, on his overthrow, was put to death with great tortures by the Romans.

AKINS, Zöe, *ay'kins* (1886–1958), American playwright, born in Humansville, Missouri. She trained as an actress in New York, but lacking the necessary ability she turned to writing light comedy and film scripts. In 1935 her dramatization of Edith Wharton's *The Old Maid* won her the Pulitzer prize. The best known of her plays are *Déclassée* (1919), and *Daddy's Gone A-Hunting* (1921).

AKSAKOV, *ak-sah'kof*, (1) **Ivan Sergeyevitch** (1823–86), Russian lyric poet and publicist, born at Nadeshdino, son of (3), best known as the representative of Panslavism.

(2) **Konstantin** (1817–60), Russian historian and philologist, son of (3), shared the slavophile ideas of his brother Ivan (q.v.) and set out in his writings to throw into relief the contrasts between Russia and the rest of Europe.

(3) **Sergei Timofeyevitch** (1791–1859), Russian novelist, father of (1) and (2), was born at Ufa in Orenburg. The son of a wealthy landowner, he held government posts at St Petersburg and Moscow before his meeting with Gogol in 1832 turned him to literature. His house became the centre of a Gogol cult, but Aksakov was temperamentally utterly different from his master. He wrote *The Blizzard* (1834), *A Family Chronicle* (1846–56), *Years of Childhood* (1858). His writing shows his love of country sports and deep feeling for nature.

ALACOQUE, Marguerite Marie, St (1647–90), a French nun at Paray-le-Monial, founder of the devotion to the Sacred Heart. She was canonized in 1920, her feast day being October 17.

ALAIN-FOURNIER, Henri, *a-li foor-nyay* (1886–1914), French writer, born in Sologne, killed at St Rémy in World War I, left a few short stories, *Miracles* (1924), and a modern fairy tale, *Le Grand Meaulnes* (1913). See his *Correspondance* (4 vols. 1926–28), and *Lettres à sa famille* (Paris, 1930).

ALAMÁN, Lucas, *a-la-man'* (1792–1853), Mexican politician and historian, born at Guanajuato. As a deputy in the Spanish Cortes he spoke for Mexican independence, and as foreign secretary under the conservative governments of Bustamante and Santa Anna he negotiated with the Vatican and France to set up a Mexican royal house. He founded the Mexican National Museum.

ALAMANNI, Luigi (1495–1556), an Italian poet, who was born at Florence and died at Amboise a political refugee, having been employed as a diplomat by Francis I. His best work was *La coltivazione* (1564), a didactic poem in the style of Vergil's *Georgics*. See H. Hauvette, *Un Exilé florentin à la cour de France* (Paris, 1903).

ALANBROOKE, Alan Francis Brooke, 1st Viscount, of Brookeborough (1883–1963), British soldier, was born at Bagnères-de-Bigorre, France, and was educated abroad and at the Royal Military Academy, Woolwich. He joined the Royal Field Artillery in 1902 and in World War I he rose to general staff officer. He commanded the 2nd Corps of the B.E.F. in France in 1940 and later became C.-in-C. Home Forces. From 1941 to 1946 he was C.I.G.S. As Churchill's principal strategic adviser he accompanied him to the conferences with Roosevelt and Stalin. He received many honours, including the O.M. and the K.G., and was created baron in 1945, viscount in 1946. See *The Turn of the Tide*, by Sir Arthur Bryant (1957), and *Triumph in the West* (1959), based on the Alanbrooke War Diaries.

ALARCÓN, Pedro Antonio de, *a-lar-kon'*, (1833–91), Spanish author, was born at Guadic. He served with distinction in the African campaign of 1859–60, and became a Radical journalist. At the Restoration in 1874, however, he became a Conservative, and served as minister to Stockholm, and councillor of state. He published a war diary, travel notes and poems, but is best known for his *Sombrero de tres picos*, on which de Falla's ballet was based. His novel *La Prodiga* proving a failure, he abandoned writing for the rest of his life.

ALARCÓN Y MENDOZA, Juan Ruiz de (*c.* 1580–1639), Spanish dramatist, ranked almost as high as Calderón and Lope de Vega, was born of good family in Mexico, and early obtained a post in the council of the Indies at Madrid, where he died. He was neglected for generations save by plagiarists, but restored to his real rank by modern critics. His heroic tragedies are almost as brilliant as his character comedies. His *La verdad sospechosa* was the model for Corneille's *Le Menteur*.

ALARIC, name of two kings of the Visigoths.
Alaric I (*c.* 370–410), appears in A.D. 394 as leader of the Gothic auxiliaries of Theodosius.

Next year, however, he invaded and ravaged Thrace, Macedon, Thessaly, and Illyria, but was driven out of the Peloponnesus by Stilicho and the troops of the western empire. In 396 he was made governor of Illyria by the eastern emperor Arcadius; in 400 he invaded Upper Italy, but was met and defeated by Stilicho at Pollentia on the Tanarus (402), whereupon he retired to Illyria. Through Stilicho's mediation he concluded a treaty with Honorius, agreeing to join in attacking Arcadius. The projected expedition did not take place, but when Honorius failed to pay the promised subsidy, Alaric invested Rome. Promises again made were again broken, and a second time he besieged Rome. Enraged by further breach of covenant, he advanced on Rome a third time (410), and his troops pillaged the city for six days, Alaric, who was an Arian Christian like his people, forbidding his soldiers to dishonour women or destroy religious buildings. When Alaric quitted Rome, it was only to prosecute the conquest of Sicily; and he seemed likely to become master of all Italy, when he died at Cosenza. Legend tells that, to hide his remains from the Romans, they were deposited in the bed of the river Busento, and that the captives who had been employed in the work were put to death.

Alaric II (ruled 484–507), eighth king of the Visigoths, reigned over Gaul south of the Loire, and most of Spain. An Arian, he was attacked, completely routed near Poitiers, and slain by the orthodox Clovis, king of the Franks.

ALAS, Leopoldo, pseud. **Clarín** (1852–1901), Spanish author, born at Zamora, was professor of Law at Oviedo, journalist and critic. He published short stories (*Cuentos morales*, 1896), a drama, *Teresa*, and the novel *La Regenta*, for which he is most famous. He also wrote treatises on law and economics. His writing is objective, sometimes cold, but always powerful and sincere.

ALASCO, John. See LASCO.

ALAVA, Don Miguel Ricardo de (1771–1843), Spanish general and statesman, served under Wellington, for a time led the anti-absolutist party in the Cortes, and alternately held office or was an exile in England or Belgium.

ALBA. See ALVA.

ALBAN, St, a Roman soldier, the proto-martyr of Britain, said to have been stoned to death at Redbourn or St Albans about 305 for sheltering a Christian priest known (by mistranslation) as Amphibalus. His feast day is June 22.

ALBANI, *al-bah'nee,* (1) a Roman family, many members of which, from the accession of Giovanni Francesco Albani as Clement XI to the papal throne in 1700, filled high positions in the church. It died out in 1852. It was Cardinal Alessandro Albani (1692–1779) who formed the famous art collection in the Villa Albani.

(2) **Dame Emma,** stage-name of **Marie Louise Emma Cécile Lajeunesse** (1852–1930), Canadian singer, born at Chambly, Quebec, and trained in music by her father, at twelve made her début at Albany, whence she assumed the professional name of 'Albani'. She studied at Paris and Milan, and in 1870

sang at Messina with a success that the leading cities of Europe and America confirmed. See her *Forty Years of Song* (1911).

(3) **Francesco** (1578–1660), a painter of the Bolognese school, studied, along with Guido Reni, first under Calvaert, and afterwards under Ludovico Caracci. He painted about forty-five altarpieces; but his bent inclined him more to mythological or pastoral subjects.

ALBANIE, Count d', the title assumed successively by two brothers, ' John Sobieski Stolberg Stuart ' (1795–1872) and ' Charles Edward Stuart ' (1799–1880), who were certainly the sons of Lieutenant Thomas Allen, R.N., and who claimed that he was the son of Prince Charles Edward. For their sojourn in the Highlands, their publications, and the younger brother's descendants, see H. Beveridge, *The Sobieski Stuarts* (1909).

ALBANY, (1) **Duke of,** the title conferred in 1398 upon Robert (1340?–1420), brother of Robert III (q.v.) of Scotland, who was succeeded by his son Murdoch (d. 1425). See JAMES I. For John (1481–1536), a grandson of James II, see JAMES V. Queen Victoria made her youngest son Leopold (1853–84) Duke of Albany in 1881. His son Leopold (b. 1884) Duke of Saxe-Coburg (1905–18) forfeited his British titles in 1917.

(2) **Louisa, Countess of** (1752–1824), was born at Mons, the daughter of Prince Gustav Adolf of Stolberg, who fell at Leuthen (1757). In 1772 she married Prince Charles Edward, no longer 'bonny', and no longer 'young', but a selfish worn-out sot. No children came of the marriage; and in 1780, to escape from ill-usage, she sought refuge in a nunnery. Four years later she obtained a formal separation; and, both before and after her husband's death (1788), she lived with the poet Alfieri (q.v.), and on his death (1803), with a French painter, Fabre. See works by Von Reumont (2 vols., Berl. 1860), Vernon Lee (1884) and M. Crosland (1963).

ALBEE, Edward (1928–   ), U.S. dramatist, educated at Laurenceville and Choate schools in Washington, and at Columbia Univ. His major works include *The Zoo Story* (1958), a one-act duologue on the lack of communication in modern society, *The American Dream* (1960) and *Who's Afraid of Virginia Woolf?* (1962, filmed 1966), a searing analysis of a failing marriage.

ALBEMARLE, the English form of Aumale, in Normandy, whose first earl, Odo, was the Conqueror's brother-in-law. The title reverted by marriage to the royal family in 1269, and was conferred in 1419 on Richard Beauchamp, Earl of Warwick, and in 1660 (a dukedom) on his *soi-disant* descendant, General Monk (q.v.). It expired with his son in 1688; and in 1696 Arnold Joost van Keppel (1669–1718), a devoted follower of William III, was made Earl of Albemarle. Among his descendants have been William, second earl (1732–54), soldier and diplomatist; George, third earl (1724–72), who captured Havana; and George Thomas Keppel, sixth earl (1799–1891), who fought at Waterloo, and rose to be a general in 1874. Of several works by him, the most interesting is *Fifty Years of My Life* (1876).

ALBÉNIZ, Isaac, *al-bay'neeth* (1860–1909), born at Camprodón, Catalonia, studied under Liszt, and became a brilliant pianist and prolific composer, especially of picturesque works for the piano based on Spanish folk music. He also wrote several operas.

ALBERONI, Giulio (1664–1752), cardinal and statesman, was born at Firenzuola, near Piacenza, May 21. The son of a poor vinedresser, he accompanied the Duc de Vendôme, as secretary, to France and Spain. In 1713 the Duke of Parma employed him as his agent in Madrid; and quickly gaining the favour of Philip V, in 1714 he became prime minister of Spain, and in 1717 was made a cardinal. His internal administration was liberal and wise, and he did much to develop the resources of Spain, while he remodelled the army and fleet, and increased the foreign commerce. To gratify the queen, he suddenly invaded Sardinia, in violation of the Peace of Utrecht —an unexpected audacity that made England, France, Austria, and Holland form, in 1719, the ' Quadruple Alliance '. But Alberoni was not dismayed, even when the Spanish fleet in the Mediterranean was destroyed by an English one. He patronised the Pretender to annoy England, and the French Protestants to annoy Louis. He sought to unite Peter of Russia and Charles XII with him, to plunge Austria into a war with the Turks, to stir up an insurrection in Hungary, and to bring about the downfall of the Regent in France. But Philip lost courage, and concluded a treaty, its chief condition the dismissal of the cardinal. He was ordered to leave Spain without delay, and fled to a monastery at Bologna. On the death of the pope in 1721, he repaired to Rome, and took part in the election of Innocent XIII, who, like his two successors, befriended the great exile. He soon retired to Piacenza, where he died. See Italian Life by Bersani (1862).

ALBERT (1819–61), **Prince Consort of England,** was born at the Schloss Rosenau, near Coburg, on August 28, 1819, the youngest son of the Duke of Saxe-Coburg-Gotha, by his marriage with Louisa, daughter of the Duke of Saxe-Gotha-Altenburg. Studious and preternaturally earnest, the Prince's studies in Brussels and Bonn did not entirely eradicate the provincialism of his early life; while it is questionable if he ever fully apprehended the unabashed opportunism underlying the high principles of his political mentor, Baron Stockmar. He was a willing party to Leopold of Belgium's plan for his marriage to an infatuated Queen Victoria, whom he wed in the February of 1840. He was made Consort in 1842 and Prince Consort in 1857. Ministerial distrust and public misgiving combined to obstruct his interference in politics, although his counsel, percolating through to the Cabinet, was—save on the question of Germany's future status in Europe—invariably found to be temperate and often far-sighted. The Prince developed a congenial sphere of self-expression in the encouragement of the arts and in the promotion of social and industrial reforms. It was largely due to him that the Great Exhibition of 1851 took practical form. He died at Windsor Castle on December 14. See Life by

Sir Theodore Martin (5 vols. 1875–80), Vitzhum's *Reminiscences* (trans. 1887), the *Panmure Papers* (2 vols.), and works by Chancellor Bolitho (1932), Fulford (1949) and Eyck (1959).

ALBERT, Ger. **Albrecht**, *al'breкнt*, the name of 5 Dukes of Austria of whom the following became kings of Germany:

Albert I (*c.* 1250–1308), was crowned German king at Aix-la-Chapelle in 1298. He ruled with vigour and success, and reduced his unruly nobles to obedience; but was murdered while crossing the Reuss in a boat, by his own nephew, John, whose claim to the duchy of Swabia he had refused.

Albert II (1397–1439), succeeded as Duke in 1404, became King of Hungary and Bohemia in 1438, and died of dysentery while fighting the Turks. He was the first of the Hapsburg dynasty.

ALBERT, Ger. **Albrecht**, called the **Pious** (1559–1621), Archduke of Austria, was the third son of the Emperor Maximilian II. Brought up at the Spanish court, in 1577 he was made cardinal, in 1584 Archbishop of Toledo, and during 1594–96 was viceroy of Portugal. He was next appointed Stadtholder of the Netherlands, where he displayed a moderation unwonted among the proud proconsuls of Spain. He relinquished his orders, and in 1598 married the infanta Isabella. In 1599 he was defeated by Maurice of Nassau, and in 1609 made a twelve years' truce with him.

ALBERT, Ger. **Albrecht** (1817–95), Archduke of Austria, son of the Archduke Charles, fought under Radetzky in 1849, and as fieldmarshal commanded in Italy at Custozza, &c., in 1866. He reorganized the Austrian army, and wrote on military subjects. See Life by C. von Duncker (Vienna, 1897).

ALBERT I (1875–1934), King of the Belgians, succeeded his uncle, Leopold II, in 1909. His bearing when his kingdom was in German hands (1914–18) and in subsequent restoration was much admired. He was killed by a fall in the Ardennes.

ALBERT, called the **Bear** (1100–70), Count of Ballenstädt from 1123, and founder of the House of Ascania which ruled in Brandenburg for two hundred years. In 1134, in return for service in Italy, Albert was invested by the Emperor with extensive lands between the Elbe and the Oder. Brandenburg itself was left to Albert by a treaty made in 1140 with the Count Pribislav.

ALBERT, called **Alcibiades** (1522–57), Margrave of Brandenburg, Prince of Kulmbach-Bayreuth, was born, a Hohenzollern, at Ansbach. He was a restless military adventurer with no constant allegiance. In 1543, although a Protestant, he allied himself to Charles V against France, but by the Treaty of Chambord in 1552 conspired with the French to overthrow the Emperor. Defeated in a territorial claim, in 1554 he fled to France, where he died.

ALBERT III, called **Achilles** (1414–86), Elector of Brandenburg from 1470–86, was third son of Frederick I. In 1440 he inherited Ansbach from his father and in 1470 succeeded his brother, who had abdicated. His most important legacy to Brandenburg was

the *Dispositio Achillea* of 1473, which established the rule of primogeniture, so that when he died Brandenburg stayed undivided.

ALBERT (1490–1568), first Duke of Prussia, last grand master of the Teutonic Order, was a younger son of the Margrave of Ansbach. Elected grand master in 1511, he embraced the Reformation, and, by Luther's advice, declared himself secular Duke of Prussia.

ALBERT, called the **Bold** (1443–1500), Duke of Saxony. The son of Frederick the Gentle, he was joint ruler with his brother Ernest from 1464 until 1485 when, by the Treaty of Leipzig, they divided their inheritance between them. The two branches of the Wettin family then became known as the Albertine and Ernestine lines.

ALBERT, *al-bayr*, (1) **Eugen Francis Charles d'** (1864–1932), pianist and composer, born at Glasgow, the son of a French musician, studied at London and abroad, composed operas (*Tiefland*, &c.), a suite, a symphony, many songs, and much music for the piano.

(2) *al'bert*, **Heinrich** (1604–51), German composer, born at Lobenstein, did much to develop the *lied* as we know it, composed many airs, songs, chorals, and hymn tunes. He studied at Leipzig, and became organist in Königsberg, where he died.

ALBERTI, (1) **Domenico** (*c.* 1710–40), Italian composer, born in Venice. His work is almost entirely forgotten, but he is remembered as the inventor of the ' Alberti Bass ', common in 18th-century keyboard music, in which accompanying chords are split up into figurations based upon each chord's lowest note.

(2) **Leon Battista** (1404–72), Italian architect, born at Genoa, one of the most brilliant figures of the Renaissance, worked in Florence from 1428 and died at Rome. Influenced by Vitruvius, he wrote *De Re Aedificatoria* (10 vols. 1485), which stimulated interest in antique Roman architecture, and his own designs, which include the churches of S. Francesco at Rimini and S. Maria Novella at Florence, are among the best examples of the pure classical style. He was skilled also as musician, painter, poet, and philosopher. See study by W. Flemming (1916) and A. Stokes, *Art and Science* (1949).

ALBERTUS MAGNUS, St, Count of Bollstädt (*c.*1200–1280), the *Doctor Universalis*, canonized in 1931, was born at Lauingen, studied at Padua, and, entering the newly-founded Dominican order, taught in the schools of Hildesheim, Ratisbon, and Cologne, where Thomas Aquinas was his pupil. In 1245–54 he lectured at Paris, in 1254 became provincial of the Dominicans in Germany, and in 1260 was named Bishop of Ratisbon. But in 1262 he retired to his convent at Cologne to devote himself to literary pursuits, and there he died in 1280. Of his works (1651 : 1890–99) the most notable are the *Summa Theologiae* and the *Summa de Creaturis*. Albertus excelled all his contemporaries in the wideness of his learning, and in legend appears as a magician. He was to the best of his ability a faithful follower of Aristotle as presented by Jewish, Arabian, and western commentators, and did more than any one to bring about that union of theology and Aristotelianism which is the basis of scholasticism. See works by Sighart (1857; trans. 1876), Wilms (1929; trans. 1933) and S. M. Albert (1948).

ALBIKER, Karl, *al'bi-ker* (1878–1961), German sculptor, born at Uhlingen. He studied at Karlsruhe, and his work shows the influence of Rodin and classical sculpture.

ALBINONI, Tommaso (1674–1745), Italian composer, born at Venice, wrote 48 operas, and a number of concertos which have been revived in recent times.

ALBOIN (ruled 561–574), king of the Lombards (in Pannonia), fought against the Ostrogoths, and slew Kunimond, king of the Gepidae, with his own hand (566), marrying his daughter Rosamond. In 568 he invaded Italy, subdued it to the Tiber, and fixed his residence at Pavia. He was a just ruler; but at a feast at Verona he made his queen drink from her father's skull, and she incited her paramour to murder him (574).

ALBONI, Marietta (1826–94), Italian contralto opera singer, was born at Città di Castello in Umbria, and died near Châlons.

ALBORNOZ, Gil Alvarez Carillo (1300–67), Spanish prelate, born at Cuenca, became Archbishop of Toledo, but fought against the Moors, and was dubbed a knight. For denouncing Peter the Cruel, he had to flee to Pope Clement VI at Avignon, who made him a cardinal; and he died at Viterbo, papal legate to Bologna.

ALBRECHT. See ALBERT.

ALBRECHTSBERGER, Johann Georg *al'breKHts-* (1736–1809), Austrian composer and writer on musical theory, born at Klosterneuburg, was court organist at Vienna. Hummel and Beethoven were his pupils.

ALBRET, Jeanne d'. See JEANNE.

ALBUMAZAR, properly **Abu-Mashar,** *al-byoo-maz'ér* (805–885), Arab astronomer, was born at Balkh. He spent much of his life in Baghdad, and died at Wasid. Despite his fantastic theories as to the beginning and end of the world, he did valuable work on the nature of tides. He was the subject of *L'Astrologo,* a play revived by Dryden in 1748 under the title *Albumazar.*

ALBUQUERQUE, Affonso d', *al-boo-ker'kay* (1453–1515), called 'the Great', Portuguese viceroy of the Indies, was born near Lisbon. Appointed viceroy of the new possessions in India, he landed on the Malabar coast in 1503, and conquered Goa, which he made the seat of the Portuguese government, besides Ceylon, the Sunda Isles, Malacca, and (in 1515) the island of Ormuz. He was active, far-seeing, wise, humane, and equitable; but through his enemies at court he was superseded in his office—a blow that gave a severe shock to his shattered health. A few days after, he died at sea near Goa. His *Commentaries* were translated by Birch for the Hakluyt Soc. (4 vols. 1875–84). See Lives by Morse Stephens (1891), Prestage (1929).

ALBUZJANI, or **Abul-Wafa** (940–998), Persian mathematician, a pioneer of trigonometry.

ALCAEUS, one of the greatest Greek lyric poets, flourished in Mitylene about 600 B.C. He was the inventor of Alcaic verse, which Horace, the best of his imitators, transplanted into the Latin language. Of the ten books of Alcaeus's odes, only fragments remain. See Page, *Sappho and Alcaeus* (1955).

ALCAMENES, *al-kam'en-eez* (fl. 420 B.C.), Greek sculptor, the pupil and rival of Phidias (q.v.). A Roman copy of his *Aphrodite* is in the Louvre. See a book by Sir C. Walston.

ALCESTER, Frederick Beauchamp Paget Seymour, 1st Baron, *awl'stér* (1821–95), British admiral, was educated at Eton, entered the navy in 1834, served in Burma, in the Baltic against Russia, and in New Zealand, and received his peerage for the bombardment of Alexandria in 1882.

ALCIBIADES, *al-si-bī'a-deez* (c. 450 B.C.– 404 B.C.), Athenian statesman, born at Athens, lost his father, Clinias, in the battle of Coronea (447), and so was brought up in the house of his kinsman Pericles. Socrates gained great influence over him, but was unable to restrain his love of magnificence and dissipation, especially after his marriage to the wealthy Hipparete. He first bore arms in the expedition against Potidaea (432 B.C.), but took no part in political matters till after the death of the demagogue Cleon, when, jealous of Nicias, he persuaded the Athenians to ally themselves with Argos, Elis, and Mantinea (420) against Sparta. It was at his suggestion that, in 415, they engaged in the Sicilian expedition, of which he was a commander. But while preparations were making, one night all the statues of Hermes in Athens were mutilated. Alcibiades' enemies threw on him the blame of this sacrilege, and after he had set sail, he was recalled to stand his trial. Passing to Lacedaemon, and conforming to Spartan manners, he induced the Lacedaemonians to send assistance to Syracuse, to form an alliance with Persia, and to encourage Ionia and the islands, whither he now went, to revolt against Athens. But the not unjust suspicions of Agis and other Spartans led him to flee to Tissaphernes, the Persian satrap, to whom he soon became indispensable. And now he began to plot the overthrow of democracy in Athens, and secured Persian support for the oligarchical council established in 411, which did not, however, recall him. Thereupon he took the command of the Athenian (democratic) army at Samos, and during the next four years defeated the Spartans at Cynossema, Abydos, and Cyzicus, recovered Chalcedon and Byzantium, and restored to the Athenians the dominion of the sea. He then returned home (407) and was enthusiastically received, but, failing in an expedition to Asia, he was superseded (406) and went into exile in the Thracian Chersonesus. Emerging after the great Spartan victory at Aegospotami, he made for the Persian court, but by procurement of the Spartans, who knew he was seeking Persian help for the Athenians against them, his house was fired and he was assassinated (404). See Lives by E. F. Benson (1928) and J. Hatzfeld (1940).

ALCIPHRON (fl. A.D. 180), Greek writer of 118 imaginary letters from ordinary people (farmers, fishermen, &c.) affording glimpses into everyday life in the 4th century B.C. See translation by Wright (1923).

ALCMAEON, *alk-mee'on* (fl. 520 B.C.), Greek

physician and philosopher of Croton, southern Italy, true discoverer of the Eustachian tubes and pioneer of embryology, held that health was a condition in which opposite sensible properties cancelled each other out. He recognized the importance of experiment and formulated a medical theory, from which an empirical theory of knowledge was derived. Burnet described him as ' the founder of empirical psychology '. See Burnet, *Early Greek Philosophy* (4th. ed. 1952).

ALCMAN (fl. 620 B.C.), Greek poet, was born at Sardis, in Lydia, but lived, first as a slave, and afterwards as a freedman, in Sparta. The first to write erotic poetry, he composed in the Doric dialect *Parthenia*, or songs sung by choruses of virgins, bridal hymns, and verses in praise of love and wine. Of his scanty fragments, which are given in Bergk's *Poetae Lyrici*, the most important is a *Parthenion*, discovered on an Egyptian papyrus at Paris in 1855.

ALCOCK, (1) **Sir John William** (1892–1919; kt. 1919), English airman, born at Manchester, on June 14, 1919, with Arthur Whitten Brown, first flew the Atlantic (Newfoundland to Ireland) in a Vickers-Vimy machine. He died of injuries received in an aeroplane accident. See a book by G. Wallace (1955).

(2) **Sir Rutherford** (1809–97), British diplomat, born in London, studied medicine there at King's College, and was consul and British minister in China and Japan. He wrote *The Capital of the Tycoon* (1863), *Art in Japan* (1878), &c.

ALCOTT, (1) **Amos Bronson** (1799–1888), American educationist, father of (2), born near Wolcott, Conn., having failed to make a living as a pedlar, started a school run on ' advanced ' lines with no more success, then established a vegetarian co-operative farming community which also ran at a loss. His ideas on education, however, were brilliant and ahead of his time, and in 1859 he became superintendent of the Concord schools. An ardent transcendentalist, he established the Concord School of Philosophy and Literature in 1879. See Life by Shepard (1938).

(2) **Louisa May** (1832–88), American children's writer, daughter of (1), was born at Germantown, Philadelphia, and died at Concord. Her *Little Women* (1868–69), *Old-fashioned Girl* (1870), *Little Men* (1871) and *Jo's Boys* (1886), have charmed generations of children and are firmly established among the classics. See her *Life, Letters, and Journals*, ed. Cheney (1889) and Life by K. Antony (1938).

ALCOVER, Joan, *al-ko-ver'* (1854–1926), Spanish poet, was born and died at Palma, Majorca. Although his first writings were in the Castilian language, he is chiefly known as a poet in Catalan. He presided over a literary *salon* in Majorca, where he was known as a precise literary critic and brilliant talker. His poetry reflects the tragedy of his private life (he lost his wife and four children in rapid succession) and a deep feeling for his native landscape. He published *Poesias* (1887), *Metereos* (1901), *Poèmes Biblics* (1919).

ALCUIN, originally **Ealhwine,** or **Albinus** (735–804), the adviser of Charlemagne, was born at York and educated at the cloister

school, of which in 778 he became master. In 781, returning from Rome, he met Charlemagne at Parma, and on his invitation attached himself to the court at Aix-la-Chapelle. Here he devoted himself first to the education of the royal family itself, and through his influence the court became a school of culture for the hitherto almost barbarous Frankish empire. In 796 he settled at Tours as abbot; and the school here soon became one of the most important in the empire. Till his death he still corresponded constantly with Charlemagne. His works comprise poems; works on grammar, rhetoric, and dialectics; theological and ethical treatises; lives of several saints; and over two hundred letters. See monographs by Werner (1881), West (1892), Gaskoin (1904), Wilmot-Buxton (1922), and Duckett (1951).

ALDHELM, or **Ealdhelm, St** (c. 640–709), educated at Malmesbury and Canterbury, became Abbot of Malmesbury about 675, and first Bishop of Sherborne in 705. A skilled architect, he built a little church still standing (some say) at Bradford-on-Avon; a great scholar, he wrote Latin treatises, letters, and verses, besides English poems that have perished. See Life by G. F. Browne (1903), and his works in Giles's *Patres Eccles. Angl.* (1844).

ALDINGTON, Richard, *awld'-* (1892–1962), English poet, novelist, editor, and biographer, born in Hampshire. He was educated at London University, and, himself an Imagist, in 1913 became editor of *Egoist*, the periodical of the Imagist school. The first World War, in which he served, left him broken in health and with a great deal of resentment, seen especially in his novel, *Death of a Hero* (1929). As well as other novels, he published several volumes of poetry, including *A Fool i' the Forest* (1925) and *A Dream in the Luxembourg* (1930). At the beginning of World War II he went to America, where he published his *Poetry of the English-Speaking World* (1941) and many biographies, including *Wellington* (1946; awarded James Tait Black memorial prize), a study of D. H. Lawrence (1950), the controversial *Lawrence of Arabia* (1955), and a study of Robert Louis Stevenson (1957). He married Hilda Doolittle (q.v.), also a poet, in 1913, and they were divorced in 1937. See his autobiographical *Life for Life's Sake* (1940).

ALDOBRANDINI, a noble Florentine family: (1) **Cinzio** (1551–1610), cardinal and art patron, owner of the famous antique Roman frescoes named after him.

(2) **Ippolito** (1536–1621), became Pope Clement VIII (q.v.).

(3) **Silvestro** (1499–1588), law teacher, rebelled against the Medici and opposed Charles V.

ALDRED, or **Ealdred,** or **Alred** (d. 1069), became Abbot of Tavistock (1027), Bishop of Worcester (1044), and Archbishop of York (1060). He undertook several diplomatic missions to the Continent, and was the first English bishop to visit Jerusalem (1058). It has been alleged that he crowned Harold in 1066; he certainly crowned William the Conqueror, and proved a faithful servant to the Norman king. He was active and courageous, but ambitious, greedy, and self-seeking. Aldred died at York.

ALDRICH, (1) **Henry** (1647–1710), English cleric, born at Westminster, passed in 1662 from Westminster School to Christ Church, Oxford, of which he became a canon in 1682, and dean in 1689. He designed the Peckwater Quadrangle, and wrote the well-known catch, ' Hark, the bonny Christ Church Bells '; but he is less remembered as architect or composer, or even as an inveterate smoker, than as the author of the *Artis Logicae Compendium* (1691).

(2) **Thomas Bailey** (1836–1907), American poet and novelist, born at Portsmouth, N.H., was from 1881 to 1890 editor of the *Atlantic Monthly. The Story of a Bad Boy* (1870) was his most successful novel.

ALDROVANDI, Ulisse (1522–1605), Italian naturalist, was born at Bologna, and educated there and at Padua. Imprisoned at Rome in 1549 as a heretic, he graduated in medicine at the university of his native city (1553), occupied successively its chairs of Botany and Natural History, and established its Botanical Garden in 1567. All his studies and collections were made subservient to his great work on birds, insects, and mollusca (1599–1642).

ALDUS MANUTIUS, or Aldo Manucci or Manuzio (1450–1515), Venetian printer, born at Bassiano, after whom are named the Aldine editions of the Greek and Roman classics and of the great Italian writers that for about a hundred years were printed at Venice by himself and his successors (his son, **Paolo Manuzio,** 1512–74; and *his* son, **Aldus** the younger, 1547–97). He was the first to print Greek books. He had beautiful founts of Greek type and Latin type made, and first used italics on a large scale. In all 908 works were issued, of which the rarest and most valuable are those from 1490 to 1497, the *Virgil* of 1501, and the *Rhetores Graeci.* See Horatio F. Brown's *The Venetian Printing-Press* (1891), M. Ferrigni, *Aldo Manuzio* (Milan 1925).

ALEANDER, Hieronymus (1480–1542), Italian cardinal, born at Motta, rector of Paris University and later Vatican librarian, but chiefly remembered as an opponent of Luther.

ALEARDI, Aleardo, Count (1812–78), Italian poet, who was born and died at Verona, was popular in his time as a writer of patriotic lyrics. See B. Croce, *La lettera della nuova Italia* (1940).

ALECSANDRI. See ALEXANDRI.

ALEKHINE, Alexander (1892–1946), chess champion of the world for many years, was born in Russia, but became a French citizen.

ALEMÁN, Mateo (1547–1610 or 1620), a Spanish novelist, was born at Seville, and died in Mexico. His great work is *Guzmán de Alfarache* (1599).

ALEMBERT, Jean le Rond D', *a-lā-bayr* (1717–1783), French philosopher and mathematician born in Paris, November 16, was found the day after his birth near the church of St Jean le Rond, whence his name—the surname he himself added long after. He was the illegitimate son of Madame de Tencin and the Chevalier Destouches, and was brought up by the wife of a poor glazier; but his father secured him 1200 francs a year. At the Collège Mazarin the boy showed his lifelong passion for mathematics. On leaving college, he returned to his kind foster-mother, and pursued his favourite studies for thirty years, broken only by two ineffectual attempts to earn a living by law and medicine. In 1741 he was admitted to the Academy of Sciences; in 1743 appeared his epoch-making *Traité de dynamique.* Later works were *Le Cause générale des vents* (1747); *La Précession des équinoxes* (1749); and *Différents Points importants du système du monde* (1754). Frederick the Great offered him the presidency of the Academy of Berlin in 1752, but he declined to leave France, while accepting a pension of 1200 francs; the French king granted him a similar sum. In 1762 Catharine II of Russia invited him, but in vain, to undertake the education of her son. D'Alembert was tenderly attached to Mademoiselle L'Espinasse (q.v.), with whom he lived in platonic affection (1765–76), and whose death was a crushing blow to him. His *Opuscules mathématiques* (8 vols. 1761–80) contain an immense number of memoirs; his *Oeuvres littéraires* were edited by Bidot (5 vols. 1821), and his *Oeuvres et correspondances inédites* by C. Henry (1887). For Diderot's great *Encyclopédie* he wrote the famous *Discours préliminaire,* a noble tribute to literature and philosophy. Besides numerous articles in the *Encyclopédie* (the mathematical portion of which he edited), he published books on philosophy, literary criticism, the theory of music, and a treatise *Sur la destruction des Jésuites* (1765). He became secretary to the Academy in 1772, and wrote lives of all the members deceased since 1700. See Life by Bertrand (Par. 1889).

ALENÇON, *a-lā-sŏ,* title of a ducal family, a branch of the house of Valois, representatives of which fell at Crecy and Agincourt, and held high command at Pavia. Subsequently the title was given to a brother of Charles IX, who fought against the Huguenots, to the grandson of Louis XIV, to a brother of Louis XIV, and to a grandson of Louis-Philippe.

ALESIUS, Alexander (1500–65), Scottish reformer, was born in Edinburgh, April 23, studied at St Andrews, and became a canon there. Won over to the Reformation, he had to flee to the Continent (1532), and, settling at Wittenberg, signed the Augsburg Confession, and gained the friendship of Melanchthon. In 1535 he came over to England, was well received by Cranmer and Cromwell, and lectured for a time on theology at Cambridge; but the persecuting ' Six Articles ' compelled him to return to Germany. He was successively appointed to a theological chair in the universities of Frankfurt-on-the-Oder and Leipzig, where he died March 17, 1565.

ALESSI, Galeazzo (1512–72), Italian architect, born at Perugia. After studying ancient architecture, he gained a European reputation by his designs for palaces and churches at Genoa and elsewhere. He was a pupil of Caporali and a friend of Michelangelo. See Rossi's *Di Galeazzo Alessi memorie* (1873).

ALEXANDER. The name of three kings of Scotland.

Alexander I (*c.* 1078–1124), the fourth son of Malcolm Canmore, in 1107 succeeded his brother, Edgar, but only to that part of the kingdom north of the Firths of Forth and Clyde (see DAVID I). He married Sibylla, a natural daughter of Henry I of England; initiated a diocesan episcopate; and about 1115 had to quell an insurrection of the northern clans.

Alexander II (1198–1249), born at Haddington, succeeded his father, William the Lion, in 1214. He early displayed that wisdom and strength of character, in virtue of which he holds so high a place in history among Scottish kings. His entering into a league with the English barons against King John drew down upon him and his kingdom the papal excommunication; but two years later the ban was removed, and the liberties of the Scottish Church were even confirmed. On Henry III's accession to the English throne, Alexander brought the feuds of the two nations to a temporary close by a treaty of peace (1217), in accordance with which he married Henry's eldest sister, the Princess Joan (1221). The alliance thus established was broken after her death without issue (1238), and the second marriage of Alexander with the daughter of a noble of France. In 1244 Henry marched against Scotland, to compel Alexander's homage; but a peace was concluded without an appeal to arms. While engaged in an expedition to wrest the Hebrides from Norway, Alexander died of fever on Kerrera, near Oban.

Alexander III (1241–86), in 1249 succeeded his father, Alexander II, and in 1251 married the Princess Margaret (1240–75), eldest daughter of Henry III of England. Very shortly after he had come of age, his energies were summoned to defend his kingdom against the formidable invasion of Haco, king of Norway (1263), whose utter rout at Largs secured to Alexander the allegiance both of the Hebrides and of the Isle of Man. The alliance between Scotland and Norway was strengthened in 1282 by King Eric's marriage to Alexander's only daughter, Margaret (1261–83); the untimely death of their infant daughter, Margaret, commonly designated the Maid of Norway, on her way to take possession of her throne, was the occasion of many calamities to Scotland. During the concluding years of Alexander's reign, the kingdom enjoyed a peace and prosperity which it did not taste again for many generations. His only surviving son died without issue in 1284; and next year Alexander contracted a second marriage with Joleta, daughter of the Count de Dreux. The hopes of the nation were soon after clouded by his untimely death. Riding on a dark night between Burntisland and Kinghorn, he fell with his horse, and was killed on the spot, March 12, 1286. A monument (1887) marks the scene of his death.

ALEXANDER, the name of three emperors of Russia.

Alexander I (1777–1825), was born at St Petersburg, December 23. Educated on Rousseauesque principles, in 1793 he married Elizabeth of Baden, and in 1801 succeeded his father, the murdered Emperor Paul. Many reforms were at once initiated, as to education, serfdom, press censorship, and the administration generally. In 1805, joining the coalition against Napoleon, he was present at the battle of Austerlitz, where the allied armies of Austria and Russia were defeated, and retired with the remains of his forces into Russia. Next year he came forward as the ally of Prussia, but in 1807, after the battles of Eylau and Friedland, he was obliged to conclude the peace of Tilsit. In 1808 he declared war on England, and, attacking her ally Sweden, wrested therefrom the province of Finland. In the war of France against Austria in 1809, he took only a lukewarm part; against Turkey he renewed hostilities, which were continued till the peace of Bucharest in 1812. The unnatural alliance of Alexander with France could not, however, be maintained; and though he was not with his troops during the French invasion of Russia (1812), he took an active part in the great struggles of 1813 and 1814. At the occupation of Paris after the downfall of Napoleon in 1814, Alexander was the central figure, and he was received with equal enthusiasm in London. At the Congress of Vienna he laid claim to Poland, but promised to confer on it a constitution. On Napoleon's return from Elba, Alexander urged the energetic renewal of the war; yet on this occasion, too, France owed much to his generosity. At Paris he had met Madame de Krudener (q.v.), who gave a new direction to his mind, and his French ideas gave place to a decided pietism, with sympathies for Protestant and English ways of thinking. The most important political outcome of this period was the Holy Alliance, founded by Alexander, and accepted by all the Christian powers of Europe, except Britain. Many causes contributed to force him into a reactionary course, especially the influence of Metternich; and the revolt in Greece brought his policy into complete opposition to the deepest sympathies of the nation. The death of his only and much-loved natural daughter, the terrible inundation of St Petersburg in 1824, and a Russo-Polish conspiracy against the house of Romanoff, contributed to break the heart of the emperor, who died at Taganrog, December 1, 1825. See Rambaud's *Histoire de la Russie* (Paris 1879; Eng. trans. 1879), Sutherland-Edwards *The Romanoffs* (1890), and Clarence Ford's *Madame de Krudener* (1893).

Alexander II (1818–81), was born at St Petersburg, April 29. He was carefully educated by his father, Nicholas I, but was subjected to such a life of manoeuvring, reviewing, and military parade, as at last injured his health. He then travelled through Germany to recruit his energies, and there in 1841 married the Princess Marie (1824–80), daughter of the Grand-duke of Hesse. He succeeded to the throne, March 2, 1855, a year before the end of the Crimean war. The grand achievement of his reign, which was in great measure his own deed, was the emancipation of the serfs in 1861. Legal and municipal reforms followed; and in 1865

Alexander established elective representative assemblies in the provinces. He resisted strenuously all foreign interference with Polish affairs during the insurrection of 1863, which was suppressed with great severity. During his reign, the Russian empire was widely extended in the Caucasus and in Central Asia. In the Franco-German war of 1870–71, Alexander maintained a sympathetic attitude towards Germany, a policy which was continued in subsequent alliances both with that country and Austria. In 1874 his only daughter Marie married the Duke of Edinburgh (from 1893 Duke of Saxe-Coburg and Gotha). The tsar shared the national sympathy with the Slavonic races under Turkish rule, and took the field with the army during the victorious war between Russia and Turkey in 1877–78. But the most remarkable feature of the second half of his reign was the struggle with the Nihilists. Like his uncle, Alexander I, he was personally a liberal monarch, but his government repressed the revolutionists severely, and they sought vengeance by attacking the tsar and his officers. On March 13, 1881, he was injured by a bomb thrown at him near his palace, and died a few hours after. See works by Laferté (1882), Paléologue (trans. 1926).

Alexander III (1845–94), born March 10, in 1866 married the Princess Marie Dagmar of Denmark (1847–1928; as Dowager Empress she escaped from Russia to England in May 1919). After the death of his father, Alexander II, through fear of assassination he shut himself up in his palace at Gatschina, but was crowned in 1883 with extraordinary magnificence at Moscow. During his reign, Russia steadily pursued her policy of conquest, and of the consolidation of her dominions, the subjugation of the Turkomans in Central Asia being completed by the fall of Merv. In 1885 hostilities with Britain, with regard to the defining of the frontier between the Russian territories and Afghanistan, for a time seemed imminent; as regards European affairs, he appeared inclined to break away from the triple alliance between Russia, Germany, and Austria, and to look rather to France. From 1887 there were repeated attempts by the revolutionary party on the life of the emperor, who died, however, at Livadia, November 1, 1894, and was succeeded by his son Nicholas II (q.v.). See a Life by Charles Lowe (1894), and a work by Samson-Himmelstierna (Eng. trans. 1893).

ALEXANDER, the name of eight popes, of which the following are noteworthy:

Alexander II, Anselm of Luccu (pope 1061–73), born in Baggio, undertook reforms and campaigned against immorality and corruption in the church. He was a founder of the Patarine party, which opposed the marriage of priests.

Alexander III, Orlando Bandinelli (pope 1159–81), born at Siena, taught law at Bologna, became adviser to Adrian IV. After his election as pope he was engaged in a struggle with the Emperor Frederick Barbarossa who refused to recognize him and set up antipopes, until defeated and compelled to sign the Treaty of Venice (1177). He was

also involved in the quarrel between Henry II of England and Becket.

Alexander VI, Rodrigo Borgia (1431–1503), born at Játiva in Spain. The beautiful Rosa Vanozza bore him Caesar, Lucretia, and other children. In 1455 he was made a cardinal by his uncle, Calixtus III, and in 1492, on the death of Innocent VIII, was elevated to the papal chair, which he had previously secured by flagrant bribery. The long absence of the popes from Italy had weakened their authority and curtailed their revenues. To compensate for this loss, Alexander endeavoured to break the power of the Italian princes, and to appropriate their possessions for the benefit of his own family, employing the most execrable means to gain this end. He died August 18, 1503, most likely of fever, but there is some evidence for the tradition that he was accidentally poisoned by wine intended for Cardinal da Corneto, his host. He apportioned the New World between Spain and Portugal; whilst under his pontificate the censorship of books was introduced, and Savonarola was executed as a heretic. See Creighton's *History of the Papacy*, vols. ii and iii (1882–87), and books by Mathew (1912), Portigliotti (trans. Miall, 1928).

ALEXANDER, (1) **Albert Victor, 1st Earl Alexander of Hillsborough** (1885–1965), English Labour politician, born at Weston-super-Mare, the son of an engineer, first entered parliament as Co-operative member for the Hillsborough division of Sheffield in 1922, becoming in 1924 parliamentary secretary to the Board of Trade. He was three times first lord of the Admiralty (1929–1931), (1940–45) and (1945–46), and in the Labour government (1946-50) he was minister of defence. Created viscount in 1950 and earl in 1963, he became in 1955 leader of the Labour peers in the House of Lords. He became a C.H. in 1941, and a K.G. in 1964.

(2) **Archibald** (1772–1851), American Presbyterian preacher and theologian, born in Virginia, was professor at Princeton Theological Seminary, as were also his sons **James Waddell Alexander** (1804–59), a noted preacher, and **Joseph Addison Alexander** (1809–60), distinguished as preacher, linguist and exegete.

(3) **Cecil Frances**, *née* **Humphreys** (1818–1895), Irish poet and hymn writer, wife of (9), born in County Wicklow. She published her *Verses for Holy Seasons* in 1846, and two years later her *Hymns for Little Children*, which included the well known ' All things bright and beautiful ', ' Once in Royal David's city ', and ' There is a green hill far away '.

(4) **Sir George** (1858–1918), actor, born at Reading, made his début at Nottingham in 1879. He played in *Lady Windermere's Fan, The Second Mrs Tanqueray, Prisoner of Zenda*, &c. See Life by Mason (1935).

(5) **Sir Harold Rupert Leofric George Alexander, 1st Earl Alexander of Tunis** (1891–1969), British soldier, was born at Caledon, Co. Tyrone and was educated at Harrow and Sandhurst. In World War I he commanded a battalion on the Western Front when he was 24 and gained many mentions and awards. From 1932 to 1934 he

was general staff officer, Northern Command, and in 1935 served on the North-West Frontier. In 1940 he was the last officer out of Dunkirk; later as G.O.C. Southern Command he originated battle training schools. In 1942 he was G.O.C. Burma, and from 1942–43 C.-in-C. Middle East, his North African campaign being one of the most complete victories in military history. Appointed field marshal on the capture of Rome in June 1944, he became Supreme Allied Commander, Mediterranean Theatre, for the rest of the war. From 1946 to 1952 he was governor-general of Canada and from 1952 to 1954 minister of defence. He was created viscount in 1946, earl in 1952, and was awarded the O.M. in 1959. See Life by N. Hillson (1952) and *Memoirs* (1962).

(6) **John White** (1856–1915), American painter, born at Allegheny. He was influenced by the work of Whistler, and specialized in portraits, painting Rodin, Mark Twain, Thomas Hardy and R. L. Stevenson among others. In 1874 he became an illustrator for *Harper's Magazine*. He kept a studio in Paris from 1890 to 1901, when he was made a Chevalier of the Légion d'Honneur.

(7) **Samuel** (1859–1938), Australian philosopher, born at Sydney, was professor of Philosophy at Manchester 1893–1924. His writings include *Moral Order and Progress* (1889), *Space, Time, and Deity* (1920), *Beauty and other Forms of Value* (1933).

(8) **William.** See STIRLING, EARL OF.

(9) **William** (1824–1911), Irish preacher and poet, Bishop of Derry and Raphoe from 1867, Archbishop of Armagh and Primate 1896–1910, was born at Londonderry, and educated at Oxford. He married Cecil Frances Humphreys (see (3) above) in 1850.

(10) **William** (1826–94), Scottish writer, was editor of the *Aberdeen Free Press* and author of the dialectal *Johnny Gibb of Gushetneuk* (1871), a series of realistic sketches of the remote country folk and places of northeastern Scotland.

ALEXANDER NEVSKI (1218–63), a Russian hero and saint, received his surname for his splendid victory over the Swedes on the Neva (1240).

ALEXANDER of Battenberg. See BATTENBERG.

ALEXANDER OF HALES (d. 1245), English schoolman, the 'Irrefragable Doctor', originally an ecclesiastic of Hailes, Gloucestershire, became a professor of Philosophy and Theology in Paris, and later entered the Franciscan order. His chief and only authentic work is the ponderous *Summa Universae Theologiae.*

ALEXANDER OF TRALLES, Greek physician, was born in Tralles in Hydra about the middle of the 6th century B.C., and is best known for his *Twelve Books on Medicine.*

ALEXANDER SEVERUS (A.D. 205–235), Roman emperor, was the cousin and adopted son of Heliogabalus, whom he succeeded in 221. His virtues but made him an object of hatred to the unruly praetorian guards; and, though his first expedition (231–33) against Artaxerxes of Persia, was successful, during one against the Germans an insurrection broke out, headed by Maximinus, in which

Alexander was murdered with his mother not far from Mainz.

ALEXANDER THE GREAT (356 B.C.–323 B.C.), King of Macedonia, son of Philip of Macedon and Olympias, daughter of Neoptolemus of Epirus, was born at Pella, and was trained by Aristotle in every branch of human learning. He was only sixteen when his father marched against Byzantium, and left him regent in his absence; and he displayed singular courage at the battle of Chaeronea (338 B.C.). Philip, being appointed generalissimo of the Greeks, was preparing for a war with Persia, when he was assassinated (336 B.C.), and Alexander, not yet twenty years of age, ascended the throne. Having crushed the rebellious Illyrians, and razed Thebes to the ground (to prevent a coalition with Athens), Alexander crossed the Hellespont in 334 B.C., and obtained a great victory over the Persians at the river Granīcus; whereupon most of the cities of Asia Minor at once opened their gates to him. At a pass near Issus, in Cilicia, he met Darius, who had advantage in numbers, and utterly defeated him. The family of Darius, as well as his treasure, fell into the hands of the conqueror, who treated them with the greatest magnanimity. Alexander now occupied Damascus, and took and destroyed Tyre, after seven months of incredible exertion (332 B.C.). Thence he marched victoriously through Palestine. Egypt, weary of the Persian yoke, welcomed him as a deliverer; and there he restored native institutions and founded Alexandria (331 B.C.). After consulting the oracle of Ammon in the Libyan Desert, he again set out to meet Darius, and near Arbela in 331 B.C. won another decisive victory over an even greater army than at Issus. Darius escaped on horseback. Babylon and Susa, and the treasure houses of the East, opened their gates to Alexander, who also entered in triumph Persepolis, the capital of Persia. That, in a fit of drunkenness, and at the instigation of Thaïs, an Athenian courtesan, he set fire to Persepolis, the wonder of the world, and reduced it to a heap of ashes, is mere legend. In 329 he overthrew the Scythians on the banks of the Jaxartes; and next year he subdued the whole of Sogdiana, and married Roxana, whom he had taken prisoner. The murder of his foster-brother, Clitus, in a drunken brawl, followed. In 326 B.C., proceeding to the conquest of India, hitherto known only by name, Alexander crossed the Indus near to the modern Attock, and at the Hydaspes (Jhelum) overthrew Porus, after a bloody contest, in which he lost his charger Bucephalus; thence he marched through the Punjab establishing Greek colonies. Having hence fought his way to the ocean, he ordered Nearchus to sail to the Persian Gulf, while he himself marched back through Gedrosia (Baluchistan). Of all the troops which had set out with Alexander, little more than a fourth part arrived with him in Persia (325 B.C.). At Susa he married Stateira, the daughter of Darius. At Babylon he was busy with gigantic plans of conquest and civilization, when he was taken ill after a banquet, and died eleven days later. His body was deposited in a golden coffin at

Alexandria by Ptolemaeus. His empire soon broke up, and was divided amongst his generals (see PTOLEMY SELEUCIDAE). Alexander was more than a conqueror. He diffused the language and civilization of Greece; and to him the ancient world owed a vast increase of its knowledge in geography and natural history.

See *Cambridge Ancient History* (vol. vi, 1927), Lives by Droysen (1885 ; new ed. 1931), Karst (1929), and Tarn (2 vols. 1948). Alexander the Great became the hero of a romance, which arose in Egypt about A.D. 200 and, carried through Latin translations to the West, was widely popular in the middle ages, and was worked into poetic form in French and German, translated into English (Scots probably by Barbour), &c.; see works by Paul Meyer (Paris 1886), Budge (1890, &c.), Heer (1931) and J. F. C. Fuller (1958).

ALEXANDERSON, Ernst F. W. (1878–), Swedish-American electrical engineer and inventor was born in Uppsala, Sweden. In 1901 he went to the U.S.A. He invented the Alexanderson alternator for transoceanic communication; antenna structures ; radio receiving and transmitting systems. By 1930 he had perfected a complete television system. He has 300 patents to his credit.

ALEXANDRA, Queen. See EDWARD VII.

ALEXANDRA FEODOROVNA, *fyod'-* (1872–1918), Empress of Russia upon her marriage with Nicholas II (1894), was Princess of Hesse-Darmstadt and grand-daughter of Queen Victoria. She came under the influence of Rasputin (q.v.), and meddled disastrously in politics, being eventually imprisoned and shot, with her husband and children, by revolutionaries. See B. Pares, *Fall of the Russian Monarchy* (1939).

ALEXANDRI, or Alecsandri, Vasilio (1821– 1890), Rumanian poet and patriot, born at Jassy, was educated and died in Paris.

ALEXEI, (1) *è-lek'sĭ,* or **ALEXIS,** called **Mikhailovich** (1629–76), the second Russian tsar of the house of Romanoff, succeeded his father Michael in 1645. In his two campaigns against the Poles (1654–67), he took Smolensk and conquered almost all Lithuania. He also gained a part of the Ukraine; but his war with Sweden (1656–58) was unfortunate. By his second wife he was the father of Peter the Great.

(2) called **Petrovitch** (1690–1718), the eldest son of Peter the Great, was born at Moscow. Having opposed the emperor's reforms, he was excluded from the succession, and escaped to Vienna, and thence to Naples. Induced to return to Russia, Alexei was condemned to death, but pardoned, only to die in prison a few days after. His son became tsar, as Peter II.

ALEXEIEV, Mikhail Vasilevich, *è-lek-sah'yef* (1857–1918), Russian chief of staff 1914–17, directed the great retreat from Warsaw, 1915.

ALEXIS, Willibald. See HÄRING, GEORG.

ALEXIUS COMNENUS (1048–1118), Byzantine emperor, born at Constantinople, was the nephew of the Emperor Isaac Comnenus, and in 1081 was elevated by his soldiers to the throne. Everywhere he was encompassed with foes. The Scythians and Turks were pouring down from the north and northeast;

the fierce Normans were menacing his western provinces; and, in 1096, the myriad warriors of the first crusade burst into his empire on their way to Palestine. His daughter, Anna Comnena (q.v.), wrote a biography. See essay by F. Chalandon (Paris 1900).

ALFARABI, an Eastern philosopher and encyclopaedic writer, born at Farab, across the Oxus, studied at Baghdad, travelled widely, and died at Damascus in 950. See study by Madkour (Paris 1934).

ALFIERI, Vittorio, Count, *al-fyay'ree* (1749– 1803), Italian poet, was born at Asti, in Piedmont, January 17. His education was very defective, but at fourteen he found himself master of a vast fortune. The chief interest of his youth was a passion for horses, which he retained through life. The years 1767–72 he spent in travelling through Europe, after which, at Turin, he devoted himself to literary pursuits, renouncing idleness and unworthy amours. The applause which his first attempts received encouraged him to win fame as a dramatist, so at a mature age he began to learn Latin, and also to study the Tuscan dialect in Tuscany. At Florence in 1777 he made the acquaintance of the Countess of Albany (q.v.), wife of Prince Charles Edward; and she having quitted her husband in 1780, and been formally separated from him in 1784, from that time onward the two lived together, chiefly in Alsace or Paris, until the Revolution drove them first to England, and next to Florence. Here Alfieri died, October 8, 1803. Their ashes repose in the church of Santa Croce, in Florence, under a beautiful monument by Canova, between the tombs of Michelangelo and Macchiavelli. Alfieri published twenty-one tragedies, six comedies, and the ' tramelogedia ' *Abele,* a mixture of tragedy and opera. His *Opere* (22 vols. Pisa 1805–15) also include an epic in four cantos, an autobiography (3rd ed. 1903; trans. 1801), many lyrical poems, sixteen satires, &c. See his Life by Centofanti (1842) and Teza (1861), and his Letters, edited by Mazzatini (1890).

ALFONSO, the name of five kings of Aragon, including:

Alfonso I, called **el Batallador** (d. 1134), succeeded in 1104, became involved in a conflict with Castile and Leon, exercising sovereignty over the latter by reason of his marriage with its queen, Urraca. He liberated Saragossa from Moorish rule in 1118.

Alfonso V, called the **Magnanimous** (*c.* 1390–1458), also king of Sicily, succeeded his father, Ferdinand I, in 1416, and in 1442, after a long contest, made himself king also of Naples.

ALFONSO, the name of eleven kings of Leon and Castile including:

Alfonso III, called **the Great** (d. 910), king of Leon, Asturias, and Galicia from 866 till his death, fought over thirty campaigns and gained numerous victories over the Moors, occupied Coimbra, and extended his territory as far as Portugal and Old Castile. His sons conspired against him more than once.

Alfonso X, called **the Astronomer,** or the **Wise** (1221–84) king of Leon and Castile born at Burgos, succeeded his father, Ferdinand III, in 1252. His victories over the Moors enabled him to unite Murcia with Castile, and in 1271 he crushed an insurrection headed by his son Philip; but a second rising under another son Sancho in 1282 deprived him of his throne. Alfonso was the founder of a Castilian national literature. He caused the first general history of Spain to be composed in Castilian, as well as a translation of the Old Testament to be made by Toledo Jews. His code of laws and his planetary tables are famous; and he wrote several long poems, besides works on chemistry and philosophy. See study by Procter (1951).

ALFONSO, Port. Affonso. Name of six Portuguese kings of whom the following are noteworthy:

Alfonso I, or **Affonso Henriques** (1110–85), earliest king of Portugal, was only two years old at the death of his father, Henry of Burgundy, conqueror and first Count of Portugal, so that the management of affairs fell to his ambitious and dissolute mother, Theresa of Castile. Wresting the power from her in 1128, he turned his sword against the Moors, defeated them at Ourique, July 25, 1139, and proclaimed himself king on the field of battle. He took Lisbon (1147), and later, all Galicia, Estremadura, and Elvas.

Alfonso V, called **Affonso o Africano** (1432–1481), was called 'the African' in honour of his victories over the Moors in Algiers. Attempting to seize Castile and Leon, he was defeated and abdicated in 1476, but was forced to ascend the throne again. He died of plague.

Alfonso VI (1643–83), succeeded his father, John IV, in 1656, and in 1667 was forced to surrender both his crown and queen to his brother Pedro.

ALFONSO. The name of two kings of Spain:

Alfonso XII (1857–85), after the expulsion of his mother, Isabella II (1868), was educated at Vienna and in England. On the waning of the Carlist cause he was proclaimed king (Dec. 1874), and, mainly through the talents of his minister, Cánovas del Castillo, his reign of eleven years was a time of relative prosperity.

Alfonso XIII (1886–1941), was posthumous son of Alfonso XII, his mother, Maria Cristina of Austria, acting as regent until 1902. He was deposed on the establishment of the second republic in 1931 and died in exile. See Life by R. Sencourt (1942).

ALFORD, Henry (1810–71), English divine, born in London, fellow of Trinity College, Cambridge (1834), Dean of Canterbury (1857), was first editor of the *Contemporary Review* (1866–70), wrote on the classics and published poems and hymns, including the favourite ' Come ye thankful people, come '. See Life by his widow (1873).

ALFRED, called **the Great** (849–99), king of the West Saxons (Wessex), was born at Wantage, Berkshire, and in 853 was taken to Rome. The fifth and youngest son of King Ethelwulf, he succeeded to the crown in 871, on the death of his brother Ethelred. By that time the Danes had overrun most of England north of the Thames. The victory of Ashdown, won chiefly by Alfred's bravery,

just before his accession, gave only a temporary check to their incursions into Wessex; and in that same year the West Saxons fought eight other battles against them. After that, there was some respite, till early in 878, Guthrum, king of the Danes of East Anglia, suddenly burst into Wessex. Alfred could make no effectual resistance, and, seeking refuge in the marshes of Somerset, raised a fort at Athelney. In May he defeated the Danes at Edington, Wiltshire; and by the peace of Wedmore, Guthrum had to receive baptism, and to acknowledge the supremacy of Alfred, who retained the country south of the Thames and most of Mercia, while ceding to the Danes East Anglia and the rest of Mercia. In 884 Alfred sent a fleet against the Danes of East Anglia; in 886 he took and fortified London; and about the same time Northumbria made submission to him—thus he became overlord of all England. On the whole, he enjoyed a much-needed period of peace, till 893, when a fresh swarm of Danes, under Hasting, invaded the country. They were supported by their fellow-countrymen in East Anglia and Northumbria, and for four years gave much trouble. Alfred died October 26 (or 28), 899 (or 900; or 901), and was buried at Winchester.

As a leader, his great work consisted in repelling the Danes, who at his accession threatened to subdue the whole country, and in helping towards the consolidation of England into a united monarchy. It is absolutely unhistorical to regard him as establishing trial by jury, as having divided England into counties and hundreds, or as the founder of the university of Oxford; as legislator, he simply compiled or collected the best among the enactments of earlier kings. The aim of all his work was practical; to promote the good of his people; and his writings bear the same character of sagacious usefulness. They include translations of Boethius' *Consolation of Philosophy*, of the Histories of Bede and Orosius, and of the *Pastoral Care* of Gregory the Great (ed. by Sweet 1871). See Lives by Asser (q.v.), Pauli (1851), Conybeare (new ed. 1914), Besant (1901), Harrison (1901), Plummer (1902), Lees (1919), Williams (1951).

ALFRED OF BEVERLEY. See ALURED.

ALGARDI, Alessandro (1602–54), Italian sculptor, born at Bologna. His chief work is a colossal rilievo, in St Peter's, of ' Pope Leo restraining Attila from marching on Rome '.

ALGAROTTI, Francesco (1712–64), an Italian author, patronized by Frederick the Great and Augustus III of Poland, wrote on popular science, art, and the classics.

ALGAZEL. See GHAZALI.

ALGER, Horatio (1834–99), American writer, born at Revere, Mass., educated at Harvard, became a Unitarian minister, and wrote boys' adventure stories on the ' poor boy makes good ' theme, as *From Canal Boy to President* (1881), &c.

ALHAZEN (*c.* 965–1038), Arab mathematician, born at Basra, wrote a work on optics (in Latin, 1572) giving the first account of atmospheric refraction and reflection from curved surfaces. He constructed spherical and parabolic mirrors and spent a period of his life feigning madness to escape a boast he had made that he could prevent the flooding of the Nile.

ALI (d. 661), the first convert to Mohammedanism, and fourth khalif, was the son of Abu Taleb, the Prophet's uncle. He was the bravest follower of the Prophet, whose daughter Fatima he married. Made khalif in A.D. 656, in place of the murdered Othman, he was himself assassinated.

ALI, (Chaudri) Mohamad (1905–), Pakistani politician, born at Jullundur, India, was educated at Punjab University. In 1928 he left a chemistry lectureship at Islamia College, Lahore, for the Indian Civil Service. Four years later when he was made accountant-general of Bahawalpur State he re-established its finances. In 1936 he became private secretary to the Indian finance minister and in 1945 was the first Indian ever to be appointed financial adviser of war and supply. In 1947, on the partition of India, he became the first secretary-general of the Pakistan Government, in 1951 finance minister, and in 1955 prime minister. He resigned on September 8, 1956, because of lack of support from members of his own party, the Moslem League. Of powerful intellect, he was often described in Pakistan as the 'brains trust' of the post-partition governments.

ALI BEY (1728–73), Egyptian ruler, was a Caucasian slave who in 1763 rose to be chief of the Mamelukes in Egypt, slaughtered the other beys in 1766, and was proclaimed sultan in 1768. He made himself independent of Turkey, and had conquered Syria and part of Arabia, when one of his sons-in-law raised an army against him in Egypt, and defeated him. He died a few days after of his wounds or of poison.

ALI IBN HUSEIN (1879–1935), ruler of the Hejaz, was born at Mecca, the eldest son of King Hussein of the Hejaz, whom he succeeded in 1924 when his father was forced off the throne in the Wahabi Rebellion, but himself had to abdicate in 1925. For the rest of his life he lived in exile in Baghdad.

ALI PASHA, surnamed **Arslan**, 'the Lion' (1741–1822), ruler of Albania, after a youth of brigandage, murder, and warfare, was in 1787 made pasha of Trikala, in 1788 of Janina, and in 1803 governor of Rumili. The ally successively of France and Britain, he deemed his power securely established, but in 1820 was deposed by Sultan Mahmoud, and put to death in 1822.

ALICE MAUD MARY (1843–78), Grand-duchess of Hesse, was born April 25, the second daughter of Queen Victoria. In 1862 she married Prince Louis of Hesse (1837–92), who succeeded his uncle as Grand-duke in 1877; and she died at Darmstadt, December 14, 1878. Of her daughters one married Prince Louis of Battenberg, one the Grand-duke Sergius of Russia, a third Prince Henry of Prussia, and a fourth the Tsar Nicholas II of Russia. See her *Letters* (1884), with memoir.

ALISON, (1) **Archibald** (1757–1839), Scottish Episcopal minister, born in Edinburgh, father of (2), author of *Essays on the Nature and Principles of Taste* (1790).

(2) **Sir Archibald** (1792–1867), Scottish historian, son of (1), father of (3), born at Kenley, Salop, wrote the *History of Europe during the French Revolution* (10 vols. 1833–1842), and its continuation to the accession of Louis Napoleon (9 vols. 1852–59). He was created a baronet in 1852. See his Autobiography (1883).

(3) **Sir Archibald** (1826–1907), Scottish soldier, son of (2), born in Edinburgh, served in the Crimea, the Indian Mutiny, and the Ashanti expedition, and led the Highland Brigade at Tel-el-Kebir. He wrote a treatise *On Army Organization* (1869).

ALLAN, (1) **David** (1744–96), Scottish painter, Wilkie's forerunner, born at Alloa, studied in Glasgow; and in Rome, where in 1773 he gained the gold medal of St Luke's Academy. In 1777 he came to London, where he painted portraits; in 1780 he removed to Edinburgh, and in 1786 succeeded Runciman at the head of the art academy there. See study by T. C. Gordon (1951).

(2) **Sir Henry Havelock.** See HAVELOCK.

(3) **Sir Hugh** (1810–82), Canadian-Scottish shipowner, was born at Saltcoats in Ayrshire, settled in 1824 in Canada, where his firm became eminent as shipbuilders, and founded the Allan Line of steamers. He was knighted in 1871.

(4) **Sir William** (1782–1850), Scottish historical painter, was born in Edinburgh, where he studied with Wilkie as a fellow-pupil, subsequently proceeding to the Royal Academy schools in London. In 1805 he went to St Petersburg and, before his return to Edinburgh in 1814, toured southern Russia and Turkey. In 1835 he was elected R.A., in 1838 became president of the Royal Scottish Academy, and on Wilkie's death in 1841 was appointed limner to Her Majesty for Scotland and knighted.

ALLARD, Jean François (1785–1839), French soldier, adjutant in 1815 to Marshal Brune, after whose assassination he went, by way of Egypt and Persia, to Lahore (1820), where Ranjit Singh made him generalissimo of the Sikh army.

ALLARDICE. See BARCLAY-ALLARDICE.

ALLBUTT, Sir Thomas Clifford (1836–1925), English physician, born at Dewsbury, educated at Cambridge, studied medicine at London and Paris, practised at Leeds, and became regius professor of Medicine at Cambridge in 1892. In 1867 he introduced the short clinical thermometer, a great advance on the old pattern, which was a foot long and had to be kept in position for twenty minutes. He wrote many medical works and books on the history of medicine.

ALLECTUS (c. A.D. 250–296), Roman-British insurgent, murdered Carausius (q.v.) and set up in Britain, against Constantius Chlorus, as Roman ruler.

ALLEINE, Joseph, *al'in* (1634–68), English Puritan writer, born at Devizes, was educated at Lincoln and Corpus Christi colleges, Oxford, and from 1654 till his ejection in 1662 was assistant minister at Taunton. Thenceforth an itinerant preacher, he was often fined and imprisoned. His *Alarm to the Unconverted* (1672) was long read. His interesting *Remains* appeared in 1674.

ALLEN, (1) **Charles Grant Blairfindie** (1848–1899), English philosophical writer and novelist, born at Kingston in Canada, graduated from Merton College, Oxford, in 1871. After four years at Queen's College, Jamaica, as professor of Logic and principal (1873–77), he returned to England, and, adopting a literary career, published *Physiological Aesthetics* (1877), *Colour Sense, Evolutionist at Large, Darwin,* and several clever novels—*Babylon, In all Shades, The Woman who Did* (1895), *An African Millionaire* (1897), &c. See *Life* by Clodd (1900).

(2) **Ethan** (1738–89), American soldier, born at Litchfield, Connecticut, distinguished himself early in the revolutionary war by the surprise and capture of Fort Ticonderoga (May 10, 1775). He next did good service in Montgomery's expedition to Canada, but was taken prisoner and not exchanged till 1778. He wrote a famous deistical work (1784). See *Life* by Holbrook (1940).

(3) **George** (1832–1907), English publisher and engraver, born at Newark. A pupil of Ruskin, for whom he engraved many plates, and whose publisher he subsequently became, he started a business in Bell Yard, Fleet Street, which ultimately merged with others and became the well-known house of Allen and Unwin.

(4) **Sir Hugh Percy** (1869–1946), English musician, born in Reading. A church organist from the age of eleven, he was elected organ scholar of Christ's College, Cambridge, in 1892, three years after gaining a doctorate of music from Oxford. After posts at Ely and St Asaph's Cathedrals, in 1901 he became organist of New College, Oxford, and was active in the musical life of the city and university. As university *choragus*, after 1909, he had a considerable influence on musical education at the university. From 1918 Allen was director of the Royal College of Music and professor of Music at Oxford, posts in which his powerful personality and insistence on practical music-making had a profound effect. Knighted in 1920, he was active in the administration of the Royal Choral and Royal Philharmonic Societies until his retirement from the R.C.M. in 1937. He retained his chair at Oxford until his accidental death. See *Life* by Bailey (1948).

(5) **James Lane** (1849–1925), American novelist, born in Kentucky, wrote *The Kentucky Cardinal, Aftermath, The Choir Invisible,* and other novels. See study by G. C. Knight (1935).

(6) **Ralph** (1694?–1764), English philanthropist, the ' Man of Bath ', the friend of Pope, Fielding, and Chatham, made a fortune by his post-office improvements. He built the mansion of Prior Park, near Bath. See his *Life and Times* by Peach (1895).

(7) **Walter** (1911–   ), English novelist, born in Birmingham. After working as a schoolmaster and university lecturer (in the United States), Allen became a journalist. His first novel, *Innocence is Drowned*, was published in 1938, and he scored a considerable success with *Dead Man over All*, in 1950. He has written several critical works, including *The English Novel—A short critical history* (1954).

(8) **William** (1532–94), English cardinal, was born at Rossall, Lancashire, in 1532, and in 1550 was elected fellow of Oriel College, Oxford. In 1556 he became principal of St Mary's Hall, and, Catholic though he was, he retained this office till 1560, but next year had to seek refuge in Flanders. Even then he stole back home in 1562, that his native air might cure a wasting sickness; but when, in 1565, he landed once more in the Low Countries, it was never to return to England. He received priest's orders at Mechlin, in 1565 founded the English college at Douai to train missionary priests for the reconversion of England to Catholicism, and later founded similar establishments at Rome (1575-58) and Valladolid (1589). In 1587 he was created a cardinal during his fourth visit to Rome, where he died October 16, 1594. At the time of the Armada, Allen signed, if he did not pen, the *Admonition*, urging the Catholics to take up arms. See his *Letters* (1882), and a study by Martin Haile (1914).

(9) **William Hervey** (1889–1949), American author, born in Pittsburg and trained for the American navy, in which he became a midshipman. In World War I, however, he fought with distinction as a lieutenant in the Army, and later (1926) published his war diary *Towards the Flame*. His best-known novel *Anthony Adverse* (1933) sold a million and a half copies; others are *Action at Aquila* (1938), *The Forest and the Fort* (1943), *Bedford Village* (1945), and *The City of the Dawn* which was unfinished at his death. Allen also wrote a study of Edgar Allan Poe under the title *Israfel* (1926).

ALLENBY, Edmund Henry Hynman, 1st Viscount (1861–1936), British general, was educated at Haileybury and R.M.C. Sandhurst, joining the Inniskilling Dragoons. He saw service in South Africa in 1884–85, 1888, and 1899–1902, ending as a column leader. In 1914 he commanded the 1st Cavalry Division B.E.F. In 1917 the attack of Allenby's 3rd Army captured the important Vimy Ridge, but stalled against obstinate resistance. Transferred to Palestine, where stalemate had supervened, Allenby's vitality and confidence swiftly reanimated the whole front. Cleverly deluding the Turks as to the real point of attack, ' the Bull ' launched his cavalry to carry Beersheba; cutting off the enemy's retreat from Gaza. By December 9, Allenby had redeemed his promise to give the British people Jerusalem as a Christmas present. The fall of Damascus in October 1918 brought the campaign to a successful close. When he was high commissioner in Egypt Allenby's strong hand and firm measures undoubtedly averted a subversive uprising. Methodical, scholarly—he could quote the Greek classics in the original—Allenby was a field commander who combined thorough preparation with great drive in execution. G.C.B. and G.C.M.G. 1918, G.C.V.O. 1934, peerage conferred 1919. See biography by Wavell (1940).

ALLEYN, Edward (1566–1626), English actor, stepson-in-law of Philip Henslowe, with whom he acted ; contemporary with Shakespeare, founded Dulwich College. See his *Memoirs* by Collier (1841), and Young's *Dulwich*

College (2 vols. 1891). See Life by Hosking (1952).

ALLIBONE, Samuel Austin (1816–89), American bibliographer, born in Philadelphia, in 1879 became head of the Lenox Library, New York, and compiled an invaluable *Dictionary of English Literature* (3 vols. 1858–70–71).

ALLINGHAM, (1) Margery (1904–66), English detective story writer, born in London, author of *Flowers for the Judge* (1936), *The Tiger in the Smoke* (1952), &c.

(2) **William** (1824–89), Irish poet, born of English origin at Ballyshannon in Donegal, was in the Irish Customs 1846–70, and in 1874 succeeded Froude as Editor of *Fraser's Magazine*. In 1874 he married Helen Paterson (1848–1926), who, born near Burton-on-Trent, made a name by her book illustrations and water colours, and edited his *Diary* (1907), &c. His works (6 vols. 1890) include *Day and Night Songs* (1855), illustrated by Rossetti and Millais; *Laurence Bloomfield in Ireland* (1864), and *Irish Songs and Poems* (1887).

ALLISON, Fred (1882–), American physicist, born at Glade Spring, Virginia, was professor at Alabama Polytechnic Institute (1922), discovered the elements francium (1930) and astatine (1931) and sixteen isotopes of lead by means of his magneto-optic method.

ALLORI, Alessandro (1535–1607), Florentine mannerist painter, was adopted and trained by Bronzino (q.v.) whose name he and his son, **Cristofano** (1577–1621) later adopted. They both were portrait painters at the Medici court and executed religious works for the churches of Florence.

ALLSOPP, Samuel (1780–1838), English philanthropist, a member of the great brewing establishment of Allsopp & Sons, Burton-on-Trent, was noted for the charities of his public and private life. The youngest of his three sons, **Henry** (1811–87), to whom the development of the firm was largely due, represented Worcestershire (1874–80), and in 1880 was created a baronet, in 1886 Lord Hindlip.

ALLSTON, Washington (1779–1843), American painter, was born at Waccamaw, South Carolina; graduated at Harvard in 1800, and came next year to London to study art. In 1803 he went to Paris, and in 1805 on to Rome, where he formed a close intimacy with Thorvaldsen and Coleridge. Elected an A.R.A. in 1819, he had the year before returned finally to America, and fixed his residence at Cambridge Port, near Boston, where he died. He was author of a poem, *The Sylphs of the Seasons* (1813), the art novel, *Monaldi* (1842), and *Lectures on Art* (ed. by Dana 1850). See his Life by Flagg (1893).

ALMACK, William (d. 1781), founder of Almack's, of either Yorkshire or Scottish origin (possibly originally McCall), came at an early age to London where he was successively valet and innkeeper. He opened a gaming club in Pall Mall in 1763, and assembly rooms in King Street, St James's, in 1765. These became centres of London society. The club was acquired by Brooks in 1778, and the rooms on his death passed to his niece, Mrs Willis, whose name they bore for many years. Almack amassed great wealth and retired to Hounslow.

ALMAGRO, Diego de (1464 or 1475–1538), Spanish *conquistador*, was a foundling. He had marched on Chile in 1536, and dispersed the Peruvian army before Cuzco, when, on April 6, 1538, he was defeated in a desperate engagement with the Spaniards under Pizarro near Cuzco, and on the 26th was strangled in prison. His half-caste son, Diego, collecting some hundreds of followers, stormed Pizarro's palace, and slew him (1541); then proclaimed himself captain-general of Peru; but, defeated at Chupas (September 16, 1542), was executed with forty companions.

ALMANSUR, i.e., 'the victorious' (d. 775), the title assumed by the cruel and treacherous khalif Abu-Jafar, who succeeded his brother in 754 and founded Baghdad in 764. See Nöldeke's *Sketches of Eastern History* (trans. 1892).

ALMA-TADEMA, Sir Lawrence, *al'ma tad'e-ma* (1836–1912), Dutch-English painter of classical subjects, knighted in 1899, O.M. in 1905, was born at Dronryp, Friesland. Destined originally to be a doctor, in 1852 he entered the Antwerp Academy of Art. In 1873 he settled permanently in England and in 1876 was elected an A.R.A., in 1879 an R.A. See Life by F. G. Stephens (1895).

ALMEIDA, *al-may'i-THa,* (1) **Brites de** (fl. 1385) Portuguese heroine, born in Aljubarotta. Little is known of her except that she was a baker and that, about 1385, during the war between John I and the king of Cadiz, she advanced on the Spanish forces attacking her village and killed seven of them with her baker's shovel. The incident was celebrated by Camoens in a poem. The shovel is believed to have been preserved as a relic in Aljubarotta for several generations, though some doubt is now thrown on her actual existence.

(2) **Francisco de** (c. 1450–1510), Portuguese viceroy of the Indies, appointed in 1505, and superseded in 1509 by Albuquerque. He was slain in an affray with savages where Cape Town now stands.

ALMEIDA-GARRETT, João Baptista da Silva Leitão, *al-may'eeTHa-ga-ret'* (1799–1854), Portuguese author and politician, born at Oporto and brought up in the Azores, was exiled after the 1820 revolt, returned and supported Dom Pedro and became Minister of the Interior. A pioneer of the romantic movement and of modern Portuguese drama, he wrote the historical play *Gil Vicente* (1838), the epic *Camões* (1825), and many ballads. See Life by Gomes de Amorim (3 vols. Lisb. 1881–88).

ALMOHADES, a Moslem dynasty in Africa and Spain during the 12th and 13th centuries.

ALMORAVIDES (Arabic *al murabathin*, 'dedicated to God's service'), an Arab dynasty in Africa and Spain in the 11th and 12th centuries.

ALMQVIST, Karl Jonas Ludvig (1793–1866), Swedish author, was born at Stockholm and died at Bremen, after a singular career, in which (though apparently innocent) he once had to flee as a suspected forger and would-be poisoner to America, where he became

Lincoln's secretary. See Life by E. B. Almqvist (Stockholm 1914).

A.L.O.E. See TUCKER, CHARLOTTE MARIA.

ALONSO (1) **Dameso** (1898–), Spanish poet and philologist, was born in Madrid, where he studied under Pidal before travelling widely in Europe and America as teacher and lecturer. He became professor of Romance Philology at Madrid University, and established his reputation as an authority on Góngora. In addition to studies of Góngora, Medrano, San Juan de la Cruz, and Erasmus, he has published poetry, of which *Hijos de la Ira* is the best known. It is religious in inspiration, powerful and emotional in expression.

(2) **Mateo** (1878–), Argentinian sculptor. He studied at the Escuela de Bellas Artes, Barcelona, and is best known for his statue of Christ the Redeemer, erected in 1904 at the top of the Uspallata Pass, in the Andes, to commemorate the settlement of disputes between Chile and the Argentine.

ALOYSIUS, St. See GONZAGA (1).

ALP-ARSLAN (1029–72), Persian sultan from 1059 to his death. He took and plundered the city of Caesarea, in Cappadocia, in 1064 added Armenia and Georgia to his dominions, and in 1071 gained a decisive victory over the Greek emperor at Manzikert. Marching to the conquest of Turkestan, he was stabbed by a captive enemy.

ALPHONSO. See ALFONSO.

ALPINI, Prospero, *al-pee'nee,* Latin **Prosper Alpinus** (1553–1617), Italian physician and botanist, was born in Marostica in the Republic of Venice. He spent three years as physician to the Italian consul in Cairo, and during this period he made a special study of the palm tree. His work led him to the doctrine of the sexual differences in plants, the basis of the Linnaean system. In 1593 he became professor of Botany in Padua. His main work *De Plantis Aegypti Liber* was published in 1592. His *De Medicina Egyptiorum* (1591) brought attention to the coffee plant for the first time in a European book.

ALRED. See ALDRED.

ALTDORFER, Albrecht (c. 1480–1538), German painter, engraver, and architect, leading member of the ' Danube School ' of German painting, was born and died at Regensburg. His most outstanding works are biblical and historical subjects set against highly imaginative and atmospheric landscape backgrounds. He was also a pioneer of copperplate etching. See W. B. Scott, *Little Masters* (1879), and study by von Baldass (1941).

ALTEN, Karl August, Graf von (1764–1840), Hanoverian general, came to England in 1803, entered the German Legion, fought through the Peninsular war, and commanded at Quatre-Bras and Waterloo. After his return to Hanover, he became minister of war.

ALTER, David (1807–81), American physicist, born at Freeport, Pa. one of the earliest investigators of the spectrum.

ALTHORP, Lord. See SPENCER.

ALUNNO, Niccolo, called **Niccolo di Liberatore** (c. 1430–1502), Umbrian painter, born at Foligno. His works, which show the influence of Fra Angelico, may be seen in Florence, Foligno, and Terni. See Berenson, *Central Italian Painters of the Renaissance* (1909).

ALURED, or **Alfred, of Beverley,** an English chronicler whose *Annales,* coming down to 1129, was published at Oxford in 1716 by Hearne.

ALVA, or **Alba, Ferdinand Alvarez de Toledo, Duke of** (1508–82), Spanish general and statesman, was born at Piedratita on October 29, and gave such proofs of his courage and capacity in the battle of Pavia (1525), in and Hungary against the Turks, in Charles V's expedition to Tunis and Algiers, and in Provence, that he became general at twenty-six, and commander-in-chief at thirty. His skilful defence of Navarre and Catalonia (1542) gained him his ducal title ; and in 1547 he contributed greatly to Charles V's victory at Mühlberg over the Elector of Saxony. He took part in the unsuccessful expedition against Henry II of France, who had seized Metz; but was more fortunate in 1555 in Italy against the combined armies of the pope and the French king. After the abdication of Charles V in 1556, Alva overran the States of the Church, but was obliged by Philip II to conclude a peace, and restore all his conquests. On the revolt of the Netherlands, Philip sent Alva in 1567 with unlimited power and a large military force; his first step was to establish the 'Bloody Council'. As many as 100,000 artisans, mechanics, merchants, &c., emigrated to England, while others enlisted under the banners of the proscribed Princes of Orange. Alva, infuriated by the defeat of his lieutenant the Duke of Aremberg sent Counts Egmont and Horn to the block. He afterwards defeated Prince Louis, and compelled William of Orange to retire to Germany; upon which he entered Brussels in triumph, December 22, 1568. The pope presented him with a consecrated hat and sword, as Defender of the Catholic faith; an honour which, hitherto conferred only on crowned heads, increased his insolence to the highest degree. But Holland and Zeeland renewed their efforts against him, and succeeded in destroying his fleet, until, recalled by his own desire in 1573, he left the country, of which, as he boasted, he had executed 18,000 men. Soon after conquering Portugal, he died at Thomar, December 12, 1582.

ALVARADO, Pedro de, *al-va-rah'THŌ* (c. 1495–1541), Spanish general, after sharing with Cortés (q.v.) in the conquest of Mexico, was appointed governor of Guatemala.

ALVAREZ QUINTERO, Serafín, *al'va-rayth keen-tay'rō* (1871–1938), and **Joaquín** (1873–1944), Spanish playwrights, both born in Utrera. These brothers were the joint authors of well over a hundred modern Spanish plays, all displaying a characteristic gaiety and sentiment—and sometimes accused of being a little too stagily Spanish. Some are well known in the translations of Helen and Harley Granville-Barker: *Fortunato, The Lady from Alfaqueque,* and *A Hundred Years Old* (all produced in 1928), and *Don Abel Writes a Tragedy* (1933). In addition may be mentioned *El patio* (1900), *Las flores* (1901), *El genio allegre* (1906), and *Pueblo de mujeres* (1912).

ÁLVAREZ, José (1768–1827), Spanish sculptor of the classical school, was imprisoned in Rome for refusing to recognize Joseph Bonaparte as King of Spain, but was later released and employed by Napoleon to decorate the Quirinal Palace. In 1816 he became court sculptor to Ferdinand VI in Madrid, where he executed *Antilochus and Memnon* (Royal Museum) and portraits and busts of the nobility and of Rossini.

ALVARO, Corrado, *al-vah'rō* (1895–1956), Italian novelist and journalist, born in Reggio. Sometime editor of *Il Mondo*, he was the author of several novels and collections of essays. His best novels are *I maestri del diluvio* (1935) and *L'Uomo è forte* (1934), both set in Soviet Russia, though the author declared that his criticisms were of Fascist and not Communist society.

ALYPIUS (dates unknown), Ancient Greek writer on music, said to have worked before either Euclid or Cassiodorus. His surviving work, published in 1652 by Mark Meibomius, consists of a list of symbols for the notation of the Greek modes and scales.

AMADEUS, *a-ma-day'oos*, the name of several rulers of Savoy, among them:

Amadeus V, called the Great (1249–1323), founder of the Italian royal house, born at le Bourget, ruled from 1285, died at Avignon.

Amadeus VI, called the Green (1334–83), born at Chambéry, succeeded in 1343, founded the Order of the Annunziata, added Vaud to the possessions of Savoy.

Amadeus VIII (1383–1451), had Savoy made a duchy (1416), and in 1418 Piedmont chose him as ruler; but in 1434 he retired to a hermitage beside Lake Geneva. In 1439 as Felix V he was elected pope (i.e., antipope in opposition to Eugenius IV); but he resigned in 1449, and died at Geneva.

AMADEUS I (1845–90), king of Spain, a member of the house of Savoy, second son of Victor-Emmanuel of Italy, was elected king in 1870, but had to abdicate in 1873, and, as Duke of Aosta, returned to Italy.

AMALIA, Anna (1739–1807), Duchess of Saxe Weimar, was left a widow in 1758, and as the prudent regent for seventeen years of her son, attracted to Weimar, Herder, Goethe, Musaeus and Schiller. A patron of the arts, she founded the Weimar museum. The battle of Jena broke her heart. See Life by Bornhak (Berl. 1892).

AMANULLAH KHAN (1892–1960), amir and king of Afghanistan (1919–29), established Afghan independence (1922) after an Indian war, but, overzealous in westernizing, was deposed in 1929.

AMARA-SINHA, a celebrated Hindu grammarian, whose date is variously put at 56 B.C., the 5th cent. A.D., and the 11th cent.

AMARI, Michele, *a-mah'ree* (1806–89), Italian politician and orientalist, was born at Palermo. A member of the Carbonari, he was mostly in exile in 1841–59, then professor of Arabic at Pisa and Florence, and minister of Public Instruction (1862–64). He wrote *La Guerra del Vespro Siciliano* (1841).

AMASIS, *a-may'sis*. Two Kings of Egypt.

Amasis I, born not long before Moses, founded the 18th dynasty and freed Egypt from the alien Shepherd Kings.

Amasis II, ruled from 569 to 525 B.C., cultivated the friendship of the Greeks, and greatly promoted the prosperity of Egypt. He built the temple of Isis at Memphis.

AMATI, *a-mah'tee*, Italian family of Cremonese violin-makers, whose famous members were Andrea (*c.* 1520–80) whose earliest known label dates from 1564; his younger brother Nicola (fl. 1568–86), Andrea's two sons, Antonio (fl. 1550–1638), and Geronimo (1551–1635); and the latter's son, Niccolò (1596–1684), the master of Guarneri and Stradivari. Geronimo (1649–1740) was the last important Amati.

AMBEDKAR, Bhimrao Ranji (1893–1956), Indian politician and champion of the depressed castes, was born in a Ratnagiri village on the Konkan coast of Bombay, the son of an Indian soldier. Educated at Elphinstone College, Bombay, Columbia University, New York, and the London School of Economics, he became a London barrister and later a member of the Bombay Legislative Assembly and leader of 60,000,000 Untouchables. In 1941 he became a member of the Governor-General's Council. Appointed law minister in 1947, he was the principal author of the Indian Constitution.' He resigned in 1951. With some thousands of his followers he publicly embraced the Buddhist faith not long before his death. His dedicated work for the outcastes strengthened the Indian public opinion which secured a better life for them. His publications include: *Annihilation of Caste* (1937). See Life by Keer (1954).

AMBERLEY, Viscount. See RUSSELL Family (3).

AMBOISE, George d', *ã-bwaz* (1460–1510), French cardinal and prime minister under Louis XII, to secure his election as pope encouraged a schism between the French Church and Rome, and convened a separate council, first at Pisa, then at Milan and Lyons. He left a vast fortune. See Life by Hardouin (1875).

AMBROSE, St (*c.* 339–397), was born at Trier, son of the prefect of Gaul. He studied at Rome, and in 369 was made consular prefect of Upper Italy, which had suffered much from the controversy between Arians and Catholics. His fairness commended him so much to both parties, that on the death of the Bishop of Milan in 374, Ambrose was unanimously called to succeed him. He long refused to accept this dignity, and even left the city; yet he soon returned, was baptized, as hitherto he had been only a catechumen, and was consecrated eight days afterwards. He sold his goods for the poor, and fitted himself for his new office by theological studies. As a bishop, he won universal reverence; but he was severe and stern against wickedness, even in high places. Thus, he repulsed the Emperor Theodosius himself even from the door of the church, on account of his having caused the rebellious Thessalonians to be massacred, excommunicated him, and restored him only after severe penance. His unflinching defiance of the court party enabled him to save the churches in his diocese from the Arian heretics. Ambrose's most valuable legacy to the church is his hymns, and the improvements he introduced into the service—the Ambrosian ritual and the Ambrosian chant. The Ambrosian Library at Milan, founded by Cardinal Borromeo in 1609, was named in honour of Milan's patron saint. See Lives by Thornton (1879), Dudden (1935).

AMENOPHIS, or **Amen-hotep,** name of four Egyptian pharaohs of the 18th Dynasty, of whom the most noteworthy were:

Amenhotep II (c. 1447–1420 B.C.), the son of Thothmes III (q.v.) and Queen Hatshepsut (q.v.), fought successful campaigns in Palestine and on the Euphrates.

Amenhotep III (c. 1411–1375 B.C.), consolidated Egyptian supremacy in Babylonia and Assyria and built his great capital city, Thebes, the colossi of Memnon, &c.

Amenhotep IV. See AKHNATON.

AMERY, Leopold Charles Maurice Stennett (1873–1955), English Conservative politician, was born at Gorakpur, India, and was educated at Harrow and Oxford. A member of *The Times* staff from 1899 to 1909, he became M.P. for Sparkbrook, Birmingham, in 1911, holding the seat throughout his 34 years in the House of Commons. In 1919 he was Colonial Office under-secretary, in 1922 first lord of the Admiralty. From 1924 to 1929 he was colonial secretary and from 1925 dominions secretary as well. In the 1940 Churchill administration he was secretary of state for India and Burma, a post he held till 1945. A lifelong champion of the British Commonwealth as 'a new political, economic, and spiritual conception', he believed profoundly that the future of the world depended largely on the development of 'welfare Imperialism'. His publications include *My Political Life* (3 vols. 1953–1955).

AMES, (1) **Fisher** (1758–1808), American politician, born at Dedham, Mass., member of congress and orator.

(2) **Joseph** (1689–1759), English bibliographer, the historian of printing, known for his *Typographical Antiquities* (1749), was a London ironmonger, born at Yarmouth.

(3) **Lat. Amesius, William** (1576–1633), English Puritan theologian, who wrote mostly in Latin, and spent the later half of his life in Holland, where he became a professor of Theology, celebrated for his exposition of the Calvinist doctrine.

AMHERST, (1) **Jeffrey, 1st Baron Amherst** (1717–97), English general, was born at Riverhead, Kent, and at the age of fourteen entered the army. In 1758 Pitt gave him the command of the expedition against the French in Canada; and Canada was won by the autumn of 1760, thanks to his prudence and to Wolfe's enthusiasm. This was the great achievement of his life, though in 1772 he became commander-in-chief, and in 1796 a field-marshal, having been raised to the peerage in 1776. He died August 3, 1797. See Life by Mayo (1916).

(2) **Nicholas** (1697–1742), English Whig poet, expelled from St John's College, Oxford (1719), and editor of *The Craftsman* (1726–1737).

(3) **William Pitt, 1st Earl Amherst of Arakan** (1773–1857), nephew of (1), was born at Bath, and succeeded as second baron in 1797. His embassy to China (1816) failed through his refusal to 'kowtow' to the emperor; but, in spite of that failure, he received in 1823 the governor-generalship of India. For the successful first Burmese war, and for the capture of Bhurtpore, he was rewarded with an earldom in 1826. He returned to England two years later, and died at Knole Park, Kent, March 13, 1857.

AMICI, Giovanni Battista, *a-mee'chee* (1784–1863), Italian optician, astronomer and natural philosopher, born in Modena. He constructed optical instruments, perfecting his own alloy for telescope mirrors and, in 1827, produced the dioptric, achromatic microscope that bears his name. He became director of the Florence observatory in 1835 and won a high reputation as an astronomer.

AMICIS, Edmondo de, *a-mee'chis* (1846–1908), Italian novelist, born in Oneglia. Intended for the army, and becoming director of the Italia Militare, Florence, in 1867, he turned to literature and recorded his experiences as a soldier in *La vita militare* (1868). He is chiefly remembered for his alliance with Manzoni in an attempt to 'purify' the Italian language. *L'Idioma gentile* (1905) presents his views on this subject. His most popular work is the sentimental *Il Cuore* (1886), translated into English as *An Italian Schoolboy's Journal* and into more than twenty-five other languages. His interest in education is reflected in *Il romanzo d'un maestro* (1890), and he also travelled widely, producing several books about his adventures.

AMIEL, Henri Frédéric, *a-myel* (1821–81), Swiss writer, born at Geneva, from 1849 till his death was professor at the Academy (University) of Geneva. He published some essays and poems, but his wide culture and critical power were first made known after his death by his *Journal intime* (1883).

AMIOT. See AMYOT.

AMIS, Kingsley, *ay'mis* (1922–), English novelist and poet, born in London, educated at the City of London School and at St John's College, Oxford, served as an officer in the Royal Signals (1942–45) and from 1948 lectured in English Literature at the University College of Swansea. He has published verse, articles on 'classical' jazz and on science fiction, and achieved a reputation by his second novel, *Lucky Jim* (1954), which added a new comic hero to English fiction, an unruly but kind-hearted cad who suffers exasperating struggles with his social environment. A history lecturer in the above, he reappears as small-town librarian in *That Uncertain Feeling* (1956) and as a provincial author abroad in *I Like It Here* (1958). Later works on wider themes include *One Fat Englishman* (1963), *The Anti-Death League* (1965), &c. After Ian Fleming's death, Amis wrote a James Bond novel, *Colonel Sun* (1968), under the pseudonym of Robert Markham, as well as *The James Bond Dossier* (1965). His second wife **Elizabeth Jane Howard** (b. 1923) is also a novelist.

AMMANATI, Bartolommeo, *am-an-ah'tee* (1511–92), Italian architect and sculptor, born at Settignano. Working in the late Renaissance style he executed the ducal palace at Lucca; also part of the Pitti palace and the

Ponte della Trinità (destroyed in World War II) at Florence, where he died.

AMMIANUS MARCELLINUS (*c.* A.D. 330-390), Roman historian, born of Greek parents at Antioch, after fighting in Gaul, Germany, and the East, settled at Rome, and devoted himself to literature. He wrote in Latin a history of the Roman empire in 31 books, of which only 18 are extant, comprising the years 353-378. This part of his work, however, is the most valuable, as it treats of affairs with which he was contemporary.

AMMON, Christoph Friedrich von (1766-1850), German rationalist theologian, born at Bayreuth, was professor of Theology at Erlangen and Göttingen.

AMMŌNIUS, *am-mō'nee-us*, (1) (*c.* 175-242), Greek philosopher, surnamed Saccas, because in youth he was a sack-carrier in Alexandria, was the founder of the Neoplatonic philosophy, and teacher of Plotinus. See W. B. Inge, *The Philosophy of Plotinus* (1918).

(2) (fl. 400), Alexandrian grammarian, who taught at Constantinople.

(3) (5th cent.), Alexandrian Neoplatonist, a disciple of Proclus.

AMORY, *ay'mė-ree*, (1) **Derick Heathcoat, 1st Viscount Amory** (1899-), English Conservative politician, born at Tiverton, educated at Eton and Christ Church College, Oxford, entered parliament in 1945, was minister of pensions (1951-53), at the Board of Trade (1953-54), minister of agriculture (1954-58) chancellor of the Exchequer (1958-1960), when he was made viscount.

(2) **Thomas** (*c.* 1691-1788), an eccentric author of Irish descent, who was living in Westminster about 1757, seldom stirred out till dark, and was doubtless somewhat insane. His chief works are *Lives of Several Ladies of Great Britain, A History of Antiquities, Productions of Nature,* &c. (1755), and the *Life of John Buncle* (1756-66)—an odd combination of autobiography, fantastic descriptions of scenery, deistical theology, and sentimental rhapsody.

AMOS, the peasant prophet of Tekoa, near Bethlehem of Judea, prophesied in the kingdom of Israel against idolatry about 800 B.C.

AMPÈRE, (1) **André Marie**, *ā-payr* (1775-1836), French mathematician and physicist, father of (2), was born at Lyons, and became a teacher in the Polytechnic School of Paris, a professor in the Collège de France, and a member of the Academy. Among his works are *Observations électro-dynamiques* (1822) and *Théorie des phénomènes électro-dynamiques* (1830). His name was given to the unit of electrical current. See Life by Valson (1886).

(2) **Jean Jacques Antoine** (1800-64), French writer and philologist, son of (1), after a spell of foreign travel, lectured on the history of literature at Marseilles, and after 1830 was professor in the Collège de France. He was elected to the Academy in 1847. Ampère was deeply read in German literature, and wrote on China, Persia, India, Egypt, and Nubia. His chief work was *Histoire littéraire de la France avant le XIIe siècle* (3 vols. 1840).

AMPTHILL, Lord. See RUSSELL Family.

AMRU, or **Amr** (d. 664), Arab soldier, joined the Prophet about 629; took part in the conquest of Palestine; in 641 took Alexandria

after a fourteen months' siege (that he burnt the famous library is false); and died governor of Egypt.

AMUNDSEN, Roald Engelbregt Gravning (1872-1928), Norwegian explorer, born at Borge, early abandoned his medical studies in favour of a life at sea. In 1897 he served as first mate of the *Belgica* with the Belgian Antarctic expedition. In 1903 he sailed the Northwest passage in the smack *Gjöa*, an enterprise taking three years to complete. Amundsen's Antarctic expedition of 1910 reached the pole in December 1911, one month ahead of Scott. In 1926 he flew over the pole from Spitzbergen to Telfer in Alaska. In 1928, flying to assist in the search for Nobile, he was lost at sea. See his *My Life as an Explorer* (1927) and L. Ellsworth, *Beyond Horizons* (1938).

AMYOT, Jacques, *am-yō* (1513-93), French humanist, born at Melun, died Bishop of Auxerre. One of the most lucid of French prose writers, he translated many classical texts, the most important being his French version of Plutarch's *Lives*, which was the basis of North's translation into English, and hence of Shakespeare's *Julius Caesar*, &c. See books by Zangroniz (Paris 1906), Stivel (Paris 1909) and Cioranescu (1941).

AMYRAUT, Lat. Amyraldus Moyse, *a-mi-rō* (1596-1664), French theologian, born at Bourgueil, professor of Protestant Theology at Saumur, departed from the doctrine of predestination in the direction of 'hypothetical universalism'.

ANACHARSIS, a witty Scythian prince, travelled widely in quest of knowledge, and visited Athens in Solon's time.

ANACREON (late 6th cent. B.C.), Greek lyric poet, born at Teos, an Ionian city in Asia Minor. With his fellow townsmen he emigrated to Abdera, in Thrace, on the approach of the Persians, and lived at the court of Polycrates of Samos, at Athens, and elsewhere, singing in flowery and graceful strains the praises of the muses, of wine, and of love. He left Athens on the fall of the Pisistratids, and seems to have died, eighty-five years old, in Teos, choked by a grape-stone, according to legend. Of the five books of his poems, only a few genuine fragments have been preserved. The elegant *Odes*, translated by Cowley and Moore, which have given us the word anacreontic, are admittedly of later origin, though scraps of Anacreon's verse may have been worked into them.

ANASTASIA, Grand Duchess Anastasia Nikolaievna Romanov (1901-?1918), daughter of the Tsar Nicholas II, was believed to have perished when the Romanov family were executed by the Bolsheviks in the cellar of the Ipatiev House in Ekaterinburg on July 19, 1918. A woman now living in the Black Forest as Anna Anderson has for more than thirty years claimed to be Anastasia. Conflicting opinions as to her identity by members of the Romanov family and others failed to establish the truth of her assertion, and her claim was finally rejected by a Hamburg court in May 1961. The mystery has been the theme of books, plays and films, including an autobiography, *I, Anastasia*, with notes by R. K. von Nidda (1958).

ANAXAGORAS, *an-ak-zag'o-ras* (500 B.C.– 428 B.C.), Ionic philosopher, born at Clazomenae, taught for thirty years at Athens, where he had many illustrious pupils, among them Pericles, Euripides, and Archelaus (supposed teacher of Socrates). At last his explanations of physical phenomena by natural causes exposed him to accusation of impiety, and withdrawing to Lampsacus, on the Hellespont, he died there. He held that all matter existed originally in the condition of atoms; and that order was first produced out of chaos through an infinite intelligence (Gr. *nous*). See a monograph by Heinze (1890).

ANAXIMANDER, *-man'-* (611–547 B.C.), Ionic philosopher and successor of Thales, was born at Miletus. He held the principle of the world to be the infinite or indeterminate (*apeiron*).

ANAXIMENES, *an-ak-zim'en-eez* (d. *c.* 500 B.C.), Ionic philosopher, was born at Miletus. He held *air* to be the primary form of matter, from which all things were formed by compression.

ANCKARSTRÖM. See ANKARSTRÖM.

ANCRE, Baron de Lussigny, Marquis d', orig. **Concino Concini** (d. 1617), Italian-born French marshal, was a Florentine who came to the French court in 1600, in the train of Maria de' Medici, the wife of Henry IV. After Henry's death, he became chief favourite of the queen-regent, and was made a marquis, and, in 1614, even marshal of France, though he had never seen war. His prodigality was immense, and he squandered vast sums on the decoration of his palaces. Hated alike by nobility and populace, he was assassinated in the Louvre. His wife was executed for influencing the queen by witchcraft.

ANCUS MARCIUS (640–616 B.C.), fourth king of Rome, is said to have conquered the neighbouring Latin tribes, and settled them on the Aventine.

ANDERS, Władysław (1892–1970), Polish general, commanded Polish troops in the tsarist army in World War I and a cavalry division fighting against the Soviets in the Russo-Polish War of 1919–20. On the outbreak of World War II he commanded the Nowogrodek Cavalry Brigade, fighting both Germans and Russians, was captured by the Russians and in July 1941 was released to become c.-in-c. of the Polish ex-P.O.W. forces organized in Russia. In 1943 he became commander of the 2nd Polish Corps in Italy. After the war, deprived of his nationality by the Polish Communist Government in 1946, he was a leading figure in the 140,000-strong Free Polish community in Britain and inspector-general of the Polish forces-in-exile. He wrote *An Army in Exile* (1949).

ANDERSEN, Hans Christian (1805–75), Danish author, one of the world's great story-tellers, was born April 2, at Odense in Fünen. The son of a poor shoemaker, after his father's death he worked in a factory, but early displayed a talent for poetry. Hoping to obtain an engagement in the theatre, he found his way to Copenhagen, but was rejected for his lack of education. He next tried to become a singer, but soon found that

his physical qualities were quite unfitted for the stage. Generous friends, however, helped him; and application having been made to the king, he was placed at an advanced school. Some of his poems, particularly *The Dying Child*, had already been favourably received, and he now became better known by his *Walk to Amager*, a literary satire in the form of a humorous narrative. In 1830 he published the first collected volume of his *Poems*, and in 1831 a second, under the title of *Fantasies and Sketches*. A travelling pension granted him by the king in 1833 bore fruit in his *Travelling Sketches* of a tour in the north of Germany; *Agnes and the Merman*, completed in Switzerland; and *The Improvisatore*, a series of scenes inspired by Rome and Naples. Soon afterwards he produced *O.T.* (1836), a novel containing vivid pictures of northern scenery and manners, and *Only a Fiddler* (1837). Many more works might be mentioned, but it is such fairy tales as ' The Tin Soldier ', ' The Emperor's New Clothes ', ' The Tinderbox ', ' The Snow Queen ' and ' The Ugly Duckling ' that have gained him lasting fame and delighted children throughout the world. He died at Copenhagen, August 4, 1875. See his genially egotistic *Story of My Life* (trans. Mary Howitt 1847), his *Correspondence with the Grand-Duke of Saxe-Weimar* (Eng. trans. 1891), E. Bredsdorff, *H. C. Andersen og England* (Copenhagen 1954), Life by Nisbet Bain (1895), and *Life and Work*, 150th anniversary publication by Committee for Danish Cultural Activities (Copenhagen 1955).

ANDERSON, (1) **Carl David** (1905–), American physicist, born in New York, did notable work on gamma and cosmic rays, positrons (Nobel prize, 1936), and mesons.

(2) **Elizabeth Garrett** (1836–1917), English physician, was born in London, and was brought up at Aldeburgh, Suffolk. In 1860 she entered on the study of medicine; owing to opposition to the admission of women, she had difficulty in qualifying, but in 1865 passed the Apothecaries' Hall examination. In 1870 she was made a visiting physician to the East London Hospital, and headed the poll for the London School Board; and the university of Paris gave her the degree of M.D. Marrying (1871) J. G. S. Anderson (died 1907), she practised regularly as a physician for women and children. A sister of Dame Millicent Fawcett, she was elected mayor of Aldeburgh in 1908—the first woman mayor in England. She died December 17, 1917. Her daughter **Louisa** (1878–1943), C.B.E., organized hospitals in France in World War I, and wrote her mother's life (1939).

(3) **James** (1662–1728), Scottish antiquary and W.S., was born at Edinburgh, and in 1705 published a treatise vindicating the independence of Scotland; thenceforward to the close of his unhappy life, he was employed on his *Selectus Diplomatum et Numismatum Scotiae Thesaurus* (1739).

(4) **James** (1739–1808), Scottish writer on political economy and agriculture, was born at Hermiston, near Edinburgh; had a farm in Aberdeenshire; invented the ' Scotch plough '; edited *The Bee* at Edinburgh (1790–93); and settled in London in 1797. His *Recreations of*

Agriculture anticipated Ricardo's theory of rent.

(5) **Sir John.** See WAVERLEY.

(6) **John** (1726–96), Scottish scientist, born in Rosneath manse, Dunbartonshire, studied at Glasgow, and from 1756 to 1760 was professor of Oriental Languages, and then of Natural Philosophy. He also established a biweekly class for mechanics, and at his death left all he had to found Anderson's College in Glasgow. The author of *Institutes of Physics* (1786), &c., he also invented the balloon post, and a gun which, in 1791, he presented to the French National Convention.

(7) **Sir Kenneth Arthur Noel** (1891–1959), British general, born in India. He fought under Allenby in Palestine in 1917–18 and was c.-in-c. of British troops there 1930–32. In World War II he held commands in France, North Africa, and in Britain, and after the war in East Africa. He was governor-general of Gibraltar from 1947 to 1952 when he retired.

(8) **Mary** (1859–1940), American actress, was born at Sacramento, California. Her début as Juliet at Louisville in 1875 was successful and she played with growing popularity in America and (after 1883) in England. In 1890 she married A. de Navarro (d. 1932), retired (apart from charity), and settled in England. See her *A Few Memories* (1896), *A Few More Memories* (1936).

(9) **Maxwell** (1888–1959), American playwright, important in the development of modern American drama. His plays, some of which are in a free form of blank verse, include *What Price Glory* (1924, in collaboration with Laurence Stallings), *Elizabeth the Queen* (1930), first of several historical dramas, *Both Your Houses* (1933, Pulitzer prize), *High Tor* (1937), and *The Bad Seed* (1955).

(10) **Robert** (1806–71), American general, served in the Black Hawk war, the Mexican war, and the beginning of the Civil War, defending Fort Sumter.

(11) **Sherwood** (1876–1941), American author, born at Camden, Ohio, left his family and his lucrative position as manager of a paint factory to devote his entire time to writing. His first novel was *Windy McPherson's Son* (1916), but his best known work is *Winesburg, Ohio* (1919). See Life by Howe (1952).

(12) **Thomas** (1819–74), Scottish organic chemist, studied at Edinburgh and Stockholm, became professor of Chemistry at Glasgow, and is remembered for his discovery of pyridine.

ANDERSSON, Karl Johan (1827–67), Swedish explorer, in 1850 went with Francis Galton to Damaraland, in 1853–54 continued alone; and published *Lake Ngami, or Discoveries in South Africa* (1856). In 1858 he explored the Okavango, in 1866 set out for the Cunene. He came within sight of the stream, but had to retrace his steps, and died on the homeward journey.

ANDRADA E SILVA, José Bonifacio de, *an-drah'da ay seel'va* (1763–1838), Brazilian statesman and geologist, was leader of the movement for Brazilian independence under Dom Pedro in 1822.

ANDRADE, Edward Neville da Costa, *an'drayd* (1887–1971), English physicist, born in London, after studying at London, Heidelberg, Cambridge, and Manchester, became professor of Physics at Woolwich (1920–28), and from 1928 to 1950 at London University. He was known for his work on metals and liquids. He was director of the Royal Institution and the Davy-Faraday laboratory 1950–1952. He was elected F.R.S. in 1935 and was president of the Physical Society (1943–45).

ANDRÁSSY, (1) Julius, Count (1823–90), Hungarian statesman, father of (2), born at Volosca. A supporter of Kossuth, he was prominent in the struggle for independence (1848–49), after which he remained in exile until 1858. When the Dual Monarchy came into being in 1867, he was made prime minister of Hungary. See Life by Wertheimer (1910–13).

(2) **Julius, Count** (1860–1929), Hungarian statesman, son of (1), born at Toketerebes, became minister of the interior in 1900, and foreign minister in 1918. In 1921 he attempted to restore the monarchy, and was imprisoned, but after his release became leader of the royalist opposition. He wrote several historical works.

ANDRÉ, John (1751–80), British officer, was born in London, of French-Swiss descent; took over his father's business; but in 1774 joined the army in Canada, and became aide-de-camp to Sir Henry Clinton, and adjutant-general. When in 1780 Benedict Arnold (q.v.) obtained the command of West Point, André was selected to make the arrangements for its betrayal. Arnold and André met on September 20, near Haverstraw on the Hudson; then André began his dangerous journey to New York. As he was nearing the British lines he was captured and handed over to the American military authorities. The papers found on him proved him a spy; a military board convened by Washington declared that 'agreeably to the laws and usages of nations he ought to suffer death'; and he was hanged at Tappantown. In 1821 his remains were interred in Westminster Abbey. See his *Journal* (1904), Life by Sargent (1902), and Lossing's *Two Spies* (1886).

ANDREÄ, Johann Valentin (1586–1654), German theologian, was born near Tübingen, and died at Stuttgart, the Protestant court-chaplain. Long regarded as the founder or restorer of the Rosicrucians, he wrote *Chymische Hochzeit Christiani Rosenkreuz* (1616).

ANDREA DEL SARTO. See SARTO.

ANDRÉE, Salomon August (1854–97), Swedish engineer, born at Gränna, started from Danes' Island in a balloon for the North Pole in 1897. His body was found on White Island in 1930.

ANDREEV, Leonid (1871–1919), Russian dramatist and novelist, born at Orel, suffered much from poverty and ill-health as a student, and attempted suicide, before taking to writing and portrait painting. Many of his works have been translated into English, as *The Seven that were Hanged* (1909), *The Red Laugh* (1905), &c.

ANDREW, St. One of the twelve apostles, brother of Simon Peter, a fisherman converted by John the Baptist. He is traditionally supposed to have preached the gospel in Asia Minor and Scythia, and to have been crucified in Achaia by order of the Roman governor. The belief that his cross was X-shaped dates only from the 14th century. The patron saint of Scotland and of Russia, he is commemorated on November 30.

ANDREW, name of three kings of Hungary:

Andrew I (?–1060), cousin of King Stephen (q.v.). He reigned from 1046–60, when he was overthrown by his brother Bela I, whose right of succession he had denied.

Andrew II (1175–1235), son of Bela III. His long reign (1205–1235) was made turbulent by anarchic nobles, and in 1222 he was compelled to sign the Golden Bull, the Hungarian equivalent of Magna Carta.

Andrew III (?–1301), called the **Venetian**. Grandson of Andrew II, he was the last of the Arpàd dynasty. He was one of several contestants for the throne after the murder of Ladislas IV. By defeating Charles Martel, the Papal candidate, at the battle of Agram in 1291, he was able to make good his claim.

ANDREW, John Albion (1818–67), American anti-slavery statesman, four times governor of Mass. See Life by H. G. Pearson (1904).

ANDREWES, Lancelot (1555–1626), English prelate, was born at Barking in 1555, and educated at Ratcliffe, Merchant Taylors' School, and Pembroke Hall, Cambridge, of which he was in 1576 elected fellow. Taking orders in 1580, he accompanied the Earl of Huntingdon to the north; and in 1589, through Walsingham's influence, he was appointed a prebendary of St Paul's and master of Pembroke Hall. In 1597 Elizabeth made him a prebendary, and in 1601 dean, of Westminster. He rose still higher in favour with King James, who appreciated his learning and peculiar oratory. He attended the Hampton Court Conference, and took part in the translation of the Bible. In 1605 he was consecrated Bishop of Chichester; in 1609 he was translated to Ely, and in 1618 to Winchester, having the year before accompanied the king to Scotland as one of the royal instruments for persuading the Scots of the superiority of episcopacy over presbytery. He died September 27, 1626. His works fill 8 vols. of the *Library of Anglo-Catholic Theology* (1841–54) and he is considered one of the most learned theologians of his time. See Lives by Russell (1863), Ottley (1894), Macleane (1910) and Welsby (1958); and T. S. Eliot's book (1928).

ANDREWS, (1) **Roy Chapman** (1884–1960), American naturalist and explorer, born in Beloit, Wis. He is popularly known as the discoverer, in Mongolia, of fossil dinosaur eggs, though his many and valuable contributions to palaeontology, archaeology, botany, zoology, geology, and topography have assured him a more lasting reputation. He explored Alaska before World War I, and was on several expeditions to Central Asia, sponsored by the American Museum of Natural History, of which he became honorary director. His published works include *Across Mongolian Plains* (1921), *Ends of Earth* (1929), *Meet Your Ancestors* (1945), *Heart of Asia*

(1951), and two volumes on whaling.

(2) **Thomas** (1813–85), Irish physical chemist, was born in Belfast. He practised as a physician at Belfast, where from 1849 to 1879 he was professor of Chemistry. He is noted for his discovery of the critical temperature of gases, above which they cannot be liquefied, however great the pressure applied. See his *Scientific Papers*, ed. with a memoir, by Tait and Crum Brown (1889).

ANDRIĆ, Ivo (1892–   ), Yugoslav author and diplomat, born near Travnik, was minister in Berlin at the outbreak of war in 1939. His chief works, *The Bridge on the Drina* (1945) and *Bosnian Story* (1945), won for him the Nobel prize for literature (1961) and the sobriquet ' the Yugoslav Tolstoy '.

ANDRIEUX, François Guillaume Jean Stanislas, *ā-dree-yœ* (1759–1833), French scholar and dramatist, born at Strasburg, became professor of French Literature at the Collège de France (1814) and secretary of the Académie (1829). His works are classical in style, for he was antagonistic to the rising influence of Romanticism. They include *Les Étourdes* (1788), *La Comédienne* (1816), &c.

ANDRONICUS, *-nī'-*, the name of four Byzantine emperors:

Andronicus I Comnenus (1110?–85), grandson of Alexius I, in his youth served against the Turks, was imprisoned for treason for twelve years, but escaped to Russia. Pardoned and employed again, he fell once more into disfavour; and after his scandalous seduction of Theodora, the widow of Baldwin, king of Jerusalem, he settled among the Turks in Asia Minor, with a band of outlaws. After the death of Manuel in 1182, he was recalled to become first guardian, then colleague, of the young Emperor Alexius II. Soon after, he caused the empress-mother to be strangled, and then Alexius himself, marrying his youthful widow. His reign was vigorous, and restored prosperity to the provinces; but tyranny and murder were its characteristics in the capital.

Andronicus II Palaeologus (1260–1332), during his reign (1282–1328) withdrew from the negotiations for the union of the Greek and Roman communions, and restored the Greek ritual in full. He and the empire suffered much from Spanish mercenaries, hired for the wars with the Turks.

Andronicus III Palaeologus (1296?–1341), grandson of the foregoing, excluded from the succession for the murder of his brother, compelled his grandfather to make him his colleague in the empire and then to abdicate (1328). Meanwhile the Turks occupied the southern shores of the Bosporus, and the Serbians conquered Bulgaria, Epirus and Macedonia.

Andronicus IV Palaeologus (d. 1385), leagued himself with the Turks to dethrone his father, John V (son of Andronicus III), but was blinded and imprisoned, escaped in 1376, and took possession of the capital. Ultimately he made a treaty with his father.

ANDRONICUS, called **Cyrrhestes** (1st cent. B.C.), Greek architect, born at Cyrrhus. He constructed the Tower of the Winds at Athens, known in the Middle Ages as the Lantern of Demosthenes.

ANDRONICUS, Livius. See LIVIUS ANDRONICUS.

ANDRONICUS OF RHODES (fl. 70–50 B.C.), Greek Peripatetic philosopher, who lived at Rome in Cicero's time and edited the writings of Aristotle.

ANEURIN (fl. 6th–7th cents. A.D.), a Welsh poet, whose principal work, the *Gododin*, celebrates the British heroes who fell in conflict with the Saxons in the bloody battle of Cattraeth, now usually identified with the battle the Saxons called Degsastan (Dawstane in Liddesdale?), and fought in A.D. 603. See the editions and translations by Williams ab Ithel (1852), Skene (in *The Four Ancient Books of Wales*, 1866), and T. Stephens (1885).

ANGAS, George Fife (1789–1879), English shipowner, a founder of South Australia after 1851, was born at Newcastle-on-Tyne, and died at Adelaide. See *Life* by Hodder (1891).

ANGELICO, Fra, real name **Guido di Pietri,** monastic name **Giovanni da Fiesole** (1387–1455), Italian painter, was born at Vicchio in Tuscany. In 1407 he entered the Dominican monastery at Fiesole, in 1436 he was transferred to Florence, and in 1445 was summoned by the pope to Rome, where thenceforward he chiefly resided till his death, March 18, 1455. His most important frescoes are those in the Florentine convent of San Marco (now a museum), at Orvieto, and in the Nicholas Chapel of the Vatican. Others were painted at Cortona and Fiesole. Of his easel pictures, the Louvre possesses a splendid example, *The Coronation of the Virgin,* and the London National Gallery (since 1860) a *Glory,* or Christ with 265 saints—both of which were originally at Fiesole. There are fine examples of his art in the Uffizi at Florence. Fra Angelico's constant aim is to arouse devotional feeling through the contemplation of unearthly loveliness; the ethereal beauty of his angelic figures gave him his new name. He was beatified after his death. See works by Hausenstein (1924; trans. 1928), Schneider (Paris 1925), Bazin (Paris 1941), Argan (1955).

ANGELL, Norman, in full, **Sir Ralph Norman Angell Lane** (1872–1967), English pacificist (Nobel peace prize, 1933), born at Holbeach, wrote *The Great Illusion* (1910; trans. in many languages) to prove the economic futility of war even for the winners.

ANGELLIER, Auguste Jean, *ā-zhel-yay* (1848–1911), French poet and critic, born at Dunkirk, was English professor at Lille, and wrote a masterly *Life of Robert Burns* (1893).

ANGELO, Michael. See MICHELANGELO.

ANGELUS SILESIUS, properly **Johann Scheffler** (1624–77), German philosophical poet, born at Breslau, was a Protestant physician who became a Catholic priest. See *Life* by Ellinger (1927).

ANGERSTEIN, John Julius, *an'gèr-stīn* (1735–1823), a London underwriter of Russian origin, whose thirty-eight pictures, bought in 1824 for £57,000, formed the nucleus of the National Gallery.

ANGERVILLE. See AUNGERVILLE.

ANGIOLIERI, Cecco, *an-jō-lyay'ree* (c. 1260–c. 1312), Italian poet, born in Siena. Nothing is known of his life except from his sonnets, the only kind of verse he wrote, which reveal a drinker, lecher and gambler with a cynical, sardonic character and a heartless wit. He attacked Dante in three poems. The master's replies are unrecorded.

ANGLESEY, Henry William Paget, 1st Marquis of (1768–1854), born in London, May 17, from Westminster passed to Christ Church, Oxford, sat in parliament off and on from 1790 to 1810; and in 1812 succeeded his father as Earl of Uxbridge. He served in the army with distinction in Flanders (1794), Holland (1799), and the Peninsular war (1808); and for his splendid services as commander of the British cavalry at Waterloo, where he lost a leg, he was made Marquis of Anglesey. In 1828 he was appointed lord-lieutenant of Ireland, advocated Catholic emancipation, and was recalled by Wellington in 1829. In 1830–33 he held the same office under Lord Grey's administration; but lost his popularity through coercive measures against O'Connell. To him Ireland is indebted for the Board of Education. In 1846–52, now field-marshal, he was master-general of the ordnance. See Anglesey, *One-Leg* (1961).

ANGOULÊME, Louis Antoine de Bourbon, Duc d', *ā-goo-laym* (1775–1844), eldest son of Charles X of France. He retired from France along with his father after the Revolution, and lived in various places, including Holyrood. In 1799 he married his cousin, Marie Thérèse (1778–1851), only daughter of Louis XVI, ' the only man in the family ', in the words of Napoleon. After the Restoration, he made a feeble effort, as lieutenant-general of France, to oppose Napoleon on his return from Elba; and in 1823 he led the French army of invasion into Spain. On the revolution in July 1830, he accompanied his father into exile, and died at Görz. See works on the duke by Vte. de Guichen (1909), on the duchess by Lenotre (trans. 1908) and Turquan (trans. 1910).

ÅNGSTRÖM, Anders Jonas (1814–74), Swedish physicist, born at Lödgö, was *privatdozent* (1839), keeper of the observatory (1843), and professor of Physics (1858), and from 1867 secretary to the Royal Society at Uppsala. He wrote on heat, magnetism, and especially optics; the ångström unit, for measuring wavelengths of light, is named after him. His son, **Knut J. Ångström** (1857–1910), was also a noted Uppsala physicist, important for his researches on solar radiation.

ANGUS, Marion (1866–1946), Scottish poet, born in Aberdeen. Her volumes of verse include *The Lilt and Other Verses* (1922), *Sun and Candlelight* (1927), *The Singin' Lass* (1929), and *Lost Country* (1937). Her selected poems were published posthumously, with a memoir, in 1950.

ANIMUCCIA, Giovanni, *an-i-moot'cha* (c. 1500–71), Italian composer, born in Florence. No records of his early life exist, but in 1555 he became choirmaster at the Vatican, a post he held until his death, when he was succeeded by Palestrina. A man of deep religious feeling, he was influenced by St Philip Neri, for whose oratory he composed the *Laudi*—semidramatic religious pieces in popular style from which oratorio developed.

ANJOU, Duke of. See HENRY II.

ANKARSTRÖM, Johan Jakob (1762–92), the assassin of Gustavus III of Sweden, was a page at court, served in the bodyguard, but after settling on his estates (1783), was tried for treason, though released for want of evidence. Soon after he formed a plot with a ring of discontented nobles to murder Gustavus, and, the lot falling on him, wounded the king mortally with a pistol at a masked ball. He was publicly flogged for three days, and then executed.

ANKER-LARSEN, Johannes (1874–1957), Danish novelist and dramatist, born in Langeland. He left theology and the law for the theatre and literature. After acting for eight years, he became stage-director at various theatres, including the Royal Theatre, Copenhagen. His work reflects the religious unrest of his time and his characters tend to try to escape from life by flights into fantasy. He was awarded the Gyldendal prize for his novel *Vises Sten* (' The Philosopher's Stone ') in 1923.

ANNA CARLOVNA (1718–46), niece of the Empress Anna Ivanovna (q.v.), and wife of a Duke of Brunswick, was regent during the one year's reign (1740–41) of her infant son Ivan. He was murdered, and she herself died in prison.

ANNA COMNENA (1083–1148), Byzantine princess, was the daughter of the Emperor Alexius I (Comnenus). She tried in vain to secure the imperial crown, and failed in her attempt to overthrow or poison her brother (1118), her husband Bryennius being either too timid or too virtuous to back her. Disappointed and ashamed, she withdrew from the court, and sought solace in literature. On the death of her husband (1137), she retired into a convent. Her life of her father, though a rhetorical panegyric, is one of the better class of Byzantine histories. See Oster's *Anna Comnena* (1868–71), books by Naomi Mitchison (1928) and Georgina Buckler (1929).

ANNA IVANOVNA (1693–1740), Empress of Russia, was the second daughter of Ivan, elder brother of Peter the Great. She married in 1710 the Duke of Courland, who died next year. The throne of Russia was bestowed on her by the Supreme Council in 1730, on her accepting constitutional limitations. But she soon declared herself autocrat; her paramour, Biron (q.v.), established a reign of terror, and is said to have banished 20,000 persons to Siberia.

ANNE, St, wife of St Joachim, and mother of the Virgin Mary, is first mentioned in the *Protevangelium* of James, in the 2nd century. She is the patron saint of carpenters. Her feast day is July 26.

ANNE (1665–1714), Queen of Great Britain and Ireland, the last Stuart sovereign, was born at St James's Palace. She was the second daughter of James II (then Duke of York), by his first wife, Anne Hyde, the daughter of Clarendon. Her mother died in 1671, and in 1672 her father joined the Church of Rome; but his daughters were brought up members of the Church of England, to which Anne always retained an ardent if not a very enlightened attachment. In 1683 she was married to the indolent and good-natured Prince George of Denmark (1653–1708), when Sarah Jennings (1660–1744), the wife of Lord Churchill (afterwards Duke of Marlborough), was appointed a lady of her bedchamber. As Anne needed someone on whom she could lean, Lady Churchill speedily acquired supreme influence over her, which she exerted in favour of her husband. In their correspondence, Anne went by the name of Mrs Morley, and Lady Churchill by that of Mrs Freeman. During her father's reign, Anne lived in retirement, taking no part in politics. On the landing of the Prince of Orange, she soon joined his party; but quarrelled presently with her sister, and by 1692 was drawn into intrigues, in which both the Churchills were engaged, for the restoration of her father, or to secure the succession to his son. She was herself childless when, on the death of William III· on March 8, 1702, she succeeded to the throne. She had borne, indeed, seventeen children; but one only, William, Duke of Gloucester (1689–1700), survived infancy. The influence of Marlborough and his wife was most powerfully felt in all public affairs during the greater part of her reign, the chief event of which was the union of England and Scotland (1707). The strife of parties was extremely violent, and political complications were increased by the queen's anxiety to secure the succession for her brother. In so far as she had any political principles, they were opposed to that constitutional liberty to which she owed her occupancy of the throne. These principles and her family attachment tended to alienate her from the Marlboroughs, whose policy, from the time of her accession, had become adverse to Jacobitism, and who now, along with Godolphin, were at the head of the Whig party. The duchess also offended the queen by presuming too boldly upon the power she had so long possessed. In 1710 they parted, never to meet again. Anne had found a new favourite in Abigail Masham, a cousin of the duchess, who herself, about 1704, had introduced her into the royal household. To Mrs Masham's influence the change of government in 1710 was in great measure due when the Tories came into office, Harley (afterwards Earl of Oxford) and St John (Lord Bolingbroke) becoming the leaders of the ministry. But, although concurring more or less in a design to secure the succession of the throne to her brother, the new ministers had quarrels among themselves which prevented its successful prosecution, and kept the poor queen in a state of constant unrest. She died August 1, 1714. See works by J. H. Burton (1880), McCarthy (1902), H. Paul (1907), P. F. W. Ryan (1908), G. M. Trevelyan (1930–34).

ANNE BOLEYN. See BOLEYN.

ANNE OF AUSTRIA (1601–66), eldest daughter of Philip III of Spain, in 1615 became the wife of Louis XIII of France. The marriage was so far from being a happy one, that the royal pair lived for the first twenty-two years in a state of virtual separation—a result due chiefly to the influence of Richelieu. In 1643 Anne became queen-regent for the baby Louis XIV. Her minister

Mazarin (q.v.) died in 1661, and she retired to the convent of Val de Grâce. See works by M. W. Freer (1864, new ed. 1912; 1866), Mme de Motteville's *Mémoires* (trans. 1902), and Mrs C. Grant's *Queen and Cardinal* (1906).

ANNE OF BOHEMIA (1366–94), in 1382 married Richard II (q.v.).

ANNE OF BRITTANY (1476–1514), wife of Charles VIII and Louis XII of France, was an admirable Duchess of Brittany, her hereditary dominion.

ANNE OF CLEVES (1515–57), a Lutheran princess, plain of feature, who in 1540 married as his fourth queen, Henry VIII, a marriage declared null and void six months afterwards.

ANNE OF DENMARK (1574–1619), in 1589 married James VI of Scotland, the future James I of England (q.v.).

ANNIGONI, Pietro, *an-i-gō'nee* (1910–), Italian painter, born at Milan. After studying at the Accademia delle Belle Arti at Florence, he held his first one-man show at Florence in 1932. During the 1950s he worked in England, and held a London exhibition in 1954. He is one of the few 20th-century artists to put into practice the technical methods of the old masters, and his most usual medium is tempera, although there are frescoes by him in the Convent of St Mark at Florence (executed in 1937). His Renaissance manner is shown at its best in his portraits, e.g., of H.M. The Queen (1955). See *Pietro Annigoni* (1954), ed. C. R. Cammell.

ANNING, Mary (1799–1847), English palaeontologist, was born at Lyme Regis, the daughter of a carpenter and vendor of specimens, who, dying in 1810, left her to make her own living. In 1811 she discovered in a local cliff the fossil skeleton of an ichthyosaurus, now in the British Museum. She also discovered the first plesiosaurus and, in 1828, the first pterodactyl.

ANNUNZIO. See D'ANNUNZIO.

ANOUILH, Jean, *an-wee* (1910–), French dramatist, born in Bordeaux of French and Basque parentage. He began his career as a copywriter and as a gag-man in films. His first play, *L'Hermine* (1931) was not a success; but his steady output soon earned him recognition as one of the leading dramatists of the contemporary theatre. He was influenced by the neoclassical fashion inspired by Giraudoux, but his very personal approach to the re-interpretation of Greek myths is less poetic and more in tune with contemporary taste. Among his many successful plays may be mentioned *Le Voyageur sans bagage* (1938), *Le Bal des voleurs* (1938) (in English as *Thieves' Carnival*, 1952), *La Sauvage* (1938), *Eurydice* (1942) (in English as *Point of Departure*, 1950), *Antigone* (1946), *Médée* (1946), *L'Invitation au château* (1948) (adapted by Christopher Fry as *Ring Round the Moon*, 1950), *L'Alouette* (1953) (in English as *The Lark*, 1955), *Becket* (in London, 1961), and *Poor Bitos* (in London, 1963-64). See study by Gignoux (Paris 1946).

ANQUETIL-DUPERRON, Abraham Hyacinthe, *ã-kě-teel dü-pe-rõ* (1731–1805), French orientalist, born in Paris, studied in India, translated the *Zend-avesta* into French (1771), and a Persian version of the *Upanishads* into Latin. His brother, **Louis-Pierre Anquetil** (1723–1806), was a notable historian.

ANSCHÜTZ, Ottomar, *an'shüts* (1846–1907), German photographer, born in Yugoslavia. He was a pioneer of instantaneous photography, and was one of the first to make a series of pictures of moving animals and people, so making a substantial contribution to the invention of the cinematograph.

ANSCHÜTZ-KÄMPFE, Hermann, *an'shütskemp'fè* (1872–1931), German engineer, born at Zweibrücken. In 1902 he began experiments with the gyroscope as the basis for the mariners' compass, and in 1908 brought out the gyrocompass, which has been in general use since.

ANSDELL, Richard (1815–85), English animal and genre painter, born at Liverpool, became an R.A. in 1870.

ANSELM, St (1033–1109), Archbishop of Canterbury, was nobly born at or near Aosta, in Piedmont. At fifteen he ardently desired to embrace the monastic life, but his father refused his consent; and about 1056, his mother being dead, he left home, and, after three years in Burgundy and France, was attracted by Lanfranc's fame to the abbey of Bec, in Normandy. In 1063 he succeeded his master as prior, and in 1078 became Abbot of Bec, the most famous school of the 11th century. Lanfranc, who had meantime become Archbishop of Canterbury, died in 1089; and the diocese remained four years vacant till in 1093 Anselm was appointed. He was distinguished both as a churchman and a philosopher. His numerous embroilments with William Rufus and his successor, and the unbending spirit which he displayed, indicate the vigour and resoluteness of his character, as much as his writings exhibit the depth and acuteness of his intellect. Exiled by Rufus, Anselm returned at Henry's urgent request; but the new monarch's demand that he should renew his homage, and be again invested with his archbishopric, was met with an absolute refusal, and led to a second exile of two years' duration. In 1107, however, Anselm's threat of excommunication led to a reconciliation, and the compromise was devised which, in 1122, was accepted by pope and emperor at Worms. Embracing without question the doctrines of the church mostly as stated by Augustine, and holding that belief must precede knowledge and must be implicit and undoubting, Anselm yet felt the necessity of a religious philosophy, and for this purpose wrote his *Monologion, Proslogion*, and *Cur Deus Homo* (Eng. trans. by Prout 1887). Besides his philosophical treatises, his *Meditations* and *Letters* have come down to us, revealing his humble fervent faith, and the tender sympathy of his nature. He died April 21, 1109, and was buried next to Lanfranc at Canterbury; in 1494 he was canonized. See Rémusat's *Anselme* (2nd ed. 1868); R. W. Church's *Anselm* (1870); *Life and Times of St Anselm* (1883) by Martin Rule and his Rolls edition of Eadmer's two Lives of Anselm (1884); and monographs by J. M. Rigg (1896) and McIntyre (1954).

ANSGAR, St (801–865), the Apostle of the North, was a native of Picardy, and monk of

Corbie, who in 826 went, with his colleague Autbert, to preach Christianity to the heathen Northmen of Schleswig. In 832 the pope established an archbishopric in Hamburg (transferred to Bremen in 848), and Ansgar was appointed the first archbishop. See his Life by Tappehorn (Münst. 1863).

ANSON, (1) George, Baron Anson (1697–1762), English admiral, born April 23, at Shugborough Park, Staffs., entered the navy in 1712, and was made a captain in 1724. In 1739, on the outbreak of war with Spain, he received the command of a pacific squadron of six vessels, and sailed from England in September 1740. With only one ship, and less than two hundred men, but with £500,000 of Spanish treasure, he returned to Spithead, June 15, 1744, having circumnavigated the globe in three years and nine months. Anson was made rear-admiral of the blue (1744); and in 1747, having utterly defeated the French off Cape Finisterre, and captured £300,000, he was made Baron Anson of Soberton, and, four years later, first lord of the Admiralty. In 1761 he received the high dignity of admiral of the fleet. He died June 6, 1762. Of the popular *Voyage round the World* (1748), whether edited by Walter or Robins, he himself was virtually the author. See Lives by Sir J. Barrow (1839) and W. V. Anson (1912).

(2) **Sir William Reynell** (1843–1914), English jurist, born at Walberton, Sussex, was warden of All Souls College (from 1881) and M.P. for Oxford University (from 1899). His *Principles of the English Law of Contract* (1884) and *Law and Custom of the Constitution* (1886–92) are standard works.

ANSPACH, Elizabeth, Margravine of (1750–1828), English writer, was the daughter of Lord Berkeley, first married (1767) to Lord Craven, but separated from him (1780). After travelling awhile, she settled in the house of the Margrave of Anspach and Bayreuth, whom on Lord Craven's death (1791) she married. She wrote books of travel, plays, and entertaining *Memoirs* (1826). An earlier Margravine of Anspach and Bayreuth was the witty **Wilhelmine** (1709–58), sister of Frederick the Great.

ANSTEY, (1) Christopher (1724–1805), English writer, author in 1766 of the *New Bath Guide*, was educated at Bury St Edmunds, Eton, and King's College, Cambridge, of which he was a fellow (1745–54).

(2) **F.**, pseudonym of **Thomas Anstey Guthrie** (1856–1934), English writer, born in London, who studied at Trinity Hall, Cambridge, and in 1880 was called to the bar. A whimsical humorist, he wrote *Vice Versa* (1882), *The Tinted Venus* (1885), *The Brass Bottle* (1900), &c.

ANTALCIDAS, *an-tal'si-das*, a Spartan politician, chiefly known by the treaty concluded by him with Persia at the close of the Corinthian war in 386 B.C.

ANTAR, more fully **Antara Ibn Shaddad el-Absi** (6th cent.), Arab-Negro poet and warrior, born of a famous Absite chieftain and a black slave somewhere in the desert near Medina, Saudi Arabia. The author of one of the seven Golden Odes of Arabic literature, and the subject of the 10th-century *Romance*

of *Antar*, he is regarded as the symbol of Bedouin heroism and chivalry and by some as ' the father of knights '. See T. Hamilton, *Antar: A Bedoueen Romance* (1820), and A. J. Arberry, *The Seven Odes* (1957).

ANTENOR, *an-tee'nor*, Athenian sculptor, active about 500 B.C., and known to have executed bronze statues of *Harmodius* and *Aristogiton*, and a statue of *Kore* in the Acropolis.

ANTHEIL, George, *an'tīl* (1900–59), American composer of Polish descent, born in New Jersey. Antheil studied in Philadelphia and under Ernest Bloch, spending some years in Europe as a professional pianist before becoming known as the composer of the *Jazz Symphony* (1925), the *Ballet Mécanique* (1927), and the opera *Transatlantic* (1930). The sensation caused by the ballet, written for ten pianos and a variety of eccentric percussion instruments, overshadowed his more traditional later works, which include five symphonies, concertos, several more operas, and chamber music. See his autobiographical *Bad Boy of Music* (1945).

ANTHONY, St. See ANTONY, ST.

ANTHONY, Susan Brownell (1820–1906), U.S. women's suffrage leader, was born at Adams, Mass. Early active in temperance and antislavery movements, she became the champion of women's rights in 1854. From 1869 she was a leader of the National Woman Suffrage Association. She organized the International Council of Women (1888) and the International Woman Suffrage Alliance (1904).

ANTIGONUS, called Cyclops, or the One-eyed, *-tig'-* (d. 301 B.C.), Greek soldier, one of the generals of Alexander the Great, received, after the latter's death, the provinces of Phrygia Major, Lycia, and Pamphylia. On Antipater's death in 319, he aspired to the sovereignty of Asia, and waged incessant wars against the other generals, making himself master of all Asia Minor and Syria. In 306 he assumed the title of king, but was defeated and slain by Lysimachus, Cassander, and Seleucus at Ipsus in Phrygia.

ANTIGONUS GONATAS (d. 239 B.C.), king of Macedon, did not mount his throne until 276, seven years after the death of his father, Demetrius Poliorcetes. Pyrrhus of Epirus overran Macedonia in 274, but Antigonus soon recovered his kindgom, and kept it.

ANTINOÜS, *-tin'-* (d. 122), Bithynian youth of matchless beauty, a native of Claudiopolis, the favourite of the Emperor Hadrian, and his companion in all his journeys. He was drowned in the Nile, near Besa, perhaps through suicide, either from weariness of the life he led, or from a belief that his voluntary death would avert disaster from the emperor. The emperor enrolled him among the gods.

ANTIOCHUS, *an-tī'o-kus*, the name of thirteen kings of Syria of the Seleucid dynasty of whom the following are noteworthy:

Antiochus I (323–261 B.C.), called **Sōter**, was the son of Seleucus, one of Alexander's generals, whose murder in 280 gave him the whole Syrian empire, but left him too weak to assert his right to Macedonia. He gained the name of Sōter (' Saviour ') for a victory over the Gauls, but fell in battle with them.

Antiochus II (286–247 B.C.), called **Theos** (' God '), his successor, was thus named by the Milesians, whom he freed from their tyrant Timarchus. He married Berenice, daughter of Ptolemy II, exiling his first wife, Laodice, and her children. On his death there followed a struggle between the rival queens; Berenice and her son were murdered and Laodice's son, Seleucus, succeeded. That Antiochus and Laodice were reconciled, and that Laodice poisoned Antiochus, are probably inventions.

Antiochus III (242–187 B.C.), **the Great**, grandson of the foregoing, who in 223 succeeded his father, Seleucus Callinicus, was the most distinguished of the Seleucidae. He waged war with success against Ptolemy Philopator, and though defeated at Raphia near Gaza (217), he obtained entire possession of Palestine and Coele-Syria (198), dowering therewith his daughter Cleopatra on her betrothal to the young king Ptolemy of Egypt. He afterwards became involved in war with the Romans, who had conquered Macedonia; but he declined to invade Italy at the instigation of Hannibal, who had come to his court for refuge. He crossed over into Greece, but was defeated in 191 at Thermopylae, and in 190 or 189 by Scipio at Magnesia. Peace was granted him only on condition of his yielding all his dominions west of Mount Taurus, and paying a heavy tribute. To raise the money, he attacked a rich temple in Elymais, when the people rose against him, and killed him (187 B.C.).

Antiochus IV (d. 163 B.C.), called **Epiphanes**, son of the foregoing, succeeded his brother in 175, fought against Egypt and conquered a great part of it. He twice took Jerusalem; and, endeavouring there to establish the worship of Greek gods, excited the Jews to a successful insurrection under Mattathias and his heroic sons, the Maccabees.

Antiochus XIII, called **Asiaticus** (ruled 69–64 B.C.), was deprived of his kingdom by Pompey, who reduced Syria to a Roman province.

ANTIPATER, *-tip'-*, (1) (398–319 B.C.), Macedonian general, highly trusted by Philip and Alexander the Great, left by the latter as regent in Macedonia, 334 B.C. He discharged the duties with great ability, both before and after the death of Alexander, in 322 defeating an alliance of the Greek states.

(2) (d. 43 B.C.), the father of Herod the Great, appointed by Julius Caesar procurator of Judaea in 47 B.C. He died by poisoning.

(3) (d. 4 B.C.), the son of Herod the Great by his first wife, a worthless prince, who was perpetually conspiring against the life of his brothers, but was executed in prison five days before Herod died.

ANTIPHON (480–411 B.C.), the earliest of the ten Attic orators, born at Rhamnus in Attica, belonged to the oligarchical party; and to him, according to his pupil Thucydides, was mainly due the establishment of the government of the Four Hundred. On its fall six months later, he was condemned to death, in spite of his noble defence. Of his fifteen extant orations, the best edition is by Blass (Leip. 1881).

ANTISTHENES, *an-tis'thē-neez* (c. 444–370

B.C.), Greek philosopher, founder of the Cynic school, was the son of an Athenian father and a Thracian mother. He fought at Tanagra (426 B.C.), was first a disciple of Gorgias, afterwards a friend of Socrates, and died at Athens.

ANTOINE, André, *ã-twan* (1858–1943), French actor-manager, born at Limoges, as actor, founder of the Théâtre Libre (1887), and director of the Odéon (from 1906), greatly influenced the French stage.

ANTOKOLSKI, Mark Matveevich, *-kol'-* (1843–1902), Russian sculptor, born at Wilno of Jewish parentage. From 1880 he lived and worked in Paris, but most of his works are in the Alexander III Museum at Leningrad. *Ivan the Terrible* and *Turgeniev* are the most famous of his portrait statues.

ANTOMMARCHI, Francesco, *an-tom-mahr'-kee* (1780–1838), Napoleon's physician at St Helena from 1818, was a native of Corsica. Napoleon ultimately gave him his full confidence, and left him 100,000 francs. After his return to Europe, he published *Les Derniers Moments de Napoléon* (1823). During the Polish revolution he did duty at Warsaw as director of military hospitals. He afterwards went to the West Indies, and died in Cuba.

ANTONELLI, Giacomo (1806–76), Italian cardinal, born at Sonnino, son of a woodcutter. In 1819, his birthplace having been demolished as a nest of bandits, Antonelli came to Rome, and entered the Grand Seminary, where he gained the favour of Pope Gregory XVI. In 1847 he was made cardinal-deacon by Pius IX, and in 1848 was president and minister of foreign affairs in a Liberal cabinet, which framed the famous *Statuto* or Constitution. He accompanied the pope in his flight to Gaeta, and, returning with him to Rome, supported the reactionary policy. In 1855 an attempt was made upon his life. In the Vatican Council of 1869–70 Antonelli showed great tact and ability. After his death, the vast property, £1,600,000, bequeathed to his three brothers, was vainly disputed by a *soi-disant* daughter (1877–79).

ANTONELLO DA MESSINA (c. 1430–79), Italian painter, who is said to have introduced into Italy the Flemish methods of oil-painting, which he had learned from the Van Eycks. His *St Jerome* is in the National Gallery.

ANTONESCU, Ion, *-nes'-* (1882–1946), Rumanian general and dictator, born at Pitesti. He was military attaché in Rome and London, and became chief of staff in 1937. The following year he was suspended from the army and imprisoned as one of the leaders of an unsuccessful revolt, but was soon released and made minister of war. In 1940 he was made premier, assumed dictatorial powers, forced the abdication of King Carol, and till 1944 was dictator. In 1946 he was executed for his part in bringing Rumania into the war on the side of Germany.

ANTONINUS, M. Aurelius. See AURELIUS.

ANTONINUS PIUS, Titus Aurelius Fulvus (A.D. 86–161), Roman emperor, inherited great wealth, and in 120 was made consul. Sent as proconsul into Asia by the Emperor Hadrian, in 138 he was adopted by him and the same year came to the throne. His reign was proverbially peaceful and happy. In his private character he was simple, temperate, and benevolent; while in public affairs he acted as the father of his people. The persecution of Christians was partly stayed by his mild measures, and Justin Martyr's *Apologia* was received by him with favour. In his reign the empire was extended, and the wall named after him built between the Forth and Clyde. The epithet *Pius* was conferred on him for his defence of Hadrian's memory. By his muchloved but worthless wife Faustina he had four children; one married Marcus Aurelius, his adopted son and successor. See works by Lacour-Gayet (Par. 1888) and E. C. Bryant (1894).

ANTONIUS, Marcus (*c.* 83 B.C.–30 B.C.), Roman triumvir, on his mother's side was related to Julius Caesar. His youth was dissipated, and, pressed by creditors, he escaped to Athens in 58 B.C. In Palestine and Egypt he ingratiated himself with the soldiery; and, after assisting Caesar in Gaul, he went to Rome in 50 B.C., to uphold his great kinsman, and was appointed quaestor, augur, and tribune of the plebs. Next year he was expelled from the curia, and fled to Caesar, who made this a pretext for his war against Pompey. Antony was appointed commander-in-chief in Italy; at Pharsalia he led the left wing of Caesar's army. In 47 B.C. he was made master of the horse by Caesar, who left him to govern Italy during his absence in Africa. Antony, as usual, disgraced himself. He drank, he divorced his wife, and took up with an actress. In 44 B.C., as consul, he vainly endeavoured to prevail on the Romans to recognize Caesar as emperor. On Caesar's assassination, he played the part so finely described by Shakespeare, and the flight of the conspirators from Rome left him with almost absolute power. Next, we find him in dispute with Octavian (see AUGUSTUS), besieging Mutina, and denounced by Cicero. The defeat of Mutina (43 B.C.) drove him a fugitive beyond the Alps; but in Gaul he visited the camp of Lepidus, and gained the favour of the army, of which he took the command. Plancus and Pollio joined him; and Antony returned to Rome at the head of seventeen legions and 10,000 cavalry. Octavian now threw off the mask, and held a consultation with Antony and Lepidus, near Bononia, when it was determined that these ' triumvirs ' should share the whole Roman world. Returning to Rome, they began their course of proscription and plunder. Among their first victims was Cicero; and, in all, 300 senators and 2000 *equites* are believed to have fallen. After securing Italy, and raising an enormous sum of money, Antony and Octavian led their troops into Macedonia, and defeated Brutus and Cassius. Antony next paid a visit to Athens, and then passed over to Asia, to arrange his dispute with Cleopatra, queen of Egypt, who captivated him by her beauty and address. He followed her into Egypt, and lived in idleness and luxury, until he was aroused by tidings of a quarrel in Italy between his own kindred and Octavian. This dispute gave rise to a short war, which came to an end before he arrived in Italy. A new division of the Roman world was now

arranged, Antony taking the East, and Octavian the West, while Lepidus had to put up with Africa. Antony had married Octavian's sister, Octavia; but, returning now to Cleopatra, he resumed his voluptuous life, and was guilty of acts of the grossest injustice. Octavian used these facts to excite the indignation of the Roman people; and in the naval engagement of Actium (31 B.C.) Antony was defeated. He now went back again to Egypt, where, deserted by the Egyptian fleet, as by his own army, and deceived by a false report of Cleopatra's suicide, he killed himself by falling upon his sword.

ANTONY, St, called **the Great,** or Antony of Thebes (251–356), the father of Monachism, was born at Koman in Upper Egypt. Having sold his possessions for the poor, he withdrew into the wilderness, and took up his abode in an old ruin on the top of a hill, where he spent twenty years in the most rigorous seclusion. In 305 he was persuaded to leave this retreat by the prayers of numerous anchorites, and then founded a monastery, at first only a group of separate and scattered cells near Memphis and Arsinoë. In 355 the venerable hermit, then over a hundred years old, made a journey to Alexandria to dispute with the Arians; but feeling his end approaching, he retired to his desert home, where he died. Athanasius wrote his Life.

ANTONY OF PADUA, St (1195–1231), born at Lisbon, August 15, was at first an Augustinian monk, but in 1220 he entered the Franciscan order, and became one of its most active propagators. He preached in the south of France and Upper Italy, and died at Padua, June 13, 1231. He was canonized by Gregory IX in the following year. According to legend, he preached to the fishes when men refused to hear him; hence he is the patron of the lower animals, and is often represented as accompanied by an ass. See *Chronicle of St Anthony of Padua*, edited by the Rev. H. J. Coleridge (1883).

ANTRAIGUES, Emanuel Delaunay, Comte d', *ä-trayg* (1755–1812), French politician, born at Villeneuve de Berg. His *Mémoires sur les États-généraux* (1788) was one of the first sparks of the French Revolution; but in 1789, when Antraigues was chosen a deputy, he defended the hereditary privileges and the kingly veto, and ranked himself against the union of the three estates. After 1790 he was employed in diplomacy at St Petersburg, Vienna, and Dresden. In England he acquired great influence with Canning. On July 22, 1812, he was murdered, with his wife, near London, by an Italian servant. See L. Pingaud, *Un Agent secret* (1893).

ANVILLE, Jean Baptiste Bourguignon d', *ä-veel* (1697–1782), a geographer and mapmaker, was born and died in Paris.

ANWARI, a celebrated Persian poet and astrologer, who died between 1191 and 1196.

ANZENGRÜBER, Ludwig (1839–89), Austrian playwright and novelist, born in Vienna. Coming of peasant stock, he had been a bookshop assistant, a touring actor and a police clerk before the success of his play, *Der Pfarrer von Kirchfeld* (1870), enabled him to devote the rest of his life to writing. He was the author of several novels, of which the best is *Der Sternsteinhof* (1885), and about twenty plays, mostly about Austrian peasant life, with a strong propagandist bias. See Life by Strobl (1921).

AOSTA, Duke of. See AMADEUS.

APELLES, *a-pel'leez* (fl. 325 B.C.), Greek painter, was probably born at Colophon, on the Ionian coast of Asia Minor. He was trained at Ephesus and Sicyon, visited Macedon, where he became the friend of Alexander the Great, and is said to have accompanied him on his expedition to Asia, and settled at Ephesus. None of his work has survived, but his fame lives in ancient writings.

APICIUS, Marcus Gabius, a Roman epicure in the time of Augustus and Tiberius. It is said that when he had spent £800,000 upon his appetite, and had only some £80,000 left, he poisoned himself to avoid the misery of plain diet.

APOLLINAIRE, Guillaume, orig. *Apollinaris Kostrowitzky* (1880–1918), French poet, born in Rome of Polish descent, in Paris became a leader of the movement rejecting poetic traditions in outlook, rhythm, and language. His work, akin to the cubist school in painting, is expressed chiefly in *Les Alcools* (1913) and *Calligrammes* (1918). See studies by Fabureau (Paris 1932), Giedion-Welcker (1945), and Adéma (1954).

APOLLINARIS THE YOUNGER (d. 390), Bishop of Laodicea, was one of the sternest opponents of Arianism. His father, **Apollinaris the Elder,** who was presbyter at Laodicea, was born at Alexandria, and taught grammar, first at Berytus, and afterwards at Laodicea. Apollinaris himself upheld a doctrine condemned by the Council of Constantinople (381), as denying the true human nature of Christ. He must not be confused with Claudius Apollinaris, Bishop of Hierapolis, in Phrygia (A.D. 170), who wrote an *Apology* for the Christian faith, and several other works, all lost. See also SIDONIUS.

APOLLODORUS, *-daw'-*, (1) (fl. *c.* 408 B.C.), Athenian painter, alleged inventor of chiaroscuro.

(2) (fl. *c.* 140 B.C.), Athenian grammarian, author of a work on mythology (tr. Frazer 1921).

(3) Roman architect, executed in A.D. 129 for his fearless criticism of the emperor Hadrian's design for a temple. He was the architect of Trajan's column.

APOLLONIUS, called **Dyskolos** ('ill-tempered'), Alexandrian grammarian of the 2nd century, the first to reduce Greek syntax to a system.

APOLLONIUS OF PERGA (fl. 250–220 B.C.), Greek mathematician, author of a famous work on conic sections which laid the foundations of modern teaching on the subject.

APOLLONIUS OF TYANA (3 B.C.–*c.* A.D. 97), Greek philosopher, born at Tyana in Cappadocia, was, according to Philostratus, a zealous neo-Pythagorean teacher, who travelled to India via Asia Minor, meeting the Magi at Babylon on his way. When he returned, his fame as a wise man was greatly increased; the people regarded him as a worker of miracles and a divine being, and

princes were glad to entertain him. He was patronized by Vespasian, and followed him into Egypt. After travels in Spain, Italy and Greece, he was accused of conspiring against Domitian; ultimately he appears to have settled in Ephesus. His history, partly apocryphal, was written more than a century after his death by Philostratus (q.v.). See *Life and Times* by F. W. G. Campbell (1908), and study by Mead (1901).

APOLLONIUS RHODIUS (b. *c.* 295 B.C.), Greek scholar, born in Alexandria, but long resident in Rhodes, wrote many works on grammar, and an epic poem, the *Argonautica*, marked by learning and industry rather than by poetic genius. Greatly admired by the Romans, it was translated into Latin by Varro and imitated by Valerius Flaccus.

APPELBEE, Leonard (1914–), English artist, born in London. He studied at Goldsmith's College and the Royal College of Art. He is best known for his landscapes, in an adaptation of post-impressionist technique, giving a 'cut-paper' effect. His landscape of *Meadle* is in the Tate Gallery.

APPERLEY, Charles James, pseud. Nimrod (1777–1843), English sporting writer, was born near Wrexham, and educated at Rugby. He devoted himself to hunting, and in 1821 began to contribute to the *Sporting Magazine*, but in 1830 had to retire to France, where he thenceforth chiefly resided. See his *Life and Times*, completed by Cuming (1927).

APPIA, Adolphe (1862–1928), Swiss scene designer and theatrical producer, born at Geneva. He was one of the first to plead for the substitution of simple planes instead of rich stage settings, and for the symbolic use of lighting, particularly in the presentation of opera. See his *Die Musik und die Inscenierung* (1899) and *La Mise-en-scene du drame Wagnérien* (1895).

APPIAN, Gr. Appianos (2nd cent.), Roman historian, eleven of whose twenty-four books of Roman history, written in Greek, survive. He was a native of Alexandria, and flourished during the reigns of Trajan, Hadrian, and Antoninus Pius.

APPIANI, Andrea, *ap-pyah'nee* (1754–1817), Italian artist, known as 'the Painter of the Graces', was born and died at Milan. He was court painter to Napoleon. His best known work is the set of frescoes depicting *Psyche* in the Monza palace.

APPIUS CLAUDIUS. See CLAUDIUS, APPIUS.

APPLEGATH, Augustus (1788–1871), English inventor, made important improvements on the steam printing-press and in the manufacture of bank-notes.

APPLETON, (1) Daniel (1785–1849), American publisher, born at Haverhill, Mass., founded the famous New York publishing house.

(2) **Sir Edward** (1892–1965), born in Bradford. He was trained at St John's College, Cambridge. He was appointed assistant demonstrator in experimental physics at the Cavendish Laboratory in 1920. He became famous as a young man through his researches on the propagation of wireless waves, and he was appointed Wheatstone professor of Physics at London University. In 1936 he returned to Cambridge as Jacksonian professor of Natural Philosophy. In

1939 he became secretary of the Department of Scientific and Industrial Research, where he remained until his appointment as principal and vice-chancellor of Edinburgh University in 1949. In 1947 he reached the peak of his success when he was awarded the Nobel prize for physics for his contribution 'in exploring the ionosphere'. He was president of the British Association in 1953. His work revealed the existence of a layer of electrically charged particles in the upper atmosphere (the Appleton layer) which plays an essential part in making wireless communication possible between distant stations, and is also fundamental to the development of radar. He published papers on electricity and the problems of wireless telegraphy.

APPONYI, Albert Georg, Count, *op'on-yė* (1846–1933), Hungarian statesman, born at Vienna. He entered the Hungarian Diet in 1872, and, a brilliant orator, soon became leader of the moderate opposition which became the National party in 1891. In 1899 he and his supporters went over to the Liberal Government party, and from 1901–03 he was president of the Diet. From 1906 to 1910 he was minister of culture and, a devout Catholic, gave asylum to the expelled French Jesuits. He introduced free public education. In 1920 he led the Hungarian peace delegation, protested bitterly against the terms imposed under the Treaty of Trianon and resigned. He frequently represented his country at the the League of Nations.

APRAXIN, (1) Fyodor Matveyevich, Count (1671–1728), Russian admiral, the creator of the Russian navy, and long all-powerful in the court of Peter the Great.

(2) **Stephen Fyodorovich, Count** (1702–58), Russian general, nephew of (1), defeated the Prussians at Grossjägersdorf (1757) but died next year a prisoner in disgrace.

APULEIUS, Lucius, *ap-ū-lay'us* (2nd cent.), Latin satirist, was born about A.D. 125 at Madaura, in Numidia, and studied at Carthage and Athens. The fortune bequeathed him by his father enabled him to travel; he visited Italy, Asia, &c., and was initiated into numerous religious mysteries. The knowledge which he thus acquired of the priestly fraternities he made abundant use of afterwards in his *Golden Ass.* Having married a wealthy middle-aged lady, he was charged by her relations with having employed magic to gain her affections. His *Apologia*, still extant, was an eloquent vindication. After this, his life appears to have been devoted to literature and public oratory, in both of which he attained great eminence. His romance, *The Metamorphoses* or *Golden Ass,* is a satire on the vices of the age, especially those of the priesthood and of quacks. The most exquisite thing in it is the episode of Cupid and Psyche.

AQUAVIVA, Claudius, *a-kwa-vee'va* (1543–1615), fifth general of the Jesuits (1581), born at Naples. His *Ratio Studiorum* was the basis of later Jesuit education.

AQUILA, Ponticus, *ak'wil-a* (fl. 130), translator of the Old Testament into Greek, a native of Sinope, is said to have been first a pagan, then a Christian, and finally a Jew.

AQUINAS, St Thomas, *a-kwī'nas* (1225–74),

Italian scholastic theologian, was of the family of the Counts of Aquino, and was born in the castle of Roccasecca, near Aquino, a small town between Rome and Naples. He was educated by the Benedictines of Monte-Cassino, and at the University of Naples; and, against the will of his family, entered (1243) the Dominican order. His brothers carried him off by force, and kept him a prisoner in the paternal castle for two years; ultimately escaping through France to Cologne, he became there a pupil of the great Dominican luminary, Albertus Magnus (q.v.). In 1248 the heretofore ' Dumb Ox ' was appointed to teach under Albert, and began to publish commentaries on Aristotle. In 1252 he went to Paris, obtained great distinction as a philosophic theologian, and taught till, in 1258, now a doctor, he was summoned by the pope to teach successively in Anagni, Orvieto and Rome. He enjoyed the highest consideration throughout the church, and his voice carried almost decisive weight. Like most of the other scholastic theologians, he had no knowledge of Greek or Hebrew, and was almost equally ignorant of history; but his numerous writings display intellectual power of the highest order. He was the first among 13th-century metaphysicians to stress the importance of sense-perception and the experimental foundation of human knowledge, and reinterpreted the doctrine of transubstantiation. His *Summa Theologiae,* the first attempt at a complete theological system, remains to this day substantially the standard authority in the Roman Church. The *Summa contra Gentiles* deals chiefly with the principles of natural religion. His commentaries on Scripture and devotional treatises also have a high reputation. His influence on the theological thought of succeeding ages was immense. He refused all high ecclesiastical appointments, even the archbishopric of Naples. Gregory X, who had called a general council to effect the union of the Greek and Latin churches, summoned Aquinas to defend the papal cause at Lyons. He set out, though suffering from fever, and died on the road at the Cistercian abbey of Fossanuova, March 7. All Europe mourned his loss; universities, religious orders, and princes contended for the honour of possessing his body, which was finally bestowed by the pope on Toulouse. Aquinas was canonized in 1323. The only scholastic theologian who in any degree rivalled Aquinas, already known as the ' Angelic Doctor ', was the Franciscan 'Subtle Doctor', Duns Scotus (q.v.). The Franciscans followed Scotus, and the Dominicans Thomas, and henceforward mediaeval theologians were divided into two schools, Scotists and Thomists, whose divergencies penetrate more or less every branch of doctrine. Thomism represents, with few exceptions, the general teaching of the Catholic Church; its rivals now being not the Scotists but the eclectic school of Jesuits. St Thomas was the author of the famous *Pange lingua gloriosi* and other eucharistic hymns. See studies by Grabmann (1928), G. K. Chesterton (1933), Patterson (1933), Carroll (1948), Copleston (1955), D'Arcy (1955).

ARABELLA STUART. See STEWART (14).
ARABI PASHA. See AHMED ARABI.
ARAGO, (1) **Dominique François Jean** (1786–1853), French scientist and statesman, was born February 26, at Estagel near Perpignan. At seventeen he entered the Polytechnic, and in 1804 became secretary to the Observatory, in 1830 its chief director, having at twenty-three been elected a member of the Academy of Sciences. He took a prominent part in the July Revolution (1830), and as member of the Chamber of Deputies voted with the extreme left. In 1848 he was a member of the provisional government, and opposing Louis Napoleon, refused to take the oath of allegiance after the events of 1851–52. His achievements, mainly in the fields of astronomy, magnetism, and optics, are recorded in his works (ed. by Barral, 17 vols. 1854–62). See Audiganne's *Arago, son génie et son influence* (2nd ed. 1869).

(2) **Emmanuel** (1812–96), French statesman, son of (1), was also an opponent of Louis Napoleon, and was ambassador to Switzerland (1880–94). He was born and died in Paris.

(3) **Étienne** (1802–92), French author and politician, born in Paris, brother of (1), was a staunch republican, was mayor of Paris (1870), and wrote successful comedies and *vaudevilles*.

(4) **Jacques Étienne Victor** (1790–1855), French author of travel books, novels and plays, brother of (1), achieved fame with *Voyage autour du monde*.

ARAGON, Louis, *a-ra-gŏ* (1897–ㅤ), French writer, born at Paris. At first one of the most brilliant of the surrealist group (*Le Paysan de Paris*, 1926), he became a convert to Communism, wrote some dull novels and later some war poems, admirable for their sincerity and consummate command of the language (*Crève-Cœur; Les Yeux d'Elsa*).

ARAM, Eugene (1704–59), English scholar and murderer, was born at Ramsgill, in Yorks. Though a gardener's son, and self-taught, he became a schoolmaster, first at Ramsgill, and in 1734 at Knaresborough, where he became intimate with one Daniel Clark, a shoemaker. The sudden disappearance of the latter in 1745, at a time when he happened to be in possession of valuable goods, threw suspicion on Aram, not as Clark's murderer but as his confederate in swindling. His garden was searched, and in it was found a portion of the missing property. Aram was arrested and tried, but acquitted for want of evidence. He now left his wife at Knaresborough, and acted as a schoolmaster at various places in England, acquiring, in spite of his nomadic mode of life, a knowledge of botany, heraldry, Chaldee, Arabic, Welsh, and Irish, and amassing considerable materials for a comparative lexicon and postulating the relationship between Celtic and Indo-European tongues. His secret was betrayed by a confederate, who excited suspicion by the loudness of his protestations that a skeleton found near Knaresborough was not Clark's. The accomplice was at last driven to confess where the murdered man had been buried; the bones were exhumed and identified, and Aram was suddenly dragged from his ushership at Lynn in Norfolk. He was tried at York, August 3, 1759, and hanged on the 6th. At the trial he conducted his own defence, attacking with great acumen the doctrine of circumstantial evidence. After his condemnation he confessed his guilt, wrote a defence of suicide, but failed in an attempt to illustrate his essay. A factitious interest attaches to his story from Lord Lytton's romance and Hood's ballad. See E. R. Watson's *Eugene Aram* (1913).

ARANDA, Pedro Pablo Abarca y Bolea, Count of (1718–99), Spanish statesman and general, born at Sietano, was made ambassador to Poland in 1760, but in 1766 was recalled to Madrid and made prime minister, with the task of restoring order after risings. He procured the expulsion of the Jesuits, alleged perpetrators of the disorder, from Spain in 1767, but in 1773 fell from power and was sent to France as ambassador. Returning in 1787, he became prime minister again in 1792, but antagonized Godoy (see ALCUDIA), and died in Aragon in enforced retirement.

ARANY, János, *aw'ron-y'* (1817–82), Hungarian poet, born at Nagy-Szalonta of peasant stock. With Petöfi (q.v.) he was a leader of the popular national school, and is regarded as one of the greatest of Hungarian poets. He was chief secretary of the Academy from 1870–79. His satire *The Lost Constitution* (1845) won the Kisfaludy Society prize, but his chief work is the *Toldi* trilogy (1847–54). He also published successful translations of Aristophanes and Shakespeare. See study by F. Riedl (Ger. 1920).

ARATUS OF SICYON (c. 271–213 B.C.), a Greek statesman who liberated Sicyon from its tyrant in 251, and whose great object was to unite the Greek states, and so form an independent nation.

ARATUS OF SOLI (1st half 3rd cent. B.C.), Greek poet, wrote about 270 B.C. two astronomical poems, *Phainomena* and *Diosemeia*, from one of which St Paul quoted when preaching at Athens.

ARBER, Edward (1836–1912), English scholar, born in London, deserted the Civil Service for a literary career and became professor of English at Birmingham (1881–94). He issued a series of 'English Reprints' (30 vols. 1868–80) with the purpose of making available accurate versions of important texts of the 15th-18th centuries at low cost; and he also produced *An English Garner* (8 vols. 1877–96), a miscellany of old and rare tracts and poems. Important to bibliographers and historians were his transcripts of the records of the Stationers' Company.

ARBLAY, Madame d'. See BURNEY (2).

ARBUTHNOT, John (1667–1735), Scottish physician and wit, the much-loved friend of Swift and Pope, was born at Arbuthnott, Kincardineshire. His father was the (Episcopal) parish priest, who was ejected after the Revolution. One of John's brothers fought under Dundee at Killiecrankie, and another in Mar's rebellion; John was, according to Chesterfield, 'a Jacobite by prejudice, a republican by reflection and reasoning'. He studied at Aberdeen and University College, Oxford, but took his M.D. degree at St Andrews (1696). Settling in London, where before this he had taught mathematics, in 1697 he attracted notice by his *Examination of Dr Woodward's Account of the Deluge*. Accident called him into attendance on Prince George of Denmark; in 1705 he was appointed physician to the queen, and her death in 1714 was a severe blow to his prosperity. In 1715, along with Pope, he assisted Gay in *Three Hours after Marriage*, a farce that proved to be an absolute fiasco. He delivered the Harveian oration in 1727, and died February 27, 1735. Utterly careless of literary fame, Arbuthnot was the chief, if not sole author of the brilliant *Memoirs of Martinus Scriblerus*, first published in Pope's works (1741); and his too was the celebrated *History of John Bull* (1712). See his *Life and Works*, by G. A. Aitken (1892).

ARC. See JOAN OF ARC.

ARCADIUS (A.D. 377–408), first emperor of the East alone, was born in Spain, and after the death of his father, the Emperor Theodosius, in A.D. 395, received the eastern half of the Roman empire, the western falling to Honorius. Arcadius lived in oriental state and splendour, and his dominion extended from the Adriatic to the Tigris, and from Scythia to Ethiopia; but the real rulers over this vast empire were the Gaul Rufinus, the eunuch Eutropius, and the Empress Eudoxia, who exiled Chrysostom in 404.

ARCESILAS, or **Arcesilaus** (316–241 B.C.), Greek philosopher, founder of the New Academy, born at Pitane in Aeolia, was an opponent of the Stoics and a supporter of the doctrines of Plato.

ARCH, Joseph (1826–1919), English preacher and reformer, was born at Barford, Warwickshire, and whilst still a farm labourer became a Primitive Methodist preacher. In 1872 he founded the National Agricultural Labourers' Union, and later was M.P. for Northwest Norfolk. See his *Autobiography* (1898).

ARCHELAUS, *ar-ki-lay'us*, (1) Greek philosopher of the Ionic school who flourished about 450 B.C. He was the first to maintain the spherical form of the earth and is reputed to have taught Socrates.

(2) King of Macedonia from 413 to 399 B.C.

(3) Pontic general sent by Mithridates the Great to Greece to oppose the Romans in 87 B.C. He was defeated by Sulla at Chaeronea and at Orchomenos in 86. Unjustly suspected of treason, Archelaus went over to the Romans at the outbreak of the second war in 83.

(4) High priest of Comana and king of Egypt, son of (3), married Berenice, daughter of King Ptolemy Auletes, in 56 B.C., and ruled over Egypt for six months during Ptolemy's banishment.

(5) called **Sisines**, grandson of (4), King of Cappadocia (40 B.C.–A.D. 17), assisted Mark Antony, was deposed by Tiberius and died in prison at Rome, Cappadocia becoming a Roman province.

(6) Ethnarch of Judaea, son of Herod the Great, succeeded his father in A.D. 1, and maintained his position against an insurrection raised by the Pharisees. His heirship being disputed by his brother Antipas, Archelaus went to Rome, where his authority was confirmed by Augustus, who made him Ethnarch of Judaea, Samaria, and Idumaea, while his brothers, Antipas and Philip, were made tetrarchs over the other half of Herod's dominions. After a nine years' reign, he was deposed by Augustus for his tyranny, and banished to Vienne, in Gaul, where he died.

ARCHER, (1) **Frederick James** (1857–86), English jockey, was born at Cheltenham, January 11; rode his first race in 1870; in all had 2746 mounts, winning the Derby five times, the Oaks four, the St Leger six, the Two Thousand Guineas five, &c.; and shot himself, whilst temporarily insane, at his house in Newmarket.

(2) **Thomas** (1668–1743), English architect, born at Tanworth, designed the churches of St John's, Westminster, and St Paul's, Deptford; also Roehampton House and part of Chatsworth.

(3) **William** (1856–1924), Scottish dramatic critic, dramatist, and apostle of Ibsen, born at Perth, went up from Edinburgh to London in 1878. His most successful play was *The Green Goddess* (1921). See Life by C. Archer (1931).

ARCHILOCHUS OF PAROS, *ar-kil'o-kus* (fl. 714–676 B.C.), Greek poet, regarded as the first of the lyric poets, by the ancients being ranked with Homer, Pindar, and Sophocles. Even Plato calls him ' the very wise ', but much of his renown is for vituperative satire. Only fragments of his work are extant.

ARCHIMEDES, *ar-ki-mee'deez* (c. 287–212 B.C.), Greek scientist, the most celebrated of ancient mathematicians, was born at Syracuse, and perished in the capture of that city by the Romans. He alone of the ancients contributed anything of real value to the theory of mechanics and to hydrostatics, first proving that a body plunged in a fluid loses as much of its weight as is equal to the weight of an equal volume of the fluid. Among the numerous inventions ascribed to him are the endless screw, and the Archimedes screw or spiral pump for raising water. His works, in Doric Greek, were edited by Torelli (1792), Heiberg (1880–81), and Sir T. L. Heath (1897–1912), who wrote a Life of him (1920).

ARCHIPENKO, Alexander (1880–1964), Ukrainian sculptor, born in Kiev, studied there and at Moscow and Paris, where he was influenced by cubism. After 1923 he lived in America and taught in the new Bauhaus at Chicago. His work is characterized by extreme economy of form, and shows the influence of Brancusi (q.v.). See study by Hildebrand (1923).

ARCHYTAS OF TARENTUM, *ar-ki'tas* (fl. 400 B.C.), Greek general, mathematician, and Pythagorean philosopher, first doubled the cube, recognized the various types of mathematical progression, and according to Horace was drowned in the Adriatic.

ARCOS, René (1880–), French poet and novelist, was born at Clichy. In 1906 he was associated with Georges Duhamel in the literary group L'Abbaye. He wrote *L'Âme essentielle* (1903), *Ce qui naît* (1910), *Autrui* (1926), and an essay on Romain Rolland published in 1950. Arcos has been described as inflated with optimism, but expresses a genuine idealism.

ARCULFUS. See ADAMNAN.

ARDITI, Luigi, *ar-dee'tee* (1822–1903), Italian composer, born near Turin, studied music at Milan. Famous first as a violinist, he conducted the Italian opera at New York (1852–1856), and was musical director at Her Majesty's Theatre, London (1857–78). His operas, *I Briganti* (1841) and *La Spia* (1856), are less known than some of his songs, violin duets, and waltzes such as *Il Bacio.* See his *Reminiscences* (1896).

ARENSKY, Anton Stepanovich (1861–1906), Russian composer, born at Novgorod, studied under Rimsky-Korsakov, and from 1895 conducted the court choir at St Petersburg. His compositions, which show the influence of Tchaikovsky, include 3 operas, 2 symphonies, and vocal and instrumental pieces.

ARETAEUS, *a-re-tee'us* (fl. A.D. 100), a Greek physician of Cappadocia, considered to rank next to Hippocrates. The first four books of his great work, preserved nearly complete, treat of the causes and symptoms of diseases; the other four, of the cure. There is an edition by Adams (1856), and an English translation (1837).

ARETINO (1). See BRUNI and SPINELLO.

(2) **Pietro,** *a-re-tee'nō* (1492–1557), Italian poet, was born at Arezzo, Tuscany, April 20, the natural son of a nobleman named Luigi Bacci. Banished from his native town, he went to Perugia, where he worked as a bookbinder, and afterwards wandered through Italy in the service of various noblemen. At Rome he distinguished himself by his wit, impudence, and talents, and secured even the papal patronage, which, however, he subsequently lost by writing his sixteen shameless *Sonetti Lussuriosi.* He now won the friendship of Giovanni de' Medici and gained an opportunity of ingratiating himself with Francis I at Milan in 1524. A few years later he settled at Venice, there also acquiring powerful friends. The Bishop of Vicenza not only soothed the irritation of the pope, but recommended Aretino to the Emperor Charles V. The latter, as well as Francis, pensioned the fortunate wit, besides enriching him with splendid presents. It is said that while laughing heartily at a droll adventure of one of his sisters, he fell from a stool, and was killed on the spot (1557). His poetical works include five witty comedies and a tragedy of some merit. See Lives by Chasles (Paris 1873), Sinigaglia (Naples 1882), Samosch (Berl. 1881), Lucio (Turin 1888), Schultheiss (Hamb. 1890), Hutton (1922).

ARFE. Family of Spanish 16th-century carvers, of whom:

(1) **Henrique de,** and his son **Antonio de,** carved in silver many of the finest tabernacles and crucifixes in the Spanish cathedrals and monasteries.

(2) **Juan de, y Villafane** (1535–c. 1603), born at León, was one of Spain's finest metal engravers.

ARGAND, *ar-gã,* (1) **Aimé** (1755–1803), Swiss physician and chemist, inventor of the Argand lamp, was born at Geneva, and lived for a time in England.

(2) **Emile** (1879–1940), Swiss geologist, born at Geneva, known for his geological maps of the Alps.

(3) **Jean-Robert** (1768–1822), Swiss mathematician, born at Geneva, after whom is named the 'Argand diagram, a diagram with rectangular axes, on which complex numbers can be represented by a point. A pioneer in the use of complex numbers, he showed by means of them that all algebraic equations have roots.

ARGELANDER, Friedrich Wilhelm August, *ar-ge-lan'der* (1799–1875), a German astronomer, was born at Memel and died at Bonn. With Schönfeld and Krüger between 1852 and 1861 he plotted the position of all stars of the northern hemisphere above the ninth magnitude.

ARGENS, Jean Baptiste de Boyer, Marquis d', *ar-zhã* (1704–71), a French philosophical writer whose works fill 38 volumes, was born at Aix in Provence and died near Toulon, having resided from 1744 to 1769 at the court of Frederick the Great. See his *Mémoires* (new ed. Paris 1807).

ARGENSOLA, Bartolomé Leonardo de, *ar-*KHen-*sō'la* (1562–1631), and **Lupercio de** (1559–1613), Spanish poets, born at Barbastro, were both educated at Huesca University and both entered the service of Maria of Austria. Their poems led them to be styled the 'Spanish Horaces', but they were also successively historiographers of Aragon. Lupercio also wrote some tragedies.

ARGENSON, René Louis, Marquis d', *ar-zhã-sō* (1694–1757), French statesman, was the son of the Marquis d'Argenson (1652–1721) who created the secret police and established the *lettres de cachet.* He fell a victim in 1747 to the machinations of Madame de Pompadour, as ten years later did his brother, **Marc Pierre,** Comte d'Argenson (1696–1764), who became war minister in 1743. See works by Zevort (1880), the Duc de Broglie (2 vols. 1891), and Ogle (1893).

ARGYLL, *ar-gīl',* title of the chiefs of the Campbells, the powerful West Highland clan. They had achieved knighthood in the 13th century and obtained the barony of Lochow in 1315. From 1445 the chief was styled Lord Campbell, until, in 1457, the earldom of Argyll was conferred upon Colin, Lord Campbell. The following are noteworthy:

(1) **Archibald, 2nd Earl** (d. 1513), son of Colin, 1st Earl, was killed at Flodden.

(2) **Colin, 3rd Earl** (d. 1530), son of (1), was justiciar of Scotland, and this office became hereditary in the family in 1528.

(3) **Archibald, 4th Earl** (d. 1558), was the first of the Scottish nobility to embrace the Reformation.

(4) **Archibald, 5th Earl** (1530–73), son of (3), was a follower of Mary Queen of Scots and was involved in the assassination of Darnley, but later supported James VI and became lord high chancellor (1572).

(5) **Archibald, 7th Earl** (c. 1576–1638), as king's lieutenant was defeated by Errol and Huntly at Glenlivet in 1594; he was later largely responsible for ' breaking ' the Macgregors (1613) and suppressing the Macdonalds (1615).

(6) **Archibald, Marquis and 8th Earl** (1598–1661), son of (5), created Marquis in 1641, was a leading covenanter, and was heavily defeated by Montrose at Inverlochy in 1645.

Arrested at the Restoration for compliance with the usurpation, he was beheaded at Edinburgh.

(7) **Archibald, 9th Earl** (1629–85), son of (6), attempted to assist Monmouth by raising Scotland against James VII and II, but was taken prisoner and beheaded at Edinburgh.

(8) **Archibald, 1st Duke** (d. 1705), son of (7), an active promoter of the Revolution, was created Duke of Argyll in 1701.

(9) **John, 2nd Duke** (1678–1743), son of (8), was a prominent Unionist and Hanoverian, whose generalship, learned under Marlborough, was the main cause of the defeat of the Jacobite insurgents in 1715–16.

(10) **George John Douglas, 8th Duke** (1823–1900), was a Liberal cabinet minister and author of *Scotland As It Was and As It Is* (1887), and of *Autobiography and Memoirs* (1906).

(11) **John Douglas Sutherland, 9th Duke** (1845–1914), married Princess Louise and was governor-general of Canada.

ARGYROPULOS, (1) **Joannes** (1416–*c*. 1486), Greek scholar, a professor at Florence under the Medici, one of the earliest teachers of Greek learning in the West, was born at Constantinople and died in Rome.

(2) **Perikles** (1809–60), Greek publicist, born at Constantinople, became professor of Jurisprudence at Athens (1837), and in 1854–1855 was foreign minister.

ARIAS, Benito, called **Montano**, *ah'ree-ahs* (1527–98), Spanish theologian and linguist, born at Fregenal de la Sierra, became a Benedictine monk and was delegate to the council of Trent (1562–64). He edited for Philip II the famous Antwerp Polyglot edition of the Bible (1568–73).

ARIBAU, Bonaventura Carles, *ah-ree-bah'oo* (1798–1862), Catalan writer and economist, born in Barcelona. He achieved a double success in his life, becoming director of the Mint and of the Spanish Treasury, and being decorated by the Prince Consort for his work on the industrial section of the Great Exhibition of 1851. In addition, he became editor of the *Biblioteca de autores españoles,* and was the author of the *Oda a la Patria* (1833), one of the earliest and best modern poems in Catalan. This had a tremendous influence on contemporary Catalan writers.

ARIOSTO, Ludovico (1474–1533), one of the greatest of Italian poets, was born at Reggio nell'Emilia, September 8. He was bred to the law, but abandoned it for poetry. However, in 1500 he was compelled by his father's death to exert himself for the support of a large family. In 1503 he was introduced to the court at Ferrara of the Cardinal Ippolito d'Este, who employed him in many negotiations, but was extremely niggardly in his rewards. Here, in the space of ten years, Ariosto produced his great poem, *Orlando Furioso* (1516), the Roland epic that forms a continuation of Boiardo's *Orlando Innamorato.* When the cardinal left Italy (1518), the duke, his brother, invited the poet to his service, and acted to him with comparative liberality. In 1522 he was commissioned to suppress an insurrection in the wild mountain district of Garfagnana, an arduous task which he successfully accomplished; and after remain-

ing three years governor of the province, he returned to Ferrara. It was now that he composed his comedies, and gave the finishing touch to his *Orlando.* At length, in 1532, that poem made its appearance in a third edition, enlarged to its present dimensions. Ariosto died July 6, 1533, and was buried in the church of San Benedetto, at Ferrara, where a magnificent monument marks his resting place. He is described in the Latin verses of his brother Gabrielle as a man of noble personal appearance and amiable character. Besides his great work, Ariosto wrote comedies, satires, sonnets, and a number of Latin poems. Of these the sonnets alone show the genius of the poet. His Latin poems are mediocre indeed, and his comedies, besides lacking interest, are disfigured by licentious passages. Of the *Orlando* there are many English translations: by Harrington (1607 and 1634), Croker (1755), Huggins (1757), Hoole (1783), and Stewart Rose (1823). In the last only is there to be found a fair representation of the feeling and spirit of the original. One of Ariosto's comedies had been rendered into English by Gascoigne as early as 1566. See books by J. Shield Nicholson (1914), Edwards (1924), Catalano (Geneva 1930), E. G. Gardner's *King of Court Poets* (1906), and Ferrazzi's *Bibliografia Ariostesca* (1881).

ARIOVISTUS, German chief who invaded Gaul and was defeated by Caesar near Vesontium (Besançon), 58 B.C. See Caesar's *De Bello Gallico.*

ARISTARCHUS OF SAMOS (fl. 280–264 B.C.), Alexandrian astronomer who seems to have anticipated Copernicus, maintaining that the earth moves round the sun.

ARISTARCHUS OF SAMOTHRACE, Alexandrian grammarian and critic who lived *c*. 215–143 B.C., known for his revision of Homer's epics.

ARISTIDES, *a-ris-tī'deez,* (1) (*c*. 550–468 B.C.), Greek general, at the battle of Marathon (490 B.C.) was appointed one of the ten leaders, but induced his companions to make Miltiades commander-in-chief. Next year he was chief archon, and secured the general respect of the citizens, earning for himself the title 'the Just'; but about 483 the jealousy of Themistocles procured his banishment. Three years later came Xerxes' invasion, when, on the eve of Salamis, Aristides, hearing that the Greek fleet was hemmed in by that of the Persians, made his way from Aegina to offer his aid to Themistocles. He did good service in that great sea fight; and, as Athenian general, he divided with Pausanias the glory of Plataea (479). In 477 B.C. he introduced a sweeping change into the constitution, by which all citizens, without distinction of rank, were admitted to the archonship. Through him, too, about the same time, Athens, not Sparta, became the ruling state of a maritime confederacy. He was an old man when he died (most likely in 468), and so poor, it is said, that he had to be buried at the public cost. See Vom Berg, *Das Leben des Aristides* (Gött. 1871).

(2) Second-century Christian apologist, whose work, mentioned by Eusebius and Jerome, was discovered in the later 19th

century. A fragment in an Armenian translation was published first; in 1889 J. R. Harris published a Syriac version from the convent of St Catherine on Mount Sinai; and from it J. A. Robinson recognized that the Greek speech in the mediaeval legend of Barlaam and Josaphat is, in a modified form, the original Greek of his apology.

ARISTIPPUS, -*tip'*-, founder of the Cyrenaic or Hedonistic philosophy, was a native of Cyrene in Africa. He became a pupil of Socrates at Athens, and remained with him almost up to the master's death, 399 B.C. He himself taught philosophy both at Athens and Aegina, and was the first of the pupils of Socrates to take money for his instruction. Much of his life was passed in Syracuse, at the court of Dionysius the tyrant, where he acquired the reputation of a philosophic voluptuary. He lived some time at Corinth, in intimacy with the famous Laïs, but towards the close of his life he is supposed to have retired to Cyrene. He taught his doctrines to his daughter Arete, by whom they were communicated to her son Aristippus the Younger.

ARISTOBULUS, -*boo'*-, an Alexandrian Jew and Peripatetic philosopher, who lived about 170 B.C., was considered by the early fathers as the founder of the Jewish philosophy in Alexandria.

ARISTOGEITON. See HARMODIUS.

ARISTOPHANES, *a-ris-tof'a-neez* (*c.* 448– *c.* 388 B.C.), the greatest of Attic, if not of all, comedians. Of his personal history we have nothing recorded, except that he had three sons—Philippos, Araròs, and Nikostratos— all comic poets. He is said to have written fifty-four plays, but eleven only are extant, which may be ranged under the categories of political, philosophical, social, and literary; and again under three periods, ending respectively 425, 406, and 388 B.C., about which last date he died. To the first period belong the *Acharnians, Knights, Clouds,* and *Wasps,* the poet's four masterpieces, named from their respective choruses, and the *Peace,* in all of which full rein is given to political satire; to the second, the *Birds, Lysistrata, Thesmophoriazusae,* and *Frogs,* in which we find less political rancour, and more reticence and caution; to the third, the *Ecclesiazusae* and *Plutus,* comedies of a tamer type, known as that of the middle comedy, in which political allusions and the distinctive characteristic of the old comedy, the *parabasis,* disappear. The first printed edition, the Aldine (Venice 1498), contains nine plays; Junta (1515) added two. See translations of some of the plays by Mitchell (1822), Walsh (1837), B. H. Kennedy (1874), Tyrrell (1883), Rogers (1852–1916), and a study by Gilbert Murray (1933).

ARISTOTLE, *ar'*- (384–322 B.C.), Greek philosopher and scientist and physician, born at Stagira, a Greek colony on the peninsula of Chalcidice, the son of the friend and physician of Amyntas II, king of Macedon, father of Philip, and grandfather of Alexander the Great. In his eighteenth year he left Stagira for Athens, and, three years later, became Plato's pupil. During his twenty years' sojourn in Athens he established a

school of rhetoric and prepared the work with that title. To this period belong some of his dialogues, including *Eudemus,* which confirm that Aristotle began as a firm disciple of Plato. On the death of Plato (347), Aristotle left Athens—either because he was chagrined that Plato had not appointed him his successor as head of the ' Academy ' or Platonic school of philosophy, or because Athens and Philip of Macedon were now at feud. He stayed three years with an old friend, now despot of Lesbos, at Atarneus in Asia Minor, and married his niece; and after his friend had been assassinated, retired to Mitylene. In 342 he was invited by Philip to Macedon, to educate his son Alexander, who for at least three years was his pupil. The two parted finally when Alexander set out on his expedition into Asia (334 B.C.). Aristotle's works, particularly the dialogue *On Philosophy,* began to show marked divergence from his former Platonism, and the *Eudemian Ethics,* parts of the *De Anima, Metaphysics* and *Politics* are usually assigned to this middle period. On his return to Athens in 335, Aristotle opened a school called the 'Lyceum', from its proximity to the temple of Apollo Lyceius. His followers were called the ' Peripatetics ', either from his practice of walking up and down in the garden during his lectures, or because the place was known as ' The Walk ' (*Peripatos*). After the death of Alexander the anti-Macedonian party at Athens accused Aristotle of impiety. With the fate of Socrates before his eyes, he made a timely escape (322 B.C.) to Chalcis in Euboea, where he died. To this last period belong his distinct contributions to philosophy, particularly the relevant sections in his *Metaphysics* and *De Anima,* as well as that classic of moral philosophy, the *Nicomachian Ethics.* The unequal style, irregular sequence and concentrated argument of his works indicate that they were lecture notes. It is probably true that they were buried in a cellar at Scepsis for 200 years and not published until the 1st century B.C. Only the logic of Aristotle was known in Europe during the Dark Ages. The remainder became known to the learned in the West mainly through Arabian translations, which in their turn were translated into Latin. At the time when what was supposed to be the Aristotelian system was (especially through the influence of Thomas Aquinas) dominant in western Europe, Aristotle's works were hardly known to any one in the original. Aristotle, trained as a physician, brought to his philosophy a due respect for fact, on which, with the aid of his analytical methods, he based his doctrines, whereas Plato's philosophy in his middle dialogues was a system based on the supersensible world of the forms or ideas. Both, however, were concerned with the logical problem of predication; Plato groping his way forward, Aristotle supplying a solution. Aristotle brought Platonism down to earth and ' codified ' it. He was the first to work out a theory of reasoning which, with amplification, through the addition of modern symbolic logic, has survived to the present day as deductive logic. His *Organon* was the name given to his treatises on logic, of which the most notable were that on the *Categories* (on substance, quality, quantity); *Prior Analytics* (syllogistic moods and figures); and *Posterior Analytics* (the theory of knowledge and of scientific method). The name *Metaphysics* (i.e., ' after the Physics ') was given to Aristotle's discussions on ' first philosophy ', because they were placed by his editors *after* his books about nature; they treat of the relations of matter and form, the actual and potential, the four causes, &c. It can fairly be admitted that the pre-occupation with Aristotelian metaphysics, especially during the Middle Ages, held up the advance of empirical science. Something of the spirit of the Aristotelian approach to philosophy survived in the work of the modern British Linguistic school of philosophy. Again, his *Poetics* has remained a classic of aesthetic philosophy and, although based entirely on Sophoclean drama, has given rise to a school of dramatic criticism. Aristotelian type of tragedy emphasizes the plot, not characterization, the ' tragic flaw ' propelling the estimable hero to disaster, to bring about not an aesthetic experience, but rather the *catharsis* or purging of potentially socially harmful emotions of the audience. Aristotle appears to have projected what may be called an Encyclopaedia of Philosophy, though the scheme is only imperfectly carried out in his works. See edition of his works in English with commentaries by W. D. Ross (1927 ff.), and studies by Zeller (1897), Jaeger (trans. 1934), Mure (1932), Taylor (1943), also the *Poetics*, trans. with commentary by S. H. Butcher (1896).

ARISTOXENUS OF TARENTUM, -*tox'*-, Greek writer upon music, a pupil of Aristotle, flourished about 350 B.C. See books by C. F. A. Williams (1911), and G. Urbain (Paris 1924).

ARIUS, Gr. Areios (*c.* 250–336), the founder of Arianism, was born in Libya, trained in Antioch, and became a presbyter in Alexandria. Here about 319 he maintained, against his bishop, that the Son was not co-equal or co-eternal with the Father, but only the first and highest of all finite beings, created out of nothing by an act of God's free will. He secured the adherence of clergy and laity in Egypt, Syria, and Asia Minor, but was deposed and excommunicated in 321 by a synod of bishops at Alexandria. Eusebius, Bishop of Nicodemia, absolved him, and in 323 convened another synod in Bithynia, which pronounced in his favour. At Nicomedia, Arius wrote a theological work in verse and prose, called *Thaleia*, some fragments of which remain. The controversy became fierce, and to settle it the Emperor Constantine convoked the memorable Council of Nicaea, or Nice, in Bithynia, 325. Three hundred and eighteen bishops, especially from the East, were present, besides priests, deacons, and acolytes. Arius boldly expounded and defended his opinions. It was principally by the reasoning of Athanasius (q.v.) that the Council was persuaded to define the absolute unity of the divine essence, and the absolute equality of the three persons. All the bishops subscribed it except

two, who were banished, along with Arius, to Illyricum. Arius was recalled in 334, but Athanasius refused to readmit him to church communion, and the controversy went on all over the East. In 336 Arius went to Constantinople, and the Emperor commanded the bishop to admit him to the sacrament. But a day or two before the Sunday appointed for the purpose, he died suddenly—poisoned by the orthodox, said his friends; by the direct judgment of God, according to his enemies. After his death the strife spread more widely abroad: the Homoousian doctrine (identity of essence in Father and Son) and the Homoiousian (similarity of essence) seemed alternately to prevail; and synods and counter-synods were held. The West was mainly orthodox, the East largely Arian or semi-Arian. There was a good deal of persecution on both sides; but Julian the Apostate (361–363) and his successors extended full toleration to both parties. Arianism at last was virtually suppressed in the Roman empire under Theodosius in the East (379–395), and Valentinianus II in the West. Among the Germanic nations, however, it continued to spread through missionary efforts, the Lombards being the last to come round (in 662). Milton held Arian or semi-Arian views. The Arian controversy was revived in England by Dr Samuel Clarke (1675–1729), and Whiston (1667–1752); but Arianism was superseded by Unitarianism. See Gwatkin, *Studies in Arianism* (1882) and *The Arian Controversy* (1889).

ARKWRIGHT, Sir Richard (1732–92), English cotton-spinning inventor, was born at Preston in Lancashire. Of humble origin, the youngest of thirteen children, he settled about 1750 as a barber in Bolton, and became also a dealer in hair, a secret process of his own for dyeing hair increasing the profits of his trade. About 1767, assisted by a Warrington clockmaker, John Kay, he seems to have given himself wholly up to inventions in cotton-spinning. Next year he removed to Preston, where he set up his celebrated *spinning-frame*—the first machine that could produce cotton-thread of sufficient tenuity and strength to be used as warp. The same year, to escape the popular rage against machinery, he removed to Nottingham, and set up his first mill, driven by horses; in 1771, entering into partnership with Jedidiah Strutt of Derby, the celebrated improver of the *stocking-frame*, he set up a larger factory, with water-power, at Cromford, Derbyshire. In 1775 he took out a fresh patent for various additional improvements in machinery. His success stimulated rivals to invade his patent; and to such an extent did other cotton-spinners use his designs that he was obliged, in 1781, to prosecute nine different manufacturers—the outcome, however, was that in 1785 his letters patent were cancelled. Popular animosity was also excited against him on the ground that his inventions diminished the demand for labour; and in 1779 his large mill near Chorley was destroyed by a mob in the presence of a military and police force. In 1786 he was knighted, in 1787 became high-sheriff of Derbyshire, and in 1790 introduced the steam engine into his works at

Nottingham. See Life by Crabtree (1923) and R. S. Fillon and A. P. Wadsworth, *The Strutts and the Arkwrights 1758–1830* (1959).

ARLEN, Michael, orig. **Dikran Kouyoumdjian** (1895–1956), English novelist, born at Ruschuk, Bulgaria, of Armenian parents, was educated in England and naturalized in 1922. He made his reputation with *Piracy* (1922), *The Green Hat* (1924), and his short story collections, *The Romantic Lady* (1921) and *These Charming People* (1923). Set mostly against a background of London society in the 'twenties and 'thirties of the present century, his tales have now almost a period flavour.

ARLINGTON, Henry Bennet, 1st Earl of (1618–85), was born at Arlington, Middlesex, and from Westminster School proceeded to Christ Church, Oxford. During the Civil War, at Andover he got a lifelong scar on the nose; afterwards at Madrid, as Charles's agent, he acquired an equally lasting pomposity. The Restoration brought him back to England. Created Lord Arlington in 1663 and Earl of Arlington in 1672, he was not the most scrupulous member of the unscrupulous Cabal. In 1674 he was impeached as a 'promoter of popery, a self-aggrandizer, and a betrayer of trust'—in brief, as the 'conduit-pipe' of Charles's evil policy. The impeachment fell through; but Arlington found it desirable to exchange the office of secretary of state for that of lord chamberlain, and finally he retired to his Suffolk seat, and died, July 28, 1685. See study by Barbour (1914).

ARLISS, George (1868–1946), English actor, born in London. He first appeared on the stage at the Elephant and Castle in 1887; but his reputation as an actor was made in America, where he lived for twenty-two years from 1901, returning to London to play the rajah in *The Green Goddess* in 1923. His film career began in America in 1920. He is remembered for his successful representations of famous historical characters, such as Disraeli, Wellington, Richelieu and Voltaire, which were always coloured by his own individual personality. See his autobiography, *Up the Years from Bloomsbury* (1940).

ARMFELT, Gustaf Mauritz (1757–1814), Swedish general, born in Finland, a favourite of Gustavus III, and ambassador in Austria under Gustavus IV, after whose deposition he fell foul of the new régime and fled in 1811 to Russia, for whom he subsequently governed Finland, newly acquired from Sweden. See his Autobiography (Stock. 1830), and Life by Tegner (Stock. 1883–87).

ARMINIUS (18 B.C.–A.D. 19), a famous chief of the German Cherusci, who in A.D. 9, in a three days' battle in the 'Teutoburg Forest', probably near Detmold, annihilated the whole Roman army. 'Varus, Varus, give me back my legions!' was the cry of the Emperor Augustus, now old and weak, on hearing the fatal news. The Germans, who had only their own liberation in view, prosecuted their victory no further; but when Germanicus (q.v.) assumed the command on the Lower Rhine he resolved to crush the barbarians. In two successive campaigns (A.D. 15–16) he reduced Arminius to great straits; but in A.D. 17 he was recalled to Rome by the Emperor Tiberius. No sooner, however, was the foreign enemy expelled than internal feuds broke out, in the course of which Arminius was slain by his own kinsmen. See BANDEL, and German works by Böttger (1874) and Kemmer (1893).

ARMINIUS, Jacobus, properly **Jakob Hermandszoon** (1560–1609), Dutch theologian, born at Oudewater, studied at Utrecht, Leyden, Geneva and Basel, and was ordained in 1588. Despite early opposition to the doctrine of predestination he was made professor of Theology at Leyden in 1603. In 1604 his colleague Gomar (q.v.) attacked his doctrines and thenceforward he was engaged in a series of bitter controversies. Arminius asserted that God bestows forgiveness and eternal life on all who repent of their sins and believe in Christ; he wills that all men should attain salvation, and only because he has from eternity foreseen the belief or unbelief of individuals has he from eternity determined the fate of each—thus rejecting the high Calvinistic doctrine of absolute predestination or election. In 1608 Arminius himself besought the States of Holland to convoke a synod to settle the controversy; but, worn out with care and disease, he died on October 19, 1609, before it was held. Arminius was less Arminian than his followers, who continued the strife for many years and influenced the development of religious thought all over Europe. In England Laudians and Latitudinarians were alike Arminian in tendency; Wesleyans and many Baptists and Congregationalists are distinctly anti-Calvinist. See Life by Brandt (Eng. tr. by Guthrie, 1854).

ARMITAGE, (1) Edward (1817–96), English painter, born in London, studied under Delaroche, was elected R.A. in 1872, and became professor at the Royal Academy schools in 1875. He produced chiefly historical and biblical subject-paintings, including the frescoes *Death of Marmion*, and *Personification of the Thames* in the House of Lords.

(2) **Kenneth** (1916–), English sculptor, born in Leeds. He studied at the Royal College of Art and the Slade School (1937–39) and exhibited at the Venice Biennale in 1952 with other British sculptors. His bronzes are usually of semi-abstract figures, united into a group by stylized clothing. In 1958 he won the Venice Biennale Gold Medal for foreign sculptors.

ARMSTEAD, Henry Hugh (1828–1905), English sculptor, born in London, began as a designer of gold and silver work, but from 1863 specialized in sculpture; his best known works are reliefs and bronze statues for the Albert Memorial, the fountain at King's College, Cambridge, and the reredos at Westminster Abbey.

ARMSTRONG, (1) Archy (d. 1672), Scottish court-jester of James I and Charles I, gained much wealth and influence, but was dismissed in 1637 for insolence to Archbishop Laud, and withdrew in 1641 to Arthuret in Cumberland, where he died at a great age.

(2) **John** (*c.* 1709–79), Scottish physician and poet, was born in Castleton manse, Liddesdale, Roxburghshire. He took the

Edinburgh M.D. in 1732, and soon after commenced practice in London. In 1736 he published the indelicate *Oeconomy of Love;* in 1744 his principal work, *The Art of Preserving Health,* a didactic poem in blank verse. In 1746 he was appointed physician to the London Soldiers' Hospital, in 1760 physician to the forces in Germany, whence he returned on half-pay in 1763, to resume practice. With Fuseli, the painter, he made a Continental tour (1771); and he died in London from a fall. He wrote several medical books and papers.

(3) **John** (1784–1829), English physician, was born near Bishop-Wearmouth. He graduated from Edinburgh (1807), commenced practice at Bishop-Wearmouth, in 1811 was chosen physician to Sunderland Infirmary, and, having extended his reputation by a work on *Typhus* (1816), in 1818 removed to London, where he was physician to the Fever Hospital (1819–24). See Life by Dr Boott (2 vols. 1833). His son, **John** (1813–1856), in 1853 became Bishop of Grahamstown, South Africa.

(4) **John** (1893–   ), English painter, born at Hastings. He studied at the St John's Wood School of Art, and he was a member of Unit One (1933). His paintings, represented in the Tate Gallery, London, have usually been of a symbolic, almost surrealist character, in a precise tempera technique, but he is equally well known for his designs for the film, the theatre and the ballet.

(5) **Johnnie,** of Gilnockie, near Langholm, a Border freebooter, hero of several Border ballads, was hanged, with thirty-six followers, by James V at Caerlanrig, in 1529.

(6) **(Daniel) Louis** (1900–71), popularly known as ' Satchmo ', American Negro trumpeter, born in New Orleans. Having learnt to play the cornet in a waifs' home, he moved to Chicago in 1922, changed from cornet to trumpet, and in 1925 formed his own band. He made his first tour abroad in 1932 and soon became internationally known as an outstanding jazz virtuoso. Later, he turned to some extent from the traditional improvisatory style of jazz to ' swing ', with regularly scored pieces and academically trained performers. See his *My Life in New Orleans* (1955), R. Goffin's *Horn of Plenty.*

(7) **Sir Walter** (1850–1918), Scottish writer of works on Velázquez, Gainsborough, Reynolds, Raeburn, Lawrence, &c., born in Roxburghshire, was director of the National Gallery of Ireland, 1892–1914.

(8) **William,** the 'Kinmont Willie' of the Border ballad, a Dumfriesshire moss-trooper, rescued in 1596 by Scott of Buccleuch from Carlisle Castle.

(9) **William George, Baron Armstrong** (1810–1900), English inventor, born at Newcastle, was articled to a solicitor, and became a partner; but in 1840 he produced a much improved hydraulic engine, in 1842 an apparatus for producing electricity from steam, and in 1845 the hydraulic crane. He was elected an F.R.S. in 1846; and shortly afterwards erected the Elswick Engineworks, Newcastle. This large establishment at first chiefly produced hydraulic cranes, engines, accumulators, and bridges, but was

soon to be famous for its ordnance, and especially the Armstrong gun, whose barrel is built up of successive coils of wrought-iron. From 1882 shipbuilding was included. In 1887 Armstrong was created a baron. In 1897 the firm amalgamated with Joseph Whitworth & Co., and the firm of Armstrong, Whitworth & Co. came into being.

ARNAL, Étienne (1794–1872), French actor, born at Meulan, appeared regularly from 1815–68, first in tragedy, and later, with outstanding success, as a comedian.

ARNASON, Jón (1819–88), ' the Grimm of Iceland ', was national librarian, and made a great collection of Icelandic legends (trans. 1864–66).

ARNAUD, ar-nō (1) **Arsène.** See CLARETIE.

(2) **Henri** (1641–1721), French pastor and military leader of the Waldenses, wrote in exile at Schönberg his famous *Histoire de la rentrée des Vaudois dans leurs vallées* (1710).

ARNAULD, ar-nō, (1) **Angélique** (1624–84), daughter of (5), entered the convent of Port-Royal, was successively subprioress and abbess; and during the persecution of the Port-Royalists, sustained by her heroic courage the spirits of the sisterhood and their friends. See works on her by F. Martin (1873), G. Dall (Paris 1893), A. K. H. (1905), M. Trouncer (1957), and Sainte-Beuve's *Port-Royal* (4th ed. 6 vols. 1878).

(2) **Antoine** (1560–1619), French lawyer, father of (3), (4), and (5), the greatest advocate of his time in France, won a wide celebrity by his zealous defence of the University of Paris against the Jesuits in 1594.

(3) **Antoine** (1612–94), French theologian, twentieth and youngest son of (2), studied at the Sorbonne, became doctor and priest, and, living mostly in seclusion, became famous for his brilliant controversial writings, mainly against the Jesuits and in defence of the Jansenists. He became the religious director of the nuns of Port-Royal des Champs, the convent of which his sister was abbess. Here he and his friends, Pascal, Nicole, and other ' Port-Royalists ' living near him, produced many books, including treatises on grammar, geometry, and logic. He also wrote in defence of transubstantiation and against Calvinism. Under Jesuit influence, the king issued an order for his arrest. Arnauld hid himself for some time, but finally withdrew to Brussels, where he died. His works were published in 45 vols. (1775–83).

(4) **Marie-Angélique** (1591–1661), sister of (3), was made abbess of Port-Royal at eleven, ultimately reformed the convent by her holy example and severe discipline, resigned, and returned to be prioress under her sister Agnes (1593–1671).

(5) **Robert** (Arnauld d'Andilly) (1588–1674), son of (2) and father of (1), retired to the seclusion of Port-Royal des Champs, and published graceful translations of Josephus, Augustine, St Teresa, and others.

ARNAULT, Antoine-Vincent, *ar-nō,* (1766–1834), French poet, was born in Paris, suffered four years' exile as an Imperialist (1815–19), and died, secretary of the Academy, near Havre, September 16, 1834. A rigid classicist, he produced seven dramas—the best *Les Vénitiens* (1799), but all inferior to his *Fables et Poésies* (1812). See his *Souvenirs d'un sexagénaire* (1833).

ARNDT, (1) Ernst Moritz (1769–1860), German poet and patriot, was born in the then Swedish island of Rügen, December 26. The son of a former serf, he yet received an excellent education at Stralsund, Greifswald, and Jena, with a view to the ministry; but in 1805, after travelling extensively over Europe, he became professor of History at Greifswald. His *Geschichte der Leibeigenschaft in Pommern und Rügen* (1803) led to the abolition of serfdom; and in his *Geist der Zeit* (1807) he attacked Napoleon with such boldness that, after Jena, he had to take refuge in Stockholm. *Was ist des deutschen Vaterland?* and others of his fiery songs, did not a little to rouse the spirit of Germany. In 1817 he married a sister of Schleiermacher's and in 1818 became professor of History in the new University of Bonn; but, aiming steadily at constitutional reforms, he was suspended in 1819 for participation in so-called 'demagogic movements', and was not restored till 1840. He was elected a member of the German national assembly in 1848, but retired from it in 1849. Vigorous in mind and body, beloved and revered by the whole German people as 'Father Arndt', he died at Bonn, January 29, 1860. His works comprise an account of the Shetland and Orkney Islands (1826), numerous political addresses, some volumes of reminiscences, two of letters (1878–92), and his poems. See German Lives of him by Langenberg, Baur, Schenkel, Meinhold (1910), and Fahrner (1937), and an English one, with preface by Seeley (1879).

(2) Johann (1555–1621), German Lutheran divine, whose semimystic *Wahres Christenthum* (' True Christianity ') has been called the Protestant *Imitatio*. There are two English translations—by Boehm (1720) and by Jaques (1815).

ARNE, Thomas Augustine (1710–78), English composer, was born in London, March 12, and educated at Eton. His father, an upholsterer, intended him for the bar, but young Arne became skilful as a violinist, forming his style chiefly on Corelli; and his zeal in the study of music induced his sister (the actress, Mrs Cibber, 1714–66) to cultivate her excellent voice. He wrote for her a part in his first opera, *Rosamond*, which was performed with great success in 1733. Next followed his comic operetta, *Tom Thumb* ; and afterwards his *Comus* (1738). He married a singer, Cecilia Young (1736); and after a successful visit to Ireland, was engaged as composer to Drury Lane Theatre, for which he composed his famous settings of Shakespearean songs, *Under the Greenwood Tree*; *Where the Bee Sucks*; *Blow, Blow, thou Winter Wind*; &c. He also wrote many vocal pieces for the Vauxhall concerts. *Rule, Britannia*, originally given in *The Masque of Alfred*, is his; as well as two oratorios and two operas, *Eliza* and *Artaxerxes*. He died in London, March 5, 1778. His son Michael (1740–86) was also a musician and composer, remembered for his lovely ' Lass with the delicate air '.

ARNIM, (1) Harry, Graf von (1824–81), German diplomat, from 1864 to 1870 was Prussian ambassador at Rome, where he backed up the anti-Infallibilists during the Vatican Council. Ennobled, he went as ambassador to France (1872–74), but fell into disfavour, was charged with purloining state documents, and died in exile at Nice. His son Henning (d. 1910) married Mary A. Beauchamp (1866–1941), of Sydney, who wrote *Elizabeth and her German Garden* (1898), &c., and married the 2nd Earl Russell in 1916. See Life of Mary by L. de Charms (1958).

(2) Jürgen, Baron von (1889–), German general, born of an old Silesian military family, served at first in the infantry in World War I, then became a tank expert and in World War II was given command of a Panzer Division in the Russian campaign. He took over the 5th Panzer Army in Tunisia in January 1943. A fanatical Nazi and Britain-hater, he was captured in May 1943.

(3) Ludwig Achim von (1781–1831), German writer of fantastic but original romances, stirred up a warmer sympathy for old popular poetry, and published over 20 volumes, mainly tales and novels. His wife, **Bettina** (1785–1859), a sister of Clemens Brentano (q.v.), was in her girlhood enthusiastically attached to Goethe, and afterwards published a (largely fictitious) *Correspondence* with him, besides 10 vols. of tales and essays. See Life of Bettina by A. Helps and E. J. Howard (1957).

ARNOBIUS THE ELDER (d. 330), a teacher of rhetoric at Sicca, in Numidia, became a Christian about 300, and wrote a defence of Christianity, translated in vol. xix of the *Ante-Nicene Library*.

ARNOBIUS THE YOUNGER (fl. 5th cent.), Gaulish bishop who wrote commentaries on the Psalms.

ARNOLD, (1) Benedict (1741–1801), American general and turncoat, was born at Norwich, Connecticut, January 14. At fourteen he ran away, joined the provincial troops then engaged in the old French war, but soon deserted, and became a merchant in New Haven. On the outbreak of the War of Independence he joined the colonial forces, assisted in the capture of Fort Ticonderoga, and in 1775, for his gallantry at the (unsuccessful) siege of Quebec, was made a brigadier-general. Though greatly admired by General Washington, he had bitter and influential enemies; to his great chagrin, in 1777 five of his inferiors in rank were promoted by congress over his head. At the battle of Ridgefield, his horse was killed under him, and for his gallantry he was made a major-general. He fought with distinction in the eventful battles of Saratoga (having his horse killed, and being himself severely wounded). In 1778 he was placed in command of Philadelphia. In 1780 Arnold sought and obtained the command of West Point, which, through a conspiracy with André (q.v.), he agreed to betray. On the capture of André, Arnold fled to the British lines, and was given a command in the royal army. In 1781 he led an expedition against his native state; and after the war lived in obscurity in London, where he died June 14, 1801. See the Life by Sparks; also works by I. N

Arnold (1880; extenuating his treason), J. G. Taylor (1931), Sherwin (1931).

(2) **Sir Edwin** (1832–1904), English poet, born at Gravesend, won the Newdigate prize at Oxford in 1852, taught at King Edward's School, Birmingham, and in 1856 became principal of the Government College at Poona. Returning in 1861, he joined the staff of the *Daily Telegraph*, of which he became editor in 1863. He wrote *The Light of Asia* (1879) on Buddhism, and other poems coloured by his experience of the East.

(3) **John** (1736–99), English horologist, son of a Bodmin watchmaker, worked in Holland, set up business in London, made improvements in construction and production methods to the chronometer, invented shortly before by John Harrison (q.v.).

(4) **Joseph** (1782–1818), English botanist, born at Beccles, Suffolk, studied medicine at Edinburgh and accompanied Sir Stamford Raffles (q.v.) as naturalist to Sumatra, where he died. He discovered the largest flower known, *Rafflesia arnoldi*, measuring a yard across and weighing fifteen pounds.

(5) **Malcolm** (1921–), English composer, born in Northampton. He won a scholarship to the Royal College of Music at the age of sixteen, and studied under Ernest Hall and Gordon Jacob. He played the trumpet in the London Philharmonic Orchestra. His compositions achieved immediate success for their spontaneous lyrical sincerity, high spirits and unusual professional skill in matters of structure as well as orchestration: they include five symphonies, ten concertos, five ballets, including *Homage to the Queen*, two one-act operas, and other orchestral and chamber pieces.

(6) **Mary Augusta.** See WARD (8).

(7) **Matthew** (1822–88), one of the greater English poets, and the Sainte-Beuve of English criticism, eldest son of Dr Arnold of Rugby, was born at Laleham, near Staines, December 24, 1822, was educated at Winchester, Rugby, and Balliol College, Oxford, and, graduating with honours in 1844, was next year elected a fellow of Oriel. After acting for four years as private secretary to Lord Lansdowne, he was appointed one of the lay inspectors of schools in 1851, an office from which he retired in 1886. During 1857–67 he was professor of Poetry at Oxford. He was frequently sent by the government to inquire into the state of education on the Continent, especially in France, Germany, and Holland; and his masterly reports, with their pregnant hints and downright statement of English deficiencies, attracted much attention in England. So, too, did his audacious application to Scripture of the methods of literary criticism. In 1883 a pension of £250 was conferred on him, and in the same year he lectured in the United States. He died suddenly at Liverpool, April 15, 1888, and was buried at Laleham. His works, some forty in number, include a Rugby prize poem on Alaric (1840), the Newdigate prize poem on Cromwell (1843), *Poems* (1853–54), *Essays in Criticism* (1865, 1888), *On the Study of Celtic Literature* (1867), *New Poems* (1867), *Culture and Anarchy* (1869), *St Paul and Protestantism*

(1870), *Literature and Dogma* (1872), *Last Essays on Church and Religion* (1877), *Mixed Essays* (1879), *Irish Essays* (1882), and *Discourses on America* (1885). See his *Letters* (ed. 1895, 1932), *Note-books* (1952), and books by Saintsbury (1899), G. W. E. Russell (1904), Trilling (1949), Baum (1958).

(8) **Samuel** (1740–1802), English composer, became organist to the Chapels Royal (1783) and to Westminster Abbey (1793). He is best remembered by his valuable collection of cathedral music (1790). His son, **Samuel James** (1774–1852), was a playwright and manager.

(9) **Thomas** (1795–1842), English scholar, father of (7), headmaster of Rugby, was born at East Cowes, Isle of Wight. In 1807 he went to Winchester, whence in 1811 he was elected a scholar of Corpus Christi College, Oxford. Having taken a first-class in classics (1814), he was the next year elected a fellow of Oriel, and he gained the chancellor's prizes for the Latin and English essays in 1815 and 1817. He took deacon's orders in 1818, and the year after settled at Laleham, near Staines, where he prepared pupils for the university. In 1820 he married Mary Penrose, daughter of a Nottinghamshire rector, and sister of one of his earliest friends; in August 1828 he entered on the task of regenerating Rugby, where he had the tact to make himself both loved and feared. In 1832 he purchased for his vacations Fox How, between Rydal and Ambleside; in 1841 he received from Lord Melbourne his regius professorship of Modern History at Oxford. He died suddenly of angina pectoris, June 12, 1842, and was buried in Rugby Chapel. His principal works are six volumes of Sermons (best ed. 1848); an edition of Thucydides (3 vols. 1830–35); the *History of Rome* (3 vols. 1838–1843), broken off at the end of the second Punic war; and his Oxford *Lectures on Modern History* (1842). 'These', in the words of the *Edinburgh Review*, 'are all proofs of his ability and goodness. Yet the story of his life is worth them all.' And that story has been admirably told by Dean Stanley in his *Life of Arnold* (1845, 12th ed. 1881). See too works by Findlay (1897), Worboise (1897), Wymer (1953) and T. W. Bamford (1960). His second son, **Thomas** (1823–1900), wrote a *Manual of English Literature* (1862), and edited *The Select Works of Wyclif* (1869), *Beowulf* (1876) and, with E. W. Addis, the *Catholic Dictionary* (1883). For his daughter, Mrs Humphry Ward, see WARD (9).

ARNOLD OF BRESCIA, *bray'sha* (*c.* 1100–1155), Italian churchman and politician, educated in France under Abelard, adopted the monastic life; and having by his preaching exasperated the people of Brescia against their bishop, was banished from Italy by the Lateran Council (1139). In France he met with bitter hostility from St Bernard, and took refuge in Zürich, where he remained five years. Meanwhile an insurrection against the papal government had taken place in Rome, and thither in 1143 Arnold repaired, and struggled for ten years to found amongst disorderly and disunited masses a republic on ancient Roman lines. Pope Adrian IV (Nicholas Breakspear) laid the city under an interdict, when Arnold, whose party fell to pieces, retired to Campania. On the arrival of the Emperor Frederick Barbarossa, in 1155, Arnold was arrested, brought to Rome, and hanged, his body burned, and the ashes thrown into the Tiber. But he is remembered alongside Rienzi and Savonarola. See *Life* by Greenaway (1931).

ARNOLD OF WINKELRIED, a Swiss of Unterwalden, who, according to tradition, made a way for his comrades into the enemy's ranks at Sempach (1386) by grasping an armful of Austrian spearheads and plunging them into his own bosom.

ARNOLFO DI CAMBIO (1232–1301), Florentine architect, designed the church of Santa Croce and the rebuilt cathedral.

AROUET, the family name of Voltaire (q.v.).

ARP, Jean or Hans (1888–1966), Alsatian sculptor, born at Strasbourg. He was one of the founders of the Dada movement in Zürich in 1916. During the 'twenties he produced many abstract reliefs in wood, but after 1928 he worked increasingly in three dimensions, and he was second only to Brancusi (q.v.) in his influence on organic abstract sculpture, based on natural forms. In 1948 he wrote *On My Way.* See study by C. Giedion-Welcker (1958).

ARPAD (d. 907), the national hero of Hungary, under whom the Magyars first gained a footing in that country about 884.

ARRAN, Earl of. See HAMILTON.

ARREBO, Anders Christiansen (1587–1637), Danish clergyman, Bishop of Trondheim (1618–22), made his name as a translator of the Psalms (1623), but his greatest work was the *Hexaëmeron,* a monumental epic in the vernacular about the six days of Creation.

ARRHENIUS, Svante (1859–1927), Swedish scientist, born near Uppsala, became professor of Physics at Stockholm in 1895, a director of the Nobel Institute in 1905. He did valuable work in connection with the dissociation theory of electrolysis, and was awarded the Nobel prize for chemistry in 1903.

ARRIAGA, *ar-yah'ga,* (1) **Juan** (1806–26), Spanish composer, who died at the age of 20, but whose compositions show remarkable maturity, the symphony in D being reminiscent of Beethoven.

(2) **Manoel José de** (1840–1917), Portuguese statesman, took part in the revolution of 1910, and was president of the republic 1911–15.

ARRIAN, Lat. Flavius Arrianus (c. A.D. 95–180), Greek historian, a native of Nicomedia in Bithynia, who in 136 was appointed prefect of Cappadocia. He edited the *Encheiridion* of his friend and master Epictetus, whose lectures (*Diatribai*) he wrote out in eight books. Only four have been preserved. His chief work, however, is the *Anabasis Alexandrou,* or history of the campaigns of Alexander the Great, which has come down to us almost entire. His accounts of the people of India, and of a voyage round the Euxine, are valuable for ancient geography. See edition with Eng. trans. by Robson (Loeb Library, 1930–1933).

ARROL, Sir William (1839–1913), Scottish engineer, rose from a blacksmith to be head of the great firm who were contractors for the second Tay Bridge (rail), the Forth Bridge, &c. He was knighted in 1890.

ARROWSMITH, Aaron (1750–1823), English cartographer, born at Winston, Durham, about 1770 came up to London, and by 1790 had established a great map-making business. His nephew, **John** (1790–1873), was also an eminent cartographer.

ARSACIDAE, a dynasty of Parthian kings, so called from the founder, Arsaces, who wrested a kingdom for himself from the feeble grasp of the Seleucid Antiochus II about 250 B.C., which ultimately extended from Bactria to the Euphrates, and included Persia. Its greatest kings were Mithradates, Phraates, Mithradates 'the great', Volagases I, and Artabanus, who fell at Hormizdján in A.D. 226 attempting to stem the conquering career of Ardashír, founder of the Sassanian dynasty of Persia.

ARSINOË, *ar-sin'ō-ee* (316–271 B.C.), Egyptian princess, daughter of Ptolemy I, married first, about 300 B.C., the aged Lysimachus, king of Thrace, and finally, in 279, her own brother, Ptolemy II, Philadelphus.

ARSONVAL, Jacques-Arsène d', *ar-sō-vahl* (1851–1940), French physicist, born at Borie, was director of the laboratory of biological physics at the Collège de France from 1882, and professor from 1894. He invented the reflecting galvanometer named after him, and he also experimented with high-frequency oscillating current for electromedical purposes.

ARTABAZUS, *-bay'-,* the name of several Persian generals under the dynasty of the Achaemenidae.

ARTAXERXES, *ar-ta-zerk'zeez,* anc. Pers. **Artakshathra,** the name of several Persian kings.

(1) **Artaxerxes I,** called **Longimanus** (' longhanded '), the second son of Xerxes (q.v.), reigned from 465 to 425 B.C.

(2) **Artaxerxes II,** called **Mnemon** (' the mindful '), reigned from 404 to 359 B.C.

(3) **Artaxerxes III,** called **Ochus,** son of (2), found the empire disintegrating, but did much to build it up again. He was poisoned in 338 by his favourite eunuch, Bagoas.

(4) **Artaxerxes, or Ardashir** (d. 242), founder of the new Persian dynasty of the Sassanidae, overthrew Ardavan (Artabanus), the last of the Parthian kings in A.D. 226. He next conquered Media and a large part of the Iranian highlands, but was defeated by Alexander Severus in 233.

ARTEDI, Peter, *ar-tay'dee* (1705–35), a Swedish ichthyologist and botanist, wrote *Ichthyologia,* the first systematic study of fishes, edited by Linnaeus after the author had been accidentally drowned in a canal near Amsterdam.

ARTEMISIA, (1) **Queen of Caria** (352–350 B.C.), erected a magnificent mausoleum at Halicarnassus to the memory of her brother and husband, Mausolus. It was one of the traditional seven wonders of the world.

(2) **Queen of Halicarnassus,** accompanied Xerxes, with five ships, in his expedition against Greece, and distinguished herself at Salamis (480 B.C.); an unfortunate love affair made her leap from a rock into the sea.

ARTEVELDE, Jacob van (1290–1345)

Flemish statesman, a wealthy and highborn brewer of Ghent, who, in 1335, when war was raging between England and France, gave his support to the former power, while the Count of Flanders sided with the latter, and who actually concluded a treaty with Edward III. Proclaimed governor of Flanders, for nine years he was almost absolute ruler; but he went too far when he proposed that the Black Prince should be elected Count of Flanders, and was killed in a popular insurrection, July 24, 1345. His son **Philip van Artevelde** in 1381 headed a new revolt of the people of Ghent, and gained a victory over the Count of Flanders, the son of his father's old enemy. The count therefore sought the assistance of Charles VI of France, and Philip was defeated and slain at Roosbeke, 1382. His history forms the theme of a fine drama by Sir Henry Taylor. See Hutton, *James and Philip van Artevelde* (1883).

ARTHUR, a half-legendary king of the Britons—Cymri driven into the west of England by the Saxons—is represented as having united the British tribes in resisting the pagan invaders, not only of his people, but also of Christianity. He is said to have lived in the 6th century, and to have maintained a stubborn contest against the Saxon Cerdic, but the *Anglo-Saxon Chronicle* is suspiciously silent as to his warfare and as to his existence. Indeed the Welsh bards of the earliest period do not assert that he was a contemporary, and it is more than doubtful whether he is an historic personage. It is worthy of remark that the fame of Arthur is widely spread; he is claimed alike as a prince in Brittany, Cornwall, Wales, Cumberland, and the lowlands of Scotland; that is to say, his fame is conterminous with the Brythonic race, and does not extend to the Goidels or Gaels. The story of Arthur passed into literature and a multitude of fascinating legends became interwoven with it, including those of the Round Table and the Holy Grail, both introduced near the turn of the 12th–13th century. See texts (some in translation) of Nennius, Geoffrey of Monmouth, Wace, Layamon, Chrétien de Troyes, Malory, and *The Mabinogion*; also books by Glennie (1869), Rhys (1891), Bruce (1928), Lewis (1932), Loomis (1949, 1956), and Lindsay (1958).

ARTHUR, Prince (1187–1203), the posthumous son of Geoffrey (Henry II's fourth son) by Constance, Duchess of Brittany. On Richard's death in 1199, Arthur by the law of primogeniture should have succeeded to the English crown; and the French king, Philip II, upheld his claims, until John (q.v.) bought him over to a disgraceful treaty. Arthur soon after fell into his uncle's hands, and was imprisoned, first at Falaise, afterwards at Rouen, where, on April 3, 1203, he is supposed to have perished, either by assassination or by drowning, in an attempt to escape. The story of John's orders to Hubert to put out his eyes was current as early as 1228.

ARTHUR, Prince (1486–1502), the eldest son of Henry VII, was born at Winchester, September 19. When he was still under two years old a marriage was arranged between him and Catharine of Aragon in order to provide an alliance between England and Spain. The wedding took place in November 1501, but Arthur, a sickly youth, died next April at Ludlow.

ARTHUR, (1) **Chester Alan** (1830–86), twenty-first president of the United States, was born at Fairfield, Vermont, October 5, the son of a Baptist minister from Antrim. He became the head of a very eminent law firm and leader of the Republican party in New York state. He was made vice president of the United States when Garfield became president in 1881; and, after Garfield's death, he was president from September 1881 to March 1885. He died November 18, 1886.

(2) **Sir George** (1785–1854), British diplomat, born near Plymouth, was governor of British Honduras (1814–22), Van Diemen's Land (1823–36), Upper Canada (1837–41), and Bombay (1842–46). He was created a baronet in 1841.

ARTZYBASHEV, *art-si-ba′shef,* (1) **Boris** (1899–), American artist. His illustrations have a vivid and repetitive brilliance of pattern, reminiscent of the early Ballets Russes *décors.* He has also written stories for children, based on Russian folklore.

(2) **Mikhail Petrovich** (1878–1927), Russian author. His liberalist novel *Sanin* had an international reputation at the turn of the century. It was translated by P. Pinkerton in 1907, who also translated *Breaking Point* (1915), and with I. Ohzol, *Tales of Revolution* (1918). He was the great-grandson of the Polish patriot Kosciusko.

ARUNDEL, Thomas, *ar′-* (1353–1413), English prelate, third son of Robert Fitzalan, Earl of Arundel, in 1373 became Archdeacon of Taunton and Bishop of Ely, in 1388 Archbishop of York, and in 1396 of Canterbury. Banished by Richard II (1397), he helped to seat Henry of Lancaster on the throne (1399). He was a bitter opponent of the Lollards.

ARUNDEL AND SURREY, Earl of. See HOWARD.

ASBJÖRNSEN, Peter Christian (1812–85), Norwegian folklorist, born at Christiania, studied at the university there, then for four years was a tutor in the country. In long journeys on foot he collected a rich store of popular poetry and folklore, and, with Jörgen Moe (1813–82), Bishop of Christiansand, published the famous collection of Norwegian folk tales, *Norske Folkeeventyr* (1841–44); followed in 1845–48 by *Norske Huldreeventyr og Folkesagn* which he brought out alone. From 1856 to 1858 he studied forestry, subsequently becoming inspector of forests for the Trondhjem district. See translations of his tales by Dasent and Braekstad.

ASBURY, Francis (1745–1816), the first Methodist bishop consecrated (1784) in America, was born at Handsworth, Staffordshire, August 20; in 1771 was sent as a missionary to America; and died at Richmond, Virginia, March 31, 1816. See Lives by Larrabee (1853) and Strickland (1858).

ASCH, Sholem (1880–1957), Jewish writer, born at Kutno in Poland, emigrated to America in 1914 and became naturalized in

1920. His prolific output of novels and short stories, most of them originally in Yiddish but many since translated, includes *The Mother* (1930), *The War Goes On* (1936), *The Nazarene* (1939), *The Apostle* (1943), *East River* (1946) and *Moses* (1951). His early work includes the plays *Mottke the Thief* (1917) and *The God of Vengeance* (1918).

ASCHAM, Roger, *as'kĕm* (1515-68), English humanist, was born at Kirby Wiske near Thirsk, in Yorkshire. He graduated in 1534 at St John's College, Cambridge, and, in spite of his avowed leaning to the Reformed doctrines, obtained a fellowship. His reputation as a classical scholar soon brought him numerous pupils; and about 1538 he was appointed Greek reader at St John's. In defence of archery, he published, in 1545, *Toxophilus*, the pure English style of which ranks it among English classics. In 1546 he was appointed university orator. He was tutor to the Princess Elizabeth (1548-50), and later became Latin secretary to Queen Mary. His prudence and moderation preserved him from offending by his Protestantism; and after Mary's death Elizabeth retained him at court as secretary and tutor, which offices he held till his death, December 30, 1568. His principal work, *The Scholemaster*, a treatise on classical education, was published in 1570. See monographs by Katterfeld (1879) and Weidemann (1900).

ASCHE, John Stanger Heiss Oscar (1872-1936), Australian actor, playwright and theatrical manager, born at Geelong. He wrote *Chu Chin Chow* (1916), and managed the Adelphi theatre, London (1904), and His Majesty's (1907).

ASCLEPIADES, *as-klep'i-a-deez* (fl. 1st cent. B.C.), a Greek physician, born at Prusa in Bithynia. He seems to have wandered about as a not very successful teacher of rhetoric before he finally settled at Rome, where, by the practice of medicine, he had risen in Cicero's time to considerable fame and wealth.

ASCOLI, Graziadio Isaia, *as'-* (1829-1907), Italian philologist, was born of Jewish parentage at Görz, and was destined for a mercantile career, but early devoted himself to comparative philology. In 1861 he obtained a chair of Philology at Milan, and in 1889 was created a senator.

ASELLIO, Gasparo (1581-1626), an Italian physician, the discoverer of the lacteal vessels.

ASGILL, John (1659-1738), English pamphleteer, born at Hanley Castle, Worcestershire, was called to the bar in 1692. Having got into difficulties, he sailed in 1699 for Ireland, where his talents gained him a lucrative practice; and in 1703 he obtained a seat in the Irish parliament. Three years before, however, he had published a paradoxical pamphlet to prove that by the rules of English law the redeemed need not die. Much to his surprise, the Irish parliament voted this a blasphemous libel, and expelled its author. In 1705 he returned to England, and became M.P. for Bramber, in Sussex. But the fame of his unlucky pamphlet haunted him; for the English House condemned it to be burned by the common hangman, and expelled Asgill in 1707. Ultimately he was imprisoned for debt in the Fleet, where he died.

ASHBEE, Charles Robert (1863-1942), English architect, designer and writer, born at Isleworth. He was educated at King's College, Cambridge, and was the founder of the Guild of Handicrafts, the London Survey Committee and the Essex House Press. As an architect, he undertook (among other work) church restoration, and his publications include *The Book of Cottages and Little Houses* (1906) and *Caricature* (1928). He also wrote a number of books of verse. There are several examples of silverwork designed by him in the Victoria and Albert Museum, London.

ASHBOURNE, Edward Gibson, 1st Baron (1837-1913), Lord Chancellor of Ireland, was born in Dublin, educated there at Trinity College, and called to the Irish bar in 1860. Entering parliament in 1872, he rose through various posts in successive Conservative administrations to the chancellorship (1885, 1886, 1895), carrying (1885) a measure facilitating the purchasing clauses of the Land Act.

ASHCROFT, Dame Peggy, properly **Edith Margaret Emily** (1907-), English actress, born in London. She first appeared on the stage with the Birmingham Repertory Company in 1928, and scored a great success in London as Naomi in *Jew Süss* in 1929. In 1930 she played Desdemona to Paul Robeson's Othello, and acted leading parts at the Old Vic in the season of 1932-33. In Sir John Gielgud's production of *Romeo and Juliet* (1935), she was a memorable Juliet. She has worked both in films and on the British and American stage, and was created D.B.E. in 1956.

ASHLEY, Lord. See SHAFTESBURY.

ASHMEAD-BARTLETT, Sir Ellis (1849-1902), born at Brooklyn, in 1880 entered parliament as a Conservative, and in 1892 was knighted. An ardent Turcophil, he—with his son Ellis (1881-1931), later a noted war correspondent—was captured by the Greeks in 1897. See BURDETT-COUTTS.

ASHMOLE, Elias (1617-92), English antiquary, born at Lichfield, qualified as a lawyer in 1638 and subsequently combined work for the Royalist cause with the study of mathematics, natural philosophy, astronomy, astrology, and alchemy, entering Brasenose College, Oxford. In 1646 he became acquainted with Lilly and other famous astrologers; and in 1650 he edited a work of Dr Dee's to which he subjoined a treatise of his own. In 1652 he issued his *Theatrum Chymicum*, and in 1672 his major work, a *History of the Order of the Garter*. After the Restoration he mainly devoted himself to heraldic and antiquarian studies. In 1682 he presented to the University of Oxford a fine collection of rarities, bequeathed him by his old friend Tradescant, thus founding Ashmolean Museum. Among his friends were Selden and Dugdale, whose daughter became his third wife. See his *Diary* (1717; ed. Gunther 1927).

ASHMUN, Jehudi (1794-1828), American philanthropist, the founder in 1822 of the colony of Liberia for liberated Negroes on the west coast of Africa, was born at Champlain, New York, and died at New Haven, Connecticut. See *Life* by Gurley (1835).

ASHTON, (1) Frederick William Mallandaine (1906–), English dancer and choreographer, born in Guayaquil, Ecuador. He trained as a dancer under Massine and Marie Rambert, first appeared in public in 1926, and in 1935 became choreographer to Sadler's Wells Ballet. His *Cinderella* was produced at Covent Garden in 1948. He also worked with the New York City Ballet and the Royal Danish Ballet Company. He became co-director, with Ninette de Valois, of Sadler's Wells Ballet, and was created C.B.E. in 1950 and knighted in 1962.
(2) **Winifred**. See DANE, CLEMENCE.

ASINIUS. See POLLIO.

ASKE, Robert (d. 1537), English rebel, a Yorkshire attorney at Gray's Inn, who was hanged at York for having in the previous autumn headed the Catholic rising known as the Pilgrimage of Grace.

ASKEW, Anne (1521–46), English Protestant martyr, was born of gentle parentage near Grimsby. Early embracing the Reformed doctrines, she was turned out of doors by her husband, and thereupon went up to London to sue for a separation; but in 1545 she was arrested on a charge of heresy. After examination and torture by the rack, she was burned in Smithfield, July 18, 1546.

ASNYK, Adam (1838–97), Polish lyric poet and dramatist, born at Kalisz, died at Cracow.

AŚOKA, *a-sō'ka*, an Indian king 264–223 B.C., a convert to Buddhism, organized it as the state religion.

ASPASIA (fl. 5th cent. B.C.), the mistress of Pericles (q.v.) after his separation from his Athenian wife, was born at Miletus. Intellectual and vivacious, she was lampooned in Greek comedy and satire, but was held in high regard by Socrates and his followers, and was a great inspiration to Pericles, who successfully defended her against a charge of impiety. After his death she lived with Lysicles, a cattle dealer who had risen to power and influence.

ASPLUND, Erik Gunnar (1885–1940), Swedish architect, born in Stockholm. In 1924–27 he designed the Stockholm City Library, and he was responsible for most of the buildings in the Stockholm Exhibition of 1930. Their design was acclaimed for the new gaiety and imagination with which the architect used simple modern forms and methods, e.g., the cantilever and glass walls.

ASQUITH, Herbert Henry, 1st Earl of Oxford and Asquith (1852–1928), British Liberal statesman, born at Morley, studied at Balliol, Oxford, took a first-class in classics, won the Craven, and a fellowship. Called to the bar in 1876, Q.C. in 1890, M.P. for East Fife 1886–1918, in 1892–95 he was home secretary, in 1905–08 chancellor of the Exchequer. In April 1908 he succeeded Campbell-Bannerman as premier. Winning two general elections in 1910, he held the premiership continuously for eight years and eight months, a record unequalled since Liverpool's time (1812–27). His régime was notable, *inter alia*, for the upholding of Free Trade, the great budget of 1909, old age pensions, national insurance, payment of M.P.s, the Parliament Act, Irish home rule, Welsh disestablishment, 'suffragette'

troubles, declaration of war (August 4, 1914), Coalition ministry (May 1915), Sinn Fein rebellion. Member for Paisley 1920–24, created an earl in 1925, he resigned the Liberal leadership in 1926. See his *Memories and Reflections* (1928). His second wife Margot, daughter of Sir Charles Tennant, Bart. (1865–1945), wrote a lively *Autobiography* (1922; rev. ed. 1962). See Lives by Spender and Asquith (1932) and by Roy Jenkins (1964). Of the five children of his first marriage, **Raymond** (1878–1916), his brilliant eldest son, was killed in action; **Herbert** (1881–1947) was a poet; and for his elder daughter, see BONHAM-CARTER. Of the two children by his second wife, **Elizabeth** (d. 1945) married Prince Antoine Bibesco in 1919, and wrote lively novels; and **Anthony** (1902–68) was a notable film director, whose works included *Pygmalion*, *The Browning Version*, *The Way to the Stars* and *Orders to Kill*.

ASSEMANI, Joseph Simon, *as-e-mah'nee* (1687–1768), Syrian orientalist, was born of Maronite family at Tripoli and died keeper of the Vatican Library.

ASSER, Welsh monk of St David's, known for his biography of King Alfred. He resided at intervals (885–901) at Alfred's court, assisting him in his studies, and worthily enjoying an affectionate confidence. Alfred promoted him to various dignities, and prior to 900 made him Bishop of Sherborne. He died in either 909 or 910. His Latin life of Alfred was first published, with various interpolations, in 1572 by Archbishop Parker.

ASSURBANIPAL. See SARDANAPALUS.

ASTAIRE, orig. Austerlitz, **Fred** (1899–), American actor and dancer, was born in Omaha. When he and his elder sister Adele began to exhibit an unusual talent for dancing they were sent to New York to study, and in 1916 they launched out as a brother and sister team, rising to stardom in the 'twenties in *Lady be Good*, *Funny Face*, &c. Adele having retired on her marriage to Lord Charles Cavendish (1932), with various partners, but especially with Ginger Rogers, Fred revolutionized the film ' musical ' with original and carefully worked out tap-dance routines designed by himself, as in *Gay Divorce*, *Roberta*, *Top Hat*, &c. In 1959 he appeared in a straight acting rôle in the nuclear war film *On the Beach*. See his Autobiography (1960).

ASTELL, Mary (1668–1731), English religious writer, a Newcastle merchant's daughter, who lived at Chelsea, and in 1694 projected an Anglican sisterhood with an academic bias, which was strongly criticized by Bishop Burnet and by the *Tatler*, and did not materialize. See Life by Florence M. Smith (1916).

ASTLEY, Philip (1742–1814), English theatrical manager, equestrian, and the best horsetamer of his time, in 1770 started a circus at Lambeth, and built Astley's Amphitheatre (1798), once one of the sights of London.

ASTON, Francis William (1877–1945), English scientist, born at Birmingham, was educated at Malvern and at Birmingham and Cambridge. Noted for his work on isotopes, he invented the mass spectrograph, with which he investigated the isotopic structures of elements. The Aston dark space, in electronic discharges, is named after him.

ASTOR, (1) **John Jacob** (1763–1848), American millionaire, founder of the American Fur Company, was born near Heidelberg, and helped on his father's farm until, in his sixteenth year, he went to London and worked with his brother, a maker of musical instruments. In 1783 he sailed to America and invested his small capital in furs. On his death in New York he left about twenty million dollars, and a legacy of $350,000 to found a public library in New York.

(2) **John Jacob** (1864–1912), a great-grandson of (1), served in the Spanish-American war, built part of the Waldorf-Astoria hotel in New York, and went down with the *Titanic*.

(3) **John Jacob, 1st Baron Astor of Hever** (1886–1971), British newspaper proprietor, son of (6), educated at Eton and New College, Oxford, was elected M.P. for Dover in 1922, and became chairman of the Times Publishing Company after the death of Lord Northcliffe, resigning his directorship in 1962. His eldest son **Gavin** (b. 1918) became a director in 1952 and chairman in 1959.

(4) **Nancy Witcher Langhorne, Viscountess** (1879–1964), wife of (7), born in Virginia, U.S.A., succeeded her husband as M.P. for Plymouth in 1919, and was the first woman to take a seat in the House of Commons. She was known for her interest in social problems, especially temperance. See her *My Two Countries* (1923), and Life by Collis (1960).

(5) **William** (1792–1875), son of (1), augmented his inherited wealth and is said to have left fifty million dollars. He added to his father's library bequest, and on account of his great property interests was known as the ' landlord of New York '.

(6) **William Waldorf, 1st Viscount Astor** (1848–1919), a great-grandson of (1), was U.S. minister to Italy in 1882–85, and in 1892 settled in England. Made a baron in 1916, viscount in 1917, he owned the *Pall Mall Gazette* (1893–1916).

(7) **William Waldorf, 2nd Viscount Astor** (1879–1952), English politician, son of (6), educated at Eton and New College, Oxford, was elected M.P. for Plymouth in 1910. On passing to the House of Lords in 1919 he became parliamentary secretary to the Local Government Board (subsequently Ministry of Health) and his wife (see (4)) succeeded him in the lower house. He was proprietor of the *Observer*.

(8) **William Waldorf, 3rd Viscount Astor** (1907–66), English politician, son of (7), educated at Eton and New College, Oxford, sat as M.P. for East Fulham (1935–45) and for Wycombe (1951–52).

ASTORGA, Emanuele, d' (1680–1757), Italian composer, born at Agosta in Sicily; died at Madrid or Lisbon. His masterwork is a *Stabat Mater* (1707). See study by Volkmann (1911–19).

ASTRUC, Jean (1684–1766), French biblical scholar and medical professor, born at Sauve, wrote a work on Moses which laid the foundation for modern criticism of the Pentateuch.

ASTYAGES, *as-tī'a-jeez*, son of Cyaxares, the last king of Media, ruled from 584 B.C. until 550 B.C. when he was dethroned by Cyrus the Great (q.v.).

ATAHUALPA (d. 1533), last of the Incas, on his father's death in 1525 received the kingdom of Quito, and in 1532, overwhelming his elder brother, Huascar, seized Peru. Meanwhile the Spaniards had disembarked; and Atahualpa, made a captive, agreed to great ransom, but was accused of plotting against Pizarro, tried, and strangled.

ATATÜRK. See MUSTAFA KEMAL ATATÜRK.

ATHALIAH (d. 837 B.C.), daughter of Ahab and Jezebel, and wife of Jehoram, King of Judah, secured the throne of Judah to herself after the death (843 B.C.) of her son, Ahaziah, at the hands of Jehu, by the slaughter of all the royal children save Ahaziah's son, Joash. Her support of Baal-worship led, after six years, to an insurrection headed by the priests; Joash was made king, and Athaliah put to death. Her fate is the subject of a play by Racine, to which Mendelssohn added incidental music.

ATHANARIC (d. 381), a prince of the Western Goths, who fought three campaigns with the Emperor Valens, but was finally defeated in 369, and who, driven by the Huns from the north of the Danube, died at Constantinople.

ATHANASIUS, St (c. 296–373), Christian leader, born in Alexandria, in his youth often visited the celebrated hermit St Antony, and himself for a time embraced an anchorite's life. He was only a deacon when he distinguished himself at the great Council of Nicaea or Nice in 325. In 326 he was chosen Patriarch of Alexandria and Primate of Egypt, and was but newly installed when Arius, banished on the condemnation of his doctrine at Nice, was recalled, and recanted. Athanasius refused to comply with the will of the Emperor Constantine that the heretic should be restored to communion. Hence, and on other charges brought by the Arians, he was summoned by the emperor to appear before the synod of Tyre, in 335, which deposed him. The sentence was confirmed by the synod of Jerusalem in 336, when he was banished to Trèves. In 338, he was restored; but in 341 he was again condemned by a council of ninety-seven (mainly Arian) bishops at Antioch. Orthodox synods at Alexandria and at Sardica protested in his favour, and he was again replaced in his office (349). Under the Arian Emperor Constantius, he was again condemned and forcibly expelled, whereupon he retired to a remote desert in Upper Egypt. Under Julian the Apostate, toleration was proclaimed to all religions, and Athanasius became once more Patriarch of Alexandria (361). His next controversy was with the heathen subjects of Julian, by whom he was compelled again to flee from Alexandria, and he hid in the Theban desert until 363, when Jovian ascended the throne. After holding office again for a short time, he was expelled again by the Arians under the Emperor Valens, who, after petitions from the orthodox Alexandrians, soon restored the patriarch to his see, in which he continued till his death. Athanasius was the great leader during the most trying period in the history of the early Christian church. His conscientiousness, his wisdom, his fearlessness, his commanding intellect, his activity and patience, all mark him out as an ornament of his age. His writings, polemical, historical, and moral, are simple, cogent, and clear. The polemical works treat chiefly of the Trinity, the Incarnation, and the divinity of the Holy Spirit. See also the church histories, Lives by Bush (1888), Reynolds (1889), Bardy (Paris 1925), and study by F. L. Goss (1945). See ARIUS. The so-called *Athanasian Creed* (representing Athanasian beliefs) is little heard of till the 7th century.

ATHELING. See EDGAR.

ATHELSTAN (*c.* 895–939), son of King Edward the Elder, and grandson of Alfred the Great, was crowned king of the Mercians and West Saxons at Kingston-upon-Thames in 924. He conquered portions of Cornwall, Wales, and Northumbria, and, a league being formed against him in 937 of Welsh, Scots, and Danes, completely routed them at Brunanburh. After this his fame spread to the Continent; and one of his sisters married Otho the Great, afterwards emperor; another, Hugh, Duke of the French, father of Hugh Capet. At home he improved the laws, built monasteries, and promoted commerce.

ATHENAEUS, *ath-en-ee'us*, a Greek writer, born at Naucratis in Egypt. He lived first at Alexandria and afterwards at Rome about the close of the 2nd century. His *Deipnosophistae* (' Banquet of the Learned '), in fifteen books, but of which we possess only the first two, and parts of the third, eleventh, and fifteenth, is very interesting as one of the earliest collections of *Ana.*

ATHENAGORAS, *-ag'-* (2nd cent.), a Christian philosopher who taught first at Athens, and afterwards at Alexandria. Of his two extant treatises one is on the Resurrection, the other is a petition to Marcus Aurelius on behalf of the Christians.

ATHENAIS. See EUDOCIA.

ATHERTON, Gertrude Franklin, *née* Horn (1857–1948), American novelist, born in San Francisco. Left a widow in 1887, she travelled extensively, living in Europe most of her life and using the places she visited as backgrounds for her novels—which range from Ancient Greece to California and the West Indies. She was made Chevalier of the Legion of Honour for her relief work during World War I and in 1934 became president of the American National Academy of Literature. The most popular of her many novels are *The Conqueror* (1902), a fictional biography of Alexander Hamilton, and *Black Oxen* (1923), which is concerned with the possibility of rejuvenation.

ATKINSON, Thomas Witlam (1799–1861), English architect and travel-writer, born at Cawthorne, Yorks., became successively quarryman, stonemason, and architect; then, in 1848–53, travelled some 40,000 miles in Asiatic Russia, sketching and keeping journals which formed the basis of several works on that part of the world.

ATTALUS, the name of three kings of Pergamos, of whom the last, dying in 133 B.C., left his kingdom to Rome.

ATTERBOM, Per Daniel Amadeus (1790–1855), Swedish Romanticist poet, born at Åsbo, professor at Uppsala of Logic (1828) and of Aesthetics (1835).

ATTERBURY, Francis (1663–1732). English prelate, was born March 6 at Milton-Keynes, near Newport-Pagnell, and educated at Westminster, whence in 1680 he passed to Christ Church, Oxford. In 1687 he answered a pseudonymous attack on Protestantism by Obadiah Walker, master of University College; and, taking orders about the same time, won such reputation as a preacher, that he was appointed lecturer of St Bride's (1691), a royal chaplain, and minister to Bridewell Hospital. Boyle's *Examination of Bentley's Dissertations on the Epistles of Phalaris* (1698), a clever but shallow performance, was really by Atterbury, who had been the young nobleman's tutor at Christ Church. In 1704 he was promoted to the deanery of Carlisle; in 1710 he was chosen prolocutor of Convocation; in 1712 became Dean of Christ Church; and in 1713 was made Bishop of Rochester and Dean of Westminster. To Atterbury is ascribed, with great likelihood, Dr Sacheverel's famous defence (1710) before the Lords; and he was author of the scarcely less famous *Representation of the State of Religion* (1711). He may well have aspired to the primacy; but the death of Queen Anne extinguished his hopes in that direction. His known character and Jacobite leanings made him no favourite with George I. In 1715 he refused to sign the bishops' declaration of fidelity, and in 1722 he was committed to the Tower for complicity in an attempt to restore the Stuarts. A bill of pains and penalties was passed; and Atterbury, who had defended himself with great ability, was deprived of all his offices, and for ever banished the kingdom. In 1723 he quitted England, and after a short stay at Brussels, settled in Paris, where he died, February 15, 1732. He was laid in a nameless grave in Westminster Abbey. His works comprise sermons, and letters to Pope, Swift, Bolingbroke, and others of his friends. See Beeching's *Life* (1909) and Williams' *Memoirs and Correspondence of Atterbury* (2 vols. 1869).

ATTICUS, Titus Pomponius (109–32 B.C.), Roman philosopher and writer, born in Rome, was educated with Cicero and the younger Marius. In 85 B.C. he withdrew to Athens; and, after 65 B.C., when Sulla induced him to return to Rome, he still devoted himself chiefly to study and the pleasures of friendship. In 32 B.C. he was informed that a disorder he suffered from was mortal, and died after five days of voluntary starvation. A man of large wealth, and an Epicurean in philosophy, he was intimately acquainted with both Greek and Roman literature, and his taste was so good that Cicero used to send him his works for revision. None of his own writings have been preserved, but we have 396 epistles addressed to him by Cicero, ranging from 68 to 44 B.C. His Life by Cornelius Nepos is a panegyric rather than a biography.

ATTILA, Ger. Etzel, Hung. Ethele, *at'-* (*c.* 406–453), Hunnish king, called the ' Scourge of God ', became in 434 king (jointly at first with a brother) of countless hordes of Huns from Asia scattered from the north of the Caspian to the Danube. Attila soon had Vandals, Ostrogoths, Gepidae, and Franks fighting under his banner, so that his dominion extended over Germany and Scythia from the Rhine to the frontiers of China. In 447 he devastated all the countries between the Black Sea and the Mediterranean. The Emperor Theodosius was defeated in three bloody engagements, and Constantinople owed its safety solely to its fortifications and the ignorance of the enemy in the art of besieging; Thrace, Macedon, and Greece were overrun, and Theodosius was compelled to cede a territory south of the Danube, and to pay tribute. In 451 Attila invaded Gaul, but Aëtius, the Roman commander, and Theodoric, king of the Visigoths, compelled him to raise the siege of Orleans, and, after a fearful and bloody contest, utterly defeated him on the Catalaunian Plain, near Châlons-sur-Marne. He retreated to Hungary, but next year made an incursion into Italy, devastating Aquileia, Milan, Padua, and other cities, Rome itself being saved only by the personal mediation of Pope Leo I, who bought off the city with large sums. He died in 453, soon after his return to Pannonia, immediately after his marriage to the beautiful Burgundian Ildeco; and the Hunnish empire decayed. See Gibbon's *Decline and Fall*, and works by Hutton (1915) and Brion (1929).

ATTLEE, Clement Richard, 1st Earl Attlee (1883–1967), English Labour statesman, born at Putney, was educated at Haileybury and University College, Oxford, and was called to the bar (1905). Through Haileybury House, a boys' club in the Stepney slums, he developed a practical interest in social problems which, fortified by the works of Ruskin and William Morris, made him a convert to Socialism. In 1910 he became secretary of Toynbee Hall. His lectureship at the newly founded London School of Economics (1913–23) was interrupted by service in the war, in which he was wounded, and attained the rank of major. In 1919 he was elected mayor of Stepney, and in 1922 he entered parliament and became Ramsay MacDonald's parliamentary secretary (1922–24), under-secretary of state for war (1924), served on the Simon commission on India (1927–30) and was postmaster-general (1931). He did not become a member of MacDonald's coalition government. One of the few Labour M.P.s to retain his parliamentary seat in the following election, he became deputy leader of the opposition (1931–35) under Lansbury, whom he succeeded as leader in 1935, and he paved the way for Churchill's war-time premiership by refusing to commit his party to a coalition under Chamberlain. He was dominions secretary (1942–43) and deputy prime-minister (1942–1945) in Churchill's war cabinet. As leader of the opposition he accompanied Eden to the San Francisco and Potsdam conferences (1945), and after the huge Labour electoral victory returned to the latter conference as prime minister. During his six years in office, Attlee carried through, despite severe economic handicaps aggravated by America's precipitate ending of Lend-Lease, a vigorous programme of reform. The Bank of England, the coal mines, civil aviation, cable and wire-less services, railways, road transport and steel were nationalized, the National Health Service was introduced and independence was granted to India (1947) and Burma (1948). Labour's foreign policy of support for N.A.T.O. in the face of Russian intransigence, particularly the necessity for rearming the Germans and the manufacture of British atom bombs, precipitated continuous party strife which at times taxed even Attlee's considerable gifts of shrewd chairmanship. He earned affection and respect by his sheer lack of dogma, oratorical gifts or showmanship and by his balanced judgment and quiet, yet unmistakable authority which belied the public image of ' Little Clem '. He was leader of the Opposition from 1951 until 1955 when he resigned and accepted an earldom. He became C.H. (1945), was awarded the O.M. (1951) and was created K.G. (1956). His many books include *The Labour Party in Perspective* (1937), with supplement *Twelve Years Later* (1949), and an autobiography, *As It Happened* (1954). See Lives by R. Jenkins (1948) and V. Brome (1949).

ATTWELL, Mabel Lucie, married name **Mrs Harold Earnshaw** (1879–1964), English artist and writer, born in London. She studied at Heatherley's and other art schools, and was noted for her child studies, both humorous and serious.

ATTWOOD, Thomas (1765–1838), English musician and composer, a pupil of Mozart, organist of St Paul's from 1796 till his death.

ATWOOD, George (1746–1807), English mathematician, tutor of Trinity College, Cambridge, invented a machine to illustrate the motion of a body falling under the action of gravity.

AUBANEL, Théodore, ō-*ban-el* (1829–86), a Provençal playwright and lyric poet, by calling an Avignon printer. See monographs by Saint-Rémy (1882) and Mariéton (1883).

AUBER, Daniel-François-Esprit, ō-*bayr* (1782–1871), French composer of operas, was born at Caen, January 29, and studied under Cherubini. His best-known works are *La Muette de Portici*, usually entitled *Masaniello* (1828), and *Fra Diavolo* (1829). He died in Paris. See studies by Pougin (Par. 1873) and Malherbe (Par. 1911).

AUBIGNÉ. See D'AUBIGNÉ.

AUBLET, Jean Baptiste Christophe Fusée, ō'*blay* (1720–78), French botanist and humanist, born at Salon near Arles, spent over ten years in Mauritius and the French West Indies, where he established gardens of medicinal plants and made extensive collections and so founded forest botany in tropical America. He was also the first secular slavery abolitionist and his interest in ethnic problems gave the name *ethnora maripa*, to the famous Maripa palm which he discovered.

AUBREY, John (1626–97), English antiquary and folklorist, born at Easton Percy near Chippenham, was educated at Malmesbury, Blandford, and Trinity College, Oxford. He entered the Middle Temple in 1646, but was never called to the bar; in 1652 he succeeded to estates in Wiltshire, Herefordshire, and Wales, but was forced through lawsuits to part with the last of them in 1670, and with his books in 1677. His last years were passed, in 'danger of arrests', with Hobbes, Ashmole, and other protectors. Only his quaint, credulous *Miscellanies* (1696) was printed in his lifetime; but he left a large mass of materials. Of these, his Wiltshire and Surrey collections have in part been published; his *Brief Lives* (Hobbes, Milton, Bacon, &c.), given to Antony à Wood, appeared in *Letters by Eminent Persons* (1813), and were edited by A. Clark (2 vols. 1898); his *Remains of Gentilism and Judaism* was issued by the Folk-lore Society in 1880. See studies by Collier (1931) and Powell (1948).

AUBUSSON, Pierre d' (1423–1503), of noble French family, entered the service of the Emperor Sigismund, and fought against the Turks. Returning to France, he served with the Armagnacs against the Swiss, and covered himself with glory at their defeat near St Jacob (1444). He next joined the order of the Knights Hospitallers of St John of Jerusalem, and became grandmaster in 1476. Mohammed II's career of conquest, which threatened to spread over Western Europe, was stayed alone by d'Aubusson and his little colony of Christian soldiers in Rhodes. In May 1480 an army of 100,000 Turks invested the town, but were forced to raise the siege after a month's desperate fighting.

AUCHINLECK, Sir Claude John Eyre, oᴋʜ′*in-lek* (1884–   ), British field-marshal, was educated at Wellington College, and joined the 62nd Punjabis in 1904. In World War I he served in Egypt and Mesopotamia, becoming a brevet-colonel. In World War II his unrewarding command in North Norway was followed by the command-in-chief in India. This he exchanged for Wavell's Middle East theatre in July 1941, when the eighth army was in a depleted state after the ill-fated Greek campaign. Though his armour and antitank guns were inferior in range and fire-power and though nearly twenty of his subordinate generals became casualties through various misfortunes, he made a successful advance into Cyrenaica, but was later thrown back by Rommel. His regrouping of the eighth army on El Alamein is now recognized as a successful defensive operation which paved the way for ultimate victory, but at the time Auchinleck was made a scapegoat for the retreat and replaced by General Alexander (q.v.) in August 1942. In June 1943 he returned to India as c.-in-c.; serving subsequently as Supreme Commander India and Pakistan (1947). He was created field-marshal 1946, C.B. in 1934, G.C.B. in 1945. See Life by P. Connell (1959).

AUCHMUTY, Sir Samuel, oᴋʜ′*moo-tee* (1758–1822), British general, son of a New York clergyman, entered the British army as a volunteer in 1777, and during the Revolutionary War served three campaigns against the American colonists. Having attained to a captaincy, he served in India (1783–97) at Seringapatam, &c. A lieutenant-colonel and G.C.B., he was one of Baird's chief lieutenants in the desert march to support Abercromby at Alexandria. He captured Montevideo in 1806, and afterwards commanded in the

Carnatic, in Java, and in Ireland, where he died.

AUCKLAND. See EDEN (2).

AUDEBERT, Jean Baptiste, ō-dė-*bayr* (1759–1800), a French naturalist and artist, best known by his *Histoire naturelle des singes.*

AUDEN, Wystan Hugh (1907–   ), English poet, born at York, was educated at Gresham's School, Holt, and Christ Church, Oxford, where he was an exhibitioner. Being of an adventurous temper he gathered round him a group of friends—Stephen Spender, C. Day Lewis, Rex Warner, Christopher Isherwood—who felt deeply the impact of the unemployment blizzard which struck England in the early thirties and who developed a social conscience which looked like near-Communism to their contemporaries. This is reflected in the early poems of Auden and has gained for him the title 'Poet of the Thirties'. He is thus of importance for an understanding of the social and ideological background of that critical decade. After Oxford he taught for a time at Sedbergh. As the decade wore to its tragic close questions of international concern displaced social problems. The cause of the Spanish Republic first engaged the support of Auden and his friends. Auden acted on that side in a civilian capacity and wrote his lovely and passionate *Spain* in 1937. The house of Faber now commissioned him and his friend Isherwood to go to China and report on the Japanese aggression there. The result was their *Journey to a War* (1939), the prose of which was written by Isherwood while the verse, consisting of 34 sonnets and a verse *Commentary*, expressed Auden's humanistic view of the human situation from the dawn of history onward. Auden emigrated to New York early in 1939 where in due time he became a naturalized American citizen. He was appointed associate professor at Michigan University and in 1954 became a member of American Academy of Arts and Letters. That he also made his peace with England is shown by his appointment to the chair of Poetry at Oxford two years later. To speak now of his works—his first volume *Poems* (1930), contained the work by which he is generally known, the poetry of revolt, and which was to be reissued in various editions but with significant changes down to *Collected Shorter Poems* (1950). *The Orators* appeared separately in 1932, an obscure and puzzling work, part prose, part verse. In the thirties also he collaborated with Isherwood in three plays—*The Dog Beneath the Skin* (1935), *The Ascent of F6* (1936), and *On the Frontier* (1938). He also wrote the libretto for *Ballad of Heroes* (composer Benjamin Britten) on the eve of the war. His *Collected Poems* (1945) included three long poems which enable us to trace his conversion from Liberal-humanism to Anglicanism. These are *New Year Letter* (1941), *The Sea and the Mirror*, and *For the Time Being*, the two last being published as *For the Time Being* (1944). *The New Year Letter* is a brilliant talk in octosyllabics on the philosophy of religion but definitely Christian only in the Invocation. *The Sea and the Mirror*, based on Shakespeare's *Tempest*, a philosophic discussion of the human situation, is remarkable for Caliban's prose disquisition (a parody of the manner of Henry James) on art in an age of unbelief. *For the Time Being: a Christmas Oratorio* is definitely Christian but displays too much of music-hall wit to please the religious. The converted Auden, in contrast to Eliot, never wrote a truly devotional poem—no doubt his native bent for irony and mental acrobatics stood in the way. There never was a danger that his return to orthodoxy would suppress his high spirits, but *Nones* (1951), and *The Shield of Achilles* (1955) are in more sober vein. It is by the shorter poems, the bulk of which are in the original volume of 1930, where he expressed the resentment of middle-class youth at the rotting away of a generation through war and unemployment, that Auden is known. It is the fashion to regard that outburst as irresponsible, but it has its place in the story no less than the religious mysticism of Eliot and Muir. If we talk of his verbal and rhythmic acrobatics we should remember that equivalent skill is very rare—perhaps Byron is the closest analogy both for irreverence and technical dexterity. The critics agree, however, that in Auden's case this goes with an ardent moral passion. All the more regrettable was his tinkering with his early poems to bring them into line with his later ideology. Auden married in 1935 the authoress Erika Mann, daughter of Thomas Mann (q.v.). See studies by Scarfe (1942), Hoggart (1951, 1955); John Lehmann, *The Whispering Gallery* (1955) and Joseph Warren Beach, *The Making of the Auden Canon* (1957), which deals with the emendations made by Auden to the earlier versions in *Collected Poems* (1945).

AUDLEY, (1) Sir James (*c.* 1316–86), one of the original knights of the Garter (1344), in 1350 fought at Sluys, and in 1354 attended the Black Prince, who declared him the bravest knight on his side at Poitiers. Audley in 1367 was governor of Aquitaine, in 1369 was great seneschal of Poitou, and took part in the capture of La-Roche-sur-Yon. He died at Fontenay-le-Comte.

(2) **Thomas, Baron Audley of Walden** (1488–1544), English lord chancellor, was educated for the law, becoming attorney for the Duchy of Lancaster in 1530 and king's serjeant in 1531. Active in furthering the King's designs, Audley profited abundantly by ecclesiastical confiscations, 'carving for himself in the feast of abbey lands the first cut, and that a dainty morsel' (Fuller). In 1529 he was appointed Speaker of the House of Commons, and in 1532 lord chancellor. He was named in the Commission for the trial of Anne Boleyn, and for the examination of Catherine Howard. He was created Baron Audley of Walden in 1538.

AUDOUIN, Jean Victor, ō-doo-ĭ (1797–1841), French entomologist, in 1833 became professor of Entomology at the Jardin des Plantes, and made a study of muscardine (a silkworm disease), parasites infecting the vine, and other pests.

AUDOUX, Marguerite, ō-doo (1880–1937), French novelist, born in Saucoins. The daughter of a village carpenter, she was brought up by public assistance from the age of three, and became, until ill-health compelled her to give up, a sempstress and then a farmworker. She started writing for *Le Matin* and other papers, and in 1910 published *Marie Claire*, her only memorable work. It had an introduction by Octave Mirbeau, won the *Femina Vie Heureuse* prize and attained an international success which she was never able to repeat. She died in poverty and neglect. *Marie Claire* was translated into English by J. N. Raphael.

AUDRAN, Gérard, ō-drä (1640–1703), French engraver, like his nephews, **Benoît** (1661–1721) and **Jean** (1667–1756). See Duplessis, *Les Audran* (1892).

AUDUBON, John James (1785–1851), American ornithologist, born at Les Cayes, Santo Domingo, illegitimate son of a Creole and a French mariner, who adopted him and took him to France, where he studied painting under David and developed a taste for natural history. He was sent to America in 1804 to occupy a property near Philadelphia, which his father had purchased. Here he married Lucy Bakewell, daughter of an English settler. In 1807 he sold his land and migrated westward to become a merchant, but as he was chiefly engaged in bird hunting, business did not thrive; and for a time he supported his family by painting portraits at Louisville, Cincinatti, and elsewhere. In 1820 he voyaged down the Ohio and Mississippi, stopping at the principal towns, drawing portraits, and adding to his already wonderful collection of bird illustrations. In 1821 he visited Europe. Exhibitions of his drawings in Liverpool and Edinburgh proved successful, and in 1827 he issued the prospectus of *The Birds of America* (1827–38; new ed. 1966), which contains coloured figures of 1065 birds, natural size, and is said to have cost £20,000 to produce. *The Viviparous Quadrupeds of North America* (1845–49), on which he worked with John Bachman, was completed by his sons. See his *Journal* (ed. 1929), and studies by F. H. Herrick (1917) and C. Rourke (1936).

AUE, Hartmann von. See HARTMANN.

AUENBRUGGER, Leopold, ow'ĕn-broog-ĕr (1722–1809), Austrian physician, born at Graz, the discoverer of percussion in medical diagnosis.

AUER, Karl, Freiherr von Welsbach (1858–1929), chemist, born at Vienna, invented the incandescent gas-mantle and the osmium lamp. He also discovered the cerium-iron alloy known as Auer metal or mischmetal, now used as flints in petrol lighters.

AUERBACH, Berthold, ow'ĕr-baкн (1812–82), German novelist, born of Jewish parentage at Nordstetten in the Black Forest, studied at the universities of Tübingen, Munich, and Heidelberg, in 1836 suffering imprisonment in the fortress of Hohenasperg as a member of the students' Burschenschaft. Destined for the synagogue, he abandoned theology for law, then law for history and philosophy, especially that of Spinoza, on whose life he based a novel (1837), and whose works he translated (1841). In his *Schwarzwalder Dorfgeschichten* (1843), on which his fame chiefly rests, he gives charming pictures of Black Forest life, though his peasants are too often peasant Spinozas. Of his longer works the best known are *Barfüssele* (1856) and *Auf der Höhe* (1865). He died at Cannes. See his Correspondence (2 vols. 1884), and studies by Bettelheim (1907) and Weber (1923).

AUERSPERG, Anton Alexander, Graf von, pseud. **Anastasius Grün,** *ow'ĕrs-perg* (1806–1876), an Austrian poet, distinguished by his Liberalism and ultra-German sympathies. He was one of the German epic and lyrical poets, among whom he holds a high rank. His Collected Works fill 7 vols. (1877). See Life by Radicz (2 vols. 1876–78).

AUGEREAU, Pierre François Charles, *ō-zhĕ-rō* (1757–1816), French soldier. Born of humble parentage, he enlisted in the ranks, practised as a fencing master, and achieved rapid promotion under Napoleon in Italy. Dismissed by Madame Junot as ' a blockhead and a cypher ', he was nonetheless a *rusé* tactician and an impetuous leader who, despite his avarice, won the admiration of high and low alike. Prominent at Lodi, Jena, Eylau, and Leipzig, in 1804 he was created Marshal of the Empire, in 1808 Duke of Castiglione. A turncoat in 1815, he retired into private life. See *Napoleon and His Marshals,* Macdonnel (1934).

AUGIER, Guillaume Victor Emile, *ō-zhee-ay* (1820–89), French dramatist, was born at Valence. His *Théâtre complet* (1890) fills 7 vols., and includes fine social comedies, as *Le Gendre de M. Poirier* (1854, with Sandeau) and *Les Fourchambault* (1878). See study by Gaillard de Champris (1910).

AUGUSTINE, St (1) **Aurelius Augustinus** (354–430), the greatest of the Latin fathers, was born at Tagaste in Numidia, November 12. His father, a magistrate, was a heathen till advanced in years; his mother was St Monica. The gifted boy was sent to Carthage to complete his studies, but yielded to the temptation of the city. Before he had reached his eighteenth year, his mistress bore him a son, Adeodatus. What seems to have first stirred his deeper being was a passage in the *Hortensius* of Cicero on the value of philosophy; and fascinated by the pretensions of the Manichaean sect to supply ' a satisfactory solution of all things human and divine ', he became a professed Manichaean. He afterwards lectured on literature, first at Tagaste and then at Carthage. Here he wrote, in his twenty-seventh year, his first work, a (lost) treatise on aesthetics. His spiritual nature became more imperative in its demands, and he forsook the Manichaeans in disgust. In 383 he went to Rome, but soon settled in Milan as a teacher of rhetoric, and became a friend of the bishop, the eloquent and devout St Ambrose. He was now an enthusiastic student of Plato, and also zealously studied the Bible. At last he became a decided Christian, and was baptized by Ambrose in 387, along with his natural son Adeodatus. Before leaving Italy for Africa, Augustine wrote treatises against the Manichaeans and on Free Will; other works he wrote after his return. In 391 he was ordained a priest by Valerius, Bishop of Hippo in Numidia, whose colleague he became in 395. Then ensued the great Donatist and Pelagian controversies; and Augustine proved a most formidable and relentless antagonist to both heretical schools. In 397 appeared his *Confessions*—a sacred autobiography of one of the greatest intellects the world has seen. In 413–426 he produced his *De Civitate Dei,* a profound and masterly vindication of the Christian church, conceived of as a new order rising on the ruins of the old Roman empire—though here as elsewhere the powerful intellect is frequently misled by defective scholarship, for of Greek ' Augustine knew little, and of Hebrew nothing '. In 428 Augustine published his *Retractationes,* in which he frankly acknowledges the errors and mistakes in his works. In 430 the Vandals, under Genseric, besieged Hippo; and Augustine died on August 28, in the third month of the siege. The central tenets of his creed were the corruption of human nature through the fall of man, the consequent slavery of the human will, predestination, election and reprobation, and the perseverance of the saints. It was not by his controversial writings merely, but by his profound conception of Christianity and the religious life, and by his personal fervour and force of character that Augustine moulded the spirit of the Christian church for centuries, so that at the Reformation Protestants and Catholics alike appealed to his authority. Calvinism is by many regarded as little more than a reassertion of Augustinianism, though this is denied by the Catholic Church; and Jansenism professed to be the true expression of Augustine's views. See Harnack's *Monasticism* (trans. 1901); monographs by Cloth (1840), Bindemann (1844–69), Dorner (1873), Böhringer (1878), Reuter (1887); French by Poujoulat (6th ed. 1875), Bertrand (1912), Bardy (1940), Gilson (1943); W. Cunningham's Hulsean Lecture for 1885; McCabe's *St Augustine and his Age* (1902); W. Montgomery's *St Augustine: Aspects of his Life and Thought* (1914); Burnaby, *Amor Dei* (1938) and Lives by Marrou (tr. Hepburne-Scott, 1958) and Brown (1967).

(2) **St** (d. 604), first Archbishop of Canterbury, was prior of the Benedictine monastery of St Andrew at Rome, when, in 596, he was sent, with forty other monks, by Pope Gregory I, to convert the Anglo-Saxons to Christianity, and establish the authority of the Roman see in Britain. Landing in Thanet, the missionaries were kindly received by Ethelbert, king of Kent, whose wife Bertha, daughter of the Frankish king, was a Christian. A residence was assigned to them at Canterbury, where they devoted themselves to monastic exercises and preaching. The conversion and baptism of the king contributed greatly to the success of their efforts among his subjects, and it is recorded that in one day Augustine baptized 10,000 persons in the river Swale. In 597 he went to Arles, and there was consecrated Bishop of the English. His efforts to extend his authority over the native British (Welsh) church, with whose bishops he held a conference in 603 at Aust on the Severn, were less successful. He died May 26, 604, and in 612 his body was transferred to his abbey of SS. Peter and Paul, its site now occupied by St Augustine's Missionary College (1848). See works by Cutts (1895), Mason (1897), and Sir H. H. Howorth (1913).

AUGUSTULUS, Romulus (ruled A.D. 475–476), last emperor of the western half of the old Roman empire. His father, Orestes, a Pannonian, had risen to high rank under the Emperor Julius Nepos, on whose flight he conferred the vacant throne on Augustus (the diminutive *Augustulus* was a nickname), retaining all substantial power in his own hands. Orestes failing to conciliate the barbarians who had helped him against the emperor, they, under Odoacer, besieged him in Pavia and killed him. Augustulus yielded at once, and being of too little consequence to be put to death, was dismissed to a villa near Naples with an annual pension of 6000 pieces of gold.

AUGUSTUS, Gaius Julius Caesar Octavianus (63 B.C.–A.D. 14), first Roman emperor, was the son of Gaius Octavius, senator and praetor, and Atia, Julius Caesar's niece. His grand-uncle adopted him as his son and heir. At the time of Caesar's assassination (44 B.C.) Augustus was a student under the orator Apollodorus, at Apollonia in Illyricum, but returned at once to Rome. Mark Antony at first refused to surrender Caesar's property; but after some fighting, in which Antony was forced to flee across the Alps, Augustus obtained the consulship, and carried out Caesar's will. When Antony returned from Gaul with Lepidus, Augustus threw off the republican mask, and joined them in establishing a triumvirate. He obtained Africa, Sardinia and Sicily; Antony, Gaul; and Lepidus, Spain. Their power was soon made absolute by the massacre of those unfriendly to them in Italy, and by the victory at Philippi over the republicans under Brutus and Cassius. Difficulties between Augustus and Antony, raised by Fulvia, Antony's wife, were removed by her death and Antony's marriage with Octavia, sister of Augustus. Shortly afterwards the Roman world was divided anew, Augustus taking the western half, and Antony the eastern, while Lepidus had to content himself with Africa. While Antony was lost in dissipation at the court of Cleopatra, Augustus was striving to gain the confidence of the Roman people. War was at length declared against the Egyptian queen, and by the naval victory at Actium (31 B.C.) Augustus became sole ruler of the Roman world. Antòny and Cleopatra committed suicide; Antony's son by Fulvia, and Caesarion, son of Caesar and Cleopatra, were put to death; and in 29 B.C., after regulating affairs in Egypt ,Greece, Syria, and Asia Minor, Augustus returned to Rome in triumph, and closing the temple of Janus, proclaimed universal peace. His subsequent measures were mild and prudent, and he reformed many abuses. Republican names and forms still remained, but they were mere shadows; and Octavian, henceforward known by the new title of Augustus (' sacred ', ' venerable '), was, in all but name, absolute monarch. After a course of victories in Asia, Spain, Pannonia, Dalmatia, and Gaul, he suffered the one crushing defeat of his long rule (9 B.C.), when the Roman army under Varus was annihilated by the Germans under Arminius (q.v.). Thenceforth he confined himself to domestic improvement and reform, and so beautified Rome, that it was said, ' Augustus found the city built of brick, and left it built of marble '. He also built cities in several parts of the empire; altars were raised to commemorate his beneficence; and the name Augustus was given to the month *Sextilis*. Age, domestic sorrow, and failing health warned him to seek repose in Campania; but his infirmity increased, and he died at Nola in A.D. 14. He was succeeded by his stepson, Tiberius. Augustus had consummate tact as a ruler, and skilfully used the passions and talents of others; but his best measures originated mostly with himself. Horace, Virgil, Ovid, Propertius, Tibullus, and Livy were the glory of the *Augustan Age*, a name given in France to the reign of Louis XIV, in England to that of Queen Anne. See books by Shuckburgh (1903), Firth (1903), Rice Holmes (1931), Buchan (1937).

AUGUSTUS. The name of three electors of Saxony, two of whom were also kings of Poland.

(1) **Augustus** (1526–86), Elector of Saxony, is chiefly notable as having first used his utmost influence in favour of the Calvinistic doctrine of the sacraments; and then, becoming Lutheran, in 1574 persecuted the Calvinists. But he gave a great impetus to education, agriculture, manufactures, and commerce. The Dresden library and most of the galleries owe their origin to him.

(2) **Augustus II of Poland** (1670–1733), nicknamed **the Strong**. After fighting the Turks with credit, he became a candidate for the throne of Poland, and, adopting the Catholic faith, was elected king by the venal nobles (1697). His efforts to recover the provinces lost to Sweden led to his defeat, his deposition from the kingdom, and the election of Stanislaus Leszcynski (1704). On the defeat of Charles XII at Pultowa, in 1709, he marched into Poland, formed a fresh alliance with the czar, and recommenced a war with Sweden, which raged till the death of Charles XII (1718). The rival king had disappeared, and Augustus kept the crown of Poland till his death. The Saxon court became known as the most dissolute in Europe. Maurice of Saxony was one of his illegitimate children (said to number 300).

(3) **Augustus III of Poland** (1696–1763), son of (2), by help of Russia drove out Stanislas once more and became king of Poland (1734). He took Maria Theresa's side, and was vanquished by Frederick the Great. Count Brühl (q.v.) was his minister.

AUKRUST, Olav Lom, *ow'kroost* (1883–1929), Norwegian poet. He was a schoolmaster who wrote large quantities of religious and patriotic verse. *Himmelvarden* (1916) consists of three long cycles in New Norwegian containing many passages of great lyric power. *Hamar i Hellom* (1926), of which the chief poem is *Emme*, summons the people of Norway to use the power of their great traditions to achieve present security and progress. His final collection of poems, *Solrenning*, is incomplete and was published posthumously in 1930.

AULNOY, Marie Catherine Jumelle de Berneville, Comtesse d', *ō-nwa* (c. 1650–1705),

wrote many tedious romances, but is remembered by her charming *Contes des Fées* (1698).
AULUS GELLIUS. See GELLIUS.
AUMALE, *o-mahl*, French countship in Normandy, held in the Middle Ages by the Guises, became a dukedom in 1547, and from 1675 was customarily bestowed on a prince of the French royal family.

(1) **Charles de Lorraine, Duc d'** (1556–1631), French statesman, one of the leaders of the League against the Huguenots, was defeated by Henry IV at Arques and Ivry, went over to the Spaniards, and was condemned to be broken alive at the wheel, a fate which he evaded by remaining in exile till his death.

(2) **Henri-Eugène-Philippe-Louis d'Orléans, Duc d'** (1822–97), fourth son of King Louis-Philippe, was born at Paris, January 16, and greatly distinguished himself in the campaigns in Algeria, where in 1847 he succeeded Marshal Bugeaud as governor-general. On the revolution of 1848 he retired to England. Here he became known by his contributions to the *Revue des deux mondes*, his incisive pamphlets against Louis Napoleon, and his great works, *Histoire des princes de Condé* (1869–97) and *Les Institutions militaires de la France* (1867). In 1871 elected to the Assembly and the Academy, in 1886 he bequeathed his magnificent château of Chantilly to the Institute. The decree expelling him from France was revoked in 1889. He died May 6, 1897, through the shock of the burning of his niece, the Duchess d'Alençon, at the Paris bazaar.
AUNGERVILLE, or **de Bury, Richard** (1287–1345), English churchman, born at Bury St Edmunds. He studied at Oxford, became a Benedictine monk at Durham, and having been tutor to Edward III, was made successively Dean of Wells and Bishop of Durham, besides acting for a time as high chancellor, as ambassador to the Pope and to France and Germany, and as commissioner for a truce with Scotland. He had a passion for collecting manuscripts and books; and his principal work, *Philobiblon*, intended to serve as a handbook to the library which he founded in connection with Durham College at Oxford (afterwards suppressed), describes the state of learning in England and France. See E. C. Thomas's edition of the *Philobiblon* (1888).
AURANGZIB. See AURUNGZEBE.
AURELIAN, properly **Lucius Domitius Aurelianus** (*c.* 212–275), Roman emperor, was born, a husbandman's son, in Dacia or Pannonia, and enlisting early as a common soldier rose rapidly to the highest military offices. On the death of Claudius (270), Aurelian was elected emperor by the army, with whom his great stature, strength, and courage had made him very popular. He repulsed the Alemanni and Marcomanni, and erected new walls round Rome. He resigned Dacia to the Goths, and made the Danube the frontier of the empire. He defeated Zenobia (q.v.), besieged her in Palmyra, and took her prisoner. When an insurrection broke out again in Palmyra, he returned in 273, and destroyed the city. Aurelian quelled a rebellion in Egypt, and recovered Gaul from Tetricus. By restoring good discipline in the army, order in domestic affairs, and political

unity to the Roman dominions, he merited the title awarded him by the senate—' Restorer of the Roman Empire'. He was assassinated near Byzantium during a campaign against the Persians.
AURELIUS, properly **Marcus Aurelius Antoninus** (121–180), Roman emperor, and one of the noblest figures in history, was the son of Annius Verus and Domitia Calvilla, and was born at Rome, April 26. His original name was Marcus Annius Verus. When only seventeen years of age he was adopted by Antoninus Pius, who had succeeded Hadrian, and whose daughter Faustina was selected for his wife. From A.D. 140, when he was made consul, to the death of Pius in 161, he discharged his public duties with the utmost fidelity, and maintained the kindliest relations with the emperor; while at the same time he still devoted himself with zeal to the study of law and philosophy, especially the Stoic philosophy. On his accession to the throne, with characteristic magnanimity he voluntarily divided the government with his brother by adoption, Lucius Aurelius Verus, who in 161 was sent to take command against the Parthians. The generals obtained a victory—not final—in spite of the self-indulgence and luxury of Verus; and the victorious army brought back with it a plague that long scourged Rome. The peaceful Marcus Aurelius was throughout his reign destined to suffer from constant wars, and though in Asia, in Britain, and on the Rhine the barbarians were checked, permanent peace was never secured. Rome was suffering from pestilence, earthquakes, and inundations when the imperial colleagues led the Roman armies against the northern barbarians on the Danube. The Marcomanni were humbled in 168, and in 173 almost annihilated in retreating across the Danube. Verus had died in 169. The victory over another Germanic tribe, the Quadi, in 174, was attributed by the Christians to the prayers of what afterwards became known as the ' Thundering Legion ' (because of a fierce and unexpected thunderstorm which confounded the enemy). He was next summoned to the East by a rebellion of the governor, Avidius Cassius, who, before Aurelius arrived, had fallen by an assassin's hand. Meanwhile, his wife Faustina (q.v.), whom the emperor tenderly loved in spite of stories to her discredit, died in an obscure village at the foot of Mount Taurus. On his way home he visited Lower Egypt and Greece. At Athens he showed his catholicity by founding chairs of philosophy for each of the four chief sects—Platonic, Stoic, Peripatetic, and Epicurean. Towards the close of 176 he reached Italy, and next autumn departed for Germany, where fresh disturbances had broken out. Victory again crowned his arms; but his constitution, never robust, at length gave way, and he died either at Vienna or at Sirmium in Pannonia, March 17, 180. Marcus Aurelius was the flower of the Stoic philosophy; and few books have had such a potent charm as his *Meditations*. His sentences reveal the loneliness of his soul, but they show us that he did not allow himself to be embittered as well as saddened by his

experience of life. His death was felt to be a national calamity; he became almost an object of worship to the citizens of the empire, and was believed to appear in dreams like the saints of subsequent Christian ages. Aurelius twice persecuted the Christians. He doubtless believed that what he regarded as Christian fanaticism and superstition were dangerous to true philosophy, to society, and to the empire. There are editions of the *Meditations* (which were written in Greek) by Gataker (1652) and Stich (1882); and English translations by Jeremy Collier (new ed. 1887), G. Long (1869), Rendall (1898); but definitive, both for text and translation, is Farquharson (1945). See Renan's *Marc Aurèle* (1882); Farrar's *Seekers after God* (1868); Matthew Arnold's *Essays in Criticism* (1888).

AURIC, Georges, ō-*reek'* (1899–   ), French composer, born at Lodève, Hérault, studied under d'Indy, became one of ' Les Six ', was successively music critic of *Marianne* and *Paris Soir*, and since 1962 has been administrator of the Paris Opéra and Opéra Comique. His compositions range widely from full orchestral pieces to songs, and he has been particularly successful with incidental music to films, beginning with René Clair's *A nous la liberté* (1932), and including several British films, as *It Always Rains on Sunday* (1947) and *Passport to Pimlico* (1949). His music, exciting and colourful, influenced by Satie and Stravinsky, shows the modern return to counterpoint at its best.

AURIOL, ō-*ryol,* (1) **Jacqueline** (1917–   ), French woman aviator, the daughter-in-law of (2). She broke the women's jet speed record in 1955 by flying at 715 miles per hour in a French *Mystère*.

(2) **Vincent** (1884–1966), French politician, a Socialist deputy from 1914, was president from 1947 to 1953.

AURUNGZEBE, or **AURANGZIB,** *aw'rung-zeb* (1618–1707), ' Ornament of the Throne ', the most magnificent of the Mogul emperors of India, was the third son of Shah-Jehan, who in 1657 was seized with a serious illness. The reins of power were at once grasped by the eldest son, Dara, who was attacked by another brother, Shuja, governor of Bengal. Aurungzebe's policy was to let the two fight it out, and then play off his next brother against the victor. By this time, however, Shah-Jehan had somewhat recovered; so Aurungzebe, professing the utmost loyalty, made him a prisoner; and the old man, still in confinement, died in the seventh year of his undutiful son's reign. Aurungzebe ultimately seized and confined his too confiding brother Murad; and after a struggle of three years, Dara and Shuja also fell into his power, and all three were put to death. The sceptre was now firmly within his grasp. His long reign of half a century was distinguished by great outward prosperity; but the empire was diseased at its heart. Everywhere there was distrust; the emperor, who had established his throne by fraud, was naturally enough distrusted by all. His sons imitated him in his disobedience to his father, and the Hindus, whom he treated with great harshness, excited the Mahrattas against him in the south. Some of the minor Mohammedan princes were subdued, but the Hindu states were gathering strength for the overthrow of the Mogul power. Most of his enterprises failed; and he may be said to have ruined the empire. His later years were passed in the fear of receiving the measure he had meted to others, and he died, a fugitive before the Mahrattas, at Ahmednagar. See *Lives* by Stanley Lane-Poole (1893) and Sir J. Sarkar (1912–16, 1933).

AUSONIUS, Decius Magnus (*c.* 309–392), foremost Latin poet of the 4th century, was born at Burdigala (Bordeaux). He was appointed by Valentinian tutor to his son Gratian; and he afterwards held the offices of quaestor, prefect of Latium, and consul of Gaul. On the death of Gratian, Ausonius retired to his estate at Bordeaux, where he occupied himself with literature and rural pursuits until his death. It is most probable that he was a Christian. His works include epigrams, poems on his deceased relatives and on his colleagues, epistles in verse and prose, and idylls. In spite of his grace of expression, Ausonius is a poor poet.

AUSTEN, Jane, *aws'tèn* (1775–1817), English novelist, born in Steventon, Hants., of which her father was rector. She spent the first twenty-five years of her life there and afterwards lived in Bath, Southampton, Chawton, and Winchester, where she died. Her life was completely uneventful. The youngest of a family of seven, her domestic relations were always harmonious, but her mind was alert and her senses sharp. She began writing for family amusement as a child, her *Love and Freindship* (*sic*; pub. 1922) dating from this period. Her early published work satirized the sensational fiction of her time—Mrs Radcliffe and other ' gothick ' novelists—and applied the canons of common sense to apparently melodramatic situations. Later she developed this technique in evaluating ordinary human behaviour. All her characters are ' ordinary ', but her psychological insight, her sensitive ear, her inimitable muted irony and her rich but selective detail present them as three-dimensional individuals who are nevertheless archetypal. Of her six great novels, four were published anonymously during her lifetime and two under her signature posthumously. *Sense and Sensibility*, published in 1811, was begun in 1797; *Pride and Prejudice* appeared in 1813; *Mansfield Park*, begun in 1811, appeared in 1814; *Emma* in 1815. Her posthumous novels were both published in 1818; *Persuasion* had been written in 1815, and *Northanger Abbey*, begun in 1797, had been sold in 1803 to a publisher, who neglected it, and reclaimed in 1816. The standard edition of her works is that edited by R. W. Chapman (5 vols. 1923, with a sixth containing juvenilia and fragments, such as *Lady Susan, The Watsons, Sanditon,* &c., in 1954). A *Memoir of Jane Austen* by her nephew, J. E. Austen-Leigh, appeared in 1870, reprinted in 1871 with some of her unfinished work. See studies by M. Lascelles (1939) R. W. Chapman (1949) and M. Kennedy (1958).

AUSTIN, (1) Alfred (1835–1913), English poet, born of Catholic parents at Leeds, was educated at Stonyhurst and Oscott, graduated at London University in 1853, and was called to the bar in 1857. He published *The Season: a Satire* (1861), *The Human Tragedy* (1862), *The Conversion of Winckelmann* (1897), and a dozen more volumes of poems, and an Autobiography (1911). In 1883–93 he edited the *National Review*; in 1896 he became poet laureate. He died at Swinford Old Manor, near Ashford, Kent, where he had lived since 1867. See Life by Crowell (1955).

(2) **Herbert, 1st Baron Austin of Longbridge** (1866–1941), English motor-car manufacturer, born in Bucks. After managing several engineering works in Australia, he returned to England and joined the Wolseley Sheep-Shearing Company. In 1895, with the Wolseley Company, he produced his first car, and in 1905 he opened near Birmingham his own works, which rapidly developed and whose enormous output included, in 1921, the popular 'Baby' Austin 7. He was created a baron in 1936.

(3) **John** (1790–1859), English jurist, husband of (5), born at Crecting Mill, Suffolk. In 1818 he was called to the bar, and in 1826 was appointed professor of Jurisprudence in the newly founded University of London (now University College). The subject was not recognized as a necessary branch of legal study, and from lack of students, Austin resigned the chair (1832). His *Province of Jurisprudence Determined*, defining (on a utilitarian basis) the sphere of ethics and law, was at first little read; but by-and-by it practically revolutionized English views on the subject, and introduced a definiteness of terminology hitherto unknown. He died at Weybridge. His *Lectures on Jurisprudence* were published in 1863. See studies by W. J. Brown (Boston 1910), Eastwood and Keeton (1929); also Holdsworth, *Some Makers of English Law* (1938).

(4) **John Langshaw** (1911–60), English philosopher, educated at Shrewsbury and Balliol College, Oxford, served in the Intelligence Corps (1939–45) and was awarded the Legion of Merit, Croix de Guerre, and O.B.E. in 1945. He became White's professor of Moral Philosophy at Oxford in 1952. He extended the modern philosophical appeal to ordinary linguistic usage for the solution of philosophical perplexities, as in his performatory theory of knowledge, to a systematic study of the workings of language itself.

(5) **Sarah,** *née* **Taylor** (1793–1867), English writer, wife of (3), mother of Lady Duff-Gordon (q.v.), known for her translations of Ranke's *Popes* and Guizot's *Civilization*; wrote also on Germany and on education. See Janet Ross, *Three Generations of Englishwomen* (1889).

(6) **Stephen Fuller** (1793–1836), American pioneer, founder of Texas State. See Life by Beals (1953).

AUTOLYCUS, a Greek astronomer and mathematician of Pitane in Aeolia, about 330 B.C.

AUVERGNE, Martial d', *ō-vern'y* (1430?–1508), French author and poet, born in Paris. His *Arrets d'amour* are humorous romantic stories containing many passages dealing with contemporary customs. His verse is of a more serious character and shows the influence of Chartier.

AVEBURY, Lord. See LUBBOCK.

AVEMPACE, or Ibn Bajjah (d. 1138), an Arabian philosopher, born in Spain, who lived mainly at court in Morocco, and died at Fez.

AVENTINUS, properly Johannes Thurmayr, (1477–1534), German scholar and historian, born at Abensberg (Lat. *Aventinum*), Bavaria, who taught Greek and mathematics at Cracow, wrote a history of Bavaria, &c., died at Ratisbon. See Dollinger's *Studies in European History* (Eng. trans. 1890).

AVENZOAR, properly Ibn Zohr, *a-ven-zō'ėr* (*c.* 1072–1162), Arabian physician and author on medicine at Seville in Spain, praised by his pupil Averrhoës.

AVERCAMP, Hendrick (1585–1634), Dutch painter. He was a pupil of Pieter Isaacsz and was influenced by the elder Breughel. This can be seen in his winter landscapes, by which he is chiefly known, where his skating peasants reflect a Breughelian exuberance.

AVERRHOËS, or Averroës, properly Ibn Ruoshd, *a-ver'ō-eez* (1126–98), the most famous of the Arabian philosophers, was born at Cordova, son of the Kadi there. He himself was Kadi successively in Cordova, Seville, and Morocco; and though for a time stripped of all honours and banished, he was restored again by a new khalif to his dignities at Morocco, where he died. He was an indefatigable and acute commentator on Aristotle's writings, and hence was called 'the Expositor'. It was, however, to Alexandrian or Neoplatonic influences that he owed his doctrine of a Universal Reason (other than the individual reasons), indivisible, but shared in by all; he denied, too, the immortality of individual men. He expounded the Koran according to Aristotle, and so founded a Moslem philosophy of religion, the cause of many heresies. He profoundly influenced many of the great scholastics, though ultimately Averroists were condemned by Leo X. Most of his writings are known to us only through Latin translations; the great edition being that of 1552 (11 vols. folio, Venice). Averrhoës also wrote a sort of medical system, which, under the name of *Colliget*, was translated into Latin, and repeatedly printed. See Renan's *Averroès* (4th ed. 1882), and Lafinio's *Studii sopra Averroe* (1875).

AVIANUS, Flavius (4th cent.), Latin author of fables in poor elegiac verse. See vol. III of Hervieux' *Les Fabulistes Latins* (1893).

AVICEBRÓN, properly ibn Gabirol (1020–*c.* 1070), Jewish poet and philosopher, was born at Malaga, and died at Valencia. His great work, *Fons Vitae*, translated, from the Arabic, is largely Neoplatonist.

AVICENNA, Arabic **ibn Sina,** *-sen'-* (980–1037), Arab philosopher and physician, born near Bokhara, was physician to several sultans, and for some time vizier in Hamadan, in Persia, where he died. His philosophy was Aristotelianism modified by Neoplatonism; his medical system was long the standard. See Life and Works by S. M. Afnan (1958).

AVIENUS, Rufus Festus, *a-vi-ay'nus* (fl. *c.* 375),

Latin descriptive poet, wrote on natural and geographical topics, translated the *Phainomena* of Aratus. See Holder's edition (Innsbruck 1887).

ÁVILA, *ah'vi-la,* (1) **Gil González de** (1577–1658), Spanish historian, royal historiographer for Castile, known for his account of the reign of Henry III.

(2) **Juan de** (1500–69), Spanish writer and preacher, born at Almodóvar del Campo. The ' Apostle of Andalusia ', beatified by Leo XIII (1894), he has left numerous ascetic works, notably *Audi, Filia,* and several volumes of spiritual letters. He was also a trusted counsellor of St Teresa.

ÁVILA Y ZÚÑIGA, Luiz de, *thoo'nyi-ga* (*c.* 1490–1550), Spanish general, diplomatist, and author of a history of Charles V's German wars. Charles V entrusted him with embassies to Popes Paul IV and Pius IV; and he accompanied the emperor against the German Protestant princes. His *Comentarios* (1547) were translated into several languages.

AVISON, Charles (*c.* 1710–70), composer, was born and died at Newcastle. Also known as a critic, he wrote an *Essay on Musical Expression* (1752), and he figures in Browning's *Parleyings.*

AVOGADRO, Amedeo, *-gah'-* (1776–1856), Italian scientist, born at Turin, was professor of Physics there (1834–50), and in 1811 formulated the hypothesis, known as Avogadro's law, that equal volumes of gases contain equal numbers of molecules, when at the same temperature and pressure.

AVON, First Earl of. See EDEN (1).

AXEL, or Absalon (1128–1201), Archbishop of Lund from 1177, was also minister to Valdemar I and Canute VI of Denmark and founder of Copenhagen.

AYALA, *a-yah'la,* (1) **Adelardo López de** (1829–79), Spanish poet and statesman, born at Guadalcanal, wrote a number of plays.

(2) **Pedro López de** (1332–1407), Spanish soldier and statesman, who held high office under several kings of Castile, and wrote the *Crónicas de los Reyes de Castilla* and a didactic and satirical poem begun during his captivity in England (1367).

AYER, Alfred Jules (1910–), British philosopher, was educated at Eton College and Christ Church College, Oxford, where he also lectured. During World War II he was commissioned into the Welsh Guards and in 1945 was attaché at the British embassy in Paris. He became Grote professor at University College, London, in 1947. His antimetaphysical *Language, Truth, and Logic* (1936) is an extremely lucid and concise rendering in English of the doctrines of the logical positivist ' Vienna Circle ' of philosophers whom he visited in 1932. This ' young man's book ' he modified by a new introduction in 1946. His best later work is *Problems of Knowledge* (1956). He was elected F.B.A. in 1952 and in 1959 became Wykeham professor of Logic at Oxford. He edited *Logical Positivism* (1960).

AYESHAH, or Aïsha (*c.* 610–677), the favourite of the nine wives of Mohammed, bore him no children. On Mohammed's death on June 8, 632, she resisted Ali, the Prophet's son-in-law, and secured the khalifate for her

father, Abu-Bekr (q.v.). Again opposing Ali, she was defeated and taken in 656.

AYLMER, John (1521–94), English prelate, born probably at the ancestral Aylmer Hall, Tilney St Lawrence, Norfolk. In 1541 graduated B.A. of Cambridge; became tutor to Lady Jane Grey; in 1553 was installed Archdeacon of Stow, in 1562 of Lincoln, having lived abroad during the Marian persecution; and finally, in 1577, was consecrated Bishop of London. The ' Morrell ' of Spenser's *Shepheard's Calendar,* the ' proude and ambitious pastoure ' is a fair enough estimate of one who showed equal rigour to Catholics and Puritans, and was always quarrelsome and arbitrary.

AYRER, Jacob, *ī'-* (*c.* 1540–1625), German dramatist, next to Hans Sachs the most prolific of the 16th century. He was a citizen of Nuremberg in 1594, and a procurator in the courts of law. See study by Wodick (1912).

AYRTON, (1) Michael (1920–), British artist, author and art teacher, born in London. See his essays, *Golden Section* (1957).

(2) **William Edward** (1847–1908), English engineer, born in London, was professor of Electrical Engineering at the Central Technical College, S. Kensington. His first wife was a pioneer woman doctor, Matilda Chaplin (1846–83); his second, Hertha Marks (1854–1923), continued his work on the electric arc, &c.

AYTON, Sir Robert (1570–1638), a Scottish poet and courtier to whom have been ascribed ' I do confess thou'rt smooth and fair ' and the prototype of ' Auld Lang Syne '.

AYTOUN, William Edmonstoune (1813–65), Scottish poet, born in Edinburgh, was educated at the Academy and the University, and in 1840 was called to the Scottish bar. He entered in 1836 on his lifelong connection with *Blackwood's*; in 1845 was appointed professor of Rhetoric and Belles-Lettres in Edinburgh University, and in five years quintupled the number of his hearers. In 1849 he married a daughter of Professor John Wilson (q.v.); in 1852 was made sheriff of Orkney. His works include *Poland, Homer, and Other Poems* (1832); *Lays of the Scottish Cavaliers* (1848); *Firmilian, a Spasmodic Tragedy* (1854); *Bon Gaultier Ballads* (1855), and *Poems of Goethe* (1858), conjunctly with Theodore Martin; *Bothwell* (1856); and *Norman Sinclair* (1861), a semi-autobiographical novel. See Lives by Sir T. Martin (1867) and Miss R. Masson (1898).

AZAÑA, Manuel, *a-thah'nya* (1880–1940), Spanish statesman, was a barrister, author, and lecturer in Madrid University. War minister in 1931, and prime minister in 1931–33 and 1936 as leader of the Republican Left, in 1936–39 he was president.

AZEGLIO, Massimo Taparelli, Marchese d', *a-dzay'lyō* (1798–1866), Italian statesman, landscape painter, publicist, and romance writer, born at Turin, a son-in-law of Manzoni (q.v.), took a leading part in the risorgimento and the 1848 revolution. See his autobiographical *I Miei Ricordi* (1873).

AZIKIWE, Nnamdi, *a-zee'kwee* (1904–), Nigerian politician, was born at Zungeri, N. Nigeria, and was educated at American universities. In 1937 he began to take a leading part in the Nigerian nationalist movement, founding a series of newspapers and becoming, during World War II, president of the National Council of Nigeria and the Cameroons and vice-president of the Nigerian National Democratic Party. From 1952 to 1953 he was a member of the Western House of Assembly and from 1954 to 1959 of the Eastern House. He became prime minister of the Eastern region (1954–59), governor-general of Nigeria

(1960–63), and was elected first president of the Nigerian republic in Nov. 1963. In Britain during the military uprising of 1966, his office was suspended, although he returned privately to Nigeria.

AZORÍN, pseud. of **José Martinez Ruiz** (1873–1967), Spanish novelist and critic, born at Monóvar, educated at Valencia. His novels include *Don Juan* (1922) and *Dona Inés* (1925). See studies by Mulertt (Halle, 1926) and Mendoza (1933).

B

BAADER, Franz Xaver von, *bah'der* (1765–1841), a Roman Catholic theologian and mystical philosopher, was born and died at Munich. A follower of Boehme (q.v.), he regarded Hume's philosophy as atheistic and opposed Kant by maintaining that the true ethical end is not obedience to a moral law, but a realization of the divine life. See study by D. Baumgardt (1927).

BAAL-SCHEM-TOV, properly **Israel ben Eliezer** (1699–1760), Jewish teacher and healer in Poland, the founder of modern Chasidism.

BABBAGE, Charles (1792–1871), English mathematician, born at Totnes, Devon, was educated at Trinity and Peterhouse Colleges, Cambridge, where he was Lucasian professor of Mathematics (1823–39). He did valuable work on the theory of logarithms and built a calculating machine, which in an unfinished state is preserved in the Science Museum, London. He was elected F.R.S. in 1816, helped to found the Statistical and Astronomical Societies, and in his later years was chiefly known as a fierce enemy of organ-grinders. See H. P. Babbage, *On the Calculating Machine* (1889) and Life by M. Moseley (1964).

BABBITT, Irving (1865–1933), American writer, born at Dayton in Ohio, professor of French at Harvard (1894–1933). Primarily moralist and teacher, he was a leader of the ' new humanism ' which flourished in America in the 1920s. His books include *Literature and the American College* (1908), *The New Laokoön* (1910), *Rousseau and Romanticism* (1919), *On Being Creative* (1932).

BABCOCK, Harold Delos (1882–1968), American physicist, born at Edgerton, Wisconsin, was on the staff of the Mount Wilson observatory (1909) when he measured the magnetic field of the star 78 Virginis, which provided a link between the electromagnetic and the relativity theories.

BÁB-ED-DIN (d. 1850), the title, meaning 'gate of righteousness', assumed by **Mirza Ali Mohammed,** who in 1843 formed a new faith composed of Mohammedan, Christian, Jewish, and Parsee elements '(still known as Babism), and after a long imprisonment was put to death.

BABER, or **Babur,** properly **Zahir ud-Din Mohammed,** *bah'bèr* (1483–1530), first Great Mogul in India, a descendant of Timur, was

barely twelve when he succeeded his father in the sovereignty of the countries lying between Samarkand and the Indus. Having made himself master of Kashgar, Kunduz, Kandahar, and Kabul, in April 1526 he routed at Panipat the vast army of the Afghan emperor of Delhi, and entered the capital; Agra next month surrendered. See his autobiography (trans. A. S. Beveridge 1912), studies by Lane-Poole (1899), S. M. Edwardes (1926), F. Grenard (trans. 1931), and E. D. Ross's edition of his *Poems* (1911).

BABEUF, François Noel, *ba-bœf* (1760–97), French communist, born at St Quentin, during the Revolution, as ' Gracchus Babeuf', in his *Tribun du peuple,* advocated a rigorous system of Communism. A conspiracy to destroy the Directory and establish an extreme democratic and communistic system was discovered, and Babeuf guillotined. See Bax's *Last Episode of the Revolution* (1911) and the study by D. Thomson (1947).

BABINET, Jacques, *ba-bee-nay* (1794–1872), French physicist, standardized light measurement by using the red cadmium line's wavelength as the standard for the ångström unit. Babinet's principle, that similar diffraction patterns are produced by two complementary screens, is named after him.

BABINGTON, Antony (1561–86), English conspirator, born of an old and rich Catholic family at Dethick, Derbyshire, had served as a page to Queen Mary of Scotland, then a prisoner at Sheffield, when in 1586, some seven years after his marriage, he was induced by Ballard and other Catholic emissaries to put himself at the head of a conspiracy that had for its object Elizabeth's murder and Mary's release. Cipher messages were intercepted by Walsingham in which Mary warmly approved the plot and these were later used against her. Anticipating Walsingham, Babington fled, was captured at Harrow and executed with the others on September 20.

BABINSKI, Joseph François Felix (1857–1932), French neurologist, born in Paris, who described a reflex of the foot symptomatic of organic hemiplegia, and a reflex of the forearm believed to be due to a lesion in the spinal chord. Both reflexes are known as Babinski's Sign. In association with **Alfred Fröhlich** (1871–1953), a Viennese pharmacologist, he investigated an endocrinal disorder, adiposogenital dystrophy, or Babinski-Fröhlich disease.

BABITS, Mihály, *bah'beech* (1883–1941), Hungarian poet of the 20th-century literary renaissance, also a novelist and the best modern translator of Dante, Shakespeare, and the Greek classics.

BABRIUS, Greek fabulist, who has been assigned to various periods between 250 B.C. and A.D. 250. He collected Aesopic fables, which he turned into popular choliambic verse. These had been almost all lost, till in 1842 a Greek discovered at Mount Athos 123 of them. See editions by Rutherford (1883) and Crusius (1897).

BACCHELLI, Riccardo, *bat-chel'li* (1891–), Italian novelist, born at Bologna. His principal works are *Il diavolo al Pontelungo,* a humorous tale of Bakunin's (q.v.) efforts to introduce socialism into Italy, and the three-volume family chronicle of the Risorgimento, *Il mulino del Po* (1938–40). See P. Pancrazi, *Scrittori Italiani del novecento* (1939 ed.).

BACCHYLIDES, *ba-kil'i-deez* (5th cent. B.C.), Greek lyric poet, nephew of Simonides and contemporary of Pindar (qq.v.) at the court of Hicro of Syracuse. Fragments of his epinikian odes (written to celebrate victories in the Great Games), discovered in 1896, were edited by Kenyon (1897) and Jibb (1905). See also study by Severyns (1933).

BACCIOCHI, Maria Anna Elisa, *née* **Bonaparte,** *bat-cho'kee* (1777–1820), eldest sister of Napoleon, born at Ajaccio, married Felice Bacciochi, and was created by her brother in 1805 Princess and in 1809 Grand-duchess of Tuscany.

BACCIO DELLA PORTA. See BARTOLOMMEO.

BACH, *baKH,* name of a German family of musicians connected with church and town music since the early 16th century. Its most prominent members were:

(1) **Carl Philipp Emanuel** (1714–88), German composer, known as the ' Berlin ' or ' Hamburg ' Bach, son of (4), born at Weimar, educated at the Thomas-school, Leipzig, where his father was cantor, and at Frankfurt University, showed remarkable musical precocity at an early age, became in 1740 cembalist to the young Frederick (later ' the Great '), who was himself a proficient flautist, but proved too conservative in his musical tastes for Carl. Through the Princess Amalia, he found employment first at Zittau (1753) and later as *kapelmeister* at Hamburg, where he died of a lung condition. He was left-handed and therefore only unimpeded in the playing of the organ and clavier, for which his best pieces were composed. He published *The True Art of Clavier Playing* (1753; trans. 1949), the first methodical treatment of the subject, introduced the sonata form, wrote numerous concertos, keyboard sonatas, church and chamber music. He bridged the transitional period between his father and Haydn, by his homophonic, formal yet delicate, compositions. See *Life* by O. Vrieslander (1923), and Burney, *Present State of Music in Germany,* vol. 2 (1775).

(2) **Johann Christian** (1735–82), known as the ' Milan ' or ' London ' Bach, German

composer, eleventh son of (4), born in Leipzig, studied under his brother (1) in Berlin and from 1754 in Italy. After turning Catholic, he was appointed organist at Milan in 1760, for a time composed only ecclesiastical music, including two masses, a ' Requiem ' and a ' Te Deum ', but developed an interest in and began to compose opera. In 1762 he was appointed composer to the London Italian opera, became musician to Queen Charlotte and later collaborated with Abel (q.v.). The young Mozart on his London visit took to him greatly and was influenced by his style. Christian developed symphonic form. He was buried at St Pancras, London. He was twice painted by Gainsborough. See *Life* by C. S. Terry (1929).

(3) **Johann Christoph Friedrich** (1732–95), known as the ' Bückeburg ' Bach, ninth son of (4), born at Leipzig, educated there at the Thomas-school, where his father was cantor, and at Leipzig University, became in 1750 *kapelmeister* at Bückeburg. He was an industrious but undistinguished church composer.

(4) **Johann Sebastian** (1685–1750), German composer, one of the supremely great musicians of the world, father of (1), (2), (3), and (5), was born at Eisenach, March 21. An orphan before he was ten, he was placed in the care of his elder brother, **Johann Christoph** (1671–1721), organist at the town of Ohrdruf. Sebastian showed precocious ability at the local school, and was taught the organ and clavier by his brother. The latter placed his music library out of bounds to Sebastian, who soon acquired the nocturnal habit of copying out scores, a habit which he continued throughout his life and which eventually ruined his eyesight. In 1700 he became a church chorister at St John's church, Lüneburg. When his voice broke, he served as a violinist and harpsichord accompanist. In 1703 he was given a court appointment at Weimar, but in 1704 he became organist at Arnstadt, where many of his early church cantatas were written, including the flamboyant ' Easter ' cantata No. 15 and a humorous capriccio to mark the departure of a brother for the Swedish service. But he found his official duties as choirmaster exceedingly irksome. In 1705 he took a month's leave, which he overstayed, to journey on foot to Lübeck to hear the organist Buxtehude (q.v.). This and his innovations in the chorale accompaniments infuriated the authorities at Arnstadt. After marrying a cousin, **Maria Barbara Bach,** whom he had introduced into the choir, in 1707 he left to become organist at Mühlhausen. The prevailing Calvinism there condemned his elaborate anthems, but his imposing inaugural cantata,' God is my King ', was recommended for publication. In 1708 he transferred to the ducal court at Weimar and remained ' here nine years. The two toccatas and fugues ı D minor, the fantasia and fugue in G minor, ιhe preludes and fugues in C and G, and the *Little Organ Book* of short preludes belong to this period. In 1716 the duke gave the senior post of *kapelmeister* to a musical nonentity: Sebastian promptly resigned, flushed by his moral victory over the French harpsichordist,

Jean Louis Marchand, who had failed to appear at a greatly publicized musical contest with Sebastian at Dresden. The duke confined Sebastian for a month, before letting him take up his post of *kapellmeister* to Prince Leopold of Anhalt-Cöthen. At Cöthen, four overtures, the six French and six English suites, several concertos for one and two violins, and more for various ensembles were written. Six of the latter, now known as the 'Brandenburg' Concertos, were sent in 1721 to the margrave of Brandenburg, who had commissioned them. In *The Well-tempered Clavier* (1722), which profoundly influenced Mozart, Bach transformed the conventional structure of preludes and fugues written in each major and minor key. In 1720 Marie died suddenly. Of their seven children, four had survived. In 1722 he married **Anna Magdalena Wilken**, an accomplished singer, harpsichordist, and copyist, for whom Sebastian wrote a collection of keyboard pieces. Of the thirteen children born to them, seven died in infancy. For his children, Sebastian wrote a keyboard instruction book, and with Anna he completed a second *Notebook*. In 1723 he was appointed cantor of the Thomas-school in Leipzig, a post which he retained, despite acrimonious disagreements with the authorities and his colleagues, for the remainder of his life. To make it more difficult for them to overrule his decisions, Sebastian solicited the title of court composer to the elector of Saxony, and for his sponsor he wrote the thirty 'Goldberg Variations'. Goldberg was a pupil of his, and of his son (5). Sebastian's house became a centre of musical pilgrimage, and many eminent musicians, who included several relations, became his pupils. He became conductor of the *Collegium Musicum*, a society composed mainly of students, in 1729, but in 1743 refused to join the newly sponsored concert society, from which originated the famous *Gewandhaus* concerts. At Leipzig he wrote nearly three hundred church cantatas, of which two hundred survive. In the majority, the choruses have the lion's share, as in 'Sleepers Awake', 'We Praise Thee, Lord God', 'I cry to Thee, Thou Shepherd of Israel' but there are a few memorable ones for solo voice, as 'O joyous Light', 'I am a good Shepherd', &c. His 'Christmas' Oratorio is an assembly of six cantatas connected by a common narrative. The 'St Matthew Passion' (1729) and the Mass in B Minor (1733 ff.) are two of the greatest choral works ever written. In 1747, Sebastian visited Berlin and was unexpectedly invited to Potsdam by Frederick the Great, who asked him to try his latest Silbermann pianofortes. After much improvisation, Sebastian departed with a subject given to him by Frederick which he developed into a trio for flute, violin, and clavier, entitled *The Musical Offering*. He died two years later, almost totally blind, of apoplexy on July 28. At the time of his death he was engaged on his masterly series of fugues for keyboard, *The Art of Fugue*. His work stands midway between the old and the new, his main achievement being his remarkable development of polyphony. To his contemporaries he was known mainly as an organist, and a century was to pass before he

was to be adequately recognized as composer. See works by Forkel (trans. 1920), P. Spitta (trans. 1899), A. Pirro (1906), C. H. H. Parry (revised 1934), A. Schweitzer (trans. 1911), C. S. Terry (1928), A. E. F. Dickinson (1936), David and Mendel (1945), F. Blume (1950), H. Keller (1950) and Hindemith (1952).

(5) **Wilhelm Friedemann** (1710–84), known as the 'Halle' Bach, German composer, eldest and most gifted son of (4), was born at Weimar, educated at the Thomas-school and Leipzig University, where he showed a bent for mathematics. In 1733 he became organist at Dresden and in 1747 at Halle. But his way of life became increasingly dissolute and from 1764 he lived without fixed occupation at Brunswick, Göttingen and Berlin, where he died. He was the greatest organ player of his time, but very few of his compositions, which include church cantatas and several instrumental pieces, were published, as he very rarely bothered to write them down. See Life by M. Falk (Leipzig 1919) and novel by A. E. Brachvogel (Berlin 1941).

BACHE, *baych*, (1) **Alexander Dallas** (1806–1867), American physicist, grandson of Benjamin Franklin, born at Philadelphia, became professor of Natural Philosophy at Pennsylvania University (1828–41), and as president of the coast survey mapped the entire coastline.

(2) **Francis Edward** (1833–58), English violinist, organist, and composer for the piano, was born and died in Birmingham. His brother **Walter** (1842–88) popularized Liszt's piano works, and taught piano at the Royal Academy of Music.

BACHMAN, John, *bak'-* (1790–1874), an American naturalist and Lutheran pastor, co-author with Audubon (q.v.) of *The Viviparous Quadrupeds of North America*.

BACHOFEN, Johann Jakob, *baⰽⰽ'ō-fen* (1815–1887), Swiss jurist and historian, professor of Roman Law at Basel from 1841, known for his work on the theory of matriarchy (*Das Mutterrecht*, 1841). See studies by Bernoulli (1924) and Burckhardt (1943).

BACK, Sir George (1796–1878), English Arctic explorer, was born at Stockport, and entering the navy in 1808, next year was taken prisoner by the French in Spain. With Franklin (q.v.) he had already shared in three Polar expeditions—to the Spitzbergen Seas (1819), the Coppermine River (1819–22), and Mackenzie River (1822–27)—when he volunteered to go in search of Captain (Sir John) Ross, who was supposed to be lost. He left London in February 1833, and on June 28, started from a station of the Hudson Bay Company on his journey north. After passing a terrible winter with his companions near the Great Slave Lake, he discovered, in 1834, Artillery Lake and the Great Fish River, or Back's River, which he traced to the Frozen Ocean. Hindered by the ice from proceeding along the coast, he returned by the river, reaching England in the autumn of 1835. In 1836–37 he further explored the Arctic shores. He was knighted in 1839, and made admiral in 1857; but his hardships had disabled him from further active service. See his two *Narratives* (1836) and (1838).

BACKHUYSEN, or **Bakhuizen, Ludolf,** *bak'hoy-sèn* (1631–1708), Dutch marine painter, born at Emden, is best known for his *Rough Sea at the Mouth of the Maas* (Louvre) and several seascapes in London, Amsterdam, and The Hague.

BACON, (1) Delia Salter (1811–59), American authoress, sister of (6), was born at Tallmadge, Ohio; spent the years 1853–58 in England to prove the theory that Shakespeare's plays were written by Lord Bacon, Raleigh, Spenser, &c. She did not originate the idea herself, but eloquent and almost insane, was the first to give it currency in her *Philosophy of the Plays of Shakespeare Unfolded* (1857), with a preface by Hawthorne. See *Delia Bacon, a Biographical Sketch* (1888).

(2) Francis, Baron Verulam of Verulam, Viscount St Albans (1561–1626), English philosopher and statesman, born at York House in the Strand, London, January 22, the younger son of (8). With his elder brother **Anthony** (1558–1601), the future diplomatist, Bacon passed his boyhood under the stern discipline of his mother, a zealous Calvinist. In 1573 the brothers entered Trinity College, Cambridge, and in 1576 Gray's Inn, Francis being called to the bar in 1582. At Cambridge he had recognized the barrenness of scholastic philosophy and the need of educational reform. He became M.P. in 1584; and sought to attract the queen's attention by addressing to her a paper advocating tolerance in the treatment of recusants. In 1593 he offended her by opposing in parliament the grant of a subsidy. Failing in his efforts to obtain any favour from Burghley (who had married his mother's sister), Bacon attached himself to the Earl of Essex, from whom he accepted a gift of land at Twickenham. He advised his patron in 1598 (although he afterwards denied having done so) to undertake the suppression of Tyrone's rebellion in Ireland, and when the earl returned in disgrace (1599) and was tried, Bacon acted with the prosecuting counsel—in the hope, he said, of aiding his patron. When in 1601 Essex broke into open rebellion, Bacon voluntarily endeavoured to secure his conviction on the charge of treason, and after the execution drew up the official declaration of Essex's treasons. In the last years of Elizabeth's reign he tried to act the part of mediator between crown and commons, and recommended a tolerant policy in Ireland. On James I's accession (1603) he sought royal favour by extravagant professions of loyalty; by planning schemes for the union of England and Scotland, and for pacifying the Church of England on comprehensive lines; and by making speeches in parliament to prove that the claims of the king and parliament could be reconciled. For these services he was knighted (1603) and was made a commissioner for the union of Scotland and England. In 1605 Bacon published the *Advancement of Learning*; in 1606 he married a London alderman's daughter; in 1607 he became solicitor-general. In 1612 he offered to manage parliament for the king, and to obtain supplies without concerting undignified bargains. In 1613 he was promoted to the attorney-

generalship. In 1615 he examined under torture an old clergyman, Edmund Peacham, charged with preaching treason, and undertook to confer privately with each judge of the King's Bench in order to secure a conviction. In 1616 he prosecuted Somerset, with whom he was intimate, for the murder of Overbury. In 1616 Bacon became a privy councillor, in 1617 lord keeper, and in 1618 lord chancellor, being raised to the peerage as Lord Verulam, a title taken from *Verulamium*, the Latin name of St Albans, near which lay Bacon's estate of Gorhambury. His obsequiousness was now more marked than ever; he even accepted the king's policy of the Spanish marriage. A word from Buckingham influenced his behaviour to suitors in the Court of Chancery; in one case, when Buckingham expressed his surprise, Bacon cancelled his decision. He was on the side of severity in the case of Raleigh (1618). In 1620 he published his *Novum Organum*, and in 1621 was created Viscount St Albans. But his fall was at hand. Complaint was made that Bacon was in the habit of taking bribes from suitors in his court, and in 1621 charges were sent to the House of Lords by the Commons for inquiry. That he took presents from suitors was undeniable, but that he allowed these gifts to influence his judicial decisions is disputed. Bacon was arraigned before his fellow peers, offered no defence and was fined, imprisoned in the Tower, and banished from parliament and the court. After a few days he was released, and retired to Gorhambury; three months later the king pardoned him, but declined to allow him to return to parliament or the court. In March 1626 he caught cold while stuffing a fowl with snow near Highgate, in order to observe the effect of cold on the preservation of flesh; taken to a friend's house, he died there on April 9, and was buried in St Michael's Church, St Albans. He died deep in debt. Bacon's philosophy is chiefly to be studied in (i) *The Advancement of Learning* (1605), a review of the state of knowledge in his own time, and its chief defects; (ii) *De Augmentis Scientiarum* (1623), a Latin expansion of the *Advancement*, and (iii) *Novum Organum* (1620). Bacon abandoned the deductive logic of Aristotle and the schoolmen, and stressed the importance of experiment in interpreting nature and the necessity for proper regard for any possible evidence which might run counter to any held thesis. He described heat as a mode of motion, and light as requiring time for transmission, but was behind the scientific knowledge of his time. His greatness consists in his insistence on the facts that man is the servant and interpreter of Nature, that truth is not derived from authority, and that knowledge is the fruit of experience; and in spite of the defects of his method, the impetus he gave to future scientific investigation is indisputable. He was the practical creator of scientific induction. An unparalleled belief in himself, which justified to himself his ignoring of all ordinary laws of morality, is the leading feature in the character of this ' wisest, brightest, meanest of mankind '. As a writer of English prose and a student of human nature, Bacon is seen to best advantage in his essays, ten of which were published in 1597, the number being increased to 58 in 1625. His *History of Henry VII* (1622) shows scholarly research, besides a direct and nervous style. In his fanciful *New Atlantis* he suggests the formation of scientific academies. The *Apophthegms* (1625) are a disappointing collection of witticisms. His religious works included prayers and verse translations of seven Psalms (1625). The professional works embrace *Maxims of the Law* (1630), *Reading on the Statute of Uses* (1642), &c. The standard edition of Bacon's works is that by Spedding, Ellis, and Heath (1857–74). See Macaulay's *Essay* (1837) and works by Kuno Fischer (trans. 1857), Abbott (1885), Nichol (1890), Williams (1933), F. H. Henderson (1948) and J. G. Crowther (1960). For the theory that Bacon wrote the plays attributed to Shakespeare, see BACON (DELIA).

(3) **Francis** (1909–), Irish artist, born in Dublin, began painting at the age of 19 and without formal art education. He treated religious subjects in a highly individual manner, but made little impact until 1945, when his *Three Studies for Figures at the Base of a Crucifixion* won praise. Since then many successful works have emerged, but these are a small proportion of the total output of the artist, who destroys all paintings which do not satisfy him. His style derives from surrealism, often with a tendency towards the macabre; examples are in the Tate Gallery and the Museum of Modern Art, New York. See study by J. Rothenstein and R. Alley (1964).

(4) **John**. See BACONTHORPE.

(5) **John** (1740–99), English sculptor, was born in London, became one of the first students of the Royal Academy Schools and is responsible for the monuments to Chatham in Westminster Abbey and the Guildhall, the statue of Dr Johnson in St Paul's, &c. His second son, John (1777–1859), was also a sculptor. See *Life* by Richard Cecil (1801).

(6) **Leonard** (1801–81), American Congregationalist divine, brother of (1), was professor of Theology at Yale, and wrote many works on theology and against slavery.

(7) **Nathaniel** (*c.* 1642–76), American colonial leader, a native of Suffolk, who, emigrating to Virginia, made himself prominent by his raids against the Indians and his opposition to the governors, culminating in Bacon's rebellion, the capture and burning of Jamestown in 1676.

(8) **Sir Nicholas** (1509–79), English statesman, father of (2), attained high legal offices which, as a Protestant, he lost under Mary, but in 1558, on her accession, Elizabeth made him lord keeper of the Great Seal, and left to him and Cecil the management of church affairs. A staunch anti-Catholic, he was an implacable enemy of Mary, Queen of Scots.

(9) **Roger** (*c.* 1214–92), known as 'doctor mirabilis', English Franciscan philosopher, probably born at Ilchester, Somerset, seems to have studied at Oxford and before 1236 proceeded to Paris, where he wrote his commentaries on Aristotle's physics and metaphysics. He resigned his chair there in 1247 to devote himself to experimental science, returning to Oxford about 1250, and

may have entered the Franciscan order. About 1256, 'owing to many infirmities', he went into retirement (banishment or confinement, according to some) for ten years in Paris. Among the few clear-sighted men who admired Bacon was Guy de Foulques. He had desired to see Bacon's writings; and, on his ascent of the papal throne as Clement IV in 1265, Bacon wrote to him expressing his readiness to furnish him with whatever he desired. Clement repeated the request to see his works; and Bacon accordingly drew up his *Opus Majus*, which he sent to the pope by his favourite pupil, John of London. How Clement received it is not known; but it could only have reached him about the time of his last illness in 1268. In 1277 the general of the Franciscans declared himself against Bacon, forbade the reading of his books, summoned their author for 'suspected novelties', and issued an order for his imprisonment—an imprisonment that lasted almost till his death. When in 1288 Jerome himself became Pope Nicholas IV, Bacon sent him a treatise on the means of warding off the infirmities of old age, but in vain. He had just recovered his freedom when he died at Oxford. Despite his invention of the magnifying glass, his valuable optical researches, defining reflection and refraction, his knowledge of gunpowder (1248), and of astronomy and medicine he still reflected the prejudices of his time in his search for the philosopher's stone. He suggested a revised calendar and a lighter-than-air machine, and emphasized the importance of mathematics. See works on him by A. G. Little (1914, 1928), J. H. Bridges (1914), R. Carton (1924), D. E. Sharp (1930), and T. Crowley (1950).

BACONTHORPE, or **Bacon, John** (d. 1346), called 'the resolute doctor', a diminutive Norfolk Carmelite, scholar, grandnephew of Roger Bacon, and expositor of the Arab philosopher, Averroës. He anticipated Wycliffe's teaching that priests should be subordinate to kings.

BACSÁNYI, János (1763–1845), Hungarian poet and patriot, imprisoned by the Hapsburgs for his nationalism, as expressed in *The Valour of the Magyars* (1785).

BADDELEY, née Snow, Sophia (1745–86), English actress and singer, eloped in 1763 with Robert Baddeley (1732–94), the actor. While she played Ophelia, he specialized in low comedy rôles. See *Memoirs* by Mrs Steele (1781).

BADEN-POWELL, Robert Stephenson Smyth, 1st Baron Baden-Powell (1857–1941), British general, born in London, son of Baden Powell, Savilian professor of Geometry at Oxford. Educated at Charterhouse, he joined the army, served in India and Afghanistan, was on the staff in Ashanti and Matabeleland, and won fame as the defender of Mafeking (1899–1900). He is chiefly known, however, as the founder (1908) of the Boy Scouts and (1910), with his sister **Agnes** (1858–1945), of the Girl Guides. See *Lives* by Fletcher (1900), R. J. B. Smith (1900), W. F. Aitken (1913), Reynolds (1942), and Bond (1955).

BADER, Douglas Robert Stuart (1910–), British aviator, born in London, was commissioned from Cranwell in 1930. He lost both legs in a flying accident in 1931 and was invalided out, but overcame his disability and returned to the R.A.F. in 1939. He commanded the first R.A.F. Canadian Fighter Squadron, evolving tactics that contributed to victory in the Battle of Britain, but was captured in August 1941 after a collision with an enemy aircraft over Béthune. Thrice mentioned in despatches, holder of the D.S.O. and D.F.C. with bars, the Legion of Honour and the Croix de Guerre, he left the R.A.F. in 1946. A great pilot and leader of 'the few', he set an example of fortitude and heroism that became a legend. See Paul Brickhill's *Reach for the Sky* (1954).

BADÍA-Y-LEBLICH, Domingo, *bah-*THee*'ah-ee-lay-bleek'* (1766–1818), Spanish traveller, was born in Barcelona and studied Arabic. Disguised as a Moslem, he visited (1803–07) Morocco, Tripoli, Cyprus, Egypt, and Mecca (the first Christian to be there since the spread of the Islamic faith), also Syria and Constantinople. See his *Voyage* (1814).

BADOGLIO, Pietro, *bah-dol'yō* (1871–1956), Italian marshal, born at Grazzano Monferrato, Piedmont, served with distinction in Tripoli; with Diaz took command after the disaster of Caporetto (1917); superseding de Bono, completed the conquest of Abyssinia (1935–36); and, on Italy's entry into World War II in June 1940, was made commander-in-chief, but in December resigned on the Greek humiliation of Italian arms in Albania. Following Mussolini's downfall (1943), he formed a non-Fascist government, negotiated an armistice, declared war on Germany, and, not without democratic and republican opposition, held power till 1944, when, after the king's delegation of his powers to his son, he was unable to form a government and resigned.

BAECK, Leo (1873–1956), German-Jewish religious leader, born at Lissa, Prussia, was rabbi (1912–42) in Berlin, and when the Nazis came to power became the political leader of German Jewry and spent 1942–45 in the Theresienstadt concentration camp. After the war he lectured in Britain. His chief publications were *The Essence of Judaism* (1936), *The Pharisees and Other Essays* (1947), &c.

BAEDA. See BEDE.

BAEDEKER, Karl, *bay'-* (1801–59), German publisher, born at Essen, started his own publishing business in 1827 at Coblenz, and is best known for the admirable guidebooks which bear his name, published since 1872 at Leipzig.

BAEKELAND, Leo Hendrik, *bayk'land* (1863–1944), Belgian-American chemist, born at Ghent, emigrated to the U.S.A. in 1889, invented photographic printing paper usable with artificial light, discovered the first synthetic phenolic resin (Bakelite), and was a founder of the plastics industry.

BAER, Karl Ernst von, *bayr* (1792–1876), Estonian naturalist, a pioneer in embryology, was born at Piep in Estonia. After studying medicine at Dorpat and later at Würzburg, Baer was professor at Königsberg and from 1834 at St Petersburg. He discovered the mammalian egg in the ovary and the notochord, formulated the 'biogenetic law' that in embryonic development general characters appear before special ones. His studies were used by Darwin in his theory of evolution, which Baer, however, discounted.

BAEYER, Johann Friedrich Wilhelm Adolf von, *bī'-* (1835–1917), German organic chemist, born in Berlin, discovered when he was twelve years old a new double salt of copper and sodium. In 1855 he went to Heidelberg University, where he studied under Bunsen and Kekule (qq.v.). From 1860, he taught in the Berlin Technical Institute until he was appointed professor of Chemistry at Strasbourg (1872) and Munich (1875–1915). He devoted much time to establishing a modern system of instruction. His researches covered many aspects of chemistry, notably the synthesis of the dye indigo and the elucidation of its structure, the mechanism of photosynthesis, condensation of phenols and aldehydes, the polyacetylenes, the stability of polymethylene rings, the terpenes and the basicity of organic oxygen compounds. He was awarded the Nobel prize for chemistry in 1905. See his *Memoirs* and W. H. Perkin's Memorial Lecture (Chemical Society Memorial Lectures, vol. 3).

BAFFIN, William (c. 1584–1622), English navigator, was probably born in London, and in 1612–16 was pilot in several expeditions in search of the Northwest Passage, during which he carefully examined Hudson Strait (1615), discovered Baffin Bay (1616), and discovered also and named Lancaster, Smith, and Jones Sounds (1616). His latter voyages (1616–21) were to the East, and at the siege of Ormuz he was killed in 1622. See his *Voyages* (ed. Markham 1881).

BAGEHOT, Walter, *baj'ot* (1826–77), English economist and journalist, born at Langport, Somerset, graduated in mathematics at University College, London, was called to the bar in 1852 and after a spell as banker in his father's firm at Langport, succeeded his father-in-law, James Wilson, as editor of the *Economist* in 1860. His *English Constitution* (1867) is still considered a standard work. He followed Green and others in applying the theory of evolution to politics, as in *Physics and Politics* (1872). Other works include *Lombard Street* (1875), *Literary Studies* (1878), and *Economic Studies* (1880). He advocated many constitutional reforms, including the introduction of life peers. See Works and Life, ed. Hutton (1915), and studies by W. Irvine (1939), W. St J. Stevens (1959) and A. Buchan, *The Spare Chancellor* (1959).

BAGFORD, John (1650–1716), English antiquary, born in London, was a bootmaker who made scrapbook collection of English broadside ditties and verses in 64 volumes. These, the 'Bagford Ballads', were edited by J. W. Ebsworth (1878).

BAGGESEN, Jens, *bag'e-sen* (1764–1826), Danish poet and satirical humorist, born at Korsör, travelled extensively in France and Germany and engaged in literary feuds with romanticists. He was the author of *Comical Tales* (1785), &c. See Lives by Clausen (Copenhagen 1895) and Rubow, *Dansk Literaer Kritik* (Copenhagen 1921).

BAGIMONT. See BAJIMONT.

BAGLIVI, properly **Armero, Giorgio**, *bah-lyee'vee* (1669–1707), Italian physician, born at Ragusa, became professor of Anatomy at the papal university in 1696. A brilliant clinician, who was uninfluenced in his practical work by his own theories, which stemmed from the iatrophysical school of Borelli (q.v.), he assumed, however, that disease is located in the solid parts of the body.

BAGNACAVALLO, *ban-yah-kah-val'lo*, pseudonym and birthplace of **Bartolommeo Ramenghi** (1484–1542), Italian painter, pupil of Francia, studied Raphael's works in Rome and assisted him in the decoration of the Vatican. He also came under the influence of Dosso Dossi. His *Circumcision* (Louvre) and the *Crucifixion* at St Peter's, Bologna, where he eventually settled, show him as a mannerist painter echoing the styles of the three masters.

BAGRATION, Peter Ivanovich, Prince, *bagrah-tee-yon'* (1765–1812), Russian general, descended from the royal Bagratidae of Georgia, entered the Russian service in 1783, and, after much active service, in November 1805, with 6000 troops, stood for six hours against 30,000 French under Murat. He fought, too, at Austerlitz, Eylau, Friedland, and the siege of Silistria (1809). He was mortally wounded in the battle of Borodino, October 7, 1812. See Tolstoy, *War and Peace* (1868).

BAHA ULLAH, *bah-hah' ool-lah'*, the name, meaning 'splendour of God', given to **Mirza Huseyn Ali** (1817–92), successor of Bâb-ed-Din (q.v.), founder of the new Bahai sect. See books by G. Townshend and P. Esslemont.

BAHR, Hermann (1863–1934), Austrian dramatist, novelist, and critic, was born at Linz, studied at Vienna, Berlin, &c., took a leading part in the literary movements, naturalism and expressionism, of the Hapsburg empire period and published social novels such as *Die schöne Frau* (1899) and comedies such as *Die gelbe Nachtigall* (1907). See his autobiography (1923).

BAHRDT, Karl Friedrich (1741–92), German theologian and freethinker, born at Bischofswerda in Saxony, was a professor at Leipzig (1766–68) and Giessen (1771–75). From these posts he was expelled for his loose living, and so for the last ten years of his life kept a public house on the Weinberg near Halle. His 'model version' of the New Testament (1775) infuriated Goethe.

BAÏF, Jean Antoine de, *ba-eef* (1532–89), French poet, born at Venice, was a member of the Pléiade, author of *Amours* (1552), *Passe-Temps*, &c. He attempted to introduce blank verse into French poetry, and experimented with combinations of poetry and music. See H. Chamard, *Histoire de la Pléiade* (1940).

BAIKIE, William Balfour, *bay'kee* (1825–64), Scottish explorer, naturalist, and linguist, was born at Kirkwall, Orkney. He studied medicine at Edinburgh, and in 1848 became a naval surgeon. Appointed surgeon and naturalist to the Niger expedition in 1854, he succeeded through the captain's death to the command of 'the *Pleiad*', and penetrated 250 miles higher than any previous traveller. In a second expedition in 1857 'the *Pleiad*' was wrecked, and he was left to continue his work single-handed from Lukoja. Within five years he had opened the navigation of the Niger, constructed roads, collected a native vocabulary, translated parts of the Bible and Prayer Book into Hausa, and founded a city state. See his *Narrative* (1856).

BAILEY, (1) Sir Donald Coleman (1901–), British engineer, was born at Rotherham and graduated at Sheffield. During World War II he designed the prefabricated, mobile, rapidly-erected bridge which bore his name. He was knighted in 1946.

(2) **James Anthony**. See BARNUM.

(3) **John** (1750–1819), English agriculturalist and mathematician, born at Blades Field, Yorkshire, from 1819 land agent to Lord Tankerville at Chillingham, published an essay on plough construction (1795) in which he proposed certain alterations in the light of mathematical calculations he had made.

(4) **Nathan**, or **Nathaniel**, English lexicographer, the compiler of *An Universal Etymological English Dictionary* (1721–27; 30th ed. 1802), used by Dr Johnson in compiling his own dictionary, was a 'Seventh-day Baptist', and kept a boarding-school at Stepney, where he died in 1742.

(5) **Philip James** (1816–1902), English poet, founder of the 'spasmodic' school, born at Basford, Nottingham, the son of the historian of Nottinghamshire, **Thomas Bailey** (1785–1856). After studying at Glasgow University, he was called to the English bar in 1840, but never practised. *Festus: a Poem* (1839) reached, greatly altered, an 11th (Jubilee) edition in 1889. His reputation stood high in his own day.

(6) **Samuel** (1791–1870), English philosopher, was born in Sheffield, where afterwards he became a banker. He twice contested his native city as a 'philosophical radical' without success, and left £80,000 to the town. His *Essays on the Formation and Publication of Opinions* (1821) constitute an able defence of the proposition that a man's opinions are independent of his will. His works on mental philosophy and economics are of less value.

BAILLIE, (1) Lady Grizel (1665–1746), Scottish poetess, daughter of the Scottish Jacobite, Sir Patrick Hume (q.v.), in 1684 supplied him with food during his concealment in the vault beneath Polwarth church. She shared her parents' exile at Utrecht and in 1692 married the son of Baillie of Jerviswood. She is remembered by her songs, best of which is 'And werena my heart licht I wad dee'.

(2) **Joanna** (1762–1851), Scottish poetess and playwright, sister of (3), was born in Bothwell manse. In 1806 she and her sister, Agnes, settled at Hampstead, London. Her tragedy *De Montfort*, produced at Drury Lane in 1800 with Kemble and Mrs Siddons in the leading parts, achieved a popular success, as did her *Family Legend* in Edinburgh in 1810 under Scott's auspices. See Life by M. Carhart (1923).

(3) **Matthew** (1761–1823), Scottish physician and anatomist, brother of (2), was born in

Shotts manse. After seven years at Glasgow and Oxford (1773–80) he studied anatomy under the famous William Hunter, his mother's brother, and in 1783 succeeded to his uncle's lucrative practice and lectureship. He was the author of the first treatise in English on morbid anatomy (1793).

(4) **Robert** (1599–1662), Presbyterian divine, was born in Glasgow and educated at the university there. In 1622 he received episcopal ordination, and was shortly after presented to the parish of Kilwinning. In 1637 he refused to preach in favour of Laud's service book, in 1638 sat in the famous General Assembly which met in Glasgow to protest against episcopacy. In 1639 he served as chaplain in the Covenanting army at Duns Law, and in 1640 was selected to go to London with other commissioners and draw up charges against Archbishop Laud. On his return to Scotland in 1642 he was appointed joint professor of Divinity at Glasgow. In 1643 he was a delegate to the Westminster Assembly, in 1649 was chosen by the church to proceed to Holland to invite Charles II to accept the Covenant and crown of Scotland. He performed his mission skilfully; and, after the Restoration, was made principal of Glasgow University. See his historically valuable *Letters and Journals*, edited by David Laing (1842).

(5) **Robert, of Jerviswood** (d. 1684), Scottish conspirator, was a native of Lanarkshire, who in 1683 entered into correspondence with, and subsequently joined, Monmouth's supporters in London. On the discovery of the Rye-house Plot, he was arrested and sent to Scotland, was tried at Edinburgh, condemned to death on insufficient evidence, and hanged. His son married (1).

BAILLY, Jean Sylvain, *bah-yee* (1736–93), French astronomer, born in Paris, from art turned to literature, and then to astronomy, writing his great *Histoire de l'astronomie* (1775–87). He was elected a member of three academies, an honour that had fallen to no one before him except Fontenelle. As president of the National Assembly and mayor of Paris during the Revolution in 1789, he conducted himself with great integrity; but lost his popularity by allowing the National Guard to fire on crowds who were demanding the dethronement of the king. He withdrew from public affairs and went to live first at Nantes, and afterwards with his friend Laplace at Melun. There he was seized by Jacobin soldiers and brought to Paris, where he was guillotined. See Nourrisson's *Turgot, Necker, Bailly* (1885).

BAILY, (1) Edward Hodges (1788–1867), English sculptor, born at Bristol, executed many of the well-known London statues, including that of Lord Nelson in Trafalgar Square.

(2) **Francis** (1774–1844), English astronomer, born at Newbury, Berks, made a large fortune as a stockbroker and on his retirement in 1825 devoted himself to astronomy and was president of the Royal Astronomical Society when he died. He detected the phenomenon known as ' Baily's beads ' during an eclipse of the sun in 1836, and calculated the mean density of the earth. He also wrote

a life of the first astronomer royal, John Flamsteed (1835). See Memoir by Sir J. Herschel (1845).

BAIN, Alexander (1818–1903), Scottish writer on mental philosophy of the empirical school, was born in Aberdeen, where he was professor of Logic (1860–81), and then was elected rector. His most important works are *The Senses and the Intellect* (1855), *The Emotions and the Will* (1859), *Mental and Moral Science* (1868), *Logic* (1870), and books on the two Mills. His psychology was based on physiology, but he considered the human organism capable of originating impulses, instead of being merely, as in the works of previous empiricists (Locke, Berkeley, Hume) capable of receiving and responding to impressions. See his Autobiography (1904).

BAINES, Edward (1774–1848), English politician and journalist, from 1801 proprietor of the *Leeds Mercury*, Liberal M.P. for Leeds 1834–41, championed separation of church and state, opposed governmental control over education and wrote a history of Lancashire. See Life by his son, **Sir Edward Baines** (1800–90), who also sat for Leeds, held the same ideas as his father, and wrote a history of the cotton industry (1835).

BAIRAKDAR, Mustafa, *bī-rak-dahr'* (1755–1808), Turkish grand vizier, as pasha of Rustchuk in 1806 fought against the Russians, and after the revolt of the janissaries in 1807, by which Selim III was deposed in favour of Mustapha IV, marched his troops to Constantinople, where they found the dead body of Selim lying in the seraglio. Bairakdar executed the murderers, deposed Mustapha, and proclaimed his brother, Mahmoud II, sultan (1808). As grand vizier, he endeavoured to carry out Selim's reforms and to annihilate the janissaries, who, however, rebelled, and, backed by the fleet, demanded the restoration of Mustapha. Bairakdar defended himself bravely, until, strangling Mustapha, he threw his head to the besiegers, and then blew himself up.

BAIRD, (1) Sir David, Bart. (1757–1829), British soldier, born at Newbyth, East Lothian, in 1779 sailed to India as captain in a Highland regiment at the height of the 2nd Mysore war. He was thrown into a dungeon at Seringapatam and endured captivity for nearly four years, after the British army had been ambushed by Hyder Ali and a French-trained force in 1780. He was released in 1784, took part in several sieges and attacks and returned in 1799, a major-general, and led the victorious attack on Seringapatam. He commanded an expedition in Egypt against the French in 1801, was knighted and made a K.C.B. in 1804. In 1805–06 he commanded an expedition which successfully wrested the Cape of Good Hope from the Dutch. He was at the siege of Copenhagen (1807), and in 1809 distinguished himself and lost an arm in the battle of Coruña (1809) in the Peninsular war, succeeding Sir John Moore (q.v.). He received the thanks of parliament four times and was created a baronet for his services. See Lives by T. Hook (1832) and W. H. Wilkin (1912).

(2) **John Logie** (1888–1946), Scottish tele-

vision pioneer, born at Helensburgh, studied electrical engineering at Glasgow University. Poor health compelled him to give up the post of engineer to the Clyde Valley electric power company, and after a brief business career bedevilled by illness he settled in Hastings (1922) and began research into the possibilities of television. Later, in Soho, London, his experiments reached a practicable stage, and in 1926 he gave the first demonstration of a television image. His 240-line mechanically-scanned system was adopted by the B.B.C. (at first experimentally) in 1929, but was superseded in 1937 by a rival 405-line system with electronic scanning. Baird continued his research up to the time of his death and succeeded in producing three-dimensional and coloured images (1944) as well as projection on to a screen and stereophonic sound.

(3) **Spencer Fullerton** (1823–87), American naturalist, became professor of Natural History at Carlyle, Pa., made a vast collection of North American fauna, compiled *A History of North American Birds*, and was a commissioner of fish and fisheries. See *Life* by W. H. Dall (1915).

BAIRNSFATHER, Bruce (1888–1959), British soldier and cartoonist, born at Murree, India. He served in France during World War I, and became famous for his war cartoons featuring the character ' Old Bill '. During World War II, he was an official war cartoonist attached to the U.S. Army. His drawings have appeared in various periodicals, in war books, and in his *Fragments from France* (1916, &c.) in six volumes, and *Jeeps and Jests* (1943).

BAJAZET, or **Bajazid,** *baj-a-zet'*, name of two sultans in the Ottoman Empire:

Bajazet I (1347–1403), in 1389 succeeded his father, Murad I, who was slain on the battlefield of Kossovo. In three years he conquered Bulgaria, with parts of Serbia, Macedonia, and Thessaly, and most of Asia Minor. His rapid conquests earned him the name of Ilderim—' Lightning '. He for ten years blockaded Constantinople, to rescue which King Sigismund of Hungary (afterwards emperor) assembled a large army, including 2000 French nobles, and laid siege to Nikopolis, on the Danube. Bajazet hastened to meet him, and gained a decisive victory (1396). Bajazet would have entirely destroyed the Greek empire if he had not in 1402 been completely defeated by Timur (q.v.) near Angora. Bajazet himself fell into the hands of the conqueror, who treated him with great generosity (the iron cage is a myth), and in whose camp he died. He was succeeded by his son Soliman I.

Bajazet II (1446–1512), succeeded his father, Mohammed II, the conqueror of Constantinople, in 1481. His 32 years' reign was a succession of wars against Hungary, Poland, Venice, Egypt, and Persia, which served on the whole to establish the Ottoman power.

BAJIMOND, Bagimont or Boiamond, a canon of Asti in Piedmont, was sent by Pope Gregory X in 1274 to Scotland to collect the tithe of all the church livings for a crusade. Bajimond's roll was used as the papal system of taxation in Scotland until the Reformation.

BAJUS, or **De Bay, Michael,** *bah'yoos* (1513–1589), Flemish Catholic theologian, born in Hainault, in 1551 became professor of Theology at Louvain. He was a devoted student of St Augustine, and seventy-six of his propositions were condemned by a papal bull in 1567. He may be regarded as the precursor of the Jansenists. See Linsenmann, *Michael Bajus* (Tüb. 1867).

BAKER, (1) **Sir Benjamin** (1840–1907), English engineer, born at Frome, in 1861 entered his long association with John Fowler (q.v.) as consulting engineer. They together constructed the London Metropolitan railway, Victoria station, and bridges. Their greatest achievement, however, was the Forth Rail Bridge, built on the cantilever principle and opened in 1890, when Baker was knighted and Fowler received a baronetcy. Baker was also consulting engineer for the Aswan dam and its subsequent heightening. He also designed the vessel which carried Cleopatra's Needle to London, and many miles of the London underground railways.

(2) **Bryant** (1881–1970), American sculptor, born in London, England. He studied in London, and later went to the U.S., where he made busts of President Wilson, President Hoover, and others.

(3) **Henry** (1698–1774), English naturalist, born in London, from a bookseller's apprentice became a teacher of deaf-mutes, and, making a largish fortune, in 1729 married Defoe's youngest daughter. In 1740 he was elected F.R.S. and F.S.A. and he wrote works on microscopy and philosophical poems.

(4) **Sir Herbert** (1862–1946), English architect, born in Kent, designed Groote Schuur, near Cape Town, for Rhodes, the Union Government buildings at Pretoria, and, with Sir E. L. Lutyens, the new Delhi; in London, the new Bank of England, South Africa House, &c. He was knighted in 1926 and became R.A. in 1932. See his *Architecture and Personalities* (1944).

(5) **Herbert Brereton** (1862–1935), English chemist, born at Livesey, near Blackburn, as professor at the Imperial College of Science investigated the influence of water on chemical change and was an expert on poison gases during World War I.

(6) **Ray Stannard,** pseud. **David Grayson** (1870–1946), American journalist and author, born in Lansing, Michigan. He worked on the editorial staff of various journals from 1892 to 1915, and in 1940 received a Pulitzer prize for his eight-volume authoritative biography of Woodrow Wilson. Under his pseudonym he wrote essays on rural life, including *Adventures in Contentment* (1907) and *The Countryman's Year* (1936). See his autobiography, *Native American* (1941).

(7) **Sir Richard** (c. 1568–1645), English historian, born in Kent, was knighted in 1603. High-sheriff of Oxfordshire in 1620, in 1635 he was thrown into the Fleet Prison for debt. Here he wrote his *Chronicle of the Kings of England* (1643), which was once a standard work in any country gentleman's library, but which nevertheless contained many errors.

(8) **Sir Samuel White** (1821–93), British traveller, born in London, in 1845 went to

Ceylon (where he established an agricultural settlement at Nuwara Eliya), and afterwards superintended the construction of a railway across the Dobrudja. In 1860 he married a Hungarian lady, and with her undertook the exploration of the Nile sources. Setting out from Cairo in 1861, at Gondokoro they were joined by Speke and Grant coming from the south, who told Baker of the Victoria Nyanza, which they had discovered; they also mentioned that the natives had described to them another great lake, named Luta Nzige. Baker resolved to reach this lake; and after many adventures they beheld, on March 14, 1864, from a lofty cliff, the great inland sea to which Baker gave the name of the Albert Nyanza. In 1869–73 he commanded an expedition, organized by the pasha of Egypt, for the suppression of slavery and the annexation of the equatorial regions of the Nile Basin. He thoroughly explored Cyprus in 1879, and afterwards visited Syria, India, Japan, and America. Knighted in 1866, he died at his home near Newton Abbot. His works include *The Rifle and the Hound in Ceylon* (1854), *The Albert Nyanza* (1866), *Ismailia* (1874), *Cyprus as I saw it* (1879). See *Life* by Murray and White (1895).

BAKEWELL, Robert (1725–95), English stock breeder, was born at Dishley, Leicestershire, and by selection and inbreeding improved the standard and methods of management of sheep, cattle, and draught horses. He established the Leicester breed of sheep, aroused a wide interest in breeding methods, made a great deal of money, but died in poverty. See *Life* by H. C. Pawson (1957).

BAKHUIZEN. See BACKHUYSEN.

BAKST, Leon, *bahkst* (1866–1924), Russian painter, born at St Petersburg, and later lived in Paris. He was associated with Diaghilev from the beginnings of the Russian ballet, designing the décor and costumes for numerous productions (1909–21). His rich, exuberant colours, seemingly uncontrolled, in reality produced a powerful theatrical effect, which revolutionized fashion and decoration generally.

BAKUNIN, Mikhail, *bah-koo'nin* (1814–76), Russian anarchist, born near Moscow of aristocratic descent, took part in the German revolutionary movement (1848–49) and was condemned to death. Given up to Russia, and sent to Siberia in 1855, he escaped to Japan, and arrived in England in 1861. In September 1870 he attempted an abortive rising at Lyons. As the leader of anarchism Bakunin was in the Communist International the opponent of Karl Marx; but at the Hague Congress in 1872 he was outvoted and expelled. Bakunin believed that Communism, with its theoretical 'withering away of the state', was an essential step towards anarchism. See *Life* by E. H. Carr (1937).

BALAGUER Y CIRERA, Victor, *ba-la-gayr'ee thee-ray'ra* (1824–1901), Spanish poet, politician, and historian. A leading figure of the Catalan renaissance, he wrote a *History of Catalonia*, a *Political and Literary History of the Troubadours*, and poems in both Catalan and Spanish.

BALAKIREV, Mili Alexeivich, *ba-la-kee'ryef* (1836–1910), Russian composer, born at Nijni Novgorod, became the leader of the national Russian school of music. Cui, Mussorgsky, Rimsky-Korsakov, Borodin, and Tchaikovsky were all influenced by him. His compositions were derived from folk music.

BALARD, Antoine Jérôme, *ba-lahr* (1802–1876), French chemist, born at Montpelier, Hérault, discovered bromine, hypochlorous acid, and chlorine monoxide.

BALASSA, Bálint, Angl. Valentine, *baw'law-shaw* (1555–91), Hungarian knight and Magyar lyric poet, born at Kékkö, who died fighting the Turkish invaders, and whose poetry was inspired by military heroism, love, and religion. He also experimented in drama (*Credulus and Julia*). See his *Little Garden for Diseased Minds*, published in Cracow in 1572.

BALBI, (1) **Adriano** (1782–1848), Italian geographer and statistician, born in Venice, author of *Atlas ethnographique du globe* (1826) and *Abrégé de géographie* (1832).

(2) **Gasparo** (16th cent.), a Venetian merchant who, on a journey from Aleppo to India, visited Baghdad, Basra, Goa, Cochin, and Pegu, and a Latin translation of whose *Viaggio* (1590) was printed at Frankfurt in 1594.

BALBO, (1) **Cesare, Count** (1789–1853), Italian statesman and author, born at Turin. A prime minister in the first Piedmontese constitutional ministry, he published a biography of Dante in 1839 and an historical essay demonstrating his view that Italy had only prospered when free from foreign domination. See CAVOUR, and *Life* by U. Biscottini (1926).

(2) **Italo, Count** (1896–1940), Italian aviator and politician. One of the leaders of the 'March on Rome', he was the first minister of aviation in Italy, and led mass flights to Brazil (1929) and the U.S.A. (1933). In 1933 he became governor of Libya; in 1940 he was killed when his plane was brought down at Tobruk.

BALBOA, Vasco Nunez de (1475–1517), Spanish explorer, born at Jerez-de-Los-Caballeros, settled in San Domingo in 1501 and in 1511 joined the expedition to Darien, commanded by Francisco de Enisco, as a stowaway. Taking advantage of an insurrection, he took command in place of Enisco, founded a colony at Darien and extended Spanish influence. Yet the governorship was granted in 1514 to Pedrarias Davila, for whom Balboa undertook many successful expeditions and whose daughter he married. On their first disagreement Balboa was unjustly beheaded. See study by A. Strawn (1929).

BALBUENA, Bernardo de, *bal-bway'na* (1568–1627), Spanish poet, born in Valdepenas, but spent his working life in Central America, where all his poetry was written. Of this the best is *Bernardo o la victoria de Roncesvalles*, excellently and powerfully constructed and full of allegory. See *Life* by Van Horne (Mexico 1940).

BALDENSPERGER, Fernand, pseud. F. **Baldenne** (1871–1958), French literary historian, born in Saint Dié, was professor of Literature at the Sorbonne, and also taught in the U.S.A. His works include studies of Goethe, Balzac, and 18th-century literature.

BALDI, Bernardino (1553–1617), Italian Renaissance author, born at Urbino. Secretary to various prelates and to the Duke of Urbino, he was abbot of Guastalla, wrote eclogues, a didactic poem on seafaring called *La nautica* (1590), prose dialogues, &c. See Life by Zaccagnini (1908).

BALDINI, Antonio (1889–1962), Italian humorist, born at Rome. *Nostro purgatorio* (1918) recounts his war experiences, but his most characteristic works are *Michelaccio* (1924), *La dolce calamita* (1929), *Amici allo spiedo* (1932). He became editor of the *Nuova Antologia* in 1931.

BALDINUCCI, Filippo, *bal-di-noot'chee* (1624–96), Italian art historian, born at Florence, was entrusted by Cardinal Leopoldo Medici with the arrangement of the Medici collection. He wrote six volumes on Italian artists since Cimabue.

BALDOVINETTI, Alessio (1427–99), Italian painter, one of the leading artists of the early Florentine Renaissance. His frescoes, noted for their landscape backgrounds, are mostly poorly preserved as a result of his experiments in new methods of colour mixing, but he also executed mosaics of great beauty. See study by Kennedy (1938).

BALDUNG, or **Grün, Hans** (*c.* 1476–1545), German painter and engraver, born at Weiersheim near Strasbourg, may have been a pupil of Dürer. His mature works display deliberate exaggeration of late Gothic styles to obtain often morbid quasi-Expressionist effects in the manner of Grünewald, as in *Die Frau und den Tod* (Basle) and *Die Eitelkeit* (Vienna). See monographs by H. Curjel (1923) and O. Fischer (1940).

BALDWIN, kings of Jerusalem:

Baldwin I (1058–1118), youngest brother of Godfrey de Bouillon (q.v.), with whom he took part in the first Crusade.

Baldwin II (d. 1131), cousin of Baldwin I, reigned from 1118 to his death.

Baldwin III (1129–62), succeeded his father, Foulques of Anjou, successor of Baldwin II, and was himself succeeded by his brother Amalric, who died in 1174.

Baldwin IV (1161–85), ' the Leper ', son and successor of Amalric, nephew of Baldwin III, reigned till 1185.

Baldwin V (1178–86), nephew of Baldwin IV, was crowned as a young child in 1185 when Baldwin IV abdicated in his favour.

BALDWIN, name of two emperors of Constantinople:

Baldwin I (1171–1206), born at Valenciennes, succeeded his parents as Count of Hainault and Flanders in 1195. In 1200 he joined the fourth Crusade, and in 1204 was chosen the first Latin emperor of Constantinople. The Greeks, invoking the aid of the Bulgarians, rose and took Adrianople. Baldwin laid siege to the town, but was defeated and taken prisoner, and died a year after (1206) in captivity.

Baldwin II (1217–73), nephew of Baldwin I, succeeded as emperor in 1228. The Greeks took Constantinople in 1261, and he fled to Italy. So ended the Eastern Roman Empire.

BALDWIN (d. 1190), Archbishop of Canter-

bury, born at Exeter in poor circumstances, became Bishop of Worcester in 1180, and Archbishop of Canterbury in 1184. He crowned Richard Cœur-de-Lion, made a tour of Wales preaching in favour of the Crusades, and himself died on a Crusade.

BALDWIN, (1) James (Arthur), (1924–), American Negro writer, born and brought up in a poor section of Harlem, N.Y. After a variety of jobs he moved to Europe, where he lived (mainly in Paris) for some years. His novels, in which autobiographical elements appear, include *Go Tell it on the Mountain* (1954), *Giovanni's Room* (1957), *Another Country* (1963), and *Tell Me How Long The Train's Been Gone* (1968); other works include collections of essays (*Notes of a Native Son*, 1955; *The Fire Next Time*, 1963) and plays—*The Amen Corner* (1955) and *Blues for Mr Charlie* (1964).

(2) **James Mark** (1861–1934), American psychologist, born at Columbia, S.C., graduated at Princeton (1884). He deserted experimental psychology for evolutional, genetic, and social studies.

(3) **Oliver Ridsdale, 2nd Earl Baldwin of Bewdley** (1899–1958), British Labour politician, son of (5), was imprisoned by the Bolsheviks (1921), was Labour M.P. for Dudley (1929–31) and Paisley (1945–47), and governor of the Leeward Islands (1948–50).

(4) **Robert** (1804–58), premier of Upper Canada 1842–43, was born in Toronto and after a successful legal and political career founded with Lafontaine the Reform party. See study by S. Leacock (1926).

(5) **Stanley, 1st Earl Baldwin of Bewdley** (1867–1947), British Conservative statesman, father of (3), born at Bewdley, educated at Harrow and Trinity College, Cambridge, became vice-chairman of the family iron and steel business. M.P. in 1906, he became president of the Board of Trade (1921), and after taking part in the Washington financial talks (1923) he unexpectedly succeeded Bonar Law as premier. His period of office included the General Strike (1926) and was interrupted by the MacDonald Coalition (1931–35), in which he served as lord president of the Council. He skilfully avoided a party split by his India Act (1935), but the Hoare-Laval pact and the policy of non-intervention in Spain (1936) came to be regarded as betrayals of the League of Nations. His reluctance to re-arm Britain's defences is to be compared with his tact and resolution during the constitutional crisis culminating in Edward VIII's abdication (1937). He had the party politician's sure touch in domestic matters, but was not equal to the ruthless challenge of dictatorships abroad. He resigned and was made an earl in 1937. See Lives by W. Steed (1930), A. Bryant (1937), G. M. Young (1952), and Somervell (1953).

BALE, John (1495–1563), English Protestant ecclesiastic and dramatist, born at Cove, near Dunwich, obtained the Suffolk living of Thorndon, though married and turned Protestant. In 1540 he had to flee to Germany. Recalled by Edward VI, he was made Bishop of Ossory in Leinster. Here 'Bilious Bale' made himself so obnoxious to Catholics that they attacked his house and killed five servants. On Elizabeth's accession he was made a prebendary of Canterbury. His fame rests partly on Latin biographical catalogues of British authors (from Adam and Seth downwards), partly on his plays, which are mere doggerel, though his *King John* links such moralities as his own *John Baptist* with the masterpieces of the Elizabethan stage.

BALEWA, Sir Abubakar Tafawa (1912–66), Nigerian politician, born at Bauchi, the son of a butcher and minor official who later removed to Tafawa Balewa. A member of the Northern People's Congress, he entered the Federal Assembly in 1947, was minister of works (1952), transport (1953) and premier (1957) and was knighted when Nigeria became independent in 1960. A reluctant federalist at first even in his own country, he was assassinated in the military uprising of 1966.

BALFE, Michael William (1808–70), English composer, was born in Dublin. In his ninth year he made his début as a violinist, having begun to compose two years earlier; in 1823 he came to London, and during 1825–26 studied in Italy under Paer, Galli, Federici, and Rossini. In 1826 he wrote the music for a ballet, *La Pérouse*, performed at Milan; and in 1827 he sang in the Italian Opera at Paris with great applause, his voice being a pure rich baritone. In 1833 he returned to England, and in 1846 was appointed conductor of the London Italian Opera. He died at Rowley Abbey, his estate in Hertfordshire. Of his numerous operas, operettas, and other compositions, the most permanently successful has been *The Bohemian Girl* (1843), which though trivial in theme and undistinguished in technique, abounds in melody of the sentimental ballad type. The well-known 'Harp that once through Tara's Halls' is his. See works by Kenney (1875) and Barrett (1882).

BALFOUR, (1) Sir Andrew, 1st Bart. (1630–1694), Scottish physician, born at Denmiln, Fife, studied at St Andrews, London, Blois and Paris and with Sir Robert Sibbald helped to establish a ' physic garden ' near Holyrood House (1676–80), the second oldest botanic garden in Britain and the forerunner of the present Royal Botanic Garden in Edinburgh (1822–24). He was third president (1685) of the Royal College of Physicians of Edinburgh.

(2) Arthur James, 1st Earl of Balfour (1848–1930), British statesman and philosopher, brother of (3), (4), and (5), was born, on his father's side, into an ancient Scottish family and succeeded to the family estate in Haddingtonshire in 1856. His mother was sister of Lord Robert Cecil (q.v.). Educated at Eton and Trinity College, Cambridge, he entered parliament in 1874 as Conservative member for Hertford, and from 1878 to 1880 was private secretary to his uncle, Lord Salisbury, whom he accompanied to the Berlin Congress. In 1879 he published *Defence of Philosophic Doubt*, a plea for intellectual liberty in the face of the encroaching dogmatism of science. For a while an unattached member of Lord Randolph Churchill's ' Fourth Party ', he led off the attack on the ' Kilmainham Treaty ' (1882), negotiated with Lord Hartington the franchise compromise (1884), was returned for East

Manchester (1885), and was appointed president of the Local Government Board (1885), secretary for Scotland (1886), chief secretary for Ireland (1887), and first lord of the Treasury and leader in the Commons (1892–93). His premiership (1902–06) saw the end of the South African war (1905), the Education Act (1905), and the establishment of the Committee of Imperial Defence. He had been president of the British Association (1904). In 1911 he resigned the leadership of the House owing to the constitutional crisis and delivered the Gifford Lectures in 1915 on *Theism and Humanism*. He followed Churchill to the admiralty (1915) and served under Lloyd George as foreign secretary (1916–19). He was responsible for the famous Balfour Declaration (1917), which promised Zionists a national home in Palestine, keenly supported the League of Nations, and as lord president of the Council (1921) was responsible for the controversial note cancelling Allied war debts to America. He resigned in 1922, was created an earl, but served in the same office (1925–29). He had received the O.M. in 1916 and was chancellor of Cambridge University (1919) and president of the British Academy (1921). See Life by his niece, B. Dugdale (1936), and studies by Rayleigh (1930) and Pattison (1933).

(3) Eleanor Mildred. See SIDGWICK (1).

(4) Francis Maitland (1851–82), British embryologist, brother of (2), born at Edinburgh, educated at Harrow and Trinity College, Cambridge, where he became the first professor of Animal Morphology in 1882 after publishing his *Comparative Embryology* in 1880. F.R.S. in 1878, he lost his life on Mont Blanc.

(5) Gerald, 2nd Earl of Balfour (1853–1945), British statesman, brother of (2), was educated at Eton and Trinity College, Cambridge, of which he became a fellow (1878). He was chief secretary for Ireland (1895–96), president of Board of Trade (1900–05), of Local Government Board (1905–06), and succeeded his brother as Earl in 1930.

(6) Jabez Spencer (1843–1916), British financier, born at Leith, first mayor of Croydon (1883), M.P. for Burnley (1889), in 1895 was sentenced to fourteen years hard labour for his infamous Liberator Building Society and other frauds, but was released in 1906.

(7) Sir James (d. 1583), Scottish political intriguer and judge, one of Cardinal Beaton's murderers, was taken prisoner with Knox after the surrender of the castle of St Andrews (1547) and sent to France. Released in 1549, he returned to Scotland and ' served with all parties, deserted all, and yet profited by all '. He was commissioned to compile the *Practicks of Scots Law* by Morton, but how much of it is his is doubtful, because he left it and withdrew to France (1580).

(8) John, of Kinloch (fl. 1675), Scottish conspirator, chiefly responsible for Archbishop Sharp's assassination in 1679. He fought at Drumclog and Bothwell Bridge and is said to have escaped to Holland. Scott in his *Old Mortality* confused him with **John Balfour**, 3rd Lord Balfour of Burleigh, who died in 1688.

BALIOL, *bayl'yol,* an Anglo-Norman family, whose founder, Guido or Guy, held Bailleul, Harcourt, and other fiefs in Normandy, and from Rufus received large possessions in Durham and Northumberland. Bernard, his son, built the fortress of Barnard Castle; and *his* great-grandson, John, about 1263 founded Balliol College, Oxford. He died in 1269, and was survived till 1290 by his widow, Devorgilla, the daughter and co-heiress of Alan, Lord of Galloway, the great-great-granddaughter of David I, and the founder in 1275 of Sweetheart Abbey, Kirkcudbright. Their most distinguished descendants were:

(1) **Edward** (d. 1367), son of (2), in 1332 accompanied by the ' disinherited barons ', who were bent on recovering their forfeited Scottish estates, landed with 3400 followers at Kinghorn in Fife; defeated the Earl of Fife; and at Dupplin Moor in Perthshire, on the night of August 12, surprised and routed 30,000 men under the new regent Mar, who himself was slain, with 13,000 besides. On September 24, he was crowned king of Scotland at Scone. Less than three months after, he was surprised in his camp at Annan by Archibald Douglas, and nearly lost life as well as crown. He died near Doncaster, and with him ended the house of Baliol.

(2) **John de** (1249–1315), nicknamed ' Toom Tabard ' or ' Empty Jacket ' by the Scots, son of the founder of Balliol College, Oxford, who succeeded in his mother's right to the Lordship of Galloway as well as to his father's vast possessions in England and Normandy. On the death of the Maid of Norway in 1290, he became a competitor for the crown of Scotland, and his claim was pronounced superior to that of Robert Bruce, Lord of Annandale. The arbiter was Edward I of England, to whom Baliol swore fealty before and after his coronation at Scone (1292). He was soon made to feel that his sovereignty was merely nominal, and the indignities which he experienced at length roused him to an assertion of his rights as king. In 1295 he resolved to conclude an alliance with France, then at war with England; Edward thereupon invaded Scotland, took Baliol prisoner, and compelled him formally to surrender his crown, July 7, 1296. Baliol was confined for three years at Hertford and in the Tower; in 1302 he was permitted to retire to his estates in Normandy, where he died.

BALL, (1) **John** (d. 1381), a priest who was executed as one of the leaders in the rebellion of Wat Tyler (q.v.).

(2) **John** (1818–89), Irish alpinist, was born in Dublin, was the first president of the Alpine club, author of the *Alpine Guide* (1863–68), was colonial under-secretary (1855–57), and wrote on the botany, &c., of Morocco and South America.

(3) **Sir Robert Stawell** (1840–1913), Irish astronomer, was born in Dublin and studied at Trinity College. Royal astronomer for Ireland in 1874 and Lowndean professor at Cambridge in 1892, he contributed to the theory of screws and published much on astronomy and mechanics. See *Reminiscences and Letters,* ed. by his son (1915).

BALLA, Giacomo (1871–1958), Italian artist, born in Turin. He was largely self-taught, and was the master of the Futurists Boccioni and Severini. He was identified with the Futurist movement until the 'twenties, but later returned to normal representation.

BALLANCHE, Pierre Simon, *bal-lãsh* (1776–1847), French philosopher, was born at Lyons. His works are a strange medley of mysticism, socialism, and the philosophy of history. See his *Life* by Ampère (1848).

BALLANTINE, (1) **James** (1808–77), Scottish artist and poet, born in Edinburgh, was originally a housepainter, but learned drawing under Sir William Allen, and was one of the first to revive the art of glass-painting. Two prose volumes, *The Gaberlunzie's Wallet* (1843) and *Miller of Deanhaugh* (1845), contain some of his best-known songs and ballads.

(2) **William** (1812–86), English lawyer with a large practice, chiefly in criminal cases. He was created a serjeant in 1856. Amongst the famous trials with which he was associated were the Müller murder trial, Tichborne case, and the defence of the Gaekwar of Baroda. See his *Experiences of a Barrister's Life* (1882) and his *Old World and the New* (1884).

BALLANTYNE, (1) **James** (1772–1833) and **John** (1774–1821), Scott's printers, were the sons of a merchant of Kelso, where in 1783 they were both at school with Sir Walter. James was bred for the law, but in 1797 started the Tory *Kelso Mail;* and in 1802, having already printed some ballads for Scott, he produced the first two volumes of the *Border Minstrelsy.* At Scott's suggestion he moved the firm to Edinburgh, and in 1805 Scott became a secret partner in the business, which in 1808 expanded into the printing, publishing, and bookselling firm of John Ballantyne & Co., Scott having one-half share, and each of the brothers one-fourth. ' Aldiborontiphoscophornio ' and ' Rigdum-funnidos ' were Scott's nicknames for pompous James and sporting John. As early as 1813 bankruptcy threatened the firm, and it was hopelessly involved in Constable's ruin (1826). John had died bankrupt five years earlier; and James was employed by the creditors' trustees in editing the *Weekly Journal* and in the literary management of the printing office. See *History of the Ballantyne Press* (Edin. 1871) and D. Carswell, *Sir Walter* (1930).

(2) **Robert Michael** (1825–94), Scottish author of boys' books, was born at Edinburgh, a nephew of (1). He wrote his first stories on his experiences in the backwoods of northern Canada, a visit to Norway, &c. *Coral Island* is his most famous work. See his *Personal Recollections* (1893). His elder brother **James Robert Ballantyne** (1813–64), born at Kelso, was from 1845 to 1861 principal of the Sanskrit college at Benares.

BALLARD, John (d. 1586), a Jesuit executed for his connection with Babington's conspiracy.

BALLIN, Albert (1857–1918), German-Jewish shipping magnate, born in Hamburg, became a director-general of the Hamburg-America Line in 1900, a close adviser of the Kaiser, and improved Germany's mercantile marine.

BALLOU, Hosea (1771–1852), the chief founder of the Universalist Church, originally a Baptist minister, was born at Richmond, New Hampshire.

BALMER, Johann Jakob (1825–98), Swiss physicist, born at Lausen, derived a formula for frequencies of hydrogen lines in the visible spectrum. The Balmer series is the atomic spectrum of hydrogen in the visible and near ultraviolet regions of the spectrum.

BALMERINO, Arthur Elphinstone, 6th Baron (1688–1746), Scottish Jacobite, was beheaded on Tower Hill for his share in the '45. See J. Campbell's History of Balmerino (Edin. 1867).

BALMES, Jaime Luciano, bal'mays (1810–1848), Spanish writer, ecclesiastic and philosopher, born at Vich in Catalonia. He attempted to revive a Spanish school of philosophy.

BALMONT, Konstantin Dmitryevitch (1867–1943), Russian poet, translator and essayist, born in Gumische, Vladimir province, one of the greatest of the Russian symbolists. Balmont's work was coloured by the wide travelling he did during his periodic exiles, which added a vein of exoticism to his work.

BALNAVES, Henry, bal-nav'is (1512?–79), Scottish Reformer, was born at Kirkcaldy, and in 1538 was made a lord of session by James V. In 1543 the regent Arran appointed him secretary of state. Shortly after, however, he suffered a six-months' imprisonment in Blackness Castle on account of his Protestantism; and in 1546, like Knox, he joined Beaton's murderers in the castle of St Andrews. When the castle was captured by the French (1547), Balnaves, with Knox and others, was sent to Rouen. While in prison there, he wrote a treatise on Justification, which, with notes and a preface by Knox, was published in 1584 as The Confession of Faith. In 1556 he was allowed to return to Scotland and took an active part on the side of the Lords of the Congregation.

BALTIMORE, George Calvert, 1st Baron (c. 1580–1632), English statesman, born at Kipling, Yorks., entered parliament in 1609, was knighted in 1617, and in 1619 became secretary of state. In 1625 he declared himself a Catholic, and resigning office, was created Baron Baltimore in the Irish peerage, and retired to his Irish estates. As early as 1621 he had dispatched colonists to a small settlement in Newfoundland, and in 1627 he visited the place. Next spring he returned with his family, and stayed till the autumn of 1629. The severe winter induced him to sail southward in search of a more genial country; but his attempts to settle in Virginia led to disputes, and he returned home to obtain a fresh charter. He died before the grant was made final and the patent passed to his son, Cecil, 2nd Baron (c. 1605–75). The territory was called, in honour of Charles I's queen, Maryland, of which Leonard, Cecil's younger brother, became first governor (1634–47). See Life by Neill (Balt. 1869).

BALY, Edward Charles Cyril (1871–1948), English chemist, a professor of Chemistry at Liverpool, showed how a mixture of carbon dioxide, water, and ammonia can yield small quantities of organic substances under the influence of light. Elected F.R.S. in 1909.

BALZAC, (1) Honoré de (1799–1850), French novelist, born at Tours, May 20, was educated at the Collège de Vendôme, and studied law at the Sorbonne. His father wished him to become a notary, but he left Tours in 1819 to seek his fortune as an author in Paris. From 1819 to 1830 he led a life of frequent privation and incessant industry, producing stories which neither found nor deserved to find readers, and incurring—mainly through unlucky business speculations—a heavy burden of debt, which harassed him to the end of his career. He first tasted success with Les Derniers Chouans (1829), which was followed in the same year by Peau de chagrin. After writing several other novels, he formed the design of presenting in the Comédie humaine a complete picture of modern civilization. In attempting to carry out this impossible design, he produced what is almost in itself a literature. The stories composing the Comédie humaine are classified as ' Scenes de la vie privée, de la vie Parisienne, de la vie politique, de la vie militaire ', &c. Among the masterpieces which form part of Balzac's vast scheme may be mentioned Le Père Goriot, Les Illusions perdues, Les Paysans, Les Marana, La Femme de trente ans, and Eugénie Grandet, in which observation—in meticulous detail—and imagination are the main features. The Contes drolatiques (1833) stand by themselves—a series of Rabelaisian stories. Balzac's industry was phenomenal. He worked regularly for fifteen and even eighteen hours a day, and wrote eighty-five novels in twenty years. His work did not bring him wealth; his yearly income rarely exceeded 12,000 francs. During his later years he lived principally in his villa at Sèvres. In 1849, when his health had broken down, he travelled to Poland to visit Madame Hanska, a rich Polish lady, with whom he had corresponded for more than fifteen years. In 1850 she became his wife, and three months later, on August 18, Balzac died at Paris. See studies by A. Le Breton (1905), A. Bellesort (1924), and S. Zweig (trans. 1947).

(2) Jean Louis Guez de (1594–1654), French author, born at Balzac near Angoulême. After studying in Paris, at Leyden, and visiting Rome, he became historiographer royal and lived in Paris, before retiring to his estates. Balzac made his reputation by his Lettres (1624), &c., by which he tried to popularize the Latin authors, creating a rhythmic and balanced style, capable of expressing abstractions. See works by Vogler (1906) and Desclareuil (1908).

BAMFORD, Samuel (1788–1872), English reformer, born at Middleton, Lancs., was weaver, journalist, and messenger in turn and imprisoned for taking part in the 'Manchester massacre ' (1819). He wrote Passages in the Life of a Radical (1843) and Early Days (1849).

BAMPTON, John (c. 1690–1751), a Salisbury prebendary who founded the Oxford Bampton Lectures.

BANCROFT, (1) George (1800–91), American historian and statesman, born at Worcester, Massachusetts, studied divinity at Harvard, history at Göttingen. He lectured in Greek at Harvard for a while, did some preaching and established a school using advanced European methods. He wrote both poetry and prose and in 1834 published his *History of the United States*. A democrat, he was secretary to the navy (1845–46) and established the Naval academy at Annapolis. He was U.S. minister in Britain (1846–49) and Germany (1876–74). See *Life and Letters* by Howe (1908).

(2) **Hubert Howe** (1832–1918), American historian, born in Ohio, settled in San Francisco in 1852, started a bookshop, and amassed a fortune. He collected and transferred to the University of California (1905) 60,000 volumes, mainly on American history and ethnography, and published *The Native Races of the Pacific States* (1875–76), &c. See his autobiographical *Literary Industries* (1891) and *Retrospection* (1912).

(3) **Richard** (1544–1610), Archbishop of Canterbury, was born at Farnworth, Lancashire. Sent to Cambridge, he graduated in 1567, and after a series of preferments was consecrated Bishop of London in 1597. He attended Elizabeth during her last illness, and took the lead at the Hampton Court Conference. He succeeded Whitgift as archbishop in 1604. He strove to make the Roman Catholics faithful to the crown by cherishing the secular clergy as against the Jesuits, and assisted in re-establishing Scottish episcopacy.

(4) **Sir Squire** (1841–1926), English actor-manager, born in London, made his début at Birmingham (1861) and in London (1865). In 1867 he married Miss Marie Wilton (1840–1921), a distinguished actress born at Doncaster. From 1865 to January 1880 the Prince of Wales's Theatre witnessed their triumphs in Robertson's comedies, in *School for Scandal, Masks and Faces*, &c., and until 1885 they were successful lessees of the Haymarket. In 1897 he was knighted. See his *The Bancrofts: Recollections of Sixty Years* (1909) and *Empty Chairs* (1925).

BANDA, Hastings Kamuzu (?1905–), Malawi politician, achieved an education by self-help in South Africa, graduating in philosophy and in medicine in the U.S.A. and L.R.C.P. at Edinburgh (1941). His opposition to the Central African Federation caused him to give up his successful London practice (1955) and return via Ghana to Nyasaland (1958). Leader of the Malawi African Congress, he was gaoled in 1959, became minister of national resources (1961), prime minister (1963), and president of the Malawi (formerly Nyasaland) republic (1966).

BANDARANAIKE, Solomon West Ridgeway Dias, *ban-da-ra-nī'kē* (1899–1959), Ceylonese statesman, born at Colombo, was educated at St Thomas' College there and at Christ Church, Oxford. Called to the bar in 1925, he returned home to a troubled situation than urged him into the Ceylon National Congress, of which, after a series of municipal and state appointments, he became president. He established the Sinhalese Maha Sabha (Great Assembly) as a foil to growing Tamil power, helped to found the United National Party, which formed the government of Ceylon from 1948 to 1956, and as leader of the House

in Ceylon's first parliament and minister of health he brought Ceylon the distinction of being the first Asian country to rid itself of malaria. In 1951 he resigned from the Government and organized the Sri Lanka Freedom Party, which returned him to parliament as leader of the opposition and in 1956 as prime minister on a policy of nationalization and neutralism. See his *The Spinning Wheel and the Paddy Field*. He was assassinated by a Buddhist monk. His wife, **Sirimavo** (1916–), was prime minister from 1960 to 1965.

BANDEL, Ernst von (1800–76), German sculptor, born at Ansbach, took forty years to complete his colossal bronze statue of Arminius, 84 feet high, on the Grotenberg near Detmold. See Life by H. Schmidt (Han. 1892).

BANDELLO, Matteo (*c.* 1480–1562), Italian writer of *novelle* or tales, was born at Castelnuovo in Piedmont. For a while a Dominican, he was driven from Milan by the Spaniards after the battle of Pavia (1525), and settling in France, was in 1550 made Bishop of Agen. His 214 tales (1554–73) gave themes to Shakespeare, Massinger, &c., and are valuable for the social history of the period. See Life by D. Morellini (1900).

BANDIERA, Attilio, *ban-dee-ay'ra* (1817–44), and **Emilio** (1819–44), Italian revolutionaries, born in Venice, were lieutenants in the Austrian navy, where their father (1785–1847) was an admiral. Having attempted a rising in favour of Italian independence, they were shot at Cosenza.

BANDINELLI, Baccio (1493–1560), Florentine sculptor, was born and died at Florence, the son of a famous goldsmith. A rival of Michelangelo, he executed the statues of Hercules and Cacus outside the Palazzo Vecchio, *Adam and Eve* (National Museum, Florence), and the exquisite bas-reliefs in the cathedral choir.

BANÉR, Johan (1598–1641), a Swedish general of Gustavus Adolphus, gained victories at Wittstock (1636) and Chemnitz (1639) in the Thirty Years' War.

BANERJEA, Sir Surendrenath, *ban'ėr-jee* (1848–1925), Indian politician and journalist, born at Calcutta, son of a doctor. A fervent nationalist, he founded the Calcutta Indian Association in 1876 and was editor of *The Bengali* newspaper from 1879 to 1921. He was one of the initiators of the Indian National Congress and was twice returned to the Central Legislature. He welcomed the Montagu-Chelmsford reforms for the government of India, but subsequently broke with Congress because of its extremism. He accepted a knighthood in 1921. See his autobiography, *A Nation in the Making*.

BANERJEE, Satyendranath (1897–), Indian artist, born in West Bengal, domiciled in Calcutta. Talented as a child, he became a protégé of Rabindranath Tagore, and a teacher at the Calcutta College of Arts. Examples of his work are hung in art galleries throughout India and in private collections.

BANG, (1) Bernhard (1848–1932), Danish veterinary surgeon, was born at Sorö in Zeeland and studied medicine. He later became interested in the healing of animals, and in 1880 was appointed professor of Veterinary Surgery at Copenhagen, where he investigated bacillary diseases, mainly of cattle. He is known particularly for his work on bovine tuberculosis, known as Bang's disease, which has made the control of this disease possible.

(2) **Hermann Joachim** (1857–1912), Danish novelist, born in Adserballe, Isle of Als. Bang was an impressionistic writer whose work makes difficult reading, being full of affectation and lacking in any powerful characterization. Among his novels are *Stille Eksistenser* (1886) and *De uden Fædreland* (1906). See P. A. Rosenberg, *Hermann Bang* (1912).

BANIM, John (1798–1842), and **Michael** (1796–1874), Irish novelist brothers, were born at Kilkenny. John studied art at Dublin and became a miniature painter; Michael, a postmaster. Having achieved some success as a playwright when a tragedy was produced at Covent Garden in 1821, John, with the collaboration of Michael, published such novels as the *Tales of the O'Hara Family* (1826), characterized by a faithful portrayal of humble Irish folk. John's illness and poverty were alleviated by a state pension. See P. J. Murray, *Life of John Banim* (1857).

BANKES, Lady Mary (d. 1661), English Royalist, defender of Corfe Castle in 1643 and 1646 against the Parliamentarians, who on the second occasion captured it through treachery. See works by G. Bankes (1853) and T. Bond (1884).

BANKHEAD, Tallulah (1903–68), American actress, born in Huntsville, Ala., educated in New York and Washington, made her stage début in 1918 and appeared in many plays and films. She won Critic Awards for her two most famous stage rôles, Regina in *The Little Foxes* (1939) and Sabina in *The Skin of Our Teeth* (1942). Her most outstanding film portrayal was in *Lifeboat* (1944), and she also performed on radio and television.

BANKS, (1) Isabella, *née* Varley (1821–72), English novelist, was born at Manchester, and in 1846 married George Linnaeus Banks (1821–81), poet, orator, and journalist. The most popular of her numerous novels was *The Manchester Man* (1872).

(2) **Sir Joseph** (1744–1820), English botanist, born in London, and educated at Harrow, Eton, and Christ Church College, Oxford, in 1766 made a voyage to Newfoundland, collecting plants. In 1768–71 accompanied Cook's expedition round the world in a vessel equipped at his own expense (*Journal*, ed. by Hooker, 1896, and by Beaglehole, 1963). In 1772 he visited the Hebrides and Iceland, and made known the wonders of Staffa. In 1778 he was elected president of the Royal Society, an office which he held for 41 years; in 1781 he was created a baronet, and in 1802 a member of the French Institute. Banks founded the African Association; and the colony of New South Wales owed its origin mainly to him. Through him the bread-fruit was transferred from Tahiti to the West Indies, the mango from Bengal, and many fruits of Ceylon and Persia. See works by Maiden (1909) and Smith (1911).

(3) **Nathaniel Prentiss** (1816–94), American politician and soldier, was a factory worker, but studied law, and became successively a member of the state and national legislatures. He was speaker of congress in 1856, and in 1857, 1859, and 1861 was elected governor of his native state, Massachusetts. In the Civil War he commanded on the Potomac, and received the thanks of congress for the capture of Fort Hudson (1863). He was a member of congress till 1873.

(4) **Thomas** (1735–1805), English sculptor, born at Lambeth, was apprenticed to an ornament carver, and married wealth. From 1772 to 1779 he lived in Rome and visited Russia in 1781. His work, in the neoclassical manner, is unequal, the best known being his monuments to Captains Burgess and Westcott in St Paul's. See Life by Bell (1938).

BANNATYNE, George (1545–1608), native of Forfarshire and an Edinburgh burgess, whose MS., compiled during the plague of 1568, preserved much of the poetry of the 15th and 16th centuries. The Bannatyne Club was founded in 1823.

BANNISTER, (1) John (1760–1836), English comedian, was born at Deptford, the son of the actor and vocalist, Charles Bannister (c. 1738–1804).

(2) **Roger Gilbert** (1929–), English athlete, born at Harrow, educated at University College School, Exeter and Merton Colleges, Oxford, and St Mary's Hospital School, London. He won the Oxford-Cambridge Mile Event (1947–50), ran in the Olympic Games (1952), and in 1954 captured the European 1500 metres record. At Oxford, on May 6, 1954, he was the first man to run the mile in under four minutes (3 minutes 59·4 seconds). See his *First Four Minutes* (1955).

BANTING, (1) Sir Frederick Grant (1891–1941), Canadian physiologist, born at Alliston, Ontario, studied at Toronto, became professor there in 1923 and with Professor J. J. R. Macleod discovered insulin, for which they were jointly awarded the Nobel prize that year. He was killed in an aeroplane accident on a mission connected with aviation medicine.

(2) **William** (1797–1878), a London undertaker, who in 1863 published a pamphlet describing how he had reduced his obesity, hence the term ' banting ' for slimming.

BANTOCK, Sir Granville (1868–1946), English composer, was born in London. He was professor of Music at Birmingham University (1908–34), being knighted in 1930. His inspiration was often drawn from oriental life, as in his *Omar Khayyám*. His works include the choral work *Atlanta in Calydon* and *Hebridean Symphony*.

BANVILLE, Théodore Faullin de, *bã-veel* (1823–91), French poet and dramatist, was born at Moulins. From *Les Cariatides* (1841) to *Dans la fournaise* (1892), he showed himself one of the most musical of lyrists, one of the wittiest of parodists. The title ' roi des rimes ' was given him from his ingenuity in handling the most difficult forms of verse—the mediaeval ballades and rondels. His *Gringoire* (1866) holds an established place in French repertory. See his *Souvenirs* (1882), studies by Baudelaire (1861) and Mallarmé (1897), whom he influenced greatly.

BAO DAI, *bow dī* (1913–), Indo-Chinese ruler, born in Annam, was educated in Paris. After succeeding his father, the Emperor Khai Dai of Annam, in 1925, he ascended the throne in 1932. He collaborated with the Japanese during World War II and after it found temporary favour with Ho Chi-minh. He abdicated in 1945, but returned to Saigon in 1949, having renounced his hereditary title, as Chief of the State of Vietnam within the French Union. In 1955 he was deposed and South Vietnam became a republic.

BÄR, Karl E. von. See BAER.

BARAGUAY D'HILLIERS, Louis, *ba-ra-gay'deel-yay'* (1764–1813), French general, commanded Napoleon's armies in Italy, Egypt, and Spain. His son Achille (1795–1878), also a general, was a marshal of France (1854).

BÁRÁNY, Robert, *bah'rah-ny'* (1876–1936), Austrian physician, born in Vienna, investigated the balancing apparatus in the inner ear and was awarded the Nobel prize in 1914.

BARATYNSKI, Evgeny Abramovich, *-tin'-* (1800–44), Russian lyric poet, a soldier in early life, wrote melancholy, tender, but pessimistic verse, including *The Gypsy Girl*, *The Ball*, and *The Steamboat*.

BARBARA, St, suffered martyrdom at Nicomedia, in Bithynia, in 240 or 306. It is said that her own father, a fanatical heathen, beheaded her for her conversion to Christianity and was immediately struck dead by lightning. She is the patron saint of artillery-men.

BARBAROSSA, (1). See FREDERICK I.

(2) Horuk and Khair-ed-din, two brothers, renegade Greeks, natives of Mitylene, who as Turkish corsairs were the terror of the Mediterranean. The former was captured and beheaded in 1518; the latter, with thousands of captives, returned in triumph to Constantinople, where he died July 4, 1546. See S. L. Poole's *Barbary Corsairs* (1890).

BARBAROUX, Charles Jean Marie, *- roo* (1767–94), French revolutionary, one of the greatest of the Girondists, born at Marseilles, was guillotined at Bordeaux.

BARBAULD, Anna Letitia, *née* Aikin, *-bawld* (1743–1825), minor English author, was born at Kibworth-Harcourt, Leicestershire. Encouraged by the success of her *Poems* (1773), she in the same year, conjointly with her brother, John Aikin (q.v.), published *Miscellaneous Pieces in Prose*. She married a dissenting minister, the Rev. Rochemont Barbauld, in 1774 and during the next ten years published her best work, including *Early Lessons for Children*. Again with her brother she began the well-known series *Evenings at Home* in 1792. See Lives by Le Breton (1874) and Grace Ellis (U.S. 1874); also B. Rodgers, *Georgian Chronicle* (1959).

BARBER, Samuel (1910–), American composer, born at West Chester, Penn., studied at the Curtis Institute, Philadelphia, and carried off two Pulitzer travelling scholarships (1935, 1936) as well as the American *Prix de Rome*. His early music, which includes the setting for voice and string quartet of Matthew Arnold's *Dover Beach* (1931), the overture to *The School for Scandal* (1931), the first symphony (1936) and the well-known *Adagio for Strings*

(an arrangement of the slow movement of his string quartet op. 11; 1936) is in the traditional neo-Romantic vein, but after 1939–40 a more individual idiom began to colour his compositions, with more emphasis on chromaticism and dissonance and an occasional excursion into atonality, as in the piano sonata of 1949. Among the works of this later period are the *Capricorn Concerto* (1944), the ballet *Medea* (1946), and several vocal compositions including *Nuvoletta* (1947) from Joyce's *Finnegans Wake* and *Hermit Songs* (1952–53). His first full-length opera *Vanessa* was performed at the Salzburg Festival (1958). See Life by Broder (N.Y. 1954).

BARBERINI, *bar-ber-ee'nee*, a Tuscan family that acquired wealth by trade in the 16th century, and rose to the front rank among the Roman nobility on the elevation of Maffeo Barberini as Urban VIII to the papal chair in 1623. His brother Antonio became cardinal; Carlo, general of the papal troops; while to a son of the latter, Taddeo, was given the principality of Palestrina. Francesco (1597–1679), brother of Taddeo, cardinal and vice-chancellor, founded the Barberini Library; another brother, Antonio (1608–71), was cardinal and high chamberlain under Urban VIII. The power and ambition of the Barberini excited the jealousy of the neighbouring princes, and led to the defeat of the papal troops by the Duke of Parma (1641–1644). The Barberini then fled to France, but returned in 1652.

BARBEY D'AUREVILLY, Jules, *bar-bay dor-vee-yee* (1808–89), French Romantic writer, born at St Sauveur-le-Vicomte, was extreme in his rejection of 18th-century values. His best-known novels were *La Vieille maîtresse* (1851) and *L'Ensorcelée* (1854), and he also published poetry and literary criticism. See study by H. Bordeaux (1925).

BARBIER, *barb-yay*, (1) Henri Auguste (1805–1882), French poet, born in Paris, satirized prominent social types in French life after the July revolution. See Life by Philon (1905).

(2) Paul Jules (1825–1901), French dramatist, born in Paris, wrote the libretto for Offenbach's *Tales of Hoffman*.

BARBIROLLI, Sir John, *bahr-bee-rol'ee* (1899–1970), British violoncellist and conductor, was born in London of Franco-Italian origin. He served in World War I, played in several leading string quartets (1920–24), succeeded Toscanini (q.v.) as conductor of the New York Philharmonic (1937), and returned to England as permanent conductor (1943–58) of the Hallé Orchestra which, under his direction and with his promotion of the works of modern composers, regained its place among the world's finest. He married Evelyn Rothwell (b. 1911), the oboist, in 1939. Knighted in 1949, he was awarded the Gold Medal of the Royal Philharmonic Society in 1950 and given the Freedom of Manchester in 1958, when he became Hallé's principal instead of permanent conductor. He retired from the conductorship in 1968, and was created C.H. in 1969. See Life by Reid (1971).

BARBOU, a French family of printers, whose founder, Jean Barbou of Lyons, issued in 1539 the beautiful edition of the works of

Clement Marot. His son **Hugues** moved to Limoges, where his edition of *Cicero's Letters to Atticus* appeared in 1580. **Joseph Gérard** settled in Paris, and continued in 1755 the series of Latin duodecimo classics—rivals to the earlier Elzevirs—which had been begun in 1743 by Coustelier. The House continued until 1824. See P. Ducourtieux (1896).

BARBOUR, John (c. 1316–96), the father of Scottish poetry and history; paid several visits to England and France; and was Archdeacon of Aberdeen from 1357, or earlier, till his death. His national epic, *The Brus*, first printed at Edinburgh in 1571, is a narrative poem in octosyllabic couplets, on the life and deeds of King Robert the Bruce (q.v.), having as its climax the Battle of Bannockburn, and preserving many oral traditions. To him some have ascribed *Legends of the Saints*, fragments of a Troy book, and a translation of the French *Alexander* romance. See G. Neilson's *John Barbour, Poet and Translator* (1900).

BARBUSSE, Henri, bar-büs' (1873–1935), French novelist, was born of an English mother at Asnières. A volunteer, he fought in World War I, which inspired his masterpiece, *Le Feu* (1916). A powerful realism is accompanied by a deep feeling for all human suffering. Other works include *Le Couteau entre les dents* (1921) and *Le Judas de Jésus* (1927). A Communist sympathizer, he died in Moscow.

BARCLAY, (1) **Alexander** (1475?–1552), Scottish poet and author, was born most probably in Scotland, may have studied at universities in England, France, and Italy, and in 1508 was chaplain of Ottery St Mary, Devon. Perhaps about 1511 he became a monk of the Benedictine monastery of Ely; later he assumed the Franciscan habit; and he died at Croydon. His famous poem, *The Shyp of Folys of the Worlde* (1509), is partly a translation and partly an imitation of the German *Narrenschiff* by Sebastian Brant (q.v.). He also published *Egloges* (Eclogues), a translation of Sallust's *Jugurthine War,* &c.

(2) **Sir George,** the contriver of the Assassination Plot (1696) against William III.

(3) **John** (1582–1621), Scottish neo-Latin writer, the son of a Scots father and a French mother, was born at Pont-à-Mousson in Lorraine, lived in London and Rome and wrote, mostly in Latin, politico-satirical novels including *Euphormio* (1603), directed against the Jesuits, and *Argenis* (1621) on allegory. See Life by Dupond (1875).

(4) **John** (1734–98), a Scottish Presbyterian minister, who in 1773 founded the sect of the Bereans.

(5) **John** (1758–1826), Scottish anatomist, born in Perthshire, was mainly instrumental in founding the Dick Veterinary College in Edinburgh. The Barcleian museum of the Edinburgh College of Surgeons was founded from his anatomical collection.

(6) **Robert** (1648–90), Scottish Quaker Apologist, was born at Gordonstown. His father, Col. David Barclay (1610–86), had served under Gustavus Adolphus, and in 1666 became a convert to Quakerism. Robert was educated at the Scots College at Paris, of which his uncle was rector, and withstood every temptation to embrace Catholicism. He returned to Scotland in 1664, and in 1667 joined the Society of Friends. He married a Quakeress in 1670, and began publishing tracts. In 1672 he startled Aberdeen by walking through its streets in sackcloth and ashes. He suffered much persecution and was frequently imprisoned, but at last found a protector in the Duke of York, afterwards James II. He made several journeys into Holland and Germany, the last in company with William Penn and George Fox. He became one of the proprietors of East New Jersey in 1682, and was appointed its nominal governor. His collected works, *Truth Triumphant* (1692), reveal closely-reasoned, scholarly arguments endeavouring to harmonize Quakerism with the great religious conceptions of his day. See Life by M. C. Cadbury (1912).

(7) **Robert** (1843–1913), English banker, under whom in 1896 the merger of twenty banks took place to form Barclay and Company Limited. In 1917 the name was changed to Barclay's Bank Limited. Robert was descended from James (fl. 1736), who was admitted into partnership with his brother-in-law Joseph Freame, a goldsmith who had set up business in Lombard Street in 1728.

BARCLAY-ALLARDICE, Robert, known as **Captain Barclay** (1779–1854), Scottish soldier and sportsman, succeeded to the estate of Urie, near Stonehaven, in 1797. He entered the army (1805), and served in the Walcheren expedition (1809), but afterwards devoted himself to agriculture, cattle-breeding, and the claiming of earldoms (Airth, Strathearn, and Menteith). His great feat of walking 1000 miles in 1000 consecutive hours took place at Newmarket in June to July 1809, and he is also remembered as the sponsor and trainer of Tom Cribb (q.v.) in his rise to pugilistic stardom.

BARCLAY DE TOLLY, Michael, Prince (1761–1818), Russian soldier, descended from the same Scottish family as Barclay (1) and (5), born at Luhde-Grosshof, Livonia, entered a Russian regiment, where he gained rapid promotion. He commanded Bennigsen's advance guard at Pultusk in 1806 and lost an arm at Eylau (1807). In the war against Finland he defeated the Swedes and forced a surrender by crossing the frozen Gulf of Bothnia in strength. The Emperor Alexander appointed him minister of war in 1810. Forced to give battle to Napoleon at Smolensk (1812), he was defeated and was superseded by Kutusov. He was again promoted commander-in-chief after the battle of Bautzen (1813) and in that capacity served at Dresden and Leipzig (1813) and in France. In 1815 he was made a prince and a field-marshal. He died at Imsterburg, Prussia. Statues were erected at St Petersburg and Dorpat.

BAR COCHBA, Simon, the leader of the Jews in their great but fruitless insurrection against the Emperor Hadrian, from A.D. 130 to 135.

BARCROFT, Sir Joseph (1872–1947), Irish physiologist, born at Newry, Co. Down, a professor of Physiology at Cambridge and director of animal physiology for the Agricultural Research Council. He devised an apparatus for blood-gas analysis, studied the oxygen-carrying function of haemoglobin, and led an expedition to the Andes to study acclimatization. A F.R.S. in 1910, he was awarded the Copley medal in 1944. See *Life* by Franklin (1953).

BARDESANES, *bar-de-sah'neez,* properly **Bar-Daisan** (154–222), a Syrian, the 'last of the Gnostics', was born at Edessa. Life by Hilgenfeld (Leip. 1864) and study by F. Haase (1910).

BAREBONE, or **Barbon, Praise-God** (*c.* 1596–1679), an Anabaptist leather merchant of London, famous solely for having given nickname to Cromwell's 'Little Parliament' of 1653, of which he was one of the 139 members.

BARENTZ, or **Barents, William** (d. 1597), Dutch navigator, was pilot to several Dutch expeditions in search of the Northeast passage, and died off Novaya Zemlya. Captain Carlsen found his winter quarters undisturbed in 1871, after 274 years, and in 1875 part of his journal was recovered by another explorer. See Van Campen's *Barents' Relics* (1877).

BARÈRE DE VIEUZAC, Bertrand, *bar-ayr de vyœ-zak* (1755–1841), French revolutionist and regicide, the 'Anacreon of the guillotine', born at Tarbes who, originally a monarchist, went over to Robespierre's camp. See his lying *Mémoires* (1842; trans. 1897), and Lives by Launay (1929) and Gershoy (1962).

BARETTI, Giuseppe Marc Antonio, *ba-ret'tee* (1719–89), Italian critic, born at Turin, in 1751 established himself as a teacher of Italian in London. He revisited the Continent (1760–66), where he published a readable book of travels, and in Venice started the *Frusta Letteraria,* or 'literary scourge', in which he criticized many Italian literary fashions. In 1769 he stabbed a Haymarket bully in self-defence, and was tried for murder, but acquitted—Dr Johnson, Burke, and Garrick testifying to his character. He died in 1789. His thirty-six works included an Italian and English Dictionary (1760) and a pamphlet in French defending Shakespeare against Voltaire's criticisms. See study by A. Devalle (1932).

BARHAM, (1) **Francis Foster** (1808–71), founder of a new mystic religion called 'Alism', was born near Penzance. See Memorial by Sir I. Pitman (1873).

(2) **Richard Harris** (1788–1845), English humorist, was born at Canterbury. In 1795 he succeeded to the manor of Tappington, and in 1802 he met with an almost fatal coach accident while on his way to St Paul's School, an accident that partially crippled his right arm for life. He entered Brasenose College, Oxford (1807), was ordained (1813), and in 1821 received a minor canonry of St Paul's Cathedral. After unsuccessful attempts at novel writing, in 1837 he began his series of burlesque metrical tales under the pen-name of Thomas Ingoldsby, which, collected under the title of *Ingoldsby Legends* (1840), at once became popular for their droll humour, fine irony and esoteric learning. His lyrics were published in 1881. See *Life and Letters* (1880) by his son.

BAR-HEBRAEUS. See ABULFARAJ.

BARIATINSKI, Alexander Ivanovich, Prince, *bar-yat'yin-skee* (1814–79), a Russian field-marshal, who distinguished himself against the famous Shamyl (q.v.).

BARING, a great financial and commercial house established in London in 1770 by the two sons of **John Baring** (1697–1748), a German cloth manufacturer, who in 1717 started a small business at Larkbear, near Honiton, Devon. These two sons were **John** (1730–1816) and **Francis** (1740–1810), who was created a baronet by Pitt in 1793, and who at the time of his death had amassed a fortune of nearly seven millions. See Hidy, *The House of Baring* (1949).

(1) **Alexander, 1st Baron Ashburton** (1774–1848), second son of Francis (see family entry), was for several years engaged in the United States in the service of the great London mercantile house established by his father. In 1810 he succeeded him as head of Baring Brothers & Co., having four years before been elected member for Taunton. He represented that place, Callington, and Thetford in the Liberal interest till 1832, and in 1833 was returned for North Essex as a moderate Conservative. In Peel's brief administration (1834–35) he was president of the Board of Trade, and was created Baron Ashburton in 1835. In 1842, as special ambassador to the United States, he concluded the Washington or Ashburton Treaty, defining the frontier line between Maine and Canada. He opposed free trade, but strongly supported the penny postage system when it was proposed in 1837.

(2) **Charles Thomas** (1807–79), fourth son of (6), Bishop of Durham, was a strong Evangelical, noted for his piety and personal kindness.

(3) **Sir Evelyn, Baron Howick of Glendale** (1903–), British administrator, educated at Winchester and Oxford, entered the Indian Civil Service in 1926. In 1942 he became governor of Southern Rhodesia and from 1944 to 1951 was U.K. high commissioner and governor of the High Commission territories of Bechuanaland, Basutoland, and Swaziland. In 1952 he became governor of Kenya, quelling by 1956 the Mau-Mau rebellion. He retired in 1959 and was raised to the peerage in 1960.

(4) **Sir Francis Thornhill, 1st Baron Northbrook** (1796–1866), eldest son of (6), was educated at Oxford, where in 1817 he took a double first. He was M.P. for Portsmouth from 1826 to 1865. Under successive Whig governments he was lord of the Treasury, secretary to the Treasury, chancellor of the Exchequer, and first lord of the Admiralty.

(5) **Maurice** (1874–1946), fourth son of Edward Charles Baring (Baron Revelstoke), educated at Eton and Trinity, Cambridge, held diplomatic posts, was a war correspondent, air officer, author of short stories, poems, novels, and books on Russia.

(6) **Sir Thomas** (1772–1848), eldest son of Francis (see family entry), father of (2), (4) and (7), was chiefly remarkable as a patron of art.

(7) **Thomas** (1799–1873), a son of (6), devoted himself early to commercial pursuits,

picture collecting, and politics, becoming M.P. for Huntingdon (1844–73).

(8) **Thomas George, 2nd Baron Northbrook** (1826–1904), son of (4), was successively a lord of the Admiralty, under-secretary of state for India, under-secretary for war, governor-general of India (1872–76), first lord of the Admiralty (1880–85), and was created an earl in 1876.

(9) **William Bingham, 2nd Baron Ashburton** (1799–1864), son of (1), is chiefly remembered through his first wife, who made their house a meeting place of politicians and men of letters, among them Thackeray and Carlyle.

BARING-GOULD, Sabine,-*gold*(1834–1924), English author and Anglican clergyman, born at Exeter, of an old Devon family, wrote novels, topographical, mythological, theological studies, and hymns, among them ' Onward, Christian Soldiers '.

BARKE, James (1905–58), Scottish novelist, born at Kincardine-on-Forth. Starting out as an engineer, he soon gravitated to writing novels. He is chiefly remarkable for his devoted research on the life of Robert Burns, resulting in a five-volume cycle of novels (1946–54), an edition of *Poems and Songs of Robert Burns* (1955) and the posthumous *Bonnie Jean*, about Burns and Jean Armour.

BARKER, (1) Harley Granville-. See GRAN-VILLE-BARKER, HARLEY.

(2) **Robert** (1739–1806), Irish portrait painter, born at Kells, who in 1788 exhibited the earliest known panorama of Edinburgh, where he resided.

(3) **Thomas, of Bath** (1769–1847), English painter of rural and other scenes, was born near Pontypool, and died at Bath. His eldest son, **Thomas Jones Barker** (1815–82), was born at Bath, and died in London. A painter of battle scenes, he has been styled the ' English Horace Vernet '.

BARKHAUSEN, Heinrich, *bahrk'how-sen* (1881–1956), German physicist, born in Bremen. In 1911 he was appointed professor of Low Current Technology in the Technische Hochschule, Dresden, and in 1928 was awarded the Heinrich Herz medal for his work in this field. He did fundamental research on electron tubes and electrical oscillations and wrote comprehensive books on both subjects. In 1919 he discovered that the magnetization of iron proceeds in discrete steps and he devised a loudspeaker system to render this discontinuity audible. This phenomenon is now known as the Barkhausen effect.

BARKLA, Charles Glover (1877–1944), English physicist, born at Widnes, Lancashire, became professor of Physics in London and in 1913 professor of Natural Philosophy at Edinburgh. He conducted notable researches into X-rays and other short wave emissions and was awarded the Nobel prize (1917). He was elected F.R.S. (1912).

BARLACH, Ernst, *bar'lakh* (1870–1938), German artist, sculptor, playwright, and poet, born at Wedel. He was identified with the German Expressionist school of both art and drama. While he was best known as a sculptor in wood (his work in this medium being influenced by Gothic sculpture and Russian folk-carving), his greatest achievement was his war memorial at Güstrow Cathedral, a great bronze Angel of Death, which was removed by Hitler as subversive. Barlach's plays include *Der tote Tag* (1912), *Der arme Vetter* (1918), and *Die Sündflut* (1924). See study by Carls (1931).

BARLOW, (1) Jane (1860–1917), Irish novelist, born at Clontarf, author of stories, sometimes in verse, of Irish village life, such as *Irish Idylls* (1892), *Bogland Studies*, &c.

(2) **Joel** (1754–1812), American poet and politician, born at Redding, Conn., served as military chaplain during the War of Independence, spent 16 years abroad, mostly in France in political, literary, and mercantile pursuits, was American consul at Algiers and ambassador to France in 1811. His *Columbiad* (1807) is a historical review of events from the time of Columbus to the French Revolution. Other works include the would-be humorous poem, ' Hasty Pudding ' (1796). See Lives by Todd (1886), Zunder (1943), and Howard, *The Connecticut Wits* (1943).

(3) **Thomas** (1607–91), English divine, born at Orton in Westmorland, was educated at Appleby and Queen's College, Oxford, of which he became provost in 1657. Throughout the ecclesiastical controversies of the time, he secured his advancement by casuistry, always modifying his arguments so as to be on the winning side. This earned him the name of ' the trimmer '. His advancement to the bishopric of Lincoln (1675) was so unpopular that he avoided the cathedral. He was, if anything, a Calvinist and an opponent of Jeremy Taylor.

(4) **William** (d. 1568), English divine who opposed Wolsey in a number of polemical tracts, apologized and became a favourite at court. During Queen Mary's reign he was imprisoned in the Tower, but gained his release on the strength of his tracts against Wolsey. By his constant changes of front, he held the sees of St Asaph, St Davids, Bath, and Chichester. His son **William** (d. 1625), Archdeacon of Salisbury, wrote on the compass and magnetism.

BARMECIDES, or Barmekides, *bar'me-sīdz*, a Persian family descended from Barmak, a physician and priest of Balkh, in Khorassan. Khálid bin Bermek became prime minister of the first Abbaside calif; and his virtuous and able son, Yáhyá, was in 786 made vizier by Haroun-al-Raschid, who, fearful of their power, in 803 exterminated the family.

BARNARD, (1) Lady Anne (1750–1825), Scottish writer, author of ' Auld Robin Gray ', eldest daughter of James Lindsay, fifth Earl of Balcarres, in 1793 married Andrew Barnard (1763–1807), colonial secretary at the Cape from 1797. The famous lyric was written in 1772 to be sung to an old melody. Her Letters were published as *South Africa a Century Ago* (1904). See Lives by Lord Crawford (1849) and Masson (1948).

(2) **Edward Emerson** (1857–1923), American astronomer, born at Nashville, Tenn., made a systematic photographic survey of the sky and correctly concluded that those areas devoid of stars which he called ' black nebulae ' were clouds of obscuring matter. He discovered the fifth satellite of Jupiter in 1892.

(3) **Henry** (1811–1900), American educa-

tionist, born at Hartford, Conn., educated at Yale, became after several academic appointments the first U.S. commissioner of education (1867). He advocated centralization of school control, teacher training at the universities, &c. See *Henry Barnard on Education*, ed. J. S. Brubacher (1931).

BARNARDO, Thomas John (1845–1905), British founder of homes for destitute children, born in Dublin, was a clerk when he was converted in 1862, and after a spell of preaching in the Dublin slums came to London in 1866 to study medicine with the aim of becoming a medical missionary. Instead, he founded, while still a student, the East End Mission for destitute children in 1867 and a number of homes in greater London, which came to be known as the ' Barnardo Homes '. See *Memoirs* by S. L. Barnardo and Marchant (1907) and Lives by Bready (1930) and A. E. Williams (1954).

BARNATO, Barney (1852–97), South African millionaire, was born in Whitechapel of Jewish parentage, went out to Kimberley with a small circus in 1873, made a fortune in diamonds there and after engineering the Kaffir boom (1895) committed suicide at sea. See Life by Raymond (1897).

BARNAVE, Antoine (1761–93), French Revolutionist, born at Grenoble, brought back the royal family from Varennes, but, subsequently advocating more moderate courses, was guillotined.

BARNBY, Sir Joseph (1838–96), English composer and conductor, born at York, wrote hymns, other sacred music, and part-songs, and became principal of the Guildhall School of Music, London, in 1892, in which year he was knighted.

BARNES, (1) Djuna (1892–), U.S. author, poet and illustrator, born in Cornwall-on-Hudson, N.Y., began her career as reporter and illustrator for magazines, then writer of one-act plays and short stories, published in a variety of magazines and anthologies. Her works, many of which she has illustrated, range from the outstanding novel *Nightwood* (1936) to her verse play *The Antiphon* (1958), both included in *Selected Works* (1962). Although little known to the general public, her brilliant literary style has been acclaimed by many critics, including Eliot.

(2) **Ernest William** (1874–1953), British prelate, born in Birmingham, was educated at King Edward's School there and at Trinity College, Cambridge, where, as one of the most outstanding mathematical scholars of his time, he became a lecturer in 1902. He was ordained in 1908, became F.R.S. in 1909, and master of the Temple in 1915. He became Bishop of Birmingham in 1924. His strongly-held modernist and pacifist views involved him in continued controversy within the Church of England. He wrote *The Rise of Christianity* (1947).

(3) **Thomas** (1785–1841), English editor and journalist, born in London and educated at Christ's Hospital and Pembroke College, Cambridge, excelled in classical studies, Italian literature, mathematics, law, athletics, and good living. In 1809, he became dramatic critic of *The Times*, in 1817 editor, a post which he held for twenty-four years.

His leading principle was that a newspaper should not be a servant of the state but an independent means of its best development. He made *The Times* ' the thunderer '.

(4) **William** (1800–86), England's best purely pastoral poet, was born at Rushay, near Sturminster-Newton. In spite of early difficulties, he acquired remarkable learning, and after some time in a solicitor's office, taught a school at Dorchester with success. He became curate of Whitcombe in 1847, and rector of Winterborne Came in 1862. Meantime he had become widely known by his fine idyllic poetry in the Dorset dialect, ' the bold and broad Doric of England '. His three volumes of poetry were collected in 1879 as *Poems of Rural Life in the Dorset Dialect*. He wrote several philological works. See Life (1887) by his daughter, L. Baxter (' Leader Scott ', 1837–1902), who wrote much on Italian themes, and Quiller-Couch, an essay in *The Poet as Citizen* (1934).

BARNETT, (1) John Francis (1837–1916), English composer, nephew of John Barnett (1802–90), likewise a composer, was best known for his cantatas, particularly *The Ancient Mariner* (1867).

(2) **Samuel Augustus** (1844–1913), English clergyman and social reformer, was born in Bristol and educated at Wadham College, Oxford. In 1873 he went to a Whitechapel parish, where his interest in and sympathy with the poor of London were aroused. Discussions with Arnold Toynbee (q.v.) led Barnett to found (1884) in his memory the first university settlement, for university men to live in close contact with their East End neighbours, to study their problems and to help them. He also took part in advocating other educational reforms, poor relief measures, and universal pensions. In 1894 he became canon of Bristol, and from 1906 until his death was canon of Westminster. See Life by H. Barnett (1918).

BARNEVELDT, Jan van Olden (1547–1619), Dutch statesman and lawyer, was born at Amersfoort. Through Barneveldt's influence, Prince Maurice succeeded his murdered father as stadtholder (1584); but Barneveldt opposed his warlike schemes by concluding (1609) a truce with Spain. This caused a political rift which intensified the religious controversies of the time. To prevent a civil war, Barneveldt proposed an ecclesiastical assembly to underwrite toleration. Prince Maurice's party, however, represented the proposers as secret friends of Spain. Barneveldt was illegally arrested, condemned as a traitor, and executed. Of his two sons, the elder escaped to Antwerp, the younger was executed. See Motley's Life (1874).

BARNFIELD, Richard (1574–1627), English poet, born at Norbury, Shropshire, studied at Brasenose College, Oxford, and died, a country gentleman, at Stone, in Staffordshire. His pastoral poems are quaint, rhythmic, dainty, but over-luxuriant.

BARNUM, Phineas Taylor (1810–91), American showman, born at Bethel, Conn., ran a museum in New York, introducing freak shows, at which he sponsored the famous dwarf ' General Tom Thumb ' (1842), using for the first time the flamboyant publicity now considered typical of American show business. He managed the American tour of Jenny Lind (q.v.) in 1847, and in 1881 joined with his rival James Anthony Bailey (1847–1906) to found the famous Barnum and Bailey circus. He died worth 5 million dollars. See his Autobiography (ed. Browne, 1927) and Wallace, *The Fabulous Showman* (1959).

BAROCCI, or **BAROCCIO**, **Federigo**, *ba-rot'chi* (1528–1612), Italian painter, born in Urbino. In 1548 he went to Rome, and came under the influence of Correggio. He later developed a very personal colour scheme of vivid reds and yellows, and his fluent pictorial style had considerable influence on Rubens and his school. His *Madonna del Popolo* is in the Uffizi Gallery, Florence, and his *Christ Crucified* in Genoa Cathedral.

BAROJA Y NESSI, Pio, *ba-rō'ha* (1872–1956), Spanish writer, born in San Sebastian. He wrote more than seventy volumes of novels and essays, distinguished by quiet humour and a vivid style derived from the 19th-century Russian and French masters. His best novels are those with a Basque setting.

BARONIUS, Caesar, properly **Cesare Baronio** (1538–1607), Italian church historian, born at Sora, in Naples. Coming to Rome at nineteen, he was one of the first pupils of St Philip Neri, and attached himself to his Congregation of the Oratory, of which in 1593 he became superior. He wrote the first critical church history, the *Annales Ecclesiastici* (1588–1607), as a reply to the Protestant *Magdeburg Centuries*, proving that the church of Rome was identical with the Christian church of the 1st century. The pope made him his confessor, he became cardinal in 1596 and Vatican librarian, and might have been elected pope in 1605 but for his opposition to Spain's claim to Italy. See also his *Martyrologium Romanum* (1596), and Lives by Sarra (1862) and Kerr (1899).

BARR, Archibald (1855–1931), Scottish engineer, born near Paisley. As an engineering apprentice he graduated at Glasgow University. He was professor of Civil and Mechanical Engineering at Leeds from 1884 to 1889, when he succeeded his teacher, Thomson, in the regius chair of Civil Engineering at Glasgow; he set up the James Watt research laboratories in 1900. With William Stroud he founded the firm of scientific instrument makers who were pioneers of naval range-finding and later invented height finders for anti-aircraft gunnery.

BARRAS, Paul Jean François Nicolas, Comte de, *bar-rah* (1755–1829), French Revolutionary, was born at Fos-Emphoux in Var. In his youth he served against the English in India; then, returning home, plunged into reckless dissipation at Paris. An original member of the Jacobin Club, he represented Var in the National Convention, voted for the king's execution, and had a share in the Girondists' downfall. He conducted the siege of Toulon, and suppressed, with great cruelty, the revolt in the south of France. Hated by Robespierre, he played the chief part in the tyrant's overthrow, and was appointed virtual dictator by the terrified Convention. As such he crushed the intrigues of the Terrorists. On subsequent occasions he acted with decision against both Royalists and Jacobins; and in 1795, being again appointed dictator, he called his young friend Bonaparte to his aid, who assured his due future with the historical 'whiff of grape-shot'. The Directory being appointed, Barras was nominated one of the five members. Once more dictator in 1797, he guided the state almost alone, until his covetousness and love of pleasure had rendered him so unpopular that Bonaparte, with Sieyès' help, overthrew him easily on 18th Brumaire (November 9), 1799. After travelling abroad he died at Paris-Chaillot. See his *Mémoires*, edited by G. Duruy (trans. 1896), and Lives by H. d'Alméras (1929) and J. Vivent (1927).

BARRAULT, Jean-Louis, *ba-rō'* (1910–), French actor and producer, born in le Vesinet. From 1940–46 he was a member of the Comédie-Française, making his début there as Roderigue in *Le Cid*. In 1946, with his wife, Madeleine Renaud, he founded his own company, le Troupe Marigny, which became celebrated for its performances of Molière, Claudel, and the Gide translation of *Hamlet*. His films include *Les Perles de la Couronne*, *La Symphonie fantastique*, *Les Enfants du paradis*, and *Le Cocu magnifique*. Barrault's acting is sensitive and poetic, with a fluidity that springs from his training in mime. His theories of dramatic art are expressed in his autobiographical *Reflexions sur le théâtre* (1949, trans. 1951).

BARRÉ, Isaac, *bar- ay* (1726–1802), British soldier and politician, was born at Dublin, rose under Wolfe to be lieutenant-colonel, and was wounded at Quebec (1759). He sat in parliament from 1761 .to 1790, and held office successively under Lord Bute, Pitt, Rockingham, and Lord Shelburne.

BARRÈS, Maurice, *bar-res* (1862–1923), French novelist, literary artist, politician, apostle of nationalism, individualism, provincial patriotism and national energy, was born at Charmes-sur-Moselle, and admitted to the Academy in 1906. See his *L'Appel au soldat* (1906), *Colette Baudoche* (1909), &c., and Life by H. L. Miéville (1934).

BARRETT, (1) Sir William Fletcher (1844–1925), British physicist, born in Jamaica, professor of Physics at Dublin from 1873, made some early experiments in telepathy, and did important work on magnetic alloys.

(2) **Wilson** (1846–1904), English actor, theatre manager and writer, born in Essex, was best known for his part in the dramatic adaptation of his novel, *The Sign of the Cross* (1896), a religious melodrama.

BARRIE, Sir James Matthew, Bart. (1860–1937), Scottish novelist and dramatist, born May 9, at Kirriemuir, Angus, was educated there and at Dumfries Academy, graduating at Edinburgh University in 1882. After a year and a half as a journalist in Nottingham, he settled in London, and became a regular contributor to the *St James's Gazette* and *British Weekly* (as 'Gavin Ogilvy'). He wrote a series of autobiographical novels, including *A Window in Thrums* (1889), and *The Little Minister* (1891, dramatized 1897), set in his native village ' Thrums ', after which from 1890 onwards he wrote for the theatre, beginning with the successful *Walker, London* (1893). *Quality Street* (1902) and *The Admirable Crichton* (1902), a good-humoured social satire, established his reputation. It is, however, as the creator of *Peter Pan* (1904) that he will be chiefly remembered. An unfailing romantic, Barrie continued his excursions into fairyland in such later plays as *Dear Brutus* (1917) and *Mary Rose* (1920) and in his last play, *The Boy David* (1936), essayed a biblical theme which despite some of his finest writing won no laurels in the theatre. Despite his shyness, he became something of a public figure with his famous rectorial address on ' Courage ' delivered at St Andrews University (1919). He received his baronetcy (1913), O.M. (1922), and became rector of Edinburgh University (1930–37). He died June 20. See his *Greenwood Hat* (1937), and Lives by W. A. Darlington (1938), Asquith (1954), and study by G. Blake (1951).

BARRINGTON, (1) **Daines** (1727–1800), English lawyer and naturalist, son of (3), attained position at the bar and published *Observations on the Statutes* (1766).

(2) **George,** real name **Waldron** (1755–1804), Irish writer, was born at Maynooth. In London he turned pickpocket, was in 1790 transported to Botany Bay and set free in 1792, rising to the position of high constable of Parramatta, New South Wales. He published historical works on Australia.

(3) **John Shute Barrington, 1st Viscount** (1678–1734), English politician, was born at Theobalds, and, after four years' study at Utrecht, was called to the bar in 1699. His *Rights of Protestant Dissenters* (1704) gained him the confidence of the Presbyterians; his *Dissuasive from Jacobitism* (1713) recommended him to George I, and in 1720 he was raised to the Irish peerage as baron and viscount, having ten years before assumed the name Barrington. He was expelled from the House of Commons in 1723 for his connection with the lottery of Harburg. See Life prefixed to his theological works (1828). Of his six sons, **Samuel** (1729–1800) was a distinguished admiral, and see (1), (4) and (5).

(4) **Shute** (1734–1826), English prelate, son of (3), became a fellow of Merton College, Oxford, was ordained in 1757 and by 1760 was Bishop of Llandaff. As Bishop of Salisbury (1782–91), he was responsible for laying out its beautiful setting. From 1791 he was Bishop of Durham.

(5) **William Wildman Shute Barrington, 2nd Viscount** (1717–93), English politician, son of (3), held political office for nearly forty years. See Life by Shute Barrington (1814).

BARROS, João de, *bah'rōsh* (1496–1570), a Portuguese historian, born at Viseu, known for his *Decades* (1552–1615), the history of the Portuguese in the East Indies.

BARROW, (1) **Isaac** (1630–77), English mathematician and divine, born in London, was educated at Charterhouse and Trinity College, Cambridge, where he became a fellow in 1649. His Royalist sympathies and leanings towards Arminianism prevented him from obtaining the professorship of Greek until 1660. He travelled abroad (1655–59),

became professor of Geometry at Gresham College, London (1662), and the same at Cambridge (1663), but he resigned in 1669 to make way for his celebrated student, Isaac Newton. He founded the library of Trinity College, Cambridge, when he became master in 1673. He published on trigonometry, optics, and the Pope's supremacy, and became known for the length of his sermons. At Westminster Abbey he once detained a congregation so long that they got the organ to play ' till they had blowed him down '. See *Life* by P. H. Osmond (1944).

(2) **Sir John** (1764–1848), English explorer, born at Dragley Beck, Lancashire, made his first voyage in a Greenland whaler (1781), and after teaching mathematics became in 1792 private secretary to the ambassador to China, Lord Macartney, whom he followed to the Cape Colony when he became governor in 1797. Barrow made extensive explorations wherever he went and wrote valuable accounts of his journeys. He became secretary to the Admiralty in 1804, promoted Arctic expeditions, was a founder and vice-president of the Geographical Society (1830). Barrow Strait, Cape Barrow, and Point Barrow preserve his memory. See his *Autobiography* (1847), and the *Memoir* by Staunton (1852).

BARRY, (1) **Ann.** See (6).

(2) **Sir Charles** (1795–1860), English architect, born in London and educated privately, was apprenticed to a firm of surveyors before going to Italy (1817–20). On his return, he designed the Travellers' Club (1831), the Manchester Athenaeum (1836), the Reform Club (1837), and the new Palace of Westminster (1840), completed after his death by his son **Edward Middleton** (1830–80). His work showed the influence of the Italian Renaissance. He was elected R.A. (1841) and knighted in 1852. See *Life* (1867) by his second son, **Alfred** (1826–1910), Bishop of Sydney. Another son, **Charles** (1823–1900), was also an architect; his fifth son, **Sir John Wolfe-Barry,** Bart. (1836–1918), was engineer of the Tower Bridge and Barry Docks.

(3) **Comtesse du.** See DU BARRY.

(4) **Elizabeth** (1658–1713), a London actress, introduced to the stage by the Earl of Rochester. Her many rôles included the chief characters of Otway's and Congreve's plays.

(5) **James** (1741–1806), Irish historical painter, born at Cork. A protégé of Burke, he studied in Italy (1766–70), and in 1782 was appointed professor of Painting to the Royal Academy, from which his irritable temper brought about his expulsion (1799). He decorated the Great Room of the Society of Arts with a series of pictures illustrating human progress. See J. Comyns Carr, *Papers on Art* (1885).

(6) **Spranger** (1719–77), British actor, Garrick's rival, born at Dublin, in 1768 married the actress Mrs Ann Dancer, *née* Street (1734–1801).

BARRYMORE, (1) **Ethel** (1879–1959), American actress, sister of (2) and (3), born in Philadelphia, daughter of the actor-playwright Maurice Barrymore and the actress Georgina Drew Barrymore. In 1897–98 she scored a great success in London with Sir Henry Irving in *The Bells*. Other noteworthy appearances were in *Trelawney of the Wells* (1911), *The Second Mrs Tanqueray* (1924), *Whiteoaks* (1938) and *The Corn is Green* (1942). She also acted in films, including *Rasputin and the Empress* (1932), the only production in which all three Barrymores appeared together, and on radio and television.

(2) **John** (1882–1942), American actor, brother of (1) and (3), born in Philadelphia. He spent some time studying art, but eventually returned to the family profession, making his name in Shakespearean rôles, his *Hamlet* being particularly famous, and appearing in many films. His classical nose and distinguished features won for him the nickname of 'The Great Profile'. See G. Fowler, *Goodnight Sweet Prince* (1942).

(3) **Lionel** (1878–1954), American actor, brother of (1) and (2), born in Philadelphia, played small parts and appeared in the early films of D. W. Griffith before making a name for himself in Gerald du Maurier's *Peter Ibbetson* (1917) and in *The Copperhead* (1918), thereafter taking many rôles in films and radio plays, notably *Grand Hotel, David Copperfield, Dinner at Eight*. For a short time he was a director with M.G.M. After twice accidentally breaking a hip he was confined to a wheelchair, but undeterred he scored a great success as Dr Gillespie in the original *Dr Kildare* film series. He had etchings exhibited and was a talented musician, his arrangements and original compositions having been performed by orchestras of the first rank. See L. Barrymore and C. Shipp, *We Barrymores* (1942).

BARSANTI, Francesco, *-san'-* (*c*. 1690–*c*. 1775), Italian composer and performer, born in Lucca. In 1714 he accompanied Geminiani to London, where he played flute then oboe at the Opera. Going to Edinburgh in 1742, he became prominent in the musical life of the town, both as performer and composer; while there he published (1742) *A Collection of Old Scots Tunes*. He wrote flute and violin sonatas, concerti grossi, an overture and other chamber works.

BARTAS, Guillaume de Salluste du (1544–90), French soldier, diplomat and poet, was born at Montfort in Armagnac. A Huguenot, he fought in the religious wars, went on missions to the English court, and died of wounds received at the battle of Ivry. His chief poem, *La Sepmaine*, gives an account of the creation, and is said to have influenced Milton's *Paradise Lost*. See Pellissier's *Vie* (1883) and translation of his poems (1592 ff.).

BARTH, *bahrt*, (1) Heinrich (1821–65), German traveller, was born at Hamburg, studied at Berlin, and visited Italy and Sicily, and in 1845 North Africa, Sinai, Palestine, Asia Minor, and Greece. He was next appointed by the British government, along with Dr Overweg, scientific companion to Mr James Richardson charged with a mission to central Africa. Starting from Tripoli early in 1850, they crossed the Great Desert. Barth soon separated from his friends, who both succumbed to the climate, and continued his explorations, which extended to Adamáwa in the south, and from Bagirmi in the east to Timbuktu in the west, nearly 12,000 miles, which he described in *Travels and Discoveries in Central Africa* (5 vols. 1857–58). Afterwards he made several journeys in Greece, Turkey, and Asia Minor. See *Life* by von Schubert (1897).

(2) or **Bart, Jean** (1651–1702), French sailor of fortune, was born, a fisherman's son, at Dunkirk, and served first in the Dutch navy under De Ruyter, but on the outbreak of the war with Holland passed over to the French service. For a while the captain of a privateer, in 1691 he commanded a small squadron in the North Sea, where he destroyed many English vessels, and made a descent on the coast near Newcastle. In 1694, after a desperate struggle with a superior Dutch fleet, he recaptured a large flotilla of cornships, and brought them safely into Dunkirk. Soon after he was taken prisoner and carried to Plymouth, but escaped in a fishing-boat to France. The king received him with distinction at Versailles, and in 1697 appointed him to the command of a squadron. See Laughton's *Studies* (1887) and Malo's *Corsaires dunkerquois* (1912).

(3) **Karl** (1886–1968), Swiss theologian, born at Basel on May 10, studied at Berne, Berlin, Tübingen and Marburg. Whilst pastor at Safenwil, Aargau, he wrote a commentary of St Paul's epistle to the Romans (1919, trans. 1930) which established his theological reputation. He became professor at Göttingen (1921), Münster (1925), Bonn (1930), refused to take an unconditional oath to Hitler, was dismissed and so became professor at Basel (1935–62). His theology begins with the realization of man's wickedness; the principal sin being man's endeavour to make himself rather than God the centre of the world. Barth therefore re-emphasized the finiteness of man and made God's grace once again the pivot and goal of man's life. God's unquestionable authority and 'otherness' was the key to his theology. But Barth was criticized in that his own reasoned exposition of antiphilosophical theology itself constituted philosophy and that he prescribed belief in a Divinity who failed to explain the nature of man's humanity. His many works include *Knowledge of God and the Service of God* (trans. 1938) and the monumental *Church Dogmatics* (Eng. trans. ed Bromiley and Torrance, 1958). See studies by C. Van Til (1946), S. Spencer (1947), and Berkouwer (1957).

BARTHÉ, Richmond, *bartay* (1901–63), American Negro sculptor, born at Bay St Louis, Miss., studied at Chicago Art Institute. Among his best works are the busts of Booker T. Washington in the Hall of Fame and of Dessalines in Haiti.

BARTHÉLEMY, *bar-tel-mee,* (1) **Auguste Marseille** (1796–1867), a French poet and political satirist, was born and died at Marseilles, where he was librarian.

(2) **Jean Jacques** (1716–95), French abbé and antiquary, best known by his *Voyage du jeune Anacharsis en Grèce* (1788). See Villenave's edition of his works, with a biography (1821).

BARTHÉLEMY SAINT-HILAIRE, Jules,

sï-tee-layr (1805–95), French scholar and statesman, born in Paris, best known by his translation of Aristotle and his writings on Indian philosophy, was French foreign minister (1880–81).

BARTHOLDI, Auguste (1834–1904), French sculptor, was born at Colmar, Alsace, and specialized in enormous monuments such as the *Lion of Belfort* and the colossal bronze Statue of Liberty on Bedloe's Island, New York Harbour, unveiled in 1886, a present of the French Republic to the United States, for which he was decorated with the *Légion d'honneur* (1887).

BARTHOLINUS, a Danish family of distinguished physicians.

(1) **Casper,** senior (1585–1629), father of (3), was born at Malmö in Sweden, studied at many universities, refused professorships in philosophy, anatomy, and Greek, but accepted one in medicine at Copenhagen (1613) and in theology there (1624).

(2) **Casper,** junior (1655–1738), son of (3), was born at Copenhagen and was physiologist there. He described the larger duct of the sublingual gland and the greater vestibular glands, both of which bear his name.

(3) **Thomas** (1616–80), son of (1), was born in Copenhagen, studied extensively abroad, disliked lecturing and in 1661 retired to his country house, which was destroyed by fire along with his library and unpublished manuscripts in 1670. Best known for his work on the lymphatic system, he confirmed Pecquet's discovery of the thoracic duct.

BARTHOLOMAEUS ANGLICUS. See GLANVILLE.

BARTHOLOMÉ, Paul Albert (1848–1928), French sculptor and painter, born at Thiverval, achieved some recognition as an Impressionist painter before in 1866 devoting himself almost exclusively to sculpture. He is best known for the group of statuary inspired by his wife's death, *Aux morts* (1895), and for the monument to Rousseau in the Panthéon.

BARTHOLOMEW, John George (1860–1920), Scottish cartographer, born in Edinburgh, son of John Bartholomew (1831–93), map-engraver and publisher. After graduating at Edinburgh University he entered his father's firm, and published the *Survey Atlas of Scotland* (1895–1912), followed by a similar atlas of England and Wales, a *Physical Atlas of the World* (two volumes, 1889–1911), and the *Times Survey Atlas of the World* which appeared (1921) after his death. He is best known for his system of layer colouring of contours. He died at Cintra, Portugal.

BARTHOU, Jean Louis, *bahr-too'* (1862–1934), French politician, born at Oloron-Sainte-Marie, practised law and after several ministerial appointments became prime minister (1913), when he introduced three-year conscription. He held several cabinet posts during World War I, was minister of justice (1922, 1926, 1928), president of the Reparations Committee and as foreign minister (1934) attempted to negotiate an eastern 'Locarno' treaty. He was assassinated with king Alexander I of Yugoslavia at Marseilles, October 9.

BARTLETT, Sir Frederic Charles (1886–1969), English psychologist, born at Stow-on-the-Wold, Glos., professor of Experimental Psychology at Cambridge (1931–52), wrote *The Problem of Noise* (1934), and devised tests for servicemen in World War II.

BARTÓK, Béla (1881–1945), Hungarian composer, born in Nagyszentmiklós. He learnt the piano from his mother, and first appeared in public in 1891, subsequently studying in Pressburg and Budapest. His early compositions are in a conventional 19th-century style, but a growing interest in folk song led him to study and collect Hungarian folk music—for which gypsy music had previously been mistaken—and Balkan folk music generally. The rhythms and primitive scale forms of these traditions became the greatest influence upon his own works. In 1907 he was appointed professor of Pianoforte in Budapest Conservatory, but he was driven into exile by World War I and the Nazi occupation of Hungary, and settled in the United States. After the war he became a major figure in world music, where he won attention with the directness, violence, and originality of his work. In America he composed his Violin Concerto, his Third Piano Concerto, and the Concerto for Orchestra, which show his development of a broader and more conciliatory style. His other works include the opera *Bluebeard's Castle*, the ballet *The Miraculous Mandarin*, and six string quartets, as well as much music for orchestra and piano works. See study by H. Stevens (1953), and A. Fassett, *The Naked Face of Genius* (1958).

BARTOLI, *bar'to-lee,* (1) **Daniello** (1608–85), Italian writer, born at Ferrara, became rector of the Jesuit College in Rome. He wrote in an extravagant baroque style of the Jesuit missions in the East.

(2) **Pietro Santo,** sometimes called **Perugino,** (1635–1700), Italian painter and archaeologist, devoted his life to drawing the archaeological remains which were being discovered in Italy during his lifetime. His son **Francesco** helped him in his work.

(3) **Taddeo** (1362–1422), Italian painter of the Sienese school. The earliest specimen of his art is an altarpiece representing St Peter (1390) in the Louvre. Most of his early work was executed in Pisa, where he was responsible for the frescoes of Paradise and Hell in the cathedral, and paintings in the Palazza Publico. A *Descent of the Holy Ghost* (1403) in the church of S. Agostino at Perugia is his masterpiece. He returned to Siena in 1404 and continued his work in the cathedral and churches there, as well as in Volterra. He followed the subdued and agreeable style of the Sienese school, and was more successful in his smaller pictures.

BARTOLINI, Lorenzo, *-lee'nee* (1777–1850), Italian sculptor, born at Vernio in Tuscany, went early to Florence, and in 1797 to Paris, where he began to study art in his leisure hours and became a friend of Ingres. A bust of Napoleon executed by him, as well as a relief for the Vendôme column depicting the battle of Austerlitz, brought him recognition, and in 1808 Napoleon sent him to Carrara to found a new school of sculpture. After Waterloo, Bartolini removed to Florence, where he succeeded Ricci as professor of the academy in 1839. His aim to enliven strict classicism through the study of nature was not adequately realized in his work. His best works are *Charity*, *Macchiavelli*, and the Demidoff monument, as well as busts of Madame de Staël, Lord Byron and Liszt.

BARTOLOMMEO, Fra, properly **Baccio della Porta** (1475–1517), Italian painter, one of the most distinguished masters of the Florentine school, was born near Florence. His first teacher was Cosimo Rosselli; but he owed his higher cultivation to the study of the works of Leonardo da Vinci. His subjects are mostly religious, and by far the greater part of his pieces belong to the later years of his life. He was a warm adherent of Savonarola, at whose death he gave up painting and became a Dominican novice. The visit of the young Raphael to Florence in 1504 seems to have been instrumental in stimulating him to resume his art. He imparted to Raphael his knowledge of colouring, and acquired from him a more perfect knowledge of perspective. The two remained constant friends—Bartolommeo on one occasion finishing certain of Raphael's unfinished works, Raphael performing a like kindness for him at another time. The greater number of his works are to be seen at Florence, but the Louvre possesses a fine *Annunciation* by him. See works by Frantz (Ratisbon 1879), Leader Scott (1880), Gruyer (Paris 1886), Knapp (Halle 1903), and von der Gabelentz (1922).

BARTOLOZZI, Francesco, *bar-to-lot'see* (1727–1815), Italian engraver, was born in Florence, settled in London in 1764 at the request of Dalton, librarian to George III. Here Bartolozzi produced his exquisite line engravings of *The Silence*, *Clytie*, &c. In 1769, on the formation of the Royal Academy, he was nominated an original member, and executed, from a design by his friend Cipriani, the diploma, still in use. In 1802 he accepted a flattering invitation from the Prince Regent of Portugal, to become superintendent of a school of engravers at Lisbon, where he resided until his death. His prints, said to be more numerous than those of any engraver, include line engravings and stippled works, printed in brown and red, called ' Bartolozzi red '. See Life by Tuer (1882).

BARTON, (1) Andrew (d. 1511), Scottish naval commander who cleared the Scottish coast of pirates and in 1506 sent James IV three barrels full of Flemish pirates' heads, and who was killed in an engagement with two English ships in the Downs.

(2) **Bernard** (1784–1849), English Quaker poet, was born at Carlisle. A bank clerk throughout his life, he was a friend of Lamb and his *Metrical Effusions* (1812) interested Southey. His *Poems* (1820) include devotional lyrics in the style of George Herbert. See Life by E. V. Lucas (1894).

(3) **Clara** (1821–1912), born at Oxford, Mass., founded the U.S. Red Cross Society (1882). See Life by Epler (N.Y. 1915).

(4) **Sir Edmund** (1849–1920), Australian statesman, born at Sydney, first prime minister of the Australian Commonwealth (1901–03). See Life by Reynolds (1948).

(5) **Elizabeth** (1506?–34), the Maid of Kent, a domestic servant at Aldington, began to utter prophetic utterances, go into trances, &c., after an illness in 1525. Archbishop Warham sent two monks to examine her. One of these, Edward Bocking, persuaded her to claim that she was directly inspired by the Virgin Mary, and became her confessor at the priory of St Sepulchre at Canterbury. She denounced Henry VIII's divorce and marriage to Anne Boleyn, was made by Cranmer to confess her pretence and was hanged at Tyburn with Bocking and four other accomplices.

BARUCH, Bernard Mannes, *bah'rook* (1870–1965), American financier and public servant, born in South Carolina, educated in New York, began life as an office boy, but made a fortune by speculation. Like Beaverbrook, he became a powerful political influence, ' the adviser of presidents ' and of Churchill, served on many commissions, particularly the American Atomic Energy Commission to which he submitted in 1946 his plan for international control of atomic energy. See his *My Own Story* (1958) and *The Public Years* (1961), and Life by Coit (1958).

BARY. See DE BARY.

BARYE, Antoine Louis, *bah-ree* (1796–1875), French sculptor, distinguished for his bronze statues of animals. See French monographs by Alexandre (1889) and Chaunier (1926).

BASALDELLA, Mirko (1910–), Italian sculptor and painter, born at Udine. He studied in Venice, Florence, and Milan, and held an exhibition in Rome in 1936. Later he designed the bronze memorial doors for the Ardeatine caves near Rome. In 1953 he won the second prize in the international *Unknown Political Prisoner* sculpture competition, and in 1957 he held his first London exhibition of sculptures, which show an affinity with primitive and prehistoric forms.

BASEDOW, Johann Bernhard, *bah'ze-dō* (1723–90), German educationist who tried to put into practice the maxims of Rousseau and Comenius, was born at Hamburg. See his Life by Meyer (2 vols. 1792), and works by Hahn (1885) and Pinloche (Paris 1890).

BASEVI, George (1794–1845), English architect, born in London, became a pupil of Sir John Soane, travelled in Greece and Italy (1816–19), designed in classic revivalist style the Fitzwilliam Museum in Cambridge, laid out part of London's Belgravia, and designed country mansions and Gothic churches. He fell to his death while surveying Ely Cathedral.

BASHKIRTSEV, Marie (1860–84), Russian artist and diarist, born of noble family at Pultowa, South Russia, kept from childhood a diary in French, selections of which were published posthumously. She became a painter of some promise but died of consumption in Paris. See her *Journal* (Eng. trans. 1890) and *Letters* (trans. 1891).

BASIL, St, surnamed **The Great** (*c*. 329–79), one of the greatest of the Greek fathers, was born at Caesarea, in Cappadocia, and in 370 succeeded Eusebius as bishop of his native city. The best editions of his works are the Benedictine (Paris 1739) and Migne's (Paris 1866 trans.), B. Jackson, *Nicene and Post-Nicene Fathers* (vol. 8 1895).

BASIL I, called the **Macedonian**, Byzantine

emperor (867–886), founded the Macedonian dynasty after having been companion of, joint ruler with, and assassin of Michael III.

BASILE, Giambattista, *bah'zee-lay* (1575–1632), Italian compiler of the *Pentamerone* (Naples 1637), a collection of fifty Neapolitan folk tales, edited by Liebrecht (Breslau 1846) and translated by Sir R. Burton (1893).

BASILIDES, *ba-si-lī'deez* (fl. *c.* 125), Alexandrian philosopher, one of the greatest of the Gnostics, claimed apostolic sanction for a system which combined Platonic transcendentalism, Christology, cosmogony, and a theory of illumination.

BASIRE, *bah-zeer'*, (1) **Isaac** (1607–76), English divine, Archdeacon of Northumberland and rector of Stanhope, was born of Huguenot parentage either at Rouen or in Jersey. Ousted by the parliamentarians, he visited the Levant (1647–61) to establish communion between the English and Greek churches. See Life by Darnell (1831).

(2) **James** (1730–1802), a London engraver, the son, father, and grandfather of three engravers—**Isaac** (1704–68), **James** (1769–1822), and **James** (1796–1869).

BASKERVILLE, John (1706–75), English printer, was born at Sion Hill, Wolverley, Worcestershire. He began as a footman, became a writing master in Birmingham, and from 1740 carried on a successful japanning business there. About 1750 he began to make costly experiments in letter founding, and produced types which have scarcely been excelled. The quarto *Virgil* (1756) was, in Macaulay's words, ' the first of those magnificent editions which went forth to astonish Europe ', and which, 55 in number, included Milton, Juvenal, Congreve, Addison, the Bible, a Greek New Testament, Horace, and Catullus. In 1758 he became printer to Cambridge University. He manufactured his own paper and ink. A foe to ' superstition ', he chose to be buried in his own garden, but his remains were exhumed. See study by J. H. Benton (1944).

BASNAGE, Jacques, *bah-nazh* (1653–1723), French Protestant theologian, diplomat and historian, driven from France to Holland by the revocation of the Edict of Nantes. See French Life by Mailhet (1880).

BASOV, Nikolai (1922–), Russian physicist, professor at Lebedev Physics Inst., Moscow. Joint winner of Nobel prize for physics in 1964 with Prokhorov and Townes, for work on the development of laser beams.

BASS, (1) **George** (d. 1812), English naval surgeon who in 1796–98 explored the strait that bears his name between Tasmania and Australia. He died a South American miner.

(2) **Michael Thomas** (1799–1884), English brewer, was born at Burton-on-Trent and was trained in the family business (founded by his grandfather, William Bass, in 1777) which he expanded considerably. He helped to improve the lot of the working man both as employer and as Liberal M.P. (1848–83). His son, **Michael Arthur** (1837–1909), became Baron Burton in 1886.

BASSANO, Jacopo da, *ba-sah'nō*, properly **Giacomo da Ponte** (1510–92), Venetian painter, founder of genre painting in Europe, was born at Bassano. His best paintings are of peasant life, biblical scenes, &c., and include the altarpiece of the Nativity at Bassano, *Jacob's Return to Canaan* and *Portrait of a Gentleman*. His four sons were also painters.

BASSE, William, English poet, who published between 1602 and 1653 his best-known piece, an elegy on Shakespeare.

BASSENDYNE, Thomas (d. 1577), Edinburgh bookseller, who in 1576 reprinted the second Geneva version of the New Testament (the first published in Scotland). See Dobson's *History of the Bassendyne Bible* (Edin. 1887).

BASSOMPIERRE, François de, *ba-sõ-pyer* (1579–1646), French soldier, born at Harouel, Lorraine, was raised to the rank of marshal of France in 1622. He took an active part in the siege of La Rochelle; but was imprisoned by Richelieu in the Bastille from 1631 to 1643. He was an accomplished courtier, extravagant in luxury, and excessively addicted to gallantries. His *Mémoires*, written in the Bastille, contain interesting sidelights on his sojourn in London as ambassador.

BASTIAN, (1) **Adolf** (1826–1905), German anthropologist, born at Bremen, studied at Berlin, Heidelberg, Prague, Jena, and Würzburg, and in 1851 sailed to Australia as a ship's doctor, and collected firsthand material for his ethnological studies in most continents. He stressed the importance of the psychological aspects of folk cultures.

(2) **Henry Charlton** (1837–1915), English biologist, was born at Truro, Cornwall, educated privately and at University College, London, where he became professor of Pathological Anatomy (1867), hospital physician (1871), and professor of Clinical Medicine (1887–95). He championed the doctrine of spontaneous generation, and became one of the founders of British neurology through his work on aphasia, &c.

BASTIAT, Frédéric, *bast-yah* (1801–50), political economist, born at Bayonne, published works against protectionism and socialism. See works by G. de Nouvion (1905), Ronce (1905), and Bidet (1906).

BASTIDE, Jules, *bas-teed* (1800–79), French Radical journalist, minister of foreign affairs in 1848, and member of the Constituent Assembly, was born in Paris, took part in the Paris revolt (1832), was condemned to death, escaped, and was later pardoned.

BASTIEN-LEPAGE, Jules, *bas-tyī-lė-pahzh* (1848–84), French painter, was born at Damvillers, Meuse. His pictures are mostly of rustic scenes, but there are portraits of Sarah Bernhardt, the Prince of Wales (Edward VII), &c. See monographs by Theuriet (trans. 1892) and Cartwright (1894).

BATA, Tomas, *bah' ya* (1876–1932), Czechoslovakian industrialist. He was born at Zlín, in Moravia, where, from a small shoemaking business, he built up the largest leather factory in Europe, in 1928 producing 75,000 pairs of shoes a day. Bata was killed when an aircraft struck one of his factory chimneys.

BATAILLE, Félix Henry, *bat-tah'y'* (1872–1922), French poet and dramatist, born at Nîmes. The predominant theme in his works is inner conflict, as in *Maman Colibri* (1904), *La Marche nuptiale* (1905), &c., sometimes verging on melodrama.

BATE, Stanley (1913–), English composer

and pianist, born in Plymouth, where, in 1930, he composed, produced, and conducted his first opera. After studying under Vaughan Williams, Nadia Boulanger, and Hindemith, Bate first made his mark as a composer for the theatre, but a tour of Australia followed by some years in America drew attention to his works in symphonic and concerto form.

BATEMAN, (1) **Henry Mayo** (1887–1970), Australian cartoonist, born at Sutton Forest, New South Wales, lived in England from childhood. From 1906 much of his work appeared in *Punch* and other periodicals. He is best known for a series of humorous drawings depicting situations such as *The Guardsman Who Dropped His Rifle*. See his *The Art of Drawing* (1926) and *Himself* (1937).

(2) **Kate Josephine** (1842–1917), American actress, daughter of **Hezekiah Linthicum** (1812–75) the theatrical manager, born at Baltimore, began acting at the age of four and after successful tours in America, acted in London with Henry Irving in Shakespearean plays (1875–77). She married Dr George Crowe in 1866. Her sisters, **Isabel** (1854–1934) and **Virginia** (1853–1940) were both distinguished actresses. The latter married Edward Compton. For their children, see COMPTON and MACKENZIE.

BATES, (1) **Henry Walter** (1825–92), British naturalist and traveller, born at Leicester. With his friend Alfred R. Wallace (q.v.), in April 1848 he left to explore the Amazons, and remained there till 1859. In 1861 he published his distinctive contribution to the theory of natural selection in a paper explaining the phenomena of mimicry. In 1864 he became assistant secretary of the Royal Geographical Society. See Memoir by E. Clodd prefixed to fourth ed. of his *Naturalist on the Amazons* (1892).

(2) **Herbert Ernest** (1905–), British novelist, playwright, and short-story writer, born at Rushden, Northants. He began his working life as a journalist and was later a warehouse clerk. His first play, *The Last Bread*, and his first novel, *The Two Sisters*, appeared in 1926. In his early days he benefited from the advice of Edward Garnett and later came under the influence of Stephen Crane. He is one of the greatest exponents of the short-story form, with a gift for the sensitive portrayal of character with the maximum economy. His essay in literary criticism, *The Modern Short Story*, is regarded as a classic. Best-known works: *Fair Stood the Wind for France* (1944), *The Jacaranda Tree* (1949), *The Darling Buds of May* (1958), &c.

BATESON, William (1861–1926), English biologist, born at Whitby, Yorkshire, was educated at Rugby and Cambridge, where he became professor of Biology in 1908. In 1912 he transferred to the Royal Institution and was president of the British Association in 1914. His *Mendel's Principles of Heredity* (1902) and *Problems of Genetics* (1913) made Mendel's work better understood.

BATHORI, name of a Polish family of Transylvanian origin:

(1) **Elizabeth,** niece of (2) and wife of the Hungarian Count Nádasdy, was discovered in 1610 to have murdered 650 young girls, that she might renew her own youth by bathing in their warm blood. Her accomplices were burnt; but she was shut up for life in her fortress of Csej. See Baring-Gould's *Book of Werewolves* (1865).

(2) **Stephen.** See under STEPHEN, King of Poland.

BATHURST, *bath'-ėrst,* (1) **Allen Bathurst, 1st Earl** (1684–1775), English Tory statesman, created baron in 1722, earl 1762, father of (2) and friend of Pope, Swift, Congreve, Prior, and Sterne.

(2) **Henry, 2nd Earl** (1714–94), son of (1), from 1778 was lord chancellor—' one of the weakest, though one of the worthiest ' that ever sat on the Woolsack. His son **Henry, 3rd Earl** (1762–1834), was colonial secretary (1812–28).

(3) **Henry** (1744–1837), English divine, nephew of (1), from 1805 Bishop of Norwich, the ' only Liberal bishop ' of his day. His son **Benjamin** (1784–1809) disappeared mysteriously between Berlin and Hamburg as he was travelling with dispatches from Vienna.

BATISTA Y ZALDIVAR, Fulgencio, *bah-tees'tah ee sahl-dee'vahr* (1901–73), Cuban dictator, born in Oriente province, rose from sergeant-major to colonel in the army *coup* against President Machado (1931–33) and himself became president (1940–44). In 1952 he overthrew President Prio, and, with himself as sole candidate, was re-elected president in 1954. He ruled as dictator until his overthrow by Fidel Castro (q.v.) in January 1959, when he found refuge in the Dominican Republic.

BATMAN, John (1800–40), the ' Founder of Victoria ', born at Parramatta, in May 1835 colonized the shores of Port Phillip from Tasmania.

BATTENBERG, name of a family of German origin, derived from the title of Countess of Battenberg conferred in 1851 on the Polish countess **Julia Theresa von Hauke** (1825–95), the morganatic wife of **Prince Alexander of Hesse.** Their children included:

(1) **Prince Alexander of** (1857–93), was chosen prince of Bulgaria in 1879, proclaimed the union of Eastern Rumelia with Bulgaria (1885) without consulting Russia, and thereby also provoked the jealousy of the Serbians, whom he defeated in a fortnight's campaign. But in August 1886 partisans of Russia overpowered him in his palace at Sofia, forced him to abdicate, and carried him off to Reni, in Russian territory. Set free in a few days, he returned; but after a futile attempt to conciliate the tsar, he abdicated finally (Sept. 8), and as Count Hartenau retired to Darmstadt. See Life (trans. 1955) by Corti.

(2) **Prince Henry of** (1858–96), in 1885 married the Princess Beatrice (1857–1944), youngest daughter of Queen Victoria, and died at sea of fever caught in the Ashanti campaign. See D. Duff, *The Shy Princess* (1958).

(3) **Prince Louis Alexander of.** See MOUNTBATTEN.

BATTHYÁNYI, *bat-yan'yee,* one of the oldest and most powerful of the noble families of Hungary:

(1) **Casimir, Count** (1807–54), died an exile in Paris, having shared in the Hungarian insurrection of 1849.

(2) **Louis, Count** (1809–49), was shot by

martial law for his part in the Hungarian insurrection of 1849. His estates were confiscated, but were restored to his family in 1867; and in 1870 his body was removed and interred anew with great solemnity.

BATUTA. See IBN BATUTA.

BATYUSHKOV, Konstantin Nikolaievitch, *bat'yoosh-kof* (1787–1855), Russian poet, was born at Vologda. He served in the Napoleonic wars, but became insane in 1821 and was confined in an asylum for the remaining 34 years of his life. Profoundly influenced by French and Italian writers, his work was much admired by Pushkin. His most important work was *The Death of Tasso.*

BAUDELAIRE, Charles Pierre, *bō-dè-layr* (1821–67), French Symbolist poet, born in Paris, spent an unhappy childhood quarrelling with his soldier-diplomat stepfather, Colonel Aupick, was educated at Lyons and in Paris and was sent off on a voyage to India. But he stopped off at Mauritius, where Jeanne Duval, a half-caste, became his mistress and inspiration. On his return to Paris in 1843 he spent much of his time in the studios of Delacroix, Manet, and Daumier, and wrote art criticisms, *Le Salon de 1845* and *Le Salon de 1846.* He sided with the revolutionaries in 1848, although he was by nature aristocratic and Catholic. His masterpiece is a collection of poems, *Les Fleurs du mal* (1857), for which author, printer, and publisher were prosecuted for impropriety in 1864, but which earned the praise of critics and was to exert an influence far into the 20th century. Later works include *Les Paradis artificiels* (1860) and *Petits Poèmes en prose* (1869). He was greatly attracted by de Quincey and Edgar Allan Poe, whose works he translated (1856–1865). Baudelaire substituted self-analysis for the 'attitudinizing' of the Romantics. His was the dilemma of a religious nature without religious beliefs, a continued search for the good and the significant with which every flower, every smell, every colour, every part of life was imbued. His Satanism, his preoccupation with the macabre, the perverted, and the horrid was an essential feature of this search. The school of 'Decadents', unlike the modern Existentialists, spotlighted the 'Satanism' and ignored the reason for it. Having written a critical work on his literary associates Balzac, Gautier, and de Nerval, published posthumously in 1880, Baudelaire took to drink and opium, was struck down with paralysis and poverty, and after two years in Brussels (1864–66), he died in Paris. See works by E. Raynaud (1922), A. Thibaudet, *Intérieurs* (1924), P. Valéry (1924), J. P. Sartre (1946), and E. Starkie (1957).

BAUDOUIN I, *bō-dwī'* (1930–), king of the Belgians, elder son of Leopold III and his first wife, Queen Astrid. He succeeded to the throne in July 1951 on the abdication of his father over the controversy of the latter's conduct during World War II. In 1960 he married the Spanish Dona Fabiola de Mora y Aragon.

BAUDRY, Paul Jacques Aimé, *bō-dree* (1828–1886), French painter, was born at La Roche-sur-Yon, studied at L'École des Beaux-Arts, Paris, and in Italy. He exhibited five paintings in the Salon in 1857, but is chiefly known for the thirty large panels, illustrative of music and dancing, executed with great skill and imaginative power, with which he decorated the foyer of the Paris Opera (1866–1876). He was also responsible for the frescoes in the Cour de Cassation at the Paris law courts and ceilings at Chantilly.

BAUER, (1) **Caroline,** *bow'ér* (1807–78), German actress, born at Heidelberg, in 1829 she married Prince Leopold, afterwards King of the Belgians. Their morganatic union was as brief as it was unhappy; in 1831 she returned to the stage, which she quitted only in 1844, on her marriage to a Polish count. See her *Memoirs* (trans. 1884).

(2) **Georg.** See AGRICOLA.

BAUM, Vicki, *bowm* (1896–1960), Austrian novelist, born in Vienna, wrote *Grand Hotel* (1930), *Helene, Grand Opera* (1942), &c., short stories, and plays.

BAUMÉ, Antoine, *bō-may'* (1728–1804), French chemist, born at Senlis, invented the hydrometer named after him and many dyeing processes.

BAUMEISTER, Willi, *bow'mīs-ter* (1889–1955), German painter, born at Stuttgart. For some years he was a professor at the Frankfurt School of Art, but the Hitler régime prohibited him from teaching and he turned to scientific research on colour and to prehistoric archaeology. These interests are reflected in his work (cf. African *Histories,* a series of paintings depicting strange organic forms, dun-coloured on white background). His series of paintings, from the *Mauerbilder* murals, through *Painter with his Palette* to the *Montaru* and *Monturi* experiments, show wide variety of theme and style and continuously novel treatment. See monograph by W. Grohmann (1952).

BAUMGARTEN, Alexander Gottlieb, *bowm' gar-tén* (1714–62), German aesthetic philosopher, a clear and acute thinker of the school of Wolff, was born in Berlin, and in 1740 became professor of Philosophy at Frankfurt-on-the-Oder. His *Aesthetica* (1750–58) influenced Kant, and the *Metaphysica* (1739) is a systematic rendering of Wolff's rationalistic philosophy. See Life by G. F. Meier (1763), and studies by J. Schmidt (Halle 1874) and H. G. Peters (1934).

BAUR, Ferdinand Christian, *bowr* (1792–1860), German theologian and New Testament critic, was born at Schmiden, near Stuttgart, and held the Tübingen chair of Theology from 1826. He founded the 'Tübingen School' of theology, the first to use strict historical research methods in the study of early Christianity. See studies by R. Mackay (1863) and A. Schweitzer (1912).

BAX, (1) **Sir Arnold Edward Trevor** (1883–1953), English composer, was born in London and studied at the Royal Academy of Music. A visit to Russia in 1910 directly inspired such piano pieces as *Gopak* (1911) and *In a Vodka Shop* (1915), but much more influential on Bax was the Celtic revival. His love and admiration for all things Celtic was expressed early in Irish short stories, which he wrote under the name of Dermot O'Byrne, and musically in orchestral pieces (1912–13), in many songs set to the words of revival poets, in the choral

St Patrick's Breastplate (1923-24), and in *An Irish Elegy* (1917), for English horn, harp and strings. Between 1921 and 1939 Bax, a self-styled ' brazen romantic ', wrote his seven symphonies, expressing moods from bitterness to serenity; in 1921 his *Mater Ora Filium* assured his place in the great English choral tradition; and his vast output in most other fields—tone poems such as *In the Faery Hills* (1909) and *Tintagel* (1917), chamber music, piano solos and concertos—attests to the validity of his appointment in 1942 as Master of the King's (from 1952 Queen's) Musick. He was knighted in 1937, and died in Cork in 1953. See his autobiography, *Farewell my Youth* (1943). His brother **Clifford** (1886-1962) was a playwright and author.

(2) **Ernest Belfort** (1854-1926), a founder of English Socialism, born in Leamington. A barrister, he founded with William Morris the Socialist League and wrote much on Socialism, history, and philosophy. See Life by R. Arch (1927).

BAXTER, (1) **George** (1804-67), English engraver and print maker, born in Lewes, son of (3), developed a method of printing in oil colours, using copper or steel plates for his outlines, with neutral tones on the same plate obtained by aquatint or stipple. His process, patented in 1835, required a combination of between ten and twenty wood and metal blocks for each reproduction.

(2) **Gregory Paul** (1876-1953), American chemist, was born at Somerville, Mass. A professor at Harvard, he helped to determine the atomic weight of lead.

(3) **John** (1781-1858), English printer, father of (1), was born in Surrey, settled in Lewes and published the illustrated ' Baxter's Bible ' and the first book of cricket rules.

(4) **Richard** (1615-91), English Nonconformist divine, was born at Rowton, Shropshire. His education was irregular, but he acquired immense knowledge by private study. In 1638 he was made deacon by the Bishop of Worcester. Originally, like his family and friends, a Conformist, he found himself led to adopt some of the Nonconformist views. In 1642, on the outbreak of the Civil War, he retired to Coventry, and ministered for two years to its garrison and inhabitants. His sympathies were almost wholly with the Puritans, and after Naseby he acted as army chaplain, and was present at the sieges of Bridgwater, Bristol, Exeter, and Worcester. He went to Kidderminster (1647), but his uncertain health caused him to retire to Rouse-Lench, Worcestershire, where he wrote the first part of *The Saints' Everlasting Rest* (1650). At the Restoration he was appointed a royal chaplain, but in 1662 the Act of Uniformity drove him out of the English Church. The Act of Indulgence in 1672 permitted him to return to London, where he divided his time between preaching and writing. But in 1685 he was brought, for alleged sedition in his Paraphrase of the New Testament, before Judge Jeffreys, who treated him in the most brutal manner, calling him a dog, and swearing it would be no more than justice to whip such a villain through the city. Condemned to pay 500 marks, and to be

imprisoned till the fine was paid, he lay in King's Bench Prison for nearly eighteen months. See his autobiographical *Reliquiae Baxterianae* (1696), Life by Powicke (1924), and studies by Ladell (1929) and H. Martin (1954).

BAYARD, *bī'ard,* American family of Democrat politicians:

(1) **James Asheton** (1767-1815), father of (2) and (3), a lawyer, was elected to congress in 1796, a conspicuous member of the Federal party. He was in the senate from 1804 to 1813, opposed the War of 1812, and was one of the negotiators of the treaty which followed.

(2) **James Asheton** (1799-1880), son of (1), also a distinguished Democratic senator.

(3) **Richard Henry** (1796-1868), son of (1), was long a senator, and represented the United States in Belgium.

(4) **Thomas Francis** (1828-98), son of (2), qualified for the bar, and entering the senate (1869), acted with the Democrats. He was proposed for the presidency in 1880 and 1884, and, secretary of state 1885-89, was in 1893-97 ambassador to Great Britain.

BAYARD, Pierre du Terrail, Chevalier de, *bah-yahr* (1476-1524), ' the knight without fear and without reproach ', was born at the Château Bayard, near Grenoble. Accompanying Charles VIII to Italy in 1494-95, he won his spurs at the battle of Fornovo, where he captured a standard. Early in Louis XII's reign, in a battle near Milan, he followed the defeated forces with such impetuosity that he entered the city with them, and was made a prisoner, but the Duke Ludovico Sforza released him without ransom. At Barletta, in 1502, Bayard and ten other French knights fought an equal number of Spaniards; and although seven Frenchmen were thrown in the first charge, the result, chiefly through Bayard's bravery, after a six hours' combat, was declared equal. He fought bravely in Spain, and against the Genoese and Venetians. In 1515 Bayard was sent into Dauphiné to make a way for the army over the Alps and through Piedmont; in this expedition he took Prosper Colonna prisoner. Next, at Marignano, he gained a victory for Francis I, who, in consequence, submitted to receive the honour of knighthood from Bayard. When Charles V invaded Champagne with a large army, Bayard defended Mézières. He was mortally wounded by a shot from an arquebus while defending the passage of the Sesia, and died facing the foe, reciting the *Miserere.* His body was sent home and buried in the Minorities' church near Grenoble. The best Life is by J. Joffrey, probably Bayard's secretary, ' Le Loyal Serviteur ', (1527, trans. 1825). See also Lives by C. Hare (1911) and Shellabarger (1929).

BAYAZID I. See BAJAZET.

BAYER, Johann, *bī'ėr* (1572-1625), German astronomer, was born at Rhain, in Bavaria, and died an advocate at Augsburg. His *Uranometria* (1603) depicts the positions of 500 stars in addition to those given by Tycho Brahe (q.v.). His designations by the letters of the Greek alphabet in preference to the Arabic proper names is stil used for the brighter stars.

BAYLE, Pierre (1647-1706), French philosopher and critic, was born at Carlat, near Foix, in Languedoc. Although a Protestant pastor's son, he studied philosophy under the Jesuits at Toulouse, and for a year and a half turned Catholic. To escape censure, he went to Geneva, where he studied the philosophy of Descartes. After a few years he returned to France, and in 1675 was elected to the chair of Philosophy at Sedan, in 1681 at Rotterdam. In 1684 he started *Nouvelles de la république des lettres*, one of the most successful attempts at a popular journal of literary criticism. The revocation of the Edict of Nantes led Bayle to write a strong defence of toleration; but accusations brought forward by the theologian Jurieu, who regarded Bayle as an agent of France and the enemy of Protestantism, led to his dismissal in 1693. Bayle now devoted his leisure to the *Dictionnaire historique et critique* (Rotterdam 1696). In it he discussed the great speculative themes and the literature of his day in a detached and comprehensive manner. His detachment was the basis of his scepticism, which greatly influenced the literature and philosophy of the coming age of enlightenment. His touchstone is the Cartesian principle of ' clear and distinct ideas '. The article on ' Zeno ' in his dictionary examines masterfully the concepts of space and time. His claim that morality is independent of religion caused him to be persecuted to the end of his life. See Lives and studies by A. Cazes (1905), J. Devolve (1906), and E. Lacoste (1929).

BAYLIS, Lilian Mary (1874-1937), English theatrical manager, born in London, the daughter of musicians. In 1890 the family emigrated to South Africa, where she became a music teacher in Johannesburg. Returning to England in 1898, she helped with the management of the Royal Victoria Hall (afterwards the Old Vic), becoming manager in 1912; under her the theatre became a joint home of Shakespeare and opera. In 1931 she acquired Sadler's Wells Theatre for the exclusive presentation of opera and ballet. She was made a C.H. in 1929. See *The Work of Lilian Baylis* ed. E. G. Harcourt Williams (1938), and Life by the Thorndikes (1938).

BAYLY, Thomas Haynes (1797-1839), English songwriter, was born at Bath, and was trained for the church. He wrote 'I'd be a Butterfly', 'She wore a Wreath of Roses', 'Oh, no, we never mention her', and other songs, verse, tales and plays. See A. Lang's *Essays in Little* (1891).

BAYREUTH, Margravine of. See ANSPACH.

BAZAINE, *ba-zen*, (1) François Achille (1811-1888), marshal of France, born at Versailles. Entering the army in 1831, he served in Algeria, Spain, the Crimea, the Italian campaign of 1859, and the French expedition to Mexico (1862), but surrendered at Metz (October 27, 1870), and 3 marshals, over 6000 officers, and 173,000 men became prisoners of war. For this, in 1873, he was court-martialled, and sentenced to degradation and death, a sentence commuted to 20 years' imprisonment. But in 1874 he escaped from the fortress on the Île Ste Marguerite, near Cannes, and he died at Madrid.

(2) Jean René (1904-), French painter, born in Paris. His style has developed through Cubism to abstract art, and he has produced a number of very successful tapestry designs.

BAZALGETTE, Sir Joseph William, *baz'él-jet* (1819-90), the engineer of London's drainage system and the Thames embankments, was knighted in 1874.

BAZARD, Saint-Amand, *ba-zahr'* (1791-1832), French Socialist, born at Paris, in 1820 founded an association of French Carbonari, and in 1825 attached himself to the school of Saint-Simon, he and Enfantin becoming its ' Pères Suprêmes '.

BAZIN, René,-*zi'*(1853-1932), French novelist, born at Angers, depicted with charm and colour the life of peasant folk in the various French provinces, and in some of his novels, such as *Les Oberlé* (1901), dealt with the social problems of his time.

BEACH. See Le Caron

BEACONSFIELD, Earl of. See DISRAELI, BENJAMIN.

BEALE, (1) Dorothea (1831-1906), English pioneer of women's education, was born in London, and from 1858 was principal of Cheltenham Ladies' College. An advocate of higher education for women, she sponsored St Hilda's Hall, Oxford, in 1894 and later became a suffragette. See Lives by E. Raikes (1908) and E. H. Shillito (1920); also J. Kamm, *How Different From Us* (1958).

(2) Lionel Smith (1828-1906), English physiologist, born in London, a professor of King's College, London (1853-96), he discovered ' Beale's cells '.

BEARD, George Miller (1839-83), an American neurologist, born at Montville, Conn., distinguished for his work in neurasthenia and mental illness.

BEARDSLEY, Aubrey (1872-98), English illustrator, born at Brighton, was in an architect's and fire-insurance offices, but became famous by his fantastic posters and illustrations for *Morte d'Arthur*, Wilde's *Salome, Rape of the Lock, Mlle de Maupin, Volpone*, as well as for the *Yellow Book* magazine (1894 ff.) and his own *Book of Fifty Drawings*, mostly executed in black and white, in a highly individualistic asymmetrical style. With Wilde (q.v.) he is regarded as leader of the 'Decadents' of the 1890s. He died of consumption at Mentone, having embraced the Catholic faith. See studies by Marillier (1900) and Ross (1909), and Life by A. Symons (1949).

BEATON, Cecil (1904-), British photographer and designer, born in London and educated at Harrow and Cambridge. He designed scenery and costumes for many ballet, operatic, theatrical and film productions, including *My Fair Lady* and *Gigi*. His publications include *My Royal Past* (1939), *The Glass of Fashion* (1959) and *My Fair Lady* (1964), and he provided the drawings and illustrations for many other books. In 1957 he received the C.B.E.

BEATON, or Bethune, (1) David (1494-1546), Scottish statesman and prelate, nephew of (2), was born at Balfour, Fife, and educated at the universities of St Andrews, Glasgow, and Paris. He was at the French court (1519) as Scottish ' resident ' and twice later as ambassador to negotiate James V's marriages. He was given French rights of citizenship and appointed Bishop of Mirepoix by Francis I (1537). In 1525 he took his seat in the Scots Parliament as Abbot of Arbroath and was appointed Privy Seal. On the death of (2) in 1539, he succeeded him as Archbishop of St Andrews, and soon began persecuting the Protestants, obtaining from the pope the appointment of *legatus a latere* in Scotland. On James's death, after the disastrous rout at Solway Moss (1542), Beaton produced a forged will, appointing himself and three others regents of the kingdom during the minority of the infant Queen Mary. The nobility, however, elected the Protestant Earl of Arran regent. Beaton was arrested, but soon regained favour with the regent and as chancellor (1543) induced the latter to follow a pro-French policy and publicly to abjure Protestantism. In 1546 he had George Wishart (q.v.) burnt at St Andrews, and witnessed his sufferings from a window. Three months later he was himself assassinated by a band of conspirators in his castle of St Andrews, May 29. His mistress, Marion Ogilvy, had borne him at least two sons and one daughter—the last married an Earl of Crawford. See Life by Herkless (1891).

(2) **James** (1470?–1539), uncle of (1), took his M.A. at St Andrews in 1493, and rose rapidly to be Archbishop of Glasgow (1509), and of St Andrews (1522). One of the regents during James V's minority, he upheld the Hamilton against the Douglas faction; and in 1526 he had 'to keep sheep in Balgrumo', while the Douglases plundered his castle. He was soon, however, reinstated in his see, and figured as a zealous supporter of France, and an opponent of the Reformation, Patrick Hamilton and three other Protestants being burnt during Beaton's primacy.

(3) **James** (1517–1603), nephew of (1), an Archbishop of Glasgow from 1552 until the death of the queen-regent, Mary of Lorraine, when he withdrew to Paris as Scottish ambassador.

BEATRICE, Princess. See BATTENBERG.

BEATTIE, James (1735–1803), Scottish poet and essayist, was born at Laurencekirk, studied at Marischal College, Aberdeen, and after some years as a schoolmaster became in 1760 professor of Moral Philosophy there. His overrated *Essay on Truth* (1770) attacked Hume, but he is chiefly remembered for his poem, *The Minstrel* (1771–74), a forerunner of Romanticism. See Life by Mackie (1908), study by Aldrich (1931), and his London Diary (ed. Walker 1946).

BEATTY, David Beatty, 1st Earl (1871–1936), British admiral, was born at Nantwich, Cheshire, entered the navy and served in the Sudan (1896–98) and was promoted to commander and awarded the D.S.O. As commander of a battleship he took part in the China War (1900) and was promoted to captain, for his leadership in shore operations, at the early age of 38. In 1912 he was appointed to command the 1st Battle Cruiser Squadron. At the outbreak of World War I he steamed into Heligoland Bight, and destroyed three German cruisers. In January 1915 he encountered and pursued German

battle cruisers near the Dogger Bank, sinking the *Blücher*. At the battle of Jutland (May 31, 1916) he fought the hardest action of the war, losing two of his ships, but badly mauling his opponents. He succeeded Lord Jellicoe as commander-in-chief of the Grand Fleet in 1916 and became first sea lord in 1919, when he was created an earl and awarded the O.M. He was a skilled tactician and a great leader. See Life by Chalmers (1951).

BEAUCHAMP, Mary. See ARNIM (1).

BEAUCLERK, Topham, *bō'klahr* (1739–80), English dandy, descendant of Charles II and Nell Gwynn, only son of Lord Sydney Beauclerk, and the friend of Samuel Johnson. In 1768, two days after her divorce from Lord Bolingbroke, he married **Diana** (1734–1808), daughter of the 2nd Duke of Marlborough, and an artist of some ability, still known through Bartolozzi's engravings. See Birkbeck Hill's *Dr Johnson, his Friends and Critics* (1878).

BEAUFORT, *bō'fort*, name of an English family descended from John of Gaunt (q.v.) and Katharine Swynford:

(1) **Henry** (1377–1447), English cardinal, natural son of the above who were married in 1396 and their children legitimized next year by Richard II. He studied at Oxford and Aix-la-Chapelle; was consecrated Bishop of Lincoln in 1398; in 1405 succeeded William of Wykeham in the see of Winchester; thrice filled the office of chancellor; and at the Council of Constance (1417) voted for the election of Pope Martin V, by whom in 1426 he was made a cardinal. He strongly opposed Henry V's proposition to levy a new impost on the clergy for the war against France; but he lent the king (1416–21), out of his own private purse, £28,000—a sum which justifies the belief that he was the wealthiest subject in England. In 1427 the pope sent him as legate into Germany, to organize a crusade against the Hussites. This undertaking failed; and the cardinal fell from papal pleasure. In 1431 he conducted the young king, Henry VI, to Paris, to be crowned as king of France and England. He died at Winchester.

(2) **Jane.** See JAMES I OF SCOTLAND.

(3) **Margaret** (1443–1509), daughter of John, 1st Duke of Somerset, married in 1455 Edmund Tudor, Earl of Richmond. The Lancastrian claim to the English crown was transferred to her with the extinction of the direct line and it was in the right of his mother that her son, Henry VII (q.v.), ascended the throne in 1485. She married twice more, Henry Stafford and the Earl of Derby. She was a benefactress of Oxford and Cambridge. See Life by Routh (1925), and H. Durant, *The Somerset Sequence* (1951).

BEAUFORT, Duke of, a title conferred in 1682 on Henry Somerset, the son of the Marquis of Worcester (q.v.). The succeeding earls were courtiers in Tudor and Stuart times, but Henry, the 7th Duke (1792–1853), and his son Henry, the 8th Duke (1824–1899), were famous sportsmen, the latter an editor of *Badminton Library*, Badminton House in Gloucestershire being the family residence. The second son of the last-named, **Lord Henry** (1849–1932), was a songwriter. See H. Durant, *The Somerset Sequence* (1951).

BEAUFORT, Sir Francis (1774–1857), British admiral and hydrographer, born at Navan, Co. Meath, son of a clergyman. Entering the navy in 1787, he saw active service, including the retreat of Cornwallis (1795), and was severely wounded near Malaga. After a period working on shore telegraphs in Ireland he held three commands, and was dangerously wounded while surveying the coast of Asia Minor and suppressing piracy. From 1829 to 1855 he was hydrographer to the navy, devising the Beaufort scale of wind force and a tabulated system of weather registration.

BEAUHARNAIS, *bō-ahr-nay*, ancient French family, of which the important members are:

(1) **Alexandre, Vicomte de** (1760–94), French army officer, was born in Martinique, served in the American War of Independence, and in 1789 eagerly embraced the French Revolution. He was made secretary of the National Assembly, but was guillotined July 23, 1794. In 1779 he had married **Josephine** (q.v.), afterwards wife of Napoleon, and his daughter **Hortense** in 1802 married Napoleon's brother Louis; Beauharnais was thus the grandfather of Napoleon III.

(2) **Eugène** (1781–1824), son of (1), French general, after his mother's marriage (1796) with Napoleon, accompanied him to Italy and Egypt. He rapidly rose to the highest military rank; and in 1805 was made a prince of France and viceroy of Italy. In 1806 he married the Princess Amelia Augusta of Bavaria (1788–1851), and in 1807 was created Prince of Venice, and declared by Napoleon his adopted son, and heir of the kingdom of Italy. Wise, honourable, and virtuous, he showed great military talent in the Italian campaigns, in the wars against Austria, and in the retreat from Moscow. He organized the defence of his kingdom until Napoleon's abdication in 1814. He then settled in Bavaria and was created Duke of Leuchtenberg. See Lives by Aubriet (1825), Baudoncourt (1827), Prinz Adalbert von Bayern (1940), C. Oman (1967), and his *Mémoires et Correspondance* by Du Casse (1858–60). His second son, **Max Eugène Joseph Napoléon** (1817–52), who in 1835 succeeded his elder brother as Duke of Leuchtenberg, married a daughter of the Emperor Nicholas of Russia; and his descendants bear the name of Romanovski, and ranked among the members of the Russian imperial family.

BEAUMARCHAIS, Pierre Augustin Caron de, *bō-mahr-shay* (1732–99), French playwright, next to Molière the greatest French comic dramatist, the son of a Paris watchmaker named Caron, was born on January 24. Brought up in his father's trade, he invented, at twenty-one, a new escapement which was pirated by a rival. The affair brought him to notice at court, where his handsome figure and fine address quickly procured him advancement. He was engaged to teach the harp to Louis XV's daughters, and in 1756 the wealthy widow of a court official married him, whereupon he assumed the title by which he was known thenceforward. Duverney, a rich banker of Paris, also helped him to some speculations which realized a handsome fortune, largely increased in 1768 by another prudent marriage with a wealthy widow. His first plays, *Eugénie* (1767) and *Les Deux Amis* (1770), scored only a moderate success. The death of Duverney in 1770 involved him in a long lawsuit with his heir, Count Lablache, in the course of which he became the idol of the people, as the supposed champion of popular rights against the corrupt tribunals of the old régime. Beaumarchais appealed to the public by publishing his famous *Mémoires du Sieur Beaumarchais par lui-même* (1774–78; new ed. by Sainte-Beuve, 1873), a work which united the bitterest satire with the sharpest logic, and gained for him a reputation that made even Voltaire uneasy. The same brilliant satire burns in his two famous comedies, *Le Barbier de Séville* (1775) and *La Folle Journée, ou le mariage de Figaro* (1784). The latter had a most unprecedented success; and both are still popular plays in France, but in England are chiefly known through Mozart's and Rossini's adaptations. The Revolution cost Beaumarchais his vast fortune, and, suspected of an attempt to sell arms to the *émigrés*, he had even to take refuge in Holland and England (1793). Stone deaf in his last years, he died in Paris of apoplexy, May 19. See Lives and monographs by Loménie (4th ed. 1880), Paul Lindau (Berl. 1875), Lintilhac (1887), P. Frischauer (1936), and C. Cox (1962).

BEAUMONT, Fr. *bō-mõ*, Eng. *bō'mont*, (1) Éon de. See ÉON DE BEAUMONT.

(2) **Francis** (*c.* 1584–1616), English Elizabethan dramatist associated with John Fletcher (q.v.), was born, the third son of Francis Beaumont, a judge of the common pleas, at Gracedieu, Leicestershire, was educated at Broadgates Hall (now Pembroke College), Oxford, and entered the Inner Temple in 1600. He soon became an intimate friend of Ben Jonson and the other men of genius who met at the Mermaid Tavern, among them John Fletcher. With the latter, Beaumont was to be associated closely until he married Ursula Isley (1613). They are said to have shared everything in common, work, lodgings, and even clothes. Their dramatic works, compiled in 1647, contained 35 pieces; another folio, published in 1679, 52 works. Modern research finds Beaumont's hand in only about 10 plays, which include, however, the masterpieces. Fletcher's verse avoids enjambment, rhyme and prose while Beaumont uses all three devices. Fletcher also makes more frequent use of the feminine ending than any other contemporary poet. *The Woman Hater* (1607) is attributed solely to Beaumont, and he had the major share in *The Knight of the Burning Pestle* (1609), a burlesque of knight errantry in the Cervantes vein and a parody of Heywood's *Four Prentices of London. Philaster, The Maid's Tragedy* and *A King and no King* established their joint popularity. Other works include *The Scornful Lady* and *Cupid's Revenge. The Masque of the Inner Temple*, was written by Beaumont in honour of the marriage of the elector palatinate and the princess Elizabeth (1613). He was buried in Westminster Abbey. See studies by G. C. Macaulay (1883), E. H. C. Oliphant (1927),

B. Maxwell (1939), Appleton (1956) and M. Greaves (1966).

(3) **Sir George Howland** (1753–1827), English landscape painter and art patron, was born at Stonehall, Dunmow, Essex, and studied at Eton and New College, Oxford. He was an intimate friend of Reynolds; at his Leicestershire seat, Coleorton, entertained Wordsworth, Scott, Rogers, Byron, Wilkie, Haydon, &c.; and presented his valuable collection of pictures to the National Gallery. See Knight's *Memorials of Coleorton* (1887).

(4) **Jean Baptiste Élie de** (1798–1874), French geologist, born at Canon, Calvados, assisted in making a great geological map of France (1840).

(5) **Sir John** (1582–1627), English poet, was the elder brother of (2). His *Bosworth Field*, in which the heroic couplet makes its first appearance in English poetry, and sacred poems (1629) have been edited by Dr Grosart (1869).

(6) **Joseph** (1616–99), English poet, born at Hadleigh, Suffolk, from 1663 was master of Peterhouse, Cambridge. He wrote the long epic poem *Psyche* (1648).

(7) **William** (1796–1853), American doctor, whose work on Digestion (1833) was based on experiments with a young Canadian, Alexis St Martin, suffering from a gunshot wound, which had left a permanent opening in his stomach, which Beaumont had treated. See Life by J. S. Myer (1939), and study by G. Rosen (1942).

BEAUNE, Florimond de, *bōn* (1601–52), French mathematician and friend of Descartes, was born at Blois. His work anticipated the integral calculus.

BEAUREGARD, Pierre Gustave Toutant, *bō-ré-gahr* (1818–93), American Confederate general, was born near New Orleans, graduated at West Point in 1838, served with distinction in the Mexican war, and was appointed by the Confederate government to the command at Charleston, S.C., where, April 12, 1861, he commenced the war by the bombardment of Fort Sumter. He was virtually in command at the first battle of Bull Run, July 21, 1861; and, sent to the West in the spring of 1862 as second to General A. S. Johnston, he succeeded to the command when the latter was killed in the first day's battle of Shiloh or Pittsburg Landing. Defeated on the second day's fighting, he retreated to Corinth, Miss., where he reorganized his division; but on the approach of the Union troops he evacuated the place, and was superseded by General Bragg. In 1864 he commanded the military division of the West, but failed to check Sherman's march to the sea.

BEAVERBROOK, William Maxwell Aitken, 1st Baron (1879–1964), Canadian-born, British newspaper magnate and politician, born at Maple, Ontario, the son of a Presbyterian minister, early went into business, was a stockbroker in 1907 and by 1910 with characteristic forcefulness and shrewdness had made a fortune out of the amalgamation of Canadian cement mills. He came over to Britain, entered Parliament, became private secretary to Bonar Law, and was knighted in 1911. He was an observer at the Western Front early in World War I and wrote *Canada in Flanders* (1917). When Lloyd George became premier, he was made minister of information, and a baronet. In 1919 he plunged into journalism and took Fleet Street by storm by taking over the *Daily Express*, which he made into the most widely-read daily newspaper in the world. He founded the *Sunday Express* (1921) and bought over the *Evening Standard* (1929). The ' Beaverbrook press ' fully expressed the ebullient, relentless, and mission-laden personality of its owner. Always shrewd, if often verging on the sensational, it talked with and never down to its reading public. From 1929 its mission was Empire Free Trade. In World War II Churchill successfully harnessed Beaverbrook's dynamic administrative powers to the production of much-needed aircraft. Beaverbrook was made minister of supply (1941–42), lord privy seal, and Lend-Lease administrator in the U.S.A. He became chancellor of the university of New Brunswick in 1947. His rise to wealth and power was one of the success stories of the time, but he failed to realize his political aims. See his *Politicians and the War* (1928–32), *Men and Power* (new ed. 1956), *The Decline and Fall of Lloyd George* (1963), &c., the severe portrait of him by Sutherland in the Tate Gallery, Life by T. Driberg (1956) and study by A. Wood (1965).

BEBEL, Ferdinand August, *bay'bel* (1840–1913), German Socialist, born at Cologne, became a master turner, and rose by 1871 to be a leader of the German Social Democrat movement and its chief spokesman in the Reichstag. Imprisonment more than once added to his popularity. He wrote much on Socialism, on the Peasants' War, on the status of women, and an autobiography (trans. 1912).

BECCARIA, Cesare, Marchese de, *bek-ka-ree'a* (1735 or 1738–94), Italian political and philanthropic writer, born at Milan, in 1764 published anonymously his *Dei delitti e delle pene* (' On Crimes and Punishments '). Denouncing capital punishment and torture and early advocating prevention of crime by education, the work had a widespread influence on the punishment and prevention of crime. In 1768 he was made professor of Political Philosophy at Milan and in 1791 a member of the board for reform of the judicial code. See Life prefixed to Farren's translation of the *Dei delitti* (1880) and C. Phillipson, *Three Criminal Law Reformers* (1923).

BECHE. See DE LA BECHE.

BECHER, (1) Lady. See O'NEILL, ELIZA.

(2) **Johann Joachim,** *beKH'ér* (1635–82), German chemist, born at Speyer, whose *Physica Subterranea* (1669) was the first attempt made to bring physics and chemistry into close relation.

BECHSTEIN, Karl, *beKH'stīn* (1826–1900), born at Gotha, in 1856 founded in Berlin his famous piano factory.

BECK, or Beek, David (1621–56), a Dutch portrait painter and assistant of Van Dyck, worked mostly at foreign courts.

BECKER, (1) George Ferdinand (1847–1919), American geologist, took part in the 40th parallel survey, and achieved renown for his work on mineral deposits.

(2) **Nikolaus** (1809–45), German poet, wrote in 1840 the *Rheinlied* ('Sie sollen ihn nicht haben '), which called forth Alfred de Musset's answer ('Nous l'avons eu, votre Rhin allemand ').

(3) **Wilhelm Adolf** (1796–1846), German classical archaeologist, born in Dresden, in 1842 became professor at Leipzig. In his novel *Charicles* (1840) he ventured to reproduce the social life of old Greece; and in *Gallus* (1838) of the Augustan age at Rome.

BECKET, (1) Isaac (1653–1719), one of the earliest English mezzotint engravers, was born in Kent, apprenticed to calico printing, but learnt from Lutterel the art of mezzotint engraving and executed many plates from the portraits of Kneller, including that of Charles II, the Duke of York, and Kneller's self-portrait.

(2) **Thomas à** (1118–70), English saint and martyr, Archbishop of Canterbury, was born in London of Norman parentage, the son of a wealthy merchant. Educated at Merton Priory and in London, he was trained in knightly exercises at Pevensey Castle, studied theology at Paris, and became a notary. About 1142 he entered the household of Theobald, Archbishop of Canterbury, who sent him to study canon law at Bologna and Auxerre. At the papal court in 1152 he prevented the recognition of Stephen's son Eustace as heir to the throne; in 1155, the year after Henry's accession, he became chancellor and the first Englishman since the Conquest who had filled any high office. A brilliant figure at court, personifying the manly virtues of his time, he showed his knightly prowess in the Toulouse campaign (1159) and was also a skilled diplomat and a consummate host. The change, then, was all the more drastic when in 1162 he was created Archbishop of Canterbury. He resigned the chancellorship, turned a rigid ascetic, showed his liberality only in charities, and in short became as zealous a servant of the church as ever before of king or archbishop. He figured soon as a champion of her rights against the king and had courtiers, several nobles and other laymen excommunicated for their alienation of church property. Henry II, who, like all the Norman kings, endeavoured to keep the clergy in subordination to the state, in 1164 convoked the Council of Clarendon, where were adopted the so-called 'Constitutions', or laws relative to the respective powers of church and state. To these, the primate at first declared he would never consent; but afterwards he was induced to give his unwilling approval. Henry now began to perceive that Becket's notions and his own were utterly antagonistic, and clearly exhibited his hostility to Becket, who tried to leave the country. For this offence Henry confiscated his goods, and sequestered the revenues of his see. A claim was also made on him for 44,000 marks, as the balance due by him to the crown when he ceased to be chancellor. Becket appealed to the pope, and escaped to France. He spent two years at the Cistercian abbey of Pontigny in Burgundy; and then went to Rome, and

pleaded personally before the pope, who reinstated him in the see of Canterbury. Becket now returned to France, and wrote angry letters to the English bishops, threatening them with excommunication. Several futile efforts were made to reconcile him with Henry; but in 1170 an agreement was reached. The result was that Becket returned to England, entering Canterbury amid the rejoicings of the people, who regarded him as a shield from the oppressions of the nobility. Fresh quarrels soon broke out and excommunications were renewed. Henry's impetuously voiced wish to be rid of 'this turbulent priest' led to Becket's murder in Canterbury cathedral on December 29, 1170, by four knights, Hugh de Merville, William de Tracy, Reginald Fitzurse, and Richard le Breton. Becket's martyrdom forced concessions from the king. He was canonized in 1172, and Henry II did public penance at his tomb in 1174. In 1220 his bones were transferred to a shrine in the Trinity chapel. Until it was destroyed in 1538, this was the popular place of pilgrimage which Chaucer described in the prologue to the *Canterbury Tales*. See Lives by J. Morris (1859), Robertson and Shephard (1875–85), Hutton (1889), Duggan (1952), studies by Stubbs, *Constitutional History*, Vol. I (1874), Brooke (1931), and plays, *Murder in the Cathedral* by T. S. Eliot (1938) and *Becket* by J. Anouilh (1961).

BECKETT, (1) Sir Edmund. See GRIMTHORPE.

(2) **Samuel** (1906–), Irish author and playwright, born in Dublin, became a lecturer in English at the École Normale Supérieure in Paris and later in French at Trinity College, Dublin. From 1932 he lived mostly in France and was, for a time, secretary to James Joyce, with whom he shared the same tantalizing preoccupation with language, with the failure of human beings to communicate successfully mirroring the pointlessness of life which they strive to make purposeful. His early poetry and first two novels, *Murphy* (1938) and *Watt*, were written in English, but not the trilogy *Molloy*, *Malone Meurt* (trans. 1958), and *L'Innommable*, or the plays *En attendant Godot* (trans. *Waiting for Godot*, 1956), which took London by storm, and *Fin de partie* (trans. *End Game*, 1957), all of which first appeared in French. *Godot* best exemplifies the Beckettian view of the human predicament, the poignant bankruptcy of all hopes, philosophies, and endeavours. He was awarded the 1969 Nobel prize for literature. See studies by Kenner (1962) and Cohn (1962).

BECKFORD, (1) William (1709–70), father of (2), born in Jamaica, in 1723 was sent to England, and educated at Westminster. Elected an alderman (1752) and member for the City of London (1753), he was twice lord mayor. As such he showed himself an outspoken Whig, a rival almost of Wilkes, a man who dared to speak face to face with a king. A petition from the London corporation, presented by him to George III, being treated as unconstitutional, he delivered a dignified remonstrance, and, the king's answer being still unconciliatory, proceeded to argue the point, but died four weeks later.

(2) **William Thomas** (1760–1844), English

writer and collector, son of (1), was born at Fonthill, Wiltshire, and in 1770 inherited a fortune. Already in his seventeenth year he revealed remarkable intellectual precocity in his satirical *Memoirs of Extraordinary Painters*. From 1777 he spent much time on the Continent, meeting Voltaire in 1778, and later making a grand tour in Flanders, Germany, and Italy. In 1784 he entered parliament, but he became involved in a scandal and was excluded from society. In 1787 *Vathek*, an Arabian tale of extraordinary and gloomy imaginative splendour, appeared in French in two editions, the graceful style being modelled on Voltaire's, and was translated and published by Samuel Henley in defiance of Beckford's wishes in 1786. Revisiting Portugal in 1793, he settled in that ' paradise ' near Cintra which Byron commemorates in *Childe Harold*. He returned to England in 1796, and proceeded to erect a new palace, Fonthill Abbey, its chief feature a tower, which fell in 1800, but was rebuilt (276 feet high). In 1822 Beckford sold Fonthill Abbey, moved to Bath, and there built Lansdown Tower. In 1834 he published *Italy, with Sketches of Spain and Portugal* (incorporating, in modified form, *Dreams, Waking Thoughts*, and *Incident*, suppressed in 1783), and in 1835 another volume of *Recollections* of travel. He died May 2. See Grimsditch's translation of *Vathek* (1929), and Lives by J. W. Oliver (1930) and G. Chapman (1937).

BECKINGTON. See BEKYNTON.

BECKMANN, Ernst (1853-1923), German organic chemist, born at Solingen, a professor at Erlangen and Leipzig, discovered the molecular transformation of the oximes of ketones into acid amides, invented apparatus for the determination of freezing and boiling points, and the sensitive thermometer which bears his name.

(2) **Johann** (1739-1811), professor of Political Economy at Göttingen, is remembered chiefly for his *History of Inventions* (1780-1805; trans. 1814).

(3) **Max** (1884-1950), German painter and engraver, born at Leipzig. He was one of several German Expressionist painters who were forced to flee by the Nazis, and a brilliantly-coloured triptych entitled *Departure* in the New York Museum of Modern Art is typical of his work. He also executed a large number of self-portraits in various graphic media, including drypoint and lithograph.

BECKWITH, a family of soldiers:

(1) **Sir George** (1753-1823), uncle of (2), as governor of Barbadoes (1808-14) captured Martinique and Guadeloupe.

(2) **John** (1789-1862), nephew of (1) and (3), was wounded at Waterloo and reached the rank of major-general (1846). In later life he settled among the Waldenses in Piedmont.

(3) **Sir Thomas Sydney** (1772-1831), brother of (1), earned fame in India and the Peninsula.

BECQUE, Henry (1837-99), French dramatist, born in Paris, is known by two plays, *Les Corbeaux* (1882) and *La Parisienne* (1885), both dramatic portrayals of bourgeois life and character.

BÉCQUER, Gustavo Adolfo, *bek'ker* (1836-1870), Spanish romance writer and lyric poet, born at Seville. His *Legends* are written in a weirdly musical prose, but he is best known for his troubadour love verses. See Life by F. Schneider (Leipzig 1914).

BECQUEREL, *bek-er-el*, French family of physicists:

(1) **Alexander Edmond** (1820-91), son and assistant of (2), and father of (3), succeeded his father as professor and researched into solar radiation, diamagnetism, &c., and constructed a phosphoroscope.

(2) **Antoine César** (1788-1878), father of (1), was born at Châtillon-sur-Loing, was the first to use electrolysis as a means of isolating metals from their ores. In 1837 he was awarded the Copley medal, elected F.R.S., and became professor at the Museum Histoire Naturelle.

(3) **Antoine Henri** (1852-1908), son of (1), shared the Nobel prize with the Curies in 1903 for discovering the ' Becquerel rays ', emitted from uranium salts, which led to the isolation of radium and to the beginnings of modern nuclear physics. His son, **Jean**, was also a physicist.

BEDAUX, Charles Eugène, *bé-dō* (1887-1944), American industrialist, was born in France and emigrated to America in 1908. He originated an efficiency system which provoked much controversy, and became controller of companies providing efficiency surveys throughout the world. He returned to live in France, and the Duke and Duchess of Windsor were married at his home in 1937. Under the German occupation he acted as intermediary between Vichy and Berlin; but at the liberation was arrested by the Americans on suspicion of treason and committed suicide.

BEDDOE, John, *bed'ō* (1826-1911), a pioneer English anthropologist, born at Bewdley, served as a civil surgeon during the Crimean War, and afterwards practised at Clifton. He was a keen observer of physical characters, especially of hair and eye colour and his *Races of Britain* (1886) laid the foundations of British anthropology.

BEDDOES, *bed'ōz,* (1) **Thomas** (1760-1808), English physician, father of (2), born at Shifnal, studied medicine and became reader in Chemistry at Oxford, but his sympathies with the French Revolution led to his resignation (1792). During 1798-1801 he carried on at Clifton a ' pneumatic institute ' for the cure of diseases by the inhalation of gases, with Humphry Davy for his assistant. He wrote on political, social, and medical subjects and edited the works of John Brown (q.v.), founder of the Brunonian movement. See Life by Stock (1811).

(2) **Thomas Lovell** (1803-49), English poet and physiologist, eldest son of (1), was born at Clifton, and educated at Charterhouse and Oxford. In 1822 he published *The Bride's Tragedy*, which was a success. In 1825 he went to Göttingen to study medicine, and then led a strange wandering life as doctor and democrat, in Germany and Switzerland, with occasional visits to England. From 1825 he was engaged in the composition of a drama, *Death's Jest-book*, which appeared in 1850,

a year after his suicide in Basel. See books by Donner and his edition of the *Works* (1935).

BEDE, Cuthbert. See BRADLEY, EDWARD.

BEDE, or Baeda, the Venerable (*c.* 673–735), the greatest name in the ancient literature of England, was born near Monkwearmouth, in Durham. He studied at the Benedictine monastery there under Benedict Biscop, and was later transferred to the daughter monastery at Jarrow. Here he devoted himself to study, while he was diligent in observing the discipline of his order, as well as in the daily service of the monastery church, having been successively ordained deacon and priest. His industry was enormous, and he was continually employed in reading, writing, and teaching. Besides Latin and Greek, classical as well as patristic literature, he studied Hebrew, medicine, astronomy, and prosody. He wrote homilies, lives of saints, hymns, epigrams, works on chronology and grammar, and commentaries on the Old and New Testament. He had just finished dictating a translation of St John into Anglo-Saxon, when he died, May 26, 735. He was buried at Jarrow; but in the 11th century his bones were removed to Durham. His most valuable work is the *Historia Ecclesiastica Gentis Anglorum*, to which we are indebted for almost all our information on the ancient history of England down to A.D. 731. Bede gained the materials for this work partly from Roman writers, but chiefly from native chronicles and biographies, records and public documents, and oral and written communications from his contemporaries. King Alfred translated it into Anglo-Saxon. His *De Sex Aetatibus Mundi* was an important book on chronology. See *Bede, His Life, Times and Writings*, ed. A. H. Thompson (1935).

BEDELL, William (1571–1642), Anglican divine, born at Black Nottley, Essex, was from 1629 Bishop of Kilmore, resigned in 1633, and devoted himself to conciliation with the Roman Catholic Church and translation of the Old Testament into Irish. See Life by his son and A. Clogy, ed. by Shuckburgh (1903).

BEDFORD, John of Lancaster, Duke of (1389–1435), third son of Henry IV, in 1403 was made governor of Berwick-upon-Tweed and warden of the east marches. In 1414 his brother, Henry V, created him Duke of Bedford, and during the war with France he was appointed lieutenant of the kingdom. After Henry's death (1422), Bedford became guardian of the kingdom, and regent also of France; and, on Charles VI's death two months later, he had his nephew proclaimed King of France and England as Henry VI. In the wars with the dauphin which followed, Bedford displayed great generalship, and defeated the French in several battles—especially at Verneuil in 1424. But, owing to the way in which men and money were doled out to him from England, and the withdrawal of the forces of the Duke of Burgundy, he could not profit fully by his victories. The appearance of Joan of Arc was followed by disaster to his arms; and in 1435 a treaty was negotiated at Rouen between Charles VII

and the Duke of Burgundy, which ruined English interests in France. He died at Rouen just prior to the signing of this treaty and was buried in the cathedral there. See also RUSSELL family.

BÉDIER, Joseph, *bed-yay* (1864–1938), French scholar and mediaevalist, was born in Paris. In 1893 he was appointed professor of Mediaeval French Language and Literature at the Collège de France, and received his doctorate for *Les Fabliaux* (1893). His *Roman de Tristan et Iseult* in 1900 gained him a European reputation, and *Les Légendes épiques* (1908–13) developed in exquisite French his theory of the origin of the great cycles of romance. See E. Vinaver's *Hommage à Bédier* (1942).

BEDLOE, William (1650–80), English informer, born at Chepstow, befriended the Jesuits in London and spied for them in Europe. In 1678 he profited by the example of Titus Oates by giving an account of the ‘ popish plot ’ and providing details of the murder of Sir Edmund Godfrey. His financial rewards encouraged him to continue in the profitable denunciation of Roman Catholics. He died at Bristol. See R. W. Postgate, *Murder, Piracy and Treason* (1926).

BEDMAR, Alfonso de Cueva, Marquis de (1572–1655), Spanish conspirator, was sent in 1607 as Spanish ambassador to Venice, and in 1618 plotted the overthrow of the republic. One of the conspirators betrayed the plot, which forms the theme of Otway's *Venice Preserved*. Bedmar was dismissed, and went to Flanders, where he became president of the council. In 1622 he was made a cardinal, and finally Bishop of Oviedo.

BEE, or Begha, St, Irish princess, founded the nunnery of St Bees in Cumberland, *c.* 656.

BEEBE, Charles William (1877–1962), American naturalist, born at Brooklyn, curator from 1899 of ornithology for the New York Zoological Society, wrote many widely-read books, including *Galapagos* (1923) and *The Arcturus Adventure* (1925), and explored ocean depths in a bathysphere. See his *Exploring with Beebe*.

BEECHAM, Sir Thomas, 2nd Bart. (1879–1961), British conductor and impresario, son of **Sir Joseph, 1st Bart.** (1848–1916), the famous pill millionaire, was born at St Helens, Lancashire, educated at Rossall School and Wadham College, Oxford, and travelled extensively. He did not study at any school of music before starting his career as conductor with the New Symphony Orchestra at the Wigmore Hall in 1906. He soon branched out as impresario and producer of opera, introducing 60 works unknown to British audiences, as well as Diaghilev's Russian ballet. He was principal conductor (1932) and artistic director (1933) of Covent Garden, and in 1943 was conductor at the Metropolitan Opera House, New York. In 1944 he returned to Britain, having married **Betty Humby** (d. 1958), the pianist. In 1947 he founded the Royal Philharmonic orchestra and conducted at Glyndebourne (1948–49). Beecham did much to foster the works of Delius, Sibelius, Richard Strauss, and Stravinsky, and as a foremost conductor of his time was noted for his candid pronouncements on musical matters, for his ' Lollipop ' encores, and after-concert speeches. See his auto-biographical *A Mingled Chime* (1944), E. Smyth, *Beecham and Pharaoh* (1935), and Lives by Reid (1961) and Cardus (1961).

BEECHER, name of an American family of preachers and writers whose English founder settled in 1638 at New Haven, Connecticut. See L. B. Stowe, *Saints, Sinners, and Beechers* (1935). The following are noteworthy:

(1) **Catherine** (1800–78), American educationist, eldest daughter of (4), became principal of a Hartford seminary and wrote on female education and the duties of women.

(2) **Harriet**. See STOWE.

(3) **Henry Ward** (1813–87), American Congregationalist preacher, son of (4), was born at Litchfield, Conn., graduated at Amherst College, Mass., preached the (first) Indianapolis, and in 1847 became the (first) pastor of Plymouth (Congregational) Church, in Brooklyn, New York, and preached what he held to be the gospel of Christ, contended for temperance, and denounced slavery to an immense congregation. He favoured the free-soil party in 1852, and the Republican candidates in 1856 and 1860; and on the outbreak of the Civil War, his church raised and equipped a volunteer regiment. On the close of the war in 1865 he became an earnest advocate of reconciliation. For many years he wrote for *The Independent*; and after 1870 edited *The Christian Union*. A charge of adultery (1874) was not proved. He repeatedly visited Europe and lectured in Britain. His many writings include *Summer in the Soul* (1858), *Yale Lectures on Preaching* (1874), *Evolution and Religion* (1885), &c.

(4) **Lyman** (1775–1863), American Presbyterian minister, father of seven sons and seven daughters, including (1), (2), and (3), was born at New Haven, Connecticut, studied at Yale, and became minister at Boston (1826–32). Responding to the call to evangelize, he was president of Lane Seminary, near Cincinnati (1832–52). Though a professed Calvinist, he was charged with heresy but acquitted. He then became leader of the New School Presbyterians. See his autobiography, correspondence, &c., ed. C. Beecher (1863–65).

BEECHEY, (1) **Frederick William** (1796–1856), son of (2), rear-admiral and geographer, accompanied three polar expeditions and published geographical works.

(2) **Sir William** (1753–1839), English portrait painter, father of (1), born at Burford, Oxfordshire, entered the Royal Academy as a student in 1772, became a competent painter in the Reynolds tradition and was made R.A. with a knighthood in 1798. Two other sons, **George** and **Henry William**, were both painters, and died, one in India, the other in New Zealand; and his youngest son, **Richard Brydges** (1808–95), became an admiral, and after leaving the navy in 1857, took to painting as a profession.

BEERBOHM, Sir (Henry) Max(imilian), ' the Incomparable Max ' (1872–1956), English writer and caricaturist, born in London, the half-brother of Sir Herbert Beerbohm Tree (q.v.), he was educated at Charterhouse and Merton College, Oxford. Characteristically,

he published his very first volume of essays under the title *The Works of Max Beerbohm* (1896), some of which had appeared in the *Yellow Book*. He succeeded Bernard Shaw as drama critic of *The Saturday Review*, until 1910, when he married an American actress, **Florence Kahn** (d. 1951), and retired, except during the two world wars, to Rapallo, Italy. His delicate, unerring, aptly-captioned caricatures were collected in various volumes beginning with *Twenty-five Gentlemen* (1896), *Poet's Corner* (1904), &c. Further volumes of parodying essays appeared, including *The Happy Hypocrite* (1897), *A Christmas Garland* (1912), in which Thomas Hardy, Arnold Bennett, and others are taken off with gentle humour, elegance, and rare wit, and ending with *And Even Now* (1920). His best-known work was, however, the delightfully fantastic novel on Oxford undergraduate life, love, and death, *Zuleika Dobson* (1912). His broadcast talks from 1935 were another of his singularly brilliant stylistic accomplishments. He was knighted in 1939 and a month before his death married **Elizabeth Jungmann**, who had been his deceased wife's greatest friend. See Life by Lord D. Cecil (1964), and studies by J. G. Riewald (The Hague 1953) and by S. N. Behrman (1960); also *Max's Nineties*, a collection of his drawings, ed. O. Lancaster (1958).

BEERBOHM TREE. See TREE.

BEESLY, Edward Spencer (1831–1915), English positivist and Radical, born at Feckenham, Worcestershire, was professor of History at University College, London, 1860–93. He wrote on Catiline, Clodius and Tiberius, Queen Elizabeth, Comte, &c.

BEETHOVEN, Ludwig van, *bay'tō-vĕn* (1770–1827), German composer, was born of Flemish ancestry at Bonn, December 16. His childhood was made miserable by the ruthless determination of his father, an undistinguished tenor at the court of the Elector of Cologne at Bonn, to turn young Ludwig into a profitable Mozartian infant prodigy, even postdating his birth to 1772. Ludwig joined the elector's orchestra, first as accompanist, then as second organist. In 1787 he spent some weeks in Vienna, had lessons from Mozart, but his mother's last illness compelled his return to Bonn. He next played viola in the same orchestra and began to compose, but without much promise. In 1792, when the French troops approaching, he was again sent to Vienna, where he stayed, except for a few excursions, for the remainder of his life. He first established himself in Prince Lichnowsky's household and studied under Haydn, Albrechtsberger, and Salieri. Haydn's comments on the C minor piano trio caused a permanent breach. Beethoven's music is usually divided into three periods. In his first (1792–1802), which includes the first two symphonies, the violin sonata in C minor and the ' Pathétique ' and ' Moonlight ' sonatas, Beethoven's style does not markedly differ from that of Mozart and Haydn. Beethoven was tolerated by Vienna society despite his unruly manner, untidiness, arrogance, and repulsive appearance, for he was stocky, his face full of pockmarks, his broad hands excessively hairy, and his laughter overloud. Just as he was beginning to make a reputation as composer, he detected his increasing deafness. In a letter to his brothers, known as the *Heiligenstadt Testament* (1802), Beethoven movingly describes his predicament and prescribes for himself patience and determination. But the encroaching malady did not impede his inconclusive love affairs with his pupils. Giulietta Guicciardi, Therese and Josephine von Brunswick might each of them have been 'the immortal beloved' referred to in a letter which was discovered after his death. Beethoven shows increased emotional range, but still within the pale of contemporary music, in his second period (1802–12). His 3rd symphony, the 'Eroica' (1803), twice the hitherto normal length for a symphony, was originally intended for Napoleon, but Beethoven angrily tore out the dedication when he heard of Napoleon's self-coronation. The dazzlingly difficult 'Kreutzer' sonata (1803), the popular 4th and 5th Symphonies (1805), the violin concerto, the overture 'Leonore' 3 (1806) appeared in rapid succession and were followed by the contrastingly quiet 6th (1808), the music to *Egmont* and Goethe's songs, which brought about his meeting with Goethe's Bettina von Brentano (see ARNIM), whose recorded conversations with the composer have led to so much speculation as to his 'philosophy'. The 'Archduke' trio (1811), dedicated to his friend and pupil the Archduke Rudolph, the first five quartets and the 7th and 8th Symphonies, both short, light and exuberant, complete the second period. From 1812 Beethoven was increasingly assailed by health, business, and family worries. There was the mechanical genius Maelzel whose metronome had inspired the *allegretto* of the 8th Symphony. He had constructed a 'panharmonicon' or mechanical wind band for which he commissioned Beethoven to compose. The result was the tasteless but popular 'Battle Symphony', written to commemorate Wellington's victory at Vittoria (1813). Maelzel considered the cancellation of a small loan to Beethoven and the gift of a pair of useless earphones adequate commission and a violent quarrel ensued. There was the meeting with Goethe at Töplitz (1813) at which he was disappointed by Goethe's excessive civility and lack of artistic fervour. There was the prolonged litigation to obtain custody of his deceased brother's son, Carl. The last great period begins in 1817. There are three piano sonatas, the 'Diabelli' variations, the Mass and the Choral (9th) Symphony (1823). In the last, three magnificent symphonic movements precede the chorale finale of Schiller's *Ode to Joy*. The introduction of the choral movement fails to do justice to Beethoven's conception. But it is a failure on the grandest possible scale. The last four quartets stand on their own. They represent Beethoven's last and supreme achievement. The fourth of these, in F major, was finished at Gneixendorf, where Beethoven stayed in October 1826 with his nephew at Johann's farm. Johann, the composer's brother, refused him a fire in his room and eventually charged for board and lodging. Carl had failed his university examinations,

had bungled a suicide attempt, and was there convalescing. Beethoven developed a severe chill and the drive back to Vienna in an open chaise was the death blow to his constitution. But his last quartet is beyond grief or suffering. The motto of the last movement 'Must it be? It must be!'—is treated with an exultant confident joviality. The conflict was over, he was 'above the battle'. He died March 26. Beethoven's music is difficult to assess without reference to Beethoven, the man. One critical school extols his work for that reason. Others maintain that in striving to express 'extramusical' conceptions, he did violence to musical forms. Where Mozart preserves, embellishes and perfects, Beethoven bends and strains to his will. He enlarged the introduction and the coda; he introduced episodes in the 'working out'; he changed the minuet into the scherzo; he multiplied the key relations of the movements; he introduced the chorus into the finale of a symphony; he invented the 'cycle of songs'; he put variations on a new footing, which has been adopted and extended by his successors; and he initiated the modern use of 'programme music'. See Lives by Schwindler (1840, ed. by McArdle, 1966), Newman (1927), Turner (1933), Ludwig (trans. 1945), Grove (1951), and studies by Sullivan (1927), Tovey (1936), and Thayer (ed. E. Forbes, 1964).

BEETON, Mrs, *née* **Isabella Mary Mayson** (1836–65), English writer on cookery, was educated at Heidelberg and became an accomplished pianist; in 1856 she married Samuel Orchard Beeton, a publisher, and her *Household Management*, published in parts (1859–60), covering cookery and other branches of domestic science, made her name a household word. She died after the birth of her fourth son. See Lives by N. Spain (1948) and Montgomery Hyde (1951).

BEETS, Nicolaas, *bayts* (1814–1903), Dutch poet and writer, was born at Haarlem. A professor of Theology at the University of Utrecht, he published under the pseudonym 'Hildebrand' *Camera Obscura* (1839), a series of quietly humorous sketches of everyday Dutch life, and *Volkshliedjes* (1842), a collection of simple verses. See Life by Chantepic de La Saussaye (1906).

BEGGARSTAFF, J. and W. See NICHOLSON (5).

BEGHA, ST. See BEE.

BEHAIM, *bay'him,* (1) **Martin** (*c.* 1459–1507), German geographer, born at Nuremberg, settled in Portugal about 1484 and was associated with the later Portuguese discoveries along the coast of Africa. He revisited Nuremberg in 1490 and there, with the help of the painter Glockenthon, constructed the oldest extant terrestrial globe. See study by Ravenstein (1908).

(2) **Michael** (1416–74), a German *meistersinger*, a native of Sulzbach (Württemberg), by profession a weaver.

BEHAM, *bay'ham,* **Hans Sebald** (1500–50) and **Barthel** (1502–40), two brothers, natives of Nuremberg, painters and engravers. They are reckoned amongst Dürer's seven followers, the 'Little Masters'. See Monographs by W. B. Scott (1879) and G. Pauli (1927).

BEHAN, Brendan, *bee'-* (1923–64), Irish author, born in Dublin slums, was expelled from school, served a borstal sentence for attempting to blow up a Liverpool shipyard as a member of the I.R.A. (1939), was given fourteen years by a Dublin military court (1942) for the attempted murder of two detectives but was released by a general amnesty (1946). He was in prison in Manchester (1947) and deported in 1952. The prison atmosphere prior to a hanging he starkly dramatised in the play *The Quare Fellow* (1956; filmed 1962). His exuberant Irish wit, spiced with balladry and bawdry and a talent for fantastic caricature, found rein in his masterpiece *The Hostage* (1959), another play. It is also evident in the autobiographical novel, *Borstal Boy* (1958) and in *Brendan Behan's Island* (1963). Like Dylan Thomas, he was lionized to death in the U.S. succumbing finally in a Dublin hospital. See study by Jeffs (1966). His brother **Dominic** is a folksinger.

BEHM, Ernst, *baym* (1830–84), a German geographer, compiler, with H. Wagner, of the *Bevölkerung der Erde* (1872–82).

BEHMEN. See BOEHME, JAKOB.

BEHN, Aphra, *bayn* (1640–89), the first English professional authoress, was born at Wye, in Kent, but was brought up in Surinam, where she made the acquaintance of the slave Oroonoko, the subject afterwards of one of her novels, in which she anticipated Rousseau's ' noble savage '. Returning to England in 1663, she married a merchant called Behn, who died within three years. She then turned professional spy at Antwerp, sent back political and naval information, but received little thanks, and on her return was imprisoned for debt, and began to write poetry and plays in the coarser Restoration style. She was buried in Westminster Abbey. See studies by V. Sackville-West (1927), G. Woodcock (1948), and E. Hahn (1951).

BEHRENS, Peter, *bay'rens* (1868–1940), German architect and designer, born at Hamburg. He began as a painter, but in 1909 he was responsible for the ' first modern building ', the A.E.G. turbine factory in Berlin, making considerable use of steel in the construction. His appointment as the designer of A.E.G. electrical products (and also their advertisements) was a landmark in the history of industrial design. He trained several leading modern architects, including Walter Gropius and Le Corbusier (qq.v.). See studies by Fritz Hoeber (1913, 1928).

BEHRING, *bay-ring*, **(1) Emil von** (1854–1917), German bacteriologist, born at Hansdorf, W. Prussia, was director of Marburg Hygiene Institute, discovered diphtheria and tetanus antitoxins, was ennobled, and awarded the first Nobel prize in medicine (1901). See Life by Engelhardt (1940).

(2), Vitus. See BERING.

BEIJERINCK, Martinus Willem (1851–1931), Dutch botanist, noted for his work on galls and plant bacteria.

BEILBY, *beel'bi*, **(1) Sir George Thomas** (1850–1924), Scottish industrial chemist, born in Edinburgh, improved the method of shale oil distillation and invented a manufacturing process for synthesizing alkaline cyanides.

F.R.S. in 1906, he founded the Fuel Research station at East Greenwich.

(2) Ralph. See BEWICK, THOMAS.

BEIT, Alfred, *bit* (1853–1906), and **Sir Otto** (1865–1930), British financiers and philanthropists, born in Hamburg. Alfred was associated with Cecil Rhodes and accumulated a great fortune in diamond mining.

BEITH, John Hay. See HAY, IAN.

BEK, Antony (d. 1311), Bishop of Durham from 1283, took a prominent part in the Scottish wars of Edward I, and from 1300 was involved in ecclesiastical disputes. His brother, **Thomas** (d. 1293), was Bishop of St Davids from 1280.

BEKE, Charles Tilstone (1800–74), British explorer and biblical critic, born in London, studied ancient history, philology and ethnography. His *Origines Biblicae* (1834) gained him a Tübingen doctorate. During his Abyssinian explorations (1840–43), he fixed the latitude of over seventy stations, mapped 70,000 sq. miles, and collected fourteen vocabularies. In 1865 he undertook a fruitless mission to Abyssinia, to obtain the release of Emperor Theodore's British captives; in 1874 he explored the region at the head of the Red Sea. He wrote *Abyssinia* (1845), *The Sources of the Nile* (1860), &c.

BÉKÉSY, Georg von (1899–1972), Hungarian physiologist, born in Budapest, was led to study of the human ear through his work as a telecommunications engineer. From 1945 he carried on his researches in Stockholm and in 1949 became a senior research fellow at Harvard. The world's greatest expert on aural physiology, he was awarded the Nobel prize for medicine in 1961.

BEKHTEREV, Vladimir Mikhailovich, *byek'-tyi-ryef* (1857–1927), Russian neuropathologist, born in Viatka province, as professor at Kazan researched into neural electricity and founded the psychoneurological institute in Leningrad.

BEKKER, (1) Balthasar (1634–98), Dutch Protestant pastor, was suspected of rationalism and Socinianism, and was promptly deposed and excommunicated on the publication of *De Betooverde Wereld* (' The World Bewitched ', 1691–93), contesting the belief in witchcraft and magical powers.

(2) Immanuel (1785–1871), German editor of the Greek classics, in 1811 became professor of Philology in his native city, Berlin.

BEKYNTON, or **Beckington, Thomas** (1390–1465), English prelate, educated at Winchester and Oxford, was a fellow of New College (1408–20), prebendary of York (1423), master of St Katherine's Hospital, London, went on diplomatic missions to France (1432–42), became king's secretary and lord privy seal, and as Bishop of Bath and Wells from 1443 was a great benefactor of the city of Wells, rebuilding the bishop's palace and sponsoring the erection of other buildings.

BELCHER, (1) Sir Edward (1799–1877), English admiral, entered the navy in 1812, and from 1836 to 1842 explored the western coast of America. Knighted in 1843, in 1852 he commanded an unfortunate expedition sent out to search for Sir John Franklin, and in 1872 became rear-admiral.

(2) **George** (1875–1947), English cartoonist, was a frequent contributor to *Punch*, but was also a serious painter of cockney types and was elected R.A. in 1945.

BELINSKY, or **Bielinski, Vissarion Grigorievich** (1811–48), Russian literary critic and journalist, born at Fribourg. He edited the *Moscow Observer* (1838–39), and afterwards became principal critic of *The Annals of the Fatherland*, and of *Sovremennik* in 1846. His influence on subsequent critics in Russia was profound. His *Survey of Russian Literature since the 18th Century* was published in 1834, and a complete edition of his works in 1859–1862 (12 vols.). See *Life* by Bowman (1954).

BELISARIUS, *-sah'-* (A.D. 505–565), Byzantine general under the Emperor Justinian, was born at Germania in Illyria, defeated a great Persian army in 530, and in 532 suppressed a dangerous insurrection in Constantinople by the destruction of 30,000 of the ' Green ' faction. Sent to Africa next year to recover the provinces overrun by the Vandals, he twice defeated them. He next took the field in Italy against the Ostrogoths in 535, endured a siege in Rome by the Gothic king, Vitiges, and in 540 captured the Ostrogothic capital, Ravenna. In 542 he drove back the Persian king, Chosroes; in 544 made another, but less successful, campaign against the Goths in Italy; and in 559 repelled an assault of the Huns on the capital. In 562, falsely accused of conspiracy against the emperor, he was for a short time imprisoned; but in 563 he was again restored to honour. That he was blinded and died a beggar is mere legend. See *Lives* by Diehl (1901) and R. Graves (1938), and study in J. B. Bury's, *Later Roman Empire* (2nd ed. 1923).

BELL, (1) **Acton, Currer, Ellis**. See BRONTË.

(2) **Alexander Graham** (1847–1922), Scottish-American inventor, son of (3), was born at Edinburgh, and was educated there and in London. He went to Canada, and in 1871 became professor of Vocal Physiology at Boston, devoting himself to the teaching of deaf-mutes and to spreading his father's system of ' visible speech '. His inventions, the articulating telephone in 1872–76, the photophone in 1880, the graphophone in 1887, brought him wealth and fame. See Blake, *History of Radio-telegraphy* (1926).

(3) **Alexander Melville** (1819–1905), Scottish-American educationalist, father of (2), born at Edinburgh, where he became a teacher of elocution, but in 1865 removed to London, and in 1870 to Canada, settling finally at Washington. Of his numerous works connected with phonetics may be mentioned *Visible Speech* (1867).

(4) **Andrew** (1753–1832), British educationist, founder of the ' Madras System ' of education, was born at St Andrews. After taking Episcopal orders, he went to India in 1787 and in 1789 became superintendent of the Madras military orphanage. Finding it impossible to obtain teaching staff, he taught with the aid of the pupils themselves by introducing the monitorial system. His pamphlet entitled *An Experiment in Education* (1797) had attracted little attention in Britain until in 1803 Joseph Lancaster (q.v.) also published

a tract recommending the monitorial system. Lancasterian schools began to spread over the country; the Church grew alarmed, and in 1811 founded the National Society for the Education of the Poor, of which Bell became superintendent, and whose schools soon numbered 12,000. See *Lives* by Southey (1844) and Meiklejohn (1881).

(5) **Sir Charles** (1774–1842), Scottish anatomist and surgeon, brother of (7) and (14), famous for his neurological discoveries was born at Edinburgh. In 1804 he proceeded to London, where he lectured with great success on anatomy and surgery. In 1807 he distinguished between the sensory and motor nerves in the brain. In 1812 he was appointed surgeon to the Middlesex Hospital, which his clinical lectures raised to the highest repute. To study gunshot wounds he went to Haslar Hospital after Corunna in 1809, and after Waterloo took charge of a hospital at Brussels. In 1824 he became senior professor of Anatomy and Surgery to the College of Surgeons, and in 1826 head of the new medical school (University College), but soon resigned. Knighted in 1831, he was professor of Surgery at Edinburgh from 1836. His works include *Anatomy of Expression in Painting* (1806), *Anatomy of the Brain* (1811) and *Nervous System of the Human Body* (1830). The type of facial paralysis known as Bell's palsy is named after him. See Pichot's *Vie et travaux de Sir Charles Bell* (1859), and his *Correspondence* (1870). To the same family belonged the Edinburgh surgeon, **Joseph Bell** (1837–1911), the original of ' Sherlock Holmes '.

(6) **(Arthur) Clive (Howard)** (1881–1964), English art and literary critic, studied at Trinity College, Cambridge, and stated his aesthetic theory of *Significant Form* in *Art* (1914), another version of which was formulated in 1920 by Roger Fry (q.v.), a fellow-member of those arbiters of taste known as the ' Bloomsbury Set ', described in his *Old Friends* (1956). His best critical essays are *Since Cézanne* (1922), *Civilization* (1928), *Proust* (1929), and *An Account of French Painting* (1931). He was made Chevalier of the *Légion d'honneur* (1936). He married **Vanessa** (d. 1961), daughter of Sir Leslie Stephen, in 1907. Their son **Julian** (1908–37), also a writer, was killed in the Spanish Civil War.

(7) **George Joseph** (1770–1843), Scottish lawyer, brother of (5) and (14), was born in Edinburgh. Professor of Scots Law at Edinburgh University, he drafted the report of the commission on Scottish judicial proceedings (1823) which resulted in the Scottish Judicature Act (1825).

(8) **Gertrude Margaret Lowthian** (1868–1926), British traveller, granddaughter of (11), was born at Washington Hall, travelled much in the Middle East, was political officer in Baghdad during World War I, and published *Safar Nameh* (1894), *Amurath to Amurath* (1911), &c. See her *Letters* (2nd ed. 1947), and *Life* by E. Burgoyne (1958).

(9) **Henry** (1767–1830), Scottish pioneer of steam navigation, born at Torphichen Mill, Linlithgow, in 1812 successfully launched the 30-ton *Comet* on the Clyde.

(10) **Henry Glassford** (1803–74), Scottish lawyer and poet, vindicator of Mary Queen of Scots in verse and prose, and author of *Summer and Winter Hours* (1931), &c. See a Memoir by Stoddart (1892).

(11) **Sir Isaac Lowthian, Bart.** (1816–1904), Scottish industrialist, grandfather of (8), founded in 1852, with his brothers, great iron-smelting works on the Tees. He was M.P. for Hartlepool (1875–80).

(12) **James** (1769–1833), Scottish geographer, born in Jedburgh, author of the first critical geography (1830).

(13) **John** (1691–1780), Scottish traveller, born at Antermony in Campsie parish, Stirlingshire, studied for the medical profession, and in 1714 went to St Petersburg, and was physician to Russian embassies to Persia (1715–18), went to China through Siberia (1719–22), and again to Persia (1722). In 1737 he settled at Constantinople as a merchant, but about 1746 returned to Scotland. His *Travels* were published in 1763.

(14) **John** (1763–1820), Scottish anatomist and surgeon, brother of (5) and (7), was born at Edinburgh. His *Principles of Surgery* (1801–1807) was re-edited by (5) in 1826.

(15) **John** (1797–1869), American statesman, born in Tennessee, was speaker of the House of Representatives (1836), and a senator (1847–59). Moderate in his views, he was nominated for the presidency in 1860 by the newly formed Constitutional Union Party, but received only 39 electoral votes. He fought desperately but hopelessly to keep Tennessee out of the Civil War, which sealed the doom of his party.

(16) **John** (1811–95), English sculptor, born at Hopton, Suffolk, produced the Guards' Memorial (1858) in Waterloo Place, and the American group in the Hyde Park Albert Memorial (1873). He popularized carved wooden breadknives and trenchers.

(17) **John Jay** (1871–1934), Scottish humorous writer, best known for his *Wee MacGreegor* (1902). Other works include *Mistress M'Leerie* (1903), *Courtin' Christina* (1913), &c.

(18) **Sir Robert** (1800–67), Irish journalist and author, born at Cork, in 1828 came to London. He is best known by his annotated edition of the English poets from Chaucer to Cowper (1824–57).

(19) **Thomas** (1792–1880), British naturalist, was born at Poole, Dorsetshire. A dental surgeon at Guy's Hospital (1817–61), he lectured in and became professor of Zoology in King's College, London, in 1836. He was secretary of the Royal Society, president of the Linnaean Society and first president of the Ray Society (1844). His *British Stalk-eyed Crustacea* (1853) remains a standard work on British crabs and lobsters. He edited the *Natural History of Selborne*, by Gilbert White, whose house he purchased.

(20) **Vanessa.** See (6).

BELLA, Stefano della (1610–64), a Florentine designer and engraver, especially of battles and sieges for Richelieu.

BELLAMY, (1) **Edward** (1850–98), American novelist, born at Chicopee Falls, Mass., achieved immense popularity with his Utopian romance *Looking Backward* (1888), a work which predicted a new social order and influenced economic thinking in the United States and Europe. See Life by A. E. Morgan (1944).

(2) **George Anne** (*c.* 1727–88), English actress, the natural daughter of a Quaker schoolgirl and Lord Tyrawley, first appeared at Covent Garden and, despite a brilliant theatrical career, through profligacy and extravagance spent her last years in poverty. She published an autobiographical *Apology* (1785).

BELLARMINE, Robert Francis Romulus, St, *bel'lahr-min* (1542–1621), Jesuit cardinal and theologian, was born at Montepulciano, near Siena. He entered the order of Jesuits at Rome in 1560, and studied theology at Padua and Louvain. In 1570 he was appointed to the chair of Theology at Louvain, but returned to Rome in 1576 to lecture in the Roman College on controversial theology. In 1592 he became rector of the Roman College, was made a cardinal in 1599 against his own inclination, and in 1602 Archbishop of Capua. After the death of Clement VIII, he evaded the papal chair, but was induced by Pius V to hold an important place in the Vatican from 1605 till his death. Bellarmine, not canonized till 1931, was the chief defender of the church in the 16th century. He informed Galileo of the pope's prohibition of his teaching of the heliocentric system (1616), yet his learning and moderation gained him the praise even of Bayle. Lives have been written by the Jesuits Fuligatti (in Italian, Rome 1624) and Brodrick (Lond. 1928); a Latin autobiography, previously suppressed by the Jesuits, was edited in 1887, with a German translation, by Döllinger and Reusch.

BELLAY, Joachim du (1522–60), French poet and prose writer, next to his friend and fellow-student Ronsard (q.v.) the most important member of the Pléiade, was born at Lire in Anjou. His *Deffence et Illustration de la langue françoise* (1549), the manifesto of the Pléiade, advocating the rejection of mediaeval linguistic traditions and a return to classical and Italian models, had a considerable influence at the time. It was accompanied by an example in the form of a set of Petrarchian sonnets, *l'Olive*, dedicated to an unknown lady. Du Bellay went to Rome in 1553 as secretary to his kinsman, Cardinal du Bellay, but was not a success as a diplomat, though the visit inspired more sonnets, including the collections *Les Antiquités de Rome* and *Les Regrets*. See Pater, *Studies in the Renaissance* and R. V. Merrill, *The Platonism of du Bellay* (1926).

BELLEAU, Rémy, *bel-ō* (1528–77), French poet, born in Nogent le Rotrou. He was a member of the Pléiade and published in 1556 a translation of Anacreon that was at first believed to be an original imitation. *Bergerie* (1565 and a second edition in 1572) is a medley of delicately descriptive prose and verse, of which *Avril* still holds a place in anthologies. *Amours* (1576) is a collection of poems concerned with the appearance and arcane powers of precious stones. See study by Delacourcelle (1945).

BELLEISLE, Charles Louis Fouquet, Duc de, *bel-eel* (1684–1761), marshal of France, in the War of the Austrian Succession stormed Prague, and led the skilful retreat to Eger.

BELLENDEN, (1) or **Ballantyne, John** (d. 1587), Scottish writer, was born towards the close of the 15th century, and in 1508 matriculated at St Andrews and completed his theological studies at the Sorbonne. His translations in 1533 of Boece's *Historia Gentis Scotorum*, and of the first five books of Livy, are interesting as vigorous specimens of early Scottish prose. The *Croniklis of Scotland* is a very free translation, and contains numerous passages not found in Boece, so that it is in some respects almost an original work. Bellenden enjoyed great favour at the court of James V, at whose request he executed the translations. As a reward, he received considerable grants from the treasury, and afterwards was made Archdeacon of Moray and Canon of Ross. Becoming involved, however, in ecclesiastical controversy, he went to Rome, where he died.

(2) **William** (*c.* 1555–1633), Scottish author, was a professor in the university, and an advocate in the parliament, of Paris, and was employed in a diplomatic capacity by James VI, who, about 1610, made him Master of Requests. His principal works were *De Statu Libri Tres* (1616) and *De Tribus Luminibus Romanorum* (1634), the ' three luminaries ' being Cicero, Seneca, and Pliny, out of whose works he intended to compile a digest of the civil and religious history and the moral and physical science of the Romans. His works furnished the materials for Middleton's *Life of Cicero*. Warton first denounced the theft, which Dr Parr made clear in his edition of the *De Statu* (1787).

BELLINGHAM. See PERCEVAL.

BELLINGSHAUSEN, Fabian Gottlieb von, *-how′zèn* (1778–1852), Russian explorer, born in Oesel, in 1819–21 led an Antarctic expedition to 70° S. lat.

BELLINI, *bel-lee′nee*, (1) **Gentile** (*c.* 1429–1507), Venetian painter, son of (3), brother of (2), worked in his father's studio and was chosen to paint the portrait of Sultan Mohammed II in Constantinople. This portrait, together with his *Adoration of the Kings*, is in the National Gallery, London.

(2) **Giovanni** (*c.* 1430–1516), the greatest Venetian painter of his time, son of (3) and brother of (1), left Venice for Padua in 1464. Strongly influenced by the severe classical style of his brother-in-law Mantegna (q.v.), as in his *Pietà* at Rimini, he soon blossomed out with a novel sensuous consciousness of light and colour, aided by the clear oil varnishes which A. da Messina (q.v.) had introduced from Holland, as in the S. Giobbe altar (1489) now in the Venice Academy. He returned to Venice and continued to paint the ' Pietà ' and ' Madonna ' themes, altarpieces, pagan allegories, among the latter of which *The Feast of the Gods* (1513) is the best. Giovanni's innovations of light and colour became the hallmark of Venetian art, continued and enriched by his pupils Giorgione and Titian. See monographs by Roger Fry (1909), Hendy (1947), and Fiocco (1960).

(3) **Jacobo** (*c.* 1400–70), father of (1) and

(2), studied under Gentile da Fabriano (q.v.), painted a wide range of subjects; but only a few ' Madonnas ' in Italy and drawings in the Louvre and the British Museum remain, which show his interest in architectural and landscape setting.

(4) **Vincenzo** (1801–35), Italian operatic composer, was born at Catania in Sicily. An organist's son, he was sent by a Sicilian nobleman to the Conservatorio of Naples. His two earliest operas were *Adelson e Salvina* (1824) and *Bianca e Fernando* (1826). *Il Pirata* (1827) immediately carried the composer's name beyond Italy, and was followed by *I Capuleti ed i Montecchi* (1830) and his two masterpieces of lyrical expression *La Sonnambula* (1831) and *Norma* (1832). In 1833 he went to Paris and London, whither he had accompanied the famous Italian soprano, Pasta. *I Puritani* (1834) shows the influence of the French school, but without servile imitation. He died near Paris. See works by Pougin (1868) and Lloyd (1908).

BELLMAN, Karl Michael (1740–95), Swedish poet, was born in Stockholm, in 1757 entered the Riksbank, but fled to Norway to escape his creditors. In 1776 he was given a court pension by Gustav III. He began to write verse to popular tunes as a young civil servant. He founded a drinking club, the *Bacchi orden*, and versified his impressions of his friends and other characters. His *Fredmans Epistlar* (1772), full of minute detail of Swedish life and enriched by humour and sympathy, entitles the watchmaker Fredman to a place beside Don Quixote and Falstaff.

BELLOC, (Joseph) Hilaire (Pierre) (1870–1953), Anglo-French writer and poet, born at St Cloud near Paris, the son of a French barrister, Louis Belloc, and his English wife, was naturalized in 1903. He was educated at the Oratory School, Birmingham, under Newman, and Balliol College, Oxford, but did military service in the French army. He became Liberal M.P. in 1906, but, disillusioned with politics, did not seek re-election in 1910. Disapproving of modern industrial society and Socialism, he wrote *The Servile State* (1912) advocating a return to the system of mediaeval guilds. He was best known, however, for his delightfully nonsensical verse for children, *The Bad Child's Book of Beasts* (1896) and the *Cautionary Tales* (1907), his numerous travel books, including *Path to Rome* (1902) and *The Old Road* (1910), reconstructing the Pilgrims' Way, his historical studies *Marie Antoinette* (1910), *Richelieu* (1929), *Wolsey* (1930), *Napoleon* (1932), &c., and his religious books, including *Europe and the Faith* (1920) and *The Great Heresies* (1938). A devoted Roman Catholic, as were his friends and literary collaborators, the Chesterton brothers, he was fearlessly, sometimes fanatically, outspoken. In 1934 the pope conferred upon him the rank of Knight Commander of the Order of St Gregory. He was a master of light English prose. See study by J. B. Morton (1955) and Life by R. Speaight (1957).

BELLOC LOWNDES, Marie Adelaide (1868–1947), English novelist, sister of Hilaire Belloc (q.v.), wrote crime stories, including

The Lodger (1913) and *The Chink in the Armour* (1912). See her autobiographical *I too have Lived in Arcadia* (1942).

BELLOT, Joseph René, *bel-lō* (1826–53), French Arctic explorer, born in Paris, served with distinction at Tamatave in 1845, and in 1851 joined the expedition searching for John Franklin. He discovered Bellot Strait in 1852, and was lost during Inglefield's expedition. See his *Journal* (trans. 1855).

BELLOW, Saul (1915–), American writer, born at Lachine in Quebec, spent his childhood in Montreal. In 1924 his family moved to Chicago and he attended university there, and at Northwestern Univ. He abandoned his post-graduate studies at Wisconsin Univ. to become a writer, and his first novel, *The Dangling Man*, a study of a noncombatant in the war, appeared in 1944. He became an associate professor at Minnesota Univ., and after being awarded a Guggenheim Fellowship in 1948 travelled to Paris and Rome. Other works include *The Victim* (1947), *The Adventures of Augie March* (1953), *Henderson the Rain-King* (1959) and *Herzog* (1964). In 1962 he was appointed a professor at Chicago University. See study by Opdahl (1968).

BELLOWS, George Wesley (1882–1925), American painter and lithographer, born at Columbus, Ohio. His lithographs of boxers (of which the most famous is *Dempsey and Firpo*, in the Museum of Modern Art, New York) have a crude vigour, and he became one of the leaders of the American realists. See Life by P. Boswell (1942).

BELLOY, Dormont de, *bel-wah*, properly **Pierre Laurent Buyrette** (1727–75), a French dramatist, was one of the first to introduce on the French stage native instead of classical heroes. His first success, *Zelmire* (1762), was followed by *Le Siège de Calais* (1765), *Gaston et Bayard* (1771) and *Pierre le cruel* (1772).

BELON, Pierre, *bė-lō* (1517–64), French naturalist, in 1546–49 travelled in Asia Minor, Egypt, and Arabia. He was murdered by robbers whilst gathering herbs in the Bois de Boulogne. Belon wrote valuable treatises on trees, herbs, birds, and fishes. He was one of the first who established the homologies between the skeletons of different vertebrates; he planted the first cedar in France; and he formed two early botanical gardens.

BELZONI, Giovanni Battista, *-tsō'nee* (1778–1823), Italian explorer and archaeologist, born at Padua. He was intended for a monastery, but in 1803 came to England, where, 6 feet 7 inches tall, he gained a living by exhibiting feats of strength and models of hydraulic engines. In 1812 he went to Spain, in 1815 to Egypt, and there was commissioned by Mehemet Ali to construct a hydraulic machine. He devoted himself henceforth, through the traveller Burckhardt, to the exploration of Egyptian antiquities, and removed from Thebes the colossal bust of Rameses, which, together with the sepulchre of Sati I from the tombs of the kings which he had opened up in 1817, he sent to the British Museum. He explored the temple of Idfu, cleared the temple of Abu Simbel, opened the second pyramid of Giza and discovered the ruins of Berenice on the Red Sea. He returned to Europe in 1819 and published his discoveries. He died of dysentery on the way to Timbuktu at Gato, Benin. See Life by S. Mayes (1959).

BEM, Joseph (1795–1850), a Polish leader of the unsuccessful Hungarian insurrection of 1848–49, after which he escaped into Turkey, turned Mohammedan and received a command at Aleppo, where he died of fever ten months later.

BEMBO, Pietro (1470–1547), Italian poet, born at Venice, in 1513 was made secretary to Leo X, and in 1539 a cardinal by Paul III, who appointed him to the dioceses of Gubbio and Bergamo. Bembo was the restorer of good style in both Latin and Italian literature. Notable works are the *Rerum Veneticarum Libri XII* (1551; Italian ed. 1552), his little treatise on Italian prose, which marked an era in Italian grammar, and his *Letters*. See Life by M. Santoro (1937).

BENAVENTE, Jacinto, *-ven'tay* (1866–1954), Spanish dramatist, born at Madrid, was intended for the law, but turned to literature. After publishing some poems and short stories he won recognition as a playwright with his *El nido Ajeno* (1893), which was followed by some brilliantly satirical society comedies. His masterpiece is *Los intereses creados* (1907), an allegorical play in the *commedia dell' arte* style. He also wrote some excellent children's plays. See studies by M. Starkie (1924), I. S. Estevan (1954).

BENBOW, John (1653–1702), British admiral, born at Shrewsbury, entered the navy in 1678, and by 1696 had risen to be rear-admiral. In the West Indies, on August 19, 1702, he came up with a superior French force under Du Casse. For four days he kept up a running fight, almost deserted by the rest of his squadron, until, his right leg smashed by a chain shot, he was forced to return to Jamaica, where he died at Port Royal, November 4.

BENCKENDORFF, Alexander, Count (1849–1917), Russian ambassador in London (from 1903), greatly promoted Anglo-Russian friendship.

BENDA, Georg (1722–95), Bohemian musician was born at Alt-Benatek, *kapellmeister* to the Duke of Gotha (1748–78). He composed operettas, cantatas, and melodramas, and introduced music drama with spoken text. His brothers, **Franz** (1709–86) and **Joseph** (1724–1804), were both in turn Konzertmeister of Frederick II of Prussia.

BENEDEK, Ludwig von (1804–81), an Austrian general, born at Oedenburg, in Hungary, distinguished himself in Galicia in 1846, in Italy in 1847, in Hungary in 1849, and in 1859 drove back the Piedmontese at Solferino. He was governor of Hungary in 1860. In 1866 he commanded the northern Austrian army in the war with Prussia; but after the defeat of Sadowa, he was superseded. See Life by J. Presland (1934).

BENEDEN, Eduard van (1845–1910), Belgian cytologist, born at Liège, demonstrated in 1887 the constancy of the number of chromosomes in the cells of an organism, decreasing during maturation and restored at fertilization.

BENEDETTI, Vincent, Count (1817–1900), French diplomat, born at Bastia in Corsica, ambassador in Berlin in 1864, proposed a secret treaty with Prussia. He made the demand at Ems in 1870 that gave Bismarck the *casus belli* for the Franco-Prussian war. See his *Studies in Diplomacy* (trans. 1895).

BENEDICT, St (*c*. 480–*c*. 547) the founder of Western monachism, was born at Nursia near Spoleto, and, convinced while at the schools of Rome that the only way of escaping the evil in the world was in seclusion and religious exercise, he, a boy of fourteen, withdrew to a cavern or grotto near Subiaco, where he lived three years. The fame of his piety led to his being appointed the abbot of a neighbouring monastery at Vicovaro, nominally observing the oriental rule; but he soon left it, as the morals of the half-wild monks were not strict enough. Multitudes still sought his guidance; and from the most devoted he founded twelve small monastic communities. He ultimately established a monastery on Monte Cassino, near Naples, afterwards one of the richest and most famous in Italy. In 515 he is said to have composed his *Regula Monachorum*, which became the common rule of all Western monachism. In addition to the usual religious exercises, the rule directs that the monks shall employ themselves in manual labours, imparting instruction to youth, copying manuscripts for the library, &c. See works on the order and its founder by Mabillon (Paris 1703–39), Butler (1919), Chapman (1929), McCann (1937), Lindsay (1949).

BENEDICT, the name of fifteen popes, of which the following are noteworthy:

Benedict VIII (d. 1024), uncle of IX, elected in 1012, and driven from Rome by the Antipope Gregory, was restored to the papal chair by the Emperor Henry II, and afterwards defeated the Saracens and the Greeks. He was a reformer of the clergy.

Benedict IX, nephew of VIII, obtained the papal throne by simony in 1032, while still a youth; but in 1036 the Romans banished him on account of his licentiousness. Several times reinstalled, he was as often deposed. He died in the convent of Grotta Ferrata, probably before 1065.

Benedict XIII is a title assumed by two popes, **Pedro de Luna,** a Spaniard, chosen by the French cardinals in 1394, and recognized only by Spain and Scotland up to his death in 1424; and **Pietro Francesco Orsini** (1724–1730), a learned man of simple habits and pure morals, who unfortunately placed himself under the guidance of the unscrupulous Cardinal Coscia.

Benedict XIV (Prospero Lambertini) (1675–1758), born at Bologna, distinguished by his learning and ability, became pope in 1740. He founded chairs of Physic, Chemistry, and Mathematics in Rome, revived the academy of Bologna, rebuilt churches, and encouraged literature and science.

Benedict XV (Giacomo della Chiesa) (1854–1922), born of noble Italian family, was ordained at twenty-four, became secretary to the Papal Embassy, Spain, in 1883, then secretary to Cardinal Rampolla, bishop (1900), Archbishop of Bologna (1907), cardinal (May, 1914). Although junior cardinal, he was elected (September 3, 1914) to succeed Pius X. He made repeated efforts to end World War I and organized war relief on a munificent scale.

BENEDICT, Sir Julius (1804–85), German musician and composer, born at Stuttgart, studied under Hummel and Weber, and was at twenty conductor at a Vienna opera house, and then at the San Carlo in Naples. He became distinguished as a pianist, and in 1836 settled in London. After some success with his *opéra bouffe* on the continent, he attempted English opera with *Lily of Killarney* (1862), composed an oratorio, cantatas, &c., technically excellent and pleasing but without individuality. He was knighted in 1871.

BENEDICT BISCOP, St (*c*. 628–689), a great Anglo-Saxon churchman, five times journeyed to Rome, and in 669–671 was Abbot of St Peter's, Canterbury. In 674 he founded a monastery at Wearmouth, endowing it richly with books; and in 682 founded a second monastery at Jarrow. He is said to have introduced stone edifices and glass windows. Bede (q.v.) was his pupil.

BENEKE, Friedrich Eduard, *bay'nek-ė* (1798–1856), German philosopher, was born at Berlin, where he lectured from 1820 to 1822, when his lectures were interdicted by the Prussian government for their opposition to Hegel. He removed to a lectureship at Göttingen and returned to a professorship at Berlin after Hegel's death in 1832. In March 1854 he disappeared and in June 1856 his body was found in the canal at Charlottenburg. His chief work was in empirical psychology, which he considered was the basis of all true philosophy.

BENELLI, Sem, *bay-nel'lee* (1877–1949), Italian dramatist, born at Prato, Tuscany, wrote plays in prose and verse. Outstanding successes were *Tignola*, a light comedy, and *La cena della beffe*, a powerful tragedy in verse. For several years Benelli was consistently praised for dramatic innovation and poetical virtuosity, but his reputation has suffered eclipse, and though critics now allow him ' a sense of theatre ', they deplore his philosophy and his fustian style. As a librettist, however, his *L'Amore dei tre re* (Love of Three Kings) still survives.

BENEŠ, Eduard, *ben'esh* (1884–1948), Czechoslovak statesman, born at Kožlany, became professor of Sociology at Prague. As a refugee during World War I he worked in Paris with Masaryk for Czechoslovak nationalism, and in 1918–35 was foreign minister of the new state, and was premier also in 1921–22. In 1935 he succeeded Masaryk as president, but resigned in 1938 and left the country, resuming office, however, in 1939 on the setting up, after the outbreak of World War II, of an exile government, first in France and then in England. In 1945 he returned to his country, and in 1946 was re-elected president, but resigned after the Communist coup of 1948.

BENÉT, Stephen Vincent, *bė-nay'* (1898–1943), American poet, known especially for his poem on the Civil War, *John Brown's Body*, which was awarded the Pulitzer prize in 1929.

BENFEY, Theodor, *ben'-fī* (1809–81), a great Sanskrit scholar and comparitive philologist, was born of Jewish parents near Göttingen.

BENGEL, Johann Albrecht (1687–1752), German theologian, born at Winnenden, in

Württemberg, was the first Protestant author who treated the exegesis of the New Testament critically. See Lives by Burk (1831–37), Wächter (1865), Nolte (1913), and study by Reiff (1882).

BEN-GURION, David (1886–ㅤ), Israeli statesman, born David Green at Plonsk, Poland. Attracted to the Zionist Socialist movement, he emigrated to Palestine in 1906, working as a farm labourer and forming the first Jewish trade union in 1915. Expelled by the Turks for pro-Allied sympathies, he helped to raise the Jewish Legion in America and served in it in the Palestine campaign against Turkey. From 1921 to 1933 he was general secretary of the General Federation of Jewish Labour. In 1930 he became leader of the Mapai (Labour) Party, which became the ruling party in the state of Israel, whose birth he announced in May 1948. In 1953 he retired from the premiership, resuming it in 1955, and finally retiring in 1963. A Messianic, visionary, yet realist figure, this battle-dress creator of Israel has been acclaimed the greatest Jewish leader since Moses. See his *Rebirth and Destiny of Israel* (1959) and Life by R. St John (1959).

BENJAMIN, (1) Arthur (1893–1960), Australian composer, born at Sydney, studied in London, and served in World War I. He was professor of Pianoforte at Sydney Conservatorium from 1919–21, but returned to England, becoming an examiner for the Associated Board, and (1926) a teacher at the Royal College of Music. The unfailing craftsmanship of his lighter works is joined to an appealingly romantic style in his Symphony (1945) and his opera *A Tale of Two Cities* (first produced 1957).

(2) **Judah Philip** (1811–84), American lawyer, was born at St Croix, West Indies, the son of Jewish parents then en route from England to the United States. A lawyer in New Orleans, he early engaged in politics, serving first with the Whigs, and afterwards with the Democrats. He sat in the U.S. senate from 1852 till 1860, and in 1861 joined Jefferson Davis's cabinet as attorney-general. He was for a few months secretary of war, and then secretary of state until Davis's capture in 1865, when he escaped to England. Called to the English bar in 1866, he became a Q.C. in 1872.

(3) **René**, bǎ-zha-mǐ (1885–1948), French writer, born in Paris, was the grandson of an engraver on precious stones. His first book, *Madame Bonheur* (1909), had no success; but *Gaspard* (1915), a novel about a Paris urchin who becomes a soldier in World War I, based on his own experiences, established his reputation. Other works include *Les Justices de paix* (1913), *Les Plaisirs du hasard* (1922), a comedy, &c. In 1940 Benjamin allied himself with Pétain and as a result was arrested and imprisoned for a year in 1944. *L'Enfant tué* (1946) mourns the death of his son, killed at Mulhouse, fighting with the American forces. *La Galère des Goncourt* (1948) satirizes the members of l'Académie Goncourt who ostracized him and his works.

BENJAMIN OF TUDELA (d. 1173), a Spanish rabbi, born in Navarre, the first European traveller to describe the Far East.

In 1159–73 he made a journey from Saragossa through Italy and Greece, to Palestine, Persia, and the borders of China, returning by way of Egypt and Sicily. See his *Itinerary* (1907).

BENN, (1). See STANSGATE.

(2) **Gottfried** (1886–1956), German poet, born at Mansfeld in West Prussia. Though the son of a clergyman he embraced the philosophy of Nihilism as a young man, but later became one of the few intellectuals to favour Nazi doctrines. Trained in medicine as a venereologist, he began writing Expressionist verse dealing with the uglier aspects of his profession, such as *Morgue* (1912). Later his outlook became more mature and his poetry more versatile, though still pessimistic, and after 1945, matching the mood of despondency in defeat, won him a place among the leading poets of the century.

BENNET, (1) Abraham (1750–99), English physicist, invented the gold-leaf electroscope and constructed a simple induction machine in 1789.

(2) **Henry**. See ARLINGTON.

BENNETT, (1) (Enoch) Arnold (1867–1931), English novelist, born near Hanley, Staffs. Educated locally and at London University, he became a solicitor's clerk in London, but quickly transferred to journalism, and in 1893 became assistant editor (afterwards editor) of the journal *Woman*. In 1900 he went to live in Paris for eight years and from then on he was engaged exclusively in writing, journalistic and creative. His claims to recognition as a novelist rest mainly on *The Old Wives' Tale* (1908), the *Clayhanger* series—*Clayhanger* (1910), *Hilda Lessways* (1911), *These Twain* (1916), subsequently issued (1925) as *The Clayhanger Family*—in all of which novels the 'Five Towns', centres of the pottery industry, feature not only as background, but almost as *dramatis personae*. He excels again with *Riceyman Steps*, a picture of drab life in London, and he has a genial, humorous streak which finds outlet in works like *The Card* (1911), *The Grand Babylon Hotel* (1902), *Imperial Palace* (1930), and the play *The Great Adventure* (1913). Attention to detail is Bennett's distinguishing trait, nothing being too trivial to be investigated and described. At his least inspired this can be tedious, but he is usually engagingly readable. The play *Milestones* (1912), written in collaboration with E. Knoblock, was much performed. He was a sound critic and, whatever the subject, the epitome of common sense. As 'Jacob Tonson' on *The New Age* he was a discerning reviewer. His *Journals*, edited by N. Fowler, were published posthumously. See books by M. Bennett (1933), W. Allen (1948), F. Swinnerton (1950), R. Pound (1952), J. Hepburn (1963), and his *Letters* (vol. 1, ed. by Hepburn, 1966).

(2) **James Gordon** (1795–1872), Scottish journalist, father of (3), was born at Keith, Banffshire, emigrated to America, where, in 1835, he issued the first number of the *New York Herald*.

(3) **James Gordon** (1841–1918), son and successor of (2), sent Stanley in 1870 to find Livingstone and with *The Daily Telegraph* financed Livingstone's Congo journey (1874–

1878). He also promoted polar exploration, storm warnings, motoring, and yachting.

(4) **John Hughes** (1812–75), English physician, from 1848 to 1874 professor of the Institutes of Medicine in Edinburgh University, was pioneer in the use of the microscope in clinical pathology.

(5) **Richard Bedford, 1st Viscount** (1870–1947), Canadian statesman, born in New Brunswick, Conservative leader from 1927, and prime minister in 1930–35, convened the empire economic conference in Ottawa in 1932 from which resulted a system of empire trade preference known as the Ottawa agreements. He was made a peer in 1941.

(6) **Sir William Sterndale** (1816–75), English pianist and composer, was born at Sheffield, studied at the Royal Academy, London, and at Leipzig, and attracted Mendelssohn's notice at the Düsseldorf Musical Festival. In 1838 he was elected member of the Royal Society of Music, founded the Bach Society in 1849, and in 1856 became professor of Music at Cambridge, and in 1868 principal of the Royal Academy of Music. He was knighted in 1871. His earlier compositions, piano pieces, songs, and the cantatas *The May Queen* (1858) and *The Women of Samaria* (1867) are his happiest. See Life by his son (1908).

BENNIGSEN, Levin August Theophil, Count (1745–1826), German soldier in the Russian service, was born at Brunswick, fought at Pultusk (1806), commanded at Eylau (1807), the Russian centre at Borodino, and defeated Murat at Tarutino (1812). He fought victoriously at the battle of Leipzig (1813) and was created count by the emperor Alexander in the field. His son, **Alexander Levin** (1809–1893), was a distinguished Hanoverian statesman.

BENOIS, Alexandre Nikolaevich, *bye-nwah'* (1870–1960), a St Petersburg painter of Italian, French and German origins, greatuncle of Peter Ustinov (q.v.), was intimately connected with the rise of the Diaghilev ballet and designed many of the sets. See *Memoirs* (trans. 1960).

BENOIT DE SAINTE-MAURE, *ben-wah* (fl. *c*. 1150), French poet, born in either Sainte-Maure near Poitiers or Sainte-More near Tours. His vast romance *Roman de Troie* was a source book to many later writers, notably Boccaccio, who in turn inspired Chaucer and Shakespeare to use Benoit's episode of Troilus and Cressida. See R. K. Gordon, *The Story of Troilus* (1934).

BENSERADE, Isaac de, *bã-sė-rad* (1613–91), French poet and dramatist, born in Paris. He is remembered as the librettist for Lully's ballets and as the author of a sonnet, *Job*, which, regarded as a challenge to Voiture's *Uranie*, sharply divided court opinion.

BENSON, (1) Arthur Christopher (1862–1925), English author, son of (3) and brother of (2) and (6), master of Magdalene College, Cambridge, he wrote studies of Rossetti, Fitzgerald, Pater, Tennyson, and Ruskin, a memoir of (6), and a biography of (3). His poems include *Land of Hope and Glory*, &c.

(2) **Edward Frederic** (1867–1940), English author, son of (3) and brother of (1) and (6), was educated at Wellington and King's College, Cambridge. After some archaeo-

logical research in Greece and Egypt (1892–1895) he published several light novels with a scholarly or historical background as well as three autobiographical studies of Edwardian and Georgian society.

(3) **Edward White** (1829–96), Archbishop of Canterbury (1882), father of (1), (2), and (6), and uncle of (4), was born in Birmingham, became assistant master at Rugby (1852), was ordained priest (1857), and appointed headmaster of the newly founded Wellington College (1858). A friend of Gladstone, he was a zealous churchman and upholder of the establishment principle. See Life by (1).

(4) **Sir Frank Robert** (1858–1939), Shakespearian actor-manager, nephew of (3), born at Alresford, Hants., first appeared in Irving's production of *Romeo and Juliet* in 1882 at the Lyceum and was knighted by King George V on the stage of Drury Lane during a Shakespeare tercentenary matinee with a sword fetched from a local costumier (1916). See study by Trewin (1960).

(5) **Frank Weston** (1862–1951), American artist, born at Salem, studied in Paris, where he was a pupil of Boulanger and Lefebvre. He painted women and children, sensitive etchings and wash drawings of wild fowl, and murals in the Library of Congress.

(6) **Robert Hugh** (1871–1914), English author, son of (3) and brother of (1) and (2), was educated at Eton and Trinity College, Cambridge, turned Roman Catholic in 1903 and rose to private chamberlain to Pope Pius X (1911). A dynamic preacher and prolific author, he wrote such novels as *Come Rack! Come Rope!* (1912). See Life by Martindale (1916).

(7) **Stella** (1892–1933), English author, led an adventurous life in London, America, and China, and wrote *Tobit Transplanted* (1931), &c.

BENTHAM, (1) George (1800–84), English botanist, born at Stoke, Plymouth, was nephew of and secretary to (2) from 1826 to 1832. Abandoning law for botany, he compiled, with Sir Joseph Hooker, the great *Genera Plantarum* (1862–83). President of the Linnaean Society in 1863–74, he was made a C.M.G. in 1878. See a book by B. D. Jackson (1906).

(2) **Jeremy** (1748–1832), English writer on jurisprudence and Utilitarian ethics, uncle of (1), was born, an attorney's son, in London, educated at Westminster School and at the age of twelve entered Queen's College, Oxford. From 1763 he studied law at Lincoln's Inn, London, was called to the bar in 1772. More interested in the theory of the law, he never practised but published *A Fragment on Government* (1776), an acutely critical examination of a passage in Blackstone's *Commentaries*, which contains the germs of most of his later writings. Bentham held that laws should be socially useful and not merely reflect the *status quo*; that men inevitably pursue pleasure and avoid pain; that desires may be broadly classified into self- and other-regarding and that the function of law is to award punishment and rewards to maintain a just balance between them. That all actions are right and good when they promote ' the happiness of the greatest number ' is

the principle of utility, a phrase coined by Hutcheson or Priestley, but popularized by Bentham. As an ethical theory, Utilitarianism was crude and full of inconsistencies, basing itself on purely quantitative considerations. But as a principle of legal reform Bentham's 'calculus' met with greater success, as in his *Introduction to the Principles of Morals and Legislation* (1789) and his other legal works. Bentham early attracted the friendship of Lord Shelbourne, travelled on the continent, including Russia (1785–88), met James Mill in 1808 and founded the politically and philosophically radical sect of the Benthamites. He was a founder of University College, London, where his skeleton, dressed up in his clothes, is preserved. He also founded the *Westminster Review*. See Life by Bowring in the Collected Works (1838–43), Lives by Atkinson (1905), G. Wallas (1922), studies by C. K. Ogden (1932) and J. S. Mill, ed. F. R. Leavis (1950), and G. W. Keeton and G. Schwarzenburger, *Jeremy Bentham and the Law* (1948).

BENTINCK, the name of an ancient noble family which had migrated from the Palatinate to the Netherlands in the 14th century and to England with William of Orange in 1689:

(1) **Lord George** (1802–48), English Tory politician, and sportsman, son of the 4th Duke of Portland, was born at Welbeck Abbey, joined the army in 1819 and (1822–25) was private secretary to his uncle, George Canning, then foreign secretary. He entered parliament in 1828, supported Catholic emancipation and the Reform Bill, but left the Whigs in 1834 to form a separate parliamentary group with Lord Stanley. On Peel's third betrayal of his party in introducing free trade measures, Bentinck, supported by Disraeli who idolized him, led the Tory opposition to Peel. A great lover of racing and field sports, he stamped out many dishonest turf practices. See Lives by B. Disraeli (1851), and C. Kirby (1937).

(2) **William, 1st Earl of Portland** (1649–1709), Dutch courtier, was born in Holland. The friend from boyhood of William III, he was entrusted with the secrets of his foreign policy, and after the revolution was created an English peer, and given large estates. See Life by Mrs Grew (1924).

(3) **William Cavendish, 3rd Duke of Portland** (1738–1809), English statesman, entered Lord Rockingham's cabinet in 1765, and succeeded him as leader of the Whig party. He was twice prime minister—April to December 1783, and 1807–09; but his best work was done as home secretary under Pitt, with charge of Irish affairs (1794–1801).

(4) **Lord William Cavendish** (1774–1839), English statesman, after serving in Flanders and Italy became governor of Madras (1803–07). He was recalled, however, when his prohibition of sepoy beards and turbans caused the massacre of Vellore. He served in the Peninsular War (1808–14), in 1827 became governor-general of Bengal and in 1833 first governor-general of India. His administration resulted in better internal communications, substituted English for other Persian and Sanskrit, brought about other educational reforms with the help of Macaulay

(q.v.), and prohibited the *suttee*. See Life by Boulger (1892).

BENTLEY, (1) Edmund Clerihew (1875–1956), English journalist and novelist, born in London. He is chiefly remembered as the author of *Trent's Last Case* (1913), which is regarded as the milestone in the transformation of the detective novel from the romantic concept of the Conan Doyle era to the more realistic modern school. Bentley originated and gave name to the type of rhyming tag known as the 'clerihew'. See his autobiographical *Those Days* (1940).

(2) **Richard** (1662–1742), English classical scholar, was born at Oulton near Leeds, was educated at Wakefield Grammar School and in 1682 at St John's College, Cambridge, and in 1682 he was appointed by his college headmaster of Spalding Grammar School, but resigned to become tutor to the son of Dr Stillingfleet, then Dean of St Paul's. In 1689 he accompanied his pupil to Oxford, where he had full scope for the cultivation of classical studies, and where he was twice appointed to deliver the Boyle Lectures on the Evidences of Religion. He had taken orders in 1690, and to Stillingfleet he owed various good ecclesiastical preferments, with the post of royal librarian at St James's. His *Letter to Mill* (1691) on the Greek chronicler John Malelas is itself a masterpiece; but it was the *Dissertation upon the Epistles of Phalaris* (1699), an expansion of an earlier essay, that established his reputation throughout Europe. In 1700 Bentley was appointed Master of Trinity College, Cambridge; and in the following year he married Joanna Bernard, the daughter of a Huntingdonshire knight. The history of his mastership is an unbroken series of quarrels and litigations, provoked by his arrogance and rapacity, for which he was fully as well-known during his lifetime as for his learning. He contrived, nevertheless, in 1717, to get himself appointed regius professor of Divinity, and by his boldness and perseverance managed to pass unscathed through all his controversies. He edited various classics—among others, Horace (1711) and Terence (1726). Emendations were at once his forte and foible—the latter conspicuously in his edition of *Paradise Lost* (1732). The proposal (1720) to print an edition of the Greek New Testament, in which the received text should be corrected by a careful comparison with the Vulgate and all the oldest existing Greek MSS., was then singularly bold, and evoked violent opposition. He left behind him one son, **Richard** (1708–82), who inherited much of his father's taste with none of his energy, and two daughters, one of whom was the mother of Richard Cumberland the dramatist. See Lives by Monk (1833) and Jebb (1882).

(3) **Richard** (1794–1871), a London publisher, founder of *Bentley's Miscellany* (1837–68). The firm was absorbed by Macmillan in 1898.

BENTON, Thomas Hart (1782–1858), American statesman, known as 'Old Bullion' from his opposition to the paper currency, was born near Hillsborough, N.C. See Life by Roosevelt (1887).

BENYOWSKY, Maurice Augustus, Count de,

ben-yof'skee (1741–86), an unscrupulous Hungarian adventurer, who, while fighting for the Polish Confederation, was taken prisoner in 1769, banished to Kamchatka, and there made tutor in the governor's family. He gained the affections of the daughter of the house, and was assisted by her to escape, but not without a struggle, in which the governor was killed. Benyowsky, with ninety-six companions, set sail in a ship well armed and provisioned, and with a considerable amount of treasure, and reached France in 1772. Invited by the French government to found a colony at Madagascar, he arrived there in 1774, and was made king in 1776 by the chiefs. His relations with the French were now not always friendly, and as a result of a quarrel with the government of Mauritius, he was killed in battle. See his *Memoirs* (trans. by Nicholson, 1790).

BENZ, Karl Friedrich (1844–1929), German engineer, born in Karlsruhe. In 1879 he constructed a two-stroke engine model and founded a factory for its manufacture, leaving it when his backers refused to finance a mobile engine. He then founded his second company, Benz & Co., Rheinisch Gasmotorenfabrik, at Mannheim. His first car—one of the earliest petrol-driven vehicles—was completed in 1885 and sold to a French manufacturer, Roger. For a time he joined the firm of Panhard and Lavasseur. In 1926 his firm was merged with the Daimler-Motoren-Gesellschaft.

BEN-ZVI, Itzhak (1884–1963), Israeli statesman, born at Poltava (U.S.S.R.). Having migrated to Palestine in 1907 he became a prominent Zionist, and was a founder of the Jewish Labour party. He was elected president of Israel on the death of Dr Weizmann (q.v.) in 1952. A prominent scholar and archaeologist, he wrote on the history of the Middle East.

BÉRANGER, Pierre Jean de, *bay-rã-zhay* (1780–1857), French poet, born in Paris, August 19, after a scanty education left regular employment for an impecunious literary life in 1798. His lyrics, coloured by his politics—a curious compound of republicanism and Bonapartism—led to spells of imprisonment in 1821 and 1828, but their vivacity, satire, and wit endeared them to the masses. See his *Ma Biographie* (trans. 1858), correspondence (1859–60), and Lives by Pilon (1900) and Maigret (1904).

BÉRARD, Christian, *bay-rahr* (1902–49), French painter and designer. His attitude to his own work was curiously oversensitive. He was always a reluctant exhibitor, disliked having his paintings reproduced, and even when designing for the theatre began with an infectious dissatisfaction, so that last minute repaintings were not uncommon. Nevertheless, his fame rests mainly on his stage décor, especially for the productions of Molière by Barrault.

BERCEO, Gonzalo de, *ber-thay'õ* (*c.* 1180–*c.* 1246), earliest known Castilian poet, born in Verceo. He became a deacon and wrote more than thirteen thousand verses on devotional subjects, of which the best is a Life of St Oria. He was also the author of *Milagros de la Virgen*, a collection of legends

of the Virgin's appearances on earth. His poems were not discovered and published until the late 18th century.

BERCHEM, or **Berghem, Nicholas**, *ber'-*кнеm (1620–83), Dutch landscape painter, was born at Haarlem. His work is represented in most European collections.

BERCHET, Giovanni, *ber-ket'* (1783–1851), Italian poet, born in Milan, began by translating foreign, especially English, literature, and through his translation of *The Vicar of Wakefield* (1809) became interested in ballads. In 1816 he published a pamphlet, *Lettera semiseria di Grisostomo*, which became a manifesto of the Romantic movement in Italy. In 1821 he left Italy to avoid arrest, and lived in exile, mainly in England, until the abortive Revolution of 1848. He was received in Milan with enthusiasm and made director of education, but had to flee again to Piedmont, where he died. His best-known works are *I Profughi di Parga* (1821), *Il Romito del Cenisio*, and *Il Trovatore*. See study by E. Li Gotti (Florence 1933).

BERDYAEV, Nikolas, *byer-dyah'yef* (1874–1948), Russian Idealist philosopher, born at Kiev, became a revolutionary and an ardent student of Marx, prophesied and welcomed the 1917 Revolution and was rewarded with a professorship at Moscow. But a crisis developed between his Marxian social ideals and his spiritual ideals which ended in his dismissal in 1922. He settled in Berlin and founded there an Academy of the Philosophy of Religion, which he later transferred to Clamart near Paris, where he died. His numerous essays restate the tenets of a former school of Russian thought, combining a messianic nationalism with a claim for church unity. Communism is a failure because it is nonspiritual. Of his works published in English are *Freedom and the Spirit* (1935), *The Meaning of History* (1936), *The Origin of Russian Communism* (1937), and *Slavery and Freedom* (1944).

BERENGAR, *ber'-*, names of two kings of Italy:

Berengar I, grandfather of II, succeeded his father, a count of Frankish origin, as Duke of Friuli, and in 887 was crowned king of Italy, in 915 emperor. He was assassinated in 924.

Berengar II, grandson of I, succeeded his father as Count of Ivrea in 925, and was crowned king in 950. In 961 he was dethroned by the emperor, and after three years' refuge in a mountain fortress, was sent as a prisoner to Bamberg, in Bavaria, where he died in 966.

BERENGAR OF TOURS (999–1088), scholastic theologian, in 1031 was appointed preceptor of the cathedral school at Tours, and about 1040 Archdeacon of Angers. An opponent of the doctrine of transubstantiation, he was finally, in 1078, cited to appear at Rome, where he repeatedly abjured, but apparently never abandoned his ' error '. He spent his last years in a cell on an island in the Loire, near Tours. See A. J. Macdonald's study (1930).

BERENGARIA. See RICHARD I.

BERENICE, *ber-e-nī'see*, the name of several women of the house of Ptolemy, none of them so celebrated as the Jewish Berenice—the daughter of Herod Agrippa, who, having been four times married (to an uncle, her brother, &c.) gained the love of Titus during the Jewish rebellion (A.D. 70), and followed him to Rome. She is the heroine of Racine's tragedy.

BERENSON, Bernhard (1865–1959), American art critic, was born at Vilna, studied at Harvard, and became a leading authority on Italian Renaissance art, producing a vast critical literature which apart from standard works on each of the Italian schools includes *The Study and Criticism of Italian Art* (1901–1916), *Aesthetics and History* (1950), and the autobiographical *Sketch for a Self Portrait* (1949). See also extracts from his diaries (1947–56), *Selected Letters* (ed. by McComb, 1965), *The Passionate Sightseer* (1960), and *Life* by S. Sprigge (1960).

BERESFORD, (1) **Charles William de la Poer, 1st Baron** (1846–1919), British admiral, was born at Philipstown, Offally, Ireland, son of the fourth Marquis of Waterford. He entered the navy in 1859, and was promoted captain in 1882 for his services at the bombardment of Alexandria. He served, too, in the Nile expedition (1884). He was a lord of the Admiralty (1886–88), but resigned, sat in parliament as a Conservative and commanded the Mediterranean Fleet (1905–07), Channel Fleet (1907–09). A trenchant naval critic, he published *Memoirs* in 1914.

(2) **John Davys** (1873–1947), English novelist, wrote the *History of Jacob Stahl* (1911–15), novels, and short stories.

(3) **William Carr Beresford, 1st Viscount** (1768–1854), British soldier, was a natural son of the first Marquis of Waterford. He distinguished himself at the Cape (1806) and at Buenos Aires, where, having surrendered, he managed to escape (1807). In the Peninsula he took the command (1809) of the Portuguese army. For his services at Busaco (1810) he was made a Knight of the Bath; and for his victory over Soult at Albuera (1811) he received the thanks of parliament. He was present at Badajoz, and at Salamanca was severely wounded. In 1814 he was created Baron, and in 1823 Viscount Beresford. He left Portugal in 1822; and in the Wellington administration (1828–30) he was master-general of the ordnance. He bore the title of Duke of Elvas in Spain, and of Conde de Trancoso in Portugal.

BERG, Alban (1885–1935), Austrian composer, born in Vienna. He studied under Schönberg, and after service in the Austrian war ministry during World War I, he taught privately in Vienna. His music, which welds the twelve-note system of Schönberg to a deeply traditional style, has been influential in helping to popularize his master's teachings and he is best known for his opera *Wozzeck* (1924), his violin concerto, and the *Lyric Suite* for string quartet. His unfinished opera, *Lulu*, was posthumously produced. See studies by W. Reich (Vienna 1937) and H. F. Redlich (1957).

BERGENROTH, Gustav Adolf, *ber'gen-rōt* (1813–69), the editor of the Simancas archives, was born in East Prussia, and died at Madrid, having had to quit Germany in 1850 as a revolutionist, first for California, and then

for England, where he devoted himself to the Tudor state papers. See Memoir by Cartwright (1870).

BERGERAC, Savinien Cyrano de, *ber-zhė-rak'* (1619–55), French author, was born in Paris, and fought more than a thousand duels, mostly on account of his monstrously large nose. His works, often crude, but full of invention, vigour, and wit, include the *Histoire comique des états de la lune et du soleil* (trans. Aldington 1923), which suggested ' Micromégas ' to Voltaire and ' Gulliver ' to Swift. See ROSTAND.

BERGIUS, Friedrich, *ber-gee-oos* (1884–1949), German industrial chemist, born at Goldschmieden near Breslau, made notable researches in coal hydrogenation and the hydrolysis of wood to sugar. He shared the Nobel prize with Bosch in 1931.

BERGK, Theodor (1812–81), German classical scholar and philologist, born at Leipzig, from 1842 to 1869 was professor at Marburg, Freiburg, and Halle. His chief work is his *Poetae Lyrici Graeci* (1843).

BERGMAN, (1) **Bo Hjalmar** (1869–1967), Swedish writer, born at Stockholm, studied law at Uppsala University and later became a critic. His poetry—for example, *Marionetterna* and *Trots allt*—reveals him as an observant solitary, with a tinge of pessimism in his outlook. *Skyar*, his memoirs, shows compassionate understanding of man caught in the maze of life's complexities. *Transmattan* is a later volume of memoirs. See Stock, *Anthology of Swedish Lyrics* (1930).

(2) **Hjalmar Fredrik Elgerus** (1883–1931), Swedish novelist, short-story writer and dramatist, the outstanding Swedish writer of his period, often compared with Strindberg. *Markurells i Wadköping* (1919; trans. *God's Orchid,* 1924), a satire, and *Swedenhielms* (1925), a comedy, are his best-known works. He also wrote a series of stories, many of which are set in his native Örebro.

(3) **Ingmar** (1918–), Swedish film director, won many international prizes with such films as *Summer with Monika* (1953), *The Seventh Seal* (1956), *Wild Strawberries* (1957), *The Face* (1959), &c., outstanding for their photographic craftsmanship and subtle exploitation of facial characteristics and pictorial metaphor. Recent films include *The Silence* (1963), *Persona* (1966) and *Shame* (1968). See study by R. Wood (1969).

(4) **Torbern Olof** (1735–84), a Swedish chemist, from 1758 a professor at Uppsala, prepared, by using carbon dioxide, artificial mineral waters, and discovered hydrogen sulphide in mineral springs.

BERGSMA, William (1921–), American composer, born in California, has composed works in American folk music style—notably *Paul Bunyan* and *Pioneer Saga* (orchestral suites)—as well as chamber music, a symphony and *The Fortunate Islands,* a musical study of the West Indies.

BERGSON, Henri, *-sõ* (1859–1941), French philosopher, born in Paris, son of a Jewish musician and a British mother, became professor at the Collège de France (1900–24), was elected academician (1914), and awarded the Nobel prize (1927). Bergson, like Heraclitus, argued that change was the stuff of reality. In his *Essai sur les données immédiates de la conscience* (1889; translated as *Time and Free Will*, 1910) and *L'Evolution créatrice* (1907), he contrasted the ever-changing, yet complex, unity of consciousness with the world of things in space, discrete, subject to rearrangement, but not to change. The latter may be adequately grasped by the intellect, but not the nature of duration, which requires instead immediate intuition. The creative urge or *élan vital* (duration) is at the heart of evolution and not natural selection. Since change is basic, there can be no guiding principles of conduct, but free will. Bergson's vision was poetical rather than philosophical; he worked by analogy and suggestion rather than by rigorous argument. He had, however, a great influence on biology and psychology, on such writers as Samuel Butler, Shaw, and Proust. His *Le Rire* (1900) was a significant contribution to aesthetics. See studies by D. Lindsay (1911), J. McK. Stewart (1911), D. Balsillie (1912), H. M. Kallen (1914), and J. MacWilliam (1928).

BERIA, Lavrenti Pavlovich (1899–1953), Soviet secret police chief, born at Mercheuli, Georgia, became organizer of a Bolshevik group at a Baku college in 1917. From 1921 to 1931 he was a member of the O.G.P.U. in the Caucasus, becoming first secretary of the Georgian Communist Party in 1931. In 1938 he became Kremlin commissar for internal affairs. During World War II he was vice-president of the State Committee for Defence, services recognized by the title of Marshal of the Soviet Union in 1945. In March 1953, after the death of Stalin, he belonged briefly with Malenkov and Molotov to the 'Dictatorship of the Three'. Denounced as 'a thrice-accursed Judas', he was shot after a brief 'treason' trial on December 23, 1953. Behind a mild, parsonical façade, the 'Himmler of Russia' was a plotter of ruthless ambition and a skilled organizer of forced labour, terror, and espionage.

BERING, or Behring, Vitus (1681–1741), Danish navigator, born at Horsens in Denmark, early entered the newly-formed navy of Peter the Great, and for his bravery in the wars with Sweden was appointed to lead an expedition of discovery in the Sea of Kamchatka. Sailing in 1728 from a port on the east of Kamchatka, he followed the coast northward until, from its westward trend, he believed he had reached the northeast point of Asia. In 1741 he sailed from Ohkotsk towards the American continent, and sighting land about 58½° N. lat., followed the coast northward; but sickness and storms forced him to return, and he was wrecked on the desert island of Avatcha (now Bering Island), where he died. Bering Sea and Bering Strait are named after him. See Life by Lauridsen (trans. Chicago 1889).

BERKELEY, *bahrk'-*, (1) George (1685–1753), Anglican bishop and philosopher, born near Kilkenny, March 12, studied at Trinity College, Dublin, where he published his *Essay towards a New Theory of Vision* (1709), in which he argued that the having of 'ideas' was the habitual association of visual, tactual, and other sensations. His analysis of sense perceptions in his *Treatise* (1710) and three *Dialogues between Hylas and Philonous* (1713) resolved itself into the subjectivist principle that *esse est percipi* which Samuel Johnson sought to refute by striking his foot against a stone. The continued existence of unobserved objects, such as the celebrated 'tree in the quad' was explained by God's universal perceptions. Berkeley's phenomenalism was later refined and systematized by 19th- and 20th-century empirical philosophers. In 1713 Berkeley went to London, and then spent the best part of seven years in travel in France and Italy, first as chaplain to the brilliant and eccentric Earl of Peterborough, and afterwards as tutor to a son of the Bishop of Clogher. On his return to Ireland in 1721 he was distressed by the social corruption and disorder occasioned by the South Sea mania, and published a short *Essay towards Preventing the Ruin of Great Britain*. In 1724 he was made Dean of Derry, but having received promise of a government grant in support of his romantic scheme 'of founding a college at the Bermudas for the Christian civilization of America' he sailed for America in September 1728, taking with him his newly-married wife. To prepare for Bermuda, he made a temporary home for nearly three years in Rhode Island; and as the promised grant was in the end withdrawn, in 1731 he returned to England. *Alciphron, or the Minute Philosopher* (1732), is a religious interpretation of nature. Next came a *Vindication* (1733) of his early phenomenalism and a theological, philosophical work, the *Analyst* (1735). Meanwhile he was made Bishop of Cloyne, where he found opportunities for his ardent devotion to Irish social problems, on which he published the *Querist* (1736). In 1744 he published *Siris*, or a chain of philosophical reflections on the virtues of tar water. In 1752 he resigned his episcopate, settled in Oxford, but died January 14, 1753. Through Hume, his philosophy profoundly influenced Kant as well as Reid and the Scottish psychologists. See new edition of his works, ed. Luce and Jessop (1944–58), and studies by G. Dawes Hicks (1933), J. O. Wisdom (1953), and G. J. Warnock (1953).

(2) **Lennox Randal Francis** (1903–), English composer, born in Oxford. He began the serious study of music, under Nadia Boulanger in Paris, only after the completion of his studies at Oxford University. His early compositions, the largest of which is the oratorio *Jonah* (1935), show the influence of his French training in their conciseness and lucidity, and later works, notably the *Stabat Mater* (1946) and the operas *Nelson* (1953) and *Ruth* (1956), have won him wide recognition for their combination of technical refinement with lyrically emotional appeal.

BERLAGE, Hendrick Petrus, *ber'lah-gĕ* (1856–1934), Dutch architect, born at Amsterdam. He designed the Amsterdam Bourse (completed in 1903) in a neo-Romanesque style, but he was later influenced by Frank Lloyd Wright, and was largely responsible for the spread of his theories in Holland. He became architectural adviser to the authorities of Amsterdam, The Hague, and Rotterdam.

BERLICHINGEN, Götz von. See GÖTZ.

BERLIN, (1) Irving, real name Israel Baline (1888–   ), American composer, born in Russia and taken to the United States as an infant. He worked for a time as a singing waiter, introducing some of his own songs, such as ' Alexander's Ragtime Band '. A ' soldier show ' in 1918 led to musical comedy, but between *As Thousands Cheer* (1933) and *Louisana Purchase* (1940), most of his work was done for films. His greatest success came in 1946, with *Annie get your Gun*, and in 1954 he received a special presidential citation as a composer of patriotic songs. ' God Bless America ' achieved worldwide popularity in World War II.

(2) Sir Isaiah (1909–   ), British philosopher, fellow of All Souls, Oxford, 1932–38 and from 1950, Chichele professor of Social and Political Theory since 1957, and master of Wolfson College since 1966. He exemplifies the modern empirical approach to political philosophy in his works on *Karl Marx* (1939), *Historical Inevitability* (1954), and *Two Concepts of Liberty* (1959).

BERLIOZ, Hector, *bayr-li-ōz* (1803–69), French composer, born in Côte-Saint-André, Isère. As a child he learned to play the flute and the guitar, but studied medicine until 1823, when he overcame his family's objection to music as a career and studied under Lesueur, rapidly producing a number of large-scale works before entering the Paris Conservatoire in 1826. During his studies he fell in love with the Shakespearean actress, Harriet Smithson, whom he subsequently married, and the *Symphonie Fantastique* expresses his devotion to, and a temporary disillusionment with, her. Gaining the Prix de Rome in 1830, he spent two years in Italy. After his marriage, in 1833, he combined the composition and production of his works with music criticism until a gift from Paganini, for whom he wrote his symphony *Harold en Italie* (1834), made him temporarily independent. After 1842 he won a brilliant reputation in Germany, Russia, and England, but on his return to France his failure to gain a hearing for his major works drove him back to criticism. The deaths of his second wife and his son, ill-health, and his fruitless struggle to win a regular place in French music, clouded his later years. His compositions include the *Grande Messe des morts* (1837), the dramatic symphony *Roméo et Juliette* (1838), the overture *Le Carnaval romain* (1843), the cantata *La Damnation de Faust* (1846), which is perhaps Berlioz's most representative composition, and his comic opera *Béatrice et Bénédict* (1860–62). As well as being the first great orchestral specialist among composers, Berlioz was one of the founders of 19th-century programme music, showing his genius as much in his lightly-scored miniatures as in his more monumental works, such as his final opera *Les Troyens*. A brilliantly incisive prose writer, Berlioz produced seven books, including a treatise on orchestration and an autobiography. See also studies by W. J. Turner (1934) and T. S. Wotton (1935), and bibliography by C. Hopkinson (1951).

BERNADETTE, St (1844–79), French visionary, born at Lourdes, Hautes-Pyrénées. The daughter of François Soubirous, a miller, and baptized Marie Bernarde, she claimed to have received in 1858 eighteen apparitions of the Blessed Virgin at the Massabielle Rock, which has since become a notable place of pilgrimage. She became a nun at Nevers, and beatified in 1925, was canonized in 1933. Her feast day is February 18. *The Song of Bernadette* by F. Werfel (1942) was filmed; see also Life by M. Trouncer (1958).

BERNADOTTE, (1) Count Folke (1895–1948), nephew of Gustavus V of Sweden, acted as mediator during both world wars. Appointed by U.N.O. to mediate in Palestine, he produced a partition plan, but was assassinated by Jewish terrorists on September 17.

(2) Jean. See CHARLES XIV of Sweden.

BERNANOS, Georges (1888–1948), French writer, born in Paris. He did not begin to write seriously until he was thirty-seven and had taken degrees in Law and Letters. Like all his generation of French Catholic writers, he attacked indifference and was preoccupied with problems of sin and grace. His most memorable novels are: *Sous le soleil de Satan* (1926) and *Le Journal d'un curé de campagne* (1936). The latter, a sensitive study of a young priest, was translated by P. Morris (1937). Bernanos also wrote a play, *Dialogues des Carmélites*, and *Diary of My Times* (1938), also translated by P. Morris.

BERNARD, *ber-nahr*, (1) Claude (1813–78), French physiologist, born near Villefranche. A pharmacist's assistant at Lyons, and failing in his ambition of a literary career, he studied medicine at Paris, and in 1841 became assistant at the Collège de France to Magendie, with whom he worked until his own appointment in 1854 to the chair of General Physiology, and whom he succeeded in 1855 as professor of Experimental Physiology. He was elected to the Academy in 1868, and died at Paris. His earliest researches were on the action of the secretions of the alimentary canal, the pancreatic juice, the connection between the liver and nervous system, &c., for which he received prizes from the Academy (1851–53). Later researches were on the changes of temperature of the blood, the oxygen in arterial and in venous blood, the opium alkaloids, curarine, and the sympathetic nerves. His *Leçons de physiologie expérimentale* (1865) is a standard work. See works on him by Sir M. Foster (1899), J. M. D. Olmsted (1939), and H. Bergson (1939).

(2) Tristan (*né* Paul) (1866–1947), French novelist and dramatist, was born at Besançon. His first success came with a gay novel, *Les Mémoires d'un jeune homme rangé* (1899). In the same year he wrote a comedy, *L'Anglais tel qu'on le parle*, and from then on produced a number of light-hearted pieces with stock comic situations, which proved very popular —*Daisy* (1902), *Triplipatte* (1905), *Le Petit Café* (1911), and *Le Prince Charmant* (1921).

BERNARD OF CLAIRVAUX, St (1090–1153), theologian and reformer, was born of a noble family at Fontaines, near Dijon, in Burgundy; in 1113 entered the Cistercian monastery of Cîteaux; and in 1115 became the first abbot of the newly-founded monastery of Clairvaux, in Champagne. He was canonized in 1174. His studious, ascetic life and stirring eloquence made him the oracle of Christendom; he founded more than seventy monasteries; and the ' Mellifluous Doctor ' is regarded by the Catholic Church as the last of the fathers. He drew up the statutes of the Knights Templars in 1128; he secured the recognition of Pope Innocent II; and it was his glowing eloquence at the council of Vézelay in 1146 that kindled the enthusiasm of France for the second Crusade. The influence of St Bernard as a spiritual teacher through his fervid piety and living grasp of Christian doctrine was a wholesome antidote to the dry and cold scholasticism of the age. Yet he showed a harsh severity towards Abelard and others whose views he rejected. His writings comprise more than 400 epistles, 340 sermons, a Life of St Malachy, and 12 distinct theological treatises. The monks of his reformed branch of the Cistercians are often called Bernardines. See Lives by Cotter Morison (1877), Eales (1890), Storrs (1893), and W. W. Williams (1953).

BERNARD OF MENTHON, St (923–1008), ' Apostle of the Alps ', born in Savoy, as Archdeacon of Aosta founded the hospices in the Alpine passes that bear his name, and died at Novara.

BERNARD OF MORVAL, a monk of Cluny about 1140, is said to have been born of English parents at Morval. He is the author of the remarkable poem *De Contemptu Mundi,* in 3000 long rolling, ' leonine-dactylic' hexameters, some of which were translated by John Mason Neale (q.v.) into hymns, among them ' Jerusalem the Golden ' and ' The World is Very Evil '.

BERNARD OF WEIMAR. See BERNHARD.
BERNARDIN DE SAINT-PIERRE. See SAINT-PIERRE (2).
BERNARDINO. See PINTURICCHIO, ROSSI.
BERNARDINO OF SIENA, St (1380–1444), born at Massa di Carrara of a distinguished family, made himself famous by his rigid restoration of the primitive Franciscan rule. He entered the order in 1404, and in 1438 was appointed its vicar-general for Italy. He founded the *Fratres de Observantia,* a branch of the Franciscan order, which already numbered over 300 monasteries in Italy during his day. Bernardino was canonized in 1450. His eminently mystical works were published at Venice in 1591, at Paris in 1636. See Lives by Thureau Dangin (1912) and Howell (1913).

BERNAUER, Agnes, *bern'ow-er* (d. 1435), the beautiful daughter of a poor surgeon of Augsburg, was secretly married in 1432 to Duke Albrecht of Bavaria, only son of the reigning Duke Ernst, who, in her husband's absence, had her drowned as a witch at Straubing, in the Danube. Albrecht took up arms against his father; but after a year of war he consented to marry Anna of Brunswick.

BERNAYS, Jakob (1824–81), Jewish classical scholar, born at Hamburg. Professor and librarian at Bonn, he wrote much on the Greek philosophers.

BERNERS, (1) Gerald Hugh Tyrwhitt-Wilson, 14th Baron (1883–1950), British composer, born at Bridgnorth. His early works appeared under the name of Gerald Tyrwhitt. His total output was small, but includes an orchestral fugue and several ballets, of which the best known are *The Triumph of Neptune* and *Wedding Bouquet* (after a play by Gertrude Stein). All his work is distinguished by a delicate and witty sense of pastiche.

(2) **John Bourchier, 2nd Baron** (1467–1533), deputy of Calais, where he translated Froissart (1523–25).

(3) or **Barnes, Dame Juliana,** according to tradition was the daughter of Sir James Berners who was beheaded in 1388, the prioress of Sopwell nunnery at St Albans, and the author of the *Treatyse perteynynge to Hawkynge, Huntynge, Fysshynge, and Coote Armiris.* Probably, however, she wrote only the treatise on hunting, and part of that on hawking; the heraldry is certainly not hers. The treatise on fishing, wanting in the St Albans edition (1486), first appears in Wynkyn de Worde's edition (1496).

BERNHARD, Duke of Weimar (1604–39), Protestant general in the Thirty Years' War, distinguished himself in 1622 at the battle of Wimpfen. In 1631 he was one of the first to support Gustavus Adolphus. He commanded the left wing at Lützen, and after the king's death had the chief command. He took a very important part in the war; but after a sudden illness died at Neuburg on the Rhine. See Life by G. Droysen (1885).

BERNHARD LEOPOLD (1911–), prince of the Netherlands, born at Jena, son of Prince Bernhard Casimir of Lippe. He married Juliana (q.v.), only daughter of Wilhelmina, Queen of the Netherlands, in 1937 and the title of Prince of the Netherlands was conferred on him. The marriage has issue of four daughters.

BERNHARDI, Friedrich von (1849–1930), German general of cavalry, exponent of militarism, champion of Prussianism, wrote *Germany and the Next War* (1912) and other similar works.

BERNHARDT, Sarah, properly **Henriette Rosine Bernard** (1844–1923), the greatest *tragédienne* of her day, was born in Paris. Entering the Paris Conservatoire in 1859, in 1862 she made her début as ' Iphigénie ' at the Théâtre Français, but attracted little notice. In 1867 she played minor parts at the Odéon, won fame as ' Zanetto ' in Coppée's *Le Passant* (1869), and as ' Queen of Spain ' in *Ruy Blas* (1872), and was recalled to the Théâtre-Français. After 1876 she made frequent appearances in London, America, Europe, &c. In 1882 she married M. Jacques Daria or Damala (d. 1889), a Greek actor, from whom she was divorced shortly afterwards. In 1916 her French nationality was restored. She founded the Théâtre Sarah Bernhardt in 1899. In 1915 she had a leg amputated, but did not abandon the stage. A legendary figure in the theatre world, she died probably the most versatile actress of any age. See her Autobiography (1907), and Lives by Sir G. Arthur (1923), Maurice Baring (1933), L. Verneuil (1942), her grandson, L. Bernhardt (trans. 1949), M. Agate (1945) and J. Richardson (1959).

BERNI, or Bernia, Francesco, *ber'nee* (c. 1497–1535), Italian poet, was born at Lamporecchio

in Tuscany, and in 1517 went from Florence
to Rome. He entered successively the service
of his uncle, Cardinal Bibbiena, of Ghiberti,
chancellor to Clement VII, and in 1532 of
Cardinal Ippolito de' Medici. This he
quitted a year later, and went to Florence,
where, refusing to poison Cardinal Salviati,
he was himself poisoned. His recast or
rifacimento of Boiardo's *Orlando Innamorato*
(1542) is still read in Italy (and justly so) in
preference to the original. He had a large
share in establishing Italian as a literary
language. See Life (1881) by Virgili.

BERNIER, François, *bern-yay* (d. 1688),
French traveller, born at Angers, about 1654
left France for Syria, Egypt, Arabia and
India, where for twelve years he was physician
to Aurungzebe. He published a delightful
account of his travels (1670–71; trans. 1893).

BERNINI, Giovanni Lorenzo, *bayr-nee'nee*
(1598–1680), Italian baroque sculptor, architect and painter, the son of a sculptor, **Pietro**
(1562–1629), born at Naples, came to Rome
at an early age, attracted the notice of Cardinal
Scipione Borghese, for whom he executed his
early statues and who introduced him to
the papal court. His statue *David* (before
1620), in utter contrast to Michelangelo's
grim, heroic treatment, presents a scowling
young rogue ready to take advantage of
Goliath's clumsiness. Similarly his *Apollo
and Daphne* (1625, in the Borghese Gallery),
presenting a pretty young damsel, completely
fails in the conception of the legend. Bernini
had all the theatrical flourish of his style. In
1633 he completed the bronze baldacchino in
St Peter's, having been appointed architect,
but his structurally unsound towers on the
façade caused his removal from papal favour
until 1647, when he designed the fountain of
the four river gods in the Piazza Navona.
In 1656 he decorated the apse of St Peter's
with the so-called *Cathedra Petri*, a *tour de
force* of decorative and theatrical inventiveness, designed the colonnade in front of the
cathedral, and in 1663 the grand staircase to
the Vatican. In 1665 he made a triumphal
journey to Paris to improve upon the designs
for the Louvre, but his own were also rejected.
His last works were the tomb to Alexander VII
in St Peter's (1678), and the small Jesuit
church of S. Andrea al Quirinale. He was
buried in the church S. Maria Maggiore.
See monographs by S. Fraschetti (1900),
M. Reymond (1911), R. Norton (1914), and
Wittkower (1955).

BERNOULLI, *ber-noo-yee*, a Swiss family of
mathematicians and scientists which had its
origin in Antwerp, but because of its dissenting views settled first in Frankfurt (1583) and
later in Basel. See French family history by
E. Doublet (1914). Its most distinguished
members were:

(1) **Daniel** (1700–82), Swiss mathematician,
son of (3), born at Basel, studied medicine
and mathematics and became professor of
Mathematics at St Petersburg (1723). In 1733
he returned to Basel to become professor
first of Anatomy, then Botany, finally Physics.
He shared with Euler the distinction of
having gained the French Academy prize ten
times and was elected F.R.S. in 1750. He did
work on trigonometrical functions, continued

fractions, and the kinetic theory of gases, and
solved an equation proposed by Riceti, now
known as ' Bernoulli's equation '.

(2) **Jacques** (1654–1705), Swiss mathematician, brother of (3), born at Basel, where
he became professor in 1687, investigated
infinite series, the cycloid, transcendental
curves, equiangular spiral, and the catenary.
In 1698 he published his essay on the differential calculus and its application to geometry,
first using the term *integral*. He established
the principles of the calculus of probability
and described the numbers which bear his
name. A logarithmic spiral was at his
request engraved on his tombstone in Basel
cathedral.

(3) **Jean**, or **Johann** (1667–1748), Swiss
mathematician, brother of (2) and father of
(1), born at Basel, did mathematical and
chemical research and was professor at
Groningen (1695) and at Basel (1705). He
wrote on differential equations, rectification
and quadrature of curves, isochronous curves
and curves of the quickest descent. The
exponential calculus is claimed for him. He
had a habit of claiming his brother's work as
his own and expelled his son (1) because the
latter had won a competition in which he had
also been competitor. Another son, **Nicho-
laus** (1695–1726), was professor at St Petersburg. Yet another, **Jean** (1710–90), professor
at Basel, was interested chiefly in physics.
Of the latter's sons, **Jean** (1744–1807) was at
the Berlin academy and wrote on indeterminate equations, **Jacques** (1759–89), became
professor successively at Basel, Verona, and
St Petersburg.

BERNSTEIN, *-stīn*, (1) **Eduard** (1850–1932),
German Socialist leader, born in Berlin, lived
in England from 1888 to 1901. An associate
of Engels, he was an advocate of revisionism,
an evolutionary form of Marxism, and a
member of the Reichstag periodically (1902–
1928). See his *My Years of Exile* (1921).

(2) **Henry** (1876–1953), French dramatist,
born in Paris of Jewish extraction and educated at Cambridge. His first play, *Le
Marché* (1900), was followed by *Le Détour*
(1902), *La Rafale* (1906), *Israël* (1906), *Le
Voleur* (1907), *Samson* (1909), &c. A pronounced enemy of socialism and anti-
Semitism, he fought a number of duels with
critics and anti-Semites. His greatest triumphs
were *Le Secret* (1913) and *Judith* (1922). He
produced many of his plays in his own
theatres. A pacifist in his youth, he fought
in World War I in the British artillery and
the French Air Force. He escaped to New
York in 1940 and returned to France after
the liberation in 1945. His brilliant, breathless, brutal plays depend to a great extent on
stage effects. See Life by L. de Sidaner
(1931).

(3) **Leonard** (1918–), American conduc-
tor, pianist, and composer, born in Lawrence,
Mass., educated at Harvard and the Curtis
Institute of Music. Bernstein reached fame
suddenly in 1943 by conducting the New
York Philharmonic as a substitute for Bruno
Walter. His compositions include two
symphonics—*Jeremiah* (1942) and *The Age of
Anxiety* (1949)—a television opera, *Trouble
in Tahiti*, and the musical comedies *On the*

Town, which incorporated music from his ballet *Fancy Free*, and *West Side Story* (1958), based on the Romeo and Juliet theme.

BEROSUS, or **Berossus** (fl. *c.* 260 B.C.), a priest of Babylon, who wrote in Greek three books of Babylonian-Chaldean history, in which he made use of the archives in the temple of Bel at Babylon, and of which unfortunately only a few fragments have been preserved by Josephus, Eusebius, and Syncellus.

BERRI, Charles Ferdinand, Duc de, *ber-ree* (1778–1820), second son of the Comte d'Artois (afterwards Charles X), was born at Versailles. In 1792 he fled with his father to Turin; fought with him under Condé against France; afterwards visited Russia, and lived for some time in London and Edinburgh. In 1814 he returned to France, in 1815 was appointed commander of the troops in and around Paris, and in 1816 married **Caroline Ferdinande Louise** (1798–1870), eldest daughter of Francis, afterwards king of the Two Sicilies. Assassinated by the fanatic Louvel in front of the Opéra (February 13, 1820), he left only a daughter; but the same year the widowed duchess gave birth to the Comte de Chambord (q.v.). After the July revolution, 1830, she, with her son, followed Charles X to Holyrood; in 1832 she landed from Italy near Marseilles, but, after many adventures, was betrayed by a Jew at Nantes, and imprisoned in the citadel of Blaye. Her confession that she had formed a second marriage with the Neapolitan marquis, Lucchesi-Palli, at once destroyed her political importance, and the government set her at liberty. She died in Styria. See works by Ménière (1882), Nauroy (1889), Imbert de Saint Amand (trans. 1892–93), Noel Williams (1911), Praviel (1929), and Fabre (1938).

BERRY, (1) **James Gomer**. See KEMSLEY.

(2) **Mary** (1763–1852), English author, was born at Kirkbridge in Yorkshire, travelled on the Continent (1783–85), and in 1788 first met Horace Walpole (q.v.), whose literary executor she became, and who induced her to settle at Little Strawberry Hill with her younger sister and lifelong companion, **Agnes**. See her *Journal and Correspondence* (1865), Houghton's *Monographs* (1873), and the *Berry Papers* (1914), ed. by Lewis Melville.

(3) **William Ewert**. See CAMROSE.

BERT, Paul, *bayr* (1833–86), French physiologist and republican statesman, was born at Auxerre. A professor of the Sorbonne (1869), he did pioneer work in studying blood gases, the toxic effects of oxygen at high pressure, and anaesthetics generally. His *La Pression barométrique* (1878) was translated in 1943 because of its importance for aviation medicine. As minister of education, Bert founded the Universities of Lyons and of Lille.

BERTHA. See AUGUSTINE, or AUSTIN, ST.

BERTHELOT, Marcellin, *ber-tė-lō* (1827–1907), French chemist, born in Paris, became the first professor of Organic Chemistry at the Collège de France (1865), was put in charge of Paris defences in 1870, was foreign minister (1895–96), and an Academician (1900). He helped to found thermochemistry, introduced

a standard method for determining the latent heat of steam, discovered many of the derivatives of coal tar, and his syntheses of many fundamental organic compounds help to destroy the classical division between organic and inorganic compounds. He studied the mechanism of explosion and wrote many scholarly works on the history of early chemistry.

BERTHIER, Alexandre, *bert-yay* (1753–1815), Prince of Neuchâtel and Wagram, Marshal of the French empire, was born at Versailles, and, entering the army in 1770, fought with Lafayette in the American War of Independence. In the French Revolution he soon rose to be chief of the staff in the Army of Italy (1795), and in 1798 proclaimed the republic in Rome. He became chief of staff to Napoleon, on whose fall he had to surrender the principality of Neuchâtel, but was allowed to keep his rank as peer and marshal. Napoleon made overtures to him from Elba; but he retired to Bamberg. On July 1, 1815, at the sight of a Russian division marching towards the French frontier, he threw himself from a window. His *Mémoires* appeared in 1826.

BERTHOLLET, Claude Louis, Comte, *ber-to-lay* (1748–1822), French chemist, was born at Talloires in Savoy, studied at Turin, came to Paris in 1772, and in 1781 was elected a member of the Academy of Sciences. He aided Lavoisier in his researches on gunpowder and in forming the new chemical nomenclature, and accepted his antiphlogistic doctrines; in 1785 he showed the value of chlorine for bleaching. Following Priestley, he showed ammonia to be a compound of hydrogen and nitrogen. He was made a senator and a count by Napoleon, yet voted for his deposition in 1814, and on the Bourbon restoration was created a peer.

BERTILLON, Alphonse, *ber-tee-yõ* (1853–1914), a Paris police officer who in 1880 devised a system of identifying criminals by measurements. See *Life* by Rhodes (1956).

BERTIN, Louis François, *ber-tĩ* (1766–1841), the founder in 1799 of the *Journal des Débats*, edited afterwards by his sons, **Louis Marie Armand** (1801–54) and **Édouard** (1797–1871).

BERTRAM, C. See RICHARD OF CIRENCESTER.

BERTRAND, *ber-trã*, (1) **Henri Gratien, Comte** (1773–1844), one of Napoleon's generals, was born and died at Châteauroux. He shared the emperor's banishment to St Helena, and, on his death, returned to France, where in 1830 he was appointed commandant of the Polytechnic School.

(2) **Louis Marie Émile** (1866–1941), French author, born at Spincourt, spent some years in Algeria, which provides a setting for *Sang des races* (1898), *La Cina* (1900), and other realistic novels and travel books. He also wrote historical novels and biographical studies of Flaubert and Louis XIV. He was elected to the Academy in 1925. See study by M. Ricord (1947).

BERTRAND DE BORN. See BORN.

BÉRULLE, Pierre de (1575–1629), French cardinal and theologian, born near Troyes, was a leader of the Catholic reaction against Calvinism. He founded the French Congregation of the Oratory (1611) and introduced the

Carmelite order into France. He was ambassador to Spain in 1626, was minister of state until dismissed by Richelieu, and was made a cardinal in 1627. Many of his pupils became famous, he widely influenced French religious teaching, being dubbed by Pope Urban VIII ' Apostolus Verbi Incarnati '. See studies by Houssaye (1873–75) and Pottier (1929).

BERWICK, James Fitzjames, 1st Duke of (1670–1734), a great French general, was the natural son of James II, by Arabella Churchill, sister of the Duke of Marlborough. Born at Moulins, he was educated in France as a Catholic, served in Hungary under Duke Charles of Lorraine, in 1687 was created Duke of Berwick, and fled from England at the Revolution. He fought through his father's Irish campaign (1689–91) and then in Flanders and against the Camisards. In 1706 he was created a marshal of France, and in 1707 in Spain established the throne of Philip V by the decisive victory of Almansa. After several years of inactivity, he received the command in 1733 of an army intended to cross the Rhine. While besieging Philippsburg, he was killed by a cannon ball, June 12, 1734. He left descendants in both Spain and France—the Dukes of Liria and Fitzjames. See his *Mémoires* (1778), and two works by C. T. Wilson (1876–83).

BERZELIUS, Johan Jakob (1779–1848), Swedish chemist, was born in East Götland, Sweden, studied at Uppsala and died at Stockholm. His accurate determination of atomic weights established the laws of combination and the atomic theory. He introduced modern symbols, an electrochemical theory, discovered the elements of selenium, thorium, and cerium, and first isolated others. His great work was rewarded with the gold medal of the Royal Society.

BERZSENYI, Daniel, *ber'shen-yi* (1776–1836), Hungarian lyric poet, born in Heteny. Educated by his father, he won fame as a patriotic poet with his *Ode to Magyarokhoz*, inspired by the Magyar nobility's successful opposition to Napoleon on the Styrian Alps. Collections of his verse appeared in 1813 and in 1830, when he was elected a member of the Hungarian Academy. His complete works, edited by his friend Dobrentei, were published in Pesth in 1842 and in a definitive edition in 1864.

BESANT, *bez'ĕnt*, (1) **Annie**, *née* **Wood** (1847–1933), British theosophist, sister-in-law of (2), born in London of Irish parentage, brought up at Harrow, at twenty married the Rev. Frank Besant, but was separated from him in 1873. From Secularism and Bradlaugh she passed in 1889 to Madame Blavatsky and Theosophy, herself its high priestess from 1891, and in her later years championed nationalism and education in India. See her *Autobiography* (1893), and studies by Geoffrey West (new ed. 1933) and Besterman (1934).

(2) *bé-zant'*, **Sir Walter** (1836–1901), English novelist, brother-in-law of (1), born at Portsmouth, studied at King's College, London, and at Christ's College, Cambridge. After a few years as a professor in Mauritius, he devoted himself to literature. His first work, *Studies in French Poetry*, appeared in 1868; and in 1871 he entered into a literary partnership with James Rice (1844–82), a native of Northampton, and editor of *Once a Week*. Together they produced many novels, including *Ready-Money Mortiboy* (1872), *The Golden Butterfly* (1876), *By Celia's Arbour*, *The Chaplain of the Fleet*, *The Seamy Side* (1881). After Rice's death, Besant himself wrote *All Sorts and Conditions of Men* (1882), and other novels advocating social reform, resulting in the establishment of the People's Palace in the east end of London. He was also the author of some biographical studies and works on the history of London, &c. He was secretary of the Palestine Exploration Fund (some of whose works he edited), and first chairman of the Incorporated Society of Authors. See his *Autobiography* (1902).

BESS OF HARDWICK. See CAVENDISH.

BESIER, Rudolf (1878–1942), British playwright, remembered for *The Barretts of Wimpole Street* (1930).

BESSARION, or **Basilius, John**, *bessah'ree-on* (1389/1400–72), one of the earliest scholars who transplanted Greek literature and philosophy into the West, was born at Trebizond, and died at Ravenna. As Archbishop of Nicaea, he accompanied the Greek emperor, John Palaeologus, to Italy in 1438, to effect a union between the Greek and the Roman churches. Soon afterwards joining the Roman church, he was made cardinal by Pope Eugenius IV. Ten years later, Nicholas V created him Bishop of Frascati; and for five years he was also papal legate at Bologna. After the fall of Constantinople, of which he had been titular patriarch, he visited Germany and endeavoured to promote a crusade against the Turks. Twice he was nearly elected pope.

BESSEL, Friedrich Wilhelm (1784–1846), German mathematician and astronomer, was born at Minden, and starting as a ship's clerk, was in 1810 appointed director of the observatory and professor at Königsberg. He catalogued stars, predicted a star beyond Uranus as well as the existence of dark stars, investigated Kepler's problem of heliocentricity and systematized the functions involved, which bear his name.

BESSEMER, Sir Henry (1813–98), British inventor, born at Charlton, Herts, patented in 1856 an economical process by which molten pig iron disturbed by a current of air is turned directly into steel. He was knighted in 1879. See his *Autobiography* (1924).

BESSIÈRES, Jean Baptiste, *bes-see-ayr* (1768–1813), Duke of Istria and Marshal of the French empire, was born of poor parents at Preissac, Lot; became a private in 1792; in less than two years rose to be captain; distinguished himself at St Jean d'Acre, Aboukir, Austerlitz, Jena, Eylau, in Spain and the Russian campaign; was killed by a stray shot near Lützen on the eve of battle.

BEST, Charles Herbert (1899–), Canadian physiologist, born at West Pembroke, Maine, became professor at Toronto in 1929. In 1922 he was associated with Banting and Macleod in their joint discovery of insulin. F.R.S.(1938), he was created C.H. (1971).

BETHAM-EDWARDS. See EDWARDS (1).

BETHELL, Richard. See WESTBURY (LORD).

BETHLEN, (1) Gabriel, or **Bethlen Gabor** (1580–1629), born of a noted Protestant family of Hungary, in 1613 was elected prince of Transylvania. In 1619, with the Bohemians, he invaded Hungary, and next year was chosen its king, but in 1621 concluded peace with Ferdinand II, and resigned his claims to Hungary, while obtaining large accessions of territory. In 1622 and 1626 he renewed hostilities with the emperor.

(2) **István (Stephen), Count** (1874–1951), Hungarian statesman, born at Gernyeszeg (Cornesti), Transylvania, was a leader of the counter-revolutionary movement after World War I, and as prime minister in 1921–31 promoted Hungary's economic reconstruction.

BETHMANN HOLLWEG, Theobald von (1856–1921), German statesman, born at Hohenfinow, Brandenburg, studied law, and rose in the service of Brandenburg, Prussia, and the Empire, till in 1909 he became imperial chancellor. He treated the Belgian neutrality treaty as a ' scrap of paper ', and played an invidious rôle before and after the outbreak of war in 1914.

BETHUNE, John. See DRINKWATER.

BETJEMAN, Sir John (1906–), British author, educated at Marlborough and Oxford, known for his light verse (*Mount Zion* (1933), *New Bats in Old Belfries* (1940), *Collected Poems* (1958), *Summoned by Bells* (1960, a verse autobiography), &c.), much of which satirizes modern taste, for his essays and guidebooks, and for his championship of Victorian and Edwardian art and architecture. He was awarded the C.B.E. in 1960 and was knighted in 1969. He was made poet laureate in 1972. See study by D. Stanford (1961).

BETTERTON, Thomas (*c.* 1635–1710), English actor and adapter of dramas, born in London, in 1661 joined Davenant's theatrical company. Addison, Cibber, Dryden, Pepys, &c., bear admiring witness to his dramatic powers, which overcame the natural disadvantages of a low voice, small eyes, and an ungainly figure. His wife, an actress, shared his stage triumphs. In an unfortunate speculation in 1692 Betterton lost all his savings. He was buried in Westminster Abbey. See Life by Lowe (1891).

BETTI, Ugo (1892–1954), Italian dramatist and poet, born in Camerino, was a judge by profession. His collections of verse include *Re pensieroso* (1922), of short stories *Caino* (1929) and *Le Case* (1937), and the best of his plays *La Padrona* (1929), in which life appears symbolically in the person of a cynical, masterful and attractive woman. His own profession was not spared in *Corruzione al Palazzo di Giustizia* (1944, trans. 1957), in which one of the characters exclaims: ' We judges are all hypocrites '. See study by E. de Michelis (1937).

BETTY, William Henry West (1791–1874), English actor, better known as the Young Roscius, was born at Shrewsbury, made his début at the age of eleven, and sustained the heaviest parts with considerable success. He quitted the stage in 1808, but after studying for two years at Cambridge, returned to it in 1812. He retired finally in 1824, and lived on the fortune he had so early amassed.

BEUST, Friedrich Ferdinand, Count von, *boyst* (1809–86), Austrian statesman, was born at Dresden, and died at Schloss Altenberg, near Vienna, having been Imperial Chancellor (1867–71) and ambassador at London (1871–1878) and Paris (1878–82). His chief achievement was the reconciliation of Hungary to Austria. See his *Memoirs* (trans. 1887).

BEVAN, Aneurin (1897–1960), British Labour politician, born at Tredegar, Mon., one of thirteen children of a miner, began work in the pits at thirteen on leaving school. Six years later he was chairman of a Miner's Lodge of more than 4000 members. Active in trade unionism in the South Wales coalfield, he led the Welsh miners in the 1926 General Strike. I.L.P. member for Ebbw Vale in 1929, he joined the more moderate Labour party in 1931. He established a reputation as a brilliant, irreverent, and often tempestuous orator. During World War II he was frequently a ' one-man Opposition ' against Sir Winston Churchill. Appointed minister of health in the 1945 Labour government, he introduced in 1948 the revolutionary National Health Service. He became minister of labour in 1951, but resigned the same year over the National Health charges proposed in the Budget. From this period dated ' Bevanism ', the left-wing nagging movement to make the Labour party more Socialist and less ' reformist '. It made Bevan the centre of prolonged and often bitter disputes with his party leaders, but the movement began to wither late in 1956 when he became shadow foreign secretary. He ceased to be a Bevanite at the 1957 Brighton Party Conference when he opposed a one-sided renunciation of the hydrogen bomb by Britain. The most publicized Labour politician of his time, he brought to the Commons Radical fervour, iconoclastic restlessness and an acute intellect. He published *In Place of Fear* (1952). See Life by M. Foot (1962). In 1934 he married **Jennie Lee** (1904–), fiery daughter of a Scottish miner and convinced Socialist advocate ; Labour M.P. from 1929–31, and since 1945, she was responsible for the Arts as a member of the Dept. of Education and Science from 1965.

BEVERIDGE, William Henry Beveridge, 1st Baron (1879–1963), British economist, best known as the author of the *Report on Social Insurance and Allied Services* (1942), was born of Scottish descent at Rangpur, India, was educated at Charterhouse and Balliol College, Oxford, taught law, served as leader writer on the *Morning Post*, made himself the leading authority on unemployment insurance, and compiled his notable report, *Unemployment* (1909, rev. 1930). He entered the Board of Trade (1908) and became director of labour exchanges (1909–16). He was director of the London School of Economics (1919–37) and master of University College, Oxford (1937–1945). From 1941 to 1943 he was president of the Royal Statistical Society. From 1934 he served on several commissions and committees, and ultimately on that of experts of several government departments (1941–42), out of which grew the ' Beveridge Report '. Its main feature was a comprehensive scheme of social insurance. covering the whole community without income limit. Published at the height of the war, it was remarkable testimony to Britain's hopes for the future, and has since formed the basis of much social legislation. Goebbels even made a study of it. Beveridge was elected to parliament as a Liberal in 1944, but was defeated in 1945. See his autobiographical, *Power and Influence* (1953), and other writings. He was raised to the peerage in 1946.

BEVIN, Ernest (1881–1951), British Labour statesman, born at Winsford, Somerset, of poor parents, who left him an orphan before he was seven years old. In 1894 he moved to Bristol to earn his living as a van boy and later as van driver. He educated himself and came early under the influence of trade unionism and the Baptists, and was for a time a lay preacher. At the age of thirty he was a paid official of the dockers' union. In 1920 he earned himself a national reputation by his brilliant handling of his union's claims before a wage tribunal at which he was opposed by an eminent barrister. He won acceptance for most of the claims and the title ' the dockers' K.C.' Bevin was the pioneer of modern trade unionism. Out of 32 separate unions he built up the gigantic National Transport and General Workers' Union and became its general secretary (1921–40). He was one of the leaders in the General Strike (1926), served on the Macmillan Committee on finance, and furthered the work of the International Labour Organization, In 1940 he became minister of labour and national service in Churchill's coalition government. He successfully attained complete mobilization of Britain's manpower by 1943 and was a significant member of the war cabinet. He began to take a keen interest in foreign affairs and became foreign secretary in the Labour government (1945–51). In this office he was responsible for the satisfactory conclusion of peace treaties with Southeast European countries and with Italy, despite growing Soviet disinclination to cooperate. He accepted the necessity for the Western powers to establish a federal government in Western Germany and by the Berlin air lift (June 1948–May 1949) accepted and met the Soviet challenge for the control of that city. He was largely responsible for the successful conclusion of mutual assistance (1948) and defence agreements (1949) with other European powers and America. He opposed, however, total integration of European states, believing that Britain had special Commonwealth obligations. Only with reluctance did he acquiesce in the formation of a Council of Europe. He failed to settle the difficult problem of Palestine, which he handed over to the United Nations. He concluded a new treaty with Egypt (1946) and arranged on his own initiative the meeting of the Commonwealth Foreign ministers (1950) out of which emerged the ' Colombo Plan '. Ill-health made him relinquish office in March 1951, and he died a month later. His wife, **Florence Anne** (d. 1968), was made D.B.E. in 1952, largely as a recognition of her husband's services. Bevin was essentially a skilled and moderate negotiator, robust, down-to-earth, a ' John Bull ' of trade unionists. He believed that he might be able to achieve world peace and conciliation in the manner he had successfully applied in union affairs. But he was essentially a realist, and his realism earned him the censure of the more left-wing elements in his party as well as the esteem of many of his political opponents. See his *The Job to be Done* (1942) and Lives by T. Evans (1946) and A. Bullock (2 vols. 1960, 1967).

BEWICK, Thomas, *byoo'ik* (1753–1828), English wood engraver, was born, a farmer's son, at Cherryburn House, Ovingham, Northumberland, and early evinced a strong love of nature and drawing. At fourteen he was apprenticed to Ralph Beilby (1744–1817), a Newcastle engraver, became his partner in 1776, and, taking his brother John (1760–95) as an apprentice, in his woodcuts for *Gay's Fables* (1779), *Select Fables* (1784), and his own *History of Quadrupeds* (1790), established his reputation, his famous *Chillingham Bull*, a large woodcut (1789), being regarded as his masterpiece. Finer even than the *Quadrupeds* was his *History of British Birds* (1797–1804), in which the figures are rendered with the utmost accuracy, and are powerful and finely decorative arrangements of black and white; the tailpieces are vivid renderings of landscape and of rustic life, frequently touched with humour. Chief of later works was the *Aesop's Fables* (1818), in which he was assisted by William Temple, William Harvey, and his son, **Robert Elliott** (1788–1849), who became his partner in 1812, and also took part in the cuts for an unfinished *History of British Fishes*. See his charming *Autobiography* (1862, new ed. 1924); Hugo's *Bewick Collector* (1866), and ' Supplement ' (1868); *Life*, by Thomson (1882); Dobson's *Bewick and his Pupils* (1884); J. Boyd's *Bewick Gleanings* (1887), and D. C. Thomson, *The Watercolour Drawings* (1930).

BEYLE, Marie-Henri. See STENDHAL.

BEZA, Theodore, *bee'zĕ* (1519–1605), French religious reformer, was born of the noble family of De Besze at Vézelay, in Burgundy, and studied Greek and law at Orleans. He became known as a writer of witty (but indecent) verses, settled with brilliant prospects in Paris, and lived for a time in fashionable dissipation. But after an illness, he took a serious view of life, and, marrying his mistress, in 1548 went with her to Geneva; and from 1549 to 1554 was Greek professor at Lausanne, publishing a drama on *The Sacrifice of Abraham*. In 1559 he was appointed a theological professor and president of the college at Geneva, and became Calvin's ablest coadjutor. In a work on the punishment of heretics (1554) he had approved of the burning of Servetus. During the civil war in France he was chaplain to Condé, and later to Coligny. In 1563 he once more returned to Geneva, and on Calvin's death (1564) the care of the Genevese church fell upon Beza's shoulders. He presided over the synods of French reformers held at Rochelle in 1571 and at Nimes in 1572. His best known work is the Latin New Testament. See Lives by Baird (1899) and Picard (1906).

BHABHA, Homi Jehangir (1909–66), Indian physicist, did much original work on cosmic rays. Elected F.R.S. in 1941, he became professor of Theoretical Physics at Bombay in 1945. He died in an air crash.

BHARTRIHARI, *bahr'tri-hah'ree* (fl. 7th cent.), Hindu poet and philosopher, author of three *satakas* (centuries) of stanzas on practical conduct, love, and renunciation of the world, and Sanskrit grammarian. See translated selections by A. Ghose (1924), J. M. Kennedy (1913), and D. Scott (1940).

BHASA (fl. 3rd cent.), Sanskrit dramatist, author of plays on religious and legendary themes. See study by A. D. Pusalker (1940).

BHAVABHŪTI, *bah'vah-boo'tee*, surnamed ' Sri-kanṭha ', a great Indian dramatist, who flourished in A.D. 730.

BHAVE, Vinoba, *bah-vay* (1895–   ), Indian land reformer, was born in a Maharashtra village. Mahatma Gandhi took him under his care as a young scholar, an event which changed his life. Distressed in 1951 by the land hunger riots in Telengana, Hyderabad, he began a walking mission throughout India to persuade landlords to give land to the peasants. A barefoot, ascetic saint, his silent revolution led to 4,000,000 acres of land being redistributed in four years. He was claimed to be the most notable spiritual figure in India after the death of Gandhi, whose ardent disciple he was. See *Man and his Mission*, ed. Tandon (1954), and book by Vasto (1956).

BIANCHI, Luigi, *byan'kee* (1856–1928), Italian mathematician, professor at Pisa, known especially for his work on surface geometry. His *Lezioni di geometria differenziale* (1894) is a standard work.

BIANCHIFERRARI, Francesco de', *byan'kee-fer-rah'ree* (1460–1510), Italian religious painter of the Modenese school.

BIANCHINI, Francesco, *byan-kee'nee* (1662–1729), Italian antiquary and astronomer, was born at Verona, became librarian to Pope Alexander VIII, established an observatory at Albano, discovered three comets, and observed the moon's surface.

BIANCONI, Charles, *byan'kō-nee* (1786–1875), a native of Lombardy who came to Dublin in 1801 and started the first public conveyance between Clonmel and Cahir in 1815; forty years later his cars were working over 4000 miles of road daily. See Life by his daughter, Mrs O'Connell (1878).

BIAS OF PRIENE (fl. *c.* 570 B.C.), one of the Seven Wise Men of Greece, famous for his eloquence, his nobility of character, and his apothegms.

BIBESCO, Princess. See ASQUITH.

BICHAT, Marie François Xavier, *bee-shah* (1771–1802), French physician, was born at Thoirette, Jura, and studied at Lyons and Paris. In 1797 he began giving lectures, and in 1801 was appointed physician to the Hôtel-Dieu. He was the first to simplify anatomy and physiology by reducing the complex structures of the organs to their simple or elementary tissues.

BICKERSTAFFE, Isaac (*c.* 1735–*c.* 1812), Irish playwright, was page to Lord Chesterfield, the lord-lieutenant. Later he was an officer of marines, but was dismissed from the service, and in 1772 had to flee the country. Of his numerous pieces, produced between 1766 and 1771, the best known is *The Maid of the Mill.*

BICKERSTETH, Edward (1786–1850), English evangelical clergyman, born at Kirkby Lonsdale, Westmorland, compiled over 700 hymns in his *Christian Psalmody* (1833). His son **Edward Henry** (1825–1906), Bishop of Exeter, wrote hymns and poems, and his grandson **Edward** (1850–97) became Bishop of Japan in 1886.

BIDAULT, Georges, *bee-'dō* (1899–   ), French statesman, born and educated in Paris, where he became a professor of History and edited the Catholic *L'Aube.* He served in both world wars, was taken prisoner in the second, released, and took part in the French resistance movement. He became leader of the M.R.P. (Movement Républicaine Populaire) and was prime minister in 1946 and in 1949–50, deputy prime minister (1950, 1951), and foreign minister (1944, 1947, 1953–54). Although devoted to French interests, he supported many measures of European cooperation.

BIDDER, George Parker (1806–78), British engineer and mathematician, was born at Moreton-Hampstead, showed early his remarkable gift for arithmetical calculations, was educated at Camberwell and Edinburgh, and became a civil engineer, inventing the railway swing bridge and designing the Royal Victoria Docks, which were opened in 1856. The ' Calculating Boy ' gave public demonstrations of his gift, which also gave him a great advantage over his opponents when acting as parliamentary adviser.

BIDDLE, John (1615–1662), the founder of English Unitarianism, was born at Wotton-under-Edge, Gloucestershire, and in 1634 entered Magdalen Hall, Oxford, in 1641 was elected master of the Gloucester free school, but in 1645 was thrown into jail for rejecting in his preaching the deity of the Holy Ghost. The Westminster Assembly undertook in vain to ' settle ' Biddle's case; a work by him (1647) was burnt by the hangman as blasphemous; and during the Commonwealth he was in 1655 banished to the Scilly Isles. In 1658 he was released, and continued to preach in London till after the Restoration. In 1662 he was again apprehended and fined £100. He could not pay it, so was sent to jail where he died. See Life by T. P. Govan (1959).

BIDPAI, also **Pilpay,** *bid'pī,* the reputed author of an Indian collection (now lost) of fables and stories widely circulated both in the East and West, of which the earliest extant form exists in an Arabic version of about A.D. 750.

BIDWELL, Shelford (1848–1909), English barrister and physicist, known for his work in electricity, magnetism, and optics. He was president of the Physical Society (1897–1899).

BIELA, Wilhelm von, *bee'la* (1782–1856), Austrian officer who in 1826 observed the comet named after him, although it had already been seen in 1772.

BIER, August, *beer* (1861–1949), German surgeon, born at Helsen, Waldeck, became successively professor of Surgery at Kiel, Greifswald, Bonn, and Berlin. He invented new methods, researched into spiral anaesthesia, and was the first to use cocaine. See his *Hyperämic als Heilmittel* (trans. 1906).

BIERCE, Ambrose Gwinett (1842–?1914), American journalist, and author of collections of sardonically humorous tales such as *In the Midst of Life* (1898,) &c., disappeared in Mexico. See Lives by C. McWilliams (1929) and R. O'Connor (1968).

BIERSTADT, Albert, *beer'shtat* (1830–1902), American artist, born at Solingen, near Düsseldorf, was well known for his Rocky Mountains scenes.

BIFFEN, Sir Rowland (1874–1949), in 1908 first professor of Agricultural Botany at Cambridge, was a pioneer in breeding hybrid rust-resistant strains of wheat.

BIGELOW, *big'ĕ-lō*, (1) **Erastus Brigham** (1814–79), born at West Boylston, Mass., invented looms for various kinds of material, a carpet loom, and a machine for making knotted counterpanes.

(2) **Jacob** (1787–1879), physician and botanist, born in Massachusetts, held several professorships at Harvard, and was associated with the compilation of the single-word nomenclature of the *American Pharmacopoeia* of 1820, afterwards adopted in England.

(3) **John** (1817–1911), writer and diplomat, born at Malden, N.Y., was managing editor of the *New York Evening Post* from 1850 to 1861, when he went as consul to Paris. From 1865 to 1866 he was U.S. Minister in France. In 1875 he was elected secretary of state for New York. He published a biography of Benjamin Franklin (1874) and edited his works, &c. His son **Poultney** (1855–1954), was an international journalist and traveller, and friend of Kaiser Wilhelm II.

BIGGE, Sir John (Amherst) Selby-Bigge (1892–   ), English painter. He studied at Oxford and the Slade School, and was associated with the surrealist movement for a time. In 1933, when he joined Unit One, he was producing abstracts based on mechanical forms. He has lived in Europe since 1936, being awarded the O.B.E. in 1946, and succeeding to his title in 1951.

BIGGERS, Earl Derr (1884–1933), American novelist, born at Warren, Ohio, and educated at Harvard, created the famous character Charlie Chan in his series of detective novels starting with *The House without a Key* (1925).

BIGOD, a family founded by a poor Norman knight, which in 1136 acquired from Stephen the earldom of Norfolk. The second earl, **Roger,** took a prominent part in securing Magna Carta; in 1306 the earldom became extinct.

BILDERDIJK, Willem, *bil'der-dīk* (1756–1831), Dutch poet and philologist, was born at Amsterdam. His voluminous poetry, a blend of rhapsody and neoclassical style, ranges from light verse to epic. See Life appended to his poems (ed. by Da Costa, 1856–79).

BILLAUD-VARENNE, Jean Nicolas, *bee-yō va-ren* (1756–1819), a notorious Terrorist in the French Revolution, was born at La Rochelle, in 1795 was transported for twenty years to Cayenne, and died in Haiti.

BILLINGER, Richard (1893–   ), Austrian poet, born at St Marienkirchen, author of collections of lyrics, also novels coloured by peasant life in Upper Austria.

BILLINGS, (1) **Josh,** pseud. of **Henry Wheeler Shaw** (1818–85), a land agent at Poughkeepsie, New York, who published facetious almanacs and collections of witticisms, the wit, however, mainly due to deliberate misspelling. See Life by Clemens (1932).

(2) **Robert William** (1813–74), English architect, was born in London, and for seven years was apprenticed to John Britton (q.v.). He himself produced *Baronial and Ecclesiastical Antiquities of Scotland* (1845–52), with 240 illustrations.

BILLROTH, Theodor, *bil'rōt* *(1821–94), Austrian surgeon, born at Bergen (Rügen), professor of Surgery at Zürich (1860–67) and Vienna (1867–94), a pioneer of modern abdominal surgery, performed the first successful excision of the larynx (1874) and the first resection of the intestine (1881). A brilliant musician, he was a friend of Brahms.

BILLY THE KID. See BONNEY.

BILNEY, Thomas (1495?–1531), English martyr, studied at Trinity Hall, Cambridge, and was ordained in 1519. He was opposed to the formal ' good works ' of the schoolmen, and denounced saint and relic worship; and influenced Hugh Latimer and other young Cambridge men by his reforming views. He was cautioned by Wolsey (1526), made to recant by Tunstall (1527), but imprisoned in the Tower for a year. When he eventually resumed his preaching, he was burned at Norwich (August 19, 1531).

BINDING, (1) **Karl** (1841–1920), German criminal lawyer, father of (2), born at Frankfurt, professor at Basel, Freiburg, Strassburg, and Leipzig, known for his *Die Normen und ihre Übertretung* (6 vols. 1872–1920).

(2) **Rudolf Georg** (1867–1938), German poet, born at Basel, son of (1), author of lyrics and short stories, became a devotee of Hitler.

BINET, Alfred, *bee-nay* (1857–1911), French psychologist, born at Nice, director of Physiological Psychology at the Sorbonne from 1892, with Theodore Simon established a standard for the measurement of intelligence. He also studied hypnotism. See Life by R. Martin (1925).

BINYON, (Robert) Laurence (1869–1943), English poet and art critic, born at Lancaster. On leaving Oxford, he took a post in the British Museum printed-books department and from 1913 to 1933 was in charge of Oriental prints and paintings. His study *Painting in the Far East* (1908), was the first European treatise on the subject. *Japanese Art* followed in 1909, while other titles— *Botticelli* (1913), *Drawings and Engravings of William Blake* (1922), &c.—show the wide range of his cultural interests. Meanwhile he had achieved a reputation as a poet untouched by *fin de siècle* ideas, but strongly in the tradition of Wordsworth and Arnold. Beginning with *Lyric Poems* (1894), he issued volumes at intervals up to his *Collected Poems* (1931). His *Odes* (1901) contain some of his best work, challenging comparison with major poets; ' The Sirens ' and ' The Idols ' are the two odes nearest perfection. He also wrote plays —*Paris and Oenone*, *Attila*, *Arthur*—which had successful runs, and his one-act pieces are frequently performed by amateurs. He translated Dante into terza rima, and this discipline shows in his later work. Created C.H. in 1932, he was Norton professor of Poetry at Harvard, 1933–34. The poet of affecting melancholy and imaginative reflection, he is forever himself commemorated in his lines ' For the Fallen ' (set to music by Elgar), extracts from which adorn war memorials throughout the British commonwealth.

BION, one of the three Greek bucolic poets, seems to have flourished about 100 B.C., a native of Smyrna, settled in Sicily, and is said to have been poisoned by a jealous rival. Little of his work has survived except his *Lament for Adonis*.

BION OF BORYSTHENES (fl. 280 B.C.), at first perhaps a slave, studied philosophy at Athens, and lived at the court of Antigonus Gonatas.

BIOT, Jean Baptiste, *bee-ō* (1774–1862), French physicist and astronomer, was born and died in Paris. Professor of Physics in the Collège de France, he made a balloon ascent with Gay-Lussac (q.v.) to study magnetism at high altitudes in 1804. He travelled to Spain with Arago (q.v.) in 1806 to determine the length of a degree of longitude. He invented a polariscope and established the fundamental laws of the rotation of the plane of polarization of light by optically active substances. His son, **Édouard Constant** (1803–50), was a Chinese scholar.

BIRCH, (1) Jonathan (1783–1847), till 1803 a Baltic timber merchant, translated *Faust* and the *Nibelungenlied*.—His son, **Charles Bell Birch** (1832–93), was a sculptor, an A.R.A. in 1880.

(2) **Samuel** (1757–1841), English merchant, the son of a London pastrycook, rose to become an alderman and as such saw his proposal to join volunteer regiments at first rejected, later accepted, with him as colonel of the 1st Loyal London Volunteers. He was twice voted the freedom of Dublin for his support for Irish Protestantism and in 1814 became Lord Mayor of London. He was also a popular dramatist and wrote poetry. The front of his original shop in Cornhill, known as Birch's, is in the Victoria and Albert Museum.

(3) **Samuel** (1813–85), English Egyptologist, was born in London, in 1861 he became keeper of the Egyptian and Oriental antiquities in the British Museum. He helped to decipher the Cretan syllabic inscriptions, and was an early authority on the hieroglyphics.

(4) **Samuel John Lamorna,** R.A., R.W.S. (1869–1955), English painter, born at Egremont. He produced many water colours of English (especially Cornish) and Australian landscapes in a charming, realistic manner.

(5) **Thomas** (1705–66), English historian and biographer of Boyle, Tillotson, Queen Elizabeth, Prince Henry, &c., was born at Clerkenwell, and in 1730 took Anglican orders.

BIRD, (1) Edward, R.A. (1772–1819), English *genre* painter, was born at Wolverhampton. His *Good News, Choristers Rehearsing, The Will* and *Chevy Chase* had considerable repute in the 19th century.

(2) **Isabella.** See BISHOP.

(3) **Robert Montgomery** (1805–54), American author, was born at Newcastle, Delaware. Besides two successful tragedies, he wrote *Calavar, a Mexican Romance* (1834), *Nick of the Woods* (1837), and other novels.

BIRDE, William. See BYRD.

BIRDWOOD, (1) Sir George Christopher Molesworth (1832–1917), born at Belgaum, Bombay, graduated M.D.(Edin.), held public posts in Bombay till 1868, in the India Office (1871–1902). He was an authority on Indian art and the East.

(2) **William Riddell, 1st Baron Birdwood** (1865–1951), British soldier, nephew of (1) and son of **Herbert Mills** (1837–1907), Anglo-Indian judge, and educationist, was born at Kirkee, educated at Clifton and Sandhurst. He was transferred from India for service in the South African war, was brigade major at the relief of Ladysmith (1900), and became Lord Kitchener's military secretary for the remainder of the war. He commanded the Anzac Corps in the Gallipoli Landing (1915) and in France until the end of World War I. From 1925, when he was promoted field-marshal, he was commander-in-chief of the Indian army. From 1930 to 1938, when he was created baron, he was master of Peterhouse, Cambridge. He was appointed Captain of Deal Castle in 1935. See his memoirs, *Khaki and Gown* (1941).

BIREN, Ernst. See BIRON, ERNST.

BIRKBECK, George (1776–1841), the founder of mechanics' institutes, was born at Settle, Yorkshire. In 1799, as professor of Natural Philosophy at Anderson's College, Glasgow, he delivered his first free lectures to the working classes. In 1804 he became a physician in London. He took a leading part in the formation of the London Mechanics' or Birkbeck Institute (1824)—the first in the kingdom, which developed into Birkbeck College, a constituent college of London University. See Life by T. Kelly (1957) and Burns, *Birkbeck College* (1924).

BIRKELAND, Kristian, *beer'kĕ-lahn* (1867–1917), Norwegian physicist, born at Oslo, became a professor of Physics at the university there. He demonstrated the electromagnetic nature of the aurora borealis and with Eyde in 1903 developed a method for obtaining nitrogen from the air.

BIRKENHEAD, Frederick Edwin Smith, 1st Earl of (1872–1930), English Conservative statesman and lawyer, born at Birkenhead, where he attended the Grammar School, studied at Wadham College, Oxford, being elected fellow of Merton in 1896, and called to the bar in 1899. He entered Parliament in 1906 and by his provocative maiden speech established himself as a brilliant orator and wit. In the Irish crisis (1914) he vigorously supported Lord Carson's organized resistance to Home Rule. By 1911 he was P.C., attorney-general in 1915, and sat on the Woolsack by the time he reached forty-seven. His extraordinary ability was seen at its best in the Casement trial (1916), when he appeared for the Crown. Despite his earlier convictions, he played a major part in the Irish settlement of 1921 and was created earl. Baldwin appointed him secretary of state for India (1924–28), but his conduct caused much criticism and he resigned to devote himself to a commercial career. His greatest achievements as a lawyer were his *Law of Property Act* (1922) and a textbook on international law. He also wrote *Famous Trials* (1925), &c. See *Life* by his son (revised ed. 1959).

BIRKETT, William Norman, 1st Baron Birkett (1883–1962), English lawyer and politician, born at Ulverston, studied at Emmanuel College, Cambridge, was called to the bar (1913) and earned a brilliant reputation as counsel in such notable murder trials as the Rouse case (1930). A judge of the King's Bench (1941–50), he was chairman of the advisory committee on the famous Defence Regulation 18B during World War II and figured notably in the summing up of the Nuremberg Trials (1945–46), in which he was the British alternate judge to Lord Justice Lawrence. A Lord Justice of Appeal (1950–57), he was knighted in 1951 and raised to the peerage in 1958. He was a Liberal M.P. (1923–24, 1929–31).

BIRMINGHAM, George A. See HANNAY (2).

BIRNEY, James Gillespie (1792–1857), an American antislavery statesman, was leader of the Liberty party, founded in 1840, and was nominated as presidential candidate in 1844. See *Life* by W. Birney.

BIRON, *bee-rō*, the title of a family that has given several marshals to France:

(1) **Armand de Gontaut, Baron de** (1524–92), father of (3), fought against the Huguenots at Saint-Denis and Moncontour, but early joined and rendered great service to Henry IV. He was killed at the siege of Épernay. See his *Correspondance* (ed. by Barthélemy, 1874).

(2) **Armand Louis de Gontaut, Duc de Lauzun, Duc de** (1749–93), fought with Lafayette in America, joined the Revolutionists in France and defeated the Vendeans at Parthenay in 1793; but was guillotined. See his *Mémoires* (trans. 1928).

(3) **Charles de Gontaut, Duc de** (1562–1602), son of (1), by his valour gained the affection of Henry IV, and the nickname of ' Fulmen Galliae '; but, being convicted of correspondence with Spain, he was beheaded in the Bastille.

(4) orig. **Bühren, Ernst Johann** (1690–1772), Duke of Courland, assumed the name and arms of the French dukes De Biron, when, as favourite of Anna Ivanovna, he became the real ruler of Russia on her ascent to the Russian throne in 1730. He was blamed for most of the ills which befell Russia at this time, but introduced vigour into the administration. In 1737 Anna made him Duke of Courland. On the death of the empress (1740) Biron assumed the regency and acted with great moderation, but he was arrested and banished for a time to Siberia. Peter III in 1762 allowed him to return and he was eventually given back his titles.

BIRRELL, Augustine (1850–1933), British politician and author, born at Wavertree,

Liverpool, was educated at Amersham and Trinity Hall, Cambridge, and called to the bar (1875). Liberal M.P. for W. Fife (1889–1900) and N. Bristol (1906–18), as minister of education he introduced the bill of 1906. Irish secretary (1907–16), he resigned after the Sinn Fein rebellion. A shrewd wit and charming essayist, he wrote *Obiter Dicta* (1884–87) and *Res Judicatae*, on Charlotte Brontë, Hazlitt, Marvell, &c. To ' birrell ' is to comment on life gently and allusively, spicing good nature with irony.

BISCOE, John. See ENDERBY.

BISCOP. See BENEDICT BISCOP.

BISHOP, (1) Sir Henry Rowley (1786–1855), English composer, was born in London, exercised considerable influence in his lifetime by his glees and 88 operas, few of which have survived, though some songs from them have remained popular, including ' Home, Sweet Home ', and ' Lo!, Here the Gentle Lark '. He was musical director at Covent Garden (1810–24), and received the first knighthood conferred upon a musician in 1842. He held professorships at Edinburgh and Oxford.

(2) **Isabella, *née* Bird** (1832–1904), British writer and traveller, born in Edinburgh, from 1854 visited Canada and the United States, the Sandwich Islands, the Rocky Mountains, Yezo, Persia and Kurdistan, Tibet, and Korea, and wrote travel books. See *Life* by A. M. Stoddart (1906).

(3) **William Avery** (1894–1956), Canadian aviator, was born in Owen Sound. He joined the Royal Flying Corps in 1915, and by 1918 he was a lieutenant-colonel. Credited with the destruction of 72 enemy aircraft, he was awarded the V.C., M.C., D.S.O., D.F.C., Legion of Honour, and Croix de Guerre with Palm. By 1938 he was an air marshal and chairman of the Air Advisory Committee to the ministry of national defence. Throughout World War II he was director of the Royal Canadian Air Force. His books include *Winged Warfare* (1918) and *Winged Peace* (1944).

BISMARCK, Otto Edward Leopold von, Prince Bismarck, Duke of Lauenburg (1815–1898), Prusso-German statesman, was born on the ancestral estate at Schönhausen in Brandenburg on April 1, and studied law and agriculture at Göttingen, Berlin, and Greifswald. In 1847 he became known in the new Prussian parliament as an ultra-royalist, and opposed equally the constitutional demands of 1848 and the scheme of a German empire, as proposed by the Frankfurt parliament of 1849. In 1851, as Prussian member of the resuscitated German diet of Frankfurt, he resented the predominance of Austria, and demanded equal rights for Prussia. In 1859 he was sent as minister to St Petersburg, and in 1862 to Paris. Recalled the same year to take the foreign portfolio and the presidency of the cabinet, and not being able to pass the military reorganization bill and the budget, he closed the chambers, announcing that the government would be obliged to do without them. For four years the army reorganization went on, when the death of the king of Denmark (1863) re-opened the Schleswig-Holstein question, and excited a fever of national German feeling, which led to the defeat of Denmark by Austria and Prussia, and the annexation of the duchies. This again brought about the quarrel between Prussia and Austria and the 'seven weeks' war', which ended in the humiliation of Austria at the battle of Königgratz (1866), and the reorganization of Germany under the leadership of Prussia. Bismarck was throughout the guiding spirit, and, from being universally disliked, became the most popular man in Germany. The action of France in regard to the candidature of Prince Leopold of Hohenzollern for the throne of Spain gave Bismarck the opportunity of carrying into action the intensified feeling of unity amongst Germans. During the Franco-Prussian war which he deliberately provoked (1870–71) Bismarck was the spokesman of Germany; he it was who in February 1871 dictated the terms of peace to France. Having been made a count in 1866, he was now created a prince and chancellor of the new German empire. After the peace of Frankfurt the sole aim of Bismarck's policy, domestic and foreign, was to consolidate the young empire and secure it, through political combinations, against attack from without. The long and bitter struggle with the Vatican, called the Kulturkampf, was a failure, the most oppressive of the antipapal Falk or May Laws being ultimately repealed. Otherwise, his domestic policy was marked by universal suffrage, reformed coinage, codification of law, nationalization of the Prussian railways, repeated increase of the army, a protective tariff (1879), and various attempts to combat socialism and to establish government monopolies of tobacco, &c. In 1884 he inaugurated the career of Germany as a colonizing power. To counteract Russia and France, he formed in 1879 the Austro-German Treaty of Alliance (published in 1888), which Italy joined in 1886; and he presided over the Berlin Congress in 1878. The phrase 'man of blood and iron' was used by the 'Iron Chancellor' in a speech in 1862. Two attempts were made on his life (1866, 1874). Disapproving the policy of the Emperor William II, along with his son Herbert (1849–1904), foreign secretary, he resigned the chancellorship in March 1890, becoming Duke of Lauenburg. Long a caustic critic of imperial measures, he was reconciled to his sovereign in 1894. He died at Friedrichsruh, July 30. See *His Reflections and Reminiscences* (trans. 1898), the 'Friedrichsruh' edition of his speeches, letters, and dispatches (1924 ff.), and Lives by E. Ludwig (trans. 1927), E. Eyck (1941–44) and A. J. P. Taylor (1955).

BISSEN, Herman Vilhelm (1798–1868), Danish sculptor, born in Copenhagen, became director of the Academy of Arts there in 1850. His early work, influenced by Thorwaldsen, includes the *Flowergirl* (1829) in the Carlsberg, and the Gutenberg monument (1834) at Mainz. In front of the Kristianborg palace is his equestrian statue of Frederick VII, which, together with the bronze monument at Fredericia (1855) and other war memorials, testifies to his more heroic middle period. He later turned to classical and Nordic mythological subjects. See Life by Plon (1871).

BITZIUS, Albert, properly **Jeremias Gotthelf** (1797–1854), Swiss author, was born at Morat, in Freiburg canton, studied at Bern, and became in 1832 pastor of Lützelfluh, in Emmenthal, and wrote many novels of Swiss village life, including *Käthi* (1847) and *Uli* (trans. 1888), &c. See studies by Altheer (1913) and Guggisberg (1935).

BIXIO, Girolamo Nino (1821–70), Italian merchant captain, one of Garibaldi's most trusted followers, was born at Chiavari near Genoa, and died of cholera in the East Indies.

BIZET, Georges, properly **Alexandre Césare Léopold,** *bee-zay* (1838–75), French composer, was born in Paris, where he studied at the Conservatoire under Halévy, whose daughter he married in 1869, and in Italy. Although he won the Prix de Rome in 1857 with *Le Docteur Miracle*, his efforts to achieve a reputation as an operatic composer with such works as *Les Pêcheurs de Perles* (1863) and *La Jolie Fille de Perth* (1867) were largely unsuccessful. His charming incidental music to Daudet's play *L'Arlésienne* (1872) was remarkably popular and survived in the form of two orchestral suites. On these and on his masterpiece, the four-act opera *Carmen*, completed just before his untimely death of heart disease, Bizet's reputation is based. *Carmen,* derived from Mérimée's story, proved too robust at first for French society and achieved its reputation via the English Channel. By its delicate orchestration and truly remarkable operatic intensity it successfully survived the current criticisms of being too Wagnerian and not sufficiently Spanish and gypsylike for its theme. A symphony in C was first performed in 1935. See Lives by D. C. Parker (1957) and W. Dean (1965), and M. Curtiss, *Bizet and his World* (1959).

BJERKNES, Jakob Aall Bonnevie, *byerk'nays* (1897–), Norwegian meteorologist, son of Vilhelm (1862–1951) the physicist, was born in Stockholm, and eventually became professor of the Geophysical Institute at Bergen. With his father he formulated the theory of cyclones on which modern weather forecasting is based. In 1940 he became professor in the university of California, U.S.A., and was naturalized in 1946. He was awarded the Symons gold medal by the Royal Meteorological Society in 1940.

BJÖRNSON, Björnstjerne, *byœrn'son* (1832–1910), Norwegian novelist and playwright, was born at Kvikne, in Österdalen, where his father was pastor; was educated at Molde, Christiania, and Copenhagen; and from 1857 alternated visits to Rome (1860–62) and Paris (1882–88) with theatrical management and newspaper editing at Bergen and Christiania, whilst constantly writing and taking an active part in politics as Home Ruler and Republican. His first successful drama, *Mellem Slagene* (1856), deals with the Norwegian civil wars. Björnson repudiated the ideal of 'art for art's sake'. His *Peasant Tales,* such as *Arne* (1859) and *En Glad Gut* (1860), as well as the saga-inspired dramas, such as *Kong Sverre* (1861) and the trilogy dealing with the pretender *Sigurd Slembe* (1862), were intended to provide an image of Norwegian life, recognizable and yet in some measure idealized to constitute an incentive Under Ibsen's influence he turned to writing plays on social themes, such as sexual equality and the social aspects of religion, as in his greatest play, one of two under the common title *Over Aevne* (1883), in which a clergyman capable of working miracles cannot respond to his wife's love. One of a collection of songs (1870) is Norway's national anthem. Björnson was more typical of Norway and of greater influence on Norway's culture and destiny than his great contemporary Ibsen. He was awarded the Nobel prize in 1908. See *Three Dramas*, trans. R. F. Sharp (1914), Life by C. Collin (1924), and *Breve til Karoline*—letters to his wife Caroline—(Oslo 1958).

BLACK, (1) Adam (1784–1874), Scottish publisher, born in Edinburgh, was twice lord provost, and Liberal M.P. for the burgh (1856–65). The two enterprises which, above all else, gave position, fortune, and success to his firm, were the purchase of the *Encyclopaedia Britannica* in 1827 after Constable's failure; and that of Scott's novels from Cadell's representatives in 1851 for £27,000. See *Memoirs* by Nicolson (1885) and *A. & C. Black (1807–1957)*, by A. & C. Black (1957).

(2) **John** (1783–1855), Scottish editor of the *Morning Chronicle* (1817–43), was born near Duns, Berwickshire. His fearless advocacy of progress led to his duel with Roebuck in 1835. Dickens and James Mill were among his friends and contributors. He wrote a *Life of Tasso* (1810), and translated German, French, and Italian works.

(3) **Joseph** (1728–99), Scottish chemist, was born, a wine merchant's son, at Bordeaux, and educated at Belfast, Glasgow, and Edinburgh. In an extension of his M.D. thesis (1756) he showed that the causticity of lime and the alkalies is due to the absence of the 'fixed air' (carbon dioxide) present in limestone and the carbonates of the alkalies. On Cullen's removal in 1756 to Edinburgh, Black succeeded him as professor of Anatomy and Chemistry in Glasgow, but soon after exchanged duties with the professor of the Institutes of Medicine, practising also as a physician. Between 1756 and 1761 he evolved that theory of 'latent heat' on which his scientific fame chiefly rests. In 1766 he succeeded Cullen in the chair of Medicine and Chemistry in Edinburgh, and henceforward devoted himself to teaching. See Black's *Lectures* (1803), *Life and Letters*, by Sir Wm. Ramsay (1918).

(4) **William** (1841–98), Scottish novelist, born in Glasgow, studied art but became a journalist, went to London in 1864 and was a war correspondent during the Austro-Prussian war. *A Daughter of Heth* (1871) established him as a novelist; the best of his twenty novels being *A Princess of Thule* (1873), which led him to abandon journalism altogether. See Life by W. Reid (1902).

BLACKADDER, John (1615–86), Scottish Covenanting minister of Troqueer near Dumfries, died a prisoner on the Bass Rock. See *Memoirs* (1823). His fifth son, **John** (1664–1729), was colonel of the Cameronians. See his *Life and Diary* (1824).

BLACKBURN, Robert (1885–1955), British aircraft designer, born at Leeds, designed his first plane in 1910, and founded the Blackburn Aircraft Company in 1914 under contract to build military biplanes.

BLACKBURNE, (1) Francis (1782–1867), lord chancellor of Ireland, was born at Great Footstown, County Meath, and in 1798 entered Trinity College, Dublin. Attorney-general for Ireland from 1830, he prosecuted O'Connell. He was lord chancellor in 1852 and 1866. See Life by his son (1874).

(2) **Lancelot** (1658–1743), in 1717 became Bishop of Exeter, and in 1724 Archbishop of York, having previously, according to his enemies, been chaplain on a buccaneer.

BLACKETT, Baron Patrick Maynard Stuart 1897–), English physicist, educated at Dartmouth College, served in the Royal Navy during World War I. He then entered Magdalene College, Cambridge, and studied physics at the Cavendish Laboratory. He was the first to photograph, in 1925, nuclear collisions involving transmutation, in 1932, independently of Anderson, he discovered the positron; he pioneered research on cosmic radiation, and in World War II operational research. He was elected F.R.S. in 1933 (president 1965–70), was awarded the Nobel prize for physics in 1948, was professor at the Imperial College of Science (1953–65), was president of the British Association (1957), became a C.H. (1965), was awarded the O.M. (1967) and made a life peer (1969). See his *The Military and Political Consequences of Atomic Energy* (1948).

BLACK HAWK (1767–1838), a famous chief of the Sauk and Fox Indians, who joined the British in 1812, and opposing the removal west of his tribe, fought against the United States in 1831–32. See Lives by Patterson (1834) and Snelling.

BLACKIE, (1) John (1782–1874), Scottish publisher, founded in 1809 the Glasgow firm which still bears the name.

(2) **John Stuart** (1809–95), Scottish scholar, was born in Glasgow, was educated at Aberdeen, Edinburgh, and briefly abroad, and in 1834 was called to the Scottish bar and published a metrical translation of Goethe's *Faust*. His magazine articles on German subjects became widely known and he became professor of Humanity at Aberdeen (1841–52) and of Greek at Edinburgh till 1882. He helped to reform the Scottish universities, was a keen advocate of Scottish nationality, and raised funds for the endowment of a Celtic chair at Edinburgh. He published much on philosophy, history, and legal subjects, and fine metrical translations of the works of Aeschylus (1850) and the *Iliad* (1866). See Lives by Stoddart (1895) and his nephew (1895).

BLACKLOCK, Thomas (1721–91), blind Scottish minister and poet, born at Annan. Blind from smallpox in infancy but educated at Edinburgh, he is remembered for a letter of encouragement to Burns, which helped persuade the latter to remain in Scotland.

BLACKMORE, Richard Doddridge (1825–1900), English novelist, born at Longworth, Berkshire, educated at Blundell's School,

Tiverton, and Exeter College, Oxford, was called to the bar at the Middle Temple in 1852, practised for a while, but poor health made him take to market gardening and literature at Teddington. After publishing several collections of poetry, he found his real bent in fiction. *Clara Vaughan* (1864) was the first of fifteen novels, mostly with a Devonshire background, of which *Lorna Doone* (1869) is his masterpiece and an accepted classic of the West Country. Other novels include *The Maid of Sker* (1872), *Alice Lorraine* (1875), *Tommy Upmore* (1884), &c. See K. Budd, *The Last Victorian* (1960)

BLACK PRINCE. See EDWARD III.

BLACKSTONE, Sir William (1723–80), English jurist, was the posthumous son of a London silk mercer, and was born in London. In 1738 he obtained a scholarship from the Charterhouse to Pembroke College, Oxford; in 1741 entered the Inner Temple; in 1744 was elected a fellow of All Souls; and in 1746 was called to the bar, but failed to attract either notice or practice. In 1749 he succeeded an uncle as recorder of Wallingford, Berkshire; and in 1753 he delivered lectures at Oxford on the law of England. In 1758, a Mr Viner having left £12,000 to endow a chair of English law at Oxford, Blackstone was appointed first Vinerian professor. Next year he returned to Westminster; and as the doctrines which he taught had commended him to the Tory government, he was made a king's counsel in 1761. Member for Hindon, in Wiltshire, and principal of New Inn Hall, Oxford, he was in 1763 made solicitor-general to the queen. In 1765–69 he published his celebrated *Commentaries on the Laws of England*, which earned him a fortune. This work became the most influential exposition of English law in point of style and accuracy, although its author failed on the level of explanation. He died February 14, 1780, and was buried at Wallingford.

BLACKWELL, (1) Alexander (*c.* 1700–47), Scottish adventurer, seems to have been born in Aberdeen soon after 1700, and to have been a younger son of the Rev. Thomas Blackwell (1660–1728), principal of Marischal College. He may, or may not, have studied medicine under Boerhaave at Leyden; anyhow, about 1730, he was a printer in London, and becoming bankrupt in 1734, was supported in prison by his wife, who published a *Herbal* (2 vols. folio, 1737–39) with 500 cuts, drawn, engraved, and coloured by herself, her husband adding their Latin names and a brief description of each. Next, in 1742, Blackwell turns up in Sweden, where, having cured the king of an illness, he was appointed a royal physician, and undertook the management of a model farm. While still in the full enjoyment of court favour, he was charged with complicity in a plot against the constitution, and after being put to the torture, was beheaded, August 9, 1747, protesting his innocence to the last.

(2) **Sir Basil Henry** (1889–   ), British publisher and bookseller, son of Benjamin Henry Blackwell, chairman of the famous Oxford bookshop founded in 1846, was born in Oxford, educated there at Magdalen College School and Merton College, joined the family business in 1913, but also published independently, founding the Shakespeare Head Press (1921). He succeeded to the chairmanship in 1924 and henceforth conjoined the family bookselling interest with that of publishing, mostly on academic subjects. He was president of the International Association of Antiquarian Booksellers in 1925 and was knighted in 1956.

(3) **Elizabeth** (1821–1910), the first woman doctor in the United States, was born at Bristol. Her father emigrated to the States in 1832, and died six years later, leaving a widow and nine children. Elizabeth helped to support the family by teaching, devoting her leisure to the study of medical books. After fruitless applications for admission to various medical schools, she entered that of Geneva, in New York State, and graduated in 1849. She next visited Europe, and after much difficulty was admitted into the *Maternité* hospital at Paris, and St Bartholomew's Hospital in London. In 1851 she returned to New York, and there established herself in a successful practice; after 1868 she lived in England till her death. See her autobiography (1896).

BLACKWOOD, (1) Adam (1539–1613), an adversary of Buchanan and champion of Queen Mary, was born at Dunfermline, and lived mostly at Poitiers.

(2) **Algernon Henry** (1869–1951), English novelist, born in Kent, son of Sir Arthur Blackwood, was educated at Wellington and Edinburgh University before tramping and working his way through Canada, as related in his *Episodes before Thirty* (1923). His novels, which reflect his taste for the supernatural and the occult, include *John Silence* (1908), *The Human Chord* (1910), *The Wave* (1916), *Tongues of Fire* (1924), and a volume of short stories, *Tales of the Uncanny and Supernatural*, which appeared in 1949, the year he was made C.B.E.

(3) **William** (1776–1834), Edinburgh publisher, established himself as a bookseller—principally of old books—in 1804, and in 1817 started *Blackwood's Magazine*, and from the seventh number took over the editorship himself with Wilson (' Christopher North '), Lockhart, Hogg, &c., as contributors. His place was filled during 1834–52 by his sons, **Alexander** and **Robert** and then by **John** (1818–79). Blackwood published all except one of George Eliot's novels, and novels by Trollope, Mrs Oliphant, Blackmore, Reade, and Kinglake. See Mrs Oliphant, *Annals of the Publishing House* (1897–98).

BLAEU, *blah-ü* (spelt also **Blaeuw** and **Blauw**, Lat. **Coesius**) **Willem Janszoon** (1571–1638), Dutch mapmaker, mathematician, and astronomer, was born at Alkmaar and founded a publishing firm in Amsterdam, specializing in globes. His son **Jan** (d. 1673) started his own business, but later entered into partnership with his brother, **Cornelis** (d. 1650). His *Atlas Major*, in 11 volumes, is extremely valuable from the light the maps throw on local history. The volume on Scotland contains forty-nine maps, prepared by Timothy Pont (q.v.), and local details by Sir John Scott. Jan further published topographical plates and views of towns. Two of his sons carried on the business until 1700.

BLAINE, James Gillespie (1830–93), American journalist and statesman, born at West Brownsville, Pa., was speaker (1869–75) and was defeated in the Republican nominations for the presidency in 1876, 1880, 1884, and 1892.

BLAINVILLE, Henri Marie Ducrotay de, *blī-veel* (1778–1850), zoologist and anatomist, Cuvier's successor in 1832 as professor of Comparative Anatomy in the Museum of Natural History, Paris.

BLAIR, (1) Eric. See ORWELL.

(2) **Hugh** (1718–1800), Scottish preacher, born and educated in Edinburgh, licensed as a preacher in 1741 and was promoted in 1758 to one of the charges of the High Church, Edinburgh. In 1762 he was appointed to a new regius chair of Rhetoric and Belles Lettres. His discourses, sermons and lectures enjoyed a reputation beyond their merit, and George III bestowed a pension on him in 1780. See Life by J. Hill (1807).

(3) **Robert** (1699–1746), Scots minister and poet, was born at Edinburgh, and in 1731 was ordained minister of Athelstaneford, Haddingtonshire, where he lived in easy circumstances till his death. He is best known as the author of *The Grave* (1743), a blank-verse poem which heralded the ' churchyard school ' of poetry. The 1808 edition was finely illustrated with rare imaginative power by Blake.

BLAIZE. See BLASIUS.

BLAKE, (1) Nicholas. See DAY-LEWIS, CECIL.

(2) **Robert** (1599–1657), next to Nelson the greatest of English admirals, was born at Bridgwater in August 1599, the eldest of a merchant's twelve sons. From Bridgwater grammar school he passed in 1615 to St Alban Hall and Wadham College, Oxford, where he remained till 1625. He seems not to have continued his father's business, but may from time to time have made voyages to distant seas. He led the life of a quiet country gentleman until he was forty. Returned for Bridgwater in 1640 to the Short Parliament, he cast in his lot unhesitatingly with the parliamentarians, but did not become a member of the Long Parliament till 1645. An ardent Republican, and a man of blunt manners, devoid of fear, and of inflexible character, he was much respected by Cromwell, but they never became very intimate. He served under Popham in Somerset, and attracted notice at the siege of Bristol and by his obstinate defence of Lyme in 1644 against Prince Maurice. His defence of Taunton for nearly a year against overwhelming odds proved a turning point in the war. In 1649 he was appointed with two others to command the fleet, then in a state of disaffection and weakness. Within two years he had blockaded Lisbon, destroyed the squadron of Prince Rupert, and forced the royalists to surrender the Scilly Isles and Jersey, their last stronghold. Early in 1652 began the struggle with the Dutch for the supremacy of the seas, and Blake found himself pitted against Tromp, De Ruyter, and De Witt. In the first engagement on May 19 Tromp

retreated under cover of darkness with the loss of two ships. On September 28, Blake gave battle to De Ruyter and De Witt off the mouth of the Thames; the fight ended with the flight of the Dutch next day. On November 29, eighty vessels under Tromp encountered Blake with scarcely forty off the Goodwin Sands. After a two-day hotly contested fight, victory remained with the Dutch. Blake lost six ships, but brought the remainder in a shattered state into safety. In February 1653 he was again at sea with nearly eighty ships; and on the 18th Tromp was sighted near Portland with about an equal force. In the long running fight from Portland to Calais, Blake was severely wounded, but gained a complete victory, sinking five ships and capturing four, as well as some thirty merchantmen. His ill-health prevented him from taking part in the engagement of July 31, which finally shattered the naval supremacy of Holland. In 1654 he sailed into the Mediterranean and made the English flag respected at Cadiz, Leghorn, and Naples. In 1655 he sailed under the guns of Tunis, a nest of pirates, and burned nine ships. The terrified dey of Algiers submitted to his terms; and in September, Stayner, one of his lieutenants, fell in with the Plate fleet and captured it—a loss to Spain of nearly two millions in treasure alone. But the crowning exploit of Blake's career was his last. Hearing in April 1657 that a fleet from America had arrived off Tenerife, at once sailed thither, and on the 20th he arrived in the bay, where sixteen ships were lying at anchor. Before night he completely destroyed the fleet and the town of Santa Cruz, and drew off with a loss of 50 killed and 120 wounded; then, his health failing fast, he returned homewards, and died as his ship entered Plymouth Harbour, August 7, 1657. Cromwell buried him in Westminster Abbey, but his body was removed at the Restoration. See Hannay's *Admiral Blake* (1886).

(3) **William** (1757–1827), English poet, painter, engraver, and mystic, was born in London, November 28, the son of a hosier. In 1771 he was apprenticed to James Basire, the engraver; and after studying at the Royal Academy School, he began to produce water colour figure subjects and to engrave illustrations for the magazines. His first book of poems, the *Poetical Sketches* (1783), was followed by *Songs of Innocence* (1789) and *Songs of Experience* (1794), which include some of the purest lyrics in the English language and express his ardent belief in the freedom of the imagination and his hatred of rationalism and materialism. His mystical and prophetical works include the *Book of Thel* (1789), *The Marriage of Heaven and Hell* (1791), *The French Revolution* (1791), *The Song of Los* (1795), *Vala,* and many others, which mostly have imaginative designs interwoven with their text, printed from copper treated by a peculiar process, and coloured by his own or his wife's hand. Among his designs of poetic and imaginative figure subjects are a superb series of 537 coloured illustrations to Young's *Night Thoughts* (1797) and 12 to Blair's *Grave* (1808). Among the most important of his paintings

(in a kind of tempera) is *The Canterbury Pilgrims*, which the artist himself engraved; *The Spiritual Form of Pitt guiding Behemoth* (now in the National Gallery); *Jacob's Dream*; and *The Last Judgment*. Blake's finest artistic work is to be found in the *21 Illustrations to the Book of Job*, published in 1826, when he was verging upon seventy, but unequalled in modern religious art for imaginative force and visionary power. At his death Blake was employed on the illustrations to Dante. He is also known as a wood engraver by cuts in Thornton's *Virgil*, rude in execution, but full of the very spirit of idyllic poetry. During his life Blake met with little encouragement from the public; but Hayley, Flaxman, and Samuel Palmer were faithful friends, and by John Linnell's generosity Blake was in his last days saved from financial worry. And all through his life he was upheld by the most real and vivid faith in the unseen, guided and encouraged—as he believed—by perpetual visitations from the spiritual world. He died in London, August 12. See books by Gilchrist (1863; new ed. 1942), Swinburne (1868), Ellis (1907), Symons (1907), Selincourt (1909), Russell (1912), Berger (trans. 1914), T. Wright (1929), Middleton Murry (1933), Bronowski (1944), Davis (1948), Wilson (1948), Erdman (1954), Plowman (1955), Rudd (1956) and Digby (1957).

BLAKESLEE, Albert Francis (1874–1954), American botanist, born at Geneseo, N.Y., in 1936 became director of the Carnegie Station for• experimental evolution and in 1937 established that colchicine can produce polyploidy in plants.

BLAMEY, Sir Thomas (1884–1951), Australian general, born at Wagga, won the D.S.O. in World War I and played an important part in the evacuation of Gallipoli. He became chief of staff of the Australian Corps in 1918. On the outbreak of World War II he was given command of the Australian Imperial Forces in the Middle East, and organized the withdrawal from the Balkan area. On the establishment of the S.W. Pacific command he became c.-in-c. of Allied Land Forces in Australia (1942) and received the Japanese surrender in 1945. In 1950 he was made a field-marshal, the first Australian soldier to receive this rank.

BLAMIRE, Susanna, *bla-mīr'* (1747–94), English poetess, ' the Muse of Cumberland ', author of north-country lyrics and poems in Scots dialect, collected in 1842.

BLAMPIED, Edmund, *-peed* (1886–1966), British artist, born in Jersey, a watercolourist, etcher, and engraver. During the German occupation he designed the Jersey occupation stamps.

BLANC, Jean Joseph Louis, *blā* (1811–82), French Socialist statesman and historian, was born at Madrid. In 1830 he came to study in Paris, then for two years was a private tutor at Arras, and in 1834 returned to Paris, where in 1839 he founded the *Revue du progrès*. Here appeared his chief work on Socialism, the *Organisation du travail*, which in book form (1840) made him very popular among French workmen. The book denounces the principle of competitive industry, and pro-

poses the establishment of cooperative workshops, subsidized by the state. Blanc next published his *Histoire de dix ans 1830–1840* (1841–44), which had a deadly effect on the Orleans dynasty. After the revolution of February 1848, Blanc was appointed a member of the provisional government, and placed at the head of the commission for discussing the problem of labour. But accused without reason of a share in the disturbances of the summer of 1848, he escaped to London, where he finished his *Histoire de la révolution* in 1862, and wrote much for the French press. On the fall of the Empire, Blanc returned to France, and was elected in 1871 to the National Assembly, in 1876 to the Chamber of Deputies, always supporting the extreme Left. He died at Cannes, December 6. See studies by C. Robin (1851), Golliet (1903), and Renard (1923).

BLANCHARD, Jean Pierre François, *blā-shahr* (1753–1809), French balloonist, inventor of the parachute, born in Les Andelys, was the first to cross the English Channel by balloon, from Dover to Calais, in 1785. He was killed at La Haye during practice jumps from a balloon.

BLANDRATA, or Biandrata, Giorgio (*c.* 1515–1590), Italian founder of Unitarianism in Poland and Transylvania, was nobly born at Saluzzo, Piedmont. The freedom of his religious opinions compelled him to flee to Geneva in 1556, but in 1558 Calvin's displeasure at his anti-Trinitarianism drove him to Poland. Finally, in 1563, he became physician to John Sigismund, Prince of Transylvania. He is supposed to have been strangled in his sleep by his nephew.

BLANE, Sir Gilbert (1749–1834), Scottish physician, was born at Blanefield, Ayrshire, in 1779 sailed with Rodney to the West Indies. As head of the Navy Medical Board, he was instrumental in introducing the use of lemon juice on board ship to prevent scurvy. In 1812 he was made a baronet.

BLANQUI, *blā-kee*, (1) **Jérôme Adolphe** (1798–1854), French economist, brother of (2), was born at Nice; in 1833 became a professor in the Conservatoire des Arts et des Métiers. He was a follower of Say, and in favour of free trade. His chief work is the *Histoire de l'économie politique en Europe* (1838).

(2) **Louis Auguste** (1805–81), French revolutionary leader, brother of (1), born at Puget-Théniers (Alpes Maritimes), was sentenced (1872) for his share in the Commune to be transported to New Caledonia, a sentence commuted to life imprisonment, from which he was released in 1879. A passionate extremist and master of insurrection, he spent thirty-seven years of his life in prison. See Life by N. Stewart (1939).

BLASCO IBÁÑEZ, Vicente. See IBÁÑEZ.

BLASIUS, St, Bishop of Sebaste, Cappadocia, suffered martyrdom in 316. Woolcombers claim him as their patron, and he is invoked in case of throat trouble and cattle diseases.

BLASS, Friedrich (1843–1907), German scholar, born at Osnabrück, became professor of Greek at Kiel (1881) and at Halle (1892). He edited a great number of classical texts and was chiefly known for his study of Greek oratory.

BLATCHFORD, Robert (1851–1943), British Socialist journalist (' Nunquam '), was born at Maidstone. In turn brushmaker, soldier, clerk, writer, he founded the weekly *Clarion* (1891). See *My 80 Years* (1931).

BLAUW. See BLAEU.

BLAVATSKY, née Hahn, Helena Petrovna (1831–91), Russian theosophist, born at Ekaterinoslav, Russia, travelled widely in the East, including Tibet, founded in 1875 the Theosophical Society in New York and later carried on her work in India. Her psychic powers were widely acclaimed but did not survive investigation by the Society for Psychical Research, but this did not deter her large following. Her writings include *Isis Unveiled* (1877), &c. See Lives by A. P. Sinnett (1913), A. L. Cleather (1922), A. T. Barker (1925) and J. Symonds (1959).

BLAZE DE BURY, Henri, *blahz dè bü-ree'* (1813–88), French interpreter of German authors. His wife, **Marie Pauline Rose Stuart** (1814–94), born at Oban, Scotland, and brought up in France, was also an author.

BLEEK, Friedrich, *blayk* (1793–1859), German biblical scholar, born at Ahrensbök in Holstein, professor of Theology at Bonn (1829), is chiefly remembered for his commentary on the book of Hebrews. His son, **Wilhelm** (1827–75), German philologist, went out to Natal, became keeper of the Grey Library at Cape Town (1861), and wrote on native languages and folklore.

BLÉRIOT, Louis, *blayr-yō* (1872–1936), French airman, made the first flight across the English Channel on July 25, 1909, from Baraques to Dover in a small 24-h.p. monoplane.

BLESSINGTON, Marguerite, Countess of (1789–1849), Irish writer, was born near Clonmel, and at fourteen was forced into marrying a worthless Captain Farmer. She quitted him in three months' time, and in 1818, shortly after his death, married the Earl of Blessington. With him in 1822 she set out on a long tour on the Continent, where, as well as in London, she gathered around her all the most distinguished men of the time. In Genoa she formed an intellectual friendship with Lord Byron; afterwards she resided in Paris, until the death of her husband in 1829. He left her a large fortune; and she held a little court at her Kensington mansion, Gore House. Her connection with Count d'Orsay (q.v.), which dated from 1822, placed her in an equivocal position, and her lavish expenditure overwhelmed her in debt, though for nearly twenty years she was making an extra income of over £2000 per annum as author of a dozen most trashy novels, *The Idler in France, The Idler in Italy,* and *Conversations with Lord Byron* (1834; new ed. 1894). At length in April 1849 she and d'Orsay had to flee to Paris, where on June 4 she died of apoplexy. See Lives by Madden (3 vols. 1855) and Molloy (1896).

BLEULER, Eugen, *bloy'lèr* (1857–1939), Swiss psychiatrist, born at Zollikon, near Zürich, where he was professor (1898–1927), carried out research on epilepsy and other physiological conditions, then turned to psychiatry,

and in 1913 published an important study on schizophrenia. His wife, **Hedwig Bleuler-Waser** (1869–1940), was a well-known writer and social worker in the field of temperance.

BLICHER, Steen Steensen, *blee-ker* (1782–1848), Danish poet and novelist, was born in Jutland near Viborg, which forms the background of much of his work. He became a teacher and clergyman, was unhappily married, and took a great interest in the social and spiritual problems of his day. His collection *The Migratory Birds* ranks among the purest of Danish lyrical poetry, with its pervasive note of resignation and sorrow. But his short stories, often in dialect, such as *E Bindstouw*, are among the gems of Danish literature. See the translation, *Twelve Stories*, with an introduction by S. Undset (1945), and Lives by Kristensen and Lund (Copenhagen 1882), and Aakjaer (Copenhagen 1903–04).

BLIGH, William (*c.* 1753–1817), British sailor, born at Plymouth, sailed under Captain Cook in his second voyage round the world (1772–1774), and in 1787 was sent as commander of the *Bounty* to Tahiti to collect plants of the bread-fruit tree with a view to acclimatization in the West Indies. During their six-month stay on the island, his men had become completely demoralized, and on the return voyage mutinied under the harsh treatment of their commander. On April 28, 1789, Bligh, with eighteen men, was cast adrift in an open boat only 23-feet long, with a small stock of provisions, and without a chart; while the mutineers returned to Tahiti, and ultimately settled on Pitcairn Island. After almost incredible hardship, Bligh arrived at Timor, near Java, on June 14, having sailed his frail craft for 3618 miles. ' Bread-fruit Bligh ' was again sent out to collect bread-fruit plants, and in 1805 was appointed governor of New South Wales. Here, too, his conduct was so overbearing that in 1808 he was arrested, and kept in prison for two years. The officer who arrested him was tried in England and cashiered. Bligh was promoted admiral in 1811, and died in London, December 7, 1817. See his *Second Voyage*, ed. by Ida Lee (1920), and Lives by Mackaness (1931), Rutter (1936), and H. V. Evatt, *Rum Rebellion* (1938).

BLIND, Karl, *blint* (1826–1907), German political agitator, was born at Mannheim, and studied law at Heidelberg. For his share in the risings in South Germany in 1848 he was sentenced to eight years' imprisonment, but while being taken to Mainz was set free by the people, and from 1852 lived in England. He wrote on politics, history, mythology, &c. His stepdaughter, **Mathilde** (1847–96), championed women's rights and published poems, &c.

BLIND HARRY. See HARRY.

BLISS, (1) **Sir Arthur** (1891–   ), English composer, born in London. He studied under Holst, Stanford and Vaughan Williams at the Royal College of Music, and had attracted considerable attention before World War I, in which he served. In 1921 he became professor of Composition at the Royal College, but resigned his post after a year to devote himself to composition. From 1942–44 he was music director of the B.B.C. On the death of Bax in 1953 he became Master of the Queen's Musick. His film music includes that for Wells's *Things to Come* and *Men of Two Worlds*; his other compositions include the ballets *Checkmate* (1937) and *Miracle in the Gorbals* (1944), the opera *The Olympians* (1948), chamber music, and piano and violin works. He was knighted in 1950.

(2) **Philip Paul** (1838–76), American evangelist and hymnwriter, best known for such favourites as ' Hold the Fort ', ' Down Life's Dark Vale We Wander ', ' Jesus Loves Me ', ' Let the Lower Lights Be Burning ' and ' Pull for the Shore ', contained in *Gospel Songs* (1874). He was killed in the Ashtabula train disaster. See his *Memoirs* (1877).

BLIXEN, Karen, Baroness, pseud. **Isak Dinesen** (1885–1962), Danish novelist and story teller. Educated in Denmark, England, Switzerland, Italy, and France, she married in 1914 her cousin, Baron Bror Blixen Finecke, and went with him to Kenya. In 1931 she returned to Denmark to live at the old family home of Rungstedlund, once the home of the 18th-century romantic Ewald. She wrote *Seven Gothic Tales* (1934), which she later translated into Danish. Other works include *Out of Africa* (1938), *Winter's Tales* (1942), and *Last Tales* (1957).

BLOCH, *bloкн*, (1) **Ernest** (1880–1959), Swiss-American composer, born, of Jewish descent, in Geneva. He studied in Brussels, Frankfurt, and Munich before settling in Paris, where his opera *Macbeth* was produced in 1910, after his return to Switzerland. In 1915 he became professor of Musical Aesthetics at Geneva Conservatory. In 1916 he went to America, where he held several teaching posts, adopted U.S. citizenship (1924), and won a high reputation which rapidly spread to Europe, where he returned for eight years in 1930. His compositions include *Trois Poèmes juifs* (1913), the Hebrew *Sacred Service* (1930–33) for baritone, chorus, and orchestra, and numerous other chamber and orchestral works; his symphonies include the *Israel* (1912–16), and the ' epic rhapsody ' *America* (1926). See study by M. Tibaldi-Chiesa (Turin 1933).

(2) **Felix** (1905–), Swiss-German-American physicist, born at Zürich, professor of Theoretical Physics at Stanford University, U.S.A., from 1934. He shared the 1952 Nobel award for physics with Purcell (q.v.) for work in nuclear physics. The *Bloch bands* are sets of discrete but closely adjacent energy levels arising from quantum states when a nondegenerate gas condenses to a solid.

(3) **Jean de** (1836–1902), a Polish Jew of poor parentage, made a fortune in Russian railways, sought to reconcile Russian and Polish interests, and wrote to prove that modern warfare must become impossible.

(4) **Jean-Richard** (1884–1947), French novelist and critic. His reputation stands by his novel *Et Compagnie* (1918), which belongs to the school of writing derived from Zola and Pierre Hamp.

(5) **Konrad Emil** (1912–), American biochemist, born in Germany, educated at Technische Hochschule, Munich, and Columbia University, emigrating to U.S.A. in 1936. In 1954 he was appointed as first professor of

Biochemistry at Harvard University. He won with Lynen the Nobel prize for medicine in 1964 for work on the mechanism of cholesterol and fatty acid metabolism, discovering the complex sequence of the molecule in the human body, important in finding a cure for arteriosclerosis.

(6) **Martin** (1883–1954), British painter, born at Neisse in Silesia, and naturalized in 1947. After studying at Berlin and Munich, he was forced to leave Germany by the Nazis in 1934, went to Denmark, and later to England, where he opened a school of painting with Roy de Maistre. His brilliant colours and expressionist technique were used to interpret the England landscape.

BLOCK, (1) **Alexander.** See BLOK.

(2) **Maurice** (1816–1901), political economist, was born at Berlin of Jewish parentage, settled in Paris, and in 1880 was elected to the Academy.

BLOEMAERT, Abraham, *bloo'mahrt* (1564–1651), a Dutch landscape painter, father of the copper engraver, **Cornelius Bloemaert** (1603–88).

BLOK, Alexander Alexandrovich (1880–1921), Russian poet, born at St Petersburg, in 1903 married the daughter of Mendeleyev. His first book of poems, *Songs about the Lady Fair* (1904), was influenced by the mysticism of Soloviev, a Tolstoian vision of reality beyond appearances, where truth is embodied in ideal womanhood. In *Nocturnal Hours* (1911) the ideal has given way to the realism of city squalor. Blok welcomed the 1917 Revolution and in 1918 wrote two poems, *The Twelve* (trans. 1920), a symbolic sequence of revolutionary themes, and *The Scythians*, an ode, inciting Europe to follow Russia. Blok was soon disillusioned, however, and suffered greatly in the hard times which followed the revolution. Other works include the romantic verse drama *The Rose and the Cross*. See Bowra, *The Heritage of Symbolism* and *A Book of Russian Verse* (1943), French Life by N. Berberova (1947), and study by C. Kisch (1961).

BLOM, Eric (1888–1959), British musicologist, born in Switzerland of Danish descent, became a distinguished music critic in England. He edited the *Master Musician* series of biographies, the quarterly *Music and Letters*, the fifth edition of Grove's *Dictionary of Music* and wrote monographs on Mozart (1935), on Beethoven's piano sonatas (1938), *Music in England* (1943), &c. He became a C.B.E. in 1955.

BLOMEFIELD, Francis, *bloom'-* (1705–52), author of the *History of Norfolk* (1739–75), was born at Fersfield, became rector of Brockdish, and died in London of smallpox.

BLOMFIELD, *bloom'-*, (1) **Charles James** (1786–1857), Bishop of London (1828), grandfather of (2), was born at Bury St Edmunds, and studied at Trinity College, Cambridge. During his episcopate about 200 new churches were consecrated in London, mainly through his efforts. His classical reputation rests on his editions of Aeschylus, Callimachus, Euripides, &c. He resigned his see in 1856 because of paralysis. See Life by his son (1863).—His fourth son, **Sir Arthur William** (1829–99), was an architect who assisted with the erection of the London Law Courts (1881).

(2) **Sir Reginald** (1856–1942), English architect, grandson of (1), designed the Menin Gate and Lambeth Bridge, and wrote books on architecture and garden designs. See his *Memoirs* (1932).

BLOMMAERT, Philip, *blom'mahrt* (1809–71), Flemish scholar, with Conscience (q.v.), a reviver of the Flemish tongue, was born and died at Ghent.

BLONDEL (fl. 12th cent.), French minstrel who is said to have accompanied Richard Cœur de Lion to Palestine and to have located him when imprisoned in the Austrian prison of Dürrenstein (1193) by means of a song they had jointly composed. The poems attributed to one Blondel of Nesle in Picardy are uninteresting. See Sir Walter Scott's novel *The Talisman*.

BLONDEL, Maurice (1861–1939), French philosopher, born at Dijon, became professor at Aix-Marseille. In *L'Action* (1893) he sought to show that knowledge of facts was dependent upon a kind of faith, derived from action.

BLONDIN, Charles, *blŏ-dĭ*, properly **Jean François Gravelet** (1824–97), French rope-dancer, born at Hesdin near Calais, and trained at Lyons. In 1859 he crossed Niagara on a tightrope; and later did the same with variations (blindfold, with a wheelbarrow, with a man on his back, on stilts).

BLOOD, Thomas (*c.* 1618–80), Irish adventurer, was a Parliamentarian during the Civil War. Deprived of his estate at the Restoration, he put himself in 1663 at the head of a plot to seize Dublin Castle and Ormonde, the lord-lieutenant. The plot was discovered and his chief accomplices executed; but he himself escaped to Holland. In 1666, he was in Scotland fighting for the Covenanters at Rullion Green. On the night of December 6, 1670, he seized the Duke of Ormonde in his coach, and attempted to hang him at Tyburn; on May 9, 1671, disguised as a clergyman, with three accomplices he entered the Tower, with the intention of stealing the regalia. After nearly murdering the keeper of the jewels, he succeeded in getting off with the crown, while one of his associates bore away the orb. They were pursued, however, and captured; but at the instigation of Buckingham, who was accused of having hired Blood to attack Ormonde, King Charles visited the miscreant in prison, pardoned him, took him to court, and restored him his estate. For several years Colonel Blood was an influential medium of royal patronage, until, quarrelling with Buckingham, he was committed by the King's Bench. He was bailed out, but died on August 24, 1680. See Life by W. C. Abbott (1911).

BLOOM, Ursula, professional name of Mrs **Gower Robinson** (1892–), British novelist, and playwright, born in Chelmsford. Her novels, which include *Pavilion* (1951) and *The First Elizabeth* (1953), are mainly historical romances, and most of her plays were written for radio production.

BLOOMER, Amelia, *née* **Jenks** (1818–94), American champion of women's right to wear trousers, &c., was born at Homer, New York, and in 1840 married a lawyer.

She herself for demonstration wore the full trousers which came to be called 'bloomers'.

BLOOMFIELD, Robert (1766–1823), English versifier, was born at Honington, near Bury St Edmunds. A shoemaker's apprentice, he wrote his *Farmer's Boy* in a garret. Published in 1800 with the assistance of Capel Lofft, it proved very popular. Bloomfield subsequently published *Rural Tales*, &c., was given a small allowance by the Duke of Grafton, but half-blind, died in poverty. See his *Remains* (1824).

BLORE, Edward (1787–1879), English artist and architect of the Gothic revival, the son of **Thomas** (1764–1818), the topographer, was born at Derby and built Sir Walter Scott's Abbotsford (*c.* 1816).

BLOUET, Paul, *bloo-ay*, pseud. **Max O'Rell** (1848–1903), French author, born in Brittany; served in the Franco-German war and against the Commune, being severely wounded; in 1873 came to England as a newspaper correspondent; was French master at St Paul's School (1876–84); and from 1887 lectured in the U.K., U.S., and colonies. His works include *John Bull and his Island* (1883), *A Frenchman in America* (1891), *John Bull & Co.* (1894), &c.

BLOUNT, *blunt*, (1) **Charles** (1654–93), English deist, was born at Upper Holloway, London, the son of **Sir Henry Blount** (1602–1682), traveller in the Levant. He became noted for his contributions (often flippant) to the political, literary, and theological controversies of the times. Despairing of marriage with his deceased wife's sister, he committed suicide.

(2) **Martha** (1690–1762), the friend of Pope from 1710 or earlier until his death in 1744.

(3) **Thomas** (1618–79), English lexicographer and antiquarian, was author of *Ancient Tenures and Jocular Customs of some Manors* (1679), a dictionary of obscure legal terms, and other works.

BLOW, John (*c.* 1648–1708), English composer born at Newark, sang in the Chapel Royal choir, was appointed organist at Westminster Abbey (1668), Master of the Children at the Chapel Royal (1674) and subsequently organist there, and Master of the Children at St Paul's (1687). Much of his vast output of anthems and church services is uninspired, but the best, e.g., the Ode for St Cecilia's Day, 'Begin the Song', has a nobility which places Blow high among 17th-century English composers. He wrote a small amount of instrumental music and a masque, *Venus and Adonis* (1687), which was performed before Charles II.

BLOY, Léon (1846–1917), French author, born in Périgeux, wrote novels, essays, and religious and critical studies with a strong Roman Catholic bias, containing bitter and sometimes uncalled-for castigation of political and social institutions, which brought him unpopularity in his day but has contributed to the revival of interest in his works since 1940. His *Le Désespéré* (1886) and *La Femme pauvre* (1897, Eng. trans. 1939) are autobiographical; other books include *Le Pélerin de l'absolu* (1914, Eng. trans. 1947). See his journal (1924), and studies by Polimeni (1947), Bollery (1947–49) and Beguin (1949).

BLÜCHER, Gebhard Leberecht von, Prince of

Wahlstadt, *blüKH'ĕr* (1742–1819), Prussian field-marshal, was born at Rostock, in Mecklenburg, December 16, 1742. After two years in the Swedish service, he distinguished himself in the Prussian cavalry, but retired from the service in disgust at troubles brought about by his own dissipation and insubordination, and for 15 years farmed his own estates. In 1793 he fought, as colonel of hussars, against the French on the Rhine, and in 1806, as lieutenant-general, at Auerstädt, and was distinguished, though not successful, at Lübeck, Stralsund, and elsewhere. When the Prussians rose against France in 1813, Blücher took chief command in Silesia, and at the battles of Lützen, Bautzen, Haynau, displayed heroic courage. At the Katzbach he cleared Silesia of the enemy, and at Leipzig won very important successes; in January 1814 he crossed the Rhine, and though once routed by Napoleon, gained several battles, and, on March 31, entered the French capital. In England, he received the freedom of the city of London, and Oxford made him D.C.L. After Napoleon's return in 1815, Blücher assumed the general command, suffered a severe defeat at Ligny, but completed Wellington's victory at the battle of Waterloo by his timely appearance on the field, and his Prussians pursued the fleeing enemy all through the night. At the second taking of Paris, Blücher wanted to inflict on Paris what other capitals had suffered, but was restrained by the Duke of Wellington. He died on September 12, at his estate of Krieblowitz, in Silesia, presented to him by the king. 'Marshal Forwards' was not a great tactician, his victories being due mainly to dash and energy; in speech and behaviour he was rough and uncultivated. See Lives by Scherr (1863), Unger (1908), and E. F. Henderson (1911).

BLUM, *bloom,* (1) **Léon** (1872–1950), French Socialist statesman, was born in Paris. A lawyer, he was elected to the chamber in 1919 and became one of the leaders of the Socialist party. In 1924 he lent his support to Herriot, a policy which resulted in great electoral advances by the Left, and the elections of May 1936 gave France the first Socialist prime minister since 1870. In 1938 Blum formed a second 'popular front' government which had a stormy existence. During World War II he was interned in Germany. He remained the leader and adviser of the Socialists on his return and in December 1946 was elected prime minister of the six-week caretaker government and originated the Anglo-French treaty of alliance and methods to deal with the rise of prices. See Life by Fraser and Natanson (1937).

(2) **Robert** (1807–48), German Liberal agitator, born at Cologne in 1807, was successively theatre secretary and bookseller. When the revolutionary movement broke out in 1848, Blum was one of its most energetic leaders. Joining the Vienna insurgents, to whom he was bearer of a congratulatory address, he was arrested, and shot on November 9. See Life by his son (Leip. 1878).

BLUMENBACH, Johann Friedrich, *bloom'ĕn-baKH* (1752–1840), German anthropologist, was born at Gotha, studied at Jena and Göttingen, where he became extra-ordinary professor of Medicine in 1776. By his study of comparative skull measurements, he founded anthropology by introducing race classification on a quantitative basis. See Memoir by Marx (1840) and *Göttinger Professoren* (1872).

BLUMENTHAL, *bloo'mĕn-tahl,* (1) Jacob (1829–1908), German composer of popular songs, born at Hamburg, was pianist to Queen Victoria.

(2) **Leonhard, Graf von** (1810–1900), Prussian general, greatly distinguished himself in the wars of 1866 and 1870–71.

BLUNCK, Hans Friedrich, *bloonk* (1888–1961), German novelist, poet and folklorist, was born at Altona. After studying law he was successively propagandist, university official and farmer. Steeped in the folklore of the North German plain, Blunck's writings lent colour to the racial theories of National Socialism. His poetical works include *Sturm überm Land* (1915), *Der Wanderer* (1925), *Erwartung* (1936), and his novels *Werwendes Volk* (1933) and *Die Urvätersaga* (1934). He published his autobiographical *Unwegsamezeiten* in 1953.

BLUNDELL, Peter (1520–1601), a kersey manufacturer of Tiverton, founded Blundell's School.

BLUNDEN, Edmund Charles (1896–), English poet and critic, was born at Yalding, Kent, educated at Christ's Hospital and Queen's College, Oxford. He served in France in World War I and won the M.C. He was professor of English Literature at Tokyo (1924–27), fellow of Merton College, Oxford, from 1931, joined the staff of *The Times Literary Supplement* in 1943, returned to the Far East and from 1953 lectured at the University of Hong Kong. Blunden, a lover of the English countryside, of cricket on the village green, of the early 19th-century writers, is essentially a nature poet, as is evident in *Pastorals* (1916) and *The Waggoner and Other Poems* (1920), but his prose work *Undertones of War* (1928) is perhaps his best. Other works include *The Bonadventure* (1922), on his visit to America, a Life of Leigh Hunt, books on Lamb, Keats, &c., and he edited Clare, Christopher Smart, Shelley, Keats and Collins. See study by Hopkins (1950).

BLUNT, Wilfrid Scawen (1840–1922), English poet and traveller, born at Petworth, Sussex, was educated at Stonyhurst and Oscott, and served in the diplomatic service (1859–70). He travelled in the Near and Middle East, espoused the cause of Arabi Pasha and Egyptian nationalism (1882), stood for parliament and was imprisoned in 1888 for activity in the Irish Land League. He wrote fierce political verse, charming love poems, and bred Arab horses. See *My Diaries* (1922) and Lives by Finch (1938) and Lytton (1961).

BLUNTSCHLI, Johann Kaspar, *bloont'shlee* (1808–81), Swiss legal scholar, born at Zürich, in 1833 became professor there and later at Munich (1848) and Heidelberg (1871). His reputation rests on his *Allgemeines Staatsrecht* (1852). He helped to found the Institute of International Law, Ghent (1873). See his autobiography (1884).

BOABDIL, properly **Abu-Abdallah** (d. c. 1493), the last Moorish king of Granada, dethroned his father, Abu-l-Hasan, in 1481, and two years later was defeated and taken prisoner by the Castilians near Lucena. He was set free on condition of paying tribute, and returned to Granada to struggle with his father and with his uncle for the throne. The fall of Málaga was only the prelude to the siege of the capital itself, which was finally starved out in 1491, in spite of the reckless courage of the Moors and of Boabdil, who, usually weak and vacillating, became resolute in battle. The spot from which he last saw Granada after surrendering to Ferdinand of Spain the keys of the city, still bears the name of *el último sospiro del Moro*, ' the last sigh of the Moor '. He lost his life in battle in Africa.

BOADICEA, *bō-a-di-see'a* (better **Boudicca** or **Bonduca**) (1st cent. A.D.), British warrior-queen, wife of Prasutagus, king of the Iceni, a tribe inhabiting the part of Britain now occupied by Norfolk and Suffolk. On her husband's death (c. A.D. 60), the Romans seized her territory, and treated the inhabitants, herself, and her daughters brutally. Boadicea gathered a large army, destroyed the Roman colony of Camulodunum (Colchester), took Londinium and Verulamium (London and St Albans), and put to death, according to Tacitus, as many as 70,000 Romans. Suetonius Paulinus, the Roman governor of Britain, who had been absent in Mona (Anglesey), now advanced against her, and she suffered an overwhelming defeat and took poison. See Collingwood and Myres, *Roman Britain* (1936) and Dudley and Webster *The Rebellion of Boudicea* (1962).

BOBBIN, Tim. See COLLIER, JOHN, (3).

BOCAGE, Manoel Barbosa du, *boo-kahzh'é* (1765–1805), Portuguese lyric poet, was born in Sebutal, served in the army and the navy, sailed in 1786 to India and China, returning to Lisbon in 1790, where, recognized as a poet, he joined the literary coterie *Nova Arcadia*. Bocage is essentially a romantic, but his sonnets are classical in form. He often satirizes, as in *Pina de Talião*.

BOCCACCIO, Giovanni, *bok-kaht'chō* (1313–1375), Italian writer, most probably born in Tuscany, was the illegitimate son of a merchant of Certaldo, who launched him on a commercial career, during which he spent some time in Paris. But the young Giovanni abandoned commerce and the study of canon law. At Naples he gave himself to story-writing in verse and prose, mingled in courtly society, and fell in love with the noble lady whom he made famous under the name of Fiammetta. Up to the year 1350 Boccaccio lived alternately at Florence and at Naples, producing prose tales, pastorals, and poems. The *Teseide* is a graceful version in *ottava rima* of the mediaeval romance of Palamon and Arcite, which was partly translated by Chaucer in the *Knight's Tale*, and is the subject of Shakespeare and Fletcher's *Two Noble Kinsmen*. The *Filostrato*, likewise in *ottava rima*, deals with the loves of Troilus and Cressida, also in great part translated by Chaucer. After 1350 Boccaccio became a diplomat entrusted with important public affairs, and a scholar devoted to the cause of the new learning. During this period, in which he formed a lasting friendship with Petrarch, Boccaccio, as Florentine ambassador, visited Rome, Ravenna, Avignon, and Brandenburg. In 1358 he completed his great work, the *Decameron*, begun some ten years before. During the plague at Florence in 1348, seven ladies and three gentlemen, leaving the city and betaking themselves to a country villa, while away ten days (whence the name *Decameron*) by each in turn telling stories, a hundred in all, in the garden. Many of these are licentious; others are full of pathos and poetical fancy; several are masterpieces of imaginative creation; all are related in exquisitely graceful Italian. Boccaccio selected the plots of his stories from amid the floating popular fiction of the day, and especially from the *fabliaux* which had passed into Italy from France, the matter being mediaeval, while the form is classical. Boccaccio's originality lies in his consummate narrative skill, and in the rich poetical sentiment which transforms his borrowed materials. The two great tendencies which run through European literature, the classical and the romantic, are seen working together in the *Decameron* as they are hardly to be seen elsewhere. The influence of the book on European literature has been lasting, not merely in Italy, but in France and England. Chaucer borrowed largely from it; as, to a lesser degree, did Sidney, Tourneur, Marston, Fletcher, and Shakespeare. None of Dryden's works has had more enduring popularity than his *Tales from Boccaccio*. In later days, Keats (in *Isabella*), Tennyson (in *The Falcon* and *The Lover's Tale*), Longfellow, Swinburne, and George Eliot are among those who have turned for their subjects to the *Decameron*. Boccaccio for some time held a chair founded for the elucidation of the works of Dante, on whose *Divina Commedia* he produced a commentary. During his last years he lived principally in retirement at Certaldo, and would have entered into holy orders, moved by repentance for the follies of his youth, had he not been dissuaded by Petrarch. He wrote in Latin an elaborate work on mythology, *De Genealogia Deorum*, and treatises such as *De Claris Mulieribus* and *De Montibus*. He died at Certaldo, December 21, 1375. See works on him (in older English literature called John Bochas) by Baldelli (1806), Landau (Stuttg. 1877), Koerting (Leip. 1880), Crescini (1887), J. A. Symonds (1894), E. Hutton (1909), C. G. Osgood (1930), MacManus (1947), and study by H. G. Wright (1958).

BOCCAGE, Marie Anne Fiquet du, *bok-ahzh*, née Le Page (1710–1802), French poetess, was born at Rouen. Her *Paradis terrestre* (1748), an imitation of Milton, *La Colombiade* (1756), &c., gave her an exaggerated fame, perhaps on account of their author's great beauty, but her letters to her sister, written while travelling through England, Holland, and Italy, have historical interest.

BOCCHERINI, Luigi, *bok-ker-ee'nee* (1740–1805), Italian composer, born at Lucca, a cellist and prolific composer at the courts of the Infante Don Luis in Madrid and Frederick II of Prussia. He is best known for his chamber music, the famous minuet which holds its own among the most popular of classical tunes being from his string quintet in E, and for his cello concertos and sonatas. The great similarity of his work to that of his greater contemporary earned him the nickname 'Haydn's wife'. He died in poverty. See works by Picquot (Paris 1851), Bonaventura (Milan 1932), and de Rothschild (France 1962, trans. 1965).

BOCCIONI, Umberto, *bot-chŏ'nee* (1882–1916), Italian artist and sculptor, born at Reggio. He was the most original artist of the Futurist school, and its principal theorist. After working with Balla, Severini, and Marinetti in Rome and Paris from 1898 to 1914, he wrote a comprehensive survey of the movement, *Pittura, scultura futuriste* (1914). An important bronze sculpture, *Unique Forms of Continuity in Space* (1913), is in the Museum of Modern Art, New York. See studies by Marinetti and Longhi (1914).

BOCHART, Samuel, *bo-shahr'* (1599–1667), French Huguenot theologian and philologist, born at Rouen, after extensive studies, especially in the Semitic languages, became Protestant pastor at Caen. In 1646 he published his *Geographia Sacra*, in 1663 *Hierozoicon, sive de Animalibus Scripturae Sacrae*; and in 1652 visited the Swedish court.

BOCHAS, John. See BOCCACCIO.

BOCK, Fedor von (1880–1945), German fieldmarshal, born at Küstrin, was a staff-officer and was decorated with the *Pour le Mérite* in World War I. He commanded the German armies invading Austria (1938), Poland (1939) and of the Lower Somme, France (1940). Promoted field-marshal, he participated in the invasion of Russia (1941), but was dismissed by Hitler for failing to capture Moscow (1942).

BÖCKH. See BOECKH.

BÖCKLIN, Arnold (1827–1901), Swiss painter, mainly of mythological subjects, born at Basel, combined classical themes of nymphs and satyrs with dark romantic landscapes, rocks, and castles, characteristic of 19th-century German painting. See study by M. F. Schneider (1943).

BODE, *bŏ'dĕ,* (1) **Johann Elert** (1747–1826), German astronomer, born at Hamburg, was director of Berlin observatory. The arithmetical relation subsisting between the distances of the planets from the sun is called Bode's Law. This does not hold for the most distant planet, Pluto, and has no theoretical foundation.

(2) **Wilhelm von** (1845–1929), German art critic, born in Brunswick, became general director of the Prussian royal museums in 1905, and wrote much on Rembrandt and on the history of art, especially in the Renaissance period. See study by Winkler (1935).

BODENSTEDT, Friedrich Martin von (1819–1892), German writer, born at Peine in Hanover, lived for a while at Moscow, travelled in the Middle East, was a professor at Munich University and director of the Meiningen court theatre. He translated into German many Russian, English, and Persian texts, and published poetry. His best known work is *Lieder des Mirza Schaffy* (1851),

alleged to be a translation from the Tatar. See his Autobiography (1890) and Life by G. Schenk (1893).

BODENSTEIN, Ernst August Max, *-shtin* (1871–1940), German chemist, born at Magdeburg, was professor in Berlin (1923–36) and did original work in reaction kinetics, equilibria, and photochemistry.

BODICHON, *née* **Leigh Smith, Barbara,** *bod-ee-shŏ* (1827–90), English advocate of women's rights, a founder of Girton College, and a water-colour landscape painter, was the daughter of a Norwich M.P., and died in Algeria, having in 1857 married **Eugène Bodichon, M.D.** (1810–85).

BODIN, Jean, *bo-dĭ* (c. 1530–96), French political philosopher, was born at Angers and died of the plague at Laon, having been appointed king's attorney there in 1576. According to Bodin's greatest work, *Les Six Livres de la République* (1576), property and the family form the basis of society, and a limited monarchy is the best possible form of government. In opposition to certain Protestant writers, he held that under no circumstances are citizens justified in rebelling against their ruler. One prince, however, may interfere in behalf of the oppressed subjects of another. His *Methodus ad Facilem Historiarum Cognitionem* (1566) is a noteworthy contribution to the philosophy of history. His famous *Colloquium Heptaplomeres,* first published by Noack in 1857, is a conversation between a Jew, a Mohammedan, a Lutheran, a Zwinglian, a Roman Catholic, an Epicurean, and a Theist, who come to the conclusion that they will leave off disputing on religion, and live together in charity. Bodin, though so liberal in his opinions as to earn the reputation of an atheist, was not in advance of his age in his notion about witchcraft as evidenced by his *Demonomanie des sorciers* (1580). See Baudrillart's *Jean Bodin et son temps* (1853), and J. W. Allen, *History of Political Thought in the 16th century* (1928).

BODLÄNDER, Guido (1855–1904), German chemist, professor at Breslau, worked on the electrolytical and optical properties of solutions.

BODLEY, Sir Thomas (1545–1613), English statesman and bibliophile, was born at Exeter. His family, forced to flee during the persecutions of Mary, settled at Geneva, where Bodley studied languages and divinity. In 1558 he entered Magdalen College, Oxford, gained a Merton fellowship (1564), was elected a proctor, and officiated as public orator. He devoted himself to the study of Hebrew, and, spending the years 1576–80 in Italy, France, and Germany, became proficient in modern languages. He was now employed by the queen in diplomatic missions to Denmark, France, and Holland; married a wealthy widow in 1587; and returned to his favourite city, Oxford, in 1597, where he devoted himself to literature, especially to the extension of the university library, originally established by Humphrey, Duke of Gloucester, and now called the Bodleian. He was knighted by King James in 1603, and died at Oxford, January 28, 1613. His Autobiography, with his letters, is published in

Trecentale Bodleianum (1913). See also Macray's *Annals of the Bodleian Library* (1868) and *Letters*, ed. G. W. Wheeler (1926).

BODMER, Johann Jakob (1698–1782), Swiss writer, was born at Greifensee near Zürich, and died at Zürich, having been professor of History from 1725 to 1775. The study of the classical authors convinced him of the poverty and tastelessness of existing German literature. His own efforts as poet and author, if not as critic, were a failure, but he helped to spread knowledge of early German literature by his editions of the *Minnesänger* (1748) and the *Nibelungenlied* (1757). See studies by L. Meister (1783) and M. Wehrli (1936).

BODONI, Giambattista, *bo-dō'nee* (1740–1813), Italian printer, born at Saluzzo, designed a modern type face still widely used today. His press at Parma published editions of the classics widely admired for their elegance. See Lives by Bernardi (1873) and Cleland (1916).

BOÉ, Franz de la. See SYLVIUS (1).

BOECE, *bō-ees*, **Boyis,** or **Boethius, Hector** (*c.* 1465–1536), Scottish historian, was born at Dundee, and studied at Montaigu College, Paris, where *c.* 1492 to 1498 he was a regent or professor of Philosophy, and where he made the friendship of Erasmus. Bishop Elphinstone then invited him to preside over his newly-founded university of Aberdeen. Boece accepted the office, and he was at the same time made a canon of the cathedral. In 1522 he published his lives, in Latin, of the bishops of Mortlach and Aberdeen; in 1527 the Latin *History of Scotland*, which, though proved to contain a large amount of fiction, was deemed distinctly critical at the time of its publication. The king awarded him a pension until he was promoted to a benefice in 1534. See BELLENDEN, JOHN; and J. Moir's edition and translation of the *History* (New Spalding Club 1895).

BOECKH, Philipp August (1785–1867), German classical antiquary, was born at Karlsruhe, became professor of Rhetoric and Ancient Literature at Berlin in 1811, where he lectured for more than forty years. His four great works are his edition of Pindar (1811–1821); *Die Staatshaushaltung der Athener* (1817, trans. 1828); *Metrologische Untersuchungen* (1838); and *Das Seewesen des Attischen Staats* (1840). His lesser works have been collected (1858–74); and his Correspondence with **K. O.** Müller was published in 1883. See Life by M. Hoffman (1901).

BOEHM, (1) **Sir Joseph Edgar, Bart.** (1834–1890), British sculptor, born in Vienna, was educated in England, and finally settled there in 1862. He was made an R.A. in 1882 and a baronet in 1889. The queen's effigy on the coinage issued in 1887 was from his designs, and he executed the well-known seated statue of Thomas Carlyle (1875).

(2) **Theobald** (1794–1881), German flautist and inventor, born in Munich, became a member of the Bavarian Court Orchestra in 1818 while working at his father's trade as a goldsmith. In 1828 he opened a flute factory in Munich, and after hearing the English player Nicholson in 1831 he determined to make a flute which would be acoustically perfect. As this involved making holes in places where they could not be fingered, he devised a key mechanism to overcome the problem, and in 1847 produced the model on which the modern flute is based. Attempts to use his key system on the oboe and bassoon have been largely unsuccessful, though certain features have been applied to the clarinet. See Rockstro's *Treatise on the Flute* (1890) and Welch's *History of the Boehm Flute* (1896).

BOEHME, Jakob, *bœ'mě* (1575–1624), German theosophist and mystic, was born of poor parents at Altseidenberg near Görlitz in Upper Lusatia, and in boyhood tended cattle. He became a shoemaker, but devoted much of his time to meditation on divine things. About 1612 he published *Aurora*. It contains revelations and meditations upon God, Man, and Nature, and shows a remarkable knowledge of Scripture and of the writings of alchemists. It was condemned by the ecclesiastical authorities of Görlitz, and he suffered much persecution. His chief aim is to explain the origin of things, especially the existence of evil. God is the *Ungrund* or *Urgrund*, the original and undistinguished unity, at once everything and nothing, which, however, has in itself the principle of separation whereby all things come into existence. It is through the principle of negation, which in a way is identified with evil, that creation is explained. Boehme's philosophy is in fact an application of the principle of contradiction to explain the great problems of philosophy and religion; but the difficulties are only concealed or shifted about under a cloud of mystical language, in which a system of triads, suggested by the Christian doctrine of the trinity, have an important place. His influence spread beyond Germany to Holland and England. Newton studied him; Henry More was influenced by him; William Law might be called a disciple; John Pordage (1608–98) and Jane Leade (1623–1704) were leaders of the Philadelphians, a Behmenist sect. Points of contact with Spinoza, Fichte, Schelling, and Hegel revived interest in his speculations in Germany in the 19th century. See works by Hamberger (1844), Martensen (trans. 1885), Boutroux (1888), Hartmann (Lond. 1890), Deussen (Leip. 1911), A. J. Penny (1912), and H. Bornkamm (1925).

BOËLLMAN, Léon, *bō-el-man* (1862–97), French composer and organist, born at Ensisheim, Alsace. Boëllman became noted first as a child prodigy, and from 1881 until his death was organist at the Church of St Vincent de Paul, Paris, and much admired for his skill in improvisation. As a composer, he worked in all fields except dramatic music, and is remembered for his *Gothic Suite* for organ and his *Symphonic Variations* for cello and orchestra.

BOERHAAVE, Hermann, *boor-hah'vě* (1668–1738), Dutch physician and botanist, was born at Voorhout, near Leyden; in 1682 he went to Leyden, where he studied theology and oriental languages, and took his degree in philosophy in 1689; but in 1690 he began the study of medicine, and in 1701 was appointed lecturer on the Theory of Medicine, in 1709 professor of Medicine and Botany. The two works on which his great fame chiefly rests, *Institutiones Medicae* (1708) and *Aphorismi de Cognoscendis et Curandis Morbis* (1709), were translated into various European languages, and even into Arabic. Though so industrious in his own profession, he also undertook in 1718 the professorship of Chemistry, and his *Elementa Chemiae* (1724) occupies a high place in the history of chemistry. Meanwhile patients came from all parts of Europe to consult him, so that he made a fortune of two million florins. See Lives by Burton (2 vols. 1743) and Johnson (1834).

BOETHIUS, (1) **Anicius Manlius Severinus** (*c.* 475–524), Roman statesman and philosopher, was born of a consular family, and studied with enthusiasm philosophy, mathematics, and poetry. Soon after 500 he was appointed a court minister by the Gothic king, Theodoric, now ruling Italy from Rome; and his Roman countrymen owed it to him that the Gothic rule was so little oppressive. He was made consul in 510, and his two sons shared the same honour in 522. But his bold uprightness of conduct at last brought down upon his head the vengeance of those whom he had checked in their oppressions. He was accused of treasonable designs against Theodoric, was stripped of his dignities, and, after imprisonment at Pavia, was executed in 524. During his imprisonment he wrote his famous *De Consolatione Philosophiae*, in which the author holds a conversation with Philosophy, who shows him the mutability of all earthly fortune, and the insecurity of everything save virtue. The work, which in style happily imitates the best Augustan models, is theistic in its language, but affords no indication that its writer was a Christian. Boethius was the last great Roman writer who understood Greek; his translations of Aristotle were long the only means of studying Greek philosophy; and his manuals on arithmetic, astronomy, geometry, and music were generally used in the schools. Peiper's (1871) is a standard edition of the *Consolatio,* which was often translated—as by King Alfred into Anglo-Saxon, and by Chaucer into English prose (printed by Caxton in 1480). See studies by H. F. Stewart (1891) and H. R. Patch (N.Y. 1935).

(2) **Hector.** See BOECE.

BOEX. See ROSNY.

BOGARDUS, James (1800–74) American inventor, born in Catskill, New York, was apprenticed to a watchmaker, and early showed the bent of his mind by improvements in eight-day clocks, by the invention of a delicate engraving machine, the dry gasmeter, the transfer machine for producing banknote plates from separate dies, a pyrometer, a deep-sea sounding machine, a dynamometer, and in 1839 a method of engraving postage stamps, which was adopted by the British government. He also erected the first cast-iron building in America.

BOGATZKY, Karl Heinrich von, *bō-guts'kee* (1690–1774), German hymnwriter, was born at Jankowe in Lower Silesia. His chief work is his *Golden Treasury* (trans. 1775). See his Autobiography, and Life by Kelly (1889).

BOGLE, George (1746–81), British diplomat, born near Bothwell, Lanarkshire, entered the service of the East India Company, and in 1774 was selected by Warren Hastings to act as envoy to the Lama of Tibet. Bogle was the first Briton to cross the Tsanpu in its upper range, established commercial links with Tibet and became a personal friend of the Lama. He returned in 1775, and died at Calcutta. See Clements R. Markham's narrative of his mission (1876).

BOGUE, David, *bōg* (1750–1825), Scottish congregational minister and one of the founders of the London Missionary Society, was born at Coldingham, Berwickshire, became an Independent minister and tutor at a Gosport seminary, out of which grew the London Missionary Society. He also was a founder of the British and Foreign Bible Society and the Religious Tract Society and with Dr James Bennet wrote a *History of Dissenters* (1809).

BOHEMOND, *bō-ay-mõ*, name of several Norman princes of Antioch. The most noteworthy were:

Bohemond I (*c.* 1056–1111), eldest son of Robert Guiscard (q.v.) and father of Bohemond II, distinguished himself in his father's war against the Byzantine emperor, Alexius Comnenus (1081–85). After his father's death he was excluded from the throne of Apulia by his brother Roger, and only gained the principality of Tarentum after a long struggle. He joined the crusade of 1096, and took a prominent part in the capture of Antioch (1098). While the other crusaders advanced to storm Jerusalem, Bohemond established himself as prince in Antioch. He was taken prisoner, however, in 1100 by a Turkish emir, and remained two years in captivity, Tancred meanwhile looking after his interests in Antioch. He then returned to Europe to collect troops, and after defeating Alexius was acknowledged by him as prince of Antioch. See Life by R. B. Yewdale (1924).

Bohemond II (1108–31), younger son of Bohemond I, assumed the government of Antioch in 1126 and was killed in battle.

BÖHM. See BOEHM.

BÖHME. See BOEHME.

BOHN, Henry George (1796–1884), British publisher, was born of German parentage in London, in 1831 started as a secondhand bookseller. In 1841 he issued his famous ' guinea catalogue ', containing 23,208 items. In 1846 he started the cheap libraries of standard reprints, which bear his name. An accomplished scholar, he translated several of the foreign classics volumes himself, besides compiling a dictionary of quotations, &c.

BOHR, Niels Henrik David (1885–1962), Danish physicist, born and educated in Copenhagen, became professor there in 1916 after working under J. J. Thomson at Cambridge and Lord Rutherford at Manchester. He greatly extended the theory of atomic structure when he explained the spectrum of hydrogen by means of an atomic model and the quantum theory (1913). During World War II he escaped from German-occupied Denmark and assisted atom bomb research in America, returning to Copenhagen in 1945. He was founder and director of the Institute of Theoretical Physics at Copenhagen, was awarded the Nobel prize in 1922 and elected F.R.S. in 1926. See studies, ed. Pauli (1955).

BÖHTLINGK, Otto (1815–1904), German Sanskrit scholar, was born at St Petersburg; from 1835 to 1842 studied oriental languages, especially Sanskrit, at Berlin and Bonn; and lived in Jena and Leipzig. His works include the first European edition of the Indian grammarian Panini (1839) and a Sanskrit dictionary (1855–75).

BOHUN, *boon,* a family founded by the Norman Humphrey de Bohun, whose fourth descendant, Henry, in 1199 was made Earl of Hereford. Humphrey, fourth Earl of Hereford (1276–1322), was taken prisoner at Bannockburn, and fell at Boroughbridge. In 1380 the heiress of the earldoms of Hereford, Essex, and Northampton married Henry Bolingbroke (Henry IV).

BOIAMOND. See BAJIMOND.

BOIARDO, Matteo Maria, Count of Scandiano, *bo-yahr'dō* (1434–94), one of the greater Italian poets, was born at Scandiano, a village at the foot of the Lombard Apennines. He studied at Ferrara, and in 1462 married the daughter of the Count of Norellara. He lived at the court of Ferrara on intimate terms with Dukes Borso and Ercole; by the latter he was employed on diplomatic missions, and appointed governor in 1481 of Modena, and in 1487 of Reggio. As an administrator he was distinguished for his clemency, and opposition to capital punishment. He died at Reggio, December 21. Boiardo has been called the ' Flower of Chivalry '. His fame rests on the *Orlando Innamorato* (1486), a long narrative poem in which the Charlemagne romances are recast into *ottava rima*. Full of rich and graceful fancy, this is the only work in which the spirit of chivalry is found in union with the spirit of the Renaissance. Ariosto adopted Boiardo's characters, and brought his narrative to a close in the *Orlando Furioso,* by which the fame of the earlier poem has been unfairly obscured. After going through sixteen editions before 1545, Boiardo's work became almost forgotten, its vigorous but rough and provincial style being uncongenial to the Florentine taste. His other works comprise Latin eclogues, a versification of Lucian's *Timon,* translations of Herodotus, the *Ass* of Lucian, and the *Golden Ass* of Apuleius, and a series of sonnets and *Canzoni* (Reggio 1499). See Lives by Reichenbach (1929), Procacci (1931), and Renda (1941).

BOIELDIEU, François Adrien, *bwahl-dyœ* (1775–1834), French composer, was born at Rouen and achieved success with his opera *Le Calife de Bagdad* (1800) in Paris. He conducted at St Petersburg (1803–10) and on his return produced his two masterpieces, *Jean de Paris* (1812) and *La Dame blanche* (1825). His strength lies in bright and graceful melody. See works on him by Pougin (Paris 1875) and Faure (Paris 1945). His son **Adrien** (1816–83) also composed operas.

BOIGNE, Count Benoît de, *bwahn'y',* properly **La Borgne** (1751–1830), French military adventurer, was born at Chambéry, served in the Irish Brigade in France, was in the Russian army for a time, arrived in India in 1778, joined the East India Company's Madras army, and entering Sindhia's service, won an empire for his master. He resigned in 1795 and returned to France, where he died.

BOILEAU, or Boileau Despréaux, Nicolas, *bwah-lō* (1636–1711), French critic, was born in Paris, November 1, 1636, studied law and theology at Beauvais, but as a man of means devoted himself to literature. His first publications (1660–66) were satires, some of which brought him into trouble; in 1677 the king appointed him, along with Racine, royal historiographer. *L'Art poétique,* imitated by Pope in the *Essay on Criticism,* was published in 1674, along with the first part of the clever serio-comic *Lutrin.* In 1669–77 Boileau published nine epistles, written, like his satires, on the Horatian model. His ode on the capture of Namur (1692, burlesqued by Prior) is a glaring example of servile flattery and bad verse. In his last years Boileau retired to Auteuil, where he died on March 13, 1711. His works include several critical dissertations in prose, a collection of epigrams, a translation of Longinus *On the Sublime,* a *Dialogue des héros de roman,* and a series of letters (many to Racine). His verse has wit and vigour, but he never rises to the level of the great satirists. His influence as a critic has been profound. The 16th century had flooded French literature with new words and new ideas. He set up good sense, sobriety, elegance, and dignity of style as the cardinal literary virtues, discountenancing the conceits of the salon coteries and the grossness and grotesqueness of the earlier writers. Through the influence of the ' lawgiver of Parnassus ', French prose became almost identical with clear, precise, and polished composition; but for more than a hundred years verse was robbed of fire and melody and suggestiveness, and the drama was divorced from real life. While he refined he impoverished the vocabulary—the language lost its old pith, colour, and flexibility. See works on him by Morillot (1890), Lanson (1892), C. J. Revillout (1899) and D. Mornet (1942), and studies by M. Hervier (1938) and Haley (1938).

BOISBAUDRAN, Paul Émile Lecoq de, *bwah-bō-drā* (1838–1912), French physical chemist, was born at Cognac, Charente. A founder of spectroscopy, he discovered gallium, samarium and dysprosium.

BOISGOBEY, Fortuné du, *bwah-gō-bay* (1824–91), a prolific French detective-story writer, was born at Granville in Normandy.

BOIS-REYMOND, Emil du, *bwah-ray-mō* (1818–96), German physiologist, born in Berlin of French parentage, professor of Physics at Berlin, discovered neuro-electricity. His brother, **Paul** (1831–89), a mathematician, wrote on the theory of functions.

BOISSERÉE, Sulpice, *bwah-sě-ray* (1783–1854), German art historian, born at Cologne, with his brother **Melchior** (1786–1851) collected at Stuttgart two hundred pictures, sold in 1827 to the king of Bavaria.

BOISSIER, Gaston, *bwahs-yay* (1823–1908), French classical scholar, secretary (from 1895) and historian of the Académie.

BOISSONADE, Jean François, *bwahs-on-ahd* (1774–1859), French scholar, born at Paris, in 1828 became professor of Greek Literature in the Collège de France.

BOISSY D'ANGLAS, François Antoine de, *bwah-see-dã-glah* (1756–1826), French statesman, a member of the States-General (1789), he joined the successful conspiracy against Robespierre, was elected secretary of the Convention, and a member of the Committee of Public Safety, in which capacity he displayed remarkable talent. He was later called to the Senate by Napoleon; and made a peer by Louis XVIII.

BOITO, Arrigo, *bō-ee'tō* (1842–1918), Italian composer and poet, was born at Padua, and studied at the Milan Conservatorio. His first important work was the opera *Mefistofele* (1868), which survived its initial failure and later grew in popularity. Another opera, *Nerone* (1916), was not produced till 1924. He wrote his own and other libretti, including those for Verdi's *Otello* and *Falstaff.*

BOIVIN, Marie, *bwah-vĩ* (1773–1841), a French nun who devoted herself to midwifery and was superintendent of the Maternité at Paris. Marburg University gave her the degree of M.D.

BOJARDO. See BOIARDO.

BOJER, Johan, *bo-yer* (1872–1959), Norwegian novelist, born at Orkedalsören, turned author after military service and extensive travel in western Europe. His first and successful novel *Et folketog* (1896) was followed by *The Great Hunger* (trans. 1918), *The Power of a Lie* (trans. 1919), and many other novels and plays. See Life by La Chenais (1930).

BOKER, George Henry (1823–90), American poet, playwright, and diplomat, born in Philadelphia, won belated recognition for his 400 sonnets and for *Francesca da Rimini* (1855), a romantic verse tragedy and the best American play before the Civil War. Boker's propaganda for the North secured him the post of minister to Turkey (1871–75) and Russia (1875–78). See Life by E. S. Bradley (1927).

BOLDREWOOD, Rolf, the pseudonym of **Thomas Alexander Browne** (1826–1915), Australian novelist, was born in London, but taken to Australia as a young child. A squatter and later an inspector of goldfields, his exciting, romantic and didactic novels depict life at the cattle stations and diggings. They include *Robbery under Arms* (1888), *Babes in the Bush* (1900), &c.

BOLEYN, Anne, *bool'in* (*c.* 1504–36), English queen, second wife of Henry VIII, the daughter of Sir Thomas Boleyn, by Elizabeth Howard, daughter of the Duke of Norfolk. She was at the French court (1519–21), and on her return her suitors included Henry Percy, the heir to the Earl of Northumberland, and King Henry himself, who began to shower favours upon her father, having already had an affair with her sister. Anne did not apparently favour him until negotiations for the divorce from Catharine of Aragon began in 1527, but, as these dragged on, their association became shameless and they were secretly married in January 1533. Cranmer declared her Henry's legal wife in May and she was crowned with great splendour in Westminster Hall on Whitsunday; but within three months Henry's passion had cooled. It was not revived by the birth, in September 1533, of a princess, the famous Elizabeth, still less by that of a stillborn son, on January 29, 1536. On May Day that year the king rode off abruptly from a tournament held at Greenwich, leaving the queen behind, and the next day she was arrested and brought to the Tower. A secret commission investigated charges of Anne's adultery with her own brother, Lord Rochford, and four commoners. The latter on the 12th, and Anne and her brother on the 15th, were tried and convicted of high treason. Her own uncle, the Duke of Norfolk, presided over her judges, and pronounced the verdict. On May 19, on Tower Green, Anne was beheaded, the others having suffered two days earlier. Henry the next day married Jane Seymour. See Hepworth Dixon's *History of Two Queens* (1874), Paul Friedmann's *Anne Boleyn* (1884), Sergeant's (1923), and works cited under HENRY VIII.

BOLINGBROKE, (1). See HENRY IV.

(2) **Henry St John, 1st Viscount** (1678–1751), English statesman, was born at Battersea on October 1, and educated at Eton. Whether he went on to Oxford is not definitely known. After travelling on the Continent, he entered parliament in 1701 as Tory member for Wootton Bassett, became successively secretary for war (1704) and foreign secretary (1710), and shared the leadership of the party with Harley. He was made a peer in 1712 and in 1713 he brilliantly negotiated the treaty of Utrecht. After intriguing successfully for Harley's downfall, he was plotting a Jacobite restoration when Queen Anne died, and George I succeeded. Bolingbroke fled to France, was attainted in 1715, and acted for some time as secretary of state to the Pretender. While living abroad he wrote his *Reflections on Exile.* In 1723 he obtained permission to return to England, settled at Dawley, near Uxbridge, and became the associate of Pope, Swift, and other men of letters. A series of letters attacking Walpole in the *Craftsman* were reprinted as *A Dissertation on Parties.* Disappointed in his hope of readmission to political life, he returned to France, where he remained from 1735 to 1742 and wrote his *Letters on the Study of History.* His last years were spent at Battersea, where he wrote his *Letters on the Spirit of Patriotism* and his *Idea of a Patriot King,* which was to have a profound political influence. George III disastrously endeavoured to act according to its maxims and Disraeli quoted from it with approval. The monarchy, as conceived by Bolingbroke, was to stand above faction and represent the nation. A brilliant orator and writer, Bolingbroke suffered as a public figure through his egotism and rakishness. He was twice married and died December 12, 1751, at Battersea. See works on him by MacKnight (1863), Collins (1886), Sichel (1902), A. Hassall (rev. 1915), and C. Petrie (1937).

BOLÍVAR, Simón, *bo-lee'vahr* (1783–1830), South American revolutionary leader, ' the Liberator ' of South America from the Spanish yoke, was born in Caracas, of noble family, studied law at Madrid, and was in Paris during the Revolution. After the declaration of independence by Venezuela in 1811, he obtained command of an army, and in 1813, entering Caracas as conqueror, proclaimed himself dictator of western Venezuela. Fortune, however, soon deserted him; but driven out in 1814, he made repeated descents on Venezuela from the West Indies, and in 1817 began to make headway against the Spaniards. Owing to dissensions among the patriots, it was only in June 1821 that the victory of Carabobo virtually ended the war; and it was not till 1824 that the royalist troops were finally driven out. In 1821 Bolívar was chosen president of Colombia, comprising Venezuela, Colombia, and New Granada. In 1822 he added Ecuador to the republic, and in 1824 drove the Spaniards out of Peru, and made himself dictator there for a time. Upper Peru was made a separate state, and called Bolivia in his honour, while he was named perpetual protector; but his Bolivian constitution excited great dissatisfaction, and led to the expulsion of the Colombian troops. His assumption of supreme power, after his return to Colombia in 1828, roused the apprehension of the republicans there; and in 1829 Venezuela separated itself from Colombia. Bolívar, in consequence, laid down his authority in 1830, and died the same year. Although his life ended in dictatorship, his ideal of a federation of all Spanish-speaking South American states continued to exert a lively influence. See Life by F. L. Petre (1910), and studies by J. B. Trend (1946) and S. de Madariaga (1952).

BOLLAND, John van, *bol-lä'* (1596–1665), an Antwerp Jesuit, the founder and first editor of the Bollandist *Acta Sanctorum.*

BOLOGNA, Giovanni, *bo-lon'ya* (1524–1608), Flemish sculptor and architect, was born at Douai, and died at Florence, having lived in Italy from 1551. He won great popularity and executed much work in Florence for the Medici, including the *Flying Mercury* (1564) and various fountains in the Boboli gardens, the *Rape of the Sabines* (1580), and *Hercules and the Centaur* (1599). His bronzes can be seen in the Wallace Collection, &c. See Life by Desjardins (Paris 1884).

BOLSEC, Hieronymus (d. *c.* 1584), an ex-Carmelite friar who opposed Calvin's doctrine of predestination at Geneva (1551), causing him to reformulate it, then returned to Catholicism and wrote a libellous Life of him (Paris 1577).

BOLTWOOD, Bertram Borden (1870–1927), American physicist, born at Amherst, Mass., and educated in Europe, became professor at Yale (1910–27). He discovered the radio-active element ionium.

BOLTZMANN, Ludwig, *bolts-mahn* (1844–1906), Austrian physicist, was born in Vienna, and after many professorships elsewhere became professor there in 1895. He did important work on the kinetic theory of gases and established Boltzmann's law, or the principle of the equipartition of energy. He committed suicide.

BOLYAI, János, *bo'lyoy* (1802–60), Hungarian mathematician, was born at Kolozsvar, and became, after criticisms of Euclid's parallel axiom, one of the founders of non-Euclidian geometry, so continuing the work of his father Farkas (1775–1856).

BOLZANO, Bernhard, *bolt-sah'no* (1781–1848), a Catholic theologian, philosopher, and mathematician, was born at Prague of Italian ancestry. He formulated the modern mathematical theory of functions.

BOMBA. See FERDINAND II (of Naples).

BOMBARD, Alain Louis (1924–), French physician and marine biologist, born at Paris. In 1952 he set out across the Atlantic alone in his rubber dinghy *L'Hérétique* to prove his claim that shipwreck castaways could sustain life on nothing more than fish and plankton. He landed at Barbados on December 24, 1952, emaciated, but vindicated in his theories. He now runs a marine laboratory—' La Coryphene '—at Saint-Malo, for the study of the physiopathology of the sea. See *The Bombard Story,* tr. B. Connell (1953).

BOMBOIS, Camille, *bō-bwa* (1883–), French primitive painter, born at Venarey-les-Laumes, Côte d'Or. Without academic training, he worked in a travelling circus, and as a labourer, painting as a hobby. After distinguished service during World War I, he took a job at night, and painted during the day. By 1923 he had been discovered by collectors and was able to devote all his time to painting his very personal landscapes (e.g., of the *Sacré Cœur*) and pictures of wrestlers and acrobats. They are uncompromisingly realistic, with a childlike frankness and simplicity of technique.

BONALD, Louis Gabriel Ambroise, Vicomte de, *bon-ahl* (1754–1840), French writer, emigrated to Heidelberg during the French Revolution and wrote *Théorie du pouvoir politique et religieux* (1796), advocating the system of monarchy and prophesying the return of the Bourbons. He was appointed by Napoleon minister of instruction in 1808, in 1815 supported the ultramontane party and was ennobled by Louis XVIII. His son, Louis Jacques Maurice (1787–1870), became Archbishop of Lyons in 1839, and cardinal in 1841.

BONAPARTE, (in Ital. four syllables, in Fr. and Eng. three, and spelt *Buonaparte* by Napoleon till 1796) is the name of an ancient family of Ajaccio in Corsica. From it descended **Charles** (1746–85), father of the Emperor Napoleon, who assisted Paoli in defending Corsica against the French, but ultimately took the French side, held various appointments in Corsica, and was ennobled by Louis XVI. As a Corsican commissioner he resided in Paris, where he gained for his son, Napoleon, a free admission into the military school at Brienne.—His wife, **Maria Letizia Ramolino** (1750–1836), mother of Napoleon I, and stepsister of Cardinal Fesch, lived to see her family placed on the thrones of Europe, and also to witness their downfall, submitting to her change of fortune with remarkable dignity. See Lives by Tschudi (trans. 1900) and Decaux (trans. 1963). Besides the Emperor Napoleon (q.v.) and the sons named below, she had three daughters, **Marie Anne Elisa** (1777–1820)—wife of Felix Bacciochi—Princess of Lucca and Grand Duchess of Tuscany; **Marie Pauline** (1780–1825), wife of Prince Camillo Borghese (q.v.), Duchess of Guastalla; and **Maria Annunciata Caroline** (1782–1839), wife of Joachim Murat (q.v.). See works on the marriages by Bingham (1881), and Lives of Napoleon's sisters by Turquam (trans. 1908), H. N. Williams (1908), and collective works on the Bonaparte family by F. Masson (1897–1914), F. Wekner-Wildberg (1939), and on Napoleon's brothers below by du Casse (1883), A. H. Atteridge (1909), and their memoirs. See also NAPOLEON I and III. Napoleon's brothers were:

(1) **Jerome** (1784–1860), youngest brother of Napoleon, served as naval lieutenant in the expedition to Haiti, and lived in New York, where he married (1803) Elizabeth Patterson (1785–1879), daughter of a merchant in Baltimore. He served in the war against Prussia, in 1807 was made king of Westphalia, and fought at Waterloo. He lived long in Florence, but in 1848 was appointed governor of the Invalides, and in 1850 was made a French marshal. His marriage with Elizabeth Patterson having been declared null by Napoleon, Jerome, then king of Westphalia was forced to marry Catharine, daughter of the king of Württemberg. By his first wife Jerome left one son, **Jerome Bonaparte-Patterson** (1805–70), who married a wealthy wife and had one son (1830–93), a soldier. By his second wife he had three children—**Jerome Napoleon Charles** (1814–47), Comte de Montfort; **Mathilde** (1820–1904), who married Prince Demidov; and **Napoleon Joseph Charles Paul** (1822–91), who was born at Trieste and passed his youth in Italy; entered the military service of Württemberg in 1837; and was expelled from France (1845) for republicanism. In 1848 (having on his brother's death taken the name of Jerome) he was elected to the Legislative National Assembly. He commanded at the battles of Alma and Inkermann. In 1859 he married the Princess Clotilde, daughter of Victor Emmanuel of Italy, by whom he had two sons and a daughter. After the fall of the empire he took up his residence in England, but returned to France in 1872, and sat in the Chamber of Deputies. On the death of the Prince Imperial in 1879, the eldest son of Prince Napoleon became the heir of the Bonapartist hopes; and in 1886 father and son were exiled as pretenders to the throne. He died at Rome, March 18, 1891. His eldest son, **Victor** (1862–1926), settled at Brussels, and was succeeded as head of the Bonaparte family by his son **Louis** (1914–).

(2) **Joseph** (1768–1844), king of Naples and Spain, eldest brother of Napoleon, born in Corsica, studied for the bar at Marseilles. Plenipotentiary to the United States in 1800, he signed the treaties of Lunéville (1801) and Amiens (1802); assisted in the *concordat* negotiations; in 1805 was made ruler of the Two Sicilies; and in 1806, king of Naples. A humane and accomplished man, but an ineffective ruler, in 1808 he was summarily transferred by his brother to the throne of Spain, but found himself unprepared to cope with the Spanish insurgents, and after the defeat of the French at Vitoria in 1813

returned to his estate at Morfontaine in France. After Waterloo he accompanied Napoleon to Rochefort and escaped to America, became an American citizen, lived for some years at Bordentown, in New Jersey, U.S., as a farmer, but in 1832 returned to Europe, and died at Florence. See Life by Abbott (1869). His wife, **Julia Marie Clary** (1777–1845), daughter of a wealthy citizen of Marseilles, and sister-in-law of Bernadotte, king of Sweden, bore him two daughters.

(3) **Louis** (1778–1846), third brother of Napoleon, fought in the army, becoming king of Holland in 1806 after his marriage with Hortense de Beauharnais, Napoleon's stepdaughter. The war between the Dutch and the French led to his abdication (1810). He wrote some unimportant literary works. One of his sons, **Louis Napoleon**, became the emperor Napoleon III (q.v.). See *Mémoires* (trans. 1928) of his wife, Life of his wife by Wright (1963), and article on MORNY.

(4) **Lucien** (1775–1840), prince of Canino, and a younger brother of Napoleon, was born at Ajaccio, and was educated at Autun, Brienne, and Aix. In 1798 he was made a member of the Council of Five Hundred, and just before the 18th Brumaire he was elected its president. He was successful as minister of the interior; and as ambassador to Madrid (1800) undermined British influence. On condition that he would divorce his second wife (the widow of a stockbroker) the crowns of Italy and Spain were offered him; but he refused them, and lived on his estate of Canino, in the States of the Church, being created by the pope Prince of Canino. He had never wholly shaken off his early strong republicanism; and having denounced the arrogant policy of his brother towards the court of Rome, he was 'advised' to leave Roman territory, and in 1810, on his way to America, was captured by the English and kept a prisoner at Ludlow and Thorngrove, Worcestershire, till 1814. He returned to Italy and published his memoirs (Jung 1882–1883). One of his sons, **Charles** (1803–57), won a European reputation as a botanist. A second, **Louis Lucien** (1813–91), philologist, born at Thorngrove, was granted a civil list pension for his 222 linguistic works in 1883; and the third, **Pierre** (1815–81), became notorious for killing Victor Noir, a journalist, in a duel.

BONAR, Horatius, D.D., *bo'nahr* (1808–89), born in Edinburgh, minister at Kelso (1837–1866) and at Edinburgh. Wrote well-known hymns—' I lay my sins on Jesus ', ' I heard the voice of Jesus say ', &c.

BONAVENTURE, or **Bonaventura, St,** originally **John of Fidanza** (1221–74), was born near Orvieto, Tuscany. In 1243 he became a Franciscan, in 1253 a teacher at Paris, in 1256 general of his order, and in 1273 Cardinal Bishop of Albano. During the Council of Lyons he died, July 14, 1274, from sheer ascetic exhaustion. In 1482 he was canonized by Sixtus IV, and in 1587 was ranked by Sixtus V as the sixth of the great doctors of the church. His religious fervour procured for him the title of ' Doctor Seraphicus ', and his mysticism attracted Luther, though he promoted Mariolatry, celibacy, and a high view of transubstantiation. His most important works are the *Breviloquium* (a dogmatic); the *Itinerarium Mentis in Deum*, *De Reductione Artium ad Theologiam*, a commentary on Peter Lombard; and his *Biblia Pauperum*, or 'Poor Man's Bible'. See his works (8 vols. Rome, 1588–96; new ed. Freiburg, 1882–92), and books about him by Richard (1873), Da Vicenza (1874), Prosper (1886), and Gilson (tr. 1938).

BONCHAMP, Charles, Marquis de, *bŏ-shã* (1760–93), French soldier, born at the château of Jouverteil in Anjou, fought in the American War of Independence, and after the French Revolution, a Vendean leader, was killed at the battle of Cholet on October 19.

BOND, William Cranch (1789–1859), American astronomer, born at Portland, Maine, from 1840 director of Harvard University observatory, a pioneer of celestial photography. His son, **George Philips** (1825–65) succeeded him. Together (and simultaneously with Lassell) they discovered Hyperion, the seventh satellite of Saturn.

BONDFIELD, Margaret Grace (1873–1953), British Labour politician and trade unionist, was born in Somerset, became chairman of the T.U.C. in 1923 and as minister of labour (1929–31) was the first woman to be a British cabinet minister. She was made C.H. in 1948.

BONDI, Clemente, *bon'dee* (1742–1821), Italian Jesuit and poet, quarrelled with his order and fled to Austria. He wrote love poems and satires.

BONE, (1) Henry (1755–1834), English enamel painter, was born at Truro, in London enamelled watches and fans, and made enamel portraits, brooches, &c. In 1801 he became enamel painter to George III. Elected R.A. in 1811, he exhibited his large enamel, *Bacchus and Ariadne*, after Titian. His son, **Henry Pierce** (1779–1855), was also an enamel painter.

(2) **Sir Muirhead** (1876–1953), Scottish painter, father of (3), born in Glasgow, trained at the School of Art there and went to London in 1899 and exhibited at the New English Art Club and the Royal Academy. His etchings, drawings, and paintings combine a meticulous realism with a strong sense of composition. He was an official artist on land and sea in both world wars, his *View of St Paul's* being one of the most striking records of war devastation in London. His most important collection of drawings and watercolours is *Old Spain* (1936). He was knighted in 1937.

(3) **Stephen** (1904–58), British artist, critic, and illustrator, son of (2), was born in Chiswick, London, and educated at Bedales and the Slade School of Art. He married a fellow-student, **Mary Adshead** (1904–), with whom he collaborated in a delightful children's book *The Little Boy and his House* (1936). He executed a mural scheme for the Piccadilly underground station (1928). He was naval artist (1943–45) and the *Manchester Guardian* art critic from 1948.

BONER, Ulrich, one of the oldest Swiss fabulists, was a preaching friar of Bern in 1324–49. His *Edelstein*, a collection of fables and jokes was one of the first German books printed.

BONGHI, Ruggero, *bong'gee* (1828–95), Italian conservative statesman, from 1870 professor of Ancient History at Rome, and author of an edition of Plato's works (1858), was born at Naples.

BONHAM-CARTER, Lady Violet, Baroness Asquith of Yarnbury (1887–1969), Liberal politician and publicist, daughter of H. H. Asquith (q.v.) by his first marriage. She married in 1915 Sir Maurice Bonham-Carter (d. 1960), scientist and civil servant. She was prominent in cultural and political movements, serving as president of the Liberal Party Organization in 1944–45 and as governor of the B.B.C. (1941–1946). She was created a life peeress in 1964, and published *Winston Churchill as I Knew Him* in 1965. Jo Grimond (q.v.) is her son-in-law. Her eldest son **Mark** (1922–), stood unsuccessfully as a Liberal in 1945 and 1964 and was Liberal M.P. for Torrington (1958-59). He became director of the Royal Opera House, Covent Garden (1958), and first chairman of the Race Relations Board (1966). He edited Margot Asquith's *Autobiography* (1962).

BONHEUR, Rosa, *bon-œr* (1822–99), French animal painter, born at Bordeaux, studied under her father, **Raymond** (d. 1853) and in 1841 exhibited at the Salon. Her *Ploughing with Oxen* (1849) is in the Luxembourg, her famous *Horse Fair* (1853) in the N.Y. Gallery. See book by Laruelle (1885).

BONIFACE, St, *bon'i-fas* (c. 680–754), 'the Apostle of Germany', whose original name was Wynfrith, was born in Wessex (probably at Crediton in Devon). From childhood a Benedictine monk in Exeter, he taught in the monastery of Nursling near Romsey, was elected abbot (717). He declined this dignity in order to spread Christianity among the Frisians, but a war put an end to his immediate plans. He returned to Nursling, but set out again in 718 with a commission from Pope Gregory II to preach the gospel to all the tribes of Germany. He met with great success in Thuringia, Bavaria, Friesland, Hesse and Saxony, everywhere baptizing multitudes, and was consecrated bishop (723), archbishop and primate of Germany (732). He founded many bishoprics. His chief life work was bringing everything in the Frankish kingdom into accordance with Roman Catholic order and suppressing the irregularities of Irish or Columban Christianity. In 747 Mainz became his primatial seat; but in 754 he resigned the archbishopric, and had resumed his missionary work among the Frisians, when he was killed at Dokkum, near Leeuwarden, by heathens, June 5, 754. See his correspondence (trans. 1940) and earliest Life by Willibald included in Levison, *Vitae* (1905), trans. 1916, also works by Müller (1870), Browne (1910), and F. M. Stenton, *Anglo-Saxon England* (1943).

BONIFACE, the name of nine popes, of which two are noteworthy:

Boniface VIII, real name **Benedetto Gaetani,** pope (1294–1303), a noble of Anagni. His tenure of the Roman see was marked by the most strenuous assertion of papal authority, in the bull *Unam Sanctam* of 1302 he claimed supreme power in temporal and spiritual affairs. He failed, however, to assert a feudal superiority over Sicily, and sought without success to call Edward I of England to account. Philip the Fair of France, supported by his states and clergy, maintained the independence of his kingdom; disregarded many bulls and briefs, and even excommunication; and, with the aid of Italian enemies of Boniface, took him prisoner at Anagni. Boniface died at Rome soon afterwards in 1303. For his simony Dante placed him in the *Inferno*. See Life by Boase (1933).

Boniface IX, real name **Pietro Tomacelli**, pope (1389–1404), was chosen to succeed Urban VI in opposition to the Avignonese Clement VII. He was notoriously inexperienced in papal administration but acquired despotic power in Rome.

BONILLA, Manuel, *bo-neel'ya* (1849–1913), Honduran politician and revolutionary, born in Jutacalpa. He was twice president of Honduras (1903–07 and 1911–13), on each occasion his presidency being achieved by revolt against the holder of the office.

BONINGTON, Richard Parkes (1802–28), English painter, was born near Nottingham. About 1817 his family moved to Calais, and there and at Paris he studied art and began a friendship with Delacroix, who introduced Bonington to oriental art, while the latter showed Delacroix his watercolour techniques. Bonington's first works were exhibited in the Salon in 1822, mostly sketches of Le Havre and Lillebonne. He also began to work in lithography, illustrating Baron Taylor's *Voyages*. From 1824 he experimented increasingly in romantic subjects taken from history, and studied armour. His best-known works followed: *Francis I and Marguerite of Navarre*, *Henry IV receiving the Spanish Ambassador*, *Entrance to the Grand Canal*, and *Ducal Palace*. His work forms an important link between French and English art. He excelled in light effects achieved by the use of a large expanse of sky, broad areas of pure colour and the silhouetting of dark and light masses, as well as his rich colouring of heavy draperies and brocades. After a sunstroke, he fell seriously ill and died in London. See monographs by G. S. Sandilands (1929) and Hon. A. Shirley (1940).

BONIVARD, François de, *bo-nee-vahr* (1493–1570), Swiss divine and politician, prior of the abbey of St Victor, opposed the Duke of Savoy. His imprisonment in the dungeons of Chillon castle (1532–36) was celebrated in many popular folksongs and in Byron's legendary poem, *Prisoner of Chillon*. A convert to the protestant faith, Bonivard, after his liberation by the Bernese, wrote an important *Chronicle*, amended by Calvin. See Lives by Berghoff (1923) and Bressier (1944).

BONNARD, *bo-nahr*, (1) **Abel** (1883–1968), French poet, novelist, essayist, was born at Poitiers in 1883, and won the national poetry prize with his first collection of poems, *Les Familiers* (1906). He took up the psychological novel with *La Vie et l'amour* (1913). An Academician since 1932, he was minister of education in the Vichy government (1942–45). He was exiled to Spain in 1945, returned to France (1958) and was banished (1960).

(2) **Pierre** (1867–1947), French painter and lithographer, was born in Paris and trained at the Académie Julien. He joined the group called 'Les Nabis', which included Denis and Vuillard, with whom he formed the Intimiste group. His style was formed under the influence of impressionism, Japanese prints and the works of Gauguin and Toulouse-Lautrec. Ignoring the movements towards abstraction, he continued to paint interiors and landscapes, in which everything is subordinated to the subtlest rendering of light and colour effects. See Life by Vaillant (1966) and book by A. Fermigier (1970).

BONNAT, Léon Joseph Florentin, *bon-nah* (1833–1922), French painter, born at Bayonne, was well-known as a painter of religious pictures, such as his *Adam and Eve finding the Body of Abel* (1860), and as a portrait painter of Hugo, Pasteur, Dumas, &c.

BONNER, Edmund (*c.* 1500–69) Bishop of London. The reputation he gained at Oxford recommended him to Wolsey, who made him his chaplain. His zeal in King Henry's service after Wolsey's fall earned him due promotion; and in 1533 he was deputed to appear before the pope at Marseilles, to appeal to a general council. His language on this occasion is said to have suggested to His Holiness the fitness of having him burned alive, or thrown into a caldron of molten lead, so that Bonner judged it prudent to depart. In 1540 he was made Bishop of London, and as such pronounced sentence on several Protestant martyrs, though it is certain he did his best to befriend Anne Askew. After Edward VI's accession, he gave proofs of his lukewarmness in the cause of reformation, and at length, in 1549, was committed to the Marshalsea, and deprived of his bishopric. The accession of Queen Mary (1553) restored him to office; and his part in the persecutions of the Protestants made him thoroughly unpopular. On Elizabeth's accession (1558), Bonner accompanied his episcopal brethren to salute her at Highgate, but was excepted from the honour of kissing her hand. In May 1559 he refused the oath of supremacy, so was deposed and again imprisoned in the Marshalsea, where he died.

BONNET, *bon-nay*, (1) **Charles** (1720–93), Swiss naturalist and philosopher, born at Geneva, distinguished himself by researches on parthenogenesis, polypi, the tapeworm, the respiration of insects, the use of leaves, &c. Failing sight made him abandon his experiments and turn to philosophy. He was critical of vitalistic theories and pointed out that the nonexistence of the soul can never be proved. He held a catastrophic theory of evolution. See studies by J. Trembley (1794), A. Lemoine (1850), de Caraman (1859), and E. Claparède (1909).

(2) **Georges** (1889–1973), French politician, born at Basillac in Dordogne, was elected to the Assembly in 1924, became ambassador to the United States in 1937, and was foreign minister at the time of the Munich crisis of 1938.

BONNEVAL, Claude Alexandre, Comte de, *bon-vahl* (1675–1747), French adventurer, served with distinction in Italy and the Netherlands, but for extortion and insolence was condemned to death by a court martial. Fleeing to Austria, he fought against his native country, and performed daring exploits under Prince Eugene in the war against Turkey. As master-general of ordnance in the Netherlands, he quarrelled with the governor, and was again condemned to death by a court martial. His sentence commuted, he went to Constantinople, became a Mohammedan, and achieved success as general in the war of the Porte with Russia, and in Persia, but was ultimately banished. See works by the Prince de Ligny (1817) and Vandal (1885).

BONNEVILLE, Nicholas de, *bon-veel* (1760–1828), French writer, appointed president of a Paris district during the French Revolution (1789). A student of English and German literature, he translated Shakespeare, founded several newspapers, and wrote a history of modern Europe (1792).

BONNEY, William H., ' Billy the Kid' (1859–81), American bandit, born in New York, achieved legendary notoriety for his hold-ups and robberies in the southwestern states.

BONNIVARD. See BONIVARD.

BONO, Emilio de (1866–1944), Italian general and Fascist politician, born at Cassano d'Adda, was in 1922 a quadrumvir of the Fascist ' March on Rome ', was made governor of Tripolitania in 1925, colonial minister in 1929, and was commander-in-chief at the commencement of hostilities against Abyssinia in 1935. In 1943 he opposed Mussolini in the Fascist Grand Council, and in 1944 was executed for treason.

BONOMI, Joseph, *bo-nō'mee* (1739–1806), Italian architect, was born at Rome, and settled in England in 1767. He revived Greek renaissance style. His son, **Joseph** (1796–1878), illustrated important works by Egyptologists, and wrote on Nineveh. He was curator of Soane's Museum.

BONONCINI, or Buononcini, Giovanni Maria, *bō-non-chee'nee* (1642–78), Italian composer, born near Modena, where in 1671 he became a violinist in the court orchestra, and subsequently chapelmaster of the cathedral. Between 1666 and his death he published a great quantity of chamber and vocal music, together with a treatise, the *Musico prattico,* which was influential in its day. His sons **Giovanni Battista** (1670–1755) and **Marc Antonio** (1675–1726) were notable composers, the former specially remembered for his rivalry with Handel.

BONPLAND, Aimé, *bō-plã* (1773–1858), French botanist, born at Rochelle, travelled with Humboldt in South America (1799–1804) and collected and described 6000 new species of plants. Named professor of Natural History at Buenos Aires in 1816, he undertook a journey up the Paraná; but Francia, dictator of Paraguay, arrested him, and kept him prisoner for nine years. See Life by Brunel (3rd ed. Paris 1872).

BONSTETTEN, Karl Victor von (1745–1832), Swiss statesman, who studied at Leyden, Cambridge, and Paris, lived much in Italy and at Copenhagen, and wrote books of travel, letters, a work on the imagination, &c.

BONVALOT, Pierre Gabriel, *bō-va-lō* (1853–1933), French explorer, was born at Épagne (Aube), travelled extensively in Central Asia.

BOOLE, George (1815–64), English mathematician and logician, born at Lincoln, where he started a school before becoming professor of Mathematics at Cork in 1849. He did important work on the mathematical theories of analytic transformations, of differential equations, &c., but is primarily known by his *Mathematical Analysis of Logic* (1847) and *Laws of Thought* (1854). In these he employed mathematical symbolism to express logical processes, thus being an outstanding pioneer of modern symbolic logic, greatly influencing the subsequent work of Frege and Bertrand Russell among others. He was awarded the Royal Medal by the Royal Society in 1844 and was elected fellow in 1857. His wife, **Mary Everest** (d. 1916), was a niece of Sir George Everest (q.v.). The youngest of their five daughters, **Ethel Lillian,** achieved fame under her married name, **E. L. Voynich,** as a writer of popular period novels, including *The Gadfly* (1897), set against the romantic background of the Young Italy movement. See study by Cobham (1951).

BOONE, Daniel (1735–1820), American pioneer, born in Pennsylvania, went to Kentucky, and from 1769 lived in the forest and explored much of the country with his brother. He was twice captured by Indians, and repeatedly repelled (1775–78) Indian attacks on a stockade fort, which he had erected, now Boonesboro. See Lives by Addington Bruce (1910) and Gulliver (1916).

BOORDE, or Borde, Andrew (*c.* 1490–1549), Carthusian monk, born near Cuckfield, who from 1527 studied medicine at Orleans, Toulouse, Montpellier, and Wittenberg, visited Rome and Compostela, and for Thomas Cromwell carried through a confidential mission in France and Spain. He practised medicine in Glasgow (1536), travelled through Europe to Jerusalem, and died in the Fleet prison in London. Boorde's chief works are his *Dyetary* and the *Fyrst Boke of the Introduction of Knowledge,* which contains the first known specimen of gypsy language, and the *Itinerary of England* (1735).

BOOS, Martin, *bōz* (1762–1825), a Bavarian Catholic priest, the founder about 1790 of a religious movement closely akin to that of the Protestant Pietists, Bitterly persecuted, he accepted in 1817 an appointment at Düsseldorf, and died near Neuwied.

BOOT, Sir Jesse, 1st Baron Trent (1850–1931), British drug manufacturer, was born in Nottingham. At thirteen, he inherited his father's herbalist's shop and studied pharmacy in his leisure hours. In 1877 he opened his first chemist's shop in Nottingham. In 1883 he controlled ten branches, and by mass selling at reduced prices introduced the modern chain store. In 1892 he began large-scale drug manufacture and soon after the turn of the century he was controlling the largest pharmaceutical retail trade in the world, which numbered more than a thousand branches in 1931. He was raised to the peerage in 1929. His benefactions to Nottingham totalled £2,000,000. See Cecil Roberts, *Achievement* (1950).

BOOTH, (1) **Barton** (1681–1733), English actor, the son of a Lancashire squire, was educated at Westminster, but, turning actor, played with success for two seasons at Dublin, and in 1700 appeared in Betterton's company in London. His performance of Cato in Addison's tragedy in 1713 brought him wealth and fame.

(2) **Charles** (1840–1916), English shipowner, statistician, and social reformer, born at Liverpool, joined his brother Alfred in founding the Booth Steamship Company and the allied leather factories of Alfred Booth & Co. An ardent radical in his youth, he settled in London in 1875 and devoted 18 years to the preparation of his great *Life and Labour of the People in London* (1903), the prototype of the modern social survey, based on organized on-the-spot investigation. He also wrote on social questions. He became president of the Royal Statistical Society (1892–94), served on several commissions, was made privy councillor (1904), F.R.S., and received many honorary degrees. See *Life* by T. S. and M. B. Simey (1960).

(3) **Edwin Thomas** (1833–93), American actor, son of (6), born in Harford county, Maryland, played Tressel at the age of 16 to his father's Richard III and rose to the top of his profession, visiting England (1861–1862), and in 1864 produced *Hamlet* in New York for a record run. Ruined by opening a theatre in New York in 1869, he was able to settle his debts by 1877. He visited Germany and Britain (1880–82) and played Othello to Henry Irving's Iago. See *Lives* by Winter (1893), Grossman (1894), and Lockridge (1932).

(4) **Sir Felix** (1775–1850), London distiller, who contributed £17,000 for Ross's Arctic expedition (1829–33), and after whom the Boothia Felix peninsula was named. He was made a baronet in 1835.

(5) **John Wilkes** (1839–65), American assassin, son of (6), was born at Baltimore and was an unsuccessful actor. In 1865 he entered into a conspiracy to avenge the defeat of the Confederates and shot President Lincoln (q.v.) at Ford's Theatre, Washington, on April 14. He broke his leg, managed to escape to Virginia, but was tracked on April 26, and, refusing to surrender, was shot. See works by Stern (1939) and Bryan (1940).

(6) **Junius Brutus** (1796–1852), English actor, father of (3) and (5), was born in London, went on the stage at 17, and achieved fame as Richard III at Covent Garden. In 1821 he emigrated to the United States, where for thirty years he was famous in spite of his eccentricity, even insanity, aggravated by his drunkenness.

(7) **William** (1829–1912), English founder and 'general' of the Salvation Army, born at Nottingham, was minister of the Methodist New Connexion (1855–61), but the foundation of the Salvation Army on military lines began in 1865 with mission work in London's East End. He was the mainspring of the Army, so named in 1878, and directed its growth at home and abroad. See his *Darkest England* (1890) and *Lives* by Railton (1912), Begbie (1920), and St John Ervine (1934). His wife, **Catherine** (1829–90), was fully associated with him. See *Life* by Booth-Tucker (1892). His son **Bramwell** (1856–1929) and his daughter **Evangeline** (1865–1950) succeeded him. See study by P. W. Wilson (1940).

BOOTHBY, (1) **Guy Newell** (1867–1905), novelist, born in Adelaide, Australia, but long resident in England, wrote over fifty novels, many on Australian life. His 'Dr Nikola' novels were particularly successful.

(2) **Sir Robert John Graham, 1st Baron Boothby of Buchan and Rattray Head** (1900–), Scots Conservative politician, was educated at Eton and Oxford. In 1924 he was elected M.P. for East Aberdeenshire, the seat he held until 1958. 'Discovered' in 1926 by Winston Churchill, he became his parliamentary private secretary till 1929. From 1940 to 1941 he was parliamentary secretary to the ministry of food and later served in the R.A.F. He became in 1948 an original member of the Council of United Europe and was a British delegate to its Consultative Assembly (1949–54). He was made an officer of the Legion of Honour in 1950, was knighted in 1953, and raised to the peerage in 1958. He has been an outstanding commentator on public affairs on radio and TV. He brought to political argument a refreshing candour, a robust independence and a talent for exposing the easy hypocrisies of public life. See his *The New Economy* (1943), *I Fight To Live* (1947) and *My Yesterday, Your Tomorrow* (1962).

BOOTHE, Clare (1903–), American authoress, born in New York, was on the editorial staff of *Vogue* and other periodicals, wrote *European Spring* &c., but was most successful with her plays, which include *The Women* (1936) and *Kiss the Boys Goodbye* (1938). She was elected to the House of Representatives as a Republican in 1942, and was U.S. ambassador to Italy (1953-57). She married (1935) Henry Robinson Luce (q.v.).

BOPP, Franz (1791–1867), German philologist, born at Mainz, studied oriental languages, and at Paris wrote *The Conjugation of the Sanskrit Verb* (1816), in which he showed the common origin of the Indo-European languages. His great work is *A Comparative Grammar of Sanskrit, Zend, Greek, Latin, Lithuanian, Old Slavonic, Gothic, and German* (6 vols. 1833–52; trans. by Eastwick).

BÓR. See KOMOROWSKI.

BORA, Katharina von (1499–1552), having adopted Lutheran doctrines, ran away from the Cistercian convent of Nimptschen, near Grimma, in 1523, and married Luther in 1525.

BORAH, William Edgar (1865–1940), American senator, advocated disarmament but opposed the entry of the U.S.A. into the League of Nations.

BORCHGREVINK, Carsten Egeberg, *bor*KH'-*gra-vink* (1864–1934), Norwegian explorer, born at Oslo, emigrated to Australia, was the first to set foot on the Antarctic continent (1894), and first to winter there (1898–99).

BORDA, Jean Charles de (1733–99), French mathematician and astronomer, born at Dax, helped to measure the arc of the meridian and to establish the metric system.

BORDE, Andrew. See BOORDE.

BORDEAUX, Henry, *bor-dō* (1870–1963), French novelist and Academician (elected 1919), born in 1870 at Thonon, studied law before he took to writing novels, concerned with the defence of family life, often with a Savoy background, such as *La Peur de vivre* (1902), *Les Roquevillard* (1906), *La Maison* (1913), &c. See study by Ligot (Paris 1925).

BORDEN, Sir Robert Laird, G.C.M.G. (1854–1937), Canadian statesman, born at Grand Pré, Nova Scotia, practised as barrister, became leader of the Conservative party in 1901, in 1911 overthrew Laurier's ministry on reciprocity with the U.S.A., and was prime minister of the Dominion till 1920. He organized Canada for war, and was the first overseas premier to attend a Cabinet meeting in London (1915).

BORDET, Jules, *bor-day* (1870–1961), Belgian physiologist, born at Soignies, Nobel prize winner (1919), was an authority on sera, discovered *alexine* and the microbe of whooping cough.

BORDONE, Paris, *bor-dō'nay* (1500–71), Italian painter of the Venetian school, was born at Treviso and worked there, in Vicenza, Venice, and Paris. He was strongly influenced by his greater contemporary, Titian, his most celebrated work being the *Fisherman presenting the Ring of St Mark to the Doge,* in the Venice Accademia.

BORELLI, Gian Alfonzo, *bor-el'lee* (1608–79), Italian mathematician and physiologist, was born at Naples, where he held a professorship as well as at Pisa and Messina. He founded the iatrophysical school of medicine, which sought to explain all bodily functions by physical laws.

BORENIUS, Tancred (1885–1948), Finnish art historian, professor of the History of Art at University College, London, from 1922, is known for his writings on Italian and early English painting.

BORGHESE, *bor-gay'zay,* a great family of Siena, afterwards at Rome.—**Camillo Borghese** ascended the papal throne in 1605 as Paul V. A marriage with an heiress of the house of Aldobrandini brought the Borghese family into the possession of great wealth.—**Prince Camillo Filippo Ludovico Borghese** (1775–1832) joined the French army, in 1803 married Pauline, Napoleon's sister, and became governor-general of Piedmont. He sold the Borghese collection of art treasures to Napoleon for 13,000,000 francs, receiving in part-payment the Piedmontese national domains; when these were reclaimed by the king of Sardinia in 1815, he received back part of the collection. The Borghese Palace still contains one of the finest collections of paintings in Rome, though some of its treasures were sold in 1892–93. See J. H. Douglas, *The Principal Noble Families of Rome* (1905).

BORGIA, *bor'jah,* the Italian form of **Borja,** the name of an ancient family in the Spanish province of Valencia. Alfonso de Borja (1378–1458), bishop, accompanied Alfonso of Aragon to Naples, and was chosen pope as Calixtus III. Rodrigo de Borja (1431–1503), his nephew, ascended the papal throne in 1492 as Alexander VI (q.v.). Before this he had had a number of children by a Roman girl,

Giovanna Catanei, known as Vanozza. Two of these children became especially notorious.

(1) **Cesare** (1476–1507), ambitious and energetic, was a brilliant general and administrator. At seventeen a cardinal, he was suspected, perhaps rightly, of procuring the assassination of his elder brother, whom he shortly after succeeded as captain-general of the Church, for which post he readily doffed the purple. He married Princess Charlotte d'Albret, sister of the king of Navarre (1499), and in two successive campaigns made himself master of Romagna, Perugia, Siena, Piombino, and Urbino; he went so far as to threaten Florence itself, and was planning the reconstruction of a kingdom of Central Italy with himself at its head. He was menacing Bologna when, on the eve of his departure for his third campaign, both he and his father were taken seriously ill at a farewell banquet given by the Cardinal of Corneto. There was talk of poison. Cesare survived, but his father died and his enemies now rallied. The succession to the papacy of Julius II, his bitterest enemy, after Pius's brief reign of twenty-seven days, was fatal to him. Cesare surrendered at Naples, under the promise of a safe conduct; but Gonsalvo di Cordova broke his oath, and (1504) had him carried to Valencia. In 1506, however, he made his escape to the court of Navarre, took command of the royal forces against the rebellious constable of Navarre, and fell at the siege of the citadel of Viana, March 12, 1507. Despite attempts to rehabilitate it, his memory remains in execration. Yet amongst the peoples whom he governed he left the reputation of a just prince, upright and severe. He encouraged art, and was the friend of Pinturicchio, and the protector of Leonardo da Vinci. See Lives by Garner (1912), Sabatini (1912), and Woodward (1913).

(2) **Lucrezia** (1480–1519), born in Rome, married Sforza, Lord of Pesaro (June 1493); but her father annulled this marriage (1497), and gave her (1498) to a nephew of the king of Naples. Father and brother having secured the assassination of the new husband (1500), Lucrezia now became the wife of Alfonso, son of the Duke of Este, who inherited the duchy of Ferrara. Lucrezia has been represented as outside the pale of humanity by her wantonness, vices, and crimes; and as a too pliant instrument in the hands of Alexander or of Cesare Borgia. She died, enjoying the respect of her subjects, a generous patroness of learning and of art, besung by Ariosto and other poets. See Life by Gregorovius (1874, trans. 1903); Fyvie, *Story of the Borgias* (1912), Portigliotti, *The Borgias* (trans. 1928), and books by N. Balchin (1948), Collison-Morley (1932), Bellonei (1939), Pepe (1946), and Dubreton (1954).

BORGLUM, (John) Gutzon (de la Mothe) (1867–1941), American sculptor, born in Idaho of Danish descent, won renown for works of colossal proportions, such as the famous Mount Rushmore National Memorial portraying Washington, Lincoln, Jefferson, and Theodore Roosevelt, hewn out of the solid rock of the mountainside. His brother **Solon Hannibal** (1868–1922) also won fame as a sculptor, especially of horses and 'wild west' subjects. See studies by C. H. Caffin (1913) and A. Adams (1929).

BORGOGNONE, Ambrogio, *bor-gon-yō'nay* (*c.* 1445–1523), Milanese painter whose work is characterized by a graceful treatment conveying a feeling of genuine piety. *Virgin Crowned* in the Brera Gallery in Milan and the frescoes at the Certosa di Pavia are good examples of his work. See Pater's *Miscellanies* (1895).

BORIS GODUNOV. See GODUNOV.

BORLASE, William (1695–1772), Cornish antiquary, was for fifty years rector at Ludgvan. He published *The Antiquities of Cornwall* (1754), &c.

BORMANN, Martin (1900–?45), German Nazi politician, born at Halberstadt, one of Hitler's closest advisers, became *Reichsminister* (1941) after Hess's flight to Scotland and was with Hitler to the last. His own fate is uncertain, but he was possibly killed by Russian snipers in the mass breakout by Hitler's staff from the Chancellory (May 1, 1945). He was sentenced to death *in absentia* by the Nuremberg Court (1946).

BORN, (1) Bertrand de (*c.* 1140–*c.* 1215), French troubadour, born in Périgord, played a conspicuous part in the struggles of the English king Henry II and his sons, and died a monk at Dalon, near Limoges. See study by C. Appel (1931).

(2) **Max** (1882–1970), German physicist, born at Breslau (Wrocław). Professor of Theoretical Physics at Göttingen (1921–33), lecturer at Cambridge (1933–36), professor of Natural Philosophy at Edinburgh (1936–1953), he shared the 1954 Nobel prize with Walther Bothe (q.v.) for work in the field of quantum physics.

BÖRNE, Ludwig, *bœr'nè* (1786–1837), German political writer and satirist, born at Frankfurt of Jewish descent, baptized in 1818, edited various journals (1812–21), establishing his reputation as a vigorous opponent of the Prussian government, and inciting the German people to revolution and social reform. The French Revolution of July 1830 drew him to Paris, where he finally settled in 1832, and died of consumption. He and Heine became bitterly hostile to each other. See his *Briefe aus Paris* and his Life by Gutzkow (1840), and other works by Gervinus (1838), Beurmann (1841), and Holzmann (1888).

BORODIN, Alexander Porphyrevich, *bo-ro-dyeen'* (1833–87), Russian composer and scientist, an illegitimate son of Prince Gedeanov, who registered him as the child of a serf. Although Borodin showed a precocious aptitude for music, beginning to compose at the age of nine, he was trained for medicine and distinguished himself as a chemist. His first systematic musical studies were undertaken in 1862, under Balakirev, who conducted his First Symphony in 1869. From 1872 onwards, Borodin lectured on Chemistry at the St Petersburg School of Medicine for Women. His compositions include the unfinished opera, *Prince Igor*, three symphonies, the last of which was also left unfinished, and the symphonic sketch, *In the Steppes of Central Asia*. See study by G. E. H. Abraham (1927).

BOROUGH, (1) Steven (1525–84), English navigator, born at Northam, Devon, captained a vessel on the first voyage to northern Russia via North·Cape in 1553, and became chief pilot to the newly founded Muscovy Company. He discovered the entrance to the Kara Sea.

(2) **William** (1536–99), younger brother of (1), was also an expert navigator of Russian waters, drew up charts of the northern ocean (1560) and the north Atlantic (1576). He was vice-admiral in Drake's Cadiz adventure and commanded a ship against the Armada. See Hakluyt's *Navigations*.

BORROMEO, St Carlo, *bor-ro-may'o* (1538–1584), cardinal and Archbishop of Milan, canonized in 1610, was born in 1538 at his father's castle of Arona, on the Lago Maggiore. He did much to bring the Council of Trent to a successful conclusion, and had the principal part in drawing up the famous *Catechismus Romanus*. He was renowned for his determined efforts to maintain ecclesiastical discipline and for his poor relief during the famine of 1570 and the plague of 1576. He founded in 1570 the Helvetic College at Milan; and he brought about an alliance of the seven Swiss Catholic cantons for the defence of the faith. See Lives by Sailer, Dieringer, Sala (Milan 1857–59), Giussano (Eng. trans. 1884), and E. H. Thompson (1893). His nephew, Count **Frederico Borromeo** (1564–1631), from 1595 Archbishop of Milan, founded the Ambrosian Library.

BORROMINI, Francesco, *bor-rō-mee'nee* (1599–1667), Italian architect, was the chief representative of the baroque style. See study by E. Hempel (Vienna 1924).

BORROW, George Henry (1803–81), English author, was born at East Dereham, Norfolk. His father, a captain of militia, during the Napoleonic war moved about with his regiment to Scotland, Ireland, and many parts of England, then settled at Norwich, where young Borrow attended the grammar school (1816–18), and for the next five years was articled to a firm of solicitors. Already he deserved his Romany title 'Lavengro' ('wordmaster'), having picked up a knowledge of Irish, French, German and Danish (these two under 'Taylor of Norwich'), Welsh, Latin, Greek, even of Romany, the language of that strange race of which he was almost an adopted member. On his father's death in 1824 he came up to London to seek his fortune, and fared ill as hack writer to Sir Richard Phillips the publisher. From 1825 to 1832 he wandered in England, sometimes in Gypsy company as described in *Lavengro* and *The Romany Rye* in which autobiography and fiction overlap, and was nearly poisoned by a Romany beldame, fought and vanquished the Flaming Tinman, with Isopel Berners tented in Mumper's Dingle, and met with other accidents. Next, as agent of the Bible Society he visited St Petersburg (1833–35), Portugal, Spain, and Morocco (1835–39). In 1840 he married a well-to-do widow, and settled down on a small estate of hers at Oulton, near Lowestoft, where, after travels in southeastern Europe (1844), a tour in Wales (1854), and a residence of some years in London, he ended his days a lonely man, sensitive to criticism, brusque of speech, and yet a giant in strength and stature. Among his chief works are *The Zincali, or Gypsies of Spain* (1840); *The Bible in Spain* (1843), which was an instant success; *Lavengro* (1851); its sequel, *The Romany Rye* (1857); *Wild Wales* (1862); and *Romano Lavo-Lil, or Word-book of the English-Gypsy Language* (1874), written unsuccessfully to forestall a similar work by Charles Godfrey Leland. All but the first and last are autobiographical. His *Letters to the British and Foreign Bible Society* appeared in 1911, his *Welsh Poems* in 1915. See Watts-Dunton's *Old Familiar Faces* (1916); Lives by Knapp (1899), Jenkins (1912), Thomas (1912), C. K. Shorter (1920), who edited the complete works (16 vols. 1924), Stephen (1927), and Elam (1929).

BOSANQUET, Bernard, *bōz'an-ket* (1848–1923), English idealist philosopher, born at Rock Hall, near Alnwick, was lecturer at University College, Oxford (1871–81), professor at St Andrews (1903–08), and wrote on most philosophical topics. Hegelian in inspiration, he rejected Hegel's ' objective logic ', but was less extreme and rigorous than Bradley. His best works are *Implication and Linear Inference* (1920) and the *Three Lectures on Aesthetic* (1915), a masterly critique of Croce's theory. His wife, Helen **Dendy** (1860–1925), wrote on poor law and social subjects, and a Life (1924) of her husband.

BOSCÁN-ALMOGAVER, Juan, *bos-kahn' al-mō-ga-vayr'* (c. 1495–1542), Spanish poet, a native of Barcelona, said to have introduced the Italian school of poetry into Spain.

BOSCAWEN, Edward (1711–61), English admiral, known as ' Old Dreadnought ', was the third son of Viscount Falmouth. He highly distinguished himself at the taking of Porto Bello (1739) and at the siege of Cartagena (1741), and in command of the *Dreadnought*, in 1744, captured the French *Médée*, with 800 prisoners. He had an important share in the victory off Cape Finisterre (May 3, 1747), where he was wounded in the shoulder; and in command of the East Indian expedition displayed high military skill in the retreat from Pondicherry. He returned in 1750. In 1755 he intercepted the French fleet off Newfoundland, capturing two 64-gun ships and 1500 men; in 1758, now admiral of the blue, he was appointed commander-in-chief of the successful expedition against Cape Breton. Boscawen crowned his career by his signal victory over the French Toulon fleet in Lagos Bay, August 18, 1759. He received the thanks of parliament, a pension of £3000 a year, a seat in the privy council, and the command of the marines.

BOSCH, (1) Carl (1874–1940), German chemist, born in Cologne, brother-in-law of Haber (q.v.), became president of the I. G. Farben Industrie, shared a Nobel prize with Bergius 1931 for his part in the invention and development of chemical high pressure methods, e.g., the ' Bosch process ', by which hydrogen is obtained from water gas and superheated steam.

(2) or **van Aken, Hieronymus** (c. 1460–

1516), Dutch painter, born at Hertogenbosch. He was a pupil of Ouwater, and is noted for the macabre devils, freaks, and monsters which appear in his works. One of his best-known pictures is the *Temptation of St Anthony* at Lisbon. He has had considerable influence on the surrealists, and this has led to a revival of interest in his work. See studies by Philip (1956), Combe (1957) and Liupert (1959), and detailed analyses of single pictures by W. Fränger, e.g., *The Millennium of Hieronymus Bosch* (1952).

BOSCOVICH, Roger Joseph, *bos'-* (1711–87), a Jesuit mathematician and astronomer, born at Ragusa, wrote on optics and astronomy and was elected F.R.S. in 1761. See *Life* by Gill (1941).

BOSE, *bōs*, (1) Sir Jagadis Chandra (1858–1937), Indian physicist and botanist, professor at Calcutta, known for his study of electric waves, their polarization and reflection, and for his experiments demonstrating the sensitivity and growth of plants.

(2) **Subhas Chandra** (1895–?1945), Indian Nationalist leader, president of the All-India Congress (resigned 1939), supported the Axis in the war and became c.-in-c. of the Japanese-sponsored Indian National Army. He was reported killed in Formosa (1945). See H. Toye, *The Springing Tiger* (1959).

BOSIO, François Joseph, Baron (1769–1845), French sculptor, was born at Monaco. For Napoleon he carved the bas-reliefs for the Column of the Place Vendôme in Paris, and he also sculpted the Quadriga of the Arc de Triomphe du Carrousel and other well-known Paris statues. He died director of the Academy of Fine Arts in Paris.

BOSSUET, Jacques Bénigne, *bos-way* (1627–1704), churchman, controversialist, France's greatest pulpit orator, was born at Dijon, and educated in the Jesuits' School there and at the Collège de Navarre in Paris. He received a canonry at Metz in 1652, and in 1661 preached before Louis XIV. His reputation as an orator spread over France, and he became the recognized chief of the devout party at court. In 1671 he entered the French Academy. For his pupil, the Dauphin, he is said to have written his *Discours sur l'histoire universelle* (1679); as Bishop of Meaux (1681) he took a leading part in the Gallican controversy, and wrote the *Doctrine de l'Église catholique*. He attacked with excessive violence the mysticism of Fénelon. His greatest works are the *Histoire Universelle*, regarded by many as the first attempt at a philosophy of history; the *Oraisons funèbres*; and the *Histoire des variations des Églises protestantes* (1688). His *Politique tirée de l'écriture sainte* (1709) upholds the divine right of kings. See works by Mrs Lear (1881), Lanson (1890), Rébelliau (1900), Dimier (1916), and Sanders (1921).

BOSTON, Thomas (1676–1732), Scottish theologian, from 1707 until his death, minister of Ettrick, is remembered chiefly for his *Fourfold State* (1720), long recognized as a standard exposition of Calvinistic theology. *The Crook in the Lot* and his posthumous *Autobiography* were favourites with the Scottish country folk. See *Life* by A. Thomson (1895).

BOSWELL, (1) Alexander, 1st Bart. (1775–1822), Scottish songwriter and printer, son of (2), educated at Westminster and Oxford, set up at Auchinleck a private press, at which he printed many rare books in early English and Scottish literature, besides a volume of vigorous poems in the Ayrshire dialect (1803); in 1817 he contributed twelve songs to Thomson's *Select Collection*, of which ' Good night, and joy be wi' ye a' ', ' Jenny's Bawbee ', and ' Jenny dang the Weaver ' were very popular. He was created a baronet in 1821, and died March 27, of a wound received the day before in a duel with James Stuart of Dunearn, who had challenged him as the author of anonymous political pasquinades. His younger brother, James (1778–1822), edited the third *Variorum Shakespeare* (1821).

(2) James (1740–95), Scottish man-of-letters and biographer of Dr Johnson (q.v.), father of (1), was born October 18 in Edinburgh, the eldest son of a judge, Lord Auchinleck. He was educated at the Edinburgh High School and University, where he struck up a friendship with William Johnson Temple, to whom he later addressed many of his self-revelatory letters. He then studied civil law at Glasgow, but his true goal was literary fame and the friendship of great men. At eighteen he had begun to keep an astonishingly frank and self-probing journal. In spring 1760 he ran away to London and turned Catholic. To discourage such religious fervour, Lord Eglinton, a friend of Boswell's father in London, saw to it that Boswell became more of a libertine than ever and he reverted to his original faith. Young Boswell hobnobbed with the young Duke of York, with Sheridan's father, made plans to join the army, and skilfully resisted all attempts to lure him into matrimony. He first met Johnson on his second visit to London, on May 16, 1763, at Tom Davies's bookshop in Russell Street. By the following year they were on such cordial terms that Johnson accompanied him as far as Harwich. Boswell was on his way to Utrecht to continue his legal studies, but stayed only the winter and then toured Germany, France, Switzerland, and Italy. By an astounding process of literary gatecrashing he introduced himself to Voltaire and Rousseau. To the latter, for example, he had written: ' Open the door to a man who dares to assure you that he deserves to enter '. From Rousseau, he procured an introduction to Paoli (q.v.), hero of Corsica, whom he ' Boswellized ' in *Account of Corsica* (1768), which had an immediate success and was translated into several languages. Wherever Boswell went, he acquired temporary mistresses. There was the serious and high-minded affair with ' Zélide ' of Utrecht, with the Irish Mary Anne Montgomery, and with numerous others in London, Rome, and elsewhere, including the disreputable episode with Rousseau's Thérèse Le Vasseur. The great lover finally married in 1769 a cousin, Margaret Montgomerie, a prudent, amiable woman who bore with his shortcomings. He returned from the continent in 1766, was admitted advocate, in 1773 was elected to Johnson's famous literary club, and took the great doctor on the memorable journey to the Hebrides. A major literary enterprise (1777–83) was a series of seventy monthly contributions to the *London Magazine* under the pseudonym ' The Hypochondriak '. After Johnson's death appeared *The Journal of the Tour of the Hebrides* (1785). Its great success made Boswell plan his acknowledged masterpiece the *Life of Samuel Johnson* (1891), of which *The Journal* served as a first instalment. On Croker's calculation he had met Johnson on 276 occasions. Meanwhile Boswell had entered the Inner Temple and had been called to the English bar in 1786. He hardly practised, however, except to publish anonymously *Dorando, a Spanish Tale*, a thinly disguised summary of a topical case, at the time of publication still *sub judice*. Boswell's wife died in 1789, leaving him six children. His drinking habits gained the better of him, but the *Life* was not, as Macaulay believed, the haphazard by-product of drink, debauchery, and flattery, but the work of a conscious artist, born journalist, and biographical researcher. The discoveries of Boswell's manuscripts, at Malahide Castle in Ireland in 1927 and at Fettercairn House in Scotland in 1930, which have been assembled by Yale University, are proof of Boswell's literary industry and integrity, whatever else he might have lacked. He died in London, May 19. See *Private Papers*, ed. F. A. Pottle (1928–34), also *Boswell's London Journal* (1950), *Boswell in Holland* (1952), *Boswell on the Grand Tour* (1955), and Lives by W. K. Leask (1897), Tinker (1922), Vulliamy (1932), and Wyndham Lewis, *The Hooded Hawk* (1946).

BOSWORTH, Joseph (1789–1876), Anglo-Saxon scholar, born in Derbyshire, was professor of Anglo-Saxon at Oxford from 1858, and in 1867 gave £10,000 for a chair of Anglo-Saxon at Cambridge.

BOTHA, Louis, *bō′ta* (1862–1919), South African statesman and soldier, born at Greytown in Natal, was a member of the Transvaal Volksraad, succeeded Joubert (1900) as commander-in-chief of the Boer forces during the war, and in 1907 became prime minister of the Transvaal colony under the new constitution. In 1907 and 1911 he attended imperial conferences in London; in 1910 he became the first premier of the Union of South Africa. He suppressed De Wet's rebellion in 1914, conquered German Southwest Africa in 1914–15. See Lives by Earl Buxton (1924) and Engelenburg (1929).

BOTHE, Walther, *bō′tė* (1891–1957), German physicist, born at Oranienburg, from 1934 head of the Max Planck Institute for Medical Research at Heidelberg. His work on the development of coincidence technique in counting processes brought him the Nobel physics award for 1954, shared with Max Born (q.v.).

BOTHWELL, James Hepburn, Earl of (c. 1537–78), in 1556 succeeded his father as fourth earl and as hereditary Lord High Admiral. One of the greatest nobles in Scotland, he professed adherence to the Reformation, but stood staunchly by Mary of Guise, the queen regent, who in 1558 made him warden of the Border Marches, and in 1560 sent him on a mission to France. Then it was that he

first saw Queen Mary, and then that Throckmorton described him to Elizabeth as 'a
glorious, rash, and hazardous young man '.
In 1561, shortly after her landing at Leith,
Mary made him a privy councillor; but his
own turbulence and Moray's jealousy made
the next three years of his life a period of
captivity or exile—captivity first at Edinburgh
Castle, and then for more than a year in
England. Not till her marriage with Darnley
did Mary recall him from France; but, on
September 20, 1565, she restored him to all his
dignities; and five months later he married at
Holyrood, with Protestant rites, the Catholic
sister of the Earl of Huntly. By hostile
accounts, he had many mistresses previously,
and was addicted to far fouler vices. Then
came the murder of Rizzio by Darnley
(March 9, 1566), Bothwell's appointment as
keeper of Dunbar, Mary's visit to him at
Hermitage Castle where he was lying badly
wounded by the outlaw Jock Elliot (October
16), Darnley's murder by Bothwell (February
9, 1567), the mock trial and acquittal (April
12), Mary's abduction to Dunbar (April 23),
Bothwell's divorce (May 3 and 7), his elevation to the dukedom of Orkney (May 12), his
marriage to Mary (May 15), and the last
parting at Carberry Hill (June 15). On the
27th he sailed from Dunbar, and driven by a
storm over to Norway, on September 2,
was brought by a Danish warship into Bergen.
He never regained his freedom, but from 1568
was imprisoned at Malmö, and from 1573,
more rigorously, at Dragsholm in Sjaelland,
where he seems to have gone mad before his
death, on April 14, 1578. See Lives by
Schiern (Danish 1863; Eng. trans. 1880) and
R. Gore-Browne (1937).

BOTOLPH, St (d. c. 680), Saxon abbot,
founded a monastery in 654 at Icanhoe (Ox
Island), usually identified as Boston, Lincs.

BOTTESINI, Giovanni, *bot-te-zee'nee* (1823–
1889), Italian musician, the greatest master
of the double bass, was born at Crema in
Lombardy. He was also successful as a
conductor and composer.

BÖTTGER, Johann Friedrich, *bœt'yer* (1682–
1719), established and perfected the manufacture of porcelain at Meissen, Saxony.

BOTTICELLI, Sandro, *bot-tee-chel'lee* (1444–
1510), originally **Alessandro Filipepi,** Florentine painter, was born at Florence, a tanner's
son. Botticello was the nickname of his
elder brother Giovanni, a broker. Showing
signs of genius for painting, he was sent about
1458 to the school of Fra Lippo Lippi. He
produced many works on classical subjects—
the finest his *Birth of Venus,* in the Uffizi, and
his *Primavera* (Spring) in the Florence
Academy. His numerous devotional pictures
are marked by much imaginative refinement
—the *Coronation of the Virgin,* in the Florence
Academy, and the large circular *Madonna and
Child,* in the Uffizi, being famous examples.
The *Assumption of the Virgin,* in the National
Gallery, is not by him, but by Francesco
Botticini. Other great works are *Mars and
Venus,* in the National Gallery; a *Nativity,*
also there; and three frescoes, representing
the *Life of Moses,* the *Destruction of Korah,
Dathan, and Abiram,* and the *Temptation of
Christ,* executed in 1481–82, in the Sistine

Chapel at the Vatican. Botticelli was powerfully impressed by the teaching of Savonarola;
apart from paintings, Botticelli's art is seen
at its most inventive in the pen and silver-
point illustrations of Dante's *Divina Commedia* drawn 1492–97. See works by
Ullmann (1894), Streeter (1903), Horne (1908),
Anderson (1912), Binyon (1913), Bode (tr.
1925), Yashiro (1925), Mesnil (1938), and
della Chiesa (1960).

BOTTOMLEY, (1) **Gordon** (1874–1948),
English poet and playwright, born at Keighley, is best remembered for his *Poems of
Thirty Years* (1925) and his collections of
plays, *King Lear's Wife and Other Plays* (1920),
&c., which, although they mostly constituted
an unhappy blend of poetry and rhetoric,
won him much critical approval. His poetry
anticipated Imagism.
(2) **Horatio William** (1860–1933), journalist
and financier, born in Bethnal Green, reared
in an orphanage, became, successively, an
errand boy, a solicitor's clerk and a shorthand
writer in the Supreme Court. In 1884 he
started a local paper, *The Hackney Hansard.*
He was a brilliant journalist and a persuasive
speaker, with a consuming desire for a life of
luxury. By 1900 he had promoted nearly fifty
companies with a total capital of £20,000,000.
In 1891 and 1909 he was charged with fraud
and acquitted, and between 1901 and 1905
had had sixty-seven bankruptcy petitions and
writs filed against him. Meanwhile he had
founded *John Bull* and become Member of
Parliament for South Hackney in 1906. In
1911 he presented a petition in bankruptcy
and applied for the Chiltern Hundreds.
During World War I he received subscriptions
of nearly £900,000 for various enterprises, and
in 1918 paid his creditors and was discharged
from his bankruptcy, but in 1922 he was
charged for the third time in his career with
fraudulent conversion, found guilty and
sentenced to seven years' penal servitude.
He died in poverty. See *Horatio Bottomley*
by Julian Symons (1957).

BOTZARIS. See BOZZARIS.

BOUCH, Sir Thomas (1822–80), the engineer
of the Tay Bridge (1878), whose fall the next
year hastened his death.

BOUCHER, François, *boo-shay* (1703–70),
French painter at the court of Louis XV, was
born in Paris. He was the purest representative of the rococo style in painting. Many
of his paintings are in the Wallace collection,
the most accomplished being his portraits of
Madame de Pompadour. See works by H.
Macfall (1908) and Mrs Bearne (1913).

**BOUCHER DE CRÈVECŒUR DE
PERTHES, Jacques** (1788–1868), French
archaeologist, whose discoveries at Moulin
Quignon of chipped stones shaped like a
human hand were at first received as evidence
of the antiquity of man with incredulity and
later accepted by the Royal Society.

BOUCICAULT, Dion, *boo'si-kō* or *-kōlt*
(1822–90), dramatist and actor, was born at
Dublin, was educated at University College,
London, and died in New York. Among his
original and adapted pieces were *The Colleen
Bawn* (1860), *The Octoroon* (1861), &c.

BOUDICCA. See BOADICEA.

BOUDIN, (Louis) **Eugène,** *boo-dĩ* (1824–98),

French painter, born at Honfleur. A precursor of Impressionism, he is noted for his seascapes, which include *Deauville* (Tate Gallery), *Harbour of Trouville* (National Gallery), and *Corvette russe* (Luxembourg, Paris). See monograph by G. Cohen (1900).

BOUFFLERS, *boo-flayr,* (1) **Louis François, Duc de** (1644–1711), served under Condé, Turenne, and Catinat in the wars of Louis XIV with such distinction that he received the marshal's baton in 1693. His famous defence of Namur against William III in 1695, and of Lille against Prince Eugene in 1708, made him a duke and peer of France. After the defeat of Malplaquet in 1709, he conducted the French retreat with great skill.

(2) **Stanislas, Marquis de** (1737–1815), the ' Chevalier de Boufflers ', was born at Lunéville, the son of the witty Marquise de Boufflers, who played a brilliant part at the court of Stanislaus, the exiled king of Poland. He rose to be *maréchal de camp*, became governor of Senegal in 1785, entered the French Academy (1788), corresponded with and married Mme de Sabran, and was a poet and literary man much admired in French *salons*. See Life by N. Webster (1916).

BOUGAINVILLE, Louis Antoine de, *boo-gī-veel* (1729–1811), French navigator, was born at Paris. In 1756 he served with distinction in Canada as Montcalm's aide-de-camp, as also in the campaign of 1761 in Germany. Then entering the naval service, he accomplished the first French circumnavigation of the world (1766–69), which he described in his valuable *Voyage autour du monde.* In the American war he commanded several ships of the line, and in 1779 was made *chef d'escadre,* in 1780 a field-marshal in the army. After the outbreak of the Revolution he devoted himself solely to scientific pursuits. By Napoleon I he was made a senator, count of the empire, and member of the Legion of Honour.

BOUGH, Samuel, *bow* (1822–78), Scottish landscape painter, born at Carlisle, was a scene painter in Manchester and Glasgow (1845–49). In 1855 he settled in Edinburgh, where he died, having been elected R.S.A. in 1875. Strongly influenced by David Cox, he is best known for his watercolours. See book by S. Gilpin (1909).

BOUGHTON, Rutland (1878–1960), English composer, born at Aylesbury, founded the Glastonbury Festival (1914–25), wrote the successful opera *The Immortal Hour,* the choral drama *Bethlehem,* and many other works. See Life by M. Hurd (1962).

BOUGUER, Pierre, *boo-gayr,* (1698–1758), French physicist, born at Croisic in Brittany, in 1735 was sent with others to Peru to measure a degree of the meridian at the equator. There in 1735–42 they investigated the length of the seconds pendulum at great elevations, the deviation of the plumbline through the attraction of a mountain, the limit of perpetual snow, the obliquity of the ecliptic, &c. Bouguer's views on the intensity of light laid the foundation of photometry; in 1748 he invented the heliometer.

BOUGUEREAU, William Adolphe, *boog-rō* (1825–1905), French painter, born at La Rochelle, studied art while engaged in business at Bordeaux, and proceeding to Paris in 1850 gained the *Grand Prix de Rome.* He returned from Italy in 1855, having the year before first made his mark with *The Body of St Cecilia borne to the Catacombs,* which, with his *Mater Afflictorum* (1876), is now in the Luxembourg.

BOUILHET, Louis, *boo-yay* (1821–69), French poet and dramatist, friend of Flaubert (q.v.), was born at Cany in Seine Inférieure, and died at Rouen. In his *Fossiles* (1856) he attempted to use science as a subject for poetry. Of his many plays, *Conjuration d'Amboise* (1866) met with success. See Lives by Angot (1885), De la Ville de Mirmont (1888), and Frère (1908).

BOUILLÉ, François Claude Amour, Marquis de, *boo-yay* (1739–1800), French general, was born at the castle of Cluzel in Auvergne, entered the army at fourteen, and served with distinction during the Seven Years' War. In 1768 he was appointed governor of Guadeloupe, and afterwards commander-in-chief in the West Indies. When war broke out in 1778 he took from the British Dominica, Tobago, St Eustache, Saba, St Martin, St Christopher, and Nevis. Louis XVI nominated him a member of the Assembly of Notables in 1787–88; in 1790 he was made commander-in-chief of the army of the Meuse, Saar, and Moselle. Forced to flee from France for his share in the attempted escape of Louis XVI, in 1791 he entered the service of Gustavus III of Sweden, and afterwards served under the Prince of Condé. He refused in 1793 to take the chief command in La Vendée; and went to England, where he wrote his *Mémoires sur la Révolution.* See Gabriel's *Louis XVI, Bouillé, et Varennes* (1874).

BOUILLON, Godfrey of. See GODFREY.

BOUILLY, Jean Nicolas, *Boo-yee* (1762–1842), a prolific French dramatist, the ' poète lacrymal ', and writer for the young, was born at La Coudraye near Tours, and died at Paris. See Life by Carré de Busserolles (Tours 1875).

BOULAINVILLIERS, Henri, Comte de, *boo-lĭ-vee-yay* (1658–1722), born at St Saire in Normandy, resigned the military profession and devoted himself to writing (posthumously published) works on the ancient families of France.

BOULANGER, Georges Ernest Jean Marie, *boo-lā-zhay* (1837–91), French general, was born at Rennes, and educated at St Cyr. He served in Italy, China, the Franco-German war, and against the Commune, being several times wounded, and through radical influence was minister of war from January 1886 to May 1887. As such he urged the expulsion of his former patron, the Duc d'Aumale, and the other Orleans princes, and through the introduction of some army reforms and the appearance of a fortunate music-hall song in his praise, was adopted as the embodiment of the ' revenge ' policy by the Parisians, who for some months suffered from what was termed the Boulanger fever. In 1887, while commanding at Clermont-Ferrand, he was, for remarks on the then war minister, ordered under arrest; in 1888, for disobedience to orders, he was deprived of his command, but immediately elected deputy for Dordogne and

Nord. He was wounded in a duel with M. Floquet, the minister-president, in the same year. Boulangism became really formidable in 1889, and was supported with large sums of money by leading Royalists for their own ends. But when the government prosecuted Boulanger he lost courage and fled the country. He was condemned in absence; his schemes wholly collapsed, and he shot himself in Brussels.

BOULAY DE LA MEURTHE, Antoine, Comte, *boo-lay-de-la-mœrt* (1761–1840), a French statesman who espoused the Revolution but opposed Jacobinism, and under the Empire had an important part in preparing the *Code civil.*

BOULE, Pierre Marcellin, *bool* (1861–1942), French palaeontologist, born at Montsalvy (Cantal), known for his work on the geology of the mountains of central France and for his *Les Hommes fossiles* (1921), &c.

BOULLE, or Boule. See BUHL.

BOULLIAU, Ismael, *boo-yō* (*c.* 1650), constructed the first known mercury thermometer in 1659.

BOULT, Sir Adrian Cedric (1889–   ), English conductor, born in Chester. After studying at Oxford and Leipzig, he conducted the City of Birmingham Orchestra from 1924 until 1930, when he was appointed musical director of the B.B.C. and conductor of the newly formed B.B.C. Symphony Orchestra. Extensive tours in Europe and America won Boult a high reputation for his wide sympathies and championship of English music, and these qualities had a profound influence upon the musical policy of the B.B.C. After his retirement from broadcasting in 1950, Boult was conductor in chief of the London Philharmonic Orchestra until 1957 and its president from 1965. He was created C.H. in 1969.

BOULTON, Matthew (1728–1809), engineer, was born at Birmingham, where his father was a silver stamper. Matthew extended the business by the purchase of a piece of barren heath at Soho, near Birmingham, his works there being opened in 1762. He entered into partnership with James Watt (q.v.), and in 1774 they established a manufactory of steam engines, which proved remunerative only after eighteen anxious years. They also improved coining machinery—it was only in 1882 that a Boulton press at the Mint was finally discarded. Boulton died at Soho. See Smiles's *Lives of Boulton and Watt* (1865).

BOURBAKI, Charles Denis Sauter, *boor-bah-kee* (1816–97), French general, born at Pau, fought in the Crimea and Italy. In 1870 he commanded the Imperial Guard at Metz; and under Gambetta he organized the Army of the North, and commanded the Army of the Loire. His attempt to break the Prussian line at Belfort, though ably conceived, ended in disaster; in a series of desultory attacks on a much inferior force, January 15–17, 1871, he lost 10,000 men. In the retreat to Switzerland that followed he attempted suicide. See Life by Grandin (1897).

BOURBON, *boor-bõ*, a French family which for generations occupied the thrones of France and Naples, and till 1931 that of Spain. It took its name from the castle

of Bourbon (now Bourbon-l'Archambault, 12 miles NW. of Moulins in dep. Allier). Adhémar, sire of Bourbon in the 10th century, traced his descent from Charles Martel. After several changes the seignory of Bourbon devolved upon an heiress, who in 1272 married Robert, the sixth son of Louis IX of France, and the name and possessions of the house thus passed to a branch of the royal family of the Capets. From Duke Robert sprang two lines. The elder ended with the famous Constable de Bourbon (see BOURBON, CHARLES). A representative of the younger line inherited the possessions of the Constable, and became Duke of Vendôme. His son, Antoine, obtained by marriage the throne of Navarre, and Antoine's son was the famous Henry of Navarre (Henry IV) who in 1589, on the extinction of the male line of Valois, fell heir to the crown of France. See the articles on Henry IY, Louis XIII–XVIII, Charles X, and Chambord (Comte de). From a younger son of Louis XIII the Orleans branch (see ORLEANS, DUKE OF) descends. From Louis XIV descend also the branches that formerly held the thrones of Spain, Parma, and Naples. A younger brother of Antoine (Henry IV's father) founded the houses of Condé (q.v.) and Conti (q.v.). The branch of Montpensier was founded in the 15th century. The sons and grandsons of Louise Philippe held titles derived from Paris, Chartres, Nemours, Eu, Joinville, Aumale, and Montpensier. See works by Achaintre (1825), Coiffier de Moret (1828), Mure (1860–1868), Dussieux (1869), and Bingham (1889).

BOURBON, Charles (1490–1527), known as ' Constable de Bourbon ', was son of Gilbert de Bourbon, Count of Montpensier, and the only daughter of the Duke of Bourbon. He thus united the vast estates of both these branches of the Bourbon family; and for his bravery at the battle of Marignano in 1515 he was made constable of France. But powerful enemies strove to undermine him in the favour of Francis I; and, threatened with the loss of some of his lands and dignities, he renounced the service of France, and concluded a private alliance with the Emperor Charles V, and with Henry VIII of England. At the head of a force of German mercenaries he joined the Spanish army in Lombardy in 1523, and, invading France in 1524, failed at the siege of Marseilles. Next year, however, he was chief commander at the great victory of Pavia, in which Francis I was taken prisoner. But Charles V distrusted him, though he made him Duke of Milan and Spanish commander in Northern Italy. Along with George of Frundsberg he led the mixed army of Spanish and German mercenaries that stormed and plundered Rome in 1527. Bourbon was struck down in the fierce struggle—by a bullet fired by Benvenuto Cellini, as the latter asserted.

BOURCHIER, Thomas (*c.* 1404–86), Archbishop of Canterbury, became Bishop of Worcester in 1434, of Ely in 1444, Archbishop in 1454, and a cardinal in 1473, having also been lord chancellor (1455–56). See vol. v of Hook's *Lives of the Archbishops.*

BOURDALOUE, Louis, *boor-da-loo* (1632–1704), pulpit orator, was born at Bourges, and filled in succession the chairs of Rhetoric, Philosophy, and Moral Theology in the Jesuit College of his native place, but was chiefly memorable as a powerful and eloquent preacher in Paris and at court. The year after the revocation of the Edict of Nantes, he was sent to Montpellier to bring back the Protestants to the Roman Catholic Church. In his later years he relinquished the pulpit, and devoted his time to hospitals, prisons, and pious institutions. See his works (1900), Life by F. Castets (Paris 1901–04), and study by R. Daeschler (1927).

BOURDELLE, Émile Antoine, *boor-del* (1861–1929), French sculptor, painter, and teacher, born at Montauban. He studied at the École des Beaux-Arts, Paris, and under Rodin. He found inspiration in Greek art, relating its style to his own time. He illustrated a number of books, and his teaching had considerable influence. His sculpture *Hercules* (1909) is in the Museum of Modern Art, Paris; his *La Sculpture et Rodin* was published in 1937. See the monograph by P. Lorenz (1947).

BOURDON DE L'OISE, François Louis, *boor-dõ-dè-lwahz* (1760?–97), French revolutionary, took part in storming the Tuileries, sat in the Convention, voted for the execution of Louis XVI, but in 1797 was transported by the Directory to Cayenne, where he died.

BOURGELAT, Claude, *boorzh-lah* (1712–99), veterinary surgeon, born in Lyons, founded there in 1761 the first veterinary school in Europe.

BOURGEOIS, *boorzh-wah*, (1) **Jeanne**. See MISTINGUETTE.

(2) **Léon Victor Auguste** (1851–1925), French socialist statesman, born in Paris, studied law and served as minister of public instruction (1890–92, 1898), labour (1912–13, 1917) and was prime minister (1895–96). A delegate to the Hague conference (1907), he was one of the founders of the League of Nations and in 1920 was awarded the Nobel peace prize. He advocated a form of socialism called solidarism.

BOURGET, Paul, *boor-zhay* (1852–1935), novelist and Academician (1894), born at Amiens, first wrote striking verse: *La Vie inquiète* (1875), *Edel* (1878), and *Les Aveux* (1881). His *Essais* (1883) indicated his true strength; the second series, *Nouveaux Essais de psychologie contemporaine* (1886), was a singularly subtle inquiry into the causes of pessimism in France. Bourget's first novel, *L'Irréparable* (1884) was followed by a steady stream of works which placed him in the front rank of modern French novelists. *L'Étape* (1902) marked the crystallization of his talent. His works after 1892 showed a marked reaction from realism and scepticism towards mysticism.

BOURIGNON, Antoinette, *boo-ree-nyõ* (1616–80), French religious fanatic, born at Lille, believing herself called to restore the pure spirit of the gospel, fled from home, entered a convent, had charge of a hospital at Lille, at Amsterdam (1667) gathered followers and printed enthusiastic works, but was driven out, founded a hospital in East Friesland, and died at Franeker. Bourignan-

ism about 1720 so prevailed in Scotland that till 1889 a solemn renunciation was demanded from every entrant into the ministry. Her works were edited by Poiret (25 vols. Amsterdam 1676–84; 2nd ed. 1717). See book by MacEwen (1910).

BOURMONT, Louis de Ghaisnes, Comte de, *boor-mõ* (1773–1846), French marshal, the conqueror of Algiers, was born and died at his paternal castle of Bourmont, in Anjou. He went into exile at the Revolution, but from 1794 to 1799 was engaged in the struggle in La Vendée. Subsequently he obtained the favour of Napoleon, and for his brilliant services in 1813–14 was made general. In 1814 he declared for the Bourbons; yet, on Napoleon's return from Elba, he went over to him, only once more to desert on the eve of Ligny. His evidence went far to bring about Ney's execution. He was appointed minister of war in 1829, and in 1830 received the command of the expedition against Algiers. His rapid success won him the marshal's baton, but on the July Revolution he was superseded, and went to England to share the exile of Charles X. In 1833 Dom Miguel of Portugal placed him at the head of his troops, but the brief campaign was unsuccessful.

BOURNE, (1) **Francis Alphonsus** (1861–1935), English cardinal, born at Clapham. He was educated at Ushaw College, St Edmund's College, St Sulpice, Paris, and Louvain University. Ordained a priest in 1884, he was successively curate at Blackheath, Sheerness, Mortlake, and West Grinstead. In 1889 he was appointed rector of Southwark Diocesan Seminary, and became Bishop of Southwark in 1897. He was made a domestic prelate to Pope Leo XIII in 1895. In 1903 he succeeded Vaughan as Archbishop of Westminster, and was created a cardinal in 1911. A great pastor, he travelled widely, and is best remembered for his zeal for education, and his organization of the International Eucharistic Congress in 1908. His chief works are *Ecclesiastical Training* (1926) and *Occasional Sermons* (1930). See Life by E. Oldmeadow (2 vols. 1940–44).

(2) **Hugh** (1772–1852), the founder of the Primitive Methodists, was born at Fordhays, Stoke-upon-Trent, and died at Bemersley. His zeal as a Wesleyan preacher for large open-air meetings, carried on once from 6 a.m. till 8 p.m., received no approbation from the leaders of the denomination; and in 1808 he was cut off from the Wesleyan connection. But he quickly gathered round him many devoted adherents; and in 1810 a committee of ten members was formed at Standley, near Bemersley. The title of Primitive Methodists was adopted in 1812; by the people they were sometimes called Ranters. Bourne and his brother founded the first chapel of the body at Tunstall in 1811. For the greater part of his life he worked as a carpenter and builder, but found time to visit Scotland, Ireland, and the United States. Amongst his writings was a *History of the Primitive Methodists* (1823). See Life by Wilkinson (1952).

(3) **Vincent** (1695–1747), English writer of Latin verse, was until his death a master at his old school, Westminster. Cowper, one

of his pupils, thought highly of him, and Lamb called him ' a sweet, unpretending, pretty-mannered, matterful creature. . . . His diction all Latin and his thoughts all English! ' See Mitford's edition, *Poemata* (1734), with a memoir.

BOURRIENNE, Louis Antoine Fauvelet de, *boor-ree-en* (1769–1834), French statesman, was born at Sens, studied at the military school of Brienne, where he was on friendly terms with the young Bonaparte. In 1797 he became Napoleon's secretary, accompanied him to Egypt (1799), but was dismissed in 1802 for being implicated in the dishonourable bankruptcy of the house of Coulon, army contractors, and appointed to a post in Hamburg until 1813. Having been recalled and fined for embezzlement, he joined the supporters of the Bourbons after whose restoration he was elected a deputy and figured as an anti-liberal. He died in an asylum at Caen. His *Mémoires* (trans. 1893) are not always reliable.

BOUSCAREN, Juliette. See FIGUIER.

BOUSSINGAULT, Jean Baptiste, *boo-sĭ-gō* (1802–87), French agricultural chemist, was born and died in Paris, studied at the school of Mines and at St Étienne, served under Bolívar in the South American war of independence and became professor of Chemistry at Lyons. He demonstrated that plants absorb nitrogen from the soil and showed that carbon is assimilated by plants from the carbon dioxide of the atmosphere.

BOUTET, Anne Françoise Hippolyte. See MARS.

BOUTS, Dierick, or Dirk, or Thierry, *bowts* (c. 1415–75), Dutch painter, born at Haarlem, but usually placed with the Flemish school. He worked at Louvain and Brussels, coming under the influence of Roger van der Weyden, and produced austere religious paintings, with rich and gemlike colour. His *Resurrection* is in the Munich Pinakothek. See study by Max Friedlander (1925).

BOWDICH, Thomas Edward (1791–1824), African traveller, born at Bristol, conducted a successful mission to Ashanti (1816); and on his return (1818) studied mathematics and other subjects in Paris and was awarded a Cambridge prize of £1000. Aggrieved at his treatment by the African Company, he exposed their management in a book which led the government to take over their possessions. In 1822 he began a trigonometrical survey of the Gambia, where he died of fever. See his *Mission to Ashanti* (1819), and the narrative of his last voyage, edited by his wife (1825).

BOWDLER, Thomas (1754–1825), English man of letters, was born at Ashley, Bath, unhappily immortalized as the editor of the ' Family Shakespeare ', in which ' those words and expressions are omitted which cannot with propriety be read aloud in a family '. ' Bowdlerizing ' has become a synonym for prudish expurgation.

BOWEN, Elizabeth Dorothea Cole (1899–1973), Anglo-Irish author, born in County Cork and brought up in Dublin. *Encounters* (1923), a book of short stories, was followed by *Ann Lee's* (1926) and a series of novels, of which *The Death of the Heart* (1938) and *The Heat of the Day* (1949), a war story, are the best known. She was a sensitive writer with a fine feeling for landscape and light. See her *Bowen's Court* (1942), and Life by J. Brooke (1952).

BOWER, (1) **Archibald** (1686–1766), ex-Jesuit author of a *History of the Popes* (1748–66), was born at Dundee and died in London.

(2) **Frederick Orpen** (1855–1948), botanist, born at Ripon, professor at Glasgow University in 1885–1925, wrote *The Origin of a Land Flora* (1908), *Ferns* (1923 *et seq.*), besides textbooks and works of a more popular nature, and improved upon the system of classification.

(3) or **Bowmaker, Walter** (1385–1449), abbot of Inchcolm in the Firth of Forth, continued the Latin *Scotichronicon* of Fordun (q.v.) from 1153 to 1437. See Goodall's edition (Edinburgh 1759).

BOWES, Marjory, the first wife of John Knox (q.v.).

BOWIE, Colonel Jim, *boo'ay* (c. 1790–1836), inventor of the curved dagger or sheathknife named after him, killed in the Texan war.

BOWLES, (1) **Caroline Anne.** See SOUTHEY.

(2) **William Lisle** (1762–1850), English clergyman and poet, was born at King's Sutton vicarage. A prebendary of Salisbury from 1804, he was a forerunner of the romantic movement in English poetry. His *Fourteen Sonnets, written chiefly on Picturesque Spots during a Journey* (1789) had Coleridge, Wordsworth, and Southey among their enthusiastic admirers. His best poetical work is *The Missionary of the Andes*. In 1806 he published an edition of Pope, and an opinion which he expressed on Pope's poetical merits led to a rather memorable controversy (1809–25) in which Campbell and Byron were his antagonists. See the Memoir by Gilfillan prefixed to his collected poems (Edinburgh 1855), and his correspondence (*A Wiltshire Parson and his Friends*), edited by G. Greever in 1926.

BOWMAN, Sir William, 1st Bart. (1816–92), English oculist, was born in Nantwich, and published with R. B. Todd (1809–60) *Physiological Anatomy* (1845–56), and gained a high reputation by his *Lectures on Operations on the Eye* (1849), describing the ciliary muscle. His *Collected Papers* appeared in 1892.

BOWRING, Sir John (1792–1872), British diplomat, born in Exeter, on leaving school entered a merchant's office, and acquired knowledge of 200 languages. In 1821 he formed a close friendship with Jeremy Bentham (q.v.), and in 1824 became the first editor of his radical *Westminster Review*. He visited Switzerland, Italy, Egypt, Syria, and the countries of the Zollverein, and prepared valuable government reports on their commerce. He sat in parliament from 1835 to 1849, and actively promoted the adoption of free trade. From 1849 he was British consul at Hong Kong; in 1854 he was knighted and made governor. In 1856 an insult having been offered to a Chinese pirate bearing the British flag (the ' affair of the lorcha *Arrow* '), Bowring ordered the bombardment of Canton, a proceeding which nearly upset the Palmerston ministry. In 1855 he concluded a commercial treaty with

Siam, in 358 made a tour through the Philippines. See his autobiography (1877).

BOWYER, William (1699–1777), London printer and classical scholar, studied at St John's College, Cambridge, and in 1722 went into partnership with his father, William Bowyer (1663–1737). In 1767 he was nominated printer to the two Houses of Parliament. He published several philological tracts, translated Rousseau's paradoxical *Discourse* (1751), and wrote two essays on the *Origin of Printing* (1774); but his chief production was a Greek New Testament. See J. Nichols, *Anecdotes* (1778).

BOYCE, William (1710–79), English composer, born in London, in 1736 was appointed composer to the Chapel Royal, in 1758 organist. He holds a high rank as a composer of church music; his works include the song 'Hearts of Oak', the serenata of *Solomon* (1743), and a valuable collection of *Cathedral Music* (1760).

BOYCOTT, Charles Cunningham (1832–97), the agent for Lord Erne in County Mayo, as one of the first victims in 1880 of Parnell's system of social excommunication, gave, in the verb 'to boycott', a new word to most European languages.

BOYD, (1) Benjamin (*c.* 1796–1851), from 1841 a great Australian squatter, was born at Merton Hall, Wigtownshire, failed in his scheme to make 'Boyd Town' in New South Wales a great commercial port, and disappeared in the Solomon Islands on his way back from California.

(2) **Zachary** (*c.* 1585–1653), Scottish divine, studied at Glasgow and St Andrews and became a regent of the Protestant college of Saumur in France. Returning to Scotland in 1621, he was appointed (1623) to the Barony parish, Glasgow, and was thrice elected rector of the University. He wrote *The Last Battel of the Soule in Death* (1629), a prose work and *Zion's Flowers* (1644), some metrical versions of Scripture history, popularly known as 'Boyd's Bible'.

BOYD ORR, John, 1st Baron Boyd Orr (1880–1971), Scottish biologist, born at Kilmaurs, Ayrshire, educated at Glasgow University, served with distinction in World War I, winning the D.S.O. and M.C. He became director of the Rowett Research Institute and professor of Agriculture at Aberdeen (1942–45), and was first director of the United Nations Food and Agriculture Organization (1945–48). His pessimistic prognostications on the world food situation got him a reputation as an apostle of gloom, but his great services in improving that situation brought him the Nobel peace prize in 1949, in which year he was made a peer. His works include *Minerals in Pastures and their Relation to Animal Nutrition* (1928), *Food and the People* (1944), *The White Man's Dilemma* (1952) and *As I Recall* (1966). He was created C.H. in 1968.

BOYDELL, John (1719–1804), English illustrator, was born at Dorrington, Shropshire, in 1741 travelled to London, where he learned engraving, started a print-shop, and in 1790 was lord mayor. From his 'Shakespeare Gallery' of 162 pictures by Opie, Reynolds, Northcote, West, &c., was engraved a superb

volume of plates (1803) to accompany a splendid edition of Shakespeare's works (9 vols. fol. 1792–1801). The immense sums of money he spent on these illustrations brought him into difficulties.

BOYER, bwah-yay, (1) Alexis, Baron de (1757–1833), a great French surgeon, was born a tailor's son at Uzerches in Limousin, and in 1805 was appointed first surgeon to Napoleon, whom he accompanied on his campaigns.

(2) **Jean Pierre** (1776–1850), president of Haiti, was born a mulatto at Port-au-Prince. Sent early to France, in 1792 he entered the army, and distinguished himself against the British on their invasion of Haiti, and established an independent republic in the western part of the island. President Pétion on his deathbed recommended him as his successor (1818). After the death of Christophe, he united the Negro district with the mulatto in 1820, next year added also the eastern district, hitherto Spanish, and in 1825, for 150,000,000 francs, obtained recognition of independence from France. He governed Haiti well for fifteen years, but his partiality to the mulattoes made the pure Negroes rise in 1843. Boyer fled, and died in Paris.

BOYLE, name of an Irish family of Hereford origin, members of which were created earls of Cork and Orrery:

(1) **Charles, 4th Earl of Orrery** (1676–1731), Jacobite soldier and man of letters, grandson of (5) and father of (2), edited the *Letters of Phalaris*, which were shown to be spurious by Richard Bentley and satirized by Swift in his *Battle of the Books* (1704). He fought at the battle of Malplaquet (1709), helped to negotiate the Treaty of Utrecht (1713), and was imprisoned in the Tower of London as a Jacobite (1721). The 'orrery', a kind of planetarium, was so named in his honour by the inventor, George Graham.

(2) **John, 5th Earl of Cork and of Orrery** (1707–62), Irish writer, son of (1), is remembered more by his rancorous *Remarks on Swift* (1751) than by an excellent translation of the *Letters of Pliny* (1751).

(3) **Richard, 1st Earl of Cork**, 'the Great Earl' (1566–1643), Irish administrator, father of (4) and (5), was born at Canterbury. After studying at Cambridge and the Middle Temple, he went over to Ireland in 1588 to make his fortune. He married an heiress, purchased large estates in Munster and improved them, promoted the immigration of English Protestants, and won the favour of Queen Elizabeth. He built bridges, founded harbours and towns, erected thirteen strong castles, and from his ironworks reaped £100,000. About 4000 persons found employment on his vast plantations. He was knighted in 1603; in 1620 became Viscount Dungarvan and Earl of Cork; and in 1631 was made lord high treasurer, an office which remained hereditary in his family. In his old age the Munster rebels compelled him to turn his castle into a fortress, but he soon raised a little army, and quenched rebellion in his borders. See *Life and Letters* by D. Townshend (1904).

(4) **The Hon. Robert** (1627–91), Irish physicist and chemist, seventh son of (3), was

born at Lismore Castle in Munster, studied at Eton and went to the Continent for six years. On his return he settled on the family estates at Stalbridge, Dorset, and devoted himself to science. He was one of the first members of the ' invisible college ', an association of Oxford intellectuals opposed to the prevalent doctrines of scholasticism, which became the Royal Society in 1645. Settling at Oxford in 1654, with Robert Hooke (q.v.) as his assistant, he carried on experiments on air, vacuum, combustion, and respiration. In 1661 he published his *Sceptical Chymist*, in which he criticized the current theories of matter, and defined the chemical element as the practical limit of chemical analysis. In 1662 he arrived at Boyle's Law, which states that the pressure and volume of a gas are inversely proportional. He also researched into calcination of metals, properties of acids and alkalis, specific gravity, crystallography, refraction, and first prepared phosphorus. As a director of the East India Company (for which he had procured the Charter) he worked for the propagation of Christianity in the East, circulated at his own expense translations of the Scriptures, and by bequest founded the ' Boyle Lectures ' in defence of Christianity. In 1668 he took up residence in London with his sister, Lady Ranelagh, and gave much of his time to the Royal Society. In 1688 he shut himself up, in order to repair the loss caused by the accidental destruction of his MSS. Boyle was surprisingly an alchemist, but his alchemy was a logical outcome of his atomism. If every substance is merely a rearrangement of the same basic elements, transmutations should be possible. Modern atomic physics has proved him right. See Lives by Birch (1744), F. Masson (1914), L. T. More (1944) and M. Boas (1958).

(5) **Roger, 1st Earl of Orrery** (1621–79), Irish soldier and statesman, the third son of (3), was in childhood made Baron Broghill. In the Civil War he first took the royalist side, but after Charles's death came under the personal influence of Cromwell, and distinguished himself in the Irish campaign. He became one of Cromwell's special council, and a member of his House of Lords. On Cromwell's death, he tried to support Richard, but after his abdication crossed to Ireland, and secured it for the king. Four months after the Restoration he was made Earl of Orrery. He wrote poems, eight heroic plays, two comedies, a romance and a *Treatise of the Art of War* (1677). See his *Dramatic Works*, ed. W. S. Clark (1937).

BOYLESVE, properly **Tardivaux, René**, *bwa-lev* (1867–1926), French novelist and Academician (1918), was born and brought up at La Hayte-Descartes and completed his studies in Paris. He established his reputation by *Le Parfum des îles Borrommées* (1898) and *Mademoiselle Cloque* (1899), a novel of provincial life.

BOYS, Sir Charles Vernon (1855–1944), English physicist, was born in Rutland. His many inventions include an improved torsion balance, the radio-micrometer, a calorimeter, and a camera with moving lens, with which he photographed lightning flashes. He was knighted in 1935.

BOZZARIS, Marcos, *bot-tzah'rees* (1788–1823), Greek patriot, was born at Suli in Epirus, and in 1803 was forced to retreat to the Ionian Isles by Ali Pasha (q.v.). In 1820 at the head of 800 expatriated Suliotes he gained several victories for Ali against the sultan; in 1822 he skilfully defended Missolonghi, but was killed in an attack on the Turkish-Albanian army at Karpenisi.

BRABAZON, (1) **Hercules** (1821–1906), English watercolour painter, born in Paris, executed many sketches on his travels in Europe and Egypt, his later work being in the style of Turner. A pure amateur, he was loth to exhibit or sell his work, examples of which are in the Tate Gallery and British Museum, London, and the Metropolitan Museum of Art, N.Y. See Life by Hind (1912).

(2) **John Theodore Cuthbert Moore-Brabazon, 1st Baron Brabazon of Tara** (1884–1964), British aviator and politician, the first holder of a flying licence, was educated at Harrow and Cambridge. He was a keen motorist and in 1907 won a 360-mile race. During World War I he served with the R.F.C., reaching the rank of lieutenant-colonel and winning the M.C. He was responsible for several innovations in aerial photography. In 1918 he entered Parliament and became private parliamentary secretary to Churchill at the War Office. Between 1923 and 1927 he served two periods of office as parliamentary secretary to the ministry of transport. He was a prominent member of the enquiry into the R.101 airship disaster. In 1940 he became minister of transport, in 1941 of aircraft production, but resigned at public displeasure of his outspoken criticism of the ally, Russia. In 1942, he was created baron, and in 1953 received the G.B.E. See his *The Brabazon Story* (1956).

BRACCIO DA MONTONE, *bratch'yō da mon-tō'nay*, otherwise **Brancaccio**, or **Forte-bracci** (1368–1424), Italian freelance, born at or near Perugia. In 1416 he obtained the sovereignty of Perugia; in 1417 he held Rome for a time. Next he commanded the troops of Queen Joanna of Naples, and was created Count of Foggia and Prince of Capua. In 1423, by the queen's command, he was crowned Prince of Aquila and Capua, and he then coveted the throne of Naples. He over-ran Campania and Apulia, and advanced into Calabria, but in a battle before Aquila was wounded and taken prisoner. Three days later he died.

BRACE, Charles Loring (1826–90), American social reformer, was born at Litchfield, Connecticut, and died in the Engadine. He founded the Children's Aid Society in 1853, and wrote notes of visits to Hungary (1852), Germany (1853), Norway (1857), and California (1869), &c.

BRACEGIRDLE, Anne (c. 1663–1748), English actress, renowned for her beauty and virtue, and for her performances (1688–1707) in the plays of Congreve at Drury Lane under Betterton.

BRACHET, Auguste, *bra-shay* (1844–98), French philologist, was born at Tours, trained under Diez and Littré, and was attached to the Bibliothèque Nationale in 1864. Of his many works on philology, the best known are his *Grammaire historique* (1867, trans. 1869), and the *Dictionnaire étymologique* (1870, trans. 1873).

BRACKEN, Brendan, 1st Viscount Bracken (1901–58), Irish journalist and Conservative politician, born at Kilmallock, educated at Sydney and at Sedbergh, was associated with the *Financial News*, of which he became chairman, and the *Economist*, of which he became managing director, from 1928 to 1945. He was elected to parliament in 1929, was minister of information in 1941–45, and first lord of the admiralty in the 1945 'caretaker' government. He was created a viscount in 1952.

BRACTON, Henry de (d. 1268),English ecclesiastic and jurist, was a 'justice itinerant', in 1264 became Archdeacon of Barnstaple and Chancellor of Exeter Cathedral. His *De Legibus et Consuetudinibus Angliae*, the earliest attempt at a systematic treatment of the body of English law, was first printed entire in 1569 (edited by Sir Travers Twiss, 1878–83; by G. E. Woodbine, 1915 *et seq.*); and in 1887 F. Maitland published a *Collection of Cases*, with proof that this was the actual collection on which Bracton's treatise was founded.

BRADBURY, Sir John Swanwick Bradbury, 1st Baron (1872–1950), British government official, born at Winsford, Cheshire. As secretary to the Treasury (1913–19) he was responsible for the substitution of £1 and 10s. notes for gold coins. Treasury bills bearing his signature are often called 'Bradburys'.

BRADDOCK, Edward (1695–1755), a British general, born in Perthshire, entered the Coldstream Guards in 1710, and, appointed to command against the French in America, on July 8, 1755, reached the Monongahela. On the 9th he pushed forward to capture Fort Duquesne (now Pittsburgh), when, 7 miles from it, he was attacked by a party of 900 French and Indians, who, firing from cover, offered no target, whereas the British, unused to forest warfare, did. After two hours' fighting, in which Braddock had four horses shot under him and was mortally wounded, the survivors made a hasty retreat under Washington, the only one of Braddock's staff who escaped unhurt. No less than 63 out of 86 officers, and 914 out of 1373 men engaged, were killed or wounded. The French loss was trifling. Braddock died July 13, at Great Meadows, about 60 miles from the scene of his fatal surprise. See Winthrop Sargent's monograph (Philadelphia 1855), study by L. McCardell (1958), and Parkman's *Montcalm and Wolfe* (1884).

BRADDON, Mary Elizabeth (1837–1915), novelist, was born in London and attained popularity with *Lady Audley's Secret* (1862), the story of a golden-haired murderess. Of some seventy-five novels, perhaps the best is *Ishmael* (1884), which depends not so much on sensation as on character. She married in 1874 the publisher, John Maxwell (1825–95), and the novelist, W. B. Maxwell (d. 1938), was her son.

BRADFORD, (1) William (1590–1656), a 'Pilgrim Father', was born at Ansterfield, near Doncaster, and, having in 1608 escaped to Amsterdam, in 1620 sailed in the *Mayflower*,

and in 1621 succeeded Carver as governor of Plymouth colony.

(2) **William** (1663–1752), an early American printer, was a Leicestershire Quaker.

BRADLAUGH, Charles, *brad'law* (1833–91), English social reformer, but vigorous anti-socialist, was born in London. He was in turn errand boy, small coal-merchant, and trooper at Dublin. Buying his discharge, he returned to London in 1853, became timekeeper to a builder, clerk to a solicitor, and before long a busy secularist lecturer, and pamphleteer under the name of 'Iconoclast'. His voice was heard in all popular causes, whether on platforms throughout the country or in the pages of his *National Reformer*; in 1880 he was elected M.P. for Northampton. He claimed the right as an unbeliever to make affirmation of allegiance in lieu of taking the parliamentary oath; but the House refused to allow him either to make oath or to affirm. He was thrice re-elected, and at length, in 1886, having taken the oath, was allowed to take his seat. In parliament he gained respect by his debating power, and he earned wide popularity by his agitation against perpetual pensions. Of his writings the best known is the *Impeachment of the House of Brunswick*. His republication, in conjunction with Mrs Annie Besant (q.v.), of a pamphlet, *The Fruits of Philosophy*—advocating birth control—led in 1876 to a sentence of six months' imprisonment and a £200 fine, but the conviction was quashed on appeal. See Life by his daughter and J. M. Robertson (2 vols. 1894), and the centenary volume (1933).

BRADLEY, (1) Andrew Cecil (1851–1935), English critic, brother of (3) and half-brother of (4), the most influential commentator of his generation, was professor of Poetry at Oxford (1901–06) and published *Poetry for Poetry's Sake* (1901), *Commentary on In Memoriam* (1901), *Shakespearean Tragedy* (1904), and *Oxford Lectures* (1909).

(2) **Edward**, pseud. **Cuthbert Bede** (1827–1889), English author and clergyman, was born at Kidderminster, and educated at Durham University. His facetious description of Oxford life in *Adventures of Mr Verdant Green* (1853–57) was the first and most popular of 26 works.

(3) **Francis Herbert** (1846–1924), English Idealist philosopher, brother of (1) and half-brother of (4), born at Glasbury, Brecknock-shire, dogged by lifelong ill-health, was elected in 1870 fellow of Merton College, Oxford. His ethics were Hegelian in inspiration, but his metaphysics a monism derived from the principle that truth must always be the whole truth. His system greatly influenced the early Bertrand Russell and thus indirectly Wittgenstein, whose logical atomism could be described as 'Bradley turned upside down'. His chief works were *Principles of Logic* (1883), *Ethical Studies* (1876), and *Appearance and Reality* (1893). He was awarded the O.M. in 1914. See study by R. Wolheim (1959).

(4) **George Granville** (1821–1903), English divine and Dean Stanley's biographer, half-brother of (1) and (3), from Rugby passed to University College, Oxford, became a fellow

(1844), a master at Rugby, in 1858 head-master of Marlborough, in 1870 master of University College, and in 1881 dean of Westminster. His daughter was the writer Margaret Louisa Woods (q.v.).

(5) **Henry** (1845–1923), English philologist, became joint editor of the Oxford English Dictionary in 1889, senior editor in 1915.

(6) **James** (1693–1762), English astronomer, was born at Sherborne, Gloucestershire, and from Northleach Grammar School passed in 1711 to Balliol College, Oxford. His genius for mathematics and astronomy soon won him the friendship of Halley and Newton, and secured his election to the Royal Society in 1718. In 1721 he was elected to the Savilian professorship of Astronomy at Oxford, and in 1742 he succeeded Halley as regius professor of Astronomy at Greenwich. In 1729 he published his discovery of the aberration of light, providing the first observational proof of the Copernican hypothesis. In 1748 he discovered that the inclination of the earth's axis to the ecliptic is not constant. He died at Chalford, Gloucestershire. His 60,000 astronomical observations fill two folio vols. (1798–1805). See Rigaud's *Works and Correspondence of Bradley, with Memoir* (1832), and H. H. Turner, *Astronomical Discovery* (1905).

(7) **Katharine Harris.** See FIELD (6).

(8) **Omar Nelson** (1893–   ), American general, served in World War I, and in the 2nd played a prominent part in Tunisia and Sicily. In 1944 he led the U.S. invading armies through France. He became chairman of the joint chiefs of staff in 1949 and was promoted general of the army in 1950.

BRADMAN, Sir Donald George (1908–   ), Australian cricketer, born in New South Wales, stock- and share-broker by profession, played for Australia 1928–48, captain of the XI from 1936. He set up many batting records, including the highest score, and he made the greatest number of centuries in England *v.* Australia test matches. He was knighted in 1949.

BRADSHAW, (1) George (1801–53), English printer, born at Salford, originator in 1839 of railway guides, was a Manchester Quaker mapmaker, and died of cholera at Christiania.

(2) **John** (1602–59), regicide, born near Stockport, was called to the bar in 1627, and held various appointments until in 1649 he was appointed president at the trial of Charles I. On that solemn occasion his manners were as short as his speeches were lengthy. As a reward he was made permanent president of the Council of State and chancellor of the Duchy of Lancaster, with a grant of estates worth £2000 per annum. His ' stiff republicanism ' estranged him from Cromwell. He was buried in Westminster Abbey, but at the Restoration his body was dug up and hanged, as were Cromwell's and Ireton's.

BRADSTREET, *née* **Dudley, Ann** (1612–72), Puritan poetess, the first American woman writer, born probably at Northampton, in 1628 married Simon Bradstreet (1603–97), afterwards governor of Massachusetts. In 1630 they emigrated with the Winthrops (q.v.). Her first volume of Phineas Fletcher-like poems was published in London in 1650.

BRADWARDINE, Thomas (1290–1349), English theologian, born at Chichester, studied with distinguished success at Merton College, Oxford, and in 1325 was one of the proctors of the university. His fame was founded on his theological lectures *De Causa Dei contra Pelagium* (edited by Sir Henry Savile, 1618), an able defence of the Augustinian doctrines of grace, fully proving his right to the title of ' Doctor profundus '. Called about 1335 to London, he became chancellor of St Paul's, a prebendary of Lincoln, and confessor to Edward III, whom he accompanied on his campaigns in France. In 1348 Bradwardine was elected Archbishop Stratford's successor by the chapter of Canterbury, and, in spite of a dispute with the king, he was consecrated at Avignon in July 1349. When he returned to England, he died of the Black Death at Lambeth.

BRADY, Nicholas (1659–1726), Anglican clergyman, born at Bandon, Co. Cork, educated at Westminster, Christ Church, Oxford, and Dublin. The metrical version of the Psalms by him and Nahum Tate (q.v.) was authorized in 1696, but with the strong opposition of many of the Tory clergy.

BRAGA, Theophilo (1843–1924), born in the Azores, was president of the Portuguese republic, Oct. 1910–Aug. 1911 (provisional) and May–Oct. 1915. Poet and savant, he wrote a history of Portuguese literature.

BRAGG, (1) Braxton (1817–76), Confederate general, born in North Carolina, commanded in several great battles of the Civil War, but though successful at Chickamauga, the hardest fought battle in the war, his tenure of command was an unfortunate one. See *Life* by D. C. Seitz (1924).

(2) **Sir William Henry** (1862–1942), English physicist, Quain professor of Physics, London (1915–23), studied radioactivity, X-rays, crystals, &c., Nobel prize (1915) shared with his son, **Sir William Lawrence** (1890–1971). The latter was Fullerian professor of Chemistry at and director of the Royal Institution till 1966, knighted 1941, and created C.H. 1967.

BRAHAM, (i.e., Abraham), John, *bray'am* (1774–1856), tenor, born in London of German-Jewish parents, had his first great success at Drury Lane (1796), and for half a century held the reputation of one of the greatest tenors. He squandered a fortune by purchasing the Colosseum in Regent's Park and building the St James's Theatre.

BRAHE, Tycho, *brah'e* (1546–1601), Danish astronomer, was born of noble family at Knudstrup in South Sweden—then under the Danish crown—December 14, and was sent to study law at Copenhagen, Leipzig, Wittenberg, Rostock, and Augsburg, but devoted himself to astronomy. In 1563 he discovered serious errors in the astronomical tables, and in 1572 carefully observed a new star in Cassiopeia. In 1576 he received from the king, Frederick II of Denmark, the offer of the island of Hveen in the Sound, as the site for an observatory, with an endowment; and the foundation stone of his Uraniborg (or Castle of the Heavens) was laid. Here for 20 years Brahe carried out his observations with success—but he rejected the Copernican theory for a modification of the Ptolemaic system. After the death of Frederick in 1588 he was involved in many disputes and quarrels, partly provoked by his neglect of the duties of some of his many appointments— notably that of prebendary of Roskilde. He became unpopular with the government, lost some of his revenues, and in 1597 left the country. After residing at Rostock and at Wandsbeck near Hamburg, he accepted in 1599 an invitation of the emperor Rudolf II to Benatky near Prague (where he had Kepler as assistant); and there he died, October 24, 1601. His complete works appeared at Prague in 1611; his Letters have been edited by Frijs (Copenhagen 1876); and see also the Life (Edinburgh 1890) by J. L. E. Dreyer, who also edited the *Opera Omnia* (Copenhagen 1913 *et seq.*).

BRAHMS, Johannes (1833–97), German composer, born at Hamburg, was the son of a poor orchestral musician. A gifted pianist, he was compelled by family poverty to earn his living as a young boy playing in the dockside inns of Hamburg, and though his reputation spread rapidly it was not until 1853 that he was able to concentrate on composition. This was after he had met the flamboyant Hungarian refugee violinist Reményi, with whom he went on tour, and from whom he probably absorbed much of the spirit which went into the *Hungarian Dances* and *Zigeunerlieder*. During the tour he met Joachim (q.v.), who became a lifelong friend and fellow-antagonist of Romanticism, and Liszt (q.v.), who successfully charmed Reményi into becoming a devotee of the ' New German ' music. The solidly classical Brahms, however, was not impressed, and he parted from Reményi and went to Göttingen to visit Joachim, who gave him an introduction to Schumann. The enthusiasm of Schumann for his early works, especially his assistance in publishing the piano sonatas, was influential in establishing Brahms's reputation, and Brahms's devotion to the older composer expressed itself in his lifelong care for Schumann's widow and children. He never married, and after 1863, when he settled in Vienna, his life was uneventful except for occasional public appearances in Austria and Germany at which he played his own works. He was adopted by the anti-Wagnerian faction as the leader of traditional principles against ' modern ' iconoclasm, and his fame as a composer spread rapidly. Firmly based on classical foundations, his works contain hardly any programme music apart from a few pieces such as the *Tragic Overture* and the C minor quartet (inspired by Goethe's *Werther*). His great orchestral works are comparatively late, the first, *Variations on a Theme of Haydn*, appearing when he was 40, and his first symphony when he was 43. The *Academic Festival Overture*, also dating from this period, was composed in honour of his honorary doctorate at Breslau University. His greatest choral work is the *German Requiem*, which had its first full performance in 1869. Prolific in all fields except opera, he shows an extraordinary evenness in quality, due to his ruthless destruction of his early efforts and of all else which failed to measure up to his self-imposed standards of excellence. See Lives by May (1905), Geiringer (1936), and Culshaw (1948).

BRAID, James (1870–1950), Scottish golfer, born at Earlsferry, became a joiner and went to ply his trade in St Andrews, where he was able to indulge his passion for golf and develop into an outstanding player. In 1893 he went to London as a clubmaker at the Army and Navy Stores, but became a professional in 1893 at Romford, then, from 1904 until his death, at Walton Heath.

BRAIDWOOD, Thomas (1715–98), after studying at Edinburgh University, opened a school there, and from 1760 onwards became famous as a teacher of the deaf and dumb. His school, which was visited by Dr Johnson in 1773, was ten years later transferred to Hackney, London.

BRAILLE, Louis, *brah'y'*, angl. *brayl* (1809–1852), born at Coupvray near Paris, at three became blind, and at ten entered the Institution des Jeunes Aveugles at Paris, where, as pupil and (from 1826) professor, he worked with success to invent a system which the blind could both read and write in relief.

BRAILSFORD, Henry Noel (1873–1958), English Socialist author and political journalist, born in Yorkshire. Educated at Glasgow University, he became assistant professor of Logic there, leaving to join the Greek Foreign Legion in the war with Turkey in 1897. He described his experiences in *The Broom of the War God* (1898). His Socialism was pre-eminently international in outlook and was the key to everything he did (see *The War of Steel and Gold*, 1914). He joined the Independent Labour Party in 1907 and edited (1922–26) its weekly organ *The New Leader*. He was a leader writer to several influential papers, including the *Manchester Guardian* and the *Daily Herald*. His literary work includes *Shelley, Godwin and their Circle* (1913).

BRAIN, (1) **Aubrey Harold** (1893–1955), English horn player, born in London, father of (2). He studied at the Royal College of Music and became chief horn player in the New Symphony Orchestra (1911) and London Symphony Orchestra (1912). In 1923 he became professor of his instrument at the Royal Academy of Music, and from 1930 to 1945 was principal horn of the B.B.C. Symphony Orchestra. His elder son, **Leonard** (1915–), is an oboist.

(2) **Dennis** (1921–57), English horn player, born in London, second son of (1). He studied under his father at the Royal Academy of Music, also becoming a fine organist. He worked with the Royal Philharmonic and Philharmonia Orchestras as chief horn player. His mastery of his instrument won him fame throughout Europe, and amongst the composers who wrote works specially for him are Britten, Hindemith, and Malcolm Arnold. He met his death in a motor accident.

BRAINERD, David (1718–47), missionary, was born at Haddam, Conn., studied three years in Yale College, where his opinions caused doctrinal disputes and his expulsion, worked successfully among the American Indians from 1742, and his devotion found expression in his *Journal* (1746). See Life by J. Edwards (1749).

BRAITHWAITE. See BRATHWAITE.

BRAKELONDE. See JOCELIN DE BRAKE-
LONDE.

BRAMAH, (1) **Ernest,** pseud. of Ernest
Bramah Smith (1867–1942), English author,
gave up unsuccessful farming and lived for a
while in China, which forms the background
of the ' Kai Lung ' stories (*Wallet of Kai Lung*
(1900), &c.) for which he is best remembered.
In 1914 he wrote *Max Carrados*, first of
several books with a blind detective hero,
which also achieved considerable popularity.

(2) **Joseph** (1748–1814), inventor, was born
at Stainborough near Barnsley, Yorkshire.
A farmer's son, he was lamed in his sixteenth
year, so was apprenticed to the village
carpenter, and presently became a cabinet-
maker in London, where he distinguished
himself by the number, value, and ingenuity
of his inventions and improvements, including
a beer machine used at the bar of public-
houses, a safety lock (patented 1788) and a
very ingenious machine for printing bank-
notes (1806). He was one of the first to propose the application of the screw-propeller.

BRAMANTE, Donato, *bra-man'tay* (1444–
1514), Italian architect, was born near
Urbino, and, at first a painter, resided in
Milan from 1472 to 1499, then went to Rome,
where he was employed by Popes Alexander
VI and Julius II. The greatest work he
undertook was the rebuilding of St Peter's
(begun 1506). When only a small portion of
his plans had been realized, he died, and
succeeding architects departed widely from
the original design of a grand cupola over a
Greek cross. See Life by C. Baroni (1945).

BRAMHALL, John (1594–1663), a great anti-
Puritan Irish prelate, was educated at Sidney
Sussex College, Cambridge. Going to
Ireland as Wentworth's chaplain in 1633, he
became Bishop of Derry in 1634, actively
reformed the established church and repressed
its enemies, notably Ulster Presbyterians.
When the Civil War broke out, for safety's
sake he crossed to England; in 1644 the
Royalist disasters drove him to the Continent.
The Restoration gave him the see of Armagh.
He imitated Laud in policy and resembled
him in person, but was far his inferior in
intellect. See his Collected Works (1842–45)
and Life by W. J. S. Simpson (1927).

BRAMPTON, Baron. See HAWKINS (2).

BRANCACCIO. See BRACCIO.

BRANCUŞI, Constantin, *bran-koo'zi* or
brin'koosh (1876–1957), Rumanian sculptor
born at Pestisani, near Turgujiu, won a
scholarship to the Bucharest Academy and
arrived in Paris in 1904, where he remained for
the rest of his life. From 1906 he worked in
Rodin's atelier. His *The Kiss* (1908) was
the most abstract sculpture of the period,
representing two blocklike figures. His
Sleeping Muse (1910) shows Rodin's influence,
but is the first of his many characteristic,
highly-polished egg-shaped carvings. *The
Prodigal Son* (Philadelphia 1925) shows the
influence of African sculpture. His aim was
simplification, to get to the essence of the
thing, the essence being objective, and he was
therefore outside the subjective Expressionist
schools of the day. Other works include
several versions of *Mademoiselle Pogany*

(1913–31), *Bird in Space* (N.Y. 1925) and *The
Sea-Lions* (1943). See monograph by D.
Lewis (1958) and study by Jianou (1963).

BRAND, (1) **Hennig,** a 17th-century German
alchemist who discovered phosphorus in 1669.

(2) **Sir Jan Hendrik** (1823–88), president
of the Orange Free State from 1864 till his
death, was born in Capetown. He defeated
the Basutos (1865–69), and favoured friendship with Britain.

(3) **John** (1744–1806), English antiquary,
born at Washington, Co. Durham, graduated
at Lincoln College, Oxford, and in 1784
became resident secretary of the Society of
Antiquaries. His *Popular Antiquities* (1777;
expanded by Ellis, 1813) is a standard work.

BRANDAN, St. See BRENDAN.

BRANDES, Georg Morris Cohen, *brand-'ez*
(1842–1927), Danish literary critic, was born
in Copenhagen, where he graduated at the
university in 1864. He brought to Denmark
a new outlook on literature by his *Main
Currents of 19th Century Literature* (6 vols.
1901–05) which bears the fruits of a European
tour on which he met Renan, Taine, Mill and
others, and imbibed doctrines of realism and
radicalism which evoked opposition as well
as acclaim and kept him out of the chair of
Literature at Copenhagen. For a while he
lived in Berlin, where he came under the
influence of Nietzsche and his radicalism
moved further to the Right, as is seen in his
works on Shakespeare, Goethe (1915), Voltaire, &c. See his *Recollections* (1906), and
Lives by Boyesen (1895) and Moritzen (1922).

BRANDL, Alois (1855–1940), German scholar,
born at Innsbruck, became professor of
English Philology at Berlin in 1895, and wrote
on English romanticism, on Old and Middle
English literature, and on the pre-Shakes-
pearean drama.

BRANDO, Marlon (1924–), U.S. film and
stage actor, born Omaha, Neb., a product of
the famous New York Actors' Studio, with its
emphasis on ' method ' acting. He appeared
in several plays, before achieving fame in
Williams' *A Streetcar Named Desire* (1946), as
the arrogant and brutal, but magnetic
Kowalski, which rôle he also played on film
(1951). Gifted with tremendous versatility, he
has created as widely differing film parts as
Mark Antony (*Julius Caesar*, 1953), a
Western hero (*One-eyed Jacks*, 1959, which he
also directed and produced), and a convincingly English Fletcher Christian (*Mutiny on the
Bounty*, 1962). His most outstanding rôle,
however, for which he won an Oscar in 1954,
was as the confused but courageous dockland
hero, Terry Malone, in *On the Waterfront*.

BRANDON, (1) **Charles** (*c.* 1484–1545), the
son of Henry VII's standard-bearer who fell
at Bosworth (1485), was in 1514 created Duke
of Suffolk. Next year he married Mary,
Henry VIII's sister, and widow of Louis XII
of France, and so was the grandfather of
Lady Jane Grey.

(2) **Richard,** the executioner of Charles I,
as well as of Strafford, Laud, &c., succeeded
his father, Gregory Brandon, in 1640, and
died, full of remorse, June 20, 1649.

BRANDT, Georg (1694–1768), Swedish chemist, born at Riddarhytta, Sweden, and
discovered (*c.* 1730) cobalt.

BRANGWYN, Sir Frank (1867–1956), British artist, born at Bruges. He was apprenticed to William Morris for four years, and then went to sea and travelled widely. Although he excelled in many media, particularly in etching, he was most famous for his vigorously coloured murals, e.g., the *British Empire Panels* (1925) for the House of Lords. They were rejected and are now in the Swansea Guildhall. In 1936 a Brangwyn Museum was opened in Bruges and a retrospective exhibition was held at the Royal Academy in 1952. He was elected R.A. in 1919 and knighted in 1941. See study by C. G. E. Bunt (1949).

BRANNER, H. C. (Hans Christian) (1903–66), Danish novelist and short-story writer, held in high regard for his simplicity of style and his skilled psychoanalytical writing. His novels include *Ryttern* (1949; trans. *The Riding Master*, 1951) and *Ingen kender Natten* (1956; ' Nobody knows the Night '). *Om lidt er vi borte* (1939; ' In a little while we are gone ') and *To Minutters Stilhed* (1944; ' Two Minutes of Silence ') are collections of short stories.

BRANT, (1) **Joseph** (1742–1807), Mohawk chief, fought for the British in the Indian and Revolutionary wars, exerting his immense influence to bring about a general Indian peace. In later years an earnest Christian, he translated St Mark's Gospel and the Prayer Book into Mohawk, and in 1786 visited England, was received at court, entertained by Boswell, painted by Romney, and a bronze statue of him was unveiled at Brantford, Ontario, in 1886.

(2) **Sebastian** (1458–1521), German poet and humanist, was born at Strasbourg; studied and lectured at Basel; and died in his native city. His *Narrenschiff* (Basel 1494), or ' Ship of Fools ', a satire on the follies and vices of his times, is not very poetical, but is full of sound sense and good moral teaching. It was translated into English by Alexander Barclay (q.v.) and Henry Watson, both in 1509.

BRANTING, Hjalmar (1860–1925), founder of the Swedish Socialist party, premier in 1920, 1921–23, and 1924–25, shared the Nobel peace prize in 1921.

BRANTÔME, Pierre de Bourdeilles, Seigneur de, brā-tōm (c. 1530–1614), French author, born in Périgord, was educated at Paris and at Poitiers. In his sixteenth year the abbacy of Brantôme was bestowed on him by Henry II, but he never took orders, and spent most of his life as a courtier and freelance. In 1561 he accompanied Mary Stuart to Scotland, and in 1565 he joined the expedition sent to Malta to assist the Knights of St John against the sultan. He served in Italy under the Maréchal de Brissac, in Africa under the Spaniards, and in Hungary as a volunteer against the Turks. He was made chamberlain to Charles IX and Henry III, and fought against the Huguenots. About 1594 he began to write his memoirs, and henceforth lived in retirement until his death. His works, first published in 1659, comprise *Vies des grands capitaines, Vies des dames galantes,* and *Vies des dames illustres,* and provide a detailed picture of the Valois court. Their literary merit and historical interest are considerable. Their matter is often of the most scandalous description, but they give a wonderfully vivid picture of their author's times. See Life and edition of his works by L. Lalanne (1896).

BRAQUE, Georges (1882–1963), French painter, born at Argenteuil. He was one of the founders of classical Cubism, and worked with Picasso from 1908 to 1914. After World War I (in which he was wounded) he developed a personal nongeometric semi-abstract style. In 1924 and 1925 he designed scenes for two Diaghilev ballets—*Les Fâcheux* and *Zéphyr et Flore*. His paintings are mainly of still life, the subject being transformed into a two-dimensional pattern, and they are among the outstanding decorative achievements of our time, with a pervasive influence on other painters which has not been approached by more violently controversial artists. He was a Grand Officier of the *Légion d'honneur* and he was awarded an honorary doctorate of Oxford University in 1956. See Jean Paulhan's *Braque, le Patron* (1946), and monographs by André Lejard (1949) and J. Richardson (1959).

BRASIDAS, the great Spartan general who from 431 B.C. distinguished himself in the Peloponnesian war, and who in 422 at Amphipolis, with a handful of helots and mercenaries, had to encounter the flower of the Athenian army under Cleon. In the battle both generals were killed, but the Athenians were completely beaten.

BRASSEY, (1) **Thomas** (1805–70), British engineer, born a farmer's son at Buerton near Chester, was articled to a land surveyor, in 1834 obtained, through George Stephenson, contracts for a viaduct and in 1836 settled in London as a railway contractor. His operations soon extended to all parts of the world; for his contract of the Great Northern Railway (1847–51) he employed between 5000 and 6000 men. He died at Hastings. See Helps's *Life and Labours of Brassey* (1872).

(2) **Thomas, 1st Earl** (1836–1918), son of (1), was born at Stafford, educated at Rugby and University College, Oxford, and called to the bar in 1866. As civil lord of the Admiralty (1880–84), and secretary (1884–1885), he made his influence felt in naval questions and in 1895–1900 was governor of Victoria. In *The ' Sunbeam ', R.Y.S.* (1917), and other works, he tells of the 300,000 miles he sailed in forty years in the yacht which he gave as a hospital ship during World War I. He founded and edited (1886–90) *The Naval Annual,* and published works on political and naval questions.

BRATBY, John (1928–), English artist and writer, born at Wimbledon. He studied at the Royal College of Art and is one of the leading representatives of the English Realist School. With Jack Smith he represented Great Britain at the Venice Biennale in 1956. His *Baby in Pram* is in the Walker Art Gallery, Liverpool. He has written several novels, including *Breakdown* (1960) with illustrations by himself.

BRATHWAITE, Richard (1588–1673), English minor poet, satirist, and essayist, was born near Kendal. He wrote *The Golden Fleece* (1611), *The Poet's Willowe* (1614), a book of pastorals, and *A Strappado for the Divell* (1615), a collection of satires. *Barnabee's Journall* (1638) is his best known work. See Life by M. W. Black (1928).

BRATIANU, *bra-ti-ah'noo*, Rumanian family of statesmen:
(1) **Ion** (1821–91), father of (2), with his brother **Demeter** (1818–92), founded the Rumanian Liberal party. He was premier in 1876–88, Demeter holding the office for a short time in 1881.
(2) **Ion** (1864–1927), son of (1), who as premier brought Rumania into World War I against the Central Powers. His brother, **Vintila** (1867–1930), was premier (1927–28).

BRAUER, Adrian. See BROUWER.

BRAUN, *brown*, (1) **Eva** (1910–45), secretary to Hoffmann, Adolf Hitler's staff photographer, became Hitler's mistress and is said to have married him before they committed suicide together in the air-raid shelter of the Chancellery during the fall of Berlin in 1945. See H. Hoffmann, *Hitler was my Friend* (1957), and H. Trevor Roper, *Last Days of Hitler* (1955).
(2) **Ferdinand** (1850–1918), German physicist, born at Fulda, shared a Nobel prize in 1909 with Marconi (q.v.) for his work on wireless telegraphy and cathode rays.
(3) **Lili**, *née* von Kretschmann (1865–1916), German Socialist authoress and feminist, born at Halberstadt, married the Socialist writer and politician **Heinrich Braun** (1854–1927). Her best known book is *Im Schatten der Titanen* (1908). See her autobiographical *Memoiren einer Sozialistin* (1909–11), and study by J. Vogelstein (1923).
(4) **Wernher von** (1912–), German-born American rocket pioneer, born in Wirsitz, studied engineering at Berlin and Zürich and, infatuated by space travel, founded in 1930 a society for space travel which maintained a rocket-launching site near Berlin by charging an admission fee to spectators. Since rockets were outside the terms of the Versailles Treaty, the German army authorities became interested and in 1936, with Hitler's backing, von Braun was director of a properly organized rocket research station at Peenemünde, where he perfected and launched the famous V-2 rockets against Britain in September 1944. At the end of the war, von Braun hid from Himmler's henchmen in Bavaria and surrendered to the Americans. He became a naturalized American and a director of the U.S. Army's Ballistic Missile Agency at Huntsville, Alabama, and was chiefly responsible for the manufacture and successful launching of the first American artificial earth satellite, the *Explorer*, at Cape Canaveral on January 31, 1958. See D. Lang, *The Man in the Thick Lead Suit* (1958).

BRAUNER, Bohuslav (1855–1935), Czech chemist, born in Prague, noted for his work on the Periodic Table, rare elements and their properties.

BRAWNE, Fanny. See KEATS.

BRAXFIELD, Robert Macqueen, Lord (1722–1799), Scottish judge, noted for his harshness towards political prisoners, was born near Lanark. Hard-headed, hard-hearted, harddrinking, he was the original Lord Weir of R. L. Stevenson's unfinished novel, *Weir of*

Hermiston (1896), adapted for the stage by R. J. B. Sellar (1958).

BRAY, Thomas (1656–1730), English divine and philanthropist, born at Marton, in Shropshire, and died incumbent of St Botolph Without, Aldgate, having published *Catechetical Lectures*, &c., and been the means of establishing eighty parochial libraries in England, and thirty-nine in America—his home from 1699 to 1706. Out of his library scheme grew the S.P.C.K.; and he may also be regarded as the founder of the S.P.G.

BRAYLEY, Edward Wedlake. See BRITTON (1).

BRAZIL, Angela, *braz'él* (1868–1947), English writer of school stories, born at Preston, was a governess for some years before beginning to write tales notable for their healthy realism. Her works include the *Fortunes of Philippa* (1906) and *The School by the Sea* (1914).

BRAZZA, Pierre Savorgnan de, *brat'za* (1852–1905), French-Italian French explorer, born of Italian descent at Rio de Janeiro. He entered the French navy in 1870, served on the Gabun, and in 1876–78 explored the Ogowe. In 1878 the French government gave him 100,000 francs for exploring the country north of the Congo, where he secured vast grants of land for France, and founded stations, including that of Brazzaville on the north shore of Stanley Pool. In 1883 he returned, largely subsidized by the French government; and by 1886 he had established twenty-six stations. He continued to explore till 1897, being in 1890–91 governor of French Congo. See works by Neuville (1884) and Ney (1888).

BREADALBANE. See CAMPBELL.

BREAKSPEAR, Nicolas. See ADRIAN.

BRÉAL, Michel, *bray-ahl* (1832–1915), French comparative philologist and mythologist, born in Rhenish Bavaria, in 1859 settled in Paris, and eventually in 1866 became professor of Comparative Grammar at the Collège de France. He founded the science of semantics with his *Essai de Sémantique* (1897), an exposition of principles for the study of the meaning of words.

BRECHT, Bertholt Eugen Friedrich, *breKHt* (1898–1956), German playwright and poet, perhaps Germany's greatest dramatist, born at Augsburg, studied medicine and philosophy at Munich and Berlin Universities and won the *Kleist* drama prize in 1922 for his first two Expressionist plays, *Trommeln in der Nacht* and *Baal*, followed by *Mann ist Mann* (1926) with its clownish, inhuman soldiery. He was keenly interested in the effects produced by combining drama and music and consequently collaborated with Weill, Eisler and Dessau in his major works. It was the *Dreigroschenoper* (1928) with music by Kurt Weill that established Brecht's reputation. An adaptation of Gay's *Beggar's Opera* but in a sham Victorian London setting, it is a remarkable portrayal of the indolence, greed, and crazy bewilderment of human beings, and a satirical presentation of a bourgeois materialistic society. A Marxist, he regarded his plays as social experiments, requiring detachment, not passion, from the observing audience. To achieve this, Brecht introduced the 'epic' theatre, where the audience is required to see the stage as a stage, actors as actors, and not the traditional make-believe of the theatre. Thus, to prevent the audience from identifying themselves with a principal actor, the camp-following *Mutter Courage* (1938) is deliberately made to muff her lines and *Puntilla* (1940) is given an increasingly ugly make-up. With Hitler's rise to power in 1933, Brecht sought asylum in Denmark, Sweden, Finland, journeyed across Russia and Persia, and in 1941 settled in Hollywood, U.S.A. His abiding hatred of Nazi Germany found expression in a series of short, episodic plays and poems collected under the title of *Furcht und Elend des dritten Reiches* (1945). He denied membership of the Communist party before a Senate subcommittee on un-American activities in 1946 and in 1948 accepted the East German government's offer of a theatre in East Berlin. The *Berliner Ensemble* was founded, producing under his direction his later plays such as *Der kaukasische Kreidekreis* and *Der gute Mensch von Sezuan*, as well as touring in Western Europe, visiting London shortly after his death with Helene Weigel, his widow, as the company's leading actress. Brecht, although apparently antipathetic towards the East German anti-Communist uprising in 1953 and a recipient of the Stalin Peace prize (1954), proved as artist and thinker to be an embarrassment to the East German authorities. His opera *Lukullus* (1932-51), in which the Roman general has to account for his deeds before a tribunal-of-the-shadows, was withdrawn by order after the first night. *Galileo* underlined the moral that however much the intellect may be oppressed, truth will out. Brecht's moral pessimism was out of tune with Marxist materialistic optimism. But it is by his great lyrical and dramatic powers, stemming from such diverse influences as Luther's biblical language, Elizabethan drama, the works of Rimbaud, Villon, and Kipling, as well as the Japanese *Nō* theatre, his incredible range of poetic language from the bawdy to the sublime, as in his several volumes of ballads, poems, and plays, and not by his early political pieces, that he will be remembered. See his *Versuche*, and studies by G. Serreau (Paris 1955), R. Wintzen (Paris 1955), J. Willett (1959) and M. Esslin (1959).

BRECKINRIDGE, (1) **John** (1760–1806), American statesman, born near Staunton, Va., became a member of congress in 1792 and as attorney-general of Kentucky (1795–1797) was largely responsible for the state's reformed penal code. He was a staunch supporter of Jefferson, who made him attorney-general of the U.S. in 1805.

(2) **John Cabell** (1821–75), vice-president of the United States, was born near Lexington, Kentucky, where he practised law until 1847, when he was chosen major of a volunteer regiment for the Mexican war. He sat in congress 1851–55, and in 1856 was elected vice-president, with Buchanan as president. In 1860 he was the proslavery candidate for the presidency, but was defeated by Lincoln. A U.S. senator from March to December 1861, he then was appointed a Confederate major-general in 1862, held important commands, was secretary of war in Jeff

Davis's cabinet, and escaped to Europe, whence he returned in 1868. He died at Lexington.

BREE, Matthias Ignatius van, *bray* (1773–1839), Flemish painter, sculptor, and architect, was born at Antwerp, studied there and at Paris and painted the empress Josephine. Among his best works is the *Death of Rubens* in Antwerp museum. He taught the most eminent later Flemish painters, Wappers and De Keyser. His brother, **Philipp Jacob** (1786–1871), was also an historical painter.

BREHM, Alfred Edmund, *braym* (1829–84), German naturalist, born at Renthendorf, travelled in Africa, Spain, Norway, Lapland, Siberia, and Turkestan, and became keeper of the Hamburg Zoological Garden in 1863. His *magnum opus* is the *Illustriertes Thierleben* on which many other natural histories are largely based.

BREITINGER, Johann Jakob, *brīt'ing-er* (1701–76), Swiss critic and literary theorist, born in Zürich. He was an adherent of the Anglo-German Romantic movement and a friend of Bodmer, though of much narrower vision.

BREITMANN, Hans. See LELAND (1).

BREMER, Fredrika, *bray'mer* (1801–65), Swedish novelist, was born near Åbo in Finland, and was brought up near Stockholm. She varied her literary labour by long journeys in Italy, England, the United States, Greece, Palestine, which supplied the material for her *Homes of the New World* (1853) and *Life in the Old World* (1862). Latterly she devoted herself to the education and emancipation of women, and this aim is very apparent in her later novels, *Hertha* and *Father and Daughter* (1859). Her religious views she set forth in her *Morning Watches* (1842). Of the stories, perhaps the best is *The Neighbours* (1837). She is the first writer to paint a genuine picture of Swedish family life. See her Life and Letters, edited by her sister (trans. 1868).

BREMOND, Henri, *bray-mõ* (1865–1933), French critic and theologian, born in Aix-en-Provence. For twenty-two years a Jesuit (1882–1904), Bremond came under the influence of Newman, Tyrrell and the 'modernist' thinkers in the Catholic Church, gradually moving away from an orthodox religious position. His most extensive work is the *Literary History of Religious Feeling in France*, the final volumes of which were published after his death, and amongst his other books are *Sainte Chantal*, placed on the Index by the church, and numerous literary studies.

BRENDAN, St (484–577), an Irish ecclesiastic who, after seven years' fruitless voyaging in search of 'the mysterious land far from human ken', once more set sail with sixty friends, and at length reached 'that paradise amid the waves of the sea'. He afterwards founded the monastery of Clonfert. The *Navigation of St Brendan* (ed. Waters 1928) was popular in Western Europe from the 11th century. In old maps 'St Brendan's country' is placed west of the Cape Verde Islands.

BRENTANO, von, *-tah'no,* (1) **Bettina.** See ARNIM.

(2) **Clemens** (1778–1842), German poet, uncle of (3) and (5) and brother of (1), was born at Ehrenbreitstein. Save for the six years (1818–24) he passed with the ' Nun of Dülmen ', recording her revelations, he led a restless, unsettled life, and showed plain signs of derangement some years before his death at Aschaffenburg. In his earliest poems the peculiarities of the Romantic school of his time are carried to excess. His dramatic productions, the best of which is *Die Grün-dung Prags*, are characterized by great dramatic power, amusing though rather far-fetched wit, and a wonderful humour. He was most successful in his smaller novels, particularly in the *Geschichte vom braven Kaspar*, &c. His later work showed strong Catholic tendencies. See Life by W. Schell-berg (1922), and study by G. Müller (1922).

(3) **Franz** (1838–1917), German philosopher and psychologist, brother of (5) and nephew of (2), born at Marienberg, became a Catholic priest in 1864 and professor of Philosophy at Würzburg in 1872. Opposed to the doctrine of papal infallibility, he abandoned the priesthood in 1873 and was made to resign the professorship when he married in 1880. From 1880 to 1895 he was *Privatdozent* at Vienna. He spent his later years in Florence and Zürich. In his *Psychology from an Empiricist Standpoint* (1874), a misleading title because he was a rationalist, he went beyond Aristotelian and scholastic philo-sophy, arguing that psychology was the study of the mental acts of conception, judgment, and will. Each mental act had an ' inten-tional object ', i.e., the concept, the judgment or the attitudes of love and hate respectively. Elaborate psychological classifications in a further work (1911) developed the doctrine in detail. He was the precursor of ' Gestalt Psychology ' of the Würzburg, Graz, and Prague schools, and Husserl, Meinong, von Ehrenfels, Masaryk, and Rudolf Steiner numbered among his students. See Life by O. Kraus (1919).

(4) **Heinrich** (1904–64), West German statesman, born at Offenbach, became a successful lawyer. One of the founders of the Christian Democratic Party, he went into politics in Hesse in 1945 and was elected in 1949 to the Federal Diet at Bonn and played a prominent part in drafting the Constitution. He became foreign minister in 1955, aligning West Germany closely with the policies of the Atlantic Alliance, but resigned in 1961 to facilitate the formation of a coali-tion government of Dr Adenauer's parties with the Free Democrats.

(5) **Lujo** (1844–1931), German political economist, nephew of (2) and brother of (3), born at Aschaffenburg in Bavaria, in 1868 went to England to study the condition of the working classes, and especially trades associations and unions. The outcome of this was his *English Guilds* (1870) and *Die Arbeitergilden der Gegenwart* (2 vols. 1871–1872). He became professor of his subject in five universities and wrote on wages (1877), labour in relation to land, compulsory insurance for workmen, and an *Economic History of England* (1929). He was awarded the Nobel peace prize in 1927.

BRENTFORD. See JOYNSON-HICKS.

BRENZ, Johann (1499–1570), German Lutheran reformer, born in Swabia, died at Stuttgart. He was co-author of the Württem-berg Confession of Faith, and his Catechism (1551) stands next to Luther's in Protestant Germany. See Life by Hartmann (1862).

BRETON, *brẽ-tõ̃*, (1) **André** (1896–1966), French poet, essayist and critic, born at Tinchebray, Normandy. In 1919 he joined the Dadaist group, and collaborated with Philippe Soupault to write *Les Champs magnétiques*, which was described as ' an experiment in automatic writing '. In 1924 he published his Surrealist manifesto and *Le Poisson soluble*, and became editor of *La Révolution surréaliste*, and in 1930 he joined the Communists. He spent the war years in the U.S.A. His writings include *Qu'est-ce que le surréalisme?* (1936).

(2) **Jules Adolphe** (1827–1906), French painter, born at Courrières, near Arras, studied in Ghent and Paris, became a follower of Millet, but with added sentimen-tality and sophistication in his portrayal of peasant life. His *Harvest* pictures in the Louvre are representative of his work. See his *Life of an Artist* (trans. 1892) and *La Peinture* (1904).

(3) **Nicholas,** *bret'ẽn* (c. 1545–c. 1626), English poet, writer of lyrical, pastoral, satirical, religious, romantic, and humorous verse and prose, was the son of a London merchant and stepson of George Gascoigne (q.v.). Walton drew from his *Wits Trench-mour* (1597) for the *Compleat Angler*. See studies by Monroe (1929) and Blunden in *Votive Tablets* (1931).

BRETÓN DE LOS HERREROS, Don Manuel, *bre-tõn' THay los er-ray'rõs* (1796–1873), Spanish dramatist, author of some 360 plays, mostly social comedies in which caricature rather than character is portrayed.

BRETONNEAU, Pierre, *bre-ton-nõ̃* (1778–1862), French physician, born at Tours, was the first to name diphtheria and described typhoid fever.

BRETSCHNEIDER, Karl Gottlieb, *bret'shnī-der* (1776–1848), German theologian, was born at Gersdorf in Saxony, lectured in theology at Wittenberg (1804–06) and eventually became superintendent at Gotha, where he died. In his treatise on the gospel of St John (1820) he examines the arguments against St John's authorship. His *Manual of the Religion and History of the Christian church* (trans. 1857) reveals his dogmatic position. He allows full and reasoned criticism of the Christian dogmas while still recognizing the inspired nature of the Bible. See Autobiography (Gotha 1851).

BREUER, Josef, *broy'er* (1842–1925), Austrian neurologist. See FREUD (3).

BREUGHEL, or **Brueghel,** *brǣ'gel*, (1) **Jan** (1568–1625), younger son of (2), called ' Velvet ' Breughel, painted still life, flowers, landscapes and religious subjects generally on a small scale. His son, **Jan** (1601–78), imitated him closely.

(2) **Pieter** (c. 1520–69), the most original of all 16th-century Flemish painters, father of (1) and (3), was probably born in the village of Breughel, near Breda, and died in Brussels.

In 1551 he travelled through France and Italy, but was curiously unaffected by the Italian mannerism. His genre pictures of peasant life reach their finest expression in his last works, *The Blind Leading the Blind* (Naples 1568), the *Peasant Wedding*, and the *Peasant Dance* (Vienna *c.* 1568), in which his affectionate gusto and bucolic relish in peasant life is portrayed with unswerving truthfulness and feeling. His principal works are in Vienna, but his *Adoration of the Kings* (1564) and *Death of the Virgin* are in the National Gallery. See monographs by Tolnai (1935), Glück (1958) and Delevoy (1959).

(3) **Pieter** (*c.* 1564–1637), son of (2), called ' Hell ' Breughel because he painted *diableries*, scenes with devils, hags or robbers.

BREUIL, Henri, *brœ'y*, (1877–1961), French archaeologist. As a young abbé he discovered some cave paintings at Les Eyzies in the Dordogne, and succeeded in proving their authenticity to the experts, who had hitherto refused to accept as genuine either the famous Altamira paintings discovered in 1875, or the newly-found set at La Mouthe. This marked the beginning of the study of palaeolithic art; and the findings of a lifetime of research in the subject, not only in Europe, but also in Africa, are embodied in his *Four Hundred Centuries of Cave Art.*

BREWER, (1) **Ebenezer Cobham** (1810–97), born in London, took a first class in the law tripos from Trinity Hall, Cambridge, in 1835, and the year before received orders. He then became a London schoolmaster. Of thirty compilations by him the best known is his *Dictionary of Phrase and Fable* (1870), still a standard work of reference.

(2) **John Sherren** (1809–79), English scholar, born at Norwich, was appointed professor of English in King's College, London, in 1841. For nearly twenty years he was occupied in the Record office, editing the *Monumenta Franciscana* (1858), works of Roger Bacon (1859) and Giraldus Cambrensis (1861), vols. i-iv of the *Calendar of Papers of the Reign of Henry VIII* (1862–72), &c. See Memoir prefixed to his *English Studies* (1880).

BREWSTER, Sir David (1781–1868), Scottish physicist, was born at Jedburgh and educated for the Church; but a constitutional nervousness disinclining him for a clerical life, he became editor in 1802 of the *Edinburgh Magazine*, and in 1808 of the *Edinburgh Encyclopaedia*. Previous to this he had been interested in the study of optics. The kaleidoscope was invented by him in 1816, and years later he improved Wheatstone's stereoscope by introducing refracting lenses. In 1819 the *Edinburgh Philosophical Journal* took the place of the *Magazine*; and in 1831 Brewster was one of the chief originators of the British Association. In 1815 he was elected an F.R.S. and Copley medallist; in 1818 the Rumford gold and silver medals were awarded him for his discoveries on the polarization of light; in 1832 he was knighted, in 1838 he was appointed principal of St Salvator and St Leonard's, St Andrews. He was principal of Edinburgh University from 1859 See *Home Life of Brewster*, by his daughter, M. M. Gordon (1869).

BREZHNEV, Leonid Ilyich (1906–), Russian politician, born in the Ukraine, early career as party official in Ukraine and Moldavia. Member (1952–57) and president of the praesidium (1960–64), he became first secretary of the central committee in succession to Khruschev in 1964.

BŘEZINA, Otakar, *běr-zhe'zi-na*, properly **Václav Jebavy,** *ye'ba-vee* (1868–1929), Czech poet, born at Pocatky, leading exponent of symbolism in Czech poetry in his collections *Polar Winds* (1897), *Temple Builders* (1899), *The Hands* (1901), &c. See studies by P. Selver (1921) and A. Vesely (Brno 1928).

BRIALMONT, Henri Alexis, *bree-al-mŏ* (1821–1903), a Belgian general, engineer, and authority on fortification, &c., was born at Venloo. He designed the fortifications of Antwerp, Liège, Namur, Bucharest, &c.

BRIAN (926–1014), a famous king of Ireland, the Brian Boroimhe or Boru (' Brian of the tribute ') of the annalists, in 976 succeeded his murdered elder brother as chief of the Dal Cais; and, after much fighting, made himself king of Cashel two years later. Having established his rule over all Munster, he marched into Leinster, and was acknowledged as king by its chiefs in 984. With the help of Maelsechlainn Mac Domhnaill, chief king of Ireland, he crushed an outbreak of the Leinster men in 1000; then, aided by the Danes of Dublin, he overpowered his late ally. He subdued the Connaughtmen, and the men of the north; and after marching from Meath to Armagh, made a circuit of Ireland, taking hostages everywhere. He thus became Ardrigh na Erenn, chief king of Ireland. The aged hero was killed after defeating the Danes of Dublin at Clontarf.

BRIANCHON, Charles Julien, *bree-ã-shŏ* (1785–1864), French mathematician, born at Sèvres, wrote on curves of the second order, and on the theory of transversals. A theorem in conic sections bears his name.

BRIAND, Aristide, *bree-ã* (1862–1932), French socialist, born at Nantes, framer of the law for the separation of church and state (1905), was eleven times French premier, and foreign minister 1925–32. He shared the 1926 Nobel prize for peace with Gustav Streseman and advocated a United States of Europe. See Lives by Daniélou (1935) and Hesse (1939).

BRIDE, St. See BRIDGET.

BRIDGE, Frank (1879–1941), English composer and conductor, was born at Brighton and studied under Stanford (q.v.) as Britten (q.v.) was later to study under him. He played the viola in leading quartets and conducted the New Symphony Orchestra, from its inception, at Covent Garden and often at the ' Proms '. He is best known for his string quartets, but his full orchestral works were less successful, except perhaps his ' Sea ' suite. See Howells, *Music and Letters XXII* (1941).

BRIDGES, Robert Seymour (1844–1930), English poet, born at Walmer, studied at Eton and Corpus Christi, Oxford, qualified in medicine at St Bartholomew's and practised in that and other London hospitals till he retired in 1882. Meantime he had published three volumes of graceful lyrics (1873, 1879, 1880), some of them with a charm hardly equalled since Elizabethan days.

Settling at Yattendon, Berks, he wrote several plays, including *Nero* (1885), *Achilles in Scyros* (1890) and *The Feast of Bacchus* (1889), the narrative poem *Eros and Psyche* (1885) and other works, and he collaborated in the *Yattendon Hymnal* (1895–99), a pioneer in the trend away from contemporary sentimentalism in church music. He showed rare sympathy and insight as a critic in his essay on Keats; and by his examination of Milton's prosody and other studies on verse forms he shed much light on the mysteries and fascinations of the subtlest metrical rhythms and harmonies. He was also a keen advocate of spelling reform. From 1907 he lived in cloistered seclusion at Boar's Hill, Oxford, publishing comparatively little until, in 1929, on his eighty-fifth birthday, he issued *The Testament of Beauty*, his masterpiece, a magnificent poem enshrining the gathered wisdom of his long career. A lifelong friend since his Oxford days was Gerard Manley Hopkins (q.v.), whose poetry, then neglected, he edited and did much to promote. See studies by O. Elton (1932), E. Thompson (1944) and Ritz (1960).

BRIDGET, or **Bride, St** (453–523), patron saint of Leinster, entered a convent at Meath in her fourteenth year, and founded four monasteries, the chief at Kildare, where she was buried. Her legendary history is a mass of astonishing miracles, some of which were apparently transferred to St Bridget from the Celtic goddess Ceridwen. She was regarded as one of the three great saints of Ireland, the others being St Patrick and St Columba, and was held in great reverence in Scotland. See Life by Curtayne (1955).

BRIDGET, or **Brigitta, St** (*c.* 1302–73), Swedish visionary, born of noble family at Finstad in 1302 or 1303, married a judge, by whom she had eight children, was for some years mistress of the Swedish royal household; and after pilgrimages to Compostella and elsewhere, and the death of her husband, founded the monastery of Wadstena, in East Gothland, the cradle of a new order (of St Bridget or of St Salvator), which flourished in Sweden until the Reformation. It had seventy-four establishments scattered throughout Europe, and has still a few representatives in Spain, Bavaria, and Belgium. In 1349 St Bridget went to Rome, where she founded a Swedish hospice, and having made a pilgrimage to Palestine, died at Rome on her return, July 23, 1373. She was canonized in 1391. Her daughter, St Catharine of Sweden (1335–81), was canonized in 1489. The *Revelationes Stae. Brigittae*, written by her confessors, has passed through many editions. See Life by Jorgensen (trans. 1954).

BRIDGEWATER. See EGERTON.

BRIDGMAN, (1) **Frederick Arthur** (1848–1927), American painter, was born at Tuskegee, Alabama; for a time was a banknote engraver at New York, but meanwhile studied art, and in 1866 went to Paris. He painted in Brittany, the Pyrenees, Algiers, Egypt, mostly oriental subjects such as *Market Scenes in Nubia* (1883), *Pharoah's Progress through the Red Sea*, &c., exhibited in the international exhibition in Paris in 1900.

(2) **Laura Dewey** (1829–89), was born in Hanover, New Hampshire. At the age of two a violent fever utterly destroyed sight, hearing, smell, and in some degree taste. Dr Samuel Howe (q.v.) educated her at the Perkins institution, and she became a skilful teacher of blind deaf-mutes. See Lives by the Misses Howe (1903) and Elliott and Hall (1904), and Charles Dickens, *American Notes* (1842).

(3) **Percy Williams** (1882–   ), American physicist, born in Cambridge, Mass., educated at Harvard, where he became professor of Physics and Mathematics. He obtained under high pressure a new form of phosphorus, proved experimentally that viscosity increases with high pressure, and was awarded the Nobel prize in 1946 for his work on high-pressure physics and thermodynamics.

BRIDIE, James, pseud. of **Osborne Henry Mavor** (1888–1951), Scottish dramatist, born in Glasgow. He qualified as a doctor at Glasgow University and became a successful general practitioner and consultant. Always interested in the theatre, he seized his chance when the Scottish National Players produced his *Sunlight Sonata* in 1928 under the pseudonym of Mary Henderson. After that, he wrote a stream of plays, among them *The Anatomist* (1931), *A Sleeping Clergyman* (1933), *Mr Bolfry* (1943), *Dr Angelus* (1947) —always amusing, extravagant, thought-provoking, and entertaining, though uneven in quality. His wit has been described as Shavian—but he was not so good a craftsman, though he had more heart. He served in both world wars in the R.A.M.C. and after the second he became head of the Scottish Committee of C.E.M.A. and played a leading part in the foundation of the Glasgow Citizen's Theatre. See *James Bridie and His Theatre* by Winifred Bannister (1955).

BRIDPORT, Lord. See HOOD (1).

BRIEUX, Eugène, *bree-œ'* (1858–1932), French dramatist and Academician, was born in Paris of poor parents and experienced many of the social evils which his powerful, didactic plays, leavened by wit, expose. His works include *The Evasion* (1896), *Maternity* (1903), &c.

BRIGGS, Henry (1561–1631), English mathematician, was born at Warley Wood, near Halifax, and in 1588 became a fellow of St John's College, Cambridge. In 1592 he was appointed reader of the Physic Lecture, in 1596 first reader in Geometry at Gresham House, London, and in 1619 first Savilian professor of Astronomy in Oxford. Briggs made an important contribution to the theory of logarithms, introducing the decimal base instead of the Napierian, and also invented the method of long division in use today.

BRIGHAM YOUNG. See YOUNG (4).

BRIGHT, (1) **Henry** (1814–73), English watercolour painter, was born at Saxmundham, was a dispenser at a hospital in Norwich but eventually became the last of the ' Norwich school '. He toured the British Isles and the Continent, on occasions in the company of Turner and Ruskin.

(2) **James Franck**. See (4).

(3) **John** (1811–89), British Radical statesman and orator, son of a Quaker cotton-

spinner at Rochdale, was born there, and educated at a Friends' school at Ackworth, and afterwards at York and Newton. While in his father's factory he took a great interest in public questions; and after a tour of the Near East (1835) he lectured at Rochdale on his travels, as well as on commerce and political economy. When the Anti-Corn-Law League was formed in 1839 he was a leading member, and, with Cobden, engaged in free trade agitation throughout the kingdom. In 1843 he became M.P. for Durham, and strongly opposed the Corn Laws until they were repealed. In 1845 he obtained the appointment of select committees on the Game Laws, and on cotton cultivation in India. In 1847 he was elected a member for Manchester; in 1852 aided in the temporary reorganization of the Corn-Law League. Like Cobden a member of the Peace Society, he energetically denounced the Crimean war (1854). Elected in 1857 for Birmingham, he seconded the motion (against the Conspiracy Bill) which led to the overthrow of Palmerston's government; and he advocated the transference of India to the direct government of the crown. During the Civil War in America he warmly supported the cause of the North. His name was closely associated with the Reform Act of 1867. In 1868 he accepted office as president of the Board of Trade, but in 1870 retired through illness. He supported the disestablishing of the Irish Church (1869) and the Irish Land Act of 1870. He took office in 1873, and again in 1881, as chancellor of the duchy of Lancaster, but retired from the Gladstone ministry in 1882, being unable to support the government in its Egyptian policy. He strenuously opposed Gladstone's Home Rule policy (1886–88) and exerted a great influence on the Unionist party, being then as always recognized as one of the most eloquent speakers of his time. He was lord rector of Glasgow University in 1880. See his *Speeches* (1868), *Letters* (1885), *Diaries* (ed. Walling, 1930); and Lives by Robertson (1877), Vince (1898), O'Brien (1910), Trevelyan (1913).

(4) **Richard** (1789–1858), physician, was born at Bristol, and studied at Edinburgh, London, Berlin, and Vienna, and from 1820 was connected with Guy's Hospital. He made many important medical observations (' Bright's disease ' of the kidneys is named after him) and wrote numerous dissertations. His *Travels through Lower Hungary* (1818) contains a valuable account of the Gypsies. His son, James Franck (1832–1920), was from 1881 to 1906 master of University College, Oxford. He was author of a *History of England* (5 vols. 1875–1904).

(5) **Timothy** (c. 1551–1615), Yorkshire doctor and clergyman, the originator in 1588 of modern shorthand.

BRIGIT, BRIGITTA. See BRIDGET.

BRIL, (1) Mattys (1550–84), Flemish landscape painter, born at Antwerp, died in Rome, brother of (2). ·

(2) **Paul** (1556–1626), brother of (1), was taught by Mattys in Rome and soon excelled him, raising the prestige of landscape painting by his frescoes in Rome.

BRILLAT-SAVARIN, Anthelme, *bree-yah-sa-va-rí* (1755–1826), French gastronome, born at Belley, was a deputy in 1789, and mayor of Belley in 1793; took refuge in Switzerland, and afterwards in America, where he played in the orchestra of a New York theatre; and from 1796 until his death was a member of the Court of Cassation. His *Physiologie du goût* (1825), an elegant and witty compendium of the art of dining, has been repeatedly republished and translated; an English form is *A Handbook of Gastronomy*, with 52 etchings by Lalauze (1884).

BRINDLEY, James (1716–72), English engineer, was humbly born at Thornsett near Chapel-en-le-Frith. Apprenticed to a millwright, he became an engineer, and in 1752 contrived a water engine for draining a coalmine. A silk mill on a new plan, and several others of his works, recommended him to the Duke of Bridgewater (see EGERTON (1)), who employed him (1759) to execute the canal between Worsley and Manchester—a difficult enterprise crowned with complete success (1772). He also commenced the Grand Trunk Canal, and completed the Birmingham, Chesterfield, and others; in all, constructing 365 miles of canals. Up till the last he remained illiterate; most of his problems were solved without writings or drawings; and when anything specially difficult had to be considered, he would go to bed and think it out there. He died at Turnhurst, Staffordshire. See Life by Meynell (1956).

BRINELL, Johann August (1849–1925), Swedish engineer, invented the Brinell machine for measuring the hardness of alloys and metals.

BRINK, (1) Bernard ten (1841–92), philologist, was born at Amsterdam, and became professor in 1870 of Modern Languages and Literature at Marburg, in 1873 of English at Strasburg. Invaluable to English philologists are his *Chaucer-Studien* (1870), *Geschichte der englischen Literatur* (1874; Eng. trans. 1883–1893), &c.

(2) **Jan ten** (1834–1901), a Dutch critic, born at Appingedam, after a short residence at Batavia became in 1862 Dutch master at The Hague, and in 1884 professor of Dutch Literature at Leyden, having earned for himself a foremost place as a critic of acuteness and insight, especially in the department of fiction and belles-lettres.

BRINTON, Daniel Garrison (1837–99), writer on North American ethnology, was born at Thornbury, Pa.

BRINVILLIERS, Marie Madeleine, Marquise de, *brí-vee-yay* (c. 1630–76), French murderess, daughter of Dreux d'Aubray, lieutenant of Paris, in 1651 married the Marquis de Brinvilliers, who introduced her to a handsome young officer, Sainte Croix, who became her lover and was sent to the Bastille by her father. There he learned about arsenic, and on his release the couple set about poisoning the marquise's family. Her father, brothers, and sisters succumbed, and eventually Sainte Croix himself, an accidental victim of his own poison. He left incriminating documents, and the marquise fled, but was arrested in Liège, taken to Paris, and executed. Scribe made her the subject of a comic opera, and Albert Smith of a romance. See also works by Bauplein (1871), Toiseleur (1883), and Stokes (1924).

BRION, Friederike Elisabeth, *bree'on* (1752–1813), the pastor's daughter at Sesenheim, near Strasbourg, who in 1770–71 was loved by, and still more loved, Goethe. She never married. See works by Düntzer (Stuttgart 1893) and Bode (1920).

BRISBANE, General Sir Thomas Makdougall (1773–1860), soldier and astronomer, was born at Brisbane House, Largs, Ayrshire; at sixteen entered the army, and served with distinction in Flanders, the West Indies, Spain, and North America; from 1821 to 1825 was governor of New South Wales; in 1836 was made a baronet, in 1837 a G.C.B. He catalogued in Australia 7385 stars, and received the Copley medal from the Royal Society. Brisbane, the capital of Queensland, was named after him.

BRISCOE, Henry Vincent Aird (1888–1961), English physical chemist, born at Hackney, London, investigated the chemistry of the elements boron, rhenium, and selenium.

BRISSOT DE WARVILLE, Jacques Pierre, *brees-sō dė var-veel* (1754–93), French revolutionary politician, born near Chartres, after completing his studies at Paris abandoned the legal profession for that of authorship. His *Théorie des lois criminelles* (1780) was followed by his *Bibliothèque des lois criminelles* (1782–86), which established his reputation as a jurist. He was imprisoned for four months in the Bastille on the false charge of having written a brochure against the queen; to escape from a new term there he retired in 1787 to London, and next year visited North America as representative of the *Société des Amis des Noirs*. In 1789 he was elected representative for Paris in the National Assembly, where he exercised a predominant influence over all the early movements of the Revolution. He also established *Le Patriote français*, which became the organ of the earliest Republicans. As the Revolution proceeded, Brissot was recognized as the head of the Girondists or Brissotins. He contributed powerfully to the fall of the monarchy, strongly enjoining war against Austria and England, and the diffusion of republican principles. In the Convention his moderation made him suspected, and, with twenty other Girondists, was guillotined. See his Memoirs (1830), Ellery's *Brissot de Warville* (1916), and study by Goez-Bernstein (1942).

BRITANNICUS, or in full, **Claudius Tiberius Britannicus Caesar**, the son of the Emperor Claudius and Messalina, was born A.D. 41 or 42. Claudius' fourth wife, Agrippina, caused her husband to adopt her son Nero, and treat Britannicus as an imbecile; and Nero, after his accession, had his half-brother poisoned in 55. He is the subject of a tragedy by Racine.

BRITTAIN, Vera (*c.* 1893–1970), English writer, was born at Newcastle-under-Lyme. After studying at Oxford she served as a nurse in World War I, recording her experiences with war-found idealism in *Testament of Youth* (1933). Besides writing a number of novels, she made several lecture tours in the United States, in 1925 married George Catlin, professor of Politics at Cornell, and wrote the sequels, *Testament of Friendship* (1940) and *Testament of Experience* (1957).

BRITTEN, (Edward) Benjamin (1913–), English composer, born in Lowestoft. Britten studied the piano under Harold Samuel and composition under Frank Bridge before winning a scholarship to the Royal College of Music, where he worked under John Ireland; he was already a prolific composer, and certain of his student works have survived to stand beside more mature compositions: notable among these is the set of choral variations, *A Boy was Born*. During the 1930s Britten supplied a great deal of incidental music for plays and documentary films, collaborating at times with W. H. Auden, whose poetry provided texts for the song cycles *Our Hunting Fathers* and *On This Island*. From 1939–42 Britten worked in America, producing his large-scale instrumental works, the Violin Concerto and the *Sinfonia da Requiem*. After his return to Britain, his works were almost exclusively vocal and choral, apart from the Second String Quartet and the Variations and Fugue on a Theme of Purcell (*The Young Person's Guide to the Orchestra*). As well as the choral ' Spring ' Symphony and many vocal and choral works, after 1945, when his first opera *Peter Grimes* won an immediate success, Britten wrote two further operas on a large scale, *Billy Budd* and *Gloriana*, the latter for the coronation of Queen Elizabeth II, and five, including *The Turn of the Screw*, on a smaller scale he calls ' chamber operas ', with a basic orchestra of twelve players. Amongst his gifts is the skill to write with a simplicity that attracts amateur performers while losing nothing of its artistic and dramatic effectiveness; this quality is especially marked in the ' children's operas ', *The Little Sweep*, incorporated in *Let's Make an Opera!* (1949), and *Noye's Fludde* (1958), a musical rendering of a 14th-century miracle play. In addition to his enormous activity as a composer, Britten is an accomplished pianist, usually heard as an accompanist, particularly of Peter Pears (q.v.), with whom and Eric Crozier he founded in 1948 the annual Aldeburgh Festival, where several of his own works have had their first performances in company with rarely heard works of all periods. He became a C.H. in 1953, and received the O.M. in 1965. See *Benjamin Britten*, by E. W. White (1954), and *Benjamin Britten: a commentary on his works*, ed. by D. Mitchell and H. Keller (1956).

BRITTON, (1) John (1771–1857), English topographer and antiquary, was born at Kingston St Michael near Chippenham. At sixteen he went to London, and was in turn cellarman, clerk, and compiler of a song book and a dramatic miscellany. He was employed with Edward Wedlake Brayley (1773–1854) to compile *The Beauties of Wiltshire*; its success led to *The Beauties of England and Wales* (15 vols. 1803–14).

(2) **Thomas** (1654?–1714), ' the musical small-coal man ', founded a fashionable musical club in London, patronized by Handel, Pepusch and others. A student of the

occult and a bibliophile, he helped to form the Harleian library and collected the Somers tracts.

BRIZEUX, Julien Auguste Pélage, *bree-zœ* (1803–58), French poet, born in Lorient. Much of his work, including a translation of Dante's *Divina Commedia*, was influenced by Italian styles, but he wrote much poetry in which the folklore, and sometimes the dialect, of Brittany found a place. His *Histoires poétiques* was crowned by the French Academy in 1855.

BROAD, Charlie Dunbar (1887–1971), English philosopher, born in London, was professor of Moral Philosophy at Cambridge (1933–53). He excelled in analysis of ideas and theories, as in *Scientific Thought* (1923), *Five Types of Ethical Theory* (1930), and *Examination of McTaggart's Philosophy* (1933–38), &c.

BROADWOOD, John (1732–1812), founder, with the Swiss Burkhardt Tschudi, of the great London pianoforte house, was born at Cockburnspath, Berwickshire, and walked down to London to become a cabinetmaker there. His grandson, **Henry Fowler Broadwood** (1811–93), was likewise a great improver of the piano.

BROCA, Paul (1824–80), French surgeon and anthropologist, born at Sainte-Foy-le-Grande, Gironde, first located the motor speech centre in the brain and did research on prehistoric surgical operations.

BROCCHI, Giovanni Battista, *brok'kee* (1772–1826), Italian mineralogist and traveller, born at Bassano, wrote on the structure of the Apennine mountain range and disproved the view that Rome occupies the site of an extinct volcano. He died at Khartum while on a geological expedition to the Sudan. See Life by Stoppani (1874).

BROCKHAUS, Friedrich Arnold, *brok'hows* (1772–1823) founder of the firm of Brockhaus in Leipzig and publisher of the famous *Konversations-Lexikon*, begun by Löbel in 1796 and completed in 1811. An improved edition was begun in 1812 edited by Brockhaus. The business was carried on by his descendants. The first illustrated edition of the *Lexikon* was published in 1892–97; *Der Grosse Brockhaus* was begun in 1928.

BROD, Max (1884–), Austrian writer, born in Prague, emigrated, a Zionist, to Palestine in 1939, wrote light popular fiction but developed into an author of deeply moralistic poems and novels, which include *Tycho Brahes Weg zu Gott* (1916), *Das Buch der Liebe* (1921), and a Life of Kafka (1937, trans. 1947).

BRODIE, (1) **Sir Benjamin Collins, 1st Baronet,** F.R.S. (1783–1862), surgeon, was born at Winterslow Rectory, Wiltshire. He studied at St George's Hospital, of which he became assistant surgeon and surgeon. He advocated milder treatment of diseases of joints than amputation. See *Autobiography*, in his *Collected Works* (3 vols. 1865), and Life by T. Holmes (1898). His son, **Sir Benjamin Collins** (1817–80), the discoverer of graphitic acid, in 1855 became professor of Chemistry at Oxford.

(2) **William** (d. 1788), deacon of the Edinburgh Wrights' Incorporation, was hanged for burglary. See R. L. Stevenson and W. E. Henley's play, *Deacon Broc* (1880).

(3) **William** (1815–81), Scottish sculpto was born at Banff, began life as a plumber mate but took up sculpture in his leisur hours. A portrait bust of Lord Jeffrey brought him recognition and he was given the means to study at Rome (1853). His major works include statues of Sir David Brewster, Lord Cockburn in the Parliament House, Edinburgh, and Queen Victoria in Windsor Castle.

BROGAN, Sir Denis William (1900–), British historian, born at Rutherglen of Irish descent, educated at Glasgow, Oxford, and Harvard, became a fellow of Corpus Christi, Oxford, in 1934, and professor of Political Science at Cambridge in 1939. He is known for his books on historical and modern America as well as more general works, such as *The English People* (1943) and *The French Nation* (1957). He was knighted in 1963.

BROGLIE, *brol'yay*, a prominent French family of Piedmontese origin:

(1) **Achille Charles Léonce Victor** (1785–1870), grandson of (6), and son of Prince Claude Victor (b. 1757, guillotined 1794), was distinguished as a Liberal politician and advocate of the abolition of slavery, foreign secretary and prime minister (1835–36) under Louis-Philippe. An Academician, he published *Écrits et discours* (1863) and his *Souvenirs* (1866).

(2) **François Marie, Duc de** (1671–1745), marshal of France, took part in every campaign from 1689.

(3) **Jacques Victor Albert** (1821–1901), son of (1), early entered the field of literature, was elected an Academician in 1862, ambassador at London and twice premier (1873, 1877). His works include *L'Église et L'Empire romain au IVe siècle* (1856), two hostile works on Frederick the Great, &c.

(4) **Louis César Victor Maurice, Duc de** (1875–1960), grandson of (3), physicist, famed for his researches in X-ray spectra, became an Academician in 1934.

(5) **Louis Victor** (1892–), younger brother of (4), also a physicist, won a Nobel prize in 1929 for his pioneer work on the undulatory theory of matter.

(6) **Victor François** (1718–1804), son of (2), was the most capable French commander in the Seven Years' War. Entered Russian service after the revolution.

BROKE, Sir Philip Bowes Vere, *brook* (1776–1841), English rear-admiral, born at Broke Hall, Ipswich, entered the service in 1792, was made captain in 1801, and appointed to the *Shannon* frigate, 38 guns, in 1806. In her he fought the memorable duel with the American *Chesapeake* frigate, off Boston, June 1, 1813, which made ' brave Broke ' a hero in popular song. The Americans were confident of success, but proved no match for Broke's thoroughly disciplined men, who, after delivering two terrific broadsides, sprang across the bulwarks, and ran up the British colours fifteen minutes after the commencement of the action. A blow received in boarding seriously affected Broke's health, and he retired from active service with a baronetcy. See Life by Dr Brighton (1866).

BROME, Richard (d. *c.* 1652), dramatist, of whom little is known except that he had been in his earlier days servant to Ben Jonson, and that he wrote as many as twenty-four popular plays, the best being *The Northern Lass* and *The Jovial Crew*.

BROMFIELD, Louis (1896–1956), American novelist, was born at Mansfield, Ohio, the son of a farmer. Educated at Cornell Agricultural College and Columbia University, he joined the French Army in 1914, was awarded the *croix de guerre*, and returned to journalism in America. His novels include *The Green Bay Tree* (1924), *Early Autumn* (Pulitzer prize, 1926), *The Strange Case of Miss Annie Spragge* (1928), *The Rains Came* (1937), *Until the Day Break* (1942), *Colorado* (1947), *Mr Smith* (1951). His short stories include *Awake and Rehearse* (1929), and his plays *The House of Women* (1927). See study by M. Brown (1956).

BRONGNIART, Alexandre, brŏ-nyahr′ (1770–1847), French naturalist and geologist, from 1800 director of the porcelain manufactory at Sèvres, was born and died in Paris. He introduced the term *Jurassic* for the limestones and clays of the Cotswolds. His son, **Adolphe Théodore** (1801–76), was a botanist.

BRONN, Heinrich Georg (1800–62), German naturalist and palaeontologist, was born at Ziegelhausen near Heidelberg, and did important research on rock formations.

BRONTË, bron′tay, originally **Brunty** or **Prunty**, the name of three sisters remarkable in English literary history, born at Thornton, Yorkshire, the daughters of **Patrick Prunty** (1777–1861) a clergyman of Irish descent and his Cornish wife **Maria** (1783–1821), and sisters of **Maria** and **Elizabeth**, who both died in childhood and **Branwell** (1817–48), a brother who squandered his many-sided talents. See studies by du Maurier (1960) and Gerin (1961). The family removed to Haworth, now part of Keighley, in 1820 when their father became rector there. After the mother's death from cancer, his sister came to look after the children. Their childhood, spent in the sole companionship of one another on the wild Yorkshire moors, was happy enough. Branwell's twelve toy soldiers inspired them to construct two fantasy worlds of their own, *Gondal* and *Angria*, which contained all the exotic places and was peopled by all the great figures they had read about. Incidents in these were described by the children in verse and prose in rival collections of notebooks. Such escapism ill-fitted them for their harsh schooling at Cowan Bridge, but Roe Head, their second school, proved more attractive. Branwell's debts caused them to leave home and find employment, but they always returned to their beloved Haworth. See joint Lives and studies by Mackay (1897), Gosse (1903), Shorter (1907), Sinclair (1914), Sugden (1929), Romicu (trans. 1931), Bradby (1932), Cooper Willis (1933), B. White (1939), P. Bentley (1948), and L. and E. M. Hanson (1949). Their biographies from the time they left home are treated separately as follows:

(1) **Anne**, pseud. **Acton Bell** (1820–49)

went as governess to Inghams at Blake Hall in 1839 and to Robinsons at Thorpe Green (1841–45), a post she had to leave because of Branwell's importunate love for Mrs Robinson. She shared in the joint publication, under pseudonyms, of the three sisters' *Poems* (1846), only two volumes of which were sold. Her two novels *Agnes Grey* (1845) and *The Tenant of Wildfell Hall* (1848) although unsuccessful at the time, show a decided talent, if less vivid than that of her sisters. See Lives by A. Harrison and D. Stanford (1959) and W. Gerin (1959).

(2) **Charlotte**, pseud. **Currer Bell** (1816–55), returned in 1835 to her old school, Roe Head, as teacher, but dreams of *Angria* forced her to give up this post and two others, both as governess. Back at Haworth, the three sisters planned to start a school of their own and, to augment their qualifications, Charlotte and Emily (3) attended the Héger Pensionat in Brussels (1842). Their plans foundered, however, and Charlotte returned to Brussels as English teacher (1843–44) and formed a hopeless and unreciprocated attachment to the married M. Héger, whom she later scornfully satirized in *Villette* (1852). Her chance discovery of Emily's remarkable poems in 1845 led to the abortive joint publication, under pseudonyms, of the three sisters' *Poems* (1846) of which only two copies sold. This turned them all to novel writing. *The Professor*, which did not achieve publication until Charlotte's death, dwells on the theme of moral madness, possibly inspired by Branwell's degeneration. It was rejected by her publisher but with sufficient encouragement for her to complete her masterpiece, *Jane Eyre* (1847). This in essence, through the master-pupil love relationship between Rochester and Jane, constituted a magnificent plea for feminine equality with men in the avowal of their passions. Such sublime frankness horrified the Victorians and foreshadowed the 20th century. It was followed in 1849 by *Shirley*, a novel set in the background of the Luddite riots. She married her father's curate, Mr Nicholls in 1854 and died during pregnancy in the following year, leaving the fragment of another novel, *Emma*. See Lives by Mrs Gaskell (1877), Swinburne (1877), Birrell (1887), Shorter (1906), McDonald (1914), Goldring (1915), Langbridge (1929), and Benson (1932) and study by Gerin (1967).

(3) **Emily Jane**, pseud. **Ellis Bell** (1818–48), in 1837 became a governess in Halifax, attended the Héger Pensionat in Brussels with Charlotte (2) and in 1845 embarked upon a joint publication of poems after the discovery by the latter of her *Gondal* verse, including such fine items as *To Imagination*, *Plead for Me*, and *Last Lines*. Her single novel, *Wuthering Heights* (1847), has much in common with Greek tragedy. The wild, brutal, heroic theme of the destructive power of thwarted love (in Heathcliff for Catherine and in Earnshaw for his dead wife) finds expression in an intensely lyrical prose, coloured by season and locality, in which word and action rather than introspection, as in Charlotte's writing, predominate. See Lives and studies by A. F. M. Robinson (1883),

Law (1925), Wilson (1928), Simpson (1930), and V. Moore (1936).

BRONZINO, Il, properly Agnolo di Cosimo di Mariano (1502–72), Florentine painter, born at Monticelli, was a pupil of Rafaello del Garbo and of Pontormo, who adopted him. He decorated the chapel of the Palazzo Vecchio in Florence, and painted the *Christ in Limbo* in the Uffizi (1552). His *Venus, Folly, Cupid and Time* is in the National Gallery, and his portraits include most of the Medici family, also Dante, Boccaccio, and Petrarch. His nephew and nephew's son, both Florentine painters, adopted his name. See ALLORI, also study by McComb (1928).

BROOKE, Lord. See GREVILLE.

BROOKE, (1) Sir Basil Stanlake. See BROOKEBOROUGH.

(2) Henry (*c.* 1703–83), Irish dramatist and novelist, was born at Rantavan, County Cavan. He became the friend of Pope and married his cousin and ward. His poem, *Universal Beauty* (1735), is supposed to have suggested Erasmus Darwin's *Botanic Garden*. His novel, *The Fool of Quality* (1766), is the sole survivor of his numerous works. See Life by Scurr (1927).

(3) Sir James (1803–68), rajah of Sarawak, was born at Benares, and educated at Norwich, sailed in 1838 in a schooner-yacht from London for Sarawak, a province on the northwest coast of Borneo, with the object of putting down piracy, and was made Rajah of Sarawak (1841) for assistance rendered to the Sultan of Borneo against rebel tribes. Brooke instituted free trade, framed a new code of laws, declared the Dyak custom of head-hunting a capital crime, and vigorously set about the extirpation of piracy. In 1857 Brooke, superseded in the governorship of Labuan, but still acting as Rajah of Sarawak, sustained successfully, with his native forces, a series of attacks by a large body of Chinese, who were irritated at his efforts to prevent opium-smuggling. See Brooke's own *Letters* (1853), Lives by Jacob (1876) and St John (1879), and study by Runciman (1960).

(4) Rupert Chawner (1887–1915), English poet, was born and educated at Rugby and at King's College, Cambridge, travelled in Germany and visited the U.S.A. and Tahiti. He died a commissioned officer on Skyros on his way to the Dardanelles and was buried there. His *Poems* appeared in 1911, *1914 and Other Poems* in 1915, after his death. If lacking the insight of a maturer poet, his poetry was characterized by a youthful, self-probing honesty, a fresh perception, a gentle lyricism and comedy. These, together with his handsome appearance and untimely death, made him a favourite poet among young people in the interwar period. See his *Letters from America* and *John Webster* (1916), and life by Hassall (1964).

(5) Stopford Augustus (1832–1916), a brilliant preacher and author, born in Letterkenny, Donegal, was appointed a royal chaplain in 1872 but through inability to continue to believe in miracles, he seceded from the Church of England, but continued to preach in his proprietary chapel as Unitarian minister. He published *Theology in the English Poets* (1874), *Primer of English Liter-*ature (1876), *English Literature to the Conquest* (1898), &c. See Life by Jacks (1917).

BROOKEBOROUGH, Basil Stanlake Brooke, 1st Viscount (1888–1973), Irish statesman, was elected to the Northern Ireland parliament in 1929, became minister of agriculture in 1933, of commerce in 1941, and prime minister from 1943 till his resignation in 1963. A staunch supporter of Unionist policy he exhibited an unswerving determination to preserve the ties between Northern Ireland and the U.K. He was created viscount in 1952, and became a K.G. in 1965, retiring from politics in 1968.

BROOKS, (1) Charles William Shirley (1816–1874), editor of *Punch*, was born in London, wrote dramas and newspaper articles; in 1870 he succeeded Mark Lemon as editor of *Punch*. His novels include *Aspen Court* (1855), *The Gordian Knot* (1860), &c. See Lives by Johnson (1897) and Layard (1907).

(2) Phillips (1835–93), American Protestant Episcopal bishop, was born at Boston, studied at Harvard, and after serving cures in Philadelphia and Boston, was consecrated Bishop of Massachusetts in 1891. A keen thinker and powerful preacher, he opposed the theory of apostolical succession but is best known for his Yale *Lectures on Preaching* (1877). See Life by Allen (1900).

(3) Van Wyck (1886–1963), American author and critic, wrote biographical studies of Mark Twain (1920), Henry James (1925), and Emerson (1932), attacked American materialism and won the Pulitzer prize with his *Flowering of New England* (1936), a study in literary history.

BRORSON, Hans Adolf (1694–1764), Danish poet. Brorson was a fervent follower of the Pietist movement in Protestant thought, and is remembered for the mystical fervour of much of his work. Several of his hymns are still in use.

BROSCHI, Carlo, *bros'kee* (1705–82), under the name ' Farinelli ' was the most famous of castrato singers. He was born at Naples and died at Bologna; visited London in 1734; and in Spain was made a grandee, with a pension of £2000 a year.

BROSSE, Salomon de (1565–1626), French architect of the Luxembourg in Paris (1615–1620), and of Louis XIII's hunting lodge (1624–26), the nucleus of Versailles.

BROSSES, Charles de, *bros* (1709–77), French historian, was born at Dijon, and died president of the parliament of Burgundy. Among his works were: *Lettres sur Herculaneum* (1750); *Histoire des navigations aux terres australes* (1756); *Du culte des dieux fétiches* (1760, the word *fétich* being first used by him in the sense now usual); &c. Lord R. Gower translated selections from his *Letters* (1897). See Life by Marnet (1875).

BROTHERS, Richard (1757–1824), English religious fanatic and ex-naval officer, born in Newfoundland, announced himself in 1793 as the ' nephew of the Almighty ', apostle of a new religion, the Anglo-Israelites. In 1795, for prophesying the destruction of the monarchy, he was sent to Newgate and subsequently to an asylum, but not before he had acquired a number of disciples, some of them men of influence and standing.

BROUGHAM, Henry, 1st Baron Brougham and Vaux, *broom, vawks* (1778–1868), was born in Edinburgh, his father being of an old Westmorland family, and his mother a niece of Robertson, the historian. Educated at the High School and Edinburgh University, in 1800 he was admitted to the Scottish bar; and in 1802 helped to found the *Edinburgh Review,* to whose first twenty numbers he contributed eighty articles. His Liberal views shut him out from the hope of promotion in Scotland; in 1805 he settled in London; in 1806 was secretary to a mission to Lisbon; and in 1808 was called to the English bar. Entering parliament in 1810 he carried an act making participation in the slave trade felony. In 1812 he carried the repeal of the Orders in Council; but contesting Liverpool against Canning, was defeated, and remained without a seat till 1816, when he was returned for Winchelsea. He never acquired a very large practice at the bar, but he repeatedly distinguished himself by speeches of great vigour and ability—his most famous appearance being in defence of Queen Caroline (1820). His eloquence and boldness, though they forfeited for him the favour of the crown, gained him that of the people, and in 1820–30 Brougham was the popular idol. In 1822 he used his power, though in vain, in support of a scheme of national education; and he did much for the establishment of London University, of the first Mechanics' Institute, and of the Society for the Diffusion of Useful Knowledge. In 1830 he was returned for the county of York. The aristocratic Whigs would, had they dared, have excluded Brougham from the Reform ministry, but found him indispensable; he was persuaded to accept a peerage and the chancellorship (1830), and assisted materially in carrying the Reform Bill. But his arrogance, self-confidence, and eccentricities rendered him as unpopular with his colleagues as he was on the bench. He went out with the Whig government in 1834, and on its reconstruction was shelved, never to hold office again. He was founder of the Social Science Association (1857); but it is as a law reformer that Brougham will be best remembered. In 1816 he introduced a bill amending the law of libel, and in 1827 made proposals for dealing with law reform on a large scale. After he left office, he secured great changes in the law of evidence. As an orator and as a debater in parliament, Brougham was inferior only to Canning, though fiery declamation and fierce invective were carried beyond bounds. His miscellaneous writings, numbering 133, are upon an almost incredible variety of subjects, but have little permanent value. Rogers remarked of him, 'There goes Solon, Lycurgus, Demosthenes, Archimedes, Sir Isaac Newton, Lord Chesterfield, and a great many more in one post-chaise'; and O'Connell's gibe ran. 'If Brougham knew a little of law, he would know a little of everything'. While not engaged in parliament, Brougham chiefly resided at Cannes, where he died, May 7. His own *Life and Times* (3 vols. 1871), written in extreme old age, is very untrustworthy. The brougham (carriage) is named after him. See Atlay's *Victorian Chancellors* (vol. i. 1906), Aspinall, *Lord B. and the Whig Party* (1927), and Lives by F. Howes (1957) and C. New (1961).

BROUGHTON, *braw'tĕn,* (1) **Lord.** See HOBHOUSE (1).
(2) **Rhoda** (1840–1920), English novelist, was born near Denbigh. Her first two, and perhaps best, novels, *Not Wisely but Too Well* and *Cometh up as a Flower* (both 1867), considered daring at the time, were followed by many others.

BROUNKER, William, 2nd Viscount Brounker of Castle Lyons, *brung'ker* (1620–84), Irish mathematician, educated at Oxford, a founder member and first president of the Royal Society. He first expressed indeterminable quantities in terms of infinite series.

BROUSSAIS, François Joseph Victor, *broo-say* (1772–1838), French physician, founder of a theory of medicine which strongly resembles the Brunonian system of John Brown, was born at St Malo, served as a surgeon in the navy and army, and in 1820 was appointed a professor at Val-de-Grâce, in 1830 in the Academy of Medicine in Paris. See monograph by Reis (Paris 1869).

BROUWER, or Brauwer, Adriaen, *brow'wĕr* (c. 1605–38), painter, was born at Oudenarde, studied at Haarlem under Frans Hals, and about 1630 settled at Antwerp, where he died of the plague. His favourite subjects were scenes from tavern life, country merrymakings, card players, smoking and drinking groups, and roisterers generally. See Lives by Schmidt (1873) and Bode (1924).

BROWN, (1) Alexander Crum, F.R.S. (1838–1922), Scottish chemist, half-brother of (14), was born in Edinburgh, and in 1869 became professor of Chemistry there. The rule of substitution for benzene derivatives bears his name.
(2) **Sir Arthur Whitten** (1886–1948; kt. 1919), born in Glasgow of American parents, was companion of Alcock (q.v.) on the first transatlantic flight (1919). See G. Wallace, *The Flight of Alcock and Brown* (1955).
(3) '**Capability**'. See BROWN (17).
(4) **Charles Brockden** (1771–1810), American novelist, born of Quaker ancestry at Philadelphia, the first professional American writer. *Wieland* (1798), *Ormund* (1799), *Jane Talbot* (1804), &c., are Gothic romances, full of incident and subtle analysis, but extravagant.
(5) **Ford Madox** (1821–93), British historical painter, grandson of (12), was born at Calais. His earlier studies were conducted at Bruges, Ghent, and Antwerp; in Paris he produced his *Manfred on the Jungfrau* (1841), a work intensely dramatic in feeling, but sombre in colouring. He contributed to the Westminster cartoon competitions. A visit to Italy (1845) led him to seek a greater variety and richness of colouring as in *Chaucer reciting his Poetry* (1851). He contributed verse, prose, and design to the pre-Raphaelite *Germ*, and in his youth Rossetti worked in his studio. Among his maturer works are *Christ washing Peter's Feet, The Entombment,* &c. He had just completed twelve frescoes for the Manchester Town Hall, when he died. See Life by Ford Madox Hueffer (1896).

(6) **George Alfred, Lord George-Brown**
(1914–   ), British Labour politician, born at
Southwark, London, left school at fifteen,
attended further education classes, was an
official of the Transport and General Workers
Union before entering parliament as M.P. for
Belper division in 1945. After holding minor
posts in the Labour government of 1945–51,
he became opposition spokesman on defence
(1958–61), when he supported Gaitskell in
opposing unilateral disarmament. He unsuccessfully contested Wilson for Party leadership in 1963. Vice-chairman and deputy
leader of the Labour Party from 1960, he was
first secretary of state and secretary of state
for economic affairs (1964–66), when he instigated a prices and incomes policy, which fell
victim to the later freeze on wages and prices.
He resigned in July 1966, but resumed his
post, becoming foreign secretary in August.
A flamboyant, impetuous and controversial
figure, Brown finally resigned and returned
to the back benches in March 1968 during the
gold crisis. Having lost his seat in the 1970
general election, he was created a life peer.

(7) **George Douglas** (1869–1902), born in
Ayrshire, wrote as ' George Douglas ' *The
House with the Green Shutters* (1901), a
powerfully realistic novel, an antidote to the
' Kailyard School '.

(8) **George Loring** (1814–89), American
painter and etcher, born in Boston, gained a
high reputation as a landscape painter.

(9) **Henry Kirke** (1814–86), American
sculptor, returned in 1846 from Italy to
Brooklyn and executed statues of Lincoln and
Washington in Union Square, New York.

(10) **John** (*c.* 1627–85), Scottish Covenanter
martyr, known as the ' Christian carrier ', of
Priesthill, Ayrshire, shot by Claverhouse.

(11) **John** (1722–87), of Haddington,
Scottish author of the *Self-interpreting Bible*
(1778) and preacher, was born at Carpow,
near Abernethy, Perthshire. He had little
schooling, but taught himself Greek, Latin
and Hebrew. For a time he was a pedlar;
during the '45 served in the Fife militia;
taught in several schools; and having studied
theology in connection with the Associate
Burgher Synod, was in 1751 called to the congregation of Haddington. In 1768 he accepted
the Burgher chair of Divinity. See his Memoirs
(1856) and study by Mackenzie (1918).

(12) **John** (*c.* 1735–88), British physician,
founder of the Brunonian system of medicine,
born of poor parents, in Bunkle parish,
Berwickshire, taught at Duns and in Edinburgh, and after studying medicine became
assistant to Professor Cullen (q.v.). Conceiving himself slighted by the latter, he
began to give lectures himself upon a
new system of medicine, according to which
all diseases are divided into the sthenic,
depending on an excess of excitement, and
the asthenic; the former to be removed by
debilitating medicines, and the latter by
stimulants. In 1779 he took his M.D. at St
Andrews. In debt, he went to London in 1786.
His works were edited, with a memoir, by his
son (1804).

(13) **John** (1800–59), American abolitionist,
was born in Torrington, Connecticut, of
Pilgrim descent. He was successively tanner

and land surveyor, shepherd and farmer;
and, a strong abolitionist, wandered through
the country on antislavery enterprises. He
was twice married and had twenty children.
In 1854 five of his sons removed to Kansas,
and joining them after the border conflict
had begun, Brown became a leader in the
strife. In reprisal, he once ordered five pro-
slavery men at Pottawatomie to be shot.
Osawatomie, Brown's home, was burned
in 1856, and a son killed. When the war in
Kansas ceased, Brown began to drill men in
Iowa. His scheme next was to establish a
stronghold in the mountains of Virginia as a
refuge for runaway slaves, and he now made
his harebrained attack on the U.S. armoury
at Harper's Ferry in Virginia. In 1859 he
assembled twenty-two men (six of them
coloured) and boxes of rifles and pikes on his
farm near the town; and on the night of
October 18, with eighteen men, he broke
into the armoury and took several citizens
prisoner. The citizens shot some of the
invaders, and next day Colonel Robert E. Lee
(afterwards famous), with a company of
marines, arrived from Washington. Brown
and six men, barricading themselves in an
engine-house, continued to fight until his two
sons were killed and he was severely wounded.
Tried by a Virginia court for insurrection,
treason, and murder, he was convicted and
hanged at Charlestown, Virginia. Four of his
men were executed with him, and two others
later. The song ' John Brown's body lies a-
mouldering in the grave ', commemorating
the Harper's Ferry raid, was highly popular
with the Republican soldiers in the Civil War.
See Lives by Redpath (1860) and Villard
(1910); and Benét's poem *John Brown's Body*
(1928).

(14) **John** (1810–82), great-grandson of (11),
Scottish essayist, was born at Biggar, attended
the High School at Edinburgh and studied
arts and medicine at the university there,
becoming M.D. in 1833. Almost all his
writings comprise only three volumes, the
two *Horae subsecivae* (' Leisure Hours ')
(1858–61) and *John Leech and other Papers*
(1882). Humour and pathos are the chief
features of his genius, as exemplified in his
sketches of ' Rab ' and ' Marjorie '—the
uncouth mastiff and the dead child. His
essays rank with those of Lamb. See Peddie's
Recollections (1893), Taylor Brown's *Life*
(1903), and his own *Letters* (1907).

(15) **Sir John** (1816–96), founder of the
Atlas Works at Sheffield, employing 4500
hands, invented the method of rolling plate-
armour, and first made steel rails.

(16) **John** (1826–83), for thirty-four years
personal attendant of Queen Victoria, born at
Craithenaird, Balmoral, died at Windsor
Castle.

(17) **Lancelot** (1715–83), the landscape-
gardener, famous as ' Capability Brown ', was
born at Kirkharle, Northumberland, laid out
gardens at Blenheim and Kew. See Life by
D. Stroud (1950).

(18) **Oliver Madox** (1855–74), British author
and artist, son of (5), was born at Finchley.
At twelve, he executed a watercolour of
considerable merit. In 1871, he wrote his
first novel *Gabriel Denver*, reprinted in his

Literary Remains (1876) under its first title *The Black Swan.* He died prematurely of food poisoning. See Life by Ingram (1883).

(19) **Peter Hume** (1850–1918), Scottish Historiographer Royal (from 1908), was born in Haddingtonshire, and studied at Edinburgh. Author of Lives of Buchanan (1890), John Knox (1895), Goethe (1920), a *History of Scotland* (1898–1909), &c., in 1898 he became editor of the Privy Council Register of Scotland; in 1901 professor of Ancient Scottish History, Edinburgh.

(20) **Robert** (1773–1858), Scottish botanist, son of the Episcopal clergyman at Montrose, was educated at Aberdeen and Edinburgh, and served in a Scottish regiment. In 1798 he visited London, and in 1801 went as naturalist with Captain Flinders to the Australian coasts; in 1805 he brought home nearly four thousand species of plants. Appointed librarian to the Linnean Society, he published the *Prodromus Florae Novae Hollandiae* (1810). His adoption of Jussieu's natural system led to its general substitution in place of the Linnean method; Humboldt called him ' facile princeps botanicorum '. In 1810 Brown received charge of Banks's library and splendid collections; and when, in 1827, they were transferred to the British Museum, he became botanical keeper there.

(21) **Robert** (1842–95), Scottish botanist and geographer, born at Campster, in Caithness, studied at Edinburgh University, travelled in Greenland, subarctic Canada, the West Indies, and the Barbary States, and wrote *The Countries of the World*, &c.

(22) **Thomas** (1778–1820), a Scottish metaphysician, born at Kirkmabreck manse, Kirkcudbrightshire, in 1792 entered Edinburgh University, abandoned law for medicine, but found that his real bent was for literature and philosophy. He contributed to the *Edinburgh Review*; and in 1804 appeared his *Cause and Effect*, in which he showed that Hume's doctrine was not incompatible with religion. In 1810 he became a colleague to Dugald Stewart, professor of Moral Philosophy. He was a forerunner of associationist psychology. See his *Lectures* (1860).

(23) **Tom** (1663–1704), ' of facetious memory ' in Addison's phrase, was born at Shifnal or, more probably, Newport, Shropshire. His studies at Christ Church, Oxford, probably cut short by his irregularities, are remembered by his extempore adaptation of Martial's epigram, ' Non amo te, Sabidi ': ' I do not love thee, Dr Fell '. After teaching at Kingston-on-Thames, he settled in London, where he made an uncertain living by writing scurrilous satirical poems and pamphlets. He is principally interesting now as the assailant of Dryden, Sherlock, D'Urfey, &c. He was buried in the Westminister cloisters near his friend, Mrs Aphra Behn. See a book by Boyce (1939).

(24) **Ulysses.** See BROWNE (10).
BROWNE, (1) Charles Farrar, pseud. **Artemus Ward** (1834–67), American humorist, was born at Waterford, Maine, wrote for the *Cleveland Plaindealer* a description of an imaginary travelling menagerie, followed by letters in which grotesque spelling and a mixture of business platitudes and sermonizing served to convey sound sense and shrewd satire. In 1861 ' Artemus Ward ' entered the lecture field, and started a panorama, whose artistic wretchedness furnished occasion for countless jokes. In 1864 he contracted tuberculosis; but in 1866, having rallied somewhat, he went to London, where he contributed to *Punch*, and was very popular as ' the genial showman ', exhibiting his panorama at the Egyptian Hall. His publications were *Artemus Ward, His Book* (1862), *Artemus Ward, His Panorama* (1865), &c.

(2) **Edward Granville** (1862–1926), English Oriental scholar, devoted himself chiefly to Persian, and wrote a monumental *Literary History of Persia* (1902–24).

(3) **Edward Harold** (1811–91), became Norrisian professor of Divinity at Cambridge and Bishop of Winchester in 1873. His *Exposition of the Thirty-Nine Articles* (1850) is a standard work.

(4) **Felicia Dorothea.** See HEMANS.

(5) **Hablot Knight,** pseud. **Phiz** (1815–82), was born at Kennington, London. He was apprenticed to a line engraver, but soon took to etching and watercolour painting, and in 1833 gained a medal from the Society of Arts for an etching of ' John Gilpin '. In 1836 he became illustrator of *Pickwick* and maintained his reputation by his designs for other works. His son, **Gordon F.** (1858–1932), was a well-known book illustrator. See Life by Thomson (1884); *Phiz and Dickens,* by Edgar Browne (1913).

(6) **Robert** (*c.* 1550–*c.* 1633), founder of the Brownists, was born at Tolethorpe, Rutland, and after graduating at Cambridge in 1572, was a schoolmaster in London, and an open-air preacher. In 1580 he began to attack the Established Church, and soon after formed a distinct church on congregational principles at Norwich. Committed to the custody of the sheriff, he was released through the influence of his kinsman, Lord Burghley; but in 1581, with his followers, was obliged to take refuge at Middelburg, in Holland. In 1584 he returned, via Scotland, to England, and reconciling himself to the Church, in 1586 became master of Stamford grammar school, in 1591 rector of Achurch, Northamptonshire. Of a very violent temper, he was, when eighty years old, sent to Northampton jail for an assault on a constable, and in jail he died. The Brownists may be said to have given birth to the Independents or Congregationalists.

(7) **Sir Samuel James** (1824–1901), an Indian general, who lost an arm and gained the V.C. in the Mutiny, and served before in the Punjab campaign of 1848–49, as afterwards in the Afghan one of 1878–79. He invented the sword-belt named after him, ' Sam Browne '.

(8) **Sir Thomas** (1605–82), English author, was born in London, and educated at Winchester College and at Broadgate Hall (now Pembroke College), Oxford. He next studied medicine, travelled in Ireland, France, and Italy, continued his medical studies at Montpellier and Padua, graduated as Doctor of Medicine at Leyden and at Oxford, and settled in 1637 at Norwich. He lived calmly throughout the Civil War, maintained a

large medical practice and active correspondence with antiquaries and scientists, and was knighted by Charles II on his visit to Norwich in 1671. He was buried in the church of St Peter Mancroft. His greatest work is his earliest, the *Religio Medici*, written about 1635—a kind of confession of faith, revealing a deep insight into the dim mysteries of the spiritual life. The surreptitious publication of two editions in 1642 obliged him to issue an authorized edition in 1643; *Pseudodoxia Epidemica, or Enquiries into . . . Vulgar and Common Errors* (1646), a strange and discursive amalgam of humour, acuteness, learning, and credulity, is by far the most elaborate of his works. *Hydriotaphia; Urn Burial* (1658), mainly a discussion of burial customs, shows all the author's vast and curious learning set in language of rich and gorgeous eloquence. The *Garden of Cyrus* (1658), the most fantastic of Browne's writings, aims to show that the number five pervaded not only all the horticulture of antiquity, but that it recurs throughout all plant life, as well as the ' figurations ' of animals. After his death appeared *Miscellany Tracts* (1683), *Letter to a Friend* (1690), and *Christian Morals* (1716), an incomplete work, evidently intended to be a continuation of the *Religio Medici*. Browne's favourite theme is the mystery of death. His style is too idiomatic and difficult to be popular, and his studied brevity often falls into obscurity. Charles Lamb boasted that he was the first ' among the moderns ' to discover Sir Thomas Browne's excellences. De Quincey ranks him with Jeremy Taylor as the most dazzling of rhetoricians, and Lowell calls him ' our most imaginative mind since Shakespeare '. See studies by Gosse (1905), G. Keynes (1924), Leroy (Paris 1931) and Dunn (1950).

(9) **Thomas A.** See BOLDREWOOD, ROLF.

(10) **Ulysses Maximilian, Count von** (1705–1757), born at Basel, of an Irish Jacobite family, became one of the foremost field-marshals in Maria Theresa's army and commanded the Austrians at Lobositz (1756) in the Seven Years' War. He was mortally wounded at the battle of Prague.

(11) **William** (1591–1643), pastoral poet, was born at Tavistock; from Exeter College, Oxford, proceeded to the Inner Temple; and then was tutor to Robert Dormer, the future Earl of Carnarvon. According to Wood, he was taken into the household of the Herberts at Wilton, and there ' got wealth and purchased an estate '. His finest poetry is to be found in the long pastoral similes of *Britannia's Pastorals* (1616) and in the *Inner Temple Masque* (1615).

BROWNING, (1) **Elizabeth Barrett** (1806–61), English poet, wife of (3), was born at Coxhoe Hall, Durham, March 6, but spent her girlhood mostly on her father's estate, near Ledbury, in Herefordshire. At ten she read Homer in the original, and at fourteen wrote an epic on *The Battle of Marathon*. About 1821 she seriously injured her spine, in an accident while saddling her pony, and was long an invalid. The family ultimately settled in London. Her *Essay on Mind, and Other Poems*, was published when she was nineteen.

In 1833 she issued a translation of the *Prometheus Bound*. This was succeeded by *The Seraphim, and Other Poems* (1838), in which volume was republished the fine poem on Cowper's grave. When she was staying at Torquay, her brother and a party of friends were drowned there in a boating expedition, and the shock confined her for many years to a sickroom. In 1844 appeared the *Poems*, which contained ' The Cry of the Children ', a noble outburst against the employment of young children in factories. In 1845 she first saw Robert Browning, who freed her from her sickroom and a possessive father by marrying her the following year. The *Poems* of 1850 contained an entirely new translation of the *Prometheus Bound*. In *Casa Guidi Windows* (1851) she expressed her sympathy with the regeneration of Italy. *Aurora Leigh* (1856) is a poem into which all the treasures of its writer's mind and heart have been poured. In *Poems before Congress* (1860) she again manifested her interest in Italian freedom. She died at Florence, June 30. Her so-called *Sonnets from the Portuguese* are not translations at all, but express her own love (' my little Portuguese ' was Browning's pet name for her). See her *Letters to R. H. Horne* (1876), her *Letters*, ed. by Kenyon (1897), her and her husband's *Letters 1845–46* (1899); Lives by Ingram (1889), Willis (1928), Shackford (1935), Taplin (1957), and the play by Besier, *The Barretts of Wimpole Street* (1931).

(2) **Oscar** (1837–1923), English historian, born in London, lectured on history at Cambridge, and wrote on Dante, George Eliot, &c., and volumes of reminiscences. See Life by H. E. Wortham (1927).

(3) **Robert** (1812–89), English poet and husband of (1), born at Camberwell, May 7, attended lectures at University College, and then travelled abroad. *Pauline*, a dramatic poem, written at the age of nineteen, was published in 1833; *Paracelsus* (1835), won him some recognition in literary circles, but the general public did not show any interest in him until the appearance of *Men and Women* (1855). *Bells and Pomegranates* (1841–46) included the dramatic lyrics *How they Brought the Good News from Ghent to Aix, Saul, The Lost Leader*, and *The Pied Piper of Hamelin*—poems which still remain the most popular of all Browning's writings. In 1846 he married Elizabeth Barrett, and with her he settled at Florence; their son, Robert Barrett (1849–1912), the sculptor, was born there. After the death of his wife (1861) he settled permanently in London with his only son. His masterpiece, *The Ring and the Book* (1869), is an epic dealing most searchingly with the passions of humanity, and has for its basis the narrative of a murder by an Italian count, as related by the various persons concerned. Browning brought an almost journalistic approach to the profession of poetry, and a sense of the bizarre rather than the beautiful, both in character and situation, and totally unspoiled by any preconceptions. His realism was healthy at a time when poetry was tending to become stereotyped in a hackneyed Romantic mould, but where he dealt with the past his thought and language

were of the 19th century. He was also addicted to a certain verbal frivolity which manifested itself in ill-timed puns and too-clever rhymes. Browning's poetry is nevertheless distinguished for its depth of spiritual insight and power of psychological analysis; and he invented new kinds of narrative structure which have taken the place of the epic and the pastoral. In his play, *Pippa Passes* (1841), for example, a girl's song binds together a variety of scenes. His other chief works are *Sordello* (1840), *Dramatis Personae* (1864), *Fifine at the Fair* (1872), *The Inn Album* (1875), *Pacchiarotto* (1876), *Asolando* (1889). See his Letters edited by T. L. Hood (1933), Lives by W. H. Griffin and H. C. Minchin (revised 1938), G. K. Chesterton (1903), Miller (1952), and studies by P. de Reul (1929) and W. C. De Vane (1935).

BROWNRIGG, (1) Elizabeth, a midwife hanged at Tyburn in 1767 for the barbarous murder of a workhouse apprentice, Mary Clifford.

(2) **Sir Robert** (1759–1833), conquered in 1814–15 the Kandyan kingdom in Ceylon.

BROWN-SÉQUARD, Édouard, *-se-kahr* (1817–94), French physiologist, was born at Port Louis, Mauritius, the son of a Philadelphia sea captain and a lady called Séquard. He studied at Paris, graduated M.D. in 1846, devoted himself to physiological research, and received many prizes for his experiments on blood, muscular irritability, animal heat, the spinal cord, and the nervous system. He was professor of Physiology at Harvard (1864), at the School of Medicine in Paris (1869–73), and the Collège de France (from 1878). See Éloy, *La Méthode de Brown-Séquard* (Paris 1893).

BROWNSON, Orestes Augustus (1803–76), a versatile American writer, was born at Stockbridge, Vermont, and died at Detroit, having in turn been a Presbyterian, a Universalist, a Unitarian pastor and, from 1844, a Roman Catholic.

BRUCE, a family illustrious in Scottish history; descended from—

(1) **Robert de Bruis** (d. *c.* 1094), a Norman knight, who accompanied William the Conqueror to England in 1066. The name is traced to the domain of Bruis near Cherbourg. This Robert received extensive lands in Yorkshire. The more important members of this family are:

(2) **Robert** (*c.* 1078–1141), son of (1), a companion in arms of Prince David of Scotland, afterwards David I, from whom he got the Lordship of Annandale. Robert renounced his allegiance to David in the war in England between Stephen and Matilda, niece of the King of Scots, resigning his lands in Annandale to (3).

(3) **Robert** (fl. 1138–*c.* 1189), son of (2), who fought on the Scottish side and whose brother, Adam, inherited the English estates.

(4) **Robert** (d. 1245), grandson of (3), 4th Lord of Annandale, married Isabel, second daughter of David, Earl of Huntingdon and Chester, brother of William the Lion, and thus founded the royal house of Bruce.

(5) **Robert de** (1210–95), 5th Lord of Annandale, son of (4), did homage to Henry III in 1251, on the death of his mother, for her

lands in England, and was made sheriff of Cumberland and constable of Carlisle. On the Scottish throne becoming vacant at the death in 1290 of the 'Maid of Norway', granddaughter of Alexander III, Baliol and Bruce claimed the succession, the former as great-grandson of David, Earl of Huntingdon, by his eldest daughter, Margaret; the latter as grandson, by his second daughter, Isabel. Edward I of England as umpire decided in favour of Baliol in 1292. To avoid swearing fealty to his successful rival, Bruce resigned Annandale to his eldest son (6).

(6) **Robert de** (1253–1304), eldest son of (5), is said to have accompanied Edward I of England to Palestine in 1269. In 1271 he married Marjory, Countess of Carrick, and in her right became Earl of Carrick. In 1292 he resigned the earldom to his eldest son, Robert, the future king. On the death of his father in 1295 he did homage to Edward for his English lands, was made Constable of Carlisle, and fought for the English king against Baliol. On Baliol's defeat he applied to Edward for the crown, but was refused it.

(7) **Robert** (1274–1329), eldest son of (6), hero of the Scottish War of Independence, was born at Lochmaben or Turnberry or in Essex. In 1296, as Earl of Carrick, he swore fealty to Edward I at Berwick, and in 1297 renewed his oath of homage at Carlisle. Shortly after, with his Carrick vassals, he joined the Scottish revolt under Wallace, but by the Capitulation of Irvine made his peace with the English monarch. In 1298 Bruce again rose against Edward, and after Falkirk had his lands wasted by the English. He was one of the four regents of Scotland in 1299, but did not again fight against Edward till the final rising in 1306. With John Comyn, the nephew of Baliol, he seems to have made an agreement as to their rival claims to the throne. They met in the church of the Minorite Friars, Dumfries (February 10, 1306); a quarrel took place; and Bruce in passion stabbed Comyn, who was dispatched by Kirkpatrick. Bruce now assembled his vassals and asserted his rights to the throne, and two months later was crowned king at Scone. An English army under the Earl of Pembroke took Perth and drove Bruce into the wilds of Athole. At Dalry, near Tyndrum, Bruce was defeated by Macdougal, the Lord of Lorn, Comyn's uncle, and by and by took refuge in Rathlin, off the north coast of Ireland. In the spring of 1307 he landed in Carrick, surprised the English garrison in his own castle of Turnberry, and later in the year defeated the English under the Earl of Pembroke at Loudon Hill. After the death of King Edward in 1307, the English were cleared out of the country and all the great castles recovered except Stirling, which the governor promised to surrender if not relieved before June 24. This led to the memorable battle of Bannockburn, June 24, 1314, when the English under Edward II, amounting, it is said, to 100,000 men, were totally routed by Bruce with 30,000. In 1317 Bruce went over to Ireland to assist his brother Edward, and defeated the Anglo-Irish at Slane. Until

the truce of 1323 the Scots repeatedly invaded England; and on the accession of Edward III in 1327 hostilities recommenced with a great Scottish inroad into the northern counties. The war was at last closed by the Treaty of Northampton (1328), recognizing the independence of Scotland, and Bruce's right to the throne. Bruce died of leprosy at Cardross Castle, on the Firth of Clyde. His heart was to be carried to Palestine and buried in Jerusalem, but Douglas, who bore it, was killed fighting against the Moors in Spain, and the sacred relic was brought to Scotland, and buried in Melrose Abbey. Bruce's body was interred in the Abbey of Dunfermline, where in 1818 his bones were discovered. Marjory, his daughter by his first wife (a daughter of the Earl of Mar), married Walter the High Steward, and their son afterwards ascended the throne as Robert II. His immediate successor, David II (q.v.), was the son of his second wife, a daughter of the Earl of Ulster. See studies by Sir H. Maxwell (1897), Linklater (1934) and A. M. Mackenzie (1956). His brother **Edward** was actively engaged in the struggle for Scotland's independence. In 1315 the chieftains of Ulster tendered to him the crown of Ireland. With 6000 men he embarked at Ayr, and by a series of victories over the English made himself master of Ulster. He was crowned king of Ireland in 1316, but was slain at the battle of Dundalk in 1318.

BRUCE, (1) **Charles Granville** (1866–1939), British mountaineer, was in the regular army (1888–1920), retired with the rank of brigadier-general and led the Everest expeditions of 1920 and 1924.

(2) **Sir David** (1855–1931), British physician, born in Australia, discovered that the tsetse fly was the carrier of sleeping sickness.

(3) **James** (1730–94), Scottish explorer, known as ' the Abyssinian ', was born at Kinnaird House, Stirlingshire, studied at Harrow and Edinburgh University, was a wine merchant in London (1754–61) and consul-general at Algiers (1763–65). In 1768 he set out from Cairo on his famous journey to Abyssinia by the Nile, Assouan, the Red Sea, and Massowah. In 1770 he was at Gondar, had many adventures, and held for a time a government appointment. He reached the source of the Abai, or headstream of the Blue Nile, then considered the main stream of the Nile (Nov. 14, 1770); and having remained till the end of 1771, he returned, through great hardships, by way of Sennaar, Assouan, Alexandria, and Marseilles. In France he visited Buffon and other distinguished men, and in 1774 he was back in Scotland. His long-expected *Travels to Discover the Sources of the Nile* were published in 1790. The work contained such curious accounts of the manners of the Abyssinians that by many—as by Dr Johnson —his tales were set down as fabrications. Modern travellers have strongly confirmed his general accuracy. Bruce, who was a huge, self-assertive, dictatorial man, died at Kinnaird. See the Life by Murray in the later editions of the Travels, and that by Sir Francis Head (1844).

(4) **James.** See ELGIN (2).

(5) **Michael** (1746–1767), Scottish poet, was born at Kinnesswood near the eastern shore of Loch Leven. A weaver's son, he tended sheep in his boyhood, but in 1762 attended Edinburgh University to study for the Secession ministry. He became schoolmaster, however, and died penniless, of consumption, aged twenty-one. His poems were published by the Rev. John Logan (q.v.) a college friend, who claimed authorship of the ' Ode to the Cuckoo ' and other poems. See *Poems on Several Occasions* (1770), and *Life and Works* by Barnet (1927), Mackenzie (1905), and Snoddy (1947).

(6) **Robert.** See BRUCE, FAMILY OF.

(7) **Robert** (1554–1631), from 1587 to 1600 was a Presbyterian minister in Edinburgh, and thereafter suffered much for his opposition to James VI's attempts to introduce Episcopacy.

(8) **Stanley Melbourne, 1st Viscount Bruce of Melbourne** (1883–1967), Australian politician, entered parliament in 1918, and represented Australia in the League of Nations Assembly. He was premier of Australia 1923–29 and from 1933 to 1945 was high commissioner in London.

(9) **Sir William of Kinross** (d. 1710), Scottish architect, rebuilt Holyrood in 1671–1679.

(10) **William Speirs** (1867–1921), Scottish zoologist and explorer, made voyages to the Antarctic (1892), the Weddell Sea (1902–04), and Spitsbergen, and wrote the volume on *Polar Exploration* (1911) for the Home University Library. See study by R. N. Rudmose Brown (1923).

BRUCE-JOY, Albert (1842–1924), Irish sculptor, born at Dublin, studied under Foley, executed portrait busts of Matthew Arnold, King Edward VII, and enormous statues of John Bright, Alexander Balfour, and Gladstone.

BRUCH, Max, *brook*H (1838–1920), German composer, was born in Cologne, became musical director at Coblenz in 1865 and conducted the Liverpool Philharmonic Society (1880–83), introducing many of his choral works. He is best known, however, for his violin concerto in G minor, the *Kol Nidrei* variations in which he employs the idioms of Hebrew and Celtic traditional melodies, and the *Konzertstück*. See work by H. Pfitzner (Munich 1938).

BRUCKNER, Anton, *brook'nėr* (1824–96), Austrian composer, born in Ansfelden. After the death of his father, Bruckner became a choir boy at the monastery of Saint Florian, where he learned the organ and was appointed assistant organist (1845) and organist (1848). Dissatisfied with his early compositions, he studied in Vienna in 1855, and in the following year became organist of Linz Cathedral. The first performance of *Tristan and Isolde*, in 1865, converted him to Wagnerism and led to the composition of the nine symphonies, the last of which is unfinished, upon which his fame chiefly rests. From 1867 until 1891 he was professor of Composition at Vienna Conservatory, but also won considerable fame as an organist and played in Paris and London. Regarded in Germany and Austria as the greatest 19th-century symphonist, Bruckner was easily and too often persuaded to make extensive cuts and modify the orchestration of his works for the sake of performances and publication, so that it is difficult to establish the authentic versions, but his music has recently begun to make considerable headway in Britain. Amongst his other works are four impressive masses, a large number of smaller sacred works, and many choral works. See studies by G. Engel (N.Y. 1931) and R. Haas (1934), also H. Redlich, *Bruckner and Mahler* (1955).

BRUDENELL, James Thomas. See CARDIGAN.

BRUEGHEL. See BREUGHEL.

BRUGMANN, Karl (1849–1919), German philologist, born at Wiesbaden, wrote an *Indo-Germanic Grammar* (1886–1900). He was directed towards linguistic study by the teachings of Curtius, from whose doctrines he deviated into the stricter criteria of the ' Young Grammarian ' school, stressing the fixity of sound laws.

BRUGSCH, Heinrich Karl, *broogsh* (1827–94), German Egyptologist, was born at Berlin. In 1853 he first visited Egypt, and subsequently alternated between Egypt and Germany as professor or fulfilling missions for Germany. He was successively bey and pasha. Of over thirty books on Egyptology, including a grammar, dictionary, &c., and written in French, German, and Latin, the best known in England is *Egypt under the Pharaohs* (1879).

BRÜHL, Heinrich, Count von (1700–63), the unworthy prime minister of Augustus III, king of Poland and elector of Saxony. With the basest sycophancy, he humoured the whims of his luxurious master, draining the coffers of the state, and burdening the country with debt. He himself meanwhile maintained a most splendid and costly establishment.

BRUMMELL, George Bryan, called Beau Brummell (1778–1840), was born in London, the son of Lord North's private secretary, and grandson of a gentleman's gentleman. At Eton, and during a brief sojourn at Oxford, he was less distinguished for studiousness than for the exquisiteness of his dress and manners; and after four years in the army, having come into a fortune, he entered on his true vocation of arbiter of elegancies. His success was brilliant; but the pace was too hot, and his wit was, moreover, too fine for his twenty years' patron and admirer, the Prince Regent. They quarrelled in 1813, and gambling debts three years later forced Brummell to flee to Calais. He struggled on there, reckless as before, for fourteen years; from 1830 to 1832 held a sinecure consulate at Caen; and, after three years of imbecility, died there in the pauper lunatic asylum. See books by Jesse, De Monval (1906), Melville (1928), Connely (1940), and Campbell (1948).

BRUNCK, Richard François Philippe (1729–1803), French classical scholar, was born and died at Strasbourg, having been educated under the Jesuits in Paris, a military commisary during the Seven Years' War, and a prisoner during the Terror. He is best known for his *Greek Anthology* (1772–76).

BRUNE, Guillaume Marie Anne, *brün* (1763–1815), French marshal of the First Empire, was born at Brives-la Gaillarde. Appointed in 1799 to the command of the army in Holland, he defeated the Duke of York at Bergen, and forced him to capitulate at Alkmaar. On the return from Elba he had joined the emperor and was brutally murdered by a royalist mob at Avignon.

BRUNEAU, Alfred, *brü'-nō* (1857–1934), French composer, born in Paris, studied there at the Conservatoire with Massenet (q.v.). Although he wrote a choral symphony, lieder, &c., of a high order, he is best known for his operas based on Zola's works, such as *Le Rêve* (1891) and *Messidor* (1897). On its first production, the latter suffered because of the composer's and Zola's unpopularity for championing Dreyfus (q.v.). He excelled as a music critic. See his three volumes of criticisms (1900–03), and studies by Boschot (Paris 1913) and Hervey (1907).

BRUNEL, *broo-nel'*, family of distinguished engineers:

(1) **Isambard Kingdom** (1806–59), only son of (2), was born at Portsmouth, and in 1823, after two years spent at the Collège Henri Quatre in Paris, entered his father's office. He helped to plan the Thames Tunnel, and himself, in 1829–31, planned the Clifton Suspension Bridge, which was completed only in 1864 with the materials of his own Hungerford Suspension Bridge (1841–45) over the Thames at Charing Cross. He designed the *Great Western* (1838), the first steamship built to cross the Atlantic, and the *Great Britain* (1845), the first ocean screw-steamer. The *Great Eastern*, then the largest vessel ever built, was built under his sole direction in 1853–58. In 1833 he was appointed engineer to the Great Western Railway, and constructed all the tunnels, bridges, and viaducts on that line. Among docks constructed or improved by him were those of Bristol, Monkwearmouth, Cardiff, and Milford Haven. See Noble's *The Brunels* (1938), and Lives by his son (1878), L. T. C. Rolt (1957).

(2) **Sir Marc Isambard** (1769–1849), father of (1), born at Hacqueville near Rouen, escaped from Paris to the United States in 1793; in 1794 he was appointed to survey for the canal from Lake Champlain to the Hudson at Albany. He was afterwards an architect in New York, and chief engineer for the city. Returning to Europe in 1799, he married and settled in England. A plan submitted by him to the government for making block-pulleys by machinery was adopted in 1803, and on its completion in 1806 the saving on the first year was about £24,000. He received £17,000 as a reward. He constructed public works in Woolwich arsenal, Chatham dockyard, &c., and made experiments in steam navigation on the Thames in 1812, but his scheme for steam-tugs was declined by the navy board. The destruction of his sawmills at Battersea by fire (1814) led to his bankruptcy (1821), when he was thrown into prison for debt. He was released on a grant of £5000 being made by the government. His most remarkable undertaking was the Thames Tunnel (1825–1843). He was knighted in 1841; and died in London. See Life by Beamish (1862).

BRUNELLESCHI, Filippo, *broo-nel-les'kee* (1377–1446), one of the greatest Italian architects, was born and died at Florence. A goldsmith first, then a sculptor, he finally devoted himself to architecture, at Rome became imbued with classical traditions, and, soon after his return to Florence in 1407, offered his plan for completing the cathedral, founded in 1296, and now lacking only a dome. Brunelleschi's dome (1420–61) is, measured diametrically, the largest in the world, and served as a model to Michelangelo for that of St Peter's. Besides this masterpiece he also executed the churches of Spirito Santo and San Lorenzo.

BRUNET, Jacques Charles, *brü-nay* (1780–1867), French bibliographer, compiler of a great bibliographical dictionary (1810), a standard work, was born and died in Paris.

BRUNETIÈRE, Ferdinand, *brün-tyayr* (1849–1906), French critic, was born at Toulon, was editor of the *Revue des deux mondes* from 1893, became professor at the École Normale, and in 1894 an academician. He held an evolutionary theory of the development of literary form and opposed naturalism in fiction. He published *Histoire et littérature* (1884–87), &c.

BRUNHILDA (567–613), the daughter of the Visigothic king Athanagild, married King Sigbert of Austrasia, and afterwards as regent for her two grandsons, Theodebert II, king of Austrasia, and Theodoric II, king of Burgundy, divided the government of the whole Frankish world with her rival Fredegond, who governed Neustria for the youthful Clotaire II. On Fredegond's death in 598 she seized Neustria, and for a time united under her rule the whole Merovingian dominions, but was overthrown by the Austrasian nobles under Clotaire II, and put to death by being dragged at the heels of a wild horse.

BRUNI, Leonardo, *broo'nee* (1369–1444), Italian humanist, a native of Arezzo, and hence styled **Aretino.** Papal secretary in 1405–15, he then wrote his *Historia Florentina*, and was made chancellor of Florence in 1427. Bruni aided the advance of the study of Greek literature mainly by his literal translations into Latin of Aristotle, Demosthenes, Plato, &c.; he also wrote Lives of Petrarch and Dante in Italian. See Life by Baron (1928).

BRÜNING, Heinrich (1885–1970), German statesman, born at Münster, studied at Bonn and the London School of Economics, was leader of the Reichstag centre party from 1929, and chancellor in 1930–32, when he was forced to resign by the Nazis. In 1934 he left Germany. He was professor of Government at Harvard (1939–52), professor of Political Science at Cologne (1951–55). See his *Memoirs (1918–1934)* (1971).

BRUNNE. See ROBERT OF.

BRUNNER, (1) **Arnold William** (1857–1925), American architect and town planner, designer of Pennsylvania capitol building, Cleveland Civic Centre, &c. See study by R. I. Aitken (1926).

(2) **Sir John Tomlinson** (1842–1919), British industrialist, founder in 1873 with Ludwig Mond of the chemical firm Brunner, Mond & Co., which merged with I.C.I. in 1926.

BRUNNOW, Philipp Ivanovich, Count von, *broon'nō* (1797–1875), born at Dresden, entered the Russian service in 1818, and was Russian ambassador in London both before and after the Crimean war.

BRUNO, (1) St (925–65), the third son of Henry the Fowler, became Archbishop of Cologne

in 953, and Duke of Lorraine in 954, and was distinguished both for piety and learning.

(2) **St** (970–1009), was martyred by the heathen Prussians.

(3) **St** (*c.* 1030–1101), founder of the Carthusian order, was born at Cologne, became rector of the cathedral school at Reims, but, oppressed by the wickedness of his time, withdrew in 1084 to the wild mountain of Chartreuse, near Grenoble. Here with six friends he founded the austere Carthusians. In 1091 he established a second Carthusian monastery at Della Torre in Calabria, where he died.

(4) **Giordano** (1548–1600), a restless speculative thinker, was born at Nola near Naples, was at first a Dominican, but doubting the dogmas, fled to Geneva, whence Calvinist suspicion of his scepticism drove him to Paris, where he lectured. Here the zeal of the orthodox Aristotelians forced him to withdraw to London (1583), where he knew Sidney, and Oxford, where he repeatedly gave lectures. In 1585 he was in Paris again, in 1586 in Wittenberg, in 1588 in Prague, then in Helmstedt, Frankfurt, Padua; and in 1592 in Venice he was arrested by the officers of the Inquisition and after a seven-year trial was burnt at Rome. His philosophy, which was strongly anti-Aristotelian, was a pantheistic, poetic, monistic system based on the Copernican astronomy, Nicolaus of Cusa, Neoplatonism, Stoicism, Epicureanism. He influenced Spinoza and Leibniz. Of his works, the most famous is the *Spaccio della bestia trionfante.* See studies in Italian by Gentile (1921), in English by McIntyre (1903), Boulting (1916), and Yates (1964).

BRUNOT, Ferdinand, *brü-nō* (1860–1938), French philologist, a dean of the Faculty of Letters at the University of Paris, wrote a history of the French language (1905–34) in relation to successive states of society.

BRUNSWICK, (1) **Charles William Ferdinand, Duke of** (1735–1806), fought in the Seven Years' War, commanded the Prussian and Austrian troops in France and at Valmy, and died of wounds soon after his sore defeat by Napoleon at Auerstädt. See Life by Fitzmaurice (1901).

(2) **Frederick William** (1771–1815), son and successor of (1), came to England in 1809, and with his ' Black Brunswickers '—so called from their uniform, in mourning for the losses at Auerstädt—entered the British service, fighting in the Peninsular war; he was killed at Quatre Bras.

BRUSILOV, Alexei, *broo-syee'loff* (1856–1926), Russian commander-in-chief, June to August 1917, served against Turkey 1877, and won fame (1915–17) in the invasion of Galicia and in the Carpathians. His troops mutinied, and Kornilov took his place.

BRUTUS, (1) **Lucius Junius** (fl. 500 B.C.), legendary hero who established Republican government at Rome. The son of a rich Roman, on whose death Tarquin the Proud seized the property and killed an elder brother, he himself escaped only by feigning idiocy, whence the name *Brutus* (' stupid '). When popular indignation was roused at the outrage on Lucretia, he drove the royal family from Rome. He was elected one of the first two consuls (509 B.C.). He sentenced to death his own two sons for conspiring to restore the monarchy, and fell repelling an attack led by one of Tarquin's sons.

(2) **Marcus Junius** (85–42 B.C.), sided with Pompey when the civil war broke out, but after Pharsalia submitted to Caesar, and was appointed governor of Cisalpine Gaul. He divorced his wife to marry Portia, the daughter of Cato, his master. Cassius prevailed on him to join the conspiracy against Caesar (44 B.C.); and, defeated by Antony and Octavian at Philippi, he killed himself.

BRUYÈRE. See LA BRUYÈRE.

BRY, Théodor de, *bree* (1528–98), Flemish engraver and goldsmith, born at Liège, settled in Frankfurt-am-Main about 1570, and established a printing house there. A well-known print of his is *The Procession of the Knights of the Garter under Queen Elizabeth*, the result of a visit to England.

BRYAN, (1) **Michael** (1757–1821), born at Newcastle, published a *Dictionary of Painters and Engravers* (1813–16).

(2) **William.** See O'BRYAN.

(3) **William Jennings** (1860–1925), lawyer and politician, born at Salem, Ill., graduated from Illinois College in 1881, studied law at Chicago, and practised at Jacksonville and in Nebraska. Elected to congress in 1890, as Democratic candidate for the presidency he was crushingly defeated by McKinley in 1896 and 1900, by Taft in 1908. A great stump-orator, founder and editor of *The Commoner*, he was appointed secretary of state by Wilson (1913), but as an ardent pacifist, resigned in June 1915 over America's second *Lusitania* note to Germany. He was leading an anti-Darwinian campaign when he died. See his *Memoirs* (1925) and Life by Hibben (1929).

BRYANT, William Cullen (1794–1878), poet and journalist, was born at Cummington, Massachusetts, and at thirteen published a satirical poem. The majestic blank verse of *Thanatopsis* (1817) surpassed anything previously written by an American. Although Bryant was practising at the bar, he continued to contribute to the newspapers in prose and verse, becoming editor of the *Evening Post* in 1829. The paper was Democratic, but, inclining to antislavery views, assisted in 1856 in forming the Republican party. Bryant's public addresses and letters to his paper on his visits to Europe and the West Indies were published in book form. He died at New York. See complete works (1883–84) and Lives by Parke Godwin (1883), Bigelow (1890) and Bradley (1905).

BRYCE, (1) **David** (1803–76), an Edinburgh architect, whose speciality, 'Scottish Baro-nial', is exemplified in Fettes College and the Royal Infirmary, Edinburgh.

(2) **James, 1st Viscount** (1838–1922), British statesman, born at Belfast, was educated at Glasgow High School and University, and Trinity College, Oxford, where he graduated in 1862 as double first. Elected a fellow of Oriel, and called to the bar in 1867, he was regius professor of Civil Law at Oxford from 1870 to 1893, and entered parliament in 1880. In 1905 he was made Irish secretary, and in 1907–13 was ambassador to the United States, signing the

Anglo-American Arbitration Treaty in 1911. A strong home-ruler, he took an active interest in university reform, the Eastern question, &c. He wrote *The Holy Roman Empire* (1864), *Transcaucasia and Ararat* (1877), *The American Commonwealth* (1888), &c. In 1907 he was awarded the O.M. and became president of the British Academy. See his Life by H. A. L. Fisher (1927).

BRYDGES, Sir Samuel Egerton, Bart. (1762–1837), English bibliographer and author of genealogical works, was born at Wootton House, Kent, failed to establish his claim to the barony of Chandos, but was gratified with a Swedish knighthood in 1808 and an English baronetcy in 1814. He represented Maidstone in 1812–18, and printed privately at the 'Lee Priory Press' small editions of many rare Elizabethan books. See his *Autobiography* (1834) and a book by Wood-worth (1935).

BRYSKETT, Lodowick (*c.* 1545–*c.* 1612), English writer, learned Greek from his friend Edmund Spenser (q.v.), whose conversations he records in *A Discourse of Civill Life* (1606). See his *Life and Correspondence*, by Plomer and Cross (1927).

BRYUSSOV, Valery Yakovlevich (1873–1924), Russian poet, critic and translator, born in Moscow. He was one of the leaders of the Russian Symbolist movement which looked to France for its inspiration. Like Balmont (q.v.), his best work was done before 1910, but unlike him his technique remained unimpaired to the last. He became an enthusiastic Bolshevist in 1917 and worked tirelessly for that cause until his death. See S. Graham, *The Republic of the Southern Cross* (1918).

BUBER, Martin, *boo'* (1878–1965), Jewish theologian and philosopher, born in Vienna, was early introduced to Chasidism, to study which he retired after a few sceptical years of philosophical studies at Vienna, Berlin, and Zürich. From 1916 to 1924 he was editor of *Der Jude*. He became professor of Com-parative Religion at Frankfurt (1923–33), after which he directed the Central Office for Jewish Adult Education until 1938 when he fled to Palestine to become professor of Social Philosophy at Jerusalem. Buber published profusely, but his most impor-tant works as one of the main figures of religious existentialism are *Between Man and Man* (1947), in which he discusses social problems, *Eclipse of God* (1952), in which the Chasidic as well as existentialist 'I-Thou' theme is discussed from a religious as distinct from a philosophical standpoint, and *God and Evil* (1953), in which the basic evil is seen to be that of having no direction, or refusing to take the only possible path—towards God. See books by Cohen (1957), Diamond (1960).

BUCCLEUCH, Duke of. See SCOTT.

BUCER, or Butzer, Martin, *boots'èr* (1491–1551), German Protestant reformer, was born at Schlettstadt, in Alsace, entered the Dominican order, and studied theology at Heidelberg. In 1521 he quitted the order, married a former nun, and in 1523 settled in Strasburg. In the disputes between Luther and Zwingli, Bucer adopted a middle course. At the Diet of Augsburg he declined to subscribe to the proposed Confession of Faith, and afterwards drew up the *Confessio Tetrapolitana* (1530). At Wittenberg, however, he made an agreement in 1536 with the Lutherans, but when attacked for his refusal to sign the *Interim* in 1548, he came to England on Cranmer's invitation (1549), to teach theology at Cambridge, where he made many friends. In Mary's reign his remains were exhumed and burned. His chief work was a translation and exposition of the Psalms (1529). Lenz edited (1880–87) his correspondence with the Landgrave of Hesse, whose ' second ' marriage Bucer defended. See studies by Baum (1860), Lang (1900), Pauck (1928), and Hopf (1946).

BUCH, Leopold von, *book*KH (1774–1853), a German geologist and traveller, investigated volcanic processes and upheld the theory of Elevation Craters, since discarded.

BUCHAN, Earls of. See under COMYN, ERSKINE, and STEWART.

BUCHAN, (1) Alexander (1829–1907), Scottish meteorologist, was born at Kinnesswood, near Kinross, became secretary of the Scottish Meteorological Society in 1860. He postulated the theory, based on earlier statistics, that the British climate is subject to successive warm and cold spells falling approximately between certain dates each year.

(2) **Elspeth,** *née* **Simpson** (1738–91), the wife of a potter, in 1784 founded at Irvine a fanatical sect, the Buchanites, announcing herself to her forty-six followers as the Woman of Rev. xii.

(3) **John, 1st Baron Tweedsmuir** (1875–1940), Scottish author and statesman, born at Perth, was educated at Glasgow University and at Brasenose College, Oxford, where he won the Newdigate prize in 1898. In 1901 he was called to the bar and became private secretary to Lord Milner, high commissioner for South Africa. He returned in 1903 to become a director of Nelson's, the publishers. During World War I he served on H.Q. staff until 1917, when he became director of information. He wrote *Nelson's History of the War* (1915–19), and became president of the Scottish History Society (1929–32). He was M.P. for the Scottish Universities (1927–35), and was raised to the peerage in 1935, when he became a most popular governor-general of Canada. In 1937 he was made a privy councillor, and chancellor of Edinburgh University. Despite his busy public life, Buchan wrote over fifty books, beginning with a series of essays, *Scholar Gipsies* (1896). He found his forte as a writer of fast-moving adventure stories. *Prester John* (1910) is set in South Africa; the Scottish Highlands form the scene of *Huntingtower* (1922), *John MacNab,* and *Witch Wood* (1927). He became best known for his exciting counter-espionage thrillers *The Thirty-nine Steps* (1915), *Greenmantle* (1916), and *The Three Hostages* (1924). Of his biographical works, which include *Cromwell* (1934) and *Augustus* (1937), his *Montrose* (1928) and *Sir Walter Scott* (1932) are the best. See his autobiography, *Memory Hold-the-Door* (1940), G. P. Insh, *An Empire's Homage* (1940), and Life by S. C. Buchan (1947). His son, **John Norman Stuart, 2nd Baron** (1911–

) was a distinguished soldier in World War II, whose wife, **Priscilla Jean Fortescue, Lady Tweedsmuir** (1915–), was Conservative M.P. for South Aberdeen from 1946 to 1966.

(4) **William** (1729–1805), physician, born at Ancrum, Roxburghshire, author of the popular *Domestic Medicine* (1769).

BUCHANAN, *bě-kan'ĕn,* (1) **Claudius** (1766–1815), born at Cambuslang near Glasgow, in 1797 became chaplain to the East India Company at Barrackpur; translated the Gospels into Persian and Hindustani, and made two tours through southern and western India. Returning in 1808 to England, he excited so much interest in Indian missions that before his death the first English bishop had been appointed to Calcutta.

(2) **George** (1506–82), Scottish humanist and reformer, born near Killearn, in Stirlingshire, of poor but well-connected parents, received his senior education in France, where most of his life was passed. Having been imprisoned by Cardinal Beaton in the Castle at St Andrews for his *Franciscanus,* a satirical poem on the friars, Buchanan escaped to France in 1539 and until 1542 he was a professor at Bordeaux, where he had Montaigne as a pupil, at Paris, and in 1547 at Coimbra in Portugal, where he was arrested by the Inquisition as a suspected heretic. During his confinement he began his Latin paraphrase of the Psalms which, published in 1566 with a dedication to Mary, Queen of Scots, was in use as a textbook until the end of the 19th century. Back in Scotland for the last time in 1561, he was appointed classical tutor to her, although he was a member of the Church General Assembly at the same time. But the respect which John Knox had for him clears him of any charge of duplicity. He abandoned Mary after the death of Darnley, and in his *Detectio Mariae Reginae* Buchanan stated with undue violence the case of the insurgent lords against her. He now became tutor to the young king, James VI, and in 1570–78 was keeper of the privy seal. His last years he gave to the completion of his Latin *History of Scotland* (1582). In his own day, his European reputation rested mainly on his skill in Latin poetry, as also on his *History of Scotland,* still valuable for its partisan but acute, view of his own time. Buchanan's influence after his death was chiefly through his tract *De Jure Regni,* in which he states with boldness the doctrine that kings exist by the will, and for the good, of the people. See Lives by P. H. Brown (1890) and J. M. Aitken (1939).

(3) **James** (1791–1868), fifteenth president of the United States, was born at Stony Batter, near Mercersburg, Pennsylvania, the son of an immigrant Irish farmer. He was educated at Dickinson College, and in 1812 was admitted to the bar, where he enjoyed a large practice. He was sent in 1832 to negotiate the first commercial treaty with Russia; became secretary of state in 1845 and till the close of Polk's presidency in 1849 succeeded in settling the Oregon boundary question. On the nomination of the Democratic party, he was elected president in 1856.

During his administration the slavery question came to a head. Buchanan himself was strongly in favour of the maintenance of slavery; and he freely supported the attempt to establish Kansas as a slave state. As the close of his term approached, it became evident that a conflict was impending, and the election of Lincoln precipitated the outbreak. After his retirement in March 1861, Buchanan took no part in public affairs; but he published in 1866 a defence of his administration. See his Life by G. T. Curtis (2 vols. New York 1883).

(4) **Robert** (1802–75), Scottish divine, a leader in the Free Church Disruption, was born at St Ninians near Stirling, and died in Rome, after forty-two years' ministry in Glasgow. See his *History of the Ten Years' Conflict* (1849), and his Life by the Rev. N. L. Walker (1877).

(5) **Robert Williams** (1841–1901), British poet, novelist and playwright, born at Caverswall, Staffordshire, was educated at Glasgow High School and University, where his closest friend was David Gray (q.v.), with whom he set out for London in 1860, but they had a hard time of it and success came too late for Buchanan. He attacked Swinburne (q.v.) in the *Spectator* and the pre-Raphaelites under the pseudonym of 'Thomas Maitland' in another article entitled 'The Fleshly School of Poetry' (1871). *London Poems* (1866) was his first distinct success. He also wrote novels and plays. See Life by H. J. Jay (1902), and study by L. Hearn (1916).

BUCHEZ, Philippe Benjamin Joseph, *bü-shay* (1796–1865), French physician and socialist, born at Matagne-la-Petite, published works on social science, history, and philosophy, striving to weld Communism and Catholicism, and began the *Histoire parlementaire de la Révolution française* (1833–38). In 1848 he was president of the National Assembly. See study by G. Castella (Paris 1911).

BUCHHÓLTZ, Johannes, *booKH'-* (1882–1940), Danish novelist, born at Odense in 1882, wrote *Egholm and his God* (trans. 1921), *Susanne* (1931), &c.

BUCHMAN, Frank Nathan Daniel, *book'man* (1878–1961), American evangelist, founder of the 'Group' and 'Moral Rearmament' movements, born at Pennsburg, Pa., was minister in charge of a hospice for under-privileged boys in Philadelphia (1902–07), travelled extensively in the East, and in 1921, believing that there was an imminent danger of the collapse of civilization, founded at Oxford the 'Group movement', and for its propagation led parties of young men, including some Oxford undergraduates, to many parts of the world. The movement was misleadingly labelled the 'Oxford Group', until 1938, when it began to rally under the slogan 'Moral Rearmament'. The Buchmanites did not regard themselves as a new sect, but as a catalyst for existing religious institutions. They emphasized divine guidance, constant adherence to the four cardinal principles of honesty, purity, unselfishness, and love, fostered by compulsory, public 'sharing' of their shortcomings. After World War II the movement emerged in a more political guise as an alternative to Capitalism and Communism. See Buchman's *The Oxford Group and its Work of Moral Rearmament* (1954) and *America Needs an Ideology* (1957).

BUCHNER, *booKH'nér,* (1) **Eduard** (1860–1917), German chemist, born in Munich, winner of Nobel prize in 1907 for demonstrating that alcoholic fermentation is not due to physiological but to chemical processes in the yeast. (2) **Hans** (1850–1902), bacteriologist, brother of (1), discovered that blood serum contains protective substances against infection.

BÜCHNER, (1) **Georg** (1813–37), German poet, brother of (2), born at Goddelau near Darmstadt, studied medicine, became involved in revolutionary politics, and fled to Zürich, where he died. His best-known works are the poetical dramas *Dantons Tod* (1835) and *Wozzek* (1837), the latter used by Berg (q.v.) for his well-known opera (1926). See studies by Pfeiffer (1934), Schmid (1940).

(2) **Ludwig** (1824–99), German physician and materialist philosopher, was born at Darmstadt, lectured at Tübingen (1852), but his controversial *Kraft und Stoff* (1855) brought about his forced resignation and made him take up private practice at Darmstadt. His sister **Luise** (1821–77), was poetess and novelist, and see (1).

BUCK, (1) **Dudley** (1839–1909), organist and composer, mainly of church music, was born at Hartford, Conn.

(2) **Pearl Sydenstricker** (1892–1973), American novelist, born in Hillsboro, W. Virginia, lived in China from infancy. Her earliest novels are coloured by her experiences while living in China. *The Good Earth* (1931), the best of this period, earned her the 1938 Nobel prize. In 1935 she returned to America, and most of her output after that date was concerned with the contemporary American scene. Her novels include *The Patriot* (1939) and *Dragon Seed* (1942), and amongst other works are *What America Means to Me* (1944) and *My Several Worlds* (1955). See Life by T. F. Harris (vol. i 1970, vol. ii 1972).

(3) **Sir Percy Carter** (1871–1947), English musical educationist, born in West Ham. He held successive posts at Wells and Bristol Cathedrals, was director of Music at Harrow School, and from 1910–23 held the chair of Music at Dublin University. In the latter year he became professor of Music at London University. The author of several sound textbooks, Buck was responsible for the inauguration of the Teachers' course at the Royal College of Music, was president of the Royal College of Organists, and music adviser to the Education Committee of the L.C.C. He was knighted in 1935.

BUCKHURST, Lord. See SACKVILLE.

BUCKINGHAM, Dukes of, (1) **George Villiers, 1st Duke** (1592–1628), English statesman, second son of Sir George Villiers, was born at his father's seat of Brooksby, Leicestershire. In 1614 he was brought under the notice of James I, and was soon received into high favour, as successor to the Earl of Somerset. He was knighted, raised to the peerage as Viscount Villiers in 1616, and became Earl of Buckingham in 1617, Marquis in 1618. Offices and lands were heaped on him so profusely that, from a threadbare hanger-on at court, ' Steenie ' became, with a single exception, the wealthiest noble in England. In 1623, while the Spanish match was in progress, Buckingham persuaded Charles to go to Madrid and prosecute his suit in person; the ultimate failure of the negotiations was largely owing to his arrogance. On his return Buckingham, now a duke, was made lord-warden of the Cinque Ports. He negotiated the marriage of Charles with Henrietta Maria of France, and maintained his ascendancy after Charles's accession in 1625. But the abortive expedition against Cadiz exposed him to impeachment by the Commons, and only a dissolution rescued him. His insolence in making love to the queen of France next made mischief. In 1627 he appeared with an armament before Rochelle; but the Huguenots refused him admission within the harbour; and when his troops made an ill-supported descent on the neighbouring Île de Rhé, they were defeated, in spite of his brave conduct. For a second expedition to Rochelle he had gone down to Portsmouth, but was assassinated by a discontented subaltern, John Felton, on August 23. See Lives by Sir P. Gibbs (1908) and C. R. Cammell (1939).

(2) **George Villiers, 2nd Duke** (1627–87), son of (1), was born at Wallingford House (on the site of the Admiralty), January 30, and, after his father's assassination, was brought up with Charles I's children. On the outbreak of the Civil War he hurried from Cambridge to the royalist camp, and lost, recovered, and once more lost his estates—almost his life, too, during Lord Holland's unfortunate rising in Surrey (1648), when his younger brother met a hero's death. He went with Charles II to Scotland, and after the battle of Worcester and an escape more amazing even than his master's, went again into exile. Returning secretly to England, he married, in 1657, the daughter of Lord Fairfax, to whom his forfeited estates had been assigned. At the Restoration he got them back and for the next twenty-five years he excelled the other courtiers in debauchery and wit. In 1667 he killed in a duel the Earl of Shrewsbury, whose countess, his paramour, looked on, disguised as a page. He was mainly instrumental in Clarendon's downfall; was a member of the infamous ' Cabal '; and, fooled by the king in the secret treaty of Dover, went over to the popular side. He died on April 16, at Kirby Moorside, miserably, if not, indeed, ' in the worst inn's worst room '. He was author and partauthor of several comedies, the wittiest *The Rehearsal* (1671), a travesty of Dryden's tragedies, but he is better remembered as the ' Zimri ' of Dryden's *Absalom and Achitophel*. See Lives by Lady Burghclere (1903) and H. W. Chapman (1949).

BUCKINGHAM, James Silk (1786–1855), English traveller, journalist and lecturer, was born at Flushing near Falmouth, started a number of newspapers in India and in Britain, and published travel books. See his unfinished Autobiography (1855).

BUCKINGHAMSHIRE, Duke of. See SHEFFIELD.

BUCKLAND, (1) **Francis Trevelyan** (1826–80), English surgeon and naturalist, son of (2), studied at Oxford and St George's Hospital, was assistant surgeon to the 2nd Life Guards (1854–63), became known for his researches in fish culture and was in 1867 appointed inspector of salmon fisheries, in 1870 special commissioner on salmon fisheries in Scotland. See Life by Bompas (1885) and study by G. Burgess (1967).

(2) **William** (1784–1856), father of (1), English geologist, born at Tiverton, was educated at Oxford, where he became reader in Mineralogy. He is known for his description of Kirkdale Cave. An F.R.S. in 1818, he became in 1845 Dean of Westminster. See Life by his daughter, Mrs Gordon (1894).

BUCKLE, (1) **George Earle** (1854–1935), editor of *The Times* from 1884 to 1912, was born at Twerton vicarage, Bath. He completed Monypenny's *Life of Disraeli* (1914–1920), and edited six volumes of Queen Victoria's *Letters* (1926–32).

(2) **Henry Thomas** (1821–62), English historian, was born at Lee, in Kent. Mostly self-educated, he mastered eighteen foreign languages and amassed an enormous library to assist him in his *History of Civilization in England* (1857–61), only two volumes of which saw the light of day and in which he practised a scientific method of writing history, taking into account a country's climate, &c. He excelled as a chess player. See Lives by A. H. Huth (1880), J. M. Robertson (1896), and G. St Aubyn (1958).

BUCKLEY, William (1780–1856), born near Macclesfield, was a bricklayer first, then a private, and, for conspiring with other soldiers at Gibraltar to shoot the Duke of Kent, was transported to Australia in 1802, but escaped, and lived thirty-two years with the aborigines of Victoria. See Life by J. Morgan (1852).

BUCKSTONE, John Baldwin (1802–79), English comedian, actor-manager and playwright, was born at Hoxton, played at the Surrey, Adelphi, Drury Lane, and Lyceum Theatres, mostly as comedian, visited the U.S.A. in 1840 and then played at the Haymarket, where he was actor-manager (1853–1878). He wrote 150 pieces for the stage.

BUDAEUS, Latinized form of **Guillaume Budé** (1467–1540), French scholar, born in Paris. Of his works on philology, philosophy, and jurisprudence, the two best known are one on ancient coins (1514) and the *Commentarii Linguae Graecae* (1519). Louis XII and Francis I also employed him in diplomacy. At his suggestion Francis founded the Collège de France. Though suspected of a leaning towards Lutheranism, he was royal librarian and founded the royal collection at Fontainebleau, which, moved to Paris, became the Bibliothèque Nationale. See his collected works (1557); monographs by Rebitté (1846), De Budé (1884), Delaruelle (1907); and his *Lettres inédites* (1887).

BUDD, George (1808–82) and **William** (1811–1880), two brothers, born at North Tawton, Devonshire, were both of them celebrated physicians, the one in London, the other in Bristol. The latter, William, advocated disinfection against contagious diseases, such as typhoid fever, cholera, and rinderpest. See E. W. Goodall, *William Budd* (1936).

BUDDHA (' the enlightened '), the founder of Buddhism, was born, perhaps about the year 568 B.C., the son of the rajah of the Sakya tribe ruling at Kapilavastu, 100 miles north of Benares. His personal name was Siddhartha; but he was also known by his family name of Gautama, and by many epithets, such as Sakya Muni, &c. When about thirty years old he left the luxuries of the court, his beautiful wife, and all earthly ambitions for the life of an ascetic; after six years of self-torture he saw in the contemplative life the perfect way. For some forty years he taught, gaining many disciples and followers, and died about eighty years old at Kusinagara in Oudh. His system was perhaps rather a revolutionary reformation of Brahmanism than a new faith; the keynote of it being that existence is necessarily miserable, and that ' Nirvana ', or nonexistence, the chief good, is to be attained by diligent devotion to Buddhistic rules. The death of the body does not bring Nirvana: the unholy are condemned to transmigration through many existences. Buddhism spread steadily over India, and in the 3rd century B.C. was dominant from the Himalayas to Cape Comorin. In the earlier centuries of our epoch it began to decline, was relentlessly persecuted by triumphant Brahmanism in the 7th and 8th centuries, and stamped out of continental India (except Nepal) by invading Mohammedanism. But it had spread to Tibet, Ceylon, Burma, Siam, China, and Japan, where it is still powerful. See works by Prof. and Mrs Rhys-Davids, Williams (1889), Waddell (1895), Stcherbatsky (1923), A. B. Keith (1923) and M. Perchenson (1959); and the Lives by Oldenberg, E. J. Thomas (1927) and T. C. Humphreys (1951).

BUDDHAGHOSA (5th cent. A.D.), Indian Buddhist scholar, born near Buddh Gaya, or Ghosa, East India, the place of the Buddha's enlightenment, studied the Buddhist texts in Ceylon and is best known for the *Visuddhimagga*, ' The Path of Purity ', a compendium of the Buddhist doctrines.

BUDÉ. See BUDAEUS.

BUDENNY, Simeon Mikhailovich, *boo-dyen'ni* (1883–   ), Russian general, fought in the Russo-Japanese war, became a revolutionary propagandist and a Bolshevik in 1919. He commanded the Red Cavalry against the White Army and against Poland, was made a marshal in 1935, and in 1941 commanded the S.W. sector against the German invasion.

BUDGE, Sir Ernest Alfred Wallis (1857–1934), English orientalist and archaeologist, was keeper of Egyptian and Assyrian antiquities in the British Museum in 1893–1924, wrote many books, and conducted excavations in Egypt, the Sudan, &c.

BUDGELL, Eustace (1686–1737), English writer, born at Exeter, a cousin of Addison's, lost £20,000 by the South Sea Bubble, and from a contributor to the *Spectator* degenerated to a Grub Street writer, and drowned himself in the Thames.

BUFF, Charlotte. See GOETHE.

BUFFALO BILL. See CODY (2).

BUFFON, Georges Louis Leclerc, Comte de *bü-fõ* (1707–88), French naturalist, was born at Montbard, in Burgundy, the son of a wealthy lawyer. After studying law at the Jesuit college in Dijon, he devoted himself to science, and while on a visit to England (1733) translated into French Newton's *Fluxions*. Admitted to the Academy, he was in 1739 appointed director of the Jardin du Roi, and formed the design of his *Histoire Naturelle* (1749–67), in which all the known facts of natural science were discussed in language of the loftiest eloquence. Though he may be ranked among the *philosophes*, Buffon was not one of the leaders or militant members of the party. After receiving various high honours, he was made Comte de Buffon by Louis XV. Although his work exhibits his overconfidence, he invested natural science with new dignity and interest and foreshadowed the theory of evolution. See his *Correspondance* (1860), and works on him by Flourens (1844), Nadault de Buffon (1863), and Lebasteur (1889).

BUGATTI, Ettore (1882–1947), Italian motor-manufacturer, born at Milan, began designing cars in 1899 and set up his works in Strasbourg (1907). World War I caused him to move to Italy and later to France, where his racing cars won international fame in the 1930s.

BUGEAUD, Thomas, *bü-zhõ'* (1784–1849), French marshal, was born at Limoges, and served in the Napoleonic campaigns, and with great distinction in Algeria and Morocco (1836–44), his victory at Isly in 1844 over the emperor of Morocco's forces gaining him the title Duc d'Isly. In the February revolution of 1848 he commanded the army in Paris, where he later died of cholera. See works by Count d'Ideville (1882) and Roches (1885).

BUGENHAGEN, Johann, *boo'gën-hah-gën* (1485–1558), German Lutheran reformer, born near Stettin, helped Luther in the Reformation and with the translation of the Bible. See Lives by Bellermann (1859), Vogt (1868), Zitzlaff (1885), Hering (1888), and Legge (1925).

BUGGE, Sophus Elseus, *boog'gë* (1833–1907), Norwegian philologist, born at Laurvik, studied at Christiania, Copenhagen, and Berlin, and in 1866 was appointed professor of Comparative Philology and Old Norse at the University of Christiania. Author of many critical works, notably on the Edda songs.

BUHL, properly Boulle, **Charles André** (1642–1732), a Parisian cabinetmaker in the service of Louis XIV. Introduced *buhlwork*, a style of decorating furniture by inlaying metals, shells, pearls, &c., on ebony, which was carried on by his sons, **Jean, Pierre, André,** and Charles.

BULGANIN, Nikolai, *bool-gah'neen* (1895–   ), Soviet politician, born at Nizhni-Novgorod (now Gorki). An early member of the Communist party, he was mayor of Moscow (1933–37) and a member of the Military Council during World War II. Created a marshal at the end of the war, he succeeded Stalin as minister for defence in 1946. After Stalin's death he became vice-premier in Malenkov's government and was made premier after the latter's resignation in February 1955, a constitutional façade with Khrushchev wielding real power as a first secretary of the party. 'B and K', unlike their predecessors, travelled extensively abroad in Yugoslavia, India, and Britain, and conducted propaganda by means of lengthy letters addressed to Western statesmen, particularly over the disarmament question. Khrushchev ousted Bulganin from his nominal position in March 1958 and he suffered total political eclipse in August 1958, retaining only the minor post of chairman of the Soviet State Bank

BULGARIN, Thaddeus, *bool-gah'reen* (1789–1859), Russian author and journalist, a zealous supporter of reaction and of absolutism. His best novel is *Ivan Vyzhigin* (1829).

BULL, (1) George, D.D. (1634–1710), English divine, was born at Wells, and studied at Exeter College, Oxford, whence he retired in 1649, having refused to take the commonwealth oath. Ordained in 1655, he took the small parish of St George's, Bristol, and eventually obtained the bishopric of St Davids (1705). His greatest work, the *Defensio Fidei Nicenae* (1685), was directed against Arians and Socinians; for his *Judicium Ecclesiae Catholicae* (1694) thanks of the French clergy were sent to him through Bossuet. See a translated edition of his works with a Life in the *Library of Anglo-Catholic Theology* (Oxford 1842–55).

(2) **John** (*c.* 1563–1628), English musician, born in Somerset about 1563, was appointed organist in the Queen's Chapel in 1591, first music lecturer at Gresham College in 1596, and organist to James I in 1607. A Catholic, he fled abroad in 1613, and at Brussels entered the archduke's service; in 1617 he became organist of Antwerp Cathedral, and there he died. He seems to have been, appropriately, the composer of the air of 'God save the King'. He was essentially an instrumental composer and may be considered as one of the founders of contrapuntal keyboard music.

(3) **Olav Jacob Martin Luther** (1883–1933), Norwegian lyric poet, born in Christiania. Bull has been called the Keats of Norway, probably because of the love of nature evident in all of his work. He was, however, a pronounced individualist, his most outstanding work being *Metope* (1927). See *Amer.-Scand. Rev.* (1925), pp. 653–65.

(4) **Ole Bornemann** (1810–80), Norwegian violinist, was born at Bergen. After some changes of fortune he rose to fame in Paris as a violinist. He was enthusiastically received in Italy, and after visiting England, Scotland, and Ireland, made a triumphal tour through Russia, Germany, and Norway. From 1843 he was repeatedly in America, making enormous sums by his concerts, but losing heavily by land speculations, especially an attempt to found a Scandinavian colony in Pennsylvania. He died at his villa near Bergen. He was as much an eccentric as a great artist. See Memoir by Sara C. Bull (1886).

BULLEN, (1) Arthur Henry (1857–1920), English editor, born in London, edited John Day, Thomas Campion, and other Eliza-

bethans, and founded at Stratford-on-Avon the Shakespeare Head Press (1904).

(2) **Frank Thomas** (1857–1915), English writer, till 1883 a sailor, made notable additions to the literature of the sea, including *Cruise of the Cachalot* (1898). See his *Recollections* (1915).

BULLER, Sir Redvers Henry (1839–1908), entered the army in 1858, and was promoted lieutenant-general in 1894, having served in the Chinese war of 1860, the Red River expedition, the Ashanti and Kaffir wars, Zulu war (winning a V.C.), the Egyptian war, and the Sudan expedition. He was commander-in-chief in the Boer war (1899–1900) and raised the siege of Ladysmith, but was succeeded by Roberts when he replied to criticism of British failures in South Africa. See Melville's *Life* (1923).

BULLETT, Gerald (1893–1958), British author, was born in London and was educated at Jesus College, Cambridge. From 1914 his published work included fiction, poems, essays, biographies, anthologies, children's books, literary criticism, and plays. His novels include *The Pandervils*, *The Jury*, and *The Snare of the Fowler*.

BULLINGER, Heinrich, *bool'ling-er* (1504–1575), a Swiss Reformer, son of a priest, married in 1529 a former nun, became Zwingli's successor as leader of the reformed party in its struggle with the Catholics, as well as with the Zealots and the Lutherans. See Lives by Pestalozzi (1858) and Christoffel (1875).

BÜLOW, (1) Prince Bernhard Heinrich von, *bü'lö* (1849–1929), German statesman, born at Flottbeck, Holstein, was chancellor (1900–1909), foreign secretary (1897), count (1899), prince (1905), he wrote *Imperial Germany* (trans., new ed. 1916), *Memoirs* (trans. 1931–1932). See studies by P. Herre (1931), and V. Wegerer (1931).

(2) **Hans Guido von** (1830–94), German pianist and conductor, was born at Dresden, studied law, but under the influence of Wagner made himself the musico-political spokesman of the new German school. In 1851 he took pianoforte lessons from Liszt, married his daughter, Cosima (1857), and made himself into an outstanding conductor. In 1864 he became court pianist and director of the music school at Munich, but resigned when his wife deserted him for Wagner in 1869. Henceforward an opponent of Wagner and his school, he undertook extensive conducting tours in England and America, and died in Cairo. See studies by M. von Bülow (1921, 1925).

BÜLOW VON DENNEWITZ, Friedrich Wilhelm, Count (1755–1816), Prussian general, in 1813 commanded in the first successful encounter with the French at Möckern. His victories at Grossbeeren and Dennewitz saved Berlin; he was prominent in the battle of Leipzig, and by taking Montmartre finished the campaign of 1814. In 1815 he joined Blücher by forced marches, and came to Wellington's aid at Waterloo. See Life by Varnhagen von Ense (Berlin 1854). His brother, **Dietrich Adam Heinrich** (1757–1807), satirized the Prussian army system in *Der Feldzug von 1805* (1806).

BULWER, Henry Lytton (1801–72), diplomatist and author, was born in London, the elder brother of Lord Edward Bulwer Lytton (q.v.). Educated at Harrow and Cambridge, he entered the diplomatic service in 1827, and was attaché at Berlin, Brussels, and The Hague. An advanced Liberal M.P., he became secretary of embassy at Constantinople in 1837, where he negotiated a very important commercial treaty. As minister plenipotentiary at Madrid, he negotiated the peace between Spain and Morocco (1849). His outspokenness resulted in his expulsion, and in 1849 he proceeded to Washington, where he concluded the Clayton-Bulwer Treaty He was ambassador to the Ottoman Porte (1858–1865), and ably carried out Palmerston's policy on the Eastern Question. Created Lord Dalling and Bulwer in 1871, he died at Naples. Among his works were *An Autumn in Greece* (1826), *Historical Characters* (1868–70), and an unfinished *Life of Palmerston* (1870–74).

BULWER LYTTON. See LYTTON.

BUNAU-VARILLA, Philippe Jean, *bü-nō va-ree-ya* (1859–1940), French engineer, chief organizer of the Panama Canal project, was instrumental in getting the waterway routed through Panama instead of Nicaragua, worked to bring about the sale of the canal to the U.S.A., incited the Panama revolution (1903) to further this end, was made Panamanian minister to the U.S.A. and negotiated the Hay-Bunau-Varilla Treaty (1903) giving the U.S.A. control of the Canal Zone. See his *From Panama to Verdun* (1940).

BUNBURY, Henry William (1750–1811), caricaturist, born at Mildenhall, Suffolk, early became distinguished for his humorous designs, which entitle him to rank after Rowlandson and Gillray.

BUNCHE, Ralph Johnson (1904–71), American administrator, born, the grandson of a slave, at Detroit, studied at Harvard, Capetown, the London School of Economics and became assistant-professor of Political Science at Howard University, Washington (1928). During World War II he advised the government on African strategic questions, and as an expert on trusteeship territories drafted the appropriate sections of the U.N. Charter. As director (1947–54) of the U.N. Trusteeship department, he followed Count Folke Bernadotte, after the latter's assassination (1948), as U.N. mediator in Palestine and arranged for a cease-fire. Awarded the Nobel peace prize (1950), he became a U.N. under-secretary (1954–67) and played an important role in Suez, the Congo, and the Indo-Pakistan war of 1965. He was under secretary-general from 1968.

BUNGAY, Thomas (c. 1290), a Franciscan mathematician and philosopher, accounted a magician, born at Bungay, and buried at Northampton.

BUNIN, Ivan Alexeievich, *boo'neen* (1870–1953), Russian author, born at Voronezh, wrote lyrics and novels of the decay of the Russian nobility and of peasant life, among them *The Village* (trans. 1923), *The Gentleman from San Francisco* (trans. 1922), his best-known work with its theme the vanity of all things earthly, and the autobiographical

The Well of Days (trans. 1933). He lived in Paris after the Revolution, and received the Nobel literature prize in 1933.

BUNN, Alfred (c. 1796–1860), the ' Poet Bunn ', from 1833 to 1840–48 was the quarrelsome manager of Covent Garden and Drury Lane theatres. Wrote and translated libretti.

BUNSEN, *boon'sen,* (1) **Christian Karl Josias, Baron** (1791–1860), Prussian diplomat, theologian and scholar, was born at Korbach, in Waldeck, and studied at Marburg, Göttingen, Copenhagen, Berlin, Paris, and Rome, where he was appointed (1818) secretary to the Prussian embassy at the papal court (Niebuhr being ambassador), and in 1827 resident minister. He gave much time to Plato, Egyptology, and published much on church history, liturgical history, and biblical criticism, and was a great supporter of the Archaeological Institute. In 1841 he was sent to London on a special mission about an Anglo-Prussian bishopric in Jerusalem, and next year was appointed ambassador at the English court. In 1844 he drew up a constitution for Prussia closely resembling the English. In the Schleswig-Holstein question Bunsen strongly advocated the German view. Differing from the court on the Eastern Question, he resigned in 1854, and lived at Heidelberg and Cannes. See his *Memoir* (1868) by his widow, Frances Waddington (1791–1876), and her own *Life and Letters* by Hare (1879).

(2) **Robert Wilhelm** (1811–99), chemist and physicist, was born at Göttingen, and studied there and at Paris, Berlin, and Vienna. After holding several lectureships and professorships he became professor of Chemistry at Heidelberg in 1852. He shares with Kirchhoff the discovery, in 1859, of spectrum analysis, which facilitated the discovery of new elements. He partially lost the sight of one eye, which caused him to forbid the study of organic chemistry in his laboratories. He invented the Bunsen burner, the grease-spot photometer, a galvanic battery, an ice calorimeter, and, with Roscoe, the actinometer.

BUNYAN, John (1628–88), English author of the *Pilgrim's Progress*, was born at Elstow near Bedford, son of a ' braserer ' or tinker, in which craft John was duly trained. In 1644 he was drafted into the army, in June 1645 returned to Elstow, and there about 1649 married a poor girl who brought with her two books which had belonged to her father, the *Plain Man's Pathway to Heaven* and the *Practice of Piety.* About this time Bunyan began to pass through those deep religious experiences which he has described so vividly in his *Grace Abounding.* In 1653 he joined a Christian fellowship which had been organized by a converted royalist major, and about 1655 he was asked by the brethren to address them. This led to his preaching in the villages round Bedford; and in 1656 he was brought into discussions with the followers of George Fox, which led to his first book, *Some Gospel Truths Opened* (1656), a vigorous attack on Quakerism. To this Edward Burrough, the Quaker, replied, and Bunyan gave rejoinder in *A Vindication of*

Gospel Truths Opened. In November 1660 he was arrested while preaching in a farmhouse near Ampthill. During the twelve years' imprisonment in Bedford county gaol which followed, Bunyan wrote *Profitable Meditations, Praying in the Spirit, Christian Behaviour, The Holy City, The Resurrection of the Dead, Grace Abounding,* and some smaller works. He was released after the Declaration of Indulgence of 1672, under which he became a licensed preacher, and pastor of the church to which he belonged; but in February 1673 the Declaration of Indulgence was cancelled, and on March 4, a warrant, signed by thirteen magistrates, was issued for his arrest. Brought to trial under the Conventicle Act, Bunyan was sent to prison for six months in the town gaol. It was during this later and briefer imprisonment, and not during the twelve years in the county gaol, that he wrote the first part of the *Pilgrim's Progress.* When first issued (1678) it contained no Mr Worldly Wiseman. Many passages were added in the second and third editions (1679). It is essentially a vision of Life recounted allegorically as the narrative of a journey, told with such an eye to detail and conversational invention that, despite its spiritual meanings, it is a realistic story, contemporary, and authentic. There followed the *Life and Death of Mr Badman* (1680), the *Holy War* (1682), and the second part of the Pilgrim, containing the story of Christiana and her children (1684). Bunyan had been pastor at Bedford for sixteen years, when, after a ride through the rain from Reading to London, he died at the house of a friend in Holborn, August 31, 1688, and was buried in Bunhill Fields, the *Campo Santo* of the Nonconformists. Despite the narrowness of his religious outlook, he was a master of plain, yet beautiful, English prose, the supreme example of the ' proletarian ' writer, and by his realism and psychological insight the precursor of the modern novelist. See Lives by J. A. Froude (1880), Brown (1885), White (1905), Harrison (1928), J. Lindsay (1937), Sharrock (1954), and Talon (1956); also studies by T. B. Macaulay in *Edinburgh Review* (1830), G. B. Shaw (1907), and Firth (1938).

BUOL-SCHAUENSTEIN, Karl Ferdinand, Count, *boo-ol-show'en-shtin* (1797–1865), Austrian prime minister and foreign minister who signed the Treaty of Paris 1856.

BUONAPARTE. See BONAPARTE.

BUONARROTI. See MICHELANGELO.

BUONDELMONTI, *bwon'dayl-mon'tee,* a Guelph leader at Florence in the first half of the 13th century, whose assassination on Easter Sunday 1215 set off the civil war between Guelphs and Ghibellines.

BUONONCINI. See BONONCINI.

BURBAGE, Richard (*c.* 1567–1619), English actor, the son of James Burbage, himself an actor, and the builder of the Shoreditch and Blackfriars theatres. Richard made his debut early, and had earned the title of ' Roscius ', when the death of his father in 1597 brought him a share in the Blackfriars Theatre. In 1599, together with his brother Cuthbert, he pulled down the Shoreditch house, and built the famous Globe Theatre

as a summer playhouse, while the Blackfriars was to be a winter one. He took as partners Shakespeare, Heminge, Condell, and others. See C. C. Stopes, *Burbage* (1913).

BURBANK, Luther (1849–1926), American horticulturalist, born at Lancaster, Mass., by indefatigable experiment bred new fruits and flowers at Santa Rosa, California. The city of Burbank, California, is named after him.

BURCHELL, William John (*c.* 1782–1863), botanist and naturalist, born at Fulham, travelled in S. Africa (1810–15), S. America (1826–29). Many plant families are named after him.

BURCKHARDT, (1) Jacob (1818–97), Swiss historian, born at Basel, studied theology and later art history in Berlin and Bonn, became editor of the *Basler Zeitung* (1844–45), and from 1858–93 was professor of History at Basel University. He is known for his works on the Italian Renaissance and on Greek Civilization. See the biography by W. Kaegi (Basel 1958) and *Judgements on History and Historians* (trans. H. Zohn, intro. H. R. Trevor-Roper, 1959).

(2) **Johann Ludwig** (1784–1817), Swiss traveller, born at Lausanne, was educated at Neuchâtel, Leipzig, and Göttingen. In 1806 he was sent by the African Association to explore the interior of Africa. By way of Malta he went, disguised as an oriental, to Aleppo, where he studied for more than two years; then he visited Palmyra, Damascus, Lebanon, and in 1812 Cairo. But hindered from going by Fezzan to the Niger, he went to Nubia, and thence in 1814 to Mecca, where he was accepted not only as a true believer, but as a great Moslem scholar. In 1815 he returned to Cairo, and in 1816 ascended Mount Sinai. When on the point of joining the Fezzan caravan, for which he had waited so long, he died of dysentery at Cairo. His collection of oriental manuscripts was left to Cambridge University. His journals of travel were published in 1819-30 by the African Association.

BURDER, George (1752–1832), English Congregationalist minister in Lancaster, Coventry, and from 1803 London. His *Village Sermons* had a vast circulation.

BURDETT, Sir Francis, Bart. (1770–1844), the most popular English politician of his time, was educated at Westminster and Oxford, spent three years (1790–93) on the Continent, and witnessed the French Revolution. In 1793 he married Sophia Coutts, of the great banking family. Entering the House of Commons in 1796, he made himself conspicuous by opposing the war with France, and advocating parliamentary reform, Catholic emancipation, freedom of speech, prison reform, and other liberal measures. His candidature for Middlesex in 1802 involved him in four years' costly and fruitless litigation; in May 1807 he fought a duel with a Mr Paull. Burdett having in 1810 published, in Cobbett's *Political Register*, a Letter to his Constituents, declaring the conduct of the House of Commons illegal in imprisoning a radical orator, the Speaker's warrant was issued for his arrest. For two days he barricaded his house; the people supported him, and in a street contest between them and the military one life was lost; but after two days an entry was forced, and Burdett conveyed to the Tower. The prorogation restored him to liberty. In 1820 a letter on the 'Peterloo massacre' brought three months' imprisonment and a fine. In 1835 he joined the Conservatives. See Patterson's *Life* (1931).

BURDETT-COUTTS, Angela Georgina, Baroness, *bèr-det' koots* (1814–1906), English philanthropist, daughter of Sir Francis Burdett, inherited much of the property of her grandfather, Thomas Coutts (q.v.), and used it to mitigate suffering. In 1871 she received a peerage, in 1872 the freedom of the City of London. In 1881 she married William Ashmead-Bartlett (1851–1921), who assumed her name.

BURDON-SANDERSON, Sir John, 1st Bart. (1828–1905), born at Jesmond, Newcastle, held chairs of Physiology and Medicine in London and Oxford, and did much to advance pathology and physiology. See his *Life* by Burdon-Sanderson (1911).

BÜRGER, Gottfried August (1747–94), German lyric poet, was born at Molmerswende, near Halberstadt, the son of the Lutheran pastor. In boyhood he displayed no inclination to study, but a relish for verse. In 1764 he began to study theology; but in 1768 he migrated to Göttingen, and entered on a course of jurisprudence. His life here was wild and extravagant, and he might have sunk into obscurity but for the intimacy which he happily formed with Voss, the two Stolbergs, and others. He studied closely the ancient and modern classics; Shakespeare and Percy had as great an influence on him as he in turn had on Sir Walter Scott, who translated his *Lenore*. He married unhappily three times, speculated unwisely, and favourite poet though he was of the German nation, he was left to earn his bread by translations and similar hack-work. See his *Life* by Döring (1826), Pröhle (1856), and Von Wurzbach (1900), and his *Letters* (1802–74).

BURGESS, John Bagnold (1830–97), English genre painter, was born at Chelsea, painted mostly scenes from Spanish life, bullfights, gypsies, *Kissing Relics in Spain,* &c. He became R.A. in 1889.

BURGH, Hubert de (d. 1243), from 1215 to 1232 was the patriotic Justiciar of England, virtual ruler for the last four years, but now is chiefly remembered as the gaoler of Prince Arthur (q.v.). He was created Earl of Kent in 1227, and died at Banstead, Surrey. Walter de Burgh, Earl of Ulster, who died at Galway in 1291, was his grand-nephew.

BURGHLEY. See CECIL.

BÜRGI. See BYRGIUS.

BURGKMAIR, Hans, *boork'mīr* (1473–1531), German painter and wood-engraver, was born and died at Augsburg. The father-in-law of the elder Holbein and the friend of Dürer, he is best known by his woodcuts, amounting to nearly 700. See book by A. Burkhard (Berlin 1932).

BURGOYNE, (1) John (1723–92), English general and dramatist, entered the army in 1740, eloped later with a daughter of the Earl of Derby, and resided nine years in France (1747–56). Then he distinguished himself by the capture of Valencia de Alcántara (1762), and sat in parliament as a Tory, till in 1774 he was sent out to America. In 1777 he led an expedition from Canada; on July 6, he took Ticonderoga; but on October 17, after two engagements, was forced to surrender to General Gates (q.v.) at Saratoga. Having gone over to the Whigs, he was commander-in-chief in Ireland in 1782–83. He was the author of pamphlets in his own defence, of *The Maid of the Oaks* (1775), and of *The Heiress* (1786), a most successful comedy. See his *Life* by F. J. Hudleston (1928).

(2) **Sir John Fox** (1782–1871), English engineer officer, natural son of (1), was with Moore at Coruña, served under Wellington through the Peninsular war. In the Crimean war he was chief of the British engineering department, was unjustly recalled, but was made a baronet (1856), constable of the Tower (1865), and a field marshal (1868). See his *Life* by Wrottesley (1873).

BURIDAN, Jean, *boor-rèe-dā,* 14th-century French scholastic philosopher, born at Béthune in Artois about 1300, studied at Paris under Ockham, became himself a teacher of the Nominalist philosophy, and was rector of the university of Paris in 1327. He was alive in 1358. His works treat of logic, metaphysics, physics, ethics, and politics. The sophism known as ' Buridan's ass ' (which is bound to starve between two bundles of hay of exactly equal size and attractiveness) does not occur in his works, but is suggested in Aristotle and in Dante.

BURKE, (1) Edmund (1729–97), British statesman and philosopher, born in Dublin, January 12, educated at a Quaker boarding-school and at Trinity College, Dublin. In 1750 he entered the Middle Temple, London, but soon abandoned law for literary work. His *Vindication of Natural Society*, in which, with well-concealed irony, he confutes Bolingbroke's views of society by a *reductio ad absurdum*, was published anonymously in 1756, as also was his *Philosophical Inquiry into the Origin of our Ideas of the Sublime and Beautiful.* From 1761 to 1763 he was back in Dublin as private secretary to ' Single-speech Hamilton', then secretary for Ireland. In 1765 he became private secretary to the Marquis of Rockingham, at that time premier, and entered parliament for the pocket borough of Wendover. His eloquence at once gained him a high position in the Whig party. Rockingham's administration lasted only about a year; but though he held no office till the downfall of the North ministry in 1782, Burke's public activity never ceased till his death. Lord North's long administration (1770–82) was marked by the unsuccessful coercion of the American colonies, by corruption, extravagance, and reaction. Against this policy Burke and his Whig friends could only raise a strong protest. The best of Burke's writings and speeches belong to this period, and may be described as a defence of sound constitutional statesmanship against prevailing abuse and misgovernment. *Observations on the Present State of the Nation* (1769) was a reply to George Grenville; *On the Causes of the Present Discontents*

(1770) treats of the Wilkes controversy. Perhaps the finest of his many efforts are the speech on *American Taxation* (1774), the speech on *Conciliation with America* (1775), and the *Letter to the Sheriffs of Bristol* (1777) —all advocating wise and liberal measures, which would have averted the troubles that ensued. Burke never systematized his political philosophy. It emerges with inconsistencies out of the writings and speeches mentioned above. Opposed to the doctrine of ' natural rights ', he yet takes over the concept of ' social contract ' and attaches to it divine sanction. But his support of the proposals for relaxing the restrictions on the trade of Ireland with Great Britain, and for alleviating the laws against Catholics, cost him the seat at Bristol (1780), and from that time till 1794 he represented Malton. When the disasters of the American war brought Lord North's government to a close, Burke was paymaster of the forces under Rockingham (1782), as also under Portland (1783). After the fall of the Whig ministry in 1783 Burke was never again in office, and misled by party feeling, he opposed Pitt's measure for Free Trade with Ireland and the Commercial Treaty with France. In 1788 he opened the trial of Warren Hastings by the speech which will always rank among the masterpieces of English eloquence. His *Reflections on the French Revolution* (1790) was read all over Europe and strongly encouraged its rulers to resist, but his opposition to it cost him the support of his fellow Whigs, notably that of Fox. In his *Appeal from the New to the Old Whigs*, *Thoughts on French Affairs*, and *Letters on a Regicide Peace*, he goes further, urging the government to suppress free opinions at home. He died July 9, 1797, and was buried in the little church at Beaconsfield, where in 1768 he had purchased the estate of Gregories. During his whole political life Burke was financially embarrassed, despite two pensions granted him in 1794. He ranks as one of the foremost political thinkers of England. He had vast knowledge of affairs, a glowing imagination, passionate sympathies, and an inexhaustible wealth of powerful and cultured expression; but his delivery was awkward and ungainly, and speeches which captivate the reader only served to empty the benches of the House of Commons. Although himself a Whig, Burke's political thought has become, with Disraeli's, the philosophy of modern Conservatism. See Lives by J. Morley (1867), A. P. Samuels (1923), R. H. Murray (1931), P. Magnus (1939), Copeland (1950), and studies by A. Cobban (1929), D. Wecter (1939), Osborn (1940), and Parkin (1956).

(2) **John** (1787–1848), Irish genealogist, compiler of *Burke's Peerage*—the first dictionary of baronets and peers in alphabetical order, published in 1826.

(3) **Sir John Bernard** (1814–92), son of (2), took over *Burke's Peerage* from his father and published it annually from 1847, as well as anecdotes of the aristocracy, &c., was an expert in heraldry, Ulster King of Arms (1853), and keeper of the state papers of Ireland (1855).

(4) **Robert O'Hara** (1820–61), Irish traveller, one of the first to cross the Australian continent from south to north, was born at St Cleram, County Galway, and educated in Belgium, served in the Austrian army (1840), joined the Irish Constabulary (1848), and emigrated to Australia in 1853. While inspector of police in Victoria he accepted the leadership of an expedition, and after many hardships, reached with Wills the tidal waters of the Flinders River. Burke died of starvation on the return journey, June 28, and Wills a day or two later. An expedition brought their remains to Melbourne. See Wills's *Exploration of Australia* (1863).

(5) **Thomas** (1886–1945), English writer, born in London. He is possibly best known for his *Limehouse Nights* (1916); but he is the author of about thirty books, mostly on aspects of London or about inns. These include *Nights in Town* (1915), *The Streets of London* (1941), and *The English Inn* (1930). He also made a fine reconstruction of the Thurtell and Hunt case in *Murder at Elstree* (1936). See his autobiographical *The Wind and the Rain* (1924).

(6) **Thomas Henry** (1829–82), from 1868 permanent Irish under-secretary, was brutally murdered with Lord Frederick Cavendish (q.v.) in Phoenix Park, Dublin.

(7) **William** (1792–1829), was an Irishman, like **William Hare**, his partner in a series of infamous murders, committed at Edinburgh, to supply dissection subjects to Dr Robert Knox, the anatomist. Hare, the more villainous of the two, was admitted king's evidence, and, according to Serjeant Ballantine, died some time in the 'sixties a blind beggar in London; while Burke was hanged, to the general satisfaction of the crowd. See Bridie's play *The Anatomist*, and Roughead, *The Trial of Burke and Hare* (1948).

BURLEIGH. See BURGHLEY, and BALFOUR (8).

BURLINGAME, Anson (1820–70), American diplomat, born at New Berlin, New York. He was sent as U.S. minister to China by Lincoln; and when returning was made Chinese envoy to the U.S. and Europe. He negotiated the Burlingame treaty between China and the U.S. (1868), establishing reciprocal rights of citizenship.

BURLINGTON, Richard Boyle, 3rd Earl of (1695–1753), was an enthusiastic architect, a great admirer of Palladio, and patron of the arts generally. He refashioned the Burlington House of his great-grandfather, the first earl, in Piccadilly and by his influence over a group of young architects was responsible for fostering the Palladian precept which was to govern English building for half a century.

BURMANN, *boor'mann,* a Dutch family of scholars, originally from Cologne:

(1) **Peter** ' the elder ' (1668–1741), studied law at Utrecht and Leyden, and became professor of History and Rhetoric at Utrecht, afterwards of Greek at Leyden. His chief works are editions of the Latin classics.

(2) **Peter** ' the younger ' (1714–78), nephew of (1), studied at Utrecht, and became professor at Franeker, then at Amsterdam, and keeper of the public library there. He edited

Virgil, Aristophanes, Claudian, Propertius, and a Latin anthology.

BURN, (1) **Richard** (1709–85), English legal writer and historian, born at Winton, in Westmorland, was educated at Oxford and from 1736 was vicar of Orton and compiled *Justice of the Peace* and *Ecclesiastical Law*, which works passed through many editions.

(2) **William** (1789–1870), Scottish architect, was born in Edinburgh, and trained under Smirke in London. He founded a successful business first in Edinburgh, and then, after 1844, in London. His unhappy ' restoration ' of St Giles, Edinburgh (1829–33), has been as far as possible undone.

BURNABY, Frederick Gustavus (1842–85), English soldier and traveller, was born at Bedford, joined the Royal Horse Guards Blue in 1859, attaining the rank of colonel in 1881. His experiences in Central and South America, in the Carlist camp in 1874, and with Gordon in the Sudan in 1875, prepared him for the great exploit of his life—his ride in the winter of 1875 across the Russian steppes. His brightly written *Ride to Khiva* (1876) at once made him famous. In 1876–78 he travelled in Asia Minor and Armenia, writing thereafter *On Horseback through Asia Minor*. In Graham's expedition to the Eastern Sudan he was badly wounded at El Teb; and in 1884 he made his way without leave to join Sir Herbert Stewart's column in the Nile expedition, and was killed by an Arab spear-thrust at Abu Klea. Burnaby crossed the Channel to Normandy in 1882 in a balloon. See *Life* by Ware and Mann (1885).

BURNAND, Sir Francis Cowley (1836–1917), English dramatist and journalist, was called to the bar in 1862, but the success of some early dramatic ventures altered his plans. He helped to start *Fun*, but in 1863 left that paper for *Punch*, of which he was editor 1880–1906. He was knighted in 1902. See his *Reminiscences* (1903).

BURNE-JONES, Sir Edward, Bart. (1833–98), British painter, was born at Birmingham of Welsh ancestry, studied at Exeter College, Oxford, where he became the intimate friend of William Morris. Through the encouragement of Rossetti, he relinquished the church for art. His early works, mostly in watercolour, as *The Merciful Knight* (1864) and *The Wine of Circe* (1867), attain a greater brilliancy and purity of hue even than his later oils which, inspired by the early art of the Italian Renaissance, are characterized by a romantic and contrived mannerism. His subjects, drawn from the Arthurian romances and Greek myths, include *The Days of Creation, The Beguiling of Merlin, The Mirror of Venus* (1877), *Pan and Psyche* (1878), &c. He became D.C.L. in 1881, A.R.A. in 1885 (resigned 1893), and a baronet in 1894. His *Love and the Pilgrim* is in the Tate. His son, **Sir Philip** (1861–1926), was also a painter. See monographs by Bell (1892), Mackail (1900), and *Memorials* by his wife (1904).

BURNES, Sir Alexander (1805–41), Scottish traveller and official, was born at Montrose, distantly related to Robert Burns. In 1821 he entered the Indian army, and his knowledge of oriental languages gained him rapid promotion. Starting from Lahore in 1832, and adopting the Afghan dress, he passed through Peshawar and Kabul, and crossed the Hindu Kush to Balkh. From there he passed on to Bokhara, Astrabad, and Tehran, and journeying through Isfahan and Shiraz, embarked at Bushire for India. Returning to England in 1833 he received high honours; and in 1839 he was appointed political resident at Kabul, where he was murdered by the Afghan mob. See his *Travels into Bokhara* (1834), and *Kabul* (1842).

BURNET, (1) **Gilbert** (1643–1715), the Whig broad-church Bishop of Salisbury, was born in Edinburgh. At ten he entered Marischal College, Aberdeen, applied himself first to law and then to divinity with such diligence that in 1661 he was admitted a probationer. In 1663 he visited Cambridge, Oxford, and London, and next year perfected his Hebrew under a rabbi of Amsterdam. In 1669, he was appointed professor of Divinity at Glasgow; but in 1674, having brought on himself the enmity of his old patron Lauderdale, he resigned his chair, and settled in London, where he was made chaplain to the Rolls Chapel, and afterwards lecturer at St Clements, publishing several works, including in 1679–81 the first two volumes of his *History of the Reformation*. In 1680 he declined the bishopric of Chichester; in 1683 he attended the execution of his friend Russell. Charles II exhibited his unkingly spite by depriving him of his lectureship; and on James's accession Burnet went to the Continent, and travelled through Europe, eventually taking Dutch nationality. In 1684 he met the Prince of Orange, with whom he became a great favourite. When William came over, Burnet accompanied him as royal chaplain, and in 1689 was appointed Bishop of Salisbury. His first pastoral letter, founding William's right to the throne on conquest, gave so much offence to parliament that it was burned by the hangman. In 1699 he published his *Exposition of the Thirty-nine Articles*, which was condemned as heterodox by the Lower House of Convocation. In 1714 appeared vol. iii of his *History of the Reformation*. He died at Clerkenwell. His first wife was remarkable for her beauty, the second for her fortune, and the third for her piety. See his *History of My Own Time* (1724–34), the essential *Supplement* (1902), and the *Life* by Clarke and Foxcroft (1907).

(2) **John** (1863–1928), Scottish classical scholar, born at Edinburgh, professor of Greek at St Andrews (1892–1926), known for his works on Greek philosophy and his editions of Plato and Aristotle.

(3) **Sir Macfarlane** (1899–   ), Australian physician, born at Traralgon, Victoria, became in 1928 assistant director and later director of the Institute for Medical Research, Melbourne. A world authority on viral diseases, he shared the Nobel prize in 1960 with Medawar (q.v.) for researches on immunological intolerance in relation to skin and organ grafting. He received a knighthood in 1951 and the O.M. in 1958.

(4) **Thomas** (c. 1635–1715), English clergyman, born at Croft, Yorkshire, became clerk of the closet to William III, but had to resign

the post in 1692 on account of his *Archaeologia Philosophica*, which treated the Mosaic account of the Fall as an allegory. His *Telluris Theoria Sacra* (1680–89), recomposed in English by the author, is a mere fanciful cosmogony. See Life by Heathcote prefixed to its seventh edition (1759).

BURNETT, (1) Frances Hodgson (1849–1924), English novelist, born at Manchester, in 1865 emigrated with her parents to Tennessee. Her first literary success was *That Lass o' Lowrie's* (1877). Later works included plays and *Little Lord Fauntleroy* (1886—by far her most popular story), *The One I Knew Best of All* (1893, autobiographical) and *The Secret Garden* (1909).

(2) **James.** See MONBODDO.

(3) **Sir William** (1779–1861), physician-general of the navy, was born at Montrose, and died at Chichester. 'Burnett's fluid', a strong solution of zinc chloride used as a wood preservative, is named after him.

BURNEY, (1) **Charles** (1726–1814), English musicologist, father of (2), was born at Shrewsbury, studied music there, at Chester, and under Dr Arne in London, later giving lessons himself. After composing three pieces, *Alfred*, *Robin Hood*, and *Queen Mab* for Drury Lane (1745–50), he went as organist to King's Lynn, Norfolk (1751–60). He travelled (1770–72) in France, Italy, Germany, and Austria to collect material for his *General History of Music* (1776–89), his *Present State of Music in France and Italy* (1771), and later volumes on Germany and Holland being amusing diaries of his tour. His *General History* was for long considered a standard work, superseding that of Sir John Hawkins, but its value was stultified by its bias towards the then popular Italian style, to the neglect of Bach and his contemporaries. Burney also wrote a *Life of Metastasio*, and nearly all the musical articles in *Rees's Cyclopaedia*. In 1783 he became organist to Chelsea Hospital, where he died. He knew intimately many of the eminent men of his day, including Burke, Dr Johnson and Garrick. He became F.R.S. in 1773. See Lives by his daughter (2) (1832) and Lonsdale (1965), and studies by Glover (1927) and Scholes (1948) who also edited *Burney's Musical Tours in Europe* (1959). His son **Charles** (1757–1817), was a schoolmaster and classical critic; another son, **James** (1750–1821), was a rear-admiral in the navy, and wrote *Voyages* (see Manwaring's Life, 1931); and a daughter of his second marriage, **Sarah Harriet** (*c.* 1770–1844), wrote novels.

(2) **Fanny**, or **Frances**, afterwards **Madame D'Arblay** (1752–1840), English novelist and diarist, daughter of (1), was born at King's Lynn and educated herself by reading English and French literature and observing the distinguished people who visited her father. Already at ten she had begun her incessant scribbling of stories, plays, and poems; on her fifteenth birthday, in a fit of repentance for such waste of time, she burned all her papers, but she could not erase from her brain the plot of *Evelina*, her first and best novel, published anonymously in 1778, which describes the entry of a country girl into the gaieties of London life. Her father at once

recognized his daughter's touch, and soon confided the secret to Mrs Thrale, who, as well as Dr Johnson, petted the gifted young authoress. The praises of Johnson, Burke, and Reynolds for this work seem strangely excessive. *Cecilia* (1782), though more complex, is less natural, and her work gradually declines. In *Camilla* (1796) she has developed a cumbersome syntax, and in *The Wanderer* (1814) her style has become impossible. She was appointed a second keeper of the robes to Queen Charlotte in 1786, but her health declined, she retired on a pension and married a French émigré, General d'Arblay, in 1793. Her *Letters and Diaries* (1846) show her skill in reporting dramatically. As a portrayer of the domestic scene she was a forerunner of Jane Austen, whom she influenced. See Lives by Seeley (1889), Dobson (1903), Johnson (1926), Lloyd (1936), and Hemslow (1958).

BURNHAM, **Harry Lawson Webster Lawson, 1st Viscount** (1862–1933), was born in London, educated at Eton and Oxford, was Liberal and later Unionist M.P., succeeded his father as director of the *Daily Telegraph* in 1903 and helped to frame the Representation of the People Act of 1918. He was president of the International Labour Conference and the Empire Press Union for several years. He is chiefly known, however, as chairman of the committees which inquired into the salaries of teachers and which recommended the Burnham Scales.

BURNOUF, *bür-noof,* a French family of distinguished philologists and orientalists:

(1) **Emile Louis** (1821–1907), philologist, cousin of (2), directed the French school at Athens, and wrote on Sanskrit, Greek, the science of religion, Japanese mythology, and Latin hymnology.

(2) **Eugène** (1801–52), a great orientalist, son of (3), was born in Paris. He became a member of the Académie des Inscriptions in 1832, and from then till his death was professor of Sanskrit at the Collège de France. His first works were on Pali (1826–27) and Zend MSS. His lithographed edition (1829–43) of the Vendidad-Sadé, part of the *Zend-Avesta*, and his *Commentaire sur le Yaçna* (1833) revealed the language and doctrine of Zoroaster to the western world. He attempted to decipher the cuneiform inscriptions of Persepolis (1836). In 1840 he published text and translation of the *Bhâgavata Purâna*, a system of Indian mythology, and in 1844 his *Histoire du Bouddhisme*. See his Correspondence (1891), and Lives by Barthélemy Saint-Hilaire (1892) and Berger (1893).

(3) **Jean Louis** (1775–1844), philologist, father of (2), was professor of Rhetoric at the Collège de France (1817), inspector and librarian of the university, and member of the Académie des Inscriptions (1836). He translated Tacitus (1827–33).

BURNS, (1) **Edson Louis Millard** (1897–   ), United Nations official, Canadian Government official, and major-general. Following a distinguished career in World War II and subsequent service as minister of veterans' affairs in the Canadian Government, as a United Nations official he became widely known for his tact and diplomacy in his efforts to maintain peace in the Middle East.

(2) **Sir George** (1795–1890), a Glasgow philanthropist and founder of the Cunard (q.v.) Company, was created a baronet in 1889. See *Life* by Hodder (1890).

(3) **John** (1858–1943), British Labour politician, born of Scottish parentage in London, worked as an engineer, took to Socialism, and, elected M.P. for Battersea in 1892, became president of the Local Government Board in 1905, of the Board of Trade 1914, but resigned when war began. He was the first working-man Cabinet minister in Britain.

(4) **Robert** (1759–96), Scottish poet, was born at Alloway near Ayr, January 25, the son of a small farmer. The boy's education, begun at a school at Alloway Mill, and continued by one John Murdoch, was thoroughly literary. Unlike Hogg, Burns had always more or less consciously studied the *technique* of his art. Among early influences were the popular tales and ballads and songs of Betty Davidson, an old woman who lived with the poet's family. He read Allan Ramsay, and began to write a little. Acquaintance with sailors and smugglers broadened his outlook, and he became a kind of rural Don Juan, though he had too much heart for the rôle. The death of Burns's father in 1784 left him to try to farm for himself. Farming without capital was, even then, like gambling without capital—one reverse meant ruin. Burns's husbandry at Mossgiel near Mauchline went ill; the entanglement with Jean Armour (1767–1834) began; and out of his poverty, his passion, his despair, and his desperate mirth, came the extraordinary poetic harvest of 1785. To this year belong the ' Epistle to Davie ', ' Death and Dr Hornbook ', ' The Twa Herds ', ' The Jolly Beggars ', ' Halloween ', ' The Cotter's Saturday Night ', ' Holy Willie's Prayer ', ' The Holy Fair ', and ' The Address to a Mouse '. No poet perhaps of any language has ever attained such a wild perfection as he reaches in the reckless merriment of ' The Jolly Beggars '. The next year was another *annus mirabilis*, though much of the verse is satirical. ' The Twa Dogs ' is a masterpiece of humour; ' The Lament ' and ' Despondency ' remind one of Régnier. In this year there was abundant trouble with Jean Armour; there was the Highland Mary (Mary Campbell) episode, and her death. Looking about him for money to emigrate to Jamaica, Burns published the famous Kilmarnock edition of his poems (1786). Their fame spread, Burns got a few pounds, and was just about to sail, when the praises and promises of admirers induced him to stay in Scotland. In winter he went to Edinburgh, met the wits and the great, and was lionized. On returning to the country, he ' fell to his old love again ', Jean Armour; then, after a Highland tour, went back to Edinburgh, and began the epistolary flirtations with ' Clarinda ' (see MACLEHOSE). By this date Johnson had set about publishing his *Scots Musical Museum*, to which we owe all that is briefest and brightest of Burns. He contributed an astonishing number of the most beautiful, tender, passionate, and vivacious songs in any language, chiefly adapted

to old Scottish airs, and moulded now and then on old Scots words. In 1788 Burns married Jean Armour. He took a lease of Ellisland farm, on the Nith, above Dumfries, and next year received an appointment in the Excise. ' Tam o' Shanter ' (1790) was written in one day; by this time Ellisland had proved a failure. He left his farm, withdrew to Dumfries, flirted with the French Revolution, drank, wrote songs, expressed opinions then thought Radical, and made himself unpopular with the local lairds. But in 1795 he turned patriot again. He died on July 21, of endocarditis induced by rheumatism, at Dumfries, and there is buried. His humble origin, his identification with the Scottish folk tradition, which he rescued, refurbished, and in part embellished, provide the reasons for unwaning popularity as the national poet of Scotland. But the Burns cult did Burns, the poet, grievous harm. Burns' night orators, philosophizers, and imitators found the lesser sentimental pieces better suited for their purposes. Yet it is not the self-conscious ' Heaven-taught Ploughman ' but the satirical poet, the ironical observer of men, manners, religion, politics, and human nature, and the unromantic love poet of the folk tradition that will continue to command a foremost place in the literature of the world. See *Letters* ed. J. de L. Ferguson (1931); Lives by J. G. Lockhart (1829), C. Carswell (1930), F. B. Snyder (1932), H. Hecht (trans. 1950), and M. Lindsay (1954); and critical studies by D. Daiches (1952) and (1957).

BURNSIDE, Ambrose Everett (1824–81), American general, born at Liberty, Indiana, served an apprenticeship to a tailor, but graduated at West Point in 1847. As colonel of volunteers in 1861, he commanded a brigade at Bull Run, and in February 1862 captured Roanoke Island. Reluctantly superseding McClellan, he crossed the Rappahannock on December 13, and attacked Lee near Fredericksburg, but was repulsed with a loss of over 10,000 men. In 1863 he successfully held Knoxville, and in 1864 led a corps under Grant through the battles of the Wilderness and Cold Harbor. He was elected U.S. senator in 1875. He lent his name to a style of side-whiskers. See *Life* by Poore (1882).

BURR, Aaron (1756–1836), an American statesman, born at Newark, New Jersey, graduated at Princeton. Called to the bar in 1782, he was attorney-general 1789–91, U.S. senator 1791–97, and vice-president of the U.S. 1800–04. His defeat in a contest for the governorship of New York led him to force a duel (July 11, 1804) on Alexander Hamilton, his personal rival, who fell mortally wounded. Burr fled to South Carolina, and though indicted for murder, returned and completed his term as vice-president. He now prepared to raise a force to conquer Texas, and establish there a republic, and ultimately (said his enemies, unjustly) dismember the Union. This enterprise was proclaimed by the president, and Burr tried for treason (1807). Acquitted, but bankrupt in reputation, he spent some wretched years in Europe, and in 1812 resumed his law practice in New York. Here, shunned by society, he died. See his *Journal* (1903), and Lives by Merwin (1900) and Wandell (1925).

BURRA, Edward (1905–), English artist, born in London. He studied at the Chelsea School of Art and the Royal College of Art, and travelled widely in Europe and the U.S. He is well known as a colourist, and his surrealist paintings of figures against exotic (often Spanish) backgrounds are invariably in water colour. His picture *Soldiers* in this vein is in the Tate Gallery, London. He has also designed for the ballet. See the monograph by John Rothenstein (1945).

BURRELL, Sir William (1861–1958), Scottish shipowner and art collector, born in Glasgow. He entered his father's business at the age of fifteen, and during his lifetime he accumulated a valuable collection of works of art, including modern French paintings, which he gave in 1944 to his native town, with provision for a gallery. In 1949 he gifted an art gallery and a number of pictures to Berwick-on-Tweed.

BURRITT, Elihu (1810–79), 'the learned blacksmith', was born at New Britain, Conn. He worked as a blacksmith in his native place and at Worcester, Mass., but devoted all his leisure to mathematics and languages. Through his published works and through his travels in the U.S.A. and Europe he was known as an apostle of peace. He founded the *Christian Citizen* in 1844. In 1865–70 he was U.S. consul in Birmingham, England.

BURROUGHS, *bur′rōz,* (1) **Edgar Rice** (1875–1950), American novelist, born at Chicago, known for his 'Tarzan' stories, beginning with *Tarzan of the Apes* (1914).

(2) **John** (1837–1921), American writer, born at Roxbury, New York, settled down in 1874 on a farm, to divide his time between literature, fruit-growing and periodic duties as a bank-examiner. His books mostly deal with country life, and include *Wake-Robin* (1871), *Winter Sunshine* (1875), *Birds and Poets* (1877), *Locusts and Wild Honey* (1879).

(3) **William Seward** (1857–98), American inventor of adding and calculating machines.

BURROWS, Montagu (1819–1905), English historian, born at Hadley, near Barnet, rose in the navy to commander (1852), and then, going up to Oxford, took a double first, and in 1862 became Chichele professor of Modern History. Among his works are *Wiclif's Place in History* (1882), *Autobiography* (1908), &c.

BURT, (1) **Sir Cyril Lodowic** (1883–1971), English psychologist, born in London, educated at Christ's Hospital and Jesus College, Oxford, and at Würzburg, became professor of Education at London (1924–31) and professor of Psychology (1931–50). He was also psychologist to the London County Council, was consulted by the War Office and the Civil Service Commission on 'Personnel Selection' and was largely responsible for the theory and practice of intelligence and aptitude tests, ranging from the psychology of education to the problems of juvenile delinquency. He was knighted in 1946. See his *Factors of the Mind* (1940).

(2) **Edward** (d. 1755), General Wade's agent in road-making through the Highlands (1725–26), in 1754 published his *Letters from the North of Scotland.*

BURTON, (1) **Decimus** (1800–81), English architect, son of a London builder, planned at the age of 23 the Regent's Park colosseum, an exhibition hall with a dome larger than that of St Paul's, and in 1825 designed the new layout of Hyde Park and the triumphal arch at Hyde Park Corner.

(2) **John Hill** (1809–81), Scottish historian, was born at Aberdeen. He was in 1854 appointed secretary to the Prison Board of Scotland, and was a prison commissioner, and historiographer royal for Scotland. He was best known for his *Life of Hume* (1846), and wrote much on Scottish life, history, law, and letters.

(3) **Lord Michael.** See BASS (2).

(4) **Sir Richard Francis** (1829–90), English traveller, was born at Torquay, son of a colonel. His education, on the Continent and in England, was irregular and included expulsion from Oxford. In 1842 he served in Sind under Sir Charles Napier; and having mastered Hindustani, Persian, and Arabic, made a pilgrimage to Mecca disguised as a Pathan (1853). In 1856 he set out with Speke (q.v.) on the journey which led to the discovery (1858) of Lake Tanganyika, and afterwards travelled in North America. In 1861 he was consul at Fernando Pó, and went on a mission to Dahomey. He was subsequently consul at Santos in Brazil, at Damascus, and (1872) at Trieste. In 1876–78 he visited Midian, and in 1882 Guinea; and he was knighted in 1886. Among Burton's many works are *First Footsteps in East Africa* (1856), *Wanderings in West Africa* (1863), &c., including books on Sind, Goa, Brazil, Syria, Iceland, and translations of Camoens, &c. Burton amassed a vast store of notes, sociological, anthropological, often simply erotological; and for some of his translations (*The Perfumed Garden, Kama Sutra,* and his monumental annotated edition of the *Arabian Nights,* 16 vols., 1885–88) he resorted to private publication, so avoiding prosecution and making a considerable fortune in his last years. Lady Burton, *née* Isabel Arundell (1831–96), shared in much of his travelling and writing; a devoted wife, she denied posterity her husband's last (incompleted) work, *The Scented Garden Men's Hearts to Gladden,* and his journals, by burning the manuscript after his death. See her Life of Sir Richard (1893), a criticism of this by G. M. Stisted (1896); Lives by Wright (1906), Downey (1931) and Brodie (1967); Penzer's *Bibliography* (1923); and J. Burton's *Life of Lady Burton* (1942).

(5) **Robert** (1577–1640), English author of the *Anatomy of Melancholy,* was born at Lindley, Leicestershire, was educated at Nuneaton, Sutton Coldfield, and Brasenose College, Oxford, and in 1599 was elected a student of Christ Church. In 1616 he was presented to the Oxford vicarage of St Thomas, and about 1630 to the rectory of Segrave. Both livings he kept, but spent his life at Christ Church, where he died, January 25, 1640. Little is known of the life of 'Democritus Junior'; but according to Anthony à Wood: 'He was an exact mathematician, a curious calculator of nativities, a general read scholar, a thro' paced philologist, and one that understood the surveying of

lands well. . . . His company was very merry, facete, and juvenile'. Not unnaturally, it was rumoured—falsely—that the author of the *Anatomy of Melancholy* died a suicide's death. The first edition of the great work appeared in quarto in 1621. Four more editions in folio were published within the author's lifetime, each with successive alterations and additions; the final form of the book was the sixth edition (1651–52). One of the most interesting parts of the book is the long preface, 'Democritus to the Reader', in which Burton gives indirectly an account of himself and his studies. This strange book is a farrago from all, even the most out-of-the-way, classical and mediaeval writers, yet not one quotation but lends strength or illustration to his argument. Every page is marked by keen irony, profound and often gloomy humour, and by strong and excellent sense; while throughout there runs a deep undertone of earnestness that at times rises into a grave eloquence of quite singular charm. Milton, Dr Johnson, Sterne, Byron, and Lamb were all influenced or impressed by the book. See C. Whibley, *Literary Portraits* (1904), and Middleton Murry, *Countries of the Mind* (1931).

BURY, (1) Blaze de. See BLAZE.

(2) Lady Charlotte Susan Maria (1775–1861), Scottish novelist, youngest child of the fifth Duke of Argyll, married in 1796 Colonel John Campbell (d. 1809), and in 1818 the Rev. Edward John Bury (1790–1832). Beautiful and accomplished, she published sixteen novels, including *Flirtation*, *Separation*, &c., and was reputedly the anonymous author of the spicy *Diary illustrative of the Times of George IV* (1838).

(3) John Bagnell (1861–1927), British historian, born in Co. Monaghan, professor of Modern History (1893–1902) and Greek (1899–1902) in Dublin and thereafter of Modern History in Cambridge, wrote histories of Greece, the Later Roman Empire, and edited Pindar and Gibbon. See Memoir and bibliography by Baynes (1929).

(4) Richard de. See AUNGERVILLE.

BUSBECQ, Ogier Ghiselin de, *büs-bek'* (1522–1592), a Flemish diplomatist, in 1556–62 the Emperor Ferdinand's ambassador at Constantinople. He wrote two works on Turkey. See his *Life and Letters* by Forster and Daniell (2 vols. 1880).

BUSBY, Richard (1606–95), English schoolmaster, born at Lutton-Bowine, Lincolnshire, from Westminster School passed to Christ Church, Oxford, and from 1640 till his death was headmaster of Westminster. He is the model 17th-century headmaster, notable alike for learning, assiduity, and unsparing application of the birch; none the less for his own loyalty and integrity, and the affection of his pupils. Among them were Dryden, Locke, South, and Atterbury. See Life by Russell Barker (1895).

BUSCH, (1) Moritz (1821–99), a German publicist, born at Dresden, who from a Radical became an adherent of Bismarck's.

(2) Wilhelm (1832–1908), German comic artist, was born near Hanover, and began in 1859 to draw for the *Fliegende Blätter*. See study by Dangers (1937).

BÜSCHING, Anton Friedrich (1724–93), German geographer, founder of statistical geography, was born in Schaumburg-Lippe, and died the director of a gymnasium in Berlin. His son, Johann Gustav (1783–1829), published many works on German antiquities, literature, and art.

BUSENBAUM, Hermann, *boo'sen-bowm* (1600–68), Jesuit theologian, was born in Westphalia, and died rector of the Jesuit College at Münster. His *Medulla Theologiae Moralis* (1645) became a standard authority in Jesuit seminaries, though several of its propositions were condemned by the popes. An ill-expressed sentence seems to mean (but does not), ' When the end is lawful, the means also are lawful'.

BUSH, Alan Dudley (1900–), English composer, born in London. President of the Workers' Music Association, which he founded in 1936, Bush was a convinced Communist who simplified his work in accordance with the principles governing Soviet music, and suggested that political ideas underlay many of his orchestral works, which included two symphonies and concertos for violin and piano, and an opera, *Wat Tyler*, which won an Arts Council award in 1951.

BUSHNELL, Horace (1802–76), American divine, was born at New Preston, Conn., and died at Hartford, where from 1833 to 1859 he was a famous Congregational pastor, and where the city park is named after him. His works had considerable influence in Britain as well as the U.S.A. See Life by his daughter (1880).

BUSK, Hans (1815–82), one of the chief originators of the volunteer movement, at Cambridge founded a rifle club; and he helped in 1858 to revive the only existing volunteer corps, the Victoria Rifles. His sister, Rachel Harriette (1818–1907), folklorist and traveller, published *Folk-songs of Italy* (1886), and collections from Spain, Tirol, and the East.

BUSONI, Ferruccio Benvenuto, *boo-sō'nee* (1866–1924), Italian pianist and composer, was born at Empoli, Tuscany. An infant prodigy, he played in public at the age of nine, and at fifteen made a successful concert tour. In 1889 he became professor of the Pianoforte at Helsinki, met Sibelius (q.v.), and married (1890) Gerda Sjöstrand. He subsequently taught and played the pianoforte in Moscow, Boston, Berlin, Weimar, and Zürich, returning to Berlin in 1920. The influence of Liszt is apparent in his great pianoforte concerto. His opera *Doktor Faust*, completed posthumously by a pupil in 1925, is, despite its severely intellectual character, his greatest work. Its superbly scored ballet music shows his debt to Bizet (q.v.). See the biography by E. J. Dent (1933).

BUSS, Frances Mary (1827–94), English pioneer of higher education of women, and founder of the North London Collegiate School for Ladies. See Lives by Ridley (1896), Holmes (1913), and Burstall (1938); also J. Kamm, *How Different from Us* (1959).

BUSSY-RABUTIN, Roger, Comte de, properly Roger de Rabutin, Comte de Bussy, *bü-see-*

ra-bü-tï' (1618–93), French soldier who ruined his brilliant military prospects by getting himself imprisoned and exiled for his *Histoire amoureuse des Gaules*, a book of partly fictitious court scandals (1666). See his *Mémoires* and his letters to his cousin, Mme de Sévigné.

BUTCHER, Samuel Henry (1850–1910), Greek scholar and M.P. for Cambridge University from 1906, was born in Dublin. Educated at Marlborough and Trinity College, Cambridge, he was senior classic and chancellor's medallist in 1873, gained a fellowship, was elected to an extraordinary fellowship at University College, Oxford, and in 1882 became professor of Greek at Edinburgh. He collaborated with Andrew Lang in one of the best prose translations of the *Odyssey* (1879) and is also well known for his work on Aristotle's *Poetics* (1895).

BUTE, John Stuart, 3rd Earl of (1713–92), British statesman, succeeded his father in 1723, and about 1737 was made one of his lords of the bedchamber by Frederick, Prince of Wales. On the prince's death (1751), Bute became groom of the stole to his son, afterwards George III, whom he strongly influenced. In 1761 he was appointed one of the principal secretaries of state; and from May 29, 1762, to April 8, 1763, he was prime minister. His government was one of the most unpopular that ever held office, its fundamental principle being the supremacy of the royal prerogative. Bute may have been incapable; but, worse than that, he was deemed by the popular verdict ' unfit to be prime minister of England, as (1) a Scotsman, (2) the king's friend, and (3) an honest man '. For some time he retained his influence over the king, but from 1768 his life was chiefly spent in the country, where he engaged in botany and science study. See Life by Lovat Fraser (1912).

BUTENANDT, Adolf Friedrich Johann (1903–), German organic chemist, born at Bremerhaven-Lehe, was offered the Nobel prize for chemistry in 1939 for his work on sex hormones, but declined in obedience to a Nazi decree. He isolated androsterone and investigated the chemical structure of progestin.

BUTLER, (1) Alban (1710–73), English Catholic hagiographer, was born at Appletree, Northampton; was educated at Douai, and became professor there; was for some time chaplain to the Duke of Norfolk; and at his death was head of the English College at St Omer. His great work, the *Lives of the Saints* (1756–59), primarily intended for edification, makes no distinction between fact and fiction. His nephew, **Charles** (1750–1832), a lawyer, wrote on legal and theological subjects.

(2) **Benjamin Franklin** (1818–93), American lawyer, general, and congressman, was born at Deerfield, New Hampshire. Graduating at Waterville College, Maine, in 1838, and admitted to the bar in 1840, he became noted as a criminal lawyer, a champion of the working classes, and an ardent Democrat, both in the legislature and in the state senate. In 1861 he was appointed major-general of volunteers, and in 1862 took possession of New Orleans (May 1), where prompt and severe measures crushed all opposition. In December ' Beast Butler ', as the Confederates called him, was superseded, but in November 1863 received a command in Virginia, and next year made an expedition against Fort Fisher, near Wilmington. Elected to Congress in 1866, he was prominent in the Republican efforts for the reconstruction of the southern states and the impeachment of President Johnson. In 1878 and 1879 he was nominated for governor of Massachusetts by the National Party, and endorsed by Democrats, in 1882 elected, but in 1883 again defeated. His nomination for president in 1884 was not taken seriously. See his *Autobiography* (1892).

(3) **Lady Eleanor** (1745–1829), and Miss Sarah Ponsonby (1755–1831), two Irish recluses, known as the ' Maids of Llangollen ' or ' Ladies of the Vale '. They settled about 1774 at Plas Newydd, Llangollen, and were visited there by Mme de Genlis, Miss Seward, De Quincey, &c.

(4) **Elizabeth.** See (16).

(5) **Frances Pierce.** See KEMBLE (3).

(6) **George.** See (9).

(7) **James.** See ORMONDE.

(8) **Joseph** (1692–1752), English moral philosopher and divine, was born May 18, at Wantage, Berkshire. Destined for the Presbyterian ministry, he attended an academy for dissenters at Gloucester, and later at Tewkesbury, where the future Archbishop Secker was a fellow pupil. But he joined the Church of England and in 1714 entered Oriel College, Oxford. He corresponded with the philosophical theologian, Samuel Clarke, seeking rational confirmation of Christian doctrine and objecting to the latter's *a priori* arguments for the existence of God. In 1718 he graduated, took orders and was appointed preacher at the Rolls Chapel, where he preached the *Fifteen Sermons* (1722, published 1726) which comprised his ethical theory of objective intuitionism. For Butler, human psychology is divisible into three main elements: the passions; the reflective principles of cool self-love and benevolence; and the supreme principl, conscience. He identified virtue not with any one of these elements but with the proper relation between them. A man is virtuous when he acts according to nature, meaning ideal nature, where the three elements are working in harmony. Butler became prebendary of Salisbury (1721), rector of Haughton-le-Skerne near Darlington (1722), and of Stanhope (1725), where he lived in complete retirement, busy on his *Analogy of Religion Natural and Revealed* (1736), the aim of which was to show that objections against revealed religion may also be levelled against the whole constitution of nature. Secker desired to see him promoted to some more important position, and mentioned his name once to Queen Caroline. The queen thought he had been dead, and asked Archbishop Blackburne. ' No, madam,' said the Archbishop, ' he is not dead, but he is buried '. In 1733 Butler became chaplain to his friend Lord Chancellor Talbot, and in 1736 a prebendary of Rochester, and clerk of the closet to Queen

Caroline. In 1738 he was made Bishop of Bristol, in 1740 Dean of St Paul's; in 1747 he is said to have been offered the primacy; and in 1750 he was translated to Durham. He died at Bath, June 16, 1752, and was buried in Bristol Cathedral. See Gladstone's edition of his works (2 vols. 1896), and his *Subsidiary Studies* (1896), and Lives by Spooner (1902), Baker (1924), E. C. Broad (1936), and study by A. Duncan-Jones (1952).

(9) **Josephine Elizabeth**, *née* **Gray** (1828–1906), English social reformer, was born at Milfield and successfully crusaded against the white-slave traffic and the Contagious Diseases Acts which placed loose women in seaports and military towns under police jurisdiction, often subjecting them to much injustice. She was married to **George Butler** (1819–90), Canon of Winchester and author of educational works. See her *Personal Reminiscences of a Great Crusade* (1896), and studies and Lives by Fawcett and Turner (1928), G. W. and L. A. Johnson (1928), and Bell (1963).

(10) **Nicholas Murray** (1862–1947), born in New Jersey, became professor of Philosophy in Columbia University in 1889, president in 1902–1945. He received the Nobel peace prize in 1931, and was the author of books on public questions, mostly on the philosophy of education.

(11) **Reginald Cotterell** (1913–), English sculptor, born at Buntingford, Herts. He was a lecturer at the Architectural Association School of Architecture from 1937 to 1939, and technical editor of the Architectural Press from 1946 to 1951, when he was appointed the Gregory fellow of Sculpture at Leeds University. In 1953 he won 1st prize in the international *Unknown Political Prisoner* sculpture competition. He is recognized as one of the leading exponents of 'linear' sculpture, and has produced many constructions in wrought iron, although he has recently turned to a more realistic style.

(12) **Lord Richard Austen** (1902–), British Conservative politician, born at Attock Serai, India, the son of a distinguished administrator. He was educated at Marlborough and Cambridge, was president of the University Union in 1924 and fellow of Corpus Christi College from 1925 to 1929, when he became M.P. for Saffron Walden, Essex. After a series of junior ministerial appointments from 1932, he was minister of education (1941–45). His name will always be closely associated with the forward-looking Education Act of 1944 which reorganized the secondary school system and introduced the '11-plus' examination for the selection of grammar school pupils. In Churchill's 1951 Government he was chancellor of the Exchequer, and in 1955 introduced the emergency 'credit squeeze' budget, which was to be his last. In December he became lord privy seal (until 1959) and leader of the House of Commons (until 1961). Though 'tipped' for the premiership after Eden's resignation in 1957, Macmillan was chosen and Butler became home secretary (until 1962). First secretary of state and deputy prime minister (1962–63), he again narrowly lost the premiership to Douglas-Home in 1963, and became foreign secretary (1963–

1964). Once described as 'both irreproachable and unapproachable', he will go down as one of the most progressive, thoughtful, and dedicated of Tory leaders. In 1965 he was appointed Master of Trinity College, Cambridge, and was made a life peer. See Francis Boyd, *Richard Austen Butler* (1956).

(13) **Samuel** (1612–80), English satirist, author of *Hudibras*, the son of a small farmer, was baptized at Strensham, Worcestershire. He was educated at Worcester grammar school, and perhaps Oxford or Cambridge. As secretary to a Mr Jeffreys, a justice of the peace, of Earls-Croome, Worcestershire, he is said to have occupied his leisure with music and painting. He was afterwards in the service of the Countess of Kent, and became intimate with Selden. There is no ground for saying he was in the service of Sir Samuel Luke, of Cople Hoo, near Bedford, who is supposed to have sat for Hudibras. After the Restoration, he became secretary to the Earl of Carbery, Lord President of Wales, by whom he was appointed steward of Ludlow Castle. About this time he took a wife whose fortune was lost in 'ill securities'. The first part of *Hudibras* appeared in 1663, the second in 1664, and the third in 1678. The poem, a burlesque satire on Puritanism, secured immediate popularity, and was a special favourite of Charles II's, who, however, rewarded its author with only a solitary grant of £300, by Butler distributed among his creditors. From the Earl of Dorset, who introduced *Hudibras* to the king, he received some kindness; but his best friend was William Longueville of the Temple. He died in Rose Street, Covent Garden, of consumption, on September 25, and was buried, at Longueville's expense, in the churchyard of St Paul's, Covent Garden. The *Posthumous Works* (1716) are mainly spurious, unlike his *Genuine Remains in Verse and Prose* (1759). See studies by Veldkamp (1923) and E. A. Richards (1937).

(14) **Samuel** (1774–1839), English divine, grandfather of (15), born at Kenilworth, was headmaster of Shrewsbury then Bishop of Lichfield and Coventry. He edited Aeschylus (1809–16). See Life (1896) by (15).

(15) **Samuel** (1835–1902), English author, painter and musician, grandson of (14), born at Langar Rectory, near Bingham, Nottinghamshire, was educated at Shrewsbury and St John's College, Cambridge. Forever quarrelling with his clergyman father, he gave up the idea of taking orders and became instead a sheep farmer in New Zealand. Passages from his *A First Year in Canterbury Settlement* (1863) reappeared in *Erewhon* (1872), a Utopian satire ('Erewhon' is an inversion of 'nowhere') in which many of the conventional practices and customs are reversed. For example, crime is treated as an illness and illness as a crime. Machines have been abolished for fear of their mastery over men's minds, &c. The dominant theme of its supplement, *Erewhon Revisited* (1901), is the origin of religious belief. Butler was greatly influenced by Darwin's *Origin of Species*, and accepted the latter's theory of evolution, but not of natural selection. He returned to Britain in 1864, and thereafter

lived in London until his death. For a time, he studied painting, and his picture *Mr Heatherley's Holiday* is in the Tate Gallery. In a series of writings he tried to revive the ' vitalist ' or ' creative ' view of evolution, as in *Luck or Cunning* (1886), in opposition to Darwin's doctrine of natural selection. He began to suspect a dogmatism in the march of science as narrow as, but more invidious than, that of the church. He loved music, especially Handel's, and composed two oratorios, gavottes, minuets, fugues, and a cantata. In his later years he turned to Shakespearean scholarship and published translations of the *Iliad* (1898) and the *Odyssey* (1900). His essay *The Humour of Homer* (1892) is a remarkable piece of literary criticism. He is best known, however, for his autobiographical novel *The Way of All Flesh*, published posthumously in 1903, a work of moral realism on the causes of strife between different generations which left its mark on Shaw and much 20th-century literature. See memoir by his collaborator H. Festing Jones (1920), and Lives by C. E. M. Joad (1924), C. G. Stillman (1932), J. B. Fort (1935), M. Muggeridge (1936), Furbank (1948), and Harkness (1955).

(16) **Sir William Francis** (1838–1910), British general and author, born at Suirville, Tipperary, served on the Red River Expedition (1870–71), on the Ashanti Expedition (1873), in the Sudan (1884–85), and in South Africa (1888–99), and published several books on his experiences. See his *Autobiography* (1911) and study by E. McCourt (1968). In 1877 he married **Elizabeth Southerden Thompson** (1850–1933), battle-painter, born at Lausanne, who made her reputation with the *Roll Call* (1874), *Inkermann* (1877), &c. See her *Autobiography* (1923).

BUTLIN, Sir William Edmund (1899–), holiday camp promoter, born in South Africa. He moved with his parents to Canada, and after serving in World War I, he worked his passage to England with only £5 capital. After a short period in a fun fair he went into business on his own. In 1936 he opened his first camp at Skegness, followed by others at Clacton and Filey. During World War II he served as director-general of hostels to the ministry of supply, and was awarded the M.B.E. in 1952. After the war more camps and hotels were opened both at home and abroad. He sponsored a mass walk from John o' Groats to Land's End in February 1960. He was knighted in 1964.

BUTT, (1) **Dame Clara** (1872–1936), English contralto singer, born at Southwick, made her début in 1892. Elgar's *Sea Pictures* were especially composed for her. See Life by W. Ponder (1928).

(2) **Isaac** (1813–79), Irish politician, the first ' Home Ruler ', was the son of the Protestant rector of Stranorlar, and was born at Glenfin, County Donegal. Educated at Raphoe and at Trinity College, Dublin, he gained a brilliant reputation for his accomplished scholarship, edited the *Dublin University Magazine* from 1834 to 1838, and filled the chair of Political Economy from 1836 to 1841. He was called to the Irish bar in 1838, and before long became a foremost

champion of the Conservative cause, actively opposing O'Connell's Repeal Association in 1843. But from 1852 to 1865 he represented Youghal as a ' Liberal Conservative ', and he defended Smith O'Brien and others in the state trials of 1848 and all the Fenian prisoners between 1865 and 1869. In 1871 he was returned for Limerick to lead the Home Rule party in the House of Commons, but soon found, to his mortification, that he could not control the forces he had formed. See Thornley, *Isaac Butt and Home Rule* (1964).

BUTTERFIELD, William (1814–1900), English architect, was born in London and was the architect of Keble College, Oxford; St Augustine's College, Canterbury; the chapel and quadrangle of Rugby; All Saints', Margaret Street, London; and St Albans, Holborn. He was also responsible for many controversial ' restorations '.

BUTTERICK, Ebenezer (1826–1903), American tailor, inventor of standardized paper patterns for garments.

BUTZER. See BUCER.

BUXTEHUDE, Diderik, Ger. **Dietrich,** *books-tė-hoo'dė* (1637–1707), Danish organist and composer, was born at Helsingborg (now in Sweden), and in 1668 was appointed to the coveted post of organist at the Marienkirche, Lübeck. Here he began the famous *Abend-musiken*—evening concerts during Advent of his own sacred choral and orchestral music and organ works. In 1704 Bach walked two hundred miles across Germany from Arnstadt and Handel travelled from Hamburg to attend the concerts and to meet Buxtehude, outstanding in his time as an organist and as a composer, the principles of whose ' free ' organ and pure instrumental works were later to be developed by Bach. See the Life by H. J. Moser (Berlin 1957).

BUXTON, Sir Thomas Fowell, 1st Bart. (1786–1845), English brewer and social reformer, born at Earls Colne, Essex, was educated at Trinity College, Dublin, and married into the Gurney family of Norwich. As M.P. for Weymouth (1818–37) he worked for modification of the criminal law, abolition of the slave trade, and prison reform, succeeding Wilberforce as head of the antislavery party in 1824. See his Memoirs by his son, **Charles** (1823–71), an independent Liberal M.P., published in 1848.

BUXTORF, Johann (1564–1629), German Hebraist, was born at Kamen, in Westphalia; in 1591 became professor of Hebrew at Basel, and died there of the plague. His *Lexicon Chaldaicum, Talmudicum et Rabbinicum* was completed by his son (1639). See Life by Kautzsch (1879). That son, **Johann** (1599–1664), succeeded to the Hebrew chair, as also did his son, **Jakob** (1645–1704), and *his* nephew, **Johann** (1663–1732).

BUYS-BALLOT, Christoph Henrik Diedrik, *bīz-bal-lot* (1817–90), Dutch meteorologist, the inventor of the aeroklinoscope and of a system of weather signals, was born at Kloetingen in Zeeland, and died at Utrecht.

BYNG, (1) **George, 1st Viscount Torrington** (1663–1733), English sailor, father of (2), was born at Wrotham, Kent, at fifteen entered the navy, and in 1688 recommended himself to William of Orange by his zeal in the cause of the Revolution. Made rear-admiral in 1703, he next year captured Gibraltar, and for his gallant conduct at the sea fight of Málaga was knighted by Queen Anne. In 1708 he commanded a squadron fitted out to oppose invasion by the Pretender. He pursued the French fleet to the Firth of Forth, took one ship, and forced the rest back to Dunkirk. For his services during the '15 he was created a baronet; and in 1718 he commanded the fleet sent to Sicily, on July 31 utterly destroying the Spanish fleet off Messina. In 1721 he was created viscount. See *The Torrington Diaries*, ed. C. B. Andrews (1954).

(2) **John** (1704–57), English sailor, fourth son of (1), joined the navy at fourteen, and in 1745 had risen to the rank of rear-admiral in the Mediterranean fleet. In 1756, the year he was promoted admiral, he was sent with a poorly equipped squadron to relieve Minorca, at that time blockaded by a French fleet. Off the Castle of St Philip on May 20, he gave the signal to engage the enemy's fleet. The van under Rear-admiral West at once attacked, but the rear, under Byng, got into some disorder and hardly came within gunshot. The van suffered great loss, and Byng sailed away to Gibraltar and left Minorca to its fate. In England the public was furious, and Byng was brought home under arrest. Acquitted of cowardice or disaffection, he was found guilty of neglect of duty, and condemned to death, but recommended to mercy. The king, however, refused to pardon him, and Byng was shot on ' the *Monarque* ' at Portsmouth, March 14, ' pour encourager les autres ' in Voltaire's phrase. See study by Tunstall (1928) and *The Byng Papers* (1930 ff.).

(3) **Julian Hedworth George, 1st Viscount Byng of Vimy** (1862–1935), British general, commanded the 9th Army Corps in Gallipoli (1915), the Canadian Army Corps (1916–17), and the 3rd Army (1917–18). Governor-general of Canada (1921–26), he was commissioner of the metropolitan police (1928–1931), and was made a viscount in 1926 and a field-marshal in 1932.

BYRD, bird, (1) **Richard Evelyn** (1888–1957), American rear-admiral, explorer, and aviator, made the first aeroplane flight over the North Pole, May 9, 1926; he flew over the South Pole, November 28–29, 1929. From his base, ' Little America ', near Ross Sea, he carried out Antarctic exploration in 1933–34 and he led another expedition in 1939–41. See his *Discovery* (1935) and *Alone* (1938).

(2) **William** (1543–1623), English composer, born probably in Lincoln. His early life is obscure, but it is likely that he was one of the Children of the Chapel Royal, under Tallis, and at the age of twenty he became organist of Lincoln Cathedral, where he remained until 1572, when he was made joint-organist with Tallis of the Chapel Royal. Three years later, Queen Elizabeth granted Byrd and Tallis an exclusive licence for the printing and sale of music, and their joint work of that year, *Piae Cantiones*, was dedicated to her. Byrd was associated with

John Bull and Orlando Gibbons in *Parthenia* (1611), the first printed music for virginals. A firm Catholic, Byrd, who is often regarded as the greatest of the Tudor composers, was several times prosecuted as a recusant, but he wrote music of great power and beauty for both the Catholic and the Anglican services, as well as madrigals, songs, and music for strings. See studies by F. Howes (1928) and E. H. Fellowes (1948).

(3) **William** (1674–1744), American tobacco planter, colonial official and diarist, born in Virginia, the son of William Byrd (1652–1704), pioneer planter and early Virginian aristocrat. During two periods in London (1697–1705 and 1715–26) as a student of law and colonial agent, he showed himself an elegant socialite, a man of learning and many amours. In 1728 he took part in surveying the boundary line between Virginia and Carolina, in 1737 he founded the town of Richmond, and in 1743 he became president of the council of state, of which he had been a member since 1709. Indicative of his cultural and intellectual interests were a large library, a fine collection of paintings, and a fellowship of the Royal Society of Great Britain. His published works include *The Western Manuscripts* (1841), and see *The London Diary (1717–1721) and Other Writings* (ed. Wright and Tinling, 1958) and the study by R. C. Beatty (1932).

BYRGIUS, Justus, or **Jost Bürgi**, *bür'gi-oos* (1552–1633), Swiss inventor of celestial globes and compiler of logarithms, was born in the Swiss canton of St Gall.

BYRNE, Donn, pseud. of **Brian Oswald Donn-Byrne** (1889–1928), Irish-American novelist and short-story writer, born in Brooklyn and educated at Dublin, the Sorbonne, and at Leipzig. A cowpuncher in South America and garage hand in New York, he wrote *Messer Marco Polo* (1921), *Hangman's House* (1926), &c.

BYROM, John (1692–1763), English poet and stenographer, was born at Broughton, near Manchester, studied medicine at Montpellier, returned to London to teach his new system of shorthand, but in 1740 succeeded to the family estates. See his *Diary* (ed. 1854–57) and *Poems* (ed. 1894–1912).

BYRON, George Gordon, 6th Baron Byron of Rochdale (1788–1824), English poet, was born in London, son of the irresponsible and eccentric Captain John Byron (1756–91) and Catherine Gordon of Gight, Aberdeen, a Scottish heiress, and grandson of **Admiral John Byron** (1723–86), author of the classical account of the *Wager* disaster. The poet's first ten years were spent in his mother's lodgings in Aberdeen, her husband having squandered her fortune in France. The boy was lame from birth, and the shabby surroundings and the violent temper of his foolish, vulgar and deserted mother produced a repression in him which explain many of his later actions. In 1798 he succeeded to the title on the death of ' the wicked lord ' his great-uncle. He was educated at Aberdeen grammar school, then privately at Dulwich and at Harrow School, proceeding to Trinity College, Cambridge, in 1805, where he read much, swam and boxed, and led a dissipated life. An early collection of poems under the title of *Hours of Idleness* were reprinted with alterations in 1807 and were ' savagely cut up ' by the *Edinburgh Review* in 1808. Byron replied with his powerful Popian satire *English Bards and Scotch Reviewers* (1809), and set out on his grand tour, visiting Spain, Malta, Albania, Greece, and the Aegean, returning after two years with ' a great many stanzas in Spenser's measure relative to the countries he had visited ', which appeared under the title of *Childe Harold's Pilgrimage* in 1812 and were widely popular. This was followed by a series of oriental pieces such as the *Giaour* (1813), *Lara* (1814), and the *Siege of Corinth* (1816). During this time he dramatized himself as a man of mystery, a gloomy romantic figure, derived from the popular fiction of the day and not least from *Childe Harold*. He became the darling of London society, and of Lady Caroline Lamb, and gave to Europe the concept of the ' Byronic hero '. In 1815, he married an heiress, Anne Isabella Milbanke, who left him in 1816 after the birth of a daughter, Ada. He was also suspected of a more than brotherly love for his half-sister, Augusta Leigh, and was ostracized. The poet left for the Continent, travelled through Belgium and the Rhine country to Switzerland, where he met Shelley, and on to Venice and Rome, where he wrote the last canto of *Childe Harold* (1817). He spent two years in Venice and met the Countess Teresa Guiccioli, who became his mistress. Some of his best works belong to this period, including *Beppo* (1818), *A Vision of Judgment* (1822), and *Don Juan* (1819–24), written in a new metre (ottava rima) and an informal conversational manner which enabled him to express the whole of his complex personality, poems in which he ' stripped the tinsel off sentiment ' and spoke with the voice of a completely free mind,

rejoicing in the richness and variety of human experience and conscious of its absurdity, cruelty, boredom, and its glory. He gave active help to the Italian revolutionaries and founded with Leigh Hunt a short-lived journal, *The Liberal*. In 1823, he joined the Greek insurgents who had risen against the Turks, and died of marsh fever at Missolonghi. His body was brought back to England and buried at Hucknall Torkard in Nottingham. Byron was not, however, ' Childe Harold ' and his greatness lies not so much in that he created a world of fantasy but that he learnt to escape back to reality. He belongs more to the humorists and realists such as Voltaire and Swift than to his contemporaries, the romantic poets, to which fact W. H. Auden in his *Letter to Lord Byron* (1937) attests. His reputation declined after his death despite the championship of Matthew Arnold. On the Continent he had a far-reaching influence both as the creator of the ' Byronic hero ' and as the champion of political liberty, leaving his mark on such writers as Hugo, De Musset, Leopardi, Heine, Espronceda, Pushkin, and Lermontov. The best edition of his works is by E. H. Coleridge and R. E. Prothero (1899–1904). See Lives by T. Moore (1830), E. C. Mayne (1912), A. Maurois (1930), H. Nicolson (1924), P. C. Quennell (1935, 1941), D. Gray (1945), L. A. Marchand (1958), and D. L. Moore (1961). See also critical studies by Arnold (1888), Swinburne (1866, 1884), Henley (1890), Ker (1925), R. Escarpit (Paris 1958), and on the Augusta Leigh controversy, see Murray (1906) and Fox (1924).

BYWATER, Ingram (1840–1914), English humanist, born in London, was Greek professor at Oxford 1893–1908, and translated Aristotle's *Poetics*, &c. See Memoir by W. W. Jackson (1917).

C

CABALLERO, Fernán, pseud. of Cecilia Francesca de Arrom (1797–1877), daughter of Nikolaus Böhl von Faber (1770–1836), a German merchant in Spain, who wrote on the history of Spanish literature. Born at Morges in Switzerland, she spent most of her childhood in Germany, but returned to Spain in 1813. Three times widowed, she died at Seville. She introduced in Spain the picturesque local-colour novel. The first of her fifty romances was *La Gaviota* (1849); others are *Elia, Clemencia, La Familia de Alvareda*. She also collected Spanish folk tales.

CABANEL, Alexandre (1823–89), French painter, was born at Montpellier, and died in Paris. A strict classicist, he won great popularity as a portrait painter and as a teacher, many of his pupils becoming famous, among them Bernard and Constant.

CABANIS, Pierre Jean Georges, *ka-ba-nees* (1757–1808), French physician and philo-

sophical writer, born at Cosnac, Charente-Inférieure, attached himself to the popular side in the Revolution. He furnished Mirabeau with material for his speeches on public education; and Mirabeau died in his arms. During the Terror he lived in retirement, and was afterwards a teacher in the medical school at Paris, a member of the Council of Five Hundred, then of the senate. He died near Meulan. His chief work is his once-famous *Rapports du physique et du moral de l'homme* (1802).

CABELL, James Branch, *kab'-* (1879–1958), American novelist and critic, born at Richmond, Va., made his name by *Jurgen* (1919), the best known of a long sequence of works set in the imaginary mediaeval kingdom of Poictesme and written in an elaborate, sophisticated style made even more precious by the author's fondness for archaisms. See *Collected Works* (18 vols. 1927–30), including short stories and verse, and autobiographical essays, *Quiet, Please* (1952); also bibliography by F. J. Brewer (1958).

CABET, Étienne, *ka-bay* (1788–1856), French communist, was born at Dijon, and died at St Louis, having gone out to Texas in 1849 to found (unsuccessfully) an 'Icarian community', so named after his *Voyage en Icarie* (1840), a 'philosophical and social romance', describing a communistic Utopia.

CABEZÓN, Antonio de, *ka-bay-*THon (1510–1566), Spanish composer, blind from birth, noted for his keyboard pieces and vocal works.

CABLE, George Washington (1844–1925), American author, born in New Orleans, at nineteen volunteered as a Confederate soldier. After the war he earned a precarious living in New Orleans, before taking up a literary career in 1879. In 1884 he went to New England. His Creole sketches in *Scribner's* made his reputation. Among his books are *Old Creole Days* (1879), *The Grandissimes* (1880), *The Silent South* (1885), *Bylow Hill* (1902), *Kincaid's Battery* (1908), *Lovers of Louisiana* (1918). See Life by L. L. C. Biklé (1928).

CABOT, or Caboto, (1) **John, or Giovanni** (1425–*c*.1500), discoverer of the mainland of North America, was a Genoese pilot, who was naturalized at Venice in 1476, and about 1490 settled in Bristol. Under letters-patent from Henry VII he set sail from Bristol in 1497 with two ships, accompanied by his three sons, and on June 24 sighted Cape Breton Island and Nova Scotia.

(2) **Sebastian** (1474–1557), second son of (1), was born probably at Venice, and is commonly said to have sailed in 1499 with two ships in search of a Northwest Passage, following the American coast from 60° to 30° N. lat. According to Harrisse, however, this expedition was really commanded by the elder Cabot, for the whole of whose work Sebastian calmly took credit. In 1512 he entered the service of Ferdinand V of Spain as a cartographer, but returned to England in 1517, where he seems to have been offered by Henry VIII, through Wolsey, the command of an expedition which 'tooke none effect'. In 1519 Cabot returned to Spain, and, as pilot-major for Charles V, examined in 1526 the coast of Brazil and the Plate River. An attempt to colonize ending in failure, he was imprisoned, and banished for two years to Africa. In 1533 he obtained his former post in Spain; but in 1548, again in England, he was made inspector of the navy by Edward VI, to whom he explained the variation of the magnetic needle. He seems to have died in London. Of his famous map (1544) a copy exists in the Bibliothèque Nationale at Paris. See Winsor's *History of America* (1885), works by Nicholls (1869), Harrisse (1882–96), Weare (1897), Beazley (1898), Williamson (1929), and Bibliography by Winship (1900).

CABRAL, or Cabrera, Pedro Alvarez (*c*. 1467–*c*. 1520), the Portuguese discoverer, in the same year as Pinzon (q.v.), of Brazil, in 1500 sailed from Lisbon in command of a fleet of thirteen vessels bound for the East Indies. Falling into the South American current of the Atlantic, he was carried to the unknown coast of Brazil, which he claimed on behalf of the king of Portugal. He then made for India; but losing seven of his ships, he landed at Mozambique, of which he was the first to give clear information, and, sailing thence to Calicut, established the first commercial treaty between Portugal and India. He returned to Lisbon in 1501. See study by J. R. McClymont (1914) and account of voyages to Brazil and India (Hakluyt Soc. 1937).

CABRERA, Don Ramón, *ka-bray'ra* (1810–77), a Carlist leader in 1833–40 and 1848–49, was born at Tortosa, and died at Wentworth near Staines, having married a wealthy English lady. In 1839 Don Carlos created him Count of Morella.

CABRINI, St Francesca Xavier (1850–1917), American nun, born near Lodi, Italy, founded the Missionary Sisters of the Sacred Heart (1886), emigrated to the U.S.A. in 1887 and became renowned for her social and charitable work. Canonized in 1946, she became the first American saint. See Life by Borden (1951).

CACCINI, Giulio, *kat-chee'nee* (*c*. 1550–1618), Italian composer and singer, born at Rome, with Jacopo Peri paved the way for opera by setting to music the dramas *Dafne* and *Euridice*.

CADALSO VASQUEZ, José de, *vas'keth* (1741–82), Spanish writer, born at Cadiz. By profession an army officer, he wrote for diversion. He is best known for a prose satire—*Los eruditos a la violeta*—which ridicules pedantry. His work has lasted through the charm of the underlying personality rather than any degree of authentic poetry. He was killed at the Siege of Gibraltar.

CADAMOSTO, Aloys da, *ka-da-mos'to* (*c*. 1432–80), Venetian explorer, who was born and died in Venice, for Prince Henry the Navigator undertook, in 1455, a voyage to the Canaries and as far as the mouth of the Gambia. See account of his voyage (Hakluyt Soc. 1937).

CADBURY, famous English Quaker family of industrialists and social reformers, descended from **Richard Tapper Cadbury**, who settled in Birmingham in 1794. Important members include:

(1) **George** (1839–1922), son of (2), in partnership with his brother **Richard** (1835–1899) expanded his father's business, moved the factory out of town and established for the workers the model village of Bournville, a prototype for modern methods of housing and town planning. George also became proprietor of the *Daily News* in 1902. The firm amalgamated with J. S. Fry and Sons in 1919. See Life by A. G. Gardiner (1923).

(2) **John** (1801–89), son of Richard Tapper Cadbury, founded the cocoa and chocolate business of Cadburys.

(3) **Richard** (1835–99). See (1).

CADE, Jack (d. 1450), leader of the insurrection of 1450, was by birth an Irishman. After an unsettled early career he established himself in Kent as a physician, and married a squire's daughter. Assuming the name of Mortimer, and the title of Captain of Kent, he marched on London with upwards of

40,000 followers, and encamped at Blackheath. He entered London, where for two days he maintained strict order, though he forced the Lord Mayor to pass judgment on Lord Say, one of the king's detested favourites whose head Cade's men straightway cut off in Cheapside. On the third day some houses were plundered; and that night the citizens held London Bridge. A promise of pardon now sowed dissension among the insurgents; they dispersed, and a price was set upon Cade's head. He attempted to reach the coast, but was killed in a garden near Heathfield in Sussex. See J. Clayton's *True Story of Jack Cade* (1910).

CADELL, *kad'-*, (1) **Francis** (1822–79), Scottish explorer in Australia, born at Cockenzie, in 1850–59 explored the Murray River. He was later murdered by his crew.

(2) **Robert** (1788–1849), partner from 1811 in the Edinburgh publishing house of Constable & Co., after whose failure in 1825 he began business again, and realized a handsome fortune by his editions of Scott's works.

CADET DE GASSICOURT, Louis Claude, *ka-day dè gas-see-koor* (1731–99), French chemist, member of the Académie des Sciences, was in 1760 responsible for one of the worst smells in chemistry when he produced what was later called cacodyl.

CADILLAC, Antoine de la Mothe, Sieur, *ka-dee-yak* (1656–1730), French colonial administrator, born in Gascony, went to America with the French army in 1683, founded in 1701 the settlement which became the city of Detroit. In 1711 he was appointed governor of Louisiana but returned to France in 1716 and died in his native Gascony.

CADMAN, Samuel Parkes (1864–1936), American preacher, born in England, became pastor of the Central Congregational Church in Brooklyn (1901), was president (1924) of the Federal Council of Churches of Christ in America, and attained worldwide fame as a radio preacher.

CADOGAN, *ka-dug'ĕn,* (1) **Sir Alexander George Montagu** (1884–1968), English diplomat, son of (2), educated at Eton and Oxford, was minister plenipotentiary at Peking (1933–35) and U.K. representative on the Security Council of the United Nations (1946–50). From 1952 to 1957 he was chairman of the British Broadcasting Corporation.

(2) **George Henry, 5th Earl** (1840–1915), father of (1), English statesman, born at Durham, son of the 4th Earl, became undersecretary for war (1875) and for the colonies (1878) under Disraeli, but is best remembered as lord-lieutenant of Ireland (1895–1902), when, though criticized for weakness, he showed himself an able and unbiased administrator.

(3) **William, 1st Earl Cadogan,** *ka-dug'an* (1675–1726), English general, born in Dublin, after service as a ' volunteer ' at the Battle of the Boyne, was commissioned in the Inniskilling Dragoons. In 1703, with the rank of colonel, he was entrusted with his first confidential mission by the Duke of Marlborough; subsequently being appointed quartermaster-general of the forces.

Cadogan led the march into Bavaria which ended in the victory of Blenheim; and so perfect became the understanding between the Duke and his subordinate that the Irishman could interpret his leader's designs without a word being exchanged between them. At the head of his own Regiment of Horse at the Helexem-Neerwinden river crossing, at Oudenarde, and at the forcing of Villars' ' impregnable ' *Ne Plus Ultra* lines, Cadogan's services were outstanding. With Marlborough's political disgrace, Cadogen prudently resigned all his appointments; but on the accession of George I was restored to favour. In 1715 he succeeded the sluggish Argyll in Scotland, his success in quelling the Jacobite rebellion bringing him a peerage. On Marlborough's death Cadogan was appointed commander-in-chief and mastergeneral of the Ordnance. See Coxe's *Memoirs of the Duke of Marlborough* (1847), Marlborough's *Letters and Dispatches* (ed. Murray, 1845) and W. S. Churchill's Life of Marlborough (1948).

CADORNA, Count Luigi (1850–1928), Italian chief of staff (1914) and commander-in-chief against Austria (1915–17), the son of General Count Raffaele Cadorna (1815–97), who took Rome in 1870.

CADOUDAL, Georges (1771–1804), French insurgent, a miller's son from Auray in Lower Brittany, from 1793 to 1800 led the Royalist Chouans against the Republicans, and was guillotined for conspiring, with Pichegru, against Napoleon. See a work by his nephew (Paris 1887).

CADWALADR (d. 1172), a Welsh prince, who resisted Henry II although blinded by Irish pirates.

CAEDMON, *kad'mon* (d. *c.* 680), is the first English poet of known name. Bede tells us that, unlearned till mature in years (later accounts make him a cowherd), Caedmon became aware in a semimiraculous way that he was called to exercise the gift of religious poetry, was educated, became a monk at Whitby, and spent the rest of his life in composing poems on the Bible histories and on religious subjects. The ' Paraphrase ' ascribed to Caedmon is extant in a single MS. of the 10th century in the Bodleian, consisting of 229 folio pages, 212 of which contain the account of the creation and story of Genesis down to the offering of Isaac, the Exodus of Israel, and part of the book of Daniel; the remaining pages comprise a poem of Christ and Satan. It is certain that this poetry, at least in its present form, is due to various authors, and probably to different times. The extant MS. was presented by Archbishop Ussher to Franciscus Junius, by whom it was printed at Amsterdam in 1655. Whether any part of the extant paraphrase is the work of Bede's poet is extremely doubtful. The fine Northumbrian poem known as ' The Dream of the Rood ', part of which is inscribed in runic letters on the Ruthwell cross, the whole being found in a MS. at Vercelli, was formerly ascribed to Caedmon. See Howorth, *The Golden Days of the Early English Church* (1917), and Crawford (in *Anglia* 1925).

CAESALPINUS. See CESALPINO.

CAESAR, (1) Gaius Julius (100 or 102 B.C.–44 B.C.), was the son of a Roman praetor. His aunt was wife of Marius; and in 83 B.C. Julius himself married Cornelia, daughter of Cinna, and thus incurring the wrath of Cinna's enemy, Sulla, went to Asia (81) till Sulla's death (78). Elected pontifex in 74, he became the leader of the democratic party in overthrowing Sulla's constitution (70). After a year in Spain as quaestor, he married (67) Pompeia, a relative of Pompey. In 65, as curule aedile, he lavished vast sums of money on games and public buildings, and was subsequently pontifex maximus and praetor. There is slight ground for believing he was indirectly concerned in Catiline's conspiracy. In 61 he obtained the province of Hispania Ulterior, and on his return he was elected consul. With rare tact and sagacity he reconciled Pompey and Crassus, and formed with them the First Triumvirate (60 B.C.). Caesar gave Pompey his daughter Julia in marriage, while he married Calpurnia. Next he obtained the province of Gallia Cisalpina, Gallia Transalpina, and Illyricum; and passing into Gaul (58) for nine years conducted those splendid campaigns by which he completed the subjugation of the West to Rome. In his first campaign he vanquished the Helvetii and Ariovistus; in 57 the Belgic confederacy and the Nervii; and in 56 the Veneti and other peoples of Brittany and Normandy. He next drove two invading German tribes across the Rhine; and (55 B.C.) invaded Britain. In 54, on a second invasion of Britain, he crossed the Thames, and enforced at least the nominal submission of the southeast of the island. On his return to Gaul, he was himself defeated by the rebellious Eburones, but exacted a terrible vengeance on their leaders. Visiting northern Italy, he had hastily to return in midwinter to quell a general rebellion, headed by young Vercingetorix. The struggle was severe; at Gergovia, the capital of the Arverni, Caesar was defeated. But by the capture of Alesia (52) he crushed the united armies of the Gauls. In the meantime Crassus had fallen in Asia (53), and Pompey gone over to the aristocrats. Under his direction the senate called upon Caesar, now in Cisalpine Gaul, to resign his command and disband his army, and entrusted Pompey with large powers. His forces far outnumbered Caesar's legions, but they were scattered over the empire. Enthusiastically supported by his victorious troops, Caesar crossed the Rubicon (a small stream which separated his province from Italy proper), and moved swiftly southwards. Pompey fled to Brundusium, pursued by Caesar, and thence to Greece (49); and in three months Caesar was master of all Italy. After subduing Pompey's legates in Spain, he was appointed dictator. Pompey had gathered in Egypt, Greece, and the East a powerful army, while his fleet swept the sea. Caesar, crossing the Adriatic, was driven back with heavy loss from Dyrrhachium. But in a second battle at Pharsalia, August 9, 48 B.C., the senatorial army was utterly routed, and Pompey himself fled to Egypt, where he was murdered. Caesar, again appointed dictator for a year, and consul for five years, instead of returning to Rome, went to Egypt, where out of love for Cleopatra (who subsequently bore him a son) he engaged in the successful 'Alexandrine War' (47). He overthrew a son of Mithridates in Pontus, and, after a short stay in Rome, routed the Pompeian generals, Scipio and Cato, at Thapsus (April 6, 46 B.C.) in Africa. After his victories in Gaul, Egypt, Pontus, and Africa had been celebrated by four great triumphs, he had still, in spite of wise and noble generosity, to quell an insurrection in Spain by Pompey's sons. He now received the title of 'Father of his Country', and also of *imperator*, was made dictator for life, and consul for ten years; his person was declared sacred, and even divine; his statue was placed in the temples; his portrait was struck on coins; and the month Quintilis was called Julius in his honour. He proposed to make a digest of the whole Roman law, to found libraries, to drain the Pontine Marshes, to enlarge the harbour of Ostia, to dig a canal through the Isthmus of Corinth, and to quell the inroads of the barbarians on the eastern frontiers; but in the midst of these vast designs he was cut off by assassination on the Ides (15th) of March, 44 B.C. The alleged motive of the sixty conspirators—mostly aristocrats, headed by Brutus and Cassius—was that Caesar was aiming at a hereditary monarchy. Caesar was of a noble presence, tall, thin-featured, bald, and close-shaven. As general and statesman he takes a foremost place in the annals of the world; and, excepting Cicero, he was the greatest orator of his time. As a historian, he has never been surpassed in simplicity, directness, and dignity. He was, in addition, a mathematician, philologist, jurist, and architect. The main outcome of his life work was the transformation of the Roman republic into a government under a single ruler. Of Caesar's works the Commentaries on the Gallic and Civil wars alone have been preserved. See the Roman histories of Merivale, Arnold, Mommsen, Ihne, and Ferrero (trans. 1907); and works on Caesar by Napoleon III (1865–66), Froude (1879), Stoffel (Paris 1888–91), Fowler (1892), Dodge (1893), Holmes (1931), Buchan (1932), and Adcock (1956).

(2) **Sir Julius** (1558–1636), English judge, was born at Tottenham, the son of Cesare Adelmare, physician to Queen Mary. Judge of the Admiralty Court in 1584, chancellor of the Exchequer in 1606, master of the rolls in 1614, he sat in six parliaments, and was knighted in 1603.

CAGLIARI, Paolo, *kal'ya-ree.* See VERONESE.

CAGLIOSTRO, Count Alessandro di, *kal-yos'tro* (1743–95), Italian charlatan, born at Palermo, of poor parentage, his true name Giuseppe Balsamo. When thirteen years old he ran away from school, and was afterwards sent to the monastery of Caltagirone, where, a novice among apothecary monks, he picked up his scanty knowledge of chemistry and medicine. He soon made the monastery too hot for him, and in 1769 he set out to seek his fortune; in company with the Greek sage Althotas, he is vaguely represented as travelling in parts of Greece, Egypt, and Asia.

At Rome he married a very pretty woman, Lorenza Feliciani, who became a skilful accomplice in his schemes; and in 1771 the pair set out on their wanderings, visiting Germany, London, Paris, Spain, Warsaw, and other European centres. Successful alike as physician, philosopher, alchemist, and necromancer, he carried on a lively business in his 'elixir of immortal youth', founded lodges of 'Egyptian freemasons' and at Paris in 1785 played a part in the affair of the Diamond Necklace, which lodged him for a while in the Bastille. In May 1789 he revisited Rome; on December 20, the Inquisition detected him founding 'some feeble ghost of an Egyptian lodge'. He was imprisoned, and condemned to death for freemasonry. His sentence was commuted to life imprisonment in the fortress of San Leone, near Urbino, where he died. Such is the usual account, made familiar by Carlyle's *Miscellanies*; but his early history is somewhat obscure. See books by Trowbridge (1910), Photiadès (1932). His *Mémoires* (1785) are *not* authentic.

CAGNIARD DE LA TOUR, Charles, *ka-nyahr dè la toor* (1777–1859), French physicist, born in Paris, invented a siren for measuring the frequency of sounds.

CAGNOLA, Luigi, Marchese, *ka-nyō'la* (1762–1833), Italian architect, a follower of Palladio (q.v.), born at Milan, whose masterwork was the triumphal *Arco della Pace*, of white marble, in Milan.

CAHOURS, Auguste, *ka-oor* (1813–91), French scientist, a professor of Chemistry at Paris, discovered amyl alcohol, allyl alcohol, anisol and tin tetraethyl.

CAILLAUX, Joseph, *kī-yō* (1863–1944), born at Le Mans, became French finance minister in 1899, 1906, 1911, 1913, and 1925, premier in 1911. Arrested in 1918, he was convicted (1920) of corresponding with Germany during the war. Reprieved in 1924, he took part in war debt negotiations with the U.S.A. In 1914 his second wife shot M. Calmette, editor of *Figaro*, but was acquitted. See *Mémoires* (3 vols. 1942–48), and T. Wolff, *Das Vorspiel* (1919).

CAILLETET, Louis Paul, *kah-y'tay* (1832–1913), French ironmaster of Châtillon-sur-Seine, member of the Academy of Sciences, while engaged in research on the liquefaction of gases in 1877 liquefied for the first time hydrogen, nitrogen, oxygen, and air by compression, cooling, and sudden expansion. This was also done by Pictet (q.v.) at about the same time.

CAILLIAUD, Frédéric, *kah-yō* (1787–1869), French traveller in Egypt, the White Nile region, &c., was born and died at Nantes, where in 1827 he became keeper of the Natural History Museum.

CAILLIÉ, René, *kah-yay* (1799–1838), French explorer, born at Mauze in Poitou, in 1827–28 by his adventurous journey from Sierra Leone to Timbuktu and Tangier gained a prize of 10,000 francs offered by the geographical society of Paris.

CAÏN, Auguste Nicolas, *ka-ĩ* (1822–94), French animal sculptor, was born and died in Paris. His son, George (1853–1919), painted *Mort des derniers Montagnards*, &c.

CAINE, Sir (Thomas Henry) Hall (1853–1931), British novelist, born (of Manx blood on his father's side) at Runcorn, was trained as an architect, and wrote *Recollections of Rossetti* (1882), *My Story* (1908), *The Deemster* (1887), *The Eternal City* (1901), *The Prodigal Son* (1904), and other popular novels; and a *Life of Christ* (1938). See S. Norris, *Two Men of Manxland* (1948).

CAIRD, (1) Edward (1835–1908), Scottish Idealist philosopher, born at Greenock, Renfrewshire, became professor of Moral Philosophy at Glasgow in 1886 and master of Balliol College, Oxford (1893–1907). He is best known for his monumental commentary, *The Critical Philosophy of Immanuel Kant* (1889). Other works include *The Evolution of Religion* (1893). See study by H. Jones and J. H. Muirhead (1922).

(2) **John** (1820–98), brother of (1), was a great Scottish preacher. His *Religion in Common Life*, preached before the Queen at Crathie in 1855, was said by Dean Stanley to be the greatest single sermon of the century. D.D. in 1860, he was appointed professor of Divinity in 1862, and was principal of Glasgow University 1873–98. He published *Sermons* (1858), *An Introduction to the Philosophy of Religion* (1880), and *Spinoza* (1888).

CAIRNES, John Elliot (1823–75), Irish economist, was born at Castle Bellingham, County Louth. He was placed in his father's brewery; but, much against his father's will, went to Trinity College, Dublin, where he graduated in 1848. In 1856 he was appointed professor of Political Economy at Dublin, in 1859 at Queen's College, Galway, and in 1866 at University College London. He resigned his chair in 1872 for health reasons, and died at Blackheath. His ten works include *Character and Logical Method of Political Economy* (1857), *The Slave Power* (1862), *Essays on Political Economy* (1873), and *Some Leading Principles of Political Economy* (1874). Cairnes may be regarded as a disciple of Mill, though differing from him on many points.

CAIRNS, (1) Hugh MacCalmont Cairns, Earl (1819–85), born in County Down, N. Ireland, educated at Belfast and Trinity College, Dublin, was called to the bar at the Middle Temple in 1844, entered parliament for Belfast in 1852, and quickly made his mark in the House as a debater. He became Q.C. in 1856, in 1858 solicitor-general, in 1866 attorney-general under Lord Derby and a judge of appeal, and in 1867 Baron Cairns. Under Disraeli he was made lord chancellor in 1868, and again in 1874, and was created Viscount Garmoyle and Earl Cairns in 1878. For some years he led the Conservatives in the Upper House. He prepared measures for simplifying the transfer of land, and projected that fusion of law and equity which was carried out by Lord Selborne.

(2) **John** (1818–92), Scottish theologian, born at Ayton Law, Berwickshire, was from 1867 professor of Theology in the United Presbyterian seminary. He became principal in 1879. He published a Memoir of Dr John Brown (1860), and *Unbelief in the 18th Century* (1881). See Life by MacEwen (1895).

CAIROLI, Benedetto, *kī-rō'lee* (1825–89), Italian statesman, born in Pavia. In youth a revolutionary and a Garibaldian, he was in 1878 and 1879 Radical prime minister of Italy.

CAIUS, John, *keez* (1510–73), English physician and scholar, was born at Norwich, Caius being a Latinized form of Kayes or Keys. In 1529 he entered Gonville Hall, Cambridge, where in 1533, he was elected a fellow, having just before been appointed principal of Fiswick's Hostel. In 1539 he went abroad, in 1541 was created an M.D. of Padua; returning to England in 1544, he lectured on anatomy in London, then practised at Shrewsbury and Norwich. In 1547 he was admitted a fellow of the College of Physicians, of which he was subsequently nine times elected president. He also became physician to Edward VI, Queen Mary, and Queen Elizabeth. Gonville Hall, founded in 1348 by Edmund Gonville, rector of Thelnetham, Suffolk (d. 1351), was by Caius in 1557 elevated into a college, which took the name of Gonville and Caius College, and of which in 1559 he became master. A loyal Catholic, he had great trouble with his Protestant fellows, who burned his Mass vestments, and whom in return he put in the stocks. He was author of *A Boke or Counseill against the Sweatyng Sicknesse* (1552), and of other works (collected in 1912) on subjects critical, antiquarian and scientific.

CAJANDER, Aino Kaarlo, *ka-yan'dĕr* (1879–1943), Finnish politician and forestry expert, became professor of Forestry at Helsinki, and was three times prime minister of Finland (1922, 1924, 1937–40).

CAJETAN, Ital. Gaetano, Cardinal, properly **Thomas de Vio** (1469–1534), born at Gaeta, in 1508 became general of the Dominicans, in 1517 cardinal, in 1519 bishop of Gaeta, and in 1523 legate to Hungary. In 1518 he sought to induce Luther to recant at Augsburg. He died at Rome.

CALAME, Alexandre (1810–64), Swiss painter of Alpine scenery, born at Vevey, died at Mentone. See monograph by Rambert (Paris 1884).

CALAMITY JANE, nickname of **Martha Jane Burke** (*c.* 1852–1903), American frontierswoman, of eccentric character, usually dressed in man's clothes, was celebrated for her bravery and her skill in riding and shooting, particularly during the gold rush days in the Black Hills of Dakota. She is said to have threatened ' calamity ' for any man who tried to court her. See study by D. Aikman (N.Y. 1927).

CALAMY, family of English Puritan divines:
(1) **Benjamin** (1642–86), son of (2), prebendary of St Paul's, published *A Discourse about a Scrupulous Conscience*, dedicated to Judge Jeffreys.
(2) **Edmund** (1600–66), father of (1), studied at Pembroke Hall, Cambridge (1616–19); and afterwards became domestic chaplain to Felton, Bishop of Ely. In 1626 he was appointed lecturer at Bury St Edmunds, but resigned when the order to read the *Book of Sports* was enforced (1636); in 1639 he was chosen minister of St Mary Aldermanbury, London. He had a principal share in

Smectymnuus (1641), a reply to Bishop Hall's *Divine Right of Episcopacy.* He disapproved of the execution of Charles, and of Cromwell's protectorate, and was one of the deputation to Charles II in Holland. His services were recognized by a royal chaplaincy and the offer of the bishopric of Coventry and Lichfield, which he refused through conscientious scruples (his wife's, according to Tillotson). Ejected for nonconformity in 1662, he continued to attend service in his old church, till, heart-broken by the Great Fire, he died. He published nineteen sermons, &c.
(3) **Edmund** (1671–1732), grandson of (2), studied three years at Utrecht, and, declining Carstares' offer of a Scottish professorship, from 1694 was a Nonconformist minister in London. He visited Scotland in 1709, when Edinburgh, Glasgow, and Aberdeen all conferred degrees on him. His forty-one works include *Account of the Ejected Ministers* (1702) and an interesting Autobiography, first published in 1829.

CALAS, Jean, *ka-lahs* (1698–1762), French Protestant, a tradesman of Toulouse, who was broken on the wheel on the monstrous charge of having murdered his eldest son (who had hanged himself) ' because he had contemplated conversion to Catholicism '. A revision of the trial followed, and the parliament at Paris in 1765 declared Calas and all his family innocent. Louis XV gave them 30,000 livres, but neither the parliament of Toulouse nor the fanatical monks were ever brought to account. See Voltaire's *Sur la tolérance*; a French monograph by Coquerel (2nd ed. 1870), an English one by F. H. Maugham (1928); and essays by Mark Pattison (1889) and Kegan Paul (1891).

CALDARA, kal-dah'ra, (1) **Antonio** (1670–1736), Italian composer, was born in Venice, and died in Vienna, where he was vice-kapellmeister. Amongst his choral works are some outstanding examples of the polyphonic style. He also wrote many operas and oratorios, and some trio-sonatas in the style of Corelli.
(2) **Polidoro.** See CARAVAGGIO (2).

CALDECOTT, Randolph (1846–86), English artist and book-illustrator, was a bank-clerk at Whitchurch and Manchester, then moved to London to follow a successful artistic career. Until his health gave way he contributed to *Punch* and the *Graphic*, and illustrated many books for children. The Caldecott medal has been awarded annually since 1938 to the best American artist illustrator of children's books. See *Memoir* by Blackburn (1886).

CALDERON, Philip Hermogenes (1833–98), British painter, son of a Spanish Protestant refugee, painted historical and genre pictures, was elected R.A. in 1867 and in 1887 became keeper of the Royal Academy.

CALDERÓN DE LA BARCA, Pedro (1600–1681), one of Spain's greatest dramatists, was born of good family at Madrid. After schooling under the Jesuits, he studied law and philosophy at Salamanca (1613–19), and during ten years' service in the Milanese and in Flanders saw much of men and manners that he afterwards utilized. On Lope's death in 1635, he was summoned by Philip IV to Madrid, and appointed a sort of master of the revels. In 1640 the rebellion in Catalonia roused him once more to take the field; but in 1651 he entered the priesthood, and in 1653 withdrew to Toledo. Ten years went by, and he was recalled to court and to the resumption of his dramatic labours, receiving, with other preferments, the post of chaplain of honour to Philip; and he continued to write for the court, the church, and the public theatres till his death. Castilian and Catholic to the backbone, Calderón wrote with perfect fidelity to the Spanish thought and manners of his age. Schlegel pronounced him ' the fourth in a mighty quaternion', with Homer, Dante, and Shakespeare '. His *autos sacramentales*, outdoor plays for the festival of Corpus Christi, number 72, and have been divided into seven classes—biblical, classical, ethical, ' cloak and sword plays ', dramas of passion, and so forth; the finest of them is *El divino Orfeo*. Of his regular dramas 118 are extant. About a score of them are known to English readers through the following translators: Shelley (a fine fragment from *The Magician*); Denis McCarthy (10 plays, 1853–73); Edward FitzGerald (8 plays, 1853 *et seq.*); Archbishop Trench (2 plays, with essay on ' Life and Genius ', 1856; 2nd ed. 1880). See Fitzmaurice-Kelly, *Spanish Literature* (1898), Menéndez y Pelayo, *Calderón* (Madrid 1881), A. A. Parker, *The Allegorical Drama of Calderón* (1943).

CALDERWOOD, (1) **David** (1575–1650), Scottish ecclesiastical historian, in 1617 joined in a protest against granting the power of framing new church laws to an ecclesiastical council appointed by the king, and was imprisoned and banished. In Holland he published (1625) the *Altare Damascenum* against Episcopacy. After King James's death (1625), he returned to Scotland, and spent years in collecting materials for his history of the Church of Scotland.

(2) **Henry** (1830–97), Scottish philosopher, from 1856 to 1868 was minister of Greyfriars, Glasgow, and then became professor of Moral Philosophy at Edinburgh. He was the author of *The Philosophy of the Infinite* (1854), *Vocabulary of Philosophy* (1894), *David Hume* (1898), &c. See Life by his son and by the Rev. D. Woodside (1898).

CALDWELL, (1) **Anne.** See MARSH (1).

(2) **Erskine** (1903–), American author, born at White Oak, Ga., worked amongst the ' poor whites ' in the southern states, where he absorbed the background for his best-known work *Tobacco Road* (1932), of which the dramatized version by Jack Kirkland (1933) had a record run in New York. Other books include *God's Little Acre* (1933), *Sure Hand of God* (1947), *A Lamp for Nightfall* (1952), and *Love and Money* (1954).

CALEPINO, Ambrogio, *kal-e-pee'nō* (1435–1511), an Augustinian monk, born at Bergamo, compiled a polyglot dictionary.

CALETTI-BRUNI. See CAVALLI.

CALHOUN, John Caldwell, *kal-hoon'* (1782–1850), American statesman, of Irish Presbyterian descent, was born in Abbeville County, South Carolina, studied at Yale, and became a successful lawyer. In Congress he supported the measures which led to the war of 1812–15 with Great Britain, and promoted the protective tariff. In 1817 he joined Monroe's cabinet as secretary of war, and did good work in reorganizing the war department. He was vice-president under John Q. Adams (1825–29), and then under Jackson. In 1829 he declared that a state can nullify unconstitutional laws; and his *Address to the People of South Carolina* (1831) set forth his theory of state rights. On the passing by South Carolina in 1832 of the nullification ordinance he resigned the vice presidency, and entered the Senate, becoming a leader of the states-rights movement, and a champion of the interests of the slave-holding states. In 1844, as secretary of state, he signed a treaty annexing Texas; but once more in the senate, he strenuously opposed the war of 1846–47 with Mexico. He, Henry Clay, and Daniel Webster were ' the great triumvirate ' of American political orators. See the Life by M. L. Coit (1950).

CALIGULA, Gaius Caesar Augustus Germanicus, *-lig'-* (A.D. 12–41), Roman emperor, the youngest son of Germanicus and Agrippina, was born at Antium. Educated in the camp, he was nicknamed Caligula from his soldier's boots (*caligae*). He ingratiated himself with Tiberius, and, on his death in A.D. 37, was found to have been appointed co-heir along with the emperor's grandson Gemellus; the senate, however, conferred imperial power on Caligula alone. At first he seemed lavishly generous; but when illness, the result of his vicious life, had weakened his faculties, the lower qualities of his nature obtained the complete mastery. Besides squandering in one year the enormous wealth left by Tiberius (£5,625,000), he banished or murdered his relatives, excepting his uncle Claudius and sister Drusilla (with whom he is said to have carried on incestuous intercourse); filled Rome with executions and confiscations; amused himself while dining by having victims tortured and slain in his presence; and uttered the hideous wish that all the Roman people had but one neck, that he might strike it off at a blow! His favourite horse he made a member of the college of priests and consul. Finally, he had declared himself a god, when he was assassinated. See study by Balsdon (1935).

CALIXTUS, the name of three popes:

Calixtus or **Callistus I** (from A.D. 218 to 222), according to Hippolytus, his bitter opponent, was originally a slave, and had twice undergone severe punishment for his crimes before he became a priest under Zephyrinus, whom he succeeded.

Calixtus II (1119–24), formerly **Guido,** Archbishop of Vienne, in 1121 overcame the antipope Burdinus (Gregory VIII), who was supported by the emperor Henry V, and in 1122 concluded with the emperor the concordat of Worms, which settled the Investiture Controversy.

Calixtus III (1455–58), formerly **Alfonso de Borja** (Ital. *Borgia*), born at Jativa in Spain, was successively counsellor to Alfonso V of Aragon, Bishop of Valencia, and cardinal. He laboured in vain to organize a crusade against the Turks, and raised to the cardinalate his nephew, Rodrigo Borgia (afterwards Alexander VI). The name Calixtus III was also assumed by an antipope whom Frederick Barbarossa set up in 1168 against Alexander III.

CALIXTUS, Georg (properly **Callisen**) (1586–1656), Lutheran theologian, was born at Medelbye in Schleswig and from 1603 to 1609 studied at Helmstedt, where, after travelling for four years he was professor of Theology. Although acknowledged by learned Romanists to be one of their ablest opponents, he was, for some statements in his works which seemed favourable to Catholic dogmas, and others which approached too near to the Calvinistic standpoint, declared guilty of abominable heresy. Having at the conference of Thorn in 1645 been on more intimate terms with the Calvinistic than the Lutheran theologians, he was accused of apostasy. His friends in Brunswick, however, stood firmly by him, and he retained his chair till his death.

CALLAGHAN, James (1912–), British politician, educated at Portsmouth Northern Secondary School, joined the staff of the Inland Revenue Department in 1929. In 1945 he was elected Labour M.P. for South Cardiff and from 1950 represented South-east Cardiff. One of the chief contenders for the party leadership after the death of Gaitskell, in 1964 he was appointed Chancellor of the Exchequer in Wilson's government. In this capacity he introduced some of the most controversial taxation measures in British fiscal history, including the corporation and selective employment taxes. In 1967 he changed posts with Roy Jenkins to become Home Secretary.

CALLAS, Maria Meneghini, *kal'-* (1923–), American operatic soprano, born in New York of Greek parents. She studied at Athens Conservatory, and in 1947 appeared at Verona in *La Gioconda,* winning immediate recognition. She has sung with great authority in all the most exacting soprano rôles, excelling in the intricate *bel canto* style of pre-Verdian Italian opera.

CALLCOTT, (1) Sir Augustus Wall (1779–1844), English landscape painter, husband of (3), brother of (2), born in Kensington. R.A. (1810), he was knighted in 1837.

(2) **John Wall** (1766–1821), English composer, brother of (1), born in Kensington, in 1866 published a *Musical Grammar.* He was especially celebrated for his glees, the best of which were published (1824), with a memoir by his son-in-law, W. Horsley.

(3) **Lady Maria** (1785–1842), wife of (1), wrote *Little Arthur's History of England.* See Life by R. B. Gotch (1937).

CALLENDAR, Hugh Longbourne (1863–1930), English physicist, born at Hatherop, Glos., educated at Cambridge, professor of Physics, McGill University, Montreal (1893), University College London (1898), Imperial College of Science (1902), devised a constant-pressure air thermometer which could measure up to 450° C., and also an accurate platinum resistance thermometer.

CALLES, Plutarco Elías, *kah'yayz* (1877–1945), Mexican general and politician. An ex-schoolmaster, he took part in the revolt against Porfirio Diaz (1910), became governor of Sonora (1917) and from 1924 to 1928 was president of Mexico. Known for his fanatical anticlericalism and for his efforts to restrict foreign influence in the oil industry, he was defeated by Cardénas and in 1936 was exiled to the U.S.A.

CALLIMACHUS, *-lim'-,* an Alexandrian poet, grammarian, and critic of the 3rd century B.C., was born at Cyrene in Libya, and became head of the Alexandrian Library. The mere fragments that represent most of his eight hundred works have been edited by A. W. Mair (Loeb Library 1921); his six extant Hymns and sixty-four Epigrams by Wilamowitz-Möllendorff (1897).

CALLISTRATUS, an Athenian orator whose eloquence is said to have fired the imagination of the youthful Demosthenes. For his Spartan sympathies he was condemned to death in 361 B.C., and on his return from exile in Macedonia was executed. Another Callistratus was a grammarian and critic.

CALLISTUS. See CALIXTUS I.

CALLOT, Jacques, *kal-lō* (c. 1594–1635), French engraver, was born at Nancy and early devoted himself to art in opposition to his father's wishes. A boy of twelve, he attached himself to a band of gypsies, and wandered with them to Florence; thence a gentleman sent him on to Rome, where, however, some Nancy merchants recognized him, and induced him to return home. He twice revisited Italy, and in 1612 was studying in Rome; afterwards he repaired to Florence, where, by numerous spirited etchings, he gained great fame. In 1621 he returned to Nancy, there to be favourably received by the Duke of Lorraine. For Louis XIII, who invited him to Paris, he executed etchings of the siege of Rochelle, but refused to commemorate the capture of his native town. His 1600 realistic engravings cast vivid light on the manners of the 17th century. His *Miseries of War* and his *Gypsies* are especially celebrated. See works on him by Bouchot (Paris 1890), Plan (Brussels 1911), Levertin (Brussels 1935) and Bechtel (1956).

CALMET, Augustin, *kal-may* (1672–1757), French Benedictine, entered the order in 1689, and was successively appointed teacher of philosophy in the Abbey Moyen-Moutier (1698), subprior at Münster in Alsace (1704), prior at Lay (1715), abbot of St Leopold (1718), and abbot of Senones in Lorraine (1728). He wrote biblical works and a *History of Lorraine* (4 vols. 1728). See Lives by Digot (Nancy 1861) and Guillaume (Nancy 1875).

CALMETTE, (Léon Charles) Albert (1863–1933), French bacteriologist, born at Nice, was a pupil of Pasteur and founder of the Pasteur Institute at Saigon, where he discovered an antisnakebite serum. He became head of the Pasteur Institute at Lille in 1895, but is best known for the vaccine BCG (Bacillus Calmette-Guérin), for inoculation against tuberculosis, which he jointly discovered with Dr Guérin.

CALOMARDE, Don Francisco Tadeo, Duke (1775–1842), a reactionary Spanish statesman, who died in exile at Toulouse.

CALONNE, Charles Alexandre de, *ka-lon*

(1734–1802), French statesman, born at Douai, studied law, and in 1783 was made controller-general of finance. As such he gained favour among the courtiers, who had complained of Turgot and Necker, by showering on them sums obtained by borrowing and increased taxation. In 1786, when the people could bear this no longer, Calonne advised the king to convoke the Assembly of the Notables, and distribute the burden of taxation more equally. In opening the Assembly (1787), he described the general prosperity of France, but confessed that the annual deficit of the treasury had risen to 115 million francs, and that during 1776–86 the government had borrowed 1250 millions! The Notables demanded a statement of accounts; and failing to satisfy them, he was banished to Lorraine. After this, he resided chiefly in England, until in 1802 Bonaparte permitted him to return. He died very poor.

CALOVIUS, or Kalau, Abraham (1612–86), Lutheran controversialist, was born at Mohrungen in East Prussia, and became successively professor at Königsberg (1637), preacher at Danzig (1643), and professor at Wittenberg (1650). He was six times married.

CALPRENÈDE, Gautier des Costes de la (1610–63), French author, officer of the guards and royal chamberlain of France, wrote tragedies, tragi-comedies, and the clever but tedious ' heroic romances ', *Cléopâtre, Cassandre*, &c.

CALPURNIUS SICULUS, Titus, a Latin bucolic poet of the middle of the 1st century A.D. His Eclogues are in Postgate's *Corpus* (1904), and were translated by E. J. L. Scott (1891).

CALVAERT, Denis, or Dionisio Fiammingo (c. 1540–1619), Flemish painter, was born at Antwerp, and settled at Bologna. There he opened a school, among whose students were Guido Reni, Domenichino, and Albani, who afterwards, however, were pupils of the Caracci.

CALVÉ, Emma (1866–1942), a French operatic singer, famous as ' Carmen ', made her début at Brussels in 1882, and appeared in London in 1892.

CALVERLEY, Charles Stuart (1831–84), English parodist, born in Worcestershire, educated at Harrow, Oxford and Cambridge. In 1858 he was elected a fellow, and in 1865 called to the bar, and settled in London. A fall on the ice in the winter of 1866–67 put an end to a brilliant career; and his last years were spent as an invalid. One of the most gifted men of his time, Calverley will be remembered by his two little volumes, *Verses and Translations* (1862) and *Fly Leaves* (1872), whose gem, ' Butter and Eggs ', appeared first in *Chambers's Journal* for Nov. 1869. His rendering of Theocritus (1869) shows at once his scholarship and his facile mastery of English verse. See Memoir by Sendall, prefixed to his *Literary Remains* (1885).

CALVERT, (1) Edward (1799–1883), English pastoral artist and friend of Blake, born at Appledore, Devon. See a memoir by his son (1893), and Binyon's *The Followers of William Blake* (1925).

(2) **Frederick Crace** (1819–73), English chemist, was born in London, resided in France (1836–46), and then settled as a consulting chemist in Manchester. He was largely instrumental in introducing carbolic acid as a disinfectant.

(3) **George.** See BALTIMORE.

(4) **George Henry** (1803–89), American author, great-grandson of Lord Baltimore, was born in Maryland, studied at Harvard and Göttingen, and from 1843 lived at Newport, Rhode Island. His works embrace poems, tragedies, comedies, essays, translations from the German, and studies of Goethe (1872), Wordsworth (1878), Shakespeare (1879), and Coleridge, Shelley, and Goethe (1880).

CALVET, Jean, *kal-vay* (1874–1965), French literary historian, especially from the Catholic standpoint, was professor at Toulouse and Paris.

CALVIN, (1) John (1509–64), born at Noyon, in Picardy, where his father, Gérard Caulvin or Cauvin, was procureur-fiscal and secretary of the diocese. He studied Latin at Paris (from 1523) under Corderius; subsequently as a law student in Orléans he received from the Scriptures his first impulse to theological studies. From Orléans he went to Bourges, where he learned Greek, and began to preach the reformed doctrines. After a short stay (1533) at Paris, now a centre of the ' new learning ' and of religious excitement, he visited Noyon. We next find him at Saintonge; at Nerac, the residence of the queen of Navarre; at Angoulême, with his friend Louis du Tillet; then at Paris again. Persecution raged so hotly that Calvin was no longer safe in France; at Basel he issued in 1536 his *Christianae Religionis Institutio*, with the famous preface addressed to Francis I. After a short visit to Italy, to Renée, Duchess of Ferrara, he revisited his native town, sold his paternal estate, and set out for Strasbourg, by way of Geneva, where Farel (q.v.) persuaded him to remain and assist in the work of reformation. The citizens had asserted their independence against the Duke of Savoy; and magistrates and people eagerly joined with the reformers. A Protestant Confession of Faith was proclaimed, and moral severity took the place of licence. The strain, however, was too sudden and extreme. A spirit of rebellion broke forth under the ' Libertines ', and Calvin and Farel were expelled from the city (1538). Calvin, withdrawing to Strasbourg, devoted himself to critical labours on the New Testament; and here in 1539 he married the widow of a converted Anabaptist. But in 1541 the Genevans, wearying of the Libertine licence, invited Calvin to return; and after some delay, he acceded to their request. By his College of Pastors and Doctors, and his Consistorial Court of Discipline, he founded a theocracy, which was virtually to direct all the affairs of the city, and to control the social and individual life of the citizens. His struggle with the Libertines lasted fourteen years, when the reformer's authority was confirmed into an absolute supremacy (1555). During that long struggle occurred also Calvin's controversies with Castellio (q.v.), Bolsec (q.v.), and Servetus (q.v.). The last, whose speculations on the Trinity were abhorrent to Calvin, was apprehended at Vienne by the Catholic authorities (to whom Calvin forwarded incriminating documents), and was sentenced to be burned, but effected his escape, and at Geneva, on his way to Italy, was subjected to a new trial, condemned, and burnt to death (1553). Calvin's intolerance was approved by the most conspicuous Reformers, including the gentle Melanchthon. Through Beza he made his influence felt in the great struggle in France between the Guises and the Protestants. None can dispute Calvin's intellectual greatness, or the powerful services which he rendered to the cause of Protestantism. Stern in spirit and unyielding in will, he was never selfish or petty in his motives. He rendered a double service to Protestantism: he systematized its doctrine, and he organized its ecclesiastical discipline. His commentaries embrace the greater part of the Old Testament and the whole of the New except the Revelation. The first collected edition of Calvin's works is that of Geneva (12 vols. fol. 1617). A complete critical edition by Baum, Cunitz, Reuss, &c., appeared at Brunswick (59 vols. 1863–1900). By the Calvin Translation Society in Edinburgh, his works were collected and translated into English (52 vols. 1844–1856). His letters were published by Bonnet (2 vols. Paris 1854); in an English translation by Constable and Gilchrist (1855 et seq.). The libraries of Geneva and Zürich contain about 3000 MSS. of sermons and other short writings by Calvin. Beza's life of him appeared in French in 1564, and in Latin in 1576. See studies by E. Doumergue (7 vols. 1899–1927) and Werdel (1963), J. McKinnon, *Calvin and the Reformation* (1936), Hunter, *Teaching of Calvin* (1950), McNeill, *History and Character of Calvinism* (1954), and Niesel, *Theology of Calvin* (1956).

(2) **Melvin** (1911–), American chemist, professor of Chemistry at California University from 1947, known for his researches on photosynthesis. He won the Nobel prize in 1961.

CAM, Port. **Cão, Diogo,** 15th-century Portuguese explorer, in 1482 discovered the mouth of the Congo, near whose bank an inscribed stone erected by him as a memorial was found in 1887.

CAMARGO, Maria Anna de (1710–70), French dancer, born at Brussels, won European fame for her performances at the Opera (1730–50). She was responsible for the shortening of the traditional ballet skirt and for the introduction of new steps. There are paintings of her by Lancret and Quentin de la Tour.

CAMBACÉRÈS, Jean Jacques Régis de, *kã-ba-say-res* (1753–1824), Duke of Parma and archchancellor of the Empire from 1804, was born at Montpellier. The *Projet de Code Civil*, published in his name, formed the basis of the *Code Napoléon*.

CAMBERT, Robert, *kã-bayr* (c. 1628–77), French operatic composer, born in Paris, was a pioneer of French national opera, but fell foul of Lully (q.v.) and came to London (1673), where he died. See Pougin, *Les Vrais créateurs de l'opéra français*.

CAMBIO. See ARNOLFO DI CAMBIO.

CAMBON, *kã-bõ,* (1) **Joseph** (1756–1820),

French revolutionary, born at Montpellier, was a financial expert and originator of the 'Great Book of the Public Debt'. Although a moderate, he voted for the king's death and was banished as a regicide in 1815, dying near Brussels.

(2) **Jules** (1845–1935), was French ambassador in Berlin from 1907 to 1914.

(3) **Paul** (1843–1924), brother of (2), as French ambassador in London, 1898–1921, greatly promoted the Entente Cordiale.

CAMBRENSIS. See GIRALDUS.

CAMBRIDGE, George William Frederick Charles, Duke of (1819–1904), was born at Hanover, the only son of George III's seventh son, **Adolphus Frederick** (1774–1850), who was created first duke in 1801. Promoted major-general in 1854, he fought at Alma and Inkermann; in 1862 was made field-marshal; and from 1856 to 1895 was commander-in-chief. He married an actress, Miss Farebrother, their children bearing the name Fitzgeorge. See Lives by Verner (military; 1905) and Sheppard (private; 1906).

CAMBYSES, Pers. **Kambujiya** (d. 522 B.C.), second king of the Medes and Persians, succeeded his father, Cyrus, in 529 B.C. He put his brother Smerdis to death, and in 527 or 525 invaded and conquered Egypt. He meditated further conquests, but the Tyrian mariners refused to serve against Carthage; an army sent to seize the temple of Ammon perished in the desert; and one which he led in person to Nubia purchased some conquests dearly at the price of myriads of lives. He had given himself up to drunkenness and hideous cruelties, when news came, in 522, that Gaumáta, a Magian, had assumed Smerdis' character, and usurped the Persian throne. Cambyses marched against him from Egypt, but died in Syria by accident or suicide.

CAMDEN, (1) **Sir Charles Pratt, 1st Earl** (1713–94), was educated at Eton and Cambridge, and called to the bar in 1738. Lord chancellor from 1766 to 1770, he was president of the Council (1782–94), and was created Earl Camden in 1786.

(2) **William** (1551–1623), English scholar, antiquary, and historian, was born in London, where his father was a painter, and educated at Christ's Hospital, St Paul's School, and Oxford. Appointed second master of Westminster School in 1575, and headmaster in 1593, he undertook his survey of the British Isles, the famous *Britannia* (1586; 6th ed. 1607). It was first translated from the Latin by Philemon Holland in 1610. In 1597 Camden was made Clarencieux King-at-arms, an appointment which gave him more leisure for his favourite studies. His other most important works, all in Latin, are a list of the epitaphs in Westminster Abbey (1600), a collection of old English historians (1603), a narrative of the trial of the Gunpowder plotters (1607), and *Annals of the Reign of Elizabeth to 1588* (1615). He died at Chislehurst (his house was afterwards Napoleon III's), and was buried in Westminster Abbey.

CAMERARIUS, (1) **Joachim** (1500–74), German scholar, changed his original name Liebhard into Camerarius, because his forefathers had been *Kämmerer* (chamberlains) to the bishops of Bamberg. His works include an excellent biography of his friend Melanchthon (1566), a collection of letters by that reformer (1569), and *Epistolae Familiares* (3 vols. 1583–95).

(2) **Joachim** (1534–98), son of (1), was one of the most learned physicians and botanists of his age.

(3) **Rudolf Jakob** (1665–1721), was also a physician and botanist.

CAMERON, (1) **(George) Basil** (1884–   ), English conductor, born at Reading. He conducted the municipal orchestras of Torquay, Hastings, and Harrogate, before going in 1930 to the United States, where he was conductor of the San Francisco and Seattle symphony orchestras. On his return he became, in 1940, one of the principal conductors of the Henry Wood Promenade concerts. He was created C.B.E. in 1957.

(2) **Charles H.** See (5).

(3) **Sir David Young,** R.A. (1865–1945), Scottish painter and etcher, belonged to the ' Glasgow school '. Works may be seen in the Tate Gallery and the National Gallery of Scotland.

(4) **John** (*c.* 1579–1625), the ' walking library ', was born in Glasgow, and educated at its university. In 1600 he went to the Continent, where his erudition secured him appointments at Bergerac, Sedan, Saumur, &c.; and returning to Britain in 1620, he was two years later appointed principal of Glasgow University. In less than a year, however, he returned to Saumur, and thence to Montauban, where he received a Divinity professorship, and where, as at Glasgow, his doctrine of passive obedience made him many enemies. He was stabbed by one of them in the street, and died from the wound. His eight theological works, in Latin and French (1616–42), are said to be the foundation of Amyraut's doctrine of universal grace (1634).

(5) **Julia Margaret,** *née* Pattle (1815–79), born at Calcutta, married in 1838 the Indian jurist, Charles Hay Cameron (1795–1880), and died, like him, in Ceylon. She took admirable photographs of Tennyson, Darwin, Carlyle, Newman, &c.

(6) **Richard** (1648–80), Scottish Covenanter, was born in Falkland, where, having studied at St Andrews 1662–65, he became precentor and schoolmaster under an Episcopal incumbent, but was subsequently ' converted by the field preachers '. In 1678 he went to Holland, and returned in 1680 in time to publish the Sanquhar Declaration. Retiring then, with some sixty armed comrades, to the hills between Nithsdale and Ayrshire, he succeeded in evading capture for a month. On July 20, 1680, however, the band was surprised by a body of dragoons on Airds Moss, near Auchinleck, and, after a brave fight, Cameron fell. His hands and head were fixed on the Netherbow Port, Edinburgh. See *Life* by J. Herkless (1897).

(7) **Simon** (1799–1889), American statesman, born in Pennsylvania, was a journeyman printer and newspaper editor, in 1845 became a senator, was Lincoln's secretary of war (1861–62), and minister plenipotentiary to Russia (1862–63), and died at New York.

(8) **Verney Lovett** (1844–94), African explorer, was born at Radipole near Wey-

mouth, entered the navy in 1857, and served in the Mediterranean, West Indies, Red Sea, and on the east coast of Africa, taking part in the Abyssinian expedition, and in the suppression of the slave trade. In 1872 he was appointed to the command of an east-coast expedition to relieve Livingstone, and starting from Bagamoyo in March 1873, in August at Unyanyembe met Livingstone's followers bearing his remains to the coast. At Ujiji he found some of Livingstone's papers; and then he made a survey of Lake Tanganyika. In the belief that the Lualaba was the upper Congo, he resolved to follow its course to the west coast; but native hostility prevented him from forestalling Stanley's discoveries in 1877, and striking southwest he reached Benguela on November 7, 1875. Made C.B. and commander, in 1878 he travelled overland to India, to satisfy himself of the feasibility of a Constantinople-Baghdad railway; and in 1882, with Sir Richard Burton, he visited the Gold Coast. He wrote *Across Africa* (1877), *Our Future Highway to India* (1880), several boys' books, &c. He died from a hunting accident. See Foran's *African Odyssey* (1937).

CAMERON OF LOCHIEL, (1) **Donald** (*c.* 1695–1748), ' Gentle Lochiel ', a Highland chieftain, whose reluctant support of the young Pretender in 1745 encouraged that of other chieftains, died in exile in France.

(2) **Sir Ewen** (1629–1719), grandfather of (1), fought at Killiecrankie (1689). He is said to have slain the last wolf in Scotland.

CAMILLUS, Marcus Furius (447–365 B.C.), a Roman patrician who first appears as censor in 403 B.C. He took Veii in 396, after a ten years' siege; and in 394 his magnanimity induced Falerii to surrender unconditionally. Condemned on a charge of misappropriating the booty, but really because of his patrician haughtiness, he went into banishment at Ardea (391); but, Brennus having captured and destroyed all Rome except the Capitol, he was recalled and appointed dictator, appeared according to the legend just as the garrison were about to purchase the Gauls' departure, and drove the invader from the town. He routed the Aequi, Volsci, and Etrusci; and in 367 B.C., though eighty, he became for the fifth time dictator, and defeated the Gauls near Alba. He died of the plague.

CAMMAERTS, Émile, *kam'ahrts* (1878– 1953), Belgian (French-writing) poet and patriot, born in Brussels, lived in England from 1908 as professor of Belgian Studies at London University.

CAMOENS, Port. Camões, *ka-mō'ĕsh*, **Luis de** (1524–80), the greatest poet of Portugal, born at Lisbon, studied for the church as an ' honourable poor student ' at Coimbra, but declined to take orders. His *Amphitriões* was acted before the university. Returning to Lisbon, probably in 1542, he fell in love with Donna Caterina Ataíde, who returned his affection; but her father was against the marriage, and the poet had to content himself with passionate protestations in his *Rimas*— short poems after the model of the Italians. For reasons not ascertained Camoens was banished from Lisbon for a year, and joining a Portuguese force at Ceuta, served there for two years, losing his right eye by a splinter. In 1550 he again returned to Lisbon, where for the next three years he seems to have led a somewhat discreditable life; and having been thrown into prison for his share in a street affray, was released only on his volunteering to proceed to India. At Goa (1553–1556) he engaged in two military expeditions, but his bold denunciations of the Portuguese officials at length led to an honourable exile in a lucrative post at Macao (1556). Returning to Goa (1558), he was shipwrecked and lost everything except his poem, *The Lusiads*. At Goa he was thrown into prison through the machinations of his former enemies; but at length, after an exile of sixteen years, Camoens returned to Portugal to spend the remainder of his life at Lisbon in poverty and obscurity. In 1572 he published *The Lusiads*, which had an immediate and brilliant success, but did little for the fortunes of its author, who died in a public hospital. In *The Lusiads* (*Os Lusiados*, ' the Lusitanians '), Camoens did for the Portuguese language what Chaucer did for English and Dante for Italian—besides making himself the interpreter of the deepest aspirations of the Portuguese nation. It has been called ' The Epos of Commerce ', and the Portuguese regard it as their national epic. Of Camoens' sonnets, 70 have been well translated by Aubertin (1881); and the whole by Sir R. Burton (1885). There is an English rendering of *The Lusiads* by Sir R. Fanshawe (1655; ed. J. D. M. Ford, 1940). See Burton's *Camoens* (1882), Aubrey F. G. Bell's monograph (1923), and a Portuguese Life by A. de Oliveira Matos (1943).

CAMPAGNOLA, *kam-pa-nyō'la*, (1) **Domenico** (*c.* 1490–*c.* 1564), Italian painter, pupil of (2) and assistant of Titian, known for his religious frescoes in Padua, also for masterly engravings and line drawings in the manner of Titian.

(2) **Giulio** (1482–*c.* 1515), Italian engraver, born at Padua, designed type for Aldus Manutius, and produced fine engravings after Mantegna, Bellini, and Giorgione.

CAMPAN, **Jeanne Louise Henriette**, *kā-pā* (1752–1822), French writer, born in Paris, confederate of Marie Antoinette (1770–92), after Robespierre's fall opened a boarding-school at St Germain-en-Laye at which Hortense de Beauharnais was a pupil; and in 1806 Napoleon appointed her head of the school at Ecouen for the daughters of officers of the Legion of Honour. She wrote *Vie privée de Marie Antoinette* (1823), *Journal anecdotique* (1824), and *Correspondance avec la Reine Hortense* (2 vols. 1835). See works by Flammermont (1886) and V. M. Montague (1914).

CAMPANELLA, **Tommaso** (1568–1639), Italian philosopher, was born at Stilo in Calabria, entered the Dominican order in his fifteenth year, was as a theological or political heretic confined in a Neapolitan dungeon for twenty-seven years, and seven times racked, and died in the Dominican monastery of St Honoré, near Paris. An opponent of the schoolmen, he wrote over fifty works, chiefly in Latin, among them *Philosophia Sensibus*

Demonstrata (1591), *Universalis Philosophia* (1638), and *Civitas Solis* (1623), an imitation of Plato's *Republic*. His sonnets, first published by his German disciple, Tobias Adami, in 1622, were translated into rhymed English by J. A. Symonds in 1878. See Life by Amabile (3 vols. 1882), and study by Mattei (Florence 1934).

CAMPBELL, *kam'bĕll*, a Scottish family name, to which genealogists have chosen to assign an Anglo-Norman origin, deriving it from the Latin *De Campo Bello*. An alternative theory makes it purely Celtic, of Scoto-Irish origin; and *Cambel*, as the name was always formerly written, is just the Celtic *cam beul*, ' curved mouth '. Sir Duncan Campbell of Lochow, created Lord Campbell in 1445, and his descendants, the ducal house of Argyll (q.v.), have been noticed there. From his younger son, Sir Colin Campbell of Glenorchy (*c.* 1400–78), are descended the earls and marquises of Breadalbane (creations 1681 and 1831–35); and from the younger son of the second Earl of Argyll, who fell at Flodden in 1513, the earls of Cawdor (cr. 1827).

(1) **Alexander** (1788–1866), American minister, leader of the ' Disciples of Christ ', otherwise known as ' Campbellites ', was born near Ballymena, Antrim, and emigrated to the States with his father, **Thomas** (1763–1854), in 1807. They advocated a return to the simple church of New Testament times, and in 1826 Alexander published a translation of the New Testament, in which the word ' baptism ' gave place to ' immersion '. In 1841 he founded Bethany College in West Virginia, and there he died. He wrote much. See Life by Richardson (1868).

(2) **Sir Colin, Baron Clyde** (1792–1863), was born in Glasgow. His father was a carpenter, named Macliver, but Colin assumed the name of Campbell from his mother's brother, Colonel John Campbell, who in 1802 put him to school at Gosport. He was gazetted an ensign in 1808, and by 1813 had fought his way up to a captaincy, serving on the Walcheren expedition (1809), and through all the Peninsular war, where he was twice badly wounded. He took part in the expedition to the United States (1814), and then passed nearly thirty years in garrison duty at Gibraltar, Barbados, Demerara, and various places in England, in 1837 becoming lieutenant-colonel of the 98th foot. For the brief Chinese campaign of 1842 he was made a C.B. and for his brilliant services in the second Sikh war (1848–49) a K.C.B., thereafter commanding for three years at Peshawar against the frontier tribes. On the outbreak of the Crimean war in 1854 he was appointed to the command of the Highland Brigade; the victory of the Alma was mainly his; and his, too, the splendid repulse of the Russians by the ' thin red line ' in the battle of Balaklava. He was rewarded with a K.G.C.B., with a sword of honour from his native city, and with several foreign orders, and in 1856 was appointed inspector-general of Infantry. On the outbreak of the Mutiny (July 1857), Lord Palmerston offered him the command of the forces in India: he effected the final relief of Lucknow in November, was

created Baron Clyde in July 1858, and brought the rebellion to an end by December. Returning next year to England, he was made a field-marshal. He died at Chatham, and was buried in Westminster Abbey. See Lives by Lieutenant-General Shadwell (2 vols. 1881) and Archibald Forbes (1895).

(3) **Donald.** See (11).

(4) **Duncan** (c. 1680–1730), a deaf-and-dumb London soothsayer, born in Lapland, of an Argyllshire father. See his Life by Defoe (1720; new ed. by Aitken, 1895).

(5) **George** (1719–96), Scottish divine, was born at Aberdeen, and educated there at the grammar school and Marischal College. Abandoning law for divinity, he was in 1748 ordained minister, and in 1759 was appointed principal of Marischal College, in 1771 professor of Divinity. His works included the famous *Dissertation on Miracles* (1762) in answer to Hume, *Philosophy of Rhetoric* (1776), and *Lectures on Ecclesiastical History* (1800), with a memoir by G. S. Keith.

(6) **James Dykes** (1838–95), Coleridge's biographer, was for many years a successful merchant in Mauritius.

(7) **John, 1st Baron Campbell** (1779–1861), lord chancellor of England, born at Cupar, Fife, studied for the church at St Andrews, turned to law and journalism, and was called to the bar in 1806. A Whig M.P. (1830–49), he was knighted and made solicitor-general in 1832, and became attorney-general in 1834. Created a baron in 1841, he was appointed successively lord chancellor of Ireland, chancellor of the duchy of Lancaster (1846), [chief justice of the Queen's Bench (1850), and lord chancellor (1859). His *Lives of the Chief Justices* (1849–57) and *Lives of the Lord Chancellors* (1845–47) are disfigured by the obtrusion of himself, and in later volumes by inaccuracy. See Life by his daughter, Mrs Hardcastle (1881).

(8) **John Francis,** of Islay (1822–85), folk-lorist, was educated at Eton and Edinburgh University, held offices at court, and was afterwards secretary to the lighthouse and coal commissions. He travelled much, and died at Cannes. An enthusiastic Highlander and profound Gaelic scholar, he is chiefly remembered by his *Popular Tales of the West Highlands* (4 vols. Edinburgh 1860–62).

(9) **John McLeod** (1800–72), Scottish theologian, was born at Kilninver, Argyllshire, entered Glasgow University at eleven, and was ordained minister of Row, near Helensburgh, in 1825. His views on the personal assurance of salvation and on the universality of the atonement led to his deposition for heresy in 1831. For two years he laboured in the Highlands as an evangelist, and then for six and twenty, from 1833, preached quietly without remuneration to a congregation that gathered round him in Glasgow. From 1870 he lived at Rosneath, and died there. He wrote *Christ the Bread of Life* (1851), *The Nature of the Atonement* (1856), and *Thoughts on Revelation* (1862). See the *Memorials* by his son (2 vols. 1877).

(10) **Lewis** (1830–1908), Scottish classical scholar, born in Edinburgh, and educated there, at Glasgow, and Oxford, took Anglican orders, and was professor of Greek at St Andrews 1863–92. He is known especially for his editions of Sophocles and Plato.

(11) **Sir Malcolm** (1885–1949), British racing motorist, born in Chislehurst, Kent, from 1927 onwards established successive world speed records in motor and speed-boat racing. Knighted in 1931, he was the first motorist to exceed 300 m.p.h. (at Bonneville Salt Flats, Utah, 1935). His son **Donald** (1921–67) broke the world water speed record on Ullswater in 1955, and breaking his own record yearly, reached 276·33 m.p.h. on Lake Dumbleyung, W. Australia, in 1964. He was killed at Lake Coniston in a later attempt.

(12) **Mrs Patrick,** *née* Beatrice Stella Tanner (1865–1940), born at Kensington of mixed English and Italian parentage, married in 1884, went on the stage in 1888. Though her mercurial temperament made her the terror of managers, she possessed outstanding charm and talent, and leapt to fame in *The Second Mrs Tanqueray* (1893). Her first husband died in South Africa in 1900; in 1914 she married George Cornwallis-West. She played Eliza in Shaw's *Pygmalion* (1914) and formed a long friendship with the author.

(13) **Reginald John** (1867–1956), born at London, entered the Congregational ministry, was pastor of the City Temple, London (1903–15), and in 1907 startled the evangelical world by his exposition of an 'advanced' *New Theology*.

(14) **(Ignatius) Roy (Dunnachie)** (1901–57), South African poet and journalist, born in Durban. The violence of his personality and his enthusiasms give his work a brilliance quite distinct from its merit. He became an ardent admirer of things Spanish and fought with Franco's armies during the Civil War. His books include *The Flaming Terrapin* (1924), *The Wayzgoose* (1928), *Adamastor* (1930), *The Georgiad* (1931), *Mithraic Emblems* (1936), and *Flowering Rifle* (1939). A collected edition of his poems appeared in 1949 and he published two autobiographical volumes: *Broken Record* (1934) and *Light on a Dark Horse* (1951).

(15) **Thomas** (1777–1844), Scottish poet, was born and educated in Glasgow, and in 1797 repaired to Edinburgh nominally to study law; but he was more and more drawn to the reading and writing of poetry. *The Pleasures of Hope*, published in 1799, ran through four editions in a year. During a tour on the Continent (1800–01) Campbell visited Hohenlinden, at Hamburg fell in with the prototype of his 'Exile of Erin', and sailed past the batteries of Copenhagen. In 1803 he married and settled in London, having refused the offer of a chair at Wilna, and resolved to adopt a literary career. He contributed articles to *The Edinburgh Encyclopaedia,* and compiled *The Annals of Great Britain from George II to the Peace of Amiens.* In 1809 appeared *Gertrude of Wyoming*; in 1818 Campbell was again in Germany, and on his return he published his *Specimens of the British Poets.* In 1820 he delivered a course of lectures on poetry at the Surrey Institution; and from this date to 1830 he edited *The New Monthly Magazine,* contributing thereto *The Last Man* and other

poems. In 1827–29 he was thrice elected lord rector of the university of Glasgow. He died at Boulogne, and was buried in Westminster Abbey. 'Hohenlinden', 'Ye Mariners of England', and 'The Battle of the Baltic' are among his best-known poems. See his *Life and Letters* by Beattie (1849), Cyrus Redding's *Reminiscences* (1859), a short Life by Hadden (1900), and editions of the poems by Allingham (1890), Lewis Campbell (1904), and Logie Robertson (1908).

(16) **William Wallace** (1862–1938) American astronomer, born in Hancock County, Ohio, worked at the Lick observatory, California, from 1891, becoming director in 1930, and is known for his work on the velocity of stars.

(17) **William Wilfred** (1860–1919), Canadian poet, born at Kitchener, Ontario, author of *Lake Lyrics* (1889), &c., and editor of the *Oxford Book of Canadian Verse*.

CAMPBELL-BANNERMAN, Sir Henry (1836–1908), was the second son of Sir James Campbell, lord provost of Glasgow in 1840–43. He assumed the name Bannerman in 1872. Educated at Glasgow and Trinity College, Cambridge, he became Liberal M.P. for the Stirling burghs in 1868, was chief secretary for Ireland in 1884, and, having been converted to Home Rule for Ireland, war secretary in 1886, G.C.B. in 1895, Liberal leader in 1899, prime minister in 1905. He resigned April 4, 1908, and died April 22. A 'pro-Boer', he granted the ex-republics responsible government; and he launched the campaign against the House of Lords. See the Life by Spender (1923).

CAMPE, Joachim Heinrich (1746–1818), German educationist, born near Holzminden, after serving with Basedow (q.v.) founded an institution of his own, and in 1787 reorganized the school system in Brunswick, where he also established a large publishing house. He wrote some works on education, and a German Dictionary (5 vols. 1807–11); but his books for the young were specially popular—e.g., *Robinson der Jüngere*. See study by Leyse (1896).

CAMPEGGIO, Lorenzo, *kam-ped'jō* (1472–1539), Italian cardinal, born at Bologna, studied law, married early, and after his wife's death took orders. He was made Bishop of Feltri (1512), a cardinal (1517), papal legate to England to incite Henry VIII against the Turks (1518), and Bishop of Salisbury and Archbishop of Bologna (1524). Joint judge with Wolsey in the divorce suit against Catharine of Aragon, he ended by displeasing all parties (1529).

CAMPENDONCK, Heinrich (1889–1957), German Expressionist painter, born at Krefeld, a member of the 'Blue Rider' group founded by Marc and Kandinsky (qq.v.).

CAMPENHOUT, François von (1779–1849), Belgian composer, wrote *La Brabançonne* (the Belgian national anthem).

CAMPER, Peter (1722–89), Dutch anatomist, born at Leyden and died at the Hague, wrote a series of works on mammalian anatomy, and was professor at Franeker (1749–61), Amsterdam (1761–63), and Groningen (1763–1773).

CAMPHAUSEN, Wilhelm, *kamp-how'zen* (1818–85), German painter of battle-pieces, was born and died at Düsseldorf.

CAMPHUYSEN, Dirk Rafelsz, *-hoy'-* (1586–1627), Dutch painter, minister, and religious poet, born at Gorinchem. His son **Govert** (1624–74), court painter at Stockholm, and his nephew **Raphael** (1598–1657), are now believed to have painted many pictures formerly attributed to him.

CAMPI, a family of artists at Cremona:

(1) **Antonio** (*c.* 1536–*c.* 91), brother of (3) and (4), was a successful imitator of Correggio.

(2) **Bernardino** (1522–*c.* 92), the son of a goldsmith, and possibly a kinsman of (1), imitated Titian with such success that it has been difficult to distinguish the copies from the originals. His works may be seen in Mantua and Cremona.

(3) **Giulio** (1502–72), elder brother of (1) and (4), studied under Giulio Romano and has left a fine altarpiece at Cremona.

(4) **Vincenzo** (1536–91), brother of (1) and (3), excelled in small figures; also painted portraits.

CAMPIN, Robert (*c.* 1375–1444), Dutch artist, called the **Master of Flémalle** from his paintings in the Abbey of that name near Liège. He was identified by M. Georges Hulin in 1909. About 1400 he settled at Tournai, where Roger van der Weyden and Jaques Daret were his pupils, and he is thought to have learnt technical secrets from Hubert van Eyck. His *Madonna* and the pair of portraits of a man and his wife in the National Gallery, London, show him to have been a painter of rude vigour.

CAMPION, (1) **Edmund** (1540–81), the first of the English Jesuit martyrs, was the son of a London tradesman, and from Christ's Hospital passed to St John's College, Oxford. He became the most popular man at the university, but hankered after the old religion, although he was made a deacon in the Church of England in 1569, in which year he attempted to help re-establish Dublin University. Suspected of leanings towards Rome, and fearing arrest, he escaped to Douai, and in 1573 joined the Society of Jesus in Bohemia. In 1580 he was recalled from Prague, where he was professor of Rhetoric, to accompany Parsons on the Jesuit mission into England. The audacity of his controversial manifesto known as Campion's 'Brag and challenge', which was followed by his *Decem Rationes*, or 'Ten Reasons', greatly irritated his opponents. In July 1581 he was caught near Wantage, and sent up to London, tied on horseback, with a paper stuck on his hat inscribed ' Campion, the seditious Jesuit '. Thrice racked, he was tried on a charge of conspiracy of which he was innocent, hanged on December 1, 1581, and, with other sufferers in the same cause, beatified by Leo XIII in 1886. See Lives by Richard Simpson (1867; new ed. 1896) and E. Waugh (1936).

(2) **Thomas** (1567–1620), physician, poet, and composer, was born at Witham in Essex, studied at Cambridge and abroad, and died in London. He set his own lyrics to music, and as well as poetry in Latin and English he left

several books of ' ayres ' for voice and lute. See study by Kastendieck (1938).

CAMPOAMOR, Ramón de (1817–1901), Spanish poet, born in Navia. He gave up a medical career for literature; but after some success during his lifetime, his work is now neglected. Modern taste finds him pretentious and shallow, in spite of a certain superficial wit. His short, epigrammatic poems, *Doloras, Pequenos poemas* and *Humoradas*, are still readable. See *Obras completas* (8 vols. 1901–03).

CAMPOLI, Alfredo, *cam'-pō-* (1906–), Italian violinist, born in Rome, in London from 1911, won an early reputation as a soloist, but during the lean years of the 1930s became better known for his salon orchestra, disbanded at the beginning of the war, after which he emerged as one of the outstanding violinists of the time.

CAMPOMANES, Pedro Rodriguez, Count of, *kam-pō-mah'nays* (1723–1802), Spanish statesman and writer on political economy.

CAMROSE, William Ewert Berry, 1st Viscount (1879–1954), British newspaper proprietor, was born at Merthyr Tydfil, son of an alderman of that town. After working on local newspapers, he founded (in 1901), with his brother Gomer (see KEMSLEY), *The Advertising World*. In 1915 the brothers Berry acquired the *Sunday Times* and during the 1920s gained control of more than a hundred national and provincial publications. They also bought large paper mills. In 1928 Berry became managing editor of the *Daily Telegraph* and denounced as bribes the gifts offered in the circulation war of the 1930s. He was raised to the peerage in 1941, and in 1947, at the time of the Royal Commission on the Press, published *British Newspapers and their Controllers*.

CAMUCCINI, Vincenzo, *ka-moo-chee'nee* (1771–1844), Italian painter of biblical and classical subjects, was born and died at Rome.

CAMUS, *kah-müs*, (1) Albert (1913–60), French writer, born a farm-labourer's son at Mondovi, Algeria, studied philosophy at Algiers and, interrupted by long spells of ill-health, turned actor, schoolmaster, playwright and journalist there and in Paris. Active in the French resistance during World War II, he became co-editor with Sartre of the left-wing newspaper *Combat* after the liberation until 1948, when he broke with the latter and ' committed ' political writing. Having earned an international reputation with his nihilistic novel, *L'Étranger* (1942; trans. 1946), ' the study of an absurd man in an absurd world ', Camus set himself in his subsequent work the aim of elucidating some values for man confronted with cosmic meaninglessness. The essays *Le Mythe de Sisyphe* (1942; trans. 1955), on suicide, and *L'Homme révolté* (1951; trans. 1953), on the harm done by surrendering to ideologies, the magnanimous letters to a German friend (1945), a second masterpiece *La Peste* (1947; trans. 1948), in which the plague-stricken city Oran symbolizes man's isolation, were followed by a return to extreme ironical pessimism in *La Chute* (1956; trans. 1957). *Le Malentendu* and *Caligula* (both 1945;

trans. 1947) are his best plays. His political writings are collected in *Actuelles I* (1950) and *II* (1953). He was awarded the Nobel prize (1957) and was killed in a car accident. See studies by R. de Luppé (1951), P. Thody (1957), G. Brée (1959), J. Cruikshank (1959) and J. Grenier (1969).

(2) Armand Gaston (1740–1804), French revolutionary, born in Paris, was sent in 1793 to make Dumouriez prisoner, but was himself with four colleagues seized and delivered over to the Austrians. After an imprisonment of two and a half years, he was exchanged for the daughter of Louis XVI, and on his return to Paris was made member, and afterwards president, of the Council of Five Hundred, but resigned in 1797, and devoted his time to literature.

CANALETTO, properly **Canale**, **(1) Antonio** (1697–1768), Venetian painter, studied at Rome, painted a series of views in Venice, spent most of the years 1746–56 in England, where he painted excellent views of London and elsewhere, but died in his native city. See Life by F. J. B. Watson (1950) and study by W. G. Constable (1962).

(2) Bernardo Bellotto, surnamed **Canaletto** (1720–80), nephew of (1), attained high excellence as a painter, and also as an engraver on copper. He practised his art in Venice, Rome, Verona, Brescia, Milan, Dresden, and England, where he painted a masterly interior of King's College Chapel, Cambridge. He died in Warsaw. See R. Meyer, *Die beiden Canaletti* (Dresden 1878), and monograph by K. T. Parker (1948).

CANDACE, *kan'da-see*, the name (or rather title) of the queens of Ethiopia in the first Christian century.

CANDLISH, Robert Smith (1806–73), Scottish ecclesiastic, born in Edinburgh, was minister from 1834 of St George's, Edinburgh. After the Disruption he co-operated with Dr Chalmers in organizing the Free Church, and from Chalmers' death was its virtual leader. He was made moderator of the Free Assembly in 1861, principal of the New College in 1862, and a D.D. of Edinburgh. See Life by W. Wilson (1880).

CANDOLLE, *kã-dol*, **(1) Alphonse de** (1806–1893), French botanist, son of (2), published the great *Géographie botanique* (2 vols. 1855) and *L'Origine des plantes cultivées* (1883); he also edited his father's *Mémoires* (1862).

(2) Augustin Pyrame de (1778–1841), French botanist, was born at Geneva, February 4, and there and in Paris studied chemistry, physics, and botany. His earliest work, on lichens (1797), was followed by *Astragalogia* (1802) and *Propriétés médicales des plantes* (1804). He first lectured on botany in the Collège de France in 1804. His *Flore française* appeared in 1805. For the government he traversed France and Italy in 1806–1812, investigating their botany and agriculture. He was appointed in 1807 to a chair at Montpellier; in 1816 he retired to Geneva, where a professorship of Botany was founded for him. He died September 9, 1841. His greatest work, *Regni Vegetabilis Systema Naturale* (vols. i.–ii. 1818–21), was on a smaller scale continued in the *Prodromus Systematis Naturalis Regni Vegetabilis* (17 vols. 1824–73, the last ten by his son and others).

CANINA, Luigi, *ka-nee'na* (1795–1856), Italian architect and antiquary, was born at Casale, lived in Turin and Rome, and died at Florence.

CANNABICH, Christian (1731–98), German composer, born at Mannheim, studied under Stamitz, whose successor he became as *konzertmeister* at the ducal court of Karl Theodor at Mannheim, and later at Munich. He composed over 100 symphonies as well as ballets, chamber works, &c. See studies by Kloiber (Munich 1928) and H. Hofer (Munich 1921).

CANNING, (1) Charles John, 1st Earl (1812–1862), third son of George Canning (3), was born in London, and was educated at Eton and Christ Church, Oxford, where he obtained high honours. He entered parliament in 1836 as Conservative member for Warwick, but next year was raised to the Upper House as Viscount Canning by his mother's death, both his elder brothers having predeceased her. In 1841 he became under-secretary in the Foreign Office. Under Lord Aberdeen he was postmaster-general; and in 1856 he succeeded Lord Dalhousie as governor-general of India. The war with Persia was brought to a successful close in 1857. In the same year (May 10), the Indian Mutiny began with the outbreak at Meerut. Canning's conduct was decried at the time as weak—he was nicknamed 'Clemency Canning'; but the general opinion later was that he acted with courage, moderation, and judiciousness. In 1858 he became the first viceroy, and in 1859 was raised to an earldom. He had married in 1835 Charlotte, elder daughter of Lord Stuart de Rothesay, and sister to Lady Waterford; and she having died at Calcutta on November 18, 1861, he retired from his high office, and died in London. See Life by H. S. Cunningham (1892), and A. J. C. Hare's *Story of Two Noble Lives* (3 vols. 1894).

(2) Elizabeth (1734–73), a London domestic servant who in January 1753 disappeared for four weeks, and then alleged she had been seized by two men and carried to a house at Enfield Wash, where she had been ill-used by an old woman, and starved in an upper room, to compel her to an immoral life. She identified Susannah Wells and an old gypsy named Mary Squires as her persecutors; and Squires was sentenced to be hanged, Wells to be burned in the hand. The lord mayor made further investigations, which resulted in Squires' free pardon; and the case now became the excitement of the town. On April 29, 1754, Canning was tried at the Old Bailey for perjury, and after an eight days' trial, in which the jury seem to have been completely puzzled between the thirty-eight witnesses who swore that Squires had been seen in Dorsetshire, and the twenty-seven who swore to her having been in Middlesex, was sentenced to seven years' transportation. She died at Weathersfield, Connecticut. See Paget's *Paradoxes and Puzzles* (1874), and book by Machen (1925).

(3) George (1770–1827), English statesman, born in London. His father, who claimed descent from William Canynges of Bristol (q.v.), displeased his family by marrying beneath his station, and died in poverty when his son was one year old. The boy's education was provided by his uncle, Stratford Canning, a banker. From Eton he passed in 1788 to Christ Church, Oxford, and thence in 1790 to Lincoln's Inn. But in 1794, at Burke's suggestion, he entered parliament for Newport, Isle of Wight, as a supporter of Pitt; in 1796 he was appointed an under-secretary of state; and in 1798 he established his reputation by his speeches against the slave trade and Tierney's motion for peace with the French Directory. He gave valuable assistance to the ministry, not only by his voice in parliament, but by his pen in the *Anti-Jacobin* (1797–98); the 'Needy Knife-grinder' is one of his happiest efforts. In 1800 he married Joan Scott, who was sister to the Duchess of Portland, and had £100,000. Pitt resigned office in 1801; when he again became premier, Canning was treasurer of the navy until Pitt's death (1804–06). In the Portland ministry (1807) Canning as minister for foreign affairs planned the seizure of the Danish fleet, which did so much to upset the schemes of Napoleon; and he recommended the energetic prosecution of hostilities in Spain under both Moore and Wellesley. His disapproval of the Walcheren expedition led to a misunderstanding with Castlereagh (q.v.), secretary-at-war, which resulted in a duel. After the Portland ministry fell, Canning held no high office for many years. All his eloquence was enlisted in favour of Catholic emancipation in 1812, when he was elected for Liverpool, a seat exchanged for Harwich in 1822. In 1814 he went as ambassador to Lisbon, in 1816 was made president of the Board of Control, and supported the Liverpool ministry in all their repressive measures until 1820, when he resigned in consequence of the action of the government against Queen Caroline. Nominated governor-general of India in 1822, he was on the eve of departure when Castlereagh's suicide called him to the head of Foreign Affairs. He infused a more liberal spirit into the cabinet, he asserted British independence against the Holy Alliance, and gave a new impetus to commerce by a gradual laying aside of the prohibitive system. He arranged the relations of Brazil and Portugal; drew the French cabinet into agreement with the British respecting Spanish-American affairs; was the first to recognize the free states of Spanish America; promoted the union of Britain, France, and Russia in the cause of Greece (1827); protected Portugal from Spanish invasion; contended earnestly for Catholic emancipation; and prepared the way for a repeal of the corn laws. In February 1827 paralysis forced Lord Liverpool to resign, and Canning formed an administration with the aid of the Whigs. His health, however, gave way under the cares of office, and he died at the Duke of Devonshire's Chiswick villa, in the room where Fox had died twenty-one years earlier. He was buried, near Pitt, in Westminster Abbey. His widow next year was created Viscountess Canning. As a parliamentary orator Canning was remarkable for acuteness,

power of expression, and well-pointed wit; on the whole, however, he was inferior to Pitt, Burke, and Fox. See his Speeches edited by Therry (6 vols. 1828); A. Stapleton's *Political Life of Canning* (1831) and *George Canning and his Times* (1859); Dalling's *Historical Characters* (1867); Petrie's *Life of George Canning* (1930); a study by P. J. Rollo (1965); and his *Official Correspondence*, ed. by Stapleton (2 vols. 1887).

(4) **Sir Samuel** (1823–1908), engineer-in-chief of the Atlantic cables of 1865–69, was born at Ogbourne St Andrew, near Marlborough.

(5) **Sir Stratford.** See STRATFORD.

CANNIZZARO, Stanislao (1826–1910), Italian chemist, professor of Chemistry at Genoa, Palermo, and Rome. In 1860, while at Genoa, he marched with Garibaldi's thousand. He was the first to appreciate the importance of Avogadro's work in connection with atomic weights. He coordinated organic and inorganic chemistry, and discovered the reaction named after him.

CANO, (1) Alonso (1601–67), Spanish painter, born in Granada, in 1639 was appointed court painter and architect. Accused (falsely, it seems) of having murdered his wife, he was racked; but no confession having been elicited, he was acquitted and taken back into the royal favour, and spent his last years in acts of devotion and charity. See study by Wethey (1955).

(2) **Juan Sebastian del** (d. 1526), the first circumnavigator, was born at Guetaria on the Bay of Biscay. In 1519 he sailed with Magellan (q.v.), and, after his death, safely navigated the *Victoria* home to Spain, September 6, 1522. He died in a second expedition. See Life by M. Mitchell (1958).

(3) **Melchior** (1509–60), Spanish theologian, born at Tarancón. A Dominican, he became professor of Theology at Valladolid, Alcalá de Henares, and Salamanca. His *Loci Theologici* (1563) laid the foundations of theological methodology.

CANOVA, Antonio (1757–1822), Venetian sculptor, was born at the village of Possagno, and studied at Venice and Rome. After his *Theseus* (1782), he was regarded as the founder of a new school. He did not rigorously adhere to the severe simplicity of the antique, but infused into his works a peculiar grace such as characterized his *Cupid and Psyche*, which was produced soon after he had completed in 1787 the monument of Pope Clement XIV. Other works were a *Winged Cupid*, *Venus and Adonis*, a *Psyche holding a Butterfly*, *Penitent Magdalen*, and *Perseus with the head of the Medusa*, a second famous papal monument, and one at Vienna to an archduchess. In 1802 he was appointed by Pius VII curator of works of art, and was called to Paris to model a colossal statue of Napoleon. In 1815 the pope sent him again to Paris to recover the works of art taken there, and he visited England. Created Marquis of Ischia, he died in Venice, October 13, 1822. See Lives by Missirini (1824), Cicognara (1823), Colosanti (1927), and his *Memorie* (1885).

CÁNOVAS DEL CASTILLO, Antonio (1828–1897), Spanish Conservative statesman and historian, born at Malaga, became a member of the Cortes in 1854, and was premier 1875–81, 1884–85, 1890–92, and from 1895 till August 8, 1897, when, at the bath of Santa Agueda, Vitoria, he was shot by an anarchist in the presence of his wife. See study by C. Benoist (1930).

CANROBERT, François Certain, *kã-ro-bayt* (1809–95), marshal of France, born at St Céré in Lot, supported the *coup d'état* of 1851, commanded in the Crimea in 1854, and was wounded at the Alma. On St Arnaud's death Canrobert assumed the chief command. He commanded at Magenta and Solferino (1859); in the Franco-German war of 1870 he was shut up in Metz with Bazaine, and became a prisoner in Germany.

CANT, Andrew (c. 1590–1663), Scottish Covenanting minister, in 1638 was sent to Aberdeen to persuade the inhabitants to subscribe the Covenant; and in November of that same year he was a member of the Glasgow Assembly which abolished Episcopacy. He was nevertheless a zealous royalist, and in 1641 preached before Charles I at Edinburgh. His son, **Andrew**, was principal of Edinburgh University 1675–85.

CANTACUZENUS, Johannes, *-zee'-* (d. 1383), Byzantine soldier and statesman in the reigns of Andronicus II and III, the latter of whom in 1341 left him guardian of his son, Johannes V, then nine years old. Cantacuzenus, however, proclaimed himself the child's colleague, and after a five years' civil war secured his recognition, as well as the marriage of one daughter to the young emperor, and of another to the Sultan Orchan. A second war, during which the Turks occupied Gallipoli, caused his retirement in 1355 to a monastery, where he died. **Matthias,** his son, was also made a colleague in the empire in 1353, and on his father's abdication began a war which ended in his own deposition. He too died in 1383.

CANTARINI, Simone, *kan-ta-ree'nee* (1612–1648), an Italian painter, born at Pesaro, and hence called ' Il Pesarese ', studied under Guido Reni at Bologna. His intolerable arrogance made him numerous enemies; and after a quarrel with his chief patron, the Duke of Mantua, he died at Verona, perhaps having poisoned himself.

CANTELLI, Guido (1920–56), became permanent conductor at La Scala, Milan, and achieved international fame after World War II; he was specially applauded for his performances of 19th-century music. Cantelli met his death in an air disaster.

CANTELUPE, St Thomas de, or **St Thomas of Hereford** (c. 1218–82), born at Hambleden near Henley-on-Thames, studied at Oxford, Paris, and Orleans, and was made chancellor of Oxford University (1262), chancellor of England by Simon de Montfort (1264–65), and Bishop of Hereford (1275). He died at Orvieto, and was canonized in 1320. His relics were brought to Hereford, where his shrine became almost as revered as that of Becket at Canterbury.

CANTH, Minna, née **Johansson** (1844–97), Finnish playwright and feminist, born at Tampere. Her writings assail social evils and show the influence of Ibsen.

CANTILLON, Richard, *kã-tee-yõ* (1697–1734),

French economist, born in Ireland, became a prosperous financier in Paris and London, and wrote the authoritative *Essai sur la nature du commerce en général* (1755), which in many respects anticipated Adam Smith and Malthus. See the *Essai*, translated by Higgs (1931).

CANTON, John (1718–72), English scientist, born at Stroud, settled as a schoolmaster in London, and was elected a fellow of the Royal Society in 1749. He invented an electroscope and an electrometer; originated experiments in induction; was the first to make powerful artificial magnets; and in 1762 demonstrated the compressibility of water.

CANTOR, Georg (1845–1918), Russian-born German mathematician, born at St Petersburg, studied at Berlin and Göttingen and in 1877 became professor of Mathematics at Halle. He worked out a highly original arithmetic of the infinite which resulted in a theory of sets for irrational numbers, adding a new and important branch to mathematics. See his *Contributions to the Founding of a Theory of Transfinite Numbers* (1895–97; trans. 1915), Bertrand Russell, *Introduction to Mathematical Philosophy* (1919), and E. T. Bell, *Development of Mathematics* (1945).

CANTÚ, Cesare (1804–95), Italian author, born at Brivio in the Milanese territory. Imprisoned as a liberal in 1833, he described the sorrows of a prisoner in a historical romance, *Margherita Pusterla* (1838), which was only less popular than Manzoni's *I promessi sposi*. To his *Storia universale* (35 vols. 1836–42) succeeded a multitude of works on Italian history and literature, as well as lighter works, and *Manzoni: Reminiscenze* (2 vols. 1883).

CANUTE, or Cnut (*c.* 994–1035), king of the English, Danes, and Norwegians, was the son of Sweyn, king of Denmark, by his first wife Gunhild, a Polish princess. His father died in England in his career of conquest (1014), and Cnut was at once chosen by his fleet king of England, while his elder brother, Harold, succeeded as king of Denmark. But the Witan sent for Ethelred to be king, and Cnut was soon obliged to flee back to Denmark, first cutting off the hands, ears, and noses of the English hostages, and landing them at Sandwich. In 1015 he put to sea again with a splendid fleet, landed in Dorsetshire, ravaged the country far and wide, and by Christmas had made himself master of Wessex. Early next year he marched to York, and overawed all Northumbria into submission. Already he was master of England, save London, when Ethelred's death and the election by the Londoners of his vigorous son Edmund to be king gave a new turn to the struggle. Twice Cnut failed to capture London; the final struggle took place at Assandun, or Ashingdon, when, after a desperate battle, the English fled. Edmund and Cnut met at the isle of Olney, in the Severn, and divided the country between them: Cnut taking the northern part, and Edmund the southern. Edmund's death in 1016 gave the whole kingdom to the young Danish conqueror. His first act was to put to death some of the more powerful English chiefs, and to send

Edmund's two little sons out of the kingdom. In 1018 he levied a heavy Danegeld, with which he paid off his Danish warriors, keeping only the crews of forty ships. The kingdom he divided into the four earldoms of Mercia, Northumberland, Wessex, and East Anglia. From this time onwards till his death Cnut's character seems to have become completely changed. At once he laid aside his ruthless temper to become a wise, temperate, devout, and law-abiding ruler. He strove also to govern England according to English ideas, restored the equal rights that had prevailed in Edgar's time, and gradually replaced the Danish earls with native Englishmen. Aethelnoth became Archbishop of Canterbury; Godwine, Earl of Wessex. He himself married Emma, the widow of Ethelred. He was liberal to monasteries and churches, and reverent to the memory of the native saints. He had a high conception of the duty of a king. The death of Harold in 1018 had given him the crown of Denmark; that of Olaf in 1030 secured him in the possession of Norway. He died at Shaftesbury. See Larson's study (1912).

CANYNGES, William (*c.* 1399–1474), a great Bristol merchant, mayor, and M.P., who rebuilt St Mary Redcliffe, and, having taken orders, in 1469 became dean of the college of Westbury.

CAPABLANCA (Y GRANPERRA), José Raúl (1888–1942), Cuban chess-master, became world champion when he defeated Lasker in 1921. He retained the title until his defeat by Alekhine in 1927.

CAPEK, (1) Karel, *cha'pek* (1890–1938), Czech author, born at Schwadonitz, is above all remembered for his play *R.U.R.* (Rossum's Universal Robots), produced in 1921, showing mechanization rampant. With his brother (2) he wrote the *Insect Play* (1921), one of several pieces foreshadowing totalitarianism, also short stories on crime and mystery, prophetic science-fiction, and travelbooks, as *Letters from England* (tr. 1925). His brilliant writings which are pregnant with social and political satire, are often reminiscent of H. G. Wells or George Orwell, and have been translated into English almost in their entirety.

(2) **Josef** (1887–1945), elder brother of (1), regarded himself primarily as a painter. His early literary works written in collaboration with his brother include the allegorical *Insect Play*. From such anxious visions of the future he progressed to a philosophy of sceptical humanism which found expression in his one novel, *Stin Kapradiny* (1930), and in his essays. He died in Belsen.

CAPEL, *kay'-*, (1) **Arthur, Lord** (1610–49), was raised to the peerage in 1641, and fought for the king through the Great Rebellion. Captured at Colchester in 1648, he escaped from the Tower, but was retaken and beheaded.

(2) **Arthur** (1631–83), eldest son of (1), was created Earl of Essex in 1661. Viceroy of Ireland (1672–77), and first lord-commissioner of the Treasury (1679), on the discovery of the Rye House Plot he was sent to the Tower, where he was found with his throat cut—probably by his own hand.

From him the present Earl of Essex is descended.

(3) Monsignor **Thomas John** (1836–1911), a Roman Catholic churchman, celebrated till about 1878 as a London pulpit orator. He figures as ' Catesby ' in *Lothair*.

CAPELL, Edward (1713–81), English scholar, was born near Bury St Edmunds, and published an edition of Shakespeare (10 vols. 1768) and *Notes and Various Readings to Shakespeare* (3 vols. 1783).

CAPELLA, Martianus Mineus Felix (fl. A.D. 480), a native of Africa, whose *Satiricon*, a kind of encyclopaedia, highly esteemed during the middle ages, is a medley of prose and verse, full of curious learning. See editions by Kopp (1836), Eyssenhardt (1866), and Dick (1925).

CAPET, Hugo (*c.* 938–996), king of France, founder (987) of the third Frankish dynasty, which continued to rule France till 1328.

CAPGRAVE, John (1393–1464), chronicler, theologian, and provincial of the Augustine Friars in England, was born and died at Lynn, studied probably at Cambridge, and was ordained priest about 1418, having already entered his order at Lynn. His works include Bible commentaries, sermons, *Nova legenda Angliae*, *De illustribus Henricis*, the lives of twenty-four emperors of Germany, kings of England, &c., and *Vita Humfredi Ducis Glocestriae*. Among his English works are a life of St Katherine in verse (ed. by Horstmann, Early Eng. Text Soc. 1893), and *A Chronicle of England from the Creation to 1417* (' Rolls Series ', 1858). *Ye Solace of Pilgrimes*, a description of Rome, was traced to him, and edited by Mills (1911).

CAPISTRANO, Giovanni da, *ka-pis-trah'nō* (1386–1456), born at Capistrano in the Abruzzi, entered the Franciscan order at thirty. From 1426 he was employed as legate by several popes, and acted as inquisitor against the Fraticelli. In 1450 he preached a crusade in Germany against Turks and heretics, and opposed the Hussites in Moravia. His fanaticism led to many cruelties, such as the racking and burning of forty Jews in Breslau. When Belgrade was besieged by Mohammed II in 1456, he led a rabble of 60,000 to its relief; but he died at Ilak, on the Danube. He was canonized in 1690.

CAPITO, or Köpfel, Wolfgang Fabricius (1478–1541), reformer, born at Hagenau in Alsace, entered the Benedictine order, and in 1515 became professor of Theology at Basel. He approved of Luther's action, but in 1519 entered the service of Archbishop Albert of Mainz; and did not till later declare for the Reformation. See *Capito und Butzer*, by J. W. Baum (1860).

CAPO D'ISTRIAS or D'Istria, Ioannes Anto-nios, Count (1776–1831), president of the Greek republic, was born in Corfu, and in 1809, after holding a high position in the Ionian Islands, passed to the diplomatic service of Russia. In 1828 he entered on a seven years' presidency of Greece; but imbued as he was with Russian ideas, his autocratic measures aroused discontent; and on October 9, 1831, he was assassinated in a church at Nauplia. See Lives by Mendels-sohn-Bartholdy (Berlin 1864), and Dragoumis

(Paris 1891). His feeble brother, **Iony Augostinos** (1778–1857), succeeded him, but resigned the following April.

CAPONE, Al, properly **Alphonse,** *ka-pōn'* (1899–1947), American gangster, born in Brooklyn, achieved worldwide notoriety as a racketeer during the prohibition era in Chicago. Such was his power that no evidence sufficient to support a charge against him was forthcoming until 1931, when he was sentenced to 10 years' imprisonment for tax evasion.

CAPOTE, Truman, *ka-po'tay* (1924–   ), U.S. author, born in New Orleans of Spanish descent, spent much of his childhood in Alabama. He won several literary prizes while at school in New York but showed little ability in other subjects. His short story *Miriam*, published in the magazine *Made-moiselle*, was selected for the O. Henry Memorial Award volume in 1946. *Other Voices, Other Rooms* (1948), his first novel, revealed his talent for sympathetic delineation of small-town life in the deep South, while *The Grass Harp* (1951) is a fantasy enacted against a background of the Alabama of his childhood. Other works are *Breakfast at Tiffany's* (1958), which was highly successful as a film, and *In Cold Blood* (1966), a ' non-fiction novel '.

CAPPELLE, Jan van der (1624/5–79), Dutch marine painter, noted for his atmospheric seascapes.

CAPPELLO, Bianca (1548–87), the Venetian mistress, and from 1579 wife, of Francesco de' Medici, Duke of Florence (1541–87), with whom she was supposed, but falsely in all likelihood, to have been poisoned by his brother, the Cardinal Ferdinando. See books by Saltini (1863) and Bax (1927).

CAPPONI, Gino, Marchese (1792–1876), Italian Liberal politician, historian, and Dante scholar, blind from 1844, was born and died at Florence. See Lives by Montazio (1872) and Von Reumont (1880).

CAPRA, Frank (1897–   ), American film director, born at Palermo. His *Mr Deeds Goes to Town* (1936) and *You Can't Take it with You* (1938) won academy awards; other successes include *It Happened One Night* (1934) and *Lost Horizon* (1937).

CAPRIVI, Georg Leo, Graf von, *ka-pree'vee* (1831–99), German imperial chancellor, was born in Berlin. Entering the army in 1849, he fought in the campaigns of 1864 and 1866, and in the Franco-German war of 1870 was chief of staff to the 10th Army Corps. In 1883–88 he was at the head of the Admiralty and then commander of his old army corps, till, on Bismarck's fall in 1890, he became imperial chancellor and Prussian prime minister. His principal measures were the army bills of 1892–93 and the commercial treaty with Russia in 1894, in the October of which year he was dismissed. See Life by Gothein (1918).

CAPUS, (Vincent Marie) Alfred, *ka-pü* (1858–1922), French writer, born at Aix-en-Provence, turned from engineering to journa-lism, wrote *Qui perd gagne* (1890) and other novels, but is best remembered for his comedies of the Parisian bourgeoisie, *La Veine* (1901), &c. He was elected to the

Académie in 1910. See study by Noël (1909).

CARACALLA (176–217), Roman emperor, the son of the Emperor Septimius Severus, was born at Lyons. He was originally named Bassianus, from his maternal grandfather, but his legal name was Marcus Aurelius Antoninus. Caracalla was a nickname given him from his long hooded Gaulish tunic. After his father's death at Eboracum (York), in 211 he ascended the throne as coregent with his brother Publius Septimius Antoninus Geta, whom he murdered. He next directed his cruelty against all Geta's adherents, killing twenty thousand of both sexes—including the great jurist Papinianus. After almost exhausting Italy by his extortions, he turned to the provinces. In 214 he visited Gaul, Germany, Dacia, and Thrace; and after a campaign against the Alemanni, assumed the surname Alemannicus. He was assassinated on the way from Edessa to Carrhae.

CARACCI, or **Carracci**, *ka-rat'chee*, family of Italian painters:

(1) **Agostino** (1557–1602), born in Bologna, dabbled in poetry and literature, and was a brilliant engraver on copper. His brother's jealousy is said to have driven him from Rome (where they did the frescoes in the Farnese palace) to Parma, where he died.

(2) **Annibale** (1540–1609), brother of (1), born in Bologna, was bred a tailor, but rapidly became a great painter. His style was influenced by that of Correggio and Raphael.

(3) **Antonio Marziale** (1583–1618), natural son of (1), was a pupil of (2).

(4) **Ludovico** (1555–1619), son of a butcher, was born at Bologna, studied at Venice and Parma, and with his cousins (1) and (2) established in Bologna an ' eclectic ' school of painting. His works, which may still be seen at Bologna, include the *Madonna and Child Throned* and the *Transfiguration.*

CARACCIOLO, Prince Francesco, *ka-rat'chō-lō* (1752–99), had risen to the supreme command of the Neapolitan navy, when in December 1798 he fled with King Ferdinand before the French from Naples to Palermo. Learning, however, of the intended confiscation of the estates of all absentees, he obtained permission to return to Naples, and there entered the service of the ' Parthenopean Republic '. For two months he ably directed the operations of the revolutionists, and not till their cause seemed hopeless did he quit the capital. He was captured in peasant disguise, and on June 29, was brought on board Nelson's flagship, tried by a court martial of Neapolitan officers, and hanged from the yard-arm of a Neapolitan frigate. See NELSON; Paget's *Paradoxes and Puzzles* (1874); Gutteridge, *Nelson and the Neapolitan Jacobins* (1903).

CARACTACUS, Caratâcos, or **Caradoc** (d. A.D. 54), a British king, warred gallantly against the Romans (A.D. 43–50), but at length was completely overthrown by Ostorius near Ludlow. His wife and daughters fell into the hands of the victors; his brothers surrendered; and he himself was delivered up by Cartismandua, queen of the Brigantes. He was carried to Rome,

A.D. 51, and exhibited in triumph by the emperor Claudius. According to tradition he died at Rome about A.D. 54; but there is absolutely no ground for supposing that the Claudia of 2 Tim. iv. 21 was his daughter, and introduced Christianity into Britain.

CARAFFA, Carlo (1517–61), Italian cardinal, member of an ancient Neapolitan family, to which several cardinals and Pope Paul IV (q.v.) belonged. He fought in the Netherlands, joined the Knights of Malta, and was made cardinal by his uncle, Paul IV, who, however, had ultimately to banish the cardinal and his brothers from Rome for extortion. Pius IV caused him to be put to death.

CARAN D'ACHE, *ka-rā dash,* pseud. of **Emmanuel Poiré** (1858–1909), French caricaturist, born in Moscow. The name comes from the Russian word for ' pencil '.

CARAUSIUS (*c.* 245–293), Roman emperor in Britain from 287 till his murder by Allectus, was originally a Batavian pilot.

CARAVAGGIO, *-vad'jō,* (1) **Michel Angelo Merisi** or **Amerighi da** (1569–1609), Italian painter, was born at Caravaggio. His father, a mason, employed him in preparing plaster for the fresco painters of Milan, and, after studying the works of the great masters there for five years, and afterwards in Venice, he went to Rome, where at length Cardinal del Monte noticed one of his pictures. But his quarrelsomeness soon involved him in difficulties. Having killed a man he fled to Malta, and there obtained the favour of the Grand Master; in making his way back to Rome, he was wounded, lost all his baggage, caught a violent fever, and on reaching Porto Ercole, lay down on a bank and died. Caravaggio gave in his paintings expression to his own wild and gloomy character; his *Christ and the Disciples at Emmaus* is in the National Gallery. See study by Friedlander (1955).

(2) **Polidoro Caldara da** (*c.* 1492–1543), was murdered by his servant at Messina. He aided Raphael in his Vatican frescoes. His *Christ bearing the Cross* is in Naples.

CARCO, Francis, pseud. of **Francis Carcopino-Tusoli** (1886–1958), French author, born at Nouméa in New Caledonia, first gained recognition with his volume of poems *La Bohème et mon coeur* (1912), and added to his reputation with a series of novels chiefly set in Paris's Latin Quarter.

CARDAN, Jerome, Ital. **Geronimo Cardano,** Lat. **Hieronymus Cardanus** (1501–76), Italian mathematician, naturalist, physician, and philosopher, born at Pavia, became professor of Mathematics at Padua, and of Medicine at Pavia and Bologna. In 1571 he went to Rome, where Gregory XII pensioned him, and where he died a few weeks after finishing his candid autobiography *De Propria Vita.* He wrote over a hundred treatises on physics, mathematics, astronomy, astrology, rhetoric, history, ethics, dialectics, natural history, music, and medicine. See *Lives* by Henry, Morley (2 vols. 1854) and Waters (1899).

CÁRDENAS, (1) García Lopez de (mid 16th cent.), Spanish explorer, while on Coronado's expedition to New Mexico discovered the Grand Canyon of the Colorado in 1540.

(2) **Lázaro** (1895–1970), Mexican general, born in the Michoacán area, president of the

republic (1934–40). Left-wing in sympathies, he introduced many social reforms.

CARDI. See CIGOLI.

CARDIGAN, James Thomas Brudenell, 7th Earl of (1797–1868), sat in the House of Commons from 1818 until 1837, when he succeeded his father. He entered the army in 1824, and rapidly bought himself into the command of the 15th Hussars, which he resigned in 1833, on the acquittal of an officer whom he had illegally put under arrest. From 1836 to 1847 he commanded the 11th Hussars, on which he spent £10,000 a year, and which he made the crack regiment in the service. His treatment of his officers brought about a duel with Captain Harvey Tuckett, for which in 1841 Cardigan was tried before the House of Lords, but escaped through a legal quibble. He commanded a cavalry brigade under Lord Lucan in the Crimea, and led the Six Hundred at Balaklava. He was inspector-general of cavalry 1855–60. The woollen jacket known as a cardigan is named after him. See *Crimea*, C. E. Vulliamy *passim* (1939).

CARDONNEL, Adam de (*c.* 1667–1719), English politician, at an early age entered the War Office as a clerk. In 1692 he became private secretary to the Duke of Marlborough, serving him with tactful skill and unswerving fidelity throughout all his campaigns. Elected M.P. for Southampton in 1701, at the Duke's instigation he was appointed secretary-at-war. Involved in Marlborough's political downfall, he was removed from his ministerial appointment and expelled from the House of Commons. See Coxe's *Memoirs of the Duke of Marlborough* (1848) *passim*.

CARDUCCI, Giosuè, *kar-doot'chee* (1835–1907), Italian poet, was born, a physician's son, at Valdicastello, Pisa province. In 1860 he became professor of Italian Literature at Bologna, in 1876 was returned to the Italian parliament as a Republican, and in 1890 was nominated a senator. He was awarded a Nobel prize in 1906. See complete edition of his *Poems* (Bologna, 20 vols. 1889–1909); his *Correspondance* (1913–14); studies by Chiarini (1903), A. Jeanroy (Paris 1911), Benedetto Croce (1920); and A. N. Bickersteth's selection and verse translations (1913).

CARDWELL, Edward, 1st Viscount Cardwell (1813–86), English statesman, born in Liverpool, at Oxford obtained a double first and a fellowship. From a Peelite gradually becoming a Liberal, he was president of the Board of Trade (1852–55), chief secretary for Ireland (1859–61), chancellor of the Duchy of Lancaster (1861–64), colonial secretary (1864–66), and secretary for war (1868–74). Reorganizer of the British army, he was raised to the peerage in 1874.

CARÊME, Marie Antoine, *ka-rem'* (1784–1833), French *chef de cuisine* and author, wrote *La Cuisine française*, &c. As Talleyrand's cook, he played an important part at the Congress of Vienna.

CAREW, (1) Bamfylde Moore (1690–*c.* 1759), son of the rector of Bickleigh, near Tiverton, and 'king of the gipsies'. See reprint (1931) of 2 books (1745, 1749) ed. by Wilkinson.

(2) **George, 1st Baron Carew of Clopton and 1st Earl of Totnes** (1555–1629), English

soldier and administrator, educated at Broadgates Hall, Oxford, fought in the Irish wars (1575–83), interrupted in 1578 by a voyage with Sir Humphrey Gilbert. As lieutenant-general of English ordnance he accompanied Essex to Cadiz (1596) and Azores (1597), and as president of Munster (1600–03) repressed the earl of Tyrone's rebellion. Master-general of ordnance (1608–17), he received, jointly with Buckingham and Cranfield, the monopoly for gunpowder manufacture (1621). He was governor of Guernsey (1610–21). A friend of Raleigh, he left important historical and antiquarian documents relating to Ireland.

(3) **Thomas** (1595–1639), English poet, born at West Wickham, after quitting Oxford without a degree, studied in the Middle Temple. Between 1613 and 1619 he visited Italy, Holland, France; afterwards he rose into high favour with Charles I. A friend of Ben Jonson and Donne, he wrote polished lyrics in the Cavalier tradition. See his *Poems* (ed. Dunlap, 1949).

CAREY, (1) Henry (*c.* 1690–1743), English poet and musician, is believed to have been an illegitimate son of some member of the Savile family. He published his first volume of poems in 1713. He wrote innumerable songs, witty poems, burlesques, farces, and dramatic pieces, sometimes composing the accompanying music. His best-known poem is 'Sally in our Alley'; there is no sufficient ground for attributing 'God save the King' to him. He died suddenly, by his own hand apparently. See his *Poems* (ed. Wood, 1930).

(2) **Henry Charles** (1793–1879), American political economist, was born at Philadelphia. Hither his father, **Mathew Carey** (1760–1839), a journalist who had been thrown into prison for Nationalist opinions, had emigrated from Ireland in 1784, to become a successful publisher and author, known especially for his *Vindiciae Hibernicae*, written to confute Godwin and other English misrepresenters of Ireland. Henry Charles early became a partner in his father's bookselling business; and when in 1835 he retired from business to devote himself to his favourite study, he was at the head of the largest publishing concern in the United States. He died October 13, 1879. Among his works were *Principles of Political Economy* (3 vols. 1837–40) and *Principles of Social Science* (3 vols. 1858–59). Originally a zealous free-trader, he came to regard free trade as impossible in the existing state of American industry; it might be the ideal towards which the country should tend, but a period of protection was indispensable. See Memoirs by Elder (Philadelphia 1880) and Kaplin (1931).

(3) **James** (1845–83), a Dublin builder and town councillor, who joined the Fenians about 1861, and helped to found the 'Invincibles' in 1881. He betrayed his associates in the murder of Lord Frederick Cavendish (q.v.) and Mr Burke, the Phoenix Park murders, and on the voyage between Capetown and Natal was shot dead by a bricklayer, Patrick O'Donnell, who was hanged in London.

(4) **Sir Robert** (*c.* 1560–1639), youngest son

of Lord Hunsdon, for the last ten years of Elizabeth's reign was English warden on the Border marches. He was present at her deathbed (1603), and in sixty hours galloped with the news to Edinburgh. Charles I created him Earl of Monmouth.

(5) **William**, D.D. (1761–1834), English missionary and orientalist, was born at Paulerspury, near Towcester. Apprenticed to a shoemaker, he joined the Baptists in 1783, and three years later became a minister. In 1793 he and a Mr Thomas were chosen as first Baptist missionaries to India, where he founded the Serampur mission in 1799, and from 1801 to 1830 was Oriental professor at Fort William College, Calcutta. See Lives by Culross (1881) and G. Smith (1884).

CARGILL, Donald (c. 1619–81), Scottish Covenanter, was born at Rattray, near Blairgowrie, studied at Aberdeen and St Andrews, and in 1655 was ordained minister of the Barony parish in Glasgow. Ejected for denouncing the Restoration, he became an indefatigable field preacher, fought at Bothwell Bridge, and took part with Richard Cameron in the famous Sanquhar declaration (1680). Having excommunicated the king, the Duke of York, and others at Torwood, Stirlingshire, he was seized, and executed at the cross of Edinburgh.

CARISSIMI, Giacomo (1604/5–74), Italian composer, was organist in Tivoli, Assisi, and from 1628 in Rome. He did much to develop the sacred cantata, and his works include the oratorio *Jephthah*. See study by Vogel (Prague 1928).

CARL. See CHARLES.

CARLÉN, Emilie (1807–92), Swedish novelist, was born at Strömstad, and died at Stockholm. The first of her novels (31 vols. 1869–75) appeared in 1838; many have been translated into English. See her Reminiscences (1878).

CARLETON, (1) Guy, 1st Baron Dorchester (1724–1808), British general, born at Strabane, Co. Tyrone, served under Cumberland on the Continent, under Wolfe in Canada. Governor of Quebec 1766–70, 1775–77, 1786–91, 1793–96, he successfully defended the city against the Americans, whom he defeated at Lake Champlain in 1776. In 1782–83 he was British commander-in-chief in America. As soldier and statesman he did much to save Canada for Britain. See *Life* by A. G. Bradley (' Makers of Canada ', 1907).

(2) **Will** (1845–1912), American author of *Farm Ballads* (1873), *City Ballads* (1885), &c., born in Hudson, Michigan, graduated at Hillsdale College, Michigan.

(3) **William** (1794–1869), Irish writer, born at Prillisk, Co. Tyrone, of peasant birth, the youngest of fourteen children. He became a tutor and writer in Dublin, contributing sketches to the *Christian Examiner*, republished as *Traits and Stories of the Irish Peasantry* (1830). A second series (1833) no less well received; and in 1839 appeared *Fardorougha the Miser*. His tales are mostly pathetic. See his Autobiography (2 vols. 1896).

CARLI, Giovanni Rinaldo, *kar'lee* (1720–95), Italian economist and archaeologist, best known by his *Della Moneta* (1754–60).

CARLILE, (1) Richard (1790–1843), English journalist, born at Ashburton, Devon, became a chemist's boy and a tinman's apprentice, sold the Radical *Black Dwarf* through London, next sold thousands of Southey's *Wat Tyler*, reprinted Hone's *Parodies*, and wrote a series of imitations of them, for which he got eighteen weeks in the King's Bench. This was the first of a series of imprisonments whose total amounted to nine years and four months. See Holyoake's *Life and Character of R. Carlile* (1848).

(2) **Wilson** (1847–1942), Anglican clergyman, born at Buxton, founded the Church Army in 1882 and was made a prebendary of St Paul's in 1905. See Reffold's *Wilson Carlile* (1947).

CARLISLE, (1) George William Frederick Howard, 7th Earl of, K.G. (1802–64), was educated at Eton and Christ Church, Oxford, took in 1821 the Chancellor's and Newdigate prizes, and graduated with a first class in Classics. M.P. for Morpeth in 1826, he at once attached himself to the cause of parliamentary reform. In 1830 he was elected for Yorkshire, and after the Reform Bill, for the West Riding, a seat which he lost in 1841, but recovered in 1846. Under Melbourne he was chief-secretary for Ireland (1835–41), and under Russell (1846–52) chief-commissioner of woods and forests, and afterwards chancellor of the duchy of Lancaster. In 1848 he succeeded to the peerage, and was lord-lieutenant of Ireland in 1855 and 1859. He wrote a *Diary in Turkish and Greek Waters* (1854), *Poems* (1866), &c.

(2) **Lucy, Countess of** (1599–1660), second daughter of the ninth Earl of Northumberland, in 1617 married James Hay, afterwards Earl of Carlisle (d. 1636). Witty and beautiful, she was the friend of Strafford, and, after his fall, played an intricate game of intrigue, which in 1649 brought her for some months to the Tower.

CARLO DOLCI. See DOLCI.

CARLOMAN (751–71), Charlemagne's younger brother, ruled the Franks from 754. At his death Charlemagne took over his lands.

CARLOMAN (828–80), son of Louis the German, king of Bavaria, Moravia, Pannonia, and Carinthia from 876, and of Italy from 877.

CARLOMAN (d. 884), son of Louis II, ruled France with his brother, Louis III (d. 882), from 879.

CARLOS, (1) Don (1545–68), son of Philip II by his first wife, Maria of Portugal, was born at Valladolid. He was sent to study at Alcala de Henares, where he profited so little that the king invited a nephew, the Archduke Rudolf, to Spain, intending to make him his heir. Weak, vicious, and cruel, he early conceived a strong aversion towards the king's confidants, and in confession to a priest, on Christmas Eve 1567, betrayed his purpose to assassinate a certain person. As the king was believed to be the intended victim, this confession was divulged; and Don Carlos was tried and found guilty of conspiring against the life of his father. The sentence was left for the king to pronounce. Philip declared that he could make no exception in favour of such an unworthy son; but sentence of death was not formally recorded. Shortly afterwards Don Carlos died. The suspicion that he was poisoned or strangled has no valid evidence to support it.

(2) **Don** (1788–1855), second son of Charles IV of Spain, on the accession of his niece Isabella in 1833, asserted his claim to the throne—a claim reasserted by his son, **Don Carlos** (1818–61), Count de Montemolin, and by *his* nephew, **Don Carlos** (1848–1909). Carlist risings, whose strength lay in the Basque provinces, occurred in 1834–39 and 1872–76.

(3) or **Careless, William** (d. 1689), a royalist officer who hid with Charles II (q.v.) in the oak at Boscobel.

CARLSTADT, properly **Andreas Rudolf Bodenstein** (d. 1541), reformer, born prior to 1483 at Carlstadt in Bavaria, in 1517 joined Luther, who in 1521 rebuked his iconoclastic zeal, and whom he afterwards opposed on the question of the Eucharist. Accused of participation in the Peasants' War, he fled to Switzerland, and became professor of Theology at Basel.

CARLTON, Richard (*c.* 1560–*c.* 1638), English composer. He was educated at Cambridge and spent most of his life as vicar of St Stephen's, Norwich, and a minor canon of Norwich Cathedral. In 1601 he published a volume of madrigals and was a contributor to *The Triumphs of Oriana*, the volume of madrigals presented to Queen Elizabeth in 1603.

CARLYLE, (1) **Alexander**, of Inveresk (1722–1805), Scottish divine, was minister of Inveresk from 1748 till his death. The friend of Hume, Adam Smith, Smollett, John Home, &c., with Robertson the historian he led the moderate party in the Church of Scotland; he was Moderator of the General Assembly in 1770, and was made Dean of the Chapel Royal in 1789. His imposing presence earned him the name of ' Jupiter Carlyle '. ' He was ', says Sir Walter Scott, ' the grandest demigod I ever saw '. See his interesting *Autobiography*, first edited in 1860 by John Hill Burton (new ed. 1910).

(2) **Jane Welsh**. See (3).

(3) **Thomas** (1795–1881), was born at Ecclefechan in Dumfriesshire. He was the second son of James Carlyle (1758–1832), a stonemason of fearless independence and strong natural faculty; but his first son by his second wife, Margaret Aitken (1771–1853). From the Ecclefechan school he proceeded in 1805 to Annan Academy; and in 1809 he entered Edinburgh University, where he excelled in geometry. In 1813 he began preparation for the ministry of the Church of Scotland; but in 1814 he competed successfully at Dumfries for the mathematical mastership of Annan Academy, and in 1816 accepted the post of assistant at the parish (or grammar) school of Kirkcaldy. Teaching soon became intolerable, and when at the end of 1818 he removed to Edinburgh, he had abandoned all thoughts of the ministry. Here he obtained private teaching; for Brewster, editor of the *Edinburgh Encyclopaedia*, he wrote many articles, chiefly biographical and geographical; and he translated Legendre's *Elements of Geometry*.

In 1819 he began the study of Scots Law, but found law as uncongenial as divinity. Till 1822 he lived in Edinburgh, absorbed in German literature, especially Goethe, who had an abiding influence on him. In 1821 he was introduced through his friend Edward Irving to Irving's pupil, **Jane Baillie Welsh** (1801–66), only daughter of Dr John Welsh, medical practitioner in Haddington, who had left his daughter sole heiress of the small estate of Craigenputtock, 16 miles from Dumfries. In 1822 Irving, entering on the pastorate of the Caledonian Chapel in London, recommended Carlyle as tutor to Charles Buller. Carlyle found his duties pleasant, and was now able to give substantial pecuniary aid to his family, particularly as regarded the education of his younger brother **John Aitken Carlyle**, M.D. (1801–79), the translator in 1840 of Dante's *Inferno*. Now also he arranged to write a *Life of Schiller* and a translation of the *Wilhelm Meister* of Goethe. He paid his first visit to London in 1824, and remained there till the publication in book form of his *Schiller* (1825). At this time he received the first of a series of letters from Goethe, and made the acquaintance of Coleridge, Thomas Campbell, Allan Cunningham, Procter, and other notabilities. In 1825 he removed to the farm of Hoddam Hill, near his father's farm of Mainhill, which he had leased, his brother Alexander doing the farming, while he translated German romances. In 1826 his father and he had removed to Scotsbrig farm, when in October he married Miss Welsh, and settled in Edinburgh. Here he completed four volumes of translations from Tieck, Musäus, and Richter (*German Romance*, 1826), and sent his first article on Jean Paul Richter to the *Edinburgh Review* in 1827. In 1828 they removed to Craigenputtock, and there they lived for six years, Carlyle writing meanwhile magazine articles on Burns, Samuel Johnson, Goethe, Voltaire, Diderot, Schiller, &c. He also wrote a *History of German Literature*, the best parts of which were subsequently published in the form of essays; and in 1833–34 there appeared in *Fraser's Magazine* his most characteristic work, *Sartor Resartus*, the fantastic hero of which, Teufelsdröckh, illustrates in his life and opinions the mystical ' Philosophy of Clothes '. In *Sartor* he abandoned the simple diction of his earlier essays for the thoroughly individual style of his later works—eruptive, ejaculatory, but always powerful. In 1834 Carlyle, resolved to try his fortune in London, established himself in the house, 5 Cheyne Row, Chelsea, in which he lived till the day of his death. His *French Revolution*, which established his reputation as a literary genius of the highest order, appeared in 1837. In 1837, 1838, 1839, and 1840 he lectured on ' German Literature ', ' The History of Literature ', ' The Revolutions of Modern Europe ', and ' Heroes and Hero-worship '. In 1838 appeared *Sartor* in book form, and the first edition of his *Miscellanies*; in 1839 *Chartism*, the first of a series of attacks on the shams and corruptions of modern society; in 1843 *Past and Present*, and in 1850 *Latter-day Pamphlets*. *Cromwell's Letters and*

Speeches (1845) completely revolutionized the public estimate of its subject. In 1851 he published a biography of his friend John Sterling. From this time Carlyle gave himself up entirely to his largest work, *The History of Friedrich II commonly called Frederick the Great* (1858–65). As Lord Rector of Edinburgh University he delivered an address in which he embodied his moral experiences in the form of advice to the younger members of his audience (1866). Three weeks later his wife died very suddenly. Carlyle's grief developed into remorse when he discovered from her letters and journal that during a period of their married life his irritability and unconscious want of consideration for her wishes had caused her much misery and even ill-health. The *Letters and Memorials of Jane Welsh Carlyle* prove Mrs Carlyle to have been one of the keenest critics, most brilliant letter writers, and most accomplished women of her time. In 1867 there appeared in *Macmillan's Magazine* Carlyle's view of British democracy, under the title of ' Shooting Niagara '. He prepared a special edition of his collected works, and added to them in 1875 a fresh volume containing ' The Early Kings of Norway ' and an ' Essay on the Portraits of John Knox '. In 1874 he accepted the Prussian Order of Merit, bestowed in recognition of his life of Frederick the Great, who founded the Order. When Disraeli offered him a G.C.B. and a pension, he declined both. He died at his house in Chelsea, and was laid in the churchyard of Ecclefechan beside his kindred. As a prophet in the guise of a man of letters, Carlyle exerted a greater influence on British literature during the middle of the nineteenth century, and on the ethical, religious, and political beliefs of his time, than any of his contemporaries. Irritable and intolerant though he was, he was incapable of conscious injustice, vindictiveness, or insincerity. See his *Reminiscences* (Froude's and Norton's editions); Froude's *Life* (4 vols. 1882–84); his wife's *Letters and Memorials* (1883); his and her *Love Letters* (1909); his *Correspondence* with Emerson (1883), *Early Letters* (1886–88); *Bibliography*, by Shepherd (1881); books by Masson (1885), Garnett (1887), Nichol (1892), Duffy (1892), Chesterton (1902), Craig (1908), Ralli (1920), and D. A. Wilson (6 vols. 1923–34). The controversy about his relations with his wife, reopened in 1903 by *New Letters* of Mrs Carlyle's, prefaced by Crichton-Browne, and Froude's *My Relations with Carlyle*, was continued by Alex. Carlyle (1903) and D. A. Wilson (1913). See also Lives of Jane Welsh Carlyle by Hanson (1952) and Bliss (1954).

CARMAGNOLA, Francesco, *kar-man-yō'la* (1390–1432), condottiere and commander-in-chief of the Venetian forces, beheaded for failure.

CARMAN, William Bliss (1861–1929), Canadian nature poet born at Fredericton, New Brunswick, contributed poems to the *Atlantic Monthly*, *Century*, &c. His *Collected Poems* appeared in 1905, and *Later Poems* in 1921. He collaborated with the American poet Richard Hovey (1864–1900).

CARMEN SYLVA (1843–1916), the pen-name of Elizabeth, queen of Rumania, who was born the daughter of Prince Hermann of Wied Neuwied, and married King (then Prince) Charles of Rumania in 1869. Her only child, a daughter, died in 1874, and out of her sorrow arose her literary activity. Two poems, printed privately at Leipzig in 1880 under the name ' Carmen Sylva ', were followed by *Stürme* (1881), *Leidens Erdengang* (1882; trans. as *Pilgrim Sorrow* by H. Zimmern, 1884), *Pensées d'une reine* (1882), *Meister Manole* (1892), and other works. In the war of 1877–78 she endeared herself to her people by her devotion to the wounded. See her *From Memory's Shrine: Reminiscences* (1911), and Life by her collaborator, Mme Kremnitz (new ed. 1903).

CARMONA, Antonio (1869–1951), became a general in 1922, and was president of Portugal from 1926 to his death.

CARNAP, Rudolf (1891–1970), German-born American philosopher, born at Wuppertal, was lecturer at Vienna (1926–31), professor at Prague (1931–35) and later at Chicago and California. One of the leaders of the ' Vienna Circle ' of logical positivists, as in his *Der Logische Aufbau der Welt* (1923), he later embarked upon a more comprehensive study in his *Logical Syntax of Language* (trans. 1937) and became the leader of the semantic school with his *Meaning and Necessity* (Chicago 1948) and his semantic studies of induction and probability (1950).

CARNARVON, (1) George Edward Stanhope Molyneux Herbert, 5th Earl of (1866–1923), Egyptologist, son of (2), with Howard Carter (q.v.) excavated tombs of the 12th and 18th dynasties at Thebes, dying during the exploration of Tut-ankh-amen's.

(2) **Henry Howard Molyneux Herbert, 4th Earl of** (1831–90), took a first class in Classics at Oxford in 1852. Lord Derby's colonial secretary (1866), he resigned office upon the Reform Bill of 1867. When Disraeli returned to power in 1874, Carnarvon became colonial secretary but resigned (1878) on the despatch of the British fleet to the Dardanelles. In 1885–86 he was lord-lieutenant of Ireland. See his *Essays* (1896) and Life by Sir A. Hardinge (1925).

CARNEADES, *kar-nee'a-deez* (*c*.213–129 B.C.), Greek philosopher, founder of the Third or New Academy, was born at Cyrene, and died at Athens.

CARNEGIE, Andrew (1835–1918), Scottish ironmaster, was born in Dunfermline, whence his father, a weaver, emigrated in 1848 to Pittsburgh. Factory hand, telegraphist, and railway clerk, he invested his savings in oil lands, and after the Civil War in the business which grew into the largest iron and steel works in America. He retired in 1901, a multimillionaire, to Skibo Castle in Sutherland, and died at Lenox, Mass. His benefactions exceeded £70,000,000, including public libraries throughout U.S.A. and Britain, Pittsburgh Carnegie Institute, Washington Carnegie Institution, Hero Funds, Hague Peace Temple, Pan-American Union Building, and great gifts to Scottish and American universities, Dunfermline, &c. Besides an Autobiography (1920), he wrote *Triumphant Democracy, The Gospel of Wealth.*

Problems of Today. See Life by Hendrick (1933).

CARNOT, *kar-nō*, (1) **Lazare Hippolyte** (1801–88), French politician, born at St Omer, in early life a disciple of St Simon, left that school protesting against Enfantin's ' organization of adultery ', and devoted himself to the inculcation of a more orthodox and virtuous socialism. After the February Revolution (1848) he was appointed minister of public instruction, but soon resigned. In 1863 he entered the Corps Législatif, and the National Assembly in 1871. Elected a life senator in 1875, he died March 16, 1888. He wrote an *Exposé* of St Simonianism and *Mémoires* of his father, Grégoire, and Barère.

(2) **Lazare Nicolas Marguerite** (1753–1823), father of (1) and (4), ' organizer of victory ' during the French Revolution, was born at Nolay, Côte d'Or, entered the army as engineer, in 1791 became a member of the Legislative Assembly, and in the Convention voted for the death of Louis XVI. During a mission to the army of the north, he took temporary command and gained the victory of Wattignies. Elected into the Committee of Public Safety and entrusted with the organization of the armies of the Revolution, he raised fourteen armies, and drew up a plan of operations by which the forces of the European reaction were repelled from the frontier. Though he endeavoured to restrict the power of Robespierre, he was accused after the Reign of Terror; but the charge was dismissed. Having as a member of the Directory opposed, in 1797, the extreme measures of Barras, his colleague, he was sentenced to deportation as a suspected royalist. Escaping to Germany, he wrote a defence which conduced to the overthrow of his colleagues in 1799. The 18th Brumaire brought him back to Paris, where in 1800, as minister of war, he helped to achieve the brilliant results of the Italian and Rhenish campaigns. He retired when he understood the ambitious plans of the emperor, but on his reverses hastened to offer his services, and received the command of Antwerp in 1814, which he heroically defended. During the Hundred Days he was minister of the interior; and after the second restoration retired first to Warsaw, and next to Magdeburg, where he died. He wrote much on mathematics, military tactics, &c. See his son's *Mémoires* (2 vols. 1861–64; new ed. 1907; his *Correspondance*, ed. by Charavay (1892 *et seq.*); Lives by Arago (1850), Dupré (1940), and Watson (1955).

(3) **Marie François Sadi** (1837–94), son of (1), president of the French Republic, was born at Limoges. He studied at the École Polytechnique, and became a civil engineer. In 1871 he was chosen to the National Assembly, and was finance minister in 1879 and 1887. In 1887 he was chosen president of the Republic, but was stabbed at Lyons by an anarchist, June 24, 1894.

(4) **Nicolas Léonard Sadi** (1796–1832), son of (2), founder of the science of thermodynamics, was born at Paris, became a captain of engineers, but died of cholera. He wrote *Réflexions sur la puissance du feu* (1824).

CARO, (1) **Annibale** (1507–66), Italian poet and prosewriter, was secretary to a succession of cardinals, and died at Rome.

(2) **Elme Marie** (1826–87), ' le philosophe des dames'—from the popularity of some of his lectures with society ladies—born at Poitiers, became in 1857 a lecturer at the École Normale, in 1864 professor at the Sorbonne, and in 1874 was elected to the French Academy.

CAROL I (1839–1914), of the house of Hohenzollern, was made Prince of Rumania in 1866, king in 1881. His grandnephew **Carol II** (1893–1953), renounced (1925) his right of succession, became king by a *coup* in 1930, was deposed in 1940, and left Rumania.

CAROLINE, Amelia Elizabeth (1768–1821), wife of George IV, was the second daughter of Charles William, Duke of Brunswick-Wolfenbüttel, and of George III's sister, Augusta. In 1795 she married the Prince of Wales. The marriage was disagreeable to him, and although she bore him a daughter, the Princess Charlotte (q.v.), he let her live by herself at Shooters Hill and Blackheath, the object of much sympathy. Reports to her discredit led the king in 1806 to cause investigation to be made into her conduct, which was found to be imprudent, but not criminal. When George came to the throne in 1820, she was offered an annuity of £50,000 to renounce the title of queen and live abroad; when she refused, and made a triumphal entry into London, the government instituted proceedings against her for adultery. Much that was very reprehensible was proved; but her husband's usage, and the splendid defence of Brougham, caused such a general feeling in her favour, that the ministry gave up the Divorce Bill. She assumed the rank of royalty, but was turned away from Westminster Abbey door at George IV's coronation, July 19, 1821. On August 7, she died. See books by Clerici (trans. 1907), L. Melville (1912), Sir E. Parry (1930), Greenwood's *Hanoverian Queens* (1911), and J. Richardson's *The Disastrous Marriage* (1960).

CAROLINE OF ANSPACH (1683–1737), the queen of George II (q.v.), upheld Walpole and humoured the king. See Greenwood's *Hanoverian Queens* (1909), and P. Quennell's *Caroline of England* (1939). For her granddaughter Caroline Matilda, see STRUENSEE.

CAROLUS-DURAN, properly **Charles Auguste Émile Durand** (1838–1917), French painter, born at Lille, was strongly influenced by Velasquez and the Spanish school. He was the teacher of Sargent.

CAROSSA, Hans (1878–1956), German writer and doctor, born at Tölz, became prominent with his autobiographical *Eine Kindheit* (1922). Other writings include *Rumänisches Tagebuch* (1924), and *Das Jahr der schönen Täuschungen* (1941). See studies by A. Haueis (1935) and G. Clivio (1935).

CAROTHERS, Wallace Hume (1896–1937), American chemist, born in Burlington, Iowa, experimented in plastics, and discovered nylon.

CAROVÉ, Friedrich Wilhelm (1789–1852), liberal Catholic philosopher, born at Coblenz.

CARPACCIO, Vittore, -pat'-chō (c. 1455–1522), Italian painter, was born in Venice. His most characteristic work is seen in the nine subjects from the life of St Ursula which he painted, 1490–95, for the school of St Ursula, Venice (now in the Accademia). The nine subjects from the lives of the Saviour, and Saints Jerome, George, Tryphonius, 1502–08, painted for the school of San Giorgio de Schiavoni are still preserved there. In 1510 he executed for San Giobbe his masterpiece, the *Presentation in the Temple*, now in the Accademia. His later works show a marked decline. See studies by Ludwig and Molmenti (trans. Cust, 1947), and Pignatti (1958).

CARPEAUX, Jean Baptiste, kar-pō (1827–75), French sculptor, born at Valenciennes, in 1854 obtained the *Prix de Rome*. His *chef d'œuvre* was the marble group, *The Dance*, in the façade of the Paris Opera House of 1866. See study by A. Mabille de Poncheville (Paris 1925).

CARPENTER, (1) Edward (1844–1929), social reformer and poet, born at Brighton, wrote *My Days and Dreams: an Autobiography*, in 1916.

(2) Mary (1807–77), philanthropist, was born at Exeter, the eldest child of Lant Carpenter, LL.D. (1780–1840), Unitarian minister. Trained as a teacher, she took an active part in the movement for the reformation of neglected children, and founded a ragged school and several reformatories for girls. Besides her reformatory writings she published *Our Convicts* (1864), *The Last Days of Rammohun Roy* (1866), and *Six Months in India* (1868). See *Mary Carpenter*, by J. E. Carpenter (1879).

(3) William Benjamin (1813–85), brother of (2), biologist, born at Exeter, studied medicine at Bristol, London, and Edinburgh. His graduation thesis (1839) on the nervous system of the invertebrates led up to his *Principles of General and Comparative Physiology* (1839). Removing to London in 1844, he was appointed Fullerian professor of Physiology at the Royal Institution, lecturer at the London Hospital and University College (1849), examiner at the University of London, and its registrar (1856–79), and, on his retirement, C.B. He did valuable research on the Foraminifera, &c. Other works are *Principles of Human Physiology* (1846), *The Microscope and its Revelations* (1856), *Principles of Mental Physiology* (1874), and *Nature and Man* (1888), with a memoir by his son, Joseph (1844–1927), theologian, lecturer at, then principal (1906–15) of, Manchester College.

(4) William Boyd (1841–1918), born at Liverpool. A favourite of Queen Victoria, he was made a royal chaplain (1879), canon of Windsor (1882) and bishop of Ripon 1884–1911, then canon of Westminster. K.C.V.O. (1912), he wrote *Some Pages of my Life* (1911) and *Further Pages* (1916), and was a great pulpit orator.

CARPINI, or Johannes de Pian del Carpine (c. 1182–c. 1253), a Franciscan monk, was born in Umbria and died Archbishop of Antivari. He was head of the mission sent by Pope Innocent IV to the emperor of the Mongols, whose warlike advances had thrown Christendom into consternation. A big, fat man, more than sixty years old, he started from Lyons in April 1245, and, crossing the Dnieper, Don, Volga, Ural, and Jaxartes, in the summer of 1246 reached Karakoram, beyond Lake Baikal, thence returning to Kiev in June 1247, and so back to Lyons. Hakluyt copied much of the Latin narrative of his travels into his *Navigations and Discoveries* (1598). See study by Beazley.

CARPOCRATES OF ALEXANDRIA, kar-pok'ra-teez, flourished in the first decades of the 2nd century A.D., and founded the Gnostic sect of Carpocratians.

CARPZOV, (1) Benedict (1595–1666), writer on law, held high offices at Dresden and Leipzig.

(2) Johann Benedict (1607–57), brother of (1), professor of Theology at Leipzig, published his *Systema Theologicum* in 1653.

CARR, (1) Edward Hallett (1892–   ), British diplomat and writer, was a member of the British delegation at Versailles in 1919, and was at the foreign office from 1922 to 1926, from when until 1947 he was professor of International Politics at the University of Wales. He is known for his books on international relations, for his studies of Dostoevsky (1931) and Marx (1937), and for his monumental *History of Soviet Russia* (1950 ff.).

(2) Joseph Williams Comyns (1849–1916), critic, playwright, and director of the New Gallery, was called to the bar in 1872.

(3) Robert. See OVERBURY.

CARRA, Carlo (1881–1966), Italian painter, born at Quergneto, Alexandria. He studied at the Brera Academy, Milan, and aligned himself at first with the Futurists, being one of the signatories of the Futurist Manifesto at the Exhibition in Paris in 1911. In 1915 he met Giorgio di Chirico and was influenced by his 'metaphysical painting' movement. Carra's aim from that time was, broadly, to synthesize the past and present; he sought, so to speak, a bridge between Giotto and Cézanne. Noteworthy canvases are *Funeral of an Anarchist*, *Metaphysical Muse*, *Penelope*, and *Le Canal*, perhaps the most famous, housed in the Zürich Museum of Modern Art.

CARRACCI. See CARACCI.

CARRANZA, Bartholomaeus de (1503–76), Spanish theologian, born at Miranda in Navarre, entered the Dominican order, became professor of Theology at Valladolid, and in 1554 accompanied Philip II to England, where he was confessor to Queen Mary, and where his zealous efforts to re-establish Catholicism gained him the confidence of Philip and the archbishopric of Toledo. Here, however, he was accused of heresy, and imprisoned by the Inquisition in 1559. In 1567 he was removed to Rome, and confined in the castle of St Angelo. He died a few days after his release.

CARREL, (1) Alexis (1873–1944), French biologist, born at Ste Foy-lès-Lyon and educated at Lyon University, member of the Rockefeller Institute in New York, winner of the Nobel prize for physiology and medicine (1912), discovered a method of suturing blood-vessels which made it possible to replace arteries. He did much research on the prolongation of the life of tissues. He died in Paris.

(2) **Armand** (1800–36), French publicist and Republican, was born at Rouen, in 1830 became editor of the *National*, and, wounded in a duel with Émile de Girardin, died two days later, July 24, 1836. Littré and Paulin edited his *Œuvres politiques et littéraires* (5 vols. 1857–58).

CARREÑO DE MIRANDA, Juan, *karrayn'yō* (1614–85), Spanish painter, born at Avilés, the successor of Velázquez at the Spanish court, painted religious pictures and frescoes.

CARRER, Luigi (1801–50), Italian poet, best known for his *Ballads* (1834), was born and died in Venice. See Life by Venanzio (1854).

CARRIER, Jean Baptiste, *kar-yay* (1756–94), infamous French revolutionist, was born at Yolai, near Aurillac. In the National Convention he helped to form the Revolutionary Tribunal, voted for the death of the king, demanded the arrest of the Duke of Orleans, and assisted in the overthrow of the Girondists. At Nantes in 1793 he massacred in four months 16,000 Vendean and other prisoners, chiefly by drowning them in the Loire (the *noyades*), but also by shooting them, as in a battue. After the fall of Robespierre, Carrier was tried, and perished by the guillotine.

CARRIERA, Rosalba (1675–1757), Italian painter, born in Venice, famed for her portraits and miniatures, some of them in pastel.

CARRIÈRE, *kar-yayr,* (1) **Eugène** (1849–1906), French artist, born at Gournay-sur-Marne, resided at Paris, and was called by E. de Goncourt ' the modern Madonna painter '. His portraits are remarkable. See study by E. Faure (1908).

(2) **Moriz** (1817–95), philosopher, born at Griedel, in Hesse, in 1853 became professor of Philosophy at Munich. Among his works (13 vols. 1886–91) are *Ästhetik* (1859) and *Kunst und Kulturentwickelung* (1863–74).

CARRINGTON, Richard Christopher (1826–1875), English astronomer, born in Chelsea and educated at Cambridge, made an important catalogue of stars at his private observatory at Redhill.

CARROLL, (1) James (1854–1907), physician, early emigrated from England to Canada and the U.S.A., was a surgeon in the American army, and in association with Reed did valuable research on yellow fever, deliberately infecting himself with the disease in the process. In 1902 he became professor of Bacteriology and Pathology at Columbia and the Army Medical School.

(2) **John** (1735–1815), first U.S. Roman Catholic Bishop. A native of Maryland, he entered the Jesuit Order in 1753 and was ordained priest in 1769. The Maryland priests petitioned Pius VI for a bishop in the U.S. and Carroll was appointed (1789) to the see of Baltimore. In 1808 he was made archbishop and the diocese was divided into four sees.

(3) **Lewis.** See DODGSON, CHARLES.

(4) **Paul Vincent** (1900–68), Irish dramatist,

born in Dundalk, became a teacher in Glasgow, where he helped to found the Citizens' Theatre. His plays include *Shadow and Substance* (1938), *The White Steed* (1939), and *The Wayward Saint* (1955).

CARSON, (1) Christopher or ' **Kit** ' (1809–68), born in Kentucky, in Missouri became a trapper and hunter. His knowledge of Indian habits and languages led to his becoming guide in Frémont's explorations, and Indian agent in New Mexico (1853). See Life by Burdett (1869).

(2) **Edward Henry, Baron** (1854–1935), lord of appeal (1921–29), was born in Dublin. Conservative M.P. (1892–1918) for Dublin University and (1918–21) for the Duncairn division of Belfast, Q.C. of the Irish Bar (1880) and English Bar (1894), solicitor-general for Ireland (1892), for England (1900–06), attorney-general (1915), first lord of the admiralty (1917), he was a member of the War Cabinet, July 1917–Jan. 1918. He organized the Ulster Volunteers, and violently opposed Home Rule. See Life by Marjoribanks and Colvin (1932–36).

CARSTAIRS, John Paddy (1914–), British novelist, film director, filmscript writer, and artist. He studied art at the Slade School, and painted a number of light-hearted landscapes in various media. His best-known novel is *Love and Ella Rafferty* (1947), and he also wrote the autobiographical *Honest Injun* (1943).

CARSTARES, William (1649–1715), Scottish divine, born near Glasgow, studied at Edinburgh and Utrecht, and became friend and adviser to the Prince of Orange. Coming to London in 1672, he was arrested in 1675, and imprisoned in Edinburgh till 1679. In 1683 he was again arrested, and put to the torture of the boot and thumbscrew. After an imprisonment of a year and a half, he returned to Holland to be chaplain to the Prince of Orange, and afterwards secured good relations between the new king and the Scottish church. From 1693 to the death of the king in 1702 he could not have had more influence in Scottish affairs if he had been prime minister; he was popularly called ' Cardinal Carstares ' by the Jacobites. He was elected principal of Edinburgh University in 1703, and in 1705–14 four times Moderator of the General Assembly. His influence helped to pass the Treaty of Union. See *Life of Carstares*, by Story (1874).

CARSTENS, Asmus Jakob (1754–98), Danish painter, was born near Schleswig, and studied art at Copenhagen; in 1783–88 barely supported himself by portrait painting in Lübeck and Berlin before his *Fall of the Angels* gained him a professorship in the Academy. He was a precursor of Overbeck and Cornelius.

CARTE, (1) Richard D'Oyly (1844–1901), a London musical instrument maker, who built the Savoy Theatre, where he produced Gilbert and Sullivan operas.

(2) **Thomas** (1686–1754), English historian, was born near Rugby, educated at both Oxford and Cambridge, and took holy orders. In 1714, however, he resigned rather than take the oaths to the Hanoverian government. In 1722 he was suspected of complicity in the

conspiracy of Atterbury, whose secretary he was, but he escaped to France, where he remained till 1728. After his return, he published a *Life of James, Duke of Ormonde* (2 vols. 1736), and a *History of England to 1654* (4 vols. 1747–55), whose prospects were blighted by an unlucky note, ascribing to the Pretender the gift of touching for the king's evil.

CARTER, (1) **Elizabeth** (1717–1806), English scholar, poet, &c., best known by her translation of Epictetus, was born at Deal, and died in London. Among her friends were Dr Johnson, Sir Joshua Reynolds, Burke, and Horace Walpole. See memoir by Gaussen (1917).

(2) **Henry.** See LESLIE, FRANK.

(3) **Howard** (1873–1939), English archaeologist, born at Swaffham, Norfolk. See CARNARVON, and his joint archaeological account with A. C. Mace (1923–33).

CARTERET, (1) **John, 1st Earl Granville** (1690–1763), English orator, diplomatist, and statesman, son of Baron Carteret, studied at Westminster School and Christ Church College, Oxford. On the accession of George I, he became, as a Whig, a Lord of the Bedchamber. In 1719 he was ambassador extraordinary to Sweden, and arranged treaties of peace between Sweden, Denmark, Hanover, and Prussia. In 1721 he was appointed one of the two foreign secretaries, and as such attended in 1723 the congress of Cambrai. As lord-lieutenant of Ireland (1724–30) he ordered the prosecution of the author, printer, and publisher of *Drapier's Letters*; on his recommendation Wood's coinage was abandoned (1725). In spite of the Drapier prosecution, Swift and he became warm friends. In 1730–42 he led in the House of Lords the party opposed to Walpole, and became the real head of the next administration, although nominally only secretary of state—his foreign policy being to support Maria Theresa. He was with George II at the battle of Dettingen (1743). Now become Earl Granville, he was driven from power by the Pelhams in 1744, though from 1751 till his death he was president of the Council under Henry Pelham, and twice refused the premiership. See Lives by Ballantyne (1887) and Pemberton (1936), and the Carteret Papers in the British Museum.

(2) **Philip** (d. 1796), English navigator, sailed as lieutenant in John Byron's voyage (1764–66), and commanded the second vessel in Wallis's expedition (August 22, 1766). Separated from Wallis next April while clearing the Strait of Magellan, he discovered Pitcairn and other small islands (one of the Solomons bears his name), and returned round the Cape of Good Hope to England, March 20, 1769. He retired in 1794, a rear-admiral, and died at Southampton.

CARTESIUS. See DESCARTES.

CARTIER, *kar-tyay*, (1) Sir **Georges Étienne** (1814–73), became attorney-general for Lower Canada in 1856, and was prime minister from 1858 to 1862. See Life by John Boyd (1915).

(2) **Jacques** (1491–1557), French navigator, discoverer of the St Lawrence, was born and died at St Malo. Between 1534 and 1541

he made three voyages of discovery to North America. See Life by Joüon des Longrais (Paris 1888), and *Memoir* with Bibliography by J. P. Baxter (N.Y. 1906).

CARTOUCHE, properly **Louis Dominique Bourgnignon** (*c.* 1693–1721), the head of a Paris band of robbers, was broken on the wheel. See work by Maurice (Paris 1859).

CARTWRIGHT, (1) **Edmund** (1743–1823), English inventor of the power loom, was born at Marnham, Notts. Educated at Wakefield and University College, Oxford, he became rector of Goadby-Marwood, Leicestershire (1779), where on his glebe he made improvements in agriculture. A visit in 1784 to Arkwright's cotton-spinning mills resulted (1785–90) in his power loom. Attempts to employ it at Doncaster and Manchester met with fierce opposition; it was not till the 19th century that it came into practical use. Cartwright also took out patents for wool-combing machines (1790) and various other inventions; he even joined Robert Fulton in his efforts after steam navigation. All these labours brought him no direct gain, but in 1809 government made him a grant of £10,000. He died at Hastings. See his Life (1843).

(2) **John** (1740–1824), the 'Father of Reform', and elder brother of (1), served in the navy (1758–70) under Howe; in 1775 he became major to the Notts militia. He now began to write on politics, advocating annual parliaments, the ballot, and manhood suffrage, and afterwards taking up reform in farming, abolition of slavery, the national defences, and the liberties of Spain and Greece. Fined £100 for sedition in 1820, he died in London. Of his eighty books and tracts a list is given in the Life by his niece (1826).

(3) **Peter** (1785–1872), Methodist preacher, born in Virginia, was ordained in Kentucky in 1806, and in 1823 removed to Illinois. In 1846 he was defeated by Abraham Lincoln in an election for congressman. See his *Autobiography* (1856), and *The Backwoods Preacher* (London 1869).

(4) **Thomas** (1535–1603), English Puritan divine, born in Hertfordshire, became in 1569 Lady Margaret professor of Divinity at Cambridge, but was deprived for his nonconforming lectures and later several times imprisoned.

(5) **William** (1611–43), English playwright, poet, and preacher, was born at Northway, near Tewkesbury, and died at Oxford. See Life by R. C. Goffin (1918).

CARUS, *kah'roos*, (1) **Julius Victor,** (1823–1903), zoologist, born at Leipzig, from 1849 to 1851 was keeper of the museum of comparative anatomy at Oxford. In 1853 he became professor of Comparative Anatomy at Leipzig.

(2) **Karl Gustav** (1789–1869), German scholar, physiologist, physician, and artist, born at Leipzig. See his *Lebenserinnerungen* (1865–66).

CARUSO, **Enrico** (1873–1921), Italian operatic tenor, was born and died at Naples. He made his first appearance in *Faust* (1895), first appeared in London in 1902 and in New York the following year. The extraordinary power and musical purity of his voice, combined with his acting ability, won him recognition as one of the greatest tenors of all time. See Life by D. Caruso (1946).

CARVER, (1) George Washington (?1860–1943), American Negro scientist, renowned for his researches on agricultural problems and on synthetic products.

(2) John (c. 1575–1621), was the leader of the Pilgrim Fathers, and died at New Plymouth, Massachusetts, within five months of their landing.

CARY, (1) Alice (1820–71), American poet, storyteller, &c., was born near Cincinnati, and removed in 1852 to New York. Her sister, Phoebe (1824–71), also wrote verse. See Mrs Ames's Memorial (1873).

(2) (Arthur) Joyce (Lunel) (1888–1957), English novelist, born at Londonderry of English parents, was educated at Tunbridge Wells and Clifton College and later studied art in Edinburgh and Paris, graduating (1912) at Oxford. He then served with the Red Cross in the Balkan war of 1912–13 and was decorated by the king of Montenegro. In 1913 he joined the Nigerian Political Service and fought in a Nigerian regiment in World War I. War injuries and ill-health dictated his early retirement after the war to Oxford, where he took up writing. Out of his African experience emerged such novels as Aissa Saved (1932), African Witch (1936), and Mister Johnson (1939), this last a high-spirited, richly humorous study of a native clerk. In 1941 he was awarded the Tait Black Memorial Prize for The House of Children, and with the trilogy, Herself Surprised (1940), To be a Pilgrim (1942), and The Horse's Mouth (1944), Cary established himself. These were followed by Moonlight (1946) and A Fearful Joy (1949), and a later trilogy on the life of Chester Nimmo, a politician, Prisoner of Grace (1952), Except the Lord (1953), and Not Honour More (1955), and The Captive and the Free (1959). Like Thomas Hardy, Cary respects the exigence of fate and reveals a compassionate despair at the muddled thinking, misconceptions, and consequent mismanagement in human relationships. He is a tough-minded realist who does not hesitate to accept what he sees—a humpty-dumpty world of which the pieces cannot be put together again; but he is too rational to indulge in hysteria, while a Dickensian gift of comedy and charity keeps him kin with his creations. See his essays Art and Reality (1958) and the study by A. Wright (1958).

(3) Henry Francis (1772–1844), English translator of Dante, was born at Gibraltar. He was educated at Rugby, Sutton Coldfield, and Birmingham, in 1790 entered Christ Church, Oxford, and in 1796 took holy orders. In 1805 he published a translation of the Inferno, in 1814 of the whole Divina Commedia. He afterwards translated Pindar's Odes and Aristophanes' Birds, and wrote memoirs in continuation of Johnson's Lives of the Poets. He was buried in Westminster Abbey. See Memoir by his son (2 vols. 1847), and Life by R. W. King (1925).

(4) John (c. 1754–1835), English cartographer, began as an engraver in London and c. 1783 became a publisher and land surveyor. His New and Correct English Atlas appeared in 1787. He prospered, and county atlases followed, with a large New Universal Atlas in 1808. In 1794, at the request of the postmaster-general, he undertook a road survey of England and Wales, the results of which were embodied in Cary's New Itinerary (1798). He was responsible for the Improved Map of England and Wales etc. (1832) on the scale of half an inch to the mile. His total output was probably not less than 1000 publications. See Sir H. G. Fordham, John Cary, map-, chart-, and print-seller and globe-maker (1925).

(5) Lucius. See FALKLAND.

(6) Sir Robert. See CAREY.

CASA, Giovanni della (1503–56), Italian author and Archbishop of Benevento, was born near Florence, and died in Rome. He is remembered for lyric verse and Galateo, a book of etiquette.

CASABIANCA, Louis (c. 1755–98), a French naval officer, born at Bastia, was captain of the flagship L'Orient at the battle of the Nile, August 1, 1798. He was mortally wounded; the ship caught fire; his ten-year-old son would not leave him; and both perished in the final explosion. The story is the subject of Mrs Hemans's famous poem.

CASALS, Pau (Pablo), ka-sals' (1876–), Spanish cellist, conductor and composer, born at Vendrell, Tarragona. He studied at the Royal Conservatory, Madrid, returning to Barcelona as professor of the Cello at the Conservatory. After playing as leading cello in the Paris Opera from 1895 to 1898, he began to appear as a soloist. With Thibaud and Cortot he formed, in 1905, a trio famed for its performance of classical works. In 1919 he founded the Barcelona Orchestra, which he conducted until he left Spain at the outbreak of the Spanish Civil War in 1936, after which he did not return. In 1950 he founded at Prades, France, an annual festival of classical chamber music. His own compositions consist of choral and chamber works. See biography by Lilian Littlehales (1948).

CASANOVA DE SEINGALT, -sī-gal', (1) Francesco (1727–1805), Italian painter, famous for his battle pieces.

(2) Giovanni Battista (1728–95), brother of (1), also a painter, from 1764 director of the Dresden Academy.

(3) Giovanni Jacopo (1725–98), brother of (1) and (2), Italian adventurer, was born at Venice, and by 1750 had been abbé, secretary to Cardinal Aquaviva, ensign, and violinist at Rome, Constantinople, Corfu, and his own birthplace, where he cured a senator of apoplexy. His irregularities drove him from Venice, but after roaming through Northern Italy and France he was back there in 1755, and was then condemned to five years' imprisonment in the 'Piombi'. In fifteen months' time he effected a daring escape, and for nearly twenty years wandered through Europe, visiting most of its capitals, and making the acquaintance of the greatest men and women of the day, from the pope to Madame de Pompadour, and from Cagliostro to Frederick the Great. Alchemist, cabalist,

knight of the papal order of the Golden Spur, and spy, he was everywhere introduced to the best society, and had always to ' vanish ' after a brief period of felicity. In 1785 he established himself with the Count of Waldstein, at his castle of Dux in Bohemia, and there he died. His clever, cynical *Mémoires écrits par lui-même* (12 vols. Leipzig 1828–38) were edited by the French poet Jean Laforgue who, set to expurgate their pornographic content, finished by embellishing them instead. The original MS., jealously guarded from human eyes by Brockhaus, the publishers, survived by lucky chance both the Napoleonic Wars, and the bombing of the firm's premises in 1943, and was finally published in the original text in 1960–61. See books by Le Gras (trans. 1923), Bleakley (1923), and Life by Maynial (trans. 1911).

CASAS, Las. See LAS CASAS.

CASAUBON, *ka-zō-bō,* (1) **Isaac** (1559–1614), French humanist, born at Geneva, was often hampered in his incessant labours by broken health and narrow means. In 1583 he became professor of Greek at Geneva; in 1586 he married the daughter of the famous Henri Stephens (q.v.). He was made Greek professor at Montpellier in 1596, and royal librarian at Paris in 1598. After the death of Henry IV his Protestantism exposed him to risk; and removing in 1610 to London, he was made a prebendary of Canterbury, and died in London. His works include *De Satyrica Graecorum Poësi et Romanorum Satira* (1605), *De Libertate Ecclesiastica* (1607), the *Exercitationes contra Baronium* (1614), and editions of Aristotle, Theophrastus, Persius, Suetonius, &c. See Life by Mark Pattison (2nd ed. 1892).

(2) **Méric** (1599–1671), son of (1), born at Geneva, studied at Oxford, and died rector of Ickham, near Canterbury. He edited Marcus Aurelius, &c., and vindicated his father in two Latin works.

CASELLA, Alfredo (1883–1947), Italian composer and musician, born in Turin, studied piano at Paris Conservatoire and first came to notice as a composer in 1908. His work, which is varied but mainly neoclassical in character, includes 3 operas, 2 symphonies, concertos for cello, violin, organ, &c., as well as chamber music, many piano pieces and songs. He produced some noteworthy editions of classical composers and wrote books on Stravinsky, Bach and Beethoven. See a study by L. Cortesi (1930).

CASEMENT, Sir Roger David (1864–1916), British consular official, born in Kingstown (now Dun Laoghaire) near Dublin, denounced Congo and Putumayo rubber atrocities. Knighted in 1911, he was degraded, and executed for high treason, having been arrested on landing in Ireland from a German submarine to head the Sinn Fein rebellion. His controversial ' Black Diaries ', revealing, among other things, homosexual practices, were long suppressed by the government but ultimately published in 1960. See study by R. MacColl (1956).

CASEY, Richard Gardiner, Baron Casey (1890–   ), Australian statesman, born in Melbourne, won the D.S.O. in 1918, and was elected to the House of Representatives in 1931. He became first Australian minister to the U.S.A. in 1940, minister of state in the Middle East (a War Cabinet rank) in 1942, and minister for external affairs in 1951. A life peerage was conferred on him in 1960.

CASIMIR, the name of many Polish sovereigns. Under Casimir I in 1041, Christianity was established. Casimir III, the Great (1310–70), king from 1333, founded Cracow university (1364).

CASIMIR-PÉRIER, *ka-zi-meer-per-yay,* **Jean Pierre Paul** (1847–1907), born at Paris, son of Casimir Périer (q.v.), was a moderate Republican deputy from 1874, became under-secretary for instruction and for war, vice-president and president of the Chamber (1885–93), premier, December 1893 to May 1894, then again president of the Chamber. On Carnot's assassination (June 1894), he was elected president of the Republic, but resigned January 15, 1895.

CASLON, William (1692–1766), English typefounder, born in Cradley, Worcestershire, set up in business as a gun engraver and toolmaker in London in 1716, but soon began cutting type for printers. The fame of his skill became widespread, and his graceful ' old face ' types were extensively used in Europe and America until the end of the 18th century, when they went out of fashion. Revived fifty years later, they have retained their popularity to the present day. His son **William** (1720–78) carried on the business.

CASORATI, Felice (1886–   ), Italian painter, born at Novara, Piedmont. A pupil of Vianello, he is one of the exponents of Italian neoclassicism and is noted for his series of portraits of women, from which may be singled out the character studies of *The Heiress* and *The Cousin.* Examples of his art are to be found throughout Italy, in Milan, Rome, Florence, &c., and also in Boston, U.S.A. See study by J. Cremona (Turin 1942).

CASPARI, Karl Paul, *kas-pah'ree* (1814–92), German theologian, born at Dessau, professor of Theology at Christiania (Oslo), wrote an Arabic grammar, works on Isaiah, Micah, Daniel, and a church history.

CASS, Lewis (1782–1866), American statesman, born at Exeter, New Hampshire, was called to the Ohio bar in 1803, but rose to be general in the war of 1812. He was then for eighteen years civil governor of Michigan, which under his skilful administration became a settled state. In 1831–36 he was secretary of war, and in 1836–42 minister at Paris. He twice failed in a try for the presidency, sat in the senate 1845–57, and was secretary of state in 1857–60. He died at Detroit. His position was generally one of compromise, but he was bitterly hostile to Britain. He published works on the Indians (1823) and France (1840).

CASSAGNAC, *ka-sa-nyak,* (1) **Adolphe Granier de** (1806–80), French journalist, came to Paris in 1832, where his vehement writing in the journals brought him many duels and law-suits. In 1840 he went to the West Indies and married a Creole. Until 1848 a zealous Orleanist, he became a strenuous imperialist, and as such represented his native department from 1852 to 1870. He became editor of the semi-official *Le Pays.*

(2) **Paul Adolphe Marie de** (1843–1904), son of (1), joined him on *Le Pays* (1866), and fought at Sedan in 1870. Violently imperialist, and as deputy (from 1876) troublesome to friends and foes, he edited the ' Victorist ' organ *Autorité.*

CASSANDER (*c.* 354–297 B.C.), from 318 ruler, from 305 king of Macedonia, son of Antipater.

CASSATT, Mary, *-sat'* (1845–1926), American impressionist painter, born at Allegheny, Pittsburgh. She studied in Spain, Italy and Holland, but worked mainly in France, where she was a pupil and close follower of Degas. Her *Woman and Child Driving* in the Philadelphia Museum is a typical work.

CASSEL, Gustav (1866–1945), Swedish economist, born at Stockholm and professor there from 1904, became known as an authority on monetary problems.

CASSELL, John (1817–65), the son of a Manchester innkeeper, came to London in 1836 as temperance advocate, in 1847 started as a tea and coffee merchant, and, turning author and publisher, in 1859 entered into partnership with Messrs Petter & Galpin. See History by S. Nowell-Smith (1958).

CASSIAN, John (360?–*c.* 435), monk, spent some years as an ascetic in the Egyptian deserts, was ordained by Chrysostom at Constantinople in 403, and afterwards instituted several monasteries in the south of France, including the Abbey of St Victor at Massilia (Marseilles), which served as a model for many in Gaul and Spain. Cassianus was one of the first of the ' semi-Pelagians '. There is an edition of his works by Gazaeus (1616). See Wiggers' *De Johanne Cassiano* (1822), and Life by Gibson in vol. xi of *Nicene and Post-Nicene Fathers* (1895).

CASSINI, Italian-French family of scientists:

(1) **Alexandre Henri Gabriel de, Vicomte** (1784–1832), son of (5), specialized in botany and wrote *Opuscules phytologiques* (1820).

(2) **César François** (1714–84), son of (4), is noted for his topographical map of France, begun 1744.

(3) **Giovanni Domenico (Jean Dominique)** (1625–1712), astronomer, father of (4), was born near Nice, in 1650 became professor of Astronomy at Bologna, and in 1669 took charge of the observatory at Paris, where he died. He greatly extended our knowledge of the sun's parallax, the periods of Jupiter, Mars, and Venus, the zodiacal light, &c.

(4) **Jacques** (1677–1756), son and successor of (3), father of (2), wrote on astronomy and electricity.

(5) **Jacques Dominique de, Comte** (1748–1845), son and successor of (2), completed his father's map. Ennobled, he was imprisoned for a time during the Revolution.

CASSIODORUS, Flavius Magnus Aurelius (*c.* 485–*c.* 580), Roman author and monk, born at Scylaceum (Squillace) in Calabria, was secretary to the great Ostrogothic king, Theodoric, quaestor and praetorian prefect, sole consul in 514, and after Theodoric's death (526) chief minister to Queen Amalasontha. His history of the Goths we possess only in Jordanes' epitome. His *Institutiones* is an encyclopaedic course of study for the monks of the Vivarium, which he founded and to which he retired.

CASSIUS, or in full, **Gaius Cassius Longinus** (d. 42 B.C.), conspirator, was quaestor to Crassus in the Parthian war (54 B.C.), saved the credit of Roman arms after the commander's disastrous defeat and death, and as tribune of the people (49) attached himself to Pompey. After Pharsalia he was taken prisoner and pardoned by Caesar. In 44 B.C. as praetor he allied himself with the aristocrats who resented Caesar's supremacy, and won over M. Brutus; and the same year Caesar was murdered. But popular feeling blazed out, and Mark Antony seized his opportunity. Cassius fled to the east, united his forces with those of Brutus, and at Philippi being routed, compelled his freedman to kill him.

CASSIUS. See DION CASSIUS.

CASSIVELLAUNUS, a British chief who fought against Caesar on his second invasion, 54 B.C.

CASSON, (1) **Sir Hugh** (1910–), British architect, educated at Cambridge, professor of Interior Design, Royal College of Art, from 1953, wrote *Homes by the Million* (1947), *Permanence and Prefabrication* (1947), *Victorian Architecture* (1948), &c., and was knighted in 1952.

(2) **Sir Lewis** (1875–1969), British actormanager and producer, born in Birkenhead, known especially for his productions of Shakespeare and Shaw, married Sybil Thorndike (q.v.) in 1908, was director of drama to C.E.M.A. (1942–45), and was knighted in 1945.

CASTAGNO, Andrea del, *kas-ta'nyō* (1409–1480), Italian painter, born at Castagno, in Tuscany. After early privations, he attracted the attention of Bernardetto de Medici, who sent him to the masters in Florence. Of his work, which is similar to Uccello's in style, the most noted example remaining is in the Hall of Justice at Florence, representing the execution of the conspirators against the house of Medici.

CASTAÑOS, Francisco Xaver de, Duke of Bailén, *kas-tan'yos* (1756–1852), a Spanish general, who in July 1808 compelled 18,000 French to surrender at Bailén, but was defeated by Lannes at Tudela. Under Wellington he took part in the battles of Albuera, Salamanca, and Vitoria.

CASTELAR, Emilio (1832–99), Spanish orator, statesman, and writer, was born at Cadiz, studied at Madrid, and in 1856 became professor there of History and Philosophy. A leader of the republicans, he fled to Paris in 1866 but returned at the 1868 revolution, and in 1873 helped to bring about the downfall of Amadeus I. For a while he held dictatorial power, but was forced to resign in 1874, and fled on Alfonso XII's accession. He returned to Spain in 1876, and till his withdrawal from public life in 1893, he often spoke in the Cortes with all his old fire and eloquence. His writings include *La civilisación en los cinco primeros siglos* (2nd ed. 1865), *Vida de Byron* (1873), and political works. See Lives by Sánchez de Real

(Madrid 1874), Araco (1900), and Varagnac (1920).

CASTELLI, Ignaz Franz (1781–1862), an Austrian poet, was born and died in Vienna. He wrote *Kriegesliedes für die österreichische Armee* (1809), which was banned by Napoleon.

CASTELLIO, Sebastianus (1515–63), a theologian, born in Savoy, studied at Lyons, and about 1540, on Calvin's recommendation, was appointed rector of a school at Geneva. His humanistic views embroiled him with the reformer; and in 1544 he was forced to migrate to Basel, where in 1553 he became Greek professor. He translated the Bible into Latin and French.

CASTELLO BRANCO, Camillo, Visconde de Correia Botelho (1825–90), Portuguese novelist. An illegitimate child whose love of literature and longing for adventure grew from his reading, Castello Branco became one of the most important of modern Portuguese novelists, with a deep understanding of the life of his people. His work ranges from romances in the style of Victor Hugo, like *The Mysteries of Lisbon*, to closely observed, imaginative interpretations of the everyday Portuguese scene, like *The Crime of Father Amara*. He was created viscount for his services to literature in 1885, and died by his own hand.

CASTELNAU, -nō, (1) Michel de (1520–92), French soldier and diplomat in the service of Henry II, ambassador in England (1575–85). See his *Memoirs*.

(2) **Noel Marie Joseph Edouard, Vicomte de Curières de** (1851–1944), born at Aveyron of a military, royalist, Catholic family, served in 1870–71, was a member of the Conseil de Guerre in 1913, took command of the Army of Lorraine in 1914, directed the Champagne offensive Sept. 1915, and (Dec.) became Joffre's chief of staff.

CASTELNUOVO-TEDESCO, Mario (1895–), Italian composer, born at Florence, studied under Pizzetti, began composing as a boy, and in 1926 brought out his opera *La Mandragola*, based on Machiavelli's book. In addition to two other operas he produced orchestral and instrumental works, but is probably best known for his songs, especially his complete series of the lyrics from Shakespeare's plays. See Von Weber, *The Book of Modern Composers* (1942).

CASTI, Giambattista (c. 1721–1803), Italian poet, born at Prato, Tuscany, took orders, but in 1764 went to Vienna, where he became poet laureate. On Joseph II's death he returned to Florence, and in 1798 removed to Paris. He wrote the *48 Novelle galanti* (Paris 1793), and *Gli animali parlanti* (1802), a political satire, freely rendered by W. S. Rose in 1819.

CASTIGLIONE, kas-teel-yō'nay, (1) Baldassare, Count (1478–1529), Italian author, was born near Mantua, and in 1505 was sent by the Duke of Urbino as envoy to Henry VII of England, who made him a knight. He lived much in Rome, and died at Toledo on an embassy for Clement VII. His chief work, *Il Cortegiano* (Eng. trans. 1561), a manual for courtiers, and his Italian and Latin poems are models of elegance; and his

Letters (1769–71) illustrate political and literary history.

(2) **Carlo Ottavio, Count** (1784–1849), numismatist, editor of Ulfilas, &c., was born at Milan and died at Genoa.

CASTILLEJO, Cristóval de, kas-teel-yay'hō (c. 1490–1556), last of the Spanish court poets, was born at Ciudad Rodrigo, and died in Vienna.

CASTLE, William Ernest (1867–1962), American biologist, educated at Harvard, professor of Geology there (1897) and later of Genetics (1908–36), carried out important research in the field of natural selection.

CASTLEREAGH, Robert Stewart, Viscount, kas'l-ray (1769–1822), was the son of an Ulster proprietor, who in 1789 was created Baron Londonderry, in 1795 Viscount Castlereagh, in 1796 Earl, and in 1816 Marquis, of Londonderry. Robert was educated at Armagh, and, after spending a year at St John's College, Cambridge, was making the Grand Tour of Europe when in 1790 he was returned to the Irish parliament as Whig member for County Down—the election cost his father £60,000. He turned Tory in 1795, and next year became keeper of the Privy Seal; but he continued a steadfast supporter of Catholic emancipation. As Irish chief-secretary from 1797, he bent his whole energies to forwarding Pitt's measure of Union—a measure carried in 1800, largely through Castlereagh's skill in buying up the borough-mongers; but Pitt's pledges to the Catholics were defeated by George III's bigotry, and Castlereagh, with Pitt, retired from office. In the weak Addington ministry (1802) he was president of the Board of Control; however, he held the post of war minister from July 1805 to January 1806, and again from April 1807 to September 1809. The bombardment of Copenhagen and seizure of the Danish fleet, the extension of the war to the Peninsula, and selection of Wellesley for general, may be set off against the Walcheren expedition, whose failure was due to the mistaken policy of giving Lord Chatham its command. Castlereagh was made the scapegoat, and the shilly-shally behaviour of his colleagues caused him to challenge his great rival, Canning. On September 21, 1809, they met upon Putney Heath, and, at the second fire, Canning received a slight wound in the thigh. Castlereagh's real greatness began in March 1812, when, as foreign secretary under Lord Liverpool, he became the soul of the coalition against Napoleon in 1813–14. He represented England at the congresses of Châtillon and Vienna in 1814–15, at the treaty of Paris in 1815, at the congress of Aix-la-Chapelle in 1818; and he was preparing to start for a congress at Verona, when he committed suicide with a penknife at Foots Cray, his Kentish seat. England and Europe owe much to Castlereagh for the forty years' peace that succeeded Napoleon's downfall. Yet no statesman, save Strafford, was ever pursued with more rancorous hatred—a hatred that raised a shout of exultation as he was borne to his grave in Westminster Abbey. He had succeeded his father as second marquis in 1821, and was himself succeeded by his half-brother, **Sir Charles Stewart** (1778–1854), a gallant soldier, diplomatist, and statesman, who edited Castlereagh's *Correspondence and Despatches* (12 vols. 1847–53). See works by Alison (3 vols. 1861), Lady Londonderry (1904), A. Hassall (1909), Webster (2 vols. 1925–31), H. M. Hyde (1933 and 1959), and Leigh (1951); and Lord Salisbury's essay.

CASTNER, Hamilton Young (1859–99), American analytical chemist, educated at Columbia, came to Britain and invented a new process for the isolation of sodium from brine by electrolysis.

CASTRÉN, Matthias Alexander (1813–52), Finnish philologist, born at Tervola, a pioneer in the study of Finno-Ugrian, and Ural-Altaic, carried out ethnographic researches in Lapland, Siberia, and China. See his *Life* by Shellman (1870). A son, **Robert** (1851–83), wrote on Finnish history.

CASTRIOT, George. See SKANDERBEG.

CASTRO, (1) **Cipriano** (*c.* 1858–1924), Venezuelan dictator, born near San Antonio, became supreme military leader (1899) and president (1902–08). His dictatorship involved Venezuela in financial troubles and a blockade of its ports (1902). Deposed in 1908, he died in exile.

(2) **Eugenio de** (1869–1944), Portuguese poet, born in Coimbra. He became professor of Portuguese Literature at his native town and travelled widely in Europe. In Paris he became influenced by symbolism, which, through him, influenced Portuguese literature —especially with his *Oaristos* (1890).

(3) **Fidel** (1927–), Cuban revolutionary, son of a successful sugar planter, studied law and practised in Havana, fighting cases on behalf of the poor and against the official corruption and oppression which were rife under President Batista. In July 1953, with his brother Raul, also an ardent revolutionary, he led an unsuccessful rising and was sentenced to 15 years' imprisonment, but, released under an amnesty within a year, he fled to the U.S.A. and thence to Mexico, all the time organizing anti-Batista activities. In 1956 he landed in Cuba with a small band of insurgents, but was betrayed and ambushed, barely escaping into the Sierra Maestra mountains, whence he waged a relentless guerrilla campaign. The degeneration of Cuba into a police state brought many recruits to his cause, and in December 1958 he mounted a full-scale attack and Batista was forced to flee. Castro, prime minister from February 1959, proclaimed a ' Marxist-Leninist programme ' adapted to local requirements. He set about far-reaching reforms in agriculture, industry, and education, not all immediately successful, but sufficiently so to enable his regime to gather strength. His overthrow of U.S. dominance in the economic sphere and routing of the U.S. connived emigré invasion at the Bay of Pigs (April 1961) was balanced by consequent dependence on Communist (mainly Russian) aid and the near-disaster of the ' missiles crisis ' of 1962.

(4) **Guillen de** (1569–1631), dramatist, was born in Valencia, commanded a Neapolitan fortress, but later lived in Madrid, and died in poverty. To his *Las Mocedades del Cid* Corneille was deeply indebted. See Lord Holland's *Lives of Lope de Vega and Castro* (1817).

(5) **Inez de** (d. 1355), the daughter of a Spanish nobleman, in 1340 came to Portugal in the train of her cousin Costança, the bride of the Infante, Dom Pedro. Her beauty captivated him, and, after Costança's death in 1345, he made her his mistress, in 1354 his wife. But by authority of his father, Alfonso IV, she was stabbed to death.

(6) **João de** (1500–48), Portuguese soldier, born at Lisbon, volunteered against the Moors at Tangiers, accompanied Charles V to Tunis, and had already fought and travelled in the East, when in 1545 he sailed to India at the head of a small expedition. Here, after his heroic relief and defence of Diu, he was appointed Portuguese viceroy, but died in the arms of Francis Xavier.

CATALANI, Angelica, *ka-ta-lah'nee* (1779–1849), Italian singer, born at Sinigaglia, was educated in a convent near Rome, where at six she displayed wonderful vocal powers. She made her début at Venice in 1797, and had a succession of triumphs in every country in Europe for over thirty years.

CATALDI, Pierre Antoine, *ka-tal'dee* (1548–1626), Italian mathematician, professor of the University of Bologna, founded there one of the first mathematical academies.

CATESBY, *kayts'-,* (1) **Mark** (*c.* 1679–1749), naturalist, was probably born and died in London, and travelled in North America in 1710–19 and 1722–26.

(2) **Robert** (1573–1605), was a Northamptonshire Catholic of good fortune and lineage, being sixth in descent from Richard III's Catesby, hanged three days after Bosworth. Robert had suffered much as a recusant both by fines and imprisonment, when in 1604 he engaged in the Gunpowder Plot. He was shot dead in the defence of Holbeach House.

CATHARINE, St, (1) a virgin of royal descent in Alexandria, who publicly confessed the gospel at a sacrificial feast appointed by the Emperor Maximinus, and was beheaded, after they had vainly attempted to torture her on a toothed (later known as a ' catherine ') wheel, A.D. 307.

(2) **St Catharine of Siena** (1347–80), was the daughter of a dyer in Siena. She became a Dominican, and so is their patron saint. Her enthusiasm converted hardened sinners, and she prevailed on Pope Gregory XI to return from Avignon to Rome. Christ's stigmata were said to be imprinted on her body. She was canonized in 1461. She wrote devotional pieces, letters, and poems (ed. by Tomasseo, 1860); her *Dialogue* was translated in 1896. See books by Antony (1916) and Undset (trans. 1954) and Keyes, *Three Ways of Love* (1964). Other saints are **Catharine of Bologna** (1413–63). **Catharine of Sweden** (see St Bridget), and **Catharine Ricci** (1522–89), a Tuscan prioress.

CATHARINE, name of two empresses of Russia:

Catharine I (*c.* 1684–1727), was the daughter of a Lithuanian peasant, her original name being Martha Skavronska. Left an orphan, she was brought up by a Lutheran pastor at Marienburg in Livonia. In 1702 she married a Swedish dragoon, but Marienburg being taken by the Russians, she became the mistress of Prince Menshikov, and then of Peter the Great, being in 1703 baptized into the Greek Church as Catharine Alexievna. She was married to the emperor in 1712, and on Peter's death in 1725 was acknowledged Empress of Russia, when she surrendered herself to Menshikov's direction.

Catharine II (1729–96), 'the great', was born at Stettin, daughter of the Prince of Anhalt-Zerbst, and was married to Peter, heir to the Russian throne, in 1745. She soon quarrelled with her husband, and became notorious for her intimacy first with Saltykov and then with Poniatowski. After Peter III's accession in 1762, the conjugal differences became continually wider. Catharine was banished to a separate abode, till Peter was dethroned by a conspiracy, and Catharine made empress. A few days afterwards Peter was murdered (July 1762). Catharine now made a show of regard for the Greek Church, although her principles were those of the French philosophers. The government was carried on with great energy; and the dominions and power of Russia rapidly increased. When discontent was manifested, the young prince Ivan, the hope of the disaffected, was murdered in the castle of Schlüsselburg. From that time internal politics consisted of court intrigues for and against one favourite or another, Potemkin (q.v.) being the best known. The first partition of Poland in 1772 and the Turkish war (1774) vastly increased the empire; so did a war with Sweden (1790) and another Turkish war (1792). The second and third partitions of Poland, and the incorporation of Courland with Russia, completed the triumphs of Catharine's reign. She was a woman of great ability, though she had in full the vices of her time and station. See her *Memoirs* (trans. 1927); also works by Waliszewski (trans. 1894), Princess Lucien Murat (trans. 1929), and G. Scott-Thomson (1947).

CATHARINE DE' MEDICI (French **Médicis**) (1519–89), wife of one king of France, and mother of three, was the daughter of Lorenzo de' Medici, Duke of Urbino, and was born at Florence. In her fourteenth year she was married to Henry, second son of Francis I, but was slighted at the French court, even after the accession of her husband. On the accession of her eldest son, Francis II, in 1559, she found some scope for her ambition; and on the accession of her second son, Charles IX, in 1560, the government fell entirely into her hands. She sought to rally the Huguenot leaders around the throne to serve as a counterpoise to the Guises. But after the peace of Amboise, she became alarmed at the increase of the Protestant power, and entered into a secret treaty with Spain, and into a plot with the Guises, which resulted in the fearful massacre of St Bartholomew's Day. She got her third son elected to the Polish throne. But her tyrannical administration at home roused a Catholic party, headed by her fourth son, the Duke of Alençon; and it was believed that she was privy to the machinations that led to his

death. When, after Charles IX's death, Henry III returned from Poland to be king of France, his mother still ruled the court; but having betrayed all who trusted them, she and her son were abhorred by Catholic and Protestant alike. She died at Blois. See works by E. Sichel (1905 and 1908), L. Romier (1925), J. E. Neale (1943), and her letters (1880–99).

CATHARINE HOWARD. See HOWARD Family (5).

CATHARINE OF ARAGON (1485–1536), queen of England, was the first wife of Henry VIII, and fourth daughter of Ferdinand and Isabella. Married on November 14, 1501, when scarcely sixteen, to Arthur (1486–1502), Prince of Wales, she was left a widow on April 2, and on June 25, was betrothed to her brother-in-law Henry, as yet a boy only eleven years old. The pope's dispensation enabling such near relatives to marry was obtained in 1504, and the marriage took place in June 1509, seven weeks after Henry's accession to the crown. Between 1510 and 1518 she bore him five children, one only of whom, the Princess Mary, survived; but, though Henry was very far from being a model husband, and though he had conceived a passion for Anne Boleyn (q.v.) as early as 1522, he appears to have treated Queen Catharine with all due respect until 1527. He now expressed doubts as to the legality of his marriage, and set about obtaining nullification, which, all other means failing, was at length pronounced by Cranmer in May 1533. Queen Catharine, who had offered a dignified passive resistance, lived at Ampthill, in Bedfordshire, and afterwards at Kimbolton Castle, Hunts, where she led an austere religious life until she died—apparently of cancer of the heart. See Froude's *Divorce of Catharine of Aragon* (1891) and G. Mattingly, *Catharine of Aragon* (1950).

CATHARINE OF BRAGANZA (1638–1705), was the daughter of the Duke of Braganza, who in 1640 became John IV of Portugal. In May 1662 she was married at Portsmouth to Charles II (q.v.), seven years after whose death—she mourned it deeply—she returned to Portugal. See Life by L. L. Davidson (1908).

CATHARINE OF VALOIS (1401–37), the youngest daughter of Charles VI of France, in 1420 was married at Troyes to Henry V (q.v.) of England; in 1421 gave birth to Henry VI; and, after Henry V's death (1422), married Owen Tudor, a poor Welsh squire, her son by whom, Edmund, was Henry VII's father. Catharine died at Bermondsey Abbey. See vol. iii. of Miss Strickland's *Queens of England.*

CATHARINE PARR. See PARR (1).

CATHCART, (1) Charles Murray, 2nd Earl (1783–1859), eldest son of (3), long known as Lord Greenock, served with high distinction in Spain and at Waterloo, and in 1846–49 was commander-in-chief in British North America.

(2) **Sir George** (1794–1854), a younger son of (3), served with the Russians in the campaigns of 1812 and 1813, and as aide-de-camp to Wellington was present at Quatre Bras and Waterloo. After helping to suppress the

Canadian rebellion of 1835, and being deputy-lieutenant of the Tower, in 1852 as governor at the Cape he brought to a successful end the Kaffir war. He fell as a general of division at Inkermann (November 5). He wrote valuable *Commentaries on the War in Russia and Germany in 1812–13* (London 1850).

(3) **William Schaw, 1st Earl Cathcart** (1755–1843), son of the ninth Baron Cathcart, was educated for the bar at Eton and Glasgow, but entering the army, served in the wars in America, Flanders, and Germany. In 1803–1805 he was commander-in-chief in Ireland; in 1807 commanded the land forces at Copenhagen, and was made Viscount Cathcart. Sent in 1813 as ambassador to St Petersburg, he accompanied the Tsar Alexander in his campaigns; in 1814 he was made an earl.

CATHELINEAU, Jacques, *ka-tė-lee-nō* (1759–93), Vendean leader, was born at Pin-en-Mauge, Lower Anjou. In 1793, at the head of a handful of recruits, he became famous for his exploits, the greatest of them the storming of Cholet, and supreme command was forced upon him after the victory of Saumur. He was mortally wounded while attacking Nantes.

CATHER, Willa Sibert, *ka'THėr* (1876–1947), American authoress, born at Winchester, Va., brought up on a Nebraska ranch, excelled in descriptions of the Middle West. Her first great success was *O Pioneers* (1913), other novels include the Pulitzer prizewinner *One of Ours* (1922), *A Lost Lady* (1923), *Death Comes for the Archbishop* (1927), and *Sapphira and the Slave Girl* (1940). See study by Daiches (1951).

CATHERINE. See CATHARINE.

CATILINA, Lucius Sergius, angl. **Catiline,** *kat-i-lī'na* (c. 108–62 B.C.), Roman conspirator, born of an impoverished family, fell into profligacy and crime. An adherent of Sulla, he was elected praetor in 68, and next year governor of Africa, but was disqualified for the consulship in 66 by charges of maladministration. Disappointed and burdened with debts, he entered into a conspiracy with other Roman nobles like himself; but the plot was revealed to Cicero by Fulvia, mistress of one of them. In November 63 Catiline explained to his confederates a plan for assassinating Cicero and the hostile senators, and other details of a complete revolution—details soon made known to Cicero. When the chosen assassins came to the house of the consul, they were repulsed; and when two days later Catiline appeared in the senate, Cicero made his famous speech against him. Catiline's reply was drowned in cries of execration. He escaped from Rome, but Lentulus, Cethegus, and others of the conspirators were arrested and executed. Insurrections in several parts of Italy were suppressed; and in January 62 Catiline encountered the forces of the republic at Pistoria (now Pistoia), and after a desperate battle was defeated and slain. Sallust's *Bellum Catilinarium* is a historical masterpiece.

CATINAT, Nicolas, *ka-tee-na* (1637–1712), marshal of France, born in Paris, died near St Denis. He defeated Amadeus II of Savoy at Staffarda (1690) and Marsaglia (1693).

CATLIN, George (1796–1872), American ethnologist, was born at Wilkes-Barre, Pa., and bred to the law, but soon turned to drawing and painting. During 1832–40 he was studying the Indians of the Far West, everywhere painting portraits (470 full length) and pictures illustrative of life and manners, now in the National Museum at Washington. Catlin spent eight years in Europe with a Far West show; travelled (1852–57) in South and Central America; and again lived in Europe until 1871. He died at Jersey City. His works include *Manners of the North American Indians* (2 vols. 1841), *The North American Portfolio* (1844), and *Last Rambles in the Rocky Mountains* (1868).

CATO, (1) **Dionysius,** the name prefixed to a 4th-century volume of 164 moral precepts in Latin dactylic hexameters, which was a great favourite during the Middle Ages. The author is unknown. An English version by Benedict Burgh was printed by Caxton before 1479; see text and translation in *Minor Classical Poets* (Loeb 1934).

(2) **Marcus Porcius** (234–149 B.C.), ' the Elder ', was born at Tusculum. He distinguished himself at the capture of Tarentum (209), and in the second Punic War; and became successively quaestor, aedile, praetor, and consul (195). In Spain he crushed a formidable insurrection; and in 191 he gained glory in the campaign against Antiochus. Meanwhile, he strove to stem the tide of Greek refinement and luxury, and advocated a return to a simpler and stricter social life after the ancient Roman pattern. In 184 elected censor, he discharged so rigorously the duties of his office that ' Censor ' became his permanent surname. He repaired watercourses, paved reservoirs, cleansed drains, raised the rents paid by the tax-farmers and reduced the contract prices paid by the state. More questionable reforms were those in regard to the price of slaves, dress, furniture, equipages, and the like. Good and bad innovations he opposed with equal intolerance. Sent on a mission to Carthage in 175, he was so impressed with the dangerous power of the Carthaginians that afterwards he ended every speech in the senate with the words: ' Moreover, I vote that Carthage must be destroyed '. He wrote several works, of which only the *De Re Rustica* (ed. by Keil, Leipzig 1884–1902), and a few fragments of his *Origines*, a summary of the Roman annals, have been preserved. We possess his life by Cornelius Nepos, Plutarch, and Aurelius Victor.

(3) **Marcus Porcius** (95–46 B.C.), ' the Younger ', great-grandson of (2), called **Uticensis** from the place of his death, was born 95 B.C., and served in the campaign against Spartacus. Military tribune in 67, he brought back with him from Greece the Stoic philosopher Athenodorus. As quaestor he carried through a rigorous reform into the treasury offices. As tribune (63) he delivered a famous speech denouncing Caesar as an accomplice of Catiline, and began a course of strenuous opposition to Crassus, Pompey, and Caesar, which hastened the formation of the first triumvirate. He was

afterwards forced to side with Pompey, and after the battle of Pharsalia (48) escaped into Africa, and undertook the defence of Utica. When he had tidings of Caesar's decisive victory at Thapsus (46), he resolved to die rather than surrender; and, after spending the night reading Plato's *Phaedo*, committed suicide by stabbing himself in the breast.

CATROUX, Georges, *kat-roo* (1879–1969), French general, born in Algiers, served in World War I, was governor-general of Indo-China (1939–40), commanded the Free French forces in Syria and the Near East in 1940–41, and became governor-general of Algeria in 1943. In 1945–46 he was ambassador in Russia.

CATS, Jacob (1577–1660), Dutch statesman and poet, was born at Brouwershaven in Zeeland, and after studying law at Leyden and Orleans, settled at Middelburg. He rose to high office in the state, and was twice ambassador in England (1627 and 1652). From this time till his death, 'Father Cats' lived at his villa near the Hague, writing the autobiography printed in the 1700 edition of his Poems.

CATTERMOLE, George (1800–68), English watercolour painter and book illustrator, born at Dickleborough, Norfolk, known for his antiquarian and architectural paintings, and for his illustrations of the Waverley Novels.

CATULLUS, Gaius Valerius, *-tul'-* (*c.* 84–*c.* 54 B.C.), greatest lyric poet of ancient Italy, born at Verona. He lived mainly at Rome, where he settled about 62 B.C., and at his villas at Tibur and Sirmio. He began to write verses when a boy of sixteen. In Rome he became intimate with Cicero, the Metelli, Hortensius, and probably Lucretius; and in Rome he met the 'Lesbia' to whom he sang in verses unequalled in the lyric poetry of passion. A final rupture seems to have happened in 57 B.C., and in that year Catullus accompanied Memmius to his province of Bithynia. He returned to Rome disappointed in his hopes of enriching himself, and entered impetuously as an aristocrat into the contest of parties. A fiery, unscrupulous partisan, he assailed his enemies, including Julius Caesar, with equal scurrility and wit. In all probability he did not survive the year 54 B.C. His extant works comprise 116 pieces, many of them extremely brief, while the longest contains only some 400 lines. But in this slender body of poetry, there are, besides the magnificent love poems, graceful, playful verses of society, fierce, satiric poems, elaborate descriptive and mythological pieces (some of them adapted from the Greek), and the strange, wild, imaginative *Attis*. The text of the works, lost for more than three hundred years, was discovered in the 14th century at Verona; three important MSS. survive. See studies by Munro (1905), and Quinn (1960).

CAUCHY, Augustin Louis, Baron, *kō-shee* (1789–1857), French mathematician, the founder with Bolzano of the theory of functions, was born in Paris. His *Mémoire sur la théorie des ondes* (1815) helped to establish the undulatory theory of light; at Prague, where he resided as tutor to the Comte de Chambord, he published his *Mémoire sur la dispersion de la lumière* (1837). He was professor of Astronomy at Paris (1848–52), but refused the oath of allegiance to Napoleon III. See his Life by Valson (1868).

CAULAINCOURT, Armand de, *kō-lĭ-koor* (1772–1827), was made a general of division in 1805, and shortly after created Duke of Vicenza. Faithful to the last to Napoleon, he was minister for foreign affairs in 1813, and during the Hundred Days resumed the office, receiving a peerage of France, of which he was deprived after the restoration. See his *Souvenirs* (1837–40).

CAUS, or Caulx, Salomon de, *kō* (1576–1626), a Huguenot engineer, who was born at Dieppe, and died in Paris, but spent much of his time in England and Germany. His *Les Raisons des forces mouvantes avec diverses machines* (1615) has led some to claim for him the invention of the steam engine.

CAVAIGNAC, Louis Eugène, *ka-vay-nyak* (1802–57), French general, born in Paris, was a son of General Jean Baptiste Cavaignac (1762–1829), a member of the National Convention. Exiled to Algeria as a republican (1832), he became governor-general there in 1848, but was soon called to Paris and became minister of war. As military dictator he quelled the formidable insurrection of June. On the *coup d'état* of December 1851 he was arrested but soon released; and though he refused to adhere to the Empire, he was permitted to reside in France. See Life by Deschamps (2 vols. 1870).

CAVALCANTI, *-kan'tee*, (1) **Bartolommeo** (1503–62), a noble Florentine, led a revolt against the Medici, and was afterwards employed by Pope Paul III.

(2) **Guido** (*c.* 1230–1300), Italian poet and friend of Dante, married a Ghibelline, and was banished by the Guelphs. He returned to Florence only to die. See works by Capasso (Pisa 1879) and Ercole (Milan 1885).

CAVALCASELLE, Giovanni Battista, *-sel'lay* (1820–97), Italian art writer, born at Legnano, known for his joint authorship, with Sir J. A. Crowe, of *Early Flemish Painters* (1856), *History of Painting in Italy* (1864–71), and other authoritative works.

CAVALIER, Jean, *ka-val-yay* (1681–1740), a baker of Anduze, who in 1702 became a famous leader of the Huguenot Camisards, being a prophet and preacher. He surrendered to Villars in 1704, and entered the service of Savoy. He settled with a British pension in England, and died at Chelsea, governor of Jersey.

CAVALIERI, (1) Emilio de' (*c.* 1550–99), Italian composer, born in Rome, lived mainly at the Florentine court of the Medici.

(2) **Francesco Bonaventura** (1598–1647), Italian mathematician, born at Milan, whose 'method of indivisibles' began a new era in geometry and paved the way for the introduction of integral calculus.

CAVALLI, Francesco, *née* Caletti-Bruni (*c.* 1600–76), Italian composer, born at Crema, assumed the name of his patron. A pupil of Monteverdi, he was organist and *maestro di capella* of St Mark's in Venice, where he died. As a dramatic composer he prepared the way for Scarlatti. See studies by T. Wiel (Venice 1914) and H. Prunières (Paris 1931).

CAVALLINI, Pietro, *ka-va-lee'nee* (1259–1344), Roman painter and artist in mosaic, a contemporary of Giotto. His mosaics in S. Maria in Trastevere are notable.

CAVAZZOLA, Paolo (1486–1522), painter, was born and died at Verona.

CAVE, (1) Edward (1691–1754), ' Sylvanus Urban ', born at Newton near Rugby, set up a small printing office in London, and in 1731 started the *Gentleman's Magazine.* Samuel Johnson became its parliamentary reporter in 1740.

(2) **William** (1637–1713), English church historian, born at Pickwell, died a canon of Windsor.

CAVEDONE, Giacomo, *ka-ve-dō'nay* (1577–1660), painter, was born at Sassuolo, assisted Guido Reni at Rome, and settled in Bologna.

CAVELL, Edith, *kav'él* (1865–1915), English nurse, second daughter of rector of Swardeston, Norfolk, tended friend and foe alike in Brussels in 1914–15, yet was ruthlessly executed (October 12) by the Germans for helping Belgian and Allied fugitives. See Life by A. A. Hoehling (1958).

CAVENDISH, the surname of the ducal house of Devonshire, a family directly descended from the chief-justice Sir John Cavendish, who in 1381 was beheaded at Bury St Edmunds by Jack Straw's followers; and from Sir William Cavendish of Cavendish, Suffolk (*c.* 1505–57), a brother of Wolsey's biographer. His third wife, the celebrated ' Bess of Hardwick ', afterwards Countess of Shrewsbury, brought Chatsworth into the family; and William, their second son, was in 1618 made Earl of Devonshire. See E. C. Williams, *Bess of Hardwick* (1959).

(1) **William, 1st Duke** (1640–1707), succeeded as 4th earl in 1684. A steadfast Whig under the last two Stuarts, he was made Duke of Devonshire and Marquis of Hartington (1694) in recognition of his services to the Revolution.

(2) **William, 4th Duke** (1720–64), great-grandson of (1), succeeded in 1755, and was prime minister 1756–57.

(3) **William, 5th Duke** (1748–1811), wrote poetry. His beautiful duchess, Lady Georgiana Spencer, is immortalized in the paintings of Gainsborough and Reynolds.

(4) **William, 6th Duke** (1790–1858), was chiefly distinguished by his sumptuous embassy to St Petersburg (1826).

(5) **William, 7th Duke** (1808–91), had for twenty-four years been Earl Burlington when he succeeded his cousin (4) as duke.

(6) **Spencer Compton, 8th Duke** (1833–1908), eldest son of (5), but for thirty-three years known as Marquis of Hartington, was educated at Trinity College, Cambridge, and entered parliament in 1857. The representative of a great Whig house, he was chosen as early as 1859 to move the vote of want of confidence that overthrew the Derby government, and between 1863 and 1874 held office as a lord of the admiralty, under-secretary for war, war-secretary, postmaster-general, and, from 1871, chief-secretary for Ireland. Neither a born statesman nor great orator, he yet showed an ' infinite capacity

for taking pains ', when, in February 1875, on Mr Gladstone's temporary abdication, he was chosen leader of the Liberal opposition. He led it admirably, and in the spring of 1880, on the downfall of the Beaconsfield administration, was invited by the Queen to form a ministry. He rejected the offer, and served under Mr Gladstone, first as secretary of state for India, and then as war-secretary from 1883 to 1885. But disapproving Irish Home Rule, he became head of the Liberal Unionists from 1886, and served in the Unionist government as lord president of the Council from 1895 till 1903, when as a free trader he withdrew. See Life by Holland (1911). His younger brother, **Lord Frederick Cavendish** (1836–82), was Liberal M.P. for the northern division of the West Riding of Yorkshire from 1865 till the spring of 1882, when he was appointed chief-secretary for Ireland, but immediately after arrival in Dublin was murdered by ' Irish Invincibles ' in Phoenix Park (see CAREY (3)).

'CAVENDISH'. See JONES (7).

CAVENDISH, (1) George (*c.* 1500–*c.* 1562), the biographer of Wolsey, became Wolsey's gentleman-usher at least as early as 1527. In attendance upon his great master till the end (November 28, 1530), he afterwards retired to his house at Glemsford, in Suffolk, where he lived quietly with his wife, a niece of Sir Thomas More, till the close of his own life. He wrote a *Life of Cardinal Wolsey,* first published in 1641.

(2) **Henry** (1731–1810), natural philosopher, eldest son of Lord Charles Cavendish, and a grandson of the second Duke of Devonshire, was born at Nice. From a school at Hackney he passed in 1749 to Peterhouse, Cambridge, but quitted it three years later without a degree; thereafter he devoted the whole of his long life to scientific investigations, having had a large fortune bequeathed him by an uncle. A silent, solitary man, he had his magnificent library in London, four miles from his residence on Clapham Common, so that he might not encounter persons coming to consult it. His female domestics had orders to keep out of his sight, on pain of dismissal. His dinner he ordered daily by a note placed on the hall table. He died, unmarried, leaving more than a million sterling to his relatives. Cavendish may almost be called the founder of pneumatic chemistry. In 1760 he discovered the extreme levity of inflammable air, now known as hydrogen gas—a discovery which led to balloon experiments; and later, he ascertained that water resulted from the union of two gases—a discovery which has erroneously been claimed for Watt. The famous Cavendish Experiment was an ingenious device for estimating the density of the earth. Cavendish also wrote on astronomical instruments; his *Scientific Papers* were edited by Clerk Maxwell, Larmor, and Thorpe (1921). The Cavendish Physical Laboratory at Cambridge was named after him and contains most of his apparatus. See Life by G. Wilson (1846), and *A History of the Cavendish Laboratory* (1910).

(3) **Thomas** (*c.* 1555–92), circumnavigator, was born at Trimley St Martin, near Ipswich,

and, after squandering his patrimony at court, shared in Grenville's expedition to Virginia (1585). On July 21, 1586, he sailed from Plymouth with 123 men and three ships of 40, 60, and 140 tons, and, by Sierra Leone and Brazil, reached the Strait of Magellan. During the nine months on the Pacific he burned three Spanish towns and thirteen ships; then, with a rich booty, but only his largest vessel, he returned by the Cape of Good Hope to England, September 10, 1588. Elizabeth knighted him. A second expedition (1591) ended in utter disaster, and Cavendish died broken-hearted off Ascension.

(4) **William, Duke of Newcastle** (1592–1676), son of Sir Charles Cavendish, and nephew of the first Earl of Devonshire, was educated at St John's College, Cambridge. James I in 1610 created him Knight of the Bath, and in 1620 Viscount Mansfield. Charles I, who was splendidly entertained by him at Welbeck and Bolsover, in 1628 created him Earl of Newcastle, and in 1638 appointed him governor to his son, afterwards Charles II. His support of the king in the Civil War was munificent. As general of all the forces north of the Trent, he had power to issue declarations, confer knighthood, coin money, and raise men; the last function he executed with great zeal. After Marston Moor (1644) he lived on the Continent, at times in great poverty, till the Restoration. In 1665 he was created Duke of Newcastle. He was author of two works on horsemanship, and of several poor plays. See his Life by his second wife (1667; new editions, 1886, 1915). She, **Margaret Lucas** (1624–74), the daughter of an Essex house, where ' all the brothers were valiant, and all the sisters virtuous ', had married him in 1645, and herself wrote a dozen folio volumes of poems, plays, letters, &c. See E. Jenkins, *The Cavalier and his Lady* (new ed. 1893).

CAVENTOU, Joseph Bienaimé, *ka-vã-too* (1795–1878), French chemist, professor at the École de Pharmacie, Paris, in 1817 in collaboration with Pelletier introduced the term *chlorophyll*. They also discovered quinine (1820), strychnine, brucine, and cinchonine.

CAVOUR, Count Camillo Benso di (1810–61), Italian statesman and restorer of Italian nationality, was born at Turin, of an ancient Piedmontese house. His liberal opinions led him in 1831 to retire from the army; and devoting himself to agriculture, he vastly improved the family estates. He widened his economic and political knowledge by travel in France and England. In conjunction with Count Cesare Balbo, he in 1847 established a newspaper, *Il Risorgimento*, in which he advocated a representative system; and on his suggestion, the king was petitioned for a constitution, which was granted in February 1848. Cavour strenuously opposed the ultrademocrats, and counselled alliance with England. In D'Azeglio's ministry he had an important place; and from 1852, when he succeeded D'Azeglio as premier, till his resignation in 1859, he was the originator and director of the Sardinian policy. Superintending also finance, commerce, agriculture, home office, and foreign affairs, he greatly improved the financial condition, introduced free-trade measures, consolidated constitutionalism, weakened clerical influence, and made Sardinia a power in Europe. Through his advice Sardinia took part in the Crimean war, and so he managed to bring the Italian question before the Congress of Paris in 1856. In 1858 he planned with Napoleon to drive Austria out of Italy, and in 1859 he conducted with masterly tact and astuteness a diplomatic contest with Austria. The peace of Villafranca, leaving Venetia Austrian, was a bitter disappointment, and Cavour resigned; returning, however, to his great task in 1860. Popular feeling in central Italy declared for union with the north, and thus Parma, Modena, and Tuscany came under the sway of Victor Emmanuel; but Cavour had to purchase the acquiescence of France by the surrender of Nice and Savoy. He secretly encouraged the expedition of Garibaldi, which in 1860 achieved the deliverance of Sicily and southern Italy. In 1861 an Italian parliament was summoned, and Victor Emmanuel was declared king of Italy, though Rome and Venetia still were wanting. Thus had Cavour achieved his task, but not without a fearful strain on his health, and he died June 6, 1861. See works by De la Rive (trans. 1863), Bianchi (1885), Whyte (1925, 1930), D. M. Smith (1954), his *Lettere* (1883–87).

CAXTON, William (c. 1422–c. 1491), the first English printer, was born in the Weald of Kent, possibly at Tenterden. In 1438 he was apprenticed to Robert Large, a London mercer who was lord mayor in 1439–40 and died in 1441. Caxton then went to Bruges, where he prospered and was in 1462–70 acting ' governor of the English nation ', i.e. of the Merchant Adventurers. He had diplomatic dealings with Burgundy and the Hanse. In 1471 he attached himself to the household of Margaret, Duchess of Burgundy, Edward IV's sister. The art of printing he probably learned when he was in Cologne in 1471–72. In Bruges he joined with Colard Mansion; and in 1474 and 1475 he put through the press there the first book printed in the English tongue, the *Recuyell of the Historyes of Troye. The Game and Playe of the Chesse* was another of his earliest publications. Apparently about the end of 1476 he set up his wooden press at Westminster, where Tothill Street now is. The *Dictes or Sayengis of the Philosophres* (1477) is the first book proved to have been printed in England. Of about 100 books printed by him over a third survive in unique copies or fragments only. He was diligent in printing or in translation till within a few hours of his death. See works by C. Knight (1854), W. Blades (1861–82), Plomer (1925), Aurner (1926); Crotch's introduction to the *Prologues and Epilogues* (E.E.T.S. 1929); a paper by G. P. Winship (1909); S. de Ricci's *Census of Caxtons* (1909); and E. Gordon Duff's *English 15th Century Books* (1918).

CAYLEY, (1) Arthur (1821–95), English mathematician, born at Richmond, Surrey. He was educated at King's College, London, and Trinity College, Cambridge, and graduated as senior wrangler and first Smith's prizeman in 1842. He was called to the bar at Lincoln's Inn in 1849, and established a practice as a conveyancer. In 1863 he was elected first Sadlerian professor of Pure Mathematics at Cambridge, and in 1875 a fellow of Trinity. He was president of the Royal Astronomical Society (1872–73), and of the British Association at its Southport meeting in 1883, where his address on the ultimate possibilities of mathematics attracted much attention. Among his many contributions to science are his origination of the theory of invariants and covariants, his work on the theories of matrices and analytical geometry, and in the field of theoretical astronomy. His chief book is an *Elementary Treatise on Elliptic Functions* (1876); his Mathematical Papers were published (1889–1898) in 13 vols. with index vol.

(2) **Sir George** (1773–1857), English pioneer of aviation, born in Scarborough, constructed and flew in 1808 a glider with a wing area of 300 square feet, probably the first heavier-than-air machine. In 1853 he constructed the first successful man-carrying glider. He also interested himself in railway engineering, allotment agriculture, and land reclamation methods, invented a new type of telescope, artificial limbs, the caterpillar tractor, and the tension wheel. He helped to found the Regent Street Polytechnic, London. See C. H. Gibbs-Smith, *Sir George Cayley's Aeronautics* (1962).

CAYLUS, Anne Claude Philippe de Tubières, Comte de, -lüs' (1692–1765), an archaeologist, who was born and died in Paris, and after serving in the Spanish War of Succession, travelled in Italy and the Levant, returning to Paris in 1717 to devote himself to the study of antiquities and the promotion of the fine arts.

CAZALÈS, Jacques Antoine Marie de (1752–1805), a leader of the French monarchists in the early Revolution times, from 1791 to 1803 an émigré in Coblenz and in England.

CEADDA, St. See CHAD.

CECCHI, *chek'ee,* (1) **Emilio** (1884–1966), Italian writer, born at Florence, known for essays and critical works in the sensitive and stylistic *prosa d'arte* manner.

(2) **Giammaria** (1518–87), Italian dramatist, was born and died at Florence, and wrote plays modelled on ancient classical comedy.

CECIL, name of an English family of statesmen, descended from **David Cecill,** a sheriff of Northamptonshire (1532–33) and M.P. The earldoms of Exeter and Salisbury characterize two branches of the family founded by two sons, (2) and (3), of (1) respectively. They became marquisates in 1789 (Salisbury) and 1801 (Exeter). See *Hist. MSS. Commission, Hatfield MSS.* (1923); Dennis, *The House of Cecil* (1915). Its most distinguished members in chronological order were:

(1) **William, 1st Baron Burghley or Burghleigh** (1520–98), one of England's greatest statesmen, father of (2) and (3), was born at Bourn, Lincolnshire, September 13, the son of Richard Cecil of Burghley, Northamptonshire, who rose high in favour with Henry VIII, and left large estates at his death in 1552. Educated at Stamford and Grantham,

young Cecil passed in 1535 to St John's College, Cambridge, where he was remarkable for his diligence and aptitude, and where he formed an attachment for a wineseller's daughter, Mary, sister of Sir John Cheke (q.v.). They were married in 1541, a few months after his entering Gray's Inn, but she died not long afterwards, leaving him one son. At Gray's Inn he studied not merely law, but history, genealogy, and theology. In 1547 Henry VIII appointed him *custos brevium.* His second marriage (1545), to the daughter of Sir Anthony Cooke, procured him the patronage of the Protector Somerset, who made him Master of Requests (1547), and his secretary (1548). He shared in Somerset's disgrace, even to two months' imprisonment in the Tower; but in 1550 his pre-eminent abilities secured for him the post of secretary of state, and in 1551 the honour of knighthood. With a sagacity far beyond the spirit of his age, he endeavoured to throw trade open, and did succeed in abolishing some monopolies. During Mary's reign he conformed to Catholicism. Prior to Mary's death, he had entered into correspondence with Elizabeth, who in 1558 appointed him chief secretary of state. For the next 40 years he was the chief architect of Elizabethan greatness. His policy at home and abroad was at once shrewd and cautious, liberal and comprehensive, while he displayed decision, ready and stern, when necessity demanded. He was above animosities and favouritism. His employment of an army of spies is perhaps excusable on the ground that he was matched by equally determined schemers, bent on restoring papal power in England. The queen created him Baron Burghley (1571), K.G. (1572), and lord high treasurer (1572)—an office he held till his death. His emoluments were as nothing to his expenditure, which was lavish in the building and beautifying of his mansions—Burghley, Theobalds in Herts, and Cecil House in the Strand. He died August 4 and was buried in St Martin's, Stamford. See Lives by E. Nares (1828–31), M. A. S. Hume (1898), A. Jessopp (1904), and C. Read, *Mr Secretary Walsingham* (1925) and *Lord Burghley and Queen Elizabeth* (1960).

(2) **Thomas, 1st Earl of Exeter, 2nd Baron Burghley** (1542–1623), English soldier, son of (1) by his first wife, served in the Scottish war (1573), against the Armada (1588), and crushed Essex's rebellion (1601).

(3) **Robert, 1st Earl of Salisbury** (c. 1563–1612), English statesman, son of (1), was made 1st Viscount Cranborne by James I (1604) and earl (1605) in return for his services, as Elizabeth's secretary of state, in securing James's succession to the English crown. Lord treasurer from 1608, he remained James's chief minister till his death. See Lives by A. Cecil (1915) and P. M. Handover (1959).

(4) **Sir Edward, 1st Baron Wimbledon** (1572–1638), English courtier, son of (2), commanded in the Low Countries (1596–1610) and the abortive Spanish expedition (1625), but was exonerated by Buckingham's favouritism.

(5) **Robert Arthur Talbot Gascoyne, 3rd Marquis of Salisbury** (1830–1903), English

Conservative statesman, father of (6), (7), and (8), was born at Hatfield House, February 3, educated at Eton and Christ Church, Oxford, was elected fellow of All Souls' (1853) and Conservative member for Stamford. In 1865 he became Viscount Cranborne and heir to the marquisate on the death of his elder brother, and he proved one of the most effective opponents of Gladstone's Reform Bill of that year. In the Derby ministry (1866), Lord Cranborne became Indian secretary; but Lord Derby and Disraeli proceeding to concoct a Reform Bill, Lord Cranborne (like others) resigned, and fought against the measure with extreme pertinacity. In 1868 he succeeded his father as third marquis, and was the strongest opponent of the disestablishment of the Irish Church. In 1869 he was elected chancellor of the University of Oxford. In 1870 he supported the Peace Preservation Bill, but disapproved the Irish Land Act. The bill for abolishing religious tests in the universities gave him much trouble. In January 1874 parliament was dissolved, and the Conservatives came in with a great majority. Lord Salisbury again became secretary for India; but before the end of the year he had again come into collision with his chief on the Public Worship Regulation Act, being described by Disraeli as ' a great master of gibes and flouts and jeers '. In 1878 he succeeded Lord Derby as foreign secretary and accompanied Disraeli (Lord Beaconsfield) to the Berlin Congress. On the death of the latter, he succeeded to the leadership of the Conservative Opposition; in June 1885 he became prime minister and secretary of state for foreign affairs, and settled the ' Penjdeh incident '. The contentious Irish Home Rule Bill defeated the Liberals and Lord Salisbury, backed by Liberal Unionists, was premier again in 1886 and in 1895, when a succession of foreign complications brought the country several times to the verge of war, only averted by the firm, and at the same time conciliatory, attitude of the British government. Turkish massacres in Armenia led to the reopening of the Eastern Question in an acute form, nearly resulting in a European conflagration. Hostilities with the United States seemed imminent owing to the interference of the latter country in a boundary dispute between British Guiana and Venezuela. Dr Jameson's filibustering expedition into the Transvaal at New Year 1896 led to critical relations with the republic, and revealed antagonism on the part of Germany. The jealousy of France at the British occupation of Egypt was actively aroused by Lord Salisbury in April 1896 entering upon the reconquest of the Sudan. And the Cretan insurrection, with the consequent crushing defeat of Greece by Turkey (1897), severely tested the Concert of the Powers. He resigned the foreign secretaryship in 1900; and having remained at the head of the Government during the Boer war (1899–1902), retired from public life in July 1902, receiving the Victorian Order. He died August 22, 1903. See Lives by his daughter, Lady Gwendolen (1921), and A. L. Kennedy (1953).

(6) **James Edward Hubert Gascoyne, 4th Marquis** (1861–1947), English Conservative politician, son of (5) and father of (9) and (10), served in the Boer war, was lord president of the Council (1922–23), lord privy seal (1924–29), and leader of the House of Lords (1925–29).

(7) **Robert, 1st Viscount Cecil of Chelwood** (1864–1958), English Conservative statesman, son of (5), educated at Eton and University College, Oxford, was called to the bar in 1887, and entered parliament (1903). He was minister of blockade (1916–18), and as under-secretary for foreign affairs (1918) helped to draft the League of Nations Covenant and was British representative at various disarmament conferences. He was president of the League of Nations Union (1923–45) and thereafter an honorary life president of U.N.A. He resigned from the Cabinet because of the cruiser question with the United States (1927) and was awarded the Nobel peace prize (1937) and made C.H. in 1956. He wrote books on commercial law, the church, and peace (1928 ff.), and his autobiography, *All the Way* (1949).

(8) **Lord Hugh Richard Heathcote, 1st Baron Quickswood** (1869–1956), English Conservative politician, son of (5), joined a group of Parliamentary Independents under Churchill, served in the Royal Flying Corps (1915), interested himself in prayer-book revision proposals, and was provost of Eton (1936–44). He was created baron in 1941.

(9) **Robert Arthur James Gascoyne-, 5th Marquis of Salisbury** (1893–1972), English Conservative statesman, son of (6), was born at Hatfield House and educated at Eton and Oxford. He won the Croix de Guerre with the Grenadier Guards in France during World War I. He became M.P. for South Dorset in 1929, and in 1935 as Viscount Cranborne became foreign under-secretary. He resigned with his chief, Anthony Eden, in February 1938 over the ' appeasement ' of Mussolini. In the Churchill government of 1940 he became paymaster general and was dominions secretary till 1941 when he was called to the Lords. He was colonial secretary, and lord privy seal, and represented Britain at the founding conference of UNO at San Francisco. As leader of the Opposition in the House of Lords (1945–51), he counselled acceptance by the Tory majority of most of the legislation of the political and economic revolution. In the Churchill government of 1951 he became secretary of state for commonwealth relations and in 1952 lord president of the Council. From 1951 to 1957 he was leader of the House of Lords. In January 1957 he (and Churchill) advised the Queen on the choice of Harold Macmillan (rather than R. A. Butler) as prime minister to succeed Anthony Eden. In March 1957 he resigned the lord presidency in protest against the Government's action in releasing unconditionally Archbishop Makarios of Cyprus from his Seychelles exile. He conducted the affairs of the House of Lords—which he wished to see reformed (within limits)—with notable distinction and un-

matched authority as one of the heads of 'the Establishment'.

(10) **Lord (Edward Christian) David (Gascoyne)** (1902–ʹ), English biographer, younger son of (6), held the professorship of English Literature at Oxford from 1948, becoming a C.H. in 1949. Known chiefly as a literary biographer—*Cowper* (1929), *Sir Walter Scott* (1933), *Jane Austen* (1935), *Max* (1964)—he also wrote an effective political biography: the life of William Lamb, in two volumes—*The Young Melbourne* (1939) and *Lord M.* (1954). There is nothing of the debunking attitude in his treatment of his subjects. Rather they are handled with delicate understanding and clear-sighted appraisal which does not preclude warmth. His style is polished and elegant and lends a pervasive charm to all his writings. *The Stricken Deer* (1930), a second appraisal of William Cowper, is probably Cecil's most sympathetically penetrating study, for, without having the poet's morbidity, he, too, is profoundly religious and reflective. A collection of essays, *The Fine Art of Reading* (1957), demonstrates clearly both his range and his limiting preferences.

(11) **David George Brownlow, 6th Marquis of Exeter**, known as **Lord Burghley** (1905–ʹ), English athlete, won the Olympic gold medal for the 400 metre hurdles (1928) and eight Empire championships. From 1936 he presided over the Amateur Athletic Association and the British Olympic Association, which was responsible for organizing the 1948 Olympic Games in London.

CECILIA, St (d. A.D. 230), the patroness of music, especially church music, was a convert to Christianity, and is said to have suffered martyrdom.

CECROPS, traditionally the first king of Attica and the founder of Athens.

ČELAKOVSKÝ, *chel'a-kov-ski*, (1) **František Ladislav** (1799–1852), Bohemian poet, died at Prague, professor of Slavonic Philology.

(2) **Ladislav** (1834–1902), son of (1), was from 1880 professor of Botany at Prague.

CELANO, Thomas of, *che-lah'nō* (d. *c.* 1255), author of the *Dies Irae*, born at Celano in the Abruzzi, was an early disciple of St Francis of Assisi, on whose life he is a leading authority. He spent the years 1221–28 in the Rhineland. See *The Dies Irae* by Warren (1897), and *The Lives of St Francis*, trans. by Howell (1908).

CELESTINE was the name of five popes: Celestine I (422–32); II (1143–44); III (1191–98); IV (1241); and V, the Neapolitan Pietro da Morrone (1215–96), who, after a long life of ascetic severities, was reluctantly elected pope in 1294. He resigned his office after five months—'the great refusal', for which Dante places him at the entrance of hell. He was imprisoned by his successor, Boniface VIII. He founded the Celestines, and was canonized in 1313.

CELLINI, Benvenuto, *chel-lee'nee* (1500–71), Italian goldsmith, sculptor, and engraver, author of one of the most interesting autobiographies ever written, was born in Florence, a city which he had to quit in early life after having taken part in 'an affray'. He then travelled to Rome, where his skill as an artist in metalwork gained him the favour of the highest nobles and prelates. By his own account he was as expert with sword and dagger as with his goldsmith's tools, and he had apparently no scruple in murdering or maiming any who endeavoured to thwart him. He states that at the siege of Rome in 1527 it was he who killed the Constable Bourbon, and that he afterwards shot down the Prince of Orange before the castle of St Angelo. He stood in high favour with Pope Clement VII, but was eventually flung into prison for the murder of a rival goldsmith. In 1534 he was pardoned and set free by Paul III, who wished him to engrave dies in the mint; soon afterwards, having spoken contemptuously of the pope's artistic tastes, he was cast into an *oubliette* of St Angelo. He escaped through his knowledge of the castle's vaults, but was immediately recaptured, and was only saved from the pope's vengeance by the intercession of Cardinal d'Este. For some years he lived alternately in Rome and Florence, Mantua and Naples. In 1537 he was honourably received at the court of Francis I of France, but soon returned to Florence, where he worked under the patronage of Cosimo de' Medici, and where he executed his famous bronze *Perseus with the head of Medusa*. He began to write his autobiography in 1558, and died at Florence. The autobiography was translated by Roscoe (1822), J. A. Symonds (1887), A. Macdonell (1903), and Cust (1910). Examples of his work are in the Louvre and the Victoria and Albert Museum.

CELSIUS, Anders (1701–44), Swedish astronomer, the constructor in 1742 of the centigrade thermometer, was born at Uppsala. He was the grandson of Magnus Celsius (1621–79), astronomer and decipherer of the Helsing runes, and nephew of Olof Celsius (1670–1756), professor of Theology and author of the *Hierobotanicon*. Anders became in 1730 professor of Astronomy at Uppsala, where in 1740 a splendid observatory was erected for him.

CELSUS, (1) (2nd cent. A.D.), a philosopher and friend of Lucian, who wrote, about 176–180, during the persecution of Marcus Aurelius, under the title *Logos Alēthēs* ('true word'), the first notable polemic against Christianity. The book itself has perished; but fragments of high interest occur as quotations in Origen's *Contra Celsum*. See studies by R. Bader (1940) and A. Wifstrand (Lund 1942).

(2) **Aulus Cornelius** (fl. A.D. 50), a Latin physician, wrote on medicine, rhetoric, history, philosophy, war, and agriculture. His only extant work is the *De Medicina* (trans. Spencer 1935–38).

CENCI, Beatrice, *chen'chee* (1577–99), according to Muratori, was the youngest of the twelve children by his first marriage of Francesco Cenci, a Roman nobleman of colossal wealth. After his second marriage, he treated the children of his first wife in a revolting manner; and the beauty of Beatrice inspired him with an incestuous passion, so with her stepmother and her brother Giacomo, she planned his murder, and two hired assassins drove a nail into his brain (September 9, 1598). The crime was discovered, and both she and Giacomo were racked; Giacomo confessed, but Beatrice maintained her innocence. All, however, were beheaded (September 10, 1599). Thus Muratori, while others allege that Beatrice was the victim of an infernal plot. Bertolotti's (1879) and later investigations, however, deprived the story of some of the romantic elements on which Shelley's tragedy mainly turns. Beatrice was not sixteen, but twenty-two years of age, was far from beautiful, and before her trial bore an illegitimate son. And the sweet and mournful picture in the Barberini palace in Rome cannot possibly be a portrait of Beatrice by Guido, who never painted in Rome till some nine years after her death. See *Edinburgh Review* for January 1879, Swinburne's *Studies* (1894), Marion Crawford in *Century Magazine*, January 1908, and *Beatrice Cenci* (2 vols. trans. 1926), by C. Ricci.

CENTLIVRE, Susannah, *sent-leev'èr* (c. 1667–1723), dramatist, born probably in Ireland, her surname either Freeman or Rawkins, is said to have been the wife or mistress of two or three gentlemen. In 1700 she produced a tragedy, *The Perjured Husband*, and subsequently appeared on the stage at Bath. In 1706 she married Joseph Centlivre, head cook to Queen Anne, with whom she lived happily till her death. Her nineteen plays (with Life, 3 vols. 1761; later ed. 1872) include *The Busybody* (' Marplot ' its leading character, 1709) and *A Bold Stroke for a Wife* (1717).

CERDIC (d. 534), landed in Hampshire in 495, and founded the kingdom of Wessex.

CERINTHUS (c. A.D. 100), a Judaico-Gnostic heretic born at Alexandria, who is said to have lived in Ephesus contemporaneously with the aged apostle John.

CERVANTES SAAVEDRA, Miguel de, Sp. *ther-vahn'tays* (1547–1616), Spanish author of *Don Quixote*, was born at Alcalá de Henares, the fourth of seven children born to Rodrigo de Cervantes (d. 1585), a poor medical practitioner, and his wife, Leonor de Cortinas (d. 1593). The story of his having studied at Salamanca is improbable; the first known productions of his pen appeared in 1569 in a collection of pieces on the death of the queen. Early in the same year he travelled to Italy in the service of Cardinal Giulio Acquaviva, but shortly afterwards enlisted as a soldier; and at the battle of Lepanto he received three severe gunshot wounds, in the chest and in the left hand, which was almost entirely lost. After having seen further service against the Turks in Tunis, he was returning to Spain in 1575 when the galley he sailed in was captured by Algerine corsairs, and with his brother Rodrigo and others he was carried into Algiers, where he remained in captivity five years, during which he made four daring attempts to escape. In 1580 he was ransomed by the efforts of Trinitarian monks, Algiers traders, and his devoted family. Finding no permanent occupation at home, he drifted to Madrid, and essayed a literary career. In December 1584 he married Catalina

de Salazar y Palacios (1565–1626). The marriage was childless, but Cervantes had an illegitimate daughter, Isabel de Saavedra (c. 1585–1652). His first important work was the *Galatea*, a pastoral romance, printed at Alcalá in 1585. For some years he strove to gain a livelihood by writing for the stage. He produced by 1587 between twenty and thirty plays, of which two only, *La Numancia* and *Los tratos de Argel*, have survived. In 1587 he became commissary to the fleet at Seville. In 1594 he was appointed a collector of revenues for the kingdom of Granada; but in 1597, failing to make up the sum due to the treasury, he was sent to prison at Seville, released on giving security, but not reinstated. Local tradition maintains that he wrote *Don Quixote* in prison at Argamasilla in La Mancha. In 1603 he was living at Valladolid; in September 1604 leave was granted to print the first part of *Don Quixote*, and early in January 1605 the book came out at Madrid. It leapt into popularity at once, though Lope de Vega wrote sneeringly of it; but instead of giving his readers the sequel they asked for, Cervantes busied himself with writing for the stage and composing short tales, or ' exemplary novels ' as he called them. His *Viage del Parnaso*, a poem of over 3000 lines in *terza rima*, reviews the poetry and poets of the day. In 1613 he published his twelve *Novelas.* In 1614 a pseudonymous writer brought out a spurious second part of *Don Quixote*, with an insulting preface, which served to spur Cervantes to the completion of the genuine second part (1615). While it was in the press he revised his various plays and interludes, and a little before his death, at Madrid, finished the romance of *Persiles and Segismunda.* In right of *Don Quixote* Cervantes ranks as one of the great writers of the world; but his short novels also are the best of their kind; and if a good deal of his poetry is weak, there is much that only a poet could have written. *Numancia* is a powerful and original drama; *Don Quixote* is the most carelessly written of all great books. Cervantes wrote it by fits and starts, and he neglected it for his other works. But it may be that we owe more to this carelessness than we think. In his other works Cervantes studied recognized models; in *Don Quixote* he followed the bent of his own genius alone, and wrote only as instinct prompted him. Written in a desultory fashion, it had time to grow and ripen under his hand; Don Quixote and Sancho, outlines at first, became by degrees flesh and blood realities to his fancy, beings that he loved; and the story—the second part especially—served him as a kind of commonplace-book. The first complete edition of Cervantes' works was Rivadeneyra's (12 vols. Madrid 1863–64). The oldest translation of *Don Quixote* is the English by Shelton (1612–20). See books by Pérez Pastor (1897–1902), L. Ruis (bibliography, 1895–1904), Calvert (1905), Fitzmaurice-Kelly (1913), editor of the *Complete Works* in English (8 vols. 1901–03), and S. de Madariaga (1935).

CESALPINO, Andrea, Lat. **Caesalpinus** (1519–1603), botanist and physiologist, born at Arezzo, propounded a theory of the circulation of the blood and evolved a system of plant classification.

CESARI, Giuseppe, or **Il Cavaliere d'Arpino,** *chay'za-ree* (c. 1568–1640), Italian painter, born at Arpino, honoured by five popes, is best known for the frescoes in the Capitol at Rome, where he died.

CESAROTTI, Melchiore, *chay-za-rot'tee* (1730–1808), Italian poet, was born at Padua, where in 1768 he became professor of Greek and Hebrew. His translations of Macpherson's *Ossian* (1763) and the *Iliad* threw fresh life into Italian literature. His *Filosofia delle lingue* and *Filosofia del gusto* are the best of his works.

CESNOLA, Count Luigi Palma di, *chayz-nō'la* (1832–1904), archaeologist, was born near Turin, fought in the Austrian, Crimean, and American Civil wars, and, having taken American citizenship, became U.S. consul in Cyprus. He was for 25 years director of the N.Y. Metropolitan Museum, to which he presented his collection of antiquities.

CÉSPEDES, Pablo de, *thays'pe-*THAys (1536–1608), Spanish painter, born at Córdoba, studied at Rome under Michelangelo and Raphael, and in 1577 became a canon at Córdoba, where he established a school of art, and was also active as an architect and writer.

CETEWAYO, (d. 1884), ruler of Zululand from 1873, in 1879 defeated the British at Isandhlwana, but was himself defeated at Ulundi. He was restored in 1883 to part of his kingdom, but was soon driven out by his subjects, and died at Ekowe. See C. T. Binns, *The Last Zulu King.*

CEULEN, Ludolph van, *kœ'-* (1540–1610), Dutch mathematician, born at Hildesheim, professor of Fortification at Leyden, devoted himself to finding the value of π. By 1610 he had worked it out to 35 decimal places (' Ludolph's number '). He died at Leyden.

CEVA, *chay'-,* (1) **Giovanni** (1647?–1734), Italian mathematician, gave name to a theorem connected with the concurrency of straight lines through the vertices of a triangle.

(2) **Tommaso** (1648–1736), brother of (1), and also a mathematician, published *Opuscula Mathematica* (1699).

CÉZANNE, Paul, *say-zan* (1839–1906), French artist, born at Aix-en-Provence. A contemporary and friend of Zola, with whom he shared an interest in literature, from 1859–61 he studied law at Aix, entered his father's bank, and in 1862, persuaded by Zola, went to Paris, and studied at the Académie Suisse. In Paris he met the circle of painters centred on Manet, but found ,himself not truly in accord with them, and thereafter worked mainly at Aix and l'Estaque, with occasional visits to Paris, where he exhibited at the first and third Impressionist exhibitions in 1874 and 1877. He was influenced by Pissarro, with whom he worked at Auvers and Pontoise (1872–73). He abandoned his former sombre expressionism for the study of nature, as in the famous *Maison du Pendu* of this period in the Louvre, and began to use his characteristic glowing colours. In his later period (after 1886, when he became financially independent of his father) he emphasized the underlying forms of nature—' the cylinder, the sphere, the cone '—by constructing his pictures from a rhythmic series of coloured planes, painting not light but plastic form, and thus becoming the forerunner of Cubism. In 1886 he married Hortense Fiquet, with whom he had had a secret liaison since 1870; she is reputed to have had the occasional task of retrieving completed canvases, abandoned by her husband wherever he happened to have been working on them—for his passion was the actual painting of them, not the possession. Also in 1886, his friendship with Zola was ended by the publication of the latter's novel, *L'Œuvre,* in which the central figure, an unsuccessful and unbalanced Impressionist painter, is in many respects identifiable as Cézanne. Cézanne, who himself described his aim as being ' to make Impressionism something solid and durable like the art of the old masters ', obtained recognition only in the last years of his life, and two exhibitions of his work were held by Vollard, in 1895 and 1899. His *L'Homme au chapeau de paille* (c. 1871) is in the Metropolitan Museum, New York; his *Aix: Paysage rocheux* (c. 1887) and *Le Jardinier* (c. 1906) are in the Tate Gallery, London; and *La Vielle au chapelet* (c. 1897–98) is in the National Gallery, London. See the monographs by B. Dorival (trans. 1949), J. Rewald (1950), M. Raynal (1954), and M. Schapiro (N.Y. 1954), and the *Letters,* edited by J. Rewald (1941).

CHABANEAU, François, *sha-ba-nō* (1754–1842), French chemist, born at Nontron, began as a student of theology but was expelled on account of his views on metaphysics. Professor of Mathematics at Passy when only seventeen and with no knowledge of the subject, he turned to the study of physics and chemistry. Later he became professor of Mineralogy, Physics and Chemistry at Madrid, where he carried out the researches on platinum which resulted in 1783 in an ingot of malleable platinum.

CHABAS, François (1817–82), French Egyptologist, born at Briançon, while in commerce became a learned linguist, and from 1851 gave himself up to hieroglyphics.

CHABRIER, Alexis Emmanuel, *sha-bree-yay* (1841–94), French composer, was born at Ambert. His operas are *Gwendoline* (1886), *Le Roi malgré lui* (1887), *Briséis* (unfinished), but the piece most performed today is perhaps his orchestral rhapsody *España.*

CHAD, O.E. Ceadda, St (d. 672), born in Northumbria, was a pupil of St Aidan, spent part of his youth in Ireland, and in 664 became abbot of Lastingham, in 666 Bishop of York. Doubt having been cast on the validity of his consecration, he withdrew in 669, but was immediately made Bishop of Mercia, fixing the see at Lichfield.

CHADWICK, (1) **Sir Edwin** (1801–90), social reformer, born near Manchester, was called to the bar in 1830. Appointed an assistant poor-law commissioner, in his report (1833) he laid the foundation of the later systems of government inspection; and he became secretary of the new Poor Law Board. See studies by Finer (1952) and R. A. Lewis (1952).

(2) Sir James (1891–), English physicist, studied at Manchester, Berlin, Cambridge, worked on radioactivity and discovered the neutron. He was a Nobel prizewinner in 1935, was knighted in 1945 and created C.H. in 1970.

CHAGALL, Marc, *sha-gal'* (1889–), Russian artist, born at Vitebsk. He studied at St Petersburg and in Paris. In 1914 he held a one-man show in Berlin, and for a short time was commissar of Fine Arts at Vitebsk, but in 1922 he left Russia and settled near Paris. He spent the years 1941–1947 in the U.S.A. Books illustrated by him include Gogol's *Dead Souls* and La Fontaine's *Fables*, but he is most famous for his fanciful painting, in which a visual potpourri of animals, objects, and people from the artist's past life, from his dreams and from Russian folklore, is presented in an arbitrary colour scheme of blues, greens, yellows, and pinks, e.g. *Bouquet of Flying Lovers* (1947) in the Tate Gallery, London. The word ' surrealist ' is said to have been coined by Apollinaire to describe the work of Chagall. See his autobiography *Ma Vie* (1931, trans. 1965), studies by L. Venturi (1956), Meyer and Bolliger (1957), and W. Erben (trans. 1957).

CHAILLU, Paul du. See DU CHAILLU.

CHAIN, Sir Ernest Boris (1906–), born in Berlin of Russian extraction, fled from Germany to Britain in 1933, and, for his part in the development of penicillin, shared with Fleming and Florey the Nobel 1945 award for medicine. He was made K.B. in 1970.

CHALIAPIN, Fedor Ivanovich, *sha-lya'peen* (1873–1938), a Russian bass singer of great power, born at Kazan, sang in opera at Tiflis in 1892, Moscow in 1896, and London in 1913. He left Russia after the Revolution. See *Chaliapin* by Gorky (reprinted 1968).

CHALKONDYLAS, (1) **Demetrios** (1424–1511), an Athenian, came after the Turkish conquest from Athens to Italy, and at Florence and Milan taught Greek, published grammars, and edited Homer, Isocrates and Suidas.

(2) **Nikolaos,** brother of (1), wrote, about 1450, a history of the Turks and the fall of the Greek Empire.

CHALLEMEL-LACOUR, Paul Armand, *shal-mel-la-koor* (1827–96), French politician, born at Avranches, one of the most gifted representatives of republicanism and anticlericalism. Foreign minister, senator, ambassador at Berne and in London, vice-president (1890), and president (1893) of the Senate, he wrote on philosophy, edited Madame d'Épinay's works, and was an Academician.

CHALLIS, James (1803–82), English astronomer, born at Braintree, graduated in 1825 at Cambridge, where in 1836 he became professor of Astronomy. In August 1846 he twice unconsciously noted the planet Neptune before its discovery at Berlin on September 23.

CHALLONER, Richard (1691–1781), English prelate, born at Lewes, turned Catholic as a boy, went to the English College at Douai in 1704 and was ordained in 1716, remaining there as a professor until 1730. He then served as a missionary priest in London, until in 1741 he was consecrated Bishop of Debra and coadjutor of Bishop Petre, whom

he succeeded as Vicar Apostolic of the London district in 1758. During the ' No Popery ' riots of 1780 he was secreted near Highgate. Among his thirty-four works are the *Catholic Christian Instructed* (1737), an answer to Conyers Middleton's *Letters from Rome*; the *Garden of the Soul* (1740), still a most popular prayer book with English Catholics; his revision of the Douay version of the Bible (5 vols. 1750), *Memoirs of Missionary Priests,* 1577–1684 (2 vols. 1741), and *Britannia Sancta* (2 vols. 1745). See his *Life and Times* by E. H. Burton (2 vols. 1909), by Cardinal Griffin and others (1946).

CHALMERS, (1) **Alexander** (1759–1834), was born at Aberdeen, studied medicine there, but about 1777 became an active writer for the press in London, and the busiest of booksellers' hacks. His reputation depends mainly on the *General Biographical Dictionary* (32 vols. 1812–14).

(2) **George** (1742–1825), Scottish antiquary, born at Fochabers, studied law, practised in Baltimore till the breaking out of the War of Independence and then settled in London (1775). Of his thirty-three works the chief is *Caledonia: an Account, Historical and Topographical, of North Britain* (1807–24); lives of Defoe, Paine, Ruddiman and Mary, Queen of Scots; and editions of Allan Ramsay and Lyndsay.

(3) **George Paul** (1833–78), was born at Montrose, served as errand boy to a surgeon, and apprentice to a shipchandler; but in 1853 came to Edinburgh, and studied art under Scott Lauder. Elected R.S.A. in 1871, he is represented in the National Gallery of Scotland by *The Legend*.

(4) **James** (1782–1853), a Dundee bookseller, born in Arbroath, for whom has been claimed the invention of adhesive stamps.

(5) **Thomas** (1780–1847), Scottish divine, born at Anstruther, educated at St Andrews, was in 1803 ordained minister of Kilmany. He carried on mathematical and chemistry classes at St Andrews in 1803–04, and in 1808 published an *Inquiry into National Resources*. In 1815 he became minister to the Tron parish in Glasgow, where his magnificent oratory, partly published as *Astronomical Discourses* (1817) and *Commercial Discourses* (1820), took the city by storm. In 1823 he accepted the Moral Philosophy chair in St Andrews, where he wrote his *Use and Abuse of Literary and Ecclesiastical Endowments* (1827). In 1827 he was transferred to the chair of Theology in Edinburgh, and in 1832 published a work on political economy. In 1833 appeared his Bridgewater treatise, *On the Adaptation of External Nature to the Moral and Intellectual Constitution of Man*. Meanwhile, the struggles in regard to patronage became keener, until in 1843 Chalmers, followed by 470 ministers, left the church of his fathers, and founded the Free Church, whose swift and successful organization was mainly due to his indefatigable exertions. He spent the close of his life as principal of the Free Church College, and in completing his *Institutes of Theology*. His works, in 34 vols., deal especially with natural theology, apologetics and social economy. As a

religious orator Chalmers was unrivalled. See *Memoirs,* by his son-in-law, Dr Hanna (4 vols. 1849–52); *Correspondence* (1853); and books by Dean Ramsay (1850), Mrs Oliphant (1893) and H. Watt (1943).

CHAM, *shã,* pseud. of Amédée de Noé (1819–79), French caricaturist, son of the Comte de Noé by an English mother, born in Paris, in 1843 began his famous connection with the *Charivari.* *Cham* is French for *Ham,* the son of Noah. See *Life* by Ribeyre (Paris 1885).

CHAMBERLAIN, (1) Sir (Joseph) Austen (1863–1937), eldest son of (3), was chancellor of the Exchequer 1903–06, 1919–21, secretary for India 1915–17, a member of Lloyd George's War Cabinet, lord privy seal, leader of the House and Unionist leader 1921–22. As foreign secretary 1924–29, he was made K.G. in 1925 and received also a Nobel peace prize for negotiating the Locarno Pact. See *Life and Letters* by C. Petrie (1939–40).

(2) Houston Stewart (1855–1927), a British admiral's son, married Richard Wagner's daughter, and wrote in German on music, Wagner, Kant and philosophy. Rabidly anti-English, he was naturalized as a German in 1916.

(3) Joseph (1836–1914), British statesman, born in London, was educated at University College School, entered Nettlefold's screw factory at Birmingham, and retired in 1874 with a fortune. A Radical politician, in 1868 he became a Birmingham town councillor, and in 1873–76 was mayor. Returned unopposed for Birmingham in 1876, he soon made his mark in Parliament, and in 1880 was appointed president of the Board of Trade, with a seat in the Cabinet. To his exertions was due the passing of the Bankruptcy Bill. Regarded as the leader of the extreme Radical party, he enunciated schemes for the regeneration of the masses, and during the general election of 1886 produced an ' unauthorized ' programme, which included the readjustment of taxation, free schools, and the creation of allotments by compulsory purchase. In February 1886 he became president of the Local Government Board, but resigned in March because of his strong objections to Gladstone's Home Rule Bill, of which he became the most strenuous opponent. From 1891 he was leader of the Liberal Unionists, and in the Coalition Government of 1895 took office as secretary for the colonies, here acquiring a great reputation as a colonial administrator, enhanced even during and after the South African War (1899–1902). In September 1903 he resigned office to be free to advocate his scheme of tariff reform, giving preferential treatment to colonial imports and protection for native manufactures. Subsequently, in 1919 and especially 1932, the scheme was carried out by his sons. In 1906 he practically withdrew from public life in consequence of ill-health. He was the first chancellor of Birmingham University, whose welfare he did much to promote. See his *Speeches,* ed. by C. W. Boyd (1914), and Lives by Miss Marris (1900), J. L. Garvin (1932), C. Petrie (1938), J. Amery (1951).

(4) (Arthur) Neville (1869–1940), son of (3) by his second marriage, lord mayor of Birmingham 1915–16, chancellor of the exchequer 1923–24, 1931–37, minister for health 1924–29, became prime minister in 1937. For the sake of peace, and with the country unprepared for war, he essayed ' appeasement ' of Italy and Germany, but in the end, having meantime pressed on with rearmament, was constrained to go to war (1939). Criticism of his war leadership accompanied initial military reverses, and in 1940 he yielded the premiership to Churchill; and in ill-health relinquished all office shortly before his death. See *Life* by Feiling (1946).

(5) Owen (1920–   ), American physicist, born in San Francisco, became a professor at the University of California after working on nuclear weapons and at the Argonne National Laboratory. In 1959 he was awarded the Nobel prize jointly with his colleague Segrè (q.v.) for research on the antiproton.

CHAMBERLAND, Charles Edouard, *shã-ber-lã* (1851–1908), French bacteriologist, a collaborator with Pasteur, invented the unglazed porcelain filter.

CHAMBERLAYNE, William (1619–89), English poet, practised as a physician at Shaftesbury, and fought as a royalist at Newbury. His works are *Love's Victory, a Tragi-Comedy* (1658), and *Pharonnida, an Heroick Poem* (1659).

CHAMBERLIN, Thomas Chrowder (1843–1928), American geologist, born at Mattoon, Ill., educated at Beloit College, where he became professor of Geology, was chief geologist of the Wisconsin Geological Survey and later professor of Geology at Chicago, where he died. His best-known work was in connection with the fundamental geology of the solar system. Books include *The Origin of the Earth* (1916) and *The Two Solar Families, The Sun's Children* (1928).

CHAMBERS, (1) Sir Edmund Kerchever (1866–1954), British critic, born in Berks, educated at Marlborough and Corpus Christi, Oxford, was an official of the Board of Education (1892–1926). He wrote importan books on the mediaeval (1903) and Elizabethan (1923) stage, Shakespeare (1925, 1930, 1944, 1946), and Arthur (1927).

(2) Ephraim (c. 1680–1740), English encyclopaedist, born at Kendal, while apprentice to a globemaker in London conceived the idea of a cyclopaedia (2 folio vols. 1728) that should surpass Harris's *Lexicon Technicum* (1704). A French translation gave rise to the great French *Encyclopédie.*

(3) Raymond Wilson (1874–1942), English scholar, was educated at University College, London, where he became professor of English. His numerous very learned works include studies of *Widsith* and *Beowulf,* an essay on *The Continuity of English Prose* (1932), and editions of Berners's Froissart (6 vols. 1901–03, with W. P. Ker), and other texts.

(4) Robert (1802–71), Scottish publisher, younger brother of (7), born in Peebles, began business as a bookseller in Edinburgh in 1818, and gave his leisure to literary

composition. In 1824 he produced the *Traditions of Edinburgh*; and between 1822 and 1834 he wrote twenty-five volumes. The success of the *Journal* was materially promoted by his essays and his literary insight. In 1844 he published anonymously the pre-Darwinian *Vestiges of Creation*. The authorship, ascribed to him in the *Athenaeum* of December 2, 1854, was first announced in Mr Ireland's introduction to the 12th ed. (1884). He received the degree of LL.D. from St Andrews in 1863. The labour of preparing the *Book of Days* (2 vols. 1863) broke his health, and he died at St Andrews. Other works by Robert are *Popular Rhymes of Scotland* (1826), a *History of the Rebellions in Scotland*, *Life of James I*, *Scottish Ballads and Songs* (1829), *Dictionary of Eminent Scotsmen*, *Ancient Sea Margins* (1848), *The Life and Works of Robert Burns* (4 vols. 1851; new ed. by W. Wallace, 1896), *Domestic Annals of Scotland* (3 vols. 1858–61), and *Songs of Scotland prior to Burns* (1862).—His son Robert (1832–88) became head of the firm in 1883, and conducted the *Journal* till his death. See W. Chambers's *Memoir of William and Robert Chambers* (1872; 13th ed., with supplementary chapter, 1884).

(5) **Robert William** (1865–1933), American novelist and illustrator, born at Brooklyn.

(6) **Sir William** (1726–96), architect, was born of Scottish ancestry at Stockholm, but brought up in England. He designed Somerset House (1776) and the pagoda in Kew Gardens, and wrote a *Treatise of Civil Architecture* (1759).

(7) **William** (1800–83), Scottish publisher, brother of (4), was born at Peebles, where his father was a cotton manufacturer. In 1814 he was apprenticed to a bookseller in Edinburgh, and in 1819 started business for himself, to bookselling afterwards adding printing. Between 1825 and 1830 he wrote the *Book of Scotland* and, in conjunction with his brother Robert, a *Gazetteer of Scotland*. In 1832 he started *Chambers's Edinburgh Journal*, six weeks in advance of the *Penny Magazine*; and soon thereafter he united with Robert in founding the business of W. & R. Chambers. In 1859 William founded and endowed an institute in his native town. Lord Provost of Edinburgh (1865–69), he promoted a successful scheme for improving the older part of the city; and he carried out at his own cost a restoration of St Giles' Cathedral. Shortly before his death he received the offer of a baronetcy. He was made LL.D. of Edinburgh in 1872. Besides many contributions to the *Journal*, he wrote a *Youth's Companion*, a *History of Peeblesshire* (1864), *Ailie Gilroy*, *Stories of Remarkable Persons*, *Stories of Old Families*, and a *Historical Sketch of St Giles' Cathedral* (1879).

CHAMBORD, Henri Charles Dieudonné, Comte de, *shã-bor* (1820–83), claimant to the French throne, grandson of Charles X, was born in Paris, seven months after the assassination of his father, the Duc de Berri (q.v.). When Charles X abdicated in 1830, the people insisted on the 'citizen king', and the elder Bourbons were driven into exile. They fixed their Court successively at Holyrood, Prague, Görz and Frohsdorf.

The Count was trained in clerical and absolutist ideas by his aunt, the Duchesse d'Angoulême. A good, dull, timid soul, whom D'Orsay likened to 'a palace with no room furnished but the chapel', 'Henry V' fooled away three chances of regaining the crown—in 1848, 1870 and 1873. Lamed by a fall from his horse (1841), he passed forty years of blameless inertia. See BOURBON; the Comte de Falloux's *Mémoires d'un Royaliste* (1888); and Lives by Nouvion (1884), Dubosc de Pesquidon (1887), P. de Luz (1931).

CHAMFORT, Nicolas Sébastien Roch, *shã-for* (1741–94), French writer, gaining an entrance into the literary circles of Paris, lived for years 'by his wit, if not by his wits', and at the Revolution was hailed in the clubs as 'La Rochefoucauld-Chamfort'. After a time, however, certain incisive witticisms—such as, 'Be my brother or I will kill you'—drew down on him the anger of the Jacobin leaders. Threatened with arrest, he tried to commit suicide, and died after several days' suffering. His works (ed. by Auguis, 5 vols. 1824–25) include tales, dramas, *éloges*, brilliant maxims and even more admirably observed anecdotes.

CHAMINADE, Cécile Louise Stéphanie (1861–1944), French composer, born in Paris, best known in England for her piano pieces.

CHAMISSO, Adelbert von (Louis Charles Adelaide de) (1781–1838), lyric poet and biologist, was born at the château of Boncourt, in Champagne, of French parents. The French Revolution driving his parents to settle in Prussia in 1790, he became a page of the queen, and entered the army. But in 1806 he returned to France, for though no admirer of Napoleon, he would not fight against his native land. In the circle of Madame de Staël at Coppet he began that study of natural science which he afterwards pursued at Berlin. In 1815–18 he accompanied a Russian exploring expedition round the world as naturalist; and on his return was appointed keeper of the Botanical Garden of Berlin. In 1819 he was the first to discover in certain animals what he called 'alternation of generations' (the recurrence in the life cycle of two or more forms). In 1835 he was elected to the Academy of Science; and, after a happy domestic life, he died at Berlin. He wrote several works on natural history, but his fame rests partly on his poems, still more on his quaint and humorous *Peter Schlemihl* (1813), the story of the man who lost his shadow. See his Life by Fulda (Leipzig 1881), and in English by Lentzner (1893).

CHAMPAIGNE, Philippe de (1602–74), portrait and religious painter, born in Brussels, worked in Paris. Works may be seen in the National Gallery and the Wallace Collection.

CHAMPFLEURY, *shã-flœ-ree*, assumed name of Jules Fleury-Husson (1821–89), French author, who was born at Laon, and died at Sèvres, head of the Porcelain Museum there. In early pieces for the theatre, and later romances, he achieved some distinction as a realistic writer. Works of greater value, however, are those on the history of caricature, literature, art, pottery, &c.

CHAMPLAIN, Samuel de, *shã-plĩ* (1567–1635), French governor of Canada, was born at Brouage in Saintonge, and in 1603 made his first voyage to Canada. In 1604–07 he explored the coasts, and on his third voyage in 1608 he founded Quebec. In 1612 he was appointed lieutenant of Canada, and he had a busy time with attacks on the Iroquois, explorations of the interior, and journeys to France, until 1629, when he had to surrender to an English fleet, and was taken to England. Liberated in 1632, he returned to Canada in 1633. See Lives by Dionne (trans. 1905), Flenley (1924), and Syme (1953). His works were ed. by Biggar (Toronto, 1922–36).

CHAMPNEYS, Basil (1842–1935), architect of Newnham College (Cambridge), Rylands Library (Manchester), &c., was the son of William Weldon Champneys (1807–75), who was dean of Lincoln from 1868.

CHAMPOLLION, *shã-pol-yõ,* (1) **Jean François** (1790–1832), French archaeologist, brother of (2), founder of modern Egyptology, born at Figeac. Educated at Grenoble, he devoted himself from his boyhood to the study of oriental languages, especially Coptic. In 1807 he went to Paris, and in 1809–16 was professor of History at Grenoble. He had already published (1811–14) two volumes of *L'Égypte sous les pharaons*, when he was expelled from his chair for his Bonapartist sympathies. His decipherment of the hieroglyphics was set forth in three works (1821–1828). He was sent by the king on a scientific mission to Italy in 1824–26, and in 1826 was appointed conservator of the Egyptian collections. In 1828–29 he accompanied a scientific expedition to Egypt; on his return he was made a member of the Académie des Inscriptions (1830), and a chair of Egyptology was founded for him in the Collège de France. See Life by Hartleben (1906).

(2) **Jean Jacques Champollion-Figeac** (1778–1867), French archaeologist, brother of (1), was born at Figeac. After holding at Grenoble the offices of librarian and professor of Greek, he was appointed in 1828 conservator of MSS. in the Royal Library in Paris, but after the February revolution was deposed from office by Carnot. In 1848 he was appointed librarian of the palace of Fontainebleau. His works include *Annales des Lagides* (2 vols. 1819), *Les Tournois du Roi René* (1827–28), and numerous French historical documents. After his brother's death, he prepared, with the help of his MSS., *L'Égypte ancienne et moderne* (1840) and *L'Écriture démotique égyptienne* (1843). See *Les deux Champollion* (Grenoble 1887) by his son, **Aimé** (1812–94), himself an archaeologist.

CHANCELLOR, Richard (d. 1556), English seaman, was brought up in the household of the father of Sir Philip Sidney, and was chosen in 1553 as 'pilot-general' of Sir Hugh Willoughby's expedition in search of a northeast passage to India. The ships were parted in a storm off the Lofoten Islands, and Chancellor, after waiting seven days at Vardöhus, proceeded alone into the White Sea, and travelled thence overland to the court at Moscow, where he concluded a treaty giving freedom of trade to English ships. His interesting account of Russia is in Hakluyt's *Navigations*. Next spring he returned to England, where his hopeful reports led to the establishment of the Muscovy Company. In 1555 he made a second voyage to the White Sea and to Moscow. In July 1556 he set sail homewards, but on November 10 was lost in Aberdour Bay, Aberdeenshire.

CHANCOURTOIS, Alexandre Emile Béguyer de, *shã-koor-twah* (1819–86), French geologist, professor of Geology at the School of Mines in Paris, was one of the first to suspect periodicity in the elements. His work went unnoticed at the time.

CHANDLER, (1) **Charles Frederick** (1836–1925), American chemist, was born at Lancaster, Mass., and studied at Harvard, Göttingen and Berlin. He was influential in establishing the American Chemical Society, and is noteworthy for his contributions to industrial chemistry and public health reform.

(2) **Richard** (1738–1810), English archaeologist, was born at Elson, Hants, and educated at Winchester and at Queen's and Magdalen Colleges, Oxford. His *Marmora Oxoniensia* (1763) is an elaborate description of the Oxford marbles. He afterwards travelled through Greece and Asia Minor for the Dilettanti Society. The materials collected were given to the world in *Ionian Antiquities* (1769), *Inscriptiones Antiquæ* (1774), *Travels in Asia Minor* (1775), and *Travels in Greece* (1776). Chandler, made D.D. in 1773, held preferments in Hants and at Tilehurst, near Reading.

CHANDOS, a great English family, descended from a follower of William the Conqueror. Its greatest member was Sir John Chandos, the Black Prince's follower, who fell in battle, January 1, 1370; and its last representative in the direct male line was another Sir John (d. 1428), whose sister married one Giles Brydges. Their descendant, Sir John Brydges, was lieutenant of the Tower under Queen Mary, and was created Baron Chandos in 1554. James Brydges (1673–1744), eighth Lord Chandos, sat in parliament for Hereford from 1698 to 1714, and was created Duke of Chandos in 1719. In 1796 the title passed by marriage to the family of Grenville, till 1889 dukes of Buckingham and Chandos. See J. R. Robinson, *The Princely Chandos* (1893).

CHANDOS, Oliver Lyttelton, 1st Viscount (1893–1972), belonged to a family with many political connexions. After Eton and Cambridge, where he gained a blue for golf, Lyttelton served in the Grenadier Guards in World War I, winning the D.S.O. By 1928 he was managing director of the British Metal Corporation, and during the years of depression played a big part in organizing international cartels in the metal world to mitigate the effects of the slump. On the outbreak of war in 1939 he became controller of Non-Ferrous Metals, and in 1940 was made president of the Board of Trade, a seat in the House of Commons being found for him at Aldershot. He was subsequently minister of state in Cairo, and minister of production. When the Conservatives were returned to office in 1951

Lyttelton went to the Colonial Office, until his resignation from politics to return to business in 1954, when he was raised to the peerage. His period of office was a difficult one, with outbreaks of violence in Kenya and Malaya to contend with, and a constitutional crisis in British Guiana. However, he played a leading part in drawing up plans of constitutional reform and advance for many of the African colonial territories. See *Memoirs* (1962).

CHANDRAGUPTA, or **Sandrakottos**, Hindu king of Pâtaliputra or Palibothra, to whom Megasthenes was sent by Seleucus Nicator (*c.* 300 B.C.).

CHANEY, Lon (1883–1930), American film actor, born at Colorado Springs, famous for spine-chilling deformed villains and other horrific parts, as in *The Hunchback of Notre Dame* and *The Phantom of the Opera.*

CHANGARNIER, Nicolas Anne Théodule, *shā-garn-yay* (1792–1877), French general, born at Autun, served in Algeria (1830–48; governor-general 1848), but returned to Paris to take command of the Paris garrisons and of the National Guard. After the *coup d'état* in 1851 he went into exile; in the Franco-Prussian war he was shut up in Metz with Bazaine. He died at Versailles. See Life by Comte d'Antioche (1891).

CHANNING, William Ellery (1780–1842), born at Newport, R.I., graduated at Harvard in 1798, and in 1803 was ordained to a Congregational church in Boston, where his sermons were famous for their ' fervour, solemnity, and beauty '. He was ultimately the leader of the Unitarians. In 1821 he received the degree of D.D. from Harvard University, and next year he visited Europe, and made the acquaintance of Wordsworth and Coleridge. Among his Works (6 vols. 1841–46) were his *Essay on National Literature, Remarks on Milton, Character and Writings of Fénelon, Negro Slavery*, and *Self-culture.* See Lives by W. H. Channing (1880) and Chadwick (1903).

CHANTREY, Sir Francis Legatt (1781–1841), English sculptor, was born at Norton, in Derbyshire. His father, who was a carpenter, and rented a small farm, died when Chantrey was only twelve, and the boy was in 1797 apprenticed to a carver and gilder in Sheffield. His efforts at modelling and drawing were encouraged by J. R. Smith, the engraver, and in 1802 he was able to cancel his indentures. He studied for a short time at the Royal Academy, and in 1805 received his first commission, a marble bust for Sheffield parish church. This was followed by busts for Greenwich Hospital; in 1808 he won the competition for the statue of George III for the Guildhall, and during the rest of his life he was largely employed on works of portraiture. His head of Satan, and his *Plenty* designs for Sheaf House, Sheffield, and his *Penelope* at Woburn, are examples of his treatment of ideal and imaginative subjects. In 1818 he became an R.A.; and in 1835 he was knighted. He left the bulk of his fortune of £150,000 to the Royal Academy with life rent to his widow (d. 1875) to purchase native works of art. The collection is now in the Tate Gallery. See books by G.

Jones (1849), J. Holland (1851), A. Fish (1904).

CHANZY, Antoine Eugène Alfred, *shā-zee* (1823–83), French general, born at Nouart, served in Algeria, Lombardy, &c. Placed in December 1870 at the head of the second Army of the Loire, he resisted the invaders. In 1873–79 he was governor-general of Algeria. Chosen a life senator in 1875, he was put forward for the presidency in 1789. He was ambassador at St Petersburg in 1879–81.

CHAPELAIN, Jean, *sha-pli* (1595–1674), a learned, industrious French writer, who passed for a poet and critic, and was an original member of the Académie. His unreadable epic, the *Pucelle*, in twenty-four books, was gibbeted by Boileau.

CHAPLIN, (1) Charles Spencer (1889–   ), film actor and director, was born at Kennington, London, of theatrical parents. His father died when he was a child, leaving the family in straitened circumstances, and Chaplin's first regular education was in the school at Hanwell poor law institution. These hard times are often mirrored in the poignant contrasts of humour and sadness which are a feature of his early films. At eight years old he was a seasoned stage performer, but his skill in comedy developed under Fred Karno, as a member of whose company he went to Hollywood in 1914 and entered the motion picture business, then in its infancy, making 35 films in his first year. In these early comedies he adopted the bowler hat, out-turned feet, moustache and walking-cane which became the hallmark of his consummate buffoonery in *The Kid, The Gold Rush, The Champion, Shoulder Arms*, &c. His art was essentially suited to the silent film and, realizing this, he experimented with new forms when sound arrived, as in *City Lights* (1931), with music only, and *Modern Times* (1936), part speech and part mime. Eventually he entered the orthodox sound film field with the satirical *Great Dictator* (1940). In *Limelight* he acted, directed and composed the music and dances. His left-wing sympathies caused him to fall foul of the rabid anti-Communist factions of post-war America, and led to the biting satire of *A King in New York* (1957) which mocks at the American way of life. See Life by Huff (1952), Minney, *The Immortal Tramp* (1954) and *Autobiography* (1964).

(2) **Henry, Viscount** (1841–1923), became Conservative M.P. for Sleaford (1868) and Wimbledon (1907). He several times held office in the Government, acting as leader of the Opposition, 1915–16. See Life by his daughter Lady Londonderry (1926).

(3) **Matilda.** See AYRTON, W. E.

CHAPMAN, (1) George (*c.* 1559–1634). English dramatist, was born near Hitchin, Hertfordshire, and is supposed to have studied at Oxford and Cambridge. To Lawrence Keymis's *Second Voyage to Guiana* (1596) he prefixed a spirited poem. His earliest extant play, *The Blind Beggar of Alexandria*, was produced in February 1595–96. The comedy, *All Fools*, printed in 1605, was probably produced in 1599. In 1598 he completed Marlowe's *Hero and Leander.* After partial translations from the

Iliad in 1598 and 1610, the complete translation of *The Iliads of Homer, Prince of Poets*, appeared in 1611. Having finished the *Iliad*, he set to work on the *Odyssey* (1616), followed (about 1624) by the minor works. In spite of all harshnesses, obscurities, conceits, and mistakes in Greek, Chapman's translation of Homer is a noble achievement. He joined Jonson and Marston in the composition of *Eastward Ho* (1605), and in 1606 published a graceful comedy, *The Gentleman Usher*. In 1607 appeared *Bussy d'Ambois*, and in 1613 *The Revenge of Bussy d'Ambois*—tragedies containing much bombast intermingled with exalted poetry. *The Conspiracie* and *Tragedie of Charles, Duke of Byron* (1608) are also undramatic, but abound in fine poetry. Chapman's other plays are *The May Day* (1611), *The Widow's Tears* (1612), and *Caesar and Pompey* (1631). Two posthumous tragedies (1654), *Alphonsus* and *Revenge for Honour*, bear his name with doubtful right. *The Ball*, a comedy, and *The Tragedie of Chabot* (1639) were the joint work of Chapman and Shirley. Among Chapman's nondramatic works are *Enthymiæ Raptus* (1609), *Petrarch's Seven Penitentiall Psalmes* (1612). *The Divine Poem of Musæus* (1616), and *The Georgicks of Hesiod* (1618). Minto detected in him the rival poet of Shakespeare's sonnets. See his plays, ed. Parrott (1910–14); J. M. Robertson, *Shakespeare and Chapman* (1917); Swinburne *Contemporaries of Shakespeare* (1919); H. Ellis, *George Chapman* (1934), F. S. Boas, *Introduction to Stuart Drama* (1946).

(2) **Walter.** See CHEPMAN.

CHAPONE, Hester, *née* Mulso (1727–1801), born at Twywell, Northants, wrote for the *Rambler* (No. 10), *Gentleman's Magazine*, &c., but is chiefly remembered for her *Letters on the Improvement of the Mind* (1772). See her *Works* with Life (4 vols. 1807).

CHAPPELL, William, F.S.A. (1809–88), was a member of a great London music publishing house. His *Collection of National English Airs* (2 vols. 1838–40) grew into *Popular Music of the Olden Time* (2 vols. 1855–59). Chappell took a principal part in the foundation in 1840 of the Musical Antiquarian Society, the Percy Society, and in 1868 of the Ballad Society. He published in 1874 vol. i of a *History of Music*.

CHAPTAL, Jean Antoine (1756–1832), French statesman and chemist, born at Nogaret, was in 1811 made Comte de Chanteloup by Napoleon. As a member of the Senate he introduced the metric system of weights and measures.

CHARCOT, *shahr-kō*, (1) **Jean Baptiste** (1867–1936), son of (2), born at Neuilly, a doctor, commanded South Polar expeditions in the *Français* (1903–05) and *Pourquoi Pas?* (1908–1910), and later went down with the *Pourquoi Pas?* off Iceland.

(2) **Jean Martin** (1825–93), father of (1), pathologist, was born at Paris, studied at Paris, where he became a professor, doctor at the Salpêtrière, and a member of the Institute. Freud was among his pupils. He contributed much to our knowledge of chronic and nervous diseases, and made hypnotism a scientific study.

CHARD, John Rouse Merriott (1847–97), born near Plymouth, as lieutenant won the V.C. when he heroically held Rorke's Drift a whole night (January 22, 1879) against 3000 Zulus, with eighty men of the 24th Regiment.

CHARDIN, *shahr-di*, (1) **Jean Baptiste Siméon** (1699–1779), French painter, born in Paris, a son of the king's billiard-table maker, showed such promise as a student that he was selected to assist in the restoration of the royal paintings at Fontainebleau, and he later attracted attention as a signpainter. In 1728 he exhibited at the ' Exposition de la jeunesse ', a series of still-life paintings which were so successful that he was elected to the Academy in the same year. He now emerged as a genre painter and produced many superb pictures of peasant life and domestic scenes. *Grace before Meat* (1740; Louvre), perhaps his masterpiece in this vein, earned the extravagant praises of Diderot. In 1755 he was appointed treasurer of the Academy, with an apartment in the Louvre. As an exponent of still life and genre Chardin is without equal in French painting, his composition and colouring is comparable with that of the best Dutch and Flemish masters, and he is free from both satire and sentimentality. An unassuming, serious bourgeois, he never travelled further than Fontainebleau, but spent the whole of his long, placid life in Paris. See studies by Furst (1911), and G. Wildenstein (1933).

(2) **Sir John** or **Jean** (1643–1713), traveller, born in Paris, went to India in 1663 to buy diamonds; resided in Persia; visited France in 1670, and returned to India and Persia. In 1681 he settled as a Protestant in England, became court jeweller, and was knighted by Charles II. His *Journal du voyage*, and an English translation appeared in 1686–1711.

CHARDONNE, Jacques, pseud. of **Jacques Boutelleau** (1884–   ), French writer, born at Barbezieux, of domestic novels mainly set in his native Charente, among them *Claire* (1931), *Les Destinées sentimentales* (1934–36) and *Romanesques* (1937). He also wrote essays and a chronicle of the French collapse in 1940.

CHARDONNET, Hilaire, Comte de, *shahr-don-nay* (1839–1924), French chemist, born at Besançon, was a pioneer of the artificial-silk industry.

CHARLEMAGNE, or Charles the Great (742–814), king of the Franks and Roman emperor, was born perhaps at Aachen, and was the eldest son of Pepin the Short and grandson of Charles Martel. On Pepin's death (768) Charles and his brother Carloman jointly succeeded to the throne; and on Carloman's death (771) Charles became sole king, and in 772 fought against the Saxons. At the request of Pope Adrian I, he crossed the Alps in 773, and overthrew the Lombard kingdom, confirming Ravenna to the papal see. In 775 he was again reducing the Saxons; in 776 he suppressed an insurrection in Italy; and in 777 secured the submission of the Saxon chiefs. From Spain, whither he had gone to fight the Moors and Arabs (778), he was summoned to crush the Saxons; in 781 he was in Rome. The Saxons, rising in arms once more, destroyed a Frankish army in 782, which Charlemagne fearfully avenged. A more general rising followed, but in 783–785 the Frankish monarch persuaded the chiefs to submit to baptism and become his faithful vassals. In 788 Bavaria was absorbed in his dominions, and next the country of the Avars to the Raab; the eastern ' mark ', the nucleus of the Austrian empire, being established to defend the frontier there (798). In 800 he marched into Italy to support Pope Leo III against the rebellious Romans, and on Christmas Day 800, in St Peter's Church, was crowned by the pope, and saluted as Carolus Augustus, emperor of the Romans. The remaining years of his reign were spent in further consolidating his vast empire, which extended from the Ebro to the Elbe. Bishoprics were founded in the Saxon country; many of the Slavs beyond the Elbe were subjugated. The emperor zealously promoted education, agriculture, arts, manufactures and commerce. He built sumptuous palaces, particularly at Aachen and Ingelheim near Bingen, and many churches. Learned men were encouraged to come to his court, and he himself could speak Latin and read Greek. His fame spread to all parts of the world; in 798 Haroun Al-Raschid sent ambassadors. The emperor, who was of most commanding presence, was buried at Aachen. His reign was a noble attempt to consolidate order and Christian culture among the nations of the West; but as his successors were weaklings, his empire fell to pieces. Besides his Capitularies or collection of laws, there are letters and Latin poems ascribed to him. His Life was written in Latin by his secretary, Eginhard (q.v.). See Lives by Cutts (1882), Mombert (1889), Hodgkin (1897), Davis (1900); Calmette (1945); and H. Fichtenau *The Carolingian Empire* (trans. 1957).

CHARLES. Two kings of Great Britain and Ireland:

Charles I (1600–49), born at Dunfermline, was a sickly child, unable to speak till his fifth year, and so weak in the ankles that till his seventh he had to crawl upon his hands and knees. Except for a stammer, he outgrew both defects, and became a skilled tilter and marksman, as well as an accomplished scholar and a diligent student of theology. He was created Duke of Albany at his baptism, Duke of York in 1605, and Prince of Wales in 1616, four years after the death of Prince Henry had left him heir to the crown. The Spanish match had been mooted as early as 1614; but it was not till February 17, 1623, that, with Buckingham, Charles started on the romantic incognito journey to Madrid. Nothing short of his conversion would have satisfied the Spanish and papal courts; and on October 5, he landed again in England, eager for rupture with Spain. The nation's joy was speedily dashed by his betrothal to the French princess, Henrietta Maria (1609–1669); for the marriage articles pledged him to permit her the free exercise of the Catholic religion, and to give her the upbringing of their children till the age of thirteen. On March 27, 1625, Charles succeeded his father, James I; on June 13 he welcomed his little bright-eyed queen at Dover, having married her by proxy six weeks earlier. Barely a twelve-month was over when he packed off her troublesome retinue to France—a bishop and 29 priests, with 410 more male and female attendants. Thenceforth their domestic life was a happy one; and during the twelve years following the murder of Buckingham (1592–1628), in whose hands he had been a mere tool, Charles gradually came to yield himself up to her unwise influence, not wholly indeed, but more than to that of Strafford even, or Laud. Three parliaments were summoned and dissolved in the first four years of the reign; then for eleven years Charles ruled without one, in its stead with subservient judges and the courts of Star Chamber and High Commission. In 1627 he had blundered into an inglorious French war; but with France he concluded peace in 1629, with Spain in 1630. Peace, economy and arbitrary taxation were to solve the great problem of his policy—how to get money, yet not account for it. The extension of the ship tax to the inland counties was met by Hampden's passive resistance (1637); Laud's attempt to anglicize the Scottish Church, by the active resistance of the whole northern nation (1639). Once more Charles had to call a parliament: two met in 1640—the Short Parliament, which lasted but three weeks, and the Long, which outlasted Charles. It met to pronounce Strafford's doom; and, his plot with the army detected, Charles basely sacrificed his loyal servitor to fears for the queen's safety, at the same time assenting to a second bill by which the existing parliament might not be dissolved without its own consent. That pledge, as extorted by force, Charles purposed to disregard; and during his visit to Edinburgh, in the autumn of 1641, he trusted by lavish concessions to bring over the Scots to his side. Instead, he got entangled in dark suspicions of plotting the murder of the Covenanting lords, of connivance even in the Ulster massacre. Still, his return to London was welcomed with some enthusiasm, and a party was forming in the Commons itself of men who revolted from the sweeping changes that menaced both church and state. Pym's ' Grand Remonstrance ' justified their fears, and Charles seemed to justify the ' Grand Remonstrance ' by his attempt to arrest the five members (January 4, 1642); but that ill-stricken blow was dictated by knowledge of an impending impeachment of the queen herself. On August 22 he raised the royal standard at Nottingham; and the four years' Civil War commenced, in which, as at Naseby, he showed no lack of physical courage, and which resulted at Naseby in the utter annihilation of his cause (June 14, 1645). Quitting his last refuge, Oxford, he surrendered himself on May 5, 1646, to the Scots at Newark, and by them in the following January was handed over to the parliament. His four months' captivity at Holmby House, near Northampton; his seizure, on June 3, by Cornet Joyce; the three months at Hampton Court; the flight on November 11; the fresh captivity at Carisbrooke Castle, in the Isle of Wight—these lead up to the 'trial' at Westminster of the 'tyrant, traitor, and murderer, Charles Stuart'. He had drawn the sword, and by the sword he perished, for it was the army, not parliament, that stood at the back of his judges. Charles faced them bravely, and with dignity. Thrice he refused to plead, denying the competence of such a court; and his refusal being treated as a confession, on January 30, 1649, he died on the scaffold in front of Whitehall, with a courage worthy of a martyr. On the snowy 7th of February they bore the 'white king' to his grave at Windsor in Henry VIII's vault; in 1813 the Prince Regent had his leaden coffin opened. Six children survived him—Charles and James, his successors; Mary, Princess of Orange (1631–60); Elizabeth (1635–50); Henry, Duke of Gloucester (1639–60); and Henrietta, Duchess of Orleans (1644–70), the last born ten weeks after Charles's final parting from his queen. See the articles HENRIETTA MARIA, LAUD, STRAFFORD, ELIOT, HAMPDEN, PRYNNE, PYM, CROMWELL, BRADSHAW, &c.; I. Disraeli's *Commentaries on the Life and Reign of Charles I* (5 vols. 1828–30); *Letters of Charles I to Henrietta Maria* (Camden Soc. 1856); Chancellor's *Life of Charles I, 1600–25* (1886); Muddiman's *Trial of Charles I* (1928); the Lives by Sir John Skelton (1898), Allan Fea (1904) F. M. G. Higham (1932), and John (1952); and, specially, S. R. Gardiner's *History of England, 1603–42* (10 vols. 1863–1882), and *History of the Great Civil War* (3 vols. 1886–1891); also Mathew, *The Age of Charles I* (1951); C. V. Wedgwood, *The Great Rebellion*, (2 vols. 1955—1958).

Charles II (1630–85), was born at St James's Palace, May 29. Created Prince of Wales in his ninth year, on the outbreak of the Civil War he accompanied his father at the battle of Edgehill. By 1644 the Royalist cause had declined so sharply that Charles was forced into exile, first to Scilly and Jersey—where James, Duke of Monmouth, was begotten of his liaison with Lucy Walter —and finally to France. His offer to agree to any conditions that would preserve his father's life having been rejected, on the execution of the latter Charles assumed the title of king. In 1650 he agreed to the terms laid down by the Scottish Commissioners, and having subscribed to the Covenant was crowned at Scone on January 1, 1651. He speedily found himself the prisoner of rancorous politico-religious factions far too busy quarrelling amongst themselves to combine to assert the king's title. Marching into England at the head of a scratch force lacking in all cohesion and control, he suffered such grievous defeat at Worcester (September 3, 1651) that flight was inevitable. With £1000 set on his head by parliament, for forty-four days he stole through the Western counties, only preserved from capture by the unswerving devotion of the many loyalists, of all classes, who risked their lives to help him on his way. Finally smuggled aboard a coal-brig at Shoreham, he was safely landed in Normandy. Nine years of wandering, indigent exile ensued before a distracted and impoverished England, in dread of a revival of military despotism, summoned Charles to take up the reins of government; a recall very largely engineered by General George Monck. Landing at Dover, Charles entered London in triumph on May 29, 1660. Two years later he married the Portuguese Princess Catherine of Braganza, but the union was childless. The first seven years of the reign were characterized by a loyal parliament and widespread constitutional support for a Church and State as anti-Catholic as it was anti-Puritan, although Clarendon's control of policy exhibited an inflexible authoritarianism dangerously at variance with the prevailing climate of opinion. The intransigent attitude of the extremist Catholic-Presbyterian 'Cabal' was ultimately reduced to impotence by the provisions of the Test Act of 1673. But failure to appreciate that the retention of Dunkirk without Calais to support it was no more than an empty gesture, rendered Charles's sale of the former Cromwellian incubus extremely unpopular; while the limited success attending the attempt to win back the valuable transoceanic carrying trade from the Dutch by the war of 1665 aroused general dissatisfaction. This was further exacerbated by de Ruyter's destructive raid on shipping in the Medway and Thamesmouth, where much of the Fleet had been 'laid up in ordinary' for want of an adequate parliamentary grant to fit it out and the necessary seafarers to man it—this last a consequence of the Great Plague. Clarendon's alleged mismanagement of the war led to his dismissal, hard on the conclusion of the Peace of Breda (1667). This was the outcome of the exhaustion of both belligerents, and left France free to pursue her design for an Anglo-Gallic combination against the States-General. This aim was temporarily checked by Sir William Temple's negotiations for a triple alliance between Britain, Holland and Sweden, a sop to the party of the 'Cabal'. But denied the requisite funds— particularly for the upkeep of the Navy—by Shaftesbury's intemperate 'Country Party', Charles, believing that a king's only morality is the welfare of his people, and that an Anglo-French alliance against Holland was the only alternative to a dangerously powerful Franco-Dutch coalition against Britain, signed the secret Treaty of Dover (1670). If by this pact the British sovereign became in some sort the pensioner of Louis of France, he sinuously contrived to evade the services expected of him in return, including the forcible conversion of his realm to Roman Catholicism, while sedulously devoting £76,000 of his first subsidy of £84,700 to the build-up of a fighting marine powerful enough to exact wary respect from Frenchman and Hollander alike. The Dutch War of 1672 sufficiently avenged the Medway raid; but Gallic cooperation therein was so half-hearted that public opinion refused to support a conflict in which ' the French only accompanied their allies to the scene of action to see if the British Navy earned its pay '. Peace with Holland was concluded and cemented by the marriage of Charles's niece, Mary, to the Prince of Orange. With

Shaftesbury heading an Opposition intent on making the utmost political capital out of Titus Oates's trumped-up ' Popish Plot ', Charles steered an astutely prudent course. Pretending to be duly impressed by reported machinations too infeasible to beguile any but the most gullible, he nonetheless steadfastly refused to tamper with the succession to exclude his brother James. The immoderate violence of the Whig leaders, together with the unmasking of the Rye House Plot to assassinate the king and his brother, turned the tide in Charles's favour. With his implacable opponents vanquished, for the last three years of his life Charles reigned tranquilly and without obstruction. Stricken with apoplexy, he died on February 6, 1685. Shrewd, supple and of great political acumen, Charles was ' an exact knower of mankind ' and one who ' had a world of wit and not a grain of ill-nature in him ' (Defoe). Above all, he was determined to restore his country's prosperity and safeguard it by building the most powerful Navy afloat. Inheriting a tremendous load of debt and an Exchequer containing exactly £11. 2s. 10d., by 1685 he had wrought so well that ' there were more men to be found on the Exchange worth £10,000 than in 1651 had been worth £1,000 ' (Sir Josiah Child). Indeed, ' England has rarely been so prosperous as under Charles II ' (Sir Charles Petrie), and the rise in living standards was shared by all classes. The Fleet was stronger than at any time under the Parliament, while 300,000 tons of merchant shipping wore the English flag. Men's liberty had been underwritten by the passage of the Habeas Corpus Act of 1679; science had been advanced by the construction of Greenwich Observatory and the production of the Nautical Almanac. Charles sharply differentiated between his duties as a sovereign and his indulgences as a man; and if his numerous amours expanded the ranks of the nobility with a dozen natural offspring, no woman who had granted him her favours could justly accuse him of ingratitude or neglect. See works by Hallam, Clarendon and Ranke, the Diaries of Pepys and Evelyn, and Lives by O. Airey (1904), E. Scott King, R. Crawfurd (1909), John Drinkwater and Sir Arthur Bryant (1954) and Hesketh Pearson (1960).

CHARLES (Karl Ludwig Johann) (1771–1847), Archduke of Austria, third son of the Emperor Leopold II, was born at Florence. Entrusted in 1796 with the chief command of the Austrian army on the Rhine, he defeated Moreau and Jourdan in several battles, drove the French over the Rhine, and took Kehl. In 1799 he was again victorious over Jourdan. Next year ill-health compelled him to accept the governor-generalship of Bohemia. Recalled after Hohenlinden to the chief command, he checked the progress of Moreau. In 1805 he commanded against Masséna in Italy; then, upon bad tidings from Germany, made a masterly retreat to Croatia. In 1809 he won the great battle of Aspern; but Napoleon soon retrieved his fortunes at Wagram. See his *Ausgewählte Schriften* (6 vols. Vienna 1893–94).

CHARLES (1887–1922), Emperor of Austria

(Karl I) and King of Hungary (Károly IV), succeeded his grand uncle, Francis Joseph (q.v.), in 1916. The elder son of Archduke Otto (d. 1906), son of Francis Joseph's brother, the Archduke Carl Ludwig, Charles became heir presumptive on the assassination at Sarajevo (June 28, 1914) of his uncle, Archduke Franz Ferdinand. In November 1918 he was compelled to abdicate. Two attempts at restoration in Hungary (1921) failed.

CHARLES. Ten kings of France:

Charles I, called **the Bald** (823–77), was king of France from 843 and emperor (as **Charles II**) of the West from 875.

Charles II, called **the Fat** (839–88), king from 884, had become emperor in Germany (as **Charles III**) in 881, but was deposed for making a disgraceful treaty with the Northmen in 887.

Charles III, called **the Simple** (879–929), king from 893, made peace with the Northmen, and was deposed in 922.

Charles IV (1294–1328), was king from 1322.

Charles V, called **the Wise** (1337–80), succeeded his father, John II, in 1364, and regained most of the territory lost to the English.

Charles VI, called **the Foolish** (1368–1422), son of the foregoing, lost the battle of Agincourt, and died insane.

Charles VII (1403–61), on succeeding his father, Charles VI, in 1422, held with his army the southern provinces; Paris and the north being in the hands of the English, who proclaimed Henry VI of England king of France, and appointed the Duke of Bedford regent. Charles was compelled to evacuate Champagne and Maine; but in 1426 at Montargis Dunois gained the first victory over the English, who in 1427 laid siege to Orleans. Joan of Arc roused the fervour of both nobles and people; the siege of Orleans was raised in May 1429; the English gradually lost all they had gained in France; and their cause became hopeless after the treaty concluded at Arras (1435) between the French king and the Duke of Burgundy. Bayonne fell in 1451, and with the death of Talbot under the walls of Castillon in 1453, the whole south finally passed to France, and the Hundred Years' War came to an end. In 1436 Charles entered Paris. He devoted himself to the reorganization of the government, and under his rule France recovered in some measure from her terrible calamities. His last years were embittered by the conduct of his son, the Dauphin, afterwards Louis XI. He died at Mehun-sur-Yèvre. See the work by Du Fresne de Beaucourt (6 vols. 1881–92).

Charles VIII, called **the Affable** (1470–98), succeeded his father, Louis XI, in 1483; in 1495–96 he failed in an attempt to secure the kingdom of Naples.

Charles IX (1550–74), the second son of Henry II and Catharine de' Medici, was born at St Germain-en-Laye, and succeeded his brother, Francis II, in 1560. He was proficient in manly exercises, and possessed much physical energy, with some literary accomplishments. But, weak and wavering with all his cruelty and cunning, he was completely subject to his mother, whose counsels drove him to authorize the atrocious massacre of St Bartholomew, August 24, 1572. Its consequences were far from favourable to the Catholic cause, while scarce two years later the wretched king died miserably. See works by Desjardins (1874) and De la Barre-Duparcq (1875).

Charles X (1757–1836), third surviving son of the Dauphin Louis, and grandson of Louis XV, born at Versailles, received the title of Comte d'Artois, and in 1773 married Maria Theresa of Savoy. The first emigration was headed by him and Condé. After taking a small part in the war of 1792, Charles went to St Petersburg; thence in 1793 to England. In spite of the failure of the expedition to Quiberon Bay in June 1795, another was attempted under Artois in October, but he had not courage to land and head the insurgents, whom he basely left to the vengeance of Hoche. After this he lived partly at Holyrood and partly at Hartwell, until the allies entered Paris in 1814, when he appeared in France as lieutenant-general of the kingdom. After the second restoration, in alliance with the priests, he headed the Ultras in their struggle with the Constitutionalists. The death of his brother Louis XVIII (1824) brought him to the throne. He swore adherence to the Charte, and was at first popular, but soon showed signs of restoring the absolutism of the old French monarchy. Popular discontent rapidly increased; but in 1829 Charles called Prince Polignac to the head of affairs. A threatening royal speech, on March 2, 1830, was followed by a remonstrance, signed by 221 deputies, upon which the king dissolved the chambers. The deputies who signed the address were all re-elected, but the celebrated five ordinances of July 25 were signed by the king, putting an end to the freedom of the press, and dissolving the recently elected chamber. Paris took up arms, and the king, as a last resource, with his elder son, the Duc d'Angoulême (q.v.), abdicated on August 2, 1830, in favour of his grandson, the little Comte de Chambord. But it was too late; the Revolution was completed, and Louis-Philippe was chosen king of the French. Charles resided for some time at Holyrood again, and afterwards at Prague. He died of cholera at Görz, November 6, 1836. See works by Védrenne (1879), Petit (1886), Lucas-Dubreton (1927) and P. de la Gorce (1928).

CHARLES. Seven Holy Roman Emperors:

Charles I. See CHARLEMAGNE.

Charles II. See CHARLES I of France.

Charles III. See CHARLES II of France.

Charles IV (1316–78) was the son of John of Bohemia, and held his court mainly at Prague.

Charles V (1500–58), was born at Ghent. From his father Philip, son of the Emperor Maximilian and Mary of Burgundy, he inherited the Low Countries, the county of Burgundy, and a claim to the imperial crown; from his mother, Joanna, daughter of Ferdinand and Isabella, he inherited Spain, Naples and Spanish America. In 1517 he went to Spain, and was made joint ruler with his mother, now insane; and in 1519 he was elected to the Holy Roman Empire. Next year he was crowned emperor at Aachen, and a few months later (1521) presided at the Diet of Worms, which condemned Luther's opinions.

The history of Western Europe was now largely the rivalry of Charles and Francis I of France. Henry VIII of England and the popes favoured now the one and now the other; and the result was almost continuous war, broken by the Treaty of Madrid (1526), the Ladies' Peace of Cambrai (1529) and the Peace of Crespy (1544). Charles claimed the duchy of Burgundy and the duchy of Milan. Francis asserted his right to these, and demanded homage of Charles for Flanders and Artois. At first the war—mainly in Italy—was altogether in Charles's favour. Henry VIII aided the emperor, and Francis's greatest subject, the Constable Bourbon, leagued with Charles and Henry. In 1524 Charles's troops drove the French out of Italy and invaded Provence; and next year Francis was defeated and taken prisoner at Pavia, being released in 1526 only on yielding to Charles on all the points in dispute. Straightway the Holy League was formed against Charles by Pope Clement VII, Henry VIII, Francis and the Venetians; but in 1527 a motley army of Spaniards, Italians and Germans, led by Bourbon, who fell in the assault, sacked Rome, and imprisoned the pope. Charles, denounced as the author of the sacrilege, disclaimed all part in it. The Peace of Cambrai (1529) left Charles master of Italy.

During these years Charles had been resident in Spain, where it required all his tact to suppress discontent and extort the funds needed for his foreign schemes. In 1529 he proceeded to Italy, and at Bologna was crowned by the pope king of Lombardy and emperor of the Romans. In vain he urged the pope to call a general council for settling the Lutheran problem. At the Diet of Augsburg (1530) Charles confirmed the Edict of Worms, and the Protestants formed the League of Schmalkald. The threat of an invasion by the Sultan forced Charles to make concessions. In 1535 Charles in person crushed the corsair Barbarossa, and captured Tunis. In 1536 he invaded Provence from Italy, but accomplished nothing; Francis, in desperation, called in the aid of the Turk. In 1538 the pope (Paul III), Francis and Charles agreed at Nice to a ten years' truce. In 1539 Charles travelled through France to the Low Countries, quelled an insurrection at Ghent, and stripped the town of all its privileges; and held another diet in Germany. In 1541 he conducted against the pirates of Algiers a fleet which was utterly wrecked by storms. The war with Francis about Milan went on again for three years; the Turkish fleet wintered at Toulon, whereat Henry VIII was so indignant that he concerted with Charles an invasion of France; it forced Francis to make the unfavourable peace of Crespy (1544). Charles's league with the pope drove the Protestants to arms, but two campaigns saw their power broken, and the Augsburg Interim (1548) followed. Charles's severe enforcement of the Interim, his cruel treatment of his prisoners, the Landgrave of Hesse and the Elector of Saxony, and his evident design to make himself absolute master of Germany, led to the overthrow of all his plans. Maurice of Saxony, who, although a Protestant, had hitherto supported Charles, worsted the emperor and was soon in a position to command the most favourable conditions for the Protestants, and by the Treaty of Passau (1552) and the Peace of Augsburg (1555), Protestantism received legal recognition. He had tried in vain to persuade his brother Ferdinand to waive his claims to the empire in favour of his son Philip, and the princes of Germany, Catholic as well as Protestant, refused to entertain Charles's suggestion. Disappointed in his dearest hopes, and broken in health by gout, Charles laid down his imperial dignity and resigned the kingdom of Spain to his son (1555), who had married Mary of England. Retiring to the monastery of Yuste, in Estremadura, he spent the rest of his life in complete seclusion. Don John (q.v.) of Austria was an illegitimate son of Charles V. See Robertson's *Life of Charles V*, and Prescott's continuation; Ranke's *History of the Reformation in Germany*; Sir W. Stirling-Maxwell's *Cloister Life of Charles V*; Lives by C. Hare (1917), E. Valvekens (1945), J. Babelon (1947) and Tyler (1956).

CHARLES. Four kings of Spain:

Charles I. See CHARLES V, Holy Roman Emperor.

Charles II (1661–1700), who succeeded his father, Philip IV, in 1665, went to war against France in the Grand Alliance and precipitated the War of Spanish Succession by choosing Philip of Anjou as his successor. See J. Nada, *Carlos the Bewitched* (1962).

Charles III (1716–88), was a younger son of Philip V, and succeeded his half-brother, Ferdinand VI, in 1759.

Charles IV (1784–1819), son of the foregoing, was the king whose fleet Nelson destroyed at Trafalgar, and who had to abdicate in Napoleon's favour in 1808.

CHARLES. Fifteen kings of Sweden, of which the first six are semilegendary:

Charles VII, ruled 1161–67, fought the Russians.

Charles VIII (1408–70), ruled from 1448 to 1457, when he was driven out by the Danes, but came back temporarily (1464–65) and eventually permanently (1467–70).

Charles IX (1550–1611), was elected regent in 1595 and became king in 1600. He restored the Protestant faith and went to war against Poland and Denmark.

Charles X (1622–60), the son of the Count Palatine by Gustavus-Adolphus' sister, took part in the Thirty Years' War, and on the abdication of his cousin, Queen Christina (1654), succeeded to the throne of a kingdom impoverished by her extravagance. He overran Poland in 1655; forced the Great Elector to acknowledge his lordship over Prussia; and crushed the forces of the Polish king anew in a terrible three-day battle at Warsaw (July 28–30, 1656). His next war was with the Danes, when he crossed the Great and Little Belt on the ice, and extorted

the Treaty of Roskilde (1658), which gave to Sweden the southern parts of the Scandinavian peninsula, heretofore Danish. In 1659 he was driven from a new attack on Copenhagen by help of the Brandenburgers and Dutch; and he died suddenly at Gothenburg, being succeeded by his infant son, Charles XI (1655–97).

Charles XII (1682–1718), the son of Charles XI, was born June 17, 1682, and on the death of his father in 1697 was declared of age. Denmark, Poland and Russia thought this a favourable time for combining to humble Sweden. The young king at once flung an army into Sjælland, and in concert with Sir George Rooke's Anglo-Dutch squadron speedily compelled the Danes to sue for peace. Charles now hastened to meet the Russians, 50,000 strong, at Narva, stormed their camp with but 8000 Swedes, and routed them with great slaughter, November 30, 1700. He next dethroned Augustus II, and procured the election of Stanislaus Leszczynski as king of Poland. Augustus was pursued to Saxony, his hereditary dominion, and forced to sign a humiliating peace (1706). In 1707 Charles had collected an army of 45,000 men in Saxony, and in the January of the following year suddenly burst into Russia, and almost captured Peter the Great at Grodno. He drove the Russians before him, and had won a battle at Smolensk, when he suddenly turned southwards to the Ukraine, trusting to the promises of the Cossack *hetman* Mazeppa. But Mazeppa failed to bring forward his 30,000 Cossacks, and, after a winter of fearful hardship, Charles, with 23,000 men, laid siege to Pultowa, where the Czar defeated him (July 8, 1709). Charles fled across the Turkish frontier to Bender. The Czar and the king of Denmark assailed the Swedish territories, but Charles stirred up the Porte to war with Russia. Soon, however, the Turks became suspicious of Charles and imprisoned him; but escaping, he made his way through Hungary and Germany in sixteen days, till he reached Stralsund in November 1714. A month later the town was forced to capitulate to an allied army of Danes, Saxons, Prussians and Russians, Charles having escaped four days before. Nothing daunted, he attacked Norway in 1716; and soon after he formed a highly ambitious scheme. He was to make terms with the Czar by surrendering the Baltic provinces of Sweden, then conquer Norway, next land in Scotland and replace the House of Stuart on the throne, with the help of the Jacobite party within and that of Cardinal Alberoni without. No sooner had he purchased his peace with the Czar than he burst into Norway; and during the siege of Halden was killed by a musket-shot from the fortress—not, as was long alleged, by a treacherous shot from his own ranks. Charles was brave to the pitch of reckless folly, determined to the point of foolish obstinacy. His hardy frame defied alike fatigue, heat and cold: he shared the coarsest food and severest labour of the common soldier with a winning cheerfulness. He was able and sagacious in counsel. But his ambition was fatal to his country; and after his death, Sweden, exhausted by his wars, ceased to be numbered among the great powers. Voltaire's *Histoire de Charles XII* remains, despite errors, the best life; there are also good sketches by King Oscar II (Eng. trans. 1879), Nisbet Bain (1896), Oscar Browning (1899), E. Godley (1928), and E. Bengtsson (trans. 1960).

Charles XIV (1763–1844), originally JEAN BAPTISTE JULES BERNADOTTE, was born, a lawyer's son at Pau. He entered the French army in 1780 as a common soldier, became an ardent partisan of the Revolution, and fought his way up to the command of a division in 1794, and a marshal's baton in 1804. He distinguished himself greatly in the German campaigns in 1796 and the year after under the eye of Napoleon himself in Italy. In 1799 he was minister of war, and for his conduct at Austerlitz was named in 1805 Prince of Pontecorvo. In the campaigns of 1806 he commanded the first army corps. After Jena he pursued the Prussians to Halle, and Blücher to Lübeck, compelling him to surrender (November 7). He received the command of the French troops in North Germany and Denmark, and led the Saxon troops at Wagram. But he had never been liked or trusted by Napoleon, whose jealousy now became so apparent that Bernadotte returned to Paris. In 1810 he was elected heir to the throne of Sweden. He turned Protestant, and changed his name to Charles John; and the health of the Swedish king, Charles XIII, failing next year, the reins of government came almost entirely into his hands. He refused to comply with Napoleon's demands, which were opposed to Swedish interests, and was soon involved in war with him. He took part in the final struggle at Leipzig, but showed much reluctance to join in the invasion of France. He became king of Sweden on Charles's death in 1818, and won for himself the character of a wise and good king. He died March 8, 1844, and was succeeded by his son Oscar. See Life by Sarrans (1845), and a series of books by Sir D. Plunket Barton (1914, 1921, 1925, abr. 1929).

CHARLES, Jacques Alexandre César (1746–1823), French physicist, born at Beaugency (Loiret), the discoverer of Charles's Law connecting the expansion of gas with its rise in temperature, was one of the first to make a balloon ascent. He was professor of Physics in Paris, where he died.

CHARLES ALBERT (1798–1849), king of Sardinia, in 1800 succeeded his father, Prince Charles Emmanuel of Savoy-Carignan. In 1817 he married Maria Theresa, daughter of the Archduke of Tuscany. When the revolution took place in Piedmont in 1821, he was temporarily regent, in 1829 was appointed viceroy of Sardinia, and on the death of Charles Felix in 1831 ascended the throne. His moderation earned Mazzini's denunciations but the applause of all farsighted men. In 1848 he declared war against Austria; but after the fatal battle of Novara, March 24, 1849, he had to abdicate in favour of his son, Victor Emmanuel II. He died brokenhearted in Portugal.

CHARLES D'ORLÉANS (1391–1465). See ORLEANS.

CHARLES EDWARD. See STEWART.

CHARLES, Martel (' the Hammer ') (c. 688–741), was the natural son of Pepin of Heristal, mayor of the palace under the later Merovingian kings. Chosen duke in 714 by the Austrasian Franks, he became in 720 mayor of the palace and real ruler of all the Franks. He had much hard fighting with the Saxons, Alemanni and Bavarians, and he it was who rolled back the tide of Moslem conquest, in a desperate battle between Tours and Poitiers (732). Charles finished his work by driving the Saracens out of Burgundy and Languedoc (737). He died in 741, leaving the kingdom to be divided between his sons—Carloman and Pepin.

CHARLES OF ANJOU (1225–1285), youngest son of Louis VIII of France, received the crown of Naples and Sicily from Pope Urban IV, slew Manfred, and provoked the rising against the French known as ' the Sicilian Vespers '.

CHARLES THE BOLD (1433–77), Duke of Burgundy, was born at Dijon. From his youth he was a declared enemy of Louis XI of France, nominally feudal superior of Burgundy, and he early formed an alliance with the Duke of Brittany and some of the great nobles of France. Their united forces ravaged Picardy, threatened Paris, defeated the king at Montlhéry, and extorted from him favourable terms. In 1467 Charles succeeded his father, Philip the Good, as Duke of Burgundy. Richer and more powerful than any prince of his time, he conceived the design of restoring the old kingdom of Burgundy, and conquering Lorraine, Provence, Dauphiné and Switzerland. Louis invited him to a conference, and while he hesitated, stirred up the citizens of Liège to revolt. At the news Charles seized the king, and but for Comines (q.v.), would have put him to death. He compelled Louis to accompany him to Liège, and sanction by his presence the cruelties which he inflicted on the citizens. War raged between them till 1475, when Charles turned anew to his favourite scheme of conquest, and soon made himself master of Lorraine. Invading Switzerland, he stormed Granson, and hanged and drowned the garrison; but was terribly defeated by the Swiss near that place (March 1, 1476). Presently he besieged Morat, but sustained a more terrible defeat (June 22). The news that Duke René of Lorraine was attempting to recover his territories roused him from despair. He laid siege to Nancy; but his army was small, and his Italian mercenaries went over to the enemy. Charles fought with all his wonted recklessness, and perished in the battle. His daughter Mary married the Emperor Maximilian I. See Lives by Kirk (3 vols. 1863) and Putnam (1908).

CHARLES THE GREAT. See CHARLEMAGNE.

CHARLET, Nicolas Toussaint (1792–1845), French painter and engraver, born at Paris, held a clerkship under the Empire, but lost it at the Restoration (1815), and betook himself to art. A pupil of Gros, he is known for his humorously-treated genre pictures and his lithographs of the Napoleonic wars. See Lives by Lacombe (1856) and Dayot (1892).

CHARLEVOIX, Pierre François Xavier de, *shar-lĕ-vwa* (1682–1761), French Jesuit, born in St Quentin, twice visited Canada, and voyaged down the Mississippi to New Orleans. He published his journal, histories of San Domingo, Japan and Paraguay, and a *Histoire de la nouvelle France* (1744; Eng. trans. New York, 6 vols. 1865–72).

CHARLOTTE, Princess (1796–1817), born at Carlton House, London, was the only child of the future George IV and Caroline of Brunswick, who parted immediately after her birth. A bright, lively, warm-tempered girl, she was brought up in strict seclusion, seeing her father rarely, and her mother only for two hours a week. Her six months' engagement to Prince William of Orange she herself broke off in June 1814, greatly to George's fury. On May 2, 1816, she married Prince Leopold of Saxe-Coburg; but the marriage, a happy one, was cut short on November 5, 1817, by her death after giving birth to a stillborn boy. See works by Lady R. Weigall (1874), Mrs H. Jones (1885), C. E. Pearce (1911) and D. M. Stuart, *Daughter of England* (1951).

CHARLOTTE ELIZABETH (1652–1722), only daughter of the Count Palatine, and granddaughter of Elizabeth of Bohemia, in 1671 became second wife of Philip, Duke of Orleans (1640–1701). See *Life and Letters* (1889), and Life by A. Barine (trans. 1909).

CHARLOTTE SOPHIA (1744–1818), niece of the Duke of Mecklenburg, married George III (q.v.), and had fifteen children. Her eldest daughter, Charlotte Augusta Matilda (1766–1828), in 1797 married the future king of Württemberg. See P. Fitzgerald's *Good Queen Caroline* (1899) and Greenwood's *Hanoverian Queens* (1911).

CHARNOCK, (1) Job (d. 1693), the founder in 1686–90 of Calcutta by the removal thither from Húglí of the factories of the East India Company.

(2) **Robert** (c. 1663–96), the Romanist exfellow of Magdalen College, Oxford, who was hanged at Tyburn for his share in Barclay's plot to assassinate William III.

CHARPENTIER, Gustave, *shar-pã-tyay* (1860–1956), French composer, born at Dieuze, Lorraine, composed both music and libretto of *Louise* (1900) and *Julien* (1913), and succeeded his teacher, Massenet, in the Académie des Beaux Arts.

CHARRON, Pierre (1541–1603), French theologian, born at Paris, assailed the League in *Discours chrétiens* (1589), vindicated Catholicism in *Les Trois Vérités* (1594), and in his chief work, *De la sagesse* (1601), took a sceptical attitude towards all forms of religion. He was a friend of Montaigne.

CHARTERIS, *chart'èrz*, (1) **Francis** (1675–1732), colonel, cardsharper, thief and scoundrel generally, was a native of Dumfriesshire, and purchased an estate in East Lothian. His only daughter married the fourth Earl of Wemyss. Coupled with the devil, he is mentioned by Pope in his *Moral Essays*. He was depicted by Hogarth in *A Harlot's Progress*.

(2) **Leslie** (1907–), English crime story writer educated at Cambridge, known for his books with a criminal hero ' the Saint '.

CHARTIER, Alain, *shar-tyay* (1385–c. 1435), French author, born at Bayeux, was secretary to Charles VI and VII and went on diplomatic missions to Germany, Venice and Scotland (1425–28). His much imitated *La belle dame sans merci* (1424) is a piece of escapism in the midst of his preoccupation with the plight of France in the Hundred Years' War, which forms the backcloth of his two best works, the *Livre des quatre dames* (1415–16) in which four ladies on the morrow of Agincourt weep for their lost lovers, and the *Quadrilogue invectif* (1422), a debate apportioning the blame for France's ills between the people and the nobility. Chartier also showed skill in handling the *ballade* and other lyrical forms. See E. J. Hoffman, *Alain Chartier, his Work and Reputation* (1942).

CHASE, (1) James Hadley, pseud. of René Raymond (1906–), British novelist, started the vogue for tough realism in gangster stories with his *No Orchids for Miss Blandish* (1939), the first of a number in similar vein.

(2) **Salmon Portland** (1808–73), American statesman, born at Cornish, New Hampshire, in 1830 settled as a lawyer in Cincinnati, where he acted as counsel for the defence of fugitive slaves. In 1841 he helped to found the Liberty party, which in 1844 brought about Clay's defeat. Chase was returned to the senate in 1849 by the Ohio Democrats, but separated from the party in 1852 when it committed itself to slavery. He was twice governor of Ohio (1855–59), and in 1861–64 was secretary of the treasury. In 1864 Lincoln appointed him chief justice of the U.S.; as such he presided at the trial of President Johnson (1868). He died at New York.

(3) **William Merritt** (1849–1916), American painter of landscapes, portraits and still-life, born in Indiana, from 1872–78 studied at Munich under Piloty. See study by K. M. Roof (1917).

CHASLES, *shahl*, (1) **Michel** (1793–1880), French geometrician, was born near Chartres. He entered the École Polytechnique in 1812, and in 1829 addressed to the Brussels Academy a memoir on duality and homography in geometry. Its introduction expanded into the *Origine et développement des méthodes en géométrie* (1837). In 1841 he became a professor at the École Polytechnique, and in 1846 at the Sorbonne. In 1852 appeared his *Traité de géométrie supérieure*; in 1860, *Porismes d'Euclide*; in 1865, *Sections coniques*; in 1870, the *Progrès de la géométrie*. He died at Paris. In 1867 he reported to the Academy that he had come into possession of autographs of Pascal's which proved that he had anticipated Newton's greatest discoveries. Ultimately, however, he had to admit that these and about 27,000 other autographs (of Julius Caesar, Dante, Shakespeare, &c.) were forgeries. The forger, Vraïn-Lucas, was convicted.

(2) **Philarète** (1798–1873), French savant and essayist, born at Mainvilliers, near Chartres, was jailed as a Jacobin and fled on his release to England, where he acquired

the knowledge which he used as a reviewer of English books on his return. In 1837 he became librarian of the Bibliothèque Mazarine, in 1841 professor of Northern Languages at the Collège de France. He died at Venice. See his *Mémoires* (2 vols. 1876–78).

CHASSÉ, David Hendrik, Baron (1765–1849), Dutch soldier, born at Thiel, in Guelders, took French service in 1787. 'General Baïonette', as Napoleon nicknamed him because of his fondness for bayonet charges, afterwards fought with great distinction in Germany and Spain; he was made a baron by Louis Bonaparte in 1809. As lieutenant-general of the Dutch forces in 1815 he fought at Waterloo against his old comrades, the French; as governor of Antwerp he for three weeks held the citadel with 5000 men against 60,000 Belgians and French (1832).

CHASSEPOT, Antoine Alphonse, *shas-pō* (1833–1905), was an employee in the Paris arsenal, and in 1863 produced the model of his rifle, adopted in 1866. He subsequently became a hotelkeeper in Nice.

CHASSÉRIAU, Théodor, *sha-say-ree-ō* (1819–1856), Creole-French painter, born at Samana, San Domingo, studied under Delaroche and Ingres, executed murals and historical subject paintings. His *Tepidarium at Pompeii* and *Susanna* are in the Louvre. See studies by Bouvenne (Paris 1884) and Bénédite (Paris 1931).

CHASTELARD, Pierre de Boscosel de (c. 1540–63), grandson of the chevalier Bayard (q.v.), as page in the household of Marshal Damville came to Scotland with Queen Mary (1561). Madly in love with the queen, he ventured to conceal himself under her bed, was discovered and forgiven, but on a repetition of his offence was hanged at St Andrews. He is the subject of a tragedy by Swinburne.

CHATEAUBRIAND, François René, Vicomte de, *sha-tō-bree-ã* (1768–1848), French writer and politician, born of a noble Breton family at St Malo. He served for a short time as an ensign, and in 1791 sailed to North America, spending eight months in the travels recounted in his *Voyage en Amérique*. Returning to France, he married, but forthwith joined the army of the émigrés, and was left for dead near Namur. From 1793 to 1800 he maintained himself in England, chiefly in London, by teaching and translation; in 1797 he published an *Essai sur les Révolutions*. *Atala*, a love story of savage life (1801), established his literary reputation; and the *Génie du christianisme* (1802), a vindication of the Church of Rome, raised him to the foremost position among the French men of letters of the day. He was in 1803 appointed secretary to the embassy at Rome, where he wrote his *Lettres sur l'Italie*, and in 1804 was sent as envoy to the little republic of Valais. But on the murder of the Duc d'Enghien, Chateaubriand refused to hold office under Napoleon. He set out to the East in 1806, visited Greece, Palestine and Egypt, and returned to France in 1807. Two years later he issued *Les Martyrs*, a prose epic of Diocletian's persecutions. From 1814 to 1824 he gave a thoroughgoing support to the Restoration

monarchy. He was made a peer and minister, and in 1822–24 was ambassador extraordinary at the British court. Disappointed in his hope of becoming prime minister, from 1824 to 1830 he figured as a Liberal; but on the downfall of Charles X went back to the Royalists. During the reign of Louis-Philippe he occupied himself in writing his celebrated *Mémoires d'outre-tombe*. Parts of this eloquent autobiography appeared before his death; the whole, in 6 vols., not till 1902 (translated in 1902). His writings also include the *Itinéraire de Paris à Jerusalem*; *Les Natchez*, a prose epic dealing with savage life in North America; and two works of fiction, *René* and *Le Dernier des Abencérages*. See works by Sainte-Beuve (1877), Biré (1902–03), Cassagne (1911 *et seq.*), Giraud (1904–12), Lemaître (1912), Madame Durry (1933), Martin-Chauffier (1943), Marshall and Stock (1958), F. Sieburg (tr. 1961), and his *Correspondance* (1912 *et seq.*).

CHÂTELET-LOMONT, Gabrielle Émilie, Marquise du, *shat-lay-lo-mō* (1706–49), talented French beauty, studied Latin and Italian with her father the Baron de Breteuil, and subsequently mathematics and the physical sciences. Her marriage with the Marquis du Châtelet-Lomont did not hinder her from forming, in 1733, a *tendresse* for Voltaire, who came to reside with her at her château of Cirey, on the borders of Champagne and Lorraine. In 1747 the philosopher had to make room for M. Saint-Lambert, a captain of the Lorraine Guards. The Marquise wrote *Institutions de physique* (1740), and translated Newton's *Principia*. See Life by Maurel (1930).

CHATELIER, Henry le, *shat-lyay* (1850–1936), French chemist, in 1888 discovered the law of reaction governing the effect of pressure and temperature on equilibrium. He devised a railway water-brake, an optical pyrometer, and made contributions to metallurgy and ceramics.

CHATHAM, William Pitt, 1st Earl of (1708–1778), often spoken of as 'the elder Pitt', orator and statesman, was the younger son of Robert Pitt of Boconnoc, in Cornwall, and was born in Westminster. Educated at Eton and Trinity College, Oxford, he obtained a cornetcy in the Blues (1731), and in 1735 entered parliament for the family borough, Old Sarum. He sided with Frederick, Prince of Wales, then at deadly feud with the king, and offered, as leader of the young 'Patriot' Whigs, a determined opposition to Walpole. The latter being driven from power, the king found it necessary, in 1746, to allow Pitt's admission to the Broad-bottom administration; subsequently he was paymaster-general, but resigned in 1755. The Duchess of Marlborough had left him £10,000 in 1744; and Sir William Pynsent left him £3000 a year and the Somerset estate of Burton-Pynsent, the family seat thenceforward of the Pitts. In 1756 Pitt became nominally secretary of state, but virtually premier. He immediately put into execution his own plan of carrying on the war with France, raised the militia, and strengthened the naval power; but the king's old enmity and German predilections led him to resign in April

1757, to be recalled in June, in obedience to the loud demands of the people. His war policy was characterized by unusual vigour, sagacity and success. French armies were beaten everywhere by Britain and her allies—in India, in Africa, in Canada, on the Rhine—and British fleets drove the few French ships they did not capture or destroy from almost every sea. But the prime mover of all these brilliant victories found himself compelled to resign (1761) when, through Lord Bute, the majority of the cabinet refused to declare war with Spain. Pitt received a pension of £3000 a year; and his wife, sister of George Grenville, was created Baroness Chatham. In 1766 he formed a new ministry, choosing for himself the almost sinecure office of privy seal, with a seat in the House of Lords as Viscount Pitt and Earl of Chatham. Ill-health prevented Chatham from taking any active part in guiding his weak and embarrassed ministry, and he resigned in 1768, to hold office no more. He spoke strongly against the arbitrary and harsh policy towards the American colonies, and warmly urged an amicable settlement of the differences. But when it was proposed to make peace on any terms, ill though he was, Chatham came down to the House of Lords (April 2, 1778), and by a few broken words secured a majority against the motion. But exhausted by speaking, on rising again to reply to a query, he fell back into the arms of his friends, and died May 11, 1778. He was honoured with a public funeral and a statue in Westminster Abbey; government voted £20,000 to pay his debts, and conferred a pension of £4000 a year on his descendants. His imposing appearance and his magnificent voice added greatly to the attractions of his oratory. His character was irreproachable, though his haughtiness irritated even his friends. See Lives by F. Thackeray (1827), Frederic Harrison (1905), A. von Ruville (trans. 1907), Rosebery (1910), B. Williams (1913); and books by Winstanley (1912), Hotblack (1917), Sherrard (3 vols., 1952–58) and Brooke (1956).—His eldest son, **John, 2nd Earl of Chatham** (1756–1835), commanded the luckless Walcheren Expedition (1809). For his second son, see PITT.

CHATRIAN. See ERCKMANN.

CHATTERJI, Bankim Chandra (1838–94), Indian writer, born at Katalpura, Bengal, one of the most influential figures in 19th-century Indian literature, wrote *Durges Nandini* (1864) and *Ananda Math* (1882), a novel of the Sannyasi rebellion of 1772 from which the Nationalist song *Bande Mataram* (' Hail to thee, Mother '), was taken.

CHATTERTON, Thomas (1752–70), English poet, was born at Bristol. His father, a subchanter in the cathedral, and master of a charity school, had died in the August before the poet was born. The mother, a poor schoolmistress and needlewoman, brought up her boy and his sister beneath the shadow of St Mary Redcliffe, where their forefathers had been sextons (more probably masons) since the days of Elizabeth. He seemed a dull, dreamy child till his seventh year; then, quickly learning to read from a black-letter Bible, he began to devour every book that fell in his way. He was a scholar of Colston's bluecoat hospital 1760–65, and then was bound apprentice to Lambert, an attorney. In December 1762 he wrote his first poem, ' On the Last Epiphany '; in the summer of 1764, the first of his pseudo-antiques, ' Elinour and Juga ', which he professed to have got from Canynge's Coffer in the muniment room of St Mary's. Next, early in 1767, for one Burgum, a pewterer, he concocted a pedigree of the De Bergham family (this brought him five shillings); and in 1768 he hoaxed the whole city with a description, ' from an old manuscript ', of the opening of Bristol Bridge in 1248. His life at Lambert's was a sordid one; he slept with the footboy, and took his meals in the kitchen. Yet, his duties over—and he discharged them well—he had ample leisure for his studies, poetry, history, heraldry, music, antiquities. An attempt to draw Dodsley had failed, when, in 1769, he sent Horace Walpole a ' transcript ' of ' The Ryse of Peyncteyne yn Englande, wroten by T. Rowleie 1469, for Mastre Canynge '. Walpole, quite taken in, wrote at once to his unknown correspondent, expressing a thousand thanks for the manuscript. Back came a fresh batch of manuscript, and with it a sketch of Chatterton's own history. The poems, however, being shown to Mason and Gray, were pronounced by them to be forgeries; and Walpole's next letter was a letter of advice to stick to his calling. A ' Last Will and Testament of Thomas Chatterton . . . executed in the presence of Omniscience this 14th of April 1770 ', falling into his master's hands, procured the hasty cancelling of his indentures; and ten days later the boy quitted Bristol for London. There he arrived with his poems, and perhaps five guineas in his pocket, and lodged first in Shoreditch; next, from the middle of June, at Brooke Street, Holborn. Abstemious, sleepless, he fell to work as with a hundred hands, pouring forth satires, squibs, stories, political essays, burlettas, epistles in Junius' style (for ' Wilkes and liberty '), and the ' Balade of Charitie '. For a while his prospects seemed golden. Publishers spoke well of him; he obtained an interview with the Lord Mayor Beckford; in the first two months he earned eleven guineas (at the rate of from a farthing to twopence a line); and he sent home glowing letters, with a box of presents for his mother and sister. Then Beckford died; the ' patriotic ' publishers took fright; the dead season set in; he had overstocked the market with unpaid wares; a last desperate application failed for the post of surgeon to a Bristol slaver. He was penniless, starving, yet too proud to accept the meal his landlady offered him, when, on August 24, 1770, he locked himself into his garret, tore up his papers, and was found next morning poisoned. They buried him in the paupers' pit of the Shoe Lane Workhouse. For eighty years the Rowley controversy was waged with no less bitterness than ignorance, the Rowleyans including Jacob Bryant (1781), Dean Milles (1782), and Dr S. R. Maitland (1857); the anti-Rowleyans, Tyrwhitt (1777–82) and Warton

(1778–82). The subject was laid to rest by Skeat in his edition of *Chatterton* (1871); the bogus ' early English ' is the boy poet's own invention. See *Chattertoniana*, by Hyett and Bazeley (1914). The Rowley Poems were edited by Steele (1899) and Hare (1911), the complete poetical works by H. D. Roberts (1906). See Watts-Dunton's essay in Ward's *English Poets* (1880); Sir H. Croft's *Love and Madness* (1780); books by Dix (1837), Sir D. Wilson (1869), Masson (new ed. 1900), H. Richter (1900), J. H. Ingram (1910), E. H. W. Meyerstein (1930). The story was dramatized by Alfred de Vigny in 1835.

CHAUCER, Geoffrey (*c.* 1345–1400), English poet, was the son of John Chaucer, a vintner and tavern keeper in London, perhaps the John Chaucer who was deputy to the king's butler. It is possible he may have gone to Oxford or to Cambridge; certainly in 1357 and 1358 he was a page in the service of the wife of Lionel, Duke of Clarence; whence he would seem to have been presently transferred to the king's household. In 1359 he served in the campaign in France, and was taken prisoner at ' Retters ' (Réthel), but was soon ransomed, the king contributing £16 towards the required amount. He returned home in 1360. In 1367 the king granted him a pension. He is described as ' our beloved yeoman ', and as ' one of the yeomen of the king's chamber ', and in 1368 is one of the king's esquires. In 1368 one Philippa Chaucer appears amongst the ladies of the queen's bedchamber, and there is no good reason for doubting that this is the poet's wife. She seems to have had two sons and a daughter. In the year 1369 Chaucer comes certainly before us as a poet, with his *Book of the Duchess*, on the death of John of Gaunt's wife. In 1370 he went abroad on the king's service; in 1372–73 on a royal mission to Genoa, Pisa, Florence; in 1376, abroad, it is not known where; in 1377, to Flanders and to France; in 1378, to Italy again. Meanwhile in 1374 he was appointed comptroller of the Customs and Subsidy of Wools, Skins, and Tanned Hides in the port of London; in 1382, comptroller of the Petty Customs; and in 1385 he was allowed to nominate a permanent deputy. In 1374 the king granted him a pitcher of wine daily; and John of Gaunt conferred on him a pension of £10 for life. In 1375 he received from the crown the custody of lands that brought him in £104. In 1386 he was elected a knight of the shire for Kent. The following writings certainly belong to the period 1369–87: *The Parliament of Fowls, The House of Fame, Troilus and Cressida*, and *The Legend of Good Women;* also what ultimately appeared as the Clerk's, Man of Law's, Prioress's, Second Nun's, and Knight's Tales in the *Canterbury Tales*. Chaucer's earlier writings, including his translation of part of the *Roman de la Rose*, followed the current French trends, but the most important influence acting upon him during this middle period of his literary life was that of Italy. Much of his subject matter he derived from his great Italian contemporaries, especially from Boccaccio, but it was the spirit, not the letter of these masters

which he imitated. And in the heroic heptastich, and presently in the heroic couplet, he found metrical forms that satisfied the highest ideal. The crowning work of the middle period of his life is certainly *Troilus and Cressida*—a work in which his immense power of human observation, his sense of humour, and his dramatic skill are lavishly displayed. The *Legend of Good Women* has an admirable prologue, but was never finished. His next great subject was the Canterbury Pilgrimage. But about the end of 1386 he lost his offices, possibly owing to the absence abroad of John of Gaunt, and fell upon hard times. In 1389 he was appointed clerk of the King's Works, but two years afterwards we find him superseded. Thrift was not one of his virtues, and no sort of provision seems to have been made against a ' rainy day '. In 1394 King Richard granted him a pension of £20 for life; but the advances of payment he applied for, and the issue of letters of protection from arrest for debt, indicate his condition. On the accession in 1399 of Henry IV, son of his old patron, he was granted a pension of 40 marks (£26. 13s. 4d.), and we may believe his few remaining months were spent in comfort. He seems to have died on October 25, 1400, and was laid in that part of Westminster Abbey which through his burial there came afterwards to be called the Poet's Corner. In spite of all his reverses and troubles, it was during this last period of his life that Chaucer's genius shone brightest. The design of the *Canterbury Tales* was indeed too huge for completion; and no doubt his troubles interfered with his progress. His greatest achievement is the Prologue (1387) to the *Tales*, which for its variety, humour, grace, reality and comprehensiveness is, as a piece of descriptive writing, unique in all literature. Chaucer is in order of time the first great poet of the English race; and in order of merit he is amongst the first of all our poets. In the Middle Ages in England he stands supreme. Many works have been ascribed to Chaucer, and were long printed in popular editions, that are certainly not his—e.g., *The Court of Love, Chaucer's Dream, The Complaint of the Black Knight, The Cuckoo and Nightingale, The Flower and the Leaf*, and much of the extant *Romaunt of the Rose*. See works by Ward, Ten Brink, Skeat, Lounsbury, Legouis (trans. 1913), Brusendorff (1925), Manly (1926), Lowes (1944), H. S. Bennett (1947), W. W. Lawrence (1951); Chaucer Society publications; bibliography (1908–53), by D. D. Griffith.

CHAULIAC, Guy de, *shō-lee-ac* (*c.* 1300–68), French surgeon, born at Chauliac in Auvergne. The most famous surgeon of the Middle Ages, he wrote *Chirurgia Magna* (1363), which was translated into French over a century later and used as a manual by generations of doctors.

CHAUMETTE, Pierre Gaspard, *shō-met* (1763–94), a French Revolutionist, was born a shoemaker's son at Nevers. At the Revolution he joined with Camille Desmoulins, and soon gained such popularity by his extreme sansculottism that he was appointed procurator of the Paris commune. His extravagances disgusted Robespierre, and he perished on the scaffold.

CHAUSSON, Ernest, *shō-sõ* (1855–99), French composer, born in Paris, studied under Massenet and César Franck. Several of his orchestral works, including the *Poème* for violin and orchestra, and the symphony in B♭ (1891), as well as a number of attractive songs, have kept their popularity.

CHAVANNES. See PUVIS DE CHAVANNES.

CHÁVEZ, Carlos, *chah'vays* (1899–   ), Mexican composer, born in Mexico City. He supplemented casual musical teaching by study in New York and Europe, and, returning to Mexico, formed the Mexican Symphony Orchestra in 1928, becoming director of the National Conservatoire. As an official in the Ministry of Fine Arts, Chávez's influence on every aspect of Mexican music is extremely great. His works are little known outside his own country, partly owing to their large size and demands for grandiose orchestral forces, but are influenced by Mexican folk music and include ballets, symphonies and concertos and an unusual *Toccata for Percussion* (1942).

CHEHOV, Anton Pavlovitch, *che'hof* (1860–1904), Russian author, born in Taganrog, the son of an unsuccessful shopkeeper and the grandson of a serf. He studied medicine at Moscow University and qualified as a doctor in 1884. As a student, he had written articles for various comic papers, and his first book, *Motley Stories* (Pëstrye Rasskazy), appearing in 1886, was successful enough for Chehov gradually to adopt writing as a profession. He continued to regard himself as a doctor rather than a writer, though he practised very little except during the cholera epidemic of 1892–93. His magazine articles led to an interest in the popular stage of vaudeville and French farce, and, after the failure of his first full-length play, *Ivanov* (1887), he wrote several one-acters, such as *The Bear* (1889) and *The Proposal* (1889). His next full length plays, *The Wood Demon* (1889) and *The Seagull* (1896), were also failures and Chehov had decided to concentrate on his stories, by which his reputation was already made and which had introduced him to his admired Tolstoy and Gorky, when Nemirovich-Danchenko persuaded him to let the Moscow Art Theatre revive *The Seagull* in 1898. Produced by Stanislavsky, who revealed its quality and originality, its reception encouraged him to write for the same company his masterpieces: *Uncle Vanya* (1900), *The Three Sisters* (1901) and *The Cherry Orchard* (1904). Meanwhile he continued to write short stories. In 1891 he wrote *Saghalien Island*, after a visit to a penal settlement, which had a considerable effect on subsequent criminal legislation. In 1897 he was threatened with tuberculosis and lived thereafter either abroad or in the Crimea. In 1900 he was elected fellow of the Moscow Academy of Science, but resigned when his fellow-member, Gorky, was dismissed by order of the Czar. In 1901 he married the actress Olga Knipper, who remained for many years after her husband's death the admired exponent of female parts

in his plays. He died, at the height of his powers, in Badenweiler.

Chehov is perhaps the most popular Russian author outside his own country. His stories have strongly influenced an entire school of writers, beginning with James Joyce and Katharine Mansfield; and his plays are firmly established in the classical repertoires of Europe. His technique is impressionistic—almost *pointilliste*: he builds a low toned atmosphere out of tiny patches of brightly coloured personalities. In all his work he equates worldly success with loss of soul. It is the sensitive, hopefully struggling people, at the mercy of forces almost always too strong for them, who are his heroes. For this reason his work, though presenting a convincing picture of Russian middle-class life at the end of the 19th century, has a timeless quality, since it reflects the universal predicament of the ' little man '.

Among his many short stories, the following are outstanding: *The Chorus Girl, The Duel, Ward No. 6, The Darling, The Lady with the Dog, In the Ravine* and *The Bishop.* His plays are all available in more than one translation, together with *My Life* (1895), *The Tales of Anton Chehov*, translated by Constance Garnett, 13 vols. (1916–23), *The Life and Letters of Anton Chehov*, translated and edited by S. Koteliansky and P. Tomlinson (1925). See also study by W. H. Bruford (1948) and Lives by I. Nemirosky (1950), Hingley (1950) and E. J. Simmons (1963).

CHEKE, Sir John (1514–57), English classical scholar, was born at Cambridge, and in 1529 obtained a fellowship of St John's College, where he embraced the Reformed doctrines. He laboured earnestly to advance Greek studies, and in 1540 was appointed first regius professor of Greek. His new mode of pronouncing Greek was assailed by Bishop Gardiner, but established itself in England. In 1544 he became tutor to the Prince, afterwards Edward VI, whose accession secured Cheke a seat in parliament (1547), the provostship of King's College (1548) and a knighthood (1552). He was stripped of everything at Mary's accession, and went abroad, but in 1556 was treacherously seized in Belgium, and brought to the Tower. Fear of the stake induced him to abjure Protestantism, but his recantation preyed on his mind, and he died September 13, 1557. See Life by Strype (1821 edition).

CHEKHOV. See CHEHOV.

CHELCICKY, Petz, *chel-chit'skee* (*c.* 1390–*c.* 1460), Czech reformer, born probably at Chelčice in Bohemia, founded the sect which became the Moravian Brothers, and the Christian doctrine of his *The Net of True Faith* (*c.* 1450) was later promulgated by Tolstoy.

CHELMSFORD, (1) **Frederic Thesiger, 1st Baron** (1794–1878), was a midshipman in the navy, but exchanged the sea for law, and was called to the bar in 1818. He was knighted and made solicitor-general in 1844, attorney-general in 1845 and 1852, and lord chancellor in 1858 and 1866.

(2) **Frederic Augustus Thesiger, 2nd Baron** (1827–1905), son of (1), served through the Crimea, the Mutiny, and the Abyssinian

campaign of 1868. He commanded in the Kaffir war of 1878 and in the Zulu war of 1879, having resigned the governorship of Cape Colony. He was lieutenant of the Tower (1884–89).

(3) **Frederick John Napier Thesiger, 1st Viscount** (1868–1933), son of (2), was governor of Queensland (1905–09), of New South Wales (1909–13), viceroy of India (1916–21), first lord of the Admiralty in 1924.

CHEMNITZ, Martin (1522–86), Lutheran theologian, was born at Treuenbrietzen, in Brandenburg. His skill in astrology led to his appointment as ducal librarian at Königsberg in 1549, and thenceforth he devoted himself to theology. His opposition to Osiander led him to Wittenberg (1553); and he was appointed a preacher at Brunswick in 1554, and ' superintendent ' in 1567. His works include *Examen Concilii Tridentini* (1565–73) and *De duabus Naturis in Christo* (1571).

CHÉNIER, Marie André, *shen-yay* (1762–94), French poet, was born at Constantinople, the third son of the French consul-general and a Greek woman. At three he was sent to France, and at twelve was placed at the Collège de Navarre, Paris, where Greek literature was his special subject. At twenty he entered the army, and served for six months in Strasburg; but disgusted with the frivolity of military life, returned to Paris, and gave himself up to strenuous study. To this period belong his famous idylls, *Le Mendiant* and *L'Aveugle*. His health giving way, he travelled in Switzerland, Italy and the Archipelago. In 1786 he returned to Paris, and began several ambitious poems, most of which remained fragments. The most noteworthy are *Suzanne*, *L'Invention* and *Hermès*, the last being in plan and spirit an imitation of Lucretius. In 1787 he went to England as secretary to the French ambassador, but his residence there proved uncongenial; in 1790 he returned to Paris to find himself in the ferment of the Revolution, which at first he supported; but alarmed by its excesses he mortally offended Robespierre by pamphlets. He was thrown into prison, and after six months was executed on July 25, 1794, just three days before the close of the Reign of Terror. See French works by Becq de Fouquières (1881), Faguet (1902). His younger brother, **Marie Joseph** (1764–1811), was an ardent republican, sat in the Legislative Assembly, and wrote satires and heavy plays.

CHEN NING YANG. See YANG.

CHEOPS, Grecized form of Khufu (*c.* 3000 B.C.), king of Memphis in Egypt, of the fourth dynasty, famous as the builder of the largest pyramid. A son and successor Chephren (Khafra) built the next largest pyramid.

CHEPMAN, Walter (*c.* 1473–1538), was an Edinburgh notary, who, with a bookseller, Andrew Myllar, in 1507 received a patent from James IV to set up the first Scottish printing press.

CHERBULIEZ, *sher-bü-lyay*, a French family at Geneva whose founder, Abraham Cherbuliez, a prosperous bookseller, left three sons:

(1) **André** (1795–1874), professor of Ancient Literature at the Geneva Academy.

(2) **Antoine Élisée** (1797–1869), an eminent publicist, professor of Law and Political Economy at Geneva, at Paris the redoubtable antagonist of Proudhon and the socialists, and finally professor at Zürich.

(3) **Joel** (1806–70), who succeeded to his father's business, and edited the *Revue critique* (1833 *et seq.*). His *Lendemain du dernier jour d'un condamné* (1829) was a clever burlesque and more upon Victor Hugo's well-known *tour-de-force*, while his *Genève* (1867) was a solid contribution to the history of the city.

(4) **Victor** (1829–99), son of (1), was born at Geneva, and studied there, at Paris, Bonn and Berlin, first mathematics, then philology and philosophy; after which he lived in Geneva as a teacher, until his call to Paris in 1864 to join the staff of the *Revue des Deux Mondes*. Naturalized (1880), he was elected to the French Academy in 1881. Cherbuliez began his literary career with compounds between fiction and criticism, from which he turned to work which really proved his powers. The strong and striking *Comte Kostia* (1863) was followed by a series of novels, among the best of which are: *Le Roman d'une honnête femme* (1866), *Meta Holdenis* (1873), *Samuel Brohl et Cie* (1877), *L'Idée de Jean Têterol* (1878), *Noirs et rouges* (1881), *La Vocation du Comte Ghislain* (1888), and *Le Secret du précepteur* (1893). He wrote also as ' G. Valbert ' in the *Revue des Deux Mondes* many literary and political articles. See Saintsbury's *French Novelists* (1891) and Faguet's *éloge* (1899).

CHERENKOV, Pavel Alekseevich (1904–), Soviet physicist, who in 1934 noted the emission of blue light from water and other transparent media when atomic particles, moving at a speed greater than light, are passed through it. Subsequent researches by Professors Tamm and Frank led to a definite explanation of the ' Cherenkov effect ' for which all three Soviet physicists shared the Nobel prize in 1958. The principle was adapted in constructing a cosmic-ray counter mounted in *Sputnik III*. Lucien Mallet, a French physicist, claimed to have discovered the effect in 1926.

CHERNYAKHOVSKY, Ivan Danilovich, *cher-nyah-kof'skee* (1908?–45), Soviet soldier, probably born in the western Ukraine, who after his liberation in 1944 of Vitebsk from the Germans was promoted by Stalin to become the youngest general in the Soviet army, captured Minsk with Rokossovsky, Vilna and led the invasion of East Prussia, where he died from wounds received in action.

CHERNYSHEVSKI, Nicolai Gavrilovich (1828–89), Russian critic and novelist. A follower of the French socialists, he wrote on political and social matters such as Nihilism as well as literature, and was imprisoned in Siberia from 1862–83 for revolutionary activities. His *Aesthetic Relationship between Art and Reality* deals with his theory of the place of art in life, and his propagandist novel, *A Vital Question*, was written in imprisonment.

CHERRY-GARRARD, Apsley (George Benet) (1886–1959), English explorer and author, accompanied Scott (q.v.) to the Antarctic (1910–13) as assistant zoologist and wrote *The Worst Journey in the World* (1922), an account of the ill-fated expedition. He chose the quotation from Tennyson's *Ulysses* which was used as epitaph for the Polar party.

CHERUBINI, Maria Luigi Carlo Zenobio Salvatore, ke-roo-bee′nee (1760–1842), Italian composer, was born at Florence, showed early promise in church pieces, studied at Bologna and Milan, and wrote a succession of operas, at first in Neapolitan, later (having moved to Paris) in French style, of which little is now heard apart from some of the overtures, e.g., that of *The Water-Carrier* (1800), his best opera. His later work was mainly ecclesiastical. In 1822 he became director of the Paris Conservatoire, and raised it to greatness. His work on counterpoint and fugue (1835) was a standard book. See Lives by Bellasis (1874) and Crowest (1915).

CHERWELL, Frederick Alexander Lindemann, chahr′-, **1st Viscount** (cr. 1956) (1886–1957), British scientist, was born at Baden-Baden and was brought up at Sidmouth, Devon. He was educated at the University of Berlin and at the Sorbonne, where his work on the problems of atomic heat attracted the attention of distinguished physicists. In 1914 he became director of the R.F.C. Experimental Physics Station at Farnborough. He was the first to evolve the mathematical theory of aircraft spin and put it into practice in a daring flight. In 1919 he became professor of Experimental Philosophy at Oxford. As director of the Clarendon Laboratory, he made it one of the best on low-temperature research in Britain. A close friend of Sir Winston Churchill, he became his personal assistant in 1940. Under his leadership British scientists produced answers to many of the new weapons of war. He was created a baron in 1941 and was paymaster-general in 1942–45 and again in the 1951 government, advising on nuclear research and scientific matters generally. He resigned in 1953 to resume his professorship. Aloof and of decided opinions, he was respected rather than acclaimed, but his immense knowledge and resource heightened the prestige of science and contributed significantly to the nation's military survival. See *The Prof*, by R. F. Harrod (1959).

CHESELDEN, William (1688–1752), English surgeon, born at Somerby near Melton Mowbray, was the first to perform operations for lateral lithotomy and iridectomy. He wrote a manual of anatomy.

CHESHIRE, Geoffrey Leonard (1917–), English bomber pilot and philanthropist, educated at Stowe School and Merton College, Oxford. An outstanding pilot and leader, he was awarded the D.S.O. (1940), D.F.C. (1941) and the V.C. (1944) on completing a hundred bombing missions, often at low altitude, on heavily defended German targets. He was with Penney (q.v.) official British observer of the destruction caused by the atomic bomb over Nagasaki (1945). This experience together with his new-found faith in Roman Catholicism made him decide to devote the rest of his life to tending the sick, by founding ' Cheshire Homes ' in many countries.

CHESNEY, (1) Col. Charles Cornwallis (1826–1876), was author of the *Waterloo Lectures* (1861) delivered at Sandhurst.

(2) **Francis Rawdon** (1789–1872), uncle of (1), the explorer of the Euphrates, was born at Annalong, County Down, and was gazetted to the Royal Artillery in 1805. In 1829 he inspected the route for a Suez Canal; after 1831 he four times explored a route to India by Syria and the Euphrates. He commanded the artillery at Hong Kong in the 1843–47. In 1850 he published his *Survey of the Euphrates and Tigris*, and in 1868 a *Narrative of the Euphrates Expedition*. See Life by his wife and daughter (1893).

(3) **Gen. George Tomkyns** (1830–95), younger brother of (1), became a member of the Council of the Viceroy of India in 1886, and in 1892 Conservative M.P. for Oxford. He was the author of *The Battle of Dorking* (1871), *The Private Secretary* (1881), *The Lesters* (1893), &c.

CHESSMAN, Caryl (1922–60), American convict-author, was sentenced to death in 1948 on seventeen charges of kidnapping, robbery and sexual assault, but was granted eight stays of execution by the governor of California amounting to a record period of 12 years under sentence of death, without a reprieve. During this period Chessman conducted a brilliant legal battle from prison, learnt four languages and wrote the best-selling books against capital punishment *Cell 2455 Death Row* (1956), *Trial by Ordeal* (1956) and *The Face of Justice* (1958). His ultimate execution provoked worldwide criticism of American judicial methods.

CHESTERFIELD, Philip Dormer Stanhope, 4th Earl of (1694–1773), English statesman, orator, wit and man of letters, was born in London. He studied at Cambridge, made the Grand Tour, was member for St Germains in Cornwall from 1715 to 1722, for Lostwithiel from 1722 to c. 1723. In 1726 he succeeded his father as 4th Earl of Chesterfield. In 1730 he was made lord steward of the household. Until then, as a Whig, he had supported Walpole; but being ousted from office for voting against an excise bill, he went over to the Opposition, and was one of Walpole's bitterest antagonists. He joined the Pelham ministry in 1744, made an excellent Irish lord-lieutenant in 1745, and was in 1746 one of the principal secretaries of state. Intimate with Swift, Pope and Bolingbroke, he drew from Johnson his famous indignant letter. Besides the well-known *Letters to his* [natural] *Son*, he also wrote *Letters to his Godson and Successor*. His *Letters to Lord Huntingdon* appeared in 1923, his verse in 1927. See *Letters of Chesterfield* ed. B. Dobrée (1932), *Unpublished Letters* ed. Gulick (1937); and books by Craig (1907), Coxon (1925); essays by Sainte-Beuve, C. Collins, Austin Dobson.

CHESTERTON, Gilbert Keith (1874–1936), English critic, novelist and poet, born in London, was educated at St Paul's and studied art at the Slade School, though he never practised it professionally. His first writings were for periodicals, and all through his life much of his best work went into essays and articles in *The Bookman, The Speaker, The Illustrated London News,* and his own *G. K.'s Weekly,* which was born in 1925 of the *New Witness* inherited from his brother a few years earlier. Tremendous zest and energy, with a mastery of paradox, a robust humour and forthright devotion characterize his entire output. He became a Roman Catholic in 1922, but this decision is clearly foreshadowed in his works, the best of which were published before that date. His two earliest books were the collections of poetry *The Wild Knight* and *Greybeards at Play* (both 1900); the works which followed include *The Napoleon of Notting Hill* (1904), liberal and anti-Imperialist in outlook, brilliant studies of Browning (1903), G. F. Watts (1904), Dickens (1906) and R. L. Stevenson (1907); and the provocative *Heretics* (1908) and *Orthodoxy* (1908). The amiable detective-priest Father Brown, who brought Chesterton popularity with a wider public, first appeared in *The Innocence of Father Brown* (1911). Soon after his conversion Chesterton published his well-known Life of St Francis of Assisi, also one of St Thomas Aquinas (1933). His *Collected Poems* appeared in 1933, and his *Autobiography* posthumously in 1936. An ebullient personality, with a figure of Johnsonian proportions, absent-minded but quick-witted, he will go down as one of the most colourful and provocative writers of his day. See Life by M. Ward and bibliography by J. Sullivan (1958). His brother, **Cecil Edward** (1879–1918), wrote anti-liberal books and started, with Hilaire Belloc, the anti-bureaucratic paper *New Witness* (see above) in 1912. He married **Ada Elizabeth Jones,** journalist and writer, who pioneered the Cecil Houses for London's homeless women.

CHETHAM, Humphrey (1580–1653), a Manchester merchant and cloth manufacturer, the founder of a bluecoat hospital and of a public library at Manchester.

CHETTLE, Henry (d. *c.* 1607), English dramatist and pamphleteer, edited Greene's *Groat's-worth of Wit* (1592), wrote thirteen plays of considerable merit, and was part author of thirty-five others, including *Robin Hood, Patient Grisel, The Blind Beggar of Bethnal Green* and *Jane Shore.*

CHEVALIER, *shě-val-yay,* (1) **Albert** (1862–1923), composer and singer of costermonger ballads, was born the son of a French teacher at the Kensington Grammar School. He appeared as an actor at the old Prince of Wales's in 1877, and in 1891 came before the public as a music-hall singer. Writing, composing and singing his songs of the humour and pathos of coster life (of fifty well-known ones, forty are his own creations), he immortalized such songs as ' My Old Dutch ' and ' Knocked 'em in the Old Kent Road '. See his *Before I Forget* (1901).

(2) **Maurice** (1888–1972), French film and vaudeville actor, born in Paris. He began as a child singing and dancing in small cafés, and became dancing partner to Mistinguett at the Folies Bergères from 1909 to 1913. He was a prisoner during World War I,

won the Croix de Guerre, and became a member of the Legion of Honour. He first appeared in London in 1919 and forty years later his individual, straw-hatted, *bon-viveur* personality was yet capable of scoring a popular success in the musical film *Gigi.* Among the best of his earlier films were *The Innocents of Paris* and *The Love Parade.* See his autobiography, *Ma route et mes chansons,* (trans. as *The Man in the Straw Hat* in 1949), and *I Remember it Well* (1971).

(3) **Michel** (1806–79), French economist, was born at Limoges, and trained as an engineer. An ardent St Simonian, he attached himself to Enfantin, and helped to compile the propagandist *Livre nouveau.* After six months' imprisonment in 1832, he retracted all he had written in the *Globe* against Christianity and marriage. He was sent by Thiers to inquire into water and railway communication in the United States; was made a councillor of state in 1838; and in 1840 professor of Political Economy at the Collège de France. In 1845 he was returned by Aveyron to the Chamber of Deputies. After the revolution of 1848 he made onslaughts that were never met upon Louis Blanc's socialism in articles collected as *L'Organisation du travail* (1848) and *Questions politiques et sociales* (1852). As a free-trader he aided Cobden in carrying into effect in 1860 the commercial treaty between France and England, becoming a senator and grand officer of the Legion of Honour. He died at Montpellier.

CHEVALLIER, Gabriel, *shě-val-yay* (1895–1969), French novelist, born in Lyons. He won wide acclaim with his *Clochemerle* (1934, English translation 1936), an earthy satire on petty bureaucracy, after a series of less successful psychological novels. Other books include *La Peur* (1930), *Clarisse Vernon* (1933), *Sainte-Colline* (1937), *Les Héritiers Euffe* (1945), *Le Petit général* (1951) and *Clochemerle Babylone* (1954).

CHEVREUL, Michel Eugène (1786–1889), French chemist, born at Angers, studied chemistry at the Collège de France in Paris. He lectured at the Collège Charlemagne, and held a technical post at the Gobelins. In 1826 he entered the Academy of Sciences, and in 1830 became director of the Museum of Natural History. Early discoveries were those of margarine, olein and stearin; and these studies and his theory of saponification opened up vast industries. Between 1828 and 1864 he studied colours. This patriarch of the scientific world, ' le doyen des étudiants de France ', died April 9, 1889, his hundredth birthday having been celebrated three years before with great enthusiasm.

CHEYNE, (1) **George,** *chayn,* Scots *cheen* (1671–1743), Scots physician, born at Methlick, Aberdeenshire, after studying at Edinburgh, started a London practice in 1702. Full living made him enormously fat (thirty-two stone weight), as well as asthmatic, but from a milk and vegetable diet he derived so much benefit that he recommended it in all the later of his twelve medical treatises. His *Essay of Health and Long Life* was eulogized by Dr Johnson. He died at Bath.

(2) **Thomas Kelly,** *chay'nee* (1841–1915),

English biblical critic, chief editor of the *Encyclopædia Biblica* (4 vols. 1900–03) and author of *Critica Biblica* and a number of works on the Old Testament, was born in London. Educated at Merchant Taylors' School and Worcester College, Oxford, he became fellow of Balliol in 1868. He was (1885–1908) Oriel professor of the Interpretation of Scripture at Oxford and canon of Rochester, and a member of the Old Testament Revision Company.

CHIABRERA, Gabriello, *kya-bray'ra* (1552–1637), Italian poet, was born and died at Savona. Educated at Rome, he served Cardinal Cornaro, but was obliged to leave for revenging himself upon a Roman nobleman. An enthusiastic student of Greek, he skilfully imitated Pindar and Anacreon, while his *Lettere Famigliari* introduced the poetical epistle into Italian.

CHIANG KAI-SHEK (1887–), Chinese general and statesman, born in Fenghwa, Chekiang, received his military training at Tokio, where he fell under the influence of Sun Yat-sen (q.v.), for whom he fought in the 1911 revolution, and by whom he was put in charge of the Whampoa Military Academy, an establishment for training Kuomintang officers on the Russian model. In 1926 he commanded the army which set out to accomplish by military means the unification of China, a task which he completed by 1928. During this time he had opposed the infiltration of Communism and rid the Kuomintang of its influence. As president of the republic (1928–31), he consolidated the Nationalist régime by force of arms, but dangerous left-wing splinter groups retained a foothold in several areas and it was their survival which led to Chiang's ultimate downfall. Head of the executive in 1935–45, he was also commander-in-chief of China united against Japanese aggression. During and after the war he allowed corrupt right-wing elements to become dominant in the Kuomintang, and the split with the Communists was intensified. In 1948 he again became president, but in 1949 the Kuomintang collapsed before the Communist advance and Chiang was forced to withdraw with the remnant of the Nationalist army to Formosa where he has since retained the office of president. There the Chinese National government, 'White China', trains new forces, aided by the U.S.A., and breathes threats against the mainland, causing more consternation among Western politicians than among its enemies. See his *Summing up at Seventy* (1957), and Life by Hsiung (1948). His second wife, **Mayling Soong** (1898–), was educated at American universities, and distinguishes herself in social and educational work, and as author of a number of works on China.

CHIARELLI, Luigi, *kya-rel'lee* (1884–1947), Italian playwright, born in Trani. A journalist who took to the stage, he had his first play, *Vita intima*, performed in 1909 and he continued to write, experimenting with combinations of violent realism and his own somewhat grotesque humour. His only big success, however, was *La Maschera e il volta* (1916), a farcical comedy translated into nearly every European language. It was produced in London in an English translation by C. B. Fernald in 1923 and has been revived several times. Two other plays have been translated and produced in this country: *Money, Money!* (1931) and *One Plus Two* (translated by Frederick May, 1957).

CHICHELE, Henry, *chich'-lay* (c. 1362–1443), English prelate, in 1408 became Bishop of St Davids, and in 1414 Archbishop of Canterbury. He founded at Oxford the colleges of St John's and All Souls. See vol. v. of Hook's *Archbishops of Canterbury.*

CHIESA, Francesco, *kyay'sa* (1871–), Swiss-Italian author, born at Sagno in Ticino, studied law at Pavia, and was for over 30 years director of the cantonal college at Lugano. His poetry includes *La Cathedrale* (1903), *La Reggia* (1904), *Calliope* (1907) and *Consolazioni* (1921). Of his novels *Tempo di Marzo* (1925) and of his short stories *Racconti puerili* (1920) are probably the best known. Chiesa's art is inward and spiritual, and his prose has moments of lyricism. See study by G. Zoppi (Milan 1921).

CHIFLEY, Joseph Benedict (1885–1951), Australian politician, in early life an engine driver, entered parliament in 1928, became defence minister the following year, and was Labour prime minister 1945–49.

CHIGI, *kee'jee,* a princely Italian family, whose founder, Agostino Chigi (d. 1512) of Siena, in Rome became banker to the popes, and was noted for his pomp and encouragement of art. See Cugnoni's *Agostino Chigi il Magnifico* (Rome 1881).—A descendant, **Fabio Chigi,** became pope as Alexander VII (1655–67).—**Flavio Chigi** (1810–85) was a nuncio and cardinal.

CHILD, (1) Francis James (1825–96), American scholar, the most learned of ballad editors, was born in Boston, Mass. He graduated at Harvard in 1846, and, after a year or two spent in Europe, was in 1851 appointed to the chair of Rhetoric, which he exchanged in 1876 for that of Anglo-Saxon and Early English Literature. His first work was *Four Old Plays* (1848); but more important were his annotated *Spenser* (5 vols. 1855) and *English and Scottish Ballads* (8 vols. 1857–59).

(2) **Sir Josiah** (1630–99), writer on commerce, was the second son of a London merchant. He himself made a fortune of £200,000 as a navy victualler at Portsmouth and a director of the East India Company. In 1678 he was made a baronet. In his *Brief Observations concerning Trade and Interest* (1668; 3rd ed. 1690) he explains his plans for the relief and employment of the poor, substituting districts or unions for parishes, and transporting paupers to the colonies. His brother, **Sir John,** was governor of Bombay, where he died, February 4, 1690.

(3) **Lydia Maria,** *née* Francis (1802–80), American author, born in Medford, Mass., published her first novel in 1821, and in 1828 married David Lee Child (1794–1874), a journalist, with whom she edited the *Anti-slavery Standard* in New York in 1843–44. Her works, nearly thirty in number, include novels, the best of them relating to early New England history, and an ambitious but inaccurate work on the history of religion (1855).

(4) **William** (c. 1606–97), English composer, born in Bristol, was organist at St George's Chapel, Windsor, from 1632, with an interlude during the Cromwellian régime, and was buried there. He wrote anthems and church services.

CHILDERS, (1) **Hugh Culling Eardley** (1827–1896), British politician, born in London, the son of a Yorkshire clergyman, was educated at Cheam and Trinity College, Cambridge. After seven years in Australia, he returned to England in 1857, and sat as a Liberal for Pontefract 1860–85, and for South Edinburgh 1886–92, holding office as first lord of the Admiralty 1868–71, chancellor of the Duchy of Lancaster 1872–1873, war secretary 1880–82, chancellor of the exchequer 1882–85 and home secretary 1886. He died in London.

(2) **Robert Cæsar** (1838–76), British orientalist, was born at Nice, held a Civil Service post in Ceylon (1860–64), and in 1873 became Pali professor at University College London.

(3) **Robert Erskine** (1870–1922), son of (2), served in the South African and First World wars, wrote a spy story, *The Riddle of the Sands* (1903), became a Sinn Fein irreconcilable, and was executed by the Irish Free State authorities.

CHILDS, George William (1829–94), American publisher, born in Baltimore, was proprietor from 1864 of the *Public Ledger* newspaper. His benefactions included memorials in England to Cowper, George Herbert, Leigh Hunt and Shakespeare. See his *Recollections* (1890).

CHILLINGWORTH, William (1602–43), theologian, was born at Oxford, the son of a prosperous citizen, and in 1618 became a scholar, in 1628 a fellow of Trinity. He embraced Catholicism, and in 1630 went to Douai, where he was led to renounce that faith by examination of the questions at issue. He became thereafter involved in controversies with several Catholic divines, and his answers are contained in his *Additional Discourses*. In the quiet of Lord Falkland's house at Great Tew in Oxfordshire he wrote *The Religion of Protestants, a Safe Way to Salvation* (1637). He left also nine sermons, and a fragment on the apostolical institution of episcopacy. In 1638 he took orders, and was made chancellor of Salisbury. In the Civil War he accompanied the king's forces, and before Gloucester devised a siege engine like the old Roman *testudo*. At Arundel Castle he fell ill, and after the surrender was lodged in the bishop's palace at Chichester, where he died. See Rashdall's *Typical English Churchmen* (1902).

CHINGIS KHAN. See GENGHIS KHAN.

CHIN SHIH HUANG TI. See SHIH HUANG TI.

CHIPIEZ. See PERROT.

CHIPPENDALE, Thomas (1718–79), English cabinet-maker born at Otley, Yorks., moved to London, set up a workshop in St Martin's Lane in 1753, and soon became famous for his graceful neoclassical furniture, especially chairs, which he made mostly from mahogany, then a newly introduced wood. His *Gentleman and Cabinet-maker's Director*

(1754), the first comprehensive trade catalogue of its kind, set forth his designs for the perusal of patrons, but had widespread influence on the designs of other craftsmen. His son Thomas carried on the business after his death until 1813. See Life by O. Brackett.

CHIRICO, Giorgio de, *ki-ree'ko* (1888–), Italian artist, born at Volo, Greece. He studied at Athens and Munich, working later in Paris, and with Carrà in Italy, where he helped to found the *Valori Plastici* review in 1918. About 1910 he began to produce a series of dreamlike pictures of deserted squares, e.g., *Nostalgia of the Infinite*, dated 1911, in the Museum of Modern Art, New York. These have had considerable influence on the surrealists, with whom he exhibited in Paris in 1925. His whole style is often called 'metaphysical painting', a term which he reserved for his work after 1915, including semi-abstract geometric figures and stylized horses. In 1929 he wrote *Hebdomeros*, a dream novel, but in the 'thirties he denounced all his previous work and reverted to an academic style, and to his study of the techniques of the Old Masters. See his autobiography *Memorie della mia vita* (1945) and studies by J. Thrall Soby (1941) and J. Faldi (1949).

CHISHOLM, *chiz'ĕm,* (1) **Alexander** (c. 1792–1847), Scottish historical and portrait painter, was born at Elgin, and died in Rothesay, having in 1818 settled in London.

(2) **Erik** (1904–65), Scottish composer, born in Glasgow, studied under Tovey. From 1930, as conductor of the Glasgow Grand Opera Society, he produced many rarely heard works, including *The Trojans*, by Berlioz. In 1945 he was appointed professor of Music at Capetown. His works include two symphonies, concertos for piano and violin, other orchestral music and operas.

CHITTENDEN, Russell Henry (1856–1943), American physiologist, born at New Haven, Conn., educated at Yale and Heidelberg, was one of the founders of the study of physiological chemistry in America. He was professor of this subject at Yale and later director of the Sheffield Scientific School. See his *Physiological Economy in Nutrition* (1905) and *Nutrition of Man* (1907).

CHLADNI, Ernst Florens Friedrich, *klad'nee* (1756–1827), founder of the science of acoustics, was born at Wittenberg, and died at Breslau. He invented the euphonium. His study of the vibration of solid bodies resulted in the patterns known as Chladni figures.

CHLODOVECH. See CLOVIS.

CHLODWIG. See CLOVIS.

CHLOPICKI, Joseph, *klo-pitz'kee* (1771–1854), Polish soldier and patriot, who served under Napoleon, was made a general by the Emperor Alexander, but became dictator in the Polish insurrection of 1830, and died in exile at Cracow.

CHOATE, (1) **Joseph Hodges** (1832–1917), nephew of (2), an eminent lawyer and accomplished orator, born at Salem, was U.S. ambassador to Britain 1899–1905.

(2) **Rufus** (1799–1859), American lawyer, was born in Essex, Mass., and admitted to the bar in 1823. He sat in congress from 1830

to 1834, and then settled in Boston, where he rose to be leader of the bar. He sat in the U.S. senate 1841–45. Sailing for Europe in ill-health, he died at Halifax, Nova Scotia. See Memoir by Brown, prefixed to his writings (1862), and Neilson's *Memories of Choate* (1884).

CHODOWIECKI, Daniel Nikolaus, *ko-do-vyet'skee* (1726–1801), painter and copper-plate engraver, was born at Danzig and became director of the Academy of Sciences at Berlin. See Life by F. Meyer (Berlin 1887) and Austin Dobson's *Eighteenth Century Vignettes* (2nd series, 1894).

CHOISEUL-AMBOISE, Étienne François, Duc de, *shwa-zœl* (1719–85), minister of Louis XV, served with credit in the Austrian Wars of Succession, and, through Madame de Pompadour, became lieutenant-general in 1748, and Duc de Choiseul in 1758. He arranged in 1756 the alliance between France and Austria against Frederick the Great, and made himself popular by the terms he obtained in 1763 at the close of a disastrous war, as also by his opposition to the Jesuits. He improved the army and navy, developed trade and industry, and reopened intercourse with India. He had spies in every court, and Catharine of Russia nicknamed him *Le Cocher de l'Europe*. His power survived the death of his patroness in 1764, but Madame du Barry alienated Louis from his able minister, who retired in 1770 to his estate of Chanteloup.

CHOPIN, Frédéric, *shop-ĭ* (1810–49), Polish composer and pianist, born at Żelazowa Wola, a village near Warsaw, where his father, a Frenchman, had settled. The boy played in public at the age of eight; in 1825 he published his first work, a Rondo in C minor; from 1826–29 he studied at Warsaw Conservatoire under Elsner; he then visited Vienna and made a brilliant impression. In 1831 he went to Paris, where he found fame, and lost his health. Here he became the idol of the *salons*, giving lessons to a select clientèle of pupils, and employing his leisure in composition. In 1836 he was introduced to George Sand (Madame Dudevant) by Liszt, spent the winter of 1838–39 with her in Majorca and lived at her home at Nohant until 1847, when they became estranged. Chopin visited England in 1837 and 1848, playing in London, Manchester, Edinburgh and Glasgow. Long enfeebled by consumption, he died at Paris. On a groundwork of Slavonic airs and rhythms, notably that of the mazurka, Chopin raised superstructures of the most fantastic and original beauty; his style is so strongly marked as to amount to a mannerism. He seldom composed for the orchestra; but for the piano he wrote a great deal of music superlatively artistic in form, impregnated with subtle romance, and full of exuberant fancy. His compositions comprise 50 mazurkas, 27 *études*, 25 *préludes*, 19 nocturnes, 13 waltzes, 12 polonaises, 4 ballades, 4 impromptus, 3 sonatas, 2 piano concertos, and a funeral march. See Ganche's edition of his works (1932); Opiénski's of his *Letters* (trans. Voynich, 1932); also Lives by Niecks (1888), Liszt (Eng. tr. 1879), and Hedley (1947); George Sand's *Histoire de*

ma vie (Vol. X, 1856), and Gerald Abraham's *Chopin's Musical Style* (1939).

CHORLEY, Henry Fothergill (1808–72), English music critic, born near Wigan, musical editor of the *Athenaeum*, is remembered for his *Thirty Years' Musical Recollections* (1862) and other musical literature, rather than for his verse, drama and novels. He was a rabid anti-Wagnerian. See *Autobiography* (2 vols. 1873).

CHOSROES, or Khosru, reigned over Persia A.D. 531–579, waged war with Rome for twenty years, and at home promoted agriculture, commerce and science. His grandson, **Chosroes II** (591–628), inflicted on the Byzantine empire great disaster, conquering Syria and Egypt.

CHOU EN-LAI, *choo-en-lī* (1898–), Chinese politician, born near Shanghai. Educated at an American missionary college in Tientsin, he was imprisoned for rioting in 1919 and thereafter spent some time in Europe, particularly at Paris, and probably also in Moscow, receiving training as a revolutionary. In 1924 he was at Whampoa Military Academy in Canton, headquarters of the Kuomintang, as assistant to the Soviet military adviser. He organized the typical Communist revolt which secured Shanghai in 1927, but shortly afterwards, when the Kuomintang turned against the Communists, he was arrested, but escaped to organize further Moscow-inspired insurrections, among them the abortive rising at Canton in the same year. Thereafter he undertook the task of spreading Communist doctrine in the towns, while Mao Tse-tung (q.v.) strengthened the cause in the country districts. The two joined forces in 1931 after Mao had set up his provincial government in the SE. Chou En-lai was largely responsible for persuading Chiang Kai-shek to bury the hatchet temporarily in order to present a united front against Japan, and his knowledge of the West brought him a number of diplomatic missions in the service of Mao Tse-tung. He was made premier and foreign minister in the new Communist government in 1949. He visited Moscow for political discussions in 1952 and secured the transfer to China of the Manchurian Railway. He was re-elected prime minister in 1955 when the new Constitution was introduced.

CHRÉTIEN DE TROYES, *kray-tyĭ dĕ trwah* (d. c. 1183), greatest of mediaeval French poets, born at Troyes, enjoyed the patronage of Marie de Champagne, daughter of Louis VII. His extant early works, *Philomena* (from Ovid's *Metamorphoses*) and the epic *Guillaume d'Angleterre* are less important than his great metrical Arthurian romances *Érec et Énide, Cligès, Lancelot, Yvain* and *Perceval*, which introduce all the fantastic ingredients of Celtic legend woven into a tapestry intricate and fascinating though somewhat tortuous to the modern reader. *Érec et Énide* (c. 1160) is the earliest known Arthurian romance, while *Cligès* (c. 1164) contains elements of the legend of Tristan and Isolde used in an antithetical manner which has caused the poem to be styled an 'Anti-Tristan'. Chrétien himself is widely believed to have been the author of a lost

version of the Tristan story mentioned by later poets. In *Perceval*, his last work, of which all but the first 9000 out of 32,000 lines were completed by others after his death, we find the first interweaving of the legend of the Holy Grail with Arthurian material. See the romances (except *Perceval*) tr. W. W. Comfort (1914), study by G. Cohen (1931), and W. A. Nitze, *Perceval and the Holy Graal* (1949).

CHRISTIAN. Scandinavian kings, of whom the following are noteworthy:

Christian II (1481–1559), king of Denmark, Norway and Sweden, mounted the throne of Norway and Denmark in 1513. His marriage in 1515 to a sister of the Emperor Charles V did not extinguish his love for his mistress Dyveke (q.v.). In 1520 he overthrew Sten Sture, the regent of Sweden, and thereafter was crowned king. But his treacherous massacre in the Stockholm ' blood-bath ' of the foremost men in Sweden (November 8–10, 1520) roused such a spirit that he was speedily driven out by Gustavus Vasa. In Denmark a popular revolt drove him for refuge to the Netherlands, and placed his uncle, Frederick I, on the throne. Assisted, however, by Charles V, Christian landed in Norway in 1531, but at Akershus next year was totally defeated, and spent his remaining years in imprisonment.

Christian IV (1577–1648), king of Denmark and Norway, and duke of Schleswig-Holstein, was elected successor to his father, Frederick II, in 1588. He assumed the government of the duchy in 1593, of the kingdom in 1596. His first war with Sweden (1611–13) ended in an advantageous peace; his second (1643–45) cost him much of his territory across the Sound. In the Thirty Years' War he became chief (1625) of the Protestant Union, but his disasters so damped his ardour that in 1629 he was glad to make room for Gustavus Adolphus. On sea and land he greatly increased his country's trade. The well-known ballad, ' King Christian stood by the lofty Mast ', commemorates his heroism in the sea-fight with the Swedes before Kiel in 1644.

Christian VIII (1786–1848) from 1839 was king of Denmark.

Christian IX (1818–1906), king of Denmark from 1863, in 1864 lost Schleswig-Holstein. His daughter Alexandra married King Edward VII (q.v.).

Christian X (1870–1947), king of Denmark from 1912, lost Iceland (1918, 1944), regained northern Schleswig (1920), and during the German occupation (1940–45) remained in Denmark with his people.

CHRISTIAN, (1) **Fletcher** (fl. 18th century), the ringleader in the mutiny on the *Bounty* (see ADAMS, JOHN; and BLIGH). His brother, Edward, was a Law professor at Cambridge from 1788 till his death in 1823.

(2) **William** (1608–63), from 1648 receiver-general of the Isle of Man, was shot for treason committed in 1651 against his feudal sovereign the Countess of Derby.

CHRISTIANSEN, Christian (1843–1917), Danish physicist, born at Lorborg, became professor of Physics at Copenhagen in 1886 after having verified Sellmeier's theory of anomalous dispersion by experiments on the refractive index of fuchsine (magenta).

CHRISTIE, (1) family of London auctioneers. The founder of the firm, in 1766, was **James** (1730–1803), two of whose sons were **James** (1773–1831), antiquary and auctioneer, and **Samuel Hunter** (1784–1865), student of magnetism and professor of Mathematics at Woolwich (1806–50). Samuel's son, Sir **William Henry Mahoney** (1845–1922), was astronomer royal (1881–1910). See Roberts's *Memorials of Christie's* (1897).

(2) **Agatha Mary Clarissa**, *née* **Miller** (1891–), English author, born in Torquay. Under the surname of her first husband (Colonel Christie, divorced 1928), she wrote more than seventy detective novels, featuring the Belgian detective, Hercule Poirot, or the inquiring village lady, Miss Marple. In 1930 she married **Max E. L. Mallowan** (1904–), noted archaeologist, professor at London University (1947–62), C.B.E. 1960, knighted 1968. Between December 1953 and January 1954, she achieved three concurrent West End productions, *The Spider's Web*, *Witness for the Prosecution* and *The Mousetrap* (record-breaking run).

(3) **John Reginald Halliday** (1898–1953), English murderer, born in Yorkshire. He was hanged for the murder of his wife and confessed to the murder by strangulation of five other women. He also confessed to the murder of Mrs Evans, wife of Timothy John Evans, who lived in the same house. Evans had been convicted and hanged for the murder of his infant daughter in 1950. He had been charged at the same time with the murder of his wife, but this was never heard. After a special inquiry instigated by the Home Office, and several fierce debates in the House of Commons, no definite conclusion was reached; but there was an increasing body of opinion that Evans was technically innocent and that Christie killed both Mrs Evans and the child, and in 1966 Evans was granted a free pardon. The trial of Christie, therefore, played an important part in altering legislation affecting the death penalty. See *Trials of Evans and Christie*, edited by F. Tennyson Jesse (1957).

CHRISTINA (1626–89), queen of Sweden, succeeded her father, Gustavus Adolphus, in 1632. Clever and beautiful, she received a man's rather than a woman's education. During her minority the kingdom was governed mainly by Chancellor Oxenstjerna. In 1644 she assumed the reins of power, and in 1650 was crowned with the title of ' king '. For four years thereafter she ruled with vigour, and patronized learned men, such as Grotius, Salmasius and Descartes. In 1654, however, weary of the personal restraint which royalty imposed on her, she abdicated in favour of her cousin, Charles Gustavus, reserving to herself sufficient revenues, entire independence and supreme authority over her suite and household. Leaving Sweden, she embraced Catholicism at Brussels, and entered Rome on horseback in the costume of an Amazon. At Fontainebleau in 1657 she caused her grand equerry, Monaldeschi, to be executed in her own household for treason. The death of the king in 1660 made

her hasten from Rome to Sweden; but, failing in her attempt to be reinstated on the throne, she again left the country. In 1666 she aspired to the crown of Poland. The remainder of her life was spent at Rome. See Hollingworth's history of her *Intrigues and Gallantries* (1697; reprinted 1928); and books by Gribble (1913), Mrs Compton Mackenzie (1931) and C. Weibull (1936).

CHRISTINA OF SPAIN. See MARIA CHRISTINA.

CHRISTINE DE PISAN (c. 1363–1431), a French poetess, born in Venice, was daughter of an Italian who was court astrologer to Charles V. Brought up in Paris, she married in 1378 Étienne Castel, who became the king's secretary, but died in 1389. Left with three children and no money, she was obliged to call upon her literary talents and between 1399 and 1415 produced a number of brilliant works in both prose and verse, including a Life of Charles V for Philippe, Duke of Burgundy; *Cité des dames*, a translation from Boccaccio; and *Livre des trois vertus*, an educational and social compendium for women. Her love poems have grace and charm, but lack depth. Christine is noteworthy for her defence of the female sex, hitherto a target for satirists. Saddened by the misfortunes of the Hundred Years' War she withdrew to a nunnery in about 1418 but lived to write in celebration of Joan of Arc's early successes in 1429. See studies by Pinet (1927) and J. Moulin (1964).

CHRISTISON, Sir Robert (1797–1882), Scottish toxicologist, was born at Edinburgh, the son of the professor of Humanity. After graduating in 1819, he studied toxicology in Paris under Orfila. He was in 1822 appointed professor of Medical Jurisprudence at Edinburgh, and from 1832 to 1877 held the chair of Materia Medica. He became physician to Queen Victoria (1848), president of the Edinburgh Royal Society (1868–73) and a baronet (1871). In old age he could walk, run or climb better than his coevals. Besides contributing to medical journals, Christison wrote a *Treatise on Poisons* (1829), &c. See *Life*, edited by his sons (1885–86).

CHRISTOPHE, Henri (1767–1820), king of Haiti, was born a slave on the island of Grenada. Coming to Haiti, he joined the black insurgents against the French in 1790, and, with his gigantic stature and courage, soon became a leader among them, and by Toussaint l'Ouverture was appointed brigadier-general. In 1802 he gallantly defended Cape Haiti against the French. He and Pétion overthrew Dessalines in 1806; and in 1807 he was appointed president. Civil war commenced between him and Pétion; but Christophe was proclaimed king of Haiti as Henri I in 1811, and ruled with vigour. But his avarice and cruelty led to an insurrection; and he shot himself. See Aimé Césaire, *La Tragédie du Roi Christophe*.

CHRISTOPHER (Gr. *Christophŏros*, ' Christ-bearer ' from the legend of his carrying the Christ child across a river), a Syrian saint, said to have been 12 feet high, and to have suffered martyrdom under the Emperor Decius (249–251). For the legends about him see monographs by Sinemus (Hanover 1868) and Mainguet (Tours 1891). See also H. C. Whaite, *St Christopher in English Medieval Wallpainting*.

CHRISTY, (1) **Edwin P.** (1815–62), American entertainer, originator of the minstrel show, was singing with two assistants at a public house in Buffalo in 1842, but steadily increased the reputation of his troupe, and the success of his enterprise in New York and London, till, becoming insane during the Civil War, he threw himself out of a window.

(2) **Henry** (1810–65), wealthy English ethnologist, explored and excavated prehistoric caves in southern France.

CHRYSANDER, Friedrich (1826–1901), German musical historian, biographer and editor of Handel.

CHRYSIPPUS (c. 280–207 B.C.), Stoic philosopher, was born at Soli in Cilicia. He came as a youth to Athens, and devoted himself to philosophy under Cleanthes. Of his works, which are said to have exceeded 700, only a few fragments remain. See monographs by Petersen (Altona 1827) and Gercke (Leipzig 1884).

CHRYSOLORAS, Manuel (c. 1355–1415), the first to transplant Greek literature into Italy, was born at Constantinople. About 1391 he was sent by the Byzantine emperor, John Palaeologus, to England and Italy to entreat assistance against the Turks, and in 1397 he settled at Florence and taught Greek literature. He was afterwards employed by Pope Gregory XII in an attempt to promote a union of the Greek with the Roman Church, and in 1413 went with John XXII to the Council of Constance, where he died. His chief work was a Greek grammar, *Erotemata* (Venice 1484). His nephew, **John**, also taught Greek in Italy.

CHRYSOSTOM, St John (c. 347–407) (from Gr. *Chrysostomos*, ' golden-mouthed ', so named from his eloquence), was born at Antioch, and trained by his pious mother Anthusa. He studied oratory for the career of advocate; but, in his twenty-third year, was baptized and ordained an *anagnōstēs* or ' Reader '. After six years spent as a monk in the mountains, illness forced him to return in 380 to Antioch, where he was ordained deacon in 381 and priest in 386. The eloquence and earnestness of his preaching secured for him the reputation of the greatest orator of the church; and in 398 the Emperor Arcadius made him archbishop of Constantinople. Chrysostom bestowed much of his revenues on hospitals, sought to reform the lives of the clergy, and sent monks as missionaries into Scythia, Persia and other lands. His faithful reproof of vices moved the Empress Eudoxia to have him deposed and banished in 403—first to Nicaea, and then to the Taurus mountains, and finally to Pityus on the Euxine. Compelled to travel hither on foot, with his bare head exposed to a burning sun, the old man died on the way at Comana, in Pontus. His body was brought to Constantinople and reburied with honour in 438. His works are numerous, and consist of *Homilies*, *Commentaries* on the whole Bible, part of which have perished, *Epistles*, *Treatises* on Providence, the Priesthood, &c., and *Liturgies*. See works by

Neander (tr. 1838), Busk (1885), Puech (trans. 1902), Meyer (1933), Attwater (n.e. 1964), and Baur (2 vols.).

CHUBB, (1) **Charles** (1772–1846), English locksmith, patentee of improvements in ' detector ' locks, originally (1818) patented by his brother, Jeremiah, of Portsea, was in the hardware business at Winchester and Portsea, previous to his settlement in London. Under his son, John Chubb (1816–72), further patents were taken out.

(2) **Thomas** (1679–1747), English deist, was born at East-Harnham near Salisbury. Brought up in poor circumstances, he had little formal education, but had already contrived to pick up considerable learning, when a perusal of the ' historical preface ' to Whiston's *Primitive Christianity Revived* impelled him to write his own tract, *The Supremacy of the Father Asserted* (1715). Encouraged by Jekyll and others, he continued to write; and a quarto volume of his tracts, published in 1730, made his name widely known. His opinions drifted near to deism, yet he went to church, and regarded the mission of Christ as divine. See his *Posthumous Works* (2 vols. 1748).

CHUDLEIGH, **Elizabeth** (1720–88), Countess of Bristol, and mistress and bigamous wife of the Duke of Kingston—prototype of ' Beatrix ' in *Esmond*. See Pearce's *Amazing Duchess* (1911).

CHUNDER SEN, Keshub (1838–84), a Hindu, the chief developer after 1858 of the Theistic society called the ' Brahma Samaj of India ', which originated with Rammohun Roy (q.v.). He visited Europe in 1870. See Max Müller's *Biographical Essays* (1884), and a Life by Mozoomdar (1888).

CHUQUET, Nicolas, *shü-kay* (1445–1500), French mathematician, took a degree in medicine at Paris, but is best known for his book on arithmetic, *Tripartie en la science des nombres*.

CHURCH, (1) **Frederick Edwin** (1826–1900), American landscape painter, born at Hartford, Conn., painted in South America, the Arctic Regions, and the East.

(2) **Sir Richard** (1785–1873), born at Cork of Quaker parentage, had served with distinction in the British and Neapolitan services, and been made a C.B. (1815) and K.C.H. (1822), when in 1827 he was appointed generalissimo of the insurgent Greeks, whose success was due largely to his strategy. See Lives by Stanley Lane-Poole (1890) and E. M. Church (1895).

(3) **Richard Thomas** (1893–1972), author, born in London, made his name first as a poet, but he is known also for his novels, literary criticism, travel books and stories for children, especially *A Squirrel called Rufus*. His novel *The Porch* (1937) won the Femina Vie-Heureuse prize. He published three volumes of autobiography, *Over the Bridge* (1956, *Sunday Times* Prize for Literature), *The Golden Sovereign* (1957) and *The Voyage Home* (1964). His work, both poetry and prose, is characterized by a quietly reflective spirit.

(4) **Richard William** (1815–90), English scholar, nephew of (2), born at Lisbon, was educated at Wadham College, Oxford, in

1838 was elected a fellow of Oriel, and in 1871 Dean of St Paul's. A close friend of Newman, he wrote sermons, essays, historical works and studies of Dante, Spenser and Bacon. See Life by his daughter (1894), and a shorter one by D. C. Lathbury (1905).

(5) **William**, inventor, patented in England in 1822 the first typesetting machine.

CHURCHILL, (1) **Charles** (1731–64), English satirical poet, was born in Westminster and educated at Westminster School. At seventeen he made a Fleet marriage, in 1756 was ordained priest, ' through need, not choice ', and at his father's death in 1758 succeeded him as curate of St John's, Westminster. But after a bankruptcy, a formal separation from his wife and a course of unclerical dissipation, he gave up the church (1763). His *Rosciad* (1761) had already made him famous and a terror to actors. *The Apology* (also 1761) was a savage onslaught on his critics, particularly Smollett. In *Night* (1762) he lengthily replied to criticisms of his life. *The Ghost* (1762) ridiculed Dr Johnson and others in over 4000 lines. Churchill next helped Wilkes in the *North Briton*, and heaped ridicule upon the Scots in *The Prophecy of Famine* (1763), an admirable satire. For *The Epistle to Hogarth* (1763) the artist retaliated with a savage caricature. Other works include *Independence*, and, unfinished, *The Journey* and the masterly *Dedication*. He lacked the chief essential of true satire, a real insight into the heart of man, but possessed volubility in rhyming, boisterous energy, and an instinctive hatred of wrong. See Laver's edition of his poems (1933).

(2) **John**. See MARLBOROUGH.

(3) **Lord Randolph Henry Spencer** (1849–1895), father of (5), third son of the 7th Duke of Marlborough, was born at Blenheim Palace, and educated at Eton and Merton College, Oxford. Returned for Woodstock in 1874, in which year he married **Jeanette (Jennie) Jerome**, the beautiful daughter of a New York businessman, he became conspicuous in 1880 as the leader of a guerilla band of Conservatives known as the ' Fourth Party '; and soon had a considerable following among the younger Conservatives, who regarded him as the future leader of the Tory Democracy. After a plucky attempt to defeat Mr Bright at Birmingham in 1885, Lord Randolph was returned for South Paddington. He was secretary for India in Lord Salisbury's first ministry (1885–86), and then, in his second, chancellor of the Exchequer and leader of the House of Commons from July to December 1886, when he resigned. See studies by Lord Rosebery (1906), Winston Churchill (1906) and R. R. James (1959).

(4) **Randolph Frederick Edward Spencer** (1911–68), British journalist, son of (5), educated at Eton and Christ Church College, Oxford. He served in the war in North Africa and Italy and in the Middle East as an intelligence officer on the General Staff. He was Conservative M.P. for Preston (1940–45) and contested seats in Liverpool and Ross and Cromarty. A pugnacious and forthright commentator on current affairs, fearless in his criticisms even of the press for which

he wrote, he achieved recognition as the author of *The Rise and Fall of Sir Anthony Eden* (1959), &c., *Twenty-one Years*, his autobiography (1965), and also as the editor of some of Sir Winston's speeches. He published 2 vols. of a full-length biography of his father (1966, 1967).

(5) **Sir Winston Leonard Spencer** (1874–1965), British statesman, was born on November 30, at Blenheim Palace, Woodstock, Oxon, the eldest son of (3). He was educated at Harrow and Sandhurst and was gazetted to the 4th Hussars in 1895. His early army career included service with the Malakand Field Force in 1897 and with the 1898 Nile Expeditionary Force, when he fought hand-to-hand with the Dervishes at Omdurman. Acting as a London newspaper correspondent in the Boer War, he was captured in an ambush but successfully escaped with a £25 price on his head. In 1900 he became Conservative M.P. for Oldham, but his differences with the party widened and he joined the Liberals in 1906, becoming colonial under-secretary and from 1908 to 1910 president of the Board of Trade, when he introduced the labour exchanges. He became home secretary in 1910 and was involved in the 'Siege of Sidney Street' controversy in 1911. In that year of the threatening German 'Agadir incident' he became first lord of the Admiralty. He developed a War Staff, became the 'father of naval aviation' and generally organized the Navy for the war he foresaw. In 1915 he was made the scapegoat for the Dardanelles disaster and joined the Army in France. In 1917 he became Mr Lloyd George's minister of Munitions, concentrating on the production of thousands of tanks (largely his own 'brain-child'). From 1919 to 1921 he was secretary of state for war and air and from 1924—when he was returned for Epping as a 'Constitutionalist' supporter of the Conservatives—till 1929 he was chancellor of the Exchequer. His spare-time occupations ranged from bricklaying (for which he held a union card) to editing the *British Gazette* during the 1926 General Strike. In the 'thirties he brooded in the political wilderness, increasingly angry at the National Government's supineness in face of the arming dictators. Munich he prophetically called ' a total and unmitigated defeat '. When war came again he was back at the Admiralty. Then, in May 1940, when power slipped from the hands of Neville Chamberlain, he formed a Coalition Government, the beginning of his 'walk with destiny' for which he considered all his earlier life but a preparation. He offered the British people nothing but 'blood, toil, tears and sweat' and with steely resolution led Britain alone against Germany and Italy, incomparably expressing the national spirit of resistance. During the war he worked round the clock, travelled 150,000 miles, always making vital decisions, from shaping the Atlantic Charter in 1941 to devising the strategy of Alamein in 1942, from giving the highest priority to the battle against the U-boats and repelling the Luftwaffe assault on Britain to inspiring tortured Europe with his voice. He was on close personal terms with President F. D. Roosevelt while sustaining the often difficult alliance with the Soviet Union. Defeated in the July 1945 election at the height of his wartime fame, he became a pugnacious leader of the Opposition. In international speeches he warned about the tyranny behind the Iron Curtain (his own phrase) and fostered the conception of European and Atlantic unity, later to bear fruit in NATO and other supranational organizations. In 1951, he became prime minister again at the age of 77, and when he laid down his office in 1955 he was the last surviving member of the great Allied war-winning triumvirate. Sir Winston, who called himself ' a child of the House of Commons ', remained in old age a back-bencher who was looked on almost with veneration. In the last phase of his crowded years of public service—recognized by countless honours and decorations—he was often described as ' the greatest living Englishman '. He achieved a world reputation not only as an all-seeing strategist and inspiring war leader, but as the last of the classic orators with a supreme command of English; as a writer with an Augustan style, great breadth of mind and a profound sense of history; as a painter of no little talent; as the shrewdest—and sometimes the most impish—of political tacticians; as the seer who said (when the Commons was considering the perils and opportunities of the H-bomb age), ' the nations stand at this hour of human history before the portals of supreme catastrophe and measureless reward '; as a zestful social reformer who believed that there could be ' shining uplands ' of welfare before mankind; as a figure who incarnated in himself the tumultuous sweep of modern history; and as an intensely human, rich and vivid personality whose abiding qualities were courage and imagination, passion and magnanimity, all in the service of a limitless patriotism. Publications include: *The World Crisis* (4 vols. 1923–29); *Marlborough* (4 vols. 1933–38); *The Second World War* (6 vols. 1948–54); *History of the English-Speaking Peoples* (4 vols. 1956–58). See Guedalla, *Mr Churchill* (1941); Eade (ed.), *Churchill: By His Contemporaries* (1953); Cowles, *Winston Churchill: The Era and the Man* (1953); Coote and Bunyan (eds.), *Sir Winston Churchill: A Self-Portrait* (1954); Rowse, *The Later Churchills* (1958); and two vols. of Life by his son Randolph Churchill (1966, 1967).

(6) **Winston** (1871–1947), American historical novelist, was born at St Louis, Missouri. His works include *Richard Carvel* (1899) and *The Crisis* (1901).

CHURCHYARD, Thomas (1520–1604), English soldier, poetaster, &c., born at Shrewsbury, served in Scotland, Ireland and the Low Countries under the Earl of Surrey, published many verse and prose pieces, the best being *The Legend of Shore's Wife* (1563, in *A Mirror for Magistrates*). See study by H. W. Adnitt (1884).

CHURRIGUERA, Don José, *choo-ree-gay'ra* (1650–1725), Spanish architect, born in Salamanca. He was royal architect to

Charles II and developed the extravagant style which has come down to us as Churrigueresque. See Stirling-Maxwell's *Annals of the Artists of Spain* (1848).

CHUTE, Anthony (d. 1595?), a minor Elizabethan poet, author of *Beawtie Dishonoured* (1593), largely plagiarized from Churchyard's (q.v.) *Legend of Shore's Wife*. He was patronized by Gabriel Harvey and assailed by Thomas Nash the satirist.

CHUTER-EDE, Baron of Epsom. See EDE.

CHU TEH, *choo de* (1886–), Chinese soldier-statesman, born in Szechuan Province, was educated at the Yunnan Military Academy, graduated in 1911, joined the Sun Yat-sen Revolution and was brigadier-general in 1916 but succumbed to opium. Cured in 1922, he left China to study political science at Göttingen, but was expelled from Germany in 1926 for Communist activities. As commandant of the Nanchang Military Training School, he took part in the Nanchang Army Revolt (1927), from which there emerged a nucleus of the Chinese Red Army. He was elected commander-in-chief (1928) of the Fourth Army and led it in the famous long march (1934–36). In 1949, as commander-in-chief, he was elected a vice-chairman of the People's Republic of China. See the rather biased work, *The Great Road*, by A. Smedley (1958).

CIALDINI, Enrico, *chal-dee'nee* (1811–92), Duke of Gaeta, born at Castelvetro, studied medicine at Parma, fled after the insurrection of 1830, but fought again for the national cause in 1848, 1849 and 1859–61, gaining two victories in the latter war, besides capturing Gaeta and Messina. In 1864 he became a senator, and in the war of 1866 occupied Venice.

CIANO, Count Galeazzo, *chah'nō* (1903–1944), Italian politician, son-in-law of Mussolini and a leading Fascist. As minister of propaganda (1935) and of foreign affairs (1936–43), he supported his father-in-law's expansionist and war policy, but, on early signs of its failure, opposed it; and in 1943 he contributed his vote to the fall of the régime. He was dragged from hiding by the now republican Fascists and after trial shot. See his *Diary, 1939–43* (trans. 1947).

CIARAN, the name of two Irish 6th-century saints, the one the founder of Clonmacnoise, and the other Bishop of Ossory.

CIBBER, *sib'ber*, (1) **Colley** (1671–1757), actor and dramatist, was born in London, son of the Schleswig sculptor, Caius Gabriel Cibber (1630–1700), known for his *Melancholy* and *Raving Madness.* In 1690 he joined the Theatre Royal in Drury Lane, and there, except for short intervals, spent his whole career. In 1696 his first comedy, *Love's Last Shift*, established his fame both as dramatist and actor. As manager and playwright, he greatly improved the decency of the theatre. From 1730 he was poet laureate. See his famous *Apology for the Life of Mr Colley Cibber, Comedian* (1740); and books by Habbema (Amsterdam 1928), F. D. Senior (1928).

(2) **Theophilus** (1703–58), son of (1), actor and dramatist, married the actress Susannah Maria Arne, sister of T. A. Arne (q.v.).

CICERO, Marcus Tullius (106–43 B.C.), orator, statesman, and man of letters, was born at Arpinum in Latium, of good family. At Rome he learned law and oratory, Greek philosophy, and Greek literature. His first important speech, in his twenty-sixth year, was the successful defence of a client against a favourite of the dictator Sulla. After a visit to Athens, and a tour in Asia Minor, he was (76) elected quaestor, and obtained an appointment in Sicily; at the request of the Sicilians he undertook his successful impeachment of the infamous Verres in 70 B.C. In 66 he was praetor, and supported in a great speech (*Pro Lege Manilia*) the appointment of Pompey to conduct the war with Mithridates. In 63 he was consul, and foiled the plot of Catiline. The 'father of his country' was now for a brief space the great man of the day. But the tide soon turned. Cicero might have saved the country, but had violated the constitution—a Roman citizen could not be capitally punished save by the sentence of the people in regular assembly. Clodius, now tribune, pressed the charge, and after Cicero in 58 had taken refuge at Thessalonica, he was condemned to exile, and his house at Rome and his country houses at Formiae and Tusculum were plundered. But in 57 the people almost unanimously voted his recall. Now, however, he was no longer a power in politics; and, nervously sensitive to the fluctuations of public opinion, he could not decide between Pompey and the aristocracy and Caesar and the new democracy. Thus, though he ultimately inclined to Caesar, he lost the esteem of both parties, being regarded as a trimmer and time-server. In 52 he composed his speech in defence of Milo, who had killed Clodius in a riot. Next year he was in Asia, as governor of Cilicia. In 49–48 he was with Pompey's army in Greece, but after Pharsalia threw himself on the mercy of the conqueror. In 46–44 he wrote most of his chief works on rhetoric and philosophy, living in retirement and brooding over his disappointments. In 43, after Caesar's death, his famous speeches against Antony were delivered, and cost him his life. As soon as Antony, Octavian and Lepidus had leagued themselves in the triumvirate, they proscribed their enemies, and Cicero's name was on the fatal list. Old and feeble, he fled to his villa at Formiae, pursued by the soldiers of Antony, and was overtaken as he was being carried in a litter. With calm courage he put his head out of the litter and bade the murderers strike. He was in his sixty-third year. As orator and pleader Cicero stands in the first rank; of his speeches the most famous are those against Verres and Catiline. As a politician he failed. As an essayist and letter-writer he is most attractive. His essays on ' old age ', ' friendship ' and ' duty ' (*De Officiis*) are still good reading; and his Tusculan disputations, his treatises on the ' nature of the gods ' and ' true ends of human life ' (*De Finibus*), illustrate the various ancient philosophies. For his Works, see Teubner and Loeb editions, and Oxford Classical Texts. See Lives by Middleton (1741), Trollope (1880), Lucas Collins (1885), Strachan-Davidson (1894), Sihler (1914).

CID, El, sid (c. 1043–99), Spanish hero, was born at Burgos. His name was Rodrigo or Ruy Diaz, and Cid is the Moorish Sidi (' my lord '); Campeador (' champion ') is often added. A compound of condottiere and patriot, he was constantly fighting from 1065; his great achievement the capture of Valencia (1094). See works by H. B. Clarke (1897) and Pidal (1930).

CIDENAS (c. 343 B.C.), Babylonian astronomer, head of an astronomical school at Sippra, discovered the precession of the equinoxes.

CIERVA, Juan de la, thyer'va (1895–1936), Spanish aeronautical engineer, invented the autogiro in 1923.

CIGOLI, properly **Ludovico Cardi** (1559–1613), Italian painter and architect of the later Florentine school, was born at Cigoli, near Florence, and was invited to Rome by Clement VII.

CILIAN, St (d. 697), the Irish apostle of Franconia, martyred at Würzburg.

CIMABUÉ, Giovanni, chee-ma-boo'ay (c. 1240–c. 1302), Italian painter, was born at Florence, into a period when the fine arts were practised in Italy chiefly by Byzantines, and painting had degenerated into a mechanical conventionalism. He at first adopted traditional forms, but soon turned to nature, and led the way to the naturalism of his great pupil Giotto (q.v.). In his stiff draperies he made little progress, but he softened his outlines, improved his flesh-tints, and gave projection and rotundity to his forms. He executed several important frescoes in the church of St Francis at Assisi; and in his later years he was capo maestro of mosaics of the Duomo of Pisa. His mosaic of Christ in glory in the apse was probably his last work. Dante refers to him in Purgatorio, xi, ll. 94–6. See studies by Bankard (1917) and A. Nicholson (Princeton 1932).

CIMA DA CONEGLIANO, Giovanni Battista, chee'ma da kon-ay-lyah'nō (c. 1460–1508), a religious painter of the Venetian school, born at Conegliano. His David and Jonathan is in the National Gallery. See study by Burckhardt (1905).

CIMAROSA, Domenico, chee-ma-rō'sa (1749–1801), Italian composer of operas, was born at Aversa, studied music at Naples, and produced his first opera there in 1772. In 1789 he was summoned to St Petersburg by Catharine II, in 1792 to Vienna; and in 1793 he returned to Naples, where his comic opera, Il Matrimonio segreto, was repeated seventy times. He died at Venice.

CIMON (d. 449 B.C.), Athenian commander, was the son of Miltiades, the conqueror at Marathon. Unable to pay the fine of 50 talents from which his father escaped by dying, he was kept in prison until it was discharged by his wealthy brother-in-law Callias. By 476 B.C. he was in supreme command of the Athenian forces in the patriotic struggle against the Persians, and effected the important conquest of Eïon, a town on the river Strymon. His greatest exploit was his encounter with a Persian fleet at the river Eurymedon (466 or 467), when he destroyed or captured most of the ships, and defeated the land forces on the same day. He likewise drove the Persians from Thrace, Caria, and Lycia; and expended much of the money which he had obtained by the recovery of his patrimony in Thrace upon the improvement of Athens. He advocated a close alliance with Sparta; and when the Helots revolted, led an army to support the Spartans; but having lost the confidence of his allies, he was ignominiously dismissed. At Athens he was opposed by the democracy, headed by Ephialtes, who procured his ostracism. He was recalled in 454, and may have been instrumental in obtaining a five years' armistice with Sparta. Cimon died at the siege of a Cyprian town.

CINCINNATUS, Lucius Quinctius (c. 519 B.C.–438 B.C.), a favourite hero of the old Roman republic, in 460 B.C. was chosen consul, and two years later dictator. When the messengers came to tell Cincinnatus of his new dignity they found him ploughing on his small farm. He rescued the consul Minucius, who had been defeated and surrounded by the Æqui. Sixteen days later, he laid down his dictatorship and returned to his farm. In 439, at the age of eighty, he was once more made dictator to deal with a Plebeian conspiracy.

CINEAS (d. c. 270 B.C.), a Thessalian, the friend and minister of Pyrrhus, was the most eloquent man of his time.

CINNA, Lucius Cornelius (d. 84 B.C.), a Roman patrician who supported Marius. Sulla, after driving Marius from Rome, and before setting out against Mithradates, allowed Cinna to be elected consul on his swearing not to disturb the existing constitution. No sooner, however, had he entered on office (87 B.C.) than he impeached Sulla, and agitated for Marius' recall. Cinna and Marius next declared themselves consuls after a cruel massacre. Marius died a few days later; and Cinna in 84 B.C. prepared to meet Sulla, but was slain by his own disaffected troops at the coast. During his fourth consulate his daughter Cornelia had been married to Julius Caesar.

CINQ-MARS, Henri Coiffier de Ruzé, Marquis de, sĭk- (1620–42), was the second son of the Marshal Marquis d'Effiat. At nineteen he was chief equerry to Louis XIII, but already in his dreams he was a duke and peer of France, and husband of the Princess Maria of Gonzaga. Finding his projects derided by Richelieu, his former patron, he conspired with the king's brother, Duke Gaston of Orleans, to murder the cardinal. With this was combined a wider plot with Spain; but the conspiracy was discovered, and Cinq-Mars, with De Thou, was executed at Lyons. See De Vigny's well-known romance Cinq-Mars (1826).

CIPRIANI, Giambattista (1727–85), Italian historical painter, born at Florence, received some instruction there from an English painter, Hugford, and then studied in Rome. In 1755 he accompanied Sir William Chambers to London, where his graceful drawings, engraved by Bartolozzi, gained great popularity. He was a member of the St Martin's Lane Academy, and in 1768 was elected a foundation member of the Royal Academy, to whose exhibitions he contributed till 1779, and whose diploma he designed in 1768. He married in 1761 an English lady of fortune, and died at Hammersmith.

CIRENCESTER, Richard of. See RICHARD.

CITRINE, Walter McLennan, 1st Baron Citrine of Wembley, *sit-reen'* (1887–   ), British trade union leader, born at Wallasey. An electrician by trade, he held office in the E.T.U. 1914–23 and was general secretary of the T.U.C. 1926–46. From 1928 to 1945 he was president of the International Federation of Trades Unions, and was a member of the National Coal Board and chairman of the Miners' Welfare Commission 1946–47. Knighted in 1935 and created a peer in 1946, he became chairman of the Central Electricity Authority in 1947. Efficient and versatile, a skilled trade-union diplomat, he was one of the more significant figures of the postwar social-democratic ' managerial revolution '.

CIVITALI, Matteo (1435–1501), an Italian architect and sculptor, who was born and died at Lucca, where his best work is seen in the cathedral. See Life by Yriarte (Paris 1886).

CLAIR, René, pseud. of René Chomette (1898–   ), French film producer, born in Paris, notable for his light touch and whimsical irony, evident in many successful films, produced at first in France, later in America, including *Sous les toits de Paris* (1930), *Le Million* (1931), *The Ghost goes West* (1935), *It happened Tomorrow* (1944). See his *Comédies et commentaires* (Paris 1959).

CLAIRAUT, Alexis Claude, *klay-rō* (1713–65), French mathematician, was born and died in Paris. Admitted at eighteen to the Academy of Sciences, he is remembered by his *Figure de la terre* (1743), his theory of the lunar apogee, and his computation of the return of Halley's comet.

CLAIRMONT, ' Claire '. See GODWIN.

CLAIRON, properly Claire Josephe Hippolyte Leyris de la Tudi (1723–1803), a French tragic actress, born near Condé in Flanders. See Life by E. de Goncourt (Paris 1890) and George Moore's *Impressions and Opinions* (1891).

CLAPARÈDE, (1) **Edouard** (1832–71), a Swiss naturalist, professor of Comparative Anatomy at Geneva.

(2) **Edouard** (1873–1940), Swiss psychologist and educationist, studied at Geneva, Leipzig and Paris, and with his cousin Flournoy founded the journal *Archives de psychologie* (1901). He was director of the experimental psychology laboratory at Geneva University, founder of the J. J. Rousseau Institute for the study of educational science, and secretary of the International Congress of Psychology. Publications include *L'Education fonctionelle* (1921) and *Morale et politique* (1940).

CLAPPERTON, Hugh (1788–1827), Scottish explorer, born at Annan, went to sea at thirteen, and was sent in 1821 with Oudney and Denham to discover the source of the Niger. They reached Kuka on Lake Chad in 1823; and Clapperton proceeded westward with Oudney, who died by the way. He still pushed on alone to Sokoto, but from here returned to England in 1825. The journey had thrown light on Bornu and the Houssa country, but the great problem of the source of the Niger was untouched. To solve it, Clapperton, now a commander, started again from the Bight of Benin in December 1825, in company with Captain Pearce, R.N., Lander (q.v.), &c. The others died early on the journey, but Clapperton and Lander reached Sokoto. Here his detention by the Sultan, joined to the hardships of the journey, so affected his health that he died. See the *Narrative* of the first journey (1826), the *Journal* of the second (1829), and the *Records of Clapperton's Last Expedition*, by Lander (1830).

CLARE, St (1194–1253), born of a noble family of Assisi. In 1212, moved by the teachings of St Francis, she gave up her possessions and went into a Benedictine convent. In 1215, when other women also wanted to live the Franciscan life, St Francis, with St Clare, founded the order of Franciscan nuns, ' Poor Clares '. She was canonized in 1255, and in 1958 was designated patron saint of television, on the ground that at Christmas 1252, while in her cell in the Convent of San Damiano, she both saw and heard the service in the Church of St Francis at Assisi. See Life by E. G. Smith (1915).

CLARE, John (1793–1864), English peasant poet, the son of a poor labourer, was born at Helpstone, near Peterborough. Though almost without schooling, he studied Thomson's *Seasons*, and began to cultivate verse writing. His *Poems Descriptive of Rural Life* (1820) had a good reception; but though the Marquis of Exeter and other patrons secured him £45 a year, he continued poor, and died insane at Northampton. Blunden edited his *Poems* (1920) and his *Sketches* (1931); see Life by J. and A. Tibble (1932).

CLARENCE, an English ducal title, conferred for the first time in 1362 on Lionel, third son of Edward III and Philippa. The most notable Dukes of Clarence, all royal, are **Thomas,** the second son of Henry IV, who fell at the battle of Beaugé (1421); **George** (1449–78), the third surviving son of Richard of York, and brother of King Edward IV (Shakespeare's Clarence), who perished in the Tower—in a butt of malmsey, according to three contemporary writers; **William IV,** who was Duke of Clarence before his accession; and **Prince Albert Victor** (1864–92), who was born at Frogmore Lodge, Windsor, and died at Sandringham, having in 1890 been created Duke of Clarence. See Memoir by Vincent (1893).

CLARENDON, (1) **Edward Hyde, 1st Earl of** (1609–74), was born at Dinton, near Salisbury, the third son of a Wiltshire squire. Destined for the church, he went up to Magdalen Hall in 1622; but the death of his elder brothers left him heir to the property, so in 1625 he quitted Oxford for the Middle Temple, of which his uncle, Sir Nicholas Hyde, the chief-justice, was then treasurer. Though he rose in his profession, he loved letters better than law; for his friends he chose such brilliant spirits as Falkland, Ben Jonson and Chillingworth. He married twice: in 1629, Ann, daughter of Sir George Ayliffe; in 1632, Frances, daughter of

Sir Thomas Aylesbury, Master of Requests and of the Mint, who bore him four sons and two daughters. In 1640 he was returned for Wootton-Bassett to the Short Parliament, for Saltash to the Long; and up to the summer of 1641 he acted heartily with the popular party. Then he drew back. Enough, he deemed, had been done; a victorious oligarchy might prove more formidable than a humbled king; nor could he conceive ' a religion without bishops '. Charles's answer to the Grand Remonstrance was of Hyde's composing, so were most of the subsequent able manifestoes; and though in a midnight interview with the king he declined to take St John's post of solicitor-general, thenceforward, with Falkland and Colepeper, he formed a veritable privy council. He headed the royalist opposition in the Commons till, in May 1642, he slipped away, and followed Charles into Yorkshire. He witnessed Edgehill; in 1643 was knighted, and made chancellor of the Exchequer; in March 1645 attended the Prince of Wales to the west of England; and with him a twelve-month later passed on to Scilly and Jersey. In Scilly, on May 18, 1646, he commenced his History; in Jersey he tarried two whole years. From November 1649 till March 1651 he was engaged in a fruitless embassy to Spain; for the next nine years was the most loyal and helpful adviser to Charles II in his needy, greedy and factious court. Charles had made him high chancellor in 1658, and at the Restoration he was confirmed in that dignity, in November 1660 being created Baron Hyde, and in the following April Earl of Clarendon. In November 1659 his daughter Anne (1638–71), then lady-in-waiting to the Princess of Orange, had entered into a secret marriage contract with the king's brother, James, Duke of York; and nine months later they were privately married at her father's house. As a statesman, Clarendon was unpopular. He could not satisfy the Cavaliers, who contrasted his opulence with their own broken fortunes; he did more than enough to irritate the Puritans. The sale of Dunkirk, the Dutch war, even the Plague and Great Fire, all heightened his unpopularity; and in 1667 he fell an easy victim to a court cabal. The great seal was taken from him; impeachment for high treason followed; and on November 29, at Charles's bidding, he quitted the kingdom for France. All but murdered at Évreux by some English seamen, at last the old man settled at Montpellier, where and at Moulins he spent nearly six tranquil years. Then moving to Rouen, he sent a last piteous entreaty that Charles would permit him to ' die in his own country '; but it was at Rouen that he died. No monument marks his grave in Westminster Abbey. The failings and merits of the statesman are mirrored in his great *History of the Rebellion in England* (3 vols. 1704–07), with its supplement and continuation, more faulty and less valuable—the *History of the Civil War in Ireland* (1721), and the *Life of Edward, Earl of Clarendon* (3 vols. 1759). Among other writings are 3 vols. of his state papers (1767–86; calendared, 1872–76). See Ranke's able analysis of the History, works cited under CHARLES I

and CHARLES II, the Lives by Lister (1838), Craik (1911), and Henslowe, *Anne Hyde* (1915).

(2) **George William Frederick Villiers, 4th Earl of** (1800–70), was born in London. His grandfather, Thomas Villiers, second son of the Earl of Jersey, having married in 1752 the heiress of the last Lord Clarendon of the Hyde family, was made Baron Hyde (1756) and Earl of Clarendon (1776). Having studied at Cambridge, he early entered the diplomatic service, and in 1833 was appointed ambassador at Madrid, where he employed his great influence in helping Espartero to establish a constitutional government. In 1838 he succeeded his uncle as 4th Earl, and in 1840 was made lord privy seal under Melbourne. When the Whigs fell (1841) he became an active member of the opposition; but warmly supported Peel and his own brother, Charles Pelham Villiers, in the abolition of the Corn Laws. Under Russell he became president of the Board of Trade in 1846 and from 1847 to 1852 was Irish viceroy. His impartiality helped to reconcile party exasperations, though it did not avert the bitter hatred of the Orangemen. He was thanked in the speech from the throne in 1848, and in 1849 received the Garter. Secretary of state for foreign affairs (1853), he incurred the responsibility of the Crimean war, and Roebuck's resolution in 1855 cost him his office, which he resumed at Palmerston's desire. He resumed his old office in 1865 and 1868. See Life by Maxwell (1913), and *A Vanished Victorian*, by Villiers (1938).

CLARETIE, Jules, properly **Arsène Arnaud** (1840–1913), French novelist, was born at Limoges. While a schoolboy in Paris he published a novel, and soon became a leading critic and political writer. His short story *Pierrille* (1863) was praised by George Sand. His novels also were generally popular. During the Franco-German war he sent a series of remarkable letters to the *Rappel* and *Opinion nationale*, and acquired the materials for a later series of bright and vigorous anti-German books of an historical character. He first made a hit on the stage with his Revolution plays, *Les Muscadins* (1874), *Le Régiment de Champagne* (1877) and *Les Mirabeau* (1878); in 1885 he became director of the Théâtre Français, and in 1888 an Academician.

CLARIN. See ALAS.

CLARK, (1) Sir Andrew (1826–93), Scottish physician, was born at Wolfhill, near Coupar-Angus, and educated at Aberdeen and Edinburgh. In 1854 he settled in London, where he acquired a high reputation for his skill in the treatment of diseases affecting the respiratory, renal and digestive organs. Among his patients were ' George Eliot ' and Mr Gladstone. He was created a baronet in 1883. He published several medical works. See Life by Canon MacColl and Dr Allchin (1896).

(2) **Sir James** (1788–1870), Scottish physician, born at Cullen, took his M.A. at Aberdeen, studied medicine at Edinburgh and London, was a naval surgeon 1809–15, practised eight years at Rome, and in 1826 settled in London. In 1837 Clark, who had been

physician to the Duchess of Kent, was appointed physician-in-ordinary to Queen Victoria.

(3) **James (Jim)** (1936–68), Scottish racing driver, educated at Loretto, won his first motor race in 1956, becoming Scottish National Speed Champion in 1958 and 1959. After joining the Lotus Team in 1960, he won major prizes in various countries and was World Champion Racing Driver in 1963 and 1965. He won in all 25 Grands Prix, thus breaking the record of 24 held by Fangio. His awards included the British Automobile Racing Club Gold Medal and the Ferodo Trophy, and in 1964 he received the O.B.E. He was killed during a race at Hockenheim, West Germany, in April 1968.

(4) **Josiah Latimer** (1822–98), English electrical engineer, born at Great Marlow, in 1854 patented a pneumatic delivery tube, and made important inventions in connection with submarine cables. He also invented a single-lens stereo-camera.

(5) **Kenneth Mackenzie, Baron** (1903–), British art historian, educated at Winchester and Trinity College, Oxford, became keeper of the Department of Fine Art in the Ashmolean Museum (1931–33), director of the National Gallery (1934–45) and Slade professor of Fine Art at Oxford (1946–50). From 1954 until 1957 he was chairman of I.T.A. He has written on Leonardo da Vinci (1939), on Piero della Francesca (1951) and on various aspects of painting. He was created K.C.B. in 1953, C.H. in 1959 and awarded a life peerage in 1969.

(6) **Mark Wayne** (1896–), American general. Born of a military family, he graduated from West Point Military Academy in 1917 and was wounded while on active service in Europe. Assiduous study at the Command and General Staff College and the National War College brought him a Staff appointment in 1942, and then the command of the U.S. Ground Forces in Europe. Prior to the Allied landings in North Africa Clark was secretly landed in Algeria to make contact with friendly French officials, narrowly escaping capture by the Vichy Security Police. In command of the 5th Army in Italy, Clark strongly, but vainly, supported Churchill's strategic design to forestall the Russians in the Balkans. Commanding general of the U.S. Forces in Austria, he ceded nothing to Soviet hectoring. Subsequently commanding general of the U.S. Forces in the Far East, his good work was rewarded by appointment as president of the Citadel (Military College), Charleston, S.C. See his *Calculated Risk* (1950) and *From the Danube to the Yalu* (1954).

(7) **William George** (1821–78), English man of letters, educated at Sedbergh, Shrewsbury and Trinity College, Cambridge. He took orders in 1853, but resigned them in 1869, and published a remarkable pamphlet, *The Present Dangers of the Church of England*. He was public orator from 1857 to 1869. Clark travelled in Spain, Greece, Italy and Poland, and published his experiences. He edited the *Cambridge Essays* (1855), and was long an editor of the *Journal of Philology*. Other works were his *Lectures on the Middle Ages and the Revival of Learning* (1872), and

the famous *Cambridge Shakespeare* (9 vols. 1863–66), in collaboration with Glover and afterwards Aldis Wright.

(8) **William Mansfield** (1884–1964), American chemist, educated at Johns Hopkins University, where he later became professor of Physiological Chemistry. He did important research on hydrogen-ion concentration and on oxidation reduction equilibria.

(9) **William Tierney** (1783–1852), English engineer, constructor in 1839–49 of the suspension-bridge at Budapest, was born at Bristol.

CLARKE, (1) **Adam,** LL.D. (c. 1762–1832), Wesleyan divine, born near Portrush, author of *Bibliographical Dictionary* (8 vols. 1802–1806); and a well-known edition of the Holy Scriptures (8 vols. 1810–26) with a commentary. Clarke denied the eternal sonship of Christ, though maintaining his divinity, held that Judas repented unto salvation, and that the tempter of Eve was a baboon. See his *Life* (3 vols. 1833).

(2) **Alexander Ross** (1828–1914), Scottish geodesist, began as an army engineer and was later attached to the Ordnance Survey. He is remembered for his work on the principal triangulation of the British Isles, and for his book *Geodesy* (1880).

(3) **Austin** (1896–), Irish poet, born in Dublin, author of *The Vengeance of Fionn* (1917) and other verse works. See his *Collected Poems* (1936)

(4) **Charles Cowden** (1787–1877), English Shakespearean scholar, was born at Enfield, Middlesex, where his father kept a school. Keats was a pupil, and in a poetical epistle (1816) addresses Clarke as 'you who first taught me all the sweets of song'. He formed the friendship of Leigh Hunt, Shelley, Hazlitt, Charles and Mary Lamb. In 1820, he became a bookseller in London and soon a partner as music publisher with Alfred Novello, whose sister, Mary Victoria (1809–98), he married in 1828. A year later Mrs Cowden Clarke began her famous *Concordance to Shakespeare's Plays* (1845). In 1834 Clarke entered on a twenty years' course of public lectures on Shakespeare and other dramatists and poets which brought him much celebrity and profit. Some of them were published, as his *Shakespeare Characters, chiefly those Subordinate* (1863), and *Molière Characters* (1865). The joint productions of the pair were the valuable *Shakespeare Key* (1879); an annotated edition of Shakespeare (1869), reissued as *Cassell's Illustrated Shakespeare*; and *Recollections of Writers* (1878), full of reminiscences of Keats, Lamb, Dickens, &c. See Life by his wife (1887) and her *Autobiographic Sketch*.

(5) **Sir Edward** (1841–1931), K.C., P.C., English lawyer, born in London, had a brilliant career of fifty years (1864–1914) at the bar. In 1880–1900 he sat for Plymouth as Conservative M.P.; in 1886–92 he was solicitor-general. He published works on the Bible, an autobiography (1918), &c.

(6) **Edward Daniel** (1769–1822), English traveller and author, born at Willingdon Vicarage, Sussex, passed from Tonbridge School to Jesus College, Cambridge, and from 1790 to 1799, as tutor in noblemen's

families, travelled in Europe. In 1799–1802 he thus traversed Finland, Russia, Scandinavia, the Middle East and Greece. In 1808 he was appointed first professor of Mineralogy at Cambridge. His *Travels* (6 vols. 1810–23) were received with extraordinary favour; his other works were chiefly on antiquarian subjects and mineralogy. See Life by Bishop Otter (1825).

(7) **Frank Wigglesworth** (1847–1931), American geologist, professor of Physics at Howard University and at Cincinnati (1874–1883), chief chemist to the U.S. Geological Survey (1883–1925), did much work on the recalculation of atomic weights.

(8) **James Freeman** (1810–88), American theologian, studied at Harvard, became a Unitarian pastor, in 1841 founded the Church of the Disciples at Boston, and held a chair of Natural Theology at Harvard (1867–71). He wrote many books, including an Autobiography (1891).

(9) **Jeremiah** (*c.* 1659–1707), English composer, born probably in London. He studied under Blow at the Chapel Royal and became organist of Winchester College in 1692 and of St Paul's Cathedral three years later, following his master at the Chapel Royal in 1704. He committed suicide as the result of an unhappy love affair. The real composer of the *Trumpet Voluntary* long attributed to Purcell, Clarke wrote operas, theatre music, religious and secular choral works, and music for harpsichord.

(10) **Marcus** (1846–81), son of a London barrister, went at eighteen to Australia, where he became the principal prose author; his chief work, *For the Term of his Natural Life* (1874), a story of the convict settlements. See Life by B. Elliott (1958).

(11) **Mary Anne**, *née* **Thompson** (1776–1852), was mistress during 1803–07 to Frederick, Duke of York (1763–1827), and trafficked in commissions. Imprisoned for libel in 1813, she settled in Paris.

(12) **Samuel** (1675–1729), English philosopher, born at Norwich, studied at Caius College, Cambridge. Descartes' system then held almost universal sway; but he adopted the views of Newton, and expounded them in his edition of Rohault's *Physics*. Along with philosophy he studied theology and philology. Chaplain from 1698 to Bishop Moore of Norwich, in 1706 he became chaplain to Queen Anne, and in 1709 rector of St James's, Westminster. By his work on the Trinity (1712), in which he denied that that doctrine was held by the early church, he raised the controversy in which Waterland was his chief opponent. His famous *Discourse concerning the Being and Attributes of God*, originally the Boyle Lectures of 1704–05, was in answer to Hobbes, Spinoza, Blount and the free-thinkers, and contained the famous demonstration of the existence of God, often, but inaccurately, called an *a priori* argument. Clarke's keen correspondence with Leibniz (published in 1717) dealt with space and time and their relations to God, and moral freedom. See Lives by Hoadly, prefixed to his collected works (4 vols. 1738–42), Whiston (1741), and R. Zimmermann (Vienna 1870).

(13) **William Branwhite** (1798–1878), English minister and geologist, born at East Bergholt, Suffolk, was educated at Dedham and Cambridge, took orders, in 1839 went out to New South Wales, and in 1841 discovered gold in the alluvium of the Macquarie.

CLARKSON, Thomas (1760–1846), English philanthropist, was born at Wisbech, and educated at St Paul's School, and St John's College, Cambridge. He gained a prize for a Latin essay in 1785, on the question, ' Is it right to make slaves of others against their will ? ' which in an English translation (1786) was widely read. He now devoted himself to an indefatigable crusade against African slavery, and, after the passing of the anti-slavery laws (1807), wrote a *History of the Abolition of the African Slave-trade* (2 vols. 1808). He became a leading member of the Anti-slavery Society, formed in 1823 for the abolition of slavery in the West Indies, and saw the object of its efforts attained in 1833. See Lives by Taylor (1839 and 1876) and E. L. Griggs (1936).

CLAUDE, Georges (1870–1960), French chemist and physicist, member of the Academy of Sciences, noted for his work on gases, and credited with the idea of the use of electromagnetic wave measurement and neon lighting for signs.

CLAUDE LORRAINE, *klōd*, properly **Claude Gelée** (1600–82), French landscape painter, was born at Chamagne, near Mirecourt, in Lorraine, went with a relative when still a boy to Italy, and in Rome ground colours for Agostino Tassi, a landscape painter. He seems also to have studied under Godfrey Waals at Naples, and after some travels finally settled at Rome in 1627. From 1629, when he drew four landscapes for Pope Urban VIII, his works were much sought after. Claude's landscapes, which number about four hundred, are found in Italy, France, Spain, and Germany, and in particular England—see paintings in the National Gallery and drawings in the British Museum. He was somewhat restricted in his range of subjects and effects, and had little sympathy with nature in her wilder and sterner moods. His composition, if rather formal, is always graceful and well considered, and his colour is singularly mellow and harmonious. Claude produced about thirty etchings; Hamerton pronounced *Le Bouvier* ' the finest landscape etching in the world '. See Ruskin, *Modern Painters*; Grahame, *The Portfolio* (March 1895); Hind, *The Drawings of Claude Lorraine* (1925).

CLAUDEL, Paul, *klō-del* (1868–1955), French poet, essayist and dramatist, born in Villeneuve-sur-Fère. Now regarded as one of the major figures in French Catholic literature, it was long before he was recognized, even by his countrymen. He joined the diplomatic service and held posts in many parts of the world. This experience, with the early influence of the Symbolists, adds quality and richness to his work. His eight dramas, of which the most celebrated are *L'Annonce fait à Marie* (1892), *Partage de Midi* (1905), *L'Otage* (1909) and *Le Soulier de satin* (1921) (translated into English by

Fr. John O'Connor), have a Wagnerian grandeur and, in many cases, an anti-Protestant violence that render them antipathetic to popular taste. He has also written some memorable poetry—*Cinq Grandes Odes* (1922) and *Corona Benignitatis Anni Dei* (1913)—and the libretti for two operas: *Jeanne d'Arc au bûcher* by Honegger and *Christophe Colombe* by Milhaud. He was elected to the French Academy in 1946. See *Claudel* by Wallace Fowlie (1958).

CLAUDIANUS, Claudius (4th cent. A.D.), the last of the great Latin poets, came from Alexandria to Rome in A.D. 395, and obtained patrician dignity by favour of Stilicho, whose fall (408) he seems not to have long survived. A pagan, he wrote first in Greek, though he was of Roman extraction. We have several epic poems by him, panegyrics on Honorius, Stilicho and others, invectives against Rufinus and Eutropius, occasional poems, and a Greek fragment, *Gigantomachia*.

CLAUDIUS I (10 B.C.–A.D. 54), fourth Roman emperor, whose full name was Tiberius Claudius Drusus Nero Germanicus, was the younger son of Drusus, brother of the Emperor Tiberius, and was born at Lyons. His supposed imbecility saved him from the cruelty of Caligula; but in his privacy he had studied history, and wrote in Latin and Greek several works now lost. After Caligula's assassination (A.D. 41), Claudius was found by the soldiers hiding in the palace, and proclaimed emperor. By giving largess to the troops who had raised him to the throne, he commenced the practice which subjected Rome to a military despotism. His first acts gave promise of just government, but he later appeared to condone the behaviour of his third wife, Messalina, who practised cruelty, extortion and profligacy without restraint. The emperor lived in scholarly retirement, and expended enormous sums in building, especially the Claudian Aqueduct. Abroad his arms were victorious. Mauritania was made a Roman province, the conquest of Britain was commenced, and the frontier provinces in the east were settled. Messalina at last married herself publicly to a young lover, on which the emperor put her to death. He next married his niece, Agrippina, who is believed to have poisoned him to secure the succession of Nero, her son by an earlier husband. See novels by R. Graves, *I, Claudius* and *Claudius the God* (1934).

CLAUDIUS, Appius, a Roman decemvir (451 and 450 B.C.), who gained the favour of the citizens by his ability, but began to show his real aims towards absolute power. The indignation of the populace reached a height on his gaining possession of Virginia, daughter of a plebeian, Lucius Virginius, who was with the army, by pretending that she was the born slave of one of his clients. Her lover Icilius summoned Virginius from the army, but another mock-trial again adjudged the girl to the decemvir. To save her from dishonour, the father seized a knife and slew her. Public indignation and the father's appeal to the army overthrew the decemviri, and Appius died in prison by his own hand.

CLAUDIUS, Matthias (1740–1815), a German poet and prose writer, who shared in the movement for the return to simplicity in lyric poetry. See study by Roedl (1934).

CLAUS, Karl (1835–99), German zoologist, born at Cassel, became professor at Würzburg (1860), Marburg, Göttingen and Vienna (1873). He wrote a famous textbook of Zoology (1880) revised by Grobe (10 vols. 1932); also works on Copepods and other invertebrates. See his Autobiography (1899).

CLAUSEL, Bertrand, *klō-zel* (1772–1842), French marshal, born at Mirepoix, obtained distinction in the Italian and Austrian campaigns, but more especially as commander in Spain in 1812. Condemned to death as a traitor on the return of the Bourbons, he was in 1819 permitted to come back from America to France; and from 1835 to 1837 was governor of Algeria.

CLAUSEN, Sir George, *klow'sėn* (1852–1944), R.A. (1908), kt. (1927), landscape and figure painter, born in London. Several works are in the Tate Gallery.

CLAUSEWITZ, Karl von, *klow'ze-vits* (1780–1831), Prussian general, who revolutionized the theory of war, was born at Burg. He served with distinction in the Prussian and in the Russian service, in 1815 became chief of a Prussian army corps, and was ultimately director of the army school, and Gneisenau's chief of staff. He died of cholera at Breslau. His *Vom Kriege* ('On War', trans. 1873, 4th ed. 1940) was very popular in Germany. See Lives by Schwartz (Berlin 1877) and Camon (Paris 1911).

CLAUSIUS, Rudolf (1822–88), German physicist, born at Köslin, studied at Berlin, and in 1869 became professor of Natural Philosophy at Bonn. He studied optics and electricity, and shared the honour of establishing thermodynamics on a scientific basis. See a monograph by Riecke (Göttingen 1889).

CLAUSSEN, Sophus Niels Christen, *klow'sėn* (1865–1931), Danish poet, born in Heletoft. He is generally regarded as the greatest symbolist poet of his country. He lived for many years in France, where he was influenced by the French symbolists, but brought a personal eroticism to nearly everything he wrote. He also translated Heine and Shelley. His *Samlede Vaerker* were published in seven volumes in 1910. See Life by E. Frandsen in 1950.

CLAVERHOUSE. See DUNDEE.

CLAVIJERO, Francisco Xavier, *klav-ee-hay'rō* (1721–87), Jesuit, was born at Vera Cruz, and died at Bologna. His valuable Italian *History of Mexico* was translated by C. Cullen in 1787.

CLAY, Henry (1777–1852), American statesman and orator, was born in ' the Slashes ', Hanover county, Virginia. He was the son of a Baptist preacher who died in 1781, and from his employment in a grist-mill was nicknamed ' the mill-boy of the Slashes '. At fifteen he became an assistant clerk in the chancery court of Virginia; and in 1797 he was licensed to practise law, and went to Lexington, Kentucky, where he soon acquired a high reputation. He entered the lower house of congress in 1811, and was chosen its speaker, a post he filled for many years. He was active in bringing on the war of 1812–15 with Great Britain, and was one of the commissioners who arranged the treaty of Ghent which ended it. By his course in regard to the ' Missouri Compromise ' of 1821, he won the title of ' the great pacificator '. In 1824, 1831 and 1844 he was an unsuccessful candidate for the presidency. The compromise of 1850 between the opposing free-soil and pro-slavery interests was largely Clay's work. He died at Washington. See *Life* by Schurz (Boston 1887).

CLAYTON, (1) **John** (*c.* 1650), English scientist, educated as a theologian, first discovered that gas could be distilled from crude coal and stored, but did not realize the commercial importance of his discovery. He also did work on stained glass.

(2) **John Middleton** (1796–1856), American statesman, was born in Sussex county, Delaware, studied at Yale, and practised as a lawyer. In 1829 he became a United States senator, and, while secretary of state in 1849–50, he negotiated the Clayton-Bulwer Treaty with Britain.

CLEANTHES (*c.* 300–220 B.C.), a Stoic philosopher, born at Assos in Troas, studied under Zeno for nineteen years, and, on his death, succeeded him. He died of voluntary starvation. His principal extant writing is the *Hymn to Zeus*. See his *Fragments* and Zeno's, edited by Pearson (1891).

CLELAND, (1) **John** (1709–89), English novelist, educated at Westminster, after a spell in the consular service and in the East India Company, followed by vagrant travel in Europe, published in 1750 *Fanny Hill, or the Memoirs of a Woman of Pleasure*, a best-seller in its time which achieved a second *succés de scandale* on its revival and prosecution under the Obscene Publications Act in 1963. *Memoirs of a Coxcomb* (1751), though better literature, was less successful, so Cleland turned to journalism and playwriting, excelling at neither, and dabbled in Celtic philology.

(2) **William** (*c.* 1661–89), Scottish Covenanting poet, studied at St Andrews and Utrecht, and had fought at Drumclog, Bothwell Brig and in Argyll's expedition, when, as colonel of the Cameronians, he fell in the defence of Dunkeld against the Jacobite clansmen.

CLEMENCEAU, **Georges**, *klem-ã-sõ* (1841–1929), French statesman, born in La Vendée, became a Paris physician, lived in U.S.A. 1865–69, in 1871 was in the French National Assembly, and, sent in 1876 to the Chamber, was a leader of the extreme left. The destroyer of many ministries, he was himself premier 1906–09, 1917–20. ' The Tiger ', as he was called, presided at the Peace Conference in 1919 and his intransigent hatred of Germany at that time may have contributed towards World War II. A brilliant journalist, he founded *L'Aurore*, &c., and from 1918 was an Academician. See studies by Hyndman (1919), Daudet (1938) and Szeps (1945).

CLEMENS, **Samuel Langhorne**. See TWAIN, MARK.

CLEMENT, or **Clemens**, is the name of seventeen popes, of whom three, as schismatics, are not usually reckoned.

(1) **Clemens Romanus**, was one of the Apostolic Fathers, and is reckoned variously as the second or third successor of St Peter in the see of Rome. According to Lightfoot, he was a freedman of Jewish parentage belonging to ' Caesar's household '. The second of the two epistles attributed to him is certainly not by Clement; but the first is generally accepted as his, and was probably written about A.D. 95. It is addressed to the Corinthian Church, and treats of social dissensions and of the resurrection. The first edition was edited by Patrick Young in 1633, from the incomplete Alexandrian MS. then in the king's library. This was the only copy known until in 1875 Bryennios (q.v.) published a complete MS. (dated 1056) found at Constantinople; and in 1876 a complete Syriac MS. came into the possession of Cambridge University. See Lightfoot's exhaustive edition (1869–77), where the second epistle will also be found. The other works attributed to Clement—the Apostolic Constitutions and Canons, two Syriac epistles on Virginity, the *Clementinae* (the *Recognitions* and *Homilies*), and two epistles to James are all undoubtedly spurious.

(2) **Clement III** (1187–91) allayed an old feud between the Romans and the popes.

(3) **Clement IV**, named **Gui Foulques**, pope in 1265–68, supported Charles of Anjou and encouraged Roger Bacon.

(4) **Clement V** (1305–14), formerly archbishop of Bordeaux, suppressed the Templars, and removed the seat of the papacy to Avignon (1308), a movement disastrous to Italy.

(5) **Clement VI** (1342–52), also French, was the fourth of the Avignon popes, a patron of art and learning, but no saint.

(6) **Clement VII** (1523–34), Giulio de' Medici, was a cunning diplomatist but a most unlucky pope, allied himself with Francis I against Charles V, was besieged by the Constable Bourbon and became his prisoner, and refused to sanction Henry VIII's divorce.

(7) **Clement VIII** (1592–1605), an Italian, secured peace between France and Spain, and extended the States of the Church.

(8) **Clement XI** (1700–21), issued the bull *Unigenitus* against the ' Gallican liberties ' of the French church.

(9) **Clement XIV**, named **Ganganelli** (1769–74), an excellent and accomplished but much calumniated pope, suppressed in 1773 the Jesuit order.

CLEMENT OF ALEXANDRIA, Lat. **Clemens Alexandrinus** (*c.* 150–*c.* 215), a Church father, was born probably at Athens, of heathen parents, and lived chiefly in Alexandria. In his earlier years he devoted himself to philosophy. After coming to Alexandria he was made a presbyter, and about 190 became head of the celebrated Catechetical school. In 203 the persecution under Severus compelled him to flee to Palestine. His most distinguished pupil was Origen. The chief writings of Clement that have survived, besides a practical treatise, *Who is the Rich Man that is Saved*, are the *Missionary*, the *Tutor* and the *Miscellanies*, which form a connected series, probably continued in his lost *Outlines*, which was an investigation of the canonical writings. They exhibit a man of pure and gentle spirit, sincere piety, wide reading, and wider sympathies; but his learning is undigested, his style verbose, and his method desultory. See editions by Dindorf (4 vols. Oxford 1868); Stählin (Leipzig 1905 *et seq.*); the translation in Clark's *Ante-Nicene Library* (1877–79); monographs by J. Patrick (1914) and R. B. Tollinton (1914).

CLÉMENT, Jacques (1564–89), the Dominican who stabbed Henry III (q.v.) of France.

CLEMENTI, Muzio (1752–1832), pianist and composer for the pianoforte, was born at Rome, and was brought to England in 1766 by Peter Beckford, M.P. He conducted the Italian Opera in London (1777–80), toured as a virtuoso in 1781, and later went into the piano-manufacturing business. In 1817 he wrote the *Gradus ad Parnassum*, on which subsequent piano methods have been based. He can be regarded as the father of pianoplaying, having been a pioneer of that instrument when it began to supersede the harpsichord; and he left many charming and tuneful pieces. See Life by Unger (1913).

CLEMENTIS, Vladimir (1902–52), Czech politician, was born at Tesovec, Slovakia, in 1902 and studied at Prague University. He became a Czech Communist M.P. in 1935 and in 1945 vice-minister of foreign affairs in the first Czech postwar Government. A chief organizer of the 1948 coup, he succeeded Jan Masaryk as foreign minister, but was forced to resign in 1950 as a ' deviationist '. Following a purge, he was hanged.

CLEON (d. 422 B.C.), a loud-voiced Athenian demagogue and leader of the war party at the time of the Peloponnesian war, was originally a tanner. He advocated (427 B.C.) the slaughter of the Mytilenean prisoners, but his first great success was the reduction of Sphacteria, in which a Lacedaemonian force had long held out. Perhaps this exploit was really due to his colleague Demosthenes, but many of his countrymen must have credited Cleon with military genius, for in 422 he was sent to oppose the Spartan Brasidas in Macedonia, but was killed at Amphipolis.

CLEOPATRA (69–30 B.C.), should by the will of her father, Ptolemy Auletes (d. 51 B.C.), one of the Macedonian kings of Egypt, have shared the throne with her younger brother, Ptolemy. But she was ousted by Ptolemy's guardians, and was about to assert her rights, by help of Syrian troops, when Julius Caesar arrived in Egypt in pursuit of Pompey. Caesar, captivated by her charms, warmly espoused her cause, and, after the Alexandrine war, in which Ptolemy fell, replaced her upon the throne. Cleopatra bore him a son, who was called Caesarion (afterwards killed by Augustus), and soon followed her lover to Rome. After Caesar's murder and the battle of Philippi, Antony summoned her to appear before him at Tarsus in Cilicia. She was then in her twenty-eighth year, the perfection of Greek beauty (she was pure Greek by descent); and the splendour of her loveliness and her wit fascinated Antony. They spent the next winter in Alexandria. Antony then went to Rome to marry Octavia, the sister of Octavian, but soon returned to the arms of Cleopatra, who met him in Syria (36 B.C.), and accompanied him on his march to the Euphrates. From this time his usual residence was with her at Alexandria, where he heaped upon her and her children extravagant gifts and honours; his infatuation cost him all his popularity in Rome. It was at Cleopatra's instigation that he risked the great sea-fight of Actium; and when she fled with sixty ships, he flung away half the world to follow her. When Octavian (Augustus) appeared victorious before Alexandria, Cleopatra entered into private negotiations with him. Antony, told that she had killed herself, fell upon his sword; but on learning that the report was false, he had himself carried into her presence, and died in her arms. Finding that she could not touch Octavian, and scorning to grace his triumph at Rome, she took poison, or, as it is said, killed herself by causing an asp to bite her breast. See books by Sergeant (1909), Weigall (1914), Von Wertheimer (trans. 1931) and H. Volkmann (1958).

CLERK, John (1728–1812), Scottish writer on naval tactics, was a son of the antiquary, Sir John Clerk of Penicuik (1676–1755). Retiring in 1773 from a prosperous business in Edinburgh, he devoted himself to the study of naval tactics at his newly purchased estate Eldin, Lasswade. In 1782 he printed 50 copies of his *Essay on Naval Tactics*, which was published in 1790 and started a controversy as to whether Rodney owed his West Indies successes to it.—His son, **John** (1757–1832), was raised as Lord Eldin to the Scottish bench in 1823.

CLERKE, Charles (1741–79), English naval captain, who succeeded to the command of Cook's expedition, but himself died soon after off Kamchatka.

CLERK-MAXWELL, James (1831–79), Scottish physicist, born in Edinburgh on June 13, was educated at Edinburgh Academy and University and at Cambridge. As a schoolboy of fifteen he devised a method for drawing certain oval curves which was published by the Royal Society of Edinburgh. At Cambridge he graduated as second wrangler. He was appointed professor at Aberdeen (1856), at King's College, London (1860), and became the first professor of Experimental Physics at Cambridge (1871), and organized the Cavendish Laboratory. In 1873 he published his great *Treatise on Electricity and Magnetism* which treats mathematically Faraday's theory of electrical and magnetic forces considered as action in a medium rather than as action at a distance. Clerk-Maxwell also contributed to the study of colour vision, and to the kinetic theory of gases, but his greatest work was his theory of electromagnetic radiation. He was awarded the Adams prize for an essay on the stability of Saturn's rings. He died on November 5. See Lives by Campbell and Garnett (1882), Glazebrook (N.Y. 1896) and Sir J. J. Thomson (1931).

CLEVE, van. The name of several Flemish painters.

(1) **Cornelis** (1520–67), son of (3), born at Antwerp, specialized in portraits of the rich Flemish bourgeoisie. In 1554 he went to

England, hoping for the patronage of Philip of Spain, who was there for his marriage to Mary Tudor, but his arrival unfortunately coincided with that of a collection of pictures by Titian and others from Italy, which ousted the Flemish school from royal favour. The disappointment mentally deranged Cornelis, who never entirely recovered, being known thereafter as ' Sotte (i.e., mad) Cleve '. Some of his work is at Windsor Castle.

(2) **Jan** (1646–1716), painted religious works at Ghent.

(3) **Joos van der Beke** (c. 1480–1540), father of (1), was born and died at Antwerp, where most of his work was done, though he also worked at Cologne and was invited to Paris to paint portraits of Francis I and his family. He is best known for his religious pictures and is sometimes called ' the Master of the Death of the Virgin ' from two tryptichs of that subject at Munich and Cologne. See study by von Baldass (1925).

CLEVELAND, (1) **Barbara Villiers, Duchess of** (1640–1709), mistress of Charles II. As the youthful wife of Roger Palmer, about 1659 she became the willing mistress of Charles II; Palmer being made Earl of Castlemaine by way of solatium. Hectoring and spendthrift, her amours were notorious, one of her lovers being a professional strong man, another the future Duke of Marlborough. In 1670 she was created Duchess of Cleveland. Settling in France, in 1705 she married ' Beau ' Fielding, but the marriage was annulled as bigamous. Her sons by Charles were created, respectively, Dukes of Cleveland, Grafton and Northumberland. See Rowse, *The Early Churchills* (1957).

(2) **John** (1613–58), English Cavalier poet, was born at Loughborough, Leicestershire, son of a poor clergyman, who was ousted by parliament from the living of Hinckley in 1645. In 1627 he entered Christ's College, Cambridge, graduated B.A. four years later, and then migrated to St John's, where he was elected to a fellowship in 1634, and lived nine years ' the delight and ornament of the society '. He vigorously opposed Cromwell's election to the Long Parliament for Cambridge, and was for his loyalty himself ejected from his fellowship in 1645. He betook himself to the king's army, and was appointed judge advocate at Newark, but was obliged to surrender with the garrison. In 1655 he was arrested at Norwich, but was released by Cromwell, who could admire the courageous manliness of the poor poet's letter addressed to him. In 1656 he published a volume containing thirty-six poems—elegies on Charles I, Strafford, Laud and Edward King, also some stinging satires. Cleveland now went to live at Gray's Inn, where he died. In 1677 was published, with a short Life, *Clievelandi Vindiciae*. See *Caroline Poets* (vol. 3, 1921), with *Life* by G. Saintsbury, and Dame Rose Macaulay's novel, *They were Defeated* (1932).

(3) **Stephen Grover** (1837–1908), the twenty-second and twenty-fourth president of the United States, was born at Caldwell, New Jersey, the son of a Presbyterian minister. In 1859 he was admitted to the bar, and began to practise at Buffalo. From 1863 to 1866 he was assistant district attorney for Erie County, and in 1870 was chosen sheriff. After filling the office of mayor of Buffalo, he was in 1882 elected governor of New York by a majority of 190,000 votes. In 1884 he was nominated by the Democrats for the presidency, and took his seat as president in 1885. In a message to congress in 1887 he strongly advised a readjustment of the tariff on certain manufactured articles of import, and the admission duty-free of some raw materials. Protectionists classed the president's message as a free-trade document, but this was denied by the Democrats, and its doctrines were adopted at the convention of that party in 1888. In the following August, on the rejection of the proposed Fisheries Treaty with Canada by the Republican majority in the senate, the president sent a message to congress, declaring a policy of ' retaliation ' against Canada to be necessary. At the election in November he was defeated by the Republican candidate, General Harrison, over whom, however, he secured a large majority in November 1892. In 1895 he evoked intense excitement throughout the whole civilized world by his application of the ' Monroe Doctrine ' to Britain's dispute with Venezuela over the frontier question. See studies by A. Nevins (1932) and H. S. Merrill (1958), and his *Writings and Speeches*, edited by Parker (1892).

CLEVELEY, John (1747–86), and **Robert** (1747–1809), twin brothers, born at Deptford, from 1764 were both marine painters.

CLIFFORD, a family descended from **Walter** (fl. 12th cent.), Richard FitzPonce's son, who by marriage, prior to 1138, acquired Clifford Castle on the Wye, 17 miles W. of Hereford, and who thence assumed the surname Clifford. He was the father of Fair Rosamond, Henry II's mistress, who seems to have died about 1176, and to have been buried at Godstow Nunnery, near Oxford. The legend of her murder by Queen Eleanor appears first in the 14th century; the Woodstock maze, the clue, the dagger and the poisoned bowl belong to a yet later age. Among Walter's descendants were the soldier-judge **Roger de Clifford** (d. c. 1285), who by marriage with Isabella de Vipont got Brougham Castle in Westmorland (c. 1270); **John** (1435–61), the savage Lancastrian; **Henry** (1455–1523), the ' shepherd lord '; **Henry** (1493–1542), 15th Lord Clifford and 1st Earl of Cumberland; **George**, 3rd earl (1558–1605), naval commander, whose daughter, **Anne** (1590–1676), married first the Earl of Dorset, and then the Earl of Pembroke; and **Henry**, 5th and last earl (1591–1643). To a cadet branch belonged **Thomas** (1630–73), a Catholic member of the Cabal, who in 1672 was created Lord Clifford of Chudleigh.

CLIFFORD, (1) **John** (1836–1923), English divine, born at Sawley near Derby, studied at the Baptist College in Nottingham and at University College London, and in 1858–1915 was pastor of a charge in Paddington. A leading passive resister to the Education Act of 1902 and a strong Nonconformist Liberal, he was created C.H. in 1921.

(2) **William Kingdon**, F.R.S. (1845–1879), mathematician, was born at Exeter. In 1860 he passed to King's College, London, and thence in 1863 to Trinity College, Cambridge, where he excelled in gymnastics, and came out second wrangler in 1867, next year being elected a fellow. In 1871 he was elected to the chair of Mathematics and Mechanics at University College London, which he retained until his untimely death at Madeira. In 1878 he published part i. of *Elements of Dynamics*; a further instalment appeared in 1887. His *Common Sense of the Exact Sciences* was completed by Professor Karl Pearson in 1885; his *Mathematical Papers* were issued in 1881; his lectures on *Seeing and Thinking* in 1879; and his *Lectures and Essays* were edited, with a memoir, by Stephen and Pollock (1879; 2nd ed. 1886).—His wife (*née* Lucy Lane, a Barbadian), who died in 1929, was the author of *Mrs Keith's Crime* (1885), &c.

CLINTON, (1) **De Witt** (1769–1828), American politician, son of (5), admitted to the New York bar in 1788, was private secretary to his uncle (2) in 1790–95. He sat in the state legislature (1797) and in the state senate (1798–1802); and in 1802 he was elected to the U.S. senate, but resigned in the same year on being appointed mayor of New York by his uncle. In this office he continued, save for two short intervals, until 1815; he was defeated by Madison in the presidential contest of 1812. He pressed the Erie Canal scheme, was elected governor of the state in 1817, and in 1825 opened the canal. He died in office at Albany. See Life by Campbell (1849).

(2) **George** (1739–1812), born in Ulster County, New York State, fought with his father and brother (5) in the expedition against Fort Frontenac, sat in the New York assembly, in 1775 was sent to the second Continental Congress, and in 1776 as general of militia served against his namesake Sir Henry (3). In 1777 he was chosen first governor of New York, to which post he was re-elected in 1780 and 1801; and to him was due the conception of the Erie Canal. In 1804 he was elected vice-president of the United States, and in that office he died at Washington.

(3) **Sir Henry** (c. 1738–95), British general, born in Newfoundland, was the son of the Hon. George Clinton, governor of Newfoundland, and afterwards of New York. He first entered the New York militia, then in 1751 the Guards, served with conspicuous gallantry in the Seven Years' War, and was promoted major-general in 1772. Sent to America in 1775, he fought at Bunker Hill, and in 1776 was repulsed in an attack on Charleston, but was shortly afterwards knighted for his services under Howe. After Burgoyne's surrender in 1778, Clinton succeeded Howe as commander-in-chief. In 1780 he captured Charleston and the entire southern army; but after Cornwallis' capitulation at Yorktown in 1781, Clinton resigned his command and returned to England, where in 1783 he published a *Narrative* of the campaign. In 1794 he was appointed governor of Gibraltar, where he

died. His two sons, **Sir William Henry** (1769–1846) and **Sir Henry** (1771–1829), both rose to be generals and G.C.B.s, the younger being one of Wellington's favourite officers.

(4) **Henry Fynes** (1781–1852), scholar, was born at Gamston, Notts; was educated at Southwell, Westminster, and Christ Church, Oxford, where he graduated B.A. in 1803; represented Aldborough in parliament from 1806 till 1826; and died at Welwyn. His principal works, on Greek and Roman chronology, are the *Fasti Hellenici* (1824–34) and *Fasti Romani* (1845–50).

(5) **James** (1736–1812), American soldier, was the third son of **Charles Clinton** (1690–1773), who emigrated from Ireland to New York State in 1729. He fought with distinction against the French and as a brigadier-general during the War of Independence.

CLISSON, Olivier de (1336–1407), a famous French knight, a comrade of du Guesclin.

CLITHEROW, Margaret, *née* **Middleton** (c. 1556–86), a Catholic martyr, called the ' Pearl of York ', the wife of a York butcher, was pressed to death, March 25, 1586. See Life by M. Monro (1948).

CLIVE, (1) **Kitty** (1711–85), comic actress, was born in London, the daughter of William Raftor, a Jacobite lawyer from Kilkenny. She came out at Drury Lane about 1728, and chiefly at Drury Lane she continued to play till 1769, when she quitted the stage and retired to Twickenham. About 1731 she had married George Clive, a barrister, but they soon parted. She died at Little Strawberry Hill. Garrick, Handel, Horace Walpole and Dr Johnson all liked her, the last remarking to Boswell that ' in the sprightliness of humour he never had seen her equalled '. See her Life by Percy Fitzgerald (1888).

(2) **Robert** (1725–74), soldier and administrator, was born at the manor house of Styche, near Market Drayton. He was the eldest of thirteen children; his father, a lawyer and small landowner, of a very old Shropshire family. The boy was brought up by an uncle near Eccles. There, and at all his four schools—Lostock, Market Drayton, Merchant Taylors' and Hemel Hempstead—he proved a much better fighter than scholar. In 1743 he was packed off to India as a writer in the service of ' John Company '. He reached Madras penniless, and the drudgery of his life there moved him to suicide. But the pistol snapped twice, and he flung it from him, exclaiming: ' It appears I am destined for something; I will live '. The capture of Madras by the French (1746), Clive's escape thence to Fort St David, his share in its defence, in the fruitless siege of Pondicherry (1748), and in the storming of Devikota (1749)—these events bring us up to Clive's daring dash upon Arcot (1751). He seized it, and held its enormous citadel for eleven whole weeks against 7000 natives and 120 French soldiers. His own little force was reduced to 80 Englishmen and 120 sepoys; but, after a last desperate assault, the siege was raised (November 14), and Clive followed up his success by the victories of Arni and Kaveripak and the capture of Kovilam and Chingalpat In 1753 he married Margaret Maskelyne, sister to the astronomer, and sailed with her

for England, where he was presented with a diamond-hilted sword, cleared his father's estate, stood for St Michaels, but was unseated, and otherwise got through a very fair fortune. So in 1755 he was back in India, and a twelvemonth later was summoned from Madras to avenge the tragedy of the Black Hole. Calcutta was soon retaken; Chandernagore, the French settlement, captured; and at Plassey, on June 23, 1757, Clive's 3200 men (two-thirds of them sepoys) victoriously encountered Suraj ud Dowlah's 50,000 *plus* 50 French gunners. For three years sole ruler in all but name of Bengal, Clive, in 1760, with a fortune of more than £40,000 a year, returned to England, to be hailed by Pitt as ' a heaven-born general '. In 1761 he entered parliament as member for Shrewsbury; in 1762 was raised to the Irish peerage as Baron Clive of Plassey; in 1764 was created a Knight of the Bath. But meanwhile in India the Company's affairs had fallen into the utmost disorder; and Clive was the only man who could set them right. He arrived at Calcutta in 1765, and at once applied himself wisely and firmly to reform the civil service and re-establish the military discipline. Early in 1767 Clive quitted India, never to return; in all he had spent there less than a dozen years. This time he came back to England poorer than he last left it; but this time he came back to encounter a storm of obloquy. His drastic measures had raised up a host of influential enemies, who stirred up ill-feeling against him. His early proceedings in India were in 1772 made the subject of animadversion in parliament and next year matter for the inquiry of a select committee. He was examined and cross-examined ' like a sheep-stealer '. The censure implied in the ultimate resolution was hardly wiped out by its rider, that he ' did at the same time render great and meritorious services ' (May 21, 1773). Sickness, opium, mental depression—on November 22, 1774 Clive died by his own hand (perhaps not intentionally).—His eldest son, **Edward** (1754–1839), was governor of Madras 1798–1803, and in 1804 was made Earl of Powis, having married (1784) the daughter of the last Earl of Powis of the Herbert line.—See Lives of Clive by Sir John Malcolm (1836, with Macaulay's essay thereon), Malleson (1882, 1893), Sir C. Wilson (1890), Sir A. J. Arbuthnot (1899), Sir G. Forrest (1918), R. Gatty (1927), R. J. Minney (1931).

CLODD, Edward (1840–1930), British anthropologist, born at Margate, was secretary of the London Joint-Stock Bank (1872–1915), and early became known as a rationalist thinker. Among his writings are *Childhood of the World* (1873), *Myths and Dreams* (1885), *Story of Creation* (1888), *Huxley* (1902), *Memories* (1916), and *The Question* (1917). See McCabe's *Memoir* (1931).

CLODIUS, Publius C. Pulcher (d. 52 B.C.), a Roman tribune (58 B.C.), who brought about Cicero's banishment, and tyrannized with his gladiators till he was slain by Milo.

CLOOTZ, Jean Baptiste du Val de Grâce, Baron, called **Anacharsis Clootz** (1755–94), was born at Schloss Gnadenthal, near Cleves, and educated in Paris. While still young he

traversed Europe under the name of Anacharsis, lavishing his money to promote the union of all nations in one family. In the French Revolution he saw the fulfilment of his dreams. He constituted himself the ' orator of the human race ', and wearied the National Assembly with his ravings against Christianity. With all its folly his enthusiasm was honest, and he was both hated and feared by Robespierre, who involved him in Hébert's downfall. He was guillotined, March 23, 1794. Of his absurd books may be named: *Certitude des preuves du Mohammédisme* (London 1780) and *La République du genre humain* (1793). See Lives by Avenel (Paris 1865) and Stern (Berlin 1915).

CLOPINEL. See MEUNG.

CLOPTON, Sir Hugh (d. 1497), a London mercer, benefactor of his birthplace, Stratford-on-Avon, built (*c.* 1483) New Place, which was Shakespeare's home from 1597 to 1616, and was lord mayor of London in 1492.

CLOSTERMAN, John (1656–1713), German painter, was born at Osnabrück, and in 1681 settled in England as a portraitist, notably of Queen Anne.

CLOTAIRE I, or Hlothar, or Chlotar (6th cent.), son and successor of Clovis (q.v.), first king of the Franks in Gaul, reigned as sole king from 558 to 561. **Clotaire II** reigned from 584 to 628.

CLOTILDE, St (474–545), daughter of Chilperic, king of Burgundy, in 493 married Clovis (q.v.). After his death she lived a life of austerity and good works at the abbey of St Martin at Tours, where she died.

CLOUET, kloo-ay. A family of French portrait painters of Flemish origin (**Clowets** or **Cloets**), most important of whom were:

(1) **François** (*c.* 1516–72), son of (2), born probably at Tours, succeeded his father as court painter to Francis I and continued in that office under Henry II, Francis II and Charles IX. His masterpiece, the Louvre portrait of Elizabeth of Austria, is one of the finest examples of the period; that of Mary Queen of Scots in the Wallace Collection is attributed to him.

(2) **Jean, Jehan, or Janet** (d. 1540-41), father of (1), was probably the son of Jehan Clouet (*c.* 1420-*c.* 1480), a Flemish painter who came to France as court painter to the Duke of Burgundy. He became court painter to Francis I, whose portrait in the Louvre is supposed to be by him.

CLOUGH, kluf, (1) **Ann Jemima** (1820–92), English educationist, sister of (2), became in 1871 first principal of the first hall for women students at Cambridge, later called Newnham College.

(2) **Arthur Hugh** (1819–61), English poet, was born at Liverpool, son of a cotton merchant who emigrated to Charleston, U.S.A. The boy was sent back to England in 1828 and entered Rugby, where he became Dr Arnold's most promising pupil and where he commenced his friendship with Matthew Arnold. Though he only got a ' second ' at Balliol, 1841, he was elected a fellow of Oriel and there lived through the crisis which resulted in Newman's conversion to Rome. His own difficulties with the Thirty-nine Articles led to his resignation in 1848. He

became for a time principal of the new University Hall, attached to University College, Gower Street, which had a Unitarian bias little to Clough's liking (' the Sadducees ', he called them). He had thus had experience of religious extremes from Puseyism or Newmanism to Unitarianism and he hints in a letter that it may be for him a case of ' no Christianity at all '. On his dismissal from University Hall he obtained an examinership in the Education Department. Before taking up that appointment he spent some months in Boston, Mass., where he met all the Boston Brahmins. Financial worries added to his religious troubles; in the year he got his fellowship at Oriel his father became a bankrupt. He does not seem to have enjoyed much family life—the letters to his sister Anne are revealing—before his marriage to Miss Blanche Smith in 1854. The last years of his short life were relatively happy. He enjoyed not only the friendship of the great Victorians, Ruskin, Arnold, Carlyle, &c., but also of distinguished Americans of the Boston connection. At Oriel Clough was the self-confident leader of a group, members of the Decade, and conducted reading parties in vacation to the Lakes and in Scotland. The latter resulted in a ' Long-vacation pastoral ' called *The Bothie* (1848), which delighted those of his friends whom it did not outrage. For one thing it broke the class barrier (the Oxford student marries a ' Scotch lassie '), for another it is written in loose and conversational hexameters. His only other long poems were *Amours de voyage*, also in hexameters, written at Rome in 1849; and *Dipsychus*, 1850, both published posthumously and neither calculated to reassure his friends. Arnold hesitated for ten years to write his commemorative poem *Thyrsis*. The two-volume *Correspondence* published in 1957 shows that Clough's dilemma was not confined to the Thirty-nine Articles (to which after all he subscribed) but to the whole of what is now called the Establishment. He imbibed the revolutionary doctrines of George Sand, called himself a republican, disliked class distinction (' your aversion, the Gentleman ') and the capitalist system. In short, he anticipates the ' Angry Young Men ' of the post-war era and this is no doubt the reason for revived interest in him. Palgrave's edition of the poems (1862) prefixed a memoir, as did Clough's widow's *Poems and Prose Remains* (1869). See also Dr Lowry's *Letters of Matthew Arnold to Arthur Clough* and monographs by S. Waddington (1883), J. L. Osborne (1920), *Memoir of Anne Clough* (1897), and study by K. Chorley (1962). *Correspondence*, ed. Mulhauser (1957), is his best memoir.

CLOVIO, Giulio, or Jurni Glovichisch (1498–1578), miniaturist, was born in Croatia, and died at Rome, having for fifty years been a monk. See Life by J. W. Bradley (1890).

CLOVIS, old Ger. **Chlodwig or Chlodovech** (465–511), Merovingian king, succeeded his father, Childeric (481), as king of the Salian Franks, whose capital was Tournai. His first achievement was the overthrow of the Gallo-Romans under Syagrius, near Soissons.

He then took possession of the whole country between the Somme and the Loire, and established himself in Soissons. In 493 he married Clotilda (q.v.). She was a Christian, and earnestly desired his conversion. In a great battle with the Alemanni near Cologne, Clovis as a last resource invoked the God of Clotilda, offering if victorious to turn Christian. The Alemanni were routed, and on Christmas Day Clovis and several thousands of his soldiers were baptized by Remigius, Bishop of Rheims. In 507, love of conquest concurring with orthodox zeal, Clovis marched against the Arian Visigoth, Alaric II, whom he defeated and slew at Vouglé, near Poitiers, taking possession of the whole country as far as Bordeaux and Toulouse; but he was checked at Arles by the Ostrogoth Theodoric. Clovis now took up his residence in Paris, where he died.— **Clovis II**, son of Dagobert, reigned over the Franks from 638 to 656.

CLOWES, (1) William (*c.* 1540–1604), English surgeon, served with Leicester in the Low Countries and on board the fleet that defeated the Armada. He became surgeon to the queen, and after a prosperous practice in London retired to Plaistow in Essex. He wrote five books in clear and vigorous English.—His son, **William** (1582–1648), was also a well-known surgeon.

(2) **William** (1779–1847), English printer, born at Chichester, in 1803 started the London printing business carried on by his son, **William** (1807–83), and was the first printer to use steam-driven machines.

(3) **William** (1780–1851), English nonconformist, born at Burslem, became a potter, and in the course of a dissolute youth achieved an ephemeral reputation as a champion dancer, but in 1805 was converted to Methodism, becoming in 1810 a co-founder with Hugh Bourne (q.v.) of the Primitive Methodists. See Life by Wilkinson (1951).

CLUSÉRET, Gustave Paul, *kloo-zè-ray* (1823–1900), French soldier, born in Paris, served in the June insurrection of 1848, the Crimea, Algeria, under Garibaldi, and the American Civil War on the Federal side, becoming a general in 1862, and after the war founding the New York *New Nation*. He returned to Paris in 1868, took a prominent part in the Commune (1871), escaped to England, America and Switzerland, returned to France under the amnesty (1880), and in 1888 was elected to the Chamber of Deputies. He published *Mémoires* (1888).

CLUSIUS. See LECLUSE.

CLUVERIUS, or Clüver, Philipp (1580–1622), the founder of historical geography, was born at Danzig, studied law at Leyden, and visited Norway, England, Scotland, France, Italy, &c. See Life by Partsch (Vienna 1891).

CLYDE, Lord. See CAMPBELL, SIR COLIN.

CLYNES, Joseph Robert (1869–1949), English Labour politician, born at Oldham, worked in a cotton mill from the age of ten and educated himself. Organizer of the Lancashire Gasworkers' Union (1891), he was president (1892) and secretary (1894–1912) of Oldham's Trade Council and, entering parliament (1910), was food controller (1918), vice-chairman (1922) and lord privy seal in Britain's first Labour cabinet (1924). As home secretary (1929–31), he refused to allow Trotsky to settle in Britain. He became a privy councillor (1918). See his *Memoirs* (1937).

CLYTAEMNESTRA, in Homeric legend, the wife of Agamemnon.

CNUT. See CANUTE.

COATES, (1) **Eric** (1886–1958), English composer, born at Hucknall, Notts. He studied in Nottingham and at the Royal Academy of Music, working as violist in chamber music groups until, in 1912, he became leading violist in the Queen's Hall Orchestra under Sir Henry Wood, who produced several of his early works at Promenade Concerts. Success as a composer of attractive light music enabled Coates to devote himself to composition after 1918. Among his best-known compositions are the *London Suite* (1933), *The Three Bears* (1926), the suites *Four Centuries* (1941) and *The Three Elizabeths* (1944), and a number of popular waltzes and marches.

(2) **Wells Wintemute** (1895–1958), English architect, born in Tokyo. He was one of the principal figures of the modern movement in architecture, and practised as an architect from 1929. He studied in Canada and London, and in 1933 formed the MARS group of architects. He was responsible for the design of B.B.C. studios, the EKCO laboratories, and many other buildings in Great Britain and in Canada, and he also played an important part in the development of industrial design.

COATS, Sir Peter (1808–90), and **Thomas** (1809–83), Scottish industrialists, two brothers, thread manufacturers at Paisley, of which they were both munificent benefactors. The former was knighted in 1869.

COBBE, Frances Power (1822–1904), British social worker and feminist, born at Newbridge near Dublin, travelled in Italy and the East, and wrote *Cities of the Past* (1864) and *Italics* (1864). A strong theist, a supporter of women's rights, and a prominent anti-vivisectionist, she published more than thirty works, mostly on social questions. See her autobiography (1894).

COBBETT, William (1763–1835), born at Farnham, Surrey, was the son of a small farmer, and grandson of a day labourer. From scaring crows the boy rose to be ploughman; but a visit to Portsmouth and a sight of the fleet had spoiled him for farming, when, in May 1783, a sudden freak took him to London. He reached it with just half a crown, and for nine months was quill-driver to a Gray's Inn attorney. Enlisting then in the 54th Foot, he first spent a year at Chatham, where he mastered Lowth's *English Grammar*, and read through a whole lending library—Swift's *Tale of a Tub* had been his boyhood's delight. Next he served as sergeant-major in New Brunswick (1785–91), meanwhile studying rhetoric, geometry, logic, French and fortification. On his return he obtained a most flattering discharge; in February 1792 he married; but in March went to France to get out of a court

martial on three of his late officers, whom he had taxed with peculation. Six months later he sailed for America. At Philadelphia he taught English to French refugees; and, as 'Peter Porcupine', wrote fierce onslaughts on Dr Priestley, Tom Paine and the native Democrats. Twice he was prosecuted for libel, and in 1800 he returned to England. The Tories welcomed him with open arms and in 1802 he started his famous *Weekly Political Register*, which, with one three-months' break in 1817, continued till his death. But, Tory first, it altered its politics in 1804, till at last it became the most uncompromising champion of Radicalism. A great lover of the country, Cobbett settled at Botley in Hampshire, where he planted, farmed and went in for manly sports; a true soldiers' friend, he got two years in Newgate (1810–12) for his strictures on the flogging of militiamen by German mercenaries. In 1817 money muddles and dread of a second imprisonment drove him once more across the Atlantic; and he farmed in Long Island till, in 1819, he ventured back again. Botley had to be sold, but he started a seed-farm at Kensington and stood for Coventry (1821) and Preston (1826). Both times he failed; but his ill-advised trial for sedition (1831) was followed next year by his return for Oldham. He died at Normanby farm, near Guildford, and was buried at Farnham. The *Rural Rides* (new ed. with notes by Pitt Cobbett, 1885) are unsurpassable. They were a reprint (1830) from the *Register*, and followed or were followed by *Porcupine's Works* (12 vols. 1801), the excellent and entertaining *English Grammar* (1818), the savage *History of the Reformation* (1824–27), the *Woodlands* (1825), the shrewd, homely *Advice to Young Men* (1830), and forty or fifty more works. Cobbett was the originator of Hansard's *Debates* (1806), and Howell's *State Trials* (1809). See Lives by E. Smith (1878), E. I. Carlyle (1904), Cole (1924), Chesterton (1925), Pearl (1953); *Life and Letters* by Lewis Melville (1913).

COBBOLD, Richard (1797–1877), English author of *Margaret Catchpole* (1845) and other works, was born at Ipswich, and for fifty years was rector of Wortham, near Diss. —His mother, **Elizabeth** (1767–1824), wrote poetry; and his third son, **Thomas Spencer** (1828–86), lectured in London on botany, zoology, comparative anatomy, geology and helminthology. He wrote *Entozoa* (1864), *Tapeworms* (1866), *Human Parasites* (1882), &c.

COBDEN, Richard (1804–65), English economist and politican, 'the Apostle of Free Trade', was born at Heyshott, near Midhurst, Sussex. His father had to sell his farm in 1814; and Richard, the fourth of his eleven children, was sent for five years to a 'Dotheboys' school in Yorkshire. In 1819 he was received into an uncle's warehouse in London, where he showed great aptitude both as clerk and commercial traveller. In 1828 he and two friends entered into a partnership for selling calicoes by commission in London. They set up an establishment for calico-printing in Lancashire in 1831, and in 1832 Cobden settled in Manchester. In 1835 he visited the United States, and in 1836–37 the Levant. The result was two pamphlets, *England, Ireland, and America* (1835), and *Russia* (1836), the former preaching free trade and non-intervention, the latter directed against ' Russophobia '. He contested Stockport unsuccessfully on free-trade principles in 1837. In 1838 seven merchants of Manchester founded the Anti-Corn-Law League; its most prominent member was Cobden. His lectures all over the country and his speeches in parliament (to which Stockport returned him in 1841) were characterized by clear, quiet persuasiveness; and to them was in great part due, as Peel acknowledged, the abolition of the Corn Laws in 1846. Cobden's zeal for free trade in corn had, however, to such a degree withdrawn his attention from private business that he was now a ruined man, and a subscription of £80,000 was raised in recognition of his services; with this in 1847 he re-purchased Dunford, the farmhouse in which he was born. As his health, too, had suffered he travelled for fourteen months in Spain, Italy, Russia, &c., and during his absence was elected for both Stockport and the West Riding; he chose the latter constituency. He shared Bright's unpopularity for opposing the Crimean war; and on Palmerston's appeal to the country to support him in his Chinese policy, of which Cobden was a strenuous opponent, he retired from the West Riding and contested Huddersfield, where, however, he was defeated (1857). In 1859 he revisited America, and meanwhile was elected for Rochdale. Palmerston offered him the presidency of the Board of Trade; but Cobden felt bound to decline. Ill-health forbade his taking further part in parliamentary proceedings, but in 1859–60 he arranged the treaty of commerce with France. Cobden spoke out strongly in favour of the North during the American Civil War, and in 1864 strenuously opposed intervention in favour of Denmark. He died in London, and was buried at Lavington, Sussex. His *Speeches on Questions of Public Policy* were edited by John Bright and Thorold Rogers (1870). See Life by Lord Morley (2 vols. 1881; 14th ed. 1920), and books by J. A. Hobson (1918), and W. H. Dawson (1926).

COBDEN-SANDERSON, Thomas James (1840–1922), English printer and bookbinder, born at Alnwick, a leader of the 19th century revival of artistic typography, worked with William Morris (q.v.) and in 1900 founded the Doves Press from which was issued the famous *Doves Bible* (1903). In 1916 the press closed and Cobden-Sanderson threw the type into the Thames. See his *Journals, 1879–1922* (1926), and study by A. W. Pollard (San Francisco, 1929).

COBET, Carel Gabriel (1813–89), a Dutch Hellenist, born in Paris, and from 1846 a professor at Leyden.

COBHAM, Lord. See OLDCASTLE.

COBORN, Charles, stage-name of **Colin Whitton McCallum** (1852–1945), Cockney comedian of Scottish descent, spent his childhood in London's East End, went on the stage in 1875 and immortalized the songs ' Two Lovely Black Eyes ' (1886) and ' The Man who Broke the Bank at Monte Carlo '

(1890). See his autobiographical *The Man who Broke the Bank* (1928).

COCCAIO, Merlino. See FOLENGO.

COCCEIUS, or Koch, Johannes (1603–69), German theologian, born at Bremen, in 1636 became professor of Hebrew at Franeker, and in 1650 of Theology at Leyden. His Hebrew Lexicon (1669) was the first tolerably complete one.

COCCEJI, Heinrich Freiherr von, *kok-say'yee* (1644–1719), German jurist, born at Bremen, professor of Law at Heidelberg (1672), Utrecht (1689) and Frankfurt an der Oder (1690). His work on civil law (*Juris Publici Prudentia*, 1695) was long a textbook. His youngest son, **Samuel** (1679–1755), born at Heidelberg, also became professor at Frankfurt an der Oder in 1703, and was ultimately Frederick the Great's chancellor. He reformed the Prussian administration of justice, and wrote on law. See a monograph by Trendelenburg (Berlin 1863).

COCHLAEUS, or Dobneck, Johann (1479–1552), Luther's opponent, was born near Nürnberg, and died a canon of Breslau. See German monographs by Otto (1874) and Getz (1886).

COCHRAN, Sir Charles Blake (1872–1951), British theatrical producer, born at Lindfield in Sussex, began as an actor, then turned impresario, becoming agent for Mistinguett, Houdini and other famous figures. His spectacular presentation of *The Miracle* (1911) won him renown as a producer, but after a number of successes, the failure of the Wembley rodeo venture in 1924 made him bankrupt. However, he made a rapid comeback with the brilliant Noel Coward musicals *This Year of Grace* (1928), *Bitter Sweet* (1929) and *Cavalcade* (1931). His most successful production was *Bless the Bride* by Herbert and Ellis (1947), which ran for 886 performances. He was knighted in 1948. See Life by C. Graves (1951).

COCHRANE, Lord. See DUNDONALD.

COCKBURN, *kō'burn,* (1) **Sir Alexander,** G.C.B. (1802–80), British judge, in 1822 entered Trinity Hall, Cambridge, in 1829 was called to the bar, and soon became distinguished as a pleader before parliamentary committees. In 1847 he became Liberal M.P. for Southampton, in 1850 a knight and solicitor-general, in 1851 attorney-general, in 1856 chief justice of the Common Pleas, in 1858 a baronet (in succession to an uncle), and in 1859 lord chief justice. He prosecuted in the Palmer case, and presided over the Wainwright and Tichborne cases. He represented Britain in the *Alabama* arbitration at Geneva.

(2) **Alison,** *née* **Rutherford** (1713–94), poetess, was born in Selkirkshire. For over sixty years she was a queen of Edinburgh society. Of her lyrics the best known is the exquisite version of ' The Flowers of the Forest ' (' I've seen the smiling of Fortune beguiling '), commemorating a wave of calamity that swept over Ettrick Forest, and first printed in 1765. In 1777 she discerned in Walter Scott ' the most extraordinary genius of a boy '; in 1786 she made Burns's acquaintance. See her Letters (edited by Craig-Brown, 1900).

(3) **Henry** (1779–1854), Scottish judge, was born perhaps at Cockpen, but more probably in the Parliament Close of old Edinburgh. He entered the High School in 1787, and the university in 1793. Through a debating club he became the companion of Jeffrey, Horner and Brougham. He was called to the Scottish bar in 1800; and in 1807 his uncle, the all-powerful Lord Melville, gave him an advocate-deputeship—a non-political post, from which, on political grounds, he ' had the honour of being dismissed ' in 1810. He rose, however, to share with Jeffrey the leadership of the bar. A zealous supporter of parliamentary reform, he became solicitor-general for Scotland in 1830; had the chief hand in drafting the Scottish Reform Bill; was elected lord rector of Glasgow University (1831); in 1834 was made, as Lord Cockburn, a judge of the Court of Session; and three years later a lord of justiciary. He contributed to the *Edinburgh Review*, and was author of an admirable *Life of Jeffrey* (1852), *Memorials of his Time* (1856), *Journal, 1831–44* (2 vols. 1874). See also *Some Letters of Lord Cockburn* (1932).

(4) **Piers**, a freebooter of Henderland, near St Mary's Loch, whose execution at Edinburgh in 1529 suggested the *Border Widow's Lament*.

COCKCROFT, Sir John Douglas (1897–1967), English nuclear physicist, born in Yorkshire, was educated at Manchester and Cambridge, where he became Jacksonian professor of Physics (1939–46). He and Walton succeeded in disintegrating lithium by proton bombardment (1932) and shared the Nobel prize (1951). He assisted in the design of much special experimental equipment for the Cavendish Laboratory, including the cyclotron. During World War II, he was director of Air Defence Research (1941–44) and of the Atomic Energy division of the Canadian National Research Council (1944–46). He became the first director of Britain's Atomic Energy Establishment at Harwell in 1946. He was knighted in 1948, awarded the O.M. in 1957 and appointed master of Churchill College, Cambridge, in 1959.

COCKER, Edward (1631–75), a London schoolmaster, whose *Arithmetick* (1678), was the first English work really adapted to commerce. His reputation for accuracy gave rise to the expression ' according to Cocker '.

COCKERELL, (1) **Charles Robert** (1788–1863), a London architect, son of (3), who travelled in the Levant and Italy (1810–17), was professor of Architecture in the Royal Academy 1840–57, and designed the Taylorian Institute at Oxford.

(2) **Sir Christopher Sydney** (1910–   ), English radio-engineer, born in Cambridge and pioneer of the amphibious hovercraft which rides on a cushion of jet-generated air (1953). A prototype made the Calais-Dover crossing in 1959. He was knighted in 1969.

(3) **Samuel Pepys** (1754–1827), father of (1), laid out Brunswick and Mecklenburg Squares and designed the tower of St Anne's, Soho.

COCKERILL, John (1790–1840), English industrialist, was born at Haslingden, Lancashire, the son of William Cockerill (1759–1832), an inventor who in 1807 established a machine factory at Liège. John and an elder brother, having in 1812 taken over their father's business, in 1815 started a woollen factory at Berlin, and in 1817 the famous iron works at Seraing.

COCTEAU, Jean, *kok-tō* (1889–1963), French poet, playwright and film director, born at Maisons-Lafitte, near Paris. Success came early with *La Lampe d'Aladin* (1909), and he exploited it. He postured and preened and ran the gamut of experience—a spectacular conversion to Roman Catholicism through Jacques Maritain—a derisive repudiation of his mentor—recourse to opium—search for salvation through solitude—yet met with astonishing success in whatever he touched. He figured as the sponsor of Picasso, Stravinsky, Giorgio di Chirico and the musical group known as *Les Six*, in complete accord with the surrealist and dadaist movements. He was actor, director, scenario writer, novelist, critic, artist, all of his work marked by vivacity and a pyrotechnic brilliance. He was elected to the French Academy in 1955. Significant works are his novels *Le Grand Écart* (1923), *Thomas l'Imposteur* (1923), *Les Enfants terribles* (1929), and plays *Les Mariés de la Tour Eiffel* (1921), *Orphée* (1926), *L'Aigle à deux têtes* (1946). His films include *Le Sang du poète* (1932), *La Belle et la bête* (1945), *Orphée* (adapted from his play, 1949) and *Le Testament d'Orphée* (1960). See his autobiographical *Maalesh* (1950), *Journals* (ed. and tr. by W. Fowlie 1957) and Life by E. Sprigge and J.-J. Kihm (1968).

CODRINGTON, Sir Edward (1770–1851), English admiral, born at Dodington, Glos., entered the navy in 1783. In 1794 he was lieutenant of Lord Howe's flagship in the action off Ushant, and at Trafalgar, in 1805, he was captain of the *Orion*, and leader of a squadron. He rose to the rank of vice-admiral in 1821, and in 1826 was appointed commander-in-chief of the Mediterranean squadron, taking a leading part in the battle of Navarino (1827). He was admiral of the red in 1837, and in 1839 commander-in-chief at Portsmouth. See *Memoir* by his daughter, Lady Bourchier (2 vols. 1873).—One son, **Sir William John**, G.C.B. (1804–84), was commander-in-chief in the Crimea from November 11, 1855.—Another, **Sir Henry John**, K.C.B. (1808–77), admiral, took part in the destruction of St Jean d'Acre, and served in the Baltic in 1854–55.

CODY, (1) **Samuel Franklin** (1862–1913), aviator, born in Texas, came to England in 1896 and acquired British nationality. He experimented with man-lifting kites, participated in the planning and construction of the first British dirigible, and built an early aeroplane in 1908. He was killed in a flying accident.

(2) **William Frederick** (1846–1917), American showman, born in Iowa, was known as ' Buffalo Bill ' after killing nearly 5000 buffalo in 18 months in pursuance of a contract to supply the workers on the Kansas Pacific Railway with meat. He served as a scout in the Sioux wars, but from 1883 toured with his famous Wild West Show. The town of Cody in Wyoming stands on part of his

former ranch. See study by R. J. Walsh (1928).

COEHOORN, Menno, Baron van (1641–1704), soldier and fortification expert, the ' Dutch Vauban ', was born near Leeuwarden, and died at The Hague.

COELLO, (1) **Alonso Sánchez** (c. 1515–90), Spanish portrait painter, court painter to Philip II, whose portrait by him is in the National Gallery.

(2) **Claudio** (1621–93), Spanish religious painter, is known for the sacristy altarpiece in the Escorial and many other church-paintings in Toledo, Saragossa and Madrid.

COGGAN, Frederick Donald (1909–), English prelate, born in London, educated at Merchant Taylors' school and St John's College, Cambridge, was a lecturer in Semitic languages at Manchester (1931–34), professor of the New Testament at Wycliffe College, Toronto (1937–44), principal of London College of Divinity (1944–56), and Bishop of Bradford from 1956 until 1961, when he was consecrated Archbishop of York. He is the author of several theological works.

COGGESHALL, Ralph de, abbot from 1207 to 1218 of the Cistercian abbey of Coggeshall, was a native of Cambridgeshire, and wrote a Latin Chronicle (edited by J. Stevenson in 1875).

COGSWELL, Joseph Green, LL.D. (1786–1871), American bibliographer, born at Ipswich, Mass., was professor of Geology at Harvard 1820–23, established the Round Hill School with Bancroft (q.v.), edited the *New York Review* (1836–42), and from 1848 was superintendent of the Astor Library.

COHN, Ferdinand Julius (1828–98), German bacteriologist, professor of Botany at Breslau, the father of bacteriology in that he was the first to account it a separate science. He did important research in plant pathology, and worked with Koch on anthrax.

COHORN. See COEHOORN.

COKE, *kook,* (1) **Sir Edward** (1552–1634), English jurist, was born of an old Norfolk family, at Mileham. From Norwich school he passed in 1567 to Trinity College, Cambridge, in 1571 to Clifford's Inn, in 1572 to the Inner Temple; and he was called to the bar in 1578. His rise was rapid—from recorder of Coventry (1585), to member for Aldeburgh (1589), solicitor-general (1592), Speaker of the House of Commons (1593), attorney-general (1594), chief justice of the Common Pleas (1606), chief justice of the King's Bench and privy councillor (1613). The rancour which he demonstrated in his prosecutions of Essex, Raleigh, and the Gunpowder conspirators (1600–03–05) has gained him little credit with posterity; but from 1606 he stands forth as a vindicator of the national liberties, opposing, unlike Bacon, every illegal encroachment on the part of both church and crown. Alone of twelve judges, he resisted the royal prerogative; and in the Overbury case he showed an indiscreet zeal to come at the real truth. His removal from the bench on most trivial grounds (November 1617) was aggravated by a quarrel with his wife; and though ten months afterwards he was recalled to the council, his conduct in parliament from 1620 as a leader of the popular party, an opponent of Spain and of monopolies, estranged him for ever from the court. In 1621–22 he suffered nine months' imprisonment in the Tower; still, though old, he carried his opposition into the next reign, the Petition of Right (1628) being largely his doing. Coke's four *Institutes* (1628–44) deal with tenures, statutes, criminal law and the jurisdiction of the several law courts. The first of these is the so-called *Coke upon Littleton*—a commentary that, in spite of its puerile etymologies, has still a real, if mainly historical, value. Eleven of the thirteen parts of his epoch-making Law Reports were published during his lifetime (1600–15); and the whole, translated out of the original French and Latin, fills 6 vols. in Thomas and Fraser's edition (1826). See Lives by Woolrych (1826), C. W. Johnson (1837) and C. W. James (1929).

(2) **Thomas** (1747–1814), English Methodist bishop, born at Brecon, graduated in 1768 at Oxford, and became a curate in Somerset, but in 1777 joined the Methodists, and was attached to the London circuit. He visited America nine times, and died in the Indian Ocean on a missionary voyage to Ceylon. He published, besides religious works, extracts from his American *Journals* (1790), a *History of the West Indies* (3 vols. 1808–11), and, with Henry Moore, a Life of Wesley (1792).

(3) **Thomas William.** See LEICESTER OF HOLKHAM.

COLARD, Mansion (d. 1484), the first printer of Bruges, was of French extraction.

COLBERT, Jean Baptiste, *kol-bayr* (1619–1683), French statesman, was born at Rheims, obtained a post in the War Office, and in 1651 entered the service of Mazarin. When in 1661 he became the chief minister of Louis XIV, he found the finances in a ruinous condition, and immediately began his reforms. Dishonest administrators were imprisoned; farmers of the state revenues were forced to yield up the resources of the crown; the debts of the state were reduced by arbitrary composition; and in all the departments of finance order and economy were introduced so that in ten years the revenue was more than doubled. He reorganized the colonies in Canada, Martinique and St Domingo, and founded others at Cayenne and Madagascar. In a few years he provided France with one of the strongest fleets in the world, with well-equipped arsenals, and a splendid body of seamen. He improved the civil code, and introduced a marine code. The Academies of Inscriptions, Science and Architecture were founded by him. In short, Colbert was the patron of industry, commerce, art, science and literature—the founder of a new epoch in France. His aim was to raise the strength of France by developing every side of the national life. In this—often by arbitrary measures—he entirely succeeded during the early part of Louis's reign, but the wars and the extravagance of the court undid all that had been accomplished. Colbert died bitterly disappointed, and hated by the people as the cause of their oppressive taxes. See his *Lettres, instructions et mémoires* (8 vols. 1862–82); Lives by Clément (3rd ed. 1892),

Neymarck (1877), Gourdault (6th ed. Tours 1885), Dussieux (1886), La Roncière (1919–1920); books by Cosnac (1892), Cole (1939).

COLBURN, (1) **Henry** (d. 1855), a London publisher, in 1814 started the *New Monthly Magazine*. He published Disraeli's first novel. In 1841 his business was taken over by Messrs Hurst and Blackett.

(2) **Zerah** (1804–40), American child prodigy, born in Vermont, displayed such powers of calculation that in 1810 his father left Vermont to exhibit him. He answered in twenty seconds such questions as ' How many hours in 1811 years? ' and a few years later solved much more complicated problems with equal rapidity. He was shown in Great Britain and Paris; from 1816 to 1819 he studied at Westminster School at the expense of the Earl of Bristol. His father died in 1824, and he returned to America; here he was a Methodist preacher for nine years, and from 1835 professor of Languages at Norwich, Vt. His remarkable faculty disappeared as he grew to manhood.

COLCHESTER, Charles Abbot, 1st Baron (1757–1829), Speaker of the House of Commons, was born at Abingdon. He was educated at Westminster and Christ Church, Oxford, and in 1779 entered the Middle Temple. Returned to parliament as a strong Tory in 1795, he improved in his first session the legislation regarding temporary and expiring laws; and it is due to his exertions that municipal bodies receive a copy of all new acts as soon as they are printed. To him too we mainly owe the Private Bill Office and the royal record commission, whose proceedings he for many years superintended. But his greatest service was in the Act (1800) for taking the first census. He was Speaker from 1802 until 1817, when he retired with a peerage. See his *Diary and Correspondence* (3 vols. 1861), edited by his son Charles, second Lord Colchester (1798–1867), who was postmaster-general in 1858.

COLE, (1) **George**. See (5).

(2) **George Douglas Howard** (1889–1958), English economist, historian and detective-story writer, born in London, was educated at St Paul's School and Balliol College, Oxford, where in 1925 he became reader in Economics and in 1944 Chichele professor of Social and Political Theory. Historian, chairman (1939–1946, 1948–50) and president from 1952 of the Fabian Society, he wrote numerous books on Socialism, including Lives of William Cobbett (1925) and Robert Owen (1925) and a history of the British working-class movements, 1789–1947 (1948), often in collaboration with his wife, Margaret Isobel Cole and her brother, Raymond Postgate. The Coles also collaborated in writing detective fiction. See D. Mirsky, *The Intelligentsia of Great Britain* (1935).

(3) **Sir Henry** (1808–82), British writer and art critic, born at Bath, became assistant-keeper of the Records in 1838. He wrote for the newspapers, and, as ' Felix Summerly ', produced children's books. Chairman of the Society of Arts, he did valuable service on the committee of the Great Exhibition of 1851, founded the South Kensington Museum and in 1860 became its director. He was

created K.C.B. in 1875. See his Auto-biography (1884).

(4) **Thomas** (1801–48), born at Bolton, removed to America in 1819, where he became one of the best known landscape painters. In 1830 two of his pictures appeared in the Royal Academy, and he afterwards made sketching tours through England, France, and Italy; but all his best landscapes were American.

(5) **Vicat** (1833–93), landscape painter (especially of Surrey scenes), was born at Portsmouth, the son of the painter, George Cole (1810–83). He was elected an R.A. in 1880. See Life by Chignell (3 vols. 1889).

COLEBROOKE, Henry Thomas (1765–1837), English orientalist, born in London, became an official in India, made a study of Sanskrit and aroused interest in Asiatic language and culture by his essays and his *Sanskrit Grammar* (1805). See Life by his son, Sir T. E. Colebrooke (1873), and Max Müller's *Biographical Essays* (1884).

COLENSO, John William (1814–83), Bishop of Natal, was born at St Austell, and graduated in 1836 from St John's College, Cambridge, of which he became a fellow. He published *Miscellaneous Examples in Algebra* in 1848, *Plane Trigonometry* in 1851, and *Village Sermons* in 1853, in which same year he was appointed first Bishop of Natal. He soon mastered the Zulu language, prepared a grammar and dictionary, and translated the Prayer Book and part of the Bible. His *The Pentateuch and the Book of Joshua Critically Examined* (1862–79), which cast doubts upon biblical accuracy, was regarded as heretical and his Metropolitan, Bishop Gray of Capetown, went to great lengths in attempting to have him deposed, even publicly excommunicating him. Colenso also earned disfavour by championing dispossessed Negroes. He died at Durban. See Life by G. W. Cox (2 vols. 1888).

COLEPEPER, John (d. 1660), a native of Sussex, served abroad, and was returned for Kent in 1640 to the Long Parliament. There he pursued a course much the same as Hyde's (see CLARENDON), and in 1642 was created chancellor of the Exchequer, in 1643 master of the Rolls, and in 1644 Lord Colepeper.

COLERIDGE, (1) **Hartley** (1796–1849), eldest son of (3), born at Clevedon, Somerset, was brought up by Southey at Greta Hall, and was educated at Ambleside school and Merton College, Oxford. His scholarship was great but unequal; his failures to win the Newdigate filled him with ' a passionate despondency '; and he forfeited an Oriel fellowship by intemperance. He spent two years in London, tried taking pupils at Ambleside, occasionally writing for *Black-wood's Magazine*, lived some time at Grasmere, and then went to live at Leeds with one Bingley, a publisher, for whom he wrote biographies, published under the titles of *Biographia Borealis* (1833) and *Worthies of Yorkshire and Lancashire* (1836). Bingley also printed a small volume of his poems in 1833. Hartley subsequently lived at Grasmere, with two short intervals of teaching at Sedbergh. Provided for by an annuity, he continued to write poetry, and edited Ford and Massinger. His days were spent in fitful study, lonely reverie, and wanderings over the Lake Country, with occasional lapses into intemperance. His poetry was graceful, tender and sincere. His *Poems* were collected by his brother Derwent, with a Memoir (2 vols. 1851); also his *Essays and Marginalia* (2 vols. 1851). See Lives by Griggs (1929), Hartman (1931).

(2) **John Duke, 1st Baron Coleridge** (1821–1894), was the eldest son of the judge Sir John Taylor Coleridge (1790–1876), the nephew of (3) and Keble's biographer. Educated at Eton and Oxford, he became successively solicitor-general (1868), attorney-general (1871), chief justice of the Common Pleas (1873), and lord chief justice of England (1880).

(3) **Samuel Taylor** (1772–1834), English poet, son of a vicar of Ottery St Mary, Devon, was educated at Christ's Hospital and at Jesus College, Cambridge. In his essay on Christ's Hospital (Essays of Elia), Charles Lamb described the impression made on him by his senior there. Coleridge's university career was interrupted by a runaway enlistment in the 15th Dragoons. Apparently, it was at Cambridge that he imbibed revolutionary views at about the time when Southey was giving concern to the authorities at Balliol College, Oxford, for a like reason. The two young poets met at Bristol in 1794 and planned a 'pantisocracy' or communist society on the banks of the Susquehanna, which came to nothing. Coleridge now became immersed in lecturing and journalism of various sorts, activities which were to engage his attention for the greater part of his working career. Bristol was the centre of these activities, which included itinerant preaching at Unitarian chapels. In his essay 'My First Acquaintance with Poets', Hazlitt has a memorable description of one of these occasions. The Bristol circle provided Coleridge with generous friends—Cottle the bookseller bore the loss arising from the publication of his first book of poems (1796), which is chiefly interesting now for the 'Ode to France', in which he recants revolutionary views. Thomas Poole, another 'friend of liberty', lent him and his newly married wife, Sara Fricker (Southey's sister-in-law), a cottage at Nether Stowey, where they enjoyed the intimate friendship of the Wordsworths, William and Dorothy. The result was momentous for English poetry—from their discussions emerged a new poetry which represented a revulsion from neo-classic artificiality and, as a consequence, the renovation of the language of poetry. *Lyrical Ballads* (1798), which opened with Coleridge's magical 'Ancient Mariner' and closed with Wordsworth's 'Tintern Abbey', was thus in the nature of a manifesto. A visit to Germany with the Wordsworths (1798–99) gave Coleridge a permanent bent for German philosophy and criticism, and he was a means of passing this into the current of English thought and taste. In 1800 he went north to Keswick and for a time, with the Wordsworths at Grasmere and Southey already resident at Keswick, it looked as if a fruitful career was opening out for him, but his moral collapse, due partly to opium, made the next few years a misery to him and his friends. His 'Ode to Dejection' (1802) is both a recantation of Wordsworth's animistic view of Nature and a confession of failure. Henceforth his association with Wordsworth was strained; his relations with Dorothy were constant only through her devotion to him. A brief stay in Malta as secretary to the Governor (1804–06) may well have directed him to orthodoxy, though he seems to have retained his Unitarian attitude as late as 1809 when he began his weekly paper, *The Friend* (1809), published as a book in 1818. Settled in London, finally as the guest of the Gillmans in Highgate (from 1816), he engaged in various activities—miscellaneous writing, lecturing at the Royal Institution (his lectures on Shakespeare alone survive of this activity) and the stage (*Remorse* (1813) had a mild success at Drury Lane). In 1816 he published 'Christabel' and that wonderful fragment, 'Kubla Khan', both written in his earlier period of inspiration. He had long relinquished the idea of renewing that inspiration and resigned himself, as he indicates in the close of 'Dejection' to philosophical speculation. In this he succeeded to the extent of impressing contemporaries who were glad to have a reasoned defence of orthodoxy and resistance to demagogic politics. His critical writing in these middle years is important also as (so Saintsbury thought) the finest 'creative' criticism in the language. It has to be collected from various works—from *Biographia Literaria* (1817), *Aids to Reflection* (1825) which is largely philosophical, and *Anima Poetae* (1895). Coleridge's small corpus of inspired poetry written during his intimacy with Wordsworth is at once a perfect illustration of that gift of imagination which the romantics exalted and a marvel of verbal music. In our day, however, for these things are taken for granted, his theological and politico-sociological works have been read (despite their awkward style) with a fresh interest. His Tory-democratic attitude appeals to many and his defence of orthodoxy, which is always philosophical, has influenced modern 'neo-Christianity'. It might be said that the religious 'reaction' which he represented in the early 19th century has its counterpart in the modern 'reaction' which looks to religion and authority as a remedy for social evil. His *Biographia Literaria* (1817), despite its personal divagations, which are always interesting, is one of our great critical documents. It reviews his literary relations with Wordsworth, and while indicating blemishes in the great poet—chiefly excessive 'accidentality' and a mistaken notion of the language of real life—leaves no doubt of his essential greatness. Some, however, have found it carping, and even an act of treachery to his former collaborator.

Standard editions of the works are *Poetical Works* ed. J. D. Campbell (1893 and 1899), and *Complete Poetical Works*, ed. E. H. Coleridge (1912), who also edited the *Letters* in 1895. See also *Unpublished Letters*, ed. E. L. Griggs 1932, and *Collected Letters*

(1956). Studies of Coleridge include those by Fausset (1926), S. Potter (1935), E. K. Chambers (1938), House (1953) and J. B. Beer (1959). The standard biography is by J. D. Campbell (1894).

(4) **Sara** (1802–52), daughter of (3), was born December 23 at Greta Hall, Keswick, and brought up in Southey's household. In 1822 she translated Dobrizhoffer's *Historia de Abiponibus*, and in 1825 the ' Loyal Servitor's' memoirs of the Chevalier Bayard. In 1829 she married her cousin, Henry Nelson Coleridge, and helped to edit her father's writings. She died May 3, 1852. Her own works were *Pretty Lessons for Good Children* (1834) and *Phantasmion* (1837), a fairy tale. Her Memoirs and Letters were edited by her daughter in 1873. Her son, **Herbert Coleridge** (1830–61), educated at Eton and Balliol, was called to the bar, but, devoting himself to comparative philology, worked for the Philological Society's dictionary, and wrote a *Thirteenth Century Glossarial Index* (1859) and an essay on King Arthur.

COLERIDGE-TAYLOR, Samuel (1875–1921), English composer, born in London, the son of a West African doctor and an Englishwoman, composed *Hiawatha* (1898–1900) and other cantatas and orchestral works.

COLET, John (*c.* 1467–1519), born in London, was the son of Sir Henry Colet, twice Lord Mayor. Colet studied at Oxford, and about 1493 travelled to Italy. Here he became acquainted with the views of Savonarola, which subsequent study and experience led him to regard with increasing approval. Having returned to England in 1496, and been ordained priest, he lectured at Oxford on the Epistles of St Paul, and attracted great attention, his principles of interpretation being at every point opposed to those of the scholastic theologians. In 1498 Erasmus came to Oxford, and it is one of Colet's chief claims to remembrance that he powerfully influenced that scholar's opinions on the proper methods of scripture interpretation and on the value of the scholastic philosophy. In 1505 Colet was made Dean of St Paul's, and continued to deliver lectures on different books of Scripture, which gave rise to much diversity of opinion; charges of heresy were brought against him, but Archbishop Warham refused to support them. With the large fortune Colet inherited from his father he founded St Paul's School in 1509–12. He died of dropsy. See Seebohm's *Oxford Reformers* (2nd ed. 1869), and Lives by the Rev. J. H. Lupton (1887) and Sir J. A. R. Marriott (1933).

COLETTE, Sidonie Gabrielle (1873–1954), French novelist, born at Saint-Sauveur-en-Puisaye. Her early books were written in collaboration with her first husband, Henri Gauthier-Villars (pen-name Willy); after their divorce in 1906 she appeared in music-halls in dance and mime, and out of this period came *L'Envers du music-hall* (1913). Her work is characterized by an intense, almost entirely physical preoccupation with immediate sense experiences. Her novels include the *Claudine* series (1900–05; trans. in part 1953), *Chéri* (1920; trans. 1930), *La Fin de Chéri* (1926; trans. 1933), *La Chatte* (1933; trans. 1953), *Gigi* (1945; trans. 1953) and *The Stories of Colette* (trans. 1958). In 1912 she married Henry de Jouvenel, and in 1935, Maurice Goudeket. She was president of the Académie Goncourt. See three vols. of her letters (1958, 1959, 1962), and studies by Goudeket (1957), le Hardouin (1958) and M. Davies (1962).

COLFAX, Schuyler (1823–85), American statesman, was born at New York and died at Mankato, Minnesota. Originally a newspaper editor, in 1868 he was elected vice-president of the United States, in Grant's first term. Implicated, apparently unjustly, in the Crédit Mobilier charges of 1873, he spent the rest of his life in political retirement. See Life by Hollister (1886).

COLIGNY, Gaspard de, *kol-een-yee* (1519–72), French Huguenot leader, born at Châtillon-sur-Loing, early distinguished himself in the wars of Francis I and Henry II. In 1552 he was made admiral of France, though he never commanded at sea; in 1557 he saved his country by holding St Quentin with a handful of men for seventeen days against the army of Spain. It was during his imprisonment, after the capture of this town, that he embraced Protestantism, to the furtherance of which the rest of his life was dedicated. After the defeat of Dreux (1562), where Condé was taken prisoner, Coligny drew off the Huguenot remnant into Normandy; in the second Huguenot war, on Condé's death (1569), he was appointed generalissimo and brought about the favourable peace of St Germain (1570). Catharine de Medici, however, alarmed at the growing power of the Huguenots and at Coligny's ascendancy over young Charles IX, determined by one desperate stroke to regain her power; and Coligny was one of the first victims in the massacre of St Bartholomew, August 24, 1572. He was the noblest Frenchman of his time. His religious zeal was purely disinterested, and he had France's welfare deeply at heart. His great aim was to make the Huguenots a national party, and to defeat the schemes of Spain. See Lives by Blackburn (Philadelphia 1869), Bersier (trans. 1884), Delaborde (Paris 1880) and Whitehead (1904).

COLINS, Alexander (*c.* 1526–1612), Flemish sculptor of the Emperor Maximilian's tomb at Innsbruck, was born at Mechlin, and died at Innsbruck.

COLLARD, Frederick William (1772–1860), a London piano-manufacturer, born at Wivelis-combe, Somerset, like his brother and partner, **William Frederick** (1776–1866).

COLLE, Raffaello del (*c.* 1490–1566), an Italian religious painter, pupil of Raphael.

COLLEONI, Bartolommeo (1400–75), Italian condottiere, born near Bergamo, fought on both sides in the strife between Milan and Venice, where he finally settled in 1454, becoming generalissimo. He is the subject of a famous Venetian equestrian statue by Verrochio (q.v.). See Lives by Oscar Browning (1891) and Belotti (1923).

COLLETT, Jacobine Camilla, *née* **Wergeland** (1813–95), Norwegian novelist, born in Kristiansand. A sister of the more famous

Henrik Wergeland, she championed the rights of women and social justice. Her novels mark the beginning of realism in Norwegian fiction.

COLLEY, Sir George (1835–81), British soldier, joined the army in 1854, and served in Cape Colony and China. He ably managed the transport service in the Ashanti expedition, in 1875 accompanied Sir Garnet Wolseley to Natal and from 1876 to 1880 he was mostly in India as secretary to the viceroy. Appointed governor and commander-in-chief of Natal in April 1880, he commanded against the Boers at Laing's Nek and Ingogo, and fell, shot through the forehead, at Majuba Hill. See Life by Sir W. Butler (1899).

COLLIER, (1) Arthur (1680–1732), English philosopher, was born at Steeple Langford rectory, Wilts, where he himself became rector in 1704. At Balliol he had studied Descartes and Malebranche; and his *Clavis Universalis* (1713, but written 1703) coincides remarkably with Berkeley's *Theory of Vision* (1709). See Life by R. Benson (1837).

(2) **Jeremy** (1650–1726), English nonjuror, was born at Stow cum Quy, Cambridgeshire. His father was a clerical schoolmaster at Ipswich, and here and at Caius College, Cambridge, he was educated, afterwards becoming rector of Ampton near Bury St Edmunds, and lecturer at Gray's Inn. His reply to Burnet's *Inquiry into the State of Affairs* (1688) cost him some months in Newgate. He next waged warfare on the crown with incisive pamphlets, and was arrested in 1692 on suspicion of being involved in a Jacobite plot. In 1696 he gave absolution to the would-be assassins Friend and Parkyns on the scaffold, for which offence he was outlawed. In 1697 he published his *Short View of the Immorality of the English Stage*, which fell like a thunderbolt among the wits. Congreve and Vanbrugh answered angrily, and were crushed anew by Collier. Dryden in the preface to his *Fables* (1700) acknowledged that he had been justly reproved. Collier continued to preach to a congregation of nonjurors, and was consecrated bishop in 1713. He upheld the 'usages', and laid himself open to a charge of holding Romish views. His largest works were the *Great Historical, Geographical, Genealogical, and Poetical Dictionary* (4 vols. folio, 1701–21), and *An Ecclesiastical History of Great Britain* (2 vols. folio, 1708–14).

(3) **John** (1708–86), the Lancashire poet, 'Tim Bobbin', was born at Urmston, near Manchester, the son of the curate of Stretford, and from 1729 was usher or master of a school at Milnrow, near Rochdale. His rhyming satire, *The Blackbird*, appeared in 1739, and his *View of the Lancashire Dialect* (in humorous dialogue) in 1775. See his Works, with Life (Rochdale 1895).

(4) **John** (1850–1934), English painter, the son of Lord Monkswell the judge, painted portraits and subject pictures, including the much-reproduced *Fallen Idol*, and *The Last Voyage of Henry Hudson* (Tate Gallery).

(5) **John Payne** (1789–1883), English journalist and Shakespearean author, born in London, became in 1809 a parliamentary reporter, but his real literary career commenced in 1820 with *The Poetical Decameron*. From 1825 to 1827 he issued a new edition of *Dodsley's Old Plays*, and in 1831 his *History of English Dramatic Poetry, and Annals of the Stage to the Restoration*. Appointed librarian by the Duke of Devonshire, he from 1835 to 1839 published *New Facts* regarding Shakespeare, followed by an edition of the plays (8 vols. 1842–44), and *Shakespeare's Library* (1844), a reprint of the histories, novels and early dramas on which Shakespeare drew. In 1852 he announced his discovery of an extensive series of marginal annotations in a 17th century hand on a copy of the second Shakespeare folio (1631–1632) he had bought—the ' Perkins folio '. These he published as *Notes and Emendations to Shakespeare*, and calmly lifted them into his 1853 edition of Shakespeare. The emendations were furiously applauded or furiously assailed; the best Shakespearian students were more or less sceptical. Collier's alleged discovery of the suspiciously long-lost notes of Coleridge's lectures on Shakespeare and Milton, delivered in 1811, was also called in question. When at last in 1859 the folio was sent to the British Museum for examination, it was conclusively proved that the boasted emendations were recent fabrications. Collier died at Maidenhead, and after his death some manipulated books were discovered in his own library. See Dr Ingleby's *Complete View of the Shakspere Controversy* (1861); Collier's own *An Old Man's Diary* (1871–72); and Life and Bibliography by Wheatley (1885).

COLLINGS, Jesse (1831–1920), English politician, was born at Littleham-cum-Exmouth in Devonshire. Elected Radical M.P. for Ipswich in 1880, he sat for Bordesley as a Unionist (1886–1918), and was specially identified with the Agricultural Labourers' Union and measures for promoting allotments and small holdings (' three acres and a cow '). P.C. (1892), he was under-secretary for the Home Office in 1895–1902. See Life by himself and Sir J. L. Green (1920).

COLLINGWOOD, (1) Cuthbert, Lord (1750–1810), English admiral, was born at Newcastle upon Tyne. He entered the navy at eleven, and from 1778 his career was closely connected with that of Nelson, whom he followed up the ladder of promotion step by step. Among the great naval victories in which he bore a prominent part, were those of Lord Howe off Brest in 1794; of Lord Jervis off Cape St Vincent in 1797; and of Trafalgar in 1805, where he held the second command. A peerage was his reward. After several years' uneventful service in the Mediterranean, he died at sea, and was buried beside Nelson, in St Paul's. See his Correspondence and Life (1828), and shorter Lives by W. Davies (2nd ed. 1878) and Clark Russell (1891).

(2) **Robin George** (1889–1943), English philosopher, archaeologist and historian, born at Coniston, Waynflete professor of Metaphysical Philosophy at Oxford (1934–1941), a leading authority on the archaeology of Roman Britain, was greatly influenced by Croce's idealism as in *Essay in Philosophical*

Method (1933), &c., but developed his own more empirical *Principles of Art* (1937). See his *Autobiography* (new ed. 1951).

COLLINS, (1) **Anthony** (1676–1729), English deist, was born at Heston near Hounslow. He passed from Eton to King's College, Cambridge, and became the disciple and friend of John Locke. In 1707 he published his *Essay concerning the Use of Reason*; in 1709 *Priestcraft in Perfection*. In 1711 he visited Holland, where he became friendly with Le Clerc; in 1713 appeared his *Discourse on Free-thinking*, best known of all his works, to which Bentley replied in his famous *Remarks*. In 1713 Collins made a second visit to Holland, in 1718 he became treasurer for Essex, and in 1724 issued his *Grounds and Reasons of the Christian Religion*.

(2) **Charles Allston** (1828–73), second son of (6), in early life painted pre-Raphaelite pictures which are valued by collectors. In 1860 he married the younger daughter of Charles Dickens, and having already turned his attention to literature, produced *The Eye-witness* essays (1860), two novels, &c.

(3) **John Churton** (1848–1908), English scholar, who graduated from Balliol College, Oxford, in 1872, was a learned critic and editor of English classics, and in 1904 became professor of English Literature at Birmingham. See Life by his son (1911).

(4) **Michael** (1890–1922), Irish politician and Sinn Fein leader, born near Clonakilty, was largely responsible for the negotiation of the treaty with Great Britain in 1921. He was killed in an ambush between Bandon and Macroom. See Life by R. Taylor (1958).

(5) **William** (1721–59), English poet, was born at Chichester, the son of a hatter, who was twice mayor. From the prebendal school of his native city he passed in 1733 to Winchester, and thence in 1741 to Oxford, as a demy of Magdalene. He took his B.A. in 1743; and having been pronounced ' too indolent even for the army ', and dissuaded from entering the church, as the sole alternative he came to London and sought to make a living by literature. He now fell into ' irregular habits ', and was at times reduced to the greatest straits; Dr Johnson once rescued him from the bailiffs by obtaining an advance from a bookseller on the promise of Collins to translate the *Poetics* of Aristotle. It was during this period, however, that he wrote his Odes, upon which his fame as a poet now rests. They attracted no notice at the time of their publication (1747), and they were little valued even by Gray and Dr Johnson. By the death of an uncle in 1749, Collins inherited £2000, which enabled him to retire to Chichester, and apparently to pursue a regular course of study. It was about this time that he met Home, the author of *Douglas*, and gave him his ' Ode on the Superstitions of the Highlands ', a poem in which, says Lowell, ' the whole Romantic School is foreshadowed '. It was first published in the Transactions of the Royal Society of Edinburgh (1788). Before 1753 Collins felt the approaches of the mental disease to which he finally succumbed, and sought relief in a visit to France. On his return he gradually became worse, and his

reason completely gave way, though he sometimes had lucid intervals. He died so unknown to fame that no newspaper of the day had any notice of his death. See H. W. Garrod's *Collins* (1929) and Edmund Blunden's edition of the *Poems* (1929).

(6) **William** (1788–1847), English landscape and figure painter, father of (2) and (8), was born in London, of a Wicklow family, and studied at the Royal Academy. He is remembered for his subject pictures of country scenes, such as *Blackberry Gatherers* and *The Bird-catchers* (1814). He was elected an R.A. in 1820; studied and sketched in Italy in 1836–38; and died in London. See Life (1848) by Wilkie Collins.

(7) **William** (1789–1853), Scottish publisher, founder in 1820 of the famous firm of that name in Glasgow.

(8) **William Wilkie** (1824–89), novelist, elder son of (6), was born in London. He was educated partly at Highbury, but during 1836–39 was with his parents in Italy. After his return he spent four years in business, and then entered Lincoln's Inn, but gradually took to literature, the Life of his father (1848) being his earliest production. Other works include *Antonina, or the Fall of Rome* (1850), *Basil* (1852), *Hide and Seek* (1854), *The Dead Secret* (1857), *The Woman in White* (1860; the first detective story), *The Moonstone* (1868), *The New Magdalen* (1873), &c.—in all, fully a score of novels and collections of novelettes. See study by S. M. Ellis (1931), and T. S. Eliot's *Selected Essays 1917–32* (1932).

COLLINSON, (1) **Peter** (1694–1768), English botanist and naturalist, was born at Hugal Hall, near Windermere, and became a manufacturer of hosiery. He introduced American plant species into Britain, and *vice versa*, thereby assisting agricultural progress in both countries.

(2) **Sir Richard** (1811–83), British admiral and arctic navigator 1850–54, was born at Gateshead. See *Journal of H.M.S. Enterprise*, with a memoir by his brother (1889).

COLLOT D'HERBOIS, **Jean Marie**, *kol-lō-der-bwah* (1751–96), French revolutionary, born in Paris, had been a provincial actor, but was attracted by the Revolution back to Paris, where his impudence, his loud voice and his *Almanach du Père Gérard* secured his election to the National Convention. In 1793 he became president of the Convention and a member of the murderous Committee of Public Safety. Sent by Robespierre to Lyons, he took bloody revenge by guillotine and grapeshot on the inhabitants for having once hissed him off the stage. He joined in the successful plot against Robespierre (1794), but himself was expelled from the Convention, and banished to Cayenne (1795), where he died.

COLMAN, **St** (d. 676), an Irish monk of Iona, who in 661 became Bishop of Lindisfarne, but in 664 withdrew to Iona on the defeat of the Celtic party at the Council of Whitby. He died in County Mayo.

COLMAN, (1) **George** (1732–94), ' the Elder ', playwright and manager, was born at Florence, the son of the English envoy. He was educated at Westminster and Oxford, and called to the bar in 1755. In 1760 his first piece, *Polly Honeycombe*, was produced at Drury Lane with great success; next year came *The Jealous Wife*, and in 1766 *The Clandestine Marriage*, written in conjunction with Garrick. In 1767 he purchased, with three others, Covent Garden Theatre, and held the office of manager for seven years, until he sold his share. In 1776 he purchased the Haymarket Theatre from Foote, but was paralysed by a stroke from 1785.

(2) **George** (1762–1836), ' the Younger ', son of (1), was educated at Westminster, Oxford and Aberdeen. During his father's illness he acted as manager of the Haymarket and on his death the patent was transferred to him. As Examiner of Plays from 1824 he showed himself both arrogant and finical. In industry he rivalled his father, and he made money by his *John Bull, Iron Chest, Heir at Law* and other comedies, and by songs like ' Mynheer Van Dunck '. See his *Random Records of My Life* (1830).

(3) **Samuel** (1832–1920), American painter, born in Portland, Maine, studied in Europe in 1860–62, was elected a member of the National Academy in 1862, and first president (1866–71) of the American Society of Painters in Watercolours. His pictures include scenes from Algeria, Germany, France, Italy and Holland.

COLOMB, Sir John Charles Ready (1838–1909), English authority on naval matters, was the son of Gen. G. T. Colomb, and rose to be captain in the Royal Marine Artillery 1854–69. He was Conservative M.P. for Bow and Bromley 1886–92, and for Yarmouth 1895–1906; in 1888 he was made a K.C.M.G.

COLONNA, a Roman family, which took its name from a village among the Alban Hills. From it have sprung a pope (Martin V, q.v.), several cardinals, generals, statesmen and noted scholars, and **Vittoria Colonna** (c. 1492–1547). The daughter of the constable of Naples, at four years old she was betrothed to a boy of the same age; at seventeen they were married. After her husband's death in the battle of Pavia (1525), Vittoria found her chief consolation in solitude and the writing of poetry. During seven years of her widowhood she resided alternately at Naples and Ischia, and then in the convents of Orvieto and Viterbo. Later she lived in Rome, where she died. She was the loved friend of Michelangelo, admired by Ariosto, and the intimate associate of the reforming party at the papal court. Her poems appeared at Parma in 1538; the best edition is by Visconti (Rome 1840). See her *Correspondence* (Turin 1888), Mrs H. Roscoe's *Vittoria Colonna, her Life and Poems* (1868), and A. Bernardy's *Vittoria Colonna* (1928).

COLQUHOUN, *ko-hoon'*, (1) **Archibald Ross** (1848–1914), born off the Cape, travelled extensively for engineering, political and journalistic purposes. First administrator of Mashonaland, he wrote many works of travel and politics.

(2) **John** (1805–85), second son of Sir James Colquhoun of Luss, was born in Edinburgh, studied at Edinburgh University, served in the Dragoons 1829–34, and became a supreme authority on sport in Scotland. His *Moor and Loch* (1840) was much extended and improved in the 4th (1878) and 5th (1884) editions. *Rocks and Rivers* appeared in 1849, *Salmon Casts and Stray Shots*, 1858, and *Sporting Days*, 1866. He died in Edinburgh.

(3) **John Campbell** (1785–1854), uncle of (2), wrote much on mesmerism. He was sheriffdepute of Dunbartonshire from 1815.

(4) **Patrick** (1745–1820), born at Dumbarton, became in 1782 provost of Glasgow, and in 1792 a London police magistrate. He was indefatigable in forwarding reforms, and wrote innumerable pamphlets, besides *Police of the Metropolis* (1795) and *Population and Wealth of the British Empire* (1814).

(5) **Robert** (1914–62), Scottish artist, born at Kilmarnock. He studied at the Glasgow School of Art, and in Italy, France, Holland and Belgium. His enigmatic, dreamlike figures (e.g., *Girl with a circus goat*) are usually presented in a characteristic colour scheme of reds and browns.

COLSTON, Edward (1636–1721), a Bristol merchant and philanthropist, Tory and highchurchman. He bestowed over £70,000 in establishing or endowing almshouses, schools and other public benefactions. From 1689 he lived chiefly at Mortlake.

COLT, Samuel (1814–62), American inventor, born in Hartford, Conn., ran away to sea in 1827, and about 1832 travelled over America, lecturing on chemistry. In 1835 he took out his first patent for a revolver, which after the Mexican war was adopted by the U.S. army. He also worked on submarine mines. He expended over $2,500,000 on an immense armoury in Hartford, where he died, and where his widow erected a handsome Episcopal church to his memory.

COLTON, (1) **Charles Caleb** (c. 1780–1832), clergyman, sportsman, gambler, suicide and author of the aphoristic *Lacon* (2 vols. 1820–22).

(2) **Gardner Quincy** (1814–98), American chemist, in 1844 was the first, with Horace Wells, to make use of nitrous oxide (' laughing gas ') in the extraction of a tooth.

COLUM, Padraic (1881–1972), Irish poet and playwright, born in County Longford, educated at Trinity Coll., Dublin, a leader of the Irish literary revival, wrote for the Abbey Theatre *The Land* (1905), *Fiddler's House* (1907), *Thomas Muskerry* (1910), &c., and was for a short time editor of the *Irish Review*. From 1914 he lived in the U.S.A., and published two studies on Hawaiian folklore (1924 and 1926), the result of governmentsponsored research. He wrote a number of volumes of verse, also children's stories.

COLUMBA, Colum-cille or **Colm, St** (521–97), was born at Gartan, County Donegal, the son of a chief related to several of the princes then reigning in Ireland and in the west of Scotland. He studied under St Finnian at Moville on Strangford Lough and under another St Finnian at Clonard; in 546 he founded the monastery of Derry, and in 553 that of Durrow. The belief that he had caused the bloody battle of Culdremhne in 561 led to his excommunication and exile from his native land. Accompanied by twelve disciples, he found a resting-place in the little island of Hy (Iona or I Colum-cille), and having founded a monastery there (563), he set himself to convert the Northern Picts; and he and his followers founded monasteries on the Pictish mainland, the Western Islands, and the Orkneys. The parent house of Iona exercised supremacy over all these, as well as over the Columban churches in Ireland and those afterwards established in the north of England. In his system the bishops were subordinate to the abbots, though episcopal orders were recognized and bishops only could ordain. The Columban churches kept Easter on a different day from the Roman churches, and their clergy had a peculiar tonsure. Columba's health began to fail in 593, and he died June 9, 597. An *Altus* published by Dr Todd in the *Liber Hymnorum* has been ascribed to him by unbroken tradition. On the night before his death he was engaged on a transcript of the Psalter, and the *Annals of Clonmacnois* state that he wrote three hundred books with his own hand. See the Life by Adamnan (q.v.); the *Life of Columcille*, compiled by Manus O'Donnell (1532), trans. by O'Kelleher and Schoepperle (Illinois Univ. Press, 1918); works by Douglas Simpson (1927), J. A. Duke (1932).

COLUMBAN, or Columbanus, St (543–615), ' the younger Columba ', born in Leinster, studied under St Comgall at Bangor in Down, about 585 went to Gaul with twelve companions, and founded the monasteries of Anegray, Luxeuil and Fontaine in the Vosges country. His adherence to the Celtic Easter involved him in controversy; and the courage with which he rebuked the vices of the Burgundian court led to his expulsion. After a year or two at Bregenz, on Lake Constance, he went to Lombardy, and in 612 founded the monastery of Bobbio, in the Apennines, where he died. His writings, all in Latin, comprise a monastic rule, six poems on the vanity of life, seventeen sermons and a commentary on the Psalms (1878). See Life by Mrs T. Concannon (1915), Latin Life by the monk Jonas (trans. 1896), Montalembert's *Monks of the West*, and L. Gougaud's *Christianity in Celtic Lands* (trans. 1932).

COLUMBUS, Christopher; Ital. **Cristoforo Colombo;** Span. **Cristóbal Colón** (1451–1506), discoverer of the New World, was born at Genoa, the son of a woolcomber, and was bred to the same trade. But at fourteen he went to sea, fought with Tunisian galleys, and about 1470, shipwrecked in a fight off Cape St Vincent, reached the shores of Portugal on a plank. In Lisbon he married Filippa Moniz. As early as 1474 he had conceived the design of reaching India by sailing westward—a design in which he was encouraged by the Florentine astronomer Toscanelli; in 1477 he ' sailed 100 leagues beyond Thule ', probably to or beyond Iceland; and, having also visited the Cape Verde Islands and Sierra Leone, he began to seek a patron for his intended expedition. He applied to John II of Portugal; later by letters to Henry VII of England; then to the powerful Duke of Medina Celi, who referred him to Isabella the Catholic, queen of Castile. After an adverse judgment from a board of

advisers, mainly ecclesiastics, his plans were rejected, but afterwards reconsidered; and finally, after seven years of alternate encouragement and repulse, they were accepted by Ferdinand and Isabella in April 1492.. On Friday, August 3, Columbus set sail from the bar of Saltes, an island near Palos, in command of the small *Santa Maria*, with 50 men, and attended by two little caravels, the *Pinta* and the *Niña*, the whole squadron comprising only 120 adventurers. He first made the Canary Islands; and though he found it hard to keep up the courage and patience of his crews, new land was descried on Friday, October 12—now believed to have been Watling's Island in the Bahamas. He then visited Cuba and Hispaniola (Haiti), planted a small colony, and set sail with his two caravels (for the flagship had been wrecked). After an exceedingly tempestuous voyage, he re-entered the port of Palos, March 15, 1493, and was received with the highest honours by the court. He sailed on his second voyage on September 25, with three carracks and seventeen small caravels, and on November 3 sighted Dominica in the West Indies. After a succession of wretched quarrels with his associates, and a long and desperate illness in Hispaniola, he returned to Spain much dejected in 1496. His third voyage, begun in 1498, resulted in the discovery of the South American mainland. In 1500 Columbus and his brother were sent home in irons by a newly appointed royal governor; but the king and queen repudiated this action, and restored Columbus to favour. His last great voyage (1502–04), along the south side of the Gulf of Mexico, was accomplished in the midst of great hardships and many distresses, Spanish jealousy of the foreigner working against him on sea no less than at court. He died at Valladolid, in Spain, and was buried in a monastery near Seville, whence in 1536 his remains and those of his son Diego were removed to Santo Domingo, in Hispaniola. In 1796 they were said to have been transferred to the cathedral at Havana; and, brought to Spain in 1899, they were deposited (1902) in Seville cathedral. A man of ardent impulse and poetical imagination, Columbus was hardly the stuff that leaders are made of; consequently he failed to control the turbulent and adventurous spirits among his followers. Irritable and impetuous, he was, nevertheless, magnanimous and benevolent.—His brother **Bartholomew**, who died in Cuba in 1514, assisted him effectively in his labours.— Another brother, **Giacomo** (called in Spain Diego), also assisted him in his West Indian government.—Christopher's eldest son, **Diego** (c. 1480–1526), was the heir to his honours, merits and misfortunes; while a natural son, **Don Fernando** (1488–1593), wrote an important Life of his father (Italian trans., Venice 1571). See the Lives by Irving (1831), St John (1850), Crompton (1859), Helps (1868), Traducci (Eng. trans. 1891), Elton (1892), C. K. Adams (1892), and Markham (1892); his letters, edited by Major (1870); the *Journal* of his first voyage (ed. Markham, 1893, C. Jane, 1931); Winsor's *Columbus* (1891); and works by Harrisse (1895–1900), Thacher 1904), F.

Young (1906), S. E. Morison (1942 and 1956) and B. Landström (1967).

COLUMELLA, L. Junius Moderatus (fl. *c.* 60 B.C.), Roman writer on agriculture, was born at Gades in Spain. *De Re Rustica*, in 12 books, treats of arable and pasture lands, culture of vines, olives, &c., care of domestic animals, &c., gardening (in dactylic hexameters), arboriculture, &c. Editions are Schneider's in *Scriptores Rei Rusticae* (1794), and Postgate's (1904).

COLVILLE, David (1813–97), founder of Colville's Steel Works, Glasgow, was born in Campbeltown and began in 1871, employing 200 men, making plates and angle iron for Scottish shipbuilders. In 1880 he obtained the contract to supply the iron bars for the rebuilding of the Tay Bridge. In 1879 he built five of the largest Siemens furnaces and at once gained a worldwide reputation. In 1885 he took his three sons into partnership, but two of them died in 1916 and the third, John, became an M.P. Thus the chairmanship passed to a former office boy, John Craig, who made the firm the fourth largest steel concern in Great Britain.

COLVIN, (1) **Sir Auckland** (1838–1908), British colonial administrator, was educated at Eton and Haileybury, entered the Indian Civil Service in 1858, in 1880 was appointed English controller-general in Egypt, in 1881 was made a K.C.M.G. and in 1887–92 was lieutenant-governor of the N.W. Provinces of India.

(2) **John Russell** (1807–57), British colonial administrator, father of (1), born at Calcutta, was educated at St Andrews and the East India College at Haileybury, and in 1826 went out to Bengal. Private secretary to Lord Auckland from 1836 to 1842, in 1854 he became lieutenant-governor of the North-Western Provinces. He died in the fort of Agra, then besieged by the mutineers. See the Life in the ' Rulers of India ' series by (1).

(3) **Sir Sidney** (1845–1927), English scholar, born at Norwood, Surrey, studied at Trinity College, Cambridge, where he gained the chancellor's medal for English verse (1865), and, graduating in 1867 as third classic, became a fellow in 1869. He was elected Slade professor of Fine Art at Cambridge in 1873, and director of the Fitzwilliam Museum in 1876, a post which he resigned on becoming keeper of the Department of Prints and Drawings in the British Museum (1884–1912). His writings, for periodicals or in book form, are marked by accurate scholarship and poetic feeling, and deal with Dürer, Flaxman, Landor, Keats, R. L. S., &c. See his *Memories* (1921), and E. V. Lucas, *The Colvins and their Friends* (1928).

COMBE, (1) **Andrew** (1797–1847), M.D., was born in Edinburgh, and in 1823 began to practise there. In 1836 he received the appointment of physician to the king of the Belgians, but his health failing, he returned to Scotland, where in 1838 he became a physician to Queen Victoria. He died at Gorgie, Edinburgh. Combe's *Principles of Physiology* (1834) reached a 15th edition in 1860. See Life by George Combe (1850).

(2) **George** (1788–1858), elder brother of (1), Scottish phrenologist and moral philosopher, was born, a brewer's son, in Edinburgh. He became a writer to the signet in 1812, and practised till 1837. Through Spurzheim (q.v.) he became a convert to phrenology, and wrote *Essays on Phrenology* (1819) and *The Constitution of Man* (1828; 10th ed. 1893), which was violently opposed as inimical to revealed religion. He travelled and lectured in the United Kingdom, Germany and America, and published *Notes on the United States* (1841). Combe married in 1833 Cecilia (1794–1868), daughter of Mrs Siddons. Combe's ideas on popular education were carried out for some years in a school which he founded in Edinburgh in 1848. See Life by C. Gibbon (1878).

(3) **William** (1741–1823), author of *Dr Syntax*, was born at Bristol, and educated at Eton and Oxford, which he quitted without a degree. ' Godson ' (or natural son) of a rich London alderman, who died in 1762, leaving him £2150, he led for some years the life of an adventurer, but was later imprisoned as a debtor. Of his eighty-six works published between 1774 and 1824, the *Three Tours of Dr Syntax* (1812–21) alone are remembered.

COMBERMERE, Stapleton-Cotton, Viscount (1772–1865), field marshal, son of Sir Robert Salusbury Cotton, Bart., of Combermere Abbey, Cheshire, was born at Llewenny Hall, Denbighshire. Educated at Audlem and Westminster School, he entered the army in 1790, and in 1794 was made lieutenant-colonel of a new regiment of light dragoons, with whom he served four years in India. In 1808 he proceeded to the Peninsula; in 1809 succeeded to the baronetcy; and in 1810 was appointed to the command of the whole allied cavalry. In 1814 he was created Baron Combermere. Though not at Waterloo, he commanded the cavalry of the army of occupation in France. He was commander of the forces in the West Indies, 1817–20; commander-in-chief in Ireland, 1822–25; and commander in India, 1825–30, where in 1827 he captured the Jat fortress of Bhartpur. He was made a viscount in 1827, constable of the Tower in 1852, and a field-marshal in 1855. See his *Correspondence* (2 vols. 1866).

COMENIUS, or Komenský, John Amos (1592 1670), Czech educational reformer, was born in Moravia, apparently at Uherský Brod. His parents belonged to the Moravian Brethren. He studied at Herborn (1612) and then at Heidelberg, became rector of the Moravian school of Prerau (1614–16) and minister at Fulnek, but lost all his property and library in 1621, when that town was taken by the Imperialists. Settling at Lissa in Poland (1628), he there worked out his new theory of education, wrote his *Didactica Magna*, and was chosen bishop of the Moravian Brethren in 1632. In 1631 he published his *Janua Linguarum Reserata*, and in 1639 his *Pansophiæ Prodromus*. In 1641 he was in England by invitation of parliament, planning a Baconian College of all the Sciences; but the Civil War drove him to Sweden (1642). He returned to Lissa in 1648, and in 1650 went to Saros-Patak, Hungary. Here he composed his *Orbis Sensualium Pictus* (Nuremberg 1658), the first picture book for children. Finally, he settled in Amsterdam, and died at Naarden. See Lives by Laurie (1881) and Kvacsala (German, 1892), Keatinge's translation of *The Great Didactic* (1896), and studies by Young (1932) and Needham (1942).

COMGALL, St (*c.* 515–602), founded about 558 the great abbey of Bangor, in County Down.

COMINES, Philippe de, *kom-een'* (1445–1509), a French statesman and historian, born at the castle of Comines near Courtrai, in 1463 entered the court of Burgundy, but in 1472 passed over to the service of Louis XI of France. He was rewarded with the rich fief of Talmont, wedded the heiress of Argenton and became one of Louis's most trusted advisers. Louis's death brought him the loss of much property, and even eight months' imprisonment in an iron cage; but in 1493 he was restored to a measure of favour. He accompanied Charles VIII on his Italian expedition (1494), was present at the battle of Fornovo, and met Machiavelli. His *Mémoires* (1524; ed. by Chantelauze, 1881, by Calmette, 1925), are the earliest French example of history as distinguished from the chronicle; Danett's translation (1601) was edited by C. Whibley in 1897. See his *Lettres et négotiations*, edited by Kervyn de Lettenhove (Brussels 1867-68), and Whibley's *Literary Portraits* (1904).

COMMODUS, Lucius Aurelius (A.D. 161–192), from 180 Roman emperor, was the son of the great Marcus Aurelius and the profligate Faustina. He was carefully educated, but lived to become one of the most worthless and bloody wretches that ever disgraced a throne. At his father's death he was fighting the Marcomanni on the upper Danube, but at once concluded a treaty, and hastened to Rome. After the discovery of his sister Lucilla's plot against his life in 183, he gave uncontrolled vent to his savagery. At length his mistress, Marcia, had him strangled by Narcissus, a famous athlete.

COMNENUS, a family, originally Italian, of which many members occupied the Byzantine throne from 1057 to 1185 and that of Trebizond from 1204 to 1461. See ALEXIUS, ISAAC, and ANNA COMNENA.—**David Comnenus,** the last in Trebizond, was executed at Adrianople in 1462, with all his family, by Mohammed II. The attempted derivation of the Bonaparte family from a branch of the Comneni settled in Corsica is baseless.

COMMON, Andrew Ainslie (1841–1903), astronomer at Ealing, was born at Newcastle-upon-Tyne. In 1881 he was the first to apply photography to the study of nebulae, and in 1885 he was elected F.R.S.

COMPARETTI, Domenico (1835–1927), Italian classical scholar, born at Rome, in 1859 was appointed to the chair of Greek at Pisa and subsequently at Florence and at Rome. Among his works are *Virgil the Magician* (1872; Eng. trans. 1895), *Homer and Pisistratus* (1881), *Canti e racconti del popolo italiano* (1869 *et seq.*, with D'Ancona), and *Book of Sindibad* (Folklore Soc. 1882).

COMPTON, (1) **Arthur Holly** (1892–1962), American physicist, was born at Wooster, Ohio. After a distinguished career he became chancellor of Washington University, St Louis, in 1945. He was a leading authority on nuclear energy, X-rays, and quantity production of plutonium. He was awarded the Nobel prize for physics in 1927.

(2) **Fay** (1894–   ), English actress, born in London, daughter of the actor Edward Compton (1854–1918) and sister of Sir Compton Mackenzie (q.v.), first appeared on the stage in 1911. After a successful U.S. visit in 1914 she won acclaim in London as *Peter Pan* (1918), subsequently playing many famous parts, especially in plays by Barrie and in comedies such as Dodie Smith's *Autumn Crocus* and *Call it a Day*.

(3) **Henry** (1632–1713), youngest son of the 2nd Earl of Northampton, in 1662 entered the church; in 1674 he became Bishop of Oxford, and in 1675 of London. Suspended for two years under James II, he cordially welcomed William of Orange. See Life by E. Carpenter (1956).

COMPTON-BURNETT, Ivy (1892–1969), English novelist, born in London, graduated in classics at London University. A prolific writer, her rather stylized novels have many features in common. They are set in upper class Victorian or Edwardian society; the characters, many of whom are rather stock-like, usually belong to a large family, spanning several generations, some of whose members are guilty of varying degrees of tyranny, ruthlessness or amorality; the plots often have elements of melodrama; realism usually triumphs over poetic justice as wickedness is allowed to go unpunished. Her novels contain few descriptive or narrative passages and few images. She was noted for her skilful use of dialogue, not because the language is appropriate to character but because it conveys the secret thoughts and understanding of the characters. Her works include *Brothers and Sisters* (1929), *Parents and Children* (1941), *Mother and Son* (1955, Tait Black Memorial Prize), *A Father and his Fate* (1957), *The Mighty and their Fall* (1961), *A God and His Gifts* (1963). See studies by P. H. Johnson (1951), R. Liddell (1955) and F. Baldanza (1964).

COMTE, Auguste (1798–1857), French philosopher and sociologist, the founder of Positivism, was born at Montpellier. At the École Polytechnique in Paris (1814–16) he led a protest of the students against the manners of one of the tutors, and was expelled. A few months were spent with his parents, and then Comte returned to Paris, where for a time he made a scanty living by teaching mathematics. Already, it seems, he had freed himself from the influence of all existing social and religious theories, and a reforming zeal was beginning to possess his mind, when in 1818 he came into contact with Saint-Simon, by whom his inclination towards the reconstruction of thought and life was strengthened. Comte remained for six years the disciple and collaborator of the older thinker; but there gradually became apparent a disagreement of aim and method, and the necessity felt by Comte of asserting the independence of his own conceptions led to a violent rupture. In 1825 Comte married, but the union proved unhappy, and ended in a separation. In 1826 Comte began a course of lectures in exposition of his system of philosophy, which was attended by several eminent men of science, but the course was for a few months interrupted by an attack of insanity. His labours were afterwards resumed, and during the publication of his *Philosophie positive* (6 vols. 1830–42) he made his livelihood chiefly as examiner and tutor in the École Polytechnique. After these positions were taken from him, owing to the prejudices of his colleagues, he resumed the private teaching of mathematics, but in his later years he was supported entirely by a ' subsidy ' from J. S. Mill, Grote and other friends. In 1845 Comte became acquainted with Clothilde de Vaux, and until her death less than a year after a close intimacy was maintained between them. On Comte's side it was a pure and passionate attachment, and its influence is clearly shown in his later works, especially in the most important of these, the *Politique Positive*. Comte died September 5, 1857, and was buried in Père-Lachaise. The aim of the Positive philosophy is to organize our knowledge of the world, of man, of society into a consistent whole. All human conceptions are regarded as having passed through a theological and then a metaphysical stage into a positive or experiential stage. The abstract sciences form a hierarchy—mathematics, astronomy, physics, chemistry, biology, sociology. The sociological development is from militarism to industrialism; the fullest life, according to the Positive polity, is that which rests on the fullest knowledge. The main office of a reorganized spiritual power is to strengthen the social tendencies of man at the expense of the person or individual. In the Positive religion (it being impossible to affirm or deny the idea of a Deity) the object of reverence and love is Humanity, a unity consisting of all men and women, past, present and to come, whose lives are devoted to the well-being and progress of the race. Comte's works are *Cours de philosophie positive* (6 vols. 1830–42; freely translated into English and condensed by Harriet Martineau, 2 vols. 1853), *Traité elémentaire de géométrie analytique* (1843), *Traité d'astronomie populaire* (1845), *Discours sur l'ensemble du positivisme* (1848), *Système de politique positive* (4 vols. 1851–54; Eng. trans. 1875–1877), and *Catéchisme positiviste, ou sommaire exposition de la religion universelle* (1852; trans. 1883). See Comte's *Testament* (1884), his *Lettres* (1902–05); and books by Ingram, Hutton, Gruber, Deherme, Ostwald, Gould (1920).

COMYN, Cumming, or Cumyn, a family which took its name from the town of Comines near Lille, on the Franco-Belgian frontier. While one branch remained there, and gave birth to Philippe de Comines (q.v.), another followed William of Normandy to England. In 1069 the Conqueror made Robert of Comines, or Comyn, Earl of Northumberland; his younger son, William, became chancellor of Scotland about 1133. By 1250 his descendants in Scotland included four Earls (Buchan, Menteith, Angus and Athole) and thirty-two belted knights of the name of

Comyn; but seventy years afterwards this great house was overthrown. See BRUCE, and Mrs Cumming-Bruce's *Family Records of the Bruces and the Comyns* (Edinburgh 1870).

CONANT, Thomas Jefferson (1802–91), American biblical scholar, filled chairs of Languages in various colleges. He made new versions of both Old and New Testaments, translated Gesenius' Hebrew grammar, and was one of the American committee for the revision of the Old Testament.

CONDAMINE, C. M. de La. See LA CONDAMINE.

CONDÉ, (1) Louis I de Bourbon, Prince de (1530–69), was the younger brother of Antony of Bourbon, king of Navarre. During the wars between Henry II and Spain, he distinguished himself at the siege of Metz, the battle of St Quentin and the capture of Calais from the English. On Francis II's accession (1559), Condé, like his brother, joined the Huguenots, took part (1560) in the unlucky Conspiracy of Amboise against the Guises, and escaped execution only by the death of the king. The regent, Catharine de' Medici, the Guises' bitter enemy, made concessions to the Huguenots, and Condé became governor of Picardy. The massacre of Huguenots at Vassy by Guise (1562) led to the first civil war, and Condé and Coligny gathered a Huguenot army; but at Dreux Condé was defeated and taken prisoner. In the second Huguenot war (1567–69) Condé had coins struck with the inscription: ' Louis XIII, first Christian king of France '; but at Jarnac (1569) he was defeated, taken prisoner, and shot.

(2) **Louis, Prince de** (1621–86), great-grandson of (1), known as ' the Great Condé ', was educated by the Jesuits at Bourges. In 1643, as generalissimo of the French forces, he defeated the Spaniards at Rocroi; and in 1644 and 1645 he defeated the Bavarians at Freiburg and Nördlingen. The capture of Dunkirk followed in 1646, and a great victory at Lens in 1648 over the famous Spanish infantry. The court party came to terms with the Fronde by his help; but Condé gave such offence to the queen and Mazarin by his arrogance that they imprisoned him and his brothers for a year. But popular feeling forced Mazarin to leave Paris and set Condé at liberty. He soon raised an army and began the third war of the Fronde. At Bleneau he defeated the royal troops, but was at length forced by Turenne to Paris, where he was defeated, and a peace was concluded (1653). Condé would not accept its terms, however, and going over to Spain, served for six years against his country. The battle of the Dunes, near Dunkirk, where Turenne, aided by 6000 of Cromwell's Ironsides, defeated the Spaniards, put an end to the war. Yet so formidable was Condé still, that the young king found it advisable to restore him to all his honours and estates. In the next war with Spain, Franche-Comté was overrun by his advice and help (1668). In 1674 he fought his last battle at Seneffe, against William of Orange. It lasted seventeen hours, and both sides claimed the victory. On Turenne's death in 1675, Condé succeeded him in the command of the army on the

Rhine, but his health now rendered him unfit for active service. Retiring to Chantilly, he lived there till his death, associating much with Molière, Racine, Boileau and La Bruyère. He had always scoffed at religion, but the year before his death he announced his conversion, and took especial pleasure in the society of Bossuet. He had no political genius, and as a commander he owed his successes more to fiery energy than to military talent. See Lives by Mahon (trans. 1845), Fitzpatrick (2nd ed. 1874), and E. Godley (1915); and the Duc d'Aumale's *Histoire des Princes de Condé* (7 vols. 1869–1896).

CONDER, (1) Charles (1868–1909), cousin of (2), British painter on silk (fans, etc.), was born in London, worked for a time in Australia, and was later influenced by the Impressionists. See study by F. Gibson (1914).

(2) Claude Reignier (1848–1910), cousin of (1), was employed in the Palestine Exploration survey 1872–77, afterwards serving in Egypt and Bechuanaland, and in the Ordnance Survey at home.

(3) Josiah (1789–1855), grandfather of (1) and (2), a London bookseller, editor, author.

CONDILLAC, Étienne Bonnot de Mably de, *kŏ-dee-yak* (1715–80), a French philosopher, the founder of Sensationalism, was born of a noble family at Grenoble. As a child his delicate health delayed his progress in education; but in youth he numbered among his friends Rousseau, Diderot, Duclos, &c. Many of his works were composed for his pupil, the Duke of Parma, grandson of Louis XIV, and he was titular Abbé de Mureaux. He was elected a member of the French Academy in 1768. He withdrew to his estate of Flux, near Beaugency, where he died. He based all knowledge on the senses. Among his works were *Essai sur l'origine des connaissances humaines* (1746), *Traité des systèmes* (1749), *Traité des sensations* (1754), *Logique* (1781), and *Langue des calculs* (1798). The first of several editions of his *Œuvres complètes* appeared in 1798. See monographs by Robert (Paris, 1869), Réthoré (1864), Dewaule (1892), Saltykow (1901) and Lenoir (1924).

CONDORCET, Marie Jean Antoine Nicolas Caritat, Marquis de, *kŏ-dor-say* (1743–94), French mathematician, was born, the son of a cavalry officer, at Ribemont, near St Quentin. At thirteen, after distinguishing himself in the Jesuit school at Rheims, he began his mathematical studies at the College of Navarre in Paris. His success was rapid and brilliant; and the high approval of Clairaut and D'Alembert determined his future. His *Essai sur le calcul intégral* (1765) won him a seat in the Academy of Sciences; in 1781 he entered the French Academy. He took an active part in the *Encyclopédie*. On the outbreak of the Revolution he made eloquent speeches and wrote famous pamphlets on the popular side, was sent by Paris to the Legislative Assembly in 1791, and in 1792 became president of the Assembly. He voted that the king should receive the most severe punishment except death, and, as deputy for Aisne in the National Convention, he sided usually with the Girondists. Accused

and condemned by the extreme party, he found refuge in the house of a generous lady, Madame Vernet, for eight months; but, driven to change his place of concealment, was recognized and lodged in the jail of Bourg-la-Reine, where he was found dead the next morning. In his *Progrès de l'esprit humain* (1794), written in hiding, he insisted on the justice and necessity of establishing a perfect equality of civil and political rights between the individuals of both sexes, and proclaimed the indefinite perfectibility of the human race. His complete works were issued in 1804 (21 vols.) and in 1847–49 (12 vols., with a Life by Arago). See his Correspondence with Turgot (1883), and Lives by Robinet (1893) and Cahen (1904).

CONEGLIANO. See Cima.

CONFUCIUS, Lat. for K'ung Fu-tse, 'the Master K'ung' (551–479 B.C.), Chinese philosopher, was born in the state of Lu, a part of the present province of Shantung. His lineage is traced through the dukes of Sung to the kings of the Shang or Yin dynasty. His father, a distinguished soldier, died in the child's third year, leaving the mother in straitened circumstances. The sage tells us that ' at fifteen his mind was set on learning, and at thirty he stood firm in his convictions '. He married at nineteen, and had a son Li and two daughters. About the time of his marriage we find him in charge of the public stores of grain and of the public herds; in 531 he commenced his career as a teacher. In 501 the duke of Lu appointed him governor of the town of Chung-tu, where a marvellous reformation in the manners of the people speedily took place. The next year saw him first minister of works, and next minister of crime; and for three years Confucius was the idol of the people. But this success did not last long. The prosperity of the state awakened the jealousy and fears of its neighbours, who brought about a breach between Confucius and his duke; and in 497 Confucius left Lu, not returning till 485 or 484. During this long period he visited many states, attended always by a company of his disciples. On his final recall to Lu by a new duke, he was well received, but did not re-enter political life. In his last years he is said to have put the finishing hand to his labours on the ancient writings. He himself tells us that he reformed the music to which the ancient odes were sung, and edited the odes themselves; probably then also he wrote the only classical work assigned to him—the *Ch'un Ch'iu*, which embraces the events in the history of Lu from 722 to 481 B.C. In the *Confucian Analects*, or memorabilia compiled soon after his death, we have abundant information of the Master's sayings and doings. It is often said that Confucianism is a system of morality without religion. That Confucius was emphatically a moral teacher is true; his greatest achievement as such was his formulating the golden rule, ' What you do not wish done to yourself, do not do to others.' And though this high morality was not without a religious sanction, we do not find in Confucius the expressions of a fervent piety, and his model or ideal man does not commune with God or implore forgiveness. Duke Ai, who had been unable to follow his counsels, caused a temple to be built, where sacrifices or offerings should be presented to the sage from generation to generation. Succeeding dynasties did honour to him by titles and offerings; and none more so than the late Manchu-Tatar dynasty. The lineal representative of the sage, with the title of *kung* or duke, ranked next to the members of the imperial house. See Legge's *Chinese Classics*, vol. i (1861), and *Confucius' Life and Teaching* (6th ed. 1887); Alexander's *Confucius the Great Teacher* (1891); *Confucianism and its Rivals*, by Prof. H. A. Giles (1915); *The Ethics of Confucius*, with Commentary by M. M. Dawson (1915); R. Wilhelm's *Confucius and Confucianism* (1931); Shryock's *Origin and Development of the State Cult of Confucianism* (1932); A. Rygaloff's *Confucius* (1946); and studies by H. Creel Kaizuka (trans. 1957) and Lin Yutang (1958).

CONGREVE, (1) Richard (1818–99), English Positivist, was born at Leamington, and educated under Arnold at Rugby. Of Wadham College, Oxford, he was a scholar, fellow and tutor, but resigned after having become definitely a disciple of Comte. In 1855 he published a good edition of Aristotle's *Politics*. Later works include *Elizabeth of England* (1862) and *Essays* (1874), besides many Positivist sermons and addresses.

(2) **William** (1670–1729), English dramatist and poet, was born at Bardsey near Leeds. He was educated at Kilkenny and at Trinity College, Dublin, where he was a fellow student of Swift; and in London he entered the Middle Temple. His first publication was *Incognita, or Love and Duty Reconciled* (1692), a novel of cross-purposes and disguises which, though written in a fortnight, appears to have enjoyed considerable popularity; and his translation of the eleventh satire of Juvenal came out soon after in Dryden's *Juvenal and Persius*. In January 1693 his comedy *The Old Bachelor*, produced under Dryden's auspices, with the celebrated Mrs Bracegirdle (q.v.) as heroine, achieved brilliant success at a time when the theatre had been suffering a slump. His second comedy, *The Double Dealer* (November 1693), was in every way stronger than *The Old Bachelor*, but the satire on the heartless sexual morals of the time was aimed too directly at the theatre's best customers, and it failed to please. *The Mourning Muse of Alexis* (1695), a poetic dialogue on Queen Mary's death, was as full of artificial conceits as *Incognita*. *Love for Love*, generally regarded as Congreve's stage masterpiece, was first produced in 1695. It is more satirical, more vital and stronger in feeling than its predecessors; it also has a more coherent plot and truer characterization. In 1697 Congreve's one tragedy, *The Mourning Bride*, appeared. The eulogies it received in the 18th century from Dr Johnson and others were as excessive as the contempt it met with in the 19th, though it bears comparison with most other tragedies in the contemporary fashion, and is remembered for the two overworked quotations ' music hath charms to soothe the savage breast ' and ' hell hath no fury like a woman

scorned '. Congreve was next occupied busily in the famous Jeremy Collier (q.v.) controversy, defending the morality of the new stage. His last play, *The Way of the World*, was produced in 1700. Its dialogue is masterly, and the writing possibly more accomplished than in any of its predecessors, but it is deficient in action. Congreve wrote no more for the stage, unless one includes in his dramatic works the words of a masque of *The Judgment of Paris*, set to music by John Eccles (q.v.) for a musical competition in 1701, and the undistinguished libretto of *Semele*, also to the music of Eccles, but later used by Handel. He was now almost blind owing to cataract, but his support of the Whig party brought him a few sinecure offices—commissioner for wine licences, &c., which enabled him to live comfortably, writing occasional poems, until his death after a coach mishap. He was buried in Westminster Abbey. See Lives by Gosse (1924), Taylor (1931) and Hodges (1941) and his *Letters and Documents* (ed. by Hodges, 1965).

(3) **Sir William** (1772–1828), English scientist, eldest son of Sir William Congreve, Bart., comptroller of the Woolwich Laboratory, passed through Woolwich Academy, and in 1808 invented the Congreve rocket, first used in the Napoleonic wars. The first friction matches, called ' Congreves ' (alluding to the rockets) were not invented by him but by John Walker (q.v.). He became an F.R.S. and M.P. for Gatton.

CONINGTON, John (1825–69), English classical scholar, born at Boston, educated at Rugby and Magdalen, became Latin professor at Oxford in 1854. His greatest work is his edition of *Virgil* (3 vols. 1861–68). He published, among other translations, a metrical version of Horace's *Odes* (1863); *Æneid* (1866), in Scott's ballad metre; *Iliad* (1868), in Spenserian stanza; and Horace's *Satires* and *Epistles* (1869), in the couplet of Pope. In 1872 appeared his edition of *Persius* and his *Miscellaneous Writings*, with a short Life by Prof. H. J. S. Smith.

CONKLING, Roscoe (1829–88), American politician, born in Albany, N.Y., sat in congress as a Republican, 1858–62, 1864–66; in the senate, 1867, 1873, 1879. In 1876 he received 93 votes for the presidential nomination; in 1880, supporting Grant and opposing Blaine, he split the Republican party.

CONNAUGHT, Arthur William, Duke of (1850–1942), third son of Queen Victoria, was born at Buckingham Palace, entered Woolwich Academy in 1866, in 1879 married the Princess Louise Margaret of Prussia (1860–1917). F.M. (1902), inspector-general of the Forces (1904–07), he was commander-in-chief in the Mediterranean (1907–09). In 1911–16 he was governor-general of Canada. Of his children, Margaret (1882–1920) married (1905) Gustaf Adolf, Crown Prince of Sweden; Prince Arthur (1883–1938) married the Duchess of Fife (1913), and was governor-general of South Africa, 1920–23; Patricia (b. 1886) married Adm. Sir Alex. Ramsay, K.C.V.O., D.S.O., in 1919.

CONNELLY, Marcus (Marc) Cook (1890–), American writer and dramatist, born in McKeesport, Pa. As a journalist who took to the theatre, he achieved several outstanding successes in collaboration with George S. Kaufman. These include *To the Ladies* (1922), the amusing ' expressionist ' *Beggar on Horseback* (1924), and *Hunter's Moon* (1958). His greatest individual success was *Green Pastures* (1930) adapted from Negro stories of the Deity and a Negro heaven. It won the Pulitzer prize.

CONNOLLY, (1) Cyril (1903–), British author and journalist, educated at Eton and Oxford; he has contributed to the *New Statesman* and other periodicals since 1927 and now writes regularly for the *Sunday Times*. He was founder/editor of *Horizon* (1939–50) and briefly literary editor of the *Observer*. Editor of *The Golden Horizon* and of *Great English Short Novels*, he is better known for such works as *The Unquiet Grave* (1944–45), *Ideas and Places* (1953), *Missing Diplomats* (1953) and *Previous Convictions* (1963).

(2) James (1870–1916), Irish Labour leader, spent some time in the United States and in 1913 with Larkin (q.v.) organized the great transport strike in Dublin. He organized socialist ' armies ' and when the nationalist movement Sinn Fein took part in the Easter rebellion (1916), was arrested and executed May 12. See Life by D. Ryan (1924).

CONOLLY, John (1794–1866), English physician, born at Market Rasen, Lincolnshire, graduated at Edinburgh in 1821, and in 1827 settled in London, where he was for two years a professor in University College. From 1839 to 1844 he was resident physician at Hanwell Asylum; afterwards he was visiting physician. Under him mechanical restraint of the insane was discontinued. See Memoir by Sir James Clark (1869).

CONRAD. Four German kings, one of whom was also Holy Roman emperor.

Conrad I (d. 918), was the son of the Count of Franconia, and nephew of the Emperor Arnulf. Elected king on the extinction of the direct Carlovingian line in 911, he gradually re-established the imperial authority over most of the German princes, carried on an unsuccessful war with France, and at last fell mortally wounded at Quedlinburg in a battle with the Hungarians.

Conrad II (*c.* 990–1039), elected in 1024, was the son of the Duke of Franconia. In 1026 he crossed the Alps, crushed a rebellion in Italy, was crowned at Milan and was anointed Roman emperor by the pope. He was soon recalled to Germany to put down four revolts, which he achieved by 1033. In 1032 he succeeded to the kingdom of Burgundy; in 1036 a fresh rebellion recalled him to Italy; but this time he was forced to grant various privileges to his Italian subjects. Shortly after his return he died at Utrecht.

Conrad III (1093–1152), the first Hohenstaufen king of the Germans, was the son of Frederick of Swabia. While under twenty, he had bravely supported Henry V, who in return granted him the duchy of Franconia. He unsuccessfully contested the crown of Italy with the Emperor Lothair of Saxony, on whose death the princes of Germany, fearing the growing preponderance of the Guelph party, offered Conrad the throne, and he was crowned at Aix-la-Chapelle, February 21, 1138. He was immediately involved in a quarrel with Henry the Proud, Duke of Bavaria and Saxony, and head of the Guelphs in Germany, the struggle being continued under Henry's son, Henry the Lion (q.v.). When St Bernard of Clairvaux preached a new crusade, Conrad set out for Palestine with a large army (1147). A new Bavarian rebellion was defeated before his death.

Conrad IV (1228–54), son of Frederick ii, was involved in constant struggles in Germany, and later invaded Italy to establish his right to the Sicilian crown.

CONRAD, Joseph (1857–1924), novelist, was born of Polish parents at Berdichev, by then Russian. His father was a revolutionary of literary gifts—he translated Victor Hugo's *Les Travailleurs de la mer*—who was exiled to Vologda. In 1878 Joseph joined an English merchant ship and was naturalized in 1884 when he gained his certificate as a master. In the ten years that followed, the boats he sailed in plied between Singapore and Borneo, and this gave him an unrivalled background of mysterious creeks and jungle for the tales to follow. There was also an interlude on the Belgian Congo which provided exotic colour for his *Heart of Darkness*, one of his three finest short stories, the others being *Youth* and *Typhoon*. In 1896 he married and settled at Ashford in Kent, where he lived a somewhat reclusive life for the rest of his days. Conrad's first novel was *Almayer's Folly* (1894), and then followed *An Outcast of the Islands* (1896). These are technically rather crude in motivation and are overpainted. *The Nigger of the Narcissus* (1897) and *Lord Jim* (1900) achieved a limited success before *Chance* (1914) made him famous, when readers turned back to discover that *Lord Jim* was the masterpiece it is, though the plot lapses badly in the middle and the oblique manner of narration may have deterred readers who like straight narrative and plenty of incident. For these Conrad did not cater—' I insist not on the events but on their effect on the persons of the tale ',—that is, after the sea his chief interest was psychological. Perhaps his sense of honour on which the tale turns (Lord Jim at a crucial moment loses nerve and abandons his ship) is rather conventional, but Conrad had a rigorous view of loyalty and of ' the brotherhood of the sea '. No doubt, in spite of *Lord Jim* and *Chance*, the short story was his true medium—*Tales of Unrest* (1898), *Youth* (1902) and *Twixt Land and Sea* (1912). One can measure his progress in this genre from his very early *Lagoon*, which is in his own words ' second-hand Conradese ', to *Typhoon*, with its unforgettable picture of Captain MacWhirr fighting the hurricane. His semi-autobiographical *The Mirror and the Sea* and his *Personal Record* testify to his high artistic aims. *Nostromo* (1904) is his most elaborate effort and it may be a masterpiece, but having forsaken the mysterious East he had to fabricate a new milieu and new situations in his story about silver mines in South America. Again the intrigue is too slowly developed. He returned to the East in *Victory* (1919), but his later works, *The Arrow of Gold* (1919) and *The Rescue* (1920), owed their popularity largely to his earlier work. See Jessie Conrad, *Joseph Conrad As I Knew Him* (1926); Curle, *Joseph Conrad: The Last Twelve Years*, and *Joseph Conrad and His Characters* (1957); Lohf and Sheehy (1957) and Baines (1960); also studies by Hueffer (1924), Warner (1951), Visak (1955), Guerard (1960), and Leavis, *The Great Tradition* (1948).

CONRAD of Montferrat (d. 1192), held Tyre against Saladin, and was stabbed by an assassin, after having been elected king of Jerusalem.

CONRAD VON WÜRZBURG (d. 1287), German poet, died at Basel. His unfinished *Trojan War*, in 60,000 lines, is inferior to his smaller narrative poems.

CONRADIN of Swabia (1252–68), the last Hohenstaufen emperor, was the son of Conrad IV (1228–54). His uncle, Manfred (q.v.), had assumed the crown of Sicily on a rumour of Conradin's death, and Pope Urban IV's hatred of the Hohenstaufens led him to offer the crown of the Two Sicilies to Charles of Anjou, who invaded Italy and slew Manfred at Benevento (1266). Conradin, invited by the Neapolitans to assert his rights, appeared in Italy with 10,000 men, but was defeated near Tagliacozzo, August 22, 1268, taken prisoner, and executed.

CONS, Emma (1838–1912), English social worker, bought in 1880 the Royal Victoria Hall in Waterloo Road, London, familiarly known as the ' Old Vic ', and launched it on its long career as a Shakespearean theatre.

CONSALVI, Ercole (1757–1824), Italian statesman and prelate, who was born and died at Rome, was made cardinal and secretary of state by Pope Pius VII (1800), and concluded the concordat with Napoleon (1801). At the Congress of Vienna he secured the restoration of the Papal States; as papal secretary he suppressed all monopolies, feudal taxes and exclusive rights. He was a liberal patron of science and art. See Life by E. Daudet (Paris 1866).

CONSCIENCE, Hendrik (1812–83), Flemish novelist, was born at Antwerp, and died at Brussels, director from 1866 of the Wiertz Museum. His *Phantazy* (1837), a fine collection of tales, and his most popular romance, *De Leeuw van Vlaenderen* (1838), early endeared him to his fellow countrymen; but it was his series of pictures of Flemish life, beginning with *Hoe man schilder wordt* (1843), that, through translations, carried his name over Europe. A complete edition appeared at Antwerp (1867–80), another in 1912. See Lives by Eekhoud (Brussels 1881) and Pol de Mont (Haarlem 1883).

CONSIDÉRANT, Victor Prosper (1808–93), French Socialist, was born at Salins, dep. Jura, and entered the army, which, however, he soon left to promulgate Fourier's doctrines. On the death of his master (1837), Considérant became head of his school, and edited the *Phalange*. An Englishman, Mr Young, having advanced money, Considérant established a socialist colony or *Phalanstère* in Eure-et-Loir; but the experiment failed, and with it the *Phalange*. Of his numerous writings, the chief is the *Destinée Sociale*. In 1849 he was accused of high treason, and fled from France. In Texas he founded a community, *La Réunion*, which flourished for a time. He returned to France in 1869, and died there. See Life by Coignet (1895).

CONSTABLE, (1) Archibald (1774–1827), Scottish publisher, was born at Carnbee, Fife, and became a bookseller's apprentice in Edinburgh (1788–95). He then started as a bookseller at the Cross of Edinburgh, and quickly gathered round him the chief book-collectors of the time. He drifted into publishing, bought the *Scots Magazine* in 1801, and was chosen as publisher of the *Edinburgh Review* (1802). He published for all the leading men of the time, and his quick appreciation of Scott became the envy of the book trade. In 1812 he purchased the copyright of the *Encyclopaedia Britannica* for over £13,000. In the crisis of 1826 Constable & Co. failed for over £250,000. His only noteworthy issue after this failure was his celebrated *Miscellany*. See *Archibald Constable and his Literary Correspondents*, by his son, Thomas Constable (3 vols. 1873).

(2) **Henry** (1562–1613), English poet, the son of Sir Robert Constable of Newark, at sixteen entered St John's College, Cambridge, early turned Catholic, and betook himself to Paris. He was pensioned by the French king, and seems to have been employed in confidential missions to England and Scotland. He died at Liège. In 1592 was published his *Diana*, a collection of twenty-three sonnets; two years later, the second edition, containing seventy-six, but some by his friend, Sir Philip Sidney, and other poets. See editions by W. C. Hazlitt (1859), J. Gray (1897) and J. Gundy (1961).

(3) **John**, R.A. (1776–1837), English landscape painter, was born at East Bergholt, Suffolk, where his father was a landowner and miller. Educated at Lavenham and Dedham, he assisted his father for a year in the mill (1794); but his love of art was irrepressible, and Sir George Beaumont prevailed on his family to send him to London. Here he arrived in 1795; and, after a year spent in his old employment, he entered in 1799 the schools of the Royal Academy, to whose exhibition he sent a work in 1802. In 1816 he married Mary Bicknell; and in 1828, on the death of her father, solicitor to the Admiralty, an inheritance of £20,000 enabled Constable to devote himself exclusively to his beloved but unremunerative landscape work. In 1821 he won the best artistic triumph of his life, in the applause which greeted his *Haywain* in the Paris Salon. Not less marked was the impression produced by his *White Horse*, at Lille in 1825. Both gained gold medals and exercised a powerful influence upon Delacroix and other French artists. In 1819 he was elected A.R.A., in 1829 R.A. His later years were saddened by the deaths of his wife and his friend Archdeacon Fisher, by ill-health, and by great depression of spirits; but he worked steadily at his art, though his landscapes still were frequently unsold. Some of his finest landscapes, including the *Valley Farm*, *Cornfield* and *Haywain*, and over a score of

other works, are in the National Gallery; nearly as many in the Tate Gallery; *Salisbury Cathedral* at South Kensington, where, and in the British Museum, his work in water colour and pencil may be studied. See books by Leslie (1843, ed. Mayne 1951), Holmes (1902), Lord Plymouth (1903), Lucas (1925), Peacock (1965); *Letters 1826–1837*, ed. Leslie (1931) and *Correspondence* (3 vols. 1962, 1965, 1966, ed. by Becket); and Lives by Shirley (1944) and Key (1947).

CONSTANS II, in full **Flavius Heraclius Constans** (630–668), elder son of Constantine III, as Emperor of the East from 641 made himself odious by cruelty, and was found drowned in his bath. His reign was marked by Saracen inroads in the Middle East and Asia Minor.

CONSTANS, Flavius Julius (c. 320–350), youngest of Constantine the Great's three sons, in A.D. 337 received Illyricum, Italy and Africa as his share of the empire. After the defeat and death of his elder brother Constantine (340), Constans became sole ruler of the West till his death.

CONSTANT, Benjamin, *cõ-stã* (1845–1902), a lifelong Parisian, was a painter first of Eastern subjects, latterly of portraits. See studies by Nicolson (1949) and Holdheim (1961).

CONSTANT DE REBECQUE, Henri Benjamin (1767–1830), author and politician, was born of French Huguenot ancestry at Lausanne. Educated at Oxford, Erlangen and Edinburgh, he settled in Paris in 1795 as a publicist. He entered the Tribunate in 1799, but was banished from France in 1802 for denouncing the despotic acts of Napoleon. After travelling in Germany and Italy with Madame de Staël, he settled at Göttingen. On Napoleon's fall in 1814 he returned to Paris; during the Hundred Days became one of Napoleon's councillors, though previously he had styled Napoleon a Genghis Khan; and after the second restoration of the Bourbons wrote and spoke in favour of constitutional freedom. He was returned to the Chamber of Deputies in 1819, and became the leader of the liberal Opposition. He wrote *De la religion* (5 vols. 1824–31); but more important is a remarkable psychological novel, *Adolphe* (1816). His Correspondence appeared in 1844, his *Œuvres politiques* in 1875, his Letters to Madame Récamier and his family In 1882–88, and his *Journal intime* in 1895. See the Life by Shermerhorn (1924), and H. Nicolson, *Benjamin Constant* (1949).

CONSTANTINE I, called **the Great,** properly **Flavius Valerius Aurelius Constantinus** (c. 274–337), Roman emperor, was born at Naissus, in Upper Moesia. He was the eldest son of Constantius Chlorus and Helena, and first distinguished himself as a soldier in Diocletian's famous Egyptian expedition (296), next under Galerius in the Persian war. In 305 the two emperors Diocletian and Maximian abdicated, and were succeeded by Constantius Chlorus and Galerius. Constantine joined his father, who ruled in the West, at Boulogne on the expedition against the Picts, and before Constantius died (306) he proclaimed his son his successor. Galerius did not dare to quarrel with

Constantine, yet he granted him the title of Caesar only, refusing that of Augustus. Political complications now increased, until in 308 there were actually no less than six emperors at once—Galerius, Licinius and Maximin in the East; and Maximian, Maxentius his son, and Constantine in the West. Maxentius drove his father from Rome, and after some intrigues, Maximian died by suicide (309). Maxentius threatened Gaul with a large army. Constantine, crossing the Alps by Mont Cénis, thrice defeated Maxentius, who was drowned after the last great victory at the Milvian Bridge near Rome (312). Before the battle a flaming cross inscribed ' In this conquer ' was said to have caused Constantine's conversion to Christianity; and the edict of Milan (313), issued conjointly with Licinius, gave civil rights and toleration to Christians throughout the empire. Constantine was now sole emperor of the West; and by the death of Galerius in 311 and of Maximin in 313, Licinius became sole emperor of the East. After a war (314) between the two rulers, Licinius had to cede Illyricum, Pannonia and Greece; and Constantine for the next nine years devoted himself vigorously to the correction of abuses, the strengthening of his frontiers and the chastising of the barbarians. Having in 323 again defeated Licinius, and put him to death, Constantine was now sole governor of the Roman world. He chose Byzantium for his capital, and in 330 inaugurated it under the name of Constantinople (' City of Constantine '). Christianity became a state religion in 324, though paganism was not persecuted. In 325 was held the great Church Council of Nicaea, in which the court sided against the Arians. Yet it was only shortly before his death that Constantine received baptism. The story of his baptism at Rome by Pope Sylvester in 326, and of the so-called *Donation of Constantine*, long treated as an argument for the temporal power of the papacy, is utterly unhistorical. His later years were stained with bloodshed, especially the execution of his eldest son Crispus (326) for treason and of his own second wife Fausta (327) on some similar charge. He proposed to divide the empire between his three sons by Fausta, Constantius, Constantine and Constans; but in 340 Constantine II lost his life in war with Constans. Constantine the Great died on May 22, 337. See works by Cutts (1881), Firth (1905), Schwartz (1913), Coleman (1915), and the *Cambridge Ancient History* vol. 12 (1939).

Constantine III reigned part of 641 only; **Constantine IV,** emperor in 668–685, gave up much territory to the Bulgarians, Serbs, and Croats; **Constantine V,** called Iconoclast and other uncomplimentary names, was a capable but unscrupulous ruler from 741 to 775, always at feud with the monks; **Constantine VI** was nominally ruler from 780 to 797; **Constantine VII,** called Porphyrogenitus (912–959), favoured peace, literature and learning, and wrote historical and political works; **Constantine VIII–X** were insignificant; **Constantine XI** (1403–53), last emperor of the Eastern Empire, came to the crown as a Palaeologus in 1448, and fell fighting the Turks at the great siege of Constantinople.

CONSTANTINE, two kings of Greece:

Constantine I (1868–1923), led the Greeks to victory in the Balkan wars (1912–13), and succeeded his father, George I, in 1913. William II's brother-in-law, he thwarted Venizelos, was deposed 1917, recalled 1920, deposed 1922.

Constantine II (1940–   ), succeeded his father Paul I in 1964, married Princess Anne-Marie of Denmark (b. 1946) in 1964 (daughter, b. 1965, son, b. 1967). He fled to Rome in December 1967 after an abo rtive *coup* against the military government which had seized power in April.

CONSTANTINE NIKOLAEVICH (1827–92), second son of Tsar Nicholas I, in the Crimean war commanded the Russian fleet, and held the British and French in check before Kronstadt. In 1865 and 1878 he became president of the council; in 1882 he was dismissed for revolutionary views.

CONSTANTIUS (317–361), third son of Constantine I, was Eastern Roman emperor 337–361. He fought against the Persians, and after the death in 350 of his brother Constans, became sole emperor.

CONSTANTIUS CHLORUS (*c.* 250–306), nephew of Claudius II and father of Constantine (q.v.), became Caesar in A.D. 292, had Britain, Gaul and Spain as his government, and, after re-establishing Roman power in Britain and defeating the Alemanni, became Augustus in 305. Died at York in 306.

CONTARINI, *kon-ta-ree'nee*, a Venetian family, one of the twelve that elected the first doge, furnished between 1043 and 1674 eight doges, four patriarchs, and many generals, statesmen, artists, poets and scholars.

(1) **Gasparo** (1483–1542), cardinal, was Venetian ambassador at the court of Charles V and papal legate at the Diet of Ratisbon (1541), where he displayed great moderation.

(2) **Ludovico** (1629–53), was ambassador in Paris.

(3) **Simone** (1563–1633) was Venetian ambassador at several Italian courts, in Spain, in Constantinople, &c., and was a Latin poet.

CONTI, House of, a younger branch of the Bourbon House of Condé (q.v.).

(1) **Armand de Bourbon** (1629–66), founder of the house, brother of the great Condé, took his title from the little town of Conti, near Amiens. Though feeble and deformed, and set aside for the church, he took with ardour to the career of arms, but after 1657 retired from the world.

(2) **François Louis** (1664–1709), son of (1), Prince de la Roche-sur-Yon et de Conti, was educated under the eyes of Condé, and in his first campaign in Hungary covered himself with glory, but falling into disgrace with the court, was banished to Chantilly. Subsequently he served under the Duc de Luxembourg, and took a brilliant part in the victories of Steinkirk and Neerwinden. In 1697 he narrowly escaped being made king of Poland. On his return to France he was still coldly received by Louis, but in 1709 received command of the army of Flanders, only to die in the same year.

(3) **Louis Armand** (1661–85), eldest son of (1), died childless after a short but promising career in arms.

(4) **Louis François Joseph** (1734–1814), was the last of the line.

CONWAY, (1) Henry Seymour (1721–95), field-marshal and statesman, Horace Walpole's friend.

(2) **Hugh** (1847–85), pseudonym (taken from the school frigate *Conway*, on which he spent some time) of **Frederick John Fargus**, a Bristol auctioneer, who also wrote clever newspaper verse and tales. His greatest success was the melodramatic, *Called Back* (1884), also popular as a play.

(3) **Moncure Daniel** (1832–1907), American divine, born in Virginia, entered the Methodist ministry in 1850, but, after a course at Cambridge, became a Unitarian preacher in Washington in 1854, and in Cincinnati in 1857. He was a strong opponent of slavery, and in 1863 came to England to lecture on the war. In London he became head of the South Place Institute (for advanced religious thought), which he finally gave up in 1897, wrote much for the press, and published *Demonology and Devil-lore* (1879), *Thomas Carlyle* (1881), *Life of Paine* (1892), an autobiography, and other books.

(4) **William Martin, Baron Conway of Allington** (1856–1937), English mountaineer and art critic, born at Rochester, and educated at Trinity, Cambridge, was Art professor at Liverpool 1885–88, at Cambridge 1901–04, M.P. for the English Universities 1918–31. He wrote several works on mountaineering and on the Van Eycks, Dürer, Giorgione, &c. Knighted in 1895, he became a peer in 1931.

CONYBEARE, William John (1815–57), English religious writer, joint author with Dean Howson of a widely known *Life and Epistles of St Paul* (1851), was the eldest son of William Daniel Conybeare (1787–1857), the geologist, who in 1844 became dean of Llandaff. He was educated at Westminster and Trinity, Cambridge, became a fellow, and in 1842 was appointed principal of Liverpool Collegiate Institution, which ill-health compelled him to exchange in 1848 for the vicarage of Axminster. *Essays* (1856) and a novel were his only other works.

COOK, (1) Arthur James (1885–1931), labour leader, born at Wookey, near Wells, became secretary of the National Miners' Federation in 1924, and led the miners in the 1926 strike.

(2) **Edward Dutton** (1829–83), English writer, born in London, a solicitor's son, studied painting and engraving, wrote a successful melodrama, acted as dramatic critic for the *Pall Mall* (1867–75) and then for the *World* till his death. Among his sixteen works were half a dozen novels, *A Book of the Play* (1876) and *On the Stage* (1883).

(3) **Eliza** (1818–89), English minor poetess, daughter of a London tradesman, contributed to magazines from an early age, and issued volumes of poetry in 1838, 1864 and 1865. She conducted *Eliza Cook's Journal* (1849–1854), much of it republished as *Jottings from my Journal* (1860). She obtained a civil list pension in 1864.

(4) James (1728–79), English navigator, was born at Marton, in Cleveland, Yorkshire, the son of an agricultural labourer. After a short time in a haberdasher's shop at Staithes, he was bound apprentice to Whitby ship-owners, and spent several years in the coasting and Baltic trade. In 1755 he entered the navy, and in 1759 became master. He was for eight years engaged in surveying about the St Lawrence and the shores of Newfoundland. In 1768–71, in command of the *Endeavour*, he conveyed to the Pacific the expedition for observing the transit of Venus. On the return, New Zealand was circumnavigated and charted; the east coast of Australia was surveyed and taken possession of for Britain; the strait between Australia and New Guinea was sailed through, and the voyage completed by way of Java and the Cape of Good Hope. Cook, now a commander, was given the command of a second voyage of discovery in the *Resolution* and *Adventure*, in 1772–75, to discover how far the lands of the Antarctic stretched northwards, and sailed round the edge of the ice, reaching 71° 10′ S., in long. 110° 54′ W. During the intervals between the Antarctic voyages, Cook visited Tahiti and the New Hebrides, and discovered New Caledonia and other groups. Owing to Cook's precautions, there was only one death among his crews during all the three years. Captain Cook's next and last voyage (1776–1779) was to discover a passage round the north coast of America from the Pacific, and was by way of the Cape, Tasmania, New Zealand, the Pacific Islands, the Sandwich Islands (now discovered), and the west coast of North America, which he surveyed from 45° N. as far as Icy Cape in Bering Strait, where he was compelled to turn back, reaching Karakakoa Bay in Hawaii, in January 1779. The natives, at first friendly, suddenly changed their attitude; and on February 14, when Cook landed with a party to recover a stolen boat, set upon them with sudden fury, Cook being clubbed and stabbed to death. Cook did more than any other navigator to add to our knowledge of the Pacific and the Southern Ocean. An account of the first voyage originally appeared in Hawkesworth's *Voyages* (vols. ii and iii, 1773); the narrative of the second was written by Cook himself (2 vols. 1777); that of the third was partly by Cook and partly by King (3 vols. 1784). His own journal of the first voyage was edited by Wharton (1893). See Lives by Kippis (1788, repr. 1883), Besant (1890), Kitson (1907), Carruthers (1930) and Williamson (1946).

(5) Sir Joseph (1860–1947), once a Staffordshire miner, was Australian prime minister in 1913–14, high commissioner in London in 1921–27.

(6) Stanley Arthur (1873–1949), English bible scholar, born at King's Lynn, from 1932 to 1938 professor of Hebrew at Cambridge, wrote on Old Testament history. Works include *The Place of the Old Testament in Modern Research* (1932) and *An Introduction to the Bible* (1945). He was joint editor of the *Cambridge Ancient History*.

(7) Thomas (1808–92), British railway excursion and tourist pioneer, was born at Melbourne, Derbyshire, his first railway trip (a temperance one) being made from Leicester to Loughborough in 1841. See Fraser Rae, *The Business of Travel* (1891), and J. A. R. Pimlott, *The Englishman's Holiday* (1947).

COOKE, (1) Benjamin (1734–93), English composer of glees, anthems, &c., was organist of Westminster Abbey from 1762, as from 1802 was his son, **Robert**, who drowned himself in 1814.

(2) George Frederick (1756–1811), English actor, born in Westminster, made his début at Brentford in 1776, and between 1784 and 1800 attained a front rank in his profession in spite of drinking habits. From 1801 to 1810 he played at Covent Garden both in comedy and in tragedy, and rivalled Kemble in the public favour. In 1810 he visited America, and died in New York. A monument marks his grave, erected in 1821 by Edmund Kean, who regarded Cooke as the greatest of actors. See Life by William Dunlap (1813).

(3) Josiah Parsons (1827–94), American chemist, educated at Harvard, where he became professor of Chemistry and Mineralogy (1850–94). He investigated the atomic weights of elements.

(4) Thomas (1703–56), hack writer and translator of Hesiod, &c., was born at Braintree. His criticisms of Pope earned him a place in the *Dunciad* (II. 138).

(5) Thomas Simpson (1782–1848), a tenor singer and composer, born in Dublin, and from 1815 connected with Drury Lane, London.

(6) Sir William Fothergill (1806–79; kt., 1869), British inventor, born at Ealing, studied medicine, took up telegraphy, and in 1837 became Wheatstone's partner. In 1845 they patented the single needle apparatus; in 1846 Cooke formed a company, which paid £120,000 for the partners' earlier patents. In 1867 he got the Albert gold medal.

COOKWORTHY, William (1705–80), English porcelain manufacturer, the discoverer of kaolin near St Austell, was a Plymouth druggist and Quaker, born at Kingsbridge, Devon.

COOLIDGE, (1) Calvin (1872–1933), thirtieth president of U.S.A. (1923–29), was born at Plymouth, Vt., became a lawyer, was governor of Massachusetts 1919–20. Vice-president 1921–23, then president on Harding's death, he was triumphantly re-elected by the Republicans in 1924.

(2) Susan, pseudonym of **Sarah Chauncy Woolsey** (1835–1905), American children's writer and literary critic, born in Cleveland, Ohio. She wrote the *Katy* books and other stories for girls, in an easy natural style, free from contemporary sentimentality.

(3) William Augustus (1850–1926), American alpinist, born in New York, between 1865 and 1898 ascended some 1220 peaks and passes of the Alps, many for the first time.

COOMARASWÁMY, Ananda, *koo-mah′ra-swah′mee* (1877–1947), Ceylon-born author, a leader of the 20th-century cultural revival in India, especially in the field of art. See *Art and Thought* (1947, ed. Bharathe Iyer).

COOPER, (1) Abraham (1787–1868), English painter of battle scenes, also known for equestrian and sporting pictures, R.A. from 1820, was born in London.

(2) **Sir Alfred Duff, 1st Viscount Norwich** (1890–1954), British politician, educated at Eton and Oxford, served with the Grenadier Guards in the 1914–18 war and was elected to parliament as a Conservative in 1924, becoming secretary for war in 1935–37. He resigned from the office of first lord of the Admiralty in 1938 in protest against Chamberlain's ' appeasement ' policy, but became minister of information under Churchill in 1940–42, and ambassador to France (1944–1947). He wrote lives of Talleyrand (1932), Haig (1935) and King David (1943), and other books. In 1919 he married Lady Diana Manners, daughter of the Duke of Rutland, who acted a leading rôle in Max Reinhardt's famous *The Miracle* (1911–12). See her *Rainbow Comes and Goes* (1958), *The Light of Common Day* (1959) and *Trumpets from the Steep* (1960).

(3) **Ashley.** See SHAFTESBURY.

(4) **Sir Astley** (1768–1841), surgeon, was born, a clergyman's son, at Brooke Hall, Norfolk. From sixteen a medical student in London and Edinburgh, he lectured on anatomy at St Thomas's Hospital (1789) and at the College of Surgeons (1793), in 1800 became surgeon to Guy's, and in 1813 professor of Comparative Anatomy in the College of Surgeons. An essay on the loss of the *membrana tympani* gained him, in 1802, the Copley medal of the Royal Society, of which he was elected a fellow in 1805. In 1804–07 appeared his great work on *Hernia*, which was followed by *Dislocations and Fractures* (1822), *Anatomy and Diseases of the Breast* (1829–40), *Anatomy of the Thymus Gland* (1832). In 1820 he removed a tumour from the head of George IV, and was made a baronet. In 1827 he became president of the College of Surgeons, in 1828 sergeant-surgeon to the king, and in 1830 vice-president of the Royal Society. He raised surgery from its primitive state to a science. See study by Brock (1953).

(5) **Charles Henry** (1808–66), English antiquary, born at Great Marlow, from 1849 was town clerk of Cambridge, and wrote on its annals, worthies, &c.

(6) **Dame Gladys** (1888–1971), English actress, born in London, made her début in 1905 and leapt to fame as Paula in *The Second Mrs Tanqueray* (1922). She achieved success in films as well as on the stage. Created D.B.E. in 1967.

(7) **James Fenimore** (1789–1851), American novelist, was born at Burlington, New Jersey. His father, a wealthy Quaker and Federalist member of congress, removed to Cooperstown, New York, then in a wild frontier region of great natural beauty. Cooper entered Yale College in 1803, was expelled during his third year, in 1806 shipped as a common sailor, and in 1808 entered the navy as a midshipman. He rose to the rank of lieutenant, but in 1811 resigned his commission and married Susan, a sister of Bishop De Lancey of New York. His first novel, *Precaution* (1819), was a failure; and the thirty-two which followed it were of extremely unequal quality. The best were the stories of the sea and of Red Indians— *The Spy* (1821), *The Pilot* (1823), *The Last*

of the Mohicans (1826), *The Prairie* (1826), *The Red Rover* (1827), *The Bravo* (1831), *The Pathfinder* (1840), *The Deerslayer* (1841), *The Two Admirals* (1842), *Wing-and-Wing* (1842) and *Satanstoe* (1845). His other writings include a meritorious *Naval History of the United States* (1839; abridged edition, 1841), and *Lives of Distinguished American Naval Officers* (1846). After visiting England and France, he was U.S. consul at Lyons (1826–1829), and then travelled in Switzerland and Italy till 1831. His later years were much disturbed by literary and newspaper controversies and actions for libel, in nearly all of which he was successful. See Lives by Lounsbury (1882), Boynton (1931), Grossman (1950); editions of his *Letters* by Morse (1914) and Cooper (1922).

(8) **John,** also called **Giovanni Coperario** (*c.* 1570–*c.* 1627), English composer who studied in Italy and retained his Italianized name after his return to England in 1604. Winning a high reputation for his compositions, which include masques, songs and instrumental works as well as church music, ' Coperario ' became music master to the children of James I and to the composers William and Henry Lawes.

(9) **Peter** (1791–1883), manufacturer and philanthropist, was born and died in New York. He erected large ironworks in Baltimore in 1828, and in 1830 constructed the first locomotive engine ever built in America. He afterwards built an iron-wire factory in New York and blast-furnaces in Pennsylvania; and promoted the laying of the Atlantic cable. To provide the working classes with educational advantages, he erected and endowed the Cooper Union (1854–59) in New York. See Life by Mrs Carter (1889).

(10) **Samuel** (1609–72), English miniaturist, is represented by several portraits of monarchs and nobility in the royal collection. His work is in the true oil portrait style, as distinct from the tinted drawing of earlier schools.

(11) **Thomas** (1805–92), the Chartist poet, born at Leicester, was apprenticed to a shoemaker at Gainsborough, taught himself Latin, Greek, Hebrew and French, and at twenty-three turned schoolmaster and Methodist preacher. He became leader of the Leicester Chartists in 1841, and got two years for sedition in Stafford jail. Here he wrote *The Purgatory of Suicides*, a poem in the Spenserian stanza, and *Wise Saws and Modern Instances* (1845). He published two novels, *Alderman Ralph* (1853) and *The Family Feud* (1854), and in 1855, relinquishing sceptical opinions he had held since his imprisonment, became a Christian lecturer. See his Autobiography (1872) and *Thoughts at Fourscore* 1885); and R. J. Conklin, *Thomas Cooper the Chartist* (1936).

(12) **Thomas Sidney** (1803–1902), English animal painter, born at Canterbury, was successively coach painter, scene painter and drawing master, lived three years at Brussels (1827–30), and was elected R.A. in 1867. See his *My Life* (2 vols. 1890).

COOTE, Sir Eyre (1726–83), British general, born at Ash Hill, Co. Limerick, entered the army early, and from 1754 to 1762 served in

India. It was he who induced Clive to risk the battle of Plassey (1757); in 1760 he defeated Lally at Wandiwash; and his capture of Pondicherry in 1761 completed the downfall of the French in India. Made a K.B. in 1770, Coote in 1779 assumed the command-in-chief in India, and in 1781, by his rout of Hyder Ali at Porto Novo, a second time saved the presidency. He died at Madras. See Life by H. C. Wylly (1922).

COPE, (1) **Charles West** (1811–90), English subject painter, born at Leeds, the son of a landscape painter, studied at the Royal Academy and in Italy. He was elected R.A. in 1848; and from 1867 to 1874 was professor of Painting. See his son's *Reminiscences* (1891).

(2) **Edward Drinker** (1840–97), American naturalist and palaeontologist, born in Philadelphia, from 1891 held chairs in the university of Pennsylvania. As a hunter of vertebrate fossils he ranks with his rival Marsh (q.v., 3); and he contributed materially to the discussion of evolution. See Osborn's Life (1931).

(3) **Sir John,** K.B. (d. 1760), was a cornet in 1707, and in 1742 commanded the troops sent to assist Maria Theresa. On the landing of Prince Charles Edward in 1745, he was appointed commander-in-chief of the forces in Scotland. After a fruitless march to the Highlands, he returned by sea to Dunbar, and on September 21 was routed at Preston-pans. Cope was described as ' a little, dressy, finical man ', and as a commander he is held to ridicule in the song ' Hey, Johnny Cope '. See Life by Cadell (1899).

COPEAU, Jacques, *kop-ō* (1879–1949), French theatrical manager, as co-founder of the *Nouvelle Revue française* in 1908 and manager of the Théâtre du Vieux-Colombier, had a profound influence on French dramatic art.

COPELAND, William Taylor (1797–1868), English china manufacturer, born probably at Stoke, was son of William Copeland, the partner of Spode. He managed the Spode concerns in Stoke and London, from 1827 to 1833, later gaining control, and from 1846 onwards produced Parian (imitation marble) groups and statuettes, and bone china. He also invented a filter press for working clay, and was one of the founders of the North Staffordshire Railway. In 1835 he was Lord Mayor of London, and from 1837 to 1852 and 1857 to 1865 M.P. for Stoke-on-Trent.

COPERARIO. See COOPER (8).

COPERNICUS, Nicolas (1473–1543), founder of modern astronomy, was born at Toruń, Poland. His father was a Germanized Slav, his mother a German; and Poland and Germany both claim the honour of producing him. Brought up under his uncle, the prince-bishop of Ermeland, from 1491 on he studied mathematics, optics and perspective at Cracow university, and in 1496 canon law at Bologna. In 1497 he was appointed canon of Frauenburg, the cathedral city of Erme-land, on the Frisches Haff. The year 1500 he spent at Rome, where he lectured on astronomy, and (November 6) ' observed an eclipse of the moon '. In 1501 he began the study of medicine at Padua; in 1503 he was

made doctor of canon law at Ferrara; in 1505 he left Italy for Prussia. ' Scholasticus ' of Breslau till 1538, and canon of Frauenburg, yet he never became a priest. As medical attendant on his uncle, he lived with him from 1507 till 1512 in the princely castle of Heilsberg, 46 miles from Frauenburg, where he had onerous duties. After his uncle's death in 1512, he lived at Frauenburg, not merely studying the stars, but executing with vigour and success the offices of bailiff, military governor, judge, tax collector, vicar-general, physician and reformer of the coinage. His difficulties were increased by the intrigues and wars by which West Prussia was restored to the Teutonic Knights and incorporated with Brandenburg. The *De Revolutionibus*, proving the sun to be the centre of the universe, he completed in 1530; in 1542 he was seized with apoplexy; and on May 24, 1543, the first printed copy of the work was touched by his dying hands. Copernicus also published a Latin translation of the Epistles of Theophylactus Simocatta and a treatise on trigonometry. See Lives by Gassendi (Paris 1654), Von Hipler (1873), Polkovski (Warsaw 1873), Dr Prowe (3 vols. Berlin 1883–84) and Rudnicki (1943).

COPLAND, Aaron, *kōp'land* (1900–), American composer, was born in Brooklyn, New York, where he studied under Rubin Goldmark, the teacher of Gershwin. Three years of study in France, under Nadia Boulanger, followed, and his music quickly gained appreciation after his return to America in 1924; a Guggenheim Fellowship —the first to be awarded to a composer—in 1925 marked the progress of his reputation. A series of early works influenced by Stravin-sky, neoclassical in outlook and employing jazz idioms, was followed by compositions in which he tapped a deeper vein of American tradition and folk music, of which the ballets *Billy the Kid* (1938) and *Appalachian Spring* (1944), and *A Lincoln Portrait* (1942), for orator and orchestra, are typical. As well as ballets and impressive film scores, Copland has composed two operas and three sym-phonies. See his autobiography, *Composer from Brooklyn*, and study by Berger (1953).

COPLESTON, (1) **Edward** (1776–1849), English scholar, born at Offwell rectory, Honiton, became professor of Poetry at Oxford (1802), provost of Oriel (1814), dean of Chester (1826), and Bishop of Llandaff and dean of St Paul's (1828). His *Advice to a Young Reviewer* is a piece of admirable irony.

(2) **Frederick Charles** (1907–), English philosopher, born near Taunton, educated at Marlborough and St John's College, entered the Society of Jesus in 1930 and was ordained in 1937. He became professor of the History of Philosophy at Heythrop College in 1939 and of metaphysics at the Gregorian Univer-sity, Rome, in 1952. His publications include *Nietzsche* (1942), *Schopenhauer* (1946), *A History of Philosophy*, (8 Vols. 1946–66), *Aquinas* (1955) *Existentialism* (1948) and a critique of *Contemporary Philosophy* (1956).

COPLEY, (1) **Sir Godfrey** (d. 1709), a York-shire baronet, left one hundred pounds in trust to the Royal Society (of which he was a fellow); the fund has been applied since 1736 to the provision of the annual 'Copley Medal' for philosophical research.

(2) **John Singleton** (1737–1815), portrait and historical painter, was born at Boston, Mass., of Anglo-Irish parents, lately of Limerick. At sixteen he was executing portraits; in 1755 Washington sat to him. In 1766–67 he sent over works for exhibition in London; and in 1774 he left for England. He was well received by Reynolds, West and Strange, and was commissioned to paint the king and queen for Governor Wentworth. He studied in Italy, and returned to London at the end of 1776. *The Death of Chatham* (1779–80) and the still finer *Death of Major Peirson* (1783) are both in the Tate Gallery. Other works include an enormous canvas of the Siege of Gibraltar painted for the City of London (1786–91) and a group of the royal princesses in Buckingham Palace. Elected an R.A. in 1779, he died in 1815, leaving a son, the future Lord Lyndhurst (q.v.). See his *Letters and Papers* (Mass. Hist. Soc. 1915), and Lives by Perkins (1873), a granddaughter, Mrs Amory (1882), and B. N. Parker (1938).

COPPARD, Alfred Edgar (1878–1957), English short story writer and poet, born at Folkestone. His schooling ceased when he was nine, and after being an office boy, then an accountant, he became a professional writer in 1919. In 1921 he published *Adam and Eve and Pinch Me*, and soon became celebrated for his tales of country life and character. His prose is remarkable for its minuteness of observation and poetic quality. Other volumes of stories include *The Black Dog* (1923), *The Field of Mustard* (1926) and *Lucy in Her Pink Jacket* (1954). His *Collected Poems* appeared in 1928. See his autobiographical *It's Me, O Lord!* (1957), and bibliographies by J. Schwartz (1931) and G. H. Fabes (1933).

COPPÉE, François, *kop-pay* (1842–1908), French poet, was born in Paris. For three years a war-office clerk, he early gave himself to poetry, and with *Le Reliquaire* (1866) and *Les Intimités* (1867) gained the front rank of the 'Parnassiens'. Later volumes of poetry were *Les Humbles*, *Le Cahier rouge*, *Olivier* (his one long poem), *Les Récits et les élégies* and *Contes en vers*. His earliest dramatic poem, *Le Passant* (1869), owed much to Sarah Bernhardt, and was followed by *Deux Douleurs*, *L'Abandonnée*, *Le Luthier de Crémone*, *La Guerre de Cent Ans*, *Madame de Maintenon* (1881), *Severo Torelli* (1883), *Les Jacobites* (1885), *Le Pater* (1890), *Pour la couronne* (1895). Coppée entered the Academy in 1884, and won fame in yet another field by his *Contes en prose*, *Vingt Contes nouveaux*, and *Contes rapides*. See French studies by H. Schoen (1909) and L. le Meur (1932).

COQUELIN, *kok-lǐ*, (1) **Benoît Constant** (1841–1909), French actor known as Coquelin *aîné*, born a baker's son at Boulogne, was admitted to the Conservatoire in 1859, and made his début at the Théâtre Français, December 7, 1860. Here, and after 1897 at the Porte St Martin, he played with unbroken success, both in classical pieces and in rôles created by himself, standing without a rival in the broader aspects of comedy.

(2) **Ernest Alexandre** (1848–1909), brother of (1), also a member of the Comédie Française, died a fortnight after Coquelin *aîné*.

(3) **Jean** (1865–1944), son of (1), was likewise an actor.

COQUEREL, (1) **Athanase Josué Laurent** (1820–75), son of (2), born in Amsterdam, was a still more ' advanced ' theologian, and in 1862 was through Guizot's influence ousted from the ministry. He died at Fismes, in Marne. Among his works were an edition of Voltaire's letters on toleration (1863) and *Jean Calas* (1857). See Life by Stroehlin (Paris 1885).

(2) **Athanase Laurent Charles** (1795–1868), from 1830 an eloquent minister of the French Reformed Church in his birthplace, Paris. His writings, all marked by earnestness and liberal sympathies, include a reply to Strauss (1841), six collections of sermons (1842–56), and *Christologie* (1858).

CORAÏS, or **Coray, Adamantios** (1748–1833), Hellenist, born at Smyrna, abandoned mercantile pursuits, and in 1785 settled as a doctor in Paris. He published editions of Greek classics, *Atakta, ou Mélanges sur la littérature grecque moderne* (5 vols. Paris 1828–35), &c. See his Autobiography (Paris 1829–33) and posthumous papers and letters (5 vols. Athens 1881–91); and a Greek Life by Therianos (3 vols. Trieste 1889–90).

CORAM, Thomas (*c.* 1668–1751), philanthropist, was born at Lyme Regis, Dorsetshire. A shipwright seemingly, in 1694 he was settled at Taunton, Massachusetts, and in 1719 in London, after suffering shipwreck off Cuxhaven. In London he interested himself in the settlement of Georgia and in planting English artisans in Nova Scotia; and he had already begun his long agitation for the foundation of a foundling hospital. Children were first admitted in 1741. More thoughtful for others than for himself, Coram fell into poverty, so in 1745 his friends raised an annuity of £161. His portrait was painted by Hogarth, a warm patron of his scheme. See Life by Compston (1918).

CORBET, Richard (1582–1635), English poet-bishop, the son of a gardener at Ewell, Surrey, from Westminster School passed to Oxford, and in 1620 was made dean of Christ Church. In 1624 he was consecrated to the see of Oxford, and in 1632 translated to Norwich. Corbet's Poems (1647) reflect the jovial temper of the man. His longest piece is *Iter Boreale*, a holiday tour of four students; the best and best known is the *Fairies' Farewell*.

CORBETT, James John (1866–1933), American boxer, born in San Francisco. He won the world's heavyweight championship by knocking out John L. Sullivan in the twenty-first round. Nicknamed 'Gentleman Jim', he made several appearances on stage, in films and on radio. He introduced a ' science' into the art of pugilism it had never before known.

CORBOULD, English family of painters:

(1) **Edward Henry** (1815–1905), historical painter.

(2) **Henry** (1787–1844), father of (1), landscape painter.

(3) **Richard** (1757–1831), grandfather of (1),

versatile painter especially noted as a book illustrator.

CORBUSIER, Le, pseud. of **Charles Édouard Jeanneret,** *kor-bü-zyay* (1887–1965), Swiss architect, born at La Chaux-de-Fonds. After working in Paris with the architect Auguste Perret (q.v.), he associated with Peter Behrens in Germany (1910–11). In 1919 he published (with Ozenfant, q.v.) in Paris the Purist manifesto and began to work on his theory of the interrelation between modern machine forms and the techniques of contemporary architecture. His books, *Vers une architecture* (1923), *Le Modulor* (1948) and *Le Modulor 2* (1955), &c., have had worldwide influence on town planning and building design. His first building, based on the technique of the Modulor (a system using standard-sized units, the proportions of which are calculated according to those of the human figure), was the *Unité d'habitation*, Marseilles (1945–50), which was conceived as one of a number of tall buildings which, when the overall scheme (' la Ville radieuse ') had been completed, would form a pattern projecting from the ' carpet ' of low buildings and open spaces. This was his favourite type of town-planning concept, used again in designing Chandigarh, the new capital of the Punjab. Some of his buildings are raised on stilts or *piloti,* an innovation first used by him in the Swiss Pavilion in the Cité Universitaire at Paris. See his *My Work* (trans. by Palmes, 1961) and monograph ed. by Papadaki (1948).

CORDAY, Charlotte (1768–93), Frenchwoman whose full name was Marie Charlotte Corday d'Armont, was born at St Saturnin, near Sées (Orne). Of a noble family, she yet welcomed the Revolution, for from Voltaire she had imbibed ' philosophic ' theories, from Plutarch ideas of antique heroism. But the Jacobins horrified her; and her hatred of their acts was intensified by converse with Girondists who had fled to Caen. She resolved to rid her country of one of the heads of the Jacobins, and came with that view to Paris. Whether to slay Robespierre or Marat was decided by the demand of the latter for two hundred thousand more victims. Twice she failed to obtain an audience, but on the evening of July 13, 1793, she was admitted on the plea of important news from Caen. She found Marat in his bath, and her pretended denunciation of the fugitive Girondists called forth the remark: ' I will have them all guillotined at Paris '. She immediately drove her knife into his heart. Charlotte was brought before the Revolutionary Tribunal, but showed no repentance. In the Conciergerie she sat to the artist Hauer; on the evening of July 17 she was guillotined. See works by Dubois (1838), Vatel (1872), Van Alstine (1889), Austin Dobson (1890), Mary Jeaffreson (1894), E. Defrance (1909) and H. d'Almeras (1910).

CORDOVO. See GONSALVO.

CORELLI, (1) **Arcangelo** (1653–1713), Italian composer, surnamed ' Il divino ', was born at Fusignano near Bologna; visited Paris and Germany as a violin player; and ultimately settled at Rome. His Concerti grossi and his solo and trio sonatas for violin mark an epoch in chamber music, and had great influence on Bach and on contemporary string technique. See H. Engel, *Das Instrumenten konzert* (1932).

(2) **Marie** (1855–1924), English popular novelist, trained for a musical career. She wrote *A Romance of Two Worlds* (1886), *Thelma* (1887), *Wormwood* (1891), *The Soul of Lilith* (1892), *Barabbas* (1893), *The Sorrows of Satan* (1895), *The Mighty Atom* (1896), *God's Good Man,* (1904) &c. See Life by W. S. Scott (1955).

CORI, Carl Ferdinand (1896–   ), biochemist, born in Prague, educated there and at Trieste, American citizen since 1922, professor of Pharmacology and Biochemistry at Washington since 1931, became an authority on carbohydrate metabolism and enzymes of animal tissues. With his wife, Gerty T. Cori (d. 1957), he was awarded the 1947 Nobel prize for medicine with Houssay.

CORINTH, Louis, *ko'rint* (1858–1925), German painter, born at Tapiau, East Prussia, the son of a tanner, studied at Königsberg, Munich and under Bouguereau in Paris. Deeply influenced by the heritage of Rembrandt, Hals and Rubens, he yet stoutly defended the claims of the impressionists. From conventional nude, landscape painting and especially portraiture, e.g., his study in ' blimpish ' arrogance, *Carl von Gayling* (1893; private), *The Freemasons* (1898; Munich), and the delicate *Eduard Count Keyserling* (1900; Munich) his style became markedly impressionistic, as in *Under the Chandelier* (1905; private), *After a Bathe* (1906; Hamburg) and his many *Waldensee* views, his later work, e.g., *Georg Brandes* (1924; Antwerp), executed under the restricting after-effects of a stroke (1911), verging on expressionism. From 1900 he lived in Berlin and with Liebermann and Slevogt led the secession movement, of which he became president (1915) against the Berlin academic school. He died at Zandvoort, Holland, and was buried at Stahnsdorf near Berlin. See his *Das Erlernen der Malerei* (1908), his Life of a fellow secessionist, Leistikow (1910), and studies by A. Kuhn (1925) and G. von der Osten (Munich 1955).

CORIOLANUS, Gaius or **Gnaeus Marcius** (5th cent. B.C.), a legendary Roman patrician, so surnamed from the heroism he showed at the capture of the Volscian town of Corioli (493 B.C.). The plebeians having refused to elect him to the consulship, he argued during a famine against the gratuitous distribution of the corn from Sicily unless the plebeians should give up their tribunes, recently instituted. For this he was banished. He took refuge with the Volscians, and aided them against Rome. His victories alarmed the Romans, who on his approach (488 B.C.) sent deputations to plead with him. He was deaf to every entreaty. At last, the noblest matrons, headed by his mother Veturia, and his wife Volumnia, leading her two children, came to his tent. Their tears moved him, and he led back the Volsci.

CORK, Earl of. See BOYLE.

CORNARO, a Venetian noble family, two of whose members were:

(1) **Caterina** (1454–1510), married King James II of Cyprus in 1472, after whose death eight months later she was kept in mild imprisonment by the Venetians until 1489, when she set up a kind of court for poets and scholars at Asolo, near Bassano.

(2) **Luigi** (1475–1566), at forty finding his health much impaired by intemperance, adopted strict rules both in meat and drink, living to a cheerful old age. At eighty-three he published his famous *Discorsi della vita sobria* (Eng. trans. 1779).

CORNEILLE, *kor-nay,* (1) **Guillaume,** properly **Cornélis van Beverloo** (1922–), Belgian painter, born at Liège, a leading European exponent of ' action ' painting. His works include *Drawing in Colour,* belonging to the ' and the country loses itself in Infinity ' series (1955); Henriette le Gendre, Paris), *Summer Flowers* (1958; Moltzau collection, Norway), &c.

(2) **Pierre** (1606–84), French dramatist, was born at Rouen, where he tried to obtain a barrister's practice, but in 1629 removed to Paris, where his comedy *Mélite,* already performed at Rouen, proved highly successful. It was followed by *Clitandre, La Veuve, La Galerie du Palais, La Suivante* and *La Place Royale.* In these early pieces intricate and extravagant plots are handled with ingenuity, but the writer's poetic genius flashes out only in occasional verses. For a time Corneille was one of Richelieu's ' five poets ', engaged to compose plays on lines laid down by the cardinal; among the pieces thus produced were *Les Tuileries, L'Aveugle de Smyrne* and *La Grande Pastorale.* Corneille, however, was too independent to retain Richelieu's favour. *Médée* (1635) showed a marked advance on his earlier works; and in 1636 *Le Cid* took Paris by storm. Richelieu ordered his literary retainers to write it down; but adverse criticism was powerless against the general enthusiasm. *Horace,* founded on the story of the Horatii, and *Cinna,* appeared in 1639; *Polyeucte,* a noble tragedy, in 1640; and *La Mort de Pompée* in 1641. *Le Menteur* (1642) entitles Corneille to be called the father of French comedy as well as of French tragedy. *Théodore* was brought out in 1645, and *Rodogune* in 1646. Between 1647—when he was made an academician—and 1653 Corneille produced *Héraclius, Don Sanche d'Aragon, Andromède, Nicomède,* and *Pertharite.* These pieces, of which the last was damned, show a decline in dramatic and poetic power; and Corneille occupied himself with a verse translation of the *Imitatio Christi.* He returned to the stage in 1659 with *Œdipe,* which was followed by *La Toison d'or, Sertorius, Sophonisbe, Othon, Agésilas, Attila,* and *Tite et Bérénice* (1670). In 1671 he joined Molière and Quinault in writing the opera *Psyché.* His last works were *Pulchérie* (1672) and *Suréna* (1674). After his marriage in 1640 he lived habitually in Rouen until 1662, when he settled in Paris. During his later years his popularity waned before that of Racine, whose cause was espoused by Boileau and the king. Corneille died in Paris. See works by Guizot (1852; trans. 1857), Taschereau (1828; new ed. 1855), Trollope (London 1881), Faguet (8th ed. 1901),

Segall (N.Y. 1902), Dorothy Canfield (N.Y. 1904), Rivaille (1936) and Turnell (1948).

(3) **Thomas** (1625–1709), brother of (2), was born at Rouen, and himself was a dramatist of merit, his tragedies—*Camma, Laodice, Pyrrhus, Bérénice, Timocrate, Ariane, Bradamante,* &c.—being in general superior to his comedies. He also wrote a verse translation of Ovid's *Metamorphoses.* See Reynier's *Thomas Corneille, Sa Vie et ses ouvrages* (1893).

CORNELIA. See GRACCHUS.

CORNELISZ, (1) **Cornelis** (1562–1638), known as Cornelisz van Haarlem, was a Dutch historical and portrait painter.

(2) **Jakob** (d. *c.* 1530), known as Cornelisz van Amsterdam, Dutch painter.

(3) **Lucas** (1495–*c.* 1552), painter, born at Leyden, the son of Cornelis Engelbrechtsen, Lucas van Leyden's master, was taught by his father, but had to act as a cook to support his large family, whence his sobriquet *Kok.* Visiting England about 1527, he was appointed by Henry VIII royal painter. About 1532 he went to Italy.

CORNELIUS, (1) **Peter** (1824–74), German composer, born at Mainz, was the nephew of (2). Going to Weimar in 1852, he became devoted to Liszt, Wagner and the New German school, and produced his famous comic opera, *The Barber of Baghdad* (a failure in 1858), and his grand opera, *Der Cid* (1865).

(2) **Peter von** (1783–1867), German painter, born at Düsseldorf in 1783, in 1811 joined the group of Veit, Schadow and Overbeck in Rome. While there he aided in the decoration of the Casa Bartoldi. From Rome he went to Düsseldorf, where he became director of the academy; in 1819 he was called to Munich. Here he remained till 1841, and executed the large frescoes of Greek mythology in the Glyptothek and the New Testament frescoes in the Ludwigskirche, which was built to give scope for his genius. In 1841 he was appointed director of the Berlin Academy. Among his productions at Berlin are the frescoes for the Campo Santo, or royal burial place, the finest his *Four Riders of the Apocalypse.* See Life by Förster (2 vols. 1874).

CORNELIUS NEPOS. See NEPOS.

CORNELL, (1) **Ezra** (1807–74), American telegraph contractor, who founded Cornell University (opened 1868) at Ithaca, N.Y.

(2) **Katharine** (1898–), American actress, producer and manager, born in Berlin of American parents, educated in New York, she made her first stage appearance in 1916. She appeared in many stage productions such as *The Green Hat, The Letter* and *The Age of Innocence* before embarking on a career as producer. Her own productions include a number of Shakespearian and Shavian classics, *The Constant Wife, The First-Born* and *Dear Liar.*

CORNUTUS, L. Annaeus (1st cent. A.D.), a Libyan Stoic philosopher, banished from Rome by Nero, A.D. 68.

CORNWALL, Barry. See PROCTER.

CORNWALL, Duke of. See ELIZABETH II.

CORNWALLIS, (1) **Caroline Frances** (1786–1858), daughter of a Kentish clergyman, mastered Latin and Greek thoroughly, and corresponded with many eminent persons. Her refusal to wed Sismondi did not forfeit his friendship, and she lived much in Italy. Her *Philosophical Theories* (1842) was the first of twenty ' Small Books on Great Subjects '—Ragged Schools, Criminal Law, Greek Philosophy, &c. She died at Lidwells, Kent. See her *Letters and Remains* (1864).

(2) **Charles, 1st Marquis Cornwallis** (1738–1805) son of the 1st Earl Cornwallis, was born in London, and was educated at Eton and the Military Academy of Turin. He served as aide-de-camp to the Marquis of Granby during part of the Seven Years' War, and been returned for the family borough of Eye (1760), in 1766 he was made a colonel, in 1770 constable of the Tower, and in 1771 a major-general. Though personally opposed to taxing the American colonists, he accepted a command in the war, and with an inferior force defeated Gates at Camden in 1780, and more than held his own at Guildford (1781). But his operations were hampered by the incapacity of Howe and Clinton; and at length he was forced to surrender at Yorktown, Virginia, October 19, 1781—a disaster that proved the ruin of the British cause in America. In 1786 he was appointed governor general of India and commander-in-chief, and distinguished himself by his victories over Tippoo Sahib and by unwearying efforts to promote the welfare of the natives. He returned from India in 1793, to be made marquis. As lord-lieutenant of Ireland, with Castlereagh for secretary, he crushed the '98 rebellion, and showed a rare union of vigour and humanity. As plenipotentiary to France he negotiated the peace of Amiens in 1802. Reappointed governor-general of India in 1804, he died at Ghazipur. See his Correspondence, edited by Charles Ross (3 vols. 1859), and studies by Seton-Kerr (1890), Aspinall (1931).

CORNYSHE, William (*c.* 1465–*c.* 1523), English composer at the courts of Henry VII and Henry VIII, where he was employed as musician, actor and producer of entertainments. In 1510 he became master of the Children of the Chapel Royal, and was in charge of the music at the Field of The Cloth of Gold, 1520. He composed religious and secular choral works.

CORONADO, Francisco Vázquez de (*c.* 1510–1554), Spanish explorer of Mexico, born at Salamanca, commanded an expedition in 1540 which penetrated into what is now the southwest of the U.S.A. and discovered the Grand Canyon of the Colorado. See his *Journey*, ed. Winship (1904).

COROT, Jean Baptiste Camille, *ko-rō* (1796–1875), French landscape painter, was born at Paris, and educated at Rouen. He became an assistant in a Paris drapery establishment, but in 1822 took up the systematic study of art. In 1825 he settled in Rome; in 1827 returned to Paris, and contributed his *Vue prise à Narni* and his *Campagne de Rome* to the Salon. His main sketching ground was at Barbizon, in the Forest of Fontainebleau; but he made two other visits to Italy in 1835 and 1843. It was not until about 1840 that he developed fully

his style, characterized by great breadth and delicacy, and sacrificing accuracy of detail to unity of impression and harmony of general effect. At the Salon, he won medals in 1833, 1848, 1855 and 1867; in 1846 he received the Cross of the Legion of Honour, and in 1867 became an officer of the order. Among his masterpieces are *Danse de nymphes, Homère et les bergers, Orphée, Joueur de flûte* and *Le Bûcheron*. See works by Moreau-Nélaton (1905), D. C. Thomson (1892, 1914), J. W. Mollett (*Painters of Barbizon*, 1890), A. Robaut (Paris 1905), E. Meynell (1908), Fosca (1930).

CORREGGIO, Antonio Allegri da (*c.* 1494–1534), was so styled from a small town 20 miles E. of Parma, where he was born, and studied art under his uncle and three other masters. In 1514 he painted for the Franciscan convent a *Virgin Enthroned*, now in the Dresden Gallery; in 1518 he began his great series of mythological frescoes for the convent of San Paolo at Padua. From 1521 to 1524 he was engaged upon *The Ascension* in the cupola of the Benedictine church of San Giovanni. The decoration of the cathedral of Parma was commissioned in 1522. Meanwhile Correggio was also much occupied with easel pictures. Among these are the *Ecce Homo* (National Gallery, London) and his very celebrated version of the shepherds at Bethlehem, commissioned in 1522, now in the Dresden Gallery, a work of marvellous softness and delicacy. Five years later he painted *Il Giorno*, an exquisite picture of St Jerome (Parma Gallery). In 1530 Correggio removed from Parma to his native town, and purchased an estate. The *Jupiter and Antiope* of the Louvre, the *Education of Cupid* of the National Gallery, the *Danae* of the Borghese Gallery, and the *Leda* of the Berlin Museum, have been assigned to the painter's later years; the *Reading Magdalene*, of which the picture in the Dresden Gallery is now regarded as merely a 17th century copy, was completed in 1528. He died at Correggio. His only son Pomponio was born in 1521, and was alive in 1593. He also was a painter, and an altarpiece by him is in the Academy at Parma. See works by Corrado Ricci (1896; 1930) and Sturge Moore (1906).

CORRENS, Karl (1864–1933), German botanist, born in Munich, from 1914 director of the Kaiser Wilhelm Biological Research Institute at Berlin, was one of the rediscoverers of Mendelism.

CORRI, Domenico (1746–1825), composer, was born in Rome, in 1771 came to Edinburgh, and in 1787 removed to London, where he entered into partnership with his son-in-law Dussek (q.v.).

CORSSEN, Wilhelm Paul (1820–75), German philologist, was born at Bremen, studied under Boeckh and Lachmann, was professor at Schulpforta from 1846 to 1866, and then settled in Berlin. His earliest great work is his treatise on the pronunciation of Latin (2 vols. 1858–59); the second (2 vols. 1874–1875) tried to prove against the world that Etruscan was cognate with Latin.

CORT, Henry (1740–1800), English ironmaster, navy agent in London, was also the inventor of ' puddling ' processes. Ruined by a prosecution for debt, he was ultimately pensioned.

CORTÉS, Hernando (1485–1547), the Spanish conqueror of Mexico, was born of noble family at Medellín, in Estremadura, and studied at Salamanca. He sailed for San Domingo in 1504, and accompanied Velázquez in his expedition to Cuba. Fired by discoveries of Alvarado and others, Velázquez fitted out an expedition against Mexico, the command of which he gave (1518) to Cortés. The armament with which he entered on the conquest of the vast and civilized empire consisted of 550 Spaniards, some 250 Indians, twelve or fifteen horses, and ten brass guns. Refusing to obey orders sent from Velázquez to supersede him, he landed first in the Yucatán, and fought his first battle at Tabasco. At San Juan de Ulua, messengers from Montezuma, king of Mexico, reached him, bringing presents. Having founded Vera Cruz, and burnt his ships, he marched to Tlascala, whose warlike inhabitants, subdued after hard fighting, became henceforward his faithful allies. After some delay he started on his march to Mexico, with his Tlascalan allies; and at Cholula an ambuscade, prompted by Montezuma, was frustrated by his sleepless vigilance. On November 8, 1519, he reached the capital, a city situated in a great salt lake, and approached by three long causeways, with drawbridges at the ends. At the lowest estimate its inhabitants exceeded 300,000. Montezuma was audaciously carried off to the Spanish quarters, and constrained to submit to a public act of vassalage to Spain, as well as to give gold to the value of 100,000 ducats. But meantime the Mexican hatred of the invaders was beginning to surmount their fear, and in the sixth month of his imprisonment Montezuma asked Cortés to depart. The conqueror craved delay; and learning that eighteen ships under Narváez had arrived in the bay of San Juan, dispatched against him by Velázquez, Cortés left Alvarado in command, and hastened with a handful of men to meet Narváez, whose 800 men he easily defeated and induced to embrace his cause. And now he heard from Alvarado that the Spaniards were besieged in their quarters in Mexico. Cortés at once marched to his lieutenant's relief, and found himself face to face with a whole nation in arms under Montezuma's brother. A general attack was made upon him, and not repulsed without a desperate struggle. Montezuma died during the fighting. Cortés burned the two great idols of Mexico, but saw that he must leave the capital. The start was made at midnight, July 1, 1520; but in the difficult passage by pontoons over the gaps in the causeways, the Spaniards were assailed by such furious and overwhelming multitudes that the retreat became a confused and hopeless rout. In that awful night Cortés lost 450 Spaniards, forty-six horses, his artillery, 4000 Indian allies, and most of the Mexican prisoners. At Otumba, where the miserable survivors retreated, they were once more surrounded by an innumerable host, but a desperate battle ended in victory. The exhausted Spaniards were kindly received by their Tlascalan allies, and Cortés proceeded to repair his disaster. He had still 550 foot soldiers, with forty horsemen and eight or nine cannon. Supported by 10,000 Indian allies, and with a fleet of brigantines built at Tlascala, he began the formal siege of Mexico. After destroying innumerable canoes on the lakes, he made a series of simultaneous incursions along the causeways. The Mexicans were filled with the fury of despair, and although famine and pestilence fought for the Spaniards—fifty thousand Mexicans perishing during the siege—the city had to be destroyed before it could be taken. It fell at length, August 13, 1521, after a siege of several months. Cortés was formally appointed governor and captain-general of New Spain in 1522. He next sent out Alvarado to the conquest of Guatemala, Sandoval to the north, and Cristóbal de Olid to Honduras. The last rebelled, and Cortés set out to subdue him; but before his arrival Cristóbal had been assassinated, so he returned to New Spain (1526), to find Ponce de León invested with the powers of government. In May 1528 he arrived in Spain, was received with honour by Charles V, and created a marquis. He returned in July 1530 as captain-general, but not as civil governor, of New Spain. Poor and broken in health, he returned to Spain in 1540, accompanied Charles in his unhappy expedition against Algiers, and died neglected near Seville. His body was translated to Tezcuco in 1562, to Mexico City in 1629. See Lives by Helps (1871), MacNutt (1909), Prescott's *History* and S. de Madariaga, *Hernán Cortés* (1940).

CORTONA, Pietro Berrettini da (1596–1669), Italian architect and painter, born in Cortona, is known for his frescoes in the Barberini palace at Rome and the Pitti palace at Florence. He also designed several Roman churches. See study by Muñoz (Rome 1921).

CORTOT, Alfred, *kor-tō* (1877–1962), French pianist and conductor, was born in Nyon, Switzerland, of French parents. After winning the first prize for piano-playing at the Paris Conservatoire in 1896, he became known in France as an outstanding player of Beethoven's concertos. In 1902 he formed the Société de Festival Lyrique, which gave the first Paris performance of *Götterdämmerung* under his baton. In 1905, with Thibaud and Casals, he founded a trio whose chamber music performances won great renown. Principally known in later years as an exponent of Chopin's music, he was professor of the Pianoforte at the Paris Conservatoire from 1917 to 1920 and author of several books on musical appreciation, interpretation and piano technique.

CORVINUS, Matthias. See MATTHIAS.

CORVISART-DESMARETS, Jean Nicolas, Baron de, *day-mar-ay* (1755–1821), professor at the Collège de France, and introducer of percussion in studying heart diseases, was born at Vouziers in Champagne.

CORY, William Johnson (1823–92), English poet, born at Torrington, Devon, was author of *Ionica, Poems* (1858, enlarged 1891) and assistant-master at Eton in 1845–72. See *Extracts from the Letters and Journals* (1897).

CORYATE, Thomas (c. 1577–1617), English traveller, born at Odcombe Rectory, Somerset, entered Gloucester Hall, Oxford, in 1596, but left without a degree, and after James I's accession lived by his wits, or rather his wit, about court. In 1608 he set out on a journey on foot of 1975 miles through Paris, Lyons, Turin, Venice, Zürich and Strasbourg, and in 1611 published *Coryat's Crudities: Hastily gobled up in Five Moneths' Travels* (new ed. 1905). Dedicating his travel-worn shoes in Odcombe church, he started for Constantinople, Greece, Smyrna, Alexandria, Palestine, Mesopotamia, Persia, Afghanistan and Agra. He died at Surat.

COSGRAVE, (1) Liam (1920–), Irish politician, son of (2), was educated at St Vincent's College, Castleknock, Dublin. He was called to the bar in 1943 and has been a member of the Dail since 1948 and leader of the Fine Gael party since 1965. From 1954 to 1957 he was minister for external affairs.

(2) **William Thomas** (1880–1965), Irish politician, was first president of the Executive Council of the Irish Free State (1922–32), and then leader of the Opposition (1932–44).

COSIMO, (1) Agnolo di. See BRONZINO.

(2) **Piero di.** See PIERO DI COSIMO.

COSIN, John (1594–1672), Bishop of Durham, was born at Norwich. Educated there and at Caius College, Cambridge, he became a fellow, and after various preferments, master of Peterhouse, Cambridge (1635), and dean of Peterborough (1640). An intimate friend of Laud, he had already come into collision with the Puritans about his ritualistic reforms, and, deprived in 1641 of his benefices and ejected by order of the House of Commons from Peterhouse (1644), he retired to Paris. At the Restoration he recovered his preferments, and in December 1660 he was consecrated Bishop of Durham. During his first seven years he spent £34,500 upon his two castles, his cathedral, the library at Durham, and deeds of general benevolence. Imperious in temper, he sternly repressed Puritan and Roman Catholic recusancy alike; for, however devoted to ancient ritual and order, he hated Popery, and never ceased to regret the perversion of his own ' lost son ' who had turned Roman Catholic. He died in London. All Cosin's writings are inconsiderable save his *Collection of Private Devotions* (1627), which was denounced by Prynne in his *Brief Survey of Mr Cozen's Cozening Devotions*. A lasting service to the church was his contribution, invaluable from his profound liturgical learning, to the final revision (1661) of the Prayer Book. Cosin's works are collected in the ' Library of Anglo-Catholic Theology ' (5 vols. 1843–55). His *Correspondence* was edited by Ornsby (1868–72). See Life by P. H. Osmond (1913).

COSMAS (fl. 6th cent. A.D.), surnamed Indicopleustes, a merchant of Alexandria who after much travel in India, &c., returned to Egypt about A.D. 550, and in monastic retirement wrote a Greek work on Christian Topography (ed. by Montfaucon 1706, and by Winstedt 1910; trans. with notes by McCrindle, Halk. Soc. 1898).

COSMAS and **DAMIAN, SS.** (d. A.D. 303), Arabian brothers, said to have been physicians at Ægæa in Cilicia, who were cast into the sea as Christians, but rescued by an angel. Thereafter, burning and stoning having proved ineffectual, they were beheaded.

COSQUIN, Emmanuel, *kos-kĩ* (1841–1922), French folklorist, was born at Vitry-le-François in Marne, where his father was a notary. In his great *Contes populaires de Lorraine* (2 vols. 1886) he contends for the transmission of European folk tales from India within the historical period.

COSSA, Francesco del (?1435–77), Italian artist, born at Ferrara. His work was similar to that of Tura (q.v.), and often equally austere, but in his most famous work, the frescoes in the Palazzo Schifanoia at Ferrara, which were commissioned by Borso d'Este, he produced a number of gay mythological and court scenes. He also worked at Bologna. See *The Painters of Ferrara* by B. Nicolson (1950).

COSTA, (1) Isaac Da. See DA COSTA.

(2) **Joaquin** (1846–1911), Spanish historian and writer, was born at Monzon, Huesca. He was a crusader for the political and economic regeneration of Spain and an investigator of Spain's oldest traditions. His work includes *Juridical and Political Studies* (1884) and *Agrarian Collectivism in Spain* (1898).

(3) **Lorenzo** (c. 1460–1535), Italian painter, was born at Ferrara, and died at Mantua. His *Madonna and Child Enthroned* is in the National Gallery in London.

(4) **Sir Michael** (1810–84), conductor and composer, was born at Naples. Trained at the conservatorio there, he settled in England (1828), and in 1831 his ballet of *Kenilworth* was produced with success. He was conductor at the King's Theatre (1832), at Covent Garden (1846), to the Philharmonic Concerts (1846) and to the Sacred Harmonic Society (1848). His oratorio *Eli*, produced at the Birmingham Festival of 1855 (where he conducted till 1879), raised him to eminence; *Naaman*, less successful, was first sung at Birmingham in 1864. From 1857 till 1877 he conducted at the Handel Festival, and in 1871 he became director of Her Majesty's Opera. He was knighted in 1869. Costa composed ballets and operas, including *Malek Adhel* (1838) and *Don Carlos* (1844). He died in Brighton.

COSTELLO, (1) John Aloysius (1891–), Irish politician, was born in Dublin and educated at University College, Dublin. Called to the bar in 1914, he became attorney-general in 1926–32. In 1948 he became prime minister of a government of several parties of which his own Fine Gael party was the chief. As a foremost constitutional lawyer, one of his first acts was to repeal the External Relations Act, which paved the way that year for the formal change from the State of Eire to the Republic of Ireland. On the defeat of his government by Mr De Valera's Fianna Fail party in 1951, he became leader of the opposition in the Dail, from 1954 to 1957 was premier, and again opposition leader until 1959.

(2) **Louisa Stuart** (1799–1877), authoress, was born in Ireland, and in Paris and London painted miniatures from about 1814 to 1835,

when she published *Specimens of the Early Poetry of France*, in which she was aided by her brother **Dudley** (1803–65). But it was her bright descriptions of travel in Auvergne, the Pyrenees, Wales, Tirol, &c., that made her really popular. Her semi-historical novels were read in their day.

COSTER (1). See JANSZOON.

(2) **Charles de** (1827–79), Belgian story-teller, born in Munich, studied at Brussels. His most famous work, the prose epic *The Legend of Tyl Ulenspiegel* (trans. 1918), took ten years to write.

(3) **Dirk** (1889–1950), Dutch physicist, professor of Physics and Meteorology at Groningen, in 1923 while working in Copenhagen discovered the element *hafnium*.

COSWAY, Richard (*c.* 1742–1821), English miniaturist, born at Tiverton, studied art in London, and was elected A.R.A. in 1770, R.A. in 1771. Cosway painted in oils *à la* Correggio, but it was in portraiture that he made his mark, and soon his miniatures were ' not only fashionable, but the fashion itself '. The Prince of Wales appointed him painter-in-ordinary, and Mrs Fitzherbert and all the beauties sat to him. His small female full-lengths with the faces finished in water-colour, though slight in execution, are full of exquisite grace; and his ivory miniatures are delicate and valuable. See Daniell's *Catalogue raisonné* (1890), and the Life by Williamson (1905). In 1781 he married the Irish-Italian **Maria Hadfield** (1759–1838), herself a skilful artist, who established a conventual school at Lodi, and was made a baroness by Francis I.

COTES, Roger (1682–1716), English mathematician, born at Burbage, near Leicester, went from St Paul's School, London, to Trinity College, Cambridge, where he became a fellow in 1705, and Plumian professor of Astronomy and Natural Philosophy in 1706. He was elected F.R.S. in 1711, and took orders in 1713. His admirable preface explaining the Newtonian philosophy, and answering objections to gravitation, is prefixed to the second edition (1713) of Newton's *Principia*. ' Had Cotes lived ', said Newton, ' we might have known something '.

COTGRAVE, Randle (d. 1634?), English lexicographer, the author of our earliest French dictionary, was a native of Cheshire; was admitted scholar of St John's College, Cambridge, in 1587; became secretary to Lord Burghley; published his dictionary in 1611 and was alive to see the second edition through the press in 1632.

COTMAN, John Sell (1782–1842), English water-colourist, was born and educated at Norwich. His well-to-do parents sent him to study art in London, whence he made journeys all over Britain sketching architecture and the countryside. In 1806 he went back to his birthplace and became a leading member of the ' Norwich School ', but in 1811–23 lived at Yarmouth, where he executed some fine oil paintings and etchings. Lack of success brought on fits of depression, and having sold up his pictures and possessions, he left Norwich in 1834 and became, thanks to the good offices of Turner, drawing master of King's College, London. His work exhibits a variety of styles, the best being characterized by masterly arrangement of masses of light and shade, with a minimum of modelling, giving an effect reminiscent of a Japanese print or a modern poster, as in his famous *Chirk Aqueduct* and *Greta Bridge*. See studies by Kitson (1937) and Rienaecker (1953). His sons **Miles Edmund** (1810–58) and **Joseph John** (1814–78) were competent landscape painters.

COTTA, a publishing-house established at Tübingen in 1640. The family came originally from Italy. Its most prominent members have been **Johann Friedrich** (1701–79), theological professor at Tübingen, Göttingen and Jena; and his grandson, **Johann Friedrich, Freiherr Cotta von Cottendorf** (1764–1832). Educated at Tübingen, and for some time an advocate, in 1787 he undertook the family business, and in 1795 established the famous *Horen*, a literary journal, under Schiller's editorship. Already in 1793 he had sketched out the plan for the *Allgemeine Zeitung* (1798). The *Almanach für Damen* (1798) and other periodicals were no less successful. Cotta now likewise published the works of Schiller, Goethe, Herder, Fichte, Schelling, Jean Paul, Tieck, Voss, the Humboldts, &c. In 1810 he moved to Stuttgart, and in 1824 introduced the first steam printing press into Bavaria. In the diet of Württemberg, and as president of the Second Chamber, he was ever the fearless defender of constitutional rights. He was the first Württemberg proprietor to abolish serfdom on his estates. He was succeeded by his son, **Georg** (1796–1863); and he by his son **Georg Astolf** (1833–76).

COTTIN, Sophie, *née* Risteau, *kot-tĭ* (1770–1807), married at seventeen a Parisian banker, who left her a childless widow at twenty. For comfort she turned to letters, wrote verses and a lengthy history, and romantic fiction. She had already written *Claire d'Albe* (1799), *Mathilde* (1805), &c., when in 1806 she wrote her most successful work, *Élisabeth, ou les exilés de Sibérie.*

COTTLE, (1) **Amos Simon** (1768–1800), educated at Bristol and Cambridge, wrote various works, including *Icelandic Poetry* (1797).

(2) **Joseph** (1770–1853), younger brother of (1), from 1791 to 1799 a Bristol bookseller, remembered as the first publisher of Southey, Coleridge and Wordsworth. His own verses are forgotten, but his *Early Recollections* (1837; 2nd ed. 1847) is still a chief source for our knowledge of the Lake poets.

COTTON, (1) **Charles** (1630–87), English writer, the friend of Izaak Walton and translator of Montaigne, was born at his father's estate of Beresford in Staffordshire. His father, himself a man of great ability, was a warm friend of Ben Jonson, Selden, Donne and other illustrious men. The boy travelled on the Continent, and early wrote verses which were handed about among his friends. In 1656 he married his cousin Isabella, half-sister of the famous Col. Hutchinson (q.v.). Though a sincere loyalist, he seems to have lived securely enough under the Commonwealth, and the decay of his father's estate was due mainly to unprosperous lawsuits. In 1664 Cotton issued anonymously his burlesque poem, *Scarronides, or* the First Book of Virgil Travestie, added to in later editions in grossness as well as in bulk. Later works are his *Voyage to Ireland in Burlesque* (1670), *Burlesque upon Burlesque* (1675), *Planter's Manual* (1675), and a treatise on fly-fishing contributed in 1676 to the fifth edition of Walton's *Compleat Angler*. His translation (1685) of Montaigne's *Essays* is a masterpiece. See his *Life and Poetry* by Sembower (1911), his *Poems* ed. Beresford (1923).

(2) **George Edward Lynch** (1813–66), was educated at Westminster and Trinity College, Cambridge, and from 1836 was a master at Rugby under Arnold and Tait; in *Tom Brown's School Days* he appears as 'the young master'. In 1852 he became head of Marlborough College, which he raised to a position among the first schools of England, and in 1858 Bishop of Calcutta, where he founded schools for the children of the poorer Anglo-Indians and Eurasians. He was drowned in the Ganges. See Memoir (1871).

(3) **John** (1585–1652), English divine, born in Derby, was a tutor at Cambridge, and from about 1612 held a charge at Boston, Lincolnshire. Cited for his Puritan views before Laud, he in 1633 fled to Boston, Mass., where he preached till his death. His works, nearly fifty in number, include a catechism, forms of prayer, and his defence against Roger Williams of the civil authority in religious matters.

(4) **Sir Robert Bruce** (1571–1631), English antiquary, was born at Denton, Hunts. From Westminster School (the famous Camden his master) he passed to Jesus College, Cambridge, where he graduated B.A. in 1585. At Cotton House in Westminster, on the site of the present House of Lords, he accumulated books, manuscripts, coins, &c., and practised large hospitality. His papers read before the Antiquarian Society spread wide the reputation of his learning; King James knighted him in 1603, created him a baronet in 1611, and frequently consulted him. But he kept the scholar in prison for eight months in connection with the Overbury case (1615–16). Cotton, returned to parliament in 1604, from about 1620 identified himself with the constitutional opposition to the crown. His protest against the proposed debasement of the coinage (1626), his frank criticism of kingcraft in his *Raigne of Henry III* (1627), his *Dangers wherein the Kingdom now Standeth* (1628), and the frequent meeting in his house of Eliot, Pym, Selden and Coke, marked him out to the court as an enemy. A seemingly ironical tract, *A Proposition to Bridle the Impertinency of Parliaments*, having fallen into Wentworth's hands, it was found on inquiry that the original was in Cotton's library, from which a copy had been made, though without his knowledge. Cotton was flung into prison, but released on the occasion of the birth of an heir to the throne (May 29, 1630). His library, however, was not restored to him; and he pined and died. Fourteen of his tracts were collected as *Cotton's Posthuma* in 1651.—His son, **Sir Thomas** (1594–1662), had the books

restored to him; and his great-grandson, **Sir John** (1679–1731), in 1700 bestowed them on the nation.

(5) **Sir Stapleton**. See COMBERMERE.

COTY, (1) **François** (1874–1934), French industrialist and newspaper proprietor, born at Ajaccio in Corsica, built up the famous perfumery firm which bears his name, obtained control of *Figaro* in 1924 and founded the *Ami du Peuple* in 1928. He was a member of the Corsican Senate.

(2) **René** (1882–1962), French statesman, the last president of the French Fourth Republic (1953–59), born at Le Havre, a barrister, was elected a Left Republican deputy in 1923, entered the Senate in 1935 and was minister of reconstruction in 1947, and in 1953 president of France. After the constitutional crisis precipitated by the generals in Algeria in May 1958, he powerfully assisted the return to power of General de Gaulle and the consequent birth of the new constitution and 5th Republic in January 1959, with de Gaulle as his successor.

COUCH, (1) **Sir Arthur Quiller-** (1863–1944), English man of letters, grandson of (2), born at Bodmin, was educated at Clifton College and Trinity College, Oxford, where he was lecturer in Classics (1886–87). After some years of literary work in London and in his native county, where he lived from 1891, he became in 1912 professor of English Literature at Cambridge. He edited the *Oxford Book of English Verse* (1900) and other anthologies, and published volumes of extremely entertaining and illuminating essays, criticism, poems, parodies, &c., among them *From a Cornish Window* (1906), *On the Art of Writing* (1916), *Studies in Literature* (compiled from some of his lectures, 1918–29), and *On the Art of Reading* (1920). By many readers, however, he is remembered for a series of delightfully humorous novels set in a Cornish background, written under the pseudonym 'Q'. See Life by F. Brittain (1947).

(2) **Jonathan** (1789–1870), Cornish naturalist, father of (3), for sixty years doctor at Polperro, his native village, achieved a reputation as an ichthyologist.

(3) **Richard Quiller** (1816–63), son of (2), naturalist, antiquary and expert on old Cornish, was from 1845 a doctor at Penzance.

COUCI, Raoul or **Renaut, Châtelain de** (13th cent.), a French trouvère of about 1207–18.

COUÉ, Émile, *koo-ay* (1857–1926), French doctor, of Nancy, whose system of cures by 'autosuggestion' (Couéism) brought worldwide renown. See C. H. Brooks, *The Practice of Autosuggestion* (1926).

COUES, Elliot, *kowz* (1842–99), American ornithologist, author of *Key to North American Birds* (1872).

COULANGES. See FUSTEL DE COULANGES.

COULEVAIN, Pierre de, pen-name of **Augustine Favre de Coulevain**, *koo-lĕ-vĭ* (1838–1913), whose *L'Île inconnue* (1906; trans. 1911) contained kindly criticism of England and English ways.

COULOMB, Charles Augustin de, *koo-lõ* (1736–1806), born at Angoulême, experimented on friction, and invented the torsion balance for measuring the force of magnetic and electrical attraction. The coulomb, the unit of quantity in measuring current electricity, is named after him.

COULTON, George Gordon (1858–1947), born at King's Lynn, became a lecturer at Cambridge, and vigorously and learnedly wrote *Five Centuries of Religion* (1923 *et seq.*), *Life in the Middle Ages* (1928–29), &c. See his *Fourscore Years* (1943).

COUPERIN, *koo-pě-rĭ*, (1) **Charles** (1638–79), French organist and composer, born at Chaumes-en-Brie, one of the first generation of a celebrated family of musicians. He succeeded his brother (3) as organist of the church of Saint-Gervais, Paris.

(2) **François**, known as ' le Grand ' (1668–1733), son of (1), was born in Paris. He was taught by his father, whom he eventually followed as organist of Saint-Gervais in 1685, holding the post until his death. In 1693 he became organist to Louis XIV, and in 1717 composer-in-ordinary of chamber music to the king, having previously been harpsichord teacher of the royal children. Internationally famous as a harpsichord composer whose principles are enunciated in his textbook *L'Art de toucher le clavecin*, he had a profound influence on Bach. His other compositions include many chamber concertos as well as motets and other church music. See *Couperin and the French Classical Tradition*, by Wilfrid Meller (1956).

(3) **Louis** (1626–61), violinist, organist and composer, brother of (1). He was introduced to Paris and the court by Chambonnières, and was appointed organist of Saint-Gervais.

COUPERUS, Louis, *kow'pěr-üs* (1863–1923), Dutch poet and novelist, born at The Hague, wrote a powerful tetralogy, *The Books of the Small Souls*.

COURBET, Gustave, *koor-bay* (1819–77), French painter, born at Ornans, the son of a farmer, was sent to Paris to study law, but turned to painting. He had little formal art training and scorned the rigid classical outlook, preferring Flemish and Spanish models, especially Velasquez. The founder of Realism, he began exhibiting in 1844 pictures in which everyday scenes were portrayed with complete sincerity and absence of idealism, as *Peasants of Flazey* and *Funeral at Ornans*, both of which were condemned as ' socialistic ' though not painted with any political intent. Perhaps his most famous canvas is the large *Studio of the Painter: an Allegory of Realism*, in the Louvre, a kind of synthesis of his outlook, containing the various types of model which he favoured, some of his friends, and the painter himself. Republican in sympathies, he joined the Commune in 1871, and on its suppression was imprisoned and fined for his part in the destruction of the Vendôme Column. On his release in 1873 he fled to Switzerland and died there at Vevey. See G. Boas, *Courbet and the Naturalistic Movement* (1938).

COURIER, Paul Louis, *koor-yay* (1772–1825), a brilliant French writer, a polished translator from Greek, and a master of irony, was born in Paris. In 1816 he issued the *Pétition aux deux chambres*, a scathing exposure of the wrongs of the peasantry. His masterpiece, *Simple Discours de Paul Louis, Vigneron*

(1821), derided the scheme to purchase Chambord for the Duc de Bordeaux by a ' national offering ', and he was imprisoned. He was assassinated on his estate in Touraine. See memoir in Gaschet's edition (2 vols. 1925), and works by Gaschet.

COURNAND, André Frédéric (1895–), Franco-American surgeon, born in Paris, educated at the Sorbonne, emigrated to the U.S.A. in 1930 and became an American citizen in 1941. A specialist in heart surgery, he was awarded the Nobel prize for medicine in 1956, jointly with Forssmann and Richards. In 1960 he became professor of Clinical Physiology at Columbia University.

COURTAULD, Samuel (1876–1947), as chairman of Courtaulds Limited (founded in 1825 by Samuel Courtauld, descendant of a Huguenot family) promoted the British rayon and nylon industry, and was a patron of art and music.

COURTELINE, Georges, pseud. of **Georges Moinaux** (1860–1929), French dramatist, born at Tours, wrote satirical comedies, many of them one-acters, including *Boubouroche* (1893), *Un Client sérieux* (1897) and *Le Commissaire est bon enfant* (1900). He also published novels, as *Le Train de 8ʰ47* (1888, later dramatized) and *Messieurs les Ronds-de-cuir* (1893).

COURTENAY, Sir William (*c.* 1796–1838), the name assumed in 1832 by a crazy Cornishman, John Nichols Thom, who claimed to be a Knight of Malta and heir to the earldom of Devon. A political and religious maniac, and sometime inmate of Kent County lunatic asylum, he gathered about a hundred scythe-armed followers, asserted that he was the Messiah and possessed the stigmata and the power to work miracles. He was killed with eight of his disciples in Blean Wood, near Canterbury, in a skirmish with troops sent from the city to apprehend him.

COURTHOPE, William John (1842–1917), English poet and critic, born at South Malling vicarage, near Lewes, was educated at Harrow and Oxford, where (1895–1901) he was professor of Poetry. In 1892–1907 he was first civil service commissioner. Among his works are *Addison* (1883), *Pope* (1889) and *History of English Poetry* (6 vols. 1895–1909).

COURTNEY, Leonard Henry, 1st Baron Courtney of Penwith (1832–1918), was born, a banker's son, at Penzance. Educated at St John's Coll., Cambridge, made a fellow (1856), he was called to the bar, and from 1872 to his visit to India (1875–76) was professor of Political Economy at University College London. He wrote for *The Times*, and his pamphlets and magazine articles placed him among the ablest and most advanced *doctrinaire* Liberals, an early advocate for proportional representation and a wide extension of local government. He represented Cornish constituencies 1876–1900, and held minor offices. Created a baron in 1906, he died in 1918. See Life by Gooch.

COURTOIS, Bernard, *koor-twa* (1777–1838), French chemist who in 1811 discovered iodine while studying the liquor obtained in leaching the ashes of burnt kelp. For this he was given a government award, but died in poverty.

COUSIN, *koo-zĭ,* (1) **Jean** (1501–*c.* 1590), French sculptor, glass-stainer and painter, was born at Soucy, near Sens. He was responsible for the stained glass in the church of Saint-Gervais in Paris, in Sens Cathedral, and the Sainte Chapelle in Vincennes. See two works by Didot (1872).

(2) **Jean,** a navigator of Dieppe, for whom, and not Pinzon, has been claimed the discovery of Brazil in 1500. See article by Captain Gambier in *Fortnightly* for January 1894.

(3) **Victor** (1792–1867), French philosopher, was born in Paris. Appointed in 1815 assistant professor to Royer-Collard, he threw himself heartily into the reaction against the sensualistic philosophy of the 18th century, and became an exponent of the Scottish metaphysicians. In 1817 he visited Germany, and studied Kant, Jacobi, Fichte, Schelling and Hegel. For his liberalism he was in 1821 deprived of his offices; and on a second visit to Germany in 1824–25 he was arrested as a Carbonarist at Dresden, and detained for six months at Berlin. On his return to France he took a decided stand against the reactionary policy of Charles X, and, reinstated at the Sorbonne in 1827, exerted great influence on numerous devoted pupils. During 1820–27 he published his editions of Proclus and Descartes and part of his celebrated translation of Plato. After the revolution of 1830, when his friend Guizot became prime minister, Cousin was made a member of the Council of Public Instruction, and in 1832 a peer of France and director of the École Normale. In 1830 he was elected a member of the Academy; in 1840 he became minister of public instruction under Thiers. The revolution of 1848 found in Cousin a friend, and he aided Cavaignac's government. After 1849 he disappeared from public life, living for many years in the Sorbonne; he died at Cannes. His philosophy is eclecticism; sensationalism, idealism, scepticism and mysticism he held to be incomplete rather than false. His brilliant lectures and attractive personality revived the study of philosophy in France. Cousin's chief works are *Fragments philosophiques* (1826), three works on the history of philosophy and ethics (1827–41), a treatise on Kant's philosophy (1842), *Études sur les femmes et la société du XVIIᵉ siècle* (1853), his famous *Du vrai, du beau, et du bien* (1854); books on Aristotle, Locke, Kant and Pascal, and his editions of Abelard and Pascal's *Pensées.* See works by Janet (1885), and Barthélemy St Hilaire (3 vols. 1895).

COUSINS, (1) **Frank** (1904–), British trade-union leader, born at Bulwell, Nottingham, a miner's son, worked in the pits at fourteen, turned lorry driver and by 1938 was a full-time union organizer. In 1955 he was appointed general secretary of the Transport and General Workers' Union. He played a controversial part in the London transport strike (1958) and defying the T.U.C. and the leaders of the Labour Party, aligned his union behind a near unilateral nuclear disarmament policy in 1958. In 1965 he was elected M.P. for Nuneaton, having been appointed minister of technology (1964), a post he resigned in 1966 because of

the government's economic policy, resuming his former union post. He also gave up his parliamentary seat the same year.

(2) **Samuel** (1801–87), English engraver, born at Exeter, in 1814 was apprenticed to S. W. Reynolds, the mezzotinter, and in 1826 started on his own account, and produced the ' Master Lambton ' after Lawrence, which at once established his reputation. It was followed by a long series of plates after Reynolds, Lawrence, Landseer, Millais, &c. Elected an A.R.A. in 1835 and a R.A. Engraver in 1855, he retired in 1880. To the Academy he presented £15,000 to found annuities for poor artists. See Memoir by G. Pycroft (1887).

COUSTEAU, Jacques Yves, *koos-tō* (1910–), French naval officer and underwater explorer, born at Saint-André, Gironde. He invented the Aqualung diving apparatus (1943), and a process of underwater television. In 1945 he founded the French Navy's Undersea Research Group, and became commander of the oceanographic research ship *Calypso* in 1950. He has published *Par 18 mètres de fond* (1946), *La Plongée en Scaphandre* (1948) and *The Silent World* (1953). His film *The Golden Fish* won him an Oscar.

COUSTOU, the name of a French family of sculptors.

(1) **Guillaume** (1678–1746), was the sculptor of the *Chevaux de Marly* at the entrance of the Champs Elysées, Paris.

(2) **Guillaume** (1716–77), son of (1), left works including the bronze bas-relief *Visitation* at Versailles, and the mausoleum of the dauphin (father of Louis XVI) in the cathedral at Sens.

(3) **Nicolas** (1658–1733), brother of (1), was the sculptor of the *Descente de Croix* at Notre Dame.

COUTHON, Georges, *koo-tō* (1756–94), French revolutionary, born at Orcet, near Clermont, in Auvergne, was an advocate at the outbreak of the Revolution. Sent by Puy de Dôme to the National Convention, he demonstrated his shrieking hatred of the priesthood and the monarchy. He became in July 1793 a member of the *Comité de Salut Public.* At Lyons he crushed the insurrection with merciless severity, and outdid himself after his return to the Convention with his frothy ravings against Pitt and England. Robespierre's fall brought down Couthon also; he was thrown into prison, delivered by the mob with whom he was popular, recaptured by the soldiers of the Convention, and executed, with St Just and Robespierre.

COUTTS, Thomas (1735–1822), banker, was the son of an Edinburgh merchant and banker, who was lord provost in 1742–44. He founded the London banking-house of Coutts & Co. with his brother James, on whose death in 1778 he became sole manager. Keen and exact in matters of business, he left £900,000. By his first wife, a servant of his brother's, he had three daughters, who married the Earl of Guilford, the Marquis of Bute and Sir Francis Burdett; in 1815 he married Harriot Mellon (q.v.). See BURDETT-COUTTS; books by Robinson (1929); and a Life by Coleridge (1919).

COVENTRY, Sir John (d. 1682), a staunch Cavalier who had sat in the Long Parliament (1640), and at the Restoration was made a Knight of the Bath. Elected for Weymouth in 1667, he asked, during a debate on playhouses (October 1670) a question reflecting on the king's amours. Charles and his minions were furious, and one December night Coventry was pulled from his coach and his nose slit to the bone. The ' Coventry Act ' made maiming a capital offence.

COVERDALE, Miles (1488–1568), English biblical scholar, born in Yorkshire, studied at Cambridge, was ordained priest at Norwich in 1514, joined the Augustinian Friars at Cambridge, and probably imbibed his liking for the new doctrines from the prior Robert Barnes, who was burned as a Protestant in 1540. According to Foxe, Coverdale was at Hamburg with Tyndale in 1529. His own translation of the Bible appeared in 1535, with a dedication to Henry VIII, and secured the royal licence in 1537. The Prayer Book retains the Psalms of this translation, and many of the finest phrases in our authorized version of 1611 are directly due to Coverdale. In 1538 Coverdale was sent by Cromwell to Paris to superintend another English edition of the Scriptures. Francis I had granted a licence, but during the printing an edict was issued prohibiting the work. Many of the sheets were burned, but the presses and types were hastily carried over to London. Grafton and Whitchurch, the noted printers of that day, were thus enabled to bring out in 1539, under Coverdale's superintendence, the ' Great Bible ', which was presented to Henry VIII by Cromwell. The second ' Great Bible ', known also as ' Cranmer's Bible ' (1540), was also edited by Coverdale, who on Cromwell's fall found it expedient to leave England. While abroad he married, received the degree of D.D. from Tübingen, and acted as Lutheran pastor in Rhenish Bavaria. In March 1548 he returned to England, was well received through Cranmer's influence, and in 1551 was made Bishop of Exeter. On Mary's accession he was deprived of his see, but was suffered to leave the country, at the earnest intercession of the king of Denmark, whose chaplain, Dr Macchabaeus (MacAlpine), was Coverdale's brother-in-law. Returning to England in 1559, he did not resume his bishopric, but was made D.D. by Cambridge in 1563, and in 1564 was collated by Grindal to the living of St Magnus, near London Bridge, which he resigned from growing Puritan scruples about the liturgy in 1566. Most of his works, including letters, were edited for the Parker Society by the Rev. George Pearson (2 vols. 1844–46). See F. Fry, *The Bible by Coverdale* (1867).

COWAN, Sir Walter (1871–1956), British admiral. His earlier naval career included the Brass River and Benin expeditions, the Nile campaign—which brought him a D.S.O. —South Africa and Jutland. Offering his services ' in any rank ' in 1939, he was appointed liaison officer with an Indian cavalry formation, ultimately being captured. Exchanged as ' too old to be dangerous ', he promptly joined a Commando unit, winning another D.S.O. 46 years after the award of the first. He was created K.C.B. in 1919. See L. Dawson, *Sound of Guns* (1949).

COWARD, Sir Noël (1899–1973), English actor, dramatist, and composer of light music, born in Teddington. At the age of fourteen he appeared in *Peter Pan*, and thereafter in other plays, including many of his own. His first play *I'll Leave It to You* (1920), was followed by many successes, including *The Vortex* (1924), *Hay Fever* (1925), *Private Lives* (1930), *Blithe Spirit* (1941), *This Happy Breed* (1943) and *Nude With Violin* (1956), all showing his strong satiric humour and his unique gift for witty dialogue. He wrote the music for, among others, his operetta *Bitter Sweet* (1929) and his play *Cavalcade* (1931), and for a series of revues, including *Words and Music* (1932), with its ' Mad Dogs and Englishmen ', *This Year of Grace* (1928) and *Sigh No More* (1945). He produced several films based on his own scripts, including *In Which We Serve*, *Blithe Spirit* and *Brief Encounter*. He was knighted in 1970. See his autobiographical *Present Indicative* (1937) and *Future Indefinite* (1954), Life by Morley (1969) and study by Greacon (1953).

COWELL, (1) Edward Byles (1826–1903), English Sanskrit scholar, born at Ipswich, from 1856 filled the chair of History in the new Presidency College at Calcutta, becoming also soon after principal of the Sanskrit College. He was from 1867 professor of Sanskrit at Cambridge.

(2) **Henry Dixon** (1897–   ), American composer, born in Menlo Park, Cal. Noted as a leader of the *avant-garde* in American music, he developed many of the idiosyncrasies of his style in youth, before undertaking orthodox studies in the Universities of California and New York. His book, *New Musical Resources*, and *The New Musical Quarterly*, of which he was founder, reflect his interest in experimental composition perhaps more than his own works, where ' progressive ' styles appear with more traditional types of material. He composed more than a dozen symphonies and a large number of other orchestral works.

(3) **John** (1554–1611), English jurist, born at Ernsborough, Devon, was educated at Eton and King's College, Cambridge, where he became regius professor of Civil Law in 1594. His *Interpreter* (1607), a glossary of the legal meanings of words, was assailed by Coke (to whom motives of jealousy have been attributed) for its controversial interpretation of the monarchy, and Parliament ordered it to be burnt by the common hangman.

COWEN, Sir Frederic Hymen (1852–1935), composer, born at Kingston, Jamaica, was brought as a child to England. His early talent was cultivated by study under Benedict and Goss, and at Leipzig and Berlin. He composed operas, cantatas, oratorios, half-a-dozen symphonies, a number of overtures, pianoforte pieces, and minor works, and some 300 songs. In 1888–92 and 1900-07 he was conductor to the Philharmonic, in 1900–10 of the Scottish Orchestra. He was knighted in 1911, and published *My Art and My Friends* in 1913.

COWLEY, (1) Abraham (1618–67), in his own

day considered the greatest of English poets, was born in London, the seventh and posthumous child of a stationer. Attracted to poetry by the *Faërie Queen*, he wrote excellent verses at ten, and at fifteen published five poems. From Westminster School he proceeded in 1637 to Trinity College, Cambridge, and while there wrote, among many other pieces, a large portion of his epic the *Davideis*, its hero King David. During the Civil War he was ejected from Cambridge (1644), but studied at Oxford for another two years. In 1646 he accompanied and followed the queen to Paris, was sent on Royalist missions, and carried on her correspondence in cipher with the king. He returned to England in 1654 and 1655, was arrested, released on £1000 bail, and, perhaps as a blind, took the Oxford M.D. (1657). On Cromwell's death he again went to Paris, returned to England at the Restoration, and, after disappointment, at last received a comfortable provision. He died at Chertsey. Cowley's *Davideis, Pindarique Odes, Mistress*, and graceful essays are in Grosart's edition (1881), and Waller's (1905–06); Gough edited his *Prose Writings* (1914); see also, besides Sprat's and Johnson's *Lives*, studies by Nethercot (1931) and Loiseau (1932).

(2) **Henry Richard Charles Wellesley, Earl** (1804–84), nephew of Wellington, was secretary or ambassador to Vienna, Constantinople, Switzerland (1848), the Germanic Confederation (1851) and Paris (1852–67). He was created Earl Cowley in 1857 and a K.G. in 1866.

COWPER, *koo'per*, (1) **Spencer** (1669–1727), M.P. and judge, brother of (2), was tried in 1699 for the murder of a Quakeress, Sarah Stout. He was acquitted. See Paget, *Paradoxes* (1874).

(2) **William Cowper, Earl** (*c.* 1664–1723), brother of (1), became a barrister in 1688, M.P. for Hertford in 1695, lord keeper of the Great Seal in 1705, Baron Cowper in 1706, lord chancellor in 1707 and 1714, and Earl Cowper in 1718, in which year he resigned, and from a Whig became a leader of the opposition.

(3) **William** (1666–1709), surgeon and anatomist, was born at Petersfield, in Sussex, settled as a surgeon in London, and wrote *The Anatomy of Human Bodies* (1698). See F. J. Cole, *History of Comparative Anatomy* (1944).

(4) **William**, *koo'pèr* (1731–1800), English poet, son of a Great Berkhamstead rector, was educated at Westminster School where Warren Hastings and Churchill the poet were contemporaries. In 1752 he took chambers in the Middle Temple and was called to the bar in 1754. A mental crisis occurred in 1763 when a clerkship in the House of Lords involving an appearance at the bar of the Lords was offered him. Cured temporarily from the resulting collapse, he was received into the household of Morley Unwin, who with his wife Mary contrived to make the poet's stay at Huntingdon happy. On the death of Mr Unwin his widow removed to Olney, which was henceforth to be associated with the name of Cowper. Unfortunately the curate of Olney, John Newton, was precisely the person to undo the work of tranquillizing the sick man. His gloomy piety, imposed on the poet, eventually caused a recurrence of his malady (1773), but the fruit of their association was the *Olney Hymns* (1779), to which Cowper contributed some hymns which are still congregational favourites. In 1779 Newton accepted a charge in London and his absence was at once reflected in a restoration of the poet's spirits. Mrs Unwin (for he needed a directress) suggested to him the writing of a series of moral satires which were published in 1782 along with some occasional pieces which show the lighter side of his talent. Further to engage him in literary activity, Lady Austen now appeared on the scene (1781) as the occupant of Newton's vicarage. It is not known why her friendship with the poet was interrupted two years later, but *The Task*, published in 1785, was the fruit of her suggestion. Cowper's cousin, Lady Hesketh, took her place as literary directress (1786), but Cowper seems to have exhausted himself as a creative poet and now turned only to translations—the Homer, which was not successful (1791), Milton's Latin poems and some French and Italian translations. His genius, however, still shone in the short or occasional piece. 'On Receiving My Mother's Picture' and 'To Mary' owe more perhaps to sentiment than art, but 'Yardley Oak' (1791) is a direct and powerful precursor of the Romantic movement; and out of the darkest period, after Mrs Unwin's death in 1796, comes the wonderful, if tragic, 'Castaway'. The lighter side of Cowper's genius—'John Gilpin', 'Table Talk', the burlesque opening of *The Task*—should not be overlooked, but we think of him as the poet of the evangelical revival and as the precursor of Wordsworth as a poet of Nature. The evangelical revival involved humanitarian ideals in a hard age and these Cowper expressed in such a way as to impress the new middle class with its notions of gentility and piety. His public is Jane Austen's public and he anticipated the humanitarian zeal of the Clapham sect and the 19th-century movement for reform generally. That apart, *The Task* survives for its faithful pictures of the English park (the Throgmortons' little estate) as it existed in the 18th century. Wordsworth is obviously indebted to him, but there is a complete absence of the animism which inspires the greater poet's nature studies. No account of Cowper's works is complete without a reference to his letters, which have charmed generations of readers with their intimacy. They are not all of this kind—those to Newton are morbidly pious and indicate the conflict which lacerated his mind. The most sensitive study of the poet is by Lord David Cecil (1929), but see also those by Fausset (1928) and N. Nicholson (1951).

COX, (1) **David** (1783–1859), English landscape painter, was born at Deritend, a suburb of Birmingham. His father was a blacksmith, and he worked at the forge for a time; after studying drawing under Joseph Barber, he was a travelling scene-painter. He next took lessons in London from John Varley; in 1805–06 visited North Wales, which to the end of his life was his favourite sketching-ground; and taught as a drawing-master from 1814 to 1826 in Hereford, publishing *A Treatise on Landscape Painting*. In 1813 he joined the Society of Painters in Water-colours, to whose exhibitions he was a regular contributor. From 1827 till 1841 London was his headquarters, but he was constantly sketching in the country, and occasionally made brief visits to the Continent. In 1839 he turned his attention seriously to oil-painting, and executed about a hundred works in oil. These are less widely known than his watercolours, but they are of at least equal quality. In 1841 he settled at Harborne, near Birmingham, where he died. It was during this period that he produced his greatest works. They mainly owe their inspiration to the scenery of North Wales, and especially of Bettws-y-Coed, which he visited every autumn. The Birmingham Art Gallery has many examples of his work both in oil and watercolour, as also has the Tate Gallery. See Lives by Solly (1875), Hall (1881), F. G. Roe (1924) and T. Cox (1947).

(2) **David** (1809–85), the younger, son of (1), was also a watercolour painter.

(3) **Edward William** (1809–79), English barrister, recorder of Helston and Portsmouth, spiritualist, and originator or proprietor of the *Law Times*, *Field*, *Queen*, and *Exchange and Mart*, was born at Taunton, and died very rich at Moat Mount, Middlesex. He published much on law, Conservatism, dreams, &c.

(4) **George William** (1827–1902), English mythologist, educated at Rugby School and Trinity College, Oxford, took orders in 1850. Among his works are *Tales of Ancient Greece* (1868), *Aryan Mythology* (1870), *History of Greece* (1874), *Comparative Mythology and Folklore* (1881), *Lives of Greek Statesmen* (1886), and *Life of Colenso* (1888). In 1877 he assumed his uncle's title of baronet, which had not been ratified, and his right to it was subsequently disallowed.

(5) **Richard** (1500–81), English reformer, born at Whaddon, Bucks, and educated at Eton and King's College, Cambridge, became headmaster of Eton, dean successively of Ely, Osney, Christ Church and Westminster (1549), a refugee in Frankfurt (1555–58), where he contended bitterly with Knox, and Bishop of Ely (1559).

COXE, (1) Henry Octavius (1811–81), English librarian, born at Bucklebury, Berks, educated at Westminster and Oxford, entered the British Museum in 1833, and in 1838 the Bodleian Library, of which he became head in 1860. In 1857 he had toured the Levant, discovering many codices. He was rector of Wytham near Oxford, from 1868. Among his works were editions of Roger of Wendover's *Chronicle* (1841–44) and Gower's *Vox Clamantis*; also catalogues of MSS. in the Oxford Colleges and the Bodleian. See Burgon, *Lives of Twelve Good Men* (1888).

(2) **William** (1747–1828), English historian, author of *History of the House of Austria* and thirteen other works of history and travel, was born in London, and from Eton passed to King's College, Cambridge, of which he

became a fellow in 1768. He spent much of twenty years on the Continent, and died a prebendary of Salisbury and archdeacon of Wilts.

COXIE, Coxcie or Coxius, Michiel (1499–1592), Flemish painter, born at Mechelen, introduced the Italian classical style into Flanders. Frescoes in Santa Maria dell' Anima at Rome are his work. He was court painter to Philip II. His son **Raphael** (1540–1616) was also a painter.

COXWELL, Henry Tracey (1819–1900), English aeronaut, born at Wouldham rectory, near Rochester, was educated for the army but settled as a surgeon-dentist in London. From boyhood he had taken a keen interest in ballooning, and in 1845 established the *Aerostatic Magazine*, after then making some 700 ascents—the most remarkable in 1862, when he reached, with Glaisher, a height of seven miles. See his *My Life and Balloon Experiences* (2 vols. 1887–88).

COZENS, (1) Alexander (d. 1786), English watercolour painter, was believed to be one of the two natural sons of Peter the Great by a woman from Deptford who accompanied the Tsar to Russia. After studying in Italy, he came to England in 1746, and died in London.

(2) **John Robert** (1752–*c*. 1799), son of (1), also a watercolour landscape painter, in 1776 visited Switzerland, and in 1783 returned from Italy. In 1794 his mind gave way, and in his later days he was befriended by Sir George Beaumont and Dr Munro. Turner and Girtin copied his drawings, and Constable pronounced that ' his works were all poetry ', that he was ' the greatest genius that ever touched landscape '.

COZZENS, James Gould, *kuz'-* (1903–), American writer, born at Chicago, published his first novel, *Confusion*, at the age of nineteen. He fought in the U.S. Air Force in World War II, and on his release from service wrote the Pulitzer prizewinning *Guard of Honour* (1948). Among his other works are *S.S. San Pedro* (1931), *Ask Me Tomorrow* (1940), *The Just and the Unjust* (1942), *By Love Possessed* (1958) and *Children and Others* (1965).

CRAB, Roger (*c*. 1621–80), English hermit, served (1642–49) in the Parliamentary army and then set up in business as a ' haberdasher of hats ' at Chesham, Bucks; but in 1651 sold off his stock-in-trade, distributing the proceeds among the poor, and took up his residence in a hut, his sole drink water, and his food bran, turnip-tops, dock-leaves and grass. He published *The English Hermite, Dagon's Downfall* and a tract against Quakerism; and died at Bethnal Green.

CRABBE, George (1754–1832), English poet, was born at Aldeburgh on the Suffolk coast, son of a ' salt-master ' and warehousekeeper. His father's violence was offset by his mother's piety. Two of his three brothers perished at sea. His environment was therefore ideally suited for the literary work he was to engage in. Such schooling as he got was irregular, but he managed to pick up enough surgery in a nine months' course in London to enable him to set up poorly as a surgeon in Aldeburgh. This could not be his chosen career, for already literary ambitions had quickened in the lad—he had published *Inebriety, a Poem* in 1775 and *The Candidate.* He ventured to throw himself on the literary world in London in 1780, but penury, unrelieved by appeals to various patrons of letters, was his lot till a lucky application to Burke changed the course of his life. As the guest of Burke at Beaconsfield, he met the noted men of the day and patronage flowed in. He was ordained in 1782 and the next year was established in the Duke of Rutland's seat at Belvoir with the prospect of various livings to follow his chaplaincy there. After his marriage he spent happy years in charges in Suffolk, 1792–1805; returned to Muston in Leicestershire; and finally settled in Trowbridge, Wilts. In 1783 his *The Village* sponsored by Burke and Dr Johnson brought him fame. Twenty-four years passed before *The Parish Register* revealed his gifts as a narrative poet. He followed this up with *The Borough*, a collection of 24 tales in letter-form. *Tales* followed in 1812, showing no diminution of his powers of narrative and character-drawing. *Tales of the Hall* (1819) concluded this remarkable output of narrative genius. Crabbe's manner suited all tastes—he is still read because of his veracity and his masterly genre painting of humble and middle class life. His strict moralism—the miseries of the poor are due to sin and insobriety—no doubt repels us, but we return to grim stories of madness as in ' Sir Eustace Grey ' (*Parish Register*) and the comic wooing in ' The Frank Courtship ' (*Tales*), where his craft is at its best. Masefield revived the manner in *The Everlasting Mercy* and other poems. The *Complete Works*, prefaced by an excellent Life by his son, were issued in 1834, and re-edited with an introduction by E. Blunden in 1947. The Cambridge University Press issued a complete edition of the poems, 1905–07. See also Lives by Ainger (1903) and Huchon (1907).

CRADDOCK, Charles Egbert, pseud. of **Mary Noailles Murfree** (1850–1922), American writer who, born at Murfreesboro, Tenn., wrote from 1884 many tales of mountain backwoods life.

CRAIG, (1) Alexander (*c.* 1567–1627), a worthless Scottish poet, was born at, and died near, Banff.

(2) **Edward Gordon** (1872–1966), English actor and stage designer, the son of Ellen Terry. He was for eight years an actor under Irving, retiring from the stage in 1897; but it was his understanding of the actor's point of view that gave him his special approach to theatrical design. His aim of simplifying the scene and emphasizing the actors was too advanced for England, where his three productions for his mother were failures; but he was acclaimed in Germany, Italy and Russia, where he produced *Hamlet* (1912) at the Moscow Arts Theatre. In 1905 he met Isadora Duncan, with whom he travelled through Europe. He settled in Italy in 1906, published a quarterly, *The Mask*, from 1908 to 1929, and founded a theatrical art school in Florence in 1913. He greatly influenced scenic design in America and Europe, and his published works include *On the Art of the*

Theatre (1911), *Towards a New Theatre* (1913), *Ellen Terry and Her Secret Self* (1931), and the autobiographical *Index to the Story of My Days* (1957).

(3) **Sir James Henry** (1748–1812), a British general who served with distinction in America, the Netherlands, the Cape, Sicily, &c. He was governor of Canada, 1807–11.

(4) **John** (1512–1600), Scottish Reformer, lost his father at Flodden, and was educated at St Andrews. He joined the Dominicans there, but fell under suspicion of heresy, and after a brief imprisonment (1536) went to Rome. Through Cardinal Pole he gained admission to the Dominican convent of Bologna; but Calvin's *Institutes* converted him to Protestantism. On August 18, 1559, he was lying in the dungeon of the Inquisition, condemned to suffer next morning at the stake, when Pope Paul IV died, and the mob set the prisoners at liberty. A bandit befriended him; a dog brought him a purse of gold; he escaped to Vienna, and there preached in his friar's habit, one of his listeners being the Archduke Maximilian. Presently the new pope, learning his whereabouts, demanded his surrender; but Maximilian gave him a safe conduct, and in 1560 he returned to Scotland. In 1563 he was appointed coadjutor to Knox; in 1567 incurred some censure for proclaiming, under strong protest, the banns between Mary and Bothwell: and in 1572 was sent to ' illuminate the dark places ' in Angus and Aberdeenshire. He came back to Edinburgh in 1579 as a royal chaplain, had a share with Melville in the Second Book of Discipline, and drew up the ' Confession of Faith '. See Memoir by T. G. Law prefixed to facsimile reprint of his *Short Summe of the whole Catechisme* (1883).

(5) **Sir Thomas** (1538–1608), Scottish writer on feudal law, was born either at Craigfintray (Aberdeenshire) or in Edinburgh. From St Andrews he passed in 1555 to Paris, and in 1563 was admitted a Scottish advocate, being next year appointed justice-depute of Scotland, and in 1573 sheriff-depute of Edinburgh. Besides an epithalamium on Queen Mary's marriage with Darnley, several more Latin poems, and the masterly *Jus Feudale* (1608; 3rd ed. 1732), he wrote *De Unione Regnorum* (Scottish Hist. Soc. 1910), and Latin treatises on James VI's right to the English throne and on the homage controversy between Scotland and England. See Life by P. F. Tytler (1823).

CRAIGAVON, James Craig, 1st Viscount (1871–1940), Ulster statesman, resolute opponent of Home Rule and the first prime minister of Northern Ireland (1921–40). He was created a baron in 1927.

CRAIGIE, Sir William Alexander (1867–1957), Scottish scholar, born in Dundee, was professor of Anglo-Saxon at Oxford in 1916–25, of English at Chicago 1925–35. He was joint-editor from 1901 of the *New English Dictionary*, editor of the *Dictionary of the Older Scots Tongue* (1931 *et seq.*), &c.

CRAIK, (1) George Lillie (1798–1866), Scottish scholar, born at Kennoway, Fife, studied for the Church at St Andrews, but went to London in 1826, and in 1849 became professor of History and English Literature at Queen's College, Belfast. He wrote much on literary history. His youngest daughter, **Georgiana Marion** (1831–95; Mrs May), was a popular novelist.

(2) **Dinah Maria**, *née* **Mulock** (1826–87), English authoress, was born at Stoke-upon-Trent. Settling in London at twenty, she published *The Ogilvies* (1849), *Olive* (1850), *The Head of the Family* (1851), and *Agatha's Husband* (1853). She never surpassed or even equalled her *John Halifax, Gentleman* (1857), which has been translated into French, German, Italian, Greek and Russian. In 1865 she married George Lillie Craik, nephew of (1) and a partner in the publishing house of Macmillan, and spent a period of quiet happiness and literary industry at Corner House, Shortlands, Kent, where she died. Much of her verse is collected in *Thirty Years' Poems* (1881). She produced in all forty-six works—viz., fourteen more novels and several volumes of prose essays, including *A Woman's Thoughts about Women* (1858) and *Concerning Men, and other Papers* (1888).

CRAMER, Johann Baptist, *krah'mer* (1771–1858), German pianist, was born at Mannheim, the son of Wilhelm Cramer (1745–99), a musician who settled in London in 1772. From 1788 the son undertook concert tours on the Continent, and gained a high reputation. He founded in 1828 a musical publishing firm, and, after some years' residence in Paris, died in London. Most of his compositions are forgotten, but his *Studies* is an important work.

CRAMPTON, Thomas Russell (1816–88), British engineer, born at Broadstairs, was a pioneer of locomotive construction and was responsible for the first successful cross-channel submarine cable, between Dover and Calais, in 1851.

CRANACH, Lucas (1472–1553), German painter, so named from Kronach, near Bamberg, where he was born. He seems to have been instructed by his father, and, becoming in 1504 court painter at Wittenberg to the Elector Frederick, was ennobled. In 1509 he accompanied an embassy to the Emperor Maximilian, and while in the Netherlands portrayed the future Charles V. In 1537, and again in 1540, he was elected burgomaster of Wittenberg. He repaired to Augsburg in 1550 to share the captivity of John Frederick, and on the Elector's release (1552) went with him to Weimar, where he died. His paintings include sacred and a few classical subjects, hunting scenes and portraits. He was closely associated with the German Reformers, many of whom (including Luther and Melanchthon) were portrayed by himself and his pupils. A *Crucifixion* in the Stadtkirche, Weimar, is his masterpiece. His wood engravings are numerous. Of three sons, all painters, the second, **Lucas the Younger** (1515–86), painted so like his father that their works are difficult to distinguish. See German works by Heller (1821), Schuchardt (3 vols. 1851–71), Warnecke (1879), Lindau (1883) and Rosenberg (1932).

CRANBORNE, Viscount. See CECIL.

CRANBROOK, Gathorne Gathorne-Hardy, 1st Earl (1814–1906), British politician, born at Bradford, educated at Shrewsbury and at Oriel College, Oxford, was called to the bar in 1840, and in 1856 was returned as a Conservative M.P. by Leominster. In 1865 he defeated Gladstone in the famous Oxford University election; in 1878 he was made Viscount and in 1892 Earl Cranbrook. He was under-secretary for the Home Department (1858–59), president of the Poor Law Board (1866–67), home secretary (1867–68), war secretary (1874–78), secretary for India (1878–80) and lord president of the Council (1885–92). See Life by his son (1910).

CRANE, (1) **Harold Hart** (1899–1932), American poet, was born in Garrettsville, Ohio. He shows the influence of Walt Whitman, and his most important work is contained in *The White Buildings* (1926), a collection on New York life, and *The Bridge* (1930), an epic using Brooklyn Bridge as its focal point.

(2) **Stephen** (1870–1900), American writer and war correspondent, born at Newark, N.J., became known as a novelist through *The Red Badge of Courage* (1895), a vivid story of the Civil War. See *War Dispatches* (1964) and Life by T. Beer (1936).

(3) **Thomas Frederick** (1844–1927), American folklorist, born in New York City, was educated at Ithaca, New York, and graduated at Princeton in 1864. He was assistant professor of Modern Languages at Cornell in 1868–73, professor of Spanish and Italian there in 1873–84, professor of Romance Languages in 1884–1909. His best-known work is *Italian Popular Tales* (1885).

(4) **Walter** (1845–1915), English painter, poet and socialist, was born at Liverpool, the son of a portrait painter, **Thomas Crane** (1808–59). He was well known as an illustrator of children's books. In 1862 he exhibited *The Lady of Shalott* at the Academy, and he was a constant contributor to the Grosvenor from its foundation in 1877. His work shows the influence of the pre-Raphaelites and of Botticelli. Principal of the Royal College of Art, South Kensington (1898–99), he wrote textbooks on the art of illustration. See his *An Artist's Reminiscences* (1901), and a study by P. G. Konody (1902).

CRANMER, Thomas (1489–1556), Archbishop of Canterbury, was born at Aslacton or Aslockton, Notts, July 2. By his widowed mother he was sent in 1503 to Jesus College, Cambridge, where in 1510 he obtained a fellowship. He forfeited it by his marriage with ' black Joan ' of the Dolphin tavern, but regained it on her death before the year's grace was up; and taking orders in 1523, proceeded D.D. and became a divinity tutor. In 1529 the plague was raging in Cambridge, and Cranmer removed with two pupils to Waltham. Here he met Fox and Gardiner; and their talk turning on the royal divorce, Cranmer suggested an appeal to the universities of Christendom. The suggestion pleased Henry VIII; so Cranmer became a counsel in the suit. He was appointed a royal chaplain and archdeacon of Taunton; was attached to the household of Anne Boleyn's father (Anne at the time being Henry's paramour); and was sent on two embassies, to Italy in 1530 and to Germany in 1532. At Rome the pope made him grand penitentiary of England; at Nuremberg he had married a niece of the reformer Osiander, when a royal summons reached him to return as Warham's successor in the see of Canterbury. He sent his wife secretly over, and himself following slowly, was consecrated on March 30, 1533. He took the oath of allegiance to the pope, with a protest that he took it ' for form's sake '. In May Cranmer pronounced Catharine's marriage null and void *ab initio*, and Anne's, four months earlier, valid; in September he stood godfather to Anne's daughter Elizabeth. It was the same throughout the entire reign. Cranmer annulled Henry's marriage with Anne Boleyn (1536), divorced him from Anne of Cleves (1540), informed him of Catharine Howard's prenuptial frailty and strove to coax her into confessing it (1541). Sometimes he raised a voice of timid entreaty, on Anne Boleyn's behalf, on Cromwell's; still, if Henry said they were guilty, guilty they needs must be. He did what he dared to oppose the Six Articles (1539), one of which made the marriage of priests punishable with death; but he failed to stick to his opposition, and sent away his own wife to Germany, whence he did not recall her till 1548.

A kindly, humane soul, yet he was not ahead of his compeers—More, for instance, or Calvin—in the matter of religious toleration. We cannot acquit him of complicity in the burning of Frith and Lambert for denying Transubstantiation (1533–38), of Friar Forest for upholding the papal supremacy (1538), of two Anabaptists (1538), of Joan Bocher for denying Christ's humanity (1550), and of a Dutch Arian (1551). With the dissolution of the monasteries he had little to do; but he bestirred himself in promoting the translation of the Bible and a service-book, in curtailing the number of holy days, and in negotiating an eirenicon with foreign reformers. On the path, indeed, towards Protestantism, he was ever in advance of Henry VIII, though to Henry he surrendered his right of private judgment as completely as ever Ultramontane to Pope. Henry repaid him with implicit confidence, and twice saved him from the plots of his enemies (1543–45). In 1547 Henry died, and Cranmer sang mass of requiem for his soul. He had been slowly drifting into Protestantism; but now the inrushing tide swept him onward through all those religious changes by which the mass was converted into a communion—changes stereotyped in the Second Prayer Book of 1552. During this as during the preceding reign he meddled little with affairs of state though he was one of the council of regency. What he did do was not too creditable. In gross violation of the canon law he signed Seymour's death warrant; he had a chief hand in the deposition and imprisonment of Bishops Bonner, Gardiner and Day; and won over by the dying boy-king's pleading, he reluctantly subscribed the instrument diverting the succession from Mary to Lady Jane Grey (1553). Herein he was guilty of conscious perjury, yet, the twelve days' reign over, he made no attempt to flee. On

September 14 he was sent to the Tower, on November 13 was arraigned for treason, and, pleading guilty, was condemned to die. In March 1554 he was removed to Oxford. He bore himself bravely and discreetly in a scholastic disputation, as also upon his trial before the papal commissioner, whose jurisdiction he refused to recognize. In October from the jail he witnessed Latimer's and Ridley's martyrdom; and on February 14, 1556, he was formally degraded. And now in rapid succession he signed seven recantations, each more submissive than its predecessor. The last he transcribed on March 21, and forthwith they brought him to St Mary's Church. If not before, he learned at least now from the sermon that he must burn; anyhow, when they looked for him to read his recantation, instead he retracted all that he had written. With a cheerful countenance he then hastened to the stake, and, fire being put to him, thrust his right hand into the flame, and kept it there, crying: ' This hath offended !　Oh this unworthy hand! ' Among Cranmer's forty-two writings, the chief of which have been edited by Jenkyns (4 vols. 1833) and Cox (2 vols. Parker Society, 1844–46), may be noticed his prefaces to the Bible (1540) and the First Prayer Book (1549); the *Reformatio Legum Ecclesiasticarum* (1571); and *A Defence of the Doctrine of the Sacrament* (1550). See *Narratives of the Reformation*, edited by Nichols (Camden Society, 1859), with a sketch of Cranmer by Ralph Morice, his secretary; and books by Dean Hook (*Lives of the Archbishops*, vols. vi.–vii. 1868), Pollard (1905), C. H. Smyth (1926), Deane (1927), Belloc (1931), Maynard (1956), Bromiley (1956).

CRASHAW, Richard (*c.* 1613–49), English religious poet, was born in London, the only son of the Puritan poet and clergyman William Crashaw (1572–1626). From the Charterhouse he proceeded in 1631 to Pembroke Hall, Cambridge, and *c.* 1636 became a fellow of Peterhouse. His Catholic leanings prevented him from receiving Anglican orders, and by 1644 he lost his fellowship for refusing to take the Covenant. He went to Paris, embraced Catholicism, and suffered great distress, until after 1646, through Cowley, he was introduced to Queen Henrietta Maria, who recommended him at Rome; and in April 1649 he became a subcanon at Loretto, but died four months afterwards. In 1634 Crashaw published a volume of Latin poems, *Epigrammatum Sacrorum Liber* (2nd ed. 1670), in which occurs the famous line on the miracle at Cana: ' *Nympha pudica Deum vidit et erubuit* ' (the modest water saw its God and blushed); in 1646 appeared his *Steps to the Temple*, republished at Paris in 1652, under the title *Carmen Deo Nostro*, with 12 vignette engravings designed by Crashaw. See studies by R. C. Wallerstein (1935) and A. Warren (1939).

CRASSUS, (1) **Lucius Licinius** (140–91 B.C.), Roman orator, in 95 was elected consul, along with Quintus Scaevola; and during their consulship was enacted a rigorous law banishing from Rome all who had not the full rights of citizens, which was one of the chief causes of the Social War. Crassus is one of the speakers in Cicero's *De Oratore*, and indeed represents the writer's own opinions.

(2) **Marcus Licinius** (*c.* 115–53 B.C.), surnamed *Dives*, the triumvir, the son of a partisan of Sulla, who on the return of Marius and Cinna to Rome in 87 made away with himself. Cinna subjected the boy to a jealous surveillance, to escape which he went to Spain. He afterwards joined Sulla (83), and distinguished himself in the battle against the Samnites at the gates of Rome. As praetor he crushed the Servile revolt by the conquest of Spartacus at the battle of Lucania (71), and in 72 was made consul with Pompey, a colleague whom he hated. Caesar valued the friendship of Crassus, the richest of Roman citizens. Plutarch estimates his wealth at over 7000 talents, and Pliny states that his lands were worth 8000 talents (say £2,000,000). About 60, Caesar, Pompey and Crassus entered into the first triumvirate. In 55, as consul with Pompey, Crassus had Syria assigned him for his province, and in war against the Parthians, misled by a treacherous guide, he was utterly defeated in the plains of Mesopotamia. Retreating towards Armenia, he was beguiled into a conference with the Parthian general Surenas, and slain. His head was sent to Orodes, who poured melted gold into the lips, saying: 'Sate thyself now with that of which in life thou wert so greedy.' See Oman's *Seven Roman Statesmen* (1902).

CRATINUS (*c.* 519–423 B.C.), a Greek comic poet. Next to Eupolis and Aristophanes, he best represents the Old Attic comedy. He limited the number of actors to three, and was the first to add to comedy the interest of pungent personal attack; even Pericles did not escape. Of his twenty-one comedies, nine of which obtained the first public prize, on one occasion over Aristophanes, we possess only some fragments, collected in Meineke's *Fragmenta Comicorum Graecorum* (Berlin 1840). A younger **Cratinus**, a contemporary of Plato, belonged to the Middle Comedy.

CRATIPPUS (1st cent. B.C.), a Peripatetic philosopher, a native of Mitylene, and a contemporary of Cicero, whose son Marcus he instructed at Athens in 44 B.C. Pompey visited him after Pharsalia, and Brutus turned aside to Athens to hear him, even while making preparations to meet Octavian and Antony. Nothing that he wrote has survived.

CRAVEN, (1) **Lady**. See ANSPACH.

(2) **Mrs Augustus**, *née* **Pauline de la Ferronays** (1808–91), Catholic novelist, was born in London, the daughter of a French emigré, who after the Restoration was French ambassador at St Petersburg and Rome, and for a time French foreign minister. In 1834 she married the young diplomatist, Augustus Craven (d. 1884), a grandson of the Margravine of Anspach. Her best-known work was *Récit d'une sœur* (1865). See Life by Mrs Bishop (1895).

(3) **William, Earl of Craven** (1606–97), English soldier, son of Sir William Craven (1548–1618), a merchant taylor, who became lord mayor of London. Served in the Low Countries on behalf of Elizabeth of Bohemia, and was taken prisoner with Prince Rupert, purchasing his liberty in 1639 and subsequently attaching himself to the exiled queen's court at The Hague. A man of great wealth, he assisted Charles I financially, and his estates were sequestered in 1652 but returned at the Restoration. He had been created a baron in 1627, and was made an earl by Charles II in 1664 and a number of offices were bestowed upon him, including that of lord-lieutenant of Middlesex, but he retained his attachment to Elizabeth of Bohemia.

CRAWFORD, (1) **Francis Marion** (1854–1909), novelist, son of (3), was born in Tuscany. He had his education at Concord, N.H., Trinity College, Cambridge, Karlsruhe and Heidelberg. At Rome he devoted himself to the study of Sanskrit, and during 1879–80 was engaged in press work at Allahabad, where he was admitted to the Catholic church. His first novel, *Mr Isaac*, (1882), was succeeded by *Dr Claudius* (1883), *A Roman Singer* and *An American Politician* (1884), *Zoroaster* (1885), *Saracinesca* (1886), *Marzio's Crucifix* (1887), *With the Immortals* (1888), *The Ralstons* (1895), *Casa Braccio* (1896), *The Heart of Rome* (1903), &c.

(2) **Thomas** (*c.* 1530–1603), of Jordanhill, Renfrewshire, in 1570 captured Dumbarton Castle from Queen Mary's adherents by escalade.

(3) **Thomas** (1814–57), father of (1), sculptor, born in New York City, in 1834 went abroad for his studies, and settled in Rome, where he at first worked under Thorvaldsen. Many of his earlier groups have found a place in Boston collections; his later works include the fine Washington monument at Richmond and the bronze figure of Liberty surmounting the dome of the capitol at Washington. Stricken with blindness in 1856, Crawford died in London.

(4) **William Harris** (1772–1834), American politician, born in Virginia, practised law at Lexington, Georgia, and was elected to the state senate in 1802 and to the U.S. senate in 1807 and 1811. Appointed minister to France in 1813 and secretary of the treasury in 1816, he was a Democratic candidate for the presidency in 1824.

CRAWFORD AND BALCARRES, *bal-kar'is*, (1) **Alexander William Crawford Lindsay, 25th/8th Earl of** (1812–80), born at Muncaster Castle, Cumberland, and educated at Eton and Trinity, Cambridge, succeeded his father in 1869. His researches enabled him in 1848 to establish his father's claim to the Crawford title (the premier earldom of Scotland; cre. 1398). A great book-collector, he wrote *Letters on the Holy Land* (1838), *Progression by Antagonism* (1846), *Sketches of the History of Christian Art* (1847), *Lives of the Lindsays* (1849) and *The Earldom of Mar* (1882). He died in Florence; his body, stolen from the mausoleum at Dunecht, near Aberdeen, was after some months found in a wood close by in July 1882.

(2) **David Alexander Edward Lindsay** (1871–1940), **27th Earl**, grandson of (1), held various portfolios, 1916–22, and became chancellor of Manchester University, 1923.

(3) **James Ludovic Lindsay**, F.R.S., LL.D. (1847–1913), son and successor of (1), president of the Royal Astronomical Society in 1878–80, in 1888 presented to the nation the admirably equipped observatory at Dunecht; the apparatus and library were transferred to the Royal Observatory, Blackford Hill, Edinburgh.

CRAWFURD, (1) **George** (d. 1748), Scottish genealogist, published a Scottish peerage in 1716.

(2) **John** (1783–1868), Scottish orientalist, was born in Islay, and died in London, having served (1803–27) as an East Indian army doctor. He was envoy to Siam, and in 1823 succeeded Sir Stamford Raffles as administrator of Singapore.

CRAYER, Caspar de (1584–1669), a Flemish historical and portrait painter, born at Antwerp, lived at Brussels and at Ghent.

CREASY, Sir Edward Shepherd, *kree'sie* (1812–78), born at Bexley, Kent, from Eton passed to King's College, Cambridge, and in 1834 was elected a fellow. Called to the bar in 1837, he went on the home circuit for over twenty years, and in 1840 was appointed professor of History at London University, in 1860 chief-justice of Ceylon, and knighted. In 1870 he came home invalided on a year's leave of absence, in 1871 went out again, but had to return finally in 1873. He died at Hampton Wick. He was author of *The Fifteen Decisive Battles of the World* (1851), *Invasions of England* (1852), *History of the Ottoman Turks* (1854–56), &c.

CRÉBILLON, *kreb-ee-yõ*, (1) **Claude Prosper Jolyot de** (1707–77), French novelist, younger son of (2), was born in Paris. After writing a number of slight pieces for the stage, he acquired great popularity as an author of licentious stories. In 1740 he married an Englishwoman, Lady Stafford. The indecency of his *Le Sopha, conte moral*, having offended Madame de Pompadour, he was banished from Paris for five years, but on his return in 1755 was appointed to the censorship. He died forgotten.

(2) **Prosper Jolyot de** (1674–1762), French dramatist, was born at Dijon, and educated in Paris for the law. His tragedy of *Idoménée* was successfully produced in 1703. It was followed by *Atrée et Thyeste* (1707), *Électre* (1709), and *Rhadamiste et Zénobie* (1711), his masterpiece. After writing several other pieces, Crébillon fell into neglect and produced nothing for over twenty years. He was then pushed forward as a dramatic rival to Voltaire by Madame de Pompadour, elected to the Academy, awarded a pension of 1000 francs, and appointed royal censor and a royal librarian. His *Catilina* was brought out with great success in 1748. Among his other works were *Xerxès*, *Sémiramis*, *Pyrrhus*, and *Le Triumvirat*. There are editions of his works by Perelle (2 vols. 1828) and Vitu (1885).

CREDI, Lorenzo di (1459–1537), Italian painter, was the fellow-pupil, lifelong friend, and executor of Leonardo da Vinci, and lived and died at Florence. He painted mainly Holy Families, and executed his works with great care. Examples may be seen in the National Gallery and the Louvre.

CREECH, (1) **Thomas** (1659–1700), English translator of Lucretius, was born at Blandford, became headmaster of Sherborne and rector of Welwyn, Herts, and hanged himself for love or penury.

(2) **William** (1745–1815), an Edinburgh bookseller, lord provost in 1811–13, who published the first Edinburgh edition of Burns, the works of Blair, Beattie and Dugald Stewart, and Mackenzie's *Mirror* and *Lounger*.

CREED, Frederick George (1871–1957), inventor, born in Nova Scotia, came to Glasgow in 1897 and there perfected the Creed teleprinter, used in news offices all over the world.

CREEVEY, Thomas (1768–1838), English minor politician remembered for the *Creevey Papers*, a journal important as a source of Georgian social history.

CREIGHTON, Mandell, *krī'tèn* (1843–1901), English historian, born at Carlisle, a fellow of Merton College, Oxford, from 1866, became first professor of Ecclesiastical History at Cambridge in 1884, Bishop of Peterborough in 1891, and of London (1896). His chief works are *Simon de Montfort* (1876), *History of the Papacy during the Reformation Period* (5 vols. 1882–94) and *Queen Elizabeth* (1897). See *Life* (1904) by his wife (1850–1936), herself an educational and social worker.

CREMER, Sir William Randal (1838–1908), English politician, born at Fareham. An active trade unionist and pacifist, he was a strong advocate of British neutrality in the Franco-Prussian war, and founded the Workmen's Peace Association, the germ of the International Arbitration League. In 1903 he won the Nobel peace prize.

CRÉMIEUX, *krem-yœ*, (1) **Benjamin** (1888–1944), French writer and critic, born at Narbonne, is known for his works on modern European literature, including the *XXᵉ siècle* (1924) and for his translation of the plays of Pirandello. He died in Buchenwald concentration camp.

(2) **Isaac Adolphe** (1796–1880), French jurist and politician, born of Jewish parents at Nîmes, became a Paris advocate in 1830, in 1842 entered the Chamber, and in 1848 was a member of the provisional government. Imprisoned at the *coup d'état*, in 1876 he was made a senator. He founded the *Alliance Israélite Universelle*.

CRESPI, (1) **Giovanni Battista** (c. 1557–1633), Italian painter, born at Cerano, regarded by many as second only to Tintoretto as a painter of the high Renaissance period. He also worked as an architect and sculptor. His best works are in Milan, where he died.

(2) **Giuseppe Maria**, called **Lo Spagnuolo** (1665–1747), an Italian painter of the Bolognese school, was born at Bologna, painted religious and mythological subjects showing the influence of the Eclectic school of the Carracci (q.v.).

CRESTIEN DE TROIES. See CHRÉTIEN.

CRESTON, Paul, real name Joseph Guttoveggio (1906–), American composer, born in New York. His musical education did not include any training in composition, but his considerable body of work, including five symphonies and a dozen concertos as well as smaller orchestral and chamber compositions, is firmly classical in its regard for form and abstract musical self-sufficiency.

CRESWICK, Thomas (1811–69), English landscape painter and book illustrator, R.A. 1851, was born at Sheffield. The figures in his paintings were often from the brush of Ansdell, Cooper, Frith, &c.

CREUZER, Georg Friedrich, *kroyt'zèr* (1771–1858), German historian, born at Marburg, from 1804 to 1845 was professor of Philology and Ancient History at Heidelberg. His first and greatest work was his perversely ingenious *Symbolik und Mythologie der alten Völker, besonders der Griechen* (4 vols. Leipzig 1810–12). See Life by B. Stark (Heidelberg 1874).

CRIBB, Tom (1871–1848), English prize-fighter, was born at Bitton, Gloucestershire. His first public contest (Jan. 1805) ended in victory after 76 rounds, but his real progress to the championship began two years later when he was taken in hand by the famous sportsman Captain Barclay-Allardyce (q.v.). He twice defeated both the redoubtable Jem Belcher and the American Negro Molineaux, ultimately retiring unbeaten to a peaceful existence as a London publican.

CRICHTON, James, *krī-tên* (1560–82), the 'Admirable', son of the Scottish lord advocate, Robert Crichton, was born at Elliock, Sanquhar, and educated at St Andrews, where George Buchanan was his tutor, and where he graduated M.A. in 1575. He was for two years in France, apparently in the French army. In 1579 at Genoa he delivered a Latin oration before the senate; in 1580 at Venice he addressed a Latin poem to the then Aldus Manutius, who issued a handbill announcing a great scholastic disputation in which Crichton, athlete, scholar, poet and linguist, was to take part. In 1581 (according to Aldus) Crichton went to Padua and overcame all the scholars there in public disputations. Later he was in Mantua in the service of the duke and here in 1582 (not 1585, as confusion with another James Crichton then in Italy has made out) he was killed in a nocturnal brawl by the duke's son. Johnston in his *Heroes Scoti* (1603) first used the epithet 'admirable' ('*omnibus in studiis admirabilis*'); but Crichton owes his popular reputation mainly to Sir Thomas Urquhart, who wrote a fantastic account of him (*Discovery of a most exquisite Jewel*, 1652)—largely accepted by later biographers, including P. F. Tytler (1819) as well as by Harrison Ainsworth in a novel (1837). Even Aldus, as customarily panegyrical, must be somewhat discounted. Crichton's extraordinary memory is, however, corroborated in Burchelati's *Epitaphiorum Dialogi Septem* (1583); and there is no reason to doubt his linguistic facility or his skill as a fencer. But his printed Latin verses and essays are not brilliant.

CRICK, Francis Harry Compton (1916–), British scientist, educated at Mill Hill and the universities of London and Cambridge, from 1949 carried on research in molecular biology at the Cavendish Laboratory. With J. D. Watson in 1953 he constructed a molecular model of the complex genetic material deoxyribonucleic acid (DNA); later researches on the nucleic acids have led to far-reaching discoveries concerning the genetic code. With Watson (1) and Wilkins he was awarded the Nobel prize for medicine and physiology in 1962.

CRILLON, Louis des Balbes de Berton de, *kree-yõ* (1541–1615), French general, called 'Le Brave', was born at Murs in Provence, and, still a boy, covered himself with glory at the siege of Calais and the capture of Guines —later at Dreux, Jarnac and Moncontour. Wounded at Lepanto (1571), he was yet sent to carry the news of the victory to the pope and the French king. He abhorred the massacre of St Bartholomew, but took part in the siege of La Rochelle in 1573, and eventually died at Avignon. See Life by Montrond (5th ed. 1874).

CRIPPEN, Hawley Harvey (1862–1910), American murderer, born in Michigan, studied medicine and dentistry there and in London (1883), and in 1896 came again to London, eventually settling there with his second wife, Cora Turner, originally Kunigunde Mackamotski, who had an unsuccessful career as 'Belle Elmore', opera singer and music hall star, and led her husband an impossible domestic life. Having transferred his affections to his secretary, Ethel le Neve, Crippen, on January 31st, 1910, after a party at their home at Hilldrop Crescent, Holloway, poisoned his wife, dissected the body, and, having destroyed the bones by fire, interred the remains in the cellar. He told his wife's friends that she had left for America and had suddenly died there. After the police had investigated, albeit unsuccessfully, Ethel, now installed in the house, took fright, and the pair fled to Antwerp, where they boarded an Atlantic liner as Mr and Master Robinson. The suspicious captain, who had read reports of the second and successful search at Hilldrop Crescent, contacted Scotland Yard by radio-telegraphy (the first use of radio for police purposes), a detective disguised as a pilot was dispatched by a faster vessel, and the couple were arrested. They were both tried at the Old Bailey, and Crippen was executed at Pentonville on November 23. See account of the trial by F. Young (2nd ed. 1950).

CRIPPS, (1) Charles Alfred (1852–1941), 1st Baron Parmoor (1914), English lawyer and statesman, wrote a standard work on the law of compensation (1881); sat as a Conservative in 1895–1900, 1901–06, 1910–14; in the war of 1914–18 upheld the right of conscientious objection; afterwards championed the League of Nations; and, as lord president of the Council, was in the Labour governments of 1924 and 1929–31. See his *A Retrospect* (1936).

(2) **Sir Richard Stafford** (1889–1952), British Labour statesman, economist, chemist and patent-lawyer, son of (1) and of Theresa, sister of Beatrice Webb (q.v.), was born in London. At Winchester, he won a scholarship to New College, Oxford, his chemistry papers attracting the attention of Sir William Ramsay, who persuaded him to work in his laboratory at University College London instead. At 22 he was part-author of a

paper read before the Royal Society. He also pursued legal studies and was called to the bar in 1913, became the youngest barrister in the country in 1926 and made a fortune in patent and compensation cases. In 1930 he was appointed solicitor-general in the second Labour government, but refused to serve in MacDonald's Coalition. From then until the outbreak of World War II, Cripps was associated with a succession of extreme left-wing movements, at first pacific in character, but later, as the Nazi threat increased, concerned with rallying everyone, and not only Socialists, to active opposition to Chamberlain's policy of appeasement, in a 'Popular Front' which brought about his expulsion from the Labour Party in 1939 and forced him to sit as independent M.P. throughout the war. In 1940 he became ambassador to Moscow. The year 1942, however, under Churchill's leadership, saw his extraordinary rise to political power. In February he became lord privy seal and leader of the Commons, during the summer he was sent to India with the famous 'Cripps offer' of dominion status for a united India, rejected by both Gandhi and Jinnah, and finally in November he succeeded Beaverbrook in the vital post of minister of aircraft production which he held for the remainder of the war. When Labour came to power in July 1945, Cripps was readmitted to the party and appointed president of the Board of Trade. In 1947 he became the first minister of economic affairs and within a few weeks succeeded Dalton as chancellor of the Exchequer. In this last office Cripps established a moral and intellectual ascendancy over Parliament and the country, scarcely known since Gladstone. His at first unpopular policy of 'austerity' caught the public conscience. The trade unions took the unprecedented step of imposing a voluntary wage freeze. He only began to be challenged when he devalued the pound in September 1949. Illness from overwork forced his resignation in October 1950, leaving behind a number of brilliant disciples in Gaitskell, Wilson and Jay. Cripps firmly believed that politics was a proper sphere for the practice of Christianity. He was elected rector of Aberdeen University (1942–45), F.R.S. in 1948 and made C.H. in 1951. See his *Towards a Christian Democracy* (1945), &c., and Lives by E. Estorick (1949) and C. Cooke (1957).

CRISPI, Francesco (1819–1901), Italian statesman, born at Ribera, Sicily, was called to the bar, but, joining the revolutionary movement of 1848, had to flee to France. He organized the successful movement of 1859–60, and re-entered Sicily with Garibaldi. In the restored kingdom of Italy he became deputy, president of the chamber, minister, and in 1887–90, and again in 1894, premier—a member of the Left, strongly anticlerical, and maintaining the alliance with Germany at the cost even of alienating France. Bank scandal vilification failed, but in 1896 the Abyssinian disaster of Adowa compelled his resignation.

CRISPIN, St (martyred 287), under the reign of Diocletian fled, with his brother St Crispinian, from Rome and worked as a shoemaker in Soissons, while striving to spread Christianity. He and his brother suffered martyrdom by being thrown into molten lead.

CRISTOFORI, or Cristofali, Bartolommeo, -*tof'*- (1655–1731), harpsichord-maker, the inventor about 1710 of the pianoforte, was born at Padua, and died at Florence. See Life by Puliti (Florence 1874).

CRITIAS (5th cent. B.C.), a pupil of Socrates, but rather a hearer than a doer of his word. On his return to Athens from banishment, he headed the oligarchical party, and was afterwards the worst of the thirty tyrants set up by the Spartans (404 B.C.). In the same year he fell at Munychia, resisting Thrasybulus and the exiles. He had a high reputation as an orator, and wrote poetry.

CRIVELLI, Carlo (*c.* 1435–93), painter, born at Venice, worked much at Ascoli. His *Annunciation* is in the National Gallery. See study by G. Rushforth (1900).

CROCE, Benedetto, *krō'chay* (1866–1952), Italian idealist, philosopher, historian, critic and senator, born at Pescasseroli, Aquila, was buried and lost his parents and sister in an earthquake on the island of Ischia (1883), studied at Rome, and in Naples devoted himself at first to literature and antiquarian studies, founding the bimonthly review, *La Critica*, in 1903. He developed a phenomenology of the mind (*Lo Spirito*) in which the four principal activities of the mind, art and philosophy (theoretical), political economy and ethics (practical), do not oppose, as they do for Hegel, but complement each other. His theory of aesthetics with its denial of the physical reality of the work of art, is set out in the first volume of *Lo Spirito* and considerably influenced Collingwood (q.v.). In 1910, Croce became senator and was minister of education (1920–21) when with the rise of Mussolini he had to resign his professorship at Naples. His opposition to totalitarianism continued to find expression in many anti-Hegelian, anti-Marxian and anti-Fascist articles and studies, not least in *History as the Story of Liberty* (trans. Sprigge 1941), for which he was severely censured by his pro-Fascist colleague, Gentile (q.v.). With the fall of Mussolini in 1943, he played a leading rôle in resurrecting Liberal institutions in Italy. He also wrote literary studies of Goethe, Dante, Ariosto and Corneille. See his *Autobiography* (trans. Collingwood, 1927), study by R. Piccoli (1922), and collected studies, ed. Schilpp (1947).

CROCKETT, (1) David (1786–1836), American backwoodsman, distinguished himself against the Creek Indians in Andrew Jackson's campaign of 1814, in 1821 was elected to the Tennessee state legislature, and in 1826 to congress. He died fighting for Texas at the battle of the Alamo. Highly embellished stories of his exploits have assumed mythological proportions. See his autobiography, and Lives by C. Rourke (1934) and J. A. Shackford (1956).

(2) **Samuel Rutherford** (1860–1914), Scottish 'kailyard' novelist, born near New Galloway, Kirkcudbright, became in 1886 Free Church minister at Penicuik, but resigned for a literary career in 1895. In 1893 he

attained fame with his sketches, *The Stickit Minister*. *The Raiders* (1894) had a great success, and was followed by *The Lilac Sunbonnet*, *Men of the Moss Hags*, &c.

CROCKFORD, William (1775–1844), a London fishmonger, founded a famous gaming club (1827).

CROESUS, *kree'-sus* (reigned 560–546 B.C.), the last king of Lydia, succeeded his father, Alyattes, in 560 B.C. He made the Greeks of Asia Minor his tributaries, and extended his kingdom eastward from the Aegean to the Halys. His conquests, his mines, and the golden sand of the Pactolus made his wealth proverbial. Cyrus defeated and imprisoned him (546) but his death is a mystery.

CROFT, (1) Sir Herbert, Bart. (1751–1816), from 1786 vicar of Prittlewell, Essex, but from 1802 a bankrupt debtor on the Continent, wrote a memoir of Dr Young for Johnson's *Lives of the Poets*, besides *Love and Madness* (1780), &c.

(2) **William** (1677–1727), English organist and composer, born at Nether Eatington, Warwickshire, in 1700 became a chorister in the Chapel Royal, in 1704 joint organist, and in 1707 sole organist. In 1708 he succeeded his old teacher, Dr Blow (q.v.), as organist of Westminster Abbey and choirmaster of the Chapel Royal; and in 1713 he took his Mus.Doc. at Oxford. Thirty of his anthems for state ceremonies were printed in 1724.

CROFTS, Ernest (1847–1911), English battle painter, born at Leeds, was educated at Rugby, studied art in London and at Düsseldorf, and became keeper of the Royal Academy.

CROKE, (1) Richard (1489–1558), English Greek scholar, who was born and died in London, studied at Cambridge, Oxford, and Paris, lectured on Greek at Leipzig and at Cambridge after his return (1517) to England. Ordained a priest in 1519, he was sent to Italy (1529–30) to further Henry VIII's divorce, and in 1531 became rector of Long Buckby, near Daventry.

(2) **Thomas William** (1824–1902), born near Mallow, in 1874 became R.C. Bishop of Auckland, New Zealand, and in 1870 Archbishop of Cashel. He was a strong Nationalist.

CROKER, (1) John Wilson (1780–1857), British politician, was born at Galway, the son of the surveyor-general of Irish customs. After four years at Trinity College, Dublin, in 1800 he entered Lincoln's Inn, but in 1802 was called to the Irish bar. Two satires on the Irish stage and on Dublin society (1804–1805) proved brilliant hits; so did his *Sketch of Ireland Past and Present* (1807), a pamphlet advocating Catholic emancipation. In 1809 he helped to found the *Quarterly*, to which he contributed 260 articles. He had entered parliament for Downpatrick in 1807; and now in 1809 he was rewarded with the lucrative secretaryship of the Admiralty for his warm defence of the Duke of York *in re* Mary Anne Clarke (q.v.). That post he held till 1830, and then retired with a pension of £1500. After 1832, he refused to re-enter parliament; he would not even take office under Peel, his old friend (1834); and with Peel he broke utterly on the repeal of the

Corn Laws (1846). Among the seventeen works that he wrote or edited were his *Stories for Children from English History* (1817), which suggested the *Tales of a Grandfather*; the *Suffolk Papers* (1823); his *Boswell's Johnson* (1831); and *Essays on the Early French Revolution* (1857). He is better remembered for his onslaught on Keats, and Macaulay's onslaught on him (Macaulay 'detested him more than cold boiled veal'); and as the originator of the term Conservative, a founder of the Athenaeum Club, and the 'Rigby' of Disraeli's *Coningsby*—the jackal of 'Lord Monmouth' (the Marquis of Hertford). See his *Correspondence and Diaries*, edited by Jennings (3 vols. 1884), and Life by Brightfield (1951).

(2) **Thomas Crofton** (1798–1854), Irish folklorist, born at Cork, was from 1818 to 1850 a clerk at the Admiralty. As a boy of fourteen he had begun to collect songs and legends of the Irish peasantry; in 1818 he sent Moore nearly forty old Irish melodies; and in 1825 published anonymously his *Fairy Legends and Traditions of the South of Ireland*, a work which charmed Scott and was translated into German by the brothers Grimm (1826). A second series followed in 1827, and the whole reached a 6th edition in 1822. Of nearly twenty more works the best were *Researches in the South of Ireland*, (1824), *Legends of the Lakes* (1829) *The Adventures of Barney Mahoney* (1832) and *Popular Songs of Ireland* (1839). See Life by his son, prefixed to *Fairy Legends* (1859).

CROLL, James (1821–90), Scottish physicist, was born at Little Whitefield, near Coupar-Angus. He received an elementary school education, but in science was wholly self-trained. Successively millwright, insurance-agent and keeper of the museum of Anderson's College, Glasgow, he was on the Scottish Geological Survey 1867–81. Made an F.R.S. and LL.D. in 1876, he died at Perth in 1890. Among his works were *Climate and Time* (1875) and *The Philosophical Basis of Evolution* (1890). See his *Autobiography* (1896).

CROLY, George (1780–1860), Irish poet, romance-writer, biographer and preacher, was born at Dublin, and educated at Trinity College. He took orders in 1804, and coming in 1810 to London, in 1835 became rector of St Stephen's, Walbrook. From 1817 he published some forty works—the best-known the romance of *Salathiel*. See Memoir prefixed to his *Book of Job* (1863).

CROME, (1) John ('Old Crome') (1768–1821), English landscape painter, the chief of the 'Norwich School', was born in that city, the son of a poor weaver. After serving as an errand-boy to a physician, he was apprenticed to a housepainter (1783); but procured employment as a drawing-master. He was mainly influential in founding, in 1803, the Norwich Society of Artists, of which he was president in 1808. He occasionally visited London, where he exhibited in the Academy and the British Institution; and a tour through Belgium and France in 1814 resulted in *The Fishmarket on the Beach*, *Boulogne* and *The Boulevard des Italiens*, *Paris*. But his subjects were nearly always derived from the scenery of his native county, which, though founding on the Dutch landscapists, he treated in a singularly direct and individual fashion. His works realized only most moderate prices during his lifetime; but he is now recognized as one of the great English landscapists. He practised, though rarely, as a watercolour painter; and his etchings of *Norfolk Picturesque Scenery* were published in 1834. See studies by Binyon (1897), Baker (1921), Mottram (1931).

(2) **John Bernay** (1794–1842) (' Young Crome '), son of (1), likewise painted landscapes.

CROMEK, Robert Hartley (1770–1812), English engraver, born in Hull, published Blair's *Grave* with Schiavonetti's engravings after Blake. He visited Scotland to collect and publish the *Reliques of Burns* (1808) and *Select Scottish Songs* (1810), and meeting Allan Cunningham, published his fabrications in *Remains of Nithsdale and Galloway Song* (1810).

CROMER, Evelyn Baring (1841–1917), **Earl** (1901), was born at Cromer, and entered the Royal Artillery in 1858. Secretary to his cousin, Lord Northbrook, when viceroy of India (1872–76), controller-general of Egyptian finance (1879–80), and finance minister of India (1880–83), in 1883–1907 he was agent and consul-general in Egypt. G.C.B., K.C.S.I., O.M., he was made a baron in 1892, a viscount in 1899. See Life by Marquess of Zetland (1932), and his own *Modern Egypt* (1908), *Abbas II* (1915), *Political and Literary Essays* (1908–16).

CROMPTON, Samuel (1753–1827), English inventor of the spinning-mule, was born, the son of a small farmer, at Firwood near Bolton, Lancashire. When he was old enough, he assisted his mother (a widow from 1759) on the farm, wove, and fiddled at Bolton theatre. At twenty-one he was so much annoyed at the breaking ends of yarn that he set to work to invent a spinning-machine better than Hargreaves'. After five years' labour, in 1779 he framed a machine which produced yarn of such astonishing fineness that the house was beset by persons eager to know the secret. His machine was such that any mechanic who saw it could carry away the leading features, so he could not leave the house for fear of his discovery being stolen. He had spent every farthing he had; he had no funds wherewith to obtain a patent; and a Bolton manufacturer persuaded him to disclose the invention to the trade, under the promise of a liberal subscription: all that he got was £67. 6s. 6d. Soured by this treatment, in the course of time he saved money enough to begin manufacturing on a small scale at Oldhams, near Bolton, and latterly at Bolton, but not till his rivals had already outpaced him. After the use of the mule had told distinctly on British manufacturing prosperity, a sum of between £400 and £500 was raised for him by subscription, and efforts were made to procure him a national reward. Five thousand pounds was all he obtained in 1812, and he returned to Bolton almost broken hearted. He tried bleaching at Over Darwen, then failed as partner in a cotton firm. Some friends purchased him an annuity of £63. He died at Bolton. See Life by French (2nd ed. 1860).

CROMWELL, (1) Oliver (1599–1658), was born at Huntingdon, the son of Robert Cromwell, younger son of Sir Henry Cromwell of Hinchinbrook, whose father was a Welshman, Richard Williams, who took the surname of his uncle and patron, Thomas Cromwell, Earl of Essex. Oliver's mother was a daughter of Sir Thomas Steward of Ely. He was first cousin to John Hampden. Educated at Huntingdon grammar school and at Sydney-Sussex College, Cambridge, he seems to have carried away a modest share of classical and general culture, and went to London to study law. In 1617 his father died, leaving him a moderate estate at Huntingdon; and in 1620 he married Elizabeth, daughter of Sir James Bourchier, a London merchant. He embraced Puritanism in its most enthusiastic form, and supported the ministry of its proscribed preachers. In 1628 he sat for Huntingdon in the stormy third parliament of Charles, raising his voice against Romanizing ecclesiastics; and then returned to farming at Huntingdon, whence he removed to St Ives and afterwards to Ely, where property had been left him by his uncle. He appears to have come into collision as a local patriot with the king's commissioners for the drainage of the Fens. He sat for Cambridge in the Short and Long Parliaments (1640); in the latter, though no speaker, he was vehement on the Puritan side. When war broke out (1642) he vigorously organized his district for the parliament; and as captain of a troop of horse fought at Edgehill. Now he formed his unconquerable Ironsides, combining rigid discipline with strict morality and organized enthusiasm. While the cause of the parliament was depressed elsewhere, his constancy, capacity and courage upheld it in the eastern counties, which had formed themselves into an association. In 1644 he, under Manchester, joined the Scots before York, and at Marston Moor the charges of his cavalry decided the day. He now stood forth as the leader of the Independent and thoroughgoing party against the Presbyterian moderates; and while the Presbyterian and aristocratic generals were set aside by the Self-denying Ordinance, he, under Fairfax, led the new model army to decisive victory at Naseby, June 14, 1645. As representative of the army in its contest with the Presbyterian parliament, he marched on London, and coerced the parliament. It was no doubt under his directions that Joyce carried off the king from Holmby, though it seems that Cromwell desired to make terms with the king. As a prisoner in the Isle of Wight, the king, while he was negotiating with the parliament, was carrying on intrigues with his partisans in England and Scotland, which brought on the second Civil War and the invasion of England by Hamilton. After swiftly quelling the insurrection in Wales, Cromwell marched northwards, and totally destroyed the invading army of Hamilton at Preston. The soldiery now clamoured for justice on the king; and Cromwell, despairing of any arrangement with the faithless Charles, brought him to trial, and signed the death-warrant (January 1649). The Commonwealth having been established, Cromwell suppressed the Levellers, and was next sent to Ireland to end the Civil War still raging there. This he did effectually, and on the whole humanely, though it cost some strokes of sanguinary severity, the necessity for which he himself deplored. On his return from Ireland he (Fairfax having declined) took the command against the Scots, who had called in Charles II. Invading Scotland, he was out-generalled by Leslie, and was in extreme peril, when a false move of the Scots enabled him to win the decisive victory of Dunbar. The Royalists proper having marched into England, he followed, and on September 3, 1651, at Worcester, gained his victory which ended the Civil War—his ' crowning mercy '. He now declared for a constitutional settlement and an amnesty; while the parliament, reduced by revolutionary expulsions to the ' Rump ', was bent on perpetuating its own power. After fruitless negotiations Cromwell turned it out with unwise violence and contumely. Supreme power being now in the hands of himself and the other chiefs of the army, he called the Puritan convention, nicknamed the Barebones Parliament; but the Barebones Parliament proving too visionary and revolutionary, it was dismissed, and supreme power reverted to Cromwell and his officers. Cromwell was now declared Protector under an instrument which provided for government by a single person with one (reformed) House of Parliament and a Council of State, the Protector's nominees to which required election by the parliament (December 16, 1653). The Protector's power of legislating by ordinance till parliament should meet was largely used by Cromwell for reorganization and reform. But when parliament met, it fell to questioning his authority, and he was compelled to exclude the disaffected by a test. His second parliament, from which the recalcitrants were excluded at the outset, offered him the title of king. Cromwell wavered; but the stubborn resistance of the republican soldiers decided him to decline the offer. The Upper House was, however, restored; the Protector was empowered to name his successor; fixed revenue was voted to him; and he was installed as Protector with a ceremonial resembling a coronation. When parliament met again, its two Houses fell into a collision which compelled Cromwell to dissolve it; and his power thenceforth rested upon the army, though it was his constant desire to revert to constitutional government. His protectorate was a perpetual conflict with republican resistance on the one hand and with royalist plots and risings on the other, while his life was constantly threatened by royalist assassins. Yet he was able to inaugurate a great policy, home and foreign. He reorganized the national church on the principle of comprehension, including all but Papists, Prelatists and Antitrinitarians, while the ministry was weeded by commission. He upheld toleration as far as he could, and curbed the persecuting tendencies of parliament. For law reform he did his best. He united Scotland and Ireland to England, giving them both representation in parliament. Scotland, having free trade with England, enjoyed great prosperity under his rule. Ireland he sought to make a second England in order and industry, though his measures were high-handed. He saved the universities from the fanatics, put good men at their head, and encouraged letters. But his foreign policy brought him most renown. Under him the Commonwealth became the head and protectress of Protestant Europe. He made peace with Holland, tried to form a league of all the Protestant states, and protected the Waldenses. In the interest of religious liberty and commerce he allied himself with France against Spain. He took Jamaica, and Blake's naval victories over the Spaniards brought at once glory and treasure. His troops, with those of France, won the battle of the Dunes, and he obtained Dunkirk. He sedulously fostered British commerce, and by the hand of Blake chastised the pirate states of Barbary. His boast that he would make the name of Englishman as respected as that of Roman had been was justified. His court was simple and frugal, yet dignified; and though there was a strain of coarseness in his character (as illustrated in occasional horseplay), his bearing in public upheld the majesty of the state. His speeches are very rough and unmethodical, but they are marked by sense, force and intensity. He was fond of music, and not without regard for art. It seems that his government was striking root; but disease and care, together with grief at the death of his favourite daughter, Lady Claypole, cut short his life. He died September 3, 1658, and the fabric of government which his mighty arm had sustained fell speedily to the ground. Of his greatness as a soldier and statesman there can be no question, but it is difficult to pronounce how far ambition mingled with higher motives; religious enthusiasm is often associated with fanaticism and self-deception. He was laid with great pomp in the tomb of the kings at Westminster, but after the Restoration his body was gibbeted at Tyburn and afterwards buried there. See Noble (1787) and Waylen (1892; new ed. by J. G. Cromwell, 1897) for the family history; Carlyle, *Cromwell's Letters and Speeches* (1846); Lives or studies by Goldwin Smith (1867), F. Harrison (1888), R. F. D. Palgrave (1890), Church (1894), S. R. Gardiner (1897), Roosevelt, Firth, Morley (1900), Buchan (1934), C. V. Wedgwood (1939), M. Ashley (1957), P. Young (1962) and works at CHARLES I and II.

(2) **Richard** (1626–1712), was the third son of (1), but by the deaths of two elder brothers, Robert and Oliver, became his father's heir. He was an amiable and popular but weak man, devoted to field-sports and pleasure. When the Protector had been empowered to nominate his successor, an effort was made to train Richard to the work of government, but in vain. Scarcely had he entered on the Protectorship when the forces of anarchy, both parliamentary and military, broke loose; finding himself unable to restrain them, and deep in debt, he abdicated in May 1659. After the Restoration he lived abroad as

John Clarke; but he returned to England about 1680, and lived and died at Cheshunt.

(3) **Thomas** (*c.* 1485–1540) (*malleus monachorum*, ' the hammer of the monks '), was the son of a Putney blacksmith, cloth-shearer, brewer and innkeeper. During eight or nine years passed on the Continent (1504–1512) he seems to have served as a common soldier, to have been befriended at Florence by Frescobaldi the banker, to have acted as clerk at Antwerp and to a Venetian merchant, to have visited Rome, and to have traded on his own account at Middelburg. Anyhow, by 1513 he was back in England and married; there, step by step, he rose to wealth and importance as a wool-stapler and a scrivener, half-usurer, half-lawyer, having originally been bred to the law. Wolsey employed him as early as 1514; through Wolsey, probably, he got into parliament (1523); he was Wolsey's chief agent in the unpopular work of suppressing certain smaller monasteries for the endowment of his colleges at Ipswich and Oxford (1525); and finally he became his factotum and secretary. He was cheaply faithful to the cardinal, aiding him not only by quick-witted advice and by pleading his cause in parliament, but even with £5 out of his own savings. Withal, he made himself friends of Wolsey's enemies; and his fidelity ingratiated him with Henry VIII. Him Cromwell promised to make the richest king ever in England, and counselled him to cut the knot of the divorce by declaring himself supreme head of the church. Counsel and promise were carried into effect by the Act of Supremacy (1534) and by the dissolution of the monasteries (1536–39). To abolish papal authority, break the power of the church, humble the nobility and make the king absolute were Cromwell's aims; in their accomplishment he stuck at nothing. At heart, it would seem, still a Catholic—for so late as 1535 he bequeathed £46 for a priest to sing mass for his soul—he yet did his utmost to Protestantize the English Church; and that English ' Terror ', in which perished More and Fisher and hundreds of lowlier victims, set in with Cromwell's rise and ebbed with Cromwell's fall. Among the posts and honours showered on him were those of privy councillor (1531), chancellor of the Exchequer (1533), secretary of state and master of the rolls (1534), vicar-general (1535), lord privy seal and Baron Cromwell of Oakham (1536), knight of the Garter and dean of Wells (1537), lord great chamberlain (1539), and finally Earl of Essex (1540). But the hatred of all, the Catholic reaction, and Henry's aversion to Anne of Cleves, consort of Cromwell's choosing, combined to effect his ruin; within eight weeks he was sent to the Tower. His abject entreaties and his revelations of Henry's discourse with him touching Anne of Cleves availed him nothing. Condemned under a bill of attainder, he was bunglingly beheaded on Tower Hill, July 28, 1540. See Lives by Merriman (1902) and Wilding (1935).

CRONIN, Archibald Joseph (1896–   ), Scottish novelist, born at Cardross, graduated in medicine at Glasgow (1919), but in 1930 abandoned practice for literature and at

once was successful with *Hatter's Castle* (1931). Subsequent works include *The Citadel* (1937), *The Keys of the Kingdom* (1941), *Beyond this Place* (1953), *Crusader's Tomb* (1956) and *A Song of Sixpence* (1964).

CRONJE, Piet (1835–1911), Boer general (1881 and 1899–1900) in the wars with Britain, defeated Methuen at Magersfontein but surrendered to Lord Roberts at Paardeberg (1900).

CRONSTEDT, Axel Fredrik, Baron (1722–1765), Swedish metallurgist who first isolated nickel (1751) and noted its magnetic properties. He made a useful chemical classification of minerals and also discovered a zeolite (a water-softening silicate).

CROOK, George (1829–90), American soldier, born in Ohio, served in the Civil War as Federalist and in 1866–77 against the Indians in Idaho, Arizona, and, crushing the great rising, in Wyoming and Montana.

CROOKES, Sir William (1832–1919), O.M., born in London, was a pupil and assistant of Hoffmann at the Royal College of Chemistry, next superintended the meteorological department of the Radcliffe Observatory, Oxford, and from 1855 lectured on Chemistry at the Science College, Chester. In 1859 he founded the *Chemical News*, and in 1864 became also editor of the *Quarterly Journal of Science*. F.R.S. in 1863, in 1880 he was awarded by the *Académie des Sciences* 3000 francs and a gold medal. In 1898 he was president of the British Association, in 1887 of the Chemical Society, and in 1913 of the Royal Society. He was a high authority on sanitation; discovered the metal thallium in 1861, the sodium amalgamation process in 1865, &c.; improved vacuum tubes and promoted electric lighting; invented the radiometer (1873–76) and the spinthariscope; and was the author of *Select Methods of Chemical Analysis* (1871), and of works on diamonds, beetroot sugar, wheat, dyeing, calico-printing and psychical research. He was knighted in 1897.

CROSBY, Harry, better known as **Bing** (1904–   ), American singer and film star, born in Tacoma, Washington. Specializing in light comedy rôles, with his distinctive style of crooning he is one of the best-known names in the entertainment world. By the end of 1933 he was among the ten most popular stars in motion pictures and held an undisputed lead among radio singers. The following year he came into his own in the field of gramophone records, and thereafter maintained his popularity in all three spheres. He began his career playing the drums in the evenings while he was still at school and later became one of the trio known as Paul Whiteman's Rhythm Boys. See his *Call Me Lucky* (1953).

CROSS, (1) Charles Frederick (1855–1935), English chemist (F.R.S. 1917), who with Edward John Bevan (1856–1921) invented the modern method of producing artificial silk.

(2) **Henri Edmond.** See SIGNAC, P.

(3) **Marian.** See ELIOT, GEORGE.

CROSSE, Andrew (1784–1855), English electrician, born at Fyne Court, Somerset, was educated at Bristol and at Brasenose, Oxford.

His principal researches concerned the artificial formation of minerals by processes of electrical deposition and the improvement of wines, cider, &c., by electricity. His announcement in 1837 that under certain circumstances organisms (of the genus Acarus) appeared in solutions of inorganic substances excited much attention but more ridicule. See Memoir (1857) by his second wife (d. 1895), and her *Red Letter Days of my Life* (1892).

CROSSLEY, Sir Francis (1817–72), English carpet manufacturer and philanthropist, was born and died at Halifax, for which he was Liberal M.P. from 1852 till 1859 (then for the West Riding), and to which he presented a public park (1857) at a cost of £41,000, besides almshouses and an orphanage. He was made a baronet in 1863.

CROTCH, William (1775–1847), English composer, was born at Norwich. A carpenter's son, at two he could play *God Save the King*, and in 1779 was performing in London as a musical prodigy. In 1797 he became professor of Music at Oxford, and in 1822 first principal of the Royal Academy of Music. He composed many pieces for the organ and piano, two oratorios, ten anthems, &c., and wrote *Elements of Musical Composition* (1812) and *Styles of Music of all Ages* (1807–18). He died suddenly at Taunton.

CROWE, (1) **Catherine**, *née* Stevens (1800–70), English writer, born at Borough Green, Kent, in 1822 married Lt.-Col. Crowe, and spent great part of her later life in Edinburgh. Her mind was morbid and despondent, ever hovering on the borderline of insanity, which it crossed once in one violent but brief attack. Her translation of Kerner's *Seeress of Prevorst* (1845) prepared the way for her well-known *Night-side of Nature* (1848), a collection of stories of the supernatural. She wrote also tragedies, juvenile books and novels—the best *Susan Hopley* (1841) and *Lilly Dawson* (1847).

(2) **Mrs.** See BATEMAN (2).

(3) **Sir Joseph Archer** (1825–96), English art-writer, born in London, studied art for seven years in Paris and travelled on the Continent, where in 1847 he met Cavalcaselle (q.v.). He was a special correspondent in the Crimea, Indian Mutiny and the Franco-Austrian war; and in 1857–59 was director of the School of Art at Bombay. In 1860 he was appointed consul-general at Leipzig and afterwards at Düsseldorf; in 1882 commercial attaché at Paris. C.B. in 1885, K.C.M.G. in 1890, he died at Gamburg (Baden). See his *Reminiscences* (1895).

CROWQUILL, Alfred. See FORRESTER.

CROWTHER, Samuel Adjai (1812–91), bishop of the Niger territory, born in Ochugu, to the east of Dahomey, was carried off as a slave in 1819, and sold more than once, but taken by a British man-of-war and landed at Sierra Leone in 1822. He was baptized in 1825, taking the name of a London vicar; conducted a mission school at Regent's Town; accompanied the Niger expeditions of 1841 and 1854; was ordained in London in 1842, and consecrated bishop in 1864. A D.D. of Oxford, he translated the Bible into Yoruba. See J. Page's *The Black Bishop* (1908).

CRUDEN, Alexander (1701–70), born at Aberdeen, took his M.A. at Marischal College, and, after ten years' tutoring, in 1732 started as a bookseller in London. In 1737 appeared his admirable *Concordance of the Holy Scriptures*. It was dedicated to Queen Caroline, who promised to 'remember him', but died a few days later. Cruden now lapsed into insanity, and for ten weeks was kept in a madhouse, as again for a fortnight in 1753. Earning meanwhile his livelihood as a press-reader, he assumed the title of 'Alexander the Corrector', and in 1755 began to go through the country reproving Sabbath-breaking and profanity. But many a good and kindly action was interwoven with his crackbrained courtships, his dreams of knighthood and a seat in Parliament. Just back from a visit to Aberdeen, he died at his prayers in his Islington lodgings. See *Lives* by A. Chalmers, prefixed since 1824 to the *Concordance*, and by E. Olivier (1934).

CRUFT, Charles (1852–1939), English showman, was for many years general manager of James Spratt, dog-biscuit manufacturers. He organized the first dog show in 1886, and the annual shows since then have become world-famous. Through his influence the popularity of dogs has increased and the standards of dog-breeding have been greatly improved.

CRUIKSHANK, George, *krook'shank* (1792–1878), caricaturist and illustrator, was born in London, the son of Isaac Cruikshank (c. 1756–1811), who, as well as his eldest son, **Isaac Robert** (1789–1856), was also a caricaturist. He thought at first of the sea as a profession, but, some of his sketches having come under the notice of a publisher, was induced to illustrate children's books and songs. *The Scourge* (1811–16) afforded scope for his genius, and from thenceforth he pursued this, his true vein. His illustrations for Hone's political squibs attracted attention; but in the exquisite series of coloured etchings contributed to the *Humorist* (1819–1821), and in the etchings to the *Points of Humour* (1823–24), his fine artistic power began to be visible. This best period of his art culminated in the etchings to *Peter Schlemihl* (1823) and to Grimm's *German Popular Stories* (1824–26), which latter, now extremely scarce, was reproduced in 1868, with a preface by Ruskin. Similar in artistic aims and in method are the spirited little woodcuts contributed to *Italian Tales* (1824), *Mornings at Bow Street* (1824–27), and Clark's *Three Courses and a Dessert* (1830). His numerous plates in *Bentley's Miscellany* and *Ainsworth's Magazine* mark a third period, in which he aimed at greater elaboration and completeness, and frequently attained great power of tragic design. The finest specimens of this period are the great series to Dickens's *Oliver Twist* and Ainsworth's *Jack Sheppard*, *Guy Fawkes, The Tower of London, Windsor Castle* and *The Miser's Daughter*, of which, as of *Oliver Twist*, he thirty years afterwards claimed the chief authorship. Among the best productions of his later years are the large and elaborate etchings to Brough's *Life of Sir John Falstaff* (1858). As a water-colourist he left work marked by considerable skill and delicacy; and in his later years he

devoted himself to oil-painting, showing more humour, fervour and inventive ability than artistic power. His *Worship of Bacchus* (1862) is a vigorous protest against drunkenness; and to the cause of temperance he also devoted many of his designs, especially the powerful series of *The Bottle* (1847). He died February 1, 1878, and is buried in St Paul's. There are collections of his works in the British Museum, and in the Victoria and Albert Museum. See A. M. Cohn's Catalogue (1914), Marchmont's *The Three Cruikshanks* (1898), and Lives by Bates (2nd ed. 1879), Jerrold (2nd ed. 1883), Stephens (1891) and Douglas (1903).

CRUM BROWN, Alexander. See BROWN (1).

CRUSIUS, Christian August (1715–75), German philosopher, a forerunner of Kant, died a professor at Leipzig. See study by Heimsoeth (1926).

CRUVEILHIER, Jean, *krü-vayl-yay* (1791–1874), French anatomist, pioneer of the descriptive method, born at Limoges, became professor of Pathology at Montpellier in 1824 and of Pathological Anatomy in Paris in 1836.

CSIKY, Gregor, *chi'kee* (1842–91), Hungarian dramatist, born at Pankota, Vilagos, Hungary. A professor of Theology at Temesvar seminary, he published some tales from religious history (Photographs from Life), and in 1875 a comedy, *Jaslot* (The Oracle), which was a success. Other plays followed, comedies like *Mirkány Kariar* and *Anna*, and tragedies, *Janus, The Magician, Theodora*. Csiky also translated Sophocles, Plautus, and Molière into Hungarian, as well as several English plays. *Az Ellenallhatatlan* (The Irresistible), which won a prize from the Hungarian Academy, typifies his talent for a direct, fresh approach to his subject.

CSOKONAI VITEZ, Mihaly, *cho'ko-noy vi'tays* (1773–1805), Hungarian poet, born at Debrecen, Hungary, and professor of Poetry at the university there until his dissipated way of life lost him the post. His fame persists, however, chiefly through his lyrics, which stem from the brimming source of Hungarian folksong. Among his works are *Magyar-Musa* (1797); *Anacreontic Poems* (1903); and *Dorottya* (1804), a mock-heroic poem. See his collected works (ed. Maxton; 1831).

CSOMA DE KÖRÖS, Alexander, *chö'mö* (1784–1836), a Hungarian traveller, born in the Transylvanian village of Körös. In 1820 he started for Central Asia, finding his way in Asiatic dress by Baghdad and Tehran to Bokhara, thence by Kabul and Lahore to Kashmir and Tibet, which he visited for the third time (1827–31). At Calcutta he completed his Tibetan grammar and dictionary and was appointed librarian to the Asiatic Society, but in January 1836 he started on another journey to Tibet, only to die of fever six days after reaching Darjeeling. See English Life by Dr Theodore Duka (1885).

CTESIAS, *tes'ee-as* (5th cent. B.C.), a Greek historian of Persia, was physician to Artaxerxes Mnemon, and accompanied him in the expedition against his rebellious brother Cyrus, 401 B.C. See Gilmore's edition of *The Fragments of Ktesias' Persika* (1888).

CTESIBIUS, *tes-ib'ee-oos* (fl. 2nd cent. B.C.), a Greek inventor in mechanics, was the teacher of Hero of Alexandria.

CUBITT, (1) Thomas (1788–1855), English builder, born at Buxton, revolutionized trade practices in the building industry, and was responsible for many large London projects, including Belgravia, and the East front of Buckingham Palace.

(2) **Sir William** (1785–1861), English inventor, born at Dilham, Norfolk, had been a miller, cabinetmaker and millwright until 1812, and then chief engineer in Ransome's works at Ipswich, in which he was a partner 1821–26. He removed to London in 1823. The Bute Docks at Cardiff, the Southeastern Railway and the Berlin waterworks were by him. He also invented the treadmill; and for his services in connection with the Great Exhibition buildings he was knighted in 1851.

CUDWORTH, Ralph (1617–88), chief of the 'Cambridge Platonists', was born at Aller, in Somerset, in 1632 entered Emmanuel College, Cambridge, in 1639 was elected a fellow, and became a popular tutor. In 1645 he was appointed master of Clare Hall and regius professor of Hebrew; in 1650 rector of North Cadbury, Somerset, and in 1654 master of Christ's College; in 1662 rector of Ashwell, Hertfordshire; and in 1678 prebendary of Gloucester. He died at Christ's College. His *True Intellectual System of the Universe* (1678), portentously learned, ample and discursive, aimed to establish the reality of a supreme divine Intelligence against materialism. His sermon before the House of Commons (1647) shows the best features of the Latitudinarian school. His important *Treatise Concerning Eternal Morality* was published in 1731. See monographs by Lowrey (1884), W. R. Scott (1891), G. Aspelin (1943).

CUEVA, Juan de la (*c.* 1550–1607), a Spanish poet and dramatist, born at Seville, and known especially for his use of new metrical forms and his introduction of historical material into the drama.

CUGNOT, Nicolas Joseph (1725–1804), French engineer, about 1770 invented a three-wheeled steamdriven carriage with a speed of almost 2½ m.p.h.

CUI, César Antonovich, *koo-ee'* (1835–1918), Russian composer, was born at Vilna, the son of a French teacher. An expert on fortification, he became lieutenant-general of engineers. Practically a self-taught musician, he composed *William Ratcliff* (1861) and other operas, &c.

CUJACIUS, properly **Jacques de Cujas** or **Cujaus** (1522–90), French jurist, was born at Toulouse, and died a professor at Bourges. His complete works were edited by Fabrot (10 vols. 1658). See study by P. F. Girard (1916).

CULLEN, (1) Countée (1903–46), American Negro poet, born in New York, began his literary career with *Color* (1925), a book of poems in which classical models such as the sonnet are used with considerable effect. He published several subsequent volumes of verse, a novel *One Way to Heaven* (1932), and collaborated with Arna Bontemps in the play *St Louis Woman* (1946).

(2) **Paul** (1803–78), Irish cardinal, was born near Ballitore, County Kildare. After a brilliant course in the Propaganda College at Rome he was ordained priest in 1829, and was successively vice-rector and rector of the Irish College in Rome and rector of the Propaganda College. In 1850 consecrated Archbishop of Armagh and Primate of Ireland, he commenced a vigorous reign of twenty-eight years. His denunciations of Fenianism made him many enemies among the more hot-headed Irishmen but greatly increased the respect of English Protestants. Translated to Dublin in 1852, he was created a cardinal priest in 1866, the first Irishman to attain that dignity. He died at Dublin.

(3) **William** (1710–90), Scottish physician, was born at Hamilton. After some experience as an apprentice apothecary in Glasgow, on board ship and in London, he studied at Edinburgh under Munro, and started practice in his native town. William Hunter (q.v.) was a pupil. In 1740 Cullen graduated M.D. at Glasgow, established himself there as a physician, and lectured on medicine. In 1751 he was appointed to the chair of Medicine, but in 1755 removed to Edinburgh, where for thirty-five years he occupied successively the chairs of Chemistry, Institutes of Medicine, and Medicine, besides teaching clinically in the Infirmary. To him is largely due the recognition of the important part played by the nervous system in health and disease. He bitterly opposed the Brunonian system (see BROWN, JOHN). Cullen's chief works are *Synopsis Nosologiae Methodicae* (1769); *Institutions of Medicine* (1772); *Practice of Physic* (1776–84); *Treatise of Materia Medica* (1789). See Life by Thomson and Craigie (2 vols. 1832–59).

CULPEPER, (1) **John**. See COLEPEPER.

(2) **Nicholas** (1616–54), English physician, born in London, studied at Cambridge, and started in 1640 to practise astrology and physic in Spitalfields. In 1649 he published an English translation of the College of Physicians' Pharmacopoeia, *A Physical Directory*, renamed in 1654 *Pharmacopoeia Londinensis, or the London Dispensatory*. This infringement of a close monopoly, together with his Puritanism, brought Culpeper many enemies. In 1653 appeared *The English Physician Enlarged, or the Herbal*. Both books had an enormous sale, and both are included in Dr Gordon's collective edition of his Works (4 vols. 1802).

(3) **Sir Thomas** (1578–1662), born of good Kentish family, studied at Hart Hall, Oxford, and at one of the Inns of Court, was knighted in 1619, and bought Leeds Castle in Kent, where, or at Greenway Court, near Hollingbourn, he mostly lived. His *Tract against Usurie* (1621) contended for the reduction of interest to six per cent.

(4) **Sir Thomas** (1626–97), third son of (3), studied at University College, Oxford, and having made the Grand Tour, and been knighted soon after the Restoration, retired to Greenway Court. Besides editing his father's treatise in 1668, he himself wrote pamphlets on usury. He wrote also *Essayes or Moral Discourses* (1655–71).

CULVERWEL, Nathanael (d. 1651?), one of the Cambridge Platonists, born in Middlesex, entered Emmanuel College in 1633 and was elected fellow in 1642. His vigorous *Light of Nature* (1652) was edited in 1857 by John Brown, D.D., of Edinburgh, with an essay by Cairns. See Campagnac's *Cambridge Platonists* (1902) and G. P. H. Pawson's *Cambridge Platonists* (1930).

CUMBERLAND, Dukes of (1). See Ernest Augustus, king of Hanover.

(2) See George V, king of Hanover.

(3) **William Augustus** (1721–65), second son of George II, adopting a military career, was wounded at Dettingen in 1743, and defeated, not ingloriously, at Fontenoy by Marshal Saxe in 1745. Sent next to crush the Young Pretender's rebellion, he did so effectually at Culloden (1746), and by his cruelties earned the lasting title of ' Butcher ' to set off against his reward of £25,000 a year. In 1747 he was defeated by Saxe at Laffeld, and in 1757 had to surrender at Kloster-Zeven, after which he retired. See works by Campbell-Maclachlan (1876), E. Charteris (1913). Also see CLIFFORD.

CUMBERLAND, Earls of. See CLIFFORD.

CUMBERLAND, (1) **Richard** (1631–1718), philosopher, born in London, was educated at St Paul's School and Magdalen College, Cambridge, and became rector of Brampton, Northamptonshire (1658), vicar of All Saints, Stamford (1667), and bishop of Peterborough (1691). His *De Legibus Naturae* (1672), written in reply to Hobbes, founds morality on a utilitarian basis.

(2) **Richard** (1732–1811), playwright, was born in the lodge of Trinity College, Cambridge. He was the great-grandson of Bishop Cumberland and maternal grandson of Dr Richard Bentley. From Bury St Edmunds and Westminster, where he was contemporary with Cowper, Churchill and Warren Hastings, he passed to Trinity College, Cambridge, and was a fellow at twenty. Becoming private secretary to Lord Halifax, he gave up his intention of taking orders. As secretary to the Board of Trade (1776–82), he undertook a secret mission to Spain (1780) which cost him £4500, a sum that ministers refused to reimburse when the Board was suppressed. Having obtained a compensation allowance of about half his salary, Cumberland retired to Tunbridge Wells, where he wrote farces, tragedies, comedies, pamphlets, essays and two novels, *Arundel* and *Henry*. Of his comedies may be named *The West Indian, The Brothers, The Fashionable Lover, The Jew* and *The Wheel of Fortune*. Cumberland is alluded to in Goldsmith's *Retaliation* with not unkindly satire as ' the Terence of England, the mender of hearts '; in Sheridan's *Critic* he is gibbeted as ' Sir Fretful Plagiary '. See his rambling Memoirs (2 vols. 1807).

CUMMINGS, Edward Estlin (1894–1962), American writer and painter, born at Cambridge, Mass., was educated at Harvard. His best-known book, *The Enormous Room* (1922), describes his wartime internment in France. Other successful works were *Tulips and Chimneys* (1923), *Eimi* (1933) and collections of poems in modern style employing unorthodox rhythmic and linguistic devices such as the omission of capitals. He studied art in Paris, and a collection of his drawings and paintings was published in 1931.

CUMMINS, Maria Susanna (1827–66), American writer, born at Salem, Mass., with her first novel, *The Lamplighter* (1854), scored enormous popular success.

CUNARD, Sir Samuel (1787–1865; bart. 1859), born at Halifax, Nova Scotia, succeeded early as a merchant and shipowner, came to England in 1838, and, for the new steam rail service between Britain and America, joined with George Burns, Glasgow, and David McIver, Liverpool, in founding (1839) what became the Cunard Line. The first passage (1840) was that of the *Britannia*, in 14 days 8 hours.

CUNNINGHAM, (1) Sir Alan Gordon (1887–), British general, brother of (3), from Kenya in 1941 struck through Italian Somaliland and freed Abyssinia and British Somaliland from the Italians. He was high commissioner for Palestine (1945–48).

(2) **Allan** (1784–1842), Scottish poet and man of letters, was born in Keir parish, Dumfriesshire. His father was neighbour to Burns at Ellisland; and Allan, a boy of twelve, followed at the poet's funeral. At ten he was apprenticed to a stonemason brother, but continued to pore over songs and stories. His first publications were his sham-antique verse and prose contributions to Cromek's *Remains of Nithsdale and Galloway Song* (1810). Hogg he already knew, and these gained him the acquaintance of Scott, with whom ' Honest Allan ' was always a great favourite. He now removed to London, and became one of the best-known writers for the *London Magazine*, as well as manager in Chantrey's studio (1815–41). Among his works were *Traditional Tales of the English and Scottish Peasantry* (1822); *Songs of Scotland, Ancient and Modern* (1825); *Lives of British Painters, Sculptors, and Architects* (6 vols. 1829–33); and *Life of Wilkie* (3 vols. 1843). Of his five sons, Captain **Joseph Davey** (1812–51) and Major-General **Sir Alexander** (1814–93) both served in the Indian army; the former wrote a good history of the Sikhs (1849), and the latter many books on Indian architecture and statistics; **Peter** (1816–1869) is remembered by his *Handbook of London* (1849; recast by H. Wheatley, 3 vols. 1891); and **Francis** (1820–75), also an Indian soldier, edited Marlowe, Massinger and Ben Jonson.

(3) **Andrew Browne, 1st Viscount Cunningham of Hyndhope** (1883–1963), British admiral, was educated at Stubbington and Dartmouth, entering the Royal Navy in 1898. Service in the 1914–18 war brought him a D.S.O. and two bars. Duty as deputy-chief of the Naval Staff (1938–39) was followed by appointment as c.-in-c. Mediterranean, where his victory in the battle of Cape Matapan virtually eliminated the Italian battle fleet from the war. His intrepidity and resource were equally valuable in the evacuation of Crete. He was promoted to first sea lord in 1943. A peerage and the O.M. were conferred on him in 1946. See his memoirs, *A Sailor's Odyssey* (1951).

(4) **William**, D.D. (1805–61), Scottish divine, a chief leader of the Disruption, was born at Hamilton, and, educated–at Edinburgh, became minister at Greenock (1830) and Edinburgh (1834), then professor (1843) and principal (1847) at the Free Church College. He wrote on theology and church history. See Life by Rainy and Mackenzie (1871).

(5) **William** (1849–1919), Scottish economist, author of the pioneer *Growth of English Industry and Commerce* (1882), which in revised form remained a standard work for many years, reaching a 6th edition in 1929. He was born in Edinburgh and, educated there and at Cambridge, taught history at Cambridge, economics at King's College, London, and in 1907 was made archdeacon of Ely.

CUNNINGHAME GRAHAM, (1) Robert, originally Robert Graham (d. 1797), Scottish laird and songwriter, grandfather of (2), born on the family estates at Gartmore, Stirlingshire. His mother was a daughter of the 12th Earl of Glencairn. He was educated at Glasgow University, became a planter and receiver-general in Jamaica, was chosen rector of Glasgow University on his return in 1785 and was M.P. (1794–96). He warmly supported the French Revolution, moved an abortive bill of rights and composed ' If doughty deeds my lady please ' and other lyrical poems. On the death of the last Earl of Glencairn in 1796, he succeeded to the latter's estates and changed his name to Cunninghame Graham.

(2) **Robert Bontine** (1852–1936), Scottish author and politician, grandson of (1), was born in London, educated at Harrow and from 1869 was chiefly engaged in ranching and adventuring in the Argentine, until he succeeded to the family estates in 1883. In 1879 he had married a Chilean poetess. He was M.P. (1886–92) and was imprisoned with John Burns, the Socialist Leader, for 'illegal assembly ' in Trafalgar Square in 1887. He was the first president of the Scottish Labour party in 1888. He travelled extensively in Spain and Morocco (1893–98), where an incident described in his *Mogreb-El-Acksa* (1898) inspired Shaw's *Captain Brassbound's Conversion*. He wrote a great number of travel books, but is best known for his highly individual, flamboyant essays and short stories, collections of which are entitled *Success* (1902), *Faith* (1909), *Hope* (1910), *Charity* (1912) and *Scottish Stories* (1914). He was elected the first president of the Scottish National party in 1928 and died in Buenos Aires. Conrad and Hudson were among his close literary friends. See A. F. Tschiffely, *Don Roberto* (1937), and *The Essential Cunninghame Graham*, ed. Bloomfield (1952).

CUNOBELINUS. See CYMBELINE.

CUREL, François, Vicomte de (1854–1928), French dramatist, novelist and Academician (1918), born at Metz, was trained as an engineer.

CURETON, William, D.D., LL.D. (1808–64), English Syriac scholar, born at Westbury, Shropshire, in 1837 entered the British Museum as assistant-keeper of MSS. Here he brought to light a Syriac version of the Epistles of Ignatius (q.v.) and other MSS. He was a canon of Westminster.

CURIE, Pierre (1859–1906), French physicist, and his wife, **Marie**, née **Sklodowska** (1867–1934), born at Warsaw, worked jointly at Paris on magnetism and radioactivity, and discovered radium. Son of a Paris physician, M. Curie became professor of Physics at the Sorbonne in 1901, shared a Nobel prize with his wife and Becquerel in 1903, and was run over and killed in Paris. Mme Curie, who succeeded to his chair, isolated polonium and radium in 1910, and got a Nobel prize in 1911. She was appointed honorary professor of Radiology at Warsaw in 1919. See also JOLIOT-CURIE, and Life by Ève Curie (Eng. tr. 1938). Their second daughter **Ève** (1904–), born in Paris, became well known as a musician and writer, and during World War II worked in the U.S.A. on behalf of the French resistance movement.

CURLL, Edmund (1675–1747), a London bookseller, gibbeted by Pope in the *Dunciad*. He was twice (1716 and 1721) at the bar of the House of Lords for publishing matter regarding its members; was tried and convicted for publishing obscene books (1725), fined (1728) for the issue of *Nun in Her Smock* and *De Usu Flagrorum*, and pilloried for his *Memoirs of John Ker of Kersland*. His announcement of *Mr Pope's Literary Correspondence* (1735) led to the seizure of the stock, and furnished Pope (who instigated its publication) with a sufficient excuse for the issue of an authentic edition (1737–41). Curll did not deal solely in garbage, as a list of his contains 167 standard works. His *Curliad* (1729) is styled a 'hypercritic upon the Dunciad Variorum'. It was of Curll's biographies that Arbuthnot wittily said they had added a new terror to death.

CURRAN, John Philpot (1750–1817), Irish orator, was born at Newmarket in County Cork. At Trinity College, Dublin, he was as idle and reckless as he had been at school, but yet learnt something of law; and the boisterous taproom debates of his life in Dublin and London shaped him into an orator. After two years at the Middle Temple, London, he was called to the Irish bar in 1775. Here his conviviality, wit and eloquence soon made him a prominent figure, and led to his being employed in many of the greatest causes of the time. In 1782 he became king's counsel, and in 1783 was returned to the Irish parliament for Kilbeggan. He became a strong supporter of Grattan, but his eloquence proved less effective in the House than before an Irish jury. His sarcastic retorts involved him in duels, of which, in the course of his career, he fought five, all fortunately without serious harm. Although a staunch Protestant, Curran had a warm sympathy with his suffering Catholic countrymen, and was constant in his unavailing appeals on their behalf to government. With his defence of Archibald Hamilton Rowan in 1792 commenced the long series of defences in state trials which have shed such a lustre on his name. Curran flung himself into the defence of the rebels of 1798 with heroic energy. Then came the Union, which Curran had always opposed as 'the annihilation of Ireland'. His own health was now shattered

and domestic troubles darkened his later years. His wife eloped with a clergyman, and his youngest daughter, Sarah, died in Sicily a few months after the hapless fate of her lover, Robert Emmet. (MacDonagh's *Viceroy's Postbag*, 1904, deals with Curran as a 'heartless and inhuman scoundrel' in her regard.) In 1806–14 he was master of the rolls in Ireland. From London his remains were re-interred in Glasnevin Cemetery, Dublin, in 1834. See Lives by his son, W. H. Curran (1819), and L. Hale (1958).

CURRIE, James (1756–1805), Scottish physician, the earliest editor of Burns, born at Kirkpatrick-Fleming manse, Dumfriesshire, studied medicine at Edinburgh and Glasgow, and from 1780 practised in Liverpool. His chief medical work was the able *Reports on the Effects of Water in Febrile Diseases* (1797); but he is best remembered by his edition of Burns (1800; 7th ed. 1813), with a Life and criticism of the writings, undertaken solely for the benefit of Burns's family. See Life by his son (1831).

CURTIN, John (1885–1945), Australian trade-union leader, journalist and Labour politician, born at Creswick, Victoria, in 1941 became Commonwealth premier and in the Japanese war proved a far-seeing and intrepid national leader.

CURTIS, (1) **Benjamin Robbins** (1809–74), and (2) **George Ticknor** (1812–94), two brothers, born at Watertown, Mass., both writers on legal subjects, and the latter also a biographer. See *Memoir* of the former (2 vols. 1879).

(3) **George William** (1824–92), American man of letters, born in Providence, Rhode Island, after four years in Europe (1846–50) joined the staff of the New York *Tribune*, and was one of the editors of *Putnam's Monthly* from 1852 to 1869. He commenced the 'Editor's Easy Chair' papers in *Harper's Monthly* in 1853, and became principal leader-writer for *Harper's Weekly* on its establishment in 1857. A novel, *Trumps* (1862), and most of his books appeared first in these journals. He died at New York. See *Lives* by Winter (1893), Chadwick (1893) and Cary (1894).

CURTIUS, (1) **Ernst** (1814–96), German archaeologist, born at Lübeck, studied at Bonn, Göttingen and Berlin, visited Athens with Brandis in 1837, and next accompanied Ottfried Müller in his travels through Greece. Tutor (1844–49) to the Crown Prince Frederick of Prussia, in 1856 he succeeded Hermann as professor at Göttingen, whence he was recalled in 1868 to Berlin. From 1853 a member of the Academy of Sciences, he was one of its permanent secretaries 1871–93. He died July 11, 1896. Among his works are *Naxos* (1846), *Peloponnesos* (1851–52), *Olympia* (1852), *Die Topographie Kleinasiens* (1872), *Ephesos* (1874), *Griechische Geschichte* (1857–61; 5th ed. 1881 *et seq.*; Eng. trans. by A. W. Ward, 1868–73). See Life by F. Curtius (1913).

(2) **Georg** (1820–85), brother of (1), one o the greatest Greek scholars, was born a Lübeck, and studied at Bonn and Berlin After teaching at Dresden and Berlin, he became in 1849 extraordinary, in 1851

ordinary, professor of Classical Philology at Prague, at Kiel in 1854, at Leipzig in 1862. The chief of his many works were *Griechische Schulgrammatik* (1852; Eng. trans. 1863); *Erläuterungen* to the foregoing (1863; trans. by Abbott, 1870); *Grundzüge der griechischen Etymologie* (1858; trans. by Wilkins and England, 1875–76); and *Das griechisches Verbum* (1873–76; trans. by same, 1880). See monograph by Windisch (1887).

(3) **Mettus** or **Mettius** (4th cent. B.C.), a noble Roman youth who in 362 B.C. is said to have leapt on horseback into a chasm which had opened in the forum, and which the soothsayers declared could only be filled by throwing into it the most precious treasure of Rome.

(4) **Quintus** (fl. 1st cent. A.D.), a Roman historian, who about A.D. 41–54 wrote *De Rebus Gestis Alexandri Magni*, in ten books, of which the first two have been lost and the text of the remainder is imperfect. It has little value as history; but its style, if mannered, is elegant. The *editio princeps* was published at Venice about 1471. See a French monograph by Bosson (1887), and W. W. Tarn, *Alexander the Great*, vol. 2 (1947).

(5) **Theodor** (1857–1928), German organic chemist, professor at Heidelberg from 1897, known especially for his discovery of hydrazine (1887) and other organic compounds.

CURWEN, John (1816–80), the apostle of the Tonic Sol-fa system, was born at Heckmondwike, Yorkshire, the son of an Independent minister, and himself in 1844 was settled as Independent minister at Plaistow. In 1841 he began to advocate the sol-fa system; in 1843 his *Grammar of Vocal Music* appeared; in 1864 he resigned his ministry and gave himself wholly to the cause. He died at Heaton Mersey, Lancashire. See *Memorials* (1882).

CURWOOD, James Oliver (1878–1927), American writer, born at Owosso, Mich., author of popular novels of outdoor life, as *The Courage of Captain Plum* (1908), *The Grizzly King* (1917), *The Alaskan* (1923), &c.

CURZON, (1) George Nathaniel, Marquis Curzon of Kedleston (1859–1925), English statesman, was born at Kedleston Hall in Derbyshire, eldest son of Baron Scarsdale. After a promising career at Eton, he failed to take a first in classics at Oxford, but his subsequent brilliance gained him a fellowship of All Souls in 1883. In 1886 he was elected M.P. for Southport, and the following year began extensive travels all over the East which gave him the extraordinary insight into oriental affairs and the personal contact with eastern rulers which fitted him for his later work at the Foreign Office and in India. Three authoritative books, on Asiatic Russia (1889), on Persia (1892) and on problems of the Far East (1894), were the outcome of his journeys. He became under-secretary for India in 1891, and for foreign affairs in 1895. In 1898, aged only 39, he was chosen viceroy of India and was given an Irish barony, having been unwilling to accept an English peerage with its accompanying bar from the House of Commons. A controversial and often turbulent viceroy, constantly at war with his officials, he introduced many reforms, both social and political, including the establishment of the N.W. Frontier Province and the partition of Bengal. After the arrival of Lord Kitchener (q.v.) as commander-in-chief in 1902, a difference of opinion arose over the dual control system then in force in the Indian Army. The government, finding Curzon's régime too dynamic for its liking, manipulated this crisis in such a way as to procure his resignation, and he left India, a disappointed man, in 1905. Relegated to the political wilderness, he devoted himself to art and archaeology and to the question of university reform. He returned to politics as lord privy seal in the Coalition of 1915, and became a member of Lloyd George's War Cabinet in 1916, in which year he received the Garter. In 1919 his long-standing ambition to become foreign secretary was fulfilled, but in the unhealthy atmosphere of postwar foreign politics his optimistic planning was doomed to frustration, as in the failure of the Persian treaty (1919) and in the constant thwarting of his efforts by Lloyd George. In 1921 he was created a marquis, and as delegate to the Lausanne conference in 1922–23 he won a resounding success by his firm attitude at a time when British prestige had fallen dangerously low. On the resignation of Bonar Law in May 1923 he clearly hoped for and expected the premiership, and the choice of Baldwin was a great blow, but he offered his support and continued as foreign secretary until 1924. Curzon's handling of affairs was characterized by great self-confidence and decision and an unshakable faith in his own infallibility which brought him an unfortunate reputation for unapproachability and pomposity—his parliamentary manner was likened to that of 'a divinity addressing blackbeetles'—but his energy and ability and his courage in the face of bitter disappointments and physical handicap (he suffered from spinal curvature from an early age) stamp him as one of the outstanding figures of the century. See studies by Lord Ronaldshay (1928), Nicolson (1937), and Mosley (1960).

(2) **Robert, Lord Zouche** (1810–73), born in London, studied at Oxford, travelled in the Levant (1833–37), was an *attaché* at Constantinople, and wrote *Monasteries in the Levant* (1849).

CUSHING, (1) Caleb (1800–79), American statesman, born in Salisbury, Mass., was admitted to the bar in 1821, sat in the state legislature and senate, and was elected to congress in 1835–43. He arranged the first treaty between China and the United States in 1844; raised and commanded a regiment in the war with Mexico; and was U.S. attorney-general in 1853–57, counsel for the U.S. at the Geneva Conference in 1872, and minister to Spain in 1874–77.

(2) **Harvey Williams** (1869–1939), American neurologist, educated at Yale and Harvard (M.D., 1895), was professor of Surgery at the latter and made special study of the brain and the pituitary gland. Works include *The Pituitary Body and its Disorders* (1912), and *Life of Sir William Osler* (Pulitzer prize, 1925).

CUSHMAN, Charlotte Saunders (1816–76), an American actress, who was born and died at Boston, U.S., appeared first in opera in 1834, and as Lady Macbeth in 1835. In 1844 she accompanied Macready on a tour through the northern states, and afterwards appeared in London, where she was well received in a range of characters that included Lady Macbeth, Rosalind, Meg Merrilees, and Romeo—her sister Susan (1822–59) playing Juliet. She retired from the stage in 1875.

CUST, (1) Sir Edward (1794–1878), British general and military historian, was born and died in London, the sixth son of the first Lord Brownlow.

(2) Sir Lionel Henry (1859–1929), English art historian, director of the National Portrait Gallery (1895–1909), surveyor of the king's pictures (1901–27), author of many works, especially on Van Dyck and on the royal collections.

(3) Robert Needham, LL.D. (1821–1909), nephew of (1), born at Cockayne-Hatley, Bedfordshire, was educated at Eton, and entered the Indian civil service. He held important posts in North India, in 1864–65 was a member of the legislative council and returned to England in 1869. He published works on the modern languages of the East Indies (1878), of Africa (1882) and of Oceania, as well as *Linguistic and Oriental Essays* (3 series, 1880–91), *Pictures of Indian Life* (1881), *Evangelisation of the Non-Christian World* (1894), &c.

CUSTER, George Armstrong (1839–76), American soldier, born in Ohio, graduated at West Point in 1861, and served with distinction through the Civil War. As a cavalry commander in the west, he several times defeated the hostile Indians; but on June 25, 1876, he attacked the Sioux on the Little Big Horn, in Montana, and he and his 264 men were all destroyed. See *Life* by Whittaker (1878).

CUTHBERT, St (c. 635–87), was in one legend born in Ireland, the son of a petty king; but in another in Lauderdale, then part of Northumbria. In 651 he was certainly a shepherd boy there, and while watching his flock by night had a vision which made him resolve to become a monk. The same year he entered the monastery of Old Melrose, and in 660 accompanied its abbot Eata to Ripon. In consequence of the dispute about Easter, Eata returned to Melrose (661), and Cuthbert, having accompanied him, was elected prior. In 664 he left Melrose for the island monastery of Lindisfarne, of which he became prior, his old master, Eata, being abbot. But in 676 he quitted Lindisfarne for a hermit's cell built with his own hands on one of the Farne group. Here in 684, he was visited by Ecgfrid, king of Northumbria, who came entreating him to accept the bishopric of Hexham. He reluctantly complied, but shortly after exchanged the see of Hexham for that of Lindisfarne. Still thirsting after solitude, at the end of two years he returned to his cell, where he died March 20, 687. The fame of St Cuthbert had been great during his life; it became far greater after his death. Churches were dedicated to him from the Trent and Mersey to the Forth and Clyde.

His body remained (incorrupt, as was believed) at Lindisfarne till 875, when the monks, bearing it on their shoulders, fled inland from the Danes. After many wanderings it found a resting-place at Chester-le-Street in 883; in 995 it was translated first to Ripon and then, in 999, to Durham. Here, enclosed in a costly shrine, and believed to work miracles daily, it remained till the Reformation. The grave was opened in 1826, when inside a triple coffin his skeleton was found, still entire, wrapped in five robes of embroidered silk. Until the Reformation no woman was suffered to approach his shrine. See the ancient *Lives* by Bede, Simeon of Durham and Reginald of Durham and those by Raine (1828), Eyre (1849), Fryer (1830) and Colgrave (1940).

CUTTS, John Cutts, Baron (1661–1707), one of William III's and Marlborough's generals, who served in Ireland and the Low Countries, was probably born at Arkesden, near Saffron-Walden, and died in Dublin.

CUVIER, Léopold Chrétien Frédéric Dagobert, *kü-vyay* (1769–1832), French anatomist, better known by his adopted literary title, Georges Cuvier, was born at Montbéliard, then belonging to Württemberg, his ancestors being Huguenot refugees. He studied for the ministry at Stuttgart; and his love for zoology was confirmed by residence as a tutor on the Normandy coast (1788–94). In 1795 through Geoffroy Saint-Hilaire he was appointed assistant professor of Comparative Anatomy in the Jardin des Plantes, and elected a member of the French Institute; in 1803 he became permanent secretary of the Academy of Sciences. After the Restoration he was made chancellor of the University of Paris, admitted into the cabinet by Louis XVIII, and in 1826 created grand-officer of the Legion of Honour. His opposition to the royal measures restricting the freedom of the press lost him the favour of Charles X; but under Louis-Philippe he was made a peer of France in 1831, and next year minister of the interior. He died of paralysis. In his plans for national education, in his labours for the French Protestant Church, and in scientific work, he was alike indefatigable. He was conspicuous for an unsurpassed grasp of facts rather than for originality or power of generalization, and proved a formidable opponent of the Theory of Descent. Although his four types—Vertebrate, Mollusc, Articulate and Radiate—are now known to give a false simplicity to nature, his structural method made classification more natural. Now also palaeontology was linked to comparative anatomy. Among Cuvier's more important works are: *Leçons d'anatomie comparée* (1801–05); *L'Anatomie des mollusques* (1816); *Les Ossements fossiles des quadrupèdes* (1812); *Histoire naturelle des poissons* (1828–49), written in concert with Valenciennes. Best known is *Le Règne animal distribué d'après son organisation* (1817), which has passed through so many editors' hands. See Mrs R. Lee's *Memoirs of Baron Cuvier* (1833), Pasquier's *Éloge* (1833), Carus's *Geschichte der Zoologie* (1872), Haeckel's *History of Creation* (1876), Ducrotay de Blainville's *Cuvier et Geoffroy*

Saint-Hilaire (1890), and Dandin's *Cuvier et Lamarck* (Paris 1926).

CUYP, or **Kuyp**, (1) **Albert** (1620–91), Dutch painter, who was born and died at Dordrecht, excelled in painting cattle, moonlight, wintry landscapes, still waters with ships, horsemarkets, hunts, camps and cavalry-fights, and golden sunlight.

(2) **Jacob Gerrits**, ' Old Cuyp ' (*c*. 1575–1649), father of (1), a portrait painter of Dordrecht.

CYMBELINE, in Shakespeare's play, a king of Britain, whose original was Holinshed's half-historical Cunobelinus, who died *c*. 43 A.D., and of whom several coins are extant.

CYNEWULF, *kin'e-* (8th cent.), Anglo-Saxon poet, identified by some with Cynewulf, bishop of Lindisfarne (737–80). Four poems, *Juliana, Christ, Elene* and *The Fates of the Apostles*, have his name worked into the text in runes. See translation with notes by C. W. Kennedy (1910).

CYPRIAN, St (*c*. 200–258), **Thascius Caecilius Cyprianus**, one of the great fathers of the church, was born probably at Carthage; and, after teaching rhetoric there, became a Christian about 245. He was made a bishop in 248, when his zealous efforts to restore strict discipline soon brought him a host of enemies. In the Decian persecution he had to seek safety in flight; and after his return to Carthage in 251 the rest of his life was a constant struggle to hold the balance between severity and leniency towards the ' Lapsed ' (i.e., those who had conformed for a time to heathenism). Excommunicated by the Roman bishop Stephen for denying the validity of heretic baptism, at a synod at Carthage in 256 Cyprian maintained that the Roman bishop, in spite of Peter's primacy, could not claim a judicial authority over other bishops. On September 14, 258, he suffered martyrdom under the Emperor Valerian. See Lives by Poole (1840), Archbishop Benson (1897), and studies by H. Koch (1910, 1926, 1930).

CYRANKIEWICZ, **Jozef**, *si-ran-kyay'vits* (1911–), Polish politician, became secretary of the Socialist party in Cracow in 1935. He was taken prisoner by the Germans in 1939, escaped and organized resistance in the Cracow Province and was sent to Auschwitz in 1941. In 1945 he became secretary-general of the Socialist party and was prime minister from 1947 to 1952. He resumed the premiership in 1954.

CYRANO DE BERGERAC. See BERGERAC.

CYRENIUS (d. A.D. 21), a Grecized form of **Publius Sulpicius Quirinus**, named in Luke ii as governor of Syria. He was appointed governor in A.D. 6, but may have also held the post some years earlier.

CYRIL OF ALEXANDRIA, St (376–444), one of the fathers of the church, was born at Alexandria, and brought up under the care of his uncle Theophilus, whom, after some years spent as a monk in the Nitrian desert, he succeeded as patriarch of Alexandria in 412. He forthwith closed the churches of the Novatians, and in 415 expelled the Jews from the city. With the shameful murder of Hypatia (q.v.) he was at least indirectly connected. The latter part of his life was

spent in the relentless persecution of Nestorius (q.v.). The council of Ephesus in 431 condemned Nestorius, with his doctrine of the two natures in Christ. After this, John of Antioch and his adherents (numbering from 30 to 40 bishops), who had arrived at Ephesus too late, constituted a synod of their own, which condemned Cyril. The emperor confirmed both of these depositions; but Cyril kept his patriarchate till his death. Among his extant works are a defence of Christianity, written against the Emperor Julian in 433; and a series of homilies and treatises on the Trinity, the Incarnation, and the Worship of God in spirit and in truth. The best edition is that of Aubert (7 vols. Paris 1638). See Kopallik, *Cyril von Alexandria* (Mainz 1881).

CYRIL OF JERUSALEM, St (*c*. 315–386), ordained presbyter about 345, tried to be neutral during the Arian controversies, and in 351 was ordained Bishop of Jerusalem. He was twice expelled from his see, in 358 and by a synod at Constantinople in 360; but on the accession of Julian in 361 he returned to his flock till 367, when, by order of Valens, he was again expelled. He returned again on the death of Valens in 378, and took part, on the orthodox side, in the second Council of Constantinople. His *Katēchēseis* (instructions to catechumens) have been edited by Touttée (Paris 1720), and by Reischl and Rupp (1845–60). There is a translation in the *Oxford Library of the Fathers* (1838) and by R. M. Woolley (1930). See works by Gonnet (1876) and Mader (1891).

CYRIL (827–69), and **METHODIUS** (826–85), saints, apostles of the Slavs, were brothers, and natives of Thessalonica. Cyril had been a disciple of Photius, and was surnamed ' the philosopher '. The Tartar Khazars to the northeast of the Black Sea having about 860 asked the Emperor Michael III to send them Christian missionaries, Cyril was sent and made many converts. The Bulgarians of Thrace and Moesia were evangelized by Methodius, who baptized their king Bogoris in 861. At the request of the Duke of Moravia, the brothers went thither, prepared a Slav translation of the Scriptures and chief liturgical books, and won the hearts of the people from the Roman missionaries. The two brothers were summoned to Rome to explain their conduct, and Cyril died there in 869. Methodius, who in the same year was consecrated at Rome Bishop of the Moravians, completed the evangelization of the Slavs. Called to Rome a second time in 879 to justify his celebration of the mass in the native tongue, he gained the approval of Pope John VIII, returned to his diocese in 880, and probably died at Hradiště on the Morava. Both brothers were recognized as saints by the Roman Catholic Church, after having been condemned as Arians by several popes. The Cyrillic alphabet, modified out of the Greek by Cyril, superseded a more ancient Slavonic alphabet. See German works by Ginzel (2nd ed. 1860), Dümmler and Miklosich (1870), and Bonwetsch (1885).

CYRILLUS LUCARIS. See LUCARIS.

CYRUS THE GREAT (d. 529 B.C.), the

founder of the Persian empire, was the fourth in a line of kings of Anzan, in Susiana (called by the Hebrews *Elam*), who formed a branch of the Persian royal dynasty of the Achaemenides. According to Herodotus, Cyrus was the son of Mandane, daughter of Astyages, king of Media, and the Persian Cambyses. He was to have been killed by Astyages had not a herdsman saved him till he was old enough to be sent to Persia. This and the very different stories of Xenophon and others have been superseded by the evidence of monuments discovered in modern times. Cyrus was the son of Cambyses I, grandson of Cyrus I, and great-grandson of Teispes, who was also the great-grandfather of Hystaspes, the father of Darius (q.v.). In the third or sixth year of Nabonidus, king of Babylon (553 or 550 B.C.), Cyrus, ' king of Elam ', made Astyages, king of Media, a prisoner, and took his capital, Ecbatana, the Median army having mutinied. By 548 he was ' king of Persia '. Favoured by a revolt of the tribes on ' the Lower Sea ', or Persian Gulf, he advanced on Babylon, and, after giving battle at Opis, took Sippara (Sepharvaim) and Babylon itself ' without fighting ' in 539. The account of the siege of Babylon by Cyrus recorded by Herodotus must therefore be erroneous. Cyrus, a polytheist and an idolater, at once began a policy of religious conciliation. The nations who had been carried into captivity in Babylon along with the Jews were restored to their native countries, and allowed to take their gods with them. The empire of Lydia had fallen before the army of Cyrus some years before (in or about 546), and after the conquest of Babylonia he was master of all Asia from the Mediterranean to the Hindu Kush. The conqueror's hold over Asia Minor and Syria was much strengthened by his friendly relations with the Phoenicians and the Jews; in the Old Testament he is called the Shepherd and the Anointed of Jehovah. After he had extended his empire from the Arabian desert and the Persian Gulf in the south, to the Black Sea, the Caucasus and the Caspian in the north, he died in 529—according to Herodotus and Diodorus, during an unsuccessful struggle with Tomyris, queen of the Massagetae, on the Jaxartes. Before his death he had made his son and successor Cambyses ' king of Babylon '. The *Cyropaedia* of Xenophon is a historical romance. See Sayce's *Introduction to Ezra, Nehemiah, and Esther* (2nd ed. 1887); also his *Fresh Light from the Ancient Monuments* (1883).

CYRUS THE YOUNGER (424–401 B.C.), second son of Darius Nothus and Parysatis, conspired against his brother Artaxerxes Mnemon (404), was sentenced to death, but afterwards pardoned and even restored to his dignity as satrap of Asia Minor. In 401 he left Sardis at the head of a large army of Asiatics and Greek mercenaries, encountered his brother at Cunaxa, 500 stadia from Babylon, and was there defeated and slain. See XENOPHON.

CZARTORYSKI, Adam Jerzy, *char-to-ris'kee* (1770–1861), Polish statesman, son of Prince Adam Czartoryski (1734–1823), was born at Warsaw, and educated at Edinburgh and London. He fought against Russia in the Polish insurrection of 1794, and, sent to St Petersburg as a hostage, gained the friendship of the Grand-duke Alexander and the confidence of the Emperor Paul, who made him ambassador to Sardinia. When Alexander ascended the throne he appointed him assistant to the minister of foreign affairs. As curator of the university of Wilna (1803) he exerted all his influence to keep alive a spirit of nationality; and when some of the students were sent to Siberia, Czartoryski resigned his office. Into the Revolution of 1830 he threw himself with all his heart. He was elected president of a provisional government, and summoned a national diet which in January 1831 declared the Polish throne vacant and elected Czartoryski head of the national government. He immediately devoted half of his large estates to the public service; and, though in August he resigned his post, continued to fight as a common soldier. After the suppression of the rising, Czartoryski—excluded from the amnesty and his Polish estates confiscated—escaped to Paris, where he afterwards resided, the liberal friend of his poor expatriated countrymen. In 1848 he freed all his serfs in Galicia, and during the Crimean war he endeavoured to induce the allies to identify the cause of Poland with that of Turkey. He refused the amnesty offered to him by Alexander II, and died near Paris. See his *Memoirs*, translated by Gielgud (1888).

CZERMAK, Johann Nepomuk, *cher'mak* (1828–73), physiologist, the founder of laryngoscopy, was born in Prague, studied at Vienna, Breslau and Würzburg, and was professor successively at Cracow, Pesth, Jena and Leipzig. His collected works were published in 1879.

CZERNY, Karl, *cher'nee* (1791–1857), Austrian pianist and composer, was born and died at Vienna. He studied under Beethoven and Clementi, and himself taught Liszt, Thalberg and Döhler. His piano exercises and studies are widely used today. See *Life* by Steger (Munich 1924).

CZERNY GEORGE, Turk. **Karadjordje,** i.e., ' Black George ' (1766–1817), the leader of the Serbians in their struggle for independence, after the treaty of Slobosje (July 8, 1808) was elected governor and recognized as Prince of Serbia by the sultan. He had returned from a two years' exile in Austria when he was murdered at the instigation of his rival, Prince Milosch.

D

DĄBROWSKI, correct Polish form of DOMBROVSKI.

DA COSTA, Isaak (1798–1860), Dutch poet, was born at Amsterdam, the son of a Portuguese Jew, studied at Leyden, and in 1822, a year after taking his doctorate of philosophy, embraced Christianity. See Dutch Lives by Koenen (1861), Pierson (1865) and Ten Brink (1888).

DADDI, Bernardo (c. 1290–1350), Italian painter of the Florentine school, and a follower, perhaps a pupil, of Giotto. See study by Vitzthum (1905).

DAENDELS, Herman Willem (1762–1818), a Dutch general, born at Hattem, in Guelderland, from 1808 to 1811 was governor-general of the Dutch East Indies, and in 1815 was entrusted with the organization of the Dutch colonies on the coast of Africa, where he died.

DA GAMA. See GAMA.

DAGOBERT, the name of several Merovingian French kings.

Dagobert I (ruled 628–39), son of Clotaire II, ruled at first only over Austrasia but later over a combined Frankish kingdom. Subsequently he set his sons to rule over Neustria and Austrasia.

Dagobert II (ruled 676–79), son of Sigibert III, after whose death he was banished to an Irish monastery. He was assassinated after a short reign.

DAGUERRE, Louis Jacques Mandé (1789–1851), French photographic pioneer, born at Cormeilles, had been a scene painter in Paris, when, from 1826 onwards, and partly in conjunction with M. Niepce, he perfected his 'daguerrotype' process in which a photographic image is obtained on a copper plate coated with a light-sensitive layer of silver iodide and bromide. See Life by Gernsheim (1956).

DAHL, (1) **Anders** (18th cent.), Swedish botanist, was a pupil of Linnaeus. The genus *Dahlia* is named after him.

(2) **Johann Christian Clausen** (1788–1857), a Norwegian landscape painter, from 1821 professor of Painting at Dresden.

(3) **Michael** (1656–1743), portrait painter, born at Stockholm, in 1688 settled in London. Works may be seen in the National Portrait Gallery.

DAHLGREN, (1) **John Adolphus Bernard** (1809–70), American admiral, born in Philadelphia, joined the navy in 1826 and did much to advance the science of naval gunnery by founding an ordnance workshop at Washington, where he designed a new type of naval gun (1850). He commanded the South Atlantic Blockade squadron in the Civil War.

(2) **Karl Fredrik** (1791–1844), Swedish poet and humorist, born at Stensbruk in Ostergötland, studied at Uppsala, and from 1815 was a preacher at Stockholm. His works—novels, tales, poems, dramas, &c.—fill 5 vols. (1847–52).

DAHLMANN, Friedrich Christoph (1785–1860), German historian, was born at Wismar, studied at Copenhagen and Halle, and in 1813 became professor of History at Kiel, in 1829 of Political Science at Göttingen, where he published (1830) his *Quellenkunde der deutschen Geschichte.* Banished in 1837 by the king of Hanover, he went to Leipzig, next to Jena, where he wrote his masterpiece, *Geschichte von Dänemark* (3 vols. 1840–43). In 1842 he became professor of History at Bonn, and in the movement of 1848 headed the constitutional liberals. See Life by Springer (Leipzig 1870–72).

DAHN, Julius Sophus Felix (1834–1912), publicist, historian, poet, was born at Hamburg, the son of the actor, Friedrich Dahn (1811–89). He studied at Munich and Berlin, and became professor of German Jurisprudence at Königsberg and Breslau. See his *Erinnerungen* (1890–93).

DAIMLER, Gottlieb (1834–1900), German engineer, born at Schorndorf, worked after 1872 with Otto and Langen on improving the gas engine, designed in 1885 one of the earliest roadworthy motor cars, and founded the Daimler Automobile Company at Cannstatt in 1890.

DAKIN, Henry Drysdale (1880–1950), English chemist, was born in London. Important for his researches on enzymes and his work on antiseptics, he developed ' Dakin's ' or the ' Carrel-Dakin ' solution (a 0·5% solution of sodium hypochlorite), widely used for treating wounds in World War I. Elected F.R.S. in 1917, he was awarded the Davy Medal in 1941.

DALADIER, Édouard, *da-la-dyay* (1884–1970), French politician, born at Carpentras, became in 1927 leader of the radical socialists, and in 1933 minister of war and prime minister of a short-lived government. Again minister of war, in January 1934 he was asked to form a cabinet, but his government immediately met the full force of the repercussions of the Stavisky (q.v.) crisis, and lasted only a few weeks. In 1936 he became war minister in the Popular Front cabinet, and in 1938 again took office as premier. Pacifist in outlook, he supported ' appeasement ' and was a signatory of the Munich Pact. In 1940 he resigned, became successively war and foreign minister, and on the fall of France was arrested and interned until 1945.

D'ALBERT. See ALBERT (1).

DALCROZE. See JAQUES-DALCROZE.

DALE, (1) **David** (1739–1806), Scottish industrialist, was born at Stewarton, Ayrshire. Apprenticed to a Paisley weaver, he afterwards travelled the country, buying up the homespun linen yarn, about 1763 became clerk to a silkmercer, then an importer of French and Dutch yarns. On Arkwright's visiting Scotland it was agreed that he and Dale should engage in cotton-spinning together at New Lanark, near the Falls of

Clyde. There Dale built mills (1785) and became prosperous. In 1799 he sold these mills to Robert Owen (q.v.), his son-in-law. Dale spent his last years at Glasgow in works of benevolence and in preaching to a church of his own, the ' Old Independents '.

(2) **Sir Henry Hallett** (1875–1968), British physiologist, educated at Cambridge and London, elected F.R.S. (1914), became director of the National Institute for Medical Research, London. In 1936 he shared with Loewi the Nobel prize for medicine for work on the chemical transmission of nerve impulses. He was knighted in 1932, created G.B.E. in 1943, and awarded the O.M. in 1944.

DALÉN, Nils Gustav (1869–1937), Swedish engineer, educated at Göteborg and Zürich, invented automatic lighting for unmanned lighthouses and railway signals. Nobel prize-winner for physics in 1912, he was blinded a year later by an explosion in a chemical experiment, but continued to work till his death.

DALGARNO, George (c. 1626–87), Scottish writer, born at Old Aberdeen, studied at Marischal College, and kept a school for thirty years in Oxford, where he died. He wrote the *Ars Signorum, vulgo Character Universalis* (1661) and *Didascalocophus, or the Deaf and Dumb Man's Tutor* (1680)—both reprinted for the Maitland Club in 1834.

DALHOUSIE, James Andrew Broun-Ramsay, Marquis of (1812–60), ' greatest of Indian proconsuls ', was third son of the 9th Earl of Dalhousie, and was born at Dalhousie Castle, Midlothian. Educated at Harrow and Christ Church, Oxford, he succeeded in 1832, by the death of his only remaining brother, to the courtesy title of Lord Ramsay. In 1835 he stood unsuccessfully for Edinburgh as a Conservative; in 1837 was elected for Haddingtonshire; in 1838, on the death of his father, entered the House of Peers as Earl of Dalhousie. In 1843 Peel appointed him vice-president of the Board of Trade, and in 1845 he succeeded Mr Gladstone as president. When Peel resigned office in 1846, Lord John Russell asked Lord Dalhousie to remain at the Board of Trade in order to carry out the regulations he had framed for the railway system. In 1847 he was appointed governor-general of India—the youngest viceroy ever sent there. His Indian administration was not less successful in the acquisition of territory than in developing Indian resources and improving the administration. Pegu and the Punjab were conquered; Nagpur, Oudh, Sattara, Jhansi and Berar annexed. Railways on a colossal scale were planned and commenced; 4000 miles of telegraph were spread over India; 2000 miles of road were bridged and metalled; the Ganges Canal was opened; and important irrigation works all over India were executed. Noteworthy also are Dalhousie's energetic action against suttee, thuggee, female infanticide and the slave-trade; the organization of the Legislative Council; the improved training of the civil service, which was opened to all natural-born British subjects, black or white; the development of trade, agriculture, forestry, mining and the postal service. In 1848 he was made a K.T.; in 1849 received the marquisate and

the thanks of parliament. Broken in health, he left India in 1856, and on December 19, 1860, he died at Dalhousie Castle. See monograph by Lee Warner (1904); and his *Private Letters* (1910).

DALI, Salvador, *dah'lee* (1904–), Spanish artist, born at Figueras. After studying at the Academy of Fine Arts, Madrid, he moved to Paris and joined the Surrealists in 1928, and became one of the principal figures of the movement. He made a deep study of abnormal psychology and dream symbolism, and represented ' paranoiac ' objects in landscapes remembered from his Spanish boyhood with almost academic realism and highly finished craftsmanship. In 1940 he settled in the United States, and later became a Catholic and devoted his art to symbolic religious paintings. His publications include *The Secret Life of Salvador Dali* (1942) and the surrealist novel *Hidden Faces* (1944). He collaborated with Luis Buñuel (q.v.) in producing the surrealist films *Le Chien Andalou* (1928) and *L'Age d'Or* (1930). His painting *The Persistence of Memory* (1931) (known as the *Limp Watches*) is in the Museum of Modern Art, New York, and his *Christ of St John of the Cross* (1951) is in Glasgow Art Gallery. See study by F. Cowles (1959).

DALLAM, or Dalham, a family of English organ-builders.

(1) **Ralph** (d. 1672), built organs for St George's Chapel, Windsor, and for Greenwich church.

(2) **Robert** (1602–65), son of (3), was responsible for organs at New College, Oxford, York Minster, St Paul's Cathedral, Jesus College, Cambridge (1634), Canterbury Cathedral (1635), and St Mary Woolnoth (destroyed in the Fire of London).

(3) **Thomas** (c. 1599–c. 1630), built organs for King's College, Cambridge, and for Worcester Cathedral. See his *Diary* (Hakluyt Soc. 1898).

DALLAPICCOLA, Luigi (1904–), Italian composer and teacher, whose compositions, making wide use of twelve-note technique, include songs, a piano concerto, an opera, *The Prisoner*, a ballet, *Marsyas*, and orchestral and choral works, such as *Canti di Prigionia*.

DALLAS, (1) Alexander James (1759–1817), a lawyer of West Indian birth and Scottish descent, who went to the U.S. (1783), settled in Philadelphia, became naturalized, and was later secretary of the treasury and war-secretary under President Madison. See Life by his son G. M. Dallas (1871).

(2) **George Mifflin** (1792–1864), son of (1), was born in Philadelphia, and graduated at Princeton College in 1810. Admitted to the bar, he entered the diplomatic service, and in 1831 was sent to the U.S. senate by Pennsylvania. He was U.S. minister to Russia, 1837–39, and in 1844 was elected vice-president of the United States. In 1846 his casting vote as president of the senate repealed the protective tariff of 1842, though he had been a Protectionist. Minister to Great Britain 1856–61, he died at Philadelphia. His posthumous writings include *Letters from London* (1869), a Life of his father (1871), and his *Diary*.

DALLING, Lord. See BULWER.

DALOU, (Aimé) Jules (1838–1902), French sculptor, born in Paris. He was the pupil of Carpeaux, and after being the curator of the Louvre during the Commune, he fled to England in 1871, and taught at the Royal College of Art for some years. His realistic modelling influenced many English sculptors of the time. His well-known monument *Triumph of the Republic* is in Paris.

DALRYMPLE, (1) Alexander (1737–1808), Scottish hydrographer, brother of (2), was born at New Hailes, Musselburgh. In 1779 he became hydrographer to the East India Company, in 1795 to the Admiralty; and died three weeks after his dismissal.

(2) **Sir David, Lord Hailes** (1726–92), Scottish historian, born at Edinburgh, the great-grandson of the 1st Viscount Stair, brother of (1), a justiciary lord in 1776, he is best known for his accurate, chronological *Annals of Scotland, 1057–1371* (1776–79), &c.

(3) **Sir James** (1650–1719), second son of the 1st Viscount Stair, became a chief clerk of the Court of Session, and in 1698, a baronet. His *Collections concerning the Scottish History preceding 1153* (1705) is still of value.

DALTON, (1) Hugh, Baron Dalton of Forest and Frith (1887–1962), British Labour politician, born at Neath, Glamorgan, was educated at Eton, King's College, Cambridge, and the London School of Economics, served in the first world war and was Labour M.P. (1924–31 and from 1935). He became minister for economic warfare (1940) and president of the Board of Trade (1942) in Churchill's war-time coalition. In 1945 he became Labour chancellor of the Exchequer, nationalized the Bank of England (1946) but resigned in consequence of ' budget leakages ' to a journalist in November 1947. He was made a life peer in 1960. See his *Call back Yesterday* (1953) and his memoirs, *High Tide and After* (1962).

(2) **John** (1766–1844), English chemist, was born at Eaglesfield, near Cockermouth, the son of a Quaker weaver. After 1781 he became assistant in a boarding-school kept by a cousin in Kendal, of which in 1785 he and a brother became the proprietors. Here his love of mathematical and physical studies was developed, and here in 1787 he commenced a meteorological journal continued all his life, recording 200,000 observations. He collected butterflies and gathered a great hortus siccus and herbarium. In 1793 he was appointed teacher of mathematics and science in New College, Manchester, and later supported himself in Manchester by private tuition. In 1794 he first described colour blindness (' Daltonism ') exemplified in his own case and that of his brother. An F.R.S. and an associate of the Paris Academy, he died at Manchester. His chief physical researches were on mixed gases, the force of steam, the elasticity of vapours and the expansion of gases by heat, his law of partial pressures being also known as ' Dalton's law '; and in chemistry on the absorption of gases by water, on carbonic acid, carburetted hydrogen, &c., while his atomic theory elevated chemistry to a science. Dalton was unquestionably one of the greatest of chemists.

In his habits he was simple, in manners grave and reserved but kindly. He ' never found time ' to marry. See Lives by Dr Angus Smith (1836), Dr Henry (1854), Lonsdale (1874) and Sir H. Roscoe (1895), and W. Tilden, *Famous Chemists* (1921).

(3) **John Call** (1825–89), physiologist, was born at Chelmsford, Mass., and lived in New York.

DALY, (John) Augustin, *day'li* (1838–99), American dramatist and manager, born in Plymouth, N.C. After being a dramatic critic, he went into management, opening the Fifth Avenue Theatre, New York, in 1869, and his own theatre, Daly's, in 1879, with the company of which he visited London in 1884. In 1893 he opened the London Daly's with Ada Rehan in *The Taming of the Shrew.* He wrote and adapted nearly one hundred plays, of which the best was *Horizon* (1871), though the most popular were melodramas such as *Under the Gaslight* and *Leah the Forsaken.* He was chosen by Tennyson to adapt *The Foresters* for the stage in 1891.

DALYELL, or Dalzell, Thomas, *dee-ell'* (*c.* 1599–1685), the ' Muscovy general ', born at Binns, Linlithgowshire, served in the Rochelle expedition (1628) and in Ireland, was taken prisoner at Worcester (1651), but escaped, and in 1655 entered the service of Russia and fought against the Tatars and Turks. In 1666 appointed commander-in-chief in Scotland, he defeated the Covenanters at Rullion Green in the Pentlands. A devoted royalist, he never shaved his beard after Charles I's execution.

DALZIEL, Edward (1817–1905), English engraver, born at Wooler, fifth of the twelve sons of a Northumbrian artist, in 1839 joined his brother George in London, and gradually built up (with him and a third brother, Thomas) the great business of the ' Brothers Dalziel ', wood-engravers.

DAM, Carl Peter Henrik (1895–   ), Danish biochemist, taught in Copenhagen, went to U.S.A. (1940) and became a member of the Rockefeller Institute for Medical Research (1945). For his discovery of Vitamin K (1934) he was with Doisy awarded the Nobel prize for medicine in 1943.

DAMALA. See BERNHARDT, SARAH.

DAMASUS, the name of two popes, the first, a Portuguese, in 366–384; and the second in 1048.

DAMER, Anne Seymour, *day'mèr* (1749–1828), English sculptress and friend of Horace Walpole, was the daughter of Field-marshal Conway, and in 1767 married the worthless John Damer, who shot himself in 1776. See Life by Noble (1908).

DAMIANI, Pietro, or St Peter Damian (1007–1072), Italian cleric, born at Ravenna, herded swine in boyhood, but rose to be cardinal and Bishop of Ostia (1057). He supported the policy of Hildebrand (Gregory VII) without sharing his arrogance, and laboured strenuously to reform the clergy, then at a low ebb of immorality and indolence. He died at Faenza. His letters, speeches, &c., were collected by Cardinal Cajetan (best ed. 4 vols. Venice 1743). See Life by Neukirch (Göttingen 1875).

DAMIANUS St. See COSMAS.

DAMIEN, Father Joseph, *dam-yĭ* (1840–89), Belgian missionary renowned for his great work among the lepers of the Hawaiian island of Molokai, where he lived from 1873 until his death from the disease. See Lives by Clifford (1889) and Cooke (1889), and R. L. Stevenson's *Father Damien* (1890).

DAMIENS, Robert François, *dam-yĭ* (1714–1757), French soldier, attempted to assassinate Louis XV, allegedly at the behest of the Jesuits. On January 4, 1757, he went to Versailles, next day followed the king about everywhere, and about 6 p.m., as the king was entering his carriage, stabbed him. He was seized, and nearly three months later slowly tortured to death, being finally torn to pieces by four horses.

DAMOCLES, *dam'o-kleez* (4th cent. B.C.), a courtier of the elder Dionysius, tyrant of Syracuse, who, having extolled the happiness of royalty, was reproved in a singular manner. He was seated at a table, richly spread, but on looking upwards he saw a keen-edged sword suspended over his head by a single horse-hair.

DAMON and PYTHIAS, more correctly **Phintias** (4th cent. B.C.), two Pythagoreans of Syracuse, remembered as the models of faithful friendship. Condemned to death by the elder Dionysius, tyrant of Syracuse, Pythias begged to be allowed to go home to arrange his affairs, and Damon pledged his own life for his friend's. Dionysius consented, and Pythias returned just in time to save Damon from death. Struck by so noble an example, the tyrant pardoned Pythias, and desired to be admitted into their sacred fellowship.

DAMPIER, William (1652–1715), English navigator and hydrographer, was born near Yeovil. He gained a great knowledge of hydrography in voyages to Newfoundland, Bantam, Jamaica and Campeachy Bay. After two years among the lawless logwood cutters of Yucatán, he joined in 1679 a band of buccaneers who crossed the Isthmus of Darien and, ravaged the coast as far south as Juan Fernández. In another expedition (1683), after seizing a Danish ship at Sierra Leone, he coasted along the shores of Chile, Peru and Mexico, sailing thence across the Pacific, and touching at the Philippines, China and Australia. Marooned on Nicobar Islands (1688) he made his way in a native canoe to Atchin, and got back to England (1691), where he published his interesting *Voyage round the World* (1697). He conducted (1699–1700) a voyage of discovery to the South Seas, in which he explored the north-west coast of Australia, also the coasts of New Guinea and New Britain, giving his name to the Dampier Archipelago and Strait. On the return voyage he was wrecked off Ascension, and lived with his crew on turtles and goats for five weeks, until relieved. The old buccaneer was a better pilot than commander, and his cruelty to his lieutenant led to his being court-martialled. Yet in 1703 he was re-appointed to the command of two privateers (the master of one of them Alexander Selkirk) to the South Seas, when he was said to have been guilty of drunkenness, brutality and even cowardice. Dampier

returned home at the close of 1707, poor and broken, nor did his angry *Vindication* re-establish his reputation. Next year he sailed again as pilot to a privateer, which rescued Selkirk, and returned in 1711. See Life by Wilkinson (1929), and Masefield's edition of the *Voyages* (1907).

DAMROSCH, Leopold (1832–85), German conductor and composer, born at Posen, was leader of the Weimar court orchestra under Liszt (1857–59) and conductor at Breslau (1859–60 and 1862–71) before emigrating to New York, where he ultimately became conductor at the Metropolitan Opera House and did much to popularize Wagner in the United States. His son, **Walter Johannes** (1862–1950), born at Breslau, also became well known as a conductor and composed several operas.

DANA, (1) **Charles Anderson** (1819–97), American newspaper editor, born at Hinsdale, N.H., spent two years at Harvard, and was a member of the Brook Farm community. During 1848–62 he edited the New York *Tribune*, which opposed the extension of slavery to new territories; and from 1863 to the close of the war he was assistant-secretary of war. In 1867 he purchased the New York *Sun*, and successfully managed it on democratic lines. He published translations and anthologies, collaborated in a Life of Grant (1868), and with George Ripley, a former associate at Brook Farm, edited the *New American Cyclopaedia* (1857–63) and the *American Cyclopaedia* (1873–76), both in 16 vols. He died in New York. See J. Wilson, *Life of C. A. Dana* (1907).

(2) **James Dwight** (1813–95), American mineralogist and geologist, was born at Utica, N.Y. He graduated at Yale in 1833, and was sent out in 1838 as a scientific observer in the U.S. exploring expedition under Wilkes, visiting the Antarctic and Pacific, during which Dana's ship was wrecked. He afterwards with his father-in-law, Silliman, edited the *American Journal of Science*, and in 1846 was elected professor of Natural History and Geology at Yale. Among his works are *System of Mineralogy* (1837), *Manual of Mineralogy* (1848), two treatises on corals, *Textbook of Geology* (1864) and *Hawaiian Volcanoes* (1890).

(3) **Richard Henry** (1787–1879), American poet and prose writer, was born at Cambridge, Mass. He was educated at Harvard, and admitted to the bar at Boston in 1811. In 1818 he became associate editor of the *North American Review*, to which he contributed largely. His *Dying Raven* (1821), *The Buccaneer* (1827) and some others of his poems were warmly praised by critics; but Dana's best work was in criticism. He died at Boston.

(4) **Richard Henry** (1815–82), son of (3), author and lawyer, graduated at Harvard in 1837. During a break in his college career, occasioned in part by a weakness in the eyes, he shipped as a common sailor, and made a voyage round Cape Horn to California and back. This voyage he described in *Two Years before the Mast* (1840), the best book of its kind; in 1840 he was admitted to the Massachusetts bar, and was especially

distinguished in maritime law. Among his works are *The Seaman's Friend* (1841) and *To Cuba and Back* (1859). He also edited Wheaton's *International Law*, and was a prominent free-soiler and Republican. He died in Rome. See Life by Adams (2 vols. 1890).

DANBY, (1) **Francis** (1793–1861), Irish painter, born near Wexford, painted landscapes and large biblical and historical subject pictures.

(2) **Lord.** See LEEDS, DUKE OF.

DANCE, (1) **George** (1700–68), English architect, designed the Mansion House (1739) and many other London buildings.

(2) **George** (1741–1825), son of (1), rebuilt Newgate (1770–83), and was one of the original Royal Academicians.

DANCER, (1) **Ann.** See BARRY, SPRANGER.

(2) **Daniel** (1716–94), the Pinner miser, who lived on a few pence a day, went swathed in hay-bands, and died worth £3000 a year.

DANCKERTS, Henry (*c.* 1630–80), engraver and architectural painter, was born at The Hague and died at Amsterdam, having resided in England during 1668–79.

DANCOURT, Florent Carton (1661–1725), French dramatist, actor and court favourite, became devout in his old age, which he spent in retirement in the country. He excelled in depicting the stupidity of the peasantry and the follies of the *bourgeoisie*. See works by Barthélemy (1882) and Lemaître (1882).

DANDOLO, Enrico (*c.* 1108–1205), a Venetian, eminent in learning, eloquence and knowledge of affairs, who in 1173 was sent as ambassador to Constantinople, and in 1192 was elected doge. As such, he defeated the Pisans, and in 1201 marched at the head of the crusaders, and subdued Trieste and Zara, the coasts of Albania, the Ionian Islands and Constantinople, July 17, 1203. When the Emperor Alexius was murdered by his own subjects, Dandolo laid siege to Constantinople and took it by storm April 13, 1204. He established there the empire of the Latins, and caused Count Baldwin of Flanders to be chosen emperor. Other important members of the family include **Giovanni**, doge, 1280–1289; **Francesco**, 1328–39; **Andrea**, 1342–54.

DANE, Clemence (1891?–1965), pseud. of **Winifred Ashton**, English novelist and playwright, born in Blackheath. Her best novels are probably *Regiment of Women* (1917), *Legend* (1919), *Broome Stages* (1931) and *The Flower Girls* (1954), the last two dealing with theatrical families. Many of her plays have achieved long runs, including the near-classic *A Bill of Divorcement* (1921), the ingenious reconstruction of the poet's life in *Will Shakespeare* (1921), the stark tragedy of *Granite* (1926) and *Call Home the Heart* (1927). In 1953 she received a C.B.E.

DANGERFIELD, Thomas (1650–85), inventor of the Meal-tub Plot, was the son of a farmer at Waltham in Essex, and had been a thief, vagabond and soldier on the Continent, pseudo-convert to Catholicism, coiner, &c., when in 1679 he accused the Presbyterians of plotting to destroy the government. Imprisoned when this was shown to be a lie, he excused himself as having been deceived by a tale invented by the Roman Catholics to

screen a plot of their own against the king's life. Papers proving this would, he alleged, be found in a meal-tub in the house of a lady (who was tried and acquitted). He himself was now whipped and pilloried, and on returning from Tyburn was killed by a blow in the eye from the cane of a bystander.

DANIEL, (1) **Arnaut** (fl. late 12th cent.), Provençal poet, was born at the Castle of Rebeyrac, in Périgord, of poor but noble parents. He became a member of the court of Richard Cœur-de-Lion and was esteemed one of the best of the troubadours, particularly for his treatment of the theme of love. He introduced the sestina, the pattern of which was later adapted by Dante and Petrarch.

(2) **Samuel** (1562–1619), English poet, was the son of a music-master, and was born near Taunton. He entered Magdalen Hall, Oxford, in 1597, but left it without a degree. He was sometime tutor at Wilton to William Herbert, son of the Earl of Pembroke, afterwards at Skipton to Anne Clifford, daughter of the Earl of Cumberland. In 1604 he was appointed to read new plays; in 1607 became one of the queen's grooms of the privy chamber, and in 1615–18 had charge of a company of young players at Bristol. Retiring then to a farm which he possessed at Beckington, in Somerset, he died there in October 1619. Daniel was highly commended by Lodge, Carew, and Drummond of Hawthornden, although Ben Jonson described him as ' a good honest man . . . but no poet '. Coleridge, Lamb and Hazlitt unite in praising him. His works include sonnets, epistles, masques and dramas; but his chief production is a poem in eight books, *A History of the Civil Wars between York and Lancaster*. His *Defence of Ryme* (1602) is in admirable prose. See D. Bush, *English Literature in the Earlier 17th century* (1945).

DANIELL, John Frederic (1790–1845), English chemist, born in London, became F.R.S. in 1814, Chemistry professor in King's College, London (1831), and wrote an *Introduction to Chemical Philosophy* (1839). He invented a hygrometer (1820), a pyrometer (1830) and the Daniell electric cell.

DANNECKER, Johann Heinrich von (1758–1841), German sculptor, was born at Waldenbuch, near Stuttgart, and from 1790 was professor of Sculpture in that city. His masterpiece, ' Ariadne on the Panther ' (1816), is at Frankfurt.

D'ANNUNZIO, Gabriele (1863–1938), Italian poet, novelist, dramatist, journalist, airman, *Principe* (1924), was born at Pescara. His ' Romances of the Rose ' are *Il Piacere* (1889), *L'Innocente*, and *Trionfo della morte*; *Le Vergini delle rocce* (1896) is one of a ' Lily ' trilogy; *Il Fuoco* (1900), first of a ' Pomegranate ' series. His tragedies include *La Città morta* (1898); *La Gioconda; Francesca da Rimini*. *Le Martyre de St Sébastien* (1911) is a mystery play. Grace, voluptuousness, affectation characterize this apostle of a new Renaissance. He urged war against Austria, served, and was wounded (1916); in 1919 he seized and held Fiume, despite the Allies. See study by A. Rhodes (1959).

DANTAS, Julio, *dä'tash* (1876–1962), Portuguese dramatist, poet and short-story writer, born in Lagos. In his light lyrical poems and stories he displayed considerable talent, but his heavier work, such as historical dramas, attempted under the influence of the Norwegian and French schools, was less successful. His *A ceia dos cardeais* (1902) was translated by H. A. Saintsbury as *The Cardinal's Collation* (1927). See the study by W. Geise (Coimbra 1941).

DANTE ALIGHIERI (1265–1321), ' that singular splendour of the Italian race ', as Boccaccio, his first biographer, calls him, was born, a lawyer's son, in Florence in May 1265. He was baptized Durante, afterwards contracted into Dante; and the old biographers often remarked on the appropriateness of both names, ' the much-enduring ' and ' the giver '. In his *Vita Nuova*, the New (i.e., probably Early) Life, he relates how he first set eyes on ' the glorious lady of his heart, Beatrice ', he then being about nine years of age, and she a few months younger. To Boccaccio, and to his statement alone, we owe the generally accepted fact that she was the daughter of Folco Portinari, for Dante himself never gives the slightest clue as to her family name. That chance meeting in May 1274 determined the whole future course of the poet's life. The story of his boyish but unquenchable passion is told with exquisite pathos in the *Vita Nuova*. There is no evidence that any similar feeling was aroused in the heart of Beatrice herself. She was married early to one Simone de' Bardi, but neither this nor the poet's own subsequent marriage interfered with his pure and Platonic devotion to her, which became even intensified after her death, on June 9, 1290. Shortly after, Dante married Gemma Donati, daughter of a powerful Guelph family. That it proved an unhappy marriage is a mere conjecture, based on the fact that after Dante's exile he never appears to have seen his wife again. In 1289 Dante fought at Campaldino, where Florence defeated the Ghibellines, and was at the capitulation of Caprona. He was registered in one of the city guilds—that of the Apothecaries—being entered as ' Dante d'Aldighieri, *poeta* '. In 1300, after filling minor public offices, and possibly going on some embassies abroad, he attained to the dignity of one of the six priors of Florence—a dignity lasting for only two months. It was towards the ' White Guelphs ' or more moderate section that his sympathies tended; as prior, he procured the banishment of the heads and leaders of the rival factions, showing characteristic sternness and impartiality to Guelph and Ghibelline, White and Black, alike. Shortly afterwards the leaders of the Whites were permitted somehow to return. The partiality thus shown was a prominent feature in the accusation against Dante; but he had a complete answer in the fact that then he was no longer in office. In 1301, in alarm at the threatened interference of Charles of Valois, Dante was sent on an embassy to Rome to Pope Boniface VIII. From that embassy he never returned, nor did he ever again set foot in his native city. Charles espousing the side of the *Neri* or

Blacks, their victory was complete; and in January 1302 sentence of banishment went forth against Dante and others. This was followed by a yet severer sentence on March 10, which condemned them to be burned alive if ever caught, and which was repeated in 1311 and 1315. Dante's principal halting-places seem to have been—first Verona, in Tuscany, in the Lunigiano, near Urbino, and then Verona again. During this period he is said to have visited Paris; but some of his biographers connect that visit with the period of his early education. Among these is Serravalle, who wrote as late as 1417, and who is also the sole authority for Dante's alleged visit to England and Oxford. Those who, like Boccaccio, take him to France during his exile, suppose him to have been recalled to Italy and politics by the election of Henry of Luxembourg as emperor and his visit to Italy, where no emperor had set foot for more than fifty years. The exile's hopes were now roused to the highest pitch, but were finally crushed by Henry's unexpected death on August 24, 1313, after which Dante took refuge in Romagna, and finally in Ravenna, where for the most part he remained until his death, on September 14, 1321. He was buried with much pomp at Ravenna, and there he still lies, restored in 1865 to the original sarcophagus. Dante had seven children, six sons and one daughter, Beatrice, a nun at Ravenna; but his family became extinct in the 16th century.

The dates and sequence of his various works are matter of conjecture. Doubtless the *Vita Nuova* is the earliest. By far the most celebrated is the *Divina Commedia*, in which he purposes ' to say of Beatrice that which never yet was said of any woman '. In this vision of Hell, Purgatory and Heaven we have an encyclopaedic view of the highest culture and knowledge of the age on philosophy, history, classical literature, physical science, morals, theology, expressed in the sublimest and most exquisite poetry, and with consummate power and beauty of language. The *Divina Commedia* may be said to have made the Italian language, which was before so rude and unformed that Dante himself hesitated to employ it on such a theme, and is said to have commenced his poem in Latin. No work probably in the world, except the Bible, has given rise to so vast a literature. The next most important work is the fragment called the *Convito*, or *Banquet*, which takes the form of a commentary on some *canzoni*, or short poems, of the author, of which there are only three, though the work, if completed, would have contained fourteen. The *De Monarchia* (in Latin) expounds Dante's theory of the divinely intended government of the world by a universal emperor acting in harmony with a universal pope. Another unfinished work, *De Vulgari Eloquentia*, discusses the origin of language, the divisions of languages, and the dialects of Italian in particular. *Canzoniere* is a considerable collection of short poems, *canzoni*, sonnets, &c.; and, finally, we have a dozen epistles addressed mainly to leading statesmen or rulers. There are also some *Eclogues* and other minor works, as well as several of doubtful authenticity. See the edition by Edward Moore (4th ed. 1924); Lives by Toynbee (1910) and Zingarelli (1931); Gilson, *Dante the Philosopher* (1952), J. H. Whitfield, *Dante and Vergil* (1950), U. Cosmo, *Handbook to Dante Studies* (1950), and D. Sayers, *Introductory Papers* (1954).

DANTON, Georges Jacques, *dã-tõ* (1759–94), French politician, born of peasant stock at Arcis-sur-Aube, at the outbreak of the French Revolution was practising as an advocate in Paris. Mirabeau recognized his genius, and hastened to attach him to himself. The year before, with Marat and Camille Desmoulins, Danton had instituted the Cordeliers' Club, which soon became the rallying point of all the hotter revolutionists. There the tall brawny man, with harsh and daring countenance, beetling black brows, and a voice of enormous power, thundered against the aristocrats. His share in the march on the Tuileries (August 10, 1792) is very doubtful, but it is certain that immediately thereafter he appears as minister of justice. And now the gigantic personality of the man seemed to overshadow all around him. The advance of the Prussians for a moment struck panic to the heart of France; on September 2 Danton uttered the famous words: ' Pour les vaincre, pour les atterrer, que faut-il? De l'audace, encore de l'audace, et toujours de l'audace.' Paris was moved with resistless enthusiasm; she poured forth army after army of her sons, but the September massacres in the prisons were an outburst of cowardice and fear. Danton had, perhaps, a share in this atrocity, but Marat was mainly responsible. Danton voted for the death of the king (January 1793), was one of the nine original members of the Committee of Public Safety, and frequently went on missions to Dumouriez and other republican generals. In the Convention, he bent his giant strength to crush the Girondists, or moderate party, on whose fall (October 1793) the extremists found themselves supreme. Henceforth all his energies were devoted at once to fire the hearts of Frenchmen against the foreign enemy and to conciliate domestic hatreds. He strove to abate the pitiless severity of the Revolutionary Tribunal, which he had himself set up; but although Hébert and his party were cut off, Danton's policy of clemency failed to commend itself to the Mountain, whose ferocious instincts saw a more promising leader in Robespierre. For a while Danton went to his native Arcis, and forgot all the machinations of his enemies in the quiet of domestic happiness with his second wife. Soon his friends summoned him to Paris, there to be arrested and brought, on April 2, 1794, with Camille Desmoulins and a group of his friends, before the Revolutionary Tribunal. His defence was sublime in its audacity, its incoherence, its heroism and magnificent buffoonery. The first two days of his trial his mighty voice and passionate eloquence moved the people so greatly that the Committee concocted a decree to shut the mouths of men who had 'insulted Justice'; thus only could they send to his doom the greatest figure that fell in the Revolution

(April 5, 1794). See Lives by Bougeart, Robinet, Madelin (1914), Belloc (1899), Barthou (1932).

DA PONTE, Lorenzo, orig. **Emanuele Conegliano** (1749–1838), Italian poet, born at Ceneda near Venice, became professor of Rhetoric at Treviso until political and domestic troubles drove him to Vienna, where as poet to the Court Opera he wrote the libretti for Mozart's operas *Figaro* (1786), *Don Giovanni* (1787) and *Così fan Tutte* (1790). In London he taught Italian and sold boots; in 1805 he transferred to New York, where he sold liquor, tobacco and groceries and ended up as lecturer in Italian at Columbia College.

DAQUIN, or d'Aquin, Louis Claude, *da-kĩ* (1694–1772), French composer, organist and harpsichordist, born in Paris. A noted child prodigy, he played before Louis XIV when six years old and displaced his master, Marin de la Guerre, as organist of the Sainte Chapelle in 1706. He held many official posts, defeating Rameau in the contest for one in 1727, and became organist of the Chapel Royal in 1739. His works include religious music, and pieces for the organ and harpsichord, the most famous of which is *Le Coucou*.

D'ARBLAY, Madame. See BURNEY, FANNY.

DARBOY, Georges, *dar-bwah* (1813–71), born at Fayl-Billot, in Haute-Marne, in 1859 was made Bishop of Nancy, in 1863 Archbishop of Paris. He upheld the Gallican theory, waged a long struggle with the Jesuits and at the Vatican Council opposed the dogma of papal infallibility, but when it was adopted was one of the first to submit. During the German siege of Paris he was unceasing in labours of benevolence, and under the Commune he refused to leave his flock. Arrested as a hostage by the Communists, April 4, 1871, he was shot in the court of the prison of La Roquette, May 24. See Life by L. C. Price (1915).

DARBY, John Nelson (1800–82), English divine, the principal founder in 1830 of the Plymouth Brethren or ' Darbyites ', was born in London, was educated at Westminster School and Trinity College, Dublin, was for a year or two an Anglican clergyman, and died at Bournemouth. He wrote thirty works. See his *Personal Recollections* (1881).

D'ARC. See JOAN OF ARC.

DARCY, Thomas, Lord (1467–1537), English soldier and statesman, born in Yorkshire, held a number of offices, was ennobled in 1505 and made warden of the east marches. He was one of Wolsey's chief accusers, and lost favour with Henry VIII by speaking against the divorce. An opponent of the dissolution of the monasteries, he was beheaded for his part in the Pilgrimage of Grace.

DARGOMIZHSKY, Alexander Sergeievitch, *dar-gĕ-mish'ski* (1813–69), Russian composer, born in Tula. At the age of twenty-two he retired from government service to devote himself to music and composed his first opera, *Esmeralda*, which was regarded as a work of extreme realism. Later, under the influence of the Russian Nationalist composers, his setting of Pushkin's *The Stone*

Guest (completed by Rimsky-Korsakov) anticipated the work of Moussorgsky in dramatic power and naturalistic treatment of words. Dargomizhsky had little success in his lifetime except in Belgium, where he introduced his orchestral works in 1864. See Gerald Abraham's *Studies in Russian Music* (1935) and *On Russian Music* (1939).

DARÍO, Rubén, pen-name of **Felix Rubén García Sarmiento** (1867–1916), who, born in Nicaragua, lived a wandering life of journalism, amours and diplomatic appointments, and died of pneumonia. His *Azul, Prosas Profanas* (1896), &c., showing Greek and French (Parnassian and Symbolist) influence, gave new vitality to Spanish poetry. See his autobiography (1912), and H. G. Doyle *Bibliography of Rubén Darío.*

DARIUS. The name of three kings of Persia.

Darius I, surnamed **Hystaspis** (548–486 B.C.), was the son of Hystaspes, of the family of the Achaemenides (q.v.), and ascended the Persian throne in 521, after putting to death the Magian Gomates (' Smerdis '), who gave himself out to be Bardes, Cambyses' brother. He had for several years to contend with revolts in many parts of his dominions, especially Babylon. He then reorganized the Persian empire, making Susa the capital, while he pushed his conquests as far as the Caucasus and the Indus. In his expedition against the Scythians in 515, after carrying a large army—though 700,000 is an exaggeration—across the Bosporus on a bridge of boats, and subduing Thrace and Macedonia, he was led on by the retreating Scythians as far as the Volga, and returned to the Danube with heavy loss. He went back to Susa, leaving an army under Megabazus in Thrace. His first expedition against the Athenians miscarried through the wreck of his fleet at Mount Athos in 492; the second was decisively defeated at Marathon. He died in 486, before the Egyptian revolt (487) had been subdued and in the midst of preparations for a third expedition against the Athenians, and was succeeded by Xerxes (q.v.). Darius was a Persian by birth, and bred in the Zoroastrian faith, which under him became the state religion.

Darius II, surnamed **Ochus,** called by the Greeks **Nothos,** ' bastard ' (d. 405 B.C.), illegitimate son of Artaxerxes I, snatched the crown from Sogdianus, his also illegitimate brother, who had slain his legitimate brother, Xerxes II. He was the tool of his cruel half-sister and spouse Parysatis; and his reign was a long series of miseries, crimes and revolts ruthlessly suppressed. After the failure of the Sicilian expedition of the Athenians in 415, Darius broke the humiliating treaty of 449. He died at Babylon, and was succeeded by his eldest son, Artaxerxes II.

Darius III, surnamed **Codomannus** (d. 330 B.C.), son of a daughter of Artaxerxes II (q.v.), and king from 336, was defeated by Alexander at the Granicus (334), at Issus (333) and at Gaugamela or Arbela (331), and, during flight, treacherously slain by a satrap.

DARLAN, Jean Louis Xavier François, *dar-lã* (1881–1942), French admiral, passed through the École Navale in 1899, becoming *Capitaine de corvette* in 1918 and attaining Flag rank in 1929. A pronounced ' political ' and frequently termed 'l'Amiral des boulevardes', he became in turn minister of the Navy and Mercantile Marine, vice-president of the Council of Ministers, and secretary of state for Foreign Affairs and the Navy. In the early days of the Vichy régime he enjoyed the somewhat hollow title of minister for National Defence. In North Africa, as representative of the Vichy Administration, Darlan was bound to Pétain by the traditional but inflexible military *droit administratif.* It was therefore difficult to determine whether his professed readiness to co-operate with the victorious Anglo-American forces was sincere or mere temporizing. Speculation on this issue was ended by his assassination in late December 1942.

DARLEY, (1) Felix Octavius Carr (1822–88), American artist, born in Philadelphia, illustrator of Washington Irving, Fenimore Cooper, Dickens, &c.

(2) **George** (1795–1846), Irish poet and mathematician, born in Dublin, from *c.* 1822 lived in London, writing verse for periodicals, and collections entitled *The Errors of Ecstasie* (1822) and *Labours of Idleness* (1826). He also published mathematical textbooks. See his *Life and Letters* by Abbott (1928).

DARLING, (1) Charles John, 1st Baron Darling (1849–1936), English judge, born at Colchester, was educated privately, articled to a Birmingham solicitor, called to the bar (1874) and joined the Oxford circuit. A freelance journalist, he was Conservative M.P. (1888–97) when his appointment as a judge of the King's Bench aroused widespread controversy and ill-founded misgivings. He presided over the Steinie Morrison (1911) and Armstrong (1922), murder trials, the Romney picture (1917) and Pemberton Billing (1918) cases, heard the Crippen (1910) and Casement (1916) appeals, deputised for the Lord Chief Justice, Lord Reading, when the latter was ambassador in Washington (1914–18) and was a member of several royal commissions. In his august office his wit and humour tended to get the better of him as they enlivened his volumes of light verse, *Scintillae Juris* (1877), *On the Oxford Circuit* (1909), &c. On his retirement, he was raised to the peerage (1924). See biographical studies by E. Graham (1929), D. Barker (1936) and D. Walker-Smith (1938).

(2) **Grace** (1815–42), born at Bamburgh, Northumberland, with her father, William Darling (1795–1860), lighthouse keeper on one of the Farne Islands, on September 7, 1838, rescued the survivors of the *Forfarshire.* See the *Journal of William Darling* (1886) and Life by C. Smedley (1932).

DARLINGTON, (1) William (1782–1863), botanist, born at Birmingham, Penn., died at Westchester. The California pitcher plant (*Darlingtonia*) is named after him.

(2) **William Aubrey** (1890–　　), English playwright and dramatic critic, author of *Alf's Button.*

DARMESTETER, (1) Agnes Mary Francis, *née* Robinson (1857–1944), wife of (3), afterwards Mme Duclaux, was born at Leamington, and wrote verse, a novel, Lives of Emily Brontë, Froissart, Renan, Hugo, &c.

(2) **Arsène** (1846–88), brother of (3), was a distinguished philologist and French lexicographer.

(3) **James** (1849–94), born of Jewish parentage, at Château-Salins, Lorraine, in 1877 became professor of Zend at Paris. Besides works on the Zend-Avesta, he wrote on English literature and a French translation of his wife's poems.

DARNLEY, Henry Stewart, Lord (1545–67). See MARY, QUEEN OF SCOTS.

DART, Thurston (1921–71), English keyboard player, conductor and musical scholar. Educated in the Chapel Royal, and at the Royal College of Music and London University, he lectured on music at Cambridge from 1947 to 1964 (becoming professor in 1962), and from 1965 at King's Coll., London; from 1955 to 1959 he was director of the Boyd Neel Orchestra (now Philomusica of London). His regard for authenticity in early music was expressed in his *The Interpretation of Music* (1954) and exemplified in his editions of 16th and 17th century English music.

DARU, Pierre Antoine, Comte (1767–1829), French financier, poet and historian, born at Montpellier, at sixteen entered the army, was imprisoned during the Terror, and by Napoleon was made intendant-general in Austria and Prussia, and by Louis XVIII a peer. His son, **Napoleon** (1807–90), opposed the *coup d'état*, and was proscribed; but became a member of the National Assembly in 1871, of the senate in 1876.

DARUSMONT, Frances, *née* **Wright** (1795–1852), abolitionist and socialist, born at Dundee, lived mostly in America from 1818, in 1838 married (unhappily) a Frenchman, died at Cincinnati. See *Life* by Gilbert (1855).

DARWIN, (1) Charles Robert (1809–82), the discoverer of natural selection, was born at Shrewsbury. His grandfather was Dr Erasmus Darwin (q.v.); his father Dr Robert Waring Darwin, F.R.S. (1766–1848); and his mother was a daughter of Josiah Wedgwood. After five years at Shrewsbury grammar school, he studied medicine at Edinburgh University (1825–27), and then, with a view to the church, entered Christ's College, Cambridge, in 1828. Already at Edinburgh he was a member of the local Plinian Society; he took part in its natural history excursions, and read before it his first scientific paper— on Flustra or sea-mats. But it was at Cambridge that his biological studies seriously began. Here he became acquainted with Professor Henslow, the botanist, who also encouraged his interest in zoology and geology. In 1831 he took his B.A., and shortly after was recommended by Henslow as naturalist to H.M.S. *Beagle*, then about to start for a scientific survey of South American waters. He sailed on December 27, 1831, and did not return till October 2, 1836. Meanwhile he visited Teneriffe, the Cape Verde Islands, Brazil, Montevideo, Tierra del Fuego, Buenos Aires, Valparaiso, Chile, the Galapagos, Tahiti, New Zealand, Tasmania and the Keeling Islands, in which last he started his famous theory of coral reefs. It was during this long expedition that Darwin obtained that intimate knowledge of the fauna, flora and geology of many

climes which so admirably equipped him for the great task he was to perform. By 1846 he had published several works on the geological and zoological discoveries of his voyage, on coral reefs, volcanic islands, &c.— works that placed him at once in the front rank of scientists. He formed the friendship of Sir Charles Lyell, was secretary of the Geological Society in 1838–41, in 1839 was elected F.R.S., and in 1839 married his cousin, Emma Wedgwood (1808–96; see H. Litchfield's *Emma Darwin*, 1915). From 1842 he passed his time at Down, Kent, as a country gentleman among his garden, conservatories, pigeons and fowls. The practical knowledge thus gained (especially as regards variation and interbreeding) was invaluable; and private means enabled him to devote himself unremittingly, in spite of continuous ill-health, to science. At Down he addressed himself to the great work of his life—the problem of the origin of species. After five years' unremitting work, he ' allowed himself to speculate ' on the subject, and drew up in 1842 some short notes, which he enlarged in 1844 into a sketch of conclusions for his own use. These embodied in embryo the principle of natural selection, the germ of the Darwinian Theory; but with constitutional caution Darwin delayed publication of his hypothesis which was only precipitated by accident. In 1858 Alfred Russel Wallace (q.v.) sent home from the Malay Archipelago a memoir addressed to Darwin; and this, to his surprise, Darwin found to contain in essence the main idea of his own theory of natural selection. Lyell and Hooker persuaded him to read a letter of his own of the previous year simultaneously with Wallace's before the Linnean Society, which was accordingly done on July 1, 1858. Hereupon Darwin set to work seriously at once to condense his vast mass of notes, and put into shape his great work on *The Origin of Species by Means of Natural Selection,* published in November 1859. That epoch-making work was received throughout Europe with the deepest interest, was violently attacked and energetically defended, but in the end succeeded in obtaining recognition (with or without certain reservations) from almost all competent biologists. From the day of its publication Darwin continued to work on unremittingly at a great series of supplemental treatises. *The Fertilisation of Orchids* appeared in 1862, *The Variation of Plants and Animals under Domestication* in 1867 and *The Descent of Man* in 1871. The last-named work, hardly less famous than the *Origin of Species,* derives the human race from a hairy quadrumanous animal belonging to the great anthropoid group, and related to the progenitors of the orang-utan, chimpanzee and gorilla. In it Darwin also developed his important supplementary theory of sexual selection. Later works were *The Expression of the Emotions in Man and Animals* (1873), *Insectivorous Plants* (1875), *Climbing Plants* (1875), *The Effects of Cross and Self Fertilisation in the Vegetable Kingdom* (1876), *Different Forms of Flowers in Plants of the same Species* (1877), *The Power of Movement in Plants* (1880) and *The Formation of Vegetable Mould through the action of Worms* (1881). It is as the great leader of evolutionary biology that Darwin will be mainly remembered. Though not himself the originator of the evolution hypothesis, nor even the first to apply the conception of descent to plant and animal organisms, Darwin was undoubtedly the first thinker to gain for that conception a wide acceptance among biological experts. By adding to the crude evolutionism of Erasmus Darwin, Lamarck and others his own specific idea of natural selection, he supplied to the idea a sufficient cause, which raised it at once from a hypothesis to a verifiable theory. His kindliness, honesty of purpose, devotion to truth and attachment to his friends rendered him no less remarkable on the moral and emotional than on the intellectual side of his nature. He died suddenly, April 19, 1882, and was buried in Westminster Abbey. See his Life and Letters (1887; with *More Letters*, 1903) by his son, **Sir Francis**, F.R.S. (1848–1925), botanist, fellow of Christ's College. See his autobiography, edited by his grand-daughter, N. Barlow (1958), centenary essays, ed. Barnett (1958), *The Living Thoughts of Darwin*, ed. J. Huxley, and studies by J. Fisher (1958), L. Eiseley (1958), C. D. Darlington (1959) and G. Himmelfarb (1959). An elder son, **Sir George Howard**, K.C.B., F.R.S. (1845–1913), educated at Trinity College, from 1883 to 1912 was professor of Astronomy at Cambridge, distinguished for his work on tides, tidal friction, and the equilibrium of rotating masses. **Sir Charles Galton** (1887–1962), son of the above, was director of the National Physical Laboratory (1938–49).

(2) **Erasmus** (1731–1802), born near Newark, December 12, studied at Cambridge and Edinburgh, and at Lichfield became a popular physician and prominent figure from his ability, his radical and freethinking opinions, his poetry, his eight-acre botanical garden, and his imperious advocacy of temperance in drinking. After his second marriage in 1781, he settled in Derby, and then at Breadsall Priory, where he died suddenly. By his first wife he was grandfather of Charles Darwin; by his second of Francis Galton. His philosophy of nature is inconsequent and untenable, but many of his ideas are original and contain the germs of important truths. He anticipates Lamarck's views on evolution and also his own famous grandson's. Sometimes he is exceedingly happy in seeing analogies in nature; at other times he is quite fantastical. In his verse, too, amid frequent extravagance and incomprehensibility, there burst forth strains of genuine poetry. The ' Loves of the Plants ' (1789), a part of his *Botanic Garden*, was happily burlesqued in the ' Loves of the Triangles ' in the *Anti-Jacobin*. His chief prose works are *Zoonomia, or the Laws of Organic Life* (1794–96), and *Phytologia* (1799). See Life by Charles Darwin with Krause's essay (1879), and that by H. Pearson (1930); books by Brandl (1902–09).

DASENT, Sir George Webbe (1817–96), British journalist and folklorist, was born in St Vincent, of which his father was attorney-general. He was educated at Westminster School and King's College, London; graduated B.A. from Magdalen Hall, Oxford, in 1840; and was called to the bar in 1852, in which year also he took his D.C.L. He was (1845–70) a *Times* assistant-editor, and married a sister of its editor, Delane. He often acted as civil service examiner in English and modern languages, from 1872 to 1892 was a Civil Service commissioner, and was knighted in 1876. Among his works, besides four novels, are a translation of *The Prose or Younger Edda* (1842); *Popular Tales from the Norse* (1859) and *Tales from the Fjeld* (1874), both from the Norwegian of Asbjörnsen; and translations from the Icelandic of the *Saga of Burnt Njal* (1861) and the *Story of Gisli the Outlaw* (1866). His introduction to Asbjörnsen's *Popular Tales* was a solid contribution to folklore.

DASHKOVA, Ekaterina Romanovna (1743–1810), Russian princess, born at St Petersburg, married Prince Dashkov at fifteen, and was left a widow three years after. She was an intimate friend of Catharine II, one of the heads of the conspiracy against Peter III which had secured her the throne. Quarrelling with Catharine, she visited Germany, England, France and Italy, and made the acquaintance of Garrick, Dr Blair, Dr Robertson, &c. The empress and she were reconciled, but on Catharine's death in 1796 she was ordered by Paul III to retire to her estates at Novgorod. See autobiography (trans. 1840) and *Memoirs*, ed. K. Fitzlyon (1958).

DASHWOOD, (1) **Edmée Elizabeth.** See DELAFIELD.

(2) **Sir Francis** (1708–81), the founder of the profligate ' monks of Medmenham ' or ' Franciscans ', succeeded an uncle as Lord Le Despencer in 1762, and was postmaster-general, &c.

DAUBENTON, Louis Jean Marie, *dō-bã-tõ* (1716–99), French naturalist, born at Montbar in Burgundy, wrote much for Buffon's *Histoire naturelle* and the *Encyclopédie*.

DAUBENY, Charles Giles Bridle, *dawb'nee* (1795–1867), born at Stratton in Gloucestershire, became professor of Chemistry at Oxford in 1822, of Botany in 1834. He wrote on volcanoes (1826), the atomic theory (1831), &c.

D'AUBIGNÉ, *dō-been-yay,* (1) **Jean Henri Merle** (1794–1872), French historian of the Reformation, was born at Eaux-Vives, near Geneva, studied at Berlin under Neander, and in 1818 became pastor of the French Protestant church in Hamburg. In 1823 he was appointed court preacher at Brussels. Returning to Geneva, he took part in the institution of the new Evangelical Church, and filled its chair of Church History until his sudden death. His *Histoire de la Réformation du XVIe siècle* (1835–53) enjoyed immense popularity; other works were *Germany, England, and Scotland* (1848); a vindication of Cromwell (1848); and *Trois siècles de lutte en Écosse* (1849). See Life by Bonnet (Paris 1874).

(2) **Théodore Agrippa** (1552–1630), French scholar, was born near Pons in Saintonge. Of noble family, but poor, he distinguished himself as a soldier in 1567 in the Huguenot cause,

and by Henry IV was made vice-admiral of Guienne and Brittany. His severe and inflexible character frequently embroiled him with the court; and after Henry's assassination (1610) he withdrew to a life of literary study at Geneva. He died April 29, 1630, leaving a worthless son, Constant, who was father of Madame de Maintenon. D'Aubigné's *Histoire universelle, 1550–1601* (Amsterdam 1616–20), was burned in France by the common hangman. His biting satire is shown in his *Confession catholique du Sieur de Sancy* and his *Aventures du baron de Foenesté*. See his *Histoire secrète*, (1731); also French studies by Réaume (1883), Morillot (1884), Rocheblave (1910), Plattard (1933).

DAUBIGNY, Charles François, *dō-bee-nyee* (1817–78), French artist, a pupil of Delaroche, was born and died in Paris. A member of the Barbizon school, he painted landscapes, especially moonlight and river scenes, a number of which are to be seen in the National Gallery. See Life by Henriet (1875).

DAUBRÉE, Gabriel Auguste, *dō-bray* (1814–1896), French geologist and mineralogist, born at Metz, became professor of Mineralogy and director of the École des Mines at Paris. A pioneer of experimental geology, he wrote on that subject, and on crystalline rocks.

DAUDET, *dō-day,* (1) **Alphonse** (1840–97), French writer, born at Nîmes, after being educated at the Lyons Lycée was an usher at Alais; but, when only seventeen, set out for Paris with his older brother, **Ernest** (1837–1921), who became a journalist and novelist of some mark, and both obtained appointments as clerk or private secretary in the office of the Duc de Morny. Alphonse's poem *Les Amoureuses* (1858) was followed by theatrical pieces (written partly in collaboration), *La Dernière Idole* (1862), *L'Oeillet blanc* (1865), *Le Frère aîné* (1868), *Le Sacrifice* (1869), *Lise Tavernier* and *L'Arlésienne* (1872). In the journals appeared some of his best work, *Lettres de mon moulin* (collected 1869), *Robert Helmont* (1874), *Contes du lundi* (1873) and the charming extravaganza of *Tartarin de Tarascon* (1872), continued in *Tartarin sur les Alpes* (1885) and *Port Tarascon* (1890). *Le Petit Chose* (1868) is full of pathos and of reminiscences of his own early struggles; *Jack* (1876) is the story of a bastard; in *Fromont jeune et Risler aîné* (1874) the devotion of a man of business to his firm, his wife and his brother meets with an evil return. *Le Nabab* (1877) was a transparent caricature of Morny; the chief parts in *Les Rois en exil* (1879) are supposed to have been played also by actual persons; the hero of *Numa Roumestan* (1881) bears some resemblance to Gambetta; in *L'Évangéliste* (1883) the Salvation Army was introduced; *Sapho* (1884) is a tale of the infatuation of a young man for a courtesan; and in *L'Immortel* (1888) all the author's powers of ridicule are turned against the French Academy. Daudet has been compared with Dickens. He died December 16, 1897, and *Le Soutien de famille* came out in 1898. See Daudet's *Trente ans de Paris* (1887) and *Souvenirs d'un*

homme de lettres (1888), Ernest Daudet's *Mon frère et moi* (1882); books by R. H. Sherard (1894), Léon Daudet (trans. 1899) and Dobie (1949).
(2) **Julia Allard** (1845–1940), wife of (1), wrote *Souvenirs* (1910), poems, &c.
(3) **Léon** (1867–1942), French writer, son of (1), studied medicine but turned to journalism, and from 1908 was associated with the Royalist newspaper *Action française,* of which he became editor. He sat in the Chamber of Deputies from 1919 to 1924; in 1925 his son was assassinated and subsequently he spent some time in Belgium as a political exile. He wrote several novels, but is best remembered for his numerous memoirs and critical works, some of which have been translated into English.

D'AUMALE. See AUMALE, DUC D'.

DAUMER, Georg Friedrich, *dow'mėr* (1800–1875), German moral philosopher, was born at Nuremberg, where he taught in the gymnasium, and where Kaspar Hauser (q.v.) committed to his care. He abandoned pietism for bitter antagonism to Christianity, but in 1859 became a foremost champion of Ultramontanism. His many philosophical writings reflect his varying positions; his poetical works, especially *Mahomet* (1848), gained a high reputation. He died at Würzburg. See H. Kern, *Von Paracelsus bis Klages* (1942).

DAUMIER, Honoré, *dōm-yay* (1808–79), French painter and caricaturist, was born at Marseilles and died at Valmondois, in his old age blind and befriended by Corot. Though he won contemporary fame for satirical cartoons on the theme of government corruption and incompetence, and was imprisoned for caricaturing the king, his stature as a serious artist is now universally recognized. An opponent of artificial classicism, he painted strongly realistic subject pictures with an intense feeling for form and expression almost reminiscent of Michelangelo—indeed, we are told that Daubigny, on seeing that master's ceiling in the Sistine Chapel, said that it looked as if it were by Daumier. Among his masterpieces are *Don Quixote,* in Chicago, and *The Third Class Carriage,* in the Metropolitan Museum of Art, New York. See studies by M. Sadleir (1925), E. Fuchs (1930), J. Erényi (1946) and Wartmann (1946).

DAUN, Leopold Joseph, Graf von, *down* (1705–1766), Austrian soldier, born at Vienna, served against the Turks and through the war of the Austrian Succession, in 1754 being made a field-marshal. In the Seven Years' War (1757) he neutralized the Austrian defeat under Browne near Prague by driving Frederick the Great, who had beleaguered that city, to Kolin, and forcing him to evacuate Bohemia. On October 14, 1758, he gained another victory at Hochkirch, and came near to annihilating the Prussian army. In 1759 at Maxen he forced Fink to surrender with 11,000 men. After this, however, he gained no important successes, Frederick having grasped the tactics of ' the Austrian Fabius Cunctator '.

DAURAT, Jean, *dō-rah* (c. 1510–88), a gifted French scholar, as president of the Collège de

Coqueret superintended the studies of Ronsard, Du Bellay, Baif and Belleau. These poets, with whom he was united in the famous Pléiade, he carefully trained for the task of reforming the vernacular and ennobling French literature by imitation of Greek and Latin models.

DAVAINE, Casimir Joseph (1812–82), French biologist, a pioneer of bacteriology, whose investigations into the bacterial origin of anthrax set Robert Koch (q.v.) on the road to isolating the bacillus. He was the first to use experimental infection.

D'AVENANT, (1) **Charles** (1656–1714), eldest son of (2), studied at Balliol, sat in parliament under James II and William III, and was commissioner of excise and joint-licenser of plays, secretary to the commissioners for union with Scotland, and inspector-general of imports and exports. Among his writings are *Discourses on the Revenues of England* (1698) and *A Discourse upon Grants* (1700).

(2) **Sir William** (1606–68), English poet and playwright, father of (1), was born at Oxford, where his father kept the Crown, a tavern at which Shakespeare used to stop on the way between London and Stratford. Hence arose a baseless scandal as to D'Avenant's parentage, which D'Avenant was willing enough to foster. In his twelfth year the precocious boy penned an ' Ode in Remembrance of Master Shakespeare ', not printed, however, until 1638. After a short period of study at Lincoln College, he became page to Frances, Duchess of Richmond; next was in the household of the aged poet, Fulke Greville, Lord Brooke; and in 1628 took to writing for the stage. During the next ten years he produced many plays, the least poor of which were *The Cruel Brother* (1630) and *The Wits* (1636). In 1638, at the request of the queen, he was appointed poet laureate in succession to Ben Jonson. About the same time he lost his nose through an illness—a calamity which laid him open to the merriment of such wits as Suckling and Denham. He afterwards became manager of Drury Lane Theatre, but in the Civil War was flung into the Tower. He soon escaped to France, and returning, so distinguished himself that he was knighted by Charles at the siege of Gloucester (September 1643). D'Avenant again got into difficulties, and was confined in the Tower for two years, where he completed his tedious epic of *Gondibert* (1651). In 1656 he gave what was practically the first opera in England, with Mrs Coleman as the first actress that ever appeared on an English stage.

DAVID (Heb., ' beloved '), the first king of the Judean dynasty of Israel, was the youngest son of Jesse of Bethlehem, and distinguished himself by slaying Goliath. Saul appointed him to a military command, and gave him his daughter Michal to wife; but he had soon to flee from the king's jealousy. In the cave of Adullam, near Gath, he gathered a troop of 400 freebooters, with whom he ranged through the country between Philistia and the Dead Sea. Saul's expeditions against him put him to great straits, and for over a year David became a vassal of the Philistine king of Gath. After the death of Saul and Jonathan at Gilboa, he reigned seven and a half years in Hebron over the tribe of Judah, while Ishbosheth, Saul's son, ruled the rest of Israel. On the death of Ishbosheth, all Israel chose David as king. He conquered the independent city of Jebus (Jerusalem), and made it the political and religious centre of his kingdom, building a palace for himself on its highest hill, Zion (the ' city of David '), and placing the Ark of the Covenant there under a tent. In the course of a few years the conquest of the Philistines, Moabites, Aramaeans, Edomites and Ammonites reduced the whole territory from Egypt to the Euphrates. The last years of his long reign of thirty-two years in Jerusalem were troubled by attempted revolutions by his sons Absalom and Adonijah. The death of the greatest of the kings of Israel took place at earliest 1018, at latest 993 B.C. ' The sweet singer of Israel ' was doubtless the creator of the sublime religious lyric poetry of the Hebrews, though possibly not many of the Psalms as we have them are David's own handiwork.

DAVID, or **Dewi, St,** the patron saint of Wales, according to the *Annales Cambriae* (10th cent.) died in 601, Bishop of Moni Judeorum, or Menevia, afterwards St Davids. He presided over two Welsh Synods, at Brefi and ' Lucus Victoriae '.

DAVID. Two kings of Scotland:

David I (*c.* 1080–1153), was the youngest of the six sons of Malcolm Canmore and St Margaret (q.v.). He was sent in 1093 to England along with his sister Matilda (who in 1100 married Henry I of England), and remained for several years at the English court. In 1107, when his elder brother Alexander succeeded to the throne, David became Prince of Cumbria, with a territory which, besides part of Cumberland, included all southern Scotland except the Lothians. By his marriage in 1113 to Matilda, widow of the Norman Earl of Northampton and daughter of the Saxon Earl of Northumbria, he became Earl of Huntingdon. In 1124 he succeeded his brother on the Scottish throne; in 1127 he swore, with the other great barons of England, to maintain the right of his niece, Matilda, to the English crown. In 1135, then, he took up arms on her behalf when Stephen seized the throne, and penetrated into England as far as Durham, where peace was purchased by the confirmation of the earldom of Huntingdon to his son Henry, and the promise of that of Northumberland. In 1138 the war was, however, renewed, and David, deserted by Bruce and others of his Anglo-Norman vassals who owned large estates in England, was signally defeated at the ' Battle of the Standard ', near Northallerton. The next year a second peace was concluded, when the promised earldom of Northumberland was bestowed on Prince Henry. The rest of David's reign—which marks the end of Celtic and the beginning of Feudal Scotland—was devoted to the welding of the different races of Scotland into one nation, the civilization of the people by the erection of burghs, the promotion of trade, manufactures and commerce, and the founding or restoration of bishoprics and religious houses. According to Bellenden,

' the croun was left indegent throw ampliation of gret rentis to the kirk ', a state of matters that led James I (of Scotland) to remark, while standing by David's tomb at Dunfermline, that ' he was ane sair sanct for the crown '. He is often called ' St David ', though he was never formally canonized; but his name was inserted in the calendar prefixed to Laud's Prayer Book for Scotland (1637). He died at Carlisle, May 24, 1153, and was succeeded by his grandson, Malcolm.

David II (1324–71), only son of King Robert Bruce, was born at Dunfermline, and was married in 1328 to Edward II's daughter, Joanna. In 1329 he succeeded his father, and in 1331 was crowned, with his child queen, at Scone. In 1334 the success of Edward Baliol (q.v.) and Edward III's victory at Halidon Hill forced David's guardians to send him and his consort to France, whence he returned in 1341. Five years later he invaded England, but at Neville's Cross, near Durham, was utterly routed by the Archbishop of York, October 17, 1346. For eleven years a prisoner in or near London, and at Odiham in Hampshire, at length in 1357 he was released on promise of a ransom of 100,000 merks, whose non-payment involved him in shameful dependence on England. In 1363 he actually proposed to his parliament that Edward III's second son should succeed him on the Scottish throne; and though the proposal was curtly rejected the intrigue between the two kings was ended only by David's death at Edinburgh Castle, February 22, 1371. Queen Joanna dying in 1362, David next year had married Margaret Logie, a comely widow, whom he divorced in 1369. By neither marriage had he any issue, so was succeeded by his sister's son, Robert II.

DAVID, (1) **Félicien,** *dah-veed* (1810–76), French composer, born at Cadenet, was first a chorister in Aix cathedral, then at twenty entered the Paris Conservatoire. He became an ardent disciple of St Simon and of Enfantin; and finally, on the break-up of the brotherhood in 1833, travelled to the East. In 1835 he returned to Paris, and published his *Mélodies Orientales* for the pianoforte. They were unsuccessful; and David remained in obscurity till his *Désert* (1844), a grand 'Ode-symphonie', had a sudden and complete success. He failed to retain his popularity, but the oriental devices and motifs which he used influenced many other composers.

(2) **Ferdinand,** *dah'feet* (1810–73), German violinist, was born at Hamburg, studied under Spohr at Cassel, and was concertmeister at Leipzig from 1836 till his death at Klosters in the Grisons. Mendelssohn's violin concerto was written under his close supervision. See work by Eckardt (Leipzig 1888).

(3) **Gerhard,** *da'vit* (c. 1460–1523), Flemish painter, born at Oudewater in Holland, in 1484 entered the Painters' Guild of Bruges, of which he became dean in 1501. The National Gallery, London, contains his admirable *Canon and Patron Saints.* See *Portfolio* for December 1895.

(4) **Jacques Louis,** *dah-veed* (1748-1825), French painter, was born at Paris. He gained the ' prix de Rome ' in 1774, and at Rome devoted himself to drawing from the antique. On his return to France his *Belisarius* (1780) procured his admission to the Academy. Soon afterwards he married, and visited Italy again and also Flanders. It is in the works of this period, such as the *Oath of the Horatii* (1784), *Death of Socrates* (1788), and *Brutus Condemning his Son* (1789), that the classical feeling is first clearly visible. David entered with enthusiasm into the Revolution, and in 1792 became a representative for Paris in the Convention. He voted for the death of Louis XVI, was a member of the Committee of Public Safety, and was the artistic director of the great national fêtes founded on classical customs. After Robespierre's death he was twice imprisoned, and narrowly escaped with his life. Released in 1795, he produced his masterpiece, *The Rape of the Sabines* (1799), and in 1804 was appointed court painter by Napoleon. After the Bourbon restoration he was banished in 1816 as a regicide, and died at Brussels. See works by his grandson (1880), Cantinelli (1930), and Life by A. Maurois (1949).

(5) **Pierre Jean,** called **David d'Angers** (1789–1856), French sculptor, was born at Angers. In spite of the opposition of his father, a woodcarver, he resolved to become an artist; and, going to Paris in 1808, placed himself under Jacques Louis David (q.v.). In 1811 his *rilievo* of the *Death of Epaminondas* gained the ' grand prix ', and David proceeded to Rome, where he became intimate with Canova. In 1816 he returned to France. A statue of the Great Condé established his reputation; and in 1826 he was elected to the Institute and appointed a professor in the School of the Fine Arts. During the July revolution, David fought in the ranks of the people; in 1835–37 he executed the pediment of the Pantheon; in 1848 his republicanism procured him a seat in the Constituent Assembly. After the *coup d'état* he was exiled, but soon returned from Greece to France. In the Angers museum 200 of his works are preserved, as well as 400 of his medallions and many drawings. See Life by Jouin (1878–90).

DAVIDS, Thomas William Rhys (1843–1922), British orientalist, born at Colchester and educated at Brighton and Breslau, in 1866 entered the Ceylon civil service, in 1877 was called to the bar in London, and was professor of Pali and Buddhist Literature in University College, London, 1882–1912; of Comparative Religion in Manchester, 1904–15.

DAVIDSON, (1) **John** (1857–1909), poet, born at Barrhead, Renfrewshire, in 1890 went to London, and from 1885 until his suicide in 1909 wrote verse, plays, novels, &c., the best known being *Fleet Street Eclogues* (1893). See study by H. Fineman (Philadelphia 1916).

(2) **Randall Thomas** (1848–1930), **Baron Davidson of Lambeth** (1928), Archbishop, born at Edinburgh, studied at Harrow and Trinity College, Oxford; was chaplain to Archbishop Tait and to Queen Victoria, Dean of Windsor, Bishop of Rochester (1891) and of Winchester (1895), and Archbishop of Canterbury (1903; resigned 1928).

He wrote the life of Archbishop Tait (his father-in-law) in 1891. See Life by G. K. A. Bell (1952).

(3) **Thomas** (1838–70), poet, the ' Scottish probationer ', was born at Oxnam, studied at Edinburgh, and in 1864 was licensed as a U.P. preacher. See Life by Rev. James Brown (1877).

(4) **Thomas** (1840–1900), Scottish writer on mediaeval philosophy, Rosmini, education, art, &c., was born at Deer, Aberdeenshire, studied at Aberdeen, and from 1867 lived in the U.S.A., an indefatigable and original thinker and teacher.

DAVIES, (1) Christian, or **Mother Ross** (1667–1739), was born at Dublin and died at Chelsea Pensioners' Hospital, having in 1693 enlisted as a private, and served through Marlborough's campaigns. She was several times wounded and thrice married.

(2) **Clement** (1884–1962), Welsh politician, born at Llanfyllin, Montgomeryshire. He was educated at Llanfyllin and Trinity Hall, Cambridge, and was called to the bar in 1909. He became Liberal M.P. for Montgomeryshire in 1929, and in 1945 he was elected Leader of the decimated Liberal party in the House of Commons, holding this office until September 1956, when he resigned. He stubbornly refused all ministerial offices offered by the Conservative Governments, did not enter into any political agreements with either of the two great parties and thus kept the Liberal party a separate political entity. He conducted a brilliant parliamentary defence of Seretse Khama against the actions of successive Labour and Conservative colonial secretaries.

(3) **Sir Henry Walford** (1869–1941; kt. 1922), composer, organist and popular broadcaster on music, born at Oswestry, was professor of Music at Aberystwyth (1919–26), organist of St George's Chapel, Windsor (1927–32), master of the King's Musick (1934–41). See study by H. C. Colles (1942).

(4) **Hubert Henry** (1876–1917), playwright, born at Woodley, Cheshire, was a journalist in San Francisco, returned to England in 1901, and disappeared in 1917. He wrote *Cousin Kate* and *The Mollusc*.

(5) **John** (1565–1618), English poet and writing master, was born at Hereford. His poems, not without merit but prolix and tedious, were collected by Dr Grosart (2 vols. 1873).

(6) **Sir John** (1569–1626), poet and statesman, was born of a good family at Tisbury, Wiltshire. At sixteen he entered Queen's College, Oxford, and later entered the Middle Temple. He was called to the bar in 1595, but was disbarred three years later for breaking a stick in the dining hall over the head of a wit whose raillery had provoked him. He returned to Oxford, but in 1601, after ample apologies, was readmitted to the Middle Temple, and was returned to parliament for Corfe Castle. On the death of Elizabeth he accompanied the official commissioners to the Scottish court and quickly came into favour with James I, who sent him in 1603 as solicitor-general to Ireland. Three years later he was appointed Irish attorney-general and was knighted. He supported

severe repressive measures, and took part in the plantation of Ulster. He was for some time speaker of the Irish parliament; but was returned to the English parliament in 1614 for Newcastle-under-Lyme, and practised as king's serjeant in England. He had been nominated chief justice a month before his death of apoplexy, December 7, 1626. In 1622 he collected into one volume his three chief poems—*Orchestra, or a Poeme of Dancing* (1596); *Nosce Teipsum* (1599), a long didactic piece on the soul's immortality; and *Hymns to Astraea* (1599), a collection of clever acrostics on the name Elizabeth Regina. His complete works were collected by Dr Grosart (3 vols. 1869–76). His widow, **Eleanor Touchet,** daughter of Baron Audley, married again, and survived till 1652. She imagined herself a prophetess.

(7) **Sarah Emily** (1830–1921), English feminist, born at Southampton, campaigned as secretary of a committee for access of girls to the Cambridge local examinations, granted in 1865, helped to found Hitchin College for women (1867), which became Girton College, Cambridge (1873), of which she was secretary (1882–1904), and as a member of the London School Board (1870–73), agitated for London degrees for women, granted in 1874. See study by B. Stephen (1927).

(8) **William Henry** (1871–1940), British poet, born in Newport, Monmouthshire. Emigrating to the United States at the age of twenty-two, he lived partly as a tramp and partly as a casual workman until the loss of a leg whilst ' jumping ' a train caused him to return to England, where he began to write and lived the life of a tramp and pedlar in order to raise sufficient money to have his poems printed by a jobbing printer. A copy of this first work, *A Soul's Destroyer*, came into the hands of Bernard Shaw, who arranged for its regular publication in 1907. The success of this book was consolidated by *The Autobiography of a Super-tramp* (1908). His later works, including poetry, *Poet's Calendar* (1927) &c., the prose *Adventures of Johnny Walker, Tramp* (1926), and the essays *Beggars* (1909) and *My Garden* (1933), maintained his success. His *Collected Poems* (about 600) were published in 1943. In 1919 he was awarded a Civil List pension. See his further autobiography, *Later Days* (1925) and the studies by T. Moult (1934) and R. Stonesifer (1963).

DAVILA, Enrico Caterino, *dah'vi-la* (1576–1631), Italian historian, born near Padua, entered the service of France, and then that of Venice. He was shot near Verona by an assassin. His great work is the *Storia delle guerre civili di Francia, 1558–98* (1630; trans. 1647).

DA VINCI. See LEONARDO DA VINCI.

DAVIOT, Gordon. See MACKINTOSH, (2) ELIZABETH.

DAVIS, (1) Dwight Filley (1879–1945), American public official, born at St Louis, Missouri. In 1900 he donated an international challenge cup for lawn tennis, competed for annually. The Davis Cup signifies world team championship.

(2) **Jefferson** (1808–89), president of the

Confederate States, was born in Christian county, Kentucky, studied at West Point, and served in several frontier campaigns, but resigned his commission in 1835. He entered congress in 1845 for Mississippi, and served with distinction in the Mexican war (1846–47) as colonel of volunteers. He was sent to the senate in 1847, 1848 and 1850; and in 1853–1857 was secretary of war. Returning to the senate, he succeeded Calhoun as leader of the extreme State Rights party, and as such carried in the senate (May 1860) his seven resolutions asserting the inability of congress or the legislatures of the territories to prohibit slavery. The lower house of congress refused to concur; the failure of the Democratic National Convention at Charleston to adopt like resolutions caused the disruption of the Democratic party; and the election of Lincoln to the presidency was an immediate result. In January 1861 Mississippi seceded from the Union; a few weeks later Davis was chosen provisional president of the Confederate States, an appointment confirmed for six years in November. The history of his presidency is that of the war of 1861–65 (see the articles on Grant, Sherman, Lee and Stonewall Jackson). In May 1865, after the collapse of his government, Davis was captured by Union cavalry, imprisoned for two years in Fortress Monroe on Hampton Roads, then released on bail. Though indicted for treason, he was never brought to trial; and he was included in the amnesty of 1868. After 1879 he resided on an estate bequeathed to him in Mississippi. In 1881 he published *The Rise and Fall of the Confederate Government*. He died December 6, 1889; in 1893 his remains were translated to Richmond. See Lives by Alfriend (1868), Pollard (1869), his widow (2 vols. 1891) and McElroy (1937); also Craven's *Prison-life of Jefferson Davis* (1866).

(3) **John** (c. 1550–1605), English navigator, was born at Sandridge, near Dartmouth, about 1550, and undertook in 1585–87 three Arctic voyages in search of a Northwest passage. In the last voyage he sailed with a barque of apparently not over twenty tons as far as 73° N. lat., and discovered Davis Strait. He next made two ill-fated voyages towards the South Seas and as pilot of a Dutch vessel to the East Indies. In his last voyage as pilot of an English ship he was killed by Japanese pirates at Bintang, near Singapore. His *World's Hydrographical Description* (1595) and *The Seaman's Secrets* (1594) were edited by Captain A. H. Markham (Hakluyt Soc. 1878). See Life by Sir Clements R. Markham (1889).

(4) **John** (d. 1622), of Limehouse, a navigator to the East Indies, died at Batavia, having published in 1618 *A Ruter or Briefe Direction for Readie Sailings into the East India*.

(5) **Moll** (fl. 1669), an actress and dancer, mother by Charles II of Lady Mary Tudor, whose son was the Earl of Derwentwater (q.v.).

(6) **Richard Harding** (1864–1916), American writer, born at Philadelphia, wrote novels, short stories and plays, and was a famous war correspondent. See Life by F. D. Downey.

(7) **Thomas Osborne** (1814–45), Irish poet

and patriot, born at Mallow, studied at Trinity College, Dublin. Called to the Irish bar in 1838, he joined the Repeal Association though a Protestant, and in 1841 became joint editor with John Dillon of the *Dublin Morning Register*. In 1842, with Dillon and Duffy, he founded the *Nation* newspaper, ' to direct the popular mind to the great end of nationality '. His *Poems* and *Essays* were published in 1846 (new ed. 1915), *Prose Writings* in 1890. See *Memoirs* (1890), *Short Life* (1896) by Sir C. G. Duffy, and T. W. Moody's *Davis* (1945).

(8) **William** (1627–90), a Gloucestershire highwayman, known as the ' Golden Farmer ' from his always paying in gold. He was hanged for shooting a pursuing butcher.

(9) **William Morris** (1850–1935), American geomorphologist, was professor of Geology at Harvard, where he was educated. He introduced the term *peneplain* into physical geography to describe a rolling lowland, and was the first to formulate the doctrine of the ' cycle of erosion '.

DAVISON, William (c. 1541–1608), Queen Elizabeth's secretary in 1586–87, and her stalking-horse in the execution of Mary Stuart, after which he was imprisoned for two years in the Tower.

DAVISSON, Clinton Joseph (1881–1958), American physicist, educated at Chicago and Princeton, where he was instructor in physics before taking up industrial research at the Bell Telephone Laboratories. In 1927, with L. H. Germer, he discovered the diffraction of electrons by crystals. In 1937 he shared the Nobel prize for physics with George Paget Thomson.

DAVITT, Michael (1846–1906), founder of the Irish Land League, was born, a peasant's son, at Straid, County Mayo. Evicted from their smallholding, the family emigrated to Haslingden in Lancashire (1851); and here in 1857 the boy lost his right arm through a machinery accident in a cotton factory. In 1866 he joined the Fenian movement, and was sentenced in 1870 to fifteen years' penal servitude. He was released in 1877, and, supplied with funds from the States, began an anti-landlord crusade which culminated in the Land League (October 21, 1879). Davitt was thenceforward in frequent collision with the government, and from February 1881 to May 1882 was imprisoned in Portland for breaking his ticket-of-leave. His *Leaves from a Prison Diary* were published in 1885. A strong Home Ruler, but Socialist on the question of land nationalization, after the split in the party he opposed Parnell (q.v.), and was returned to parliament in 1892 as an anti-Parnellite, but unseated on the ground of clerical intimidation. In 1895 he was returned unopposed by South Mayo, but resigned in 1899.

DAVOUT, Louis Nicolas, *dah-voo* (1770–1823), French marshal, was born at Annoux, in Burgundy; was educated with Bonaparte at the military school of Brienne. As general he accompanied Bonaparte to the East, and mainly secured the victory at Aboukir. A marshal of the empire (1804), he acted a brilliant part at Austerlitz (1805) and Auerstädt, and was made Duke of Auerstädt

DAVY

361

DAWSON

(1808). At Eckmühl and at Wagram he checked the Austrians' attack, and in 1811 was created Prince of Eckmühl. As governor of Poland he ruled that country with the harshest despotism; in the Russian campaign of 1812 he gathered fresh laurels on the fields of Mohilev and Vitebsk. After the retreat from Moscow he became governor-general of the Hanse towns, and at Hamburg maintained a régime of repression till the first restoration of the Bourbons. On Bonaparte's return from Elba, Davout was appointed war minister; and after Waterloo he received the command of the remnant of the French army under the walls of Paris. In 1819 he was made a peer of France. See his *Correspondance* (5 vols. 1885–87), and Lives by Chénier (1886), his daughter, the Marquise Blocqueville (3 vols. 1879–80), and Montégut (1882).

DAVY, (1) **Sir Humphry** (1778–1829), English chemist, was born and educated at Penzance, where his father was a woodcarver, there and at Truro. In 1795 he was apprenticed to a Penzance surgeon, wrote verses, made chemical experiments, entered on an encyclopaedic course of study, and in 1797 seriously took up chemistry. Dr Beddoes (q.v.), who in 1798 established a Pneumatic Institute at Clifton, took him as his assistant. Here he met Coleridge and Southey, and experimented on the respiration of gases (more than once nearly losing his life), and discovered the effect of laughing gas. The account in his *Researches, Chemical and Philosophical* (1799) led to his appointment as lecturer to the Royal Institution. He delivered his first lecture in 1801; and his eloquence and the novelty of his experiments soon attracted brilliant audiences. In 1803 he began researches in agriculture, on which he delivered his epoch-making lectures—*Elements of Agricultural Chemistry* (1813). His fame chiefly rests in the views originated in his Bakerian lecture *On Some Chemical Agencies of Electricity* (1806), followed up by the grand discovery that the alkalis and earths are compound substances formed by oxygen united with metallic bases. He first decomposed potash in 1807; when he saw the globules of the new metal, *potassium*, his delight was ecstatic. In similar manner he discovered the new metals *sodium, barium, strontium, calcium* and *magnesium*. He lectured in Dublin in 1808–09, and received the LL.D. of Trinity College. In 1812 Davy was knighted, and married Mrs Apreece, *née* Jane Kerr (1780–1855), a lady of considerable wealth; in 1813 he resigned the chemical chair of the Royal Institution, when he was elected honorary professor of Chemistry. To investigate his new theory of volcanic action he visited the Continent with Faraday, and was received with the greatest distinction by the French *savants*, though England and France were at war. In 1815 he investigated fire damp and invented his safety lamp. He was created a baronet in 1818, and in 1820 succeeded Sir Joseph Banks as president of the Royal Society. In 1820–23 his researches on electromagnetism were communicated to the society. He died at Geneva. Among his writings were *Elements of Chemical Philosophy*

(1812); *On the Safety-lamp* (1818); *Salmonia, or Days of Fly-fishing* (1828); and *Consolations in Travel* (1830)—all included in his Collected Works (9 vols. 1839–40). See *Memoirs* (1836) by his brother, John Davy, M.D. (1790–1868), who also wrote on Ceylon, physiology, the Ionian Islands, &c.; Sir Humphry's *Fragmentary Remains* (1858); Lives by Thorpe (1896), Kendall (1954), and *The Scientific Achievements of Sir Humphry Davy* by J. C. Gregory (1930).

(2) **John** (1763–1824), English composer of the song 'The Bay of Biscay', &c., was born, an illegitimate child, at Creedy Bridge, near Exeter; was brought up by his uncle, a blacksmith; played and taught music at Exeter and London; and died penniless in London.

DAVYS, John. See DAVIS.

DAWES, (1) **Charles Gates** (1865–1951), Republican vice-president of U.S.A. under Coolidge, 1925–29, financier and general, born at Marietta, Ohio, was head of the commission which drew up the 'Dawes plan' (1924) for German Reparation payments. He was awarded the Nobel Peace prize for 1925.

(2) **Richard** (1708–66), Hellenist, was born near Market Bosworth. Cobet ranks him with Bentley and Porson as one of the 'three English Richards', his own masters.

(3) **Sophia** (1790–1840), English adventuress, born at St Helens in the Isle of Wight, was a fisherman's daughter, an inmate in a workhouse, an officer's mistress, a servant in a brothel, mistress to the Duc de Bourbon, wife (1818) to his aide-de-camp, the Baron de Feuchères, and perhaps the Duc's murderess (1830).

DAWKINS, Sir William Boyd (1837–1929; kt. 1919), English geologist, was born at Buttington vicarage, near Welshpool, and educated at Rossall School and Jesus College, Oxford. He joined the Geological Survey in 1861, became curator of Manchester Museum in 1870, and professor of Geology in Manchester in 1872. His books are *Cave-hunting; or, Caves and the Early Inhabitants of Europe* (1874); and *Early Man in Britain* (1880).

DAWSON, (1) **Charles** (1864–1916), English antiquarian, victim or perpetrator of the 'Piltdown skull' hoax, was a Sussex lawyer who collected downland fossils as a hobby. Cranial fragments, found by him at Piltdown in 1912, together with parts of a jawbone unearthed later, were accepted by anthropologists as Lower Pleistocene human remains, and as such one of the greatest discoveries of the age, being named after him *Eoanthropus Dawsoni*. Many experts had doubts, but it was not until 1953 that the skull was formally denounced as a fake, after scientific tests had established that the jawbone was that of a modern ape, coloured to simulate age, that the cranium had also been stained to match the gravel deposits in which it was found, and that the fragments had clearly been 'planted' on the site. See J. S. Weiner, *The Piltdown Forgery* (1955), and F. Vere, *The Piltdown Fantasy* (1955).

(2) **George Mercer** (1849–1901), Canadian geologist, son of (5), born at Pictou, educated at McGill University, did much pioneer

geological work in British Columbia and the Yukon, where Dawson City was named after him.

(3) **Henry** (1811–78), landscape painter, was born at Hull, till 1835 was a Nottingham lace-maker, then took to art, and died at Chiswick, the price of his pictures having risen from £5 or less to £800 or more. He specialized in marine and river scenes, as *The Wooden Walls of Old England*, perhaps his best-known work. See Life by his son (1890).

(4) **James** (1717–46), the son of a Manchester apothecary, studied for the church at St John's College, Cambridge, but having held a captaincy in Prince Charles Edward's army, was hanged on Kennington Green. His sweetheart died in her coach there simultaneously. The incident gave rise to Shenstone's ballad 'Jemmy Dawson'.

(5) **Sir John William** (1820–99), Canadian geologist, father of (2), born at Pictou, Nova Scotia, studied at Edinburgh, and afterwards devoted himself to the natural history and geology of Nova Scotia and New Brunswick. He was appointed superintendent of education in Nova Scotia in 1850; and from 1855 to 1893 was principal of McGill University, Montreal. He was an authority on fossil plants and was a systematic anti-Darwinian. Among his works are *Acadian Geology* (1855), *Archaia* (1858), *Story of the Earth and Man* (1872), *Dawn of Life* (1875), *Origin of the World* (1877), *Fossil Men* (1878), *Egypt and Syria* (1885), *The Meeting-place of Geology and History* (1894) and *Relics of Primeval Life* (1897).

DAWSON OF PENN, Bertrand Edward, 1st Viscount (1864–1945), English doctor, born at Purley, was physician-in-ordinary successively to Edward VII, George V, Edward VIII, George VI and Queen Mary. He became a baron in 1920, a viscount in 1936.

DAY, (1) Daniel (1683–1767), a Wapping pump and block maker, the founder of Fairlop Fair.

(2) **John** (1522–84), English printer, born at Dunwich, set up his press in London. One of the first English music printers, he produced the earliest church service book with musical notation (1560), and in the same year Parker's English version of the psalms, with music by Tallis and others. His most celebrated publication was Foxe's *Actes and Monuments* (1563), better known as the *Book of Martyrs*.

(3) **John** (1574–1640?), English dramatist, studied at Caius College, Cambridge, is mentioned in Henslowe's *Diary* in 1598 as an active playwright, and collaborated freely with Chettle, Dekker, &c. His Works, privately printed by A. H. Bullen in 1881, include a graceful comedy, *Humour out of Breath*, and *The Parliament of Bees*, an allegorical masque.

(4) **Thomas** (1748–89), English author of *Sandford and Merton*, was born in London, and thirteen months later by his father's death became heir to £900 a year. From the Charterhouse he passed to Corpus, Oxford, where he formed a close friendship with Richard Lovell Edgeworth (q.v.). In 1765 he entered the Middle Temple, in 1775 was

called to the bar, but never practised. A disciple of Rousseau, he brought up an orphan blonde and a foundling brunette, one of whom should become his wife. That scheme miscarried; 'and, admitted to the Lichfield coterie, he proposed first to Honora and next to Elizabeth Sneyd. She sent him to France to acquire the French graces; as acquired by him they but moved her to laughter. Finally in 1778 he married an appreciative heiress, Esther Milnes, and spent with her eleven happy years, farming on philanthropic and costly principles in Essex and Surrey, till on September 28, 1789, he was killed by a fall from a colt he was breaking in. Two only of Day's eleven works call for mention—*The Dying Negro* (1773) and the *History of Sandford and Merton* (3 vols. 1783–89). The poem struck the keynote of the antislavery movement; the child's book is excellent although sometimes, like its author, ridiculous. See Lives by Keir (1791), Blackman (1862) and Gignilliat (1933).

DAYE, Stephen (*c.* 1610–68), American printer, born in London, in 1639 set up at Harvard the first New England printing press. He died at Cambridge, Mass.

DAY-LEWIS, Cecil (1904–72), British poet, born in Ballintogher, Ireland. During the 'thirties, together with Auden and Spender, he was highly regarded for bringing new life to poetry with contemporary symbols and ideas. He was publicized in 1936 for his pamphlet refuting Huxley's defence of absolute pacifism, and in 1939 he broke away from Communism. He was professor of Poetry at Oxford (1951–56), and under the pseudonym of Nicholas Blake wrote excellent detective stories. His work includes *A Hope Of Poetry* (1934), *The Friendly Tree* (1936), *Overtures to Death* (1938) and a translation of the *Aeneid* (1952). He was created C.B.E. in 1950, and poet laureate in 1968. His *Collected Poems* appeared in 1954, and his autobiographical *The Buried Day* in 1960. See study by Dyment (1955).

DEÁK, Francis, *day'-ahk* (1803–76), Hungarian statesman, born in Söjtör, Zala, practised as an advocate, entered the national diet in 1832, and played the part of a moderate, becoming in 1848 minister of justice. Hailed in 1861 as leader in the Diet, by his efforts Hungary's constitution was restored in 1867 and the dual monarchy of Austria-Hungary established.

DEAKIN, (1) Alfred (1857–1919), Australian statesman, born in Melbourne, became minister of public works and water supply, and solicitor-general of Victoria, and under the Commonwealth attorney-general (1901) and prime minister (1903–04, 1905–08, 1909–1910).

(2) **Arthur** (1890–1955), British trade union leader, born at Sutton Coldfield, began work on 4s. a week at thirteen in a Dowlais, S. Wales, steel works. A full-time trades union official from 1919, he became in 1935 assistant to Ernest Bevin, general secretary of the Transport and General Workers Union, following the Bevin tradition that a trade union leader should be a first-class organizer rather than an 'agitator'. In 1945 he became general secretary of the 1,300,000-

strong union and was president of the World Federation of Trade Unions from 1945 till 1949, when he led the British withdrawal from the organization because of its Communist domination. Subsequently he was one of the founders of the International Confederation of Free Trade Unions. He became a Companion of Honour in 1949, was chairman of the T.U.C. in 1951 and continued to be one of the most influential members of its General Council till his death.

DEANE, (1) **Henry** (d. 1503), was Archbishop of Canterbury from 1501 till his death, having previously been prior of Llanthony near Gloucester, chancellor and justiciary of Ireland, Bishop of Bangor (1496) and of Salisbury (1500).

(2) **Richard** (1610–53), English admiral, born at Temple Guiting in Gloucestershire, fought through the Great Rebellion for the Parliament, sat on Charles I's trial, commanded afterwards by sea and land, and fell in the great naval battle with the Dutch off the North Foreland, June 2, 1653.

DEAT, Marcel, *day-ah* (1894–1955), French politician, born at Guerigny, founder in 1933 of the Socialist Party of France, which was Fascist in outlook. His pro-Nazi sympathies procured him the post of minister of labour in the Vichy government, and having achieved notoriety by his ruthless deportations of French workers to Germany, he fled thither himself in 1945, was sentenced to death *in absentia*, but evaded arrest until his death at Turin.

DE BARY, Heinrich Anton (1831–88), German botanist, was born at Frankfurt-am-Main, and died at Strasburg, first rector of its reorganized university. He studied the morphology and physiology of the fungi and the Myxomycetae.

DE BEAUVOIR, Simone, *bō-vwahr* (1908–), French existentialist writer and novelist, born in Paris, studied philosophy with Sartre (q.v.) as a fellow student at the Sorbonne, where she was professor (1941–43), and became closely associated with his literary activities after World War II. Her own works enrich existentialism with an essentially feminine sensibility. They include *Tous les hommes sont mortels* (1946), *L'Amérique au jour le jour* (1950; trans. 1952), *La Deuxième sexe* (1949; trans. 1956), her masterpiece *Les Mandarins* (1954; trans. 1957) which won the Prix Goncourt (1954), *The Long March* (Eng. trans. 1958) and *Memoirs of a Dutiful Daughter* (Eng. trans. 1959).

DE BONO, Emilio (1866–1944), Italian fascist politician and general, born at Cassano d'Adda, was a quadrumvir in Mussolini's march on Rome (1922), governor of Tripolitania (1925), colonial secretary (1939) and commanded the Italian forces invading Abyssinia (1935). He voted against Mussolini in the Fascist Supreme Council (1943) and was summarily tried and executed as a traitor by neofascists in Verona January 10, 1944.

DEBRETT, John (c. 1750–1822), a London publisher, known by his *Peerage* (1st ed. 1802).

DEBS, Eugene Victor (1855–1926), American politician, born at Terre Haute, Ind., was

Socialist candidate for the American presidency 1900, 1912, 1920. His pacificism brought him imprisonment 1918–21. See study by M. Coleman (N.Y. 1930).

DEBURAU, Gaspard, *de-bü-rō* (1796–1846), French actor, born in Bohemia, developed mime into a fine art and romanticized the traditional harlequinade by the introduction of the Pierrot motif.

DEBUSSY, Claude Achille (1862–1918), French composer, born on August 22 at St Germain-en-Laye, received his musical education at the Paris Conservatoire (1873–84), studying piano under Marmontel. In 1879 he travelled Europe as the ' musical companion ' of Tchaikovsky's friend Mme von Meck, and in 1884 he won the Prix de Rome with his cantata *L'Enfant prodigue.* His early work was influenced by Wagner, for whom he had a great admiration, but he branched off into a more experimental and individual vein in his first mature work, the *Prélude à l'après-midi d'un faune,* evoked by Mallarmé's poem, which first won him fame. He added further to his reputation with his operatic setting of Maeterlinck's *Pelléas et Mélisande,* begun in 1892 but not performed until 1902, and some outstanding piano pieces, *Images* and *Préludes,* in which he moved further from traditional formulae and experimented with novel techniques and effects, producing the pictures in sound which led his work to be described as ' musical Impressionism '. He extended this new idiom to orchestral music in *La Mer* (1905), the orchestrated *Images,* and other pieces, and later elaborated his piano style still further, as in the scintillating *Feux d'artifice* and the atmospheric *La Cathédrale engloutie.* In his later period he composed much chamber music, including pieces for the flute and the harp, two instruments peculiarly suited to his type of music. Debussy in his private life was shy and reserved, particularly in his last years, which were clouded by his suffering from the cancer which caused his death, but although he shunned the social round he frequented literary circles and was a friend of Verlaine and Baudelaire, some of whose poems he set to music. He married in 1899 Rosalie Texier, a dressmaker, whom he left somewhat callously in 1904 for Emma Bardac, who became his wife in 1905. His compositions, intensely individual, explored new and original avenues of musical expression, and had a profound effect on French music in general and piano music in particular at the turn of the century. See *Life and Works* (Eng. trans. 1933) and a study by Vallas (1932, reissued 1958); also Lives by M. Dietschy (1957) and Lockspeiser (2 vols., 1962, 1965).

DEBYE, Peter Joseph Wilhelm, *de-bī'* (1884–1966), Dutch-American physicist, born at Maastricht, educated at Munich (where he later lectured), professor successively at Zürich, Utrecht, Göttingen and Leipzig, was director of the Kaiser Wilhelm Institute for Physics, Berlin, 1935–40. Nobel prize winner for chemistry (1936), he went in 1940 to the U.S.A. as professor of Chemistry at Cornell. He was specially noted for his work on molecular structure. He was also a pioneer in

X-ray powder photography. He was a foreign member of the Royal Society, and a Rumford and Faraday medallist.

DECAMPS, Alexandre Gabriel, *dĕ-kã* (1803–1860), painter, was born in Paris. A pioneer of the Romantic school, he was a great colourist, specializing in Oriental scenes and biblical subjects. One of his best pictures, *The Watering Place*, is in the Wallace collection.

DECATUR, Stephen, *-kay'-* (1779–1820), American naval commander, was born in Sinepuxent, Maryland, of French descent, and became a midshipman in 1798. He served against the French, and in the war with Tripoli (1801–05) gained great distinction; his achievement of burning the captured *Philadelphia* off Tripoli, and then escaping under the fire of 141 guns, Nelson pronounced ' the most daring act of the age '. Promoted captain in 1804 and commodore in 1810, in the war with England in 1812 he captured the frigate *Macedonian,* but in 1814 surrendered, after a resistance that cost him a fourth of his crew, to four British frigates. In 1815 he chastised the Algerines for piracy, and compelled the dey to declare the American flag inviolable. He was killed in a duel by Commodore James Barron, near Bladensburg, March 22, 1820.

DECAZES, Elie, Duc, *dĕ-kahz* (1780–1860), French statesman, was called as a French advocate and judge to the Hague by the king (1806), supported the Bourbon restoration, and after 1815 was the moderate liberal minister of Louis XVIII (q.v.), who made him a duke. He was ambassador in London (1820–21), and held dignities under Louis Philippe. Later he developed the coalfields on his estates in Aveyron. His eldest son, **Louis Charles** (1819–86), was foreign minister in 1873–77.

DECIUS, Caius Messius Quintus Trajanus (*c.* 200–251), a Roman emperor. He was born at Budalia, in Lower Pannonia, and was sent in 249 by the emperor Philippus to reduce the rebellious army of Moesia. The soldiers proclaimed him emperor against his will, and Philippus encountered him near Verona, but was defeated and slain. Decius' brief reign was one of warring with the Goths, and he was killed near Abricium in 251. Under him the Christians were persecuted with great severity.

DECKEN, Karl Klaus von der (1833–65), German traveller, was born at Kotzen, Brandenburg, served (1851–60) in the Hanoverian army, and then from Zanzibar began a journey to Lake Nyasa, which failed through treachery. In 1862, with Kersten, he climbed Kilimanjaro to the height of 13,780 feet. He was murdered by a Somali on an East African expedition. See Kersten's *Von der Decken's Reisen in Ostafrika* (4 vols. 1869–79).

DECKER, (1) **Sir Matthew** (1679–1749), a political economist, born at Amsterdam, came to London in 1702, and having made a fortune in commerce, received a baronetcy in 1716, and sat in parliament. He published anonymously two pamphlets: one (1743) proposed to raise all the public supplies from a tax upon houses; the other (1744)

contained many good arguments for free trade.
(2) **Thomas.** See DEKKER.

DE COSTER. See CÓSTER.

DEE, John (1527–1608), English alchemist, geographer and mathematician, was born in London, and educated there, at Chelmsford, and from 1542 to 1545 at St John's College, Cambridge. One of the original fellows of Trinity (1546), he earned the reputation of a sorcerer by his mechanical beetle in a representation of Aristophanes' *Peace,* and next year he fetched from the Low Countries sundry astronomical instruments. This was the first of many foreign visits—to Louvain and Paris (1548–51), Venice and Presburg in Hungary (1563), Lorraine (1571), Frankfurt-on-Oder (1578), Bohemia (1583–89) and even, it is said, St Helena. He was imprisoned under Queen Mary on suspicion of compassing her death by magic (1555); but Edward VI had conferred two church livings on him, and Elizabeth showed him considerable favour, making him warden of Manchester College in 1595. For most of his life he was concerned with the search for the Northwest passage to the Far East, aiding the exploration by his navigational and geographical knowledge. He was constantly in difficulties, though he claimed to have found in the ruins of Glastonbury a quantity of the Elixir. Indeed, he appears to have been as much dupe as deceiver, the dupe of his own assistant, Edward Kelley, during 1582–88. This knave professed to confer with angels by means of Dee's magic crystal, and talked him into consenting to a community of wives. Dr Dee died wretchedly poor and was buried in Mortlake church. His eldest son, **Arthur** (1579–1651), was likewise an alchemist, a friend of Sir Thomas Browne. Dr Dee's seventy-nine works deal with logic, mathematics, astrology, alchemy, navigation, geography and the calendar (1583). See his *Private Diary,* edited by Halliwell-Phillipps (1842), and book by Hort (1922).

DEEPING, (George) Warwick (1877–1950), English novelist, born in Southend. He trained as a doctor, but after a year gave up his practice to devote himself to writing. His early novels were mainly historical, and it was not until after World War I, in which he served, that he gained recognition, with his bestseller, *Sorrell and Son* (1925), which was later filmed. Other novels include *Old Pybus* (1928) and *Roper's Row* (1929). In his stories, all of which have a sentimental flavour, good breeding is represented as the cardinal virtue, enabling its fortunate possessors to triumph over adversity with slightly class-conscious aplomb.

DEFFAND, Marie de Vichy-Chamrond, Marquise du, *def-fã* (1697–1780), French noblewoman of an old Burgundian family, was educated in a Paris convent, and as a girl became famous for her wit, audacity and beauty. In 1718 she married the Marquis du Deffand, but they soon separated; and for a number of years she led a life of gallantry and became a conspicuous figure in Paris literary society. She was a correspondent of Voltaire, Montesquieu and D'Alembert. In 1753 she became blind, and in 1754 invited Mademoiselle de Lespinasse to live with her and help her to preside over her salon. The arrangement lasted for ten years, when a quarrel broke out, and Mademoiselle de Lespinasse departed, taking away with her D'Alembert and others of the elder lady's former admirers. From 1766 Madame du Deffand corresponded with Horace Walpole, who offered help when she fell into pecuniary troubles. She died at Paris. See her *Correspondance* (new ed. 5 vols. 1865-67); her *Lettres à Horace Walpole* (3 vols. 1912; ed. by Mrs Paget Toynbee); works by Asse (1877), Perey (1893), Mme C. Ferval (1933).

DEFOE, Daniel (1660-1731), English author, born in London, son of a butcher, was educated at a dissenting academy. He appears to have travelled widely on the Continent before setting up in the hosiery trade. He took part in Monmouth's rebellion and joined William III's army in 1688. In his *Appeal to Honour and Justice* (1715), he describes his career from that time onwards with its extraordinary shifts from merchant adventurer, to projector and government spy. Down to 1704 he strenuously supported the king's party and earned William's favour by the rude vigour of his poem *The True-born Englishman* (1701). In Queen Anne's reign he ran into trouble with his famous squib *The Shortest Way with the Dissenters* (1702), the irony of which at first deceived the High Church party. The Queen being of that party, the consequences for him were serious, viz., a ruinous fine, the pillory and imprisonment during the Queen's pleasure. In Newgate he managed to continue his pamphleteering on such questions as ' occasional conformity ' and wrote a mock-pindaric *Hymn to the Pillory*. *The Review*, which he started on his release in 1704, is of importance in the history of journalism. Appearing thrice weekly down to 1713, it aimed at being an organ of commercial interests, but also expressed opinions on all sorts of political and domestic topics, thus initiating the modern leading article. The ' Scandal Club ', one of its features, anticipates the *Tatler* and *Spectator*. Besides writing *The Review* single-handed, he wrote, among much ephemeral pamphleteering, the astonishingly vivid ghost story *The Apparition of One Mrs Veal*, allegedly, like so many of his fictions, a true account of an actual happening. After 1704 his political conduct becomes highly equivocal—the *Appeal to Honour and Justice* referred to above is an attempt at justification. What is clear is that he undertook various secret commissions for the Tory minister Harley, including dubious dealings with the Scottish commissioners for Union in 1706-1707; that on Harley's fall in 1708 he supported Nottingham's ministry; and that he again changed his coat on the return of Harley in 1710. On the accession of the House of Hanover Defoe turned to domestic affairs and to the writing of fiction which—perhaps due to his dissenting conscience—was all passed off as actual history. In the first category we have such topics treated as would please the tradesman class with its stuffy piety and eye on gain. *The Compleat English Tradesman* (1725-27) has more of gain than piety in it; *Religious Courtship*

(1722) is slightly nauseating; but *Everybody's Business is Nobody's Business* still amuses. In the second category, *Robinson Crusoe* (1719-20) is of course his title to fame. The underlying idea, how to exist in solitude and debarred the necessaries of civilization, is amazingly worked out and not without a strong element of prudential piety. Among the other six fictions—the *Journal of the Plague Year* seems to have had a source in an actual diary—the most vivid is undoubtedly *Moll Flanders* (1722), which is still one of the best tales of low life. He did not repeat this triumph in *Roxana* (1724). His most prolific year was 1720, when he completed *Robinson Crusoe*. The astonishing thing is that the inferior sequel to the first part should have appeared in the same year as the famous *Memoirs of a Cavalier* and the brilliant (but unequal) *Captain Singleton*. Defoe's versatility is astounding. Apart from the social novel, for which we have to wait until Richardson, there is hardly a type of modern fiction he did not anticipate. Except for a few squibs, his political writing is forgotten and his domestic writing is only interesting to the historian of social manners. His *Review*, however, gives him an important place in the history of journalism. In 1810 Scott's edition of the novels appeared in ten vols. This was extended by an Oxford edition in 1840 to include some of the miscellaneous works. G. A. Aitken's *Romances and Travels* (1895-96), is the standard edition. Sutherland's study (1937) and Moore's (1939), are recommended.

DE FOREST, Lee (1873-1961), American inventor, born at Council Bluffs, Iowa, was educated at Yale and Chicago. A pioneer of radio, he introduced the grid into the thermionic valve, and invented the audion and the four-electrode valve. He also did much early work on sound reproduction and on television.

DEFREGGER, Franz (1835-1921), Tirolese painter, noted for his scenes of peasant life. See study by H. Hammer (1940).

DEGAS, (Hilaire Germain) Edgar, *dě-gah* (1834-1917), French artist, born in Paris. After studying at the École des Beaux-Arts under Lamothe, a pupil of Ingres (q.v.), he went to Italy, where he was influenced by the art of the Renaissance painters. On his return to Paris he associated with the Impressionists and took part in most of their exhibitions from 1874 to 1886. He was also influenced by Japanese woodcuts, and, in the seemingly casual composition of his paintings, by photography. He travelled in Spain and Italy and visited New Orleans, U.S.A., in 1872-73, but most of his paintings and pastels (in which he particularly excelled) of dancers and women at their toilet were produced in his Paris studio, often with the aid of wax and clay models. His interest lay in precision of line and the modelling of the human form in space. *Miss Lola at the Cirque Fernando* (1879) is in the Tate Gallery, *Rehearsal of the Ballet* (c. 1874) is in the Louvre, *Dancer Lacing her Shoe* (c. 1878) is in the Paris Museum of Impressionism, *Dancer at the Bar* is in the Metropolitan Museum, New York, and the well-known *Cotton-brokers Office*

(1873) is in Pau Museum. Latterly, because of failing sight, he concentrated on sculpture. See his *Letters*, edited by Halévy and Guérin (1931), and monographs by A. Vollard (trans. 1928), Fosca (1954), Cabanne (1958) and the 4-vol. study by Lemoisne (1946–48).

DE GAULLE, Charles André Joseph Marie, -gōl (1890–1970), French general and first president of the Fifth Republic, born November 22 at Lille, fought in the 1914–18 war, from which he emerged an enthusiastic advocate of the air-armour combination to which Germany was to found its *blitzkrieg* of 1940. His book, *The Army of the Future* (1940), aroused considerable comment; but his efforts to modernize and revivify the French Army made little progress. With the fall of France, June 1940, de Gaulle fled to England to raise the standard of the ' Free French '. The failure of the Gaullist attempt to capture Dakar, together with the General's prickly, unaccommodating conduct of policy, combined to render his collaboration in the North African landings, inadvisable; while his reconciliation with his military superior, the ex-prisoner of war General Giraud, was never much more than a gesture for the press cameras. Entering Paris at the head of one of the earliest liberation forces, August 1944, de Gaulle became head of the provisional government; but, being strongly suspected of aspirations towards an authoritarian rule, he withdrew to the political sidelines. He continued to exercise such widespread influence, however, that in May 1958, with the troubles in North Africa precipitating the collapse of all responsible government, he was called upon to head a temporary administration. A referendum confirmed to him powers as prime minister greater than any one Frenchman had enjoyed for decades, and he emerged triumphant as the one man able to inspire confidence after the melancholy postwar procession of vacillating leaders. In the elections which followed the adoption of his new constitution (Nov. 1958) his supporters won an overwhelming victory, though he had handed over the party leadership to Soustelle (q.v.) and was himself elected first president of the Fifth Republic in December 1958 with greater powers than that office had previously bestowed. His extremely successful, if high-handed, foreign policy encompassed the granting of independence to all French African colonies (1959–60); negotiation of the Évian agreements with strife-torn Algeria, which became independent in 1962, de Gaulle surviving repeated political crises by a lavish use of the referendum; his insistence despite U.S. pressure on developing an independent French nuclear deterrent; consolidation of a new friendship with Federal Germany; his refusal of any concessionary terms and thus effective blocking of Britain's entry into the Common Market in 1962–63 and 1967; belated recognition of the Peking government (1964); and a triumphant succession of state visits, including Russia in 1966. In 1965 he was re-elected only by a second vote. His position was confirmed by his party's overwhelming victory at the general election following the ' students' revolution ' in May 1968, but in April 1969 he was forced to resign as president

after the defeat of his referendum proposals for senate and regional reforms. See his war memoirs, in 3 vols. (1954, 1956, 1959), and studies by Funk (1959) and Crawley (1969).

DE GUBERNATIS. See GUBERNATIS.

DE HAVILLAND, Sir Geoffrey (1882–1965), British aircraft designer, built his first plane in 1908 and became director of the firm bearing his name, which produced many famous and diverse types of aircraft during and between the two world wars, including the Tiger Moth, the Mosquito (of revolutionary plywood construction) and the Vampire jet. He established a height record for light aircraft in 1928, won the King's Cup air race at the age of fifty-one, was knighted in 1944 and received the O.M. in 1962. See *Outline of de Havilland History* by Sharp (1961).

DEHMEL, Richard (1863–1920), German poet, born, a forester's son, at Wendisch-Hermsdorf, Brandenburg, wrote intellectual verse showing the influence of Nietzche. See his *Mein Leben* (1922) and study by H. Slochower (1928).

DÉJAZET, Pauline Virginie, *day-zha-zay* (1797–1875), born in Paris, from five played children's rôles with marvellous precocity, and later became famous for her soubrette and ' boy ' parts (*déjazets*). In 1859–68 she managed, with her son, the Folies-Dramatiques, renamed the Théâtre Déjazet. See Lives by Duval (1876) and Lecomte (1892).

DEKKER, (1) **Eduard Douwes,** pseud. **Multatuli** (1820–87), Dutch government official and writer, born in Amsterdam. He served for many years in the Dutch civil service in Java, and in his novel *Max Havelaar* (1860), and in many bitter satires, he protested against the abuses of the Dutch colonial system.

(2) **Thomas** (*c.* 1570–*c.* 1641), dramatist, was born in London. He was a very prolific writer, but only a few of his plays were printed. In 1600 he published two comedies, *The Shoemaker's Holiday, or the Gentle Craft*, and *The Pleasant Comedy of Old Fortunatus*. The first of these pieces is one of the pleasantest of old plays, and the second abounds in poetry of rare beauty. His next play was *Satiromastix* (1602), which held up to ridicule Ben Jonson, who in 1619 told Drummond of Hawthornden that Dekker was a knave. In 1603 Dekker published a pamphlet, *The Wonderful Year*, which gives a heartrending account of the plague. To the same date belongs the very amusing tract, *The Bachelor's Banquet*, in which he describes with gusto the ills of henpecked husbands. His most powerful writing is seen in *The Honest Whore* (1604; part ii, 1630). In 1607 he published three plays written in conjunction with Webster, the *Famous History of Sir Thomas Wyat, Westward Ho* and *Northward Ho*. The *Bellman of London* (1608) pamphlet gives a lively account of London vagabonds; and Dekker pursued the subject in *Lanthorn and Candlelight* (1608). In *The Gull's Hornbook* (1609) the life of a town gallant is racily depicted. The excellent comedy, *The Roaring Girl* (1611), was written partly by Dekker, but chiefly by Middleton. From 1613 to 1616 Dekker was confined in the King's Bench prison for debt, as previously in the Counter prison. With Massinger he composed the

Virgin Marytr; and Lamb was doubtless right in ascribing to Dekker the most beautiful scene (II, i). *The Sun's Darling*, licensed in 1624, but not printed until 1656, was written in conjunction with Ford. A powerful tragedy, *The Witch of Edmonton* (posthumously published in 1658), was written by Dekker, Ford and Rowley. We hear of Dekker in 1637, when he republished his *Lanthorn and Candlelight* as *English Villainies*, and then he drops out of notice. His plays were collected in 1873 (4 vols.), and his pamphlets in 1884–86. See Hunt's study (1912) and Brooke's *Tudor Drama* (1912).

DE KOONING, Willem or **William** (1904–), American painter, born in Rotterdam. He emigrated to the U.S.A. in 1926, and is one of the leaders of the modern American nonfigurative artists, but his painting *Woman I* (1952) in the Museum of Modern Art, New York, is an expressionist figure study.

DE LA BECHE, Sir Henry Thomas (1796–1855), English geologist, born near London, served a year in the army, and in 1817 became a fellow of the Geological Society, of which he was elected president in 1847. In 1820 he published a paper on the temperature and depth of Lake Geneva; in 1824 he visited Jamaica, and published one on its geology. Other works include a *Manual of Geology* (1831) and a *Geological Observer* (1853). In 1832 he became head of the newly constituted Geological Survey. He founded the Geological Museum and the School of Mines.

DELACROIX, Ferdinand Victor Eugène, *dĕ-la-krwah* (1798–1863), French painter, born at Charenton, was the son of **Charles** (1741–1805), who had been foreign minister under the Directory, and prefect of Marseilles. As a boy Eugène developed a love of art, and in 1861 he entered the studio of Guérin, where his fellow-pupil was Géricault, whose famous *Raft of the Medusa* gave him early inspiration. In 1822 he exhibited at the Institute *Dante and Vergil in Hell*, and in 1824 *The Massacre at Chios* (now in the Louvre). Both of these pictures, particularly the latter, with its loose drawing and vivid colouring, shocked the devotees of the austere and statuesque classical style, and aroused a storm of criticism. Constable's *Haywain*, which was hung in the same exhibition, profoundly impressed Delacroix, who moved even further away from the traditional treatment in brilliant canvases of historical and dramatic scenes, often violent or macabre in subject, among them *The Execution of Faliero*, now in the Wallace collection, and the famous *Liberty Guiding the People* (1831, Louvre). A journey to Morocco and Spain with a diplomatic mission in 1832 led to several pictures with an oriental flavour, such as *Algerian Women* (1834), and he also turned to literary themes, notably from Shakespeare and Tasso. In 1838 he began work on a series of panels for the library of the Chamber of Deputies, choosing as his subject the history of ancient civilization, but despite this official recognition and despite the fact that the Government had bought his *Massacre at Chios*, he was regarded as a rebel in the art world and was not elected to the Institute until 1857. Perhaps the greatest figure in 19th century French art, Delacroix was one of the most accomplished colourists of all time, and was responsible for shifting the emphasis away from the meticulous but pallid techniques of Ingres and David. His draughtsmanship and loose composition have been criticized, but the aberrations were often deliberately contrived in order to achieve balance of colour. A man of immense energy, he interested himself in politics and literature, and assiduously kept a daily journal from the age of twenty-three until the year of his death, recording fascinating details of his life and work. See the *Journal* (Eng. tr. by W. Pach, 1938), and studies by Meier-Graefe (1922), R. Escholier (1926–29) and H. Graber (1938).

DELAFIELD, E. M., pseud. of **Edmée Elizabeth Monica Dashwood** (1890–1943), English novelist, born in Llandogo, Mon., a writer of gay, light novels of country life, full of local colour and gossip. See her *Diary of a Provincial Lady* (1931).

DE LA MARE, Walter (1873–1956), poet and novelist, was born at Charlton in Kent. The promise of *Songs of Childhood* (1902, by ' Walter Ramal '), his prose romance *Henry Brocken* (1904), his children's story *The Three Mulla Mulgars* (1910) and his novel of the occult *The Return* (1910) was fulfilled in his volumes of poetry *The Listeners* (1912), *Peacock Pie* (1913), *The Veil* (1921), in the fantastic novel *Memoirs of a Midget* (1921), in books of short stories such as *On the Edge* (1930). Romanticist and musician in words, De la Mare has delighted children and grown-up readers alike by the delicate enchantments and humour of his *märchen* world. He became C.H. in 1948, O.M. in 1953, and in that year published a new volume of lyrics *O Lovely England*. See Sir Russell Brain, *Tea with Walter de la Mare* (1957).

DELAMBRE, Jean Joseph, *dĕ-lã'br'* (1749–1822), French astronomer, born at Amiens, studied under Lalande. He attracted attention by his tables of the motion of Uranus; and in 1792–99, with Méchain, he measured the arc of the meridian between Dunkirk and Barcelona.

DELAND, Margaret Wade, *née* **Campbell** (1857–1945), born at Allegheny, Pa., published *The Old Garden, and other Verses* (1886), *John Ward, Preacher* (1888), &c.

DELANE, John Thaddeus (1817–79), English journalist, born in London, graduated in 1839 from Magdalen Hall, Oxford, where he was more famous for horsemanship than reading. John Walter, however, his father's neighbour in Berkshire and proprietor of *The Times*, had early marked his capable character; and in May 1841, not yet twenty-four, he became joint editor of *The Times*. For thirty-six years Delane held this post, aided, however, for twenty-five of them by George Dasent (q.v.). Under him *The Times* attained a circulation and an influence unparalleled in journalism. He wrote no articles, but contributed excellent reports and letters. His exposure of the railway mania, his attacks upon the management of the Crimean war, and his strong opposition to Britain's assisting Denmark in 1864 were noteworthy. He resigned in 1877. See Lives by Dasent (1908), Sir E. Cook (1915); also *The History of the Times*, vol. 2 (1939).

DELANY, Mrs (Mary Granville) (1700–88), was born at Coulston, Wiltshire. The niece of Lord Lansdowne, she married first, in 1718, 'fat, snuffy, sulky' Alexander Pendarves (1659–1724); and secondly, in 1743, the Rev. Patrick Delany (1685–1768), an Irish divine, Swift's friend, and the author of a dozen volumes. After his death she lived chiefly in London, dying at Windsor. Her admired 'paper-mosaics', or flower work, have long since faded; but she is remembered through her patronage of Fanny Burney and by her *Autobiography and Correspondence* (6 vols. 1861–62).

DELAROCHE, Hippolyte, known as **Paul** (1797–1856), French painter, was born in Paris. He studied under Gros, from whom he absorbed the technique of the large historical subject painting. Many of the best known examples of this *genre*, as applied to English history, have come from his brush, including *Death of Queen Elizabeth* (1827) and *Execution of Lady Jane Grey* (1834). From this period until 1841 he was engaged on his grandest work—the series of paintings in the École des Beaux Arts, in the execution of which he was aided by Armitage and other of his pupils. He never fully recovered from the death of his wife, daughter of Horace Vernet (q.v.), in 1845, and his work after this shows a decline. He was professor of Painting at the École des Beaux Arts from 1833. See Rees, *Vernet and Delaroche* (1880).

DE LA ROCHE, Mazo (1885–1961), Canadian novelist, born in Toronto, wrote *Jalna* (1927), the first of a series of novels about the Whiteoak family. *Whiteoaks* (1929) was dramatized with considerable success. See her autobiography *Ringing the Changes* (1957).

DE LA RUE, Warren (1815–89), British astronomer and electrician, was born in Guernsey. He was educated at Paris, and early entered his father's business—the manufacture of paperwares—for which his inventive genius devised many new processes. He invented the silver chloride battery and did research on the discharge of electricity in gases. A pioneer of celestial photography, he invented the photoheliograph.

DELAUNAY, Robert, *dĕ-lō-nay* (1885–1941), French artist, born in Paris. He was originally apprenticed to a stage designer and turned to painting in 1905. He was associated with the Blaue Reiter Group (1911–12), but is principally known as the founder of Orphism. He painted many pictures of Paris (particularly the *Eiffel Tower*), and his researches into colour orchestration as applied to abstract art influenced many artists, especially Marc and Klee. See the monograph by F. Gilles de la Tourette (1950).

DELAVIGNE, Jean François Casimir, *dĕ-la-veen'y'* (1793–1843), French dramatist, satirist and lyricist was born at Le Havre. He became popular through his *Messéniennes* (1818), satires upon the Restoration. *Les Vêpres siciliennes* (1819), a tragic piece, was followed by *L'École des vieillards* and *Les Comédiens* (1821), *Louis XI*, partly founded on *Quentin*

Durward (1833), *La Fille du Cid* (1839), &c. He was made an Academician in 1825.

DE LA WARR, Thomas West, 3rd or **12th Baron** (1577–1618), the first governor of Virginia, arrived there from England in June 1610, but nine months later was prostrated by ill-health, and died in 1618. The state of Delaware is named after him.

DELBRÜCK, (1) Hans (1848–1929), German historian of the art of war, was a native of Rügen, in 1885–1919 professor at Berlin, in 1883–1919 editor of the *Preussische Jahrbücher*.

(2) **Martin Friedrich Rudolf** (1817–1903), for years Bismarck's right-hand man, born at Berlin, in 1864–66 reorganized the Zollverein.

DELCASSÉ, Théophile (1852–1923), French foreign minister 1898–1905, 1914–15, promoted the *entente cordiale* with Britain and figured in Moroccan crises.

DELEDDA, Grazia (1875–1936), Italian authoress, Nobel prize winner for 1926, made her name with stories of her native Sardinia.

DELESCLUZE, Louis Charles, *dĕ-lay-kluz* (1809–71), French radical and journalist, was born at Dreux. His politics drove him from France to journalism in Belgium (1835), but the February revolution (1848) brought him back to Paris, where his facile pen made him popular with the rabble but brought him imprisonment and he was ultimately transported till 1859. (See his *De Paris à Cayenne; Journal d'un transporté*, 1867). In 1868 he started the *Réveil*, to promote the International; in the Paris Commune he played a prominent part, and died on the last barricade.

DELIBES, Léo, *dĕ-leeb* (1836–91), French composer, was born at St Germain du Val, Sarthe, and died in Paris, where in 1865 he had become second director at the Grand Opera, and in 1880 a Conservatoire professor. He wrote light operas, of which *Lakmé* had the greatest success, but is chiefly remembered for the ballet *Coppélia* (1870), which has remained a prime favourite down to the present day.

DELILLE, Jacques (1738–1813), French poet, was born near Aigues-Perse in Auvergne. Educated at the Collège de Lisieux in Paris, he obtained a professorship in Amiens. His verse translation of Vergil's *Georgics* (1769) had an extraordinary vogue, and was praised by Voltaire. Delille was made an Academician in 1774, and, after holding a canonry at Moissac, was presented by the Comte d'Artois with the abbacy of Saint-Severin. *Les Jardins* (1782), a didactic poem, was generally accepted as a masterpiece. The Revolution compelling Delille to leave France, he travelled in Switzerland and Germany, and then in London spent eighteen months translating *Paradise Lost*. After his return to France in 1802 he produced a translation of the *Aeneid* (1804), *L'Imagination* (1806) *Les Trois Règnes* (1809) and *La Conversation* (1812). During his life he was regarded by his countrymen as the greatest French poet of the day, and was even declared the equal of Virgil and Homer; but his fame suffered a rapid eclipse. See Sainte-Beuve's *Portraits littéraires* vol. ii.

DELISLE, *dě-leel*, (1) **Jean Baptiste Louis Romé** (1736–90), French physicist, born at Gray in Franche-Comté, a founder of the science of crystallography.

(2) **Joseph Nicolas** (1688–1768), French astronomer, born at Paris, a pioneer in solar study and founder of a famous school of Astronomy at St Petersburg in 1726.

(3) **Leopold Victor** (1826–1910), French librarian and palaeographer, born at Valognes, entered the manuscript department of the Bibliothèque nationale in 1852, and became head of it in 1871. Three years later he was made *administrateur-general*. He made important contributions to bibliography and literary history, especially in his work on *Recueil des historiens des gaules et de la France*.

DE LISLE, Rouget. See ROUGET DE LISLE.

DELITZSCH, Franz Julius (1813–90),German Old Testament scholar, orientalist, and Hebraist, born at Leipzig, became professor of Theology at Rostock in 1846, at Erlangen in 1850, at Leipzig in 1867. One of the foremost among conservative German theologians, he exercised great personal influence over a generation of Leipzig students, and a long series of profoundly learned books extended a sound knowledge of Old Testament exegesis in Germany, England and America. See *Life* by S. I. Curtiss (1891). His son, **Friedrich** (1850–1922), in 1877 became professor of Assyriology at Leipzig, in 1893 at Breslau, in 1899 at Berlin.

DELIUS, *dee'li-us*, (1) **Frederick** (1862–1934), English composer, of German-Scandinavian descent, born in Bradford. Despite his musical gifts, his parents planned a commercial career for him, but when he was twenty he went to Florida as an orange planter, in his leisure studying music from books and scores. He entered Leipzig Conservatory in 1886, but was influenced more by Grieg, who befriended him there, than by his teachers. After 1890 he lived almost entirely in France, composing prolifically in an individual style unconnected with any traditional school. He wrote six operas, including *Koanga* (1897) and *A Village Romeo and Juliet* (1901), small orchestral works, and larger choral and orchestral pieces, *Appalachia, Sea Drift* and *A Mass of Life*, which are less familiar. In 1924 Delius, seized by paralysis, became helpless and totally blind, but with the assistance of Eric Fenby, who became his amanuensis in 1928, he produced a group of final works, including the complex *A Song of Summer, Idyll* and *Songs of Farewell*. See biographies and studies by P. Heseltine (1923), C. Delius (1935), E. Fenby (1936), A. Hutchings (1948) and Sir T. Beecham (1959).

(2) **Nikolaus** (1813–88), German Shakespearian critic, born at Bremen. He became extraordinary professor in 1855 at Bonn, professor in 1863. His early lectures were on Sanskrit and the Romance tongues, but he afterwards devoted himself to English and Shakespeare. He was responsible for the first critical edition of Shakespeare's works in Germany (7 vols. 1854–61).

DELL, Ethel Mary (1881–1939), British novelist, born in Streatham. As a writer of light romantic novels she enjoyed a tremendous vogue in the years between the wars. Her novels, which have been reprinted many times, include *The Way of an Eagle* (1912), *The Keeper of the Door* (1915) and *Storm Drift* (1930).

DELLA CASA, Lisa (1919–), Swiss soprano, born in Burgdorf near Berne. She studied in Zürich, first appeared at Solothurn-Biel in 1943, subsequently joining the company at the Stadttheater, Zürich. Her appearance at the Salzburg Festival of 1947 led to her engagement with Vienna State Opera Company. A specialist in the operas of Richard Strauss, she shares with Lotte Lehmann the distinction of having sung all three soprano rôles in *Der Rosenkavalier*.

DELLA ROBBIA. See ROBBIA.

DELOLME, Jean Louis (1740–1806), Swiss writer, born at Geneva, was an advocate there, but about 1769 came to England, where in spite of his literary activity, he lived in great poverty, always in debt and repeatedly in prison. Having inherited a small property, he returned to Geneva in 1775. He is remembered for his *Constitution of England* (Fr. 1771, Engl. 1775), *History of the Flagellants* (1782) and *Strictures on the Union* (1796). In 1816 Dr Thomas Busby tried to prove that Delolme was Junius.

DELONEY, Thomas (*c.* 1550–1600), English balladist and writer of fiction. His *Jack of Newbury, Thomas of Reading* and *Gentle Craft*, with their lively dialogue and characterization, are not far from the later novel. Mann edited his works (1912); see a study by Chevalley (Paris 1926).

DE LONG, George Washington (1844–81), American polar explorer, born in New York, commanded the *Jeannette* in an attempt to reach the North Pole via Bering Strait in 1879. Having abandoned his ship in the pack ice, he travelled 300 miles by sledge and boat to the Siberian coast, but only two of his crew reached safety. See his diary of the voyage.

DELORME, (1) Marion (1613–50), French courtesan, born at Paris, where at an early period of her life her beauty and wit gathered a group of high-born lovers round her—among them the Duke of Buckingham, Sainte-Évremond, the Duc de Brissac and the Chevalier de Grammont. Even Richelieu was not insensible to her charms, and caused her to be separated from Cinq-Mars, her love for whom was the one ennobling passion of her life. During the early days of the Fronde her house was the rallying-point of its chiefs, and Mazarin was about to imprison her when she suddenly died. See Mirecourt's imaginative *Confessions* (1851) and Péladan's study (1927).

(2) **Philibert** (*c.* 1510–70), French architect, was born at Lyons, and died in Paris. Royal architect to Henri II, he built the Tuileries for Catherine de Médicis, and the châteaux of Anet, Meudon, &c. See study by A. Blunt (1958).

DEL RIO, Andrés Manuel (1764–1849), Spanish mineralogist, born in Madrid, became professor of Mineralogy at the Mexico School of Mines in 1793, and in 1801 discovered the metal vanadium.

DELUC, Jean André, *dĕ-lük* (1727–1817), Swiss geologist, meteorologist and physicist, was born at Geneva, and, settling in England in 1773, was reader to Queen Charlotte till his death at Windsor. He tried to prove that creation as described in the Bible was consistent with science. He investigated atmosphere, the density of water, invented a hygrometer and was the first to record accurately the heights of mountains by the barometer.

DELVAUX, Paul, *del-vō'* (1897–   ), Belgian surrealist painter, born at Antheit. He has lived mainly in Brussels, where he studied, and exhibited mainly neo-impressionist and expressionist pictures until 1935. He was influenced by Chirico and Magritte, and has produced a series of paintings depicting nude and semi-nude girls in dreamlike settings (e.g., *The Call of the Night*), using a palette which has gradually increased in brightness. Exhibitions of his work were held in London and New York in 1946.

DELVIG, Anton Antonovitch, Baron von (1798–1831), Russian poet, was born in Moscow, studied with Pushkin at the Tsarskoé Sélo school and became keeper of the public library at St Petersburg. From 1825 to 1831 he published the almanac *Flowers from the North*.

DEMADES, *dem'a-deez* (c. 380–318 B.C.), an Athenian orator of great eloquence but of no principle. A bitter enemy to Demosthenes, he promoted the Macedonian interest, and was sent away in safety by Philip when taken prisoner at Chaeronea (338), but had not the grace to be honest even in his anti-patriotism, and was put to death for his treachery by Cassander.

DEMARÇAY, Eugène Anatole (1852–1904), French chemist, in 1896 discovered spectroscopically the element *europium*, and also gave spectroscopic proof of the discovery of radium.

DEMBINSKI, Henryk (1791–1864), Polish general, was born near Cracow, entered the Polish army in 1809, and fought under Napoleon against Russia and at Leipzig. In the Polish revolution of 1830 he was commander-in-chief; in 1833 he entered the service of Mehemet Ali. On the outbreak of the Hungarian insurrection, Kossuth appointed him commander-in-chief. He was hampered by the jealousy of Görgei; and after the defeat of Kapolna (February 26–28, 1849) was forced to resign. On Kossuth's resignation he fled to Turkey, but in 1850 returned to Paris. He was author of *Mémoires* (1833) and four other works.

DEMETRIUS, (1) the name of several kings of Macedonia, of whom the one surnamed Poliorcetes, ' besieger of cities ', was the son of Antigonus (q.v.), and obtained the crown in 294 B.C. He died the prisoner of Seleucus in 283. Several of the Seleucid kings of Shria were also called Demetrius.
(2) See DMITRI.

DEMETRIUS PHALEREUS (c. 345 B.C.–283 B.C.), Greek orator and statesman, was so named from the Attic seaport of Phalerum, where he was humbly born. Educated with Menander in the school of Theophrastus, he entered (c. 325) on public life, in 317 was

entrusted by Cassander with the government of Athens, and satisfactorily discharged its duties for ten years. Latterly he became dissipated; and when Demetrius Poliorcetes approached Athens with a besieging army in 307, Demetrius had to flee—first to Thebes and next to the court of Ptolemy Lagi at Alexandria. On Ptolemy's death he retreated to Busiris in Upper Egypt, and died there of snake-bite in 283.

DEMETZ, Frédéric Auguste (1796–1873), a French magistrate, the founder in 1839 of the great reformatory of Mettray, near Tours.

DEMIDOV, a Russian family descended from a blacksmith at Tula, who in the time of Peter the Great amassed an immense fortune as a manufacturer of arms. Prince Anatole (1813–70), educated in France, wrote *Voyage dans la Russie méridionale* (4 vols. Paris 1839–49).

DE MILLE, Cecil Blount (1881–1959), American film producer, born in Ashfield, Massachusetts, acted on the stage and wrote unsuccessful plays before discovering Hollywood with Samuel Goldwyn (q.v.) as a suitable place for shooting the first American feature film, *The Squaw Man* (1913). With the Gloria Swanson comedy, *Male and Female* (1919), he became the most ' advanced ' of American film directors. Through *The Ten Commandments* (1923, re-made in cinemascope dimensions in 1957), *The Sign of the Cross* (1932), *The Plainsman* (1937, his best film) and *Reap the Wild Wind* (1942) he made a reputation for box-office mastery of the vast film spectacle, on the formula of a high moral theme, enlivened by physical violence and sex, a notable exception being the filmed Passion play, *King of Kings* (1927). He also organized the first commercial, passenger airline service in the U.S.A. in 1917.

DEMOCRITUS, *-mok'-* (fl. 5th cent. B.C.), a Greek philosopher, born at Abdera in Thrace about 470 or 460 B.C., who is represented by untrustworthy tradition as continually laughing at the follies of mankind. He travelled in the East, showed ceaseless industry in collecting the works of other philosophers, and was by far the most learned thinker of his age. He lived to a great age, but the date of his death is uncertain. The few extant fragments of his numerous physical, mathematical, ethical and musical works were collected by Mullach (Berlin 1843). Democritus's *atomic system* assumes an infinite multitude of atoms, instinct with a primary motion derived from no higher principle; from their multitudinous combinations springs that vast and varying aggregate called *nature*, in which he recognizes law but not design. His system, said to have been derived from Leucippus, was developed by Epicurus and Lucretius. See works by Liard (Paris 1873), Brieger (1884), Liepmann (1885), Natorp (1893) and Solovine (1928).

DEMOGEOT, Jacques Claude, *dĕ-mō-zhō* (1808–94), a French *littérateur*, born at Paris, lectured at Beauvais, Rennes, Bordeaux and Lyons, and was professor of Rhetoric at the Lycée St Louis at Paris, and later at the Sorbonne. Among his works were *Les Lettres et les hommes de lettres au XIXᵉ* *siècle* (1856); *Histoire de la littérature française* (1857), an admirable handbook; *Tableau de la littérature française au XVIIᵉ siècle* (1859); *Histoire des littératures étrangères* (2 vols. 1880).

DEMOIVRE, Abraham, *dě-mwah'vr'* (1667–1754), French mathematician, was born at Vitry, in Champagne. A Protestant, he came to England in 1688, after the revocation of the Edict of Nantes, and supported himself by teaching. Newton's *Principia* whetted his devotion to mathematical studies, and at last he ranked among the leading mathematicians of his time. In 1697 he was elected an F.R.S.; and he helped to decide the famous contest between Newton (q.v.) and Leibniz for the merit of the invention of fluxions. Latterly deaf, blind, somnolent (he would sleep twenty hours on end), he died in London. Among his works are *The Doctrine of Chances* (1718), *Annuities* (1725) and *Miscellanea Analytica de Seriebus et Quadraturis* (1730).

DE MORGAN, (1) Augustus (1806–71), father of (2), was born at Madura, Madras Presidency, the son of an Indian army colonel. Educated at several English private schools, he 'read algebra like a novel', went up to Trinity, Cambridge, whence he came out fourth wrangler (1827), and in 1828 he became first professor of Mathematics in University College, London. In 1831 he resigned this office, but resumed it 1836–66; and he was secretary of the Astronomical Society (1831–38 and 1848–54). A mathematician of the first order, he was minutely versed in the history of the mathematical and physical sciences; he also devoted himself to the development of the Aristotelian or 'Formal' Logic. He wrote a number of works on mathematics and logic, and contributed 850 articles to the *Penny Cyclopaedia*. See Memoir (1882) and *Reminiscences* (1895) by his wife, Sophia Elizabeth Frend.

(2) **William Frend** (1839–1917), ceramic artist and novelist, son of (1), born in London, studied art at the Academy Schools, and started as a designer of tiles and stained glass, but became interested in pottery, and in 1871 established a kiln in Chelsea, where he turned out glazed ware in beautiful blues and greens which won much praise in artistic circles but made little money, and in 1905 he had to abandon the work. Thereupon, at the age of sixty-five, he began writing novels in a whimsical Dickensian manner. *Joseph Vance* (1906) was a great success, and several later books, as *Alice-for-Short* (1907) and *Somehow Good* (1908), also attained considerable popularity. His wife **Evelyn Pickering** (1855–1919), whom he married in 1887, was a pre-Raphaelite painter. See Life by H. M. W. Stirling (1922).

DEMOSTHENES, *de-mos'thĕ-neez*, (1) (d. 413 B.C.), Athenian general, in 425 B.C. assisted Cleon to reduce Sphacteria, and in 413, having been sent to Sicily to the relief of Nicias, fell, fighting bravely, into the hands of the Syracusans, and was put to death.

(2) (*c.* 383–322 B.C.), the greatest of Greek orators, lost his father at an early age. The fortune bequeathed to him was reduced by the neglect or fraud of his guardians; when he came of age he prosecuted them, and gained his cause, but most of his inheritance was irretrievably lost. This litigation compelled Demosthenes to the study of the law, and to the pursuit of it as a livelihood. Up to the age of thirty he confined himself to 'speechwriting', and gained repute as a constitutional lawyer. His most famous constitutional law speech was delivered personally in support of Ctesippus against Leptines (354). He now made his first appearance as a politician; but continued to practise as a speechwriter until he was forty, by which time he had made a fortune that allowed him to devote himself exclusively to politics. At the beginning of his political career danger threatened Greece from Philip of Macedon; Demosthenes from the outset advocated a policy which might have saved Athens and Greece. Intelligent as was the Athenian democracy, it was only when events justified Demosthenes that his policy was adopted. Philip's attack on the state of Olynthus gave occasion to the *Olynthiacs*, which, with the orations against Philip, the *Philippics*, are Demosthenes' greatest speeches. Athens made war with Philip on behalf of Olynthus; but, having failed to save the city, found peace expedient. During 346–340 Demosthenes was engaged in forming an anti-Macedonian party and in indicting Aeschines for betraying Athens. War broke out again in 340, and ended in the fatal battle of Chaeronea (338). Athens did not withdraw her confidence from Demosthenes; but the Macedonian party seized on a proposal to present him with a public crown as an occasion for his political destruction. The trial was held in 330, when in the famous speech *On the Crown* Demosthenes gloriously vindicated himself against Aeschines. In 324 Harpalus, the treasurer of Alexander the Great, absconded to Athens with an enormous sum of money. It was placed in the state treasury, under the care of Demosthenes and others, and when Alexander demanded it, half was missing. Demosthenes was accused and condemned, but escaped from prison into exile. In 323 Alexander died, and Demosthenes was recalled to head a fruitless attempt to throw off the Macedonian yoke. The battle of Crannon ended the revolt. Demosthenes fled to Calaureia, and, being there captured by Macedonian troops, poisoned himself. A. Schafer's *Demosthenes und seine Zeit* (2nd ed. 3 vols. 1885–87) eclipses all other works, good as are the handbooks of Brodribb (1877) and Butcher (1881). See too Blass's *Attische Beredsamkeit* (2nd ed. 1893); the texts of Blass (1885–89) and Butcher (1903–07); and the English translations by Kennedy (1852–63) and Vince (1926–30).

DEMPSEY, William Harrison, called **Jack** (1895–), American boxer, born at Manassa, Colorado, defeated Jess Willard in 1919 to win the world heavyweight title, which he lost to Gene Tunney in 1926.

DEMPSTER, Thomas (*c.* 1579–1625), Scottish scholar, born in Aberdeenshire, was educated at Turriff, Aberdeen, Cambridge, Paris, Louvain, Rome and Douai. A zealous Catholic, he held several provincial professorships, and at Paris was a professor for seven years; but a brawl drove him to England. He married a beautiful wife there, and then returning to the Continent, at Pisa in 1616 obtained a professorship. But his wife's infidelities marring his peace, he removed to Bologna where he became professor of Humanities, and where he died. Dempster's not too veracious autobiography forms part of his *Historia Ecclesiastica Gentis Scotorum* (Bologna, 1627)—an erudite work in which, however, his desire to magnify his country often led him to forge the names of persons and books that never existed, and to claim as Scotsmen writers whose birthplace was doubtful.

DENCK, Hans (*c.* 1495–*c.* 1527), German Anabaptist, born at Habach, Bavaria, became in 1523 rector of the Sebaldusschule in Nuremberg. From 1524 he preached a doctrine resembling Evangelical Quakerism in various parts of Germany. He wrote a commentary on the book of Micah (1531). See study by A. M. Schwindt (1924).

DENHAM, (1) Dixon (1786–1828), English traveller in Africa, the comrade of Clapperton (q.v.), was born in London and died at Sierra Leone where he was lieutenant-governor.

(2) **Sir James Steuart, Bart.** (1712–80), Scottish political economist, was born and died in Edinburgh, having returned there in 1763, after seventeen years of exile for his share in the '45. He succeeded to a Lanarkshire property in 1773, and then took the surname Denham.

(3) **Sir James Steuart** (1744–1839), only son of (2), commanded against the Irish rebels in 1798.

(4) **Sir John** (1615–69), English poet, was the only son of an Irish judge himself of English birth, and was born at Dublin. He was educated in London and at Trinity College, Oxford, where Wood tells us he was ' a slow dreaming young man, and more addicted to gaming than study ' a taste of which his own essay against gaming (1651) did not cure him. In 1634 he married and went to live with his father at Egham, an estate to which he succeeded four years later. At the outbreak of the Civil War he was high-sheriff of Surrey, and immediately joined the king. He fell into Waller's hands on the capture of Farnham Castle, and was sent prisoner to London, but soon permitted to repair to Oxford. In 1641 he produced *The Sophy*, a feeble tragedy which was acted with great applause at Blackfriars; in 1642 *Cooper's Hill*, a poetical description of the scenery around Egham, itself still read, but more famous in the merits of its greater successor, Pope's *Windsor Forest*, avowedly an imitation. In 1648, being discovered in the performance of secret services for Charles I, he fled to Holland and France. In 1650 he collected money for the young king from the Scots resident in Poland, and he several times visited England on secret service. At the Restoration he was appointed surveyor-general of works, and in 1661 created a Knight of the Bath. He was a better poet than architect, but he had Christopher Wren as his deputy. In 1665 he married a young

girl, who soon showed open favour to the Duke of York. The poor poet for a few months went crazy. About the time of his recovery his wife died suddenly (January 1667), not without suspicion of poison. Denham's last years were miserable between poverty and the satires of Butler and others.

DENIFLE, Heinrich Seuse, *den'i-flē* (1844–1905), Austrian Catholic historian, born in Tirol, compiled the *Chartularium Universitatis Parisiensis* (6 vols. 1889–97), and wrote *Geschichte der Universitäten im Mittelalter, Luther und Luthertum*, &c.

DENIKIN, Anton Ivanovich (1872–1947), Russian general, in 1918–20 headed the anti-Bolshevik forces, then went into exile and wrote books on his military experiences.

DENIS, St (3rd cent. A.D.), the traditional apostle of France and first bishop of Paris, who was sent from Rome about 250 to preach the gospel to the Gauls; in Paris he made numerous proselytes. The Roman governor ordered Denis and two other Christians to be brought before him. As they continued firm in their faith, they were cruelly tortured and beheaded in 272 or 290.

DENIS, Maurice, *dė-nee* (1870–1943), French artist, born at Grandville. He was one of the original group of Symbolist painters, the Nabis, influenced by Gauguin. Some of his comments on the aesthetics of the modern movement have obtained a wide currency. He wrote *Théories* (1913), *Nouvelles théories* (1921), *Histoire de l'art religieux* (1939) and a study of *Sérusier* (1942). In 1919 he founded, with Desvallières, the Studios of Sacred Art, devoted to the revival of religious painting, but perhaps his most famous picture is the *Hommage à Cézanne* (1900), in the Musée d'Art Moderne, Paris. See monograph by P. Jamot (1946).

DENISON, Edmund Beckett. See GRIMTHORPE.

DENMAN, (1) Right Hon. George (1819–96), seventh son of (2), called to the bar in 1846, was Liberal M.P. for Tiverton in 1859–65 and 1866–72, from which last year to 1892 he was judge, being in 1893 made a privy-councillor.

(2) **Thomas, 1st Baron** (1779–1854), born in London, was educated at Eton and St John's College, Cambridge, and entered Lincoln's Inn in 1806. With Brougham he defended Queen Caroline (1820), and shared his consequent popularity. He was Whig M.P. for Wareham and Nottingham, 1818–1826; was attorney-general in Earl Grey's administration in 1830–32; became lord chief-justice in 1832, and was raised to the peerage in 1834. He retired from the bench in 1850. See Memoir by Sir Joseph Arnould (2 vols. 1873).

(3) **Thomas 3rd Baron** (1874–1954), succeeded in 1894, and was governor-general of Australia in 1911–14.

DENNERY, Adolphe Philippe (1811–99), French playwright, born in Paris of Jewish extraction, was clerk to a notary, but from 1831 produced 133 dramas, vaudevilles, &c.— the most successful, *Marie Jeanne* (1845). He was the creator of the Norman wateringplace, Cabourg. He died in Paris.

DENNIS, John (1657–1734), English critic, was born in London, and educated at Harrow and Caius College, Cambridge. After a tour through France and Italy, he took his place among the wits and men of fashion, and brought a rancorous pen to the assistance of the Whigs. His nine plays had little success. Pope's *Essay on Criticism* (1711) contained a contemptuous allusion to one of them, *Appius and Virginia* (1709), answered by Dennis next month in *Reflections Critical and Satirical*, which commenced a long feud. Among his critical works is *An Essay on the Genius and Writings of Shakespeare* (1712).

DENT, (1) Edward John (1790–1853), chronometer-maker, was born and died in London.

(2) **Edward Joseph** (1876–1957), English musician, born in Yorkshire, was professor of Music at Cambridge 1926–41. He made translations of many libretti and has written on opera, and lives of Scarlatti, Busoni and Handel. In 1923 he helped to found the International Society for Contemporary Music.

(3) **Joseph Mallaby** (1849–1926), British publisher, worked as a bookbinder in London and later (1888) founded the publishing house of J. M. Dent & Sons, which brought out the *Temple Classics* and also *Everyman's Library*.

DENTATUS, Manius Curius (d. 270 B.C.), a Roman general famed for his noble simplicity, who between 290 and 274 B.C. defeated the Samnites and Sabines, Pyrrhus, and the Lucanians.

DEPEW, Chauncey Mitchell (1834–1928), American lawyer, railway director, politician, orator, &c., born at Peekskill, New York, wrote *Memories* (1922).

DE QUINCEY, Thomas (1785–1859), English writer, son of a Manchester merchant, was educated at Manchester Grammar School, where he proved an apt pupil. Ill-health and the romantic vagabondage which was in the air then induced him to run away from school and wander in Wales. He had expectations from his father's estate, but his guardian kept him to an allowance of a guinea a week. How he managed to exist on this sum in London, where he now went, solitary and a waif, is movingly told in his *Confessions of an Opium-eater*. Reclaimed from this vagabondage, he spent a short time at Worcester College, Oxford. It was here that he became addicted to opium. A visit to his mother at Bath brought him into contact with Coleridge, then resident at Bristol, and through him with Southey and Wordsworth. When these poets settled at the Lakes De Quincey visited them there, and after a brief sojourn in London, which enabled him to make the acquaintance of Lamb, Hazlitt and others of the ' Cockney ' school he took up his quarters at Grasmere in 1809. In 1816 he married Margaret Simpson, daughter of a ' statesman ', by whom he had three daughters and five sons, two of the latter distinguishing themselves as soldiers. De Quincey now set up as an author. Except for *The Logic of Political Economy* (1841), and an unsuccessful novel, his whole literary output, including *The Confessions*, consisted of magazine articles. The *Confessions* appeared as a serial in *The London Magazine*, 1821, and at once made him famous. Visits to London varied his existence at the Lakes, but in 1828 the lure of the Edinburgh literati drew him to the northern capital, where he lived and worked till his death in 1859. It was the flourishing age of the literary magazine, and Edinburgh rather than London was the centre of activity. For twenty years De Quincey lent distinction to *Blackwood's Magazine*, *Tait's Magazine* and, occasionally, *The Quarterly*. The brilliance of his articles was marred by an incurable tendency to digress, which, though harmless and even enjoyable in the *Confessions*, is a constant irritation in an essay on an abstract subject. His vast and curious erudition, too, got in his way and he did not know when to stop. For the general reader probably the tenth volume of Masson's edition, which contains the essay on Style and that on Rhetoric, is sufficient for the abstract writings, but the De Quincey who survives is the De Quincey of dream fugues and musical incantation, and for this we must go to the *Confessions*, both in the original version and the enlarged one of 1856; and also to the fantasies *Suspiria, Levana* and *Our Ladies of Sorrows* (1845), and the ' Dream Fugue ' at the end of *The English Mail-Coach* (1849). Those who do not mind the macabre treated jocosely may still find some entertainment in the Blackwood article *Murder Considered as a Fine Art*. Masson's edition of the works (ten vols. 1889–91) is not likely to be superseded. His *Life* also is the standard one. But see also Elton, *Survey of English Literature, 1780 to 1830*, and studies by Sackville West (1936) and Proctor (1943).

DERAIN, André, *dė-ri* (1880–1954), French artist, born at Chatou. He is most famous for his Fauve pictures, executed from 1904–1908, when he was associated with Vlaminck and Matisse. Later landscape pictures show a romantic realism influenced by Cézanne. He also designed for the theatre (notably the Diaghilev ballet) and illustrated several books. See monographs by Leymarie (1948) and Sutton (1959) and study by Diehl (1964).

DERBY, Earl of, a title conferred in 1485 on Thomas, second Lord Stanley, two months after Bosworth Field, where he had greatly contributed to Richmond's victory. The Stanleys were descended from Adam de Aldithley, who attended Duke William to England, and whose grandson, having married the heiress of Thomas Stanley, of Stafford, exchanged the manor of Thalk in that county, his wife's marriage portion, for Stoneley, in Derbyshire, and assumed the surname of Stanley. In 1405 Sir John Stanley, who had married the heiress of Lathom, got a grant of the Isle of Man, which he and his descendants ruled till 1736.

(1) **James, 7th Earl** (1606–51), fought on the royalist side throughout the Great Rebellion, and, taken prisoner after Worcester, was beheaded at Bolton; his countess, Charlotte de la Trémouille (d. 1663), is famous for her heroic defence of Lathom House (1644) and of the Isle of Man (1651).

(2) **Edward Geoffrey Smith Stanley, 14th Earl** (1799–1869), was born at Knowsley Hall, Lancashire. He was educated at Eton and

Christ Church, Oxford, where, in 1819, he gained the Latin Verse. He entered parliament for Stockbridge in 1820; and in 1830 became chief-secretary for Ireland under the Grey administration. He supported the Reform Bill, and signalized his Irish administration by two bold measures—one for National Education and another abolishing ten Irish bishoprics. In 1833 he became colonial secretary, and carried the emancipation of West Indian slaves. In 1834, alarmed by a motion for secularizing the surplus of the Irish Church temporalities, Mr Stanley seceded from the Whigs; in November he declined to join the Peel administration, and the Stanleyites maintained an independent position; but he held the colonial seals in 1841–44. In 1844 he resigned his seat for North Lancashire, for which he had sat since 1832, and was called to the Upper House in his father's barony of Stanley of Bickerstaffe, having for ten years borne the courtesy title of Lord Stanley, through his father's succession to the earldom of Derby. In December 1845, when Peel determined to repeal the corn laws, he retired from the Cabinet, and in 1846 headed the Protectionists in the Lords. He was now regarded as the Conservative leader. In 1851 he succeeded his father as Earl of Derby; in February 1852 he formed an administration, displaced in the following December by a hostile vote against Disraeli's budget. In 1858 he again became premier, and in 1859 his government brought forward a measure of reform; a hostile amendment having been carried, he dissolved and appealed to the country. When the new House met in June 1859, he resigned on a vote of want of confidence. Returning to power in 1866, he passed the Reform measure of 1867 in conjunction with Disraeli, in whose favour he resigned the premiership in 1868. His last speech in parliament was made (1869) against the Irish Church disestablishment. Lord Derby was styled by Bulwer Lytton 'the Rupert of debate', and stood in the very first rank of parliamentary speakers. An accomplished scholar, he translated the *Iliad* into blank verse (1864), and was also a keen sportsman and a popular landlord. He cared little for office (he refused in 1863 the crown of Greece), and more than once injured his party by declining to form a ministry, notably on the fall of Aberdeen in 1855. See Lives by Kebbel (1890) and Saintsbury (1892), and W. D. Jones, *Lord Derby and Victorian Conservatism* (1956).

(3) **Edward Henry Smith Stanley, 15th Earl,** K.G., D.C.L., LL.D., F.R.S. (1826–93), eldest son of (2), was born at Knowsley Hall, and educated at Rugby and Trinity College, Cambridge, where he took a double first. In 1848 he became M.P. for Lynn, and in 1852 was appointed foreign under-secretary in his father's first ministry. After declining to join Palmerston's ministry in 1855, he became secretary for India in his father's second administration (1858–59), and carried the measure transferring the government of India to the Crown. He was foreign secretary in the third Derby and first Disraeli ministries (1866–68). In 1874 he again became foreign

secretary under Disraeli; but resigned in March 1878 when the majority of the Cabinet determined to support Turkey by occupying Cyprus. In 1880 he definitely joined the Liberal party, and was colonial secretary (1882–85), but seceded on Home Rule. See his *Speeches and Addresses* (1894).

(4) **Frederick Arthur, 16th Earl** (1841–1908), brother of (3), governor-general of Canada (1888–93).

(5) **Edward George Villiers** (1865–1948), son of (4), director of recruiting (1915–16), war secretary (1916–18, 1922–24); ambassador to France (1918–20). See Life by Randolph Churchill (1960).

(6) **Oliver Frederick George** (1896–1950), second son of (5), leading Conservative politician; secretary of state for war (1940); colonial secretary (1942–45).

DERÈME, Tristan, nom-de-plume of **Philippe Huc** (1889–1941), French poet of the *fantaisiste* school. Works include *La Verdure dorée* (1922, incorporating eight previous collections of poems), *L'Enlèvement sans clair de lune* (1924), &c.

DERINGER, Henry (19th cent.), Philadelphia manufacturer of small arms, invented the pocket pistol known as a ' derringer '.

DERKOVITS, Gyula (1894–1934), Hungarian Expressionist and Cubist painter, born at Szombathely.

DE ROS, Georgiana, Lady (1795–1891), daughter of the Duke of Richmond, in 1824 married William, Lord de Ros (1797–1874). A friend of the Duke of Wellington, she knew nineteen prime ministers.

DE ROSSI, Giovanni Battista. See ROSSI.

DÉROULÈDE, Paul (1846–1914), French politician and poet, born at Paris. His writings cried for revenge on Germany and he was active in the anti-Dreyfus campaign. In 1900 he was exiled for 10 years for sedition, but returned in 1905.

DEROZIO, Henry Louis Vivian (1809–31), Eurasian poet-patriot, born at Calcutta. At nineteen he had published two books of poems and was lecturing on English history and literature at the Hindu College, Calcutta. And in the next four years he had translated De Maupertuis, lectured on philosophy, written a critique on Kant, edited four journals, become embroiled in local politics, and instigated so much freethinking and social rebelliousness that he was dismissed from the College a few months before he died. Much of his verse is imitatively ornamental, but some of his sonnets put him among the lesser Romantics. See edition of his poems and critical study by F. B. Bradley Birt (1923),

DE RUYTER. See RUYTER.

DERWENTWATER, James Radcliffe, 3rd Earl of (1689–1716), was born in London, and brought up at St Germain. He succeeded as third earl in 1705, on the death of his father, who had married Lady Mary Tudor, Charles II's daughter by Moll Davis. In 1715 warrants were issued against several gentlemen in the north, one of them against the young Catholic earl; but he fled from Dilston, his seat in Northumberland, and soon placed himself at the head of a few retainers. From this point the history of the Earl becomes the history of the Rebellion which ended in the disastrous encounter at Preston. Derwentwater bore himself with heroism, but, with most of the rebel leaders, was taken prisoner, and conveyed to the Tower. At his trial for high treason at Westminster Hall he pleaded guilty, and threw himself on the king's mercy. Every effort for a pardon failed, and he was beheaded on Tower Hill. See a Life by F. J. A. Skeet (1929).

DERZHAVIN, Gavriil Romanovich (1743–1816), Russian poet, was born at Kazan, and in 1762 entered the army as a private. His talents soon gained him promotion. In 1791 he became secretary of state, in 1800 imperial treasurer, and in 1802 minister of justice. See Life by Tharaud (Paris 1925).

DESAIX DE VEYGOUX, Louis Charles Antoine, *dĕ-say-dĕ-vay-goo* (1768–1800), born at St Hilaire-d'Ayat in Auvergne, entered the army at fifteen, and in 1796 covered himself with glory in Moreau's famous retreat through the Black Forest. Behind the ruinous fortress of Kehl Desaix resisted the Austrians for two months, only capitulating, in 1797, when his ammunition was spent. His greatest achievement was the conquest of Upper Egypt, after an eight months' campaign (1799). He was shot in the battle of Marengo.

DESARGUES, Gérard, *day-zarg* (1593–1662), French mathematician, born at Lyons, lectured on mathematics in Paris and is one of the founders of modern geometry. Most of his work was contained in his book *Brouillon Project* (1639) on conics. As an engineer he took part in the siege of La Rochelle.

DÉSAUGIERS, Marc, *day-zō-zhay* (1772–1827), French writer of songs and vaudevilles, whom some have set above Béranger, was born at Fréjus, and died in Paris, his residence from 1797, after adventurous years in San Domingo and elsewhere.

DESAULT, Pierre Joseph, *dĕ-sō* (1744–95), a French surgeon and anatomist, founded the first school of clinical surgery in France.

DESBARRES, Joseph Frederick Wallet, *day-bar* (1722–1824), born in England of Huguenot parentage, at the siege of Quebec (1759) was aide-de-camp to Wolfe. He surveyed the coast of Nova Scotia in 1763–73; was lieutenant-governor of Cape Breton and of Prince Edward Island; and died at Halifax, N.S., aged 102.

DESCARTES, René, *day-kahrt*, Latinized **Cartesius** (1596–1650), French rationalist philosopher and mathematician, rightly called ' the father of modern philosophy ', born March 31 at La Haye, near Tours, was trained at the Jesuit College at La Flèche, where he was on cordial terms with Mersenne. Although he was careful to remain a Roman Catholic all his life, he soon became dissatisfied with scholasticism and, determined ' no longer to seek any other science than the knowledge of myself or of the great book of the world ', he enlisted under Prince Maurice of Nassau (1617), but found ample time for his mathematical studies in the company of other mathematicians serving as engineers. In 1619 he joined the Bavarian army, and one winter's day he was sitting, meditating by a stove when he hit upon his new rationalism. His aim was certainty—the kind

of certainty that did not rely upon unobserved entities for the explanation of natural events nor upon the authority of learned theologians, but by submitting everything to reason, in short by extending the clearness and distinctness of mathematical ideas and proofs to all spheres of human knowledge and to knowledge itself. He began this quest by systematically doubting the evidence of his senses, by postulating a malignant demon who would falsify even mathematical and rational processes, but he found that in doubting he could not doubt that he was thinking. This led him, as it had St Augustine before him, to the basic (if, of course systematically misleading) proposition—*Cogito ergo sum* (I think, therefore I exist). This conclusion, because of its clearness and distinctness, must be true. Another such conclusion was the idea of God as the absolutely perfect Being—an idea which imperfect humanity could never originate, hence God exists—the ontological argument. God as the Perfect Being cannot deceive, therefore all rational and conceptual qualities, when presented to the mind, are indubitable, but physical properties may still deceive. Descartes embarks upon a dualism between mind and body and their properties which are for him mutually exclusive. They can only be united as in man, by the intervention of God. This dualism was later consistently worked out by Malebranche, who explained processes in the nerves and brain are merely the *occasion* of God's producing a corresponding mental result (*occasionalism*), and rather differently by Leibniz, who postulated the ' pre-established harmony ' between the mental and physical worlds. For Descartes the brain was mysteriously situated in the pineal gland. Animals, lacking rational souls, are mere automata. The Cartesian philosophy is to be found in the *Discours de la méthode* (1637), and more fully in *Meditationes de Prima Philosophia* (1641) and *Principia Philosophiae* (1644). Modern rationalism is mainly a critical development of Cartesian metaphysics and British empiricism, almost by definition, a rejection of the Cartesian approach. In astronomy, his theory of vortices held the field till Newton. But his greatest achievement was his discovery and formulation of coordinate geometry (1637). In 1649, Descartes presented himself at the Court of Queen Christine of Sweden, an ardent student of his philosophy, who insisted on having lessons from him at 5 o'clock each morning. Unaccustomed to such hours and the cold, Descartes caught inflammation of the lungs and died in February 1650. See French studies by G. Milhaud (1921) and E. Gilson (1930), English works by Kuno Fischer (trans. 1887), S. V. Keeling (1934) and especially the two outstanding studies (1902 and 1952) by N. Kemp Smith, who also edited *Selected Writings* (1952), and G. Ryle's attack upon Cartesianism, *The Concept of Mind* (1949).

DESCHAMPS, Eustache, called **Morel,** *day-shã* (c. 1345–c. 1406), French poet, born at Vertus in Champagne, was brought up by Machaut (q.v.), who may have been his uncle and who probably taught him his craft. A soldier, a magistrate, a court favourite and a traveller in Italy and Hungary, he held important posts in Champagne, but after his patron, Charles V, died, his possessions were ravaged by the English. He composed 1175 lyrics, besides the *Miroir de mariage* satirizing women, and several poems in the current fashion, deploring the miseries of the Hundred Years' War. See the *Oeuvres complètes* (11 vols. 1878–1903) edited by Queux de Saint-Hilaire and Raynaud.

DESIDERIO DA SETTIGNANO (1428–64), a Florentine sculptor in the early Renaissance style, born at Settignano near Florence, was influenced by Donatello and della Robbia.

DESMARETS, Jean, Sieur de Saint-Sorlen, *day-ma-ray* (1596–1676), French poet, author of *Comparaison de la langue et la poésie française avec la grecque et la latine* (1670), first chancellor and co-founder of the Académie française, and a protagonist in the ancients versus moderns controversy.

DESMOND, Earl of, a title conferred in 1329 on Maurice Fitzgerald, along with county Kerry, and last borne by Gerald Fitzgerald, 15th Earl, who in 1579–80 rebelled against Elizabeth, sacked Youghal by night and was proclaimed a traitor. He escaped the fate of the garrison at Smerwick, but was driven at last from his strongholds, wandered about for over two years, and was killed (1583) in a cabin in the Kerry mountains.

DESMOULINS, Camille, *day-moo-lǐ* (1760–1794), born at Guise, studied law along with Robespierre at the Collège Louis le Grand in Paris, but owing to a stutter never practised. His confused notions of classical republicanism found vent in his pamphlets, *La Philosophie au peuple français* (1788) and *La France libre* (1789), the latter published the day after the destruction of the Bastille, where he played a dramatic part. His *Discours de la Lanterne* procured him the sinister title of ' Procureur-général de la Lanterne '. In November 1789 he began the brilliantly witty, cruelly sarcastic *Révolutions de France et de Brabant,* which appeared weekly until July 1792. His *Tribune des patriotes,* however, died in its fourth number. Desmoulins had been a member of the Cordeliers' Club from its foundation, and early clung to Danton. Elected by Paris to the National Convention, he voted for the death of the king. In the struggle between the Girondists and the Mountain he took an active part, and in May 1793, urged on by Robespierre, published his truculent *Histoire des Brissotins.* On December 5, came out the *Vieux Cordelier,* an eloquent expression of Desmoulins' and Danton's longing for clemency. Robespierre took fright at the reception of the third number, and soon became actively hostile. On March 30, 1794, Desmoulins was arrested with Danton; on April 5 he died by the guillotine, not too heroically. A fortnight later his beloved wife, Lucile Duplessis (1771–1794), whom he had married in 1790, followed him to the same doom, dying with the courage of a martyr. See books by Claretie (1908); Godart (Paris 1889); Miss V. Methley (1915), Arland (1928); and P. Compton (1933).

DE SOTO, Fernando (c. 1496–1542), Spanish explorer, born at Jerez de los Caballeros,

accompanied Pedrarias Dávila to Darien in 1519, served in Nicaragua in 1527, and assisted Pizarro in the conquest of Peru, returning to Spain with 180,000 ducats. Charles V gave him permission to conquer Florida, and appointed him governor of Cuba; in May 1539 with 600 men he anchored in Tampa Bay, and the long search for gold was begun. For three years harassed by hostile Indians, lured onward by reports of wealth, the ever-decreasing company continued their toilsome march. In 1541 the Mississippi was crossed, and the third winter was spent on Washita River. Returning to the Mississippi in the spring, De Soto died of a fever on its banks; and to conceal his death from the Indians, his body was lowered at midnight into the great stream he had discovered. Hardly half of his followers finally reached Mexico. See Life by Cunninghame Graham (1903); also, the *Discovery of Florida,* ed. Rye (Hakluyt Soc. 1851).

DESPARD, (1) Charlotte, *née* **French** (1844–1939), social reformer, advocate of women's rights, and pacifist, a sister of Lord Ypres.

(2) **Edward Marcus** (1751–1803), conspirator, was born in Queen's County, Ireland, and at fifteen obtained an ensigncy. From 1772 till 1790 he did good service in the West Indies, but was then recalled on frivolous charges, proved in 1792 to be baseless. His demands for compensation brought him two years' imprisonment (1798–1800), on his release from which he engaged in a crack-brained conspiracy to assassinate the king and to seize the Tower and Bank of England. For this, with six associates, he was drawn on a hurdle, hanged and beheaded. See Oman, *The Unfortunate Colonel Despard* (1922).

(3) **John** (1745–1829), brother of (2), British general, was present at twenty-four engagements, mostly during the American War of Independence.

DESPAUTERIUS, Johannes (c. 1460–1520), a Fleming, whose Latin grammar was much used in Scotland before the Reformation.

DESPENCER, Lord le. See DASHWOOD.

DESPENSER, (1) Hugh le, justiciary of England from 1260, fell at Evesham fighting on the side of the Barons (1265).

(2) **Hugh** (1262–1326), son of (1), after Gaveston's death (1312) became head of the court party; was banished with his son, Hugh (1321), but recalled the next year by Edward II and created Earl of Winchester; and, after Queen Isabella's landing, was taken and hanged at Bristol, as was his son at Hereford.

DES PÉRIERS, Bonaventure, *day payr-yay* (c. 1500–44), French writer, born at Autun, was a member of the court of men of letters assembled by Margaret of Navarre (q.v.). In a dialogue, *Cymbalum Mundi* (1537), under the pretence of attacking the superstitions of the ancients, he satirized the religious beliefs of his own day. The book raised a storm of indignation, against which Margaret was powerless to shield him; and rather than fall into the hands of his persecutors he is said to have killed himself. His admirable *Nouvelles Récréations et joyeux devis* (1558) consists of 129 short stories, both comic and romantic. To Des Périers has often been assigned the chief authorship of Margaret's *Heptameron*. See Lacour's edition of his works (2 vols. 1856) and a monograph by Chenevière (1886).

DESPIAU, Charles, *des-pyō* (1874–1946), French sculptor, born at Mont-de-Marsan, was discovered by Rodin, who took him as a pupil. See study by Roger Marx (1922).

DESPRÉAUX. See BOILEAU.

DES PRÉS, Josquin, *day-pray* (c. 1450–1521), Dutch composer, born probably at Condé, where he died. A pupil of Okeghem (q.v.), he was Kapellmeister to Lorenzo de' Medici, Louis XII and Maximilian I. A master of polyphony, he has left a number of valuable masses and motets. Burney called him 'father of modern harmony'. See study by F. Blume (1926).

DESSALINES, Jean Jacques, *-leen* (c. 1758–1806), emperor of Haiti, born in Guinea, was imported into Haiti as a slave. He was bought by a French planter, whose name he assumed, and in the insurrection (1791) was second only to Toussaint L'Ouverture. After the first compromise he became governor of the southern part of the island, but soon renewed the war, and after infamous cruelties compelled the French to evacuate Haiti in October 1803. He was created governor in January 1804, and on October 8 was crowned emperor as Jean Jacques I. But his cruelty and debauchery soon alienated even his firmest adherents, and while trying to repress a revolt he was cut down by Christophe (q.v.), who succeeded him.

DESTOUCHES, Philippe, orig. **Néricault,** *day-toosh* (1680–1754), French playwright, born at Tours, wrote seventeen comedies, two of them admirable—*Le Philosophe marié* (1727) and *Le Glorieux,* his masterpiece (1732).

DETAILLE, Jean Baptiste Edouard, *dė-tah'y'* (1848–1912), a French battle painter of the school of Meissonier, born in Paris, painted battle scenes while serving in the Franco-Russian war, also portraits, including *Edward VII and the Duke of Connaught,* in the Royal Collection.

DEUTSCH, Emanuel Oscar Menahem, *doych* (1829–73), Jewish orientalist, born in Silesia, in 1855 became an assistant librarian at the British Museum. He wrote on the Talmud in the *Quarterly Review* (1867). See his *Literary Remains* (1874).

DE VALERA, Eamon, *de-va-lay'ra* (1882–   ), Irish statesman, was born in New York of a Spanish father and Irish mother. Brought up on an uncle's farm in County Limerick, he became a teacher of mathematics in Dublin, and there associated himself with various republican movements. A commandant in the 1916 rising, he narrowly escaped the firing squad, was sentenced instead to life imprisonment but released on an amnesty in 1917. In the same year he was elected M.P. for East Clare and became leader of Sinn Fein, the nationalist movement. Rearrested for subversive activities, he was released from Lincoln jail in Michael Collins's daring raid in 1919, fled to the U.S.A., and was elected president of Dáil Eireann. He opposed the 1921 treaty with

the British government and became leader in 1926 of Fianna Fail, the newly formed Republican opposition party, which won the 1932 elections. President of the Executive Council until 1937, he was thereafter prime minister under the remodelled constitution. He instituted a number of constitutional reforms, introduced the Irish language into the educational system, worked to remove all vestiges of British influence, and secured Irish neutrality in World War II. The swing of the political pendulum removed him in 1948 and 1954, restored him in 1951 and (1957–59) when he was elected president of Ireland. In spite of his colourful early career, his leadership has been moderate, and he has opposed extremism and religious intolerance. See Lives by M. J. MacManus (1947) and M. C. Bromage (1956).

DE VERE, Aubrey Thomas (1814–1902), Irish poet, was third son of Sir Aubrey De Vere (1788–1846), Bart., of Curragh Chase, Co. Limerick (himself a poet). In addition to many volumes of poems he published poetical dramas on Alexander the Great (1874) and Becket (1876), *Essays on Poetry* (2 vols. 1887), and works on Irish ecclesiastical politics and literary criticism. From 1851 he was a Catholic. See his *Recollections* (1897).

DEVEREUX. See ESSEX, EARL OF.

DEVILLE. See SAINTE-CLAIRE DEVILLE.

DEVORGILLA. See BALIOL.

DEVRIENT, *de-freent,* a family of German actors. Chronologically they are:

(1) **Ludwig** (1784–1832), distinguished both in comedy and tragedy, and especially in Shakespearean characters.

(2) **Carl August** (1797–1872), nephew of (1), played lovers' parts, and married the *diva,* Madame Schröder-Devrient (1805–60).

(3) **Philipp Eduard** (1801–77), brother of (2), was a baritone singer and actor, and wrote many plays and the valuable *Geschichte der deutschen Schauspielkunst* (5 vols. 1848–74); he edited Shakespeare with his son, Otto (1838–94), also an actor, manager and playwright.

(4) **Gustav Emil** (1803–72), the most gifted of the three brothers, became identified with such characters as Hamlet, Tasso, and especially Posa.

(5) **Max** (1857–1929), son of (2), upheld the family tradition.

DE VRIES, Hugo (1848–1935), Dutch botanist, born at Haarlem, professor at Amsterdam in 1878–1918, continued Mendel's work.

DEWAR, Sir James (1842–1923; kt. 1904), from 1875 professor at Cambridge and F.R.S., was born at Kincardine-on-Forth, and educated at Dollar, Edinburgh and Ghent. He liquefied and froze many gases, invented the vacuum flask and (with Sir F. Abel) discovered cordite.

D'EWES, Sir Simonds (1602–50), English antiquary, born at Coxden, near Chard, sat for Sudbury in the Long Parliament, and was expelled by Pride. His *Diaries* and his transcripts of manuscripts (which else had perished) possess high value. W. Notestein edited his *Journal* (1924).

DE WET, Christian (1854–1922), Boer general,

had acquired fame as a hunter before he became conspicuous in the Transvaal war of 1880-81; and in the war of 1899–1902 he was the most audacious of all the Boer commanders. He wrote a book on the war, and in 1907 he became minister for agriculture of the Orange River Colony. In October 1914 he joined the South African insurrection, and was taken in December. He was sentenced to six years' imprisonment, but released December 1915.

DE WETTE, Wilhelm Martin Leberecht (1780–1849), German biblical critic, born at Ulla, near Weimar, studied from 1799 at Jena, and became professor at Heidelberg in 1809, in 1810 at Berlin. A letter sent in 1819 to his friend, the mother of Sand the assassin of Kotzebue, cost him his chair. In 1822 he became professor of Theology at Basel. He wrote introductions to the Old and New Testaments, and a manual of Hebrew archaeology.

DEWEY, (1) George (1837–1917), American admiral, born at Montpelier, Vt., as commodore in 1898 destroyed or took the whole Spanish fleet at Manila Bay without losing a man.

(2) **John** (1859–1952), American philosopher, born at Burlington, Vt., became professor of Philosophy at Columbia University (New York) in 1904. A leading exponent of pragmatism, he has written *Essays in Experimental Logic* (1916), *Reconstruction in Philosophy* (1920), *The Quest for Certainty*, (1929), *Art as Experience* (1934), &c. See studies by Hook (N.Y. 1939), ed. P. Schilpp (1943), and Nathanson (1951).

(3) **Melvil** (1851–1931), American librarian, founder of the ' Dewey System ' of book classification by decimals. See Life by G. G. Dawe (1933).

(4) **Thomas Edmund** (1902–71), American politician, born at Owosso, Michigan. After studying law at the universities of Michigan and Columbia, he became district attorney for New York County in 1937, and governor of New York State in 1942, being re-elected to this office in 1946 and 1950. He was Republican nominee for president in 1944 and 1948, when by virtue of the ' Dewey machine ', his campaign organization, he appeared to be a much stronger candidate than President Truman (q.v.).

DE WITT, Jan (1625–72), born at Dort, was the son of Jacob de Witt, a vehement opponent of William II, Prince of Orange. Jan was one of the deputies sent by the States of Holland in 1652 to Zeeland, to dissuade that province from adopting an Orange policy. In 1653 he was made grand pensionary. The Orange party, during the war between England and Holland, was ever striving to increase the power of the young prince (afterwards William III); the republican, or oligarchic party, composed of the nobles and the wealthier burgesses, with De Witt at their head, on the other hand sought to abolish the office of stadhouder. In 1654, on the conclusion of the war, a secret article in the treaty drawn up between De Witt and Cromwell deprived the House of Orange of all state offices. After the restoration of Charles II, De Witt leaned

to the side of France, all the more during the two years' renewal of hostilities (1665–67), in which he saved the remnant of the Dutch fleet, and which were terminated by the Peace of Breda. The Triple Alliance (1666) for a time arrested Louis XIV's designs upon the Spanish Netherlands; but on his invasion of the United Provinces in 1672 the Orange party raised William to the family dignity of stadhouder and commander of the Dutch forces. The first campaign proved unfortunate, which did not improve the temper of the people towards De Witt, who had resigned his office of grand pensionary. His brother Cornelius, accused of conspiring against the stadhouder's life, was imprisoned and tortured. De Witt went to see him in prison, when they were attacked by an infuriated mob, and torn to pieces, August 20, 1672. Among his writings are his *Memoirs* (1709) and his *Letters* (6 vols. 1723–25). See the Lives by Simons (1832–1836), Knottenbelt (1862), J. Geddes (vol. i. London 1879), and Pontalis (Eng. trans. 2 vols. 1885).

DHULEEP SINGH (1838–93), son and successor of Ranjit Singh (q.v.), deposed and pensioned in 1849, turned Christian (until 1886 when he sought in vain to re-establish himself), and lived for years as a Suffolk squire.

DIAGHILEV, Sergei Pavlovich, *dee-ah'gee-lef* (1872–1929), Russian impresario, born in Novgorod. He obtained a law degree, but his real preoccupation, encouraged by his stepmother, Elena Panaea, was with the arts. In 1898 he became editor of *Mir Iskousstva* (World of Art) and during the next few years arranged exhibitions and concerts of Russian Art and Music. In 1908 he presented *Boris Godunov* in Paris, and the next year brought a ballet company to the Châtelet. His permanent company was founded in 1911, with Cecchetti as ballet master and remained perilously in existence for twenty years, triumphantly touring Europe, with headquarters in Monte Carlo, yet never free from financial anxiety. All the great dancers, composers and painters of his period contributed to the success of his Ballets Russes; and some, such as Tchelichev, owed their subsequent fame to their association with the company. Diaghilev was a temperamental tyrant, combining ruthlessness with charm—an aesthetic catalyst whose mere presence seemed to activate the creation of works of art. See studies by C. W. Beaumont (1933) and A. Haskell with W. Nouvel (1935).

DIANE DE FRANCE (1538–1619), Duchess of Angoulême, a natural daughter of Henry II and a Piedmontese (according to others, of Diane de Poitiers), was formally legitimized, and married first to a son of the Duke of Parma, next to the eldest son of the Constable de Montmorency. She enjoyed great influence at court under Henry IV, and superintended the education of the future Louis XIII.

DIANE DE POITIERS, *dee-an dè pwah-tyay* (1499–1566) mistress of Henry II of France, was married at thirteen, and left a widow at thirty-two; presently she won the affections of the boy dauphin, already wedded to Catharine de' Medici. On his accession (1547) Diane enjoyed great influence, and was made Duchess of Valentinois. After his death (1559) she retired to her Château d'Anet. See Life by Capefigue (1860).

DIAZ, or Dias, Bartolomeu (*c.* 1450–1500), a Portuguese navigator whose residence at the court of John II brought him into contact with many scientific men, among others the German cosmographer Behaim (q.v.). In 1486 the king gave him the command of two vessels to follow up the discoveries already made on the west coast of Africa. Diaz soon reached the limit which had been attained in South Atlantic navigation, and first touched land in 26° S. lat. Driven by a violent storm, he sailed round the southern extremity of Africa, the Cape of Good Hope, without immediately realizing the fact, and discovered Algoa Bay. The discontent of his crew compelled him to return; and arriving in Lisbon, December 1488, he was at first greeted with enthusiasm. But in the expedition of 1497 he had to act under Vasco da Gama, who even sent him back to Portugal after they had reached the Cape Verd Isles. Three years later he joined the expedition of Cabral, the discoverer of Brazil, but was lost in a storm, May 29, 1500.

DÍAZ, (1) Daniel Vázquez (1882–1969), Spanish artist, born at Nerva. He came into contact with cubism in Paris, and returned to Spain in 1918 to paint portraits, landscapes and murals in a style reminiscent of Cézanne. In 1953, he retired from his teaching post at the San Fernando Academy.

(2) **Diego Valentin** (*c.* 1585–1660), Spanish artist, born at Valladolid. He was a Familiar of the Holy Office, and painted many pictures for churches and monasteries, e.g., the *Annunciation*, in the orphanage which he founded in his native town.

(3) **José de la Cruz Porfirio** (1830–1915), president of Mexico, born at Oaxaca, fought in the Mexican War and under Juárez was instigator of several risings against the government, and was ultimately elected president in 1877 remaining in office continuously, except during 1880–84, until 1911, when Madero's revolution forced him to resign and flee into exile. Though the dictatorial nature of his régime led to his final downfall, he was responsible for a great increase in Mexico's prosperity and economic stability.

DÍAZ DE LA PEÑA, Narciso Virgilio, *dee'ath day la pay'nya* (1807–76), painter, was born at Bordeaux of Spanish parentage, and, left an orphan, was educated by a Protestant pastor at Bellevue, near Paris. At fifteen he was apprenticed to a porcelain painter; in 1831 he began to exhibit in the Salon. His favourite subjects were landscapes with nymphs, lovers and satyrs; and his *forte* was colour. He died at Mentone.

DÍAZ DEL CASTILLO, Bernal, *kas-teel'yō* (*c.* 1492–1581), the historian of the conquest of Mexico, was one of the handful of heroes who accompanied Cortés in 1519. His *Historia de la conquista de la Nueva España* (1904; trans. 1908–16), written at the age

of eighty-four, is invaluable. See Life by Cunninghame Graham (1915).

DIBDIN, (1) Charles (1745–1814), English songwriter, born at Southampton, early attracted notice by his singing, and, still a boy, composed an operetta, *The Shepherd's Artifice*, which was produced at Covent Garden in 1762. He subsequently lived an unsettled life as an actor and composer of stage music, and in 1788 began a series of musical entertainments, which enjoyed some popularity. Dibdin wrote nearly a hundred sea songs—among the best 'Poor Jack' and 'Tom Bowling'. He also wrote nearly seventy dramatic pieces. Two of his sons, **Charles** (1768–1833) and **Thomas John** (1771–1841), wrote songs and dramas. See Dibdin's Autobiography (4 vols. 1803) and *The Dibdins*, by E. R. Dibdin (1888).

(2) **Thomas Frognall** (1776–1807), English bibliographer, a nephew of (1), was born at Calcutta, orphaned at four, and brought up by an uncle. He took orders in 1804, was librarian to Lord Spencer, and held charges near Newmarket and in London. He wrote *Bibliomania* (1809); *The Bibliographical Decameron* (1817); *Bibliotheca Spenceriana* (1814–15); *Reminiscences of a Literary Life* (1836); and *Bibliographical Tour in the Northern Counties of England and Scotland* (1838).

DICEY, Albert Venn (1835–1922), English jurist, in 1882–1909 professor of Common Law at Oxford, wrote *Law of the Constitution* (1885), *Conflict of Laws* (1896), *Law and Public Opinion in England* (1905). See his *Memorials* (ed. Rait, 1925).

DICK, (1) James (1743–1828), Scottish philanthropist, a West India merchant, born at Forres, who left over £113,000 to promote higher learning in the parish schools of the counties of Elgin, Banff and Aberdeen.

(2) **Robert** (1811–66), self-taught Scottish geologist and botanist, born at Tullybody, was from 1830 a baker in Thurso. See Life by Dr Smiles (1878).

DICK-READ, Grantly (1890–1959), English gynaecologist, studied at St John's College, Cambridge, and the London Hospital. His unorthodox work, *Natural Childbirth* (1933), with its rejection of anaesthetics during childbirth and its advocacy of prenatal relaxation exercises, caused bitter controversy, but has twenty years later found common acceptance. In 1948 he emigrated to South Africa where he conducted a tour of African tribes in 1954 investigating childbirth.

DICKENS, Charles (1812–70), was born at Landport, then a little suburb of Portsmouth or Portsea, on Friday, February 7. His father was John Dickens, a clerk in the navy pay office, and at that time attached to Portsmouth dockyard; in 1814 he was transferred to London, and in 1816 to Chatham, where the boy, already a great reader, got some schooling. In 1821 the family fell into trouble; reforms in the Admiralty deprived the father of his post and the greater part of his income; they had to leave Chatham, and removed to London, where they took a small house in Camden Town. But not for long. The father was presently arrested for debt and consigned to the Marshalsea, and Charles, then only ten years of age, and small for his age, was placed in a blacking factory at Hungerford Market, where with half a dozen rough boys, he labelled the blacking bottles. Not only were his days passed in this wretched work, but the child was left entirely to himself at night, when he had four miles to walk to his lonely bedroom in Camden Town. On Sundays he visited his father in the prison; and presently they found him a lodging in Lant Street close by. On his father's release they all went back to Camden Town, and the boy was sent again to school, an academy in the Hampstead Road, for three or four years. When he was taken from school no better place could be found for him than a stool at the desk of a solicitor. Meantime, however, his father had obtained a post as reporter for the *Morning Herald*, and Charles resolved also to attempt the profession of journalist. He taught himself shorthand; and he frequented the British Museum daily to supplement some of the shortcomings of his reading. In his seventeenth year he became a reporter at Doctors' Commons; but all his ambitions were at this period for the stage. It was not until he was twenty-two that he succeeded in getting permanent employment on the staff of a London paper as a reporter; in this capacity he was sent much about the country. In December 1833 the *Monthly Magazine* published his ' Dinner at Poplar Walk '. Other papers followed, but produced nothing for the contributor except the gratification of seeing them in print. However, they did Dickens the best service possible, in enabling him to prove his power, and he presently made an arrangement to contribute papers and sketches regularly to the *Evening Chronicle*, continuing to act as reporter for the *Morning Chronicle*, and getting his salary increased from five guineas to seven a week. The *Sketches by Boz* were collected and published in the beginning of the year 1836, the author receiving £150 for the copyright; he afterwards bought it back for eleven times that amount. In the last week of March in the same year appeared the first number of the *Pickwick Papers*; three days afterwards Dickens married Catherine, daughter of his friend George Hogarth, editor of the *Evening Chronicle*. She bore him seven sons and three daughters between 1837 and 1852, three of whom predeceased him; in 1858 husband and wife separated. Success having definitely come his way, Dickens for the rest of his life allowed himself scant respite. In fulfilment of publishers' engagements he produced *Oliver Twist* (1837–39; in *Bentley's Miscellany*, which Dickens edited for a time), *Nicholas Nickleby* (1838–39), and *Master Humphrey's Clock*, a serial miscellany which resolved itself into the two stories, *The Old Curiosity Shop* (1840–41), and *Barnaby Rudge* (1841). Thereafter a great part of Dickens's life was spent abroad, especially notable being his visits to America in 1842 and 1867–68 (the latter more felicitous than the former), his stay at Genoa in 1844–45 and at Lausanne

in 1846, and his summers spent at Boulogne in 1853, 1854 and 1856. Meanwhile there came from his pen an incessant stream:— *American Notes* (1842), *Martin Chuzzlewit* (1843), *The Christmas Tales*—viz., *A Christmas Carol, The Chimes, The Cricket on the Hearth, The Battle of Life, The Haunted Man* and *The Ghost's Bargain* (1843, 1846 and 1848); *Pictures from Italy* (1845), *Dombey and Son* (1846–48), *David Copperfield* (1849–50), *Bleak House* (1852–53), *A Child's History of England* (1854), *Hard Times* (1854), *Little Dorrit* (1855–57), *A Tale of Two Cities* (1859), *The Uncommercial Traveller* (1861), the Christmas numbers in *Household Words* and *All the Year Round, Great Expectations* (1860–61), *Our Mutual Friend* (1864–65), *The Mystery of Edwin Drood* (1870, unfinished). To this long roll must be added public readings (1858–70), both in this country and in America, private theatricals, speeches, letters innumerable, pamphlets, plays, the conduct of a popular magazine—first (1850) called *Household Words* and then (1859) *All the Year Round*. Nevertheless he had taken irreparable toll of his vitality, and he died suddenly, June 9, 1870, at Gadshill, near Rochester (the place he had coveted as a boy, and purchased in 1856), and was buried in Westminster Abbey. The general style of Dickens was virile and direct. He had full command of a nervous English, reinforced by sympathy and humour, by drollery as refreshing as it was unexpected, and by a fierce indignation against wrong. Critically his work is easily assailed, but of its popularity there can be no doubt, for it has conquered the whole English-speaking world. See his *Letters* (3 vols. 1880-82); Lives by John Forster (3 vols. 1872-74; 2 vols. 1911) and J. Lindsay (1958); Studies by Gissing (1898), Chesterton (1906, 1911), Swinburne (1913), Dibelius (1920), Quiller-Couch (1925), Delattre (Paris 1927), Straus (1928), House (1941); by his daughter, Mamie Dickens (1897), and (1928) by his sixth son, Sir Henry Fielding Dickens (1849–1933; kt. 1922), Common Serjeant 1917–32; J. Butt and K. Tillotson (1957) and K. J. Fielding (1958).

DICKINSON, (1) Emily (1830–86), American poetess, born at Amherst, Mass., was daughter of a lawyer who became a Congressman. Owing, some say, to an unhappy love affair, but just as possibly because she was a mystic by inclination, she withdrew herself at twenty-three from all social contacts and lived a secluded life at Amherst, writing in secret over a thousand poems. All but one or two of these remained unpublished until after her death, when her sister Lavinia brought out three volumes between 1891 and 1896 which were acclaimed as the work of a poetic genius. Further collections appeared, as *The Single Hound* (1914), and *Bolts of Melody* (1945). Her lyrics, intensely personal and often spiritual, show great originality both in thought and in form, and have had considerable influence on modern poetry. See Life by Bianchi (1924), and studies by Whicher (1938), Anderson (1964) and Duncan (1965), and her *Letters*, ed. T. H. Johnson and T. Ward (3 vols. 1958)

(2) **Goldsworthy Lowes** (1862–1932),English philosophical writer and essayist, wrote *Letters of John Chinaman, The Greek View of Life*, a commentary on Faust (with Miss Stawell), besides (as a pacifist) works deploring war and anarchy.

DICKSEE, Sir Frank (1853–1928; kt. 1925), English painter, in 1881 became an A.R.A., in 1891 an R.A., in 1924 president of the R.A. He is remembered for several much-reproduced historical subject paintings, such as *Romeo and Juliet*, and *The Passing of Arthur*. His sister, **Margaret Isabel** (1858–1903), painted several equally well-remembered canvases, as *The Children of Charles I* and *Swift and Stella*.

DIDEROT, Denis, *dee-dĕ-rō* (1713–84), was born, a master cutler's son, at Langres in Champagne, October 15. Trained by the Jesuits at home and in Paris, he refused to become either a lawyer or a physician, was thrown upon his own resources, and led (1734–44) a life of ill-paid toil as tutor and bookseller's hack. In 1743 he married a young sempstress, who contrived to bring about a temporary reconciliation between father and son; but the marriage was not happy, and Diderot formed a series of liaisons. His *Pensées philosophiques* was burned by the Parliament of Paris in 1746, and in 1749 he was imprisoned for his *Lettre sur les aveugles*. The bookseller Le Breton now invited him to edit an expanded version of Ephraim Chambers's *Cyclopaedia* (1727). But in Diderot's hands the character of the work was transformed. He enlisted nearly all the important French writers of the time as contributors, and, in place of a compendium of useful information, produced an engine of war for the *philosophe* party. For some twenty years he stood at his post in spite of dangers and drawbacks. The sale of the book was again and again prohibited, and its editor ran a constant risk of imprisonment or exile. D'Alembert, for a time co-editor with Diderot, forsook him in despair. But his marvellous energy, his varied knowledge, and his faculty of rallying his fellow workers, enabled Diderot to carry his vast undertaking to a successful conclusion. The first volume appeared in 1751; the last in 1765. In his later years Diderot was rescued from pecuniary difficulties by Catharine II of Russia, to whom in 1773 he paid a five months' visit. He died of apoplexy, July 30, 1784. One of the most prolific and versatile, Diderot was also one of the most careless of writers. He was a novelist and a dramatist, a satirist, a philosopher, a critic of pictures and books, a brilliant letter writer; but his published works are far from embodying the results of his labours as an author. His efforts in fiction include a story in the manner of the younger Crébillon; *La Religieuse*, an exposure of conventual life; and the Sterne-like *Jacques le Fataliste*. In *Le Neveu de Rameau*, an imaginary conversation between the author and a parasite (translated by Goethe; Eng. trans. 1897), the follies of society are laid bare with sardonic humour and piercing insight. His plays were somewhat unsuccessful examples of melodrama, the happiest efforts being two short pieces

which were never acted: *La Pièce et le prologue* and *Est-il bon? Est-il méchant?* His letters to Sophie Volland (ed. Babelon 1932) form the most interesting section of his voluminous correspondence. As a critic Diderot stood far in advance of his contemporaries, and anticipated the Romanticists. The originality, shrewdness and abounding vivacity of his criticisms more than atone for lack of literary finish. His *Salons*, remarks on pictures exhibited, are the earliest example of modern aesthetic criticism. Diderot has been described as an atheist, also as a pantheist. See the edition of his works by Assézat and Tourneux (20 vols. 1875–77); the study by Rosenkranz (2 vols. Leipzig 1866); by Green (1936); and by Kemp (1937); Morley's *Diderot and the Encyclopaedists* (2 vols. 1878); Carlyle's *Miscellanies*; and monographs by Scherer (1880), Reinach (1894), Collignon (1895), and Ducros (1895); and study by A. M. Wilson (1957).

DIDOT, *dee-dō,* a family of French printers and publishers.

(1) **François** (1689–1757) had two sons, **François Ambroise** (1730–1804) and **Pierre François** (1732–1795).

(2) **Henri** (1765–1852), son of Pierre François, was an engraver and letter founder, producing very beautiful ' microscopic' types.

(3) **Pierre** (1760–1853), eldest son of François Ambroise, brought out the magnificent Louvre editions of Virgil, Horace, Racine and La Fontaine, besides Boileau's works and Voltaire's *Henriade*.

(4) **Firmin** (1764–1836), brother of (3), as a printer and, especially as an engraver and founder, raised the family name to the highest eminence. He revived and developed the stereotyping process, and produced singularly perfect editions of many classical, French and English works. He became a deputy, and obtained some reputation as an author by his tragedies, *La Reine de Portugal* and *La Mort d'Annibal*, and several volumes of metrical translations from the classics.—Firmin's sons, **Ambroise Firmin** (1790–1876) and **Hyacinthe Firmin** (1794–1880), carried on and transmitted the business, as the firm of Firmin Didot Frères. See works by Werdet (1864), Brunel (1871), and Wallon (1886).

DIEBITSCH, Hans Karl Friedrich, Count (1785–1831), a Russian field-marshal, born in Silesia, made the campaigns of 1805 and 1812–14, and in the Turkish war of 1829 won the surname of Sabalkanski (' crosser of the Balkans '). He died of cholera while suppressing the Polish insurrection.

DIEFENBACH, Lorenz (1806–83), German philologist, born at Ostheim in Hesse, studied at Giessen, travelled much, and was twelve years pastor and librarian at Solms-Laubach. In 1848 he settled at Frankfurt, where he was second librarian (1865–76). He died at Darmstadt. His industry was enormous, embracing poetry and romances, besides many philological works, especially *Celtica* (1839–40), a significant work in Celtic studies.

DIEFENBAKER, John George, *dee´-fĕn-bay-kér* (1895–), Canadian Conservative politician, was born at Normanby Township, Ontario, educated at the University of Saskatchewan and called to the Saskatchewan bar in 1919. In 1940 he entered the Canadian Federal House of Commons and became leader of the Progressive Conservatives in December 1956. In June 1957 he became prime minister of Canada when the Liberal party was defeated after 22 years in office, but lost office again in April 1963.

DIEFFENBACH, Johann Friedrich (1794–1847), German surgeon, born at Königsberg, was from 1840 professor of Surgery at Berlin. He was distinguished in transplanting noses and lips.

DIELS, Otto, *deels* (1876–1954), German chemist, born at Hamburg, professor of Chemistry at Kiel University 1916–48. With his pupil **Kurt Alder** (1902–58), he demonstrated in 1928 the 'diene synthesis' (Diels-Alder reaction), which is of far-reaching importance, especially in the plastics industry. They shared the Nobel chemistry prize in 1950.

DIEMEN, Antony Van. See TASMAN.

DIEPENBEECK, Abraham van (*c.* 1596–1675), Flemish painter, born at Bois-le-Duc, studied under Rubens in Antwerp, and after a residence in Italy returned to be his assistant. He first devoted himself to glass painting, but soon turned to oil painting and designing. He visited England in the reign of Charles I, and was much employed by the Duke of Newcastle, drawing the plates for his folio on *Horsemanship* (Antwerp 1657). He was president of the Antwerp Academy from 1641.

DIEREN, Bernard van, *dee'ren* (1884–1936), Dutch composer, critic and author, born in Rotterdam, resident in England from 1909. Trained as a scientist, he began to study music seriously in his twenties; his earliest surviving works date from 1912. His complexity of style and concentration of utterance, as well as his refusal to compromise with popular taste, leave his work little known, despite the enthusiasm of a small band of disciples. He wrote a study of the sculptor Epstein (1920) and a volume of musical essays, *Down Among the Dead Men*. His compositions include an opera, *The Tailor*, a *Chinese Symphony* for soloists, choir and orchestra as well as numerous songs and chamber compositions.

DIESEL, Rudolph, *deez'-ĕl* (1858–1913), German engineer, born in Paris, studied at the Munich Polytechnic and subsidized by Krupps set about constructing a 'rational heat motor', demonstrating the first compression-ignition engine in 1897, after solving the problem of fuel injection into the cylinder head against enormous pressures by devising a special pump. He spent most of his life at his factory at Augsburg until he vanished from an English channel steamer in September 1913. His body was never recovered.

DIESTERWEG, Friedrich Adolf Wilhelm, *dees'tĕr-vayg* (1790–1866), educationist, born at Siegen, who introduced Pestalozzi's methods into Germany.

DIETRICH OF BERN, See THEODORIC.

DIETRICH, Marlene, *deet'rikh* (1904–), German film actress, born in Berlin. She became famous in 1930 in a German film

The Blue Angel, and thereafter went to Hollywood, appearing in *Morocco*, *Blond Venus*, and others, also in British and French films. She is an international cabaret star. See L. Frewin's *Blond Venus* (1954).

DIEZ, Friedrich, *deets* (1794–1876), German Romance philologist, was born at Giessen, and educated there and at Göttingen. In 1818 he saw Goethe at Jena, and by him was directed to the study of Provençal. From 1822 he lived at Bonn, and in 1830 became professor of Romance Languages. His *Altspanische Romanzen* (1821) was followed by a series of works on Romance languages, including *Grammatik der romanischen Sprachen* (1836–38), &c.

DIGBY, (1) **Sir Kenelm** (1603–65), English diplomat and writer, was born at Gayhurst, near Newport Pagnell. His father, **Sir Everard Digby** (1578–1606), in 1592 came into a large estate, but seven years later turned Catholic, and was hanged as a Gunpowder conspirator. Kenelm himself was bred a Catholic, but in 1618, after a half-year in Spain, entered Gloucester Hall, Oxford (now Worcester College). He left it in 1620 without a degree, and spent nearly three years abroad, in Florence chiefly. At Madrid he fell in with Prince Charles, and, following him back to England, was knighted and entered his service. In 1625 he secretly married 'that celebrated beautie and courtezane', Venetia Stanley (1600–33), who had been his playmate in childhood. With two privateers he sailed in 1628 to the Mediterranean, and on June 11 vanquished a French and Venetian squadron off Iskenderun. On his beloved wife's death he withdrew to Gresham College, and there passed two hermitlike years, diverting himself with chemistry and the professors' good conversation. Meanwhile he had turned Protestant, but, 'looking back', in 1636 he announced to Laud his reconversion; and his tortuous conduct during the Great Rebellion was dictated, it seems, by his zeal for Catholicism. He was imprisoned by the parliament (1642–43), and had his estate confiscated; was at Rome (1645–47), where he finished by 'hectoring at his Holiness'; and thrice revisited England (1649–51–54), the third time staying two years, and entering into close relations with Cromwell. At the Restoration, however, he retained his office of chancellor to Queen Henrietta Maria. He was one of the first members of the Royal Society (1663). 'The very Pliny of our age for lying', said Stubbes of Digby, whom Evelyn terms 'an arrant mountebank'. Yet he was a friend of Descartes and Sir Thomas Browne. His 'powder of sympathy', really perhaps invented by Sir Gilbert Talbot, is described in one of his fifteen works. See his bombastic *Memoirs*, dealing with his courtship, ed. by Nicolas (1827), and supplemented by Bligh's *Digby and his Venetia* (1932); his *Scanderoon Voyage* (1868); *Lives* by Digby (1912) and Petersson (1956).

(2) **Kenelm Henry** (1800–80), the youngest son of the dean of Clonfert, in 1822 published *The Broad Stone of Honour*—'that noble manual for gentlemen', as Julius Hare called it. It was much altered in the 1828

and subsequent editions, its author having meanwhile turned Catholic. He died in London, where most of his long life was spent. Of fourteen other works (32 vols. 1831–74) all the last eight were poetry. See a Memoir (1919) by B. Holland.

DILKE, (1) **Charles Wentworth** (1789–1864), English critic and journalist, graduated at Cambridge, edited *Old English Plays* (6 vols. 1814–16), and served for twenty years in the navy pay office. In 1830 he became proprietor of the *Athenaeum*, and edited it until 1846, when he took over the *Daily News* and managed it for three years. See short Life by Sir Charles Dilke prefixed to *Papers of a Critic* (2 vols. 1875).

(2) **Sir Charles Wentworth** (1810–69), only son of (1), was born in London, and educated at Westminster, and Trinity Hall, Cambridge. He studied law, but never practised. One of the most active originators of the Great Exhibition of 1851, he refused a knighthood and a large reward, but in 1862 accepted a baronetcy. In 1865 he became Liberal M.P. for Wallingford, in 1869 went as English commissioner to the horticultural exhibition at St Petersburg, where he died suddenly.

(3) **Sir Charles Wentworth** (1843–1911), English radical politician, son of (2), born at Chelsea, graduated from Trinity Hall, Cambridge, as head of the law tripos in 1866, and was called to the bar. His travels in Canada and the United States, Australia and New Zealand he described in *Greater Britain* (1868). He was returned to parliament for Chelsea in 1868. A doctrinaire Radical, and once at least an avowed Republican, he yet held office as undersecretary for foreign affairs and president of the Local Government Board under Mr Gladstone. In 1885 he married the widow of Mark Pattison (*née* Emilia Frances Strong), herself the author of *Claude Lorrain, sa Vie et ses Œuvres* (1884), *The Shrine of Death* (1886), &c. His connection with a Mrs Crawford, and a divorce case led to defeat in 1886 and temporary retirement. But for this, he might have been Gladstone's successor. Author of *European Politics* (1887), *Problems of Greater Britain* (1890) and *The British Empire* (1899), he organized the labour members into an influential party, was an authority on defence and foreign relations. He returned to public life in 1892 as M.P. for the Forest of Dean. See Lives by Gwynne and Tuckwell (1917), and R. Jenkins (1958).

DILL, Sir John Greer (1881–1944), British field-marshal, educated at Cheltenham College and R.M.C. Sandhurst. In South Africa and the war of 1914–18 he served with the East Lancashire Regiment. Responsible command and staff assignments encouraged the hope of appointment as C.I.G.S., but this was perversely withheld until 1940. Endowed with profound strategical insight and outstanding organizational ability, his best work was done as the head of the British Joint Staff Mission in Washington. He died, still in harness, at Washington. G.C.B. 1942, C.M.G. 1818, D.S.O. 1915, American D.S.M. (posthumous).

DILLENIUS, Johann Jakob (1687–1747),

born at Darmstadt, from 1728 was first professor of Botany at Oxford. The tropical genus *Dillenia* is named after him. See Life by Schilling (Hamburg 1889).

DILLINGER, John (1903–34), American gangster, specializing in armed bank robberies, terrorized his native state of Indiana and neighbouring states. After escaping from Crown Point county jail, where he was held on a murder charge, he was shot dead by F.B.I. agents in Chicago.

DILLMANN, Christian Friedrich August (1823–94), German orientalist, born in Württemberg, studied at Tübingen under Ewald, and in 1846–48 visited the libraries at Paris, London and Oxford, cataloguing Ethiopic MSS., and returning to Tübingen. He became professor of Oriental Languages at Kiel in 1860, but was transferred in 1864 to the chair of Old Testament Exegesis at Giessen, and in 1869 to Berlin. The first authority on the Ethiopic languages, he became in 1877 a member of the Berlin Academy, was president of the fifth International Congress of Orientalists, and edited its *Abhandlungen* (3 vols. 1881–82).

DILLON, John (1851–1927), Irish politician, the son of John Blake Dillon (1816–66), who was a leader of the Young Ireland party, an exile in 1848–55, and member for County Tipperary in 1865–66. Born in New York, and educated at the Catholic University of Dublin, John Dillon became a doctor. He identified himself with the Parnellite movement and in 1880 was returned for County Tipperary. In parliament he distinguished himself by the violence of his language, while speeches delivered by him in Ireland led to his imprisonment in 1881, 1881–82 and in 1888. From 1885 to 1918 he sat for East Mayo. In 1896–99 he was head of the Anti-Parnellite party, in 1918 of the Nationalist remnant.

DILTHEY, Wilhelm, -*tay* (1833–1911), German philosopher, born at Biebrich, became professor of Philosophy at Berlin in 1882, but despite his massive yet fragmentary attempts to supplement Kant by a ' Critique of the historical reason ' based on the concepts of ' structural system ' in mental life and the ' positivist ' category of ' lived experience ' was more at home in literary and biographical studies on Schleiermacher (1870), the young Hegel (1905) and on Lessing, Goethe and Novalis in *Das Erlebnis und die Dichtung* (1905) than in *Systematische Philosophie* (1907). See studies by Hodges (1944, 1952).

DIMBLEBY, Richard (1913–65), British broadcaster, educated at Mill Hill School, worked on the editorial staff of various newspapers before being appointed first news observer of the B.B.C. in 1936. In 1939 he became the B.B.C.'s first war correspondent and was the first radio man in Berlin and at Belsen. In 1946 he opted to become a freelance broadcaster and gave commentaries on many major events, particularly royal occasions, and the funerals of Kennedy and Churchill. He took part in the first Eurovision relay in 1951 and in the first live TV broadcast from the Soviet Union in 1961. For his work he received many radio and T.V. awards and was the holder of the

O.B.E. and the C.B.E. See *Richard Dimbleby, Broadcaster* (ed. Miall, 1966).

DIMITROV, Georgi Mihailov, *di-mee-trof'* (1882–1949), Bulgarian politician, was born near Radomir. He became a printer, was secretary of his union and later of the Bulgarian Trade Union Federation. Imprisoned in 1917 for anti-militarist agitation, he was released, but later fled to Yugoslavia and was sentenced to death in his absence. He lived under an assumed name in Berlin, and in 1933 was charged by the Nazis, along with others, with setting fire to the Reichstag. The brilliance and courage of his defence roused the admiration of the world, and on his acquittal he became a Russian citizen. From 1934 to 1943 he was executive secretary of the Comintern. In 1945 he returned to Bulgaria and became Premier in 1946. His rule was marked by ruthless sovietization.

DIMITROV-MAISTORA, Vladimir, *di-mee-trof' mī'sto-ra* (1882–   ), Bulgarian artist, born at Kustendil. He studied in Germany, France, Belgium, Italy and the U.S.A., and is best known for his pictures of peasants and landscapes.

DIMITRY. See DMITRI.

DINDORF, Wilhelm (1802–83), German classical scholar, editor of Aristophanes, Aeschylus, Sophocles, &c., was born at Leipzig, where in 1828–33 he was professor. With Hase and his brother Ludwig (1805–71) he edited Stephanus' *Thesaurus Graecae Linguae* (1832–65).

DINES, William Henry (1865–1927), English meteorologist, who carried out exploration of the upper air by means of kites and balloons. See his *Collected Papers* (1931).

DINESEN, Isak. See BLIXEN, KAREN.

DINGAAN (d. 1840), Zulu king, fought against the Boer settlers in Natal, was defeated in 1838 and fled to Swaziland, where he was killed.

DINGELSTEDT, Franz von (1814–81), German poet, novelist, &c., born at Halsdorf, near Marburg, was royal librarian at Württemberg in 1843–50, and director of the court theatres at Munich, Weimar and Vienna. He was ennobled in 1876. His collected works fill 12 vols. (1877). See study by K. Glossy (1925).

DINIZ, Anglicized **Denis,** *dee-neezh'* (1261–1325), king of Portugal from 1279 to 1325. He founded the University of Coimbra in 1290, negotiated the first commercial treaty with England in 1294, formed the Portuguese navy in 1317, introduced improved methods of land cultivation, founded agricultural schools and was a patron of literature and music.

DINIZ DA CRUZ E SILVA, Antonio, *dee-neezh' THah krooz-* (1731–99), Portuguese poet, born at Lisbon. He took a law degree at the University of Coimbra in 1753, and became a founder member of the *Arcadia Lusitana,* a society dedicated to the revival of national poetry. He wrote the epic poem, *O Hyssope,* and *Odes Pindaricas,* lyrics which earned him the title of the ' Portuguese Pindar '. His later life was spent in Brazil. See his *Poesias* (1807–17), and the biographical study in the introduction to *O Hyssope* (1879; ed. J. R. Coelho).

DINWIDDIE, Robert (1693–1770), born in Scotland, was governor of Virginia from 1752 to 1758, when he was recalled, after precipitating the French and Indian war, and rendering himself generally unbearable to the Americans.

DIO CASSIUS. See DION CASSIUS.

DIOCLETIAN, probably **Gaius Aurelius Valerius Diocletianus** (245–313), Roman emperor, was humbly born near Salona, in Dalmatia. He served with distinction under Probus and Aurelian, accompanied Carus on his Persian campaign, and was proclaimed emperor in 284 by the army at Chalcedon. Diocletian's first years of government were so troubled by the incursions of barbarians that he took Maximian as colleague in the empire, assigning to him the western division (286). Still menaced both east and west, he subjected the Roman empire to a fourfold division, Constantius Chlorus and Galerius being proclaimed Caesars (292). Diocletian retained the East, with Nicomedia as his seat of government; Maximian kept Italy and Africa; Constantius took Britain, Gaul and Spain; while Galerius had Illyricum and the valley of the Danube. Britain, after maintaining independence under Carausius and Allectus, was in 296 restored to the empire; the Persians were defeated in 298; and the Marcomanni and other northern barbarians were driven beyond the Roman frontier. In 303 there was severe persecution of the Christians. Diocletian abdicated in 305, compelling Maximian to do likewise; and building a palace (now the heart of modern Split) near Salona on the coast of Dalmatia, devoted himself to philosophic reflection and gardening.

DIODATI, (1) Charles (*c.* 1608–38), nephew of (2), Milton's friend, the son of a refugee doctor, was educated at St Paul's School, and Trinity, Oxford, and practised medicine near Chester and in Blackfriars.

(2) **Jean** (1576–1649), Swiss Calvinist divine, born at Geneva, became professor of Hebrew there in 1597, pastor of the reformed church in 1608, and in 1609, on Beza's death, professor of Theology. He was a preacher at Nîmes (1614–17), and Genevese representative at the Synod of Dort. He is remembered by his Italian translation of the Bible (1607) and his *Annotationes in Biblia* (1607). See Lives by Budé (1869) and Betts (1905).

DIODORUS SICULUS (fl. 44 B.C.), born at Agyrium in Sicily, travelled in Asia and Europe, and lived in Rome, collecting for thirty years the materials for his immense *Bibliothēkē Historikē,* a history of the world in forty books, from the creation to the Gallic wars of Caesar. The first five books are extant entire; the next five lost; the next ten complete; and of the remainder fragments remain. The style is clear and simple, if monotonous.

DIOGENES, *dī-oj'ĕ-neez* (412–323 B.C.), Cynic philosopher, was a native of Sinope in Pontus, who, coming to Athens a rake and spendthrift, was fascinated by the teaching of Antisthenes (q.v.) and became at once an austere ascetic, his clothing of the coarsest, his food of the plainest, and his bed the bare ground. At length he found himself a permanent residence in a tub. The Athenians admired his contempt for comfort and allowed him a wide latitude of comment and rebuke. Practical good was the chief aim of his philosophy; for literature, poetry, art, music, technical philosophy and oratory he did not conceal his disdain. Seized by pirates on a voyage to Aegina, he was sold as a slave. But the slave soon ruled his master, Xeniades of Corinth, acquired his freedom, was appointed tutor to the children, and spent his old age as one of the household. It was here that he had his interview with Alexander the Great when, asked by the king in what way he could serve him, he answered: 'You can stand out of the sunshine,' and sent Alexander away saying: 'If I were not Alexander, I would be Diogenes.' See a work by Hermann (1860).

DIOGENES LÄERTIUS (fl. 2nd cent. A.D.), was born at Läerte in Cilicia. His *Lives of the Greek Philosophers*, in ten books, contains a mass of anecdotes, but is worthless in respect of plan or criticism. See edition by Cobet (1850), and English translation by Hicks (1926).

DION (409–353 B.C.), a Syracusan, both brother-in-law and son-in-law of the elder Dionysius. This connection with the tyrant brought him great wealth, but his austere manners made him hateful to Dionysius the Younger, who banished him in 366. Thereupon he retired to Athens to study philosophy under Plato. A sudden attack upon Syracuse made him master of the city (357), but his severity irritated its luxurious citizens, and he was murdered.

DION CASSIUS (c. 155–c. 230), a Greek historian, was born at Nicaea, in Bithynia. About 180 he went to Rome, held successively all the high offices of state, was twice consul, and enjoyed the intimate friendship of Alexander Severus, who sent him as legate to Dalmatia and Pannonia. About 229 he retired to his native city. Of the eighty books of his *History of Rome*, from the landing of Aeneas in Italy down to A.D. 229, only nineteen (xxxvi–liv) have reached us complete. These embrace the period 68 B.C.–A.D. 10. The first twenty-four books exist in the merest fragments; of the last twenty we have Xiphilinus' 11th-century epitome. The *Annals* of Zonaras, too, followed Dion Cassius so closely as to be almost an epitome.

DION CHRYSOSTOMUS (c. A.D. 50–117), Greek rhetorician, probably the maternal grandfather of Dion Cassius, was born at Prusa, in Bithynia, came to Rome under Vespasian, but was banished by Domitian. He next visited—in the disguise of a beggar, and on advice of the Delphic oracle—Thrace, Mysia and Scythia. On Nerva's accession (96) he returned to Rome, and lived in great honour under him and Trajan. Eighty (two perhaps spurious) orations or treatises on politics, morals, philosophy, &c., are extant, besides fragments.

DIONNE, *dee-on'*, Cécile, Yvonne, Annette, Émilie and Marie (born 1934), girl quintuplets successfully delivered to their French-Canadian parents, Ovila and Elzire Dionne in North Ontario, Canada. Émilie died in 1954.

DIONYSIUS EXIGUUS (d. 556), a Scythian abbot of a monastery at Rome. One of the most learned men of his time, he fixed the Christian era and collected canons.

DIONYSIUS OF ALEXANDRIA (c. 200–64), 'the Great', was a pupil of Origen, became Bishop of Alexandria in 247, and showed wisdom and moderation in the controversies of his time. His fragmentary writings have been published.

DIONYSIUS OF HALICARNASSUS (fl. 1st cent. B.C.), Greek critic, historian and rhetorician, came to Rome in 29 B.C., and died there. His Greek *Archaeologia*, a history of Rome down to 264 B.C., is a mine of information about the constitution, religion, history, laws and private life of the Romans. Of its twenty books, we have only the first nine complete.

DIONYSIUS THE AREOPAGITE, one of the few Athenians converted by the Apostle Paul (Acts xvii. 34); tradition makes him the first bishop of Athens and a martyr. The Greek writings bearing his name were written, not by him, but probably by an Alexandrian. They are first mentioned in 533, from which time they were generally accepted as genuine, and had a great influence on the development of theology. They include treatises *On the Heavenly and Ecclesiastical Hierarchies, On Divine Names, On Mystical Theology*, and a series of ten *Epistles*. Various dates, from 120 to 520, have been assigned to them. See works by Hipler (1861), Niemeyer (1869), Schneider (1884), Vidieu (1888) and Cahn (1889).

DIONYSIUS THE ELDER (431–367 B.C.), tyrant of Syracuse, had been a clerk and then a soldier, when in 405 he made himself absolute ruler of his native city. After suppressing with ferocity several insurrections and conquering some of the Greek towns of Sicily, he began war with the Carthaginians in 398. At first successful, he soon after suffered calamitous reverses; but a pestilence breaking out in the Carthaginian fleet, Dionysius suddenly attacked his enemies and obtained a complete victory. In 392 the Carthaginians renewed hostilities, but were defeated, and Dionysius concluded a most advantageous peace. He now turned his arms against Lower Italy, and in 387 captured Rhegium. From this time he exercised the greatest influence over the Greek cities of Lower Italy, while his fleets swept the Tyrrhenian and Adriatic seas. In 383 and again about 368 he renewed war with the Carthaginians, whom he wished to drive out of Sicily, but died suddenly next year, not without a suspicion of poison. He was a poet and patron of poets and philosophers.

DIONYSIUS THE YOUNGER, son of the foregoing, succeeded in 367 B.C. His education had been purposely neglected, and he had grown up indolent and dissolute. Dion (q.v.) sought to improve him by bringing Plato to Syracuse, but his endeavours were frustrated by Philistus the historian. Dion was banished, but ten years afterwards expelled Dionysius. He fled to Locri, and made himself master of the city, which he ruled despotically, till in 346 dissensions in

Syracuse enabled him to return there. But in 343 Timoleon came to free Sicily, and Dionysius was exiled to Corinth.

DIONYSIUS THRAX (fl. *c.* 100 B.C.), a native of Alexandria, who taught at Rhodes and at Rome. His *Technē Grammatikē* is the basis of all European works on grammar.

DIOPHANTUS (fl. 3rd cent. A.D.), a Greek mathematician, lived at Alexandria about A.D. 275. Of his three works, *Arithmetics, Polygonal Numbers* and *Porisms*, the first is the earliest extant treatise on algebra, but only six of the original thirteen books are extant. *Polygonal Numbers*, a mere fragment, is not analytical but synthetical; in it numbers are represented by lines. The *Porisms*, entirely lost, were probably a collection of propositions on the properties of certain numbers. Diophantine Analysis is that part of algebra which treats of the finding of particular rational values for general expressions under a surd form. See Heath's *Diophantos of Alexandria* (1885; enlarged 1910).

DIOR, Christian, *dee-or'* (1905-57), French couturier, born at Granville, Normandy. He was the founder of the international fashion house of that name, and first began to design clothes in 1935. After working for Piguet and Lelong in Paris, he founded his own Paris house in 1945, and in 1947 he achieved world-wide fame with his long-skirted 'New Look'. See his *Memoirs* (trans. 1958).

DIOSCORIDES, Pedanius, *di-os-kor'id-eez* (fl. 1st cent. A.D.), a Greek physician from Anazarba in Cilicia, left a great work on materia medica.

DIPPEL, Johann Konrad (1673-1734), a German theologian and alchemist, born at Burg Frankenstein, near Darmstadt, invented the loathsome and discarded panacea, 'Dippel's Animal Oil', a distillation of animal bone and offal. He also discovered Prussian blue. See study by W. Bender.

DIRAC, Paul Adrien Maurice (1902-), English physicist, was born in Bristol, and in 1932 became professor of Mathematics at Cambridge. He has done important work in the field of quantum mechanics. He received the Nobel prize for physics in 1933.

DIRCEU. See GONZAGA, TOMÁS.

DIRCKS, Henry (1806-73), English civil engineer, was the author of works on perpetual motion (1861) and electrometallurgy, of *The Ghost* (1863, in which he describes his invention, commonly called 'Pepper's Ghost'), on the Marquis of Worcester (1865), and of *Inventors and Inventions*.

DISNEY, Walt(er Elias) (1901-66), American artist and film producer, born in Chicago. Universally known as the creator of Mickey Mouse (who first appeared as a sound cartoon in 1928), he had previously produced several series of animated cartoons. He is also remembered for his Silly Symphonies and his full-length coloured cartoon films, of which the first was *Snow White and the Seven Dwarfs* (1937), and which included *Pinocchio* (1940), *Dumbo* (1941), *Bambi* (1942), *Lady and The Tramp* (1955), *Sleeping Beauty* (1959), &c., and also, in 1940, *Fantasia*, the first successful attempt to realize music in images. In 1948 he began directing his series of coloured nature films, including *The Living Desert* (1953). He also directed several swashbuckling colour films for young people, including *Treasure Island* (1950), *Robin Hood* (1952), &c. See Life by D. D. Miller (1958).

DISRAELI, Benjamin, 1st Earl of Beaconsfield, *diz-ray'lee* (1804-81), British statesman and novelist, was born December 21, in London, the eldest son of Isaac D'Israeli (q.v.), who, lax in the Jewish faith, had him baptized in 1817. He was educated at a private school kept at Walthamstow by a Unitarian minister, was articled to a solicitor and kept nine terms at Lincoln's Inn. In 1826 he became the talk of the town with his first novel, *Vivian Grey*. Returning from his grand tour in 1831, he fought four elections unsuccessfully before entering parliament for Maidstone in 1837. His maiden speech, too ornate, was drowned in shouts of laughter except the closing words ' ay and though I sit down now, the time will come when you will hear me '. A reckless back-bencher at first, his marriage to Mrs Wyndham Lewis, the widow of a fellow M.P. steadied him somewhat and by 1842 he was head of the ' Young England ' group of young Tories. Peel did not reward Disraeli's services with office and on the former's third ' betrayal ' of his party on the repeal of the Corn Laws (1846) Disraeli made a savage onslaught on his leader in the name of the Tory Protectionists and brought about his political downfall. At the same time he wrote two political novels, *Coningsby* (1844) and *Sybil* (1846), in which his respect for tradition is blended with ' Young England ' radicalism. As chancellor of the Exchequer and leader of the Lower House in the brief Derby administration of 1852, he coolly discarded Protection, and came off on the whole with flying colours; still, his budget was rejected, mainly through Mr Gladstone's attack on it; and Mr Gladstone succeeded him, in the Aberdeen coalition ministry. In 1858 he returned, with Lord Derby, to power, and next year introduced a petty measure of parliamentary reform—his ' fancy franchise ' bill—whose rejection was followed by his resignation. For seven years the Liberals remained in office; and Disraeli, in opposition, displayed talents as a debater, and a spirit and persistency under defeat that won for him the admiration of his adversaries. As chancellor of the Exchequer in the third Derby administration (1866), he introduced and carried a Reform Bill (1867). In February 1868 he succeeded Lord Derby as premier; but, in the face of a hostile majority, he resigned in December. On this occasion Mrs Disraeli was raised to the peerage as Viscountess Beaconsfield. She died in 1872. Disraeli returned to power in 1874 and from this time his curious relationship with the queen began. In 1875 he made Britain half-owner of the Suez Canal; and in 1876 he conferred on the Queen the new title of Empress of India, himself the same year being called to the Upper House as Earl of Beaconsfield. The Bulgarian insurrection which was brutally put down by the Turks did not move Disraeli as it did Gladstone. The Russians threatened Constantinople and at length a British fleet was dispatched to the Dardanelles, but war was averted by Disraeli's diplomacy at the Congress of Berlin (1878). Russia agreed to respect British interests, the Turkish empire was drastically reduced and Britain's share was ' Peace with honour ' and Cyprus. Bismarck was full of admiration for Disraeli: ' Der alte Jude, das ist ein Mann.' But the increase of taxation and loss of trade brought about a catastrophic defeat of the Tories at the polls in 1880. Disraeli retired to novel writing and died April 19, 1881. He was buried at Hughenden, near High Wycombe. See Lives by Thursfield (1898), Monypenny and Buckle (1910), Maurois (1927), Lever (1942), Blake (1966), and study by Somervell (1925).

D'ISRAELI, Isaac (1776–1848), English man of letters, the son of a Jewish merchant and father of Benjamin Disraeli (q.v.), was born at Enfield and in 1801 became a British subject. His *forte* was in literary illustrations of persons and history, as in his *Curiosities of Literature* (1791–1834), *Calamities of Authors* (1812) and a commentary on Charles I (1831) which won him an Oxford D.C.L. See Memoir by his son prefixed to the 1849 edition of the *Curiosities*.

D'ISTRIA, Dora. See GHIKA.

DITTERSDORF, Karl Ditters von (1739–99), Viennese composer and violinist, a friend of Haydn. He wrote 13 Italian operas, and much orchestral and piano music. See his Autobiography (Eng. trans. 1896), and D. Krebs *Dittersdorfiana* (1900).

DIX, (1) **Dorothea Lynde** (1802–87), American humanitarian, born at Hampden, Maine, devoted her life to prison reform and to the improvement of the lot of the feeble-minded throughout the United States.

(2) **John Adams** (1798–1879), American politician, born at Boscawen, New Hampshire, from 1833 was successively secretary of state, U.S. senator, and secretary of the treasury. In the Civil War as major general he rendered effective service to the cause of the Union. He became minister to France in 1866, and governor of New York in 1872.

(3) **Otto** (1891–1969), German realist painter, was born at Gera-Unternhaus. He was noted for his peasant-life scenes, and for his leadership (1922) of the German ' New Realist ' movement.

DIXON, (1) **Jeremiah.** See MASON, CHARLES.

(2) **Sir Pierson John** (1904–65), British diplomat, born at Englefield Green, Surrey, became, after a distinguished career in the foreign service, ambassador to Czechoslovakia from 1948 until 1953, when he was made permanent U.K. delegate to the U.N. He was ambassador to France from 1960. See Life by his son, P. Dixon (1968).

(3) **Richard Watson** (1833–1900), English poet, author of seven volumes of poetry and of a *History of the Church of England* (6 vols. 1877–1902), was born at Islington, studied at Pembroke College, Oxford, and became an hon. canon of Carlisle in 1874 and vicar of Warkworth in 1883.

(4) **William Hepworth** (1821–79), English writer, was born in Manchester, and came to London in 1846. Two series of papers in the *Daily News* on ' The Literature of the Lower Orders ' and ' London Prisons ' attracted attention, and in 1850 he published *John Howard, and the Prison World of Europe*. *William Penn* (1851) is a defence against Macaulay's onslaught. From 1853 to 1869 Dixon was editor of the *Athenaeum*. He wrote a number of works on political history.—His second son **Harold Baily** (1852–1930), chemist, known for his work on gases, was professor of Chemistry at Manchester in 1886–1922.

DJILAS, Milovan, *jee'las* (1911–), Yugoslav politician, born in Montenegro. A lifelong friend of Tito, Djilas rose to a high position in the Yugoslav Government as a result of his wartime exploits as a partisan. He was discredited and imprisoned as a result of outspoken criticism of the Communist system as practised in Yugoslavia, but was released from prison under amnesty at the end of 1966. See his *The New Order* (1957) and *Land without Justice* (1958).

DMITRI or Demetrius (1583–91), youngest son of Tsar Ivan the Terrible, was murdered by the regent Boris Godunov, but about 1603 was personated by a runaway Moscow monk, Grigoriy Otrepieff, the ' false Demetrius ', who was crowned tsar and killed in 1606 in a rebellion. A second and a third ' false Demetrius ' arose within the next few years, but their fate was no better.

DOBBIE, Sir William George Shedden (1879–1964), British general, born at Madras, governor of Malta in 1940–42 during its famous resistance to incessant German and Italian air attack.

DOBELL, (1) **Bertram** (1841–1914), English bookseller and bibliophile, discovered and edited the works of Traherne and Strode, and edited the poems of Thomson, ' poet of despair '.

(2) **Sydney Thompson** (1824–74), poet, born at Cranbrook, Kent, was associated with his father as a wine merchant in London and Cheltenham, but, owing to delicate health, lived much in the Scottish Highlands and abroad. His chief works were in the overstrained style of the Spasmodic School the first of them *The Roman* (1850) appearing under the pseudonym Sydney Yendys. Professor Nichol edited his collected poems in 1875 and his prose works in 1876 as *Thoughts on Art, Philosophy, and Religion*. See his *Life and Letters* (2 vols. 1878) and the memoir by W. Sharp prefixed to his selected poems (1887).

DÖBEREINER, Johann Wolfgang (1780–1849), German chemist, born at Bug bei Hof in Bavaria, professor at Jena from 1810, is remembered as the inventor of ' Döbereiner's Lamp ', in which hydrogen, produced in the lamp by the action of sulphuric acid on zinc, burns on contact with a platinum sponge.

DOBRÉE, (1) **Bonamy** (1891–), English scholar, professor of English Literature, Leeds (1936–55), has written on Restoration Comedy (1924) and Tragedy (1929), Chesterfield (1932), Wesley (1933), Pope (1951), Kipling (1951), Dryden (1956), &c.

(2) **Peter Paul** (1782–1825), British classical scholar, Greek professor at Cambridge from 1823, was born in Guernsey and educated at Trinity, Cambridge.

DOBROLYUBOV, Nikolai Alexandrovich, *-yoo'-* (1836–61), Russian literary critic, born at Nijni Novgorod, was influenced by Belinski and Chernichevski and became the most influential figure in 19th century Russian criticism of the 'socio-utilitarian' school. See his diary (1910).

DOBROVSKY, Joseph (1753–1829), Czech scholar, the founder of Slavonic philology, born at Gyermet near Raab in Hungary, studied at Prague, in 1772 became a Jesuit, and was teacher, tutor and editor of a critical journal. In 1792 he visited Denmark, Sweden and Russia to search for Bohemian books and MSS. carried off in the Thirty Years' War. See *German Life* by Palacky (1883).

DOBSON, (1) **Frank** (1888–1963), English sculptor, born in London. He studied under Sir W. Reynolds, and in 1914 he held his first one-man show of drawings. He was associated with the London Group for many years, and was professor of Sculpture at the Royal College of Art until 1953. His sculptures show an extraordinary feeling for plastic form, and his very individual style (with simplified contours and heavy limbs) is shown at its best in his female nudes. A bronze, *Truth*, is in the Tate Gallery, London. He was elected R.A. in 1953.

(2) **Henry Austin** (1840–1921), English poet, was born at Plymouth. He was educated at Beaumaris, Coventry, and Strasbourg as a civil engineer like his father, but in 1856–1901 was a Board of Trade clerk. His earliest poems, published in 1868 in *St Paul's Magazine*, were followed by *Vignettes in Rhyme, Proverbs in Porcelain, Old World Idylls, At the Sign of the Lyre, The Story of Rosina* and *Collected Poems* (1923). Often in rondeau, ballade or villanelle form, these poems are marked by rare perfection. In prose Dobson published monographs of Fielding (1883), Steele, Thomas Bewick (and his pupils), Horace Walpole, Hogarth, Goldsmith, Fanny Burney, Richardson (1902); and *Eighteenth Century Vignettes* (1892–96), *Four Frenchwomen*, and other collections of graceful and erudite essays.

(3) **William** (1610–46), English portrait painter, was born in London in 1610. He succeeded Van Dyck in 1641 as serjeant-painter to Charles I, and painted portraits of him, the Prince of Wales, and Prince Rupert. His affairs got into confusion, and he was imprisoned for debt, and died in poverty shortly after his release.

(4) **William Charles Thomas** (1817–98), painter, born at Hamburg, the son of an English merchant, was elected an R.A. in 1872.

DOCKWRA, or **Dockwray, William** (d. 1716), a merchant who in 1683 devised a new penny postal system in London, was alternately favoured and persecuted by the authorities.

DOD, Charles Roger Phipps (1793–1855), Irish journalist, born at Drumlease vicarage in Leitrim, came to London in 1818, and for twenty-three years worked on *The Times*. He started the *Parliamentary Companion* (1832) and a *Peerage* (1841).

DODD, William (1729–77), English forger, born at Bourn in Lincolnshire, graduated from Clare Hall, Cambridge (1750), married

took orders and became a popular preacher. He published a series of edifying books, edited the *Christian Magazine*, and was made a king's chaplain (1763), LL.D. (1766) and tutor to Philip Stanhope, Lord Chesterfield's nephew. But, despite his large income, his expensive habits drifted him hopelessly into debt. He purchased Charlotte Chapel in Pimlico, but a simoniacal attempt to buy the rich living of St George's, Hanover Square, led to his name being struck off the list of chaplains (1774). Dodd left England, and was well received by his pupil, now Lord Chesterfield, at Geneva, and presented to the living of Wing in Buckinghamshire. But sinking deeper and deeper into debt, he sold his chapel, and in February 1777 offered a stockbroker a bond for £4200 signed by Lord Chesterfield. It proved to be a forgery, and Dodd, though he refunded a great part of the money, was tried and sentenced to death. Extraordinary efforts were made by Dr Johnson and others to secure a pardon; but the king refused to reprieve his former chaplain, and Dodd was hanged. Of his fifty-five works, the *Beauties of Shakespeare* (1752) was long popular, and *Thoughts in Prison* is still interesting. See *A Famous Forgery*, by Percy Fitzgerald (1865).

DODDRIDGE, Philip (1702–51), English Nonconformist, born in London, determined to enter the nonconformist ministry on the advice of the famous Samuel Clarke, and from 1719 studied at Kibworth academy, Leicestershire, in 1723 became pastor of a congregation there. In 1729 he settled at Northampton as minister and president of a theological academy. He died at Lisbon, whither he had gone for his health. His *Rise and Progress of Religion in the Soul* (1745) has been translated into Dutch, German, Danish, French and even Syriac and Tamil. His hymns include 'Hark, the glad sound, the Saviour comes', and 'O God of Bethel, by whose hand'. See his *Correspondence and Diary* (1829–31) and Memoirs by Stanford (1880) and Nuttall (1951).

DODDS, Alfred Amédée (1842–1922), French general, born at Saint Louis (Senegal), served with distinction in the Franco-German war, and in 1892 led the Dahomey expedition against Béhanzin.

DODGE, (1) **Grenville Mellen** (1831–1916), American soldier and engineer, born at Danvers, Mass., fought gallantly in the Civil War, being ultimately promoted to major-general in 1864. After the war, as chief engineer of the Union Pacific railway from 1866 and of the Texas and Pacific from 1870, he was responsible for the construction of many miles of track on the most famous American railroads.

(2) **Henry** (1782–1867), American politician and pioneer, born at Vincennes, Ind., served in the war of 1812 and the Black Hawk war of 1832, and became famous as a frontiersman. He was made in 1836 governor of a large area west of the Great Lakes and became a member of the House of Representatives in 1841. See *Life* by Pelzer.

(3) **Mary,** *née* **Mapes** (1838–1905), American writer, born at New York, published after the death of her husband, a lawyer,

Hans Brinker; or, The Silver Skates (1865), which became a children's classic, &c., and edited *St Nicholas* (1873).

(4) **Theodore Ayrault** (1842–1909), American military historian, born at Pittsfield, Mass., fought in the Civil War, losing a leg at Gettysburg, and wrote *A Bird's-eye View of our Civil War* (1885), *Alexander* (1890), *Hannibal* (1891), *Caesar* (1892), &c.

(5) **William de Leftwich** (1867–1935), American artist, studied in Paris, painted murals in many public buildings, including the Congressional Library at Washington and the Folies-Bergère in Paris.

DODGSON, Charles Lutwidge, pseud. Lewis Carroll (1832–98), English author, was born at Daresbury, near Warrington, and was educated at Rugby and Christ Church, Oxford, graduating B.A. in 1854 with a first class in mathematics. He took orders in 1861, and was mathematical lecturer 1855–81 and introduced logical problems into the nursery with *Alice's Adventures in Wonderland* (1865), which, with its continuation *Through the Looking-glass* (1872) and its illustrations by Tenniel, rapidly became a nursery—indeed a household—classic and has been widely translated. ' Alice ', to whom the story was originally related during boating excursions, was the second daughter (d. 1934) of Henry George Liddell (q.v.). Dodgson also published *Phantasmagoria* (1869), *Hunting of the Snark* (1876), *Euclid and his Modern Rivals* (1879), *Sylvie and Bruno* (1889–93, illus. by Furniss), *Curiosa Mathematica* (1888–93), *Symbolic Logic* (1896) and ' What the Tortoise said to Achilles ' in *Mind* (1895). See books by his nephew, S. D. Collingwood (1899); by Isa Bowman (1899), Walter de la Mare (1932), Langford Reed (1932), F. B. Lennon (1947); and selections from his Letters (ed. Evelyn Hatch, 1933).—The original MS. of *Alice's Adventures in Wonderland* was sold (1928) to a United States buyer for £15,400.

DODINGTON, George Bubb, 1st Baron Melcombe (1691–1762), a ' person of importance in his day,' was born plain Bubb in 1691, the son of an Irish fortune-hunter or apothecary, and took the name Dodington in 1720 on inheriting a fine property from his uncle. Resolved ' to make some figure in the world ', he had got into parliament in 1715, and from 1722 to 1754 sat for Bridgwater. Otherwise, he was always changing his place, from Walpole's service to the Prince of Wales's, from his to Argyll's, then back to the Prince's, and so on, his one good action being that he spoke up for Byng. He was sometimes in office but oftener out of it. He had not long reached the goal of his ambition, a peerage, when he died at Hammersmith. A self-styled Maecenas, he passed for something of a wit and poet. See Browning's *Parleying*; his self-revelatory posthumous diary (1784), and a study by Lloyd Sanders (1919).

DODS, Marcus (1834–1909), Presbyterian divine and scholar, in 1889 became professor of New Testament Exegesis at the (United) Free Church College in Edinburgh, and in 1907 principal. He published several theological works from 1863.

DODSLEY, Robert (1704–64), born in Mansfield, Notts., was apprenticed to a stocking weaver, but, probably ill-treated, ran away and became a footman. His leisure he gave to reading, and in 1732 published *A Muse in Livery*. His *Toy Shop*, a dramatic piece, was through Pope's influence, acted at Covent Garden in 1735 with great success. With his profits, and £100 from Pope, he set up as bookseller, but still continued to write bright plays—*The King and the Miller of Mansfield* (1737), *The Blind Beggar of Bethnal Green* (1741), *Rex et Pontifex* (1745), &c., which were collected as *Trifles* (1745). In 1738 he bought *London* from the yet unknown Johnson for ten guineas; other famous authors for whom he published were Pope, Young, Akenside, Goldsmith, &c., and he started the *Annual Register* in 1759. With a tragedy, *Cleone* (1758), acted at Covent Garden with extraordinary success, he closed his career as a dramatist. He is chiefly remembered by his *Select Collection of Old Plays* (12 vols. 1744–45); ed. Haylitt (1874–1876) and his *Poems by Several Hands* (3 vols. 1748; 6 vols. 1758). See Life by Strauss (1910).

DOESBURG, van. See MONDRIAN, PIET.

DOGGETT, Thomas (d. 1721), a London actor, who was born in Dublin, founded (1715) a sculling prize, ' Doggett's Coat and Badge ', still competed for by Thames watermen on August 1.

DOHNANYI, Ernst (Erno) von (1877–1960), Hungarian composer and pianist, born at Pressburg. He achieved some success with his opera *The Tower of Voivod* (1922), but is perhaps best known for his piano compositions, especially *Variations on a Nursery Theme*, for piano and orchestra.

DOHRN, (1) **Anton** (1840–1909), German zoologist, born at Stettin, in 1870 founded the marine zoological station at Naples.

(2) **Karl August** (1806–92), German entomologist, father of (1), was born and died at Stettin.

DOISY, Edward Adelbert (1893–   ), American biochemist, held various academic posts before becoming director in 1924 of the department of biochemistry at St Mary's Hospital, St Louis. Noted for his work on sex hormones, in 1943 he was awarded (with Dam) the Nobel prize for medicine.

DOLABELLA, Publius Cornelius (*c.* 70–43 B.C.), Cicero's profligate son-in-law, in 49 sought refuge from his creditors with Caesar. Two years later, having obtained the tribuneship, he brought forward a bill cancelling all debts, which led to bloody struggles in Rome. On Caesar's murder (44) he usurped the consulate, and made a great display of republican sentiments, until Antony gave him the province of Syria. He murdered at Smyrna the proconsul Trebonius, and proceeded to wring money from the towns of Asia with a recklessness that brought about his outlawry. Laodicea, in which he had shut himself up, was taken by Cassius, and Dolabella bade one of his own soldiers kill him.

DOLCI, *dol'chee*, (1) **Carlo** (1616–86), painter, was born and died at Florence. His works which are scattered over all Europe, include many Madonnas, *St Cecilia* (Dresden), *Herodias with the Head of John the Baptist* (Dresden) and the *Magdalen* in the Uffizi at Florence.

(2) **Danilo** (1925–), Italian social worker, 'the Gandhi of Sicily', was born in Trieste, qualified as an architect, but, witnessing the death of an infant from starvation in Sicily, decided to fight poverty there. Fasting, with a mouth-organ, he managed to extract municipal funds to launch his campaign in three of Sicily's poorest towns, Trappeto, Partinico and Montalepre, building schools and community centres to teach the people the methods by which they can raise themselves by their own efforts, helped by funds and social workers from many European countries. Opposed by the government, his own church and the powerful banditry, *Mafia*, he was imprisoned in 1956 for four months for leading a gang of unemployed in repairing a road, unpaid and without permission, i.e., an 'upside down strike', and again in 1957 for obscenity in publishing the pathetic life stories of little boys who sold themselves for vice in return for food. Although neither Communist nor fellow-traveller, he was awarded the Lenin Peace prize in 1956. See his *To Feed the Hungry* (trans. 1959), and Life by J. McNeish (1965).

DOLET, Étienne, *do-lay* (1509–46), 'the martyr of the Renaissance', was born at Orleans. At the university of Paris he was set upon a lifelong study of Cicero; in Venice (1526–32) he imbibed the spirit of humanism. At Lyons, his residence from 1534, he came under strong suspicion of heresy; and killing a man in self-defence he fled to Paris, where friends intervened with the king (1537). In Lyons he set up a printing press, and was arrested more than once for publishing heretical books. In 1544 he was found guilty of heresy, on a charge mainly based on an alleged mistranslation of Plato, in which he was accused of denying the immortality of the soul, and he was burned at Paris. His chief work is *Commentaries on the Latin Language.* See Christie's *Dolet* (1880).

DOLGORUKOVA, Katharina, Princess Yuyevskaia, *-roo'kĕ-va* (1847–1922), was the favourite of Alexander II (q.v.), who married her in July 1880, after his first wife's death. Under the pseudonym of Victor Laferté, she published *Alexandre II, Détails inédits sur sa vie intime et sa mort* (Geneva 1882). Her *Mémoires* (1890) were suppressed by the Russian government. See Paléologue, *Tragic Romance of Alexander II* (trans. 1926).

DOLIN, Anton, stage name of **Patrick Healey-Kay** (1904–), British dancer and choreographer, born at Slinfold, Sussex, studied under Nijinsky and was a member of Diaghilev's ballet company from 1923. He subsequently danced many rôles with Karsavina and other famous ballerinas. He was principal in the Vic-Wells Ballet 1935–37 and afterwards formed the Markova-Dolin ballet company. He has written several books on subjects connected with the ballet.

DOLLFUSS, Engelbert (1892–1934), Austrian statesman, born at Texing, studied at Vienna

and Berlin, became leader of the Christian Socialist party, and in 1932 chancellor. In 1933 he suspended parliamentary government, drove the Socialists into revolt and crushed them. Purged of its Socialist majority, parliament then granted Dollfuss power to remodel the state. In 1934 conflict with the Nazis culminated in his murder on July 25.

DÖLLINGER, Johann Joseph Ignaz (1799–1890), German theologian, was born at Bamberg. He was professor of Ecclesiastical History and Law in the university of Munich almost continuously from 1826 to 1871, when he was elected rector. A staunch Ultramontane, he published *Die Reformation* (1846–48); but in 1857 a visit to Rome caused a change in his opinions. In 1870 the Vatican Council promulgated the decree of papal infallibility, and in March 1871 Döllinger issued a letter withholding his submission. Excommunicated, he took a leading part in the summoning of the congress at Munich out of which arose the Old Catholics. From this time Döllinger advocated the union of the various Christian churches in lectures, and, in two conferences, agreement was reached on various points with the Anglican and Orthodox churches. He published a history of moral controversies in the Catholic church since the 16th century (with Reusch, 1888), *Akademische Vorträge* (1888–91, Eng. trans. 1890–95), &c. He represented his university in the Bavarian Chamber from 1845 to 1847, and onwards from 1849, and sat in the Frankfurt Parliament of 1848–49.

DOLLOND, John (1706–61), English optician, born in London of Huguenot parentage, in 1752 from a silk weaver turned optician, and devoted himself to the invention of an achromatic telescope. His success was rewarded with the Copley Medal (1758), and in 1761 he was elected F.R.S. See Life by Kelly in the *Philosophical Magazine* (1804).—His son **Peter** (1730–1820), was also a noted optician and the firm has continued in existence to the present day.

DOLMETSCH, Arnold (1858–1940), British musician of Swiss origin, born at Le Mans, France, naturalized in 1931, known for his revival of interest in early music and early musical instruments, author of *The Interpretation of the Music of the Seventeenth and Eighteenth Centuries* (1893), a standard work. His son **Carl** (1911–), also known as an expert on early instruments and as a virtuoso on the recorder, and other members of the family have kept alive the tradition, continued the workshops at Haslemere established by Arnold, and fostered the Haslemere Festival, now an established event in the musical world. See *Personal Recollections of Arnold Dolmetsch* by Mabel Dolmetsch (1958).

DOLOMIEU, Déodat Guy Gratet de (1750–1801), French geologist and mineralogist, was born at Dolomieu in Dauphiné. Important for his researches on volcanic rocks, he gave name to 'dolomite'. See study by Lacroix (1921).

DOMAGK, Gerhard (1895–1964), German biochemist, was born in Brandenburg. He discovered the chemotherapeutic properties of sulphanilamide, and thus ushered in a new age in chemotherapy. In 1939, on instruction from the German government, he refused the Nobel prize for physiology and medicine.

DOMBROVSKI, or **Dąbrowski, Jan Henryk** (1755–1818), Polish soldier, born near Cracow, fought against Russia (1792–94), and, then taking service with France, took a distinguished part throughout the Napoleonic campaigns. On Napoleon's fall he returned to Poland, and was appointed by the Emperor Alexander a general of cavalry and Polish senator.

DOMENICHINO, or **Domenico Zampieri** (1581–1641), a painter of the Bolognese school, was born in Bologna and died at Naples. His masterpiece is the *Last Communion of St Jerome* (1614), in the Vatican. See study by L. Serra (Rome 1921).

DOMENICO VENEZIANO (*c.* 1400–61), Florentine painter, known for his altarpiece in the Uffizi at Florence, and represented in the National Gallery by a *Madonna and Child*.

DOMETT, Alfred (1811–87), poet and administrator in New Zealand, where he lived from 1842 to 1871. He was born at Camberwell, like his lifelong friend, Browning (who calls him ' Waring '); studied at St John's College, Cambridge; and was called to the bar in 1841.

DOMINIC, St (*c.* 1170–1221), the founder in 1216 of the Order of Friars Preachers, was born at Calaruega in Old Castile, and studied at Palencia. Here he acquired such a name for piety and learning that in 1193 the Bishop of Osma made him a canon, and relied mainly on his aid in reforming the whole chapter according to the Augustinian rule. The young man led a life of rigorous asceticism, and devoted himself to missionary labours among Moslems and ' heretics '. In 1204 he accompanied his bishop on a political mission, and thrice had to traverse the south of France, peopled almost entirely by Albigenses. He undertook the work of their conversion, and travelled from place to place on foot, bearing St Paul's epistles in his hands and preaching everywhere. He continued his labours for ten years, and gathered like-minded companions round him, for whom he founded the first house of his order at Toulouse. He also set up an asylum for women in danger from heretical influence, which developed into an order of nuns. Unhappily, events occurred which have left a deep stain on his memory and that of his order, associating it closely with the Inquisition. Innocent III, incensed by the murder of his legate, Peter of Castelnau, called the barons of northern France, led by Simon de Montfort, to a crusade against the heretics; and Dominic became a consenting party to these cruelties. In 1215 he went to the fourth Lateran Council, and Innocent III promised approval of his new order on condition that it adopted an old rule. Dominic chose the rule of St Augustine, and next year the authorization was given by Honorius III. Dominic became ' Master of the Sacred Palace ', an office which has continued hereditary in the order. In 1220 the Dominicans, in imitation of their Franciscan brethren, adopted a poverty so rigid that not even the order as a corporation could hold houses or lands, and thus they forced themselves to become mendicants or beggars. Dominic died at Bologna. He had lived to see his order occupying sixty houses and divided into eight provinces. It had spread to England, where from their dress they were called Black Friars; to northern France, Italy, Spain and Austria. He was canonized in 1234 by his friend Gregory IX. See Lives by Lacordaire, Archbishop Alemany, Miss Drane (1891), Herkless, Guiraud (trans. 1901), Danzas, *Études sur l'ordre de St Dominique* (4 vols. 1874–76), and Life by Mandonnet and Vicaire (Eng. trans. 1958).

DOMINICI, Gaston, *dom-een-ee'-see* (1877–), central figure in the Drummond murder case, was born at Digne, Provence. He was sentenced to death in November 1954 after prolonged inquiries and a controversial confession (afterwards retracted) for the murder in mysterious circumstances near Lurs, Provence, on August 5, 1952, of Sir Jack Drummond (a British nutrition expert), his wife and their eleven-year-old daughter. The case was officially closed on November 14, 1956, with Dominici still in a Marseilles prison hospital. On August 4, 1957, his sentence was formally commuted to life imprisonment. See Jean Giono, *The Dominici Affair* (1956).

DOMINIS, Marco Antonio de (1566–1624). born in the Dalmatian island of Arbe, when Archbishop of Spalato became involved in the quarrel between the papacy and Venice, and resigned his see for reasons given in his *Consilium Profectionis* (1616). In 1616 he came to England, in 1618 was by James I appointed master of the Savoy, and in 1619 dean of Windsor. In his *De Republica Ecclesiastica* (1617) he disputed the supremacy of the pope; in 1619 he published without authority Sarpi's *History of the Council of Trent*. His enemy Paul V died in 1620, and was succeeded by Gregory XV, a relative of de Dominis, who now began to intrigue with Rome for a return to the bosom of the Church. He left England in 1622, and while waiting at Brussels denounced in his *Consilium Reditus* the Church of England as a wretched schism. He went on to Rome, but was seized by the Inquisition, and died in prison. He wrote his *De Radiis Visus et Lucis in Vitris Perspectivis et Iride* in 1611.

DOMITIANUS, Titus Flavius (A.D. 51–96), a son of Vespasian, succeeded his elder brother Titus as Roman emperor in 81. He ruled at first well, but, after the failure of his campaigns (87) against the Dacians and Marcomanni, gave way to the most atrocious cruelties. These became so intolerable that a conspiracy was formed against him, and he was assassinated. See a French monograph by S. Gsell (1894).

DONALDSON, (1) James (1751–1830), Scottish philanthropist, an Edinburgh newspaper proprietor and bookseller, who left about £240,000 to found a ' hospital ' (school) for 300 poor children. It was built in 1842–51 from designs by Playfair at a cost of about £120,000 and subsequently became a school for deaf and dumb children.

(2) **Sir James** (1831–1915; kt. 1907), born at Aberdeen, became rector of Stirling High School (1854), classical master in Edinburgh High School (1856), its rector (1866), Humanity professor at Aberdeen (1881), principal of the United College at St Andrews (1886), and principal of its University (1890). He wrote on Greek, patristic, theological and educational subjects.

(3) **John William**, D.D., (1811–61), English philologist, was born in London, of Haddington ancestry. He entered Trinity College, Cambridge, and, graduating in 1834 as second classic and senior optime, became a fellow and tutor of his college. From 1841 to 1855 he was headmaster of Bury St Edmunds grammar school (he almost emptied it); thereafter he tutored at Cambridge with great success, till his death, from overwork, in London. Donaldson's *New Cratylus* (1839) was the first attempt on a large scale to familiarize Englishmen with German principles of comparative philology.

(4) **Sir Stuart Alexander** (1812–67), youngest brother of (3), Australian statesman.

DONAT. See DONATUS.

DONATELLO, properly **Donato di Betto Bardi** (c. 1386–1466), the greatest of the early Tuscan sculptors, was born in Florence where he also died. He may be regarded as the founder of modern sculpture, as the first producer since classic times of statues complete and independent in themselves and not mere adjuncts of their architectural surroundings. Among his works are the marble statues of SS Peter, Mark and George for the exterior of San Michele; and the tombs of Pope John XXIII in the Baptistery, of Cardinal Brancacci at Naples, and of Bartolomeo Aragazzi at Montepulciano, works in which he was aided by Michelozzi. The influence of his study of the antique is very visible in his bronze statue of David, now in the Bargello Museum, Florence, where also are his celebrated marble bas-reliefs of singing and dancing children, originally designed as a balustrade for the organ of the cathedral. At Padua is the noble bronze equestrian statue of the condottiere Gattamelata. See works by H. Kauffmann (1935), H. W. Vanson (2 vols. 1958), and the Phaidon Press *Donatello* (1941).

DONATI, Giambattista (1826–73), astronomer, was born at Pisa and died at Florence, where he was director of the observatory. He discovered the brilliant comet (' Donati's comet ') of 1858. Noted for his researches on stellar spectra, he was the first to observe the spectrum of a comet.

DONATUS, (1) **Aelius** (fl. 4th cent. A.D.), taught grammar and rhetoric at Rome about A.D. 360, amongst others to St Jerome. His treatises form a pretty complete course of Latin grammar, and in the middle ages were the only textbooks used in the schools, so that Donat came, in western Europe, to mean grammar book. He also wrote a commentary on Terence, of which we have only a part.

(2) **Tiberius Claudius** (c. 400), a later grammarian, wrote a very worthless life of Virgil.

DONATUS MAGNUS, bishop (312) of Carthage, was a leader of the Donatists, a 4th-century puritan Christian sect in North Africa.

DON CARLOS. See CARLOS.

DONDERS, Franciscus Cornelis (1818–89), Dutch oculist and professor of Physiology at Utrecht, improved the efficiency of spectacles and wrote on the physiology of the eye.

DÖNITZ, Karl, *doe'nits* (1891–   ), German naval commander, born in Grünau, near Berlin. He entered the submarine service of the German Navy in 1916, and became a staunch advocate and supporter of U-boat warfare. He was appointed commander of Hitler's U-boat fleet, which he himself had planned, and in 1943 succeeded Raeder as grand admiral and c.-in-c. of the German Navy. Becoming Führer on the death of Hitler, he was responsible for the final surrender to the Allies, and in 1946 was sentenced to ten years' imprisonment for war crimes. See his *Memoirs* (1959), and *Hitler and his Admirals* by A. Martienssen (1948).

DONIZETTI, Gaetano (1797–1848), Italian composer, was born at Bergamo, where and at Bologna he studied music. His first opera, *Enrico di Borgogna*, was produced in 1818 at Venice with success, and was followed by others in rapid succession. But the work which carried his fame beyond Italy was *Anna Bolena*, produced at Milan in 1830. *L'Elisir d'amore* (1832) and *Lucrezia Borgia* (1833) also achieved lasting popularity. On his earliest visit to Paris, in 1835, his *Marino Faliero* met with little success, but immediately afterwards *Lucia di Lammermoor* took the Neapolitan public by storm. In 1840 he revisited Paris, and brought out *La Fille du régiment*, *Lucrezia Borgia* and *La Favorita*, the last act of which is his masterpiece, and was written in three to four hours. In 1843 the comic opera *Don Pasquale* was well received; but the gloomy theme of *Dom Sébastian* almost precluded success. *Catarina Cornaro* (1844) was a failure. Stricken by paralysis, he fell into imbecility, and died at Bergamo. See studies by Donati-Petteni (Milan 1931) and H. Weinstock (1964).

DONNAY, Maurice (1859–1945), French dramatist, born in Paris. His *Amants* (1895) achieved considerable popularity, as did *Lysistrata* (1920), an adaptation of Aristophanes, and several other works showing a novel approach to contemporary social problems.

DONN-BYRNE. See BYRNE.

DONNE, John (1572–1631), English poet, was born in London, son of a prosperous ironmonger, but connected through his mother with Sir Thomas More. Though a Catholic, he was admitted to Hart Hall, Oxford, and later graduated at Cambridge, where his friendship with Sir Henry Wotton began. He decided for law and entered Lincoln's Inn in 1592. After taking part in Essex's two expeditions to Cadiz in 1597 and the Azores, 1598 (reflected in his poems ' The Storm ' and ' The Calm '), he became (1598) secretary to Sir Thomas Egerton, keeper of the Great Seal, whose justice he celebrated in his fourth satire. His daring fugitive pieces and brilliant personality pointed to a career as notable as that of his great contemporary Bacon, but his secret marriage to the Lord Keeper's niece, Anne More, caused him to be dismissed and cast in prison. Having now decided for the established faith, he lived at Mitcham in Surrey, but seems to have haunted the Court with an eye to employment. The work he undertook under the direction of Thomas (afterwards Bishop) Morton was religious polemic against the Catholics. He had already written his passionate and erotic poems, *Songs and Sonets*, his six *Satires* and his *Elegies*, but published no verse till 1611, when his first *Anniversarie* appeared, a commemorative poem for Elizabeth Drury, daughter of his benefactor, Sir Robert Drury, whose house in the Strand offered hospitality to the poet when in London. A second *Anniversarie* followed, really a ' meditatio mortis ' displaying his metaphysical genius and dazzling wit at its best. His religious temper is seen in more lyrical form in the *Divine Poems*, some of which certainly date from before 1607. These, like most of his verse, had to wait for his decease for publication, but his pieces were handed round a wide circle of learned and aristocratic friends. How difficult his journey to the Anglican faith was may be judged from the satirical ' Progresse of the Soule ' (1601). This ugly unfinished poem is antiheretical, but also sceptical in a disturbing way. Donne's hesitation over some ten years to take orders is variously explained as due to a Hamlet-like indecision, or to a sense of unworthiness having regard to his profligate youth (much exaggerated in the fashion of the day), or to his still having an eye on civil employment. The years of waiting, what Grierson calls his ' steps to the altar ', do not reflect great credit on the man, but the times excused the grossest flattery of the great. It was the age of learned women of rank, and some of the most distinguished, including Mrs Herbert and the Countess of Bedford, he now courted in verse letters of laboured but ingenious compliment. More injurious to his name was a splendid epithalamium for the marriage of the favourite, Robert Carr, to the divorced Countess of Essex, a scandalous poem for a scandalous wedding. In Funeral poems, of which the first and second *Anniversaries* are only the most brilliant, he also paid court to the great. His prose works of this period include *Pseudo-Martyr* (1610), which is an acute polemic against the Jesuits, but now unreadable. More interesting is his *Biothanatos*, which discusses the question of suicide, towards which he says in his preface, ' I have often . . . a sickly inclination '. He decides that suicide is permissible in certain cases, a conclusion at variance with that affirmed in his third *Satire*, but confirmed in a letter to his friend Sir Henry Wotton. King James put a close to this sickly period by directing him into the Church (1614), and promoting him, after several charges, to the deanship of St Paul's in 1621 when he relinquished his readership at Lincoln's Inn. Fortunately we have his sermon , which were vastly popular. In his time Donne was noted as a great

traveller. We must understand the reference in Walton's Life to his early travels in Italy and Spain to refer to 1594–95, i.e., after his legal studies. There were also his voyages to Cadiz and the Azores (his library was stocked with Spanish works), and in his middle period he accompanied his patron, Sir Robert Drury, to France and Spain. In 1619 and 1620 he was in Germany, where he preached one of his noblest sermons before the exiled Queen of Bohemia, King James's daughter. He was a careerist who could be genuinely moved by the task in hand. Donne's creative years fall into three periods: from 1590 to 1601, a time of action, marked by passion and cynicism; from his marriage to his ordination in 1614 a period of anguished meditation and flattery of the great; from then onwards, a time of acceptance pierced by occasional doubt such as the much later Manley Hopkins also experienced. In his first period, his *Songs and Sonets* and his *Elegies* show in their startling realism and passion the complete rejection of Petrarchan love verse, the major influence now being Latin erotic verse. The *Satires* are the work of a tiro— with the exception of the brilliant third (on religion) they are immature Donne and only remarkable because they share with Hall's satires the distinction of being the first on the classical model in English. The second period of adulatory verse letters, epicedes, &c., has already been noted. The third period, that is of his ministry, includes two sonnet sequences, *La Corona* and *Holy Sonnets*, the latter containing (no. xvii) an anguished tribute to his wife, died 1617. Also of this period are the fine ' Hymne to God, the Father ', ' To God My God, in my Sicknesse ', and ' The Author's Last Going into Germany '. These sonnets and hymns, which again remind us of Hopkins' ' terrible ' religious poems, prove that in transferring his allegiance from the world to God Donne retained the passion which animated his early verse. Donne's prose is often uncouth, but is also capable of rising to a subtle harmony. His sermons, like his discursive verse, show the eager mind under a load of conceit and ingenious similitude. The glory of the Anglican faith is the major theme, but the terrors of sin, death and judgment are too luridly described for modern taste. In *A Garland for John Donne* (1931) various questions are posed which show the desire to explain the present vogue of the poet. Dr Mary Ramsay defended her thesis (it appeared in French in 1917) that Donne was essentially the mediaevalist. T. S. Eliot denied this— ' Donne is the antithesis of the scholastic '. Perhaps an inclusive statement would be that in his concatenated logical method he was a scholastic; in his sceptical view of the world he belonged to the transition to modern ideas. In the same volume George Williamson made the fruitful suggestion that Donne did for his age what Eliot has done for ours. It is not quite true that Grierson's great edition of Donne in 1912 started the modern vogue—Gosse's 2-volume *Life and Letters* (1899) aroused curiosity which Desmond McCarthy in various articles intensified. Since then there have been several studies, including those of Fausset (1924), Mario Praz (1925), and Legouis (1928). In 1934 appeared two studies by Leishman and Bennett respectively. G. Keynes' bibliography appeared in 1958.

DONOGHUE, Stephen (Steve), *don'è-gyoo* or *-hyoo* (1884–1945), English jockey, born in Warrington. He won the Derby six times, on Pommern (1915), Gay Crusader (1917), Humorist (1921), Captain Cuttle (1922), Papyrus (1923) and Manna (1925), and the Queen Alexandra Stakes at Ascot for six consecutive years (1929–34) on Brown Jack.

DOOLEY, Mr. See DUNNE.

DOOLITTLE, Hilda (1886–1961), known as ' H. D.', imagist poet, born at Bethlehem, Pa., lived in London from 1911, and married Richard Aldington (q.v.) in 1913. After their divorce in 1937, she settled near Lake Geneva. See *Collected Poems* (1940).

DOPPLER, Christian (1803–53), Austrian physicist, born at Salzburg, professor of Physics at Vienna (1851). ' Doppler's principle ' explains the variation in frequency observed, higher or lower than that actually emitted, when a vibrating source of waves and the observer respectively approach or recede from one another.

DORA D'ISTRIA. See GHIKA.

DORAN, John (1807–78), English journalist and historian of the stage, born in London, brought out a melodrama, *Justice, or the Venetian Jew*, at the Surrey Theatre in 1824. This was followed by many other works, including *A Lady of the Last Century* (1873, an account of Mrs Montagu), *Mann and Manners* (1876, the letters of Sir Horace Mann to Horace Walpole), and books on kings and queens and on stage history. Dr Doran was repeatedly acting-editor of the *Athenaeum*; edited the *Church and State Gazette* (1841–1852): and was editor of *Notes and Queries*.

DORAT, Jean. See DAURAT.

DORÉ, Gustave (1833–83), French painter and book illustrator, was born at Strasbourg. He first made his mark by his illustrations to Rabelais (1854) and to *The Wandering Jew* and Balzac's *Contes drolatiques* (1856). These were followed by illustrated editions of Dante's *Inferno* (1861), the *Contes* of Perrault and *Don Quixote* (1863), the *Purgatorio* and *Paradiso* of Dante (1868), the Bible (1865–66), *Paradise Lost* (1866), Tennyson's *Idylls of the King* (1867–68), La Fontaine's *Fables* (1867), and many other series of designs, which in the end deteriorated. He also executed much in colour. See Lives by Delorme (Paris 1879), Blanchard Jerrold (1891) and M. Rose (1946).

DORIA, Andrea (c. 1466–1560), Genoese admiral, was born at Oneglia of an ancient princely house. After serving under various Italian princes he returned to Genoa in 1503. In 1513 he received command of the Genoese fleet, and in 1519 defeated the Turkish corsairs off Pianosa. In 1522 the imperial faction were restored to power in Genoa, and Doria, an anti-imperialist, transferred his allegiance to Francis I. In command of the French fleet, he defeated Charles V, blockaded Genoa, and proclaimed the independence of the republic. In 1529, fearing the predominance of Francis, Doria

went over to Charles V, entered Genoa amid popular acclamation, and established an aristocratic government which lasted to the end of the republic. The emperor gave him the order of the Golden Fleece and the princeship of Melfi. In 1531 he made a descent on the stronghold of the corsair Barbarossa, and in 1532 took Patras from the Turks. In 1535 he took part with Charles V in the bombardment of the Goletta forts and the destruction of Barbarossa's fleet. In 1538, with the combined fleets of the empire, the pope and the Venetians, Doria engaged Barbarossa (indecisively) off Prevesa. At Algiers in 1541, and at Jerba in 1560, he suffered disastrous reverses from the Turks. His later years were disturbed by the conspiracy of the Fieschi and stained by his savage revenge for the murder of his nephew Gianettino. Doria died at Genoa. He was the idol of his people and the honoured counsellor of Charles V and of his son Philip. See Lives by Guerazzi (3rd ed. Milan 1874) and Petit (Paris 1887).

DORISLAUS, Isaac (1595–1649), Anglo-Dutch diplomat, born at Alkmaar in Holland, came to England about 1627. For some months he was History lecturer at Cambridge, and in 1640 he was appointed judge-advocate. He sided with the parliament, helped to bring Charles I to his doom, and in 1649 was sent to Holland to bring about an alliance with England. He was assassinated by twelve exiled royalists.

DORN, (1) Bernhard (1805–81), orientalist, was born near Coburg, and died at St Petersburg.

(2) **Friedrich Ernst** (1848–1916), German chemist, born at Guttstadt, educated at Königsberg, known for his discovery of radon (or radium emanation).

(3) **Heinrich Ludwig Egmont** (1804–92), German conductor and composer of operas, &c., and teacher of Schumann, born at Königsberg, died in Berlin.

DORNER, Isaak August (1809–84), German evangelistic, Protestant theologian, born near Tuttlingen in Württemberg, in 1861 became a professor at Berlin. See Life by J. Bobertag (1906).—His son **August** (1846–1920), was also an evangelistic theologian, who wrote on the philosophy of religion.

DORNIER, Claude, *dor'nyay* (1884–1969), German aircraft engineer, born at Kempten, founder of the Dornier works at Friedrichshafen on L. Constance and at Altenrhein in Switzerland. He made seaplanes and flying-boats, including the famous twelve-engined Do X (1929), and the Dornier twin-engined bomber was a standard Luftwaffe type in World War II.

DOROTHEA OF ZELL. See KÖNIGSMARK.

DÖRPFELD, Wilhelm (1853–1940), German archaeologist, born in Barmen, son of **Friedrich Wilhelm Dörpfeld** (1824–93), the noted educationist, was Schliemann's collaborator and successor at Troy, professor at Jena 1923. See SCHLIEMANN.

DORREGARAY, Antonio, Marquis of Eraul (1820–82), Spanish Carlist leader in 1836 and 1872.

D'ORSAY, Alfred Guillaume Gabriel, Count (1801–52), the ' last of the dandies ', was born in Paris. In 1822 he attached himself to Lady Blessington (q.v.). In 1827 he married Lady Harriet Gardiner, Lord Blessington's fifteen-year-old daughter by a former wife. In 1829 Lord Blessington died, and d'Orsay, separated from his wife, took up his residence next door to Lady Blessington's in London, where for twenty years they defied the conventions in a society of authors, artists and men of fashion. An intimate friend and supporter of Louis Napoleon, he naturally looked for a position when the exile became prince-president and d'Orsay a bankrupt; but the directorship of Fine Arts in Paris was conferred upon him only a few days before his death.

DORSET, Earls of. See SACKVILLE.

DOS PASSOS, John Roderigo (1896–1970), American war correspondent, novelist and playwright, born in Chicago, educated in Europe and at Harvard, won renown with *One Man's Initiation* (1917) and *Three Soldiers* (1921), both novels of World War I. His best known work is a trilogy on American life, *U.S.A.* (1930–36). See his autobiography (1968).

DOSSO DOSSI, properly **Giovanni di Nicolò Lutero** (1479–1542), Italian religious painter, a friend of Ariosto, was born near Mantua and died at Ferrara. He painted some pictures jointly with his brother Battista.

DOST MOHAMMED KHAN (1793–1863), made himself ruler of Kabul in 1826, and until 1855 pursued a pro-Russian, anti-British policy.

DOSTOEVSKY, or **Dostoieffsky, Fyodor Mikhailovich** (1821–81), novelist, was born at Moscow, the son of a surgeon. Leaving the Engineers for literature, he published *Poor Folk* in 1846. Joining revolutionary circles in St Petersburg, he was condemned to death (1849), reprieved at the last moment, and sent to hard labour in Siberia. In 1854 he was enrolled in a Siberian corps. His sufferings are recorded in *House of the Dead.* In 1859 he returned to St Petersburg. His masterpiece, *Crime and Punishment* (1866), is one of the most powerful realistic works of fiction. Other important books are *The Idiot* and *The Brothers Karamazov.* Domestic trials, financial troubles and ill-health clouded his later life, spent abroad, and from 1871 in St Petersburg as a Slavophil journalist. See his *Letters and Reminiscences.* Koteliansky and Murry, 1923) and *Diary of a Writer* (begun 1876); Lives by Soloviev (trans. 1916), his daughter (trans. 1921), Carr (1931), and Troyat (1947); studies by Roe (1945), Lloyd (1947), Mackiewicz (1948).

DOU or **Douw, Gerard** (1613–75), Dutch painter, was born and died at Leyden. He studied under Rembrandt 1628–31, and at first mainly occupied himself with portraiture, but soon turned to *genre.* His 200 works include his own portrait, his wife's, and *The Poulterer's Shop,* in the National Gallery, London; and his celebrated *Dropsical Woman* (1663), with ten others, in the Louvre.

DOUGHTY, Charles Montagu (1843–1926), English travel writer and poet, born at Theberton Hall in Suffolk, studied at Caius College, Cambridge. Out of two years' travel and hardship in Arabia (1875–77), slowly grew his great book *Travels in Arabia*

Deserta (1888), a prose classic. Austere, archaic and artificial like his prose are his epics, *Dawn in Britain* (1906), *Mansoul* (1923), &c. See Life by D. G. Hogarth (1928).

DOUGLAS, orig. *doo'glas,* now *dug'las,* (1) a family whose origin is lost in obscurity, but which at the beginning of the 15th century was thought to spring from the same stock as the Murrays.—William de Douglas, who witnessed charters between 1175 and 1213, had six sons, of whom Archibald was his heir, and Brice became Bishop of Moray. Sir Archibald is a witness to charters between 1190 and 1232. Sir William de Douglas, apparently his son, figures from 1240 to 1273. His younger son, 'William the Hardy', harried the monks of Melrose, and was the first man of mark who joined Wallace in the rising against the English in 1297. It appears that he possessed lands in one English and in seven Scottish counties. His son, the Good Sir James Douglas (*c.* 1286–1330), called also 'the Black Douglas' from his swarthy complexion, was Bruce's greatest captain in the War of Independence. The hero of seventy fights, he was slain in Andalusia, bearing the heart of Bruce (q.v.). His son William fell at Halidon Hill; and the next Lord of Douglas, Hugh, brother of Sir James, and a canon of Glasgow, made over the now great domains of the family in 1342 to his nephew Sir William. See also SELKIRK.

Earls of Douglas.—The Douglases had since the time of William the Hardy held the title of Lords of Douglas; in 1358 Sir William (*c.* 1327–84) was made Earl of Douglas, and by marriage became Earl of Mar about 1374. His son, James, 2nd Earl of Douglas (*c.* 1358–88), fell at Otterburn, leaving no legitimate issue. His aunt had married for her second husband one of her brother's esquires, James of Sandilands, and through her Lord Torphichen, whose barony was a creation of Queen Mary in 1564, is now the heir general of the House of Douglas. The earldom of Douglas meanwhile was bestowed on an illegitimate son of the Good Sir James—Archibald (*c.* 1328–1400), Lord of Galloway, surnamed the Grim. By his marriage with the heiress of Bothwell he added that barony to the Douglas domains; and he married his only daughter to the heir-apparent of the Scottish crown, and his eldest son to the eldest daughter of the Scottish king. His son, Archibald, 4th Earl (*c.* 1369–1424), called 'Tyneman', was wounded and taken prisoner by Hotspur at Homildon in 1402, next year at Shrewsbury was again wounded and taken prisoner, and, repairing to France, was made Duke of Touraine, and fell at Verneuil. His son, Archibald, 5th Earl (*c.* 1391–1439), fought in the French wars. His son, William, 6th Earl (*c.* 1423–40), was decoyed into Edinburgh Castle, and beheaded, along with his brother. His Scottish earldom was bestowed on his grand-uncle (the second son of Archibald the Grim), James, the 'Gross' (*c.* 1371–1443), who in 1437 had been made Earl of Avondale. His son, William, 8th Earl (*c.* 1425–52), was for a time all-powerful with James II, who made him lieutenant-general of the realm;

he afterwards entered into a confederacy against the king, by whom he was stabbed in Stirling Castle. His brother James, 9th Earl (1426–88), in 1454 made open war against James II. The issue seemed doubtful until the Hamiltons sided with the king, and Douglas fled to England. His brothers, who still maintained the struggle, were defeated at Arkinholm (Langholm) in May 1455; and the earldom of Douglas came to an end by forfeiture. The last earl lived many years in England, leagued himself in 1484 with the exiled Duke of Albany, was defeated and taken prisoner at Lochmaben, and died in the abbey of Lindores.

Earls of Angus.—William, 1st Earl of Douglas, while securing the earldom of Mar also secured the affections of the young widow of his wife's brother, Margaret Stewart, Countess of Angus and Mar. The issue of this amour was a son, George, who in 1389 had a grant of his mother's earldom of Angus. George, 4th Earl of Angus (c. 1412–62), aided the king against the Douglases in 1454; his loyalty was rewarded by a grant of their old inheritance of Douglasdale and other lands; and so, in the phrase of the time, ' the Red Douglas put down the Black '. His son, Archibald, 5th Earl (c. 1449–1514), was nicknamed Bell-the-Cat from the lead he took against Cochrane (q.v.) at Lauder; he filled the highest offices in the state and added largely to the family possessions. His grandson, Archibald, 6th Earl (c. 1489–1557), in 1514 married Margaret, widow of James IV of Scotland. By this marriage was a daughter, Margaret, who, marrying the Earl of Lennox, became the mother of Darnley, Queen Mary's husband and James VI's father. The Earl of Angus had for a time supreme power in Scotland, but in 1528 James V escaped from his hands, and sentence of forfeiture was passed against him and his kinsmen. On James's death in 1542 Angus was restored to his estates and honours. He was succeeded by his nephew, David, whose son, Archibald, the ' Good Earl ' (1558–88), died without male issue, and the earldom passed to a kinsman, William Douglas of Glenbervie.

Marquises and Duke of Douglas, and Lords Douglas.—William, 11th Earl of Angus (1589–1660), was created Marquis of Douglas in 1633. Archibald, 3rd Marquis (1694–1761), was created Duke of Douglas in 1703, and died childless, when his dukedom became extinct, and his marquisate devolved on the Duke of Hamilton. His sister, Lady Jane Douglas (1698–1753), married in 1746 Sir John Stewart of Grandtully, and gave birth to twin sons in 1748. One of them died in 1753; the other in 1761 was served heir of entail on the Duke of Douglas. This was disputed on the ground that he was not really her son; but the House of Lords in 1771 settled the famous *Douglas Cause* in his favour. In 1790 he was made Baron Douglas of Douglas Castle, which title became extinct on the death of his son James, 4th Lord Douglas, in 1857, when the estates went to his niece, the Countess of Home.

Earls of Morton.—Sir Andrew de Douglas, who appears in record in 1248, was apparently

a younger son of Sir Archibald, the second chief of the house. His great-grandson (?), Sir William Douglas, the ' Knight of Liddesdale ' (c. 1300–53), was assassinated by his kinsman, William, 1st Earl of Douglas. The grandson of his nephew Sir James Douglas of Dalkeith, married a daughter of James I, and in 1458 was created Earl of Morton. His grandson, the 3rd earl, dying without male issue in 1553, the earldom devolved on his youngest daughter's husband, the Regent Morton (q.v.), and from him the present Earl of Morton is descended.

James, 2nd earl of Douglas and Mar, had an illegitimate son, Sir William Douglas of Drumlanrig, whose descendants were created Viscounts of Drumlanrig in 1628, Earls of Queensberry in 1633, Marquises of Queensberry in 1681, Dukes of Queensberry in 1683, Earls of March in 1697, and Earls of Solway in 1706. On the death of the 4th Duke of Queensberry (q.v.) in 1810, that title went to the Duke of Buccleuch; the title of Marquis of Queensberry went to Sir Charles Douglas of Kelhead; and that of Earl of March to the Earl of Wemyss. In 1646 the third son of the 1st Marquis of Douglas was created Earl of Selkirk; in 1651 the eldest son was created Earl of Ormond, in 1661 Earl of Forfar; and in 1675 the fourth son was created Earl of Dumbarton. In 1641 the second son of the 10th Earl of Angus was created Lord Mordington. In 1633 Sir Robert Douglas (c. 1574–1639) was created Viscount Belhaven. See the histories of the house by Hume of Godscroft (1644; 2 vols. 1748) and Sir Herbert Maxwell (2 vols. 4to, 1902); and the *Douglas Book*, by Sir W. Fraser (4 vols. 1885). Also QUEENSBERRY.

(2) **Lord Alfred Bruce** (1870–1945), English poet, son of the 8th Marquis of Queensberry, wrote a number of brilliant sonnets, collected in *In Excelsis* (1924) and *Sonnets and Lyrics* (1935). He is remembered for his association with Oscar Wilde (q.v.), to which his father objected, thereby provoking Wilde to bring the ill-advised libel action which led to his own arrest and imprisonment. See his *Autobiography* (1929), and Lives by P. Braybrooke (1931) and G. W. Freeman (1948).

(3) **David** (1798–1834), Scottish botanical traveller in North America, born at Scone, discovered many new species of flora and fauna, and introduced into this country many trees, shrub and herbaceous plants, including the Douglas fir, which is named after him. See his *Journal* (1915).

(4) **Gawain or Gavin** (c. 1474–1522), Scottish poet-bishop, was the third son of Archibald, 5th Earl of Angus, and was born at Tantallon Castle. Educated at St Andrews for the priesthood, in 1501 he was made dean or provost of St Giles, Edinburgh. From the marriage of his nephew, the 6th Earl of Angus, to James IV's widowed queen, Douglas expected rapid preferment, but when, through her influence, he had obtained the bishopric of Dunkeld (January 1515), he was imprisoned on an old statute for receiving bulls from the pope, and not consecrated until more than a year after. On the fall of Angus, the bishop fled to England to obtain the aid of Henry VIII, but

died suddenly of the plague at London in September 1522. His works include *The Palice of Honour*, most likely written in 1501, an allegory of the life of the virtuous man; a translation of the *Aeneid*, with prologues, finished about 1513, the first version of a Latin poet published in English; and *King Hart*, an allegory of disputed authorship, first printed apparently in Pinkerton's *Ancient Scottish Poems* (1786). J. Small edited his works (1874). See also L. M. Watt, *Douglas's Aeneid* (1930).

(5) **George.** See BROWN (6).

(6) **(George) Norman** (1868–1952), Scottish writer, born at Tilquhillie, near Banchory, lived much in Italy, and wrote natural history memoirs; baffling novels—*South Wind* (1917), *They Went* (1920), *In the Beginning* (1928); scholarly wayward travel books—*Siren Land* (1911), *Old Calabria* (1919), *Alone* (1921), &c. See his *Together* (1923) and *Looking Back* (1934). See also studies by Tomlinson (1931) and MacGillivray (1933).

(7) **Sir Howard, Bart.**, G.C.B. (1776–1861), British general, son of Admiral Sir C. Douglas, born at Gosport, served in Canada and the Peninsula, and was governor of New Brunswick (1823–29), where he founded Fredericton University, lord high commissioner of the Ionian Islands (1835–40), and M.P. for Liverpool (1842–46). He wrote on naval and military matters.

(8) **John** (1721–1807), Scots-born prelate, the son of a Pittenweem shopkeeper, was educated at Dunbar and Oxford; as an army chaplain was present at Fontenoy (1745), and became Bishop of Carlisle (1787), Dean of Windsor (1788) and Bishop of Salisbury (1791). He wrote much—a defence of Milton from Lauder's charge of plagiarism (1750), the famous *Letter on the Criterion of Miracles* (1754) against Hume, ironical attacks on the Hutchinsonians, and political pamphlets. See his *Select Works*, with Life by Macdonald (1820).

(9) **Norman.** See (6).

(10) **Robert** (1594–1674), a Scottish Presbyterian minister who aided the Restoration, but would not acknowledge episcopacy.

(11) **Sir Robert** (1694–1770), a Scottish baronet and genealogist, compiled a *Peerage of Scotland* (1764) and a *Baronage* (1798), published some time after his death.

(12) **Stephen Arnold** (1813–61), American political leader, born at Brandon, Vermont, became attorney-general of Illinois in 1834, member of the legislature in 1835, secretary of state in 1840, and judge of the supreme court in 1841. He was returned to congress in 1843–44–46, and to the U.S. senate in 1847–52–58. His policy was to 'make the United States an ocean-bound republic', and on the question of slavery he maintained that each territory should decide whether it should be a free or a slave state. In 1860 he was nominated for the presidency, but was defeated by Lincoln. He died at Chicago.

(13) **Sir William Fettes**, P.R.S.A. (1822–91), Scottish landscape and figure painter, born at Edinburgh, studied at the university there, and for several years was in business before devoting his time to painting. He was elected R.S.A. in 1854, and P.R.S.A. in 1882.

(14) **William Sholto, 1st Baron Douglas of Kirtleside** (1893–   ), British service chief, educated at Tonbridge school and Oxford University, served in World War I as a fighter pilot. After a brief career as a commercial test pilot, he re-entered the air force, and at the outbreak of World War II was assistant chief of air staff. He became A.O.C. successively of Fighter and Coastal Commands, and directed the successful anti-submarine campaign which played a decisive part in the later stages of the war. After the war he commanded the air force in occupied Germany, and, having been made a marshal of the R.A.F. in 1946, became military governor of the British zone of occupation. He was raised to the peerage in 1948.

DOUGLAS-HOME, Sir Alexander Frederick (1903–   ), British Conservative politician, born in London, heir to the Scottish earldom of Home, was educated at Eton and Christ Church, Oxford, entered Parliament in 1931 and was Chamberlain's secretary during the latter's abortive negotiations with Hitler and Mussolini (1937–39). Out of Parliament (1945–51), he became minister of state, Scottish Office (1951–55), succeeded to the peerage as 14th Earl (1951), was Commonwealth-relations secretary (1955–60), leader of the House of Lords and lord president of the Council (1957–60), and foreign secretary (1960–63). After Macmillan's resignation, he astonished everyone by emerging as premier (Nov. 1963). He made history by renouncing his peerage and fighting a by-election at Kinross, during which, although premier, he was technically a member of neither House. A similar situation was depicted in the play, *The Reluctant Peer* (1963) by his brother, **William** (1912–   ) British playwright, born in Edinburgh and author of *Now Barabbas, The Chiltern Hundreds, The Manor of Northstead, The Reluctant Debutante* and other plays. After Labour's win in the 1964 election, Sir Alec resigned as Conservative leader in 1965, becoming shadow minister of foreign affairs.

DOUGLASS, (1) Andrew Ellicott (1867–1962), American astronomer, born at Windsor, Vermont, became professor of Physics and Astronomy at Arizona and later director of the Steward Observatory. He investigated the history of the sun by examining the annual rings of the Arizona pines and sequoias. See his *Climatic Cycles and Tree Growth* (3 vols. 1919, 1928, 1936).

(2) **Frederick** (1817–95), American Mulatto orator, was born at Tuckahoe, near Easton, Maryland. In 1838 he escaped from a Baltimore shipyard, and changed his name from Lloyd or Bailey. He lectured on slavery (1845–47) in Great Britain, where £150 was collected to buy his freedom. In 1847 he started *Frederick Douglass's Paper* at Rochester, N.Y. He held various public offices and was U.S. minister to Haiti (1889). See his own *Life and Times* (1881), and the Life by Booker T. Washington (1907).

DOULTON, Sir Henry, dōl'tén (1820–97), English pottery manufacturer, born at Lambeth, entered his father's pottery there, and in 1846 introduced stoneware drain pipes instead of flat-bottomed brick drains; in 1848 started works, later the largest in the world, near Dudley. He furthered the revival in art pottery.

DOUMER, Paul, *doo-mayr* (1857–1932), French statesman, born at Aurillac, was a working jeweller, journalist, deputy (1888), governor-general of French Indo-China (1897–1902), president of the Chamber (1905–06), of the Senate (1927–31), of the Republic (1931–32). He was shot by a mad Russian émigré, May 6, 1932, and later died.

DOUMERGUE, Gaston, *doo-merg* (1863–1937), first Protestant president of the French Republic (1924–31), was born at Aigues-Vives. He was premier in 1913–14, 1934 (when he failed to carry constitutional changes); president of the Senate 1923–24.

DOUMIC, René (1860–1937), French critic, born in Paris, member (1909) and permanent secretary (1923) of the French Academy, and editor of the *Revue des Deux Mondes* from 1916. He wrote *Les Hommes et les idées du XIXᵉ siècle* (1903), and *Études sur la littérature française* (6 vols. 1896–1909).

DOUW. See Dou.

DOVE, Heinrich Wilhelm, *dō'vė* (1803–79), meteorologist, born at Liegnitz, in 1845 became professor of Natural Philosophy at Berlin. Besides other optical discoveries, he applied the stereoscope to the detection of forged banknotes. His *Distribution of Heat* was published in 1853 by the British Association, and his *Das Gesetz der Stürme* (1857) has also been translated.

DOVER, Thomas (1660–1742), a London physician, born in Warwickshire, the inventor of ' Dover's Powder ', who, in 1709, whilst captain of a privateer, took Alexander Selkirk off from Juan Fernández. See K. Dewhurst, *The Quicksilver Doctor.*

DOW (1) Gerard. See Dou.

(2) **Neal** (1804–97), American temperance reformer, author of the Maine Liquor Law (1851), a stringent prohibition measure, was born at Portland, Me., and was mayor there in 1851 and 1854. See his *Reminiscences.*

DOWDEN, (1) Edward (1843–1913), Irish critic, born at Cork, was educated at Trinity College, Dublin. In 1867 he became professor of English Literature there. He wrote books on Shakespeare (1875–93), *Studies in Literature* (1788–95), *Southey* (1879), *Life of Shelley* (1886), *History of French Literature* (1897), *A Woman's Reliquary* (poems, 1913), *Letters,* and *Poems* (1914).

(2) **John** (1840–1910), brother of (1), became Episcopal Bishop of Edinburgh in 1886. He wrote on the Scottish liturgy, the Celtic Church, the Mediaeval Church in Scotland, the *Bishops of Scotland* (1912), &c.

DOWDING, Hugh Caswall Tremenheere, 1st Baron (1882–1970), British air chief marshal of World War II, was born at Moffat. He served in the Royal Artillery and the Royal Flying Corps in World War I. As commander-in-chief of Fighter Command (1936–40), he organized the air defence of Britain and on the disasters to France in May-June 1940 stood for the retention of his force at home; and in August-September the German air fleet was shattered in the momentous Battle of Britain. He retired in 1942 and was created a peer in 1943. His *Many Mansions* (1943), pleading spiritualism, has communica-tions attributed to men killed in the war; an earlier book was withheld at request. See Life by B. Collier (1957).

DOWIE, John Alexander (1847–1907), born at Edinburgh, was a Congregational minister in Sydney, N.S.W., but becoming a faith healer and calling himself ' Elijah the Restorer ', founded near Chicago the prosperous industrial and banking community called ' Zion City '.

DOWLAND, John (1563–1626), English lutenist songwriter, was born possibly at Westminster. In 1588 he took a music degree at Oxford, later also graduating at Cambridge. Having failed, as a Catholic, to become a court musician to Queen Elizabeth, he entered the service of the Duke of Brunswick in 1594, and subsequently went to Italy, where he met with some English papist refugees. Fearing for his own reputation he wrote to Sir Robert Cecil denouncing them, an action which appears to have restored him to favour in England, whither he returned in 1596. His *First Books of Songes or Ayres of Foure Partes with Tableture for the Lute* appeared in 1597 and ran to five editions by 1613. In 1598 Dowland became lutenist to Christian IV of Denmark, and his second (1600) and third (1603) books of ' ayres ' appeared while he was abroad, though he was back in London by 1605, the year in which he brought out his *Lachrymae,* which contains some of the finest instrumental consort music of the period, dedicated to Anne of Denmark. Though as a lutenist he was the greatest virtuoso of the age, and his song accompaniments for that instrument are far in advance of his time, he is now remembered above all for the plaintive beauty of ' Weep you no more, sad fountains ', ' Awake, sweet love ' and many other exquisite songs, dismissed perfunctorily by the 19th century, but today numbered amongst the greatest of all time. See E. H. Fellowes, *English Lutenists* (1921).

DOWNING, (1) Sir George, 1st Bart. (*c.* 1623–1684), English soldier and diplomat, emigrated to New England with his parents in 1638, attended the newly-founded Harvard University. Returning to England, he fought for Parliament and later undertook several diplomatic missions for Cromwell, including that of ambassador to The Hague, where he associated with the royalist exiles and contrived to run with the hare and hunt with the hounds to such good effect that at the Restoration he continued as ambassador and received other offices, as well as a baronetcy (1663). As a diplomat he was an expert in commercial matters, but achieved a reputation for contentiousness and duplicity which led Charles II to use him as an instrument in provoking the Dutch to war. Downing Street in London was named after him.

(2) **Sir George, 3rd Bart.** (1684–1749), born in Cambridgeshire, grandson of (1), was founder of Downing College, Cambridge, not built, however, till 1807.

DOWSING, William (*c.* 1596–1679), English Puritan, born at Laxfield, Suffolk, in 1644 purged over 150 churches in that county of stained glass, brasses, paintings and other relics of popery. He was also responsible for much iconoclasm in Cambridgeshire. See his *Journal* (ed. C. White, 1885).

DOWSON, Ernest (1867–1900), English poet of the ' decadent ' school, studied at Oxford, was a friend of Arthur Symons and W. B. Yeats, and wrote delicate verse (collected, with Memoir, 1900). The well-known lines beginning ' I have been faithful to thee, Cynara, in my fashion ' are his. See Yeats *Autobiographies* (1926).

DOYLE, (1) Sir Arthur Conan (1859–1930), British writer of detective stories and historical romances, nephew of (3), was born of Irish parentage in Edinburgh, educated at Stonyhurst and in Germany, and studied medicine at Edinburgh. Initial poverty as a young practitioner at Southsea and as an oculist in London coaxed him into authorship. His début was a story in *Chambers's Journal* (1879), and his first book introduced that prototype of the modern detective in fiction, the super-observant, deductive Sherlock Holmes, his good-natured question-raising doctor friend and colleague in crime detection, Dr Watson, and the whole apparatus of detection mythology associated with Baker Street, the fictitious home of the former. *The Adventures of Sherlock Holmes* were serialized in the *Strand Magazine* (1891–93) when the author, tired of his popular creation, tried to kill off his hero on a cliff, but was compelled in 1903 to revive him. ' Elementary, my dear Watson! ' became household words, and the serials were published as books with the titles, *The Sign of Four* (1890), *The Hound of the Baskervilles* (1902), &c. Conan Doyle, however, set greater stock by his historical romances, *Micah Clarke* (1887), *The White Company* (1890), *Brigadier Gerard* (1896) and *Sir Nigel* (1906), which have greater literary merit. A keen boxer himself, *Rodney Stone* (1896) is one of his best novels. *The Lost World* (1912) and *The Poison Belt* (1913) are essays into the pseudo-scientifically fantastic. He served as a physician in the South African war (1899–1902), and his pamphlet, *The War in South Africa* (1902), correcting enemy propaganda and justifying Britain's action, earned him a knighthood (1902). He used his detective powers to some effect outside fiction in attempting to show that the criminal cases of the Parsee Birmingham lawyer, Edaljee (1903), and Oscar Slater (1909) were instances of mistaken identity. He wrote on spiritualism, to which he became a convert in later life. See the autobiographical *The Stark Munro Letters* and Lives by H. Pearson (1943) and J. Dickson Carr (1949).

(2) Sir Francis Hastings Charles (1810–88; 2nd Bart.), English poet, was born at Nunappleton near Tadcaster. Educated at Eton and Christ Church, Oxford, he was called to the bar, held offices in the customs, and in 1867–77 was professor of Poetry at Oxford. His two series of Oxford lectures he published in 1869 and 1877. His verse collections, 1834 (enlarged 1840) and 1866, are unmemorable save for such ballads of British military fortitude as ' The Loss of the *Birkenhead* ', The Private of the Buffs ', &c. See his *Reminiscences and Opinions* (1886).

(3) Richard (1824–83), English caricaturist, book illustrator and watercolour painter, was born in London. Trained by his father, himself the noted caricaturist ' H. B.' (John Doyle, 1797–1868), he became in 1843 a contributor to *Punch*, designing the cover and furnishing the well-known ' Ye Manners and Customs of ye Englyshe ' and the first of the famous ' Brown, Jones, and Robinson ' travel and other adventures; but in 1850 he left, resenting, as a Catholic, attacks on ' papal aggression '. He illustrated Ruskin (*King of the Golden River*), Thackeray (*Newcomes*), Dickens (*Battle of Life*), &c.

DRACHMANN, Holger Henrik Herbolt (1846–1908), Danish poet, dramatist and novelist, born at Copenhagen of German family. He travelled widely in Europe, and was a marine painter of merit, with a knowledge of seafaring life.

DRACO (7th cent. B.C.), archon at Athens in 621 B.C., reorganized the laws of Athens with admirable impartiality; but the severity of his penalty—death for almost every offence—made the strict execution of his code (since proverbial for its rigour) unpopular, and it was superseded by that of Solon (q.v.).

DRAKE, (1) Charles Francis Tyrwhitt (1846–1874), British explorer, with Palmer and Burton, of the Desert of the Wanderings and Syria, was born at Amersham, Bucks, educated at Rugby and Wellington College, and died at Jerusalem. See his *Literary Remains*, edited by Sir W. Besant (1877).

(2) Sir Francis (*c.* 1540–96), greatest of the Elizabethan seamen, was born at Crowndale, near Tavistock, followed the coasting-trade some years, but by 1565 was voyaging to Guinea and the Spanish Main. In 1567 he commanded the *Judith* of 50 tons in his kinsman John Hawkins's ill-fated expedition; and in 1570 and 1571 sailed to the West Indies to make good the losses he had then sustained from the Spaniards. In May 1572 he equipped two small ships, the *Pasha* and *Swan*, with seventy-three men, landed at Nombre de Dios, July 29, and beat off the Spaniards; his severe wound alone prevented them from carrying off the ' Treasure of the World '. He burned Porto Bello, destroyed many Spanish ships, and crossed the isthmus to the highest point of the dividing ridge. There, climbing a tree, he gazed on the vast South Seas, and ' besought Almighty God of his goodness to give him life and leave to sail once in an English ship in that sea '. Drake arrived at Plymouth August 9, 1573, and the news of his exploits raised him at once to the height of popularity. In 1577 he fitted out the *Pelican* of 100 tons, the *Elizabeth* of 80 tons, and three smaller vessels, and sailed from Plymouth on December 13; on August 20, 1578, the squadron, reduced to three ships by the burning of two, entered the Strait of Magellan, where Drake changed his own ship's name to the *Golden Hind*. On entering the Pacific violent tempests were encountered for fifty-two days, during which the *Marigold* foundered with all hands and the *Elizabeth* returned home. Drake provisioned his ship from the Spanish storehouses at Valparaiso and captured several rich prizes. Failing to find a passage into the

Atlantic he turned south from perhaps 48° N. lat., touched near the Golden Gate, struck across the Pacific, and for sixty-eight days did not sight land until he made the Pelew Islands. After refitting in Java, he held for the Cape of Good Hope, and arrived in England September 26, 1580. The queen, in the face of Spanish protests, was at first uncertain how to receive Drake, but at length (April 4, 1581) paid a visit to his ship at Deptford and knighted him. In the autumn of 1585 Drake sailed with twenty-five ships against the Spanish Indies, harrying Hispaniola, Cartagena and the coast of Florida, and, after great sufferings from sickness, brought home the 190 dispirited Virginian colonists, with tobacco and potatoes (July 28, 1586). Early in 1587 he set sail with a strong squadron, and, entering the harbour of Cadiz, destroyed thirty-three ships, and escaped unscathed. He next sailed to the Azores, capturing a Portuguese carack worth £100,000. On the sailing of the Spanish Armada, Drake's division of the English fleet was stationed off Ushant, until all the ships were blown together to Plymouth by the same storm as carried the Spaniards across the Bay of Biscay. The battle began on the morning of July 19, 1588, and raged along the Channel all that week. Drake's consummate seamanship and audacious courage covered him with fresh glory, and inspired new terror in the Spaniards. He captured the *Rosario* off Portland, whose captain, Valdés, ransomed himself for £3000 three years later. On July 29 occurred the disastrous action after which the Spaniards resolved to return home by the Orkneys. Want of ammunition forced Drake and Howard to give up the chase, but the storms of the northern seas swept the Spaniards to destruction. Next spring a great expedition under Drake and Sir John Norreys sailed for Spain and Portugal, but had little success beyond inflicting damage upon the Spanish shipping, while sickness and hunger carried off thousands on board the crowded and ill-victualled English ships. Drake spent his next few years on shore, bringing a water-supply to Plymouth, and representing the town in parliament. In August 1595 he sailed from Plymouth to the West Indies. Ill-fortune followed the fleet from the beginning. Hawkins, the second in command, died off Puerto Rico in November, and Drake himself died of dysentery off Porto Bello. See books by Corbett (1898), Runciman (1919), Sir R. C. Temple (1926), E. F. Benson (1927), A. E. W. Mason (1941), J. A. Williamson (1952) and M. E. Wilbur (1956).

(3) **Francis** (1696–1771), a York surgeon, was born at Pontefract and died at Beverley. He was author of *Eboracum* (1736), and, conjointly with the bookseller Caesar Ward, of the *Parliamentary History of England* (22 vols. 1751–60).

(4) **Friedrich**, *drah'kĕ* (1805–82), German sculptor, was born at Pyrmont. Among his works were *The Eight Provinces of Prussia* (colossal figures for the royal palace at Berlin), and *Warrior crowned by Victory*. He died at Berlin.

(5) **Samuel Gardner** (1798–1875), American antiquarian, born in Pittsfield, N.H., published many reprints and valuable works on the early history of New England.

DRAPER, (1) **John William** (1811–82), American author and man of science, was born at St Helens, near Liverpool, and in 1833 emigrated to Virginia. In 1839 he became professor of Chemistry in the University of New York, and from 1850 to 1873 was president of its medical department. Among his works are *On the Forces that Produce the Organisation of Plants* (1844), *Physiology* (1856), *History of the American Civil War* (1867–70), and *Scientific Memoirs* (1878).

(2) **Ruth** (1889–1956), American diseuse and monologuist, born at New York, made her stage début in 1915. Following successful solo appearances for the American troops in France in 1918, she toured extensively, appearing in 1926 before George V at Windsor. Her repertoire comprised 36 monologues, of her own devising, and embraced 57 characters. She was the recipient of many doctorates, including the LL.D. from Edinburgh University in 1951 when she was also made a C.B.E.

DRAYTON, Michael (1563–1631), poet, was born at Hartshill near Atherstone, Warwickshire. His earliest work was *The Harmony of the Church*, a metrical rendering of scriptural passages, which gave offence to the authorities, and was condemned to be destroyed. In 1593 he published a volume of eclogues, *Idea, the Shepherd's Garland*, which afterwards underwent considerable revision. His first important poem, *Mortimeriados* (1596), recast in 1603 as *The Barons' Wars*, abounds in fine passages. *England's Heroical Epistles* (1597) has more polish and less inequality than many of Drayton's works. In *Poems, Lyric and Heroic* (c. 1606), appeared the *Ballad of Agincourt*. The first eighteen 'songs' or books of Drayton's greatest work, *Polyolbion*, were published in 1613, with annotations by John Selden, and the complete poem, the outcome of vast learning and the labour of years, appeared in 1622. Drayton aimed at giving 'a chorographical description of all the tracts, rivers, mountains, forests, and other parts of Great Britain'. The inevitable monotony of the subject is relieved by the beauty of the pastoral descriptions. In 1619 Drayton collected in one volume all the poems (except *Polyolbion*) which he wished to preserve. Eight years afterwards he published a new volume of miscellaneous poems, among them the whimsical and delightful *Nymphidia, the Court of Fairy*, a triumph of ingenious fancy. His last work, *The Muses' Elysium* (1630), contains some pastoral poems of finished elegance. He was buried in Westminster Abbey; the inscription on his monument is probably by Ben Jonson. Drayton wrote many sonnets; one of them ('Since there's no help, come let us kiss and part') was pronounced by Rossetti to be 'almost the best in the language, if not quite'; and he had a hand in several plays. See Hooper's edition of *Polyolbion* (3 vols. 1876); the Spenser Society reprints (1885–92); his

Works, ed. J. W. Hebel, &c. (5 vols. 1931–41); and books by O. Elton (1905), B. H. Newdigate (1941).

DREISER, Theodore (1871–1945), American writer, born at Terre Haute, Ind., became a journalist in Chicago, St Louis and later in New York. His first novel *Sister Carrie* (1900), starkly realistic, was criticized for obscenity, and he did not write another until 1911, when *Jennie Gerhardt*, which also proved controversial, won success. More followed, the best being *An American Tragedy* (1925). See his autobiographical *A Book about Myself* (1922), and Life by Matthiessen (1951). Dreiser's brother, **Paul** (1857–1911) was a song composer under the name 'Paul Dresser'.

DRELINCOURT, Charles, *drĕ-lĭ-koor* (1595–1669), French divine, born at Sedan, from 1620 was a Protestant pastor at Charenton, near Paris. He wrote, among other works, *Consolations against the Fear of Death* (1651), to a fourth edition of the English translation of which was attached Defoe's *Apparition of one Mrs Veal* (1716).

DREW, (1) Andrew (1792–1878), a British admiral, who defended Cape Coast Castle with 160 men against 50,000 Ashantis (1824), and captured the rebel Canadian steamer, the *Caroline*, and sent her burning over Niagara (1838).

(2) **Samuel** (1765–1833), the 'Cornish metaphysician', was born at St Austell, and had been a smuggler and shoemaker when in 1788 he became a Wesleyan preacher. He died at Helston.

DREYFUS, Alfred (*c.* 1859–1935), born at Mülhausen in Alsace, the son of a rich Jewish manufacturer, was brought in 1874 to Paris. He was an artillery captain, on the General Staff, when in 1893–94, falsely charged with delivering to a foreign government documents connected with the national defence, he was court-martialled, degraded, and transported to the Cayenne Île du Diable. The efforts of his wife and friends to prove him an innocent victim of malice, injustice and forgery plunged France into a chaos of militarism and anti-Semitism which provoked Zola to assail the government in his celebrated *J'accuse.* Col. Picquart, who first threw doubts on the verdict, was victimized in an attempt by the authorities to prevent a retrial, but after the suicide of Col. Henry, who had falsified evidence at the original trial, the case was tried again and Dreyfus was found guilty but pardoned. It was not until 1906, when anti-Semitism in France had died down, that the verdict was reversed. Proof of Dreyfus's innocence was forthcoming on the publication of documents of the German military attaché in 1930. He fought in World War I and was awarded the Legion of Honour in 1919. See Life by his son (trans. 1937), and study by G. Chapman (1955).

DREYSE, Johann Nikolaus von, *drī'zĕ* (1787–1867), German gunsmith, born at Sömmerda near Erfurt, founded ironworks there, and invented a muzzle-loading, and in 1836 a breech-loading, needle-gun—adopted in the Prussian army in 1841.

DRIESCH, Hans, *dreesh* (1867–1941), German physiologist and professor of Philosophy at Heidelberg (1911), Cologne (1920), Leipzig (1921), was born at Kreuznach. His works on the organism, vitalism, individuality, &c., have been translated. See study by Heinichen (1924).

DRINKWATER, (1) or, later, **Drinkwater Bethune, John** (1762–1844), English historian, born at Warrington, served through the famous siege of Gibraltar (1779–83), of which he wrote a classic History (1785).

(2) **John** (1882–1937), English poet, dramatist, and critic, born in Leytonstone. He was an insurance clerk who achieved an immediate success with his play *Abraham Lincoln* (1918), which he followed with *Mary Stuart*, *Oliver Cromwell* (both published in 1921), *Robert E. Lee* (1923) and a comedy, *Bird in Hand* (1927). His first volume of poems appeared in 1926 and he also wrote critical studies of Morris, Swinburne and Byron, and of lyric poetry. He was one of the founders of the Pilgrim Players and became manager of the Birmingham Repertory Theatre. He married (1) Kathleen Walpole, an actress, in 1906, and when the marriage was dissolved in 1924, (2) Daisy Kennedy, violinist, former wife of Benno Moiseiwitsch.

DRIVER, Samuel Rolles, D.D. (1846–1914), English Old Testament scholar, born at Southampton, succeeded Pusey as regius professor of Hebrew.

DROESHOUT, Martin (17th cent.), a Flemish engraver, resident in London, widely known by his portrait of Shakespeare, prefixed to the folio edition of 1623.

DROSTE-HÜLSHOFF, Annette Elisabeth, Baroness von, *dros'tĕ hüls'hŏf* (1797–1848), German poetess, born in Westphalia. Commonly regarded as Germany's greatest woman writer, she led a retired life that was productive of a great deal of poetry in a more restrained and classical style than that of most of her contemporaries, though her long narrative poems, the greatest of which is *Die Schlacht in Loener Bruch*, were influenced by Byron. Her works were published posthumously in 1851. See studies by L. Schucking (1862), C. Heselhaus (1943).

DROUET, *droo-ay*, **(1) Jean Baptiste, Comte d'Erlon** (1765–1844), French marshal, born at Reims, served in the campaigns of Moselle, Meuse, Sambre and Peninsula. At the first restoration the Bourbons gave him a command, but on Napoleon's return he was under arrest in Lille citadel. He seized and held it for the emperor, who made him a peer of France; and at Waterloo he commanded the first *corps d'armée*. After the capitulation of Paris he fled to Bavaria, returned on the July revolution, was governor-general of Algeria 1834–35, and was made marshal in 1843.

(2) **Jean Baptiste** (1763–1824), was a revolutionist of the extreme Jacobin section.

(3) **Louis François Philippe** (1792–1873), was a famous flute-player at the French and Dutch courts, and also a composer and a manufacturer of flutes in London.

DROUOT, Antoine, Comte, *droo-ō* (1774–1847), a French general of artillery, born at Nancy, and styled by Napoleon 'le Sage de la Grande Armée'.

DROZ, Antoine Gustave (1832–95), French novelist, born in Paris, grandson of Jean Pierre Droz (1746–1823), an engraver of medals. He had devoted himself to art till he made his first and greatest success with *Monsieur, Madame, et Bébé* (1866). Later came *Entre nous* (1867), *Les Étangs* (1876), *L'Enfant* (1885), &c.

DRUMMOND, (1) Annabella (c. 1350–1402), born probably at Stobhall near Perth, about 1367 married John Stewart, afterwards Robert III of Scotland.

(2) **Henry** (1786–1860), London banker, Tory M.P. and Irvingite apostle, lived and died at Albury in Surrey.

(3) **Henry** (1851–97), Scottish theologian and biologist, born at Stirling, studied at Edinburgh, and in 1877 became lecturer on, in 1884 professor of, Natural Science at the Free Church College in Glasgow. He travelled in the Rocky Mountains, Central Africa, Japan, Australia, &c. Works include *Natural Law in the Spiritual World* (1883), *The Ascent of Man* (1894), and *Tropical Africa* (1888). See Life by Sir G. A. Smith (1899).

(4) **Sir Jack Cecil.** See DOMINICI.

(5) **James Eric, 16th Earl of Perth** (1876–1951), British statesman, born at Fulford, Yorks, was first secretary-general of the League of Nations (1919–1932), and ambassador in Rome (1933–39).

(6) **Margaret** (c. 1472–1501), youngest daughter of Lord Drummond, in 1496 became James IV's mistress, and bore him a daughter. She was poisoned, along with two of her sisters.

(7) **Thomas** (1797–1840), Scottish engineer and statesman, born at Edinburgh, educated there and at Woolwich, entered the Royal Engineers, and in 1820 joined the ordnance survey, whose work was immensely facilitated by his improved heliostat and lime-light (the 'Drummond Light'); the latter, however, was really invented by Sir Goldsworthy Gurney. He became head of the boundary commission under the Reform Bill; and under-secretary for Ireland (practically its governor) in 1835. Here he gained the affection of the people; his was the memorable saying, 'Property has its duties as well as its rights' (1838). Worn out by his labours, he died in Dublin. See Life by Barry O'Brien (1889).

(8) **William, of Hawthornden** (1585–1649), Scottish poet, was born at Hawthornden. He graduated M.A. at Edinburgh in 1605, studied law at Bourges and Paris, and by his father's death in 1610 became laird of Hawthornden. He devoted his life to poetry and mechanical experiments. He was on the point of marrying when the lady died (1614 or 1615). He married Elizabeth Logan in 1632. He had to subscribe to the Covenant but witnessed its triumph with a sinking of heart that the most sarcastic verses could not relieve. He died December 4, his death hastened by grief for Charles I's execution. Drummond enjoyed the friendship of Drayton, Montrose and Ben Jonson; the last paid him a memorable visit in 1618–19. Drummond's *Notes* of their talk is a charming chapter of literary history. His chief works

are *Tears on the Death of Moeliades* (i.e., Prince Henry, 1613); *Poems: Amorous, Funerall, Divine, Pastorall, in Sonnets, Songs, Sextains, Madrigals*, (1616); *Forth Feasting* (1617); and *Flowers of Sion* (1623). In prose are *The Cypress Grove*, and a *History of the Five Jameses*. The farcical macaronic poem *Polemo-Middinia* (1683) may be his; it has been attributed to Samuel Colvil. See Life by Masson (1873).

DRURY, (1) Alfred (1857–1944), English sculptor, born in London. Among his works are *St Agnes* (Chantrey Collection, 1896), Edward VII (1903), Sir Joshua Reynolds (Burlington House quadrangle, 1931) and the *London Troops* war memorial at the Royal Exchange. He became an R.A. in 1913.

(2) **Dru** (1725–1803), a London silversmith, devoted himself to entomology, and published *Illustrations of Natural History* (3 vols. 1770–82, with over 240 figures by Moses Harris of exotic insects). His *Exotic Entomology* was edited in 1837 by Westwood, with over 650 figures.

(3) **Robert** (1687–c. 1736), a London tavernkeeper's son, who, on the homeward voyage from the East Indies, was kept a prisoner in Madagascar for fifteen years, and published a most interesting account of his captivity (1729). Afterwards he was a slaver, and then porter at the India House.

DRUSUS, (1) M. Livius, tribune of the people in 122 B.C., opposed the democratic policy of his colleague, C. Gracchus.

(2) **M. Livius** (d. 91 B.C.), son and namesake of (1), though identified by birth and sympathy with the senators, renewed some of the most liberal measures of the Gracchi, and advocated the claims of the Italians to Roman citizenship. He was assassinated.

(3) **Nero Claudius** (d. 9 B.C.), or Drusus Senior, stepson of the Emperor Augustus, and younger brother of the Emperor Tiberius. His campaign against the Rhaeti and other Alpine tribes (15 B.C.) is celebrated by Horace (*Odes*, iv. 4). Until his death he was engaged chiefly in establishing Roman supremacy in Germany, and received the title Germanicus; the celebrated Germanicus (q.v.) was his son.

DRUTEN, John van, *droo'těn* (1901–57), English, naturalized-American playwright, born in London. He became famous with the production of his play *Young Woodley* in 1928. After several years and considerable success in the United States, he was granted American citizenship in 1944. *The Voice of the Turtle*, his most successful play with an American setting, was produced in 1943. See his autobiography, *The Way to the Present* (1938).

DRYANDER, Jonas (1748–1810), Swedish botanist, lived in London from before 1782, in which year he became librarian to Sir Joseph Banks. In 1788 he was one of the founders of the Linnean Society.

DRYDEN, John (1631–1700), English poet, was born at the vicarage of Aldwinkle All Saints, Northamptonshire, where his maternal grandfather was rector. He was educated at Westminster under Busby and at Trinity College, Cambridge, where he resided till 1657. Coming up to London in that year he attached himself to his cousin, Sir Gilbert

Pickering, Cromwell's chamberlain, in the hope of employment, which he might well expect since on both sides his people were parliamentarians. His *Heroic Stanzas*, in quatrains, on the death of Cromwell (1658), was soon followed by his *Astrea Redux* (1660), in heroic couplets, which was to be his staple measure even in the plays which soon poured from his pen for the amusement of ' a venal court '. The first of these 'heroic' verse plays to take the public taste was *The Indian Emperor* (1665), dealing with the conquest of Mexico by Cortez and his love for the Emperor's daughter. It is as good an example as any of this grandiloquent type of play at which he continued to labour down to 1676, when his last rhyming play, *Aurungzebe*, appeared. His rejection of rhyme for blank verse then proved salutary, for *All for Love* (1678) is his best play and not unworthy to be placed beside Shakespeare's *Antony and Cleopatra*. In some ways it is a better contrived play, for Dryden confines his action to the last phase of Antony's career. His adaptation of another of Shakespeare's plays *Troilus and Cressida*, the following year, was by comparison a failure. Adaptation was a means of keeping up with the demands of the theatre on his service. He had already adapted (with Davenant) *The Tempest* in 1670; Milton's *Paradise Lost* (as *The State of Innocence*), 1677; and Thomas Corneille's *The Mock Astrologer* (1668). If we turn an ungrateful eye on these forced labours, we find little relief in his original comedies. However, there are the lively prologues and epilogues to the plays which show us a Dryden sensitive to every breath of popular taste, but maintaining his integrity and in the end, like Ben Jonson, turning on the frivolity of the audiences of that day. His own taste changed—in his charming *Essay of Dramatic Poesy* (1668), which might have been written in Castelvetro's Renaissance Urbino, the argument leans to rhymed dramatic verse and is critical of Shakespearian drama (with, however, a fine appreciation of Shakespeare) and in the *Defence of the Epilogue* (to that popular play *The Conquest of Granada*, 1670), he still holds to neoclassical ideals. Buckingham's *Rehearsal*, a satire on ' heroic ' plays (1672), probably made him reconsider his attitude to Shakespearian drama and blank verse. In his later work he even attempted tragicomedy. Meanwhile his fortunes advanced. He had married in 1663 a daughter of the Earl of Berkshire, at whose house at Charlton, Wilts., he sometimes stayed. He became poet laureate and historiographer royal in 1670, and the emoluments were increased from £200 to £300 a year. He might have entertained even brighter hopes when party warfare called him to the defence of the King's party against the Whigs, who employed Titus Oates as a tool and Monmouth as a champion. The series of satires he now wrote, commencing with the most famous, *Absalom and Achitophel* (1681), and followed by *The Medal* (1682) and *Mac-Flecknoe* (1684), written some years before, did much to turn the tide against the Whigs. To this era also belong the didactic poem *Religio Laici* (1682), which argues the case for

Anglicanism, and the much finer *The Hind and the Panther*, marking his conversion to Rome, 1685. A place in the customs (1683), was his reward for his political labours. It is a relief to find that he did not change his coat again at the Revolution, but accepted the drudgery of translation as means of living. Of these his fine translation of Virgil was most profitable. That of Juvenal and Persius was prefaced by a *Discourse Concerning the Origin and Progress of Satire* which had all his old ease and urbanity. His final work, published in 1699, was *Fables, Ancient and Modern* which, with its paraphrases of Chaucer, Ovid and Boccaccio, has delighted generations of readers. These works are only the most outstanding of a lifetime's industry. What the common reader recalls is probably the famous satirical portraits in *Absalom and Achitophel* which vie with those of Pope in his *Prologue to the Satires*; his fine lyrics, many of them buried in his ' heroic ' plays; the pure entertainment of the *Fables* and his elegiac genius seen at its best in the *Ode to Mrs Ann Killigrew* (1685). Dryden himself preferred *Alexander's Feast*, an ode written for a musical society in 1697—a quieter taste may prefer the earlier ode written for the same society in 1687, the opening stanza of which Saintsbury thought the finest stave in English poetry. Dryden is transitional between the metaphysical poets of the school of Donne and the neoclassic reaction which he did so much to create. His *Annus Mirabilis* (1667), dealing with the Dutch naval war and the fire of London, with all its admirable vigour, marks the degradation of the school of metaphysical wit. Trade and politics are incompatible with a manner intended for religious discourse or aristocratic panegyric. He returned to the metaphysical manner in one or two of his later poems but clearly the stage is set for the age of reason. The standard edition of Dryden's works is that of Sir Walter Scott, 1808, and revised and corrected by George Saintsbury in 1882. W. P. Ker published a collection of his Critical Essays in 1900. Scott's Life is still the standard Life. Numerous studies of the poet have since appeared, including those by Saintsbury (1881), A. W. Verrall (1914), Allardyce Nicoll (1923), Van Doren (1931), and Osborn (1940). There are also numerous essays of which T. S. Eliot's *Homage to Dryden* (1924), is the best known.

DRYGALSKI, Erich Dagobert von (1865–1949), German geophysicist, born at Königsberg, headed expeditions to Greenland (1891–93), and in the *Gauss* to the Antarctic (1902–03).

DU BARRY, Marie Jeanne Gomard de Vaubernier, Comtesse (1741–93), favourite of Louis XV, was born at Vaucouleurs, the daughter of a dressmaker. Brought up in a Paris convent, in 1769 as Mademoiselle Lange she won the notice of Louis XV, who married her to Comte Guillaume du Barry, brother of her former protector. Her influence henceforth reigned supreme until the death of Louis in 1774, when she was dismissed from court. She was tried before the Revolutionary Tribunal for having wasted the treasures of the state and worn mourning for the late king, and was guillotined, ' vainly whimpering ', December 6, 1793. Her *Mémoires* (1829–30; trans. 1896) are unreliable; but see Lives by Vatel (1882–84), R. B. Douglas (1896), N. Williams (1904), E. and J. de Goncourt (trans. 1914), Claude Saint-André (1915) and S. Loomis (1960).

DUBOIS, *dü-bwah*, (1) **Guillaume** (1656–1723), French cardinal, born at Brives-la-Gaillarde, the son of a poor apothecary, was tutor first and then secretary to the Duc de Chartres; and when the latter (now Duke of Orleans) became regent in 1715, Dubois was virtually all-powerful. He was appointed foreign minister and Archbishop of Cambrai (1720), a cardinal (1721), and prime minister of France (1722). He died a victim to hard work and the wildest debauchery. See French works by Seilhac (2 vols. 1862), Fontaine de Rambouillet (1886), Wiesener (1891), Bliard (1901) and Bourgeois (1910).

(2) **Paul** (1829–1905), French sculptor, born at Nogent-sur-Seine, till 1856 studied law. His works include a portrait bust of Pasteur and an equestrian statue of Joan of Arc.

(3) **William Edward Burghardt** (1868–1963), American Negro writer and editor, born at Great Barrington, Mass., studied at Harvard and Berlin, and was professor of Economics and History at Atlanta University (1896–1910). Subsequently he became associated with the National Association for the Advancement of Coloured People, and edited its magazine. He wrote a number of works on slavery and the colour problem.

DU BOIS-REYMOND, **Emil** (1818–96), physiologist, was born and died in Berlin. His name is chiefly identified with animal electricity, the subject of his chief work (2 vols. 1848–84). His brother, **Paul** (1831–1889), was a mathematician.

DU BOS, *dü bō*, (1) **Charles** (1882–1939), French writer, born in Paris, wrote critical works on Byron, Mauriac, Gide, &c., and published a 7-volume collection of able critical essays under the title *Approximations* (1922–27). His *Qu'est-ce que la littérature* published posthumously in 1945, contains a ' Hommage ' by a number of writers including Charles Morgan. See his *Chiers* (1959).

(2) **René Jules** (1901–), bacteriologist, born in France, became an American citizen in 1938 and is known for his work in internal medicine, especially his discovery of the antibiotic *tyrothricin*.

DUBRICIUS, **St** (d. 612), was the traditional founder of the Welsh bishopric of Llandaff.

DU CAMP, **Maxime**, *kä* (1822–94), French poet, novelist, journalist, was born in Paris, travelled in the East, and in 1880 was elected to the Academy. He wrote books on Paris and was a founder of the *Revue de Paris*. See his *Souvenirs littéraires* (1882–83; trans. 1893).

DU CANGE, **Charles Dufresne, Sieur**, *käzh* (1610–88), French scholar, was born at Amiens, and became a parliamentary advocate in Paris, where he died. Du Cange's chief productions are *Glossarium ad Scriptores Mediae et Infimae Latinitatis* (Paris 1678) and *Glossarium ad Scriptores Mediae et Infimae Graecitatis* (1688).

DUCCIO DI BUONINSEGNA (*c.* 1260–*c.* 1320), Italian painter, founder of the Sienese school, in whose work the Byzantine tradition in Italian art is seen in its most highly-developed state. His masterpiece is the *Maestà* for the altar of Siena cathedral (1311), and the *Madonna* in S. Maria Novella at Florence, long attributed to Cimabue, is now generally considered to be his work. He is represented in the National Gallery by the *Annunciation*, *Christ healing the Blind Man*, and the *Transfiguration*. See studies by Weigelt (1911) and d'Ancona (1956).

DU CHAILLU, **Paul Belloni**, *shah-yü* (*c.* 1835–1903), French explorer, born in Paris (or New Orleans), in 1855 sailed for four years to West Africa. His *Explorations in Equatorial Africa* (1861; revised ed. 1871) made important contributions to geographical, ethnological, and zoological science, especially as to the Ogowé River, the Fans, and the gorilla, but was received at first with much distrust. *A Journey to Ashango-Land* (1867) describes another expedition (1863–65).

DUCHAMP, **Marcel**, *dü-shä* (1887–1968), French painter, brother of Jacques Villon (q.v.) and Raymond Duchamp-Villon (1876–1918), the sculptor, associated with several modern movements including Cubism and Futurism, shocked his generation with such works as *Coffee-Mill* (1911) and *Nude descending a staircase* (1912; Philadelphia), and was one of the pioneers of Dadaism, the anti-art protest, which exalted the presentation of energy and change above timeless, classical aesthetic values and fulminated against mechanization. In 1915 he left Paris for New York, where he laboured eight years on a ten-foot-high composition in glass and metal, *The Bride Stripped Bare by Her Bachelors Even* (1915–23; Philadelphia), in which many of the shapes were obtained by chance effects, dust blown on to the drawings, &c. This he described in his *Green Box* notes (1933). He edited the American art magazine, *VVV* (1942–44), and became an American citizen in 1955. See monograph by R. Lebel (trans. 1959).

DU CHÂTELET. See CHÂTELET-LOMONT.

DUCHENNE, **Guillaume Benjamin Amand**, *dü-shen'* (1806–75), French physician, educated at Douai and Paris, a pioneer in electrophysiology and the founder of electrotherapeutics. He was the first to describe locomotor ataxia. Works include *L'Electrisation localisée* (1855) and *Physiologie des mouvements* (1867).

DUCHESNE, *dü-shen*, (1) **André** (1584–1640), a French historian, in Latin called Chesnius or Quercetanus, who wrote histories of England, Scotland, and Ireland, of the popes down to Paul V, and of the House of Burgundy, and made collections of the early Norman and French histories.

(2) **Père**. See HÉBERT.

DUCIS, **Jean François**, *dü-see* (1733–1816), a French poet and playwright, who was born and died at Versailles, and who adapted Shakespeare without knowing English.

DUCK, (1) **Jacob** (*c.* 1600–60), Dutch painter of genre pictures, guardroom scenes, &c., was born and lived at The Hague.

(2) **Stephen** (1705–56), an English farm-

labourer, born at Charlton in Wiltshire, who as a poet became librarian to Queen Caroline and rector of Byfleet, but drowned himself in a fit of despondency.

DUCKWORTH, Sir John Thomas (1748–1817), British admiral, born at Leatherhead, totally defeated a superior French squadron off San Domingo, February 6, 1806. In 1807 he forced the passage of the Dardanelles; and in 1813 was created a baronet.

DUCLAUX. See DARMESTETER.

DUDDELL, William du Bois (1872–1917), British engineer, worked on radiotelegraphy and in 1897 invented an improved version of the oscillograph. He was elected F.R.S. in 1912 and the Physical Society instituted the Duddell Medal in his honour.

DUDEVANT, Madame. See SAND.

DUDLEY, (1) **Dud** (1599–1684), a natural son of the 5th Baron Dudley, was the first to smelt iron with coal, at his father's ironworks at Pensnet in Worcestershire (1619) and at Bristol (1651). See his *Metallum Martis* (1665).

(2) **Edmund** (c. 1462–1510), English lawyer and privy councillor, was Empson's partner in carrying out the detested policy of Henry VII, whose son and successor sent him to the block. He was also father of the Duke of Northumberland. See GREY (LADY JANE) and LEICESTER.

(3) **Lord Guildford.** See GREY, LADY JANE.

(4) **Sir Robert** (1573–1649), a son of the Earl of Leicester by Lady Sheffield, studied at Christ Church, Oxford, made a voyage to the West Indies (1594–95), was knighted by Essex on the Cadiz expedition (1596), joined Essex's plot (1601), and, after a vain attempt to establish his legitimacy, quit England in 1605, deserting wife and daughters, and taking a mistress with him. He turned Roman Catholic, and lived chiefly at or near Florence, busy with naval inventions; in 1620 the Emperor Ferdinand created him Duke of Northumberland and Earl of Warwick in the Holy Roman Empire. See Life by J. Temple Leader (1895).

DUESBURY, William (1725–86), English china maker, born at Cannock in Staffordshire, in 1755 moved to Derby, and founded the china manufacture there.

DUFAURE, Jules Armand Stanislas, *dü-fōr* (1798–1881), French statesman, premier of France 1876, 1877–79, was born at Saujon, Charente Inférieure. See Life by Picot (1883).

DU FAY, Charles François de Cisternay (1698–1739), French chemist, superintendent of gardens to the king of France, discovered the two kinds of electricity, positive and negative, and carried out research on phosphorus and double refraction.

DUFF, (1) **Alexander** (1806–78), born near Pitlochry, in 1829 became the first Scottish missionary to India. His plan of combining religious teaching with Western science caused opposition; but his school flourished, and in time he was encouraged by government officials. In 1843 Duff cast in his lot with the Free Church, and had to give up his college; but he began anew, and soon his work was on a greater scale than before. In 1844 he helped to start the *Calcutta Review*. He was moderator of the Free Church Assembly in 1851, and again in 1873; and was LL.D. of New York, and D.D. of Aberdeen. Duff was one of the founders of the University of Calcutta, but was obliged by persistent ill-health to leave India permanently in 1863. A gift of £11,000, presented to him, he gave to a fund for invalided Free Church missionaries. He raised £10,000 to endow a missionary chair in the New College, Edinburgh, of which he was the first occupant. See Lives by G. Smith (1879) and T. Smith (1883).

(2) **Sir Mountstuart Elphinstone Grant** (1829–1906), born at his father's estate of Eden in Aberdeenshire and educated at Edinburgh and Balliol, in 1854 was called to the bar, was Liberal M.P. for the Elgin Burghs 1857–81, and then was governor of Madras till 1886, when he was made a G.C.S.I. See his *Notes from a Diary* (1897–1905).

(3) **Sir Robert William** (1835–95), Liberal M.P. for Banffshire 1861–93, when he was appointed governor of New South Wales.

DUFFERIN AND AVA, Frederick Temple Hamilton Temple Blackwood, 1st Marquis of (1826–1902), was born at Florence, succeeded his father as 5th Baron Dufferin in 1841, and from Eton passed to Christ Church, Oxford. His *Letters from High Latitudes* (1859) is an account of a yachting cruise to Iceland and Spitzbergen. In 1860 he was sent by Lord Palmerston to inquire into the religious massacres in Syria, and on his return was created a K.C.B. He was under-secretary for India (1864–66 and for war) (1866); chancellor of the Duchy of Lancaster (1868–72); and governor-general of Canada (1872–78), having been created an earl in 1871. From 1879 to 1881 he was ambassador at St Petersburg, whence he was transferred to Constantinople. After the collapse of the rebellion of Arabi Pasha, he went to Cairo to restore order in Egypt; to him was due the abolition of the Dual Control. In 1884 he succeeded Lord Ripon as viceroy of India; his tenure of office was made memorable by measures for strengthening the Indian frontier and by the annexation of Upper Burma in December 1885. He was successively ambassador at Rome, marquis (1888), and ambassador to France (1891–96). He suffered by the bankruptcy of the Globe Co. See his Life by Lyall (1904). The Marchioness wrote on their life and work in India, Canada, Russia and Turkey.

DUFF-GORDON, Lady Lucie (1821–69), English authoress, the only child of John Austin (q.v.), was born in London. A playmate of John Stuart Mill, she married in 1840 Sir Alexander Duff-Gordon (1811–72). A brilliant literary hostess and friend of Heine, she translated German authors such as Meinhold, Niebuhr and Ranke, paid health visits to the Cape and to Egypt and gained a reputation by her vivacious *Letters* (1865) and (1875). See books by her daughter Janet Ross (1888), Waterfield (1937).

DUFFY, Sir Charles Gavan (1816–1903), Irish nationalist, made K.C.M.G. in 1873, was born in County Monaghan, helped to start the *Nation* (1842), the Young Ireland organ, and for twelve years engaged in agitation, being tried for sedition and treason-felony. On the break-up of the Independent Irish party, he emigrated in 1856 to Australia, where, after the establishment of the Victorian constitution, he became in 1857 minister of public works, of lands in 1858 and 1862, and prime minister in 1871. In 1877 he was elected speaker of the Legislative Assembly. His *Ballad Poetry of Ireland* became a household book in his native country. In 1880, when he returned to Europe, appeared his *Young Ireland, 1840–50* (final ed. 1896), followed in 1883 by *Four Years of Irish History, 1845–49*, and in 1898 by *My Life in Two Hemispheres*.

DUFOUR, Guillaume Henri (1787–1875), a Swiss general and writer on military matters, served in the French army and commanded the new Swiss federal forces against the Sonderbund in 1847. He was also responsible for a topographical map of Switzerland and was a founder of the Red Cross. See French Lives by Sayous (Geneva 1884) and Chapuisat (1944).

DUFRESNE, Charles. See Du Cange.

DUFY, Raoul, *dü-fee* (1877–1953), French artist and designer, born at Le Havre. In 1900 he won a scholarship to the École des Beaux-Arts, and was much influenced by Fauvism, which he later abandoned; but he retained his singing blues and reds. From 1907 to 1918 he produced many fabric designs and engraved book illustrations, and in 1919 he went to the Riviera, and began a long series of swift calligraphic sketches in oils, gouache and watercolour of seascapes, regattas and racecourse scenes. See the studies by P. Courthion (1951) and J. Lassaigne (1954).

DUGDALE, Sir William (1605–86), English antiquary, was born at Shustoke, near Coleshill, Warwickshire. He studied law and history under his father, to please whom he married before he was eighteen, and soon after whose death he purchased the neighbouring manor of Blythe (1625). In 1638 he was created a pursuivant-at-arms extraordinary, and in 1640 Rouge Croix pursuivant. During the Great Rebellion he adhered to the Royalist cause, and from 1642 to 1646 was at Oxford, the king's headquarters, being made an M.A. and Chester herald, while pursuing his antiquarian researches. He lived in obscurity during the Commonwealth, but on the Restoration received the office of Norroy, and in 1677 was promoted to be Garter Principal King of Arms, at the same time receiving knighthood. His works include the *Monasticon Anglicanum* (1655–1661–73), a history of English religious foundations (Eng. ed. 6 vols. 1817–30); *Antiquities of Warwickshire* (1656); *History of Imbanking and Drayning* (1662); and *Baronage of England* (3 vols. 1675–76). his *Life, Diary, and Correspondence*, edited by William Hamper (1827).

DU GUAY-TROUIN, René, *dü gay troo-ĩ* (1673–1736), French sailor, born at St Malo, for his daring exploits as a privateer was given the command of a frigate in 1697. In 1707 he engaged a British fleet at the entrance to the Channel, burning one ship, and

capturing three others and sixty transports. For the capture, in 1711, of Rio de Janeiro he was ennobled. In 1731 he was sent into the Levant. See his *Mémoires* by Beauchamps (4 vols., Paris 1740; Eng. trans. 1742); French Lives by La Landelle (2nd ed. 1876), De Bona (1890), and Philipps (1892); and Sir J. K. Laughton's *Studies in Naval History* (1887).

DUHAMEL, Georges (1884–1966), French novelist, poet and man of letters, originally studied medicine and became an army surgeon. This gave the background for *La Vie des martyrs* (1917) and *Civilisation* (1918, awarded Prix Goncourt). Many of his fifty volumes of vigorous, skilful writing have been translated. They include *News from Havre* (1934), *The Pasquier Chronicles* (1937), *Why France fights* (1940) and *Light on my Days* (1948, autobiographical). He edited *Mercure de France* and was elected to the Académie française in 1935.

DÜHRING, Karl Eugen (1833–1921), German philosopher and political economist, was born at Berlin, and became quite blind before he was thirty. As a philosopher he was positivist and anti-Hegelian; as an economist he was influenced by Henry Charles Carey (q.v.).

DUILIUS, Gaius (fl. 3rd cent. B.C.), as consul in 260 B.C. won Rome's first great naval victory over the Carthaginians off Myle, mainly by his grappling-irons.

DUJARDIN, Félix, *dü-zhar-dĩ* (1801–60), French zoologist, investigator of Foraminifera, Protozoa, &c., was born at Tours and died at Rennes.

DUKAS, Paul *dü-kah* (1865–1935), French composer, born in Paris. Some of his work is classical in approach, but he tends mainly towards musical Impressionism. His best-known work is the symphonic poem *L'Apprenti sorcier* (1897); the opera *Ariane et Barbe-Bleue* is also noteworthy. He wrote some musicological books, and edited works by Rameau and Scarlatti.

DULAC, Edmund (1882–1953), French-born, naturalized-British artist and book illustrator, mainly of fairy tales. He designed the coronation stamp (1937).

DULLES, John Foster (1888–1959), U.S. politician, was born in Washington, D.C., and was educated at Princeton University and the Sorbonne. As a young lawyer from a family with a diplomatic tradition he attended the Hague Conference of 1907. At the Conference of Versailles he was adviser to President Wilson and was principal U.S. spokesman on the Reparations Commission. In the interwar years he combined legal work in America with international conferences of churchmen and others concerned with advancing Christian ideals in world affairs. During World War II he was a strong advocate of a world governmental organization. In 1945 he was adviser to Senator Vandenberg at the Charter Conference of the United Nations. In 1946, in 1947 and in 1950 he was U.S. delegate to the General Assembly. In January 1953 he became U.S. secretary of state, opening a vigorous diplomacy of personal conferences with statesmen in other countries. By the end of 1954 he had travelled nearly 180,000 miles and had visited more than 40 countries, signing treaties and agreements and drawing the attention of the Western nations more strongly to the threat of Communism. In 1954 he launched the concept of S.E.A.T.O. and backed the plan to bring Western Germany into N.A.T.O. In 1956, after the nationalization of the Suez Canal by President Nasser of Egypt, he proposed the Suez Canal Users' Association. Later he opposed the Anglo-French military intervention and was himself strongly opposed by much British Conservative opinion. Though President Eisenhower hailed him in 1957 as ' one of the greatest of our secretaries of state ', the Western world was apt to criticize his inflexible thinking and his occasional rashness and to consider him a tactician rather than a creator of memorable policies; but no one questioned his dedicated belief that a moral purpose should inform international affairs. He was awarded the highest American civil decoration, the Medal of Freedom, shortly before his death from cancer. He published *War, Peace and Change* (1939), *War or Peace* (1950).

DULONG, Pierre Louis (1785–1838), French chemist, born at Rouen, trained first as a doctor and later became professor of Chemistry and then of Physics in Paris. In 1813 he discovered the explosive nitrogen trichloride. With Petit he did research on heat and enunciated the law of the constancy of atomic heats (1819). In 1826 he was elected foreign member of the Royal Society.

DUMAS, *dü-mah,* (1) Alexandre (in full, Alexandre Dumas Davy de la Pailleterie) (1802–70), French novelist and playwright, born at Villers-Cotterets (Aisne), was the grandson of Count Alexandre Davy de la Pailleterie and Marie-Cessette Dumas, a Haitian Negress, and the son of General Alexandre Davy-Dumas and Marie Labouret, daughter of a tavernkeeper and small landowner at Villers-Cotterets. After an idle, irregular youth, he went to Paris in 1823; obtained a clerkship in the bureau of the Duc d'Orléans; but spent some years in reading and in learning the art of writing. A volume of short stories and a couple of farces, however, were his only productions when, at twenty-seven, he became famous by his *Henri III* (1829), performed at the Théâtre-Français. He had operated that revolution in historical drama which admirers of Hugo ascribe to the poet of *Hernani* (1830). In 1831 he did the same for domestic tragedy with *Antony*, failed in verse with *Charles VII chez ses grands vassaux*, and scored a tremendous success (in collaboration with Goubaux and Dinant) with *Richard Darlington*; in 1832 he carried the romantic ' history ' to its culmination in *La Tour de Nesle* (in collaboration with Gaillardet). In that same year he fell ill of cholera, went to Switzerland to recuperate, and wrote for the *Revue des Deux Mondes* the first of his famous and delightful *Impressions de voyage*. A prodigious worker, he would, after months of production, refresh himself with a round of travel, and he always published his experiences. Hence *En Suisse* (1832), *Le Midi de la*

France (1840), *Le Caucase* (1859), &c. But it was as a storyteller that Dumas was destined to gain enduring success. As to his own share in his own work, he exhausted, it appears, some ninety collaborators, and his debates with some of them by no means reflected to his credit. He took whatever he could get from whomsoever he could get it, and gave it his own immense and radiant personality. Still, it is undeniable that his thefts were many and flagrant. Trelawny's *Adventures of a Younger Son*, for instance, appears in his collected works; and it is said that he was with difficulty restrained from signing a book of the *Iliad* which some one else had run into prose. From the first it was his purpose to put the history of France into novels, and his earliest attempt was *Isabelle de Bavière* (1836). It was followed by *Pauline* (1838), *Acté* (1839), *Othon l'archer* (1840)—and others all on different lines; then the historical vein cropped up anew in *Le Chevalier d'Harmenthal* and *Ascanio* (1843). For the amazing decade that followed there is no parallel in literature except the first ten years of the author of *Waverley*. In 1844, with a number of digressions into new provinces—as *Cécile, Fernande, Amaury, Monte Cristo*—appeared *Les Trois Mousquetaires*; in 1845, *Vingt ans après, La Fille du régent*, and *La Reine Margot*; in 1846, *La Guerre des femmes, Maison rouge, Le Bâtard de Mauléon, La Dame de Monsoreau*, and *Les Mémoires d'un médecin*; in 1848, *Les Quarante-cinq* and the beginnings of *Bragelonne*—finished in 1850; and in 1849, *Le Collier de la reine*. The next two years witnessed productions as varied as *La Tulipe noire* and *Le Trou de l'enfer* (1850), and *La Femme au collier de velours* (1851); in 1852 the historical masterpiece *Olympe de Clèves* was produced. Between that year and 1854 were produced the ten delightful volumes of *Mes Mémoires*, with *Ange Pitou* and *La Comtesse de Charny*. Other achievements in the romance of French history were *Ingénue* (1854), *Les Compagnons de Jéhu* (1857), *Les Louves de Machecoul* (1859), and *Les Blancs et les bleus* (1867–68), with which last the sequence ended. The list is nothing like complete, and we can only refer in passing to the cloud of drama (the great historical novels were dramatized—the *Mousquetaires* cycle supplied at least three plays—as also were *Monte Cristo* and others), history, *causerie*, journalism, &c., in whose midst this enormous production went on. Dumas took a conspicuous part in the Days of July; in 1837 he received the red ribbon; in 1842 he married Mlle Ida Ferrier, from whom he promptly separated; in 1855 he went for two years into exile at Brussels; from 1860 to 1864 he was helping Garibaldi in Italy, and conducting and writing a journal; and in 1886 he produced the last but one of his plays. By this time the end was near; he sank under his work. He had got rid of a series of fortunes, and he quitted Paris for the last time with only a couple of napoleons in his pocket. He went to his son's villa at Dieppe, and there he died. See Lives by Fitzgerald (1873), Blaze de Bury (1885), Glinel (1885), Parigot (1901), Lecomte (1903), A. F.

Davidson (1902), Lucas-Dubreton (1928); also the *Memoirs* (trans. 1907–09); and A. Maurois, *The Three Musketeers* (1957).

(2) **Alexandre** (1824–95), natural son of (1), was born in Paris, when his father was but twenty-two years old. He was soon legitimized, and at sixteen, after a course of training at the Institution Goubaux and the Collège Bourbon, he left school for the world of letters and the society to which his father, then almost at his apogee, belonged. He was essentially respectable, however, and, having sown a certain quantity of wild oats and made a few experiments in literature, he settled down to serious work. He started in fiction and succeeded; he went on to drama; he took to theorizing about art, morals, politics, religion even, and succeeded. His novels—from *La Dame aux camélias* (1848) to *L'Affaire Clémenceau* (1864)—are all readable, and the former was a great success in dramatic form (1852). His essays, letters, speeches, prefaces, and prelections generally are brilliant and admirable in form, and daring, paradoxical, suggestive in a very high degree. Of his sixteen plays, *Le Demi-Monde* (1855), *Le Fils naturel* (1856), *Les Idées de Mme Aubray* (1867), *Une Visite de noces* (1871), *Monsieur Alphonse* (1873), *Denise* (1885) are masterpieces. Other famous dramas in which he had a share are *Le Supplice d'une femme* (1865), whose chaotic original is due to Émile de Girardin; *Héloïse Paranquet* (1866), in collaboration with Durantin; and *Les Danicheff* (1876). He may have assisted George Sand in preparing several of her works for the stage, and he completed and produced his father's *Joseph Balsamo* (1878). Elected to the Academy in 1874, he died November 27, 1895. See study by J. Claretie (1883); also A. Maurois, *The Three Musketeers* (1957).

(3) **Jean Baptiste André** (1800–84), French chemist, was born at Alais, Gard. He studied at Geneva, and coming to Paris in 1821, was first a lecturer in the École Polytechnique, then professor of Chemistry in the Athénée, the École Centrale (founded by himself), and finally, the Sorbonne. He came forward into public life (1849), was appointed master of the Mint (1868), and elected to the Academy (1875). His chief works are *Traité de chimie appliquée aux arts* (1828) and *Leçons sur la philosophie chimique* (1838). See forty-page memoir by A. W. Hofmann in *Nature*, February 6, 1880.

DU MAURIER, *mōr-yay*, (1) **George Louis Palmella Busson** (1834–96), artist and illustrator, was born in Paris, but was the grandson of *émigrés* who fled to England at the Revolution. In 1851 he came himself to London and studied chemistry, but returning to Paris adopted art as a profession, and studied there and at Antwerp and Düsseldorf. In England he rapidly acquired reputation as a designer of exceptional dexterity. He illustrated new editions of Thackeray's *Esmond* and *Ballads*, Foxe's *Book of Martyrs*, &c.; and much of his work appeared in *Once a Week* and the *Cornhill Magazine*. Finally he joined the staff of *Punch*, and became *par excellence* the gentle, graceful satirist of fashionable life (see his *English

Society at Home, 1880). He wrote and illustrated three novels, *Peter Ibbetson* (1891), *Trilby* (1894; extraordinarily successful), and *The Martian* (1897). See books by F. Moscheles (1896), T. A. Armstrong (1912), T. M. Wood (1913).

(2) **Sir Gerald** (1873–1934), British actor-manager, younger son of (1), was educated at Harrow, left a business career for the stage, made a reputation in criminal rôles, beginning with *Raffles* (1906). He became joint manager of Wyndham's theatre (1910–1925), and was knighted in 1922 for his services to the stage. He was manager of the St James's theatre from 1926 until his death. See *Gerald; a Portrait* (1934) by (3).

(3) **Daphne** (1907–), British novelist, daughter of (2), author of a number of successful period romances and adventure stories, including *Jamaica Inn* (1936), *Rebecca* (1938), *Frenchman's Creek* (1942), and *My Cousin Rachel* (1951). She has also published a family history, *The Du Mauriers* (1937), and a biography of her father.

DUMONT, *dü-mõ*, (1) **Augustin Alexandre** (1801–84), French sculptor, one of a long artist line, was born and died in Paris. The statue of Napoleon on the Vendôme column is his work. See two works by Battier (1885–90).

(2) **Pierre Étienne Louis** (1759–1829), the apostle of Benthamism, was born at Geneva, and in 1783 accepted the charge of the French Protestant Church at St Petersburg. In 1785 he became tutor in London to the sons of Lord Shelburne, afterwards Marquis of Lansdowne, his talents and liberalism recommending him to the Whigs. During the early years of the French Revolution he was at Paris, and became attached to Mirabeau, regarding whom he has given much information in his *Souvenirs sur Mirabeau* (1832). In 1791 he returned to England, and met Jeremy Bentham. This was the event of his life. Convinced of the value of Bentham's views on legislation, he obtained permission to edit his unpublished writings. The results appeared in his *Traité de législation civile et penale* (1802), *Théorie des peines et des récompenses* (1811), &c. Dumont returned to Geneva in 1814, and became a member of the representative council. He died at Milan.

DUMONT D'URVILLE, Jules Sébastien César (1790–1842), French admiral, born at Condé in Calvados, entered the navy in 1807, and in 1826–29 sailed in search of La Pérouse (q.v.), and made coast surveys of Australasia. In 1837–40 he made a voyage of Antarctic exploration, discovering Joinville Island and Adélie Land. He was killed in a railway accident near Versailles. See the forty-nine volumes of text and maps recording his voyages, and a Life by Joubert (Tours, 1885).

DUMOURIEZ, Charles François, *dü-moor-yay* (1739–1823), French general, born at Cambrai, from 1757 served with distinction during the Seven Years' War. A year or two of secret diplomacy in Poland and Hamburg brought him three years' imprisonment in the Bastille and at Caen (1772), but Louis XVI in 1778 made him commandant of Cherbourg. In 1790 he became one of the Jacobins, and was appointed commandant at Nantes. He now attached himself to the Girondists, and held for a short time the ministry of Foreign Affairs, which he resigned to take the field. The allies were advancing in great force. By a series of bold and rapid manœuvres Dumouriez prevented them from sweeping over Champagne, defeated the Prussians at Valmy (September 20, 1792), and overthrew the Austrians at Jemappes. The campaign of 1793, aiming at the conquest of the Netherlands, opened with the siege of Maestricht; Breda and other places were taken by the French; but at Neerwinden (March 18, 1793), Dumouriez sustained a severe defeat from the Austrians. His leanings towards constitutional monarchy excited the jealousy of the revolutionists; and soon he was denounced as a traitor and summoned to Paris. To save his head he went over to the Austrian camp. After wandering through many countries of Europe, he finally settled in England, and died at Turville Park near Henley-upon-Thames. Besides pamphlets, Dumouriez wrote *Mémoires* (1794).

DUNANT, Jean Henri, *dü-nã* (1828–1910), Swiss philanthropist, born at Geneva, inspired the foundation of the International Red Cross after seeing the plight of the wounded on the battlefield of Solferino. His efforts brought about the conference at Geneva (1863) from which came the Geneva Convention (1864). In 1901, with Frédéric Passy, he was awarded the first Nobel peace prize.

DUNBAR, (1) Paul Lawrence (1872–1906), American poet, born at Dayton, Ohio, the son of an escaped Negro slave. He gained a reputation with *Lyrics of Lowly Life* (1896), many of which were in dialect. His *Complete Poems* appeared in 1913. See studies by L. K. Wiggins (1907) and B. G. Brawley (1936).

(2) **William** (*c.* 1460–*c.* 1520), Scottish poet, born probably in East Lothian between 1460 and 1465, seems to have entered St Andrews University in 1475, and taken his M.A. in 1479. He became a Franciscan novice, and visited every flourishing town in England between Berwick and Calais; preached at 'Dernton' and Canterbury; crossed the sea at Dover, and instructed the inhabitants of Picardy; but he divested himself of the habit. He appears next to have been secretary to some of James IV's numerous embassies to foreign courts. In 1500 he obtained from the king a pension of £10, afterwards increased to £20, then to £80. In 1501 he visited England, probably with the ambassadors sent to arrange the king's marriage. Early in 1503, before the queen's arrival, he composed in honour of the event his most famous poem, *The Thrissill and the Rois*, perhaps the happiest political allegory in English literature. He seems now to have lived chiefly about court, writing poems, and sustaining himself with the vain hope of church preferment. In 1508 Chepman printed seven of his poems—the earliest specimen of Scottish typography. He visited the north of Scotland in May 1511, in the train of Queen Margaret, and his name

disappears altogether after Flodden. He was certainly dead in 1530; and David Laing argues that he must have died before 1522. As a poet, Dunbar is at times as rich in fancy and colour as Spenser in the *Faerie Queen*; as homely and shrewd and coarse as Chaucer in the *Miller's Tale*; as pious and devotional as Cowper in his hymns; and as wildly grotesque in satire as Burns. He reaches his highest level in his satires, *The Twa Marriit Wemen and the Wedo*, and *The Dance of the Sevin Deidly Synnis*. His *Lament for the Makaris* is a masterpiece of pathos. See *Poems*, ed. W. M. Mackenzie (1932), and study by R. A. Taylor (1932).

DUNCAN I, king of Scotland. See MACBETH.

DUNCAN, (1) Adam, Viscount (1731–1804), British admiral, was born at Dundee; and, entering the navy in 1746, commanded the *Valiant* at Havana (1762). He distinguished himself at Cape St Vincent (1780), and as admiral took command in 1795 of the North Sea Squadron to watch the Dutch fleet—Holland and France being at war with Britain. His blockade of the Texel was most effective, and Dutch trade was almost ruined. In the spring of 1797 the mutiny of the Nore spread to Duncan's seamen, and his position was for some weeks critical. On October 11 he gained the brilliant victory of Camperdown and was rewarded with a pension of £2000 and the title of Viscount Duncan of Camperdown. He died suddenly at Coldstream; his elder son was in 1831 made Earl of Camperdown. See Life by third Earl (1898).

(2) **Henry** (1774–1846), Scottish clergyman, from 1798 minister of Ruthwell, Dumfriesshire, in 1810 established there the first savings bank. He restored the 7th-century runic cross now in Ruthwell Kirk.

(3) **Isadora** (1878–1927), American dancer, travelled widely in Europe demonstrating her new style of dancing, based on the figures in Greek vase-painting, and influenced the development of the ballet. She founded schools in Berlin, Salzburg, Vienna and elsewhere. Her private life gave rise to considerable scandal, particularly after her children had been tragically killed in a motor accident. She herself was accidentally strangled when her scarf caught in the wheel of her car. See her *My Life* (1928), and monograph by P. Magnici (1948).

(4) **Thomas** (1807–45), Scottish painter, born at Kinclaven, Perthshire, was elected an A.R.S.A., an R.S.A., and in 1843 an A.R.A. He is best known for historical and genre works, many with a Jacobite flavour, as *Prince Charles's Entry into Edinburgh after Prestonpans*. He died in Edinburgh.

DUNCKER, Maximilian Wolfgang (1811–86), German historical writer, was born at Berlin, the son of a well-known bookseller, **Karl Duncker** (1781–1869). He became extraordinary professor of History at Halle in 1842; sat in the National Assembly (1848); and as a Liberal in the Prussian chamber (1849–52); was called to a Tübingen chair in 1857, and thence recalled in 1859 to Berlin to fill a post in the ministry of state. From 1867 to 1874 he was director of the state archives of Prussia. His greatest work is his *History of Antiquity* (1852–57; Eng. trans.

1877–82). In 1883–86 was published the translation of his history of Greece to the end of the Persian war. See Life by Haym (1891).

DUNCKERLEY, Thomas (1724–95), a natural son of George II, who was present at the taking of Quebec, and devoted himself to the promotion of Freemasonry. See Life by H. Sadler (1891).

DUNCOMBE, Thomas Slingsby (1796–1861), English politician, Radical M.P. for Hertford (1826–32), and for Finsbury from 1834, was born near Boroughbridge, and educated at Harrow. In 1842 he presented the Chartist petition to Parliament. See Life (1868).

DUNDAS (of Arniston), a Scottish family distinguished for legal and political talent. Sir James Dundas, the first of Arniston, was knighted by James VI, and was governor of Berwick. His son, Sir James, was a judge of the Court of Session, under the title of Lord Arniston (1662), but was deprived of his office for refusing to abjure the Covenant. He died in 1679. His eldest son, Sir Robert, who also rose to the bench, died in 1726.

(1) **Henry, 1st Viscount Melville** and **Baron Dunira** (1742–1811), brother of (3), was admitted to the Scottish bar in 1763. His assiduity, ability and family influence soon procured him advancement, and he was successively depute-advocate and solicitor-general. In 1774 he became M.P. for Midlothian, in 1775 lord advocate, in 1777 keeper of the signet for Scotland. Dundas's career in parliament was highly successful, though not very creditable to his consistency. Elected in opposition to the ministry, he soon became a strenuous supporter of Lord North, and one of the most obstinate defenders of the war with America. When North resigned in 1781, Dundas continued lord advocate under Rockingham. On the formation of the Coalition he passed over to Pitt, and became his ablest coadjutor. When Pitt returned to power in 1784, Dundas was appointed president of the Board of Control, and he introduced a bill for restoring the Scottish estates forfeited after the '45. Secretary of state for the Home Department (1791), he also held a number of other offices; and many of the most important public measures originated with or were promoted by him. He resigned with Pitt in 1801, and in 1802, under the Addington administration, was made Viscount Melville and Baron Dunira. In 1805 he was impeached of ' gross malversation and breach of duty ' as treasurer of the navy. The fortnight's trial before his peers acquitted him on all charges involving his honour. Thereafter he lived mostly at Dunira, his seat near Comrie. See Lives by Lovat Fraser (1916), Furber (1931), and Matheson (1933), and Omond's *Arniston Memoirs* (1887).

(2) **Robert** (1685–1753), son of Sir Robert, in 1717 became solicitor-general, in 1720 lord advocate, and as M.P. for Midlothian from 1722 distinguished himself by his attention to Scottish affairs. Sir Robert Walpole coming into power in 1725, Dundas resigned his office, when he was elected dean of the Faculty of Advocates. In 1737 he was raised to the bench, also as Lord Arniston. He became president of the Court of Session in 1748.

(3) **Robert** (1713–87), son of (2), was admitted to the Scottish bar in 1738, and rose to be Lord Advocate (1754) and president of the Court of Session (1760).

DUNDEE, **John Graham of Claverhouse, 1st Viscount** (c. 1649–89), Scottish soldier, spent three years at St Andrews, then four perhaps soldiering under Turenne. In 1672 he entered the Prince of Orange's horse-guards as cornet. In 1674 at the battle of Seneff he saved (according to the *Grameid*) William's life; in 1677 he returned to Scotland, and became lieutenant in a troop of horse commanded by his cousin, the Marquis of Montrose. At this time the government of Charles II was forcing Episcopacy upon Scotland and persecuting the Covenanters with the utmost rigour. In this service Claverhouse, now sheriff-depute of Dumfriesshire, was employed. At Drumclog, on Sunday, June 1, 1679, he was routed by an armed body of Covenanters, some forty of his troopers being slain and himself forced to flee. Three weeks later he commanded the cavalry at Bothwell Brig, where the Covenanters were defeated, about 400 being killed, chiefly by Claverhouse's dragoons. He hunted down the Covenanters and finding arms near the home of John Brown (q.v.), ' the Christian Carrier ' asked the latter to declare his loyalty to King James II, and when Brown refused had him executed. He became colonel, in 1682 sheriff of Wigtownshire, in 1683 a privy councillor, in 1684 was gifted the estate of Dudhope, and made constable of Dundee. In 1688, on his march to London to stem the Revolution, Claverhouse was made Viscount Dundee; next, being joined by the Jacobite clans and three hundred Irish, he raised the standard for James against William and Mary. After various movements in the north he seized Blair Castle, and General Mackay marched against him. On the evening of July 27, 1689, the two armies met at the head of the Pass of Killiecrankie. Dundee fell by a musketball while waving on his victorious clansmen; he was taken to Blair Castle, where he expired, and was buried in the church of Old Blair. ' Bloody Claverse ', ' Bonnie Dundee '—the two names illustrate the opposite feelings borne towards one whom the malice of foes and the favour of friends have invested with a factitious interest. Bonnie at least he was in outward form, with the ' long dark curled locks ' and the ' melancholy haughty countenance ' which we know by his portraits and by Scott's matchless description. Mark Napier's *Memorials and Letters of Dundee* (1859–62), partisan and not accurate, are still well worth sifting. See also lives of him by M. Morris (1887), ' A Southern ' (1889), L. Barbé (1903), S. Terry (1905), M. Barrington (1911), G. Daviot (1936) and A. S. H. Taylor (1939).

DUNDONALD, **Thomas Cochrane, 10th Earl of** (1775–1860), British seaman, was the eldest son of Archibald, 9th Earl (1749–1831), who beggared himself over chemical discoveries. Born at Annsfield, Hamilton, he entered the navy in 1793, and in 1800 received the command of a sloop, with which he took in fifteen months over fifty prizes; his most dashing achievement the capture of a Spanish 32-gun frigate with a loss of but 3 killed and 18 wounded. He was captured shortly afterwards by the French, but was speedily exchanged, and promoted to post-captain. After protecting the Orkney fisheries for fifteen months, he returned (February 1805) to prize-taking, and by April had made £75,000 of prize money for his own share. The next four years were mainly spent in harassing the enemy's coasts, and in 1808, with a small force, defending for twelve days the almost untenable Fort Trinidad at Rosas. Meanwhile in 1805 he had stood unsuccessfully for Honiton, but by judicious *largesse* was elected next year. In 1807 he was returned for Westminster, and at once proceeding to war against naval abuses, was ordered off to the Mediterranean. In April 1809 he was selected to burn the French fleet then blockaded in Aix Roads by Lord Gambier. On the night of the 11th the boom at the entrance was shattered. Explosion vessels and fireships caused a panic, and daylight showed almost all the French fleet aground. Gambier, however, was miles away, and Cochrane's signals met with no response. Consequently only four of the enemy's ships were destroyed. Cochrane received the Knighthood of the Bath, and Gambier the thanks of parliament, after an acquittal by the court martial which ensued on Cochrane's protest against the vote of thanks. Discredited and on half-pay, Cochrane pursued his crusade against naval corruption, until in 1814 he was arrested on a charge of fraud. A rumour of Napoleon's overthrow had sent up the funds, and he, with two others, was tried for propagating it and selling out upwards of a million sterling with a gross profit of £10,000. The others were guilty; Cochrane, by some held innocent, was sentenced to pay a fine of £1000, to suffer a year's imprisonment, and to stand for an hour in the pillory. This last was remitted, but he was struck off the navy list, expelled from parliament, and degraded from his knighthood. Westminster re-elected him; and in March 1815 he broke out of jail and reappeared in the House, to be forcibly removed and reimprisoned for the remaining three months of his sentence, and further fined £100. In 1818 he proceeded to aid Chile and Peru in their war of freedom; and in command of Chile's little navy he stormed the fifteen strong forts of Valdivia (1819), and cut out a frigate from under the batteries of Callao (1820), in two and a half years making Chile mistress of her own waters. He squabbled over his reward, as also over that (including the marquisate of Maranhão) for his brilliant services on behalf of the infant empire of Brazil (1823–25). For the cause of Greek independence he could do little through lack of ships and men (1827–28); so, returning to England, he devoted himself to procuring his reinstatement in the navy. But it was not till 1832 that a 'free pardon' was granted to the Earl of Dundonald—he had succeeded to the title ten months earlier—and that he was gazetted a rear-admiral.

Restored to the honour of knighthood (1847), commander-in-chief on the North American station (1848–51), and rear-admiral of the United Kingdom (1854), he died at Kensington, and was buried in Westminster Abbey. Lord Dundonald advocated the application of steam power to warships. His 'secret war plan' (to overwhelm fleets and fortresses by sulphur-fumes, &c.) was in 1812 and 1846 condemned as too inhuman, though infallible, and was not revealed till 1908 (in 'Panmure Papers'). See his own (nominally) *Narrative of Services in the Liberation of Chili, Peru, and Brazil* (1859), and *Autobiography of a Seaman* (1860–61), which breaks off in 1814, and is completed in the Life by the eleventh Earl and Fox-Bourne (2 vols. 1869). See also books by Fortescue (1896) and Twitchett (1931), Lord Ellenborough, *The Guilt of Lord Cochrane in 1814* (1914), J. W. P. Mallalieu, *Extraordinary Seaman* (1957) and H. Cecil, *A Matter of Speculation* (1965).

DUNÉR, Nils Christofer (1839–1914), Swedish astronomer, educated at Lund, professor of Astronomy at Uppsala and director of the observatory there (1888–1909). He made a study of variable and double stars, and was an expert on stellar spectroscopy. He died at Stockholm.

DUNFERMLINE, Lord. See ABERCROMBY.

DUNGLISON, Robley (1798–1869), American physician, born at Keswick, studied medicine in London, Edinburgh, and Erlangen, and from 1824 held chairs in the United States, where he was the friend of Presidents Jefferson and Madison. See Life (1870).

DUNHILL, Thomas Frederick (1877–1946), English composer and teacher, born in London, studied under Stanford and taught at the Royal College of Music. In 1907 he organized concerts to publicize the works of younger British composers. He first made his name with chamber works and songs, but his greatest success was the light opera *Tantivy Towers* (1931) to words by A. P. Herbert. He wrote a short biography of Elgar (1948).

DUNLOP, (1) John Boyd (1840–1921), Scottish inventor, born at Dreghorn, Ayrshire, was a flourishing veterinary surgeon near Belfast, when, before 1889, he invented the pneumatic tyre.

(2) **Ronald Ossory, R.A., R.B.A.** (1894–   ), Irish painter, born in Dublin. He studied at the Manchester and Wimbledon Schools of Art, and is a member of the London Group and the New English Art Club, being best known for his palette-knife painting, with rich impasto and glowing colour. His work is represented in the Tate Gallery, London, and many provincial galleries, and his writings on art include *Landscape Painting* (1954) and the autobiographical *Struggling with Paint* (1956).

DUNNE, (1) Finley Peter (1867–1936), American humorist, born at Chicago, edited papers there, and as 'Mr Dooley' became from 1900 the exponent of American-Irish humorous satire on current personages and events, in *Mr Dooley in Peace and War*, &c.

(2) **John William** (1875–1949), English inventor and philosopher, designed the first British military aeroplane (1906–07), and

wrote the best-selling philosophical works, *An Experiment with Time* (1927), *The Serial Universe* (1934), *The New Immortality* (1938) and *Nothing Dies* (1940).

DUNNING, John Ray (1907–), American physicist who in 1940 was one of the team of scientists which prepared the way for the atomic bomb by obtaining experimental verification of uranium–235 fission by slow neutrons.

DUNOIS, Jean, *dün-wah* (1402–68), the 'Bastard of Orleans', Count of Dunois and Longueville, was born in Paris, the natural son of Louis, Duke of Orleans, brother of Charles VI. His first great achievement was the defeat of the English at Montargis (1427); next he threw himself into Orleans with a small force, and defended it till its relief by Joan of Arc forced the English to raise the siege. In 1429 Dunois and the Maid of Orleans won the battle of Patay, after which he marched through the provinces overrun by the English, and took the fortified towns. Shortly after Joan's tragical death, Dunois took Chartres, the key of Paris, forced Bedford to raise the siege of Lagny, chased the enemy from Paris, and soon deprived them of all their conquests except Normandy and Guienne. In 1448–50 he drove them from Normandy, and in 1455 from Guienne also, and secured the freedom of France. For joining the league of the nobles against Louis XI he was deprived of all his possessions, which were, however, restored to him under the treaty of Conflans (1465). Although he never commanded a force large enough to win a victory to balance Agincourt or Crécy, his numerous petty successes served the cause of France better than greater and more dearly-bought victories would have done.

DUNOYER DE SEGONZAC, A. See SEGONZAC.

DUNRAVEN, Windham Thomas Wyndham-Quin, 4th Earl of (1841–1926), born at Adare Manor, Limerick, studied at Christ Church, Oxford, acted as *Daily Telegraph* correspondent in Abyssinia and the Franco-German war, and succeeded as fourth earl in 1871. He was under-secretary for the Colonies (1885–87), an Irish Free State senator from 1922. In addition to Reminiscences, he wrote on Irish Reform and Devolution, *The Great Divide* (1874), *Self-Instruction in Navigation,* &c.; and in 1893 and 1895 contested the America Cup with his yachts *Valkyrie II* and *III*.

DUNSANY, Edward John Moreton Drax Plunkett, 18th Baron (1878–1957), novelist, poet and playwright of Irish descent, educated at Eton and Sandhurst, served in the Boer War with the Coldstream Guards and in World War I as an officer of the Inniskilling Fusiliers. By World War II, he was Byron professor of English Literature at Athens. His literary works are highly poetic and imaginative. They began in 1905 with the novel *The Gods of Pegana*. At Yeats's invitation he wrote many plays for the Abbey Theatre, including *The Glittering Gate* (1909) and *The Laughter of the Gods* (1919). His verse is contained in *Fifty Poems* (1930) and *Mirage Water* (1939). See his autobiographical series *Patches of Sunlight*

(1938), *While the Sirens Slept* (1944), *The Sirens Wake* (1945) and *To Awaken Pegasus* (1949).

DUNS SCOTUS, Johannes (*c.* 1265–1308), one of the greatest of the mediaeval schoolmen, was born apparently at Maxton, Roxburghshire, in or before 1265. Joining the Franciscan order, he studied at Oxford, and lectured there on philosophy and theology; the report that 30,000 students then thronged to Oxford may be taken as an exaggerated testimony to his fame. He was also at intervals in Paris, and in 1308 in Cologne, where he died in November of the same year. His works are chiefly commentaries on the Bible, on Aristotle, and on the *Sentences* of Peter Lombard. The first are not contained in the collected edition (edited by Luke Wadding, Lyons 1639). The last occupy seven out of its twelve vols. (vols. v–x called *Opus Oxoniense*, vol. xi called *Opus Parisiense*—the latter edited from students' notebooks). Duns Scotus was the critic of preceding scholasticism, and the founder of a new type of thought. The schoolmen of the 13th century, especially Thomas Aquinas, had systematized and defended the Christian theology by means of the philosophy of Aristotle. On certain points Aquinas diverged from Aristotle, but the disagreement of Duns Scotus went much deeper. He contended that Aquinas was wrong in subordinating the practical to the theoretical, and seeking in speculation instead of in practice for the foundation of Christian theology. This contention struck at the root of the whole Aristotelico-Christian philosophy. Theology, he held, rests in faith, and faith is not speculative but practical—an act of will. The system of theology built up by Aquinas is subjected by Duns Scotus to a searching criticism, conducted with consummate dialectical skill, and abounding in refined distinctions, which gained him the title of 'Doctor Subtilis'. He maintained a strict orthodoxy, and against the Dominicans (Aquinas' order), zealously defended the Immaculate Conception. See works by Harris (1927) and (in French) by Longpré (1924, &c.); also Little in *English Historical Review* (October 1932.).

DUNSTABLE, John (d. 1453), English composer, a native of Dunstable (perhaps in Herts), who, it has been exaggeratedly claimed, 'invented the art of musical composition'. An early exponent of counterpoint, he wrote motets, masses and secular songs including the three-part *O Rosa bella*.

DUNSTAN, St (*c.* 909–88), Archbishop of Canterbury, was the son of a West Saxon noble, and was born near Glastonbury. Educated at the abbey, he lived for some time at the court of Athelstan, but his companions procured his banishment for practising unlawful arts. He took the monastic vows and retired to Glastonbury, where he gave himself up to study. The accession of Athelstan's brother, Edmund, recalled him to court, and he was appointed Abbot of Glastonbury in 945. He began a great work of reformation, and soon the abbey became a centre of religious teaching. At the same time he became the treasurer and adviser of Edmund, whose death in 955 led to the accession of Edwy and the fall of Dunstan's power. He took refuge in Flanders, and at Ghent he first saw the strict Benedictine discipline he was yet to introduce into England. In 957 he was recalled by Edgar, who had become king of the country north of the Thames, and was created Bishop of Worcester, in 959 of London also. In that year Edwy's death made Edgar king of the whole country, and one of his first acts was to appoint Dunstan to the see of Canterbury. The wise measures that made Edgar's reign so peaceful and prosperous were in great part due to the counsels of Dunstan. With Oswald, Archbishop of York, he solemnly crowned Edgar at Bath (973)—a formal declaration of the unity of the kingdom. Dunstan laboured to elevate the lives of the clergy, raise their social status, and make them the real teachers of the people in secular as in religious matters. He made obligatory the payment of tithes by landowners, while he did not entirely surrender the liberties of the church to Rome. On Edgar's death in 975, Dunstan declared for Edward, elder son of the late king, and crowned him at Winchester. On Edward's murder in 978, the two archbishops crowned Ethelred, whose hostility put an end to the great churchman's political career. See the six early biographies collected in Bishop Stubbs' *Memorials of St Dunstan* (' Rolls ' series, 1875), and Life by Duckett (1955).

DUNSTERVILLE, Lionel Charles (1865–1946), British soldier, a schoolmate, at Westward Ho College, of Rudyard Kipling (q.v.), who based his famous schoolboy character ' Stalky ' on him. He commanded the Baku expedition of 1918, which he described in *The Adventures of Dunsterforce* (1920).

DUNTON, John (1659–1733), English bookseller, born at Graffham, Hunts, refused to make the fourth in a direct line of clergymen, so was apprenticed to a London bookseller. He took a shop, married happily, made some lucky ventures, but was ultimately involved in financial troubles. He visited America, Holland, and Cologne, settled somehow with his creditors, and kept shop for ten years with fair prosperity; his *Athenian Gazette* being specially successful. He married a second time unhappily, and under the real and imaginary troubles of his later years his mind became deranged. See his extraordinary *Life and Errors of John Dunton* (1705), which throws interesting sidelights on the book trade of the time.

DUPANLOUP, Félix Antoine Philibert, *dü-pā-loo* (1802–78), French prelate, born at St Félix in Savoy, became vicar-general of Paris in 1838 and Bishop of Orleans in 1849. Though he had advocated tolerance for the Jesuits, and defended the temporal authority of the pope, he protested openly against the infallibility dogma; once, however, it was published, he signified his acceptance of it. In 1871 he was elected deputy for Orleans to the National Assembly; and from this time until his death, he struggled manfully against the constant attacks upon the church both in the Assembly and outside. H entered the Senate in 1876, and the French Academy in 1854, but resigned his *fauteuil*. He wrote on education, marriage, &c. See Lives by Lagrange (trans. 1885), M. Salomon (1904), Faguet (1914); his *Journal intime* (1902); and *Lettres choisies* (2 vols. 1888).

DUPARC, Henri, in full **Marie Eugène Henri Fouques-Duparc** (1848–1933), French composer, studied under César Franck, and is remembered for his songs, which, though only 15 in number, rank among the world's greatest. See study by Northcote (1949).

DUPIN, (1) **André** (1783–1865), French statesman and lawyer, wrote legal works and memoirs (4 vols. 1855–61).

(2) **François Pierre Charles, Baron** (1784–1873), younger brother of (1), author of *Voyages dans la Grande Bretagne* (1820–24), was made a baron in 1824, a peer in 1837, and filled several posts, which he resigned in 1852.

DUPLEIX, Joseph François, *dü-playks* (1697–1763), born at Landrecies, in 1720 was appointed to a seat in the French East India Council at Pondicherry. In 1730 he became superintendent at Chandernagore, in 1741 governor-general of all the French Indies; and his skilful diplomacy among the native princes almost made the Carnatic a French province. His power alarmed the English Company. When war broke out in Europe between France and England, Labourdonnais, who had taken Madras, was bribed with £40,000 to restore it to the English on payment of a ransom. This Dupleix refused to accede to, and violent disputes resulted in Labourdonnais' recall. Several brilliant engagements took place between the French and the Nawab of the Carnatic, who endeavoured to seize Madras, but was forced to raise the siege. An attack on the English at Fort St David failed, but Dupleix's science and courage were displayed in the defence of Pondicherry, which Admiral Boscawen in vain attacked for five weeks. But Dupleix's ambitious project of founding a French empire in India on the ruins of the Mogul monarchy was frustrated by Clive; though the struggle continued until Dupleix's recall in 1754. The French Company refused to reimburse him for the vast sums he had spent out of his (alleged) private fortune, and he died in poverty and neglect in 1763. See Hamont, *Dupleix d'après sa correspondance;* Martineau, *Dupleix et l'Inde française* (5 vols. 1920–29); a work by Cultru (1901); also Lives by Malleson (1890), Guérin (1908), Biddulph (1910).

DUPONT, Pierre (1821–70), French popular poet and songwriter, author of *Le Chant des ouvriers*, was born and died at Lyons.

DU PONT, Samuel Francis (1803–65), American naval officer, commanded a vessel in the Mexican War, and in the Civil War organized the blockade of the South Atlantic area by Federal naval forces.

DU PONT DE NEMOURS, famous French-American family.

(1) **Eleuthère Irénée** (1771–1834), younger son of (2), industrialist, established (*c.* 1804) in Wilmington, Del., a gunpowder factory which developed into one of the world's largest chemical concerns.

(2) **Pierre-Samuel** (1739–1817), a disciple of Quesney, after a stormy political life settled in U.S.A.

(3) **Victor-Marie** (1767–1827), son of (2), aide-de-camp to Lafayette (1789–91), settled in U.S.A. after 1800 and became a business-man but without his brother's success. Samuel Francis Du Pont (q.v.) was his son.

DUPRÉ, (1) Giovanni (1817–82), sculptor, was born of French ancestry at Siena, and died at Florence. His works include *Cain and Abel* at Florence, and the Cavour monument in Turin. See *English Life* by Frieze (1886).

(2) **Jules** (1812–89), French landscape painter of the Barbizon school, was born at Nantes, and died in Paris. See study by Claretie (Paris 1879).

(3) **Marcel** (1886–1971), French organist, born at Rouen, won the Prix de Rome for composition in 1914, and won fame all over Europe for his organ recitals.

DUPUIS, Charles François, *dü-pwee* (1742–1809), was professor of Rhetoric in the Collège de France, member of the Académie des Inscriptions, and during the Revolution a member of the Convention, of the Council of Five Hundred, and of the legislative body, of which he became president. His *Origine de tous les cultes* (10 vols., 1795) originated the commission appointed by Napoleon to explore Upper Egypt.

DUPUYTREN, Guillaume, Baron, *dü-pwee-trĭ* (1777–1835), from 1812 professor of Clinical Surgery in Paris, invented many surgical instruments. See *Life* by Cruveilhier (1841).

DUQUESNE, Abraham, Marquis, *dü-kayn* (1610–88), French naval officer, born at Dieppe, distinguished himself in 1637–43 in the war with Spain. In the Swedish service he rose to vice-admiral; and then returning to France, reduced Bordeaux, which had declared for the Fronde. He defeated De Ruyter and Van Tromp several times in 1672–73, and the united fleets of Spain and Holland off Sicily in 1676. On the revocation of the Edict of Nantes, Duquesne was the only Protestant excepted. See *Life* by Jal (1872).

DURAN. See CAROLUS-DURAN.

DURAND, (1) Sir Henry Marion (1812–71), the son of a cavalry officer, was trained at Addiscombe, served in the Afghan war (bursting in the gates of Ghazni, 1839) and the Sikh war. As agent in Central India he rendered very valuable service during the mutiny; and was subsequently a member of the Indian Council, K.C.S.I., major-general, and governor-general of the Punjab.

(2) **Sir Henry Mortimer**, K.C.S.I., G.C.M.G. (1850–1924), second son of (1), did valuable work, military and diplomatic, in the East, and was ambassador to Spain and the U.S.

(3) **Madame.** See GRÉVILLE (HENRY).

DURANDUS, (1) Gulielmus (1237–96), French jurist, born at Puimisson near Béziers, studied canon law at Bologna and Modena, and had held various offices under several popes, when in 1286 he became Bishop of Mende, still, however, remaining in Rome, where he died. His *Speculum Judiciale* (1271; first printed 1474) is his most famous work; of his *Rationale Divinorum Officiorum*

(Mainz 1459), book i was translated by J. M. Neale and B. Webb as *The Symbolism of Churches* (1843).

(2) **Gulielmus** (d. 1332), from 1327 Bishop of Puy-en-Velay, was called ' Doctor Resolu-tissimus '; he first supported and then opposed Thomas Aquinas.

DURANTE, Francesco (1684–1755), a Nea-politan composer of church and chamber music, born at Fratta Maggiore.

DÜRER, Albrecht (1471–1528), was born at Nuremberg, the son of a goldsmith from Hungary. In 1486 he was apprenticed to Michael Wolgemut, the chief illustrator of the Nürnberg Chronicle, and in 1490 started on his four years' travels. Then, having married the beautiful Agnes Frey, who was certainly not the Xanthippe of tradition, and having visited Italy, he worked again for a while under Wolgemut, and in 1497 started on his own account, and, aided by Schäufelein, Baldung, and others, executed many paintings, among them the Dresden triptych, and the Paumgartner altarpiece at Munich. In 1498 he published his first great series of designs on wood, the illustrations of the Apocalypse, which like Dürer's other work of the kind, were cut by a professional engraver. The copperplates of this period include *The Prodigal Son* (1500) and *Adam and Eve* (1504). In 1505–06 Dürer visited Venice, and there produced the *Feast of the Rosaries*, now the property of Strahow monastery, Prague. On (or before) his return he painted *Adam and Eve* (1507), now at Madrid; and *Assumption of the Virgin*—a triptych, whose centre was destroyed by fire at Munich in 1674. It was followed in 1511 by the *Adoration of the Trinity*, in the Vienna Gallery. Dürer was much employed by Maximilian I, of whom he executed several portraits, for whose prayer book he made forty-three pen and ink drawings, and in whose honour he drew the *Triumphal Car* and (with others) the *Triumphal Arch*, which were engraved on wood, the latter on ninety-two blocks, forming a surface of 100 square feet—the largest known woodcut. In 1520–21 Dürer visited the Netherlands. At Antwerp he made the acquaintance of Erasmus; and he was present at the coronation of Charles V, who appointed him his court painter. He died at Nuremberg. During his later years Dürer manifested great sympathy with the Reformation. Dürer's drawings and studies are very numerous, and are to be found in most public collections, those of the Albertina in Vienna and of the British Museum being the richest. As an engraver on metal and a designer of woodcuts he ranks even higher than as a painter. His work is distinguished by an unerring perception of the capabilities of the material, his metalplates being executed with extreme finish and refinement; while his woodcuts are boldly drawn with a broad expressive line, such as could be easily followed by the engraver. His copperplates, over 100 in number, include the *Little Passion* (16 plates, 1508–13); the *Knight, Death, and the Devil* (1513); *St Jerome in his Study*, and *Melancholia* (1514). Dürer may also be regarded as the inventor of etching, as he produced several plates in which all the lines are bitten with acid. His woodcuts are about 200 in number, including the *Greater Passion*, 12 subjects; *The Little Passion*, 37 subjects; and *The Apocalypse*, 16 subjects. Of his various scientific writings the *Instructions in Measurement* (1525), *Treatise on Fortification* (1527), and *Treatise on Human Proportion* (1528) are the most important. See his Correspondence (*Briefe*, Brinckmann and Birkner 1911); his *Schriftlicher Nachlass* (Heidrich 1908), and Dürer's *Writings* (trans. and ed. W. M. Conway 1959); Lives by L. Cust (1897), Nüchter (trans. 1911); monographs by Ephrussi (Paris 1882), A. von Eye (1892), T. S. Moore (1905), Knackfuss (trans. 1900), H. Wölfflin (Munich 1905); works by C. Dodgson (1926), Panofsky (4th ed. 1955), H. and E. Tietze (3 vols. 1928–1938), F. Winkler (Berlin 1959) and M. Levy (1964).

DUREY, Louis, *dü-ray* (1888–   ), French composer, born in Paris. His musical education did not begin until he was twenty-two, and in 1916 under the influence of Erik Satie, he became one of the group of young French composers known as ' The Six ', but broke with them in 1921. He has written large orchestral and choral works, but is chiefly known for his songs and chamber music.

D'URFEY, Thomas (1653–1723), British dramatist and songwriter, was born at Exeter of Huguenot ancestry, a nephew of Honoré d'Urfé (1568–1625), author of the famous romance of *Astrée*. He early became a busy playwright, his comedies especially being popular. Among these were *The Fond Husband* (1676), *Madame Fickle* (1677), and *Sir Burnaby Whig* (1681). In 1683 he published his *New Collection of Songs and Poems*, which was followed by a long series of songs, collected as *Wit and Mirth, or Pills to Purge Melancholy* (6 vols. 1719–20). Meanwhile he had been busy with plays, for whose morals he suffered like the rest from the heavy hand of Jeremy Collier. His fortunes declined as his comedies ceased to please.

DURHAM, John George Lambton, Earl of (1792–1840), British statesman, was born in London, and on his father's death in 1797 inherited Lambton Hall, Durham, which had been in the family for over six centuries. Educated at Eton, he served for two years in the dragoons, and in 1813 was returned as a Whig for his native county. He was a strong liberal, and in 1821 brought forward a scheme for parliamentary reform much more advanced than that of 1832. In 1828 he was created Baron Durham. In the administration of his father-in-law, Lord Grey (1830), he was lord privy seal, and one of the four persons who drew up the Reform Bill. Resigning office in 1833, he was made an earl, and from 1835 to 1837 was ambassador-extraordinary to St Petersburg. In 1838 he was appointed governor-general of Canada, where, owing to the revolt of the French in Lower Canada, the constitution had been suspended. His measures were statesmanlike but dictatorial, and the House of Lords voted disapproval of some of his acts. Thereupon in five months' time he returned to England without being recalled. Lord

Durham's famous report on Canada was ascribed by Brougham and many contemporaries to his secretary, Charles Buller (q.v.) —erroneously, according to Reid in the *Life and Letters* (1906) of Durham. See New's study (1929); Lucas's edition of the Report (1912).

DURONCERAY, Marie. See FAVART.

DURRELL, Lawrence George (1912–   ), British novelist and poet, was born at Darjeeling, India, educated at King's School, Canterbury, eloped with his future wife to Paris and began writing novels there. The second World War found him teaching English in Athens, but he escaped from the Germans in a fishing boat (1941), served in the Foreign Office in Cairo, Athens and Belgrade, and settled in 1953 in Cyprus, where political and terrorist upheavals inspired *Bitter Lemons* (1957). As a writer he first made his name with *Prospero's Cell* (1945), followed by the cosmopolitan multi-love story comprising the ' Alexandria Quartet ', *Justine, Balthazar, Mountolive* and *Clea* (1957–60), as well as *Selected Poems* (1956) and the novels *Tunc* (1968) and *Numquam* (1970). His brother **Gerald Malcolm** (1925–   ), is a noted zoologist, traveller, writer and broadcaster. His popular animal stories include *The Drunken Forest* (1956), and *A Zoo in My Luggage* (1960). See his reminiscences, *My Family and Other Animals* (1956) and *Birds, Beasts and Relatives* (1969).

DÜRRENMATT, Friedrich (1921–   ), Swiss author, born at Konolfingen, Bern, the son of a pastor; studied there and at Zürich and turned from painting to writing. The theme which recurs in all his work is that life is a calamity which has to be accepted for what it is but without surrender. His novels include the detective story *Der Richter und sein Henker* (1952), *Der Verdacht* (1953), *Die Panne* (1956), and his plays *Romulus der Grosse* (1949), and *Die Ehe des Herrn Mississippi* (1952), which established his international reputation. *Ein Engel kommt nach Babylon* (1953) is a parable in which an angel brings chaos instead of happiness, and *Der Besuch einer alten Dame* (1956) describes the return of an old lady to her native village to revenge herself on a seducer.

DURUY, Victor, *dü-rwee* (1811–94), French historian and educationist, was born and died in Paris. He became professor of History in the Collège Henri IV (1833), minister of public instruction (1863–69), and an Academician (1884). See his *Notes et souvenirs* (1901), and Life by Lavisse (1895).

DUSE, Eleonora, *doo'zay* (1859–1924), Italian actress, born near Venice, rose to fame in Italy, then triumphed (1892–93) at Vienna, Berlin, New York, London, &c. She died at Pittsburgh, having returned to the stage in 1921 after years of retirement. D'Annunzio owed much to her histrionic genius. The Duse ranks among the greatest actresses of all time. See Life by Signorelli (trans. 1959).

DUSHAN. See STEPHEN DUSHAN.

DUSSEK, Jan Ladislav (1761–1812), Czech composer and pianist, born at Czaslau in Bohemia. At Amsterdam he produced his earliest works for the piano; in London (1788–1800) he was very popular. In 1803–06

he was instructor to Prince Louis Ferdinand of Prussia; in 1808 he entered Talleyrand's service.

DUTENS, Louis, *dü-tä* (1730–1812), historian, born at Tours of Huguenot parentage, came to England, went to Turin as chaplain to the English embassy (1758–62), and remained as *chargé d'affaires*. He held a pension of £300, in 1766 was presented to the rich sinecure living of Elsdon in Northumberland, travelled much, and was made historiographer royal. He undertook the first comprehensive edition of Leibniz's works (1768). See his *Mémoires d'un voyageur* (3 vols. 1806).

DUTROCHET, René Joachim Henri, *dü-tro-shay* (1776–1847), French physiologist, born at Poitou, qualified in medicine at Paris, and became physician to Joseph Buonaparte of Spain. He was the first to study and to name osmosis. See his *Nouvelles Recherches sur l'endosmose et l'exosmose* (1828) and *Mémoires* (1837).

DUTT, (1) Michael Madhu Sudan (1824–73), Indian poet, born at Sagandari, Bengal, absorbed European culture, became a Christian and wrote poetry and drama in English and Bengali, as the plays *Sarmishtha* (1858), *Padmavati* (1859), and the blank verse epics *Tillotama* (1860) and *Meghanad-Badha* (1861).

(2) **Toru.** See Toru Dutt.

DUUN, Olav (1876–1939), Norwegian novelist, born in Namsdal, made a reputation with the saga-like *Juvikingar* and its five sequels (1918–23).

DUVAL, Claude (1643–70), highwayman, was born at Domfront, Normandy, and came to England at the Restoration in the train of the Duke of Richmond. Taking soon to the road, he pursued a successful career till, having been captured drunk, he was hanged at Tyburn.

DUVEEN, Joseph, 1st Baron Duveen of Millbank (1869–1939), English art dealer. A benefactor of the National Gallery, he gifted a gallery for the Elgin marbles.

DVOŘÁK, Antonin, *dvor'zhak* (1841–1904), Czech composer, was born near Prague on September 8. His father was a butcher, and Antonin worked for a while in the business, but showed such musical talent that he was sent to the organ school in Prague in 1857. In 1859 he began to earn his living playing the viola in an orchestra and giving lessons, but all the while he was composing in secret. It was not until 1873 that he attracted attention with his *Hymnus*, a nationalistic cantata based on Halek's poem *The Heroes of the White Mountain.* In 1873 he married, and from 1874 to 1877 was organist at St Adalbert's church in Prague, during which time he made a name for himself with several compositions which were promising enough to bring him to the notice of the authorities and gain for him a state grant. In 1877 Brahms became a member of the committee which examined the compositions of grant holders, recognized Dvořák's promise, and introduced his music to Vienna by sponsoring the publication of the *Klänge aus Mähren,* which were followed by the *Slavonic Dances,* a commissioned work. Brahms's friendship was a great influence and stimulus in the life

of the young composer. His work, basically classical in structure, but leavened with colourful Slavonic motifs, won increasing recognition, culminating in European acclaim for his *Stabat Mater,* first performed in London in 1883. He had now written six symphonies and much chamber and piano music, and enjoyed a worldwide reputation which brought him in 1891 the offer of directorship of the New York Conservatoire. It was in America that he wrote his ninth symphony, the ever-popular ' From the New World ', containing themes redolent of American folk music yet retaining a distinct Slavonic flavour. The beautiful solo for cor anglais in the slow movement is firmly established as a world favourite among classical melodies. At this time he also wrote some of his best chamber music. He returned to Prague in 1895. The last period of his life was spent composing chiefly orchestral music, but he also wrote three more operas, including *Rusalka* (1901) and *Armida* (1904) which, like their predecessors, were not highly successful. Dvořák's music possesses all the qualities calculated to preserve for it a permanent place in the concert repertoire. Rich in melodic interest and variety of ingredients, it represents a successful blend of Brahmsian classicism and folk elements from a diversity of sources. See studies by Hoffmeister (trans. 1928), Stefan (trans. 1941) and Alec Robertson (1944).

DWIGHT, (1) John, an early English potter at Fulham in 1671–98, a native of Oxfordshire, patented a ' transparent earthenware ', thus pioneering the English pottery industry.

(2) **Theodore** (1764–1846), American journalist and politician, brother of (3), sat in the House of Representatives 1806–07, wrote in support of the Federalist party, edited the Albany *Daily Advertiser* (1815–17), and founded its New York namesake, which he edited in 1817–36. His son **Theodore** (1796–1866) edited *Dwight's American Magazine* (1845–52), and wrote travel books.

(3) **Timothy,** LL.D. (1752–1817), American divine, grandfather of (4), born at Northampton, Mass., was a chaplain during the War of Independence; became minister of Greenfield Hill, Conn. (1783), where he also successfully conducted an academy; and in 1795 was elected president of Yale College and professor of Divinity. His principal works are his *Theology Explained and Defended* (1818), *The Conquest of Canaan* (1785), an ambitious epic poem, and *Travels in New England and New York* (1821).

(4) **Timothy,** D.D., LL.D. (1828–1916), grandson of (3), born at Norwich, Conn., was president of Yale in 1886–99, and was a member of the American committee for revising the English Bible.

DYCE, (1) Alexander (1798–1869), Scottish critic, born at Edinburgh, was educated at the High School, and graduated from Exeter College, Oxford, in 1819. He took orders, but in 1825 settled in London as a man of letters. With rare learning and sagacity he edited Peele (1828–39), Webster (1830; new ed. 1857), Greene (1831), Shirley (1833), Middleton (1840), Beaumont and Fletcher (1843–46), Marlowe (1850), Shakespeare

(1857), &c., besides writing *Recollections of the Table-talk of Samuel Rogers* (1856).

(2) **William** (1806–64), historical and religious painter, was born at Aberdeen, and went in 1825 to Rome, where he developed pre-Raphaelite sympathies. From 1844 professor of Fine Arts in King's College, London, he executed frescoes in the new House of Lords, Osborne House, Buckingham Palace, and All Saints', Margaret Street. He was elected R.A. in 1848, and died at Streatham.

DYCK, Sir Anthony Van. SEE VAN DYCK.

DYER, (1) Sir Edward (*c.* 1545–1607), poet and diplomatist, was born at Sharpham Park, Somerset, studied at Oxford, was knighted in 1596, and died in London. ' My Mind to Me a Kingdom is ' is the best-known of his poems, which Grosart collected in 1872. See R. M. Sargent, *At the Court of Queen Elizabeth* (1935).

(2) **George** (1755–1841), Charles Lamb's friend, was born in London, and from Christ's Hospital passed to Emmanuel College, Cambridge, taking his B.A. in 1778. In 1792 he settled in Clifford's Inn, London, and, with ' poems ' and a vast mass of hack work, produced the *History of the University of Cambridge* (1814) and *Privileges of the University of Cambridge* (1824). He contributed ' all that was original ' to Valpy's classics (141 vols. 1809–31), and became totally blind soon after his life's work was done. Simple, slovenly, but kindly, he afforded Lamb much innocent amusement.

(3) **John** (1699–1757), Welsh poet, born in Llanfynydd parish, Carmarthenshire, and educated at Westminster, abandoned law for art, and in 1725 published *Grongar Hill*, remarkable for simplicity, warmth of feeling, and exquisite descriptions of scenery. He next travelled in Italy, published the *Ruins of Rome* (1740), took orders, and in 1741 became vicar of Catthorpe, Leicestershire, which he exchanged later for the Lincolnshire livings of Belchford, Coningsby, and Kirkby-on-Bain. *The Fleece* (1757), a didactic poem, is praised by Wordsworth in a sonnet.

(4) **Sir William Turner Thistleton** (1843–1928), English botanist, was director of Kew Gardens in 1885–1905.

DYKES, John Bacchus (1823–76), English composer, born at Hull, graduated at Cambridge, was ordained in 1847, and became precentor of Durham Cathedral (1849), Mus.Doc. of Durham (1861), and vicar of St Oswald's there (1862). A joint-editor of *Hymns Ancient and Modern*, he composed services, anthems, and many hymn tunes, including ' Lead, Kindly Light ', ' Nearer, my God ', and ' Jesus, Lover of my Soul '. See Life by Fowler (1897).

DYMOKE, Sir John, *dim'uk* (d. 1381), by his marriage about 1350 with the heiress of the Marmions got the Lincolnshire manor of Scrivelsby, and became king's champion at Richard II's coronation. The function was last exercised at George IV's coronation by Henry Dymoke (1801–65), but Dymokes bore the standard of England at the coronations of Edward VII, George V, George VI, and Queen Elizabeth. See Lodge's *Scrivelsby* (1893).

DYMPNA (9th cent.), an Irish princess, said to have been slain by her father at Gheel in Belgium for resistance to his incestuous passion. She is the patron of the insane.

DYSON, Sir Frank Watson (1868–1939; kt. 1915), astronomer-royal in 1910–33, born at Measham, then in Derbyshire, known for his work on the distribution of stars and on solar eclipses. See Life by M. Wilson (1951).

DYVEKE (' little dove ') (1491–1517), Scandinavian adventuress, born at Amsterdam, in 1507 met the future Christian II of Denmark at Bergen, where her mother had an inn, and became his mistress. In Denmark her mother gained great influence, hateful to the nobles; and in 1517 Dyveke died suddenly, probably by poison.

DZERZHINSKY, Felix Edmundovich (1877–1926), Russian revolutionary, was exiled to Siberia at the age of twenty, fought in the 1905 revolution, and in 1917, as one of the organizers of the *coup d'état*, became chairman of the secret police and a member of the Bolshevik central committee. After 1921 he reorganized the railway system, and was chairman of the Supreme Economic Council in 1924–26. See study by Bromage (1956).

DZIERZON, Jan, *jer'zon* (1811–1906), Polish apiculturalist, born at Lowkowitz in Upper Silesia, discovered parthenogenesis in bees and introduced a new type of hive. His *Rationelle Bienenzucht* (1861) was translated in 1882 by C. N. Abbott.

E

EACHARD, Laurence. See ECHARD.

EADGAR. See EDGAR.

EADIE, John (1810–76), Scottish theologian, born at Alva, LL.D. Glasgow (1844), D.D. St Andrews (1850), wrote *Biblical Cyclopaedia* (1848), *Ecclesiastical Encyclopaedia* (1861) and a number of commentaries. See Life by Dr James Brown (1878).

EADMER, *yad'mer* (d. *c.* 1124), a learned monk of Canterbury, the devoted friend of Archbishop Anselm, to whom he had been sent by Pope Urban. In 1120 at Alexander I's request he became Bishop of St Andrews. His *Historia Novorum*, printed in 1623, and his *Vita Anselmi* (1551) were both edited (1884) in the ' Rolls ' series by Martin Rule. His lives of SS. Dunstan, Bregwin, and Oswald were printed by Wharton in part ii of his *Anglia Sacra* (1691). Most of his MSS. are in the library of Corpus Christi College, Cambridge.

EADS, James Buchanan (1820–87), American

engineer, born at Lawrenceburg, Ind., in 1861 built in a hundred days eight ironclad steamers for the government, followed by other ironclads and mortar-boats. His steel arch bridge (1867–74) across the Mississippi at St Louis, with a central span of 520 feet, is one of the finest in America. His works for improving the Mississippi mouth were completed in 1875–79. He died at Nassau, Bahamas.

EAKINS, Thomas (1844–1916), American painter, born at Philadelphia, studied in Paris under Gérôme, and became known for his portraits and genre pictures, especially sporting scenes.

EALDHELM. See ALDHELM.

EALDRED. See ALDRED.

EALHWINE. See ALCUIN.

EARHART, Amelia, *ayr'-* (1898–1937), American airwoman, born in Atchison, Kansas. She was the first woman to fly the Atlantic—Newfoundland to Burry Point, Wales, on June 17, 1928. Her plane was lost over the Pacific in July 1937. Her autobiography, *Last Flight* (1938), was edited by her husband, George Palmer Putnam. See Goerner, *The Search for Amelia Earhart* (1966).

EARLE, (1) John (*c.* 1601–65), born at York, became tutor to Charles II, then Prince of Wales, in 1641 and also served him as chaplain during his exile in France. He became Bishop of Worcester (1662), and of Salisbury (1663). He published anonymously (1628) *Microcosmographie,* a set of witty ' characters' and epigrammatic essays (ed. Murphy 1928).

(2) **William** (1833–85), British major-general, born in Liverpool. He commanded the garrison of Alexandria in 1882–84, and was killed while leading a column of the Gordon rescue expedition.

EARLOM, Richard (1743–1822), mezzotinter, born in London, engraved over sixty admirable plates after Claude's *Liber Veritatis,* and was responsible for the well-known set of Hogarth's *Marriage à la Mode.*

EARLY, Jubal Anderson (1816–94), American general, born in Virginia, commanded a Confederate brigade at Bull Run, and a division at Fredericksburg and Gettysburg. In 1864, after some successes, he was thrice defeated by Sheridan and Custer, and, relieved of his command (March 1865), he returned to his former profession as a lawyer.

EAST, (1) Sir Alfred (1849–1913), English painter and etcher, born at Kettering. He studied at the Glasgow School of Art, and is best known for his landscapes of Japan, which he visited in 1889. From 1902 he produced a large number of etchings, and in 1906 he wrote *The Art of Landscape Painting in Oil Colour.* He was knighted in 1910 and elected R.A. in 1913.

(2) **Michael** (*c.* 1580–1648), English composer and organist who probably spent several years in the service of Sir Christopher Hatton and was subsequently organist of Lichfield Cathedral. His works include church music and madrigals, and he was a contributor to *The Triumphes of Oriana,* the madrigal collection dedicated to Queen Elizabeth I in 1603.

EASTLAKE, Sir Charles Lock (1793–1865), English historical painter, born at Plymouth, studied under Haydon. R.A. (1830), P.R.A. (1850), and director of the National Gallery from 1855, he is also remembered for his *Materials for the History of Oil Painting* (1847). His collected papers (1848–70) contain a memoir by Lady Eastlake (1810–1893), the authoress of *Letters from the Baltic* and the venomous reviewer of *Jane Eyre* in the *Quarterly.* See her *Journals* (1896).

EASTMAN, George (1854–1932), American inventor and philanthropist, born at Waterville (N.Y.), turned from banking to photography, producing a successful roll-film (1884), the 'Kodak' camera (1888), and joining with Edison in experiments which made possible the moving-picture industry. He died by his own hand.

EASTWICK, Edward Backhouse (1814–83), English orientalist, born at Warfield, Berkshire, after service with the East India Company was appointed (1845) professor of Hindustani at Haileybury College, and assistant political secretary in the India Office (1859); and was secretary of legation in Persia in 1860–63. He was M.P. for Penryn and Falmouth (1868–74); financial difficulties then enforced his retirement, and he devoted the rest of his life to literary work. He produced many translations from the Persian, notably the *Gulistan* of Sádi; a *Hindustani Grammar* (1847); *Journal of a Diplomate in Persia* (1864); and translated Bopp.

EATON, Margaret, *née* O'Neill, known as ' Peggy ' (*c.* 1796–1879), the daughter of a Washington innkeeper, for her second husband married in 1829, John Henry Eaton, secretary of state for war under President Jackson. The wives of the other cabinet-ministers refused to mix with her because of her alleged premarital intimacy with Eaton and because of her birth, forcing Eaton to resign (1831) despite the strenuous efforts of Jackson, who even transferred his support to a presidential candidate, Van Buren, favourably disposed towards her. A great social success in Europe when her husband became ambassador to Spain (1836), she married a young dancing instructor after the former's death.

EBBA, St (d. *c.* 670), a Northumbrian princess, who founded the double monastery of Coldingham, and ruled it as abbess till her death.

EBBINGHAUS, Hermann (1850–1909), German psychologist, carried out researches on memory to investigate higher mental processes, and published his findings in 1885.

EBERS, Georg Moritz, *ay'bèrs* (1837–98), German Egyptologist and novelist, was born at Berlin. Lecturer (1865) and professor (1868) at Jena, he visited the East in 1869, and from 1870 to 1889 was professor of Egyptology at Leipzig. He discovered and published (1875) the celebrated hieratic medical *Papyrus Ebers*; wrote on Goshen, Sinai and Egypt; but is best known as author of numerous historical novels. See his *Story of My Life* (trans. 1893).

EBERT, *ay'bèrt,* **(1) Friedrich** (1871–1925), first president of the German Republic (elected February 1919), was born at Heidelberg, a tailor's son. A saddler at Heidelberg, he became a Social Democrat journalist and Reichstag member (1912). Chairman of his party (1913), he was a Majority Socialist leader in the Revolution of 1918.

(2) **Karl Egon** (1801–82), Bohemian poet, was born and died at Prague. His poems include the national epic *Vlasta* (1829).

EBERZ, Josef, *ay'berts* (1880–1942), German artist, born at Limbourg. He studied at Karlsruhe and Düsseldorf and worked at Stuttgart, painting mainly religious pictures.

ECCLES or EAGLES, *ek'ēlz,* (1) **John** (*c.*1650–1735), son of (2), is celebrated as a theatre composer. He became master of the King's Band of Musick in 1700, composed the music for the coronation of Queen Anne and published many volumes of theatre music, songs and masques. Two other brothers, **Henry** (*c.* 1652–1742) and **Thomas** (after 1652–after 1735), were violinists. The former achieved success in Paris; little is known of the latter, except that he played in London taverns.

ECCLES, Sir John Carew (1903–   ), Australian scientist, educated at Melbourne and Oxford, director of the Kanematsu Institute of Pathology at Sydney (1937), professor of Physiology at Otago University (1944–51), then at the Australian National University, Canberra. A specialist in neurophysiology, he was knighted in 1958, and was awarded with Hodgkin (1) and Huxley (2) the Nobel prize for medicine in 1963 for discoveries concerning the functioning of nervous impulses.

(2) **Solomon** (1618–83), English musician, father of (1), born in London. He taught the virginals and viols until he became a Quaker in 1660, when he burned his instruments and books and became a shoemaker. During the Great Plague he ran naked through the streets with a brazier of burning sulphur on his head, prophesying disaster. In 1667 he published *A Musick Lector,* a discussion on whether music was from God or not. He accompanied Fox to the West Indies in 1671 to spread Quakerism, and was prosecuted for sedition at Barbados in 1680. See monograph by J. Jeffreys, *The Eccles Family* (1951).

ECHEGARAY Y EIZAGUIRRE, José, *aychay-gah-rī' ee ay-ee-tha-gee'ray* (1833–1916), Spanish dramatist, born of Basque descent at Madrid in 1833, taught mathematics, held portfolios in various ministries (1868–1874), then won literary fame by many plays in prose and verse, received a Nobel prize (1904), returned to politics as minister of finance (1905), and to science as professor of Physics, Madrid University (1905). His masterpiece was *The Great Galeoto* (1881).

ECK, Johann Mayer von (1486–1543), German Catholic theologian, born at Egg in Swabia, became professor of Theology at Ingolstadt (1510), and was the ruling spirit of that university until his death. After his Leipzig disputation with Luther, Eck wrote his *De Primatu Petri,* and went to Rome in 1520, to return with the bull which declared Luther a heretic. See *Life* by Wiedemann (1865); his German writings are edited by Meister and Zöpfl (1929).

ECKART. See ECKHART.

ECKENER, Hugo (1868–1954), German aeronautical engineer, born at Flensburg, became a friend of Count Zeppelin and in 1911 was made a director of his airship company. In 1924 he piloted the ZR3, later called the *Los Angeles,* from Friedrichshafen to Lakehurst, N.J., on the first flight by an airship directly from continental Europe across the Atlantic. He made many other notable flights. See his *My Zeppelins* (1958).

ECKERMANN, Johann Peter (1792–1854), German author, born at Winsen in Hanover, and studied at Göttingen. The publication of his *Beiträge zur Poesie* (1823) led to his removal to Weimar, where he assisted Goethe in preparing the final edition of his works. He achieved fame by his *Conversations with Goethe* (1837), Eng. trans. by Fuller (1839), Oxenford (1850). See a German work by Houben (1925–28).

ECKFORD, Harry (1775–1832), American naval architect, was born at Irvine, went out to Quebec in 1790, and died at Constantinople. He built the famous early steamship *Robert Fulton* (1822).

ECKHART, Johannes, called **Meister Eckhart** (*c.* 1260–1327), German mystic, born at Hochheim near Gotha, entered the Dominican order, studied and taught in Paris, acted as prior of Erfurt and as vicar of his order for Thuringia, was Dominican provincial in Saxony 1303–11, in 1307 was also appointed vicar-general of Bohemia and from 1312 preached at Strasbourg, Frankfurt and Cologne. Eckhart's teaching is a mystic pantheism, and influenced later religious mysticism and speculative philosophy; in 1325 he was arraigned for heresy by the Archbishop of Cologne, and two years after his death his writings were condemned by Pope John XXII. His extant works consist of Latin and German sermons and tractates. See Life by J. Ancelet-Hustache (Eng. trans. 1958).

EDDINGTON, Sir Arthur Stanley (1882–1944; kt. 1930; O.M. 1938), astronomer, professor (1913), and observatory director (1914) at Cambridge, born at Kendal, was considered by many the greatest of modern English astronomers. His most notable works are *Space, Time and Gravitation* (1920), *Stars and Atoms* (1927) and *The Expanding Universe* (1933). See Life by Douglas (1956).

EDDY, Mary Baker Glover (1821–1910), American founder of the Christian Scientists, was born at Bow, N.H. Given up because of supposedly fatal injuries after a fall, she read about the palsied man in Matthew's Gospel, and claimed to have risen from her bed similarly healed. Thereafter she devoted herself to developing her spiritual discovery, stating its principles in *Science and Health with Key to the Scriptures* (1875), which taught the illusory nature of disease. In 1879 she organized at Boston the Church of Christ, Scientist, and became a minister. See study by Peel (1966).

EDE, James Chuter (1882–1965), **Baron Chuter-Ede of Epsom** (having adopted this style on receipt of a life peerage in 1964), British Labour politician, born at Epsom and educated at Dorking High School and Christ's

College, Cambridge. A Surrey elementary schoolmaster from 1905 to 1914, he entered parliament as M.P. for Mitcham in 1923 and for South Shields in 1929. He was chairman of the Surrey County Council from 1933 to 1937. From 1940 to 1945 he was parliamentary secretary to the ministry of education and became home secretary in the 1945 Labour government. In 1951 he was also leader of the House of Commons. A humanitarian reformer at the Home Office, he was responsible for the Criminal Justice Act of 1948. In 1953 he was made C.H. In parliament Chuter-Ede was a quiet, shrewd debater with a Nonconformist passion for political liberty.

EDELFELT, Albert Gustav (1854–1905), Finnish artist, born at Porvoeo, worked in many different media in a naturalistic style. Among his best works are a portrait of Pasteur, *Christ and the Magdalene* and *Women in the Churchyard.*

EDELINCK, Gerard (1649–1707), Flemish copper engraver, born at Antwerp, in 1665 went to Paris, where he died. His portrait of Dryden, after Kneller, is well known. See Life by Delaborde (Paris 1886).

EDEN, (1) Sir (Robert) Anthony, 1st Earl of Avon (1897–   ), British statesman, born on June 12 at Windlestone Hall, Bishop Auckland, was educated at Eton and Christ Church, Oxford. He won the M.C. in 1917, and became Tory M.P. for Warwick and Leamington in 1923, holding the seat till his resignation in 1957. In 1931 he became foreign under-secretary, in 1934 lord privy seal and in 1935 foreign secretary. He resigned in 1938 following differences with the prime minister, Neville Chamberlain, principally on policy towards Fascist Italy. On the outbreak of World War II he became dominions secretary. In 1940 he was Sir Winston Churchill's secretary of state for war, issuing the historic appeal that brought the Home Guard into being. In December 1940 he was foreign secretary again. Strenuous wartime work, which included negotiations for a 20-year treaty of alliance with the Soviet Union in 1942, culminated in his leadership of the British delegation to the 1945 San Francisco conference which established the United Nations. With Labour in power in 1945–51, he was deputy leader of the Opposition, returning to the Foreign Office once more in 1951 in Sir Winston Churchill's government. His peak year of patient negotiation was 1954, marked by settlements in Korea and Viet Nam (Indo-China), by the emergence of a new political pattern in Western Europe backed by a British military guarantee, and by a new agreement with Egypt for the withdrawal of British forces from the Suez Canal Zone. He succeeded Sir Winston Churchill as prime minister on April 6, 1955, in a year marked by the ' summit ' conference at Geneva with the heads of America, France and the Soviet Union. In November 1956 he ordered British and French forces to occupy the Suez Canal Zone ahead of the invading Israeli army. His action was condemned by the United Nations and caused a bitter and prolonged controversy in Britain which did not subside when

he ordered a withdrawal. In failing health, he abruptly resigned the premiership on January 9, 1957. He was created an earl in 1961. Eden's gracious, debonair manner concealed strong political convictions and fixity of purpose. Regarded as one of the Western world's most experienced statesmen, his supreme aim was world peace based on respect for law. History has yet to pronounce whether his premiership enlarged his reputation. He has written *Places in the Sun, Foreign Affairs* (1939), *Freedom and Order* and *Days for Decision* (1949) and his memoirs (3 vols. 1960-65). See also studies by Lewis Broad (1955), William Rees-Mogg (1956) and Randolph Churchill (1959).

(2) **George, 1st Earl of Auckland** (1784–1849), English statesman, son of (3), born at Eden Farm, Beckenham, succeeded as 2nd baron in 1814. A steadfast supporter of reform, he held two or three offices, and in 1835 was appointed governor-general of India. He plunged into the unhappy Afghan war in 1838, and was superseded in 1841. He was created an earl in 1839. See Life by Trotter (1893).

(3) **William, 1st Baron** (1744–1814), English statesman and diplomat, third son of Sir Robert Eden, Bart., of West Auckland, Durham, was educated at Eton and Oxford, and called to the bar in 1768. In 1772 he was appointed under-secretary of state, and afterwards president of the Board of Trade, commissioner to treat with the American insurgents, chief secretary to the Irish viceroy, minister-plenipotentiary to France (negotiating Pitt's commercial treaty with that country in 1786), ambassador to Spain, ambassador to Holland, and postmaster-general. In 1788 he was raised to the Irish peerage, and in 1793 to the British peerage. See his *Journal and Correspondence* (4 vols. 1860–1862).

EDGAR, or **Eadgar** (944–975), king of the English, was the younger son of Edmund the Magnificent. In 957 he became ruler over Northumbria and Mercia, and in 959, on his brother Eadwig's death, king of Wessex also. His reign, whose policy was largely shaped by Dunstan (q.v.), was one of peace and prosperity.

EDGAR ATHELING (*c.* 1050–*c.* 1125), grandson of Edmund Ironside, was born probably in Hungary. The heir of Edward the Confessor, he was kept from the throne by William the Conqueror (1066); and having engaged in revolts against the Norman, he sought refuge in Scotland (1068) with Malcolm Canmore, who married his sister Margaret. Edgar embraced the cause of Robert, Duke of Normandy, against William Rufus, and was again driven (1091) to Scotland, where in 1097 he reseated his nephew Edgar on the throne, which had been usurped by Donald Bane. In 1099 he embarked on an unprofitable crusading expedition to the East; and finally was taken prisoner at Tinchebrai (1106) fighting for Duke Robert against Henry I.

EDGERTON, (1) Harold Eugene (1903–   ), American electrical engineer, born at Fremont, Neb., became in 1934 professor of Electrical Engineering at the Massachusetts

Institute of Technology. A specialist in high-speed photography, he has produced a krypton-xenon gas arc which was employed in the photographing of the capillaries in the white of the eye without hurting the patient. See his *Flash!* (1939).

(2) **Sidney** (1818–1900), American politician, born in New York, sat in Congress (1859–63), became first chief justice of Idaho Territory and as such was a founder of the new state (1864) of Montana, of which he was made the first governor.

EDGEWORTH, (1) **Francis Ysidro** (1845–1926), British economist, nephew of (3), born at Edgeworthstown, professor of Political Economy at Oxford (1891–1922), editor of the *Economic Journal* (1891–1926), was perhaps the most outstanding mathematical economist of his time. Best known for his *Mathematical Psychics* (1881), he also carried out important work in the field of statistical theory, on which he wrote no books, but contributed a host of articles, pamphlets and reviews. See A. L. Bowley's *Edgeworth's Contribution to Mathematical Statistics* (1928).

(2) **Henry Essex** (1745–1807), the 'Abbé Edgeworth', was the son of the Protestant rector of Edgeworthstown in Ireland, who, turning Catholic, settled at Toulouse. Ordained priest, young Edgeworth took the surname De Firmont from Firmount, the family property. In 1791 he became confessor to the Princess Elizabeth, in 1793 to her brother, Louis XVI, just sentenced to death. He attended him to the scaffold; but the 'Son of St Louis, ascend to heaven', was an invention, it seems, of the journalist Lacretelle. He got safely to England (1796), and as chaplain attended Louis XVIII to Mitau, where he died. See his Memoirs by C. Sneyd Edgeworth (1815), and his Letters (1818); and V. M. Montagu, *Abbé Edgeworth and his Friends* (1913).

(3) **Maria** (1767–1849), eldest daughter of (4), was born at Blackbourton, Oxon., and as a child achieved story-telling fame. Chiefly for her father's sake she sacrificed in 1802 her one romance—with the Swedish Count Edelcrantz. Greatly lionized in London, she was at Abbotsford in 1823, a visit returned by Scott at Edgeworthstown in 1825. To the literary partnership between father and daughter we owe directly *Practical Education* (1798) and the *Essay on Irish Bulls* (1802). But most of her other works were inspired by her father, and gained or lost by his revision. Published between 1795 and 1847, they filled over 20 volumes. Besides the *Tales from Fashionable Life* and *Harrington* (an apology for the Jews), there are her three Irish masterpieces, *Castle Rackrent* (1800), *The Absentee* (1812), and *Ormond* (1817). Her novels may be too didactic, but for wit, pathos, lively dialogue and simple directness, for bright vivacity and healthy realism, as a mirror, moreover, of the age when they were written and of that 'most distressful country' in which their best scenes are laid, they still deserve to be read. The *Memoirs of Richard Lovell Edgeworth* (1820; 3rd ed. 1844) is autobiographical up to 1782; the completion, less interesting,

is by Miss Edgeworth. See her *Life and Letters* (1867; ed. by Hare, 1894); Lives by Miss Zimmern (1883) and the Hon. Emily Lawless (1904); C. Hill, *Maria Edgeworth and her Circle* (1910); *The Edgeworths,* by A. Paterson (1914); and E. I. Jones, *The Great Maria* (1959).

(4) **Richard Lovell** (1744–1817), Irish inventor, educationist and eccentric, father of (3), was born at Bath. With his great friend Thomas Day (q.v.) he studied at Corpus Christi, Oxford, and while there made the first of his four marriages. He then studied law for a time, but following a stay in France, where he took part in the attempted diversion of the Rhône, he returned in 1773 to live mainly on the family estate at Edgeworthstown, Co. Longford, an energetic and intelligent landlord. From boyhood 'irrecoverably a mechanic', he was ever inventing something—a semaphore, a velocipede, a pedometer, &c.; and through his inventions he came in touch with Erasmus Darwin and so with the Lichfield circle and with his second and third wives, Honora and Elizabeth Sneyd. The father of nineteen children, the eldest educated on Rousseau's system, he held noteworthy theories of education and published these in *Professional Education* (1808) and in another book (see above) written in collaboration with his daughter. He wrote much also on mechanical subjects. In politics he advocated parliamentary reform and Catholic emancipation, and, a member of the last Irish parliament (1798–1799), spoke for union but voted against it.

EDINBURGH, Prince Philip, Duke of (1921–), son of Prince Andrew of Greece, was born at Corfu and educated at Cheam, Gordonstoun and Dartmouth. Entering the Royal Navy in 1939 as Lieut. Philip Mountbatten (his mother was Princess Alice of Battenberg), in 1941 he joined H.M.S. *Valiant,* on which he fought in the battle of Cape Matapan, subsequently serving in the Pacific on H.M.S. *Whelp.* Having become a naturalized British subject, on November 20, 1947, he was married to the Princess Elizabeth. Seriously interested in science and the technology of industry, as well as in youth adventure training and awards, he is also a keen sportsman, a yachtsman, and a qualified airman. He received the O.M. in 1968. See Life by Wulff (1947) and SAXE-COBURG-GOTHA.

EDISON, Thomas Alva (1847–1931), American inventor, born at Milan, Ohio, at the age of twelve became a railroad newsboy, and began to experiment in chemistry. Gaining the exclusive right of selling newspapers on his line, and purchasing some old type, he published the *Grand Trunk Herald,* the first newspaper printed in a train. A stationmaster taught him telegraphy, and he invented an automatic repeater, by which messages could be sent from one wire to another without the intervention of the operator. He developed his system of duplex telegraphy while he was a telegraph operator in Boston. In 1871 he invented the printing-telegraph for quotations, for whose manufacture he established a workshop at Newark, N.J., removed to Menlo Park, N.J., in 1876, and to West Orange, N.J., in 1887. His faculties now getting full play, he took out patents in connection with telegraphy, including quadruplex and sextuplex systems, megaphone, phonograph, adaptations of electric light, kinetoscope, metallurgic methods, benzol plants, and hundreds of other inventions. See Lives by Simonds (1934) and Josephson (1961).

EDITH. See EDWARD THE CONFESSOR.

EDMONDS, Thomas Rowe (1803–89), English economist and statistician, advocate of the abolition of private ownership in industry and a two-hour day for workers, compiled life tables (1832) and wrote on political economy (1828) and the principle of population (1832).

EDMUND (*c.* 922–946), king of the English, in 940 succeeded his brother Athelstan. He conquered Mercia and the 'Five Boroughs' of the Danish confederacy in 941 or 944, and also Cumbria, which he entrusted to Malcolm of Scotland; but was slain by an outlaw at Pucklechurch, Gloucestershire.

EDMUND, St (1) (*c.* 841–870), said to have been born in Franconia, the son of King Alkmund, in 855 succeeded Offa, king of the East Angles, as his adopted heir. In the Danish invasion of 866–70 he was defeated and shot to death with arrows at Hoxne, Suffolk, because he refused to abjure his faith. In 903 his remains were translated from Hoxne to Bury St Edmunds. See Life by F. Hervey (1929).

(2) **St Edmund Rich**, born at Abingdon about 1170, studied and taught at Oxford and Paris. He acquired fame as a preacher, was commissioned by the pope to preach the sixth crusade throughout England (*c.* 1227), and in 1234 was made Archbishop of Canterbury. He attached himself to the national party, whose spokesman he became against Henry III, even threatening him with excommunication if he did not dismiss foreign favourites. But his gentleness, generosity, austerity and purity put him out of joint with the age; and in 1240 he retired to the abbey of Pontigny in France, and died the same year, November 16, at Soisy. See Lives by Dom W. Wallace (1893), F. de Paravicini (1899) and C. H. Lawrence (1960).

EDMUND IRONSIDE (*c.* 981–1016), king of the English, was son of Ethelred the Unready, and was chosen king by the Londoners on his father's death (April 1016), while Canute was elected at Southampton by the Witan. Edmund hastily levied an army in the west, defeated Canute twice, raised the siege of London, and again routed the Danes. Levying a fresh army, he defeated them at Otford—his last victory. At Assandûn (Ashingdon, in Essex), after a desperate fight, he was routed. By a compromise with Canute, the latter retained Mercia and Northumbria, Edmund all the south and the headship, the survivor to succeed to the whole. A few weeks later Edmund died.

EDMUNDS, George Franklin (1828–1919), American senator, born at Richmond, Vt., sat in the state legislature and senate, and in the U.S. senate (1866–91), of which he was president *pro tempore* after Arthur became president. He took an active part in the prosecution of President Johnson, and was author of the 'Edmunds Act' for the suppression of polygamy in Utah.

EDRIC STREONA (d. 1017), the wicked ealdorman from 1007 of the Mercians, who, a traitor and murderer, was himself at last slain by Canûte's order.—His nephew, **Edric Silvaticus**, in 1067–70 opposed the Conqueror.

EDRISI or **Idrisi**, *id-ree'see* (*c.* 1100–64), Arabic geographer, was born at Ceuta, studied at Córdoba, and travelled in Spain, Barbary and Asia Minor. He then settled at the court of Roger II of Sicily, who invited him to write a description of the earth. For this end travellers were sent on journeys of exploration, and were directed to send him an account of all they had seen or heard. This occupied many years, and Edrisi's Description of the World (*Nuzhat-el-Mushtâk*), or 'Book of Roger', as it was also called, was not completed till 1154. Unequal in execution, it yet stands in the very first rank of mediaeval geographies.

EDSCHMID, Kasimir, pseud. of **Eduard Schmidt** (1890–1966). German writer, born at Darmstadt, a pioneer of Expressionism in his novel *Die sechs Mündungen* (1915). In addition to other novels, travel books, and a study of Byron, he wrote *Über den Expressionismus in der Literatur* (1919).

EDWARD. English kings of the Saxon line:

(1) **Edward the Elder** (*c.* 870–*c.* 924), about 901 succeeded his father, Alfred the Great, and raised the supremacy of Wessex into something little short of an imperial authority, extending his sway over Mercia, East Anglia and Northumbria.

(2) **Edward the Martyr** (*c.* 963–978), in 975 succeeded his father, Edgar, as king, and was murdered at Corfe Castle by his stepmother, Elfrida.

(3) **Edward the Confessor** (*c.* 1003–66), the last Anglo-Saxon king of the old line, was born at Islip in Oxfordshire, the elder son of Ethelred the Unready, by his marriage in 1002 with Emma, daughter of Richard the Duke of the Normans. On the death of Ethelred in 1016, Canute obtained possession of the throne, and next year married the widowed Queen Emma, by whom he had two children, Gunhild and Hardicanute. He lived in Normandy, but was invited to his court by his half-brother Hardicanute in 1041, and next year succeeded him as king. This was brought about mainly by the great Earl Godwin, whose only daughter, Edith, Edward married in 1045. He was perpetually influenced by his foreign favourites, and the history of his reign is merely the record of the struggle of the Norman or court party with the national party, led by Godwin and his son Harold. Edward died January 5, 1066, and was canonized for his monklike virtues by Pope Alexander III in 1161. See early lives of Edward, edited by H. R. Luard ('Record' series, 1858), and Stenton's *Anglo-Saxon England* (1947).

EDWARD, kings of England:

Edward I (1239–1307), the elder son of Henry III and Eleanor of Provence, was born at Westminster, June 17, 1239. In 1254 he married Eleanor of Castile, receiving from his father Gascony, Ireland and Wales, where in fighting the turbulent Welshmen he learned his first lessons in warfare. At the Parliament of Oxford (1258) he supported his father against the barons, but then sided with Simon de Montfort, still, however, maintaining personal loyalty to his father. Rashness lost him the battle of Lewes (1264), he was held hostage for his father's pledges, but escaped, and the struggle ended in 1265 with Simon's death on Evesham field. Joining the last crusade, Edward won renown as a knight, but failed to save the Frankish kingdom in the East. His father died in November 1272, but the new king did not return to England till August 1274. At his coronation he received the homage of Alexander III of Scotland for his lands in England, but Prince Llewelyn of Wales paid his homage only in 1276. Edward at once began that wise policy of domestic consolidation and financial as well as legal reform that makes his reign so important an epoch. After the defeat and death of Llewelyn in 1282, by the famous Statute of Wales (1284) the principality was finally annexed to the English crown. Finding most of his judges corrupt, he punished them ruthlessly, then in 1290 banished all the Jews (16,000) on the ground of extortionate usury. (He had earlier hanged 280 for money-clipping and forgery.) The death of the young Scottish queen, the Maid of Norway, that same year gave Edward a chance of reasserting a tenuous claim to the overlordship of Scotland. He decided against Bruce (q.v.) and in favour of John Baliol, who on his accession paid homage for the whole kingdom of Scotland. Meantime the ambitions of the French king, Philip IV, forced Edward to take measures to preserve his French possessions, and in 1295 he summoned an assembly of the estates, practically the first representative parliament. The growing exasperation of the Scots flared into open warfare in 1296. Edward marched north, captured Berwick, penetrated to Aberdeen, Banff and Elgin, accepted Baliol's surrender of the crown at Montrose, and returned to Berwick with the coronation stone. Here he received the fealty of the Scottish clergy, barons and gentry, whose names fill the Ragman Roll. He could now turn to France, but the clergy and the great barons refused to take part in foreign war, and Edward had to compromise, especially since Wallace (q.v.) had begun guerrilla warfare, won a great victory at Stirling Bridge, and ravaged England from Newcastle to Carlisle. Edward patched up his Continental differences and defeated Wallace at Falkirk in 1298. In 1305, the year of Wallace's execution, Edward prepared a new constitution for Scotland, divided it into sheriffdoms, and arranged for Scots representation in the English parliament. But Scotland was not subdued; Robert Bruce, who had hitherto played a dubious game, murdered his rival Comyn in 1306, was crowned at Scone, and kept up an incessant struggle. Edward, old and infirm, marched north, but died July 7, 1307, at Burgh-on-Sands near Carlisle. He charged his son Edward to carry his bones with the army until he had utterly subdued the Scots; but the young prince buried him in Westminster, where a slab is inscribed: ' Eduardus

primus, Scotorum malleus, hic est'. See Seeley's *Life and Reign of Edward I* (1871); vol. ii of Stubbs' *Constitutional History*, his *Early Plantagenets* (1876), and his prefaces to the *Chronicles of Edward I and Edward II* (1882–83); Tout's *Edward I* (1893); Sir J. H. Ramsay's *Dawn of the Constitution* (1908).

Edward II (1284–1327), son of the preceding, was born at Caernarvon, April 25, 1284, and in 1301 was created Prince of Wales, the first English heir-apparent who bore that title. In 1297, as regent in his father's absence, he signed the famous *Confirmatio Cartarum*. He accompanied his father on his Scottish expeditions, but was absent at his death, and, instead of carrying out his dying behest, returned to London and the companionship of his favourite, the Gascon, Piers de Gaveston. He created him Earl of Cornwall, and on his departure for France in 1308 to marry Isabella, daughter of Philip IV, left him guardian of the kingdom. The indignant nobles demanded his banishment; twice he was forced to leave England; at length they rose, captured Gaveston, and executed him in 1312. In 1314 Edward invaded Scotland with a large army. At Bannockburn, however, on June 24, he was defeated with immense slaughter by Bruce, who thus secured the final independence of his kingdom, and who by the capture of Berwick in 1318 undid every trace of the conquest of Edward I. This disaster was followed by risings in Wales and Ireland, and two seasons of unexampled famine and pestilence. From this time the influence of Lancaster was supreme, but in 1321, with the aid of his new favourites, Hugh le Despenser and his son, Edward overthrew Lancaster, and put him to death. He then invaded Scotland for the last time with no particular success, and in 1323 concluded a truce for thirteen years. A dispute now arose with Charles IV of France, brother of his wife, Isabella, in regard to Edward's territories in that country. Charles seized these, whereupon Edward sent Isabella to effect an amicable arrangement. She despised her husband, hated the Despensers, and had contracted a guilty passion for Mortimer, one of the disaffected nobles; so, having obtained possession of the young Prince Edward, she landed with a large body of malcontents on the coast of Suffolk, September 24, 1326. The Despensers were executed, and Edward, taken captive, had to abdicate. He was murdered in Berkeley Castle, September 21, 1327. See Tout's *The Place of the Reign of Edward II in English History* (1914).

Edward III (1312–77), son of the preceding, was born at Windsor, November 13, 1312, and was crowned January 29, 1327. During his minority the country was really governed by Mortimer and Isabella. In 1328 Edward married Philippa of Hainault, and two years later put Mortimer to death, and banished his mother to Castle Rising. Invading Scotland to assist Edward Baliol, who, on the death of Bruce, had got himself crowned at Scone, he defeated the Scots at Halidon Hill, near Berwick, in 1333, whereupon Baliol did homage to Edward for his possessions, but a few months later had to flee the kingdom. Despite successive English invasions the Scots rallied each time. Charles IV of France having died without a son, Edward claimed the crown in right of his mother, Isabella, sister of Charles; but as the law of France excluded females from the throne, his claim was utterly groundless. Edward admitted that his mother could not inherit the crown, but affirmed that he, as her son, might. He declared war against Philip in 1337, raising money by tallages, forced loans, and by seizing wool. Despite the brilliant sea victory at Sluys in 1340, he was at first unsuccessful, and soon found himself compelled to purchase the grants of money necessary for the war with concessions of privileges, which he occasionally evaded. At length in 1346, accompanied by his eldest son, the Black Prince, he again invaded France, conquered a great part of Normandy, marched to the gates of Paris, and on August 26, 1346, inflicted a terrible defeat on the French at Crécy. After some further successes, and the fall of Calais after a year's siege, a truce for a few months was concluded, afterwards from time to time extended. Meanwhile the Scots, in 1346, had been defeated at Neville's Cross near Durham, and their king, David II, taken prisoner, while in 1349 the Black Death had carried off a third of the population of England, and permanently changed the whole relations between labourer and master. The war began anew in 1355, and next year, on September 19, the Black Prince obtained a brilliant victory at Poitiers, where King John of France was taken prisoner. The Scottish king was released under promise of a ransom of 100,000 merks in 1357, and King John in 1360, when a peace was concluded. John, finding it impossible to raise his proposed ransom, returned to captivity, and died in London in 1364. Shortly before this date, David of Scotland made a secret agreement with Edward, by which his kingdom, if he died without male issue, was to be handed over to the English sovereign. The Black Prince was obliged in 1374 to conclude a truce for three years; and, for all his brilliant victories, Edward was at the last unsuccessful. Neither in Scotland nor in France did he realize his desires. Affairs at home were no less unsatisfactory in his last years, and public finance drifted hopelessly into ruin. He quarrelled with his parliaments, and saw public discontent sap loyalty, while he gave himself up to the influence of the rapacious Alice Perrers, his mistress from 1366, and let the government slip into the hands of his fourth son, John of Gaunt. The Black Prince, who had headed a party opposed to his father's policy, died June 8, 1376, and the king himself expired almost alone on June 21, 1377. See Lives by Longman (1869), Warburton (1875) and Mackinnon (1900).

Edward IV (1442–83), son of Richard, Duke of York, and Cicely Nevill, daughter of the first Earl of Westmorland, was born at Rouen, April 28, 1442, and bore the title of Earl of March. On his father's defeat and death at Wakefield (December 30, 1460), he found himself head of a strong party. He at once set out from Gloucester, defeated the

Lancastrians at Mortimer's Cross (February 2, 1461), lost in the person of Warwick the second battle of St Albans (February 17); but on the 26th, taking advantage of the reaction of the south, entered London in triumph as king. On March 29, he secured the crown by the battle of Towton, near York. Queen Margaret kept up the struggle in the north, but her defeats at Hedgeley Moor and Hexham (1464) and the capture of Henry VI (1465) in the meantime crushed her hopes. The young Edward was handsome and frank in manners, and quickly became popular. The commons granted him the wool tax and tonnage and poundage for life. But he imperilled his popularity by his licentiousness; and his ill-advised marriage (1464) with Elizabeth Woodville displeased Warwick and many of his nobility, whose disaffection was increased by the honours heaped upon the queen's relations. Warwick won over the king's brother, the Duke of Clarence, and married him to his daughter Isabel. Meantime popular discontent culminated in insurrections in the north. Warwick crossed to France, and made friends with his ancient enemy, Queen Margaret, and cemented the alliance by marrying his daughter Ann to her son, Prince Edward. In September 1470 Warwick landed in England, and Edward, deserted on every side, fled to Flanders; six months later he landed at Ravenspur to meet Warwick. Clarence now came over to his side, and in the battle at Barnet, April 14, 1471, the ' Kingmaker ' fell on the field of his defeat. Edward put an end to the war by the victory over Queen Margaret at Tewkesbury (May 4). He showed his savagery in the murder of Prince Edward and his vengeance upon the other captives. The night of his arrival in London Henry VI died in the Tower—of a broken heart, as was given out; and Edward used his power to extort money by forced loans. In 1478 he stained his name by the private execution of Clarence in the Tower. Edward's partisanship of Burgundy against France brought no glory; he died suddenly, April 9, 1483, worn out by his debaucheries. See Lives by Stratford (1910), Scofield (1923), and Gairdner's *Houses of Lancaster and York* (1874).

Edward V (1470–83), son of the preceding, was born in the Westminster Sanctuary, November 3, 1470. At the death of his father, his maternal uncle, Earl Rivers, set out with him from Ludlow for London. But Richard, Duke of Gloucester, got possession of him at Northampton, brought him to the capital on May 4, 1483, and the same month was appointed Protector. In June his brother, the young Duke of York, also fell into Richard's hands. The two boys were removed to the Tower, and never more heard of. In 1674 some bones were discovered and re-interred as theirs in Westminster Abbey. There is at least no doubt that they were murdered. See Gairdner's *Richard III* (1878), and Tanner and Wright, *Recent investigations regarding the Fate of the Princes in the Tower* (1935).

Edward VI (1537–53), born at Hampton Court, October 12, 1537, was Henry VIII's son by his third queen, Jane Seymour. On

January 21, 1547, he succeeded Henry, when Edward Seymour, Earl of Hertford, his uncle, got himself made Protector, allied himself with the Reformed party, and invaded Scotland to enforce the marriage contract between Edward and Mary, Queen of Scots. At Pinkie the Scots were defeated, and Scotland lay at the mercy of Seymour, now self-created Duke of Somerset. Two rebellions—of Catholics in Devon, and of agrarian malcontents, under Ket the tanner, at Norwich—were suppressed in 1549; but soon afterwards the Protector was accused of over-ambition, and executed (January 22, 1552), John Dudley, Earl of Warwick, being created Duke of Northumberland. The people regretted Somerset, for Dudley was a worse and a weaker man. Indifferent in matters of religion (though he died a professed Catholic), he too let the Reformation take its course under Cranmer. Aiming to secure the succession for his family, he married his fourth son, Lord Guildford Dudley, to Lady Jane Grey (q.v.); and he worked upon the dying boy king to exclude his sisters and nominate Lady Jane as his successor. Edward consented, and died on July 6, 1553, probably from the effect of quack nostrums on a consumptive frame. See his *Literary Remains* (1857), study by Sir C. Markham (1907) and H. W. Chapman, *The Last Tudor King* (1958).

Edward VII (1841–1910), eldest son (Albert Edward) of Queen Victoria, was born at Buckingham Palace, November 9, 1841. He was educated privately, and at Edinburgh, Oxford (Christ Church), and Cambridge (Trinity). In 1860 he visited the United States and Canada; in 1862 travelled with Dean Stanley in the East; and on March 10, 1863, married Alexandra (born December 1, 1844; died November 20, 1925), eldest daughter of Christian IX of Denmark. Three sons and three daughters were born: these were Albert Victor (1864–92), Duke of Clarence (q.v.); George (1865–1936; see GEORGE V); Louise (1867–1931), Princess Royal; Victoria (1868–1935); Maud (1869–1938), who married Haakon VII of Norway; Alexander (born and died 1871). In 1871–72 the Prince of Wales had a severe attack of typhoid. He made a visit to India in 1875–76. He assisted in promoting the Royal College of Music; and the Imperial Institute was due to his suggestion. In 1900 he was shot at in Brussels. On January 22, 1901, he succeeded his mother as Edward VII. His coronation, delayed by illness, was carried out on August 9. By visits to Continental capitals the King strove to allay international animosities. He was much interested in sport. He died May 6, 1910. See Lives by Sir S. Lee (1925–27) and E. F. Benson (1933).

Edward VIII (1894–1972), born at White Lodge, Richmond, Surrey, June 23, eldest son of George V, was educated at Osborne, Dartmouth, and Magdalen College, Oxford. As Prince of Wales he was in the navy and (in World War I) the army, travelled much, and achieved considerable popularity. He succeeded his father, January 20, 1936, but abdicated December 11 on account of general disapprobation of his proposed marriage to Mrs Ernest Simpson (see below). He was thereupon given the title of Duke of Windsor, and the marriage took place on June 3, 1937. In 1940–45 he was governor of the Bahamas. See his *A King's Story* (1951), and Life by Bolitho. His wife, the **Duchess of Windsor** (1896–   ), was born Bessie Wallis Warfield at Blue Ridge Summit, Pa. In 1916 she married Lieut. E. W. Spencer of the U.S. Navy, but in 1927 the marriage was dissolved. The following year she married in London Ernest Simpson, an American-born Englishman. Well known in London society in 1930, she met the Prince of Wales at a country house party. In 1936, the year of the Prince's accession, she obtained a divorce in England, and the king subsequently made clear to Stanley Baldwin and his government his determination to marry her even if it meant giving up the throne. See her *The Heart has its Reasons* (1956).

EDWARD THE BLACK PRINCE (1330–76), eldest son of Edward III, was created Earl of Chester (1333), Duke of Cornwall (1337) and Prince of Wales (1343). In 1346, boy though he was, he fought at Crécy, and is said to have won from his black armour his popular title—a title first cited in the 16th century. In 1355–56 he undertook two marauding expeditions in France, the second signalized by the great victory of Poitiers. In 1361 he married his cousin, Joan the 'Fair Maid of Kent' (1328–85), who bore him two sons, Edward (1365–70) and the future Richard II; in 1362 his father created him Prince of Aquitaine, and next year he departed to take possession of his principality. In 1367 he espoused the cause of Pedro the Cruel (q.v.), and at Navarrete won his third great victory, taking Du Guesclin prisoner; in 1370, worn out by sickness, he mercilessly sacked Limoges. A great soldier, he was a failure as an administrator. See Lives by G. P. R. James (1822), Dunn-Pattison (1910) and H. D. Sedgwick (1932).

EDWARDES, (1) **George** (1852–1915), English theatrical manager, born in Clee, Lincs, the son of a customs officer. In 1881 he became business manager at the Savoy Theatre, leaving in 1885 to enter into partnership with John Hollingshead at the Gaiety; in 1886 he took over the sole management. In 1893 he built Daly's theatre for Augustin Daly. He is known as the father of musical comedy, the form of which he standardized by his gift of foreseeing public taste and recognizing and developing talent. His lovable personality was intensified by his good looks, his generosity and his characteristically slow, plaintive voice. His many successes include *The Geisha*, *The Merry Widow*, *The Gaiety Girl* and *The Quaker Girl*.

(2) **Sir Herbert Benjamin** (1819–68), entered the East India Company's army in 1840, became assistant to Sir Henry Lawrence and distinguished himself in the Sikh wars and the Mutiny. Edwardesabad in Northwest Frontier Province was named after him. See memoir by his wife (1886).

EDWARDS, (1) **Amelia Blandford** (1831–92), English novelist, born in London, author of *My Brother's Wife* (1855), *Debenham's Vow* (1869) and *Lord Brackenbury* (1880). She was founder of the Egyptian Exploration Fund, and contributed papers on Egyptology to the principal European and American journals.

Her cousin **Matilda Barbara Betham-Edwards** (1836–1919), also wrote novels, poems and stories, many of which have been translated into French and German. See her *Reminiscences* (1898) and *Mid-Victorian Memories* (1919).

(2) **Bryan** (1743–1800), English writer, born at Westbury, Wilts, spent some thirty years in Jamaica, in 1796 became M.P. for Grampound, and wrote *History of the British West Indies* (1793), &c.

(3) **Edward** (1812–86), English pioneer librarian, born in London, helped in the reorganization of the British Museum Library in 1839, became first librarian of Manchester Free Library (1850–58), and wrote books on library history.

(4) **Jonathan** (1703–58), American theologian and metaphysician, was born at East Windsor, Conn., graduated at Yale in 1720, and was ordained in 1727 colleague to his grandfather, Solomon Stoddard (1643–1729), at Northampton, Mass. The happiness and success of his first seventeen years was broken by a bitter dispute with his people about the circulation of certain books which he considered immoral; he advocated a return to the earlier Congregational rule of refusing to admit persons to communion who were not consciously converted, and resigned his ministry in 1750. He next laboured as missionary to the Housatonnuck Indians until he was called to the presidency of Princeton College, but he died thirty-four days after his installation, March 22, 1758. Edwards is among America's most original thinkers in metaphysics, in virtue of his rigidly Calvinist treatise on the *Freedom of the Will* (1754). Other works were *Original Sin* (1758), *Christian Virtue* (1788) and *The End for which God created the World* (1789). See Lives by A. V. G. Allen (1889), O. E. Winslow (1940) and P. Miller (N.Y. 1949), who also edited the *Works* (1957 *et seq.*).

(5) **Jonathan** (1745–1801), second son of (4), born in Northampton, Mass., graduated at New Jersey in 1765. He became in 1769 pastor at White Haven, Conn., in 1796 at Colebrook, Conn., and in 1799 president of the new college at Schenectady, New York. His works include *A Dissertation concerning Liberty and Necessity* (1797) and *On the Necessity of the Atonement* (1785).

(6) **Oliver** (1835–1904), American Federal general, born at Springfield, Mass., distinguished himself in the Battle of the Wilderness (1864), and at Sailor's Creek, where he captured Generals Custis, Lee and Ewell.

(7) **Richard** (c. 1523–66), English playwright, was born in Somerset, studied at Corpus Christi College, Oxford, and became choirmaster of the Chapel Royal.

EDWIN, St (585–633), king of Northumbria, was the son of Ella, king of Deira, who died in 588, whereupon Ethelric, king of Bernicia, seized his territories. He was brought up in North Wales, and at length found refuge with Redwald, king of East Anglia, who took up arms on his behalf against Ethelfrith, the son

of his oppressor, who was defeated and killed in a great battle (617). Edwin now obtained Deira, and overrunning Bernicia, formed a united Northumbria, extending to Edinburgh, which he fortified, and which is traditionally linked with his name. He next conquered the West Riding, and pushed his power westward as far as Anglesea and Man. After Redwald's death he obtained the overlordship of East Anglia, and by a victory over the West Saxons, that of all England, save Kent. Edwin had already married Ethelburga, daughter of Ethelbert, the convert of Augustine. Under Paulinus' influence he was converted to Christianity, and baptized with his nobles in 627. He fell in battle with Mercians and Welsh at Heathfield (probably Hatfield Chase, Yorkshire), and was afterwards canonized. See Alexander Smith's poem, *Edwin of Deira* (1861).

EECKHOUT, Gerbrand van den, *ayk'howt* (1621–74), Dutch religious painter, a pupil of Rembrandt, was born and died at Amsterdam.

EEDEN, Frederik Willem van, *ay'dĕn* (1860–1932), Dutch poet and writer, born at Haarlem, left a promising medical career for literature. In addition to lyrical verse he wrote plays, including the social satire *IJsbrand* (1908) and the tragedy *De Heks van Haarlem* (1915), also novels such as *Johannes Viator* (1892) and *De Kleine Johannes* (1886–1906), of which the latter has been translated into English. See studies by L. J. M. Feber (1922) and G. Kalff (1927).

EGAN, (1) **Maurice François** (1852–1924), American diplomat and writer, born at Philadelphia, minister to Denmark from 1907, wrote interesting reminiscences, particularly of the First World War period, as well as poetry, short stories, &c.

(2) **Pierce** (1772–1849), English writer born in London, was the author of many works, including *Boxiana* (1818–24) and *Life in London* (1821). The last, immortalized in Thackeray's *Roundabout Papers*, had coloured illustrations by the brothers Cruikshank. His son, **Pierce** (1814–80), wrote innumerable novels, chiefly for *Reynolds' Miscellany* and the *London Journal*.

EGBERT (d. 839), king of the West Saxons, was son of Ealhmund of Kent. For laying claim to the West Saxon kingship after the death of Cynegils (786), he was driven to Charlemagne's court, whence he returned in 802 to fill the throne of Wessex. After twelve years came a war with the Cornish, and one with the Mercians, in which the great victory of Ellandune (probably near Winchester) secured him the over-lordship of Mercia. In 829 the Northumbrians also accepted him as their suzerain, and thus Egbert became the first real king of England, though he did not assume that style. In 835 Egbert was defeated by Scandinavian pirates in a battle in Dorsetshire, but in 837 he defeated, at Hengestdune near the Tamar, a huge northern host allied with Cornish insurgents.

EGBERT, St (639–729), a Northumbrian who lived much in Ireland, and died in Iona.

EGEDE, Hans, *ay'gĕ-dĕ* (1686–1758), the apostle of Greenland, was born in Norway and was pastor of Vagen 1707–17. In 1721, after studying the language, he embarked for Greenland, with his wife, two sons and some companions. He remained there fifteen years and secured a permanent footing for the Christian mission. The death of his wife in 1736 drove him from Greenland, but at Copenhagen he was busy promoting the Greenland mission, of which in 1740 he became bishop. See his *Det gamle Grönland's nye Perlustration* (1729 and 1741).—His son, **Paul** (1708–89), born in Norway, succeeded him, and, as bishop, completed in 1766 the translation of the New Testament, besides a catechism (1756) and prayer book (1783).

EGERTON, *ej'-*, an English family including Earls and Dukes of Bridgewater, Earls of Ellesmere and their descendants, among them the following:

(1) **Francis, 3rd Duke of Bridgewater** (1736–1803), known as the 'father of British inland navigation', constructed, after the plans of the celebrated Brindley (q.v.), the earliest canal in England, 42 miles long, uniting Worsley with Manchester and Runcorn on the Mersey above Liverpool. See Malet, *The Canal Duke* (1961).

(2) **Francis, 1st Earl of Ellesmere** (1800–57), English statesman, second son of the 1st Duke of Sutherland, was born in London, and educated at Eton and Christ Church, Oxford. He was Irish secretary (1828–30) and secretary for war (1830). In 1833, on succeeding to the Bridgewater estates, he assumed the name of Egerton, and in 1846 was created Earl of Ellesmere. He translated *Faust*, &c.

(3) **Francis Henry, 8th Earl of Bridgewater** (1756–1829), son of John Egerton, Bishop of Durham, was a prebendary of Durham, but lived in Paris for many years and kept his house and garden full of animals dressed up like manikins, because he was fond of shooting. He left £8000 to be paid to the author of the best treatise on the subject of God manifested in Creation, which was eventually awarded to eight authors of the 'Bridgewater Treatises', by the Royal Society.

(4) **John, 1st Earl of Bridgewater,** son of (5), whose induction as lord-lieutenant of Wales at Ludlow Castle (1634) provided the occasion for Milton's *Comus*.

(5) **Sir Thomas, Baron Ellesmere and Viscount Brackley** (1540–1617), English lawyer and statesman, father of (4), was educated at Brasenose College, Oxford, and Lincoln's Inn and was called to the bar in 1572. Acquiring a large practice in chancery, he became solicitor-general in 1581, a confidant of Queen Elizabeth and James I despite Lord Burghley, a friend of Francis Bacon and Essex, took part in the trial of Mary, Queen of Scots (1586) and of Essex (1600–01), and became lord chancellor in 1603. He helped to draft the Act of Union of England and Scotland (1606) and in the struggle with Coke and the courts of common law, maintained the supremacy of his own court, Coke's friends corrupting his title to 'Break-Law'.

EGGE, Peter Andreas, *ay'gė* (1869–1959), Norwegian novelist, born at Trondheim. Of humble peasant stock and too poor to pursue his education, he was a discovery of

Knut Hamsun (q.v.), who arranged for the publication of his first novel, *Common People* (1891). His first real success was with *The Heart* (1917), which is a serious and penetrating study of marriage between two dissimilar personalities, and *Hansine Solstad* (1926), a delicate, sympathetic delineation of a woman wrongfully accused of theft in her youth, whose supposed crime dogs her through life. Egge also wrote plays in which he followed Ibsen in creating drama from defects of character.

EGGLESTON, Edward (1837–1902), American author, born at Vevay, Ind., was Methodist minister, editor, and wrote *The Hoosier Schoolmaster* (1871) and *The Faith Doctor* (1891).

EGIDIUS. See GILES, ST.

EGINHARD. See EINHARD.

EGINTON, Francis (1737–1805), a reviver in 1781 of glass-painting at Birmingham.

EGLINTON AND WINTON, Archibald William Montgomerie, 13th Earl of (1812–61), twice lord-lieutenant of Ireland, was a well-known patron of the turf and field-sports, and is chiefly remembered for his splendid reproduction of a tournament at Eglinton Castle in 1839. Among the knights was Louis Napoleon. See Fraser's *Memorials of the Montgomeries* (1859).

EGMONT, Lamoral, Count of, Prince of Gavre (1522–68), Flemish statesman and soldier, was born at the castle of La Hamaide, in Hainault. He accompanied Charles V to Algiers in 1541 and in all his later campaigns, distinguished himself at St Quentin (1557) and Gravelines (1558), for which he was made governor of Flanders and Artois. He now sided with the party in the Netherlands that was dissatisfied with Philip's Catholic policy, and from a courtier became a hero of the people; but it is doubtful whether he was actuated by high motives or by self-interest and disappointed ambition. At any rate, when insurrections took place, he broke with the Prince of Orange and the 'Beggars' League'. He seemed to have restored order and to have gained the confidence of the Duke of Alva, now (1567) lieutenant-general to the Netherlands; but suddenly he and Count Horn were seized, condemned to death, and beheaded at Brussels. See a work by Juste (1862) and Motley's *Dutch Republic* (1856).

EHRENBERG, Christian Gottfried (1795–1876), naturalist, born at Delitzsch in Prussian Saxony, travelled in Egypt, Syria, Arabia and Central Asia. His works on microscopic organisms founded a new branch of science, and he discovered that phosphorescence in the sea is caused by living organisms.

EHRENBURG, Ilya (1891–1967), Russian writer, born in Moscow, worked for many years in Paris as a journalist. Among his best works are *The Adventures of Julio Jurenito* (Eng. tr. 1930), a satire on the aftermath of World War I, *The Fall of Paris* (1941) and *The Storm* (1947), both novels about World War II, for which he received Stalin prizes, and *The Thaw* (1954). Among many other awards, he received two Orders of Lenin.

EHRLICH, Paul, *ayr'leeKH* (1854–1915), German bacteriologist, born of Jewish family at Strehlen, Silesia, was a pioneer in haematology, discovered salvarsan and propounded the side-chain theory in immunology. He was joint winner, with Metchnikov, of the 1908 Nobel prize for medicine.

EICHENDORFF, Joseph Freiherr von, *īkh'endorf* (1788–1857), German poet, novelist and critic, born near Ratibor, is best remembered for his romantic lyrics, though two of his novels, *Aus dem Leben eines Taugenichts* (1826) and *Das Marmorbild* (1826), have been translated into English.

EICHHORN, Johann Gottfried, *īkh'horn* (1752–1827), German biblical scholar, born at Dörrenzimmern in Franconia, became in 1775 professor of Oriental Languages at Jena, in 1788 at Göttingen. His Introductions to the Old and New Testaments (1780–1814) were the first attempt to apply the ordinary methods of literary criticism to Scripture. He derived each of the four gospels from one original Greek gospel.

EICHMANN, Karl Adolf, *īkh'mahn* (1906–62), Austrian Nazi war criminal, born at Solingen, became a member of the S.S. and organiser of anti-Semitic activities. Captured by U.S. forces in 1945, he escaped from prison some months later, having kept his identity hidden, and in 1950 reached Argentina. He was traced by Israeli agents and in 1960, seized, taken to Israel, condemned and executed. See studies by Reynolds, Katz and Adouby (1961) and by Russell of Liverpool (1962).

EIFFEL, Gustave, *ef-el* (1832–1923), French engineer, born at Dijon, designed notable bridges and viaducts. The Eiffel Tower, 985 feet high, was erected in 1887–89 on the Champ-de-Mars in Paris at a cost of £260,000 In 1893 he was condemned to two years' imprisonment and fined for breach of trust in connection with the Panamá Canal.

EIJKMAN, Christiaan, *īkh'man* (1858–1930), Dutch physician, first to produce a dietary deficiency disease experimentally and to propose the concept of ' essential food factors ', later called vitamins. He shared the Nobel prize for medicine with Hopkins in 1929.

EINAUDI, Luigi, *ay-now'dee* (1874–1961), was professor of public finance at Turin (1902–49), senator (1915–45), president of Italy (1948–55).

EINHARD, or Eginhard (*c.* 770–840), Frankish historian, born in East Franconia, was sent to the court of Charlemagne, where he became a pupil of Alcuin and a favourite (but not the son-in-law) of the emperor, as also of his successor Louis. For years lay abbot of various monasteries, he ultimately retired to Mühlheim. His Life of Charlemagne (*c.* 820) is the great biographical work of the Middle Ages (edns. by Jaffé, 1876; Holder, 1882; Garrod and Mowat, 1915; Eng. trans. by Glaister, 1877). His *Annales Francorum* embraces the period 741–829; his *Epistolæ* number sixty-two. See French edition of his works by Teulet, with translation and Life (1848).

EINSTEIN, *īn-stīn*, (1) **Albert** (1879–1955), German-born mathematical physicist, who ranks with Galileo and Newton as one of the great conceptual revisors of man's understanding of the universe. Born at Ulm, Bavaria, of Jewish parents, he was educated at Munich, moved with his parents to Milan in 1894, but completed his education at Aarau and the Zürich Polytechnic, under Minowski. Taking Swiss nationality in 1901, he was appointed examiner at the Swiss Patent Office (1902–05) and began to publish original papers on the theoretical aspects of problems in physics, such as the Brownian movement, Planck's quantum theory, &c. He became world famous by his special (1905) and general (1916) theories of relativity. The special theory provided,' by the merging of the traditionally absolute concepts of space and time into a space-time continuum, a new system of mechanics which could accommodate Maxwell's electromagnetic field theory as well as the hitherto inexplicable results of the Michelson-Morley experiments (from 1881) on the speed of light, which showed that the relative velocities of light from the sun were the same in the direction of the earth's rotation as when opposed to it. Neither of these was consistent with Newtonian mechanics with its insistence on ' action at a distance ' and a light-bearing space-referential ether. Einstein showed that in the case of rapid relative motion involving velocities approaching the speed of light, puzzling phenomena such as decreased size and mass are to be expected. Furthermore, special relativity allowed the laws of nature to be written in a mathematical form which was the same for all observers not acted upon by a force. His general theory (1916) waived this inertial requirement for observers and accounted for the slow rotation of the elliptical path of the planet Mercury which Newtonian gravitational theory failed to do. In 1909 a special professorship was created for Einstein at Zürich, in 1911 he became professor at Prague, in 1912 he returned to Zürich and from 1914 to 1933 he was director of the Kaiser Wilhelm Physical Institute in Berlin. An important consequence of Einstein's theory, that the wavelength of light emitted by atoms should be influenced by gravitational field, was substantiated in 1919 by the observations by Eddington and others conducted during the solar eclipse which show that light rays from distant stars bend when passing through the sun's gravitational field. After Hitler's rise to power, he left Germany, renounced German citizenship, lectured at Oxford and Cambridge, and from 1934 at Princeton, U.S.A. In September 1939 he wrote his historic letter to President Roosevelt advising the feasibility of a super-bomb based on atomic fission and the danger of a German lead in this field. In 1940 he became an American citizen and was appointed professor at Princeton. He refused to accept Heisenberg's indeterminacy principle and spent the remainder of his life attempting by means of his unified field theory (1950) to establish a merger between quantum theory and his general theory of relativity similar to that achieved by Dirac in 1928 with the special theory, thus bringing subatomic phenomena, which can only be treated statistically, and large-scale physical phenomena under one set of determinate laws. After the war, he urged international control of atomic weapons and protested against the proceedings of the un-American Activities Senate Subcommittee which had arraigned many of his fellow scientists. In 1960 experiments conducted at Harwell yielded some confirmation of Einstein's general theory. He wrote books, *About Zionism* (1930) and on *Why War* (1933) with Sigmund Freud. He was awarded the Nobel prize (1921), elected foreign member of the Royal Society (1921) and awarded its Copley medal in 1925 and the gold medal of the Royal Astronomical Society (1926). See his expanded fourth edition, *The Meaning of Relativity* (1950), and popular accounts by Bertrand Russell, revised Pirani (1957), and J. A. Coleman (1958).

(2) **Alfred** (1880–1952), German musicologist, born at Munich, fled the Nazi régime in 1933 and lived in Florence and London. He collaborated in several well-known musical reference books, including *Eaglefield's Dictionary of Modern Music*, but is perhaps best remembered for his work on Mozart, especially the revision of Köchel's catalogue. See his posthumous *Essays on Music* (1958).

EINTHOVEN, Willem, *aynt'hō-fen* (1860–1927), Dutch physiologist, became professor of Physiology at Leyden in 1886, invented the string galvanometer, causing great advances in electrocardiography, and was awarded the Nobel prize for medicine in 1924.

EISENHOWER, Dwight David (1890–1969), American general and 34th U.S. president, born at Denison, Texas, of immigrant stock originating in the Rhineland. He graduated from the West Point Military Academy in 1915. Taking the War College course in 1928 and gaining experience under the secretary of war, by 1939 he had become chief military assistant to General MacArthur in the Philippines. On the war's outbreak he obtained leave to return to troop duty in the U.S. Carefully groomed for the responsibility by General George C. Marshall, in 1942 he assumed command of allied forces mustered for the amphibious descent on French North Africa. Without experience of high command, but perceptive and assimilative, he rapidly learned to translate strategic theory into terms of practical action. At the same time he exhibited a rare genius for smoothly coordinating the activities of an interallied staff, perhaps his most valuable contribution to the war effort. His successful conduct of the North African venture, plus the preponderant American element in the forces earmarked for ' Operation Overlord ', led to his selection as supreme commander for the 1944 cross-channel invasion of the Continental mainland; which he resolutely launched despite unnervingly capricious weather conditions. With an acute appreciation of the psychology of his U.S. forces, his strategical preference for the drive to cross the Rhine was for a shoulder-to-shoulder advance in line; a choice of method that found some justification in the failure of the ' left-hook ' stroke at Arnhem. But his reluctance to push on beyond the Elbe and occupy Berlin, and his quiescence in the hasty dismantling of the Anglo-American armies, resulted in Russia's emergence as the leading military power in Europe. Among many

honours, he received an honorary O.M. in 1945, and in 1948 became for a while president of Columbia University. With the erection of NATO in 1950 he was made supreme commander of the combined land forces, but in 1952 the popularity which he had gained in Europe swept him to nomination and ultimate victory in the presidential elections. Standing as a Republican, he won by a large majority despite the even balance of parties in the House, and was re-elected in 1956. During his presidency the U.S. government was preoccupied with foreign policy and the campaign against Communism, and undercurrents of extremism and excess of zeal often placed the President in an invidious position, but his political inexperience was balanced by sincerity, integrity and a flair for conciliation. See his *Crusade in Europe* (1948), *Waging Peace* (1965), the autobiographical *At Ease* (1968), and study by Childs (1959).

EISENSTEIN, Sergi Mikhailovich, *ī'zen-shtīn* (1898–1948), Russian film director, born in Riga, launched into films from theatrical scene painting. His substitution of the group or crowd for the traditional hero, his consummate skill in cutting and recutting to achieve mounting impressionistic effects as in the macabre Odessa steps sequence of *The Battleship Potemkin* (1925), besides being good Marxism, greatly influenced film art and gave birth to the British documentary film. Later films were *Alexander Nevski* (1938), *The Magic Seed* (1941) and the masterpiece *Ivan the Terrible* (1944) with its sequel *The Boyars Plot*, the last named being banned in the Soviet Union for many years. See his notes on film aesthetics, translated and edited by J. Leyda, *The Film Sense* (1943) and *Film Form* (1951) and his notebooks, trans. X. Danko (1959).

EISNER, Kurt, *īs'nèr* (1867–1919), German politician, born in Berlin, leader of the Bavarian revolution of 1918–19, and first president of the Bavarian republic, was a Jewish journalist. He was assassinated in Munich. See study by F. Fechenbach (1929).

EKEBERG, Anders Gustaf, *ay'kė-berg* (1767–1813), Swedish chemist and mineralogist. Professor of Chemistry at Uppsala, he discovered the element ' tantalum ' in 1802, choosing the name because of the tantalising work involved in finding something to react with it.

EKHOF, Konrad (1720–78), German actor and playwright, born at Hamburg. He founded an experimental dramatic academy in Schwerin in 1753, and later opened a theatrical school in Hamburg, where he lived for most of his career. A leading member successively of the famous Schönemann and Ackermann companies and of the national theatre at Hamburg, he did much to raise the standard of acting in Germany. From 1774 he was co-director of the Court Theatre at Gotha.

ELAGABALUS. See HELIOGABALUS.

ELCANO. See CANO (2).

ELCHO, Lord. See WEMYSS.

ELDON, John Scott, 1st Earl of (1751–1838), English lawyer and politician, born at Newcastle, became M.P. (1782), knight and solicitor-general (1788), attorney-general (1793), chief justice of common pleas (1799), lord chancellor (1801; almost continuously till 1827), earl (1821). Eldon was a great lawyer, but no statesman; for forty years he opposed reform and religious liberty. See *Lives* by Surtees (1844) and Twiss (1846), and Campbell's *Lives of the Chancellors*.

ELEANOR OF AQUITAINE (*c.* 1122–1204), in 1137 married the future Louis VII of France, by him was divorced in 1152, and straightway married the future Henry II (q.v.) of England.

ELEANOR OF CASTILE (d. 1290), daughter of Ferdinand III, in 1254 married Edward I of England. She accompanied him to the Crusades, and is said to have saved his life by sucking the poison from a wound. She died in Nottinghamshire, and the ' Eleanor Crosses ' at Northampton, Geddington and Waltham Cross are survivors of the nine erected by Edward at the halting places of her cortège. The last stopping place was Charing Cross, where a replica now stands.

ELEANOR OF PROVENCE (d. 1291), daughter of Raymond Berenger IV, married Henry III of England (1236), and died a nun.

ELGAR, Sir Edward (1857–1934), English composer, born in Broadheath near Worcester. The son of an organist and music dealer, Elgar was, apart from violin lessons, self-taught, and in his youth, as well as composing, he worked as an orchestral violinist and became conductor of the Worcester Glee Club and the County Asylum Band, and organist of St George's Roman Catholic Church, Worcester, in succession to his father. After his marriage in 1889 he went to London, but settled two years later in Malvern, and devoted himself to composition and to winning gradual acceptance, particularly among provincial choral societies. The *Enigma Variations* (1899) and the oratorio *The Dream of Gerontius* (1900) won recognition in Germany and consolidated his position as the leading figure in English music. After the Elgar Festival, held in London in 1904, the composer was knighted, and he was awarded the O.M. in 1911. His further works included the oratorios *The Apostles* and *The Kingdom*, two symphonies and concertos for violin and 'cello as well as incidental music and, during World War I, topical occasional music. After his wife's death in 1920, Elgar composed little, leaving an opera and a symphony incomplete at his death. From 1924 he was master of the King's Musick. He was the first figure of outstanding genius produced by the English musical renaissance, and his superb command of the orchestra and his mastery of late nineteenth-century musical styles within his own personal idiom was extremely influential in bringing English music back into the world's regard. See studies by B. Maine (1933), W. H. Reed (1939), D. McVeagh (1955) and P. M. Young (1955).

ELGIN, Earls of, Scottish peers of the Bruce family, of whom the following, in chronological order, are noteworthy:

(1) **Thomas Bruce, 7th Earl of Elgin and 11th Earl of Kincardine** (1766–1841), British diplomat and art connoisseur. While ambassador to the Porte (1799–1803) he became interested in the decorated sculptures on the ruined Parthenon at Athens, and, because they were in danger of wilful damage and destruction, arranged for some of them to be transported to England. This action brought criticism and accusations of vandalism, but the earl was vindicated by a government committee and the Elgin Marbles were purchased for the nation in 1816 and ultimately placed in the British Museum.

(2) **James Bruce, 8th Earl of Elgin and 12th Earl of Kincardine** (1811–63), son of (1), was born in London. As governor of Jamaica (1842–46) and as governor-general of Canada (1847–54), he displayed great administrative abilities. While on his way to China in 1857, as plenipotentiary, he heard at Singapore of the Indian mutiny, and diverted the Chinese expedition thither—thus delaying his own operations, which, after some military operations and diplomacy, issued in the treaty of Tientsin (1858). He also negotiated a treaty with Japan, and on his return home became postmaster-general. In 1860 he was again in China to enforce the treaty, and in 1861 became governor-general of India. He died at Dharmsala in the Punjab. See his *Letters and Journals* (1872); and Lives by Bourinot and J. M. Wrong (1905), and J. L. Morison (1928).

(3) **Victor Alexander Bruce, 9th Earl of Elgin and 13th Earl of Kincardine** (1849–1917), son of (2), born at Montreal, was educated at Eton and Balliol College, Oxford. A Liberal, he was viceroy of India in 1893–98, and in 1905–08 colonial secretary.

ELHUYAR, Don Fausto d' (1755–1833), Spanish chemist, who in 1783 with his brother Don Juan extracted metallic wolfram from wolframite. He later became director of mines, first in Mexico, then in Spain.

ELIA. See LAMB, CHARLES.

ELIGIUS, St. See ELOI.

ELIJAH, Gk. Elias (fl. *c.* 900 B.C.), the greatest of the prophets of Israel, lived during the reigns of Ahab and Ahaziah. See monographs by Milligan (1887) and Cheyne (1888).

ELIOT, (1) **Charles William,** LL.D. (1834–1926), American educator, born in Boston, was president of Harvard University, 1869–1909. Under him it doubled in strength, and the old curriculum was abandoned for an optional system of studies. He published, with Storer, two manuals of chemistry.

(2) **George,** pen name of **Mary Ann** or **Marian Evans** (1819–80), English novelist, born near Nuneaton, November 22, 1819. In her father, Robert Evans, a Warwickshire land agent, a man of strong character, were seen many of the traits transferred by his daughter to Adam Bede and Caleb Garth. She lost her mother, whom she loved devotedly, in 1836, and soon afterwards took entire charge of the household. Masters came from Coventry to teach her German, Italian and music—of the last she was passionately fond throughout her life. She was also an immense reader. In 1841 her father moved to Coventry, and there she met Charles Bray, a writer on the philosophy of necessity from the phrenological standpoint, and his

brother-in-law, Charles Hennell, who had published in 1838 a rationalistic *Inquiry concerning the Origin of Christianity*. At this time a fervent evangelical, she evidently at first hoped to convert her friends; but before the end of the year she had so offended her father by refusing to go to church that he threatened to break up his household and go to live with his married daughter. Subsequently she withdrew her objection to churchgoing, and the breach was avoided. In 1844 the work of translating Strauss's *Leben Jesu* was transferred from Mrs Hennell to Marian Evans, and at this she worked laboriously and in scholarly fashion until its publication in 1846. Her father died on May 31, 1849, and in June she went abroad with Mr and Mrs Bray, who left her at Geneva. In March 1850 she returned to London, and began to write for the *Westminster Review*. She became assistant editor in September 1851, and the centre of a literary circle, two of whose members were Herbert Spencer and G. H. Lewes (q.v.). It was then that she translated Feuerbach's *Essence of Christianity*, the only book that bore her real name. Gradually her intimacy with Lewes grew, and in 1854 she formed a connection with him—the great debatable step of her life—which lasted until his death in 1878. In July 1854 she went abroad with him, staying three months at Weimar, where he was preparing for his *Life of Goethe*. After a longer stay at Berlin, they returned and took up their abode first at Dover, then at East Sheen, then at Richmond. In 1856 she attempted her first story, ' The Sad Fortunes of the Rev. Amos Barton ', the commencement of the *Scenes of Clerical Life*. It came out in *Blackwood's Magazine* in 1857, and at once showed that a new author of great power had risen. ' Mr Gilfil's Love Story ' and ' Janet's Repentance ' followed quickly. *Adam Bede* (1859) had the most marvellous success; a Mr Liggins claimed the authorship. *The Mill on the Floss* (1860), *Silas Marner* (1861), *Romola* (1863) and *Felix Holt* (1866) appeared next in succession. Her first poem, *The Spanish Gypsy* (1868), was followed next year by *Agatha*, *The Legend of Jubal* and *Armgart*; and in 1871–72 appeared *Middlemarch*, by some considered her greatest work. After that *Daniel Deronda* (1876) showed a marked falling-off; so, too, did *Impressions of Theophrastus Such* (1879), a volume of somewhat miscellaneous essays. After the death of Lewes on November 28, 1878, George Eliot, who was always exceedingly dependent on some one person for affection and support, fell into a very melancholy state, from which she was roused by the solicitous kindness of John Cross (died 1924), an old friend of her own and of Lewes's, whom she married on May 6, 1880. Their married life lasted but a few months; she died in Cheyne Walk, Chelsea, on December 22, and was buried in Highgate Cemetery, in the grave next to that of Lewes. As a novelist, George Eliot will probably always stand among the greatest of the English school; her pictures of farmers and tradesmen, and the lower middle class generally of the Midland counties, are hardly surpassed

in English literature. See her *Life*, ed. by J. W. Cross (3 vols. 1885), and works by M. Blind (1883), O. Browning (1892), Leslie Stephen (1902), J. Bennett (1948), L. and E. Hanson (1952), B. Hardy (1959), J. Thale (1959), M. Crompton (1960) and W. J. Harvey (1961); also *Letters*, ed. G. S. Haight (7 vols. 1954–56), and *A Century of G. Eliot Criticism*, ed. by Haight (1966).

(3) **Sir John** (1592–1632), English statesman born at Port Eliot, near St Germans, Cornwall, entered parliament in 1614, was knighted in 1618, in 1619 was appointed vice-admiral of Devon, and in 1624 figured as an adherent of Buckingham. But in 1625 he broke with Buckingham, and in the parliament of 1626, in which Eliot was the leading spirit, his policy, one of antagonism to the king, culminated in Buckingham's impeachment. For this he was confined for eight days in the Tower. In the parliament of 1628 Eliot denounced arbitrary taxation, and helped to force the Petition of Right from Charles. For again protesting against the king's proceedings he was, on March 4, 1629, sent with eight other members to the Tower, and, refusing to acknowledge himself in error, was kept in confinement until his death of consumption, November 27, 1632. In prison he wrote an account of Charles's first parliament, *Negotium Posterorum* (first printed in 1881); a philosophico-political treatise, *The Monarchy of Man* (1879); and *An Apology for Socrates* (1881), a vindication of his own public conduct; also *De Jure Majestatis* and his *Letter-book*, both published in 1882. See Life by John Forster (1864).

(4) **John** (1604–90), the ' Indian Apostle ', was born at Widford, Herts., graduated at Cambridge, took orders, left England on religious grounds and settled at Roxbury, Mass. In 1646 he began to preach to the Indians at Nonantum nearby, establishing his native converts, who numbered 3600 in 1674, in settlements. But the numbers diminished after the war with a native King Philip (1675) and at the hands of the English. He died at Roxbury. He translated the Bible into the native dialect and helped to prepare ' The Bay Psalm-Book ' (Cambridge, 1640), the first book to be printed in New England. See Life by Francis (1836).

(5) **Sir Thomas.** See ELYOT.

(6) **Thomas Stearns** (1888–1965), American-born British poet, critic and dramatist, was born in St Louis, Missouri. After four years at Harvard (where the chief influence upon his development was that of Irving Babbitt with his ' selective ' humanism and his resistance to modern trends) he spent a year in Paris, attending lectures and improving his command of the French language. He returned to Harvard to study philosophy for three years: William James had died but he had other distinguished teachers, such as Josiah Royce and George Santayana, and, for a time, Bertrand Russell. A travelling scholarship from Harvard took him to Oxford for a year, where he worked on a doctoral dissertation of F. H. Bradley, and read Plato and Aristotle under H. H. Joachim. Persuaded by Ezra Pound, to whom he had

shown his poems, he remained in England where he thenceforth lived, taking up naturalization in 1927. After teaching for a term in High Wycombe, and for a year at Highgate Junior School, he worked for eight years in Lloyds Bank before becoming a director of the publishing firm of Faber. The enthusiastic support of Pound led to the publication of Eliot's first volume of verse, *Prufrock and Other Observations* (1917). He was introduced by Bertrand Russell into the Bloomsbury Circle, where the quality of his work was immediately recognized. His next two small volumes, the more important of which was *The Waste Land* (1922), were published by Leonard and Virginia Woolf at the Hogarth Press. *The Waste Land* was mistakenly taken to be the cynical outpouring of frustrated postwar youth, whereas the last section clearly points to a ' resurrection '. *The Hollow Men* which followed in 1925 gave more excuse for regarding Eliot at that point as a cynical defeatist.

The Waste Land had appeared in the first number of *The Criterion*, a quarterly review which Eliot edited from its beginning to its demise early in 1939. The first article in the first number was by Saintsbury, a guarantee of the traditional character of this famous magazine. While the editorial contributions showed the marked influence of Irving Babbitt, and of the writings of Charles Maurras, *The Criterion* aimed at impartiality in presenting opposed political philosophies: finding room on the one hand for J. S. Barnes's defence of Fascism, and on the other for expositions of Marxism by A. L. Rowse and Joseph Needham, and Hugh MacDiarmid's *Second Hymn to Lenin*. *The Criterion* is indispensable for a study of ideas, political and religious, between the wars, as well as for the literary developments, both here and abroad during that period. In 1927, the year in which he became a British subject, he was baptized and confirmed, having been bred a Unitarian. The publication of a volume of essays *For Lancelot Andrewes* (1928) gave his first public statement of his adherence to the Anglo-Catholic movement within the Church of England. *Ash Wednesday* (1930) is the first fruits of this new sacramental attitude. The religious plays *The Rock* (1934) and *Murder in the Cathedral* (1935) which followed sealed his reputation as the poet who had revived the verse play in the interests of Catholic devotion. His later dramas, *The Cocktail Party* (1950), *The Family Reunion* (1939), *The Confidential Clerk* (1954) and *The Elder Statesman* (1958), were to aim at being West End successes rather than sacred plays in church precincts, but Catholic doctrine inspired all these plays, sometimes to the embarrassment of critics and audience alike. Before this incursion into the theatre world Eliot delivered himself of his greatest work, *Four Quartets* (1944), which work despite its obscurity is one of the greatest philosophical poems in the language. The most rewarding is probably the last, *Little Gidding*, which with 17th-century religious dissension in mind promises reconciliation. The influence of Dante is supreme in this

noble poem. Eliot's critical work consists of literary criticism and social criticism. The former is least controversial when he deals with individual authors—the Jacobean dramatists in *The Sacred Wood* (1920), *For Lancelot Andrewes*, the admirable *Homage to Dryden*, the introduction to a selection of Kipling and the like. When writing or lecturing on literature generally he could be very provocative, as in his *Modern Education and the Classics* (1934), where he said that the Classics were to be studied not for their own sake but as a buttress for the Faith; and in *After Strange Gods* (1936), where he tries to stretch some great writers on the Procrustean bed of ' Christian Sensibility '. In social criticisms, as in *The Idea of a Christian Society* (1939) and *Notes Towards the Definition of Culture*, he is hierarchal and undemocratic. To account for Eliot's unique position both as poet and critic we must forget these controversial writings and place ourselves in the war years, 1914–18, when it was clear that Georgian poetry, which was the last phase of Romantic poetry, was exhausted. The new poetry, as announced by Ezra Pound, T. E. Hulme and Eliot, was to be related to modern life and expressed in modern idiom, preferably in free verse. Rhetoric and romantic cliches were to be avoided. Influenced by the French poets Laforgue and Corbière and also by the Jacobean dramatists, Eliot realized the programme in his satiric verse. In the phrase he coined, ' dissociation of sensibility ', he drew attention to the loss of sensual quality in poetic language since the 17th century. Another phrase he invented, ' objective correlative ', referred to the myths or symbolism which provide a working theme for the poet—hence in his case the dense obscurity of much of his *Four Quartets*. In his late essay ' Milton II ' (*On Poetry and Poets*, 1957) he confessed that he and his friends had insisted over much on these ideas and this was a sort of recantation for his abuse of Milton. But critics today have no doubt of the salutary effect of their crusade and of Eliot's poetry as having justified it. In 1948 he was awarded the O.M. and in the same year he was awarded the Nobel prize for literature. In addition to the works mentioned above, his writings include *The Use of Poetry and the Use of Criticism* (1933), *Elizabethan Essays* (1934) and *Collected Poems* (1909–62) (1963). See studies by F. O. Matthiessen (1947), Helen Gardner (1949), M. C. Bradbrook (1950), E. Drew (1950), H. Kenner (1960) and N. Frye (1963). The symposium by N. Braybrooke (1958) besides appreciation provides some details of the life of this very reticent poet. D. Gallup published a bibliography in 1952. Eliot died in London, January 4th, 1965.

ELIOTT, George Augustus. See HEATHFIELD.
ELIZABETH. Two queens of England:

Elizabeth I (1533–1603), the daughter of Henry VIII by his second wife, Anne Boleyn, was born in Greenwich Palace, September 7, 1533. When her father married Jane Seymour in 1536, she and her half-sister Mary were declared illegitimate, and her early years were passed under a cloud, though profitably so far as intellectual discipline was concerned. Her governesses and teachers were almost all devotees of the New Learning, while some were adherents of Reformation principles. During Edward VI's reign Elizabeth was subjected to the dubious attentions of Lord Seymour, high admiral of England; on Edward's death (1553) she sided with Mary against Lady Jane Grey and the Duke of Northumberland, but her identification with Protestantism aroused the suspicion of Mary and her counsellors, and led to her being implicated in Wyatt's rebellion (1554), and imprisoned in the Tower and at Woodstock. When Mary died, November 17, 1558, Elizabeth, then twenty-five years of age, ascended the throne amid the acclamation alike of Protestants, who saw in her advent a cessation to the persecutions, and of Catholics, who had more than a suspicion of her indifference in ecclesiastical matters. But her political sagacity enabled her at once to perceive that her part in Europe must be that of a Protestant sovereign, while her courage led her to act promptly. Presumably by the advice of Sir William Cecil (afterwards Lord Burghley), whom she appointed chief secretary, she issued a proclamation to the effect that the church service be read in English, and the elevation of the host be discontinued. Pope Paul IV held that, being illegitimate, she must resign all pretensions to the crown, which he claimed a right to dispose of, England being a fief of the Holy See; the sole result was to make Protestantism and patriotism synonymous in England. The Anglican Church, with its Thirty-nine Articles, its Book of Common Prayer and its acknowledgment of the headship of the sovereign, was then and there virtually established in its present form. Of the prelates who were in office only Kitchin, Bishop of Llandaff, agreed to the innovations, but of 9000 clergy, fewer than 200 resigned their livings. The policy of Elizabeth's ministry was one of peace and economy. She found the nation at war with France and Scotland, and one of her first acts was to secure peace upon favourable terms. To strengthen her own throne, Elizabeth secretly helped the Protestants in Scotland, France and the Low Countries. To prevent foreign interference in English matters was the mainspring of her foreign policy; and she lost no opportunity of weakening any power that unduly threatened her authority. The great blot upon Elizabeth's name was the execution of Mary, Queen of Scots (q.v.). She did not pursue a straightforward course when her rival was thrown into her hands in 1568. Some of her ministers were prepared to remove a life which might be turned into a dangerous tool in the hands of the Catholics. Elizabeth shrank from that course, but had not the courage or generosity to liberate Mary. Instead, she kept her a prisoner, and thus for years gave cause for conspiracy after conspiracy among the English Catholics; one of them cost the Duke of Norfolk his head. The discovery of every new plot led to demands on the part of parliament for the execution of Mary. The plots then took a graver aspect; the assassination of Elizabeth

and the placing of Mary on the throne became their object. On the discovery of Babington's conspiracy (1586) the popular cry was irresistible, and was joined in by Cecil, Walsingham and others, who had sinned too deeply against Mary to run the risk of her succession to the throne. With apparent reluctance, Elizabeth consented, and Mary was executed at Fotheringay Castle, February 8, 1587. The participation of the Catholic party in the plots was met by persecution. Many suffered under an Act passed in 1585, making it treason for a priest to be in England, and felony to harbour one. These cruel measures brought upon England the most menacing foreign attack she had yet suffered. Philip of Spain had with growing anger watched England incite rebellion among his Netherlands subjects, and allow her sea captains to devastate the Spanish harbours. His ostensible reasons for war, however, were to restore the Catholic faith, and to avenge the death of a Catholic queen. Years had been spent in preparation. In 1588 the 'Invincible Armada' sailed from the Tagus, with 8000 sailors and 20,000 soldiers, while a land army of 100,000 men was to be transported from the Netherlands under the Duke of Parma. The news aroused all England, and every man who could carry arms—Protestant and Catholic alike—was enrolled in the forces. Elizabeth herself was slow to admit the danger, although it was apparent to all her advisers, and she hesitated lamentably as to the steps to be taken to meet it. Her parsimony in such matters as the naval commissariat led to the risk of disaster, and prevented the victory from being as complete as it could have been. But to the army assembled at Tilbury she showed the courage of her race; her speech has the true ring of patriotism. A fleet of 200 vessels and 15,000 seamen was with great difficulty gathered on the southern coasts, and awaited the attack. It came in July 1588, and was only repelled by the skill and daring of the great captains of the time, Howard, Drake, Hawkins and Frobisher, providentially assisted by the elements. Elizabeth died at Richmond, March 24, 1603. From her father she inherited physical strength, resolution, energy, hauteur, a fiery temper, an inclination to cruelty and to coarseness, and a passion for splendour; to her mother may be attributed such physical attractions as she possessed, and probably also her insincerity, jealousy and love of artifice. From her sixteenth year to her fifty-sixth, one matrimonial scheme or violent passion, not always remarkable for delicacy, succeeded another. But her heart was most profoundly touched by Robert Dudley, Earl of Leicester, a handsome and clever, though shallow and dissolute man. Beyond a doubt she would have married him but for Cecil's remonstrances. After Leicester's death, Robert Devereux, Earl of Essex, succeeded to his position as favourite. Elizabeth's relations towards him, however, were rather those of a mother towards a spoiled child. When he was beheaded for rebellion in 1601 she does not seem to have exhibited much grief. She had inherited Tudor views as to the absolute supremacy of the crown over parliament. During the last thirteen years of her reign parliament assembled in 1592, 1597 and 1601; and although, partly owing to her tact and partly to its timidity, no actual collision occurred between them, it protested against monopolies, and sought to curtail Elizabeth's expenditure. 'The golden days of good Queen Bess'—of Shakespeare and Sidney—is emphatically the period in which England took up her position as a world power, and it is impossible to believe that Elizabeth had no personal part in making it what it was. The 'Virgin Queen' was cruel, capricious, insincere, at once unpleasantly masculine and weakly feminine, but she was highly popular with her subjects, and this popularity cannot be quite explained away by circumstances outside of herself. She had unquestionably the invaluable faculty of selecting as her political advisers the most capable of the men around her. See Life by J. E. Neale (1938 ed.) and his study on Elizabeth's parliaments (1953); also works by F. A. Mumby (1909, 1914), F. Chamberlin (1921); Wiesener's *La Jeunesse d'Elisabeth* (trans. 1879), Hume's *Courtships of Queen Elizabeth* (1904), A. L. Rowse's *England of Elizabeth* (1950), *The Reign of Elizabeth* by J. B. Black (1936), and study by E. Jenkins (1958).

Elizabeth II (1926–   ), formerly **Princess Elizabeth Alexandra Mary,** born in London on April 21, 1926, was proclaimed Elizabeth II on the death of her father, George VI, on February 6, 1952, and crowned on June 2, 1953. In December 1952 were announced the styles of the royal title as applicable to the Commonwealth countries, in all of which the queen is accepted as Head of the Commonwealth; she is Queen of the United Kingdom, Canada, Australia, New Zealand, Ceylon, and of several other more recently independent countries. Her husband was created Duke of Edinburgh (q.v.) on the eve of their wedding (November 20, 1947), and styled Prince Philip in 1957. Their eldest son, Prince Charles Philip Arthur George, Duke of Cornwall, born on November 14, 1948, heir-apparent, was given the title of Prince of Wales in 1958. Educated, as was his father, at Cheam and Gordonstoun, Charles spent a term at Geelong Grammar School in 1966, and entered Trinity College, Cambridge, in 1967. Their daughter, Princess Anne Elizabeth Alice Louise, was born on August 15, 1950, Prince Andrew Albert Christian Edward on February 19, 1960, and Prince Edward Anthony Richard Louis on March 10, 1964.

ELIZABETH, Queen Consort. See GEORGE VI.

ELIZABETH (1596–1662), Queen of Bohemia, eldest daughter of James VI and I of Scotland and England, was born at Falkland, brought up from 1603 in England, and in 1613 married to Frederick V (q.v.), Elector Palatine, who in 1619 was elected to the throne of Bohemia. Next year the 'Winter King' was routed by the Catholic League, and the royal family endured sore poverty in Holland. Among their thirteen children were Charles Louis (1617–80), restored to the electorate in 1648, Rupert (q.v.), Maurice

(see under Rupert), and Sophia (q.v.). Elizabeth died in England. See Life by M. A. E. Green (new ed. 1909).

ELIZABETH, Madame (1764–94), a French princess, sister of Louis XVI (q.v.), whose fate she shared heroically, like him being guillotined. See Life by Vergne (1947).

ELIZABETH, St (1207–31), born at Sáros-Patak, the daughter of Andreas II of Hungary, at four was betrothed to Louis IV of Thuringia, and educated at his father's court, Wartburg, near Eisenach. At fourteen she was married, and a boy and two girls were the fruit of their union. Louis, who admired her for her long prayers and ceaseless almsgiving, died as a crusader at Otranto in 1227. The saintly landgravine was deprived of her regency by her husband's brother, and exiled on the plea that she wasted state treasures by her charities. After severe privations, she was received into the monastery of Kitzingen by the abbess, her aunt. When the warriors who had followed her husband to the crusade returned, steps were taken to restore to Elizabeth her sovereign rights. She retired to a cottage near the castle of Marburg and lived in cloistered simplicity for the remainder of her days. She was canonized in 1235. See monographs by Montalembert (1836), W. Canton (1912); and Kingsley's *Saint's Tragedy* (1848).

ELIZABETH OF PARMA. See FARNESE (3).

ELIZABETH OF RUMANIA. See CARMEN SYLVA.

ELIZABETH PETROVNA (1709–62), Empress of Russia, the pre-nuptial daughter of Peter the Great and Catharine I, was passed over in 1727, 1730 and 1740, but in 1741, on the deposition of Ivan VI, was raised to the throne. During her reign, in which throughout she was guided by favourites, a war with Sweden was brought to a successful conclusion by the peace of Åbo. Her animosity towards Frederick the Great led her to take part in the War of the Austrian Succession and in the Seven Years' War.

ELKINGTON, George Richards (1801–65), a Birmingham manufacturer, from 1832 the introducer of electroplating in conjunction with his cousin, **Henry Elkington** (1810–52).

ELLENBOROUGH, Edward Law, 1st Earl of (1790–1871), English politician, was eldest son of Baron Ellenborough (1750–1818), lord chief-justice from 1802. He became a Tory M.P. (1813) and held office under several administrations, becoming governor-general of India (1841). Parliament approved his Afghan policy in 1843, but his treatment of the civil servants, and his policy of conciliating the natives by apparent sanction of idolatry, led to his recall in 1844. Created Viscount Southam and Earl of Ellenborough, he was first lord of the Admiralty under Peel in 1846. In 1858 he was minister for India, but the publication of a dispatch in which he rebuked Viscount Canning forced him to resign. In 1863 he expressed strong sympathies with Poland, and in 1864 advocated British intervention in favour of Denmark. Lord Colchester edited his *Political Diary, 1828–30* (1881), Sir A. Law extracts from his papers, 1842–44 (1926).

ELLERY, William (1727–1820), American

politician, born in Newport, Rhode Island, sat in the congress of 1776, and was a signatory of the Declaration of Independence.

ELLESMERE. See EGERTON.

ELLET, Charles (1810–62), American engineer, called the ' Brunel of America ', educated in France, built a number of suspension bridges in America, including one on the Schuylkill at Fairmount (1842) and another over the Ohio at Wheeling (1849). He also constructed the James River and Kanawha Canal, and having advocated and demonstrated the use of ram-boats, built and commanded a fleet of them on the Mississippi, capturing Memphis (1862), but was killed in action.

ELLICOTT, Charles John (1819–1905), after 1897 Bishop of Gloucester (the divided see), was professor of Divinity at King's College, London (1858), Hulsean lecturer (1859) and professor (1860) of Divinity at Cambridge, Dean of Exeter (1861), Bishop of Gloucester and Bristol (1863–97). Chairman for eleven years of the New Testament Revision Committee, he published commentaries on Galatians, Ephesians, &c., and works on the Sabbath, Scripture and Scepticism.

ELLINGTON, Edward ' Duke ' (1899–   ), American Negro band-leader and composer, born in Washington, where he formed a band in 1918. Throughout his career, Ellington has specialized in works which, though in jazz style, are fully composed and do not allow for individual extemporization by the players. International concert tours established his worldwide reputation, and his works have won a high regard from many serious musicians. See Life, ed. Gammond (1958).

ELLIOT, (1) Jean (1727–1805), Scottish lyricist, the author of ' The Flowers of the Forest ', was the daughter of Sir Gilbert Elliot of Minto House, Teviotdale. She lived in Edinburgh 1756–1804, but died at the family seat, or at Monteviot.—Her eldest brother, **Sir Gilbert Elliot** (1722–77), was himself a song-writer; whilst **John** (d. 1808), the third brother, was a distinguished admiral. See MINTO.

(2) **Walter** (1888–1958), Scottish politician, Conservative M.P. for Lanark (1918–23), Kelvingrove (1924–45) and Scottish Universities (1946–49), was secretary of state for Scotland (1936–38) and minister of health (1938–40). Also known as a writer and broadcaster, he published *Toryism and the Twentieth Century* (1927). See Life by Coote (1965). His wife, **Baroness Katharine Elliot of Harwood** (1903–   ) was created Scotland's first life peeress in October 1958.

ELLIOTSON, John (1791–1868), English physician, born in London, became in 1831 professor at London University, and helped to establish University College Hospital. His conversion to mesmerism (1837) cost him his professorship in 1838, but hardly injured his large practice. One of the first to use the stethoscope, he experimented on the action of drugs, encouraged clinical study, and founded the Phrenological Society. His name will live from the dedication of Thackeray's *Pendennis*.

ELLIOTT, (1) Ebenezer (1781–1849), the ' Corn Law Rhymer ', born at Rotherham, turned to poetry while working in his father's iron foundry, published several volumes, but made a prosperous living as a bar-iron merchant. He is chiefly remembered for his denunciations of social evils, especially the Corn Laws; his *Corn Law Rhymes* was first published in 1831. There are two poor memoirs of Elliott, by his son-in-law, John Watkins, and by ' January Searle ' (George S. Phillips), both published in 1850.

(2) **Grace Dalrymple** (c. 1758–1823), the daughter of an Edinburgh advocate, Hew Dalrymple, in 1771 married Sir John Elliott, M.D. (1736–86), who divorced her in 1774. She was the mistress successively or simultaneously of Lord Valentia, Lord Cholmondley, the Prince of Wales, Charles Windham, George Selwyn, Philippe Égalité, &c. She died at Ville d'Avray near Sèvres, leaving an interesting but untrustworthy *Journal of My Life during the Revolution*, published in 1859 by her granddaughter, Miss Bentinck.

ELLIS, (1) or **Sharpe, Alexander John** (1814–90), English philologist, educated at Shrewsbury, Eton and Trinity College, Cambridge, wrote much on mathematical, musical and philological questions, and did more than any other scholar to advance the scientific study of phonetics, of early English pronunciation, and of existing English dialects.

(2) **George** (1753–1815), British satirist and poet, born in Grenada, West Indies, won early popularity with his *Poetical Tales by Sir Gregory Gander* (1778), and contributed satires on Pitt and others to the *Rolliad*, though later he was co-founder with Canning of the Tory *Anti-Jacobin*. Scott was his friend from 1801, and dedicated to him the fifth canto of *Marmion*. He edited *Specimens of the Early English Poets* (1790) and *Specimens of Early English Metrical Romances* (1805).

(3) **Sir Henry** (1777–1869), antiquary, was principal librarian at the British Museum from 1827 to 1856. He was knighted in 1833. His works include *Introduction to Domesday Book* (1833), *Original Letters Illustrative of English History* (1824–46), and an edition of Brand's *Antiquities* (1813).

(4) **Henry Havelock** (1859–1939), English writer on sex, born at Croydon, son of a sea captain, travelled widely in Australia and South America before studying medicine at St Thomas's Hospital, London. In 1891 he married Edith Lees and throughout his life had a number of female admirers, not least Olive Schreiner (q.v.). His interest in human biology and his own personal experiences led him to compile his seven-volume *Studies in the Psychology of Sex* (1897–1928, r.e. 1936), the first detached treatment of the subject unmarred by any guilt feelings, which caused tremendous controversy, but is now largely superseded by Freud's clinical studies. A brilliant literary expositor, he founded the ' Mermaid ' series of Elizabethan and Jacobean dramatists and wrote *My Life* (1940). See study by H. Peterson (1928) and Lives by A. Calder-Marshall and J. S Collis (both 1959).

(5) **William** (1794–1872), English missionary to the South Sea Islands, was born in London. The illness of his wife obliged him to return home in 1825, after which he became secretary to the London Missionary Society. Ellis published in 1838 a history of Madagascar, and after 1853 he made four visits to the island. He wrote *Madagascar Revisited* (1867), *The Martyr Church of Madagascar* (1870), &c. See Life by his son (1873).

ELLISTON, Robert William (1774–1831), English actor, born in London, in 1791 ran away and made his début on the stage at Bath. In 1796 he appeared at the Haymarket and Covent Garden; in 1804–09 and 1812–15 he was a member of the Drury Lane company; and in 1819 he became lessee and manager of the theatre, from which in 1826 he retired a bankrupt. He afterwards played in the Surrey Theatre; but dissipation shattered his health. Lamb's eulogy is well known; and to Leigh Hunt he was the ' best lover on the stage '. See Life by Raymond (1845).

ELLSWORTH, Lincoln (1880–1951), American explorer, born at Chicago, helped to build the Canadian transcontinental railway, surveyed routes, &c., went on Arctic expeditions with Amundsen, and was a leader of the polar flight in the airship *Norge* in 1926. See *Our Polar Flight* (1925) and *First Crossing of the Polar Sea* (1926), both written jointly with Amundsen, and his *Beyond the Horizon* (1938).

ELLWOOD, Thomas (1639–1713), English Quaker, born at Crowell in Oxfordshire, was converted at twenty to Quakerism; in 1662 befriended Milton, and in 1665 hired a cottage at Chalfont St Giles, where Milton might escape the plague in London. Milton gave him the MS. of *Paradise Lost* to read, and on returning it Ellwood said, ' Thou hast said much of " Paradise Lost ", but what hast thou to say of " Paradise Found "? ', thus inspiring Milton's sequel *Paradise Regained*. Ellwood, who suffered imprisonment for his beliefs, himself wrote poetry. See his Autobiography (1714), and work by Frances A. Budge (1891).

EL MALAKH, Kamal (1918–), Egyptian archaeologist, artist and art critic. In 1954 he excavated at Giza, near Cairo, a cedarwood boat, which is supposed to have carried Cheops on his journey to the sun.

ELMSLEY, Peter (1773–1825), English classical scholar, known for his editions of Euripides, Sophocles, &c., from 1798 was incumbent of Little Horkesley near Colchester. In 1823 was appointed principal of St Alban's Hall, Oxford, and Camden professor of Ancient History.

ELOI, or Eligius, St (588–658), Bishop of Noyon and apostle of Flanders, was originally a goldsmith, and so became patron of smiths.

ELPHINSTONE, (1) George Keith, Viscount Keith (1746–1823), son of the tenth Lord Elphinstone, was born at Elphinstone Tower, Stirling, entered the navy in 1761, saw service in most parts of the world, and fought in the American and French wars. He commanded the expedition (1795–97) which took Cape Town, and the fleet which landed Aber-

cromby's army in Aboukir Bay (1801). He was made Baron Keith in 1797, and a viscount in 1814. See Life by Allardyce (1882).

(2) **Mountstuart** (1779–1859), fourth son of the eleventh Lord Elphinstone, entered the Bengal civil service in 1795. In 1803 he served with distinction on Wellesley's staff, and was appointed resident at Nagpur; in 1808 was sent as envoy to Shah Shuja at Cabul; and as resident from 1810 at Poona both ended the Mahratta war of 1817 and organized the newly-acquired territory. During his governorship of Bombay (1819–1827) he founded the system of administration, and did much to advance public education. He returned to England in 1829, and, declining the governor-generalship of India, lived in comparative retirement until his death at Limpsfield, Surrey. His well-known *History of India* appeared in 1841 (7th ed. 1889). See his Life (1884) by Sir E. Colebrooke, who also edited his *Rise of British Power in the East* (1887); his *Official Writings*, with Memoir by Forrest (1884); and the Life by Cotton (' Rulers of India ' series, 1892).

(3) **William** (1431–1514), Scottish statesman, born at Glasgow, was ordained priest, spent five years in France, and lectured on law at Paris and Orleans. He returned to Scotland, held several offices, and for four months before the death of James III (1488) was chancellor. Under James IV he was ambassador to France (1491), and keeper of the privy seal from 1492. It was chiefly through his influence that the first printing-press—that of Chepman (q.v.) and Myllar—was established in Scotland. The University of Aberdeen (King's College) was founded by him in 1494. Additions to the cathedral and a stone bridge over the Dee were also due to him. The fatal battle of Flodden broke his spirit; and he died at Edinburgh not long after. His *Breviarium Aberdonense*, printed in 1509–10, was reprinted in 1853.

ELSHEIMER, Adam, *els'him-er* (1578–1610), German painter, born at Frankfurt, worked in Venice after 1598 and in Rome after 1600. Basing his style on a close study of Tintoretto and other Italian masters, he excelled in the portrayal of atmosphere and effects of light, and exerted a profound influence on the development of German landscape painting.

ELSSLER, Therese (1808–78) and **Fanny** (1810–84), two celebrated dancers, sisters, and natives of Vienna. Their first triumph was at Berlin in 1830; in 1841, after a tour through Europe, they went to America, and excited unwonted enthusiasm. Fanny retired from the stage in 1851, and Therese in 1850 married Prince Adalbert of Prussia, and became a baroness.

ELSTER, Julius (1854–1920), German physicist, collaborated with Geitel in producing the first photoelectric cell and photometer and a Tesla transformer. Among other achievements, they determined in 1899 the charge on raindrops from thunderclouds, showed that lead in itself is not radioactive, and that radioactive substances producing ionization cause the conductivity of the atmosphere.

ELSTRACKE, Renold, *el'strak-e* (c. 1590–1630), one of the earliest engravers in England, was born probably at Hasselt in

Belgium. He worked chiefly for the booksellers, and his engravings, including portraits of the kings of England, Mary Stuart, &c., are sought after for their rarity.

ELTON, (1) **Charles Isaac** (1839–1900), English jurist and ethnologist, was born at Southampton, maternal grandson of Sir Charles Abraham Elton (1778–1853), translator of Hesiod. He was called to the bar in 1865, became Q.C., and was M.P. for West Somerset 1884–85 and 1886–92. He died April 23. He wrote much on the law of property and on historical and literary topics.

(2) **Godfrey, 1st Baron** (1892–   ), English writer, educated at Rugby and Balliol, was a Fellow of Queen's College, Oxford, and lecturer on History from 1919 to 1939. He became active in the National Labour Party and stood unsuccessfully for parliament, but made a name for himself as broadcaster, poet, essayist and biographer. He was secretary of the Rhodes Trust from 1939 to 1959.

(3) **James Frederic** (1840–77), British explorer, saw service in the Indian mutiny, in China, and in Mexico, led expeditions in Mozambique and Zanzibar, explored Lake Nyasa, and died of malaria in Ugogo while seeking a route from the north end of the lake to the sea coast.

(4) **Oliver** (1861–1945), English literary historian, professor at Manchester (1890–1900) and Liverpool (1900–26), known for his *Survey of English Literature* (6 vols. 1912–1928) and critical studies of Drayton, &c.

ÉLUARD, Paul, pseudonym of **Eugène Grindal** (1895–1952), French poet, born at Saint-Denis. He associated himself closely with the surrealist theories of Breton. His first volume, *Capitale de la douleur* (1926), was followed by *La Vie immédiate* (1934), *Le Livre ouvert* (2 vols. 1941), *Poésie et vérité* (1942), *Le Lit, la table* (1944), *À Pablo Picasso* (1944), &c. See M. Raymond, *De Baudelaire au surréalisme* (Paris 1933).

ELVEY, Sir George (1816–93), English musician, born at Canterbury, from 1835 to 1882 was organist of St George's Chapel, Windsor, and in 1871 was knighted. He was a great choir trainer, and did much to improve the quality of church music. See *Life* by Lady Elvey (1894).

ELWIN, Whitwell (1816–1900), rector of Booton, Norfolk, was editor of the *Quarterly Review* (1853–60), and of the standard edition of Pope's works (completed by Courthope).

ELYOT, Sir Thomas (c. 1490–1546), English writer, born in Wiltshire, became in 1523 clerk of the king's council. In 1531–32, as ambassador to Charles V, he visited the Low Countries and Germany, having orders to procure the arrest of Tyndale. Member for Cambridge in 1542, he died at Carlton, Cambridgeshire. His chief work, *The Boke Named the Gouernour* (1531), is the earliest English treatise on moral philosophy. See study by Lehmberg (1961).

ELZE, Friedrich Karl, *el'tse* (1821–89), German Shakespearean scholar, born at Dessau, applied the strict methods of classical philology to his texts of Shakespeare and other Elizabethan dramatists.

ELZEVIR, a family of printers at Leyden, Amsterdam and elsewhere, who in 1592–1681 issued some 1600 beautiful editions of Latin, French and Italian classics—many of them bibliographical prizes. The founder of the family, **Louis** (1540–1617), was born at Louvain, and settled at Leyden. Five of his sons carried on the business—**Matthias, Louis, Aegidius (Giles), Jodocus (Joost)** and **Bonaventura;** and **Abraham** and **Isaac,** sons of **Matthias,** were also notable. A **Daniel,** another **Louis,** another **Abraham,** and **Peter,** all maintained the traditions of the house, See Andrew Lang's *Books and Bookmen* (1888), H. B. Copinger's *The Elzevir Press* (1927), and Goldsmid's *Complete Catalogue* (1888).

EMERSON, Ralph Waldo (1803–82), American poet and essayist, was born in Boston of a long line of ministers, May 25, 1803. He graduated at Harvard in 1821, and after teaching at different places, became in 1829 pastor of the Second Church (Unitarian) in Boston, and married his first wife, Ellen Louisa Tucker, who died in 1832. In that year he preached views on the Lord's Supper which were disapproved by the majority of his congregation; this led him finally to resign his pulpit. In 1833 he came to Europe, and visited Carlyle at Craigenputtock, next year beginning that thirty-eight years' correspondence which shows the two men with all their characteristics, different as optimist and pessimist, yet with many profound sympathies. In 1834 he removed to Concord, where he died, April 27, 1882, having in 1835 married his second wife, Lydia (Lidian) Jackson (1802–92). In 1836 Emerson published a prose rhapsody entitled *Nature,* which, like his earlier poems, was read by few, and understood by fewer still, but which contains the germs of many of his later essays and poems. It was followed by 'The American Scholar', an oration delivered at Harvard University. These two publications, the first in the series of his collected works, strike the keynote of his philosophical, poetical and moral teachings. The 'Address before the Divinity Class, Cambridge, 1838', which follows them, defined his position in, or out of, the church in which he had been a minister. A plea for the individual consciousness as against all historical creeds, bibles, churches, for the soul of each man as the supreme judge in spiritual matters, it produced a great sensation, especially among the Unitarians, and much controversy followed, in which Emerson took no part. In 1849 he revisited England to lecture on *Representative Men.* His *English Traits* appeared in 1856, *The Conduct of Life* in 1860, *Society and Solitude* in 1870, *Letters and Social Aims* in 1876. The idealist or transcendentalist in philosophy, the rationalist in religion, the bold advocate of spiritual independence, of intuition as a divine guidance, of instinct as a heaven-born impulse, of individualism in its fullest extent, making each life a kind of theocratic egoism—this is the Emerson of his larger utterances. For him nature was a sphinx, covered with hieroglyphics, for which the spirit of man is to find the key. See his *Journals* (10 vols. 1910–14); monographs by

J. E. Cabot (1887), O. W. Holmes (1885), R. Garnett (1888), Woodberry (1907), Firkins (1915), Van Wyck Brooks (1934), J. Dewey (1938), R. L. Rush (1958).

EMINESCU, Mihail (1850–89), Rumanian poet, born at Ipotesti, studied at Czernowitz, Vienna and Berlin, wrote lyric verse which was widely read and translated. His works were collected in 4 volumes in 1939. See study by F. Lang (1928).

EMIN PASHA, originally **Eduard Schnitzer** (1840–92), German doctor and explorer, born of Jewish parents at Neisse. He studied medicine at Breslau and Berlin, practised at Scutari (Albania), where he adopted the Moslem faith and usages, and after 1876, as Emin Effendi, was in the Egyptian service, becoming bey and pasha. Gordon appointed him chief medical officer of the Equatorial Province, employed him in diplomacy and administration, and in 1878 made him governor of the province. This post he held, cut off from the world, till 1889. A skilful linguist, he added enormously to our knowledge of African languages, anthropology, zoology, botany and meteorology: he made important surveys and wrote most valuable geographical papers, and sent to Europe rich collections of plants and animals. An enlightened ruler, and a bitter foe to the slave dealers, he did much to civilize his subjects; but, isolated and hemmed in by enemies, was ' rescued ' by Stanley's expedition in 1889. He accompanied Stanley to Zanzibar, but immediately returned to continue his labours and extend the German sphere of influence about Lake Victoria. He never regained his old influence, and was marching for the west coast when he was murdered by Arabs in the Manyema country. See *Emin Pasha in Central Africa* (his letters and journals, 1888); Stanley's *In Darkest Africa* (1890); and works by Stuhlmann (1894), G. Schweitzer (trans. 1898) and A. Symons (1928).

EMLYN, Thomas (1663–1741), English Presbyterian minister, the first in England to describe himself as ' Unitarian ', who was imprisoned and fined for blasphemy. Born at Stamford, he died in London.

EMMA. See ETHELRED and EGINHARD.

EMANUEL I, *e-man'yoo-el*, also **Manoel** (1469–1521), king of Portugal, styled ' the Great ' or ' the Fortunate ', succeeded John II in 1495. His reign, marred only by persecution of the Jews, was the golden age of Portugal. He prepared the code of laws which bears his name, and made his court a centre of chivalry, art and science. Vasco da Gama's voyage round the Cape, Cabral's discovery of Brazil and the expeditions under Albuquerque and others, encouraged by Emanuel, went far to making Portugal the first naval power of Europe and the centre of the commerce of the world.

EMMERICH, Anna Katharina, called the Nun of Dülmen, *em'er-eeKH* (1774–1824), German nun, born near Coesfeld, who bore the stigmata of Christ's passion. See BRENTANO, and Life by Schmöger (Freiburg 1885; trans. New York, 1895).

EMMET, (1) Robert (1778–1803), Irish patriot, born in Dublin, son of the viceroy's physician.

He left Trinity College to join the United Irishmen, travelled on the Continent, interviewed Napoleon and Talleyrand in 1802 on behalf of the Irish cause, and returned the next year to spend his fortune of £3000 on muskets and pikes. With a few confederates he plotted to seize Dublin Castle and secure the viceroy, but the rising resulted only in a few ruffianly murders. Emmet escaped to the Wicklow mountains, but returning for a last interview with his sweetheart, Sarah Curran, daughter of the orator, was arrested, tried on September 19, 1803, and hanged the following day. See Madden's *Lives of the United Irishmen* (1846), and Lives by Postgate (1932) and L. O'Broin (1958).

(2) **Thomas Addis** (1764–1827), brother of (1), was a very successful Irish barrister, when in 1798 he was arrested as a United Irishman. After three years' detention he went in 1802 to Holland and France, and thence in 1804 to New York. See Memoirs by Haynes (1829), and MacDonagh, *The Viceroy's Postbag* (1904).

EMPECINADO, nickname of **Don Juan Martin Diaz,** *em-pay-thee-nah'dō* (1775–1823), Spanish soldier who acquired great distinction during the Peninsular struggle, became in 1814 a general, but for petitioning Ferdinand to re-establish the Cortes was banished to Valladolid (1818). On the outbreak of the insurrection in 1820 he joined the constitutionalists; and on the absolutists' triumph in 1823 was exposed in an iron cage, and finally stabbed by a soldier.

EMPEDOCLES, *-ped'o-kleez* (d. *c.* 430 B.C.), Greek philosopher, was born at Agrigentum. Such was his fame as physician and soothsayer, that the people offered him the sovereignty; but instead he brought in a democracy. It is a myth that he threw himself into the crater of Etna, to seem to have been translated, and that Etna rejected his sandals. His philosophic thought is bound up with poetry and myth, and was determined by the influence of the Eleatic school upon the physical theories of the Ionic philosophers. He assumed four primitive independent elements, air, water, fire and earth, and two moving and operating powers, love and hate, or affinity and antipathy. His theory of the universe seems to assume a gradual development of the perfect out of the imperfect, and a periodical return of things to the elemental state. See monographs by Lommatsch (1830), Raynaud (1848), Gladisch (1858) and Baltzer (1879); also Matthew Arnold's poem.

EMPSON, (1) Sir Richard (d. 1510), English politician, in 1491 became speaker of the House of Commons, and in 1504, now a knight, high steward of Cambridge University and chancellor of the Duchy of Lancaster. Throughout Henry VII's reign he was employed in exacting taxes and penalties due to the crown. His conduct, defended by himself as strictly legal, was by the people regarded as infamous and tyrannical, and in the second year of Henry VIII's reign he was convicted of tyrannizing and of constructive treason, and beheaded on Tower Hill with his partner Dudley (q.v.).

(2) **William** (1906–), English poet and

critic, born in Howden, Yorkshire, and educated at Cambridge. From 1931–34 he was professor of English Literature in Tokyo, and at Pekin 1937–39 and 1947–53, having been in the interim with the B.B.C.'s Far Eastern Service. In 1953 he became professor of English Literature at Sheffield University. His critical works include *Seven Types of Ambiguity* (1930), *The Structure of Complex Words* (1951) and *Milton's God* (1961). His *Collected Poems*, noted for their wit, concentration and complexity of thought, were published in 1955.

ENCINA, or Enzina, Juan de la, *en-thee'na* (*c.* 1469–*c.* 1534), Spanish dramatist and poet, born near Salamanca, was successively secretary to the first Duke of Alva, musical director in Pope Leo X's chapel at Rome, and prior of León in Spain. Besides his *Cancionero* (1496), he wrote in 1521 a poetical account of his pilgrimage to Jerusalem. But his fame rests on his fourteen rather poor dramatic poems, half of them religious, but the other half secular, these last the first of the kind to be acted in Spain, in 1492.

ENCKE, Johann Franz, *en'kè* (1791–1865), German astronomer, born at Hamburg, was at Seeberg Observatory near Gotha (1815–25), and subsequently became secretary of the Academy of Sciences at Berlin and director of the Observatory. Having determined the orbit of the comet of 1680, he next solved the problem of the sun. In 1819 he proved that the comet discovered by Pons in 1818 revolves in about 1200 days, and had been already observed in 1786, 1795 and 1805; it has since been called Encke's comet. See Life by Bruhns (1869).

ENDECOTT, John (*c.* 1588–1665), Puritan governor of Massachusetts, was born at Dorchester, England, and landed as manager of a plantation near Salem in 1628. He headed a sanguinary expedition against the Indians in 1636, was deputy-governor in 1641–44, 1650 and 1654, and governor six times from 1644 to 1665. He died at Boston. See Life by C. M. Endicott (1847).

ENDERBY, Samuel (fl. 1830–39), General Gordon's grandfather, one of a firm of London merchants who in 1830–39 fitted out three Antarctic expeditions. The name Enderby Land was given in 1831 to a tract of Antarctica by its discoverer, John Biscoe, a whaler employed by the company.

ENDERS, John Franklin (1897–), American bacteriologist, born at West Hartford, Conn. With his principal collaborators, Weller and Robins, he won the 1954 Nobel prize for medicine and physiology for discoveries concerning the virus of poliomyelitis.

ENDLICHER, Stephan Ladislaus (1804–49), German botanist, born at Pressburg, was from 1840 professor of Botany at Vienna, and committed suicide there. *Genera Plantarum* (1836–40) is his great work.

ENESCO, Georges (1881–1955), Rumanian composer, born at Dorohoiu. Enesco studied in Vienna and under Massenet and Fauré in Paris. Successful as a virtuoso and teacher of the violin (his pupils included Yehudi Menuhin), Enesco was also active as a composer. His works include music in

Rumanian national style, an opera, *Oedipus* three symphonies and orchestral and chamber music.

ENFANTIN, Barthélemy Prosper, *ā-fā-tī* (1796–1864), French economist and industrialist, son of a Paris banker, was expelled from the École Polytechnique in 1814 for having with other pupils fought against the allies on Montmartre. From 1825 an ardent follower of Saint-Simon (q.v.), whom, however, he saw only once, after the July revolution of 1830 he associated himself with Bazard for the propagation of Saint-Simonism, but they soon quarrelled over the question of marriage and the relation of the sexes. Enfantin recognized two sorts of marriage, one permanent, the other temporary; the government prosecuted him, and in 1832 'Père Enfantin' was sentenced to two years' imprisonment and a fine of 100 francs. Released in a few months, he found employment in Egypt as an engineer; went out to Algiers as one of a scientific commission, and wrote *Colonisation de l'Algérie* (1843). After the Revolution of 1848 he edited the short-lived *Crédit Public*; and subsequently held an important post in a railway office. He played a prominent part in the Suez Canal project. His principal works are *Doctrine de Saint-Simon*, in conjunction with others (1830); *Traité d'économie politique* (1831); *La Religion Saint-Simonienne* (1831). See Life by Castille (Paris 1859).

ENGEL, (1) Carl (1883–1944), American composer, born in Paris, wrote piano and chamber works and songs. Also known as a musicologist, he took charge of the music department of the Library of Congress in Washington in 1922.

(2) **Ernst** (1821–96), German statistician, born near Dresden, made important contributions to the study of sociology, and formulated Engel's Law, establishing a variable ratio between household income and expenditure on necessities.

(3) **Johann Carl Ludwig** (1778–1840), Finnish architect, born in Berlin, planned the layout of Helsinki as capital of Finland, and designed many churches and public buildings.

(4) **Johann Jakob** (1741–1802), German writer of the novel *Herr Lorenz Stark* (1795) and of popular philosophical books.

(5) **Karl** (1818–82), German musicologist, born near Hanover, from 1846 lived in England and died at Kensington. He made important contributions to the history of the music and instruments of foreign (especially extra-European) countries.

ENGELS, Friedrich (1820–95), the fellow-labourer with Marx and founder of ' Scientific Socialism ', born at Barmen, from 1842 lived mostly in England, where he wrote *Condition of the Working Classes in England* (1844, new tr. 1958). He first met Marx at Brussels in 1844 and collaborated with him on the *Communist Manifesto* (1848). He died in London, after spending his later years editing and translating Marx's writings. See English Life by Bernstein (1897), German by G. Mayer (1934).

ENGHIEN, Louis Antoine Henri de Bourbon, Duc d', *ā-gī* (1772–1804), only son of Henry

Louis Joseph, Prince de Condé, was born at Chantilly. In 1792 he joined the corps of *émigrés* assembled on the Rhine, and commanded the vanguard from 1796 until 1799. At the peace of Lunéville (1801) he went to reside in Baden. When Cadoudal's conspiracy was discovered, Bonaparte chose to believe in D'Enghien's complicity, and, violating the neutral territory of Baden, captured the duke and took him to Vincennes. On March 21, 1804, he was shot in the castle moat. Fouché said of this act that it was worse than a crime—it was a blunder. Boulay de la Meurthe edited his *Correspondance* (1904–13).

ENGLEHEART, George (1750–1829), English miniature painter, born at Kew. He was a pupil of Sir Joshua Reynolds, and probably the most prolific of the 18th-century miniaturists, producing over 4800 portraits, some of which are in the Victoria and Albert Museum. See Life by G. C. Williamson and H. L. D. Engleheart (1902).

ENGLER, Adolf (1844–1930), German systematic botanist, born at Sagan, became professor at Berlin in 1889. Besides writing the *Syllabus der Pflanzenfamilien* (10th ed. 1924) and many other works, he started (1888; with Prantl) and edited *Die natürliche Pflanzenfamilien*.

ENGLISH, Thomas Dunn (1819–1902), American physician, lawyer and ballad-writer whose memory survives in his poem 'Ben Bolt'. This was a popular song during the Civil War, but gained worldwide prominence when Du Maurier introduced it in Trilby. He was also the author of more than fifty now-forgotten plays.

ENNIUS (*c.* 239–169 B.C.), a Roman poet, born at Rudiae in Calabria, and probably of Greek extraction. He is said to have served in the wars, and returned from Sardinia to Rome with Cato the Elder. Here he taught Greek, gained the friendship of Scipio Africanus the Elder, and attained the rank of Roman citizen. Ennius introduced the hexameter into Latin; his versification, if rough and unpolished, is vigorous. Of his tragedies, comedies, satires and *Annales*, an epos in eighteen books, only fragments survive ; although all, it is thought, were extant as late as the 13th century. They have been edited by Vahlen (1854), L. Müller (1885) and Steuart (1925); the dramatic fragments by Ribbeck (new ed. 1903). See Müller's *Ennius* (1844), and Sellar's *Roman Poets of the Republic* (2nd ed. 1881).

ENOCH, or Thenew. See KENTIGERN.

ENRÍQUEZ GÓMEZ, Antonio, properly Enríquez de Paz, *en-ree'keth gō'meth* (1602–*c.* 1662), Spanish playwright and poet, the son of a baptized Portuguese Jew, was born at Segovia, in 1636 fled to Amsterdam, and, having there professed the Jewish faith, was in 1660 burned in effigy at a Seville auto-da-fé.

ENSOR, James (1860–1942), Belgian painter, was born at Ostend. His landscapes, still-life studies and genre paintings are often ghostly and pale-hued, achieving subtle atmosphere effects. He also wrote stories and composed music. See study by Jedlicka (1945).

ENTRECASTEAUX, Bruni d', *ā-trė-kas-tō* (1739–93), a French admiral who in 1792 explored the D'Entrecasteaux Islands near New Guinea.

ENVER PASHA (1881–1922), a Young Turk leader in the revolution of 1908, Turkish minister for war in 1914, fled to Russia in 1918 after the Turkish surrender, and was killed in an insurrection in Turkestan.

ENZINA. See ENCINA.

ÉON DE BEAUMONT, Charles Geneviève Timothée d', *ay-õ dė bō-mõ* (1728–1810), the 'Chevalier d'Éon', born at Tonnerre, Burgundy, was sent to London in 1762 as secretary of embassy, and in 1763 was made minister plenipotentiary. In 1774 the French ministry recalled him, fearing he might betray secrets to the British government. After much negotiation Éon surrendered certain compromising papers, and submitted to the condition imposed by Louis XVI of wearing feminine garb, which he had often before assumed as a disguise. In 1785 he returned to London, where he gave exhibitions in fencing, till in 1796 he was disabled by an accidental wound, and where he died, May 21, 1810, when a post-mortem examination settled the moot question of his male sex. He published *Loisirs du Chevalier d'Éon* (13 vols. Amsterdam 1774), &c., but the *Mémoires* (1837) which bear his name are not genuine. See Life by Homeberg and Jousselin (1904; Eng. trans. 1911), and *Royal Spy* by E. Nixon (1966).

EÖTVÖS, Joseph, Baron, *æt'væsh* (1813–71), Hungarian author, was born and died at Budapest. He became an advocate in 1833, but soon devoting himself to literature, published a work on prison reform, and the novels, *The Carthusian* (1838–41), *The Village Notary* (1846; Eng. trans. 1850), &c. In the revolution of 1848 Eötvös was minister of public instruction, as again under Andrassy (1867) after three years of exile. His son Roland (1848–1919) was an eminent physicist.

EPAMINONDAS (*c.* 418–362 B.C.), the greatest of Theban generals and statesmen, led a retired life till his fortieth year. After the stratagem by which his fellow-citizens expelled the Spartans (379), he joined the patriots; and, when sent to Sparta in 371 to negotiate peace, displayed as much firmness as eloquence. When war was resumed, he defeated the Spartans and their allies at Leuctra (371). Two years later, with Pelopidas, he marched into the Peloponnesus, and incited some of the allies to desert Sparta. On his return to Thebes, he was accused of having retained the supreme power beyond the lawful time, but was acquitted in consequence of his able defence. In 368 war was renewed, and Epaminondas made a somewhat unsuccessful invasion into the Peloponnesus. To atone for this he advanced into Arcadia, and near Mantinea broke the Spartan phalanx, but was mortally wounded.

EPÉE, Charles Michel, Abbé de l', *ay-pay* (1712–89), born at Versailles, became a preacher and canon at Troyes, but was deprived as a Jansenist. In 1765 he began to educate two deaf and dumb sisters; and invented a language of signs. His attempts succeeding, at his own expense he founded a deaf and dumb institute, which was converted into a public institution two years after his death. See Life by Bélanger (Paris 1886).

EPHIALTES, *ef-i-al'teez*, an Athenian statesman, assassinated in 457 B.C., predecessor of Pericles in the leadership of the democratic party.

EPHRAEM SYRUS (*c.* 306–78), Syrian churchman, was born at Nisibis, and, after its capture by the Persians in 363, removed to a cave near Edessa, and devoted himself to prayer, fasting, and the study of the Scriptures. Ephraem's orthodoxy, asceticism, and learning were the admiration of his contemporaries; and his works, written in a fervid and popular style, sustain his reputation as an orator and poet. Part of them have come down to us in Syriac, part in Greek, Latin and Armenian translations. See study by Ricciotti (Rome 1925).

EPICHARMUS (*c.* 540–450 B.C.), Greek poet, born in Cos, spent his last years at the court of Hiero of Syracuse. We possess fragments of his works and the titles of thirty-five, on topics mythological, social and political. See German monograph by Lorenz (1864).

EPICTETUS, *-tay'-*, Stoic philosopher, born at Hierapolis about A.D. 50, was at first a slave at Rome. On being freed he devoted himself to philosophy, was banished by Domitian, and settled at Nikopolis in Epirus. He left no works, but his pupil Arrian the historian collected his maxims in the work entitled *Enchiridion* and in eight books of Commentaries, four of which are lost. His ethics teach self-renunciation. See translations by Matheson (1917) and Oldfather (1926–28), and studies by Bonhöffer (1890–1911).

EPICURUS (*c.* 341–270 B.C.), Greek philosopher, born in Samos, at eighteen visited Athens, and then returned to Asia. In 310 he opened a school at Mitylene, and taught there and at Lampsacus ; in 305 he returned to Athens, and established a school of philosophy. He was most successful ; great numbers flocked to his school from all parts of Greece and Asia Minor, most of whom became greatly attached to their master and his doctrines. Although he held that pleasure is the chief good, the life that he and his friends led was one of the greatest temperance and simplicity. According to Diogenes Laertius, he left 300 volumes on Natural Philosophy, Atoms and the Vacuum, Love, the Chief Good, Justice, &c. These are lost : the only extant writings are three letters, a few fragments from the *Volumina Herculanensia*, and a number of detached sayings. The principal sources of our knowledge of the doctrines of Epicurus are Cicero, Plutarch and Lucretius, whose great poem, *De Rerum Natura*, contains substantially the Epicurean philosophy. According to him, the great evil that afflicted men was fear—fear of the gods and fear of death. To get rid of these two fears was the ultimate aim of all his speculations on nature. He regarded the universe as corporeal, and as infinite in extent and eternal in duration. He recognized two kinds of existence—that of bodies, and that of *vacuum*. Of his bodies, some are compounds, and some atoms or invisible elements. The world, as we now see it, is produced by

the collision and whirling together of these atoms. He did not deny that there are gods ; but he maintained that as 'happy and imperishable beings' they could have nothing to do with the affairs of the universe. In psychology Epicurus was a materialist : the dissolution of the body involves that of the soul, and he argues that the most terrible of all evils, death, is nothing to us, 'since *when we are, death is not*; *and when death is, we are not*'. He held that pleasure was the chief good, but it is from misapprehension that the term Epicurean came to signify one who indulged his sensual appetites without stint. 'When we say that pleasure is the end of life, we do not mean the pleasure of the debauchee or the sensualist, as some from ignorance or from malignity represent, but freedom of the body from pain and the soul from anxiety.' In modern times Epicureanism was resuscitated in France by Père Gassendi, who in 1646–49 published a Latin Life of Epicurus and a defence of his philosophy. See Cyril Bailey's edition (1927) of the extant remains, and his *Greek Atomists and Epicurus* (1928); also works by Zeller (trans. 1880), Wallace (1880), Atanassiévitch (Paris 1927) and Witt (1954).

EPIMENIDES, *ep-i-men'i-deez*, a Greek poet and priest, was born in Crete in the 7th century B.C., and is said to have lived 299 years, during fifty-seven of which he received in sleep the divine inspiration that determined his future career. (Goethe wrote a poem on the subject, *Des Epimenides Erwachen*.) Epimenides went to Athens about 596 B.C., where he stayed a plague by mystical rites, and with Solon reformed the Athenian constitution. He was the 'prophet' quoted by St Paul in Tit. i. 12. That he wrote the epic poems ascribed to him is highly improbable. See monographs by Schultess (1877) and Demoulin (1901).

ÉPINAY, Madame d', *ay-pee-nay* (1726–83), French writer, born at Valenciennes, at nineteen married a worthless cousin, and subsequently formed liaisons with Rousseau, Grimm, &c. Her *Conversations d'Émilie* (1774), a work on education, gained her a gold medal from the French Academy. See her *Mémoires et correspondance* (1818; trans. 1899), and works by Perey and Maugras (1882–83).

EPIPHANES. See ANTIOCHUS IV.

EPIPHANIUS (*c.* 315–403), ancient Christian churchman, born in Palestine and educated by Egyptian monks, who imbued him with piety and bigotry, was Bishop of Constantia in Cyprus from 367 till his death. He proclaimed Origen a heretic, in 394 called upon John Bishop of Jerusalem to condemn him, and was intolerant to Chrysostom also. His chief work is *Panarion*, a catalogue of eighty heresies. See a monograph by Lipsius (1865).

EPISCOPIUS, or Biscop, Simon (1583–1643), born at Amsterdam, studied at Leyden under Arminius and Gomarus, and succeeded to the latter's chair in 1612. He and twelve other Arminians were banished by the Synod of Dort (1618); and in the Spanish Netherlands he wrote his famous Arminian *Confessio* (1622). On the renewal of the war between Spain and Holland, he found refuge in France, and published a series of able controversial treatises. Permitted in 1626 to return, he was from 1634 a professor at the Arminian College at Amsterdam, where he produced his *Institutiones theologicae* and *Responsio*. Episcopius lays the utmost stress on the personal responsibility of man in relation to divine grace, denies the doctrine of original sin, and treats Christian faith as the potentiality of moral conduct. The Son and the Holy Spirit are only subordinately partakers of divine power and glory—a rationalist development of Arminian doctrine far beyond the Five Articles, but finally adopted by the Arminian party. See Life by Limborch (1701).

EPSTEIN, Sir Jacob, *ep'stīn* (1880–1959), British sculptor, born, a Russian-Polish Jew, in New York, studied at the École des Beaux-Arts in Paris. He became a British subject, and his early commissions included eighteen figures for the façade of the British Medical Council building in the Strand (1907–08) and *Night* and *Day* (1929) for the London Transport Building. These and later symbolic sculptures, such as the marble *Genesis* (1930), the *Ecce Homo* (1934), and the alabaster *Adam* (1938), etc., resulted in great controversy, and accusations of in-decency and blasphemy. He was an out-standing modeller of portrait heads, cast in bronze, of celebrities, e.g., Einstein, Eliot and Shaw, and of children, e.g., *Esther* (1944), his youngest daughter. He also executed two bronze *Madonna and Child* works (1927, Riverside Church, N.Y.; 1950, Holy Child Jesus Convent, London). In the 1950s, his last two large commissioned works, *Christ in Majesty* (aluminium; Llandaff Cathedral) and *St Michael and the Devil* (bronze; Coventry Cathedral), won more immediate critical acclaim. He was created K.B.E. in 1954. See his autobiographical *Let there be Sculpture* (1940; enlarged as *An Autobiog-raphy* 1955, n.e. 1963), and studies by B. van Dieren (1920) and H. Wellington (1925).

ÉRARD, Sébastien (1752–1831), a Paris pianoforte maker, born at Strasbourg, was the inventor of the harp with double pedals and of the piano with double escapement.

ERASISTRATUS, *e-ra-sis'tra-tus* (304–c. 245 B.C.), founder of a school of medicine, was born in Ceos, settled in Alexandria, and died in Samos. He came near to anticipating Harvey's discovery of the circulation of the blood.

ERASMUS, Desiderius (1466–1536), Dutch humanist, was born at Rotterdam, apparently on October 28, 1466, the illegitimate son of a physician's daughter by a man who afterwards turned monk, and whose story forms the theme of Reade's *The Cloister and the Hearth*. He was called Gerrit Ger-ritszoon (Dutch for 'Gerard Gerardson'), but himself adopted the tautological double name by which he is known. He attended the school of the ' Brothers of the Common Life ' at Deventer. On his parents' death his guardians insisted on his entering a monastery and in the Augustinian college of Stein near Gouda he spent six years—it was undoubtedly this personal experience of the ways of

monks that made Erasmus their relentless enemy. At length the Bishop of Cambrai made him his private secretary. After taking priest's orders Erasmus went to Paris, where he studied at the Collège Montaigu. He resided in Paris till 1498, gaining a livelihood by teaching; among his pupils was Lord Mountjoy, on whose invitation probably Erasmus made his first visit to England in 1498. He lived chiefly at Oxford, and through the influence of Colet his contempt for the schoolmen was intensified. In 1500 he was again in France, and for the next six years lived chiefly in Paris; to this time belong his *Adagia* (en-larged in 1515) and his *Enchiridion Militis Christiani*. In 1506 he made a short visit to England, carried out a long-desired journey to Italy, and at Padua acted as tutor to Alexander, Archbishop of St Andrews, natural son of James IV of Scotland. His visit closed with a short stay in Rome, whence he carried away a far more friendly impression than Luther did. The accession of Henry VIII, and the invitation of Lord Mountjoy, induced Erasmus once more to make England his home. In his satire, *Encomium Moriae* (1509), we have him in his happiest vein, as the man of letters and the critic of kings and churchmen. Erasmus resided chiefly at Cambridge, where he acted as Margaret professor of Divinity and professor of Greek. After 1514 he lived alternately in Basel and England, and from 1517 to 1521 at Louvain. In 1519 appeared the first edition (afterwards greatly enlarged) of his *Colloquia*, usually regarded as his masterpiece; the audacity and incisiveness with which it handles the abuses of the church prepared men's minds for the work of Luther. In 1516 was published his annotated New Testament, virtually the first Greek text; and in 1519 his edition oɪ St Jerome in nine folio volumes. In both of these works the aim of Erasmus was to introduce a more rational conception of Christian doctrine, and to emancipate men's minds from the frivolous and pedantic methods of the scholastic theologians. But when the Lutheran revolution came he found himself in the most embarrassing position. Those of the old order fell upon him as the author of all the new troubles; the Lutherans assailed him for his cowardice and inconsistency in refusing to follow up his opinions to their legitimate conclusions. In 1521 he left Louvain, where the champions of the old faith had made his stay unendur-able; and with the exception of six years in Freiburg, he spent the rest of his life at Basel. He edited a long succession of classical and patristic writers, and was engaged in continual controversies. The most important of these were with Ulrich von Hutten, Luther, and the Sorbonne. Hutten judged Erasmus harshly for not taking his place by the side of Luther; and with Luther himself Erasmus, after long hesitation, crossed swords in his *De Libero Arbitrio* (1523). Attacked by men like Hutten on the one side, he was as fiercely assailed on the other by the Sorbonne. By his *Ciceronianus* he raised against himself new adversaries — those humanists, namely, who set style above matter. Yet during his last years Erasmus enjoyed great fame and consideration. He died July 12, 1536. Erasmus stands as the supreme type of cultivated common sense applied to human affairs. He rescued theology from the pedantries of the schoolmen, exposed the abuses of the church, and did more than any other single person to advance the Revival of Learning. An edition of his works appeared at Basel (9 vols. 1540); the standard edition is Le Clerc's (1703–06), supplemented by that of W. K. Ferguson (The Hague 1934). See works by Drummond (1873), Amiel (1889), Jebb (1890), Froude (1894), Allen (1914), Campbell (1949), Huizinga (tr. 1952); and the edition of his Letters by P. S. and H. M. Allen (1906 et seq).

ERASTUS, Thomas, properly **Liebler** or **Lieber** (1524–83), Swiss theologian, born at Swiss Baden, studied theology at Basel, philosophy and medicine in Italy, and was appointed physician to the counts of Henneberg, then (from 1558) professor of Medicine at Heidelberg and physician to the Elector Palatine. He became professor of Ethics at Basel in 1580, and died there, January 1, 1583. Erastus was a skilful physician, a vigorous writer against Paracelsus and witchcraft. In theology he was a follower of Zwingli, and represented his view of the Lord's Supper at Heidelberg in 1560 and Maulbronn in 1564. In England the name of Erastians was applied to the party that arose in the 17th century, denying the right of autonomy to the church—a right neither maintained nor denied by Erastus; Lightfoot and Selden were Erastians in this sense. See Dr R. Lee's translation (1844) of Erastus's treatise.

ERATOSTHENES, *e-ra-tos'the-neez* (*c.* 276–194 B.C.), Greek mathematician, astronomer and geographer, born at Cyrene, was called to Alexandria by Ptolemy Euergetes to superintend his great library. Here, at eighty, he died of voluntary starvation, having become blind and wearied of life. Eratosthenes measured the obliquity of the ecliptic with wonderful accuracy, made a catalogue, now lost, of 675 fixed stars, and attempted to measure the magnitude of the earth. He wrote treatises on geography, moral philosophy, history and grammar. Bernhardy edited his fragments (1822). See Berger (1880).

ERCILDOUNE. See THOMAS THE RHYMER.

ERCILLA Y ZÚÑIGA, Alonso de, *er-thee'lya ee thoo-nyee'ga* (1553–*c.* 1595), Spanish poet, born at Bermeo on the Bay of Biscay, entered the service of Philip, son of Charles V, and accompanied him in 1554 to England on the occasion of his marriage to Queen Mary. Shortly after, he joined the expedition against the Araucanians in Chile whose heroism suggested an epic poem. An unfounded suspicion of his having plotted an insurrection nearly led to his execution. Deeply hurt, he returned to Spain, but, Philip treating him with neglect, made a tour through Europe, and for some time was chamberlain to the Emperor Rudolf II. In 1580 he returned to Madrid, where he struggled with poverty till his death. Cer-

vantes compares the *Araucana* (1569–97; best ed. 1828) with the finest Italian epics.

ERCKMANN-CHATRIAN, *sha-tree-ã,* the compound name of two French writers—Lorrainers both, Émile Erckmann, born May 20, 1822, at Phalsbourg, and Alexandre Chatrian, born December 18, 1826, at Abreschwiller. Their literary partnership dates from 1848, but they had little success till the publication of *L'Illustre Docteur Mathéus* (1859). *Le Fou Yégof* (1862) is one of a series of novels, to which also belong *Histoire d'un conscrit* (1864), *Waterloo* (1865), *Le Blocus* (1867), &c. These and many more have been translated into English. Well-known plays by them are *Le Juif polonais* (1869; in English *The Bells*), *L'Ami Fritz* (1876), *Les Rantzau* (1882), and *La Guerre* (1885). After the annexation of Alsace-Lorraine to Germany, a strong anti-German feeling was manifested in several of their books—the best of these *L'Histoire d'un plébiscite* (1872). They had quarrelled latterly (on pecuniary arrangements), when Chatrian died in Paris in September 1890. Erckmann died at Lunéville in March 1899. See study by E. Hinzelin (Paris 1922).

ERDMANN, Johann Eduard (1805–92), German philosopher, born at Wolmar in Livonia, studied at Dorpat and Berlin, and became professor of Philosophy at Halle in 1839. Hegelian in outlook, he wrote a History of Philosophy (3rd ed. 1877), and also wrote on logic, psychology, &c. See study by H. Glockner (1932).

ERHARD, Ludwig (1897–   ), German economist and politician, born at Furth, professor of Economics at Munich from 1945, was in 1949 elected to the Federal Parliament at Bonn and appointed chancellor of the Exchequer in the Adenauer administration. He was the pioneer of the West German 'economic miracle' of recovery from wartime devastation. When Adenauer accepted nomination for the presidency in April 1959, Erhard was widely regarded as his most likely successor to the chancellorship, but after an acrimonious public wrangle between the two, Adenauer withdrew his nomination in 1959 and continued as chancellor. In 1963, however, Erhard succeeded Adenauer as chancellor until his own enforced resignation in 1966. See his *Prosperity through Competition* (trans. 1959).

ERIC, the name of several Danish and Swedish kings, of whom the following are noteworthy:

Eric VII (1382–1459), the son of Duke Wratislaw of Pomerania, in 1412 succeeded Queen Margaret of Denmark on the throne of Denmark, Norway and Sweden, united by the treaty of Calmar. Cruel and cowardly, he lost Sweden in 1437 through a revolt in Dalecarlia, and in 1439 was deposed also in Denmark.

Eric VIII, the Saint, became king of Sweden in 1155, did much to extend Christianity and to improve the laws, and fell in battle with the Danes in 1160.

Eric XIV (1533–77) of Sweden, succeeded his father, the great Gustavus Vasa, in 1560, and at once began to exhibit the folly that disgraced his reign. His matrimonial schemes reached even Elizabeth of England and Mary of Scotland, until at length (1567) his roving fancy found rest in the love of a peasant girl, who alone was able to control his paroxysms of blind fury. He was deposed in 1569 in favour of his brother John, and eight years later was poisoned. He had a genuine love of letters, and solaced his captivity with music and the composition of psalms.

ERIC THE RED, Norwegian sailor, explored the Greenland coast and founded the Norse colonies there (A.D. 985); his son Leif Eriksson (q.v.) landed in 'Vinland', often identified as America (1000). Both men are the subject of Icelandic sagas.

ERICSSON, John (1803–89), Swedish inventor, born at Långbanshyttan, after serving as officer of engineers in the Swedish army, removed in 1826 to England, and continued to occupy himself with inventions. In 1829 he built a formidable rival to Stephenson's *Rocket*; in 1836 patented the first successful screw-propeller. In 1839 he went to the United States, where he designed the warship *Princeton*, the first steamer with engines and boilers entirely below the water-line, and brought out his improved caloric engine and numerous other inventions. In 1861, during the Civil War, he built the ironclad *Monitor*, and in 1862 a number of similar vessels for the American navy. The *Destroyer*, a vessel with submarine guns, was tried in 1881, but failed to come up to requirements. In 1883 he erected a 'sun motor' in New York. His inventions largely revolutionized navigation and the construction of warships. See *Life* by W. C. Church (2nd ed. 1893).

ERIGENA, Johannes Scotus (c. 813–880), philosopher, was doubtless a native of Ireland (then 'Scotia'). He resided at the court of Charles the Bald in France, where he is said to have been the head of the 'court school'. He came (851) to the help of Hincmar in the Predestination controversy with the doctrine that evil is simply that which has no existence, and that therefore damnation consists only in the consciousness of having failed to fulfil the divine purpose. The Council of Valence condemned this *pultes Scotorum* ('Irishmen's porridge') as 'an invention of the devil'. Tradition says that, having become Abbot of Malmesbury, he was (c. 880) stabbed to death with their pens by his scholars. Erigena translated into Latin (860) the writing of the pseudo-Dionysius the Areopagite, and Greek scholia to Gregory Nazianzen. His chief work, *De Divisione Naturae* (c. 865), was condemned by a council at Sens and by Pope Honorius III (1225), and was placed on the Index by Gregory XIII in 1685. In it he sought to reconcile authority with reason. His system is not so much Pantheism as Monism, in which God and the world are merged in the higher unity of 'Nature'. See works by Rand (1906), Gardner (1900), Bett (1925), Samstag (1930) and Cappuyns (Paris 1933).

ERINNA, a Greek poetess, the intimate friend of Sappho, born either at Rhodes or at Telos about 600 B.C. Though she died at nineteen, she won fame by her epics, only four lines of which are extant.

ERIUGENA. See ERIGENA.

ERLANGER, Joseph (1874–1965), American physiologist, was born at San Francisco, January 5. Professor of Physiology successively at the Johns Hopkins University, Wisconsin and Washington, he shared with Gasser the Nobel prize for medicine in 1944; their work is recorded in *Electrical Signs of Nervous Activity* (1937).

ERNEST AUGUSTUS (1771–1851), king of Hanover, George III's fifth son, in 1786 was sent to the University of Göttingen; in 1790 entered the Hanoverian army; at Tournay lost his left eye (1794); in 1799 was created Duke of Cumberland; and in the House of Lords showed himself a strong Tory and staunch Protestant. In 1815 he married the Princess Frederica of Mecklenburg-Strelitz, and in 1837 under the Salic law succeeded William IV as King Ernest I of Hanover. His policy was in all respects reactionary; but in 1848 he did so far yield to the storm as just to save his throne by the unwilling concession of liberal reforms. See Wilkinson's *Reminiscences of the Court of King Ernest* (1886) and Life by G. M. Willis (1954).

ERNESTI, Johann August (1707–81), classical and biblical scholar, born at Tennstedt, was a professor at Leipzig from 1742, edited many classical texts, and was the chief founder of a correct exegesis of Scripture by the laws of grammar and history.

ERNLE, Rowland Edmund Prothero, Baron (1851–1937; cr. 1919), author and politician, born at Clifton-on-Teme, was M.P. for Oxford University (1914–19), and minister of agriculture (1916–19). His works include *The Psalms in Human Life* (1903), *English Farming, Past and Present* (1912), and editions of the letters of Dean Stanley, of Gibbon, of Byron, of Richard Ford.

ERNST, Max (1891–), German painter, was born at Brühl, near Cologne. After studying philosophy at Bonn, he turned to painting, and in 1918 founded, at Cologne, the German Dada group. Later still, at Paris, with Éluard and Breton, he participated in the surrealist movement. He settled in U.S.A. in 1941, but returned to France in 1953. He won the Venice Biennale prize (1954). See study by J. Russell (1968).

ERNULPHUS, or **Arnulf** (1040–1124), a French Benedictine, appointed Prior of Canterbury by Anselm, was subsequently Abbot of Peterborough (1107) and Bishop of Rochester (114). He was equally remarkable for skill in canon law and personal saintliness; and compiled a great collection of documents about his own church, laws and papal decrees, &c., which from the old name of the see (*Hrofe-ceaster*) was known as the *Textus Roffensis*: it is to an extract from this that he owes the invidious distinction given him in *Tristram Shandy*. Sterne makes the pious bishop the most profound master of cursing on the strength of the excerpt called *The Pope's Dreadful Curse: being the Form of Excommunication taken out of the leger-book of the Church of Rochester, writ by Ernulphus the bishop* (Harleian Miscellany, vol. vi).

EROSTRATUS. See HEROSTRATUS.

ERPENIUS, properly **Thomas van Erpen** (1584–1624), Dutch Orientalist, was born at Gorkum, September 7, 1584, studied at Leyden, and at Paris learned Arabic from an Egyptian. In 1613 he became professor of Oriental Languages at Leyden, where he erected an Arabic press in his own house. As oriental interpreter to the government, he read and wrote replies to all official documents coming from the East. His famous *Grammatica Arabica* (1613) enjoyed undisputed supremacy for two hundred years; many still think his *Rudimenta* (1620) unsurpassed. Other works are his *Proverbiorum Arabicorum Centuriae Duae* (1614), and his edition of El-Mekin (1625).

ERSCH, Johann Samuel (1766–1828), German bibliographer, born at Grossglogau, studied at Halle, and became in 1800 librarian to the University of Jena, in 1803 professor of Geography and Statistics at Halle, and in 1808 also principal librarian. In 1818, along with Gruber, he commenced the publication at Leipzig of the famous yet unfinished *Allgemeine Encyklopädie*. By his *Handbuch der deutschen Litteratur seit der Mitte des 18. Jahrh.* (1812–14) he established modern German bibliography.

ERSKINE, (1) **David Stewart, 11th Earl of Buchan** (1742–1819), brother of (3) and (8), though a vain eccentric, founded the Society of Antiquaries of Scotland and brought about a reform in the election of Scottish peers.

(2) **Ebenezer** (1680–1754), founder of the Secession Church in Scotland, brother of (7), born probably in Berwickshire. Preacher of Portmoak in Kinross-shire from 1703, on the rise of the Marrow Controversy he took a prominent part on the evangelical side; in 1731 he was translated to Stirling. In the patronage dispute he advocated the right of the people to choose their own pastors, and, with three other ministers, was in 1733 suspended and then deposed. The sentence was revoked next year, but Erskine declined to return unless the evils he contended against were removed. The invitation remained open until 1740, when he was finally deposed. On the first deposition, Erskine and his adherents at Gairney Bridge near Kinross erected themselves into the 'Associate Presbytery'. This was the origin of the Secession Church. In the division in 1747 of the Seceders into Burghers and Antiburghers, Erskine headed the Burghers. He married twice, and had fifteen children. See Lives by D. Fraser (1831) and Harper (1849); and *The Erskines*, by A. R. MacEwen (1900).

(3) **Henry** (1746–1817), Scottish jurist and writer, brother of (1) and (8), born in Edinburgh. He joined the Scottish bar in 1768, became lord advocate (1783), and dean of the Faculty of Advocates (1785), but was deposed in 1796 for supporting at a public meeting a resolution against the government's Seditious Writings Bill. Returned by the Haddington burghs in March 1806, and in November by the Dumfries Burghs, he was again lord advocate (1806–07), and died October 8, 1817. He published metrical translations from the classics, *The Emigrant* (1773), &c. The recorded fragments of his speeches justify his high reputation as an orator and a wit. See Colonel Fergusson's *Henry Erskine* (1882).

(4) **John** (1509–91), of Dun, Scottish reformer, took an active share in public affairs, steadfastly supporting the reformed preachers, especially Wishart and Knox, while his moderate and conciliatory temper gave him influence even with the Catholics and the Court. From 1560 to about 1589 he was superintendent for the reformed district of Angus and Mearns. Although a layman, he was five times moderator of the General Assembly, and was one of the compilers of the *Second Book of Discipline* (1578).

(5) **John** (1695–1768), of Carnock, Scottish jurist, father of (6), called to the bar in 1719, in 1737 became professor of Scots Law at Edinburgh. His two works are still held in deserved repute—*Principles of the Law of Scotland* (1754; 21st ed. 1911), and the more important *Institutes of the Law of Scotland* (1773; 9th ed. 1871).

(6) **John, D.D.** (1721–1803), son of (5), Scottish minister, was for many years the leader of the evangelical party in the church. See *Life* by Sir Henry Moncrieff Wellwood (1818).

(7) **Ralph** (1685–1752), Scottish minister, brother of (2), joined him in the Associate Presbytery in 1737, and also took part with the Burghers. His sermons were greatly prized, and many of them were translated into Dutch. His *Gospel Sonnets* and *Scripture Songs* are well known. See *Life* prefixed to his *Practical Works* (1764).

(8) **Thomas, 1st Baron** (1750–1823), brother of (1) and (3), was born in Edinburgh, January 21, 1750. In 1764 he was sent to sea, in 1768 bought a commission in the 1st Royals, and at Minorca (1770–72) studied English literature. Quitting the army, he entered Lincoln's Inn (1775) and Trinity College, Cambridge (1776), where he took an honorary M.A. in 1778, just before being called to the bar. His success was immediate and unprecedented. His brilliant defence (1778) of Captain Baillie, lieutenant-governor of Greenwich Hospital, who was threatened with a criminal prosecution for libel, overwhelmed him with briefs. The next year saw an equally successful defence of Admiral Lord Keppel, and in 1781 he secured the acquittal of Lord George Gordon (q.v.). In 1783 Erskine became a King's Counsel, and M.P. for Portsmouth. His first appearance in the House of Commons was a failure; and he never became a parliamentary orator. His sympathy with the French Revolution led him to join the 'Friends of the People', and to undertake the defence in many political prosecutions of 1793–94. His acceptance of a retainer from Tom Paine cost him the attorney-generalship to the Prince of Wales (held since 1786); his speeches for him and Frost (1793), Hardy (1794) and Horne Tooke (1794) are among the finest specimens of forensic skill. That for Hadfield (1800), indicted for shooting at George III, was a destructive analysis of

the current theory of criminal responsibility in mental disease. In 1802 Erskine was appointed chancellor to the Prince of Wales, an ancient office revived in his favour. In 1806 he was raised to the peerage and the woolsack, but resigned next year, and gradually retired into private life. He died at Almondell, Linlithgowshire, November 17, 1823. In 1821 he had made a second marriage, this time at Gretna Green. He published a pamphlet on army abuses in 1772; a discussion of the war with France in 1797; a political romance, *Armata*; a pamphlet in favour of the Greeks; and some poems. His decisions as lord chancellor were styled the ' Apocrypha ', and have added nothing to his fame. His reputation was solely forensic, and in this respect is unrivalled in the history of the English bar. See the *Life* by Lovat-Fraser (1932).

(9) **Thomas** (1788–1870), of Linlathen, Scottish religious writer, was admitted advocate in 1810, but ceased to practise after his elder brother's death gave him the estate of Linlathen, near Dundee. He published several religious works, his cardinal belief being ultimate universal salvation. See his *Letters* (1878), and *Life* by Henderson (1899).

ERTZ, Susan (*c.* 1894–) pen-name of Mrs **Ronald McCrindle**, American novelist, born in Walton-on-Thames. Her many popular novels include *Madame Claire* (1922), *The Galaxy* (1929), *The Prodigal Heart* (1950) and *Charmed Circle* (1956).

ERVINE, St John Greer (1883–1971), British playwright and author, born in Belfast. From 1915 to 1916 he was manager of the Abbey Theatre, Dublin, where his first play, *Mixed Marriage*, had been produced in 1911. *Jane Clegg* was produced in 1914, and after service in World War I, he won a high reputation as a dramatic critic, working on *The Observer* and *The Morning Post*, and with the B.B.C. in 1932. His most successful plays are perhaps *Anthony and Anna* (1926), *The First Mrs Fraser* (1929) and *Robert's Wife* (1937); other publications include seven novels and several biographies.

ERZBERGER, Matthias (1875–1921), German politician, born at Buttenhausen, Württemberg, became controversial when, as German propaganda minister, he began to advocate peace without annexations as early as 1917 and again (1918–19) when, as a member of the armistice delegation, he advocated acceptance, despite fierce German opposition, of the terms of the Versailles Treaty. Finance minister and vice-premier in 1919, he drastically reformed the tax system and nationalized the German railways. Unsuccessful in a libel action against an unscrupulous political opponent, he resigned in February 1921 and was assassinated by members of an extremist group on August 26. He wrote *The League oᶠ Nations, the Way to World Peace* (1918; trans. 1919), &c.

ESARHADDON (d. 669 B.C.), king of Assyria, a younger son of Sennacherib, whom he succeeded in 680 B.C., achieved the conquest of Egypt (675–671).

ESCHENBACH, Wolfram von. See WOLF-RAM.

ESCOBAR Y MENDOZA, Antonio, *men-dō'tha* (1589–1669), Jesuit casuist, born at Valladolid, wrote *Liber Theologiae Moralis* (1652–63, 7 vols.), which was publicly burnt in Paris and violently attacked by Pascal in his *Lettres à un provincial*.

ESCOFFIER, Auguste, *es-kof-yay* (*c.* 1847–1935), Parisian cook, served a Russian grand-duke, became *chef de cuisine* to the general staff of the Rhine army in the Franco-Prussian war (1871) and of the Grand Hotel, Monte Carlo, before Mr Ritz persuaded him to come to the Savoy, London, and finally to the Carlton. He invented the *bombe Nero* of flaming ice, *pêche melba*, &c., and wrote the *Guide culinaire* (1903) and *Ma Cuisine* (1934).

ESOP. See AESOP.

ESPARTERO, Baldomero, *es-par-tay'rō* (1792–1879), Spanish general, the son of a cartwright in a village of La Mancha, was in 1815–25 in South America, where he fought against the insurgents. As captain-general (1836) of the Basque provinces, he next year twice defeated the Carlists, and drove Don Carlos into France; for this he was created Duke of Vitoria. In 1841 he was made regent until Queen Isabella should reach her majority; he guided the state through Socialist and Carlist troubles, until a combination of Republicans and Moderates caused his fall in 1843. He resided for four years in England, then, returning to Spain, lived quietly at Logroño till 1854, when he was again called to the head of the government; but in 1856 he was supplanted by O'Donnell. After the revolution of 1868 Espartero supported the provisional government. In 1870 his name was put forward for the throne; but in 1875 he tendered his adhesion to Alfonso. See *Life* by Florez (1843–45).

ESPINEL, Vicente de (1551–1624), Spanish writer, born at Ronda, served as a soldier in France and Italy, meeting with some of the adventures related in his *Life of Marcos de Obregón* (1618 and 1804; Eng. trans. 1816) —a book largely drawn upon by Lesage for his *Gil Blas*. After his return to Spain he took holy orders. He also published a volume of poems (1591) and a translation of the *Ars Poetica* of Horace. He was, if not the inventor, the improver of the ten-line octosyllabic stanza, and added the fifth string to the guitar. See *Life* by Pérez de Guzmán (Barcelona 1881).

ESPRONCEDA, José de, *es-pron-thay'THa* (1808–42), Spanish poet and revolutionist, born at Almendralejo in Estremadura, wrote romantic poems in the Byronic manner and is considered by many the greatest lyricist of his time. See *Life* by Cortés (Valladolid 1942).

ESPY, James Pollard, *es'pi* (1785–1860), meteorologist, was born in Pennsylvania. His *Philosophy of Storms* (1841) was commended by the Académie des Sciences. Appointed in 1843 to the Washington Observatory, Espy laid the basis of the Weather Bureau.

ESQUIROL, Jean Étienne Dominique, *es-ki-rol* (1772–1840), French physician, born at Toulouse, served in the military lazaretto at Narbonne (1794), and was appointed physician to the Salpêtrière at Paris (1811). After 1817 he delivered clinical lectures on brain diseases; in 1818 he secured the appointment of a commission on abuses in madhouses; in 1825 he became first physician to the *Maison des Aliénés*, while managing his private asylum at Charenton. The July Revolution deprived him of his public offices. Esquirol's writings embrace the whole treatment of insanity.

ESQUIROS, Henri Alphonse, *es-kee-rōs'* (1814–76), French poet and politician, born at Paris, published poems and romances. For his *Évangile du peuple* (1840), a democratic commentary on the life of Jesus, he was fined and imprisoned; this inspired his *Chants d'un prisonnier*. His *Vierges folles, Vierges martyres*, and *Vierges sages* (1841–42) showed further his socialistic sympathies. After the Revolution of February 1848, he became a member of the Legislative Assembly, but the *coup d'état* of 1851 drove him to England, where he gathered the materials for his *English at Home, Cornwall and its Coasts*, and *Religious Life in England*. In 1870 he was administrator of Bouches-du-Rhône, and was sent to the National Assembly (1871) and the Senate (1875).

ES-SA'ID, Nuri, officially **Nouri Said Pasha,** *sah'eed* (1888–1958), Iraqi politician, was born at Kirkuk and educated at the Istanbul Staff College for the Turkish Army, but fled to Egypt when his Pan-Arab activities became suspect. In World War I he fought against the Turks under King Hussein of the Hejaz. In 1921 he became Iraq's first chief of the General Staff and a year later defence minister. From 1930 he filled the office of prime minister many times until he was assassinated in July 1958 after the *coup d'état* of Brigadier Kassem (q.v.).

ESSEX, Earl of, a title borne successively by Mandevilles, Bohuns, Bourchiers (Devereux's ancestors), Thomas Cromwell and the Devereux, of whom the following are noteworthy:

(1) **Walter Devereux, 1st Earl** (cr. 1572), **2nd Viscount Hereford** (1541–76), scion of an old Herefordshire house, colonizer of Ulster.

(2) **Robert Devereux, 2nd Earl** (1566–1601), eldest son of (1), was born at Netherwood near Bromyard, November 19, 1566, and at thirteen took his M.A. from Trinity College, Cambridge. Under Leicester, who had become his stepfather in 1580, he first saw service in the Netherlands (1585–86), and distinguished himself at Zutphen. Back at court, he quickly rose in the favour of Elizabeth, only seriously interrupted by his clandestine marriage in 1590 with Sir Philip Sidney's widow. In 1591 he commanded the forces despatched to help Henry IV against the League; in 1593 became a privy councillor, and by 1594 was acting as a sort of foreign secretary. His was the principal glory of the capture of Cadiz (1596); but his, too, largely the failure next year of the 'Islands Voyage'. In 1597 Essex became Earl Marshal, in 1598 chancellor of Cambridge; but meanwhile occurred his great quarrel with Elizabeth, when he

turned his back on her, and she boxed his ears—they were never properly reconciled. His six months' lord-lieutenancy of Ireland proved a failure; and, concluding a truce with Tyrone, he hurried back to England. Elizabeth received him not ungraciously at first; but imprisonment followed, and deprivation of all his dignities. Then he formed the mad plot for removing Elizabeth's counsellors, and on February 8, 1601, attempted to raise the earldom of London. On the 19th he was found guilty of high treason, on the 25th beheaded in the Tower. A patron of letters, Essex was himself a sonneteer. See Lytton Strachey's study (1928) and Cooper's *Athenae Cantabrigienses* (1861).

(3) **Robert Devereux, 3rd Earl** (1591–1646), eldest son of (2), was born in January 1591, and in 1604 the earldom was restored to him. From 1626 he attached himself to the popular party; in July 1642 he received the command of the parliamentary army. He was brave personally, but a very poor general; and to him the prolongation of the war was largely due. The drawn battle of Edgehill, the capture of Reading, and the relief of Gloucester were followed by his blundering march into Cornwall, whence he fled by sea. In April 1646 he resigned the command, and on September 14, he died. The title died with him; but in 1661 it was revived in favour of Arthur, Lord Capel (1631–83), ancestor of the present earl. See OVERBURY, and W. Bourchier Devereux's *Lives of the Devereux Earls of Essex* (1853).

ESTAING, Charles Hector Théodat, Comte d', *es-tĩ* (1729–94), French naval officer, served in the East Indies. In 1778 he cooperated with the American colonists against the British, and captured St Vincent and Grenada in 1779, but his efforts on the mainland were unfortunate. In 1780 he persuaded the French ministry to send 6000 men to the colonists' aid. He was guillotined as a royalist.

ESTE, *es'tay*, one of the oldest and most illustrious families of Italy. In 1097 it divided into a German and an Italian branch. The former was founded by Welf IV, made Duke of Bavaria by the Emperor Henry IV in 1070. From him are descended the Este-Guelph Houses of Brunswick and Hanover, and the sovereigns of Great Britain. The Italian branch was founded by Welf's brother, Fulco I. As heads of the Guelph or imperial party they gained possession of Ferrara, Ancona, Modena and Reggio, and were famous as patrons of art and literature. Alfonso I (d. 1534), soldier and statesman, had Lucrezia Borgia (q.v.) as second wife. By a quarrel with Popes Julius II and Leo X he forfeited his papal fiefs, which were restored by Charles V after the siege of Rome in 1527. His son, Ercole II (d. 1559), who married Renata, daughter of Louis XII of France, attached himself to Charles V. His brother, Ippolito (d. 1572), a church dignitary, erected the magnificent Villa d'Este at Tivoli. Alfonso II (d. 1597), splendid and ambitious, showed great cruelty to Tasso. Rinaldo (d. 1737) by his marriage with Charlotte of Brunswick united the German and Italian houses. The male line became extinct with Ercole III (d. 1803), whose only daughter married the Archduke Ferdinand of Austria. Their eldest son, Francis IV, by the treaty of 1814–15 was restored to the duchy of Modena. His son, Francis V (1819–75), in 1859 resigned his territories to Victor Emmanuel.

ESTELLA. See PRIMO DE RIVERA.

ESTERHÁZY, a powerful family of Hungary, divided into several branches. Count Paul Esterházy of Frakno (1635–1713), Austrian field-marshal, for his successes against the Turks was made a prince of the empire in 1687. Prince Nicholas IV (1765–1833) formed a splendid collection of pictures at Vienna, and by extravagance brought his vast estates into sequestration. Napoleon in 1809 made overtures to Prince Esterházy respecting the crown of Hungary. His son, Prince Paul Anton (1786 1866), represented Austria at London until 1842, and in 1848 was minister of foreign affairs. He added to his magnificence to the burdens on the family property, which was again sequestrated in 1860.

ESTÈVE, Maurice (1904–), French artist, born at Culan. He studied in Paris, designed textiles in Spain and about 1937 worked with Robert Delaunay. His use of pure colour in his lyrical abstract paintings, some of which are watercolours, shows something of Delaunay's influence.

ESTHER, a foster-daughter of the Jew Mordecai, according to the Book of Esther was chosen by the Persian king Ahasuerus (Xerxes) as his wife in place of the disgraced queen Vashti, and brought about the deliverance of her people.

ESTIENNE. See STEPHENS.

ESTRÉES, Gabrielle d', es-tray (c. 1570–99), mistress of Henry IV of France from about 1590, was created Marquise de Monceaux and Duchesse de Beaufort. Henry was about to divorce his queen in order to marry her, when she died suddenly at Paris. From their illegitimate offspring the house of Vendôme (q.v.) was descended.

ETHELBERT (552–616), king of Kent. In his reign Kent achieved (c. 590) the hegemony over England south of the Humber, and Christianity was introduced by St Augustine (597). To him we owe the first written English laws.

ETHELDREDA, St (630–679), daughter of the king of East Anglia, was twice married, but withdrew first to the monastery founded by her aunt, Ebba, on St Abb's Head, and then to the Isle of Ely, where in 673 she founded a nunnery. Her name was corrupted into St Audrey.

ETHELRED I, king of Wessex and Kent, elder brother of Alfred the Great, reigned from 866 till his death in 871, shortly after his victory over the Danes at Ashdown.

ETHELRED II (968–1016), the 'Unready', king of England, was seven when his father, King Edgar, died, and ten when the murder (978) of his half-brother, Edward the Martyr, placed him on the throne. From boyhood he was swayed by unworthy favourites, and his reign was a series of raids by the Northmen, and endeavours to buy them off. 'Unready'

stands for 'redeless', void of foresight. He misplaced energy enough in his treacherous massacre of the Danish settlers on St Brice's Day, November 13, 1002, a crime punished by fierce invasions until in 1014 he was forced to fly to Normandy. In 1002 he had married Duke Richard's daughter, Emma—the earliest link between England and Normandy. Sweyn's death allowed his recall, but in 1016 he himself died in London. He was succeeded by Edmund Ironside, third son by a first marriage; by Emma he was the father of Edward the Confessor.

ETHELRED OF RIEVAULX. See AILRED.

ETHEREGE, Sir George (?1635–92), a Restoration dramatist, was born probably at Maidenhead. Secretary to the ambassador at Constantinople (1668 to 1670 or 1671) he married a wealthy widow, and in 1685 was sent to be resident at the Imperial court at Ratisbon. He varied the monotony of this banishment with coursing, drinking, play, flirtation with actresses and correspondence with Middleton, Dryden and Betterton. He seems to have died in Paris. In English literature he is founder of the comedy of intrigue. He sought his inspiration in Molière, and out of him grew the legitimate comedy of manners and the dramatic triumphs of Sheridan and Goldsmith. His three plays are *The Comical Revenge; or, Love in a Tub* (1664); *She Would if She Could* (1668); and *The Man of Mode; or, Sir Fopling Flutter* (1676)—all highly popular in their day. See the edition of the Works by Brett Smith (1927 et seq.); *Notes and Queries* (December 1927, January 1928).

ÉTIENNE. See STEPHENS.

ETTMÜLLER, Ernst Moritz Ludwig, et'mül-ér (1802–77), born at Gersdorf in Saxony, and from 1863 professor of German Literature at Zürich, contributed enormously to the knowledge of Middle High and Low German. In 1840 he edited *Beowulf*; in 1851 appeared his *Lexicon Anglo-Saxonicum*. He also worked in old Norse.

ETTY, William (1787–1849), English painter, was born at York, the son of a baker, and for seven years was apprenticed to a printer in Hull, working at art during his spare time. In 1806 he went to London and studied in the Royal Academy schools; for a year he was a pupil of Lawrence. In 1822–23 he spent eighteen months in Italy, half of them at Venice, where he was deeply influenced by the Venetian masters. Renowned for his nudes, and considered by many to be the greatest English figure painter, he depicted historical and classical subjects, but was perhaps at his best when working on a less ambitious scale. See Lives by Gilchrist (1855) and Farr (1958).

ETZEL. See ATTILA.

EUCKEN, Rudolf Christoph, oy'ken (1846–1926), German philosopher, born at Aurich in East Friesland, studied at Göttingen and Berlin, became a professor at Basel (1871) and at Jena (1874), and won a Nobel prize (1908). Like Bergson's, his philosophy is an activism, nearer the ethical idealism of Kant and Fichte than the intellectualism of Hegel, and is the struggle for the spiritual control of life, a vindication of the significance and worth of life, man being a co-worker with the divine. See his *Life, Work, and Travels* (trans. McCabe, 1921).

EUCLID, Greek mathematician, taught in Alexandria about 300 B.C., and was probably the founder of its mathematical school. His chief extant work is the *Elements* in thirteen books. There are also the *Data*, geometrical theorems, *Phaenomena*, or appearances of the heavens, the *Section of the Scale*, *Optics*, and *Divisions of Superficies*. His lost works include the *Pseudaria*, or Fallacies, and treatises on *Conics*, *Surface-Loci*, and *Porisms*. The *Introductio Harmonica* and *Catoptrica*, both extant, are said not to be his. Euclid's *Elements* is probably better known than any other mathematical book, and, with extensive modifications, is still widely used as a textbook of geometry. The first printed edition of Euclid was a translation from Arabic into Latin (1482). Heiberg and Menge's standard edition is in eight volumes (Leipzig 1883–1916). See Heath's edition of the *Elements* (3 vols. 1908), and his *History of Greek Mathematics* (1921).

EUCLID OF MEGARA, founder of the Megaric philosophy (c. 399 B.C.), was a disciple of Socrates, but had studied the Eleatic system.

EUDOCIA (A.D. 401–465), a Byzantine princess, the beautiful and accomplished daughter of an Athenian sophist, was chosen by the all-powerful Pulcheria to be the wife of her brother, the weak-minded emperor, Theodosius II. She renounced paganism, took the name of Eudocia instead of Athenais, and was married to Theodosius in 421. Soon violent rivalry arose between the sisters-in-law. Eudocia supported Nestorius and was worsted; later Pulcheria was banished, and Eudocia triumphantly backed Eutyches, head of an opposite heresy. But shortly before the emperor's death (450) Pulcheria regained her influence, while Eudocia retired to Jerusalem to end her life in works of piety. She wrote a panegyric on Theodosius' victories over the Persians, paraphrases of Scripture, and a poem on St Cyprian. See F. Gregorovius, *Athenais* (1882).

EUDOXUS OF CNIDUS (408–353 B.C.), Greek geometer and astronomer, studied in Egypt.

EUGENE, Prince, properly **François Eugène de Savoie Carignan** (1663–1736), Austrian soldier, was born in Paris, October 18, 1663. He was the youngest son of the prince of Savoy Carignan and a niece of Cardinal Mazarin. After his father's death (1673), his mother's banishment from court by Louis XIV, and Louis's refusal to give him a commission, he renounced his country, and at twenty entered the service of the Emperor Leopold against the Turks. He displayed extraordinary courage and talent at the siege of Vienna in 1683 and gained rapid promotion. In the war against Louis XIV in Italy, he distinguished himself; field-marshal in 1693, he defeated the Turks with immense slaughter in 1697, putting an end to their power in Hungary. The Spanish War of Succession (1701) recalled him to the army of Italy, but though he inflicted several defeats upon the

French, he was prevented from effecting much by the smallness of his forces and the skill of the Duc de Vendôme, who defeated him at Luzzara in 1702. In command of the imperial army he helped Marlborough at Blenheim (1704). Eugene was checked at Cassano (1705) by Vendôme, but afterwards crushed the French in a defeat which closed their career in Italy. He shared with Marlborough the glory of Oudenarde (1708) and Malplaquet (1709), but, crippled by the withdrawal of Holland and England, was unable to withstand the enemy on the Rhine, and his defeat by Villars at Denain (1712) was followed by other disasters, until the peace of Rastadt (1714) ended the war. On the renewal of the war (1716) against the Turks, Eugene defeated an army of 150,000 men at Peterwardein, took Temesvar, and in 1717, after a desperate battle, carried Belgrade. In a new war with France over the crown of Poland, Eugene was only able to keep the enemy out of Bavaria. After the peace he returned to Vienna, where he died, April 21, 1736. Although a strict disciplinarian, he was worshipped by his men, and lives a hero in song. His rapidity and decision raised the prestige of the Austrian arms to unequalled eminence. See works by Dumont (1823), Kausler (1839), Arneth (1859), Malleson (1888), N. Henderson (1964) and Braubach (1966).

EUGÉNIE, Empress. See NAPOLEON III.

EUGENIUS, the name of four popes:

Eugenius I (pope 654–657), Saint, succeeded St Martin I, who had been forced into exile. Like Martin, he fell foul of the emperor on the question of Monothelism, but was saved from the consequences by the advance of the Islamic invaders.

Eugenius II (pope 824–827), though elected under doubtful circumstances in furtherance of Frankish interests, is said to have fulfilled his office with dignity and wisdom.

Eugenius III (pope 1145–53), a Cistercian monk, was born near Pisa. His predecessor having died during a rebellion against the papacy in Rome, he was obliged to flee to Viterbo immediately upon his election. Soon after his return he was again driven out by a revolt initiated by Arnold of Brescia (q.v.) and he turned his attention to promoting in France a Second Crusade.

Eugenius IV (1383–1447, pope from 1431), a Venetian, quarrelled with the reforming Council of Basel convoked by his predecessor Martin V, which sought to limit papal power. Driven from Rome in 1434 by the Colonnas, he opened a new council, first at Ferrara, next at Florence, and excommunicated the bishops assembled at Basel. The Council of Basel deposed him in 1439 and elected Amadeus, Duke of Savoy, as Felix V. At the Council of Ferrara, John Palaeologus II, emperor of Constantinople, appeared with twenty Greek bishops, and a union between the Greek and Latin churches was effected for a short time in 1439. In 1444 Eugenius again entered Rome.

EUHEMERUS (fl. 300 B.C.), a Greek philosopher, a native of Messene (probably Messana in Sicily) who saw deified heroes in the gods of mythology.

EULENBURG-HERTEFELD, Philipp, Prince of, *oy'len-boorg* (1847–1921), German diplomat and poet, born at Königsberg, confidant of Wilhelm II until scandal ruined him (1907). See Life by Haller (1924).

EULER, Leonhard, *oy'ler* (1707–83), Swiss mathematician, was born April 15, 1707, at Basel, where he studied under John Bernoulli. The Bernoullis, called to St Petersburg by Catharine I, in 1727 induced Euler to settle there, and in 1730 he was appointed to the chair of Physics, in 1733 of Mathematics. More than half the mathematical treatises in the 26 quarto volumes published by the St Petersburg Academy from 1727 to 1783 are by Euler, and at his death he left 200 treatises in MS., which were afterwards published by the Academy. In 1741 he went to Berlin, in 1766 returned to St Petersburg, where he died, totally blind, September 18, 1783. His *Lettres à une princesse d'Allemagne* (1768–72) expound the most important facts in physics. His works (Basel 1911 *et seq.*) are in Latin. See studies by Pasquier (Paris 1927), A. Speiser (1934).

EULER-CHELPIN, Hans Karl August Simon Von (1873–1964), German-Swedish chemist, who became lecturer in Physical Chemistry at Stockholm, afterwards professor of Chemistry and director of the Stockholm Biochemical Institute, and with Harden was awarded the Nobel prize for chemistry in 1929 for researches on enzymes and fermentation.

EUMENES, *yoo-mee'neez.* The name of two kings of Pergamon:

Eumenes I (reigned 263–241 B.C.) successfully drove off Antiochus I *c.* 262 B.C.

Eumenes II (reigned 197–159 B.C.), son of Attalus I. During his reign Pergamon attained the zenith of its importance. Eumenes was an ally of Rome against Antiochus III and against Macedonia. He made Pergamon a centre of learning, founded a great library, and had the famous sculptured Altar of Pergamon built (now in Berlin museum).

EUMENES OF CARDIA (*c.* 360–316 B.C.) Greek soldier, one of the ablest generals of Alexander the Great, after whose death he became governor of Cappadocia, Paphlagonia and part of Pontus. He was ultimately defeated in 316 B.C. by Antigonus and executed.

EUNOMIUS (d. *c.* 399), leader of an extreme sect of Arians, known as the Anomoeans, was born in Cappadocia, laboured under the Arian Aëtius at Alexandria, was Bishop of Cyzicum about 360, but soon had to resign.

EUPHRANOR (fl. 360 B.C.), a Corinthian painter and sculptor famed for his decorations of the Stoa Basileios at Athens.

EUPOLIS. See CRATINUS.

EURIPIDES, *yoo-rip'i-deez* (480 or 484–406 B.C.), latest of the three Greek tragedians, abandoned painting for literature. Of about eighty of his dramas known to us, we possess eighteen complete. He won the tragic prize only five times, and he died at the court of Archelaus, king of Macedonia. He did not take much part in public life; in politics he was a moderate, approving of a democracy, but not of demagogues. The names and probable order of his plays are: *Alcestis, Medea, Hippolytus, Hecuba, Andromache, Supplices, Heraclidae, Troades, Helena, Phoenissae, Orestes*; the *Bacchae* and *Iphigenia in Aulis* were put on the Athenian stage only after the author's death; and it is uncertain to what period belonged the *Ion, Hercules Furens, Iphigenia in Tauris, Electra,* and *Cyclops,* whilst it is doubtful whether the *Rhesus* is genuine. The skill of Euripides as a playwright is of the highest order; he can construct plots which are exciting beyond anything attempted by his predecessors, and he has an unerring instinct for a ' situation '. But in his desire to get on to the situation as rapidly as possible, he substitutes a bald prologue for a proper exposition, and instead of working out the dénouement, makes a *deus ex machina* cut the knot of the situation. To the same end he sacrifices consistency in character drawing. His popularity increased after his death; his plays were ' revived ' more frequently than those of Aeschylus or Sophocles; and the number that have survived is greater than both theirs put together. The oldest MSS. known to us go back only to the 12th century, and are very corrupt. The *editio princeps* (Florence 1496) contains only 4 plays; the Aldine (1503), 18. There are complete editions by Nauck (3 vols., 3rd ed. 1902–06) and Gilbert Murray (3 vols. 1901–10). See translations by E. P. Coleridge (1891), in verse by A. S. Way (1894–98), and Gilbert Murray (1902 *et seq.*), who also wrote *Euripides and his Age* (1913); and works by A. W. Verrall (1895–1910), L. H. O. Greenwood (1953), Norwood (1954).

EUSDEN, Laurence (1688–1730), English poet, born at Spofforth, became undeservedly poet laureate in 1718 after eulogizing the Duke of Newcastle, who was responsible for nominations for the position. He wrote little of value, was lampooned by Pope, and died rector of Coningsby, Lincolnshire.

EUSEBIUS OF CAESAREA, *yoo-see'bee-us* (*c.* A.D. 264–340), the Father of Church History, was born probably in Palestine, became Bishop of Caesarea about 313, and in the Council of Nicea was the head of the semi-Arian or moderate party, which, averse to discussing the nature of the Trinity, would have preferred the language of Scripture to that of theology in speaking about the Godhead. His *Chronicon,* a history of the world to A.D. 325, is valuable as containing extracts from lost works. His *Praeparatio Evangelica* is a collection of such statements in heathen authors as support the evidences of Christianity; its complement is the *Demonstratio Evangelica,* in twenty books, ten of which are extant, intended to convince the Jews of the truth of Christianity from their own Scriptures. His great work, the *Ecclesiastical History,* is a record of the chief events in the Christian church till 324. Other works, all likewise in Greek, are his *De Martyribus Palestinae,* treatises against Hierocles and Marcellus, the *Theophania* (discovered in 1839), and a Life of Constantine. The first complete edition appeared at Basel in 1542; the best modern one is that of Schwartz (1903–09). See translations by Kirsopp Lake and Oulton (1926–32), by Lawlor and Oulton (1927–28).

EUSEBIUS OF EMESA (295–359), Greek bishop, a favourite of the emperor Constantine, born at Edessa, in 341 declined the bishopric of Alexandria, vacant by the deposition of Athanasius, but was afterwards bishop of Emesa in Syria. The homilies under his name are perhaps spurious.

EUSEBIUS OF NICOMEDIA (d. 342), Patriarch of Constantinople, was bishop first of Beryta (Beyrout) in Syria, and then of Nicomedia. He defended Arius at the Council of Nicea and afterwards became the head of the Arian party. He baptized the Emperor Constantine in 337, and became Patriarch of Constantinople in 339. His enemies represented him as cunning and deceitful, but imperious and violent when he had power in his hands.

EUSTACHIO, Bartolommeo, *ay-oo-stah'kyō* (1520–74), Italian anatomist, made important discoveries regarding the ear and the heart, to which his name is attached. He died professor of Anatomy at Rome. See his *Opuscula Anatomica* (1564) and *Tabulae Anatomicae* (1714). But cf. ALCMAEON.

EUSTATHIUS, *yoo-stay'thi-oos*, Greek commentator, was born at Constantinople. Archbishop of Thessalonica from 1160 and of Myra from 1174, he died at an advanced age some time after 1198. He was a man of prodigious acquirements; and his commentary on Homer and other writings contain extracts from works no longer extant.

EUSTATHIUS OF ANTIOCH (fl. *c.* 325), became patriarch of Antioch in 324, and steadfastly opposed the Arians in the Council of Nicea, for which he was deposed in 330. See Life by Sellers (1928).

EUTROPIUS, *yoo-trō'pee-us*, a Latin historian, was secretary to the Emperor Constantine, fought against the Persians under Julian, and died about A.D. 370. His *Breviarium Historiae Romanae*, a narrative of Roman history from the foundation of the city to A.D. 364, is written in a simple style, and probably was intended for the use of schools.

EUTYCHES, *yoo'ti-keez* (*c.* 384–*c.* 456), archimandrite at Constantinople, held that after the incarnation the human nature became merged in the divine, and that Christ had therefore but one nature. He was condemned by a synod at Constantinople in 448; but the council of Ephesus (449) decided in his favour and restored him, deposing his opponents. The council of Chalcedon (451) annulled this decision, and Eutyches died in banishment. His sect was put down by penal laws.

EVAGRIUS, Scholasticus (*c.* 536–*c.* 600), Byzantine church historian, was born at Epiphania in Syria. His Greek *Ecclesiastical History, 431–594*, continuing that of Eusebius, was edited by Parmentier and Bidez (1898).

EVALD, Johannes. See EWALD (2).

EVANS, (1) Sir Arthur John (1851–1941), British archaeologist, son of (5), wrote on Illyria and Bosnia, on numismatics, and on Celtic art, and made epoch-making explorations and discoveries at Knossos and elsewhere in Crete. See a book by Joan Evans (1943).

(2) Caradoc, pseud. of David Evans (1878–1945), Welsh writer, born at Llanfihangel-ar-Arth, known for robust short stories of Welsh rural life. See Life by O. Sandys (1946).

(3) Dame Edith (1888–), English actress, born in London. She earned an enviable reputation for her versatility, appearing in many Shakespeare and Shaw plays, and in others, including *The Way of the World* (Mrs Millamant), *The Late Christopher Bean* (Gwenny), *Daphne Laureola* (Lady Pitts) and *The Importance of Being Earnest* (Lady Bracknell, also on film). During World War II she entertained the troops at home and abroad, and in 1946 was created D.B.E. In 1948 she made her first film appearance in *The Queen of Spades*. See study by Trewin (1954).

(4) Sir George De Lacy (1787–1870), British general, was born at Moig in Ireland, and served in India, the Peninsula, America and at Waterloo. An advanced Liberal, he sat for Rye 1831–32, and for Westminster 1833–65, with the exception of 1841–46. During 1835–37 he commanded the ' Spanish Legion ' for Queen Isabella against the Carlists, and performed notable exploits. In the Crimea (1854) he commanded the second division, was hotly engaged at Alma, and during the siege of Sebastopol gallantly repelled a fierce sortie. Invalided home in February 1855, he received the thanks of parliament, and was created a G.C.B.

(5) Sir John (1823–1908), born at Britwell Court, was a paper manufacturer, and from 1864 was a well-known antiquary through his *Ancient Stone Implements of Great Britain* (1872, new ed. 1897).

(6) Marian. See ELIOT, GEORGE.

(7) Merlyn (1910–), British painter, born at Cardiff, studied at the Glasgow School of Art and has travelled widely. His paintings are mainly surrealist in character, with semi-abstract figures.

(8) Oliver (1755–1819), American inventor, born at Newport, Delaware, improved flour mills, and is said to have invented the first high-pressure steam engine. His steam dredging machine (1804) is considered the first American steam land carriage.

EVARTS, William Maxwell (1818–1901), lawyer and statesman, was born in Boston. He was counsel for President Johnson in 1868, U.S. attorney-general, U.S. counsel before the Alabama Tribunal in 1872, in 1877–81 secretary of state, and sat in the senate in 1885–91.

EVATT, Herbert Vere (1894–1965), Australian statesman, born in East Maitland, South Australia, studied at Sydney University, where he became tutor in Philosophy and Legal Interpretation. He served in the New South Wales State Assembly, took silk in 1929 and was justice of the High Court of Australia from 1930 to 1940. He entered the Federal Parliament as a Labour member in 1940. As minister of external affairs between 1941 and 1949, he was a frequent visitor to Britain and delegate at international conferences. He represented Australia in Churchill's war cabinet, and was leader of the opposition in the Federal Parliament from

1951 to 1960, when he became chief justice of New South Wales until his retirement in 1962.

EVELYN, John (1620–1706), English diarist and author, born of wealthy parentage at Wotton, near Dorking, October 31, 1620, was brought up at Lewes (1625–37), then entered Balliol College, Oxford, and in 1640 the Middle Temple. He witnessed Strafford's trial and execution, and in November 1642 joined the king's army, only to leave it in three days' time, lest he and his brothers should be ' expos'd to ruine, without any advantage to his majestie '. The Covenant being pressed on him, he travelled for four years on the Continent; at Paris in 1647 married the ambassador's daughter, Mary Browne (1635–1709); and in 1652 settled at Sayes Court, Deptford. He was much at court after the Restoration; acted on public committees; in 1685–87 was one of the commissioners of the privy seal, in 1695–1703 treasurer of Greenwich Hospital; and from the first was a prominent member of the Royal Society. In 1694 he removed to his brother's at Wotton, and let Sayes Court to Admiral Benbow, who sublet it to Peter the Great (a ' right nasty ' inmate). In 1699 he succeeded his brother; and, vigorous in intellect to the last, he died at Wotton, February 27, 1706. Evelyn, as active and intelligent as he was honest, and God-fearing, was yet neither sage nor hero. He was always active in Church affairs and was especially prominent in the rebuilding of St Paul's Cathedral. His pen dealt with a multitude of subjects. Of his three dozen works the chief are *Sculptura, or the Art of Engraving on Copper* (1662); *Sylva, or a Discourse of Forest-trees* (1664); and the delightful *Diary* (discovered in an old clothes-basket at Wotton in 1817), to which he owes his celebrity. See *Life* by Austin Dobson (prefixed to 1906 ed. of *Diary*), and works by Lord Ponsonby (1934), C. Marburg (1935) and W. G. Hiscock (1952 and 1955).

EVERDINGEN, Allart van (1621–75), a Dutch landscape painter and etcher, born at Alkmaar, worked in the style of Ruysdael; his brother, **Caesar** (1606–79) was an historical and portrait painter.

EVEREST, Sir George (1790–1866), surveyor-general of India, completed the trigonometrical survey. Mount Everest is named after him.

EVERETT, (1) Alexander Hill (1790–1847), American diplomat, born at Boston, was appointed minister at The Hague in 1818, at Madrid in 1825. Proprietor and editor of the *North American Review* (1829–35), and elected to the Massachusetts legislature, in 1840 he was appointed U.S. agent in Cuba, and in 1845 commissioner to China. His principal works are two series of *Critical and Miscellaneous Essays* (1845–47).

(2) **Edward** (1794–1865), American statesman and scholar, brother of (1), born at Dorchester, Mass., graduated at Harvard in 1811, and in 1815 was elected professor of Greek there. In 1820 he became editor of the *North American Review*, and in 1824 a member of the U.S. congress. In 1835–38 he was four times governor of Massachusetts,

and in 1841–45 minister at the court of St James's. He was president of Harvard 1846–49, in 1852 succeeded Daniel Webster as secretary of state, and in 1853 was returned to the U.S. senate. He wrote *A Defence of Christianity* (1814); poems; *Orations and Speeches* (1836–59); and the memoir prefixed to Daniel Webster's works (1852). See Frothingham's *Life* (1925).

EVERSLEY. See SHAW-LEFEVRE.

ÉVREMOND. See SAINT-ÉVREMOND.

EWALD, (1) Heinrich Georg August von, *ay'valt* (1803–75), German orientalist and theologian, was born at Göttingen, where he studied and became professor both of Philosophy and of Oriental Languages, but was deprived of office in 1837 for protesting against the annulling of the Hanoverian constitution. He is best known for his *Hebrew Grammar* (1827), his *History of Israel* (1843–52, Eng. tr. 1867–86) and a number of biblical works. See *Life* by T. W. Davies (1903).

(2) **Johannes,** *i'vahl* (1743–81), Danish poet, was born at Copenhagen, spent a while as a soldier, and after a disappointment in love devoted himself solely to poetry. In his elegy on the death of Frederick V (1767) he first gave clear proof of his lyrical power. His other writings include the biblical drama, *Adam og Eva* (1769); a series of satiric plays; the prose tragedy, *Rolf Krage* (1770); and the two masterpieces, *Balders Död* and *Fiskerne*, the latter containing ' King Christian stood by the lofty mast ', which has become the national song of Denmark. Ewald was the founder of Danish tragedy, yet his noblest productions are his lyrical poems and odes. See *Lives* by Hammerich (1860), Jörgensen (1888), and Dolleris (1900) and study by W. M. Payne (N.Y. 1897).

EWART, (1) James Cossar (1851–1933), Scottish zoologist, born at Penicuik, was professor of Natural History at Aberdeen in 1879–82 and at Edinburgh in 1882–1927. From 1895 he carried out notable experiments in animal breeding and hybridization and disproved the theory of telegony.

(2) **William** (1798–1869), English politician, was Liberal M.P. from 1828 to 1868 for Bletchingly, Liverpool (his native town), Wigan, and the Dumfries Burghs. He played a leading part in humanitarian reforms, including the abolition of capital punishment for minor offences and of hanging in chains. He carried a free libraries bill in 1850. See *Life* by W. Munford (1960).

EWELL, Richard Stoddert (1817–72), American soldier, born in Georgetown, D.C., served in Mexico and against the Apaches. Confederate lieutenant-general in the civil war, he was captured with his entire force at Sailor's Creek, April 6, 1865.

EWING, (1) Sir James Alfred (1855–1935), Scottish engineer, born at Dundee, was professor of Engineering at Tokyo and Dundee, of Mechanism at Cambridge (1890–1903), director of naval education (1903–1916), principal of Edinburgh University (1916–29), and in World War I decipherer of intercepted messages.

(2) **Juliana Horatia,** *née* Gatty (1841–85), English writer for children, daughter of

Margaret Gatty (1809–73), also a children's writer. Born at Ecclesfield, Yorkshire, she early began to compose nursery plays, which are said to have suggested to her mother the starting of *Aunt Judy's Magazine* (1866), which she later edited, publishing in it many of her charming stories, *Jackanapes* and the like, which are still widely read. See Lives by Horatia Gatty (1885), C. Maxwell (1949).

EWINS, Arthur James, F.R.S. (1882–1957), British chemist, born in London, and educated at Alleyn's School, Dulwich, and at London University (Chelsea Polytechnic), in 1936–37 conducted the researches ending in the preparation of sulphapyridine (M & B 693), of great value in the treatment of pneumonia, &c.

EXETER, Earls of. See CECIL.

EXMOUTH, Edward Pellew, 1st Viscount (1757–1833), admiral, was born at Dover, entered the navy at thirteen; and attracted notice in the battle on Lake Champlain (1776). In 1793, in command of a frigate, he captured a much larger French frigate, and was knighted; in 1796, for acts of personal bravery, he was created a baronet. In 1798 he was sent to the French coast, where many of his most brilliant actions took place. In 1804 he was appointed commander-in-chief in India, from whose seas he drove the French cruisers; he was afterwards made commander-in-chief in the North Sea and in the Mediterranean. In 1814 he was created baron; in 1816 was sent to Algiers to enforce the treaty abolishing Christian slavery. With a fleet of twenty-five English and Dutch vessels he bombarded the city for nine hours, and inflicted such immense damage that the Dey consented to every demand; and he was then made a viscount. See Lives by Osler (1835) and Parkinson (1934).

EYCK, Jan van, * īk* (*c.* 1389–1441), Flemish painter, born probably at Eyck on the Maas, was successively in the service of John of Bavaria, Count of Holland, and Philip the Good, for whom he undertook some diplomatic missions and conducted his prospective bride the Infanta Isabella from Portugal. From 1431 he lived at Bruges. Three of his pictures hang in the National Gallery, London, but his most famous work is the altarpiece (1432) in the cathedral at Ghent. Commissioned by Josse Vydt, a rich burgher, it consists of 24 panels, the central motif being the *Adoration of the Lamb,* and is regarded as the greatest masterpiece of early Flemish art. In the course of a chequered career it has been hidden in the nick of time from Calvinist iconoclasts (1566), looted in the Napoleonic Wars and not replaced until after Waterloo, left in part in Berlin during 1914–18 and restored under the Versailles treaty, captured by the Nazis in World War II and ultimately retrieved by the Allies from a salt mine near Salzburg in 1945. Jan's brother **Hubert** (*c.* 1370–1426), a nebulous figure whose very existence is contested by some art historians, has been traditionally assigned a major part in painting the altar-

piece, but an international committee of art experts which superintended the overhaul and restoration of the panels in 1950–51 was inclined to attribute the whole of the work to Jan, having been unable to find any trace of another hand. No painting exists which can be definitely ascribed to Hubert. The Eyckian style derives from manuscript illumination, and miniatures in the Turin Book of Hours have been attributed to Jan. The tradition that the van Eycks invented oil painting is incorrect, though Jan's work shows improvements in technique and colour mixing. See works by Weale (1908), Conway (1921), and, for the 'anti-Hubert' theory, Renders (1933), and Brockwell (1954).

EYRE, Edward John (1815–1901), British explorer, the son of a Yorkshire clergyman, emigrated to Australia at seventeen, settled on the Lower Murray, and was appointed a magistrate. In 1840 he failed in an attempt to explore the region between South and Western Australia, though he discovered Lake Eyre; but he succeeded in spite of enormous difficulties in 1841 (*Discoveries in Central Australia,* 1845). In 1847 he became governor of New Zealand, in 1854 of St Vincent, and in 1862 of Jamaica. The Negro outbreak there in 1865 was suppressed with stern severity, martial law being proclaimed. A wealthy mulatto named Gordon, a Baptist, and member of the Jamaica House of Assembly, was court martialled, and hanged two days after, the sentence being confirmed by Eyre. A commission found that Gordon had been condemned on insufficient evidence, and Eyre was recalled. On his return he was prosecuted by a committee including J. S. Mill; Carlyle, Charles Kingsley, and Sir R. Murchison promoted the Eyre defence fund. The prosecution failed; and in 1872 the government refunded Eyre the costs of his defence. See studies by Lord Olivier (hostile; 1933) and B. Semmell (1962).

EZEKIEL, Hebrew prophet, was carried captive to Mesopotamia by Nebuchadrezzar in 597 B.C. The text of the Bible book bearing his name is accepted as mainly his, though the prophecies may have been collected by a later editor. See works by Skinner, Davidson, Lofthouse and Ellison; and commentaries by Cornill, Bertholet, Smend, Keil.

EZRA, the Scribe, was living in Babylon during the reign of Artaxerxes Longimanus, or, some would say, during that of Artaxerxes II, about seventy years later. He was commissioned to lead a band of his fellow-countrymen from Babylon to Jerusalem (458 or 397 B.C.), there to reorganize the returned Jews. He is believed to have arranged the books of the Mosaic law (the Pentateuch) as it is now. The book which bears his name was anciently and justly regarded as forming one book with Nehemiah, being simply the continuation of Chronicles. See commentaries by Ryle, Davies, Bertheau, Keil and Schultz; works by Hunter, Torrey and Cheyne; and the introduction by Sayce (2nd ed. 1887).

F

FABER, (1) Cecilia. See CABALLERO.

(2) **Frederick William** (1814–63), English hymn writer, born at Calverley, Yorks, graduated at Oxford, where he won the Newdigate prize for poetry (1836). Under the influence of Newman he turned Catholic and founded a community of converts. He wrote many theological works, but is remembered for his hymns, which include 'The Pilgrims of the Night'. See Lives by F. A. Faber (1869) and J. E. Bowden (1892 ed.).

(3) **George Stanley** (1773–1854), Anglican divine, and uncle of (2), was fellow and tutor of Lincoln College, Cambridge, Bampton Lecturer (1801), rector of Stockton-on-Tees, and master of Sherburn Hospital near Durham. Of his numerous theological works, those upon prophecy have enjoyed the greatest popularity.

(4) **John** (1684–1756), English mezzotint engraver, like his father, John Faber (c. 1660–1721). His chief works are the portraits of the *Kit-Cat Club* and *The Beauties of Hampton Court*.

FABIUS, the name of a patrician family of Rome. In 481 B.C. the Fabii were decoyed into an ambush by the Veientes, and all but one out of 306 men were killed.

(1) **Quintus Fabius Rullianus**, general in the second Samnite war, was dictator (315), censor (304), and six times consul.

(2) **Quintus Fabius Maximus Verrucosus**, five times consul and twice censor, was elected dictator (217) after the Roman defeat at Trasimenus, and by his tactics in the second Punic war was known as Cunctator ('Delayer'). Avoiding a great battle, he carried on guerilla warfare and allowed Rome to muster her forces. He died in 203.

(3) **Cunctator Fabius**, surnamed **Pictor**, executed (304) upon the temple of Salus the earliest known Roman painting.

(4) **Quintus Fabius Pictor**, grandson of (3), wrote (in Greek) the first Roman history in prose.

FABRE, *fah'br'*, (1) **Ferdinand** (1830–98), French novelist, born at Bédarieux, wrote *L'Abbé Tigrane* (1873), and other stories of rustic life in the Cévennes.

(2) **Jean Henri** (1823–1915), French entomologist (the 'Insects' Homer'), born at St Léon, Aveyron, taught at Carpentras, Ajaccio and Avignon before retiring to Sérignan in Vaucluse, where he carried on his entomological investigations and studies until his death. His *Souvenirs entomologiques* (10 vols. Paris 1925 with Life by Lenoir) are masterpieces of minute and patient observation. See studies by Legros (1921), Bicknell (1923) and Bujeau (1943).

FABRE D'ÉGLANTINE, **Philippe François Nazaire** (1750–94), French dramatist, poet, revolutionist, born at Carcassonne, wrote *Le Philinte de Molière* (1790), a sequel to Molière's *Le Misanthrope*. A member of the National Convention, he devised some of the new names of months for the Revolutionary Calendar, but, having fallen foul of Robespierre, was eventually guillotined.

FABRIANO, **Gentile da**, *fa-bree-ah'nō* (1370?–1427?), Italian painter, born at Fabriano, worked chiefly in Venice and Brescia until 1419, and thereafter in Rome, Florence and Siena. He painted religious subjects often showing Franciscan influence. See studies by Colasanti (Bergamo 1909), Molajoli (Fabriano 1929), and Berenson's *Italian Painters of the Renaissance* (1932).

FABRICIUS, (1) **David** (1564–1617), German astronomer, born at Esens, father of (3), was pastor at Resterhaave and Osteel in East Friesland, where he was murdered. He discovered the first variable star.

(2) **Hieronymus**, or **Girolamo Fabrici** (1537–1619), Italian anatomist, born at Acquapendente, was from 1562 professor of Anatomy at Padua. Harvey was one of his pupils. He described the valves of the veins. His *Opera Chirurgica* (1617) passed through seventeen editions.

(3) **Joannes** (1587–1615), son of (1), and an M.D., discovered the sun's spots and its revolution.

(4) **Johann Albert** (1668–1736), German philologist, the modern founder of the history of classical literature and bibliography, was born at Leipzig, and from 1693 lived as a schoolmaster at Hamburg.

(5) **Johann Christian** (1745–1808), Danish entomologist, one of the founders of scientific entomology, was born at Tondern in Schleswig and in 1775 became professor of Natural History at Kiel. His classification of insects is based upon the structure of the mouth.

FABRITIUS, **Carel**, *fa-bree'tsyoos* (?1624–54), Dutch painter, born at Beemster. He worked under Rembrandt about 1641 and lived mainly at Delft, where he was killed in an explosion. He is important for the influence of his sensitive experiments in composition and the painting of light (as in the tiny *View of Delft*, 1652, in the National Gallery, London) upon his pupil Vermeer. Some of his paintings have been attributed to his brother **Barent**, also a pupil of Rembrandt.

FABRY, **Marie Paul Auguste Charles** (1867–1945), French physicist, became professor at Marseilles (1904) and the Sorbonne (1920). Inventor with Perot of the Fabry-Perot interferometer, he is also known for his researches into light in connection with astronomical phenomena.

FABYAN, **Robert** (d. 1513), English chronicler, was a clothier in London, where he was sheriff in 1493. His history, *The New Chronicles of England and France* (1516), comes down in its second edition (1533) to the death of Henry VII. From the accession of Richard I it takes the form of a London chronicle, this being its chief value. The best edition is that by Sir Henry Ellis (1811).

FACCIOLATI, Jacopo, *fat-cho-lah'tee,* (1682–1769), Italian lexicographer, professor at Padua, brought out (1715–19) a new edition of the *Lexicon Undecim Linguarum,* in its first form the work of Ambrose Calepino (1502). In this he was assisted by his pupil and fellow professor, **Egidio Forcellini** (1688–1768), who is mainly responsible for the conception of a totally new Latin dictionary. Facciolati continued this till *his* death, and it finally appeared in 1771. See Lives by Ferrari (1799) and Gennari (1818).

FADEYEV, Alekandr Aleksandrovich, real name **Bulyga** (1901–56), Russian novelist of Zhandov's social realism school, deeply influenced by Tolstoy, wrote *The Rout* (1927) set in the Russian civil war, and *The Young Guard* (1945) portraying Russian resistance against the Germans in World War II. As general secretary of the Soviet Writers' Union (1946–55) he mercilessly exposed any literary 'deviationism' from the party line but became himself a target and, compelled to revise the last-named work (1951), took to drink and finally shot himself.

FADINGER, Stephan (d. 1626), leader of the Austrian peasants' revolt in 1626, in which he was killed at the siege of Linz.

FAED, fayd, (1) **John** (1819–1902), Scottish painter, born at Burley Mill, Kirkcudbrightshire, in 1841 went to Edinburgh, and was elected R.S.A. in 1851.

(2) **Thomas** (1826–1900), Scottish painter, brother of (1), was made an A.R.S.A. in 1849, when he produced *Scott and his Friends at Abbotsford,* engraved by his brother James. In 1852 he removed to London. Faed was made an R.A. in 1864, but resigned in 1893.

FAGUET, Émile, *fa-gay* (1847–1916), French literary critic, born at La Roche sur Yon, Vendée, became professor of French Literature at the Sorbonne in 1890, and was elected to the Académie in 1900. He wrote a number of great works of literary history, among them *Politiques et moralistes du XIX⁰ siècle* (1891–1900; Eng. trans. 1928). See study by Duval (Paris 1911).

FAHLBERG, Constantin (1850–1910), American chemist, in 1879 discovered saccharin by synthesis from toluene.

FAHRENHEIT, Gabriel Daniel, *fah'rèn-hīt* (1686–1736), German physicist, was born at Danzig. About 1714 he first used quicksilver instead of spirits of wine for thermometers. He fixed his freezing point at 32° to avoid negative measurements. In 1724 he was elected F.R.S.

FA-HSIEN, a Chinese Buddhist monk and traveller of the beginning of the 5th century A.D., who made a pilgrimage to India. Giles translated his book (1877; revised 1923).

FAIDHERBE, Louis Léon César, *fay-derb* (1818–89), French general, born at Lille, as governor of Senegal (1854) greatly extended the frontiers of his province (1858–1861). Commanding the army of the North he was defeated near St Quentin on January 19, 1871. After the peace he was dispatched by the French government to Egypt to study the monuments, wrote on Numidian and Phoenician inscriptions (1870–74), the anthropology of Algiers and the French Sudan

(1874–84), a work on Sénégal (1889), and treatises on the Fula (or Poul) and Berber languages (1875–77), besides *Campagne de l'armée du nord* (1871).

FAIRBAIRN, (1) **Andrew Martin** (1838–1912), Scottish Congregational theologian born at Inverkeithing, known for his brilliant essays in the *Contemporary Review,* and his *Studies in the Philosophy of Religion and History* (1876), and *Christ in Modern Theology* (1894). In 1888–1909 he was principal of Mansfield College (Congregational), Oxford. See Life by Selbie (1914).

(2) **Sir William** (1789–1874), Scottish engineer, was born at Kelso, apprenticed (1804) to an engine-wright at North Shields, where he studied mathematics, and made acquaintance with George Stephenson. In Manchester (1817) he took a lead in making iron boats; and his works at Millwall, London (1835–49), turned out hundreds of vessels. For the Menai tubular bridge (Robert Stephenson's idea) Fairbairn invented the rectangular tube ultimately adopted; and he erected a thousand bridges upon this principle. He aided Joule and Thomson (Lord Kelvin) in 1851 in investigations, and guided the experiments of the government committee (1861–65) on the use of iron for defensive purposes. A chevalier of the Legion of Honour, he was created a baronet in 1869, and died at Moor Park, Surrey. See his Autobiography (1877).

FAIRBANKS, Douglas, orig. **Douglas Ullman** (1883–1939), American film actor, born at Denver, Colorado, first appeared in stage plays in 1901, but in 1915 went into films and made a speciality of swashbuckling hero parts, as in the *Three Musketeers, Robin Hood* and *The Thief of Baghdad.*—His son **Douglas** (1909–), followed in his footsteps, starring in *Catherine the Great, The Prisoner of Zenda,* &c., and also gained a reputation as a producer. Becoming interested in international affairs, he subsequently made a name for himself as a diplomat, and also distinguished himself in World War II, winning the British D.S.C., the U.S. Silver Star Medal and other decorations. He was made an honorary K.B.E. in 1949. See a book by Connell (1955).

FAIRFAX, (1) **Edward** (*c.* 1580–1635), English scholar, translator of Tasso, was a son (perhaps a natural son) of Sir Thomas Fairfax of Denton in Yorkshire. His life was spent in literary pursuits, at Fewston, near Otley, and his translation of Tasso's *Gerusalemme Liberata* (1600) is noteworthy. His *Discourse of Witchcraft* (1621) was published in the *Miscellanies* of the Philobiblon Society (1858–59).

(2) **Thomas, 3rd Baron Fairfax of Cameron** (1612–71), parliamentary general, was the son of Ferdinando, Lord Fairfax, and was born January 17 at Denton, Yorkshire. From 1620 he served in Holland, under Lord Vere, whose daughter Anne he married (1637). In the Civil War (from 1642) he was general of parliamentary horse and, distinguished especially at Marston Moor (1644), was in 1645 appointed to succeed Essex in the supreme command. In 1650, on Fairfax's refusal to march against the Scots, who had

proclaimed Charles II king, Cromwell was appointed commander-in-chief, and Fairfax withdrew into private life. After Cromwell's death he assisted Monk against Lambert; and was head of the commission dispatched to The Hague in 1660 to arrange for the return of Charles II. He died at Nunappleton, Yorkshire, November 12, 1671. Fairfax wrote works in prose and verse, including two memoirs on the Civil War. See his *Correspondence* (1848–49); *Life* by Markham (1870).

FAIRFIELD, Cicily Isabel. See WEST (3).

FAISAL, *fī'-*. Name of two kings of Iraq.

Faisal I (1885–1933), born at Ta'if, son of Husein-ibn-Ali (q.v.), king of the Hejaz, aided Lord Allenby in the Great War, and became king of Iraq in 1921.

Faisal II, in full **Faisal ibn Ghazi ibn Faisal el Hashim,** *fī'sèl* (1935–58), king of Iraq, was born in Baghdad, great-grandson with King Hussein (q.v.) of Hussein-ibn-Ali (q.v.). He succeeded his father, King Ghazi, who was killed in an accident, in 1939. After an education at Harrow he was installed in 1953 as the third king of modern Iraq, thus ending the regency of his uncle, Emir Abdul Illah. He paid a state visit to Britain in July 1956. Although in December 1956, in the aftermath of the Suez intervention, he formally declared that Iraq would continue to stand by Egypt, rivalry later grew between the two incipient Arab blocs. In February 1958 he therefore concluded with his cousin King Hussein of Jordan a federation of the two countries in opposition to the United Arab Republic of Egypt and Syria. In July that year, he and his entire household were assassinated during a military *coup d'état* and Iraq became a republic.

FAISTAUER, Anton, *fī'shtow-èr* (1887–1930), Austrian artist and designer. After studying at Vienna, he worked mainly at Salzburg, where he executed a number of frescoes in the Festival Hall, and also various decorations for churches. His style was influenced by Cézanne, but he was noted for his lively fantasy and brilliant colouring.

FAITHFULL, Emily (1835–95), English publisher, born at Headley Rectory, Surrey, in 1860 founded in London a printing house with women compositors, and was appointed printer and publisher-in-ordinary to Her Majesty. In 1863 she started the *Victoria Magazine*, advocating the claims of women to remunerative employment; and in 1868 she published *Change upon Change*, a novel.

FAITHORNE, William (1616–91), English engraver, born in London, fought as a Royalist, and having been banished for refusing allegiance to Cromwell spent several years in Paris, where he made engravings of prints from the vast collection of the Abbé de Villeloin. Allowed home in 1650, he achieved fame as a portraitist and also engraved Newcourt's maps of London and Westminster, a work of great historical value. See Fagan's catalogue (1888). His son **William** (1656–1701?) was celebrated as a mezzotinter.

FAJANS, Kasimir, *fah'yahns* (1887–), Polish-American physical chemist, educated at Leipzig, Heidelberg and Manchester, was professor of Chemistry at Munich (1917–35), then at Michigan. He formulated the theory of isotopes, and contributed valuable research in connection with uranium X_1, the age of minerals in Norway, and the energies of hydration of ions. See his *Radio-activity and Latest Developments in the Study of Chemical Elements* (1919, Eng. ed. 1922) and *Radio-elements and Isotopes* (1931).

FALB, Rudolf (1838–1903), Austrian scientist, born at Obdach, was trained for the priesthood, but took to science, wrote on astronomy and meteorology, and till his death issued from Berlin half-yearly weather forecasts.

FALCONE, Aniello (1600–56), Italian artist, founded a school of battle painters at Naples, and was the teacher of Salvator Rosa (q.v.).

FALCONER, (1) Hugh (1808–65), Scottish botanist and palaeontologist, was born at Forres, graduated M.D. at Edinburgh in 1829, joined the Bengal medical service, became (1832) keeper of the botanic garden at Saháranpur, and discovered many fossils in the Siwálik hills. He made the first experiments in growing tea in India. Back in England for his health (1842), he wrote on Indian botany and palaeontology, arranged Indian fossils in the British Museum and East India House, and prepared his great illustrated folio, *Fauna Antiqua Sivalensis* (1846–49). He returned to India in 1847 as superintendent of the botanic garden and professor of Botany at Calcutta. He died in London. His *Palaeontological Memoirs and Notes* were published in 1868.

(2) **Ion Keith** (1856–87), British orientalist, missionary and athlete, was third son of the Earl of Kintore. While at Cambridge he began evangelistic work, continued at Mile End in London. A keen cyclist, he defeated the then fastest rider in the world (1878), and rode from Land's End to John o' Groats. Lord Almoner's professor of Arabic at Cambridge, he had settled at Shaikh Othman near Aden as a Free Church missionary, when he died of fever, May 10, 1887. In 1885 he translated the Fables of Bidpai. See *Memorials* by Sinker (1888).

(3) **William** (1732–69), British poet, was born in Edinburgh. A barber's son, he went to sea, and soon was shipwrecked off Greece, this voyage forming the subject of his *Shipwreck* (1762). He then entered the royal navy, being appointed in 1769 purser on the *Aurora* frigate, which foundered with all hands near Capetown. His *Demagogue* is a satire on Wilkes and Churchill (1764), and he was also author of the *Universal Marine Dictionary* (1769).

FALGUIÈRE, Jean Alexandre Joseph (1831–1900), French sculptor and painter, born at Toulouse, celebrated for his portrait statues rather than his larger compositions. Several sculptures and paintings are in the Luxembourg at Paris; his statue of Lafayette stands in Washington, D.C. See study by Bénédite (1902).

FALIERO, Marino, *fah-lyay'rō* (c. 1274–1355), Doge of Venice, defeated the Hungarians at Zara in 1346, captured Capo d' Istria, was ambassador to Rome and Genoa, and became Doge in 1354. Next year after conspiring unsuccessfully to overthrow the oligarchs, he was arrested and beheaded. His fate is the theme of tragedies by Byron and Swinburne and of a famous painting by Delacroix. See L. M. Ragg, *Crises in Venetian History* (1928).

FALK, (1) **Adalbert** (1827–1900), Prussian statesman, born at Metschkau, Silesia, as minister of public worship (1872–79) was instrumental in carrying the May laws (1873–1875) against the hierarchical supremacy of the Church of Rome.

(2) **Johann Daniel** (1768–1826), German writer and philanthropist, born at Danzig, founded the ' company of friends in need ' for helping destitute children, and established the Falk Institute at Weimar. Of his writings the best known are his satirical works and a study on Goethe. See books by G. Schnaubert (1912), H. Diersch (1926) and F. Reis (1930).

FALKBERGET, Johan Petter, *falk'ber-ge* (1879–1967), Norwegian novelist, born in Nordre-Rugel. A miner from the age of eight, and the son of a miner, he was almost entirely concerned with the people of the iron-ore district of Røros. His first novel, *Svarte Fjelde* (Black Mountains), appeared in 1907 and his romantic optimism soon caught the popular taste. His main work is *Christianus Sextus*, the general title for six connected novels, which appeared from 1927 to 1935. His *Works*, in ten volumes, were published in 1949.

FALKENHAYN, Erich von (1861–1922), German general, Prussian war minister (1913), chief of General Staff (December 1914 to August 1916), directed the ' push ' against Warsaw in 1915, and commanded in the invasion of Rumania, 1916–17.

FALKLAND, Lucius Cary, Viscount (1610–43), English statesman and writer, was born probably at Burford, Oxfordshire, son of Sir Henry Cary, created Viscount Falkland in the Scottish peerage in 1620, the well-meaning but unfortunate lord-deputy of Ireland from 1622 to 1629. He was educated at Trinity College, Dublin, and later crossed to Holland, but soon returned to devote himself to study, especially of Greek. His father's death in 1633 gave him the title, and after a time he settled down in his house at Tew, in Oxfordshire, to a severe course of study. The house was a centre for the brightest intellects of Oxford and London. The group included Sheldon, Morley, Hammond, Earle, Chillingworth, John Hales and Clarendon. To this period belong Falkland's poems, edited by A. B. Grosart in 1871. His *Discourses of Infallibility*, and the longer *Reply to the Answer Thereto*, are a truer index to what lay closest to his heart. In 1639 he accompanied Essex in the expedition against the Scots. Then he entered parliament as member for Newport (Isle of Wight), and distinguished himself by his ardour and eloquence on behalf of constitutional liberty. Alarmed at an intolerant Presbyterianism, he felt himself reluctantly compelled to take the king's side, although mistrusting his character; in 1642 he accepted the secretaryship of state, and when war broke out loyally supported the king. He

was killed at Newbury, September 20, 1643. Though sensitive and noble-minded, he remorselessly persecuted Strafford to death. See Clarendon, both in the *History* and the *Life*; S. R. Gardiner's *History*; Tulloch's *Rational Theology* (1872); and the *Life and Times* by J. A. R. Marriott (1907).

FALKNER, William Harrison. See FAULKNER.

FALLA, Manuel de, *fa'lya* (1876–1946), Spanish composer, born in Cadiz. He studied the piano as a child, and the failure of a comic opera in 1902 moved him to spend two years in study under Pedrell, so that by 1905 he was awarded prizes both for his piano playing and for his opera *La Vida Breve*. His seven years in Paris, up to the outbreak of World War I, led him to develop his work in the direction of a less exclusively national style, but after his return to Spain his music gradually returned to his original colourful Spanish idiom. His international fame was crowned by the success of his ballet, *The Three-Cornered Hat*, in 1919. With the outbreak of the Spanish Civil War, de Falla settled in South America. Commonly accepted as the greatest of the group of Spanish composers active in the early 20th century, his works include the opera *Master Peter's Puppet Show*, the ballet *Love the Magician* and *Nights in the Gardens of Spain*. See studies by J. B. Trend (1929) and J. Pahissa (Eng. trans. 1954).

FALLADA, Hans, pseud. of **Rudolf Ditzen** (1893–1947), German writer, born at Greifswald, who achieved international fame with his novel of postwar German social problems *Kleiner Mann–Was Nun?* (1932), translated into English as *Little Man, What Now?* Of his other less successful books, *The World Outside* (1934) appeared in English.

FALLERSLEBEN. See HOFFMANN, AUGUST.

FALLIÈRES, Armand, *fal-yayr* (1841–1931), French president (1906–13), born at Agen, became an advocate, deputy, premier (1883), and president of the senate, 1899–1906.

FALLMERAYER, Jakob Philipp, *fal'mer-ī-ér* (1790–1861), German historian, born at Tschötsch, in 1826 became professor of History and Philology at Landshut, wrote on the empire of Trebizond (1827) and on the Morea (1830–36). He insisted that the modern Greeks are mainly Slavonic in origin. See his works, with Life (1861).

FALLOPIUS, Gabriel, Ital. **Gabriele Falloppia** (1523–62), Italian anatomist, became professor of Anatomy at Pisa (1548) and Padua (1551), studied specially the bones and the organs of generation; the Fallopian tube connecting the ovaries with the uterus is named after him.

FALLOUX, Frédéric Alfred Pierre, Comte de, *fal-loo* (1811–86), French politician and writer, was born at Angers. A liberal Catholic, he drew attention to his legitimist works—*L'Histoire de Louis XVI* (1840) and *L'Histoire de Saint Pie V* (1844). Falloux was minister of Public Instruction for ten months under Louis Napoleon, but after the *coup d'état* he retired from public life. He was a member of the French Academy.

FALLS, Cyril Bentham (1888–1971), English military historian, was educated at Bradfield College, Portora Royal School, Enniskillen, and London University. He served as a staff officer in World War I and won the *Croix de Guerre.* He was military correspondent of *The Times* (1939–53) and Chichele professor of the History of War at Oxford (1946–53), when he was appointed Emeritus professor. He wrote the official history of the British Campaigns in Egypt, Palestine, Macedonia and France, studies of Rudyard Kipling and Marshal Foch, *A Short History of the Second World War* (1948), *The First World War* (1960), &c.

FALSTAFF. See OLDCASTLE and FASTOLF.

FANEUIL, Peter, popularly *fun'el* (1700–43), merchant in Boston, U.S., was born at New Rochelle, N.Y. He built the Faneuil Hall in Boston, known as ' the cradle of American liberty ' (1742), and presented it to the town.

FANGIO, Juan Manuel, *fan'jō* (1911–), Argentine racing motorist, was born at Balcarce of Italian descent. He served his apprenticeship to road racing first as a mechanic and then—with a car he built himself—in South American events. He first took part in European Grand Prix racing in 1949 and by 1957 he had won the World Championship five times. See *Life* by Molter (1956).

FANSHAWE, Sir Richard (1608–66), English scholar and diplomat, born at Ware Park, Hertfordshire, studied at Jesus College, Cambridge, and went abroad to study languages. In the Civil War he sided with the king, and while at Oxford married in 1644 the lively and brave Anne Harrison (1625–80). In 1648 he became treasurer to the navy under Prince Rupert, in 1651 was taken prisoner at Worcester, and on Cromwell's death withdrew to the Continent. After the Restoration he was appointed ambassador at the courts of Portugal and Spain, and died suddenly at Madrid. He translated Horace, Guarini's *Pastor Fido,* Camoens's *Lusiad,* &c. Lady Fanshawe's charming *Memoirs* were published in 1829.

FANTIN-LATOUR, Ignace Henri Jean Théodore, *fã-tĭ-la-toor* (1836–1904), French painter, pastellist and lithographer, was born at Grenoble. A friend of Whistler, he stayed for a while in England. His portrait groups and his flower studies are most noteworthy, especially his *Hommage à Delacroix* which contains portraits of Baudelaire, Champfleury, Legros and Whistler, and his *Atelier à Batignolles,* with Monet, Renoir and Zola. See studies by A. Jullien (Paris 1909) and G. Kahn (Paris 1926).

FARADAY, Michael (1791–1867), English chemist and natural philosopher, was born, a blacksmith's son, at Newington Butts near London, September 22. Apprenticed to a bookbinder, he devoted his leisure to science. In 1813 Sir H. Davy engaged him as his assistant at the Royal Institution and entrusted to Faraday the performance of experiments, which led to the condensation of gases into liquids by pressure. In 1827 he succeeded to Davy's chair of Chemistry in the Royal Institution; and was created D.C.L. in 1832. His treatise on *Chemical Manipulation* (1827; 2nd ed. 1842) is even now a very valuable book of reference. His suggestions as to the preparation of the lungs

for diving and the ventilation of lighthouse lamps are notable, as are also his letter on table-turning and his lecture on mental education. The most prominent of his publications on physical science were on the condensation of the gases, limits of vaporization, optical deceptions, acoustical figures, re-gelation, relation of gold and other metals to light, and conservation of force. His Christmas lectures at the Royal Institution, though the subjects were often most abstruse, charmed and attracted all classes of hearers. Besides his lectures on *The Nonmetallic Elements* and on *The Chemical History of a Candle,* we have his *Various Forces in Nature.* But the great work of his life is the series of *Experimental Researches on Electricity,* published in the *Philosophical Transactions* during forty years and more. The following are almost all discoveries of the first importance: induced electricity (1831); the electrotonic state of matter (1831); identity of electricity from different sources (1833); equivalents in electrochemical decomposition (1834); electrostatic induction—specific inductive capacity (1838); relation of electric and magnetic forces (1838); the electricity of the Gymnotus (1839); hydroelectricity (1843); magnetic rotatory polarization (1846), effected by means of the optical glass; diamagnetism (1846–49); relation of gravity to electricity (1851); and atmospheric magnetism (1851). Faraday, who had received a pension in 1835, was in 1858 given a house in Hampton Court. In 1862, as adviser to the Trinity House, he advocated the use of magnetoelectric light in lighthouses. A devout Christian, a member of the body called Sandemanians or Glassites, he died at Hampton Court, August 25, 1867. See *Lives* by Tyndall (1868; 5th ed. 1894), Jones (1870), J. H. Gladstone (1872), Jerrold (1891), Kendall (1955); Faraday's *Diary* (1932 *et seq.*).

FAREL, Guillaume (1489–1565), Swiss Reformer, was born at Gap in Dauphiné, and studied at Paris. A convert to Protestantism, he in 1524 sustained at Basel thirty Protestant theses. After being twice compelled to leave Geneva, he once more entered it in 1534; and in 1535 the town council proclaimed the Reformation. The severity of the ecclesiastical discipline imposed by Calvin produced a reaction, so that in 1538 the two Reformers were expelled from the city. In 1557, along with Beza, Farel was sent to the Protestant princes of Germany to implore their aid for the Waldenses; and he next laboured in the Jura Mountains. He died at Neuchâtel, September 13, 1565. See *Lives* by Kirchhofer (German, 1831–33), Goguel (French, 1873), F. Bevan (English, 4th ed. 1893); and two works in French and in German by E. Schmidt (1834 and 1860).

FARGUS, Frederick John. See CONWAY (2).

FARIA Y SOUSA, Manuel de, *fa-ree'a ee sō'za* (1590–1649), Portuguese poet, born near Pombeiro, went to Madrid *c.* 1613, and was in 1631–34 secretary to the Spanish embassy at Rome. He wrote on Portuguese history and on Camoens, about two hundred Portuguese sonnets and twelve eclogues, and three treatises on poetry.

FARIGOULE, Louis. See ROMAINS, J.

FARINA, Johann Maria, *fa-ree'na* (1685–1766), Italian perfumier, born in Novara, who settled in Cologne in 1709, and invented eau-de-Cologne.

FARINACCI, Roberto, *fa-ree-nat'chee* (1892–1945), Italian politician, born at Isernia, became Fascist party secretary (1924–26), a member of the Fascist Grand Council (1935) and minister of state (1938). An ardent racialist and anti-Semite, notorious for his extremism and pro-Nazi tendencies, he edited the *Regime Fascista*, the party organ. He was ultimately captured and shot, on the same day and by the same band of partisans as Mussolini, while attempting to flee to Switzerland.

FARINELLI, Carlo. See BROSCHI.

FARINGTON, Joseph (1747–1821), R.A., English painter, especially of the Lake District, born at Leigh, kept an invaluable diary, discovered in a garret in 1921. It was edited by J. Greig (1922–28).

FARINI, Luigi Carlo, *fa-ree'nee* (1812–66), Italian statesman, born near Ravenna, practised medicine, later held various public offices, finally becoming minister of commerce in Cavour's last cabinet, and premier for three months from December 1862. His *Il Stato Romano* was translated into English by Mr Gladstone (1851–54); his *Storia d'Italia* is a continuation of Botta's work.

FARJEON, *far'jĕn*, (1) **Benjamin Leopold** (1838–1903), English novelist, born of Jewish parentage in London, after quarrelling with his family went to Australia prospecting for gold, and thence to New Zealand, where he became joint editor of the *Otago Daily Times*, first daily paper produced in the country. Returning to London in 1868, he wrote many novels, mostly of crime and mystery.

(2) **Eleanor** (1881–1965), daughter of (1), wrote fantasies and children's stories, and collaborated with her brother Herbert (q.v.) in *Kings and Queens* (1932). There is a Farjeon award for outstanding work in children's books. See her *Memoirs* (1958).

(3) **Herbert** (1887–1945), son of (1), born in London, was actor, dramatic critic to the *Daily Herald*, and playwright.

(4) **Joseph Jefferson** (1883–1955), son of (1), wrote detective novels and plays, as *The Green Dragon* (1929).

FARMAN, Henri, *far-mã* (1874–1958), French pioneer aviator and aircraft manufacturer, with his brother **Maurice** (1878–1964) introduced the biplane.

FARMER, (1) **John** (*c.* 1565–*c.* 1605), English composer, was organist of Christ Church Cathedral, Dublin, and is chiefly noted for madrigals.

(2) **Richard,** D.D. (1735–97), born at Leicester, in 1757 graduated from Emmanuel College, Cambridge, and helped Johnson with Cambridge notes for his *Lives of the Poets*. His once famous *Essay on the Learning of Shakespeare* (1767) showed that the great dramatist derived his knowledge of the ancients from translations. He became master of Emmanuel (1775), chief librarian to the university (1778), and prebendary at Lichfield (1780), Canterbury (1782) and St Paul's (1788).

FARNABY, Giles (*c.* 1560–*c.* 1600), English composer, born probably in Truro. Few details of his career are known, but he spent most of his active life in London. His works include madrigals and settings of the psalms in verse paraphrases for East's Psalter, but he is best remembered for his keyboard music.

FARNBOROUGH, Lord. See MAY (3).

FARNELL, Lewis Richard (1856–1934), classical archaeologist, born at Salisbury, became a fellow and later rector of Exeter College, Oxford, and was vice-chancellor of the university (1920–23). He wrote *The Cults of the Greek States* (1896–1921), &c. See his autobiographical *An Oxonian Looks Back* (1934).

FARNESE, *far-nay'zay*, an illustrious Italian family originating from Farneto near Orvieto, of whom the following are noteworthy:

(1) **Alessandro** (1468–1549), raised to the Papal See in 1534 as Paul III, founded the duchy of Parma and Piacenza.

(2) **Alessandro** (1546–92), son of the second duke, and one of the most skilful generals of his age, distinguished himself at Lepanto (1571), as governor of the Spanish Netherlands captured Antwerp (1585), and compelled Henry IV of France to raise the siege of Paris (1590).

(3) **Elizabeth** (1692–1766), became the wife of Philip V of Spain in 1714, and warmly supported Alberoni's policy (Life by Armstrong, 1892).—The three antique sculptures (the Farnese Hercules, Flora and Bull) were removed about 1790 from the Farnese Palace at Rome to Naples.

FARNOL, John Jeffrey (1878–1952), English author, born at Aston, lived from 1902 to 1910 in America as a scene painter. His first successful novel was *The Broad Highway* (1910), and he went on to establish a reputation for romantic adventure stories in a period setting, as *The Amateur Gentleman* (1913), *The Geste of Duke Jocelyn* (1919), *Peregrine's Progress* (1922), &c.

FAROUK I, *fah-rook'* (1920–65), ex-king of Egypt, born in Cairo, was educated in England and studied at the Royal Military Academy, Woolwich. He ascended the throne in 1937, dismissed the premier, Nahas Pasha, and devoted himself to schemes of economic development and land reform for a while. In 1942, with Axis troops threatening Egypt, Britain insisted on the re-appointment of Nahas Pasha. After the war, the former 'Prince Charming' and Chief Scout of Egypt gave way increasingly to a life of pleasure. In 1948 he dissolved his first marriage with Princess Farida and married Narriman Sadek in 1951. General Neguib's *coup d'état* in July 1952 forced Farouk to abdicate. His exile in Italy and elsewhere served only to increase his hedonistic inclinations. In 1959 he became a citizen of Monaco.

FARQUHAR, George, *far'kĕr* (*c.* 1677–1707), Irish playwright, born at Londonderry, possibly in 1677 (but he is said to have fought at the Boyne), was educated at Trinity College, Dublin. He became an actor in a Dublin theatre, but proved an indifferent performer. The accidental wounding of a fellow actor so shocked him that he quitted the boards, and shortly after received a commission in a regiment stationed in Ireland. His first comedy, *Love and a Bottle* (1698), proved a success. His *Constant Couple* (1700) met with an enthusiastic reception, and to it he wrote a sequel, *Sir Harry Wildair*. In 1703 he produced *The Inconstant*, founded on Fletcher's *Wild Goose Chase*. Having married in the same year, he fell into pecuniary difficulties, and, struggling with adverse fortune, succumbed, and died in April 1707. During his last illness he wrote the best of his plays, *The Beaux' Stratagem*, and died while its wit and invention were making the town roar with delight. *The Recruiting Officer* had been produced with success in 1706. Farquhar is one of the best of our comic dramatists, and has on the whole more variety and character than any of his compeers. See Ewald's edition of his *Dramatic Works* (1893) and Lives by Schmid (1904) and Connely (1949).

FARQUHARSON, (1) **David** (1840–1907), Scottish painter, born at Blairgowrie, specialized in landscapes of the Scottish highlands and the Cornish coast. He became A.R.A. in 1904.

(2) **Joseph** (1846–1935), Scottish landscape painter, born in Edinburgh, exhibited from the age of 13, became A.R.A. in 1900, R.A. in 1915.

FARR, William (1807–83), English statistician, born at Kenley, Shropshire, studied medicine and worked at medical statistics, becoming a pioneer in the application of ' vital statistics '. In 1838, he became superintendent of the statistical department of the registrar-general and retired in 1880. See Memoir by Humphreys prefixed to his *Vital Statistics* (1885).

FARRAGUT, David Glasgow (1801–70), American seaman, was born of Spanish origin, near Knoxville, Tennessee. Entering the navy in 1810, he became captain in 1855. In the civil war he commanded the armament fitted out (1862) for the capture of New Orleans. On August 5, 1864, he destroyed the enemy's gunboats in Mobile Bay; and a few days later Mobile surrendered. He was made vice-admiral, the grade being created for him by congress, as was also that of admiral (1866). See Lives by his son (1879) and Mahan (1892).

FARRANT, Richard (1530–80), English musician, was organist of St George's Chapel and of the Chapel Royal. The well-known anthem, ' Lord, for Thy tender mercy's sake ' is attributed to him, possibly erroneously. He composed a morning and evening service, two anthems, and parts of other services.

FARRAR, Frederic William (1831–1903), English clergyman and writer, born in Bombay, was ordained in 1854, taught at Harrow, became headmaster of Marlborough (1871–76), honorary chaplain to the Queen (1869–73), and afterwards a chaplain-in-ordinary. He was made a canon of Westminster and rector of St Margaret's in 1876, archdeacon of Westminster in 1883, chaplain to the House of Commons in 1890, and Dean of Canterbury in 1895. His theological writings were many, but he is chiefly remem-

bered for the now much-maligned best seller *Eric, or Little by Little* (1858), one of several school stories from his pen.

FARRELL, James Thomas (1904–), American writer of starkly realist novels of American life, best known being the *Studs Lonigan* trilogy (1932–35) set in the slums of Chicago. See Bibliography by E. Branch (1959).

FARREN, (1) **Elizabeth** (*c.* 1759–1829), English actress, famous at Drury Lane and the Haymarket in aristocratic rôles such as Lady Teazle and Lydia Languish.

(2) **Nelly** (1848–1904), English actress, daughter of Henry Farren and granddaughter of (3), born at Liverpool, was famous as a comedienne and principal boy.

(3) **William** (1786–1861), English actor and theatre manager, celebrated for his interpretation of elderly rôles in 18th century comedy. His son **Henry** (*c.* 1826–60) was also an actor.

FARRÈRE, Claude, pseud. of Frédéric Charles Pierre Édouard Bargone (1876–1957), French novelist, born at Lyons, a naval officer who turned to writing. He made his name with novels of the exotic and tales of travel and adventure. Works include *Fumée d'opium* (1904), *Les condamnés à mort* (1920), &c.

FARSON, James Negley (1890–1960), American author, born in Plainfield, N.J. He trained as a civil engineer but came to England and thence to Russia, where he had an export business and where he witnessed the 1917 revolution. He thereafter led an adventurous life as airman, sailor and journalist which is reflected in his varied works. These include *Sailing Across Europe* (1926), *Seeing Red* (1930), *Bomber's Moon* (1941), *A Mirror for Narcissus* (1957), &c.

FASCH, Johann Friedrich (1688–1758), German composer, born at Buttelstedt, Weimar, was educated at the Thomasschule, Leipzig, and founded the *Collegium Musicum* there, the forerunner of the *Gewandhaus* concerts. After a roving life he was in 1722 appointed *Kapellmeister* at Zerbst. He wrote overtures in the style of Telemann, orchestral suites, greatly admired by J. S. Bach, three operas, since lost, and also several masses, a *requiem*, trios and sonatas. His son, **Carl Friedrich Christian** (1736–1800), born at Zerbst, a harpsichordist and composer, was appointed accompanist to the flute-playing Frederick the Great in 1756. He was twice visited by Beethoven (1796) before his death.

FASTOLF, Sir John (1378–1459), English soldier, was born at Caister. He distinguished himself at Agincourt (1415), and still more in the ' Battle of the Herrings ' (1429), so called because, while convoying supplies to the English besiegers of Orleans, he formed a *laager* of herring barrels, and beat off a whole French army. Later in the same year he was less successful against Joan of Arc, and at Patay, according to Monstrelet, displayed such cowardice that the Duke of Bedford stripped him of his Garter. This, however, is questionable; he rather seems to have retained all his honours till in 1440 he came home to Norfolk, and in 1441 was granted a pension of £20 ' for notable and praiseworthy service and good counsel ',

His Norfolk life is mirrored faithfully in the *Paston Letters*. His identification with ' Sir John Falstaff ' is at least incomplete, for Oldcastle (q.v.) was certainly Shakespeare's prototype.

FATIMA, youngest daughter of Mohammed, was the wife of Ali; from them descended the Fatimites, who ruled over Egypt and North Africa (969–1171), and later over Syria and Palestine.

FAUCHER, Léon, *fō-shay* (1803–54), French journalist and politician, born at Limoges, edited *Le Temps* and other papers (1830–42), wrote *Études sur l'Angleterre* (1845) and after the 1848 revolution became minister of Public Works and of the Interior. The *coup d'état* ended his political career.

FAUCIT, Helen. See MARTIN (9).

FAULKNER, or Falkner, William Harrison (1897–1962), American author, born at New Albany, Miss., served with the R.A.F. in World War I, began his literary career with *Soldier's Pay* (1926), a novel on the aftermath of war, and continued with a number of brilliant, though often pessimistic or horrific stories throwing the evils of society into sharp relief. With *The Sound and the Fury* (1929) he began stylistic experiments somewhat in the Joycian manner, while his *Sartoris* in the same year began a closely related series dealing with the social and racial problems of an imaginary Southern state. Other novels are *As I lay Dying* (1930), *Light in August* (1932) and *Requiem for a Nun* (1951). In 1949 he was awarded the Nobel prize. See his *Collected Stories* (3 vols. 1959), and studies by Slatoff (1960) and Vickery.

FAURE, *fōr*, (1) Edgar (1908–), French statesman, born at Béziers. Trained as a lawyer in Paris, he entered politics as a Radical-Socialist, and was minister of finance and economic affairs in 1950 and 1951, holding this office again in 1954 and in 1958. He served as président du Conseil des Ministres from February 1955 to January 1956, was professor of Law at Dijon Univ. (1962–66), and became minister of agriculture in 1966.

(2) **François Félix** (1841–99), president of the French Republic, was born in Paris. A Roman Catholic, though of Protestant ancestry, and a Moderate Republican, he was first a journeyman currier in Touraine, ultimately a merchant and shipowner at Le Havre. He served as a volunteer in the Franco-German war, in 1881 became deputy for Le Havre, and, after holding posts in several administrations, in January 1895 succeeded Casimir-Périer as president.

FAURÉ, Gabriel Urbain, *fō-ray* (1845–1924), French composer born at Pamiers, became *maître de chapelle* (1877) and organist (1896) at La Madeleine, Paris, director of the Conservatoire (1905–20). Though chiefly remembered for his songs, including the evergreen *Après un rêve*, he also wrote operas and orchestral pieces, such as *Masques et bergamasques*. See study by Jankélévitch (Paris 1938), and Life by Koechlin (1945).

FAUST, Johann. See FUST.

FAUSTINA, mother and daughter, wives of two of the noblest among the Roman emperors. The elder, Annia Galeria, usually spoken of as Faustina Senior, was the wife of Antoninus Pius, and died A.D. 141; the younger, Faustina Junior, was married to his successor, Marcus Aurelius Antoninus, and died in A.D. 175. Their reputation for promiscuity was probably fabricated for after death their memories were greatly honoured by their husbands.

FAVART, Charles Simon, *fa-vahr* (1710–92), French dramatist, born in Paris, son of a pastrycook, was early attracted to the stage. He began writing comic opera, and the success of his first production, *Deux Jumelles* (1734), obtained for him financial backing which enabled him to continue with this genre. He married in 1745 Marie Justine Benoîte Duronceray (1727–72), a talented actress of the *Opéra-Comique* with whom he pioneered a new realism in costume. At the end of 1745 the *Opéra-Comique*, which he was directing, was obliged to close, and the Favarts went to Flanders with a company of actors attached to Marshal Saxe, who made an unscrupulous attempt to procure Mme Favart as his mistress. When she fled from him he took out *lettres de cachet* against her husband, who had to remain in hiding until 1750, when the marshal's death put an end to the persecution, and Favart was able to return to Paris and write more comic operas. Among the best out of more than 100 are *Bastien et Bastienne, Ninette à la cour* and *Les Trois Sultanes*. See studies by Font (1894) and Pougin (1912); also A. Iacuzzi, *The European Vogue of Favart* (N.Y. 1932).

FAVRE, Jules Claude Gabriel (1809–80), French lawyer and politician, born at Lyons, took part in the July revolution of 1830, defended Orsini (q.v.), became a Republican leader, and after the fall of Napoleon III became foreign minister, in which capacity he negotiated the treaty of Frankfurt in 1871. See *Mélanges politiques et littéraires* (1882) and study by Reclus (1912).

FAWCETT, (1) Henry (1833–84), English political economist, born at Salisbury, educated at Cambridge, was blinded in a shooting accident, but his *Manual of Political Economy* led to his election to the chair of Political Economy at Cambridge in 1863. Elected M.P. in 1865, 1868 and 1874 as a Liberal, he was an advocate of female suffrage and other reforms, and as postmaster-general from 1880 introduced the parcel post, postal orders and sixpenny telegrams. See Lives by Stephen (1885) and Holt (1915).

(2) **Dame Millicent,** *née* Garrett (1847–1929), born at Aldeburgh, Suffolk, was wife of (1) from 1867, and wrote *Political Economy for Beginners* (1870), &c. Keenly interested in the higher education of women and the extension of the franchise to her sex, she was made president of the Women's Unionist Association in 1889, G.B.E. in 1925. A sister was Mrs Garrett Anderson (q.v.).

(3) **Percy Harrison,** *faw'set* (1867–1925), English explorer, born at Torquay. He entered the army at nineteen, rose to become lieutenant-colonel, and after service in Ceylon, Hong Kong and elsewhere was in 1906 given a border delimitation assignment on behalf of the Bolivian government. This led to several hazardous expeditions in the

Mato Grosso area in search of traces of ancient civilizations. In 1925 he, his eldest son Jack, and a friend, Raleigh Rimell, disappeared near the Xingú River. See *Exploration Fawcett*, by his younger son Brian (1953) and *The Fate of Colonel Fawcett* by G. Cummins (1955).

FAWKES, (1) **Francis** (1720–77), English poet and translator of the classics, for twenty years vicar of Orpington in Kent. The comic song ' The Brown Jug ' is his best-known piece.

(2) **Guy** (1570–1606), English conspirator, was born in York of Protestant parentage. Becoming a Catholic at an early age, he served in the Spanish army in the Netherlands 1593–1604, then crossed to England at Catesby's invitation. Inspired with fanatical zeal for his religion, he plotted with several Catholics to blow up the king, his ministers and the members of both Houses of Parliament, November 5, 1605. Caught red-handed, he was tried and hanged January 31, 1606. See works by Jardine (1857), Gerard (1896) and Gardiner (1897).

FAY, András (1786–1864), a Hungarian poet, playwright and novelist, lived and died in Budapest. He was a pioneer of the social novel and wrote a set of fables after the manner of Aesop which achieved great success. See Life by Erdélyi (1890).

FAYE, Hervé Auguste Étienne (1814–1902), French astronomer, born at Benoît-du-Sault, became in 1873 professor of Astronomy at the École Polytechnique, and in 1878 director of the Paris Observatory. In 1843 he discovered Faye's comet.

FAZY, Jean James, *fah-zee* (1794–1878), Swiss journalist and publicist, was born at Geneva, founded the *Revue de Genève*, became the leading spirit in the Radical movement (1846), and until 1861 was the real ruler of Geneva. He wrote a *History of Geneva* (1838–40) and on constitutional law.

FECHNER, Gustav Theodor (1801–87), German philosopher and psychologist, born at Gross-Särchen, became professor of Physics at Leipzig in 1834, working mainly at galvanism, electrochemistry and the theory of colour. In 1839 he turned to philosophy and the study of the relations of physiology and psychology, expounded in his *Elemente der Psychophysik* (1860). He helped to formulate the psychophysical Weber-Fechner Law that, in a series of sensations, the stimulus has to increase in geometrical proportions, if the increase is to be sensed. See his Correspondence (1890), and Lives by Kuntze (1891) and Hermann (1926).

FECHTER, Charles Albert, *feKH'tèr* (1824–1879), actor, born in London, was famed for his interpretations of Hamlet and Othello. He became lessee of the Lyceum Theatre and later went to the U.S., where he died.

FEHLING, Hermann von (1812–85), German chemist, born at Lübeck, professor of Chemistry at Stuttgart, the introducer of the solution which bears his name.

FEININGER, Lyonel, *fīn'-* (1871–1956), American painter of German origin, was born in New York, and after a spell as political cartoonist, devoted himself to painting (1907). After World War I he taught at the *Bauhaus* at Weimar and Dessau,

and adopted a style reminiscent of cubism. After the Nazi rise, he returned to the U.S. where with Gropius and Mies van der Rohe he founded the *Bauhaus* Chicago.

FEISAL II. See **FAISAL II.**

FEITH, Rhijnvis, *fīt* (1753–1824), Dutch poet, was born at Zwolle, became mayor there in 1780. His *Oden en Gedichten* (1796–1810) are lyrical. Of his tragedies the best known are *Thirza* (1784), *Johanna Gray* (1791), and *Ines de Castro* (1793). His polished prose *Brieven* (1784–94), contains much fine criticism.

FELIX, St, with his sister and fellow sufferer Regula, the patron saint of Zürich. Early in the 3rd century he preached Christ there, and was beheaded on the site of the great cathedral.—Another St Felix, a Burgundian, was first Bishop of Dunwich from 631 to 647.

FELIX, the name of five popes:

Felix I (d. 274), pope from 269, who has been put, doubtfully, amongst the martyrs.

Felix II (d. 365), was the first antipope, being consecrated when Liberius was banished (355) for refusing to condemn Athanasius. When Liberius was restored (357) Felix retired; but he was ultimately regarded as a saint and martyr.

Felix III (pope 483–492). Under him began the first disruption between the Churches of the East and West.

Felix IV (pope 526–530), was appointed by Theodoric.

Felix V. See **AMADEUS VIII.**

FELIX, Antonius, or **Claudius,** a Roman procurator of Judaea in the time of the apostle Paul (Acts xxiv), was a freedman of Claudius I and brother of his favourite Pallas. Josephus says he cleared the country of robbers and suppressed the chaotic seditions of the Jews; but his cruelty, lust and greed were unbounded. Recalled in A.D. 62, he narrowly escaped execution.

FELL, John (1625–86), Anglican divine, with three others contrived to maintain the Church of England services during the Common-wealth; after the Restoration he was made Dean of Christ Church, royal chaplain and D.D. He governed the college strictly, restored its buildings, was liberal to poor scholars, and did much to promote learning. In 1676 he became Bishop of Oxford. He rebuilt the episcopal palace at Cuddesdon. ' I do not like thee, Doctor Fell ', is ascribed to Tom Brown (q.v.).

FELLENBERG, Philipp Emanuel von (1771–1844), Swiss sociologist and rural economist, born at Bern, founded in 1799 at Hofwil, near Münchenbuchsee, an agricultural college which achieved an international reputation, and established several other educational institutions, including an orphanage. See study by G. Kuffer (1944).

FELLINI, Federico (1920–   ), Italian film director, born at Rimini, educated at Bologna, cartoonist, journalist and scriptwriter, before becoming an assistant film director in 1942. His highly individual films include *I Vitelloni* (1953), *La Strada* (1954; foreign film Oscar winner, 1957), *Le Notte di Cabiria* (1957; Oscar winner, 1958), and *Giulietta degli Spiriti* (1964). His most famous and contro-versial work, *La Dolce Vita* (1960; Cannes Festival prize winner), was a *succès de* *scandale* for its cynical evocation of modern Roman high life. *Otto e Mezzo* (1963) is his most obviously autobiographical work, setting the dreams and fantasies of its film director hero against the baroque settings of the film world. In 1943 he married the actress Giulietta Masina, star of several of his films, most notably *La Strada*.

FELLOWES, Edmund Horace (1870–1951), English musicologist, from 1900 a minor canon at St George's, Windsor, edited *The English Madrigal School* (36 vols. 1912–24) and *The English School of Lutenist Song-Writers* (31 vols. 1920–28).

FELLOWS, Sir Charles (1799–1860), British archaeologist, discovered in 1838 the ruins of Xanthus, ancient capital of Lycia, and those of Tlos, and in 1839 the ruins of thirteen cities; from these he later selected marbles, casts, &c., for the British Museum.

FELLTHAM, Owen (*c.* 1602–68), English writer, author of *Resolves, Divine, Morall, Politicall* (1620–28), was born in Suffolk, and lived at Great Billing, Northants.

FELTON, John (*c.* 1595–1628), a Suffolk captain, assassinated the Duke of Buckingham at Portsmouth with a tenpenny knife and was hanged at Tyburn.

FÉNELON, François de Salignac de la Mothe, *fay-nĕ-lõ* (1651–1715), was born August 6, at the château de Fénelon in Périgord. At twenty he entered the seminary of St Sulpice in Paris, and was ordained in 1675. After some time spent in parochial duties, he became in 1678 director of an institution for women converts to the Catholic faith. Here he wrote *Traité de l'éducation des filles*; then he became head of a mission sent, on the revocation of the Edict of Nantes (1685), to preach among the Protestants of Poitou. In 1689 he was appointed by Louis XIV preceptor of his grandson, the young Duke of Burgundy; and as such wrote the *Fables*, the *Dialogues of the Dead*, and the *History of the Ancient Philosophers*. He was presented by the king to the abbey of St Valéry (1694) and to the archbishopric of Cambrai (1695). He had formed in 1687 the acquaintance of the celebrated quietist mystic, Madame Guyon (q.v.); and, convinced of the unfairness of the outcry against her, he advised her to submit her book to Bossuet (q.v.), who condemned it. Fénelon acquiesced; but refused to join in any personal condemnation. Fénelon composed his own *Maximes des saints sur la vie intérieure* in defence of certain of Madame Guyon's doctrines. A fierce controversy ensued, and in the end the pope condemned the *Maximes des saints*. The readiness with which Fénelon accepted this decision is regarded as one of his highest titles to glory. Fénelon's *Télémaque* (1699) was considered by the king a masked satire upon his court and Fénelon was strictly restrained within his diocese. From this date he lived almost exclusively for his flock; but in the revived Jansenistic dispute he engaged earnestly on the side of orthodoxy. His works are voluminous, and on a variety of subjects. See Bausset's *Histoire de Fénelon* (1808; new ed. 1862), and monographs by Janet (1896; trans. 1914), Brémond (1910); English Lives by Lear (1876), St Cyres (1901); Duclaux, *The French*

Ideal (1911). Douen, in *L'Intolérance de Fénelon* (1872), accuses Fénelon of cruelty towards the Protestants.

FENWICK, Sir John (*c.* 1645–97), English conspirator, born in Northumberland, after serving in the army in 1688 became Tory M.P. for the county of his birth. He took part in the Assassination Plot, and in 1696, being committed to the Tower, made an artful confession involving several Whig leaders in the Jacobite intrigues. The only witness against him had been spirited out of the country, but the Whig party secured the passing of a bill of attainder under which he was beheaded.

FERBER, Edna (1887–1968), American writer, born in Kalamazoo, Michigan. A prolific novelist (*Dawn O'Hara*, 1911; *Cimarron*, 1929, &c.), she is probably best remembered as the writer of the story which inspired the musical play *Show Boat*. She also wrote plays with Kaufman (q.v.), e.g., *Stage Door*.

FERDAUSI. See FIRDAUSI.

FERDINAND I (1793–1875), emperor of Austria from 1835 to 1848, the eldest son of Francis I by his second marriage with Maria Theresa, princess of the Two Sicilies, was born at Vienna, April 19. Succeeding his father in 1835 it was expected that he would inaugurate a liberal policy, but absolutist principles triumphed, and Metternich governed. When the revolutionary movement broke out in 1847–48, Ferdinand consented to the dismissal of Metternich and the appointment of a responsible ministry, and granted the outlines of a constitution. But after the October insurrection in Vienna he abdicated in favour of Francis Joseph (q.v.). He retired to Prague, where he died.

FERDINAND, called the **Catholic** (1452–1516), V of Castile, II of Aragon and Sicily, and III of Naples, was born at Sos in Aragon, March 10, the son of John II of Navarre and Aragon. In 1469 he married Isabella, sister of Henry IV of Castile. On Henry's death in 1474 most of the nobles refused to acknowledge the legitimacy of his daughter Juana, and proclaimed Isabella and Ferdinand, who in 1479 emerged victorious from the civil war that ensued. On the death of John (1479) the crowns of Aragon and Castile were united under Ferdinand and Isabella. Isabella retaining sole authority in Castilian affairs and Ferdinand's talents finding scope in his own kingdom. The suppression of the banditti he accomplished by reorganizing the *santa hermandad*, or 'holy brotherhood', a kind of militia police, which also helped to break the power of the feudal aristocracy. The establishment of the Inquisition in 1478–80 likewise helped to lessen the nobles' influence; and Ferdinand increased his power by vesting in himself the grandmastership of the military orders. He was ably seconded by his queen and by Cardinal Ximenes. The year 1492 marked the end of the long struggle with the Moors; and in August Columbus set sail from Palos. The Jews were immediately expelled from the conquered kingdom; and, a few years after, the privileges promised to the Moors were faithlessly withdrawn, baptism or exile being offered as alternatives. By these two acts the most industrious and civilized inhabitants of the Peninsula were driven from it. The discovery of America gave Spain for a time supremacy on both sides of the Atlantic. From France Ferdinand recovered by treaty the counties of Rousillon and Cerdagne (now the Pyrénées-Orientales); in 1495 he formed the Holy League with the pope, the emperor, Milan and Venice, and ultimately England, under which Gonsalvo di Cordova twice drove the French out of Naples, the second time in 1503, after which it remained in Ferdinand's possession. In 1504 Isabella died, and Ferdinand at once had his insane daughter Juana proclaimed queen of Castile, and himself regent. In 1505 he married Germaine de Foix, a niece of Louis XII of France. After Isabella's death he was compelled to buy off French claims on Naples, though in such straits for money that he was for some time unable to complete the dowry required to secure the marriage of his daughter Catharine with Henry, Prince of Wales. But he took part in the league of Cambrai against Venice in 1508, conquered Oran in 1509, and in 1512 made himself master of Navarre—thus becoming monarch of Spain from the Pyrenees to Gibraltar. He was unsurpassed in an age of cunning diplomatists. To him and Isabella Spain owed her unity and greatness as a nation and the foundation of her imperial influence. See Prescott's *Ferdinand and Isabella* (1838); de Nervo's *Isabella the Catholic* (trans. 1897), and Plunket (1915).

FERDINAND. The name of three Holy Roman Emperors. **Ferdinand I** (1503–64), who ruled from 1556 to 1564, was born in Spain. He was the son of Philip I, and succeeded his brother, Charles V, in the empire in 1556, having been elected king of the Romans in 1531. In 1521 Ferdinand married the daughter of the king of Bohemia and Hungary; and when her childless brother Louis was killed in 1526 he claimed the crown. This involved him in a struggle with John Zápolya, who laid claim to Hungary, and who was supported by the sultan Soliman. Ferdinand bought off the Turks and secured Hungary and Bohemia. He tried to reconcile his Protestant and Catholic subjects, and urged, fruitlessly, the reformation of abuses on the Council of Trent. He was succeeded by his son, Maximilian II. See Bucholtz (1838).

Ferdinand II (1578–1637), born at Graz, July 9, was grandson of Ferdinand I, and was educated by the Jesuits. Succeeding to his own duchy of Styria, he put down Protestantism by force. He attempted the same in Bohemia and Hungary, of which countries he had been elected king during the lifetime of the childless emperor Matthias, and with the aid of the Catholic League and of the Elector of Saxony subdued them, while by merciless persecution he re-established Catholicism. Meanwhile he had been elected emperor of Germany (1619); and the war now became the terrible 'Thirty Years' War'. The imperial generals, Tilly and Wallenstein, were opposed by the Protestant states of Lower Saxony, headed

by Christian IV of Denmark; but the confederates, defeated by Tilly, were forced to conclude peace at Lübeck in 1629. Ferdinand now issued an edict taking away from German Protestants nearly all the rights they had acquired by a century of struggles; and the troops of Wallenstein and of the League were immediately set to work to carry it out— an enterprise arrested by the dismissal of Wallenstein, the opposition of Richelieu, and the advent of Gustavus Adolphus of Sweden. After the murder of Wallenstein, at which Ferdinand connived, the imperial commander, Gallas, by the victory of Nordlingen (1634) detached Saxony from the Swedish alliance; but the ability of the Swedish generals and the open part that France now took in the contest brought back the balance of victory to the Protestant arms. See German Life by Hurter (1864).

Ferdinand III (1608–57), who ruled from 1637 to 1657, was the son of Ferdinand II, and was born at Graz. He was not so much under Jesuit influence as his father, and was inclined for peace; and though the conflicting interests of the belligerents made this impossible for years, a congress met at Münster in 1643, and the Peace of Westphalia was secured in 1648.

FERDINAND. The name of two kings of the Two Sicilies.

Ferdinand I (1751–1825), third son of Charles III of Spain, was born January 12. When Charles ascended the Spanish throne in 1759 Ferdinand succeeded him in Naples, under a regency, as Ferdinand IV. After his marriage, in 1768, with Maria Carolina, daughter of Maria Theresa, he fell completely under her influence, and lost his popularity. He joined England and Austria against France in 1793, but in 1801 he was forced to make a treaty with Napoleon. A violation of this treaty compelled him in 1806 to take refuge in Sicily, under English protection. The French took possession of Naples, but Ferdinand was reinstated by the Congress of Vienna in 1815, and next year united his two states into the Kingdom of the Two Sicilies. His queen had died in 1814. A popular movement in 1820 compelled him to introduce a constitution, but with Austrian help he established a rigorous despotism. He died January 4, 1825, and was succeeded by his son, Francis I. See Cordy Jeaffreson, *The Queen of Naples and Lord Nelson* (1889).

Ferdinand II (1810–59), son of Francis I, was born January 12, 1810, and succeeded his father in 1830. His first wife, a daughter of Victor Emmanuel I, dying in 1836, he married Maria Theresa, daughter of the Archduke Charles of Austria and gave himself up to Austrian counsels. Henceforward Naples became the scene of incessant conspiracy, insurrection and political prosecutions. Ferdinand yielded to the storm of 1848, and granted a constitution, but the Sicilians mistrusted his pledges and declared that he had forfeited the Sicilian crown. He subdued the revolt in Sicily by the bombardment of its chief cities that earned him the epithet of 'Bomba'. He now set aside the constitution, while all who had taken part in reforms were subjected to those persecutions which the Letters of Mr Gladstone in 1851 held up to the execration of the world. Bomba died May 22, 1859, and was succeeded by his son Francis II (1836–94), the weak and cowardly ' Bombino ', who fell in 1860–61 before Garibaldi and Italian unity. See Nisco, *Ferdinando II* (1884).

FERDINAND III (1769–1824), Grand-duke of Tuscany and Archduke of Austria, was born at Florence, May 6. He inaugurated many reforms, encouraged commerce, opened up good roads, and was the first to recognize the French Republic, in 1792. Next year Russia and Britain constrained him to become a passive member of the coalition against France, but on the French occupation of Piedmont in 1795 he resumed friendly relations with France. In 1797, to save his states from annexation, Ferdinand concluded a very unfavourable treaty with Bonaparte. French intrigues drove him into an Austrian alliance, and Bonaparte declared war against Austria and Tuscany. In 1799 Ferdinand retired to Vienna, and at the peace of Lunéville (1801) renounced all claim on Tuscany, but the peace of Paris reinstated him, 1814.

FERDINAND I (1861–1948), ex-king of Bulgaria, born in Vienna, February 26, was the youngest son of Prince Augustus of Saxe-Coburg and Princess Clementine of Orleans, and served in the Austrian army. On the abdication of Prince Alexander of Bulgaria, Ferdinand was offered and accepted the crown in August 1887. In 1908 he proclaimed Bulgaria independent, and took the title of king or tsar. Joining the Balkan League against Turkey (1912), Bulgaria gained part of Thrace and access to the Aegean; but, breaking the league, she lost her gains in Macedonia and Adrianople, and had to cede part of the Dobrudja to Rumania (1913). Allying himself with the Central Powers, he invaded Serbia in October 1915. His armies routed, ' Foxy Ferdinand ' abdicated October 4, 1918, his son, Boris III (1894–1943), succeeding him.

FERDUSI. See FIRDAUSI.

FERGUSON, (1) Adam (1723–1816), Scottish philosopher and historian, born at Logierait in Perthshire, as chaplain to the Black Watch was present at Fontenoy (1745). In 1757 he succeeded David Hume as keeper of the Advocates' Library in Edinburgh, and was next professor, first of Natural Philosophy (1759), and subsequently (1764) of Moral Philosophy. He accompanied the young Earl of Chesterfield (1774) on his travels on the Continent, and acted as secretary to the commission sent out by Lord North to try to settle the disputes with the North American colonies (1778–79). His works include an *Essay on Civil Society* (1766), *Institutes of Moral Philosophy* (1772), *History of the Roman Republic* (1782; long a standard authority), &c. See Memoir by John Small (1864).

(2) **James** (d. 1705). See FERGUSON (5).

(3) **James** (1710–76), Scottish astronomer, was born, a farm labourer's son, at Rothiemay, Banffshire. While keeping sheep he was constantly busy in making mechanical models,

and mapping the stars. Later he took to copying pictures and drawing patterns and portraits, his leisure time being given to astronomy. In 1748 he began lecturing on astronomy and mechanics. He was elected F.R.S. in 1763, lectured throughout the country, and wrote assiduously. His principal works are *Astronomy Explained upon Newton's Principles* (1756) and *Lectures on Mechanics, Hydrostatics, Pneumatics, and Optics* (1760). See *Life* by Henderson (1867).

(4) **Patrick** (1744–80), inventor of a breech-loading rifle, was born at Pitfour, Aberdeenshire, and served in the army in Germany and Tobago. In 1776 he patented his rifle, firing seven shots a minute, and sighted for ranges of from 100 to 500 yards; and with it he armed a corps of loyalists, who helped at the battle of Brandywine (1777) to defeat the Americans. On October 7, 1780, Major Ferguson fell, defending King's Mountain, South Carolina. See James Ferguson's *Two Scottish Soldiers* (1888).

(5) **Robert** (c. 1637–1714), called the ' Plotter ', was born near Alford, in Aberdeenshire, and in 1662 was ousted as a Presbyterian from the Kentish vicarage of Godmersham. He played for ten years a leading part in every treasonable scheme against the last two Stuart kings, and twice had to flee the kingdom. But after the Revolution, of which in 1706 he published a History, he conspired as busily for the Jacobite cause. His younger brother, James (d. 1705), commanded a brigade at Blenheim, and died at Bois-le-Duc. See *Ferguson the Plotter* (1887), by James Ferguson, and his *Two Scottish Soldiers* (1888).

(6) **Sir Samuel** (1810–86), poet and Celtic scholar, was born at Belfast, and called to the Irish bar in 1838. He was appointed in 1867 first deputy keeper of Irish Records. As president of the Royal Irish Academy he gave a powerful impetus to the study of early Irish art. His spirited poems were published as *Lays of the Western Gael* (1865), *Congal* (1872), *Poems* (1880), and *The Forging of the Anchor* (1883). His edition of the *Leabhar Breac* appeared in 1876; his *Ogham Inscriptions* in 1887. See Life by his widow (2 vols. 1896).

FERGUSSON, (1) James (1808–86), Scottish art historian, was born at Ayr, studied Indian rock temples, wrote on fortifications and archaeology, and was author of a popular *History of Architecture* (1865–76).

(2) **Sir James** (1832–1907), statesman, born at Edinburgh, was Conservative M.P. for Ayrshire (1854–57; 1859–68), under-secretary of state (1867–68), governor of South Australia (1868–73), governor of New Zealand (1873–74) and governor of Bombay (1880–85). In 1885 elected for Manchester, he was foreign under-secretary in 1886–91, and postmaster general in 1891–92. He perished in the earthquake of 1907 at Kingston, Jamaica.

(3) **Robert** (1750–74), Scottish poet, born at Edinburgh, September 5, studied at St Andrews University, and was employed in the office of the commissary clerk, in Edinburgh, contributing to *Ruddiman's Weekly*

Magazine poems which gained him local fame. His company was much sought and convivial excesses permanently injured his health. Religious melancholy became complete insanity after an accidental injury to his head. He died October 16, 1774, and was buried in Canongate churchyard. Burns placed a stone over his grave in 1789. Fergusson possessed vigour, wit, fluency and humour, but lacked imagination and passion. His poems were collected in 1773; later editions by Ruddiman (1779), Irving (1880), Chambers (1840), Grosart (1851; Life, 1898), Ford (1905, 1916), Dickins (1925), Law (1947). See Fairley's Bibliography (1916).

(4) **Sir William** (1808–77), Scottish surgeon, was born at Prestonpans, studied medicine in Edinburgh, and in 1836 became a surgeon in the Infirmary. In 1840 he became professor of Surgery in King's College. In 1866 he was made a baronet, in 1867 serjeant-surgeon to the Queen, and in 1870 president of the Royal College of Surgeons, London. See Life by H. Smith (1877).

FERISHTAH, or **Firishta** (*c.* 1550–*c.* 1615), Persian historian, was born at Astrabad went as a child to India, became captain in the bodyguard of the Prince of Ahmednagar, and on his deposition went to Bijapur (1589). His great History of the Mohammedan power in India (1609) was translated by Col. Briggs (1831–32).

FERMAT, Pierre de, *fer-mah* (1601–65), French mathematician, made many discoveries in the properties of numbers, probabilities, and geometry. See Life by Taupiac (Montauban 1879).

FERMI, Enrico (1901–54), Italian nuclear physicist, born in Rome, studied at Pisa, Göttingen under Born, and Leyden, and became professor of Theoretical Physics at Rome in 1927. Between 1927 and 1933 he published his semiquantitative method of calculating atomic particles and in 1934 he and his colleagues split the nuclei of the uranium atoms by bombarding them with neutrons, thus producing artificial radioactive substances. He did not return to Italy from his Nobel prize presentation in Stockholm (1938) because the Italian anti-Semitic Laws affected his Jewish wife, but became professor at Columbia University (1939). He played a prominent part in interesting the American government in atomic energy and constructed the first American nuclear reactor (1942). He was awarded the Hughes Medal of the Royal Society in 1942. See L. Fermi, *Atoms in the Family* (1938).

FERN, Fanny. See PARTON and WILLIS (1).

FERNANDEL, stage-name of **Fernand Joseph Désiré Contandin** (1903–71), French film comedian, born in Marseilles, worked in a bank and soap factory before his début on the stage in 1922, and from 1930 appeared in over a hundred films, interrupted only temporarily by military service and Nazi occupation. He established himself internationally with his moving portrayal of the naïve country priest of *The Little World of Don Camillo* (1953) and with his versatile handling of six separate rôles in *The Sheep has Five Legs* (1953), which gave full rein to

his extraordinary facial mobility. See biography by C. Rim (1952).

FERNANDEZ, Juan, a Spanish pilot who in 1563 discovered the Pacific island named after him.

FERRABOSCO, *-bos'kō*, name of a family of Italian musicians, some of whom settled in England.

(1) **Alfonso** (1543–88), son of (3), was born at Bologna, came to England before 1562, was some time in the service of Queen Elizabeth, left England in 1578 and entered the service of the Duke of Savoy. His compositions include madrigals, motets, and music for viols.

(2) **Alfonso** (*c.* 1575–1628), son of (1), born at Greenwich, was in the service of James I and Charles I. He wrote music for masques, songs, and notably music for viol consorts, showing his mastery of counterpoint and invention.

(3) **Domenico Maria** (1513–74), father of (1), was born and died at Bologna, and composed madrigals and motets.

Other members of the family include three sons of (2), **Alfonso** (*c.* 1620–*c.* 1660), **Henry** (*c.* 1623–*c.* 1658) and **John** (1626–82), all of whom held court appointments, and of whom Henry was killed in Jamaica and John was appointed organist in 1662 of Ely Cathedral.

FERRAR, Nicholas (1592–1637), in 1625 founded at Little Gidding in Huntingdonshire, the religious community familiar to readers of J. H. Shorthouse's *John Inglesant*; next year Laud ordained him deacon. The community numbered some thirty persons, who with constant services and perpetual prayer engaged in the occupation of fine bookbinding. The 'Arminian Nunnery' was not broken up by the Puritans till 1647. See Lives of Ferrar, by his brother John, ed. Mayor (1855), *Nicholas Ferrar*, ed. Rev. T. T. Carter (1892), and by A. L. Maycock (1928).

FERRARA, Andrea (16th cent.), Italian broadsword maker, probably born in Ferrara, who with his brother was in great repute as an armourer at Belluno in 1585. It is said that he tempered sword blades by the method employed by the smiths of Damascus.

FERRARI, (1) **Gaudenzio** (*c.* 1471–1546), Italian painter, most of whose works are in the Lombard galleries. See study by E. Halsey (1904).

(2) **Paolo** (1822–89), Italian dramatist, was born at Modena, and wrote many excellent comedies, including *Goldoni* (1852) and *Parini e la satira* (1857). In 1860 he became professor of History at Modena, and afterwards at Milan. See Pater's *Miscellaneous Studies* (1895).

FERREIRA, Antonio (1528–69), Portuguese poet, born at Lisbon, introduced a classical style into Portuguese verse and drama, earning the title 'The Portuguese Horace'. See study by J. de Castillo (Rio 1865).

FERREL, William (1817–91), American meteorologist, born in Fulton County, studied the effects of the earth's rotation on wind and marine currents, and invented a tide-predicting machine.

FERRERO, Guglielmo, *fer-ray'rō* (1871–1942), Italian sociologist and historian, born at Portici, known for his works on ancient history and on modern political problems, as *The Greatness and Decline of Rome* (5 vols. 1902–07), *The Tragedy of Peace* (1923), *Peace and War* (1933), &c. He married Gina Lombroso, daughter of the famous Italian criminologist Cesare Lombroso (q.v.). His son Leo (1903–33) was also a promising dramatist and essayist.

FERRERS, Laurence Shirley, 4th Earl (1720–1760), the last nobleman to die a felon's death in England, in a paroxysm of passion killed his old land steward in January 1760, for which, being tried by his peers in Westminster Hall, he was hanged at Tyburn.

FERRIER, (1) Sir David (1843–1928), Scottish neurologist, born at Aberdeen, graduated there in 1863 and took his M.D. at Edinburgh in 1868. In 1871 he joined the staff of King's College, London, where he was appointed to the specially created chair of Neuro-pathology in 1889. Best known for his work on the localization of brain functions, he was elected F.R.S. in 1876, and was knighted in 1911.

(2) **James Frederick** (1808–64), Scottish metaphysician, was born in Edinburgh. He graduated B.A. at Oxford in 1831, and next year was admitted to the Scottish bar, but never practised. In 1842 he became professor of History at Edinburgh, in 1845 of Moral Philosophy at St Andrews. Ferrier early attracted notice by his metaphysical essays in *Blackwood's Magazine*. In his *Institutes of Metaphysics* (1854) he endeavours to construct a system of idealism in a series of propositions demonstrated after the manner of Euclid. See Life by his son-in-law, Sir Alexander Grant, prefixed to his *Lectures on Greek Philosophy* (1866) and study by E. H. Haldane (1899).

(3) **Kathleen** (1912–53), English contralto singer, born in Higher Walton, Lancs. An amateur pianist of some accomplishment, she was led by a prize for singing at a local music festival to undertake serious studies in 1940, and the range and richness of her voice, together with her remarkable technical control, rapidly won her a great reputation. In 1946 she sang Lucrezia in Britten's *The Rape of Lucrezia*, and Orpheus in Gluck's *Orfeo* at Glyndebourne; from then onwards, she was in great demand throughout Europe and America. Her greatest success, perhaps, was in Mahler's *The Song of the Earth*, at the first Edinburgh Festival (1947) and at Salzburg (1949).

(4) **Susan Edmonstone** (1782–1854), Scottish novelist, was born in Edinburgh. Her first work, *Marriage* (1818), was followed by *The Inheritance* (1824) and *Destiny* (1831). She enjoyed the friendship of Sir Walter Scott, who was by some for a time credited with the authorship of her tales. Her ' Recollections of Visits to Ashiestiel and Abbotsford ' were published, with a Memoir, in Bentley's edition of her works (1881). See Life by her grand-nephew (1899).

FERRY, Jules François Camille (1832–93), French statesman, born at Saint Dié in the Vosges, admitted to the Paris bar in 1854, identified himself with the opponents of the Empire. In 1869 he was elected to the Corps Législatif, where he voted against the war with Prussia; and during the siege of Paris (1870–71) he was mayor of the city. As minister of Public Instruction (1879) he brought forward a bill excluding Jesuits from the schools. It was rejected, but the expulsion of the Jesuits was effected by decrees founded on obsolete laws, and brought about the dissolution of the ministry in September 1880. M. Ferry then formed a cabinet, which lasted till November 1881. His last ministry (1883–85) fell through his policy of ' colonial expansion ', involving war in Madagascar and Tonking. See his *Discours* (1893–97), and studies by A. Rambaud (1903) and A. Israel (Paris 1931).

FERSEN, (1) Frederik Axel, Count von (1719–1794), Swedish general and statesman, father of (2), born at Stockholm, was a descendant of the Scottish Macphersons. He served successively in the French and Swedish armies, and was made a field-marshal in 1770. He became leader of the anti-Royalist opposition and was ultimately assassinated at Stockholm.

(2) **Hans Axel, Comte de** (1755–1810), son of (1), Swedish marshal, some time in the French service, who, disguised as a coachman, drove the royal family in the flight to Varennes (1791), and who was murdered by a Stockholm mob on the false charge of having poisoned the crown prince. See Gaulot's *A Friend of the Queen* (Eng. trans. 1893), and A. Söderhjelm's *Fersen et Marie-Antoinette* (Paris 1930).

FESCH, Joseph, Cardinal Archbishop of Lyons (1763–1839), was born January 3, at Ajaccio, the half-brother of Letizia Ramolino, Bonaparte's mother. Ordained priest, he helped on the concordat with Pope Pius VII in 1801, and was raised to be Archbishop of Lyons (1802) and cardinal (1803). At a conference of clergy in Paris in 1810 he expressed views which lost him the favour of Napoleon, who was further exasperated by his letter to the pope, then (1812) in captivity at Fontainebleau. At the approach of the Austrians in 1814 he fled to Rome, where he died. See Life by Ricard (Paris 1893).

FESTUS, (1) Porcius, Roman procurator of Judaea, who succeeded Felix A.D. 60. In 62 Paul defended himself before him. See Acts xxv.

(2) **Sextus Pompeius,** was a 2nd-century Latin grammarian. Of his alphabetical epitome of the lost work of Verrius Flaccus, *De Verborum Significatione,* in twenty books, only the latter half (M—V) survives in a mutilated MS. at Naples. There is a (9th cent.) meagre abstract of the whole. See editions by Müller (1839) and Lindsay (1912).

FÉTIS, François Joseph, *fay-tees* (1784–1871), Belgian writer on music, professor at the Paris Conservatory (1821) and director of the Brussels Conservatory (1833), produced a *Universal Biography of Musicians* (1835–44) and *General History of Music* (1868–76).

FETTES, Sir William (1750–1836), Scottish merchant, lord provost of Edinburgh, from 1804 a baronet, left £166,000 to found Fettes College (1870).

FEUCHTWANGER, Lion, *foyкнт'vang-er* (1889–1958), German writer, born at Munich, won a European reputation with the 18th-century historical novel presenting an elaborately detailed picture of the lives, sufferings and weaknesses of central European Jewry in *Jud Süss* (1925), translated by Edwin and Willa Muir (1926), as well as the 14th-century tale *Die hässliche Herzogin* (1923), which as *The Ugly Duchess* (1927) was a great success in Britain. During World War I he was interned in Tunis. His thinly disguised satire on Hitler's Munich putsch, *Erfolg* (1930), earned him the hatred of the Nazis. In 1933 he fled to France, where in 1940 he was interned by the German army, but escaped to America. He has also written numerous dramas and collaborated with Brecht in a translation of Marlowe's *Edward II*. His later works include detailed part biographies of Goya (1952) and Rousseau (1954).

FEUERBACH, *foy'ėr-ba*KH, (1) **Anselm** (1829–1880), German painter, born at Speyer, lived after 1855 chiefly in Rome and died in Venice. He produced landscape and genre paintings and large subject pieces which had considerable influence in the revival of the classical ideal in German art. See his letters to his mother (ed. Pescatore, 1939), and studies by Neumann (1929) and Zahn (1940).

(2) **Ludwig Andreas** (1804–72), German philosopher, fourth son of (3), was born at Landshut, July 28. He wrote against immortality (1830) and works on Bacon, Spinoza, Leibniz and Pierre Bayle; also *Das Wesen des Christentums* (1841), on the nature of religion, translated into English by George Eliot. Feuerbach maintains that all authority above man, and all moral obligation, is a delusion; and the highest good is that which is on the whole most pleasurable, and consists in resemblance to that ideal humanity which man creates for himself, and worships as God. The German communists degraded this into an atheism which ignored any moral or social law imposed on the individual from any other source than himself. His works were collected in ten volumes (1846–66). See books by Grün (1874), Engels (1888) and Bolin (1891), also study by Barth in *Zurischen den Zeiten* (1927).

(3) **Paul Johann Anselm von** (1775–1833), German jurist, father of (2), born at Jena, made a brilliant reputation by his *Kritik des natürlichen Rechts* (1796) and his *Anti-Hobbes* (1798); his *Lehrbuch des gemeinen peinlichen Rechts* (1801; 4th ed. 1847) placed him at the head of the new school of Rigorists. His penal code for Bavaria (1813) was taken as a basis for amending the criminal law of several other countries. In 1808–11 he published a great collection of criminal cases. In his *Geschworenengericht* (1813–25) he maintained that the verdict of a jury is not adequate legal proof of a crime. Appointed a judge at Bamberg (1814) and at Anspach (1817), he died at Frankfurt. See the Life by his son Ludwig (1852).

FEUILLET, **Octave,** *fœ-yay* (1821–90), French novelist, born at Saint Lô, one of Dumas' literary assistants, began his own career with *Le Fruit défendu*. From 1848 he published in the *Revue des deux mondes* a series collected in *Scènes et proverbes* and

Scènes et comédies (1853–56). Elected Scribe's successor in the French Academy (1862), and afterwards librarian to the emperor, he wrote many popular novels and plays. See study by Bordeaux (Paris 1922).

FEVAL, Paul Henri Corentin (1817–87), French novelist, born at Rennes. His many novels include *Les Mystères de Londres* (1844) and *Le Bossu* (1858); some had an extraordinary run when dramatized.

FEYDEAU, Ernest, *fay-dō* (1821–73), a French novelist whose stories depict the worst features of society in the time of the Empire. *Sylvie* is a novel of much more than ordinary power.

FEYNMAN, Richard (1918–), American scientist, professor at the Calif. Inst. of Technology, awarded Nobel prize for physics in 1965 with Tomonaga and Schwinger for work on quantum electrodynamics.

FIACRE, or Fiachrach, St (d. 670), an Irish anchorite, who founded a monastery in France. In 1640 one Nicholas Sauvage, a hirer of hackney carriages, lived at the Hôtel St Fiacre in the Rue St Martin, Paris; hence to cabs generally was given the name *fiacre*.

FIBICH, Zdenko, *fee-bee*KH (1850–1900), Czech composer, born at Šebořic, wrote operas, symphonies, works for solo piano, &c. He was Kapellmeister in Prague from 1878. One of his melodies, *Poème*, has remained a popular favourite.

FIBIGER, Johannes Andreas Grib (1867–1928), Danish pathologist, became professor and head of the Institute of Pathological Anatomy at Copenhagen. He is notable as the first to induce cancer experimentally, feeding rats with cockroaches carrying the parasite *spiroptera neoplastica*. He won the Nobel prize for Medicine in 1926.

FICHTE, *fiK*H'*tė*, (1) **Immanuel Hermann von** (1797–1879), German philosopher, son of (2), born at Jena, was professor at Bonn (1836) and Tübingen (1842), and was ennobled in 1867. A decided theist, he wrote works on speculative theology (1847), ethics (1850), anthropology (1856), psychology (1864) and immortality (1876).

(2) **Johann Gottlieb** (1762–1814), German philosopher, father of (1), was born at Rammenau in Upper Lusatia, studied first theology and then philosophy at Jena, made a precarious living as a tutor in Saxony, Zürich, Warsaw and Königsberg, where he met Kant, became an ardent disciple, but although Kant praised his first publication, *Kritik aller Offenbarung* (1792), he refused to lend Fichte any money. In 1794 Fichte was appointed professor at Jena, where he soon modified the Kantian system by substituting for the kingpin, the ' thing-in-itself ' as the absolute reality, the more subjective *Ego*. In the *Wissenschaftslehre* (1795), the *Ego* affirms itself, simply and unconditionally as the primitive act of consciousness, but in this self-affirmation it necessarily posits a negative, a *Non-ego*, an opposite which is not itself, i.e., the objective world, thus treated almost solipsistically. Here we have the rudiments of existentialism, culminating in the 20th century in Heidegger and Sartre. The *Grundlage des Naturrechts* (1796) and *System der Sittenlehre* (1798) exhibit the above

philosophy in its abstract and excessive terminology. In 1799 an accusation of theism led to his removal to Berlin, where he gave lectures privately. In 1805 he became professor at Erlangen, where he delivered the lectures ' On the Nature of the Scholar ' (1805–06) and published the more popular and maturer versions of his philosophy under the titles *Grundzüge des gegenwärtigen Zeitalters* and *Anweisung zum seligen Leben und Religionslehre* (both 1806). But Fichte's historical importance is as the author of *Addresses to the German Nation* (1807–08), in which he invoked a metaphysical German nationalism to resistance against Napoleon. The Fichtian ' Ego ' in this context became the German nation and this was gradually subverted into the Nazi concept of the *Herrenvolk.* In 1810 the University of Berlin was opened and Fichte, who had drawn up its constitution, became its first rector. But Fichte's wife, who attended the wounded in the Berlin hospitals, gave Fichte an infection from which he died. See Lives by his son (1), (1831), R. Adamson (1881), X. Léon (1922–1924).

FICINO, Marsilio, *fi-chee'nō* (1433–99), Italian Platonist, born at Florence, was appointed by Cosimo de' Medici in 1463 president of an academy for the diffusion of the Platonic doctrines, which Ficino held to be the basis and confirmation of Christianity. Ordained at forty, he was made rector of two churches in Florence and canon of the cathedral. His theological system is a strange medley of incongruous views. See R. L. Poole's *Mediaeval Thought in Theology* (1884); and P. Kristeller's *The Philosophy of Mersiglio Ficino* (1943).

FICK, (1) Adolph (1829–1901), German physiologist, after whom a law of diffusion in liquids was named, when he discovered that the mass of solute diffusing through unit area per second is proportional to the concentration gradient.

(2) **August** (1833–1916), philologist, born at Petershagen, professor at Göttingen (1876) and Breslau (1887). His great comparative Indo-Germanic dictionary (1870; 4th ed. 1890–94) was followed by works on Greek personal names, the original language of the *Iliad,* &c.

FIELD, (1) Cyrus West (1819–92), American paper manufacturer, brother of (2) and (8), born at Stockbridge, Mass., helped to promote the Atlantic telegraph. He organized the New York, Newfoundland, and London Telegraph Company in 1854, and the Atlantic Telegraph Company in 1856, but he died poor.

(2) **David Dudley** (1805–94), American jurist, born at Haddam, Conn., brother of (1) and (8), was admitted to the New York bar in 1828, and laboured to reform the judiciary system. In 1857 he was appointed by the state to prepare penal, political and civil codes, of which the first has been adopted by New York, and all have been accepted by some other states. He did much for international law and for law reform generally. His *Outlines of an International Code* (2nd ed. 1878) were translated into **various** tongues.

(3) **Eugene** (1850–95), **American** writer, born at St Louis, **Missouri,** became a

journalist at twenty-three, and from 1853 was a columnist with the *Chicago Morning News,* achieving a reputation as humorist and versifier. He wrote the well-known nursery lullaby ' Wynken, Blynken, and Nod '. *A Little Book of Western Verse* (1889) was notable; *With Trumpet and Drum* (1892) contains his best children's verse. See books by S. Thompson (1901 and 1927) and C. H. Dennis (1924).

(4) **John** (1782–1837), Irish composer of nocturnes and Chopin's model, was born in Dublin, became an infant prodigy, and was apprenticed to Clementi (q.v.), who used him to demonstrate the capabilities of his pianos. In 1802 he accompanied Clementi to Paris, Vienna and St Petersburg, where he settled in 1804 as music teacher, returning to London in 1832. He died at Moscow. See Memoir by Grattan Flood (1921).

(5) **Marshall** (1834–1906), American merchant, born at Conway, Mass., founder of the Chicago department store known from 1881 as Marshall Field and Company, one of the world's largest and most progressive emporia.

(6) **Michael,** pseud. of **Katharine Harris Bradley** (1846–1914) and her niece, **Edith Emma Cooper** (1862–1913), joint authors of poetic dramas and lyrics. See Life by M. Sturgeon (1922).

(7) **Nathan** (1587–1633?), English actor and dramatist, born in London, was educated at St Paul's school and in 1600 became one of the children of the Queen's Chapel. He was one of the comedians of the Queen's Revels (1604–13) and various other troupes. As playwright he collaborated with Beaumont and Fletcher and with Massinger in the latter's *The Fatal Dowry* (1632) and wrote two comedies, *A Woman is a Weathercocke* (1612) and *Amends for Ladies* (1618). See edition of his works by W. Peery (1950) and study by R. F. Brinkley (1928).

(8) **Stephen Johnson** (1816–99), American lawyer, brother of (1) and (2), helped to draw up the California state laws and became chief-justice there in 1859. He was made a judge of the U.S. supreme court in 1863.

FIELDING, (1) Anthony Vandyke Copley (1787–1855), English watercolour painter, born near Halifax, was a pupil of Varley, whose sister-in-law he married. He exhibited with the Watercolour Society from 1810 and became its president in 1831. His landscapes show technical excellence and atmosphere, but are often deficient in design. He lived for some years at Worthing, where he died, and where he had produced many of his well-known downland paintings and marine pieces.

(2) **Henry** (1707–54), English novelist, was born at Sharpham Park, Glastonbury, son of General Edmund Fielding. He went to Eton, where he was contemporary with the elder Pitt and the elder Fox. He studied literature at Leyden 1728–29, and on his return busied himself with the theatre and was successful enough with his comedies and farces to set up as author manager of the Little Theatre in the Haymarket, 1736. His tenancy of this theatre did not last long, for his two highly popular burlesques—*Pasquin*

(1736) and *The Historical Register* (1737)—led to the Licensing Act in that year, which closed his theatre. Meanwhile he had married Charlotte Cradock, the avowed model of Sophia Western, the heroine of *Tom Jones*, if not of Amelia in the novel of that title. An alternative career having to be found, he was called to the bar in 1740, but his interests lay in journalism and fiction. In the latter field his chance came when Richardson published his *Pamela* (1740), the prudential virtue of which outraged upper-class feeling generally and Fielding in particular. His prentice work in theatrical burlesque suggested the famous parody, *The History of the Adventures of Joseph Andrews and His Friend Mr Abraham Adams* (1742), in which the attempted seduction of male virtue replaces Pamela's ordeal. The burlesque intention was not pursued beyond the opening chapters and *Joseph Andrews* developed into a novel of life and manners, in which the appeal is always to common humanity as exercised generally among the lower orders and particularly in the great comic creation Parson Adams whose eccentricities involve him in all sorts of humiliations but cannot hide his real philanthropy. When his next fiction, *Jonathan Wild the Great*, was written we cannot be sure, but it appeared in his three-volume *Miscellanies* (1743), and so probably preceded *Joseph Andrews*. The mock-epic history of an actual criminal, it is a superb exercise in the ironic vein but also an example of Fielding's unsparing analysis of human motive and character. It may have been written to deflate the cult of the criminal hero as seen in Gay's *Beggar's Opera*. His means were now precarious and this, added to his wife's death and his own broken health, no doubt depressed him. His hack journalism for the Government—*The True Patriot* (1745) and *The Jacobite's Journal* (1747)—were however rewarded, at his patron Lord Lyttleton's instance, by the appointment of justice of the peace for Westminster, in which office he endeavoured to suppress the ruffianism of the day. Literature still claimed him—*Tom Jones* appeared in 1749. Unlike his previous fiction which leaned to the episodic and picaresque, *Tom Jones* has been praised for its closely-knit plot—the adventures are of the open road sort, but every detail is calculated. Jones himself is a very equivocal hero, for Fielding's philosophy of the good-natured man, the man of heart, as opposed to the conventional morality of Richardson, allowed his hero a degree of libertinage which offends the modern reader. The mock-epic episodes, too, are rather tiresome and the weighty introductory chapters (which contain some of his best writing) delay the story. Above all, his notion of the 'comic-epic' as the matrix of the social novel was mistaken. With all this, *Tom Jones, A Foundling* remains one of the great English novels, and was successfully filmed in 1962. *Amelia* (1751) shows flagging spirits, and now the realism which depicts the misery that may follow the weakness and libertinage of the husband is the theme. It is distressing to see the great novelist again engaging in the scurrilities of periodical writing in the form of *The Covent Garden Journal* (1752), in which he made a vicious attack on the new novelist Smollett. His posthumous *Journal of a Voyage to Lisbon* makes amends, for there all the generosity of his nature is revealed. See lives by Murphy (1762), Dobson (1889), and studies by Digeon (1925), E. Jenkins (1947), Dudden (1952) and Butt (1954).

FIELDS, (1) **Gracie,** stage name of **Grace Stansfield** (1898-), English music-hall singer and star, born at Rochdale, won with her sentimental songs and broad Lancashire humour a unique place in the affections of British audiences, taking part in nine Royal Command Performances to 1964. She was given the freedom of Rochdale (1937) and awarded the C.B.E. (1938).

(2) **James Thomas** (1817-81), American publisher, was born in Portsmouth, N.H., edited the *Atlantic Monthly* in 1862-70, and lectured on literary subjects; he also wrote books of verse, and volumes on Hawthorne and Dickens. His wife, **Annie Adams Fields** (1834-1915), was also an authoress.

FIESCHI, *fee-es'kee*, (1) **Count Giovanni Luigi de'** (*c.* 1523-47), Italian nobleman of an illustrious Genoese house, belonged to a race hereditarily at feud with that of the famous admiral, Andrea Doria, who had restored republican government in Genoa. Fieschi with his three brothers and others organized a plot for the overthrow of Doria and the establishment of an oligarchy. The gates of the city were forced, January 2, 1547, the fleet captured, Doria in flight. But Fieschi, stepping from one galley to another at night, fell overboard, and was drowned in the harbour. The scheme ended here, and Doria returned to wreak merciless vengeance on the other participators in the plot. See monographs by Brea (1863), Celesia (1864), Gavazzo (1886) and Callegari (1892).

(2) **Joseph** (1790-1836), Corsican conspirator, was dismissed from a minor government post for fraud. With several accomplices he constructed and fired an infernal machine at King Louis-Philippe in 1835. Eighteen people were killed, but the king escaped almost unhurt, and Fieschi was executed after trial.

FIESOLE, Giovanni da. See ANGELICO, FRA.

FIGG, James (d. 1736), English fencer and pugilist, born at Thame, who gave displays of quarterstaff, fencing and boxing in Marylebone, and ran a booth at Southwark, is regarded as one of the greatest of 18th century sporting figures. He is portrayed in Hogarth's *Rake's Progress* and *Southwark Fair*.

FIGUERAS, Estanislao, *fee-gay'ras* (1819-82), Spanish statesman, was born at Barcelona. For taking part in republican plots in 1866 he was imprisoned; but after the expulsion of Isabella he became a member of the republican government. On the abdication of King Amadeus in 1873 he became president of the Spanish republic, but soon resigned.

FIGUIER, Louis, *feeg-yay* (1819-94), French writer, born at Montpellier, became professor at the École de Pharmacie in Paris, and wrote on modern science and industry, alchemy and in defence of immortality. Many of these have been translated (*The Ocean World, The World Before the Deluge, The Day after Death, &c.*). His wife, **Juliette Bouscaren** (1829–79), wrote several novels.

FILDES, Sir Luke (1844–1927), English painter, born in Liverpool, became known as a woodcut designer for the magazines, and illustrated Dickens's *Edwin Drood* (1870). He exhibited many subject pictures, became R.A. in 1887 and was knighted in 1906.

FILICAIA, Vincenzo da, *fee-li-kah'ya* (1642–1707), Italian lyric poet, born at Florence, studied there and at Pisa, and held a post under the Grand-duke of Tuscany. He is remembered for his patriotic sonnets and his ode on the liberation of Vienna from the Turks. See monographs by Castellani (1890), and Caponi (1901).

FILLAN, St (d. 777), the son of a Munster prince, became abbot of the monastery on the Holy Loch in Argyllshire, but withdrew to Upper Glendochart (Strathfillan), where he died. In 1318 Robert Bruce re-established here an Augustinian priory. His square-shaped bronze bell, and the Quigrich, or bronze head of his pastoral staff, are in the Antiquarian Museum at Edinburgh. St Fillans, on Loch Earn, is associated with an earlier saint called ' the leper '.

FILLMORE, Millard (1800–74), from 1850 to 1853 thirteenth president of the United States, was born at Summer Hill, N.Y. A farmer's son, and bred a woolcarder, he educated himself, and became a lawyer, comptroller of New York State (1847), and vice-president (1848). On the slavery question he was a supporter of ' compromise '. See Life by Griffis (1915).

FILMER, Sir Robert (*c.* 1590–1653), English writer, born at East Sutton, Kent, was an extreme advocate of the divine right of kings (see his *Patriarcha and Other Political Works* (ed. Laslett, 1949)). He also strenuously opposed the witch mania.

FINCH, (1) Alfred William (1854–1930), Anglo-Finnish painter and ceramic artist, born at Brussels, who lived in Finland from 1897, was an exponent of Pointillism.

(2) **Heneage, 1st Earl of Nottingham** (1621–1682), lord chancellor, born in Kent, was a cousin's son of **Sir John Finch, Baron Finch** (1584–1660), speaker and lord-keeper. Educated at Westminster and Christ Church, Oxford, he was called to the bar in 1645. After the Restoration, as solicitor-general he took part in the trial of the regicides, and became attorney-general (1670) and lord chancellor (1674). As high steward he presided at the trial of Stafford in 1680. He died December 18, 1682.—His son **Daniel** (1647–1730), a Tory, but not a Jacobite, statesman, succeeded him as second Earl of Nottingham, and in 1729 became also sixth Earl of Winchilsea.

FINCK, (1) Heinrich (1445–1527), German composer, from *c.* 1490 court musician at Cracow in Poland, and later at Stuttgart, Augsburg and Salzburg, wrote church music, mostly *cantus firmus*, and influenced the development of 16th-century choral style.

(2) **Thomas** (1561–1646), Danish mathematician, whose book on geometry (1583)

used for the first time the words *secant* and *tangent*.

FINDLATER, Andrew (1810–85), Scottish editor, was born near Aberdour in Aberdeenshire, graduated at Aberdeen, and in 1842–49 was headmaster of Gordon's Hospital there. He came to Edinburgh (1853) to superintend for Messrs Chambers a new edition of the *Information for the People* (1857), edited the first edition of *Chambers's Encyclopaedia* (1860–68), and wrote manuals on astronomy, philology, physical geography.

FINGER, Godfrey, orig. **Gottfried** (fl. 1685–1717), Czech composer, born at Olomuc, came to England *c.* 1685 and was a musician at the court of James II. He wrote a number of instrumental works for flutes and violins, and composed incidental music for the plays of Congreve and others. He left England in 1701, because, we are told, of xenophobic prejudice against his work, and he became chamber musician to the queen of Prussia.

FINI, Tommaso. See MASOLINO DA PANICALE.

FINLAY, (1) George (1799–1875), Scottish classical historian, was born of Scottish parents at Faversham in Kent. After studying at Glasgow and Göttingen, he spent almost all the rest of his life in Greece. His *History of Greece* from the Roman conquest to the Greek revolution appeared in 1844–61 (new ed. 7 vols. 1877, with autobiography).

(2) **Robert Bannatyne, Viscount** (1842–1929), born at Edinburgh, studied medicine there, was called to the English bar in 1867, and was Unionist M.P. for Inverness Burghs (1855–92, 1895–1906), for Edinburgh University (1910–16). Solicitor-general (1895–1900; kt. 1895), attorney-general (1900–06), he was lord chancellor in 1916–19, and in 1920 member of the Hague Permanent Court of Arbitration. He was created a viscount in 1919.

FINNIAN, St, an Irish saint, said to have taught 3000 pupils at Clonard, died there in 549.

FINSEN, Niels Ryberg (1860–1904), Danish scientist, discoverer of the curative power of the chemical rays of light (sunlight, electric light, Röntgen rays, &c.) and founder of phototherapy, was born in the Faeroe Isles, and taught anatomy at the university of Copenhagen, where he had studied. He accomplished his epoch-making work in spite of chronic illness, and got a Nobel prize in 1903.

FIRBANK, (Arthur Annesley) Ronald (1886–1926), English novelist, born in London, wrote short witty, recherché novels on Negro and Catholic themes, among them *Caprice* (1917), *The Flower Beneath the Foot* (1922) and *Prancing Nigger* (1924).

FIRDAUSI, or **Ferdusi,** *fir-dow'zee*, the pen-name of Abú-'l Kásim Mansúr, greatest of Persian poets, was born about A.D. 940 near Tús in Khorassan, and after his fifty-eighth year spent some years at the court of Mahmúd of Ghazní. When the *Shah Náma* was finished in 1008, the poet, receiving 60,000 silver dirhams instead of the promised 60,000 gold dinars, fled from Ghazní, leaving behind him a scathing satire on the sultan. Mahmúd at length sent the 60,000 gold dinars to Firdausi at Tús, just as his remains were being carried to the grave (1020). The *Shah Náma*, based on actual events from the annals of Persia, is for the most part composed of mythological and fanciful incidents. Firdausi also wrote a number of shorter pieces, kasídas, ghazals, &c. His *Yúsuf ú Zulaykhá* is on the story of Joseph and Potiphar's wife. See Atkinson's epitome of the *Shah Náma* (1832; new ed. 1892), Miss Helen Zimmern's *Epic of Kings* (1882), and Robinson's *Life of Ferdusi* (1876). The complete text was edited by Turner Macan (1829). There is a complete French translation by Julius Mohl, with the Persian text (1838–78); and an English verse translation by A. G. and E. Warner (1905–15).

FIRENZUOLA, Agnolo (1493–1548), Italian author, born at Florence, became abbot of Prato, paraphrased the *Golden Ass* of Apuleius, and wrote a couple of comedies and some licentious poems.

FIRISHTA. See FERISHTAH.

FIRTH, (1) Sir Charles Harding (1857–1936), English historian, born at Sheffield, was professor of Modern History at Oxford in 1904–1925, wrote much on the 17th century, and particularly on such themes as *Oliver Cromwell and the Rule of the Puritans in England* (1953). He was knighted in 1922.

(2) **Mark** (1819–80), English industrialist and philanthropist, born at Sheffield, in 1849 with his father and brother established there the great Norfolk steelworks. He was a munificent benefactor to Sheffield, his gifts including almshouses, a park and the Firth College (1879), now part of the university.

FISCHART, Johann (*c.* 1545–90), German satirist whose Rabelaisian works lash with inexhaustible humour the corruptions of the clergy, the astrological fancies and other follies of the time. *Flöhhatz, Weibertratz* (1573) is outrageously comic and original. Essentially different are *Das glückhafft Schiff von Zürich* (in verse, 1576) and his spiritual songs. See study by A. Hauffen (2 vols. 1921–22).

FISCHER, (1) Emil Hermann (1852–1919), German chemist, born at Euskirchen, Rhenish Prussia, became professor of Chemistry at Berlin in 1892, a Nobel prizeman in 1902. Hydrazine, rosaniline, synthetic sugar, fermentation, the purine group, synthetic peptides, veronal were among his studies and discoveries.

(2) **Ernst Kuno Berthold** (1824–1907), German philosopher, born in Lower Silesia, was professor of Philosophy at Jena (1856) and Heidelberg (1872) and wrote (1852–93) a great history of modern philosophy and books on logic and metaphysics (1852) and on Kant, Descartes, Goethe, Lessing, Schiller.

(3) **Hans** (1881–1945), German scientist, latterly professor of Organic Chemistry and director of the Institute at Munich. His researches on haemin, the porphyrins, chlorophyll and other related compounds now him the Nobel prize for Chemistry in 1930. He died by his own hand.

(4) **Johann Kaspar Ferdinand** (1650–1746), German composer, chiefly of works for the harpsichord and the organ.

(5) **Otto Philip** (1852–1932), German

chemist, professor of Chemistry at Erlangen from 1905, and cousin of (1), with him did research on the hydrazines. He studied dyes and prepared kairine, the first synthetic alkaloid.

FISCHER-DIESKAU, Dietrich, *dees'kow* (1925–), German baritone, born in Berlin, studied under Georg Walter and Weissenborn. Soon after making his professional debut at Freiburg in 1947 he joined the Berlin Municipal Opera as a principal baritone, but he soon became one of the foremost interpreters of German Lieder, particularly the song-cycles of Schubert.

FISCHER VON ERLACH, Johann Bernard (1656–1723), Austrian architect, born at Graz, a leading exponent of the Baroque style in Vienna (Karlskirche, &c.) and Salzburg (University church, &c.). See E. Riehl, *Barocke Baukunst in Österreich* (1930).

FISH, Hamilton (1808–93), American politician, born at New York, as secretary of state under Grant (1869–77) signed the Washington Treaty of 1871, and completed the settlement of the Alabama Question.

FISHER, (1) Dr Geoffrey, Baron Fisher of Lambeth (1887–1972), Archbishop of Canterbury, 1945–61, was born at Higham-on-the-Hill, near Nuneaton, Warwick, was educated at Marlborough and Oxford and was ordained in 1912. From 1914 to 1932 he was headmaster of Repton School. He was forty-five when he took up his first ecclesiastical appointment as Bishop of Chester in 1932. In 1939 he became Bishop of London. As Archbishop of Canterbury he crowned Queen Elizabeth II in Westminster Abbey in June 1953. He was created a life peer in 1961.

(2) **Herbert Albert Laurens** (1865–1940), English historian, born in London, was a fellow, tutor and warden (1925) of New College, Oxford, and vice-chancellor of Sheffield University (1912). As education minister (1916–22) he sponsored notable Acts. He wrote on Napoleon, but is best known for his *History of Europe* (1936).

(3) **St John**, Bishop of Rochester (1469–1535), English prelate, born at Beverley, was educated at Michaelhouse, Cambridge, of which he became master (1497). Made chaplain to Margaret, Countess of Richmond, Henry VII's mother, in 1502, he was appointed first Lady Margaret professor of Divinity in 1503, and in 1504 chancellor of the university and bishop. He zealously promoted the New Learning, and advocated reformation from within; as zealously he resisted the Lutheran schism. In 1527 he pronounced firmly against the divorce of Henry VIII; and having listened to the ' revelations ' of the Holy Maid of Kent, Elizabeth Barton, in 1534 he was attainted of treason and, for refusing the oath of succession, was sent with More to the Tower. In May 1535 Pope Paul III made him a cardinal; on June 17, the old man, worn by sickness and ill-usage, was tried for denial of the king's supremacy; on the 22nd he was beheaded on Tower Hill. In 1935 he was canonized. See Bridgett's *Life of Blessed John Fisher* (1888).

(4) **John Arbuthnot** (1841–1920), **1st Baron Fisher of Kilverstone**, British admiral

of the fleet, born in Ceylon, entered the navy in 1854, and rose to be first sea lord (1904–1910, 1914–15). G.C.B., G.C.V.O., O.M., administrator, strategist, gunnery expert, seaman, racy memoir writer, he brought in 'Dreadnoughts' and 'scrapped' old ships. He was raised to the peerage in 1909. Marder edited his *Fear God and Dread Nought* (1952–59).

FISKE, John, orig. **Edmund Fisk Green** (1842–1901), American historian, born at Hartford, Conn., studied at Harvard, where he became tutor and librarian. He wrote popular books on American history, especially the colonial period; also works on Spencerian philosophy and Darwinism. See his *Life and Letters* by Clark (1920).

FITCH, (1) **John** (1743–98), American inventor, born in Connecticut, gunsmith to the American troops. In 1785 completed his model steamboat with wheels at the sides; larger vessels were built in 1788–90. In 1793 he went to France, to find his projects frustrated by the Revolution; but it is said that his plans were shown to Robert Fulton (q.v.). Penniless, Fitch worked his passage back to America, and there poisoned himself. See R. C. Fitch, *History of the Fitch Family* (1929).

(2) **Ralph** (d. 1606), English merchant, in 1583–91 travelled by way of the Euphrates to and from India, Burma and Siam. The founders of the East India Company sought his advice on Indian affairs. See Life by J. Horton Ryley (1899).

FITTIG, Rudolf (1835–1910), German scientist, professor of Organic Chemistry at Tübingen (1869) and at Strasbourg (1876), for his work on organic compounds, was awarded the Royal Society's Davy medal in 1906.

FITTON, Mary (*c.* 1578–1647), a maid of honour to Queen Elizabeth, mistress in 1600 of William Herbert, Earl of Pembroke, suggested by Thomas Tyler as the 'dark lady' of Shakespeare's Sonnets cxxvii–clvii.

FITZGERALD, (1) **Lord Edward** (1763–98), Irish politician, a younger son of the Duke of Leinster, was born near Dublin, served with distinction in the American war, was M.P. in Ireland and was drawn to Paris by the Revolution. Here he renounced his title, married, and returned to Ireland in 1793, to plunge into political conspiracy. He joined the United Irishmen in 1796, and went to France to arrange for a French invasion of Ireland. The plot was betrayed and Fitzgerald seized in Dublin, in the desperate scuffle receiving mortal wounds. See Lives by Moore (1831; new ed. 1896), G. Campbell (1904), Byrne (1955).

(2) **Edward** (1809–83), English scholar and poet, born March 31, at Bredfield House in Suffolk, graduated in 1830 at Trinity College, Cambridge. His friends included Spedding, W. B. Donne, Thackeray, Bernard Barton, whose daughter Lucy (1808–98) he married, and Tennyson, who dedicated *Tiresias* to him. He died June 14, 1883. FitzGerald published anonymously his dialogue on youth, *Euphranor*, in 1851, which was followed by *Polonius* in 1852. A translation of six of Calderón's dramas (1853) was soon withdrawn from circulation. About this time he

took up Persian, and in 1856 published an anonymous version of Jámí's *Salámán and Absál*. The quatrains of Omar Khayyám, the Persian astronomer poet of the 11th century, were then little known; but Fitz-Gerald at once recognized their beauty, and his and Omar's names will remain indissolubly linked together through his rendering of the *Rubáiyát* (1859). See his *Letters and Collected Works* (1889–1902); *Letters to Fanny Kemble* (1895); the centenary celebration volume (1909); *Lives* by Wright (1904), A. C. Benson (1905), Terhune (1947) and A. J. Arberry (1959); and Prideaux, *Omar Khayyám and his Translator* (1909).

(3) **Francis Scott Key** (1896–1940), American novelist, was born in St Paul, Minnesota. He captured the spirit of the twenties—'The Jazz Age'—in *The Great Gatsby* (1925), his best-known book. Other novels include *The Beautiful and Damned* (1922), *Tender is the Night* (1934) and *The Last Tycoon* (1941). See Lives by A. Mizener (1951), A. Turnbull (1962), H. D. Piper (1966), R. Sklar (1967) and study by J. E. Miller (1964).

(4) **George Francis**, F.R.S. (1851–1901), Irish physicist, was professor of Natural Philosophy at Dublin (1881–1901) and made important discoveries in the fields of electrolysis and electromagnetic radiation. See *The Scientific Writings of the Late George Francis Fitzgerald* (ed. Larmor, 1902).

(5) **Gerald**. See DESMOND, EARL OF.

(6) **Percy Hetherington** (1834–1925), Irish writer, author of over 200 volumes, sculptor, and friend of Dickens, born at Fane Valley, Co. Louth, was called to the Irish bar. See his *Memoirs* (1895).

FITZHERBERT, Mrs, *née* **Maria Anne Smythe** (1756–1837), a Roman Catholic widow, whom the Prince of Wales, afterwards George IV, secretly married in 1785. This marriage, contracted without the king's consent, was invalid under the Royal Marriage Act of 1772; the prince afterwards denied that there had been a marriage at all. On his marriage to the Princess Caroline in 1795 the connection was interrupted, resumed with the pope's consent, and finally broken off in 1803. See her Memoirs by Langdale (1856), and Letters (ed. Leslie, 1940); also Life by Leslie (1960).

FITZMAURICE-KELLY, James (1857–1923), professor of Spanish at Liverpool (1909–16) and at London (1916–20), wrote on Spanish literature, and edited the *Oxford Book of Spanish Verse* (1913).

FITZROY, Robert (1805–65), British admiral and meteorologist, grandson of the Duke of Grafton, was born at Ampton Hall near Bury St Edmunds, and, entering the navy, surveyed the coasts of Patagonia and Tierra del Fuego, 1828–30; this work he continued on his reappointment to the *Beagle* in 1831, when he was accompanied by Darwin, the two together publishing in 1839 a *Narrative of the Voyages of H.M.S. 'Adventure' and 'Beagle'*. Governor of New Zealand (1843–1845), he was promoted rear-admiral (1857) and vice-admiral (1863) on the retired list. In 1854 he was attached to the meteorological department of the Board of Trade. The 'Fitzroy barometer' was invented by him;

and he instituted the storm warnings that developed into daily weather forecasts. Worn out by overwork, he committed suicide.

FITZSIMMONS, Robert Prometheus (1862–1917), British boxer, born in Helston and reared in New Zealand. He won the world middleweight championship from Jack Dempsey (*not* the famous heavyweight) at New Orleans in 1891, and the world heavyweight championship from Jim Corbett at Carson City in 1897. He lost his title to James J. Jeffries at Coney Island in 1899.

FITZWILLIAM, (1) Richard, 7th Viscount Fitzwilliam of Meryon (1745–1816), an Irish peer, founder at his death of the Fitzwilliam Museum in Cambridge.

(2) **William, 2nd Earl Fitzwilliam** (1748–1833), British statesman, lord-lieutenant for three months of Ireland (1794–95), where his warm support of Catholic emancipation aroused enthusiastic hopes. Pitt thought him too liberal; and his recall was followed by the Rebellion of 1798. He was president of the Council in the Grenville ministry in 1806.

FIZEAU, *fee-zō*, Armand Hyppolyte Louis (1819–96), French physicist, was in 1849 the first to measure the velocity of light by an experiment confined to the earth's surface, in which field he later collaborated with Foucault. Fizeau demonstrated also the use of the Doppler principle in determining star velocity in the line of sight.

FLACCUS, Caius Valerius, a Roman poet of the time of Vespasian, wrote the *Argonautica*, an unfinished epic of learned mediocrity.

FLACIUS, or Vlacich, Matthias (1520–75), Lutheran theologian, was born at Albona in Illyria, became professor of Hebrew at Wittenberg in 1544, but for his attacks upon Melanchthon's compromise, known as the Leipzig Interim, was deprived of his chair. In 1557–62 he was professor of Theology at Jena, but was again deprived for teaching that original sin was inherent in man's nature. After this he led a wandering life. His principal works are *Clavis Scripturae Sacrae* (1567), *Catalogus Testium Veritatis* (1556), and *Ecclesiastica Historia* (1559–74). The church history called *Magdeburg Centuries* was only partly his. See Preger's monograph (1861).

FLAGSTAD, Kirsten (1895–1962), Norwegian soprano, born in Hamar, studied in Stockholm and Oslo, where she made her operatic début in 1913. She excelled in Wagnerian rôles, Sieglinde at Bayreuth (1934); Isolde in New York (1935, &c.), and was acclaimed in most of the world's major opera houses. In 1958 she was made director of the Norwegian State Opera.

FLAHAUT DE LA BILLARDERIE, *flah-ō dè la bee-yar-dree*, **Auguste Charles Joseph, Comte de** (1785–1870), French soldier and diplomatist, fought under Napoleon, and was the paramour of Countess Potocki and of Hortense de Beauharnais, whose son by him became Duc de Morny (q.v.). An exile after Waterloo, he married the Baroness Keith and Nairne (1788–1867). After 1830 he returned to France, was ambassador at Vienna (1842–1848) and London (1860–62), and was Grand Chancellor of the Legion of Honour.

FLAHERTY, Robert (1884–1951), American film producer, brought documentary films to the fore with *Nanook of the North* (1922) and *Moana* (1926). His last great success was *Louisiana Story*. He also produced *Man of Aran* (1932–34) and *Elephant Boy* (1935).

FLAMBARD, Rannulf or Ralph (d. 1128), justiciar of England under William II, became Bishop of Durham in 1099, but ministered to the king's vices and extravagances by oppressive extortion of the people.

FLAMENG, Léopold (1831–1911), French etcher and engraver (of the Académie des Beaux Arts), was born in Brussels of French parents. He illustrated the Paris edition of the *Decameron*, and produced wonderfully faithful engravings of old masters, portraits and contemporary paintings.

FLAMINIUS, Gaius (d. 217 B.C.), twice Roman consul (223, 217 B.C.), distributed the Ager Gallicus, built the Flaminian Way (to Rimini), defeated the Insubres at the Addua (223), and was defeated and killed at Trasimene (217; see HANNIBAL).

FLAMMARION, Camille, *fla-mah-ree-ō* (1842–1925), French astronomer, born at Montigny-le-Roi, entered the Paris Observatory in 1858. He wrote books on astronomy, ballooning, physical research, &c., and founded the observatory of Juvisy (1883).

FLAMSTEED, John (1646–1719), the first astronomer-royal of England, was born at Denby near Derby. In 1676 Greenwich Observatory was built and Flamsteed (appointed astronomer-royal the previous year) began the observations that initiated modern practical astronomy. He formed the first trustworthy catalogue of the fixed stars, and furnished those observations by which Newton verified his lunar theory. His great work is *Historia Coelestis Britannica*, an account of astronomical observation (3 vols. 1725). He took holy orders, and from 1684 till his death held the Surrey living of Burstow. See Baily's *Account of Flamsteed* (1835).

FLANDIN, Pierre Étienne, *flã-dī* (1889–1958), French politician, born in Paris, a member of the Chamber from 1914, held office in several governments and was prime minister in 1934–35.

FLANDRIN, Jean Hippolyte, *flã-drī* (1809–1864), French painter, born at Lyons, in 1832 won the *Prix de Rome*, and subsequently produced *St Clare healing the Blind*, now in Nantes Cathedral. In 1842 he began his great frescoes in the church of St Germain-des-Prés, Paris. After this he was mainly engaged in fresco painting, although he executed many fine portraits. He died at Rome. See his *Lettres et Pensées* (1865), and Lives by Poncet (1864) and Montrard (1876).

FLATMAN, Thomas (1635–88), English miniature painter and poet, born in London. He was educated at Winchester and New College, Oxford, and was called to the bar in 1662. He executed many miniature portraits in the style of Samuel Cooper, e.g., his self portrait (1673) in the Victoria and Albert Museum. In the following year he published *Poems and Songs*. See *Life and uncollected poems* (1921) by F. A. Child.

FLAUBERT, Gustave, *flō-bayr* (1821–80), French novelist, born at Rouen, December 12, the son of a doctor, studied law reluctantly at Paris, where his friendship with Victor Hugo, Maxime du Camp, and the poetess Louise Colet (his lover from 1846 to 1854) stimulated his already apparent talent for writing. When barely past his student days he was afflicted by an obscure form of nervous disease, which may have been to some extent responsible for the morbidity and pessimism which characterized his work from the very beginning. These traits, together with a violent hatred and contempt for bourgeois society are revealed in his first masterpiece, *Madame Bovary* (1857), a painful but powerful tragedy of an unhappily mated wife who lapses into vice. The book achieved a *succès de scandale* after it had been condemned as immoral and its author prosecuted, albeit unsuccessfully, but it has held its place among the classics. His second work, *Salammbô* (1862), dealt with the struggle between Rome and Carthage and is rather overweighted with archaeological detail. *L'Education sentimentale* (1869) was less effective, but in 1874 appeared the splendid phantasmagoria of *La Tentation de St Antoine*, the masterpiece of its kind. *Trois contes* (1877) reveals his mastery of the short story and foreshadows Maupassant, whom he influenced. After his death appeared *Bouvard et Pécuchet* which had not received his final revision. Though regarded as a pioneer of Realism, mainly because of the minuteness of his observation, Flaubert was in fact a pure romanticist who came late and had engrafted on the earlier Romanticism characteristics stemming from Balzac and Stendhal. His correspondence with George Sand was published in 1884; and other letters followed (1887–93). An 'édition définitive' of his works was issued in 1909–12. See books by Tarver (1895), Dumesnil (1905), Descharmes (1909), L. Bertrand (1912), Faguet (trans. 1914), Shanks (1927), P. Spencer (1952), E. Starkie (1967), and Selected Letters (ed. Steegmuller; 1954).

FLAVEL, John (*c.* 1630–91), Presbyterian divine, born at Bromsgrove, ejected from his living at Dartmouth in 1662. He continued to preach privately there, and after the Declaration of Indulgence (1687) was minister of a Nonconformist church till his death.

FLAXMAN, John (1755–1826), English sculptor, was born at York, July 6. Six months later, his father, a moulder of plaster figures, removed to London; the delicate, slightly-deformed child soon developed a taste for drawing. In 1767 he exhibited models, and in 1769 became a student of the Royal Academy. Henceforward he was constantly engaged upon sculpture; but his chief source of income was the Wedgwood house, which he furnished with exquisite designs for their pottery. By the time of his marriage in 1782 he was employed upon monumental sculpture, such as his monuments to Chatterton in St Mary Redcliffe, Bristol, and to Collins in Chichester Cathedral. From 1787 he studied at Rome for seven years, executed numerous classical groups, and began his designs to the *Iliad* and *Odyssey* (published

1793), to Aeschylus (1795) and to Dante (1797), which were engraved in Rome by Piroli. His designs to Hesiod were engraved by Blake in 1817. In England again (1794), he produced his fine monument to Lord Mansfield in Westminster Abbey. In 1797 he was elected A.R.A., in 1800 R.A., and in 1810 he became professor of Sculpture to the Royal Academy. He is outstanding among English sculptors for inventive power and purity and grace of style. See works by Colvin (1876) and Constable (1927).

FLECK, Sir Alexander, Baron Fleck (1889–1968), British industrialist, was born in Glasgow and educated at Glasgow University, where he lectured for two years, before working as a physical chemist on radium and later on the manufacture of sodium. The great series of amalgamations in the British chemical industry saw Fleck gradually working for larger organizations, and by 1931 he was managing director of the General Chemical Division of the fledgling I.C.I., having successfully centralized many of the firm's operations. During World War II, his main responsibility was to maintain supplies of high explosives. In 1944 he joined the main board of I.C.I., supervised the building of the new plant at Wilton, was chairman of the I.C.I. in 1953, was knighted and elected a F.R.S. in 1955 and was made a baron in 1961. He acted as chairman of the committee which investigated the nationalized coal industry. He was (1958) president of the British Association.

FLECKER, James Elroy (1884–1915), English poet, born at Lewisham, studied Oriental languages at Cambridge, entered the consular service, and wrote *Hassan* (staged, 1923) and other rich verse, found in such works as *The Golden Journey to Samarkand* (1913) and in his *Collected Poems* (1916, 1921). See Lives by Goldring (1922) and Hodgson (1925).

FLECKNOE, Richard (d. 1678), a Roman Catholic, possibly Irish and a priest, who, after travelling (1640–50) in Europe, Asia, Africa and Brazil, came to London, mingled in the wars of the wits, wrote plays, and was the stalking-horse over whom Dryden applied the merciless lash of his satire to Shadwell; and the victim of a good-humoured satire by Marvell. See Life and works by P. H. Doney (1931).

FLEETWOOD, Charles (*c.* 1618–92), a Cromwellian soldier, of a good Northamptonshire stock, commanded a cavalry regiment at Naseby (1645), was elected M.P. for Marlborough in 1646, was commander of the parliamentary forces in England before the battle of Worcester, and commander-in-chief in Ireland (1652–55). In 1652 he married Cromwell's daughter, widow of Ireton. He was commander-in-chief in 1659, but had to give way before Monk, and was deprived of office at the Restoration.

FLEGEL, Eduard Robert, *flay'gel* (1855–86), German explorer, born at Vilna, in 1879–83 thrice ascended the Niger, the third time discovering the sources of the Benuë.

FLEISCHER, Heinrich Leberecht, *flī'sher* (1801–88), German orientalist, born at Schandau, professor of Oriental Languages at Leipzig from 1836, edited Abulfeda

(1831–34), other Persian and Arabic works, &c.

FLÉMALLE, Master of. See CAMPIN.

FLEMING, (1) Sir Alexander (1881–1955), Scottish bacteriologist, the discoverer in 1928 of penicillin, born August 6, at Loudoun, Ayrshire, was educated at Kilmarnock, became a shipping clerk in London for five years before matriculating (1902) and embarking upon a brilliant medical studentship, qualifying as a surgeon at St Mary's Hospital, Paddington. It was only by his expert marksmanship in the college rifle team, however, that he managed to find a place in Sir Almroth Wright's bacteriological laboratory there. The young researcher became the first to use antityphoid vaccines on human beings, pioneered the use of salvarsan against syphilis and while a medical officer in France during the war discovered the antiseptic powers of lysozyme, present in tears and mucus. In 1928 by chance exposure of a culture of *staphylococci* he noticed a curious mould, penicillin, which he found to have unsurpassed antibiotic powers. Unheeded by colleagues and without sufficient chemical knowledge, he had to wait eleven years before two brilliant biochemists, Florey and Chain, with whom he shared the Nobel prize for Medicine in 1945, perfected a method of producing the volatile drug. Fleming was appointed professor of Bacteriology at London in 1938. With mass production of penicillin (1942) came recognition. He was elected F.R.S. in 1943, knighted in 1944 and received civic and academic honours throughout Europe and America. See Life by A. Maurois (1959).

(2) **Ian Lancaster** (1908–64), British author and journalist, brother of (6), educated Eton and Sandhurst, studied languages at Munich and Geneva Universities, worked with Reuters in Moscow (1929–33), then as banker and stockbroker (1933–39). He served with British Naval Intelligence during World War II, and was foreign manager of the *Sunday Times* (1945–59). He achieved worldwide fame and fortune as creator of a series of spy novels, starting with *Casino Royale* (1953), and built round the exploits of his amoral hero James Bond. Several have been made into highly successful, tongue-in-cheek, films. See K. Amis: *The James Bond Dossier* (1965), and Life by Pearson (1966).

(3) **Sir John Ambrose** (1849–1945), British physicist, born at Lancaster, in 1885–1926 professor of Electrical Engineering in University College, London, invented the thermionic valve and was a pioneer in the application of electricity to lighting and heating on a large scale.

(4) **Margaret** (1803–11), Scottish child prodigy, born at Kirkcaldy, Sir Walter Scott's ' Pet Marjorie ', and the theme of an exquisite essay by Dr John Brown. She wrote poems and diaries. See H. B. Farnie's *Pet Marjorie* (1858).

(5) **Paul** (1609–40), German lyric poet, born at Hartenstein, ranks high for *Geistliche und weltliche Poemata* (1642; ed. by Lappenberg, 1866). See studies by K. Unger (1907) and H. Pyritz (1932).

(6) **(Robert) Peter** (1907–71), British travel writer and novelist, elder brother of (2), born in London. Successively on the staff of the *Evening Standard*, *The Spectator* and *The Times*, his publications include a number of travel books, amongst the best known of which are *Brazilian Adventure* (1933, new ed. 1940) and *Travels in Tartary* (1941). Received an O.B.E. in 1945.

(7) **Sir Sandford** (1827–1915), Canadian railway engineer, chief engineer of the Intercolonial Railway (1864) and of the C.P.R. (1871), surveyed several famous routes, including Yellowhead and Kicking Horse passes. See Life by L. J. Burpee (1915).

FLEMMING, Walther (1843–1915), German biologist, born at Sachsenberg, best known for his research on cell division, to which he gave the name mitosis. He also did important work on the splitting of chromosomes, and on microscope technique.

FLETCHER, (1) Andrew (1655–1716), of Saltoun, Scottish patriot, sat in the Scots parliament in 1681, and so consistently opposed Stuart policy latterly that twice he had to flee to Holland. He returned to Scotland at the revolution. He was the first patron of William Paterson, the projector of the Darien expedition, and the bitterness caused in Scotland by the treatment of the Darien colonists gave Fletcher and the nationalist party their strength in the struggle against the inevitable union with England. His famous ' limitations ' aimed at constructing a federative instead of an incorporating union. After the Union, Fletcher retired in disgust from public life, devoting himself to promoting agriculture; he introduced fanners and the mill for pot-barley. He died in London. His writings were reprinted at London in 1732. See Life by Omond (1897).

(2) **Giles** (1588?–1623), English poet, brother of (5), cousin of (3), was educated at Westminster and Cambridge, and became rector of Alderton in Suffolk. His chief work, *Christ's Victory and Triumph* (1610), full of splendid versification and imagery, has a quickening glow of genuine enthusiasm. It was modelled on Spenser.

(3) **John** (1579–1625), English dramatist, closely associated with Francis Beaumont (q.v.), was born at Rye, Sussex, the third son of that Dean of Peterborough who disturbed the last moments of Mary Stuart. He came of a literary family, being the nephew of Giles Fletcher the elder and cousin of the Spenserian poets Giles and Phineas Fletcher. All that we know of him, apart from his work for the theatre, is that he entered Benet (now Corpus) College, Cambridge, and that he died of the plague in 1625. The problem of disentangling his own plays from those in which he collaborated with Beaumont, Massinger, Rowley and Shakespeare is very difficult but three or four certainly of his own devising are outstanding and the collaboration with Beaumont yielded some memorable plays. The best of his own plays are *The Faithful Shepherdess*, which ranks, as a pastoral, with Ben Jonson's *Sad Shepherd* and Milton's *Comus*; *The Humourous Lieutenant*, acted in 1619; and *Rule a Wife and Have a Wife* (1624), on the favourite theme of conjugal

mastery. Of the ten or so plays in which he collaborated with Beaumont the best known are *The Knight of the Burning Pestle* (attributed mainly or possibly solely to Beaumont), *Philaster* (1610), a romantic comedy, *A King and No King* (1611) and *The Maid's Tragedy* (1611), generally accounted their best work. Collaboration with Shakespeare probably resulted in *Two Noble Kinsmen*, a melodramatic version of Chaucer's *Knight's Tale*, and *Henry VIII* (or insertions therein). A vein of tender poetry in Fletcher and his relaxed type of versification are useful evidence in disentangling his various collaborations. The Collected Works of Beaumont and Fletcher appeared first in 1647, since when there have been numerous editions, including an (unfinished) Variorum in 1904. See Schelling's *Elizabethan Drama* vol. II; Swinburne, *Studies in Prose and Poetry*; and Thorndike, *Influence of Beaumont and Fletcher on Shakespeare* (1901).

(4) **John Gould** (1886–1950), American poet and essayist, born at Little Rock, followed the Imagists while living in London and Paris (1908–33), but later turned to American subjects. He won the Pulitzer prize in 1939 for his *Selected Poems*. See his autobiographical *Life is my Song* (1937).

(5) **Phineas** (1582–1650), English poet, brother of (2), cousin of (3), and son of Giles Fletcher, LL.D. (1549–1611), Queen Elizabeth's minister in Germany and Russia. He was educated at Eton and Cambridge, and in 1621 became rector of Hilgay in Norfolk. His *Purple Island, or the Isle of Man* (1633), contains an elaborate description of the human body viewed as an island, the bones being its foundations, and the veins its rivers.

FLEURY, *flœ-ree*, (1) **André Hercule de** (1653–1743), French prelate, born at Lodève, became Bishop of Fréjus, and with the accession of Louis XV in 1715 he became the boy's tutor. From the outset Fleury's subtly exerted influence on policy was pacific. The astute restraint characterizing his opposition to the Duc de Bourbon was effective, and led to his acquisition of the premiership and a cardinal's hat. Temporarily, his moderation endowed France with the tranquillity her tangled finances demanded. But he needlessly prolonged Louis' constitutional minority, and with France committed to the War of the Austrian Succession, he was cast aside. See works by Tooke (1862) and Verlaque (1879).

(2) **Claude** (1640–1725), French church historian, born at Paris, was tutor to various princes, prior of Argenteuil and confessor to young Louis XV. Among his numerous works were *Moeurs des Israélites* (1681); *Moeurs des Chrétiens* (1662); *Droit ecclésiastique* (1687); and the great *Histoire ecclésiastique* (20 vols. 1691–1720)—really the first complete church history, on which he laboured thirty years. Fleury's own work only reached to 1414; it was continued to 1778 by others.

FLIEDNER, Theodor, *fleed'ner* (1800–64), German divine, born at Eppstein, in 1822 became pastor of Kaiserswerth near Düsseldorf, where in 1836 he founded the first Protestant deaconesses' home. See Life by

Georg Fliedner (3 vols. 1908–12). His son **Fritz** (1845–1901), worked as a Protestant evangelist in Spain and wrote *Iglesia Evangélica Española*. See study by M. Gerhardt (2 vols. 1933–37).

FLINCK, Govaert (1615–60), Dutch portrait and religious painter, born in Cleves. A pupil of Rembrandt, he painted biblical and genre pictures.

FLINDERS, Matthew (1774–1814), English explorer, born at Donington, Lincolnshire, entered the navy, and, having met with Bass (q.v.) discovered Bass's Strait, was in 1801–03 commissioned to circumnavigate Australia. On his way home he was wrecked, and detained a prisoner by the French governor of Mauritius until 1810. The Flinders river in Queensland, and the Flinders range in S. Australia are named for him. See his *Voyage to Terra Australis* (1814) and Life by E. Scott (1914).

FLINT, (1) **Frank Stewart** (1885–   ), English poet and translator, born in London, joined the Imagist movement and published lyric poetry, *In the Net of the Stars* (1909), *Cadences* (1915) and *Otherworld* (1920). A brilliant linguist, he produced many translations.

(2) **Robert** (1834–1910), Scottish theologian, born at Dumfries, and ordained in 1859, was professor of Moral Philosophy at St Andrews (1864–76), and of Divinity at Edinburgh (1876–1903). His *Philosophy of History* established his reputation. Other works were the Baird Lectures, *Theism* and *Anti-Theistic Theories* (1876–77), *Vico* (1884) and *Socialism* (1895).

(3) **Sir William Russell** (1880–1969), British artist and illustrator, born in Edinburgh. He painted many watercolours to illustrate books (e.g., Chaucer, Matthew Arnold) and for exhibition. His work was noted for delicate colouring and broad washes, often granulated for effect, and for a skill in rendering the human figure rarely found in the watercolour medium. His publications include *Models of Propriety* (1951). He was elected to the Royal Academy in 1933 and was knighted in 1947.

FLITCROFT, Henry (1679–1769), English architect, was born at Hampton Court, where his father was the king's gardener. The Earl of Burlington became his patron, and he held various official appointments, becoming comptroller of the works in 1758. He designed the London churches of St Giles in the Fields and St John at Hampstead, and he rebuilt parts of Wentworth House in Yorkshire and Woburn Abbey.

FLOOD, Henry (1732–91), Irish politician, educated at Trinity College, Dublin, and Oxford, became a leader in the popular party in the Irish parliament after his election in 1759. In 1775 became vice-treasurer of Ireland, but was removed in 1781 as a strong Nationalist. Disliking Grattan's reform bills as inadequate, Flood strove without success to carry a more sweeping measure, and became involved in a bitter quarrel with his former friend. In 1783 he was returned for Winchester, and in 1785 for Seaford, but he failed to make a great mark at Westminster. See his *Life and Correspondence* (1838).

FLOQUET, Charles Thomas, *flok-ay* (1828–

1896), French radical politician, born at St Jean de Luz, strenuously opposed Napoleon III's régime, edited the *République française*, and was elected to the Chamber of Deputies in 1876. President of the Chamber in 1885–1888 and 1889–93, he belonged to the anti-Boulangist faction and wounded its leader in a duel in 1888. His political influence waned after his implication in the Panama scandal of 1893.

FLORENCE OF WORCESTER, English chronicler, a monk of Worcester, where he died in 1118, wrote a *Chronicon* which comes down to 1116, and which about 1030 becomes of some value as an independent authority. It was edited by Thorpe in 1848, and trans. by Forester (1847) and Stevenson (1853).

FLORES, Juan José, *flo'rays* (1801–64), South American statesman, born at Puerto Cabello in Venezuela, fought with distinction in the war of independence, and became first president of the republic of Ecuador in 1830–1835 and 1839–43.

FLOREY, Sir Howard Walter, Baron Florey of Adelaide (1898–1968), British pathologist, born at Adelaide, professor of Pathology at Oxford from 1935 to 1962, with Chain worked on penicillin, and shared the Nobel prize for Medicine 1945. He was provost of Queen's Coll., Oxford, from 1962, and president of the Royal Society 1960–65. He was elected F.R.S. in 1941, was knighted in 1944, was created life peer and received the O.M. in 1965.

FLORIAN, Jean Pierre Claris de (1755–94), French novelist and fabulist. He wrote two prose romances, and pastorals, plays, &c. See *Select Fables* (ed. Goldschild; 1904).

FLORIO, John (c. 1553–1625), the translator of Montaigne, was born of Italian Protestant parentage in London, about 1576 was a tutor in foreign languages at Oxford, and in 1578 published his *First Fruits,* accompanied by *A Perfect Induction to the Italian and English Tongues.* His next work was *Second Fruits,* with six thousand Italian Proverbs (1591). His Italian and English dictionary, entitled *A World of Words,* was published in 1598. In 1603 Florio was appointed reader in Italian to Queen Anne, in 1604 groom of the privy-chamber. His famous translation of Montaigne (1603) has appeared in several modern editions. See studies by Chambrun (1921) and F. A. Yates (1934).

FLORY. See FLEURY.

FLOTOW, Friedrich, Freiherr von, *flo'to* (1812–83), German composer, born at Teutendorf in Mecklenburg, made his reputation by *Le Naufrage de la Méduse* (1839), *Stradella* (1844), and *Martha* (1847), the last two characterized by pleasing melody. From 1856 to 1863 he was director of the theatre at Schwerin. See Life by his widow (Leipzig 1892).

FLOURENS, *floo-räs*, (1) **Gustave** (1838–71), French Communard, son of (3), distinguished himself by his book, *La Science de l'homme* (1865), as an ardent republican took part in the Cretan insurrection against the Turks (1866), and fell fighting for the Paris Commune.

(2) **Leopold-Émile** (1841–1920), French politician, son of (3), brother of (1), was foreign minister 1886–88.

(3) **Pierre Jean Marie** (1794–1867), French physiologist, father of (1) and (2), became secretary of the Academy of Sciences (1833), professor at the Collège de France (1855), and member of the Academy (1840). He was elected to the Chamber of Deputies in 1838 and made a peer of France in 1846. He wrote on the development and nutrition of the human body and on animal instinct.

FLOWER, Sir William Henry, F.R.S. (1831–1899), born at Stratford-on-Avon, appointed in 1861 conservator of the Hunterian Museum, in 1869 Hunterian professor of Comparative Anatomy and Physiology, in 1884–98 was natural history director at the British Museum. He revolutionized museums. See Life by Cornish (1904).

FLUDD, Robert (1574–1637), English physician, mystic and pantheistic theosophist, born at Milgate. Influenced by Paracelsus, he recognized three cosmic elements—God (archetypus), world (macrocosmos) and man (microcosmos). See study by Craven (1902).

FOCH, Ferdinand, *fosh* (1851–1929), French marshal, born at Tarbes, taught at the École de Guerre, proved himself a great strategist at the Marne (1914), Ypres, &c., and as generalissimo of the Allied armies from March 1918, directed the hammerstrokes which drove back the Germans and won the war. Member of the Académie and O.M. (1918), field-marshal (1919), he ' deserved well of his country ' and of its Allies. He wrote *Principles of War* (trans. 1919), *Memoirs* (1931), &c. See studies by Bugnet (1929), Liddell Hart (1933) and Falls (1939).

FOGAZZARO, Antonio (1842–1911), Italian novelist, born at Vicenza, excelled at lively portrayals of country and small town life. He published a long series of novels, beginning with *Miranda* (1874) and including *Il Santo* (trans. *The Saint,* 1906). See studies by Vitali (Milan 1938), Poitier (Paris 1938) and Nardi (Milan 1938).

FOIX, Gaston, *fwa* (1489–1512), French nobleman whose mother was a sister of Louis XII of France, became Duc de Nemours in 1505. In the Italian wars he displayed such brilliant genius and bravery as to earn the title of ' Thunderbolt of Italy '. He twice overthrew the Swiss, at Como and Milan (1511); chased the papal troops from Bologna; seized Brescia from the Venetians; and defeated the Spaniards at Ravenna, where, however, he was killed. The estates and title went to the king of Navarre. Finally Henry IV of Navarre attached the county of Foix to the French crown.

FOKINE, Michel, *fo-keen'* (1880–1942), Russian dancer and choreographer, born in St Petersburg. He is credited with the creation of modern ballet from the artificial, stylized mode prevalent at the turn of the century.

FOKKER, Antony (1890–1939), Dutch aircraft engineer, born at Kediri in Java, built his first plane in 1911, and in 1913 founded the Fokker aircraft factory at Schwerin in Germany, which made warplanes for the German air force in World War I. After the war he set up a factory in the Netherlands and later operated also in Britain and the U.S.A.

FOLENGO, Teofilo (1491–1554), an Italian

macaronic poet, a witty and graceless Benedictine, who wrote under the name of Merlinus Coccaius.

FOLEY, John Henry (1818–74), Irish sculptor, born in Dublin, came to London in 1834. He executed many statues of public figures, including that of the Prince Consort for the Albert Memorial. Elected A.R.A. in 1849, and R.A. in 1858, he died at Hampstead and was buried in St Paul's.

FOLGORE, *fol'go-ray*, a 13th century Italian poet, who wrote a number of sonnets, translated by Rossetti and J. A. Symonds. See Navone's *Rime di Folgore* (1880).

FOLKES, Martin (1690–1754), English numismatist, was born in London, published *A Table of English Gold Coins* (1736) and *A Table of English Silver Coins* (1745). He was P.R.S., F.S.A., and a member of the Paris Academy of Sciences.

FONBLANQUE, Albany William, *fon'blank* (1793–1872), English journalist, born in London, editor from 1830 of the *Examiner*. His best articles were reprinted as *England under Seven Administrations* (1837). In 1847 he became statistical secretary to the Board of Trade. See *Life* (1874).

FONSECA, *fon-say'ka*, (1) **Eleonora Pimentel, Marchesa di** (1758–99), a Neapolitan lady-in-waiting to Queen Maria Carolina until she forfeited her mistress's favour by remarking on her intimacy with Acton (q.v.). An active French partisan, on the fall of the Parthenopean republic she was hanged at the queen's instigation.

(2) **Manoel Deodoro da** (1827–92), Brazilian statesman, born at Alagoas, during 1889–91 was first president of Brazil.

FONTANA, (1) **Carlo** (1634 or 38–1714), Swiss architect, a pupil of Bernini, worked as papal architect in Rome and also designed Loyola College in Spain and the Palazzo Durazzo at Genoa. See U. Donati *Artisti ticinesi a Roma* (1942).—His son **Francesco** (1668–1708) worked with him.

(2) **Domenico** (1543–1607), Swiss architect, born at Melide near Lugano, was papal architect in Rome, employed on the Lateran Palace and the Vatican Library. He was afterwards royal architect in Naples, where he died. See study by J. A. F. Orbaan (1911).

(3) **Franciscus,** Italian astronomer, one of the earliest users of a telescope, and of a convex rather than a concave eye-lens in a microscope. He first saw markings on Mars (1636) and irregularities on the crescent of Venus (1643).

FONTANE, Theodor, *fon-tah'nė* (1819–98), German poet and novelist, born at Neuruppin, worked in the family chemist's business until in 1849 he took to literature at Berlin. Periods of residence in Britain between 1855 and 1859 as a newspaper correspondent led to ballads such as *Archibald Douglas* and *Die Brück am Tay* and other British-flavoured pieces. His realistic novels probably influenced Thomas Mann (q.v.); the first of them, *L'Adultera* (1882), was written when he was over sixty. See studies by K. Hayens (1920) and M. E. Gilbert (1930).

FONTANES, Louis, Marquis de, *fõ-tahn* (1757–1821), born at Niort, went in 1777 to Paris, where he acquired a reputation by his poems, among which are *Le Cri de mon coeur* (1778), *Le Verger* (1788), a metrical translation of Pope's *Essay on Man* (1783), and an imitation of Gray's *Elegy*. A member of the Institute from 1795, he was made in 1804 president of the legislative body. In 1810 he entered the senate, and was raised to the peerage by Louis XVIII.

FONTENELLE, Bernard le Bovyer de (1657–1757), French author, born at Rouen, a nephew of Corneille, began his literary career in Paris. In the great quarrel of Moderns *versus* Ancients, he sided with the Moderns, assailing the Greeks and their French imitators, and receiving in return the satiric shafts of Boileau, Racine, J. B. Rousseau and La Bruyère. After the failure on the stage of his *Aspar*, he produced an imitation of Lucian, *Dialogues des morts*, and the ' precious ' *Lettres du Chevalier d'Her....* In 1697 he was made secretary to the Académie des Sciences, of which he afterwards was president. He died at Paris in his hundredth year. He had attempted well-nigh every form of literature—idylls, satires, dialogues, critical essays, histories, tragedies, &c. His best works, *Entretiens sur la pluralité des mondes*, and *Histoire des oracles*, are still worth reading. Andrew Lang discovered the germ of his explanation of myths in Fontenelle's dissertation on Fables.

FONTEYN, Margot, stage name of **Dame Margot Fonteyn de Arias,** *née* **Margaret Hookham** (1919–), English ballerina, born in Reigate. She studied under Astafieva and others and joined the Sadler's Wells Ballet (now the Royal Ballet) in 1934, where she made her first solo appearance in *The Haunted Ballroom*. She has danced most of the classical rôles from *Giselle* onwards. She married Roberto Emilio Arias (b. 1918), then Panamanian Ambassador to the Court of St James, in 1955, and was created D.B.E. in 1956. See *Life* by E. Frank (1958).

FOOTE, (1) **Andrew Hull** (1806–63), American seaman, was born in New Haven, Conn., entered the navy in 1822, and was promoted captain in 1849. In 1856 he stormed four Chinese forts at Canton, which had fired on him. In the Civil War he organized the western flotilla, and in February 1862 stormed Fort Henry. Shortly afterwards he was wounded and resigned as rear-admiral.

(2) **Arthur William** (1853–1937), American composer, born at Salem, Mass., was a noted organist and wrote church and chamber music as well as books on harmony and keyboard technique.

(3) **Samuel** (1720–77), English wit, playwright and actor, born in Truro. His brilliant mimicry of prominent people led to legal proceedings being taken against him on several occasions. His plays, which include *Taste* (1752) and *The Minor* (1760), were mainly political satire, and have not stood the test of time. See *Lives* by P. Fitzgerald (1910) and N. M. Belden (1929).

FOPPA, Vincenzo (*c.* 1427–*c.* 1515), Italian painter, leader of a Lombard school of painting which lasted till the time of Leonardo da Vinci. See study by Foulkes and Maiocchi (1909).

FORBES, (1) **Alexander Penrose** (1817–75), was born in Edinburgh, and in 1848 consecrated Bishop of Brechin. In Scotland he laboured to further Tractarian principles. His charge (1857) on the manner of the Eucharistic Presence led to his trial before the other Scottish bishops in 1860, and a censure and admonition. He edited, with his brother, **George Hay** (1821–75), the *Arbuthnot Missal* (1864), and published *Kalendars of Scottish Saints* (1872), &c. See Memoirs by Skene (1876) and Perry (1939).

(2) **Archibald** (1838–1900), British journalist, war correspondent for the *Daily News* in the Franco-Prussian war, the Carlist revolt, the Russo-Turkish campaign and the Zulu war, wrote several books.

(3) **Duncan,** of Culloden (1685–1747), Scottish jurist, was born at Bunchrew near Inverness, November 10, and studied at Edinburgh and Leyden. Called to the bar, and appointed sheriff of Midlothian, he rose rapidly into practice and political influence through the Duke of Argyll. In 1715 he was in the north actively opposing the rebels; afterwards he protested against trying the prisoners in England, and resisted the forfeitures. In 1725 he became lord advocate, in 1737 president of the Court of Session; in 1734 he succeeded his brother in the family estates; and for long he largely ruled the destinies of Scotland and contributed to her dawning prosperity by developing her internal resources, by winning over the Jacobites, and by forming Highland regiments under loyal colonels. The '45 rather took him by surprise. He hastened to the north, and did much to check the rebels, beating off the Frasers' attack on Culloden House. But he had to take refuge in Skye, and after his return was regarded with disfavour by the government, because he advocated treating the rebels with mercy. He died December 10, 1747. See Lives by Hill Burton (1847), Menary (1936).

(4) **Edward** (1815–54), British naturalist, was born at Douglas, Isle of Man, studied medicine at Edinburgh, but from 1836 devoted himself to the natural sciences, and for a year worked at Paris. In 1841 he was naturalist on the *Beacon* during the survey of a part of Asia Minor. In 1843 he became professor of Botany in King's College, London; in 1844 palaeontologist to the Museum of Geology; in 1851 professor of Natural History to the School of Mines; in 1852 president of the Geological Society; and in 1853 professor of Natural History at Edinburgh. Forbes did much to advance and systematize special departments of natural history, especially the British starfishes; his observations on the distribution of animal and vegetable life have opened many new fields of research. See the Memoir by G. Wilson and A. Geikie (1861).

(5) **George** (1849–1936), English physicist, inventor of the carbon brush for dynamos. He made improvements in the method of measuring the velocity of light (with Young), and in the field of range-finding. In 1880 he forecast the existence of Pluto.

(6) **James David** (1809–68), Scottish scientist, grandson of (10), born in Edinburgh,

known for his work on glaciers, author of *Travelling through the Alps* (1843) and *Theory of Glaciers* (1859).

(7) **(Joan) Rosita** (1893–1967), English writer and traveller, born in Swinderby, Lincolnshire. Having visited almost every country in the world and particularly Arabia and North Africa, she used her experiences as the raw material for exciting travel books, as *The Secret of the Sahara-Kufara* (1922), *From Red Sea to Blue Nile* (1928), *The Prodigious Caribbean* (1940), *Appointment in the Sun* (1949), *Islands in the Sun* (1950), &c.

(8) **Sir John** (1787–1861), Scottish physician born at Cuttlebrae, Banffshire, was joint editor of the *Cyclopaedia of Practical Medicine* (1832–35), translated the works of Auenbrugger and Laennec and thus advocated the use of the stethoscope in this country.

(9) **Robert** (1708–75), from 1769 Bishop of Ross and Caithness, compiled the Jacobite *Lyon in Mourning* (Scot. Hist. Soc. 1895–96).

(10) **Sir William, Bart.** (1739–1806). Scottish banker, grandfather of (6), born in Edinburgh, worked and in 1761 became a partner in the Edinburgh bank of Coutts & Co., and became head of a new company in 1763. See his *Memoirs of a Banking House* (1803; ed. by Robert Chambers, 1860). His bank became in 1830 the Union Bank. His second son, **John Hay** (1776–1854), was the judge, Lord Medwyn.

FORBES MACKENZIE. See MACKENZIE (9).

FORBES-ROBERTSON, Sir Johnston (1853–1937), English actor, born in London, made his debut in 1874 and soon established himself as a West End favourite by the charm of his classical features, the beauty of his diction and his grace in costume parts. In 1895, he became actor-manager of the London Lyceum and crowned his productions there with *Hamlet* in 1897. His later years were marked by success in *The Passing of the Third Floor Back* (1913). He married Gertrude Elliott, an American actress who often partnered him, in 1900. A daughter, **Jean** (1905–62), carried on the tradition and became actress-manager in *The Lady of the Camellias* in 1934.

FORCELLINI, Egidio. See FACCIOLATI.

FORCHHAMMER, Peter Wilhelm, *forKH'-ham-mèr* (1801–94), German classical antiquary, was professor of Philology at Kiel and director of the archaeological museum founded by himself and Otto John (q.v.). His brother, **Johann Georg** (1794–1865), geologist, born at Husum, wrote on the geology of Denmark.

FORD, (1) **Edward Onslow** (1852–1901), English sculptor, born in London, best known for his portrait busts, designed the Shelley Memorial at Oxford. See his *Folly* in the Tate, London.

(2) **FORD MADOX.** See HUEFFER (1).

(3) **Henry** (1863–1947), American automobile engineer and manufacturer, born at Greenfield, Mich., produced his first petrol-driven motor car in 1893. In 1899 he founded his own company in Detroit, designing his own cars, and in 1903 the Ford Motor Company. He pioneered the modern 'assembly line' mass-production techniques for his famous T-model (1908–09), 15 million

of which were produced up to 1928. He also branched out into aircraft and tractor manufacture. A fervent pacifist who thought that ' history was bunk ', he tried to negotiate a European peace in 1915. His policy of paying his employees more than a normal rate led to violent disagreements with the code laid down in the Roosevelt recovery programme in 1931. In 1919 he was succeeded by his son **Edsel** (1893–1943), and in 1945 by his grandson **Henry** (1917–), after Henry senior had tried hard to resume absolute control in the face of President Roosevelt's opposition. The latter knew that the old man had no interest in war production. See Life by R. Burlingame (1958) and studies by A. Nevins and F. E. Hill (1958) and C. E. Sorensen (1958).

(4) **John** (*c.* 1586–*c.* 1640), English dramatist, was baptized at Ilsington, Devon, studied for a year at Oxford and entered the Middle Temple in 1602. He was expelled for debt but readmitted. He was greatly influenced by Richard Burton (q.v.) whose *Anatomy of Melancholy* (1621) turned Ford's dramatic gifts into stage presentation of the melancholy, the unnatural and the horrible in *The Lover's Melancholy* (1629), *'Tis Pity She's a Whore* (1633), *The Lady's Trial* (1639), &c. He also wrote a masterful chronicle play, *Perkin Warbeck* (1638). Ford often collaborated with Dekker, Rowley and Webster (qq.v.). See works by Swinburne (1888), Sargeant (1935), Sensabaugh (1944).

(5) **Richard** (1796–1858), English travel author from Winchester, went to Trinity College, Oxford, was called to the bar, but never practised. He spent the years 1830–34 in riding tours in Spain. See his delightful *Handbook for Travellers in Spain* (1845) and *Gatherings from Spain* (1846). He introduced the British public to works of Velasquez (q.v.).

FORDHAM, George (1837–87), English jockey, was born at Cambridge, and died at Slough. He won the Derby on Sir Bevys (1879), the Oaks and Ascot Cup five times.

FORDUN, John of, *for'd'n* (d. *c.* 1384), Scottish chronicler, may have been born at Fordoun, in Kincardineshire. He lived to write only five books of the *Scotichronicon*, bringing it down to 1153, but he left collections extending to 1384, when he is supposed to have died. Walter Bower (q.v.) in 1441 resumed and enlarged the unfinished work; but many of his alterations corrupted Fordun's narrative. The work is the chief authority for the history of Scotland prior to the 15th century. The best MSS. are in the Wolfenbüttel library. Four editions have been published, Skene's in 1871–72.

FOREL, August Henri (1848–1931), Swiss psychologist, professor of Psychiatry at Zürich (1879–98), made notable contributions in the fields of the anatomy of the brain and nerves, the psychology of ants, and on hypnotism and sex hygiene.

FOREST, (1) John (*c.* 1474–1538), English friar barbarously burnt at Smithfield by Henry VIII for upholding the papal supremacy.

(2) **Lee de.** See DE FOREST.

FORESTER, Cecil Scott (1899–1966), British writer, born at Cairo. Chiefly a novelist, he

also wrote biographical and travel books and collaborated with C. E. Bechofer Roberts on a play about Nurse Edith Cavell. He is known especially for his creation of Captain Horatio Hornblower, R.N. He won the James Tait Black Memorial Prize for Literature in 1938 with *Ship of the Line*, and several of his works have been filmed. See his autobiography, *Long before Forty* (1967).

FORMAN, Simon (1552–1611), English astrologer and quack doctor, born at Quidhampton, Wiltshire, studied at Magdalen College, Oxford, and set up a lucrative practice in 1583 in London, particularly in love potions for ladies of the Court and was constantly prosecuted by the church and the College of Physicians.

FORREST, (1) Edwin (1806–72), American actor, was born in Philadelphia, and made his début there in 1820. At twenty he appeared as Othello in New York with great success. He had successful seasons in London (1836–37), but in 1845 his Macbeth was hissed by the audience; and a resentment that prompted him to hiss Macready in Edinburgh destroyed his reputation in England and Scotland. The hissing of Macready's Macbeth by Forrest's sympathizers at New York in 1849 led to a riot which cost twenty-two lives. He retired temporarily in 1853, but returned to the stage in 1860 and made his last appearance as Richelieu at Boston in 1871; and died at Philadelphia. See Lives by Alger (1877), Barrett (1881), Harrison (1889).

(2) **John Forrest, 1st Baron** (1847–1918) Australian explorer and politician, was born at Bunbury in Western Australia, and from 1864 was a colonial surveyor. In 1869 he penetrated inland from Perth to 123° E. long., and next year reached South Australia from the west along the south coast. With his brother **Alexander** (1849–1901) he made an eastward journey in 1874, and published *Explorations in Australia* (1875). Surveyor-general for the colony from 1883, he was first premier of Western Australia (1890–1901), was postmaster-general for Australia (1900–1901), minister for defence (1901–03), for home affairs (1903–04), treasurer (1905–07, 1909–10, 1913–14, 1917–18).

FORRESTAL, James (1892–1949), U.S. politician, was born at Beacon, New York. After a business career he entered U.S. Government service in 1940. From 1944 to 1947 he was secretary of the navy and, till his suicide in 1949, secretary of defence. See *The Forrestal Diaries* (ed. Mills, 1952).

FORRESTER, the name of two brothers, **Alfred Henry** (1804–72) and **Charles Robert** (1803–50), both writers and illustrators of verse, burlesques, children's stories, &c., under the joint pseudonym of ' Alfred Crowquill '. They were born and died in London.

FORSSMAN, Werner (1904–), German surgeon, born in Berlin, graduated at Berlin University, was an army doctor until 1945, then practised at various places including Bad Kreuznach and Düsseldorf. He became known for his development of new techniques in heart surgery, including cardiac catheterization, in which he carried out dangerous experiments on himself. He was awarded jointly with Cournand and Richards (1) the Nobel prize for Medicine in 1956.

FORSTER, (1) **Edward Morgan** (1879–1970), English novelist, born in London, was educated at Tonbridge School and King's Coll., Cambridge. Misery at Tonbridge was recompensed by the perfect freedom he found at Cambridge in its Bloomsbury days of G. E. Moore, G. M. Trevelyan and Lowes Dickinson, whose biography he wrote in 1934, and with whom he founded the *Independent Review*. In his novels he examined with subtle insight the pre-1914 English middle-class ethos and its custodians the Civil Service, the Church and the Public Schools. An indictment of the latter is embodied in *The Longest Journey* (1907), and a period in Italy provided the background for *Where Angels Fear to Tread* (1905) and *A Room with a View* (1908); *Howards End* (1910) was written after he had been tutor to the children of Elisabeth of the German Garden at Nassenheide (1905). But it is in his masterpiece, *A Passage to India* (1924), that Forster puts English values and Indian susceptibilities to his finest scrutiny. Kipling's camaraderie of empire is displaced by Forster's quiet heart-searching in personal relationships. The spiritual tensions of two clashing civilizations are resolved in the strange symbolism of the Malabar Cave. No other western writer has tackled this subject on Forster's level with such gentle irony, sympathy, directness and lack of sentimentality. He was awarded the Tait Black Memorial and Femina Vie Heureuse prizes for the latter in 1925. His Indian experiences as secretary to the Maharajah of Dewas Senior (1921) he described in *The Hill of Devi* (1953). Collections of short stories include *The Celestial Omnibus* (1914) and *The Eternal Moment* (1928); of essays, *Abinger Harvest* (1936) and *Two Cheers for Democracy* (1951). His Cambridge Clark lectures, *Aspects of the Novel* (1927), expressed his literary aesthetics as firmly opposed to Aristotle. *Marianne Thornton* (1958) is a domestic biography. In 1951 he collaborated with E. Crozier in the libretto of Britten's opera, *Billy Budd*. His novel *Maurice* (written 1913–14), on the theme of homosexuality, was published in 1971 after his death. He was made C.H. in 1953. See *Life* by Ackerley (1971), Lord David Cecil, *Poets and Storytellers* (1949), and studies by Rose Macaulay (1938), L. Trilling (1944), J. McConkey (1958), J. Beer (1962) and K. Gransden (1962).

(2) **John** (1812–76), English biographer, historian and journalist, was born at Newcastle. He was educated for the bar, but in 1833 began to write political articles in the *Examiner*; he edited successively the *Foreign Quarterly Review*, the *Daily News* and (1847–56) the *Examiner*. He was the author of many admirable biographical and historical essays and an admirable series dealing with the Commonwealth—*Lives of the Statesmen of the Commonwealth* (1836–39); *Debates on the Grand Remonstrance* (1860); *Arrest of the Five Members* (1860); and *Sir John Eliot, a Biography* (1864). He is, however, best remembered for his *Life and Times of Goldsmith* (1848), *Landor* (1868), *Life of Dickens*

(1871–74), and vol. i of a *Life of Swift* (1875). See *Life* by Renton (1912).

(3) **Thomas** (*c.* 1675–1738), the Jacobite M.P. for Northumberland who in 1715 headed the Border rebels, surrendered at Preston, escaped from Newgate, and died at Boulogne.

(4) **William Edward** (1819–86), English Liberal statesman, was born of Quaker parentage at Bradpole, Dorsetshire. He abandoned the bar for the wool industry. During the Irish famine of 1845 he visited the distressed districts as almoner of a Quaker relief fund; in 1850 he married Jane, daughter of Dr Arnold of Rugby. In 1861 he became Liberal M.P. for Bradford. He rose to cabinet rank and in 1870 carried the Elementary Education Act. Under the Gladstone administration of 1880 Forster was chief-secretary for Ireland. He was attacked unceasingly in Parliament by the Irish members, and his life was threatened by the 'Invincibles' for his measures of coercion. He was a severe critic of Parnell and, determined to re-establish law and order, had him and other Irish leaders arrested. When in April 1882 a majority of the cabinet determined to release the 'suspects', Forster and Lord Cowper (the lord-lieutenant) resigned. A strong opponent of Home Rule, he died in London. See *Life* by Wemyss Reid (1888).

FÖRSTER, *fœr'stèr*, (1) **Ernst** (1800–85), German artist and critic, born at München-gosserstädt, executed frescoes at Bonn University and at Munich, discovered frescoes by Jacopo de Avanzo at Padua, and wrote on German and Italian art.

(2) **Friedrich Christoph** (1791–1868), German poet and historian, brother of (1), born near Kamburg in Saxe-Meiningen, fought in the war of liberation, in 1829 was appointed keeper of the Royal Art Museum at Berlin. Besides fiery war-songs, he wrote on the war of liberation, the history of Prussia, the courts of Europe in the 18th century, and Wallenstein.

(3) **Johann Georg Adam** (1754–94), German author, son of (4), accompanied his father on Cook's second voyage and published an account of it (1784) and a book about the Rhine. See his *Letters* (1829).

(4) **Johann Reinhold** (1729–98), German traveller and botanist, father of (3), born at Dirschau, in 1772 accompanied Cook (q.v.) on his second voyage, published his observations made on this voyage (1771) and other botanical works. He became professor of Natural History at Halle in 1780.

FORSYTH, (1) **Alexander John** (1768–1843), Scottish inventor and clergyman, minister from 1791 of Belhelvie, Aberdeenshire, in 1807 patented his application of the detonating principle in firearms, which was followed by the adoption of the percussion-cap. He was pensioned by the British Government after refusing to sell the secret to Napoleon.

(2) **Sir Thomas Douglas** (1827–86), British administrator in India, was born at Birkenhead, entered the East India Company in 1848 and was created C.B. for his services after the Mutiny. In 1870 he conducted a mission to Yarkand, and in 1874 concluded a commercial treaty with Kashgar. He

succeeded in averting war with Burma in 1875. See Autobiography (1888).

FORT, Paul, *for* (1872–1960), French poet, born at Reims, settled in Paris, where he founded in 1890 the 'Théâtre des Arts' for presenting a wide range of European drama and recitals of symbolist poetry. He is best known for his popular *Ballades françaises* (1st volume 1897), in which he brought poetry closer to the rhythms of everyday speech. He also wrote several plays, edited literary magazines and wrote *Histoire de la poésie française depuis* 1850 (1927). See also works by G. Masson (1923) and R. Clauzel (1925).

FORTEBRACCI. See BRACCIO.

FORTESCUE, *for'tes-kyoo,* (1) **Sir John** (c. 1394–1476), English jurist, was born in Somerset and educated at Exeter College, Oxford. Called to the bar, he was in 1441 made serjeant-at-law, and in 1442 lord chief-justice of the King's Bench. In the struggle between York and Lancaster he was loyal to the latter and fled with Margaret of Anjou and her son to Scotland, and there was probably appointed lord chancellor by Henry VI. In 1463 he embarked with them for Holland. During exile he wrote his *De Laudibus Legum Angliae* (printed in 1537) for the instruction of Prince Edward and of immense value to later jurists. After the final defeat of the House of Lancaster at Tewkesbury (1471) Fortescue submitted to Edward IV. See his *The Governance of England* (1714).

(2) **Sir John William** (1859–1933), English military historian, was born in Madeira and brought up near Barnstaple. He became private secretary to the governor of the Windward Islands and from 1886 to 1890 was private secretary to the governor of New Zealand. He was librarian of Windsor Castle, 1905–26. Besides his monumental 13-volume *History of the British Army* (1899–1930), his writings include *Statesmen of the Great War 1793–1814* (1911), *County Lieutenancies and the Army, 1803–1814* (1925), *Wellington* (1925), and in a different vein, *The Story of a Red Deer* (1897).

FORTIGUERRA, Niccolo, *for-tee-gwer'ra* (1674–1735), Italian poet, was bishop and papal chamberlain to Clement XI, and is remembered by his satirical epic, *Il Ricciardetto* (1738).

FORTUNE, Robert (1813–80), Scottish botanist, born at Edrom, Berwickshire, was at first employed as a gardener in the Botanic Garden of Edinburgh, and at Chiswick. From 1843 he travelled extensively in the East for the London Botanical Society, introducing many oriental plants into Britain, and planted tea successfully in India's North West Provinces, publishing accounts of his travels in 1847 and 1863.

FORTUNY Y CARBO, Mariano, *for-too'nee* (1839–74), Spanish painter, was born at Reus in Tarragona. When Spain declared war against Morocco, Fortuny followed the army, and filled his portfolios with studies of Eastern life. The best of his rococo pictures are *The Spanish Marriage, Book-lover in the Library of Richelieu,* and *Academicians choosing a Model.* See monographs by

Davillier (illus. Paris 1875), Yriarte (Paris 1885) and E. Calvi (1911).

FOSCARI, Francesco, *fos'kah-ree* (c. 1370–1457), was elected Doge of Venice in 1423, and by his great military skill carried a conflict with Milan to a successful conclusion in the Treaty of Ferrara (1433). His last years were embittered by the unjust torturing and banishment of his son Giacopo. See Alethea Wiel's *Two Doges of Venice* (1891). See Byron's tragedy *The Two Foscari.*

FOSCOLO, Ugo (1778–1827), Italian author, was born in Zante, and educated at Spalato and Venice. His bitter disappointment when Venice was ceded to Austria found vent in the *Lettere di Jacopo Ortis* (1802). Believing that France was destined to liberate Italy, he served in the French armies, but, undeceived as to Napoleon's intentions, returned to Milan, and published in 1807 his best poem, *I Sepolcri.* He translated Sterne's *Sentimental Journey,* and wrote two tragedies, *Ajace* and *Ricciarda.* In 1809 he was for a few months professor of Eloquence in Pavia. After 1814, when the Austrians entered Milan, Foscolo finally sought refuge in London. There were published his *Saggi sul Petrarca, Discorso sul testo del Decamerone, Discorso sul testo di Dante,* and various papers in the *Quarterly* and *Edinburgh Reviews.* His last years were embittered by poverty and neglect. He died at Turnham Green, and in 1871 his remains were taken from Chiswick and re-interred in Florence. See Lives by Pecchio (1836), Martinetti (1892), G. Natali (1928), F. Viglione (1910) and Vincent (1953).

FOSDICK, Harry Emerson (1878–1969), American Baptist minister, ordained in 1903, professor at Union Theological Seminary, New York, from 1915, and pastor of Riverside Baptist Church in New York from 1926 to 1946. An outstanding preacher, he was a leading 'modernist' in the controversy on Fundamentalism in the 'twenties.

FOSS, Lukas (1922–), American composer, born in Berlin, settled in America in 1937. He studied under Hindemith and first attracted attention with his cantata, *The Prairie* (1941). His largest work to date is *A Parable of Death,* for soloist, narrator, choir and orchestra, but he has also written a symphony, concertos, chamber music and an opera on Mark Twain's story *The Jumping Frog of Calaveras County.*

FOSTER, (1) **Birket.** See (4).

(2) **John** (1770–1843), English essayist, born in Halifax, Yorkshire, was trained for the ministry, but, after preaching for twenty-five years with indifferent success, devoted himself to literature. His *Essays, in a Series of Letters* (1805), were only four in number—the best-known that ' On Decision of Character '. In 1819 appeared his *Essay on the Evils of Popular Ignorance,* urging the necessity of national education. He died at Stapleton, Bristol, his home for twenty-two years. See his *Life and Correspondence* by J. E. Ryland (1846).

(3) **Sir Michael** (1836–1907), English physiologist, born at Huntingdon and educated there and at University College, London, where from 1867 he taught physiology till in 1870 he was called to Cambridge

He was knighted in 1899 and was M.P. for London University (1900–06). His *Textbook of Physiology* (1877) became a standard work.

(4) **(Myles) Birket** (1825–99), English artist, was born at North Shields, of Quaker parentage, but from 1830 lived in London. He could draw before he could speak, and from 1841 to 1846 produced a large number of subjects for wood-engravings, many of them for the *Illustrated London News*. With John Gilbert he illustrated Longfellow's *Evangeline* and many of the poets, with dainty poetic landscapes and rustic scenes, nowhere better exemplified than in his *Pictures of English Landscape* (1862). In 1859 Foster exhibited the first of many watercolours, and in 1860 was elected an associate, in 1861 a member, of the Watercolour Society. He died at Weybridge.

(5) **Stephen Collins** (1826–64), American song writer, was born in Pittsburgh and died in New York. Of his 125 compositions nearly a fourth are Negro melodies. The best-known are ' The Old Folks at Home ', ' Nelly Bly ', ' Uncle Ned ', ' Beautiful Dreamer ', ' Jeannie with the Light Brown Hair ', ' Old Kentucky Home ', ' Willie, we have missed you ', and ' Come where my Love lies dreaming ', the airs and words alike his own composition. Despite his immense success, he died in poverty and obscurity. See study by Wheeler (1945).

FOUCAULT, Jean Bernard Léon, *foo-kō* (1819–68), French physicist, was born and died in Paris. He determined the velocity of light by the revolving mirror method and proved that light travels more slowly in water than in air (1850). In 1851 he proved that the earth rotates by means of a freely suspended pendulum. In 1852 he constructed the gyroscope, in 1857 the Foucault prism and in 1858 he improved the mirrors of reflecting telescopes. He was elected a foreign member of the Royal Society in 1864. See *Life* by Lissajous (1875).

FOUCHÉ, Joseph, Duke of Otranto, *foo-shay* (1763–1820), French statesman, was born at Nantes. A revolutionary, he was elected to the National Convention in 1792, and voted for the execution of Louis XVI. Commissioned to castigate Lyons (1794), he rivalled his associates in bloodthirstiness. In 1794 he was expelled from the Convention as a Terrorist. Yet in September 1799 he was appointed minister of Police; and this post he held with interruptions till 1815, having made terms with the Bourbons when he foresaw Napoleon's downfall. But he had scarcely been appointed ambassador to Dresden when decree of banishment was pronounced against the regicides (1816), and he henceforward lived in exile. He died at Trieste. Unscrupulous, politic and sagacious, he made an admirable head of police, and helped to save France from anarchy. The *Mémoires de J. Fouché* (Eng. trans. 1892) were declared not genuine by his sons. See Lives by L. Madelin (1901) and S. Zweig (1930).

FOUCQUET. See FOUQUET.

FOULD, Achille, *foo* (1800–67), French financier and politician, was born in Paris of Jewish parents, and trained in his father's bank. Elected in 1842 to the Chamber of Deputies, after the revolution of 1848 he rendered service to the provisional government, and during the presidency of Louis Napoleon was four times minister of Finance. He stabilized the country's finances. He resigned (1852) on the confiscation of the property of the Orleans family and was again appointed minister of finance (1861–67).

FOULIS, Robert, *fowlz* (1707–76), Glasgow bookseller and printer, set up shop in 1741 and in 1743 became printer to the university and produced the well-known editions of the classics, including the ' immaculate ' *Horace* (with only six misprints). In 1744 he took his brother **Andrew** (1712–75) into partnership. In 1753 Robert established an academy at Glasgow which produced many prints, oil-paintings, &c. But the printing business declined with Andrew's death and Robert was compelled to sell off the pictures in London.

FOUQUÉ, Friedrich Heinrich Karl, *foo-kay*, **Baron de la Motte** (1777–1843), German romanticist, was of Huguenot ancestry. He served as a Prussian cavalry officer in 1794 and 1813. The interval between these campaigns was devoted to literary pursuits, and the rest of his life was spent in Paris and on his estate at Nennhausen, and after 1830 at Halle. He died at Berlin. He published a long series of romances, based on Norse Legend and old French poetry, his masterpiece being *Undine* (1811). In his later work he relied more on exploiting the supernatural and the theatrical rather than sheer literary ability.

FOUQUET, *foo-kay*, (1) **Jehan** (*c.* 1420– *c.* 1480), French painter, was born at Tours. Nothing is known of his early life, but he visited Rome between 1445 and 1448 when pope Eugenius IV commissioned a portrait from him. Returning to Tours, he opened a prosperous workshop. In 1475 he received the official title of king's painter. In a copy of the *Antiquities of the Jews* of Josephus, there are paintings which have been attributed to him; similarly the *Hours of Étienne Chevalier* at Chantilly, and several panel portraits including that of Charles VII and Agnes Sorel as the virgin. In his miniatures Fouquet combines Italian influences, such as architectural perspectives and ornamental detail with the more northern traits of realistic and unidealized portrayal. See Monographs by T. Cox (1931) and P. Wescher (1945).

(2) **Nicolas, Vicomte de Melun et de Vaux and Marquis de Belle-Isle** (1615–80), French statesman, was born in Paris. Mazarin made him *procureur-général* to the parliament of Paris (1650) and superintendent of finance (1653). He now became ambitious to succeed Mazarin, and to secure himself friends distributed money lavishly. But Louis XIV himself took up the reins of power on Mazarin's death, and, instigated by Colbert, arrested Fouquet in September 1661. After a three years' trial he was sentenced to life imprisonment in the fortress of Pignerol, where he died. He has been falsely identified with the Man with the Iron Mask, who lived until 1703. See *Lives*

by Chéruel (1865), Bonnaffe (1882) and Lair (1890).

FOUQUIER-TINVILLE, Antoine Quentin, *fook-yay tī-veel* (1747–95), French Revolutionary politician, born at Hérouelles, public prosecutor to the Revolutionary Tribunal from 1793. He superintended all the political executions during the Reign of Terror until July 1794, sending his friends, among them Robespierre, Danton and Hébert, to execution as cheerfully as he sent their enemies; at last he himself was guillotined. See Lives by Dunoyer (trans. 1914), J. de Castelnau (1937), Croquez and Loullié (1945).

FOURIER, *foor-yay*, (1) **François Marie Charles** (1772–1837), French social theorist, was born at Besançon and was educated at the local academy. He excelled in study but regretfully abandoned his studies for a business career in various French towns. As a commercial traveller he visited Holland and Germany and noted down everything of interest in climate, production and manners. He became obsessed with the abuses of commerce and set about formulating the basis for a society in which these evils, summed up in the obnoxious word, civilization, would all be abolished. During the Terror (1793) he lost nearly all he had, was imprisoned, nearly guillotined, did two years' military service and continued his commercial career. His theory is expounded in three works: *Théorie des quatre mouvements et des destinées générales* (1808), *Traité d'association domestique agricole* (1822), *Le Nouveau Monde industriel et sociétaire* (1829). There is only one way, he thought, by which mankind can pass from social chaos to universal harmony and that is by allowing free and healthy development to human talent and emotions. Certain arrangements are required to achieve this. Society was to be redistributed into social units, *phalanges*, comprising 1500 people each, housed in one common dwelling, representing every trade and profession required for self-sufficiency, each receiving a minimum wage with the surplus distributed between labour, talent and capital. Thus the communal interest and individual liking were to be reconciled. Conventional marriage was to be abandoned. There was to be continual change in occupations. An attempt was made to found a society in 1832, but without success, although Fourier had to his death a number of devoted disciples. See works by Considérant (1845), de Gamond (trans. 1842), Pellarin (1843), Poisson (1932), Friedberg (1926).

(2) **Jean Baptiste Joseph, Baron de** (1768–1830), French mathematician, accompanied Napoleon to Egypt in 1798, became governor of Lower Egypt and on his return in 1802 was made prefect of the department of Grenoble, and created baron in 1808. He discovered the theorem which bears his name —that any function of a variable can be expanded in a series of sines of multiples of the variable—in connection with his monumental work on the flow of heat (1826).

FOURNIER, Henri Alain. See ALAIN-FOURNIER.

FOURNIER D'ALBE, Edmund Edward (1868–1933), English physicist and inventor, born in London, produced in 1903 an English-Irish dictionary. He invented the optophone (whereby blind people can read by ear), and among other things was the first to transmit a portrait from London by telephotography (1923).

FOWLER, (1) **Sir Henry Hartley.** See WOLVERHAMPTON.

(2) **Henry Watson** (1858–1933), English lexicographer, born at Tonbridge, Kent, and educated at Rugby and Balliol College, Oxford, was a schoolmaster at Sedberg (1882–99), came to London and engaged in free-lance journalism and a daily run and dip in the Serpentine. His collected essays published in 1903 at his own expense fell flat. He then joined his tomato-growing brother, **Frank George** (1871–1918), in Guernsey, and their literary partnership began. Their joint reputation rests on *The King's English* (1906) and *The Concise Oxford Dictionary* (1911). After Frank's death, Henry crowned their work for the Clarendon Press with the *Dictionary of Modern English Usage* (1926), a household work for all who attempt to write good English, even though it is sometimes as mannered as the mannerisms Henry set out to eradicate. Henry stubbornly refused to speed up his method of work and mode of life, scorning ' slow suicide and quick lexicography '.

(3) **Sir John** (1817–98), English civil engineer, born at Wadsley Hall, Sheffield, engaged from an early age in railway construction, including the original ' underground ' in London. River improvement and dock construction also occupied his attention. He was made a K.C.M.G. in 1885 for his services as consulting engineer in Egypt, and a baronet on the completion of the Forth Bridge (1882–90), designed by him and Sir Benjamin Baker.

(4) **John** (1826–64), English inventor in 1850–60 of the steam-plough, was born at Melksham, and died at Ackworth near Pontefract, having in 1860 established large engineering works at Leeds.

FOX, (1) **Sir Charles** (1810–74), civil engineer, was born at Derby, and was knighted in 1851 for building the Crystal Palace which housed the Great Exhibition. He also did much railway construction with his two sons, **Sir Charles Douglas** (1840–1921) and **Sir Francis** (1844–1927), both eminent engineers.

(2) **Charles James** (1749–1806), English Liberal statesman, third son of the first Lord Holland, was born in London, January 24, and educated at Eton and Hertford College, Oxford, spending his vacations in the gayest circles of the French capital. At nineteen became M.P. for Midhurst. He later became a supporter of Lord North, and was made a lord of Admiralty. In 1772 he resigned, but next year was named a commissioner of the Treasury. North dismissed him in 1775 after a quarrel. During the American war Fox was the most formidable opponent of the coercive measures of government. After the downfall of North (1782), he was one of the secretaries of state. In 1783 the North and Fox coalition was formed, and Fox resumed his former office; but the rejection of his India Bill by the Lords led to the resignation

of his government. Now Pitt came into power, and the long contest between him and Fox began. The regency, the trial of Warren Hastings and the French Revolution gave ample scope to the talents and energies of Fox, who employed his influence to modify, if not to counteract, the policy of his great rival. He was a strenuous opponent of the war with France, and an advocate of non-intervention. After Pitt's death in January 1806, Fox, recalled to office, set on foot negotiations for a peace with France. He was on the point of introducing a bill for the abolition of the slave trade when he died at Chiswick, September 13. He was buried, near Pitt, in Westminster Abbey. Fox was a fast liver, addicted to gambling and drinking; his bearing towards his opponents was generous. Burke called him ' the greatest debater the world ever saw '. See, besides the *Life and Times* and the *Memorials and Correspondence*, by Earl Russell (1853–66), Dr Parr's *Character of the Late C. J. Fox* (1809); works by Sir George Trevelyan (1880–1914); studies by H. O. Wakeman (1890), Hammond (1903), Drinkwater (1928), Hobhouse (1934), Lascelles (1936).

(3) **George** (1624–91), founder of the Society of Friends or Quakers, was born at Fenny Drayton, Leicestershire. Apprenticed to a Nottingham shoemaker, he felt at nineteen a divine call to leave his friends, and Bible in hand he wandered about the country, on a small income. He often interrupted services, especially when conducted by formalist ' professors '. The ' inner light ' was the central idea of his teaching. He inveighed against sacerdotalism and formalism, and was equally vehement against social convention. Priests, lawyers and soldiers were all obnoxious to him. The Lord forbade him to put off his hat to any, high or low. He denounced amusements. His life is a record of insults, persecutions and imprisonments. In 1656, the year after he and his followers refused to take the oath of abjuration, they had so increased that nearly one thousand of them were in jail. He visited Wales and Scotland, and having married Margaret Fell, widow of a judge and one of his followers, went to Barbados, Jamaica, America, Holland, and Germany, latterly accompanied by Penn, Barclay, Keith, and other Quaker leaders. He died in London, November 13, 1690. Guilty of many indiscretions, Fox was an amiable man, with a heart full of love for his fellows, and a mind capable of instituting systems of registration, poor relief, education and self-help which have made the sect he founded a social power. His preaching and writings were often turgid, incoherent and mystical. As a writer he will be always remembered by his *Journal*, of which a modern edition was published in 1911. See Lives by Marsh (1848), Janney (Philadelphia 1853), J. S. Watson (1860), Bickley (1884), Budge (1893), H. Deacon (1896), Hodgkin (1896), Brayshaw (1933), Noble (1953), and Roff, *Margaret Fell* (1949).

(4) **Henry Richard, 3rd Baron.** See HOLLAND (2).

(5) **William Johnson** (1786–1864), English orator and political writer, was born at Wrentham near Southwold. Trained for the Independent ministry, he became a Unitarian, and delivered a series of rationalist addresses at his chapel in Finsbury. He aroused public feeling in favour of the anti-Corn Law League; and his *Letters of a Norwich Weaver Boy* on the necessity of free trade were widely quoted and read. From 1847 till 1863 he sat as an advanced Liberal for Oldham. His best parliamentary speeches were upon education. See Life by R. and E. Garnett (1910).

FOXE, (1) John (1516–87), English martyrologist, born at Boston in Lincolnshire, at sixteen entered Brasenose College, Oxford, and was fellow of Magdalen 1538–45. During the reign of Mary he lived on the Continent, where he met Knox, Grindal and Whittingham. On Elizabeth's accession he received a pension and a prebend of Salisbury (1563), but lived chiefly in London. He was debarred from further preferment by objection to the surplice. Foxe published numerous controversial treatises and sermons, besides an apocalyptic Latin mystery play called *Christus Triumphans* (1556). But his best known work is his *History of the Acts and Monuments of the Church*, popularly known as *Foxe's Book of Martyrs*, the first part of which was published in Latin at Strasburg in 1554 (trans. 1563). Written in vivid English prose, it is no doubt exaggerated, yet it remains a valuable source of information. See Life by Mozley (1940).

(2) **Richard** (c. 1448–1528), the founder of Corpus Christi College, Oxford, was born at Ropesley near Grantham, studied at Oxford, Cambridge and Paris, and latterly became bishop successively of Exeter, Bath and Wells, Durham and Winchester. See Thomas Fowler's *History of Corpus Christi* (1893).

FOY, Maximilien Sébastien, *fwah* (1775–1825), French soldier, was born at Ham, entered the army in 1791, and held commands in the Italian (1801) and the Austrian (1805) campaigns. In 1807 Napoleon sent him to Turkey to assist Sultan Selim against the Russians and British and hold the Dardanelles From 1808 to 1812 he commanded in Portugal and Spain and was present at all the battles of the Pyrenees. In 1815 he was wounded at Waterloo, where he commanded under Ney. In 1819 elected a deputy, he was the constant advocate of constitutional liberty. See his *Histoire de la guerre de la Péninsule* (1827) and biography by Tissot, prefixed to Foy's *Discours* (1826).

FRA ANGELICO. See ANGELICO.

FRA BARTOLOMMEO. See BARTOLOMMEO.

FRACASTORO, Girolamo, *frah-kas-to'ro* (1483–1553), Italian scholar and physician, born at Verona, became professor of Logic there, practised successfully as a physician, but also excelled as geographer, astronomer and mathematician. He wrote on the theory of music and his Latin verse was compared to that of Virgil. He wrote a Latin poem on the ' new ' venereal disease (1530) from which the name *syphilis* is derived. His work in epidemiology foreshadowed Pasteur's. See Winslow *The Conquest of Epidemic Disease* (1944).

FRA DIAVOLO, *frah dyah'-*, properly Michele Pezza (1760–1806), Italian brigand

and renegade monk, born at Itri, for years headed a band of desperadoes in the Calabrian mountains and evaded capture by skilful guerilla warfare. In 1806 he attempted to excite Calabria against France, but was taken prisoner and executed at Naples on November 12. Auber's opera has nothing in common with him but its name.

FRAGONARD, Jean Honoré, *fra-go-nahr* (1732–1806), French painter and engraver, born at Grasse, studied under Boucher (q.v.) and gained the 'prix de Rome' in 1752. A brilliant technician, he painted with a loose touch and luscious colouring, genre pictures of contemporary life, the amours of the French court and landscapes foreshadowing Impressionism. His *Bacchante endormie, La Chemise enlevée* and other works are in the Louvre and he is also represented in the Wallace Collection, London. See illustrated Lives by Portalis (Paris 1888) and de Nolhac (1918) and study by G. Wildenstein (1961).

FRAMPTON, (1) Sir George James (1860–1928), British sculptor, was born in London and studied under Frith. He was elected R.A. in 1902 and knighted in 1908. Among his works are Peter Pan in Kensington Gardens, the Lions at the British Museum, portrait busts of King George V and Queen Mary and the Edith Cavell Memorial, London.

(2) **Mary** (1773–1846), English diarist, a well-connected spinster of Dorchester, whose interesting *Journal* dealing with the society and political gossip of her time was printed in 1885.

(3) **Robert** (1622–1708), English divine, born at Pimperne near Blandford, from 1665 to 1670 was chaplain at Aleppo, Syria. A popular preacher of the day, he became in 1681 Bishop of Gloucester, but was deprived of his see on refusing to take the oath of allegiance to James II, to whose Declaration of Indulgence he had objected.

(4) **Tregonwell** (1641–1727), English racehorse trainer, the 'father of the turf', was born at Moreton near Dorchester, and from 1695 was royal trainer at Newmarket.

FRANÇAIS, François Louis, *frã-say* (1814–1897), French landscape painter of the Barbizon school, was born at Plombières, studied under Corot (q.v.). His best known picture is *The End of the Winter* in the Louvre.

FRANCE, Anatole, pseud. of **Anatole François Thibault** (1844–1924), French writer, born April 16, the son of a Parisian bookseller, began his literary career as a publisher's reader, 'blurb' writer and critic and in 1879 published his first volume of stories, *Jocaste et le chat maigre* and his first novel, *Le Crime de Sylvestre Bonnard* (1881). He had married in 1877 after being appointed keeper at the Senate Library, a position he was to lose in 1891 because of a literary quarrel with Leconte de Lisle. Under the literary patronage of Madame de Caillavet, whose love affair with him brought about his divorce (1893), he poured out a number of graceful, lively novels, critical studies and the like, such as the Parnassian *Le Livre de mon ami* (1885), a picture of unalloyed childhood happiness, which stands in strong contrast to the later satirical, solipsistic and sceptical works such as *Les Opinions de Jérôme*

Coignard (1893). Another remarkable collection of short stories was published under the title *Balthasar* (1889), and his vast classical knowledge found expression in *Thais* (1890). The Dreyfus case (1896) stirred him into politics as an opponent of church and state and champion of internationalism. His *L'Isle des pingouins* (1908), a fable of modern French history, was followed in 1912 by *Les Dieux ont soif*. Elected to the French Academy in 1896, he was awarded the Nobel prize in 1921. See studies by G. Michaut (1922), T. L. May (1924), L. Carias (1931), L.P. Shanks (1932), J. Suffel (1946), J. Levaillant (1966).

FRANCESCA DA RIMINI, *fran-chays'ka da reem'ee-nee* (d. 1285), daughter of Giovanni da Polenta, lord of Ravenna, was married to Giovanni the Lame, son of Malatesta, lord of Rimini. But she already loved Paolo, Giovanni's brother; and Giovanni, surprising the lovers together, slew them both. The story is woven into Dante's *Inferno*.

FRANCESCA, Piero della or **Franceschi, Piero de'.** See PIERO DELLA FRANCESCA.

FRANCESCO DI PAULA. See FRANCIS, Saint (2).

FRANCHEVILLE, or **Franqueville, Pierre,** *frãsh-veel* (1548–1616), French sculptor, painter and architect, born at Cambrai, was long domiciled in Italy, where he studied under Bologna. He executed the two colossal statues of Jupiter and Janus in the courtyard of the Grimaldi palace, Genoa, five statues in the Nicolini Chapel in Florence, the marble statue of David in the Louvre, Paris, and *Saturn carrying off Cybele* in the Tuileries Gardens.

FRANCIA, (1) *fran'chah*, or **Francesco Raibolini** (1450–1517), Italian goldsmith and painter, born at Bologna, achieved fame as a craftsman in metal, in niello, and designed the first *italic* type for Aldus Manutius. As a painter in oils or in fresco he is particularly noted for his madonnas. See in the National Gallery, London, and Life by Williamson (1901).—His sons, **Giacomo** (c. 1486–1557) and **Giulio** (1487–c. 1543), were also painters. See Julia Cartwright's *Mantegna and Francia* (1881).

(2) **José Gaspar Rodriguez,** *fran'sya* (1756–1840), dictator of Paraguay, was born near Asunción, studied theology, took his degree as doctor, and was a professor of Divinity. Next he practised law for thirty years with a high reputation. He was past fifty when the revolution which shattered the Spanish yoke in South America broke out. Francia took a leading part in the movement in Paraguay, and on the declaration of independence in 1811 became secretary of the national junta, in 1813 one of the two consuls, and in 1814 dictator—first for three years, and then for life. Under his firm rule, which excluded all foreign intercourse, Paraguay rapidly improved. He was an unscrupulous despot, and yet he improved agriculture, promoted education, repressed superstition, and enforced strict justice in his law-courts, however little he regarded it for himself. See *Francia's Reign of Terror* (1839) by the brothers Robertson, Carlyle's *Edinburgh* essay (1843), and Life by Bazán (Madrid 1887).

FRANCIABIGIO, or Francesco di Cristofano Bigi, *fran'chah-bee'jo* (1482–1525), Florentine painter, who worked in collaboration with Andrea del Sarto in the church of the Annunziata and the Chiostro dello Scalzo and was much influenced by him and by Raphael. His *Madonna del Pozzo* was long thought to be by Raphael.

FRANCIS, the name of four saints:

(1) **of Assisi** (1181/2–1226) founder of the Franciscan Order, born Giovanni Bernardone, the son of a wealthy merchant at Assisi. From his familiarity in his youth with the language of the troubadours, he acquired the name of *Il Francesco* (' the little Frenchman '). He was remarkable for his love of gaiety, of knightly exercises and ostentatious living. A serious illness was the first stage in his conversion, but in *c.* 1205 he joined a military expedition. Halted by a dream, he returned and devoted himself to the care of the poor and the sick. On April 16, 1206, he was inspired to rebuild the ruined church of San Damiano. He renounced his patrimony, even to his clothes, and lived as a hermit. His zeal became infectious and by 1210 he had a brotherhood of eleven for which he drew up a rule which was orally approved by Pope Innocent III. Like the older forms of monastic life, the Franciscan system is founded on chastity, poverty and obedience; with the emphasis on the second. He repudiated all idea of property even in those things retained for personal use. The order increased rapidly in membership. At the first general assembly in 1219, 5000 members were present; 500 more were claimants for admission. Francis himself went to Egypt (1223) and preached in the presence of the sultan, who promised better treatment for his Christian prisoners and for the Franciscan order the privilege they have since enjoyed as guardians of the Holy Sepulchre. It is after his return to Italy that his biographers place the legend of his receiving upon his own person, while in an ecstasy of prayer, the marks (*stigmata*) of the wounds of the Redeemer (September 17, 1224). He died October 4, and was canonized by Pope Gregory IX in 1228. His festival is kept on October 4. The works of St Francis (folio, 1739) consist of letters, sermons, ascetic treatises, proverbs and hymns—the latter among the earliest metrical works in Italian, exceedingly simple, and full of the love of God. His prose is often more poetical than his poetry. See Lives by Thomas de Celano (1229 and 1250) rather than that by St Bonaventura; also Lives by Sabatier (trans. 1901), Tamassia (trans. 1911), Jörgensen (trans. 1912), Father Cuthbert (3rd edn. 1933), G. K. Chesterton (1923), Matt and Hauser (trans. 1956).

(2) **of Paola**, or S. Francesco di Paula (1416–1507), founder of the Minims, was born at Paola in Calabria, of poor parents. A Franciscan, he retired to a cave at nineteen and was soon joined by others. He founded his order in 1436. Communities were established throughout Europe, but not in the British Isles. Louis XI of France summoned Francesco to his death-bed; and Charles VIII and Louis XII built him con-vents at Plessis-les-Tours and Amboise. He died at Plessis on Good Friday, and was canonized in 1519. His festival is kept on April 2.

(3) **of Sales** (1567–1622), French Roman Catholic bishop and writer, born at the family *château* of Sales in Savoy, educated by the Jesuits in Paris, studied civil law at Padua, took orders and became a distinguished preacher. He was successfully employed in a mission for the conversion of the Calvinistic population of Chablais, and in 1599 was appointed Bishop of Nicopolis. In 1602 at Paris he was invited to preach the Lent at the Louvre; and his lectures had so much influence in converting several Huguenot nobles, that the king offered him a French bishopric, which he declined. Soon afterwards, on the death of his colleague, he became sole Bishop of Geneva. His administration of his diocese was exemplary. His *Introduction to a Devout Life*, immediately a classic, was the first manual of piety addressed to those living in society. He established a congregation of nuns of the order of the Visitation under the direction of Madame de Chantal, with whom he long maintained a correspondence, published in 1660. He died December 28, 1622. In 1665 he was canonized by Alexander VII. His works were edited by Dom. B. Mackey (1891–1912). See French Lives by Hamon (1909), Pérennès (1879), and English by Ornsby (1857), Mrs Lear (1877), Sanders (1928), Camus (trans. 1953), M. de la Bédoyère (1960).

(4) **Xavier**, Sp. *ha-vee-ayr'*, Angl. *zay'vee-êr* (1506–52), the ' Apostle of the Indies ', was born at his mother's castle of Xavero or Xavier near Sanguesa, in the Basque country, April 7, the youngest son of Juan de Jasso, privy-councillor to the king of Navarre. At Paris, where he studied and then lectured, he was associated with Loyola (q.v.) in founding the Jesuit Society (1534). Ordained priest in 1537, he lived at Rome in the service of the society, and by John III of Portugal was sent out as missionary to the Portuguese colonies in the East. He arrived at Goa in 1542, and laboured with equal zeal and success among the corrupt Europeans and the native population. After a year he visited Travancore, where in a month he baptised 10,000 natives. He then visited Malacca, the Banda Islands, Amboyna, the Moluccas and Ceylon, where he converted the king of Kandy with many of his people. The mission he next founded in Japan (1548) flourished for a hundred years. He returned to Goa in 1552 to organize a mission to China. But the intrigues of the Portuguese merchants and difficulties caused by the governor of Malacca wore out his strength, and he died December 22, 1552, soon after reaching the island of San-chian near Canton. His body was ultimately buried in Goa. He was canonized in 1622. His only literary remains are Letters (1631) and a Catechism, with some short ascetic treatises. His Life by Père Bouhours (1684) was translated by James Dryden, brother of the poet. There are also Lives in Latin by Tursellinus (1596), in Italian by Bartoli and Maffei (1653), in French by Cros (1900), in German by De Vos

(1877), in English by Venn (1862), H. J. Coleridge (1873), M. McClean (1896), E. Stewart (1917).

FRANCIS. Two kings of France:

Francis I (1494–1547), son of Charles, Comte d'Angoulême, was born at Cognac, September 12, and succeeded Louis XII, his uncle and father-in-law, January 1, 1515. His first act was to reconquer Milan (1515), winning the victory of Marignano. On the death of Maximilian of Germany in 1519 Francis became a candidate for the imperial crown; but Charles V was elected, and Francis thereupon declared war against him. The French were driven out of Italy; Henry VIII of England and the emperor invaded France on the north; the principal Italian republics declared against Francis, who, after successfully confronting his many adversaries for some time, was defeated and taken prisoner at the battle of Pavia, February 24, 1525. Charles set him at liberty a year later, compelled him among other things to renounce Flanders, Artois, Burgundy and all his Italian possessions, and to surrender his two sons as hostages. Pope Clement VII absolved Francis from his oath; and England, Rome, Venice, Florence and Genoa all siding with him in alarm at the power of Charles, the war in Italy began again. After Rome had been sacked and the pope captured, peace was concluded at Cambrai (1529), by which Francis retained Burgundy, but lost the Milanese, Flanders and Artois. There was more war and another treaty before Charles's unfortunate expedition against Algiers induced Francis to renew the quarrel (1542); but, in spite of the victory of Cérisolles (1544), Francis was at length compelled to make peace at Crespy (September 1544), matters being left *in statu quo*. Francis died at Rambouillet, March 31. Brilliant, frivolous, changeable, licentious, he fostered learning and art, but cruelly persecuted the Protestants. See works on him by Julia Pardoe (1887), Gaston Paris (1888), Coignet (trans. 1889), Hackett (1934) and Terasse (1943).

Francis II (1544–60) in 1558 married Mary, Queen of Scots (q.v.), and in 1559 succeeded his father, Henry II, as King of France.

FRANCIS, name of two Holy Roman Emperors:

Francis I (1708–65), emperor from 1745, was the eldest son of Leopold, Duke of Lorraine and Grand-duke of Tuscany. In 1736 he married Maria Theresa (q.v.) of Austria.

Francis II of the Holy Roman Empire, I of Austria (1768–1835), in 1792 succeeded his father, Leopold II, to the former. His first war with Napoleon ended with the Peace of Campo Formio (1797), when Austria lost the Netherlands and Lombardy and received in return Venice, Dalmatia and Istria; the second ended with the Treaty of Lunéville (1801) after defeats at Marengo and Hohenlinden. Then followed the campaign of 1805 when the French victories of Ulm and Austerlitz and the capture of Vienna compelled Austria to purchase peace at Pressburg by the cession of Venetia, Tyrol and Vorarl-berg. On the foundation of the Confederation of the Rhine (1806), Francis renounced the title of German-Roman emperor, and retained that of emperor of Austria (Francis I), which he had assumed in 1804. In 1809 another attempt ended in the Treaty of Vienna with the loss of Salzburg, Carinthia, Trieste, part of Croatia, Dalmatia and Galicia. After a short alliance with France the emperor, in conjunction with the Russians and Prussians, assailed Napoleon and won the battle of Leipzig (1813). By the Treaty of Vienna (1815) Francis recovered, thanks to Metternich (q.v.), Lombardy, Venetia and Galicia. His policy was conservative and anti-liberal, but personally he was an urbane and popular ruler. He died March 2. See Lives by Meynert (1871–73) and Wolfsgruber (1899).

FRANCIS JOSEPH, properly **Franz Joseph I** (1830–1916), emperor of Austria (1848), king of Hungary (1867), was the son of the Archduke Francis (Emperor Francis I's son), and nephew of Ferdinand I (q.v.), whom he succeeded. His first task was to subdue the Hungarian revolt and pacify Lombardy. This accomplished, the aspirations of the various nationalities of the empire were rigorously suppressed, and a determined effort made to fuse them into one state; the emperor reasserted his claim to rule as an absolute sovereign; the policy of bureaucratic centralization was again reverted to; and a close alliance was entered into with the Church to combat liberal progress. In 1859 Lombardy was wrested from Austria by Sardinia; and by the war with Prussia in 1866 Austria was excluded from Germany, and compelled to cede Venetia to Sardinia, Prussia's ally. The emperor then adopted a more conciliatory policy towards the various national groups within the empire. His annexation of Bosnia-Herzegovina in 1908 agitated Europe; his attack on Serbia in 1914 precipitated the first World War. By the suicide of his son **Rudolf** (1858–89), and the murder at Sarajevo of **Ferdinand** (1863–1914), eldest son of the emperor's brother **Charles Louis** (1833–96), the crown passed to Charles I (q.v.). Elizabeth of Bavaria (1837–98), Francis Joseph's wife, was stabbed at Geneva on September 10 by an anarchist. See works by Gribble (1914), Fournier (1917), O. Redlich (1928), J. Redlich (1929), Tschuppik (trans. 1930).

FRANCIS, (1) **Francis** (1822–86), English writer on angling, and editor of the *Field*, was born at Seaton, Axminster.

(2) **John** (1811–82), English journalist, born at Bermondsey, was publisher of the *Athenaeum* from 1831, and did much for the repeal of fiscal restrictions on the press. See Life (1888) by his son and successor, **John Collins** (1838–1916).

(3) **Sir Philip** (1740–1818), British civil servant, was born in Dublin and educated at St Paul's School, London. After serving in many minor government posts he became in 1773 a member of the Council of Bengal; in 1780 he fought a duel with Warren Hastings (with whom he was always quarrelling), and was seriously wounded. In 1781 he returned home with a fortune gained at whist. He

entered parliament in 1784. He was energetic in the proceedings against Hastings, wrote many pamphlets, and was made a K.C.B. in 1806. He was devoted to the prince-regent, supported Wilberforce against the slave trade and founded the ' Friends of the People '. In 1814 he married a second wife whom he encouraged in her belief that he was the author of the Letters of Junius, printed in the *Public Advertiser* (1769–72). See his *Memoirs* by Parkes and Merivale (1867); books by Chabot and Twistleton (1871) and H. R. Francis (1894); Dilke's *Papers of a Critic* (1875); Rae (*Athenaeum*, 1888–94); *The Francis Letters* (ed. B. Francis and E. Keary, 1900).

FRANCK, (1) **César Auguste** (1822–90), French composer, born at Liège in Belgium of German family, studied at Liège conservatoire at an early age, and later at Paris, where he acquired French nationality. A student of great promise, he was in the running for the Prix de Rome when his father, who wanted him to be a virtuoso pianist, withdrew him from the conservatoire and started him on a round of concerts. He was fond of composition but his ideas were somewhat outlandish in the eyes of his teachers and it was not until his three piano trios (1842–43) had been subscribed by a number of eminent musicians that he received any recognition as a composer, and even then these pieces were hardly heard in France, being better known in Germany, where they were sponsored by Liszt. In 1848 César Franck married, and settled in Paris as a teacher and organist, composing in his leisure hours. In 1872 he was made organ professor at the conservatoire, and devoted more time to composition, finishing in 1879 his tone-poem *Les Béatitudes*, which met with no success until three years after his death. Much of César Franck's considerable output was undistinguished; his reputation rests on a few masterpieces all written after the age of fifty, the best known being his string quartet, composed in the year of his death yet the first of his works to win real public acclaim, his symphony in D minor, his *Variations symphoniques* for piano and orchestra, and his tone poem *Le Chasseur maudit*. Some of his organ music is also often performed. Though fame came late, his death after a street accident was untimely, for he was in robust health and might have gone on to consolidate his newly found reputation. See Lives by D'Indy, his most distinguished pupil (Eng. tr. 1909), and N. Demuth (1949).

(2) **James** (1882–1964), German physicist, born in Hamburg, professor of Physical Chemistry at Chicago, is noted for his work on the quantum theory, for which he was awarded (with Hertz) the Nobel prize for physics in 1925.

(3) **Richard** (c. 1624–1708), a Cromwellian soldier and angler, born at Cambridge, who visited Scotland about 1656, and wrote the euphuistic *Northern Memoirs* (1694), &c.

(4) **Sebastian** (1499–1542), German humanist, born at Donauwörth, became a priest. He was converted to Protestantism, but his insistence upon moral reform rather than dogma caused him to drift away from Luther;

in 1528 he published a treatise against drunkenness, followed in 1531 by his *Chronica*, perhaps the first attempt at a universal German history. Its advocacy of religious toleration led to his banishment from Strasbourg and in 1539 he was expelled from Ulm for his *Paradoxa* (1534). He also published one of the earliest collections of German proverbs (1541). See works by Tausch (1893), Glawe (1912), Reimann (1922).

FRANCKE, August Hermann, *fran'kĕ* (1663–1727), German Pietist and educationist, born at Lübeck, in 1692 became professor of Oriental Languages at Halle, in 1698 of Theology. A pupil of Spener, he became widely known for his philanthropic activities, founding schools, orphanages, &c.

FRANCO (BAHAMONDE), Francisco (1892–   ), Spanish military dictator, was born at El Ferrol, Galicia. He commanded the Spanish Foreign Legion in Morocco, became chief of staff in 1935, and in 1936, as politically dangerous, was sent to govern the Canaries. Thence he presently flew to Morocco, and, landing troops in Spain, in 1936–39 overthrew the socialist government with Nazi and Fascist aid and, with himself as head (*Caudillo*), established an authoritarian régime. During World War II he skilfully kept Spain neutral, although his speeches were markedly pro-German. In 1947 he intimated that after his death Spain would again become a monarchy. Despite economic difficulties and quarrels with his own party, Franco managed to remain firmly in control, and his pact with the United States for military bases in Spain in return for economic aid helped to foster tacit acceptance of his undemocratic régime by other Western powers. See Lives by Arraras (1938), Coles (1954), Crozier (1967) and Hills (1967).

FRANGIPANI, *fran-jee-pah'nee*, a noble Roman family which figured in the Guelph and Ghibelline quarrels of the 12th and 13th centuries causing a schism in the church and the election of an antipope, Gregory VIII.

FRANK, (1) **Albert Bernhard** (1839–1900), German botanist, demonstrated that with certain plants germination cannot take place without fungus companions.

(2) **Anne** (1929–45), Jewish girl concentration camp victim, born in Frankfurt-am-Main, fled from the Nazis to Holland in 1933 with her family and after the Nazi occupation of Holland hid with her family and four others in a sealed off office back-room in Amsterdam from 1942 until they were betrayed in August 1944. She perished in Belsen concentration camp. The lively, moving diary she kept during her concealment was published in 1947 (trans. 1952), was dramatized and filmed, and Anne Frank became a symbol of past suffering under the Nazis. Her name was given to villages and schools for refugee children throughout Western Europe. See E. Schnabel, *The Footsteps of Anne Frank* (1959).

(3) **Bruno** (1887–1945), German author, born at Stuttgart, wrote historical novels, as *Die Fürstin* (1915), *Aus vielen Jahren* (1937), *Die Tochter* (1943), &c., in a style reminiscent

of Thomas Mann. His lyric poetry is also noteworthy. Of Jewish descent, he fled the Nazi régime and died at Beverley Hills in California. His *Der Reisepass* (1937) was directed against National Socialism.

(4) **Hans** (1900–46), German Nazi politician, born at Karlsruhe, was minister of justice in Bavaria (1933), president of the German Law Academy (1934) and governor-general in 1939 of Poland, where he established concentration camps and conducted a policy of persecution and extermination. He was condemned as a war criminal and hanged.

(5) **Leonhard** (1882–1961), German poet and novelist, born at Würzburg, fought in World War I and conceived a horror of war which led to his strongly pacifist *Der Mensch ist gut* (1917). His *Karl and Anna* (1928), also a war story, was successfully turned into a play. He left Germany and went to live in Hollywood, where he wrote several more books, including *Von drei Millionen drei* (1932).

(6) **Waldo David** (1889–1967), American novelist and journalist, born at Long Branch, N.J., wrote novels and other works coloured by mysticism and expressionism, including *City Block* (1922), *The Unwelcome Man* (1917), *The Rediscovery of America* (1929) and *New Year's Eve* (play, 1939). See study by G. B. Munson (1923).

FRANKAU, *fran'kow,* (1) **Gilbert** (1884–1953), novelist, born in London. A son of Mrs Julia Frankau, who wrote under the name of *Frank Danby,* writing came easily to him. Success rewarded him early and stayed with him, for he was, above everything, a professional writer, with a flair for anticipating popular taste. Of his many best-sellers, the following may be singled out: *One of Us* (1912), *Peter Jackson, Cigar Merchant* (1919), *Men, Maids and Mustard-Pots* (1923), *World without End* (1943). Besides his talent for novels, he exploited a bent for narrative verse in an attempt to restore a genre of English literature that had fallen into neglect. See his *Self-Portrait* (1932).

(2) **Pamela** (1908–67), daughter of (1), inherited her father's talent. She epitomized in her early novels the era of the ' bright young things ', the action sprightly, the writing flippant (e.g., *The Marriage of Harlequin,* her first novel). Like her father, a true professional, she outgrew this phase and her later novels are serious in intent. Typical are *The Willow Cabin* (1949) and *A Wreath for The Enemy* (1954). *The Offshore Light* (1952) was written under the pseudonym Eliot Naylor. She was also well known as a broadcaster. See her autobiography *I Find Four People* (1935).

FRANKL, Ludwig, Ritter von Hochwart (1810–1893), Austrian poet of Jewish origin, a professor of Aesthetics at the Vienna conservatoire (1851), established the first Jewish school in Jerusalem (1856). He wrote epics, ballads, satirical poems, &c., many of which have been translated.

FRANKLAND, Sir Edward (1825–99), English organic chemist, born at Churchtown, Lancashire, became professor at the Royal Institution, London, in 1863. He propoun-

ded the theory of valency (1852–60) and with Lockyer discovered helium in the sun's atmosphere in 1868. He was an expert on sanitation. He was elected F.R.S. in 1853 and was awarded the Copley medal in 1894.

FRANKLIN, (1) **Benjamin** (1706–90), American statesman and scientist, youngest son and fifteenth child of a family of seventeen, was born in Boston, Massachusetts, January 17, and was apprenticed at twelve to his brother James, a printer, who about 1709 started a newspaper, the *New England Courant.* Benjamin had so repaired the deficiencies of his early education that he was able to contribute to it; and when James was imprisoned by the Speaker of the Assembly for his too free criticisms the management of the paper was confided to Benjamin, who presumed too much upon his success, and the brothers fell out. Benjamin drifted to Philadelphia, friendless and almost penniless, but was fortunate enough to find immediate employment as a printer. Accident secured him the acquaintance of Sir William Keith, the governor, who persuaded him to go to England to buy printer's stock for himself, promising to lend him money and to secure him the printing for the government. Franklin arrived in London in December 1724, but, instead of the letters of credit he expected to find awaiting him, he found that Keith had no credit to give. He soon found employment in a London printing-house, remained there for eighteen months, and then returned to Philadelphia, where, with the help of friends, he established a printing-house, and his skill, industry and personal popularity ensured him signal success. In September 1729 he bought the *Pennsylvania Gazette,* and soon laid the foundations of a reputation as a journalist. In the following year Franklin married Deborah Read, by whom he had two children, a son who died in his youth, and a daughter, Sally, who became Mrs Bache. He also had an illegitimate son, William. In 1732 he commenced the publication of *Poor Richard's Almanac,* which attained an unprecedented circulation. In 1736 Franklin was appointed clerk of the Assembly, in 1737 postmaster of Philadelphia, and in 1754 deputy postmaster-general for the colonies, being elected and re-elected a member of the Assembly almost uninterruptedly until his first mission to England. In 1746 he commenced his famous researches in electricity which made him an F.R.S. He brought out fully the distinction between positive and negative electricity; he proved that lightning and electricity are identical, and he suggested the protecting of buildings by lightning-conductors. Further, he discovered the course of storms over the North American continent; the course of the Gulf Stream, its high temperature, and the use of the thermometer in navigating it; and the various powers of different colours to absorb solar heat. In 1757 he was sent to England to insist upon the right of the province to tax the proprietors of land held under the Penn charter for the cost of defending it from the Frenchmen and Indians, succeeded in his mission, and during his five years' absence received honorary degrees from Oxford and

Edinburgh. In 1764 he was again sent to England to contest the pretensions of parliament to tax the American colonies without representation. The differences, however, between the British government and the colonies became too grave to be reconciled by negotiation, and in 1775 Franklin returned to the United States, where he participated actively in the deliberations which resulted in the Declaration of Independence on July 4, 1776. To secure foreign assistance in the war Franklin was sent to Paris in 1776. His skill as a negotiator and personal popularity, reinforced by the antipathy of French and English, favoured his mission; and on February 6, 1778, a treaty of alliance was signed, while munitions of war and money were sent from France. On September 3, 1783, his mission was crowned with success through England's recognition of the independence of the United States. Franklin was U.S. minister in Paris till 1785, when he returned to Philadelphia, and was elected president of the state of Pennsylvania, a post to which he was twice re-elected. He was also a delegate to the convention which framed the constitution of the United States. In 1788 he retired from public life, and he died in Philadelphia, April 17. See his *Autobiography* in the standard edition of his works (ed. Smith 1905–07), also Lives by Parton (1864), Franklin and Headington (1880), Hale (1887), McMaster (1887), Morse (1889), Van Doren (1938), Becker (1946).

(2) **Sir John** (1786–1847), English Arctic explorer, was born at Spilsby, Lincolnshire. He entered the navy at fourteen and was present at the battles of Copenhagen (1801) and Trafalgar (1805). In 1818 he was in a fruitless expedition to Spitsbergen and from 1819 to 1822 and again from 1825 to 1827 made extensive land journeys along the Coppermine river and the Canadian arctic coast, including the Mackenzie River. Knighted in 1829, he was governor of Van Diemen's Land (Tasmania) from 1834 to 1845, in which year he commanded the *Erebus* and *Terror* in an attempt to discover the Northwest passage. Leaving Baffin Bay via Lancaster Sound, they wintered at Beechey Island, then, following their instructions to turn south at 98° long. and work along the coast of the N. American mainland they were beleaguered by thick ice in the Victoria Strait (1846). Franklin died on June 11, 1847. The 105 survivors under Captain Crozier attempted to reach one of the Hudson's Bay Company's posts on Back's River on foot, but died of starvation and scurvy. Numerous relief expeditions were sent out, and one of them, organized by Franklin's widow, found a record of the expedition to April 1848 with definite proof that Franklin had discovered the Northwest passage. He was commemorated in Westminster Abbey (1875). See works by Markham (1891), M'Clintock (1908), Cyriax (1939), Lambert (1952), Lamb (1956) and N. Wright (1959).

FRANZ, Robert, *frants* (1815–92), German composer, was born, lived, and died at Halle. He published over 250 songs, a Kyrie, chorales, and arrangements of the vocal masterpieces of Bach and Handel. Franz's best songs rank with those of Schubert and Schumann. See works by Liszt (1872), Saran (1875) and Osterwald (1886).

FRANZ JOSEF. See FRANCIS JOSEPH.

FRANZOS, Karl Emil, *frants'ōs* (1848–1904), Austrian novelist, was born of Jewish parentage in Podolia on the Austro-Russian border. His themes and settings were taken from Galicia, the Bukovina, south Russia and Rumania; his novels, which contain vivid pictures of life among Jews and peasants, include *Aus Halbasien* (1876), *Die Juden von Barnow* (1877), *Ein Kampf ums Recht* (1882) and *Der Pojaz* (1905).

FRASCH, Hermann (1851–1914), German-born American chemist, born at Gailsdorf, Württemberg, studied at Philadelphia and is best known for the Frasch process of extracting sulphur from deep underground deposits by the use of superheated steam.

FRASER, (1) **Sir Alexander** (c. 1537–1623), the founder in 1576 of Fraserburgh on his Aberdeenshire estate of Philorth, was knighted in 1594.

(2) **Alexander Campbell** (1819–1914), Scottish philosopher, born at Ardchattan, Argyllshire. In 1844 he was ordained in the Free Church of Scotland which had been founded because of schism the preceding year. He became in 1856 professor of Logic and Metaphysics at Edinburgh. He edited Berkeley's works (1871).

(3) **Marjory Kennedy** (1857–1930), Scottish singer and folk-song collector, born in Perth. She trained in Paris as a concert singer, but is best remembered for her collection of Hebridean folk-songs, begun in 1905. She wrote the libretto of Granville Bantock's opera *The Seal Woman*.

(4) **Peter** (1884–1950), born at Fearn, Ross and Cromarty, in 1910 emigrated to New Zealand, and was Labour prime minister (1940–49).

(5) **Simon.** See LOVAT, LORD.

(6) **Sir William** (1816–98), Scottish archivist, a deputy keeper of records of Scotland (1880–92), issued a series of sumptuous family histories with original charters, valuable as sources for Scottish history. He was knighted in 1887. By his will he endowed the Edinburgh chair of Scottish History, financed the *Scottish Peerage* and founded the Fraser Homes.

FRAUNHOFER, Joseph von, *frown'hō-fèr* (1787–1826), German physicist, born at Straubing in Bavaria, in 1807 founded an optical institute at Munich, improved prisms and telescopes, which enabled him to discover the dark lines in the sun's spectrum, called Fraunhofer's lines. In 1823 he became professor and academician at Munich.

FRAZER, Sir James George (1854–1941), British social anthropologist and folklorist, born in Glasgow in 1854, graduated at Cambridge in 1878, and became a fellow of Trinity. His *Totemism and Exogamy* (4 vols. 1910) developed out of *Totemism* (1 vol. 1887); and *The Golden Bough* (1890; 2nd ed. 1900; 3rd ed. rewritten, 12 vols., 1911–15; abridged 1922), his major work, named after the golden bough in the sacred grove at Nemi, absorbed many of his separately published studies of early superstition, religion, and society. Other works include *Folklore in the Old Testament* (1918), *Belief in Immortality* (1913–24), *Fear of the Dead* (1933–36) and *Magic and Religion* (1944). He became professor of Social Anthropology at Liverpool in 1907. Knighted in 1914, he received the O.M. in 1925.

FRÉCHETTE, Louis Honoré, *fray-shet* (1839–1908), ' Canadian laureate ', was born at Levis, Quebec, called to the bar, and elected to the Dominion parliament in 1874. He published prose works and plays, and his poems *Mes Loisirs* (1863), *La Voix d'un Exilé* (1867), &c., were ' crowned ' by the French Academy. See study by M. Dugas (1934).

FREDEGOND (d. 597), Frankish queen, first mistress, then wife, of Chilperic, king of Neustria, waged a relentless feud with Brunhilda, wife of Sigbert, king of Austrasia, and sister of Chilperic of Neustria's first wife; a feud intensified by the rivalry between the two kingdoms.

FREDERIC, Harold (1856–96), American novelist, born at Utica, N.Y., after a poverty-stricken youth, became a journalist and was in 1884 appointed European correspondent of *The New York Times*. He wrote *Seth's Brother's Wife* (1887), *The Return of the O'Mahony* (1892), &c., novels depicting his own background, but his best work is *The Damnation of Theron Ware* (1896). He died at Kenley, Surrey.

FREDERICK, the name of three Holy Roman Emperors:

Frederick I (*c.* 1123–90), surnamed **Barbarossa** (Redbeard), of the Hohenstaufen family, succeeded his father, Duke Frederick of Swabia, in 1147, and his uncle, Conrad III, as emperor in 1152. His reign was one long struggle against refractory vassals at home and the turbulent civic republics of Lombardy and the pope in Italy. The capture in 1162 of Milan brought all the recalcitrant states of Italy to submission. Five years later he even seemed on the point of subduing the pope; he had taken Rome by storm, when his army was suddenly overwhelmed by a terrible plague. This was the signal for revolt in Lombardy; but it was not until 1174 that Frederick was able to undertake the reduction of his Italian subjects. He incurred a severe defeat at Legnano (1176), but this proved to be more valuable to him than his previous successes. It led him to change his previous policy to one of clemency and concession, whereby the Lombards were converted into contented subjects. In 1177 he acknowledged Alexander III as pope, and thus paved the way for the final pacification of 1183. In Germany, Frederick conciliated his strongest vassals by giving them new fiefs or by raising their titular dignities, whilst the weaker he kept in check by conferring additional rights upon the municipal communities. Thus, he elevated Austria to the rank of a duchy, created Duke Ladislaus of Bohemia king, and granted Brunswick and Lüneberg to the Guelph princes. He also quelled the rebellious spirit of Henry the Lion of Bavaria, and asserted his feudal superiority over Poland, Hungary, Denmark and Burgundy. When at the height of his power he led the third crusade against Saladin. He defeated the Moslems at Philomelium and Iconium, but died in Cilicia, June 10. He was buried in the church of St Peter at Antioch. Frederick's chief traits were a resolute will that at times degenerated into gross cruelty, administrative skill, martial ardour, a love of danger, and a magnanimous ambition. He was perhaps the greatest of the mediaeval emperors. See works by Jastrow and Winter (1901), Simonsfeld (1909) and Wahl (1941).

Frederick II, of Germany (1194–1250), grandson of Frederick I and son of the emperor Henry VI and of Constance, heiress of Sicily, was born at Jesi near Ancona, December 26. In 1198 he became king of Sicily; in 1212 he wrested the imperial crown from Otto IV; on his promising to undertake a crusade, the pope sanctioned his coronation in 1215. Frederick ardently desired the consolidation of the imperial power in Italy by reducing the pontificate to a mere archiepiscopal dignity. Crowned emperor at Rome in 1220, he devoted himself to organizing his Italian territories. He founded the university of Naples, encouraged the medical school of Salerno, patronized art and literature, and commissioned his chancellor to draw up a code of laws to suit his German and Italian subjects. His schemes were frustrated by the Lombard cities, and by the popes Honorius III and Gregory IX. His departure to the East was originally fixed for 1223, but difficulties in Italy led to a five years' delay. At last papal threats constrained him to embark. He secured from the sultan of Egypt possession of Jerusalem, together with a ten years' truce. After crowning himself king of Jerusalem (1229), he returned to Italy, where his Neapolitan dominions had been overrun by the papal allies. During the remainder of his reign Frederick was engaged in struggles with the pope, whose hands were strengthened by the accession of the rebellious Lombard cities and of several princes and towns of Germany, led by Frederick's son Henry. Disaster and misfortune were gathering around him, when he died at Fiorentino, December 13. Intellectually, Frederick was perhaps the most enlightened man of his age, as in his tolerance of Jews and Mussulmans, in free-trade policy, in his recognition of popular representation by parliaments, and in his anticipation of the later humanistic movement; but at the same time he was a persecutor of heretics, an upholder of absolute sovereignty, and a supporter of the power of princes against the cities. He not only spoke the principal languages of his extensive empire, but was one of the first to write Italian poems, took a great interest in the arts, and was a diligent student of natural science. He was not an atheist as has been maintained. See works by Schirrmacher (1859–65), Huillard Bréholles (1852–61), Kington-Oliphant (1862), Winkelmann (1889), Hampe (1899), Allshorn (1912), Kantorowicz (trans. 1931) and G. Masson (1957).

Frederick III, and IV of Germany (1415–1493), the fifth Duke of Austria of that name, was born at Innsbruck, September 21. Elected king of Germany in 1440 because of his lack of power and love of peace, he occupied the imperial throne for 53 years. In 1452 he was made Holy Roman Emperor. His reign was one of anarchy, wars raging on the frontiers of the empire, and disorders within. During its course Frederick lost his hold upon Switzerland; purchased peace from his brother Albert in Upper Austria; allowed Sforza to take Milan, George Podiebrad to seat himself on the throne of Bohemia, and Matthias Corvinus on that of Hungary; surrendered the empire to the pope by the Vienna Concordat of 1448; and remained apathetic under two Turkish invasions (1469 and 1475). Nevertheless, by the marriage of his son, Maximilian I, to Mary, daughter of Charles the Bold of Burgundy, he laid the foundation of the subsequent greatness of the Hapsburgs. Frederick died at Linz, August 19. Though he neglected the interests of the empire for alchemy, astrology and botany, he lost no opportunity of aggrandizing his own family. From his time the imperial dignity continued almost hereditary in the House of Austria. See work by Chmel (1840).

FREDERICK. The name of three kings of Prussia:

Frederick I (1657–1713), born at Königsberg, July 11, succeeded to the electorate of Brandenburg in 1688. He supported William of Orange in his attempt on England, and employed the treasure collected by his father in the purchase of minor principalities. The chief event of his reign was his elevation to the dignity of king in 1701, the title being taken from Prussia, the only independent portion of his dominions. He left the finances of his country in an embarrassed condition, founded the university of Halle, embellished Berlin, and founded there the Academies of Sciences and of Painting and Sculpture. He died February 25, 1713. See works by Hahn (3rd ed. 1876) and Heyck (1901).

Frederick II, the Great (1712–86), born at Berlin, January 24, was the son of Frederick-William I, and of Sophia-Dorothea, daughter of George I of Great Britain. His early years were spent under military training and a rigid system of education, against which he rebelled fiercely but vainly. At eighteen he made an attempt to escape to the court of Great Britain. His father saw in this an act both of political rebellion and of military insubordination, and would have punished it with death but for the intercession of the emperor. As it was, the prince was closely confined at Küstrin, while his confidant, Lieutenant Katte, was beheaded before his eyes. Frederick recognized that submission was inevitable, and threw himself with nervous alacrity into the military and civil duties with which he was after a time entrusted. He won his final restoration to favour when in 1733 he dutifully accepted as his bride the Princess Elizabeth of Brunswick-Wolfenbüttel (1715–97). From 1734 Frederick resided at Rheinsberg, where he devoted his leisure to the study of music and French literature, for which he had a keen and lasting admiration. He achieved almost professional skill on the flute, for which he composed many pieces, some of which are still played. He corresponded with Voltaire (who in 1750 visited Berlin), and studied the ' philosophical ' doctrines. On May 31, 1740, Frederick became king; and in October the accession of Maria Theresa separated the crown of Austria from the imperial diadem. Frederick, in possession of a fine army and a well-filled treasury, seized the opportunity. Reviving an antiquated claim to Silesia, he entered that province (December 1740), defeated the Austrians at Mollwitz (1741) and Chotusitz (1742), and, having concluded an alliance for fifteen years with France, forced Maria Theresa to yield him Upper and Lower Silesia by the Treaty of Breslau (1742). The second Silesian war (1744–45) left Frederick with still further augmented territories and the reputation of being one of the first military commanders of the day. The next eleven years were years of peace; but Frederick's energetic internal reforms were coloured by the expectation of renewed war. In 1756 the third Silesian war, the ' Seven Years' War ', began. Frederick anticipated attack by himself becoming the aggressor, and during all this momentous struggle displayed a courage, a military genius, and a resource in victory and defeat which entitle him to the name of ' the Great '. At the Peace of Hubertsburg (February 15, 1763), he had added a tenfold prestige to the Prussian arms. Jealousy of Austrian aggrandizement continued to influence his policy. In 1772 it induced him to share in the first partition of Poland, by which he acquired Polish Prussia and a portion of Great Poland. In 1778, it led him to take arms in a brief campaign, which ended in the acquisition of the Franconian duchies. One of his latest political actions was the formation of the ' Fürstenbund ', which was the first definite appearance of Prussia as a rival to Austria for the lead in Germany. He died at Potsdam August 17. Frederick was an able administrator, and contrived to carry on his wars without incurring a penny of debt. He regarded himself as the first servant of the state; he was his own prime minister in a very literal sense. His conviction of the immaturity of his country explains the discrepancy between his theoretical writings on government and the scant liberty he granted to his people; he justified his arbitrary actions by his good intentions and his keener insight. Prussia under him was governed as one huge camp. With a view to providing treasure for future wars he fostered woollen and other manufactures by a high protective tariff; but he made himself unpopular by the introduction of the French excise system. During Frederick's reign, however, the country rapidly recovered from the ravages of war, while the army was raised to a strength of 200,000 men. At his death the area of Prussia was doubled, and, notwithstanding the temporary eclipse under Napoleon, the foundation of Prussia's greatness was laid. Frederick was essentially a just, if somewhat austere man, and the administration of justice under his rule was pure; the press enjoyed comparative freedom; and freedom of conscience was promoted. Frederick was a voluminous writer on political, historical and military subjects. His works, written wholly in French, were published by the Berlin Academy (31 vols. 1846–57), as also his *Political Correspondence* (1879 *et seq.*). See the Prussian General Staff's volumes on his *Wars* (1890 *et seq.*); and Lives by Droysen (1874–85), Kugler (1877), Reddaway (1904), Young (1919), Koser (1925), Goldsmith (1927), Gaxotte (1941), Gooch (1947).

Frederick III (1831–88), German emperor and eighth king of Prussia, only son of William I, was born at Potsdam, October 18. In 1858 he married Victoria (1840–1901), Princess Royal of England. As Crown Prince of Prussia (from 1861) he protested against Bismarck's reactionary policy in relation to constitutional questions and the press. In the Franco-German war he commanded the third army; he was at Wissembourg, Wörth and Sedan, and was made field marshal (1870). In 1871 he became Crown Prince of the German Empire. In 1878, when the Emperor William was wounded by an assassin, the Crown Prince was appointed provisional regent. On March 9, the Emperor William died; and the Crown Prince, returning from San Remo to Prussia, was proclaimed emperor as Frederick III, but he died at Potsdam, June 15, 1888. His son, William II, succeeded him. Frederick had a great horror of war, intensely disliked autocratic ideas, and sought to liberalize German institutions. See Lives by Freytag (trans. 1890) and Philippson (2nd ed. 1908).

FREDERICK V (1596–1632), elector palatine and king of Bohemia, succeeded his father, Frederick IV, as elector in 1610. Frederick married in 1613 Elizabeth (q.v.), daughter of James I of England, put himself at the head of the Protestant union of Germany, and accepted the crown of Bohemia in 1619. His defeat at the battle of the Weisser-Berg, near Prague (1620), terminated his short-lived reign; and the 'Winter King', taking refuge in Holland, was put under the ban of the empire (1621), lost his principality, and died at Mainz, November 29.

FREDERICK, the name of nine kings of Denmark of whom the following are noteworthy:

Frederick III (1609–70), succeeded to the throne in 1648. War with Sweden and the aggrandizement of the monarchy were the chief events of his reign.

Frederick V (1723–66), ascended the throne in 1746, extended commerce and industry and encouraged science and art.

Frederick VI (1768–1839), became regent when his father, Christian VII, became insane (from 1784), and in 1808 succeeded him. In his reign feudal serfdom was abolished, the criminal code amended and the slave trade prohibited in the Danish colonies. His participation in the maritime confederation between Russia, Sweden and Prussia in 1800 led to the dispatch of a British fleet and the first battle of Copenhagen, in which the Danish fleet was destroyed. On his refusal to join Britain against Napoleon, Copenhagen was bombarded (1807) for three days, and the

docks, arsenals and shipping destroyed. This made him the ally of Napoleon, and after the overthrow of Napoleon's empire, he suffered proportionately. In 1814 Norway was taken from Denmark and given to Sweden. The state became bankrupt, and did not recover for many years. In 1831 he granted a liberal constitution to his subjects.

Frederick VII (1808–63), who succeeded in 1848, was the last of the Oldenburg line, and had to quell the revolt of Holstein and Schleswig (1848–50).

Frederick VIII (1843–1912), brother of Queen Alexandra of Britain, reigned from 1906.

Frederick IX (1899–1972), succeeded to the throne in 1947. He married in 1935 Ingrid, daughter of King Gustav VI Adolf of Sweden. Of his three daughters, Crown Princess Margrethe (1940–   ), now **Queen Margrethe II**, married a French diplomat, Count Henri de Laborde de Monpézat (1967); Benedikte married a German nobleman, Prince Richard zu Sayn-Wittgenstein (1968); and Anne-Marie is the wife of King Constantine II of Greece (q.v.).

FREDERICK, Prince of Wales (1707–51), son of George II and father of George III, quarrelled with his father, married (1736) the Princess Augusta of Saxe-Gotha, in 1737 joined the parliamentary opposition, and was banished from court.

FREDERICK-CHARLES, Prince (1828–85), Prussian field-marshal, nicknamed the ' Red Prince ' from his favourite hussar uniform, born in Berlin, was the eldest son of Prince Charles, brother of the Emperor William I. He served in the Schleswig-Holstein war (1848), commanded the right wing in the Danish war, and in 1866 helped to win the victory of Königgrätz. In the Franco-German war he commanded the second army, drove Bazaine upon Metz, which capitulated, and, promoted to field-marshal, captured Orleans, broke up the army of the Loire, and scattered Chanzy's portion of it at Le Mans. In 1879 his daughter married the Duke of Connaught.

FREDERICK-WILLIAM (1620–88), ' the Great Elector ' of Brandenburg, was born February 16. On his accession in 1640 he found the state disorganized, exhausted and devastated by the Thirty Years' War. He strenuously regulated the finances, made a treaty of neutrality with Sweden, reorganized his army, and strove to repeople his deserted towns and villages. By the Treaty of Westphalia (1648) he recovered eastern Pomerania, Halberstadt and Minden, with the reversion of Magdeburg; and out of a quarrel between Sweden and Poland he contrived to secure the independence of the duchy of Prussia from Poland (1657). After another fifteen years of peace, alarmed at the aggressions of Louis XIV on the Rhenish frontier, he induced the Emperor, the King of Denmark and the Elector of Hesse-Cassel to make a league against France. Incited by Louis, the Swedes invaded Brandenburg, but were defeated and driven from the electorate; but, unaided by the Emperor and the other German princes, the Elector was compelled to agree to the Treaty of St Germain (1679), by which he restored all his conquests to the

Swedes in exchange for 300,000 crowns. From this time he devoted himself to consolidating his dominions and developing their resources. He encouraged the immigration of exiled French Protestants (after 1685), Dutchmen and other foreigners. He founded the royal library at Berlin, reorganized the universities, opened canals, established posts and greatly enlarged Berlin. He left a well-filled exchequer and a highly-organized army. He made Brandenburg virtually an absolute monarchy only less powerful than Austria. His son became King Frederick I of Prussia. See works by Philippson (1897–1903) and A. Waddington (1905–08).

FREDERICK-WILLIAM, Ger. Friedrich Wilhelm, the name of four kings of Prussia:

Frederick-William I (1688–1740) was the son of Frederick I (q.v.), whom he succeeded in 1713 when he became embroiled in the war waged by Sweden against Russia, Poland and Denmark, at the end of which (1720) he acquired western Pomerania with Stettin. Thereafter he improved the internal condition of Prussia. He was sternly practical, blunt and determined; he despised the arts and sciences, was rigidly economical and strict in his ideas of justice. At his death, May 31, 1740, he left a treasure of £1,350,000 and an army of more than 80,000 men, the best-disciplined force in Europe, which made Prussia fourth in military power. He fostered industry and agriculture, introduced the manufacture of woollen cloth, and settled in East Prussia 17,000 Protestant refugees from Salzburg. His rule laid the foundation upon which his son Frederick the Great built the subsequent greatness of Prussia. See works by Förster (1835), Paulig (2nd ed. 1889), Ranke (2nd ed. 1879), Tümpel (1915) and Waddington (1922).

Frederick-William II (1744–97), nephew of Frederick the Great, was born September 25. The abolition of some of his predecessor's oppressive measures, including the coffee and tobacco duties, made him very popular at his accession in 1786. But he soon lost the regard of his subjects by his predilection for unworthy favourites, and by the abrogation of the freedom of the press and religion (1788). The fortune his uncle left in the treasury he dissipated in a useless war with Holland. His foreign policy was weak, while he oppressed his subjects with debt and increased taxation. He acquired large areas of Polish Prussia and Silesia by the partitions of Poland in 1793 and 1795, as also Ansbach and Bayreuth. He died November 16, 1797. See works by Paulig (new ed. 1909) and G. Stanhope (1912).

Frederick-William III (1770–1840), succeeded his father, Frederick-William II, in 1797. At first he was neutral towards Napoleon; but the truculent policy of the latter so exasperated the Prussians that, instigated by their idolized Queen Louisa (q.v.), they forced the king to declare war (1806). After the disastrous defeats of Jena and Auerstädt, Frederick-William fled into East Prussia, while Napoleon entered Berlin. By the Treaty of Tilsit (1807) Prussia was deprived of all her territories west of the Elbe, and all that she had acquired by the

partition of Poland. For the next five years Frederick-William laboured to reorganize his enfeebled government. Napoleon's disastrous termination of the Russian campaign was the beginning of the war of liberation. Although the Prussians were defeated at Lützen and Bautzen, Prussia was finally delivered by the decisive victory of Leipzig (1813). By the Treaty of Vienna (1815) Prussia recovered her possessions west of the Elbe, and acquired Berg and Jülich, parts of Saxony and Westphalia, and the whole of Pomerania; but she gave up her Polish acquisitions save Posen to Russia, Friesland to Holland, and Ansbach and Bayreuth to Bavaria. The latter part of this reign was one of reaction. The democratic movements of 1819 and 1830 were rigorously suppressed, and the freedom of the press curtailed. Nevertheless, provincial diets were established (1823); the finances were put on a better footing; the system of taxation was greatly improved; education was encouraged, and the Zollverein or customs union was established. The king was a most excellent man, but his public conduct was marked by indecision and narrowness. See works by Eylert (1842–46), Hahn (3rd ed. 1877), Duncker (1877), and Hintze (1915).

Frederick-William IV (1795–1861), succeeded his father, Frederick-William III, in 1840. He began his reign by granting minor reforms and promising radical changes, but always evaded the fulfilment of these pledges. He was possessed by vague ideas of the divine right of kings, and by a mystic pietism. He refused the imperial crown offered him by the Liberal Frankfurt Diet in 1849, and opposed the popular movement of 1848; but when the people stormed the arsenal and seized the palace of the Prince of Prussia (afterwards William I), the king granted a representative parliament (1850). In 1857, afflicted with insanity, he resigned the administration to his brother, who from 1858 acted as regent till his accession, as William I, on the death of Frederick-William, January 2, 1861. See Lives by Ranke (1878), Petersdorff (1900); and Valentin, *History of the German Revolution 1848–49* (abridged trans. 1940).

FREDERICK-WILLIAM, Duke of Brunswick (1771–1815), Prussian soldier, born October 3, fought for Prussia against France in 1792 and 1806, when he was taken prisoner and Napoleon vetoed his accession to the duchy. He raised a free corps in Bohemia, and in 1809, with his 700 'black hussars' and 800 infantry, achieved a masterly retreat to Brunswick, Elsfleth and England. He subsequently took part in the Peninsular war, and received from the British government £6000 a year, which he retained until his accession to his duchy in 1813. He joined the allied army after the return of Napoleon from Elba, and fell while leading his Black Brunswickers at Quatre Bras, June 16. See Life by Spehr (2nd ed. 1861).

FREEMAN, (1) Edward Augustus (1823–92), English historian, born at Harborne, Staffs, and educated at Trinity College, Oxford, succeeded Stubbs as regius professor of Modern History. Among his prolific output are his *History of Federal Government* (1863) and *History of the Norman Conquest* (1867–1876). His work, however, is now outdated. He died at Alicante, Spain, on one of his numerous travels abroad. See Life by Stephens (1895).

(2) **John** (1880–1929), English poet, born in London, rose from clerk to secretary and director of an insurance company (1927). His *Stone Trees* (1916) and other volumes of poetry made his reputation. He won the Hawthornden Prize with *Poems New and Old* in 1920 and wrote studies of *George Moore* (1922) and *Herman Melville* (1926).

(3) **Walter** (1895–   ), American neurologist, was born at Philadelphia. He is a leading expert on neurosurgery, and developed the operation of prefrontal lobotomy, used in the relief of certain mental illnesses.

FREEMAN-THOMAS, Freeman. See WILLINGDON.

FREGE, Gottlob, *fray'gĕ* (1848–1925), German logician, lectured in mathematics at Jena, and in his *Begriffsschrift* ' Concept-script ' (1879) outlined the first complete system of symbolic logic, incorporating that of Boole (q.v.), with the aim of demonstrating that mathematics is free from the taint of psychologism by proving it to be an extension of logic. The technical difficulties involved gave rise to his distinctive philosophical doctrines, forcefully set out in his *Grundlagen der Arithmetik* (1884; tr. J. L. Austin 1950). His final work, *Grundgesetze der Arithmetik* (1893–1903), contained a postscript acknowledging that Bertrand Russell had spotted a contradiction, the famous antinomy of classes, a solution to which Russell and Whitehead attempted to provide in their *Principia Mathematica*. Frege's distinction between the ' sense ' and ' reference ' of a proposition, necessary for his defence of the objectivity of numbers, was brilliantly countered by Russell's Theory of Descriptions, but in part resurrected in 1950 by Strawson's criticisms of the latter. See P. Geach and M. Black, *Philosophical Writings of Gottlob Frege* (1952).

FREILIGRATH, Ferdinand, *frī'lig-raht* (1810–1876), German poet and democrat, born at Detmold, abandoned commerce for literature, but became a protagonist of German democracy and his writings became more and more political. He was obliged to seek safety in Belgium and Britain, for his *Glaubensbekenntnis*. He returned to Germany in 1848 and became leader of the democratic party. He was again expelled after a trial for his poem *Die Toten an die Lebenden* (1848). He translated many English classics into German. See his poems (ed. Liddell, 1950); Lives by Schmidt-Weissenfels (1876), Buchner (1881), G. Freiligrath (1889); and a study by Gudde (1922).

FRELINGHUYSEN, *fray'ling-hī-zen,* (1) **Frederick** (1753–1804), American statesman, father of (3) and uncle of (2), raised a corps of artillery, and fought in the War of Independence, and was a member of the Continental Congress in 1778 and 1782–83, and a U.S. senator in 1793–96.

(2) **Frederick Theodore** (1817–85), American senator, nephew of (1), succeeded in 1839 to his uncle's practice. He was attorney-general

of New Jersey in 1861–66, afterwards sat in the U.S. Senate, where he carried a bill against polygamy, and was secretary of state in Arthur's cabinet, 1881–85.

(3) **Theodore** (1787–1861), American lawyer, son of (1), practised law in Newark, became state attorney-general, a U.S. senator (1829–35), and chancellor of New York University; in 1844 he was nominated for the vice-presidency. In 1850 he was chosen president of Rutgers College, New Brunswick.

FRÉMONT, John Charles, *free-mont* (1813–90), American explorer, was born at Savannah, Georgia, became in 1835 a teacher of mathematics in the navy and in 1838 started surveying. In 1842 he crossed the Rocky Mountains (where a peak is named after him), and demonstrated the feasibility of an overland route across the continent. In 1843 he explored the Great Salt Lake, advancing to the mouth of the Columbia River; and in 1845 examined the continental watershed. After participating in the annexation of Upper California in 1847, he started in 1848 upon a fourth expedition along the upper Rio Grande. In 1849 he crossed over to California, where he settled, and next year became senator of the new state. In 1853 he conducted a fifth expedition. In 1856 he was the Republican and anti-slavery candidate for the presidency; nominated again in 1864, he withdrew in favour of Lincoln. He served in the regular army as major-general (1861–62), but resigned rather than serve under General Pope. In 1873 the French authorities sentenced him in absence to imprisonment for fraud in connection with the Southern Pacific railway scheme. Frémont was governor of Arizona in 1878–82, and died in New York. He published, besides accounts of his explorations, *Memoirs of My Life* (1886). See his wife's *Souvenirs of My Time* (1887), Lives by Bigelow (1856), Bashford (1928), Nevins (1928) and Goodwin (1930).

FRÉMY, Edmond, *fray-mee* (1814–94), French chemist, prepared anhydrous hydrogen fluoride, wrote on the synthesis of rubies, and worked on the ferrates, the colouring of flowers, saponification of fats, &c.

FRENCH, John, Earl of Ypres (1852–1925), British field-marshal (1913), born at Ripple, Kent, joined the navy (like his father) in 1866, the army in 1874, distinguished himself with the 19th Hussars in Sudan 1884–85, and by an unbroken record of success as cavalry commander in S. Africa 1899–1901. Chief of Imperial General Staff 1911–14, he held supreme command of the British Expeditionary Force in France 1914–15, and then of the Home Forces. O.M. (1914), K.P. (1917), Viscount (1915), Earl (1921), lord lieutenant of Ireland 1918–21, he got a grant of £50,000 in 1919. See his *1914* (1919).

FREND, William (1757–1841), English reformer and mathematician, born at Canterbury, graduated at Cambridge as second wrangler, turned Unitarian in 1787, and became an actuary. He wrote on political economy, astronomy, &c.

FRENEAU, Philip, *-nō* (1752–1832), American

sailor and poet, commanded a privateer in the War of Independence, was captured by the British, and wrote *The British Prison Ship* (1781), and the shorter poems *The Indian Burying Ground* and *The Wild Honeysuckle*. See *Life* by L. Leary (1941).

FRENSSEN, Gustav (1863–1945), German novelist, born a carpenter's son at Barlt in Holstein, studied for the church but turned to writing and attracted attention by his *Jörn Uhl* (1901), a novel of peasant life. *Hilligenlei* (1906), a life of Christ set in a Germanic background, aroused much controversy. Other works include *Der Pastor von Poggsee* (1922) and *Lebensbericht* (1941). See studies by W. Alberts (1922) and O. Hauser (1936).

FRERE, *freer,* (1) **Sir Henry Bartle Edward** (1815–84), British colonial administrator, was born at Clydach in Brecknock, and studied at Haileybury. As chief-commissioner of Sind he kept order during the Mutiny. He was governor of Bombay (1862–67). In 1872 he signed a treaty with the Sultan of Zanzibar abolishing the slave trade. In 1877 he was appointed governor of the Cape and High Commissioner in South Africa. The proposed confederation of the South African colonies was frustrated by the action of the Boers and by the Kaffir (1877–78) and Zulu (1878–79) wars; and Sir Bartle Frere's treatment of the Zulus was keenly debated. Recalled in 1880, he devoted himself to his duties as president of various learned societies and to the promotion of missionary work. He published several works on Indian and African subjects. See *Lives* by Martineau (1895) and Worsfold (1923).

(2) **John Hookham** (1769–1841), English diplomat, wit and translator, was born in London, and educated at Eton and Caius College, Cambridge. He entered the Foreign Office, in 1796 was returned for Looe, supported Pitt's government, and contributed to the *Anti-Jacobin*; among his verse are *The Loves of the Triangles*, a parody on Darwin's *Loves of the Plants*, and *The Needy Knife-grinder*, written in collaboration with his school friend, Canning (q.v.). Under-secretary for foreign affairs (1799), he was appointed envoy to Lisbon (1800), and twice minister to Spain (1802 and 1808). Recalled after the retreat to Coruña, he retired in 1821 to Malta, where he devoted himself to Greek, Hebrew and Maltese. Frere's clever mock-heroic *Specimen of an intended National Work by William and Robert Whistlecraft* (1817) suggested its *ottava rima* to Byron for his *Beppo*; but his fame rests on his admirable translations of the *Acharnians, Knights, Birds,* and *Frogs* of Aristophanes, published in 1907. See *Memoir* prefixed to his *Works* (1871), and *Lives* by Festing (1899) and von Eichler (1905).

FRÉRON, Élie Catherine, *fray-rõ* (1718–76), French critic, was a professor in the Collège Louis le Grand, and wrote in defence of church and king against Voltaire and the Encyclopédistes. See work on him by Cornou (1922).

FRESCOBALDI, Girolamo (1583–1643), Italian composer, born in Rome, studied the organ at Ferrara cathedral, became organist at Sta Maria in Trastevere, Rome, and travelled much in the Low Countries. From 1608 until his death he was organist at St Peter's in Rome. He composed chiefly organ works and madrigals.

FRESENIUS, Karl Remigius, *-zay'-* (1818–97), German chemist, revised editions of whose tables for qualitative and quantitative analysis are still being used.

FRESNAYE, Roger de la, *fray-* (1885–1925), French artist, born at Le Mans. He studied in Paris and was influenced by Cézanne; he associated with Jacques Villon in the Section d'Or group. After 1917 he produced a number of sensitive paintings with a cubist approach, making use of elegant curves and Cézannesque colour.

FRESNEL, Augustin Jean, *fray-nel* (1788–1827), French physicist, born at Broglie, became head of the department of public works at Paris, was elected F.R.S. in 1825 and awarded the Rumford medal in 1827. He died of tuberculosis. His optical investigations contributed materially to the establishment of the undulatory theory of light; he invented the well-known compound lighthouse lens and produced circularly polarized light by means of a special prism (Fresnel's rhomb). See his *Works*, with Life by Arago (1866–70).

FREUD, *froyd,* (1) **Anna** (1895–), Viennese born British psychoanalyst, daughter of (3), became chairman of the Vienna Psycho-analytical Society and emigrated with her father to London in 1938, where she organized (1940–45) a residential war nursery for homeless children. She has made important contributions to child psychology, and was made C.B.E. in 1967. Her works include *Introduction to Psycho-analysis for Teachers* (1931; tr. 1949) and *The Ego and the Mechanism of Defence* (1937; tr. 1948).

(2) **Lucian** (1922–), British artist, grandson of (3). He was mainly self-taught, and his portraits have many affinities with the naïve, uncompromising realism of Primitive painters.

(3) **Sigmund** (1856–1939), Austrian founder of psychoanalysis, 'the Copernicus of the Mind', father of (1), was born May 6, at Freiburg, Moravia, of Jewish parentage. Inspired by Goethe's essay on nature, he studied medicine at Vienna, but original work in physiology delayed his graduation until 1881. He then specialized in neurology and, spurred on by the discovery of the Viennese physician Breuer, that hysteria can be cured by making a patient recall painful memories under hypnosis, studied under Charcot (q.v.) in Paris (1885) and changed over from neurology to psychopathology. To appease his frowning colleagues in Vienna, he published on his return two strictly neurological studies on aphasia (1891) and cerebral paralysis, before risking, with Breuer, the joint publication of *Studien über Hysterie* (1895). Finding hypnosis inadequate, Freud gradually substituted the method of 'free association', allowing the patient to ramble on with his or her thoughts when in a state of relaxed consciousness and, interpreting the data, an abundance of

childhood and dream recollections. He became convinced, despite his own puritan sensibilities, of the fact of infantile sexuality. This became the basis of his theory and cost him his friendship with Breuer (1897), lost him many patients and isolated him from the always conservative medical profession. He worked on alone, publishing in 1900 his magnum opus, *Die Traumdeutung*, ' The Interpretation of Dreams ', an exhaustive study of dream material, including his own, which showed that dreams, like neuroses, are disguised manifestations of repressed wishes of a sexual origin. Repression, which differs profoundly from mere conscious suppression, Freud explained by reference to a vast reservoir of unconscious, irrational mental activity, the *id*, comprising the crude appetites and impulses, loves and hates, particularly those connected with what he termed the *Oedipus complex*, the infant's craving for exclusive possession of the parent of the opposite sex. These impulses, at variance with civilized behaviour, are repressed by the *ego*, a portion of the *id* which at an early stage has become differentiated from it. At a later stage, the *super-ego* (conscience) develops out of the *ego*, determining what is acceptable to the *ego* and what must be repressed. Repressions disappear from consciousness but live on in the *id*. In sleep or in day-dreaming the *ego* relaxes its control and the repressed impulses may succeed in pushing themselves into consciousness, but not until the reduced powers of the *ego* have exercised a censorship, by distorting the unacceptable character of the dream material into something meaningless but acceptable. Psychoanalysis seeks to uncover these repressions for what they are and replace them by acts of judgment. In 1902, Freud was appointed to an extraordinary professorship, despite previous academic anti-Semitism in Vienna and began to gather disciples, who formed the original ' Psychological Wednesday Society '. Out of this grew the Vienna Psychoanalytical Society (1908) and in 1910, with Jung as first president, the International Psychoanalytical Association, which included such names as Adler, Jung, Steckel, Rank, Eitingon, Abraham, Ferenczi, Jones and Brill. Two further major works, Freud's *Psychopathologie des Alltagslebens*, ' Psychopathology of Everyday Life ' (1904) and *Drei Abhandlungen zur Sexualtheorie*, ' Three Essays on the Theory of Sexuality ' (1905), met with heated, uncomprehending opposition and it was not before 1930, when Freud was awarded the Goethe prize, that his work no longer aroused active opposition from public bodies. Even Adler and Jung diverged from the Freudian theory by seeking to remove the central emphasis on sexuality. Adler, who broke with Freud in 1911, developed a psychology of the *ego* and Jung, who followed in 1913, a highly complex system of basic human types and ' the collective unconscious '. Ernest Jones in 1912 formed a committee of senior collaborators pledged to uphold the basic Freudian conceptions. Psychoanalysis thenceforth was a creed as well as a science. In 1933, Hitler banned psychoanalysis. After

Austria had been overrun, Freud and his family were extricated from the hands of the Gestapo by diplomatic representations and allowed to emigrate after Freud had signed a document to the effect that no pressure had been placed upon him by the Nazi government. He settled in Hampstead and died there September 23, 1939, from cancer of the jaw which had troubled him for sixteen years. Freud's work effected a profound revolution in man's attitude towards and comprehension of his mental processes, constituting, after Copernicus and Darwin, ' a third blow to man's self-esteem '. On his eightieth birthday, Thomas Mann delivered an address in his honour and he was elected a corresponding member of the Royal Society. Other important writings are a work on humour (1905), *Totem und Tabu* (1913), *Jenseits des Lustprinzips*, ' Beyond the Pleasure Principle ' (1919–20), *Das Ich und Das Es* ' Ego and Id ' (1923), and his controversial view of religion in *Die Zukunft einer Illusion*, ' The Future of an Illusion ' (1927). He collaborated with Albert Einstein in *Why War?* (1933). See his illuminating autobiographical study (trans. Strachey, 1935) and definitive Life by E. Jones (1953–57), the standard edition of his works, trans. Strachey with Anna Freud (1953–58), memoirs by H. Sachs (1945), M. Freud (1957), E. Jones (1957), *Freud and the 20th Century*, ed. B. Nelson (1958), *Psychoanalysis and Contemporary Thought*, ed. J. D. Sutherland (1958) and study by P. Rieff (1960).

FREUND, Wilhelm, *froynt* (1806–94), German lexicographer, born at Kempen in Posen, taught at Breslau, &c. On his *Wörterbuch der lateinischen Sprache* (1834–45) most English Latin dictionaries are based.

FREYBERG, Bernard, 1st Baron Freyberg, *frī'bĕrg* (1889–1963), British general, born in London, was educated at Wellington College, New Zealand. In the 1914–18 war he served with the Royal Naval Division in Gallipoli and France, winning the V.C. at Beaumont Hamel. After experience in the Southern Command and at the War Office, in the war of 1939–45 he was given command of the New Zealand Forces. Sent to New Zealand as governor-general, on his return in 1953 he was appointed deputy constable and lieutenant-governor of Windsor Castle. He was created K.C.B. and K.B.E. in 1942, and raised to the peerage in 1951. See Life by P. Singleton-Gates (1963).

FREYCINET, Charles Louis de Saulces de, *fray-see-nay* (1828–1923), French statesman, born at Foix, Ariège, was originally an engineer. In 1870 he was called by Gambetta to the war department; his conduct there he described in *La Guerre en province* (1871). Four times premier, he wrote on engineering, sanitation, &c., and was admitted to the Academy of Sciences and to the French Academy (1890).

FREYTAG, *frī-taKH*, (1) **Georg Wilhelm Friedrich** (1788–1861), German orientalist, was born at Lüneberg, and became professor of Oriental Languages at Bonn in 1819. His reputation rests on his *Lexicon Arabico-Latinum* (1830–37) and works on Arabic literature and history.

(2) **Gustav** (1816–95), German novelist and playwright, was born at Kreuzburg in Silesia, and in 1839–47 was *privatdozent* of German in Breslau University. A deputy to the North German Diet, he attended the Prussian crown prince in the Franco-German campaign (1870). His comedies and other plays —*Die Valentine* (1846), *Die Journalisten* (1853), &c.—proved brilliant successes; but his greatest achievement is *Soll und Haben* (1855) a realistic novel of German commercial life (Eng. trans. *Debit and Credit*, 1858). It was followed, but not equalled, by *Die Verlorne Handschrift* (1864; Eng. *The Lost Manuscript*, 1865), and the series (1872–81) called *Die Ahnen*. He died at Wiesbaden. See his *Reminiscences* (Eng. trans. 1890), and study by R. Koebner (1926).

FRICK, Wilhelm (1877–1946), German politician, born at Alsenz, participated in Hitler's Munich putsch (1923), led the Nazi faction in the *Reichstag* from 1924 and as minister of the Interior from 1933 banned trade unionism and freedom of the press, and encouraged anti-Semitism. Ousted by Himmler in 1943, he became ' Protector ' of Bohemia and Moravia. He was found guilty of war crimes at Nuremberg and executed.

FRICKER, Peter Racine (1920–), English composer, born in London, was educated at St Paul's school and the Royal College of Music. He was musical director of Morley College, London, 1952–64, professor of Music at California University, 1964–65, and resident composer there from 1965. The influence of Bartók and Schoenberg is apparent in such works as the *String Quartet in One Movement* (1948), the *First Symphony* (1948–49) and the *Sonata for Violin and Piano* (1950). Later works include symphonies, the *Cello Sonata* (1956), an oratorio, &c.

FRIDA, Emil. See VRCHLICKÝ.

FRIDESWIDE, St, *frid'ē-sweed-ē* (d. *c.* 735), English abbess and the patroness of Oxford, was the daughter of Didanus, an ealdorman. Founder of the abbey which became Christ Church, Oxford, she died November 14, and was canonized in 1481. See Life by F. Goldie (1881).

FRIEDEL, Charles, *free'del* (1832–99), French chemist, latterly professor of Organic Chemistry at the Sorbonne, worked on the production of artificial minerals (diamonds); he and Crafts gave their names to a reaction for the synthesis of benzene homologues.

FRIEDLAND, Valentin, *freed-lant* (1490–1556), German educationist, more commonly known as **Trotzendorf** from his birthplace near Görlitz, studied under Luther and Melanchthon at Wittenberg. Settling at Goldberg in Silesia, he founded a school in 1531 which was run entirely by the boys themselves. See Lives by Köhler (1848), Löschke (1856), and Sturm (1889).

FRIEND, Sir John (d. 1696), English Jacobite conspirator and London brewer, knighted by James II in 1685, and executed for conspiring against William III.

FRIES, *frees,* (1) **Elias** (1794–1878), Swedish botanist, was professor at Uppsala, and keeper of the botanic garden there. He wrote on fungi, lichens and the flora of Scandinavia, and introduced a new classi-ficatory system. The genus *Freesia* is named after him.

(2) **Jakob Friedrich** (1773–1843), German philosopher, born at Barby in Prussian Saxony, lectured at Heidelberg, was deprived of his Jena professorship of Philosophy for participation in the democratic disturbances of 1819, but in 1824 was appointed to the chair of Physics and Mathematics there. He attempted to use intuitive psychology as a basis of a new critical philosophy of Kant. See works by Henke (1867), Grapengiesser (1882) and Elsenhaus (1906).

FRIESE-GREENE, William (1855–1921), British pioneer of the motion-picture, was born in Bristol. His first successful picture, using celluloid film, was shown in public in 1890, in which year his invention was patented. His experiments included three-dimensional and colour cinematography. He died almost penniless.

FRIESZ, (Émile) Othon, *frees* (1879–1949), French painter, born at Le Havre, attended the École des Beaux Arts, and studied with Bonnat and Dufy (q.v.). At first an enthusiastic impressionist, he was later influenced by Cézanne. After extensive travelling in Europe, he exhibited at the Salon des Indépendants and began teaching his art of ' measure and rhythm without regard for rules '. His work may be seen in the Luxembourg (portrait of his wife) and in many German and French galleries. See study by A. Salmon (1920).

FRIPP, the name of two English watercolour painters, both born at Bristol:

(1) **Alfred Downing** (1822–95), brother of (2), a member of the Royal Society of Painters in Watercolour (1846), he lived in Italy (1850–59) and painted many pictures of Italian, Welsh and English scenes, including *Young England* and *The Irish Mother.*

(2) **George Arthur** (1814–96), brother of (1), studied painting at Bristol and travelled in Italy before settling in London and attracting Turner's praise with *Mont Blanc* (1848, Liverpool gallery); was elected a member of the Royal Society of Painters in Watercolour (1845) and was its secretary from 1848 until his resignation in 1854. He excelled in English river scenes and Scottish and Welsh mountain scenery which he executed with delicate atmospheric effects.

FRISCH, (1) Max (1911–), Swiss playwright and novelist. His most important work is perhaps the novel *Stiller* (1954), a satire on the Swiss way of life; other books are *Homo Faber* (1957) and *Mein Name sei Gantenbein* (1964). His name is often coupled with that of Dürrenmatt as one of the two most significant post-war Swiss-German dramatists. His plays, really modern morality pieces, include *Nun singen sie wieder* (1946) and *Andorra* (1962).

(2) **Otto Robert** (1904–), Austrian physicist, born in Vienna, became in 1939 head of the nuclear physics division at Harwell, and in 1947 professor of Natural Philosophy at Cambridge. He and Meitner first used the term ' nuclear fission ' (1939). He was elected F.R.S. in 1948. See his *Meet the Atoms* (1947).

FRITH, (1) John (1503–33), English Protestant

martyr, born at Westerham, Kent, from Eton went to King's College, Cambridge, whence in 1525 Wolsey summoned him to his new foundation at Oxford. A year later suspicion of heresy drove him to Marburg, where he saw much of Tyndale and Patrick Hamilton, and wrote several Protestant treatises. Venturing back in 1532, he was burned at Smithfield.

(2) **William Powell** (1819–1909), English painter, born at Aldfield, elected A.R.A. at twenty-six. By selling both paintings and their copyright, he made himself the wealthiest artist of his time. The pre-Raphaelites, with some justification, criticized the vulgarity of his historical and genre works, but he took a new direction with his huge canvases of Victorian scenes, *Ramsgate Sands* (1854; bought by Queen Victoria for Buckingham Palace), *Derby Day* (1858, National Gallery) and *The Railway Station* (1862; Holloway College), which were hailed by Ruskin as the art of the future. They display a graphic touch and flair for composition and have, although by no means great art, acquired a period charm. Only his *The First Cigarette* (1870) outraged the sensibilities of his patrons. He was elected R.A. in 1852 and continued to exhibit until 1902. See his *Autobiography*, ed. N. Wallis (1957).

FROBENIUS, Joannes (1460–1527), German printer, founded a printing office at Basel (1491), and issued 300 works, including a Vulgate, Erasmus, Tertullian, Ambrose, and Greek New Testament (1496).

FROBERGER, Johann Jakob (1616–67), German composer, born at Stuttgart. A pupil of Frescobaldi, he was court organist at Vienna (1637–57), and made concert tours to Italy, Paris, London and Brussels. Of his many compositions, the best remembered are his suites for harpsichord.

FROBISHER, Sir Martin (c. 1535–94), English sailor, was born at Altofts near Wakefield, Yorkshire. Sent to sea as a boy, he traded to Guinea and elsewhere, and seems early to have become possessed by his dream of a Northwest Passage to Cathay. He set sail northwards, June 7, 1576, with the *Gabriel* and the *Michael* of 20 tons each and a pinnace of 10 tons, their total complement thirty-five men. The pinnace foundered, the *Michael* deserted, but Frobisher, almost lost off the coast of Greenland, reached Labrador on July 28. From two subsequent expeditions, he brought back ' black earth ' which was supposed to be gold from Frobisher bay. In 1585 he commanded a vessel in Drake's expedition to the West Indies, and was knighted for his services against the Armada. He married a daughter of Lord Wentworth, settled down for a while, but was soon again scouring the seas for the treasure-ships of Spain; at the siege of Crozon near Brest in November 1594 he received a wound of which he died at Plymouth on the 22nd. His *Three Voyages* were edited by Stefánsson (1938). See Lives by Rev. F. Jones (1878) and Dawlish (1956).

FRÖDING, Gustav, *frœ′-* (1860–1911), Swedish poet, born near Karlstad, studied at Uppsala, became a schoolmaster and journalist, became insane in 1898 and

reappeared as a pious writer in 1909. Perhaps the greatest Swedish lyric poet, he is often compared with Burns. His use of dialect and folksong rhythm in his portrayal of local characters in *Guitarr och dragharmonika* (1891) and *Räggler å paschaser* (1895) turned to tragic lyricism in his *Stänk och flikar* (1896).

FROEBEL, Friedrich Wilhelm August, *frœ′bėl* (1782–1852), German educationist, was born at Oberweissbach, studied at Jena, Göttingen and Berlin, and in 1805 began teaching at Frankfurt-am-Main. In 1816 he put into practice his educational system, whose aim, to help the child's mind to grow naturally and spontaneously, he expounded in *Die Menschenerziehung* (1826). Catholic opposition foiled his attempts to establish a school near Lucerne (1831). After starting an orphanage at Burgdorf in Bern, where he began to train teachers for educational work, he in 1836 opened his first kindergarten school at Blankenburg. The rest of his life was spent in the organizing of kindergarten schools. See his works, collected by Lange (new ed. 1874), by Seidel (1883); *Chief Writings on Education* (trans. 1912); *Autobiography* (trans. 1886); *Letters* (trans. 1891), and works by Shirreff (1887), Pappenheim (1893), Hauschmann (1900), E. R. Murray (1914), Prüfer (1927), Priestman (1946).

FRÖHLICH, Alfred. See BABINSKI.

FROHSCHAMMER, Jakob, *frō′shamm-er* (1821–93), German Catholic theologian and philosopher, born near Ratisbon, became widely known by his history of dogma (1850) which was banned by the pope. In another work, he championed freedom of science from the church. He founded the first Liberal Catholic paper, *Athenäum*, in which he gave an account of Darwin's theory. He was excommunicated in 1871. See his autobiography (1888).

FROISSART, Jean, *frwah-sahr* (c. 1333– c. 1405), French historian and poet, was born at Valenciennes, educated for the church, but at nineteen began to write the history of the wars of his time. In 1360 he went to England, where he received a gracious welcome from Philippa of Hainault, wife of Edward III, who appointed him clerk of her chamber. In 1364 he travelled in Scotland, where he was the guest of King David Bruce and of the Earl of Douglas. In 1366 he went to Aquitaine with the Black Prince; in 1368 he was in Italy, possibly with Chaucer and Petrarch, at the marriage of the Duke of Clarence. For a time he was curate at Lestines in the diocese of Liège; and was afterwards at various continental courts. About 1390 he settled in Flanders, and resumed work on his *Chronicle*. In 1395 he revisited England, and was cordially welcomed by Richard II. He then returned to Chimay, where he had obtained a canonry, and where he may have died. Froissart's famous book deals with the period 1326–1400. Mainly occupied with the affairs of France, England, Scotland and Flanders, he supplies much valuable information about Germany, Italy and Spain, and even touches occasionally on Hungary and the Balkan peninsula. He is of all mediaeval chroniclers the most vivid and entertaining, accurate and impartial in his statements. The main defects in his work are the frequent repetitions and the negligent arrangement. He likewise wrote a considerable number of verses—*ballades, rondeaux, virelais,* &c.; the Round Table metrical romance, *Méliador,* was discovered in 1894. See studies by Mary Darmesteter (trans. 1895), Newbolt (1900), F. S. Shears (1930) and M. Wilmotte (Brussels 1942).

FROMENT, Nicolas, *fro-mã* (fl. 1450–90), French painter, who has left some fine examples of the late Gothic style containing features surprisingly Flemish in appearance. He was court painter to King René, whose portrait is incorporated in his masterpiece, a tryptich in the cathedral of Aix-en-Provence, having as its centrepiece Moses and the burning bush.

FROMENTIN, Eugène, *fro-mã-tĩ* (1820–76), French painter and author, born at La Rochelle, studied law but turned to painting under Cabat in Paris. Visits to Algeria and the Near East provided him with material for brush and pen: *Chasse au faucon en Algérie* and *Halte de cavaliers arabes* (both in the Louvre) are painted in almost scientific detail, their colour and composition betraying the influence of Delacroix. His three travel books also provide vivid pictures of the Algerian scene. But he is best known as the author of *Dominique* (1862), a personal novel of great power and beauty, a psychological study of his first unhappy love-affair recalled in middle-age. *Maîtres d'autrefois* (1876), written during a tour of Belgian and Dutch art galleries, contains some brilliant art criticism. See also his *Lettres de jeunesse* (1909) and *Correspondance* (1912).

FROMM, Erich (1900–), German-American psychoanalyst, born in Frankfurt, educated at the universities of Frankfurt, Heidelberg, and Munich, and at the Berlin Institute of Psychoanalysis. After holding various university appointments he ultimately became professor at New York in 1962. A neo-Freudian, he is known for his investigations into motivation, and his works include *Psycho-analysis and Religion, Sigmund Freud's Mission, The Dogma of Christ* and *The Heart of Man.*

FRONTENAC, Louis de Buade, Comte de, *frõ-tẽ-nak* (1620–98), French-Canadian states-man, served in the army, and in 1672 was appointed governor of the French possessions in North America. He was recalled after ten years of quarrelling with the Jesuits, but he had gained the confidence of the settlers and the respect of the Indians; and in 1689, when to constant attacks from the Iroquois a war with England was added, he was again sent out. He set the Indians on New England villages, repulsed a British attack on Quebec, and completely broke the power of the Iroquois. He died at Quebec. See books by Parkman (1877) and La Sueur (1906).

FRONTINUS, Sextus Julius (c. A.D. 40–103), Roman writer, was appointed Roman governor of Britain in 75, was twice consul, and in 97 was made superintendent of the waterworks at Rome. Of works ascribed to him (ed. McElwain, 1925, with trans.), the *Strategematicon,* a treatise on war, and the *De Aquis Urbis Romae* are genuine.

FRONTO, Marcus Cornelius (c. A.D. 100–170), Roman rhetorician, born at Cirta in Numidia, was entrusted by Antoninus Pius with the education of Marcus Aurelius and Lucius Verus. In 143 he was consul. The two series of his letters to Marcus Aurelius, discovered by Mai in 1815, were edited by Niebuhr (1816), Naber (1867) and Haines (1920 *et seq.*). See study by M. D. Brock (1911).

FROST, (1) **John** (d. 1877), a tailor, draper and mayor of his native Newport, Monmouth-shire, was sentenced to be hanged, drawn and quartered for leading a Chartist riot (November 4, 1839) but instead was transported for fourteen years to Tasmania. He died at Stapleton near Bristol.

(2) **Robert Lee** (1874–1963), American lyric poet, ' the voice of New England ', born at San Francisco, the son of a New England father and Scottish mother. He studied at Harvard, but did not graduate and was teacher, cobbler and New Hampshire farmer, before coming to Britain (1912–15), where under the encouragement of Rupert Brooke, Abercrombie and Gibson he published *A Boy's Will* (1913) and *North of Boston* (1914), which gave him an international reputation. Returning in glory to the United States, he continued to write poetry which in character, background and situation is essentially New England. He created a new kind of folk speech in describing ' that which is common to experience, but uncommon in writing ' in poems which ' begin in delight and end in wisdom '. He was awarded the Pulitzer prize in 1924, 1931 and 1937, received a U.S. senate citation of honour in 1950 and honorary doctorates from Oxford and Cambridge (1957). See *Collected Poems* (1951), and studies by Cox (1929), Thornton (1937), Mertins (1947), Thompson (1961, 1967) and Jennings (1964).

FROUDE, *frood,* (1) **James Anthony** (1818–1894), English historian, brother of (2) and (3), was born at Dartington, Devon, April 23, educated at Westminster and Oriel College, Oxford, and in 1842 was elected a fellow of Exeter. He received deacon's orders in 1844, and was sometime under Newman's influence; but a change was revealed in *Shadows of the Clouds,* by ' Zeta ', a psychological novel (1847, suppressed), and still more in *The Nemesis of Faith* (1848), which cost Froude both his fellowship and an educational post in Tasmania. For the next few years he wrote for *Fraser's Magazine* (which for a while he edited) and the *Westminster Review,* and in 1856 issued vols. i–ii of his *History of England from the Fall of Wolsey to the Spanish Armada,* completed in 12 vols. in 1869. In this work Froude shows supreme literary ability; but, like Macaulay, he is a man of letters first and a historian after-wards. His views of men and motives are those of the 19th century distorted by his own highly individualistic judgment. His brilliant essays *English in Ireland in the Eighteenth Century* (1871–74) and *Caesar* (1879) provide further evidence for this criticism. Froude was rector of St Andrews in 1869. In 1874, and again in 1875, he visited the South African colonies on a mission from the home government, and published his impressions in *Two Lectures on South Africa* (1880). As Carlyle's literary executor he edited his *Reminiscences* (1881), Mrs Carlyle's *Letters* (1882) and Carlyle's own *Life* (1882–84). Later works are *Oceana* (1886), a delightful account of an Australasian voyage; *The English in the West Indies* (1888); *The Two Chiefs of Dunboy* (1889), an Irish historical romance; *The Earl of Beaconsfield* (1890); *The Divorce of Catharine of Aragon* (1891); *The Spanish Story of the Armada* (1892); *Life and Letters of Erasmus* (1894); and *Lectures on the Council of Trent* (1896). In 1892 he succeeded Freeman as professor of Modern History at Oxford. See Life by Paul (1905).

(2) **Richard Hurrell** (1803–36), English tractarian, brother of (1) and (3), became in 1827 fellow and tutor of Oriel. Tracts 9 and 63 were from his pen. See his *Remains* (1838–39).

(3) **William** (1810–79), English engineer and mathematician, brother of (1) and (2), became in 1837 an assistant to Brunel (q.v.). Retiring from professional work in 1846, he devoted himself to investigating the conditions of naval construction.

FRUMENTIUS, St (*c.* 300–*c.* 380), the apostle of Ethiopia, born in Phoenicia, was captured while on a voyage by Ethiopians, became the king's secretary, and gradually secured the introduction of Christianity. In 326 he was consecrated Bishop of Axum by Athanasius at Alexandria.

FRUNDSBERG, Georg von, *froondz-berg* (1473–1528), German soldier, leader of German *Landsknechte* during the Italian wars of Maximilian and Charles V. He fought in twenty pitched battles, and Pavia (1525) was largely won by him. See Lives by Barthold (1833), Heilmann (1868), Miller (1928) and Zoepfl (1928).

FRY, (1) **Charles Burgess** (1872–1956), British sportsman and writer, born in Croydon. He was a triple blue while at Oxford and subsequently represented Britain in soccer, cricket and athletics. For a time he held the world record for the long jump.

(2) **Christopher** (1907–), English dramatist, born in Bristol, educated at Bedford Modern School, combined schoolmastering with a love of the stage, which became a full-time occupation on his appointment as director of Tunbridge Wells Repertory Players (1932–36). In 1940 he became director of the Playhouse at Oxford, having in the meantime written two pageant-plays, *Thursday's Child* and *The Tower*, also *The Boy with a Cart*, a charming rustic play on the subject of the Sussex saint, Cuthman. After service in World War II he began a series of outstanding plays in free verse, often with undertones of religion and mysticism, including *A Phoenix too Frequent* (1946), *The Firstborn* (1946), *The Lady's not for Burning* (1949), *Thor, with Angels* (1949), *Venus Observed* (1950), *A Sleep of Prisoners* (1951) and *The Dark is Light Enough* (1954). He has also produced highly successful translations of Anouilh (q.v.) and Giraudoux (q.v.). See study by D. Stanford (1951).

(3) **Sir Edward** (1827–1918), great-grandson of (5) and father of (6), was an eminent international jurist and cryptogamic botanist. He arbitrated in important international cases, as in the dispute between the U.S.A. and Mexico over the Pious Fund (1902–03) and the Casablanca incident (1908–09) involving France and Germany.

(4) **Elizabeth** (1780–1845), English Quaker prison reformer, born May 21, was the third daughter of John Gurney, the rich Quaker banker. In 1800 she married Joseph Fry, a leading London Quaker merchant. In 1810 she became a preacher among the Friends. In 1813 she visited Newgate, and found 300 women, tried and untried, with their numerous children, herded together in filth and neglect; and thenceforward devoted her life to prison reform at home and abroad; she also founded hostels for the homeless and charity organization societies—and this in spite of her husband's bankruptcy (1828). See Lives by her daughter (1847), Susanna Corder (1853), Ashby (1892), Hare (1895) and G. K. Lewis (1903).

(5) **Joseph** (1728–87), English Quaker business-man and type-founder, great-grandfather of (3), born at Sutton Benger in Wiltshire, settled at Bristol as a doctor, but went into a pottery enterprise; founded the well-known chocolate business; and from 1764 onwards became eminent as a type-founder.

(6) **Roger Eliot** (1866–1934), English art critic, aesthetic philosopher and painter, son of (3), born in London. Although his paintings are excellent examples of design, he is mainly remembered for his responsibility for the spread of the principles of the Post-Impressionists (particularly Cézanne) in England. He organized the first London exhibition of their works in 1910. His essays and lectures on art, some of which were published in *Vision and Design* (1920), gave him international authority as an art critic and as the propounder of an extreme formal theory of aesthetics, according to which the aesthetic quality of a work of art depends on its 'significant form' or formal characteristics alone. This theory he modified later, especially in *French Art* (1932). He also wrote *Transformations* (1926), *Cézanne* (1927), *Henri Matisse* (1930) and *Reflections on British Painting* (1934). See monograph by Virginia Woolf (1940), and Clive Bell, *Old Friends* (1956).

FRYXELL, Anders, *früks'el* (1795–1881), Swedish historian, was a parish priest from 1835 to 1847, but thenceforward gave himself entirely to literary work at Stockholm. His *Narratives from Swedish History* (46 vols. 1832–80) have been translated into English (M. Howitt, 1844) and in part into many other languages.

FUAD I, *foo'ahd* (1868–1936), son of Khedive Ismail Pasha (q.v.) and father of Farouk I (q.v.), was sultan of Egypt from 1917, king from 1922, when the British protectorate was terminated.

FUAD PASHA, Mehmed (1814–69), Turkish statesman and littérateur, was the son of the poet, Izzet-Mollah, became an Admiralty physician, but in 1835 took up history and politics. After diplomatic service in London and Madrid, he became grand interpreter to the Porte, minister of foreign affairs (1852 and 1855), and Grand Vizier (1861–66). To him Turkey owed the hatti-sherif of 1856.

FUCHS, *fookhs,* (1) **Klaus Emil Julius** (1912–), former British atom spy, was born at Russelsheim near Frankfurt, Germany, the son of a Protestant pacifist pastor, and was taught a creed called 'Christian Communism'. Educated at Kiel and Leipzig Universities, he escaped from Nazi persecution to Britain in 1933. Interned on the outbreak of World War II, he was released and naturalized in 1942. From 1943 he was one of the most brilliant of a group of British scientists sent to America to work on the atom bomb. In 1946 he became head of the theoretical physics division at Harwell. In March 1950 he was sentenced to 14 years' imprisonment for disclosing nuclear secrets to the Russians over a six-year period. In February 1951 he was formally deprived of British citizenship. On his release in June 1959 he became an East German citizen. See *The Traitors* by Alan Moorehead (1952).

(2) **Leonhard** (1501–66), German botanist, professor at Tübingen, a pioneer of German botany, after whom in 1703 the fuchsia was named by Plumier.

(3) **Sir Vivien Ernest** (1908–), British Antarctic explorer and scientist, leader of the Commonwealth Antarctic Expedition (1956–58), born in Kent, the son of a farmer of German origin, was educated at Brighton College and St John's, Cambridge. After four geological expeditions in East Africa (1929–38), he served as major in West Africa and Germany during World War II and was mentioned in dispatches. As director of the Falkland Islands Dependencies Survey (1947) he set up scientific bases on Graham Land peninsula, and while marooned there for a year, conceived the plan for an overland crossing of Antarctica, which materialized when in 1955 he was appointed leader of the Commonwealth expedition. With a party of ten he set out by snow tractor from Shackleton Base, Weddell Sea, on November 24, 1957, reached the South Pole on January 19, 1958, and continuing via Depot 700 with the assistance of Sir Edmund Hillary (q.v.) and his New Zealand party, reached Scott Base, Victoria Land, on March 2 to receive news of his knighthood for successfully seeing through a full scientific programme of geological readings throughout the entire 2200 miles, despite Hillary's advice to abandon the scheme because of the late season. Fuchs was awarded the gold medal of the Royal Geographical Society (1951), and its Polar medal (1953) and clasp (1958). See his *The Crossing of Antarctica* (with Sir E. Hillary, 1958).

FUCINI, Renato, *foo-chee'nee* (1843–1921), Italian writer, born at Monterotondo, near Pisa, the son of a country doctor, studied agriculture and engineering at Pisa, and became city engineer at Florence. He had a gay wit which found outlet in dialect verse, published as *Centi Sonetti* (1872) under the pseudonym of Neri Tanfucio. When Florence ceased to be a capital city Fucini lost his post and withdrew to the country.

Le veglie di Neri (1884), a collection of tales, is his best-known work. *All' aria aperta* (1897) is reckoned the best modern collection of Italian humourous *novelle.* He also wrote books for children and personal anecdotes.

FUGGER, *foog-ger,* name of a South German family of bankers and merchants in the early 16th century which founded lines of counts and princes. **Johannes** (1348–1409), was a master-weaver, who was born near Schwabmünchen, and settled at Augsburg in 1368. His second son, **Jacob** (d. 1469), carried on an extensive business. Three of his sons extended their business to an extraordinary degree, married into the noblest houses, and were ennobled by the Emperor Maximilian, who mortgaged to them for 10,000 gold gulden the county of Kirchberg and the lordship of Weissenhorn. The house attained the height of its prosperity and influence under Charles V, when its fortunes came to rest on the sons of **George** (d. 1506), founders of the two chief lines of the house of Fugger. The brothers were zealous Catholics, opponents of Luther. Charles V made them counts, invested them with the still mortgaged properties of Kirchberg and Weissenhorn, and gave them the rights of princes. The Fuggers continued still to carry on their commerce, increased their immense wealth, and attained the highest posts in the empire. They possessed great libraries and art collections, maintained painters and musicians, and encouraged art and science. See the *Fugger Newsletters* (trans. 1924–26) and works by Geiger (1895), Stauber (1900), Strieder (1926), Ehrenberg (trans. 1928).

FÜHRICH, Joseph von (1800–76), a Viennese religious painter, born at Kratzau in Bohemia. His work can be seen in churches throughout Austria.

FULBECKE, William (1560–*c*. 1603), English jurist, born at Lincoln, author of *Direction or Preparation to the Study of the Law* (1600), one of the oldest English legal text-books, which was still in use in the 19th century.

FULGENTIUS, *fool-gen'tee-oos* (468–533), Bishop from 507 of Ruspe in Numidia, wrote Latin treatises against the Arians and semi-Pelagians (ed. by Hurter, Innsbruck 1884). See Life by Mallby (Vienna 1884).

FULLER, (1) **Andrew** (1754–1815), English Baptist pastor, born at Wicken, Cambridgeshire, whose treatise *The Gospel worthy of all Acceptance* (1784), involved him in a controversy with the ultra-Calvinists. In 1792 he became the first secretary of the newly-founded Baptist Missionary Society. His other writings include *Calvinistic and Socinian Systems Compared* (1793), *Socinianism Indefensible* (1797), &c.

(2) **George** (1822–84), American artist, born at Deerfield, Mass., best known for his landscape and figure paintings, including that of Winifred Dysart. See Life (1887).

(3) **John Frederick Charles** (1878–1966), British general, served in the South African campaign with the Oxford and Bucks Light Infantry. In the 1914–18 war he was prominently associated with the Tank Corps, becoming a perfervid advocate of the

armour-cum-fighter-plane war of movement as subsequently exploited by Hitler's *Reichswehr*. He retired in 1933 to become a brilliant, if controversial, writer on military subjects. See his *Reformation of War* (1923), *Foundations of the Science of War* (1926), *Memoirs of an Unconventional Soldier* (1936) and *Decisive Battles* (3 vols. 1956).

(4) **Sarah Margaret, Marchioness Ossoli** (1810–50), American writer and critic, was born at Cambridgeport, Mass. In Boston she edited *The Dial*, a periodical devoted to ' transcendentalism ', and wrote *Summer on the Lakes* (1843). In 1844 she published *Woman in the Nineteenth Century*, and in the same year proceeded to New York, and contributed to the *Tribune* a series of articles, republished as *Papers on Literature and Art* (1846). In 1847 at Rome she met the Marquis Ossoli, and married him. In 1849, during the siege of Rome, she took charge of a hospital; and after the capture of the city by the French she and her husband sailed with their infant for America, but perished in a shipwreck. See her Autobiography (1852), and Lives by Julia Ward Howe (1883), T. W. Higginson (1884) and K. Anthony (1922).

(5) **Thomas** (1608–61), English antiquarian and divine, was born at Aldwinkle St Peter's rectory, Northamptonshire, and graduated at Cambridge. In 1630 he became curate of St Benet's, where he preached the *Lectures on Job* (published in 1654). In 1634 he was appointed rector of Broadwindsor in Dorsetshire. His first ambitious work was a *History of the Holy War* (1639), on the Crusades. *The Holy and Profane States* (1642–48) is a collection of essays. When the Civil War broke out he adhered firmly to the royal cause, and shared in its reverses. He saw active service as chaplain to Hopton's men, and printed at Exeter in 1645 for their encouragement *Good Thoughts in Bad Times*, followed in 1647 by *Good Thoughts in Worse Times*, and by *The Cause and Cure of a Wounded Conscience*. In 1647 the Earl of Carlisle presented him to the curacy of Waltham Abbey. In 1650 he published his *Pisgah-sight of Palestine*. *Abel Redivivus* (1651) was a collection of religious biographies. In 1655 he published his long-projected *Church History of Britain*, from the birth of Christ till 1648, divided into eleven books—a twelfth being a *History of the University of Cambridge*. The work was bitterly assailed by Heylin as a rhapsody, full of ' impertinencies ' and errors, and marred by his partiality to Puritanism. Fuller replied in his witty *Appeal of Injured Innocence*. He had in 1658 received the rectory of Cranford in Middlesex, and at the Restoration he was reinstated in his former preferments. In 1660 he published his *Mixt Contemplations in Better Times*, was admitted D.D. at Cambridge, and appointed chaplain to the king. He died in London, August 16, 1661. His great *Worthies of England*, left unfinished, was published by his son in 1662; its preparation took nearly twenty years. The *Worthies* is a miscellany about the counties of England and their notable men. His style shows admirable narrative faculty, with a nervous brevity and point almost new to

English, and a homely shrewd directness, but lacking richness and depth. See Lives of him by Russell (1844), Bailey (1874), Morris Fuller (1886), Broadley (1910), Lyman (1935), and study by Roberts (1953).

FULLER-MAITLAND, John Alexander (1856–1936), English musicologist, educated at Westminster and at Trinity College, Cambridge, music critic of *The Times* from 1889 to 1911 and author of many critical works, is remembered especially for his editorship of Grove's Dictionary of Music (2nd ed.) and for his work on early music, especially the *Fitzwilliam Virginal Book*, of which he brought out an edition with W. B. Squire in 1899.

FULLERTON, Lady Georgiana (1812–85), English novelist, daughter of the first Earl Granville, was born at Tixall Hall, Staffordshire and in 1833 married Alexander Fullerton, an officer. Two years after publishing her first novel, *Ellen Middleton* (1844), she became a convert to Catholicism. The rest of her life was devoted to charitable works and religious tales—*Grantley Manor* (1847) and *Too Strange not to be True* (1852), her most popular work, and others. See Mrs Craven's French Life (trans. 1888).

FULTON, Robert (1765–1815), American engineer, was born of Irish parents in what is now Fulton township, Pennsylvania, and became a painter of miniature portraits and landscapes. In 1786 he went to London and studied under West, but gradually applied his energies wholly to mechanical engineering. In 1794 he obtained from the British government a patent for a double-inclined plane to supersede locks, and invented a mill for sawing and polishing marble. He afterwards prepared plans for cast-iron bridges, and patented a machine for spinning flax, a dredging machine, and several boats. In 1797 he went to Paris, where he devoted himself to new projects and inventions, among them a submarine torpedo boat, but neither the French nor the British government would take it up. He next turned his attention to the application of steam to navigation and in 1803 made two experiments on the Seine with small steamboats. In 1806 he returned to New York, invented torpedoes, and in 1807 launched a steam vessel on the Hudson, which accomplished the voyage (nearly 150 miles) to Albany in thirty-two hours. From this period steamers on his patent came into use on the rivers of the United States. Although Fulton was not the first to apply steam to navigation (see FITCH, JOHN, and SYMINGTON), he was the first to apply it successfully. He was employed by the U.S. government on canals and other works, and in constructing (1814) a steam warship. He died February 24. See Life by H. W. Dickinson (1913).

FUNK, *foonk*, (1) Casimir (1884–   ), American biochemist, born in Warsaw, became known for his contribution to the study of vitamins, which he named.

(2) **Walther** (1890–1960), German Nazi politician. One of Hitler's chief advisers, he succeeded Schacht as minister of economics and president of the Reichsbank, and played a leading part in planning the economic

aspects of the attack on Russia, and in the exploitation of occupied territories. Captured in 1945, he was sentenced to life imprisonment as a war criminal, but was released in 1957 on account of illness.

FURETIÈRE, Antoine, *für-tyayr* (1619–88), French scholar, Abbé of Chalivoy, was expelled (1685) from the Académie for compiling his *Dictionnaire Universel* (later pub. Rotterdam 1690). Backed by a royal edict (1674), the Académie claimed a monopoly, and accused the Abbé of pillaging its collections.

FURNESS, (1) Christopher Furness, 1st Baron (1852–1912), English shipowner, born at West Hartlepool, became a shipbroker in 1876 and soon afterwards established the Furness line. He went into partnership with Edward Withy in 1885, which marked the beginning of a huge shipbuilding and engineering business. Liberal M.P., he was one of the first to start a co-partnership scheme among his employees. He was knighted in 1895 and was created baron in 1910. He was succeeded by his son, **Marmaduke** (1883–1940), who was created a viscount in 1918.

(2) **Horace Howard** (1833–1912), American Shakespearean scholar, born at Philadelphia, is well-known for his *Variorum* edition, continued by his son **Horace Howard** (1865–1930).

FURNISS, Harry (1854–1925), caricaturist, born at Wexford, the son of an English engineer, came to London in 1873, and in 1880–94 drew for *Punch*. He illustrated Dickens, wrote *Confessions of a Caricaturist*, novels, humorous sketches and serials, &c.

FURNIVALL, Frederick James (1825–1910), English philologist, son of a doctor at Egham, studied at London and Cambridge universities, won fame as an oarsman and racing-boat designer, was called to the bar, and, influenced by F. D. Maurice and Christian socialism, taught in the Working Men's College. But it was as a philologist and editor of English texts that he became famous, giving a great impulse to Early English scholarship. He founded the Early English Text Society, the Chaucer, Ballad, New Shakespeare, Wyclif and Shelley Societies, and edited some score of texts, including the six-text Chaucer, Brunne's *Handlyng Synne*, Harrison's *England*, Stubbes' *Anatomy of Abuses*, and Hoccleve, besides writing an introduction to the 'Leopold' Shakespeare. See the biography by Munro in the memorial volume of 'personal records' published in 1911.

FURSE, Charles Wellington (1868–1904), English painter, studied at the Slade School under Legros and at Paris. An active member of the New English Art Club, his work is noted for easy, fluent brushwork. His *Diana of the Uplands* in the Tate became widely known.

FÜRST, Julius (1805–73), German orientalist, born at Zerkowo in Posen, in 1864 became professor at Leipzig. His works include books on the Jewish mediaeval philosophers (1845) and the Biblical and Jewish-Hellenic literature, and his great *Hebrew and Chaldee Lexicon* (1851–54).

FURTWÄNGLER, Wilhelm, *foort'veng-lėr* (1886–1954), German conductor, born in Berlin, son of **Adolf Furtwängler** (1853–1907), the celebrated classical archaeologist. He succeeded Nikisch in 1922 as conductor of the Gewandhaus concerts in Leipzig and of the Berlin Philharmonic. International tours established him as one of the leading musical personalities of his age, though his highly subjective and romantic interpretations of the German masters aroused controversy. His ambivalent attitude to the Hitler régime cost him some popularity outside Germany, but after the war he quickly re-established himself.

FUSELI, Henry, real name **Johann Heinrich Füssli** (1741–1825), Swiss-born British painter and art-critic, was born at Zürich, and coming to England in 1763, was encouraged by Sir Joshua Reynolds to go to Italy (1770–78). Elected R.A. in 1790, he became professor of Painting in 1799, and died at Putney. His 200 paintings include *The Nightmare* (1781) and two series to illustrate Shakespeare's and Milton's works, by which he is chiefly known. His literary works, with life, were published by Knowles (1831).

FUST, Johann (c. 1400–66), German printer, was born at Mainz, where he worked after 1450 with Gutenberg, to whom he lent money and whom he sued for debt in 1455 receiving, in lieu of payment, Gutenberg's printing plant, with which he started his own business, taking Schöffer, his son-in-law, as partner. He has sometimes been confused with the half-mythical Dr Faustus (fl. 1507–40), who was born at Knittlingen in Swabia.

FUSTEL DE COULANGES, Numa Denis, *füs-tel de koo-lãzh* (1830–89), French historian, born at Paris, was professor at Amiens, Paris,Strasbourg, and from 1875 at the École Normale, Paris. His *Chio* (1857) and *Polybe* (1858) had hardly prepared one for the exceptional brilliancy of *La Cité antique* (1864; trans. 1916), which threw fresh light on the social and religious institutions of antiquity. His *Histoire des institutions politiques de l'ancienne France* (1875–92) attacks racial theories in political history. Both are literary masterpieces. See studies by Champion (1903) and de Gérin-Ricard (1936), and Life by Guiraud (1896).

FYFE, Sir David Patrick Maxwell. See KILMUIR.

FYFFE, Charles Alan, *fīf* (1845–92), English historian, was born at Blackheath, educated at Balliol College, Oxford, elected a fellow of University College, and published *A History of Modern Europe* (1880–90).

G

GABB, William More (1839–78), American palaeontologist, born at Philadelphia, worked on the Geological Survey of California (1861–66) and is remembered for his work on marine fossils of the Cretaceous period.

GABELENTZ, Hans Conon von der (1807–74), German linguist, born at Altenburg, knew 80 languages, and is remembered for his great work on the Melanesian languages (1860–73).—His son, **Georg** (1840–93), in 1878 became Oriental professor at Leipzig, in 1889 at Berlin.

GABELSBERGER, Franz Xaver (1789–1849), German civil servant, the inventor of the chief German system of shorthand, was born and died at Munich, having in 1809 entered the Bavarian civil service. See Life by Gerber (new ed. 1925).

GABIROL, ibn. See AVICEBRÓN.

GABO, Naum (1890–), American constructivist sculptor, born in Russia. With his brother, Antoine Pevsner (q.v.), and Tatlin and Malevitch, he was associated with the Moscow Suprematist Group (1913), and in 1920 broke away with his brother and Tatlin to form the group of Russian Constructivists, who have had considerable influence on 20th century architecture and design. As their theories did not coincide with those of Russian official art circles, he was forced into exile, and lived in England for some years until 1946, when he went to the U.S.A. There are several examples of his completely non-figurative geometrical ' constructions in space ', mainly made in transparent plastics, in the Museum of Modern Art, New York. See *Gabo*, with introductory essays by Read and Martin (1958).

GABORIAU, Émile, *ga-bor-ee-ō* (1835–73), French writer of detective fiction, was born at Saujon in Charente-Inférieure, had already contributed to some of the smaller Parisian papers, when he leapt into fame with *L'Affaire Lerouge* (1866), the feuilleton to *Le Pays*. It was followed by *Le Dossier 113* (1867), *Monsieur Lecoq* (1869), *Les Esclaves de Paris* (1869), *La Corde au cou* (1873), &c.

GABRIEL, Jacques Ange (1698–1782), French architect, was born in Paris. As court architect to Louis XV he planned a number of additions to Versailles and other palaces and designed the Petit Trianon (1768). He also laid out the Place de la Concorde (1753). See study by H. B. Cox (1926).

GABRIELI, (1) Andrea (*c.* 1510–86), Italian composer, was born and died in Venice, studied under Willaert, and became organist of St Mark's church. He wrote masses and other choral works; his organ pieces include toccatas and ricercares, the latter foreshadowing the fugue.

(2) **Giovanni** (1557–1612), nephew and pupil of (1), composed choral and instrumental works in which he exploited the acoustics of St Mark's with brilliant antiphonal and echo effects, using double choirs, double ensembles of wind instruments and other devices, as in his well-known *Sonata pian e forte*.

GACHARD, Louis Prosper, *ga-shahr* (1800 1885), Belgian historian, was born in Paris, but spent most of his life as keeper of the archives at Brussels and edited many important sources of Belgian history.

GADDI, a family of Florentine religious painters and architects:

(1) **Agnolo** (*c.* 1333–96), son of (3), painted the frescoes of the *Discovery of the Cross* in S Croce at Florence and of the *Legends of the Holy Girdle* in the cathedral at Prato. His work shows the influence of Giotto. He was also an architect.

(2) **Gaddo** (*c.* 1260–1332), father of (3), worked in mosaic at Rome and Florence.

(3) **Taddeo** (*c.* 1300–66), son of (2), father of (1), was Giotto's best pupil and also his godson. His finest work is seen in the frescoes of the *Life of the Virgin* in the Baroncelli chapel of S Croce. Though the best-known of Giotto's followers, his style deviated from that of his master, whom he does not match in figure painting, but whom he excels in architectural perspective. See study by Wehrmann (1910).

GADE, Niels Wilhelm, *ge'THe* (1817–90), Danish composer, was born, lived and died at Copenhagen. He began as violinist, but on a royal grant studied at Leipzig and became a friend of Schumann and Mendelssohn, from whom he took over the Gewandhaus orchestra in 1847, but next year returned to Copenhagen. He composed eight symphonies, a violin concerto, several choral works and smaller pieces. There is a Scandinavian element in his music which distinguishes him from the Leipzig school.

GADOLIN, Johan (1760–1852), Finnish chemist, born at Åbo, where he became professor of Chemistry. He isolated the oxide of the rare element, gadolinium, named after him.

GADSDEN, (1) Christopher (1724–1805), American patriot, grandfather of (2), born in Charleston, was a member of the first Continental Congress (1774), became brigadier-general during the Revolution, and was lieutenant-governor of South Carolina.

(2) **James** (1788–1858), American soldier and diplomat, grandson of (1), served in the war of 1812 and against the Seminoles. In 1853 he was appointed minister to Mexico, and negotiated the purchase (Gadsden purchase) of part of Arizona and New Mexico for railway construction.

GAFFKY, Georg Theodor August, *gaf-kee* (1850–1918), German bacteriologist, born at Hanover, isolated and cultivated the typhoid bacillus (1884).

GAGARIN, Yuri (1934–68), Russian cosmonaut, born in the Smolensk district, joined the Soviet Air Force in 1957, and in 1961 became the first man to travel in space, completing a circuit of the earth in the *Vostok* spaceship satellite. A Hero of the Soviet Union, he shared the Galabert Astronautical Prize with Glenn (q.v.) in 1963. He was killed in a plane accident in training.

GAGE, Thomas (1721–87), English soldier, was the second son of the first Viscount Gage. He accompanied Braddock's ill-fated expedition (1755), and became in 1760 military governor of Montreal, in 1763 commander-in-chief of the British forces in America, and in 1774 governor of Massachusetts. On April 18, 1775, he sent a force to seize a quantity of arms at Concord; and next day the skirmish of Lexington took place which began the Revolution. After the battle of Bunker Hill (June 17) he resigned.

GAGERN, Heinrich Wilhelm August, Freiherr von, *gah-gern* (1799–1880), German statesman, born at Bayreuth, was a founder of the student movement (*Burschenschaft*) of 1815–1819, held office in Hesse-Darmstadt, and was president of the Frankfurt parliament (1848–49). From 1859 he again took part in grand-ducal politics, as a partisan of Austria against Prussia.

GAHN, Johan Gottlieb (1745–1818), Swedish chemist and mineralogist, born at Voxna, Gävleborg. Originally a miner, Gahn later studied mineralogy and invented a method for preparing metallic manganese on a larger scale. He shared the discovery of phosphoric acid in the bones with Scheele in 1770.

GAIDOZ, Henri, *gay-dō* (1842–1932), French Celtic folklorist and philologist, born in Paris, founded the *Revue Celtique* in 1870.

GAINSBOROUGH, Thomas (1727–88), English landscape and portrait painter, one of the great English masters and founder of the English school, was born at Sudbury. In his youth he copied Dutch landscapes and at fourteen was sent to London where he learnt the art of rococo decoration under Gravelot and Hayman. *The Charterhouse* (1748) marks the end of his apprenticeship. In 1745 he married one of his subjects, Margaret Burr, the natural daughter of the 4th duke of Beaufort, and settled as portrait painter at Ipswich. *Mr and Mrs Andrews* (1748) and several 'chimney-piece' paintings belong to this his Suffolk period. On the advice of Thicknesse, one of his patrons, he moved in 1760 to Bath, where he established himself with his portrait of Earl Nugent (1760). His portraits combine the elegance of Van Dyck with his own characteristic informality although in his later work he increasingly tends towards fashionable artificialities. There are such early masterpieces as *Lord and Lady Howe*, *Mrs Portman* (Tate) and *Blue Boy* (Huntington Collection, Pasadena), and the great landscapes *The Harvest Wagon* (1767; Barber Institute, Birmingham) and *The Watering Place* (1777; Tate) in which Rubens's influence is discernible. In 1768 he became a foundation member of the Royal Academy, at which he exhibited annually, until, somewhat discontented with the place assigned to *The King's Daughters* in 1784, he retired. A quarrel with Thicknesse, his patron, led him to move to London in 1774. To this last great period belong the superb character study *Mr Truman*, the luxuriant *Mrs Graham* (1777; Edinburgh), *George III*

and *Queen Charlotte* (1781; Windsor Castle), and his serene rendering of *Mrs Siddons*, the actress (1785), without the theatricality of other artists' rendering of her. Landscapes include *Cottage Door* (1780; Pasadena); *The Morning Walk* (1780), which is closer to his 'fancy pieces' based on Murillo's paintings than to nature; and *Cattle crossing a Bridge* (1781), the most rococo of all his work. See the critical appreciation of his art by Sir J. Reynolds in the latter's 14th *Discourse*, and Life and study by E. Waterhouse (1958).

GAIRDNER, James (1828–1912), British historian, brother of Sir William Tennant Gairdner (1824–1907), the physician, was born in Edinburgh, entered the Public Record Office in London, where he became assistant-keeper in 1859. He showed erudition, accuracy, and judicial temper in editing historical documents, as also in his own works—*The Houses of Lancaster and York* (1874); *Life of Richard III* (1878); *Lollardy and the Reformation in England* (1908–13), &c.

GAISERIC, *gī'-*, popularly but less correctly **Genseric** (c. 390–477), king of the Vandals and Alans, was an illegitimate son of Godigisel, who led the Vandals in their invasion of Gaul; in 427 he succeeded his half-brother Gunderic. Invited by Bonifacius, Count of Africa, Gaiseric crossed over from Spain to Numidia in 429, captured and sacked Hippo (430), seized Carthage (439), and made it the capital of his new dominions. He quickly built up a formidable maritime power, and his fleets carried the terror of his name as far as the Peloponnesus. A bigoted Arian, he persecuted orthodox Catholics with ferocious cruelty. Eudoxia, the widow of Valentinian III, eager for revenge upon her husband's murderer Maximus, invited Gaiseric to Rome. The Vandal fleet sailed for the Tiber; the city was taken (455), and given up to a fourteen days' sack. Gaiseric carried off the empress and her two daughters, one of whom became the wife of his son Huneric. Fleets sent against the Vandals in 457 and 468 were defeated. Gaiseric died in 477, in the possession of all his conquests, the greatest of the Vandal kings. See Life by Gautier (1932).

GAISFORD, Thomas (1780–1855), English Greek scholar, became regius professor of Greek at Oxford in 1812 and in 1831 dean of Christ Church. He produced editions of Herodotus, Hephaestion, Stobaeus and Suidas. The Gaisford Prizes were founded in his memory.

GAITSKELL, Hugh Todd Naylor (1906–63), British Labour politician, was born in London. He was educated at Winchester and at New College, Oxford, becoming a Socialist during the 1926 general strike. On leaving Oxford he became a Workers' Educational Association lecturer in economics in the Nottinghamshire coalfield. In 1938 he became reader in Political Economy in the University of London. Elected M.P. for Leeds South in 1945, he became parliamentary secretary to the Ministry of Fuel and Power in 1946 and minister in 1947. Appointed minister of state for economic affairs in 1950, he became in 1950–51 the youngest chancellor of the Exchequer since Balfour. His introduction of national health service charges led to the resignation of Aneurin Bevan as minister of health and to a long ' personality ' feud with Mr Bevan and the hostile left wing of the Labour Party. But his ascendancy in the party grew steadily and in December 1955 he was elected leader of the opposition by a large majority over Mr Bevan. He bitterly opposed Eden's Suez action (1956), attempted to modify Labour policy from total nationalization to the ' shareholder state ', and refused to accept a narrow conference vote for unilateral disarmament (1960). This caused a crisis of leadership in which he retained the loyalty of most Labour M.P.s. He wrote *Money and Everyday Life* (1939).

GAIUS, *gah'yoos,* (1) (fl. A.D. 130–180), Roman jurist, on whose *Institutes* were based Justinian's. His other works were largely used in the compilation of the *Digest.* The *Institutes,* lost until Niebuhr discovered a MS. at Verona in 1816, have been repeatedly edited; and a fragment of an older MS. was printed in *Oxyrhynchus Papyri,* vol. xvii (ed. Hunt, 1928).

(2) See CALIGULA.

GALBA, Servius Sulpicius (3 B.C.–A.D. 69), Roman emperor, became consul in A.D. 33, and administered Aquitania, Germany, Africa and Hispania Tarraconensis with courage, skill and justice. In 68 the Gallic legions rose against Nero, and in June proclaimed Galba emperor. But he soon made himself unpopular by favouritism, ill-timed severity, and avarice, and was assassinated by the praetorians in Rome.

GALBRAITH, John Kenneth (1908–), Canadian economist, born in Ontario, was educated at the Universities of Toronto, California and Cambridge. In 1939 he became Assistant Professor of Economics at Princeton University and held various administrative posts before becoming Paul M. Warburg Professor of Economics at Harvard in 1949. In 1961–63 he was U.S. Ambassador to India. His written works include *The Great Crash* (1955), *The Affluent Society* (1958), *The Liberal Hour* (1960), *Made to Last* (1964) and *The New Industrial State* (1967).

GALDÓS. See PÉREZ GALDÓS.

GALEN, or Claudius Galenus (*c.* A.D. 130–201), Greek physician, was born at Pergamus in Mysia, and studied medicine there and at Smyrna, Corinth and Alexandria. After 164 he spent four years in Rome, and in 170 was recalled by the emperor M. Aurelius. He afterwards attended Commodus, Sextus and Severus. He is supposed to have died in Sicily. Galen was a voluminous writer on medical and philosophical subjects. The works extant under his name consist of 83 genuine treatises and 15 commentaries on Hippocrates. He was a careful dissector of animals, a somewhat too theoretical physiologist, and so gathered up all the medical knowledge of his time as to become the authority from whom the subsequent Greek and Roman medical writers were mere compilers. He was the first to diagnose by the pulse. See edition by Kühn (1821– 1933), and studies of Greek medicine by

Allbutt (1921), Castiglioni (1947), Singer (1956).

GALERIUS, Galerius Valerius Maximianus (d. 311), Roman emperor, born near Sardica in Dacia, rose high in the army, was made Caesar by Diocletian (292), and on Diocletian's abdication (305) became with Constantius Chlorus joint ruler of the Roman empire, Galerius taking the eastern half. When Constantius died at York (306) the troops in Britain and Gaul transferred their allegiance to his son, Constantine; but Galerius retained the east till his death.

GALGACUS, or Calgacus, the name Tacitus gives to the Caledonian chief defeated by Agricola in the battle of the Grampians (A.D. 86).

GALIANI, Ferdinando, *gah-li-ah'nee* (1728– 1787), Italian economist, born at Chieti, lived in Paris (1760–69) as a Neapolitan secretary of legation on close terms with the Encyclopédistes, and then was a minister of the King of Naples. He wrote against both extreme protection and complete free trade. See his *Correspondance* (1818; new ed. 1881), and Lives by Mattei (Naples 1879) and Nicolini (1909).

GALIGNANI, *gah-lin-yah'nee,* **John Anthony** (1796–1873) and **William** (1798–1882), Parisian publishers, were born in London. They much improved *Galignani's Messenger,* started in Paris by their father in 1814, and made it a medium for advocating cordiality between England and France. The brothers founded at Corbeil a hospital for Englishmen; and in 1889 the Galignani Home for aged printers and booksellers was opened at Neuilly.

GALILEI, Galileo, *gahl-i-lay'ee* (1564–1642), Italian astronomer, was born at Pisa, February 18, and as a student of medicine came to disbelieve and despise the prevailing Aristotelian philosophy. Entering the university of Pisa in 1581, he inferred in 1583 from the oscillations of a suspended lamp in the cathedral (equal in time whatever their range) the value of a pendulum for the exact measurement of time. The study of mathematics led him to invent a hydrostatic balance and write a treatise on specific gravity; and, appointed professor of Mathematics in the university, he propounded and proved the theorem that all falling bodies, great or small, descend with equal velocity. The hostility of the Aristotelians led him to resign his chair (1591) and retire to Florence. When he became professor of Mathematics at Padua (1592–1610), his lectures attracted pupils from all parts of Europe. Among his discoveries were a species of thermometer and a proportional compass or sector; and he perfected the refracting telescope (a Dutch invention of 1608). Galileo pursued a series of astronomical investigations, which convinced him of the correctness of the Copernican theory. He concluded that the moon owed her illumination to reflection, and that her surface was diversified by valleys and mountains. The Milky Way he pronounced a track of countless stars. Another series of observations led to the discovery of four satellites of Jupiter (1610). He also noticed spots on the sun, from whose movement he inferred its rotation. In this year he was recalled to Florence by the Grand-duke of Tuscany. In 1611 he was received with great distinction at Rome. Yet the publication, two years later, of his dissertation on the solar spots, in which he boldly advocated the Copernican system, provoked the censure of the ecclesiastical authorities. He promised (1616) to abstain from all future advocacy of the condemned doctrines. But in 1632 he published the *Dialogo sopra i due massimi sistemi del mondo*, in favour of the Copernican system. Pope Urban VIII was led to believe that Galileo had here satirized him as a timid and blind traditionalist; and Galileo, summoned before the Inquisition, after a wearisome trial and imprisonment, was condemned to abjure his scientific creed. That he was put to the torture is now disbelieved by most authorities. Galileo was further sentenced to indefinite imprisonment by the Inquisition—a sentence commuted by Pope Urban, at the request of the Duke of Tuscany, to permission to reside at Siena, and finally at Florence. At Arcetri, near Florence, he continued his researches, even after hearing and sight were much impaired. Other discoveries of his were the law of uniformly accelerated motion towards the earth, the parabolic path of projectiles, virtual velocities, and the law that all bodies have weight. Just before he became totally blind (1637) he made yet another discovery, that of the moon's monthly and annual librations. See Lives by Viviani (1654), Chasles (1862) and H. Martin (1868); besides works about him and his trial by Wegg-Prosser (1889), Fahie (1903), O'Connor (1925), Cooper (1935), Taylor (1938), Panofsky (1954), G. de Santillana (trans. 1958).

GALITZIN, *ga-lyee-tsin*, or Golyzin, noble Russian family descended from the boyar Mikhail Ivanovich Bulgakov (d. 1554), and prominent in war and diplomacy from the 16th century onwards.

(1) Amalie, Princess (1746–1806), wife of (2) and daughter of a Prussian general, was remarkable for culture, grace and ardent Catholic piety. Having separated from her husband at Münster, she gathered round her a circle of learned companions.

(2) Dimitri (1735–1803), Russian ambassador to France and Holland, father of (3), owes his good name to his wife (1).

(3) Dimitri Augustine (1770–1841), son of (1) and (2), in 1787 became a Roman Catholic, and in 1795 was ordained a priest in the United States. He betook himself to a bleak region among the Alleghanies, where he was known as 'Father Smith', and founded a town, called Loretto. He was vicar-general of Philadelphia from 1821. He wrote *Defence of Catholic Principles* (1816), *Letter to a Protestant Friend* (1820) and *Appeal to the Protestant Public* (1834). See Lives by Heyden and Brownson.

(4) Nicholas Dmitrievitch (1856–1925), governor successively of Archangel, Kaluga and Tver, was for a short time prime minister (1917), the last of the Tsarist empire.

(5) Vasili, surnamed the Great (1643–1714), was the counsellor and favourite of Sophia, sister of Peter the Great, but was banished (1689).

GALL, St (*c.* 550–645), Irish follower of St Columban, fixed in 614 his cell at a point on the Steinach river in Switzerland, round which grew up a great Benedictine abbey and the town of St Gall.

GALL, Franz Joseph (1758–1828), German phrenologist, was born at Tiefenbrunn in Baden and settled in Vienna in 1785 as a physician. He gradually evolved theories by which he traced talents and other qualities to the functions of particular areas of the brain. His lectures on phrenology, now scientifically discredited, were a popular success, but suppressed in 1802 as being subversive of religion. He died at Montrouge near Paris.

GALLAND, Antoine, *gal-lã* (1646–1715), French orientalist, born at Rollot, Picardy, travelled in Syria and the Levant, and became professor in Arabic at the Collège de France. His translation of the *Arabian Nights* (1704–1708) is the first in any western language. See his *Journal* (1881).

GALLAS, Matthias von, Count of Campo and Duke of Lucera (1584–1647), Austrian soldier, born at Trient, became one of Wallenstein's chief commanders in the Thirty Years' War and succeeded Wallenstein after the latter's murder, in which he was implicated. He was beaten at Breitenach (1631), but won a decisive victory over the Swedes at Nördlingen (1634). After an uncertain tenure of command he was dismissed in 1645.

GALLATIN, Albert, *gal-la-ti'* (1761–1849), Swiss-American financier and statesman, a cousin of Mme de Staël, born at Geneva, graduated there in 1779. He went in 1780 to the United States, taught French at Harvard, bought land in Virginia and Pennyslvania, in 1793 was elected a senator, in 1795 a representative, and in 1801–13 was secretary of the Treasury. He took an important part in the peace negotiations with Britain in 1814, and signed the Treaty of Ghent. In 1815–23 he was minister at Paris, in 1826 at London. He wrote on finance, politics, and the Indian tribes. See Lives by Adams (1879) and Steven (1883), and the Diary (1914) of his son and secretary, James Gallatin.

GALLE, Johann Gottfried (1812–1910), German astronomer, born at Pabsthaus, near Wittenberg, discovered in 1846 the planet Neptune, whose existence had been already postulated in the calculations of Leverrier (q.v.). In 1851–57 he was director of Breslau observatory.

GALLÉN-KALLELA, Akseli Valdemar (1865–1931), Finnish painter, born at Pori. A pioneer of the national romantic style, he chose his themes mainly from Finnish mythology.

GALLI-CURCI, Amelita, *gal'lee koor'chee* (1882–1963), Italian soprano, born in Milan. Although a prize-winning piano student at Milan Conservatory, as a singer she was self-taught, and first appeared in opera in 1909. Her brilliance of style was attractive enough to compensate for deficiencies of technique, and in 1916 she joined Chicago Opera Company. From 1919 onwards, she worked principally at the Metropolitan Opera, New York, and was first heard in Britain in 1924.

GALLIÉNI, Joseph Simon, *gall-yay'nee* (1849–1916), French soldier, born at St Béat, Haute

Garonne, served in the war of 1870–71 in West Africa and Tonkin, was governor of Upper Senegal from 1886, governor-general of Madagascar 1897–1905, minister for war, and as military governor of Paris from 1914 saw to its fortifications and contributed to the victory of the Marne (1914) by his foresight and planning. He was posthumously created Marshal of France.

GALLIENNE, Richard Le. See LE GALLIENNE.

GALLIENUS, Publius Licinius (c. 218–268), Roman emperor, was from A.D. 253 colleague and from 260 successor to his father, Valerian. But his authority was limited to Italy, for throughout the provinces the legions revolted, and proclaimed their commanders Caesars. Hence the period is known as the Time of the Thirty Tyrants. In 268, while besieging one of his rivals in Milan, he was murdered by some of his officers.

GALLIO, Junius Annaeus (1st cent. A.D.), Roman proconsul of Achaia under Claudius and brother of Seneca (q.v.), dismissed the charge brought by the Jews against St Paul at Corinth in A.D. 52.

GALLUP, George Horace (1901–), American public opinion expert, was born in Iowa and became professor of Journalism in Drake University (1929–31) and Northwestern University (1931–32). After five years as director of research for an advertising agency, he became professor in the Pulitzer School of Journalism, Columbia University. In 1935, he founded the American Institute of Public Opinion, and evolved the Gallup Polls for testing the state of public opinion. He has written *Public Opinion in a Democracy* (1939), and *Guide to Public Opinion Polls* (1944 and 1948).

GALLUS, (1) C. Cornelius (c. 70–26 B.C.), Roman poet, born at Forum Julii (mod. Fréjus) in Gaul, lived at Rome in intimate friendship with Virgil and Ovid; was appointed by Augustus prefect of Egypt; but, having fallen into disfavour and been banished, killed himself. Gallus was reckoned the founder of the Roman elegy, from his four books of elegies upon his mistress Lycoris, of which but a few fragments are extant.

(2) **Trebonianus** (reigned 251–253), Roman emperor, is memorable for the dishonourable peace he purchased from the Goths. He was murdered by his own soldiers.

GALOIS, Évariste, *gah-lwah* (1811–32), French mathematician, killed in a senseless duel, is noted for his group substitutions and theory of functions.

GALSWORTHY, John (1867–1933), English novelist and playwright, was born at Combe, Surrey, of a Devonshire family and educated at Harrow and Oxford. He was called to the bar, but elected to travel and set up as a writer. From the start he was the moralist and humanitarian, but his novels were also to be documentary to the times, and this the great sequence *The Forsyte Saga* may well claim to be. The sequence began with *A Man of Property* (1906), which is highly interesting as a period piece and started a new vogue in novel writing. Along with *In Chancery* (1920) and *To Let* (1921), it formed the first

part of *The Forsyte Saga* (1922). In these novels we have recorded for all time a departed way of life, that of the affluent middle class which ruled England before the 1914 war. The class is criticized on account of its possessiveness, but there is also nostalgia, for Galsworthy as a man born into the class could also appreciate its virtues. This nostalgia deepens when the record is resumed in what was collectively entitled *A Modern Comedy* (1929) which includes *The White Monkey* (1924), *The Silver Spoon* and *Swan Song* (1928). In this second cycle of the Saga the postwar generation is in the dock, but not without the author's appreciation of their plight in an age in which their world had crashed. Apart from the brilliant portrait of Soames in old age, the characters most deeply etched in the reader's mind are the old men, Old Jolyon and Old Anthony, who are pathetic but who hold by the old standards. He is not, however, so successful with his women characters—Soames' wife Irene is a tiresome beauty—or with the servants or common folk who come in merely to serve their betters. Among Galsworthy's other well-known novels are *The Island Pharisees* (1904), *The Country House* (1907), *Fraternity* (1909), and *The Patrician* (1911). In the first named he arraigned English hypocrisy, and this raises the question how far he was prepared to question the moral basis of his class and country. The answer is probably to be found in *A Novelist's Allegory*, which is one of the pieces in his collection *The Inn of Tranquillity* (1912) where Cethru answers the charge of endangering ' the laws by causing persons to desire to change them '. Galsworthy's plays best illustrate his reforming zeal, and also his sentimentality. *Strife* (1909) shows employers and men locked in a four-month struggle, which ends through the death of the strike-leader's wife. *The Skin Game* (1920) attempts to hold the scales between the aristocratic Mr Hillcrist and the rich parvenu Hornblower, but the latter is so vulgar that sympathies are tipped against him. *The Silver Box* turns on justice as meted out to the rich and to the poor. *Justice* (1910) did help to achieve its object of humanizing the penal code. Technically these plays are first-rate theatre but marred, especially in the later ones, *A Bit o' Love* and *Loyalties* (1922), by the parsimony of the language in dialogue which did well enough in the novels but makes the plays appear rather bare. See Marrot, *Life and Letters of John Galsworthy* (1934) and R. H. Mottram, *For Some We Loved* (1956); also studies by Herman Ould (1934) and A. C. Ward in *Twentieth Century Literature* (3rd ed. 1956).

GALT, gawlt, (1) Sir Alexander Tilloch (1817–1893), Canadian statesman, son of (2), born at Chelsea, entered the Canadian parliament in 1849, and was finance minister 1858–62 and 1864–66, high commissioner in Britain 1880–83. See Life by Skelton (1920).

(2) **John** (1779–1839), Scottish novelist and Canadian pioneer, born at Irvine, and educated at Greenock, travelled for health's sake in the Levant, where he met Byron. On his return he published *Letters from the*

Levant, &c. *The Ayrshire Legatees* appeared in *Blackwood* in 1820. Its successor, *The Annals of the Parish* (1821), is his masterpiece, in which the description of events in the life of a parish minister throws interesting light on contemporary social history. He produced in quick succession *Sir Andrew Wylie, The Entail, The Steamboat* and *The Provost*. His historical romances were less successful. He went to Canada in 1826, founded the town of Guelph, and played a prominent part in organizing immigration, but returned ruined in 1829, and produced a new novel, *Lawrie Todd.* He wrote also a *Life of Byron* and an autobiography (1834), and died at Greenock. In depicting life in small towns and villages Galt is without a rival. He possesses rich humour, genuine pathos and a rare mastery of Scottish dialect. See Lives by Gordon (1920) and Aberdeen (1936).

GALTON, Sir Francis (1822–1911), British scientist and explorer, grandson of Dr Erasmus Darwin, and cousin of Charles Darwin, was born at Birmingham, and educated at King Edward's School. He studied medicine at the Birmingham Hospital and King's College, London, and graduated from Trinity College, Cambridge, in 1844. Having in 1846 travelled in North Africa, he explored in 1850 lands hitherto unknown in South Africa, publishing *Narrative of an Explorer in Tropical South Africa* and *Art of Travel* (1855). His investigations in meteorology are recorded in *Meteorographica* (1863). Latterly he devoted himself to heredity, founding and endowing the study of eugenics, and publishing *Hereditary Genius* (1869); *English Men of Science: their Nature and Nurture* (1874); *Natural Inheritance* (1889); *Finger Prints* (1892); &c. His researches into colour blindness and mental imagery were also of great value. See his *Memories of my Life* (1908), and Life by Karl Pearson (1914–30).

GALUPPI, Baldassaro, *gal-oop'pee* (1706–85), Italian light operatic composer, born near Venice, resident in London (1741–44), wrote the popular *Il filosofo di campagna*, sacred music and sonatas. See studies by Raabe (1929) and Bollert (1935).

GALVANI, Luigi, *gal-vah'nee* (1737–98), Italian physiologist, was born at Bologna, studied there, and in 1762 became professor of Anatomy. He discovered animal electricity by connecting the leg muscle of a frog to its corresponding nerve, wrongly believing the source of the current to be in the material of muscle and nerve.

GAMA, Vasco da (*c.* 1469–1525), Portuguese navigator, was born at Sines in Alemtejo. He early distinguished himself as an intrepid mariner, and was selected by King Emanuel to discover the route to India round the Cape. The expedition of three vessels with 168 men left Lisbon July 8, 1497, but was four months in reaching St Helena. After rounding the Cape, despite hurricanes and mutinies, he made Melinda early in the following year. Here he found a skilful Indian pilot, crossed the Indian Ocean, and arrived at Calicut, May 20, 1498. The ruler of Calicut soon became actively hostile, and da Gama had to fight his way out of the harbour. In

September 1499 he arrived at Lisbon, and was ennobled. Emanuel immediately dispatched a fresh squadron of thirteen ships under Cabral, who founded a factory at Calicut. But the forty Portuguese left there were murdered, and to avenge them the king fitted out a squadron of twenty ships under da Gama (1502), which founded the colonies of Mozambique and Sofala, bombarded Calicut, and reached the Tagus with thirteen richly-laden vessels in December 1503. For twenty years da Gama lived inactive at Evora, while the extended Portuguese conquests were presided over by five viceroys. The fifth was so unfortunate that John III in 1524 dispatched da Gama to India, where he succeeded in making Portugal once more respected, but died at Cochin, December 24, 1525; his body was brought home to Portugal. See Camoëns, *The Three Voyages of Vasco da Gama,* (trans. 1869), the *Journal* of his first voyage (1898), a German Life by Hümmerich (1898), and English Lives by Jayne (1911) and G. Hamilton (1951).

GAMAGE, Albert Walter (1855–1930), English merchant, born in Hereford, became a draper's apprentice in London, and in 1878 founded the famous store in Holborn which bears his name.

GAMALIEL, *ga-mayl'yel* (d. *c.* A.D. 50), St Paul's teacher, was a prominent Pharisee, and taught 'the law' early in the 1st century. Tolerant and peaceful, he seems to have placed Christianity on a par with other sects; and he encouraged long-suffering on all sides.

GAMBETTA, Léon Michel (1838–82), French politician, born at Cahors, of Genoese-Jewish extraction, April 3, became a member of the Paris bar in 1859, attracted attention by his advanced liberal views, and in 1869 was elected deputy. After the surrender of Napoleon III Gambetta was one of the proclaimers of the Republic, September 4, 1870. As minister of the Interior in the Government of National Defence, he escaped from Paris under siege by balloon to Tours, and for five months was dictator of France. In spite of the surrender of Metz he called up every man after army, and sent them against the Germans; even when Paris capitulated, he demanded that the war should be carried on to the end. His colleagues in Paris having repudiated his decree from Bordeaux disfranchising all members of royal dynasties, he resigned, and retired into Spain (1871). Elected again, he took no part in the suppression of the Commune. After its fall he became the chief of the advanced Republicans. When the Duc de Broglie took office (May 1877) in the hope of restoring the monarchy, a civil war seemed imminent, but was averted by Gambetta, and Marshal MacMahon, the president, refrained from pushing matters to an extremity. Gambetta was imprisoned and fined for having declared respecting MacMahon, '*Il faudra ou se soumettre, ou se démettre*', but two months later he was re-elected for Belleville, and in 1879 MacMahon resigned. In November 1880, on the resignation of the Ferry ministry, Gambetta, from 1879 president of the chamber, succeeded in forming a cabinet, but when in January 1882 the chamber rejected his *scrutin de liste* proposal he immediately resigned. He died December 31, from the effects of ' an accidental wound in the hand from a revolver '. See his *Discours politiques* and *Dépêches* (1880–92)—his Letters (ed. Halévy and Pilias 1938). See also studies by Bury (1936), Labarthe (1938), and Laur (trs. 1908), who says he died of appendicitis.

GAMBIER, James Gambier, 1st Baron (1756–1833), British admiral, was born in the Bahamas, and off Ushant fought with distinction under Lord Howe in 1794. He commanded the British fleet at Copenhagen in 1807, and was rewarded with a peerage. At the battle of Aix Roads in 1809 he disregarded the signals of Dundonald (q.v.), but was acquitted by a court martial.

GAMELIN, Maurice Gustave, *gam-lǐ* (1872–1958), French general, after passing through the Military Academy of St Cyr, was commissioned in the *Tirailleurs Algériens*. Appointed *aide-de-camp* to General Joffre in 1906, he became his *chef de cabinet* in 1911. He attained lieutenant-colonel's rank in 1914, but no divisional command until 1925. In 1935 seniority brought him the post of chief of staff of the army and membership of the *Conseil Supérieur de la Guerre*; but his fitness for overall command was exposed in his pronouncement that ' To attack is to lose '. In 1940, blind to the lessons of the 1939 Polish campaign, he refused to re-think his outmoded defensive strategy of ' solid fronts ', which crumbled under the German *blitzkrieg*. He was hurriedly replaced by General Weygand and retired into obscurity.

GANDHI, (1) **Indira** (1917–), Indian politician, daughter of Nehru (q.v.), born at Allahabad, education included a year at Somerville College, Oxford. She was deeply involved in the independence issue, and spent a year in prison. She married Feroze Gandhi (d. 1960) in 1942. Member of central committee of Indian Congress (1950), president of party (1959–60), minister of information (1964), she took over as prime minister in 1966 after the death of Shastri.

(2) **Mohandâs Karamchand** (1869–1948), Indian leader, born at Porbandar, Kathiawar. He studied law in London, and in 1893 he gave up a Bombay legal practice worth £5000 a year to live on £1 a week in South Africa, where he spent twenty-one years opposing discriminatory legislation against Indians. In 1914 he returned to India. While supporting the British in World War I, he took an increasing interest in the Home Rule movement (*Swaraj*), over which he soon obtained a personal dominance, becoming master of the Congress organization. His civil disobedience campaign of 1920 involved violent disorders. From 1922 to 1924 he was in jail for conspiracy and in 1930 he led a 200-mile march to sea to collect salt in symbolic defiance of the Government monopoly. He was rearrested and on his release in 1931 negotiated a truce between Congress and the Government and attended the London Round Table Conference on Indian constitutional reform. Back in India, he renewed the civil disobedience campaign and was arrested again—the pattern, along with his ' fasts unto death ', of his political activity for the next six years. He assisted in the adoption of the constitutional compromise of 1937 under which Congress ministers accepted office in the new provincial legislatures. When war broke out, Gandhi, convinced that only a free India could give Britain effective moral support, urged ' complete independence ' more and more strongly. He described the Cripps proposal in 1942 for a constituent assembly with the promise of a new Constitution after the war as ' a post-dated cheque on a crashing bank '. In August 1942 he was arrested for concurring in civil disobedience action to obstruct the war effort, and was released in May 1944. In 1946 Gandhi negotiated with the British Cabinet Mission which recommended the new constitutional structure. In May 1947 he hailed Britain's decision to grant India independence as ' the noblest act of the British nation '. His last months were darkened by communal strife between Hindu and Moslem; but his fasts to shame the instigators helped to avert deeper tragedy. He was assassinated in Delhi by a Hindu fanatic, on January 30, 1948—ten days after a previous attempt on his life. In his lifetime Mahatma ('great soul') Gandhi was venerated as a moral teacher, a reformer who sought an India as free from caste as from materialism, a dedicated patriot who gave the Swaraj movement a new quality. Critics, however, thought him the victim of a power of self-delusion which blinded him to the disaster and bloodshed his ' nonviolent ' campaigns invoked. But in Asia particularly he has been regarded as a great influence for peace whose teaching had a message not only for India—of whose nationhood he became the almost mystical incarnation—but for the world. His publications include the autobiographical *The Story of My Experiment with Truth* (republished 1949). See studies by H. S. L. Polak (1949), L. Fischer (1954), B. R. Nanda (1958) and G. Ashe (1968).

GANN, Thomas William (1868–1938), British archaeologist. His field of activity was Central America, where he was responsible for the discovery of several ancient cities. Gann was an expert on Maya architecture and the tribes of Central America.

GANSFORT, Wessel Harmens. See W<small>ESSEL</small> (2).

GARBETT, Cyril Foster (1875–1955), Archbishop of York from 1942 to 1955, was born at Tongham, near Aldershot, and was educated at Portsmouth Grammar School, Keble College and Cuddesdon College, Oxford. He was Bishop of Southwark from 1919 to 1932 and of Winchester from 1932 till his translation to York in 1942. He was one of the most outspoken leaders of the Church, a prelate of great pastoral gifts and a humanitarian remembered for his warmth of personality and strength of character. Publications include *The Church and Social Problems* (1939) and a trilogy on Church and State (1947–52). See *Life* by C. Smyth (1959).

GARBO, Greta, professional name of **Greta Lovisa Gustafsson** (1905–), Swedish film actress, born in Stockholm, went to the Royal Theatre Dramatic School, Stockholm, and starred in Stiller's *Gösta Berling's Saga* (1924); he gave his star the name Garbo, chosen before he met her. She went to the U.S. in 1925, and her greatest successes followed *Anna Christie* (1930), her first talking picture—*Queen Christina* (1933), *Anna Karenina* (1935), *Camille* (1937), and *Ninotchka* (1939). She retired from films in 1941, after the failure of *Two-Faced Woman*. She became an American citizen in 1951. See Life by Bainbridge (1955).

GARBORG, Arne (1851–1924), Norwegian 'landsmaal' storywriter (from 1881), a native of Jaeren, early became a leader of the language reform movement, editing the weekly periodical *Fedraheimen* from 1877, which was written in the popular language (*Landsmaal*). In it he serialized his first novel, *Ein Fritenkjar* ('a freethinker'), which was followed by *Bondestudentar* (1883) and *Mannfolk* (1886) in the contemporary ultra-realistic manner. But he reacted against this school in *Trette Men* ('tired men') (1891). Greatly troubled by religious problems, he wrote the drama *Laeraren* (1896), and several poems. In two controversial works (1906 and 1907) he attacked Lutheran theology. See Lives by Mortensson-Egmund (1897) and Midttun (1929).

GARCÍA, gar-thee'a, (1) Manuel (1775–1832), Spanish tenor and composer, father of (2), (3), (4), was born at Seville. After making a reputation as a tenor in Cadiz and Madrid, from 1808 onward he won great success at the Italian Opera in Paris, Italy and London. In 1825, with an operatic company, he visited New York and Mexico, where he was robbed of all his money; and after his return to Paris was compelled to teach singing. Several of his compositions, such as *Il Califo di Bagdad* were much admired.

(2) **Manuel** (1805–1906), son of (1), born at Zafra in Catalonia, taught singing in Paris and London, wrote on the art, and invented the laryngoscope.

(3) **Maria**, daughter of (1). See MALIBRAN.

(4) **Paulina Viardot-García** (1821–1910), mezzo-soprano singer, daughter of (1), composed operettas and songs.

GARCÍA GUTIÉRREZ, Antonio, goo-tyer'reth (1813–84), Spanish poet and scientist, born at Chiclana de la Frontera, Cadiz. An exponent of 19th-century romanticism, he scored an early success with *El Trovador* (1836), the play which inspired Verdi's opera. His chief claim to notice in literature lies in his versification, which reads smoothly and melodiously. He published two volumes of lyric poetry, *Luz y Tinieblas*. Plays by him worthy of mention are *La Culpa y la espacion* (1844), *Venganza Catalana* (1864) and *Juan Lorenzo* (1865), which was regarded as his masterpiece. See N. B. Adams, *The Romantic Dramas of García Gutiérrez* (N.Y. 1924).

GARCIA LORCA. See LORCA.

GARCILASO DE LA VEGA, (1) (1503–36), Spanish poet and soldier, born at Toledo, fought bravely in the wars of Charles V, and died at Nice of a wound received near Fréjus. Little as he wrote, he introduced the Petrarchian sonnet into Spain and wrote odes in imitation of Virgil. See studies by Croce (1894) and Keniston (1922).

(2) called **El Inca** (c. 1540–c. 1616), Spanish writer, born at Cuzco, son of one of the conquerors of Peru by an Inca princess, at twenty went to Spain, where he died. His account of the conquest of Florida by Fernando de Soto (1605) was followed in 1609–17 by his great *Comentarios*, in which he movingly describes the legends and beliefs of his mother's people (trans. Markham, 1869). See Lives by Mrs Fitzmaurice-Kelly (1921) and Sánchez (1939).

GARDINER, (1) Allen Francis (1794–1851), English naval commander, born at Basildon, Berks, who in 1838 became a missionary to the Chilean Indians, and died in Patagonia.

(2) **James** (1688–1745), British soldier, born at Carriden in Linlithgowshire, January 11, when fourteen obtained a commission in a Scots regiment in the Dutch service. In 1702 he passed into the English army, in 1706 was severely wounded at Ramillies, and fought in all Marlborough's other battles. In 1715 he was made captain of dragoons, and with eleven others (eight of whom were killed), fired the barricades of the Highlanders at Preston. He had been noted for his licentiousness; but in 1719 a vision is said to have converted him. He was promoted colonel in 1743. Deserted by his men at Prestonpans, he put himself at the head of a handful of infantry, and was killed. See Life by Dr Doddridge (1747).

(3) **Samuel Rawson** (1829–1902), English historian, was born at Ropley, Hants, and educated at Winchester and Christ Church, Oxford. For some years he filled the chair of Modern History at King's College, London, but resigned it in 1885 to continue his *History* at Oxford on an All Souls' fellowship. In 1882 he was granted a pension. The first instalment of his great *History of England from the accession of James I to the Restoration* appeared in 1863; and at his death he had brought the work down to 1656. He had also published *The Thirty Years' War* (1874), *Introduction to the Study of English History* (1881), written in conjunction with J. Bass Mullinger, and *The Student's History of England* (1890–1892).

(4) **Stephen** (c. 1483–1555), English prelate, born at Bury St Edmunds, studied at Trinity Hall, Cambridge, became Wolsey's secretary, and between 1527 and 1533 was sent to Rome to further Henry VIII's divorce, having been made in 1531 Bishop of Winchester. He supported the royal supremacy in his *De Vera Obedientia* (1535), helped to encompass Thomas Cromwell's downfall, and to frame the Six Articles, but opposed doctrinal reformation, and for this was imprisoned and deprived on Edward VI's accession. Released and restored by Mary in 1553 he became an arch-persecutor of Protestants. See Life by Muller (1926).

GARFIELD, James Abram (1831–81), 20th president of the United States, was born in Orange, Ohio, November 19. At ten he already added to his widowed mother's income by farm work. A graduate of Williams College, he taught in a school, served as a lay preacher, became a lawyer and was elected to the state senate in 1859. On the outbreak of the Civil War, he commanded a regiment of volunteers. His brigade gained the battle of Middle Creek, January 10, 1862, and he was promoted brigadier-general. He had been made major-general for gallantry at Chickamauga (1863), when he resigned his command to enter congress, where he sat until 1880, acting as leader of the Republican party. In 1880, now a U.S. senator, he was adopted as presidential candidate by the Republicans. After his election to the presidency (March 1881) he identified himself with the cause of civil service reform, thereby irritating a powerful section of his own party. On the morning of July 2 he was shot by a disappointed office-seeker, Charles Guiteau, and died September 19. His speeches were published in 1882. See Lives by T. C. Smith (1925) and R. G. Caldwell (1931).

GARIBALDI, Giuseppe (1807–82), Italian patriot, was born a sailor's son at Nice, July 4, and himself went early to sea. In 1834 he became involved in the ' Young Italy ' movement of Mazzini, and was condemned to death for taking part in an attempt to seize Genoa. He escaped ultimately to South America, where in the rebellion of Rio Grande against Brazil he distinguished himself as a guerilla fighter and privateer, was taken prisoner, and eloped with and married the beautiful Creole, Anita Riveira de Silva, the mother of his children Menotti, Ricciotti and Teresa. After some experiences as drover, shipbroker, and teacher of mathematics, he in 1842 joined the Montevideans, then at war with Buenos Aires, and gained renown as naval commander and as organizer of the Italian legion. In 1847 he offered his services to the reforming pope, Pius IX, but received an ambiguous reply; and Charles Albert of Sardinia, besieging the Austrians in Mantua in 1848, coldly referred him to his ministers. But after the collapse of the Sardinian army, Garibaldi and his volunteers performed notable feats against the Austrians. In 1849 he joined the revolutionary government of Rome, voted for a republic, drove back the French force, and routed the Neapolitans. Mazzini had meanwhile been inveigled into an armistice; the French, reinforced, laid siege to Rome; and Garibaldi, recalled, made a brilliant defence, but was forced to retreat, pursued by the Austrians, to the Adriatic; in this flight Anita died. Arrested by the Sardinian government and requested to leave Italy, he betook himself to New York, where he worked eighteen months as a candlemaker, and then became captain of a Pacific merchantman. He returned to Italy in 1854, and had settled down as a farmer on the island of Caprera, when in 1859 the war of Italian liberation enabled him to render valuable service to Victor Emmanuel and the French. After the peace of Villafranca he helped to annex various territories to Sardinia, but was not allowed to march on Rome. Meanwhile the Mazzinists had been conspiring against the Bourbon tyranny in the Two Sicilies, and Garibaldi, in spite of Cavour, came to their aid. ' The thousand heroes ' landed at Marsala on May 11, 1860; within three months Sicily was free; and crossing the straits (August 29) Garibaldi entered Naples (September 7) amid the cheers of King Francis' troops. When Victor Emmanuel, elected sovereign by a plebiscite, arrived at Naples, Garibaldi, refusing all reward, retired to Caprera. Rome was still the centre of his thoughts, and in 1862 he embarked on a rash expedition against the capital; but the Italian government sent troops against him, and he was taken prisoner at Aspromonte (August 28). He paid a visit to England to support the cause of Denmark, and was received by the public with wild enthusiasm, but requested to return home by the government. In the war of 1866 he once more commanded the ' Red Shirts ' in Tirol. Venice was now ceded to Italy; and next year Garibaldi made his last attempt on the Holy City. Arrested by the Italian government, he escaped from Caprera, and with his volunteers defeated the papal troops at Monterotondo, but was a few days after (November 3) utterly routed at Mentana by the Zouaves and French. Once more he retired to Caprera, whence in 1870 he published two poor novels. A third (1872) was based on the Sicilian expedition. In 1870 he came to the assistance of the French Republic, and was placed in command of the volunteers of the Vosges; but, crippled by rheumatism and hopelessly outnumbered, he had no considerable success, and, elected to the Bordeaux assembly, was so insulted as to resign at once. Henceforth he remained a helpless invalid at Caprera, except on occasions like that in 1874, when he took his seat in the Chamber of Deputies at Rome; and through the generosity of English friends he became proprietor of the island. An unlucky marriage of 1860 was annulled in 1879, and he married in 1880 the nurse of his grandchildren. On June 2, 1882, he died. He was a good commander of irregulars but his ignorance of politics sometimes did harm to his cause, yet he remains the central figure in the story of Italian independence. See Garibaldi's autobiography (trans. 1889); his letters (1885); his speeches (1882); Lives by J. T. Bent (1881), D. Larg (1934); and works on him by Mario (1884), Trevelyan (3 works, new eds. 1948), Provaglio (Florence 1950) and Mack Smith (1954).

GARLAND, Hamlin (1860–1940), American writer, born at West Salem, Wisconsin, often interrupted his schooling to help his father farm in Iowa, but in 1884 went to Boston to teach and finally to write. In short stories such as the collections, *Main Travelled Roads* (1887) and *Prairie Folks* (1892), in verse and in novels, he vividly, often grimly, described the farmlife of the Midwest. *A Daughter of the Middle Border* (1921), the sequel to his autobiographical novel *A Son of the Middle Border* (1917), won the Pulitzer prize. He also wrote a Life of General Grant (1898), critical essays and literary reminiscences.

GARNET, Henry (1555–1606), English conspirator, born at Heanor, Derbyshire, was brought up a Protestant at Winchester. He became a Jesuit in 1575, and from 1587 was provincial in England. His indiscreet zeal for his order offended the secular clergy;

while his friendship with the Spanish faction exposed him to a suspicion of treason. He knew long beforehand of Guy Fawkes's plot; on the discovery he was present at the rendezvous, and shortly afterwards was apprehended. He was executed May 3. See works cited at FAWKES.

GARNETT, (1) **David** (1892–   ), English novelist, son of (2), born at Brighton, studied botany at the Royal College of Science. His first book, *Lady into Fox* (1922), won both the Hawthornden and the Tait Black Memorial prize. *A Man in the Zoo* (1924), *The Sailor's Return* (1925), &c., were also successful. Literary adviser to the Nonesuch Press (1923–32) and literary editor of the *New Statesman* (1932–34), he joined the R.A.F. in 1939, and used his experience to write *War in the Air* (1941). See C. G. Heilburn, *The Garnett Family* (1961).

(2) **Edward** (1868–1937), son of (4), writer and critic, author of the set of critical essays *Friday Nights* (1922), and (with his wife, Constance) of translations from the Russian.

(3) **Richard** (1789–1850), father of (4), English philologist, born in Otley, was a founder of the Philological Society and an expert on Celtic subjects.

(4) **Richard** (1835–1906), English writer and bibliographer, son of (3), father of (2), born at Lichfield, was keeper of printed books at the British Museum (1890–99), and author of verse, critical works and biographies including *Shelley* (1862), *Carlyle* (1883), *Twilight of the Gods* (1888) and *The Age of Dryden* (1895).

GARNIER, *garn-yay*, (1) **Francis**, properly **Marie Joseph François** (1839–73), French explorer, was born at St Étienne and entering the navy, fought in the Chinese war (1860–62). Appointed to a post in Cochin-China, he led an expedition from Cambodia to Shanghai by Yunnan (1866–68). He aided in the defence of Paris (1870–71), and in the Tonkin war (1873) took Hanoi, but was killed in a fight. See his *Voyage d'exploration* (1873) and Life by Petit (1885).

(2) **Robert** (1534–90), French poet and playwright, the most distinguished of the predecessors of Corneille, was born in Maine, and died at Le Mans. His *Oeuvres complètes* (2 v.) include eight masterly tragedies of which perhaps the best are *Antigone* (1580) and *Les Juives* (1583). For his influence on English drama, see Witherspoon (Yale 1924).

GARNIER-PAGÈS, *-pah-zhes*, two French half-brothers, both lawyers and politicians:

(1) **Étienne Joseph Louis** (1801–41), born at Marseilles, practised as an advocate, took part in the July Revolution, and in 1831 became a prominent member of the Chamber.

(2) **Louis Antoine** (1803–78), succeeded (1) in the Chamber, leading the extreme Left. Mayor of Paris (1848) and finance minister of the provisional government, he was a member of the Corps Législatif in 1864, and of the provisional government in 1871. He wrote *Histoire de la Révolution de 1848* (1861–62) and *L'Opposition et l'Empire* (1872).

GAROFALO, *gah-ro'fah-lō*, originally **Benvenuto Tisi** (1481–1559), Italian painter, born and died at Ferrara and the last and foremost

artist of the Ferrarese school. He worked chiefly in the churches and palaces of his native city, in Bologna and in Rome. The church of San Lorenzo, Ferrara, contains his *Adoration of the Magi*, and his *Sacrifice to Ceres* is in the National Gallery, London.

GARRETT, (1) **João**. See ALMEIDA-GARRETT.

(2) **Misses**. See ANDERSON, FAWCETT.

GARRICK, **David** (1717–79), English actor, manager and dramatist, was born at Hereford, February 20, where his father, Capt. Peter Garrick, was then stationed. Lichfield, however, was the home of the Garricks, and David got his education in its grammar school. In 1736 he was sent to study Latin and Greek under Samuel Johnson at Edial, and in March 1737 master and pupil set out together to London—Garrick to study for the bar, Johnson to try his fortune with his pen. But circumstances brought Garrick's legal studies to nothing, and in 1738 he became a winemerchant with his eldest brother—a partnership dissolved in 1740. Garrick, who before this had the stage fever, now devoted his mind to preparing himself for the stage, and in 1741 he made his successful début at Ipswich as Aboan in Southerne's *Oroonoko*. On October 19 he appeared in London at Goodman's Fields; and his success as Richard III was so great that within a few weeks the two patent theatres were deserted, and crowds flocked to the unfashionable East End playhouse. But, as Goodman's Fields had no licence, the managers of Drury Lane and Covent Garden had it closed. Garrick played at both the patent theatres, and ultimately settled at Drury Lane, of which he became joint-patentee in 1747. He retired from the stage and from management in 1776. During this period Garrick was himself the great attraction and played continually, his only long rest being a trip to the Continent in 1763–65, when he fancied that his popularity was in danger of diminishing. He died January 20, and was buried in Westminster Abbey. He remains the most versatile actor in the history of the British stage. He was equally at home in tragedy, comedy or farce. His great conventional fault was that he always wanted to ' improve Shakespeare '. He has been unfairly charged with meanness, vanity and petty jealousy; Garrick's forty dramatic productions are not important, but some of his numerous prologues and epilogues are excellent. He married in 1749 Eva Marie Violetti (1724–1822), a Catholic Viennese dancer. See Lives by P. Fitzgerald (1868), Knight (1894), Mrs Parsons (1906), Hedgcock (1912), Stein (1938), Barton (1948) and C. Oman (1958).

GARRISON, **William Lloyd** (1805–79), American philanthropist, was born at Newburyport, Mass. He was apprenticed to the printing trade and in 1824 became editor of the *Newburyport Herald* and in 1828 of the *National Philanthropist*. The vigorous expression of his antislavery views led to his imprisonment for libel; but friends paid his fine. He delivered emancipation lectures in New York and other places, and returning to Boston, in 1831 started the *Liberator*, a paper which he carried on until slavery was abolished in the United States. For the first few years he was constantly threatened and was subjected to mob violence, but he persevered. In 1833, 1846 and 1848 he visited Great Britain, and on his first return organized the Antislavery Society, of which he was president. He died at New York, May 24, 1879. See Lives by his children (1893), Johnson (1881) and Swift (1911).

GARROD, (1) **Sir Alfred Baring** (1819–1907), English physician, father of (2) and (3), born at Ipswich, professor of Therapeutics at University and King's College hospitals, London (1851–74), a great authority on gout. He was knighted in 1887.

(2) **Alfred Henry** (1846–79), zoologist, son of (1), professor at King's College, London (1874–79), researched into the anatomy and myology of birds and ruminants.

(3) **Sir Archibald Edward** (1857–1936), pathologist, son of (1) and father of (4), born in London, studied at Oxford and became regius professor of Medicine there in 1920. He did research on rheumatism, urinary pigments, and rare metabolic diseases. He was vice-president of the Royal Society (1926–28) and was knighted in 1918.

(4) **Dorothy Annie Elizabeth** (1892–1968), archaeologist, daughter of (3), studied at Newnham College, Cambridge, directed expeditions to Kurdistan (1928) and Palestine (1929–34), and took part in excavations in the Lebanon (1958–64). She became the first woman professor at Cambridge in 1939.

(5) **Heathcote William** (1878–1960), English scholar, born at Wells, was educated at Oxford, where he won the Gaisford Prize (1900) and the Newdigate (1901), and became a fellow of Merton. He edited classical texts and the *Oxford Book of Latin Verse* (1912) and was professor of Poetry (1923–28). He wrote much on the art of poetry and on poets, and published essays of considerable charm and humour.

GARSHIN, Vsevolod Mikhailovich (1855–88), Russian author, born at Bachmut, wrote short stories, greatly influenced by Tolstoi, many of which have been translated, including *The Red Flower* (1883), and *The Signal* (1912). He served in the Turkish war, and was wounded and invalided home in 1878, his mind being unbalanced.

GARSTIN, Sir William Edmund (1849–1925), English engineer, born in India, was educated at Cheltenham and King's College, London, and in 1872 became an official in the Indian Public Works Department. Transferred to Egypt in 1885, he became inspector-general of irrigation in 1892 and under-secretary of state for public works. He was responsible for the plans and building of the Aswan dam and the barrages of Asyut and Esna, compiled two valuable reports on the hydrography of the Upper Nile, erected the new buildings of the National Museum of Egyptian Antiquities (1902) and initiated the geological survey of Egypt (1896). On his retirement, he became a director of the Suez Canal Company (1908) and, during World War I, served on the council of the Red Cross Society, being awarded the G.C.B. in 1918. He was created C.M.G. (1894), K.C.M.G. (1897) and G.C.M.G. (1902).

GARTH, Sir Samuel (1661–1719), English physician and poet, was born at Bowland Forest, Yorkshire. In 1700 he provided burial in Westminster Abbey for the neglected Dryden. By George I he was knighted and appointed physician in ordinary, and physician-general to the army. *The Dispensary* (1699) is a satire on uncharitable apothecaries and physicians. *Claremont* (1715) is a topographical poem in the manner of Pope's ' Windsor Forest '. He also edited a composite translation of Ovid's *Metamorphoses*, published in 1717.

GARVIN, James Louis (1868–1947), British journalist, born in Birmingham, became, after a spell as leader-writer for the *Daily Telegraph*, editor of the *Observer* (1908–42). He also edited the *Encyclopaedia Britannica* (14th ed.) and wrote a biography of Joseph Chamberlain (1932–34). See study by A. M. Gollen (1960).

GASCOIGNE, (1) **George** (*c.* 1525–77), English poet and dramatist, born at Cardington in Bedfordshire, a descendant of (2), studied at Cambridge, entered Gray's Inn, wrote poems, and sat in parliament for Bedford (1557–59), but was disinherited for his prodigality. He married Nicholas Breton's mother (to improve his finances), but, still persecuted by creditors, served in Holland under the Prince of Orange (1573–1575). Surprised by a Spanish force and taken prisoner, he was detained four months. He then settled at Walthamstow, where he collected and published his poems. He translated in prose and verse, from Greek, Latin and Italian. *The Complaynt of Phylomene* was begun in 1563. *The Supposes* is from *I Suppositi* of Ariosto; *Jocasta* (1566, with Francis Kinwelmersh), practically a translation from Dolce's *Giocasta* (based on the *Phoenissae* of Euripides), is the second tragedy in English blank verse; *The Glasse of Government* is an original comedy; *The Steele Glas* is the earliest blank-verse satire; and in the *Notes of Instruction on Making of Verse* we have the first considerable English essay on the subject. To this zealous experimenter English literature owes a deep debt, though much of his work is hopelessly tedious. See Life by Schelling (1893); and the *Works*, ed. Cunliffe (1907–10).

(2) **Sir William** (*c.* 1350–1419), English judge, born at Gawthorpe, Yorkshire, was appointed in 1400 chief justice of the King's Bench. He was evidently an independent judge, as he refused to obey the king's command to sentence to death Archbishop Scrope and Mowbray, the Earl Marshal, after the northern insurrection in 1405. Nine days after Henry IV's death a successor was appointed to his office, which disposes of the Shakespearean fiction that Henry V continued him in it.

GASKELL, Mrs Elizabeth Cleghorn, *née* **Stevenson** (1810–65), English novelist, was born at Cheyne Row, Chelsea, September 29. Her father was in succession teacher, preacher, farmer, boarding-house keeper, writer and keeper of the records to the Treasury. She was brought up by an aunt at Knutsford—the Cranford of her stories—and grew up a girl of singular sweetness of disposition and of great beauty. She married in 1832 William Gaskell (1805–84), a Unitarian minister in Manchester; here she studied working men and women. In 1848 she published anonymously *Mary Barton*, followed by *The Moorland Cottage* (1850), *Cranford* (1853), *Ruth* (1853), *North and South* (1855), *Round the Sofa* (1859), *Right at Last* (1860), *Sylvia's Lovers* (1863), *Cousin Phillis* (1865), and *Wives and Daughters* (1865). She died suddenly at Holybourne, Alton, in Hants, November 12, 1865. Besides her novels she wrote *The Life of Charlotte Brontë* (1857)—a masterpiece of English biography. See books by Payne (1900), Whitfield (1929), Elizabeth Haldane (1930).

GASPERI, Alcide de (1881–1954), Italian statesman, born in Trentino, studied at Innsbruck and Vienna, entered parliament in 1911, was imprisoned by Mussolini as an anti-Fascist, and thereafter worked in the Vatican library until 1946, when he became prime minister of the new republic and remained in office until his death.

GASQUET, Francis Aidan *gas'kay* (1846–1929), British cardinal, born in London of French ancestry, educated at Downside, became a Benedictine and was made prior of Downside Abbey in 1878. Created a cardinal in 1914, he became prefect of the Vatican archives in 1918. He helped in the revision of the Vulgate and wrote *Henry VIII and the English Monasteries* (1888–89) and *Monastic Life in the Middle Ages* (1922), both from a strongly pro-Roman standpoint.

GASSENDI, or Gassend, Pierre, *ga-sã-dee* (1592–1655), French philosopher and mathematician, was born at Champtercier in Provence, January 22, and studied and taught at Aix, but revolted from the scholastic philosophy, and applied himself to physics and astronomy. His examination of the Aristotelian system appeared in *Exercitationes paradoxicae adversus Aristoteleos* (1624). In that year he was appointed provost of Digne cathedral; and in 1645 professor of Mathematics in the Collège Royal at Paris, where he died, October 14. He controverted Fludd the mystic (1631) during his stay in the Low Countries and became an early critic of Descartes' new philosophy (1642); wrote on Epicurus (1647–49); Kepler and Galileo were among his friends. His *Institutio Astronomica* (1647) gives a clear view of the state of the science in his day. He also published biographies of Tycho Brahe, Copernicus and Regiomontanus (1654). See French studies by Martin (1853), Thomas (1889); German by Kiefl (1893), Pendzig (1908) and (1910); English by Brett (1908).

GASSER, Herbert Spencer (1888–1963), American physiologist, born at Platteville, Wis., became director of the Rockefeller Institute for Medical Research in 1935 and shared the Nobel prize for medicine in 1944 with Erlanger for their joint work on *Electrical Signs of Nervous Activity* (1937).

GASSET. See ORTEGA Y GASSET.

GASTALDI, Giacomo (16th cent.), Italian cartographer, born in Piedmont, worked in Venice, produced maps of Spain (1544), the World (1546), Germany (1552), Asia (1559–1561), Africa (1564), &c.

GASTON DE FOIX. See FOIX.

GATAKER, Thomas (1574–1654), English Puritan divine, was born in London, studied at St John's College, Cambridge, and in 1611 became rector of Rotherhithe. As member of the Westminster Assembly he opposed the imposition of the Covenant, and condemned the trial of Charles I. His twenty-five works include the once controversial *Of the Nature and Use of Lots* (1616).

GATES, Horatio (1728–1806), American general, was born at Maldon, Essex. He entered the English army, served in America under Braddock, escaped with difficulty in the defeat in which that officer was slain, and on the peace of 1763 purchased an estate in Virginia. In the War of Independence he sided with his adoptive country, and in 1775 was made adjutant-general, in 1776 commander of the army which had just retreated from Canada. In August 1777 he took command of the northern department, and compelled the surrender of the British army at Saratoga in October. This success gained him a great reputation, and he sought to supplant Washington, the commander-in-chief. In 1780 he commanded the army of the South, but was routed by Cornwallis near Camden, S.C. and was superseded. He retired to Virginia till 1790, emancipated his slaves and settled in New York, where he died.

GATHORNE-HARDY. See CRANBROOK.

GATLING, Richard Jordan (1818–1903), American inventor, born in North Carolina, studied medicine but never practised, and is known for his invention of the Gatling gun (1861–62), a revolving battery gun, with ten parallel barrels, firing 1200 shots a minute.

GATTY, Margaret. See EWING.

GAUDEN, John (1605–62), born at Mayland vicarage, Essex, from Bury St Edmunds school passed to St John's College, Cambridge, studied also at Oxford, took his D.D., and became master of the Temple in 1659, and Bishop of Exeter in 1660, of Worcester in 1662. He edited Hooker's works (1662), and may be the author of *Eikon Basilike*. He published a number of works against the Puritans including the monumental *Ecclesiae Anglicanae Suspiria* (1659). See Edward Almack's *Bibliography of the King's Book* (1894).

GAUGUIN, Eugène Henri Paul, *go-gĩ* (1848–1903), French post-Impressionist painter, born in Paris, June 7, the son of a journalist and a half-Peruvian Creole mother, went to sea at seventeen, but settled down in Paris in 1871, married a Danish girl, who bore him five children, and became a successful stockbroker with a predilection for painting and for collecting Impressionist paintings. By 1883, however, he had already exhibited his own work with the help of Camille Pissarro and, determined to give up all for art, left his uncomprehending wife and family, voyaged to Martinique (1887–88) and became the leader of a group of painters at Pont Aven, Brittany (1888–90; 1894), where he met the theorist Bernard. He quarrelled with Van Gogh at Arles (1888) and (1890–94) moved in the symbolists' circle in Paris. He gradually evolved his own style, *synthesism*, in accordance with his heartfelt hatred civilization and identification with the emotional directness of primitive peoples. Thus from his Brittany seascapes, the *Still Life with Three Puppies* (1888; Modern Art, New York), the stained-glass effects of *The Vision after the Sermon* (1888; National Gallery, Edinburgh) with its echoes of Romanesque, Japanese and Breton folk art, there is a conscious development to the tapestrylike canvases, painted in purples, greens, dark-reds and browns of native subjects on Tahiti (1891–93, 1895–1901) and at Dominiha on the Marquesas islands from 1901, e.g., *No Te Aha De Riri, Why are you angry?* (1896; Chicago), and *Faa Iheihe*, 'decorated with ornaments' (1898; Tate Gallery, London), which echoes his great allegorical painting dashed off prior to an unsuccessful arsenic suicide attempt in January 1898, *D'où venons-nous? Que sommes-nous? Où allons-nous?* (Boston). Gauguin also excelled in wood carvings of pagan idols and wrote an autobiographical novel, *Noa-Noa* (1894–1900). He never overcame his lack of early basic training, but he will be remembered not only because of the tragic choices he made, the subject of many popular novels, particularly Somerset Maugham's *The Moon and Sixpence*, but because he directed attention to primitive art as a valid field of aesthetic exploration and consequently influenced almost every school of 20th-century art. See Lives by R. Burnett (1936), R. Cogniat (Paris 1947), L. and E. Hanson (1954); studies by Malingue (trans. 1948), who also edited the Letters (trans. 1949), and Bodelsen (1965).

GAULLE. See DE GAULLE.

GAUMONT, Léon Ernest, *gō-mō* (1864–1946), French cinema inventor. He synchronized a projected film with a phonograph in 1901 and was responsible for the first talking pictures, demonstrated at the Académie des Sciences at Paris in 1910 and at the Royal Institute in 1912. He also introduced an early form of coloured cinema-film, using a three-colour separation method with special lenses and projectors.

GAUNT, John of. See JOHN OF GAUNT.

GAUSS, Johann Karl Friedrich, *gows* (1777–1855), German mathematician, born at Brunswick, in 1801 published an important work on the theory of numbers. In astronomy he invented new methods for the calculation of the orbits of planets, &c.; and, appointed in 1807 professor of Mathematics and director of the observatory at Göttingen, he issued his *Theoria Motus Corporum Coelestium* (1809). In 1821 he was appointed to conduct the trigonometrical survey of Hanover, and to measure an arc of the meridian, and for his work invented a heliograph. In 1833 appeared his *Intensitas Vis Magneticae Terrestris*; and in conjunction with Weber he invented the declination needle and a magnetometer. In applied mathematics he investigated the passage of light through a system of lenses in *Dioptrische Untersuchungen* (1840). See works by Waltershausen (1850), Schering (1887) and Bell, *Development of Mathematics*.

GAUTIER, Théophile (1811–72), French poet and novelist, born at Tarbes, August 31, from painting turned to literature, and became an extreme 'romanticist'. In 1830 he published his first long poem, *Albertus*, in 1832 the striking *Comédie de la mort*. His poetry reached its highest in *Émaux et camées* (1856). In 1835 appeared his celebrated novel, *Mademoiselle de Maupin*, with its defiant preface. He wrote many other novels and masterly short stories—*Les Jeunes-France* (1833), *Fortunio* (1838), *Une Larme du diable* (1839), *Militona* (1847), *La Peau de tigre* (1852), *Jettatura* (1857) *Le Capitaine Fracasse* (1863), *La Belle Jenny* (1865), *Spirite* (1866), &c. His theatrical criticisms were collected as *L'Histoire de l'art dramatique en France* (1859); his articles on the Salon form perhaps the best history of the French art of his day. *Caprices et zigzags, Constantinople, Voyage en Russie* and *Voyage en Espagne* contain delightful travel sketches. Gautier died at Neuilly, October 23. Other works were an enlarged edition of his *Émaux et camées* (1872); *Les Grotesques* (1844), on 16th- and 17th-century writers; *Honoré de Balzac* (1858); *Ménagerie intime* (1869), a kind of informal autobiography; *Histoire du romantisme* (1872); and the posthumous works, *Portraits et souvenirs littéraires* (1875) and *L'Orient* (1877). See works by Maxime du Camp (trans. 1893), Boschot (1933) and J. Richardson (1958).—His daughter, **Judith Gautier** (1845–1917), was a member of the Académie Goncourt, Chevalier de la Légion d'Honneur, and wrote novels, plays, poems and translations. See study by R. de Gourmont (1904).

GAVARNI, Paul, properly Sulpice Guillaume Chevalier (1801–66), French illustrator and caricaturist, was born at Paris, started life as a mechanical engineer, but became a caricaturist for *Les Gens du Monde* and *Le Charivari*. At first he ridiculed the follies of the Parisians with good-humoured irony; but later a deep earnestness showed itself in his productions. After a visit to London in 1849, he reproduced in *L'Illustration* the scenes of misery he had witnessed there. He also illustrated several books, including those of Sue, Balzac and Hoffmann. Two collections of his drawings, *Oeuvres choisies* (1848) and *Perles et parures* (1850), were published in Paris. See study by C. Holme (1904).

GAVAZZI, Allesandro, *ga-vat'zee* (1809–89), Italian priest, born at Bologna, became a Barnabite monk, supported the liberal policy of Pius IX, and on the fall of Rome in 1849 escaped to England, where he founded the (Protestant) Italian Free Church. He was with Garibaldi at Palermo in 1860, and from 1870 lived mostly in Italy.

GAVESTON, Piers de. See EDWARD II.

GAY, Delphine. See GIRARDIN.

GAY, John (1685–1732), English poet, born at Barnstaple, was apprenticed to a London silk-mercer, but soon took to letters for a livelihood. In 1708 he published his first poem, *Wine*, and in 1711 a pamphlet on the *Present State of Wit*. Appointed secretary to the Duchess of Monmouth (1712), he in 1713 dedicated to Pope the georgic *Rural Sports*. In 1714 he published *The Fan* and *The Shepherd's Week*, and accompanied Lord Clarendon, envoy to Hanover, as secretary.

At Anne's death he wrote a poem on the newly-arrived Princess of Wales. *What d'ye Call It?* (1715) was called 'a tragi-comi-pastoral farce'. *Trivia*, a clever picture of town life, came next; and later he bore the blame of *Three Hours after Marriage* (1717), a play in which Pope and Arbuthnot had the larger part. In 1720 he published his poems by subscription, clearing £1000; but this and some South Sea stock vanished in the crash of 1720. In 1724 he produced *The Captives*, a tragedy, and in 1727 the first series of his popular *Fables*. But his greatest success was *The Beggar's Opera* (1728), set to music by Pepusch, the outcome of a suggestion made by Swift in 1716. Its popularity was extra-ordinary; it ran sixty-two nights, and by the thirty-sixth, Gay had netted over £700; forthwith he set about a sequel, *Polly*, which was prohibited, but which in book form brought in £1200. After this he lived chiefly with the Duke and Duchess of Queensberry, the kindest of his many patrons. In 1732 he came from their house at Amesbury in Wiltshire to London, probably about his opera *Achilles* (produced posthumously in 1733), and here died suddenly, December 4, 1732. He was buried in Westminster Abbey. Amiable, indolent and luxurious, Gay was a charming songwriter, witness ' Black-eyed Susan '. See Lives by Irving (1940), Armens (1954), and a study by Taylor and Barker (1956).

GAY-LUSSAC, Joseph Louis (1778–1850), French chemist and physicist, was born December 6 at St Léonard in Haute Vienne. From the Polytechnic School he passed in 1801 to the department of Ponts et Chaussées, and began a series of researches on gases, temperature, hygrometry and the behaviour of vapours. With Biot, and later alone, he made balloon ascents for investigating the laws of terrestrial magnetism, and for collect-ing samples of air for analysis, which resulted in his famous memoir to the Academy of Sciences with von Humboldt (q.v.) stating that oxygen and hydrogen combine at the ratio of one to two volumes respectively to form water. This led to the discovery of the law of volumes (1808). In 1809 he became professor of Chemistry at the Polytechnic, and from 1832 in the Jardin des Plantes. He was first to prepare hydriodic and iodic acids; and in 1815 he succeeded in isolating cyanogen. His investigations regarding the manufacture of sulphuric acid led to the introduction of the Gay-Lussac tower; those on the manufacture of the bleaching chlorides, the centesimal alcoholometer and the assay-ing of silver are also important. In 1818 he became superintendent of the government manufactory of gunpowder, and in 1829 chief assayer to the mint. In 1839 he was made a peer of France. He died May 9.

GAZA, Theodorus (1398–1478), Byzantine scholar, was born at Thessalonica, fled about 1444 before the Turks to Italy, and taught Greek at Ferrara and later philosophy at Rome. Cardinal Bessarion obtained for him a small benefice in Calabria. His principal work was a Greek grammar (1495) and he translated into Latin portions of Aristotle, Theophrastus, St Chrysostom.

GEBIR, or **Geber** (*c.* A.D. 800 or *c.* 900), Arab alchemist whose name appears on several publications although his existence has been denied. He is usually identified with **Jabir ibn Haijan**, a celebrated Arabic alchemist. His principal writings include *Summa Perfectionis* and tractates in geometry.

GED, William (1690–1749), Scottish printer, began as a goldsmith in Edinburgh, and in 1725 patented a process of stereotyping. He was commissioned by Cambridge University to stereotype prayer books and bibles, but his partner's unfairness and workmen's opposition compelled him to return to Edinburgh (1733). See Memoir by Nichols (1781).

GEDDES, *ged'is*, (1) **Alexander** (1737–1802), Scottish biblical critic, born in Rathven parish, Banffshire, and educated for the priesthood at Paris (1758–64), in 1769 took a cure of souls at Auchinhalrig, Banffshire, where his sympathy with local Protestants led to his dismissal (1780). Going to London, he made a new translation of the Bible for English Catholics (1792–1800). See Life by Dr Mason Good (1803).

(2) **Andrew** (1783–1844), painter (A.R.A. 1831) and etcher, was born at Edinburgh, but studied and lived mostly in London.

(3) **Auckland Campbell, 1st Baron** (1879–1954), British politician and surgeon, brother of (4), was educated at George Watson's College, Edinburgh, studied medicine at the University, and after service in the South African war, became assistant professor of Anatomy at Edinburgh, at McGill University, Montreal, where he was president (1919–20), and at the Royal College of Surgeons, Dublin. During World War I he attained the rank of brigadier-general, was appointed director of recruiting (1916) and minister of national service in 1917, after entering Parliament as a Unionist and being knighted. He became minister of reconstruction (1919), president of the Board of Trade (1919–20) and British ambassador to the U.S.A. (1920–24). He then retired from politics, except to preside over the royal commission on food prices (1924–25).

(4) **Sir Eric Campbell** (1875–1937), British politician, brother of (3), born in India and educated in Edinburgh, engaged in lumbering and railway work in America, India and England, was director-general of Military Railways 1916–17, first lord of the Admir-alty 1917, a member of the War Cabinet 1918, first minister of Transport in 1919–21. He presided over the ' Geddes Axe ' committee on national expenditure in 1922. He was knighted in 1916.

(5) **Jenny,** a Scottish vegetable-seller, traditionally reputed to have started the riots in St Giles' cathedral, Edinburgh, when Laud's prayer book was introduced on Sunday, July 23, 1637. According to the popular legend she threw her folding-stool at Bishop Lindsay, shouting: ' Thou false thief, dost thou say mass at my lug? ' There is no historical evidence of her exploit. Sydserf in 1661 mentions ' the immortal Jenet Geddes ' as having burned ' her leather chair of state ' in a Restoration bonfire, and the story appears in full detail in Phillips's continuation

of Baker's *Chronicle* (1660). Her name is also given as Mein and Hamilton. See Sir J. Cameron Lees, *St Giles', Edinburgh* (1889).

(6) **Sir Patrick** (1854–1932), born at Perth, studied under T. H. Huxley at University College, London. After several lecturing appointments, he became professor of Botany at Dundee (1883–1920) travelled widely and took a leading part in educational and social work. He took the theory of evolution as a basis for ethics, history and sociology, and wrote, with Sir J. A. Thomson, *The Evolution of Sex* (1889). He threw himself with energy into schemes of town planning, Celtic publishing, and social, academic and economic reform.

GEERAERTS. See GHEERAERTS.

GEGENBAUR, Karl, *gay'gen-bowr* (1826–1903), German comparative anatomist, was born at Würzburg, and became professor at Jena in 1855, at Heidelberg in 1873. His chief work, *Comparative Anatomy* (trans. 1878), threw much light on the evolution of the skull from his study of cartilaginous fishes. He was a great apostle of evolution on the Continent.

GEIBEL, Emanuel von, *gī'-* (1815–84), German poet, born at Lübeck, studied at Bonn, and was tutor (1838–39) in Athens to the family of the Russian ambassador. In 1852 he became professor of Aesthetics at Munich, whence in 1868 he retired to Lübeck. He made many translations from the Greek, Spanish and Italian authors, and with Heyse founded the Munich school of poetry, which emphasized harmony and form. Besides his own poems (1840) he wrote the two tragedies, *Brunehild* (1857) and *Sophonisbe* (1868). See Lives by Gaedertz (1886), Litzmann (1887), Kleibömer (1910) and Sonntag (1922).

GEIGER, *gī'gėr,* **(1) Abraham** (1810–74), Jewish scholar, was born at Frankfurt, studied at Heidelberg and Bonn, and was rabbi successively at Wiesbaden, Breslau, Frankfurt and Berlin. He wrote on biblical criticism; but his principal work is *Das Judenthum und seine Geschichte*.

(2) **Hans** (1882–1945), German physicist born at Neustadt-an-der-Haardt, worked under Rutherford at Manchester (1906–12), investigated beta-ray radioactivity and with Müller, devised a counter to measure it. He was professor at Kiel (1925) and at Tübingen (1929).

GEIJER, Eric Gustav, *ye'yėr* (1783–1877), Swedish romantic poet and historian, born at Ransäter in Värmland, studied, lectured and eventually was appointed professor of History at Uppsala. He influenced both poetry and the writing of history in Sweden. His best poems appeared in the magazine *Iduna* of the Gothic Society which he founded in 1810. His historical works, among them the *History of the Swedish People* (trans. 1845), were all unfinished. See Swedish studies by J. Landquist (1924) and C. A. Hessler (1947).

GEIKIE, *gee'kee,* **(1) Sir Archibald** (1835–1924), Scottish geologist, brother of (2), born in Edinburgh and educated at the High School and University, in 1855 was appointed to the Geological Survey; in 1867 became director of the Survey in Scotland; from 1870 to 1881 was professor of Geology at Edinburgh; and was (1882–1901) director-general of the Survey of the United Kingdom, and head of the Geological Museum, London. Knighted (1891), K.C.B. (1907), O.M. (1914), he was president of the Royal Society (1908–1913). He did much to encourage microscopic petrography and volcanic geology and wrote several textbooks.

(2) **James** (1839–1915), Scottish geologist, brother of (1), born in Edinburgh, served on the Geological Survey of Scotland from 1861, and was professor of Geology at Edinburgh (1882–1914). Besides verse translations from Heine, a large number of geological maps, sections and memoirs published by the Geological Survey, he wrote a standard work on the glacial period (1874) and several other geological books. See *Life* by Flett and Newbigin (1917).

GEILER VON KAISERSBERG, Johann, *gī'lėr fon kī'zėrs-berg* (1445–1510), German preacher, born at Schaffhausen, in 1478 became preacher in Strasbourg Cathedral. He left many earnest, witty and original works, mainly devotional, and had a reputation as the greatest pulpit orator of his age.

GEISSLER, Heinrich, *gīs'-* (1814–79), German inventor, born in Saxony, became a glass-blower and settled in Bonn in 1854. The Geissler tube, by which the passage of electricity through rarefied gases can be seen, and an air pump are among his inventions.

GEITEL, Hans Friedrich, *gī'tėl* (1855–1923), German physicist, was born at Brunswick and became professor at the technical institute there. With Elster, he invented the first practical photoelectric cell, a photometer and a Tesla transformer.

GELASIUS, name of two popes:

Gelasius I (pope 492–96), an African by birth, was one of the earliest bishops of Rome to assert the supremacy of the papal chair. He repressed Pelagianism, renewed the ban against the oriental patriarch, drove out the Manichaeans from Rome, and wrote against the Eutychians and Nestorians.

Gelasius II (pope 1118–19), formerly John of Gaeta, was cardinal and chancellor under Urban II and Paschal II, and on the death of the latter in 1118 was chosen pope by the party hostile to the Emperor Henry V. Gelasius fled before the advancing imperialists to Gaeta, and excommunicated Henry and Gregory VIII, the antipope he had set up. Shortly after he was able to return to Rome, but in the same autumn had to flee to France, where he died in the monastery at Cluny, January 29.

GELÉE. See CLAUDE LORRAINE.

GELL, Sir William (1777–1836), English archaeologist, born at Hopton, Derbyshire, travelled in Greece and published works on the topography of Troy (1804), Ithaca (1808), Pompeii (1817–32), Rome (1834), &c.

GELLERT, Christian Fürchtegott (1715–69), German poet and moralist, born at Hainichen, Saxony, was educated at Leipzig, and in 1751 became a professor there. He was a prolific writer of stories and fables and two of his comedies *Das Loos in der Lotterei* and *Die kranke Frau* were popular favourites. His novel *Leben der schwedischen Gräfin von G—*

(1747–48) shows the influence of Richardson. See Lives by Cramer (1774), Döring (1833) and study by Coym (1899).

GELLIUS, Aulus (b. *c.* A.D. 135), a Latin author, supposed to have been born at Rome, and to have practised law there, after studying philosophy at Athens. His *Noctes Atticae* is a medley on language, antiquities, history and literature. It contains many extracts from lost authors. See edition by Rolfe (1927–28)

GELON (d. 478 B.C.), tyrant of Gela from 485 B.C., made himself later master of Syracuse, and extended his influence over half of Sicily. He refused to aid the Greeks against Xerxes, and defeated the Carthaginians at Himera (480).

GENEVIEVE, St, *zhen-è-vyayv* (*c.* 422–512), patron saint of Paris, was born at Nanterre near Paris, and taking the veil, acquired an extraordinary reputation for sanctity, increased by her assurance that Attila and his Huns would not touch Paris, and by an expedition for the relief of the starving city during Childeric's Frankish invasion. In 460 she built a church over the tomb of St Denis, where she herself was buried. See Life by Sertillanges (1917).

GENGA, Girolamo (*c.* 1476–1551), Italian architect and religious painter, was born and died at Urbino where he designed the duke's palace. Three frescoes by him are in the National Gallery, London.—His son, **Bartolommeo** (1516–59), born at Cesena, was a sculptor and engineer as well.

GENGHIS KHAN, *jen'gis kahn* (1162–1227), Mongol conqueror, was born at Deligun Bulduk on the river Onon, the son of a Mongol chief. Called at thirteen to succeed his father, he had to struggle hard for years against hostile tribes. His ambition awakening with his continued success, he spent six years in subjugating the Naimans, between Lake Balkhash and the Irtish, and in conquering Tangut, south of the desert of Gobi. From the Turkish Uigurs, who voluntarily submitted, the Mongols derived their civilization, alphabet and laws. In 1206 he dropped his name Temujin for that of Genghis (Jingis or Chingis) Khan, ' Very Mighty Ruler ', in 1211 overran the empire of North China, and in 1217 conquered and annexed the Kara-Chitai empire from Lake Balkhash to Tibet. In 1218 he attacked the powerful empire of Kharezm, bounded by the Jaxartes, Indus, Persian Gulf and Caspian, took Bokhara, Samarkand, Kharezm (now Khiva) and other chief cities, and returned home in 1225. Two of Genghis' lieutenants penetrated northwards from the southern shore of the Caspian through Georgia into southern Russia and the Crimea, everywhere routing and slaying, and returned by way of the Volga. Meanwhile in the far east another of his generals had completed the conquest of all northern China (1217–23) except Honan. After a few months' rest Genghis set out to chastise the king of Tangut; and, after thoroughly subduing the country, died on August 18. Genghis was not only a warrior and conqueror, but a skilful administrator and ruler; he not only conquered empires stretching from the

Black Sea to the Pacific, but organized them into states which outlasted the short span that usually measures the life of Asiatic sovereignties. See Lives by R. K. Douglas (1877), Vladimirtsov (trans. 1930), Fox (1936), Grousset (1941).

GENLIS, Stéphanie Felicité Ducrest de St Aubin, Comtesse de, *zhā-lees* (1746–1830), French writer, was born at Champcéri near Autun, at sixteen was married to the Comte de Genlis, and in 1770 was made lady-in-waiting to the Duchesse de Chartres, to whose husband, Orléans ' Égalité ', she became mistress, and to their children, who included the future King Louis Philippe, ' governor '. She wrote four volumes of short plays entitled *Théâtre d'éducation* (1779) for her charges and nearly a hundred volumes of historical romances and ' improving ' works. Her *Mémoires* (1825) contain interesting social sidelights on the period. See Life by V. Wyndham (1958).

GENNARO. See JANUARIUS.

GENSERIC. See GAISERIC.

GENTH, Frederick Augustus (1820–93), American mineralogist, born at Wächtersbach near Hanau, and educated at Giessen and Marburg, went to America in 1848 and became professor of Chemistry and Mineralogy at Pennsylvania (1872). He investigated the cobalt-ammonium compounds, and discovered twenty-four new minerals, one of which is named *genthite*.

GENTILE, Giovanni, *jen-tee'lay* (1875–1944), Italian Idealist philosopher, born at Castelvetrano, became successively professor of Philosophy at Palmero, Pisa and Rome, and was with Croce (q.v.) the leading exponent of 20th-century Italian Idealism. He quarrelled with Croce's complex distinctions between the theoretical and practical categories of mind, and argued that nothing is real except the pure act of thought; the subject-object distinction is thus abolished, and thought becomes action. His *Theory of Mind as Pure Art* (1916; trans. 1922) made him an excellent philosophical mouthpiece for Mussolini. He was Fascist minister of education (1922–24), director of the *Enciclopedia Italiana* (1929) and was assassinated by an anti-Fascist in Florence in 1944. See study by R. W. Holmes (1937).

GENTILE DA FABRIANO. See FABRIANO.

GENTILESCHI, *jen-ti-les'kee,* (1) **Artemisia** (1590–*c.* 1642), Italian painter, daughter of (2), visited England and left a self-portrait at Hampton Court. Her chief work is a *Judith and Holophernes* in the Uffizi, Florence. She died near Naples.

(2) **Orazio** (1563–1647), father of (1), was born at Pisa, and settled in England in 1626, the first Italian painter called to England by Charles I, having been patronized by the Vatican and the Medicis in Genoa. He is responsible for the decoration of the Queen's House at Greenwich (partly transferred to Marlborough House) and *Discovery of Moses* at Madrid, *Flight into Egypt* at the Louvre and *Joseph and Potiphar's Wife* at Hampton Court. His attempt to introduce the Italian style of decoration into England was unsuccessful, although his reputation stood very high for a time.

GENTILI, Alberico, *jen-tee'lee* (1552–1608) Italian writer on international law, politics, &c., was born at Sangenesio in the March of Ancona, and, exiled as a heretic, in 1580 settled in England and lectured at Oxford.

GENTZ, Friedrich von (1764–1832), German publicist and diplomat, born at Breslau, in 1786 entered the public service of Prussia, but in 1802 exchanged into that of Austria; he wrote bitterly against Napoleon. An adherent from 1810 of Metternich, at the Congress of Vienna in 1814 he was first secretary, as also in subsequent conferences. His writings are distinguished for elegance. The theorist and practical exponent of ' Balance of Power ' in Europe, he received liberal *douceurs* from various foreign governments. See studies by Mendelssohn-Bartholdy (1867), Fournier (1880), A. R. de Cléry (Paris 1917), C. S. B. Buckland (1933).

GEOFFREY OF MONMOUTH (*c.* 1100–54), Welsh chronicler, about 1140 became Archdeacon of Llandaff, and was consecrated Bishop of St Asaph in 1152. His *Historia Regum Britanniae*, composed previous to 1147, possesses little value as history, but has profoundly influenced English literature. Its author professes to have merely translated from a Welsh history of the kings of Britain, found in Brittany, but the *Historia* is really a masterpiece of the creative imagination working on materials found in Gildas, Nennius and other chroniclers, as well as early legends. It was translated into Norman-French by Geoffrey Gaimar *c.* 1147–50, and by Wace (*Li Romans de Brut*) with additions *c.* 1155. Layamon's *Brut* (*c.* 1205) was an English paraphrase of Wace, and Robert of Gloucester's *Chronicle* was a rhymed paraphrase of the same, which helped to make Geoffrey's legends widely known. The stories of King Lear and Cymbeline, the prophecies of Merlin, and the legend of Arthur in the form we know, owe their origin to Geoffrey of Monmouth, who still influences us in Malory, Drayton, Shakespeare, Spenser, Milton, Tennyson, Swinburne and Morris. A Yorkshire monk, William of Newburgh, denounced Geoffrey in his own time as having ' lied saucily and shamelessly ', and Giraldus Cambrensis distinctly speaks of the book as fabulous. See study by Tatlock (1950).

GEOFFRIN, Marie Thérèse, *née* Rodet, *zhof-ri* (1699–1777), French patroness of literature, born in Paris, was married at fifteen to a rich citizen, who died soon after, leaving her an immense fortune. She had a genuine love of learning and art, and her *salon* became a rendezvous of the men of letters and artists of Paris, especially the *philosophes*. She contributed funds for the publication of the *Encyclopédie*. See book by J. Aldis (1906).

GEOFFROY SAINT-HILAIRE, *zhof-rwah sī-tee-layr,* (1) **Étienne** (1772–1844), French zoologist, born at Étampes, April 15, became in 1793 professor of Zoology in the Museum of Natural History at Paris, and began the great zoological collection at the Jardin des Plantes. In 1798, he was one of the scientific commission that accompanied Bonaparte to Egypt; in 1807 was made a member of the

Academy of Sciences; in 1809 was appointed professor of Zoology in the Faculty of Sciences. He died June 19, 1844. He endeavoured to establish the unity of plan in organic structure; and he raised teratology to a science, principally in his *Philosophie anatomique* (1818–20). He also wrote *L'Histoire naturelle des mammifères* (1820–42) with F. Cuvier; *Philosophie zoologique* (1830); and *Études progressives d'un naturaliste* (1835). See Life (1847) by his son Isidore; also De Quatrefages's *Rambles of a Naturalist* (1863), and Ducrotay de Blainville's *Cuvier et Geoffroy Saint-Hilaire* (1890).

(2) **Isidore** (1805–61), French zoologist, son of (1), born in Paris, became assistant-naturalist at the zoological museum in 1824, and professor of Zoology in the Faculty of Sciences in 1850. He too made a special study of teratology, publishing in 1832–37 a work on monstrous forms. The results of his investigations on the domestication of foreign animals in France appeared in *Domestication et naturalisation des animaux utiles* (1854). In 1852 he published the first volume of his *Histoire générale des règnes organiques*, but died November 10, 1861, before completing the third volume. He was a strong advocate of the use of horse flesh as human food.

GEORGE, St, patron of chivalry and guardian saint of England and Portugal. He may have been tortured and put to death by Diocletian at Nicomedia, April 23, 303. Or he may have suffered (*c.* 250) at Lydda in Palestine where his alleged tomb is exhibited. By many writers, as by Gibbon, he has been confused with the Arian, George of Cappadocia (d. 361), who after a troubled life as army contractor and tax gatherer became Archbishop of Alexandria, and five years later was torn in pieces by a furious mob. St George of the Eastern Church was no doubt a real personage of an earlier date than George of Cappadocia, but beyond this nothing is known of him, and his name was early obscured by fable. The famous story of his fight with the dragon cannot be traced much earlier than Voragine's *Legenda Aurea*. The Crusades gave a great impetus to his cult; many chivalrous orders assumed him as their patron; and he was adopted as guardian saint by England, Aragon and Portugal. In 1348 Edward III founded St George's Chapel, Windsor, and in 1344 the Order of the Garter was instituted. See Life by Barclay (1955).

GEORGE, name of six kings of Great Britain, the first four of the house of Hanover, renamed Windsor in the case of the last two, formerly Saxe-Coburg-Gotha:

George I (1660–1727), born at Hanover, March 28. He was the eldest son of Ernest Augustus of Hanover, and of Sophia, fifth (but only Protestant) daughter of Elizabeth (q.v.) of Bohemia, so a great-grandson of James I of England; and on Queen Anne's death, August 1, 1714, he was proclaimed, according to the Act of Settlement, King of Great Britain and Ireland. He had been Elector of Hanover since 1698, and had commanded the imperial forces in the Marlborough wars. In 1682 he married his cousin, the Princess Dorothea of Zell. Twelve years later he obtained a divorce on the ground of her intrigue with Count Königsmark (q.v.), and imprisoned her in the castle of Ahlden, where she died November 2, 1726. But while punishing his consort for her frailty, he himself lived openly with mistresses. George was supported by the Whigs, and openly partial to them, while he hated the Tories and Jacobites, who clung to the banished House of Stewart. Bolingbroke and the Duke of Ormond, flying to France, were impeached, with Oxford, who had stayed behind. In Scotland a Jacobite rising, headed by the Earl of Mar, took place in 1715; the battle of Sheriffmuir on November 13, though indecisive, dispirited the rebels, who afterwards dispersed. Another body marched into England, but at Preston laid down their arms; of these Lords Derwentwater and Kenmure were executed. In 1716 parliament passed the Septennial Act, to postpone for four years the accession of the Tories to power. The failure of the South Sea Company in 1720 brought the nation to the verge of anarchy, from which it was saved by Walpole's genius. A quarrel with Spain in 1726 led to an unsuccessful expedition against her American possessions, and a fruitless attempt on Gibraltar by the Spaniards. George took little part in the government of the country, the actual ruler being Sir Robert Walpole. His affections remained with Hanover, and it was his delight to live there as much as possible. He died suddenly at Osnabrück, on his way thither, June 10. Lady Wortley Montagu styles George I ' an honest blockhead '; Carlyle, on the other hand, thinks him, in spite of appearances, a man of more human faculty, ' chiefly of an inarticulate kind ', than he generally gets credit for. He was a useful figurehead in a constitutional government, and rendered greater service than he may have intended to the country which adopted him. See studies by L. Melville (1908), Imbert-Terry (1927) and Michael (1936).

George II (1683–1760), born November 10, succeeded his father as Elector of Hanover and King of Great Britain and Ireland in 1727, having been declared Prince of Wales in 1714. In 1705 he had married Caroline (q.v.) of Anspach (1683–1737). Though George interfered more in the government of the country than his father had done, the policy pursued during the first half of the reign was that of Walpole. In 1737 a quarrel with Spain resulted in the capture of Portobello by Admiral Vernon, and the loss of 20,000 men in an attempt on Cartagena. In 1742 Britain was drawn into the war of the Austrian succession, principally on account of the supposed danger to George's Hanoverian possessions. On June 16, 1743, the British and Hanoverians gained the battle of Dettingen, at which George was present, the last occasion on which a British sovereign commanded an army in the field. In May 1745 the Duke of Cumberland, the king's second son, was defeated at Fontenoy by the French under Marshal Saxe. After nine years of warfare, in which neither

country gained any substantial advantage, peace was concluded at Aix-la-Chapelle in 1748. Meanwhile in 1745–46 Prince Charles Edward (see STEWART) had landed in Scotland, and after some successes been utterly defeated by Cumberland at Culloden. Although a nominal peace existed at home between France and Britain, in India Clive gained various victories over the French, culminating in that of Plassey in 1757, which laid the foundation of British India. In the same year Britain joined Prussia in the ' Seven Years' War ', in order to protect Hanover. She suffered reverses on the Continent; but the brilliant capture of Quebec by General Wolfe in September 1759 resulted in Canada becoming a British possession. George II died suddenly at Kensington, October 25. He had no conspicuous virtues, and his worst vice was that common to his father, a propensity for mistresses. Britain advanced under his reign, the earlier years of it, according to Hallam, ' the most prosperous period that England had ever known '. See Memoirs by Harvey (new ed. 1931) and Horace Walpole (1846); studies by Lucas (1910) and J. D. G. Davies (1938).

George III (1738–1820), was the eldest son of Frederick Louis, Prince of Wales (1707–1751), and was born in London, June 4. His father having predeceased him, he in 1760 succeeded his grandfather, George II, as King of Great Britain and Ireland and Elector of Hanover (King from 1815). He was the first of the House of Hanover who commanded general respect on becoming sovereign, and at the outset he conciliated all classes of his subjects. On September 8, 1761, he married Charlotte Sophia (q.v.), Princess of Mecklenburg-Strelitz. Four or five years before he is said to have had a daughter by Hannah Lightfoot, a Quakeress, and to have married her; it is less open to doubt that, after ascending the throne, he wished to marry Lady Sarah Lennox. Eager to govern as well as reign, George felt certain that his own way was the right one, and that were it followed all would go well; hence friction soon arose between him and his people. Pitt was the popular idol; but the king disliked Pitt and his policy, and the Earl of Bute became prime minister in May 1762 in the place of the Duke of Newcastle. If Bute had been a strong man he might have justified his promotion, but, timid and incompetent, he succumbed in April 1763 to the clamour evoked by the unpopular treaty of peace with France and Spain. During the two years' administration of Grenville, his successor, the first attempt to tax the American colonies was made. The repeal of the unpopular Stamp Act, but accompanied by a declaration of the right of Great Britain to tax the colonists, took place during the premiership of Rockingham, who held office for eleven months. The Earl of Chatham, who followed him, held office for fourteen months, and the Duke of Grafton for three years. In Lord North George III found a minister after his own heart, and North remained at the head of the government from 1770 till 1782. During his administration the American colonies, exasperated at renewed attempts at taxation, proclaimed (July 4, 1776) and achieved their independence, the treaty of peace with Great Britain being signed in February 1783. The determination of the king not to grant any concessions to those whom he deemed rebels caused the struggle to be much protracted. Lord North was succeeded by Rockingham, who died after three months in office. Among his colleagues were Fox, Burke and Sheridan, whom George detested, and who, when Lord Shelburne took Rockingham's place, refused to serve with him; but he secured William Pitt as chancellor of the Exchequer. The friends of Fox and the followers of Lord North overthrew Shelburne in ten months; and the Duke of Portland's coalition ministry lasted only eight months (1783). In the interval the king compelled his ministers to resign, called Pitt to office in December 1783, and dissolved parliament. Pitt remained in office for eighteen years. The complete victory of his party at the general election in 1784 was a triumph for the king as much as for Pitt; there was now an end to the supremacy of the old Whig families. The Tory party had been consolidated and was prepared to give effect to the policy of George III. The struggle had been long and severe. John Wilkes had taken part in it; and ' Junius ' had denounced the ministers whom the king trusted. Popular feeling ran high against the sovereign for a time, but he gradually regained the affections of his subjects. When the union between Ireland and Great Britain was proposed George III wrote to Pitt characterizing it as one of the most useful measures of his reign; but when the union was effected (January 1, 1801), and Pitt proposed carrying out his pledges as to Catholic emancipation, the king refused his assent. Pitt resigned; the king rejected his advice to form a strong administration, including Fox, and entrusted Addington with the task of forming a ministry, which held office till war with France was renewed. Pitt then resumed office, but died in 1806. A ministry was formed in which Fox and Sidmouth held office, and of which Lord Grenville was the head; it was reconstituted after Fox's death, and was succeeded in 1807 by one under the Duke of Portland. In 1809 Perceval succeeded to the premiership. In 1810 the Princess Amelia, George's favourite child, fell dangerously ill; this preyed on the king's mind, and hastened an attack of mental derangement, not the first he had had. In 1810 the Prince of Wales was appointed regent; and till his death, on January 29, 1820, George was hopelessly insane; he also lost his sight. Although of German blood, George III was a typical Englishman, well-meaning and intensely patriotic; pious and a pattern of the domestic virtues. During his reign were fought decisive battles in America, India and Europe, and many great conquests made. Great statesmen, such as Chatham, Pitt and Fox, adorned it; great captains, such as Nelson and Wellington; and many great names in modern English literature—Johnson, Gibbon, Burns, Cowper, Crabbe, Scott,

Byron, Coleridge, Wordsworth, Southey, Shelley and Keats. When George III ascended the throne the national debt was £138,000,000 sterling; before his death it was more than £800,000,000. On the other hand, trade and commerce made gigantic strides; during his reign both imports and exports had increased more than fourfold in money value. See the *Correspondence of George II 1760–83* (ed. Sir John Fortescue 1927–28) and additions and corrections to it by Namier (1937), *England in the Age of the American Revolution* (1930–57) and studies by Dobrée (1935), Trevelyan (1912), Vulliamy (1937), Sedgwick (1939), Barnes (1939), Pares (1953) and Butterfield (1957).

George IV (1762–1830), the eldest son of George III, was born August 12. Owing to his father's derangement, he became Prince Regent in 1810, and he succeeded in 1820. Till nineteen the prince had been kept under strict discipline, against which he sometimes rebelled. At eighteen he had an intrigue with Mrs Robinson, an actress; and at twenty he went through the ceremony of marriage with Mrs Fitzherbert (q.v.), a Roman Catholic, thus forfeiting his title to the crown. Out of antagonism to his father he affected to be a Whig, and much of the king's aversion to Fox, Burke and Sheridan was due to their associating with him. In 1795 he married Princess Caroline (q.v.) of Brunswick, parliament agreeing to pay his debts, £650,000. As king he sought to divorce her; but her death on August 7, 1821, terminated a struggle and scandal in which the people sympathized with the queen. In 1821 George IV visited Ireland and Hanover; and in 1822 Scotland, where a magnificent reception was organized by Sir Walter Scott. Though a professed Whig when Prince of Wales, George IV governed as his father had done with the aid of the Tories. Perceval, Liverpool, Canning, Goderich and Wellington successively held office while he was regent and king. He opposed the reform movement. An undutiful son, a bad husband and a callous father, but ' the first gentleman in Europe ', he died June 26. See Lives by Leslie (1926), Fulford (1935) and Letters (ed. Aspinall, 1938).

George V (1865–1936), born at Marlborough House, June 3, served in the navy, travelled in many parts of the Empire, was created Prince of Wales in 1901, had five sons, the youngest Prince John (1905–19), and one daughter (Victoria Alexandra Alice **Mary**, Princess Royal (1897–1965), married the 6th Earl of **Harewood** (d. 1947) (q.v.)), and succeeded his father, Edward VII, May 6, 1910. His reign was marked *inter alia* by the Union of S. Africa (May 31, 1910), his visit to India for the Coronation Durbar (December 12, 1911), the Great War (1914–18), the adoption of the surname Windsor (1917), Sinn Fein Rebellion (April 24, 1916), Irish Free State settlement (1922), the first Labour Governments (1924–25, 1929–31), general strike (1926), Scottish church union (1929), economic crisis and ' national ' government (1931), statute of Westminster (1931), Government of India Act (1935). He originated the famous Christmas Day broadcasts to the nation in 1931. He died January 20, 1936. See Life by Sir Harold Nicholson (1953). His consort, **Mary**, formerly Princess Victoria Mary Augusta Louise Olga Pauline Claudine Agnes of Teck (1867–1953), was born in Kensington Palace, London, and married Prince George in 1893. She organized women's war work (1914–18), devoted her time to the interests of women and children, continuing with many public and philanthropic activities after the death of her husband. She was known and loved as a regal and in many ways highly individual figure with a keen sense of duty. She was a keen and discerning collector of antiques and *objets d'art*. See Life by Pope-Hennessy (1959).

George VI (1895–1952), second son of George V, father of Elizabeth II and Princess Margaret Rose (qq.v.), born at Sandringham, December 14, was educated at Dartmouth Naval College and at Trinity College, Cambridge. He served in the Grand Fleet at the battle of Jutland (1916), was an air cadet at Cranwell and in 1918 on the staff of the Independent Force, R.A.F. Keenly interested in the human problems of industry, he became president of the Boys' Welfare Association and originated the summer camps for public school and working class boys. In 1920 he was created Duke of York and married Lady Elizabeth Bowes-Lyon (see below) in 1923. An outstanding tennis player, he played at Wimbledon in the All-England championships in 1926. The following year, he and the duchess toured Australia. On the abdication of his elder brother, Edward VIII, he ascended the throne in 1936. During World War II he set a personal example in wartime restrictions, continued to reside in bomb-damaged Buckingham Palace, visited all theatres of war and delivered many broadcasts, for which he mastered a speech impediment. In 1947 he toured South Africa and substituted the title of head of the Commonwealth for that of emperor of India, when that subcontinent was granted independence by the Labour government. Unnoticed by the public, his health was rapidly declining. Yet he persevered with his duties, his last great public occasion being the opening of the Festival of Britain in 1951. He died suddenly of coronary thrombosis on February 7. See selected speeches and broadcasts (1952) and official Life by J. W. Wheeler Bennett (1958). His consort, **Elizabeth** (1900–), was born Elizabeth Angela Marguerite Bowes-Lyon, the youngest daughter of the 14th Earl and the Countess of Strathmore, at Waldenbury, Herts, on August 4, and was educated privately. In 1923 she married the Duke of York and in 1926 Princess Elizabeth (later Queen Elizabeth II) was born to her. In 1927 she made a long tour of Australia and New Zealand, and in 1930 her second child, Princess Margaret, was born. In May 1937 she was crowned Queen in Westminster Abbey, and she paid an official visit to Paris in 1938, and to Canada and the U.S.A. in 1939. She stayed throughout World War II at Buckingham Palace, which was bombed, and visited hospitals, civil defence centres,

and the headquarters of women's organizations. In 1947 she toured South Africa with the king, whose death in February 1952 she bore with great fortitude. In succeeding years she undertook a heavy programme of royal occasions at home and of overseas tours, performing her duties with confidence and charm.

GEORGE, two kings of Greece:

George I (1845–1913), grandfather of George II, born at Copenhagen, second son of Christian IX of Denmark, was elected to the Greek throne in 1863, but in 1913 was assassinated.

George II (1890–1947), grandson of George I, succeeded in 1922 on the second deposition of his father, Constantine I, but was himself driven out in 1923, to be restored in 1935 after a plebiscite. When Greece, after successfully resisting the Italians, was overrun by the Germans, George withdrew to Crete, to Egypt and thence to Britain. After a plebiscite in 1946 in favour of the monarchy, he re-ascended the Greek throne.

GEORGE V (1819–78), last king of Hanover (1851–66), was born at Berlin. Blind from 1833 and a complete absolutist, by siding with Austria he lost Hanover to Prussia and died an exile in Paris. His son, **Ernest Augustus** (1845–1923), Duke of Cumberland (removed from British peerage 1917), maintained his Hanoverian claim till 1913; his son, Ernest Augustus (b. 1887; deposed 1918), Duke of Brunswick, married William II's daughter, Victoria Louisa.

GEORGE, Prince, of Denmark. See ANNE.

GEORGE, (1) **David Lloyd**. See LLOYD GEORGE.

(2) **Henry** (1839–97), American economist, born in Philadelphia, went to sea, and in 1858 arrived in California, where he became a printer and married. He conducted several papers, and took an active part in public questions. In 1870 he published *Our Land and Land Policy*, in 1879 *Progress and Poverty*. His fundamental remedy for poverty was a ' single tax ' levied on the value of land exclusive of improvements, and the abolition of all taxes which fall upon industry and thrift. Other works included *Protection and Free Trade* (1886), *The Condition of Labour* (1891). See Lives by H. George, jun. (1901) and A. Birnie (1840).

(3) **Mlle**, stage name of **Marguerite Joséphine Weimar**, *zhorzh* (1787–1867), French tragedienne, born at Bayeux, noted at the Comédie-Française for her playing in both classical tragedy and the early romantic dramas. In her *Memoirs* she has left an account of her liaison with Napoleon. See E. Saunders, *Napoleon and Mlle George* (1958).

(4) **Stefan**, *gay-or'gĕ* (1868–1933), German poet, born at Büdesheim (near Bingen), edited (1892–1919) *Blätter für die Kunst*, a journal devoted to the work of a group of advanced poets and writers to which he belonged, and wrote (besides translations from Baudelaire, Shakespeare, Dante, &c.) much verse (*Hymnen*, 1890; *Der siebente Ring*, 1907; *Der Stern des Bundes*, 1914), which shows the influence of the French Symbolists and the English pre-Raphaelites.

His poems, dispensing with punctuation and capitals, are an expression of mood, conveying an impression rather than a meaning. In *Das neue Reich* (1928) he advocated a new German culture, not in accord with that of the Nazis. See study by Bennett (1954).

GEORGE OF PODIEBRAD. See PODIEBRAD.

GÉRANDO, Joseph Marie, Baron de, *zhay-rã-dõ* (1772–1842), French statesman, philosopher and philanthropist, was born of Italian ancestry at Lyons. He held high administrative posts under Napoleon, and from 1811 was a councillor of state. His works include *Des signes et de l'art de penser* (1800), based on a prize treatise ' crowned ' by the Academy; an important *Histoire de philosophie* (1803), which gained him admission to the Academy; *Visiteur du pauvre* (1820) and *Du perfectionnement-moral* (1824), each awarded the Montyon prize.

GERARD, (1) **Alexander** (1728–95), Scottish philosopher, born at Chapel of Garioch manse, professor at Aberdeen who wrote on taste, and influenced Kant, Schiller, &c.— His son, **Gilbert** (1760–1815), succeeded him in the chair of Divinity; and three of his sons were Himalayan explorers—**Capt. Alexander** (1792–1839), **Capt. Patrick** (1794–1848) and **James** (1795–1848).

(2) **John** (1545–1612), English herbalist, born at Nantwich, kept Lord Burghley's gardens for over twenty years, practised as a barber-surgeon, and became master of the company in 1607. His *Herball* (1597) was mainly based upon Dodoens' *Pemptades* (1583).

GÉRARD, *zhay-rahr*, (1) **Étienne Maurice, Comte** (1773–1852), Marshal of France, born at Damvilliers, served on the Rhine, in Italy, La Vendée, Germany and Spain. For his services at Austerlitz (1805) he was appointed general of brigade. He fought at Jena, Erfurt and Wagram, in the Russian campaign, and at Ligny and Wavre, in 1831 drove the Dutch out of Flanders, and in 1832 compelled Antwerp to capitulate. Under Louis Philippe he was twice war minister.

(2) **François Pascal Simon, Baron** (1770–1837), French painter, was born in Rome, but brought up in Paris, and became a pupil of David (q.v.) and member of the Revolutionary Tribunal in 1793. His full-length portrait of Isabey the miniaturist (1796) and his *Cupid and Psyche* (1798), both in the Louvre, established his reputation and leading men and women of the Empire and the Restoration sat to him. He now turned to historical painting for the love of it, producing the well-known *Battle of Austerlitz* and *Entry of Henry IV*, but in this type of work he lacked vitality and began to suffer a decline in popularity before the advance of Romanticism. He was made court painter and baron by Louis XVIII. See books by Adam (1852–57) and H. Gérard (1867).

GERARDS, (1) **Balthasar,** Dutch assassin, in 1584 shot William the Silent (q.v.) at Delft, and was tortured to death.

(2) See GHEERAERTS.

GERBERT. See SYLVESTER II.

GERHARDT, (1) **Charles Frédéric,** *zhay-rahr* (1816–56), French chemist, born at Strasbourg, studied chemistry at Leipzig and

Giessen, and in 1848 settled in Paris. Between 1849 and 1855 he published his views of homologous and heterologous series and the theory of types with which his name is associated, and researched into anhydrous acids and oxides. In 1855 he became professor of Chemistry at Strasbourg. See Life by Gerhardt and Grimaux (1900).

(2) **Elena,** *gayr'hart* (1883–1961), German concert singer, who early specialized in the interpretation of German Lieder, studied under Mme Hedmondt at the Conservatory of Leipzig, her birthplace, where she made her debut in 1902. She was greatly influenced by Arthur Nikisch, under whom she later studied and who was often her accompanist. Having left Germany when the Nazis came to power, she made her home in London, taking British nationality after the war. She taught at the Guildhall School of Music for a short time.

(3) **Paul,** *gayr'hart* (1607–76), German hymnwriter, born at Gräfenhainichen in Saxony, became assistant pastor at St Nicholas in Berlin in 1657, but for opposing the elector's attempted union of the Lutheran and Reformed Churches was banished in 1666. From 1669 he was pastor of Lübben. His hymns were unique in their sincerity and simplicity in the age of baroque.

GÉRICAULT, Theodore, *zhay-ree-kõ* (1791–1824), French painter, born in Rouen, became in 1810 a pupil of Guérin, in whose studio he met and befriended Delacroix (q.v.). A great admirer of the 17th century Dutch and Flemish schools, he revolted against the current classicism, and his unorthodox approach and bold use of colour incurred the disapproval of his teacher, who advised him to give up painting. His first important exhibition piece was *Officer of Light Horse* at the Salon of 1812, which was followed by other canvases noteworthy for their realism. In his quest for authenticity Géricault spent much time studying the raw material of his pictures, thus achieving the great effectiveness of his masterpiece *The Raft of the Medusa* (1819, Louvre), based on a shipwreck which had shortly before caused a sensation in France. It was harshly criticized and Géricault withdrew to England, where he did a number of paintings of racing scenes and landscapes and conceived an admiration for Constable and Bonington, whose work he brought to the notice of the French. *The Raft of the Medusa* profoundly impressed and influenced Delacroix. See studies by L. Delteil (Paris 1924) and G. Oprescu (1927).

GERMAIN, Lord George. See SACKVILLE (2).

GERMAN, Sir Edward, orig. Edward German Jones (1862–1936), English composer, born at Whitchurch, Shropshire, studied at the Royal Academy of Music and became a fellow in 1895. In 1888 he was made musical director of the Globe Theatre, London, and became known for his incidental music to Shakespeare. In 1901 he emerged as a light opera composer, when he completed Sullivan's *Emerald Isle* after the composer's death. *Merrie England*, with its engagingly national character and its charming melodies based on folksong and traditional dance forms, followed in 1902 and has remained evergreen, but *Tom Jones* (1907) and *Fallen Fairies* (1909) did not altogether fulfil his early promise. He also displayed his craftsmanship in several symphonies, suites, chamber music and songs and the *Welsh Rhapsody* (1904). He was knighted in 1928. See Life by W. H. Scott (1932).

GERMANICUS CAESAR (15 B.C.–A.D. 19), Roman soldier, son of Nero Claudius Drusus, and of Antonia, daughter of Mark Antony and niece of Augustus. Adopted by Tiberius, he was consul in A.D. 12, and in 13 was appointed to the command of the eight legions on the Rhine, and in 14 quelled a great mutiny. Next year he marched to meet Arminius (q.v.), whom he overthrew in two desperate battles. Tiberius, jealous of his popularity, recalled him in 17, and sent him to the East, at the same time appointing as viceroy of Syria, in order secretly to counteract him, the envious Calpurnius Piso. Germanicus died at Ephidaphnae near Antioch, on October 9, probably of poison. His wife, Agrippina, and two of her sons were put to death; the third son, Caligula, was spared to be emperor. A daughter, Agrippina, became as remarkable for her vices as her mother had been for her virtues. See Tacitus' *Annals*.

GERMANUS, St (*c.* 378–448), Bishop of Auxerre, was invited over to Britain to combat Pelagianism in 429. Under him the Christian Britons won the bloodless 'Alleluia Victory' over the Picts and Saxons at Maes Garmon (Germanius' field) in Flintshire.

GEROK, Karl (1815–90), German Protestant theologian, preacher and hymnwriter, born at Vaihingen, but lived mostly at Stuttgart. See Life by G. Gerok (1892).

GÉRÔME, Jean Léon, *zhay-rōm* (1824–1904), French historical genre painter, was born at Vesoul. He began to exhibit in 1847; and in 1863 he became professor of Painting in the School of Fine Arts. His *Polytechnic Student* is in the Tate. A firstrate draughtsman, he achieved distinction as a sculptor and decorative painter.

GERONTIUS, (1) (d. A.D. 413), a Roman general of British birth who rebelled against the usurper Constantine and made Maximus emperor; but, defeated by Honorius, took his own life.

(2) **Gerontius**, deacon at Milan under Ambrose, who had an extraordinary—and singularly unedifying—dream, but instead of doing penance as commanded, went to Constantinople, won favour at court, and was made bishop of Nicomedia, but was deposed by Chrysostom (A.D. 399) in spite of popular favour. Newman's *Dream of Gerontius*, turned into an oratorio by Elgar, refers to no historical person, but (with the etymological sense of *Senex*) to an aged Christian on the verge of death, enabled by vision to see beyond the veil.

GERRY, Elbridge (1744–1814), American statesman, born at Marblehead, Mass., was sent to the first National Congress. Elected governor of Massachusetts in 1810, Gerry rearranged the electoral districts so as to secure the advantage to the Republican party —whence (from a joke on *salamander*) the word *gerrymander*. He was vice-president

of the U.S.A. (1813–14). See Life by Austin (1828–29).

GERSHWIN, George (1898–1937), American composer, born in New York. He studied music in the traditional way, but published his first popular song at the age of fourteen, and became famous as a composer of Broadway musicals, bringing unusual skill and originality to the genre. His most famous works of this style are perhaps *Lady Be Good* (1924) and *Of Thee I Sing* (1931). In 1924, a commission from the conductor Paul Whiteman led to his composition of the *Rhapsody in Blue*, a concert work mating romantic emotionalism and the jazz idiom with unusual success; this he followed by the *Concerto in F*, and *An American in Paris*, exploiting the same forces. His Negro opera, *Porgy and Bess* (1935), has won worldwide popularity. Gershwin, who described jazz as ' a very powerful American folk-music ', brought great skill and sincerity not only to ' symphonic jazz ' but to the modern popular song and musical comedy, which are no less important in his hands than the more ambitious (in a traditional sense) forms he handled. See Ewen, *Journey to Greatness* (1956).

GERSON, Jean le Charlier de, *zhayr-sõ* (1363–1429), French theologian and mystic, was born at the village of Gerson, in the diocese of Rheims, December 14. He was educated in Paris. ' Doctor Christianissimus ' was a nominalist, opposed to scholasticism, but a Christian mystic. He supported the proposal for putting an end to the schism between Rome and Avignon by the resignation of both the contending pontiffs, especially at the councils of Pisa and Constance (1414). But his own fortunes were marred by the animosity of the Duke of Burgundy, for denouncing the murder of the Duke of Orleans. Gerson prudently retired to Rattenburg in Tirol, where he composed his *De Consolatione Theologiae*. It was only after several years that he was able to return to France and settle in a monastery at Lyons. He died July 12. See studies by Connolly (1929) and Barron (1936).

GERSTÄCKER, Friedrich, *ger'stek-èr* (1816–1872), German novelist and traveller, was born at Hamburg, worked his way through the United States, South America, Polynesia and Australia, and wrote exciting and colourful adventure stories, including *Mississippi River Pirates* (1848), &c.

GERTRUDE, St (626–59), daughter of Pepin the Elder, she became abbess of Nivelles, Brabant, on the death of her mother and after refusing to marry Dagobert I.

GERTRUDE OF ALTENBURG, St (1227–1297), German mystic, prioress of the Premonstratensians at Altenburg, daughter of St Elisabeth of Hungary.

GERTRUDE OF HELFTA sometimes called the Great, St (1256–*c.* 1302), entered the convent of Helfta near Eisleben at the age of five, and when fifteen began to have visions which she described in Latin treatises. She was never formally canonized.

GERVASE OF CANTERBURY (*c.* 1141–*c.* 1210), English monk and chronicler of the reigns of Stephen, Henry II and Richard I, and author of a history of the archbishops of

Canterbury, edited by Bishop Stubbs for the Rolls series (1879–80).

GERVASE OF TILBURY (c. 1150–c. 1220), English historical writer, born probably at Tilbury, lectured on canon law at Bologna, and was marshal of the kingdom of Arles, perhaps provost of the nunnery at Ebsdorf. Of his *Otia Imperialia*, composed about 1212 for the entertainment of the emperor Otho IV, the first two books consist of an abstract of geography and history, the third (ed. by Liebrecht, 1856) contains a collection of curious beliefs about the ' Veronica ', British sirens, the magnet, etc. The whole was printed by Leibniz in vol. i of *Scriptores Rerum Brunsvicensium* (1707–10). Gervase also prepared a *Liber Facetiarum* or book of anecdotes for Henry II's son Henry, which is no longer in existence.

GERVINUS, Georg Gottfried, *ger-vee'noos* (1805–71), German critic and historian, born at Darmstadt, became in 1836 a professor at Göttingen, one of the seven who protested in 1837 against the suspension of the Hanoverian constitution. Among his works are commentaries on Shakespeare (1849–52, Eng. tr. 1862) and *Geschichte des 19ten Jahrhunderts* (1856–66). He was elected to the National Assembly in 1848. See studies by Harnach (1918) and Rychner (1922).

GESENIUS, Heinrich Friedrich Wilhelm, *ge-zay'nee-oos* (1786–1842), German biblical scholar, born at Nordhausen, became professor of Theology at Halle in 1811. His first great work was *Hebräisches u. Chaldäisches Handwörterbuch* (1810–12, trans. 1906). His *Hebr. Elementarbuch*, consisting of the *Hebräische Grammatik* (1813; trans. 1910) and the *Hebräisches Lesebuch* (1814), has contributed enormously to the knowledge of the Hebrew language. His greatest work is *Thesaurus philologico-criticus Linguae Hebraicae et Chaldaicae* (part i 1829; completed by Rödiger, 1858). His theological standpoint was rationalist. See works by Haym (Berlin 1842) and H. Gesenius (Halle 1886).

GESNER, (1) Johann Matthias (1691–1761), German classical scholar and educationist, edited Quintilian, Pliny, *Scriptores Rei Rusticae* and chrestomathies.

(2) **Konrad von** (1516–65), Swiss naturalist, born at Zürich, in 1537 became professor of Greek at Lausanne, in 1541 of Physics and Natural History at Zürich. He published seventy-two works, and left eighteen others in progress. His *Bibliotheca Universalis* (1545–1549) contained the titles of all the books then known in Hebrew, Greek and Latin, with criticisms and summaries of each. His *Historia Animalium* (1551–58) aimed at bringing together all that was known in his time of every animal. But probably botany was his *forte*. He collected over five hundred plants undescribed by the ancients, and was preparing for a third *magnum opus* at his death. He also wrote on medicine, mineralogy and philology. See Hanhart's *Gesner* (1824).

GESSLER, Hermann. See **TELL.**

GESSNER, Salomon (1730–88), Swiss pastoral poet, who also painted and engraved landscapes, was born and died at Zürich, where he was a bookseller. *Daphnis* (1754), a sentimental bucolic, was followed two years later by a volume of *Idyls* and by *Inkel und Yariko*. His *Tod Abels* (1758), a species of idyllic heroic prose poem, although the feeblest of his works, had the greatest success. Gessner's landscape paintings are all in the conventional classic style, but his engravings are of real merit. In 1772 he published a second volume of *Idyls* and a series of letters on landscape painting. See studies by Wölfflin (1889) and Leemann van Elck (1937).

GEULINCX, or Geulingx, Arnold, *gæ'links* (1625–69), Belgian philosopher, born at Antwerp, from 1646 to 1658 lectured at Louvain, was deposed for his anti-scholasticism, and, after turning Protestant and living at Leyden in great distress, became in 1665 professor of Philosophy there. His ideas are expounded in *Saturnalia, Logica, Ethica*, published in his lifetime, and in *Annotata Praecurrentia ad Cartesii Principia* (1690) and *Metaphysica Vera* (1691). A leading exponent of Descartes' philosophy, he originated the doctrine of ' Occasionalism ' as an answer to the philosophical objections to the Cartesian antithesis of mind and body. This doctrine ascribes their apparent interaction to a preordained divine arrangement, analogous to the agreement, yet mutual independence, of two synchronized clocks. See study by Land (1895).

GEZELLE, Guido, KHe-*zel'lè* (1830–99), Flemish poet, born at Bruges, was for 28 years a curé in Courtrai. He founded the West Flemish school. See *Life* by A. Walgrave (1924).

GHAZALI, Abu Mohammed al-, *ga-zah'lee*, or **Algazel** (1058–1111), Arab theologian-philosopher, who was born and died at Tus in Khurasan. He taught philosophy at Baghdad (1091–95), went to Mecca, lectured ten years at Damascus, and taught also at Jerusalem and Alexandria. His chief works are *Opinions of the Philosophers, Tendencies of the Philosophers* and *Destruction of the Philosophers*, in which he challenges the methods of the current Arabian scholasticism. He also wrote a commentary on the ninety-nine names of God, ethical treatises, and works on religion and philosophy. See studies by Wensinck (1940) and M. Smith (1944).

GHEERAERTS, *gay'rahrts*, (1) **Marcus** (c. 1510–90), Flemish-born religious and animal painter and engraver, father of (2), was driven out of Bruges for his Protestantism and settled in London (c. 1568).

(2) **Marcus** (1561–1635), son of (1), court painter to James I, specialized in portraits. Many pictures attributed to him are of doubtful authenticity, but among the best of those certainly his are *Lady Russell* (1625, Woburn), and *William Camden* and *Sir Henry Savile* (both 1621, Bodleian).

GHERARDESCA. See UGOLINO.

GHIBERTI, Lorenzo, *gee-ber'tee* (1378–1455), Florentine goldsmith, bronze-caster and sculptor, was born and died at Florence. In 1400 he executed frescoes in the palace of Pandolfo Malatesta at Rimini. He was next chosen by the Florentine guild of merchants to execute a gate in bronze, to match an older one by Andrea Pisano. When Ghiberti had completed this work (1424) he was entrusted with the execution of another gate, finished in 1452 to emulate the two already adorning the baptistery. Michelangelo called them ' the gates of Paradise '. They took fifty years to complete. The mingled grace and grandeur of these compositions is beyond all praise. Ghiberti is undoubtedly one of the most accomplished workers in metal that has ever lived. Among his other works are monuments in Santa Maria Novella and in Santa Croce at Florence, executed about 1427; a bronze relief in the Duomo (1440); and bronze statues of SS. John the Baptist, Matthew and Stephen for the Or San Michele (1414–22). See studies by Perkins (1897), L. Goldscheider (1949), and Lives by J. von Schlosser (1941) and Vasari (1949).

GHIKA, Helena, *gee'ka,* pseud. **Dora d'Istria** (1829–88), Rumanian author and traveller, a daughter of Prince Michael Ghika, was born at Bucharest, married Prince Koltzoff-Massalsky, of St Petersburg, but from 1855 lived mainly at Florence. Her works include *La Vie monastique dans l'Église orientale* (1855), *La Suisse allemande* (1856), *Les Femmes en orient* (1860), a history, &c.

GHIRLANDAIO, *geer-lan-dah'yō,* (1) **Domenico Curradi** (1449–94), Florentine painter, father of (2), was born at Florence, and apprenticed to a goldsmith, probably his father, a metal garland-maker or ' Ghirlandaio ', becoming a painter when he was thirty-one. He painted principally frescoes, and in his native city. Among these are six subjects from the life of St Francis (1485) and an altarpiece, the *Adoration of the Shepherds* (now in the Florentine Academy), in the church of S. Trinità; and in the choir of Santa Maria Novella a series illustrating the lives of the Virgin and the Baptist (1490). Between 1482 and 1484 he painted for Pope Sixtus IV, in the Sistine Chapel, the fresco *Christ calling Peter and Andrew.* His easel pictures include the *Adoration of the Magi* (1488), in the church of the Innocenti at Florence, and the *Visitation of the Virgin* (1491), in the Louvre; and mosaics in the *Annunciation* in the cathedral of Florence.

(2) **Ridolfo** (1483–1561), son of (1), was a considerable painter of altarpieces and portraits. He decorated the Cappella dei Priori in the Palazzo Vecchio, Florence. The many figures in his religious scenes are beautifully characterized, the faces full of expression and feeling, but his composition tends to be unimaginative and the grouping formal and repetitive. His work is of great historical value for its detailed portrayal of costume, domestic features, &c. He was assisted by his brothers **David** (1452–1525) and **Benedetto** (1458–97). See Life by Davies (1908).

GHULAM MOHAMMED (1895–1956), governor-general of Pakistan (1951–55).

GIACOMETTI, Alberto, *jah-ko-met'tee* (1901–1966), Swiss sculptor and painter, born at Stampa, studied at Geneva and worked mainly in Paris, at first under Bourdelle. He joined the Surrealists in 1930, producing many abstract constructions of a symbolic kind, arriving finally at the characteristic

' thin man ' bronzes, long spidery statuettes, rigid in posture yet trembling on the verge of movement, suggesting transience, change and decay, e.g., *Pointing Man* (1947; Tate).

GIACOMO, Salvatore di, *jah'ko-mō* (1860–1934), Neapolitan poet, wrote songs and lyrics in dialect. Librarian in the National Library in Naples, he also compiled several historical and bibliographical works.

GIACOSA, Giuseppe, *ja-kō'sa* (1847–1906), Italian dramatist, born at Colleretto-Parella, Piedmont, was a successful practitioner of various types of play, ranging from historical dramas and comedies in verse to contemporary social problem pieces. Representative of the former are *Il Conte Rosso* (1880), *La Contessa di Challant* (1891), and of the latter, *Resa a discrezione* (1888), *Tristi amori* (1887), *Diritti dell' anima* (1894), *Come le foglie* (1900), *Il piu forte* (1904). He was no radical, however, but emphasized bourgeois ideals of decency, the homely virtues and established institutions. Consequently, his plays have not carried over into modern repertory, though *Come le foglie,* his best piece, dealing with the disintegration of a wealthy family, has been filmed. With Luigi Illica he also collaborated on the libretti for *La Bohème, Madame Butterfly* and *Tosca.* See Life by P. Nardi (1949).

GIANIBELLI, Federigo, *jan-ee-bel'lee* (fl. 1530–88), Italian military engineer, born at Mantua about 1530, entered the service of Queen Elizabeth, and during the siege of Antwerp (1585) destroyed with an explosive ship a Spanish bridge over the Scheldt. He rendered great service in the preparations for resisting ᴕe Armada of 1588, and died in London.

GIANNONE, Pietro, *jan-nō'nay* (1676–1748), Italian antipapal historian, was born at Ischitella in Naples, and practised as a barrister. His *Storia civile del regno di Napoli* (1723) led to his banishment from Naples; at Geneva he published *Il Triregno,* a bitter attack upon the papal pretensions. Decoyed into Savoy in 1736, he was confined at Turin until his death. See Life by Nicolini (1913).

GIAUQUE, William Francis, *jee-ōk* (1895–   ), American chemist, became professor in the University of California in 1934. In 1929 he took part in the discovery of the existence of isotopes of oxygen, and he later developed the adiabatic demagnetization method for the production of very low temperatures. He was a Nobel laureate in 1949.

GIBB, Andrew Dewar (1888–   ), Scottish jurist, born at Paisley, studied at Glasgow, was called to the Scottish (1914) and English (1917) bar, and after lecturing at Edinburgh and Cambridge became regius professor of Law at Glasgow (1934–58). He has written several standard works on Scots law and on the case for Scottish home rule, and he was chairman of the Scottish National Party (1936–40), of the Saltire Society (1955–57), and president of the Covenant Association from 1957.

GIBBINGS, Robert John (1889–1958), Irish artist and author, born in Cork. He is famous for the engravings and woodcuts with which he illustrated most of his books. He was director of the Golden Cockerel Press from 1924 to 1933, and through it was instrumental in reviving the art of wood engraving. He travelled widely and was perhaps the first artist to use diving equipment to make underwater drawings. His published works include: *Iorana*, *Sweet Thames Run Softly* (1940), *Over the Reefs* (1948), *Coming Down the Seine* (1953) and *Trumpets from Montparnasse* (1955). See *Engravings*, ed. P. Empson (1959).

GIBBON, (1) **Edward** (1737–94), English historian, was born at Putney, the son of a country gentleman. Educated at Westminster and Magdalen College, Oxford, he derived little benefit from either; his *Autobiography* contains a scathing attack on the Oxford of his time. Becoming a Roman Catholic at the age of sixteen, he was sent to Lausanne, where for five years he boarded with a Calvinist pastor who by a judicious course of reading wooed him back to the Protestant faith. Full details of all this are given in the *Autobiography*, as also of the one romance in his life—his love for the minister's daughter who afterwards became the mother of Mme de Staël. In classic form he acquiesced in his father's veto on the marriage—' I sighed as a lover, I obeyed as a son '. A more fruitful result of his sojourn in Lausanne was the acquisition of immense erudition which was indispensable for the historian of the Empire. Having returned to England in 1758, he employed his leisure in his father's house on an *Essai sur l'étude de la littérature*, but his bookish solitude was interrupted for four years (1759–63) by service in the Hampshire militia, a useful preparation for the historian, as he acknowledges. It was in Rome the following year (1764) that ' musing among the ruins of the Capitol ' he was seized with the ambition of writing *The Decline and Fall of the Roman Empire*. His father had left him the means to settle in London in 1772 and so devote himself to his great task. He entered Parliament in 1774, and as a devoted follower of Lord North was made commissioner of trade and plantations. This employment also he regarded as a ' school of civil prudense ' and therefore experience for the great History, the first volume of which appeared in 1776. The general acclamation was disturbed by the scandal of the famous chapters 15–16, which showed Gibbon in the rôle of a fifth-century pagan philosopher deriding Christianity in discreet sarcasms. His *Vindication* (1779) did not reassure the learned public as the relatively cold reception of the second and third volumes (1781) proved. Perhaps he thought Lausanne a more peaceful place for the conclusion of his labours, for the last three volumes were written there though published in London (1788). He returned to England and spent much of the remainder of his days with Lord Sheffield, who published his *Miscellaneous Works* (1796), which contains the *Autobiography* pieced together from fragments left by Gibbon. The chief concept of his great work is the continuity of the Roman Empire down to the fall of Constantinople. His limitations or positive errors—his blending of sources of different periods and his consistently pessimistic view of the unrelieved bleakness and misery of the later Empire in no way detract from the greatness of his achievement. His idea of history, too, as ' little more than the register of the crimes, follies and misfortunes of mankind ' might be regarded by the objective historian as a limitation, but the *Decline and Fall* is literature as well as history and his pessimism sets the tone for the work. His detestation of enthusiasm is a mark of his age, and he is no less severe on pagan than on Christian superstition. Here again his cynicism adds a spice to the work which relates it to literature rather than history. His accuracy in the use of his sources has not been questioned. See studies by G. M. Young (1932), D. M. Low (1937), E. J. Oliver (1958), H. L. Bond (1960) and J. W. Swain (1966), also *Letters* (3 vols. ed. Norton, 1956).

(2) **Lewis Grassic**, pseud. of **James Leslie Mitchell** (1901–35), Scottish novelist and historian, born in Arbuthnott, Kincardineshire. His books include *Conquest of the Maya* (1934), a standard work on the subject, and *Scots Quair*, a fictional trilogy, *Sunset Song* (1931), *Cloud Howe* (1933) and *Grey Granite* (1934), on the eventful life, both rural and urban of his Scottish heroine, Chris, in the early part of the 20th century. See *Life* by I. Munro (1966).

GIBBONS, (1) **Grinling** (1648–1721), English sculptor and woodcarver, was born at Rotterdam. He had for some time practised his art in England, when, discovered by Evelyn carving a crucifix (1671), he was appointed by Charles II to a place in the Board of Works, and employed in the chapel at Windsor; here and in St Paul's, London, his work displays great taste and delicacy of finish. At Chatsworth, Burghley, Southwick and other mansions he executed an immense quantity of carved embellishment; the ceiling of a room at Petworth is his *chef-d'oeuvre*. His favourite nature motifs were used indiscriminately but always with an eye for design. He produced several fine pieces in marble and bronze, including the statue of James II at Whitehall. See study by Green (1964).

(2) **James** (1834–1921), American divine, born at Baltimore, U.S., became archbishop of that city in 1877, and a cardinal in 1886. He was largely responsible for the growth of the Roman Catholic Church in America. He wrote *The Faith of Our Fathers* (1876), *Our Christian Heritage* (1889), &c. See Lives by Will (1923) and Ellis (1952).

(3) **Orlando** (1583–1625), English composer, son of a professional Cambridge musician, was probably born at Oxford. In 1604 he was appointed organist of the Chapel Royal, London. In 1606 he took his Mus.Bac. at Cambridge, and in 1622 his Mus.Doc. at Oxford. In 1623 he became organist of Westminster Abbey. In May 1625 he went with the king and court to Canterbury, and died there on June 5. His compositions are not numerous, but some of them are masterpieces. The best known are his Morning and Evening Service in F; among his anthems, ' O Clap your Hands ' and ' God

is gone up ', 'Hosanna', 'Lift up your Heads ', and 'Almighty and everlasting God'; and of his madrigals, 'The Silver Swan', 'O that the learned Poets', and 'Dainty, fine, sweet Bird'. Besides these he left hymns, fantasies for viols, and virginal pieces. See a monograph by E. H. Fellowes (1925), and *Tudor Church Music*, iv (1925).

(4) **Stella Dorothea** (1902–), English writer, born in London, worked as a journalist and later began a series of successful novels. She also wrote poetry and short stories. Her *Cold Comfort Farm* (1933), a light-hearted satire on the melodramatic rural novel *à la* Mary Webb, won the Femina Vie Heureuse prize, and has established itself as a classic of parody.

GIBBS, (1) **James** (1682–1754), Scottish architect, born in Aberdeen, studied in Italy. A friend and disciple of Wren, he became in 1713 one of the commissioners for building new churches in London, but was dismissed in 1715 for his Roman Catholicism. He designed St Mary-le-Strand (1717), the steeple of St Clement Danes (1719), St Peter's, Vere Street (1724), and St Martin's-in-the-Fields (1726), the latter being perhaps his most influential and attractive work. He was also responsible for St Bartholomew's Hospital (1730), the Radcliffe Camera at Oxford (1737–47) and the Senate House at Cambridge (1730). His *Book of Architecture* (1728) helped to spread the Palladian style and influenced the design of many churches of the colonial period in America. See Life by B. Little (1955).

(2) **Josiah Willard** (1839–1903), American mathematical physicist, born in New Haven, Connecticut, graduated at Yale, where he was professor from 1871 to 1903. He contributed to the study of thermodynamics, and his most important work, first published as *On the Equilibrium of Heterogeneous Substances* (1876 and 1878), and including his 'phase rule', established him as a founder of physical chemistry.

(3) **Sir Philip** (1877–1962), English writer, spent his early working life on Fleet Street, and became war correspondent to the *Daily Chronicle* in World War I. He wrote several books on his war experiences, on current affairs and travel (*European Journey*, 1934; *The New Elizabethans*, 1953; &c.), and a number of successful novels, including *The Street of Adventure* (1909) about Fleet Street, *The Middle of the Road* (1922), *The Cross of Peace* (1933) and *The Ambassador's Wife* (1956). He was knighted in 1920. See his autobiographical *The Pageant of the Years* (1947).

(4) **Sir Vicary** (1751–1820), English judge, born in Exeter, became solicitor-general, attorney-general, lord chief-baron, and chief justice of the common pleas, having made his reputation for his defence of Horne Tooke in 1794. His bitter sarcasm and lack of humour gained him the nickname of 'Vinegar Gibbs'.

GIBSON, (1) **Charles Dana** (1867–1944), American cartoonist born at Roxbury, Mass., was a brilliant black-and-white artist and, especially strong in society cartoons, created the beautiful, well-bred 'Gibson Girl'.

(2) **Edmund** (1669–1748), English church jurist, born in Westmorland, became Bishop of Lincoln (1716), then of London (1720). He edited the *Anglo-Saxon Chronicle* and translated Camden's *Britannia*, but is best known for his great *Codex iuris ecclesiastici Anglicani* (1713). His aim was to reconcile clergy and universities to the Hanoverian dynasty. See Life by N. Sykes (1927).

(3) **Edward.** See ASHBOURNE.

(4) **Guy** (1918–44), British airman. As a wing-commander in the R.A.F. he led the famous 'dambusters' raid on the Möhne and Eder dams in 1943, an exploit for which he received the V.C. He was killed on a later operation. See his *Enemy Coast Ahead* (1946).

(5) **John** (1790–1866), British sculptor, was born a market-gardener's son at Gyffin near Conway, found a patron in Roscoe, and proceeding to Rome in 1817, studied under Canova and Thorvaldsen, and lived there permanently. His best works are *Psyche borne by Zephyrs, Hylas surprised by Nymphs* and *Venus with the Turtle*. The innovation of tinting his figures (e.g., his Venus), he defended by reference to Greek precedents. In 1836 he was elected R.A. He left his studio to the Royal Academy, which founded a Gibson Gallery. See Life by Matthews (1911).

(6) **Richard** (1615–90), English court dwarf and miniaturist, married Anne Shepherd (1620–1709), like himself 3 feet 10 inches high. Charles I gave away the bride.

(7) **Thomas Milner** (1806–84), British politician, was born in Trinidad. Returned M.P. for Manchester (1841), he was a leading anti-Corn-Law orator. While sitting for Ashton-under-Lyne (1857–68) he was president of the Board of Trade (1859–60), and also *ad-interim* president of the Poor Law Commission. It was mainly owing to him that the advertisement duty was repealed (1853), the newspaper stamp duty (1855) and the paper duty (1861).

(8) **Wilfrid Wilson** (1878–1962), English poet and playwright, born at Hexham and educated privately, wrote from 1902 numerous volumes of verse (1918, 1926, &c.). Later volumes included *The Island Stag* (1947). He also wrote plays: *Daily Bread* (1910), *Within Four Walls* (1950), &c. A realist, he was concerned with the everyday things of life, particularly with industrial poverty.

GIDDINGS, (1) **Franklin Henry** (1855–1931), American sociologist, professor at Columbia from 1894, wrote *The Principles of Sociology* (1896) and *Scientific Study of Human Society* (1924), &c.

(2) **Joshua Reed** (1795–1864), American anti-slavery statesman, was born in Athens, Pennsylvania. He sat in congress (1838–59); in 1861 he was appointed consul-general in Canada.

GIDE, *zheed,* (1) **André Paul Guillaume** (1869–1951), French writer, born in Paris. He was one of the most brilliant and most widely recognized writers of his generation and received the Nobel prize for literature in 1947. He was author of over fifty volumes of fiction, poetry, plays, criticism, biography, belles-lettres and translations. Among his best-known works are: *Les Nourritures* *terrestres* (1897), *L'Immoraliste* (1902), *La Symphonie pastorale* (1919), the autobiographical *Si le grain ne meurt* (1920), *Les Faux Monnayeurs* (1926), his translations of *Oedipus*, *Anthony and Cleopatra* and *Hamlet*, and his *Journal*, of which two volumes have been translated by Justin O'Brien. His influence on contemporary letters was great, through his personal contacts and through the *Nouvelle Revue française*, of which he was a co-founder in 1909. See studies by C. du Bos (Paris 1929; trans. 1934), K. Mann (1948), A. Guerard (1951), G. Painter (1951), L. Pierre-Quint (1952), E. Starkie (1953) and J. O'Brien (1953), and Life by J. Delay (2 vols.; Paris 1957).

(2) **Charles** (1847–1932), French economist, born at Uzès (Gard), was professor in turn at Bordeaux, Montpellier and Paris. His *Principes d'économie politique* (1883) became a standard work. He wrote also on co-operation and (with Charles Rist) on the history of economic doctrines.

GIDEON, greatest of the judges of Israel, son of Joash, suppressed Baal-worship, and put an end to the seven years' domination of the Midianites by routing them near Mount Gilboa.

GIELGUD, Sir (Arthur) John, *gil'good* (1904–), English actor and producer, a grandnephew of Ellen Terry (q.v.), made his name in *The Constant Nymph* (1926) and *The Good Companions* (1931), became a leading Shakespearian actor of the British theatre and directed many of the Shakespeare Memorial Theatre productions, as well as *The Cherry Orchard* (1954) and *The Chalk Garden* (1956) in London. He has also appeared in films, notably as Disraeli in *The Prime Minister* (1940) and as Cassius in *Julius Caesar* (1952). He was knighted in 1953.

GIESEBRECHT, Wilhelm von, *gee'zè-breKHt* (1814–89), German historian, was born in Berlin, and became professor of History at Königsberg in 1857, in 1862 at Munich. His chief works are a history of the Germanic Empire to 1181 (1855–88). It was the first history of the Middle Ages based upon a critical study of primary sources.

GIESEKING, Walter, *gee'zè-* (1895–1956), German pianist, born in Lyons, France, studied in Hanover and made his first public appearance in 1915. After World War I, in which he served as a bandsman, he established an international reputation, especially in the works of Debussy and Ravel. At his death he was engaged in recording the complete piano works of Mozart, and Beethoven's piano sonatas. See Life by Garoty (1956).

GIESEL, Friedrich, *gee'zel* (1852–1927), German chemist, discovered in 1904 the radioactive element *emanium*.

GIFFEN, Sir Robert (1837–1910), Scottish economist and statistician, born at Strathaven, at first a journalist, eventually became comptroller-general of the commercial, labour and statistical department of the Board of Trade. His works include *Essays in Finance* (1879–86), *The Growth of Capital* (1890) and *Case against Bimetallism* (1892).

GIFFORD, (1) **Adam** (1820–87), Scottish judge, born in Edinburgh, was called to the Scottish bar in 1849, and was raised to the bench as Lord Gifford in 1870. By his will he left endowments to Edinburgh, Glasgow, Aberdeen and St Andrews Universities for undogmatic lectureships in natural theology.

(2) **Robert Swain** (1840–1905). American landscape painter, was born at Naushon, Mass., travelled and painted in Europe and the Near East and settled in New York. He is best known for his sombre treatment of moorlands and seascapes.

(3) **William** (1756–1826), English editor and critic, was born at Ashburton. Left an orphan at twelve, he was enabled to resume school by a local surgeon who liked his verses. He proceeded to Exeter College, Oxford, and after graduating in 1782, travelled on the Continent with Lord Grosvenor's son. His first production, the *Baviad* (1794), was a satire on the Della Cruscans; the *Maeviad* (1796), against corrupt drama. Gifford's editorship of the *Anti-Jacobin* (1797–98) procured him favour with the Tory magnates. In 1802 appeared his translation of Juvenal, with his autobiography. He edited Massinger, Ford, Shirley and Ben Jonson, and was the first editor of Scott's *Quarterly Review* (1809–24). He possessed much satirical acerbity, but little merit as a poet, and as a critic was unduly biased. See Life by R. B. Clark (1931).

GIGLI, Beniamino, *zheel'yee* (1890–1957), Italian tenor, born in Renecanti. The son of a shoemaker, he won a scholarship to the Accademia di Santa Cecilia. He made his operatic début in Donizetti's *La Gioconda* in 1914, and by 1929 had won a worldwide reputation. A lyric-dramatic tenor of superb natural gifts, Gigli compensated for technical deficiencies and weakness as an actor by the vitality of his singing and was at his best in the works of Verdi and Puccini.

GILBERT, (1) Sir Alfred (1854–1934), English sculptor, born in London, studied in France and Italy and executed work of remarkable simplicity and grace, including his statue of Eros in Piccadilly Circus, London, and *Comedy and Tragedy* (1892). He was also a considerable goldsmith. Elected R.A. in 1892, he was professor at the Academy (1900–09).

(2) **Anne.** See TAYLOR (ISAAC).

(3) **Cass** (1859–1934), American architect, born at Zanesville, Ohio, was educated at the Massachusetts Institute of Technology. He is remembered as the designer of the first tower skyscraper, the Woolworth Building (1912), then the tallest building in the world (not counting the Eiffel Tower), and of other outstanding examples in New York, Washington and elsewhere.

(4) **Grove Karl** (1843–1918), American geologist, born at Rochester, N.Y., and educated there. He formulated many of the laws of geological processes. His report on the Henry mountains became the foundation of many modern theories of denudation and river-development. He also published a history of the Niagara river and introduced technical terms such as ' laccolith ' and ' hanging valley '.

(5) **Sir Humphrey** (1537–83), English navigator, born at Buxham, educated at Eton

and Oxford, abandoned law for arms and joined the expedition to Le Havre (1512). His good service against the Irish rebels earned him a knighthood and the government of Munster (1570), after which he saw five years' campaigning in the Netherlands. In 1576 his *Discourse on a Northwest Passage to India* was published by George Gascoigne, without his knowledge; two years later he obtained a royal patent to discover and occupy remote heathen lands, but his expedition (1578–79), which had cost all his own and his wife's estates, was frustrated by internal dissensions, tempests and a smart brush with the Spaniards. Nothing daunted, he sailed again from Plymouth in June 1583, and in August landed in Newfoundland, of which he took possession for Queen Elizabeth. But off Cape Breton he lost the largest of his three vessels left out of five, so was forced to steer homewards with the *Golden Hind* and the *Squirrel*, the latter, in which was Gilbert, only ten tons burden. On September 9, the *Squirrel* went down with all on board. See Life by Wm. G. Gosling (1911), and *Voyages* by Quinn (1940).

(6) **Sir John** (1817–97), English painter and illustrator, born at Blackheath, after two weary years in the City was allowed to follow his true vocation—art. Mainly self-taught, he began to exhibit in oil and watercolour in 1836. President of the Watercolour Society (1871), a knight (1872) and an R.A. (1876), 'the Scott of painting' is remembered for his illustrations of Shakespeare, Scott, Cervantes, &c., and for his wood-engravings in the *Illustrated London News*.

(7) **Sir (Joseph) Henry** (1817–1901), English agricultural chemist, born at Hull and educated at Glasgow and London, from 1843 was associated with Sir John Bennet Lawes in the Rothamsted Agricultural Laboratory and in 1884 became professor of Rural Economy at Oxford. He is particularly noted for his work on nitrogen fertilizers, as opposed to Liebig's mineral type.

(8) **William** (1540–1603), English physician, born at Colchester, in 1561 was elected fellow of St John's, Cambridge, and in 1573 settled in London, becoming physician to Elizabeth, and president of the College of Physicians. In his *De Magnete* (1600) he established the magnetic nature of the earth; and he conjectured that terrestrial magnetism and electricity were two allied emanations of a single force. He was the first to use the terms 'electricity', 'electric force' and 'electric attraction', and to point out that amber is not the only substance which when rubbed attracts light objects. The *gilbert*, unit of magnetomotive power, is named after him. See Life (1891) and edition of his works (1902) by S. P. Thompson.

(9) **William** (1804–89), English novelist, father of (10), born at Bishopstoke, abandoned the East India Company's service for the study of surgery, and that in turn for literature. His thirty works, published from 1858 onwards, include the delightful *King George's Middy*, a Life of Lucrezia Borgia, and several Defoe-like novels—*Dives and Lazarus, Shirley Hall Asylum, De Profundis.*

(10) **Sir William Schwenck** (1836–1911),

English parodist and librettist of the ' Gilbert and Sullivan ' light operas, born in London, November 18, the son of (9), studied at King's College, London, and became a clerk in the privy-council office (1857–62). Called to the bar in 1864, he failed to attract lucrative briefs and subsisted on magazine contributions to *Fun*, for which he wrote much humorous verse over his boyhood nickname ' Bab ', collected in 1869 as the *Bab Ballads*, and occasionally for *Punch*. He also wrote fairy comedies and serious plays in blank verse, which he alone rated highest of his literary output. But it is as the librettist of Sir Arthur Sullivan's light operas that he is remembered. Their famous partnership, begun in 1871, scored its first success with *Trial by Jury* under D'Oyly Carte's able management at the Royalty Theatre, London, in 1875. The same gay, jibing, ludicrously topsy-turvy wit, beautifully accentuated by Sullivan's scores, pervaded the procession of light operas from *H.M.S. Pinafore* (1878) to *The Gondoliers* (1889), which played first at the Opéra Comique and from 1881 in the newly built Savoy Theatre, a carpet in which, considered too costly by the ever argumentative Gilbert, touched off the famous quarrel between him and Sullivan. They created only three more pieces before Sullivan's death and Edward German's efforts to fill the gap in *Fallen Fairies* (1909) proved unsuccessful. He was knighted in 1907. See works under SULLIVAN and Lives by S. Dark and Grey (1923) and H. Pearson (1957).

GILBERT OF MORAY, St (d. 1245), the last Scot canonized, was Bishop of Caithness from 1223.

GILBERT OF SEMPRINGHAM, St (*c.* 1083–1189), in 1148 founded at his birthplace, Sempringham, Lincolnshire, the order of Gilbertines for both monks and nuns. See work by Rose Graham (1901).

GILBEY, Sir Walter (1831–1914), English wine merchant, founder of the well-known wine company, horse-breeder and agriculturist, was born at Bishop's Stortford, and created a baronet in 1893.

GILCHRIST, (1) **Alexander** (1828–61), English biographer, husband of (2), born at Newington Green, was called to the bar in 1849, but maintained himself by art criticism. His *Life of Etty* appeared in 1855, but the *Life of Blake* was completed by his wife (1863). See 2nd ed. with memoir of the author (1880).

(2) **Anne**, *née* Burrows (1828–85), English writer, wife of (1), was born in London, and married in 1851. She completed her husband's *Life of Blake*, wrote on Whitman, and on New England village life, and published a *Life of Mary Lamb* (1883). See Life by her son (1887).

GILDAS, St (*c.* 493–570), Romano-British monk and writer, wrote in Armorica (*c.* 550–560) his famous treatise *De Excidio Britanniae*, first printed at London in 1525, again in Gale's *Scriptores XV* (1691). He is a weak and wordy writer, but his work is the only contemporary British version of events from the invasion of the Romans to his own time. See Stenton, *Anglo-Saxon England* (1943).

GILDER, Richard Watson (1844–1909), American poet and editor from 1881 of the

Century Magazine, born at Bordentown, N.J.

GILES, Lat. **Aegidius, St** (d. *c.* 700), according to legend an Athenian of royal descent, devoted from his cradle to good works. After giving away his patrimony, he lived two years with St Caesarius at Arles, and then retired to a hermitage, where he lived upon herbs and the milk of a hind. The Frankish king, hunting the hind, discovered Aegidius and was so impressed with his holiness that he built a monastery on the spot and made him its abbot. Here he died. He is the patron of lepers, beggars and cripples.

GILFILLAN, George (1813–78), Scottish critic and essayist, lecturer and pulpit orator, born at Comrie, studied at Glasgow, and in 1836 was ordained to a U.P. church in Dundee. See *Memoir* by Watson (1892).

GILL, (1) **Sir David** (1843–1914), Scottish astronomer, born at Aberdeen and educated there, was H.M. Astronomer at the Cape Observatory (1879–1907) and pioneered the use of photography for charting the heavens. See monograph by G. Forbes (1916).

(2) **Eric** (i.e., **Arthur Eric Rowton Gill**) (1882–1940), English carver, engraver, writer and typographer, born at Brighton, son of a clergyman. At the age of twenty-one he forsook the profession of architecture to which he had been articled and took up letter-cutting and masonry, working under the art teacher, Edward Johnston. From this he progressed to engraving about 1906–07 and in 1909 he carved his first stone figure, *The Madonna and Child.* Through the influence of Augustus John he exhibited at the Chenil Galleries, Chelsea, in 1911, and thereafter, for the rest of his life, maintained a steady output of stone and wood carvings, engravings (for his own press, St Dominic, and also for the Golden Cockerel Press), type designs, such as Perpetua, Bunyan and Gill Sans-serif, subsequently adopted by Monotype and used all over the world; as also a stream of books dealing with his various crafts, his thoughts and beliefs. Devotion, of a starkly sincere quality, is the sign manual of all his art; works include the *Stations of the Cross*, executed in Hoptonwood stone, in Westminster Cathedral (1913), war memorials up and down the country after World War I, the gigantic figure, *Mankind* (1928), now in the Tate Gallery, the fine altarpiece at Rossall School Chapel, the sculptures at Broadcasting House, London, and many more. His books are equally the product of a mind ever searching, yet ever homing to the belief that goodness and truth are the fundamentals of both life and art. His own life was a pilgrimage; for, in pursuit of his beliefs he joined the Fabian movement, but later found the socialist ethic limited and joined the Catholic Church. He founded an ideal community at Ditchling. See *Autobiography* (1940), *Letters*, ed. Shewring (1948).

(3) **William John** (1843–82), English military engineer and traveller in the East, was awarded the Royal Geographical Society's gold medal for his map of eastern Tibet. He and E. H. Palmer (q.v.) were murdered by Arab robbers.

GILLESPIE, *gil-les'pi*, (1) **George** (1613–48),

Scottish divine, was born and died at Kirkcaldy, studied at St Andrews and in 1638 was ordained minister of Wemyss. He showed characteristic fearlessness at the Glasgow Assembly that same year, was transferred to Edinburgh in 1642, and in 1643 was sent to the Westminster Assembly, where he took a great part in the debates on discipline and dogma. His *Aaron's Rod Blossoming* (1646) is a masterly statement of the high Presbyterian claim for spiritual independence. In 1648 he was moderator of the General Assembly.

(2) **James** (1726–97), an Edinburgh snuff manufacturer who founded a hospital and school.

(3) **Sir Robert Rollo** (1766–1812), British general, at the age of seventeen joined the Carabiniers. From 1793 to 1798 he experienced gruelling service against the French in Haiti. Having successfully commanded the 20th Dragoons in Jamaica, Gillespie—after a furlough enlivened by his second duel—made his way overland to India via the Black Sea, Iskanderun, the Euphrates and Basra. At Vellore in 1806 his personal daring and initiative nipped in the bud an uprising that might well have attained the proportions of the 1857 Indian Mutiny. In command of a division in the 1811 expedition against Java, his success brought him a K.C.B. In the Gurkha War of 1812 he fell at the head of his men at the final assault on Kalunga. See *Life* by E. Wakeham (1937) and Fortescue, *A Gallant Company* (1927).

(4) **Thomas** (1708–74), Scottish divine, was born at Duddingston, and from 1741 had been minister of Carnock near Dunfermline, where in 1749 he opposed the ordination of a minister, was deposed by the General Assembly and founded in 1752 the Relief Church, which was later absorbed into the United Presbyterian Church.

GILLETTE, King Camp, *jil-let'* (1855–1932), American inventor of the safety razor, was born at Fond du Lac, Wis., founded the company in 1901 and wrote on industrial welfare, &c.

GILLIES, (1) **Sir Harold Delf** (1882–1960), British plastic surgeon, born in Dunedin, N.Z., was educated at Wanganui College and Cambridge University. In 1920 published his *Plastic Surgery of the Face*, which established this art as a recognized branch of medicine. During World War II he was responsible for the setting up of plastic surgery units throughout the country and was personally in charge of the largest one at Park Prewett Hospital, Basingstoke. In 1957 appeared his *The Principles and Art of Plastic Surgery*, the standard work on this subject. He was knighted in 1930.

(2) **John** (1747–1836), Scottish historian, born at Brechin, published a translation (1778) of Isocrates and Lysias, *History of Ancient Greece* (1786), *Frederick II of Prussia* (1789), and *History of the World from Alexander to Augustus* (1807–10). In 1793 he was appointed historiographer for Scotland.

(3) **William George** (1898–   ), Scottish artist, studied at the Edinburgh College of Art, in Italy, and under André Lhote in France. He was elected to the R.S.A. in

1947. His finely organized interpretations of Scottish landscape (many in watercolour) are well known, and his work is represented in the Tate Gallery. In 1959 he became principal of Edinburgh College of Art.

GILLOTT, Joseph, *jil'lot* (1799–1873), English inventor, born at Sheffield, shares with Sir Josiah Mason the credit for having perfected the manufacture of steel pens.

GILLRAY, James (1757–1815), English caricaturist, was born, a Lanark trooper's son, at Chelsea. He first became known as a successful engraver about 1784, and between 1779 and 1811 issued 1500 caricatures. They are full of broad humour and keen satire aimed against the French, Napoleon, George III, the leading politicians and the social follies of his day. For four years insane, he died June 1. See illustrated Life by T. Wright (1851).

GILMAN, Harold (1878–1919), English artist, born at Rode, Somerset. He studied at the Slade School and in Spain. With Ginner and Gore, he was associated with the Camden Town Group (1910), and was later the first president of the London Group. Influenced by Pissarro and Van Gogh, he used 'fauve' colouring to paint interiors and portraits, e.g., his *Mrs Mounter* in the Tate Gallery, London.

GILPIN, (1) **Bernard** (1517–83), Anglican divine, born at Kentmere Hall, Westmorland, studied at Queen's College, Oxford, and at Louvain and Paris and became archdeacon of Durham in 1556. His fearless honesty against pluralities brought accusations of heresy which, however, were unsuccessful, and on Elizabeth's succession he was appointed rector of Houghton le Spring. He turned down many lucrative offers, preferring to minister to his parish and to make preaching excursions into the remotest parts of northern England. See *Memoirs* by Collingwood (1884).

(2) **William** (1724–1804), British clergyman, a leader of the 18th-century cult of the picturesque, author of works on the scenery of Britain, illustrated by his own aquatint engravings. He was born at Scaleby, Carlisle, educated at Oxford, and in 1777 became vicar of Boldre in Hampshire. He is satirized by Combe (q.v.) in *Dr Syntax*. His brother **Sawrey** (1733–1807) was a highly successful animal painter, especially of horses. See works by C. P. Barbier (1959 and 1963).

GIL POLO, Gaspar, *heel-* (c. 1535–91), a Spanish poet, was born at Valencia, and died at Barcelona. He continued Montemayor's *Diana* in his *Diana enamorada* (1564) which was very popular throughout Europe and was used by both Cervantes and Shakespeare as a basis for a plot. It marks a stage in the history of the novel.

GILSON, Étienne, *zheel-sõ* (1884–), French historian, known especially for his works on mediaeval Christian philosophy.

GIL VICENTE. See VICENTE, GIL.

GIMIGNANO, Vincenzo da San, *jim-in-yah'nõ* properly ·Tamagni (c. 1490–1530), Italian painter, perhaps a pupil of Raphael, whose influence is apparent in all his works.

GINCKELL, or **Ginkel, Godert de** (1630–1703), Dutch soldier, who was born and died at Utrecht, and accompanied William III to England in 1688. He commanded a body of horse at the battle of the Boyne (1690), and on the king's return to England was left as commander-in-chief in Ireland. He reduced Ballymore and Athlone, defeated St Ruth at Aghrim, and finally captured Limerick. In 1692 he was created Earl of Athlone. He afterwards commanded the Dutch troops under Marlborough.

GINSBERG, (1) **Allen** (1926–), American poet, author of *Howl* (1957), which achieved a *succès de scandale* as the prototype poem of the 'beat' school.

(2) **Morris** (1889–1970), English sociologist, educated at London, professor at the London School of Economics (1929–54), wrote *The Psychology of Society* (1921), *Studies in Sociology* (1932) and essays on social philosophy (1956), &c.

GINSBURG, Christian David (1831–1914), Polish rabbinical scholar, was born at Warsaw, came early to England and established himself as an authority on the Hebrew scriptures. He discovered that the manuscripts offered by Shapiro to the British Museum were forgeries.

GIOBERTI, Vincenzo, *jo-ber'tee* (1801–52), Italian philosopher and politician, born at Turin. Exiled from 1833, he published in Brussels an *Introduzione allo studio della filosofia* (1839), *Del bello* (1841), and *Del buono* (1842). His conception of the papacy as the divinely appointed agency for Italian independence and federation of Italian states he expounded in *Del primato morale e civile degli Italiani* (1843). It was hailed with enthusiasm, and his fame was enhanced by *Il Gesuita moderno* (1846–47) against the Jesuits. Returning to Italy in 1848, he was for ten weeks prime minister, then settled in Paris, where he died. His *Rinnovamento civile d'Italia* (1851), a defence of Liberalism, influenced Victor Emmanuel II. In his philosophical writings he came near to Hegelianism. See studies by Bruers (1924), Gentile (1898) and Saitta (1927).

GIOLITTI, Giovanni, *jo-leet' tee* (1842–1928), Italian statesman, born at Mondoví and trained as a lawyer, was five times prime minister from 1892 to 1921. He introduced universal suffrage and tried unsuccessfully to keep Italy neutral during World War I. After it, he introduced vast schemes of social reforms. He was a near socialist in his political persuasions. See his *Memories* (trans. 1923).

GIORDANI, *jor-dah'nee,* (1) **Giuseppe** (c. 1744–1798), Italian composer, brother of (3), born in Naples, composed the song 'Caro mio ben', and produced his opera *Il Bacio* in London in 1774.

(2) **Pietro** (1774–1848), Italian essayist, was born at Piacenza, and wrote critical essays, pamphlets and addresses.

(3) **Tommaso** (c. 1733–1806), Italian composer, brother of (1), composed several comic operas, a Te Deum (1789) and several airs, and from 1761 lived in Dublin.

GIORDANO, Luca (1632–1705), Italian painter, was born and died at Naples. He acquired the power of working with extreme rapidity (whence his nickname Fa Presto,

'Make haste'), and of imitating the great masters. In 1692 he proceeded to Madrid, at the request of Charles II of Spain, to embellish the Escorial. His oils and frescoes are in most European collections.

GIORGIONE, *jor-jō'nay*, or **Giorgio Barbarelli** (*c.* 1478–1511), Italian painter, born near Castelfranco, probably studied at Venice under Giovanni Bellini, and soon developed a freer and larger manner, characterized by intense poetic feeling and by great beauty and richness of colouring. Several early portraits by him have disappeared, but an *Enthroned Madonna* is an altarpiece at Castelfranco. In Venice Giorgione was extensively employed in fresco painting, but some fragments in the Fondaco de' Tedeschi are all that now remain of this work. The best authorities reject by far the greater number of the easel pictures ascribed to him. *The Tempest* at Venice, with its lovely landscape, is attributed to him. *The Family of Giorgione* at Venice, *The Three Philosophers* at Vienna, and the *Sleeping Venus* in the Dresden Gallery are admittedly genuine. Many of his pictures were completed by other painters, including Titian's the *Caterina Cornaro* in the National Gallery, London. Giorgione was a great innovator; he created a new type, the small intimate easel picture with a new treatment of figures in landscape. He was the first great romantic artist. See studies by H. Cook (1900), L. Venturi (1913), M. Conway (1929), G. M. Richter (1937) and A. Stokes (1949).

GIOTTO DI BONDONE, *jot'tō* (1267–1337), Italian painter and architect, was born at Vespignano near Florence. At ten, it is said, he was found by Cimabue (q.v.) tending sheep and drawing a lamb on a flat stone, and was by him taken to Florence and instructed in art. The master had infused new life into the current Byzantine forms, and his changes were perfected by his pupil, who introduced a close imitation of nature, more varied composition, and greater lightness of colouring. Giotto's works are numerous. Among them are twenty-eight frescoes from the life of St Francis, in the Upper Church at Assisi; another series of frescoes, with portraits of Charles of Valois, his friend Dante, &c., in the Bargello at Florence; another at Padua, comprising subjects from the lives of the Virgin and Christ, a *Christ in Glory*, and a *Last Judgment*; the Peruzzi frescoes at Florence, scenes from the lives of St John the Baptist and St John the Evangelist, which mark the culminating point of the painter's genius; and the noble *Coronation of the Virgin*, in tempera upon panel, in the Baroncelli Chapel of Santa Croce. From 1330 to 1333 Giotto was employed by King Robert in Naples, where he exercised a powerful influence upon artistic production. In 1334 he was appointed master of works of the cathedral and city of Florence. Aided by Andrea Pisano he decorated the façade of the cathedral with statues and designed the campanile. Giotto shows himself as the master of simplified and unified drama. His work has the intensity which comes from absence of superfluous detail. He imparts not only a new sense of form but a new feeling for narrative. See works by

Sirén (trans. 1917), Belli (1954), Battisti (1960).

GIPPS, Sir George (1791–1847), governor of New South Wales (1838–46), was born at Ringwould, Deal, and served in the Royal Engineers. His policy of land selling by auction instead of the colonial office policy of a fixed price showed him to be an unpopular but farsighted opponent of land monopoly. Gippsland in Victoria is named after him.

GIRALDI, Giambattista, surnamed **Cynthius, Cinthio, Centeo** or **Cinzio,** *jee-rahl'dee* (1504–1573), Italian writer, born in Ferrara. He was professor of Natural Philosophy at Florence and then of *belles lettres*. Later, he held the chair of Rhetoric at Pavia. He is the author of nine plays in imitation of Seneca, of which *Orbecche* (1541) is regarded as the first modern tragedy on classical lines to be performed in Italy. His *Ecatommiti* (published in 1565) is a collection of tales that was translated into French and Spanish and gave Shakespeare his plots for *Measure for Measure* and *Othello*. Some of his stories have been translated by F. Roscoe in his *Italian Novelists* (1825).

GIRALDUS CAMBRENSIS, or **Girald de Barri** (*c.* 1147–*c.* 1223), Norman-Welsh historian and ecclesiastic, born about 1147 at Manorbier Castle, Pembrokeshire. He was brought up by his uncle, the Bishop of St Davids, took holy orders in 1172, and was appointed Archdeacon of St Davids. On the death of his uncle (1176), the chapter of St Davids elected him bishop, but Henry II refused to confirm the selection, and another bishop was appointed. Girald withdrew to Paris, and on his return (1180) was required by the Archbishop of Canterbury to administer the diocese of St Davids, mismanaged by the new bishop. Being appointed a royal chaplain, and afterwards preceptor to Prince John, he accompanied that prince in 1185 to Ireland. His well-known *Topographia Hibernica* is an account of the natural history, marvels and inhabitants of that country. His *Expugnatio Hibernica* is an account of the conquest of Ireland under Henry II. In 1188 he attended the Archbishop of Canterbury in his progress through Wales to preach a crusade, and worked up his observations into the *Itinerarium Cambriae*. On the see of St Davids again becoming vacant, he was again elected by the chapter; but the Archbishop of Canterbury interposed. He devoted the remainder of his life to study, and died at St Davids. See Life by Owen (1904).

GIRARD, (1) **Albert,** KHi'- (1592–1632), Dutch mathematician, born in Lorraine, published a trigonometrical work in 1626 in which the contractions *sin, tan* and *sec* are first used. He also introduced the convention of brackets and discovered that the number of roots of an equation is equal to its degree.

(2) **Stephen,** *ji'-* (1750–1831), French-American miser and philanthropist, was born near Bordeaux, and was successively cabin-boy, mate, captain and part owner of an American coasting vessel. In 1769 he settled as a trader in Philadelphia, where he established a bank which became the mainstay of the U.S. government during the war (1812–

1814). Girard was a sceptic, a miser and an exacting master, yet in the yellow fever epidemic in 1793 he nursed many of the sick in the hospitals, and in public matters his generosity was remarkable. Among other bequests he left $2,000,000 for founding a college in Philadelphia for male white orphans; no minister of any sect was to be on its board or visit it. See Life by Ingram (Philadelphia 1886).

GIRARDIN, zhee-rahr-dĭ, (1) Delphine de, née Gay (1804–55), French writer, first wife of (2), was born at Aix-la-Chapelle. A fashionable figure, graced by beauty, charm and wit, she was acclaimed by the outstanding literary men of the period. She contributed feuilletons to her husband's paper under the pseudonym of the Vicomte de Launay, elegant sketches of society life and wrote some poetry, plays and novels, of which Le Lorgnon (1831) is the best. See Life by L. Séché (1910), and Sainte-Beuve, Causeries du Lundi, vol. III.

(2) Émile de (1806–81), French journalist, husband of (1), was born in Paris, the illegitimate son of General Alexandre de Girardin. After the July revolution (1830) he started the Journal des connaissances utiles, and in 1836 the halfpenny Orleanist Presse; a charge that this was subsidized by government led to a fatal duel with Armand Carrel (q.v.). From this time Girardin gradually became a decided republican. He promoted Louis Napoleon's election to the presidency, but was exiled for disapproving of the coup d'état. He next threw himself into the arms of the Socialists, and during the Commune proposed a scheme for splitting France into fifteen federal states. In 1874, however, he founded La France, in which he supported the republic. He wrote some plays.

(3) François Saint-Marc (1801–73), French literary critic and politician, born in Paris, in 1834 became professor of Literature at the Sorbonne, as a leader writer for the Journal des Débats combated the democratic opposition, and was elected to the Academy in 1844, to the National Assembly in 1871. He published several large works, among them Cours de littérature dramatique (1843) and Souvenirs et réflexions (1859). See a study by Tamisier (1876) and Sainte-Beuve, Causeries du Lundi, Vol. I.

GIRARDON, François, -dŏ (1630–1715), French sculptor, was born at Troyes, studied in Rome and after 1650 settled in Paris and joined the Lebrun group. He worked on decorative sculpture in Louis XIV's galleries, gardens and palaces, mostly at Versailles, where he is noted for the fountain figures, and designed the tomb of Richelieu in the Sorbonne.

GIRAUD, Henri Honoré, -rŏ (1879–1949), French general, trained at St Cyr and joined the Zouaves. In the 1914–18 war, after his capture and escape, he rose to become chief of staff of the Moroccan Division. Following service as military governor of Metz, in early 1940 he commanded in turn the French 7th and 9th Armies, again suffering capture and internment by the Germans. Escaping his captors, in 1942 he was picked up by a British submarine and landed in North

Africa. Much diplomacy was required to win his support for the Allied cause as a subordinate of General Eisenhower, and to secure his collaboration, as joint chairman of the French Committee of National Liberation, with General de Gaulle. On the abolition of his post of commander-in-chief of the French forces, he refused the appointment of inspector-general of the forces to become a highly critical right-wing deputy in the 2nd Provisional Assembly of 1946.

GIRAUDOUX, (Hippolyte) Jean, zhee-rŏ-doo (1882–1944), French writer, born at Bellac in Limousin. After a brilliant academic career and extensive travel, he settled into diplomatic service and became head of the French Ministry of Information during the second World War, until his affiliations became suspect. As a poet and novelist, steeped in symbolism, much affected by psychoanalytic theories, he brought to literature the technique of Impressionism in painting; this is shown in Provinciales (1909), Simon le Pathétique (1918), and the reflection of his war experiences, Retour d'Alsace (1917). His plays, for which he is chiefly remembered and in which he remains essentially a poet, are mainly fantasies based on Greek myths and biblical lore, satirically treated as commentary on modern life. They include La Folle de Chaillot (1945), La Guerre de Troie n'aura pas lieu (1935) and Pour Lucrèce. The last two were translated as Tiger at the Gates (1955) and Duel of Angels (1958) by Christopher Fry. See Four French Novelists by G. E. Lemaire (1938) and study by D. Inskip (1958).

GIRTIN, Thomas (1775–1802), English painter, one of the greatest of the earlier landscape painters in watercolours, was a pupil of Edward Dayes and a contemporary of Turner, with whom he worked in the studio of J. R. Smith (q.v.), colouring prints, and with whom he formed a close friendship. He painted some of his best landscapes in the north of England and in France which he visited in 1802 for his health, symptoms of the tuberculosis from which he died having appeared. Girtin's paintings were among the first in which watercolour was exploited as a true medium as distinct from a tint for colouring drawings. His breadth of vision and noble simplicity were in sharp contrast to the detailed fussiness of the majority of early watercolourists. He influenced Constable considerably. See monographs by Binyon (1900), Stokes (1922), R. Davies (1924), and Mayne (1949).

GISSING, George Robert (1857–1903), English novelist, born at Wakefield, and educated at Owens College, Manchester, which he left in disgrace. His experiences in America, embodied in New Grub Street (1891), caused quite a sensation. Other realistic Zola-esque portraits of poverty and misery include Born in Exile (1892) and The Odd Women (1893). His later works include Charles Dickens (1898), By the Ionian Sea (1901) and his autobiographical The Private Papers of Henry Ryecroft (1903). See his Letters (1927), and studies by Swinnerton (1912), Yates (1922), Selections with an introduction by Virginia Woolf (1929), and The Private

Life of Henry Maitland, by M. Roberts (ed. M. Bishop, 1958).

GIULIO ROMANO, properly **Giulio Pippi de' Giannuzzi,** *joo'lyō ro-mah'nō* (c. 1492–1546), Italian painter and architect, born in Rome, assisted Raphael in the execution of several of his finest works, and at his death completed the *Apparition of the Cross* in the Vatican. In 1524 he went to Mantua on the invitation of the Duke. The drainage of the marshes and the protection of the city from the floods of the Po and Mincio attest his skill as an engineer; while his genius as an architect found scope in the restoration and adornment of the Palazzo del Te, the cathedral, and a ducal palace. In Bologna he designed the façade of the church of S. Petronio. Among his oil paintings are the *Martyrdom of St Stephen* (at Genoa), a *Holy Family* (Dresden), *Mary and Jesus* (Louvre) and the *Madonna della Gatta* (Naples). Giulio died at Mantua. See studies by D'Arco (1842) and Dollmayr (1901).

GIUSTI, Giuseppe, *joos'tee* (1809–50), Italian poet and political satirist, born near Pistoia, mercilessly denounced in a brilliant series of poems the enemies of Italy and the vices of the age. He was elected to the Tuscan chamber of deputies in 1848. See monographs by Fioretto (1877), Leonardis (1887) and Martini (1929).

GLADSTONE, (1) Herbert John Gladstone, 1st Viscount (1854–1930), British statesman, youngest son of (3), was Liberal M.P. for Leeds (1880–1910), was criticized for ' revealing ' his father's intentions as to the Irish question (1885), became Liberal chief whip in 1899, home secretary from 1905 to 1910, when he was appointed first governor-general of the Union of South Africa and raised to the peerage. He was head of the War Refugees Association (1914–19) and published his political reminiscences, *After Thirty Years*, in 1928.

(2) **John Hall** (1827–1902), English chemist, born at Hackney, London, became professor at the Royal Institution in 1874 and established with Dale the proportional relationship between the refractive index and density of a transparent gas.

(3) **William Ewart** (1809–98), British Liberal statesman, father of (1), was born at Liverpool, December 29, the fourth son of Sir John Gladstone (1764–1851), a well-known Liverpool merchant and M.P. of Scottish ancestry. He was educated at Eton and at Christ Church, Oxford. He had distinguished himself greatly in the Union debating society, and in 1832 was returned by Newark as a Conservative to the reformed Parliament. In December 1834 Peel appointed him a junior lord of the Treasury, and next year under-secretary for the Colonies. When Lord John Russell brought forward his motions on the Irish Church, Peel was defeated and resigned, and Gladstone went with him. When Peel returned to office in 1841, Gladstone became vice-president of the Board of Trade and master of the Mint, and in 1843 president of the Board of Trade. In February 1845 he resigned because he could not approve of the Maynooth grant; but in December in thorough sympathy with

Peel, who had adopted free-trade principles, he rejoined the government as colonial secretary. No longer, however, in political sympathy with the Duke of Newcastle, whose influence had obtained for him the representation of Newark, he gave up his seat, and did not re-enter parliament until the Corn Law struggle was over; then, at the general election of 1847 he, still as a Tory, was elected by the University of Oxford. Hitherto he had been the traditional Tory; but the Corn Law agitation set him thinking over the defects of the social system. He startled Europe by the terrible description which he gave in 1851 of the condition of the prisons of Naples under King ' Bomba ', and the cruelties inflicted on political prisoners. By the death of Peel in July 1850 Gladstone was brought more directly to the front; and he compelled the House of Commons and the country to recognize in him a supreme master of parliamentary debate. His first really great speech in parliament was made in the debate on Disraeli's budget in 1852. On the fall of the short-lived Tory administration, Lord Aberdeen formed the famous Coalition Ministry, with Palmerston for home secretary, Lord John Russell for foreign secretary and Gladstone for chancellor of the Exchequer. His speech on the introduction of his first budget was again masterly. The Crimean War broke up the Coalition Ministry; Palmerston became prime minister, and Gladstone retained his office for a short time; but when Palmerston gave way to the demand for the appointment of the Sebastopol committee, Gladstone felt bound to resign. However, he returned as chancellor in 1850 when Palmerston was again in office. In 1865 South Lancashire returned Gladstone, who, on Lord Palmerston's death and Lord Russell's accession to the premiership, became leader of the House of Commons. A minor reform bill was introduced enlarging the franchise in boroughs and counties. The Conservative party opposed it, and were supported by a considerable section of the Liberals. The bill was defeated; the Liberals went out of office (1866). The serious condition of Ireland, however, and the Fenian insurrection brought the Liberals to power with Gladstone as prime minister in 1868. In his first session he disestablished and disendowed the Irish church; and in the next session he passed a measure recognizing the right of the Irish tenant to compensation for improvements. For the first time in English history a system of national education was established. The Ballot Act was passed for the protection of voters. The system of purchase in the army was abolished by a kind of *coup d'état*. Then Gladstone introduced a measure to improve university education in Ireland. This bill was intended for the benefit of Irish Catholics; but it did not satisfy Catholic demands, Catholic members voted against it, and with that help the Conservatives threw out the bill (1873). Gladstone tendered his resignation, but Disraeli declined to undertake any responsibility, and Gladstone had to remain at the head of affairs. But the by-elections began to tell against the Liberals, Gladstone suddenly dissolved parliament and Disraeli came back to power (1874). For some time Gladstone occupied himself with his literary studies, but the Bulgarian atrocities (1876) aroused his generous anger against the Ottoman power in Europe. Parliament was dissolved in 1880, the Liberals came in with an overwhelming majority, and Gladstone (now member for Midlothian) became prime minister once more. He succeeded in carrying out a scheme of parliamentary reform, which went a long way towards universal male suffrage. But he found himself drawn into a series of wars in North and South Africa; and had to pass coercive measures for Ireland. After Gladstone's government had suffered defeat (June), Lord Salisbury came back into office for a few months; but at the general election, the first for the newly-made voters under the reform act, Gladstone was returned to office (1886). He made up his mind that the Irish people were in favour of Home Rule, but a split was caused in his party, his bill was rejected and after an appeal to the country he was defeated at the polls. But the general election of 1892 returned him again to office. In 1893 his Home Rule Bill was carried in the Commons, but was thrown out by the Lords. His advanced age made him resign in March 1894. He died at Hawarden, May 19, and was buried in Westminster Abbey. His various essays in political and literary, in ecclesiastical and theological criticism, constitute a life's work in themselves. Probably no other English minister has left behind him so long and so successful a record of practical legislation. As a parliamentary debater he never had a superior—possibly never an equal. See his *Letters on Church and Religion*, ed. Lathbury (1910), *Gleanings of Past Years* (1879) and the collected Midlothian speeches (1886); also Lives by Garratt (1936), Magnus (1954), and studies by J. L. Hammond (1938).

GLAISHER, James (1809–1903), British meteorologist, born in London, joined the ordnance survey in 1829, later became chief meteorologist at Greenwich, was elected F.R.S. in 1849 and next year founded the Royal Meteorological Society. He made a large number of balloon ascents, once reaching a height of over seven miles to study the higher strata of the atmosphere. He compiled dew-point tables and wrote on several scientific subjects.

GLAMIS, Janet Douglas, Lady, *glahmz* (d. 1537), was burnt at Edinburgh, July 17, on an unsubstantiated charge of plotting James V's death.

GLANVILL, (1) Joseph (1636–80), English philosopher, born at Plymouth, studied at Oxford. The dominant Aristotelianism there weighed on him almost as heavily as the Puritan dogmatism outside; and after the Restoration he became a Latitudinarian, vicar of Frome (1662), rector of the Abbey Church in Bath (1666), and prebendary of Worcester (1678). The second edition of his famous work, *The Vanity of Dogmatising* (1665), an appeal for freedom of thought and experimental science, was

prefaced by a warm panegyric on the newly-founded Royal Society, of which he had become a fellow. Yet his *Philosophical Considerations touching Witchcraft* (1666) shows strange credulity. See studies by Redgrove (1921) and Habicht (1936).

(2) **Ranulf de** (d. 1190), chief justiciary of England (1180–89), adviser to Henry II and reputed author of the earliest treatise on the laws of England, the *Tractatus de Legibus et Consuetudinibus Angliae* (c. 1187). Glanvill was born at Stratford St Andrew, near Saxmundham; in 1174 raised a body of knights and captured William the Lion of Scotland. He joined the crusade and died at the siege of Acre (1190). See studies, ed. Woodbine (1932).

GLAPTHORNE, Henry (1610–c. 1644), English minor dramatist, born at Whittlesey, between 1629 and 1643 wrote a few poems and some plays, including *Albertus Wallenstein*; *Argalus and Parthenia*, a poetical dramatization of part of the *Arcadia*; *The Hollander* and *Wit in a Constable*, comedies; and *The Ladies Priviledge*. *The Lady Mother* was also attributed to him.

GLAS, (1) George (1725–65), Scottish surgeon, mariner, son of (2), and settler (1764) near Cape Verde, was murdered by mutineers off the Irish coast.

(2) **John** (1695–1773), Scottish sectarian, father of (1), the founder about 1730 of the small religious sect of Glassites or Sandemanians, was born at Auchtermuchty, and from 1719 was minister of Tealing near Dundee. The name Sandemanians was from his son-in-law, Robert Sandeman (1718–71). They held that church establishments were unscriptural and that congregations should be self-governing.

GLASER, Donald Arthur (1926–   ), American physicist, born at Cleveland, Ohio. While working at the University of Michigan (1949–60) he developed the ' bubble chamber ' for observing the paths of atomic particles, an achievement which won him the Nobel prize in 1960, the year in which he became professor at the University of California.

GLASGOW, Ellen (1874–1945), American novelist, known for her stories of the South, including *The Voice of the People* (1900), *Virginia* (1913), &c.

GLASPELL, Susan (1882–1948), American writer, born at Davenport, Iowa, author of novels, including *Fidelity* (1915), *Brook Evans* (1928) and *The Fugitive's Return* (1929), also of plays, among them *Trifles* (1917) and *Alison's House* (1930), based on the life of Emily Dickinson (q.v.), which won the Pulitzer prize.

GLASSE, Hannah, a London habitmaker, the author of *The Art of Cookery* (1747). She seems to have been a Roman Catholic, to have gone bankrupt in 1754, and to have died before 1770.

GLAUBER, Johann Rudolph, *glow'bèr* (c. 1603–68), German physician, born at Karlstadt, died at Amsterdam. In 1648 he discovered hydrochloric acid; he was probably the first to procure nitric acid; and he discovered Glauber's salt (sodium sulphate), the therapeutic virtues of which he greatly exaggerated; also acetone, benzine and alkaloids. His treatises were translated by Christopher Packe (1689).

GLAZEBROOK, Sir Richard Tetley (1854–1935), British physicist, born at Liverpool, director of the National Physical Laboratory from 1900, is known for his work on electrical standards.

GLAZUNOV, Aleksandr Konstantinovich (1865–1936), Russian composer, born at St Petersburg, studied under Rimsky-Korsakov, was director of the Conservatoire there from 1906 until the revolution of 1917, when the Soviet government gave him the title of People's Artist of the Republic. But in 1927 he emigrated to Paris. Among his compositions are eight symphonies and works in every branch except opera.

GLEIG, George Robert, *gleg* (1796–1888), Scottish novelist and biographer, born at Stirling, son of the Bishop of Brechin, studied at Glasgow and Balliol College, Oxford, joined the army, and served in Spain (1813) and in America (1814). He took orders (1820), and became chaplain-general of the army (1844) and inspector-general of military schools (1846). He wrote *The Subaltern* (1825) and other novels, and books on military history and biography.

GLEIM, Johann Wilhelm Ludwig, *glīm* (1719–1803), German poet, was born at Ermsleben near Halberstadt, and died at Halberstadt. His *Lieder eines preussischen Grenadiers* contributed to the war poetry of the age of Frederick the Great. See Life by Körte (1811).

GLEN, William (1789–1826), Scottish poet and unbusinesslike business man, author of 'Wae's me for Prince Charlie' and other lyrics, was born and died in Glasgow. See memoir prefixed to Poems (1874).

GLENDOWER, or Glyndwr, Owen (*c.* 1350–*c.* 1416), Welsh chief, who figures prominently in Shakespeare's *Henry IV*, claimed descent from Llewelyn, the last Prince of Wales, was born in Montgomeryshire, studied law at Westminster, and became esquire to the Earl of Arundel, but in 1401 fell into dispute with Lord Grey over some lands, and, unable to obtain redress from Henry IV, carried on a guerilla warfare against the English marchers. In 1402 he captured Lord Grey and Sir Edmund Mortimer, both of whom married daughters of the Welsh chieftain (now proclaimed Prince of Wales), and joined him in the coalition with Harry Percy (Hotspur). That coalition ended in the battle of Shrewsbury (1403), won by King Henry. In 1404 Glendower entered into a treaty with Charles VI of France, who in 1405 sent a force to Wales; and the Welsh prince, though often defeated, kept up a desultory warfare till his death about 1416. See Lives by A. C. Bradley (1927), J. E. Lloyd (1931) and J. D. G. Davies (1934); and *Bibliography* by D. Rhys Phillips (1915).

GLENELG, Charles Grant, 1st Baron (1778–1866), British statesman, was born at Calcutta, and graduated as fourth wrangler from Magdalene College, Cambridge (1801). Entering parliament in 1807, he was chief-secretary for Ireland (1819–22), vice-president (1823–27), president of the Board of Trade under Canning (1827–28), president of the Board of Control under Earl Grey (1830–34), and colonial secretary under Melbourne (1834–39). Having approved of Lord Durham's 'ordinance' as to the Canadian rebels of 1838, he was compelled to resign in 1839, and retired from public life. Elevated to the peerage in 1835, he died a bachelor at Cannes, the title thus becoming extinct.

GLENN, John Herschel (1921–), U.S. astronaut, born in Ohio, joined the U.S. Marine Corps in 1943. In 1947 he completed a record-breaking supersonic flight from Los Angeles to New York, and in 1962 a three-orbit flight in the *Mercury* space capsule. He resigned from the Marine Corps in 1965. His many awards include the Distinguished Service Medal (1962) and the Galabert Astronautical Prize (1963) together with Gagarin (q.v.).

GLEYRE, Charles, *glayr* (1806–74), Swiss painter, was born at Chevilly in the Swiss canton Vaud, studied in Italy, travelled in Greece and Egypt and took over Delaroche's teaching school in Paris. Monet, Renoir and Sisley numbered among his pupils. Much of his work is at Lausanne. See Life by Clément (1885).

GLINKA, Mikhail Ivanovich (1803–57), Russian composer, born at Novopasskoi, Smolensk, began life as a civil servant, but a visit to Italy made him eager to study music, which he did in Berlin, returning to Russia to produce his famous opera *A Life for the Tsar* (1836). His *Russlan and Ludmilla* (1847), based on a poem by Pushkin, pioneered the style of the Russian national school of composers. See studies by Berlioz (1874), Calvocoressi (1913) and Montagu-Nathan (1916).

GLOUCESTER, Earls and Dukes of:
(1) **Gilbert de Clare, 6th Earl of** (d. 1230), father of (7), also 7th earl of Clare and 5th earl of Hertford, brought the house of Clare to the peak of its fortunes and was one of the twenty-five barons entrusted with carrying out Magna Carta.

(2) **Gilbert de Clare, 8th Earl of** (1243–95), son of (7), father of (3), also 9th earl of Clare and 7th earl of Hertford, sided with Simon de Montfort, and helped him to gain the battle of Lewes (1264); but, quarrelling with Simon, he made common cause with Prince Edward and won the battle of Evesham (1265).

(3) **Gilbert de Clare, 9th Earl of** (1291–1314), son of (2), also 10th earl of Clare and 8th earl of Hertford, was mediator between Edward II and Lancaster (1313) and was killed at the battle of Bannockburn (1314). His sister, **Elizabeth** (*c.* 1291–1360), endowed Clare College, Cambridge (1336).

(4) **Prince Henry, Duke of** (1639–60), was the third son of Charles II.

(5) **Prince Henry, Duke of** (1900–), third son of George V, was educated privately and at Eton, became a captain in the 10th Hussars and in 1928 was created duke. He married Lady Alice Montagu-Douglas-Scott in 1935. There were two children, **Prince William** (1941–72) and **Prince Richard** (1944–). He was governor-general of Australia (1945–47).

(6) **Humphrey, Duke of** (1391–1447), youngest son of Henry IV, was protector during the minority of Henry VI (1422–29), greatly increased the difficulties of his brother, Bedford, by his greed, irresponsibility and factious quarrels with their uncle, Cardinal Beaufort. In 1447 he was arrested for high treason at Bury St Edmunds and five days later was found dead in bed.

(7) **Richard de Clare, 7th Earl of** (1222–62), son of (1), father of (2), also 8th earl of Clare and 6th earl of Hertford, was envoy to Scotland (1255) and to Germany (1256), was twice defeated by the Welsh (1244, 1257) and supported Simon de Montfort, but later quarrelled with him.

(8) **Prince Richard, Duke of** (1452–85). See RICHARD III.

(9) **Robert, Earl of** (d. 1147), a natural son of Henry I, was the principal supporter of his sister Matilda against Stephen.

(10) **Prince William, Duke of** (1689–1700), was the eldest son of Queen Anne.

(11) **Prince William Frederick, Duke of** (1776–1834), son of (12), nicknamed ' Silly Billy ', died without issue.

(12) **Prince William Henry, Duke of** (1743–1805), George III's brother, was created duke of Gloucester and Edinburgh in 1764.

GLOVER, Julia, *née* **Betterton** (1779–1850), Irish comic actress, born at Newry, made her début in 1789, was sold by her father to Samuel Glover in 1798. In 1802 she appeared at Drury Lane, London, and became a leading lady of the London stage, a successful Mrs Malaprop.—Her second son, **William Howard** (1819–75), was a composer and conductor.

GLOVICHISCH. See CLOVIO.

GLUBB, Sir John Bagot (1897–), British soldier, born at Preston, Lancs, was educated at Cheltenham College and the Royal Military Academy, Woolwich. After service in the Royal Engineers in World War I, he was the first organizer of the native police force in the new State of Iraq in 1920. In 1926 he became an administrative inspector in the Iraqi Government. In 1930 he was transferred to British-mandated Transjordan, organizing her Arab Legion's Desert Patrol. In 1939 he became Commandant of the Legion, making it the most efficient Arab Army in the Middle East. He was curtly dismissed from his post in 1956 following Arab criticism With immense prestige among the Bedouin, ' Glubb Pasha ' was one of the most influential figures in Arabia in the period of British paramountcy. Publications include *The Story of the Arab Legion* (1948), *A Soldier with the Arabs* (1957), *Britain and the Arabs* (1959).

GLUCK, Christoph Wilibald, *glook* (1714–87), Austro-German composer, born in Bavaria. After teaching music at Prague, in 1736 he went to Vienna, and thence in 1738 to Milan, where he studied for four years under San-Martini. In 1741 he wrote his first opera, *Artaserse,* and seven others followed in the next four years. Having achieved some reputation, he was invited in 1745 to London, where a new opera, *La Caduta de' giganti,* was performed, and where his study of Handel's work proved to be the turning point in

his career. His next opera shows signs of this new tendency, while some of the music in *Telemacco* (Rome 1750) and *La Clemenza di Tito* (Naples 1751) he afterwards considered good enough to be incorporated in *Armide* and *Iphigénie.* But his style did not mature until he found in Florence in Calzabigi a librettist worthy of his music. In 1762 he produced *Orfeo,* which struck the keynote of modern music drama. *Alceste* followed (1766), and *Paride ed Elena* (1769), the last work written for Vienna before he went to Paris. There his *Iphigénie en Aulide* (1774), and *Orphée,* an adaptation of his earlier *Orfeo,* met with enormous success. The famous Gluck and Piccinni war divided Paris into Gluckists and Piccinnists, representing French and Italian opera styles respectively. Gluck finally conquered with his *Iphigénie en Tauride* (1779), and retired from Paris full of honour. He died at Vienna. See works by Desnoiresterres (1872), Marx (1862), Reissmann (1882), Berlioz (trans. 1915), J. d'Udine (1906), E. Newman (1896), M. Cooper (1935), A. Einstein (1936).

GLYN, Elinor, *née* **Sutherland** (1864–1943), novelist, born in Jersey, Channel Islands. Starting with *The Visits of Elizabeth* (1900), she hit the jackpot with *Three Weeks* (1907), a book which gained a reputation for naughtiness. *Man and Maid* (1922), *Did She?* (1934), *The Third Eye* (1940)—with such titles she kept her public enthralled. Nonsensical, high-faluting, faulty in construction and ungrammatical, her novels were nevertheless read with avidity. She gravitated to Hollywood (1922–27), where ' it ' (her version of sex appeal) got itself glamorized on the screen. See *Elinor Glyn* (1955) by her grandson, Anthony Glyn.

GLYNDWR. See GLENDOWER.

GMELIN, *gmay'leen,* name of a German family of botanists and chemists:

(1) **Johann Friedrich** (1748–1804), nephew of (2), wrote *Onomatologia Botanica* (1771–1777).

(2) **Johann Georg** (1709–55), uncle of (1) and (4), professor of Chemistry and Botany at St Petersburg and Tübingen, travelled in Siberia (1733–43), wrote *Flora Sibirica* (1748–1749), *Reisen durch Sibirien* (1751–52).

(3) **Leopold** (1788–1853), son of (1), born at Göttingen, from 1817 to 1850 was professor of Medicine and Chemistry at Heidelberg. He discovered potassium ferricyanide, known as *Gmelin's salt,* in 1822, introduced the terms *ester* and *ketone* into organic chemistry and published a textbook of inorganic chemistry (trans. 1849). *Gmelin's test* is for the presence of bile pigments.

(4) **Samuel Gottlieb** (1744–74), nephew of (2), became professor of Botany at St Petersburg (1767), and wrote *Historia Focurum* (1768).

GNEISENAU, August Wilhelm Anton, Graf Neithardt von, *gnī'zėn-ow* (1760–1831), Prussian general, was born at Schildau in Prussian Saxony. In 1782 he accompanied the German auxiliaries of England to America, in 1786 joined the Prussian army, and in 1806 fought at Saalfeld and Jena. His gallant defence of Colberg (1807) led to his appointment on the commission for the reorganization of the Prussian army. In the war of liberation he rendered distinguished service at Leipzig (1813); in the Waterloo campaign as chief of Blücher's staff he directed the strategy of the Prussian army. In 1831, on the outbreak of the Polish rebellion, he had been made field-marshal and commander of the Prussian army on the Polish frontier, when he died of cholera at Posen. See Lives by Pertz (1864–80), Neff (1889), von Unger (1914) and von Cochenhausen (1933).

GNEIST, Heinrich Rudolf Hermann Friedrich von, *gnīst* (1816–95), German jurist, was born in Berlin, where from 1844 he was professor of Jurisprudence. He was a Liberal member of the Prussian lower house and also of the imperial diet, and is known especially for his works on English and German comparative law, several of which have been translated.

GÖBBELS. See GOEBBELS.

GOBELIN, *go-bě-lī*, French family of dyers, probably of Reims, who, about 1450, founded on the outskirts of Paris a factory which later became famous for its tapestry.

GOBINEAU, Joseph Arthur, Comte de, *go-bee-nō* (1816–82), French orientalist, diplomatist and philosopher, born at Bordeaux, wrote *The Inequality of Human Races* (trans. 1915), called the 'intellectual parent' of Nietzsche and the real inventor of the super-man and super-morality.

GODARD, (1) Benjamin Louis Paul, *gō-dahr* (1849–95), French composer and violinist, born at Paris, a pupil of Vieuxtemps, is now remembered chiefly for the 'Berceuse' from his opera *Jocelyn*.

(2) **Jean-Luc** (1930–), French film director, born and educated in Paris, was journalist and film critic with *Cahiers du cinéma* (1957–1959). His first major film *A Bout de souffle* (1960, *Breathless*) established him as one of the leaders of *nouvelle vogue* cinema. He writes his own filmscripts on contemporary and controversial themes, and his elliptic narrative style and original use of jump cuts, freeze frames, &c., have gained him much critical attention, enthusiastic and otherwise. His prolific output includes *Une Femme est une femme* (1961), *Vivre sa vie* (1962), *Une Femme mariée* (1965), *Pierrot le Fou* (1965), and *Made in U.S.A.* (1967). See monograph by Roud (1967).

GODDARD, Rayner Goddard, Baron (1877–1971), lord chief justice of England (1946–1958), educated at Marlborough and Trinity College, Oxford, was called to the bar in 1899, appointed a High Court judge in the King's Bench division in 1932 and became a lord justice of appeal and a privy councillor in 1938. In 1944 he was made a life peer and became a lord-of-appeal-in-ordinary. A strong traditionalist and a believer in both capital and corporal punishment, he stressed that punishment must punish. See Life by A. Smith (1959).

GÖDEL, Kurt (1906–), Austrian logician, showed in 1931 that any formal logical system, such as Russell's *Principia Mathematica*, must contain propositions, not provable in that system. See A. Tarski, *Undecidable Theories* (1953), and study of his proof by E. Nagel and J. R. Newman (1959).

GODERICH, Viscount. See RIPON, EARL OF.

GODFREY, (1) Sir Dan (1868–1939), English conductor, born in London, conducted opera and symphony concerts throughout Britain and was (1893–1934) director of music to the corporation of Bournemouth and its symphony orchestra, the early regular broadcasts of which made it well-known. He was knighted in 1922. See his *Memories and Music* (1924). His father, **Daniel** (1831–1903), was bandmaster of the Grenadier Guards (1856–96). His uncle, **Charles** (1839–1904), was bandmaster of the Scots Fusiliers and the Royal Horse Guards and professor of Military Music at the Royal College of Music. Another uncle, **Adolphus Frederick** (1837–82), was bandmaster of the Coldstream Guards, as was **Charles** (1790–1863), Sir Dan's grandfather, who founded *Jullien's Journal*, devoted to military music, and was appointed musician-in-ordinary to the King (1831).

(2) **Sir Edmund Berry** (1622–78), English politician and London woodmonger and J.P., knighted in 1666, whose unsolved murder, one of the most celebrated of historical mysteries, was made by Titus Oates (q.v.) the coping-stone of his 'Popish Plot'.

GODFREY OF BOUILLON, *boo-ee-yŏ* (c. 1061–1100), Crusader, was born at Baisy in Belgian Brabant, the eldest son of Count Eustace II of Boulogne, and Ida, sister to Godfrey, Duke of Lower Lorraine and Bouillon. He served with great gallantry under the Emperor Henry IV, both against Rudolph of Swabia and in 1084 in the expedition against Rome. Godfrey joined the first Crusade, was elected one of the principal commanders, and in time became its chief leader. Eight days after the capture of Jerusalem he was proclaimed king; but his humility forbade him to 'wear a crown of gold where his Saviour had worn one of thorns', so he contented himself with the title of Defender of the Holy Sepulchre. On August 12, 1099, on the plain of Ascalon, he defeated the sultan of Egypt; this victory put him in possession of almost all of Palestine. See works by De Hody (2nd ed. 1859) and Froboese (Berlin 1879).

GODFREY OF STRASBURG. See GOTT-FRIED.

GODIVA, *go-dī'va* (d. 1080), an English lady and religious benefactress who, according to tradition, when her husband, Leofric (d. 1057), Earl of Chester, imposed a heavy tax on the townsfolk of Coventry (1040), obtained its remission by riding naked through the market place. The story occurs in Roger of Wendover (1235). Some writers assert that Godiva ordered all to remain indoors, which they did except for the famous Peeping Tom, but he is a later addition (city records, 1773). See Häfele's *Die Godivasage* (1929); also *Folklore Journal* (1890).

GODLEE, Sir Rickman John (1859–1925), English surgeon, born in London, in 1884 first removed a tumour of the brain surgically. A nephew of Lister, and his biographer, he was president of the Royal College of Surgeons (1911–13) and of the Royal College of Medicine (1916–18).

GODOLPHIN, Sidney Godolphin, 1st Earl of (1645–1712), English statesman, was born at Godolphin Hall near Helston, Cornwall.

He became a royal page in 1662, entered parliament in 1668, visited Holland in 1678, and in 1684 was made head of the Treasury and Baron Godolphin. On William of Orange's landing in 1688 Godolphin stood by James, and was sent with Halifax and Nottingham to negotiate with William; when James's flight was known, he voted for a regency. Yet in February 1689 William reinstated him as first commissioner of the Treasury. Godolphin was a Tory; and, when William began to replace his Tory ministers by Whigs, Godolphin's turn to go came in 1696. Anne on her accession made him her sole lord high treasurer (1702); in 1706 he was created earl. His able management of the finances furnished Marlborough the supplies needed for his campaigns without increasing the public debt by more than one million annually. To prevent his own overthrow, he constrained Anne to dismiss Harley (1708); but the influence of Harley's friend and relative, Mrs Masham, continuing to increase, and the power of Harley to grow, Godolphin in 1710 was himself dismissed. He died at Holywell House, Marlborough's seat, near St Albans, September 15. See the Life of him by the Hon. Hugh Elliot (1888).

GODOY, Manuel de, Duke of Alcudia (1767–1851), Spanish statesman, born at Badajoz. A member of Charles IV's bodyguard, he became the royal favourite and was made prime minister in 1792, having encompassed the deposing of Aranda (q.v.). He led Spain into a series of disasters which culminated in the French invasion of 1808, when the king was obliged to imprison him as a protection from popular fury. He subsequently intrigued with Napoleon and spent the rest of his life in exile at Rome and Paris, where he died. See his *Mémoires* (1836), and Life by Madol (1931; tr. 1934).

GODRIC, St (c. 1065–1170), English pedlar, mariner—possibly pirate, pilgrim and seer, was born in Norfolk, and died at Finchale near Durham, where he had lived as a hermit from about 1110.

GODUNOV, Boris Fyodorovich (1552–1605), tsar of Russia, came to the throne in 1598, but had been regent from 1584 for Fyodor, imbecilic elder son of Ivan IV. Ivan's younger son Dimitry had been banished to the upper Volga, where he died in 1591, murdered, according to rumour, at the behest of Boris. A pretender, claiming to be Dimitry and to have eluded the assassins, later started a revolt, overcame Boris's troops and was crowned in June 1605, Boris having meantime died suddenly, thus averting certain deposition. His rule had been able but ruthless. Moussorgsky used his story in an opera. See Life by Stephen Graham (1933).

GODWIN (d. 1053), Earl of the West Saxons, was probably son of the South Saxon Wulfnoth; but later stories make his father a churl. He ingratiated himself with Earl Ulf, Canute's brother-in-law; by 1018 he was an earl, and about 1019 became Earl of the West Saxons. In 1042 he helped to raise Edward the Confessor to the throne, and married him to his daughter Edith. He led the struggle against the king's foreign favourites,

and Edward revenged himself by heaping insults upon Queen Edith, confining her in the monastery of Wherwell, and banishing Godwin and his sons. But in 1052 they landed in the south of England; the royal troops, the navy and vast numbers of burghers and peasants went over to Godwin; and the king was forced to grant his demands, and reinstate his family. Godwin died at Winchester, April 15. His son Harold was for a few months Edward's successor. See Freeman, *Norman Conquest*.

GODWIN, (1) **Francis** (1562–1633), English bishop and author, was born at Hannington, Northants, the son of Thomas Godwin (1517–90), from 1584 Bishop of Bath and Wells. He graduated at Oxford in 1580, and became rector of Sampford, eventually becoming Bishop of Hereford in 1617. His eight works include *A Catalogue of the Bishops of England* (1601), but he is best known for *Man in the Moon, or a Voyage Thither, by Domingo Gonsales* (1638), used as a source by Bishop John Wilkins, Cyrano de Bergerac and Swift.

(2) **Mary Wollstonecraft** (1759–97), Anglo-Irish feminist, was born in London. At nineteen Mary went out to earn her own livelihood, and was in turn a companion, a schoolmistress and governess in Lord Kingsborough's family. In 1788 she became translator and literary adviser to Johnson the publisher. In this capacity she became acquainted with the literati and reformers of the day. In 1790 she produced her *Vindication of the Rights of Man*, an answer to Burke's *Reflections on the French Revolution,* and in 1792 her *Vindication of the Rights of Woman*, a talented work which, advocating equality of the sexes and the main doctrines of the later women's movement, made her both famous and infamous. In 1792 she set out for Paris. There, as a witness of the ' Terror ', she collected materials for her *View of the French Revolution* (vol i 1794); and there in 1793 she met Captain Gilbert Imlay, an American timber-merchant, the author of *The Western Territory of North America* (1792). In May 1794 she bore him a daughter, Fanny; in November 1795, after a four months' visit to Scandinavia as his ' wife ' and accredited agent, she tried to drown herself from Putney Bridge, Imlay having deserted her. But she recovered her courage and went to live with William Godwin (q.v.) in Somers-town; they had first met in 1791. She being pregnant, they married in March 1797. In August, a daughter Mary (see SHELLEY) was born and on September 10 the mother died. Among her other writings are *Original Stories from Real Life* (2nd ed. illustrated Blake, 1796). See Memoirs by Godwin (1798), and monographs by Mrs Pennell (1885) and Stirling Taylor (1911).

(3) **William** (1756–1836), English political writer and novelist, was born at Wisbech, but passed his boyhood at Guestwick in Norfolk. After three years at Hindolveston day school, three more with a tutor at Norwich, and one as usher in his former school, Godwin in 1773 entered Hoxton Presbyterian College; in 1778 left it as pure a Sandemanian and Tory as he had gone in. But during a five

years' ministry at Ware, Stowmarket and Beaconsfield, he turned Socinian and republican, and by 1787 was a 'complete unbeliever'. Meanwhile he had taken up writing. The French Revolution gave him an opening, and his *Enquiry concerning Political Justice* (1793) brought him fame and a thousand guineas, and captivated Coleridge, Wordsworth, Southey, and later and above all Shelley, who became his disciple, son-in-law and subsidizer. It was calmly subversive of everything (law and ' marriage, the worst of all laws '), but it depreciated violence, and was deemed caviare for the multitude, so its author escaped prosecution. His masterpiece, *The Adventures of Caleb Williams* (1794), was designed to give ' a general review of the modes of domestic and unrecorded despotism '; unlike most novels with a purpose, it is really a strong book. In 1801, four years after the death of Mary Wollstonecraft Godwin (q.v.), he married Mrs Clairmont, who had two children already, and a third was born of the marriage. So there were poor Fanny Imlay (1794–1816), who died by her own hand; Mary Wollstonecraft Godwin (1797–1851), who in 1816 married Shelley; Charles Clairmont; ' Claire ' Clairmont (1797–1879), the mother by Byron of Allegra; and William Godwin (1803–32). A bookselling business long involved Godwin in difficulties, and in 1833 he was glad to accept the sinecure post of yeoman-usher of the Exchequer. His tragedy, *Antonio* (1800), was hopelessly damned. The best of his later prose works are *The Enquirer* (1797) and *St Leon* (1799). See Brailsford's *Shelley, Godwin, and their Circle* (1913), studies by Monro (1953) and Grylls (1953), and Lives by Woodcock (1946) and Fleischer (1951).

GODWIN-AUSTEN, Henry Haversham (1834–1923), British soldier and surveyor, son of Robert Alfred Cloyne (1808–84), the geologist; a lieutenant-colonel and F.R.S., of the Trigonometrical Survey, after whom the second highest mountain in the world, the Himalayan ' K2 ' was named in 1888.

GOEBBELS, Joseph (1897–1945), German Nazi politician, the son of a Rhenish factory foreman, was educated at a Catholic school and the Gymnasium. A deformed foot absolving him from military service, his attainment of a number of scholarships enabled him to attend eight universities. Indigent and adrift, he became Hitler's enthusiastic supporter, and was appointed editor of the Nazi sheet *Voelkische Freiheit*. With the Fuehrer's accession to power ' Jupp ' was made head of the Ministry of Public Enlightenment and Propaganda, an assignment he fulfilled with conspicuous ability. Vain and ruthlessly ambitious, he was a less ostentatious spendthrift than Goering, while his numerous amours did nothing to impoverish his infinite capacity for work. A bitter anti-Semite, his undoubted gift of mob oratory made him a powerful exponent of the more radical aspects of the Nazi philosophy. Wartime conditions greatly expanded his responsibilities and power, and by 1943, while Hitler was running the war, Goebbels was virtually running the country. A schizophrenic, alternating wishful thinking with hard-headed realism, he retained Hitler's confidence to the last, and like his Fuehrer chose immolation for himself and his family rather than surrender. See *The Goebbels Diaries*, ed. Lochner (1948), and Life by R. Manvell and H. Fraenkel (1960).

GOEBEL, Karl von (1855–1932), German botanist, born at Billigheim, Baden, was a distinguished plant morphologist, wrote *Organographie der Pflanzen* (trans. 1900–05), and founded the botanical institute and gardens at Munich.

GOEPPERT-MAYER, Maria (1906–), German scientist, born at Kattowitz, graduated at Göttingen in 1930, emigrated to the U.S.A. and taught at Johns Hopkins University, where her husband was professor of Chemical Physics. From 1960 she held a chair at the University of California. She was awarded with Wigner and Jensen the Nobel prize in physics in 1963 for research on nuclear shell structure.

GOERDELER, Carl, *gær'-* (1884–1945), German politician, born at Schneidemühl, served under Hitler as commissar for price control (1934), but resigned from his mayoralty of Leipzig in 1937 and became one of the leaders of opposition to Hitler, culminating in Stauffenberg's unsuccessful bomb plot July 20, 1944, for which Goerdeler was executed together with a number of generals. See G. Ritter, *The German Resistance: Carl Goerdeler's Struggle Against Tyranny* (1958).

GOERING, Hermann Wilhelm (1893–1946), German politico-military leader, was born at Rosenheim, Bavaria. In the 1914–18 war he was one of the first infantry officers to fight on the Western Front. In 1915 he transferred to the Air Force, became an ace pilot and later commanded the famous ' Death Squadron '. In 1922 he joined the Nazi Party and next year commanded the Hitler storm troopers, but had to go into exile for five years after the failure of the November Munich putsch. In 1928 he became one of the 12 Nazi deputies to the Reichstag. In the troubled economic crisis years his influence increased and in 1932 he became president of the Reichstag. When Hitler assumed power in 1933 Goering entered the Nazi government, his several posts including that of Reich commissioner for air. An early exploit of his as Hitler's chief lieutenant was the instigation of the Reichstag fire, his pretext for outlawing his Communist opponents. The evil genius of Nazism, he founded the Gestapo, set up the concentration camps for political, racial and religious suspects, and, in the great purge of June 30, 1934, had his comrades murdered. Two years later the international phase of his career opened when he mobilized Germany for total war under the slogan ' Guns Before Butter '. When the Munich (' peace in our time ') Agreement was made in 1938, he thoughtfully announced a five-fold extension of the Luftwaffe. Early in 1940 he became economic dictator of Germany and in June reached the pinnacle of his power when Hitler made him marshal of the Reich, the first and only holder of the rank. But the Battle of Britain, the failure of the 1941

Nazi bombing attacks to disrupt the British ports and cities, and the mounting Allied air attacks on Germany in 1942 and 1943 led to a decline in his prestige. By the time of the Allied liberation of Normandy in 1944 he was in disgrace. As the war drew to a close, he attempted a palace revolution. Hitler condemned him to death, but he escaped and was captured by U.S. troops. In 1946 he was the principal defendant at the Nuremberg War Crimes Trial when his record of unscrupulous intrigue and merciless oppression was laid bare. He was condemned for guilt ' unique in its enormity ', but committed suicide by poison on October 15 within a few hours of his execution. The dread career and sordid destiny of this vain Nazi with his vast collection of looted works of art, his limitless ambition and tigerish instincts illustrates the depths to which the leadership of a nation may be dragged when despotic power is utterly divorced from morals. See Life by W. Frischauer (1951), Butler and Young, *Marshall without Glory* (1951) and study by Manvell and Fraenkel (1962).

GOES. See VAN DER GOES.

GOETHALS, George Washington (1858–1928), American engineer, born at Brooklyn, chief engineer of the Panamá Canal (1907–1914), civil governor of the Canal Zone (1914–16). See Life by Bishop (1930).

GOETHE, Johann Wolfgang von, *gœ'tĕ* (1749–1832), German poet, dramatist, scientist and court official, born August 28 in Frankfurt-am-Main, was educated privately and studied reluctantly for his father's profession, law, at Leipzig (1765–68), but a love affair with Käthchen Schönkopf inspired his first two plays, appropriately *Die Laune des Verliebten* (1767) and *Die Mitschuldigen,* which was, however, not staged until 1787. After a protracted illness, he continued his law studies at Strasbourg from 1770 where he came under the influence of Herder (q.v.), the pioneer of German Romanticism, read Goldsmith's *Vicar of Wakefield* and dabbled in alchemy, anatomy and the antiquities. Another love affair, with Friederike Brion, inspired ' Röslein auf der Heide' and several fine lyrics. In 1771 he qualified, returned to Frankfurt, became a newspaper critic and captured the thwarted spirit of German nationalism in that early masterpiece of *Sturm und Drang* drama, *Götz von Berlichingen,* which in the person of the chivalrous robber-knight whose values had outlived his age, epitomized the man of genius at odds with society. *Faust* was begun, and Goethe followed up his first triumph with his self-revelatory cautionary novel, *Leiden des jungen Werthers* (1774), which mirrored Goethe's hopeless affair with Lotte Buff, the fiancée of a friend. Werther is made to solve the problem of clashing obligations by nobly and romantically committing suicide. Goethe himself, however, ' saved himself by flight '. *Clavigo,* a Hamlet-like drama followed in the same vein, based on Beaumarchais' *Mémoires.* Lili Schönemann inspired the love lyrics of 1775. In the autumn he surprisingly accepted the post of court-official and privy councillor (1776) to the young Duke of Weimar. He conscientiously

carried out all his state duties, interested himself especially in a geological survey, and taken in hand, emotionally, by the young widow, Charlotte von Stein (q.v.), mustered sufficient equipoise to exert a steadying influence on the inexperienced duke. His ten-year relationship with the former, however, critics are generally agreed, did little to help his development as a creative writer, valuable as his ' anchor ' might have seemed to him psychologically. In 1782 he was ennobled and, spurred on by his geological enthusiasms, extended his scientific researches to comparative anatomy, discovered the intermaxillary bone in man (1784), formulated a vertebral theory of the skull, in botany a theory that the leaf represented the characteristic form of which all the other parts of a plant are variations and made wrong-headed attempts to refute Newton's theory of light. He wrote a novel on theatrical life, *Wilhelm Meisters Theatralische Sendung,* not discovered until 1910, which contains the enigmatic poetry of Mignon's songs, epitomizing the best in German romantic poetry, including the famous ' Nur wer die Sehnsucht kennt ', &c., but his early uncontrolled advocacy of man's genius gave way to a more philosophical objectivity in his poem on the finiteness of humanity compared with divine nature. His visits to Italy (1786–88 and 1790) cured him of his emotional dependence on von Stein and contributed to a greater preoccupation with poetical form, as in the severely classical verse version of his drama, *Iphigenie* (1789), and the other but more modern subjects *Egmont* (1788) and *Tasso* (1790). His love for classical Italy, coupled with his passion for Christiane Vulpius, whom he married in 1806, found full expression in *Römische Elegien* (1795). From 1794 dates Goethe's more amiable disposition to Schiller (q.v.), with whom he conducted an interesting correspondence on aesthetics (1794–1805) and carried on a friendly contest in the writing of ballads which resulted on Schiller's part in *Die Glocke* and on Goethe's in the epic idyll *Hermann and Dorothea* (1798). They wrote against philistinism in the literary magazine *Horen.* Goethe's last great period saw the prototype of the favourite German literary composition, the *Bildungsroman* in *Wilhelm Meisters Lehrjahre* (1796) continued as *Wilhelm Meisters Wanderjahre* (1821–29). *Wilhelm Meister* became the idol of the German romantics, of whom Goethe increasingly disapproved. He disliked their enthusiasm for the French revolution, which he satirized in a number of works, including the epic poem *Reineke Fuchs* (1794), based on a medieval theme, and the drama *Die natürliche Tochter* (1803), and their disregard for style, which he attempted to correct by example in his novel *Die Wahlverwandtschaften* (1809) and the collection of lyrics, *Westöstlicher Divan* (1819). But Goethe's and German literature's masterpiece is his version of Marlowe's drama of *Faust* on which Goethe worked for most of his life. Begun in 1775, the first part was published after much revision and Schiller's advice in 1808, and the second part in 1832. The disillusioned scholar, Faust, deserts his 'ivory tower' to seek happiness in real life, makes a pact with Satan, who brings about the love-affair, seduction and death of Gretchen, an ordinary village girl, and subtly brings Faust by other such escapades to the brink of moral degradation. Part one is generally regarded as one of the classics of world literature. But English critics have not taken kindly to the excessive symbolical and didactic content of the second part. Goethe took little part in the political upheavals of his time. Yet Napoleon made a point of meeting Goethe at the congress of Erfurt (1803), and Goethe in 1813 kept aloof from the *Befreiungskriege*, having identified Napoleon with the salvation of European civilization. Goethe died March 22, 1832, and was buried near Schiller in the ducal vault at Weimar, a towering influence on German literature and especially in the mid-20th century a symbol of German liberalism and the 'good Germany', as opposed to Prussian militarism and virulent nationalism. See his literary autobiography, *Dichtung und Wahrheit* (1811–32), Lives by G. H. Lewes (1855), H. G. Atkins (1904), P. Hume Brown (1920), B. Croce (trans. 1923), G. Brandes (1925), and J. G. Robertson (1932), and studies by Thomas Carlyle (1828–1832), and B. Fairley (1932, 1948 and 1953), and on *Faust* by A. Gillies (1957), S. Atkins (1958) and R. Peacock (1959).

GOETZ VON BERLICHINGEN. See Götz.

GOFFE, William (*c*. 1605–79), English regicide, born at Stanmer rectory, Sussex, became major-general in the Parliamentary army, sat in the House of Commons, and signed Charles I's death-warrant. In 1660 he fled to America, lived for many years in seclusion at Hadley, Mass., and died at Hartford.

GOGH, van. See VAN GOGH.

GOGOL, Nikolai Vasilievich, *gō′gul-y'* (1809–52), Russian novelist and dramatist, born at Sorochintsi in Poltava, in 1829 settled in St Petersburg, and became famous through two masterpieces, a comedy and a novel. After unsatisfactory trials of official life, and of lecturing in history at the university, Gogol left Russia and lived abroad, mostly in Rome (1836–46), when he returned to Russia and died in Moscow. His *Inspector-General* (1836), the best of Russian comedies, is a wild and boisterous satire, exposing the corruption, ignorance and vanity of provincial officials. *Dead Souls* (1837), one of the greatest novels in world literature, deals with an attempt by small landowners to swindle the government by the purchase of dead serfs whose names should have been struck off the register. He also wrote some magnificent short stories, including *The Overcoat* and *The Diary of a Madman*, which introduce a nightmarish world of Gogol's fantastic imagination, exemplifying his irrational fears, frustrations and obsessions. His characters are 'flat' and 'cartoonlike'. There is no psychological insight. His later work shows increasing obsession with his own sinfulness and he burnt many of his remaining manuscripts. See translations by C. Garnett, and Lives by J. Lavrin (1926 and 1951) and V. Nabokov (1944).

GOKHALE, Gopal Krishna, *gō′ka-lay* (1866–1915), Indian politician, born at Kolhapur, became professor of History at Fergusson College, Poona, resigning in 1904, when he was selected representative of the Bombay legislative council at the supreme council, eventually becoming president of Congress in 1905. He was a leading protagonist of Indian self-government within the empire and influenced Gandhi.

GOLDING, (1) Louis (1895–1958), English novelist and essayist, author of *Magnolia Street* (1932), the story of a typical street in a provincial city whose inhabitants were Jews on one side, Gentiles on the other, also short stories, plays, &c., was born in Manchester of Jewish parents. See *Life* by J. B. Simons (1958).

(2) **Richard** (1785–1865), English engraver after West, Lawrence, &c., born in London.

(3) **William** (1911–), English novelist, educated at Marlborough School and Oxford, he is a writer of symbolic moralistic novels which analyse various aspects of man, such as *The Inheritors* (1955), which concerns the life and extermination of Neanderthal man, *Pincher Martin* (1956), which deals with Martin's struggle and reaction to death after his destroyer has been hit, and *Free Fall* (1959), which deals with the reflections of Mountjoy on his past and his search to find a meaningful pattern. Of the same type are *Lord of the Flies* (1954), which was made into a successful film (1963), and *The Spire* (1964). See study by M. Kinkead-Weekes and I. Gregor (1967).

GOLDMARK, Carl (1830–1915), Hungarian composer, born at Keszthely, Hungary, studied in Vienna and composed *Die Königin von Saba* (1875), *Merlin* (1886) and other lavishly colourful operas, two symphonies, two violin concertos, &c. His nephew, **Rubin** (1872–1936), the American composer, taught Copland and Gershwin.

GOLDONI, Carlo, *gol-dō′nee* (1707–93), Venetian dramatist, studied for the law, but his heart was set upon writing plays. A tragedy, *Belisario* (1732), proved a hit; but he soon discovered that his forte was comedy, and set himself to effect a revolution in the Italian comic stage. He spent several years in wandering over north Italy, until in 1740 he settled in his birthplace, where for twenty years he poured out comedy after comedy. He wrote no less than 250 plays in Italian, French and the Venetian dialect. He was greatly influenced by Molière and the *commedia dell' arte*, although many of his subjects are derived from direct observation of daily life. His best-known plays are *I Rusteghi*, which provided the plot for *The School for Fathers* produced in London in 1946, *La Locandiera* and *Le Baruffe Chiozzotte*. In 1761 he undertook to write for the Italian theatre in Paris, and was attached to the French court until the Revolution. See his own *Mémoires* (1787), study by Marchini-Capasso (1912) and *Life* by Chatfield Taylor (1915).

GOLDSCHMIDT, (1) Hans (1861–1923), German chemist, born in Berlin, invented the highly inflammable mixture of finely divided aluminium powder and magnesium ribbon (thermite process). The high temperatures attained make this useful for welding and incendiary bombs.

(2) **Madame.** See LIND, JENNY.

(3) **Meier Aaron** (1819–87), Danish novelist, was born at Vordingborg of Jewish parentage, wrote *En Jōde* (1845), translated as *The Jew of Denmark, Hjemlōs* (1853–57) or *Homeless,* and his Autobiography (1877).

(4) **Richard Benedikt** (1878–1958), German-American biologist, born at Frankfurt-am-Main, was appointed biological director of the Kaiser-Wilhelm Institute, Berlin, in 1921, in 1936 became professor of Zoology at California University. He conducted experiments on X-chromosomes, using butterflies, and is author of the theory that it is not the qualities of the individual genes, but the serial pattern of the chromosomes and the chemical configuration of the chromosome molecule that are decisive factors in heredity. Among his books are *Die Lehre von der Vererbung* (1927), *Die sexuellen Zwischenstufen* (1931), *Physiological Genetics* (1938) and *The Material Basis of Evolution* (1940).

GOLDSMITH, Oliver (1728–74), playwright, novelist and poet, was born in Ireland, his father being curate of Kilkenny West. After attending various local schools he entered Trinity College, Dublin, as a ' sizar ' in June 1744, but showed no exceptional ability. In 1747 he was involved in a college riot, and finally ran away; but, matters being patched up by his elder brother, returned, and took his B.A. in February 1749. His uncle (the father was dead) wished him to qualify for orders, but he was rejected by the Bishop of Elphin; thereupon he started for America, but got no farther than Cork. He was next equipped with £50 to study law in London; this disappeared at a Dublin gaming-table. In 1752 he went to Edinburgh to study medicine, and stayed there nearly two years, but was more noted for his social gifts than his professional acquirements. He drifted to Leyden, again lost at play what money he had, and finally set out to make the ' grand tour ' on foot, returning penniless in 1756. For a time he practised as a poor physician in Southwark, then was proof reader to Richardson, and next usher in Dr Milner's ' classical academy ' at Peckham. Griffiths of the *Monthly Review* retained him (for a few months) as author-of-all-work; and in February 1758 appeared his first definite work, a translation of the Memoirs of Jean Marteilhe, a persecuted French Protestant. Dr Milner had promised to obtain for him a berth as factory surgeon on the Coromandel coast; to get funds for his outfit he set about an *Enquiry into the State of Polite Learning in Europe.* But the nomination fell through, and in December he endeavoured unsuccessfully to pass at Surgeons' Hall for the humbler post of hospital mate. After he had pawned his clothes and been threatened with a debtor's prison, the *Enquiry* (1759) attracted some notice, and better days dawned on Goldsmith. He started *The Bee* (1759), and contributed to *The Busy Body* and *The Lady's Magazine.* Then came overtures from Smollett and Newbery the bookseller. For the *British Magazine* of the

former he wrote some of his best essays; for the *Public Ledger* of the latter the *Chinese Letters* (1760–71; republished as *The Citizen of the World*). In 1764 the ' Literary Club ' was founded, and he was one of its nine original members. His anonymous *History of England* was followed in December 1764 by *The Traveller,* a poem which gave him a foremost place among the minstrels of the day. *The Vicar of Wakefield* (1766) secured his reputation as a novelist. *The Good Natur'd Man,* a comedy (1768), was a moderate success. But he again escaped from enforced compilation (Histories of Rome, &c., *History of Animated Nature*) with his best poetical effort, *The Deserted Village* (1770); and three years afterwards achieved high dramatic honours with *She Stoops to Conquer.* A year later (April 4, 1774) he died of a severe fever. He was buried in the Temple Churchyard, and the club erected a monument to him in Westminster Abbey. In the year of his death was published the unfinished rhymed sketches called *Retaliation,* and in 1776 *The Haunch of Venison.* Goldsmith died £2000 in debt. As a man, despite many obvious faults, he was warm-hearted and generous, and full of unfeigned love and pity for humanity. As a writer, in addition to the most fortunate mingling of humour and tenderness, he possessed that native charm of style which neither learning nor labour can acquire. *Collected Letters* and *New Essays* appeared in 1928. See Lives by John Forster (1854), Austin Dobson (1888), H. J. Smith (1927), S. Gwynn (1937), R. M. Wardle (1958).

GOLDSTEIN, Eugen, -*stīn* (1850–1931), German physicist, born at Gleiwitz, Silesia, worked at the Berlin Observatory, discovered in 1876 the shadows cast at right angles to cathode rays and in 1886 the ' canal rays '—which were later shown to be positively charged particles of atomic mass.

GOLDSTÜCKER, Theodor (1821–72), German-Jewish Sanskrit scholar, born at Königsberg, from 1852 was professor of Sanskrit in University College, London. He founded the Sanskrit Text Society, and among his many publications is part of a great Sanskrit dictionary.

GOLDWYN, Samuel (1882–), American film producer, born of Jewish parents in Warsaw. At the age of eleven, an orphan, he ran away to relatives in England, and again at thirteen to the United States. He founded a film company with a depressed playwright, Cecil B. de Mille, as director and produced *The Squaw Man* (1913). In 1917 he founded the Goldwyn Pictures Corporation, in 1919 the Eminent Authors Pictures and finally in 1925 the Metro-Goldwyn-Mayer Company, allying himself with the United Artists from 1926. His ' film-of-the-book ' policy included such films as *Bulldog Drummond* (1929), *All Quiet on the Western Front* (1930), *Stella Dallas* (1937) and *Wuthering Heights* (1939). He introduced Rudolph Valentino, Bebe Daniels, Pola Negri, Ronald Colman, &c., to the screen and, allegedly, quaint expressions such as ' include me out ' to the English language. See his autobiographical *Behind the Screen* (1923).

GOLGI, Camillo (1843–1926), Italian cytologist, born at Corteno, Lombardy, became professor of Pathology at Pavia. He discovered the bodies in animal cells which bear his name and which, through their affinity for metallic salts, readily visible under the microscope, opened up a new field of research into the central nervous system, sense organs, muscles and glands. He shared with Ramón y Cajal the Nobel prize for medicine in 1906.

GOLLANCZ, go-langks', (1) **Sir Hermann** (1852–1930), British-Jewish scholar, brother of (2), born in Bremen, an authority on Hebrew language and literature, became professor at University College London (1902–24), and preacher at the Bayswater synagogue (1892–1923). He was the first British rabbi to be knighted (1923), sat on several government commissions and did much philanthropic work.

(2) **Sir Israel** (18⸱⸱–1930), British scholar, brother of (1), born in London, in 1906–30 professor of English Literature at King's College, was an authority on early English texts, and first secretary of the British Academy.

(3) **Sir Victor** (1893–1967), British publisher, author and philanthropist, was born in London into a Jewish family of small business men. He was educated at St Paul's School and New College, Oxford, where he won the Chancellor's prize for Latin prose. As a young man he was in revolt against his home and against orthodox Judaism, which he eventually rejected. He was for a time a master and military instructor at Repton School, but went into publishing and in 1928 founded his own firm. But he was best known for his innumerable campaigns and pressure group activities. In 1919 he was secretary of the Radical Research Group and in 1936 he founded the Left Book Club which was to have an enormous influence on the growth of the Labour party. During the Second World War he helped to get Jewish refugees out of Germany, but as soon as the war ended he worked hard to relieve starvation in Germany and tried to oppose the view that the Germans should share in the collective guilt for the crimes committed by the Nazis. In the same spirit he founded the Jewish Society for Human Service which had Arab relief as the first of its aims. He also vigorously launched national campaigns for the abolition of capital punishment and for nuclear disarmament. He was knighted in 1965. See his autobiographical *My Dear Timothy* (1952) and *More for Timothy* (1953).

GOLTZ, Colmar, Freiherr von der (1843–1916), German field-marshal, born at Bielkenfeld, wrote *Nation in Arms* (1883), &c., reorganized the Ottoman army (1883–95), and died in command of a Turkish force.

GOMARUS, or Gomar, Francis (1563–1641), Dutch Calvinist theologian, born at Bruges. As divinity professor at Leyden (1594) he became known for his hostility to his colleague, Arminius. At the synod of Dort (1618) he secured the Arminians' expulsion from the Reformed Church. From then until his death he was professor at Groningen.

GOMBERG, Moses (1866–1947), American chemist, born at Elisabetgrad, Russia, emigrated to America and was educated at Michigan, Munich and Heidelberg, becoming professor at the first-named (1904–36). He is famous for his discovery of organic free radicals.

GOMM, Sir William Maynard (1784–1875), British soldier, born in Barbados, served in the Peninsular war from 1808 and became Wellington's assistant. He also fought under Moore and on the Walcheren expedition. He was commander-in-chief in India (1850–55) and was made field-marshal in 1868.

GOMME, Sir George Laurence (1853–1916), English antiquary, born in London, wrote on folklore and London, and edited several antiquarian journals. He was clerk of the London County Council.

GOMPERS, Samuel (1850–1924), American antisocialist labour leader, born in London, went to U.S.A. in 1863, and helped to found the American Federation of Labour, of which he was long president. See his *Autobiography* (1925) and Life by R. H. Harvey (1935).

GOMULKA, Wladyslaw, go-mool'ka (1905–), Polish Communist leader, was born at Krosno, S.E. Poland. A local trade union leader, he organized during the Second World War underground resistance to the Germans and took an active part in the defence of Warsaw. In 1943 he became secretary of the outlawed underground Communist Party. He became vice-president of the first postwar Polish government, but from 1948 was gradually relieved of all his posts for 'non-appreciation of the decisive rôle of the Soviet Union' and arrested in 1951. But for Stalin's death in 1953, he would have been executed. Later in 1954 he was released from solitary confinement. He was rehabilitated in August 1956 and returned to power as party first secretary in October—thus preparing the way for a new course for Polish society. He was re-elected to this post in 1959. Braving the risk of a 'Stalinist' military putsch, Gomulka sought to put Poland on the road to a measure of freedom and independence, allowing freer discussion within a Marxist framework. In 1971, following a political crisis, he resigned office.

GONCHAROV, Ivan Alexandrovich (1812–1891), Russian novelist, born at Simbirsk, graduated from Moscow Univ. (1834), led an uneventful life in the civil service and wrote *Oblomov* (1857; trans. 1915), one of the greatest and most typical works of Russian realism. His other two novels fail to attain the same quality.

GONCOURT, gõ-koor, Edmond de (1822–96), and **Jules de** (1830–70), French novelists, the former born at Nancy, the latter at Paris. Artists primarily, in 1849 they set out to traverse France for watercolour sketches. Their notebooks made them writers as well as artists. The important work of the de Goncourt brothers commenced when, after collaborating in studies in history and art (especially Japanese art), they took to novel-writing. Their task was to unite by means of a plot a multitude of observed facts, and to cast around these an atmosphere which should illumine them. Their subject is not so much the passions as the manners of the 19th century, and their sense of the enormous influence of environment and habit upon man necessitated a close study of contemporary life. The first of these novels, *Les Hommes de lettres* (1860; new ed. as *Charles Demailly*), was followed by *Soeur Philomène* (1861), *Renée Mauperin* (1864), *Germinie Lacerteux* (1865), *Manette Salomon* (1867), and *Madame Gervaisais* (1869). The last is their greatest novel; its sharp and painful analysis was too close a reflex of themselves. After Jules's death, Edmond issued the extraordinarily popular *La Fille Élisa* (1878), *La Faustin* (1882) and *Chérie* (1885). The interesting *Idées et sensations* (1866) had already revealed their morbid hyper-acuteness of sensation, and *La Maison d'un artiste* (1881) had shown their patient love for *bric-à-brac*; the *Lettres de Jules de Goncourt* (1885), and still more the *Journal des Goncourt* (9 vols. 1888–96), disclosed their conception of fiction and their methods. Edmond, by will, founded the Goncourt Academy to foster fiction. See Paul Bourget's *Nouveaux Essais de psychologie* (1885), and Belloc and Shedlock's *Letters and Journals of E. and J. de Goncourt* (2 vols. 1894); also Lives by A. Delzant (1889), M. Sauvage (1932) and A. Billy (trans. 1960) ; and study by P. Sabatier (1920).

GONDOMAR, Diego Sarmiento de Acuña, Conde de (1567–1626), as Spanish ambassador in England (1613–21) laboured to arrange the marriage of Prince Charles (later Charles I) with the Infanta.

GÓNGORA Y ARGOTE, Don Luis de (1561–1627), Spanish lyric poet, was born at Córdoba, studied law, but in 1606 took orders and became a prebendary of Córdoba, and eventually chaplain to Philip III. He died May 23, 1627. Góngora's earlier writings are elegant and stylish. His later works, consisting for the most part of longer poems, such as *Solidades, Polifemo, Piramo y Tisbe*, are executed in an entirely novel style, which his followers designated the *stilo culto*. It is florid, pedantic, and euphuistic. See studies by Churton (London 1862) and M. Artigas (1925).

GONSALVO DI CORDOVA, properly **Gonzalo Hernández y Aguilar** (1453–1515), Spanish soldier, was born at Montilla near Córdoba. He served with distinction against the Moors of Granada, and afterwards in Portugal. Sent to assist Ferdinand II of Naples against the French (1495), he conquered the greater part of the kingdom of Naples, and expelled the French. When the partition of Naples was determined upon in 1500, Gonsalvo again set out for Italy, but first took Zante and Cephalonia from the Turks, and restored them to the Venetians. He then landed in Sicily, occupied Naples and Calabria, and demanded from the French that they should keep the compact. This demand being rejected, war was waged with varied success; but ultimately Gonsalvo won a great battle (1503) at the Garigliano river, which by careful planning and tactics he crossed five miles above Minturno, at a spot where in 1943 the 56th British Division found a crossing. His victory

secured Naples for Spain. Recalled in 1506, and treated by the king with neglect, Gonsalvo withdrew to his estates in Granada.
GONVILLE, Edmund. See CAIUS.
GONZAGA, -zah'-, a princely north Italian family named from a small town in the province of Mantua, who ruled Mantua for three centuries, and from 1432 were marquises, from 1530 dukes of Mantua. They were the champions of the imperial interests, and were always at war with the Visconti Dukes of Milan. The tenth and last Duke of Mantua, who had sided with the French, was deprived by the Emperor Joseph I of his estates, and died in exile in 1708. The Dukes of Montferrat were a branch of the Gonzagas. See family history by S. Brinton (1927).
GONZAGA, (1) Luigi, known as **St Aloysius** (1568–91), Italian Jesuit, was born in the castle of Castiglione near Brescia, March 9, 1568. Renouncing his marquisate, he entered the Society of Jesus in 1585. In a plague at Rome he devoted himself to the care of the sick, but was himself infected and died. He was canonized in 1726. See the Italian Lives by Cepari (trans. 1891), E. H. Thompson (1893) and Aubrey de Vere's *Essays* (1888).
(2) **Tomás António** (1744–1809), Brazilian and Portuguese poet, pseudonym ' Dirceu ', born at Oporto of an English mother and a Brazilian father, studied for the law, was sent to Vila-Rica in 1782 where he met the ' Marília ' of his verses, but was exiled to Mozambique for his revolutionary activities, married a rich mulatta and became a leading citizen of Mozambique. His *Marilia de Dirceu* (1792) contains the best verses in the Arcadian tradition apart from Bocage, and they are considered masterpieces of the Mineiro school.
GOOCH, (1) Sir Daniel (1816–89), English engineer, born at Bedlington, Northumberland, was early associated with the Stephensons in railway construction, became G.W.R. locomotive superintendent (1837–64) and then distinguished himself in submarine telegraphy by laying the first Atlantic cable (1865–66). He was made a baronet in 1866. He died at his Berkshire seat, Clewer Park. See his Diaries edited by Sir Theodore Martin (1892).
(2) **George Peabody** (1873–1968), English historian, born in London, Liberal M.P. for Bath in 1906–10, editor of the *Contemporary Review* (1911–60), was author of *English Democratic Ideas in the 17th century* (1898), *Germany and the French Revolution* (1920), *Studies in Diplomacy and Statecraft* (1942) and other works on political and diplomatic history. He was made a C.H. in 1939 and awarded the O.M. in 1963.
GOODALL, Frederick (1822–1904), British artist, son of the engraver Edward Goodall (1795–1870), born in London, is remembered for his subject pictures *Raising the Maypole* (1851), *Cranmer at the Traitors' Gate* (1856), &c. He became R.A. in 1863.
GOODE, George Brown (1851–96), American ichthyologist, was born at New Albany, Indiana, was U.S. fish commissioner (1887–1888) and author of a *Catalogue* of Bermuda fishes (1876) and *Oceanic Ichthyology* (1895).

GOODRICH, Samuel Griswold, pseud. **Peter Parley** (1793–1860), American publisher, was born at Ridgefield, Conn., and edited in Boston *The Token* (1828–42), to which he contributed moralistic poems, tales and essays for children and in which the best of Hawthorne's ' Twice-told Tales ' appeared. He published some two hundred volumes, mostly for the young ; many of them became popular in Great Britain. See his *Story of my own Life* (1862).

GOODRICKE, John (1764–86), English astronomer, born at Groningen, first accounted for variable stars. He was awarded the Copley Medal in 1783 and elected F.R.S. in 1786.

GOODSIR, John (1814–67), Scottish anatomist, born at Anstruther, studied at St Andrews and Edinburgh, where he became in 1846 professor of Anatomy. He is best known for his work in cellular pathology. See *Memoir* by Sir Wm. Turner (1868).

GOODYEAR, Charles (1800–60), American inventor, born at New Haven, Conn., failed as an iron-manufacturer, and in 1834 began research into the properties of rubber. Amid poverty and ridicule he pursued the experiments which ended, in 1844, in the invention of vulcanized rubber, which led to the production of the well-known tyres named after him.

GOOGE, Barnabe, *gooj* (1540–94), English poet, was born at Alvingham in Lincolnshire, studied both at Cambridge and Oxford, travelled on the Continent, and became one of the gentlemen-pensioners of Queen Elizabeth. His best works are a series of eight eclogues and his *Cupido Conquered.*

GOOSSENS, name of a Belgian, later English, family of musicians:

(1) **Eugène** (1845–1906), Belgian conductor, father of (2), born at Bruges, studied at the Brussels Conservatoire and became a conductor of several opera companies in Belgium, France and Italy before making his name in comic opera with the Carl Rosa Company in Britain from 1873. He founded the Goossens Male-Voice Choir in Liverpool in 1894.

(2) **Eugène** (1867–1958), violinist and conductor, son of (1) and father of (3) and (4), born at Bordeaux, studied at the Brussels Conservatoire and at the Royal Academy of Music, London, played with the Carl Rosa Company under his father (1884–86) and with the orchestra at Covent Garden (1893–1894) and was principal conductor of the Carl Rosa Company (1899–1915).

(3) **Sir Eugene** (1893–1962), English composer and conductor, son of (2), born in London, studied in Bruges and London, and became associate conductor to Sir Thomas Beecham in the latter's opera seasons. In 1921 he gave a highly successful series of orchestral concerts, in which he brought out some of his own music. From 1923–45 he worked in America, as conductor of the Rochester (New York) Philharmonic Orchestra and of the Cincinnati Symphony Orchestra. Appointed conductor of the Sydney Symphony Orchestra and director of the New South Wales Conservatory in 1947, he had a profound influence in Australia

both on standards of performance and the training of musicians. His own music, which includes the operas *Judith* (1929) and *Don Juan de Mañara* (1937), a large-scale oratorio *The Apocalypse,* and two symphonies, found favour with the critics. He was knighted in 1955.

(4) **Léon** (1897–), British oboist, brother of (3), born in Liverpool. He studied at the Royal College of Music and, after 1913, held leading posts in most of the major London orchestras, retiring from orchestral work to devote himself to solo playing and teaching. His sisters **Marie** (1894–) and **Sidonie** (1899–) are well-known harpists.

GORCHAKOV, (1) **Prince Alexander Michaelovich** (1798–1883), Russian statesman, cousin of (2), born at St Petersburg in 1798, ambassador at Vienna (1854–56), succeeded Nesselrode as foreign minister. As chancellor of the empire (1863) he was, till Bismarck's rise, the most powerful minister in Europe. He secured Austrian neutrality in the Franco-German war of 1870, and in 1871 absolved Russia from the treaty of Paris (1856). After the conclusion of the Russo-Turkish war, the repudiation of the treaty of San Stefano, and the signing of the treaty of Berlin his influence began to wane, and he retired in 1882. He died at Baden-Baden. See Klaczko's *Two Chancellors* (trans. 1876).

(2) **Prince Michael** (1795–1861), Russian soldier, cousin of (1), served against the French in 1812–14 and the Turks in 1828–29. He distinguished himself during the Polish revolution of 1831, and in Hungary in 1849. On the outbreak of the Crimean war he commanded in the Danubian Principalities, and, now commander-in-chief in the Crimea (1855), was defeated on the Tchernaya, but recovered his laurels by his gallant defence of Sebastopol.

GORDIANUS, Marcus Antonius, also called **Gordian,** name of three Roman emperors:

Gordian I, surnamed **Africanus** (158–238), father of Gordian II, grandfather of Gordian III, descended from the Gracchi, was twice consul, and next proconsul of Africa. The tyranny of the Emperor Maximinus excited a rebellion in Africa, and Gordianus, then in his eightieth year, was proclaimed emperor conjointly with his son (238) and committed suicide when the latter was slain in a battle near Carthage by Capellianus, governor of Numidia, a month later.

Gordian II (192–238). See GORDIAN I.

Gordian III, known as **Gordianus Pius** (c. 224–244), grandson of Gordian I, was elevated by the Praetorians to the rank of Augustus in 238. In 242 he marched against the Persians and relieved Antioch, but was assassinated by his own soldiers.

GORDON, name of a Scottish family which takes its origin and name from the lands of Gordon in Berwickshire and whose members became Lords of Strathbogie from 1357, Earls of Huntly from 1445, Marquesses of Huntly from 1599 and Dukes of Gordon from 1684 until 1836, when the title became extinct. Its 157 branches include the Lochinvar line (Viscounts Kenmure from 1633, extinct in 1847), the Earlston branch, a cadet branch of the latter, and according to tradition the Earls of Aberdeen (q.v.) are descended from an illegitimate brother of Sir Adam of Gordon, killed at Homildon in 1402. The noteworthy members of the Gordon family are (in chronological order):

(1) **George, 2nd Earl of Huntly** (d. *c.* 1502), high chancellor of Scotland (1498–1501), married Princess Annabella, daughter of James I of Scotland. Their second son married the Countess of Sutherland and was progenitor of the Earls of Sutherland. See *History of the Earldom* (1813) written in 1630 by Sir Robert Gordon of Gordonstoun (1580–1656), the 12th Earl of Sutherland's fourth son.—Their third son was progenitor of the turbulent Gordons of Gight, from whom Byron's maternal ancestors were descended.

(2) **Alexander, 3rd Earl** (d. 1524), Scottish soldier, son of (1), led the left wing of the Scots at the Battle of Flodden (1513).

(3) **George, 4th Earl** (1514–62), Scottish high chancellor, grandson of (2), supported Cardinal Beaton (q.v.) against Arran (1543), but when stripped by the crown of his new earldom of Moray rushed into revolt and was killed at Corrichie.

(4) **George, 6th Earl and 1st Marquis of Huntly** (1562–1636), was head of the Roman Catholics in Scotland, defeated at Glenlivet a royal force under the Earl of Argyll in 1594, but, submitting to the king, was pardoned and made Marquis in 1599. His second son, **Lord John** (d. 1630), was made Viscount Melgum and Lord Aboyne in 1627 and was burnt to death in Crichton's tower of Frendraught. Viscount Aboyne was the style after 1632, Earl of Aboyne after 1660 and Marquis of Huntly after 1836. See (13).

(5) **Sir John, of Lochinvar, 1st Viscount of Kenmure** (1599–1634), descended from **William of Gordon** (1306–29), second son of Sir Adam of Gordon, was created Viscount in 1633. **William**, 6th Viscount, was beheaded in 1716 for his share in the Rebellion. The peerage, then forfeited, was restored in 1824 but died out with **Adam**, 9th Viscount, in 1847.

(6) **George, 2nd Marquis of Huntly** (d. 1649), son of (4), espoused the royal cause in the Civil War and was beheaded in Edinburgh.

(7) **Lewis, 3rd Marquis of Huntly**, son of (6), was restored to the title by Charles II in 1651.

(8) **George, 4th Marquis of Huntly and 1st Duke of Gordon** (1643–1716), held Edinburgh Castle for James VII at the Revolution of 1688.

(9) **Alexander, 2nd Duke** (*c.* 1678–1728), like his father (8) a Jacobite, led reinforcements to the Old Pretender at Perth (1715). His son, **Lord Lewis** (d. 1754), defeated the Macleod of Macleod in the '45 for the Jacobites and died an exile in Montreuil.

(10) **Cosmo George, 3rd Duke** (d. 1752), father of (11) and (12).

(11) **Alexander, 4th Duke** (*c.* 1745–1827), son of (10), was the author of the well-known song, ' Cauld Kail in Aberdeen '. His wife, the sprightly **Jane Maxwell** (*c.* 1749–1812), was known as the ' beautiful Duchess of Gordon '.

(12) **Lord George** (1751–93), anti-Catholic agitator, son of (10), was born in London, educated at Eton, entered the navy and retired as lieutenant in 1772. Elected M.P. in 1774, he attacked both sides. An act of 1778 having brought Roman Catholics relief from certain disabilities, Lord George, as president of a Protestant association, headed (June 2, 1780) a mob of 50,000 persons, who marched in procession to the House of Commons to present a petition for its repeal. For five days, serious rioting took place during which many Catholic chapels and private houses, Newgate, and the house of the chief-justice, Lord Mansfield, were destroyed. On the 7th the troops were called out, and 285 of the rioters were reported killed, 173 wounded and 139 arrested, 21 being executed. Property to the value of £180,000 was destroyed in the riots. Lord George was tried for high treason; but Erskine's defence got him off. He subsequently turned Jew, calling himself Israel Abraham George Gordon. In 1787 he was convicted for a libel on Marie Antoinette, fled to Holland, was extradited and taken to Newgate, where he died of gaol fever. See Life by R. Watson (1795), Dickens's *Barnaby Rudge*, de Castro's study (1926), and *King Mob*, by C. Hibbert (1958).

(13) **George, 5th Duke of Gordon** (1770–1836), died without issue; the title of Duke of Gordon became extinct, and that of Marquis of Huntly was adjudged to the Earl of Aboyne. The estates went to the Duke's nephew, Charles, 5th Duke of Richmond and Lennox, grandson of the 4th Duke of Gordon; and his son, the 6th Duke of Richmond, was in 1876 created also Duke of Gordon.

GORDON, (1) Adam Lindsay (1833–70), Australian poet, was born at Fayal in the Azores in 1833, the son of a retired army-captain. Educated in England, at twenty he sailed to S. Australia. There and in Victoria he occupied himself as police-trooper, horse-breaker and livery stable keeper, and was the best gentleman steeplechase rider in the colonies. A fall, financial losses and fear of failure as a poet affecting his mind, he blew out his brains at Brighton, near Melbourne, June 24. He had published *Sea-Spray and Smoke-drift* (1867), *Ashtaroth* (1867), and *Bush Ballads and Galloping Rhymes* (1870). ' The Sick Stock-rider ' is a vivid picture of bush-life; but the best verse of this so-called 'first of Australian poets' is English in subject and sentiment. See studies by Humphris and Sladen (1912) and Vidler (1926).

(2) **Charles George** (1833–85), British soldier, was born at Woolwich, January 28 and descended from a cadet branch of the House of Huntly. (See GORDON family.) He entered Woolwich Academy in 1847, and the Royal Engineers in 1852; served before Sebastopol from January 1855 to the end of the siege; and was engaged in surveying the new frontiers between Turkey and Russia (1856–57). In 1860 he went to China and took part in the capture of Peking and the destruction of the Summer Palace. In command of a Chinese force (1863–64), he

fought thirty-three actions against the Taipings and took numerous walled towns, effectually crushing the formidable rebellion —a feat that placed ' Chinese Gordon ' in the foremost rank of the soldiers of his day. From 1865 he was for six years engaged in ordinary engineering duties at Gravesend, devoting his spare moments to relieving the want and misery of the poor, visiting the sick, teaching, feeding and clothing the waifs and strays. He was on the Danube Navigation Commission (1871–72). In 1873 he accepted employment under Ismail, Khedive of Egypt, and took up Sir Samuel Baker's work of opening up the vast regions of the equatorial Nile. A chain of posts was established along the Nile, steamers were placed above the last of the rapids, and the navigation of Lake Albert was successfully accomplished; but realizing that his efforts to suppress the slave trade must remain unsuccessful unless his power extended to the vast plain countries lying west of the Nile basin, Gordon returned to England in 1876. Going out again in 1877, he was appointed governor of the Sudan, from the Second Cataract of the Nile to the Great Lakes, and from the Red Sea to the headwaters of the streams that fall into Lake Chad. During the next three years, fever-wracked and surrounded by enemies, he reconnoitred this vast territory; his feats of government and engineering astounded the world. But in 1880, his health undermined, he resigned; he made a short visit to India and China, and the close óf 1880 found him in Ireland propounding a scheme of land-law improvement. For a year he volunteered to take another officer's duty in Mauritius, and from Mauritius proceeded to the Cape in colonial employment, finally returning to England at the close of 1882. Almost the whole of 1883 was spent in Palestine in quiet and reflection. Early in 1884 he was asked by the British government to proceed once more to the Sudan to relieve the garrisons in Egypt which were in rebel territory. A month after he reached Khartoum it was invested by the troops of the Mahdi. The siege had lasted five months when a relief expedition was organized in England. In September the advance up the Nile began, and early in November the troops entered the Sudan and the advance guard arrived on January 28, 1885, in the neighbourhood of Khartoum. It was too late. The place had been taken two days earlier, and Gordon had been murdered on the palace steps. The national memorial is the Gordon Boys' School at Woking. There are memorials of him in St Paul's Cathedral and elsewhere. See Lives and studies by E. Hake (1884), W. Butler (1889), F. R. Wingate (1891), H. E. Worthum (1911), Buchan (1934), G. S. Hutchinson (1945), Elton (1954), G. French (1958).

(3) **Lord George.** See GORDON Family (12).

(4) **James.** See GORDON, ROBERT.

(5) **Sir John Watson** (1788–1864), born at Edinburgh, on Raeburn's death in 1823 succeeded him as the first portrait painter of Scotland. In 1850 he was elected P.R.S.A. and knighted, and in 1851 he became an R.A.

His portraits of Macaulay, the Prince of Wales and many others are in the Scottish National Gallery and of De Quincey in the National Portrait Gallery, London. His best-known works include *Sir Walter Scott, Earl of Dalhousie* and *Dr. Chalmers.*

(6) **Lord Lewis.** See GORDON Family (9).

(7) **Patrick** (1635–99), Scottish soldier of fortune, was born at Easter Auchleuchries, Aberdeenshire. A Catholic, he at sixteen entered the Jesuit College of Braunsberg, but absconded in 1653, eventually joining the Swedish army during the war with Poland in 1655. During the next six years he was repeatedly captured and every time fought for his captors until retaken. In 1661 he joined the Russian army and rose to high rank. Although he was sent on missions. to Britain in 1665 and 1685, he did not succeed in his desire to return to Scotland permanently. ´Under Tsar Peter the Great he was made general in 1688, crushed a conspiracy in 1689 and a serious revolt in 1698. See his abridged *Diary* (ed. Robertson, 1859).

(8) **Robert** (1580–1661), Scottish cartographer, of Straloch, along with his son, **James** (c. 1615–86), who was minister of Rothiemay, Banffshire, revised and edited Pont's Scottish maps for Blaeu's *Atlas.* The son also wrote *Scots Affairs 1624-51* (Spalding Club, 1841).—A grandson, **Robert** (1665–1732), founded a boys' school at Aberdeen.

(9) **Sir Robert** (1647–1704), Scottish inventor and reputed warlock, of Gordonstoun, Moray, corresponded with Sir Robert Boyle (q.v.) the chemist and designed a pump for raising water.

GORDON-CUMMING, (1) **Constance Frederica** (1837–1924), British traveller and author, sister of (2), born at Altyre, Moray, wrote sprightly and entertaining works including *At Home in Fiji* (1881), *China* (1885), *Memories* (1904–05), &c.

(2) **Roualeyn George** (1820–66), British lion hunter, brother of (1), educated at Eton, entered the Madras Cavalry (1838), served for a time in Canada, and joined the Cape Mounted Rifles (1843); but soon resigned his commission, and engaged in those famous hunting exploits narrated in his *Five Years of a Hunter's Life* (1850).

GORE, (1) **Catherine Grace Frances,** *née* **Moody** (1799–1861), English novelist, born at East Retford, Notts, was a prolific and immensely popular writer of novels, mainly of fashionable life, such as *The Banker's Wife* (1843), &c.

(2) **Charles** (1853–1932), Anglican theologian, nephew of the 4th Earl of Arran, was educated at Harrow and Oxford, became fellow of Trinity College, Oxford in 1875 and first principal of Pusey House in 1884. His contribution to *Lux Mundi* (1889) abandoned the strict tractarian view of biblical inspiration, and his Bampton Lectures (1891) were equally controversial. He founded at Pusey House in 1892 the Community of the Resurrection, became bishop successively of Worcester (1901), Birmingham (1904), Oxford (1911–19). See **Life** by G. L. Prestige (1935) and study by **Ramsay** (1955).

GORGAS, William Crawford (1854–1920), American military doctor, born near Mobile, established a great reputation as an epidemiologist by his extermination of yellow fever in Havana in 1898, and in the Panamá Canal Zone before and during construction of the waterway.

GÖRGEI, Arthur, *gœr'gay-ee* (1818–1916), Hungarian rebel soldier, born at Toporcz in North Hungary, during the revolt of 1848 compelled Jellachich and his 10,000 Croats to capitulate at Ozora (October 7), but was driven back by Windischgrätz. As Hungarian commander-in-chief he relieved Komorn by inflicting a series of severe defeats on the Austrians, practically driving them out of the country. Though almost constantly at feud with Kossuth and a provisional government, he in 1849 accepted the ministry of war, but by delays and jealousies the enemy gained numerous advantages, and Görgei was repeatedly defeated. On August 11, he was nominated dictator, and two days later surrendered with his army of 24,000 men to the Russian commander, Rüdiger, at Világos near Arad. Görgei was imprisoned at Klagenfurt, but eventually set free and returned to Hungary in 1868.

GORGES, Sir Ferdinando, *gor'jes* (c. 1566–1647), English colonizer in America, was born at Ashton in Somerset. He founded two Plymouth companies (1606–19 and 1620–35) for planting lands in New England, in 1639 received a charter constituting him proprietor of Maine, and died at Bristol. His grandson sold his rights to Massachusetts in 1677. See his autobiography (1847) and study by H. S. Burrage (1923).

GORGIAS, *gor'jee-as* (c. 485–c. 380 B.C.), Greek sophist, sceptical philosopher and rhetorician, born at Leontini, Sicily, came to Athens as ambassador in 427, and, settling in Greece, won wealth and fame as a peripatetic teacher of eloquence. He maintained the Eleatic paradoxes of nihilism, that nothing exists and that even if it did it would be unknowable and certainly incommunicable as knowledge from one man to another. A short summary of his treatise on nature is preserved. Plato's dialogue *Gorgias* is written against him. See Diels-Kranz, *Fragmente der Vorsokratiker* (1935).

GORHAM, George Cornelius (1787–1857), Anglican divine, born at St Neots and a fellow of Queens' College, Cambridge, was in 1847, for denying unconditional regeneration in baptism, refused institution to the living of Brampford Speke, Devon, by the Bishop of Exeter and afterwards (1849) by the Court of Arches, but in the end (1851) was instituted following reversal of the decision by the judicial committee of the Privy Council. See study by Nies (1951).

GÖRING. See GOERING.

GORKY, Maxim, is the pen-name of **Aleksei Maksimovich Peshkov** (1868–1936), Russian novelist, born at Nizhni Novgorod (now Gorky), and successively pedlar, scullery boy, gardener, dock hand, tramp and writer. His early work was in a romantic theatrical vein, glorifying the unusual, with vividly drawn characters, mostly of tramps and down-and-outs. *Foma Gordeyev* (1899) marks his transition from romanticism to realism. The subsequent social novels and dramas were greatly weakened by long tendentious discussions on the meaning of life. His autobiographical trilogy (1915) contains his best writing. Involved in strikes and imprisoned in 1905, he lived abroad until 1914 and then engaged in revolutionary propaganda. From 1922 to 1928 he lived abroad again on account of his health, but then returned, a wholehearted supporter of the Soviet régime. He sponsored ' social realism ' as the official school in Soviet literature and art. See Lives by Dillon (1902), A. Kaun (1932), Holtzman (1948).

GÖRRES, Johann Joseph von, *gœr'res* (1776–1848), German writer, born at Coblenz, in 1812 became the literary centre of the national movement. Denouncing absolutism with great energy, he angered the Prussian government, and had to flee the country (1820). In 1827 he was made professor of Literature at Munich, where he devoted himself to literature and controversial theology. His chief work was his *Christliche Mystik* (1842). See Lives by Galland (1876), Schulz (1902), Schellberg (1913), Stein (1928), and studies by Sepp (1876), Berger (1921).

GORST, (1) Sir Eldon (1861–1911), son of (3), was from 1907 consul-general in Egypt.

(2) **Harold** (1868–1950), English author, son of (3), was parliamentary correspondent, lectured and wrote biographies, religious and political essays and collaborated with Gertrude Warren in *Compromised*, a modern masque (1902).

(3) **Sir John Eldon** (1835–1916), English politician, born at Preston, became a popular civil commissioner in the Maori country in New Zealand, was called to the bar in 1865 and entered parliament, a staunch supporter of Disraeli, later joined the Fourth Party led by Randolph Churchill, was knighted in 1885 and ultimately joined the Liberal Party. He held several ministerial offices, including that of solicitor-general (1885–86).

GORT, John Standish Surtees Prendergast Vereker, 6th Viscount (1886–1946), British field-marshal (1943), served in the First World War (V.C. 1918) and in the Second was commander-in-chief of the British forces overwhelmed in the initial German victories of 1940. Afterwards he was governor of Gibraltar (1941–42) and of Malta from 1942 till 1944, when he became high commissioner for Palestine and Transjordan.

GORTON, Samuel (1592–1677), English colonist, founder of the obscure and extinct sect of ' Gortonites ', was born at Gorton, Lancashire, and emigrated in 1636 to New England, where he died at Warwick.

GORTSCHAKOFF. See GORCHAKOV.

GOSCHEN, George Joachim Goschen, 1st Viscount, *gŏ'shen* (1831–1907), British statesman, was the son of a London merchant of German extraction. In 1863 he published *The Theory of Foreign Exchanges*, and became Liberal M.P. for the City of London, holding office as vice-president of the Board of Trade (1865), chancellor of the Duchy of Lancaster (1866), president of the Poor-law Board (1868), and head of the Admiralty (1871–74).

He regulated Egyptian finances (1876), and as ambassador extraordinary to the Porte (1880) induced Turkey to fulfil her treaty obligations to Greece. Opposing Home Rule, he was Unionist chancellor of the Exchequer (1887–92), and in 1888 converted part of the National Debt; he was first lord of the Admiralty (1895–99). See Life by A. D. Elliot (1911), and *Letters* (ed. Colson, 1947). His brother, **Sir William Edward Goschen** (1847–1924), was British ambassador at Berlin (1908–14).

GOSS, Sir John (1800–80), English composer of anthems (among them ' O Taste and See '), glees, &c., was born at Fareham, Hants, and was organist of St Paul's from 1838 to 1872, when he was knighted.

GOSSE, (1) Sir Edmund William (1845–1928), English poet and critic, son of (2), whose character and beliefs he described in *Father and Son* (1907), was born in London, educated privately, became assistant librarian in the British Museum (1867–75), translator to the Board of Trade (1875–1904) and finally librarian to the House of Lords (1904–14). He published two volumes of poems, *On Viol and Flute* (1873) and *Collected Poems* (1911). His *Studies in the Literature of Northern Europe* (1879), &c., first introduced Ibsen to English readers. He also wrote on Congreve (1888), Donne (1899), Jeremy Taylor (1904), Sir Thomas Browne (1905), Swinburne (1917), and Malherbe (1920), although his special field was *Seventeenth-century Studies* (1897). He was knighted in 1925. See Life by Charteris (1931).

(2) **Philip Henry** (1810–88), English naturalist, father of (1), born at Worcester, went to North America in 1827 and became a professional naturalist in Jamaica. His *Manual of Marine Zoology* (1855–56), written on his return to England, opened up a new branch of science. His best-known work was the *Romance of Natural History* (1860–62). See Life by his son (1890).

GOT, François Jules Edmond, *gō* (1822–1901), French actor, was born at Lignerolles (Orne), and in 1844 made his début. From 1850 to 1866 he was a member of the Comédie-Française. He received the cross of the Legion of Honour in 1881.

GOTHARDT, M. See GRÜNEWALD, M.

GOTTFRIED VON STRASSBURG (fl. 1200), German poet, wrote the masterly German version of the legend of Tristan and Isolde, based on the Anglo-Norman poem by Thomas (q.v.), a work of lyrical beauty imbued with a profound psychological insight. He is also noteworthy as an early exponent of literary criticism, having left appraisals of the work of poets of the period. See editions by Closs (1944) and Ranke (1946).

GOTTHARD, or Godehard, St (*c.* 961–1038), German monk, born in Bavaria, in 1022 became Bishop of Hildesheim.

GOTTHELF, Jeremias. See BITZIUS.

GOTTSCHALK. See HINCMAR.

GOTTSCHALL, Rudolf von, *-shahl* (1823–1909), German author, was born at Breslau. A keen Liberal, he produced two volumes of political verse (1842–43). From 1864 he lived in Leipzig and edited *Brockhaus'sche Blätter* and *Unsere Zeit*. He also wrote a

comedy entitled *Pitt und Fox* (1854), tragedies and historical novels. See his autobiography (1898).

GOTTSCHED, Johann Christoph (1700–66), German man of letters, born at Judithenkirch near Königsberg, in 1730 became professor of Philosophy and Poetry at Leipzig, and in 1734 of Logic and Metaphysics. Gottsched laboured to improve his mother-tongue as a literary vehicle, and to reform the German drama by banishing buffoonery and raising the style and tone. But he became pedantic and vain, and manifested a petty jealousy of all literary authority save his own, opposing Bodmer and pooh-poohing Lessing. His drama, *The Dying Cato* (1732), notwithstanding its immense success, is sadly barren. See German works by Bernays (1880), Reicke (1892) and Krause (1894).

GOTTWALD, Klement, *got'valt* (1896–1953), Czech politician, was born at Dedice, Moravia. In the First World War he fought with the Austro-Hungarian Army. He then joined the Communist Party, whose secretary-general he became in 1927. He opposed the Munich Agreement of 1938 and later went to Moscow, where he was trained for eventual office. In 1945 he became, as a Communist leader, vice-premier in the Czech Provisional Government. Prime minister in 1946, he carried out in February 1948 the Communist *coup d'état* which averted a defeat for his party at the polls. In June he became president. Strong in the support of Moscow, whose line he followed closely, he established a complete dictatorship in Czechoslovakia.

GÖTZ VON BERLICHINGEN, *gœts fon ber'liкн-ing-en* (1480–1562), German condottiere nicknamed ' with the iron-hand ' because of a steel replacement for his right hand lost in the siege of Landshut (1505), born at Jaxthausen in Württemberg, from 1497 onwards was involved in continual feuds, in which he displayed both lawless daring and chivalrous magnanimity. Twice he was placed under the ban of the empire. He fought for Duke Ulrich of Württemberg (1519) against the Swabian league, and after his heroic defence of Möckmühl was taken prisoner. In the Peasants' War of 1525 he led a section of the insurgents, was captured by the Swabian league, kept a prisoner at Augsburg for two years, and sentenced to perpetual imprisonment. He was only freed on the dissolution of the league in 1540. In 1542 he was fighting in Hungary against the Turks, and in 1544 in France. He died in his castle of Hornberg. He wrote an autobiography, published by Pistorius (1731), on which Goethe grounded the drama translated by Scott.

GOUDIMEL, Claude, *goo-dee-mel* (1507–72), French composer of masses, motets, chansons and psalm tunes, was born at Besançon, taught music at Rome, and perished at Lyons as a Huguenot just after the massacre of St Bartholomew.

GOUGH, *gof*, (1) **Hugh Gough, 1st Viscount** (1779–1869), British soldier, born at Woodstown, County Limerick, served at the Cape, in the West Indies, through the Peninsular war, and in India; and in 1838 was made commander-in-chief of the forces sent against

China. After storming Canton and forcing the Yangtze-Kiang, he compelled the Chinese to sign the treaty of Nanking (1842). In 1843 he defeated the Mahrattas. In the Sikh war in 1845 he worsted the enemy in the battles of Mudki, Firozshah and Sobraon, for which he was given a peerage. In 1848 the Sikhs renewed the war, but were again defeated by Gough at Ramnagar, Chillianwalla, and Gujerat, victories which resulted in the annexation of the Punjab. Created a baronet in 1842, Baron Gough in 1846, Viscount Gough in 1849, and a field-marshal in 1862, he died near Dublin. See the Life by Rait (1903) and Sir C. Gough's *Sikh Wars* (1897).

(2) **John** (1757–1825), English blind botanist and mathematician, lost his sight through smallpox at three; was born and died at Kendal. John Dalton and William Whewell were his pupils.

GOUJON, Jean, *goo-zhõ* (*c.* 1510–68), the foremost French sculptor of the 16th century. His finest work includes *Diana reclining by a Stag,* in the Louvre; the reliefs for the Fountain of the Innocents, also in the Louvre; the monument to the Duke of Brézé in Rouen Cathedral; and several reliefs in the Louvre, where he worked (1555–62). He was a Huguenot, but seems to have died before the St Bartholomew massacre in 1572.

GOULD, *goold,* (1) **Benjamin Apthorp** (1824–1896), American astronomer, born in Boston, Mass., educated at Harvard and Göttingen, founded the *Astronomical Journal* (1849–61), was director of the Dudley Observatory at Albany (1856–59) and in 1866 determined, by aid of the submarine cable, the difference in longitude between Europe and America. He helped to found and was director from 1868 of the national observatory at Córdoba, Argentina. His *Uranometry of the Southern Heavens* complemented Argelander's *Atlas* of the northern.

(2) **Sabine Baring-.** See BARING-GOULD.

(3) **Sir Francis Carruthers** (1844–1925), English cartoonist and pioneer of 'picture politics' ('F. C. G.'), of the *Westminster Gazette,* was born at Barnstaple, and was knighted in 1906.

(4) **Glenn** (1932–), Canadian pianist and composer, born in Toronto, he studied at the Royal Conservatory of Music before making his début as a soloist with the Toronto Symphony Orchestra. Since then he has toured extensively in the U.S.A. and Europe and has made many recordings particularly of Bach and Beethoven works. 1956 saw the world première of his own work, *A String Quartet.*

(5) **Jay** (1836–92), American financier, was born at Roxbury, N.Y. He made a survey of parts of the state, engaged in lumbering, and in 1857 became the principal shareholder in a Pennsylvania bank. He began to buy up railroad bonds, started as a broker in New York (1859), and was president of the Erie railway company till 1872. He died unlamented, worth some $100,000,000.

(6) **John** (1804–81), English ornithologist, born at Lyme Regis, became curator to the Zoological Society's Museum in 1827. His eighteen works include *Birds of Europe* (1832–37), *Birds of Australia* (1840–48), *Birds of Great Britain* (1862), &c. His remarkably accurate drawings were transferred to stone by his wife. During his first years at the Zoological Gardens, he was assisted by Edward Lear, draughtsman to the society.

(7) **Morton** (1913–), American composer, born in New York. Gould's music is national in style and exploits the various aspects of popular music from both North and South America. He has composed three symphonies and a variety of works in more popular style, including a *Concerto for Tap-dancer.*

(8) **Nathaniel** (1857–1919), British novelist, born in Manchester, became a sports columnist on a Sydney newspaper, and is remembered for a long series of exciting novels of the turf. See his autobiography *The Magic of Sport* (1909).

GOUNOD, Charles François, *goo-nõ* (1818–1893), French composer, born in Paris, June 17, studied at the Conservatoire, and in Rome. On his return to Paris he was for a time organist of the church of the Missions Étrangères where his earliest compositions, chiefly polyphonic in style, were performed; one of them, a *Messe solennelle,* brought him into notice. His first opera, *Sapho,* was produced in 1851, and *La Nonne sanglante* in 1854. His comic opera, *Le Médecin malgré lui* (1858), was a great success; in 1859 *Faust* raised its composer to the foremost rank. *Philémon et Baucis* followed in 1860; in 1862, *La Reine de Saba* (or *Irène*); in 1864, *Mireille;* in 1867, *Roméo et Juliette.* He also published masses, hymns and anthems, and was popular as a songwriter. His oratorio *The Redemption* was produced at the Birmingham Festival in 1882; its sequel, *Mors et Vita,* at Brussels in 1886. He fled to England during the Franco-Prussian war (1870). He was a member of the Institute (1866) and a commander of the Legion of Honour (1877). See Lives by Pagnerre (Paris 1890) and de Bovet (London 1890).

GOURKO, Joseph Vasilyevich, Count (1828–1901), Russian general, distinguished himself by his defence of the Shipka Pass (1877) against the Turks.

GOURMONT, Rémy de, *goor-mõ* (1858–1915), French poet, novelist and critic, born at Bazoches-en-Houlme, Normandy. Having been dismissed from his post at the Bibliothèque Nationale, Paris, because of an allegedly pro-German article in *Mercure de France,* of which he was a co-founder, he lived the life of a recluse. His creative work—poetry and novels in the symbolist vogue—is cerebral and stylistic, betraying a 'fin de siècle' obsession with words as sound more than as sense. But his evaluative work, which includes *Le Livre des masques* (1896–1898) and *Promenades philosophiques* (1905–1909), is clear-sighted and individualistic, exhibiting scholarship and intellectual curiosity; he has been favourably compared with Sainte-Beuve. His novels include *Sixtine* (1890) and *Un Cœur virginal* (1907). See *Rémy de Gourmont* by Richard Aldington.

GOW, Niel (1727–1807), Scottish violinist and

songwriter, born near Dunkeld, composed nearly a hundred tunes; and from his singular skill with the bow his name is still a household word in Scotland.—His youngest son, **Nathaniel** (1766–1831), became king's trumpeter for Scotland, bandleader, and music-publisher of Scottish airs including his own which number over 200.

GOWARD, Mary. See KEELEY.

GOWER, John (*c.* 1325–1408), English poet, became blind about 1400. His tomb is in St Saviour's, Southwark. He was a personal friend of Chaucer, wrote *Speculum Meditantis*, in French verse, long lost and discovered at Cambridge only in 1898; the *Vox Clamantis*, in Latin elegiacs (1382–84), describing the rising under Wat Tyler; and the long poem entitled *Confessio Amantis*, written in English, perhaps in 1383. There are extant also fifty French ballads, written by Gower in his youth. The *Confessio Amantis* comprises a prologue and eight books, and largely consists of over a hundred stories strung together out of Ovid's *Metamorphoses*, the *Gesta Romanorum*, the mediaeval histories of Troy, &c. The best editions are by Pauli (1857) and G. C. Macaulay (1899–1902). See study by Dodd (1913) and C. S. Lewis, *The Allegory of Love* (1936).

GOWERS, Sir Ernest Arthur (1880–1966), English civil servant, son of **Sir William Richard** (1845–1915), the distinguished neurologist, was educated at Rugby and Clare College, Cambridge, and called to the bar in 1906. After a distinguished career in the civil service he emerged as the champion of *Plain Words* (1948) and *ABC of Plain Words* (1951), which manuals have done something to rescue the English language from the slipshod habits of its users, not least from rampant administrative jargon.

GOWING, Lawrence Burnett (1918–), English painter and writer on art, born in Stoke Newington, studied at the Euston Road School with William Coldstream, and his impressionist style is often applied to portraits e.g. *Mrs Roberts* in the Tate Gallery, London. In 1948 he was appointed professor of Fine Art in the University of Durham, and he has written studies of *Renoir* (1947) and *Vermeer* (1952). In 1965 he became Keeper of the British Collection at the Tate Gallery.

GOWRIE, Earl of. See RUTHVEN.

GOYA Y LUCIENTES, Francisco José de, *gō'ya* (1746–1828), Spanish artist, born at Fuendetodos. After travelling in Italy, he returned to Spain to design for the Royal Tapestry works. In 1798 he produced the wonderfully coloured frescoes, incorporating scenes from contemporary life, in the Church of S. Antonio de la Florida, Madrid, and at about the same time the eighty-two satirical etchings—*The Caprices*. By this period he had also become a well-known portrait painter and was made First Court Painter to Charles IV in 1799, painting the *Family of Charles IV* (in the Prado Museum) in the following year. The War of Independence of 1808 inspired another series of sardonic etchings, *The Disasters of War* (1810–20). Goya combined an intense feeling for the human drama with a great freedom and

diversity of method, his satirical aquatints and lithographs contrasting sharply with his elegant tapestry designs and fashionable, if sometimes over-characteristic, portraits. See the monographs by C. Poore (1938) and P. Gassier (1955), and the *Vida y obras de Goya* (1951) by F. J. Sánchez Cantón.

GOZZI, Count Carlo, *got'zee* (1720–1806), Italian dramatist, born at Venice, wrote *Tartana* (1757), a satirical poem against Goldoni; a very popular comedy, *Fiaba dell' amore delle tre Melarance* (1761); and several similar ' dramatic fairy-tales ', the best-known, from Schiller's translation of it, being *Turandot*. See his Memoirs (1797; trans. 1889) and Life by Mantovani (1926).—His brother, **Count Gasparo** (1713–86), edited two journals in Venice, and was press censor there. Among his works are *Il Mondo morale* (1760) and *Lettere famigliari* (1755). See Life by Magrini (1883).

GOZZOLI, Benozzo, *got'zō-lee*, properly **Benozzo di Lese** (*c.* 1420–97), Italian painter, was born at Florence and became a pupil of Fra Angelico. At Montefalco (1450–52) he painted a Virgin (now in the Lateran) and a series of frescoes for the monastery of S. Francesco. At Florence (1456–64) he adorned the Palazzo Riccardi with scriptural subjects, including his famous *Journey of the Magi* in which Florentine councillors accompanied by members of the Medici family appear, and painted similar frescoes at San Gimignano (1464–67), and in the Campo Santo at Pisa (1468–84). See monographs by Stokes (1904) and (in French) Mengin (1909).

GRAAF, Regnier de (1641–73), Dutch physician and anatomist, was born at Schoonhoven, and practised at Delft. In 1663 he wrote a famous treatise on the pancreatic juice, in 1672 discovered the Graafian vesicles of the female ovary.

GRABBE, Christian Dietrich, *grah'bĕ* (1801–1836), German dramatist, born and died at Detmold, a precursor of Realism, wrote powerful tragedies on the lives of *Don Juan und Faust* (1822), *Kaiser Friedrich Barbarossa* (1829), *Napoleon* (1831), &c. See Lives by Ziegler (1855) and Gieben (1914).

GRACCHUS, *grak'koos*, a famous Roman family to which belonged **Tiberius Sempronius** (slain 212 B.C.), a distinguished opponent of Hannibal in the second Punic war; and another **Tiberius Sempronius** (born about 210 B.C.), who conquered the Celtiberians and pacified Spain. His wife, **Cornelia**, daughter of Scipio Africanus, bore him the two famous brothers, the Gracchi:

(1) **Caius Sempronius** (*c.* 159–121 B.C.), Roman statesman, at the time of the death of his brother (2) was serving in Spain under Scipio Africanus. He was elected to the tribuneship in 123 and 122. His first measure was to renew his brother's agrarian law; and to relieve the immediate misery of the poor, he employed them upon new roads throughout Italy. But by a senatorial intrigue his colleague Livius Drusus was bribed to undermine his influence by surpassing him in the liberality of his measures, Caius was rejected from a third tribuneship, and the senate began to repeal his enactments. Caius

appearing in the Forum to make opposition, a fearful riot ensued, in which 3000 of his partisans were slain; he himself held aloof from the fight, but was compelled to flee with a single slave, who first slew his master and then himself. The commons saw too late their folly, and endeavoured to atone for their crime by erecting statues to the brothers. Their mother survived them long, and on her tomb the Roman people inscribed ' Cornelia, mother of the Gracchi '.

(2) **Tiberius Sempronius** (168–133 B.C.), in 137 served as quaestor in Spain, where the kindly remembrance of his father enabled him to gain better terms from the Numantines for 20,000 conquered Roman soldiers. The hopeless poverty of thousands of the Roman citizens weighed on the mind of Gracchus, and he began an agitation for reform. Elected tribune in 133, he reimposed the agrarian law of Licinius Stolo, requisitioned all land held in excess and distributed it in allotments to the poor. His deposition of his fellow tribune Marcus Octavius, who had vetoed his proposal, threatened to undermine the authority of the senate. When Attalus, King of Pergamus, died and bequeathed his wealth to the Roman people, Gracchus proposed that it should be divided among the poor, to enable them to stock their newly-acquired farms. But he was accused of having violated the sacred character of the tribuneship by the deposition of his colleague Caecina; thousands of the fickle mob deserted him; and during the next election for the tribuneship he, with three hundred of his friends, was murdered.

GRACE, William Gilbert (1848–1915), English cricketer, born at Downend near Bristol. By 1864 he was playing cricket for Gloucester County, and was chosen for the Gentlemen v. the Players at sixteen. The acquisition of a medical degree in 1879, and a practice in Bristol, was not allowed to inhibit his love of bat and ball. He toured Canada, the U.S. and Australia, twice captaining the English team. By 1895 he had scored a hundred centuries; and the tribute subscribed for in that year, in recognition of his services to the game, came to over £5000. See books by Brownlee (1895) and Darwin (1934) and contemporary Wisden's Almanacs.

GRACIAN, Baltasar, *grah-thyahn'* (1601–58), Spanish writer and philosopher, born at Belmonte near Calatayud, in Aragon, joined the Jesuits as a youth and became a preacher and teacher in N.E. Spain and finally head of the College of Tarragona. As one would expect, his work is didactic, imbued with Jesuit ideology, a system of practical ethics, the object being to guide the reader so that he learns how to adapt means to ends, how to shake off puerile illusions, and gradually become master of himself and his destiny. Thus *The Hero* (1637), *The Politician* (1640), *The Man of Discretion* (1646), *The Manual Oracle and Art of Prudence* (1647) reveal a contrived pattern to demonstrate the ideal qualities that go to make up these types. Gracian's most important work, however, is a long allegorical novel, *El Criticon* (1650, 1657), in which he sums up civilization as seen through the eyes of a savage. It is

written in the affected, premeditated and polished style, known as *Gorgonism*, far removed from the rhythms of everyday speech, and hence it has become mainly a work for scholars. See study by A. F. G. Bell (1921).

GRAEBE, Karl, *gray'bĕ* (1841–1927), German organic chemist, born at Frankfurt-am-Main, with Liebermann first synthesized alizarin from anthraquinone (1869).

GRÄFE, Albrecht von, *gray'fĕ* (1828–70), German oculist, was born and died in Berlin. He introduced a new classification of eye diseases.

GRAFTON, (1) Augustus Henry Fitzroy, 3rd Duke of (1735–1811), English statesman, a descendant of Charles II, came into notice in 1763 in the opposition to Bute, and was secretary of state under Rockingham (1765–66). In July 1766 Pitt became premier and Earl of Chatham, making Grafton first lord of the Treasury; but owing to Chatham's illness Grafton had to undertake the duties of premier from September 1767. He resigned in 1770, but was lord privy seal under North (1771–75) and in the new Rockingham ministry (1782–83). Though possessed of more honesty of purpose than the invectives of Junius would have us believe, he had a weakness for the fair sex and for the turf which often distracted him from more urgent business. See his *Autobiography* (ed. Anson 1898).

(2) **Richard** (*c.* 1513–*c.* 1572), English printer and historian, began as a grocer, went to Antwerp in 1537 and there printed the Matthews Bible, the revised Coverdale and the ' Great ' (folio) Bible. He became printer to Edward VI, produced the Book of Common Prayer (1549), but fell into disfavour for printing Lady Jane Grey's proclamation. He also wrote three histories of England, and sat in parliament.

GRAHAM, (1) Billy (William Franklin) (1918–), American evangelist, conducted highly organized revivalist campaigns not only in the U.S.A. but in Britain, as at Harringay (1954) and Glasgow (1955). See his *Peace with God* (1954) and Burnham, *Mission Accomplished* (1956).

(2) **Dougal** (*c.* 1724–79), Scottish ballad and chap-book writer, born at Raploch near Stirling, followed Prince Charlie's army and wrote a metrical eyewitness account of the campaign. He was appointed bellman of Glasgow about 1770. Of his rambling ballads, the best known are *John Hieland-man's Remarks on Glasgow* and *Turnim-spike.*

(3) **Ennis.** See MOLESWORTH, MARY LOUISA.

(4) **James** (1745–94), Scottish quack-doctor, born and died in Edinburgh, studied medicine there, but did not graduate although he styled himself ' Dr Graham '. After several years abroad he set up practice first in Bristol (1774) then Bath (1775) and finally also in London, where he established ' temples of health and hymen ' and pre-scribed remedies and lectured. He put his patients on a ' magnetic throne ', into electrically charged baths or into ' celestial beds '. Although denounced as a quack and

frequently imprisoned, he became fashionable, his clientele including the Prince of Wales and the Duchess of Devonshire. In 1781, it is alleged, he exhibited Emma Lyon, later Lady Hamilton, as the 'Goddess of Health'. In 1783 he was arrested in Edinburgh after writing articles in support of his lectures, which had been prohibited, under a forged eminent name. In 1790 he indulged in 'earth bathing', turned religious and styled himself 'the servant of the Lord O.W.L.' (Oh wonderful love). His pamphlets and extravagant advertisements reveal him as an 'admass' man born two centuries before his time.

(5) **Sir James Robert George, Bart.** (1792–1861), British statesman, was born at Netherby in Cumberland, June 1, and educated at Westminster and Christ Church, Oxford. In 1813 he became private secretary to the British minister in Sicily. He entered parliament as a Whig in 1826, supported Catholic emancipation and the Reform Bill. Earl Grey made him (1830) first lord of the Admiralty; but in 1834 he resigned over the Irish Church question, and in 1841 became home secretary under Peel. In 1844 he issued a warrant for opening the letters of Mazzini, and the information thus obtained was communicated to the Austrian minister. His high-handed dealing with the Scottish Church increased the troubles which ended in the Disruption of 1843. He gave Peel warm support in carrying the Corn Law Repeal Bill, and resigned (1846) as soon as it was carried. On Peel's death in 1850 he became leader of the Peelites, and in 1852–55 was first lord of the Admiralty in the Coalition ministry. He retired in 1857, and died October 26. See Lives by Torrens (1863), Lonsdale (1868) and C. S. Parker (1907).

(6) **John, of Claverhouse.** See DUNDEE.
(7) **Robert.** See CUNNINGHAME GRAHAM (1).
(8) **Robert Bontine Cunninghame.** See CUNNINGHAME GRAHAM (2).
(9) **Stephen** (1884–), British traveller and writer, travelled widely in Scandinavia, Russia, Central Asia, Middle and Near East, served in the First World War and returned to a life of travel in South America and Russia, contributing to *The Times* and publishing numerous books of his travels, particularly on Russia, including lives of Peter the Great (1929), Stalin (1931) and Ivan the Terrible (1932), *Summing up on Russia* (1951) and *Pay as You Run* (1955).
(10) **Thomas** (1805–69), Scottish chemist and physicist, born in Glasgow, became in 1830 professor of Chemistry at Glasgow, and in 1837 at University College London. In 1855 he was appointed master of the Mint. Elected an F.R.S. in 1836, he was one of the founders of physical chemistry. His researches on the molecular diffusion of gases led him to formulate the law ' that the diffusion rate of gases is inversely as the square root of their density '. He discovered the properties of colloids and their separation by dialysis. See Life by Dr Angus Smith (1884).
(11) **Thomas.** See LYNEDOCH (LORD).
GRAHAME, (1) **James** (1765–1811), Scottish

poet, was born at Glasgow, became an advocate, then curate in the Church of England at Sedgefield, Durham, and wrote *Mary Queen of Scots,* a dramatic poem (1801), *The Sabbath* (1804), &c., of which the latter in its tender devotional feeling and felicity in describing quiet Scottish scenery is not unworthy of Cowper.
(2) **Kenneth** (1859–1932), Scottish author, born at Edinburgh, entered the Bank of England in 1879, became its secretary in 1898 and retired for health reasons in 1908. His early work, *Pagan Papers* (1893), *The Golden Age* (1895) and *Dream Days* (1898), revealed a remarkably subtle, delicate and humorous sympathy with the child mind. *The Wind in the Willows* (1908), with its quaint riverside characters, Rat, Mole, Badger and Toad, has become a children's classic. His early story, *The Reluctant Dragon,* has been filmed. See Lives and studies by P. R. Chalmers (1933), D. M. Fyrth (1937) and P. Green (1959).
GRAHAME-WHITE, Claude (1879–1959), English aviator and engineer, the first to be granted a British certificate of proficiency in aviation, ran the first British flying school, formed in 1910 his company to build aircraft, and published books on the aeroplane and flying.
GRAINGER, Percy (1882–1961), Australian composer and pianist, born in Melbourne, studied under Pabst and Busoni, and settled in the U.S.A. in 1915. He was a friend and admirer of Greig, whose example he followed in championing the revival of folk-music, which forms a basis of much of his work. His *Molly on the Shore, Mock Morris* and *Shepherds Hey* are examples of his skilful use of traditional dance themes.
GRAM, Hans Christian Joachim (1853–1938), Danish bacteriologist, established in 1884 a testing method for bacteria, distinguishing the *Gram-positive* from the *Gram-negative.*
GRAMONT, or **Grammont, Philibert, Comte de,** *gra-mõ* (1621–1707), French courtier, while still young served under Condé and Turenne, and became a favourite at the court of Louis XIV, but his gallantries brought him exile from France in 1662. He found congenial society among the merry profligates of the court of Charles II of England. Here, after many adventures, he married, but not without compulsion, Elizabeth Hamilton (1641–1708), with whom he afterwards returned to France. At eighty he inspired his *Mémoires* of the ' amorous intrigues ' at Charles's court, or revised them when written by his brother-in-law, Count Anthony Hamilton (q.v.). The book is a singular revelation of a world of villainy, written with equal grace and vigour. It was first printed anonymously in 1713. See translation by P. Quennell (1930).
GRANADOS Y CAMPIÑA, Enrique (1868–1916), Spanish composer and pianist, born at Lérida, studied at Barcelona and at Paris. He composed Spanish dances, and his *Goyescas* for piano are his most accomplished works. He was drowned when the *Sussex* was torpedoed by the Germans in the English Channel on March 24. See Life by Villalba (1917).

GRANBY, John Manners, Marquis of (1721–1770), the eldest son of the Duke of Rutland, was returned as M.P. for Grantham in 1742. Hastily commissioned at the time of the '45 Jacobite rebellion, he subsequently served on the Duke of Cumberland's staff, reaching substantive major-general's rank in 1755. As colonel of ' The Blues ' and second-in-command of the British Horse at Minden (1759), he was a furious but impotent witness of Lord George Sackville's failure to lead the cavalry into action, which earned his commander the contemptuous title of ' The Great Incompetent '. In 1760 Granby, at the head of his cheering squadrons, triumphantly redeemed the cavalry's tarnished reputation with the spectacular victory of Warburg. ' The mob's hero ', in Walpole's sneering phrase, was everywhere acclaimed, and in 1763 was appointed master-general of the Ordnance, succeeding the aged Ligonier as commander-in-chief in 1766. Charitable, just and ever-diligent for the welfare of his troops—during the Seven Years' War he spent £60,000 on his command —he was still in harness at the time of his premature death in 1770. See Life by Walter Evelyn Manners (1898).

GRAND, Sarah (*née* **Frances Elizabeth Clarke**) (1862–1943), British novelist, was born of English parentage at Donaghadee. At sixteen she married an army doctor, D. C. McFall (d. 1898). In 1923 and from 1925 to 1929 she was mayoress of Bath. Her reputation rests on *The Heavenly Twins* (1893), *The Beth Book* (1898), &c., in which she skilfully handles sex problems. Her later works, including *The Winged Victory* (1916), are advocacies of feminine emancipation.

GRANDI, Dino, Count (1895–), Italian politician and diplomat, born at Mordano, studied law and became one of the Fascist quadrumvirs after the march on Rome (1922). He was Mussolini's foreign minister (1929–32), and as ambassador to London unsuccessfully warned the duce of British opposition to the Abyssinian invasion (1935). He declined in favour with the formation of the Berlin-Rome axis. He moved the vote in the Fascist grand council which brought about Mussolini's resignation (1943). He was created count in 1937.

GRANDVILLE, *grã-veel*, the pseudonym of **Jean Ignace Isidore Gérard** (1803–47), French caricaturist and book illustrator, who was born at Nancy and died in a lunatic asylum near Paris. He achieved a reputation for fantastic humorous and satirical sketches and illustrated editions of La Fontaine and Swift.

GRANGE, Rachel Chiesley, Lady (d. 1745), the drunken, half-imbecile wife of the hypocritical Scottish judge, James Erskine, Lord Grange (1679–1754), who in 1732 secretly transported her to the Hebrides, and kept her for seven years a captive on St Kilda, whence she escaped to Sutherland and Skye, where she died.

GRANGER, James, *grayn'jèr* (1723–76), English biographer, was born at Shaftesbury, and died vicar of Shiplake, Oxfordshire. He published a *Biographical History of England* (1769) and insisted ' on the utility of a collection of engraved portraits '. His advice led to extraordinary zeal in collecting portraits, and ' grangerized copies ' were embellished with engravings gathered from all quarters.

GRANIER DE CASSAGNAC. See CAS-SAGNAC (1).

GRANT, (1) Sir Alexander (1826–84), British educationist, born at New York, educated at Harrow and Balliol College, Oxford, was elected a fellow of Oriel in 1849 and edited the *Ethics* of Aristotle (1857). He succeeded as tenth baronet in 1856, became inspector of schools at Madras in 1858, professor of History in Elphinstone College, Bombay, its principal, vice-chancellor of Bombay University, and in 1868 principal of Edinburgh University, where he helped to found the medical school.

(2) **Anne** (1755–1838), Scottish poetess and essayist, born in Glasgow, the daughter of Duncan McVicar, an army officer, was in America 1758–68, and in 1779 married the Rev. James Grant, minister of Laggan. Left a widow in 1801, she published *Poems* (1803), *Letters from the Mountains* (1806), *Superstitions of the Highlanders* (1811), &c. In 1825 she received a pension of £50 through the influence of Sir Walter Scott, who when he heard that she had expected £100, observed: ' A starving dog will eat a dirty pudding '. See memoir by her son (1844).

(3) **Charles.** See GLENELG, LORD.

(4) **Duncan James Corrowr** (1885–), British painter, born at Rothiemurchus, Inverness. He studied at the Westminster and Slade Schools, in Italy and Paris, and was associated with Roger Fry's Omega Workshops, and later with the London Group. His works, mainly landscapes, portraits and still-life, owe something to the influence of Roger Fry and Cézanne, but he has also designed textiles, pottery, &c. His *Girl at the piano* is in the Tate Gallery, London. See studies by R. Mortimer (1944) and Roger Fry (1923).

(5) **Sir Francis** (1803–78), Scottish painter, brother of (8) and fourth son of Francis Grant of Kilgraston, Perthshire, was born in Edinburgh, read for the bar but became one of the leading portrait painters of his day. His portrait groups were in great demand, such as the *Meet of H.M. Staghounds* and the *Melton Hunt* executed for the Duke of Wellington. He became P.R.A. in 1866 and was knighted.

(6) **James** (1822–87), Scottish novelist, born in Edinburgh, after a childhood in Newfoundland and military service published a long series of novels and histories, illustrative mainly of the achievements of Scottish arms abroad. Among his works are *Adventures of an Aide-de-Camp*; *Frank Hilton, or the Queen's Own*; *Bothwell*; *The Yellow Frigate*, &c. He became a Catholic in 1875 and died in London.

(7) **James Augustus** (1827–92), British soldier and explorer, was born and died at Nairn. Educated at Marischal College, Aberdeen, in 1846 he joined the Indian army, eventually reaching the rank of colonel. He was rewarded for his services at the battle of

Gujerat, in the Mutiny, and in the Abyssinian campaign of 1868, by being made a C.B. and C.S.I. With Captain Speke (q.v.) he explored the sources of the Nile (1860–63). Among his publications are *A Walk across Africa*, *Botany of the Speke and Grant Expedition*, &c.

(8) **Sir James Hope** (1808–75), British general, brother of (5), born at Kilgraston, Perthshire, distinguished himself in the two Sikh wars (1845–49), the Indian Mutiny and the 1860 expedition against China, and was created G.C.B. He commanded the army of Madras (1861–65). See extracts from his journals, ed. by Col. H. Knollys, who also edited his Life (1894).

(9) **Sir Patrick** (1804–95), British soldier, born at Auchterblair, Inverness-shire, served through the Gwalior, Sutlej and Punjab campaigns and the Mutiny, and was made a G.C.B. (1861), a G.C.M.G. (1868) and field-marshal (1883).

(10) **Ulysses Simpson** (1822–85), American soldier and eighteenth president of the United States, was born at Point Pleasant, Clermont county, Ohio, April 27, as second-lieutenant he joined the army of occupation in Texas under General Zachary Taylor, was in the battles of Palo Alto and Resaca de la Palma, and was present at the capture of Monterey. Promoted captain in 1853, in 1854 he resigned his commission and settled on a farm near St Louis, Missouri. When the Civil War began in 1861 Grant was appointed colonel of the 21st Regiment of Illinois Infantry. In November, now brigadier-general, he fought the battle of Belmont. In February 1862 he captured Fort Henry, and soon after Fort Donelson. In April he fought a two days' battle at Shiloh. After various unsuccessful movements against Vicksburg, Grant crossed the Mississippi, April 1863, twice defeated the enemy, and drove them into Vicksburg, which he besieged. After many assaults the stronghold surrendered conditionally on July 4, 1863, with 31,600 prisoners. In October he fought at Chattanooga, and drove the enemy out of Tennessee. In March 1864 Grant, now a major-general in the regular army, was promoted lieutenant-general, and given the command of all the armies of the United States. His plan of campaign was to concentrate all the national forces into several distinct armies, which should operate simultaneously against the enemy, Sherman moving toward Atlanta, while Grant himself accompanied the army of the Potomac against Richmond. On May 4 he crossed the Rapidan, encountered General R. E. Lee in the Wilderness, and fought a desperate three days' battle, and pursuing the offensive, he drove the enemy within the lines of Richmond. On March 29, 1865, began a week's hard fighting, after which Lee surrendered his entire army, April 9. The fall of Richmond substantially ended the war. In July 1866 Grant was appointed full general; in 1868 and 1872 he was elected president by the Republicans. Among the events of his administration were the guaranteeing of the right of suffrage without regard to race, colour or previous servitude, and the peaceful settlement of the ' Alabama Claims '. The proposal of a third

term of presidency not having been approved, Grant became a sleeping partner in a banking-house. In May 1884 the house suspended, and it was discovered that two of the partners had robbed the general of all he possessed. In the hope of providing for his family, he had begun his autobiography, when in 1884 a sore throat proved to be cancer at the root of the tongue. The sympathies of the nation were aroused, and in March 1885 congress restored him to his rank of general, which he had lost on accepting the presidency. He died at Mount McGregor near Saratoga, July 23. See his *Personal Memoirs* (1885–86); and works by his son Jesse Grant (1925), J. F. C. Fuller (1933), W. B. Hasseltine (1935), Woodward (1958).

(11) **William** (1863–1946), Scottish lexicographer, born at Elgin. He studied in France, Belgium and Germany, and became a lecturer in English, Modern Languages and Phonetics at Aberdeen University. He was until his death editor of the Scottish National Dictionary, and published various works on Scottish dialects.

GRANT-DUFF. See DUFF.

GRANVELLE, Antoine Perrenot, Cardinal de, *grã-vel* (1517–86), Spanish diplomat, son of the jurist and diplomat, **Nicholas** (1484–1550); was born at Besançon, and in 1540 was appointed Bishop of Arras and was secretary of state to the emperor, Charles V (1550–55). On the latter's abdication, he transferred his services to Philip II. In 1559 he became prime minister to Margaret of Parma in the Netherlands, in 1560 Archbishop of Malines, and next year cardinal. His policy of repressing the Protestants provoked such hostility in the Low Countries, however, that at the king's advice he retired in 1564 to Franche-Comté. In 1570 he represented Spain at Rome in drawing up a treaty of alliance with Venice and the papal see against the Turks. In 1570–75 he was viceroy of Naples. He died at Madrid. His letters, &c., were edited by Weiss (9 vols. Paris 1842–61) and Poullet (9 vols. Brussels 1878–92). See study by Phillipson (1896).

GRANVILLE, *gran'vill*, (1). See GRENVILLE.

(2) **Earl.** See CARTERET and LEVESON-GOWER.

GRANVILLE-BARKER, Harley (1877–1946), English actor, playwright and producer, born in London. As an actor, he was distinguished by his appearance in Shaw plays—he played Marchbanks in *Candida* in 1900. In 1904 he became co-manager of the Court Theatre with Vedrenne, and there followed a four-year season that was a landmark in the history of the British theatre. First performances in England of plays by Maeterlinck, Schnitzler, Hauptmann, Yeats, Galsworthy, Masefield and Shaw were performed in circumstances that set new standards of acting and design. In 1907 he left the Court and continued his success with a series of Shakespeare plays at the Savoy. He retired from the stage in the early 'twenties. Barker wrote several plays, including *The Marrying of Ann Leete* (1902), *The Voysey Inheritance* (1905), *Waste* (performed privately in 1907, publicly in 1936) and *The Madras House* (1910). With William Archer he devised a scheme for a national theatre. He was married first to Lillah McCarthy and then to Helen Huntington Gates, with whom he made the standard translations of plays by Martinez Sierra and the Quintero brothers. His prefaces to Shakespeare's plays (four vols. 1927–45) can still be mined for original criticism and ideas on production. See *A National Theatre* by H. Granville-Barker and W. Archer (1907), and the biography by C. B. Purdom (1955).

GRASS, Günter (1927–), German writer, born in Danzig, lived in Paris and achieved a European reputation with his first novel, *Die Blechtrommel*, 'The Tin Drum' (1958; tr. 1962), a kind of 'sick' Grimm's fairy tale for adults. Other works include *Katz und Maus*, 'Cat and Mouse' (1961; tr. 1963), *Hundejahre*, 'Dog Years' (1962; tr. 1964) and volumes of poetry. A ghost-writer for the leader of the Social Democrats, Willy Brandt, he was elected member of the Berlin Academy of Arts in 1963.

GRASSI, Giovanni Battista (1854–1925), Italian zoologist, born at Rovellasca, became professor of Comparative Anatomy at Rome in 1895, did important work on worms, eels, termites and malaria.

GRATIAN, a Benedictine monk of Bologna, who between 1139 and 1150 compiled the collection of canon law known as the *Decretum Gratiani*.

GRATIANUS, Augustus (359–383), Roman emperor from 375, in 367 by his father Valentinian was made *Augustus* in Gaul. On Valentinian's death he was elevated to the throne, with his half-brother Valentinian II as colleague. Gaul, Spain and Britain fell to Gratian's share, but as his brother was only four years old he virtually ruled the whole western empire; and in 378, on the death of his uncle Valens, he suddenly became sovereign also of the eastern empire. Thereupon he recalled Theodosius from Spain, and appointed him his colleague in 379. Gratian was pious, temperate and eloquent; but his fondness for frivolous amusements and his persecution of pagans and heretics alienated his subjects; so that when Maximus was proclaimed emperor crowds flocked to his standard. Gratian was defeated by him near Paris, and fled to Lyons, where he was put to death.

GRATTAN, Henry (1746–1820), Irish statesman, born in Dublin, July 3, was educated at Trinity College, Dublin, and embraced the reforming principles of Henry Flood with such ardour that his father, the recorder of Dublin, disinherited him. At twenty-one he proceeded to the Middle Temple, London, but neglected law for the debates in the House of Commons. In 1772 he was called to the Irish bar, and in 1775 he entered the Irish parliament as member for Charlemont. Flood had lost his popularity by accepting office under government, and Grattan leapt at one bound into his place, and strove to secure the removal of the restrictions upon Irish trade. Fearing a French invasion, Lord North repealed them in 1779; thereupon Grattan plunged into a struggle for legislative independence. The popular demands were asserted by him at the Convention of Dun-

gannon (February 1782). A month later the Rockingham ministry surrendered, and the Irish parliament in gratitude voted Grattan £50,000. The history of 'Grattan's parliament' did not correspond to the patriotic dreams of its great founder. It was impossible for a parliament so little representative and so much subject to corruption to rise to real statesmanship. The urgent need of parliamentary reform and the remedy of domestic abuses soon occupied the minds of all Irish patriots. Once more at Dungannon, in September 1783, were formulated demands for parliamentary reform, which were presented to the House by Flood and rejected. Grattan devoted himself to advocating the reform of special abuses, but his bills proved abortive. Meantime continued commercial depression had produced a strong feeling in Ireland for protection, which was yet unable to arrest secretary Orde's measure for absolute free trade. This measure, however, Pitt could not carry at Westminster, except subject to a number of stipulations, one of which was that all English navigation laws were to be adopted by the Irish parliament; and to this Grattan would not accede. Pitt's mortification confirmed his determination that union was the only effective means of pacification. Grattan was returned for Dublin in 1790, and himself a Protestant, had taken up the cause of Catholic emancipation; but the corruption of the Castle government and of a parliament venal beyond all precedent, the persistent repression of the agitation for Catholic relief, and the spirit of discontent generated by the French Revolution had fomented the movement of the United Irishmen. Despairing for his country and broken by ill-health, Grattan retired on the eve of the rebellion, but returned to take his seat for Wicklow, and bravely to combat the bill for the Union. In 1805 he was elected to Westminster as member for Malton in Yorkshire, and for Dublin the following year. The remaining energies of his life were devoted to the cause of Catholic emancipation. In December 1819 his health began to give way; in the following May he crossed from Dublin, a dying man, to speak once more for the cause; and he died five days after his arrival, June 4. He was buried in Westminster Abbey. His son, Henry Grattan, collected his *Speeches* (1822), edited his *Miscellaneous Works* (1822), and wrote the standard *Life* (1839–46). See too Lecky's *Leaders of Public Opinion in Ireland*, and studies by Dunlop (1889) and Gwynn, (1939).

GRAUN, Karl Heinrich, *grown* (1701–59), German composer of thirty-four operas, a 'Passion piece', &c., was born near Torgau, and died in Berlin.—His brother **Johann Gottlieb** (1699–1771), also a composer, was a pupil of Tartini.

GRAVES, (1) Alfred Perceval (1846–1931), Irish poet, father of (3), born in Dublin, wrote much Irish folk verse and songs, including 'Father O'Flynn' and an autobiography, *To Return to All That* (1930). A leader of the Celtic revival, he founded the Irish Literary Society.

(2) **Richard** (1715–1804), English author

born at Mickleton, became a fellow of All Souls, Oxford, in 1736. Of his great output, only *The Spiritual Quixote* (1772) is remembered.

(3) **Robert Ranke** (1895–   ), poet and novelist, son of (1), born in London, was educated at Charterhouse and gained an exhibition to St John's College, Oxford, but enlisted in the Royal Welch Fusiliers. At the end of World War I, he took up his studies at Oxford, and for a short time ran a shop as a means of livelihood. In 1926, his graduation year, he accepted the professorship of English at Cairo University. Since 1929, except during the Spanish Civil War and World War II, he has lived in Majorca. Outstanding novels are *I, Claudius* (1934), which won the Hawthornden and James Tait Black prizes for that year, and its sequel, *Claudius the God*, both of them *tours de force* in imaginative reconstruction of the Roman way of life; and in complete contrast of locale and theme, there are his two novels on the experiences of a British soldier in the American revolution, *Sergeant Lamb of the Ninth* (1940) and *Proceed, Sergeant Lamb* (1941). *Wife to Mr Milton* (1943) marks still another original approach. *They Hanged My Saintly Billy* (1957) is a claim for the innocence of William Palmer, who was hanged for murder by poison. His poetry has received less acceptance than his prose. He early propounded poetry as 'a spiritual cathartic' and his later work is tough, sinewy and paradoxical (see *Collected Poems*, 1959). See his autobiographies, *Goodbye to All That* (1929), *But it still goes on* (1930) and *Occupation Writer* (1950).

GRAY, (1) **Asa** (1810–88), American botanist, born at Paris, New York, took his M.D. in 1831, but relinquished medicine for botany, and in 1842–73 was professor of Natural History at Harvard, becoming meanwhile a strong Darwinian. From 1838 to 1842 he published, with Dr Torrey, the *Flora of North America*; *Genera Florae Americae Boreali-Orientalis Illustrata* (1848–50); other works being *A Free Examination of Darwin's Treatise* (1861), &c. See Life by A. H. Dupree (1960).

(2) **David** (1838–61), Scottish poet, was born at Merkland, on the Luggie, near Kirkintilloch. Destined for the church, he took to poetry and in 1860 came to London with Robert Buchanan (q.v.), but died of consumption the following year. *The Luggie* and *In the Shadows* are his chief poetic works. See study by Buchanan (1868).

(3) **Elisha** (1835–1901), American inventor, was born at Barnesville, Ohio, and engaged in the manufacture of telegraphic apparatus. His sixty patents included several for the telephone, of which he claimed the invention, and others for a multiplex telegraph.

(4) **Robert** (1809–72), Bishop of Cape Town from 1847, was the son of **Robert Gray** (1762–1834), who was Bishop of Bristol from 1827. In 1863 he pronounced the deposition of Bishop Colenso (q.v.). See Life by Brooke (1947).

(5) **Stephen** (d. 1736), English physicist, was elected to the Royal Society in 1732 and ended his days a Charterhouse Pensioner.

He was the first experimenter in static electricity, using frictional methods to prove conduction.

(6) **Sir Thomas** (d. *c.* 1369), Northumbrian knight who wrote the *Scala-chronica* (ed. Sir Herbert Maxwell, 1907).

(7) **Thomas** (1716–71), one of the greatest of English poets, was born in London, December 26. His father, Philip Gray, a money-scrivener, was of so violent and jealous a temper that his wife (Dorothy Antrobus) was obliged to separate from him; it was mainly through her exertions that the boy was sent to Eton (1727), and afterwards to Peterhouse, Cambridge (1734). At Eton he made the acquaintance of Horace Walpole, whom in 1739 he accompanied on the grand tour. They spent two and a half years in France and Italy, but quarrelled at Reggio and parted. Walpole afterwards took the blame on himself, and by his efforts the breach was healed within three years. Gray reached England in September 1741; in 1742 he wrote his *Ode on a Distant Prospect of Eton College*, and had begun at Stoke Poges the *Elegy*. In the winter he went back to Cambridge, took his bachelorship in civil law, and became a resident there. This was perhaps the happiest period of his life; he found his relaxation and his keenest pleasure in the company of his friends, and in writing letters. The *Ode on Eton College* was printed in 1747. The *Elegy* was printed in February 1751. His mother died in 1753, and was buried at Stoke Poges, with an epitaph from her son's pen on her tombstone. In 1750 Gray began the *Pindaric Odes*. The splendidly resonant *Progress of Poesy* was finished in 1754; *The Bard*, begun at the same time, in 1757. Gray had a nervous horror of fire, and kept a rope-ladder ready at his window in Peterhouse. One night in February 1756 he was roused from sleep by a pretended alarm, but it is fictitious that he descended into a tub of water put under his window by playful undergraduates. Anyhow, he migrated to Pembroke Hall, where he spent the remainder of his life. His two odes were printed in 1757, and put their author at one bound at the head of living English poets. The laureateship was offered him in 1757, but declined. From 1760 he devoted himself to early English poetry; later he made studies in Icelandic and Celtic verse, which bore fruit in his Eddaic poems, *The Fatal Sisters* and *The Descent of Odin*—genuine precursors of romanticism. In 1765 he visited Glamis Castle, in 1769 the English Lakes; in 1768 he collected his poems in the first general edition, and accepted the professorship of History and Modern Languages at Cambridge. He was now comparatively rich, and enjoyed a reputation dear to a scholar's heart; his life glided quietly on, troubled only by fits of dejection and by attacks of hereditary gout. He died July 30, and was buried beside his mother. Gray said of his own poetry that the 'style he aimed at was extreme conciseness of expression, yet pure, perspicuous and musical'. The excellence he aimed at he attained, and in his lyrical work he reached in a high degree the Greek quality of struc-

ture. All his work bears the stamp of dignity and distinction; though little in quantity, it has been sufficient to give Gray his rank among the *dii majores* of English poetry. See his *Correspondence* (ed. P. Toynbee and L. Whibley 1935), Lives by Kelton-Cremer (1935) and W. P. Jones (1937), and studies by Reed (1924) and D. Cecil (1945).

GRAYSON, David. See BAKER (6).

GRAZIANI, Rodolfo, *grah-tsi-ah′nee* (1882–1955), Marquis of Neghelli (*cr.* 1937), Italian marshal and African administrator, conducted the conquest of Abyssinia from the south (1935–36) and in 1936–37 was its ruthless viceroy. In the Second World War he was ignominiously ejected from Egypt by British and imperial troops under Wavell (1940–41) and resigned, but after the fall of Mussolini in 1943 re-emerged as the head of continuing Fascist armed resistance, only, however, to become captive of his own countrymen on the eve of final capitulation in Italy (1945).

GREATRAKES, or Greatorex, Valentine (1629–83), Irish physician, the ' touch doctor', was born and died at Affane, Co. Waterford. In 1649–56 he was an officer in the Parliamentary army in Ireland, and from 1662 became famous for curing king's evil and all manner of diseases by ' touching ' or ' stroking '. He failed at Whitehall before the king in 1666, but his gratuitous cures were attested by Robert Boyle, Ralph Cudworth, Henry More, &c. To scepticism he replied in his *Brief Account* (1666).

GRECO, El, properly **Domenico Theotocopouli** (1541–1614), Spanish painter, born in Crete. He studied in Italy, possibly as a pupil of Titian, and he is known to have settled in Toledo about 1577, when he was commissioned to execute the decorations for the new church of Santo Domingo el Antiguo, the centre-piece being the *Assumption of the Virgin,* now at Chicago. He became a portrait painter whose reputation fluctuated because of the suspicion which greeted his characteristic distortions. His painting is a curious blend of Italian mannerism and baroque rhythm, with elongated flame-like figures, arbitrary lighting and colour, and, in his later pictures, almost impressionist brushwork. The most famous of his paintings is probably the *Burial of Count Orgaz* (1586) in the Church of Santo Tomé, Toledo. Many of his works are to be seen in Toledo, where there is also the Museo del Greco; his *Crucifixion* and *Resurrection* are in the Prado, Madrid; in New York are, among others, his *Self-portrait* and *View of Toledo*; and the National Gallery, London, has a version of the *Purification of the Temple* and *Christ's Agony in Gethsemane.* See the monographs by B. M. Cossio (3 vols. 1908), C. Aznar (1950), A. Vallentin (1954), P. Kelemen and H. Wethey (1962).

GREELEY, Horace (1811–72), American editor and politician, born at Amherst, N.H., worked as a printer, came to New York in 1831, started the weekly *New Yorker* in 1834 and in 1841 the daily New York *Tribune,* of which he was the leading editor till his death, exerting, without concern for popularity, a supreme influence on American opinion.

The *Tribune* was at first Whig, then anti-slavery Whig, and finally extreme Republican; it advocated to some extent the social theories of Fourier. Greeley at first upheld the constitutional right of the southern states to secede; but when the war began he became one of its most zealous advocates. He published in the *Tribune* the impressive ' Prayer of Twenty Millions ', and within a month the emancipation proclamation was issued. After Lee's surrender he warmly advocated a universal amnesty; and his going to Richmond and signing the bail-bond of Jefferson Davis awakened a storm of public indignation. In religious faith he was a Universalist. An unsuccessful candidate in 1872 for the presidency, he died in New York. See Life by W. A. Linn (1903) and study by J. A. Isely (1949).

GREELY, Adolphus Washington (1844–1935), American Arctic explorer, was born at Newburyport, Mass. He was a volunteer in the Civil War, after its conclusion entering the regular army as lieutenant. Selected in 1881 to conduct the American expedition to Smith Sound, he was rescued in June 1884 with the survivors of his party, when some of them had been reduced to eating the bodies of the dead. Lieut. Lockwood of this expedition travelled to within 396 miles of the pole, the farthest point reached till then. In 1887 Greely became chief of the signal service. Major-general in 1906, he retired in 1908 and was awarded the Congressional Medal of Honour in 1931. He published *Three Years of Arctic Service* (1885), *American Explorers* (1893), &c.

GREEN, (1) **Charles** (1785–1870), English balloonist, was born and died in London. From 1821 to 1852 he made 527 balloon ascents—one, in 1838, to 27,146 feet.

(2) **George** (1793–1841), English mathematician and physicist, was born and died at Sneinton near Nottingham. In 1839 he was elected a fellow of Caius College, Cambridge. He was one of the founders of the mathematical theory of magnetism, gave his name to a theorem and wrote papers on potential, wave motion and equilibrium of fluids, published 1871.

(3) **John Richard** (1837–83), English historian, was born at Oxford, and educated at Magdalen School and Jesus College there. He took orders and was in succession curate and vicar of two East-end London parishes, yet snatched time to contribute historical articles to the *Saturday Review.* In 1868 he became librarian at Lambeth, but next year developed tuberculosis, and this made all active work impossible. Thus began his *Short History of the English People* (1874), the first complete history of England from the social side related to geography and the antiquities with superb literary skill. Its instant success encouraged a larger edition, *A History of the English People* (1877–80). His *Making of England* (1881) and the *Conquest of England* (1883) are fragments of an intended history of early England. See *Memoir* by his wife (1888) and *Letters,* ed. Leslie Stephen (1901).

(4) **Julian** (1900–), French novelist, born of American parents in Paris, began a

successful series of psychological studies in melancholy vein, written in French but later translated, with *Mont-Cinère* (1925), translated as *Avarice House*. His *Léviathan (The Dark Journey)*, written in 1929, won the Harper Prize Novel contest. See his *Journals* I, II, and III (1938–46), and *Memories of Happy Days* (N.Y. 1942).

(5) **Mary Anne Everett,** *née* **Wood** (1818–1895), English historian, born at Sheffield, calendared the papers of the reigns of James I (1857–59) and Charles II (1860–68); completed the calendar of the state papers of Queen Elizabeth, with addenda (1869–74); edited the Commonwealth papers (1875–88).

(6) **Thomas Hill** (1836–82), English idealist philosopher, born at Birkin Rectory, West Riding, Yorks., was educated at Rugby and Oxford, where he became Whyte's professor of Moral Philosophy in 1877. Green's influence was primarily that of a teacher, and his intense interest in social questions drew such men as Arnold Toynbee, Asquith, Milner. His philosophical views may be garnered from his hostile *Introduction to Hume's Treatise* (1874), the posthumous *Prolegomena to Ethics* (1883) and the two ' lay sermons ' edited by A. Toynbee (1883). Although incorrectly styled ' neo-Hegelian ', Green was nearer to Plato and Kant. He took the world and society as his starting point rather than the Hegelian ' spirit '. See R. L. Nettleship's *Memoir* in his edition of Green's Collected Works (1885–88), Bosanquet's preface to Green's *Principles of Political Obligation* (1895) and studies by W. H. Fairbrother (1896) and Lamont (1934).

(7) **Valentine** (1739–1813), English mezzotinter, was born at Salford Priors, near Evesham. His prints after Sir Joshua Reynolds are his best-known works.

GREENAWAY, Kate (1846–1901), English artist, portrayer of child-life in coloured book illustrations; daughter of a London wood-engraver, she became well known in 1879. The Greenaway Medal is awarded annually for the best British children's book artist. See Life by Spielmann and Layard (1905).

GREENE (1) **Graham** (1904–), British novelist and playwright, born at Berkhamsted, educated there and Balliol Coll., Oxford. He has achieved success at two levels—in his entertainments and in his complex novels. The early novels such as *The Man Within* (1929), *It's a Battlefield* (1934) and *England Made Me* (1935) are similar to the entertainments such as *Stamboul Train* (1932), *A Gun for Sale* (1936), *The Confidential Agent* (1939) and *The Third Man* (1950). In both he uses the melodramatic technique of the thriller and displays his consummate skill as a story-teller; both have topical settings, e.g. smuggling, international or civil war; both have the recurrent themes of corruption of innocence, betrayal, pursuit, justice/injustice and death. In his major novels most of these themes remain but they are over-shadowed by the central religious issues and Roman Catholic doctrinal debates which first become apparent in *Brighton Rock* (1938) but become more explicit in *The Power and the Glory* (1940). Here Greene contrasts the

human and divine concept of right and, in a deterministic way, explores human suffering and sin in the context of divine salvation and damnation. In *The Heart of the Matter* (1948) and *The End of the Affair* (1951) this exploration is continued, the moral issue of adultery is raised and human and divine love are juxtaposed. His later works lack the religious intensity of these, for *The Quiet American* (1955) is not explicitly religious, although we are made to feel that Fowler is in need of God, and in *A Burnt-Out Case* (1961) he claims to be trying ' to give expression to various types of belief, half-belief and non-belief '. In *Our Man in Havana* (1958) he adopts a less stringent attitude to sexual behaviour, and in *The Comedians* (1966) the humour and irony outweigh the tragedy. Of his plays *The Living Room* (1933) and *The Potting Shed* (1958) are religious and *The Complaisant Lover* (1959) a romantic comedy.

(2) **Nathanael** (1742–86), American soldier, was born, a Quaker's son, at Warwick, Rhode Island. He distinguished himself at Trenton and Princeton; at the Brandywine he commanded a division and saved the American army from destruction; and at Germantown he commanded the left wing, skilfully covering the retreat. In 1780 he foiled Clinton, and in December succeeded to the command of the army of the south, which had just been defeated by Cornwallis, and was without discipline, clothing, arms or spirit. By great activity he got his army into better condition, and though on March 15, 1781, Cornwallis defeated him at Guilford Courthouse, the victory was so costly that Greene passed unmolested into S. Carolina which, with Georgia, was rapidly retaken, till at Eutaw Springs the war in the south was ended in what was virtually an American victory. A general second perhaps only to Washington, he died, June 19, at Mulberry Grove, Ga. See Lives by G. W. Greene (1890) and F. B. Greene (1893).

(3) **Robert** (1558–92), English dramatist, born at Norwich and educated at Cambridge. He wrote a stream of plays and romances. The latter are often tedious and insipid; but they abound in beautiful poetry. One of them, *Pandosto*, supplied Shakespeare with hints for the plot of *The Winter's Tale*. The most popular of his plays was *Friar Bacon and Friar Bungay*. As Greene helped to lay the foundations of the English drama, even his worst plays are valuable historically. He died September 3. After his death appeared the pamphlet entitled *The Repentance of Robert Greene, Master of Arts*, in which he lays bare the wickedness of his former life. His *Groat's Worth of Wit bought with a Million of Repentance* contains one of the few authentic contemporary allusions to Shakespeare. See critical study with bibliography by J. C. Jordan (1915).

GREENOUGH, Horatio, *gree'nō* (1805–52), American sculptor, born in Boston, Mass., studied two years at Harvard, and from 1825 to 1851 lived chiefly in Italy. His principal work is the statue of Washington as Zeus, now in the Smithsonian Inst., Washington.

GREENWOOD, (1) Arthur (1880–1954),

British politician, born at Leeds and educated at Leeds University. A wartime member of Lloyd George's secretariat, he became an M.P. in 1922 and deputy leader of the Parliamentary Labour Party in 1935, showing himself an outspoken critic of ' appeasement'. In the 1940 Government he was minister without portfolio, in 1945 he became lord privy seal, and he resigned from the government in 1947. He remained treasurer of the Labour Party, of whose national executive he became chairman in 1953. He did much to shape Labour's social policies. His son **Anthony** (1911–), also a Labour politician, entered parliament in 1946, holding various parliamentary appointments from 1964, minister of housing from 1966.

(2) **Walter** (1903–), English writer, born at Salford. His novel *Love on the Dole* (1933), inspired by his experiences of unemployment and depression in the early 'thirties, made a considerable impact as a document of the times and was subsequently dramatized. He also wrote a number of other novels with a social slant.

GREG, William Rathbone (1809–81), English essayist, born at Manchester, from manager of mills at Bury became a commissioner of customs in 1856, and was comptroller of H.M. Stationery Office (1864–77). His numerous essays on political and social history were collected in *Essays on Political and Social Science* (1854), *Literary and Social Judgments* (1869), and *Miscellaneous Essays* (1884). His *Rocks Ahead* (1874) took a highly pessimistic view of the future of England, anticipating with foreboding the political supremacy of the lower classes, industrial decline and the divorce of intelligence from religion.

GREGG, John Robert (1867–1942), born in County Monaghan, invented in 1888 while working in Liverpool the Gregg system of shorthand. He subsequently emigrated to the U.S.A. and founded a publishing firm.

GRÉGOIRE, Henri, *greg-wahr* (1750–1831), French prelate and revolutionary, born near Lunéville, took orders, and lectured at the Jesuit College of Pont-à-Mousson. His *Essai sur la régénération des juifs* (1778) became widely popular. Curé of Embermenil in Lorraine, and an ardent democrat, he was sent to the States-General of 1789 as a deputy of the clergy, attached himself to the Tiers-état party, and acted a prominent part throughout the Revolution. He was the first of his order to take the oaths, and was elected ' constitutional bishop ' of Loir-et-Cher. He exercised a stern democracy which he identified with the Christian brotherhood of the gospel. At the blasphemous Feast of Reason he refused, in the face of the infuriated rabble, to renounce Christianity. After the 18th Brumaire he became a member of the Corps Législatif; the Concordat forced him to resign his bishopric. He died in Paris, unreconciled with the church. Among his works are *Histoire des sectes religieuses* (1814) and *L'Église gallicane* (1818). See his *Mémoires*, with Life by H. Carnot (1831), and studies by Krüger (1838), Böhringer (1878), Maggiolo (1884), Hollard (1895).

GREGOR, William (1761–1817), English chemist and clergyman, born at Trewarthenick, Cornwall, was a minister in Devonshire and Cornwall and analysed local minerals, particularly the sand known as *ilmenite* in which he discovered titanium.

GREGOROVIUS, Ferdinand (1821–91), German historian, born at Neidenburg, E. Prussia, studied theology, but devoted himself to poetry and literature, settled in Rome in 1852, and died at Munich. His great standard work is the *History of Rome in the Middle Ages* (trans. 1895–1902). Among his numerous other works are *Tombs of the Popes* (trans. 1903), *Lucrezia Borgia* (1874), and histories of Athens and Corsica.

GREGORY, St (*c.* 240–332), ' the Illuminator ', the apostle of Armenia, was said to have been of the royal Persian race of the Arsacidae, brought up a Christian in Cappadocia, kept fourteen years a prisoner by Tiridates III for declining idolatrous compliance, and, after converting the king (A.D. 301), to have been made patriarch of Armenia. See Peeters, *Analecta Bollandiana* (1942).

GREGORY, the name of sixteen popes, of whom the most noteworthy are:

Gregory I, the Great (*c.* 540–604), pope (590) and saint, a father of the church, born in Rome, was appointed by Justin II praetor of Rome, but about 575 relinquished this office, distributed his wealth among the poor, and withdrew into a monastery at Rome, one of seven he had founded. It was while here that he saw one day some Anglo-Saxon youths in the slave-market, and was seized with a longing to convert their country to Christianity. He set out on his journey, but the clamour of the Romans at his loss led the pope Benedict to compel his return. Pelagius II sent Gregory as nuncio to Constantinople for aid against the Lombards. He resided there three years, writing his *Moralia*, an exposition of Job. On the death of Pelagius Gregory was unanimously called by the clergy, senate, and people to succeed him. He used every means to evade the dignity, but was forced to yield, and was consecrated September 3, 590. It is doubtful whether any pope has surpassed Gregory I as an administrator. To him the Roman Church is indebted for the complete organization of her public services and ritual, for the systematization of her sacred chants. The mission to England he entrusted to Augustine (q.v.); and the Gothic kingdom of Spain, long Arian, was reconciled with the church. Nor was his zeal for the reformation of the church inferior to his ardour for its growth. Towards heathens and Jews he was most gentle, and he used all his efforts to repress slave-dealing and to mitigate slavery. When Rome was threatened by the Lombards, he showed himself virtually a temporal sovereign; he reprobated the assumption by John, patriarch of Constantinople, of the title of Oecumenical or Universal Bishop. In his writings the whole dogmatical system of the modern church is fully developed. He left homilies on Ezekiel and on the Gospels, the *Regula* (or *Cura Pastoralis*), and the *Sacramentarium* and *Antiphonarium*. In exegesis he is a fearless allegorist; his *Letters* and *Dialogues* abound with miraculous and legendary narratives. The best editions of his works are the Benedictine (1705) and that in Migne's *Patrologia*. See works by Dudden (1905), Sir H. Howorth (1912), P. Batiffol (trans. 1929).

Gregory II (669–731), pope (715), and saint was by birth a Roman. The authority of the eastern emperors had sunk in the West into little more than a name; and the tyrannical measures of the Emperor Leo the Isaurian against image-worship weakened still more the tie. Gregory protested strongly against the imperial policy. The result of the contest was a notable aggrandizement of the political authority and influence of the popes in Italy. Under Gregory's auspices Boniface entered on his missionary work in Germany.

Gregory III, pope (731–741) and saint, born in Syria, succeeded Gregory II, and excommunicated the Iconoclasts. The encroachments of the Lombards became so formidable that, the eastern emperors being powerless to help, the Romans charged Gregory to send a deputation to Charles Martel, soliciting his aid, and offering to make him consul of Rome. This offer is of great historical importance, though it failed to enlist the aid of Charles; but it was a step towards the independence of the West.

Gregory VII (Hildebrand), saint (*c.* 1020–1085), pope (1073), the great representative of the temporal claims of the mediaeval papacy, was born near Soana in Tuscany, his original name being Hildebrand. His youth was passed at Rome, in the monastery of St Maria. On the death of Gregory VI, whose chaplain he was, he is reported (doubtfully) to have spent some time at Cluny, whence he was recalled by the new and zealous pope Leo IX, whom he accompanied to Rome in 1049, and who made him a cardinal. During the four following pontificates Hildebrand continued to exercise great influence; and he was himself elected pope three days after the death of Alexander II, and crowned July 10. He addressed himself to amend the secularized condition of the church. The feudal standing of the higher clergy, the claims of sovereigns upon temporalities, and the consequent temptation to simony were, he held, the cause of all the evils under which Europe was groaning. While he laboured to enforce the observance of all the details of discipline, it was against investiture that his main efforts were directed. In 1074 he prohibited this practice, under pain of excommunication, and in 1075 he actually issued that sentence against several bishops and councillors of the empire. The Emperor Henry IV disregarding these menaces, Gregory cited him to Rome to answer for his conduct. Henry's sole reply was defiance; and in a diet at Worms in 1076 he declared Gregory deposed. The pontiff retaliated by excommunication, which, unless removed by absolution in twelve months, involved (according also to imperial law) the forfeiture of all civil rights and deposition from every civil and political office. Henry's Saxon subjects appealing to this law against him, he was compelled to yield, and by a

humiliating penance at Canossa in January 1077 obtained absolution from the pope in person. But in 1080 Henry resumed hostilities, again declared Gregory deposed, and appointed an antipope as Clement III. After a siege of three years, Henry, in 1084, took possession of Rome. Just, however, as Gregory was on the point of falling into his hands, Robert Guiscard, the Norman Duke of Apulia, entered the city, set Gregory free, and compelled Henry to return to Germany. But the wretched condition to which Rome was reduced obliged Gregory to withdraw ultimately to Salerno, where he died, May 25, 1085. In Gregory's conception of the constitution of Christian society the spiritual power was the first and highest element. It was to direct, to command the temporal, and, in a certain sense, to compel its obedience; but the arms which it was authorized to use for the purpose of coercion were the arms of the spirit only. And he devoted his unbending efforts to suppress the vices which deformed society, and to restrain the tyranny which oppressed the subject as much as it enslaved the church. See English works by W. R. W. Stephens (1888), Dr Vincent (1897), A. H. Mathew (1910), H. X. Arquillière (1934).

Gregory VIII, Alberto di Morra, pope (1187), died within two months of his election. In 1118 there had already been an antipope who assumed the style of Gregory VIII, but who was expelled and humiliated in 1123.

Gregory IX (1148–1241), pope (1227), constantly feuded with the Emperor Frederick II, and asserted the highest view of papal power.

Gregory XIII, Ugo Buoncompagni (1502–1585), pope (1572), was born at Bologna, where he was professor of Law for several years. He settled at Rome in 1539, was one of the theologians of the Council of Trent, became cardinal in 1565, and was sent as legate to Spain. On the death of Pius V, Gregory was elected pope. He displayed extraordinary zeal for the promotion of education; many of the colleges in Rome were wholly or in part endowed by him; and his expenditure for educational purposes is said to have exceeded 2,000,000 Roman crowns. The most interesting event of his pontificate was the correction of the Calendar and the introduction of the Gregorian Computation in 1582. A grievous imputation rests on Gregory's memory from his having ordered a *Te Deum* in Rome on occasion of the massacre of St Bartholomew—on the report of the French ambassador, which represented that infamous episode as the suppression of a Huguenot conspiracy. Gregory published a valuable edition of the *Decretum Gratiani*.

Gregory XV (1554–1623), pope (1621), dealt with the Immaculate Conception and regulated ritual.

Gregory XVI (1765–1846), pope (1831), represented reaction and ultramontanism in a revolutionary period, favoured the Jesuits, and increased the papal debt by spending on buildings and museums.

GREGORY, (1) David (1661–1708), Scottish mathematician, nephew of (3), born at

Kinairdy, Banffshire, became in 1683 professor of Mathematics at Edinburgh, in 1691 Savilian professor of Astronomy at Oxford. He first suggested an achromatic combination of lenses and published a defence of Newtonian astronomy (1702). For the whole family, including (3), (4), (5) and (7), see A. G. Stewart, *The Academic Gregories* (1901).

(2) **Isabella Augusta, Lady,** *née* **Persse** (1852–1932), Irish playwright, after her marriage to Sir William Henry Gregory (1817–92), governor of Ceylon (1872–77), in 1880, became an associate of W. B. Yeats (q.v.) in the foundation of the Abbey Theatre in Dublin and the Irish Players. For these she wrote a number of short plays; her best, *Spreading the News* (1904) and *The Rising of the Moon* (1907). She also wrote Irish legends in dialect and translated Molière.

(3) **James** (1638–75), Scottish mathematician, uncle of (1) and grandfather of (5), born at Drumoak, Aberdeenshire, professor of Mathematics at St Andrews (1688), Edinburgh (1674) and an F.R.S. He distinguished between convergent and divergent series and constructed the famous Gregorian telescope (1661).

(4) **James** (1753–1821), Scottish physician, father of (7), son of (5), born at Aberdeen, professor at Edinburgh (1776), gave his name to ' Gregory's Mixture '.

(5) **John** (1724–73), Scottish physician, grandson of (3), professor at Aberdeen in 1755 and at Edinburgh in 1766, wrote medical books.

(6) **Olinthus** (1774–1841), English mathematician and biographer, born at Yaxley, Huntingdon, became a newspaper editor, then a teacher of mathematics at Cambridge and at Woolwich.

(7) **William** (1803–58), Scottish chemist, son of (4), professor of Chemistry at Glasgow (1837), in King's College, Aberdeen (1839) and at Edinburgh (1844), wrote *Outlines of Chemistry* (1845).

GREGORY OF NAZIANZUS, St (*c.* 328–390), bishop and theologian, born in Cappadocia, was educated at Caesarea, Alexandria and Athens, became a close friend of Basil the Great, was made Bishop of Sasima, but withdrew to a life of religious study at Nazianzus near his birthplace. The Emperor Theodosius made him patriarch of Constantinople (380), but this dignity also he resigned next year. His theological works were largely concerned with upholding Nicene orthodoxy and include discourses, letters and hymns. The principal edition is the Benedictine. See monographs by Ullmann (trans. 1851), Benoit (Paris 1884) and Fleury (1930).

GREGORY OF NYSSA (*c.* 331–395), Christian theologian, was by his brother Basil the Great consecrated Bishop of Nyssa in Cappadocia about 371. During the persecution of the adherents of the Nicene Creed in the reign of Valens, Gregory was deposed, but on the death of Valens was joyfully welcomed back (378). He was present at the Council of Constantinople in 381, and was appointed to share in the oversight of the diocese of Pontus. He travelled to Arabia and Jerusalem to set in order the churches

there, and was again at a synod in Constantinople in 394. His chief works are his *Twelve Books against Eunomius*, a treatise on the Trinity, several ascetic treatises, many sermons, twenty-three epistles, and his great *Catechetical Oration* (1903). See his whole works in Migne's *Patrologia* and Life `by Rupp (1834) and *Epistles*, selected by Pasquali (1925).

GREGORY THAUMATURGUS, i.e., ' wonder-worker ' (*c.* 210–270), the apostle of Pontus, was born at Neocaesarea in Pontus, became a disciple of Origen, and was consecrated Bishop of Neocaesarea. His *Ekthesis,* or *Confession of Faith,* is a summary of Origen's theology. The genuineness of two other treatises is doubtful. His *Panegyricus* (which contains an autobiography) is printed among the works of Origen. See monograph by Ryssel (1880).

GREGORY OF TOURS (538 – *c.* 594), Frankish historian, was born at Arverna (now Clermont), and belonged to a distinguished Roman family of Gaul. His recovery from sickness, through a pilgrimage to the grave of St Martin of Tours, led Gregory to devote himself to the church, and he was elected Bishop of Tours in 573. As a supporter of Sigbert of Austrasia and his wife Brunhilda against Chilperic and his wife Fredegond, he had to suffer much persecution. His *Historia Francorum* is the chief authority for the history of Gaul in the 6th century. His *Miraculorum libri vii* is a hagiographical compilation. See monographs by Löbell (1869) and Monod (Paris 1872), vol. i of Mark Pattison's *Essays* (1889), L. Halphen in *Mélanges Lot* (1925).

GREIG, *greg,* name of two Scottish naval officers who became Russian admirals:

(1) **Alexis Samuilovich** (1775–1845), son of (2), distinguished himself in the Russo-Turkish wars of 1807 and 1828–29.

(2) **Sir Samuel** (1735–88), father of (1), born at Inverness, transferred to the Russian navy in 1763 and fought against the Turks (1770) and the Swedes (1788).

GRENFELL, (1) **Julian** (1888–1915), English poet, a son of Lord Desborough, educated at Eton and Balliol, killed in World War I, is remembered for his fine war poem ' Into Battle '.

(2) **Sir Wilfred Thomason** (1865–1940), English physician, an Oxford rugby blue and house surgeon to the London Hospital, he took a master mariner's certificate and became a medical missionary in the North Sea fisheries. In 1892 he went to Labrador and founded hospitals, orphanages and other social services as well as fitting out hospital ships for the fishing grounds. See *Life* by J. L. Kerr (1959).

GRENVILLE, (1) **Sir Bevil** (1596–1643), English royalist soldier, the hero of Hawker's ballad, was born at Brinn, Cornwall, studied at Exeter College, Oxford; entered parliament in 1621, and sided for some years with the popular party; but from 1639 warmly espoused the king's cause, and fell in the royalist victory of Landsdowne near Bath, July 5, 1643. See Roger Granville's *History of the Granvilles* (Exeter 1895).

(2) **George** (1712–70), English statesman,

younger brother of Richard Grenville, Earl Temple, and father of (4), entered parliament in 1741, in 1762 became secretary of state and first lord of the Admiralty, and in 1763 prime minister. The prosecution of Wilkes and the passing of the American Stamp Act took place during his ministry. He resigned in 1765. See *Grenville Papers*, edited by W. J. Smith (1853).

(3) **Sir Richard** (*c*. 1541–91), British sailor, belonging to an ancient Cornish family, early distinguished himself by his courage on land and sea. He was admitted to the Inner Temple (1559), fought in Hungary and Ireland (1566–69), was knighted about 1577, in 1585 commanded the seven ships carrying Raleigh's first colony to Virginia (the present N. Carolina), fought and despoiled the Spaniards like others of his time. In 1591 he commanded the *Revenge* in Lord Thomas Howard's squadron of six vessels, when they met a Spanish fleet of fifty-three sail off Flores, in the Azores. While the admiral made good his escape, Grenville refused to follow him; and the great *San Philip*, of 1500 tons, engaged the little *Revenge*, which soon found herself in the midst of a ring of enemies. From three in the afternoon till next morning the battle raged. Fifteen Spanish ships were beaten off in turn; two were sunk, two disabled, and 2000 men slain or drowned. But the *Revenge* was by this time a helpless wreck, her powder spent, forty of her 100 sound men dead, and most of the rest hurt, the vice-admiral himself severely wounded. Sir Richard would have had the master-gunner blow up the ship, but was overborne by the survivors, and carried on board a Spanish ship, where he died of his wounds the second or third day afterwards. This exploit was described by Raleigh, Gervase Markham and Lindshoten, ed. Arber (1871), by Froude in his *Short Studies*, by Tennyson in a ballad. See Lives by Bushnell (1936) and A. L. Rowse (1937).

(4) **William Wyndham Grenville, 1st Baron** (1759–1834), English statesman, third surviving son of (2), studied at Eton and Oxford, became in 1782 a member of parliament, in 1783 paymaster-general, in 1789 speaker; and while home secretary (1790) was created baron. He became foreign secretary in 1791, and resigned, along with Pitt, in 1801 on the refusal of George III to assent to Catholic emancipation, of which Grenville was a chief supporter. In 1806 he formed the government of ' All the Talents ', which, before its dissolution in 1807, abolished the slave-trade. From 1809 to 1815 he acted along with Earl Grey, and generally supported Canning. He died at Dropmore. See study by E. D. Adams (1904).

GRESHAM, Sir Thomas (1519–79), English financier and founder of the Royal Exchange, probably born in London, son of Sir Richard Gresham (*c*. 1485–1549), a wealthy merchant of Norfolk ancestry, who in 1537 was elected Lord Mayor of London. From Cambridge in 1543 he passed into the Mercers' Company, and in 1551 was employed as ' king's merchant ' at Antwerp. In two years he paid off a heavy loan and restored the king's credit. As a Protestant he was dis-

missed by Queen Mary, but soon reinstated. By Queen Elizabeth he was knighted (1559) and made for a time ambassador at Brussels. The troubles in the Netherlands compelled him in 1567 to withdraw from Antwerp, to which city he had made more than forty journeys on state service; on one in 1560 he was thrown from his horse and lamed for life. In 1569, on his advice, the state borrowed money from London merchants instead of from foreigners. He made the observation, known as ' Gresham's Law ', that of two coins of equal legal exchange value that of the lower intrinsic value would tend to drive the other out of use. Having in 1564 lost his only son, Richard, in 1566–68 he devoted a portion of his great wealth to building an Exchange, in imitation of that of Antwerp; he made provision for founding Gresham College; and he left money for eight almshouses. See Lives by J. W. Burgon (1839), F. R. Salter (1925) and H. Laurent (1938).

GRÉTRY, André Ernest Modeste, *gray-tree* (1741–1813), French composer of Belgian birth, born at Liège, settled in Paris, and composed over forty comic operas, of which *Le Huron* (1768) and *Lucile* (1769) were the earliest, and *Raoul* and *Richard Coeur-de-Lion* among the best known. He became inspector of the Conservatoire and a member of the Institute. See his *Mémoires* (1796), and Lives by Grégoir (1883), H. de Curzon (1908).

GREUZE, Jean Baptiste, *grœz* (1725–1805), French genre and portrait painter, was born at Tournus near Mâcon. His first notable works were historical; after a visit to Italy (1755) he painted Italian subjects; but he is seen at his best in such studies of girls as *The Broken Pitcher* in the Louvre and *Girl with Doves* in the Wallace Collection. He died in poverty. His art, full of delicacy and grace, is marred by its triviality and pursuit of mere prettiness. See monograph by Normand (1892) and Life by Hautecoeur (1913).

GREVILLE, (1) **Charles Cavendish Fulke** (1794–1865), English memoir writer, educated at Eton and Christ Church, Oxford, became private secretary to Earl Bathurst, and was clerk of the privy council 1821–59. His position gave him peculiar facilities for studying court and public life, witness his noted *Memoirs* (1875–87); see also his *Letters* (1924), *The Greville Diary* (1927).

(2) **Sir Fulke, 1st Baron Brooke** (1554–1628), English poet, born at Beauchamp Court, Warwickshire, was educated at Shrewsbury and Jesus College, Cambridge, travelled abroad, was knighted in 1597 and created baron in 1620, and was murdered by an old servant. He wrote several didactic poems, over a hundred sonnets, and two tragedies, including *The Tragedy of Mustapha* (1609), printed in 1633 (ed. Bullough 1939). His Life of Sir Philip Sidney appeared in 1652, his *Remains* in 1670.

GRÉVILLE, Henry, pseud. of **Alice Durand,** *née* **Fleury** (1842–1902), French novelist, born in Paris, accompanied her father to St Petersburg in 1857, and wrote Russian society novels.

GRÉVY, François Paul Jules, *gray-vee* (1807–91), French statesman, born at Mont-sous-Vaudrey, Jura, as an advocate acquired distinction in the defence of republican political prisoners. Vice-president of the constituent assembly, he opposed Louis Napoleon, and after the *coup d'état* retired from politics; but in 1869 he was again returned for Jura. In February 1871 he became president of the National Assembly, being re-elected in 1876, 1877 and 1879. The monarchist schemes were attacked by Grévy (1873–76); in 1879 he was elected president of the Republic for seven years. In 1885 he was again elected for seven years, but, hampered by ministerial difficulties, resigned in December 1887. He died at Mont-sous-Vaudrey. See Life by Barbier (1893).

GREW, Nehemiah (1628–1711), English botanist and physician, author of the pioneering *Anatomy of Plants*, and of *Comparative Anatomy of the Stomach and Guts* (1681), was born at Atherstone, educated at Cambridge and Leyden, and practised at Coventry and London. He was secretary of the Royal Society from 1677.

GREY, Earls, a family of English Liberal statesmen:

(1) **Albert Henry George Grey, 4th Earl** (1851–1917), English colonial administrator, nephew of (3), M.P. (1880–86), P.C., G.C.B., G.C.M.G., administrator of Rhodesia (1896–1897), then a B.S.A. company director, and governor-general of Canada (1904–11).

(2) **Charles Grey, 2nd Earl** (1764–1845), born at Fallodon, Northumberland, March 15, and educated at Eton and King's College, Cambridge. Whig M.P. for Northumberland (1786), he was one of the managers of the impeachment of Warren Hastings, and in 1792 helped to found the Society of the Friends of the People. He introduced the motion for the impeachment of Pitt, and took a prominent part in the temporary ' secession ' of the Whigs from parliament; he also denounced the union between England and Ireland. In 1806 Grey, now Lord Howick, became first lord of the Admiralty, and on the death of Fox foreign secretary and leader of the House of Commons. He carried through the act abolishing the African slave-trade. In 1807 he succeeded his father as second Earl Grey. He opposed the renewal of the war in 1815, denounced the coercive measures of the government, condemned the bill against Queen Caroline, defended the right of public meeting, and supported the enlightened commercial policy of Huskisson. In 1830 he formed a government whose policy, he said, would be one of peace, retrenchment, and reform. The first Reform Bill was produced in March 1831; its defeat led to a dissolution and the return of a parliament still more devoted to reform. A second bill was carried, which the Lords threw out in October, and riots ensued. Early in 1832 a third bill was carried in the Commons, and it weathered the second reading in the Upper House; but when a motion to postpone the disfranchising clauses was adopted, ministers resigned. The Duke of Wellington failed to form an administration, and Grey returned to office with power to create a sufficient number of peers to carry the measure. Wellington now withdrew

his opposition, and in June the Reform Bill passed the House of Lords. Grey was **the** chief of a powerful party in the first reformed parliament. He carried the act for **the** abolition of slavery in the colonies, as well as a number of minor reforms; but dissensions sprang up, and in consequence of his Irish difficulties he resigned in July 1834. He died at Howick House, Alnwick, July 17. See Life by G. M. Trevelyan (1920).

(3) **Henry Grey, 3rd Earl** (1802–94), English statesman, son of the above, entered Parliament in 1826 as Lord Howick. He became under-secretary for the Colonies in his father's ministry, retired in 1833, but was subsequently under-secretary in the Home Department, and in 1835 secretary for war. In 1841 he opposed Peel's policy, in 1845 succeeded to the peerage, in 1846 became colonial secretary, and in 1852 published his *Defence of Lord John Russell's Colonial Policy*. He opposed the Crimean war, and condemned Beaconsfield's Eastern policy. In 1858 he issued his *Essay on Parliamentary Government as to Reform*, and in 1867 his father's *Correspondence with William IV*.

GREY, (1) Beryl, stage name of **Mrs Sven Gustav Svenson** (1927–), English ballerina, born in London, she won a scholarship to Sadler's Wells Ballet School at the age of nine, and her first solo appearance at Sadler's Wells Theatre was in the part of Sabrina, in *Comus*, in 1941. The youngest recorded dancer of Giselle, she first appeared in the part at the age of sixteen. She has danced most leading parts with the Sadler's Wells company (1942–57), and has since appeared with the Bolshoi Ballet (1957–58) and the Chinese Ballet (1964).

(2) **Sir George** (1799–1882), English statesman, nephew of 2nd Earl Grey, born at Gibraltar, took a first-class from Oriel College, Oxford, and relinquished the law after succeeding his father in the baronetcy in 1828. M.P. for Devonport (1832–47). under-secretary for the Colonies (1834–35), he ably defended against Roebuck Lord John Russell's bill for the temporary suspension of the Lower Canadian constitution. In 1839 Grey became judge-advocate, in 1841 chancellor of the Duchy of Lancaster, and in 1846 home secretary. During the Chartist disturbances he discharged his duties with vigour and discrimination. He carried the Crown and Government Security Bill, the Alien Bill, and a measure for further suspension in Ireland of the Habeas Corpus Act (1849). In 1854 he became colonial secretary, and in 1855, under Palmerston, took his old post of home secretary. From 1859 he was chancellor of the Duchy of Lancaster, and home secretary again (1861–66). See Memoir by Bishop Creighton (1901) and Lives by G. C. Henderson (1907) and J. Collier (1909).

(3) **Sir George** (1812–98), British colonial governor and premier of New Zealand, born at Lisbon, and educated at Sandhurst, between 1837 and 1839 explored in Western Australia, and published his *Journals of Two Expeditions in Australia* in 1840. In 1841 he became governor of South Australia, in 1845

of New Zealand, and in 1854 (a K.C.B. since 1848) of Cape Colony, where he allayed the irritation left by the Kaffir war; in 1858 he resigned, but was requested to resume his governorship. From 1861 to 1868 he was again governor of New Zealand, and brought the Maori war to a close. He became superintendent of Auckland in 1875; and in 1877–79 was premier of New Zealand, where he had much influence with the Maoris. He wrote an important work on *Polynesian Mythology* (1855) and published a collection of Polynesian proverbs (1858). He gave valuable libraries to Cape Town and Auckland. See Lives by Rees (1893), Henderson (1907), Collier (1909), Rutherford (1961).

(4) **Lady Jane** (1537–54), Queen of England, born at Broadgate, Leicestershire, was the eldest daughter of Henry Grey, Marquis of Dorset, afterwards Duke of Suffolk, and of Lady Frances Brandon. The latter was the daughter of Charles Brandon, Duke of Suffolk, by Mary, younger sister of Henry VIII, and widow of Louis XII of France. Lady Jane was brought up rigorously by her parents, but under her tutor Aylmer, afterwards Bishop of London, made extraordinary progress, especially in languages. In 1553 the Duke of Northumberland, foreseeing the speedy death of Edward VI, determined to secure the succession to his own family. Lady Jane, not sixteen years old, was therefore married, against her wish, to Lord Guildford Dudley, Northumberland's fourth son, on May 21, 1553; and on July 9, three days after Edward's death, the council informed her that he had named her as his successor. On the 19th, the brief usurpation over, she was a prisoner in the Tower; and four months later, pleading guilty of high treason, she was sentenced to death. She spurned the idea of forsaking Protestantism and bitterly condemned Northumberland's recantation. Queen Mary might have been merciful ; but Suffolk's participation in Wyatt's rebellion sealed his daughter's doom, and on February 12 she was beheaded on Tower Green, her husband on Tower Hill. They are buried in the Tower church of St Peter ad Vincula. See *The Chronicle of Queen Jane*, edited by Nichols (Camden Soc. 1850), and studies by I. A. Taylor (1908) and H. Chapman (1962).

(5) **John** (1785–1868), English agriculturist, of Dilston near Hexham, after a political career, devoted himself as estate-agent (1833–63) to the development of a new system of agriculture. See Life by his daughter, Josephine Butler (1874).

(6) **Zane** (1875–1939), American novelist, born at Zanesville, Ohio, began his working-life as a dentist, but after a trip out west in 1904 turned out ' westerns ' with machine-like regularity . . . a total of fifty-four novels. His best-known, *Riders of the Purple Sage*, sold nearly two million copies. His hobby of big-game fishing off the coasts of Australia and New Zealand was utilized in such books as *Tales of Fishing* (1919). His success was due to the ' escapist ' lure of his simple adventure plots and attractive, authentic settings.

GREY OF FALLODON, Edward Grey, 1st

Viscount (1862–1933), British statesman, was educated at Winchester and Balliol College, Oxford, succeeded his grandfather in 1882, and was Liberal M.P. for Berwick-on-Tweed 1885–1916, secretary for foreign affairs 1905–1916. K.G. (1912), he distinguished himself in the Balkan peace negotiations 1913, and on the outbreak of the First World War in 1914. Ambassador at Washington, 1919–20, chancellor of Oxford University from 1928, he issued Memoirs in 1925, and wrote on birds (1927) and fly-fishing (1889). See Life by G. M. Trevelyan (1937).

GRIBOYEDOV, Aleksander Sergeyevich, *gribo-yay'dof* (1795–1829), Russian writer and diplomat, born in Moscow. He wrote *Gore ot Uma* (1824; English translation 'The Mischief of Being Clever),' a comedy in rhymed iambics, which satirizes the contemporary Moscow society so aptly that it has provided household phrases for the Russian people. Involved in the Decembrist Revolt, he was, however, cleared, and in 1828 became Russian ambassador to Persia. He was killed in an anti-Russian demonstration at the embassy in Teheran. See *History of Russian Literature* by D. S. Mirsky (1927) and *The Mischief of Being Clever* by Sir B. Pares (1925).

GRIEG, (1) **Edvard Hagerup** (1843–1907), Norwegian composer, born at Bergen on June 15, was of Scots descent, his forebear Alexander Greig having emigrated from Aberdeen during the post-1745 depression. On the recommendation of the famous violin virtuoso, Ole Bull, Grieg studied at the Leipzig Conservatoire, where he came strongly under the influence of Schumann's music. The lack of openings in Norway led to his making Copenhagen his main base between 1863 and 1867. There he was in close contact with Gade, H. C. Andersen and the young Norwegian poet-composer Nordraak. Under their stimulus, he evolved from a German-trained romanticist into a strongly national Norwegian composer. After some years teaching and conducting in Christiania, the success of his incidental music for Ibsen's *Peer Gynt* (1876) on top of the award of a state pension in 1874 enabled him to settle near Bergen. In 1867, he had married his cousin, Nina Hagerup, a well-known singer. Apart from his A minor piano concerto, some orchestral suites, and three violin sonatas and one quartet, his output included little in the larger forms. In his incidental music to *Peer Gynt* and Björnson's *Sigurd Jorsalfar* and his choral music, and especially in his numerous songs and piano pieces, in which his fastidious taste, sense of the picturesque and intense awareness of his folk heritage synthesized, he expressed himself most individually and successfully. He died at Bergen, loaded with honours, national and foreign, on September 4, 1907. See H. T. Finck (1909), Monrad-Johannsen (1945), Deucher (1950) and G. Abraham (ed.), *Grieg, a Musical Symposium* (1948).

(2) **Johan Nordahl Brun** (1902–43), Norwegian poet and dramatist, born at Bergen, and related to the composer (1) studied at Oslo and Oxford and spent much of his youth travelling. His poetry mirrors

his wanderlust and his passion for personal freedom. Titles are *Stones in the Stream* (1925) and *Norway in our Hearts* (1929). *The Ship Sails On* (1924) is a novel which crystallizes his experience in shipping to Australia at nineteen as an ordinary seaman. Later he edited an anti-Fascist periodical, *Veien Frem*, and also turned to the stage, where his concern with the idea of freedom is projected in *Our Honour and Might* (1935) and *Nederlaget* (1937), dealing with the Paris Commune of 1871, and translated by E. Arkwright as *Defeat* (1945). Grieg came to England after Norway was occupied by the Germans in 1940, and through the broadcasting of his verse, kept alive Norwegian resistance to the invader. His aircraft was shot down over Berlin in 1943. See *All That is Mine Demand*, war poems trans. by Gathorne-Hardy, with biographical introduction (1945), and Life by J. Borgen (1945).

GRIERSON, (1) **Sir Herbert John Clifford** (1866–1960), Scottish critic, born in Lerwick, Shetland, educated at King's College, Aberdeen, where he was professor (1894–1915), and Christ Church, Oxford, was appointed regius professor of Rhetoric and English Literature at Edinburgh (1915–35) and rector (1936–39). He edited the poems of Donne (1912), and his studies include *Metaphysical Poets* (1921), *Cross Currents in the Literature of the 17th Century* (1929), *Milton and Wordsworth* (1937), *Essays and Addresses* (1940). He was knighted in 1936.

(2) **John** (1898–1972), British producer of documentary films, born at Kilmadock, Stirlingshire, made his name in 1929 by *Drifters*, which led the way to the development of documentaries. From 1948 to 1950 he was controller of film activities in the Central Office of Information. See study by Hardy (1946).

(3) **Sir Robert, of Lag** (c. 1655–1733), Scottish Jacobite laird, born about 1655, succeeded his cousin in the Dumfriesshire estates in 1669. He was for some years steward of Kirkcudbright, and so harried the Covenanters as to leave his name a byword for cruelty; he was one of the judges of the Wigtown martyrs. He received a Nova Scotia baronetcy in 1685, with a pension of £200. After the Revolution he was fined and imprisoned as a Jacobite, and in 1696 was arraigned on a false charge of coining. He died December 31, 1733. See Colonel Fergusson's *Laird of Lag* (1886).

GRIESBACH, Johann Jakob, *greez'baKH* (1745–1812), German New Testament scholar, born at Butzbach, studied theology at Tübingen, Halle and Leipzig, lectured at Halle, and in 1775 became a professor at Jena and devoted himself to critical revision of the New Testament text, reclassifying the MSS. into three recensions, Alexandrian, Western and Byzantine. See his *Commentarius Criticus* (1811), &c.

GRIEVE. See MACDIARMID.

GRIFFIN, (1) **Bernard** (1899–1956), English cardinal, was born in Birmingham, and was educated at the English and Beda Colleges, Rome. He became Archbishop of Westminster in 1943 and cardinal in 1946. He toured postwar Europe and America and

in 1950 was Papal Legate for the centenary celebrations of the reconstitution of the English hierarchy. See his *Seek Ye First* (1949) and Life by Bedoyere (1955).

(2) **Gerald** (1803–40), Irish novelist, born at Limerick, went to London in 1823, and failed as a dramatist, but was more successful with novels of southern Irish life—*Holland Tide* (1827), *Tales of the Munster Festivals* (1827) and *The Collegians* (1829), on which Boucicault's drama *Colleen Bawn* is founded. See Life by his brother (1843) and memoir in 1896 edition of *The Collegians*.

GRIFFITH, (1) **Arthur** (1872–1922), Irish politician, born in Dublin, was a compositor and a Rand miner before editing *The United Irishman*. He founded (1905) *Sinn Fein*, and was twice imprisoned, but signed the peace treaty with Great Britain, and was a moderate president of Dail Eireann (1922). See memoir by G. A. Lyons (1923) and Life by P. Colum (1960).

(2) **David Lewelyn Wark** (1875–1948), American film director, born in Kentucky, began with literary ambitions, but success in this field having eluded him, he tentatively entered the infant film industry, in which he saw the latent artistic possibilities. After much experiment with new techniques in photography and production he brought out in 1915–16 two masterpieces, *The Birth of a Nation* and *Intolerance*. His *Hearts of the World* (1918) incorporated war scenes actually filmed at the front. Other classic examples are *Broken Blossoms* (1919), and *Isn't Life Wonderful* (1924).

(3) **Sir Richard John, Bart.** (1784–1878), Irish geologist and civil engineer, born in Dublin, examined the Irish bogs, published his *Geological Map of Ireland* in 1855 and was consulted in all major Irish building projects, including National Gallery and Museum of Natural History, Dublin. Palmerston created him baronet in 1858.

GRIGNARD, François Auguste Victor, *gree-nyahr* (1871–1935), French organic chemist, born at Cherbourg, educated at Cherbourg and Lyons, became professor first at Nancy and then in 1914 at Lyons. He discovered the organo-magnesium compounds, which led to the introduction of the 'Grignard reaction', as a method of synthesis. He shared the Nobel prize with Sabatier in 1912.

GRILLO. See RISTORI, ADELAIDE.

GRILLPARZER, Franz (1791–1872), Austrian dramatic poet, born at Vienna, was in the imperial civil service from 1813 to 1856. He first attracted notice in 1817 by a tragedy, *Die Ahnfrau*, followed by *Sappho* (1818), *Das goldene Vlies* (1820), *Des Meeres und der Liebe Wellen* (1831), *Der Traum ein Leben* (1834), &c. He produced in lyric poetry much meritorious work; and one excellent prose novel, *Der arme Spielmann*. See *Briefe und Tagebücher* (1903); German studies by Siftenberger (1904), A. Sauer (1941) and N. Fürst (Vienna 1959); French by Ehrhard (1900); English by Pollak (1907) and D. Yates (1946).

GRIMALD, Nicholas (1519–62), English poet and playwright, was born of Genoese ancestry in Huntingdonshire, studied at both Cambridge and Oxford, and became Ridley's chaplain, but recanted under Queen Mary. He contributed 40 poems to *Songes and Sonettes* (1557), was the first, after Henry Howard, to write blank verse, and translated Virgil and Cicero. See Life by L. R. Merrill (1925).

GRIMALDI, *gri-mahl'dee*, a noble Genoese house, from 968 lords of the principality of Monaco.

GRIMALDI, (1) **Francesco Maria** (1618–63), Italian physicist, born at Bologna, became professor of Mathematics there. He discovered diffraction of light and researched into interference and prismatic dispersion. He was one of the first to postulate a wave theory of light.

(2) **Joseph** (1779–1837), the typical representative of the clown of the English pantomime, was born in London. He first appeared at Drury Lane when two years old, and in his third year he had his first engagement at Sadler's Wells Theatre, where he regularly performed (except for one season) until his retirement from the stage in 1828. See *Memoirs of Joseph Grimaldi*, edited by Charles Dickens (1838), and study by Findlater (1955).

GRIMBALD, St (*c.* 820–903), prior of a Flemish monastery near St Omer, when about 893 Alfred the Great invited him to England. He died abbot of the New Minster at Winchester.

GRIMM, (1) **Friedrich Melchior, Baron von** (1723–1807), Franco-German critic and journalist, born at Ratisbon; after studying at Leipzig, accompanied a nobleman to Paris, and became reader to the crownprince of Saxe-Gotha. He got acquainted with Rousseau in 1749, and through him with Diderot, Holbach and Madame d'Epinay. His connection with the Encyclopédistes, added to his own acquirements, opened up a brilliant career. He became secretary to the Duke of Orleans, and began to write for several German princes those famous literary bulletins which for nearly forty years gave the most trenchant criticism of all important French books. In 1776 he was made a baron by the Duke of Gotha, and appointed minister-plenipotentiary at the French court. At the Revolution he withdrew to Gotha, and afterwards to the court of Catharine II, whence he was sent in 1795 as Russian minister to Hamburg. He died at Gotha. See his *Correspondance* (1812–14), Sainte-Beuve *Études sur Grimm* (1854) and Scherer *Melchior Grimm* (Paris 1887).

(2) the brothers, **Jacob Ludwig Carl** (1785–1863) and **Wilhelm Carl** (1786–1859), German folklorists and philologists, were both born at Hanau in Hesse-Kassel and studied at Marburg. Jacob spent most of the year 1805 in Paris, became on his return a clerk in the war-office, and in 1808 librarian to Jerome Bonaparte, king of Westphalia. A work on the Meistersingers (1811) was followed in 1812 by the first volume of the famous *Kinder- und Hausmärchen*, collected by him and his brother Wilhelm (also now at Kassel)—a work which formed a foundation for the science of comparative folklore. The second volume followed in 1815; the third in 1822. In 1813–15 Grimm was secretary to the minister of the Elector of Hesse at Paris and at the Congress of Vienna. In 1829 the two removed to Göttingen, where Jacob became professor and librarian, and Wilhelm under-librarian (professor 1835). They were among the seven professors dismissed (1837) for protesting against the abolition of the constitution by the king of Hanover. In 1841 the brothers received professorships in Berlin, and were elected members of the Academy of Sciences. Jacob died September 20, 1863. His *Deutsche Grammatik* (1819; 2nd ed. entirely recast, 1822–40) is perhaps the greatest philological work of the age. His *Deutsche Rechtsalterthümer* (1828; 2nd ed. 1854) and *Deutsche Mythologie* (1835; 4th ed. by Meyer, 1875–78; Eng. trans. 1879–88) deal with German usages in the Middle Ages and the old Teutonic superstitions. Only less important is his *Geschichte der deutschen Sprache* (1848; 3rd ed. 1868) and his *Reinhart Fuchs* (1834). With his brother Wilhelm he edited many old German classics, and commenced the great *Deutsches Wörterbuch* (1854 ff.). He also formulated ' Grimm's Law ' of sound changes, an elaboration of earlier findings by the Danish scholar Rask, but an important contribution to the study of philology. Jakob's minor works (8 vols. 1867–86) contain an autobiography. Many collections of his letters have been printed. Wilhelm's chief independent work was *Deutsche Heldensage* (1829).

GRIMMELSHAUSEN, Hans Jacob Christoffel von (*c.* 1622–76), German novelist, born at Gelnhausen in Hesse-Kassel, served on the imperial side in the Thirty Years War, led a wandering life, but ultimately settled down at Renchen near Kehl, where he died Amtmann of the town. In later life he produced a series of remarkable novels. His best works are on the model of the Spanish picaresque romances. The sufferings of the German peasantry at the hands of the lawless troopers who overran the country have never been more powerfully pictured than in *Simplicissimus* (1669; trans. 1924). It was followed by *Trutz Simplex* (1669), *Springinsfeld* (1670), *Das wunderbarliche Vogelnest* (1672), &c. See Life by K. C. Hayens (1932).

GRIMOND, Jo(seph) (1913–), British Liberal politician, educated at Eton and Balliol Coll., Oxford, was called to the bar in 1937, and served during World War II with the Fife and Forfar Yeomanry. In 1945 he contested the Orkney and Shetland seat, which he ultimately won in 1950. He was secretary of the National Trust for Scotland (1947–49) and rector of Edinburgh University (1960–64). From 1956 to 1967 he was leader of the Liberal Party, during which time Liberal representation in Parliament was doubled.

GRIMTHORPE, Edmund Beckett Grimthorpe, 1st Baron (1816–1905), English lawyer, an authority on architecture and horology, and till 1881 a leader of the parliamentary bar, was born at Carlton Hall near Newark, and educated at Doncaster, Eton, and Trinity College, Cambridge. He succeeded his father as fifth baronet in 1874, in 1886 was raised to the peerage, and died in April 1905. Till 1872 he bore the name Beckett Denison. He designed Big Ben and restored St Albans Abbey. See *Life* by P. Ferriday (1957).

GRINDAL, Edmund (1519–83), Archbishop of Canterbury, was born at St Bees and educated at Cambridge, where he was in turn scholar, fellow and master of Pembroke Hall. A prebendary of Westminster under Edward VI, he lived abroad during Mary's reign, and there imbibed the doctrines of Geneva, returning to England on the accession of Elizabeth. In 1559 he became Bishop of London, in 1570 Archbishop of York, and in 1575 Archbishop of Canterbury. His Puritan sympathies soon estranged him from the court, and his refusal to put down 'prophesyings' or private meetings of the clergy for the study of Scripture led to his five years' sequestration in 1577. His few writings, with a Life, were edited for the Parker Society by W. Nicholson (1843).

GRINGORE, *grĩ-gor,* or **Gringoire,** *-gwahr* **Pierre** (*c.* 1475–1538), French poet and dramatist, born at Caen, while taking the chief rôles in a theatrical society was active in the production of pantomimic farces, and is one of the creators of the French political comedy. He abused the enemies of Louis XII and thus found cover for his freedoms against the vices of the nobility, the clergy and even the pope himself. In later life he was a herald to the Duke of Lorraine, and wrote religious poetry. His works, which include the famous *Mystère de Monseigneur Saint Loys* (*c.* 1524), have been edited by Héricault and Mont-aiglon (1858–77). Gringore figures in Victor Hugo's *Notre Dame* and in a play by Banville (adapted by Pollock and Besant). See French monographs by Picot (1878), Badel (1893), Oulmont (1911) and German study by W. Dittmann (1923).

GRINNELL, Henry (1799–1874), American shipping merchant, born at New Bedford, Mass., financed Arctic expeditions to find Franklin (q.v.), including Kane's (1853–55). Grinnell Land was named after him.

GRIS, Juan, *grees,* pseud. of **José Victoriano González** (1887–1927), Spanish painter, born in Madrid. He studied in Madrid, and went in 1906 to Paris, where he associated with Picasso and Matisse and became one of the most logical and consistent exponents of synthetic Cubism. In 1912 he exhibited with the Cubists in the Section d'Or exhibition in Paris, and in 1920 at the Salon des Indé-pendants. He settled at Boulogne and in 1923 designed the décor for three Diaghilev productions. He also worked as a book illustrator. In most of his paintings, the composition of the picture dictates the deliberate distortion and rhythmic rearrange-ment of the subjects, e.g., the *Still Life with Dice* (1922) in the Musée d'art moderne, Paris. See monographs by Kahnweiler (tr. Cooper, 1958) and Soby (1959).

GRISI, *gree'zee,* (1) **Carlotta** (1819–99), Italian ballet-dancer, cousin of (2) and (3), studied under Perrot, who became her husband, and was the original 'Giselle' in 1841 at Paris.

(2) **Giuditta** (1805–40), Italian mezzo-soprano, sister of (3), the original Romeo in Bellini's *I Capuleti ed i Montecchi,* retired on marrying Count Barni in 1833.

(3) **Giulia** (1811–69), Italian soprano, sister of (2), born in Milan, renowned for her rôles in Bellini's operas, especially *I Puritani,* which was written for her, and *Norma.*

GRISWOLD, Rufus Wilmot (1815–57), Ameri-can critic, born at Benson, Vermont, became Baptist preacher, then journalist and compiler of books in Philadelphia, Boston and New York. He was one of Poe's executors, and the Life he wrote for the edition of his works (1850) occasioned much hostile criticism. See his *Letters* (1898).

GRIVAS, George Theodorou, *gree'vas* (1898–), leader of 'EOKA', the Cypriot terrorist organization in the 1950s, was born in Cyprus. He commanded a Greek Army division in the Albanian campaign of 1940–41 and was leader of a secret organization called 'X' during the German occupation of Greece. In December 1945 he headed an extreme nationalist movement against the Communists. Some nine years later he became head of the underground campaign against British rule in Cyprus, calling himself 'Dighenis' after a legendary Greek hero. His secret diaries were found in 1956 when he had a price of £10,000 on his head. After the Cyprus settlement, February 1959, Grivas left Cyprus and acclaimed a national hero by the Greeks, was promoted general in the Greek army. In 1964 he returned to Cyprus and commanded the Cypriot National Guard till 1967. See study by W. Byford-Jones (1959) and his *Memoirs* (1964).

GROCK, stage name of **Adrien Wettach** (1880–1959), Swiss clown, world-famous for his virtuosity in both circus and theatre. See his *Ich lebe gern* (1930) and *Grock, King of Clowns* (1956, trans. Creighton).

GROCYN, William, *grõ'sin* (*c.* 1446–1519), English scholar and humanist, the first who publicly taught Greek at Oxford, was born at Colerne, Wiltshire, and from Winchester passed in 1465 to New College, Oxford. He studied in Italy (1488–91), acquiring a knowledge of Greek from the Greek exile Chalcondylas; and then settled again at Oxford, where Sir Thomas More was his pupil. Erasmus lived at Oxford in Grocyn's house, and speaks of him as his 'patronus et praeceptor'. In 1506 he became master of All Hallows' College near Maidstone.

GROFÉ, Ferde (1892–), American com-poser, born in New York. He is known for a number of orchestral suites—all named after American places—which are descriptive of the American scene. Grofé orchestrated the *Rhapsody in Blue* for Gershwin, and the modern-style orchestra based upon saxo-phones rather than strings is attributed to him.

GROLIER, Jean, *grol-yay* (1479–1565), French bibliophile, born at Lyons, was attached to the court of Francis I, went to Italy as intendant-general of the army, was long employed in diplomacy at Milan and Rome, and then became treasurer. It is his library, dispersed in 1675, that has made Grolier famous. He acquired choice copies of the best works, and had them magnificently bound, with the inscription, *Io. Grolierii et Amicorum.* Of his 3000 books, about 350 have come to light. See study by Le Roux de Lincy (1866).

GROMYKO, Andrei Andreevich (1909–), Russian statesman, born near Minsk of peasant stock, studied agriculture and economics and became a research scientist at the Soviet Academy of Sciences. In 1939 he joined the staff of the Russian embassy in Washington, becoming ambassador in 1943 and attending the famous ' big three ' conferences at Teheran, Yalta and Potsdam. In 1946 he was elected a deputy of the Supreme Soviet, and in the same year became deputy foreign minister and was made permanent delegate to the U.N. Security Council, achieving an unenviable reputation through his use of the power of veto no fewer than 25 times. For a few months (1952–53) he was ambassador to the United Kingdom. He succeeded Shepilov as foreign minister in 1957, pursuing relentlessly the ' cold war ' against the West, showing no relaxation of the austere and humourless demeanour for which he had become notorious in western diplomatic circles. Nevertheless a brilliant politician, he has been thrice recipient of the Order of Lenin.

GRONCHI, Giovanni, *gron'kee* (1887–), Italian politician, was born in Pisa. He played an important part in the organization of trade unionism in Italy, and was one of the founders of the Italian Popular Party. He held various political posts until 1923, when he retired from public life for the duration of Fascism. In 1942 he again became a political figure, and was president of the Chamber of Deputies from its foundation in 1948. He was president of Italy from 1955 until 1962.

GRONOVIUS, the Latinized form of Gronov, a family of scholars of German extraction, settled in Holland, whose principal members were:

(1) **Jacobus** (1645–1716), classical scholar, son of (2), born at Deventer, studied there and at Leyden, became professor at Pisa and in 1679 was appointed to his father's chair. His works include *Thesaurus Antiquitatum Graecorum* (1697–1702), and editions of Polybius, Herodotus , Cicero, and Ammianus Marcellinus.—His elder son, **Johann Friedrich** (1690–1760), became an eminent botanist, the younger son **Abraham** (1694–1775) librarian at Leyden university.

(2) **Johann Friedrich** (1611–71), classical scholar, father of (1), was born at Hamburg, became in 1643 professor at Deventer, and in 1658 at Leyden; he edited Livy, Statius, Tacitus, Phaedrus, Seneca, Sallust, Pliny and Plautus, and published many learned works, among them *De Sestertiis.*

(3) **Laurens Theodor** (1730–78), natural historian, grandson of (1) and son of Johann Friedrich, the botanist, was author of *Zoophylacium Gronovianum* (1781), &c.

GROOME, Francis Hindes (1851–1902), English writer, authority on gypsy language and folklore and a junior editor of the original edition of this work, was born at Monk Soham near Framlingham, and educated at Ipswich, Merton and Corpus Christi, Oxford, and at Göttingen. Having come to Edinburgh in 1876, he wrote for the *Encyclopaedia*

Britannica, and was sub-editor of *Chambers's Encyclopaedia* (1887–92). He published *In Gypsy Tents* (1880), *A Short Border History* (1887), *Two Suffolk Friends* (on his father and Edward FitzGerald, 1895), *Kriegspiel* (a novel, 1896), *Gypsy Folk Tales* (1899) and an edition of *Lavengro* (1900).

GROOTE, (1) **Geert de** (1340–84), Dutch religious reformer, the founder at Deventer about 1376 of the ' Brethren of the Common Life ' and the houses of Augustinian canons.

(2) **Huig van.** See GROTIUS.

GROPIUS, Walter (1883–1969), German-American architect, born in Berlin, studied at Munich, and after serving with distinction in World War I was appointed in 1918 director of the Grand Ducal group of schools of art in Weimar, which he amalgamated and reorganized to form the ' Bauhaus ', which aimed at a new functional interpretation of the applied arts. Gropius's revolutionary architectural methods and bold use of unusual building materials were condemned as ' architectural Socialism ' in Weimar, and the Bauhaus was transferred to Dessau in 1925, housed in a building designed by Gropius. When Hitler came to power, the Bauhaus became a Nazi training-school and Gropius worked in London (1934–37) in collaboration with Maxwell Fry designing factories and housing estates for the home counties, including a revolutionary adjunct to Christ Church College, Oxford, which was never built. From 1937 to 1952 he was professor of Architecture at Harvard. His major constructions include the pavilions for the Cologne Exhibition (1914), a factory at Alfeld (1914), theatre at Jena (1922), the *Bauhaus* at Dessau (1926), large housing estates in Stuttgart, Karlsruhe, Berlin, Aluminium City (1943) and the Harvard Graduate Center (1950). He also designed *Adler* car bodies (1929–33). His tremendous influence on modern architecture was recognized by the award of many honours, including the Royal Institute of British Architects' gold medal (1956). See his *New Architecture and the Bauhaus* (trans. 1937) and *Rebuilding Our Communities* (1946); also studies by Giedion (1954) and Fitch (1960).

GROS, Antoine Jean, Baron, *grō* (1771–1835), French historical painter, was born at Paris, studied under David and acquired celebrity by his great pictures of Napoleon's battles (1797–1811); *Charles V and Francis I* (1812); *Departure of Louis XVIII for Ghent* (1815); and *Embarkation of the Duchess of Angoulême* (1815). These works combine classicism and romanticism. Later Gros attempted a return to classicism, found his work ignored and drowned himself in the Seine. See Lives by Delestre (1867), Tripier le Franc (1880) and Dargenty (1887).

GROSE, Francis (1731–91), British antiquary, was born at Greenford, Middlesex, of Swiss extraction, squandered the family fortune, but applied himself to his *Antiquities of England and Wales* (1773–87). He toured Scotland and Ireland for antiquarian material but died suddenly in Dublin. Other works include *A Classical Dictionary of the Vulgar Tongue* (1785) and *Treatise on Ancient Armour and Weapons* (1785–89).

GROSS, (1) **Hans** (1847–1915), Austrian criminologist and lawyer, born at Graz, pioneer in the application of science to the detection of crime, was from 1905 professor of Criminal Law at Graz, where he established the first criminal museum. His *Handbuch für Untersuchungsrichter* (1893; Eng. tr. 1907) is a standard work.

(2) **Samuel David** (1805–84), American surgeon, born near Easton, Penn., became professor of Surgery in Jefferson College (1856–82), wrote several text-books.

GROSSE, Aristid (1905–), American chemist, born at Riga, educated at Berlin, went to the United States in 1930 and became research fellow at Columbia University. In 1927 he isolated protoactinium and in 1940 with others carried out successful slow neutron fission experiments with uranium-235.

GROSSETESTE, Robert (c. 1175–1253), Bishop of Lincoln, was born at Stradbroke in Suffolk, and educated at Lincoln, Oxford and Paris. He had for some years been the first teacher of theology in the Franciscan school at Oxford, and had held many preferments, when in 1235 he became Bishop of Lincoln. He undertook the reformation of abuses, embroiling himself with his own chapter and with Pope Innocent IV. The pope granted English benefices to ' rascal Romans ', who drew the revenues of their office, but seldom appeared in the country. Grosseteste set himself strongly against this, thereby incurring a temporary suspension from his bishopric and a continual menace of excommunication. In the last year of the bishop's life he refused the pope's request to promote his nephew, an Italian, to a canonry; and the pope is said—falsely, it seems—to have excommunicated him. Anyhow his clergy went on obeying him till his death at Buckden near Huntingdon. Pegge's catalogue of his works fills 25 closely-printed quarto pages, and exhibits ' treatises on sound, motion, heat, colour, form, angles, atmospheric pressure, poison, the rainbow, comets, light, the astrolabe, necromancy and witchcraft '. See Brewer's *Monumenta Franciscana* (1858), Luard's edition of his Latin letters (1862), Baur's of his philosophical works (1912), Stevenson's *Life* (1899), Powicke, *Robert Grosseteste and the Nicomachean Ethics* (1930) and studies ed. Callus (1955).

GROSSI, Tommaso, *gros'si* (1791–1853), Italian poet, born at Bellano on Lake Como. He studied law at Padua and practised at Milan. His loyalty was suspect by the Austrian authorities, and he gained no advancement in his profession. His first poem, *La Prineide* (1814), was a battle poem in the Milanese dialect. There followed several historical romances, and the epic poem for which he is best known, *I Lombardi alla prima crociata* (1826).

GROSSMITH, George (1847–1912), English comedian and entertainer, from 1877 to 1889 took leading parts in Gilbert and Sullivan's operas. With his brother, **Weedon** (1853–1919), he wrote *Diary of a Nobody* in *Punch* (1892). His son **George** (1874–1935) was a well-known musical-comedy actor (*Our Miss Gibbs, Sally, No, No, Nanette,* &c.), songwriter and manager of the Gaiety Theatre. See S. Naylor's *Gaiety and George Grossmith* (1913) and his son's *G.G.* (1933).

GROSVENOR, *grōv'nẽr,* a family said to have come to England with the Conqueror, and long settled at Eaton near Chester. It received a baronetcy (1622), and the titles of Baron Grosvenor (1761), Earl Grosvenor (1784), Marquess of Westminster (1831) and Duke of Westminster (1874).

GROSZ, George, *grōs* (1893–1959), American artist, born in Berlin. He studied at Dresden and Berlin, and was associated with the Berlin Dadaists in 1917 and 1918. While in Germany he produced a series of bitter, ironical drawings attacking German militarism and the middle classes. He fled to the U.S.A. in 1932 (becoming naturalized in 1938) and subsequently produced many oil-paintings of a symbolic nature. He returned to Berlin in 1959, where he died. See study by Baur (N.Y. 1954).

GROTE, George (1794–1871), English historian and politician, born at Clay Hill, Beckenham, Kent, was educated at Charterhouse, and in 1810 became a clerk in the bank founded in 1766 by his grandfather (a native of Bremen) in Threadneedle Street. He remained there thirty-two years, devoting all his leisure to literature and political studies; a ' philosophical Radical ', he threw himself ardently into the cause of progress and political freedom. In 1822 he conceived the idea of his *History of Greece* and in 1826 mercilessly dissected Mitford's history in the *Westminster Review*. Grote became head of the bank in 1830, and in 1832 was returned for the City of London. During his first session he brought forward a motion for the adoption of the ballot; it was lost, but Grote continued to advocate the measure until he retired from parliamentary life in 1841. In 1843 he also retired from the banking-house, and devoted himself exclusively to literature, mainly to the great *History of Greece* (1846–1856). Grote was elected vice-chancellor of London University (1862), foreign associate of the French Academy (1864), and president of University College London (1868). In 1865 he concluded an elaborate work on *Plato and the other Companions of Socrates,* which, with his (unfinished) *Aristotle,* was supplementary to the *History*. Grote was buried in Westminster Abbey. See his minor works (1873) and *Fragments on Ethical Subjects* (1876). His wife, *née* **Harriet Lewin** (1792–1878), wrote a *Memoir of Ary Scheffer* (1860), *Collected Papers in Prose and Verse* (1862), *The Personal Life of George Grote* (1873). See studies by Momigliano (1952) and M. L. Clarke (1962).

GROTEFEND, Georg Friedrich, *grō'tè-fent* (1775–1853), German epigraphist, was born at Münden in Hanover, and filled scholastic appointments at Göttingen, Frankfurt and Hanover. He wrote on Latin, Umbrian and Oscan philology, &c., but made himself famous by deciphering the cuneiform alphabet.

GROTH, Klaus (1819–99), German poet in Plattdeutsch, was born at Heide in Holstein, and in 1866 became professor of German Language and Literature at Kiel. His masterpiece, *Quickborn* (1852), is a series of poems dealing with life in Ditmarsh; but some of his work is in High German. See Life by Kröger (1904).

GROTIUS, Hugo, *grō'shi-oos,* or **Huig van Groot** (1583–1645), Dutch jurist and theologian, born at Delft, April 10, studied at Leyden, and accompanied an embassy to France. On his return he practised as a lawyer in the Hague; in 1613 he was appointed pensionary of Rotterdam. The religious disputes between the Remonstrants or Arminians and their opponents were now at their height. Grotius, like his patron the grand-pensionary Barneveldt, supported the Remonstrants. In 1618 both were arrested, tried, and condemned by the dominant party under Prince Maurice, Barneveldt to death, and Grotius to imprisonment for life. He escaped, however, with the aid of his wife, and found refuge in Paris in 1621, when Louis XIII for a time gave him a pension. In 1625 he published his great work on International Law, *De Jura Belli et Pacis* in which he appealed to ' natural Law ' and the social contract as a basis for rational principles on which a system of Laws could be formulated. His influence upon such political philosophers as Hobbes and Locke was profound. In 1634 he entered the Swedish service as ambassador at the French court. On his retirement in 1645 he proceeded to Stockholm, but, disliking court and climate, was on his way back to Holland, when he died at Rostock, August 29. Grotius also wrote Latin and Dutch verse. His tragedy, *Adamus Exsul* was one of Milton's sources. His best historical work is *Annales de Rebus Belgicis* (1657). He annotated the Bible (1641–46), and wrote the famous *De Veritate Religionis Christianae* (1627). See Lives by C. Butler (1826), W. S. M. Knight (1925) and A. P. d'Entreves, *Natural Law* (1951).

GROUCHY, Emmanuel, Marquis de, *grooshee* (1766–1847), French general, born at Paris, threw in his lot with the Revolution, and had his first taste of war during the Vendean revolt, was second to Hoche in the abortive expedition to Ireland, and greatly distinguished himself in Italy (1798). Later he fought at Hohenlinden, Eylau, Friedland, Wagram, and in the Russian campaign of 1812; and after Leipzig covered the retreat of the French. On Napoleon's escape from Elba, he destroyed the Bourbon opposition in the south of France, and helped to rout Blücher at Ligny. After Waterloo, as commander-in-chief of the broken armies of France, he led them skilfully back towards the capital; then, resigning, retired to the United States. He returned in 1819, and was reinstated as marshal in 1831. See his *Mémoires* (1873–74).

GROVE, (1) Sir George (1820–1900), English musicologist, biblical scholar and civil engineer, born at Clapham, was trained as a civil engineer, erected in the West Indies the first two cast-iron lighthouses, and assisted in the Britannia tubular bridge. He was secretary to the Society of Arts (1849–52), and then secretary and director of the Crystal Palace Company. He was editor of

Macmillan's Magazine, a major contributor to Smith's *Dictionary of the Bible,* and editor of the great *Dictionary of Music and Musicians* (1878–89; 5th ed. 1954). On a journey with Sir Arthur Sullivan to Vienna in 1867 he participated in the discovery of compositions by Schubert. His *Beethoven and his Nine Symphonies* (1896; new ed. 1956) long remained a standard work. He was knighted in 1883 on the opening of the Royal College of Music, of which he was director till 1895. See his Life by C. L. Graves (1903).

(2) **Sir William Robert** (1811–96), British judge and physicist, born at Swansea, studied at Oxford, was called to the bar, raised to the bench (1871), and knighted (1872), and in 1875–87 was a judge in the High Court of Justice. Ill-health made him retire from law for a while. In 1839 he invented a new type of cell named after him, studied electrolytic decomposition and demonstrated the dissociation of water. He was elected F.R.S. in 1840, awarded the Copley Medal in 1847 and was president of the British Association in 1866. See *Nature,* vol. 54 (1896).

GRUB, George (1812–92), Scottish church historian, author of an *Ecclesiastical History of Scotland* (1861) from the Episcopalian standpoint, was born at Aberdeen, and in 1862 became a law professor there.

GRUENBERG, Louis, *groon'bérg* (1884–1964), American composer of Russian birth who was taken to the United States at the age of two. A pupil of Busoni, Gruenberg worked as a concert pianist until 1919, and then retired to devote himself to composition. He wrote extensively for orchestra, chamber music combinations and voices, but is best known for his opera *The Emperor Jones,* based on Eugene O'Neill's play.

GRÜN, Anastasius. See AUERSPERG.

GRÜN, Hans. See BALDUNG.

GRUNDTVIG, Nikolai Frederik Severin (1783–1872), Danish poet, theologian and educationist, was born at Udby in Zealand, and graduated in theology at Copenhagen. An impossible love affair awakened his genius for poetry and historical studies. He first became known for his *Northern Mythology* (1808) and *Decline of the Heroic Age in the North* (1809). These were followed by the *Rhyme of Roeskilde* and the *Roeskilde Saga* (1814), and by a collection of patriotic songs (1815). Often doubtful of his faith, he became a curate in his father's parish. In 1815 he took his stand against the current rationalism, and became the head of a religious school which strove to free the church from state interference; but from 1825 to 1832, for an attack on a conspicuous rationalist, was suspended from preaching. In 1818 he had begun the translation of Snorri Sturluson and Saxo Grammaticus; in 1820 he published a Danish translation of *Beowulf.* During three study tours to England he formed the ideas which were to lead to the creation of the Folk High Schools, which have had a tremendous influence on Danish, especially rural, life and culture. The Folk High Schools later spread to the other Scandinavian countries. He was made titular ' bishop ' of Zealand in 1862. See Life by P. G. Lindhardt (London 1951), and

F. Skrubbeltrang, *The Danish Folk High Schools* (Copenhagen 1947).—His son, **Svend Hersleb** (1824–83) was professor of Scandinavian Philology at Copenhagen, and edited many old Danish folk tales (often translated) and ballads.

GRÜNEWALD, (1) **Isaak** (1889–1946), Swedish painter, born at Stockholm, a leader of Scandinavian Expressionism. His wife, **Sigrid Grünewald-Hjerten** (1885–1946), was also a painter.

(2) **Matthias**, real name **Mathis Nithardt**, otherwise **Gothardt** (? 1480–1528), German artist, architect, and engineer, probably born at Würzburg. Very little is known of his life, but he was court painter to the Archbishop of Mainz from 1508 to 1514 and to Cardinal Albrecht of Brandenburg from 1515 to 1525, and he designed waterworks for Magdeburg about 1526. In 1516 he completed the great Isenheim altarpiece (Colmar Museum), the nine paintings of which exhibit his rare, livid colours and his use of distortion to portray passion and suffering. Grünewald is the *Mathis der Maler* of Hindemith's opera. See studies by A. Burkhard (Cambridge, Mass. 1936), W. K. Zülch (1938) and N. Pevsner and M. Meier (1958).

GRYPHIUS, *grü'fee-oos*, (1) **Andreas** (1616–1664), the greatest German lyric poet and dramatist of the baroque period, was born and died at Glogau, Silesia. He travelled in Holland, France and Italy, studying medicine and astronomy, and returned to his native town, becoming syndicus in 1650. His early misfortunes led him to the 'all is vanity' theme of his lyrics, expressed in deep gloom, collected under the title *Sonn- und Feiertagssonette* (1639). His dramas mainly concern martyrdom and include *Leo Armenius* (1650), *Catharina von Georgien* (1657), *Papinianus* (1659), &c. But he also wrote the charming pastoral, *Die geliebte Dornrose* (1660), the comedies *Herr Peter Squentz* (1663), which resembles the Bottom scenes in Shakespeare's *A Midsummer Night's Dream*, and *Horribilicribrifax* (1663) satirizing the Thirty Years' war. He was indirectly influenced by Shakespeare and Vondel. See German studies by V. Mannheimer (1904) and F. W. Wentzhaff-Eggebert (1936), and Life by A. Strutz (1931).

(2) **Sebastian** (1493–1556), German printer, born at Reutlingen in Swabia, came in 1528 to Lyons, and there between 1528 and 1547 printed above 300 works, notable for their accuracy and clear type. Amongst the more noted are the fine Latin Bible of 1550 and Dolet's *Commentaria Linguae Latinae* (1536). Gryphius's sons, **Antoine** and **François**, were also famous French printers.

GUARDI, **Francesco**, *gwahr'di* (1712–93), Italian painter, born at Pinzolo. He was a pupil of Canaletto, and was noted for his views of Venice, full of sparkling colour, with an impressionist's eye for effects of light. His *View of the Church and Piazza of St. Marco* is in the National Gallery. See Life by G. Fiocco (1923).

GUARESCHI, **Giovanni**, *gwah-res'kee* (1908–1968), Italian journalist and writer, born at Parma, became editor of the Milan magazine *Bertoldo*. After the war, in which he was a prisoner, he returned to Milan and journalism, but it was *The Little World of Don Camillo* (1950) which brought him fame. These stories of the village priest and the Communist mayor with their broad humour and rich humanity have been translated into many languages, and have been followed by *Don Camillo and the Prodigal Son* (1952) and others. Guareschi illustrated his books with his own drawings. See *My Secret Diary* (tr. 1958).

GUARINI, **Giovanni Battista**, *gwah-ree'nee* (1538–1612), Italian poet, was born at Ferrara, and was entrusted by Duke Alfonso II with diplomatic missions to the pope, the emperor, Venice and Poland. His chief work was the famous pastoral play, *Il Pastor Fido* (1585), really an imitation of Tasso's *Aminta*. See monograph by Rossi (Turin 1886).

GUARINO DA VERONA (1370–1460), Italian humanist, born at Verona, went to Constantinople in 1388 to learn Greek under Chrysoloras; after his return (1410) taught Greek in Verona, Padua, Bologna and Ferrara; wrote Greek and Latin grammars; translated parts of Strabo and Plutarch; and helped to establish the text of Livy, Plautus, Catullus and Pliny. See Lives by Rosmini (1806) and Sabbadini (1891).

GUARNIERI, or **Guarneri**, *gwahrn-yay'ree*, name of a celebrated Italian family of violinmakers of Cremona, of whom the most important were **Andrea** (fl. 1650–95), his sons **Giuseppe** (fl. 1690–1730) and **Pietro** (fl. 1690–1725), and Giuseppe's son **Giuseppe** (fl. 1725–1745), the last especially famous, and commonly known as Giuseppe del Gesù because he signed his violins with I.H.S. after his name. See Family biographies by Pougin (1909) and W. H. Hill (1931).

GUBERNATIS, **Angelo de**, *goo-ber-nah'tis* (1840–1913), Italian orientalist, born at Turin, in 1863 became professor of Sanskrit at Florence. He resigned his chair that same year to follow the socialistic dreams of Bakunin, whose cousin he married, but soon had himself re-elected professor (1867); in 1891 he accepted a call to Rome. His works on zoological mythology, birth and funeral customs, Vedic mythology, plant lore and comparative mythology are marred by fantastic solar interpretation; he also published reminiscences, a French dictionary of contemporary authors, histories of Indian and of universal literature, &c.

GUDERIAN, **Heinz** (1888–1954), German general, a leading tank expert and exponent of the *Blitzkrieg* theory, created the panzer armies which overran Poland in 1939 and France in 1940. He was chief of general staff in 1944, and after the anti-Hitler plot in the same year was made commander on the eastern front. See his *Panzer Leader* (1952).

GUEDALLA, **Philip**, *gwe-dal'la* (1889–1944), English writer, born in London, educated at Rugby and Oxford, he was a barrister (1913–1923). Sometimes described as the most distinguished and certainly the most popular historian of his time, he was the author of *Second Empire* (1922), *Palmerston* (1926),

The Hundred Days (1934), *The Hundredth Year* (1940), *Two Marshals* (Bazaine and Pétain) (1943) and *Middle East* (1944).

GUERCINO, *gwer-chee'nō*, ' the squint-eyed ', properly **Gian-Francesco Barbieri** (1590–1666), Italian painter of the Bolognese school, was born at Cento. He painted the famous *Aurora* at the Villa Ludovisi for pope Gregory XV. In 1642 after the death of Guido Reni, he became the dominant painter of Bologna, combining in his work the liveliness and movement of the Carracci with a warmer, more Venetian colouring.

GUÉRIN, *gay-rĭ*, (1) **Charles** (1873–1907), French symbolist poet, born at Lunéville, travelled in Germany and Italy and periodically stayed in Paris. His work is confined to a few collections, including *Le Coeur solitaire* (1898) and *L'Éros funèbre* (1900). A later series *L'Homme intérieur* (1906) echoed his late conversion to the Catholic faith. See Life by de Bersaucourt (1912).

(2) **Eugénie de** (1805–48), French writer, sister of (3), to whom she was devoted, was born at the château of Le Cayla (Tarn), where she died. She is chiefly known for her *Journal* (1855), which is imbued with mysticism, but she also wrote poems and edited her brother's papers. See Lives by Zyromski (1921) and V. Giraud (1928), and M. Arnold *Essays in Criticism* (1865).

(3) **Georges Maurice de** (1810–39), French poet, brother of (2), born at the château of Le Cayla (Tarn), entered the community of Lamennais at La Chesnaye in Brittany. He followed his master in his estrangement from Rome, and, going like him to Paris (1833) to try journalism, became a teacher at the Collège Stanislas. He married a rich Creole lady in November 1838, and died of consumption. His *Reliquiae*, including the *Centaur* (a kind of prose poem), letters and poems, were published in 1860. See Lives by Zyromski (1921) and Decahors (1932).

(4) **Pierre Narcisse, Baron** (1774–1833), historical painter, born in Paris, and died in Rome, where he had been director of the French Academy of Painting (1822–29). A skilful painter of classical subjects but inclined to melodrama, he counted among his pupils Géricault and Delacroix.

GUERRA. See JUNQEIRO.

GUERRAZZI, Francesco Domenico, *gwayr-raht'zee* (1804–73), Italian writer and politician, born at Leghorn, had won a great reputation by his patriotic and political fictions, when on the Grand-duke of Tuscany's flight (1849) he was proclaimed dictator in spite of his disinclination for a republic. On the duke's restoration he was condemned to the galleys, but ultimately permitted to select Corsica as his place of banishment. Restored to liberty by later events, he sat in the parliament of Turin (1862–65). His chief works of fiction are *La Battaglia di Benevento* (1827), *L'Assedio di Firenze* (1836), *Isabella Orsini* (1844), &c. See Life by P. Miniati (1927).

GUESCLIN, Bertrand du, *gay-klĭ* (*c.* 1320–80), constable of France, was born near Dinan, and early took part in the contests for the dukedom of Brittany. After King John's capture at Poitiers in 1356, du Guesclin fought splendidly against the English, his

military skill being especially shown at Rennes (1356) and Dinan (1357); he took Melun (1359) and other fortified towns, and freed the Seine from the English. He won the battle of Cocherel against Charles the Bad of Navarre, but was defeated and taken prisoner by the English at Auray, and ransomed only for 100,000 livres. He next supported Henry of Trastamare against Pedro the Cruel, king of Castile, but was defeated and taken prisoner by the Black Prince (1367). Again ransomed, du Guesclin in 1369 defeated and captured Pedro, and placed the crown of Castile on the head of Henry of Trastamare; but was recalled by Charles V of France, then hard pressed by the English, to be made Constable of France. In 1370 he opened his campaigns against the English, and soon nearly all their possessions were in the hands of the French. He died on July 13 during the siege of Châteauneuf de Randon. See Lives by Luce (1883), Postel, (1893) and Stoddard (1897).

GUEST, (1) Lady Charlotte. See SCHREIBER.

(2) **Edwin** (1800–80), English historian, studied at Caius College, Cambridge, and in 1852 became master. His *History of English Rhythms* (1838) is a work of great erudition.

GUETTARD, Jean Étienne, *gay-tahr* (1715–1786), French geologist, born at Étampes, keeper of the natural history collections of the Duke of Orleans, studied ' weathering ' and prepared the first geological map.

GUEVARA, *gay-vah'ra*, (1) **Antonio de** (1490–1545), Spanish writer, Bishop of Mondoñedo and confessor of Charles V, employed in his book on Marcus Aurelius the exalted style which anticipated the euphuism of Lyly (q.v.). His ' Familiar Letters ' were also very popular in an English version.

(2) **Luiz Vélez de** (1570–1644), Spanish dramatist, wrote many plays after the style of Lope de Vega. His novel *El Diablo cojuelo* (1641) was the model of Le Sage (q.v.).

(3) **Ernesto (Che)** (1928–67), Argentinian-born Communist revolutionary leader, graduated in medicine (1953), played an important part in the Cuban revolution (1959) and afterwards held government posts under Castro. He left Cuba in 1965 to become a guerilla leader in S. America, and was captured and executed by government troops in Bolivia in October 1967. See his *Reminiscences of the Cuban Revolutionary War* (1968), and his *Bolivian Diary*, ed. by D. James (1968).

GUICCIARDINI, Francesco, *gwit-chahr-dee' nee* (1483–1540), Italian historian, born at Florence, became professor of Law there, and also practised as an advocate; but his real field was diplomacy. His apprenticeship served in Spain (1512–14), he became papal governor of Modena and Reggio (1515), Parma (1521), the Romagna (1523) and Bologna (1531). Retiring from the papal service in 1534, he secured the election of Cosimo de' Medici as Duke of Florence; but, disappointed of the post of mayor of the palace, withdrew to Arcetri, and busied himself with his great *Storia d'Italia*, a dispassionate analytical history of Italy from 1494 to 1532. See works by Malagoli (1939) and Ridolfi (1939).

GUICCIOLI, Teresa Gamba, Countess, *gwit' chō-lee* (1801–73), Byron's mistress (1819–23), daughter of a Ravenna nobleman, in 1817 married Count Guiccioli, aged sixty, and in 1851 the French Marquis de Boissy (1798–1866). See her *Lord Byron jugé par les témoins de sa vie* (Eng. trans. 1869).

GUIDI, *gwee'dee,* (1) **Carlo Alessandro, Count** (1650–1712), Italian poet, born at Pavia, a founder of the academy called L'Arcadia, wrote a large number of florid but uninspired lyrics. See *Life* by Rizzio (1928).

(2) **Tommaso.** See MASACCIO.

GUIDO D'AREZZO or Guido Aretino (*c.* 990–1050), Benedictine monk and musical theorist, was a monk at Pomposa near Ferrara, and he is supposed to have died prior of the Camaldolite monastery of Avellana. He contributed much to musical science; the invention of the staff is ascribed to him; and he seems to have been the first to adopt in naming the notes of the scale the initial syllables of the hemistichs of a hymn in honour of St John the Baptist (*ut, re, mi,* &c.). See monographs by Angeloni (1811), Kiesewetter (1844) and Falchi (1882).

GUIGNES, Joseph de, *geen'y'* (1721–1800), French orientalist, was born at Pontoise, and died in Paris. His great work is *L'Histoire générale des Huns, Turcs, et Mogols* (1756–1758). His son, **Chrétien Louis Joseph** (1759–1845), published a Chinese dictionary (1813).

GUILBERT, Yvette (*c.* 1869–1944), French comedienne, born in Paris, was a penniless seamstress before she turned to acting and won fame for her songs and sketches, sometimes satirical, sometimes sentimental, sometimes provocative, of all facets of Parisian life. After 1890 she became known for her revivals of old French ballads. She visited America and founded a school of acting in New York. She wrote two novels. See her *La Chanson de ma vie* (1919).

GUILLAUME, *gee-yōm,* (1) **Charles Édouard** (1861–1938), Swiss physicist, born at Fleurier, Switzerland, educated at Neuchâtel, became director of the Bureau of International Weights and Measures (Sèvres) and prepared a nickel-steel alloy ' Invar ' which does not expand and can therefore be used in precision instruments and standard measures. He was awarded the Nobel prize in 1920.

(2) **Eugène** (1822–1905), French sculptor, born at Montbard, Côte d'Or, executed busts of Napoleon, Anacreon and the Gracchi brothers.

GUILLAUME DE MACHAUT, *gee-yōm dè ma-shō* (*c.* 1300–77), French poet and musician, born at Machault, Champagne. He worked successively under the patronage of John of Luxemburg and John II of France. *Le Livre du voir-dit,* written in the form of letters from the elderly poet to a girl, influenced Chaucer. He was one of the creators of the harmonic art, and wrote masses, songs, ballades and organ music. See study by W. Eichelberg (Frankfurt 1935).

GUILLIM, or Gwillim, John (1565–1621), English antiquary, born at Hereford, studied at Brasenose, Oxford, was an official of the College of Arms in London, and in 1610 published *A Display of Heraldrie.*

GUILLOTIN, Joseph Ignace, *gee-yō-tī* (1738–1814), French physician and revolutionary, born at Saintes, proposed to the Constituent Assembly the use of a decapitating instrument, which was adopted in 1791 and was named after him though similar apparatus had been used earlier in Scotland, Germany and Italy. See A. Kershaw, *A History of the Guillotine* (1958).

GUIMERÁ, Ángel, *gee-may-rah'* (1849–1924), Catalan poet and dramatist, born in Santa Cruz, Tenerife. His work falls into three periods, of which the first and third—historical plays, for the most part—show the influence of the French romantics. His middle period owes its preoccupation with contemporary life to Ibsen. He is regarded as the greatest Catalan dramatist. His most famous play is *Terra Baixa* (1896), on which D'Albert based his opera *Tiefland.*

GUINNESS, (1) **Sir Alec** (1914–), English actor, born in London. After training for the stage while he worked as an advertising copywriter he joined the Old Vic company in 1936; he rejoined the company in 1946 after serving in the Royal Navy throughout World War II. His extraordinary versatility is seen in parts ranging from the most controversial of Hamlets to outstanding success in films both comic and serious. In 1958 he was awarded an Oscar for his part in the film *The Bridge on the River Kwai,* and the following year he was knighted. See study by K. Tynan (1953).

(2) **Sir Benjamin Lee, 1st Bart.** (1798–1868), Irish brewer, was third son of Arthur Guiness, founder of the brewery established in Dublin in 1759. Under Sir Benjamin the brand of stout became famous and the business grew into the largest of its kind in the world. It became a limited liability company in 1886. First lord mayor of Dublin in 1851 and M.P. for it in 1865–68, he restored St Patrick's cathedral in 1860–65, and was created a baronet in 1867.

(3) **Edward Cecil, 1st Earl of Iveagh** (1847–1927), third son of (2), spent much of his huge fortune on philanthropic projects, and gave the mansion of Ken Wood at Highgate, with its collection of paintings, to the nation.

GUISCARD, Robert, *gees-kahr* (*c.* 1015–85), Norman warrior, Duke of Apulia and Calabria, the sixth of the twelve sons of Tancred de Hauteville, was born near Coutances in Normandy. He won great renown in South Italy as a soldier, captured Reggio and Cosenza (1060), and conquered Calabria. As the pope's champion he, along with his younger brother Roger, waged incessant war against Greeks and Saracens in South Italy and Sicily; later he fought against the Byzantine emperor, Alexius Comnenus, gaining a great victory over him at Durazzo (1081). Marching towards Constantinople, he learned that the Emperor Henry IV had invaded Italy; he hastened back, compelled Henry to retreat, and liberated the pope, who was besieged in the castle of St Angelo (1084). Then, having returned to Epirus, he repeatedly defeated the Greeks, and was advancing a second time to Constantinople when he died suddenly in Cephalonia, July 17. See works on the Normans in Europe by C. H. Haskins (1916).

GUISE, *geez*, name of a ducal family of Lorraine, taken from the town of that name. The direct line became extinct on the death (1675) of François Joseph, the 7th Duke. See Forneron, *Les Ducs de Guise* (1893). Its noteworthy members were:

(1) **Charles** (1525–74), Archbishop of Reims, created cardinal of Guise in 1547, brother of (3), with whom he became all-powerful in the reign of Francis II, introduced the Inquisition into France and exerted a great influence at the Council of Trent.

(2) **Claude of Lorraine, 1st Duke** (1496–1550), fifth son of René II, Duke of Lorraine, and father of (1), (3) and (6), was born at the château of Condé, fought at Marignano in 1515, but after that campaign remained at home to defend France against the English and Germans (1522–23). For suppressing the peasant revolt in Lorraine (1527) Francis created him Duke of Guise.

(3) **Francis, 2nd Duke** (1519–63), French soldier and statesman, son of (2), having in 1552–53 held Metz against Charles V of Germany, added to his reputation at Renti (1554), and in 1556 commanded the expedition against Naples. Recalled in 1557 to defend the northern frontier against the English, he took Calais (1558) and other towns, and brought about the treaty of Câteau Cambrésis (1559). He and his brother (1), shared the chief power in the state during the reign of Francis II. Heading the Roman Catholic party, they sternly repressed Protestantism. Guise and Montmorency won a victory over the Huguenots at Dreux (1562), and Guise was besieging Orleans when he was assassinated by a Huguenot. His memoirs, written by himself, have much historic interest. See Lives by Brisset (1840) and Cauvin (1878).

(4) **Henry, 3rd Duke,** ' Le Balafré ' (1550–1588), French soldier and statesman, grandfather of (5), fought fiercely against the Protestants at Jarnac and Moncontour (1569), and forced Coligny to raise the siege of Poitiers. He was one of the contrivers of the massacre of St Bartholomew (1572), and was the head of the Catholic League. He was, however, ambitious to succeed to the throne of France, when Henry III procured his assassination at Blois. See Lives by Rénauld (1879) and Cauvin (1881).

(5) **Henry, 5th Duke** (1614–64), at fifteen became Archbishop of Reims, but in 1640 succeeded to the dukedom. Having joined the league against Richelieu, he was condemned to death, but fled to Flanders. He put himself at the head of Masaniello's revolt in Naples as the representative of the Anjou family, but was taken by the Spanish (1647) and carried to Madrid, where he remained five years. After another attempt to win Naples (1654) he settled at Paris. See his *Mémoires* (1669).

(6) **Mary of Lorraine** (1515–60), daughter of (2), in 1534 married Louis of Orleans, Duke of Longueville, and in 1538 James V of Scotland, at whose death (1542) she was left with one child, Mary, Queen of Scots. During the troubled years that followed, the queen mother acted with wisdom and moderation; but after her accession to the regency in 1554 she allowed the Guises so much influence that the Protestant nobles raised a rebellion (1559), which continued to her death in Edinburgh Castle.

GUITRY, **Sacha,** *gee-tree* (1885–1957), French actor and dramatist, born in St Petersburg. He wrote nearly a hundred plays, mostly light comedies, many of which have been successfully performed in English. He was the son of the actor-manager Lucien Guitry (1860–1925), and first appeared on the stage in Russia with his father's company. His first appearance in Paris was in 1902, still under his father's management. He came to London in 1920 with *Nono,* a play written when he was sixteen. It starred the second of his five wives, the enchanting Yvonne Printemps. He also wrote and directed several delightful films, including *Le Roman d'un tricheur* and *Les Perles de la couronne.*

GUIZOT, **François Pierre Guillaume,** *gee-zō* (1787–1874), French historian and statesman, was born at Nîmes, October 4, of Huguenot stock. In 1805 he went to Paris to study law, but soon drifted into literature, and in 1812 became professor of Modern History at the Sorbonne. After the fall of Napoleon he held various official posts, but as a Liberal was deprived of his appointments in 1821, and in 1825 interdicted from lecturing. With some friends he then published *Mémoires relatifs à l'histoire de France jusqu'au 13e siècle* (31 vols.) and *Mémoires relatifs à la Révolution d'Angleterre* (25 vols.), and edited translations of Shakespeare and Hallam. Restored to his chair in 1828, he began his famous lectures, later published, on the history of civilization. Elected to the Chamber (1830), he became minister first of the Interior, and then of Public Instruction, establishing a system of primary education. In 1840 he came to London as ambassador, but was recalled to replace Thiers as the king's chief adviser. To checkmate Palmerston he plunged into the indefensible ' Spanish Marriages ' and relapsed into reactionary methods of government which were partly responsible for the fall of Louis-Philippe, with whom he escaped to London. In November 1849 he returned to Paris and made efforts to rally the monarchists, but after the *coup d'état* of 1851 gave himself up entirely to his historical publications. See his Memoirs; also *Guizot in Private Life* by his daughter Mme de Witt (tr. 1880), and study by Pouthas (1923).

GULBENKIAN, **Calouste Sarkis** (1869–1955), British financier, industrialist, and diplomat, was born at Scutari, of Ottoman-Turkish nationality. In 1888 he entered his father's oil business in Baku. After becoming a naturalized British subject in 1902 he brought the Russians into the new Royal Dutch-Shell merger and in 1907 he arranged for the latter to break into the American market, thus laying the foundations of an important British dollar asset. In 1916 he organized French entry into the Turkish Petroleum Company, instead of the Germans, and between 1921 and 1928 he did the same for the Americans. In 1940 in 'Vichy' France the 5 per cent. Iraq Petroleum Company interest was confiscated by Britain, and he was declared an 'Enemy under the Act', whereupon he assumed Persian citizenship. From 1948 to 1954 he negotiated oil concessions between America and Saudi Arabia. He left $70,000,000 and vast art collections to finance an international Gulbenkian Foundation. See Life by Lodwick and Young (1958), and *Mr Five Per Cent* by Hewins (1957). His son **Nubar Sarkis** (1896–1972), philanthropist and *bon vivant*, was commercial attaché to the Iranian embassy, 1926–51 and 1956–65, and until his father's death worked with him. See his Autobiography (1965).

GULDBERG, Cato Maximilian (1836–1902), Norwegian chemist and mathematician, born at Christiania, where he became professor of Applied Mathematics and formulated with his brother-in-law, Peter Waage, the chemical law of mass action (1864) governing the speed of reaction and the relative concentrations of the reactants.

GULLSTRAND, Allvar (1862–1930), Swedish ophthalmologist, born at Landskrona, became professor at Uppsala and was awarded the Nobel prize in 1911 for his researches into the forming of optical images by the eye.

GULLY, John (1783–1863), English sportsman, born at Wick near Bristol, was butcher, prizefighter, publican, turfite, M.P. for Pontefract (1832–37) and colliery proprietor, and father of twenty-four children.

GUMILEV, Nikolai Stepanovich, *goo-meel'yéf* (1886–1921), Russian poet, a leader of the Acmeist school which revolted against Symbolism. His exotic and vivid poems include *The Quiver* (1915) with some fine verses of war and adventure, and *The Pyre* and *The Pillar of Fire*, which contain his best pieces. He also wrote criticism and translated French and English poetry. He was shot as a counter-revolutionary. His wife was the poetess Akhmatova (q.v.).

GUNDOLF, Friedrich, properly **Gundelfinger**, *goon'dolf* (1880–1931), German scholar and literary critic, born at Darmstadt. He was a brilliant disciple of Stefan George, and his studies, based on George's theories of history and art, combined with his own sensitive and imaginative style, had a marked influence on literature and literary criticism. His works include *Shakespeare und der deutsche Geist* (1911), the biographies *Goethe* (1916) and *George* (1920), and a translation of Shakespeare (1908–14). He was from 1920 professor at Heidelberg. See the study by O. Heuschele (1947).

GUNDULF (1024–1108), Bishop of Rochester from 1077, was born in Normandy, was a monk at Bec and Caen, and in 1070 followed Lanfranc to England. He built the Tower of London, rebuilt Rochester cathedral and founded St Bartholomew's hospital at Chatham. The great keep of Rochester castle is also attributed to him.

GUNGL, Josef (1810–89), Hungarian composer, known for his waltzes and light music, was born at Zsambek, made many concert tours, and died at Weimar.

GUNN, (1) Sir James (1893–1965), Scottish painter, known for his portraits of George VI,

Chesterton, Belloc and other celebrities. He was president of the Royal Society of Portrait Painters from 1953, A.R.A. 1953, R.A. 1961, and received a knighthood in 1963.

(2) **Neil Miller** (1891–1973), Scottish novelist, born at Dunbeath, Caithness, was in the Civil Service until 1937, latterly as an officer of Customs and Excise. His first novel, *Grey Coast* (1926), was immediately acclaimed, and was followed by the even more successful *Morning Tide* (1931). Other works include *Highland River* (1937, Tait Black Memorial Prize) and *The Silver Darlings* (1951). Gunn was at his best when describing the ordinary life and background of a Highland fishing or crofting community, and when interpreting in simple prose the complex character of the Celt.

(3) **Thom(son) William** (1929–), English poet, attended Trinity Coll., Cambridge, went to California in 1954 and became assistant professor of English at California Univ. One of the best known of the younger British poets, he has achieved international recognition, and won many awards, with such collections as *Fighting Terms* (1955), *The Sense of Movement* (1957), *My Sad Captains* (1961) and *Touch* (1967).

GUNNING, name of two beautiful Irish sisters, born near St Ives, Hunts, and came up to London in 1751:

(1) **Elizabeth** (1734–90), married the Duke of Hamilton in 1752 and, on his death in 1759, the future Duke of Argyll. She was created Baroness Hamilton in 1770. See Bleachley *The Beautiful Duchess* (1927).

(2) **Maria** (1733–60), married the Earl of Coventry in 1752 and was so popular that she was mobbed in Hyde Park.

GUNTER, Edmund (1581–1626), English mathematician and astronomer, born in Herts, was educated at Westminster and Christ Church, Oxford. He got a Southwark living in 1615, but in 1619 became professor of Astronomy in Gresham College, London. To him are due the invention of the surveying chain, a quadrant and a scale, and the first observation of the variation of the compass, as well as the introduction of the trigonometrical terms 'cosine' and 'cotangent'.

GUNTHER, John (1901–70), American author and journalist, born in Chicago, was a foreign correspondent for the *Chicago Daily News* and for N.B.C. He established his reputation with the bestselling *Inside Europe* (1939), followed by a series of similar works, in which sometimes much, sometimes little, firsthand material is blended with documentary information to present penetrating social and political studies. Other books include *Death Be Not Proud* (1949), *A Fragment of Autobiography* (1962), &c.

GÜNTHER, (1) Albert Charles Lewis Gotthilf (1830–1914), British zoologist, was born at Esslingen, studied at Tübingen, Berlin, and Bonn, and from 1857 was on the British Museum Staff, became a naturalized Briton in 1862 and was appointed keeper in 1985. He did work on the lower vertebrates.

(2) **Johann Christian** (1695–1723), German poet, born at Strugan in Silesia, wrote love lyrics notable for their sensitivity, and their lack of affection.

GURNEY, (1) Sir Goldsworthy (1793–1875), English inventor, born at Treator near Padstow, devised the Drummond Light, and also the steam-jet blast steam carriage which in 1829 ran from London to Bath and back at the rate of 15 miles an hour, &c. He was knighted in 1863.

(2) Joseph John (1788–1847), English philanthropist, a Quaker banker of Norwich, born at Earlham Hall, in 1818 became a minister of the Society, devoted himself to and wrote about the prison reforms of his sister, Mrs Elizabeth Fry (q.v.).

GUSTAVUS, the name of six kings of Sweden:

Gustavus I, or Gustavus Vasa (1496–1560), was born into the Swedish nobility at Lindholmen in Upland, May 12, 1496, and in 1518, during the patriotic struggle with Christian II (q.v.) of Denmark, was carried off to Denmark as a hostage. After a year he escaped to Lübeck, thence to Sweden, where he strove in vain to rouse up a spirit of resistance against the Danes. He sought refuge in Dalecarlia, wandered for months with a price set on his head, and worked on farms and in mines. At last the infamous ' Blood-bath ' of Stockholm (1520) roused the Swedes, and Gustavus soon had an army large enough to attack the enemy. The capture of Stockholm in 1523 drove the Danes from Sweden, thus ending the great Scandinavian union which had existed for 126 years, and Gustavus I was elected king. He found the whole country demoralized, but after forty years' rule he left Sweden a peaceful and civilized realm, with a full exchequer and a well-organized army. He promoted trade, fostered schools, and made roads, bridges and canals. He greatly promoted Lutheranism, and was hardly fair to the Catholic clergy. Missions were sent to the Lapps, and a Finnish Bible was printed for the Finns. He died September 29, and was succeeded by his eldest son, Eric. See works by Forssell (Stockholm 1869–75), Alberg (London 1882) and Watson (1889).

Gustavus II, or Gustavus Adolphus (1594–1632), was born at Stockholm, December 9, the son of Charles IX, and grandson of (I). When he came to the throne in 1611 he found the country involved in war and disorder; but he conciliated the nobility, reorganized the government, raised men and money, and soon recovered his Baltic provinces from Denmark. His war with Russia was ended in 1617 by the treaty of Stolbova, by which Sweden received a large part of Finland and Livonia. In 1618 he visited Berlin, and in 1620 married the daughter of the Elector of Brandenburg. The old dispute with Poland was terminated in 1629 by a six years' truce, which left Gustavus master of Pillau and Memel. This peace permitted him to turn to Germany; and leaving the government to his chancellor Oxenstiern, he crossed to Pomerania in 1630 with 15,000 men to head the Protestants of Germany in their struggle against the Catholic League and the empire. The Swedes drove the imperialists from Pomerania, and took Stettin; whilst Richelieu promised Gustavus a subsidy. The Emperor Ferdinand had dismissed the imperious

Wallenstein; but while the Swedes were besieging Spandau and Küstrin, Magdeburg was taken by Tilly with terrible atrocities. Soon after its fall Gustavus, now regarded as the champion of Protestant Germany, inflicted a severe defeat on Tilly at Breitenfeld, and took the Palatinate and Mainz; in April 1632 the Swedes gained another great victory, and Tilly was carried to Ingolstadt to die. Munich was taken next and the road to Vienna lay open, had not the emperor recalled Wallenstein, who with 60,000 men entrenched himself near Nuremberg. After withstanding a desperate assault of the Swedes Wallenstein was obliged to retire into Thuringia; but on November 6, 1632, the two armies came finally face to face at Lützen near Leipzig. The Swedes soon broke the imperial lines, but Wallenstein drove back the Swedish centre. Gustavus hurried to the rescue, got separated from his troops, and riding almost alone into a squadron of Croats, received more than one fatal shot, and fell. The Swedes, burning to revenge their king, fought furiously, and gained a hard-won victory. See Lives by Trench (new ed. 1886), Fletcher (1890), MacMunn (1930), Roberts, vol. I (1953), vol. II (1958).

Gustavus III (1746–92), succeeded his father, Adolphus Frederick, in 1771. He set himself to break the power of the oligarchy of nobles by means of a feigned revolt, and encouraged agriculture, commerce and science. But he had an inordinate love for things French, and, in his endeavour to imitate the splendour of Versailles, became financially embarrassed and had to increase taxation, thus alienating his people. The nobles tried to regain their power; and Gustavus's scheme to employ the forces of Sweden on behalf of Louis XVI of France against the Revolution led to his own assassination by Ankarström (q.v.), an emissary of the oligarchical party. See French works by Geffroy (1867) and Nervo (1876), and an English one by Bain (1895).

Gustavus IV (1778–1837), succeeded his father, Gustavus III, in 1792. He was self-willed, autocratic, tactless, and hatred of Napoleon was the ruling principle of his life. He offended Russia, lost Stralsund and Rügen to the French and Finland to the Russians (1807–08) made an unsuccessful attack upon Norway, and finally, after insulting the English, was in 1809 dethroned, his uncle, the Duke of Södermanland, succeeding as Charles XIII. He died, an exile, at St Gall.

Gustavus V (1858–1950), father of Gustavus VI and uncle of Count Folke Bernadotte (q.v.), succeeded his father, Oscar II, in 1907, and, a popular sovereign, kept Sweden neutral through both World Wars. His reign was the longest in Swedish history.

Gustavus VI (1882–1973), son of Gustavus V, a distinguished scholar and authority on Chinese art and archaeology, organized several archaeological excavations and was called in as an expert for the exhibition of Chinese art in London in 1936. In 1905 he married Princess Margaret of Connaught (d. 1920) and in 1925 Lady Louisa Mountbatten (d. 1966), sister of Earl Mountbatten of Burma. She thus became the first British-born queen in Swedish history. Gustavus succeeded to the throne in 1950. He was succeeded by his grandson, Crown Prince Carl Gustavus (b. 1946).

GUTENBERG, Johannes Gensfleisch, *goot'*, (1400–68), German printer, regarded as the inventor of printing; born at Mainz, son of a patrician, Friele Gensfleisch or Gutenberg. Between 1430–1444 he is found in Strasbourg, where he was probably a goldsmith and here (by 1439) he may have begun printing. In Mainz again by 1448 he entered into partnership *c.* 1450 with Johannes Fust who financed a printing press. This partnership ended in 1455, Fust securing a verdict against his partner for the moneys advanced, and carrying on the concern with the assistance of Peter Schöffer; while Gutenberg, aided by Konrad Humery, set up another printing press. Probably rudimentary printing, whether invented by Coster (q.v.) or not, was practised before Gutenberg's development of the art. Gutenberg is credited with the Fragment of the Last Judgment (*c.* 1445), editions of Donatus' Latin school grammar, and the 42-line Bible (*c.* 1456). See studies by A. Ruppel (1939) and D. C. McMurtrie (1941).

GUTHLAC, St (*c.* 673–714), English monk at Repton in 697, and a hermit at Crowland Abbey in 699 where he lived a life of severe asceticism.

GUTHRIE, (1) Sir James (1859–1930), Scottish painter, born at Greenock, a follower of the Glasgow School, turned from genre to portraiture, of which he became a notable exponent. He was made R.S.A. in 1892, was P.R.S.A. in 1902–19, and was knighted in 1903.

(2) **Samuel** (1782–1848), American chemist, born at Brimfield, Mass., was one of the discoverers in 1831 of chloroform, invented percussion priming powder and devised a process of rapid conversion of potato starch into sugar.

(3) **Thomas** (1803–73), Scottish divine and social reformer, born at Brechin, studied at Edinburgh, and was minister at Arbirlot and in Edinburgh. In 1843 he helped to found the Free Church, and till 1864 ministered to Free St John's, Edinburgh. In eleven months (1845–46) he raised £116,000 for providing Free Church manses; in 1847 he published his first *Plea for Ragged Schools*. He also used his singular gifts of oratory in the cause of temperance and other social reforms, and in favour of compulsory education. First editor of the *Sunday Magazine* from 1864, he died at St Leonards. See *Autobiography*, edited by his sons (1874–75) and Life by Smeaton (1900).

(4) **Thomas Anstey**. See ANSTEY (2).

(5) **Sir William Tyrone** (1900–71), English theatrical producer, born at Tunbridge Wells, educated at Wellington College and Oxford, served with the B.B.C. but made his reputation as a producer at the Westminster theatre (1930–1931). He was administrator of the Old Vic and Sadler's Wells (1939–45), director of the former (1950–51) and produced extensively abroad and at the Edinburgh Festival. He was knighted in 1961, and founded the Tyrone Guthrie Theatre in Minneapolis in 1963. See his *A Life in the Theatre* (1960).

GUTHRUM, *gooTH-room* (d. 890), Danish king of East Anglia who from 871 fought against Ethelred and Alfred the Great, but who after the Peace of Wedmore (878) was baptized as Athelstane.

GUTS MUTHS, Johann Christoph Friedrich, *gootz'mootz* (1759–1839), German physical educationist, born at Quedlinburg, from 1785 to 1837 taught gymnastics and geography at Schnepfenthal. He made gymnastics a branch of German education, and wrote several educational works. See Life by Wassmannsdorf (1884).

GUTTUSO, Renato, *gu-too'sō* (1912–), Italian artist, born at Palermo. He worked for some time in Milan and settled in Rome in 1937. He was associated with various anti-Fascist groups from 1942 to 1945, and much of his work reflects this experience. After the war he began to paint dramatic Realist pictures of the lives of the Italian peasants. See monograph by John Berger (1957).

GUTZKOW, Karl Ferdinand, *goots'kō* (1811–1878), German author, born at Berlin, was influenced by the French Revolution of 1830, and for his *Wally die Zweiflerin* (1835) got three months' imprisonment as a champion of the 'Young Germany' movement. He next became a journalist, and in 1847 director of the Court Theatre at Dresden, having meanwhile written many dramas, the most successful, *Richard Savage* (1839), *Zopf und Schwert* (1844), &c. Among his romances is *Die Ritter vom Geiste* (1850–52). See studies by Maenner (1921) and Metis (1915).

GÜTZLAFF, Karl Friedrich August (1803–51), German missionary, born at Pyritz in Pomerania, at Bangkok translated the Bible into Siamese (1828–30), &c. After 1831 he lived and worked in China, dying at Hong Kong. He wrote interesting *Journals*.

GUY, Thomas, *gī* (*c.* 1644–1724), English philanthropist, founder of Guy's Hospital, was born, a lighterman's son, at Horsleydown, Southwark. He began business in 1668 as a bookseller, importing English Bibles from Holland; and, on this being stopped, he contracted with the University of Oxford for the privilege of printing Bibles. By this means, and by selling out South Sea shares, he amassed a fortune of nearly half a million. In 1707 he built and furnished three wards of St Thomas's Hospital; in 1722 founded the hospital in Southwark which bears his name, and built and endowed almshouses. During his life he was reputed a selfish and avaricious man. See Wilks & Bettany's *History of Guy's Hospital* (1893).

GUY DE LUSIGNAN, *gee dè lü-see-nyä* (d. 1195), French crusader, married the widowed Marchioness of Montferrat, daughter of King Amalric of Jerusalem, and himself was king from 1186 till July 5, 1187, when he sustained a great defeat by Saladin. In 1193 he exchanged his shadowy crown for that of Cyprus.

GUY OF AREZZO. See GUIDO D'AREZZO.

GUYON, *gü-ee-yŏ*, (1) **Jeanne Marie Bouvier de la Mothe** (1648–1717), French mystic, was born at Montargis. She had destined herself for the cloister, but was married at sixteen to the wealthy and elderly Jacques Guyon. Left a widow at twenty-eight, she determined to devote her life to the poor and needy, and to the cultivation of spiritual perfection. The former part of her plan she began to carry out in 1681 at Geneva, but three years later she was compelled to depart on the ground that her Quietist doctrines were heretical. At Turin, Grenoble, Nice, Genoa, Vercelli and Paris, where she finally settled in 1686, she became the centre of a movement for the promotion of ' holy living '. In January 1688 she was arrested for heretical opinions, and for having been in correspondence with Molinos, the leader of Quietism in Spain; and out of a commission appointed to inquire into her teachings, a controversy arose between Fénelon and Bossuet. Released by the intervention of Madame de Maintenon, after a detention of nine months, but again imprisoned in 1695, she was not released from the Bastille until 1702; and she died at Blois, June 9, 1717. She wrote *Les Torrens spirituels*, *Moyen court de faire oraison*, a mystical interpretation of the Song of Solomon, an autobiography (trans. 1897), letters, and some spiritual poetry. See books by Upham (1905) and E. Seillière (1918).

(2) **Richard Debaufre** (1803–56), British soldier, was born at Walcot, Bath, son of a naval commander of Huguenot ancestry. He entered the Austrian service in 1823, and married the daughter of a Hungarian field-marshal in 1838. Having till the revolution lived on his estates near Komorn, he then took a prominent part in the struggle for independence. During the retreat of Görgei's army he re-established communication with the government at Debreczin; he did brilliant service at Kapolya, Komorn and elsewhere; and after the war, escaping to Turkey and entering the service of the sultan, he, as Kourshid Pasha, was governor of Damascus, and in the Crimean war organized the army of Kars. He died at Constantinople. See Kinglake's *General Guyon* (1856).

GUYOT, Arnold, *gü-ee-yō* (1807–84), Swiss geographer, born at Neuchâtel, in 1839 obtained a chair there, but in 1848 followed Agassiz to America. He lectured at the Lowell Institute on *Earth and Man* (1853), and in 1854 became professor of Physical Geography and Geology at Princeton. In charge of the meteorological department of the Smithsonian Institution, he published *Meteorological and Physical Tables* (revised ed. 1884); and he was joint editor of *Johnson's Cyclopaedia* (1874–77).

GUYS, Constantin, *geez* (1805–92), French artist, known for his sketches of the Crimean War for the *Illustrated London News*, and for his penetrating character studies.

GUZMÁN, Dominic de. See DOMINIC, ST.

GUZMÁN BLANCO, Antonio (1829–99), Venezuelan dictator, born in Carácas, after being banished and taking part in two invasions, became vice-president of Venezuela in 1863. Driven from office (1868), he headed a revolution which restored him to power (1870), and till 1889 was virtual dictator, himself holding the presidency (1873–77), (1879–84) and (1886–87).

GWILLIM. See GUILLIM.

GWYNNE, Nell (*c.* 1650–87), mistress of Charles II of England. Born presumably at Hereford, of humble parentage, she lived precariously as an orange girl before going on the boards at Drury Lane. She quickly established herself as a comedienne, especially in ' breeches parts '. ' Pretty, witty Nellie's ' first protector was Lord Buckhurst; but the transfer of her affections to Charles II was genuine. She had at least one son by the king—Charles Beauclerk, Duke of St Albans —and James Beauclerk is often held to have been a second. She remained faithful to Charles's memory, rejecting one suitor with the words, ' Shall the dog lie where the deer once couched ? ' She is said to have urged Charles to found Chelsea Hospital. See study by Cunningham (1893).

GYE, (1) Frederick (1781–1869), English impresario, father of (2), from 1821 to 1840 was proprietor of Vauxhall Gardens.

(2) **Frederick** (1810–78), son of (1), director from 1849 of the Royal Italian Opera, London, was accidentally shot at Dytchley Park, Charlbury. See ALBANI.

GYP, pseud. of the **Comtesse de Mirabeau de Martel** (1849–1932), French novelist, born at the château of Koëtsal in Brittany, wrote a series of novels, describing fashionable society, of which the best known are *Petit Bob* (1882) and *Mariage de Chiffon* (1894).

H

HAAG, Carl, *hahg* (1820–1915), German painter, born at Erlangen, depicted scenes from Tirol and Dalmatia, the Deeside life of the royal family, and Oriental subjects.

HAAKON, *haw'kon*, name of seven kings of Norway, of whom the following are most noteworthy:

Haakon I, ' **the Good** ' (?914–961), was brought up a Christian in England by Athelstan, defeated his half-brother, who had seized the Norwegian throne, proved an able ruler, but was killed in battle.

Haakon IV, ' **the Old** ' (1204–63), king of Norway from 1223, annexed Greenland and Iceland, and died at Kirkwall after his defeat at Largs by Alexander III.

Haakon VII (1872–1957), originally Prince Charles of Denmark, born at Charlottenlund, became king of Norway when Norway voted herself independent of Sweden in 1905. He dispensed with much of the regal pomp and became the ' people's king '. He carried on Norwegian resistance to Nazi occupation from England (1940–45).

HAASE, Hugo, *hah'zĕ* (1863–1919), German Socialist leader (Independent from 1916), born at Allenstein (E. Prussia) of Jewish race, studied law, entered the Reichstag in 1897, took a leading part in the revolution in November 1918, and a year later was assassinated.

HAAST, Sir Julius von (1824–87), German-born New Zealand geologist, born at Bonn, went to New Zealand in 1858, discovered coal and oil deposits (1859) and became professor at New Zealand University. He founded Canterbury Museum (1866). See Life by Haast (1948).

HABA, Alois (1893–   ), Czech composer, born at Vyzovice, studied in Prague, Vienna and Berlin and was made Professor at Prague Conservatory in 1924. He has composed prolifically, and his later music reflects his interest in the division of the scale into quarter-tones. His works include an opera, *The Mother*, and orchestral, chamber and pianoforte music.

HABBERTON, John (1842–1921), American writer, born in Brooklyn, N.Y., served through the Civil War, and afterwards turned to journalism. He wrote many popular stories about children, of which *Helen's Babies* (1876) was the most popular.

HABER, Fritz, *hah'-* (1868–1934), German chemist, born at Breslau, became professor of Chemistry at Karlsruhe and Berlin, invented the process with Bosch (q.v.) for the synthesis of ammonia from the nitrogen and hydrogen in the air, thus overcoming the shortage of natural nitrate deposits open to the German explosives industry during World War I. He was awarded the Nobel prize in 1918.

HABERL, Franz Xaver (1840–1910), German musicologist, born at Ober Ellenbach, known for his researches on 16th-century music, especially that of Palestrina, the great 33-volume edition of whose works he completed from volume X onwards.

HABINGTON, William (1605–54), English poet, was born at Hindlip, Worcestershire. His father, **Thomas** (1560–1647), antiquary, was imprisoned, and his uncle, **Edward** (1553?–86), executed, for complicity in Babington's plot. He was educated at St Omer and Paris, married Lucy Herbert, daughter of the first Lord Powis, and immortalized her in his *Castara* (1634), a collection of metaphysical lyrics uneven in quality but containing some pieces of considerable charm. He also wrote *The Historie of Edward the Fourth* (1640).

HABSBURG. See HAPSBURG.

HACHA, Emil, *haкн'a* (1872–1945), Czech politician, born at Trhové Sviny, Bohemia, became president of Czechoslovakia in 1938 on Beneš's resignation following the German annexation of Sudetenland; as such, under duress, made over the state to Hitler (1939); and of the subsequent German protectorate of Bohemia and Moravia (1939–45) he was puppet president.

HACHETTE, Louis, *ah-shet* (1800–64),

French publisher, born at Rethel in the Ardennes, in 1826 established in Paris a publishing business, intended to issue books that should elevate the general intelligence.

HÄCKEL, Ernst. See HAECKEL.

HACKLÄNDER, Friedrich Wilhelm von, *hack'len-der* (1816–77), German novelist and dramatist, mostly of military life, was born at Burtscheid, near Aix-la-Chapelle.

HACKLUYT. See HAKLUYT.

HACKMAN, James (1752–79), English assassin, successively a mercer's apprentice, army lieutenant, and clergyman, was hanged at Tyburn for shooting Martha Ray (1745–79), the Earl of Sandwich's mistress and Basil Montagu's mother.

HACKSTON, David (d. 1680), Scottish Covenanter, one of Archbishop Sharp's murderers, fought at Drumclog, Bothwell Brig and Airdsmoss, and was executed at Edinburgh, July 30.

HACKWORTH, Timothy (1786–1850), English locomotive engineer, born at Wylam, Northumberland, was manager of the Stockton-Darlington railway (1825–40), and builder of a number of famous engines, including the ' Royal George ' and the ' Sans Pareil ', rival of the ' Rocket '.

HADDINGTON, Earls of. See HAMILTON.

HADDON, Alfred Cort (1855–1940), English anthropologist, born in London, lectured there and in Cambridge, and wrote *Races of Man* (rewritten 1924), &c.

HADEN, Sir Francis Seymour (1818–1910), English etcher, born in London, became a surgeon and revived the art of etching in England and founded the Society of Painter-Etchers (1880).

HADFIELD, Sir Robert Abbott, Bart. (1859–1940), British metallurgist, born in Sheffield, entered his father's works there and became discoverer of manganese steel, silicon steel and stainless steel, as well as head of the firm in 1888. He was knighted in 1908, elected F.R.S. in 1909, and made a baronet in 1917.

HADLEY, (1) John (1682–1744), English mathematician, who invented a reflecting telescope (1720) and the reflecting (Hadley's) quadrant (1730).

(2) **Patrick Arthur Sheldon** (1899–   ), English composer, professor of Music at Cambridge (1946–62), known for his choral music.

HADOW, Sir William Henry (1859–1937), English musicologist, born at Ebrington, Glos., edited the *Oxford History of Music* (1901–06), and was president of the committee of the Board of Education which produced the ' Hadow Report ' (1931) on conditions in primary schools.

HADRIAN, Publius Aelius Hadrianus (76–138), Roman emperor, born in Rome, or, according to some sources, at Italica, in Spain, and after his father's death in 86 A.D., accompanied Emperor Trajan, his kinsman and guardian, on his wars, became prefect of Syria, and after Trajan's death was proclaimed emperor by the army (117). Insurrections had broken out in Egypt, Palestine and Syria; Moesia and Mauritania were invaded by barbarians; and the Parthians had once more asserted their independence.

Hadrian concluded a peace with the last, having resolved to limit the boundaries of the empire in the East, and after appeasing the invaders of Moesia, he established his authority at Rome, and suppressed a patrician conspiracy against his life. About 121 (or 119) he began his famous journey. He visited Gaul, Germany, Britain (where he built the wall from Solway to Tyne), Spain, Mauritania, Egypt, Asia Minor and Greece, whence he returned to Rome at the end of 126. He wintered twice (125–26, 129–30) in Athens. After crushing a major revolt in Judaea (132–134), he returned to Italy, and died July 10. He reorganized the army, ruled justly and was a lover of the arts. Among his buildings were his mausoleum (now part of the castle of St Angelo) and the magnificent villa at Tibur; and he founded Adrianopolis. See his *Life and Principate*, by B. W. Henderson (1923); German works by Gregorovius (trans. 1898), Plew (1890), Kornemann (1905) and Weber (1908). For the popes see ADRIAN.

HAECKEL, Ernst Heinrich (1834–1919), German naturalist, born at Potsdam, studied at Würzburg, Berlin and Vienna, under Müller, Virchow and Kölliker, and was professor of Zoology at Jena (1862–1909), interrupting his work only by visits to the North Sea shores, the Mediterranean, Madeira, the Canaries, Arabia, India, &c. He wrote on the radiolarians (1862), calcareous sponges (1872), and jellyfishes (1879), and *Challenger* Reports on *Deep-sea Medusae* (1882), *Siphonophora* (1888), and *Radiolaria* (1887). One of the first to sketch the genealogical tree of animals, Haeckel explained that the life history of the individual is a recapitulation of its historic evolution. He tended to make the facts fit his philosophical theory of materialistic monism. Before Darwin's *Descent of Man* Haeckel alone clearly recognized the import of sexual selection; his expository works are *Natürliche Schöpfungsgeschichte* (1868; *Creation*, 4th ed. 1892); *Anthropogenie* (1874; *Evolution of Man*, 1879), &c. See Lives by Bölsche (1906) and *Festschrift* (1914).

HAFFKINE, Waldemar Mordecai Wolff (1860–1930), Russian bacteriologist, born at Odessa, assisted Pasteur (1889–93), and as bacteriologist to the government of India (1893–1915), introduced his method of protective inoculation against cholera.

HÁFIZ, pseud. of **Shams ed-Dín Muhammed** (d. *c.* 1388), the greatest of Persian lyrical poets, was born, lived and died at Shíráz. From the charming sweetness of his poetry he was styled by his contemporaries *Chagarlab*, or Sugar-lip. His ghazals are all on sensuous subjects—wine, flowers, beautiful damsels, &c.; but, while the common people regard them simply as love songs, while his name is a household word throughout Persia, they yet possess an esoteric signification to the initiated. For Háfiz, like nearly all the greater poets of Persia, was of the sect of Súfí philosophers, the mystics of Islám. His tomb, two miles northeast of Shíráz, has been magnificently adorned by princes, and is visited by pilgrims from all parts of Persia. The earliest rendering of a selection of the ghazals of Háfiz was in Latin by Reviczki

(1771). See renderings by G. Bell (2nd ed. 1928), Street (1946) and Arberry (1947).

HAGBERG, Carl August (1810–64), Swedish philologist, born at Lund, translated Shakespeare and studied Old Norse.

HAGEDORN, Friedrich von, *hah'gĕ-* (1708–1754), German poet, born at Hamburg, in 1733 became secretary to the ' English Court ' trading company at Hamburg, and wrote satirical, narrative and ' society ' verses.

HAGENBACH, Karl Rudolf (1801–74), Swiss theologian, born at Basel, from 1824 occupied a chair of Theology there, wrote church history, a theological encyclopaedia, &c.

HAGENBECK, Carl (1844–1913), German wild-beast dealer, born at Hamburg, founded the famous circus and zoological park at Stellingen, near Hamburg. See his *Beasts and Men* (1909).

HAGGARD, Sir (Henry) Rider (1856–1925), English novelist, born at Bradenham Hall, Norfolk, was educated at Ipswich grammar school. He went out to Natal in 1875 as secretary to Sir Henry Bulwer, and next year accompanied Sir Theophilus Shepstone to the Transvaal. He returned in 1879 (finally in 1881) to England, married, and settled down to a literary life. His *Cetewayo and his White Neighbours* (1882), pleased the Cape politicians, but attracted no attention elsewhere. *King Solomon's Mines* (1885) made his work known, and was followed by *She*, *Allan Quatermain* and many other stories. Other publications include *Rural England* (1902) and *The Days of My Life* (1926). He was knighted in 1912. See study by M. Cohen (1960).

HAHN, Otto (1879–1968), German physical chemist, born in 1879 in Frankfurt, studied at Frankfurt, Marburg and Munich and also under Ramsay in London and Lord Rutherford at Montreal. He lectured in Berlin from 1907, becoming director of the Kaiser-Wilhelm Institute there in 1927. With Meitner he discovered the radioactive protactinium in 1917. In 1938, following the researches of the Joliot-Curies, he bombarded uranium with neutrons to find the first chemical evidence of nuclear fission products. The Nazi government did not grasp the potentialities of this discovery and Hahn spent the war-years doing small-scale experiments for industrial use of nuclear energy. In April 1945 he was picked up by British Intelligence Units and interned in Cambridge. From 1946–60, he was president (and from 1960 honorary president) of the Max Planck Society in Göttingen, and with seventeen distinguished scientists of the same signed the ' Göttingen Declaration ' in April 1957 refusing to cooperate in the contemplated West German manufacture of nuclear weapons. He was awarded the Nobel prize in 1944.

HAHNEMANN, Christian Friedrich Samuel (1755–1843), German physician and founder of homeopathy, was born at Meissen, studied at Leipzig, and for ten years practised medicine. After six years of experiments on the curative power of bark, came to the conclusion that medicine produces a very similar condition in healthy persons to that which it relieves in the sick. His own infinitesimal doses of medicine provoked the apothecaries, who refused to dispense them; accordingly he illegally gave his medicines to his patients gratis, and was prosecuted in every town in which he tried to settle from 1798 until 1810. He then returned to Leipzig, where he taught his system until 1821, when he was again driven out, retired to Köthen, and in 1835 to Paris, where he died. See his *Organon of the Rational Art of Healing* (1810; trans. 1913), and Lives by Bradford (1895), Hobhouse (1933).

HAHN-HAHN, Ida, Countess (1805–80), German novelist, born at Tressow in Mecklenburg-Schwerin, wrote society novels influenced by the 'Young Germany' movement, before turning Catholic and founding a convent at Mainz (1854).

HAIDAR ALI, *hī'der ah'lee* (1728–82), ruler of Mysore, by his bravery at a siege (1749) attracted the notice of the maharaja of Mysore's minister, and soon rose to be all-powerful; after 1759, though calling himself only 'regent', he left his master only the title of raja. He conquered Calicut, Bednor and Cannanore, and in 1766 his dominions included more than 84,000 sq. m. He withheld the customary tribute from the Mahrattas, and carried on war against them. He waged two wars against the British, in the first of which (1767–69) he was practically successful, and dictated peace under the walls of Madras. When Haidar was defeated by the Mahrattas in 1772 he claimed English support; and on this being refused he became the bitter enemy of the English. Taking advantage of the war between them and the French (1778), he and his son, Tippoo Sahib, descended upon the Carnatic, routed the English, and ravaged the country to within forty miles of Madras, but were ultimately defeated in three battles by Coote. See Bowring's *Haidar Ali and Tipu Sultan* (1893).

HAIG, Douglas, 1st Earl Haig of Bemersyde (1861–1928), British field-marshal, born in Edinburgh. He was educated at Clifton, Oxford University and R.M.C. Sandhurst, obtaining a commission in the 7th Hussars. Active service in Egypt and South Africa, followed by staff and command assignments in India, led to his appointment in 1911 as G.O.C. Aldershot. In August 1914 he took the 1st Corps of the B.E.F. to France; succeeding Sir John French as c.-in-c. in December 1915. With the flanks of the battle zone sealed by the sea and the Swiss Border and the Germans operating on interior lines, Haig was forced to forgo war of movement and wage a costly and exhausting war of attrition; a difficult task appreciably aggravated by the progressive deterioration of the French after the failure of the Nivelle offensive of 1917, and Lloyd George's hampering distrust and irresponsible attempts to control strategy. Patient and steadfast, Haig's reward came with his Army's successful offensive of August 1918, leading to the German plea for an armistice and the admission that their opponent's strategy had been 'careful and effective' (*Handbuch der Neuzeitlichen Wehrwissenschaft*). In postwar years Haig devoted all his energies to the care of the ex-Serviceman, dying, worn out by his labours, in 1928. He was made G.C.B.

1915, G.C.V.O. 1916, K.T. 1917, O.M. 1919, when his Earldom, with grant of £100,000, was also awarded. See his Private Papers (1952), his biographies by Charteris (1929) and Duff-Cooper (1935), and works by Charteris (1931), Dewar and Boraston (1929), Davidson (1953), and Terraine (1963).

HAIGH, John George (1909–49), English murderer, born at Stamford. A company director, he murdered a widow in February 1949 by shooting and subsequently disposed of her body by reducing it in sulphuric acid. A vital clue leading to his conviction was a plastic denture which had resisted the acid. He probably murdered five others in the same way and it is possible that he drank his victims' blood, although the motive was money. He was executed August 6. See his *Trial*, ed. Lord Dunboyne (1953).

HAILES, Lord. See DALRYMPLE (2).

HAILE SELASSIE, *hī'li-* (1891–), emperor of Ethiopia, before his coronation in 1930, Prince Ras Tafari, son of Ras Makonnen. He led the revolution in 1916 against Lij Yasu and became regent and heir to the throne. He westernized the institutions of his country. He settled in England after the Italian conquest of Abyssinia (1935–36), but in 1941 was restored after the liberation by British forces. See study by Sandford (1955) and Life by L. Mosley (1965).

HAILSHAM, (1) Douglas McGarel Hogg, 1st Viscount (1872–1950), British statesman, entered Parliament in 1922, was attorney-general in 1922–24 and 1924–28, lord chancellor in 1928–29, and secretary for war in 1931–35. He was made a baron in 1928 and a viscount in 1929. His father was Quintin Hogg (q.v.).

(2) **Quintin McGarel Hogg, 2nd Viscount** (1907–), British Conservative politician, was born in London and was educated at Eton and Oxford, where he was president of the Union in 1929 and a fellow of All Souls in 1931. In 1932 he was called to the bar and from 1938 to 1950 he was M.P. for Oxford City. He succeeded to the title in 1950, and, among several political posts, was first lord of the Admiralty (1956-57), minister of education (1957), lord president of the Council (1957–59; 1960–64), and chairman of the Conservative party (1957–59). He was minister for science and technology (1959–1964), and secretary of state for education and science (1964). In the Conservative leadership crisis of Nov. 1963, he renounced his peerage for life, and was re-elected to the House of Commons in the St Marylebone by-election. He was opposition minister for the home office from 1966. In 1970 he was created a life peer (Baron Hailsham of Saint Marylebone) and became lord chancellor. His several publications include *The Case for Conservatism* (1947) and *The Conservative Case* (1959).

HAKIM BIAMR ALLAH (d. 1044), 6th Fatimide Khalif of Egypt, a Nero in cruelty and, through his apostle Darazi, the author of the religion of the Druses, was ultimately murdered. See MOKANNA.

HAKLUYT, Richard, *-loot* (?1552–1616), English geographer, born in Herefordshire, from Westminster went in 1570 to Christ Church, Oxford, where he afterwards became lecturer on geography or cosmography. He introduced the use of globes into English schools. The publication of *Divers Voyages touching the Discovery of America* (1582) seems to have procured for him in 1584 the chaplaincy of the English embassy to Paris; there he wrote *Discourse concerning Western Discoveries* (1584). On his return to England in 1588 he began to collect materials for his *Principal Navigations, Voyages, and Discoveries of the English Nation* (1598–1600; new ed. 1903–05). Made a prebendary of Westminster in 1602, he was buried in Westminster Abbey. His unpublished manuscripts were used by Purchas in his *Pilgrims* (1625–26). The *Hakluyt Society* was instituted in 1846. See Life by Parkes (N.Y. 1929).

HAKON. See HAAKON.

HALDANE, name of a distinguished Scottish family of intellectuals:

(1) **Elisabeth Sanderson** (1862–1937), British author, sister of (4) and (5), studied nursing, for a while managed the Royal Infirmary, Edinburgh, became the first woman justice of the peace in Scotland (1920). Wrote a Life of Descartes (1905) and with Ross edited his philosophical works, translated Hegel and wrote commentaries on George Eliot (1927) and Mrs Gaskell (1930).

(2) **James Alexander** (1768–1851), Scottish minister, brother of (6), born at Dundee and educated there and at Edinburgh, served in the navy (1785–94). With Simeon of Cambridge he made an evangelistic tour of Scotland; and in 1799 he was ordained independent pastor of a church in Edinburgh, in which he preached gratuitously for fifty years, and which in 1808 he led into the Baptist fold. His pamphlets were widely read. See Memoir by A. Haldane (1852).

(3) **John Burdon Sanderson** (1892–1964), British biologist, son of (4), born at Oxford, became after Eton, a fellow of New College, Oxford. After service in the Black Watch during World War I, he became reader of Biochemistry at Cambridge (1922–32), professor of Genetics, London (1933–57), and of Biometry, London (1937–57). He then emigrated to India, adopting Indian nationality, and was appointed professor of the Indian Statistical Institute, Calcutta, from which he resigned in 1961 in protest against criticism by the Indian government. He became head of Orissa State Genetics and Biometry Laboratory in 1962. His numerous works include *Animal Biology* (with J. S. Huxley, 1927), *Fact and Faith* (1934), &c. He was chairman of the editorial board of the *Daily Worker* (1940–49), but left the British Communist party in 1956, because of 'Stalinist interference in science'. Elected F.R.S. in 1932, he became Chevalier, of the Légion d'honneur (1937), won the Darwin medal of the Royal Society (1953), and received the Feltrinelli prize for Biology in 1961.

(4) **John Scott** (1860–1936), English physiologist, grand-nephew of (6), father of (3) and Naomi Mitchison (q.v.), born in Edinburgh, was elected fellow of New College, Oxford. He made a study of the effects of industrial occupations upon physiology and served as a director of a mining research laboratory at Birmingham.

(5) **Richard Burdon, 1st Viscount Haldane** (1856–1928), British Liberal statesman, philosopher and lawyer, grand-nephew of (6), was educated at Edinburgh and Göttingen, was called to the bar in 1879, entered Parliament in 1879 as a Liberal, supported the Boer war and as secretary of state for war (1905–12) remodelled the army and founded the Territorials. He was lord chancellor (1912–15) and minister of Labour (1924). He was awarded the O.M. in 1915. He gave the Gifford Lectures at St Andrews (1902–04) and published three philosophical treatises. See his autobiography (1929) and Life by F. Maurice (1937–39).

(6) **Robert** (1764–1842), British preacher, grand-uncle of (5) and brother of (2), born in London, was in the navy at the relief of Gibraltar, but settled on his estates, near Stirling, in 1783. The French Revolution brought about a spiritual revolution within him, and he founded the Society for Propagating the Gospel at Home (1797), built tabernacles for itinerant preachers and lectured to theological students at Geneva and Montauban (1817).

HALDIMAND, Sir Frederick (1718–91), Swiss-born British soldier, born in the canton of Neuchâtel, from 1756 commanded British regiments or garrisons in the American colonial wars with French and Indians. In 1778–84 he was governor of Canada. See Life by McIlwraith (1905).

HALE, (1) Edward Everett (1822–1909), American Unitarian minister, grand-nephew of (4), born in Boston, Mass., where he became minister in 1856, did much philanthropic work. His book *Ten Times One is Ten* (1870) originated numerous 'Lend a Hand' clubs. He edited religious and other journals, and documents on the founding of Virginia, and wrote short stories. See Life by his son (1917).

(2) **George Ellery** (1868–1938), American astronomer, born at Chicago, was director at the Yerkes Observatory 1895–1905, and at Mount Wilson (1904–23). He earned fame by his brilliant researches on sunspots and invented the spectroheliograph.

(3) **Sir Matthew** (1609–76), English judge, born at Alderley in Gloucestershire, studied at Oxford, entered Lincoln's Inn in 1628, and in 1637 was called to the bar. A justice of the common pleas from 1654 till Cromwell's death, he was after the Restoration (which he zealously promoted) made chiefbaron of the Exchequer and knighted, and in 1671 chief justice of the King's Bench. Devout, acute, learned and sensible, although a believer in witchcraft, he wrote histories of the *Pleas of the Crown* and of *Common Laws* besides religious works. See Lives by Burnet (1682), Williams (1835), Roscoe (1838).

(4) **Nathan** (1755–76), American soldier, grand-uncle of (1), born at Coventry, Conn., became captain in the Continental army, and, having volunteered to penetrate the British lines and procure intelligence for Washington, was detected, and executed as a spy in New York City, September 22, 1776. See books by Lossing (1886) and H. P. Johnston (1915).

(5) **Sarah Josepha** (1788–1879), American writer, reputed author of ' Mary had a Little Lamb ', which appeared in her *Poems for our Children* (1830), born at Newport, N.H., became in 1828 editor of the *Ladies' Magazine*. She wrote poems, cookery books, novels, &c. Her son Horatio (1817–97) was ethnologist to the U.S. Pacific exploring expedition.

HALES, (1). See ALEXANDER OF HALES.

(2) **John** (1584–1656), English divine, the ' Ever-memorable ', was born at Bath, was educated at Corpus Christi College, Oxford, and became fellow and lecturer at Merton College. In 1616 he went to The Hague as chaplain to the ambassador, Sir Dudley Carleton, for whom he made a report of the famous synod of Dort, which convinced him of the futility of extreme dogma and so ' he bid John Calvin good-night '. In 1619 he returned to Eton to study. His too liberal *Tract concerning Schism and Schismatics* displeased Laud, who was, however, satisfied after a personal conference and an apologetic letter, and appointed him to a canonry at Windsor (1639). The Puritan supremacy reduced him to great want. See Life by A. Kennedy (1929).

(3) **Stephen** (1677–1761), English botanist and chemist, born at Beaksbourn, Canterbury, entered Corpus Christi College, Cambridge, in 1696, was elected fellow in 1702, and became in 1709 perpetual curate of Teddington. His *Vegetable Staticks* (1727) is the starting point of our true knowledge of vegetable physiology; *Haemastaticks* (1733) treats of the circulation of the blood. Besides a work on dissolving stone in the bladder, he wrote in the *Philosophical Transactions* on ventilation, electricity, analysis of air, &c. He also invented machines for ventilating, distilling sea water, preserving meat, &c. See Life by Clark-Kennedy (1909).

(4), or **d'Hèle**, **Thomas** (*c.* 1740–80), an English naval officer, who in 1763 became a successful French dramatist, and died of drink after his separation from an actress.

HALEVI, Jehuda, *hah-lay'vee* (*c.* 1080–1141), Jewish poet and philosopher, born at Toledo. Reports of the First Crusade and his own experiences as a physician at Cordova stimulated him to respond to anti-Semitism in richly symbolical verse and prose which challenged Islam and Christianity, rejected Aristotle and the sensuality of Hellenism, extolled the moral supremacy of his own faith, and encouraged the feeling of exclusiveness that led centuries later to Zionism. See his poems, ed. N. Salaman (1928), and his *Book of the Khazars*, ed. H. Hirschfeld (1931) and I. Heinemann (1947).

HALÉVY, *ah-lay-vee*, (1) **Daniel** (1872–1962), French historian, an authority on the history of the 3rd Republic, son of (6), was born in Paris, wrote Lives of Nietzsche (1909), Vauban (1923), Michelet (1928) and numerous historical works.

(2) **Élie** (1870–1937), French historian, brother of (1), born at Étretat, became professor of Political Science at Paris in 1898 and wrote *La Formation du radicalisme philosophique* (1901–04), *Histoire du peuple anglais au XIXᵉ siècle* (1912 ff.) and

L'Ère des tyrannies (1938). See *Correspondance*, ed. Alain (Paris 1958).

(3) **Jacques François Fromentale Elias** (1799–1862), French composer, brother of (5), born in Paris. His first successful opera was *Clari* (1828), followed by the comic opera, *Le Dilettante d'Avignon* (1829). His masterpiece, *La Juive* (1835), carried his name over Europe. His next best work is the comic opera, *L'Éclair* (1835), but he produced about a dozen other operatic works. He worthily carried on the succession of the great school of French opera, midway between Cherubini and Meyerbeer. Admitted to the Academy of Fine Arts in 1846, he became perpetual secretary in 1854. His *éloges* were collected as *Souvenirs et Portraits* (1861–63). Bizet and Gounod studied under him. See Lives by (5) (1863), and Pougin (1865).

(4) **Joseph** (1827–1917), French orientalist, born at Adrianople, in 1868 travelled in northern Abyssinia, next crossed (1869–70) Yemen in quest of Sabaean inscriptions for the French Academy. His books describe his journeys or deal with the dialects of the Falashas, Sabaean and cuneiform inscriptions, &c.

(5) **Léon** (1802–83), French writer, brother of (3) and father of (6), born in Paris, became professor of Literature at the Polytechnic School. He wrote the introduction to Saint-Simon's *Opinions* (1825), also histories, poetry, fables, novels, dramatic poems, and translations of *Macbeth*, *Clavigo*, &c. His best books are *Résumé de l'histoire des juifs* (1827–28), *Poésies européennes* (1837), *La Grèce tragique* (1845–61).

(6) **Ludovic** (1834–1908), French playwright and novelist, son of (5) and father of (1) and (2), born in Paris, in 1861 became secretary to the Corps Législatif. With Meilhac (q.v.) he wrote libretti for the best-known operettas of Offenbach (q.v.), and for Bizet's *Carmen*, and produced vaudevilles and comedies. His *Madame et Monsieur Cardinal* (1873) and *Les petites Cardinal* (1880) are delightful sketches of Parisian theatrical life; *L'Invasion* (1872) was personal recollections of the war. His charming *L'Abbé Constantin* (1882) was followed by *Criquette*, *Deux Mariages*, *Princesse*, and *Mariette* (1893). He was admitted to the Academy in 1884.

HALFORD, Sir Henry, 1st Bart. (1766–1844), English physician to George III, George IV and William IV, born at Leicester, who in 1809 changed his name from Vaughan, helped to identify the body of Charles I at Windsor in 1813. See Life by W. Munk (1895).

HALIBURTON, (1) **Hugh**, Scottish poet, feigned to be a shepherd of the Ochil Hills, was really **James Logie Robertson** (1846–1922). Born at Milnathort, he studied at Edinburgh and was first English master in Edinburgh Ladies' College (1891–1914). Besides *Horace in Homespun: A Series of Scottish Pastorals* (1886) he wrote *Ochil Idylls* (1891), and prose essays, and edited Thomson.

(2) **Thomas Chandler** (1796–1865), American writer, born at Windsor, Nova Scotia, was called to the bar in 1820, and became a

member of the House of Assembly, chief justice of the common pleas (1828), and judge of the supreme court (1842). In 1856 he retired to England, and in 1859–63 was Conservative M.P. for Launceston. He is best known as the creator of Sam Slick, a sort of American Sam Weller, in newspaper sketches collected in 1837–40 as *The Clockmaker, or Sayings and Doings of Samuel Slick of Slickville*, continued as *The Attaché, or Sam Slick in England* (1843–44). Other works include *Traits of American Humour* (1843) and *Rule and Misrule of the English in America* (1850). See Memoir by Crofton (1889) and study by Chittick (1924).

HALIFAX, (1) **Charles Montagu, 1st Earl of** (1661–1715), English statesman and poet, a nephew of the Parliamentary general, the Earl of Manchester, was born at Horton, Northamptonshire, and from Westminster passed in 1679 to Trinity College, Cambridge. His most notable poetical achievement was a parody on Dryden's *Hind and Panther*, entitled *The Town and Country Mouse* (1687), of which he was joint author with Matthew Prior. M.P. for Maldon (1688) and a lord of the treasury (1692), he in that year proposed to raise a million sterling by way of loan—establishing the National Debt. In 1694 money was again wanted, and Montagu supplied it by originating the Bank of England, as proposed by William Paterson three years earlier. For this service Montagu was appointed chancellor of the Exchequer. He was responsible for the recoinage in 1695, the appointment of his friend Isaac Newton as warden of the Mint, and raising a tax on windows to pay the expense; he first introduced exchequer bills. In 1697 he became premier, but his arrogance and vanity soon made him unpopular, and on the Tories coming into power in 1699 he was obliged to accept the auditorship of the Exchequer and withdraw from the Commons as Baron Halifax. He was unsuccessfully impeached in 1701, and again in 1703. He strongly supported the union with Scotland and the Hanoverian succession. On Queen Anne's death he was appointed a member of the council of regency, and on George I's arrival became an earl and prime minister. See Life by Foxcroft (1946).

(2) **Sir Charles Wood, 1st Viscount** (1800–1885), English Liberal statesman, grandson of (1) and grandfather of (3), was chancellor of the Exchequer (1846–52) and secretary for India (1859–66).

(3) **Edward Frederick Lindley Wood, 1st Earl of** (2nd creation) (1881–1959), English Conservative statesman, grandson of (2), was (as Baron Irwin 1925) viceroy of India (1926–31), foreign secretary (1938–40) under Neville Chamberlain, whose 'appeasement' policy he implemented, and ambassador to the U.S. (1941–46). He was created Earl in 1944 and awarded the O.M. (1946). See his autobiography, *Fullness of Days* (1957).

(4) **George Savile, 1st Marquis of** (1633–95), English statesman, was created viscount (1668) for his share in the Restoration. In 1675 he opposed Danby's Test Bill, and in 1679 by a display of extraordinary oratory procured the rejection of the Exclusion Bill.

Three years later he was created a marquis and made lord privy seal. On the accession of James II he became president of the council, but was dismissed in 1685 for his opposition to the repeal of the Test and Habeas Corpus Acts. One of the three commissioners appointed by James II, to treat with William of Orange after he landed in England, on James's flight he tendered his allegiance to William and resumed the office of lord privy seal; but, joining the Opposition, he resigned his post in 1689. His defence is to be read in his *Character of a Trimmer*. His *Miscellanies* show him a witty epigrammatist. See *Life* by Foxcroft (1898); *Complete Works*, ed. by Sir W. Raleigh (1912).

HALKETT, (1) **Elizabeth.** See WARDLAW.

(2) **Hugh, Baron von** (1783–1863), Hanoverian general, born at Musselburgh, Scotland, fought in the Peninsula and at Waterloo. See German Life by Knesebeck (1865).

(3) **Samuel** (1814–71), Scottish scholar, from 1848 the Advocates' librarian, Edinburgh, compiler of the *Dictionary of Anonymous Literature* (4 vols. 1882–88) completed by the Rev. **John Laing** (1809–80), from 1850 librarian of New College, Edinburgh.

HALL, (1) **Anna Maria.** See (18).

(2) **Asaph** (1829–1907), American astronomer, born at Goshen, Conn., from 1862 to 1891 held a post in the naval observatory at Washington. In 1877 he discovered the two satellites of Mars.

(3) **Basil** (1788–1844), Scottish travel writer, born in Edinburgh, son of (12), served (1802–23) in the navy. His works on Korea (1818), Chile, Peru and Mexico (1824) were very popular; *Travels in North America* (1829), still valuable as description, was resented in the U.S.; also wrote *Fragments of Voyages and Travels* (1831–40), and novels and short stories. He died insane.

(4) **Charles Francis** (1821–71), American Arctic explorer, born in Rochester, New Hampshire, in 1821, was successively blacksmith, journalist, stationer and engraver, and became interested in the fate of Franklin. He made two search expeditions (1860–62 and 1864–69), living alone among the Eskimos, and bringing back relics and the bones of one of Franklin's men. In 1871 he sailed in command of the *Polaris* on an 'expedition to the North Pole', and on August 29 reached, via Smith's Sound, 82° 16′ N., then the highest latitude reached; next turning southward, he went into winter quarters at Thank God Harbour, Greenland (81° 38′ N.). Here he was taken ill, and died November 8. His companions left in August 1872, and after many hardships and the abandonment of the *Polaris*, reached home in the autumn of 1873. Hall published *Arctic Researches, and Life among the Esquimaux* (1864); and largely from his papers was compiled the *Narrative of the Second Arctic Expedition* (1879).

(5) **Charles Martin** (1863–1914), American chemist, born at Thompson, Ohio, discovered in 1886 the first economic method of obtaining aluminium from bauxite electrolytically. He helped to found the Aluminium Company of America, of which he became vice-president in 1890.

(6) **Chester Moor** (1703–71), English inventor, a gentleman of Essex who in 1733 anticipated Dollond in the invention of the achromatic telescope.

(7) or **Halle, Edward** (c. 1499–1547), English historian, born in London, educated at Eton and King's College, Cambridge, where he was elected fellow, and at Gray's Inn. He became a common serjeant in 1532. His *Union of the Noble Famelies of Lancastre and Yorke* (1542) was only brought down to 1532; the rest, down to 1546, was completed by the editor, Grafton. Hall's stately dignity and the reality of his figures had a charm for Shakespeare; and to the student of Henry VIII's reign the work is really valuable as the intelligent evidence of an eye witness, though too eulogistic of the king.

(8) **Sir Edward Marshall** (1858–1927), English lawyer, born at Brighton, was called to the bar in 1888 after an unpromising scholastic career at Rugby and Cambridge. He made a great public reputation in a number of sensational cases, including the Seddon poisoning case (1912) and the Russell divorce (1923); though his successes were often triumphs of personality rather than of academic legal brilliance. He was M.P. for Southport (1900–06) and East Toxteth (1910–16), and was knighted in 1917.

(9) **George Henry, 1st Viscount** (1881–1965), British Labour politician who rose from miner to M.P. (1922), colonial secretary (1945) and first lord of the Admiralty (1946). He was created a viscount in 1946.

(10) **Granville Stanley** (1844–1924), American psychologist, born at Ashfield, Mass., studied at Leipzig under Wundt, and in 1882 introduced experimental psychology on a laboratory scale in Johns Hopkins University. Founder of the *American Journal of Psychology*, he exercised a profound influence on the development of educational psychology in the U.S.A. In 1887, immediately after its foundation, he was made first president of Clark University, achieving for it an international reputation.

(11) **James** (1811–98), American geologist, born at Hingham, Mass., as New York State geologist from 1831 pioneered the study of U.S. geology with his *Geology of New York* and *New York State Natural History Survey*.

(12) **Sir James, Bart.** (1761–1832), Scottish geologist, of Dunglass, a Haddingtonshire baronet, father of (3), sought to prove the geological theories of his friend and master Hutton (q.v.) in the laboratory, and so founded experimental geology.

(13) **John** (1739–97), English engraver after West, Gainsborough, &c., was born at Wivenhoe.

(14) **Joseph** (1574–1656), English divine, born at Ashby-de-la-Zouch, became a fellow of Emmanuel College, Cambridge, in 1595. In 1617 he was made dean of Worcester and accompanied James I to Scotland to help establish episcopacy. As Bishop of Exeter (from 1627) he was suspected by Laud of Puritanism, and after being translated to Norwich in 1641 protested with other prelates against the validity of laws passed during their enforced absence from parliament, and spent seven months in the Tower. Soon

after, he was deprived of his living, and in 1647 retired to a small farm in Higham. Among his works are *Contemplations*, *Christain Meditations*, *Episcopacy*, and *Mundus Alter et Idem*. His poetical satires *Virgidemiarum* (1597–98) Pope called ' the best poetry and the truest satire in the English language '. See Lives by G. Lewis (1886) and Kinloch (1951).

(15) **Marguerite Radclyffe** (1886–1943), British writer, born in Bournemouth, began as a lyric poet with several volumes of verse, some of which have become songs, but turned to novel writing in 1924 with *The Forge* and *The Unlit Lamp*. Her *Adam's Breed* (1926) won the Femina Vie Heureuse and the Tait Black Memorial prizes, but *The Well of Loneliness* (1928), which embodies a sympathetic approach to the problem of female homosexuality, caused a prolonged furore and was banned in Britain, though not in the U.S.A.

(16) **Marshall** (1790–1857), English physician and physiologist, was born at Basford, Notts. After studying at Edinburgh, Paris, Göttingen and Berlin, he settled at Nottingham in 1817, and practised in London from 1826 until 1853. He did important work in regard to the reflex action of the spinal system (1833–37); his name is also associated with a standard method of restoring suspended respiration. He wrote on diagnosis (1817), the circulation (1831), *Respiration and Irritability* (1832), &c. See *Memoirs* by his widow (1861).

(17) **Robert** (1764–1831), English Baptist preacher, born at Arnsby near Leicester, was educated at a Baptist academy at Bristol and at Aberdeen and was appointed assistant minister and tutor in the Bristol Academy. There and at Cambridge from 1790, his preaching drew huge congregations. In 1806 he settled in Leicester. He wrote *Apology for the Freedom of the Press* (1793), &c. See his works with memoir by O. Gregory (1831–33), and Life by Hughes (1945).

(18) **Samuel Carter** (1800–89), Irish-born editor and author, born at Geneva Barracks, Waterford, came to London in 1822 to study Law, but edited the *Amulet* annual (1826–36), the *New Monthly Magazine*, *John Bull*, and founded and edited the *Art Journal* (1839–80), as well as writing, with his wife, 500 works including *Ireland, its Scenery* (1841–43), *The Book of Gems*, &c. See his *Retrospect of a Long Life* (1883). His wife **Anna Maria**, *née* **Fielding** (1800–81), Irish novelist, born in Dublin, wrote nine novels and many short stories, including *The Buccaneer* (1832), *Lights and Shadows of Irish Character* (1838), and *Marian* (1839). Her *Stories of the Irish Peasantry* came out in *Chambers's Journal*. Both are buried at Addlestone, Surrey.

HALLAM, Henry (1777–1859), English historian, born at Windsor, was educated at Eton and Christ Church, Oxford, and called to the bar in 1802. A private income, however, as well as various appointments found for him by his Whig friends, permitted him the pursuit of his literary interests. His three main works, written with painstaking accuracy, if lacking in colour, *Europe during the Middle Ages* (1818), *The Constitutional*

History of England from Henry VII to George II (1827) and the *Introduction to the Literature of Europe in the 15th, 16th and 17th Centuries* (1837–39), established his reputation even among later historians, despite his Whig prejudices. He edited the *Remains in Prose and Verse* (1834) of his son **Arthur Henry** (1811–33) of *In Memoriam*, who died abroad. See also unpruned edition by Motter (1943).

HALLE, Adam de la, *ahl* (*c.* 1235–87), French poet and composer, nicknamed ' le bossu d'Arras ', although he was not misshapen, was born at Arras, and died at Naples, having followed Robert II of Artois thither in 1283. He originated the comic opera (in *Le Jeu de Robin et de Marion*) and the modern comedy (in the half-autobiographic composition called *Le ju Adan ou de la fuellie*). Of these, the former has hardly a trace of roughness; the latter contains no hint of classical inspiration. He also wrote poems in the usual mediaeval verse forms. See editions by Langlois (1911, 1924).

HALLÉ, Sir Charles, *hal'lay* (1819–95), German-born British pianist and conductor, born at Hagen in Westphalia, studied first at Darmstadt, and from 1840 at Paris, where his reputation was established by his concerts of classical music. But the Revolution of 1848 drove him to England, and he ultimately settled in Manchester, where in 1858 he founded his famous orchestra, which did much to raise the standard of musical taste by familiarizing the British public with the great classical masters. He was knighted in 1888.—**Lady Hallé,** *née* **Wilhelmine Neruda** (1839–1911), the violinist, was born at Brünn, made her début in Vienna in 1846, and three years later played first in London at the Philharmonic. She married in 1864 the Swedish musician Ludvig Normann, and in 1888 Sir Charles. See Sir C. Hallé's *Life and Letters* (1897) and Life by Rigby (1952).

HALLECK, (1) **Fitz-Greene** (1790–1867), American poet, born at Guilford, Conn., became a clerk in New York, and in 1832 private secretary to John Jacob Astor; in 1849 he retired, on an annuity left him by Astor, to Guilford. His long mock-Byronic poem, *Fanny* (1819), is a satire on the literature, fashions and politics of the time.

(2) **Henry Wager** (1815–72), American general, born at Westernville, N.Y., served in the Mexican war. Having taken a leading part in organizing the state of California, in the Civil War (1861) he was appointed commander of the Missouri. In May 1862 he captured Corinth; in July became general-in-chief; but in March 1864 he was superseded by General Grant. Chief of staff until 1865, he commanded the military division of the Pacific until 1869, and that of the South until his death. He published *Elements of Military Science* (1846), books on mining laws, &c.

HALLER, Albrecht von (1708–77), Swiss anatomist, botanist, physiologist and poet, was born at Bern, and started practice in 1729, but in 1736 was called to a chair at Göttingen. Here he organized a botanical garden, an anatomical museum and theatre, and an obstetrical school, helped to found the Academy of Sciences, wrote anatomical and physiological works, and took an active part in the literary movement. In 1753 he resigned and returned to Bern, where he became magistrate. After this he wrote three political romances, and prepared four large bibliographies of botany, anatomy, surgery and medicine. His poems were descriptive, didactic and (the best of them) lyrical. See H. E. Sigerest, *Great Doctors* (1933), and studies by Henry (1783) and Jenny (1902).

HALLEY, Edmond (1656–1742), English astronomer and mathematician, born at Haggerston, London, November 8, from St Paul's School went in 1673 to Queen's College, Oxford. In 1766 he contributed papers to the *Philosophical Transactions* on the orbits of the planets and on a sunspot; at St Helena (1676–77) he made a catalogue of the stars in the southern hemisphere (*Catalogus Stellarum Australium*, 1679). Now F.R.S., he made observations with Cassini at Paris (1680) on a great comet (not that which goes by his name). He published in 1683 (*Phil. Trans.*) his theory of the variation of the magnet; in 1684 he conferred with Newton as to whether the centripetal force in the solar system varies inversely as the square of the distance; in 1686 he wrote on the trade winds and monsoons. He embodied in a chart (1701) the results of a voyage he undertook to test his theory of the magnetic variation of the compass; in 1702 surveyed the coasts of the English Channel and made a chart of its tides. In 1703 he became Savilian professor of Geometry at Oxford, and in 1705 published his researches on the orbits of the comets. He was secretary of the Royal Society (1713–21); in 1720 invented a diving bell and became astronomer-royal; and died at Greenwich, January 14. His *Tabulae Astronomicae* appeared in 1749. Halley was the first to predict the return of a comet, and to recommend the observation of the transits of Venus with a view to determining the sun's parallax.

HALLIWELL-PHILLIPPS, James Orchard (1820–89), English Shakespearean scholar and antiquary, was born at Chelsea, studied at Jesus College, Cambridge, contributed much to Shakespearean studies by his *Outlines of the Life of Shakespeare* (1848). He also published *Nursery Rhymes and Tales of England* (1845) and *Dictionary of Archaic and Provincial Words* (1847).

HALS, Franz (*c.* 1580–1666), Dutch portrait and genre painter, known as ' the Elder ' to differentiate him from his son, ' the Younger ' (fl. 1637–69), also an artist. The elder was born at Mechlin and little is known of his early life except that he studied under Karel van Mander and settled permanently in Haarlem *c.* 1603. He was twice married, led a ramshackle domestic life with many children, but, despite many commissions, was constantly overshadowed by poverty. Among his early ceremonial portraits are those of *Paulus von Berestyn* and his wife *Catherine* (1620), *Jacob Pietersz Olyean* and *Aletta Hanemans* (1625); all four in the Louvre. Also the dignified, sumptuously costumed *Portrait of a Man* (1622) in the Duke of Devonshire's collection. But it is by his studies of every nuance of smile from the vague, arrogant amusement of the *Laughing*

Cavalier (Wallace Collection, London) to the broad grins and outright vulgar leers of the low life sketches, the *Gypsy Girl* (Louvre), the *Hille Bobbe* (Berlin), the *Jolly Toper* (Amsterdam) which belong to the period 1625–35 that Hals achieved his perennial popularity. Another formal masterpiece is *Pieter van den Broecke* (1633; Kenwood, London). But from 1640 onwards, the virile, swaggering colours give way to more contemplative, sombre blacks and greys. His own struggles and disappointments no doubt contributed to the bitter psychological study of old age, *The Seated Man* (Kassell), as well as the last of the eight magnificent portrait groups in the Franz Hals Museum at Haarlem, *The Women Guardians of the Haarlem Almshouse* (1664), who sat for him out of charity and whom he portrays with bitter irony in all their prim, cold, starchy ' do-gooderdom '— a world apart from an earlier group, the *Banquet of the Company of St Adrian* (1627), in which the mood of robust merrymaking is symbolized by the upturned glass in the hand of one of the officers, the whole assembly a feast of many-splendoured colour. See studies by W. Bode (trans. 1914), W. Martin (1935) and N. S. Trivas (Phaidon, 1941). His brother, **Dirk** (d. 1656) was also a genre painter.

HALSBURY, Hardinge Stanley Giffard, 1st Earl of (1823–1921), English lawyer, born in London and called to the bar in 1850, became solicitor-general (1875), Conservative M.P. (1877), lord chancellor (1885, 1886–92, 1895–1905). He led the ' Die-Hards ' in defence of the Lords' Veto (1911); and he supervised the digest, *The Laws of England* (1905-16).

HALSTED, William Stewart (1852–1922), American surgeon, professor at Johns Hopkins University from 1886, first used cocaine injection for local anaesthesia, and devised successful operative techniques for cancer of the breast and inguinal hernia. He pioneered the use of rubber gloves in surgery. See Life by McCallum (1930).

HAMANN, Johann George, ' the Magus of the North ' (1730–88), German philosopher and theologian, was born at Königsberg, and died at Münster, having been in turn a student of philosophy, theology and law, private tutor, merchant, tutor again, commercial traveller, student of literature and the ancient languages, clerk and an excise official. His writings are, like his life, desultory, but they influenced Jacobi, Herder, Goethe and Jean Paul. Symbolical and oracular in style, they are rich in suggestive thought, encrusted with paradox and sarcasm, and bristle with literary allusions. See editions by Roth (1821–45) and Gildemeister (1857–1873), Lives by Poel (1874–76) and Unger (1911) and studies by H. Weber (1904) and H. Hillner (1924–25).

HAMERTON, Philip Gilbert (1834–94), English writer on art, born at Laneside, Oldham, began as an art critic by contributing to the *Saturday Review*, published *A Painter's Camp in the Highlands* (1862), *Etching and Etchers* and *Contemporary French Painters* (1868), and *Painting in France after the Decline of Classicism* (1869). From 1869 he edited the *Portfolio*. *The Intellectual Life* (1873) is letters of advice addressed to literary aspirants and others; *Human Intercourse* (1884) is a volume of essays on social subjects; *The Graphic Arts* (1882), finely illustrated, is a treatise on drawing, painting and engraving; *Landscape* (1885), a superbly-illustrated volume, sets forth the influence of natural landscape on man. Among his other works are two Lives of Turner (1878 and 1889), *Portfolio Papers* (1889), *French and English* (1889), *Man in Art* (1893), *The Mount* (1897) and two novels. He died at Boulogne-sur-Seine. See his *Autobiography* (1896).

HAMILCAR (*c.* 270–228 B.C.), Carthaginian soldier, next to Hannibal the greatest of the Carthaginians, was surnamed Barca (Hebrew *Barak*) or ' Lightning '. When a young man, he came into prominence in the sixteenth year of the First Punic War (247 B.C.). After ravaging the Italian coast, he landed in Sicily near Panormus, and, seizing the stronghold of Ercte with a small band of mercenaries, waged war for three years against Rome. He occupied Mount Eryx (244–42) and stood at bay against a Roman army. When at the close of the First Punic War (241) Sicily was yielded to Rome, the Carthaginian mercenaries revolted; but Hamilcar crushed the rebellion after a terrible struggle in 238. His master conception was to redress the loss of Sicily by creating in Spain an infantry capable of coping with Roman legionaries. He entered Spain in 237, and before his death in the winter (229–28) he had built up a new dominion. The conceptions of the great Hamilcar were carried out by his mightier son Hannibal (q.v.).

HAMILTON, name of a Scottish noble family, believed to be of English origin, which can be traced back to Walter Fitz-Gilbert, called Hamilton, who in 1296 held lands in Lanarkshire, swore fealty to Edward I, and in 1314 held Bothwell Castle for the English. His surrender of it, with the English knights who had fled there from Bannockburn, was rewarded by Robert Bruce with knighthood and grants of lands in Clydesdale, West Lothian and elsewhere. His grandson, Sir David of Hamilton of Cadzow, was the first to assume the surname of Hamilton. The Earls of Haddington are descended from a younger son of Sir David. Other titles apart from those appearing below conferred on members of the house were those of Lord Belhaven, Viscount Boyne, Baron Brancepeth, Viscount Clanboy and Earl of Clanbrassil. See Gilbert Burnet's *Memoirs of James and William, Dukes of Hamilton* (1677); works on the House by J. Anderson (1825) and G. Hamilton (1934); the *Hamilton MSS.* (Hist. MSS. Report, 1887). The most noteworthy members were:

(1) **Sir James, 1st Baron** (d. 1479), great-grandson of Sir David, was created baron in 1445. Allied by marriage and descent to the Douglases, he followed them in the beginning of their struggle with the crown, but forsook them in 1454, and for reward got large grants of their forfeited lands. After the death of his first wife he received in marriage the Princess Mary, eldest daughter of James II, formerly the wife of the attainted Earl of

Arran. His son **James** (c. 1477-1529) was created earl of Arran in 1503.

(2) **James, 2nd Earl of Arran, 3rd Baron** (1515?-75), grandson of (1) by the niece of Cardinal Beaton, was a young man when the death of James V in 1542 left only an infant a few days old between him and the throne. He was chosen regent and tutor to the young queen, and held these offices till 1554. He received in 1548, from Henry II of France, a grant of the duchy of Châtelherault.—His fourth son, **Claud** (c. 1543-1622), was made commendator of the abbey of Paisley in 1553, and Lord Paisley in 1587. His descendants obtained successively the titles of Lord Abercorn (1603), Earl of Abercorn (1606), Viscount Strabane (1701), Marquis of Abercorn (1790), and Duke of Abercorn (1868). On the death of the 2nd Duke of Hamilton in 1651, the 2nd Earl of Abercorn claimed the male representation of the House of Hamilton; and in 1861 the 2nd Marquis and 10th Earl of Abercorn was declared sole heir of the 1st Duke of Châtelherault under protest by the Duke of Hamilton. **James, 3rd Duke of Abercorn** (1869-1953) was, by three successive renewals of his term, governor of Northern Ireland (1922-45).

(3) **James, 3rd Earl of Arran, 4th Baron** (1530-1609), son of (2), was proposed as the husband both of Queen Mary of Scotland and of Queen Elizabeth of England, but went mad in 1562, and was succeeded by (4).

(4) **John, 1st Marquis of** (1532?-1604), second son of (2), succeeded his insane brother (3) and was created marquis in 1599. He was a loyal adherent of Mary, Queen of Scots.

(5) **James, 1st Earl of Cambridge and 2nd Marquis of** (1589-1625), was elevated to the English peerage in 1619.

(6) **James, 3rd Marquis and 1st Duke of** (1606-49), son of (5), led an army of 6000 men to the support of Gustavus Adolphus in 1631-32, and later played a conspicuous part in the contest between Charles I and the Covenanters. Created duke in 1643, he led a Scottish army into England (1643) but was defeated by Cromwell at Preston, and beheaded.

(7) **William, 2nd Duke of** (1616-51), brother and successor of (6), was in 1639 created Earl of Lanark, and died of wounds received at Worcester. The duchy of Hamilton now devolved on the eldest daughter of the first Duke, **Lady Anne** (1636-1717), whose husband, Lord William Douglas, Earl of Selkirk (1635-94), was in 1660 created 3rd Duke of Hamilton for life. One of her sons was in 1688 created Earl of Selkirk; another in 1696 Earl of Orkney; another Earl of Ruglen in 1697.

(8) **James Douglas, 4th Duke of** (1658-1712), was created 1st Duke of Brandon in 1771, a title challenged by the House of Lords. He fought against Monmouth, led Scottish opposition to the Union, but discouraged bloodshed. He helped to negotiate the Treaty of Utrecht (1713) and was killed, as described in Thackeray's *Henry Esmond*, in a duel with Lord Mohun.

(9) **James George, 7th Duke of** (1755-69), great-grandson of (8), succeeded to the title at the age of three. On the death of the Duke of Douglas in 1761, the male representation of the Angus branch of the Douglases, with the titles of Marquis of Douglas, Earl of Angus, &c., devolved on the Dukes of Hamilton as descendants of the Earl of Selkirk, third son of the first Marquis of Douglas.

(10) **Douglas Douglas-, 14th Duke of** (1903-1973), was chief pilot of the Mount Everest flight expedition (1932), M.P. for East Renfrew (1930-40) and lord high commissioner to the Church of Scotland (1953-55 and 1958).

HAMILTON, (1) Alexander (1757-1804), American statesman, was born in the West Indian island of Nevis. When a student in New York he wrote a series of papers in defence of the rights of the colonies against Great Britain; and on the outbreak of the war, as captain of artillery, he served in New York and New Jersey, and in 1777 became Washington's aide-de-camp. In 1781, after a quarrel, Hamilton resigned his appointment, but he continued with the army and distinguished himself at Yorktown. After the war, he studied law and became one of the most eminent lawyers in New York; in 1782 he was returned to congress. In 1786 he took the leading part in the convention at Annapolis, which prepared the way for the great convention that met at Philadelphia in 1787. In the same year he conceived the series of essays afterwards collected as *The Federalist*, and himself wrote fifty-one out of the eighty-five. On the establishment of the new government in 1789, Hamilton was appointed secretary of the treasury and restored the country's finances to a firm footing. In 1795 he resigned his office, but remained the actual leader of the Federal party until his death, and was foremost in the party strife of 1801. His successful effort to thwart the ambition of his rival, Aaron Burr, involved him in a mortal duel with him, July 11, and he died the next day. See Lives by his son (1834-40), Schachner (1946) and B. Mitchell (2 vols., 1962), F. S. Oliver's essay (1906) and his *Papers* (vols. I and II, ed. by Syrett and Cooke, 1962).

(2) **Count Anthony** (c. 1646-1720), Irish writer, was probably born at Roscrea, Tipperary. At twenty-one he went to France, and there got a captain's commission; in 1685 he was appointed governor of Limerick, and fought at the Boyne (1690); thereafter he lived at the exiled court of St Germain-en-Laye. His writings are full of wit and talent, particularly his *Contes de féerie* (1730-49; Eng. trans. 1760). For his *Mémoires du Comte de Gramont*, see GRAMONT; also translation by P. Quennell (1931) and Life by A. Clark (1921).

(3) **Elizabeth** (1758-1816), Scottish author of *The Cottagers of Glenburnie* (1808), &c., was born at Belfast, and from 1804 lived at Edinburgh.

(4) **Emma, Lady** (c. 1765-1815), Lord Nelson's mistress, was born Emily Lyon, most likely at Ness, in Cheshire. Her girlhood was passed at Hawarden. She had had three places in London, had borne two children to a navy captain and a baronet, and had posed as Hygieia in the 'Temple of

Health ' of James Graham (q.v.) the famous quack, when in 1782 she accepted the protection of the Hon. Charles Greville (1749–1809), to exchange it in 1786 for that of his uncle, Sir William Hamilton (15). After five years at Naples, in 1791 she was married to the latter, and was admitted to the closest intimacy by Maria Caroline, queen of Ferdinand I. Her ' eminent services ' to the British fleet during 1796–98 in furnishing information and procuring supplies were much overrated, but not imaginary. Nelson had first met her in 1793; four months after the trio's return to England, she gave birth to a daughter (1801–81), ' our loved Horatia ', so Nelson writes of her in a holograph letter to ' my own dear Wife, in my eyes and the face of Heaven '. Her husband's death, and two years and a half later Nelson's, left Emma mistress of £2000 a year; but by 1808 she was owing £18,000, and in 1813 was arrested for debt. Next year she fled to Calais, where she died. Her loveliness lives in nearly fifty portraits by Romney. See the spiteful *Memoirs of Lady Hamilton* (1815), Jeaffreson's *Lady Hamilton and Nelson* (1888), her *Life and Letters* (ed. by H. Tours, 1963) and Lives by W. Sichel (1905), E. H. Moorhouse (1912), O. Warner (1960).

(5) **Iain Ellis** (1922–), Scottish composer, born in Glasgow. Originally trained as an engineer, in 1947 he entered the Royal College of Music, first attracting attention when his clarinet quintet was played at a concert of the Society for the Promotion of New Music. In 1951, Hamilton won the Royal Philharmonic Society's prize for his clarinet concerto, and an award from the Koussevitsky Foundation for his second symphony, which was followed by the symphonic variations (1953). Since then, his works, which are original in technique and highly expressive, have attracted universal interest.

(6) **Sir Ian Standish Monteith** (1853–1947), British general, born in Corfu, entered the army 1873, served with distinction in Afghanistan (1878), Boer wars (1881, 1899–1901), and led the disastrous Gallipoli Expedition (1915). G.C.B., G.C.M.G., he was lieutenant of the Tower (1918–20). See his *Gallipoli Diary* (1920), &c.

(7) **James.** See MORAY.

(8) **James** (1769–1829), English educationist, born in London, introduced in America (1815) and England a new system of learning languages, discarding grammar, and using instead a literal word for word translation, with interlinear textbooks. His system resembles that of Jacotot (q.v.).

(9) **Patrick** (?1498–1528), ' the protomartyr of the Scottish Reformation', was the son of Sir Patrick Hamilton and Catherine Stewart, the illegitimate daughter of the Duke of Albany, second son of James II. Born about 1499 in the diocese of Glasgow, he took his M.A. at Paris in 1520, then proceeded to Louvain, and in 1523 was at St Andrews, whence, to escape troubles on account of his Lutheranism, he returned to the Continent (1527). After a brief stay at Wittenberg, he settled for some months in Marburg, where he wrote (in Latin) a series of

theological propositions known as ' Patrick's Places ', propounding the doctrines of the Lutherans. He returned that same autumn to Scotland, and married. Next year he was summoned to St Andrews by Archbishop Beaton, and on a renewed charge of heresy was burned before St Salvator's College, February 29. His death did more to extend the Reformation in Scotland than ever his life could have done. See Lives by Lorimer (1857), A. Cameron (1930), and D. H. Fleming *Reformation in Scotland* (1910).

(10) **Terrick** (1781–1876), Scottish linguist and orientalist, translator (1820) of the first four volumes of *Sirat Antarah*, narrative of the poet Antar (q.v.), after service with the East India Company became secretary of the British embassy at Constantinople.

(11) **Thomas** (1789–1842), author in 1827 of *Cyril Thornton*, was a younger brother of (16), studied three years at Glasgow University, served eight years in the army, joined *Blackwood's* staff, and died at Pisa.

(12) **Walter Kerr** (1808–69), the Bishop of Salisbury, first of the Tractarians to become a diocesan bishop (from 1854) in England, was born in London and educated at Eton, Laleham (under Arnold), and Christ Church, Oxford. A member of the Oxford Movement, he founded Salisbury Theological College (1860) and advocated cathedral reform.

(13) **William** (*c*. 1665–1751), Scottish minor poet, of Gilbertfield near Glasgow, the friend and correspondent of Allan Ramsay, modernizer of Blind Harry (q.v.).

(14) **William** (1704–54), Scottish poet, born at Bangour, contributed to Ramsay's *Teatable Miscellany* (1724). He joined in the Jacobite rising of the '45, and on its collapse escaped to Rouen, but was permitted to return in 1749 and to succeed to the family estate of Bangour, Linlithgowshire. He died at Lyons. The first collection of his poems was edited by Adam Smith in 1748. He is best known by ' The Braes of Yarrow '. See James Paterson's edition of the poems (1850) and Life by N. S. Bushnell (1957).

(15) **Sir William** (1730–1803), British diplomat and antiquary, grandson of the third Duke of Hamilton, and a husband of (4), was British ambassador at Naples (1764–1800), and in 1772 was made a knight of the Bath. He took an active part in the excavation of Herculaneum and Pompeii, and formed rare collections of antiquities, one of them purchased in 1772 for the British Museum. He wrote several works on Greek and Roman antiquities. He may have condoned his wife's intimacy with Nelson, for the latter was present at his death.

(16) **Sir William, Bart.** (1788–1856), Scottish philosopher, was born at Glasgow, where his father and grandfather held the chairs of Anatomy and Botany; in 1816 he made good his claim to the old baronetcy which the Covenanting heir lost in 1688 for refusing the oath of allegiance. After gaining high distinction at Glasgow, he went in 1809 to Balliol College as Snell exhibitioner and graduated in 1810. He was called to the Scottish bar in 1813, but had almost no practice; in 1820 he stood unsuccessfully for the chair of Moral Philosophy in Edin-

burgh; in 1821 he became professor of History. In 1829 he published in the *Edinburgh Review* a famous critique of Cousin's doctrine of the Infinite; this and other articles were collected in 1852 as *Discussions in Philosophy and Literature.* In 1836 he became professor of Logic and Metaphysics. His lectures were published (1859–61) by Mansel and Veitch; his principal work was his edition of Reid (1846; with notes 1862), defending what he believed to be Reid's philosophical doctrine of common sense, i.e., common reason. Ill-health diminished his power of work; but he edited Dugald Stewart's works (1854–55), and was generally able with an assistant to perform the duties of his class till his death. See Life by Veitch (1869), monographs by Veitch (1882), Monck (1881), Rasmussen (1924), and Seth's *Scottish Philosophy* (1885).

(17) **William Gerard** (1729–96), English politician, entered parliament for Petersfield in 1755, and was known as ' single-speech Hamilton ', though his brilliant maiden effort had successors.

(18) **Sir William Rowan** (1805–65), Irish mathematician, the inventor of quaternions, born in Dublin, at fifteen knew thirteen languages, had read Newton's *Principia*, and commenced original investigations. In 1827, while still an undergraduate, he was appointed professor of Astronomy at Dublin and Irish astronomer-royal; in 1835 he was knighted. His earlier essays connected with caustics and contact of curves grew into the *Theory of Systems of Rays* (1828; new ed. 1833), which helped to confirm the undulatory theory of light. His *General Method in Dynamics* (*Philos. Trans.* 1834) made a profound impression and his memoir on *Algebra as the Science of Pure Time* was one of the first steps to his grand invention of quaternions. On this subject he published in 1853 a large volume of *Lectures*; another was edited by his son the year after his death. See Life by Graves (1882–89), with *Addendum* (1891).

HAMLET, the doubtfully historical hero of Shakespeare's tragedy, first appears in the legend of Amleth in the third and fourth books of the 12th century Latin history of Denmark by Saxo Grammaticus. See works by J. Schick (1913–15), I. Gollancz (1926); R. Walker, *The Time is out of Joint* (1948), and bibliography, R. Walker (1936).

HAMLEY, Sir Edward Bruce (1824–93), British soldier, born at Bodmin, served in Ireland, Canada and the Crimea, and was commandant of the Staff College (1870–77). He commanded the second division in the Egyptian campaign of 1882, and had a difference with Lord Wolseley over Tel-el-Kebir; was created a K.C.M.G. in 1880, a K.C.B. in 1882; and was Conservative M.P. for Birkenhead (1885–92). He wrote on *The War in the Crimea* (1855), *The Operations of War* (1866, the standard textbook), *Voltaire* (1877), &c. See Life by Shand (1895).

HAMLIN, Hannibal (1809–91), American statesman, born in Paris, Maine, practised law (1833–48), was speaker of the Maine house of representatives, and was returned to congress in 1842 and 1844. He sat in the U.S. senate as a Democrat (1848–57), when he was elected governor by the Republicans, having separated from his party over his anti-slavery opinions. In the same year, 1857, he resigned to return to the senate; and in 1861 became vice-president under Lincoln. He was in the senate again (1869–81); and was minister to Spain (1881–82). See his Autobiography (1894).

HAMMARSKJÖLD, Dag Hjalmar Agne Carl, *ham′mêr-shœld* (1905–61), secretary-general of the United Nations from 1953, was born at Jönköping, Sweden. In 1933 he became an assistant professor at Stockholm University, in 1935 secretary and from 1941 to 1948, chairman of the Bank of Sweden. He was Swedish foreign minister (1951–53), a delegate to O.E.E.C., U.N.I.S.A.N., the Council of Europe and the U.N. General Assembly. Hammarskjöld, who once described himself as ' the curator of the secrets of 82 nations ', played a leading part in the setting up of the U.N. Emergency Force in Sinai and Gaza in 1956, in conciliation moves in the Middle East in 1957-58 and in sending observers to the Lebanon in 1958. He was awarded the Nobel peace prize for 1961 after his death in an air crash near Ndola in Zambia in Sept. 1961, while engaged in negotiations over the Congo crisis. See Life by J. P. Lash (1962).

HAMMER-PURGSTALL, Joseph, Freiherr von (1774–1856), Austrian orientalist, was born at Graz, studied at Vienna, and was an interpreter at Constantinople (1799–1806). He wrote on Middle East history and literature. See Life by Schlottmann (1857).

HAMMERSTEIN, *-stīn,* (1) **Oscar** (*c.* 1847–1919), American theatre manager, uncle of (2), born in Berlin, emigrated to the United States, made a fortune by inventing a machine for spreading tobacco leaves, while employed in a cigar factory, and founded and edited the *United States Tobacco Journal.* He leased, built or opened numerous theatres in New York, Philadelphia and London.

(2) **Oscar** (1895–1960), American librettist, nephew of (1), author of a large number of musical plays, often in collaboration with the composer, **Richard Rodgers** (1902–), of which the most popular were *Rose Marie* (1924), *Desert Song* (1926), *Music in the Air* (1932), *Oklahoma!* (1943), *Carmen Jones* (1943), *South Pacific* (1949), *The King and I* (1951), and *The Sound of Music* (1959).

HAMMETT, Dashiel (1894–1961), American writer, born in Maryland. His early career was spent with the Pinkerton Detective Agency in New York, where he obtained the experience which enabled him to become the first U.S. author of authentic ' private eye ' crime stories. His best known books are *The Maltese Falcon* (1930) and *The Thin Man* (1934).

HAMMOND, Henry (1605–60), English divine, was born at Chertsey, and educated at Eton and Magdalen College, Oxford. In 1633 he became rector of Penshurst, and in 1643 archdeacon of Chichester. His loyalty to Charles I cost him his living; yet he officiated as chaplain to the king till 1647, when he returned to Oxford, and was chosen sub-dean of Christ Church. Deprived by the parliamentary commissioners in 1648, he retired to Westwood in Worcestershire, where he died. His celebrated *Paraphrase and Annotations on the New Testament* was published in 1653. See Life by Bishop Fell prefixed to his *Miscellaneous Theological Works* (' Anglo-Catholic Library ', 1847–50).

HAMMURABI (18th cent. B.C.), Babylonian king, the 6th of the Amorite 1st dynasty, extended the Babylonian empire and set up a remarkably efficient administration, as his letters to his governors testify. A tablet inscribed with the code of Hammurabian Law, surprisingly advanced for one of the earliest known legal codes, is in the Louvre.

HAMP, Pierre, pseud. of **Pierre Bourillon, â** (1876–1962), French author, born at Nice of humble parentage and in every sense a self-made and self-educated man, brought to bear in his novels a realism bred of firsthand experience. Among his works are *Marée fraîche* (1908), *Le Rail* (1912), *Les Métiers blessés* (1919), *Le Lin* (1924) and *La Laine* (1931), his novels of industrial life forming a cycle which he called *La Peine des hommes.*

HAMPDEN, (1) **John** (1594–1643), English parliamentarian and patriot, the eldest son of William Hampden of Hampden, Bucks, was educated at Magdalen College, Oxford, and in 1613 at the Inner Temple, London. In 1621 he was returned by Grampound to parliament, and subsequently he sat for Wendover. Although he was no orator, his judgment, veracity and high character secured for him a leading position in the opposition party. In 1626 he helped to prepare the charges against Buckingham; next year, having refused to pay his proportion of the general loan which Charles attempted to raise on his own authority, he was imprisoned. His leading associates were Pym and Eliot. When Charles dissolved parliament in 1629, Hampden retired to his seat in Buckinghamshire, and gave himself up to the life of a country gentleman. In 1634 Charles resorted to the import of ship-money, and in 1636 he extended it to inland places. Hampden refused to pay his share, and in 1637 he was prosecuted before the Court of Exchequer. Seven of the twelve judges sided against him, but the prosecution made Hampden the most popular man in England. He was member for Bucks both in the Short Parliament and the Long, where he took part in almost all its leading transactions, especially those which ended in Strafford's death. He had never any faith in the king, and when it seemed not impossible that Charles would be able to crush the liberties of his country, Hampden, like Cromwell, meditated self exile to New England. He was one of the five members whose attempted seizure by Charles (1642) precipitated the Civil War. When hostilities broke out, Hampden subscribed £2000 to the public service, took a colonel's commission, and raised a regiment of infantry for the Parliamentary army; at Edgehill and Reading he exhibited personal bravery and generalship. On June 18, 1643, while endeavouring, on Chalgrove Field, to check a marauding force under Prince Rupert, he was wounded in the shoulder and died on the 24th at Thame. He was the most moderate, tactical, urbane and single-minded of the leaders of the Long Parliament. See Lord Nugent's *Memorials of Hampden* (1831), Macaulay's *Edinburgh* article thereon (1831), Life by H. R. Williamson (1933).

(2) **Renn Dickson** (1793–1868), English divine, born in Barbados, took a double first at Oxford in 1813, and became a fellow and tutor of Oriel. His famous Bampton lectures on the *Scholastic Philosophy* (1832) raised a controversy that threatened to break up the Church of England; his appointments to the principalship of St Mary's Hall (1833), and to the chairs of Moral Philosophy (1834) and Divinity (1836), were denounced by the High Church party; and his elevation to the see of Hereford in 1847 was regarded as a death blow to Trinitarian religion. See *Memorials* by his daughter (1871).

HAMPOLE, Richard Rolle de (c. 1290–1349), English hermit and poet, the ' Hermit of Hampole ', near Doncaster, was born at Thornton in Yorkshire, and was sent to Oxford, but at nineteen turned hermit. He wrote English lyrics and religious books in Latin and English, and translated and expounded the Psalms in prose. *The Pricke of Conscience (Stimulus Conscientiae)* is no longer thought to be his. See studies by Horstmann (1896), Hope Emily Allen (1928). Miss Allen edited his *English Writings* (1931).

HAMPTON, (1) **Wade** (1754–1835), American soldier, grandfather of (2), born in S. Carolina, served in the revolutionary war, and in 1813, now major-general, made an unsuccessful attempt to invade Canada.

(2) **Wade** (1818–1902), American soldier, grandson of (1), born in Columbia, in 1861 raised ' Hampton's Legion '. As brigadier-general he commanded a cavalry force in 1862–63, was wounded at Gettysburg, received the command of Lee's cavalry in 1864, and in 1865 served in S. Carolina against Sherman. He became state governor (1876), and was U.S. senator (1878–91).

HAMSUN, Knut, *ham'soon,* pseudonym of **Knut Pedersen** (1859–1952), Norwegian writer, born at Lom in the Gudbrandsdal. He had no formal education, and spent his boyhood with his uncle in the Lofoten Islands. He was in turn shoemaker, coal-trimmer and country schoolmaster, and emigrated twice to America, working at one time as tram conductor in Chicago. He sprang to fame with *Sult* (1888; later translated as *Hunger*), but his best-known book is *The Growth of the Soil* (1917), which was mainly responsible for his Nobel prize for Literature in 1920. Hamsun was something of a recluse in his later years, but his German philosophy of primitive forces led him to welcome the Nazi invasion of 1940, and he was fined for collaboration in 1948.

HANCOCK, (1) **John** (1737–93), American statesman, born at Quincy, Mass., as president (1775–77) of the Continental Congress, first signed the Declaration of Independence.

(2) **Winfield Scott** (1824–86), American general, was born near Philadelphia, studied at West Point, served through the Mexican

war, and was captain when the Civil War broke out. In 1861 he organized the army of the Potomac, was prominent at South Mountain, Antietam and Fredericksburg, and in 1863 took command of the 2nd corps. At Gettysburg he was in command until Meade's arrival; and on July 3 was severely wounded. In 1864 he was conspicuous in the battles of the Wilderness, Spottsylvania and Cold Harbor, and in 1864 was created brigadier-general, but was disabled for active service by a wound. Democratic candidate for the presidency in 1880, he was defeated by Garfield. He died in New York. See *Lives* by Junkin and Norton (1880), Goodrich (1886), his widow (1887), and General Walker (1890).

HANDEL, properly Händel, George Frederick (1685–1759), German-English composer, was born at Halle, February 23. Persisting in his application to music against the wishes of his barber-surgeon father, he became organist of Halle Cathedral at the age of seventeen whilst also studying law at the University. From 1703 to 1706 he gained invaluable experience as a violinist and keyboard player in the Hamburg opera orchestra, during which time he tried his hand at writing Italian operas, e.g., *Almira*. The next four years were spent in Italy, where as 'il caro Sassone' he established a great reputation as a keyboard virtuoso and had considerable success as an operatic composer. Appointed in 1710 to the court of the Elector of Hanover, he took frequent leaves of indefinite absence to try his fortune in London, introducing himself with the opera *Rinaldo* (1711). This persistent absenteeism displeased his master, and the succession of the Elector to the English throne as George I led at first to some awkwardness; the *Water Music*, composed for a river procession, is said to have been a peace offering. Attached to the households of the Earl of Burlingham and subsequently to that of the Duke of Chandos between 1713 and 1720, he then went into opera promotion at the King's Theatre, Haymarket, under the auspices of the newly founded Royal Academy of Music 'to secure a constant supply of operas by Handel to be performed under his direction'. The satisfying of the fickle taste of the fashionable London world with Italian opera involved him in extremes of fortune (the Royal Academy of Music came to an end in 1728, was resuscitated temporarily, but collapsed again, after which Handel went into partnership with Rich at Covent Garden). Artistic and political intrigues, and opposition composers and companies, not to mention the success of the parodistic *Beggar's Opera*, induced him to experiment with a new form, the English oratorio. Though leaning on operatic models, and performed in theatres usually during Lent, this venture proved enormously popular. In 1735, Handel conducted fifteen oratorio concerts in London. After a stroke in 1737 he rallied and in the next five years produced *Saul* (1739), *Israel in Egypt* (1739) and *Messiah* (1742), the latter having been first performed in Dublin. *Samson* followed in 1743, succeeded by *Joseph, Semele, Judas Maccabeus, Solomon,* &c., his last *Jephthah*, appearing in 1750. He died in London on April 4, 1759, his eyesight having failed in the final years, and he was buried in Poet's Corner, Westminster Abbey. A sociable, cultivated, cosmopolitan figure, and a very prolific composer like his exact contemporary J. S. Bach, Handel wrote for the most part in the Italianate style of the day, though in his settings of English words there are reflections of Purcell. His output included 46 operas, 32 oratorios, large numbers of cantatas, sacred music, concerti grossi and other orchestral, instrumental and vocal music. See works by Chrysander (1858–67), Flower (1923), Leichtentritt (1926), Dent (1934), P. M. Young (1947) and W. C. Smith (1949).

HANDLEY, Thomas Reginald (1892–1949), British comedian, born in Liverpool, served in World War I, worked in variety and concert parties, in the infancy of radio became known as a regular broadcaster, and in 1939 achieved nationwide fame through his weekly programme ITMA (It's That Man Again), which, with its endearing mixture of satire, parody, slapstick, wit and verbal gymnastics, became a major factor in the boosting of wartime morale and continued a prime favourite until brought to an untimely end by his sudden death.

HANDY, William Christopher (1873–1958), American Negro composer, born in Florence, Alabama. Overcoming the opposition of his father, a Methodist preacher, to his choice of a musical career, Handy joined a minstrel show as a cornet player, and in 1903 formed his own band in Memphis, subsequently moving to Chicago and to New York, where he formed his own publishing company. He was the first to introduce the Negro 'blues' style to printed music, his most famous work being the *Saint Louis Blues* (1914). See his autobiographical *Father of the Blues* (1958).

HANNAY, (1) James (1827–73), Scottish writer, born at Dumfries, after five years in the navy, was dismissed at eighteen by a court martial sentence, afterwards quashed as irregular. He edited the *Edinburgh Courant* 1860–64, and from 1868 was British consul at Barcelona, where he died. Of his novels, the best are *Singleton Fontenoy* (1850) and *Eustace Conyers* (1855). He also published *Lectures on Satire and Satirists* (1854) and *Studies on Thackeray* (1869).
(2) **James Owen**, pen-name **George A. Birmingham** (1865–1950), Irish novelist, born in Belfast, was canon of St Patrick's cathedral, Dublin, rector of Wells (1924) and Kensington Gore (1934), wrote a number of humorous novels on Irish life including *Spanish Gold* (1908), *The Inviolable Sanctuary* (1912), *Good Intentions* (1945), &c.

HANNIBAL, 'the grace of Baal' (247–182 B.C.), Carthaginian soldier, the son of Hamilcar Barca (q.v.). In his ninth year his father bade him swear eternal enmity to Rome. He served in Spain under Hamilcar and Hasdrubal; and as general reduced all southern Spain up to the Ebro (221–219) with the exception of the Iberian town of Saguntum. That town fell in 218, and the

Second Punic war began. In 218 he left New Carthage, crossed the Pyrenees, gained the Rhone, defeated the Gauls, and crossed the Alps in fifteen days, in the face of almost insuperable obstacles. His troops, used to the African and Spanish climate, perished in thousands amid ice and snow; but he overcame the Taurini, forced Ligurian and Celtic tribes to serve in his army, and at the Ticinus drove back the Romans under Scipio. The first great battle was fought in the plain of the Trebia, when the men of the Roman consular army were either cut to pieces or scattered in flight. Wintering in the valley of the Po, in spring Hannibal crossed the Apennines, wasted Etruria with fire and sword, and marched towards Rome. He awaited the consul Flaminius by Lake Trasimene, where he inflicted on him a crushing defeat; the Roman army was annihilated. Passing through Apulia and Campania, he wintered at Gerunium, and in the spring at Cannae on the Aufidus utterly destroyed another Roman army. But after Cannae the tide turned. His niggardly countrymen denied him necessary support. As his veterans were lost to him he had no means of filling their places, while the Romans could put army after army into the field. But through the long years during which he maintained a hopeless struggle in Italy he was never defeated. He spent the winter of 216-215 at Capua. When he again took the field the Romans wisely avoided a pitched battle, though the Carthaginians overran Italy, took towns, and gained minor victories. But Capua fell in 210. In 207 his brother Hasdrubal, marching from Spain to his aid, was defeated and slain at the Metaurus by the consul Nero. For four years Hannibal stood at bay in the hill-country of Bruttium, till in 203 he was recalled to Africa to repel the Roman invasion. In the next year he met Scipio at Zama; his raw levies fled, his veterans were cut to pieces, and Carthage was at the mercy of Rome. So ended the Second Punic war. Peace being made, Hannibal turned his genius to political reforms, but raised such virulent opposition that, a voluntary exile, he betook himself to the court of Antiochus at Ephesus, then to that of Prusias, king of Bithynia. The Romans demanding his surrender, he took poison, and died at Libyssa. See Hennebert's *Annibal* (1870-92), Lives by Dodge (1891), Morris (1897), and book by Groag (1929).

HANNINGTON, James (1847-85), English missionary, born at Hurstpierpoint, studied at Oxford, and in 1882, after a seven years' curacy in his native parish, went out to Uganda under the Church Missionary Society. Fever and dysentery forced him to return to England; but he was in June 1884 consecrated first Bishop of Eastern Equatorial Africa, and in January 1885 came to Mombasa. In July he started thence for Uganda, where he was slain by King Mwanga, October 29. See Life by Dawson (1887), and his *Last Journals* (1888).

HANNO (6th-5th centuries B.C.), Carthaginian navigator, undertook a voyage along the west coast of Africa. He founded colonies, and reached Cape Nun or the Bight of Benin.

We have a Greek translation of his *Periplus*. See monographs by Mer (Paris 1885) and Fischer (Leipzig 1893).

HANOTAUX, Gabriel, an-ō-tō (1853-1944), French historian and statesman, born at Beaurevoir, Aisne, held minor government offices, and was twice foreign minister. (1892-98). An Academician (1897), he wrote *Richelieu, Jeanne d'Arc*, &c., and a great history of *Contemporary France* (trans. 1904), *Maréchal Foch* (1929), &c.

HANSARD, Luke (1752-1828), English printer, came from Norwich to London, and entered the office of Hughes, printer to the House of Commons, becoming acting manager in 1774, and in 1798 succeeding as sole proprietor of the business. He and his descendants printed the parliamentary reports from 1774 to 1889; and Cobbett's *Parliamentary History 1066-1800* was continued from 1806 by his son and successors. See *Memoir* (1829).

HANSEN, (1) **Armauer** (1841-1912), Norwegian bacteriologist, a physician of Bergen, discovered the leprosy bacillus in 1879.

(2) **Martin Alfred** (1909-55), Danish novelist, of farming stock, worked on the land and as a teacher, but after 1945 devoted himself to writing. His early novels deal with social problems in the 1930s (*Nu opgiver han* ' Surrender ', 1935; *Kolonien* ' The Colony ', 1937). Later he developed a more profound style in *Jonathans Rejse* ' Jonathan's Journey ' (1941) and *Lykkelige Kristoffer* ' Lucky Christopher ' (1945), outwardly picaresque novels but in reality closely related to his work for the Danish underground press during the Occupation. With *Løgneren* ' The Liar ' (1950), a psychological novel intended first for broadcasting as a serial, he reached a wider public than ever. In 1952 appeared his most original work, the metaphysical *Orm og Tyr* ' The Serpent and the Bull '. Other writings include *Tornebusken* ' The Thorn Bush ' (1946, short stories) and *Tanker i en Skorsten* ' Thoughts up a Chimney ' (1948, essays).

HANSLICK, Eduard (1825-1904), Austrian music critic and writer on aesthetics, professor from 1861 at Vienna, supported Schumann and Brahms against Wagner in his critical writings and propounded a form theory of aesthetics in his *Vom Musikalisch-Schönen* (1854; trans. 1891), which did for music what the Bell-Fry theories later did for painting. See study by S. Deas (1940).

HANSOM, Joseph Aloysius (1803-82), English inventor and architect, born at York, invented the ' Patent Safety (Hansom) Cab ' in 1834 and designed Birmingham town hall and the R.C. cathedral at Plymouth.

HANSON, Howard (1896-), American composer, born in Wahoo, Nebraska. He was awarded the American Prix de Rome in 1921, and after three years' study in Italy became director of the Eastman School of Music, which, under his leadership, has become one of the most important centres of American musical life. His compositions, firmly in the tradition of 19th century romanticism, include an opera, *The Merry Mount*, and five symphonies.

HANSSON, Ola (1860-1925), Swedish poet,

novelist, and critic, born at Hönsinge, lived in Germany, wrote mostly in German, deserting naturalism for Nietzsche's idealism.

HANSTEEN, Christoph, *hahn'stayn* (1784–1873), Norwegian astronomer, was born at Christiania, where he became professor of Mathematics in 1814. He investigated terrestrial magnetism, discovered the ' law of magnetic force ' (1821) and made a scientific journey to Eastern Siberia (1828–1830).

HAN SUYIN (1917–), Chinese-born English novelist, born Elizabeth Chow in Peking, studied medicine there, at Brussels and at London, where after the death in the civil war of her husband, General Tang, she completed her studies. She then practised in Hong Kong, which with its undercurrents of pro-Western and anti-Western loyalties, Old China versus the New, White versus Yellow, provided the background for her first partly-autobiographical novel *A Many-splendoured Thing* (1952), which in the love-affair of an emancipated Chinese girl and an English journalist symbolizes the political and ideological climate of the British colony. In 1952 she married an English police officer in Singapore, where she practised in an anti-tuberculosis clinic. Other novels include *Destination Chungking* (1953), *The Mountain is Young* (1958) and *Four Faces* (1963).

HANTZSCH, Arthur (1857–1935), German organic chemist, born at Dresden, professor at Leipzig, investigated the arrangement of atoms in the molecules of nitrogen compounds and the electrical conductivity of organic compounds.

HANWAY, Jonas (1712–86), English traveller and philanthropist, was born at Portsmouth. Apprenticed at seventeen to a Lisbon merchant, he afterwards traded at St Petersburg, and travelled through Russia and Persia (1743–50). He published an account of his travels in 1753, and spent the rest of his life mostly in London as a navy victualling commissioner (1762–83). He was an unwearying friend to chimney sweeps, waifs and down-and-outs, and advocated solitary confinement for prisoners and milder punishments. The author of seventy-four works, he wrote against the practice of giving gratuities, and was the first Englishman to carry an umbrella. His attack on tea drinking was met by Dr Johnson. See Life by Pugh (1787) and Austin Dobson's *Eighteenth Century Vignettes* (1892).

HAPSBURG, or **Habsburg,** name of the Austrian imperial family, from the castle of Habsburg, or Habichtsburg (' Hawk's Castle '), on the Aar, in the Swiss canton of Aargau. The founder of the family was Albert, Count of Hapsburg in 1153. Under him and his son, **Rudolf I,** the family became one of the most powerful in Swabia. **Rudolf III** (Rudolf I of Austria), who was elected emperor (1273), by wresting Upper and Lower Austria, Styria and Carniola from Ottocar of Bohemia, greatly increased the power of his family. Carinthia and Tirol were added (1336–64). From 1440 to 1806 the Hapsburgs almost uninterruptedly wore the imperial crown; thereafter, till exiled in

1918, they wore that of Austria. The original family possessions were absorbed by the Swiss confederated cantons (1386–1474). See studies by Colquhoun (1906), H. Wickham Steed (1919), A. J. P. Taylor (1948), and *Memoirs of Princess Fugger* (trans. 1932).

HARCOURT, Sir William Vernon (1827–1904), British Liberal statesman, born in York, graduated from Trinity College, Cambridge, in 1851. Called to the bar in 1854, Q.C. in 1866, he acquired distinction by his contributions to the *Saturday Review*, and by his letters in the *Times* signed ' Historicus ', and collected in 1863. Liberal M.P. for the city of Oxford (1868), in 1869 he was elected professor of International Law at Cambridge; he was solicitor-general (1873–74); in 1880 he became home secretary. In 1885 he went out of office with Gladstone, but returned with him for six months in 1886, when he was chancellor of the Exchequer—an office he resumed in 1892. On Gladstone's retirement in 1893 Sir William became leader of the Lower House. His principal work was the revision of the death duties and his 1894 budget. His lukewarm support of his chief led to Lord Rosebery's resignation in 1896. After a crusade against Ritualism in 1898, he resigned the Liberal leadership, remaining a private member of the party. His second wife (1876) was Motley's daughter **Elizabeth** (1841–1928). See Gardiner's *Life* (1923).—His son, **Lewis Vernon** (1863–1922), Viscount (1916), was first commissioner of works 1905–10, 1915–16; colonial secretary, 1910–1915.

HARDEN, (1) Sir Arthur (1865–1940), English chemist, born at Manchester, professor of Biochemistry at the Lister Institute, was awarded the Nobel prize in 1929 for his work (with Euler-Chelpin) on alcoholic fermentation and enzymes. F.R.S. in 1909, he was knighted in 1936.

(2) **Maximilian** (1861–1927), German journalist, born at Berlin, founded and edited the weekly *Die Zukunft* (1892–1922). He exposed court scandals. A fearless critic with a powerful pen, he was silenced and called up as an army clerk in 1917. See Life by H. F. Young (1959).

HARDENBERG, (1) Heinrich von. See Novalis.

(2) **Karl August, Fürst von** (1750–1822), Prussian statesman, born at Essenrode in Hanover, after holding appointments in Hanover, Brunswick, Ansbach and Bayreuth, became a Prussian minister on Bayreuth's union with Prussia in 1791, and in 1803 first Prussian minister. His policy was to preserve neutrality in the war between France and Britain; but in 1806, under Napoleon's influence, he was dismissed. In 1810 he was appointed chancellor, and addressed himself to the task of completing the reforms begun by Stein. In the war of liberation he played a prominent part, and after the treaty of Paris (June 1814) was made a prince. He took part in the congress of Vienna, and in the treaties of Paris (1815). He reorganized the council of state (1817), of which he was appointed president, and drew up the new Prussian system of imposts. To Hardenberg (with Stein) Prussia owed the improvements

in her army system, abolition of serfdom and the privileges of the nobles, encouragement of municipalities, and reform of education. See *Life* by Ranke (1877).

HARDICANUTE, *hahr'di-kah-noot'*, or **Harthacnut** (*c*. 1019–42), King of Denmark (1035–42) and of England (1040–42), son of Cnut by Emma. At Cnut's death (1035) the throne was given to Harold, an elder son. Wessex, however, was reserved for Hardicanute, who was elected king of England on Harold's death (1040). He imposed a very heavy *danegeld*.

HARDIE, James Keir (1856–1915), Scottish Labour leader, one of the founders of the Labour party, born near Holytown, Lanarkshire, worked in a coalpit from childhood. Victimized as champion of the miners (whom he organized) he removed to Cumnock and became a journalist. The first of all Labour candidates, he was defeated (1888) in Mid-Lanark, sat for West Ham, South (1892–95), and Merthyr Tydfil (1900–15), and in and out of parliament worked strenuously for Socialism and the unemployed. He started and edited *The Labour Leader*, handed it over in 1903 to the Independent Labour party, of which, founded in 1893, he was chairman till 1900 and again in 1913–14. He strenuously opposed Liberal influence on the Trade Unions and strongly advocated the formation of a separate political party, as distinct from the existing Labour Representation League. A strong pacifist, he lost his seat through opposing the Boer War. The first World War probably hastened his death. See *Lives* by W. Stewart (1921) and E. Hughes (1956).

HARDING, (1) John. See HARDYNG.

(2) **Sir John** (1896–   ), **1st Baron of Petherton**, British field-marshal, was born at South Petherton, Somerset. A subaltern in World War I, he rose to chief of staff of the Allied Army in Italy in 1944. From 1955 to 1957 as governor-general of Cyprus during the political and terrorist campaign against Britain, he re-organized the security forces to combat terrorism, re-established order through the imposition of martial law and press control, banished Archbishop Makarios (q.v.), and, although he failed to bring about a political settlement, was widely respected for his straightforward, soldierly approach. He was awarded C.B.E. in 1940, D.S.O. in 1941, became K.C.B. in 1944, G.C.B. in 1951, and was created baron in 1958.

(3) **St Stephen** (d. 1134), English divine, born at Sherborne in Dorset, from 1109 to 1133 was the third abbot of Cîteaux, and endeavoured to restore the Cistercian rule to its original simplicity.

(4) **Warren Gamaliel** (1865–1923), American statesman, born, a doctor's son, at Corsica, Ohio, in 1865, became a journalist, a newspaper owner, senator (1900–04) and lieut.-governor (1904–06) of Ohio, Republican senator (1915) and 29th President of the United States (1921), but his administration foundered at the hands of his corrupt officials and he fell sick and died.

HARDINGE, Henry Hardinge, 1st Viscount (1785–1856), British soldier, governor-general of India, was born at Wrotham, Kent. Twice wounded in the Peninsular war, from 1809 to 1813 he was deputy-quartermaster-general of the Portuguese army. After Napoleon's escape from Elba, Hardinge was appointed commissioner at the Prussian headquarters, and was severely wounded at Ligny. From 1820 to 1844 he took an active share in parliamentary life, being secretary of War under Wellington in 1828, and afterwards chief secretary for Ireland. In 1844 he was appointed governor-general of India. During the first Sikh war he was present at the battles of Mudki, Firozshah and Sobraon as second in command to Lord Gough. After the peace of Lahore (1845) he was created a viscount, and granted pensions by the East India Company and by parliament. Returning in 1848, he succeeded (1852) Wellington as commander-in-chief, and in 1855 was made field-marshal. See *Life* by his son (1891), whose second son, **Charles, 1st Baron Hardinge of Penshurst** (1858–1944), was viceroy of India (1910–16), permanent under-secretary for Foreign Affairs, ambassador in Paris (1920–22).

HARDOUIN, Jean, *ahr-doo-* (1646–1729), French classical scholar, born at Quimper, entered the Jesuit order, and from 1683 was librarian at the Collège de Louis le Grand in Paris. He maintained that the entire body of classical literature, with very few exceptions, had been written by the monks of the 13th century. He rejected all the reputed remains of ancient art, as well as the Septuagint and the Greek New Testament. His edition of Pliny (1689), his *Collectio Conciliorum* (1715), a commentary on the New Testament, and several volumes on numismatics and chronology are of value.

HARDWICK, Philip (1792–1870), British architect, like his father Thomas (1752–1829), born in London, designed Euston railway station, the hall and library of Lincoln's Inn, Goldsmiths' Hall and Limerick Cathedral.

HARDWICKE, (1) Earl of. See YORKE.

(2) **Sir Cedric Webster** (1893–1964), English actor, born at Lye, Worcestershire served in World War I and made his name in Birmingham repertory company's productions of Shaw's plays and in *The Barretts of Wimpole Street* (1934). He also played leading rôles in a number of films, including *Dreyfus*, *Things to Come*, *The Winslow Boy*, &c. He was knighted in 1934 and was Cambridge Rede Lecturer in 1936. See his *Let's Pretend* (1932) and *A Victorian in Orbit* (1962, as told to J. Brough).

HARDY, (1) Alexandre (*c*. 1570–*c*. 1631), French dramatist, born in Paris. His over 500 melodramatic pieces are largely lifted from Spanish authors, but he reduced the rôle of the chorus in French drama. See study by Rigal (1890).

(2) **Sir Alister Clavering** (1896–   ), English marine biologist, born at Nottingham, professor of Zoology and Comparative Anatomy at Oxford (1946–61), made quantitative researches into marine vegetation, invented a plankton recorder and studied the diet of the herring. He was knighted in 1957.

(3) **Gathorne.** See CRANBROOK.

(4) **Thomas** (1752–1832), Scottish Radical politician, born at Larbert, Stirlingshire,

originally a shoemaker, founded in 1792 the London Corresponding Society for Parliamentary and Social Reform, and was acquitted of high treason in 1794.

(5) **Thomas** (1840–1928), English novelist and poet, was born in Higher Bockhampton, in the parish of Stinsford. His father was a stonemason who led the church choir and transmitted to his son a feeling for music. Hardy attended the village school and, later, schools in Dorchester to the age of sixteen, when he began to study under an architect much engaged in church restoration. He was twenty-two when he went to London to pursue his profession under Blomfield (q.v.), but the idyllic rural life he left behind began to find expression in poems which the publishers did not want and so, while still continuing his work as an architect, he turned to the novel as a means of expression and then, with the success of *Far from the Madding Crowd*, as both a means of expression and a livelihood. The twofold aim meant that certain of his novels were merely marketable commodities while others, some six or seven in all, are masterpieces. The latter by common consent are the delightful *Under the Greenwood Tree* (1872), his second in point of time and his most idyllic, *Far from the Madding Crowd* (1874), *The Return of the Native* (1878), *The Mayor of Casterbridge* (1886), *The Trumpet-Major* (1880), *Tess of the D'Urbervilles* (1891), and *Jude the Obscure* (1896). Some would add *The Woodlanders* (1887), for its lovely descriptions and local idiom but the intrigue is too melodramatic (Hardy's besetting weakness) for more severe tastes. All tragedies, except for *Under the Greenwood Tree*, they became increasingly pessimistic in tone till *Tess of the D'Urbervilles* alarmed the religious, and readers generally were revolted by the horrors of *Jude the Obscure*. The final sentence in *Tess of the D'Urbervilles*, just after Tess's hanging, viz., ' The President of the Immortals had finished His sport with Tess ', could not be explained away by saying it was a quotation from Aeschylus, and Hardy was henceforth dubbed atheist. Except for *The Well-beloved* (1897), he now abandoned the novel and returned to verse. He was now famous and in comfortable circumstances. He had married the first Mrs Hardy just before *Far from the Madding Crowd*, and after a year or two in a London suburb settled for life at Max Gate in Dorchester. His wife died when *The Trumpet-Major* was being staged at Dorchester, but two years later, in 1914, he married again. Except for the epic drama *The Dynasts*, the volumes of verse he now produced were all composed of sardonic lyrics, viz., *Wessex Poems* (1898), *Poems of the Past and Present* (1902), *Time's Laughing-stocks* (1909), *Satires of Circumstance* (1914), *Late Lyrics and Earlier* (1922), *Winter Words* (1928 posthumously). His transition to poetry was eased—for critics expressed some umbrage at the change—by the fact that he was able to take up a patriotic stand in the Boer War and World War I. His themes are significantly commonplace, expressed often awkwardly and without the sophistication of art, but perhaps for that

reason all the more telling, and his poems have gained in repute as his novels have declined. *The Dynasts* was to be his fitting monument (1903–04, 1906, 1908), and so it might have been if he had had command of the medium. The subject is ' the Great Historical Calamity, or Clash of the Peoples ' in the Napoleonic wars. It is provided with an extraterrestrial audience—the Immanent Will and various Spirits whose speeches, appropriate to their dignity, convey Hardy's ripest philosophy. The part of the common folk, Wessex folk, in the suffering and fighting is the best of it, the debates in Council and Parliament the most inflated. *The Dynasts* imposes on us by its vast size. Max Beerbohm's famous parody makes sufficient amends to the reader. The 1914 war and the aftermath shook his agnosticism; in his Apology to *Late Lyrics and Earlier* he calls for an alliance of religion and Science, poetry being the intermediary. See Life by Mrs F. E. Hardy (1928–30) and studies by E. Blunden (1941), Lord David Cecil (1942), C. M. Bowra (1946) and C. Day Lewis (1951).

(6) **Sir Thomas Duffus** (1804–78), English archivist, born at Port Royal, Jamaica, in 1819 entered the Record Office in the Tower, and quickly became an expert in reading ancient MSS. His earliest writings—illustrating the reign of King John—appeared in *Archaeologia* and the *Excerpta Historica*. In 1861 he became deputy keeper of the Public Records. He edited *Close Rolls, Patent Rolls, Norman Rolls*, and *Charter Rolls* (1833–44); *William of Malmesbury* (1840); *Catalogue* of lord chancellors, keepers of great seal, &c. (1843); *Modus tenendi Parliamentum* (1846); *Syllabus* of Rymer's *Foedera* (1869–85), &c.—His brother, **Sir William Hardy** (1807–87), succeeded him as deputy keeper, edited Jehan de Waurin's *Chroniques et Anchiennes Istories da la Grant Bretaigne* (1864–84), and translated vols. i and ii.

(7) **Sir Thomas Masterman, Bart.** (1769–1839), British sailor, born at Portisham in Dorset, was closely associated with Nelson, whom he served as flag-captain at the Battle of Trafalgar (1805). He was created baronet (1805) and from 1834 was governor of Greenwich Hospital. See Lives by Broadley and Bartelot (1909) and Gore (1935).

HARDYNG, John (1378–c. 1465), English chronicler, in 1390 entered the household of Harry Percy, ' Hotspur ', whom he saw fall on Shrewsbury Field in 1403. Pardoned for his treason, he became constable of Warkworth Castle, fought at Agincourt, and served the crown in confidential missions to Scotland. His chronicle, composed in limping stanzas, and treating the history of England from the earliest times down to Henry VI's flight into Scotland, he rewrote and presented to Edward IV just after his accession. It is poor history and poorer poetry, but the account of the Agincourt campaign has the interest of the eye witness. Richard Grafton continued it down to Henry VIII. See edition by Sir Henry Ellis (1812).

HARE, (1) Augustus John Cuthbert (1834–1903), English topographical writer, nephew of (3), born in Rome and educated at Harrow and University College, Oxford, wrote *Walks in Rome* (1871), *Wanderings in Spain* (1873), *Walks in London* (1878), *Sussex* (1894), &c. See his Autobiography (1896–1900).

(2) **Sir John** (1844–1921), English comedian and manager, born at Giggleswick in Yorkshire, acted at the Prince of Wales (1865–74) and co-managed the Court (1874–79), and managed the St James's (1879–88) and Garrick (1889–95) theatres. He was knighted in 1907.

(3) **Julius Charles** (1795–1855), English theologian, uncle of (1), born near Vincenza in Italy, educated at Charterhouse and Trinity College, Cambridge, became a fellow in 1818, ordained in 1826, and in 1853 chaplain to the Queen. His annual charges encouraged the study of German theology. Among his works are *Guesses at Truth* (with A. W. Hare 1827), *Vindication of Niebuhr's History* (1829), *Victory of Faith* (1840), &c. His *Life* and *Essays and Tales of John Sterling* (1848) prompted Carlyle's corrective biography. See *Memorials of a Quiet Life* by (1) (1872).

(4) **Robert** (1781–1858), American chemist, born in Philadelphia, was professor of Chemistry there (1818–47), devised an oxyhydrogen blowpipe, in 1816 the calorimeter and the apparatus for measuring the relative density of liquids. He published *Spiritualism Demonstrated* (1855).

(5) **Robertson** (1891–), English actor, born in London, built up his reputation as a comedian in the famous 'Aldwych farces', such as *Thark, Plunder, Rookery Nook* and *Cuckoo in the Nest*, cast invariably in 'henpecked little man' parts in which his ultimate 'debagging' became proverbial. He has also featured in many other stage comedies and films.

(6) **William.** See BURKE (7).

HAREWOOD, George Henry Hubert Lascelles, 7th Earl of, *hahr'-* (1923–), the elder son of the Princess Royal (see **George V**), and cousin of Queen Elizabeth II, was born at Harewood near Leeds, educated at Eton and King's College, Cambridge, served as captain in the Grenadier Guards in World War II, and was prisoner of war. Keenly interested in music and drama, he served on many committees connected with these and edited the magazine *Opera* (1950–53). He was president of the English Opera Group, a director of the Royal Opera House, Covent Garden (1951–53), artistic director of the Edinburgh International Festival (1960–65) and of Leeds Festival since 1958. He married (1) pianist Maria Stein (1949, div. 1967); (2) Patricia Tuckwell (1967).

HARGRAVES, Edmund Hammond (1815–91), English gold prospector, born at Gosport, went out as a youth to Australia, then to the Californian gold diggings in 1849. From similarity in geological formation he suspected that gold would be found in Australia also. Finding gold on the Blue Hills, N.S.W., in 1851, he was appointed commissioner of crown lands, and received a government reward of £10,000. In 1855, a year after his return to England, he published *Australia and its Goldfields*.

HARGREAVES, (1) **James** (d. 1778), English inventor, born probably at Blackburn, was an illiterate weaver and carpenter of Standhill. About 1764 he invented the spinning-jenny. But his fellow spinners broke into his house and destroyed his frame (1768). He removed to Nottingham, where he erected a spinning mill, but his patent proved invalid, as he had disclosed his invention. He continued to manufacture yarn till his death.

(2) **James** (1834–1915), English industrial chemist, born at Hoarstones, Lancashire, invented processes for the manufacture of hydrochloric acid, soda and soap, and constructed a gas-tar engine.

HÄRING, Georg Wilhelm Heinrich, pseud. **Wilibald Alexis,** *hayr-* (1798–1871), German writer, born at Breslau, wrote the historical romance *Walladmor* (1823–24), professedly as by Sir Walter Scott, a fraud that led to its translation into several languages (into English, very freely, by De Quincey, 1824). It was followed by *Die Geächteten* (1825), *Schloss Avalon* (1827), books of travel, sketches, dramas, &c.

HARINGTON, (1) **Sir Charles Robert** (1897–1972), English chemist, professor of Pathological Chemistry at University College, London (1931–42), and director of the National Institute of Medical Research (1942–62). He synthesized thyroxine and published *The Thyroid Gland* (1933). He became F.R.S. in 1931, was knighted in 1948, and received the K.B.E. in 1962.

(2) **Sir John** (1561–1612), English courtier, born at Kelston near Bath, from Cambridge went to the court of his godmother, Queen Elizabeth. His wit brought him into much favour, which he endangered by the freedom of his satires. In 1599 he served under Essex in Ireland, and was knighted by him on the field, much to the queen's displeasure. To fortify his amazing application to King James for the office of chancellor and archbishop of Ireland he composed in 1605 *A Short View of the State of Ireland,* an interesting and singularly modern essay (ed. by Macray, 1880). He is remembered as the metrical translator of Ariosto's *Orlando Furioso* (1591); his other writings include Rabelaisian pamphlets, epigrams (ed. McClure, 1927), *The Metamorphosis of Ajax* (1596), containing the earliest design for a water closet, and a *Tract on the Succession to the Crown* (ed. Clements Markham, Roxb. Club, 1880). See family history by I. Grimble (1958).

HARIRI, Abu Mohammed al Kasim ibn Ali (1054–1122), Arabic writer, known as 'the silk merchant', was born and died at Basra, and, besides works on Arabic grammar, syntax, &c., wrote *Makamat* (Literary Gatherings), a collection of witty rhymed tales of adventure. See the edition by Silvestre de Sacy (1822, 1847–53). Translations are by Preston (partial, 1850), Chenery and Steingass (1867–98).

HARLAND, Sir Edward James (1831–96), British shipbuilder, founder at Belfast in 1858 of the firm which became Harland and Wolff, in whose yard, largest in the world, have been built many famous Atlantic liners and warships. **Gustav William Wolff** (1834–1913), partner from 1860, was born in

Hamburg of German parents, but learned engineering at Liverpool and Manchester. He sat as M.P. for East Belfast from 1892.

HARLEY, Robert, 1st Earl of Oxford (1661–1724), British statesman, the son of Sir Edward Harley the parliamentarian, born in London, entered the Inner Temple in 1682, and the House of Commons as a Whig in 1689; in 1701 he was elected speaker, and in 1704 became also secretary of state. Shortly after, he began to intrigue with the Tories, and he found a most useful ally in his cousin, Abigail Hill (Mrs Masham). In 1708 the conviction of his secretary for treasonable correspondence with France caused Harley to resign office; he then set to work to undermine the power of the Whigs, and in 1710 Godolphin was dismissed, and Harley made chancellor of the Exchequer and head of the government. In 1711 a French priest and spy calling himself the Marquis de Guiscard was brought before the council, and suddenly stabbed Harley with a penknife. On his recovery he was made Earl of Oxford and Mortimer, a K.G., and lord high treasurer. The principal act of Harley's administration was the treaty of Utrecht. But his popularity was already on the wane; his friendship with Bolingbroke had turned to bitter hatred, and Mrs Masham sided with Bolingbroke. In July 1714 he was dismissed from office, in July 1715 sent to the Tower, but after two years was acquitted by the Peers. He spent the remainder of his life in retirement, the friend of men of letters, and founder of the Harleian collection in the British Museum. He died in London.

HARLOW, George Henry (1787–1819), English historical and portrait painter, born in London, best known for his portrait group of Mrs Siddons and others (including members of the Kemble family) in the trial scene from Shakespeare's *Henry VIII*.

HARMENSEN, Jacob. See ARMINIUS, J.

HARMODIUS (d. 514 B.C.), Athenian murderer, who with **Aristogeiton** in 514 B.C. murdered Hipparchus, younger brother of the 'tyrant' Hippias. They meant to kill Hippias also, but Harmodius was cut down, whilst Aristogeiton, who fled, was taken and executed. Subsequently they were regarded as patriotic martyrs, and received divine honours.

HARMSWORTH, the name of five brothers, distinguished as British newspaper magnates and politicians:

(1) **Alfred Charles William, 1st Viscount Northcliffe** (1865–1922), British journalist and newspaper magnate, one of the pioneers of mass circulation journalism, born near Dublin, was brought up in London and already at school edited the school magazine, complete with gossip column, and during the holidays reported for the local newspaper. Soon after leaving school, he became editor of *Youth* and with his brother (3) started *Answers to Correspondents* (1888), a rather flimsy imitation of the famous *Tit Bits*; founded *Comic Cuts* (1890) under the motto 'amusing without being vulgar' and an imitation *Chips* to discourage further competitors. In 1894 he absorbed the

Evening News and sponsored the Jackson Arctic expedition. He also published a number of Sunday magazine papers and in 1896 revolutionized Fleet Street with his *Daily Mail*, with its snappy American-style make-up and news presentation. The brothers Harmsworth also bought up the *Weekly Dispatch* and many provincial papers, in 1903 pioneered the first newspaper for women, the *Daily Mirror* (1903), founded the Amalgamated Press for periodical and popular educational literature and acquired vast forests in Newfoundland for newsprint. In 1908, after secret negotiations, Northcliffe became proprietor of *The Times*, took a gamble by lowering its price to one penny in 1914 to restore its sagging circulation and made its editorial policy a vehicle for his political ambitions. But like Beaverbrook, he found that success in journalism was not an asset to the aspiring politician. His controversies with Lloyd George raged throughout the first World War, and his attack on Lord Kitchener in the *Daily Mail* reduced its circulation by nearly 300,000. But in 1917 he led a war mission to the United States and in 1918 directed British propaganda. Suffering from ill-health and nervous strain, he made a world tour in 1921 but died soon after his return. A baronet in 1904, he was created baron in 1906 and viscount in 1917. See his *My Journey round the World* (1923), and Lives by M. Pemberton (1922), H. H. Fyfe (1930), J. A. Hamerton (1932), R. Pound and G. Harmsworth (1959), and also *History of The Times*, Vol. IV, Pt. I (1912–20).

(2) **Cecil Bishopp Harmsworth, 1st Baron** (1869–1948), British Liberal politician, was under-secretary at the Home Office (1912), at the Foreign Office (1919–22) and minister of blockade. He was created baron in 1939.

(3) **Harold Sydney, 1st Viscount Rothermere** (1868–1940), British newspaper magnate, born in London, was closely associated with his brother (1) and in addition founded the *Glasgow Daily Record*. In 1910 he established the King Edward chair of English Literature at Cambridge and received a baronetcy. He dissociated himself from his brother in 1914 and concentrated on the *Daily Mirror*, which reached a circulation of three million by 1922. He also founded the *Sunday Pictorial* (1915), was air minister (1917–18), and after his brother's death acquired control of the *Daily Mail* and *Sunday Dispatch*. He was created baron in 1914 and viscount in 1919.

(4) **Sir Hildebrand Aubrey, 1st Bart.** (1872–1929), also acquired newspapers and was created baronet in 1922.

(5) **Sir Robert Leicester, 1st Bart.** (1870–1937), was Liberal M.P. (1900–18) and was made baronet in 1918.

HARNACK, Adolf von (1851–1930), German theologian, son of the Lutheran dogmatic theologian **Theodosius** (1817–89), born at Dorpat, became a professor at Leipzig (1876), Giessen (1879), Marburg (1886) and Berlin (1889). His writings are on Gnosticism (1873), Ignatius (1878), Monasticism (2nd ed. 1882), the history of dogma, and of old Christian literature, and a history of the

Berlin Academy. From 1893 the orthodox suspected him of heresy on account of his criticism of the Apostles' Creed. In 1905–21 he was keeper of the Royal (later State) Library, Berlin.—His brother Otto (1857–1914), was professor of Literature and History at Darmstadt, then at Stuttgart, and wrote on Goethe, Schiller, Humboldt, &c.

HAROLD, the name of two kings of England: **Harold I** (d. 1040), called 'Harefoot', was the younger of Cnut's two sons by Aelfgifu of Northampton. On Cnut's death (1035) the witan gave Harold the provinces north of the Thames, and Wessex to Cnut's widow, Emma, for her son Harthacnut. But in 1037 Wessex submitted to Harold. He died March 17.

Harold II (c. 1022–1066), the second son of Earl Godwin. By 1045 he was Earl of East Anglia, and in 1053 succeeded to his father's earldom of Wessex. Henceforward he was the right hand of King Edward the Confessor, and he directed the affairs of the kingdom with unusual gentleness and vigour. His brother Tostig became Earl of the Northumbrians in 1055, and two years later two other brothers were raised to earldoms. Meantime Harold drove back the Welsh marauders, and added Herefordshire to his earldom. The death in 1057 of the Aetheling Edward, son of Edmund Ironside, opened up the path for Harold's ambitious hopes of the crown. He made a pilgrimage to Rome in 1058, and after his return completed his church at Waltham. In 1063, provoked by the fresh incursions of the Welsh king Griffith, he marched against him, traversed the country, beat the enemy at every point, and gave the government to the dead king's brothers. It is impossible to state exactly the date of Harold's visit to Duke William in Normandy, although it is put by Freeman at 1064. Probably Harold did make some kind of oath to William, most likely under compulsion. It is certain that Harold helped William in a war with the Bretons. On his return he married Ealdgyth, Griffith's widow, though Edith Swan-neck, who had borne him five children, was still alive. In 1065 the Northumbrians rebelled against Tostig, and Harold acquiesced in their choice of Morcar and Tostig's banishment. In January 1066 King Edward died; and Harold, his nominee, was chosen king, and crowned in Westminster Abbey. Duke William lost no time in preparing for the invasion of England, and Tostig, after trying the Normans and the Scots, succeeded in drawing to his side Harold Hardrada, king of Norway. In September the two reached the Humber, and Harold marched to meet them. At Stamford Bridge he won a complete victory (September 25, 1066), Tostig and Harold Hardrada being among the slain. But four days later William landed at Pevensey. Harold marched southwards with the utmost dispatch, and the two armies met at Senlac, about nine miles from Hastings. From nine in the morning, October 14, 1066, the English fought stubbornly until nightfall, when the pretended flight of the Normans drew them from their impregnable position and gave the Normans the victory. Harold himself fell

pierced through the eye with an arrow. His body was recognized by Edith Swan-neck, and was buried at Waltham. See vols. ii and iii of Freeman's *Norman Conquest* and F. M. Stenton, *William the Conqueror* (1908) and *Anglo-Saxon England* (1943).

HAROLD, the name of three kings of Norway of whom the following are noteworthy:

Harold I, surnamed **Haarfagr** ('Fairhaired') (d. 933), after a severe struggle (863–872) subdued the chiefs between Trondhjem and the Sogne Fjord, and finally the kings of the southwest. The conquered districts he placed under such jarls as were devoted to his service. This led many of the old nobles to emigrate to the Orkneys, Hebrides, and Iceland, whence they conducted piratical expeditions against Norway, until Harold sailed westwards and subdued all, except those in Iceland.

Harold III, surnamed **Hardrada** ('stern in council') (1015–66), when a boy was present at the battle (1030) in which his brother, St Olaf, king of Norway, was slain. Harold sought an asylum with his relative, Yaroslav, prince of Novgorod. Going on to Constantinople, he became captain of the Varangians or Scandinavian bodyguard of the Greek emperors, and defeated the Saracens in Sicily and Italy. He incurred the vengeance of the Empress Zoe, whose proffered love he rejected, with difficulty escaped to Russia, and married Duke Yaroslav's daughter. He returned about 1045 to Norway, where his nephew Magnus agreed to divide the kingdom with him. Magnus's death in 1047 left Harold sole king; with Svend of Denmark he waged unrelenting war until 1064. In 1066 he landed in England to aid Tostig against the English King Harold II (q.v.), but fell at Stamford Bridge.

HAROUN AL-RASCHID, *hah-roon' al rah-sheed'* (763–809), 5th Abbasside Caliph of Baghdad (786–809), born near Teheran, owed his peaceful accession to the Barmecide Yahya, whom he made grand vizier. To him and his four sons he left the administration of his extensive kingdom; and the energy of their rule and the general prosperity proved that his confidence was not misplaced. Meantime Haroun gave himself up to pleasure, and his taste and hospitality made his court at Baghdad a centre of all the wit, learning, and art of the Moslem world. Eventually a strange and deeply-rooted hatred towards the Barmecides possessed him, and in 803 he caused the vizier, his sons and all their descendants save one to be executed, not even excepting his favourite Jaafer (Giafar), his companion in his semi-apocryphal nocturnal rambles through Baghdad. To quell a rising in Khorasan, he marched against the rebels, but died of apoplexy at Tûs. The *Arabian Nights* has thrown a false halo round his memory. See Lives by Palmer (1880) and H. St. B. Philby (1933).

HARPE, LA. See LA HARPE.

HARPER and BROTHERS, a firm of New York publishers, consisted originally of **James** (1795–1869), **John** (1797–1875), **Joseph Wesley** (1801–70) and **Fletcher** (1806–77). James and John began publishing in

1818; the firm of Harper and Brothers, established in 1833, is carried on by descendants, and issues *Harper's Magazine* (monthly since 1850), &c. See J. Henry Harper's *The House of Harper* (1912).

HARPIGNIES, Henri, *ahr-pee-nyee* (1819–1916), French landscape painter, born at Valenciennes, went to Italy and later became associated with the Barbizon school. *The Edge of a Wood on the Banks of the Allier* (1861) is regarded as his best. *A River Scene* and *Ilex Trees at Menton* are in the Tate Gallery.

HARRADEN, Beatrice (1864–1936), English novelist, born at Hampstead, the youngest daughter of **Samuel Harraden** (1821–98), musical-instrument importer, graduated at London, turned suffragette and wrote *Ships that Pass in the Night* (1893), *Katharine Frensham* (1903), *Rachel* (1926), &c.

HARRIMAN, William Averell (1891–   ), American statesman, a close friend of President Franklin Roosevelt, was prominent in the National Recovery Administration in 1934. In 1941 he was his special war-aid representative in Britain. In 1943 he was appointed ambassador to the U.S.S.R. and in 1946 to Britain. He was secretary of commerce (1946–48) and special assistant to President Truman (1950–51), helping to organize N.A.T.O. From 1951 to 1953 he was director of Foreign Aid under the Mutual Security Act and was governor of New York (1955–58). He was ambassador-at-large (1961) and from 1965, and held minor political appointments from 1961 to 1964.

HARRINGTON, (1) James (1611–77), English political theorist, born at Upton, Northants, studied at Trinity, Oxford. He travelled to Rome, and, though a republican, became in 1646 a personal attendant of Charles I, and attended him to the scaffold. His semi-romance *Oceana* (1656), sets forth a commonwealth, maintains that the real basis of power is property, especially landed property, from which no one person should derive more than £3000 a year; and that the rulers should be changed every three years and their successors elected by ballot. In 1661 he was arrested for attempting to change the constitution, and in prison went temporarily insane. See Study by Russell Smith (1914) and family history by Grimble (1958).

(2) Sir John. See HARINGTON (2).

HARRIS, (1) Sir Arthur Travers (1892–   ), British airman, known as 'Bomber Harris', served in the Royal Flying Corps in World War I, and, in World War II, as c.-in-c. of Bomber Command (1942–45), organized mass bomber raids on industrial Germany. He was created G.C.B. in 1945.

(2) Frank (1856–1931), British writer and journalist, born, according to his autobiography, in Galway, but according to his own later statement, in Tenby, ran away to New York at the age of fifteen, became bootblack, labourer building Brooklyn Bridge, and worker in a Chicago hotel, but in 1874 embarked upon the study of law at the University of Kansas. About 1876 he returned to England and entered the newspaper world. Perhaps the most colourful figure in contemporary journalistic circles

an incorrigible liar, a vociferous boaster, an unscrupulous adventurer and philanderer, with the aspect and outlook of a typical melodrama ' Sir Jasper ', and an obsession with sex which got his autobiography *My Life and Loves* (1923–27) banned for pornography, he nevertheless had a considerable impact on Fleet Street as editor of the *Fortnightly Review, Saturday Review, Vanity Fair* and of the *Evening News*, which became under his aegis a pioneer in the new cult of provocative headlines and suggestive sensationalism. He is also remembered for his *Contemporary Portraits* (1915–30), a series of profiles, interesting but distorted by personal prejudice, as well as Lives of Oscar Wilde (1920) and Shaw (1931), and two original but not particularly scholarly works on Shakespeare. See Lives by Kingsmill (1932) and V. Brome (1959).

(3) George, 1st Baron Harris (1746–1829), British general, left Westminster School for the R.M.A. in 1759, served in Ireland, America and the West Indies, and in 1790 was fighting against Tippoo Sahib in India. Made a general in 1794, he won renown and the thanks of Parliament as commander-in-chief of the campaign which ended in the victory of Seringapatam and the annexation of Mysore.

(4) George Robert Canning, 4th Baron Harris (1851–1932), British statesman, under-secretary for India (1885–86), for war (1886–89) and governor of Bombay (1890–95), is remembered also as a great figure in the cricket world, an Oxford blue, captain of Kent and of England, and president of the M.C.C. in 1895.

(5) Howel (1714–73), preacher, founder of Welsh Calvinistic Methodism, born at Trevecca in Brecon, retired there in 1752 and ounded a kind of Protestant monastery, whose members he referred to as the ' family '. See his *Autobiography* (1791).

(6) James (1709–80), English scholar, born at Salisbury, studied at Wadham, Oxford, and Lincoln's Inn. On his father's death (1733) left master of an ample fortune, he devoted himself to the classics, but in 1761 entered parliament, and in 1763 became a lord of the Admiralty and of the Treasury, in 1764 secretary and comptroller to Queen Charlotte. In 1744 he published *Art and Happiness*; in 1751 *Hermes*, an inquiry into universal grammar. See his works edited in 1801–03 with a Memoir by his son, the diplomatist, **James, 1st Earl of Malmesbury** (1746–1820).

(7) Joel Chandler (1848–1908), American author, was born in Eatonton, Georgia, and was in turn printer, lawyer, and journalist. His *Uncle Remus* (1880) quickly carried his name to the Old World, at once to children and to students of folklore. Later works are *Nights with Uncle Remus* (1883), *Mingo, Daddy Jake, Aaron in the Wildwoods, Sister Jane, Tales of the Home Folks, Plantation Pageants, Minervy Ann* (1899), and a history of Georgia (1899). See Life by J. C. Harris (1919).

(8) Paul (1868–1947), American lawyer, born in Wisconsin, founder in 1905 of the Rotary movement, which began as a business men's luncheon club and expanded in 1912 into Rotary International, now a worldwide organization dedicated to the maintenance of high standards of service and integrity in commercial and professional life.

(9) **Renatus**, the elder (*c*. 1640–*c*. 1715), French-born London organ builder, came over from France with his father *c*. 1660, whom he assisted in building organs for Salisbury, Gloucester and Worcester cathedrals. He engaged in a contest with his rival, Father Smith (q.v.) (Bernhardt Schmidt), in 1684 over the commission for the Temple Church, London. Both constructed organs, each challenging the other to make improvements. In this way the vox humana, cromorna and double bassoon stops were heard for the first time. Purcell and Blow performed on Smith's and Draghi upon Harris's organ. Harris lost the contest, which lasted a year, but gained if anything in prestige. He built 39 organs, many for London churches as well as for James II's private chapels, Chichester (1678), Winchester (1681), Bristol (1685) and Hereford Cathedrals, King's College Chapel, Cambridge (1686), &c. His two sons, **John** (fl. 1737) and **Renatus** (d. 1727), were both organ builders.

(10) **Roy** (1898–   ), American composer, born in Oklahoma and brought up in California. Until the age of twenty-four, he had no specialized musical training, but studies in Los Angeles led to a Guggenheim Scholarship which enabled him to study in Paris under Nadia Boulanger. His music is ruggedly American in character and includes nine symphonies.

(11) **Thomas Lake** (1823–1906), English spiritualist, born at Fenny Stratford, Bucks, at three was taken to America, about 1845 became a Universalist pastor, in 1850 set up as a spiritualistic medium and founded the 'Church of the Good Shepherd' about 1858 on doctrines compounded of Swedenborg and Fourier. His followers included Lady Oliphant and her son Lawrence (q.v.). See Life by A. A. Cuthbert (1908).

HARRISON, (1) **Benjamin** (1833–1901), 23rd president of the United States, was born at North Bend, Ohio, the grandson of (8). Benjamin graduated at Miami University, Oxford, Ohio, in 1852, and in 1854 settled as a lawyer in Indianapolis. Entering the Union army in 1862, he was first lieutenant and then colonel of the 70th Regiment Indiana Volunteers. He served in Sherman's Atlanta campaign, distinguishing himself in the battles of Resaca, Peach Tree Creek, and Nashville, and in 1865 he became brevet-brigadier-general. He took an active part in the Grant campaigns of 1868 and 1872, and was nominated by the Republicans for the state governorship in 1876, but defeated. In 1878 he presided over the State Convention, in 1880 was chairman of his state delegation, and was elected U.S. senator for Indiana. In 1888 he was nominated for president, Cleveland being put forward by the Democrats for re-election. Contest turned on protection or free trade, and Harrison's election was a triumph for protection; but in 1892 he was defeated by Cleveland. In 1893 he became a professor at San Francisco, and he died in March 1901. See Life by Lew Wallace (1888).

(2) **Frederic** (1831–1923), English philosopher and lawyer, born in London, was educated at King's College School, London, and Wadham College, Oxford, taking a classical first class in 1853. He became fellow and tutor of his college, but was called to the bar in 1858, and practised conveyancing and in the Courts of Equity. He sat on the Royal Commission upon Trade Unions (1867–69), was secretary to that for the Digest of the Law (1869–70), professor of Jurisprudence and International Law at Lincoln's Inn Hall (1877–89), an alderman, London County Council (1889–93). A Positivist and an advanced Liberal, he wrote *The Meaning of History* (1862), *Order and Progress* (1875), *Lectures on Education* (1883), *Oliver Cromwell* (1888), *Early Victorian Literature* (1895), *William the Silent*, *Byzantine History*, *Ruskin*, *Chatham* (1905), *The Philosophy of Common Sense* (1908), *On Society* (1918), *Novissima Verba* (1920). See Memoir by his son Austin (1926).

(3) **Jane Ellen** (1850–1928), English classical scholar and anthropologist, born at Cottingham, Yorkshire, lectured on classical archaeology at Newnham College. Her most important works are the *Prolegomena to the Study of Greek Religion* (1903), *Themis, a study of the social origins of Greek Religion* (1912) and *Ancient Art and Ritual* (new ed. 1948). See Life by J. Stewart (1959).

(4) **John** (1693–1776), English inventor of the chronometer, was born at Foulby, near Pontefract. By 1726 he had constructed a timekeeper with compensating apparatus for correcting errors due to variations of climate. In 1713 the government had offered three prizes for the discovery of a method to determine longitude accurately. After long perseverance Harrison made a chronometer which, in a voyage to Jamaica (1761–62). determined the longitude within 18 geographical miles. After further trials, he was awarded first prize (1765–73). He also invented the gridiron pendulum, the going fusee, and the remontoir escapement. He wrote five works on his chronometer, &c.

(5) **Ross Granville** (1870–1959), American biologist, born at Germantown, Phil., professor of Biology at Yale, introduced the hanging-drop culture method (1907) for the study of living tissues.

(6) **Thomas** (1606–60), English regicide, born at Newcastle-under-Lyme, joined the Parliamentary army, commanded the guard which took the king from Hurst Castle to London, sat among his judges, and signed his death warrant. He did good service at Worcester, but was too uncompromising alike in religion and politics to favour Cromwell's tolerant ideas, and was deprived of his commission, and later imprisoned for his share in plots hatched by the more irreconcilable bigots. He refused to go into exile at the Restoration and was executed October 13. See Lives by C. H. Firth (1893) and by Simpkinson (1905).

(7) **William** (1534–93), English topographer,

born in London, studied at Cambridge and Oxford, and in 1586 he became canon of Windsor. His studies, and his use of Leland's MSS. resulted in the famous *Description of England*, as well as *Description of Britain*, written for Holinshed's *Chronicle*.

(8) **William Henry** (1773–1841), 9th president of the United States, grandfather of (1), was born in Charles City county, Virginia. Harrison joined the army Wayne led against the Indians, and distinguished himself at the battle on the Miami (1794). When Indiana Territory was formed (1800) he was appointed governor. He attempted to avoid war with the Indians, but was compelled to quell Tecumseh's outbreak, ending in the battle at Tippecanoe (November 7, 1811). In the war of 1812–14 he received the command in the northwest, repulsed the British under Proctor, and by the victory of Perry on Lake Erie was enabled to pursue the invaders into Canada, where, on October 5, 1813, he routed them in the battle of the Thames. In 1816 he was elected to congress, and in 1824 became U.S. senator. In 1840 he was elected president by an overwhelming majority, but died at Washington a month after his inauguration on April 4. See Lives by Dawson (1834), Hall (1836), Hildreth (1839), Burr (1840), Montgomery (1886), Goebel (1927).

HARRISSON, Tom (1911–), British ethnologist and sociologist, educated at Harrow and Pembroke College, Cambridge, curator of Sarawak museum from 1947, known especially for his exploration and research in Borneo, where he organized guerilla activities against the Japanese invaders in World War II, and for his application of the techniques of social anthropology to the study of British urban communities by ' Mass Observation '. He received the O.B.E. in 1959. Among his books are *Borneo Jungle* (1938), *Mass Observation* (1937), *Living among Cannibals* (1942), and *World Within* (1959), the last-named describing his war experiences.

HARRY, Blind (fl. 1470–92), Scottish minstrel, blind from his birth, who lived by telling tales, and in 1490–92 was at the court of James IV, receiving occasional small gratuities. His poem on Wallace exists in a MS. of 1488, copied by John Ramsay. This MS. does not ascribe the work to Blind Harry, nor is his name given to it in the earlier printed editions. The poem, which contains 11,861 lines, is written in rhyming couplets. The language is frequently obscure, but the work is written with vigour, and kindles sometimes into poetry. The author seems to have been familiar with the metrical romances, and represents himself as indebted to the Latin Life of Wallace by Master John Blair, Wallace's chaplain, and to another by Sir Thomas Gray, parson of Liberton. The poem transfers to its hero some of the achievements of Bruce, and contains many mistakes or misrepresentations, but much of the narrative can bear the test of historical criticism. It is believed to have been printed in Edinburgh in 1520, but no perfect copy is known of any earlier edition than that of 1570, *The Actis and Deidis of . . . Schir William Wallace, Knicht of Ellerslie*. Good

editions are by Jamieson (1820) and by Moir (Scot. Text Soc. 1885–89); a modernized version is by Hamilton of Gilbertfield (1722).

HART, Sir Robert (1835–1911), British diplomat, born at Portadown, Co. Armagh, and as inspector-general of Maritime Customs, Peking (1863–1908), played an important rôle in Anglo-Chinese affairs.

HARTE, Francis Bret (1836–1902), American author, was born in Albany, N.Y., went to California in 1854, and became a compositor in San Francisco. Sketches of his experiences among the miners attracted much attention. He was secretary of the U.S. Mint in San Francisco (1864–70) and during this period wrote some of his most famous poems, among them ' John Burns of Gettysburg ', ' The Society upon the Stanislau ', &c. He founded in 1868 and edited the *Overland Monthly*, to which he contributed *The Luck of Roaring Camp, The Outcasts of Poker Flat* (1870), &c. He was U.S. consul at Krefeld (1878–80) and at Glasgow (1880–85), and then lived in London until his death. See Life by Merwin (1912).

HARTHACNUT. See HARDICANUTE.

HARTINGTON, Lord. See CAVENDISH family (1).

HARTLEY, (1) David (1705–57), English philosopher, born at Luddenden, Halifax, was educated at Jesus College, Cambridge, and in 1727 became a fellow. He studied for the church but, dissenting from some points in the Thirty-nine Articles, became instead a medical practitioner of considerable eminence at Newark, Bury St Edmunds, London and Bath. His *Observations on Man* (1749) turns upon two hypotheses—one ' The Doctrine of Vibrations ', or a theory of nervous action analogous to the propagation of sound; the other the doctrine that the association of ideas explains almost all mental phenomena. See G. S. Bower, *Hartley and James Mill* (1881). His son, **David** (1732–1813), was a fellow of Merton College, Oxford, a dull M.P., and a fireproofing inventor.

(2) **Leslie Poles** (1895–1972), English writer, born near Peterborough. His early short stories, *Night Fears* (1924) and *The Killing Bottle* (1932), established his reputation as a master of the macabre. Later, he transferred his Jamesian power of ' turning the screw ' to psychological relationships and made a new success with such novels as *The Shrimp and the Anemone* (1944), *Eustace and Hilda* (1947), *The Boat* (1950)—among his finest work—and *The Go-Between* (1953). Later novels include *A Perfect Woman* (1955), *The Hireling* (1957) and *My Sister's Keeper* (1970).

HARTLIB, Samuel (c. 1600–70), German-born English educationist, was born at Elbing in Prussia, son of a Polish refugee and an English mother. Coming to England about 1628, he busied himself in trade, in agriculture, and on a school to be conducted on new principles, which inspired his friend Milton's *Tractate on Education* (1644), as well as Sir William Petty's *Two Letters* (1647–48). Cromwell gave him a pension. He wrote on education and husbandry. See Lives by Dircks (1865) and G. H. Turnbull (1920).

HARTMANN, (1) Karl Robert Eduard von (1842–1906), German philosopher, born at Berlin, served as an artillery officer (1858–65), but from 1867 lived in Berlin, working out his philosophical scheme, a synthesis of Hegel, Schelling, and Schopenhauer, in which 'the Unconscious' plays the rôle of creator and providence. His great work is *Die Philosophie des Unbewussten* (1869; Eng. trans. by Coupland, new ed. 1931), followed by books on evolutionary ethics and aesthetics.

(2) **Nicolai** (1882–1950), German philosopher, was born in Riga and became professor of Philosophy at Göttingen. His philosophy, compounded from neo-Kantianism and Husserl's phenomenology, is expressed in, among others, his *Grundzüge einer Metaphysik der Erkenntnis* (1921) and *Ethik* (1925).

HARTMANN VON AUE, *ow'é* (*c.* 1170–1215), German poet of the Middle High German period, took part in the Crusade of 1197. The most popular of the narrative poems is *Der arme Heinrich* (ed. by Robertson, 1895), which, based on a Swabian tradition, is utilized in Longfellow's *Golden Legend*. *Erec* and *Iwein* are both drawn from the Arthurian cycle, and closely follow Chrétien de Troyes. In *Gregor vom Steine* Hartmann relates how worldly passion is expiated by religious faith. The songs are mainly love songs. See studies by E. Witte (1929), H. Sparnay (1933), A. Stoeckli (1934), J. Fourquet (1944).

HARTNELL, Norman (1901–), English couturier and court dressmaker. He took a degree at Magdalene College, Cambridge, and started his own business in 1923, receiving the Royal Warrant in 1940. From 1946 to 1956 he was the president of the Incorporated Society of London Fashion Designers. Costumes for leading actresses, wartime 'utility' dresses, the W.R.A.C. uniform and Princess Elizabeth's wedding and coronation gowns have all formed part of his work. See his autobiography *Silver and Gold* (1955).

HARTUNG, Hans, *hahr'toong* (1904–), French artist, born in Leipzig. He studied in Basel, Leipzig, Dresden and Munich; although in his earlier years he was influenced by the German impressionists and expressionists, from 1928 onwards he produced mainly abstract work. During World War II he served in the Foreign Legion and gained French citizenship in 1945. His later paintings, which have made him one of the most famous French abstract painters, show a free calligraphy allied to that of Chinese brushwork. See the monograph by M. Rousseau (1950).

HARTY, Sir (Herbert) Hamilton (1880–1941), composer, born at Hillsborough, Co. Down, conducted the Hallé Orchestra (1920–33) and other orchestras from 1933, and was knighted in 1925. His arrangement of Handel's *Water Music* is well-known.

HARTZENBUSCH, Juan Eugenio (1806–80), Spanish dramatic poet, born at Madrid, director of the national library (1862), wrote mostly plays, of which the mediaeval *The Lovers of Teruel* (1837) is the best.

HARUN. See HAROUN.

HARVARD, John (1607–38), English clergyman, born in Southwark, studied at Emmanuel College, Cambridge, and in 1637, having married, went out to Charlestown, Mass., where he preached a while, but soon died of consumption. He bequeathed £779 and over 300 volumes to the proposed college since named after him. See monograph by W. Rendle (1885).

HARVEY, (1) Gabriel (*c.* 1550–1630), English poet and Cambridge don, cantankerous and arrogant, was born and died at Saffron Walden. Spenser's friend, he attacked Robert Greene and Thomas Nashe. See Grosart's edition of his works and a book by Harman (1923).

(2) **Sir George** (1806–76), Scottish painter, was born at St Ninians near Stirling, and settled in Edinburgh in 1823. He became P.R.S.A. (1864), and was knighted in 1867. He painted *Battle of Drumclog*, *A Highland Funeral*, *Bunyan in Bedford Gaol*, &c.

(3) **Sir John Martin** (1863–1944), English actor-manager. Intended to follow in his father's footsteps as a naval architect, he early developed a preference for the stage and from 1882 to 1896 he was with Irving at the Lyceum. He also toured the provinces in Shakespeare, and in 1899 under his own management produced at the Lyceum *The Only Way*, adapted from *A Tale of Two Cities*, in which he played Sydney Carton, his most successful rôle. He became world-famous as a romantic actor and manager. He married Angelita da Silva, who was his leading lady for many years. See his *Autobiography* (1933) and the Life by M. W. Disher (1947).

(4) **William** (1578–1657), English physician and the discoverer of the circulation of the blood, was born at Folkestone, April 1. After six years at King's School, Canterbury, in 1593 he entered Caius College, Cambridge, took his degree in 1597, and after studying at Padua, graduated M.D. both there and at Cambridge in 1602, then settled in London as a physician. In 1609 he was appointed physician to St Bartholomew's Hospital, and in 1615 Lumleian lecturer at the College of Physicians. In 1628 he published his celebrated treatise, *Exercitatio Anatomica de Motu Cordis et Sanguinis*, in which he expounded his views of the circulation of the blood. Successively physician to James I and Charles I, he accompanied the Earl of Arundel in his embassy to the emperor in 1636, and publicly demonstrated his theory at Nuremberg. Harvey was present at the battle of Edgehill in attendance on Charles I (October 23, 1642); afterward he resided at Oxford, being elected warden of Merton College. On the surrender of Oxford to the Parliament in July 1646, he returned to London. His *Exercitationes de Generatione Animalium* appeared in 1651. He died June 3, and was buried at Hempstead near Saffron Walden, and in 1833 reburied in the Harvey Chapel there. Harvey's works in Latin were published in 1766; a translation by Dr Willis appeared in 1847. See Willis's *Life of Harvey* (1878), Huxley's discourse (1878), D'Arcy Power's sketch (1897), Keynes's *Bibliography* (1928) and *Personality* (1949), and Life by A. Malloch (1929).

HARWOOD, (1) Harold Marsh (1874–1959),

English dramatist, born at Eccles, Lancashire, served as an army physician during World War I, and married in 1918 Fryn Tennyson Jesse (q.v.) the author with whom he collaborated on many light plays. He was best known for his political play, *The Grain of Mustard Seed* (1920). He managed the Ambassadors Theatre, London (1920–32).

(2) **Sir Henry** (1888–1959), English admiral, was created K.C.B. after commanding at the battle of the River Plate in which the pocket battleship *Graf Spee* was sunk in December 1939. He was later commander-in-chief of the Mediterranean.

HASDRUBAL, name of several Carthaginian soldiers, including a son-in-law (murdered 221 B.C.), and a son (killed at the Metaurus, 207 B.C.) of Hamilcar.

HASE, Karl August von, *hah'ze* (1800–90), German Protestant theologian, was born at Steinbach, Saxony, professor of Theology at Jena (1830–83). His work lay in the reconciliation of historical Christianity with modern thought. See his *Ideale und Irrthümer* (6th ed. 1908).

HASELRIG, Sir Arthur (d. 1661), English Parliamentarian, one of the Five Members (see HAMPDEN), sat in the Long and Short Parliaments for his native county, Leicestershire, commanded a parliamentary regiment of cuirassiers, and in 1647 became governor of Newcastle. In 1660 he half acquiesced in the Restoration, but died a prisoner in the Tower, January 7.

HASENCLEVER, Walter, *hah'zen-klay-ver* (1890–1940), German dramatist and poet, born at Aachen, wrote lyrical poems *Der Jüngling* (1913) and *Tod und Auferstehung* (1916) and pioneered German expressionism with his father-son drama *Der Sohn* (1914). *Ein besserer Herr* (1927) is one of his comedies. A strong pacifist, he committed suicide in a French internment camp.

HASSALL, John (1868–1948), British artist, born at Walmer, Kent, studied art at Antwerp and Paris, and in 1895 entered the advertising field, becoming the acknowledged pioneer of modern poster design. Among railway posters, his ' Skegness is so bracing ' probably holds the record for longevity and ubiquity. He also illustrated children's books.

HASSE, Johann Adolf (1699–1783), German composer, born near Hamburg, became famous as ' Il Sassone ' through his opera *Sesostrate* (Naples 1725); was *Kapellmeister* at Dresden; and in 1733 was brought to London to head an Italian opposition to Handel. Here *Artaserse* was produced with success; but Hasse soon returned to Dresden, and retired to Vienna and Venice. He married the Venetian singer, Faustina Bordoni (1693–1786).

HASSLER, Hans Leo (1564–1612), German composer, born at Nuremberg, studied under Andrea Gabrieli in Venice, and after 1595 was organist at Augsburg, Ulm and Dresden, as well as in his native city. He wrote choral, chamber and keyboard works, often strongly redolent of the Venetian school.

HASTED, Edward (1732–1812), English historian, educated at Eton and Lincoln's Inn, author of *The History of Kent* (4 vols. fol. 1778–99).

HASTINGS, (1) Francis Rawdon-Hastings, 1st Marquis of (1754–1826), governor-general of Bengal, was born in Dublin, and educated at Harrow. He fought with distinction in the American War of Independence (1775–81), in 1794 led reinforcements to the Duke of York at Malines, became active in politics, and in 1813 was made governor-general of India. Here he warred successfully against the Gurkhas (1814–16) and the Pindaris and Mahrattas (1817–18), purchased Singapore island (1819), encouraged Indian education and the freedom of the press, reformed the law system, and elevated the civil service; but in 1821 he resigned after apparently unfounded charges of corruption had been made against him, and from 1824 till his death off Naples he was governor of Malta. See his own (1824) and Prinsep's (1825) account of his administration, and Ross of Bladensburg's monograph (1893).

(2) **James** (1852–1922), Scottish clergyman and editor, was born at Huntly and, educated at the University and Free Church College, Aberdeen, became minister at Kinneff (1884), Dundee (1897), St Cyrus (1901–11). He founded the *Expository Times* (1889), and compiled Bible dictionaries and the notable *Encyclopaedia of Religion and Ethics* (12 vols. 1908–21; index 1927).

(3) **Sir Patrick** (1880–1952), British lawyer, served in the Boer War, was called to the bar in 1904, and became a K.C. in 1919. He made a great reputation in criminal cases, notably the trials for murder of Vaquier (1924) and Rouse (1931). M.P. for Wallsend (1922–26), he was attorney-general in the 1924 Labour Government. He also wrote plays, two of which, *Scotch Mist* (1926) and *The Blind Goddess* (1947), were successfully staged in London. He was knighted in 1924. See Life by Patricia Hastings (1959).

(4) **Warren** (1732–1818), English administrator in India, was born at Churchill, Oxfordshire, December 6, and educated at Westminster. In 1750 he went out to Calcutta as a writer in the service of the East India Company, was British resident at Murshidabad (1758–61) and then a member of council at Calcutta. He came home in 1764, in 1769 returned to India as second in council at Madras, and in 1772 became governor of Bengal and president of the council. A year later he was created governor-general, with a council of four members, three appointed from home. The majority in council led by Philip Francis was opposed to Hastings from the first; the finances were in disorder. One of Hastings' first tasks was to bring to trial the two chief fiscal ministers of Bengal on charges of embezzlement; but the case broke down. A corrupt official, Nuncomar (Nand Kumar), who had been employed in conducting it, and who had subsequently brought charges of corruption against Hastings, in 1775 was tried and executed on an old charge of forgery, a proceeding which threw obloquy on Hastings and on the chief justice, Sir Elijah Impey (q.v.). Hastings made an appraisement of the landed estates, revised the assessment, improved the administration of justice, organized the opium revenue, waged vigorous war with the Mahrattas,

and made the Company's power paramount in many parts of India. In 1777 an attempt was made to depose him, which was only frustrated by the action of the Supreme Court; that same year, his first wife having died eighteen years before, he married the divorced wife of Baron Imhoff, a German officer. In 1780 he was freed from embarrassment in the council by the retirement of Philip Francis, whom he wounded in a duel; he himself resigned office in 1784 and sailed for England, where he soon became subject to a parliamentary inquiry with a view to impeachment. Among the charges preferred against him by the Whig opposition were the aid given to the Nawáb of Oudh against the Rohilla Afghans, his punishment of the Zemindar of Benares for noncompliance with a demand for aid in the first Mahratta war, and his connivance in the forfeiture of property belonging to the Begums or dowager-princesses of Oudh. On these grounds he was impeached at the bar of the House of Lords, and the trial began February 13, 1788, in Westminster Hall, among the managers for the Commons being Edmund Burke, Fox, Sheridan, the future Lord Minto and Grey. It occupied more than seven years and 145 sittings. Finally, on April 23, 1795, Hastings was acquitted on all the charges, unanimously on all that affected his personal honour. But he left the court a ruined man, the £80,000 that he brought from India having been all but consumed in expenses. The East India Company, however, made generous provision for his declining years; and, at the ancestral seat of Daylesford, Worcestershire, which in 1788 he had bought back in pursuance of his boyhood's ambition, he passed the rest of his life as a country gentleman. In 1814 he was made a P.C.; and he received honours from the City and from Parliament. He died August 22. See studies by Gleig (1841), Trotter (1878), Lyall (1889), Strachey (1892), Forrest (1890–1910), Sir C. Lawson (1896), Monckton-Jones (1918), S. Weitzman (1929); his Letters to his wife (1905); and Lives by A. Mervyn Davies (1935) and K. Feiling (1954).

HATCH, Edwin (1835–89), English theologian, born at Derby, became professor of Classics at Toronto (1859–62), vice-principal of St Mary Hall, Oxford (1867–85), and reader in Ecclesiastical History at Oxford (1884). His Bampton Lectures (1880), on *The Organisation of the Early Christian Churches*, very hostile to High Church claims, established his reputation in England and Germany. Besides theological works he published a collection of religious poetry. *Memorials* by his brother (1890).

HATCHARD, John (1768–1849), London Evangelical publisher from 1797. See the Life by Humphreys (1893).

HATHAWAY, Anne. See SHAKESPEARE.

HATHERLEY, Sir William Page Wood, Lord (1801–81), English judge, born in London, became a Liberal M.P. and was solicitor-general (1851–52) and lord chancellor (1868–1872), with the title Baron Hatherley. His name is associated with a Bankruptcy Act (1869). See *Memoir* by his nephew, Dean Stephens (1883).

HATSHEPSUT, -*shep'soot* (1540?–1481? B.C.), a Queen of Egypt of the XVIIIth dynasty, was the daughter of Thothmes I who associated her with him (or was forced to do so) on the throne, she being the only one of the family of royal birth, and married her to Thothmes II, his son by another wife. On Thothmes II's accession in 1516, she became the real ruler; and, on his death in 1503, she acted as regent for her nephew, Thothmes III. Pursuing a peaceful policy, thereby perhaps endangering Egypt's Asian possessions, she built up the economy of the country. She opened the turquoise mines at the Wady Maghareh, built the great mortuary temple at Deir-el Bahri, sent a marine expedition to Punt (Somaliland?), and erected (1485 B.C.) two obelisks at Karmak. The fiction was maintained that she was a male ruler, and she is represented with a beard.

HATTO, the name of two archbishops of Mainz, one (891–913), the other (968–970). By some the latter is treated as an excellent man, by others as the hard-hearted and selfish bishop who was eaten by mice, as told in Southey's ballad. Possibly, however, the name of the island castle *Mäusethurm*, ' Mouse-tower ', at Bingen is only a corrupted form of *Mauth-thurm*, ' Toll-tower '. See Baring-Gould's *Curious Myths of the Middle Ages* (1869) and Max Beheim's *Die Mäusethurmsage* (1888).

HATTON, (1) **Sir Christopher** (1540–91), English courtier, born at Holdenby in Northamptonshire, from Oxford proceeded to the Inner Temple, and by 1564 had won the favour of Queen Elizabeth by his dancing, entered parliament, in 1587 was appointed lord chancellor. See Life by H. Nicolas (1847).

(2) **John Liptrot** (1809–86), English composer, was born at Liverpool, and settling in London in 1832, soon made his name known as a composer of numerous operas, cantatas, overtures, entr'actes, &c., but is remembered chiefly for his songs, such as ' Good-bye, Sweetheart ', ' To Anthea ', ' Simon the Cellarer ', &c.

HAUCH, Johannes Carsten, *howK*H (1790–1872), Danish poet, was born at Fredrikshald (Halden), and in 1846 was appointed professor of Northern Literature at Kiel. The Holstein revolution (1848) drove him to Copenhagen, where he became professor of Aesthetics. He wrote historical tragedies, lyrical poems, tales and romances, &c.

HAUFF, Wilhelm, *howf* (1802–27), German novelist, born at Stuttgart, studied at Tübingen, was a tutor, then editor of a paper. His fairy tales and short stories are admirable for their simplicity and playful fancy—*Die Bettlerin vom Pont des Arts* and *Phantasien im Bremer Ratskeller* in particular. *Lichtenstein* is an imitation of Scott.

HAUKSBEE. See HAWKSBEE.

HAUPTMANN, Gerhart, *howpt'-* (1862–1946), German dramatist and novelist, born at Obersalzbrunn, Silesia, studied sculpture in Breslau and Rome before settling down in Berlin in 1885. His first play, *Vor Sonnenaufgang,* ' Before Sunrise ' (1889), introduced the new social drama of Ibsen, Zola and Strindberg to Germany, but Hauptmann alleviated the extreme naturalism with a note of compassion. *Einsame Menschen*, ' Lonely People ' (1891), for example, in which a man is torn between his love for two women, a young girl student and a plain, self-effacing wife, portrays the latter, not the former, as the heroine. *Die Weber* (1892) deals with the broader setting of the Silesian weavers' revolt of 1844 and introduces a new theatrical phenomenon, the collective hero. *Florian Gayer*, an historical play, marks a transition to a strange mixture of fantasy and naturalism maintained in other such outstanding works as *Hanneles Himmelfahrt*, ' Little Hanne's Journey to Heaven ' (1893), *Die Versunkene Glocke*, ' The Submerged Bell ' (1896), *Fuhrmann Herschel* (1899), and *Rose Bernd* (1903). His later plays in a variety of styles offer no advance, although the comedies *Der Biberpelz*, ' The Beaverskin ' (1893), and *Der rote Hahn*, ' The Red Cock ' (1901), were later adapted and revised by Brecht to suit the East German Communist censorship. His novels include *Der Narr im Christo: Emmanuel Quint*, ' The Fool in Christ: Emmanuel Quint ' (1910), and *Atlantis* (1912). He was awarded the Nobel prize in 1912. See his autobiographical, *Buch der Leidenschaft* (1929) and *Das Abenteuer meiner Jugend* (1937), and studies by Garten (1954) and M. Sinden (1957).

HAUSER, Kaspar, *how'-* (1812?–33), German foundling, the ' wild boy ', was found in the marketplace of Nuremberg on May 26, 1828. Though apparently sixteen years old, his mind was a blank, his behaviour that of a little child. Afterwards he was able to give some account of himself. So long as he could remember he had been in a hole; he was attended by a ' man ', who had at last taught him to stand and walk, and who had brought him to the place where he was found. At first he showed a wonderful quickness of apprehension, but his moral character began to deteriorate, and he was being gradually forgotten, when on December 14, 1833, he was found with a wound in the side, dealt, he said, by ' the man '. Three days later he died. Many have regarded him as an impostor and suicide: others, as of noble birth and the victim of a hideous crime. See the *Quarterly* (1888), and works by E. Evans (1892) and the Duchess of Cleveland (1892).

HAUSSMANN, Georges Eugène, *hows'-* (1809–91), French financier and townplanner, born in Paris, entered the public service, and under Napoleon III became prefect of the Seine (1853). He then began his task of improving Paris by widening streets, laying out boulevards and parks, building bridges, &c. For these services he was made baron and senator; but the heavy burden (£35,000,000) laid upon the citizens led to his dismissal in 1870. In 1871 he was appointed director of the *Crédit Mobilier*, in 1881 was elected to the Chamber of Deputies. He died in comparative poverty, January 11, 1891. See his *Mémoires* (1890–93).

HAÜY, René Just, *ah-ü-ee* (1743–1822), French mineralogist, born at St Just, dep. Oise, discovered the geometrical law of crystallization.—His brother **Valentin** (1746–1822) devoted his life to the education of the blind.

HAVELOCK, Sir Henry (1795–1857), British soldier, was born at Bishop-Wearmouth, Sunderland, educated at Charterhouse and the Middle Temple, but entered the army a month after Waterloo, and went out to India in 1823, his interest in religion being stimulated during the voyage. He distinguished himself in the Afghan and Sikh wars, and in 1856 commanded a division in Persia. On the outbreak of the Indian mutiny he organized a column of a thousand Highlanders and others at Allahabad with which to relieve Cawnpore and Lucknow, engaged and broke the rebels at Fatehpur, and, driving them before him, entered Cawnpore. Next crossing the Ganges, he fought eight victorious battles, but through sickness in his little army had to retire upon Cawnpore. In September Outram arrived with reinforcements, and Havelock again advanced, Outram waiving his superior rank, and serving under Havelock as a volunteer. The relieving force engaged the enemy at the Alum Bagh, three miles from Lucknow; next they fought their way to the Residency, where they in turn were besieged until November when Sir Colin Campbell forced his way to their rescue. A week after the relief Havelock, now a K.C.B., died of dysentery, November 24, 1857. The rank of a baronet's widow and a pension were given to his widow, daughter of the Baptist missionary Dr Marshman, whose church Havelock joined in 1829. The baronetcy was conferred on his son, **Sir Henry Havelock Allan,** V.C. (1830–97), who from 1874 was a Liberal and Unionist M.P. for Sunderland and S.E. Durham, took the name Allan in 1880, and was killed by Afridis in the Khyber Pass. See Lives by Brock (1858), Marshman (1860), and Forbes (1890).

HAVERGAL, (1) Frances Ridley (1836–79), English hymnwriter, daughter of (3), born at Astley Rectory, Nuneaton, died near Swansea. Her *Poetical Works* appeared in 1884. See *Memorials of F.R.H.* by her sister (1880) and *Letters* (1885).

(2) **Henry East** (1820–75), eldest son of (3), was chaplain at Christ Church (1843–44) and New College (1844–47), Oxford. A talented organist and musician, he published hymns, chants and arrangements of sacred music.

(3) **William Henry** (1793–1870), father of (1) and (2), took holy orders at Oxford, composed hymn tunes, chants and songs, and published sermons and pamphlets.

HAVERS, Clopton (*c.* 1655–1702), English physician, after studying at Cambridge and taking his M.D. at Utrecht, settled in London in 1687. His *Osteologia Nova* (1691) was long a standard work, and he discovered the Haversian canals in bone.

HAVILLAND, Geoffrey de. See DE HAVILLAND.

HAWES, (1) Stephen (*c.* 1475–1525), English allegorical poet, attached to the court from 1502. He was a native probably of Aldeburgh in Suffolk. His chief work is *The Pastyme of Pleasure* (1509, ed. W. E. Mead 1928), dedicated to Henry VII.

(2) **William** (1785–1846), English musician and composer of glees, was born and died in London.

HAWKE, Edward Hawke, 1st Baron (1705–81), British sailor, born in London, in 1744 commanded the *Berwick* in the fleet watching the French and Spanish fleets at Toulon; in the disgraceful battle of February 11 she was one of the few ships handled with spirit. In 1747, a rear-admiral of the white, Hawke was dispatched with fourteen sail to intercept a French convoy for the West Indies; on October 14 off Cape Finisterre he caused six of the guarding squadron to strike, though the convoy itself escaped. For this he was knighted, and in the same year became M.P. for Bristol. In 1756, now a full admiral, he was sent out to supersede Byng; he commanded in the Channel (1757–58). During 1759 the French were preparing fleets at Brest and Rochefort to cover an invasion of England; the Brest fleet of twenty ships was watched by Hawke with a fleet of twenty-three. On November 14 the English fleet was driven off by gales, and the French admiral, De Conflans, slipped out to sea; but Hawke steered to cut him off at Quiberon. On November 20 he caught the French, and, although it was blowing a fresh gale, attacked at once. The result was the destruction of the French fleet and the collapse of the invasion scheme. First lord of the Admiralty in 1766–71, Hawke in 1776 was made Baron Hawke of Towton. He died at Shepperton, Middlesex. See the Life by Montagu Burrows (1883). **Martin Bladen Hawke, 7th Baron** (1860–1938), was a famous cricketer, captain of Yorkshire (1883–1910), and president of the M.C.C. in 1914–18. See his *Recollections and Reminiscences* (1924).

HAWKER, Robert Stephen (1803–75), English poet, was born at Plymouth, and educated at Pembroke College, Oxford, won the Newdigate prize in 1827 and in 1834 became vicar of Morwenstow, on the Cornish coast. He shared many of the superstitions of his people, as to apparitions and the evil eye. His poetry includes *Tendrils* (1821), the Cornish ballads in *Records of the Western Shore* (1832–36), *Reeds Shaken with the Wind* (1843), *The Quest of the Sangraal* (1864). None of Hawker's poems is better known than his spirited ballad based on the old Cornish refrain, ' And shall Trelawny die ? ' He died at Plymouth, having been admitted twelve hours before to the Roman Catholic Communion. There were Lives by Baring-Gould (1875) and Lee (1876); the definitive *Life and Letters* by his son-in-law, C. E. Byles, appeared in 1905; also Life by M. F. Burrows (1926).

HAWKESWORTH, John (c. 1715–73), English author, born in London, in 1744 succeeded Dr Johnson on the *Gentleman's Magazine*; and in 1752 started, with Johnson and others, *The Adventurer*, half of whose 140 numbers were from Hawkesworth's pen. He published a volume of fairy tales (1761), edited Swift, and prepared the account of Captain Cook's first voyage, which formed vols. ii–iii of Hawkesworth's *Voyages* (3 vols., 1773).

HAWKINS, (1) Sir A. H. See HOPE (1).
(2) **Henry, 1st Baron Brampton** (1817–1907), English judge, born at Hitchin, became Q.C. in 1858, was counsel for the defence and later for the crown in the Tichborne case (1871–74), became judge in 1876 and was knighted. In civil cases, fearing possible reversal of his decisions on appeal, he employed various tricks to avoid passing judgments. In the numerous murder cases which came before him, his fairness, however, did not warrant the nickname ' Hanging Hawkins ' which was given him. He was created baron in 1899.
(3) **Sir John.** See HAWKYNS.
(4) **Sir John** (1719–89), English musicologist, born in London, became an attorney, and as magistrate was knighted in 1772 for his services in riots (1768–69). He collected a valuable musical library, and produced in 1776 his *General History of the Science and Practice of Music*, which was overshadowed by that of Charles Burney (q.v.). He was Johnson's literary executor, and published (1787–89) an inaccurate Life and an edition of his works. See Life by P. Scholes (1953).—His son, **John Sydney** (1758–1842), published a history of Gothic architecture; his daughter, **Laetitia**, her own *Memoirs* (1822), with much about Dr Johnson.

HAWKSBEE, or Hauksbee, Francis (d. c. 1713), English physicist, became F.R.S. in 1705. He carried further the observations by Gilbert and Boyle on electricity, inventing the first glass electrical machine, and improved the air pump.—**Francis**, the younger (1687–1763), apparently his son, was also an electrician, and was in 1723 appointed clerk and housekeeper to the Royal Society.

HAWKSHAW, Sir John (1811–91), English engineer, born in Leeds, was mining engineer in Venezuela (1831–34) and consulting engineer in the construction of Charing Cross and Cannon Street stations and bridges and the Inner Circle underground railway in London. He also constructed the Severn Tunnel and the Amsterdam ship canal. He was elected F.R.S. in 1855 and knighted in 1873.

HAWKSMOOR, Nicholas (1661–1736), English architect, born in Nottinghamshire, became a clerk to Wren and also assisted Vanbrugh. His most individual contributions are the London churches, St Mary Woolnoth, St George's, Bloomsbury, and Christ Church, Spitalfields, as well as parts of Queen's College and All Souls, Oxford. See studies by H. S. Goodhart-Rendel (1924) and K. Downes (1959).

HAWKWOOD, Sir John de, Italianized Acuto (d. 1394), English soldier of fortune, born at Hedingham, Essex, is said to have distinguished himself at Crécy and Poitiers, was knighted by Edward III, and in 1360 led a band of mercenaries to Italy, where he at first took service with Pisa against Florence, and fought in various causes, but at last agreed to fight the battles of Florence for an annual pension. See Temple Leader and Marcotti's Life (Eng. trans. by Mrs Leader Scott, 1889), and *Quarterly Review* (January 1890).

HAWKYNS, Sir John (1532–95), British sailor, born at Plymouth, was the first Englishman to traffic in slaves (1562); his ' commercial ' career closed with his disastrous third voyage (1567). He became navy treasurer in 1573, was knighted for his services against the Armada in 1588, and thereafter made havoc of the Spanish West India Trade. In 1595, with his kinsman Drake, he commanded an expedition to the Spanish Main, but died at Porto Rico. See Froude, *English Seamen of the 16th Century* (1901), Unwin, *The Defeat of John Hawkins* (1960), and Lives by Williamson (1927) and Gorse (1930). His only son, Sir Richard (*c.* 1562–1622), was also a naval commander, from 1594 to 1602 a prisoner of Spain.

HAWORTH, Sir Walter Norman, *hahrth* (1883–1950), English chemist, born at Chorley, Lancashire, educated at Manchester and Göttingen, he was professor of Organic Chemistry at Newcastle (1920–25) and Birmingham (1925–48). He determined the constitution of vitamin C and various carbohydrates, for which he shared the Nobel prize with Karrer in 1937. He was elected F.R.S. in 1928, received its Davy Medal in 1934 and Royal Medal in 1942. He was knighted in 1947, and was vice-principal of Birmingham University (1947–48).

HAWTHORNE, Nathaniel (1804–64), American novelist and short-story writer, born July 4 at Salem, Mass., the son of a merchant captain, who died when the boy was only four years old; his mother lived afterwards in close retirement and straitened circumstances. At fourteen he went with her to a lonely farm in the woods of Raymond, Maine, and formed there a habit of solitude; at Bowdoin College, where he graduated in 1825, he began his first novel. But his progress was slow. After his return to Salem he shut himself up for twelve years 'in a heavy seclusion', writing tales and verses. In 1828 he published anonymously his first novel, *Fanshawe*, which was unsuccessful. Continuing to contribute to annuals and magazines, he edited in 1836 a short-lived periodical. Meanwhile some of his short stories had gained such favourable notice from the London *Athenaeum* that in 1837 *Twice-told Tales*, a volume of them, was published. His genius, however, was not yet appreciated in his own country. In 1839 the historian Bancroft, then collector of the port of Boston, appointed him weigher and gauger in the custom-house, a post he held until 1841; he then joined for a twelvemonth the Brook Farm idyllic, semi-socialistic community near Boston. Meanwhile he wrote and published a series of simple stories for children from New England history—*Grandfather's Chair, Famous Old People* and *Liberty Tree* (1841). Removing to Concord, Mass., he issued *Biographical Stories* (1842) for children, and brought out an enlarged edition of the *Twice-told Tales* (1842). He wrote sketches and studies for the *Democratic Review*, which formed the *Mosses from an Old Manse* (1846). The *Review* failed; and, as he lost all his savings at Brook Farm, he was forced to accept a place in the custom-house again—this time as surveyor in Salem. By the expiration of his term he had completed (1850) *The Scarlet Letter*, still the best known of his works. At Lenox, Mass., he now entered upon a phase of remarkable productiveness, writing *The House of the*

Seven Gables (1851), *Wonder Book* (1851), *The Snow Image* (1852), and *The Blithedale Romance* (1852), which drew colouring from the Brook Farm episode. He settled at Concord in 1852, and wrote a campaign biography of his old schoolfriend, President Franklin Pierce, and on the latter's inauguration became consul at Liverpool (1853–57). He completed *Tanglewood Tales* in 1853, as a continuation of *Wonder Book*. A sojourn of a year and a half in Rome and Florence, beginning in 1858, supplied him with the materials for *The Marble Faun* (1860), published in England as *Transformation*. Returning to Concord, he wrote for the *Atlantic Monthly* the brilliant papers on England collected as *Our Old Home* (1863). He began a new romance, founded on the idea of an elixir of immortality, which remained unfinished at his death, May 18, at Plymouth, N.H., where he had gone for health reasons. He was buried at Concord. With little faculty for poetry, Hawthorne had a singular command over the musical qualities of prose. Although exceptionally fitted for conveying subtleties of thought and fantasy, his style is suitable for children, being invariably clear and strongly marked by common sense. Hawthorne was only gradually recognized in his own country. See authorized edition of his works (1883), *The American Notebooks* (1932), *The English Notebooks* (1944), both ed. by R. Stewart, who has also written a Life (1949). See also study by Henry James (1879) and Lives by Van Doren (1949) and Waggoner (1955).

HAXO, François Nicholas Benoit (1774–1838), French military engineer, born at Lunéville, became a general under Napoleon and won fame for his reconstructions of Vauban's fortifications and for his brilliant direction of the siege of Antwerp citadel in 1832.

HAY, (1) Ian, pseud. of Maj.-General **John Hay Beith** (1876–1952), Scottish novelist and dramatist, educated at Fettes and Cambridge; he became a language master at his old school, served in World War I, and was awarded the Military Cross. His light popular novels, *Pip* (1907), *A Safety Match* (1911), *A Knight on Wheels* (1914), were followed by the war books *The First Hundred Thousand* (1915) and *Carrying On* (1917). Many novels and comedies followed, best known of the latter being *Tilly of Bloomsbury* (1919) and *Housemaster* (1936). He was director of Public Relations at the War Office (1938–41).

(2) **John** (1838–1905), American statesman, born at Salem, Ind., and admitted to the Illinois bar in 1861, was assistant private secretary to President Lincoln, and during the war served for some months. He was secretary of legation at Paris (1865–67) and Madrid (1868–70), and *chargé d'affaires* at Vienna (1867–68); on the staff of the *New York Tribune* (1870–75), and first assistant-secretary of state (1879–81). His *Pike County Ballads* (1871) include 'Little Breeches' and 'Jim Bludso'; he also published *Castilian Days* (1871), *The Bread-winner* (anon. 1883), and, with Nicolay, a Life of Lincoln (1891). In 1897 he became ambassador to Britain; in 1898 secretary of state to President

McKinley. See Life by T. Dennett (1934).

(3) Lucy. See CARLISLE (2).

HAYDEN, Ferdinand Vandeveer (1829–87), American geologist, born at Westfield, Mass., was employed in surveys in the northwest (1853–62). He served as Federal surgeon during the war, became professor of Geology at Pennsylvania University (1865–72) and was subsequently connected with the U.S. geological survey. He was influential in obtaining the establishment of Yellowstone National Park.

HAYDN, *hī'dn'*, **(1) Franz Joseph** (1732–1809), Austrian composer of Croatian descent, was born at Rohrau, Lower Austria, on April 1, the son of a wheelwright. Educated at the Cathedral Choir School of St Stephen's, Vienna, he earned his living initially by playing in street orchestras and teaching, but gained valuable experience from acting as accompanist and part-time valet to the famous Italian opera composer and singing teacher, Porpora, and as musical director (1759–60) for Count von Morzin, who kept a small company of court musicians for whom Haydn wrote his earliest symphonies. His marriage in 1760 to the sharp-tempered Maria Anna Keller was unhappy. Entering the service of the Esterhazy family in 1761, he remained with them on and off, first at Eisenstadt and later at Esterhazy, until 1790. As musical director of a princely establishment his duties included the performance and composition of chamber and orchestral music, sacred music and opera for domestic consumption. These favourable laboratory conditions led to a vast output, notable, technically, for Haydn's development and near-standardization of the four-movement string quartet and the ' classical ' symphony, with sonata or ' first movement ' form as a basic structural ingredient. This was to influence the whole course of European music. Though he himself rarely travelled during his Esterhazy period, his compositions gained an international reputation and were in demand in France, Germany, England, Spain and Italy. Retiring in fact though not in name from Esterhazy in 1790, he subsequently paid two visits to London, sponsored by the violinist and impresario Salomon (q.v.), during which he directed performances of the specially commissioned ' Salomon ' or ' London ' Symphonies (Nos. 93-104). He was made a Doctor of Music of Oxford in 1791. During the closing years of his life in Vienna —he died on May 31, 1809—his main works were *The Creation, The Seasons* and his final quartets. Though the most famous composer of his day, Haydn was quick to recognize the genius of the young Mozart, but was slower to appreciate the turbulent, questing spirit of Beethoven, who was his pupil in 1792. His spontaneity, melodiousness, faultless craftsmanship, and a gift for the expression of both high spirits and gravity were strongly tinged in the 1770s by the prevailing *Sturm und Drang* atmosphere as well as by related personal problems. His output includes 104 symphonies, about 50 concertos, 84 string quartets, 24 stage works, 12 masses, orchestral divertimenti, keyboard sonatas, and diverse chamber, choral, instrumental,

and vocal pieces. See studies by C. F. Pohl (Berlin 1875–87, completed by Botstiber, 1927), K. Geiringer (1947), R. Hughes (1956), H. C. R. Landon (1955) and *Werke* (ed. by J. P. Larsen, 2 vols., 1958).

(2) Joseph (d. 1856), English compiler of the *Dictionary of Dates* (1841; 25th ed. 1910) and other works, died in London.

(3) Michael (1737–1806), Austrian composer, brother of (1), born at Rohrau, was a cathedral chorister with Joseph in Vienna and ultimately became musical director and concert master to the Archbishop in Salzburg, where he remained until his death, having declined an offer of the post of assistant to his brother at Esterhazy. Some of his compositions are of considerable merit and charm; and several of his church pieces and instrumental works are still performed. Weber was among his pupils.

HAYDON, Benjamin Robert (1786–1846), English historical painter, born at Plymouth, studied at the Royal Academy. In 1807 he exhibited *Joseph and Mary resting on the Road to Egypt*, and in 1809 after studying the Elgin Marbles, *Dentatus*, whose cold reception by the Academy began the painter's feud with that body. His *Judgment of Solomon* (1814) was probably his finest production. While he was painting *The Raising of Lazarus* (1823; Tate), he was arrested for debt, and was poor thereafter; this though he took to portrait painting, though his *Mock Election* was purchased by George IV, though a public subscription was raised on his behalf, and though he delivered a series of lectures on painting and design (1836; published 1844). In 1832 Lord Grey commissioned *The Reform Banquet* and in 1834 the Duke of Sutherland bought his *Cassandra*. It was a bitter disappointment when he failed to gain employment on the decoration of the Houses of Parliament; under this and other vexations his mind gave way, and on June 20 he shot himself in his studio. His works are lofty in aim, but unequal; his execution was seldom equal to his conception. See his *Autobiography and Journals*, ed. Taylor (1853), ed. Huxley (1926), ed. Penrose (1927), ed. Blunden (1927); *Correspondence and Table Talk*, with a Memoir by his son (1876); *Diaries* (ed. by Pope, vols. 1-2, 1960, vols. 3-5, 1963); and Lives by Paston (1905) and George (1948).

HAYEK, Friedrich August von (1899–   ), Austrian political economist, born in Vienna, director of the Austrian Institute for Economic Research (1927–31), lectured at Vienna (1929–31), when he was appointed Tooke professor of Economic Science at London (1931–50). His *Prices and Production* (1931), *Monetary Theory and the Trade Cycle* (1933), and *The Pure Theory of Capital* (1941) dealt with important problems arising out of industrial fluctuations. He was appointed to a professorship at Chicago in 1950 and moved to the University of Freiburg i.Br. in 1962. His later works, *The Road to Serfdom* (1944), *Individualism and Economic Order* (1948) and *The Constitution of Liberty* (1960) show an increasing concern for the problems posed for individual values by increased economic controls. Works published during the same period on theoretical psychology and the history of ideas indicate a further broadening of interests, manifested by his *Studies in Philosophy, Politics and Economics* (1967).

HAYES, (1) **Catharine** (1690–1726), English murderess, was burnt for murdering her husband, a London carpenter. See Thackeray's *Catherine* in *Fraser's* (1839–40).

(2) **Helen** (1900–), U.S. actress, born in Washington, won fame in a wide variety of stage productions, such as *Pollyanna* (1917–1918), *Dear Brutus* (1919), and *The Wisteria Trees* (1951). She appeared in several films, including *A Farewell to Arms* (1932), *My Son John* (1951), and *The Sin of Madelon Claudet* (1931, for which she won an Academy Award (under its new name of ' Oscar ') in 1932).

(3) **Isaac Israel** (1832–81), American Arctic explorer, born in Chester county, Penn., sailed as surgeon in the Kane expedition (1853–54); see his *Arctic Boat-journey* (1860). He conducted a second Arctic expedition (1860–61), and in 1869 a third one described in *The Land of Desolation* (1871).

(4) **Rutherford Birchard** (1822–93), 19th president of the United States, was born at Delaware, Ohio, graduated at Kenyon College, Ohio, in 1842, and practised as a lawyer at Cincinnati (1849–61). In the Civil War Hayes served with distinction, retiring as major-general. He was returned to congress from Ohio in 1865 and 1866, and governor in 1867, 1869 and 1875. In 1876 he was Republican candidate for the presidency, the Democratic candidate being Samuel J. Tilden. Some of the electoral votes being disputed, a commission gave them to Hayes, thus securing him a majority. Under the Hayes administration the country recovered commercial prosperity. His policy included reform of the civil service, conciliation of the southern states, and resumption of specie payments; but the bill for the monetization of silver was carried against his veto. See *Lives* by Stoddard (1889) and Eckenrode (1930).

HAYLEY, William (1745–1820), English poet and writer, born at Chichester, wrote verse, *Essays*, plays, Lives of Milton and Romney, but his best was *The Life of Cowper* (1803). See his *Memoirs* (1823).

HAYM, Rudolf, *hīm* (1821–1901), German author, born at Grünberg in Silesia, in 1848 sat in the Frankfurt national assembly and became professor at Halle in 1860. He wrote biographies of Humboldt (1856), Hegel (1857), Schopenhauer (1864), Herder (1877–1885) and Duncker (1891), and a monograph, *Die romantische Schule* (1870).

HAYNAU, Julius Jakob, Baron von, *hī'now* (1786–1853), Austrian soldier, born at Cassel, entered the Austrian service in 1801, and gained notoriety during the Italian campaigns (1848–49) by his ruthless severity, especially at the capture of Brescia, where his flogging of women gained him the name of the ' Hyaena of Brescia '. From the siege of Venice he was summoned to the supreme military command in Hungary in 1849; and his successes at Raab, Komorn and Szegedin did much to secure Austrian supremacy. Appointed dictator of Hungary after its pacification, he was dismissed in

1850, and that same year in London was assaulted by Barclay & Perkins's draymen. See *Life* by Schönhals (3rd ed., Vienna 1875).

HAYNE, Robert Young (1791–1839), American statesman, born in South Carolina, was admitted to the bar in 1812, and served in the war with Great Britain. He became speaker of the state legislature and attorney-general of the state, and sat in the U.S. senate (1823–32). He opposed protection, and in 1832 supported the doctrine of nullification. South Carolina in 1832 adopted an ordinance of nullification, Hayne was elected governor, and the state prepared to resist the federal power by force of arms. A compromise, however, was agreed to, and the ordinance was repealed.—His nephew, **Paul Hamilton** (1830–86), the ' Laureate of the South ', was born at Charleston, and died near Augusta, Ga. His war songs, sonnets, &c., were collected in 1882.

HAYNES, Elwood (1857–1925), American inventor, constructed what is claimed to be the first American automobile (1893), preserved in the Smithsonian Institution. He also patented a number of alloys, including stainless steel (1919).

HAYTER, Sir George (1792–1871), English portrait and historical painter, was born in London, and knighted in 1842. Several of his works, including *Marriage of Queen Victoria*, are in the Royal collection.

HAYWARD, Abraham (1802–84), English essayist, was born at Wishford, Wiltshire, and called to the bar in 1832. He founded and edited the *Law Magazine*, was made a Q.C. in 1845, and delighted society by his social gifts almost down to his death. Many of his best articles were reprinted in his *Biographical and Critical Essays* (1858–73) and *Eminent Statesmen and Writers* (1880). See his *Select Correspondence* (1886).

HAYWOOD, Eliza, née **Fowler** (c. 1693–1756), English novelist, born in London, deserted by her husband, became an actress and wrote a number of society novels, in which the characters resembled living persons so closely, names being thinly concealed by the use of asterisks, as to be libellous. Pope denounced her in the *Dunciad*. Her works include *Memoirs of a Certain Island adjacent to Utopia* (1725), &c.

HAZLITT, William (1778–1830), English essayist, was born at Maidstone, April 10, the son of a Unitarian minister, who removed to Boston, U.S., in 1783, and to Wem in Shropshire in 1787. The boy was at fifteen sent to Hackney to study for the ministry, but had abandoned the notion when in 1798 he met Coleridge, and by him was encouraged to write *Principles of Human Action* (1805). Having tried portrait painting, he published in 1806 his *Free Thoughts on Public Affairs*, in 1807 his *Reply to Malthus*, and in 1812 found employment in London on the *Morning Chronicle* and *Examiner*. From 1814 to 1830 he contributed to the *Edinburgh Review*; his *Round Table* essays and *Characters of Shakespeare's Plays* appeared in 1817. Between 1818 and 1821 he delivered at the Surrey Institute his lectures on *The English Poets, English Comic Writers*, and *Dramatic*

Literature of the Age of Elizabeth. His marriage with Sarah Stoddart in 1808 had proved a failure and they got a divorce at Edinburgh in 1822. His essays in the *London Magazine* were afterwards republished in his *Table Talk* (1821) and *Plain Speaker* (1826). A passion for Sarah Walker, the daughter of a tailor with whom he lodged, found expression in the frantic *Liber Amoris* (1823). In 1824 he married a charming widow with £300 a year, who travelled with him to Italy, but left him for ever on the return journey. His *Spirit of the Age, or Contemporary Portraits* appeared in 1825; his *Life of Napoleon Bonaparte* (1828–30). His last years darkened by ill-health and money difficulties, he died with the words, ' Well, I've had a happy life '. He was a deadly controversialist, a master of epigram, invective and withering irony. His style ranges from lively gossip to glowing rhapsody; the best of his work is in his later collections of essays. See the *Memoirs* (1867) and *The Hazlitts* (1911) by his grandson, Birrell's *Hazlitt* (1902), P. P. Howe's authoritative *Life* (1922, Penguin ed. 1956), Keynes's *Bibliography* (1931), and Schneider's *Aesthetics of Wm. Hazlitt* (1933). Hazlitt's grandson, **William Carew** (1834–1913), compiled and edited many works; see his *Four Generations of a Literary Family* (1897).

HEAD, (1) **Sir Edmund Walker, 8th Bart.** (1805–68), English administrator, born near Maidstone, was educated at Oriel College, Oxford, and became a fellow of Merton. After serving as poor-law commissioner, he was lieutenant-governor of New Brunswick (1847–54), then govenor-general of Canada till 1861. He wrote on *Spanish and French Painting* (1847), *Ballads* (1868), &c. See Life by D. G. G. Kerr (1954).

(2) **Sir Francis Bond** (1793–1875), English administrator, born at the Hermitage near Rochester, entered the Royal Engineers, served at Waterloo, and as major retired in 1825. He was lieutenant-governor of Upper Canada (1835–37), where he suppressed an insurrection led by William Lyon Mackenzie, which heralded Lord Durham's mission to Canada. He was created a baronet (1836). See Life by S. Jackman (1958).

(3) **Richard** (*c.* 1637–86), English hackwriter, best known as the author of part i of *The English Rogue* (1665–71), the other three parts being by the bookseller Francis Kirkman. Head was born in Ireland, and drowned at sea.

HEALY, Timothy Michael (1855–1931), Irish Nationalist leader, born at Bantry in 1855, sat in parliament (1880–1918), headed in 1890 the revolt against Parnell, and became an Independent Nationalist. First governor-general of the Irish Free State (1922–28).

HEAPHY, Thomas (1775–1835), English portrait painter, born in London. His early works were mostly portraits, but from 1804 he turned to watercolours. He accompanied the Duke of Wellington in the Peninsular War and painted a composite portrait of the Duke and his officers. He was one of the founders and first president of the Society of British Artists (1824).—His son **Thomas** (1813–73) was also a portrait painter.

HEARN, Lafcadio (1850–1904), American journalist of Greek-Irish parents, born on the island of Leucadia, was trained as a journalist in the United States, became a naturalized Japanese and wrote enthusiastically on things Japanese. See Lives by E. Bisland (1907) and V. McWilliams (1946).

HEARNE, Thomas (1678–1735), English antiquary, born at White Waltham, Berkshire, graduated from St Edmund Hall, Oxford, and in 1712 became second keeper to the Bodleian Library—a post he had to resign as a Jacobite in 1716. Among his forty-one chief works were *Reliquiae Bodleianae* (1703), Leland's *Itinerary* (1710–12) and *Collectanea* (1715), editions of Camden's *Annals* (1717), Fordun's *Scotichronicon* (1722), etc. The *Reliquiae Hearnianae* was published by Philip Bliss, in 1857. See his autobiography in the *Lives of Leland, Hearne, and Wood* (1772).

HEARST, William Randolph (1863–1951), American newspaper owner, born at San Francisco, after studying at Harvard took over the San Francisco *Examiner* in 1867 from his father. He revolutionized journalism by the introduction of banner headlines, lavish illustrations and other sensational methods, nicknamed by critics ' the yellow press '. He took over the New York *Journal* (1895), trebled its circulation and made himself the head of a chain of newspapers and periodicals. See Life by Winkler (1928).

HEATH, (1) **Edward Richard George** (1916–), British Conservative politician, born at Broadstairs, was a scholar of Balliol College, Oxford, served in World War II and entered Parliament in 1950, one of Butler's ' One Nation ' new Tory intellectuals. He was an assistant (1953–55) and chief whip (1955–59), minister of labour (1959–60) when he became lord privy seal and the chief negotiator for Britain's entry into the European Common Market, abortive because of the French, yet earning him the German Charlemagne prize (1963). In the Douglas-Home administration (1963) he became secretary of state for industry and president of the Board of Trade (1963). Elected leader of the Conservative party in July 1965, he was Opposition leader until, on the Conservative victory in the 1970 general election, he became prime minister. See Lives by Hutchinson (1970) and Laing (1972).

(2) **Neville George** (1917–46), English murderer, born at Ilford, Essex, was thrice cashiered, from the R.A.F., R.A.S.C. and South African Air Force, before committing two notoriously brutal sexual murders in the summer of 1946 for which he was tried and executed on October 26. See his *Trial*, ed. Critchley (1951).

HEATHCOAT, John (1783–1861), British inventor, born near Derby, designed in 1808 a machine for making lace and set up a factory in Nottingham which was destroyed in 1816 by the Luddites. He then moved his business to Tiverton in Devon, where it still prospers today. Heathcoat also invented ribbon- and net-making machinery. See Life by W. Gore Allen (1958).

HEATHCOAT-AMORY. See AMORY.

HEATHFIELD, George Augustus Eliott, 1st Baron (1717–90), British soldier, born at

Stobs in Roxburghshire, educated at Leyden, the French military college of La Fère, and Woolwich, and served in the War of the Austrian Succession, the Seven Years' War and in Cuba (1762), returning lieutenant-general. When, in 1775, Britain became involved in hostilities with Spain, Eliott was sent out to Gibraltar. His heroic defence, from June 1779 to February 1783, ranks as one of the most memorable achievements of British arms. He was in 1787 created Lord Heathfield, Baron of Gibraltar. See Drinkwater's *Siege of Gibraltar* (1785).

HEATON, Sir John Henniker (1848–1914), English politician, born at Rochester, was M.P. (1885–1910), and championed successfully the penny postage rate within the British Empire and including the United States.

HEAVISIDE, Oliver (1850–1925), English physicist, born in London, made important advances in the study of electrical communications, and suggested the existence of an ionized gaseous layer (Heaviside layer) capable of reflecting radio waves.

HEBBEL, Friedrich (1813–63), German dramatist, was born at Wesselburen in Ditmarsh, studied in Hamburg from 1835 and after stays in Heidelberg, Munich, Copenhagen, settled in Vienna (1846). His only contemporary play is *Maria Magdalena* (1842), his favourite settings being of a legendary, historical or biblical character, as *Herodes und Marianne* (1852) and his masterpiece, the *Nibelungen* trilogy (1855–60), &c. Hebbel constantly portrayed the inherent Hegelian conflict between individuality and humanity as a whole. See books by Kuh (1907), T. M. Campbell (Boston 1919), E. Purdie (1932), G. Wethly (1935) and Hebbel's *Tagebücher* (1887) and *Briefe* (1908).

HEBER, Reginald (1783–1826), English divine and hymnwriter, born at Malpas, Cheshire, in 1783, wrote his prize poem *Palestine* at Oxford (1803). Inducted into the family living of Hodnet in Shropshire (1807), he was a frequent contributor to the *Quarterly Review*, and in 1812 published a volume of *Hymns*. He was appointed Bampton lecturer in 1815, a prebendary of St Asaph in 1817, and preacher of Lincoln's Inn in 1822. In 1823 he accepted the see of Calcutta; but his episcopate was terminated by his sudden death at Trichinopoly. He published sermons, *A Journey through India*, &c., and edited Jeremy Taylor's *Works* (1822). As a poet, his fame rests upon *Palestine* and his *Hymns*, which include ' From Greenland's Icy Mountains' and ' Holy, Holy, Holy'. See Lives by his widow (1830) and G. Smith (1895).—His half-brother, **Richard** (1774–1833), was a famous bibliomaniac with a collection estimated at 146,827 vols.

HEBERDEN, William, *heb'-* (1710–1801), English physician, born in London, studied and practised in Cambridge, but in 1748 set up in London. He distinguished chickenpox from smallpox, described *angina pectoris* and prescribed treatment. He attended Dr Johnson, was the last to write medical papers in Latin, was elected F.R.C.P. (1748) and F.R.S. in 1749.—His son **William** (1767–1845) was also a physician.

HÉBERT, Jacques René, *ay-bayr* (1755–94),

French revolutionary, nicknamed ' Père Duchesne ', was born at Alençon. A servant in Paris, he was dismissed more than once for embezzlement, but soon after the outbreak of the Revolution became a prominent Jacobin and editor of *Le Père Duchesne*, established to crush a constitutional newspaper of the same title. As a member of the revolutionary council, he played a conspicuous part in the September massacres. He was on the commission appointed to examine Marie Antoinette and brought up the trumped-up charge of incestuous practices with the dauphin. He and his fellows were mainly instrumental in converting Notre Dame into a temple of Reason. But he went too fast for Robespierre, who had him guillotined March 24. See Lives by Brunet (Paris 1857) and D. Mater (1888).

HECATAEUS OF MILETUS, *-tee'us* (*c.* 550–476 B.C.), Greek historian and geographer, visited Greece, Thrace, Persia and parts of Italy, Spain and Africa, and wrote the *Tour of the World*. Of this and of his *Histories*, a prose version of Greek poetical legends, only fragments remain.

HECHT, Ben, *heкнt* (1894–1964), American writer, born in New York, wrote novels, plays and filmscripts, from 1946 was dedicated to the Zionist cause and vilification of Britain as in *A Flag is Born* (1946).

HECKEL, (1) Erich (1883–1970), German painter, a founder of the expressionist school, the *Brücke* (*c.* 1905) was born at Döbeln, Saxony, and studied architecture at Dresden before turning to painting. He excelled in lithography and the woodcut, e.g., *Self-portrait* (1917; Munich). Vilified by the Nazis, he stayed in Berlin and was professor at Karlsruhe (1949–56).

(2) **Johann Adam** (*c.* 1812?–1877), German woodwind instrument maker, established his own workshop at Biebrich near Wiesbaden, in 1831 and with the guidance of a bassoon player, Carl Almenraeder (1786–1843), introduced improvements in the structure and key-system of bassoons, which, when standardized, marked off the German from the French type. His son, **Wilhelm** (1856–1909), and grandsons, **Wilhelm Hermann** (1879–1952) and **August** (1880–1914), carried on the business, which introduced several instrumental novelties such as the Heckelphone (1903).

HECKER, (1) Friedrich Karl Franz (1811–81), German political agitator, born at Eichtersheim, Baden, became an advocate, headed the republican movement of 1848, with a band of revolutionists invaded Baden, but was defeated and fled to America. In the Civil War he commanded a brigade. See Life by MacSorley (1952).

(2) **Isaac Thomas** (1819–88), American founder of the Paulists, the son of New York Germans, passed from Brook Farm socialism to Behmenite mysticism, became a Catholic (1844) and, after studies in England, a Redemptorist Father. Claiming new freedom, he was extruded from that order, but founded ' the Missionary Priests of St Paul ', and greatly extended Catholicism in America. His ' Americanism ' or tendency to democratize Catholicism created much

controversy. See his *The Church and the Age* (1888), and Life by Elliott (1898).

HEDERICUS, or **Hederich, Benjamin**, *-ree'-kus* (1675–1748), German schoolmaster at Grossenhain in Saxony from 1705, in 1722 published his Greek lexicon.

HEDIN, Sven Anders von, *hay-deen'* (1865–1952), Swedish explorer and geographer, born at Stockholm, began in 1885 an important series of travels in Central Asia, particularly in the Transhimalayas, the Gobi desert and Tibet, of which he made the first detailed map (1908). He was made an Hon. K.C.I.E. in 1909, but his pro-German sympathies made him abandon this honour during World War I. In 1923 he journeyed round the world, organized meteorological stations, &c. His numerous books include *My Life as Explorer* (1925).

HEDLEY, William (1770–1843), English inventor, a colliery ' viewer ' and lessee, born at Newburn near Newcastle, who in 1813 improved Trevithick's locomotive. See Life by Archer (3rd ed. 1885).

HEEM, Jan Davidsz de, *haym* (*c*. 1606–84), the greatest Dutch still-life painter, born at Utrecht, settled in Antwerp. His paintings are in most European galleries and in the United States. His son **Cornelis** (1631–95) was also a painter.

HEENAN. See SAYERS (3) and MENKEN.

HEEREN, Arnold Hermann Ludwig, *hay'ren* (1760–1842), German historian, born near Bremen, in 1787 became professor of Philosophy, and in 1801 of History, at Göttingen. His first great work was an economic history of the ancient world (1793–96; Eng. trans. 1833). He also wrote on the study of the classics since the Renaissance (1797–1802), a history of the states of the ancient world (1799; trans. 1840), *Political System of Europe and its Colonies* (1800; trans. 1834), &c. His economic interpretation of history foreshadowed Marx and Engels.

HEFELE, Karl Joseph von, *hay'fè-lè* (1800–1893), German Roman Catholic church historian, born at Unterkochen in Württemberg, became in 1840 Catholic professor of Church History at Tübingen. He showed himself a dangerous enemy to the dogma of papal infallibility, even after consecration as Bishop of Rottenburg in 1869, by contributions to the Honorius controversy (1870). But in 1871 he submitted to the dogma with an explanation. He wrote on the conversion of southwest Germany (1837), Ximenes (1844; Eng. trans. 1860), church history (1864–65), &c.; his great work is the *Konziliengeschichte* (1855–74).

HEGEL, Georg Wilhelm Friedrich, *hay'-* (1770–1831), with Kant, whose system he modified, the greatest of the German idealist philosophers, born at Stuttgart, August 27, studied theology at Tübingen, where he met Schelling and Hölderlin (qq.v.), was family tutor in Berne (1793) and Frankfurt-am-Main (1796), and in 1801, as *privatdozent* at Jena, edited with Schelling the *Kritische Journal der Philosophie* (1802–03), in which he outlined his system with its emphasis on reason rather than the romantic intuitionism of Schelling, which he attacked in the preface of his

Phänomenologie des Geistes (1807) ' The Phenomenology of the Mind ' (tr. 1844). He had been appointed to an extraordinary professorship at Jena, but the Napoleonic victory there (1806) closed the university and Hegel became editor of a Bamberg newspaper and, from 1808 to 1816, headmaster of a Nuremberg school, where he instructed the unfortunate boys in a potted version of his, the most abstruse of all, philosophical systems. In his second great work, *Wissenschaft der Logik* (vol. i, 1812, ii, 1816) ' Science of Logic ' (tr. 1829), he set out his famous dialectical ' Logic ' and in *Enzyklopädie der philosophischen Wissenschaften* (1817) ' Encyclopaedia of the Philosophical Sciences ', his tripartite system of logic, philosophy of nature and of mind, republished in 1821 with paragraphs of his students' lecture notes added. The last was written in Heidelberg, where Hegel became professor in 1816. In 1818 he succeeded Fichte in Berlin and to his death was virtually dictator of German philosophical thinking. Inspired by the French Revolution in youth, rejoicing with Napoleon, that ' world soul ', in his victory over Prussia at Jena, his philosophy eventually turned him into a loyal supporter of that authoritarian state and a morbid hater of democratic measures, particularly the English Reform Bill. His political philosophy is set out in *Philosophie des Rechts* (1821) ' The Philosophy of Right ' (new tr. T. M. Knox 1942), and his lectures on the History of Philosophy, Philosophy of History and of Art, the last named an important contribution to aesthetics, were published posthumously. He died in a cholera epidemic. Hegel's philosophy is a rationalization of his early mysticism, stimulated by Christian theology. He rejects the reality of finite and separate objects and minds in space and time, the Kantian ' thing-in-itself ' and establishes without Spinoza's dualism, an underlying, all-embracing unity, the Absolute. Only this rational whole is real and true. When we make statements or otherwise draw attention to a particular, we separate off this one aspect from the whole of reality, and this can therefore only be partially true. The evolutionary quest for greater unity and truth is achieved by the famous dialectic, positing something (thesis) denying it (antithesis) and combining the two half-truths ,in a synthesis which will contain necessarily a greater portion of truth in its complexity. Only the absolute is non-self-contradictory. It has something of the harmony of opposites of Heraclitus (q.v.). When applied as the underlying dynamic principle in the history of civilizations and of nations, it leads to plausible explanations, i.e., historicism, but bad history. Marx stood ' Hegel on the head ' by making matter, not reason, the ultimate reality. For Hegel the rational whole has greater claim to reality than its parts; the group more reality than the individuals who compose it. This has become the justification of extremist authoritarian creeds from Fascism to Communism. Kierkegaard, who hated rationality and worshipped the individual, yet took over something of Hegel's dialectic, which still survives in the existentialism of Heidegger and Sartre. Modified Hegelianism ruled under Bradley, Bosanquet, Green in Britain until the turn of the century, when its spell was eventually broken by logical positivism, James's pragmatism, Russell's logical atomism and finally by the linguistic approach of Moore and Wittgenstein with their ruthless exposure of many metaphysical tricks and claims. See German Lives by C. Rosenkranz (1844), R. Haym (1927), and H. Glockner in vol. i of his edition of Hegel's works (1927–32), studies by E. Caird (1883), J. G. Hibben (1902), on Hegel's early thought by W. Dilthey (1906), early theological writings H. Nohl (1907), B. Croce (1910), J. M. E. McTaggart (1910), W. T. Stace (1924), G. R. G. Mure (1940), K. R. Popper, *The Open Society and its Enemies*, vol. ii (1945), M. Hyppolite (1946) and J. N. Findlay (1958).

HEGESIPPUS, St, *-jes'-* (d. 180), one of the earliest Christian church historians, was almost certainly a Jewish convert. He made a journey by way of Corinth to Rome, and there compiled a list of the bishops of Rome to Anicetus (A.D. 156–167), so that he must have written his history about that period. It was entitled *Five Memorials of Ecclesiastical Affairs*, and unhappily survives only in a few fragments which Eusebius embodied in his own history.

HEIBERG, (1) **Gunnar Edvard Rode**, *he'i-bayr* (1857–1929), Norwegian dramatist, essayist and critic, born at Christiania (Oslo). His principal plays, *The Balcony* (1894) and *The Tragedy of Love* (1904), are in the radical and rational tradition of Norwegian literature.

(2) **Johan Ludvig**, *hī'berk* (1791–1860), a Danish dramatic poet, like his father, **Peter Andreas** (1758–1841).

(3) **Johan Ludvig** (1854–1928), Danish classical scholar, born at Aalborg, was simultaneously schoolmaster and professor of Classical Philology at Copenhagen (1896–1925). He edited a vast amount of Greek literature, especially the Greek mathematicians and medical writers. He was awarded an honorary Oxford doctorate and elected a corresponding member of the British Academy in 1904.

HEIDEGGER, Martin, *hī'-* (1889–), German philosopher, born at Messkirch in Baden, professor of Philosophy at Marburg (1923), succeeded Husserl at Freiburg (1929–1945), when he was retired for his connections with the Nazi régime. Heidegger began in his uncompleted main work *Sein und Zeit* (1927; tr. W. Brock, 1949) from Husserl's phenomenology an exhaustive ontological classification of 'Being' through the synthesis of the modes of human existence or *Dasein*, in which he was greatly influenced by the writings of Kierkegaard. He disclaimed, however, the title of existentialist, since he was not only concerned with personal existence and ethical choices but primarily with the ontological problem in general. Nevertheless, he has been a key influence in Sartre's existentialism. Some British philosophers have found his linguistic innovations such as ' Nothing noths ' insuperable. Translations of his other works, including his studies of the poet Hölderlin, have been

published under the collective titles *Existence and Being*, ed. W. Brock (1949), and *The Question of Being*, trans. W. Kluback and J. T. Wilde (1959). See studies by de Waelhens (1946), Grene (1958), Langan (1959), King (1964), and Blackham, *Six Existentialist Thinkers* (1952).

HEIDENSTAM, Verner von, *he'id-en-stam* (1859–1940), Swedish author and poet, born at Olshammer. He spent several years in southern Europe and the Middle East, and on his return published *Vallfart och Vandringsår* (*Pilgrimage and Years of Wandering*; 1888). This volume of collected poems, in marked contrast to the prevalent naturalism of Swedish literature of the time, established Heidenstam as one of the leaders of the new romantic movement in Sweden. There followed *Endymion* (1889), *Hans Alienus* (1892) and *Poems* (1895), after which much of his work is dominated by national ideas, *The Carlists* (1897–98), *Swedes and their Chieftains* (1908), &c. He was awarded the Nobel prize for literature in 1916.

HEIFETZ, Jascha, *hī'fets* (1901–), American violinist of Russo-Polish birth, born in Vilna. In 1910 he began studies under Auer at St Petersburg Conservatory, touring Russia, Germany and Scandinavia at the age of twelve. After the Russian Revolution he settled in the United States, becoming an American citizen in 1924. He first appeared in Britain in 1920. Among works commissioned by him from leading composers is William Walton's violin concerto.

HEIJN, or **Heyn, Piet**, *hīn* (1578–1629), Dutch sailor, born at Delfshaven, after an adventurous career became in 1623 vice-admiral under the Dutch East India Company. In 1624 he defeated the Spaniards near San Salvador in Brazil, and again in 1626 off Bahia, returning with an immense booty. In 1626 he captured the Spanish silver flotilla, valued at 12,000,000 guilders; in 1629 was made Admiral of Holland; and on August 20 fell in a sea-fight against the privateers of Dunkirk.

HEILBRON, Sir Ian Morris, *hīl'-* (1886–1959), Scottish chemist, born at Glasgow, professor of Organic Chemistry at Liverpool (1920), Manchester (1933) and at Imperial College, London (1938–49), was best known for his work on vitamins A and D. He was elected F.R.S. in 1931.

HEILPRIN, Angelo (1853–1907), American geologist and explorer, born of Polish ancestry in Hungary, and brought in 1856 to America. In 1885 he became a professor of Geology at Philadelphia and collected data in the Americas, the Arctic regions and in North Africa for his *Geological Evidences of Evolution* (1888), &c.

HEINE, Heinrich, *hī'nĕ* (1797–1856), German poet and essayist, was born of Jewish parents at Düsseldorf, December 13. At seventeen he was sent to Frankfurt to learn banking, and next tried trading on his own account in Hamburg, but soon failed. In 1819 he went to Bonn; there, and at Berlin and Göttingen, he studied law, taking his doctor's degree in 1825. But his thoughts were given to poetry. At Berlin in 1821 he published *Gedichte*, which at once arrested attention. A second collection, *Lyrisches Intermezzo*, appeared in 1823. The first and second volumes of the *Reisebilder* were published (1826–27) and *Das Buch der Lieder* created excitement throughout Germany. These two works are Heine's early masterpieces. Nearly all his writings are of an occasional nature—lyrical, autobiographical, journalistic, polemical. In 1825 he became a Christian to secure the rights of German citizenship and a respectable standing. But by this step he only alienated the esteem of his own people. His revolutionary opinions remained insuperable hindrances to his official employment in Germany. When his enthusiasm was roused by the July revolution in Paris, he hastened thither, going into a voluntary exile from which he never returned. Since 1825 he had travelled in England and Italy; he had worked on newspapers in Bavaria; and he wrote two more volumes of *Reisebilder* (1830–31). The July revolution seems to have awakened seriousness in Heine. He turned from poetry to politics, and assumed the rôle of leader of the cosmopolitan democratic movement. One of his chief aims was to make the French and the Germans acquainted with one another's intellectual and artistic achievements. Hence sprang the *Französische Zustände* (1833), first printed in the *Allgemeine Zeitung*; *De l'Allemagne* (1835), the French version of *Die Romantische Schule* (1836); and *Philosophie und Literatur in Deutschland*, part of the miscellaneous writings entitled *Der Salon* (4 vols., 1835–40). Heine was always an Ishmael—he would fight under nobody's flag but his own. His ambiguous attitude and his attack on Börne (q.v.) brought down upon him the enmity of his revolutionary compatriots. On the eve of a duel, which his book on Börne (1840) ultimately cost him, he married Eugénie Mirat (' Mathilde '; d. 1883), a Paris grisette, with whom he had been living seven years in free love. Then came his rich uncle Solomon's death, and a quarrel with the family, because of their refusal to continue his annuity of 4000 francs; but a compromise was effected in 1847, and the annuity resumed. From 1848 onwards he was confined to bed by spinal paralysis. He lingered on in excruciating pain, borne with heroic patience, until February 17, 1856. During these years he published *Neue Gedichte* and *Deutschland*, a satirical poem (1844); *Atta Troll*, the ' swansong ' of romanticism ' (1847); a collection of poems, *Romancero* (1851); and three volumes of *Vermischte Schriften* (1854). See editions by Strodtmann (1861–66), Karpeles (1885 and 1886–87), and Elster (1887), Strich (1924–31), and in French by himself (1852 *et seq.*); biographies by Strodtmann (3rd ed. 1884) and Karpeles, who edited *Heines Autobiographie* (1888; trans. 1910); *Heines Familienleben*, by his nephew, Baron von Embden (1892; trans. 1893); and Lives by W. Sharp (1888), Stigand (1875), Walter (1930) and Rose (1956).

HEINECCIUS, Johann Gottlieb, hī-nek'tsee-us (1681–1741), German jurist, was professor at Halle (from 1713, and again from 1733). He published in Latin a *Syntagma* of Roman legal antiquities (1718), a history of the Civil Law (1733), the elements of German law (1735), and a *Jus Naturae et Gentium* (1737; Eng. trans. 1763).—His brother, **Johann Michaelis** (1674–1722), a famous preacher in Halle, first studied seals scientifically.

HEINEMANN, William (1863–1920), English publisher, born at Surbiton, founded his publishing house in London in 1890 and established its reputation with the works of Stevenson, Kipling, H. G. Wells, Galsworthy, Somerset Maugham, Priestley, and others.

HEINICHEN, Johann David, hī'niKH-ĕn (1683–1729), German composer, born at Krössuln, near Weissenfels, died at Dresden, where he had been *Kapellmeister* since 1719. He wrote many choral and chamber works as well as operas and a manual on continuo-playing.

HEINKEL, Ernst, hīn'kel (1888–1958), German aircraft engineer, born at Grunbach, founded in 1922 the Heinkel works at Warnemünde, making at first seaplanes, and later bombers and fighters which achieved fame in World War II. See his *He 1000* (trans. 1956).

HEINSE, Johann, hīn'sĕ (1749–1803), German romance writer and poet, born in Thuringia, wrote *Ardinghello* (1787). See Life by Schober (1882).

HEINSIUS, hīn'see-us, (1) **Anthony** (1641–1720), Dutch statesman, born at Delft, in 1688 became Grand Pensionary of Holland, and was the close friend of William III (of England).
(2) **Daniel** (1580–1655), Dutch classical scholar, born at Ghent, became professor at Leyden. He edited many Latin classics, and published Latin poems and orations.—His son, **Nicolaas** (1620–81), obtained distinction as a diplomatic agent and classical scholar.

HEINZ, Henry John, hīnts (1844–1919), American food manufacturer and packer, born of German parents at Pittsburgh. At the age of eight he peddled produce from the family garden, and in 1876 became co-founder, with his brother and cousin, of F. & J. Heinz. The business was reorganized as H. J. Heinz Co. in 1888, and he was its president in 1905–19. He invented the slogan ' 57 varieties ' in 1896, promoted the pure food movement in the U.S., and was a pioneer in staff welfare work. See the biography, *The Magic Number 57*, by S. Potter (1959).

HEISENBERG, Werner Karl, hī'zen-berg (1901–), German theoretical physicist, born in Würzburg, was educated at Munich and Göttingen, becoming professor of Physics at Leipzig (1927–41) and professor at Berlin and director of the Kaiser Wilhelm Institute (1941–45). From 1945 to 1958 he was director of the Max Planck Institute at Göttingen (and from 1958 at Munich) and was one of the seventeen signatories of the ' Göttingen Declaration ' of 1957 (see HAHN). With Born (q.v.) he developed quantum mechanics and formulated the revolutionary principle of indeterminacy in nuclear physics (1925). He won the Nobel prize (1932), was a foreign member of the Royal Society (1955) and Gifford Lecturer (1955–56). In 1958, he and Pauli announced the formulation of a unified field theory, which if established would remove the indeterminacy principle and reinstate Einstein. See his *The Physicist's Conception of Nature* (trans. 1958).

HELENA, the name of three saints:
(1) (*c*. 255–330), mother of the Roman Emperor Constantine, originally (according to St Ambrose) an innkeeper, a native of Bithynia, not of Trier or Britain, the wife of Emperor Constantius Chlorus, to whom she bore Constantine the Great. She early became a Christian, but was not baptized till after the defeat of Maxentius. When Constantine became emperor he made her Empress Dowager. In 326, according to tradition, she visited Jerusalem, and founded the basilicas on the Mount of Olives and at Bethlehem;
(2) the wife of the Russian Grand-duke Igor, was baptized at Constantinople in 955;
(3) (fl. 12th century), was a native of West Gothland.

HELIODORUS (fl. 3rd and 4th cent. A.D.), earliest and best of the Greek romance writers, was born at Emesa in Syria, and was a sophist. His *Aethiopica* narrates in poetic prose, at times with almost epic beauty and simplicity, the loves of Theagenes and Chariclea.

HELIOGABALUS, -*gab'*- (A.D. 204–222), Roman emperor, was born at Emesa. His real name was Varius Avitus Bassianus, but having, when a child, been appointed high priest of the Syro-Phoenician sun god Elagabal, he assumed the name of that deity. Soon after the murder of Caracalla (217), Heliogabalus was proclaimed emperor by the soldiers; he defeated his rival Macrinus on the borders of Syria and Phoenicia in 218. His reign was infamous for his gluttony and debaucheries. He was murdered in an insurrection of the praetorians. See Life by Stuart Hay (1911).

HELLER, Stephen (1815–88), Hungarian pianist and composer of Budapest, made his début as a pianist at nine. From 1830, settling in Augsburg, he studied composition; in 1838 he removed to Paris, where he composed and taught until his death. See Life by Barbedette (1876).

HELMHOLTZ, Hermann von (1821–94), German physiologist and physicist, born at Potsdam, was successively professor of Physiology at Königsberg (1849), Bonn (1855), Heidelberg (1858). In 1871 he became professor of Physics in Berlin. Ennobled 1883, he died at Charlottenburg. Helmholtz was equally distinguished in physiology, mathematics, and experimental and mathematical physics. His physiological works are principally connected with the eye, the ear, and the nervous system. His ophthalmoscope he invented (1850) after, but independently of, Babbage (q.v.). Of a semiphysical nature are his analysis of the spectrum, his explanation of vowel sounds, and his papers on the conservation of energy with reference to muscular action. In physical science he is known by his paper on *Conservation of Energy* (1847); by two memoirs in Crelle's *Journal*, on vortex motion in fluids, and on the vibrations of air in open pipes, &c.; and by researches into

the development of electric current within a galvanic battery. See books by McKendrick (1899) and Königsberger (trans. 1906).

HELMONT, Jean Baptiste van (1577–1644), Flemish chemist, born at Brussels, studied medicine, mysticism and finally chemistry under the influence of Paracelsus. Van Helmont first emphasized the use of the balance in chemistry, and by its means showed the indestructibility of matter in chemical changes. He devoted much study to gases, and invented the word *gas*. He was also the first to take the melting-point of ice and the boiling-point of water as standards for temperature. He first employed the term *saturation* to signify the combination of an acid with a base; and he was one of the earliest investigators of the chemistry of the fluids of the human body. His works, entitled *Ortus Medicinae*, were often reprinted. See French monograph by Rommelaere (1868) and a study by Redgrove (1922).—His youngest son, Franciscus Mercurius (1614–1699), was a teacher of deaf-mutes. See French Life by Broeckx (1870).

HÉLOÏSE. See ABELARD.

HELPMANN, Robert (1909–), Australian dancer, actor and choreographer, born at Mount Gambier, made his début in Adelaide in 1923, joined Pavlova's touring company in 1929 and in 1931 came to Britain to study under Ninette de Valois. He was first dancer of the newly founded Sadler's Wells Ballet (1933–50). A master of the mime, he created with distinction the rôle of 'Master of Tregennis' in the *Haunted Ballroom* (1934). His choreographic work, of which possibly *Miracle in the Gorbals* (1944), a modern parable set in Glasgow, is his best, includes certain controversial ballet sequences in the film *Red Shoes* (1948). He became a C.B.E. in 1964, and joint artistic director of Australian ballet in 1965. See Life by Anthony (1946) and study by Brahms (1943).

HELPS, Sir Arthur (1813–75), English essayist and historian, born at Streatham, a Cambridge wrangler, became private secretary to the chancellor of the Exchequer and then to the Irish secretary. He wrote on historical, social and political topics, edited Prince Albert's *Speeches* (1862) and Queen Victoria's *Journal of our Life in the Highlands* (1868). In 1860 he was appointed clerk to the privy council and made C.B. in 1871 and K.C.B. in 1872.

HELST, Bartholomaeus van der (*c*. 1611–70), Dutch painter, born at Haarlem, was joint founder in 1653 of the painters' guild of St Luke at Amsterdam, where he flourished as a portrait painter in the manner of Franz Hals.

HELVÉTIUS, Claude Adrien, *el-vay-syüs* (1715–71), French philosopher, one of the Encyclopaedists, born at Paris, in 1738 was appointed a farmer-general, and became chamberlain to the queen's household, associating much with the French philosophers of the day. In 1751 he withdrew to a small estate at Voré (Le Perche), where he spent his life in the education of his family, philanthropy and literary pursuits. In 1758 appeared his *De l'esprit*, in which he endeavoured to prove that sensation is the source of all intellectual activity. It was denounced by the Sorbonne and condemned by the parliament of Paris to be publicly burnt. It was translated into the principal European tongues. His posthumous *De l'homme* (1772) influenced Bentham (q.v.). His gifted wife (1719–1800) settled in 1771 at Auteuil. See Morley's *Diderot and the Encyclopaedists* (1878), and French works by Guillois (1894) and Keim (1907).

HEMANS, Felicia Dorothea, *née* **Browne** (1793–1835), English poetess, was born in Liverpool, and from 1800 was brought up near Abergele. In 1808–12 she published three volumes of poems, and in 1812 married an Irishman, Captain Hemans. Her works include *The Siege of Valencia* (1823) and *Records of Women* (1828), but she is perhaps best remembered for the schoolbook perennial ' The boy stood on the burning deck ' and ' The stately homes of England '. See complete edition of her works, with a memoir by her sister (1839).

HEMINGWAY, Ernest Millar (1899–1961), American author, born at Oak Park, Illinois. A newspaper man, and by virtue of his era principally a war correspondent, Hemingway emerged as a ' hard-boiled ' character. His keen but narrow vision, his supreme gift of staccato, vernacular dialogue and technique of understatement heralded a revolution in English writing. The theme of most of his brilliant short stories and novels is that of physical courage. The latter include *Torrents of Spring* (1926), *The Sun also Rises* (1926), *A Farewell to Arms* (1929), *For Whom the Bell Tolls* (1940), on the Spanish Civil War, but it is only with the novella *The Old Man and the Sea* (1952) that Hemingway emerges with a deepened understanding of moral dignity. It won him a Pulitzer prize in 1953, and in 1954 he was awarded a Nobel prize. Fearing ill-health, he shot himself on July 2, 1961. The autobiographical *A Moveable Feast* was published in 1964. See *Writers in Crisis* by Geismar (1942); Wilson, *The Wound and the Bow* (1941); and studies by Fenton (1954), Young (1959), Baker (3rd ed., 1963), and Hotchner (1966).

HEMSTERHUIS, Tiberius, *hem'ster-hoys* (1685–1766), Dutch philologist, born at Groningen, became professor of Greek at Franeker in 1720, and of Greek History at Leyden in 1740. He created a new school of Greek scholarship. His editions of the *Onomasticon* of Pollux (1706), of Lucian's *Select Dialogues* (1708–32), and of Aristophanes' *Plutus* (1744) are his chief works. See Ruhnken's *Elogium Hemsterhusii* (1768). His son, **Frans** (1721–90), philosopher and archaeologist, was born at Groningen. See *French Life* by Grucker (1866) and German by E. Meyer (1893).

HENCH, Philip Showalter (1896–1965), American physician, born at Pittsburgh. Head of the department of rheumatics at the Mayo Clinic (Rochester) from 1926, and professor of Medicine at Minnesota University from 1947, he discovered cortisone, and shared the Nobel prize for medicine in 1950 with Kendall and Reichstein.

HENDERSON, (1) Alexander (c. 1583–1646), Scottish Covenanter, was born at Creich in Fife, and educated at St Andrews. In 1610, as an Episcopalian, he was made a professor there of Rhetoric and Philosophy, and in 1611 or 1612 was appointed to the parish of Leuchars. Embracing the popular cause, he is supposed to have had a great share in drawing up the National Covenant, and was moderator of the General Assembly at Glasgow in 1638, which restored all its liberties to the Kirk of Scotland. Moderator again in 1641 and in 1643, he drafted the famous Solemn League and Covenant, and sat for three years in the Westminster Assembly. See *Lives* by Aiton (1836) and McCrie (1846).

(2) **Arthur** (1863–1935), British Labour politician, born at Glasgow, was brought up in Newcastle, where he worked as an ironmoulder and became a lay preacher. He helped to build up the Labour Party, of which he was chairman (1908–10, 1914–17, 1931–32), served in the Coalition cabinets (1915–17), was home secretary (1924), foreign secretary (1929–31), when he refused, with the majority of the Labour party, to enter Ramsay MacDonald's National Government (1931). A crusader for disarmament, he was president of the World Disarmament Conference (1932). See *Life* by M. A. Hamilton (1938), and E. Jenkins, *From Foundry to Foreign Office* (1933).

(3) **George Hugh** (1892–1949), Canadian mathematical physicist, with Bateson, introduced a microphotometric method to determine the age of rocks.

(4) **Sir Nevile Meyrick** (1882–1942), British diplomat, born at Sedgwick, Sussex, was minister to Yugoslavia (1929–35), ambassador to Argentina (1935–37), and to Germany until the outbreak of World War II. See his *Failure of a Mission* (1940).

(5) **Thomas** (1798–1844), Scottish astronomer, born at Dundee, was destined for the law but devoted his leisure hours to astronomical calculations. In 1831 he was appointed director of the Royal Observatory at the Cape of Good Hope. In 1832 he measured the parallax of the star, alpha Centauri. In 1834 he became first astronomer royal for Scotland.

HENGIST (d. 488) and **HORSA** (d. 455), two brothers, said by Nennius and the *Anglo-Saxon Chronicle* to have led the first band of Teutonic invaders to Britain. They landed from Jutland at Ebbsfleet in the Isle of Thanet in 449 to help King Vortigern against the Picts, and were rewarded with the gift of Thanet. Soon after they turned against Vortigern, but were defeated at Aylesford, where Horsa is said to have been slain. Hengist, however, is said to have conquered Kent. Both names mean ' horse '.

HENGSTENBERG, Ernst Wilhelm (1802–69), German Protestant theologian, was born at Fröndenberg, Westphalia, and educated at Bonn. At first a rationalist, at Basel (1823) he passed to the opposite extreme, and thereafter as teacher, editor and author of many books, combated rationalism in every form, and sought to restore the orthodoxy of the 16th century. See *Life* by Bachmann and Schmalenbach (1876–92).

HENLE, Friedrich Gustav Jakob, *hen'lě* (1809–85), German anatomist, born at Fürth, held professorships at Berlin, Zürich and Heidelberg, discovered the tubules in the kidney which are named after him and wrote treatises on systematic anatomy.

HENLEIN, Konrad, *hen'līn* (1898–1945), leader of the Sudeten Germans in the agitation on the eve of the second World War leading in 1938 to Germany's seizure of Sudetenland from Czechoslovakia, and in 1939 to the institution of the German protectorate of Bohemia and Moravia and the dissolution of Czechoslovakia. Gauleiter of Sudetenland in 1938 and from 1939 civil commissioner for Bohemia, on Germany's subsequent defeat in the war he committed suicide when in American hands.

HENLEY, (1) **' Orator Henley '** (1692–1756), English clergyman, born at Melton-Mowbray vicarage, studied at Cambridge, taught in the school of his native town, compiled a grammar of seven languages, *The Complete Linguist* (1719–21), and was ordained in 1716. In 1726, he set up an ' oratory ', to teach universal knowledge in weekday lectures and primitive Christianity in Sunday sermons, but his addresses were a medley of ribaldry and solemnity, wit and absurdity. His *Oratory Transactions* contain a Life of himself.

(2) **William Ernest** (1849–1903), English poet, playwright, critic and editor, born at Gloucester. Crippled by tuberculosis, he spent months in Edinburgh Infirmary (1873–1875), where he wrote *A Book of Verses* (1888) which won him the friendship of R. L. Stevenson, with whom he collaborated in three plays, *Deacon Brodie*, *Beau Austin* and *Admiral Guinea*. Other volumes of his verse, with its unusual rhymes and esoteric words, followed: *The Song of the Sword* (1892), *Collected Poems* (1898), *For England's Sake* (1900), *Hawthorn and Lavender* (1901) and *A Song of Speed* (1903). A pungent critic, he successfully edited the *Magazine of Art*, *Scots Observer* and worked on a dictionary of slang. See Lives by L. C. Cornford (1913), Buckley (Princeton 1945) and J. Connell (1949).

HENNER, Jean Jacques, *en-er* (1829–1905), French painter, born in Alsace, best known for his religious subjects, portraits and nudes somewhat in the manner of Correggio, including *Girl Reading* in the Luxembourg.

HENNINGSEN, Charles Frederick (1815–77), Anglo-Swedish soldier of fortune, born in England of Swedish parentage, served with the Carlists in Spain, with the Russians in Circassia, with Kossuth in Hungary, and with Walker in Nicaragua. In the American Civil War he commanded a Confederate brigade, and afterwards superintended the manufacture of Minié rifles. He wrote *The White Slave* (1845), *The Past and Future of Hungary* (1852), &c.

HENRIETTA ANNE, Duchess of Orleans (1644–70), fifth daughter of Charles I and Henrietta Maria (q.v.), who left her at Exeter, taken by the parliamentarians under Fairfax in April 1646, but three months afterwards, disguised as a French beggarwoman, her governess, Lady Dalkeith, escaped with her from Oatlands to Calais. Her mother brought her up a Catholic. In 1661 she was married to Louis XIV's only brother, Philip, Duke of Orleans. As Louis's ambassadress in 1670 she wheedled Charles II into signing the secret treaty of Dover; and she had been back in France about a fortnight, when on June 30 she died, almost certainly of poison, but possibly without her husband's cognisance. See CHARLES II and works there cited; and Lives by Mme de la Fayette (1720; new ed. by Anatole France, 1882), Baillon (1887), J. Cartwright (1893), and Barine's *Madame, Mère du Régent* (1909).

HENRIETTA MARIA (1609–69), Queen of Charles I of England, born at the Louvre, the youngest child of Henry IV of France, whose assassination six months afterwards left her to the unwise upbringing of her mother, Marie de' Medici. A lovely little thing, bright of eye and wit, but spoilt and wayward, she was married in 1625 to Charles I. Her French attendants and Roman Catholic beliefs made her extremely unpopular. In February 1642, under the threat of impeachment, she fled to Holland and raised funds for the royalist cause. A year later she landed at Bridlington, and met Charles near Edgehill. On April 3, 1644, they separated at Abingdon for the last time. At Exeter, on June 16, she gave birth to Henrietta Anne (q.v.) and a fortnight later she was compelled to flee to France. The war of the Fronde (1648) reduced her temporarily to destitution, despite the liberal allowance assigned to her. She paid two visits to England after the Restoration (1660–61, 1662–65). See CHARLES I and works there cited; Lives by Miss Taylor (1905), Miss Haynes (1912), Miss Oman (1936); also Strickland's *Queens of England*.

HENRY, the name of eight kings of England:

Henry I (1068–1135), youngest and only English-born son of William the Conqueror, was born traditionally at Selby. When war broke out between his brothers, William Rufus and Robert of Normandy, Henry helped the latter to defend Normandy; yet in the treaty which followed (1091) he was excluded from the succession. Immediately after William's death (August 2, 1100) Henry seized the royal treasure, and was elected king by the Witan. He issued a charter restoring the laws of Edward the Confessor and the Conqueror, recalled Anselm, and set about great and popular reforms in the administration of justice. He strengthened his position by a marriage with Eadgyth (Matilda), daughter of Malcolm of Scotland and Queen Margaret, who was descended from the old English royal house. Robert had been granted a pension of 3000 marks to resign his claim to the English crown, but (1105–06) Henry made war against his badly-governed duchy; Robert was defeated at Tinchebrai, September 28, 1106, and was kept a prisoner for life (28 years). To hold Normandy Henry was obliged to wage nearly constant warfare. The French king took part with William, Robert's youthful son; but the first war ended in the favourable peace of Gisors (1113); and in 1114 his daughter Matilda was married to the Emperor Henry V. The second war (1116–20) was marked by the defeat of the French king at

Noyon in 1119, and Henry was able to satisfy the pope, who succeeded in bringing about a peace. In 1120 Henry's only legitimate son, William, was drowned on his way from Normandy to England. A fresh rebellion in Normandy ended in the battle of Bourg-théroulde (1124). In 1126 Matilda, now a widow, came back from Germany; Henry made the barons swear to receive her as Lady of England; and the same year she was married to Geoffrey Plantagenet, son of the Count of Anjou. Henry died near Rouen, December 1, 1135, and the crown was seized by his sister Adela's son, Stephen of Blois. Henry I was posthumously styled Beauclerc, or the Scholar, in honour of his learning, which was considerable for a king in his age. Able he was, and crafty, consistent, passion-less in his policy, but often guilty of acts of cold-blooded cruelty. Law was administered during his reign with strictness, and the mass of his subjects reaped the blessings of his firm rule. See Freeman, *Norman Conquest*, vol. v, H. W. C. Davis, *England Under the Normans and Angevins* (11th ed. 1937), G. Slocombe, *Sons of the Conqueror* (1960).

Henry II (1133–89), the son of Matilda, Henry I's daughter, and her second husband, Geoffrey Plantagenet, was born at Le Mans, March 5. At eighteen he was invested with the duchy of Normandy, his mother's heritage, and within a year became also, by his father's death, Count of Anjou; while in 1152 his marriage with Eleanor of Aquitaine, the divorced wife of Louis VII, added Poitou and Guienne to his dominions. In January 1153 he landed in England, and in November a treaty was agreed to whereby Henry was declared the successor of Stephen; he was crowned in 1154. He confirmed his grand-father's laws, re-established the exchequer, banished the foreign mercenaries, demolished the hundreds of castles erected in Stephen's reign, and recovered the royal estates. The whole of 1156 he spent in France, reducing his brother, Geoffrey of Nantes, who died in 1158, and, having secured his territories, he spent the next five years warring and organiz-ing his possessions on the Continent. Henry's object was that of all the Norman kings—to build up the royal power at the expense of the barons and of the church. From the barons his reforms met with little serious opposition; with the clergy he was less successful. To aid him in reducing the church to subjection, he appointed his chancellor, Becket (q.v.), to the see of Canterbury. Henry compelled him and the other prelates to agree to the ' Constitutions of Clarendon ', but Becket proved a sturdy churchman, and the struggle between him and his monarch was terminated only by his murder. In 1174 Henry did penance at Becket's tomb, but he ended by bringing the church to subordination in civil matters. Meanwhile he organized an expedition to Ireland. The English pope, Adrian IV, had in 1155 given Henry authority over the entire island; and a number of Norman-Welsh knights had gained a footing in the country— among them Richard de Clare, Earl of Pembroke, nicknamed Strongbow, who in 1170 married the heiress of Leinster and

assumed rule as the Earl of Leinster. Henry was jealous at the rise of a powerful feudal baronage in Ireland, and during his stay there (1171–72) he broke the power of Strongbow and the other nobles. In 1185 Prince John was appointed king of Ireland. But before the end of 1186 he was driven from the country, and all was left in confusion. The eldest of Henry's sons had died in childhood; the second, Henry, born in 1155, was crowned as his father's associate and successor in 1170. In 1173, incited by their jealous mother, Queen Eleanor, the prince and his brother Richard rebelled against their father, and their cause was espoused by the kings of France and Scotland. The latter, William the Lion, was ravaging the north of England when he was taken prisoner at Alnwick in 1174, and to obtain his liberty he submitted to do homage to Henry. In a few months Henry had re-established his authority in all his dominions. During a second rebellion Prince Henry died; and in 1185 Geoffrey, the next son, was killed in a tournament at Paris. In 1188, while Henry was engaged in a war with Philip of France, Richard joined the French king; and in 1189, Henry, having lost Le Mans and the chief castles of Maine, agreed to a treaty of peace granting an indemnity to the followers of Richard. The sight of the name of his favourite son John in the list broke his heart; he died at Chinon, July 6. On the whole, Henry was an able and enlightened sovereign, a clear-headed, unprincipled politician, and an able general; his reign was one of great legal reforms. Fair Rosamond (see CLIF-FORD) was said to have borne him two sons, William Longsword, Earl of Salisbury, and Geoffrey, Archbishop of York, but this is improbable. See Lives by Green (1888), Salzmann (1919), Appleby (1962), Barber (1964), and Ramsay's *Angevin Empire* (1903).

Henry III (1207–72), was born at Win-chester, October 1, and succeeded his father, King John, in 1216. In 1227 he declared himself of age; in 1232 he deprived Hubert de Burgh, who had ruled as regent and justiciary, of all his offices; and in 1234 he took the administration into his own hands. A war with France cost him Poitou, and might have cost him all his continental possessions but for the generosity of Louis IX. He reissued the Great Charter, with omis-sions; and he confirmed it more than once as a condition of a money grant. He was beset with favourites; his misrule and extortion roused all classes, and in 1258 parliament, headed by his brother-in-law, Simon de Montfort, Earl of Leicester, forced him to agree to the Provisions of Oxford, transferring his power to a commission of barons. But disunion among the barons enabled Henry to repudiate his oath, and after a brief war (1263) the matter was referred to Louis of France, who annulled the Provisions. De Montfort and his party took up arms against the king, defeated him, made him prisoner at Lewes (1264), and forced him to the humiliating agreement called the Mise of Lewes. Earl Simon then summoned parliament (January 1265), the first in which boroughs were represented,

Within a year the Earl of Gloucester deserted de Montfort (q.v.), and, with Prince Edward, defeated and slew him at Evesham (1265). Henry died November 16, 1272. See Freeman and Stubbs; works by Norgate (1912), Margaret Hennings (1924); Ramsay, *Dawn of the Constitution* (1908), R. F. Treharne, *The Baronial Plan of Reform* (1932), and study by F. M. Powicke (1947).

Henry IV (1367–1413), the first king of the House of Lancaster, was born April 3, the son of John of Gaunt, and was surnamed Bolingbroke, from his birthplace in Lincolnshire. His father was fourth son of Edward III, his mother daughter of Duke Henry of Lancaster. In 1386 Henry married a rich heiress, Mary de Bohun. In 1397 he supported Richard II against the Duke of Gloucester, and was created Duke of Hereford; in 1398 he was banished, and in 1399, when his father died, his estates were declared forfeit to Richard. In July Henry landed at Ravenspur in Yorkshire; on September 29 he induced Richard, deserted and betrayed, to sign a renunciation of his claims; thereupon he had himself crowned; and four months later Richard died, of starvation probably, in Pontefract Castle, February 1400. During Henry's reign rebellion and lawlessness were rife, and frequent descents were made upon the coast by expeditions from France. The king's movements were constantly hampered for want of money, and 'war treasurers' were ultimately appointed by the impatient Commons to watch the disbursement of the sums voted. In 1404 parliament proposed to confiscate the property of the clergy; but Henry not only discountenanced all such proposals, but permitted severe enactments against heretics. In 1401 William Chatrys was burnt for heresy at Smithfield. Under Owen Glendower the Welsh maintained their independence throughout this reign. Henry invaded Scotland in 1400, besieging Edinburgh Castle until compelled by famine to retire. In 1402, while the king was engaged against the Welsh, the Scots invaded Northumberland; but they were encountered by the Earl of Northumberland and his son Harry Percy, and were defeated (September 14) at Humbleton (or Homildon), where Douglas was taken prisoner. Harry Percy (Hotspur) and his house shortly after leagued with Douglas and Glendower against Henry; but the king met the Percies at Shrewsbury (July 21, 1403), where they were utterly defeated, Hotspur slain, and Douglas again taken prisoner. In 1406 Prince James of Scotland (afterwards James I) was captured on his way to France, and was detained and educated in England. The civil wars in France gave Henry an opportunity to send two expeditions (1411–12) thither; but in his later years he was a chronic invalid, afflicted with epileptic fits. He died in the Jerusalem Chamber at Westminster, March 20. See Stubbs, vol. iii; Gairdner's *Houses of Lancaster and York* (1874); Ramsay's *Lancaster and York* (1892); Wylie's *England under Henry IV* (1898).

Henry V (1387–1422), was born at Monmouth, August 9, the eldest of the six children of Henry IV by Mary de Bohun, and in 1399 was created Prince of Wales. From 1401 to 1408 he was engaged against Glendower and the Welsh rebels; in 1409 he became constable of Dover, and in 1410 captain of Calais. To this time belong the exaggerated stories of his wild youth. He was crowned on April 10, 1413, and at the outset of his reign liberated the young Earl of March, the true heir to the crown, restored Hotspur's son to his father's lands and honours, and had Richard II's body buried in Westminster. The great effort of his reign was an attempted conquest of France; and in 1414 he demanded the French crown, to which he seems to have believed that he had a valid claim through his great-grandfather, Edward III. In August 1415 he sailed with a great army, and on September 22 took Harfleur. On October 25, at Agincourt, he gained a battle against such odds as to make his victory one of the most notable in history. Two years after he again invaded France, and by the end of 1418 Normandy was once more subject to the English crown. In 1420 was concluded the 'perpetual peace' of Troyes, under which Henry was recognized as regent and 'heir of France', and married the French king's daughter, Catharine of Valois (q.v.). In February 1421 he took his young queen to England to be crowned; but in a month he was recalled by news of the defeat at Baugé of his brother, the Duke of Clarence. Henry's wonted success was attending him, when he was seized with illness, and died at Vincennes, August 31, leaving an infant to succeed him. Henry was devout, just, and pure of life; yet his religion did not make him merciful to a conquered enemy; and he persecuted the Lollards. See Works cited at HENRY IV; and books by Wylie (1914–29), Mowat (1920), Newhall (1924), E. F. Jacob (1947), and study by Wylie and Waugh (1914–29).

Henry VI (1421–71), only child of Henry V and Catharine of France, was born at Windsor, December 6. During his minority his uncle, the Duke of Bedford, was appointed to govern France, and another uncle, Humphrey, Duke of Gloucester, to be protector of England, with a council appointed by parliament. In France, the incapable Charles VI having died, the dauphin assumed the title of Charles VII, but his army was almost annihilated by the English at Verneuil (1424). In 1429 the siege of Orleans was raised by the French, inspired by Joan of Arc, and after this the English power declined steadily. Henry was crowned king of England in 1429, and king of France at Paris in 1431. Bedford, the only great English leader, died in 1435; Paris was recovered by the dauphin in 1436, Normandy was lost in 1450; and in 1453 the English were expelled from all France (Calais excepted). In 1445 Henry married the strong-minded Margaret of Anjou; in 1447 the Beaufort party and she had Gloucester arrested for treason; and five days later he was found dead in his bed, but there is no proof that he was murdered. Jack Cade (q.v.) obtained temporary possession of London, but was soon captured and executed. As a descendant of Lionel, Duke of Clarence, Edward III's third son, Richard, Duke of York, had a better title to the crown than Henry; in 1454, during the latter's mental lapse, he was appointed protector by parliament. On the king's recovery York levied an army to maintain his power, and at St Albans (1455) the Yorkists were victors and the king taken prisoner. This was the first of twelve battles between the Houses of York and Lancaster in the Wars of the Roses. A return of Henry's disorder made York again protector in 1455–1456; and on his recovery Henry vainly strove to maintain peace between the factions. Margaret headed the Lancastrian forces; but in 1461 Edward IV was proclaimed king, and in 1465 Henry was captured and committed to the Tower. In 1470 Warwick restored him to the throne, but six months later he was again in Edward's hands; and at Tewkesbury (May 4, 1471) his son was slain and Margaret (q.v.) taken prisoner. Edward returned to London on May 21; and that night Henry was murdered. Henry, the ' royal saint ', founded Eton and King's College, Cambridge. See Stubbs, Gairdner's *Lancaster and York*, and his introduction to the *Paston Letters* (1872); Blacman's *Life* (*c*. 1510; trans. 1919); and a work by Gasquet (1923).

Henry VII (1457–1509), father of Henry VIII, born at Pembroke Castle on January 28, the grandson of that Owen Tudor who married Queen Catharine, widow of Henry V, was the founder of the Tudor dynasty; his mother, a great-granddaughter of John of Gaunt, ranking as the lineal descendant of the House of Lancaster. After the Lancastrian defeat at Tewkesbury Henry was whisked away to Brittany, where all the Yorkist attempts on his life and liberty were frustrated. On August 1, 1485, Henry landed, unopposed, at Milford Haven. After the death of Richard ' Crookback ' on Bosworth Field, Parliament assented in Henry's assumption of the regal title. As monarch, his undeviating policy was to restore peace and prosperity to a warworn and impoverished land; an aim which his marriage of reconciliation with Elizabeth of York materially advanced. Minor Yorkist revolts, like the pretensions of such pinchbeck claimants to the throne as Lambert Simnel and Perkin Warbeck, were firmly dealt with; but Henry's policy in general was mercantilist and pacific, as was demonstrated by his readiness to conclude peace with France for a promised indemnity of £149,000. With the self-immolation of the feudal aristocracy in the recent war, the matrix of power had shifted from the castle to the bourse; and Henry's shipbuilding subsidies expanded his mercantile marine while giving him first call on craft speedily convertible into warships. The marriage of Henry's heir to Catharine of Aragon cemented an alliance with Spain that largely nullified the soaring aspirations of France; while long-nursed Caledonian enmity was undermined when James IV of Scotland wed the ' Huckster King's ' daughter Margaret. A widower after 1503, Henry's design to further his policy by remarriage was cut short by his death in 1509. His personal fortune of over a million and a half reflected the commercial prosperity his prudent policy had restored to the realm. See works by Hallam (1827), Bacon (1622), Temperley (1918), Pickthorn (1934), and Pollard's *Reign of Henry VII* (1913–14).

Henry VIII (1491–1547), second son of the above, born at Greenwich, June 28, ascended the throne in 1509. During the first years of his reign he held a place in the hearts of his people. In his earlier manhood he was accounted the handsomest and most accomplished prince of his time; and his accession to the throne was hailed by such men as Colet, Erasmus and More. Seven weeks later Henry married Catharine of Aragon, his brother Arthur's widow—a step of tremendous consequence. As a member of the Holy League, formed by the pope and Spain against Louis XII, in 1512 he invaded France, and next year won the so-called Battle of Spurs, and captured Terouenne and Tournay. During his absence a greater triumph was gained in the defeat of the Scots at Flodden. It was in this French war that Wolsey became prominent. As early as 1514 he was, after the king, the first man in the country. The chief aim of Wolsey and his master was to hold in equipoise France and Spain, and to win for England as arbiter an importance to which her own resources hardly entitled her. The support of England was accordingly till 1525 given to Spain against France. The struggle between Charles V and Francis proceeded with varying success till, in 1525, Francis was brought to the verge of ruin by his defeat and capture at Pavia. As the ascendancy thus gained by the emperor endangered the balance of power, England was now thrown into alliance with France. In 1521 the Duke of Buckingham, a descendant of Edward III, was executed on an almost groundless charge of treason. The same year Henry published his famous book on the Sacraments in reply to Luther, and received from Pope Leo X the title borne by all Henry's successors, ' Defender of the Faith '. To enable him to play his part in Continental affairs, Henry had frequent need of heavy supplies; and Wolsey took on himself all the odium of excessive taxation. Wolsey made himself still further odious by the suppression of all monasteries with less than seven inmates, devoting the revenues to educational purposes. In 1525 Henry's expensive foreign policy again brought him into straits, and Wolsey proposed an illegal tax, the Amicable Loan it met with the strongest opposition, and Wolsey was forced to abandon it. The turning-point in Henry's reign is the moment when he determined that his marriage with Catharine of Aragon must be nullified. All her children, except Mary, had died in infancy, and Henry professed to see in this the judgment of Heaven on an unnatural alliance; any doubt of the legitimacy of Mary might lead to a renewal of the civil wars; further, Henry had set his affections on Anne Boleyn, a niece of the Duke of Norfolk. Pope Clement VII was at first disposed to humour Henry, and in 1528 sent Cardinal Campeggio to England to try the validity of the marriage. The visit settled nothing; and the pope, under pressure from the emperor, revoked the case to the Roman curia. This proved the ruin of Wolsey, who now found himself without a friend at home or abroad. In 1529 he was stripped of his goods and honours, and dismissed in disgrace; next year he was summoned to London on a charge of high treason, but died on the way. Despite the coldness of the pope, Henry was as determined as ever on the divorce, and by humbling the clergy he thought he could bring the pope to terms. In 1531 the whole body of the clergy, on the same grounds as Wolsey, were declared guilty of treason under the law of *praemunire*, and purchased pardon only by the payment of £118,840. He extorted from them his recognition as ' protector and supreme head of the church and clergy of England ', and in 1532 abolished the annates paid to the pope. Sir Thomas More, who had succeeded to the chancellorship, and who saw the inevitable end of Henry's policy, prayed to be relieved of the Great Seal. In further defiance of Rome, Henry (1533) was privately married to Anne Boleyn. In 1534 it was enacted that all bishops should be appointed by a *congé d'élire* from the crown, and that all recourse to the Bishop of Rome should be illegal. It was also enacted that the king's marriage with Catharine was invalid, that the succession to the crown should lie with the issue of Henry's marriage with Anne Boleyn, and that the king was the sole supreme head of the Church of England. To this last act Bishop Fisher and Sir Thomas More refused to swear, and both were executed next year. The supporters of Luther were treated with the same severity as those of the church who refused to acknowledge the king in the place of the pope. To show that his quarrel was with the pope and not the church, and to proclaim his soundness in doctrine, Henry ordered (1537) the publication of the *Bishops' Book* or the *Institution of a Christian Man*, strictly orthodox save on the headship of the pope. In the famous *Statute of the Six Articles*, known as the ' Bloody Statute ', all the fundamental doctrines of the Church of Rome are insisted on, with the severest penalties, as necessary articles of belief (1539). In 1535 Henry appointed a commission under Thomas Cromwell to report on the state of the monasteries for the guidance of parliament; and the document seemed to justify the most drastic dealing. An act was passed for the suppression of all monasteries with a revenue under £200 a year —a high-handed and unpopular step. This, together with the fact that everywhere there was much misery by reason of the land being extensively converted from agricultural to pastoral purposes, caused, the year after the suppression of the smaller monasteries, a formidable insurrection in the northern counties, known as the ' Pilgrimage of Grace '. The revolt was crushed, and Henry next (1536) suppressed all the remaining monasteries. The bulk of the revenues passed to the crown and to those who had made themselves useful to the king. In 1536 Queen Catharine died, and the same year Anne Boleyn herself was executed for infidelity.

The day after her execution Henry was betrothed to Jane Seymour (*c.* 1509–37), who died leaving a son, afterwards Edward VI. Anne of Cleves was chosen as the king's fourth wife, in the hope of attaching the Protestant interest of Germany. Anne's personal appearance proved so little to Henry's taste that he consented to the marriage only on the condition that a divorce should follow speedily. Cromwell had made himself as generally detested as Wolsey. It was mainly through his action that Anne had been brought forward, and his enemies used Henry's indignation to effect his ruin. Accused of high treason by the Duke of Norfolk, he was executed on a bill of attainder, without a trial (1540); and Henry married Catharine Howard, another niece of the Catholic Duke of Norfolk. Before two years had passed Catharine suffered the same fate as Anne Boleyn, on the same charge, and in July 1543 Henry married his sixth wife, Catharine Parr, widow of Lord Latimer, who was happy enough to survive him. During all these years Henry's interest in the struggle between Francis and the emperor had been kept alive by the intrigues of France in Scotland. At length Henry and Francis concluded a peace (1546), of which Scotland also had the benefit. The execution of the young Earl of Surrey, son of the Duke of Norfolk, on a charge of high treason, completes the long list of the judicial murders of Henry's reign. Norfolk himself was saved from the same fate only by the death of Henry himself, January 28. Henry is apt to be judged simply as an unnatural monster, influenced by motives of cruelty and lust. Yet from first to last he was popular with his people, and he inspired the most devoted affection of those in immediate contact with him. In point of personal morals he was pure compared with Francis and James V of Scotland; even in the shedding of blood he was merciful compared with Francis. Only a prince of the most imperious will could have effected the great ecclesiastical revolution. See Froude's *History of England* (vols. i-iv), Brewer's *Henry VIII* (ed. Gairdner, 1884), Creighton's *Wolsey* (1888), Gasquet's *Dissolution of the English Monasteries* (1889), A. F. Pollard's *Henry VIII* (1902), Martin Hume's *Wives of Henry VIII* (1905), H. A. L. Fisher, *Political History, 1485-1547* (1910), Pickthorn, *Early Tudor Government* (1934) and Life by Bagley (1962).

HENRY, the name of four kings of France:
    Henry I (1008–60), son of Robert II, ascended the throne in 1031 and was involved in struggles with Normandy and with Burgundy, which he had unwisely granted to his rival brother Robert.
    Henry II (1519–59), father of Henry III, born March 31, married Catharine de' Medici in 1533, and succeeded his father, Francis I in 1547. Immediately after his accession he proceeded to oppress his Protestant subjects. Through the influence of the Guises he formed an alliance with Scotland, and declared war against England, which ended in 1558 with the taking of Calais, after that city had been 210 years an English possession. In 1552 he formed

alliances with the German Reformers, and sent an army to aid Maurice of Saxony against the emperor. His troops captured Toul and Verdun, while Montmorency seized Metz. In 1557 Guise's design to conquer Naples was frustrated by the generalship of Alva, while in the Low Countries Montmorency sustained a crushing defeat at St Quentin. These reverses were followed by the treaty of Cateau-Cambrésis (1559). Shortly afterwards Henry was accidentally wounded in a tournament by Montgomery, a Scottish nobleman, and died July 10. See works by Barre-Duparcq (1887), Bourgiez (1891), H. N. Williams (1910).

Henry III (1551–89), third son of the above, was born September 19. In 1569 he gained victories over the Protestants at Jarnac and Moncontour, and he took an active share in the massacre of St Bartholomew. In 1573 the intrigues of the queen-regent secured his election to the crown of Poland; but in 1575 he succeeded his brother, Charles IX, on the French throne. His reign was a period of almost incessant civil war between Huguenots and Catholics, the Duke of Guise having formed the Holy League to assert the supremacy of Catholicism and secure the reversion of the throne to the Guises. Henry showed fickleness and want of courage in his public conduct; and in private his life was spent in an alternation of dissolute excesses and wild outbreaks of religious fanaticism. In 1588 the assassination of the Duke of Guise roused the Catholics to the utmost pitch of exasperation; Henry threw himself into the arms of Henry of Navarre, and the two marched upon Paris at the head of a Huguenot army. But on August 1 Henry was stabbed by a fanatical Dominican named Jacques Clément; he died, the last of the House of Valois, on the following day, nominating Henry of Navarre as his successor. See Freer's *Henry III* (1858).

Henry IV (1553–1610), king of France and Navarre, was born at Pau, December 13, third son of Antoine de Bourbon and Jeanne d'Albret, heiress of Henry, king of Navarre and Bearn. After his father's death, his mother, a zealous Calvinist, had him carefully educated. In 1569 she took him to La Rochelle, and presented him to the Huguenot army, at whose head he fought at the battle of Jarnac. Henry was chosen chief of the Protestant party, and the third Huguenot war began. The peace of St Germain was followed by a marriage between Henry and Margaret of Valois, sister of Charles IX, in 1572, within less than a week of the massacre of St Bartholomew. Henry's life was spared on condition of his professing himself a Catholic. For three years he was virtually a prisoner at the French court, but in 1576 escaped to Alençon. Having revoked his compulsory conversion, he resumed the command of the army, and gained signal advantages and a favourable peace. The death in 1584 of the Duke of Anjou made Henry presumptive heir to the crown, the succession to which was opened to him by the murder of Henry III in 1589. As a Protestant he was obnoxious to most of the nation; and finding that the Dukes of Lorraine and

Savoy, and Philip II of Spain, were prepared to dispute his claims, he retired to the south until he could collect more troops and money. His cause gradually gained strength through the internal dissensions of the Leaguers, and in 1590 he defeated the Duke of Mayenne at Ivry. In 1593 he formally professed himself a member of the Church of Rome; this was followed by the speedy surrender of the most important cities of the kingdom, including Paris. In 1598 peace was concluded between Spain and France by the treaty of Vervins; and on April 15 of that year Henry signed an edict at Nantes by which he secured to Protestants liberty of conscience and impartial justice. Heretofore the remote provinces were at the mercy of governors and landed proprietors in the matter of taxes and compulsory services. These abuses Henry completely stopped, and by road-making opened up his kingdom to traffic and commerce, and established new sources of wealth and prosperity. His great minister Sully reorganized the finances, and in ten years reduced the national debt from 330 millions to 50 millions of livres. On May 14, the day after the coronation of his second wife, Mary de' Medici, and when about to set out to commence war in Germany, Henry was assassinated by a fanatic named Ravaillac, a tool of the Jesuits. According to Henri Martin, Henry ' remains the greatest, but above all the most essentially French, of all the kings of France '. His unbridled licentiousness was his worst fault. Besides the histories of France, Memoirs of Sully and others, see French monographs on Henry IV by Péréfixe (1661), Lescure (1873), Lacombe (1878), Guadet (1879), Anquez (1887), De la Ferrière (1890), Ritter (1944), and English ones by Freer (1860–63), Willert (1894), Blair (Philadelphia 1894), Sedgewick (1930), Slocombe (1933).

HENRY V of France, so-called. See Chambord.

HENRY, the name of seven German Holy Roman Emperors, of whom the following are especially noteworthy:

Henry III (1017–56) son of Conrad II, father of Henry IV, became king of the Germans in 1026, Duke of Bavaria in 1027, Duke of Swabia in 1038, and emperor in 1039. He resolutely maintained the imperial prerogatives of power, and encouraged the efforts of the Cluniac monks to reform the ecclesiastical system of Europe. In 1046 he put an end to the intrigues of the three rival popes by deposing all three and electing Clement II in their stead. In 1042 he compelled the Duke of Bohemia to acknowledge himself a vassal of the empire. By repeated campaigns in Hungary he established the supremacy of the empire in 1044. Henry also stretched his authority over the Norman conquerors of Apulia and Calabria. He promoted learning and the arts, founded numerous monastic schools, and built many great churches. See German monograph by Steindorff (1874–81).

Henry IV (1050–1106), elected king of the Germans in 1054, succeeded his father, Henry III in 1056, his mother being regent. About 1070 he began to act for himself. His first task was to break the power of the nobles; but his measures provoked a rising of the Saxons, who in 1074 forced upon Henry humiliating terms. In 1075 he defeated them at Hohenburg, and then proceeded to take vengeance upon the princes, secular and ecclesiastical, who had opposed him. The case of the latter gave Pope Gregory VII a pretext to interfere in the affairs of Germany. This was the beginning of the great duel between pope and emperor already recorded under Gregory VII. In 1076 Henry declared the pontiff deposed. Gregory retaliated by excommunicating Henry. The king, seeing his vassals and princes falling away from him, hastened to Italy to make submission at Canossa as a humble penitent, and in January 1077 the ban of excommunication was removed. Having found adherents among the Lombards, Henry renewed the conflict, but was again excommunicated. He thereupon appointed a new pope, Clement III, hastened over the Alps and besieged Rome, and in 1084 caused himself to be crowned emperor by the antipope. In Germany, during Henry's absence, three rival kings of the Germans successively found support. But Henry managed to triumph over them all. He had crossed the Alps for the third time (1090) to support Clement III, when he learned that his son Conrad had joined his enemies and been crowned king at Monza. Disheartened, he retired to Lombardy in despair, but at length returned (1097) to Germany. His second son, Henry, was elected king of the Germans and heir to the empire. This prince, however, was induced to rebel by Pope Pascal II; he took the emperor prisoner, and compelled him to abdicate. The emperor escaped and found safety at Liège, where he died, August 7. See German monographs by Floto (1855–57), Kilian (1886), and Meyer von Knonau (1890 *et seq.*).

HENRY, called **The Lion** (1129–95), Duke of Saxony and Bavaria, was the head of the Guelphs. After Bavaria (taken from his father) was restored to him (1154) by the Emperor Frederick I, his possessions extended from the North Sea and the Baltic to the Adriatic. His power and ambitious designs roused against him a league of princes in 1166; but Henry was able to make head against his enemies till the emperor, alarmed, deprived him of his dominions and placed him under the ban of the empire in 1180. Ultimately he was reconciled to Frederick's successor, Henry VI. He encouraged agriculture and the commerce of Hamburg and Lübeck, and founded Munich. See Life by A. L. Poole (1912).

HENRY, (1) **Joseph** (1797–1878), American physicist, born at Albany, N.Y., became instructor in Mathematics there in 1826, in 1832 professor of Natural Philosophy at Princeton, and in 1846 first secretary of the Smithsonian Institution. He discovered electrical induction independently of Faraday and constructed the first electromagnetic motor (1829), demonstrated the oscillatory nature of electric discharges (1842), and introduced a system of weather forecasting. The unit of inductance is named after him.

See *Memorial* (1880) and his *Scientific Writings* (2 vols. 1886).

(2) **Matthew** (1662–1714), English Nonconformist divine, born at Broad Oak farmhouse, Flintshire, became pastor at Chester (1687). His *Exposition of the Old and New Testament* (1710) was completed by others. See Life by Williams (1865).

(3) **O.**, pen-name of **William Sydney Porter** (1862–1910), American writer, master of the short story, born at Greenboro, N. Carolina. Brought up during the depression in the South, he 'borrowed' money from the bank to help his consumptive wife and to start a literary magazine, ran away at the height of the scandal, but returned in 1897 to his wife's deathbed. He was found technically guilty of embezzlement, spent three years in jail, where he adopted his pseudonym and began to write short stories. His second marriage came to nothing and he roamed about the New York back streets, where he found ample material for his tales. His use of coincidence and trick endings, his purple phraseology and caricature have been criticized, but nothing can detract from the technical brilliance and boldness of his comic writing. See Lives by Jennings (1922) and Langford (1957).

(4) **Patrick** (1736–99), American statesman, born in Hanover county, Va., failed in storekeeping and in farming, so turned lawyer in 1760, and first displayed his great eloquence in pleading the cause of the people against an unpopular tax (1763). A great patriot in the War of Independence, he delivered the first speech in the Continental congress (1774). In 1776 he carried the vote of the Virginia convention for independence, and became governor of the new state. He was four times re-elected. In 1791 he retired from public life. See Lives by W. W. Henry (1891) and G. Morgan (1929).

(5) **William** (1774–1836), English chemist, born at Manchester, studied medicine at Edinburgh, practised in Manchester, but soon devoted himself to chemistry. He formulated the law named after him that the amount of gas absorbed by a liquid varies directly as the pressure. He became F.R.S. (1808) and won the Copley Medal (1809).

HENRY FREDERICK (1594–1612), Prince of Wales, born at Stirling Castle, the elder son of James I, was created Duke of Rothesay in 1594, and Prince of Wales in 1610. His promising career was cut short by typhoid fever, though poisoning (even by the king his father) might have been the cause.

HENRY OF BLOIS (1101–71), bishop of Winchester from 1129, and legate from 1139, was King Stephen's brother.

HENRY OF HUNTINGDON (c. 1084–1155), English chronicler, about 1109 became archdeacon of Huntingdon, in 1139 visited Rome. His *Historia Anglorum* comes down to 1154 (ed. by T. Arnold, 1879; trans. 1853).

HENRYSON, Robert (c. 1425–c. 1508), Scottish makar, is usually designated schoolmaster of Dunfermline, and was certainly a notary in 1478. His *Testament of Cresseid* is a kind of supplement to Chaucer's poem on the same subject; *Robene and Makyne* is the earliest Scottish specimen of pastoral poetry. Other works include a metrical version of thirteen *Morall Fabels of Esope*, possibly his masterpiece. See studies by Stearn (1949), McQueen (1967), and his poems and fables, ed. H. Harvey Wood (1958).

HENRY THE MINSTREL. See HARRY (BLIND).

HENRY THE NAVIGATOR (1394–1460), Portuguese prince, fourth son of João I, king of Portugal, and the English Philippa, a daughter of John of Gaunt, distinguished himself at the capture of Ceuta in 1415. He took up his residence at Sagres, in Algarve; and during the war against the Moors his sailors reached parts of the ocean before unknown. He erected an observatory and a school for navigation, and dispatched some of his pupils on voyages of discovery, resulting in the discovery of the Madeira Islands in 1418. Henry's thoughts were now directed towards the gold-producing coasts of Guinea; and in 1433 one of his mariners sailed round Cape Nun, and touched Cape Bojador. Next year another expedition reached a point 120 miles beyond Cape Bojador; in 1440 Cape Blanco was reached. Up to this period the prince had borne the expense of these voyages himself; henceforth societies for the purpose were formed under his guidance. In 1446 Henry's captain, Nuno Tristam, doubled Cape Verde, and in 1448 González Vallo discovered three of the Azores. Henry died in 1460, after his mariners had reached Sierra Leone. See books by Major (1868–77), Martins (trans. 1914), Sanceau (1946).

HENSCHEL, Sir George (1850–1934), German-born British composer, conductor, singer and pianist, born at Breslau, came to England in 1877, was naturalized in 1890, and knighted 1914. He composed an opera, a Requiem and chamber music, conducted the Boston Symphony Orchestra and became the first conductor of the Scottish Orchestra (1893–95).—His first wife was the soprano-singer, **Lillian June Bailey** (1860–1901).

HENSEN, Victor (1835–1924), German physiologist, born at Kiel, investigated the production of marine fauna which he named *plankton*.

HENSLOWE, Philip (d. 1616), English stage-manager, was originally a dyer and starchmaker, but became in 1584 lessee of the Rose theatre on the Bankside. From 1591 till his death in 1616 he was in partnership with Edward Alleyn (q.v.), who married his step-daughter in 1592. Henslowe's business diary from 1593 to 1609, preserved at Dulwich College (ed. with interpolations, &c., by J. P. Collier, 1841; W. W. Greg, 1904–08), contains invaluable information about the stage of Shakespeare's day.

HENSON, Leslie (1891–1957), English comedian, remembered for his laughter-provoking facial elasticity, took leading rôles in *Lady Luck* (1927), *Funny Face* (1928), *It's a Boy* (1930), *Harvey* (1950), &c., and produced the famous Aldwych farces and many other plays. See his *Yours Faithfully* (1948).

HENTY, George Alfred (1832–1902), English novelist and journalist, born at Trumpington, educated at Westminster and Caius College,

became a special correspondent for the *Morning Advertiser* during the Crimean war and for the *Standard* in the Franco-Prussian war. He was best known, however, for his eighty historical adventure stories for boys, including *With Clive in India* (1884), *With Moore at Corunna* (1898), &c. See Bibliography by Kennedy and Farmer (1956).

HENZE, Hans Werner (1926–), German composer, born at Gütersloh, studied with Fortner at Heidelberg, and at Paris. Though influenced by Schoenberg, he has explored beyond the more conventional uses of the twelve-tone system. He has written operas (*Das Wundertheater, Boulevard Solitude*—based on *Manon Lescaut*), ballets, symphonies and chamber music, sometimes using jazz idiom. He became professor of Composition at the Academy Mozarteum, Salzburg, in 1961.

HEPBURN, (1). See BOTHWELL.

(2) **Katharine** (1909–), American actress, born at Hartford, Conn., educated at Bryn Mawr Coll., appeared on stage in *The Czarina* (1928, Baltimore), *Night Hostess* (1928, New York), &c., but attained international fame as a film actress, making her début in 1932. Among many of her outstanding films were *Morning Glory* (1932, Oscar award), *The Philadelphia Story* (1940), *The African Queen* (1952), and *Long Day's Journey into Night* (1962).

HEPPLEWHITE, George (d. 1786), English cabinet-maker, came from Lancaster to set up business in London. His designs are characterized by the free use of inlaid ornament and the shield shape. His *Cabinet-maker's and Upholsterer's Guide* appeared in 1788.

HEPWORTH, Dame Barbara (1903–), English sculptor, born at Wakefield, studied at the Leeds School of Art, the Royal College of Art and in Italy; and she has been married to John Skeaping, the sculptor, and to Ben Nicholson, the artist. She was one of the foremost nonfigurative sculptors of her time, notable for the strength and formal discipline of her carving (e.g., the *Contrapuntal Forms* exhibited at the Festival of Britain, 1951). Her representational paintings and drawings are of equal power. She became a C.B.E. (1958) and D.B.E. (1965). See *Barbara Hepworth: Carvings and Drawings* (1952), and monographs (1958, 1961, 1962).

HERACLITUS, *-klī′tus* (fl. 500 B.C.), Greek philosopher, with his opponent Parmenides (q.v.) the most important of pre-Socratic philosophers, was born at Ephesus, founded his own school there in the Ionian tradition and died at sixty. Known as ' the weeping philosopher ' because of his pessimistic view of the human condition and ' the dark one ' because of the mystical obscurity of his thought, he wrote *On Nature*, fragments of which are extant. The ever-living fire is the primordial element out of which all else has arisen, change, i.e., becoming and perishing, flowing, is the first principle of the universe. His follower, Cratylus (q.v.), made a typical remark: ' You cannot step twice into the same river.' Any apparent unity or stability is merely the equilibrium or harmony achieved by warring opposites, one never triumphing over another to upset the harmony. This dynamic monism is a recurring theme in Western philosophy. It gave immediate stimulus of opposition to the logic of Parmenides and Eleatic atomism and found an echo in Hegel's synthesis of opposites. See Bywater's edition of the *Fragments* (1877), studies by E. Pfleiderer (1896), H. Diels (1909), J. Burnet, *Early Greek Philosophy* (4th ed. 1948), and G. S. Kirk and J. E. Raven, *The Pre-Socratic Philosophers* (1957).

HERACLIUS, *-klī'-* (*c.* 575–641), Byzantine emperor, born in Cappadocia, in 610 headed a revolt against Phocas, slew him, and mounted his throne. At this time the Avars threatened the empire on the northwest, and the Persians invaded it. Chosroes II captured Damascus in 613, and in 614 Jerusalem; then all Syria, Egypt, and Asia Minor were conquered. At length Heraclius, having in 620 concluded a treaty with the Avars, in 622 took the field against the Persians, routed them in a series of brilliant campaigns, won back his lost provinces, and shut up Chosroes in Ctesiphon (628). But soon the followers of Mohammed won from Heraclius nearly all he gained from the Persians, he meanwhile wasting his time in self-indulgence and theological disputes. See French monograph by Drapeyron (1869).

HERBART, Johann Friedrich (1776–1841), German philosopher, born at Oldenburg, in 1805 was appointed extraordinary professor of Philosophy at Göttingen, in 1809 went to Königsberg as Kant's successor, but in 1833 returned to Göttingen. His works were collected by Hartenstein (1850–52; new ed. 13 vols. 1883–93). He continued in the Leibnizian tradition, rather than Kant's, by positing a multiplicity of ' reals ' or things which possess in themselves absolute existence apart from apperception by the mind of man. He rejected the idea of separate mental faculties, and devised a statics and a dynamics of mind amenable to mathematical manipulation. See De Garmo's *Herbart and the Herbartians* (1895), Felkin's translation of his *Science of Education* (1895), Ufer's *Introduction to Herbart's Pedagogy* (trans. 1896), and study by F. H. Hayward (1907), Life by G. Weiss (1926), G. F. Stout's essay on *Studies in Philosophy and Psychology* (1930).

HERBELOT, Barthélemy d', *ayr-bĕ-lō* (1625–1695), French orientalist, born in Paris, in 1692 became professor of Syriac in the Collège de France. His *Bibliothèque Orientale* (1697; 3rd ed. 1777–83) is a universal dictionary of oriental knowledge.

HERBERT, name of an English noble family, descended from ' Herbertus Camerarius ' who came over from France with William the Conqueror; seven or eight generations later the Herberts diverged into the Earls of Powis, the Lords Herbert of Cherbury, the Herberts of Muckross, and several untitled branches in England, Wales, and Ireland. **Sir William Herbert** of Raglan Castle, Monmouth, was knighted in 1415 by Henry V for his valour in the French wars. His descendants were Earls of Pembroke and Huntingdon, the Earls of Carnarvon (q.v.) descending from the 8th Earl of Pembroke:

(1) **Sir William, 1st Earl of Pembroke** (d.

1469), son of Sir William above, father of (2), an adherent of the House of York, was created Earl of Pembroke by Edward IV in 1468 but was captured by the Lancastrians and beheaded July 28.

(2) **William, 2nd Earl** (1460–91), son of (1), in 1479 exchanged the earldom of Pembroke for that of Huntingdon.

(3) **Sir William, 1st Earl of Pembroke** (2nd creation) (*c.* 1501–70), English soldier and diplomat, son of an illegitimate son of (1), married the sister of Catharine Parr, Henry VIII's sixth wife, supported Mary Tudor against Lady Jane Grey and put down Wyatt's rebellion (1554).

(4) **Henry, 2nd Earl** (*c.* 1534–1601), English courtier, son of (3), married first Lady Catharine Grey (1553), sister of Lady Jane, and in 1577 Mary Sidney, sister of the poet, to whom the latter dedicated his *Arcadia*.

(5) **William, 3rd Earl** (1580–1630), English poet, patron of Ben Jonson, Massinger and Inigo Jones, a lord chamberlain of the court (1615–30), became chancellor of Oxford University in 1617 and had Pembroke College named after him. Shakespeare's ' W. H.', the ' onlie begetter ' of the *Sonnets* has been taken by some to refer to the 3rd Earl.

(6) **Philip, 4th Earl** (1584–1650), English statesman, brother of (5) and a favourite of James I, strove to' promote peace between Charles I and the Scots, but left the King and joined the Parliamentarians (1641), and became vice-chancellor of Oxford (1641–50). Created 1st Earl of Montgomery (1605).

(7) **Thomas, 8th Earl** (1656–1733), English sailor, was lord high admiral under Queen Anne.

(8) **Henry, 9th Earl**, ' The Architect Earl ' (1693–1751), erected the first Westminster bridge (1739–50). See also HERBERT (2), HERBERT OF CHERBURY and HERBERT OF LEA.

HERBERT, (1) **Sir Alan Patrick** (1890–1971), English writer and politician. He was called to the bar but never practised, having established himself in his twenties as a witty versifier, joining *Punch* in 1924. His first theatrical success with Nigel Playfair in the revue *Riverside Nights* (1926) was followed by a series of brilliant libretti for comic operas, including *Tantivy Towers* (1930), a version of Offenbach's *Helen* (1932), *Derby Day* and *Bless the Bride* (1947). He was also the author of several successful novels, notably *The Secret Battle* (1919), *The Water Gipsies* (1930) and *Holy Deadlock* (1934). In *What a Word* (1935) and many humorous articles he campaigned against jargon and officialese. From 1935 to 1950 he was Independent member of parliament for Oxford University and introduced a Marriage Bill in the House of Commons that became law as the Matrimonial Causes Act, 1938, and did much to improve divorce conditions. He was knighted in 1945 and created C.H. in 1970. See his autobiography (1970).

(2) **George** (1593–1633), English clergyman and poet, was the son of Lady Magdalen Herbert, to whom Donne addressed his *Holy Sonnets*, and brother of Lord Herbert of Cherbury (q.v.). In 1609 he passed from Westminster to Trinity College, Cambridge,

where he was elected a fellow and public orator (1619). His connection with the court and particularly James's favour seemed to point to a worldly career and his poems, 'Affliction' and 'The Collar', indicate the sharpness of the decision which finally directed him to the Church. In 1630, under the influence of Laud, he took orders and wore out his few remaining years as the zealous parish priest of Bemerton in Wiltshire. Like his friend Nicholas Ferrar, but without Ferrar's mystical piety, he represents both in his life and works, the counterchallenge of the Laudian party to the Puritans. The Church was Christ's comely bride to be decked with seemly ornament and 'The mean thy praise and glory is'. This twofold conception along with his ideal of Christian humility and unwearying service pervades all his writing, verse and prose alike. His verse is almost completely included in *The Temple* (1633), which is the communing of a soul with God, sometimes in the expostulatory vein which only perfect faith dare assume, its serenity often pleasingly disturbed by dramatic touches. Most striking is the quaint homely imagery, due to his cult of humility. His chief prose work *A Priest in the Temple* containing what Izaak Walton called 'plain, prudent, usefull rules for the country parson' was published in his *Remains* (1652). See his *Works in Prose and Verse* with the Life by Izaak Walton and notes by Coleridge (1846). Modern studies are by Heall (1934), Forbes (1949) and Summers (1954).

(3) **John Rogers** (1810–90), English historical and religious painter, was born at Maldon, about 1840 turned Catholic, and was elected an A.R.A. in 1841, an R.A. in 1846. His *Sir Thomas More and his daughter* (1844) is in the Vernon collection in the National Gallery.

(4) **Victor** (1859–1924), Irish-American composer, born in Dublin. A cellist by training, he played in the orchestras of Johann Strauss and the Stuttgart Court before settling in New York as leading cellist of the Metropolitan Opera Company's Orchestra. His successful comic opera, *Prince Ananias* (1893), was followed by a long series of similar works containing such enduringly popular songs as 'Ah, sweet mystery of life' and 'Kiss me again'. His ambition to succeed as a composer of serious opera resulted in *Natoma* (1911) and *Madeleine* (1914), neither of which have remained in repertory. See Life by Waters (1955).

HERBERT OF CHERBURY, Edward Herbert, 1st Baron (1583–1648), English soldier, statesman and philosopher, brother of George Herbert (q.v.), was born March 3, at Eyton, Shropshire. In 1599, while still an undergraduate at University College, Oxford, he married an heiress four years older than himself. At James I's coronation he was made a knight of the Bath; in 1608 he visited France, and in 1610 was at the recapture of Jülich. In 1614 he was with Maurice of Orange, travelled through Germany and Italy, and got into trouble attempting to recruit Protestant soldiers in Languedoc for the Duke of Savoy. Made a member of the privy council, he was sent to France as ambassador (1619), and tried negotiation between Louis XIII and his Protestant subjects. He was in 1624 made a peer of Ireland, and in 1629 of England. When the Civil War broke out he at first sided very half-heartedly with the Royalists, but in 1644 surrendered to the Parliamentarians. His *De Veritate* is an anti-empirical theory of knowledge. His *De Religione Gentilium* (1645) proves that all religions recognize five main articles—that there is a supreme God, that he ought to be worshipped, that virtue and purity are the main part of that worship, that sins should be repented of, and that there are rewards and punishments in a future state. Hence Herbert came to be reckoned the first of the deistical writers. The *Expeditio Buckinghami Ducis* (1656) is a vindication of the ill-fated Rochelle expedition. The ill-proportioned *Life and Raigne of King Henry VIII* (1649) is by no means accurate. His *Autobiography*, a brilliant picture of the man and of contemporary manners, is a masterpiece in its kind, but is disfigured by overweening self-glory. The *Poems*, Latin and English, reveal a representative of the 'metaphysical' school. See Rémusat's monograph on him (1874), C. Güttler's on his philosophy (1897) and Life by Lord Herbert (1912).

HERBERT OF LEA, Sidney Herbert, 1st Baron (1810–61), British statesman, son of the 11th earl of Pembroke, born at Richmond, was educated at Harrow and Oriel College, Oxford, in 1832 was elected Conservative M.P. for South Wilts, and was Peel's secretary to the Admiralty from 1841 to 1845, when he became secretary-at-war. He opposed Cobden's motion for a select committee on the Corn Laws. In 1852 he was again secretary-at-war under Aberdeen, was largely blamed for the hardships of the army before Sebastopol, but sent Florence Nightingale to the Crimea. He was for a few weeks Palmerston's colonial secretary in 1855, and his secretary-at-war in 1859. Great improvements in the sanitary conditions and education of the forces, the amalgamation of the Indian with the imperial army, and the organization of the volunteer movement were results of his army administration. After his resignation, he was called (1861) to the Upper House as Baron Herbert of Lea. He died August 2, 1861. See Life by Lord Stanmore (1906).

HERCULANO DE CARVALHO, er-koolah'no THay ker-vahl'-yoo, **Alexandre** (1810–1877), Portuguese poet and prose writer, born in Lisbon, largely self-educated, came over to England and France, and returned eventually to become royal librarian at Ajuda. His best work is the *Historia de Portugal* (1846–53). See Life by F. de Almeida (1910).

HERD, David (1732–1810), Scottish anthologist, born at Marykirk in Kincardine, editor of *Ancient Scottish Ballads* (1776; new ed. by Hecht, 1905).

HERDER, Johann Gottfried (1744–1803), German critic and poet, was born at Mohrungen in East Prussia, August 25, studied at Königsberg, and there got to know

Kant and Hamann, In 1764 he became teacher in a school and assistant pastor in a church at Riga. Between 1766 and 1769 he wrote two works, in which he maintained that the truest poetry is the poetry of the people. In 1769 he made the acquaintance of Goethe at Strasbourg; in 1770 was appointed court preacher at Bückeburg, and in 1776 first preacher in Weimar. He died December 18. Herder's love for the songs of the people, for unsophisticated human nature, found expression in an admirable collection of folksongs, *Stimmen der Völker in Liedern* (1778–79), a work on the spirit of Hebrew poetry (1782–83; trans. 1833), a treatise on the influence of poetry on manners (1778); in oriental mythological tales, in parables and legends, in his version of the *Cid* (1805), and other works. The supreme importance of the historical method is fully recognized in these and a book on the origin of language (1772), and especially in his masterpiece, *Ideen zur Geschichte der Menschheit* (1784–91; trans. 1800), which is remarkable for its anticipations and adumbrations of evolutionary theories. He is best remembered for the influence he exerted on Goethe and the growing German Romanticism. His works have been edited by Suphan (32 vols. 1877–1909). See *Erinnerungen*, by Herder's widow (1830); *Herder's Lebensbild*, by his son (1846–47); various collections of his *Letters*; and books by Haym (1880–85), Joret (1875), Nevinson (1884), Kühnemann (2nd ed. 1912), Bürkner (1904), McEachran (1940), A. Gillies (1945).

HEREDIA, *ay-ray'*THee-*a*, (1) José María (1803–39), Cuban poet, cousin of (2), born at Santiago de Cuba, was exiled to the U.S.A. for anti-government activities in 1823. He is remembered for his patriotic verse and for his ode to Niagara.

(2) José María de (1842–1905), French poet, cousin of (1), was born in Cuba at Santiago but went at an early age to France, where he was educated. One of the Parnassians, he achieved a great reputation with a comparatively small output, his finest work being found in his sonnets, which appeared in the collection *La Trophée* (1893). He was elected to the Academy in 1894.

HEREFORD, Earls of. See BOHUN.

HEREWARD, called the Wake, was a Lincolnshire squire who held the Isle of Ely against William the Conqueror (1070–71). When William had succeeded in penetrating to the English camp of refuge, Hereward cut his way through to the fastnesses of the swampy fens northwards. The noble lineage assigned him in Kingsley's romance of *Hereward the Wake* (1866) has been shown by Freeman to be unfounded in fact. See a monograph by General Harward (1896).

HERGESHEIMER, Joseph, -*hīm'er* (1880–1954), American novelist, born in Philadelphia, studied art, but made his name by *Mountain Blood* (1915), *The Three Black Pennys* (1917), *Tubal Cain* (1918), *Java Head* (1919), *The Bright Shawl* (1922), *The Foolscap Rose* (1934) and other novels and short stories.

HERIOT, George (1563–1624), Scottish goldsmith and philanthropist, born in Edinburgh, started business in 1586, and was in 1597 appointed goldsmith to Anne of Denmark, and soon after to James VI. Heriot followed James to London, where, as court jeweller and banker, he amassed considerable riches. He bequeathed £23,625 to found a hospital or school in Edinburgh for sons of poor burgesses. 'Jingling Geordie' figures in Scott's *Fortunes of Nigel*. See Steven's *History of Heriot's Hospital* (1859).

HERKOMER, Sir Hubert von (1849–1914), German-born British portrait painter, was born at Waal in Bavaria, studied art at Southampton, Munich and South Kensington, and in 1870 settled in London, where, besides painting, he worked as engraver, wood carver, ironsmith, architect, journalist, playwright, composer, singer and actor. In 1889 he became Slade professor at Oxford, in 1890 R.A., and in 1907 was knighted. He was an enthusiast for ' colour music ', in which different colours instead of sounds are produced by a keyboard. See his *The Herkomers* (1910–11) and Life by J. Saxon Mills (1923).

HERMANN, Johann Gottfried Jakob (1772–1848), German classical scholar, born at Leipzig, from 1803 was professor there of Eloquence and Poetry. He wrote on classical metre, Greek grammar, &c., and left *Opuscula* (1827–77). See Lives by Jahn (1849) and Köchly (1874).

HERMAS, one of the Apostolic fathers, author of the early Christian treatise called the *Shepherd*, sometimes identified as the brother of Pius I, Bishop of Rome in 142–57. See Zahn, *Der Hirt des Hermas* (1868) and critical study by M. Dibelius (1923).

HERMES, Georg, *her'mes* (1775–1831), German Roman Catholic theologian, born at Dreyerwalde in Westphalia, became theological professor at Münster in 1807, and in 1819 at Bonn. In his works, e.g., his *Philosophische Einleitung in die Christkatholische Theologie* (1819), he sought to combine the Catholic faith and doctrines with Kantian philosophy. The Hermesian method became influential in the Rhineland, but his doctrines were condemned by a papal brief in 1835 as heretical, and his followers were deprived of their professorships.

HERMITE, Charles, *ayr-meet* (1822–1901), French mathematician, professor at the Sorbonne, proved that the base, *e*, of natural logarithms is nonalgebraic, and published works on the theory of numbers, elliptic functions, continued fractions, &c.

HERNÁNDEZ, José, *ayr-nahn'dayth* (1854–1886), Argentinian poet, born near Buenos Aires, known for his *gaucho* poetry of life in the pampas, where he had spent his early life among the cattlemen. His masterpiece is the epic *Martín Fierro* (1872–79). See Tiscornia, *Poetas gauchescos* (1940).

HERO OF ALEXANDRIA (1st cent. A.D.), Greek mathematician, invented many machines, among them Hero's fountain, the aeolipile, and a double forcing-pump suitable for a fire engine. He showed that the angle of incidence in optics is equal to the angle of reflection and devised the formula for expressing the area of a triangle in terms of its sides.

HERO THE YOUNGER (10th cent. A.D.), Greek mathematician at Constantinople, wrote on mechanics and astronomy.

HEROD, the name of a family which rose to power in Judaea in the first century B.C.; they were of Edomite descent, but Jewish in religion. See joint biographical studies by A. H. M. Jones (1938), S. Perowne (1958), and a popular account of their times by F. O. Busch (trans. 1958):

(1) **Herod the Great** (?73–4 B.C.), second son of Antipater, procurator of Judaea, in 47 B.C. was made governor of Galilee; ultimately he and his elder brother were made joint tetrarchs of Judaea. Displaced by Antigonus of the Hasmonean dynasty, he fled to Rome, where he obtained, through Antony, a full recognition of his claims, and became tetrarch of Judaea in 40 B.C. On Antony's fall he secured the favour of Augustus, and obtained the title of king of Judaea in 31 B.C.; his reign was stained with cruelties and atrocities. Every member of the Hasmonean family, and even those of his own blood, fell a sacrifice to his jealous fears; and latterly the lightest suspicion sufficed as the ground for wholesale butcheries. The slaughter of the innocents at Bethlehem is quite in keeping with his character, but is not alluded to by Josephus; so was his ordering the death of his wife Mariamne and his two sons by her. Herod's one eminent quality was his love of magnificence in architecture. He married ten wives, by whom he had fourteen children.

(2) **Herod Antipas** (d. after A.D. 40), son of (1), was by his will named tetrarch of Galilee and Peraea. He divorced his first wife in order to marry Herodias, the wife of his half-brother Philip—a union against which John the Baptist remonstrated at the cost of his life. It was when Herod Antipas was at Jerusalem for the Passover that Jesus was sent before him by Pilate for examination. He afterwards made a journey to Rome in the hope of obtaining the title of king; he not only failed, but, through the intrigues of Herod Agrippa, was banished to Lugdunum (Lyons), where he died.

(3) **Herod Agrippa I** (10 B.C.–A.D. 44), son of Aristobulus and Berenice and grandson of (1), was educated and lived at Rome until his debts compelled him to take refuge in Idumea. From this period almost to the death of Tiberius he suffered a variety of misfortunes, but, having formed a friendship with Caligula, he received from him four tetrarchies, and after the banishment of Herod Antipas that of Galilee and Peraea. Claudius added to his dominions Judaea and Samaria. He died 'eaten of worms' at Caesarea.

(4) **Herod Agrippa II** (A.D. 27–100), son of (3), was at Rome when his father died. Claudius detained him, and re-transformed the kingdom into a Roman province. In 53 he received nearly all his paternal possessions, which were subsequently enlarged by Nero. Agrippa spent great sums in adorning Jerusalem. He did all in his power to dissuade the Jews from rebelling. When Jerusalem was taken he went with his sister to Rome, where he became praetor. It was before him that Paul made his defence.

HERODAS. See HERONDAS.

HERODES ATTICUS, *hĕ-rō'deez* (c. A.D. 107–177), Greek orator, was born and died at Marathon, won Hadrian's favour, and was summoned to Rome in 140 by Antoninus Pius. See French monograph by Vidal Lablache (1871).

HERODIAN (c. A.D. 170–240), Greek historian, who was born in Syria, and lived in Rome. His *History*, in eight books, from the death of Marcus Aurelius (180) to the accession of Gordian III (238), is fairly trustworthy. See editions by Bekker (1855) and Mendelssohn (1883).

HERODOTUS, *he-rod'ō-tus* (c. 485–425 B.C.), Greek historian, born at Halicarnassus, a Greek colony on the coast of Asia Minor. When the colonies were freed from the Persian yoke, he left his native town, and travelled in Asia Minor, the Aegean islands, Greece, Macedonia, Thrace, the coasts of the Black Sea, Persia, Tyre, Egypt, and Cyrene. In 443 B.C. the colony of Thurii was founded by Athens on the Tarentine Gulf, and Herodotus joined it. From Thurii he visited Sicily and Lower Italy. On his travels, he collected historical, geographical, ethnological, mythological and archaeological material for his history which was designed to record not only the wars but the causes of the wars between Greece and the barbarians. Beginning with the conquest of the Greek colonies in Asia Minor by the Lydian king Croesus, he gives a history of Lydia, and then passes to Persia, Babylon and Egypt. In books v to ix we have the history of the two Persian wars. The work of Herodotus is to the bald, brief, disconnected notes of his predecessors what the work of Homer was to the poems of his predecessors. Cicero called him ' the father of history '. See studies by J. E. Powell (1939) and Myres (1953).

HÉROLD, Louis Joseph Ferdinand, *ay-rold* (1791–1833), French composer, born at Paris, wrote many operas, among them *Zampa* (1831) and *Le Pré aux clercs* (1832), also several ballets and piano music. See Life by Jouvin (1868).

HERONDAS, or **Herodas** (3rd cent. B.C.), Greek poet, of whose *Mimiambi*, pictures of Greek life in dialogue, some 700 verses were discovered on an Egyptian papyrus in the British Museum in 1891 (edited by Knox, 1922).

HEROPHILUS, *-rof'-* (fl. 300 B.C.), Greek anatomist, a founder of the medical school of Alexandria, born at Chalcedon, was the first to dissect the human body to compare it with that of other animals. He described the brain, liver, spleen, sexual organs and nervous system, dividing the latter into sensory and motor.

HÉROULT, Paul Louis Toussaint, *ayr-oo* (1863–1914), French metallurgist, invented the method of extracting aluminium by the electrolysis of cryolite, and a furnace for electric steel.

HERRERA, *er-ray'rah*, (1) **Antonio de** (1549–1625), Spanish historian, born at Cuellar near Segovia, wrote a history of *Castilian Exploits in the Pacific* (1601–15; trans. by John Stevens, 1725), a description of the

West Indies, a history of England and Scotland in the time of Mary Stuart, &c.

(2) **Fernando de** (*c*. 1534–97), Spanish lyric poet, born at Seville, took holy orders. Many of his love poems are remarkable for tender feeling, while his odes sometimes attain a Miltonic grandeur. He wrote a prose history of the war in Cyprus (1572), and translated from the Latin of Stapleton a Life of Sir T. More (1592).

(3) **Francisco**, ' **El Viejo** ' (the elder) (1576–1656), Spanish painter, born in Seville, painted historical pieces, wine shops, fairs, carnivals, and the like.

(4) **Francisco**, ' **El Mozo** ' (the younger) (1622–85), Spanish painter, son of (3), born at Seville, worked at Rome, but was ultimately painter to the king at Madrid. His best works are a fresco, *The Ascension*, in the Atocha church in Madrid, and *St Francis*, in Seville cathedral.

HERRICK, Robert (1591–1674), English poet, was the son of a London goldsmith. After graduating at Cambridge he was presented with a living in Devon (1629) of which he was deprived as a royalist in 1647. The year following, probably feeling absolved from priestly correctitude in London, he published *Hesperides: or the Works both Humane* and *Divine of Robert Herrick Esq.*, the latter being entitled *Noble Numbers*. Despite *Noble Numbers* he is the most pagan of English poets, vying with his Latin models in the celebration of imagined mistresses—Julia, Anthea, Corinna, &c.—but always in the dispassionate manner of the carver of jewels. ' Sealed of the tribe of Ben ', he was at his best when describing rural rites as in *The Hock Cart, Twelfth Night*, &c., and in lyrical gems such as ' Gather ye rosebuds while ye may ' and ' Cherry Ripe '. Youth and love and the pagan fields were his themes at a time when the West country was devastated by the Civil War. He resumed his living at the Restoration. See Life by F. W. Moorman (1910); also Rose Macaulay, *They Were Not Defeated* (1933), E. I. M. Easton, *Youth Immortal* (1934) and M. Chute, *Two Gentle Men* (1960).

HERRING, John Frederick (1795–1865), English stagecoach driver turned painter, was the most popular painter of sporting scenes in his day. See Muir's Catalogue (1894).

HERRIOT, Édouard, *er-yō* (1872–1957), French Radical-Socialist statesman, born at Troyes, became professor at the Lycée Ampère, Lyons, and was mayor there from 1905 until his death. He was minister of Transport during the first World War, premier (1924–25), 1926 (for two days) and 1932, was several times president of the Chamber of Deputies, a post which he was holding in 1942 when he became a prisoner of Vichy and of the Nazis, after renouncing his Legion of Honour, when that honour was conferred on collaborators with the Germans. After the Liberation, he was reinvested with the decoration and was president of the national assembly (1947–53), and was then elected life president. A keen supporter of the League of Nations, he opposed, however, the whole concept of the European Defence Community, especially German rearmament. He wrote a number of literary and biographical studies, best known of which are *Madame Récamier* (1904), *Beethoven* (1932), &c. See Life by P. Groschaude (1932).

HERSCHEL, name of a German-British family of astronomers:

(1) **Caroline Lucretia** (1750–1848), sister of (2), was born and lived in Hanover till 1772, when she joined him at Bath. Acting as his assistant she made independent observations, and discovered eight comets and several nebulae and clusters of stars. In 1798 she published a star catalogue. She returned to Germany in 1822. See her Memoir (1876).

(2) **Sir (Frederick) William** (1738–1822), German-British astronomer, brother of (1), father of (3), born at Hanover, visited England in 1755 as oboist in the Hanoverian Guards band; in 1766 he became an organist and teacher of music at Bath. Taking up astronomy, he made (1773–74) a reflecting telescope, with which in 1781 he discovered the planet Uranus, called by him ' Georgium Sidus '. In 1782 he was appointed private astronomer to George III; and at Slough near Windsor, assisted by his sister Caroline, he continued his researches. Knighted in 1816, he died August 25, 1822. He greatly added to our knowledge of the solar system, of the Milky Way, and of the nebulae; he discovered, besides Uranus and two of its satellites, two satellites of Saturn, the rotation of Saturn's ring, the period of rotation of Saturn, and the motions of binary stars; and made a famous catalogue of double stars, &c. In 1789 he erected a telescope 40 feet long. See Lives by E. S. Holden (1881), Sime (1900), Sidgwick (1953) and Armitage (1963); and Lady Lubbock's *Herschel Chronicle* (1933).

(3) **Sir John Fredrick William** (1792–1871), English astronomer, son of (2), born at Slough, was educated at Eton and St John's, Cambridge, where in 1813 he was senior wrangler and first Smith's prizeman. He continued and augmented his father's researches, discovering 525 nebulae and clusters. In 1848 he was president of the Royal Astronomical Society and master of the Mint (1850–55). He pioneered celestial photography, carried out research on photoactive chemicals and the wave theory of light, and translated from Schiller and the *Iliad*. He was buried in Westminster Abbey. See A. M. Clerk, *The Herschels* (1896).

HERSEY, John Richard (1914–), American author, born in Tientsin, educated at Yale, was correspondent in the Far East for the magazine *Time*. His novels include *A Bell for Adano* (1944), which was dramatized and filmed, *Hiroshima* (1946), the first on-the-spot description of the effects of a nuclear explosion, *The War Lover* (1959) and *The Child Buyer* (1960).

HERTER, Christian Archibald (1895–1966), American politician, educated at Harvard, was governor of Massachusetts (1953–57), and under-secretary of state to John Foster Dulles, whom he succeeded as secretary (1959–1961). His background of diplomatic experience included being acting minister to Belgium at the age of twenty-one, and personal assistant to Herbert Hoover (1921–1924). A sincere if reticent internationalist, he tended to be overshadowed by Dulles.

HERTWIG, Oscar (1849–1922), German zoologist, born at Friedberg, Hessen, professor at Jena and Berlin, demonstrated with Fol that one sperm only enters the egg in fertilization (1879).

HERTZ, (1) Gustav (1887–   ), German physicist, nephew of (2), born at Hamburg, professor of Physics at Berlin and director of the Siemens Research Laboratory, shared the Nobel prize (1925) with Franck for confirming the quantum theory by their experiments on the effects produced by bombarding atoms with electrons. He was head of a research laboratory in the U.S.S.R. (1945–54), and director of Karl Marx University, Leipzig (1954–61).

(2) Heinrich Rudolf (1857–94), German physicist, uncle of (1), born at Hamburg, studied under Kirchhoff and Helmholtz and ultimately became professor at Bonn in 1899. In 1887 he realized Maxwell's predictions, by his fundamental discovery of electromagnetic waves, which, excepting wavelength, behave like light waves.

(3) Henrik (1798–1870), Danish poet, was born and died in Copenhagen. *Gjengangerbrevene* (' Letters of a Ghost ', 1830) was a rhymed satirical poem. His best dramas are *Svend Dyrings Hus* (1837) and *Kong Renés Datter* (1845; often trans.).

(4) Joseph Herman (1872–1946), Zionist leader and writer, born at Rebrin, Czechoslovakia (then in Hungary), studied at Columbia University, U.S.A., became rabbi at Johannesburg until expelled by President Kruger for his pro-British attitude, becoming professor of Philosophy at Transvaal University College in 1906. In 1913 he became rabbi of the Hebrew Congregations of the British Empire and a C.H. in 1943. See his *The Jew in South Africa* (1905), &c.

HERTZOG, James Barry Munnik (1866–1942), Dutch South African statesman, was born at Wellington, Cape Colony. He was a Boer general (1899–1902) and in 1910 became minister of justice in the first Union government. In 1913 he founded the Nationalist party, advocating complete South African independence, and in World War I opposed cooperation with Britain. As premier (1924–1939), in coalition with Labour (1924–29), with Smuts in a United party (1933–39), he renounced his earlier secessionism, but on the outbreak of World War II declared for neutrality, was defeated, lost office, and in 1940 retired. See Lives by G. M. van den Heever (1946) and O. Pirow (1958).

HERVÉ, properly Florimond Ronger, er-vay (1825–92), French composer (from 1848) of light operas, one of the originators of *opéra bouffe*, achieved success with *L'Oeuil crevé*, *Le Petit Faust*, &c.

HERVIEU, Paul Ernest, er-vyœ (1857–1915), French dramatist, novelist and Academician (1900), born at Neuilly, wrote *L'Énigme*, *Le Dédale* and other powerful *piecès à thèse*. See study by E. Estève (1917).

HERWARTH VON BITTENFELD, Karl Eberhard, her'vahrt (1796–1884), Prussian general, served in the war of liberation

against Napoleon, in 1864 captured Alsen, and in 1866 contributed to the victories ending with Königgrätz. In 1870 he was made governor of the Rhine provinces, in 1871 a field-marshal.

HERWEGH, Georg, -vayg (1817–75), German revolutionary poet, was born at Stuttgart.

HERZ, erts, (1) Henri (1806–88), Jewish pianist and composer, born at Vienna, was professor of Music (1842–74) at the Conservatoire in Paris and a piano manufacturer there.

(2) Henriette (1764–1847), German-Jewish hostess in Berlin (Christian from 1817), of great beauty and culture, wife of Markus (1747–1803), doctor and philosopher. Her house was an intellectual centre. See Life by Fürst (2nd ed. 1858) and Börne's letters to her (1861).

HERZEN, Alexander (1812–70), Russian political thinker and writer, born in Moscow, was imprisoned in 1834 for his revolutionary socialism. In 1847 he left Russia for Paris, and in 1851 settled in London, becoming a powerful propagandist by his novels and treatises, and by the smuggling into Russia of his paper *Kolokol* (' The Bell '). He died in Paris. Mrs Garnett translated his *Memoirs* (1924–27). See also *The Romantic Exiles* (1933).

HERZL, Theodor (1860–1904), Zionist leader, born in Budapest, graduated in law at Vienna, but wrote essays and plays until the Dreyfus trial (1894) and the anti-Semitism it aroused, which he reported for a Viennese newspaper, possessed him. In the pamphlet *Judenstaat* (1896) he advocated the remedy in the formation of a Jewish state, convened the first Zionist Congress at Basel (1897) and negotiated with the Kaiser, the Sultan, the Russian premier, Joseph Chamberlain and Baron Rothschild. See his uninhibited diary, kept from the beginning of his ' mission ' (trans. 1958), and Life by A. Bein (trans. 1957).

HERZOG, (1) Johann Jakob (1805–82), Swiss theologian, born at Basel, became professor at Lausanne (1830), Halle (1847), Erlangen (1854), and edited the great *Realencyklopädie für protestantische Theologie und Kirche* (22 vols. 1854–68; English abridged ed. by Schaff, 3 vols. 1882–84).

(2) Maurice (1919–   ), French engineer and mountaineer, born at Lyons. He climbed the Alps in youth and, during the second World War, served in the Artillery and the Chasseurs Alpins, receiving the Croix de Guerre. He was chosen to lead the French Himalayan Expedition in 1950, and climbed Annapurna (26,926 ft.) the first 8000-metre peak to be scaled. On the descent, he lost several fingers and toes through frostbite. See his *Annapurna* (1953), written in hospital at Neuilly.

HESELRIGE. See HASELRIG.
HESELTINE, Philip Arnold. See WARLOCK.
HESIOD (c. 8th cent. B.C.), Greek poet, seemingly somewhat later than Homer, was born in Ascra, at the foot of Mount Helicon. The *Works and Days* is generally considered to consist of two originally distinct poems, one exalting honest labour and denouncing corrupt and unjust judges; the other containing advice as to the days lucky or unlucky for the farmer's work. The *Theogony* teaches

the origin of the universe out of Chaos and the history of the gods. Critics are not agreed whether the unity of the poems is the work of the original composer, disturbed by interpolations, or is the work of some late editor harmonizing lays originally unconnected. Hesiod's poetry is didactic. The *Works and Days* gives an invaluable picture of the Greek village community in the 8th century B.C., and the *Theogony* is of importance to the comparative mythologist.

HESS, (1) Germain Henri (1802–50), Swiss chemist, born at Geneva, professor of Chemistry at St Petersburg, formulated Hess's law (1840), which states that the net heat evolved or absorbed in any chemical reaction depends only on the initial and final stages.

(2) **Myra** (1890–1966), English pianist, born in London, studied under Matthay at the Royal Academy of Music, and was an immediate success on her first public appearance in 1907. She worked as a chamber musician, recitalist and virtuoso, achieving fame in North America as well as Britain. During World War II she organized the lunchtime concerts in the National Gallery, for which she was awarded the D.B.E. in 1941.

(3) **Rudolf** (1894–   ), German politician, born at Alexandria, Egypt, and educated at Godesberg, fought in the first World War, after which he studied at Munich University, where he fell under Hitler's spell. He joined the Nazi party in 1920, took part in the abortive Munich rising (1923) and, having shared Hitler's imprisonment and, it is said, taken down from him *Mein Kampf*, became in 1934 his deputy as party leader and in 1939 his successor-designate, after Göring, as *Führer*. In 1941, on the eve of Germany's attack on Russia, he flew alone to Scotland (Eaglesham), to plead the cause of a negotiated Anglo-German peace, which prompted Churchill's comment: ' The maggot is in the apple '. He was temporarily imprisoned in the Tower of London, then under psychiatric care near Aldershot. He was sentenced at the Nuremberg Trials (1946) to life imprisonment. At Spandau jail, where he became in 1966 the sole remaining prisoner, he was nicknamed ' Mad Rudi ' for his eccentricities. See Nuremberg Trial series, vol. vii (1948), book by J. R. Rees (1947), and *Retrospect* by Viscount Simon (1952).

(4) **Victor Francis** (1883–1964), Austrian-American physicist, born at Waldstein, Austria, became professor of Physics at Fordham University (N.Y.) in 1938. He helped to determine the number of alphaparticles given off by a gramme of radium (1918) and became a pioneer investigator of cosmic radiation. He shared the Nobel prize (1936) with C. D. Anderson. See his *Cosmic Radiation and Biological Effects* (1940).

(5) **Walter Rudolf** (1881–1973), Swiss physiologist, born in Frauenfeld, professor of Physiology at Zürich (1917–51), did much important research on the nervous system, and developed methods of stimulating localized areas of the brain by means of needle electrodes. He was awarded the Nobel prize for medicine for 1949.

HESSE, Hermann (1877–1962), German novelist and poet, born at Calw in Württemberg, was a bookseller and antiquarian in Basel from 1895 to 1902 and published his first novel, *Peter Camenzind*, in 1904. Thereafter he earned his living by his pen. *Rosshalde* (1914) examines the problem of the artist. *Knulp* (1915) is a tribute to vagabondage. *Demian* (1919; trans. 1958) is a psychoanalytic study of incest, while *Narziss und Goldmund* (1930; trans. 1958) portrays the two sides of man's nature by contrasting a monk and a voluptuary. *Steppenwolf* (1927; trans. 1929) mirrors the confusion of modern existence and *Das Glasperlenspiel* (1945, trans. as *Magister Ludi* in 1949 and as *The Glass Bead Game* in 1970) is a Utopian fantasy on the theme of withdrawal from the world. Hesse was awarded the Goethe prize in 1946 and the Nobel prize in 1947. His poetry was collected in *Die Gedichte* in 1942, and his letters, *Briefe*, appeared in 1951. *Beschwörungen* (Affirmations) (1955), confirmed that his powers were not diminished by age. Though he disclaimed any ruling purpose, the theme of his work might be stated as a musing on the difficulties put in the way of the individual in his efforts to build up an integrated, harmonious self. All this is expressed in sensitive and sensuous language rising to the majestic and visionary. See Lives and studies by Ball (1927), M. Schmid (1947) and H. Bode (1948), and Freedman, *The Lyrical Novel* (1963).

HESYCHIUS, *he-zik'ee-us* (fl. 4th cent. A.D.), Greek grammarian of Alexandria, compiled a useful Greek lexicon.

HESYCHIUS OF MILETUS (fl. 5th–6th cent. A.D.), Greek historian, wrote a work on the eminent Greek writers and a universal history down to A.D. 518.

HETTNER, (1) Alfred (1859–1941), German geographer, son of (2), brother of (3), born at Dresden, travelled and explored in Europe, Asia, Africa and the Americas, and was a pioneer of modern methods of systematic geography. Among his books are geographies of Russia and England, also *Die Geographie* (1927) and *Der Gang der Kultur über die Erde* (1929).

(2) **Hermann** (1821–82), father of (1) and (3), born at Leisersdorf, was an art historian and literary scholar.

(3) **Otto** (1875–1931), son of (2), brother of (1), born at Dresden, was a painter and sculptor in the neo-Impressionist style.

HEUSS, Theodor, *hoys* (1884–1963), German Federal president, born at Brackenheim, Württemberg, studied at Munich and Berlin and became editor of the political magazine *Hilfe* (1905–12), professor at the Berlin College of Political Science (1920–33) and M.P. (1924–28, 1930–32). A prolific author and journalist, he wrote two books denouncing Hitler, and when the latter came to power in 1933, Heuss was dismissed from his professorship and his books were publicly burnt. Nevertheless, he continued to write them in retirement at Heidelberg under the pseudonym of ' Brackenheim ' until 1946, when he became founder member of the Free Democratic Party, professor at Stuttgart and helped to draft the new federal constitution. He was president (1949–59) and in that capacity paid a state visit to Britain in October 1958, the first German head of state to do so since 1907. Albert Schweitzer officiated when Heuss in 1907 married **Elly Knapp** (1881–1951), social scientist and author. See his autobiographical *Vorspiele* (1954).

HEVELIUS, Johannes, *he-vay'lee-us* (1611–1687), German astronomer, born at Danzig, established the foremost observatory there in 1641 and built another when the first was burnt down in 1679. He catalogued 1500 stars, discovered four comets and was one of the first to observe the transit of Mercury. He gave names to many lunar features in *Selenographia* (1647) and argued with Hooke over types of telescopic sights.

HEVESY, George de, *he-vay'shee* (1885–1966), Hungarian-Swedish chemist, born in Budapest, discovered with Coster in 1923 the element *hafnium* at Copenhagen. He was a professor of Freiburg University from 1926, but during World War II went to Sweden, where he became professor at Stockholm. He was awarded the Nobel prize (1943) for his work on radioisotope indicators.

HEWITSON, William Chapman (1806–78), English naturalist, born at Newcastle-on-Tyne, from 1848 at Oatlands Park, Surrey, collected, depicted and wrote about butterflies, birds' eggs, &c. His collection is in the Natural History Museum, Kensington.

HEWLETT, Maurice Henry (1861–1923), English novelist, poet and essayist, born in London, keeper of land revenue records (1896–1900), made his name by his historical romance *The Forest Lovers* (1898); but his poem *The Song of the Plow* (1916) is perhaps his best work.

HEYDRICH, Reinhard, *hī'drikH*, ' the hangman ' (1904–42), Nazi terrorist and deputy-chief of the Gestapo, born at Halle, as a youth joined the violent anti-Weimar ' Free Corps ', in 1931 had to quit the navy, and, turning Nazi, rose to be second-in-command of the secret police, and presently was charged with subduing Hitler's war-occupied countries. In 1941 he was made deputy-protector of Bohemia and Moravia, but next year was struck down in his terror career by Czech assassins. In the murderous reprisals, Lidice village was razed and every man put to death.

HEYERDAHL, Thor, *hī'-* (1914–), Norwegian anthropologist, was educated at the University of Oslo. He served with the free Norwegian military forces from 1940 to 1945. Impressed by the fact that certain aspects of Polynesian culture recall features of that of the pre-Inca inhabitants of Peru, he set out to prove, by sailing a balsa raft from Callao, Peru, to Tuamotu Island in the South Pacific that the Peruvian Indians could have settled in Polynesia. His success in this venture, as well as his less spectacular archaeological expedition to Easter Island, won him popular fame and several distinguished awards. See his *On the Hunt for Paradise* (1938), *The Kon-Tiki Expedition* (1948), *Aku-Aku* (1958), &c., and A. Jacoby, *Senor Kon Tiki* (1968).

HEYLIN, Peter (1599–1662), English divine and historian, born at Burford, Oxfordshire, was deprived of his preferments under the Commonwealth, but after the Restoration became subdean of Westminster. He wrote a Life of Laud, cosmographies, histories of England, of the Reformation, and of the Presbyterians, and anti-Puritan pamphlets.

HEYMANS, Corneille, *hī'mahns* (1892–1968), French-Belgian physiologist, born at Ghent, where he became professor of Pharmacodynamics. He developed the technique of ' cross circulation ' of blood and was awarded the Nobel prize (1938) for his work on the sinus aorta. In 1950 he discovered that pressoreceptors (special nerve endings) monitor blood pressure.

HEYN, Piet. See HEIJN.

HEYNE, Christian Gottlob, *hī'nė* (1729–1812), German classical philologist, born at Chemnitz, in 1763 became professor of Eloquence at Göttingen, which university he made pre-eminent for classical studies. He edited Virgil, Pindar, Apollodorus and Homer's *Iliad* (1802). See Carlyle's *Miscellanies.*

HEYROVSKY, Jaroslav, *hī-rof'skee* (1890–1967), Czech chemist, discovered in 1922 polarographic analysis and developed the method for application to high-purity substances. For this he won the Nobel prize for chemistry in 1959, the first Czech national to gain a Nobel award.

HEYSE, Paul Johann von, *hī'zė* (1830–1914), German writer, was born in Berlin, and settled at Munich in 1854. In 1910 he received a Nobel prize and was ennobled. He excelled as a short-story teller, his *novellen* being marked by a graceful style, sly humour and often sensuality. These were collected in *Das Buch der Freundschaft* (1883–84) and other volumes. He also wrote novels, plays and epic poems and translations of Italian poets. See study by Mitchell (1916).

HEYWOOD, (1) **John** (*c.* 1497–*c.* 1580), English epigrammatist, playwright and musician, was born perhaps in London, perhaps at North Mimms, perhaps at Stock Harvard (Essex). After studying at Oxford, he was introduced at court by Sir Thomas More, who was a distant cousin by marriage, and made himself, by his wit and his skill in singing and playing on the virginals, a favourite with Henry VIII and with Mary, to whom he had been music teacher in her youth. He was a devout Catholic, and after the accession of Elizabeth went to Belgium, where he died. He wrote several short plays or interludes, whose individual characters represent classes, as the Pedlar, the Pardoner, and the like. They thus form a link between the old moralities and the modern drama. He is remembered above all, however, for his collections of proverbs and epigrams. His wearisome allegorical poem, *The Spider and the Flie*, contrasts Catholicism and Protestantism. He was the grandfather of John Donne (q.v.). See books by A. W. Reed (1917, 1918), De la Bère (1937).

(2) **Thomas** (*c.* 1574–1641), English dramatist and poet, born in Lincolnshire, was educated at Cambridge, and was writing plays by 1596. In 1598 he was engaged by Philip Henslowe as an actor. Down to 1633 he had a large share in the composition of 220 plays. He was also the author of an

historical poem, *Troja Britannica* (1609); an *Apology for Actors* (1612); *Nine Bookes of Various History concerning Women* (1624); a long poem, *The Hierarchie of the Blessed Angells* (1635); a volume of rhymed translations from Lucian, Erasmus, Ovid, &c.; various pageants, tracts and treatises; and *The Life of Ambrosius Merlin* (1641). Twenty-four of Heywood's plays have come down. The best is *A Woman Kilde with Kindnesse* (1607), a domestic tragedy; and with this may be coupled *The English Traveller* (1633). His work is usually distinguished by naturalness and simplicity. In the two parts of *The Fair Maid of the West* (1631), and in *Fortune by Land and Sea* (1655), partly written by William Rowley, he gives us some spirited descriptions of sea fights. *The Rape of Lucreece* (1608) is chiefly noticeable for its songs; *Love's Maistresse* (1636) is fanciful and ingenious; and there is much tenderness in *A Challenge for Beautie* (1636). In *The Royall King and Loyall Subject* (1637) the doctrine of passive obedience to kingly authority is stressed. *The Captives* (1624) was first published by Bullen (1885). See A. Melville Clark's study (1931) and bibliography (1924).

HIBBERT, Robert (1770–1849), British merchant, born in Jamaica, in 1847 founded the Hibbert Trust, whose funds, in 1878 applied to the Hibbert Lectures, also aid the *Hibbert Journal* (1902 ff.). See *The Book of the Hibbert Trust* (1933).

HICHENS, Robert Smythe (1864–1950), English novelist, son of a canon of Canterbury, studied music, but made his name as a novelist in *The Green Carnation* (1894), *The Garden of Allah* (1905), *The Call of the Blood* (1906), *The Paradine Case* (1933), *That Which is Hidden* (1939), &c.

HICKES, George (1642–1715), English nonjuror and philologist, born at Newsham, near Thirsk, was educated at Oxford, in 1683 became Dean of Worcester, as a nonjuror was deprived of his deanery in 1690, and in 1694 was consecrated nonjuring Bishop of Thetford. He published works in controversial and practical divinity, a *Thesaurus Linguarum Veterum Septentrionalium* (1705), and a grammar of Anglo-Saxon and Moeso-Gothic (1689).

HICKS, (1) Sir Edward Seymour (1871–1949), British actor-manager and author, born in Jersey, made his début at Islington in 1887 and built up a reputation as a light comedian, appearing in many successful plays written by himself, including *The Man in Dress Clothes, The Gay Gordons, Vintage Wine*, &c. He wrote several books of reminiscences. He was knighted in 1935.

(2) **Elias** (1748–1830), American Quaker preacher, born at Hempstead, Long Island, by his Unitarianism split the American Society into Orthodox and Hicksite Friends. See his *Journal* (1828) and *Letters* (1834), and Life by Forbush (1956).

(3) **William, 'Hicks Pasha'** (1830–83), British officer in command of the Egyptian forces annihilated by the Mahdi at El Obeid in November 1883.

HIERO, *hī'ér-o*, name of two tyrants (kings) of Syracuse:

Hiero I, king (478–467 B.C.), won a great naval victory over the Etruscans in 474. Though violent and rapacious, he was a lover of poetry, and the patron of Simonides, Aeschylus, Bacchylides, and Pindar.

Hiero II, king (269–215 B.C.), son of a noble Syracusan, came to the front during the troubles in Sicily after the retreat of Pyrrhus (275 B.C.), and in 269 was elected king of the Syracusans. He joined the Carthaginians in besieging Messana, which had surrendered to the Romans; but was beaten by Appius Claudius. In 263 he concluded a fifteen years' peace with Rome, and in 258 a permanent one. In the second Punic war Hiero supported the Romans with money and troops. He died in 215. He was a patron of the arts, and Archimedes was his relative and friend.

HIEROCLES, *hī-er'o-kleez* (5th cent. A.D.), Neoplatonist philosopher of Alexandria, is usually reckoned the author of a commentary on the ' Golden Verses ' of Pythagoras.

HIERONYMUS. See JEROME.

HIGDEN, Ralph (d. 1364), English chronicler, was a Benedictine monk of St Werburgh's monastery in Chester. He wrote the *Polychronicon*, a general history from the creation to about 1342, which was continued by others to 1377. An English translation of the *Polychronicon* by John Trevisa was printed by Caxton in 1482. See the edition by Babington and Lumby in the Rolls series (1865–86).

HIGGINS, (1) Matthew James, called ' **Jacob Omnium** ' (1810–68), British controversialist, was born at Benown Castle, County Meath. His intellectual force, his humour and irony, were enlisted in the warfare against the abuses and minor evils of social and public life by means of letters and articles to the press. He stood 6 feet 8 inches high. See Memoir by Sir W. Stirling Maxwell, prefixed to his *Essays on Social Subjects* (1875).

(2) **William** (1769–1825), Irish chemist, born at Sligo, professor at the Royal Dublin Society (1800), anticipated Dalton by his application of the atomic theory to chemistry (1791). He was elected F.R.S. (1806).

HIGGINSON, Thomas Wentworth (1823–1911), American writer, born at Cambridge, Massachusetts, was ordained to the ministry, from which he retired in 1858. Meanwhile he had been active in the antislavery agitation, and, with others, had been indicted for the murder of a man killed during an attempt to rescue a fugitive slave, but had escaped through a flaw in the indictment. In the Civil War he commanded the first regiment raised from among former slaves; in 1880–81 was a member of the Massachusetts legislature. His books include, besides histories of the United States, *Outdoor Papers* (1863), *Army Life in a Black Regiment* (1870), *Oldport Days* (1873), *Common-Sense about Women* (1881), *Hints on Writing and Speech-making* (1887) and *Concerning All of Us* (1892).

HILARION, St (c. 290–372), founder of the monastic system in Palestine, was educated at Alexandria, lived as a hermit in the desert between Gaza and Egypt, and died in Cyprus.

HILARY, St (c. 300–c. 368), was born of pagan parents at Limonum (Poitiers), and did not become a Christian till he was advanced in life. About 350 he was elected Bishop of Poitiers, and immediately rose to the first place in the Arian controversy. His principal work is that on the Trinity, but his three addresses to the Emperor Constantius are remarkable for the boldness of their language. His feast day is 13th January, which also marks the beginning of an Oxford term and English law sittings to which his name is consequently applied. See German Lives by Reinkens (1864) and Baltzer (1881), a French one by Barbier (1887), and an English by Cazenove (1883); also French study by P. Smulders (1944).

HILARY OF ARLES, St (c. 403–49), educated at Lerins, became Bishop of Arles in 429. He presided at several synods, especially that of Orange in 441, whose proceedings involved him in a serious controversy with Pope Leo the Great. His feast is observed on 5th May.

HILBERT, David (1862–1943), German mathematician, professor at Königsberg (1893) and Göttingen (1895), made important contributions to the theory of numbers, the theory of invariants and the application of integral equations to physical problems. He also critically examined the foundations of geometry in *Grundlagen der Geometrie* (1899).

HILDA, St (614–80), English abbess, the daughter of a nephew of Edwin of Northumbria, was baptized at thirteen by Paulinus. In 649 she became abbess of Hartlepool; in 657 founded the famous monastery at Streaneshalch or Whitby, a double house for nuns and monks, over which she ruled wisely for twenty-two years.

HILDEBRAND, (1). See BEETS.
(2). See GREGORY VII.
(3) Adolf (1847–1921), German sculptor, born at Harburg, sought a renaissance of classical realism in his public monuments to Brahms at Meiningen, Bismarck at Bremen, Schiller at Nuremberg, &c., and founded a new school of art criticism by his *Das Problem der Form* (1893).

HILL, (1) Aaron (1685–1750), English poet, dramatist and speculator, one of the victims of Pope in the *Dunciad*, was born and died in London.
(2) Archibald Vivian (1886–   ), English biochemist, born in Bristol, from 1926–51 was Foulerton research professor of the Royal Society. He was elected F.R.S. in 1918, shared the Nobel prize for physiology with Meyerhof (1922) for his researches into heat loss in muscle contraction. He organized air defence in World War II and was M.P. for Cambridge (1940–45). His works include *Muscular Movement in Man* (1927).
(3) George Birkbeck (1835–1903), English writer, nephew of (9), till 1876 headmaster of Bruce Castle School, Tottenham, was an authority on the life and works of Dr Johnson, edited letters of Boswell and Hume, and wrote on General Gordon in Africa.
(4) James Jerome (1838–1916), American railway magnate, born in Canada, moved to St Paul, Minn., in 1856, where he entered the transportation business. He took over the St Paul-Pacific line and extended it to link with the Canadian system, later gaining control of the Northern Pacific Railroad

after a stock exchange battle with Edward H. Harriman. He was also active in the construction of the Canadian Pacific Railroad. See Life by Pyle.
(5) Sir Leonard Erskine (1866–1952), English physiologist, educated in London, became director of research at the St John Clinic and devised the kata-thermometer to measure air cooling.
(6) Octavia (1838–1912), British housing reformer and founder of the National Trust, born in London, laboured amongst the London poor under F. D. Maurice, and in 1864, supported by Ruskin, commenced her great work of improving the homes of working men in the slums. She wrote *Homes of the London Poor* (1875), *Our Common Land* (1878), &c. See Lives by C. E. Maurice (1913) and E. Moberly Bell (1942).
(7) Rowland (1744–1833), English popular preacher, was the son of a Shropshire Baronet. At St John's College, Cambridge, he was influenced by Whitefield, and from his ordination in 1773 till 1783 he was an itinerant preacher; thereafter he made his headquarters at Surrey Chapel, Blackfriars Road, London, built by himself. It is said that the first London Sunday school was his. His *Village Dialogues* (1801) sold in vast numbers. See Lives by Sidney (1834) and Charlesworth (1886).
(8) Rowland Hill, 1st Viscount (1772–1842), British general, born at Prees Hall, Shropshire, distinguished himself under Abercromby in Egypt and under Wellington in the Peninsular War, at Waterloo swept the Old Guard from the field, and in 1828 succeeded Wellington as commander-in-chief at home, but resigned in 1842. See Life by E. Sidney (1845).
(9) Sir Rowland (1795–1879), English originator of penny postage, uncle of (3), was born at Kidderminster, and till 1833 was a teacher, noted for his system of school self-discipline. He was one of the founders of the Society for the Diffusion of Useful Knowledge (1826), interested himself in the socialistic schemes of Robert Owen, and took an active share in the colonization of South Australia. In his *Post-office Reform* (1837) he advocated a low and uniform rate of postage, to be prepaid by stamps, between places in the British Isles; and on January 10, 1840, a uniform penny rate was introduced. In 1846, the Liberals made him secretary to the postmaster general and in 1854 secretary to the Post Office. He established the book-post (1848), and reformed the money order office (1848) and the packet service. In 1864 he resigned and was given a pension and a parliamentary grant. In a report of 1867 he advocated national ownership of railways. He was buried in Westminster Abbey. See Lives by his daughter (1907) and his nephew (3) (1880).

HILLARY, Sir Edmund (1919–   ), New Zealand mountaineer and explorer, educated at Auckland Grammar School. After specializing as an apiarist, he took part in Himalayan climbs and in the British Cho Oyu expedition of 1952. As a member of Col. John Hunt's Everest expedition he attained, with Sherpa Tensing, the summit of Mount Everest on May 29, 1953, for which achievement he was knighted. With a New Zealand expeditionary party he reached the South Pole, the first man to do so overland since Captain Scott, on January 3, 1958. He flew back to Scott Base, then went out to join Sir Vivian Fuchs (q.v.) at Depot 700, and together they made their way overland to Scott Base, which they reached on March 2. See his joint accounts, *East of Everest* (with George Lowe, 1956) and *The Crossing of Antarctica* (with Sir V. Fuchs, 1958).

HILLEL, surnamed **Hababli** ' the Babylonian ' and **Hazaken**, ' the Elder ' (*c*. 60 B.C.–A.D. 10), one of the greatest doctors of the Jewish law, was born in Babylonia, and, at the age of forty came to Palestine, where he was chosen president of the Sanhedrin. See Delitzsch's *Jesus und Hillel* (3rd ed. 1879).

HILLER, (1) **Ferdinand** (1811–85), German pianist and composer, born at Frankfurt-am-Main, wrote books on harmony, Beethoven (1871) and Mendelssohn (1874).

(2) **Johann Adam** (1728–1804), a German composer of operettas. See Life by Peiser (1894).

HILLIARD, **Nicholas** (1537–1619), English court goldsmith and miniaturist, was born at Exeter. He worked for Queen Elizabeth and James I and founded the English school of miniature painting. See monographs by G. Reynolds (1947) and J. Pope-Hennessy (1949).

HILLIER, **Tristram Paul** (1905–   ), British artist, born in Peking. He studied at the Slade School and under André Lhote in Paris. Many of his paintings are of ships and beaches, the earlier ones of a surrealist character; he has lived much in France, particularly in Dieppe, and his craftsmanship and smooth handling of paint are such that his oil paintings are often mistaken for tempera. See his autobiographical *Leda and the Goose* (1954).

HILTON, (1) **James** (1900–54), English novelist, born at Leigh, Lancashire. Educated at Leys School, Cambridge, and Christ's College, Cambridge, he quickly established himself as a writer, his first novel, *Catherine Herself* being published in 1920. His success was dual, for many of his novels were filmed —*Knight without Armour* (1933), *Lost Horizon* (1933), awarded the Hawthornden Prize in 1934, *Goodbye, Mr Chips* (1934), *Random Harvest* (1941). He settled in the U.S. in 1935 and died in California.

(2) **Walter** (d. 1396), English mystic and writer, was an Augustinian canon of Thurgarton, Notts, author of *The Ladder of Perfection* and possibly *The Cloud of Unknowing*, two books important in the history of English prose. See R. W. Chambers, *The Continuity of English Prose* (1932).

HIMMLER, **Heinrich** (1900–45), German Nazi leader and notorious chief of police, was born in Munich, educated at the Landshut High School, and joined the army. In 1919 he studied at the Munich Technical College, found employment in a nitrate works and turned to poultry farming. An early Nazi, he was flag bearer in the Munich putsch (1923). In 1929 Hitler made him head of the S.S. (*Schutzstaffel*, protective force) which he

developed from Hitler's personal bodyguard into a powerful party weapon. With Heydrich, he used it to carry out the assassination of Röhm (1934) and other Nazis opposed to Hitler. Inside Germany and later in Nazi war-occupied countries, he unleashed through his secret police (*Gestapo*) an unmatched political and anti-Semitic terror of espionage, wholesale detention, mass deportation, torture, execution, massacre, and by his systematic ' liquidation ' of whole national and racial groups initiated the novel and barbarous crime of genocide. In 1943 he was given the post of minister of the Interior to curb any defeatism. After the attempt on Hitler by the army in July 1944, he was made commander-in-chief of the home forces, into which he henceforth recruited mere boys. His pathetic offer of unconditional surrender to the Allies, but excluding Russia, having failed, he disappeared but was captured by the British near Bremen. By swallowing a cyanide phial concealed in his mouth, he escaped the justice he so richly deserved as the pioneer of the horror of the gas oven and the concentration camp and as the cold-blooded butcher of over seven million people. See Life by W. Frischauer (1953), Lord Russell, *Scourge of the Swastika* (1954), and study by Manvell and Fraenkel (1965), and bibliography under HITLER.

HINCMAR (*c*. 806–882), French churchman of the family of the Counts of Toulouse, educated in the monastery of St Denis, was Abbot of Compiègne and St Germain, and in 845 was elected Archbishop of Reims. He helped to degrade and imprison Gottschalk (who died in 868 after eighteen years' captivity) for his predestinarian views; strenuously opposed Adrian II's attempts by church censures to compel obedience in imperial politics; and with equal firmness resisted the emperor's intruding unworthy favourites into benefices. See Life by Pritchard (1849).

HIND, **John Russell**, *hīnd* (1823–95), English astronomer, born at Nottingham, in 1844 at the George Bishop's observatory, Regent's Park, London, calculated the orbits of seventy planets and comets, noted new stars, and discovered ten minor planets (1817–54).

HINDEMITH, **Paul**, *hin'dĕ-mit* (1895–1963), German composer, born at Hanau, ran away from home at the age of eleven because of his parents' opposition to a musical career and earned a living by playing all manner of instruments in cafés, cinemas and dance halls, studied at Hoch's Conservatoire at Frankfurt and from 1915 to 1923 was leader of the Frankfurt Opera Orchestra, which he often conducted. He also played the viola in the famous Amar quartet (1922–29), with which he toured Europe. Through the Donaueschingen Festivals (1921–24) he established a reputation as composer. His early *Kammermusik*, notably his concerto for piano and five solo instruments (1925), reveals a trend towards neoclassicism, continued in the operas *Cardillac* (1926), based on a story by E. T. A. Hoffmann, in which he contrives a complete separation between music and action, and *Neues vom Tage* (1929), an operatic satire on the modern press, which inverts all the romantic associations of Wagnerian opera. One scene, set in a lady's bathroom, particularly shocked Nazi sensibilities. In 1927 he had been appointed professor at the Berlin High School for Music and in 1929 appeared as solo violist in the first performance in London of Walton's Viola Concerto, which profoundly influenced Hindemith's own *Philharmonic Concerto* (1932). With the *Konzertmusik*, comprising the violin concerto (1930), and *Das Unaufhörliche*, 'perpetual' second string trio (1933), Hindemith's work passed into a transitional phase. Although he never espoused atonality with its arbitrary divisions, he based himself on the chromatic scale, relating the notes acoustically around one key note. He also launched out into *Gebrauchsmusik*, i.e., pieces written with specific utilitarian aims such as for children's entertainment, newsreels, community singing, such as the *Plöner Musiktag* (1932), which dispenses with as many directions as possible. The Nazis banned his politically-pointed *Mathis der Maler* symphony (1934; opera 1938) despite Furtwängler's defence, and Hindemith went to live in Turkey, and in Britain, where he composed the *Trauermusik* for viola and strings (1936) on George V's death, and the ballet *Nobelissima Visione* (1938) on St Francis's conversion. He taught in the U.S.A. from 1939. His later mellower compositions include the *Symphonic Metamorphosis of Themes by Weber* (1944) and the requiem based on Walt Whitman's commemorative *For Those We Love* (1944). In 1947 he was appointed professor at Yale and in 1953 at Zürich, where he composed his great opera on Kepler's Life, *Die Harmonie der Welt* (1957). See his *The Craft of Musical Composition* (1945), and Life by H. Strobel (Mainz 1948).

HINDENBURG, Paul von Beneckendorff und von (1847–1934), German soldier and president, born at Posen of a Prussian Junker family, was educated at the cadet schools at Wahlstatt and Berlin, fought at the battle of Königgrätz (1866) and in the Franco-Prussian war (1870–71), rose to the rank of general (1903) and retired in 1911. Recalled at the outbreak of the first World War, he and Ludendorff won decisive victories over the Russians at Tannenberg (1914) and at the Masurian Lakes (1915). His successes against the Russians were not, however, repeated on the western front, and in the summer of 1918 he was obliged to supervise the retreat of the German armies. A national hero and ' father figure ', he was president of the German Republic (1925–34). He did not oppose Stresemann's enlightened foreign policy, but neither did he oppose the rise of Hitler, whom he defeated in the presidential election (1932) and who became chancellor in 1933. But such was his influence, that Hitler was unable to overthrow constitutional government until his death. See Lives by Goldsmith and Voigt (1930), Watson (1930), and studies by Olden (1948; critical) and Goerlitz (1953).

HINDLIP, Lord. See ALLSOPP.

HINKSON, Mrs. See TYNAN.

HINSHELWOOD, Sir Cyril Norman (1897–1967), English chemist, born in London,

Dr Lee's professor of Chemistry at Oxford (1937–64), and senior research fellow at Imperial College from 1964, simultaneously with Semenov investigated chemical reaction kinetics in the interwar years, for which they shared the Nobel prize for chemistry in 1956. A considerable linguist and classical scholar, he had the unique distinction of being president of both the Royal Society (from 1955) and of the Classical Association in 1960. He was knighted in 1948 and awarded the O.M. in 1960.

HINSLEY, Arthur (1865–1943), English cardinal, born at Selby, Yorks, rector of the English College at Rome from 1917 to 1928, Archbishop of Westminster from 1935, was made a cardinal in 1937.

HINTON, Sir Christopher, Baron Hinton of Bankside (1901–), English nuclear engineer, born at Tisbury, Wiltshire, when an apprentice in a railway workshop won a scholarship to Cambridge and rose to chief engineer of the alkali division of I.C.I. at Norwich (1931–1940). During World War II he supervised explosives filling stations. From 1946, as deputy director of atomic energy production, he virtually created a new industry in Britain with the construction of the world's first large-scale commercial atomic power station at Calder Hall, opened in 1956, which successfully combines the production of electricity with that of radioactive plutonium at the neighbouring gas-cooled atomic reactor at Windscale, Cumberland. From 1954 he was managing director of the newly formed industrial group of the U.K. Atomic Energy Authority. He was elected F.R.S. in 1954, knighted in 1951, became a K.B.E. in 1957, and was created a life peer in 1965.

HIPPARCHUS, hi-pahr'kus (fl. 160–125 B.C.), Greek astronomer, born at Nicaea in Bithynia, carried out observations at Rhodes. He discovered the precession of the equinoxes and the eccentricity of the sun's path, determined the length of the solar year, estimated the distances of the sun and moon from the earth, drew up a catalogue of 1080 stars, fixed the geographical position of places by latitude and longitude, and invented trigonometry.

HIPPER, Franz von (1863–1932), German admiral, commander at the Dogger Bank (1915) and Jutland (1916). See Life by H. von Waldeyer-Hartz.

HIPPIAS and HIPPARCHUS. See PISISTRATUS.

HIPPOCRATES, hi-pok'ra-teez, (1) (d. *c.* 485 B.C.), tyrant of Gela 492, made it the dominant city of Sicily.

(2) (*c.* 460?–377 or 359 B.C.), the most celebrated physician of antiquity, was born and practised in the Greek island of Cos. Of 72 ascribed works these seem genuine: *Prognostica*; *Aphorismi* (perhaps not all); *De Morbis Popularibus*; *De Ratione Victus in Morbis Acutis*; *De Aëre, Aquis, et Locis*; and *De Capitis Vulneribus*. Hippocrates seems to have gathered up all that was sound in the past history of medicine, was good at diagnosis and prognosis, and believed that the four fluids or humours of the body (blood, phlegm, yellow bile and black bile) are the primary seats of disease. His

professional ethics survive in the medical Hippocratic oath. See *Hippocratic Wisdom*, ed. Peterson (1946).

HIPPOCRATES OF CHIOS (5th cent. B.C.), Greek geometer, gives his name to the lunules of Hippocrates.

HIPPOLYTUS, St, *hi-pol'i-tus*, antipope (170–235), theological writer in Greek at Rome, defended the doctrine of the Logos and attacked the Gnostics. He was with Irenaeus in Gaul in A.D. 194, was a presbyter at Rome, and in 217 became antipope in opposition to the heretical (Monarchian) Calixtus. The schism lasted till 235, when Hippolytus and the successor of Calixtus were both deported to Sardinia, and there Hippolytus died. He is generally believed to be the author of a *Refutation of all Heresies* in ten books, discovered in 1842 in a 14th century MS. at Mount Athos. He wrote also a smaller work against heretics extant in a Latin translation. The so-called *Canons of Hippolytus* are more probably Graeco-Egyptian in origin.

HIROHITO, *hir-ō-hee'tō* (1901–), emperor of Japan, the 124th in direct lineage, was the first Japanese prince to visit the West in 1921. He acceded in 1926 and his reign was marked by rapid militarization and the aggressive wars against China (1931–32) and (1937–45) and against the United States (1941–45), which ended with the two atomic bombs at Hiroshima and Nagasaki. Under American occupation, Hirohito in 1946 renounced his legendary divinity and most of his powers. Now a democratic constitutional monarch. See Life by Mosley (1966).

HIROSHIGE Ando, *hi-ro-shee'gay* (1797–(1858), Japanese *Ukiyoye* painter, celebrated for his impressive landscape colour prints, executed in a freer but less austere manner than his greater contemporary, Hokusai (q.v.). His *Fifty-three Stages of the Tokaido* had a great influence on western Impressionist painters, but heralded the decline of *Ukiyoye* (wood block print design) art. See study by E. F. Strange (1925).

HIRSCH, (1) **Baron Maurice de** (1831–96), German Jewish financier, millionaire, and philanthropist, born in Munich, amassed a fortune in Balkan railway contracts.

(2) **Samson Raphael** (1808–88), Jewish theologian, born at Hamburg, leader of the modern revival of orthodox Judaism.

HIS, Wilhelm (1831–1904), Swiss biologist, born at Basel, professor of Anatomy at Leipzig, introduced the microtome and pioneered developmental mechanics. His son **Wilhelm** (1863–1934) discovered the bundle of nerve fibres of the heart.

HISS, Alger (1904–), American State Department official, born in Baltimore, a former secretary to Justice Wendell Holmes (q.v.) and adviser at the Yalta conference (1945), stood trial twice (1949, 1950) on a charge of perjury, having denied before a Congressional Un-American Activities Committee that he had passed to Whittaker Chambers, an editor of *Time*, in 1938 an agent for an international Communist spy ring, 200 secret state documents. Many eminent Americans, including two supreme court judges, Adlai Stevenson and John

Foster Dulles, testified to Hiss's character, but he was convicted on a majority verdict at his second trial and sentenced to five years' imprisonment. The suspicions of the public, intensified by the subsequent Fuchs case in Britain, were fully exploited politically, not least by Senator Joseph McCarthy (q.v.). See *The Strange Case of Alger Hiss* by Earl Jowitt (1953).

HITCHCOCK, (1) **Alfred Joseph** (1899–), English film producer, began as junior technician in 1920 and by 1925 had graduated to motion picture director. An unexcelled master of suspense, he directed such films as *The Thirty-Nine Steps* (1935), *The Lady Vanishes* (1938), *Rebecca* (1940), *Dial M for Murder* (1954) and *Rear Window* (1955), &c., all of which exemplify the famous ' Hitchcock touch '.

(2) **Edward** (1793–1864), American geologist, born at Deerfield, Mass., professor of Chemistry at Amherst (1825–45), explored dinosaur tracks in Connecticut Valley.

HITLER, Adolf (1889–1945), German dictator, born April 20 at Braunau in Upper Austria, the son of a minor customs official, originally called Schicklgrüber, was educated at the secondary schools of Linz and Steyr, and destined by his father for the civil service. Little Adolf, however, saw himself as a great artist and perhaps purposely disgraced himself in his school leaving examinations. After his father's death he attended a private art school in Munich, but failed twice to pass into the Vienna Academy. Advised to try architecture, he was debarred for lack of a school leaving certificate. His rabid hatred of intellectuals and his later customary sneers at the ' gentlemen with diplomas ' originated at this juncture. He lived on his wits in Vienna (1904–13), making a precarious living by selling bad postcard sketches, beating carpets, and doing odd jobs with his doss-house companions whom he, lice-ridden and draped in a long black overcoat given to him by a Jewish tailor, thoroughly despised. He worked only fitfully and spent his time in passionate political arguments directed at the money-lending Jews and the trade unions, which he thought were the tools of the former. The Nazi philosophy expressed candidly in *Mein Kampf*, with his characteristic brutality, opportunism, contempt for the masses, distrust of even the closest intimates, fanatical strength of will and advocacy of the ' big lie ', was born in the gutters of Vienna. He dodged military service, and in 1913 emigrated to Munich, where he found employment as a draughtsman. In 1914 he volunteered for war service in a Bavarian regiment, rose to the rank of corporal and was recommended for the award of the Iron Cross for service as a runner on the western front. At the time of the German surrender in 1918 he was lying wounded, and temporarily blinded by gas, in hospital. In 1919, while acting as an informer for the army, spying on the activities of small political parties, he became the seventh member of one of them, the name of which he changed to National Socialist German Workers' Party (N.S.D.A.P.) in 1920. Its programme was a convenient mixture of mild radicalism bitter hatred of the politicians who had 'dishonoured Germany' by signing the Versailles *Diktat*, and clever exploitation of provincial grievances against the weak federal government. By 1923 Hitler was strong enough to attempt with General Ludendorff's and other extreme right-wing factions the overthrow of the Bavarian government. On November 9, the Nazis marched through the streets of Munich, Mussolini-style. But the police, with whom they had a tacit agreement, machine-gunned the Nazi column. Hitler narrowly escaped serious injury, Göring was badly wounded and sixteen storm troopers were killed. After nine months' imprisonment in Landsberg jail, during which he dictated his autobiography and political testament, *Mein Kampf* (1925; trans. 1939), to Rudolf Hess (q.v.), he began, with Göbbels, to woo the Ruhr industrialists, Krupp and others, and, although unsuccessful in the presidential elections of 1932 when he stood against Hindenburg, Hitler was made chancellor in January 1933 on the advice of von Papen, who thought that he could best be brought to heel inside the Cabinet. Hitler, however, soon dispensed with constitutional restraints. He silenced all opposition, and engineering successfully the burning of the *Reichstag* building February 1933, advertising it as a Communist plot, called for a general election, in which the police, under Göring, allowed the Nazis full play to break up the meetings of their opponents. Only under these conditions did the Nazi party achieve a bare majority, Hitler arrogating to himself absolute power through the Enabling Acts. Opposition inside his own party he ruthlessly crushed by the purge of June 1934 in which his rival Röhm and hundreds of influential Nazis were murdered at the hands of Hitler's bodyguard, the S.S., under Himmler and Heydrich. Hindenburg's convenient demise in August left Hitler sole master in Germany. Under the pretext of undoing the wrongs of the Versailles treaty and of uniting the German peoples and extending their living-space (*Lebensraum*) he openly rearmed (1935), sent troops into the demilitarized Rhineland zone, established the Rome-Berlin 'axis', October 1936, with Mussolini's Italy, created 'Greater Germany' by the invasion of Austria (1938), and by systematic infiltration and engineered incidents engendered a favourable situation for an easy absorption of the Sudeten or German-populated border lands of Czechoslovakia, to which Britain and France acquiesced at Munich, September 1938. Renouncing further territorial claims, Hitler nevertheless seized Bohemia and Moravia, took Memel from Lithuania and demanded from Poland the return of Danzig and free access to East Prussia through the 'Corridor'. Poland's refusal, backed by Britain and France, precipitated the second World War, on September 3, 1939. Meanwhile Hitler's domestic policy was one of thorough nazification of all aspects of German life, enforced by the Secret State Police (*Gestapo*), and the establishment of concentration camps for political opponents and Jews, who were systematically persecuted. Strategic roads or *Autobahnen* were built, Schacht's economic policy expanded German exports up to 1936, and then Göring's 'Guns before Butter' four-year plan boosted armaments and the construction of the Siegfried Line. Hitler entered the war with the grave misgivings of the German High Command, but as his 'intuitions' scored massive triumphs in the first two years, he more and more ignored the advice of military experts. Peace with Russia having been secured by *volte face*, Poland was invaded, and after three weeks' *Blitzkrieg* (lightning war) was divided between Russia and Germany. In 1940 Denmark, Norway, Holland, Belgium and France were occupied and the British expelled at Dunkirk. But Göring's invincible *Luftwaffe* was routed in the Battle of Britain (August–September 1940) and Hitler turned eastwards, entered Rumania (October 1940), invaded Yugoslavia and Greece (April 1941), and ignoring his pact of convenience with Stalin, attacked Russia and, as ally of Japan, found himself at war with the United States (December 1941). The *Wehrmacht* penetrated to the gates of Moscow and Leningrad, to the Volga, into the Caucasus and, with Italy as an ally since 1940, to North Africa as far as Alexandria. But there the tide turned and the corporal's strategy became more and more the fantasies of a lunatic. Montgomery's victory over Rommel at El Alamein (October 1942) and Paulus's grave defeat, through Hitler's misdirection, at Stalingrad (November 1942), heralded the Nazi withdrawal from North Africa pursued by the British and Americans (November 1942–May 1943). The Allied invasion of Sicily, Italian capitulation (September 1943) and engulfing Russian victories (1943–44) followed. The Anglo-American invasion of Normandy and the breaching of Rommel's 'Atlantic Wall' (June 1944) were not countered by Hitler's V1 and V2 guided missile attacks on southern England. He miraculously survived the explosion of the bomb placed at his feet by Colonel Stauffenberg, July 19, 1944, and purged the army of all suspects, including Rommel, who was given Hobson's choice to commit suicide. Rundstedt's counter-offensive against the Allies, in the Ardennes, December 1944, under Hitler's direction failed and the invasion of Germany followed. Hitler lived out his fantasies, commanding nonexistent armies from his *Bunker*, the air-raid shelter under the chancellory building in Berlin. With the Russians only several hundred yards away, he went through a grotesque marriage ceremony with his mistress, Eva Braun, in the presence of the Göbbels family, who then poisoned themselves. All available evidence suggests that Hitler and his wife committed suicide and had their bodies cremated on April 30, 1945. His much-vaunted 'Third Reich', which was to have endured for ever, ended ingloriously after twelve years of unparalleled barbarity, in which thirty million people lost their lives, twelve million of them far away from the battlefields, by mass shootings, in forced labour camps and in the gas ovens of Belsen, Dachau, Auschwitz, Ravensbrück and other concentration camps in accordance with Nazi racial theories and the ' New Order ', not forgetting the indiscriminate torture and murder of many prisoners-of-war,or the uprooting and extermination of entire village communities in Poland, France and Russia. Such horror prompted the international trial at Nuremberg (1945–46), at which twenty-one of the leading living Nazis were tried and eleven executed for carrying out the revolting crimes of the ' blood-thirsty guttersnipe ' as Churchill so aptly described him. See the latter's War Memoirs (6 vols. 1948–56), C. Wilmot, *The Struggle for Europe* (1952), A. J. P. Taylor, *Origins of the Second World War* (1963), biographical studies by Bullock (1953), of his youth by Kupizek (trans. 1954) and Jetzinger (trans. 1958), of his *Last Days* by Trevor-Roper (1947), who also edited *Hitler's Table Talk* (1953), and by his associates Hoffmann and Hanfstängl (trans. 1957), and Wheeler-Bennett, *Nemesis of Power* (1953).

HITOMARO, Kakinomoto no. See AKAHITO.

HITTORF, Johann Wilhelm (1824–1914), German chemist, born in Bonn, became professor at Münster, did research on electrolytes and studied the discharge of rarefied gases with the Hittorf tube.

HOADLY, Benjamin (1676–1761), English divine, born at Westerham, Kent, Bishop successively of Bangor (1715), Hereford (1721), Salisbury (1723) and Winchester (1734), and controversial writer, defending the cause of civil and religious liberty against both crown and clergy, and carrying on a controversy with Dr Atterbury on the obedience due to the civil power by ecclesiastics. A sermon before the king in 1717 sought to show that Christ had not delegated His powers to any ecclesiastical authorities. It led to the fierce Bangorian Controversy and incidentally to the indefinite prorogation of Convocation. His son published his *Works* (1773).

HOARE, (1) Sir Richard (1648–1718), English banker, born in London, became a Lombard Street goldsmith *c.* 1673 and moved *c.* 1693 to Fleet Street, where he founded the bank which still bears his name. He was knighted in 1702 and was lord mayor of London in 1713.

(2) Sir Samuel. See TEMPLEWOOD.

HOBART PASHA, properly August Charles Hobart-Hampden (1822–86), British sailor, third son of the sixth Earl of Buckinghamshire, was born at Waltham-on-the-Wolds, Leicestershire. He served in the British navy (1835–63) during the American Civil War as ' Captain Roberts ', repeatedly ran the blockade of the Southern ports, and afterwards became naval adviser to Turkey (1867) and was made pasha and admiral. In the Russo-Turkish war (1878) he commanded the Turkish Black Sea fleet. He wrote *Never Caught* (1867), on his blockade-running exploits, and *Sketches from My Life* (ed. by his widow, 1887).

HOBBEMA, Meindert, hob'- (1638–1709), Dutch landscape painter, born probably at Amsterdam, studied under Ruysdael and eventually became collector of the city's wine customs. He lacked his master's genius and range, contenting himself with florid, placid and charming watermill scenes. Neverthe-less, his masterpiece, *The Avenue, Middelharnis*, in the National Gallery, is a striking exception and has greatly influenced modern landscape artists. See study by G. Brouilhet (1938).

HOBBES, Thomas (1588–1679), English philosopher, born at Malmesbury prematurely on April 5, when his mother heard the news of the approaching Armada, was brought up by his uncle (his clergyman father having fled after striking a colleague at the church door), and at the age of fourteen, having translated Euripides' *Medea* into Latin iambics, he studied at Magdalen Hall, Oxford, where the prevailing Aristotelianism nauseated him. In 1603 he began his long tutorial association with the Cavendish family which brought with it the benefits of a superb library, the acquaintance of such men as Bacon and Ben Jonson, and two tutorial journeys to Italy and France. The first of these (1610) was with William, later the 2nd Earl of Devonshire, and the second with the latter's son the 3rd Earl, during which he was introduced into the Abbé Mersenne's intellectual circle in Paris (1634), which included Gassendi and Descartes. He met in Florence (1636) that famous refuter of Aristotelianism, Galileo. But it had been Hobbes's introduction to Euclidian geometry while travelling tutor to the son of Sir Gervase Clifton (1629–31) that was his intellectual turning-point. Would it not be possible to extend such deductive certainty to a comprehensive science of man and society? Hobbes, obsessed by the civil disorders of his time, wrote in 1640 *The Elements of Law* (not published until 1650) in which he defended the king's prerogative on psychological and not on the spurious theological grounds of Divine Right. When Parliament impeached Strafford and Laud, Hobbes took himself to Paris (1640), characteristically proud to have been ' the first of all that fled '. He was soon immersed in a controversy with Descartes, arising out of his objections to the latter's *Meditations*. The two philosophers did not meet until 1648, but he was on very friendly terms with Mersenne and Gassendi. In 1642 he published *De Cive*, a fuller statement of his views on government, and in 1646, *A Minute or First Draught of the Optiques*, by which he hoped to rival Descartes' writings on optics. In 1646 he became mathematical tutor to the Prince of Wales, later Charles II, at the exiled English court in Paris, and after a grave illness (1647) during which he received the Sacrament of Unction, he began the *Leviathan* (1651), the ' greatest, perhaps the sole, masterpiece of political philosophy in the English language '(Oakeshott 1955). The basis of Hobbes' metaphysics is motion of bodies, attraction and repulsion in the wills of men. ' Good ' and ' evil ' are inconstant names applied haphazardly by different men to what attracts or repels them. This egotistical psychology makes the life of man in a pre-social state of nature, ' nasty, brutish and short ', a constant war of everyman with everyman. Rational, enlightened self-interest makes men want to escape such a predicament by the establishment of a contract in which they surrender the right of aggression, but not that of self-defence, to an absolute sovereign, whose commands are the law, freedom being relegated to the spheres not covered by the sovereign's commands. The social contract is binding only so long as the sovereign has power to enforce it. Sovereignty may be vested in a person or an assembly, but it must be indivisible, not a division of powers between King and Parliament, church and state. The *Leviathan* offended the royal exiles at Paris and the French government by its reduction of the status of religious obedience, and so in 1652 Hobbes returned to England, made his submission to Cromwell and eventually settled in London. His writings engaged him in controversy for the remainder of his life ; with Bramhall over the problem of freedom ; with the Puritan mathematician Wallis who mercilessly showed up Hobbes' defective attempts at squaring the circle in *De Corpore* (1655) ; with the experimenters of the 'Invisible College ', which possibly accounted for his failure to be elected a fellow of the Royal Society. At the Restoration, Charles II gave his old tutor a pension and probably used his influence to quash a bill, aimed at Hobbes and his writings, after the Plague and Fire of London (1665–66) had been explained as being God's wrath against England for harbouring such an atheist. Hobbes wrote an important dialogue against the defenders of Common Law, *Behemoth*, a history of the times, an autobiography in Latin verse and at eighty-six, because, as he said, he had nothing better to do, verse translations of the *Iliad* and the *Odyssey*, all published in 1682. He died at Hardwick Hall, Derbyshire. Hobbes was both empiricist and rationalist. His political influence was much smaller than that of his later opponent Locke, but his political philosophy is of greater value, not because of the conclusions reached but for the manner in which he presented his argument. See Molesworth's edition of his works (1839–45), M. Oakeshott's Introduction to his edition of the *Leviathan* (1955), and studies by G. C. Robertson (1886), L. Stephen (1904), F. Brandt (trans. 1928), J. Laird (1934), L. Strauss (1934), R. S. Peters (1956) and H. Warrender (1957).

HOBBS, Sir John Berry (1882–1963), English cricketer, one of England's greatest batsmen, was born in Cambridge. He first played in county cricket for Cambridgeshire in 1904, for Surrey (1905–35) and for England (1907–1930), when he and Sutcliffe established themselves as an unrivalled pair of opening batsmen. He captained the English team in 1926, made 3636 runs, including 12 centuries, in test matches against Australia, and a record number of 197 centuries in first-class cricket, including the highest score at Lord's with 316 in 1926. He was knighted in 1953.

HOBHOUSE, (1) John Cam, 1st Baron Broughton (1786–1869), British statesman and friend of Byron, was educated at Westminster and Trinity College, Cambridge. His *Journey through Albania with Lord Byron* he published in 1813. He entered parliament as a Radical in 1820, succeeded as baronet in 1831, and in 1832–52 held various cabinet

Offices. He coined the term 'His Majesty's opposition '. See his *Recollections* (1909–12).

(2) **Leonard Trelawney** (1864–1929), British social philosopher and journalist, born at St Ives, Cornwall. A Fellow of Merton College, Oxford (1894), he joined the editorial staff of the *Manchester Guardian* in 1897 and transferred to the editorship of the *Sociological Review* in 1903. For the same period, 1903–05, he was secretary of the Free Trade Union and became political editor of *Tribune* (1906–07). From 1907 he was professor of Sociology at London University. His best known works are *Labour Movement* (1893), *Theory of Knowledge* (1896) and *Development and Purpose* (1913). He thought the key to evolution lay in ' conditioned teleology '.

HOBSON, (1) John Atkinson (1858–1940), English economist, born at Derby, graduated at Oxford. An opponent of orthodox economic theories, he believed ' underconsumption ' to be the main cause of unemployment. He wrote *The Science of Wealth* (1911), &c. See his *Confessions of an Economic Heretic* (1938).

(2) **Thomas** (c. 1544–1631), the rich Cambridge carrier who let no one pick and choose in his livery-stables—hence ' Hobson's choice '.

HOBY, Sir Thomas (1530–66), English translator of Castiglione's *Courtyer*, was half-brother to the Protestant diplomatist, **Sir Philip Hoby** (1505–58).

HOCCLEVE, or Occleve, Thomas (c. 1368–c. 1450), English poet, was a clerk in the privy seal office. His chief work is a free but tedious version of the *De Regimine Principum* of Aegidius Romanus, in Chaucer's seven-line stanza, edited by Wright (1860). His *Minor Poems* and *Regement of Princes* were edited by Furnivall (E.E.T.S.1892–97; vol. ii for 1892, ed. Gollancz, 1925).

HOCHE, Lazare, *ōsh* (1768–97), French Republican general, born at Montreuil, defended Dunkirk against the Duke of York and drove the Austrians out of Alsace (1793), ended the civil war in La Vendée (1795), commanded attempted invasion of Ireland (1796), defeated Austrians at Neuwied (1797). See Life by Font-Réaulx (1900).

HO CHI-MINH (Nguyen Van Thann) (1892–1969), Vietnamese political leader, born in Central Vietnam. From 1912 he visited London and the U.S.A. and lived in France from 1918, where he was a founder member of the Communist Party. From 1922 he was often in Moscow. He placed himself at the head of the Vietminh independence movement in 1941, and between 1946 and 1954 directed the successful military operations against the French, becoming prime minister (1954–55) and president in 1954 of North Vietnam. Re-elected in 1960, ' Uncle Ho ' was a leading force in the war between North (Viet Cong) and South (with American support) Vietnam during the 1960's. See Lives by Lacoutoure (Paris 1967, trans. 1968) and Halberstam (1971).

HOCKING, Joseph (1855–1937), born at St Stephens, Cornwall, from 1878 a land-surveyor, in 1884–1910 a Nonconformist minister, wrote many novels of a religious tendency. His elder brother, **Silas Kitto** (1850–1935), in 1870–96 also a minister, wrote many similar novels.

HODGE, Charles (1797–1878), American theologian, born in Philadelphia, in 1822 became professor in Princeton Theological Seminary. He founded and edited the *Princeton Review*, and wrote a history of the Presbyterian Church in America (1840), and the well-known *Systematic Theology* (1871–1872). See Lives by Patton (1888), and (1880) by his son, **Archibald Alexander** (1823–86), who succeeded his father at Princeton in 1878 and wrote *Outlines of Theology* (1860), &c.

HODGES, Courtney (1887–1966), American soldier, rose from private to general, and from August 1944 commanded the 1st Army throughout the European campaign.

HODGKIN, (1) Alan Lloyd (1914–), English physiologist, fellow of Trinity Coll., Cambridge, and lecturer at Cambridge (1945–52), Royal Society research professor from 1952, worked on radar (1939–1945) and with Huxley (2) explained nerve transmissions in physicochemical terms. Elected F.R.S. in 1948, he was awarded the 1963 Nobel prize for medicine and physiology (jointly with Huxley and Eccles) for research on nerve impulses.

(2) **Dorothy Crowfoot** (1910–), English chemist, Wolfson research professor at Royal Society since 1960 and fellow of Somerville Coll., Oxford. She was awarded the Nobel prize for chemistry in 1964 for discoveries by use of X-ray techniques of structure of important biological substances.

(3) **Thomas** (1798–1866), English pathologist, born at Tottenham, held various posts at Guy's Hospital and described the glandular disease, *lymphadenoma*, named after him.

(4) **Thomas** (1831–1913), English historian, author of *Italy and her Invaders* (8 vols. 1880–99), &c., was born of Quaker stock at Tottenham, and became a banker in Newcastle. His son, **Robert Howard** (1877–1951), born at Newcastle, wrote *A History of the Anglo-Saxons* (1935), &c.

HODGKINS, Frances Mary (1869–1947), British artist, was born and educated at Dunedin, N.Z., but thereafter spent little time in her native land, preferring European travel, with long sojourns in Paris and in England. Her paintings, examples of which are in the Tate Gallery and the Victoria and Albert Museum, are characterized by a harmonious use of flat colour somewhat reminiscent of Matisse, and though older than most of her circle she was ranked as a leader of contemporary romanticism.

HODGSON, (1) Brian Houghton (1800–95), English orientalist, born near Macclesfield, entered the East India Company's service in 1818, was resident in Nepal (1820–43) and settled in England in 1858. He wrote some 170 very valuable papers on the ethnology, languages and zoology of Nepal and Tibet, sent home 354 MSS., on which our knowledge of northern Buddhism is mainly based, and made a collection of 10,500 birds. He was elected F.R.S. in 1877. See the Life by Sir William Hunter (1896).

(2) **John Evan** (1831–95), English historical and genre painter, latterly of Moorish subjects, was elected R.A. in 1879 and in 1882 became Academy librarian and professor of Painting.

(3) **Ralph** (1871–1962), English poet, born in Yorkshire, became a journalist in London and published three volumes of Georgian poems with the recurring theme of nature and England, *The Last Blackbird* (1907) and *Poems* (1907 and 1917) containing ' The Song of Honour ', ' The Moor ', ' The Journeyman ' and the polemic against the destruction of animals for feminine vanity in ' To Deck a Woman '. He lectured in Japan (1924–38) and made his home in Ohio, U.S.A. An anthology of his works appeared as *The Skylark and Other Poems* (1958). He was awarded the Order of the Rising Sun (1938) and the Queen's Gold Medal (1954).

HODLER, Ferdinand (1853–1918), Swiss painter, born at Bern, studied under Barthélemy Menn and developed a highly decorative style of landscape, historical and genre painting with strong colouring and outline, sometimes using parallel *motifs* for effect. He died at Geneva. His works include the *Battle of Marignano*, *William Tell*, *Night*, *Day*, and many others at Bern, Zürich and elsewhere.

HODSON, William Stephen Raikes (1821–58), British soldier, born at Maisemore Court near Gloucester, joined the Indian army in 1845, served in the first Sikh war, and some years later, as commandant of the Guides, did excellent service on the Northwest frontier. But in 1856 he was deprived of his command for irregularities in the regimental accounts and unjust treatment of the natives. During the Mutiny he was head of the intelligence department before Delhi, and raised the irregular cavalry known as Hodson's Horse. On the fall of Delhi he discovered the Mogul and his sons; these last he shot with his own hand. He himself was shot on March 11 at Lucknow, and died the day after. See Lives by G. Hodson (1883) and L. T. Trotter (1901).

HOFER, (1) Andreas (1767–1810), Tirolese patriot peasant leader, was born at St Leonhard, and like his forefathers kept a small inn. When in 1809 he called the Tirolese to arms to expel the French and Bavarians, they responded with enthusiasm; in seven weeks he drove the Bavarians out. As the armistice after Wagram left Tirol unsupported, the French again invaded them; but in eight days Hofer routed the foe and retook Innsbruck, and for the next two months was ruler of his native land. By the peace of Vienna (October 14) Austria again left Tirol at the mercy of her enemies. Hofer once more took up arms; but this time the French and Bavarians were too strong for him; Hofer had to disband his followers and take refuge in the mountains. Two months later he was betrayed, captured, carried to Mantua, tried by court martial, and shot, February 20, 1810. See Lives by Weidinger (3rd ed. 1861), Heigel (1874), Stampfer (1874) and H. Schmölzer (1905).

(2) **Karl**, *hö'fer* (1878–1955), German artist, born at Karlsruhe, where he studied. He

spent many years in France and Italy and his work was much influenced by his war experiences; his severe style and harsh, brilliant colours express the bitterness of the times in symbolic terms. See study by Reifenberg (1924).

HOFF, Jacobus Henricus van't (1852–1911), Dutch chemist, a founder of physical chemistry and stereochemistry, born in Rotterdam, educated at the university of Leyden, became in 1876 assistant at the Veterinary College at Utrecht, and in 1877 professor of Chemistry at Amsterdam, Leipzig (1887) and Berlin (1895). He postulated the asymmetrical carbon atom, first applied thermodynamics to chemical reactions, discovered that osmotic pressure varies directly with the absolute temperature and investigated the formation of double salts. He was elected a foreign member of the Royal Society in 1897 and won the first Nobel prize for chemistry in 1901. See Life by Cohen (1913).

HÖFFDING, Harald (1843–1931), Danish philosopher, born in Copenhagen, wrote *Psykologi i Omrids på Grundlag af Erfaringen* ' Outlines of Psychology ' (1882) and *Den nyere Filosofis Historie* ' History of Modern Philosophy ' (1894; trans. 1900), &c.

HOFFMANN, (1) August Heinrich, called ' Hoffmann von Fallersleben ' (1798–1874), German poet and philologist, was born at Fallersleben in Lüneburg, and became keeper of the university library of Breslau, and professor of the German Language there from 1835. The publication of his *Unpolitische Lieder* (1842) cost him his chair. In 1860 he became librarian to the Duke of Ratibor at Korvei, where he died. He is best known for his popular and patriotic *Volkslieder*, including ' Alle Vögel sind schon da ' and the German national anthem; also some antiquarian works, *Horae Belgicae* (1830–62), &c. See his *Autobiography* (1868–1870) and Life by Wagner (1869–70).

(2) **Ernst Theodor Wilhelm,** called ' Amadeus ' (1776–1822), German writer, music critic and caricaturist, born in Königsberg. Trained as a lawyer, he had an unsettled career until 1816, when he attained a high position in the supreme court at Berlin. A remarkable essay on Mozart's *Don Giovanni*, the composition of an opera and the direction of the Bamberg theatre for two months (1808), testify to his real interests. He was the archpriest of ultra-German romanticism. His wit bubbled over in irony, ridicule, sarcasm; and his imagination was inexhaustible, but utterly undisciplined, wild and fantastic. His shorter tales were mostly published in the collections *Phantasiestücke* (1814), *Nachtstücke* (1817) and *Die Serapionsbrüder* (1819–25). His longer works include *Elixiere des Teufels* (1816; trans. 1824), *Seltsame Leiden eines Theaterdirektors* (1818), *Klein Zaches* (1819) and *Lebensansichten des Katers Murr* (1821–22), partly autobiographical. Three of his stories provided the basis for Offenbach's opera, *Tales of Hoffmann* (1881). See works by Harich (1921), Schaukal (1923), Heilborn (1926).

(3) **Friedrich** (1660–1742), German physician, professor of Medicine at Halle, and body physician to Frederick I of Prussia, introduced various medicines, including Hoffmann's drops and anodyne.

(4) **Heinrich** (1809–94), German author and illustrator of *Struwwelpeter* (1847), was a Frankfurt doctor.

(5) **Josef** (1870–1956), Austrian architect, born in Pirnitz, a leader of the secession from the traditional Viennese style and an exponent of the rectilinear type of design. He was founder of the *Wiener Werkstätte* in 1903. Perhaps his most noteworthy building is the Stoclet palace at Brussels. See study by A. Weiser (1930).

HOFMANN, August Wilhelm von (1818–92), German chemist, born at Giessen, became assistant there to Liebig. When the Royal College of Chemistry was established in London in 1845 Hofmann was made superintendent; and from 1856 to 1865 he was chemist to the royal mint. He went to Berlin as professor of Chemistry in 1865, and was ennobled in 1888. He obtained aniline from coal products, discovered many other organic compounds, including formaldehyde (1867), and devoted much labour to the theory of chemical types. See his *Chemische Erinnerungen* (1882) and German Life by Volhard and Fischer (1902).

HOFMANNSTHAL, Hugo von (1874–1929), Austrian poet and dramatist, born into a banking family in Vienna of Austro-Jewish-Italian origins. While still at school, he attracted attention by his symbolic, neo-romantic poems or ' lyrical dramas ' such as *Gestern*, *Der Tod des Tizian* and *Leben*, in which the transitory and elusive nature of life and its short-lived pleasures compel the quest for the world of the spirit. An emotional and intellectual crisis, a sudden awareness of the drying-up of his lyrical gifts, precipitated the ' Chandos Letters ' (1902), an imaginary correspondence between Lord Bacon and a young Elizabethan nobleman, in which Hofmannsthal, in the guise of the latter, gives his reasons for abandoning poetry, his new hatred for abstract terms, his doubts of the possibility of successful communication, &c. Henceforth he devoted himself to drama, most of his works being based on that of other dramatists: *Electra* (1903), *Das gerettete Venedig* (1905), and the morality plays *Jedermann* (1912) and *Das Salzburger grosse Welttheater* (1923). One of his major works is the comedy, *Der Schwierige* (1921). Having renounced Stefan George and his circle, Hofmannsthal turned to the composer, Richard Strauss, for whom he wrote the libretti for *Der Rosenkavalier* (1911), *Ariadne auf Naxos* (1912), *Die Frau ohne Schatten* (1919), &c., and with whom and Max Reinhardt, he was instrumental in founding the Salzburg Festival after World War I. His statue there was demolished by the Nazis in 1938. See studies by Heuschele (1929), Naef (1938), Brecht (1946), and Hammelmann (1957).

HOFMEISTER, Wilhelm Friedrich, *höf'mī-stĕr* (1824–77), German botanist, professor at Heidelberg then at Tübingen, did fundamental work on plant embryology. See Life by Goebel (trans. 1926).

HOFMEYR, Jan Hendrik (1845–1909), South African statesman, born in Cape Town, took to journalism, as 'Onze Jan' rose to be political leader of the Cape Dutch and dominated the Afrikander Bond. He represented the Cape at the Colonial Conferences of 1887 and 1894. After the Jameson Raid (1895) he parted from Rhodes, and thereafter worked outside parliament. See Life (1913) by Reitz and his nephew, Jan Hendrik (1894–1948), who was deputy premier to Smuts and advocated a liberal policy towards the African natives. See *his* Life by Paton (1965).

HOFSTADTER, Robert (1915–), U.S. scientist, born in New York, taught at Pennsylvania Univ. and Stanford where he became professor of Physics in 1954. He shared the 1961 Nobel award with Mössbauer for researches into atomic structure.

HOGAN, William (Ben) (1912–), U.S. golfer, born at Stephenville, Texas, began at the age of eleven as a caddie. A professional at various country clubs, he fought his way to the top despite financial difficulties and won innumerable competitions. In 1948 he became the first man in twenty-six years to win all three U.S. major titles and in 1953, after recovering from a bad car accident in 1949, won every major world championship.

HOGARTH, (1) David George (1862–1929), English archaeologist, keeper of the Ashmolean Museum (1909–27), excavated in Asia Minor, Syria, Egypt, &c.

(2) **William** (1697–1764), English painter and engraver, chiefly known for his anecdotal art, was born in Smithfield, London, November 10, the son of a teacher. Early apprenticed to a silverplate engraver, he studied painting under Sir James Thornhill, whose daughter he married, after eloping with her, in 1729. By 1720 he already had his own business, engraving coats-of-arms, shop-bills and book plates and painting-conversation pieces and portraits, including that of *Sarah Malcolm*, the triple murderess (1732–33; Nat. Gal., Edinburgh). But tiring of conventional art forms, he resurrected the 'pictured morality' of medieval art by his 'modern moral subjects', often comprising several pictures in a series, but unlike the modern strip cartoon, each artistically and representationally self-sufficient. The first of these was *A Harlot's Progress* (1730–31), destroyed by fire (1755). With an unerring eye for human foibles, he was often forthright to the point of coarseness, but although his didactic purpose was unmistakable, seldom indulged in melodrama. A remarkable technical memory allowed him to dispense with preliminary sketches. His taste for the rococo 'serpentine line of beauty' admirably suited his crowded canvases with their revealing details and pointed 'subplots'. Single works such as *Southwark Fair* and the superbly-captured atmosphere of a stag party entitled *A Midnight Modern Conversation* (both 1733) preceded his eight pictures of *A Rake's Progress* (1733–35; Soane, London). In 1735 he opened his own academy in St Martin's Lane. Two pictures in the conventional style, *The Pool of Bethesda* and *The Good Samaritan* (1735), he presented to St Bartholomew's Hospital in the hope of attracting commissions. *The Distressed Poet*

(1735, Birmingham), *The Sleeping Congregation* (1736), *The Strolling Actresses* (1738), the *Four Times of Day* series (1738) and *The Enraged Musician* (1741; Ashmolean, Oxford) herald his return to 'pictured morality', of which his masterpiece is the *Marriage à la mode* series (1743–45; Tate). Brilliant psychological contrasts are depicted, the envy, greed that wealth inspires, the licence that it occasions and the *ennui* and arrogance that results are all epitomized in the loveless couple of the famous breakfast scene (Plate 2). In 1743 Hogarth visited Paris to enlist the help of Parisian engravers. He then extended his social commentaries to 'men of the lowest rank' by drawing attention to their typical vices with his prints of the *Industry and Idleness* series (1747), *Gin Lane*, *Beer Street* and *The Four Stages of Cruelty* (all 1751) in the British Museum. He later ventured into politics with a cartoon of Wilkes, Pitt and Temple as warmongers (1762) which earned him Wilkes's malicious retort in the *North Briton*. The latter Hogarth savagely caricatured in a portrait study, only rivalled by that massive portrayal of scheming treachery in *Lord Lovat* (1746). His liberating influence upon the art of portraiture may be gathered from the informal treatment of *Captain Coram* (1740; Foundling Hospital), his *Self-Portrait* (*c.* 1758) and that early undated study in impressionism, *The Shrimp Girl* (both in the National Gallery). Hogarth was buried in Chiswick churchyard. See his *Analysis of Beauty* (1753), studies by J. Truster (1768), Beckett (1949) and Life by P. Quennell (1955).

HOGBEN, Lancelot (1895–), English physiologist and writer, was born at Southsea and educated at Cambridge. He held academic appointments in Zoology in England, Scotland, Canada and South Africa before becoming Mason professor of Zoology at Birmingham (1941–47), and professor of medical statistics (1947–61). He is known for popular books on scientific subjects, including, in addition to many specialist publications, *Mathematics for the Million* (1936), *Science for the Citizen* (1938), &c.

HOGG, (1) James (1770–1835), Scottish poet and novelist, known as the 'Ettrick Shepherd', born near the parish church of Ettrick, Selkirkshire, tended sheep in his youth and had only a spasmodic education. He inherited, however, a rich store of ballads from his mother. On a visit to Edinburgh in 1801 to sell his employer's sheep, he had his *Scottish Pastorals, Poems, Songs*, &c., printed, but without success. He was fortunate, however, in making the acquaintance of Sir Walter Scott, then sheriff of Selkirkshire, who published in the second volume of *Border Minstrelsy* (1803) several of Hogg's ballads, written down from his mother's lips. With the proceeds of *The Mountain Bard* (1803), Hogg dabbled unsuccessfully in farming but eventually settled in Edinburgh. Another volume of poems, *The Forest Minstrel* (1810) failed, but *The Queen's Wake* (1813) at once obtained cordial recognition. A bequest of a farm at Altrive Lake (now Eldinhope) from the Duchess of Buccleuch, enabled him to marry in 1820 and to produce in rapid succession a number of works both in verse and prose. Hogg ended his days a well-known figure of Edinburgh society, a regular contributor to *Blackwood's Magazine* and was the ' Shepherd ' of John Wilson's *Noctes Ambrosianae*. He described himself as ' the king of the Mountain and Fairy School '. His poems of the supernatural are best when he avoids gothic elaboration and relies on the suggestive understatement of the ballad style, as in his ' Kilmeny ' and ' The Witch of Fife '. ' The Aged Widow's Lament ' shows the influence of the Scottish vernacular tradition. His debt to Burns is apparent in ' The Author's Address to his Auld Dog Hector ' and in the riotous ' Village of Balmaquhapple '. Of his prose works, the most remarkable is *Private Memoirs and Confessions of a Justified Sinner* (1824; new ed. with introduction by André Gide 1947), which anticipates Stevenson's *Jekyll and Hyde* with its haunting ' split personality ' theme. See his autobiography and *Memorials* ed. by his daughter, Mrs Garden (1885), Life by Douglas (1899) and critical study by E. C. Batho (1927).

(2) **Quintin** (1845–1903), British philanthropist, born in London, founded in 1882 the Youth's Christian Institute, which developed into the Regent Street Polytechnic. See also HAILSHAM (1).

(3) **Quintin.** See HAILSHAM (2).

(4) **Thomas Jefferson.** See SHELLEY.

HOHENHEIM, Theophrastus Bombastus von. See PARACELSUS.

HOHENLOHE-SCHILLINGSFÜRST, Chlodwic, Prince of (1819–1901), Prussian statesman, born at Rothenburg in Bavaria, in 1894 succeeded Caprivi as chancellor of German empire and prime minister of Prussia.

HOHENSTAUFEN, *-shtow'fen*, name of a German princely house, members of which held the Imperial throne from 1138 to 1254 as Conrad III, Frederick I, Henry VI, Philip I, Frederick II and Conrad IV. See histories of the house by Raumer (5th ed. 1878) and K. Hampe (7th ed. 1937).

HOHENZOLLERN, name of a German family descended from Count Thassilo, who early in the 9th century founded a castle on the Zollern hill in the Swabian Alb. About 1165 a separation took place into an elder or Swabian and younger or Franconian line. The elder line was subdivided, in 1576, into the branches of Hechingen and Sigmaringen. In 1415 the young line received from the Emperor Sigismund the electorate of Brandenburg, thus founding the Prussian dynasty; and in 1849 the two princes of the elder line ceded their rights to the king of Prussia. The kings of Prussia were German emperors from 1871 to 1918. See WILLIAM II; also CAROL I (Rumania), and family history by Hintze (1915).

HOHNER, Matthias (1833–1902), German mouth-organ manufacturer, established his firm at Trossingen, Württemberg, in 1857. His five sons added music publishing (1931), the manufacture of accordions, harmonicas, saxophones and (from 1945) electrical musical instruments, established an accordion school at Trossingen in 1931 and made the family business the biggest of its kind. See study by A. Lämmle (Stuttgart 1957).

HOKUSAI, Katsushika, *hŏ'koo-sī* (1760–1849), Japanese artist and wood-engraver, born in Tokyo, was early apprenticed to a wood-engraver under. whom he mastered the conventional *surimono* or commemorative paintings and book illustrations. But he soon abandoned the traditional style and academic subjects for the coloured woodcut designs of the *avant garde* Ukiyoye (' the passing world ') school, which treated in forceful expressionist manner commonplace subjects of the everyday world. From 1814 to 1819 he worked on the ten volumes of the famous *Mangwa* or ' Sketches at Random ', in which he depicts most facets of Japanese life. To work successfully on semi-transparent, absorbent paper requires quick, decisive linear brushwork, the maximum suggestion being packed into a single stroke. Hokusai delighted the passerby by feats of artistic versatility, e.g., dashing off the outline of a sparrow on a grain of corn. Living exclusively to improve his art, *Gwakiôjn* or ' Old Man mad on drawings ' studied Dutch paintings and entered his great period (1823–1830) with the wonderful *Hundred Views of Mount Fuji* published in 1835, the *Waterfalls, Famous Bridges, Large Flowers* and the *Ghost Stories*. He differs from Hiroshige (q.v.) in his superior draughtsmanship rather than in his sense of colour, and he greatly influenced the French Impressionists. See studies by E. F. Strange (1906) and B. Gray (1948).

HOLBACH, Paul Heinrich Dietrich, Baron d', *ol-bak* (1723–89), German-born French philosopher, was born at Heidelsheim in the Palatinate, and settled and died in Paris. One of the Encyclopaedists, he expounded in his *Système de la Nature* (1770) the natural principles of morality, and attempted to prove, among other things, that self-interest is the ruling motive of man. Holbach was, none the less, a man of most unselfish benevolence. See works by Cushing (1914), Hubert (1928), Wickwar (1935).

HOLBEACH, Henry. See RANDS.

HOLBEIN, Hans, ' the younger ' (1497–1543), German painter, was born at Augsburg, the son of Hans Holbein the elder (*c.* 1460–1524), also a painter of merit. He studied under his father, and was influenced by the work of Burgkmair. The finest of his early pictures was the altarpiece for the monastery of St Catharine (1515–16), now in the Pinakothek, Munich. About 1516 he was at work in Basel, but did not settle there till 1520; during the interval he was painting at Zürich and Lucerne. Among works executed at Basel are the portraits of the Burgomaster Meier and his wife, the ' Meier Madonna ', eight scenes of the Passion, painted upon a panel (and now in the Basel museum), and the doors of the organ of Basel Cathedral. Among the portraits are also two of Erasmus and one of Melanchthon. During his residence at Basel Holbein was largely employed upon designs for the woodengravers, including illustrations for various editions of Luther's Old and New Testaments (1522 and 1523), as also the large single woodcuts of *Christ bearing the Cross, The Resurrection, The Sale of Indulgences* and

The True Light. His most important woodcuts, however—the series of *The Dance of Death* and the *Old Testament Cuts*—were not issued till 1538. About the end of 1526 Holbein visited England, where he was introduced by Erasmus to Sir Thomas More, and began his great series of portraits of eminent Englishmen of his time, the studies for many of which exist in the royal collection at Windsor. Among the most notable of these portraits are those of Archbishop Warham, Sir Henry Guildford, Nicholas Kratzer, the king's astronomer, in the Louvre; and the family of Sir Thomas More, now lost, but known by copies and the original sketch. On his return to Basel (1529) Holbein painted the group of his wife and two children now in the museum there; and in 1530 resumed work in the council hall, executing pictures that are now destroyed. Probably in 1532 he again visited London, where he painted many portraits for the German merchants of the Hanseatic League. To this period are also due the great portrait group at Longford Castle known as *The Ambassadors,* the portraits of Thomas Cromwell, and the miniatures of Henry and Charles Brandon, sons of the Duke of Suffolk, in the royal collection at Windsor. In 1536 he was appointed painter to Henry VIII, and as such executed at Whitehall Palace a mural painting of the monarch and Queen Jane Seymour with Henry VII and Elizabeth of York, destroyed in the fire of 1698. His portrait of Jane Seymour is in the Belvedere, Vienna. To the same period is referable the half-length of Sir Nicholas Carew at Dalkeith Palace, and the portrait of Morett the jeweller in the Dresden Gallery. In 1538 Holbein was dispatched to the Netherlands to paint a likeness (now in the possession of the Duke of Norfolk) of Christina of Denmark, proposed as successor to Jane Seymour; and in 1539 he painted Anne of Cleves, at Cleves, a work now in the Louvre; while about 1540 he executed the portrait of the Duke of Norfolk, of which the original is at Windsor. Miniatures of this period, now in the Victoria and Albert Museum, are outstanding in quality. His last work was *Henry VIII granting a Charter to the Barber-Surgeons,* still in their Guildhall. He died of the plague in London between October 7 and November 29. A master of portraiture, Holbein had a genius for subordinating the interest in garments and accessories to heighten facial characteristics. See *Lives* by Wornum (1867), G. S. Davies (1903), A. B. Chamberlain (1913), and works by H. A. Schmid (1949) and P. Ganz (1950).

HOLBERG, Ludvig, Baron (1684–1754), Danish poet, playwright and philosopher, born at Bergen in Norway, became professor at Copenhagen of Metaphysics (1717), Eloquence (1720), and History (1730), quaestor of the university (1737), and a baron (1747). His first notable works were satirical poems, among them *Peder Paars* (1719–20), in which he ridicules the pedantic stiffness and stupidity of contemporary life and thought. In 1721 the first Danish theatre was opened at Copenhagen, and Holberg began to write many successful comedies. After 1724 he turned to history, and wrote, amongst other books, a *History of Denmark,* a *General Church History,* a *History of the Jews,* and *Comparative Biographies of Great Men and Women.* In 1741 he produced another classic, the satirico-humoristic romance *Niels Klim's Subterranean Journey;* and lastly the serious reflective works, *Moral Thoughts* (1744) and *Epistles* (1748–54), and an *Autobiography* (1727–43). Many of his works have been translated. See monographs by G. Brandes (1884) and by O. J. Campbell, jun. (1914), who also translated three of the ' Danish Molière's ' domestic comedies of character (1915).

HOLBØLL, Einar (1855–1927), Danish postmaster who originated the idea of special stamp issues for charitable purposes by his *Julemaerket* stamp (1904) for a tuberculosis prevention fund. The idea has since been adopted by countries all over the world.

HOLBORNE, Antony (d. *c.* 1602), English composer, known chiefly for a collection of pavanes, galliards and other dance movements for five instruments (1599). With his brother **William** he wrote a manual for the cittern containing a number of compositions for that instrument.

HOLBROOKE, Josef Charles (1878–1958), English composer of chamber music and opera, was born at Croydon, studied at the Royal Academy, was an accomplished pianist and composed the symphonic poems *Queen Mab* (1904), *The Bells* (1906) and *Apollo and the Seaman* (1908), as well as a trilogy of operas based on Welsh legends, the first of which, *The Children of Don* (1912), was performed at Salzburg in 1923. His variations on ' Three Blind Mice ' formed his most popular composition.

HOLCROFT, Thomas (1745–1809), English playwright and novelist, born in London, after three years as a Newmarket stable boy, then eight as a shoemaker, schoolmaster, and servant-secretary to Granville Sharpe, in 1770 turned strolling player. But settling in London (1777), he took to writing. *Alwyn, or the Gentleman Comedian* (1780), was the first of four novels. He also wrote nearly thirty plays, mostly melodramas, of which *The Follies of a Day* (1784) and *The Road to Ruin* (1792) were the best. His eldest son, **William** (1773–89), robbed his father of £40 and having been found by him on an American-bound vessel, shot himself. An ardent democrat, in 1794 Holcroft was tried for high treason with Hardy, Horne Tooke and others and acquitted, but the adverse publicity reduced him to poverty and made him go abroad to Hamburg and Paris (1799–1801). He died in London. See his *Memoirs,* continued by Hazlitt (1816), augmented by Colby (1925).

HOLDEN, Sir Isaac (1807–97), British inventor, was born at Hurlet, Renfrewshire, worked in a Paisley cotton mill, studied chemistry in his leisure hours and became an assistant teacher in Reading in 1829. He invented the Lucifer match, but was anticipated by John Walker of Stockton. In 1846 he joined with Lister, who had done much to improve woolcombing, in starting a mill near Paris. Lister retired, the firm became Isaac Holden & Sons in 1859, and the Alston works near Bradford were founded. After he had spent some £50,000 in experiments, Holden's woolcombing machinery brought him fame and fortune. He was Liberal M.P. (1865–95) and was created baronet in 1893.

HÖLDERLIN, Johann Christian Friedrich, *hæl'-* (1770–1843), German poet, born March 20 at Lauffen on the Neckar, studied theology at Tübingen and philosophy with Schelling and Hegel under Fichte at Jena. With a growing enthusiasm for poetry, he developed an aversion to the ' snug parsonage ' for which he was intended. As family tutor in Frankfurt-am-Main (1796–98) he found in the wife of his banker-employer, Susette Gontard (the ' Diotima ' of his works), the feminine embodiment of all he venerated in Hellenism. His early poetry owed far too much to Klopstock and to Schiller, who published Hölderlin's efforts in his literary magazines, but the inspiration provided by ' Diotima ' helped him to discover his true poetical self. However, the commercial philistinism, which Hölderlin roundly condemned in his philosophical novel, *Hyperion* (1797–99), and the understandable jealousy of the banker, made Hölderlin's stay finally impossible. During a temporary refuge at Homburg he wrote some splendid fragments for a verse drama on the death of Empedocles, some elegiac odes and the magnificent elegy ' Menon's Laments for Diotima ', which examines the discrepancy between the actual and the ideally possible. For a short time he tutored in Switzerland (1801), but returned to his mother at Nuremberg, where he wrote ' Brod und Wein ' and ' Der Rhein '. In July 1802, after a spell of employment by the German Consul at Bordeaux, he returned in an advanced state of schizophrenia, aggravated by the news of ' Diotima's ' death. For a short time he enjoyed the sinecure of court librarian to the landgrave of Hesse-Homburg, procured for him and paid by his friend von Sinclair. After a period in an asylum (1806–07), he lived out his life in the charge of a Tübingen carpenter. Neither Goethe nor Schiller was aware of his genius. It was the admiration of Rilke and Stefan George, who studied the collected works, ed. N. von Hellingrath and others (Berlin 1913 ff.), which first established Hölderlin as one of Germany's greatest poets, eighty years after his death. See *Selected Poems* (parallel German-English text, rev. ed. 1954) by T. B. Leishman, and studies by W. Dilthey, *Das Erlebnis und die Dichtung* (Berlin 1916), M. Montgomery (1923), S. Zweig, *Der Kampf mit dem Dämon* (Leipzig 1925), W. Böhm (1928–30), R. Peacock (1938), D. L. Gascoigne (1938), A. Stansfield (1944), M. Heidegger, *Existence and Being*, ed. W. Brock (1949), L. S. Salzberger (1952).

HOLINSHED, Raphael (d. *c.* 1580), English chronicler, born apparently of Cheshire family, came to London early in Elizabeth's reign, and became a translator in Reginald Wolfe's printing office. For Wolfe and his successors he undertook the compilation of

The Chronicles of England, Scotland, and Ireland (2 vols. fol. 1577). This together with its predecessor, *The Chronicle of Hall*, was the direct source from which Shakespeare drew materials for legendary and historical plays. Holinshed was not the only writer of the work which bears his name. He was assisted by William Harrison (q.v.); by Richard Stanyhurst, who contributed the description of Ireland; and by John Hooker, who wrote most of the history of Ireland. Holinshed had access to the manuscripts of Leland (2) (q.v.). See Boswell Stone, *Shakespeare's Holinshed* (1896).

HOLL, Frank (1845–88), English painter, the son of the engraver, **Francis** (1815–84), born in London, entered the schools of the Royal Academy, exhibited many genre subjects, usually pathetic scenes from modern life; after 1877 he attained immense popularity in portraiture. He was elected R.A. in 1884. His uncle, **William** (1807–71), was an engraver and portrait painter. See Life by A. M. Reynolds (1912).

HOLLAND, (1) Henry (1746–1806), English architect, son-in-law and pupil of Lancelot (' Capability ') Brown, designed old Carlton House, the original Brighton Pavilion, Brook's Club, &c. See Life by D. Stroud (1958).

(2) **Henry Richard Fox, 3rd Baron** (1773–1840), English Liberal statesman, nephew of Charles James Fox (q.v.), was born at Winterslow House, Wilts, and succeeded to the title in 1774. Educated at Eton and Christ Church, Oxford, he was trained for public life by his uncle, after whose death he was lord privy seal in the Grenville ministry (1806–07). He then shared the long banishment of the Whigs from office. He worked for reform of the criminal code, attacked the slave trade though himself a West India planter, and threw his whole heart into the Corn Laws struggle. Chancellor of the duchy of Lancaster (1830–34), he died at Holland House, Kensington. He wrote biographies of Guillen de Castro and Lope de Vega, translated Spanish comedies, prepared a Life of his uncle, and edited the memoirs of Lord Waldegrave. His wife, **Elizabeth Vassall** (1770–1845), daughter of a wealthy Jamaica planter, married in 1786 Sir Godfrey Webster, but the marriage was dissolved in 1797 for her adultery with Lord Holland, who immediately married her. She was distinguished for beauty, conversational gifts and autocratic ways; and till the end of her life Holland House was the meeting place of the most brilliant wits and distinguished statesmen of the time. See his *Memoirs*, ed. by his son, the 4th Baron (1852–54), and his *Further Memoirs* (1905), also *Journals* of Lady Holland (ed. Earl of Ilchester, 1908, 1910, 1946), and the Earl of Ilchester, *The Home of the Hollands* (1937).

(3) **Henry Scott** (1847–1918), English preacher and theologian, born at Ledbury, tutor at Christ Church (1870–84), became a canon of Truro in 1882, of St Paul's in 1884, of Christ Church in 1910, when he was appointed regius professor of Divinity, Oxford. He led the *Lux Mundi* group of theologians, influenced by neo-Hegelianism,

who were devoted to social reform according to Christian principles. See study by E. Lyttleton (1926).

(4) **Josiah Gilbert** (1819–81), American editor, born in Belchertown, Mass., became assistant editor of the Springfield *Republican* and part proprietor in 1851. In 1870, with Roswell Smith and the Scribners, he founded *Scribner's Monthly*, which he edited, and in which appeared his novels, *Arthur Bonnicastle* (1873), *The Story of Sevenoaks* (1875), and *Nicholas Minturn* (1876), &c. See Life by Plunkett (1894).

(5) **Philemon** (1552–1637), English scholar, ' the translator-general in his age ', was born at Chelmsford, from about 1595 practised medicine at Coventry, and in 1628 became for ten months headmaster of the free school there. He translated Livy, Pliny's *Natural History*, Suetonius, Plutarch's *Morals*, Ammianus Marcellinus, Xenophon's *Cyropaedia*, and Camden's *Britannia*, &c. His son, **Henry** (1583–*c.* 1650), a bookseller in London, published *Baziliologia* (1618) and *Heroologia Anglica* (1620).

(6) **Sir Sidney George** (1893–1961), New Zealand politician, born in Greendale, Canterbury, managing director of an engineering company before taking up politics. Entering Parliament as a member of the National party in 1935, he was leader of the Opposition (1940–49), premier (1949–1957), when he resigned to become minister without portfolio. He was made C.H. in 1951, and G.C.B. in 1957.

HOLLAR, Wenceslaus (1607–77), Bohemian engraver and etcher, born at Prague; came to London with the Earl of Arundel in 1637; served in a royalist regiment, and was taken prisoner at Basing House; from 1645 to 1652 lived at Antwerp; and then returning to London, was at the Restoration appointed ' His Majesty's designer '. He produced two magnificent plates of costume, entitled *Severall Habits of English Women* (1640) and *Theatrum Mulierum* (1643), as well as maps, panoramas, &c., preserved in the British Museum and the royal library, Windsor. His panoramic view of London from Southwark is one of the most valuable topographical records of the 17th century. See Life by A. M. Hind (1922).

HOLLES, Denzil, 1st Baron (1599–1680), English statesman, the second son of the 1st Earl of Clare, entered parliament in 1624. In 1629 he was one of the members who held the Speaker in his chair whilst resolutions were passed against Arminianism and tonnage and poundage. For this he was fined a thousand marks, and lived seven or eight years in exile. He was one of the five members whom Charles attempted to arrest in 1642, and was a leader of the Presbyterians. In the Civil War, dreading the supremacy of the army more than the pretensions of the king, he was an advocate of peace. For proposing in 1647 to disband the army he was accused of treason, but fled to Normandy. In 1660 he was the spokesman of the commission delegated to recall Charles II at Breda; in 1661 he was created Baron Holles of Ifield in Sussex. His last important public duty was the negotiation of the treaty of Breda in 1667. As Charles became more autocratic, Holles leaned more to the opposition. See his own *Memoirs* (1699).

HOLLOWAY, Thomas (1800–83), English manufacturer of patent medicines, born at Devonport, founded with his fortune at Egham, near Virginia Water, a women's college and an asylum for the insane.

HOLMAN, James (1786–1857), ' the Blind Traveller ', born at Exeter, was a lieutenant in the navy when, in 1810, the loss of sight compelled him to quit the service. Yet he travelled through France and Italy to the Rhineland (1819–21). He next started on a journey (1822–24) around the world, but at Irkutsk in Siberia was arrested as a spy and sent back. He again set off in 1827, and this time accomplished his purpose. Finally, he visited southeast Europe. He published accounts of his travels (1822, 1825, 1834–35) and died in London.

HOLMES, (1) Arthur (1890–1965), English geologist, born at Hebburn-on-Tyne, professor at Edinburgh (1943–56), investigated the ages of rocks by measuring their radioactive constituents.

(2) **Oliver Wendell** (1809–94), American writer and physician, father of (3), born in Cambridge, Mass., graduated at Harvard College in 1829, and, giving up law for medicine, spent two years in the hospitals of Europe. In 1839–41 he was professor of Anatomy and Physiology at Dartmouth College; in 1843 he discovered that puerperal fever was contagious. From 1847 to 1882 he was professor of Anatomy at Harvard. He began writing verse while an undergraduate, but twenty years passed with desultory efforts, before *The Autocrat of the Breakfast Table* (1857–58) suddenly made him famous by its fresh unconventional tone, its playful wit and wisdom, and its lovely vignettes of verse. This was followed by *The Professor at the Breakfast Table* (1858–59) and *The Poet at the Breakfast Table* (1872). *Elsie Venner* (1859–60), was the first of three novels, foreshadowing modern ' Freudian ' fiction. He also wrote *Our Hundred Days in Europe* (1887), an account of a visit made in 1886, during which he received honours from the universities of Cambridge, Oxford and Edinburgh. He died at Boston. See Lives by Kennedy (1883), Brown (1884), Morse (1896) and Townsend (1909), and E. M. Tilton, *Amiable Autocrat* (1947).

(3) **Oliver Wendell** (1841–1935), American judge, son of (2), born at Boston, educated at Harvard Law School, served in the Union army as captain in the Civil War. From 1867 he practised law in Boston, became editor of the American *Law Review*, and in 1882, Weld professor of Law at Harvard. He was associate justice (1882) and chief justice (1899–1902) of the supreme court of Massachusetts and associate justice of the U.S. supreme court (1902–32). He was one of the great judicial figures of his time and many of his judgments on common law and equity, as well as his dissent on the interpretation of the 14th amendment, have become famous. For many years he corresponded with Professor Laski (q.v.). See *Letters*, ed. Howe (1953).

HOLST, Gustav Theodore (1874–1934), English composer, born von Holst of Swedish origin in Cheltenham, conducted village choirs before entering in 1893 the Royal College of Music, London, on a scholarship. He studied under Stanford, but neuritis in his hand prevented him from becoming a concert pianist. Instead he played first trombone in the Carl Rosa Opera Company and later joined the Scottish Orchestra. In 1905 he became music master at St Paul's Girls' School, in 1907 musical director at Morley College, London, and in 1919 was appointed to a similar post at Reading College. It took him some time to find his own personal style as composer, to shake off the influence of Grieg and Wagner, and the early enthusiasm for Hindu literature reflected in the opera, *Sida*, the *opera di camera, Savitri*, and the *Hymns from the Rig-Veda*. He shared Vaughan Williams' interest in the English folksong tradition, which inspired his *St Paul's Suite for Strings* (1913). Economy and clarity became his watchwords. The seven-movement suite *The Planets* (1914–17), in which each planet's astrological associations are treated in musical terms, marked his emergence as a major composer. Sublime conceptions pervade also *The Hymn of Jesus* (1917) and his choral setting of Walt Whitman's *Ode to Death* (1919). Two comic operas followed: *The Perfect Fool* (1921) and the Falstaffian *At the Boar's Head* (1924). An abrupt change to stark austerity marked his extraordinary orchestral piece, inspired by Hardy's *Return of the Native, Egdon Heath* (1927). His dexterous essay into polytonality, the *Concerto for Two Violins* (1929), earned him the Gold Medal of the Royal Philharmonic Society. He was buried in Chichester Cathedral. See Life (1938) and study (1951) by his daughter, Imogen (1907–), like her father musical educationist, conductor and composer of folksong arrangements, associated with Britten in the Aldeburgh Festivals; and study by E. Rubbra (1947).

HOLT, Sir John (1642–1710), English judge, born at Thame, from Winchester passed in 1658 to Oriel College, Oxford, and, entering at Gray's Inn, was called to the bar in 1663. He figured as counsel in most of the state trials of that period, and in 1686 was made recorder of London and king's serjeant, and knighted. In 1689 he became lord chief justice of the King's Bench. He was a Whig, but his judicial career was entirely free from party bias or intrigue. See Life (1764).

HOLTBY, Winifred (1898–1935), English novelist and feminist, born at Rudston, Yorks, educated at Oxford, was a director from 1926 of *Time and Tide* and wrote a number of novels, but is chiefly remembered for *South Riding* (1935).

HOLTEI, Karl von, *-ti* (1798–1880), German actor and dramatic poet, was born and died at Breslau. He wrote musical plays, as *Der alte Feldherr* (1829) and *Lenore* (1829); also novels and the autobiographical *Vierzig Jahre* (8 vols., 1843–50).

HÖLTY, Ludwig Christoph Heinrich (1748–1776), German poet, born at Mariensee, Hanover, was a co-founder of the Göttingen

Hain, a literary coterie dedicated to promoting the national spirit in German verse. Some of his poetry is based on the Minnesänger.

HOLTZMANN, Adolf (1810–70), German philologist, born at Karlsruhe, in 1852 became professor of German at Heidelberg. He wrote on the connection between Greek and Indian fables (1844–47); on Celts and Germans (1855), maintaining that the two races were originally identical; and on the *Nibelungenlied* (1854), &c. His son, **Heinrich Julius** (1832–1910), German theologian, became professor of Theology at Heidelberg (1861) and at Strasburg (1874), and was ultimately a leading representative of modern New Testament criticism.

HOLYOAKE, George Jacob (1817–1906), English social reformer, the founder of Secularism, was born at Birmingham. He taught mathematics for some years at the Mechanics' Institution in Birmingham, lectured on Robert Owen's socialist system, was secretary to Garibaldi's British contingent, edited the *Reasoner*, and promoted the bill legalizing secular affirmations. Holyoake was the last person imprisoned in England on a charge of atheism (1842). He wrote histories of the Co-operative movement, on secularism, *Sixty Years of an Agitator's Life* (1892), *Public Speaking and Debate* (1895), &c.

HOLYWOOD. See SACROBOSCO.

HOLZ, Arno, *hōlts* (1863–1929), German author and critic, born at Rastenburg, East Prussia. His first writing was lyric poetry, but he is best known for his criticism. *Die Kunst, ihr Wesen und ihre Gesetze* (1890–92) inaugurated the German impressionist school; *Revolution der Lyrik* (1899) rejected all metrical devices, and *Phantasus* (1898–99) was written on this theory. *Papa Hamlet* (1889) and the drama *Familie Selicke* (1890), both written in collaboration with Johannes Schaf, are influenced by Zola.

HOME, (1) **Anne.** See HUNTER (1).

(2) **Daniel Dunglas** (1833–86), British spiritualist, born near Edinburgh, won fame as a medium, and as an exponent of table-turning and levitation in the United States (c. 1850) and in London (1855). See his *Incidents of My Life* (1863–72) and books by his widow (1888–90).

(3) **Henry.** See KAMES (LORD).

(4) **John** (1722–1808), Scottish clergyman and dramatist, born at Leith, graduated at Edinburgh in 1742. He was taken prisoner fighting on the Hanoverian side at Falkirk (1746), but made a daring escape from Doune Castle. Next year he became minister of Athelstaneford, where he wrote the tragedy *Agis*, and, in 1754 *Douglas*, founded on the ballad of Gil Morrice. Each of these was rejected by Garrick, but *Douglas*, produced in Edinburgh (1756), met with brilliant success, and evoked the oft-quoted and possibly apocryphal ' whaur's yer Wullie Shakespeare noo ' from an over-enthusiastic member of the audience. It also won great popularity in London, but it gave such offence to the Edinburgh Presbytery that the author resigned his ministry (1757), and became private secretary to the Earl of Bute and tutor to the Prince of Wales, who on his accession as

George III gave him a pension of £300 a year, to which a sinecure of equal value was added in 1763. The success of *Douglas* induced Garrick to bring out *Agis*, and to accept Home's next play, *The Siege of Aquileia*. Home's other works are *The Fatal Discovery*, *Alonzo*, *Alfred*, occasional poems, and, in prose, *A History of the Rebellion of 1745*. He married in 1770, and in 1779 settled in Edinburgh, where he died. Home had interesting plots and occasional flashes of genuine poetry; but he did not succeed in discarding the pompous declamation of his forerunners. See Lives by H. Mackenzie (prefixed to his works, 1822) and A. E. Gipson (1917).

HOMER (Gk. *Homēros*), the Greek poet to whom are attributed the great epics, the *Iliad*, the story of the siege of Troy, and the *Odyssey*, the tale of Ulysses' wanderings. The place of his birth is doubtful: Smyrna, Rhodes, Colophon, Salamis, Chios, Argos and Athens contended for the honour of having been his birthplace; his date, formerly put as far back as 1200 B.C. is, from the style of the poems attributed to him, referred to 850–800 B.C. Wolf (q.v.) in 1795 fiercely assailed the current opinions about Homer; defended the view, as old as the days of the Greek commentators, that the *Iliad* and *Odyssey* were not by the same hand; and contended that both had their origin in lays by Homer and his followers (Homeridae) in Chios, chanted and altered for centuries by the Rhapsodists, and finally digested into the poems we know by Pisistratus about 540 B.C. Even those who insist most strongly on the general unity of plan of the poems and assign the main authorship to one man, Homer, probably born in a Greek colony on the coast of Asia Minor, admit that they were doubtless based on current ballads, and have been doubtless considerably modified and extended, since they were moulded into the two great epics. The various problems of the ' Homeric question ' cannot be regarded as solved; and of the true Homer we know nothing positively, not even that he was blind. The so-called Homeric Hymns and the humorous *Batrachomyomachia* (' Battle of the Frogs and Mice ') are certainly of a later age. For the many notable modern works on Homer, see list given by H. J. Rose in *Handbook of Greek Literature* (1934). There are also numerous translations, including those by Alexander Pope, T. E. Lawrence (1932), E. V. Rieu (Penguin series 1945), &c. See studies by T. B. L. Webster (1958), Sir J. L. Myres (1959) and C. H. Whitman (1959).

HOMER, Winslow (1836–1910), American marine and genre painter, born in Boston, U.S.A., was apprenticed to a lithographer, studied in New York and Paris and during the Civil War was artist to *Harper's Weekly*. He painted rural and domestic scenes, such as *A Visit from an Old Mistress* (National Gallery, Washington) but was at his best in his seascapes, mostly painted after 1881 while staying at Prout's Neck on the Maine Coast. These include *The Gulf Stream*, *Search Light* (Metropolitan, N.Y.), &c. See Life by F. Watson (1942).

HONDIUS, or de Hondt, (1) **Abraham** (*c.* 1638–91), Flemish animal painter, born at Rotterdam, came to London *c.* 1665.

(2) **Jodocus or Josse** (1563–1612), Flemish cartographer, emigrated to London *c.* 1584 and moved from there to Amsterdam *c.* 1593. In addition to his own maps of the world and the hemispheres, he engraved much of John Speed's work.

HONE, William (1780–1842), English writer, born at Bath, at ten became a London lawyer's clerk, at twenty started a book and print shop, which, however, soon failed. He struggled to make a living by writing for various papers, started the *Traveller* (1815), and next the *Reformist's Register* (1817). In December 1817 he was acquitted on three separate trials for publishing things calculated to injure public morals and bring the Prayer Book into contempt. Among his later satires, illustrated by Cruikshank, were *The Political House that Jack built*, *The Queen's Matrimonial Ladder*, *The Man in the Moon*, and *The Political Showman*. His obscure antiquarian interests were reflected in *Apocryphal New Testament* (1820), *Every-day Book* (1826), *Table-book* (1827–28) and *Year-book* (1829). But Hone ended up in a debtor's jail, from which his friends extricated him to start him in a coffee house—also a failure. In his last years, growing devout, he became a preacher. See Life by Hackwood (1912).

HONEGGER, Arthur, *hon'-* (1892–1956), French composer of Swiss parentage, born in Le Havre. He studied in Zürich and at the Paris Conservatoire, and after the first World War became one of the group of Parisian composers known as Les Six. His dramatic oratorio *King David* established his reputation in 1921, and amongst his subsequent works, *Pacific 231* (1923), his musical picture of a locomotive, won considerable popularity. Honegger composed five symphonies, all except the first after 1941, and these, like a second dramatic oratorio, *Joan of Arc at the Stake* (1936), are works of considerable depth and power. See study by W. Tappolet (1933).

HONORIUS, name of three popes and one antipope (II):

Honorius I (d. 638), pope (625–638), had to do with the paschal controversy in Ireland and with the Anglo-Saxon Church. In the Monothelite controversy he abstained from condemning the new doctrines, and for so doing was stigmatized as a heretic at the Council of Constantinople (680). The three others, all Italians, were Honorius II (1124–1130), III (1216–27) and IV (1285–87).

HONORIUS, Flavius (A.D. 384–423), West Roman Emperor, second son of Theodosius the Great, at whose death the empire was divided between his sons Arcadius and Honorius, the latter (only ten years old) receiving the western half. Stilicho (q.v.) was the *de facto* ruler of the western empire until 408; and after his death Alaric the Goth overran Italy, and took Rome in 410. Honorius died at Ravenna, which he had made his capital in 403.

HONTHEIM, Johann Nikolaus von, *hont'hīm* (1701–90), German ecclesiastic, born at Trier, where he became bishop, wrote two works on the history of Trier (1750–57), but is chiefly memorable for a theological essay (1763) by ' Febronius ', in which he propounded a system of church government combining an exaggerated Gallicanism with the democratic element of congregationalism.

HONTHORST, Gerard van, *hont'-* (1590–1656), Dutch painter, who was born and died at Utrecht, twice visited England (1620 and 1628), and painted portraits of the royal family. He was fond of painting interiors, dimly illumined. His brother **William** (1604–1666), historical and portrait painter, worked for the court of Berlin (1650–64).

HOOCH, or **Hoogh, Pieter de,** *hōk* (*c.* 1629–*c.* 1684), Dutch genre painter, born at Rotterdam, by 1654 was living in Delft and probably came under the influence of Carel Fabritius and the latter's pupil Vermeer. His *Interior of a Dutch House* (National Gallery) and the *Card Players* in the royal collection are among the outstanding examples of the Dutch school of the 17th century, with their characteristically serene domestic interior or courtyard scenes, warm colouring and delicate light effects. About 1665 he moved to Amsterdam, but his later work became increasingly artificial. See monographs by G. H. C. Baker (1925) and Valentiner (trans. 1930).

HOOD, (1) **Alexander, 1st Viscount Bridport** (1727–1814). British sailor, brother of (4), entered the navy in 1741. In 1761 he recaptured from the French the *Warwick*, a 60-gun ship, and during the French revolutionary war he served under Howe in the Channel and the Strait of Gibraltar, sharing in the ' glorious first of June ' off Ushant (1794). He attained flag rank in 1780, and was made in 1796 Baron, and in 1800 Viscount Bridport.

(2) **John Bell** (1831–79), American soldier, born at Owingsville, Kentucky, commanded a brigade in the Confederate army, and was wounded at Gaines's Mill, Gettysburg, and Chickamauga. He commanded a corps in the retreat to Atlanta, and in July 1864 succeeded Johnston in command. On September 1 he had to evacuate the city, and leave the road free for Sherman's march to the sea. He afterwards pushed as far north as Nashville; but, defeated by Thomas, was relieved of command (1864). See his *Advance and Retreat* (1880) and D. S. Freeman, *Lee's Lieutenants* (1944).

(3) **Robin.** See ROBIN HOOD.

(4) **Samuel, 1st Viscount Hood** (1724–1816), British sailor, brother of (1), born December 12 at Thorncombe, Dorset, entered the navy in 1741, and became post-captain in 1756. In command of the *Vestal* frigate, he took a French frigate after a fiercely-contested action (1759); in 1778 he was made commissioner of Portsmouth dockyard. In 1780, promoted to flag rank, he was sent to reinforce Rodney on the North American and West Indian stations; in 1781 he fought an action with De Grasse, and was engaged in the battle off the Chesapeake. In the West Indies in 1782 he showed himself a masterly tactician in the series of manoeuvres by which he outwitted De Grasse off St Kitts; and he had a conspicuous share in the decisive

victory of Dominica on April 12. For his services he was made Baron Hood in the Irish peerage. In 1784 he stood against Fox for Westminster, and was elected; in 1788 he became a lord of the Admiralty. In 1793, appointed to the Mediterranean, he directed the occupation of Toulon and the operations in the Gulf of Lyons. In 1796 he was made Viscount Hood, and he died at Bath, June 27. See his *Letters* 1781–83, edited by D. Hannay (Navy Records Soc. 1895), and study by Rose (1922).

(5) **Thomas** (1799–1845), English poet and humorist, was born in London, the son of a Scottish bookseller from Errol. At about thirteen he was placed in a merchant's counting-house in the City, but, his health failing, was sent in 1815 to Dundee, to his father's relations, where he wrote for the local newspapers and magazines. In 1818 he returned to London, and entered the studio of his uncle, an engraver. After a short apprenticeship he worked for a while on his own account. In 1821 he was appointed subeditor of the *London Magazine*, and found himself in daily companionship with such men as Procter, Cary, Allan Cunningham, De Quincey, Hazlitt and Charles Lamb. It was, however, the intimacy with John Hamilton Reynolds, whose sister he married in 1825, that chiefly encouraged and trained Hood's poetic faculty. Between July 1821 and July 1823 Hood published in the magazine some of his finest poems—' Lycus the Centaur ', the ' Two Peacocks of Bedfont ' and the ' Ode to Autumn '. But these, issued anonymously, failed to attract notice when in 1827 he produced them and others in bookform. In 1825 Hood and Reynolds published (anonymously) a volume of *Odes and Addresses to Great People*, suggested by the success of Hood's burlesque *Ode to Dr Kitchener* in the magazine. They at once attracted notice and determined Hood's chief occupation for the remainder of his life. In the first series of *Whims and Oddities* (1826) Hood first exhibited such graphic talent as he possessed in those ' picture-puns ' of which he seems to have been the inventor. A second series appeared in 1827, followed by *National Tales*. In 1829 he edited *The Gem*, a remarkable little ' annual ', for, besides Lamb's ' Lines on a Child dying as soon as born ' (Hood's first child), it contained Hood's *Eugene Aram*. Hood and his wife left London in 1829 for Winchmore Hill, where he began the first of those comic annuals which he produced yearly and single-handed from 1830 to 1839. In 1834 the failure of a publisher plunged Hood into serious difficulties; and in 1835 the family went for five years to Coblenz and Ostend. During these years Hood, struggling against tuberculosis, wrote *Up the Rhine* (1839), which was popular but did not bring in any profit. By the kindness of friends Hood was enabled to return to England, with security from his creditors, in 1840. In 1841 he became editor of the *New Monthly Magazine*, in January 1844 he started a periodical of his own, *Hood's Monthly Magazine*. Meantime in the Christmas number of *Punch* (1843) had appeared the ' Song of the Shirt ', and in

Hood's Magazine there followed the ' Haunted House ', the ' Lay of the Labourer ', and the ' Bridge of Sighs '. In November 1844 Sir Robert Peel granted a pension to Mrs Hood. Hood died at Devonshire Lodge, Finchley Road, and was buried in Kensal Green Cemetery. His only surviving son, **Tom** (1835–74), published poems and humorous novels, in 1865 became editor of *Fun*. See his *Literary Reminiscences*, in *Hood's Own* (1839) and Life by W. Jerrold (1907).

HOOK, (1) **James** (1746–1827), English composer and organist, born in Norwich. In 1769 he became organist and composer at Marylebone Gardens, and held the equivalent post at Vauxhall Gardens (1774–1820). He wrote the music for a large number of plays, notably those of his wife, Miss Madden, and his son Theodore Edward (q.v.), as well as cantatas, odes and a vast number of popular songs, including ' The Lass of Richmond Hill '.

(2) **James Clarke** (1819–1907), English genre painter and etcher, born in London in 1846, painted Italian, Shakespearean and Biblical subjects; but, elected an R.A. in 1860, is best known for his seafaring pieces.

(3) **Theodore Edward** (1788–1841), English playwright, son of (1), born in London, achieved celebrity while still a boy as the author of thirteen successful comic operas and melodramas (1805–11), as a punster and matchless *improvisatore*, and as a practical joker—his greatest performance the Berners Street Hoax (1809). In 1812 he was given the post of treasurer to Mauritius. There Hook fared gloriously, until in 1818 a grave deficiency was detected in the public chest; he was arrested and sent, almost penniless, to England. He himself ascribed the ' unfortunate defalcation ' to a black clerk, who had committed suicide; anyhow, though criminal proceedings were dropped, in 1823 he was pronounced a crown debtor for £12,000, and was again sold up and arrested. In 1825 he was released from the King's Bench, but not from the debt; however, he made no effort to discharge it. Meanwhile, in 1820, he had started the Tory *John Bull*, and wrote a number of novels. See Lives by Barham (1849) and Brightfield (1928).

(4) **Walter Farquhar** (1798–1875), English church historian, born in London, was educated at Winchester and Christ Church, Oxford, and became vicar of Leeds in 1837. Mainly by his energy and enthusiasm twenty-one new churches were built in Leeds, as well as twenty-three parsonages and twenty-seven schools. He became dean of Chichester (1859). Among his works are *A Church Dictionary* (1842), *Ecclesiastical Biography* (1845–52) and *Lives of the Archbishops of Canterbury* (1860–76). See his *Life and Letters* (ed. W. R. W. Stephens, 1878).

HOOKE, Robert (1635–1703), English chemist and physicist, born at Freshwater, Isle of Wight, July 18, was educated at Westminster and Christ Church, Oxford. In 1662 he became curator of experiments to the Royal Society, and in 1677 its secretary; in 1665 he published his *Micrographia* on botany, chemistry, &c., and became professor of Geometry at Gresham College. He died March 3. Hooke anticipated the invention of the steam-engine, formulated Hooke's law of the extension and compression of elastic bodies, the simplest theory of the arch, the balance spring of watches and the anchor-escapement for clocks. The quadrant, Gregorian telescope and microscope are materially his inventions, and with the last he made important observations. After the Great Fire (1666) he was appointed city surveyor and designed the new Bethlehem Hospital (Moorfields) and Montague House. See his *Diary* (ed. Robinson and Adams, 1935) and Life by R. Waller (1705).

HOOKER, (1) **John**. See (4).

(2) **Joseph** (1814–79), American soldier, born at Hadley, Mass., served in the Mexican war, commanded a division of the 3rd corps in the Peninsular campaign of 1862, and it was he who compelled the enemy to evacuate Manassas. In command of the 1st corps he opened the battle at Antietam. In January 1863 he succeeded Burnside in the command of the army of the Potomac. In April, crossing the Rappahannock, he marched through the Wilderness to near Chancellorsville, where he awaited Lee's attack. But the Confederates turned the National flank, and, attacking the rear (May 2), threw part of Hooker's army into confusion. Next day the Confederates drove Hooker to the north side of the river, and he was superseded by Meade in June. In November he carried Lookout Mountain, and took part in the attack on Missionary Ridge. He accompanied Sherman in his invasion of Georgia, and served till the fall of Atlanta. He died in New York.

(3) **Sir Joseph Dalton** (1817–1911), English botanist, son of (6), born at Halesworth, Suffolk, and educated at Glasgow High School and University, succeeded his father in 1841 as director of the Royal Botanic Gardens at Kew. He went on several expeditions which resulted in works on the *flora* of New Zealand, Antarctica and India, as well as his *Himalayan Journals* (1854), *Genera Plantarum*, &c. He was awarded the O.M. in 1907. See monographs by L. Huxley (1918) and Bower (1919).

(4) **Richard** (1554–1600), English theologian, born near Exeter. At an early age he showed a ' quick apprehension of many perplext parts of learning ', and through his uncle, the antiquary, John Hooker or Vowell (1525–1601), chamberlain of the city, was brought under the notice of Jewel, Bishop of Salisbury, and sent to Corpus College, Oxford. He graduated M.A. in 1577, and got a fellowship; in 1581 he took orders, and preached at Paul's Cross. He was led into a marriage with Joan Churchman, a shrewish unlovely daughter of his landlady in London; in 1584 he became rector of Drayton-Beauchamp near Tring. Next year he obtained, through Whitgift, the mastership of the Temple, against a strong effort made to promote the Temple reader Travers, a prominent Puritan. The sermons of Travers soon became attacks upon the latitudinarianism of Hooker. When Whitgift silenced Travers, the latter appealed to the

Council with charges against Hooker's doctrine, and Hooker answered him with masterly conclusiveness and temperance. But having been drawn into controversy against his inclination, he felt it his duty to set forth the real basis of all church government, and to this end desired Whitgift to remove him to some quiet living. Accordingly, in 1591, he accepted the living of Boscombe near Salisbury, becoming also subdean and prebendary of Sarum; and here he finished four of the proposed eight books of the *Laws of Ecclesiastical Polity* (1594), the earliest great work of the kind in the English tongue, a monument of massive prose no less than of profound thought and masterly logic. It furnishes a conclusive answer to the Puritan exaggeration of the central position of Protestantism, the making of Scripture the sole guide of human conduct. It is mainly to Hooker's work that Anglican theology owes its tone and direction. The fifth book appeared in 1597 and the last three posthumously (1648, 1662, 1648 respectively). He died at Bishopsbourne, near Canterbury, where he had lived since 1595. See Life by I. Walton (1836, rev. ed. Church and Paget 1888), C. J. Sisson on his marriage (1940), and studies by Shirley (1949) and Munz (1952).

(5) **Thomas** (*c*. 1586–1647), English Nonconformist preacher, born at Markfield, Leicester, became a fellow of Emmanuel College, Cambridge, and was for three years a Puritan lecturer at Chelmsford. In 1630 he went to Holland, ejected for his Nonconformity; in 1633 sailed for Massachusetts, and received a charge at Cambridge. In 1636 he removed with his congregation to Connecticut, and founded Hartford. See Life prefixed to selection of his works (1849), and another by G. L. Walker (1891).

(6) **Sir William Jackson** (1785–1865), English botanist, father of (3), born at Norwich, collected specimens in Scotland (1806) and Iceland (1809), writing his *Recollections of Iceland* (1811). He became professor at Glasgow (1820) and director of the Royal Botanic Gardens at Kew in 1841. He was elected F.R.S. in 1810.

HOOLE, John (1727–1803), English translator of Tasso, Metastasio and Ariosto, and unsuccessful dramatist, was born in London. See Life by A. Sägesser (1922).

HOOPER, John (d. 1555), English bishop and martyr, born in Somerset about 1495, was educated at Oxford, whence in 1518 he passed to a Cistercian monastery at Gloucester. The reading of Zwingli made him a Reformer. He went in 1539 for safety's sake to the Continent, married in 1546 and settled at Zürich. After his return in 1549 he became a popular preacher in London, and in 1550 was appointed Bishop of Gloucester, but for his scruples over the oath and the episcopal habit was imprisoned for some weeks in the Fleet prison. In 1552 he received the bishopric of Worcester *in commendam*; in 1553, under Mary, was again committed to the Fleet, and on February 9 was burned for heresy at Gloucester. See his *Writings* (ed. Carr and Nevinson 1848–52).

HOOVER, Herbert Clark (1874–1964), 31st president of the United States born of Quaker parentage in 1874 at West Branch, Iowa, was trained in mining engineering, and gathered experience in the States, Australia, China (in the Boxer rising) and elsewhere. Both during and after World War I he was closely associated with relief of distress in Europe. He was secretary of commerce under Harding. As Republican he defeated ' Al ' Smith in the presidential election of 1928, but his opposition to direct governmental assistance for the unemployed after the world slump of 1929 made him unpopular and he was beaten by F. D. Roosevelt in 1932. He assisted President Truman with the various American European economic relief programmes which followed World War II. See his *Problems of Lasting Peace* (1942), &c., and *Memoirs* (in 3 vols., 1952–53 and 1955); also Life by H. G. Warren (1960).

HOPE, name of a Scottish noble family descended from John de Hope, who probably came to Scotland from France with Magdalen de Valois, Queen of James V, in 1537, and set up as a merchant in Edinburgh. Its noteworthy members were:

(1) **Sir Charles, 1st Earl of Hopetoun** (1681–1742), was elected privy councillor and a peer in 1702. A supporter of the Union (1707) with England, he became lord-lieutenant of Linlithgow in 1715 and in 1723 lord high commissioner to the general assembly of the Church of Scotland. He commissioned William Bruce in 1699 to build Hopetoun House on his estates, near Queensferry, and the building was considerably altered and completed in 1753 by the famous Scottish architects, William, and his son Robert, Adam (q.v.).

(2) **Sir John, 4th Earl of Hopetoun** (1765–1823), British general, served at the battle of Alexandria (1801), under Moore in Spain where he distinguished himself in the retreat to Corunna (1808), and finally under Wellington throughout the Peninsular war.

(3) **John Adrian Louis, 7th Earl and 1st Marquis of Linlithgow** (1860–1908), father of (4), was appointed first governor-general of Australia (1900–02) and was created marquis in 1902.

(4) **Victor Alexander John, 8th Earl and 2nd Marquis** (1887–1952), was viceroy of India (1936–43) and chancellor of Edinburgh University from 1944. His twin sons were, **Charles William, 3rd Marquis** (1912–), who won the M.C. and was taken prisoner with the 51st Highland Division in 1940, and **John Adrian, 1st Baron Glendevon** (1912–), who served in Italy during World War II, was a Conservative M.P., from 1950 to 1964, when he became a peer, and was minister of works (1959–62).

HOPE, (1) Anthony, pseud. of **Sir Anthony Hope Hawkins** (1863–1933), English novelist, born in London, called to the bar in 1887, chiefly remembered for his ' Ruritanian ' romances *The Prisoner of Zenda* (1894; dramatized 1896) and *Rupert of Hentzau* (1898). He also wrote the satirical *Dolly Dialogues* (1894), and an *Autobiography* (1927). He was knighted in 1918. See Life by Sir C. Mallet (1935).

(2) **Laurence**, pseud. of **Adela Florence Nicolson**, *née* **Cory** (1865–1904), English

poetess, born at Stoke Bishop, Glos., lived in India and wrote poems, influenced by Swinburne and coloured by the Orient, among them the *Indian Love Lyrics*, some of which are best known in their musical settings by Amy Woodford Finden.

(3) **Thomas** (1769–1831), English connoisseur and designer of furniture, born in London, while still a youth travelled in the Levant, Spain, &c., and collected many drawings, chiefly of buildings and sculptures. In England he first attracted attention by the interior decorations of his mansion in Duchess Street, Portland Place, London, a description of which with his theory of design appeared in his *Household Furniture* (1805). He introduced the vogue of Egyptian and Roman decoration into Britain.

HOPETOUN. See HOPE.

HOPKINS, (1) **Edward John** (1818–1901), English organist at the Temple Church, London (1843–98), wrote with Rimbault *The Organ, its History and Construction* (1855).

(2) **Sir Frederick Gowland** (1861–1947), English biochemist, born at Eastbourne, professor at Cambridge from 1914, was a pioneer in the study of accessory food factors, now called vitamins. He was awarded the Copley Medal in 1926, shared with Eijkman the Nobel prize for medicine (1929), was president of the Royal Society (1930–35) and of the British Association in 1933. He was awarded the O.M. in 1935. See study ed. Needham and Baldwin (1949).

(3) **Gerard Manley** (1844–89), English poet, was born at Stratford, London, and educated at Balliol College, Oxford. He was a pupil of Jowett and Pater and a disciple of Pusey. The religious ferment of the times absorbed him and finally he went over to Rome in 1866. In 1884 he was appointed to the chair of Greek at Royal Coll., now University Coll., Dublin. None of his poems was published in his lifetime, but his friend and literary executor, Dr Bridges, published a few of them in Miles's *Poets* and in 1918 he thought the time propitious for trying a full edition on the public. In a Preface to Notes, while admitting ' masterly beauties ' in this edition he warned readers of its faults of taste, chiefly oddity and obscurity. Hopkins's most famous poem, ' The Wreck of the *Deutschland*', he described as ' a great dragon ' —it came first in the volume—' to forbid all entrance '. The reception of the poems was very mixed, objection being taken mainly to Hopkins's experiments in what he called ' sprung rhythm ' which later prosodists declared was no novelty in English poetry. In 1930 with the issue of a new edition (with some new poems) the tide turned—' difficult ' poetry was now the fashion and Catholic and Anglo-Catholic critics helped in the chorus of approval led by I. A. Richards, Herbert Read and above all F. R. Leavis, the new law-giver in poetry. The former explored Hopkins's religious experience while the latter presented him as a revolutionary poet who in the heart of the Victorian era had anticipated modern *vers libre* and imagism. The publication of *Letters to Robert Bridges* and *The Correspondence of*

Gerard Manley Hopkins and Richard Watson Dixon (1935), and the *Notebooks* (1937), placed him and his poetry in a new and favourable light, setting forth as they did his ideals for poetry, and giving explanations of his prosodic experiments as well as sympathetic matter for a *Life*. At the same time they encouraged a minority view of the poet killed by the ' frustrated Jesuit ', of a ' lifelong tension between poet and priest '. The answer of W. H. Gardner, his best interpreter, is that from such tensions great poetry is born, and as for the ' terrible sonnets ' which expose the poet's struggles with unbelief, ' they are only " terrible " in the same way that the beauty of Christ is terrible '. The tendency of recent criticism is to regard Hopkins as a major poet and to make less of his revolutionary character. His influence on modern poetry can be exaggerated, but while imitation of his highly idiosyncratic manner is to be deprecated, in his hands the manner was capable of producing the lyric ecstasy of poems like ' Windhover ' and the religious tenderness of ' Felix Randall '. The definitive work on Hopkins is W. H. Gardner's *Gerard Manley Hopkins* (2 vols. 1944–49). The third edition of the *Poems* (1948) confirmed his title to be the leading Hopkins scholar. The *Sermons and Devotional Writings*, edited by Devlin, and the *Journals and Papers*, edited by House and Storey, appeared in 1959. See also studies by Pick (1942), Peters (1948) and Ritz (1960).

(4) **Harry Lloyd** (1890–1946), American administrator, born at Sioux City, was Federal emergency relief administrator in the depression of 1933, became secretary of commerce in 1938–40, and supervised the lend-lease programme in 1941. A close friend of F. D. Roosevelt, he undertook several important missions to Russia, Britain, &c., during World War II.

(5) **John.** See STERNHOLD.

(6) **Johns** (1795–1873), American merchant, a grocer in Baltimore, retired in 1847 with a large fortune. Besides a public park for Baltimore, he gave $4,500,000 to found a free hospital, and over $3,000,000 to found the Johns Hopkins University. See study by French (1946).

(7) **Mark** (1802–87), American educationist, president from 1836 to 1872 of Williams College, Williamstown, Mass., published many essays, sermons, &c., and was made a member of the Hall of Fame. See Life by Franklin Carter (1892). His brother **Albert** (1807–72) was an astronomer.

(8) **Matthew** (d. 1647), English witchfinder general appointed in 1644, discharged his duties so conscientiously that he himself naturally became suspect, and being found guilty by his own test in that he floated, bound, in water, was hanged. See novel *Witchfinder General* by Bassett (1966).

(9) **Samuel** (1721–1803), American Congregational theologian, born at Waterbury, Conn., studied at Yale, and was pastor (1743–69) of Housatonick (now Great Barrington), Mass., and then of Newport. His *System of Doctrines* (1793) maintains that all virtue consists in disinterested benevolence, and that all sin is selfishness.

HOPPNER, John (c. 1758–1810), English portrait painter, was born at Whitechapel of German parents. At first a chorister in the Chapel Royal, he entered the Royal Academy schools in 1775; was elected R.A. in 1795; and was Lawrence's only rival as a fashionable portrait painter. The Countess of Oxford is his masterpiece. See Life by McKay and Roberts (1909).

HOPTON, Ralph Hopton, 1st Baron (1598–1652), English soldier, a Somerset cavalier who commanded for the king in the south-west of England (1642–46), was created Lord Hopton in 1643, and died in exile at Bruges.

HORACE, Quintus Horatius Flaccus, hor'is (65–8 B.C.), Roman poet and satirist, was born near Venusia in southern Italy, December 8. His father was a manumitted slave, who as collector of taxes or auctioneer had saved enough money to buy a small estate. Horace was taken to Rome and taught by the best masters. About eighteen he proceeded to Athens to complete his education; and he was still there when the murder of Julius Caesar (44 B.C.) rekindled civil war. The same year he joined Brutus, who visited Athens while levying troops. He was present as an officer at the battle of Philippi, and joined in the flight that followed the Republican defeat, but found his way back to Italy. His property having been confiscated, he found employment in the civil service; but poverty, he says, drove him to make verses. His earliest were chiefly satires and lampoons; but some of his first lyrical pieces made him known to Varius and Virgil, who about 38 B.C. introduced him to Maecenas, minister of Octavianus and a munificent patron of art and letters. To his liberality Horace owed release from business and the gift of the farm among the Sabine Hills. Henceforward his springs and summers were generally spent at Rome, his autumns at the Sabine farm or a small villa at Tibur. As the unrivalled lyric poet of the time he had gradually acquired the position of poet laureate, when he died November 27. The first book of Satires, ten in number, appeared 35 B.C.; a second volume of eight satires in 30 B.C.; and about the same time the small collection of lyrics known as the Epodes. In 19 B.C. he produced his greatest work, three books of Odes. To about the same date belong his Epistles. The remainder of his writings are the Carmen Seculare; a fourth book of Odes; and three more epistles, one of which, known as the Ars Poetica, was perhaps left unfinished at his death. From his own lifetime till now Horace has had a popularity unexampled in literature. He was not a profound thinker; his philosophy is that rather of the market place than of the schools; he does not move among high ideals or subtle emotions. But of the common range of thought and feeling he is perfect and absolute master; and in the graver passages of the Epistles, as in the sad and noble cadence of his most famous Odes, the melancholy temper which underlay his quick and bright humour touches the deepest springs of human nature. His poetry supplies more phrases which have become proverbial than the rest of Latin literature put together. See works on him by W. Y. Sellar (1899),

J. F. d'Alton (1917), G. C. Fiske (1920), G. Showerman (1922), T. Frank (1928), T. R. Glover (1932), L. P. Wilkinson (1945), and Life by H. D. Sedgwick (1948).

HORATIUS, the name of three brothers chosen by King Tullus Hostilius to fight for Rome against the three Curiatii of Alba Longa. Two of the Horatii were speedily slain; the third, feigning flight, engaged each of his wounded opponents singly, and overcame them all. See Corneille's tragedy Horace (1640). It was a descendant of the survivor, Horatius Cocles, who in 505 B.C. held the bridge against the army of Lars Porsena. See Macaulay's Lays of Ancient Rome.

HORE-BELISHA, Leslie, 1st Baron Hore-Belisha (1893–1957), British barrister and politician, born at Devonport and educated at Clifton College and Oxford. After war service, he became a London journalist and in 1923, the year he was called to the bar, Liberal M.P. for Devonport. In 1931 he became first chairman of the National Liberal party. In 1934, as minister of transport, he gave his name to the ' Belisha ' beacons, drafted a new highway code and inaugurated driving tests for motorists. As secretary of state for war (1937–40) he carried out several far-ranging and controversial reforms to modernize and democratize the Army. He was minister of national insurance in the 1945 ' caretaker ' government, but lost his seat at the July election. In 1954 he received a peerage.

HORMAYR, Joseph, Freiherr von, hor'mir (1782–1848), Austrian historian, born at Innsbruck, in 1803 became keeper of the Austrian archives, and in 1816 imperial historiographer. But, having been imprisoned by Metternich for suspected complicity in a Tirolese revolt, he in 1828 entered the service of Bavaria. He published several works on the history of Tirol, an ' Austrian Plutarch ', and a general history of modern times.

HORN, (1) Charles Edward (1786–1849), English singer and composer of ' Cherry Ripe ', ' I know a bank ', as well as glees, piano-pieces, &c., was born in London of German parentage and died at Boston, U.S.
(2) Count (1518–68). See EGMONT.

HORNBY, (1) Sir Geoffrey Thomas Phipps (1825–95), English sailor, son of (3), was present at the bombardment of Acre (1840), and was created a K.C.B. in 1878, being then commander-in-chief in the Mediterranean, and a G.C.B. in 1885; three years later he was promoted Admiral of the Fleet. See Life by Mrs P. Egerton (1896).
(2) James John (1826–1910), English schoolmaster, son of (3), born at Winwick, and educated at Eton and Balliol, became headmaster of Eton in 1868, and provost in 1884.
(3) Sir Phipps (1785–1867), English admiral, father of (1) and (2), born at Winwick, Lancashire, entered the navy in 1797, commanded a frigate in Hoste's victory of Lissa (1811), was commander-in-chief in the Pacific (1847–50), and in 1852 was created a K.C.B.

HORNE, Richard Henry ' Hengist ' (1803–84), English writer, educated at Sandhurst, served in the Mexican navy and took his share in the fighting at Vera Cruz, San Juan Ulloa and elsewhere. Having survived yellow fever, sharks, broken ribs, shipwreck, mutiny and fire, he returned to England and took up writing. His famous epic *Orion* he published at the price of one farthing in 1843, to show his contempt for a public that would not buy poetry. In 1852 he went to Australia to dig for gold, and became a person of consequence in Victoria; but he returned in 1869. Among his books are *A New Spirit of the Age* (1844), in which E. B. Browning helped him; two tragedies, *Cosmo de' Medici* (1837) and *The Death of Marlowe* (1837), &c. Mrs Browning's letters to him were published in 1877.

HORNER, Francis (1778–1817), British economist, was born at Edinburgh, a merchant's son of mixed English and Scottish ancestry, was educated there, called to the Scottish bar (1797), English bar (1802), entered parliament, initiated several committees on economic matters, especially the convertibility of bullion, opposed agricultural protection and the slave trade. He helped to found, and contributed to, the *Edinburgh Review*, and in Lord Cockburn's words, he was 'possessed of greater public influence than any other private man'. He died of consumption at Pisa at thirty-eight. See his *Memoir* (1849).

HORNE-TOOKE. See TOOKE.

HORNUNG, Ernest William (1866–1921), English novelist, born in Middlesbrough. He was the creator of Raffles the gentleman burglar, hero of *The Amateur Cracksman* (1899), *Mr Justice Raffles* (1909), &c.

HORROCKS, (1) Sir Brian Gwynne (1895–), British general, was educated at Uppingham and R.M.C., joining the Middlesex Regiment in 1914. He served in France from 1914 to 1918 and in Russia in 1919. Command and staff assignments led to his appointment to command the 9th Armoured Division and then the 13th and 10th Corps in North Africa. His 30th Corps struggled gamely but unavailingly to link up with the airborne troops in Arnhem. On retirement Horrocks was made Gentleman Usher of the Black Rod. Well known as a military journalist and broadcaster, he was created K.B.E. in 1945 and K.C.B. in 1949. See his *A Full Life* (1960).

(2) **Jeremiah** (1619–41), English astronomer born at Toxteth near Liverpool, in 1632 entered Emmanuel College, Cambridge, and in 1639 became curate of Hoole, Lancashire, where he made his first observation of the transit of Venus (November 24, 1639, o.s.), deduced the solar parallax, corrected the solar diameter, and made tidal observations. See his works (ed. Wallis 1678).

HORSA. See HENGIST.

HORSLEY, (1) Samuel (1733–1806), English prelate, born in London, was educated at Westminster and Trinity Hall, Cambridge, and in 1759 succeeded his father as rector of Newington in Surrey. In 1767 he was elected F.R.S.; he published several scientific works and proposed a complete edition of Newton's works, which was published in 1785. But the chief event in his career was the controversy (1783–89) with Priestley,

who in his *History of the Corruptions of Christianity* included the orthodox doctrine of Christ's uncreated divinity. His services were rewarded with the bishopric of St Davids in 1788, Rochester in 1793, and St Asaph in 1802. See Life by H. Horsley Jebb (1909).

(2) **Sir Victor Alexander Haden** (1857–1916), English physiologist and surgeon, born in Kensington, became Fullerian professor at the Royal Institution (1891–93) and professor of Pathology at University College London (1893–96). He distinguished himself by his work on the localization of brain function, brain surgery, and the treatment of myxoedema. He died on active service in Mesopotamia. He had been elected F.R.S. in 1886, knighted in 1902 and awarded the Lannelongue international gold medal for surgery (1911). His father, **John Callcott** (1817–1903), was a genre painter, and his grandfather, **William** (1774–1858), a London organist and glee composer.

HORTENSE, Queen. See BONAPARTE, LOUIS.

HORTHY DE NAGYBÁNYA, Nikolaus, *hor'tee day nod'y'ban-ya* (1868–1957), regent of Hungary (1920–44), was born at Kenderes, rose to the post of Naval A.D.C. to Francis Joseph, and after his victory at Otranto (1917) became commander-in-chief of the Austro-Hungarian Fleet (1918). He was minister of war in the counter-revolutionary 'white' government (1919), opposing Bela Kun's Communist régime in Budapest and suppressing the latter with Rumanian help (1920). His aim of restoring the Hapsburg monarchy proved unpopular and so he allowed himself to be proclaimed regent. He ruled virtually as dictator, but allowed some parliamentary forms. He supported the Axis powers in World War II, supporting Germany's invasion of Yugoslavia and Russia until Hungary itself was overrun in March 1944. In October 1944 Horthy defied Hitler in broadcasting an appeal to the Allied powers for an armistice and was imprisoned in the castle of Weilheim, Bavaria, where he fell into American hands (1945), and was set free in 1946. He died at Estoril, Portugal, where he had lived since 1949. See his *Memoirs* (trans. 1956).

HORVÁTH, Mihály, *hor'vaht* (1809–78), Hungarian divine, author of a history of Hungary, became in 1844 professor of Hungarian at Vienna, and in 1848 Bishop of Csanad. He took an active part in the revolutionary war, was in exile condemned to death, but returned under the amnesty of 1867.

HOSIER, Francis (1673–1727), British admiral born at Deptford, who, with 4000 of his fleet, died of fever in the West Indies. He is remembered through Glover's *Hosier's Ghost* (1739).

HOSTE, Sir William (1780–1828), English admiral, was born at Ingoldisthorpe, Norfolk, served under Nelson, and on March 13, 1811, off Lissa in the Adriatic with four frigates, destroyed a Franco-Venetian squadron of eleven. He also captured Cattaro and Ragusa (1813–14) and was created a baronet. See memoir by his widow (1833).

HOSTILIUS, Tullus, third of the legendary kings of Rome, succeeded Numa Pompilius in 670 B.C. He conquered Fidenae and Veii; destroyed Alba, and removed the inhabitants to Rome; and warred against the Sabines.

HOSTRUP, Jens Christian, *hos'troop* (1818–1892), Danish lyric poet and playwright, born at Copenhagen. See his Autobiography (1893).

HOTCHKISS, Benjamin Berkeley (1826–85), American inventor, devised an improved type of cannon shell, a revolving-barrel machine gun (1872), and a magazine rifle (1875) widely used in the U.S.A., France and Britain.

HOTHAM, Sir John, *hō'thĕm* (d. 1645), English parliamentary soldier, in 1642 held Hull against Charles I, but in January 1645 was beheaded by parliament for his negotiations with the Earl of Newcastle, as was also his eldest son, John.

HOTSPUR, Harry. See PERCY.

HOUBRAKEN, Arnold, *how'brah-ken* (1660–1719), Dutch portrait and historical painter and also art historian, was born at Dordrecht. His son, Jakob (1698–1780), was a copper-engraver.

HOUDIN, Robert, *oo-dī* (1805–71), French conjurer, born at Blois, employed himself in Paris for some years in making mechanical toys and automata and gave magical soirées at the Palais Royal (1845–55). In 1856 he was sent by the government to Algiers to destroy the influence of the marabouts by exposing their pretended miracles. He wrote his Life (1857; trans. 1860).

HOUDINI, Harry, real name Erich Weiss (1874–1926), American magician, born at Appleton, Wisc., could escape from any kind of bonds or container. See Life by W. L. Gresham (1960).

HOUDON, Jean Antoine, *oo-dõ* (1741–1828), French classical sculptor, born at Versailles, in 1761 won the *prix de Rome*. He spent ten years in Rome, and there executed the colossal figure of St Bruno in Sta Maria degli Angeli. In 1805 he was appointed professor at the École des Beaux Arts. In 1785 he had visited America to execute a monument to Washington, a copy of which stands outside the National Gallery, London. His most famous busts are those of Diderot, Voltaire (foyer of the Théâtre Français, Paris) and Rousseau (Louvre). Others include Catherine II, Molière, Mirabeau and Napoleon. See French study by G. Giacometti (1928).

HOUGHTON, *hō'-*, (1) Lord. See MILNES.
   (2) William Stanley (1881–1913), English dramatist and critic, born at Ashton-upon-Mersey, after amateur dramatics in Manchester wrote *The Dear Departed* (1908), *The Younger Generation* (1910), *Hindle Wakes* (1912), &c.

HOUSE, Edward Mandell (1858–1938), American diplomat, born at Houston, Texas, during and after World War I represented America in many conferences, and was long a close associate of President Wilson. See his *Intimate Papers* (1926–28).

HOUSMAN, (1) Alfred Edward (1859–1936), English scholar and poet, born near Bromsgrove, was educated at Bromsgrove School and won a scholarship to St John's College, Oxford, where he failed in Greats finals and entered the Patent Office, which offered little leisure for the studies he had at heart.

Nevertheless the quality of his contributions to learned journals procured his return to academic life when in 1892 he was appointed professor of Latin at University College London. Nineteen years later he was elected to the Kennedy Chair of Latin at Cambridge, a post which allowed him the leisure to pursue his work, with the result that England once more boasted a textual critic of the heroic mould and temper. The temper often displayed itself in a waspish irascibility towards other scholars, especially those who uncritically accepted the earliest known text. Why he spent nearly thirty years (1903–30) on the text of a second-rate poet like Manilius, involving the sacrifice of a commentary on his beloved Propertius, has puzzled many people, but the qualities he brought to bear on the work were of the first order and his editions of Juvenal and Lucan were not open to the same objection. Housman, however, is known to the world by his English poetry, viz., *A Shropshire Lad* (1896), *Last Poems* (1922), and *More Poems*, published posthumously in 1936. The lyrics in *A Shropshire Lad* are arranged roughly to form a cyclic poem in which an uprooted country lad recalls the innocence and pleasures but also more poignantly the frustrations and local tragedies of a countryside which is only an imagined Shropshire and indeed hardly pastoral in the old sense at all. Though in ballad quatrains, the lyrics have a pregnant brevity of expression and a close-knit syntax which is purely classical. Still the sameness of mood and measure means that Housman's is a restricted vein of poetry, a minor muse. In his provocative Cambridge lecture on 'The Name and Nature of Poetry' (1933), he referred poetic inspiration to physical reaction in the nervous system, and since he himself was content with short flights and minor form he seemed to think of poetry as jets of feeling rather than sustained architectonics. Hence his exclusion of metaphysical poetry which has been the main poetic activity of our age. Modern scholarship has shown that he was accessible to several contemporary influences which relate him to his own generation—the Stevenson of *Underwoods* and *Songs of Travel* more than most. See *Collected Works* (1939), Life by Grant Richards (1941), memoir by Laurence Housman (in *A.E.H.; Some Poems, etc.*, 1937), and P. Withers, *A Buried Life* (1940); also studies by H. W. Garrod in *The Profession of Poetry* (1929), Edmund Wilson in *The Triple Thinkers* (1938), and Ian Scott-Kilvert (1955). The most exhaustive study of sources is by Norman Marlow (1958).
   (2) Laurence (1865–1959), English novelist and dramatist, younger brother of (1), born at Bromsgrove, studied art at Lambeth and South Kensington and attracted attention by his illustrations of Meredith's poem *Jump-to-Glory Jane*. He is best known for his *Little Plays of St Francis* (1922) and his Victorian biographical 'chamber plays', *Angels and Ministers* (1921), *Victoria Regina* (1937), &c. His autobiography, *The Unexpected Years* (1937), reveals a romantic Victorian figure, a conservative radical who espoused pacificism and votes for women.

HOUSSAY, Bernardo (1887–1971), Argentine physiologist, professor at Buenos Aires until 1965, investigated internal secretions and shared the Nobel prize for medicine (1947) with Carl and Gerty Cori.

HOUSTON, hoos'-, (1) **Edward James** (1847–1914), American electrical engineer, with Elihu Thomson (q.v.) invented arc lighting, patented in 1881.

(2) **Samuel** (1793–1863), American soldier and statesman, born in Rockbridge County, Va., enlisted in 1818, and was elected in 1823 and 1825 member of congress, and in 1827 governor of Tennessee. From 1829 he spent three years among the Cherokees. In the Texan war, as commander-in-chief, he defeated the Mexicans on the San Jacinto in April 1836, and achieved Texan independence. He was elected president of the republic, re-elected in 1841, and on the annexation of Texas, in 1845, returned to the U.S. senate. Elected governor of Texas in 1859, he opposed secession, was deposed in 1861, and retired to private life. See works by Bruce (1891), Williams (1893) and James (1929).

HOVEDEN, (1) **John** (d. 1275), Latin poet, chaplain to Queen Eleanor of Provence, founded Hoveden or Howden Church near Selby.

(2) **Roger of.** See ROGER OF HOVEDEN.

HOWARD, the name of the house which stands at the head of the English Catholic nobility, was founded by Sir William Howard, Chief-justice of the Common Pleas (d. 1308). His grandson, Sir John Howard, was a captain of the king's navy and sheriff of Norfolk; and his grandson married the daughter of the 1st Duke of Norfolk and coheiress of the house of Mowbray. In one or other of their widespread branches, the Howards have enjoyed, or still enjoy, the earldoms of Carlisle, Suffolk, Berkshire, Northampton, Arundel, Wicklow, Norwich, and Effingham, and the baronies of Bindon, Howard de Walden, Howard of Castle Rising, and Howard of Effingham. See Henry Howard's *Memorials of the Howard Family* (1834). Its most prominent members in chronological order were:

(1) **Sir John,** known as **Jack of Norfolk, 1st Duke of Norfolk** (c. 1430–85), father of (2), was by Edward IV made constable of Norwich Castle, sheriff of Norfolk and Suffolk, treasurer of the royal household, Lord Howard and Duke of Norfolk, earl marshal of England (a distinction still borne by his descendants), and lord admiral of England, Ireland and Aquitaine. He was slain on Bosworth field and his honours were attainted.

(2) **Thomas, 2nd Duke of Norfolk, 1st Earl of Surrey** (1443–1524), son of (1) and father of (3), was wounded at Bosworth, captured, and after three years imprisonment in the Tower, obtained a reversal of his own and his father's attainders, and, being restored to his honours, is celebrated for his defeat of the Scots at Flodden (1513).

(3) **Thomas, 3rd Duke of Norfolk** (1473–1554), son of (2) and father of (4), was attainted by Henry VIII, but was afterwards restored in blood. By his second wife (his first was a daughter of Edward IV) he was father of the Earl of Surrey executed by Henry VIII. The same sentence had been passed on the duke, when the death of Henry saved him.

(4) **Henry, Earl of Surrey.** See SURREY.

(5) **Catharine** (d. 1542), grand-daughter of (2), in the same month as Anne of Cleves was divorced (July 1540) became Henry VIII's fifth queen. In the November of the following year she was charged by Cranmer with intercourse before her marriage with a musician and a kinsman, and on February 13 she was beheaded. See Martin Hume's *Wives of Henry VIII* (1905).

(6) **Charles, Lord Howard of Effingham, Earl of Nottingham** (1536–1624), English sailor, in 1573 succeeded his father (ninth son of (2)), who in 1554 had been raised to the peerage and been made lord high admiral. In 1585 that dignity was conferred on the son, who in 1588 commanded against the Armada. For his share with Essex in the Cadiz expedition (1596) he was created an earl; in 1601 he quelled Essex's rising. There is no proof that he was a Catholic.

(7) **Thomas, 4th Duke of Norfolk, 1st Earl of Northampton** (1536–72), grandson of (3), was attainted and executed for high treason, for his communication with Mary, Queen of Scots. The family honours were again restored, partly by James I and partly by Charles II.

(8) **Thomas, 2nd Earl of Arundel and Surrey** (1586–1646), English statesman and connoisseur, was prominent in the court and public life of his day, but is remembered for his art collections, particularly for the Arundel Marbles (statues, inscribed marbles, &c.), gifted by his grandson to Oxford University (1667).

(9) **Henry Fitzalan, 15th Duke of Norfolk** (1847–1917), English politician, father of (10), was postmaster general (1895–1900), mayor of Sheffield (1895) and a member of the London County Council (1892–95).

(10) **Bernard Marmaduke, 16th Duke of Norfolk** (1908–), son of (9), earl marshal and premier duke and earl of England, a steward of the Jockey Club and, vice chairman of the Turf Board since 1965

HOWARD, (1) **Sir Ebenezer** (1850–1928), English founder of the garden city movement, emigrated to Nebraska in 1872 but returned to England in 1877 and became a parliamentary shorthand-writer. His *Tomorrow* (1898), later republished as *Garden Cities of Tomorrow* (new ed. 1946), envisaged self-contained communities with both rural and urban amenities and green belts, and led to the formation in 1899 of the Garden City Association and to the laying out of Letchworth (1903) and Welwyn Garden City (1919) as prototypes. See study by D. Macfadyen (1933).

(2) **Edward** (d. 1841), English novelist, a navy lieutenant who on his retirement wrote sea stories, including *Rattlin the Reefer* (1836), *Outward Bound* (1838), &c.

(3) **John** (1726–90), English prison reformer, was born at Hackney. The fortune left him in 1742 by his father, an upholsterer, enabled him to travel; and in 1756, the year after the death of his first elderly wife, he set sail for

Lisbon, but was captured by a French privateer, and carried to a Brest prison. A short captivity left a lasting impression of the inhuman treatment of prisoners of war. He married a second time, and settled at Cardington near Bedford. In 1773, now high-sheriff for Bedfordshire, he recognized that many prisoners were unjustly detained in prison untried, or even after being pronounced innocent, until they or their friends had paid certain fees to the jailers, and began a series of tours through Great Britain and Ireland, for the purpose of investigating the condition of prisons and prisoners. Chiefly as the result of his efforts, two acts were passed in 1774, one providing for fixed salaries to jailers, and the other enforcing cleanliness. His remaining years were principally spent in visiting the prisons of Great Britain and of the Continent. Whilst at Kherson, in Russia, he caught camp fever from attending a prisoner and died. The chief results of his observations were recorded in *The State of Prisons in England and Wales, with an Account of some Foreign Prisons* (1777); and *An Account of the Principal Lazarettos in Europe* (1780). See Lives by Baldwin Brown (1818), J. G. Rowe (1927), D. L. Howard (1958) and M. Southwood (1959).

(4) **Oliver Otis** (1830–1909), American soldier, born at Leeds, Maine, took command of a regiment of Maine volunteers in 1861. In 1864 he commanded the Army of the Tennessee, and led the right wing of Sherman's army in the march to the sea. He was commissioner of the Freedmen's Bureau (1865–74); was first president of Howard University at Washington, named after him; and conducted two Indian campaigns.

(5) **Sir Robert** (1626–98), English Restoration dramatist, son of the 1st Earl of Berkshire, wrote *The Committee* (1663) and the *Indian Queen*, the last assisted by his brother-in-law, John Dryden. His brothers **Edward** and **James** were also dramatists. See studies by Arundel (1929) and H. J. Oliver (1964).

HOWARD OF EFFINGHAM. See HOWARD (Family (6)).

HOWE, (1) Elias (1819–67), American inventor of the sewing machine, born at Spencer, Mass., worked as mechanic at Lowell and Boston, where he constructed and patented (1846) the sewing machine. He made an unsuccessful visit to England to introduce his invention, and returning in 1847 to Boston, found his patent had been infringed. Harassed by poverty, he entered on a seven years' war of litigation to protect his rights, was ultimately successful (1854) and amassed a fortune.

(2) **John** (1630–1705), English Puritan divine, born at Loughborough, studied at Cambridge and Oxford, and, after preaching for some time at Winwick and Great Torrington, was appointed domestic chaplain to Cromwell in 1656. In 1659 he returned to Torrington, but the Act of Uniformity ejected him in 1662, and he wandered about preaching in secret till 1671. In 1668 he published *The Blessedness of the Righteous*, in 1671 became domestic chaplain to Lord Massereene, of Antrim Castle in Ireland. Here he wrote his *Vanity of Man as Mortal*,

and began his greatest work, *The Good Man the Living Temple of God* (1676–1702). In 1676 he became pastor of the dissenting congregation in Silver Street, London. In 1685 he travelled with Lord Wharton on the Continent, and settled at Utrecht, till in 1687 the Declaration of Indulgence recalled him to England, where he died. See Life by Calamy prefixed to his works (1724), and those by H. Rogers (1836) and R. F. Horton (1895).

(3) **Joseph** (1804–73), Canadian statesman, born in Nova Scotia, proprietor and editor of the Halifax *Nova Scotian*, became premier of Nova Scotia (1863–70) and after federation entered the first Canadian government at Ottawa. See W. L. Grant, *The Tribune of Nova Scotia* (1914).

(4) **Julia Ward** (1819–1910), American writer, wife of (6), born in New York, became a prominent suffragette and Unitarian, and wrote several volumes of poems, including *Passion Flowers* (1854), as well as travel books and a play. She is best known for ' The Battle Hymn of the Republic' (1861), which begins ' Mine eyes have seen the glory of the coming of the Lord' to the tune of ' John Brown's body'. She was the first woman member of the American Academy.

(5) **Richard, 1st Earl** (1726–99), British sailor, brother of (7) and son of the second Viscount Howe, was born in London, March 8. He left Eton at thirteen, and, entering the navy, served under Anson against the Spaniards in the Pacific. Made postcaptain at twenty, he the same year drove from the coast of Scotland two French ships conveying troops and ammunition to the Young Pretender. After serving off the coast of Africa, Howe specially distinguished himself in the naval operations of the Seven Years' War. In 1758 he succeeded to the Irish title of viscount on the death of his brother, **George Augustus** (1724–58), the brigadier-general, who was killed before Ticonderoga. Appointed a lord of the admiralty in 1763, he became in 1765 treasurer of the Navy. In 1778 he defended the American coast against a superior French force. He was made a viscount of Great Britain in 1782, and, sent out to relieve Gibraltar, he disembarked troops and supplies, and then offered battle to the combined fleets of France and Spain, which declined an engagement. He was made first lord of the admiralty in 1783, and an earl in 1788. When war with France broke out in 1793 he took command of the Channel Fleet, and next year gained off Ushant ' the glorious first of June'. His last service was to recall to their duty the mutinous seamen at Spithead and Portsmouth in 1797. He died August 5. See Lives by G. Mason (1803) and J. Barrow (1838).

(6) **Samuel Gridley** (1801–76), American philanthropist, husband of (4), born in Boston, organized the medical staff of the Greek army (1824–27), went to America to raise contributions, and, returning with supplies, formed a colony on the isthmus of Corinth. Swamp-fever drove him from the country in 1830. In 1831 he went to Paris to study the methods of educating the blind, and

becoming mixed up in the Polish insurrection, spent six weeks in a Prussian prison. On his return to Boston he established schools for the blind (see BRIDGMAN, LAURA) and for idiots. In 1851–53 he edited the antislavery *Commonwealth*, and in 1867 revisited Greece with supplies for the Cretans. See Life by F. A. Sanborn (N.Y. 1891).

(7) **William, 5th Viscount Howe** (1729–1814), British soldier, brother of (5), joined the army in 1746, served under Wolfe at Louisburg (1758) and Quebec, where he led the famous advance to the Heights of Abraham. He became M.P. in 1758, but in the American War of Independence won the victory at Bunker's Hill (1775) and became commander-in-chief. Supported by his sailor-brother from the sea, he captured Brooklyn, New York, and, after the victory of White Plains (1776), Washington. The following year he defeated the Americans at Brandywine Creek. His subsequent lethargy marred his military career and he was superseded by Clinton in 1778.

HOWELL, (1) James (*c.* 1593–1666), English writer, studied at Oxford and travelled abroad on business and in 1627 entered parliament. From 1632 to 1642 he was mainly employed as a Royalist spy; and during the Civil War was imprisoned by Parliament (1642–50). At the Restoration the office of historiographer-royal was created for him. Besides translations from Italian, French and Spanish, Howell wrote forty-one works on history, politics and philosophy as well as *Instructions for Forreine Travell* (1642), a supplement to Cotgrave's dictionary and the witty and entertaining *Epistolae Ho-Elianae; or Familiar Letters* (1645–55). See study by W. H. Vann (1924).

(2) **Thomas Bayly** (1768–1815), English editor, a barrister who edited vols. i-xxi of the *State Trials* (1809–15), as his son, **Thomas Jones** (d. 1858), did vols. xxii-xxxiii (1815–1826).

HOWELLS, (1) Herbert (1892–   ), English composer, born in Lydney, Glos. He studied under Stanford at the Royal College of Music, where he became professor of Composition (1920) after a short time as sub-organist of Salisbury Cathedral. In 1936 he followed Holst as director of music at St Paul's Girls' School, and in 1952 became professor of Music at London Univ., retiring in 1962. He is best known for his choral works, especially the *Hymnus Paradisi*, which combine an alert sense of 20th-century musical developments with a firm foundation in the English choral tradition.

(2) **William Dean** (1837–1920), American novelist and critic, a powerful influence in the American literary world of his time, born at Martin's Ferry, Ohio, became a compositor in a printing office, and stimulated by the works of Cervantes, Pope and Heine, began to write poetry which was published in the *Atlantic Monthly* (1860–61), which he later edited (1872–81). His biography of Lincoln (1860) procured him the post of consul at Venice. His association with *Harper's Magazine* (1886–91) made him into the king of critics in America. The 'reticent realism' of his early novels, as in

the slight *Their Wedding Journey* (1872) matured in depth of feeling in *The Lady of the Aroostook* (1879) and finally gave way to Tolstoian humanitarian naturalism in *A Hazard of New Fortunes* (1890). His theories of fiction, which influenced Mark Twain, Henry James and Wendell Holmes (qq.v.), were expounded in *Criticism and Fiction* (1891). See his *Years of my Youth* (1915) and *Literary Friends* (1900), and Lives by O. W. Firkins (1924), his daughter M. Howells (1928) and V. W. Brooks (1959).

HOWIE, John (1735–93), Scottish writer, a farmer of Lochgoin, near Kilmarnock, who claimed to be descended from a Waldensian refugee, Huet (1178), and whose *Scots Worthies* (1774) chronicles the sufferings of the martyrs of the Covenant.

HOWISON, Jock, the traditional rescuer of James V (' the Gudeman of Ballengeich ') from a band of gypsies at Cramond Bridge.

HOWITT, (1) Mary, née Botham (1799–1888), English writer, wife of (2), born at Coleford, Gloucestershire, and brought up at Uttoxeter, married in 1821 and collaborated with her husband in many of his writings, but published independently poems, essays and stories, as well as *Our Four-footed Friends* (1867), a popular history of the U.S. (1859), &c., and translated the fairy tales of Andersen and Frederika Bremer. She was buried next to her husband in the Monte Testaccio cemetery in Rome. See her autobiography (1889) and Life by Britten (1890).

(2) **William** (1792–1879), English author, husband of (1), born at Heanor, Derbyshire, served four years as apprentice to a builder and carpenter, before settling down to writing in Nottingham (1823–35). He then travelled extensively on the Continent and visited Australia (1852–54). His wife had a share in his *Forest Minstrel* (1827) and *Ruinea Abbeys of Great Britain*. His own works, coloured by his reforming zeal, include *Journal of Literature and Popular Progress* (1849), *The Book of the Seasons* (1831), *Colonisation and Christianity* (1838), &c. Husband and wife left the Quakers in 1847 and he became a spiritualist. See S. C. Hall, *Retrospect of a Long Life* (1883).

HOYLE, (1) Edmond (1672–1769), English writer on card games, called the 'Father of Whist', lived and died in London. His popular *Short Treatise on Whist* (1742) ran into many editions and was ultimately incorporated with his manuals on Backgammon, Brag, Quadrille, Piquet and Chess into an omnibus volume (1748).

(2) **Fred** (1915–   ), British astronomer, mathematician, astrophysicist and writer, born in Bingley, Yorkshire. A fundamental contributor to our knowledge of outer space, he explained his theories lucidly and concisely in *Nature of the Universe* (1952) and *Frontiers of Astronomy* (1955). He made a successful début as a writer of science fiction with *The Black Cloud* (1957). Elected F.R.S. in 1957, he became Plumian professor of Astronomy at Cambridge in 1958.

HRABANUS MAURUS (*c.* 776–856), Archbishop of Mainz from 847, was born here, and was Abbot of Fulda 822–42. He wrote commentaries, homilies, &c.

HRDLIČKA, Ales, *hèr′dlich-ka* (1869–1943), American anthropologist, born at Humpolec, Bohemia, studied in America and was on the staff of the Natural History Museum, New York, and the National Museum, Washington. His anthropological studies inclined him to the view that American Indians were of Asiatic origin.

HROSWITHA, *hros-vee′tah* (*c.* 932–1002), German Benedictine nun of Gandersheim near Göttingen, wrote Latin poems and six prose Terentian comedies, edited by K. Strecker (1906), trans. C. St John (1923).

HROZNY, Bedřich (1879–1952), Czech orientalist, born at Lissa, the first to decipher the Hittite language, wrote *Die Sprache der Hethiter* (1917), &c.

HSIA KUEI, *shee′ah kway* (fl. 1180–1230), Chinese artist, a pupil of Li T'ang, executed delicate, almost impressionistic landscapes. See A. Waley, *Introduction to the Study of Chinese Painting* (1923).

HSUAN T'UNG. See Pu-yi.

HSUANG CHUANG, *shü-ang′ dzang* (*c.* 600–664), Chinese Buddhist traveller in India, born in Honan, became a Buddhist monk in 620 and made a long pilgrimage through China and India which he recounted in a book, translated into French by S. Julien (1858). See also Wu Cheng-en, *Monkey* (trans. A. Waley, 1942).

HUANG-TI. See Shih Huang Ti.

HUBBLE, Edwin Powell (1889–1953), American astronomer, born at Marshfield, Mo., worked at the Mt Wilson Observatory from 1919 and gave his name to the law making the apparent velocities of receding universes proportional to their distance.

HUBER, François (1750–1831), Swiss naturalist, born at Geneva, lost his eyesight in youth, but by help of his wife and a servant made many important observations on the habits of bees, described in several works. His son, **Jean Pierre** (1777–1841), also assisted him and wrote on ants.

HUBERT, St (656–727), son of the Duke of Guienne, lived a luxurious life, but was converted, and in 708 became Bishop of Liège. In art he is a hunter converted by the apparition of a crucifix between the horns of a stag. This story may have been borrowed from St Eustace. His festival is November 3.

HÜBNER, Julius (1806–82), German painter, born at Oels, studied at Düsseldorf, and became professor of Painting and director of the Gallery at Dresden. He specialized in Biblical and classical subjects.

HUC, *ük,* (1) **Evariste Régis** (1813–60), French Roman Catholic missionary, born at Toulouse, in 1839 joined the mission of the Lazarist Fathers to China. In 1844, with Père Gabet and a single native convert, he set out for Tibet, and in January 1846 reached Lhasa; but scarcely had they started a mission there, when an order for their expulsion was obtained by the Chinese resident, and they were conveyed back to Canton. Huc's health having broken down, he returned to France in 1852. He wrote *Souvenirs* of his great journey (1850; trans. by Hazlitt, 1852), &c. See monograph by Prince Henry of Orleans (Paris 1893).

(2) **Philippe.** See Derème.

HUCH, Ricarda, *hooᴋʜ* (1864–1947), German writer, born at Brunswick. She studied at Zürich, travelled extensively in Italy, married twice, and finally settled in Europe. A neoromantic, she rejected naturalism, and wrote novels including *Erinnerungen von Ludolf Ursleu dem Jüngeren* (1892) and *Aus der Triumphgasse* (1902), criticism including *Blütezeit, Ausbreitung und Verfall der Romantik* (1899–1902), and social and political works including *Der Grosse Krieg in Deutschland* (1912–14). She also wrote on religious themes, in *Luther's Glaube* (1915) and *Das Zeitalter der Glaubenspaltung* (1937).

HUDDLESTON, (1) **John** (1608–98), English Benedictine monk, born at Faringdon Hall near Preston. In 1651 he had aided Charles II in his escape from Worcester, and in 1685 he reconciled him on his deathbed to Catholicism.

(2) **Trevor** (1913–   ), Anglican missionary and bishop of Masasi, Tanzania, from 1960, was educated at Christ Church, Oxford, and ordained in 1937. He entered the Community of the Resurrection and in 1943 went to Johannesburg, where he ultimately became Provincial of the order (1949–55). From 1956 to 1958, he was novice-master of the Community in Mirfield, Yorkshire, and from 1958 to 1960, prior of its London House. He is distinguished by a passionate belief that the doctrine of the universal brotherhood of men in Christ should be universally applied. His book, *Naught for your Comfort* (1956), reflects this conviction in the light of his experiences in South Africa and its racial problems and policies.

HUDSON, (1) **George** (1800–71), English 'Railway King', born near York, was a linen-draper there, when, inheriting £30,000 in 1828, he went into local politics and railway speculation. He bought large estates, was thrice lord mayor of York, and was elected M.P. for Sunderland (1845). But the railway mania of 1847–48 plunged him into ruin. He was accused of having 'cooked' accounts, and of having paid dividends out of capital. Legal proceedings were instituted, and his suddenly-acquired gains were swept away. Sunderland, however, continued to elect him until 1859. See *Life* by Lambert (1934).

(2) **Henry** (d. 1611), English navigator, sailed in April 1607, in a small vessel with eleven sailors, on his first voyage for the discovery of a passage across the pole to the 'islands of spicery'. On his second voyage (1608) he reached Novaya Zemlya. He undertook a third (1609) for the Dutch East India Company, sailed for Davis Strait, then steering southwards, entered the Hudson River, and ascended it for 150 miles. Starting in April 1610, in the *Discoverie* of 70 tons, he reached Greenland in June, arrived at Hudson Strait, and passing through it, entered the great bay which now bears his name. He resolved to winter there; but food fell short, and the men mutinied and cast him adrift, with eight others, on June 23, to die, whereas the mutineers eventually reached England. George Asher's monograph (Hakluyt Society, 1860) proves that, though Hudson was a bold sailor, neither

river, strait nor sea was first discovered by him. See also Life by L. Powys (1927).

(3) **Henry Norman** (1814–86), American Shakespearean scholar, born at Cornwall, Vt., became a baker, wheelwright, teacher, clergyman, army chaplain, and editor of church periodicals. He wrote on Shakespeare and founded a chair of Shakespearean studies at Boston University.

(4) ' **Sir** ' **Jeffery** (1619–82), Henrietta Maria's dwarf, 3 feet 9 inches high, born a butcher's son at Oakham, suffered imprisonment as a Catholic over the ' Popish Plot '.

(5) **William** (c. 1730–93), English botanist, born at Kendal, a founder member of the Linnaean Society (1791), had the genus Hudsonia named after him.

(6) **William Henry** (1841–1922), British author and naturalist, born near Buenos Aires, came to England in 1869 and became a British subject in 1900. His early writings concerned the natural history of South America, but he is best known to English readers for his delightful account of his rambles in the New Forest in *Hampshire Days* (1903), and his romantic novel *Green Mansions* (1904). A bird sanctuary, containing Epstein's ' Rima ' decoration, was erected to his memory in Hyde Park, London (1925). See his autobiographical *Far away and Long Ago* (1918), *An Old Thorn* (1920), his letters ed. E. Garnett (1923), and Lives by Morley Roberts (1924), R. Hamilton (1951) and Tomalin (1954).

HUEFFER, *hüf'-*, (1) changed in 1923 to **FORD**, **Ford Madox** (1873–1939), English writer, son of (2), born at Merton. He collaborated with Conrad in *The Inheritors* (1901) and *Romance* (1903), wrote some forty books of which the best was his historical romance *The Fifth Queen* (1906), and founded and edited the *English Review* (1908). After World War I, in which he was gassed, he exiled himself to France and the U.S. He wrote some fine poetry (collected 1941), and a brilliant series of war novels, *The Good Soldier* (1915) and the tetralogy *Parade's End* (written in the 1920s, reprinted 1950). See *The Bodley Head Ford Madox Ford*, ed. by Greene (2 vols., 1962), D. Goldring's *The Last Pre-Raphaelite* (1948), and studies by Cassell, Wiley (1962) and Lid (1964).

(2) **Francis** (1845–89), British music critic, son-in-law of Ford Madox Brown (q.v.) and father of (1), born in Westphalia, settled in London in 1869 and as music critic of *The Times* championed *Richard Wagner and the Music of the Future* (1874).

HUERTA, **Vicente García de la**, *wayr'tah* (1730–87), Spanish poet and critic, born at Zafra, was head of the Royal Library at Madrid. His famous tragedy of *Raquel* (1778) was founded upon the story of Alfonso VIII's love for the fair Jewess, Rachel.

HUET, **Pierre Daniel**, *ü-ay* (1630–1721), French prelate and scholar, born at Caen, in 1652 visited the court of Queen Christina, and discovered the MS. of Origen which he edited (1668). In 1670 he was appointed with Bossuet tutor of the dauphin. Having in 1676 taken orders, he was successively Abbot of Aunay (1678), Bishop of Soissons (1685) and Avranches

(1692), and Abbot of Fontenay (1699). In 1679 appeared his *Demonstratio Evangelica*. In 1701 he withdrew to the Jesuits' house in Paris. He also wrote a critique of Cartesian philosophy and *Faiblesse de l'esprit humain*. See Latin autobiography (1713) and a French life by Bartholomess (1850).

HUFELAND, Christoph Wilhelm, *hoo'fě-lant* (1762–1836), German physician, born at Langensalza, became court physician at Weimar, in 1793 professor of Medicine at Jena, in 1798 president of the medical college at Berlin, and in 1809 a university professor. He wrote *Makrobiotik*, or the art of prolonging life (1796), and other works.

HÜGEL, Baron Friedrich von (1852–1925), Roman Catholic religious writer and biblical critic, born in Florence, son of the Austrian ambassador, settled in England in 1871. He wrote *The Mystical Element in Religion* (1908–09), &c. See *Selected Letters*, ed. with memoir by B. Holland (1929), and Life by Bedoyère (1951).

HUGGINS, (1) **Charles Brenton** (1900–), U.S. scientist, born at Halifax, Nova Scotia, worked at Chicago University from 1927, where he became professor of Surgery in 1936 and head of the Ben May Laboratory for Cancer Research in 1951. He shared the Nobel prize for medicine with Rous (2) in 1966 for work on cancer research, notably his discovery of hormonal treatment for cancer of the prostate gland.

(2) **Godfrey Martin, 1st Viscount Malvern of Rhodesia and Bexley** (1883–), Rhodesian statesman, practised medicine in London and in Rhodesia (1911–21) before entering politics in 1923, was premier of Southern Rhodesia (1933–53) and of the Federation of Rhodesia and Nyasaland (1953–56). He was created viscount in 1955.

(3) **Sir William** (1824–1910), British astronomer, born in London, in 1852 was elected a member of the Microscopical Society, and for some years studied physiology with the microscope. But having in 1855 built an observatory near London, he began the study of the physical constitution of stars, planets, comets and nebulae. By researches on the sun's spectra and the spectra of certain comets, he ascertained that their luminous properties are not the same. He determined the amount of heat that reaches the earth from some of the fixed stars. He was elected F.R.S. (1865), was P.R.S. (1900–05), was awarded the Copley Medal and the O.M. (1902) and was knighted in 1897. His wife, née Margaret Lindsay Murray (1848–1915), shared his work.

HUGH, St, (1) **of Avalon**, also called St Hugh of Lincoln (c. 1135–1200), Bishop of Lincoln, was born of noble family at Avalon in Burgundy. Priest at the Grande Chartreuse (1160–70), he joined a Carthusian monastery at Witham, Somerset, became Bishop of Lincoln (1186), and was canonized in 1220. See Lives by Thurston (1898) and Woolley (1927), and in 2 vols., ed. by Farmer and Douie (1961–62).

(2) **of Lincoln** (c. 1246–55), English boy supposed to have been murdered by the Jews of Lincoln, as told in ballads and early chronicles. See monograph by Jacobs (1894).

HUGH CAPET. See CAPET.

HUGHES, (1) Charles Evans (1862–1948), American politician, born at Glens Falls, N.Y., rose at the bar, was governor of New York (1907–10), became an associate justice, U.S. Supreme Court (1910), chief justice (1930–41). Republican candidate for the presidency in 1916, secretary of state (1921–25), he presided at the Washington Conference in 1921. See Life by Pusey (1951).

(2) **David Edward** (1831–1900), Anglo-American inventor, born in London, was brought up in Virginia and was professor of Music at Bardston College, Ky. (1850–53). In 1855 he invented a telegraph typewriter which was widely adopted and in 1878 a microphone and an induction balance. He left a large fortune to London hospitals.

(3) **Hugh Price** (1847–1902), Wesleyan minister, born at Carmarthen, was chosen to pioneer the West London mission in 1886. In his preaching he combined methodism and socialism and turned public opinion against Parnell. See Life by D. P. Hughes (1904).

(4) **Langston** (1902–67), American Negro poet and novelist, born at Joplin, Missouri, studied at Lincoln University, Penn., and after a variety of odd jobs wrote *Weary Blues* (1926), a collection of verse entitled *The Dream Keeper* (1932), *The Ways of White Folks* (1934) and *Shakespeare in Harlem* (1942). See his autobiographical *The Big Sea* (1940).

(5) **Ted** (1930–), English poet, born at Mytholmroyd, Yorks., educated at Pembroke Coll., Cambridge. His work, including *The Hawk in the Rain* (1957) and *Lupercal* (1960), as well as several collections of children's verse, has placed him among the foremost contemporary poets. In 1956 he married **Sylvia Plath** (1932–63), also an outstanding poet. See her posthumous collection *Ariel* (1965).

(6) **Thomas** (1822–96), English novelist, born at Uffington, Berks, was educated at Rugby and Oriel College, Oxford, was called to the bar in 1848 and became a county court judge in 1882. He was Liberal M.P. (1865–1874) and closely associated with the Christian Socialists, supported trade unionism and helped to found the Working Men's College and a settlement in Tennessee, U.S.A. He was principal of the former (1872–83). But he is primarily remembered as the author of the semi-autobiographical public school classic, *Tom Brown's Schooldays* (1856), based on his school experiences at Rugby under the headmastership of Arnold (q.v.). He also wrote a number of biographies and social studies. See S. Selfe's history of Rugby (1910), study by H. Hamer (1928), and Life by Mack and Armytage (1953).

(7) **William Morris** (1864–1952), Australian statesman, born in Llandudno, Wales, went to Australia (1884), entered N.S.W. and Commonwealth parliaments, and in 1915–23 was federal prime minister and attorney-general in Labour and Coalition governments, founding the United Australia party in the early 'thirties. An ardent supporter of the Commonwealth, he was made P.C. in 1916. See Life by W. F. Whyte (1958).

HUGO, Victor Marie, *ü′gō* (1802–85), French poet and author, was born at Besançon, February 26, the son of General Hugo, a soldier of the empire. He was educated in Paris at the Feuillantines (1809–11, 1813–15), in Madrid (1812), and at the École Polytechnique. At fourteen he produced a tragedy; and at twenty, when he published his first set of *Odes et Ballades* (1822), he had thrice been victor at the Floral Games of Toulouse. In 1823 he published *Han d'Islande*, that wild romance of an impossible Iceland; and followed it up with *Bug-Jargal* (1824), a second set of *Odes et ballades* (1826), and the famous *Cromwell* (1827), whose preface was greeted with enthusiasm or detestation, Hugo taking his place at the head of the Romanticists. In 1828 he published his *Orientales*, wherein he revealed himself a master of rhythms. In 1830 came *Hernani*—the first in fact and the second in time of those 'five-act lyrics' of which Hugo's drama is composed. In the year 1831 he produced *Notre Dame de Paris*, a pretentious but picturesque historical romance; *Les Feuilles d'automne*, which includes some of his best poetry; and his best play, *Marion Delorme*. *Le Roi s'amuse* (1832), which was interdicted, is superbly written, and has gone the round of the world as *Rigoletto*. The next year was that of *Lucrèce Borgia* and *Marie Tudor*; in 1834 came *Claude Gueux*, which is pure humanitarian sentimentalism, and the *Littérature et philosophie mêlées*, a collection of juvenilia in prose. In 1835 came *Angelo*, a third melodrama in prose, and the admirable *Chants du crépuscule*; in 1836 the opera of *La Esmeralda*; in 1837 *Les Voix intérieures*, in which the poet's diction is held by some to have found its noblest expression; in 1838 *Ruy Blas*, after *Hernani* the most famous of his stage rhapsodies; and in 1840 *Les Rayons et les ombres*, yet another collection of sonorous verse. He failed at the Français in 1843 with the ponderous trilogy of *Les Burgraves*. Hugo was until 1830 a Royalist, and worshipped Napoleon; between 1830 and 1848 he was a Napoleonist with a turn for humanitarianism. He sat for Paris in the Assemblée constituante, voting now with the Right and now with the Left, but on his election to the Assemblée législative threw in his lot with the democratic republicans. In 1851, after the *coup d'état*, he withdrew to Brussels, and in 1852 was banished to the Channel Islands, whence he issued *Napoléon le petit*, perhaps the least literary of all his works, and in 1853 *Les Châtiments*, certainly the greatest achievement in all literature in the fusion of pure poetry with political and personal satire. Three years later appeared *Les Contemplations*, the best of his earlier poems and perhaps his greatest poetic achievement; and three years after that the *Légende des siècles* (1859). His greatest novel, *Les Misérables* (1862), is a panoramic piece of social history. This was followed by the extraordinary rhapsody called *William Shakespeare* (1864); by *Les Chansons des rues et des bois* (1865); by *Les Travailleurs de la mer*, an idyll of passion, adventure and self-sacrifice; by *L'Homme qui rit*, a piece of fiction meant to be historical. He returned from Guernsey to Paris on September 5, 1870, and six months later was chosen to represent the Seine, but soon resigned. He stayed through the Commune; and then, departing for Brussels, protested publicly against the action of the Belgian government in respect of the beaten Communists, in consequence of which he was again expelled. Again he stood for Paris, but was defeated. In 1872 he published *L'Année terrible*, a series of pictures of the war; in 1874 his last romance in prose, the much-debated *Quatre-vingt-treize*. In 1876 he was made a senator, and published the second part of the *Légende*. *L'Histoire d'un crime* (1877) has been described as 'the apotheosis of the Special Correspondent', and *L'Art d'être grand-père* (1877) contains much charming verse. The years 1878–79 enriched us with *Le Pape*—a piece humanitarian, anticlerical, and above all theatrical—and *La Pitié suprême*, the effect of which is much the same, and which—like *L'Âne* (1880), and a great deal of *Les Quatre Vents de l'esprit* (1881), and *Torquemada* (1882)—is merely Hugo in decay. His mastery of words remains invariable; too frequently he produces antithesis under the delusion that he is expressing ideas, and mistakes preposterousness for grandeur; he is utterly wanting in humour. But the final impression is one of unsurpassed accomplishment and abounding mental and emotional activity. He died in Paris, May 22. See studies on him by A. Swinburne (1886), C. Renouvier (1893), P. Stapfer (1901), L. Guimbaud (1914), Duclaux (1921), J. S. Barrère (2 vols., 1949 and 1961) and A. Maurois (trans. 1956).

HULL, (1) **Cordell** (1871–1955), American statesman, was born at Overton, Tenn., and was educated at Cumberland University, Tenn. Under Roosevelt, he became secretary of state in 1933 and served for the longest term in that office until he retired in 1944, having attended most of the great wartime conferences. He was a strong advocate of maximum aid to the Allies. One of the architects of 'bipartisanship', he received the Nobel peace prize in 1944. See his Memoirs (1948).

(2) **Edward** (1829–1917), British geologist, was born at Antrim, and from 1869 to 1890 was director of the geological survey of Ireland, conducted explorations in the Middle East and became professor at the Royal College of Science. See his Reminiscences (1910).

(3) **Isaac** (1773–1843), American sailor, nephew of (4), born at Derby, Conn., had commanded a ship in the West Indian trade, when in 1798 he entered the American navy. He was appointed to the *Constitution* frigate, which he commanded from 1806, and on August 19, 1812, he captured the British frigate *Guerrière*. He afterwards commanded Mediterranean and Pacific squadrons. See Life by J. G. Wilson (1889).

(4) **William** (1753–1825), American soldier, uncle of (3), born at Derby, Conn., fought in the War of Independence, and was governor of Michigan territory (1805–12). In the war with Britain (1812) he was sent with 1500 men to defend Detroit, was compelled to

surrender, and was afterwards court-martialled for cowardice and sentenced to be shot— a sentence not carried out.

HULLAH, **John Pyke** (1812–84), English composer and music teacher, was born at Worcester. In 1836 he composed *The Village Coquettes* to Charles Dickens's libretto; in 1841 began popular singing classes in Exeter Hall; and was musical inspector of training schools (1872–82). Hullah opposed the 'Tonic Sol-fa' method. Among his works are a *History of Modern Music* (1862), &c. Of his songs, ' The Three Fishers ' and ' The Storm ' attained wide popularity. See Life by his wife (1886).

HULME, **Thomas Ernest** (1883–1917), English critic, poet and—in a wide sense—philosopher, born in Staffordshire, was sent down from St John's College, Cambridge, and after a stay in Canada, joined with Pound, Wyndham Lewis and Epstein as champion of modern abstract art, of the poetic movement known as ' imagism ' and of the anti-Liberal political writings of Sorel. Killed in action in France in 1917, he left a massive collection of notes, edited under the titles *Speculations* (1924) by H. Read and *More Speculations* (1956) by S. Hynes, which expose philistinism and attack what he considered to be weak and outworn Liberalism. See study by M. Roberts (1938).

HULSE, **John** (1708–90), English clergyman, born at Middlewich, studied at St John's, Cambridge, took orders, and founded the Hulsean divinity professorship and lectures at Cambridge.

HULTON, **Sir Edward George Warris** (1906–), English magazine proprietor and journalist, born at Harrogate, was educated at Harrow and Brasenose College, Oxford, and was called to the bar, Inner Temple. He succeeded to his father's newspaper interests and became chairman of Hulton Press Ltd. He was founder of *Picture Post* (demise 1957), a brilliant experiment in journalism. He was knighted in 1957.

HUMBERT, It. **Umberto**, name of two kings of Italy:

Humbert I (1844–1900), was born at Turin, March 14, married in 1868 his cousin Margherita of Savoy, in 1878 succeeded his father, Victor Emmanuel, and was assassinated at Monza, July 29. See Life of Margherita by F. Z. Salazar (1914).

Humbert II (1904–), became king in May 1946 on the abdication of his father, Victor Emanuel III, but himself abdicated a month later, after a national referendum had declared for a republic. He left Italy and in 1947 he and his descendants were banned from Italy for ever.

HUMBOLDT, (1) **Friedrich Heinrich Alexander, Baron von**, (1769–1859), German naturalist and traveller, brother of (2), born at Berlin, son of the king of Prussia's chamberlain, studied at Frankfurt an der Oder, Berlin, Göttingen, and under Werner in the Mining Academy at Freiberg, where he published *Flora Subterranea Fribergensis* (1793). He then held a post in the mining department in Upper Franconia, and produced a work on muscular irritability (1799). For five years (1799–1804) he and

Aimé Bonpland explored unknown territory in South America. At Paris he made, with Gay-Lussac, experiments on the chemical constitution of the atmosphere; and in 1807, after a visit to Italy, he came back to Paris with Prince Wilhelm of Prussia on a political mission and remained in France till 1827. In 1829, he explored Central Asia with Ehrenberg and Rose, and their examination of the strata which produce gold and platinum, magnetic observations, and geological and botanical collections are described in a work by Rose (1837–42) and in Humboldt's *Asie Centrale* (1843). The political changes of the year 1830 led to his employment in political services; and during the ensuing twelve years he was frequently in Paris, where he published his *Géographie du nouveau continent* (1835–38). *Cosmos* (1845–62) endeavours to provide a comprehensive physical picture of the universe. See Life by K. Bruhns (1872; trans. 1873), Lord Houghton's *Monographs* (1873), and his own correspondence with Varnhagen (1860), &c.

(2) **Karl Wilhelm von** (1767–1835), German statesman and philologist, elder brother of (1), was born at Potsdam. After travelling in Europe, he became a diplomat, but without official employment. In 1791 he married, and for some years lived in retirement, associating with Schiller and devoting himself to literature. In 1801 Humboldt became Prussian minister at Rome, and was a most generous patron of young artists and men of science. He returned to Prussia (1808) to fill next year the post of first minister of Public Instruction. The Berlin University owed its existence to him. In 1810 he went to Vienna as minister-plenipotentiary, and from this time took part in all important Prussian political affairs. His *Gesammelte Schriften* were issued 1903 *et seq.* Humboldt was the first to study Basque scientifically, and also worked on the languages of the East and of the South Sea Islands. See Life by Haym (1856); his correspondence with Schiller (1830), Goethe (1876), Körner (1879), Schlegel (1908) and his brother (1880); also a book (trans. 1897) on his daughter Gabriele (1791–1887), who married the Prussian statesman, Heinrich, Freiherr von Bülow (1792‑1846).

HUME, (1) Alexander Hamilton (1797–1873), Australian explorer from Sydney to Port Phillip (1824), was born at Paramatta, New South Wales.

(2) **David** (c. 1560–1630), Scottish genealogist, of Godscroft, Berwickshire, wrote *The Origin and Descent of the Family of Douglas* (c. 1633; extended 1644), &c.

(3) **David** (1711–76), Scottish philosopher and historian, the greatest of British empiricists, born in Edinburgh on April 26, studied without graduating at Edinburgh University, took up law, suffered a nervous breakdown (1729), endured commerce for a while in Bristol, but thankfully escaped in 1734 to France to La Flèche in Anjou, where Descartes had spent his youth, and living on next to nothing (he was a Stoic at the time!) completed between the ages twenty-three and twenty-five, his masterpiece, the *Treatise of Human Nature*, written with

exemplary, if sometimes misleading, lucidity and wit. Its enduring philosophical importance is that it consolidated and made consistent the empiricist legacy of Locke and Berkeley. Hume argues sceptically against the claims of metaphysicians such as Descartes that there are innate ideas and of theologians that we can know the ultimate reasons for anything, since in the last resort even our imagination is tied to the empirical world. The perceptions of the human mind resolve themselves into impressions (that of which we are immediately aware in experience), i.e., sensations, passions, emotions, and ideas, which are faint copies of the former, arising when we think and reason. Hume denies the existence of the self, because there is no specific impression which corresponds to the 'I'. Similarly he denies causation, i.e., that there is a logical or necessary connection between cause and effect. It is merely that we get into the habit of associating certain events with others. In ethics, Hume was the first to expose what later became known as the 'naturalistic fallacy', the misconceived attempts to jump syllogistically from 'is' to 'ought'. His arguments for the 'artificiality' of the principles of justice and political obligations, as arising out of the requirements of convention, directly challenged the rationalistic 'natural law' and 'social contract' theories of Hobbes, Hooker, Locke and later Rousseau, and are a direct consequence of his basic view that 'reason is, and ought only to be, the slave of the passions'. Hume had his work published in London (1739–40), expecting immediate notoriety and recognition, but despite some scant attention in learned journals, 'it fell still-born from the press'. He quickly learnt his lesson. In 1741–42 he published two elegantly written but philosophically lightweight volumes of *Essays Moral and Political*, which achieved success. His atheism, however, doomed his applications for the vacant professorships of Moral and Pneumatic Philosophy at Edinburgh (1744) and Logic at Glasgow (1752). Instead, he became tutor to a young lunatic nobleman, the Marquis of Annandale (1745). Fortunately the following year he was taken as secretary by General St Clair on an unsuccessful raid on the Brittany coast and on a secret mission to Vienna and Turin. In 1748 Hume published the simplified version of the *Treatise*, entitled *Enquiry concerning Human Understanding*. It was a translation of the latter, not, unfortunately, for philosophy, the former, which woke Kant out of his 'dogmatic slumbers'. The Kantian philosophy and the subsequent schools of Idealism originated as an attempt to answer Hume's famous argument on causation and to surmount the latter's scepticism. The brilliant *Dialogues concerning Natural Religion*, in which Hume cleverly disperses his own views among the three disputants, examine the various proofs for the existence of a deity. Although written in 1750 they were prudently left unpublished until 1779. In 1752 he became keeper of the Advocates' Library in Edinburgh, having published *Enquiry concerning the Principles of Morals* in 1751. The *Political Discourses*

(1752) gave Hume in his lifetime a greater reputation as an economist than his great contemporary, Adam Smith, His monumental *History of England* (1754–62), written retrogressively in six volumes back to Roman times is partial to the Scots and his own Tory convictions. Its fame made his secretaryship to the ambassador in Paris, that city's literary event (1763). 'Le bon David ', despite his ignorance of French and totally unscholarly appearance, was fêted by the Parisian *literati*. His warm-hearted efforts to settle the persecuted Rousseau (q.v.) in England (1766–67) ended in a tragic misunderstanding for which Hume was not to blame. In 1767 he became under-secretary of state for the Home Department and died on August 25, 1776, from cancer of the bowel, which he had borne with remarkable cheerfulness for a year. Despite his atheism, which had prompted the joke of naming his street ' St David's Street ', he was mourned by most of Edinburgh. Hume anticipated Comte's positivism by nearly a century and his outlook and manner of philosophizing is a dominant influence on 20th-century empiricist philosophers. See his short, witty autobiography to be found in most of the Lives, including those by J. Y. T. Greig (1931) and E. C. Mossner (1943; definitive Life 1954), the former edited *Letters* (1932), the latter with Kiblansky, *New Letters* (1954), and studies by T. H. Huxley (1879), J. Laird (1932), H. H. Price (1940), N. Kemp Smith (1941), D. G. C. MacNabb (1951), on political writings, ed. F. Watkins (1951), J. A. Passmore (1952), A. H. Basson (1958) and J. B. Stewart (1964).

(4) **Fergus** (1859–1932), English writer, a pioneer of the detective story in *The Mystery of a Hansom Cab* (1887), &c., was born in England, but brought up at Dunedin, and called to the New Zealand bar. He returned to England in 1888.

(5) **Joseph** (1777–1855), British radical politician, born at Montrose, studied medicine at Edinburgh, and in 1797 became assistant surgeon under the East India Company. He acquired several native languages, and in the Mahratta war (1802–07) filled important offices. On the conclusion of peace he returned to England (1808), his fortune made. A political philosopher of the school of James Mill and Bentham, he sat in parliament (1812, 1819–55). He advocated savings banks, freedom of trade with India, abolition of flogging in the army, of naval impressment and of imprisonment for debt, repeal of the act prohibiting export of machinery, and many other reforms. He denounced the Orange lodges' design to make the Duke of Cumberland king on the decease of William IV.

(6) **Sir Patrick** (1641–1724), Scottish statesman and Covenanter, lord chancellor of Scotland, in 1690 was created Lord Polwarth, and in 1697 Earl of Marchmont. See BAILLIE (LADY GRIZEL), and Miss Warrender's *Marchmont* (1894).

HUMMEL, Johann Nepomuk (1778–1837), Austrian pianist and composer, born at Pressburg, was taught by his father, the director of the School of Military Music

there, and when the family moved to Vienna his playing impressed Mozart, who gave him lessons. He began playing in public in 1787 and after a tour of Germany, Denmark, Britain and Holland he studied composition under Albrechtsberger and also received instruction from Haydn, Salieri and Clementi. In 1804 he became *kapellmeister* to Prince Esterházy, Haydn's former master, and later held similar appointments at Stuttgart (1816) and Weimar (1819–37). He wrote several ballets and operas but is best known for his piano and chamber works, among which are charming examples in the light classical style. He wrote a manual of piano technique (1828) which had considerable influence.

HUMPERDINCK, Engelbert (1854–1921), German composer, born at Siegburg near Bonn, studied music at Cologne, Frankfurt, Munich and Berlin, and travelled in France, Spain and Italy. He taught at Barcelona, Cologne, Frankfurt and Berlin, and became famous as the composer of the musical fairy play, *Hänsel und Gretel* (1893), which was phenomenally successful. *Schneewittchen*, *Königskinder* (opera, 1910), *The Miracle* (pantomime, 1912), &c., followed.

HUMPHREY, Hubert Horatio (1911–), American politician, born in Wallace, S. Dak., educated at Minnesota and Louisiana Universities, entered politics as mayor of Minneapolis in 1945, being elected as Democratic senator in 1948. He built up a strong reputation as a liberal, particularly on the civil rights issue, but, as vice-president from 1964 under the Johnson administration, alienated many former supporters by his apparent support of the increasingly-unpopular policy of continuation of the war in Vietnam. Although he won the Democratic presidential nomination in 1968 at the first ballot, a substantial minority of Democrats opposed his choice, and the general mood of disillusion with Democratic policies and a compromise candidate led to Nixon's election victory.

HUMPHREY, Duke. See GLOUCESTER (6).

HUMPHREYS, Cecil Frances. See ALEXANDER (3).

HUNT, (1) (Henry Cecil) John, Baron Hunt of Llanvair Waterdine (1910–), English mountaineer, a British army officer, after much military and mountaineering service in India and Europe, in 1953 led the first successful expedition to Everest (see HILLARY), and was knighted. He also led the British party in the British-Russian Caucasian mountaineering expedition (1958). He was made a life peer in 1966. See his *Ascent of Everest* (1953).

(2) **Henry**, called ' Orator Hunt ' (1773–1835), English radical agitator, born at Upavon, Wiltshire, became a well-to-do farmer, but in 1800 his hot temper embroiled him with Lord Bruce, the commandant of the Wiltshire yeomanry, which brought him six weeks in jail. He came out a hot Radical, and spent the rest of his life advocating the repeal of the Corn Laws and parliamentary reform. In 1819, on the occasion of the Peterloo massacre, he delivered a speech which cost him three years' imprisonment; he was M.P. for Preston (1831–33). See his memoirs (1820) and Life by Huish (1836).

(3) **James Henry Leigh** (1784–1859), English poet and essayist, was educated at Christ's Hospital. With his brother, a printer, he edited, from 1808, *The Examiner*, which became a focus of Liberal opinion and so attracted leading men of letters, including Byron, Moore, Shelley and Lamb. He was imprisoned for two years (1813–15) for a libel on the Prince Regent. *The Examiner*, however, was more a literary and social than a political forum. It introduced Shelley and Keats to the public—Keats's magnificent sonnet *On First Looking into Chapman's Homer* first appeared there in 1816, the year in which Hunt issued his own romance *The Story of Rimini*. With all its faults of taste, it influenced Keats in the direction of what later was called pre-Raphaelite poetry. It is true that Keats subsequently was on his guard against this influence, but the sensuous or over-luscious element in his poetry is due to Hunt's influence directly or to the Elizabethan models whom Hunt pressed on his notice. Aware that England was no safe country in which to advocate Liberal views, he went on the invitation of Shelley to Italy, with wife and seven children, to found a new quarterly, *The Liberal*. Shelley's tragic death by drowning that year forced him to accept the hospitality of Byron at his palace in Pisa. The association with Byron was not a happy one and Hunt returned to England in 1825 to carry on a ceaseless life of literary journalism, Liberal politics (no longer so dangerous) and poetry. His house at Hampstead attracted all that was notable in the literary world, not without envy or ridicule, however, as Dickens' caricature of him as Harold Skimpole in *Bleak House* shows. His importance is less in his works, poetic or critical, than in his being one of those invaluable people who introduce authors to each other, but his *Examiner* is not to be dismissed—Edmund Blunden's handsome selection makes lively reading—and his *Autobiography* (ed. Blunden, 1928) is a valuable picture of the times. Blunden supplemented his Hunt studies with a Life in 1930. See also Life by Landré (1936), and selections by R. B. Johnson (1907) and Priestley (1929).

(4) **Thomas Sterry** (1826–92), American chemist and mineralogist, born at Norwich, Conn., worked for the Canadian Geological Survey (1847–72), was professor of Chemistry at Laval University (1856–62) and McGill University (1862–68), and of Geology in the Massachusetts Institute (1872–78), formulated a system in organic chemistry and made important researches into the composition of rocks. He was made an officer of the Legion of Honour (1867).

(5) **William Henry** (1790–1864), English painter, a creator of the English school of watercolour painting, was born in London, the crippled child of a tinplate worker. By Ruskin ranked with the greatest colourists of the school, he chose very simple subjects—*Peaches and Grapes*, *Old Pollard*, *Wild Flowers*. Much of his work is in the Victoria and Albert Museum, London.

(6) **William Holman** (1827–1910), English painter, was born in London. In 1845 he was admitted a student of the Royal Academy and next year he exhibited his first picture, *Hark!*, followed by scenes from Dickens and Scott, and by the *Flight of Madeline and Porphyro* (1848). He shared a studio with D. G. Rossetti, and the pair, along with Millais and a few others, inaugurated the 'pre-Raphaelite Brotherhood', which aimed at detailed and uncompromising truth to nature. The first of his pre-Raphaelite works was *Rienzi* (1849); others which followed include *The Hireling Shepherd* (1852), *Claudio and Isabella* (1853), *Strayed Sheep* (1853) and *The Light of the World* (1854), now in Keble College, Oxford. The result of several visits to the East appeared in *The Scapegoat* (1856) and *The Finding of Christ in the Temple* (1860). Among other world-famous canvases are *Isabella and the Pot of Basil* (1867), *May Day, Magdalen Tower* (1891) and *The Lady of Shalott*. In 1905 he was nominated O.M. See his *Pre-Raphaelitism and the P.R.B.* (1905; revised 1914), and Lives by G. C. Williamson (1902), M. L. Coleridge (1908), and W. Gaunt, *The Pre-Raphaelite Tragedy* (1942).

HUNTER, (1) **John** (1728–93), Scottish physiologist and surgeon, founder of scientific surgery, brother of (3), was born at Long Calderwood, E. Kilbride. He became his brother's assistant in the dissecting-room (1748), studied surgery at Chelsea Hospital and St Bartholomew's, and in 1754 entered St George's Hospital, becoming housesurgeon in 1756 and lecturer for his brother in the anatomical school. In 1759 his health gave way, and in 1760 he entered the army as staff-surgeon, and served in the expedition to Belleisle and Portugal. At the peace in 1763 he started the practice of surgery in London, and devoted much time and money to comparative anatomy. In 1767 he was elected F.R.S., and in 1768 was appointed surgeon to St George's Hospital. In 1776 he was appointed surgeon-extraordinary to the king. In 1785 he built his museum, with lecture-rooms, and tried his famous operation for the cure of aneurysm. In 1786 he was appointed deputy surgeon-general to the army. He died October 16, and was buried in the church of St-Martin's-in-the-Fields, whence his remains were translated in March 1859 to Westminster Abbey. Hunter's collection, containing 10,563 specimens, was bought by the government in 1795 and presented to the Royal College of Surgeons (unfortunately destroyed by enemy action during World War II). His *Natural History of Human Teeth* (1771–78) revolutionized dentistry. He investigated a large number of subjects, from venereal disease and embryology to blood, inflammation and gunshot wounds. Jenner was his pupil. His father, Francis, was a younger son of the ancient house of Hunterston, Ayrshire. He married in 1771 **Anne Home** (1742–1821), author of 'My mother bids me bind my hair' and other songs set to music by Haydn. See Lives by D. Ottley (1835), S. Paget (1897), G. C. Peachy (1924) and Gloyne (1950), and study by Oppenheimer (1946).

(2) **Joseph** (1783–1861), English historian of Hallamshire, Shakespearean scholar, &c.,

born at Sheffield, was a Presbyterian minister at Bath (1809–33) and then entered the Record Office. See memoir by S. Hunter (1861).

(3) **William** (1718–83), Scottish anatomist and obstetrician, brother of (1), was born at Long Calderwood, East Kilbride, studied five years at Glasgow University for the church, but in 1737 took up medicine with Cullen, and, coming up to London from Edinburgh in 1741, was trained in anatomy at St George's Hospital and elsewhere. From about 1748 he confined his practice to midwifery; in 1764 was appointed physician-extraordinary to Queen Charlotte; in 1767 was elected an F.R.S.; and in 1768 became professor of Anatomy to the Royal Academy. In 1770 he built a house with an amphitheatre for lectures, a dissecting-room, a museum, and a cabinet of medals and coins. His museum was bequeathed finally, with an endowment of £8000, to Glasgow University. His chief work was on the uterus. See memoir by G. C. Peachey (1924) and study by Oppenheimer (1946).

(4) **Sir William Wilson** (1840–1900), Scottish statistician, born in Glasgow, studied there, at Paris and Bonn, and in 1862 entered the civil service of India. His post as superintendent of public instruction in Orissa (1866–69) gave him the opportunity to write the *Annals of Rural Bengal* (1868) and *A Comparative Dictionary of the Non-Aryan Languages of India* (1868). Then, after being secretary to the Bengal government and the government of India, he in 1871 became director-general of the statistical department of India; the Indian census of 1872 was his first work. In 1887 he retired and returned home to write books mostly on Indian subjects. C.S.I. from 1878, he was knighted in 1887. See Life by Skrine (1901).

HUNTINGDON, Selina, Countess of (1707–1791), English Methodist leader, daughter of Earl Ferrers, married the Earl of Huntingdon in 1728, and became a widow in 1746. Joining the Methodists in 1739, she made Whitefield (q.v.) her chaplain in 1748, and assumed a leadership among his followers, who became known as ' The Countess of Huntingdon's Connexion '. For the education of ministers she established in 1768 a college at Trevecca in Brecknockshire (removed in 1792 to Cheshunt, Herts), and built or bought numerous chapels, the principal one at Bath. She died in London, bequeathing to four persons her sixty-four chapels, most of which became identical with the Congregational churches. See Life (1840) and a monograph by Sarah Tytler (1907).

HUNTINGTON, (1) Collis Porter (1821–1900), American railway pioneer, born at Harwinton, pioneered the Central Pacific Railway, which was completed in 1869, as well as the Southern Pacific (1881), of which he became president, together with the allied steamship companies. His nephew, **Henry Edwards Huntington** (1850–1927), acquired an immense art collection and library, which he presented to the nation in 1922, together with his estate at Pasadena, Cal.

(2) **Daniel** (1816–1907), American historical and religious and portrait painter, was born

in New York, and first visited Italy in 1839.

(3) **Ellsworth** (1876–1943), American geographer, born in Galesburg, Ill., went on expeditions to Central Asia (1903–06), wrote on Asiatic subjects and carried out research on the relations between climate and anthropology.

(4) **William** (S.S., i.e., ' Sinner Saved '; 1745–1813), English preacher, tramp, coalheaver, prophet, &c., was born at Four Wents near Cranbrook and died at Tunbridge Wells.

HUNTLY. See GORDON.

HUNYADY, János, *hoon'yo-di* (*c.* 1387–1456), Hungarian statesman and warrior, apparently a Wallach by birth, was knighted and in 1409 presented by the Emperor Sigismund with the Castle of Hunyad in Transylvania. His life was one unbroken crusade against the Turks, its chief events his expulsion of them from Transylvania in 1442; his brilliant campaign south of the Danube in 1443; his defeats at Varna and Kossovo (1444–48); and his glorious storming of Belgrade (1456). Shortly afterwards (August 11) Hunyady died of dysentery. During the minority of Ladislaus V he acted as governor of the kingdom (1445–53). Hunyady left two sons, **Ladislaus,** who was beheaded on a charge of conspiracy by Ladislaus V, and **Matthias** (see MATTHIAS CORVINUS).

HURD, Richard (1720–1808), English prelate and writer, named the ' Beauty of Holiness ' on account of his comeliness and piety, was born at Congreve, Staffordshire, and became a fellow of Emmanuel College, Cambridge, in 1742. In 1750 he became a Whitehall preacher, in 1774 Bishop of Lichfield and Coventry, and in 1781 of Worcester. Among his works are *Commentary on Horace's Ars Poetica* (1749); *Dissertations on Poetry* (1755–57); *Dialogues on Sincerity,* &c. (1759); *Letters on Chivalry and Romance* (1762); and edited Warburton (1788). See *Memoir* by Kilvert (1860) and A. W. Evans, *Warburton and the Warburtonians* (1932).

HURTADO, Luis, *oor-tah'THō* (*c.* 1530–98), Spanish poet, romancer and playwright, was born at Toledo.

HUSKISSON, William (1770–1830), British statesman, born at Birts Morton Court, Worcestershire, March 11, was in Paris (1783–92), in 1795 was appointed undersecretary in the Colonial Department. Next year he entered parliament for Morpeth as a supporter of Pitt. Returned for Liskeard in 1804, he became secretary of the Treasury; and held the same office under the Duke of Portland (1807–09). In 1814 he became commissioner of the woods and forests, in 1823 president of the Board of Trade and treasurer of the navy, and in 1827 colonial secretary. But he resigned office finally in 1828. He obtained the removal of restrictions on the trade of the colonies with foreign countries, the removal or reduction of many import duties, and relaxation of the navigation laws, and was an active pioneer of free trade. He received fatal injuries at the opening of the Liverpool and Manchester Railway, September 15. See Life with his Speeches (3 vols. 1831), and Brady's study (1928).

HUSS, or Hus, John (*c*. 1369–1415), Bohemian reformer, was born the son of a Bohemian peasant, at Husinetz (of which Hus is a contraction) near Prachatitz. In 1398, two years after taking his master's degree at Prague, he began to lecture there on theology. He had come under the influence of Wyclif's writings, probably through Anne of Bohemia's retinue. In 1402 he was appointed rector of the university, and began to preach at the Bethlehem chapel; in 1408 he was forbidden to exercise priestly functions within the diocese. In 1409 Huss was re-elected rector, but the archbishop commissioned an inquisitor to investigate the charges of heretical teaching against him. And in connection with this in December Pope Alexander V promulgated a bull condemning Wyclif's teaching, ordered all his writings to be publicly burned, and forbade preaching in any except collegiate, parish and monastery churches. As Huss continued preaching, he was in July excommunicated. Popular riots followed, and Huss, backed by the people, still maintained his position; nor did he yield even after the city was laid under papal interdict in 1411. But by 1413 matters had greatly changed, Huss having spoken out yet more boldly against the church; hence some of his more influential supporters, including the university, had fallen away from him, and on the advice of King Wenceslaus of Bohemia he left Prague. He found refuge at the castles of his supporters, for nearly the whole of the nobles were with him. This enforced leisure he employed chiefly in the composition of his principal work, *De Ecclesia*, which, like many of Huss's minor writings, contains numerous passages taken almost verbatim from Wyclif. About this time a general council was summoned to meet at Constance, and Huss was called upon to present himself before it. Provided with a ' safe conduct ' from the Emperor Sigismund, he reached Constance on November 3, 1414. Three weeks later he was seized and thrown into prison. No precise charge had been lodged against him; but he had resumed preaching in Constance. An ill augury for Huss was the condemnation of Wyclif's writings by the council in May 1415. His own trial began on June 5 following; but he was not permitted to speak freely in his own defence, nor allowed to have a defender. Called upon to recant unconditionally, and to pledge himself not to teach the doctrines that were put in accusation against him, Huss categorically refused, and was burned on July 6. The rage of his followers in Bohemia led to the bloody Hussite wars, in which the two parties of Hussites under such leaders as Ziska and Podiebrad more than held their own in many battles with all the forces of the empire. They were not reduced till about the middle of the century. See his *Opera Omnia* (Prague, 1903 *et seq.*); *Letters* (Workman and Pope, 1904); books by Lützow (trans. 1909), Schaff (1915), Vischer (1940).

HUSSEIN, *hoos-sayn'* (1935–), King of Jordan since 1952, great-grandson of Hussein ibn Ali (q.v.) and cousin of King Faisal II of Iraq (q.v.), was educated at Victoria College, Alexandria, and in Britain at Harrow and Sandhurst. He succeeded his father, King Talal, who was deposed because of mental illness. His marriage in 1955 to Princess Dina, a graduate of Girton College, Cambridge, was later dissolved, and in 1961 he married an English girl, now titled Princess Muna, who in 1962 gave birth to an heir, Abdullah. The young king maintained a vigorous and highly personal rule in the face of the political upheavals inside and outside his exposed country, steering a middle course, on the one side favouring the western powers, particularly Britain, on the other pacifying Arab nationalism, e.g., by his curt dismissal of the British general, Glubb Pasha (q.v.), in 1956. His federation of Jordan with Iraq in 1958 came to an unexpected end with the Iraqi military *coup d'état* in July of the same year. See his Autobiography (1962).

HUSSEIN IBN ALI (1856–1931), King of the Hejaz (1916–24), and founder of the modern Arab Hashemite dynasty, great-grandfather of King Hussein (q.v.) and father of King Faisal I (q.v.), was emir of Mecca (1908–16), and after first siding with the Turks and Germany in the first World War, on the advice of T. E. Lawrence came over to the side of the Allies, declaring for Arab independence (1916), and was chosen first King of Hejaz. After provoking the opposition of the Wahabis and Britain, he was forced to abdicate in 1924, was exiled in Cyprus and died in Amman. See J. Morris, *The Hashemite Kings* (1959).

HUSSEINI, Haj Amin el (1900–), Arab insurgent. Educated at Cairo's El Hazar University, he headed the pan-Arab movement—provoked by the Balfour Declaration of 1917—that bitterly opposed the establishment of a Jewish national home in Palestine. Deeply involved in anti-Jewish disturbances in Jerusalem in 1920, Husseini escaped imprisonment by fleeing to Transjordan. Sanctioning his return under an amnesty, the British authorities sought to placate him by appointing him Grand Mufti of Jerusalem. Unappeased, he was prominent amongst those who engineered the pro-German revolt in Iraq in 1941. With the insurrection's collapse, Husseini fled to Rome and thence to Berlin; ultimately finding refuge—and congenial coadjutors—in Cairo.

HUSSERL, Edmund Gustav Albrecht (1859–1938), Austrian-born founder of the philosophical school known as phenomenology, born, of Jewish origin, at Prossnitz, Moravia, studied mathematics under Weierstrass at Berlin and psychology under Franz Brentano at Vienna, and in 1887 became a *privatdozent* at Berlin. Under Brentano's influence he wrote *Philosophie der Arithmetik* (1891), and its conclusion, that the laws of Logic are at bottom psychological, he spent the remainder of his life in refuting. The aim of phenomenology is the defence of the ' purity ' of logic against ' psychologism '. In 1900 he became professor of Philosophy at Göttingen and in the following year published his *Logische Untersuchungen*, which gained him the support of many empiricists. No empiricist, however, could follow him in his later writings, after the *Ideen zu einer reinen*

Phänomenologie und phänomenologischen Philosophie (1913; trans. W. R. B. Gibson 1931), in which in the manner of Descartes he arrived at, by a process of 'bracketing off', or suspending belief in, sections of the empirical world, a residual indubitable consciousness, and from this transcendental vantage point sought to re-interpret the generalizations of the sciences in philosophical purity and by a method akin to Kantian idealism. These later works include *Vorlesungen zur Phänomenologie des Inneren Bewusstseins* (1928). In 1916 he became professor at Freiburg. In Germany and the United States independent phenomenological periodicals were published by his disciples. Phenomenology gave rise to *Gestalt* psychology and influenced Heidegger. See studies ed. by M. Farber (1940 and 1943), and *Return to Reason* (ed. Wild, 1953).

HUTCHESON, Francis (1694–1746), Scottish philosopher, son of an Armagh Presbyterian minister of Scottish descent, was born probably at Drumalig, Saintfield, Co. Down. He studied for the church at Glasgow (1710–1716) but then started a successful private academy in Dublin. His *Inquiry into the Original of our Ideas of Beauty and Virtue*, &c. (1720), attracted much notice; it was followed by his *Essay on the Passions* (1728). In 1729 he was appointed professor of Moral Philosophy at Glasgow, where he died in 1746. His largest work is *A System of Moral Philosophy* (with a Life, 1755). Hutcheson was a pioneer of the 'Scottish School', i.e., the 'common-sense' school of philosophy, influenced by Locke; his ethical system is a development of Shaftesbury's 'moral sense' ethics, in which moral distinctions are in a sense intuited, rather than arrived at by reasoning. See work by T. Fowler (1882), Life by W. R. Scott (1900), and J. Bonar, *Moral Sense* (1930).

HUTCHINS, John (1698–1773), English historian of Dorset, where he was born and for fifty years was a clergyman. His *History* was published in 1774.

HUTCHINSON, (1) née Marbury, Anne (c. 1590–1643), English religious enthusiast, the daughter of a Lincolnshire clergyman, in 1634 emigrated with her husband from Lincolnshire to Boston, Mass., where she lectured and denounced the Massachusetts clergy as being 'under the covenant of works, not of grace'. Tried for heresy and sedition, and banished, she, with some friends, acquired territory from the Narragansett Indians of Rhode Island, and set up a democracy (1638). After her husband's death (1642) she removed to a new settlement in what is now New York state, where she and her family of fifteen persons were, all but one son, murdered by the Indians.

(2) **John** (1615–64), English Puritan, was born at Nottingham, studied at Peterhouse, Cambridge, and Lincoln's Inn, and married in 1638 Lucy, daughter of Sir Allen Apsley. He retired to Owthorpe, his Nottinghamshire seat, and his meditations on the theology and politics of the time led him to side with parliament. He became governor of Nottingham, and successfully held the town (1643–1645). Returned in 1646 to parliament for

Nottingham, he was one of King Charles's judges, and signed the warrant for his execution. He sat in the first council of state, but, alarmed at the ambitious schemes of Cromwell, ceased to take part in politics. At the Restoration he was included in the Act of Amnesty, but later was imprisoned in the Tower and at Sandown Castle on a groundless suspicion of treasonable conspiracy, and died. The *Memoirs*, written by his widow for her children, and first published in 1806 (best edition by C. H. Firth, 1885), revealed a delightful picture of a grave and courteous gentleman, wholly free from austerity and fanaticism.

(3) **John** (1674–1737), English theological writer, born at Spennithorne, Yorkshire, in 1724 published *Moses' Principia*, defending the Mosaic cosmogony and assailing Newton's theory of gravitation. His *Thoughts concerning Religion* affirm the 'Hutchinsonian' heresy that the Scriptures contain the elements not only of true religion, but of all rational philosophy; the 'original Hebrew' had to be strangely twisted to justify this theory. See Life by Spearman in Hutchinson's *Works* (1748–65).

(4) **Sir Jonathan** (1828–1913), English surgeon, born at Selby, Yorks, became surgeon at the London hospital (1863–83) and professor of Surgery. 'Hutchinson's triad' are the three symptoms of congenital syphilis first described by him. He was elected F.R.S. in 1882, P.R.C.S. in 1889 and knighted in 1908. See Life by H. Hutchinson (1946).

(5) **William** (1732–1814), English county historian, a Barnard Castle solicitor, author of the *History of the County of Durham* (1785), *History of Cumberland* (1794), &c.

HUTCHISON, Sir William Oliphant (1889–1970), Scottish artist, born at Collessie, Fife, known for his portraits and landscapes, was P.R.S.A. from 1950.

HUTTEN, hoot'ten, (1) Philip von (c. 1511–1546), German explorer, cousin of (2). In 1528 Charles V granted Venezuela to the Welsers, rich Augsburg merchants; Hutten sailed with one of their companies, and after various journeyings (1536–38) set out in 1541 in search of the Golden City. After several years of wandering, harassed by the natives, he and his followers were routed in an attack on a large Indian city. Severely wounded, he was conveyed back to Coro, and beheaded by a usurping viceroy. He left a narrative of his journeyings, published as *Zeitung aus Indien* (1765). See also Von Langegg's *El Dorado* (1888).

(2) **Ulrich von** (1488–1523), German humanist, cousin of (1), born April 21 at the castle of Steckelberg, was sent in 1499 to the neighbouring Benedictine monastery of Fulda, but his imperious temper drove him to flee from it (1504). He visited various universities, and then in 1512 passed into Italy. Returning to Germany in 1517, and crowned poet laureate by the Emperor Maximilian, he entered the service of Albert, Archbishop of Mainz, and shared in the famous satires against the ignorance of the monks, the *Epistolae Obscurorum Virorum*. Eager to see Germany free from foreign and priestly domination, he in 1519 took part,

along with Franz von Sickingen, in the campaign of the Swabian League against Ulrich of Württemberg. He espoused Luther's cause with his customary impetuosity and vehemence. A set of dialogues (1520) containing a formal manifesto against Rome moved the pope to have him dismissed from the archbishop's service. He found shelter in Sickingen's castle of Ebernburg in the Palatinate, where he engaged in virulent polemics against the papal party to rouse the German emperor, nobles and people. His earliest work in German, *Aufwecker der teutschen Nation* (1520), is a keen satiric poem. Driven to flee to Basel in 1522, he was coldly treated by Erasmus, and irritated into a bitter epistolary quarrel; and finally found a resting place through Zwingli's help on the island of Ufnau in the Lake of Zürich, the exact location of which was discovered in 1958. See books by Schott (1890), Szamatólski (1891), Holborn (1929; trans. 1938).

HUTTER, Leonhard (1563–1616), German champion of Lutheran orthodoxy, taught theology at Wittenberg from 1596. His *Compendium* (1610) and *Concordia concors* (1614) were long standard works. Hase (q.v.) adopted Hutter's name.

HUTTON, (1) Charles (1737–1823), English mathematician, born at Newcastle, was a teacher there 1755–73, and professor of Mathematics at Woolwich Academy 1773–1807. An F.R.S., he calculated the density of the earth from Maskeleyne's observations on Schiehallion.

(2) **James** (1726–97), Scottish geologist, born at Edinburgh, studied medicine there, in Paris and at Leyden. In 1754 he devoted himself in Berwickshire to agriculture and chemistry, which led him to mineralogy and geology; in 1768 he removed to Edinburgh. The Huttonian theory, emphasizing the igneous origin of many rocks and deprecating the assumption of other causes than those we see still at work, was expounded before the Royal Society of Edinburgh in *A Theory of the Earth* (1785; expanded, vols. i, ii 1795; iii 1899). It formed the basis of modern geology.

(3) **Sir Leonard** (1916–), English cricketer, born nr. Pudsey, Yorks, joined his county team in 1934, first played for England in 1937, made a century on his first appearance against Australia in 1938, and in the same year compiled the record score of 364 in the Oval test match. In the test series of 1953 and 1954–55 he captained the England teams which regained and retained the 'Ashes' after 20 years of Australian supremacy. He was knighted in 1956. See *Just My Story* (1956).

HUXLEY, name of an English family of distinguished scientists and writers; see *The Huxleys* by R. W. Clark (1968):

(1) **Aldous Leonard** (1894–1963), English novelist and essayist, son of (5) and brother of (4), born at Godalming, Surrey, was educated at Eton and Balliol College, Oxford, where he read English, not biology as intended because of an eye disease, which compelled him to settle (1937) in California. Some Shelleyan poetry, literary journalism and a volume of short stories *Limbo* (1920) were followed by *Crome Yellow* (1921) and *Antic*

Hay (1923), gay satires on post-war Britain. *Those Barren Leaves* (1925) and *Point Counter Point* (1928) were written in Italy, where he associated with D. H. Lawrence, who appears as Mark Rampion in the last named. Huxley shared with Lawrence a morbid preoccupation with the biological aspects of human existence. In 1932, in his most famous novel, *Brave New World*, Huxley warns of the dangers of moral anarchy in a scientific age, by depicting a repulsive Utopia, in which Platonic harmony is achieved by scientifically breeding and conditioning a society of human robots, for whom happiness is synonymous with subordination, a much more sinister prophecy than Orwell's *1984*, which still required thought control and police terror. Despite the wit and satire, Huxley was in deadly earnest, as his essay *Brave New World Revisited* (1959) shows. An alternative possibility, of bestial individualism in the degeneration of the survivors of an atomic war, is explored in *Ape and Essence* (1948). From such pessimism Huxley took refuge in the exploration of mysticism. *Eyeless in Gaza* (1936), *After Many a Summer* (1939), which was awarded the James Tait Black prize, pointed the way to *Time must have a Stop* (1944), in which Huxley attempted to describe a person's state of mind at the moment of and just after death. *The Perennial Philosophy* (1945) is an anthology of mystical philosophies. *The Doors of Perception* (1954) describes a controversial short-cut to mysticism, the drug *mescalin* which reduces the ' sublime ' mystical state to a mere function of the adrenal glands. In contrast, the novelette *The Genius and the Goddess* (1955) reverts to the earlier Huxley, the problems posed by the discrepancy between an extraordinary intellect and a deficiency in other human endowments. Huxley has written numerous essays on related topics beginning with *Proper Studies* (1927) and biographies. See studies by A. J. Henderson (1935) and J. Brooke (1954).

(2) **Andrew Fielding** (1917–), English physiologist, half-brother of (1) and (4), studied at Trinity College, Cambridge, of which he became a fellow in 1941 and assistant director of research in physiology in the University. He worked on operational research (1940–45) and with Hodgkin (1) provided a physico-chemical explanation for nerve transmission. Independently of H. E. Huxley (not of the family) he gave the first satisfying outline of a theory of muscular contraction. Jodrell professor of Physiology at University College London from 1960, he was awarded, with Hodgkin and Eccles, the Nobel prize for medicine in 1963.

(3) **Elspeth Josceline** (1907–), English novelist, born Grant at Njoro, Kenya, married in 1931 Gervas Huxley (1894–), grandson of (6), and has written many novels and essays on her native land and its problems.

(4) **Sir Julian Sorell** (1887–), English biologist, son of (5) and brother of (1), was educated at Eton and Balliol College, Oxford, where he won the Newdigate prize (1908), served in the first World War.

became professor of Zoology at King's College, London (1925–27), Fullerian professor at the Royal Institution (1926–29), secretary to the Zoological Society of London (1935–42), was elected F.R.S. in 1938, and was knighted in 1958. His writings include *Essays of a Biologist* (1923), *Religion without Revelation* (1927), *Animal Biology*, with J. B. S. Haldane (1927), *Evolutionary Ethics* (1943) and *Biological Aspects of Cancer* (1957). He extended the application of his scientific knowledge to political and social problems, formulating a pragmatic ethical theory, based on the principle of natural selection. He was the first director-general of U.N.E.S.C.O. (1946–48). His son Francis is a noted anthropologist.

(5) **Leonard** (1860–1933), English editor, son of (6), father of (1), (2) and (4), edited the *Cornhill Magazine*, wrote a life of Sir Joseph Hooker (1918), edited Jane Welsh Carlyle's *Letters* and married a niece of Matthew Arnold.

(6) **Thomas Henry** (1825–95), English biologist, father of (5), born at Ealing, Middlesex, May 4, studied medicine at Charing Cross Hospital, and in 1846–50, as assistant surgeon of H.M.S. *Rattlesnake*, surveying the passage between the Barrier Reef and the Australian coast, collected marine animals, and made them the subjects of scientific papers for the Royal and Linnean Societies—notably one on the *Medusae*. He was elected F.R.S. in 1851, published a memoir on sea-butterflies and other papers and was in 1854 appointed professor of Natural History at the Royal School of Mines. In his Croonian Lecture (1858) he attacked the vertebral theory of the skull. Huxley discounted the possibility of evolution until Darwin published the *Origin of Species* in 1859. He then accepted the theory and became the foremost expounder of Darwinism, meeting the objections to the theory of natural selection from the clergy and fellow-scientists like Owen by a detailed study of anthropology enhanced by the timely discovery of the Neanderthal man. His essays were published under the title *Man's Place in Nature* (1863). He then turned to fossils and produced a number of papers (1860–70). He sat on a number of royal commissions, influenced the teaching of biology and science generally in schools, was P.R.S. (1881–85) and also wrote a number of essays on theology and philosophy from an 'agnostic' viewpoint, a term he introduced, in the tradition of Hume. See his *Science and Education* (1899), *Lay Sermons* (1870) and Lives by his son L. Huxley (1900), P. Chalmers Mitchell (1900) and C. Bibby (1959).

HUYGENS, Christiaan, *hoy'-* (1629–93), Dutch physicist, born at The Hague, was the second son of the poet Constantyn Huygens (1596–1687), who was secretary to the Prince of Orange. Huygens studied at Leyden and Breda. His mathematical *Theoremata* was published in 1651. Next he made the pendulum clock on Galileo's suggestion (1657), and developed the latter's doctrine of accelerated motion under gravity. In 1655 he discovered the ring and fourth satellite of Saturn, along with the micrometer. In 1660

he visited England, where he was elected F.R.S. He discovered the laws of collision of elastic bodies at the same time as Wallis and Wren, and improved the air-pump. In optics he first propounded the undulatory theory of light, and discovered polarization. The 'principle of Huygens' is a part of the wave theory. He lived in Paris, a member of the Royal Academy of Sciences (1666–81). Then as a Protestant he felt it prudent to return to The Hague. See study by A. E. Bell (1947).

HUYSMANN, Roelof. See AGRICOLA (5).

HUYSMANS, *hoys'mahns,* (1) **Cornelis,** 'the second' (1648–1727), Dutch landscape and religious painter. Like his father, he was born at Antwerp. He was a relative of (2). His religious paintings, a successful blend of Italian and Flemish styles, include *Christ on the Road to Emmaus*. His *Woodland with Château* hangs in the National Gallery, London, and other landscapes may be found in New York, Edinburgh and Paris. His brother, **Jan Baptist** (1654–1716), also painted landscapes (Pinakothek, Munich and Brussels).

(2) **Jacob** (*c.* 1636–96), Dutch portrait painter, a relative of (1), born at Antwerp, came to London about 1661 and became fashionable at the Restoration court. He painted Izaak Walton, Catherine of Braganza (both National Gallery, London) and Lady Byron (Hampton Court).

(3) **Joris Karl,** Fr. *ü-ees-mã* (1848–1907), French novelist of Dutch origin, was born in Paris, and from ultrarealism, as in his *Les Soeurs Vatard* (1879), *À vau-l'eau* (1882), changed over to a devil-worshipping mysticism as in *Là-Bas* (1891), &c., but returned to the Roman church with *En Route* (1892), his autobiography. *Art Moderne* (1882) is a superb study of impressionist painting. See studies by L. Deffoux (1927), H. Trudgian (1934) and Laver (1954).

HUYSUM, Jan van, *hoy'soom* (1682–1749), Dutch painter, born at Amsterdam, studied under his father, **Justus** (1659–1716), a landscape painter. Jan too painted landscapes, purely conventional in style. But his fruit and flower pieces are distinguished for exquisite finish and are represented in the Louvre, Paris and Vienna. A brother, **Jacob** (1680–1740), also a painter, died in London. See study by M. H. Grant (1954).

HWEN-T'SIANG, or **Hiouen-Thsang,** *hü-en' dzahng'* (*c.* 605–664), Chinese Buddhist monk, born near Honan, in 629 set out on a pilgrimage to India, travelling by way of the Desert of Gobi, Tashkent, Samarkand, Bamian and Peshawar. He remained in India (631–44), visiting the sacred places and studying the sacred books. His memoirs (648; French trans. by S. Julien, 1858) are important for the history of India and Buddhism. See also the Life by his contemporary the Shaman Hwui Li (English trans. new ed. 1911).

HYACINTHE, Père, *ee-a-sît,* the name as a Carmelite of **Charles Loyson,** *lwah-zõ* (1827–1912), French preacher, who taught philosophy and theology at Avignon and Nantes, and gathered enthusiastic audiences to the Madeleine and Notre Dame in Paris. He boldly denounced abuses in the church; was excommunicated (1869); protested against the Infallibility Dogma; married (1872); and founded a Gallican Church in Paris (1879).

HYDE, (1) **Douglas** (1860–1949), Irish author and philologist, born in Co. Roscommon, educated at Dublin University, was founder and first president (1893–1915) of the Gaelic League, professor of Irish in the National University (1909–32), wrote *A Literary History of Ireland* (1899), poems, plays, works on history and folklore, in Irish and English, and was first president (1938–45) of Eire.

(2) **Edward.** See CLARENDON (EARL OF).

HYDER ALI. See HAIDAR ALI.

HYNE, Charles John Cutcliffe Wright (1865–1944), English author, born at Bibury, educated at Bradford and Cambridge, travelled extensively before establishing himself as a writer of adventure stories. He is remembered above all as the creator of 'Captain Kettle'.

HYPATIA (*c.* 375–415), Neoplatonist philosopher, daughter of Theon, an astronomer and mathematician of Alexandria. Her learning, wisdom and high character made her the most influential teacher in Alexandria, and her pupil, the Christian bishop Synesius, records that her lectures drew students from all parts of the Greek world. Her philosophy was an eclectic endeavour to combine Neoplatonism with Aristotelianism; she also taught astronomy and mechanics. She was hacked to death in a riot created by the zeal of the Bishop Cyril against heathen philosophy (415). Kingsley's romance, *Hypatia,* appeared in 1853. See German monographs by Wolff (1879) and Meyer (1886).

HYPERIDES, or **Hypereides,** *hī-pèr-ī'deez* (*c.* 390–322 B.C.), Athenian orator and statesman, became a professional advocate, and earned large sums. From the first he opposed the party which advocated peace with Philip, and so supported Demosthenes till after the death of Philip and during the early portion of Alexander's career. Only when Demosthenes endeavoured to follow an impossible *via media* did Hyperides break with him, and head that accusation of bribery against Demosthenes which not only resulted in his banishment but committed Athens to the fruitless revolt against Macedon known as the Lamian war. The leaders of this revolt were Leosthenes and Hyperides; the former perished in battle, the latter was put to death by Antipater (322 B.C.). Although Hyperides was admired and studied in Roman times, it was not until 1847 that papyri containing four of his orations were discovered by English travellers in Egypt. In his speeches Hyperides is always transparent, never monotonous, witty to a degree, refined in his raillery, and delightful in his irony. Above all, he never in his keenest attacks passes the bounds of good taste, as does Demosthenes.

HYRCANUS, the name of two Jewish high priests and princes of the Hasmonean family:

(1) **John Hyrcanus,** high priest (135–104 B.C.), son of Simon Maccabaeus, was at first tributary to the Syrians; but on the death of Antiochus VII he made himself independent, and subdued the Samaritans and Idumaeans, concluded an alliance with the Romans, and extended his territories almost to the limits of the Davidic monarchy. Hyrcanus was a just and enlightened ruler, and the country was prosperous during his reign. He left five sons, two of whom, Aristobulus and Alexander, governed with the title of king.

(2) **Hyrcanus II** (d. 30 B.C.), son of Alexander, was, on the death of his father (76 B.C.), appointed high priest by his mother Alexandra, who ruled Judaea till her death (67 B.C.). Then his younger brother Aristobulus and he warred for power (such as it was—they were pawns in a game played by others) with varying fortune till Aristobulus was poisoned (49 B.C.). In 47 Caesar made Antipater of Idumaea procurator of Judaea with supreme power; and a son of Aristobulus with Parthian help captured Hyrcanus, cut off his ears, and carried him off to Seleucia. But when Herod, son of Antipater, came to power, the aged Hyrcanus was invited home to Jerusalem, where he lived in peace till, suspected of intriguing against Herod, he was put to death in 30 B.C.

HYRTL, Joseph (1810–94), Austrian anatomist, professor of Anatomy at Vienna, researched into anatomy of the ear and comparative anatomy of fishes.

HYSLOP, James (1798–1827), Scottish poet, born at Kirkconnel, Dumfriesshire, while a shepherd wrote the poem 'The Cameronian's Dream' (1821).

I

IAMBLICHUS, *ī-am'bli-kus,* (1) (2nd cent.), Syrian-Greek author of the romance, *Babyloniaca;* (2) (*c.* 250–*c.*338), Greek philosopher, born at Chalcis in Syria, allowed Neoplatonist philosophy to degenerate into theurgy and demonology and wrote on mathematics and Pythagoras.

IBÁÑEZ, Vicente Blasco, *ee-vah'nyeth* (1867–1928), Spanish novelist, born at Valentia, dealt in realistic fashion with provincial life and social revolution. Notable works are *Blood and Sand* (trans. 1913), *The Cabin* (trans. 1919), and *The Four Horsemen of the Apocalypse* (trans. 1919), which vividly portrays the first World War and earned him world fame.

IBERT, Jacques, *ee-bayr* (1890–1962), French composer, born in Paris, studied in Paris, winning the French Prix de Rome in 1919. In 1937 he was made director of the French Academy in Rome. Ibert's works include seven operas, ballets, cantatas and chamber music, and the orchestral *Divertissement* (1928), based upon his incidental music for Labiche's play, *The Italian Straw Hat*, and *Escales* (1922) suite.

IBN 'ARABI (1165-1240), Arab mystic poet. His writings expound in obscure and recondite language a form of pantheism.

IBN BATUTA (1304-68), Arab traveller and geographer, was born at Tangiers, spent thirty years (1325-54) in travel, visiting Mecca, Persia, Mesopotamia, Asia Minor, Bokhara, India, China, Sumatra, southern Spain and Timbuktu; then settled at Fez, and wrote the entertaining history of his journeys, published with a French translation in 1855-59. See his *Travels in Asia* (1929).

IBN EZRA. See ABEN-EZRA.

IBN GABIROL. See AVICEBRÓN.

IBN KHALDUN, *-kul-doon'* (1332-1406), Arab philosopher, historian and politician, born at Tunis, engaged in every kind of political intrigue in which he systematically betrayed every master, turned to history in disgust and eventually became a college president and judge in Cairo. He wrote a monumental history of the Arabs, best known by its *Muqaddimah*, or introduction, in which he explains the rise and fall of states by the waxing and waning of the spirit of *Asabīya* (solidarity). See French translation by Baron de Slane (1852-68, vols. 19-21, 1934) and English translation of *The Muqaddimah*, by F. Rosenthal (1959).

IBN SAUD, Abdul Aziz, *sah-ood'* (1880-1953), King of Saudi Arabia, the outstanding Arab ruler of his time, born at Riyadh, followed his family into exile in 1890 and was brought up in Kuwait. In 1901 he succeeded his father and with a small band of followers set out to reconquer the family domains from the Rashidi rulers, an aim which he achieved with British recognition in 1927. His ambitions against King Hussein however, had been frustrated by British intervention (1921). He substituted patriarchal administration by the nationalistic *Ikwan* colonies (brotherhoods) and made pilgrimages to Mecca safe for all Mohammedans. He changed his title from sultan of Nejd to King of the Hejaz and Nejd in 1927 and in 1932 to King of Saudi Arabia. After the discovery of oil (1938) he granted substantial concessions to American oil companies. He remained neutral but friendly to the Allies in the 2nd world war. He had over a hundred wives. His son **Saud Ibn Abdul Aziz** (1902-69) had been prime minister for three months when he succeeded his father in October 1953. Without straining relations with Nasser's Egypt, he visited the United States in March 1957. In 1964 he was peacefully deposed by the Council of Ministers, and his brother **Faisal Ibn Abdul Aziz** (1904-) succeeded to the throne, as well as remaining prime minister and minister of foreign affairs.

IBRAHIM PASHA (1789-1848), viceroy of Egypt, adopted son, lieutenant and (for two months) successor of Mehemet Ali (q.v.). See *Life* by Crabites (1935).

IBSEN, Henrik (1828-1906), Norwegian dramatist and poet, an outstanding pioneer of social drama, born at Skien, March 20. His first play, *Catilina* (1850), was rejected, but after two years of journalism he was given a post at Ole Bull's theatre in Bergen, for which he wrote five conventional romantic dramas. His first significant play, *Kongsemnerne* ' The Pretenders ' (1857), attempted in the manner of Schiller and Scribe to treat an historical event in terms of psychological studies of the two main characters, the limited man of action who succeeds and the Hamlet-like visionary who hesitates and fails. The same year he was appointed artistic director to the National Theatre, Christiania. *Kaerlighedens Komedie* 'Love's Comedy ' (1862) points to his later development and shows a distinct anti-Hebbelian spirit in its theme of marriage as a millstone to the idealist. His theatre having plunged into bankruptcy, and he himself furious at Norway's aloofness in the struggle of Denmark with Germany (1864), he went into voluntary exile to Rome, Dresden and Munich (1864-92). The Norwegian parliament granted him a pension in 1866. The two dramatic poems *Brand* and *Peer Gynt* (1866-67) develop the theme of men chasing life-long dreams only to discover that their lives have been empty, unfulfilled and mediocre. Peer has much in common with Goethe's Faust. His last historical drama, *Kejser og Galilaer* 'Emperor and Galilean ' (1873), was his self-chosen masterpiece, but Ibsen's fame chiefly rests on the social plays which followed. *Et Dukkehjem* ' A Doll's House ' (1879), *Gengangere* ' Ghosts ' (1881) and *En Folkefiende* ' An Enemy of the People ' (1882), which on the surface deal with controversial social questions such as marriage, venereal disease, local government and corruption and were disliked for that, were concerned, on a deeper level, with the individual's delusions and pipe-dreams which shape his life. A master of stage-craft and psychological dénouement, Ibsen in his last phase tended more and more to symbolism as in *Vildanden* ' The Wild Duck ' (1884), *Rosmersholm* (1886), *John Gabriel Borkman* (1896), and most of all in *Bygmester Solness* ' The Master-Builder ' (1892), who in protest against the death of his wife and children ceases in his life's work of building churches and makes his fortune by adopting the lucrative ideal of ' homes for the people '. He falls to death from a tower which he knew he had not the head to climb. Those plays, together with *Naar Vi Döde Vaagner* ' When We Dead Awaken ' (1899), in which the sculptor hero tastes success without artistic fulfilment, portray much of Ibsen's own morbid introspections. *Hedda Gabler* (1890) was a solitary escape from symbolism, a realistic portrayal of soured idealism and intellectual superiority. Ibsen suffered a stroke in 1900 which ended his literary career and died May 23, 1906, having effected a revolution in the world of drama which was carried on by such brilliant disciples as Chehov, Shaw, Brieux and Hauptmann. See studies by G. B. Shaw (1891), B. W. Downs (1947), Tennant (1948), Northam (1953), McFarlane (1960), Meyer (vol. 1, 1967).

IBYCUS, *ib'-* (fl. mid-6th cent. B.C.), Greek poet of Rhegium in Italy, lived at the court of Polycrates, tyrant of Samos, and wrote choral lyrics in Doric anticipating Pindar. Legend has it that he was slain by robbers near Corinth, and dying called upon a flock of cranes to avenge him. The cranes went and hovered over the theatre at Corinth, and one of the murderers exclaimed, ' Behold the avengers of Ibycus! ' This led to their conviction. The story is told in Schiller's ballad.

ICTINUS (5th cent. B.C.), Greek architect, shares with Callicrates the glory of designing the Parthenon (438 B.C.). He was also architect of temples at Eleusis and near Phigalia.

IDA, *ee-dah* (d. 559), 1st King of Bernicia (Northumbria) from 547, landed at Flamborough, and founded Bamburgh.

IDDESLEIGH, Stafford Henry Northcote, 1st Earl of, *idz'lay* (1818–87), British Conservative statesman, born in London of an old Devonshire family, was educated at Eton and Balliol College, Oxford, became private secretary to Gladstone in 1842, was called to the bar in 1847 and in 1851 succeeded his grandfather as eighth baronet. In 1855 he entered parliament, was financial secretary to the Treasury under Lord Derby in 1859, and in 1866 was appointed president of the Board of Trade. While at the India Office in 1868 he had charge of the Abyssinian Expedition. In 1871 Mr Gladstone appointed him commissioner in the *Alabama* affair. He was chancellor of the Exchequer in 1874, and introduced the Friendly Societies Bill (1875). Upon the death of Beaconsfield he became joint leader of the party with the Marquis of Salisbury. In the second Salisbury ministry he was foreign secretary, but resigned early in January 1887. He was created earl in 1885. See Life by Lang (1890).

IDRISI. See EDRISI.

IFFLAND, August Wilhelm (1759–1814), German actor and author of numerous popular plays including *Die Jäger*, was born at Hanover. See German works on him by Duncker (1859), Koffka (1865) and E. Kliewer (1937).

IGNATIEV, Nikolai Pavlovich (1832–1908), Russian diplomat, born at St Petersburg, in 1856 entered the diplomatic service. In 1858 he induced China to give up the Amur province; and in 1860, while ambassador at Peking, secured another large strip of territory for the Maritime Province. With Khiva and Bokhara he concluded treaties. In 1867 he was made ambassador at Constantinople. An ardent Panslavist, he intrigued with the Balkan Slavs, and took a principal part in the diplomatic proceedings before and after the Russo-Turkish war of 1878; the treaty of San Stefano was mainly his work. Under Alexander III he was minister of the interior (1881), but was dismissed in June 1882.

IGNATIUS (*c.* 35–*c.* 107), one of the Apostolic Fathers, was reputed a disciple of St John and second Bishop of Antioch. According to the *Chronicon* of Eusebius (*c.* 320) he died a martyr in Rome. The *Ignatian Epistles*, the authenticity of which have at last been accepted, were written on his way to Rome after being arrested. The warnings against Judaism and Docetism, as well as the high doctrine of the bishop's office reflected in these epistles, were somewhat extreme, but some allowance must be made for his predicament. Two other recensions of the letters have survived, one of which, a Syriac version, is a 4th century redraft. See J. B. Lightfoot, *Apostolic Fathers* (1889), B. H. Streeter, *Primitive Church* (1929).

IGNATIUS LOYOLA. See LOYOLA.

IHRE, Johan, *ee'rė* (1707–80), Swedish philologist, born at Lund of Scottish extraction, became in 1748 professor of Belles-lettres and Political Economy. His *Glossarium Suiogothicum* (1769) was the foundation of Swedish philology.

IMHOTEP (fl. *c.* 2800 B.C.), Egyptian physician and adviser to King Zoser (3rd dynasty), was probably the architect of the famous Step-pyramid at Sakkara near Cairo. In time he came to be commemorated as a sage and during the Saite period (500 B.C.) he was worshipped as the life-giving son of Ptah, god of Memphis. The Greeks identified him with Asclepius, because of his reputed knowledge of medicine. Many bronze figures of him have been discovered.

IMLAY, Gilbert. See GODWIN (2).

IMMELMANN, Max (1890–1916), German airman, laid the foundation of German fighter tactics in World War I, and originated the ' Immelmann turn '—a half-loop followed by a half-roll. He was killed in action.

IMMERMANN, Karl Leberecht (1796–1840), German dramatist and novelist, born at Magdeburg, in 1817 entered the public service of Prussia, and served at Münster, Magdeburg and Düsseldorf. His fame rests upon his tales (*Miscellen*, 1830) and the satirical novels *Die Epigonen* (1836) and *Münchhausen* (1839). See Lives by his widow (1870) and H. Maync (1921).

IMPEY, Sir Elijah (1732–1809), British judge, born at Hammersmith, was called to the bar in 1756 and appointed chief justice to the new supreme court at Calcutta in 1774. A friend of Warren Hastings, he was recalled in 1783 and charged with corruption in 1787, defended himself and was acquitted. See Life by his son (1846).

INA, or Ine, West Saxon king from 689 to 726.

INCHBALD, Elizabeth, *née* Simpson (1753–1821), English novelist, playwright and actress, born at Bury St Edmunds, married John Inchbald, an actor in London in 1772, when she made her début at Bristol as Cordelia. After the death of her husband in 1779, she appeared at Covent Garden, but made her name as the author of 19 plays, including *The Wedding Day* (1794), and the novels *A Simple Story* (1791) and *Nature and Art* (1796). See Lives by S. R. Littlewood (1921) and W. McKee (1935).

INCLEDON, Charles Benjamin, *ink'ėl-dèn* (1763–1826), English ballad singer, born at St Keverne, Cornwall, served in the navy (1779–83), in 1784 made his début as tenor in Southampton Theatre, in 1790 appeared at Covent Garden. He excelled in sea shanties and ballads.

**INDY, Vincent d', ĭ-*dee* (1851–1931), French composer, born in Paris, an ardent student, disciple and biographer of César Franck (q.v.), founded the Schola Cantorum in Paris in 1894, published *Treatise of Composition* (1900) and composed operas, much chamber music and, notably, the *Symphonie cévenole* (1886) in the spirit of French romanticism.

INEZ DE CASTRO. See CASTRO (5).

INGE, William Ralph (1860–1954), English divine, born at Crayke, Yorks, educated at Eton and King's College, Cambridge, taught at Eton and was vicar of All Saints, Kensington, for two years before being appointed in 1907 professor of Divinity at Cambridge. From 1911 until 1934 he was dean of St Paul's, earning for himself by his pessimistic prognostications in sermons and newspaper articles the sobriquet of ' the Gloomy Dean '. Popular books include *Outspoken Essays* (1919, 1922) and *Lay Thoughts of a Dean* (1926, 1931); more serious works examined, among other things, Neoplatonism and Christian Mysticism. He was made a K.C.V.O. in 1930. See Life by Fox (1960).

INGEBORG. See PHILIP II OF FRANCE.

INGELOW, Jean, *in'jel-ō* (1820–97), English poet and novelist, was born at Boston, Lincs., wrote devotional poetry, lyrics and ballads, of which the short poem ' High Tide on the Coast of Lincolnshire 1571 ' is her best. Her tales for children include *Mopsa the Fairy* (1869), and her novels *Off the Skelligs* (1872). See Life by E. S. Robertson (1883).

INGEMANN, Bernhard Severin (1789–1862), Danish poet and novelist, born at Thorkildstrup in Falster, is best known for his idealized romantic historical novels *Valdemar Sejer* (1826), *Kong Erik* (1833) and *Prins Otto af Danmark* (1835), and historical poems *Waldemar the Great* (1824), *Queen Margaret* (1836) and *Holger Danske* (1837). From 1822 he lectured at the Royal Academy of Sorö near Copenhagen. See his two autobiographical works (1862–63) and his correspondence with Grundtvig (1881).

INGEN-HAUSZ, Jan, *eeng'ĕn-hows* (1730–99), Dutch physician, born at Breda, discovered in 1779 that carbon dioxide is absorbed by plants in the day and given out at night. He also devised a method for comparing heat conductivities.

INGERSOLL, (1) Charles Jared (1782–1862), American politician, son of (2), sat in congress 1813–15, and advocated the principle that ' free ships make free goods ', was for fourteen years U.S. district attorney for Pennsylvania, and a prominent leader of the Democrats 1841–47. He wrote poems and a drama, a political satire entitled *Inchiquin's Letters* (1810) and a *Sketch of the War of 1812* (1845–52).

(2) **Jared** (1749–1822), American jurist, father of (1), born in Connecticut, became a prominent lawyer and judge in Philadelphia. He was a member of congress in 1780–81, and in 1787 a delegate to the convention that framed the Federal constitution.

(3) **Robert Green** (1833–99), American agnostic, born at Dresden, New York State,

was the son of a Congregational minister, and became a lawyer. In 1862–65 he was colonel of a Federal cavalry regiment; in 1866 he became state attorney-general of Illinois. A successful lawyer and Republican orator, he had attracted some notice by his anti-Christian lectures, pamphlets and books.

INGLEBY, Clement Mansfield (1823–86), English philosopher and Shakespearian scholar, born at Edgbaston, graduated from Trinity College, Cambridge, in 1847, and practised a while as a solicitor, but in 1859 devoted himself to literature. His earliest works were handbooks of logic (1856) and metaphysics (1869), but his life-work began with *The Shakespeare Fabrications* (1859), and included a long series of works—the best known, *Shakespeare : the Man and the Book* (1877–81). See Life prefixed to his *Essays* (1888). He was a vice-president of the New Shakespeare Society and of the Royal Society of Literature.

INGLIS, *ing'ĕls*, (1) Elsie Maud (1864–1917), British surgeon, born at Naini Tal, India, one of the first women medical students at Edinburgh and Glasgow, inaugurated the second medical school for women at Edinburgh (1892), became for a while a housesurgeon in London, but in 1902, appalled at the lack of provision for maternity facilities and the prejudice against women doctors by their male colleagues, she founded a maternity hospital in Edinburgh, completely staffed by women. In 1906 she founded the Scottish Women's Suffragette Federation, which through her efforts sent two women ambulance units to France and Serbia in 1915. She set up three military hospitals in Serbia (1916), fell into Austrian hands, was repatriated, but in 1917 returned to Russia with a voluntary corps, which was withdrawn after the revolution. She died shortly after her return to London. See Lives by F. Balfour (1918) and S. McLaren (1920).

(2) **John, Baron Glencorse** (1810–91), Scottish judge, born in Edinburgh, established himself as a leading advocate by his brilliant defence of Madeleine Smith (q.v.) in 1857, and rose to lord justice-general in Scotland (1867). See Life by J. Crabb Watt (1893).

(3) **Sir John Eardley Wilmot** (1814–62), British soldier, born in Nova Scotia, joined the British army in 1833 and fought in India at Mooltan and Gujerat (1848–49). He commanded the British forces at Lucknow during the historic siege in the Indian mutiny (1857), was promoted major-general and knighted. See his wife's *Siege of Lucknow* (1892).

INGOLD, Sir Christopher Kelk (1893–1970), English chemist, professor of Chemistry at Leeds (1921–30) and London (1930), did important fundamental work on the structure of aromatic compounds. He was knighted in 1958.

INGOLDSBY, Thomas. See BARHAM.

INGRAHAM, *ing'grĕm*, (1) Joseph Holt (1809–60), American novelist, father of (2), born at Portland, Maine, was for some time a sailor, and then taught languages at a college in Mississippi. He published some wild romances, such as *Captain Kyd*; but after he was ordained to the Episcopal priesthood (1855), he wrote religious stories, *The Prince of the House of David* (1855), &c.

(2) **Prentice** (1843–1904), American novelist, son of (1), served as a soldier of fortune in Mexico, Austria, Africa and Cuba before writing 200 novels, with Buffalo Bill as the hero. He also wrote plays, short stories and poems.

INGRAM, Herbert (1811–60), English journalist, the founder in 1842 of the *Illustrated London News*, was born at Boston, Lincs, which he represented in parliament from 1856. He was drowned in a boat collision on Lake Michigan in the U.S.

INGRASSIA, Giovanni Filippo (1510–80), Italian physician who first differentiated scarlet fever from measles.

INGRES, Jean Auguste Dominique, *i'gr'* (1780–1867), French painter, the leading exponent of the classical tradition in France in the 19th century, born at Montauban, went to Paris in 1796 to study painting under David. In 1802 he won the Rome prize with *Achilles receiving the Ambassadors of Agamemnon* (École des Beaux Arts), but quarrelled with David and from 1806 to 1820 lived in Rome, where he began many of his famous nudes, including *Baigneuse* and *La Source* (begun in 1807 but not completed till 1859), both in the Louvre. The latter was exhibited in London at the International Exhibition of 1862. Many of the paintings he sent to Paris from Rome were adversely noticed, except by Delacroix, whose work Ingres detested. Ingres' paintings display superb draughtsmanship, but little interest in facial characteristics or colour. His motto was ' A thing well drawn is well enough painted '. He also painted historical subjects such as *Paolo and Francesca* (1819, Chantilly) and in Florence (1820–24) painted *The Oath o, Louis XIII* for Montauban cathedral, which appeased the rival schools of classicists and romantics in France. He returned to Paris and in 1826 was appointed professor at the Academy. His *Apotheosis of Homer* (Louvre ceiling) was well received, but not *The Martyrdom of St Symphorian* (1834, Autun cathedral) and Ingres went off again to Italy (1834–41), becoming director of the French Academy in Rome. His *Stratonice* (Chantilly), *Vierge à l'hostie* (Louvre) and *Odalisque à l'esclave* re-established him in favour in Paris and he returned in triumph, was awarded the Legion of Honour and made a senator (1862). The Louvre contains many of his best works and he is also represented in the National Gallery, London, by four paintings formerly owned by Degas. See Lives by H. Lapauze (1911), L. Hourtig (1926), J. Casson (1947) and J. Alazard (1950).

INGULPH (d. 1109), English secretary to Duke William of Normandy, who in 1086 made him Abbot of Crowland, was long regarded as the author of *Historia Monasterii Croylandensis*, printed in 1596–1684 and translated in 1854, when it was shown to be unreliable and in any case written in the 13th or 14th century.

INMAN, William (1825–81), British shipowner, founder in 1857 of the Liverpool ' Inman Liners ', was born at Leicester.

INNES, *in'nis,* (1) **Arthur Donald** (1863–1938),

British historian, born in India, wrote *England under the Tudors* (1905), &c.

(2) **Cosmo** (1798–1874), Scottish historian, born at Durris, was educated at the Edinburgh High School, and graduated both at Glasgow and Oxford. Called to the Scottish bar in 1822, he became sheriff of Moray in 1840, then an official of the Court of Session, and in 1846 professor of Constitutional Law and History in the University of Edinburgh. He is best known as the author of *Scotland in the Middle Ages* (1860) and *Sketches of Early Scotch History* (1861). He prepared vol. i of *Acts of the Scottish Parliament*, was a member of the Bannatyne, Maitland and Spalding Clubs, and edited for them several register-books of the old religious houses of Scotland. He published also *Legal Antiquities* (1872) and several memoirs, including one of Dean Ramsay. See Memoir by his daughter, J. Hill Burton (1874).

(3) **Thomas** (1663–1744), Scottish historian, born at Drumgask in Aberdeenshire, was educated at Paris, took holy orders in 1692, and after mission work at Inveraven (1698–1701) became prefect of studies in the Scots College in Paris, where he died. A Jacobite, he was no ultra-montane, but inclined towards Jansenism. The methods employed in his *Critical Essay on the Ancient Inhabitants of Scotland* (1729) foreshadowed those of Niebuhr (q.v.). It served as introduction to his *Civil and Ecclesiastical History of Scotland*, which was left incomplete at Columba's death (831). See memoir by Grub prefixed to the reprint of the *Critical Essay*, in *Historians of Scotland*, vol. VIII (1879).

INNESS, George (1825–94), American landscape artist, born at Newburgh, visited Italy and France and came under the influence of the Barbizon school. Among his best-known paintings are *Delaware Valley* and *Evening*, *Medfield, Mass.*, in the Metropolitan Museum at New York, and *Rainbow after a Storm* in Chicago Art Institute. See Life (1917) by his son George (1854–1926), also a landscape painter.

INNOCENT, the name of thirteen popes, of whom the following are noteworthy:

Innocent I, St, pope (402–417), a native of Albano, whose pontificate, next to that of Leo the Great, is the most important for the relations of Rome to the other churches. He enforced the celibacy of the clergy. He maintained the right of the Bishop of Rome to judge appeals from other churches, and his letters abound with assertions of universal jurisdiction. During his pontificate, Rome was sacked in 410 by Alaric. His feast day is 28 July.

Innocent III (1160–1216), pope (1198–1216), the greatest pope of this name, was born Lotario de' Conti at Agnagni and succeeded Pope Celestine III. His pontificate is regarded as the culminating point of the temporal and spiritual supremacy of the Roman see; under the impulse of his zeal for the glory of the church almost every state and kingdom was brought into subjection. He judged between rival emperors in Germany and had Otto IV deposed. He made Philip Augustus of France take back his wife.

He laid England under an interdict and excommunicated King John for refusing to recognize Stephen Langton as Archbishop of Canterbury. John's submission made England and Ireland satellites of the Holy See. In his time the Latin conquest of Constantinople destroyed the pretensions of his eastern rivals. He zealously repressed simony and other abuses of the time. He promoted the spiritual movement in which the Franciscan and Dominican orders had their origin. Under him the famous fourth Lateran Council was held in 1215. His works embrace sermons, a remarkable treatise on the *Misery of the Condition of Man*, a large number of letters, and perhaps the ' golden sequence ' ' Veni, sancte Spiritus '. See Lives by A. Luchaire (1904–08) and E. F. Jacobs in *Cambr. Med. Hist.* Vol. VI.

Innocent XI (1611–89), pope (1676–89), born Benedetto Odescalchi at Como. As pope, he proved a vigorous and judicious reformer, and strove hard to put an end to the abuse by Louis XIV of the king's claim to keep sees vacant and appropriate their revenues. But the actual conflict regarded the right of asylum enjoyed by the foreign ambassadors in Rome, which had been extended to the district round their houses. These districts had gradually become nests of crime, and of frauds upon the revenue; and the pope gave notice that he would not thereafter receive the credentials of any new ambassador who should not renounce these claims. Louis XIV instructed a new ambassador to maintain the dignity of France, and sent a large body of officers to support his pretensions. Innocent would grant no audience. Louis seized the papal territory of Avignon, but the pope died before the dispute was settled. See French work on him by Michaud (1882–83).

INÖNÜ, *i-nœ-nü'*, Ismet, adopted name of Ismet Paza (1884–), Turkish soldier and politician, was born in Izmir, Asia Minor. After a distinguished army career in the war (1914–18) he became Kemal Atatürk's chief of staff in the war against the Greeks (1919–1922), defeating them twice at the village of Inönü, which he adopted as his last name. As the first premier of Atatürk's new republic (1923–37) he signed the Treaty of Lausanne (1923), introduced many political reforms transforming Turkey into a modern state and was unanimously elected president in 1938 on Atatürk's death. From 1950 he was leader of the Opposition. He became premier again with General Gürsel as president in 1961, surviving repeated assassination attempts, an army *coup* and constitutional crisis in 1963, but resigned in 1965 after failing to govern effectively with minority support.

INVERCLYDE, Lord. See BURNS (2).

IONESCO, Eugene, *yo-nes'ko* (1912–), Rumanian-born French playwright, educated at Bucharest and Paris, where he settled in 1940. He pioneered a new style of drama with his short surrealistic plays, including *The Bald Prima Donna* (1950), *The Lesson* (1951), *The Chairs* (1952), *L'Amédée* (1954), *Victims of Duty* (1957), *The Picture* (1958) and *Le Rhinocéros* (1960), based on the highly personal material of his dreams, hidden

desires and inner conflicts on the Freudian assumption that humanity has a dream-world in common. His contempt for realism, the robot-like deficiencies of his characters, the suggestive irrationality of their outpourings, his paradoxical view that art is the attempt to communicate an incommunicable reality, have led to criticism by disciples of social realism. See his *Plays* (1958) and study by R. Coe (1961).

IONESCU, Take (1858–1922), Rumanian politician, became leader of the Conservative-Democratic party in 1907 and was foreign minister in 1917–18 and 1920–22. He was Rumanian delegate at the Versailles conference.

IPATIEV, Vladimir, *ee-pat'yef* (1867–1953), Russian chemist, born in Moscow, emigrated to the United States in 1931 and made contributions to the catalytic chemistry of unsaturated hydrocarbons, of great value to the oil industry.

IQBAL, Sir Mohammed (1875–1938), Indian poet and philosopher, born at Sialkot (now in Pakistan), taught philosophy at Lahore, studied law in England, and was knighted in 1923. He wrote poems in Urdu and Persian pregnant with a compelling mysticism and nationalism which caused him to be regarded almost as a prophet by Moslems. See study by Vahid (1959).

IPHICRATES, *i-fik'ra-teez* (419–353 B.C.), an Athenian general who served in the Corinthian war (395–387), in Egypt (374), against Sparta (372–371), &c.

IRELAND, (1) Alexander (1810–94), English bookseller of Manchester, father of (2), wrote *The Book-Lover's Enchiridion*, &c.

(2) John (1879–1962), English composer, son of (1), born in Cheshire, studied composition under Stanford at the Royal College of Music, London. His poetic feelings, inspired by ancient traditions and places, are in evidence in such works as the orchestral prelude *The Forgotten Rite* (1913) of the Channel Islands and the rhapsody *Mai-dun* (1921) of the Wessex countryside. He established his reputation with his violin sonata in A (1917) and between the wars was a prominent member of the English musical renaissance. The piano concerto (1930) and *These Things shall be* (1937) for chorus and orchestra feature strongly among his later works, which include song settings of poems by Hardy, Masefield, Housman and others.

(3) Samuel William Henry (1777–1835), English literary forger, born in London, was articled at seventeen to a London conveyancer. He was tempted by his father's enthusiasm for Shakespeare to forge an autograph of the poet on a carefully copied old lease. His audacity grew with the credulity of his dupes, and he produced private letters, annotated books, &c. Boswell, Warton, Parr and hundreds more came, saw and believed; but those, like Malone, really qualified to judge denounced the imposture. Ireland now produced a deed of Shakespeare's bequeathing his books and papers to a William-Henrye Irelaunde, an assumed ancestor. Next a new historical play entitled *Vortigern* was announced, and produced by Sheridan at Drury Lane, April 2, 1796. Vapid and

un-Shakespearean, it was damned at once; and this nipped in the bud a projected series of historical plays. His father finally began to suspect and the young man was forced to confess; he published a statement in 1796, and expanded it in his *Confessions* (1805). He produced a dozen poems, four or five novels, and ten or more biographical and miscellaneous compilations, but ended life in poverty.

IRENAEUS, St, *i-re-nay'oos* (c. 130–c. 200), one of the Christian fathers of the Greek church, born probably near Smyrna, in youth was acquainted with Polycarp. He became a priest of the Greco-Gaulish church of Lyons, under the Bishop Pothinus, after whose martyrdom in 177 he was elected to the see. Gregory of Tours states that he suffered martyrdom in the persecution under Severus in 202; but this is probably a mistake. Irenaeus was a successful missionary bishop, but is chiefly known for his opposition to Gnosticism (especially the Valentinians), and for his attempts to prevent a rupture between the Eastern and Western Churches over the computing of Easter. See his great treatise *Against Heresies*, ed. Erasmus (1526), and studies by J. Werner (1889) and Sanday and Turner (1923).

IRENE, *ī-ree'nee* (c. 752–803), Eastern Roman empress, a poor orphan of Athens whose beauty and talents led the Emperor Leo IV to marry her in 769. After 780 she ruled as regent for her son, Constantine VI. She imprisoned and blinded him and her husband's five brothers, but in 802 she was banished to Lesbos. As an opponent of the iconoclasts she was canonized by the Greek Church.

IRETON, Henry (1611–51), English soldier, born in 1611 at Attenborough, Nottingham, graduated from Trinity College, Cambridge, in 1629, and at the outbreak of the Civil War offered his services to parliament, fighting at Edgehill, Naseby and the siege of Bristol. Cromwell's son-in-law from 1646, he was one of the most implacable enemies of the king, and signed the warrant for his execution. He accompanied Cromwell to Ireland, and in 1650 became lord-deputy. On November 26, 1651, he died of the plague before Limerick, and was buried in Westminster Abbey till the Restoration, when his remains were transferred to Tyburn. See Life by R. W. Ramsay (1949).

IRIARTE Y OROPESA, Tomas de, *eer-yahr'-tay* (1750–91), Spanish poet fabulist, author of *Fábulas Literarias* (1782), was born at Orotava in Tenerife.

IRIGOYEN, Hipólito (1850–1933), Argentine politician, born in Buenos Aires, became leader of the Radical Civic Union party in 1896 and worked for electoral reform, which, when it came in 1912, ushered him into power as the first Radical president of the Argentine (1916–22). He was again elected in 1928, but deposed by a military *coup* in 1930.

IRNERIUS, the 'Lucerna Juris' (d. before 1140), Italian jurist, born in Bologna, was one of the first to devote serious study to Justinian. See monograph by Vecchio (Pisa 1869).

IRONSIDE, William Edmund, 1st Baron Ironside (1880–1959), British soldier, born at Ironside, Aberdeenshire, served as a secret agent disguised as a railwayman in the Boer war and held several staff-appointments in World War I. He commanded the Archangel expedition against the Bolsheviks (1918) and the allied contingent in North Persia (1920). He was chief of the Imperial General Staff at the outbreak of World War II, was promoted field-marshal (1940) and placed in command of the Home Defence Forces (1940). The ' Ironsides ', fast, light-armoured vehicles, were named after him. He was raised to the peerage in 1941. See his Diaries 1937–40 (1962).

IRVINE, Sir Alexander (c. 1600–58), laird of Drum, an Aberdeenshire royalist, descended from the ' gude ' Sir Alexander Irvine, a provost of Aberdeen, who fell in single combat at Harlaw (1411) as celebrated in the ballad of the battle.

IRVING, (1) Edward (1792–1834), Scottish divine and mystic, born at Annan, studied at Edinburgh University, became a schoolmaster and in 1819 was appointed assistant to Thomas Chalmers (q.v.) in Glasgow. In 1822 he was called to the Caledonian Church, Hatton Garden, London, where he enjoyed a phenomenal success as a preacher. In 1825 he began to announce the imminent second advent of Christ; this was followed up by the translation of *The Coming of the Messiah* (1827), professedly written by a Christian Jew, but really by a Spanish Jesuit. By 1828, when his *Homilies on the Sacraments* appeared, he had begun to elaborate his views of the Incarnation, asserting Christ's oneness with us in all the attributes of humanity; and he was charged with heresy as maintaining the sinfulness of Christ's nature. He was convicted of heresy by the London presbytery in 1830, ejected from his new church in Regent's Square in 1832, and finally deposed in 1833. The majority of his congregation adhered to him, and a new communion, the Catholic Apostolic Church, was developed, commonly known as Irvingite, though Irving had little to do with its development. See Lives by A. L. Drummond (1937), T. Carlyle, *Miscellaneous Essays* (4th ed. 1857), and *Reminiscences* (1881).

(2) **Sir Henry, John Henry Brodribb** (1838–1905), English actor, born at Keinton-Mandeville, Somerset, was for a time a clerk in London but made his first appearance at the Sunderland Theatre in 1856. He acted in Edinburgh (1857–60), Manchester (1860–1865), Liverpool, and in 1866 made his London début at the St James's Theatre. In 1871 he transferred to the Lyceum and with his *Hamlet* (1874), *Macbeth* (1875) and *Othello* (1876) gained his reputation as the greatest English actor of his time. Despite exaggerated mannerisms and a weak, un-modulated voice, his striking presence and flair for interpreting the subtler emotions made him more successful in the portrayal of static characters such as Shylock and Malvolio rather than in the great tragic rôles of King Lear or Hamlet, but it was hardly a case, as Shaw maintained, of ' simply no brains, all character and temperament '. In

1878 his famous theatrical partnership with Ellen Terry (q.v.) at the Lyceum, where he became actor-manager-lessee, began with her Ophelia to his Hamlet and lasted till 1902. A notable success was Wills' version of Goethe's *Faust* (1885), in which Ellen Terry played Marguerite to Irving's Mephistopheles. In April 1889 they gave a command performance of *The Bells* before Queen Victoria at Sandringham, and in 1893 produced Tennyson's play *Becket*. Irving toured the United States with his company eight times. In 1898 the failure of his son's play and the loss by fire of the Lyceum's stock of scenery compelled Irving to sell the lease of the Lyceum, which was eventually turned into a music-hall. In 1895 he became the first actor to receive a knighthood. His ashes were interred in Westminster Abbey. Irving wrote *The Drama* (1893) and published an edition of Shakespeare's plays (1888). See studies by W. Archer (1883), P. H. Fitzgerald (1893), H. A. Jones (1931), and Lives by A. Brereton (1908) and Gordon Craig (1931). Of his sons, **Laurence** (1871–1914) was a novelist and playwright who was drowned in the *Empress of Ireland* disaster, and **Henry Brodribb** (' H. B.'; 1870–1919) was also an actor.

(3) **Washington** (1783–1859), American man of letters, born in New York, April 3, studied law, but on account of his delicate health was sent in 1804 to Europe. He visited Rome, Paris, the Netherlands and London, and in 1806 returned to New York, and was admitted to the bar. His first writing was in *Salmagundi* (1807), a semi-monthly sheet in imitation of the *Spectator* which ran for twenty numbers. His first characteristically boisterous work was *A History of New York*, by Diedrich Knickerbocker (1809), a good-natured burlesque upon the old Dutch settlers of Manhattan Island. He served as officer in the 1812 war, wrote biographies of American naval heroes, became a friend of Sir Walter Scott and under the pseudonym ' Geoffrey Crayon ' wrote *The Sketch Book* (1819–20), a miscellany, containing in different styles such items as ' Rip Van Winkle ', ' The Legend of Sleepy Hollow ' and ' Westminster Abbey ', which have something of his sadness at the loss of his betrothed and his brothers' fortune. *Bracebridge Hall* (1822) was followed after three years' travel in France and Germany by another miscellany *Tales of a Traveller* (1825). His stay in Spain produced such studies as *Life of Columbus* (1828), *Conquest of Granada* (1829), *Voyages of the Companions of Columbus* (1831), &c. After leaving Spain Irving was for a short time secretary to the United States Legation in London; on his return to his native city (1832) he was welcomed enthusiastically, but the criticisms by Fenimore Cooper and others that he had written only about Europe resulted in *A Tour on the Prairie* (1832), &c. Irving reached the height of his career when he was appointed ambassador to Spain (1842–46). He survives as an inimitable essayist and stylist. See Lives by P. M. Irving (1862–64), G. S. Hellman (1925) and S. T. Williams (1936).

ISAAC, name of two Eastern Roman emperors:

Isaac I, Comnenus (d. 1061), became Emperor of Constantinople in 1057. He established the finances of the empire on a sounder footing, laid the clergy under contribution at the tax collections, and repelled the Hungarians attacking his northern frontier; and then, resigning the crown (1059), retired to a monastery, where he died in 1061. He wrote commentaries on Homer.

Isaac II, Angelus (d. 1204), emperor from 1185, after a reign of war and tumult was dethroned, blinded and imprisoned by his brother Alexius in 1195. Restored in 1203, he reigned six months, was again dethroned, and died in prison.

ISAACS, Rufus. See READING.

ISABELLA (1292–1358), daughter of Philip IV of France, in 1308 married at Boulogne Edward II (q.v.), and, after his murder by her and Mortimer, lived chiefly at Castle Rising near King's Lynn.

ISABELLA II (1830–1904), Queen of Spain, was born at Madrid. On the death of her father, Ferdinand VII, in 1833, she succeeded to the throne, with her mother, Queen Maria Christina (q.v.), as regent. She attained her majority in 1843, and married in 1846 her cousin, Francisco de Assisi. A bad queen, she was deposed and in 1868 was expelled to France, where she abdicated in favour of her son, Alfonso XII. See studies by Gribble (1913) and P. de Répide (1932).

ISABELLA OF ANGOULÊME (d. 1246), in 1200 married King John of England, and in 1220 a former lover, the Count de la Marche. She died at Fontevrault. A daughter by John, **Isabella** (1214–41), in 1235 married the Emperor Frederick II.

ISABELLA OF CASTILE (1451–1504), the daughter of John II, King of Castile and Leon, in 1469 married Ferdinand V (q.v.) of Aragon.

ISABEY, Jean Baptiste, *ee-zah-bay* (1767–1855), French portrait painter, born at Nancy, painted portraits of the Revolution notabilities, and afterwards became court-painter to Napoleon and the Bourbons. His son, **Eugène** (1804–86), was an historical painter.

ISAEUS (fl. 4th cent. B.C.), Athenian orator, of whom, though we have ten of the fifty speeches he composed, we know absolutely nothing except that his first speech was composed in 389 B.C. and his last in 353 B.C.— all in private suits.

ISAIAH, *ī-zī'ah*, Heb. *Jeshaiah*, the first in order of the major Old Testament prophets, son of Amoz, was a citizen of Jerusalem, who began to prophesy about 747 B.C. (probable death-year of King Uzziah), and exercised his office till at least the close of the century. Of his end we know nothing: a tradition exists that he was sawn to death in the persecution of Manasseh. The first to doubt the authenticity of the book of Isaiah was Aben-Ezra (q.v.); Koppe (1779) suspected that chaps. xl-lxvi were of later date; and now most critics hold this view. It is quite possible, however, that the disputed prophecies contain fragments from Isaiah himself; that, though post-exilic in the main, they contain at least pre-exilic fragments is more certain. See the Bible commentaries by G. A. Smith (1890), O. C. Whitehouse (1901), J. Skinner (1917), and Matthew Arnold, *Isaiah of Jerusalem*.

ISHERWOOD, Christopher William Bradshaw (1904–), English novelist, born at Disley, Cheshire, was educated at Repton and Corpus Christi, Cambridge, studied medicine at King's, London (1928–29), and wrote two novels, *All the Conspirators* (1928) and *The Memorial* (1932). His best known works, *Mr Norris Changes Trains* (1935) and *Goodbye to Berlin* (1939), were based on his experiences (1930–33) as an English tutor in the decadence of post-slump, pre-Hitler Berlin. In collaboration with Auden (q.v.), a school friend, he wrote three prose-verse plays with political overtones in which by expressionist technique, music hall parody and ample symbolism, the unsavoury social climate was forcefully exposed against idealist remedies: *The Dog beneath the Skin* (1935), *Ascent of F 6* (1937), *On the Frontier* (1938). He travelled in China with Auden in 1938 and wrote *Journey to a War* (1939). In 1940 he went to California to work as scriptwriter for Metro-Goldwyn-Mayer and in 1946 took American citizenship. He translated the Hindu epic poem, the Bhagavad-Gita, with Swami Prabhavananda (1944), who also collaborated in *Shan-Kara's Crest-Jewel of Discrimination* (1947) and *How to Know God; the Yogi Aphorisms of Patanjali* (1953). He also translated Baudelaire's *Intimate Journals* (1947). Later novels include *Prater Violet* (1945), *The World in the Evening* (1954), and *Meeting by the River* (1967). See his autobiographical *Lions and Shadows* (1938).

ISHMAEL, *ish'may-el*, son of Abraham by Hagar, the Egyptian handmaid of his wife Sarah, represented as the progenitor of the Arabs. Mohammed asserted his descent from Ishmael.

ISIDORE OF SEVILLE, St, or **Isidorus Hispalensis** (*c*. 560–636), Spanish ecclesiastic, encyclopaedist and historian, was born either at Seville or Carthagena, and became Archbishop of Seville in 594. His episcopate was notable for the councils at Seville in 618 or 619, and at Toledo in 633, whose canons formed the basis of the constitutional law of Spain. He also collected all the decrees of councils and other church laws anterior to his time. Isidore was a voluminous and learned writer. His works include *Etymologies* or *Origins* (ed. W. M. Lindsay, 1912), an encyclopaedia; introduction to the Old and New Testaments; a defence of Christianity against the Jews; three books of ' Sentences '; books on ecclesiastical offices and the monastic rule; and a history of the Goths, Vandals and Suevi. See E. Bréhaut, *An Encyclopaedist of the Dark Ages* (1911), and Life by P. Séjourné (1929).

ISLA, José Francisco de, *ees'lah* (1703–81), Spanish satirist, born at Vidanes, N.W. Spain. Joining the Jesuits, for some years he lectured on philosophy and theology at Segovia, Santiago and Pamplona, and became famous as a preacher, but still more as a humorist and satirist by his writings, especially his novel of *Fray Gerundio* (1758–1770). The *Letters of Juan de la Encina* (1732) are a good example of his style; a

more characteristic one is the *Dia Grande de Navarra*. What Cervantes had done with the sham chivalry and sentiment of the romances, Isla strove in *Fray Gerundio* to do with the vulgar buffooneries of the popular preachers, and especially the preaching friars of the day. It was well received by all except the friars, but the Inquisition stopped the publication of the book. In 1767 Isla shared the lot of the Jesuits in their expulsion from Spain, and betook himself to Bologna, where he died. Isla translated Lesage's *Gil Blas*, which he humorously claimed to have restored to its native language.

ISLEBIUS. See AGRICOLA (3).

ISLIP, Simon (d. 1366), English prelate, Archbishop of Canterbury from 1349, was probably born at Islip near Oxford, and in 1307 was a fellow of Merton. He founded a college at Oxford for monks and secular clergy in 1361 which later under Wolsey was absorbed into Cardinal, now Christ Church, College.

ISMAIL PASHA, *is-mah'eel* (1830–95), Khedive of Egypt, born in Cairo, was second son of Ibrahim Pasha, and grandson of the famous Mehemet Ali. Educated at St Cyr, in 1863 he succeeded Sa'id as viceroy, and in 1867 assumed the hereditary title of Khedive. In 1872 the Sultan granted him also the right (withdrawn in 1879) of concluding treaties and of maintaining an army, and virtually gave him sovereign powers. Ismail began a series of vast internal reforms, and, extending his dominions southward, annexed Dar-Fûr in 1874, thereafter endeavouring, through Sir Samuel Baker and General Gordon, governors of the Sudan, to suppress the slave trade. To provide funds for his vast undertakings he in 1875 sold to Great Britain 177,000 shares in the Suez Canal for £4,000,000. The Egyptian finances, however, were almost hopelessly involved; and after several failures a dual British and French control was established, the finances being placed under European management. A promise of constitutional government ended in 1879 in the summary dismissal of Nubar Pasha's ministry, and this brought about the peremptory interference of the European governments. The Khedive, who declined to abdicate, was deposed by the Sultan in June 1879, and Prince Tewfik, his eldest son, was proclaimed Khedive. Ismail ultimately retired to Constantinople, where he died. See Life by P. Crabites (1933), and studies by J. MacCoan (1889) and G. Douin (1933 ff.).

ISMAY, Hastings Lionel Ismay, 1st Baron (1887–1965), British general, educated at Charterhouse and R.M.C. Sandhurst, joined the 21st Cavalry, Frontier Force, in 1907. He served on India's N.W. Frontier in 1908 and in Somaliland between 1914 and 1918. His appointment in 1926 as assistant secretary to the Committee of Imperial Defence inaugurated a long and fruitful association with politico-military organizations, which culminated in his service as chief of staff to Winston Churchill as prime minister and minister of defence. ' Pug ', as he was affectionately known to his associates, acted as secretary-general to N.A.T.O. (1952–

1957), was created K.C.B. in 1940, baron in 1947. See *Memoirs* (1960).

ISMET PAZA. See INÖNÜ.

ISOCRATES, *ī-sok'ra-teez* (436–338 B.C.), Greek prose writer, an Athenian, represents the perfection of ' epideictic ' oratory, i.e., oratory in which form and literary finish count for everything, and matter for very little. He received an excellent education, in his youth heard the orator Gorgias, and joined the circle of Socrates, but abandoned philosophy for speech-writing, which also he gave up when he found, after six speeches, that he had not the practical gifts for winning cases in a law court. About 390 B.C. he set up as a teacher of oratory, though he professed also to give a general practical education. He drew to him pupils subsequently distinguished as statesmen, historians and orators. He himself composed model speeches for his pupils, such as the *Panegyricus* (*c.* 380 B.C.) and the *Plataeicus* (373). But he also wrote speeches intended to be practical; the *Archidamus* may actually have been composed for the Spartan king Archidamus. The majority, for instance the *Symmachicus*, the *Areopagiticus*, the *Panathenaicus* (342–339) and the letters to Philip of Macedon, were designed to be circulated and read—they are in fact the earliest political pamphlets known. As a politician, Isocrates' one idea was to unite all Greeks together in a joint attack upon the common foe, Persia. The outcome was the destruction of Greek freedom at Chaeronea by Philip, a blow which ' killed with report that old man eloquent '. For melody, artistic merit, perfection of form and literary finish, Isocrates stands unrivalled, though his work is laboured and his style is apt to become monotonous. But aiming always at political edification rather than factual accuracy, he began an unfortunate tradition which lasted down to the coming of modern historical scholarship. See W. Jaeger, *Paideia* (1945).

ISRÄELS, Jozef (1824–1911), Dutch genre painter, born at Gröningen, studied at Amsterdam and Paris, where he exhibited in 1855 a historical picture of William the Silent. But he soon turned to scenes from humble life, especially the portrayal of fisher folk, as in his *Children of the Sea* (1857) and *Evening on the Shore.* He also worked as an etcher. See studies by J. E. Pythian (1912) and M. Eisler (1924).

ITO, Marquis Hirobumi, *ee'to* (1838–1909), Japanese statesman, born in Choshu province, four times premier of Japan, was in London in 1863, 1871 and 1882–1901, drafted the Japanese constitution, and was assassinated by a Korean at Harbin.

ITÚRBIDE, Agustín de, *ee-toor'bi-*T 1824), Mexican general, born a made himself emperor (Agustín May 1822 to March 1823, imitating but was forced to abdicate and wa

IVAN, *ee-vahn'*, six grand dukes an Russia, of whom the following are noteworthy:

(1) **Ivan I,** called **Kalita** (moneyba duke of Moscow (1328–41), a sound trator and reformer, made Mo capital of Russia by transferring tl metropolitan cathedral. His son, reigned after him until 1359.

(2) **Ivan III,** called ' the Great ' (14 grand duke (1462–1505), succeeded i off entirely the yoke of the Tartar subjecting a number of the Russia palities to his own sway. In 1472 he Sophia, a niece of Constantine Pala assumed the title of ' Ruler of all and adopted the two-headed eagle Byzantine empire. See study by J. L (1962).

(3) **Ivan IV,** called ' the Terrible ' (I tsar of Muscovy from 1533, the assume the title of ' tsar ' subdued Ka Astrakhan, and made the first annex Siberia. He concluded a commerci with Queen Elizabeth, after the Eng discovered (1553) the way to Archa sea. In 1564 the treachery of one counsellors aroused his suspicions began to see treachery everywher embarked on a reign of terror a merciless to the boyars, to Moscov Novgorod and other towns. Ivan sorrow for his son, whom three year he had slain in a mad fit of rage. these failings he did much for Russiar and commerce. See Lives by A. (1895), Waliszewski (trans. 1904), S. (1932) and I. Grey (1964).

IVANOV, Vyacheslav Ivanovich, *e* (1866–1949), Russian poet and critic in Berlin and lived in Greece and Ita he was converted to Roman Cat His poetry was enriched by his ph studies and he wrote studies on th Dionysus, on Dostoyevsky, By Nietzsche.

IVEAGH, Lord. See GUINNESS.

IVES, Frederick Eugene (1856–1937 can inventor, born in Litchfiel experimented with the possibilities graphy as a means of illustra invented (1878) and improved (half-tone process.

IWASA MATAHEI, *ma'ta-hay* (*c.* 1 Japanese painter, founder of th school.

J

IR IBN HAIJAN. See GEBIR.

KS, Lawrence Pearsall (1860–1955), glish philosopher and Unitarian clergy- n, born at Nottingham. He entered the nistry in 1887, and was editor of the *bbert Journal* from its foundation in 1902 til 1943. In 1903 he became professor of ilosophy at Manchester College, Oxford, d principal in 1915, retiring from both sts in 1931. His works, over a long life, ve consistency of outlook and no diminu- n in vitality; they include *The Alchemy of ought* (1910), *Life and Letters of Stopford ooke* (1917), *Education through Recreation*, d the *Smokeover* books. See his auto- ographical *Confessions of an Octogenarian* 942).

CKSON, (1) Andrew (1767–1845), 7th esident of the United States, was born at axhaw, N.C., March 15. After being mitted to the bar he became public osecutor in Nashville in 1788. He helped frame the constitution of Tennessee, and came its representative in congress in 96, its senator in 1797, and a judge of its preme court (1798–1804). When war was clared against Great Britain in 1812, as ajor-general of the state militia he led 2500 en to Natchez, but was ordered to disband em. Jackson, however, marched them ick to Nashville, and in September 1813 ok the field against the Creek Indians in labama. This campaign ended in a decisive ctory at the Horseshoe Bend of the Talla- oosa, March 1814. In May ' Old Hickory ' as made major-general in the regular army, id appointed to the command of the South. ensacola in Spanish Florida being then sed by the British as a base of operations, ackson invaded Spanish soil, stormed ensacola, and successfully defended New rleans against Sir E. Pakenham (January 315). In 1818 Jackson again invaded lorida, and severely chastised the Seminoles. fter the purchase of Florida he was its first overnor, but soon resigned, and in 1823 as again elected to the U.S. senate. In 1824 s a candidate for the presidency he had the ighest popular vote, but not a majority; in 828 he was elected, having a majority of lectoral votes. He was fearless, honest, rompt to decide everything for personal easons, and swept out great numbers of ninor officials to fill their places with his artisans—on the principle (as was said of im): 'To the victor belong the spoils'. Questions of tariff 'and ' nullification ' were rominent during his presidency. The resident's veto power was much more freely sed by Jackson than by his predecessors. Ie opposed legislation for premature enewing of the charter of the Bank of the Jnited States, believing that this centralized noney power was working against him and n this issue was re-elected president by an verwhelming majority in 1832. In his dministration the national debt was fully

paid in 1835, and the surplus revenue which accumulated was distributed to the several states. In 1837 he retired, and died June 8, 1845. See Lives by Parton (1860), Bassett (1911), M. James (1933–37), and studies of the Jacksonian era by A. M. Schlesinger (1945), and G. G. Van Deusen (1959).

(2) Cyril (1746–1819), born in Yorkshire, a distinguished dean of Christ Church, Oxford (1783–1809), who tutored Canning, Sir Robert Peel and Charles Wynn.

(3) Frederick John Foakes (1855–1941), English church historian, born at Ipswich, educated at Eton and Trinity College, Cambridge, known for his *History of the Christian Church* (1891), *The Beginnings of Christianity* (5 vols. 1920–33), &c.

(4) John (1769–1845), English pugilist, ' Gentleman Jackson ', was born in London, was champion boxer for eight years (1795– 1803) although he only appeared in the ring three times. After his retirement, he took pupils. One of them, Byron, celebrated him in verse.

(5) John Hughlings (1835–1911), English neurologist, born at Providence Green, Yorks, physician at the London Hospital (1874–94) and at the National Hospital for the Paralysed until 1906, investigated unilateral epileptiform seizures and dis- covered that certain regions of the brain are associated with certain movements of the limbs. He was elected F.R.S. in 1878.

(6) Sir Stanley (1870–1947), English cricketer and politician, born near Leeds, educated at Harrow and Trinity College, Cambridge, played first for England against Australia while still at the university (1893), and was a regular test player until 1905, in which year he was captain. He also played for Yorkshire. Entering parliament in 1915, he became chairman of the Conservative party (1923) and governor of Bengal (1927).

(7) Sir Thomas Graham (1835–1924), English architect, studied under Sir George Gilbert Scott and was responsible for many restorations of and additions to libraries, public schools and colleges at Eton, Harrow and Rugby, the Inner Temple and New Examination Schools at Oxford.

(8) Thomas Jonathan, ' Stonewall Jackson ' (1824–63), American soldier, born at Clarks- burg, W. Va., in 1851 he became professor in the Virginia Military Institute. He took command of the Confederate troops at Harper's Ferry on the secession of Virginia, and commanded a brigade at Bull Run, where his firm stand gained him his sobriquet ' Stonewall '. Promoted major-general, in the campaign of the Shenandoah valley (1862), he out-generalled McDowell, Banks and Frémont, and eventually drove them back upon the Lower Shenandoah. Then, hastening to Richmond, he turned the scale at Gaines's Mills (June 27), and returned to defeat Banks at Cedar Run in August. He then seized Pope's depot at Manassas, and

his corps bore the brunt of the fighting in the victorious second battle there on August 30. On September 15, he captured Harper's Ferry with 13,000 prisoners, and next day arrived at Sharpsburg, where his presence, in the battle of Antietam, saved Lee from disaster. As lieutenant-general he commanded the right wing at Fredericksburg (December 13), and at Chancellorsville (May 1, 1863) repulsed Hooker. Next night he fell upon the right of the National army and drove it back on Chancellorsville. Returning from a reconnaissance, his party was fired on by some of his own command, and Jackson received three wounds. His left arm was amputated; but on May 10 he died. See Lives by Cooke (1866), Dabney (1866), his wife (1892), Parton (1893), Henderson (1898), H. A. White (1909), and D. S. Freeman, *Lee's Lieutenants* (1942).

(9) **William** (1730–1803), English composer, born at Exeter, where, after some twenty or more years in London, he in 1777 became organist of the cathedral. He composed two operas, musical accompaniments to Milton's *Lycidas*, Warton's *Ode to Fancy*, church music and songs.

JACK THE RIPPER, unidentified English murderer. Between August and November 1888, six women were found murdered and mutilated in Whitechapel and the adjoining Aldgate in the East End of London. All were prostitutes; five were found in the street and the sixth in a house. The murderer was never discovered. The affair roused much public disquiet, provoked a violent press campaign against the C.I.D. and the home secretary, and resulted in some reform of police methods.

JACOB, *jay'kob*, (1) (Heb. *Ya'aqób*), one of the three chief Hebrew patriarchs, second son of Isaac.

(2). See LACROIX (1).

(3) **François** (1920–), French scientist, born at Nancy, professor of Cellular Genetics at Collège de France. Worked with Lwoff and Monod at Pasteur Inst., Paris, on researches in genetics and microbiology, for which they were jointly awarded the Nobel prize for medicine in 1965.

(4) **Naomi Ellington** (1889–1964), English novelist, born at Ripon, Yorkshire. First a teacher, she later went on to the stage, then with *Jacob Ussher* (1926) she embarked on a writing career. Her novels, of the character-study type, include *Young Emmanuel* (1932), *Cap of Youth* (1941), *Private Gollantz* (1943), and *Gollantz and Partners* (1958). See her autobiographical *Me* series.

(5) **Violet**, *née* **Kennedy-Erskine** (1863– 1946), Scottish poet and novelist, born in Montrose, married Major Arthur Otway Jacob and lived for some years in India. Although she began as a novelist, she is best known for poems in Angus dialect, *Songs of Angus* (1915), *More Songs of Angus* (1918), *Bonnie Joann* (1922) and *Northern Lights* (1927). Her *Lairds of Dun* (1931) is a standard history of her native district.

JACOBA. See JACQUELINE OF HOLLAND.

JACOBI, *ya-kō'bee*, (1) **Friedrich Heinrich** (1743–1819), German philosopher, born at Düsseldorf, in 1770 became financial coun-

cillor for Jülich and Berg, devoted himself to literature and philosophy and in 1807 became president of the Academy of Sciences at Munich. Jacobi elaborated no system of philosophy, but criticized all other philosophies from his special doctrine—that by 'reason' (*not* the understanding) we have immediate conviction not only of the reality of objects perceived by the senses, but also of the reality of *a priori* truths. From this standpoint he examined Spinoza (1785), Hume, Kant and Schelling (1811), wrote philosophical romances—and an *Open Letter to Fichte* (1799), and other occasional writings. See monographs by Harms (1876), Heraeus (1928) and Bollnow (1933).

(2) **Karl Gustav Jakob** (1804–51), German mathematician, born at Potsdam, professor of Mathematics at Königsberg (1827–42), he discovered and expounded elliptic functions (1829) and made important advances in the study of differential equations, the theory of numbers, and determinants. His works were published by the Berlin Academy (1881–91). His brother, **Moritz Hermann** (1801–74), was a physicist and engineer at St Petersburg.

JACOBS, (1) **Joseph** (1854–1916), Australian Jewish folklorist and critic, born at Sydney, graduated at Cambridge (1876), and (1900) edited the *Jewish Encyclopaedia* in America.

(2) **William Wymark** (1863–1943), English short-story writer, born at Wapping, London, was a post-office official (1883–99) and began writing humorous yarns of bargees and tars, most of which were illustrated by Will Owen, such as *Many Cargoes* (1896), *The Skipper's Wooing* (1897), *Deep Waters* (1919) and *The Lady of the Barge* (1902), a collection which included *The Monkey's Paw* and other gruesome tales mingled with the humorous ones.

JACOBSEN, (1) **Carlyle** (1902–), American psychologist, born at Minneapolis, lectured in psychology at Minnesota, Yale. and Harvard and showed that extreme exertion taxes the heart and circulation no more than normal physical expenditure of energy. He also showed that the brain can cause physiological disturbances such as sweating, &c.

(2) **Jens Peter** (1847–85), Danish novelist, born at Thisted in Jutland, studied science at Copenhagen, translated Darwin and became, under the influence of Brandes, the leader of the new Danish naturalistic movement. Having contracted tuberculosis in Italy, he published, apart from some beautiful poems and short-stories such as ' Mogens ' (1872), two novels—*Fru Marie Grubbe* (1876) and *Niels Lynne* (1880)—before his death. Half realist, half dreamer, his deliberate impressionist style found many disciples, Rilke among them.

JACOBUS DE VORAGINE. See VORAGINE.

JACOPONE DA TODI. See TODI.

JACOTOT, **Jean Joseph**, *zhah-kō-tō* (1770– 1840), French educationist, inventor of the ' universal method ', born at Dijon, was successively soldier, military secretary, and professor. His system, which resembles that of James Hamilton (q.v.), postulates that the mental capacities of all men are equal; the unequal results of education depend almost exclusively upon will. He expounded his views in *Enseignement Universel* (1823). See Life by Guillard (1860).

JACQUARD, Joseph Marie, *zhah-kahr* (1752–1834), French silk-weaver of Lyons who by his invention (1801–08) of the Jacquard Loom enabled an ordinary workman to produce the most beautiful patterns in a style previously accomplished with almost incredible patience, skill and labour. But though Napoleon rewarded him with a small pension and the Légion d'Honneur, the silk weavers themselves offered such violent opposition to his machine that on one occasion he narrowly escaped with his life. At his death his machine was in almost universal use. See French Life by Grandsard (1884).

JACQUE, Charles, *zhahk* (1813–94), French painter and etcher, a prominent member of the Barbizon school, born and died in Paris, is best known for his paintings of sheep and etchings of rural scenes, many of them in the Louvre.

JACQUELINE OF HOLLAND, or **Jacoba of Bavaria** (1401–36), a beautiful but unfortunate princess, who was four times married —in 1407 to Prince John of France; in 1418 to her weak cousin, the Duke of Brabant; in 1422, bigamously, to Duke Humphrey of Gloucester; and in 1433, trigamously, to Frans van Borsselen.

JACQUEMART, Jules Ferdinand, *-mahr* (1837–80), French etcher, celebrated for his delicate renderings of old jewellers' work and illustrations for books on ceramics by his father, **Albert Jules** (1808–75), was born in Paris and died at Nice.

JAGAN, Cheddi Berrat, *jay'-* (1918–), Guyanan politician, born at Port Mourant, the son of an East Indian headman, qualified as a dentist at Chicago University and after a spell of provincial politics was elected to the House of Assembly in 1953 when his Communist-inspired People's Progressive Party secured a majority. The British Colonial Office, fearing the subversion of the colony's government, suspended the constitution, deprived Jagan and his ministers of their portfolios and sent British forces to the territory. In 1954 Jagan was imprisoned for violating an order restricting his movements to Georgetown. In 1955 he was re-elected leader of the party, which was returned to power with a two-thirds majority in August 1957. He became minister of trade and industry in an executive over which the governor of British Guiana had extensive powers of veto 'and nomination. From 1961 until 1964 he was the first premier of British Guiana (now Guyana) and is the present leader of the opposition.

JAGELLON, *yah-gel'-*, an illustrious dynasty which reigned in Lithuania, Poland, Hungary, and Bohemia in the 14th, 15th and 16th centuries.

JAGGER, Charles Sargeant (1885–1934), English sculptor, born in Yorkshire, studied at the Royal College of Art and at Rome, and executed mainly mythological and historical subjects. His most famous work is the *Royal Artillery Memorial* at Hyde Park Corner, London.

JAHANGIR (1569–1627), ' Conqueror of the World ', 3rd Mogul emperor, son of Akbar the Great, whom he succeeded in 1605, indulged in his weakness for opium, patronized art, literature and architecture, and allowed his remarkable wife, Nur Jahan, to take over the government. He is buried in a mausoleum in the Shalimar gardens in Kashmir, which he designed. See his Memoirs, trans. Rodgers and Beveridge (1909–14).

JAHN, (1) **Friedrich Ludwig** (1778–1852), Prussian physical educationist, born at Lanz in Prussia, in 1811 started the first gymnasium in Berlin and his methods soon became very popular. Jahn commanded a volunteer corps; and after the peace of 1815 resumed his teaching, and published *Die deutsche Turnkunst* (1816). But the gymnasiums began to witness political gatherings, too liberal to please the Prussian government, and they were closed in 1818. Jahn, who had taken a prominent part in the movement, was arrested in 1819, and suffered five years' imprisonment. He was elected to the Frankfurt National Assembly in 1848.

(2) **Johann** (1750–1816), German Roman Catholic Bible critic, born at Tasswitz in Moravia, became professor of Oriental Languages at Olmütz, and in 1789 at Vienna; but the boldness of his criticism led in 1806 to his retirement to a canonry. Notable works were his introduction to the Old Testament (1792), *Archaeologia Biblica* (1805; Eng. trans. 1840) and *Enchiridion Hermeneuticae* (1812).

(3) **Otto** (1813–69), German archaeologist and musicologist, born at Kiel, lectured at Kiel, Greifswald and Leipzig. Deprived of his chair in 1851 for political activities in 1848–49, he became in 1855 professor of Archaeology at Bonn. He published works on Greek art (1846), representations of ancient life on vases (1861, 1868), and the evil eye (1850), besides a Life of Mozart (4 vols. 1856–60) and essays on music.

JALAL AD-DIN RUMI, Mohammed ibn Mohammed, *ya-lahl' ahd-deen roo'mee* (1207–1273), Persian lyric poet and mystic, born at Balkh, settled at Iconium (Konya) in 1226 and founded a sect. He wrote much exquisite lyrical poetry, including a long epic on the Sufi mystical doctrine, *Masnavi y ma' navi*.

JAMES, the name of three men of importance in the early Christian church:

(1) **James, St ' the Great ',** son of the fisherman Zebedee and brother of John, was one of the three chief among the twelve apostles, and was beheaded by Herod Agrippa, A.D. 44.

(2) **James, St ' the Just ',** eldest among the ' brethren ' of Jesus, was stoned to death in A.D. 62. He was head of the Christian community of Jerusalem, and was noted for his piety. Most theologians consider him the author of the Epistle of James, although it has been ascribed to both the others. The first of the Catholic Epistles, it was put by Eusebius among the list of controverted books (*Antilegomena*), and was finally declared canonical by the third Council of Carthage (397). The Tübingen school regard it as a polemic against Paul.

(3) **James, St ' the Younger ',** son of Alphaeus, was likewise an apostle.

JAMES, the name of seven kings of Scotland, the last two of whom were also kings of England. See also under STEWART:

James I (1394–1437), King of Scotland from 1424, second son of Robert III, was born at Dunfermline in 1394. His elder brother, David, Duke of Rothesay, died at Falkland in 1402—allegedly murdered by his uncle, the Duke of Albany; and Robert in 1406 sent James for safety to France. But the vessel was seized by an English cruiser, and James was carried to London. He was detained a prisoner for about eighteen years with the connivance of the Duke of Albany, on whom the government of Scotland had devolved after Robert III's death in 1406. Henry IV made some compensation for his injustice to the young prince by having him carefully brought up. On Albany's death in 1420, his son Murdoch succeeded to the regency; under his feeble rule the country fell into disorder, till at length he took steps to procure the return of James. Previous to leaving England, James married on February 12, 1424, Jane Beaufort (d. 1445), a daughter of the Earl of Somerset, niece of Richard II. James found his kingdom demoralized and at once set himself to restore order. Eight months after his restoration he suddenly swooped down upon his cousin the late regent, two of his sons, and his aged father-in-law, the Earl of Lennox; they were all beheaded at Stirling. James then seized fifty of the Highland chiefs, and put to death the ringleaders. He deprived the Earl of March of his estates, and on the death of the Earl of Mar, the victor at Harlaw, he seized the earldom and annexed its immense estates to the crown. Meanwhile into the parliament he introduced the principle of representation. Its enactments related to the regulation of trade and the internal economy of the kingdom. He renewed commercial intercourse with the Netherlands, concluded a treaty with Denmark, Norway and Sweden, and drew closer the ancient bond of alliance with France. But he persisted in harshly carrying out his measures for curbing the power of the nobles, which excited strong discontent and apprehension; and after his confiscation of the earldom of Strathearn, a conspiracy was formed, headed by his kinsmen, the Earl of Athole, Sir Robert Stewart and Sir Robert Graham. The plot was carried into effect at Perth on February 20, 1437. The king was about to retire for the night when a band of assassins led by Graham broke into the Dominican monastery where the court was residing. The bolts had been removed from the chamber door, but Catharine Douglas is said to have thrust her arm into the staple. It was instantly broken. The king, who had sought refuge in a vault under the floor, was discovered, and after a desperate resistance cruelly murdered. The murderers were all taken, and tortured to death. By his wife he left one son and six daughters, one of whom, Margaret of Scotland (q.v.), married to the Dauphin of France, was a gifted poetess. James was unquestionably the ablest of the Stewart sovereigns. The tender, passionate collection of poems, *Kingis Quair* (' king's

quire ' or book), is still attributed to him. See Life by E. Balfour-Melville (1936).

James II (1430–60), King of Scotland from 1437, son of James I, born October 16, was six years old at his father's murder. Thereupon the queen mother took shelter in Edinburgh Castle with her son, who was put under her charge and that of Livingston of Callander. But Crichton, the Chancellor, who was governor of the castle, kept possession of the boy until the queen escaped with him, and took refuge with Livingston in Stirling Castle. Meanwhile the country was brought to the verge of ruin by the feuds of the nobles. When in 1439 the queen-dowager married Sir James Stewart of Lorn, Livingston compelled her to resign her guardianship of the king; and Crichton and Livingston, reconciled, were the sole rulers of the kingdom, till in 1449 James assumed the reins of government. He displayed great prudence and vigour. War with England was renewed on the Borders in 1448, but ended next year by a truce. In 1449 James married Mary (d. 1463), daughter of the Duke of Gueldres. He procured from the parliament a number of judicious enactments, but his efforts to promote the welfare of the people were thwarted by the nobles, especially by the House of Douglas (q.v.). As the Yorkists protected the exiled Douglases, James entangled himself in the contest between the Houses of York and Lancaster, and marched for England in 1460 with a powerful army. He laid siege to Roxburgh Castle, at that time held by the English, and was killed by the bursting of a cannon (August 3). See Sir A. H. Dunbar, *Scottish Kings* (1906).

James III (1451–88), King of Scotland from 1460, son of James II, was brought up under the guardianship of Bishop Kennedy of St Andrews, while the Earl of Angus was made lieutenant-general. Under their management the government was carried on judiciously and successfully; but the death of the earl in 1462 and of the bishop in 1466 left the country a prey to the factious and ambitious nobles, conspicuous among whom was Lord Boyd of Kilmarnock, high justiciar. His son, created Earl of Arran, obtained in 1467 the hand of the king's sister, the Princess Margaret. The ambition and arrogance of the family, however, led to their downfall, and both Boyd and Arran fled. The king had a refined and cultivated mind, but was unfitted to rule a country like Scotland and to keep in order its turbulent nobles. He spent his time in the society of architects, painters and musicians, and the rule of these favourites soon grew intolerable to the nobles, who attached themselves to the king's brothers, Albany and Mar. James became jealous of their popularity and imprisoned them; Albany escaped to France, but Mar died in confinement. In retaliation for an invasion of the country by an English fleet, James advanced with an army towards England (1482). He had reached Lauder when the disaffected nobles suddenly seized Cochrane and the other royal favourites and hanged them, Angus, hence called ' Bell-the-Cat ', taking the initiative. Returning to Edinburgh, they imprisoned the king in the castle. Soon the lowland nobles again rose in open rebellion, and induced the young heir to the throne to join them, while the king was supported by the northern barons. An encounter took place (June 11, 1488) at Sauchieburn near Bannockburn. The royal army was defeated, and James, in galloping from the field, was thrown from his horse and murdered. He married in 1469 Margaret of Denmark (*c.* 1457–86), and left three sons, the eldest of whom succeeded. See T. D. Robb, intro. to *The Thre Prestis of Peblis* (1920).

James IV (1473–1513), King of Scotland from 1488 after the murder of his father James III, after Sauchieburn, born March 17. His confederates in the rebellion took possession of the offices of state, the royal treasury and the late king's jewels, and even accused the loyal barons of treason and deprived them of their estates. When James reached maturity he exhibited much energy and good sense. He gradually withdrew his confidence from the dominant barons and transferred it to Sir Andrew Wood and other trustworthy counsellors. He vigilantly guarded against the encroachments of the papal court, and asserted the ecclesiastical independence of his kingdom. Though he supported the impostor, Perkin Warbeck, and invaded England on his behalf, in 1497 a seven-years' truce was concluded between the two kingdoms, and in August 1503 James married Margaret (q.v.), eldest daughter of Henry VII—an alliance which led ultimately to the union of the crowns. When Henry VIII joined the league against France, James adhered to the French alliance. Petty disputes arose between the Borderers, and inroads were made on both sides. James was irritated at the capture of two Scottish privateers by English men-of-war. The French king, hard pressed by the Spanish and English, made strenuous efforts to obtain assistance from the Scots, and James was induced to invade England. He lingered about the Borders until the Earl of Surrey had collected a powerful army; and on September 9, 1513, was fought the battle of Flodden, in which fell the Scottish king and the flower of his nobility. James had great accomplishments, was frank and very hospitable, but he was also headstrong, licentious and lavish. See Lives by I. A. Taylor (1913) and R. L. Mackie (1958).

James V (1512–42), King of Scotland from 1513, son of the above, born April 10, at Linlithgow, was only an infant when his father's death gave him the crown. The queen-dowager was appointed regent, but on her marriage (1514) with the Earl of Angus, the Duke of Albany, son of the younger brother of James III, was made regent in her stead. Amid the contentions of the rival French and English factions, and the private quarrels of the nobles, the country was reduced to a state of anarchy. Albany, after vain efforts to assert his authority, retired to France in 1524. Meanwhile James had been placed under the care of Sir David Lyndsay. In 1525 he fell into the hands of Angus, who kept him a close prisoner until

in 1528 he made his escape from Falkland to Stirling, and as an independent sovereign began to carry out a judicious policy. He banished the Douglases, punished the Border freebooters, chastised the insurgent Highlanders, renewed the ancient commercial treaty between Scotland and the Netherlands, instituted the College of Justice, and protected the peasantry against the tyranny of the barons. His sympathy with the common people and his habit of visiting their houses in disguise procured for him the designation of ' the king of the commons '. In 1536 James visited France, and in 1537 married Magdalene, daughter of Francis I, who died in the following July; in June 1538 he married Mary of Guise (q.v.). Meanwhile the principles of the reformed faith were making progress in Scotland, and Henry VIII tried to persuade his nephew to throw off the papal authority. But James had to rely on the support of the clergy in order to reduce the exorbitant power of the nobles. Henry invited the Scottish king to meet him at York in 1541, but waited there six days for him in vain. Other causes of offence arose, and war broke out in 1542. An army of 30,000 men under the Duke of Norfolk was ordered to invade Scotland, but the attempt ended in nothing. A levied Scottish army advanced to Fala; but the nobles refused to follow James beyond the frontier. Another army was shortly after levied by the exertions of the clergy; but the command having been given to Oliver Sinclair, a royal favourite, the nobles again refused to act. While the Scottish army thus disputed, a body of English Borderers fell upon, and completely routed, them at Solway Moss, taking many prisoners. James, overwhelmed by this shameful discomfiture, retired to Falkland Palace; and, attacked by a slow fever, died, December 14, 1542, about seven days after the birth of his ill-fated daughter Mary. See Bapst, *Les Mariages de Jacques V* (1889).

James, VI of Scotland from 1567, I of England from 1603 (1566–1625), the son of Mary, Queen of Scots, and Henry, Lord Darnley, was born in Edinburgh Castle, June 19. On his mother's forced abdication in 1567 he was proclaimed king. He was placed in the keeping of the Earl of Mar, and taught by George Buchanan. Within eleven years Moray, Lennox, Mar and Morton had successively held the regency, and when, in 1578, Morton was driven from power James nominally assumed the direction of affairs. But his advisers became unpopular, and Morton re-established himself. About this time James began to exhibit his characteristic partiality towards favourites; with the help of Captain James Stewart, created Earl of Arran, and of the Duke of Lennox, he was enabled finally to break the power of Morton. After Morton's execution (1581) James ruled the kingdom through his two favourites, not without much discontent. Hence in 1582 occurred the Raid of Ruthven, when the king was seized by a party of his nobles and obliged to sanction the imprisonment of Arran and the banishment of Lennox. In 1583 a counter-plot brought about the king's freedom, when he immediately restored Arran to power. The confederate lords fled to England, whence, in 1585, through the connivance of Queen Elizabeth, they returned, and with an army forced James to capitulate in Stirling Castle. Arran was again banished. In 1586 Queen Mary, then a prisoner in England, was condemned to be executed; James's conduct on this occasion does not admit of defence. In 1589 he went to Christiania, where he married the Princess Anne (1574–1619). The king was frequently in conflict with the Presbyterians and with the Roman Catholics. Hating Puritanism, he was therefore disposed to introduce Episcopacy into Scotland, and did ultimately (in 1600) succeed in establishing bishops. From 1591 to 1594, when James marched against them, the Roman Catholic lords in the north were in a state of semi-insurrection. In 1600 occurred the Gowrie Conspiracy, if any conspiracy there was (see RUTHVEN). On the death of Elizabeth in 1603, James ascended the English throne as great-grandson of James IV's English wife, the Princess Margaret. He was at first well received by his subjects in England, but became unpopular from his continued partiality towards favourites. He also degraded the prerogative of the crown by the sale of titles. His chief favourite at this time was Robert Carr or Ker, a Scotsman, whom he finally created Earl of Somerset. When Carr fell out of favour he was succeeded by Buckingham. In 1617 James revisited Scotland, signalizing the event by angry disputes with the clergy. Henry, Prince of Wales, having died in 1612, the succession devolved upon James's second son Charles, between whom and a Spanish princess the king was ineffectually anxious to effect a marriage. Buckingham, who was entrusted with the affair, acted rashly and unwisely, and war with Spain was the outcome. James died at Theobalds, March 27, 1625. He has been described as 'the wisest fool in Christendom'. 'He was indeed', says Macaulay, 'made up of two men—a witty, well-read scholar, who wrote, disputed, and harangued, and a nervous, drivelling idiot who acted.' By Mr Gardiner his character has been treated more broadly and mildly; perhaps the best estimate of the man is Scott's representation of him in *The Fortunes of Nigel*. See his poetical works, ed. J. Craigie (2 vols. 1955-58), and Lives by C. Steeholm (1938), H. G. Stafford (1940), and W. McElwee, *The Wisest Fool in Christendom* (1958).

James, VII of Scotland, II of England (both 1685–88) (1633–1701), second son of Charles I, was born at St James's Palace, October 12, and was created Duke of York. Nine months before his father's execution he escaped to Holland, served under Turenne 1652–55, and in 1657 took Spanish service in Flanders. At the Restoration (1660) James was made lord high admiral of England, twice commanding the English fleet in the ensuing wars with the Dutch. In 1659 he had entered into a private marriage contract with Anne Hyde, daughter of the Earl of Clarendon (q.v.); and the year after her death in 1671 as a professed Catholic he avowed his own conversion to Catholicism. In 1673 parliament passed the Test Act, and James was obliged to resign the office of lord high admiral. Shortly after, he married Mary, daughter of the Duke of Modena. The national ferment occasioned by the Popish Plot became so formidable that he had to retire to the Continent, and during his absence an attempt was made to exclude him from the succession. He returned at the close of 1679, and was sent to Scotland to take the management of its affairs. Meanwhile the Exclusion Bill was twice passed by the Commons, but in the first instance it was rejected by the Lords, and on the second was lost by the dissolution of parliament. During this period James spent much of his time in exile but after defeat of the bill he returned to England, and in direct violation of the law took his seat in the council, and resumed the direction of naval affairs. At the death of Charles in 1685 James ascended the throne, and immediately proceeded to levy, on his own warrant, the customs and excise duties which had been granted to Charles only for life. He sent a mission to Rome, heard mass in public, and became, like his brother, the pensioner of the French king. In Scotland the persecution of the Covenanters was renewed with increased severity; in England the futile rebellion of Monmouth (q.v.) was followed by the 'Bloody Assize'. The suspension of the Test Act by the king's authority, his prosecution of the seven bishops on a charge of seditious libel, his conferring ecclesiastical benefices on Roman Catholics, his violation of the rights of the Universities of Oxford and Cambridge, his plan for packing parliament, and numerous other arbitrary acts showed his fixed determination to overthrow the constitution and the church. The indignation of the people was at length roused, and the interposition of William, Prince of Orange, James's son-in-law and nephew, was formally solicited by seven leading politicians. William landed at Torbay, November 4, 1688, with a powerful army, and marched towards London. He was everywhere hailed as a deliverer, while James was deserted not only by his ministers and troops, but even by his daughter the Princess Anne. The unfortunate king, on the first appearance of danger, had sent his wife and infant son to France, and, after one futile start and his arrest at Faversham, James also escaped and joined them at St Germain. He was hospitably received by Louis XIV, who settled a pension on him. In 1689, aided by a small body of French troops, he invaded Ireland and made an ineffectual attempt to regain his throne. He was defeated at the battle of the Boyne, and returned to St Germain, where he resided until his death, September 6, 1701. He left two daughters—Mary, married to the Prince of Orange, and Anne, afterwards queen—and one son by his second wife, James Francis Edward (see STEWART). He had several illegitimate children—one of them, Marshal Berwick. See Macaulay's *History* with C. H. Firth, *Commentary* (1938), W. S. Churchill, *Marlborough* (1933-38), study by Ogg (1955), and Life by F. C. Turner (1948).

JAMES, (1) **Arthur Lloyd** (1884–1943), British phonetician, born at Pentre, graduated at Cardiff University and at Trinity College, Cambridge, became lecturer in phonetics at University College London in 1920, and in 1927 head of the phonetics department at the School of Oriental and African Studies, a position which was raised to the dignity of a professorial chair in 1933. He is chiefly remembered for his *Historical Introduction to French Phonetics* (1929) and for his work with the B.B.C., whose adviser he was in all matters concerning pronunciation, and whose well-known handbooks on the pronunciation of place names he edited. He committed suicide after taking his wife's life, as a result of a depressive psychosis brought on by the war.

(2) **George Payne Rainsford** (1801–60), English novelist, born in London, wrote numerous historical romances, such as *Richelieu* (1829), *Henry Masterton* (1832), parodied by Thackeray in *Barbazure* for his two horsemen (his stock opening). He was British consul at Richmond, Virginia (1852–1856), and at Venice. See Ellis, *The Solitary Horseman* (1927).

(3) **Henry, 1st Baron James of Hereford** (1828–1911), English lawyer, born at Hereford, educated at Cheltenham College, and called to the bar in 1852, entered parliament as a liberal in 1869 and rose to become attorney-general in 1873. He defended the case for *The Times* before the Parnell Commission. In 1895–1902 he was chancellor of the Duchy of Lancaster, with a peerage. See Life by Lord Askwith (1930).

(4) **Henry** (1843–1916), American novelist, brother of (9), born in New York, April 15, of Irish and Scottish stock, until his father's death was known as Henry James, junior, the father (1811–82) being a well-known theological writer and lecturer, an exponent of Swedenborg and Sandemanianism. After a roving youth in America and Europe and desultory law studies at Harvard, he began in 1865 to contribute brilliant literary reviews and short stories. His work as a novelist falls into three periods. To the first, in which he is mainly concerned with the 'international situation', the impact of American life on the older European civilization, belong *Roderick Hudson* (1875), *The American* (1877), *Daisy Miller* (1879), *Washington Square* (1880), *Portrait of a Lady* (1881), *Princess Casamassima*, in which he probes the shadier aspects of European political life, and finally *The Bostonians* (1886). From 1869 he made his home in England, chiefly in London and in Rye, Sussex, where he, the elderly, urbane aesthete of letters, struck up an oddly contrasted friendship with the brilliant pioneer of science fiction and self-conscious reformer of mankind, H. G. Wells, a friendship which lasted until the latter's savage attack on the Jamesian *ethos* in the novel, *Boon* (1915). His second period, devoted to purely English subjects, comprises *The Tragic Muse* (1890), *The Spoils of Poynton* (1897), *What Maisie Knew* (1897) and *The Awkward Age* (1899). James reverts to Anglo-American attitudes in his last great period, which includes *The Wings of a Dove*

(1902), *The Ambassadors* (1903), possibly his masterpiece, *The Golden Bowl* (1904) and two unfinished novels. Collections of his characteristic 'long short stories' include *Terminations* (1895), *The Two Magics* (1898) and *The Altar of the Dead* (1909). James is the acknowledged master of the psychological novel, which has profoundly influenced the 20th-century literary scene. Plot is sacrificed in the interests of minute delineation of character. Many seemingly insignificant incidents, however, subtly contribute allegorically or metaphorically to the author's intentions. James seldom listened to the end of a story told at dinner, but would silence the speaker after he had merely verbally set the scene. 'Leave the rest to the imagination', he would explain. A Jamesian 'incident' would often amount to no more than a physical gesture, the movement of the arm, a manner of standing up or of passing the bread at the table. Hence the criticism that 'nothing ever happens' in his later novels. But the never failing note of authenticity of his descriptions, the curious suggestive power of his prose, the skill with which he marshals minutely observed detail sustains the interest and catalyses continued contemplation. The outbreak of the first World War brought out his pro-English sympathies. He became a British subject and shortly before his death was fittingly awarded the O.M. He died February 28, 1916. See his critical studies, *French Poets and Novelists* (1878) and the essay, ' On the Art of Fiction' (1884), travel sketches such as *The American Scene* (1906) and three volumes of memoirs, *A Small Boy and Others* (1913), *Notes of a Son and a Brother* (1914) and the unfinished *The Middle Years* (1917); also studies by Rebecca West (1916), J. W. Beach (1918), P. Edgar (1927), F. O. Matthiessen (1946), Van W. Brooks (1947), S. Noel-Smith (1947), H. Dupée (1951), D. W. Jefferson (1960), also *Parisian Sketches*, ed. Edel and Lind (1958) and *Henry James and H. G. Wells*, correspondence, ed. Edel and Ray (1958).

(5) **Jesse Woodson** (1847–1882), American Wild West robber, born in Clay County, Missouri, led numerous bank and train robberies before being murdered by one of his fellow brigands. More recently he has been the subject of numerous Hollywood 'Westerns'.

(6) **Montague Rhodes** (1862–1936), English scholar and author, born at Goodnestone, Kent, was elected provost of his college, King's, Cambridge, in 1905, was director of the Fitzwilliam Museum (1894–1908) and vice-chancellor of Cambridge (1913–15). In 1918 he became provost of his old school, Eton College. He catalogued the manuscripts of every Cambridge college, of Aberdeen University, and several London libraries, wrote studies on the Apocrypha, the art and literature of the Middle Ages and the highly popular collection of *Ghost Stories of an Antiquary* (1905–11), *Twelve Medieval Ghost Stories* (1922), &c. He was awarded the O.M. See his autobiography, *Eton and King's* (1926).

(7) **Robert** (1705–76), English physician, born in Staffordshire, practised in London

and invented James's fever powders, which were popular in the 18th and 19th centuries. He also compiled a *Medical Dictionary* (1743).

(8) **William** (d. 1827), English naval historian, compiler of *The Naval History* (5 vols. 1822–24), which disclosed American naval superiority, was a Jamaica attorney, and from 1815 lived in England.

(9) **William** (1842–1910), American psychologist and pragmatic philosopher, brother of (4), born in New York, was educated there and in several schools in Europe, eventually graduated in medicine at Harvard, where he became lecturer in Comparative Anatomy in 1872, assistant professor of Philosophy (1882), professor (1885) and in 1889 changed his professorial title to that of Psychology. With Lange he formulated the theory that emotions are the perceptions of physiological changes rather than the reverse, e.g., we are frightened because we run. With his greatest work, *Principles of Psychology* (1890; abridged 1892), he firmly placed psychology upon a physiological foundation, encouraged experimental work at Harvard, although he practised it little himself. His other famous psychological work is *The Varieties of Religious Experience* (1902), which comprises his Edinburgh Gifford Lectures. His best philosophical work is the essay, *The Will to Believe* (1897), in which he expounded his brand of pragmatism which he called radical empiricism, opposing all metaphysical systems but unlike other empiricists allowing religious as well as scientific working hypotheses. Beliefs do not work because they are true, but true because they work. Two other notable philosophical studies are his Oxford Hibbert Lectures, *A Pluralistic Universe* (1909), in which he comments on Hegel, Fechtner and Bergson, and his posthumous *Some Problems of Philosophy* (1911). See his Letters, ed. by his son, Henry (1920), Life by A. A. Roback (1943), and studies by R. B. Perry (1935), M. Knight (1950), L. Morris (1950).

JAMESON, (1) Anna (1794–1860), Irish art critic and author, daughter of Brownell Murphy, a miniature painter, was born at Dublin. In 1825 she married Robert Jameson, a barrister; but they did not get on well together; and from 1829 when he went as a judge to Dominica she lived apart from him save for a visit to him in Canada (1836–1838). Her writings include *Diary of an Ennuyée* (1826), *Characteristics of Shakespeare's Women* (1832), *Beauties of the Court of Charles II* (1833), and works on art. See Memoirs by her niece, Gerardine Macpherson (1878), and *Letters and Friendships* by S. Erskine (1915).

(2) **Sir Leander Starr, 1st Bart.** (1853–1917), South African statesman, was born at Edinburgh, studied medicine there and at London, and began practice at Kimberley in 1878. Through Cecil Rhodes 'Dr Jim' engaged in pioneer work, was in 1891 made administrator for the South Africa Company at Fort Salisbury, and won enormous popularity. During the troubles at Johannesburg between the Uitlanders and the Boer government, Jameson, who by order of

Rhodes had concentrated the military forces of Rhodesia at Mafeking on the Transvaal frontier, started with five hundred troopers to support the Uitlanders, December 29, 1895. At Krugersdorp they were overpowered by an overwhelming force of Boers and, sleepless and famishing, were after a sharp fight compelled to surrender, January 2, 1896. Handed over to the British authorities, Dr Jameson was in July condemned in London to fifteen months imprisonment, but was released in December. In 1900 he was elected to the Cape Legislative Assembly, and in 1904–08 was (Progressive) premier of Cape Colony. A baronet from 1911, he retired from politics in 1912, and became president of the B.S.A. Company in 1913. See Life by I. Colvin (1922) and E. Pakenham, *Jameson's Raid* (1960).

(3) **(Margaret) Storm** (1897–), English novelist, born in Whitby. Her first success was *The Lovely Ship* (1927), which was followed by more than thirty books that maintained her reputation as storyteller and stylist. These include *The Voyage Home* (1930), *The Delicate Monster* (1937), *Cloudless May* (1943), *The Black Laurel* (1948), *The Writer's Situation* (1950), *The Hidden River* (1955) and *A Cup of Tea for Mr Thorgill* (1957). An autobiography, *No Time Like the Present*, appeared in 1933.

(4) **Robert** (1772–1854), Scottish geologist, born at Leith, studied at Edinburgh and (under Werner) at Freiburg. Professor of Natural History at Edinburgh from 1804, he was first a Wernerian, later a follower of Hutton.

JAMESONE, George (*c.* 1588–1644), Scottish portrait painter, was born in Aberdeen, and in 1612 was bound apprentice for eight years to John Anderson, a painter in Edinburgh. This overthrows the tradition that the 'Scottish Van Dyck', as he has absurdly been called, studied under Rubens at Antwerp. He lived latterly and died in Edinburgh. See J. Bulloch's *George Jamesone* (1885), and *Notes and Queries* for April 1894.

JAMET, Marie, *zhah-may* (1820–93), a St Servan seamstress, founder in 1840 with Jeanne Jugan, Virginie Trédaniel, and the Abbé Le Pailleur of the Little Sisters of the Poor.

JAMI (1414–92), the last great Persian poet, was born at Jam in Khorasan, and died at Herat. Among his poems were *Yusuf u Zuleikha* (trans. by A. Rogers, 1895) and *Salaman u Absal* (trans. by E. FitzGerald). He also wrote prose works.

JAMIESON, John (1759–1838), Scottish lexicographer, was a Secessionist pastor in Forfar (1781–96) and Edinburgh (1797–1830). His *Etymological Dictionary of the Scottish Language* (1808; revised by Longmuir and Donaldson 1879–87) is of value as a collection of words, but not philologically. Yet it only began to be superseded in 1931. He wrote a number of theological and antiquarian works and some poetry, and he edited Barbour's *Bruce* and Blind Harry's *Wallace*.

JAMIN, Jules Célestin, *zha-mĭ* (1818–86), French physicist, was the director of the physical laboratory in the Sorbonne from its foundation in 1868. He invented an interferometer in which interference fringes are produced by two closely parallel beams of light.

JAMMES, Francis, *zhahm* (1868–1938), French writer, born at Tournay in the Pyrenees, wrote poems of nature and religion—*De l'angélus de l'aube à l'angélus du soir* (1898), *Deuil des primevères* (1901), *Triomphe de la vie* (1904), *Géorgiques Chrétiennes* (1911–12), &c., and prose romances such as *Le Roman du lièvre* (1903). See studies by Bertschi (1938) and Guidetti (Turin 1938).

JAMNITZER, or **Jamitzer, Wenzel** (1508–85), a Nuremberg goldsmith, born in Vienna, founded a family workshop with his brother **Albrecht** and later worked with his sons as court goldsmith. His grandson, **Christoph** (1563–1618), published a book of fantastic engravings, *Groteskenbuch* (1610).

JANÁČEK, Leoš, *ya'nah-chek* (1854–1928), Czech composer, born in Moravia, the son of a village schoolmaster, at sixteen was choirmaster at Brno, where he eventually settled after studying at Prague and Leipzig. Devoted to the Czech folksong tradition, he matured late as a composer, principally of operas, of which *Jenufa* (1904, first performed 1912), *Osul* (1904), and perhaps *The House of the Dead* (1938), for which he wrote his own libretto based on Dostoievsky's autobiographical novel, are the most strikingly original in terms of rhythm and subtle melodic dependence upon language. His other compositions include eight further operas, a mass, a sextet for wind instruments and the song cycle, *The Diary of One Who Has Vanished*. See studies by M. Brod (Prague 1924) and D. Muller (Paris 1930).

JANE, Frederick Thomas (1870–1916), British naval author, journalist and artist, born at Upottery, Devon. He worked first as an artist, then as a naval correspondent on various periodicals. He founded and edited *Jane's Fighting Ships* (1898) and *All the World's Aircraft* (1909), the annuals by which his name is best known. Inventor of the Naval War Game, his non-fiction works include *Heresies of Sea Power* (1906) and *The World's Warships* (1915). Among his novels are *Ever Mohun* (1901) and *A Royal Bluejacket* (1908).

JANET, *zhan-ay*, (1) **François**. See CLOUET.

(2) **Paul** (1823–99), French anti-materialist philosopher, uncle of (3), born in Paris, was in turn preacher at Bourges, professor of Philosophy at Strasbourg, and of Logic in the Lycée Louis-le-Grand. In 1864 he was elected to the Academy of Moral Sciences, thereafter lecturing in the Sorbonne. He held that spirit exists apart from the body.

(3) **Pierre** (1859–1947), French psychologist, nephew of (2), born in Paris, studied under Charcot (q.v.), lectured in Philosophy and became the director of La Salpêtriere, the psychological laboratory, and eventually professor of Psychology at the Sorbonne (1898) and Collège de France (1902). His theory of hysteria, which linked ' dissociation ' with a lowering of psychic energy, was described by Freud as the first significant psychological theory, based as it was on

sound clinical practice. His works include *Major Symptoms of Hysteria* (1907). See study by Mayo (1951).

JANIN, Jules Gabriel, *zha-nĭ* (1804–74), French critic and novelist, born at St Etienne, took early to journalism, and his dramatic criticisms in the *Journal des Débats* made him a reputation as an opponent of romanticism and advocate of a classical revival. His strange and at least half-serious story *L'Âne mort et la femme guillotinée* (1829) was followed by *Barnave* (1831), half historical novel, half polemic against the Orleans family. He was elected to the Academy in 1870. See his *Correspondance* (12 vols. 1877), Life by Piedagnel (3rd ed. 1883).

JANNINGS, Emil (1885–1950), German actor, born at Rorschach in Switzerland, made his name in Max Reinhardt's company, and was introduced into moving pictures by Ernst Lubitsch. He worked in American films from 1925 to 1929, then returned to Germany, where he appeared with Marlene Dietrich in *The Blue Angel*, his most famous film.

JANSEN, *yahn'sen*, (1) **Cornelius** (1585–1638), founder of the Jansenist sect, was born at Acquoi, near Leerdam in Holland, October 28. He studied at Utrecht, Louvain and Paris; became professor of Theology at Bayonne and in 1630 at Louvain. In 1636 he was made Bishop of Ypres. He died May 6, 1638, just as he had completed his great work, the *Augustinus* (4 vols.), which sought to prove that the teaching of St Augustine against the Pelagians and semi-Pelagians on Grace, Free Will and Predestination was directly opposed to the teaching of the Jesuit schools. Jansen repudiated the ordinary Catholic dogma of the freedom of the will, and refused to admit merely sufficient grace, maintaining that interior grace is irresistible, and that Christ died for all. On its publication in 1640, the *Augustinus* caused a major outcry, especially by the Jesuits, and it was prohibited by a decree of the Inquisition in 1641; in the following year it was condemned by Urban VIII in the bull *In Eminenti*. Jansen was supported by Arnauld, Pascal and the Port-Royalists. The controversy raged in France with more or less violence for nearly a century, when a large number of Jansenists emigrated to the Netherlands. The Utrecht Jansenists are in doctrine and discipline strictly orthodox Roman Catholics, known by their countrymen as Oude Roomsch (' Old Roman '). See C. A. Sainte-Beuve, *Port Royal* (1840), and N. Abercrombie (1936).

(2) **Zacharias** (*c*. 1600), Dutch optician, the alleged discoverer in 1609 of the telescope.

JANSSEN, (1) **Cornelis** (1593–*c*. 1664), Dutch portrait painter, was born in London, and died at Amsterdam, having quitted England in 1643. His portraits show the influence of Van Dyck, with whom he worked at the court of Charles I. He is represented in the National Gallery, London, and at Chatsworth.

(2), or **Johnson, Geraert** (fl. *c*. 1616), sculptor of the well-known portrait bust of Shakespeare at Stratford-on-Avon, born in London of an English mother and Geraert the elder, also a noteworthy sculptor of sepulchral effigies, coats of arms, &c., who had emigrated from Holland c. 1567.

(3) **Pierre Jules César**, zhā-sen (1824–1907), French astronomer, born in Paris, came from childhood, became head of the Astrophysical Observatory at Meudon, greatly advanced spectrum analysis by his observation of the bright line spectrum of the solar atmosphere (1868). He was elected Academician in 1873.

JANSSENS, Abraham (c. 1575–1632), Flemish painter of Antwerp. His most famous pictures are the *Entombment of Christ* and the *Adoration of the Magi* at Antwerp.

JANSZOON, Laurens, often called **Coster** (c. 1370–1440), claimed by the Dutch as the inventor of printing, was born and died at Haarlem. He is supposed to have made his great invention between 1420 and 1426, to have been sacristan (*Koster*) at Haarlem, and to have died of the plague. No question has caused more discussion than that between Coster and Gutenberg; for the former's claim see Hessels' *Haarlem the Birthplace of Printing* (1888).

JANUARIUS, St, or **San Gennaro** (d. c. 305), Christian martyr, Bishop of Benevento, martyred at Pozzuoli in 305. His body is preserved in Naples cathedral, with two phials supposed to contain his blood, believed to liquefy on September 19, his feast day, and other occasions. See M. Serao's *San Gennaro* (1909).

JAQUES-DALCROZE, Émile, zhahk dahl-krōz (1865–1951), Swiss composer, born at Vienna, originated eurhythmics, a method of expressing the rhythmical aspects of music by physical movement, taught at Dresden and Geneva and composed operas, &c.

JARDINE, Douglas Robert (1900–58), British cricketer, born in Bombay, scored five centuries in 1927 and in Australia (1927–28) made 341 runs in Test Matches. He captained England (1932–34), and his championship of Larwood's 'leg-theory' or 'body-line' bowling in the Australian series (1932–1933) caused acute controversy. See his *In Quest of the Ashes* (1933).

JÄRNEFELT, Armas, yayr'- (1869–1958), Finnish opera composer and conductor, brother-in-law of Sibelius, born at Viborg, studied under Busoni and Massenet and conducted in Germany, Helsinki and Stockholm, taking Swedish citizenship in 1910. He is best known for his *Praeludium* and *Berceuse* for orchestra and choral music.

JASMIN, zhas-mĩ, pseud. of Jacques Boé (1798–1864), Provençal poet, who, born at Agen, earned his living as a barber. He was made a Chevalier of the Legion of Honour in 1846, and in 1852 his works were crowned by the Academy. Among his best pieces (collected in *Las Papillôtos*) are the mock-heroic *Charivari* (1825); *The Blind Girl of Castel-Cuillé* (1835), translated by Longfellow; *Françovneto* (1840); and *The Son's Week* (1849). See Life by Smiles (1892).

JASPERS, Karl, yas'- (1883–1969), German existentialist philosopher, born at Oldenburg, wrote on psychopathology (1913) and in 1916 became professor of Psychology and in 1921 professor of Philosophy, both at Heidelberg. His main works are *Psychologie der Weltan-schauungen* (1919) under Dilthey's influence, *Philosophie* (1932) and *Vernunft und Existenz* (1935; trans. 1956). For Jaspers, philosophy begins with science, but scientific objectivity can never give a complete description of the self. The unauthentic self, i.e., that described by science, must be supplemented by the capacity for choice, or authentic self, which has a different sort of existence, called 'being-oneself' and which alone can give meaning to the former. Philosophy, however, arises on the transcendental level of the *Umgreifende* ('Encompassing'), which embraces the rational world of science, human choice, everything. For his uncompromising attitude to the Nazis, Jaspers was awarded the Goethe prize (1947) and appointed professor at Basel (1948). See also *Der Philosophische Glaube* (1948), trans. 'The Perennial Scope of Philosophy' (1949), and studies by E. Allen (1951) and ed. P. Schillp (1958).

JAURÈS, Jean, zhō-res (1859–1914), French Socialist leader, writer and orator, born in 1859 at Castres (Tarn), lectured on philosophy at Toulouse, became a deputy (1885), founded the Socialist paper *L'Humanité* (1904), and was assassinated July 31, 1914. See Life by J. H. Jackson (1943).

JAY, John (1745–1829), American statesman and jurist, born in New York, was admitted to the bar in 1768. Elected to the Continental Congress in 1774 and 1775, he drafted the constitution of New York state in 1777, of which he was appointed chief justice; was elected president of congress in 1778; and in 1779 was sent as minister to Spain. From 1782 he was one of the most influential of the peace commissioners. In 1784–89 he was secretary for foreign affairs, and soon became chief justice of the supreme court. In 1794 he concluded with Lord Grenville the convention known as 'Jay's treaty', which, though favourable to the United States, was denounced by the Democrats as a betrayal of France. Jay was governor of New York from 1795 to 1801. There is a Life (1833) by his son, William Jay (1789–1858), a notable antislavery leader. See Life by F. Monaghan (1935).

JEANNE D'ALBRET, zhan dal-bray (1528–1572), only daughter and heiress of John II of Navarre and Béarn, married in 1548 Antoine de Bourbon, Duc de Vendôme, and in 1553 gave birth to Henry IV of France. She was a Huguenot and poetess. See Life by Freer (2nd ed. London 1861).

JEANNE D'ARC. See JOAN OF ARC.

JEANS, Sir James Hopwood (1877–1946), English mathematical physicist, astronomer and popular scientific writer, born at Ormskirk, near Southport, became a fellow of Trinity College, Cambridge, and from 1905 to 1909 was professor of Applied Mathematics at Princeton, N.J. He was secretary of the Royal Society (1919–29), president of the Royal Astronomical Society (1925–27) and of the British Association in 1934. He made important contributions to the dynamical theory of gases, radiation, quantum theory and stellar evolution, but was best known for his popular exposition of physical and astronomical theories and their philosophical bearings, such as *The New Background of Science* (1933), &c. He was knighted in 1928 and awarded the O.M. in 1939. He married Susi, *née* Hock (1911–), the Australian-born organist and harpsichordist. See study by Milne (1952).

JEBAVÝ, Václav. See BŘEZINA.

JEBB, Sir Richard Claverhouse (1841–1905), Scottish Greek scholar, born at Dundee, graduated from Trinity College, Cambridge, was elected fellow, and in 1875 appointed professor of Greek at Glasgow, and in 1889 regius professor of Greek at Cambridge. In 1891 he was elected M.P. (Unionist) for Cambridge University. His greatest work is his Sophocles (with trans., 9 vols., 1883–1917). See Life by Lady Jebb (1907).

JEEJEEBHOY. See JEJEEBHOY.

JEFFERIES, John Richard (1848–87), English naturalist and novelist, born near Swindon, started as a journalist on the staff of the *North Wilts Herald* about 1866, and became known by a letter to *The Times* (1872) on the Wiltshire labourers. His first real success, *The Gamekeeper at Home* (1878), was followed up by *Wild Life in a Southern County* (1879), *Amaryllis at the Fair* (1884), &c. *The Story of my Heart* (1883) is a strange autobiography of inner life; *After London, or Wild England* (1885), is a curious romance of the future. See works by Besant (1888), E. Thomas (1909), R. Arkell (1933), and *Jefferies' England*, ed. Looker (1937).

JEFFERSON, (1) **Joseph** (1829–1905), American comic actor, born in Philadelphia, came of a theatrical stock, his great-grandfather having belonged to Garrick's company at Drury Lane, while his father and grandfather were well-known American actors. Jefferson appeared on the stage at three, and had for years been a strolling actor, when in 1857, in New York, he made a hit as Doctor Pangloss, and in 1858 created the part of Asa Trenchard in *Our American Cousin*. In 1865 he visited London, and at the Adelphi first played his famous part of Rip Van Winkle. See his Autobiography (1890).

(2) **Thomas** (1743–1826), 3rd president of the United States, born at Shadwell, Albemarle County, Virginia, April 13, in 1767 was admitted to the bar, and practised with success. In 1769 he was elected to the House of Burgesses, where he joined the revolutionary party. He took a prominent part in the calling of the first Continental Congress in 1774, to which he was sent as a delegate; and it was he who drafted the celebrated Declaration of Independence, signed July 4, 1776. Jefferson now assisted the people of Virginia in forming a state constitution, and was governor 1779–81. In congress he secured (1783) the adoption of the decimal system of coinage. He was sent to France in 1784 with Franklin and Adams as plenipotentiary; next year he succeeded Franklin as minister there; and in 1789 Washington appointed him secretary of state. From the origin of the Federal and Republican parties, Jefferson was the recognized head of the latter, while the other members of the cabinet and the president were Federalists. In 1794 he withdrew from public life, but in 1797 was called to the vice-presidency of the United

States, and in 1801 was chosen president by the House of Representatives. The popular vote re-elected him by a large majority for the next presidential term. Among the chief events of his first term were the war with Tripoli, the admission of Ohio, and the Louisiana purchase; of his second term, the firing on the *Chesapeake* by the *Leopard*, the Embargo, the trial of Aaron Burr for treason, and the prohibition of the slave trade. In 1809 he retired, but continued to advise in the capacity of elder statesman, and helped to found the University of Virginia (1825). He died July 4. Ford edited his Works (10 vols. 1893–99) and *Autobiography* (1914). See Lives by Hiest (1926), Chinard (1929), Padover (1942), Kimball (1943), Beloff (1948), Malone (1949), Jonas (1953) and Schachner (1958).

JEFFERY, Dorothy. See PENTREATH.

JEFFREY, Francis Jeffrey, Lord (1773–1850), Scottish critic and judge, born in Edinburgh, studied at Glasgow and Oxford, and in 1794 was called to the Scottish bar, but as a Whig made little progress for many years. In the trials for sedition (1817–22) he acquired a great reputation; in 1820 and again in 1823 he was elected lord rector of Glasgow University, in 1829 dean of the Faculty of Advocates. In 1830 he was returned for Perth, and on the formation of Earl Grey's ministry became Lord Advocate. After the passing of the Reform Bill he was returned for Edinburgh, which he represented until 1834, when he was made a judge of the Court of Session. From 1815 he lived at Craigcrook. Along with Sydney Smith, Francis Horner and a few others, he established the *Edinburgh Review*, of which he was editor until 1829. His own contributions were very numerous and brilliant, if biased; his strictures of Wordsworth, Keats and Byron for example. While in the United States to marry his second wife, he dined with President Madison during the British-American War of 1812. A selection of his own articles were published in 1844. See Lives by H. T. Cockburn (1852) and J. A. Greig (1948).

JEFFREYS, (1) **George Jeffreys, 1st Baron,** the 'infamous Jeffreys' (1648–89), English judge, born at Acton near Wrexham, called to the bar in 1668, rose rapidly, and became in 1671 common serjeant of the City of London. Hitherto nominally a Puritan, he began to intrigue for court favour, was made solicitor to the Duke of York, was knighted in 1677, and became recorder of London in 1678. Actively concerned in the Popish Plot prosecutions, he was made chief justice of Chester and king's serjeant in 1680, baronet in 1681 and chief justice of King's Bench in 1683. His first exploit was the judicial murder of Algernon Sidney, but in every state trial he proved a willing tool of the crown, thus earning the favour of James, who raised him to the peerage (1685). Among his earliest trials were those of Titus Oates and Richard Baxter; then he was sent to the west to try the followers of Monmouth (q.v.), and hanged, transported, whipped and fined hundreds of them, during the 'bloody assize'. He was lord chancellor from September 1685 until the downfall of

James, and supported all the king's measures as president of the newly-revived Court of High Commission, and in the trial of the seven bishops. Yet he had rational views on witchcraft, and was too honest to turn Catholic. On James's flight he tried to follow his example, but was caught at Wapping, disguised as a sailor, and sent to the Tower to save him from the mob. There he died, April 18, 1689. See Lives by H. W. Woolrych (1827), Irving (1898), Hyde (1948) and Parry, *The Bloody Assize* (1929).

(2) **Harold** (1891–), English geophysicist, born at Birtley, Durham, became reader in geophysics at Cambridge in 1931. He was one of the first to investigate the effect of radioactivity on the cooling of the earth and on mountain formation. He estimated the age of the solar system as a few thousand million years and postulated that Mercury might once have been a satellite of Venus.

JEFFRIES, John (1744–1819), American balloonist, a Boston physician who settled in England after the American revolution, made the first balloon crossing of the English channel with Blanchard (q.v.) in 1785.

JEJEEBHOY, Sir Jamsetjee, *zhee′zhee-bah′ee* (1783–1859), Indian Parsee merchant and philanthropist, born at Bombay, was taken into partnership by his father-in-law, a Bombay merchant, in 1800. When peace was restored in Europe in 1815 Indian trade with Europe increased enormously. By 1822 he had amassed £2,000,000, with which he contributed generously to various educational and philanthropic institutions in Bombay. The Queen knighted him in 1842, and in 1857 he was made a baronet.

JELAL-UD-DIN. See JALAL AD-DIN RUMI.
JELLAČIĆ, Josef, Count, *yel′a-cheech* (1801–1859), Hungarian politician, born at Petrovaradin, became an officer in the Austrian army and a devoted servant of Austrian imperialism. He was appointed governor of Croatia and helped to suppress the Hungarian rising (1848). See M. Hartley, *The Man who saved Austria* (1912).

JELLICOE, John Rushworth Jellicoe, 1st Earl (1859–1935), British sailor, born at Southampton, the son of a sea captain. He served in the Egyptian war of 1882, was one of the survivors of the collision between the *Camperdown* and the *Victoria* in 1893, and commanded an international overland expedition to relieve the legations at Peking during the Boxer rising (1900), was severely wounded and awarded the C.B. After special courses in gunnery, he played a major part in the overdue modernization of the fleet under Fisher (q.v.), particularly in the speedy adoption of the new *Dreadnought* battleships, torpedo and submarine tactics, &c. In 1908 he became third sea lord and comptroller of the navy and at the outbreak of the first World War he was appointed c.-in-c. of the Grand Fleet with the acting rank of admiral. After two minor engagements at the Heligoland Bight (August 1914) and off the Dogger Bank (January 1915) he managed to catch the reluctant German fleet at sea off Jutland in the evening of May 31, 1916. The battle was never fully joined, but the German fleet beat a hasty

retreat favoured by poor visibility and never put out to sea again in force for the remainder of the war. Despite ill-informed criticism over Jellicoe's cautious handling of the battle and the heavier British losses sustained, Jellicoe was awarded the Order of Merit. When promoted first sea lord, he organized effective defence against German submarines, but because of a disagreement with Sir Eric Geddes he was unjustly dismissed from his post in 1917. In 1919 he was promoted admiral of the fleet, received the thanks of both Houses of Parliament and a grant of £50,000. He was governor of New Zealand (1920–24) and president of the British Legion (1928–32). Created an earl in 1925, he was buried in St Paul's Cathedral. See his *The Grand Fleet* (1919), Life by R. Bacon (1936), who wrote *The Jutland Scandal* (1924).

JENGHIZ KHAN. See GENGHIS.
JENKINS, (1) Herbert (1876–1923), English publisher and writer, born in Norwich. His humorous books about the Cockney, Bindle (1916, 1918, &c.), were amongst the first publications of the publishing house which he founded in 1912 and which bears his name.

(2) **John** (1592–1678), English composer of chamber music, born at Maidstone, Kent, served as musician to the royal and noble families and composed a great number of fantasies for strings, *In Nomines*, suites, catches, anthems and songs.

(3) **Robert,** an English merchant captain, trading from Jamaica, who alleged that in 1731 his sloop had been boarded by a Spanish *guarda costa*, and that, though no proof of smuggling had been found, he had been tortured, and his ear torn off. The said ear—some said he had lost it in the pillory—he produced in 1738 in the House of Commons and so helped to force Walpole into the ' War of Jenkins' Ear ' against Spain in 1739. Jenkins was later appointed governor of St Helena.

(4) **Roy** (1920–), British Labour politician and author, born at Abersychan, was educated at the local grammar school and at Balliol College, Oxford, where he obtained first class honours in Modern Greats. Elected M.P. for Central Southwark in 1948, he was the youngest member of the House; since 1950 he has sat for the Stetchford division of Birmingham. He introduced, as a Private Members' Bill, the controversial Obscene Publications Bill, strengthening the position of authors, publishers and printers *vis-a-vis* prosecutions for obscenity. After a successful spell as minister of aviation (1964–1965) he was made home secretary, in which office his alleged ' softness ' towards criminals provoked criticism. In 1967 he changed posts with Callaghan (q.v.) to become chancellor of the Exchequer, introducing a notably stringent Budget in March 1968. A successful journalist and author, his books include *Mr Balfour's Poodle* (1954), *Sir Charles Dilke* (1958), and *Asquith* (1964).

JENKINSON. See LIVERPOOL, EARL OF.
JENNER, (1) Edward (1749–1823), English physician, the discoverer of vaccination, was born at Berkeley vicarage, Gloucestershire, May 17. He was apprenticed to a surgeon at Sodbury, in 1770 went to London to study

under John Hunter, and in 1773 settled at Berkeley, where he acquired a large practice. In 1775 he began to examine the truth of the traditions respecting cowpox, and became convinced that it was efficacious as a protection against smallpox. Many investigations delayed the actual discovery of the prophylactic power of vaccination, and the crowning experiment was made on May 14, 1796. Yet the practice met with violent opposition for a year, when over seventy principal physicians and surgeons in London signed a declaration of their entire confidence in it. Jenner's discovery was soon promulgated throughout the civilized world. Honours were conferred upon him, and he was given in 1802 a grant of £10,000, and in 1807 a second grant of £20,000. See his Life and Correspondence, by J. Baron (1827–38), Life by Drewitt (1931), and Bio-bibliography, ed. Fanu (1951).

(2) Sir William (1815–98), English physician, born at Chatham, was educated at University College London, where he was professor 1848–79. He became physician in ordinary to the Queen in 1862, and to the Prince of Wales in 1863; was made a baronet in 1868, G.C.B., F.R.S., &c. He established the difference between typhus and typhoid fevers (1851). His brother, Charles (1810–1893), made a large fortune as an Edinburgh linen draper.

JENNINGS, (1) Herbert Spencer (1868–1947), American zoologist, born at Tonica, Ill., professor of Experimental Zoology (1906) and Zoology (1910–38) at Johns Hopkins University, wrote the standard work Contributions to the Study of the Behaviour of the Lower Organisms (1919) and investigated heredity and variation of microorganisms. He conducted a biological survey of the Great Lakes for the U.S. Fish Commission in 1902.

(2) Sarah. See MARLBOROUGH.

JENSEN, yen'-, (1) Adolf (1837–1879), German songwriter and composer for the piano, born at Königsberg, from 1856 to 1868 was a musician successively at Posen, Copenhagen and Berlin.

(2) Georg (1866–1935), Danish silversmith. Having worked as a sculptor, he founded his silversmithy in Copenhagen in 1904, and revived the high artistic traditions of Danish silver.

(3) Hans (1907–73), German scientist, born at Hamburg, taught there and at Hanover, and in 1949 became professor of Theoretical Physics at Heidelberg. With Maria Goeppert-Mayer and Wigner, he was awarded the Nobel prize for physics in 1963 for research on nuclear shell structure.

(4) Johannes Vilhelm (1873–1950), Danish novelist, essayist and poet, born at Farsö, Jutland. His native land and its people are described in his Himmerlandshistorien (1898–1910), but many of his works, such as The Forest and Madama d'Ora (1904), are based on his extensive travels in the Far East and America. In Den Lange Rejse (1908–22; tr. The Long Journey, 1922–24) the journey traced, however, is that of man through the ages, the three constituent novels being an expression of Jensen's Darwinism. His psychological study of Christian II of

Denmark, Kongens Fald (tr. The Fall of the King, 1933), his short prose works, Myter (1904–44), fourteen of which were translated into English as The Waving Rye (1959), and his lyric poetry (1901–41), all serve to vindicate Jensen's high place in modern Scandinavian literature. He was awarded a Nobel prize for Literature in 1944. See study by L. Nedergaard (1943) and Bodelsen's introduction to The Waving Rye.

(5) Wilhelm (1837–1911), German poet and novelist, born at Heiligenhafen in NE. Holstein, lived much in Munich.

JEREMIAH (7th cent. B.C.) (Heb. Jirmejâhû), the prophet, son of Hilkiah, the priest, was a native of Anathoth, 2½ miles NNW. of Jerusalem, was in Jerusalem during the siege by Nebuchadnezzar, and is said to have died a martyr's death at Tahpanhes in Egypt. The Septuagint text of his prophecies differs very greatly from the Massoretic Hebrew. See Life by Birmingham (1956).

JEROBOAM, -bō'-, the name of two Israelite kings:

Jeroboam I (10th cent. B.C.), first king of the divided kingdom of Israel, was made by Solomon superintendent of the labours and taxes exacted from his tribe of Ephraim at the construction of the fortifications of Zion. The growing disaffection towards Solomon fostered his ambition; but he was obliged to flee to Egypt. After Solomon's death he headed the successful revolt of the northern tribes against Rehoboam, and, as their king, established idol shrines at Dan and Bethel to wean away his people from the pilgrimages to Jerusalem. He reigned twenty-two years.

Jeroboam II (8th cent. B.C.), son of Joash, thrust back the Syrians, and reconquered Ammon and Moab.

JEROME, St, properly Eusebius Sophronius Hieronymus (c. 342–420), Christian ascetic and scholar, was born at Stridon. He studied Greek and Latin rhetoric and philosophy at Rome, where he was also baptized. In 370 he had settled in Aquileia with his friend Rufinus, but went hence to the East, and after a dangerous illness at Antioch, retired in 374–8 to the desert of Chalcis. In 379, ordained priest at Antioch, he went to Constantinople, and became intimate with Gregory Nazianzen. In 382 he came on a mission connected with the Meletian schism at Antioch to Rome, where he became secretary to Pope Damasus, and where he attained to great influence by his sanctity, learning and eloquence. Many pious persons placed themselves under his spiritual direction, of whom the Lady Paula and her daughter followed him to the Holy Land in 385. He fixed his residence at Bethlehem in 386, the Lady Paula founding four convents there, one of which was governed by Jerome. It was here that Jerome pursued or completed his great literary labours and issued the fiery invectives against Jovinian, Vigilantius and the Pelagians, and even against Rufinus and St Augustine. He died September 30, 420. His letters, treatises polemical and ascetical, commentaries on Holy Scripture, and a version and revision of former versions of the Bible (the Vulgate) were edited by Erasmus (1516). The best editions are those of the Benedictines (1693–1706) and Vallarsi (1734–42). St Jerome was the most learned and eloquent of the Latin Fathers. See works by Mrs Martin (1888), Largent (trans 1900), Grützmacher (1901–08).

JEROME BONAPARTE. See BONAPARTE.

JEROME, Jerome Klapka (1859–1927), English humorous writer, novelist and playwright, born at Walsall, Staffordshire, and brought up in London. Successively a clerk, schoolmaster, reporter, actor and journalist, he became joint editor of *The Idler* in 1892 and started his own twopenny weekly, *To-Day*. His magnificently ridiculous *Three Men in a Boat* (1889), the account of a boat trip up the Thames from Kingston to Oxford, established itself as a humorous classic of the whimsical. Other books include *The Idle Thoughts of an Idle Fellow* (1889), *Three Men on the Bummel* (1900), *Paul Kelver* (1902), the morality play, *The Passing of the Third Floor Back* (1907), and his autobiography, *My Life and Times* (1926). See Life by A. Moss (1929).

JEROME OF PRAGUE (c. 1365–1416), Czech religious reformer, the friend of Huss (q.v.), was born at Prague between 1360 and 1370. He studied at Oxford, became a convert there to Wycliffe's doctrines, and zealously taught them after his return home (1407). The king of Poland employed him to reorganize the University of Cracow in 1410; the king of Hungary invited him to preach before him at Budapest. Jerome entered with his whole soul into the contest carried on by Huss. When Huss was arrested at Constance Jerome hastened to his side to defend him but, being refused a safe-conduct, he set out to return to Prague, was arrested in Bavaria in April 1415, and was brought back to Constance. He recanted, but withdrew his recantation, and went to the stake May 30, 1416. See works by Helfert (1853) and Becker (1858), and works listed under Huss.

JERROLD, Douglas William (1803–57), English author, dramatist and wit, was born in London, the son of Samuel Jerrold, actor and manager. In 1813 he joined the navy as a midshipman, but on the close of the war he started life anew as a printer's apprentice, and in 1819 was a compositor on the *Sunday Monitor* but rose to become its dramatic critic. In 1825 he was engaged to write for the Coburg Theatre, and from 1829 for the Surrey Theatre. He also contributed to a number of magazines, including *Punch* and edited the *Illuminated Magazine* (1843–44), *Douglas Jerrold's Shilling Magazine* (1845–1848), and *Douglas Jerrold's Weekly Newspaper* (1846–48). In 1852 he became editor of *Lloyd's Weekly Newspaper*. A collected edition of his works (8 vols.) comprises the novels as well as *The Story of a Feather*, *Cakes and Ale*, *Punch's Letters to his Son*, *Punch's Complete Letter-writer*, *Mrs Caudle's Curtain Lectures*, &c., and about half of his dramatic works. *Other Times* (1868) is a selection from his political writings in *Lloyd's*. See books by his son (1859) and grandson (1910, 1918). The former, William Blanchard (1826–84), succeeded his father as

editor of *Lloyd's* and also wrote novels and plays.

JERVIS, Sir John. See ST VINCENT (EARL).

JESPERSEN, Otto, yes'- (1860–1943), Danish philologist, born at Randers, professor of English at Copenhagen, wrote excellent books on grammar, and invented an international language, Novial.

JESSE, jes'i, (1) **Edward** (1780–1868), English writer, born at Hutton Cranswick vicarage, Yorkshire, was successively secretary to Lord Dartmouth, commissioner of hackney coaches, and deputy surveyor-general of the royal parks and palaces. His books include *Gleanings in Natural History* (1832–35), *An Angler's Rambles* (1836), *Scenes and Tales of Country Life* (1844), *Anecdotes of Dogs* (1846), and *Lectures on Natural History* (1861); besides editions of Walton's *Compleat Angler* and White's *Selborne*. See Mrs Houstoun's *Sylvanus Redivivus* (1890). His son, **John Heneage** (1815–74), long a clerk in the Admiralty, wrote a series of court memoirs, *George III* (1867) the best.

(2) **Fryn Tennyson** (1889–1958), English novelist, dramatist and editor of several volumes of the *Notable British Trials* series, born the great-niece of Tennyson, studied painting, but during World War I took up journalism and after it served on Hoover's Relief Commission for Europe. In 1918 she married H. M. Harwood (q.v.) the dramatist and with him collaborated in a number of light plays and a series of war-time letters, *London Front* (1940) and *While London Burns* (1942). But she is best known for her novels, set in Cornwall, *The White Riband* (1921), *Tom Fool* (1926), *Moonraker* (1927), as well as *A Pin to See a Peepshow* (1934), based on the Thompson-Bywaters murder case, the collected poems, *The Happy Bride* (1920), and her remarkable accounts of the trials of Madeleine Smith (1927), Timothy Evans and John Christie (1958).

JESUS CHRIST, the founder of Christianity, was born ' the Son of God ' in Bethlehem, Judaea, according to the accounts in St Matthew's and St Luke's gospels, the first-born child of the Virgin Mary of the tribe of Judah and descendant of David and wife of Joseph, a carpenter. The birth took place in a stable, because on their way from Joseph's home town, Nazareth, in order to comply with the regulations for a Roman population census, they found ' there was no room for them at the inn '. According to St Matthew, Jesus's birth took place just prior to the demise of Herod the Great (4 B.C.), but the Roman census referred to by St Luke did not take place before A.D. 6. The only biographical sources are the four gospels of the New Testament of which St Mark, containing the recollection of Peter, is the oldest, and probably the most reliable, and it has been estimated that their entire compass covers only fifty days in the Life of Christ. But he is also mentioned by Tacitus, Suetonius and Josephus and in certain anti-Christian Hebrew writings of the time. Little is written of his early boyhood and manhood. He is believed to have followed Joseph's trade of carpentry but at the age of twelve we are told how his astonished mother saw him knowledgeably discoursing with the scribes, being assured by him that he was about his ' father's business '. But nearly eighteen years passed in obscurity, before his baptism at the hands of his cousin, John the Baptist (q.v.), gave him the first divine intimation of his mission. After forty days in the wilderness wrestling successfully with all manner of temptations, he gathered around him twelve disciples and undertook two missionary journeys through Galilee culminating in the miraculous feeding of the five thousand (Mark vi, 30-52), which, seen through the eyes of Herod, John the Baptist's executioner, had obvious dangerous political implications. Furthermore, Jesus's association with ' publicans and sinners ', his apparent flouting of traditional religious practices, the performance of miracles on the Sabbath, the driving of the money-lenders from the temple and the whole tenor of his revolutionary Sermon on the Mount (Matthew v-vii), emphasizing love, humility, meekness and charity, roused the Pharisees. Christ and his disciples sought refuge for a while in the Gentile territories of Tyre and Sidon, where he secretly revealed himself to them as the promised Messiah, and hinted beyond their comprehension at his coming passion, death and resurrection. According to Mark, he returned to Jerusalem in triumph, a week before the passover feast, and after the famous ' Last Supper ' with his disciples, was betrayed by one of them, Judas Iscariot, by a kiss and after a hurried trial condemned to death by the Sanhedrin. The necessary confirmation of the sentence from Pontius Pilate, the Roman procurator, was obtained on the grounds of political expediency and not through any proof of treason implicit in any claim to territorial kingship by Christ. Jesus was given into the hands of the mob incited by the Pharisees, and, deserted by his followers, was crucified early on either the passover or the preceding day (the ' preparation of the passover '). The chronology of the passion is a very complicated question. Jesus was buried the same day. The instrument of crucifixion, the cross, became the symbol of Christianity. The following Sunday, according to all four gospels, the disciples hiding away in an ' upper room ' suddenly took courage through receipt of the Holy Ghost and several revelations that Christ ' had risen from the dead ' and would continue his leadership for ever. The history of the church begins here with the *Acts of the Apostles* in the New Testament. The apostolic succession enshrined in the Catholic church begins with Christ's public declaration to Peter (Matthew xvi, 17-19) that on him he will build his church. Roman persecutions only served to strengthen her. In the 4th century at Nicaea, Christian theologians incorporated Platonic metaphysics into their theology. Roman empires in East and West became christianized but with distinctive liturgies formally separating in the 11th century, although common elements are to be found in them. Rome until the 16th century was the hub of western Christianity when the reformatory movements of Calvin, Luther and Zwingli, allied to local nationalism, split the western church into an increasing number of sects, depending for their individual authority on multifarious interpretations of the New Testament but all united in their opposition to papal supremacy. But a growing movement for church reunion was initiated at the beginning of the 20th century. See studies by W. Sanday (1907), J. Klausner (1925), B. W. Bacon (1928), F. C. Burkitt (1932), Goguel (trans. 1933), H. E. W. Turner, *Jesus Master and Lord* (1953), V. Taylor, *The Life and Ministry of Jesus* (1954), J. Daniélou, *The Lord of History* (1958), J. M. Robinson, *A New Quest of the Historical Jesus* (1959), G. Bornkamm, *Jesus of Nazareth* (1960), E. Stauffer, *Jesus and his Story* (1960), J. A. T. Robinson, *Jesus and his Coming* (1961), R. Bultmann, *Jesus and the Word* (1962), A. Schweitzer, *The Quest of the Historical Jesus* (3rd ed. trans. 1963), Dibelius, *Jesus* (1963), and E. Fuchs, *Studies of the Historical Jesus* (1964).

JEVONS, William Stanley (1835–82), English economist and logician, the son-in-law of John Edward Taylor (q.v.), born in Liverpool, studied chemistry and metallurgy at University College London, and became assayer to the Mint at Sydney, Australia (1854–59). He then returned to England and studied logic under De Morgan at London and in 1866 became professor of Logic at Owen's College, Manchester, and in 1876 professor of Political Economy at London. He introduced mathematical methods into economics, was one of the first to use the concept of final or marginal utility as opposed to the classical cost of production theories and wrote *Theory of Political Economy* (1871) and the posthumous *Principles of Economics* (1905). He also wrote an important practical paper, *Investigations in Currency and Finance* (1884). In his *Pure Logic and other Minor Works* (1890) he wrongly deplored Boole's extensive use of algebraic methods in his calculus of classes, attacked Mill's inductive logic and expounded alternatives in *The Principles of Science* (1874), but is chiefly remembered for his introductory textbook, *Lessons in Logic* (1870). A professorship in political economy at Manchester was endowed in his memory. See *Letters and Journals* (1886), and W. Mays and D. P. Henry, *Jevons and Logic* in the philosophical journal, *Mind* (1953).

JEWEL, John (1522–71), English divine, a father of English Protestantism, born at Berrynarbor near Ilfracombe, was educated at Barnstaple and at Merton and Corpus Christi Colleges, Oxford. He was admitted B.A. in 1540, and early imbibed Reformed doctrines. On Mary's accession he went abroad (Frankfurt, Strasbourg, &c.), but was appointed Bishop of Salisbury by Elizabeth in 1559. His controversial ability soon made him one of the foremost churchmen of his age, as in his *Apologia Ecclesiae Anglicanae* (1562) against Rome. A collected edition of his works was published in 1609, as also by Ayre (Parker Soc. 1845–50) and Jelf (1847–48). See the Life of him by Le Bas (1835), and *John Jewel as Apologist of the Church of England* by Booty (1963).

JEWETT, Sara Orne (1849–1909), American novelist, born at South Berwick, Maine, wrote *The Country of the Pointed Firs* (1896) and other novels and stories based on the provincial life of her state. See Life by F. O. Matthiessen (1929).

JEWSBURY, Geraldine Endsor (1812–80), English novelist, was born at Measham, Derbyshire, and from 1854 lived at Chelsea, to be near the Carlyles. See her *Letters to Mrs Carlyle*, edited by Mrs Ireland (1892).— Her sister, **Maria Jane** (1800–33), wrote poetry.

JEX-BLAKE, Sophia (1840–1912), English pioneer of medical education for women, sister of **Thomas William** (1832–1915), headmaster of Rugby and dean of Wells, was born at Hastings, studied at Queen's College for Women, London, and became a tutor in mathematics there (1859–61). From 1865 she studied medicine in New York under Elizabeth Blackwell (q.v.), but since English medical schools were closed to women, could not continue her studies on return. She fought her way into Edinburgh University, however, where with five other women she was allowed to matriculate in 1869, but the university authorities reversed their decision in 1873. She waged a public campaign in London, opened the London School of Medicine for Women in 1874 and in 1876 won her campaign when medical examiners were permitted by law to examine women students. In 1886 she founded a medical school in Edinburgh, where from 1894 women were finally allowed to graduate in medicine. See Life by M. Todd (1918).

JEZREEL, James Jershom, the name assumed by an ex-private, **James White** (1840–85), founder of the Southcottian subsect of ' Jezreelites ', their headquarters Gillingham near Chatham, who believed that Christ redeemed by his death only souls and that the body can only be saved by the law.

JHERING, Rudolf von, *yayr'ing* (1818–92), German jurist who founded a school of jurisprudence based on teleological principles rather than precedent, was born at Aurich, and died at Göttingen. See Life by Merkel (Jena 1893).

JIMÉNEZ, *hee-may'neth,* (1) **Francisco.** See XIMENES.

(2) **Juan Ramón** (1881–1958) Spanish lyric poet, born at Moguer, Huelva, which he made famous by his delightful story of the young poet and his donkey, *Platero y Yo* (1914; trans. 1956), one of the classics of modern Spanish literature, abandoned his law studies and settled in Madrid. His early poetry, impressionistic and rich in evocative imagery and sound, echoed that of Verlaine. *Almas de Violeta* (1901), *Arias Tristes* (1903) and *Jardines Lefanos* (1905) belong to this period. With *El Silencio de Oro* (1922) there came a mood of optimism and a zest for experimentation with styles and rhythms. In 1936 he left Spain because of the Civil War and settled in Florida. In his last period he emerges as a major poet, treating the major themes of life in novel sounds, illusions and styles in a subtly spun *vers libre*. In 1956, the year he was awarded the Nobel prize, a pilgrimage of poets riding on donkeys went

to a small village near Moguer as a gesture of homage. See the anthology of his poems, trans. J. B. Trend (1957).

JINNAH, Mohammed Ali (1876–1948), Pakistani statesman, born December 25 in Karachi, studied at Bombay and Lincoln's Inn, London, and was called to the bar in 1897. He obtained a large practice in Bombay, in 1910 was elected to the Viceroy's Legislative Council, and already a member of the Indian National Congress, in 1913 joined the Indian Muslim League and as its president brought about peaceful coexistence between it and the Congress party through the ' Lucknow Pact ' (1916). Although he supported the efforts of Congress to boycott the Simon Commission (1928), he opposed Gandhi's civil disobedience policy and, resigning from the Congress party, which he believed to be exclusively fostering Hindu interests, continued to advocate his ' fourteen points ' safeguarding Moslem minorities at the London Round Table Conference (1931). By 1940 he was strongly advocating separate statehood for the Moslems and he stubbornly resisted all British efforts, such as the Cripps mission (1942) and Gandhi's statesmanlike overtures (1944), to save Indian unity. Thus on August 15, 1947, the Dominion of Pakistan came into existence and Jinnah, *Quaid-i-Azam* ' Great Leader ', became its first governor-general and had to contend with the consequences of the new political division, the refugee problem, the communal riots in Punjab and the fighting in Kashmir. See Life by H. Bolitho (1954).

JOACHIM, Joseph, *yō'aκн-im* (1831–1907), Hungarian violinist and composer, born at Kittsee near Pressburg, first appeared in London in 1844. In 1869 he became director of the Berlin Conservatorium, composed three violin concertos and overtures to *Hamlet* and *Henry IV*. See Life by Moser (1910) and his *Letters*.

JOACHIM OF FLORIS, *jō'é-kim* (c. 1135–1202), Italian mystic, born in Calabria, became in 1177 abbot of the Cistercian monastery of Corazzo and later founded a stricter order, Ordo Florensis, at San Giovanni in Fiore, which was absorbed by the Cistercians in 1505. His mystical interpretation of history, based on historical parallels or ' concordances ' between the history of the Jewish people and that of the church, was grouped into three ages, each corresponding to a member of the Trinity, the last, that of the Spirit, which was to usher in perfect liberty to commence in 1260. This mystical historicism was widely accepted although condemned by the Lateran council in 1215, but lost influence, unlike the modern historicisms of Hegel and Marx, when its prophecies did not come to pass. See studies by J. Huck (1938), H. Grundmann (1950) and L. Tondelli, *Il Libro delle figure* (1940).

JOAD, Cyril Edwin Mitchinson (1891–1953), English controversialist and popularizer of philosophy, educated at Blundell's School and Balliol College, Oxford, was a civil servant from 1914 to 1930, when he became reader and head of the philosophy department at Birkbeck College, London. *Guide to Philosophy* (1936) and *Guide to the Philo-*

sophy of Morals and Politics (1938) are possibly the best of his 47 highly personal books, written in the manner of Shavian prefaces, revealing the great talent for exposition of this Bohemian, Fabian reformer, ' anti-ugly ' lover of the countryside, pacifist, anti-Victorian and until his last work, Recovery of Belief (1952), fashionable atheist. He upset academic circles by using the title of professor in journalism, by going up a lone alley resurrecting a version of philosophical realism in Matter, Life and Value (1929) and by throwing only quasi-philosophical stones at Professor Ayer in his Critique of Logical Positivism (1950). But his one concession to linguistic philosophy was his highly successful B.B.C. Brains Trust gimmick, ' It all depends what you mean by . . .' which prompted Max Beerbohm's reference to ' the agile, mellifluous and quodlibetarian Joad '. See his The Testament of Joad (1937) and The Book of Joad (1942).

JOAN. See EDWARD THE BLACK PRINCE.

JOAN, or Joanna, of Navarre (c. 1370–1437), married in 1386 the Duke of Brittany, and in 1403 Henry IV of England.

JOAN OF ARC, St, Fr. Jeanne d'Arc (c. 1412–1431), French patriot and martyr, one of the most remarkable women of all time, was born the daughter of well-off peasants at Domrémy, a hamlet on the borders of Lorraine and Champagne, January 6. The English over-ran the area in 1421 and in 1424 withdrew. Joan received no formal education but was richly endowed with an argumentative nature and shrewd common sense. At the age of thirteen she thought she heard the voices of St Michael, St Catherine and St Margaret bidding her rescue the Paris region from English domination. She presented herself before the local commander, Robert de Baudricourt, and persuaded him, after he had had her exorcised, to take her across English-occupied territory to the dauphin at Chinon, which they reached March 6, 1429. She, according to legend, was called into a gathering of courtiers, among them the dauphin in disguise, and her success in identifying him at once was interpreted as divine confirmation of his previously doubted legitimacy and claims to the throne. She was equally successful in an ecclesiastical examination to which she was subjected at Poitiers and was consequently allowed to join the army assembled at Blois for the relief of Orleans. Clad in a suit of white armour and flying her own standard, she entered Orleans with an advance guard on April 29 and by May 8 forced the English to raise the siege and retire in June from the principal strongholds on the Loire. To put further heart into the French resistance, she took the dauphin with an army of 12,000 through English-held territory to be crowned Charles VII in Rheims cathedral on July 17, 1429. She then found it extremely difficult to persuade him to undertake further military exploits, especially the relief of Paris. At last she set out on her own to relieve Compiègne from the Burgundians, was captured in a sortie and sold to the English by John of Luxembourg for 10,000 crowns. She was

put on trial (February 21–May 17 1431) for heresy and sorcery by an ecclesiastical court of the Inquisition, presided over by Pierre Cauchon, Bishop of Beauvais. Considering the political and religious implications, the trial was fair if judged by such modern equivalents as the Russian purge trials of the '30s and McCarthy's un-American activities investigations. Most of the available facts concerning Joan's life are those preserved in the records of the trial. She was found guilty, taken out to the churchyard of St Ouen on May 24 to be burnt, but at the last moment broke down and made a wild recantation. This she later abjured and suffered her martyrdom at the stake in the market-place of Rouen on May 30, faithful to her ' voices '. In 1456, in order to strengthen the validity of Charles VII's coronation, the trial was declared irregular. In 1904 she was designated Venerable, declared Blessed in 1908 and finally canonized in 1920. She was neither beautiful nor cultivated. Belief in her divine mission made her flout military advice—in the end disastrously, but she rallied her countrymen, halted the English ascendancy in France for ever and was one of the first in history to die for a Christian-inspired concept of nationalism. See Life by Anatole France (trans. 1909) and studies by A. Lang (1908), J. M. Robertson (1926), account of the trial by W. P. Barrett (1931) and preface and plays by Bernard Shaw (1924) and E. Garnett (1931).

JOAN, pope, a fictitious personage long believed to have been, as John VII, pope (855–58). One legend has it that she was born at Mainz, the daughter of English parents, and so well educated by her lover that she in due time became cardinal and pope. Her reign was said to have ended abruptly when she died on giving birth to a child during a papal procession between St Peter's and the Lateran, a route since avoided on such occasions.

JOASH. See ATHALIAH.

JOB. The Book of Job was regarded by the Jews as strictly historical. In the Christian Church the view gradually obtained currency either that it contained history poetically treated, or was simply a religious poem. Elihu's speeches (xxxii–xxxvii) are believed to be a later insertion. Job is assumed to have lived in the Patriarchal period, but the internal evidence points to the exile as the date of the book. See studies by C. J. Ball (1922) and W. B. Stevenson (1947).

JOCELIN DE BRAKELOND (c. 1155–1215), a Benedictine monk at Bury St Edmunds, wrote a domestic chronicle of his abbey from 1173 to 1202. The Chronica inspired Carlyle's Past and Present.

JODELLE, Étienne, zhō-del' (1532–73), French poet and dramatist, the only Parisian member of the Pléiade, wrote the first French tragedy Cléopatre captive (1552), also two comedies. See H. Chamard, Histoire de la Pléiade (1940).

JODL, Alfred, yō'dl' (1890–1946), German soldier, nephew of the philosopher Friedrich Jodl (1849–1914), born at Aachen, was an artillery subaltern in World War I and rose to the rank of General of Artillery in 1940.

For the remainder of World War II he was the planning genius of the German High Command and Hitler's chief adviser. He condemned the anti-Hitler plot (1944), counselled terror bombing of English cities and signed orders to shoot commandos and prisoners of war. From January 1945 he was Chief of the Operations Staff. He was found guilty of war crimes on all four counts at Nuremberg (1946) and executed. A Munich denazification court posthumously exonerated him on charges of being a ' major offender ' in 1953.

JOFFRE, Joseph Jacques Césaire, *zhof'r'* (1852–1931), French general, was born at Rivesaltes, entered the army in 1870, and rose to be French chief of staff (1914) and commander-in-chief (1915). Silent, patient, mathematical, he carried out a policy of attrition or ' nibbling ' against the German invaders of France. He was promoted marshal of France in 1916, in 1917 became president of the Allied War Council, in 1918 was elected to the Académie française, and awarded the O.M. in 1919. See study by C. Dawburn (1916) and Life by G. Hanotaux and J. G. A. Fabry (1921).

JOHANNES SECUNDUS, Jan Everts, or Everaerts (1511–36), Latin poet, born at The Hague, studied law at Bourges, and was secretary to the archbishop of Toledo, the bishop of Utrecht, and the Emperor Charles V. His famous work is *Basia*.

JOHANNES VON SAAZ (*c.* 1350–1415), German author, born at Schüttwa, wrote *Der Ackermann aus Böhmen* (*c.* 1400), a classic piece of German prose in which the author arraigns Death for the loss of his wife, Margarete, before the heavenly Judge.

JOHANNSEN, Wilhelm Ludwig (1857–1927), Danish botanist and geneticist, pioneered experimental genetics by his experiments with Princess beans which led to the pure line theory.

JOHN, St, one of the twelve apostles, son of Zebedee and younger brother of James, was a Galilean fisherman, probably a native of Bethsaida. Some have thought that his mother was Salome, who may have been the sister of the mother of Jesus. Early tradition represents him as having been slain by the Jews, like his brother James. But from the time of Justin (*c.* 150) he has been identified with the author of the Apocalypse, and from that of Irenaeus (*c.* 175) he has been represented as spending his closing years at Ephesus, and dying there at an advanced age, after having written the Apocalypse, the Gospel and the three Epistles which bear his name. There are various theories of the authorship of these works. There are expository works on the Johannine writings by J. E. Carpenter (1927), W. F. Howard (1943 and 1945) and C. H. Dodd (1946).

JOHN THE BAPTIST, St (fl. *c.* 27), the forerunner of Christ, was the son of the priest Zacharias and Elizabeth, the cousin of Mary, the mother of Jesus. He baptized and preached repentance and forgiveness of sins, denounced Herod Antipas for taking Herodias, his brother Philip's wife, and was imprisoned and executed at the request of Salome, daughter of Herodias. See Life by J. Steinmann tr. M. Boyes (1958).

JOHN OF BEVERLEY, St (d. 721), born at Cherry Burton near Beverley, in 687 became Bishop of Hexham, in 705 of York, and died at Beverley.

JOHN, St, Chrysostom. See CHRYSOSTOM.

JOHN OF THE CROSS, St (1542–91), founder with St Teresa of the Discalced Carmelites, was born Juan de Yepes y Álvarez at Fontiveros, Ávila, accompanied St Teresa to Valladolid, where he lived an extremely ascetic life in a hovel until she appointed him to a convent in Ávila, where he was arrested (1577), imprisoned at Toledo, escaped (1578) and lived in illness at the monastery of Úbeda. He was canonized in 1726. See his Works, tr. Allison Peers (1934), who also wrote a Life (1954), study by McNabb (1955) and Life by Crisógóno de Jesus, tr. K. Pond (1959).

JOHN OF DAMASCUS, St, or Chrysorrhoas (*c.* 676–*c.* 754), Greek theologian and hymn writer of the Eastern Church, was born at Damascus, and carefully educated by the learned Italian monk Cosmas. He replied to the iconoclastic measures of Leo the Isaurian with two addresses in which he vigorously defended image worship. His later years were spent in a monastery near Jerusalem. There, ordained a priest, he wrote his hymns, an encyclopaedia of Christian theology, treatises against superstitions, Jacobite and Monophysite heretics, homilies, and *Barlaam and Joasaph*, now known to be a disguised version of the life of Buddha. His works are included in Migne's *Patrologia* (1864). See Neale, *Hymns of the Eastern Church* (1870) and Lives by J. Langen (1879), J. H. Lupton (1882), E. Gilson, *La Philosophie au moyen âge* (1944).

JOHN OF NEPOMUK, St (*c.* 1330–93), patron saint of Bohemia, was born at Pomuk near Pilsen, studied at Prague, and became confessor to Sophia, wife of Wenceslaus IV. For refusing to betray to this monarch the confession of the queen John was put to the torture, then flung into the Moldau. In 1729 he was canonized. By some historians two personages of the same name are enumerated —one, the martyr of the confessional; the other, a victim to the simoniacal tyranny of Wenceslaus. See Wratislaw's *Life of St John Nepomucen* (1873), and works by A. L. Frind (Prague rev. ed. 1929), J. Weisskopf (Vienna 1931).

JOHN, the name of twenty-one popes and two antipopes XVI or XVII (997–8) and XXIII the former included in the papal numbering, which erroneously contained a fictitious John XV who was thought to have ruled for a few weeks immediately prior to the true John XV (985–96). The following are noteworthy:

John XII, pope (955–64), the grandson of Marozia, was elected pope by the dominant party when only eighteen. The Emperor Otto in 963 in a synod of the clergy caused sentence of deposition for scandalous life to be pronounced against him, and Leo VIII to be elected in his stead. John drove out Leo next year; but he died prematurely in debauchery.

John XXII, pope (1316–34), one of the most celebrated of the popes of Avignon, was born at Cahors in 1244, and elected in 1316. Attempting to carry out the policy of Gregory VII, he interposed his authority in the contest for the imperial crown between Louis of Bavaria and Frederick of Austria, supporting the latter and excommunicating his rival. A long contest ensued both in Germany and Italy, where the Guelph or papal party was represented by Robert, king of Naples, and the Ghibelline by Frederick of Sicily. The latter was also excommunicated by John; but in 1327 Louis entered Italy, and, crowned at Milan with the crown of Lombardy, advanced upon Rome, expelled the papal legate, and was crowned emperor by two Lombard bishops. He now caused the pope to be deposed on a charge of heresy and breach of fealty, When Louis returned to Germany, Guelphic predominance at Rome was restored; but John died at Avignon in 1334, having accumulated a vast treasure.

John XXIII, antipope (1410–15), a Neapolitan noble, born *c.* 1370, a cardinal who was recognized throughout most of Europe as the successor of Alexander V, having been elected by the Alexandrian faction in 1410. He convened the council of Constance, but was deposed in 1415 for his excesses, yet re-appointed cardinal.

John XXIII, pope (1958–63), born Angelo Giuseppe Roncalli, the son of a peasant at Sotto il Monte near Bergamo in northern Italy, in 1881. Ordained in 1904, he served as sergeant in the medical corps and as chaplain in World War I, and subsequently as apostolic delegate to Bulgaria, Turkey and Greece. In 1944 he became the first Papal Nuncio to liberated France and championed the controversial system of worker-priests. Patriarch of Venice in 1953, he was elected pope in October 1958 on the twelfth ballot. He convened the 21st oecumenical council in order to seek unity between the various Christian sects and broke with tradition by leaving the Vatican for short visits to hospitals and prisons in Rome. See Lives by A. Lazzarini (trans. 1959) and Leone (1963).

JOHN, surnamed Lackland (1167–1216), king of England, youngest son of Henry II, was born at Oxford, December 24. His father sent him to Ireland as governor in 1185, but his misconduct soon compelled his recall. He attempted to seize the crown during King Richard's captivity in Austria; but he was pardoned and nominated his successor by his brother on his deathbed. John was crowned at Westminster, May 27, 1199, although Arthur (q.v.), son of John's elder brother Geoffrey, was the rightful heir. On the Continent Arthur was acknowledged and his claims were supported by Philip of France, whom, however, in May 1200 John succeeded in buying off. In the same year he obtained a divorce from his cousin Hawisa of Gloucester, and married Isabel of Angoulême. In the war in France Arthur was taken prisoner, and before Easter 1203 was murdered by John's orders. Philip at once marched against John, and captured city after city, until by March 1204 only a portion of Aquitaine was left to John. In 1205 John entered on his quarrel with the church, the occasion being a disputed election to the archbishopric of Canterbury. In 1207 Innocent III consecrated Stephen Langton, an English cardinal, and John declined to receive him. In 1208 the kingdom was placed under an interdict. John retaliated by confiscating the property of the clergy who obeyed the interdict, and banished the bishops. He compelled the Scots king, William the Lion, who had joined his enemies, to do him homage (1209), put down a rebellion in Ireland (1210), and subdued Llewellyn, the independent prince of Wales (1212). Meanwhile he had been excommunicated (1209), and, in 1212, the pope issued a bull deposing him, Philip being charged with the execution of the sentence. John, finding his position untenable, was compelled to make abject submission to Rome, agreeing (May 1213) to hold his kingdom as a fief of the papacy, and to pay a thousand marks yearly as tribute. Philip, disappointed, turned his forces against Flanders; but the French fleet was surprised at Damme by the English, 300 vessels being captured, and 100 burned. In 1214 John made a campaign in Poitou, but it turned out ill, and he returned to enter on the struggle with his subjects. A demand by the barons, clergy, and people that John should keep his oath and restore the laws of Henry I was scornfully rejected. Preparations for war began on both sides. The army of the barons assembled at Stamford and marched to London; they met the king at Runnymede, and on June 15, 1215, was signed the Great Charter (Magna Carta), the basis of the English constitution. In August the pope annulled the charter, and the war broke out again. The first successes were all on the side of John, until the barons called over the French dauphin to be their leader. Louis landed in May 1216, and John's fortunes had become desperate, when he died at Newark, October 19. His reign, however, saw improvements in the civil administration, the exchequer and the law courts. Royal charters were granted to towns and English local government introduced into Ireland. See Life by K. Norgate (1902) and study of his reign by Painter (1949).

JOHN II (1319–64), king of France, succeeded his father, Philip VI, in 1350. In 1356 he was taken prisoner by Edward the Black Prince at Poitiers and carried to England. After the treaty of Bretigny (1360) he returned home, leaving his second son, the Duke of Anjou, as a hostage; and when the duke broke his parole, and escaped (1363), John chivalrously returned to London, and died there.

JOHN (1296–1346), the blind king of Bohemia, son of Count Henry III of Luxemburg (afterwards the Emperor Henry VII). Having married (1310) the heiress of Bohemia, he was crowned king in 1311. In the struggle between Austria and Bavaria for the imperial crown he contributed to the Bavarian victory at Mühldorf in 1322. In 1333–35 he was warring in Italy for the Guelph party. In 1334 he married a Bourbon, became an ally of the French king, and fell at Crécy August 26, 1346, and his motto *Ich Dien*, ' I serve ', was adopted by the Black Prince, in respect for his father, Edward III, who commanded the English army in the battle. John had been blind since 1337.

JOHN III (1624–96), king of Poland, was the son of James Sobieski, castellan of Cracow. After the defeat of the Poles by the Russians at Pilawiecz, John took up arms. On November 11, 1673, he defeated the Turks at Choczim, and was elected king of Poland, May 21, 1674. He raised the Turkish siege of Vienna in 1683 by a famous victory which, however, did not benefit Poland, but his later undertakings against the Turks were not equally successful. Troubles in Poland also clouded the last years of his reign. See *German Life* by Battaglia (1946).

JOHN, (1) Augustus (1878–1961), British painter, born at Tenby, studied at the Slade (1896–99) with his sister Gwen (see below), and in Paris, and made an early reputation for himself by his etchings (1900–14). Although a considerable draughtsman, John had no special predilection for pure design; Wyndham Lewis had described him as ' a great man of action into whose hands the fairies stuck a brush instead of a sword '. John's favourite themes were gipsies, fishing folk and wild, lovely, yet naturally regal women, as in *Lyric Fantasy* (1913, private). In his portraits of women, including many of his wife Dorelia, he is concerned more with unique items of individual beauty or dignity than with portrayal of character, as for example the beautifully caught posture of the scarlet-gowned cellist *Madame Suggia* (1923, Tate). But character he could portray, as the studies of Shaw (*c.* 1914), Thomas Hardy (1923, both Fitzwilliam, Cambridge) and Dylan Thomas (Cardiff) amply testify. His best purely formal portrait is *Judge Dowdall as Lord Mayor of Liverpool* (1908–09, Melbourne). He also had a Jimsonlike passion for murals. His study for a Canadian War Memorial was never translated into full size reality, but there is the magnificent *Galway* (1916) in the Tate. He was elected R.A. in 1928, resigned in 1938 and was re-elected in 1940. He was awarded the O.M. in 1942. See his autobiography *Chiaroscuro* (1952) and studies by A. Bertram (1923), J. Rothenstein (1944) and *Fifty-Two Drawings*, intro. Lord David Cecil (1957). His sister, **Gwen** (1876–1939), settled at Meudon, France, where, with intimate friendships with Rodin, Rilke and the philosopher Maritain, she became a Catholic and painted striking, sad-faced pictures of nuns, orphan children, cats and her sister-in-law, Dorelia. *Young Woman holding a Black Cat* is in the Tate, London.

(2) **Otto**, *yōn* (1909–), West German ex-security chief and defendant in the most curious postwar treason case, was chief legal adviser to the German civil aviation company *Lufthansa*. In 1944 he played, with his brother Hans, a prominent rôle in the abortive anti-Hitler plot of July 20, after which he made good his escape to Britain via Spain and worked for the British Psychological Warfare Executive. At the end of the war, he joined a London legal firm and appeared as a prosecution witness in the Nuremberg and von Manstein trials. In 1950 he was appointed to the newly formed West German Office for the protection of the constitution. His sensitivity against former Nazi influence in postwar German political life earned him the enmity of Adenauer and Schröder. Attending the annual commemorative ceremony of July 20 in West Berlin in 1954, he mysteriously disappeared and later broadcast for the East German Communists. In 1956 he returned to the West, was arrested, tried, and sentenced to four years' hard labour for treasonable falsification and conspiracy. John's case was that he was drugged by a friend, a wealthy Communist-sympathizing doctor in West Berlin, Wohlgemuth, and driven to the Communist sector where he was held a prisoner and forced to make broadcasts until he managed to escape. Released in 1958, he still protests his innocence. See W. Frischauer, *The Man Who Came Back* (1958).

JOHN OF AUSTRIA (1547–78), Spanish soldier, natural son of the Emperor Charles V and Barbara Blomberg of Ratisbon, was born at Ratisbon. He was early brought to Spain, and after the death of his father was acknowledged by his half-brother Philip II. In 1570 he was sent with an army against the Moors in Granada, whom he completely rooted out of the country. On October 7, 1571, with the fleets of Spain, the pope and Venice, he defeated the Turks in the great sea fight of Lepanto. In 1573 he took Tunis, and conceived the scheme of forming a kingdom for himself. But Philip, jealous of this design, sent him to Milan, and in 1576 as viceroy to the Netherlands. He sought to win the favour of the people by mildness; hard pressed for a time by William the Silent, he with the help of Parma's troops won the victory of Gembloux in 1577. Don John died at Namur, perhaps poisoned. See monographs by Sir W. Stirling-Maxwell (1883) and L. Coloma (1912).

JOHN OF GAUNT (1340–99), Duke of Lancaster, fourth son of Edward III, was born at Ghent (Fr. *Gand*). In 1359 he married his cousin, Blanche of Lancaster, and was created duke in 1362. She died in 1369, and in 1372 he married Constance, daughter of Pedro the Cruel of Castile, and assumed the title of King of Castile, though he failed by his expeditions to oust his rival, Henry of Trastamare. Before his father's death John became the most influential personage in the realm, and was thought to be aiming at the crown. He opposed the clergy and protected Wycliffe. Young King Richard, distrusting him, sent him in 1386 on another attempt to secure the crown of Castile; and this time he secured a treaty for the marriage of his daughter Catharine to the future king of Castile. After his return to England (1389) he reconciled Richard to his (John's) brother, the Duke of Gloucester, and by Richard was made Duke of Aquitaine, and sent on several embassies to France. On his second wife's death he had married in 1396 his mistress, Catharine Swynford, by whom he had three sons, legitimated in 1397; from the eldest descended Henry VIII. See work by Armitage-Smith (1904).

JOHN OF LEYDEN (1509–36), Dutch Anabaptist, born Beuckelszoon, Beuckels or Bockhold at Leyden, wandered about for some time as a journeyman tailor, then settled in his native city as merchant and innkeeper, and became noted as an orator. Turning Anabaptist, he in 1534 came to Münster, and, succeeding Matthiesen as head of the Anabaptists, set up a 'kingdom of Zion', with polygamy and community of goods. In June 1535 the city was taken by the Bishop of Münster, and John and his accomplices tortured to death. See Baring-Gould's *Historic Oddities* (2nd series, 1890).

JOHN OF SALISBURY (*c.* 1115–80), English scholar and divine, born at Salisbury, studied at Paris, was clerk of Pope Eugenius III, and in 1176 became bishop of Chartres. A learned classical writer, he wrote lives of Becket and Anselm, *Polycraticus* (ed. Webb 1909), on church and state diplomacy, *Metalogicon* (ed. Webb 1929), on logic and Aristotelian philosophy, *Entheticus*, *Historia Pontificalis* (ed. Poole 1927), and Letters. See studies by Schaarschmidt (1869) and Webb (1929).

JOHN OF TREVISA (1326–1412), Cornish translator of Higden, Glanville and Bartholomaeus Anglicus, was a fellow of Exeter and Queen's Colleges, Oxford, and vicar of Berkeley and canon of Westbury (probably Westbury-on-Trym).

JOHNS HOPKINS. See HOPKINS (6).

JOHNSON, (1) **Amy** (1903–41), English airwoman, born at Hull, flew solo from England to Australia (1930), to Japan via Siberia (1931), and to Cape Town (1932), making new records in each case. A pilot in Air Transport Auxilary in World War II, she was drowned after baling out over the Thames estuary. See MOLLISON; and Life by C. B. Smith (1967).

(2) **Andrew** (1808–75), 17th president of the United States, was born of humble parentage at Raleigh, N.C., December 29. In 1824 he went to Laurens, S.C., to work as a journeyman tailor, and in 1826 emigrated to Greenville, Tennessee. He served as alderman and mayor; in 1835 and 1839 became a member of the legislature; in 1841 was elected to the state senate, and in 1843 to congress. In 1853 and 1855 he was chosen governor of Tennessee, and in 1857 U.S. senator. After the Civil War broke out he became a leader of the Southern Union men, was made military governor of Tennessee (1862), and elected to the vice-presidency (March 1865). On Lincoln's assassination (April 14, 1865) he became president. He sought to carry out the conciliatory policy of his predecessor, but the assassination had provoked a revulsion of public feeling, and Johnson's policy was denounced as evincing disloyal sympathies. Soon a majority of congress were opposing his policy, and while he urged the readmission of Southern representatives, the majority insisted that the Southern states should be kept for a period under military government. Johnson vetoed the congressional measures; and congress passed them over his veto. Finally, his removal of secretary Stanton from the war department precipitated a crisis. Johnson claimed the right to change his 'constitutional advisers', and in return he was charged with violation of the 'Tenure of Office Act', in doing so without the consent of the senate. He was impeached and brought to trial, but acquitted. He retired from office in March 1869, and was elected to the senate in January 1875. See works by Dewitt (1903) and L. P. Stryker (1929).

(3) **Esther**. See SWIFT.

(4) **Hewlett**, the 'Red Dean' (1874–1966), English ecclesiastic, born of a capitalist family at Macclesfield, studied at Manchester and Oxford Universities. He began life as a 13-shillings-a-week engineering apprentice, did welfare work in the Manchester slums, joined the I.L.P. and, resolving to become 'a missionary engineer', was ordained in 1905. In 1924 he became dean of Manchester and from 1931 to 1963 was dean of Canterbury. In 1938 he visited Russia; with the publication of *The Socialist Sixth of the World* began his years of praise for Sovietism. In 1951 he received the Stalin peace prize. Though he was not a member of the Communist party, his untiring championship of Communist states and Marxist policies involved him in continuous and vigorous controversy in Britain. His sobriquet was a self-bestowed title when, during the Spanish War, he said 'I saw red—you can call me red'. Other publications include *Christians and Communism* (1956) and the autobiographical *Searching for Light* (1968).

(5) **Jack** (1878–1946), American Negro boxer, born at Galveston, knocked out Bob Fitzsimmons (1907) and won the world's heavyweight championship by beating Tommy Burns at Sydney (1908). He defeated Jeffries (1910) and lost his title to Jess Willard at Havana (1915). His arrogance and cruelty made him an unpopular champion. He served a prison sentence in 1919, and died in a car accident in N. Carolina.

(6) **James Weldon** (1871–1938), American Negro author, born in Jacksonville, Florida, where he practised at the bar (1897–1901). In 1906 he was U.S. consul at Puerto Cabello, Venezuela, and at Corinto, Nicaragua (1909–12). He was secretary of the National Association of Colored People (1916–30) and was awarded the Spingarn medal (1925). From 1930 he was professor of Creative Literature at Fisk University.

(7) **Lionel Pigot** (1867–1902), English poet and critic, born at Broadstairs, Kent. His *Poems* (1895) and *Ireland and Other Poems* (1897) draw their inspiration from his conversion to Roman Catholicism and his passion for the Irish Renaissance. 'By the Statue of King Charles at Charing Cross' is his best known piece. See also his *Reviews and Critical Papers* (1921).

(8) **Lyndon Baines** (1908–73), 36th President of the U.S.A., born at Stonewall, Texas, worked his way through college to become a teacher, then a congressman's secretary before being elected a strong 'New Deal' Democrat representative in 1937. He joined the U.S. Navy immediately after Pearl Harbour, and was decorated. 'L.B.J.' was elected senator

in 1948 and became vice president under Kennedy in 1960. A professional politician, he was majority leader in the senate. In Kennedy's motorcade at the latter's assassination in Dallas, Texas, in 1963, he was immediately sworn in as president. He was returned as president in the 1964 election with a huge majority. Under his administration the Civil Rights Act (1964), introduced by Kennedy the previous year, and the Voting Rights Act (1965) were passed, making effective, if limited, improvements to the Negro position in American society. The continuation and ever-increasing escalation of the war in Vietnam led to active protest and growing unpopularity for Johnson, however, and in 1968 he announced his decision not to stand for another presidential term of office and to retire from active politics. See works by P. L. Geyelin (1966) and R. Evans and R. Novak (1967).

(9) **Pamela Hansford.** See SNOW.

(10) **Richard Mentor** (1781–1850), vice president of the United States, was a member of congress in 1807–19, of the U.S. senate till 1829, and of congress till 1837. He was elected vice president (1837–41) by the senate, after the elections had not thrown up a majority in the electoral college for any one candidate.

(11) **Samuel** (1709–84), English lexicographer, critic and poet, was born at Lichfield, son of a bookseller. He was educated at Lichfield Grammar School and Pembroke College, Oxford, where he spent little over a year before poverty and perhaps insult drove him into the career of petty schoolmastering, first as an usher at Market Bosworth, later in a private venture at Edial, where Garrick was one of his pupils and where he wrote his frigid play *Irene*. In 1737 he came up to London. The struggle for a living there is reflected in his first poem, *London* (1738), an adaptation of Juvenal's third satire, contributed to the *Gentleman's Magazine*, which gave him a start in journalism. From 1740 to 1743 he wrote for it debates in Parliament, largely concocted by himself, in which 'the Whig dogs' got the worst of it. His famous *Dictionary* occupied him for eight years from 1747, but even this heroic labour did not exhaust his energies. To this period belongs his splendid adaptation of another satire of Juvenal, the tenth, 1749; and also the periodical *The Rambler*, afterwards published in three volumes compact of morality and keen observation of life, but now unreadable Poverty and bereavement oppressed him in those years—the former Garrick partly relieved by producing *Irene* in 1749, from which Johnson gained £300; the latter, viz., the death of his wife in 1752 and of his mother in 1759, permanently depressed him. The prose tale of Abyssinia, *Rasselas*, is said to have been written in a week to defray the burial expenses of the latter. Its theme is that the pursuit of happiness is vain, a theme congenial to him and made supportable by his strong religious faith. In 1762 he was relieved of the drudgery of hack work by the bestowal of a crown pension of £300 a year and was thereafter enabled to figure as the

arbiter of letters and the great social personality whose every recorded word and gesture have been treasured by posterity. The Literary Club, of which he was a founder member (1764), was the chief place where his genius shone amid a galaxy of other talent, but private society, especially that of the Thrales, husband and wife, did much to make him occupied and happy. The Thrales indeed are woven into the texture of his social life in this middle period and it was only when Mrs Thrale, now a widow, married Piozzi, an Italian singer (1784), that Johnson deprived himself of her sprightly acquaintance. As if to bear out his favourite theme of the vanity of human hopes, his social circle was narrowed by the death of Goldsmith, Beauclerk, Garrick and Mr Thrale within a few years of each other, but not before he had undertaken with Boswell in 1773 what is surely the most instructive and entertaining tour in literary history of which we have happily the two complementary records, Johnson's *Journey to the Western Isles* (1775) and Boswell's *Tour to the Hebrides*. *The Lives of the Poets* (1779–81) is the only other important contribution to letters in this late period; it includes *The Life of Mr Richard Savage* which had appeared more than thirty years before, in 1747, and which recorded with manly emotion the trials the friends had shared. Johnson died in 1784 and was buried in Westminster Abbey. Johnson's literary career then falls into four periods. The first includes much hack work for Cave's *Gentleman's Magazine*, but also *London* and the biography of Savage. The second (1748–60), the most fertile, contains the *Dictionary*, with its fine and discriminating *Preface*, the splendid *Vanity of Human Wishes*, and *Rasselas*. Despite the heavy moralizing and the style of his periodical essays in *The Rambler*, *The Idler*, &c., there is much in them for the student. The third period, besides his unrivalled conversations recorded by Boswell (which are after all part of his ' works '), includes his edition of Shakespeare (1765), with its masterly Preface. In his last period, from 1772 onwards—the political pamphleteering employed his pen—the full-blooded Tory appears in the *Patriot* and *Taxation no Tyranny* (1775). His *Journey to the Western Isles* is treasure trove, but *The Lives of the Most Eminent English Poets* (1779–81) is his enduring monument, and this despite his cantankerous treatment of Milton and Gray and his failure to appreciate metaphysical poetry. His reputation as man and conversationalist outweighs his literary reputation. For the picture of Johnson in society we are indebted above all to Boswell, who has painted him with all his hard sense and unreasonableness, his peremptory conclusion to argument, his humility and piety, his loveableness. The English see themselves in this picture, but foreigners have never understood the national homage. For one thing his ideas were circumscribed, he had no touch in him of the philosopher, and this no doubt makes for the fun of his verbal tussles with Boswell, who had imbibed something of philosophism but who wisely allowed himself usually to be ' corrected ' by his friend. See the Yale edition of his works (vol. I, 1959), Lives by J. Boswell (q.v.) (new ed. L. F. Powell, 1934), Sir John Hawkins (1787), Mrs Piozzi's *Anecdotes* (1786), and studies by W. Raleigh (1910), S. C. Roberts (1935), Elton, *Survey of English Literature, 1780–1830* and H. Pearson, *Johnson and Boswell* (1958).

(12) **Sir William** (1715–74), Irish merchant and administrator, born in County Down, in 1738 went to America, and as a fur-trader acquired great influence with the Red Indians, whom he led often against the French. His third wife (or mistress) was a Mohawk girl. In 1755 he was created a baronet. See Griffis's *Sir William Johnson and the Six Nations* (1891) and Life by A. Pound (1930).

(13) **William Eugene**, nicknamed **Pussyfoot** (1862–1945), American temperance propagandist, born in Coventry, N.Y. He became a journalist and a special officer in the U.S. Indian Service, where he received his nickname from his methods in raiding gambling saloons in Indian Territory. He was prominent during the prohibitionist movement in America and lectured for the cause all over Europe. In 1919 he lost an eye when he was struck and dragged from a lecture platform in London by medical students.

JOHNSTON, (1) Albert Sidney (1803–62), American soldier, born in Kentucky, served in the U.S. army until 1834. In 1836 he joined the army of Texas, and became its head, and in 1838 war secretary of Texas. He served in the Mexican war under General Taylor, who in 1849 appointed him paymaster in the U.S. army. In 1858 he brought the Mormon rebellion to an end. As brigadier-general he commanded in Utah and on the Pacific until 1861, when he passed over to the South. Appointed to the command of Kentucky and Tennessee, he fortified Bowling Green, and held the Northern army in check until February 1862, when he retreated to Nashville and later to Corinth, Mississippi. Here he concentrated 50,000 men, with which force he attacked Grant at Shiloh, April 6, 1862. The Union army was surprised, and the advantage lay with the Confederates till Johnston was mortally wounded. Next day Grant's supports came up and the Confederates, now under Beauregard, were driven back to Corinth. See Life by W. P. Johnston (1878).

(2) **Alexander Keith** (1804–71), Scottish cartographer, was born near Penicuik, and died at Ben Rhydding. His *National Atlas* (1843) procured him the appointment of geographer royal for Scotland. Other works are a *Physical Atlas* (1848) and the famous *Royal Atlas* (1861), besides atlases of astronomy, &c., a physical globe, and a gazetteer.

(3) **Alexander Keith** (1844–79), son of (2), born in Edinburgh, also wrote geographical works. He joined an exploring expedition to Paraguay in 1874, and in 1879 was appointed leader of the Royal Geographical Society's expedition to East Africa. He died between the Coast and Lake Nyasa, June 28, 1879, and his work was taken up by Joseph Thomson.

(4) or **Jonston, Arthur** (1587–1641),

Scottish physician and humanist, born at Caskieben, Aberdeenshire, graduated M.D. at Padua in 1610, and visited many seats of learning. He practised medicine in France, whence his fame as a Latin poet spread over Europe. About 1625 he was appointed physician to King Charles I. His famous translation of the Psalms of David into Latin verse was published at Aberdeen in 1637. He helped to bring out the *Deliciae Poetarum Scotorum hujus Aevi* (1637), to which he also contributed notable poems. In 1637 he became rector of King's College, Aberdeen. He died suddenly at Oxford. See works ed. by Sir W. D. Geddes (1892–95).

(5) **Sir Harry Hamilton** (1858–1927), British explorer and novelist, born at Kennington, London, from 1879 travelled in Africa, led the Royal Society's expedition to Kilimanjaro in 1884, and as commissioner for South Central Africa made possible British acquisition of Northern Rhodesia and Nyasaland. G.C.M.G., K.C.B., he wrote on the Congo, zoology, five novels and *The Story of My Life* (1923). See Life by his brother (1929), study by R. Oliver (1957).

(6) **Herrick Lee** (1898–), American chemist, born at North Jackson, Ohio, professor of Chemistry at Ohio and director of the Manhattan Project Research (1942–46), achieved with Giauque a temperature of less than one degree from absolute zero in gases.

(7) **Joseph Eggleston** (1807–91), American soldier, born in Virginia, graduated at West Point, fought in the Seminole war, became captain of engineers in 1846, served in the war with Mexico, and in 1860 was quartermaster-general. He resigned in 1861 to enter the Confederate service, and as brigadier-general took command of the army of the Shenandoah. He supported Beauregard at the first battle of Bull Run, in 1862 was disabled by a wound, in 1863 failed to relieve Vicksburg, and in 1864 stubbornly contested Sherman's progress towards Atlanta, but, being steadily driven back, was relieved of his command. In February 1865 Lee ordered him to ' drive back Sherman '; but he had only a fourth of the Northern general's strength. On Lee's surrender he accepted the same terms, afterwards engaged in railway and insurance business, was elected to congress in 1877, was a U.S. commissioner of railroads and died at Washington. See his *Narrative* (1874). Lives by Johnson (1891), Hughes (1893) and D. S. Freeman, *Lee's Lieutenants* (1942-44).

JOHNSTONE, name of a Scottish noble family taken from the lordship of Johnstone in Annandale, Dumfriesshire. In former days it was one of the most powerful and turbulent clans of the west Borders, and was at constant feud with its neighbours, especially the Maxwells. Of three branches, Johnstone of Annandale, Johnstone of Westerhall, and Johnston of Hilton and Caskieben in Aberdeenshire, the first, which retained the ancient patrimony, was ennobled by Charles I, and became successively Lords Johnstone of Lochwood, Earls of Hartfell, and Earls and Marquises of Annandale.

These titles, being limited to heirs-male, became dormant in 1792. Both the Houses of Westerhall and Caskieben had the rank of baronet, and a branch of the former was in 1881 raised to the peerage as Baron Derwent. See works by C. L. Johnstone (1889) and G. H. Johnstone (1909).

JOHNSTONE, James, Chevalier de (1719–*c.* 1800), Scottish soldier, the son of an Edinburgh merchant, as Prince Charles Edward's aide-de-camp fought at Culloden, and, then taking service with the French, was present at the capture of Louisbourg and the capitulation of Quebec. See his Memoirs (tr. from French, 3 vols. 1870–71).

JOINVILLE, *zhwĭ-veel,* (1) **François Ferdinand d'Orléans, Prince de** (1818–1900), French sailor and author, born at Neuilly, the third son of Louis Philippe, served in the French navy from 1834 to 1848, and was on McClellan's staff during the Virginian campaign in the American Civil War (1862); exiled from France in 1870, returned incognito and served in war against Prussia; in 1871-75 he sat in the National Assembly. He died in Paris. See his *Vieux Souvenirs* (1894; Eng. trans. 1896).

(2) **Jean, Sire de** (*c.* 1224–1319), French historian, born in Champagne, became seneschal to the count of Champagne and king of Navarre. He took part in the unfortunate crusade of Louis IX (1248–54), returned with him to France, and lived partly at court, partly on his estates. At Acre in 1250 he composed a Christian manual, his *Credo*; and throughout the crusade he took notes of events and wrote down his impressions. When almost eighty he undertook his delightful *Vie de Saint Louis* (1309). His style conforms closely to his character: it is veracious, flowing, naïve, often singularly expressive. See edition by de Wailly (1874) and trans. with intro. by Evans (1938).

JÓKAI, Maurus, or **Mór,** *yō'koy* (1825–1904), Hungarian novelist, born at Komáróm, was an active partisan of the Hungarian struggle in 1848. Besides dramas, humorous essays, poems, &c., he wrote many novels and romances, good examples of which are *The Turks in Hungary* (1852), *The Magyar Nabob* (1853) and its continuation *Zoltan Karpathy* (1854), *The New Landlord* (1862), *Black Diamonds* (1870), *The Romance of the Coming Century* (1873), *The Modern Midas* (1875), *The Comedians of Life* (1876), *God is One* (1877), *The White Woman of Leutschau* (1884) and *The Gipsy Baron* (1885); several have appeared in English. A jubilee edition in 100 volumes was published in 1894. Jókai was editor of several newspapers and conspicuous as a Liberal parliamentarian.

JOLIOT-CURIE, *zho-lyō-küree,* name of a French couple, both nuclear physicists:
(1) **Irène, née Curie** (1897–1956), wife (1926) of (2) and daughter of Pierre and Marie Curie (qq.v.), born in Paris, worked as her mother's assistant at the Radium Institute, taking charge of the work in 1932. In that year she discovered, with her mother, the projection of atomic nuclei by neutrons, and in 1934 she and her husband (2) succeeded in producing radioactive elements artificially, for which they received the 1935

Nobel prize for chemistry. She died of cancer, caused by lifelong exposure to radioactivity.
(2) **Jean Frédéric,** original surname Joliot (1900–58), husband (1926) of (1), born in Paris, studied under Langevin at the Sorbonne where in 1925 he became assistant to Madame Curie, mother of Irène. In 1935 he shared with his wife the Nobel prize for their discovery of artificial radioactivity. Professor at the Collège de France (1937), he became a strong supporter of the Resistance movement during World War II, and a membe of the Communist party. After the liberation he became director of scientific research and (1946–50) high commissioner for atomic energy, a position from which he was dismissed when the hitherto exclusively peaceful objectives were subordinated to defence requirements. President of the Communist-sponsored World Peace Council, he was awarded the Stalin peace prize (1951). Commander of the *Légion d'honneur*, he was given a state funeral by the Gaullist government when he died from cancer, caused by lifelong exposure to radioactivity.

JOLSON, Al, stage-name of **Asa Yoelson** (1886–1950), Russian-born American actor and singer, born in St Petersburg, son of a rabbi, emigrated to the United States in 1893 and made his stage début in *The Children of the Ghetto* (1899). He toured with circus and minstrel shows and became famous for his characteristic imitations of Negro singers in such hits as ' Mammy ' (1909), ' Sonny Boy ', &c. His recorded voice featured in the commemorative films *The Jolson Story* and *Jolson Sings Again*.

JOLY, John (1857–1933), Irish geologist and physicist, born in Offaly, Ireland, studied at Trinity College, Dublin, where he became professor of Geology and Mineralogy in 1897. He invented a photometer in 1888, calculated the age of the earth by measuring the sodium content of the sea (1899) and formulated the theory of thermal cycles based on the radioactive elements in the earth's crust. With Stevenson he evolved the ' Dublin method ' in radiotherapy, pioneered colour photography and the radium treatment of cancer. He was elected F.R.S. in 1892.

JOMINI, Henri, Baron, *zho-mee-nee* (1779–1869), Swiss soldier and strategist, born at Payerne in Vaud, after commanding a Swiss battalion attached himself to Ney, to whom he became chief of staff; he was created baron after the peace of Tilsit. He attracted Napoleon's notice by his *Traité des grandes opérations militaires* (1804). He distinguished himself at Jena, in the Spanish campaigns and during the retreat from Russia; but, offended at his treatment by Napoleon, he entered the Russian service (1814), and fought against Turkey (1828). He wrote a great history of the wars of the Revolution (1806), a Life of Napoleon (1827) and a *Précis de l'art de guerre* (1830). See E. M. Earle, *Makers of Modern Strategy* (1944).

JOMMELLI, Niccoló, *yo-mel'li* (1714–74), Italian composer of more than fifty operas, born at Aversa, germanized his style and lost his popularity after a spell as *kapellmeister* to the Duke of Württemberg.

JONAS, Justus, *yō-näs* (1493–1555), German professor at Wittenberg, sided with Luther in the Reformation. See monograph by Pressel (1863).

JONES, (1) Daniel (1881–1967), English phonetician, was called to the bar in 1907, when he was also appointed lecturer in Phonetics (professor 1921–49) at London. He collaborated with others in compiling Cantonese (1912), Sechuana (1916) and Sinhalese (1919) phonetic readers, compiled an *English Pronouncing Dictionary* (1917; new ed. 1956) and wrote *The Phoneme* (1950), *Cardinal Vowels* (1956), &c. He was secretary (1928–49) and president of the International Phonetic Association.

(2) **Ebenezer** (1820–60), English minor poet, born at Islington, was brought up a strict Calvinist and despite long hours as a clerk completed *Studies of Sensation and Event* (1843), which were admired by Browning and Rossetti. In his *Land Monopoly* (1849) he anticipated the economic theory of Henry George (q.v.) by thirty years.

(3) **Edward** (1777–1837), founder in 1800 of the Welsh Wesleyan Methodists, was born near Ruthin, and died at Leek.

(4) **Edward Burne.** See BURNE-JONES.

(5) **Ernest** (1819–69), English Chartist poet and leader, the son of Major Jones, equerry to the Duke of Cumberland, afterwards king of Hanover, was born at Berlin, and came to England in 1838. In 1841 he published his romance, *The Wood Spirit*, was called to the bar in 1844, and next year became leader of the Chartist movement, issuing *The Labourer*, *Notes of the People* and *The People's Paper*, and resigning nearly £2000 per annum, left to him on condition that he should abandon the Chartist cause. For his part in the Chartist proceedings at Manchester in 1848 he got two years' solitary confinement, and in prison composed an epic, *The Revolt of Hindostan*. After his release he wrote *The Battleday* (1855), *The Painter of Florence* and *The Emperor's Vigil* (1856), and *Beldagon Church* and *Corayda* (1860). He made several vain efforts to enter parliament. See G. D. H. Cole, *Chartist Portraits* (1941), and studies, ed. Saville (1952).

(6) **Ernest** (1879–1958), Welsh psychoanalyst, born at Llwchwr, Glamorgan, studied at Cardiff University College and qualified with gold medals as physician in London. Medical journalism and neurological research brought him into contact with the work of Freud and his new approach to neurosis. Jones learnt German in order to study this more closely and in 1908 became a lifelong disciple and personal friend of the founder of psychoanalysis, introduced it into Britain and in 1912 formed a committee of Freud's closest collaborators of which he was the only Gentile, pledged to uphold the Freudian theory in the face of detractors and deviationists. He introduced psychoanalysis into America and Britain, founding the British Psycho-Analytical Society in 1913, also in 1920 the *International Journal of Psycho-Analysis* which he edited (1920–33). He was professor of Psychiatry

at Toronto and director of the London Clinic for Psycho-Analysis. Among his numerous works and translations is a psychoanalytical study of *Hamlet* and the authoritative biography of Freud (1953–57). See his autobiography, *Free Associations* (1959).

(7) **Henry** (1831–99), English physician who as ' Cavendish ' published many books on whist and other games.

(8) **Henry Arthur** (1851–1929), English dramatist, together with Pinero the founder of the ' realist problem ' drama in Britain, born at Grandborough, Bucks, was in business till 1878, when *Only Round the Corner* was produced at Exeter. His first great hit was a melodrama, *The Silver King* (1882). This was followed by *Saints and Sinners* (1884), *Rebellious Susan* (1894), *The Philistines* (1895), *The Liars* (1897), *The Manoeuvres of Jane* (1898), *Mrs Dane's Defence* (1900), *Mary Goes First* (1913) and other social comedies. See *Life and Letters* by his daughter (1930), and study by R. A. Cordell (1932).

(9) **Sir Henry Stuart** (1867–1939), British classical scholar, born at Hunslet, Leeds, studied at Balliol College, Oxford, and in Greece and Italy, became Camden professor of Ancient History at Oxford and principal of University College, Aberystwyth, in 1927, and was knighted in 1933. He contributed to archaeological studies and ancient history, edited Thucydides (1898–1900) and edited the Greek lexicon of Liddell and Scott (9th ed. 1925–40).

(10) **Inigo** (1573–1652), the first of the great English architects, born in London July 15, studied landscape painting in Italy, and from Venice introduced the Palladian style into England. In Denmark, he is said to have designed the palaces of Rosenborg and Frederiksborg. In 1606 James I employed him in arranging the masques of Ben Jonson. He introduced the proscenium arch and movable scenery to the English stage. In 1613–14 he revisited Italy and on his return in 1615 was appointed surveyor-general of the royal buildings. In 1616 he designed the queen's house at Greenwich, completed in the 1630s. Other commissions included the rebuilding of the Whitehall banqueting hall, the nave and transepts and a large Corinthian portico of old St Paul's, Marlborough Chapel, the Double-Cube room at Wilton and possibly the York Water Gate. He laid out Covent Garden and Lincoln's Inn Fields. See Life by Cunningham (1848) and studies by J. A. Gotch (1928), R. Blomfield (1935), S. Sitwell, *British Architects and Craftsmen* (1945) and J. L. Milne (1953).

(11) **Owen** (1741–1814), Welsh antiquary, was all his life a London furrier, but early developed a taste for Welsh poetry. His *Myvyrian Archaeology of Wales* (1801–07; new ed. 1870) is a collection of poetic pieces dating from the 6th to the 14th century.— His son, **Owen Jones** (1809–74), art decorator, was superintendent of works for the London Exhibition of 1851, and director of decoration for the Crystal Palace.

(12) **Paul** (1747–92), Scottish-born American sailor, was born at Kirkbean, Kirkcud-

brightshire, July 6, the son of a gardener, John Paul. Apprenticed as sailor boy, he made several voyages to America, and in 1773 inherited a property in Virginia, having meanwhile for five years been mate on a slaver; about the same date he assumed the name of Paul Jones. When the American congress in 1775 resolved to fit out a naval force he offered his services. In April 1778, visiting the British coast in a brig of eighteen guns, he performed some daring exploits, including a descent on the Solway. The year after, as commodore of a small French squadron displaying American colours, he threatened Leith, and on September 23, fought off Flamborough Head a desperate engagement, in which he captured two British men-of-war. Louis XVI created him a Chevalier of the Order of Military Merit. In 1788 he entered the Russian service, and as rear-admiral of the Black Sea fleet served against Turkey. He died in Paris. See Lives by Sherburne (1825), Mackenzie (1841), Brady (1900), Buell (1900); *Life and Letters*, by Mrs de Koven (1914); also Sir J. K. Laughton's *Studies in Naval History* (1887).

(13) **Robert** (fl. 1600), English lutenist and composer, graduated at Oxford (1597), composed madrigals, including a six-part one in Morley's *The Triumphes of Oriana* as well as five books of ' ayres ', with lute accompaniments.

(14) **Robert Tyre (Bobby)** (1902–71), American golfer, born in Atlanta. He studied law and was called to the Georgia bar in 1928. He won the National Amateur Championship in 1924, 1925, 1927 and 1928, the National Open Championship in 1923, 1926 and 1929, and both Championships in 1930, in which year he also won the Amateur and Open Championships of Great Britain. He wrote *Down the Fairway* (1927), and in 1958 received the freedom of St Andrews.

(15) **Sir William** (1746–94), British Orientalist, born in London, was educated at Harrow and University College, Oxford, where his remarkable attainments attracted attention. In 1765 he became tutor to the son of Earl Spencer; in 1774 was called to the bar; and in 1776 became commissioner of bankrupts, publishing meanwhile a *Persian Grammar* (1772), Latin Commentaries on Asiatic Poetry (1774), and a translation of seven ancient Arabic poems (1780). In 1783 he obtained a judgeship in the Supreme Court of Judicature in Bengal, and was knighted. He devoted himself to Sanskrit, whose startling resemblance to Latin and Greek he was the first to point out in 1787. He established the Asiatic Society of Bengal (1784), and was its first president. He completed a translation of *Sakuntala*, the *Hitopadesa*, parts of the Vedas, and Manu, before his death. See Memoirs by Lord Teignmouth appended to his works (9 vols. 1799–1804), and appreciation by A. J. Arberry (1946).

JONGEN, *yong'ėn*, (1) **Joseph** (1873–1953), Belgian composer, won the Belgian *Prix de Rome* and was professor at Liège Conservatoir until the outbreak of World War I when he went to England. He became

director of the Brussels Conservatoire (1920–39). He composed piano, violin and organ works, the symphonic poem *Lalla Roukh*, an opera and a ballet.

(2) **Leon** (1885–), brother of (1), followed him in 1939 as director of the Brussels Conservatoire. He has written works for the piano, operas, and *Rhapsodia Belgia* for violin and orchestra.

JONSON, Ben (1572–1637), English dramatist, born at Westminster, probably of Border descent. He was educated at Westminster School under Camden, to whom he paid the tribute ' Camden most reverend head to whom I owe/All that I am in arts, all that I know '. After working for a while with his stepfather, a bricklayer, he volunteered for military service in Flanders before joining Henslowe's company of players. He killed a fellow player in a duel, became a Catholic in prison, but later recanted. His *Every Man in his Humour* with Shakespeare in the cast, was performed at the Curtain in 1598 to be followed not so successfully by *Every Man Out of His Humour* in 1599. The equally tiresome *Cynthia's Revels*, largely allegorical, was succeeded by *The Poetaster* which at least was salted by a personal attack on Dekker and Marston. He now tried Roman tragedy, but his *Sejanus* (1603) and his later venture, *Catiline* (1611), are so larded with classical references as to be merely closet plays. If he was trying to show Shakespeare how to write a Roman tragedy he failed badly, but his larger intent of discarding romantic comedy and writing realistically (though his theory of ' humours ' was hardly comparable with genuine realism) helped to produce his four masterpieces—*Volpone* (1606), *The Silent Woman* (1609), *The Alchemist* (1610) and *Bartholomew Fair* (1614). *Volpone* is an unpleasant satire on senile sensuality and greedy legacy hunters. *The Silent Woman* is farcical comedy involving a heartless hoax. Dryden praised it for its construction, but *The Alchemist* is better with its single plot and strict adherence to the unities. *Bartholomew Fair* has indeed all the fun of the fair, salted by Ben's anti-Puritan prejudices, though the plot gets lost in the motley of eccentrics. After the much poorer *The Devil is an Ass* (1616), Jonson turned or rather returned to the masque—he had collaborated with Inigo Jones in *The Masque of Blacknesse*, 1605—and produced a number of those glittering displays down to 1625 when James's death terminated his period of Court favour. His renewed attempt to attract theatre audiences left him in the angry mood of the ode ' Come leave the loathed stage ' (1632). Only his unfinished pastoral play *The Sad Shepherd* survives of his declining years. Ben attracted the learned and courtly, to several of whom his superb verse letters are addressed. Perhaps we should not wonder at the success of *The Sad Shepherd*, for his lyric genius was second only to Shakespeare's. ' Drink to me only with thine Eyes ' in *Volpone* (of all places) and ' Queen and Huntress chaste and fair ' and ' Slow, slow fresh Fount ' in the dreary stretches of *Cynthia's Revels* are but a few of these gemlike lyrics. His *Timber; or*

Discoveries, printed in the folio of 1640, prove him a considerable critic with a bent towards the neoclassicism which Cowley and Dryden inaugurated. His works were edited by William Gifford in 1816 and by Colonel Cunningham in 1875. These were superseded by Herford's splendid edition. There have been numerous studies, the best perhaps by J. A. Symonds (1886), Swinburne (1889) and G. Gregory Smith (1919), G. B. Johnston (1945), G. E. Bentley (1945), Partridge (1958) and Thayer (1963).

JÓNSSON, (1) **Einar** (1874–1954), Icelandic sculptor, studied at Rome and Copenhagen, and created a reputation for himself by the independence, realism and grandeur of his works (*The Outlaw, Evolution, New Life*, &c.).

(2) **Finnur** (1858–1934), Icelandic scholar, born at Akureyri, studied, lectured and became professor in 1898 at Copenhagen. He published *Den oldnorske og oldislandske litteraturs historie* (1894–1902), a history of the mediaeval literatures of Norway and Iceland.

JOOS VAN CLEVE. See CLEVE.

JOPLIN, **Thomas** (*c.* 1790–1847), English economist, born at Newcastle-on-Tyne, wrote a number of works on joint-stock banking in Scotland, advocated a merger of small provincial banks and became a director of such a scheme with the founding of the National Provincial Bank (1833) and opposed the monopoly of the Bank of England.

JORDAENS, **Jakob**, *yor'dahns* (1593–1678), Flemish painter, who was born and died at Antwerp, ranks next to Rubens amongst Flemish painters. He became a member of an Antwerp Guild in 1616 and from 1630 came under the influence of Rubens, who obtained for him the patronage of the kings of Spain and Sweden. His early paintings such as the *Four Evangelists* (1632, Louvre) show him to be deficient in the handling of chiaroscuro effects and colour generally, but he improved vastly in such later canvases as *The Triumph of Frederick Henry* (1652, House in the Wood, The Hague) although he never achieved the delicacy of Rubens. He also designed tapestries, and painted portraits. See monograph by M. Rooses (tr. 1908).

JORDAN, (1) **Camille**, *zhor-dã* (1771–1821), French Liberal politician, born at Lyons, supported the royalists during the Revolution and fled (1793). He subsequently became a member of the council of The Five Hundred (1797), opposed Napoleon and became a deputy in 1816.

(2) **Dorothea**, *née* **Bland**, *jor'dèn* (1762–1816), Irish actress, born near Waterford, made her début in Dublin (1777), soon became popular and in 1782 obtained an engagement from Tate Wilkinson at Leeds. She appeared with phenomenal success at Drury Lane in *The Country Girl* in October 1785. For nearly thirty years it was in the rôles of romps and boys that she mainly kept her hold on the public. In 1790 commenced her connection with the Duke of Clarence, afterwards William IV, which endured until 1811. After playing in London and in the provinces until 1814, she is said to have been compelled to retire to France for a debt of

£2000. She certainly lived in apparent poverty at St Cloud, where she died, though there is a legend that she returned to live in England for some years after her supposed death. In 1831 King William made their eldest son Earl of Munster. See books by Sergeant (1913), Jerrold (1914).

(3) **Marie Ennemond Camille**, *zhor-dã* (1838–1922), French mathematician, born at Lyons, became professor at the École Polytechnique and at the Collège de France. He applied group theory to geometry, wrote on the theory of linear differential equations and on the theory of functions, which he applied to the curve which bears his name.

(4) **Rudolf**, *yor-dahn* (1810–87), German painter of fisher folk, was born at Berlin, and died at Düsseldorf.

JORDANES, *-dah'neez* (fl. 530), historian, was first a notary at the Ostrogoth court in Italy, but became a monk, and finally Bishop of Crotona. He wrote two historical works in Latin—*De Regnorum ac Temporum Successione*, a compendium of history from the creation to 552 A.D., and *De Getarum Origine et Rebus Gestis* (Eng. trans. with introd. by Mierow, 1915), which, based on the earlier work (now lost) of the Roman Cassiodorus, is an important source of information about the Goths.

JÖRGENSEN, *yær'gen-sen*, (1) **Johannes** (1866–1956), Danish novelist and poet, lived most of his life in Assisi, Italy, became a Roman Catholic (1896) but returned to Svendborg, his birth-place, shortly before his death. His works include *Frans af Assisi* (1907), *Den hellige Katharina af Siena* (1915) and *Mit Livs Legende* (1916–28).

(2) **Jörgen**, ' King of Iceland ' (1779–*c.* 1845), Danish adventurer, the son of a Copenhagen watchmaker, was born in 1779. On June 21, 1809, having previously visited Iceland as interpreter, he arrived at Reykjavik in an armed London merchantman. But all trade being prohibited by the laws of the island, a few days afterwards he landed and seized the governor. He then proclaimed the independence of Iceland, ' under English protection ', and appropriated all he could lay his hands on for the ' state chest '. On August 9 a British sloop of war arrived, and he was carried to England. He lived in London for some years, but was convicted of robbery in 1820, and transported to Tasmania.

JOSEPH, the name of many biblical personages. The most important are:

Joseph, the elder of the two sons of Jacob by Rachel. His being sold into Egypt and his ultimate rise to power there are recorded in Genesis.

Joseph, husband of the Virgin, a carpenter at Nazareth, appears last in the gospel history when Jesus is twelve years old (Luke, ii. 43); he is never mentioned during his ministry, and may be assumed to have been already dead.

Joseph, one of the two persons chosen as worthy to fill the vacant place of Judas among the Twelve.

Joseph of Arimathea, a rich Israelite who went to Pilate and begged the body of Jesus, burying it in his own rock-hewn tomb.

JOSEPH, the name of two Holy Roman emperors:

Joseph I (1678–1711), succeeded his father Leopold I as emperor of Germany in 1705. He granted privileges to the Protestants, and, in alliance with Britain, prosecuted successfully the war of the Spanish succession against France.

Joseph II (1741–90), emperor of Germany, son of Francis I and Maria Theresa, was born March 13. In 1764 he was elected king of the Romans, and after his father's death (1765) emperor of Germany; but until his mother's death (1780) his power was limited to the command of the army and the direction of foreign affairs. Although he failed to add Bavaria to the Austrian dominions (1777–79 and again in 1785), he acquired Galicia, Lodomeria, and Zips, at the first partition of Poland in 1772; and in 1780 he appropriated a great part of Passau and Salzburg. As soon as he found himself in full possession of the government of Austria he declared himself independent of the pope, and prohibited the publication of any new papal bulls without his *placet*. He suppressed 700 convents, reduced the number of the regular clergy from 63,000 to 27,000, prohibited papal dispensations as to marriage, and in 1781 published the Edict of Toleration for Protestants and Greeks. He also abolished serfdom, reorganized taxation, and curtailed the feudal privileges of the nobles. In 1788 he engaged in an unsuccessful war with Turkey. See study by S. K. Padover (1934).

JOSEPH, king of Naples. See BONAPARTE.

JOSEPH, Père (1577–1638), French diplomat, Richelieu's *alter ego*, the ' Grey Eminence ', born François le Clerc du Tremblay in Paris, from a soldier turned Capuchin in 1599, and went on several important diplomatic missions for Richelieu. See books by Fagniez (Paris 1893–94) and Huxley (1941).

JOSÉPHINE, *née* **Marie Joséphine Rose Tascher de la Pagerie** (1763–1814), wife of Napoleon and French empress, was born in Martinique, June 23, and in 1779 married there the Vicomte de Beauharnais (q.v.). In 1796, two years after his execution, she married Napoleon Bonaparte, and accompanied him in his Italian campaign, but soon returned to Paris. At Malmaison, and afterwards at the Luxembourg and the Tuileries, she attracted round her the most brilliant society of France, and contributed not a little to the establishment of her husband's power. But the marriage, being childless, was dissolved December 16, 1809. Joséphine retained the title of empress, and, if allowed, would have rejoined Bonaparte after his fall. See works by Aubenas (1859), Sergeant(1908), Méneval (trans. 1912), Turquan (trans. 1913), Geer (1925), Wilson (1930) and Knapton (1964).

JOSEPHUS, Flavius, *jō-see'fus* (37–?100), Jewish historian and soldier, was born at Jerusalem, the son of a priest, while his mother was descended from the Asmonean princes. His acquirements in Hebrew and Greek literature soon drew public attention upon him, and he became conspicuous amongst the Pharisees, the national party, at twenty-six being chosen delegate to Nero. When the Jews rose in their last and fatal insurrection against the Romans, Josephus, as governor of Galilee, displayed great valour and prudence; but the advance of Vespasian (67) made resistance hopeless, and Jotapata, the city into which he had thrown himself, was taken after holding out for 47 days. Josephus was kept in a sort of easy imprisonment for three years, and was present in the Roman army at the siege of Jerusalem by Titus (70). After this he appears to have resided at Rome. He survived Agrippa II, who died in 100. His works are *History of the Jewish War*, written both in Hebrew and Greek (the Hebrew version is no longer extant); *Jewish Antiquities*, containing the history of his countrymen from the earliest times to the end of the reign of Nero; a treatise on the *Antiquity of the Jews*, against Apion; and an *Autobiography* (A.D. 37–90). The *editio princeps* of the Greek text appeared at Basel in 1544. See trans. by H. St J. Thackeray (with text; 1926 *et seq.*). Lion Feuchtwanger's historical romance *Der jüdische Krieg* was translated as *Josephus* (1932). See studies by N. Bentwich (1926) and F. Jackson (1930).

JOSHUA, son of Nun, of the tribe of Ephraim, was one of the twelve spies sent to collect information about the Canaanites, and during the forty years' wanderings acted as ' minister ' or personal attendant of Moses. After ' the Lord was angry with Moses ' Joshua was expressly designated to lead the people into Canaan. The Book of Joshua is a narrative of the conquest and settlement of Canaan under his leadership.

JOSIAH (649–609 B.C.), king of Judah, succeeded his father Amon at eight. He re-established the worship of Jehovah, and instituted the rites in the newly-discovered ' Book of the Law '. He fell at Megiddo attempting to check Pharaoh-Necho's advance against the Assyrians.

JOSIKA, Baron Miklós von, *yō'shee-kė* (1794–1865), Hungarian novelist in the romantic tradition of Sir Walter Scott, was involved in the revolution of 1848, and had to live an exile in Brussels and Dresden. See *Magyar Life* by Szaak (1891).

JOUBERT, *zhoo-bayr*, (1) **Joseph** (1754–1824), French writer and moralist, was born at Montignac in Périgord, and studied and taught at the college of Toulouse. He then went to Paris, and lived through all the fever of the Revolution. In 1809 he was nominated by Napoleon to the council of the new university. Fourteen years later, his friend Chateaubriand edited a small volume from his papers, and Joubert's fame was from that moment assured; his *Pensées* are worthy of their place beside those of La Rochefoucauld, Pascal, La Bruyère and Vauvenargues. There are translations by Calvert (1867), Attwell (1877), and Lyttelton (1899). See Sainte-Beuve's *Causeries du lundi* (vol. i), *Portraits littéraires* (vol. ii), and *Chateaubriand et son groupe*; also Matthew Arnold's *Essays in Criticism* (1865) and study by A. Beaunier (1918).

(2) **Petrus Jacobus** (1834–1900), Boer soldier and statesman, born at Cango,

Cape Colony, was conqueror of Colley in 1881 and of Jameson in 1896, organized the first Boer successes in the South African war of 1899–1902, but died after a short illness.

JOUFFROY, Théodore Simon, *zhoo-frwah* (1796–1842), French philosopher, born at Pontets in the Jura, professor of Philosophy at Paris (1817), in 1838 became university librarian. He wrote lucid commentaries on Reid and Dugald Stewart, translated their works and wrote *Mélanges philosophiques* (1833), *Cours de droit naturel* (1835), &c. See Life by Tissot (1876).

JOUFFROY D'ABBANS, Claude, Marquis de, *zhoo-frwah dab-ã* (1751–1832), French inventor of steam-navigation, served in the army, and in 1783 made a small paddle-wheel steamboat. Compelled to emigrate and ruined by the Revolution, he failed to float a company till after Fulton had made his successful experiments on the Seine in 1803. See monograph by Prost (Paris 1889).

JOULE, James Prescott, *jool* (1818–89), English physicist, famous for his experiments in heat, born December 24 at Salford, studied chemistry under Dalton and in a series of notable researches (1843–78) showed experimentally that heat is a form of energy, determined quantitatively the amount of mechanical, and later electrical, energy to be expended in the propagation of heat energy and established the mechanical equivalent of heat. This became the basis of the theory of the conservation of energy. With Lord Kelvin, he measured the fall in temperature when a gas expands without doing external work and formulated the absolute scale of temperature. He also showed that the molecular heat of a compound solid is equal to the sum of the atomic heats of its components, and was the first to describe the phenomenon of magnetostriction. He was elected F.R.S. in 1850 and awarded the Copley (1860) and Royal medals. His collected papers were published by the Physical Society (1884–87). See J. G. Crowther, *British Scientists of the Nineteenth Century* (1935).

JOURDAN, Jean-Baptiste, Comte, *zhoor-dã* (1762–1833), French marshal, born at Limoges, defeated the Austrians at Wattignies (October 16, 1793), gained the victory of Fleurus (June 26, 1794), and then drove the Austrians across the Rhine, took Luxemburg, and besieged Mainz. But on October 11, 1795, he was defeated at Höchst, and four times in 1796–99 by the Archduke Charles. Napoleon employed him in 1800 in Piedmont; in 1804 he was made marshal, and in 1806 governor of Naples. In 1813 he was defeated by Wellington at Vitoria, and in 1814 transferred his allegiance to the Bourbons, who made him a count. He supported the Revolution of 1830.

JOUVENEL, Henri de (1876–1935), French politician and journalist, husband (1910–1935) of the authoress Colette, born in Paris, attained a high position in the ministry of justice before editing *Le Matin*. Elected senator in 1921, he was delegate to the League of Nations (1922 and 1924) and was high commissioner in Syria (1925–26).

JOUVET, Louis, *zhoo-vay* (1887–1951), French theatre and film director and actor, born in Finistère, graduated as a pharmacist but took to the stage. He fought in the first World War and toured the United States with Jacques Copeau's company (1918–19). He became stage-manager (1922) and director (1924) of the Comédie des Champs Élysées. Equally at home in modern as in classical French drama, he was the first to recognize Giraudoux, all but one of whose plays (1928–46) he produced, as well as Cocteau's *La Machine infernale* (1931). In 1934 his company transferred to the Théâtre de l'Athénée and he was honoured by being the first director to be appointed professor at the Paris Conservatoire, outside the Comédie Française. At the latter, however, he directed (1936–37) outstanding productions of Molière's *L'École des femmes* and Corneille's *L'Illusion*. He was equally outstanding as an actor in such films as *Topaze*, *Carnival in Flanders* (1935), and directed *Carnet de bal* (1937), *La Fin du jour* (1939), *Volpone* (1940) and *Retour à la vie* (1949), &c. He was awarded the Legion of Honour (1926) and in 1949 was chosen best French film actor of the year. See study by B. L. Knapp (1958).

JOUY, Victor Joseph Étienne de, *zhwee* (1764–1846), French playwright, librettist, and author of *L'Hermite de la Chaussée d'Antin* (1812–14) and other prose works, was born at Jouy near Versailles; till 1797 served as a soldier in India and at home; and in 1815 was elected to the Academy.

JOWETT, Benjamin (1817–93), English Greek scholar, born at Camberwell, was educated at St Paul's School and Balliol, Oxford, where he won the Hertford in 1837, a classical first in 1839, and the Latin essay in 1841. Already a fellow in 1838, he was tutor from 1840 till his election as master in 1870; from 1855 to 1893 he was regius professor of Greek, from 1882 till 1886 vice-chancellor. As master of Balliol his Liberal influence permeated the college to a degree almost unexampled. Jowett belonged to the Broad Church party. For his article ' On the Interpretation of Scripture ' in *Essays and Reviews* (1860) he was tried but acquitted by the vice-chancellor's court. He is best known for his beautiful translation, marred somewhat for philosophers by lack of exact scholarship, of the *Dialogues* of Plato (1871; 3rd ed. 1892) and his (less happy) versions of Thucydides (1881) and the *Politics* of Aristotle (1885). See his *Life and Letters* ed. by Evelyn Abbott and Lewis Campbell (1897), and *Portrait* by G. Faber (1957).

JOWITT, William Allen, (1885–1957), 1st Earl Jowitt, Viscount Stevenage, British politician, born at Stevenage, Herts, and educated at Marlborough and Oxford. He was called to the bar in 1909 and took silk in 1922. He was Liberal M.P. for the Hartlepools (1922–24) and for five months for a Preston constituency (1929), which seat he resigned on joining the Labour party and becoming attorney-general; he was returned with an increased majority as a Socialist. In 1931 he joined the National Government, was expelled from the Labour party, returned to it in 1936, becoming M.P. for Ashton-under-Lyne in 1939. In 1945 he became lord chancellor, and piloted through the Conservative House of Lords a mass of Socialist legislation. His publications include *The Strange Case of Alger Hiss* (1953) and *Some Were Spies* (1954).

JOYCE, (1) **James Augustine Aloysius** (1882–1941), Irish writer, born at Dublin, was educated at the National University of Ireland, went in 1903 to Paris to study medicine and subsequently took up voice training for a concert platform career. Back in Dublin, he published a few stories, but, unable to make a living by his pen, he left for Trieste to tutor in English. Dublin saw him for the last time in 1912, when he started the short-lived Volta Cinema Theatre; and at the outbreak of World War I he was again in Trieste. He went to Zürich in 1915, where he formed a company of Irish players to perform his *Exiles* (an Ibsenite drama). He settled in Paris in 1920, remaining there until 1940 when he returned to Zürich, where he shortly afterwards died. His first publication was a collection of lyrics, *Chamber Music* (1907). *Dubliners*, short stories, appeared in 1914, to be followed by *Portrait of the Artist as a Young Man* (1917), originally serialized by Ezra Pound in the *Egoist* during 1914–15. His best-known book, *Ulysses*, appeared in Paris in 1922, but was banned in Britain and America for some years. *Work in Progress* began to appear in 1927, in sections and under different titles, and finally emerged as *Finnegans Wake* (1939). These novels flout the accepted conventions of the novel form prior to Joyce. The time factor becomes elastic and consciousness takes over and dictates the sequence of events. Plot and character emerge in a stream of association that carries on its ripples all the mental flotsam and jetsam that in the ordinary novel never rise to the surface. In addition, Joyce, particularly in the second novel, employs language like a musical notation, that is, the sound superficially supersedes the sense (to the average mind), but in reality communicates (like music) profundities which conventionalized words cannot express. That, at any rate, is what Joyce intends, but not many readers can go along with him all the way. Of the value of his experiment with his elaborate system of analogy there can be no doubt, and he conducts the experiment brilliantly, but it is self-evident that further analogy must turn back, in convolutions, on itself; there can, therefore, be no development after a certain point is reached, and that point is reached in *Finnegans Wake*. Joyce's peculiar achievement has been to translate to the art of writing the conception and technique of the art of musical composition. See also the *Critical Writings of James Joyce*, ed. E. Mason and R. Ellman (1959), biographical studies by Kenner (1956), his brother, S. Joyce, with a preface by T. S. Eliot (1958), K. Sullivan (1958), M. and P. Colum (1958) and C. P. Curran (1968), and studies by H. S. Gorman (1941), ed. T. S. Eliot (1942), L. A. G. Strong (1949), W. Y. Tindall (1950), Smidt (1955), Ussher (1955), L. Gillet (trans. 1958), R. Ellmann (1959).

(2) **William** (1906–46), British traitor, was born in Brooklyn, U.S.A., of Irish parentage. As a child he lived in Ireland and in 1922 his family emigrated to England. In 1933 he joined Sir Oswald Mosley's British Union of Fascists and secured a British passport by falsely claiming to have been born in Galway. Expelled from Mosley's party in 1937, he founded his own fanatical, Hitler-worshipping, British National Socialist Party. He fled to Germany before war broke out and from September 1939 to April 1945 broadcast from Radio Hamburg Goebbelasian propaganda of falsehood, abuse and threats against Britain. Each broadcast was heralded by the characteristic ' Chairmanny Calling ', in a pretentious voice which earned him the title ' Lord Haw-Haw '. He was captured by the British at Flensburg, was tried at the Old Bailey, London, in September 1945, convicted and executed. His defence was his American birth, but his British passport, valid until July 1940, established nine months of treason. See Rebecca West, *The Meaning of Treason* (1949) and Life by Cole (1964).

JOYNSON-HICKS, William, 1st Viscount Brentford (1865–1932), British Conservative politician, entered parliament in 1908 and was successively postmaster-general, minister of health and home secretary (1924–29). He played a leading part in defeating the Prayer Book Measure (1927). His second son, **Lancelot William, 3rd Viscount** (1902–), was also a Conservative politician.

JUAN DE LA CRUZ. See JOHN OF THE CROSS.

JUAN, Don. See JOHN OF AUSTRIA.

JUÁREZ, Benito Pablo, *hwah'res* (1806–72), president of Mexico, was born of Indian parents near Oaxaca. Exiled in 1853 for two years, in 1857 he was elected president of the supreme court. In 1858 he was compelled to retire to Vera Cruz, whence he issued decrees abolishing religious orders and confiscating church property. In 1861 he entered the capital, and was elected president for four years. In 1866 the French emperor declared war against him. But on the withdrawal of the French, he re-entered Mexico City in July 1867, the Emperor Maximilian (q.v.) having meanwhile been shot. Juárez was then elected president, and again in 1871. See Lives by U. R. Burke (1894), Zo Enníquez (1906), P. Martinez (1933), and C. Smart (1964).

JUBA, king of Numidia, having supported Pompey against Caesar, committed suicide, 46 B.C.

JUDAH, fourth son of Jacob and Leah, was founder of the greatest of the twelve tribes.

JUDAS, the betrayer of Jesus, surnamed Iscariot, was probably a native of Kerioth in the tribe of Judah. See the essay by De Quincey.

JUDAS MACCABAEUS. See MACCABEES.

JUDD, (1) **John Wesley** (1840–1916), British geologist, was born at Portsmouth, and entered the Royal School of Mines. In 1867 he joined the Geological Survey; in 1876 became professor at the School of Mines, in 1881 at the Royal College of Science. *Volcanoes* (1881) is by him.

(2) **Sylvester** (1813–53), American writer,

born at Westhampton, Mass., from 1840 a Unitarian pastor at Augusta, Me., wrote against slavery, war, intemperance, &c.

JUDE, St, was probably the Judas who was one of the 'brethren of the Lord' (Matt. xiii. 55; Mark vi. 3). His epistle was placed among the *Antilegomena*, or disputed books, by the primitive church. Many critics hold that it is directed against the Gnostics of the 2nd century.

JUDITH, a Jewish heroine, who, in the Apocryphal book named after her, is said to have made her way into the tent of Holofernes, general of Nebuchadnezzar, cut off his head, and so saved her native town of Bethulia.

JUDSON, Adoniram (1788–1850), American missionary, born in Malden, Mass., thought of turning playwright, but in 1812, having married, went to Burma as a Baptist missionary, and was a prisoner during the Burmese war. His Burmese translation of the Bible (1833) was followed by a Burmese-English dictionary. He died at sea. See Lives by Wayland (1853), E. Judson (his son) (1883), Mathieson (1929).

JUGURTHA (d. 104 B.C.), king of Numidia, by the murder of one cousin secured a part of the kingdom of his grandfather Masinissa, and bribed the Roman senate to support him (116 B.C.). But he soon invaded his surviving cousin Adherbal's part of the kingdom, in spite of Roman warnings, besieged him in Cirta (112), and put him and the Romans who were with him to death. Thereupon war was declared by the Romans; but, by bribery, Jugurtha contrived to baffle their power, until in 106 he had to flee to the king of Mauritania, whom Marius compelled to deliver him up. He was left to die in prison at Rome. See Sallust's history of the Jugurthine war, ed. Coleridge (1894).

JUIN, Alphonse Pierre, *zhwï* (1888–1967), French general, born at Bône, Algeria, passed out top of his class, which included de Gaulle, at the St Cyr Military Academy, fought in the Moroccan campaigns (1912–14) and World War I, and in 1938 became chief of staff in North Africa. As divisional commander in the First French Army he fought and was captured by the Germans in 1940, but was released in June 1941. Became military governor of Morocco, having declined the post of Vichy minister of war. After the Allied invasion of Tunisia, he changed sides, helped to defeat von Arnim's Afrika Corps remnants and distinguished himself in the subsequent Italian campaign. He became chief of staff of the National Defence Committee in Liberated France (1944–47), was resident-general in Morocco (1947–51) and served in senior N.A.T.O. commands (1953–56). He was made an honorary G.C.B. (1944), awarded the *Grand Croix de la Légion d'honneur*, promoted field-marshal (1952) and elected French Academician (1953). Publications include *Mémoires* (1959–60), and *La France en Algérie* (1963).

JUKES, Joseph Beete (1811–69), British geologist, born near Birmingham, in 1839 became geological surveyor of Newfoundland, and in 1842 helped to explore the coasts of Australia. He next surveyed part of North Wales for the Geological Survey (1846–50),

and in 1850 became local director of the survey in Ireland. He lectured on geology in Dublin. His chief works are *Excursions in and about Newfoundland* (1842), *Surveying Voyage of H.M.S. 'Fly', in Torres Strait, &c.* (1847), and *Student's Manual of Geology* (1858), &c. See his *Letters* (1871).

JULIA (39 B.C.–A.D. 14), daughter of the Emperor Augustus, was married at fourteen to her cousin Marcellus, a nephew of Augustus, and after his death in 23 B.C. to Marcus Vipsanius Agrippa, to whom she bore three sons and two daughters. He died in 12 B.C., whereupon Julia was married to Tiberius. The marriage was unhappy and her conduct far from irreproachable; but it was chiefly the jealous hatred of Livia, Tiberius's mother, that procured Julia's banishment first to the isle of Pandataria, and then to Reggio, where she died voluntarily of starvation. See novel by R. Graves, *I, Claudius*.

JULIAN (Flavius Claudius Julianus), 'the Apostate' (*c.* 331–63), Roman emperor (361–63), born at Constantinople, was the youngest son of Constantius, half-brother of Constantine the Great. On Constantine's death in 337, and the accession of his three sons, there was a general massacre of the males of the younger line of the Flavian family. Julian and his elder half-brother Gallus were alone spared as too young to be dangerous, when their father, brother, uncle and cousins perished. His youth was embittered by this tragedy, which stripped him of all belief in the Christian religion now established. In 355 he spent a few happy months at Athens in the study of Greek philosophy, and the same year was summoned to Milan to assume the rank of Caesar, and marry the emperor's sister, Helena. The next five years he served as soldier, overthrowing the Alemanni neas Strasbourg, and subduing the Frankish triber along the Rhine. He endeared himself to the soldiers by his personal courage, his success in war, and the severe simplicity of his life. In April 360 the emperor, alarmed at his growing popularity, demanded that he should send some of his best troops to serve against the Persians, but his soldiers rose in insurrection and proclaimed him Augustus. Next, he set out with his army for Constantinople. At Sirmium on the Danube he openly declared himself a pagan. There he learnt of the opportune death of his cousin (361), which opened up to him the government of the world. The first winter he spent at Constantinople in a course of public reforms. Towards Christians and Jews he adopted a policy of toleration, but none the less he devoted himself to restoring the dignity of the old religion. He stripped the church of its privileges by every means short of persecution. He spent 362–363 at Antioch, and made himself somewhat unpopular by fixing an arbitrary price on corn in order to stave off a threatened famine. In 363 he set out against the Persians. He crossed the Tigris, advanced to Ctesiphon, was enticed farther by a Persian traitor, and was at length forced to retreat through barren country, harassed by swarms of Persian cavalry. The enemy were repeatedly beaten off, but in one of the

JULIANA

721 JUNGE

attacks the emperor was mortally wounded by a spearthrust. Julian's extant writings are a series of *Epistles*; nine *Orations*; *Caesares*, satires on past Caesars; and the *Misopōgōn*. His chief work, *Kata Christianōn* is lost. See Life by J. Bidez (1930).

JULIANA, Louise Emma Marie Wilhelmina (1909–), queen of the Netherlands (1948–), born at The Hague and educated at Leyden University. In 1930 she passed her final examination in international law. She married in 1937 Prince Bernhard zur Lippe-Biesterfeld (q.v.), and they have four daughters: Princess Beatrix Wilhelmina Armgard (b. 1938), heiress to the throne, married West German diplomat Claus-Georg Wilhelm Otto Friedrich Gerd von Amsberg (b. 1926) in 1966; their son (b. 1967) is the first male Dutch heir in over a century; Princess Irene Emma Elizabeth (b. 1939), married Prince Hugo of Bourbon-Parma (b. 1939), son of the Carlist pretender to the Spanish throne, Prince Xavier, in 1964 (against her parents' wishes, and forfeiting her right of succession); Princess Margriet Francisca (b. 1943), married a commoner, Pieter van Vollenhoven, in 1967; and Princess Maria Christina (b. 1947). On the German invasion of Holland in 1940 Juliana escaped to Britain and later resided in Canada. She returned to Holland in 1945, and in 1948, on the abdication of her mother Queen Wilhelmina, became queen.

JULIUS, the name of three popes, of whom the following are noteworthy:

Julius II (1443–1513), pope from 1503, born Giuliano della Rovere at Albizuola, forced, after his election, Cesare Borgia to yield his conquests in Romagna. Julius's public career was mainly devoted to political and military enterprises for the re-establishment of papal sovereignty in its ancient territory, and for the extinction of foreign domination in Italy. To compel Venice to restore the papal provinces on the Adriatic, Julius entered into the league of Cambrai with the Emperor Maximilian, Ferdinand of Aragon and Louis XII of France, and placed the republic under the ban of the church. On the submission of Venice, suspecting the designs of Louis, he entered into a ' Holy League ' with Spain and England. Louis XII ineffectually attempted to enlist the church against the pope. The Council of Pisa, convened under Louis's influence, was a failure; and the fifth Lateran Council, assembled by Julius, completely frustrated the designs of the French king. A Liberal patron of the arts, he employed Bramante for the design of St Peter's begun in 1506, had Raphael brought to Rome to decorate his private apartments and commissioned Michelangelo for the frescoes on the roof of the Sistine chapel and for his own tomb. His military exploits inspired Erasmus' satire *Julius Excluus*.

Julius III (1487–1555), pope from 1550, born Gianmaria del Monte in Rome, was one of the three delegates to the Council of Trent, which he reopened after his election. He sent Cardinal Pole to organize with Mary Tudor the reunion of England with the Church of Rome.

JULLIEN, Louis Antoine, *zhü-lyī* (1812–60), French musician, born in the Basses Alpes, became conductor of concerts at Paris in 1836, but in 1838 made London his headquarters, and did much to popularize music concerts. Bankrupt in 1857, he retired to Paris, was imprisoned for debt, and died in a lunatic asylum. See Life by Carse (1951).

JUMIÈGES. See ROBERT and WILLIAM OF.

JUNG, yoong, Carl Gustav (1875–1961), Swiss psychiatrist, studied medicine at Basel, worked under Eugen Bleuler at the Burghölzli mental clinic at Zürich (1900–09). His early *Studies in Word Association* (1904–09; in them he coined the term ' complex ') and *The Psychology of Dementia Praecox* (1906–07) led to his meeting Freud in Vienna in 1907. He became Freud's leading collaborator and was elected President of the International Psychoanalytical Association (1910–14). His independent researches, making him increasingly critical of Freud's exclusively sexual definition of libido and incest, and published in *The Psychology of the Unconscious* (1911–12), caused a break in 1913. From then onwards he steadily developed his own theories ('analytical psychology') foremost among which are: a description of psychological types (' extraversion/introversion ', 1921); a theory of psychic energy (1928), emphasizing a final point of view as against a purely causal one; a dynamic concept of the symbol as ' transformer of energy ' (1928); the discovery and exploration of the ' collective unconscious ' with its ' archetypes ', an impersonal substratum underlying the ' personal unconscious '; the concept of the psyche as a ' self-regulating system ' expressing itself in the process of ' individuation '. To this latter process Jung devoted most of his later work, constantly enlarging the scope of his researches to include dreams and drawings of patients, the symbolism of religions, myths, historical antecedents as e.g. alchemy, and even modern physics (' synchronicity '). Jung's work has proved of great importance not only for psychology but also for anthropology, religion, art and literature, history, etc. Jung held professorships at Zürich and Basel, receiving many honorary degrees. Other main works: *On Psychic Energy* (1928), *Psychology and Religion* (1937), *Psychology and Alchemy* (1944), *Aion* (1951), *The Undiscovered Self* (1957). See *Collected Works* (19 vols., 1953ff.); also Jung, *Memories, Dreams, Reflections*, recorded and ed. by A Jaffé; F.lFordham, *An Introduction to Jung's Psychology* (1953), J. Jacobi, *The Psychology of C. G. Jung* (1962), G. Adler, *Studies in Analytical Psychology* (1966).

(2) **Johann Heinrich,** known as ' Jung Stilling ' (1740–1817), German mystic and writer. Though qualified in medicine, he became Professor of Political Economy at Marburg (1787–1804), then at Heidelberg, and wrote semi-mystical, semipietistic romances and works on political economy, as well as a charming autobiography including *Heinrich Stillings Jugend*, ed. Goethe (1777–1804).

JUNG BAHADUR, Sir (1816–77), prime-minister of Nepal, assisted the British with a body of Gurkhas during the Indian Mutiny.

JUNGE, yoong'ė, also **Jung** or **Jungius, Joachim** (1587–1657), German scientist, born at Lübeck, studied at Rostock and Giessen, where he became professor of Mathematics, a position he resigned in 1614 to study medicine at Padua. He returned to Rostock and founded the Societas Ereunetica in 1622, but accused of heresy, he passed the rest of his life in the minor post of rector of the Hamburg High School. An early champion of the atomic theory, he anticipated the botanical classification of Ray and Linnaeus.

JUNIUS, Franciscus (1589–1677), German-born philologist, born at Heidelberg, and brought up in Holland by his brother-in-law Vossius, from 1621 to 1651 lived in England in the Earl of Arundel's family, returned in 1674, and died near Windsor. He studied Anglo-Saxon and Gothic, and wrote also on ancient art.

JUNKER, Wilhelm, *yoong'kèr* (1840–92), German traveller, was born of German parents in Moscow, and studied medicine in Germany. In 1876–78 he travelled amongst the western tributaries of the Upper Nile; in 1879 he set off to explore the Welle. After four years among the Monbuttu and Niam-Niam, and some time with Emin Pasha, he returned in 1887. See his *Travels* (1889; trans. 1890).

JUNKERS, Hugo, *yoong'kèrs* (1859–1935), German aircraft engineer, born at Rheydt, was professor of Mechanical Engineering at Aachen (1897–1912). After the 1914–18 war he founded aircraft factories at Dessau, Magdeburg and Stassfurt, which produced many famous planes, both civil and military.

JUNOT, Andoche, *zhü-nō* (1771–1813), French general, born at Bussy-le-Grand, distinguished himself in the early wars of the republic. He was adjutant under Napoleon in Egypt. In 1806 he was made governor of Paris, and in 1807 was appointed to the command of the army for Portugal. He quickly made himself master of all the strong places in the kingdom, was created Duc d'Abrantès, and appointed governor of Portugal; but, defeated by Wellington at Vimeiro, was obliged to conclude the Convention of Cintra and retire from Portugal. He served in Germany and Russia, and, made one of the scapegoats for the Russian disaster, was sent to govern Illyria. Mentally deranged, he threw himself from a window of his father's house near Dijon and died a week later. His wife, the extravagant Duchesse d'Abrantès (1784–1838), gained a reputation by her *Mémoires* (1831–1835).

JUNQUEIRO, Abilio Guerra, *zhoong-kay'-ee-roo* (1850–1923), Portuguese lyric poet and satirist, born at Freixo, became a deputy in 1872, opposed the Braganzas and was tried for *lèse majesté* in 1907. After the revolution he was minister to Switzerland. His poetry shows the influence of Victor Hugo.

JUSSERAND, Jean Adrien Antoine Jules, *zhüs-rā* (1855–1932), French writer and diplomat, born at Lyons, served in the French embassy in London in 1887–90, and in 1902–25 was ambassador to the United States. He wrote (in French and in English) on English wayfaring life, on the literary history of the English people (new ed. 1926), on Shakespeare in France, &c.

JUSSIEU, *zhü-syœ*, name of a family of French botanists:

(1) **Antoine Laurent de** (1748–1836), nephew of (2), studied at Paris and became professor at the Jardin des Plantes. He elaborated in his *Genera Plantarum* (1778–89) his uncle's system of classification. His son **Adrien** (1797–1853) wrote a botanical textbook and memoirs.

(2) **Bernard** (*c.* 1699–1777), uncle of (1), demonstrated at the Jardin des Plantes (1722), created a botanical garden at Trianon for Louis XV and adopted a system which has become the basis of modern natural botanical classification. He first suggested that polyps were animals. His brother **Antoine** (1686–1758), a physician and professor at the Jardin des Plantes, edited Tournefort's *Institutiones Rei Herbariae* (1719).

JUSTIN, St, surnamed the **Martyr** (*c.* 100–*c.* 165), one of the Fathers of the Church, was born at Sichem in Samaria, and was successively a Stoic and a Platonist; and after his conversion to Christianity travelled about on foot defending its truths. At Rome between 150 and 160 he wrote the *Apologia* of Christianity addressed to the Emperor, followed by a second one. He is said to have been martyred about A.D. 165. There is an edition by Otto of his works, including numerous treatises falsely attributed to him (1876–81). There are two English translations. See works by Semisch (1842), Aubé (1874), Stählin (1880), Freppel (1885), Huth (1894), Veil (1895), Goodenough (1923) and A. Lukyn Williams (1930).

JUSTIN, name of two rulers of the Eastern Roman empire:

Justin I (450–527), born in Illyria, became commander in the imperial bodyguard, and in 518 was raised to the Byzantine throne by the army. Owing to his total want of learning he wisely resigned the civil administration to the quaestor Proclus. In 519 he entered into an arrangement with the pope; in 523 resigned to Theodoric, king of Italy, the right of appointing ' consuls ' in Rome; and in the same year became involved in a war with the Persians. He was succeeded by his nephew Justinian.

Justin II (d. 578), succeeded his uncle, Justinian I, in 565, and married and was ruled by Sophia, the unscrupulous niece of the Empress Theodora. He yielded part of Italy to the Lombards, was unsuccessful against the Persians and Avars, and became insane. See study by Vasiliev (1950).

JUSTINIAN, name of two rulers of the Eastern Roman empire:

Justinian I (Flavius Anicius Justinianus) (*c.* 482–565), emperor from 527, nephew of Justin I, was born at Tauresium in Illyria, the son of a Slavonic peasant, and was originally called Sabbatius. Through his uncle he was educated at Constantinople, in 521 was named consul, and in 527 was proclaimed by Justin his colleague in the empire. Justin died the same year, and Justinian, proclaimed sole emperor, was crowned along with his wife Theodora, once an actress. His reign is the most brilliant in the history of the late empire. He had the good fortune or the skill to select the ablest generals; and under Narses (q.v.) and Belisarius (q.v.) his reign may be said to have restored the Roman empire to its ancient limits, and to have reunited the East and West. His first war—that with Persia—ended in a favourable treaty. But the conflict of the Blue and Green factions in 532 was an outburst of political discontent, which went so far as to elect a rival emperor. Justinian had thought of flight, when Narses, Belisarius and Theodora repressed the tumults relentlessly; 35,000 victims fell in a single day. Through Belisarius's generalship, the Vandal kingdom of Africa was reannexed to the empire; and Belisarius and Narses restored the imperial authority in Rome, Northern Italy and Spain. Justinian constructed or renewed a vast line of fortifications along the eastern and south-eastern frontier of his empire, which, with his great public buildings, involved a burdensome expenditure. It was as legislator that Justinian gained his most enduring renown. He set himself to collect and codify the principal imperial *constitutiones* or statutes in force at his accession. The *Codex*, by which all previous imperial enactments were repealed, was published in 529. The writings of the jurists or commentators were next harmonized, and published under the title *Digesta* or *Pandectae* in 533. The direction of this work was entrusted to Tribonian, with a committee of professors and advocates, who also prepared a systematic and elementary treatise on the law—the *Institutiones* (533), based on the *Institutiones* of Gaius. A new edition of the *Codex* was issued in 534. During the subsequent years of his reign Justinian promulgated from time to time several new laws or constitutions, known as *Novellae*. The Institutes, Digest, Code and Novels together make up what is known as the *Corpus Juris Civilis*. An able ruler, Justinian died November 14, 565. See Lives by Isambert (1856), Body (6th ed. 1889); Roby, *Introduction to the Digest* (1884); Diehl, *Justinien et la Civilisation Byzantine*

(1901); Holmes, *The Age of Justinian* (1905–07), and Ure (Penguin).

JUVENAL, Decimus Junius Juvenalis (*c*. 55–*c*. 140), Roman lawyer and satirist, born at Aquinum in the Volscian country, received the usual rhetorical education, and served as tribune in the army, fulfilled some local functions at Aquinum, was in Britain, and returned home in safety. He was also for a time in Egypt. His 16 brilliant satires in verse of Roman times (*c*. 100–*c*. 128) and vices, written from his viewpoint of an angry Stoic moralist, range from exposures of unnatural vices, the misery of poverty, the extravagance of the ruling classes and the precarious makeshift life of their hangers-on, to his hatred of Jews and women. The last was the subject of his sixth satire, of which a part was not discovered until 1899. Dryden's versions of five of Juvenal's satires are amongst the best things he ever did. Johnson imitated two of the most famous in his *London* and *Vanity of Human Wishes*. See edition by A. E. Housman (1931), and H. E. Butler, *Post-Augustan Poetry* (1909), and study by Highet (1954).

JUXON, William (1582–1663), English divine, born at Chichester, was educated at Merchant Taylors' School and St John's College, Oxford, succeeded Laud as its president in 1621, and became a prebendary of Chichester and dean of Worcester (1627), Bishop of London (1633), and lord high treasurer (1635). In Charles I's vacillation about the fate of Strafford, Juxon advised him to refuse his assent to the bill. He ministered to the king in his last moments and the king gave him his insignia of the Order of the Garter with the word ' Remember ' before putting his head on the execution block. During the Commonwealth Juxon retired to his Gloucestershire seat, and after the Restoration was appointed Archbishop of Canterbury. See Life by W. H. Marah (1869).

K

KADAR, Janos, *kah'dahr* (1912–), Hungarian politician, was born at Kapoly in S.W. Hungary, began life as an instrument-maker and was early attracted to the Communist party. During the second World War he was a member of the Central Committee of the underground party, escaping from capture by the Gestapo. He emerged after the war as first party secretary and one of the leading figures of the Communist régime. In 1950, as minister of the interior, he was arrested for ' Titoist ' sympathies. He was freed in 1953, was rehabilitated in 1954 and became secretary of the Party Committee for Budapest in 1955. When the Hungarian anti-Soviet revolution broke out in October 1956 he was a member of the ' national ', anti-Stalinist government of Imre Nagy. On November 1 he declared that the Communist party had been dissolved as it had

' degenerated into perpetuating despotism and national slavery '. But as Soviet tanks crushed the revolution, he formed a puppet government which in the closing months of 1956 held Hungary in a ruthless reign of terror. The majority of his countrymen regarded him as betrayer, but a few as a helpless victim of forces beyond his control. He resigned in 1958, but became premier and first secretary of the central committee in 1961. In 1965 he lost the premiership, but remained first secretary. See Fryer, *Hungarian Tragedy* (1956).

KAFKA, Franz (1883–1924), Austrian novelist, born of Jewish parentage in Prague, where he graduated in Law, and although overwhelmed by a desire to write, found employment (1907–23) as an official in the accident prevention department of the government-sponsored Worker's Accident Insurance

Institution. A hypersensitive, almost exclusively introspective person with an extraordinary attachment for his father, he eventually moved to Berlin to live with Dora Dymant in 1923, his only brief spell of happiness before succumbing to a lung disease of long standing. His short stories and essays, including *Der Heizer* ' The Boilerman ' (1913) *Betrachtungen* ' Meditations ' (1913), *Die Verwandlung* ' The Metamorphosis ' (1916), &c., were published in his lifetime, but he refused the same for his three unfinished novels, which, through his friend Max Brod (q.v.), were published posthumously and translated by Edwin and Willa Muir. They are *Ein Prozess* (1925) ' The Trial ' (1937), *Das Schloss* (1926) ' The Castle ' (1937) and *Amerika* (1927; trans. 1938). Literary critics have interpreted the second variously, as a modern *Pilgrim's Progress* (but there is literally no progress), as a literary exercise in Kierkegaardian existentialist theology, as an allegory of the Jew in a Gentile world, or psychoanalytically as a monstrous expression of Kafka's Oedipus complex, but his solipsism primarily portrays society as a pointless schizophrenically rational organization into which the bewildered but unshocked individual has strayed. Kafka has exerted a tremendous influence on Western literature, not least on such writers as Albert Camus, Rex Warner and Samuel Beckett. See *Collected Works* (1935-37) and *Diaries, 1914-1923* (1949), both edited by M. Brod, who has written a definitive life (trans. 1947), also *Letters*, ed. W. Haas (trans. 1953), *Conversations*, by G. Janouch (trans. 1953), and studies by A. Camus (1942), Magny and Flores (N.Y. 1946), C. Neider (1949), E. Heller, *The Disinherited Mind* (1952), and R. Gray (1956).

KAGANOVICH, Lazar Moiseyevich, -nŏ'- (1893-), Russian politician, was born at Gomel, joined the Communist party in 1911 and after the Revolution became secretary of the Ukrainian central committee. In 1928 he became Moscow party secretary. From 1934 to 1942 and from 1943 to 1944 he was commissar for railways. In 1947 he became deputy chairman of the Council of Ministers. He survived the death of his brother-in-law, Stalin, in 1953, but he was dismissed in 1957. He was last heard of in August 1957, in ' a position of considerable responsibility '—a Siberian cement works.

KAGAWA, Toyohiko (1888-1960), Japanese missionary and writer, studied at Princeton University, then returned to Japan, where his work in the fields of social reform and evangelism made him one of the great figures of modern Christianity. See studies by W. Axling (1947), E. O. Bradshaw (Minnesota 1952) and C. J. Davey (1960).

KAISER, kī'zėr, (1) **Georg** (1878-1945), German dramatist, born at Magdeburg, lived at Buenos Aires and in Germany, and wrote plays, mostly expressionist. See study by M. J. Fruchter (Philadelphia 1933).

(2) **Henry John** (1882-1967), American industrialist, born in New York State. From 1914 to 1933 he worked on various civil engineering projects in the United States, Canada and the West Indies. As manager of seven highly productive shipyards on the Pacific coast of the United States during World War II, he developed revolutionary methods of prefabrication and assembly in shipbuilding—enabling his ships to be constructed and launched within six days. His vast industrial empire included a motor, a steel, and an aluminium and chemical corporation.

KÁLIDÁSA (fl. A.D. 450), India's greatest dramatist, is best known through his drama *Sákuntala*. See studies by B. S. Upadhyaya (India 1947) and G. C. Jhala (1949).

KALININ, Mikhail Ivanovich, kah-lee'-nin (1875-1946), Russian politician, born at Tver (which was renamed after him in 1932), was in early life a peasant and a metal-worker. Entering politics as a champion of the peasant class, he won great popularity, becoming president of the Soviet central executive committee (1919-38), and of the Presidium of the Supreme Soviet (1938-46). He died in Moscow.

KÁLNOKY VON KÖRÖSPATAK, Gustav Sigismund, Count (1832-98), Austrian statesman, born at Lettowitz in Moravia, entered the diplomatic service in 1850. He was sent as ambassador to Copenhagen in 1870, to St Petersburg in 1880, and in 1881 became minister of foreign affairs. He resigned in 1895.

KALTENBRUNNER, Ernst (1902-46), Austrian Nazi leader, head of the S.S. at the time of the Anschluss, became head of the security police in 1943, sent millions of Jews and political suspects to their death in concentration camps, and was responsible for orders sanctioning the murder of prisoners of war and baled-out airmen. He was condemned by the Nuremberg Tribunal and hanged.

KAMENEV, orig. Rosenfeld, Lev Borisovich (1883-1936), Russian politician, born of Jewish parentage in Moscow, was an active revolutionary from 1901 and was exiled to Siberia in 1915. Liberated during the revolution in 1917, he became a member of the Communist central committee. Expelled as a Trotskyist in 1927, he was readmitted next year but again expelled in 1932. He was shot after being arrested with Zinoviev (q.v.) for conspiring against Stalin.

KAMERLINGH ONNES. See ONNES.

KAMES, Henry Home, Lord (1696-1782), Scottish philosopher, born at Kames in Berwickshire, was called to the bar in 1723 and raised to the bench as Lord Kames in 1752. Besides books on Scots law he published *Essays on Morality* (1751), *An Introduction to the Art of Thinking* (1761), *Elements of Criticism* (his best-known work, 1762), and *Sketches of the History of Man* (1774). See critical study by H. W. Randall (Northampton, Mass., 1944).

KÄMPFER, Engelbert, kemp'fėr (1651-1716), German traveller, after visiting India, Java and Siam, spent two years in Japan (1692-94). His *History of Japan and Siam* appeared in English in 1727 and in 1906.

KANARIS, Constantine, ka-nah'rees (1790-1877), a Greek merchant-captain, born in the Isle of Ipsara, who blew up the Turkish admiral's ship in the Strait of Chios (1822), repeated a like feat in the harbour of Tenedos, and in 1824 burnt a Turkish frigate and some transport ships. He was appointed to important commands, was made senator in 1847, and was repeatedly at the head of ministries. He died at Athens.

KANDINSKY, Vasily (1866–1944), Russian painter, was born in Moscow. He spent his childhood in Italy, and his early work was done in Paris. After a stay (1914–21) in Russia, where he founded the Russian Academy and became head of the Museum of Modern Art, he spent a few years in charge of the Weimar Bauhaus. From 1923 on he lived in Paris. An individual painter, who developed his own abstract theories, he exercised great influence on young European artists and was a leader of the ' Blaue Reiter ' group. Studies by W. Grohmann (1959) and H. Rebay von Chrenwiesen (N.Y. 1945).

KANE, (1) Elisha Kent (1820–57), Arctic explorer, born in Philadephia. Entering the U.S. navy as surgeon, he visited China, the East Indies, Arabia, Egypt, Europe, the west coast of Africa and Mexico. In 1850 he sailed as surgeon and naturalist with the first Grinnell (q.v.) expedition. His account of it appeared in 1854. In 1853 he again set out as commander of an expedition (see his *Second Grinnell Expedition*, 1856). See Life by Elder (1858), the briefer one by Jones (1890), and J. Mirsky (Canada 1954).

(2) **Sir Robert** (1809–90), Irish chemist, born in Dublin, studied medicine, and became a professor of Chemistry there (1831), next year starting the *Dublin Journal of Medical Science*. In 1846 he originated the Museum of Industry in Ireland, was appointed its first director, and was knighted. He was president of Queen's College, Cork (1845–73), and in 1877 was elected president of the Royal Irish Academy. His chief books are *Elements of Chemistry* (1842) and *Industrial Resources of Ireland* (1844). Life by D. O'Raghallaigh (Cork 1942).

KANT, Immanuel, *kahnt* (1724–1804), German philosopher, the greatest of the idealist school, born April 22, in Königsberg, where he spent his entire life, the son of a saddler, reputedly of Scottish origin. Brought up in relative poverty and the puritanical strictness of Pietism, Kant studied at the university and after some years as private tutor in 1755 obtained his doctorate and was appointed *privatdozent*. His lectures, unlike his written works, were often witty, humorous and full of interesting red herrings. The same year he published an essay in Newtonian cosmology in which he anticipated the nebular theory of Laplace and predicted the existence of the planet Uranus, before its actual discovery by Herschel in 1781. At first a rationalist, he became more sceptical of metaphysics in his ' pre-critical ' works as in *Träume eines Geistersehers* (1766) ' Dreams of a Ghost-seer ' against Swedenborg's mysticism. But Kant was dissatisfied with Hume's reduction of knowledge of things and causation to mere habitual associations of sense-impressions. How for example was it possible for mathematics to apply to the objects of our sense-impressions? From 1775 he laboured on an answer to Hume, which materialized in his *Kritik der reinen Vernunft*

(1781; 2nd ed., in parts re-written, 1786) ' Critique of Pure Reason ' (2nd edn., including the sections omitted from the 1st, trans. N. Kemp Smith 1933), a philosophical classic, in which he shows that the immediate objects of perception are due not only to the evidence provided by our sensations but also to our own perceptual apparatus which orders our sense-impressions into intelligible unities. Whereas the former are rightly empirical and *synthetic*, the ordering is not dependent upon experience, i.e., *a priori*. Hence Kant's famous claim that ' though our knowledge begins with experience, it does not follow that it arises out of experience '. This has the corollary which Kant likened to a Copernican revolution in philosophy, that instead of presuming that all our knowledge must conform to objects, it is more profitable to suppose the reverse. Knowledge of objects as such, ' things in themselves ' (*noumena*), is impossible since we can only know our ordered sense-impressions (*phenomena*). Space and time are subjective particulars, *a priori* intuitions. All ordering of sense-impressions takes place in time, with the appropriate application of general concepts. Antinomies arise when general concepts (categories) are misapplied to non-experiential data or space and time are treated as if they were categories. Hence we cannot prove the existence of God, but Kant recognizes three principal ideas of reason, God, freedom and immortality, which pure reason leads us to form for practical, i.e., moral, considerations. These are developed in *Prolegomena* (1783, trans. P. G. Lucas 1953), *Grundlagen zur Metaphysik der Sitten* (1785) ' Groundwork to a Metaphysics of Morals ' (trans. H. J. Paton 1948), and *Kritik der praktischen Vernunft* (1788) ' Critique of Practical Reason '. The *Groundwork* contains his ethical theory based on the good will, enshrined in the famous Categorical Imperative: ' Act only on that maxim through which you can at the same time will that it should become a universal law.' This important if over-formal rendering of moral obligation was criticized by Jacobi as ' the good will that wills nothing '. *Kritik der Urteilskraft* (1790) ' Critique of Judgment ' (trans. J. H. Bernard 1892) completes the Kantian system. It comprises a remarkable treatment of the basic philosophical problems in aesthetics, not least the claim that the aesthetic judgment is independent of personal, psychological and moral considerations, yet singular and universally valid. Kant lived an extremely orderly life, possibly because of his delicate constitution, and many people are supposed to have set their watches by his daily walk. He was very friendly with two English businessmen, Green and Motherby, an admirer of Rousseau, the French Revolution but not the reign of terror, Liberal in his politics and theological lectures, which, interpreted as anti-Lutheran, he was asked by the Prussian government to cease giving. At the death of Frederick William II he considered himself absolved and published his lectures together with the acrimonious correspondence with the authorities. In *Zum ewigen Frieden* (1795) ' Perpetual Peace ' he advocated a world federation of free states. Kant's system is greater than any of the idealist schools to which it gave rise, although Fichte, Hegel, and Schopenhauer have been more widely influential. The philosophical questions he raised and his treatment of them will remain of permanent interest. See Life by E. Paulsen (trans. 1902), *Gesammelte Schriften*, Royal Prussian Academy (1902–38 ff.), of his critical philosophy, commentaries by A. C. Ewing (1938), T. D. Weldon (1945), S. Körner (Pelican, 1953), studies by E. Caird (1877), M. Heidegger (1929) N. Kemp Smith (1933), H. J. Paton (1935), A. H. Smith (1947), *Kantstudien* (1896–1936, 1942–44, 1953 ff.), of his theology, by A. Schweitzer (1899), science by G. Martin (trans. 1955), aesthetics, E. Cassirer (1938) and ethics, H. J. Paton (1947), A. E. Teale (1951).

KAPITZA, Peter, Russ. **Pëtr Leonidovich Kapitsa** (1894–), Russian physicist, born at Kronstadt, studied at Petrograd and under Rutherford at Cambridge, where he became assistant director of magnetic research at the Cavendish laboratory (1924–32). In 1934 he returned to Russia. He is known for his work on high-intensity magnetism, on low temperature, and on the liquefaction of hydrogen and helium.

KAPP, (1) **Friedrich** (1824–84), German politician, went to New York after the 1848 revolution, returned to Berlin in 1870, wrote a number of histories, including *Aus und über Amerika* (1876), and was a member of the Reichstag in 1871–78 and 1881–84.

(2) **Wolfgang** (1858–1922), son of (1), born in New York, in 1920 contrived a putsch against the Weimar republic in Berlin, which was baulked of success by a general strike. In 1922, on returning from Sweden, whence he had fled, he was arrested, but died while awaiting trial.

KAPTEYN, Jacobus Cornelius, *kap-tīn'* (1851–1922), Dutch astronomer, born at Barnevelt, professor at Groningen from 1878, plotted the stars of the southern hemisphere from the photographic survey of Sir David Gill (q.v.), and is celebrated for his discovery that all stars whose proper motion can be detected are part of one of two streams moving in different directions at different speeds. See Life by A. van Maenen (U.S. 1925).

KARADJORDJE. See CZERNY, GEORGE.

KARADŽIĆ, Vuk Stefanović, *ka'ra-jich* (1787–1864), Serbian poet and philologist, born at Tršić, published collections of national songs and tales, and evolved the simplified Cyrillic alphabet in order to produce literature in the vernacular. He translated the New Testament into Serbian.

KARAMZIN, Nikolai Mikhailovich, *ka-ram-zyeen'* (1766–1826), Russian historian and novelist, born at Mikhailovka in Orenburg. Among his writings are *Letters of a Russian Traveller* (1790–92), an account of his travels in Western Europe, several novels, including *Poor Lisa* (1792) and *Natalia, The Boyar's Daughter* (1792), and a great unfinished *History of Russia* (1816–29) down to 1613. His influence on the literature of Russia and its development was considerable. He modernized the literary language by his

introduction of western idioms and his writing as a whole reflected western thought. See D.ĵS. Mirsky, *History of Russian Literature* (1927).

KARL. See CHARLES.

KARLFELDT, Erik Axel, *karl'felt* (1864–1931), Swedish poet, born in Folkärna, in the historic province of Dalarna. His poetry is highly individual, mainly reflecting, in a language and style which is often deliberately archaic, the traditional life and customs of his native province. He declined the Nobel prize for literature in 1918, and was awarded it posthumously in 1931.

KARP, David (1922–), American author, born in New York of Russian-Jewish descent, served in U.S. army, worked as journalist, as radio, TV and paperback writer, and emerged as a serious novelist with *One* (1953), an Orwellian condemnation of totalitarianism. Other works include *The Day of the Monkey* (1955), on British colonialism, *All Honourable Men* (1956) and *The Sleepwalkers* (1960).

KARR, (Jean Baptiste) Alphonse (1808–90), French writer, born in Paris. His *Sous les tilleuls* (1832) by its originality and wit found its author an audience for a long series of novels, of which *Geneviève* (1838) only need be mentioned. In 1839 he became editor of *Figaro*, and started the issue of the bitterly satirical *Les Guêpes*. His *Voyage autour de mon jardin* (1845) is his best-known book. See his reminiscences, *Livre de bord* (4 vols. 1879–80).—His daughter, **Thérèse** (1835–87) published tales and historical books.

KARRER, Paul (1889–), Swiss chemist, born in Moscow, was educated at Zürich, where he became professor of Organic Chemistry (1919). He was the first to isolate vitamins A and K, and he produced synthetically vitamins B_2 and E. He shared the Nobel chemistry prize with Haworth in 1937.

KASTLER, Alfred (1902–), French scientist, of the Ecole Normale Supérieure in Paris, was awarded the Nobel prize for Physics in 1966 for his work on the development of lasers.

KÄSTNER, Erich (1899–), German writer, born in Dresden, is best known for his books for children. His writing career, however, began with two volumes of verse, *Herz auf Taille* (1928) and *Lärm im Spiegel* (1929), both cleverly satirical. His novels include *Fabian* (1931, trans. 1932), and *Three Men in the Snow* (1934, trans. 1935). His delightful children's books, which include *Emil and the Detectives* (1928), *Annaluise and Anton* (1929), and *The Flying Classroom* (1933), gained him worldwide fame. Among his later writings is the autobiographical *When I was a Little Boy* (1957, trans. 1959).

KATE, Jan Jacob Lodewijk ten, *ka'tĕ* (1819–1889), Dutch poet, celebrated for his parodies, born at The Hague, and died at Amsterdam.

KATER, Henry (1777–1835), English physicist of German descent, inventor of Kater's pendulum, became F.R.S. in 1815, and in 1817 won the Copley medal for his work on measuring instruments, which he brought to high standards of accuracy.

KATHARINE. See CATHARINE.

KATKOV, Mikhail Nikiforovich (1818–87), Russian journalist, was professor of Philosophy at Moscow, and after 1861 editor of the *Moscow Gazette*, was at first an advocate of reform, but was converted by the Polish rising of 1863 into a Panslavist leader and a supporter of reactionary government.

KAUFFMANN, Angelica, kowf'-man (1741–1807), Swiss painter, born at Chur in the Grisons, at eleven was painting portraits of notabilities in Italy, and in 1766 was persuaded to go to London. There she soon became famous as a painter of classic and mythological pictures, and as a portrait-painter, and was nominated one of the first batch of Royal Academicians (1769). After an unhappy marriage (*c.* 1767) with an adventurer, the 'Count de Horn', in 1781 she married the Venetian painter, Antonio Zucchi (q.v.), and returned to Italy. Her rather pretty paintings are well known from engravings by Bartolozzi. Her story furnishd the theme for Lady Ritchie's *Miss Angel* (1875). See Lives by Gerard (1892), Manners and Williamson (1924) and Hartcup (1954).

KAUFMAN, George Simon (1889–1961), American playwright, born in Pittsburgh. In collaboration with Moss Hart wrote *You Can't Take it with You* (Pulitzer prize 1936) and *The Man Who Came to Dinner* (1939). Other works include *The Solid Gold Cadillac* (with Howard Teichmann, 1953) and many musicals, some of which have been filmed.

KAUFMANN, Constantine Petrovich von (1818–82), Russian general, distinguished himself at Kars (1855) and in 1867 became governor of Turkestan. In 1868 he occupied Samarkand, and in 1873 conducted the campaign against Khiva. Died at Tashkent. See Boulger's *Central Asian Portraits* (1880).

KAULBACH, Wilhelm von, kowl'bakh (1805–1874), German painter, born at Arolsen, from 1849 director of the Munich Academy of Painting, painted grandiose historical subjects. See Life by H. Müller (Berlin 1892). His son Hermann (1846–1909), nephew Friedrich (1822–1903), and the latter's son Friedrich August (1850–1920) were also painters.

KAUNDA, Kenneth David, kah-oon'da (1924–), Zambian politician, born at Lubwa, became a teacher, founded the Zambian African National Congress (1958), subsequently was imprisoned and the movement banned. In 1960 elected president of the United National Independent Party, he played a leading part in his country's independence negotiations, and became premier in January 1964, the country obtaining independence in October that year. See his *Zambia Shall Be Free* (1962), *A Humanist in Africa* (1966).

KAUNITZ - RIETBERG, Wenzel Anton, Prince von, kow'nits (1711–94), Austrian statesman, distinguished himself in 1748 at the congress of Aix-la-Chapelle, and as Austrian ambassador at the French court in 1750–52 converted old enmity into friendship. In 1753 he was appointed chancellor, and for almost 40 years directed Austrian politics. Active in the ecclesiastical reforms of Joseph II, he was a liberal patron of arts and sciences. See Life by Beer (1872), and G. Küntzel, *Fürst Kaunitz-Rietberg als Staatsmann* (1923).

KAUTSKY, Karl Johann, kowt'ski (1854–1938), German Socialist leader, born at Prague, founded (1883) and edited *Die Neue Zeit*. A disciple of Marx, he wrote against Bolshevism (trans. 1918, 1931), against William II, on Sir Thomas More, &c. See Lenin's *The Proletarian Revolution and Kautsky the Renegade* (trans. 1920).

KAVANAGH, Arthur Macmorrough, kav'a-nah (1831–89), of Borris House, Co. Carlow, an Irish Conservative M.P. from 1866 to 1880, who, though all but armless and legless, rode, shot, yachted, painted, and in 1849–51 travelled overland to India.

KAY, (1) John. See ARKWRIGHT.

(2) **John** (1742–1826), born near Dalkeith, prosperous Edinburgh barber until (1785) he opened a print shop for caricatures of local celebrities etched by himself. They have little merit beyond humour and likeness. His *Original Portraits, with Biographical Sketches* is an invaluable record of Edinburgh social life.

KAY-SHUTTLEWORTH, Sir James Phillips, D.C.L. (1804–77), English educationist, born at Rochdale, studied and practised medicine. As secretary to the Committee of the Privy Council on Education he was instrumental in establishing a system of government school inspection. The pupil teacher system originated with him and he founded his own training college which later became St John's College, Battersea. On his retirement in 1849 he was created a baronet. In 1842 he married the heiress of the Shuttleworths of Gawthorpe, and assumed her surname.

KAYE, (1) Danny, professional name of **Daniel Kominski** (1913–), American stage, radio and film actor, born in New York. He intended to be a doctor, but soon began a stage career. In 1943 he made his first film, *Up in Arms*, following it with *Wonder Man* (1944), which made his reputation as a film comedian, together with international success in *The Secret Life of Walter Mitty* (1946). Other films include *The Inspector General* (1950), *Hans Christian Andersen* (1952) and *Knock on Wood* (1954). He does a great deal of work for UNICEF.

(2) **Sir John William** (1814–76), historian, served from 1832 in the Bengal Artillery, but in 1841 devoted himself to literature. A secretary from 1858 in the India Office, he wrote books on Indian history, and *Essays of an Optimist* (1870).

KAYE-SMITH, Sheila (1887–1956), born at St Leonards, wrote novels mainly of fate and Sussex soil. In 1924 she married T. P. Fry, a clergyman and heir to a baronetcy, and in 1929 became a Roman Catholic. Her writings include *Sussex Gorse* (1916), *Tamarisk Town* (1919), *Joanna Godden* (1921), *The End of the House of Alard* (1923).

KAZAN, Elia (1909–), American stage and film director, born in Constantinople, studied at Williams College and Yale. He acted in minor rôles on Broadway and in Hollywood before becoming director of plays and films influenced by 'The Method'. His Broadway productions include the works of Wilder, Miller, and Williams. Many of his films have a social or political theme, e.g., *Gentleman's Agreement* (Oscar winner, 1948), on anti-Semitism, *Pinky* (1949), on the colour problem, *Viva Zapata* (1952), *On the Waterfront* (Oscar winner, 1954), and *Face in the Crowd* (1957). The latter three deal with kinds of megalomania, the revolutionary figure without statecraft, the trades union boss turned gangster, and the TV demagogue. Other notable films include Williams' *Streetcar Named Desire* (1951) and *Baby Doll* (1956), Steinbeck's *East of Eden* (1954), Inge's *Splendour in the Grass* (1962), and *America, America* (1964), based on his autobiographical novel (1963).

KAZINCZY, Ferenc, *ko'zin-tsi* (1759–1831), Hungarian writer, born at Érsemlyén, was a leading figure in the Hungarian literary revival and a strong advocate of the reform of the language. He translated many European classics, wrote poetry, and there are 22 volumes of letters. Died of cholera.

KEAN, (1) Charles John (1809 or 1811–68), actor, born at Waterford, son of (2), educated at Eton, to support his mother and himself became an actor. He appeared at Drury Lane in 1827 as Young Norval, with ill success, but worked assiduously in the provinces until he attained a air position. In 1850 he became joint-lessee of the Princess's Theatre, and produced a long series of gorgeous ' revivals '. In 1859 he virtually retired, though he played in America and the provinces to within seven months of his death. In 1842 he married the actress, **Ellen Tree** (1805–80). See *Life* by J. W. Cole (1860), *Letters of Mr and Mrs Charles Kean* (Washington University, 1945).

(2) Edmund (*c.* 1789–1833), English actor, was born in London the son of Nance Carey (Henry Carey's granddaughter), hawker and stroller. A stage Cupid and a cabin-boy to Madeira, he himself about sixteen turned a stroller, and after ten years in the provinces, made his first appearance at Drury Lane as Shylock (January 26, 1814), and at once took rank as the first actor of the day. A period of wonderful success followed, but by his irregularities he gradually forfeited public approval, his reputation being finally ruined by the ' criminal conversation ' *cause célèbre* of Cox *v.* Kean (1825). He was cordially received in 1827 following a twelvemonth visit to America, but both mind and body gave way, and breaking down hopelessly in March, 1833, he died at Richmond on May 15th. See Lives by Barry Cornwall (1835), Hawkins (1869), Molloy (1888), Hillebrand (1933), G. Playfair (1939) and M. W. Disher (1950).

KEANE, Augustus Henry (1833–1912), ethnologist, born at Cork. He taught languages at Hameln and Southampton, and was Hindustani professor at University College, London, 1882–85.

KEATE, John (1773–1852), headmaster of Eton 1809–34, was born at Wells, and died at his Hampshire rectory of Hartley Westpall. A diminutive man, he was a stern disciplinarian and once flogged eighty boys together.

KEATS, John (1795–1821), English poet, was born in London, the son of a livery-stable keeper, and went to school at Enfield. In 1811 he was apprenticed to a surgeon at Edmonton and later (1815–17), he was a medical student in the London hospitals. Though he did creditably there his mind was set on the arts. His friends were painters, he appreciated ' divine ' Mozart, but above all, poetry claimed him. Leigh Hunt, his neighbour in Hampstead, introduced him to other young romantics, including Shelley, and published his first sonnets in his *Examiner* (1816). His first volume of poems (1817), is ' sicklied o'er ' with Hunt's sentimentality and the long mythological poem *Endymion* (1818) combines Hunt's influence with Elizabethan lusciousness in word and image. Nevertheless, it contains some felicitous descriptions and the ' Hymn to Pan ' and the ' Bacchic procession ' anticipate the great odes to come. Keats returned from a walking tour in Scotland (1818), which exhausted him, to find the savage reviews of *Endymion* in *Blackwood's Magazine* and the *Quarterly.* To add to his troubles his younger brother Tom was dying of consumption and his love affair with Fanny Brawne seems to have brought him more vexation than comfort. It was in these circumstances that he braced himself for the supreme effort which makes the volume of 1820, *Lamia and Other Poems*, a landmark in English poetry. Except for the romantic poem ' Isabella or The Pot of Basil ', a romance based on Boccaccio's *Decameron*, and the first version of his epical poem, ' Hyperion ', all the significant verse in this famous volume is the work of 1819, viz., the two splendid romances ' The Eve of St Agnes ' and ' Lamia ' and the great odes—' On a Grecian Urn ', ' To a Nightingale ', ' To Autumn ', ' On Melancholy ' and ' To Psyche '. Jeffrey, who had not joined in the denigration of *Endymion* praised the volume in the *Edinburgh Review* and Shelley, who had been somewhat critical of his earlier poetry, hailed ' Hyperion ' as a noble work. That this poem in its two versions is only a magnificent fragment is due partly to the allegory and partly to the Miltonic cast of the diction, which he had come to regard as inimical to his art. The romances and odes better suited his genius, which he now perceived was more Shakespearian or Elizabethan than Miltonic. The former, particularly ' The Eve of St Agnes ', display a wealth of sensuous imagery almost unequalled in English poetry. In ' Lamia ', the best told of the tales, he turns from stanza form to the couplet as used by Dryden in his romantic *Fables*. The odes are the perfect expression of his genius. Critics have toyed with the notion that had he lived he would have gone on to something truly dramatic and tragical as Shakespeare did after his decorative ' first fruits '. The ' Grecian Urn ' and ' Psyche ' are the full expression of the charm exercised on him by the Greek myths. ' Autumn ' may be hardly an ode, rather a seasonal vignette, but has any poet, Shakespeare apart, so invoked the sensuous beauty of the season? And to show the variety of his genius in different modes, the fragmentary ' Ode to Maia ', written in 1818, instinct with the feeling for the Greek, vies with ' La Belle Dame Sans Merci ' which is as pre-Raphaelite as ' The Eve of St Mark ' is in another way. Keats's letters are regarded in some quarters as equally important with his poems (see Lionel Trilling, *The Opposing Self*), and they certainly throw a valuable light on his poetical development no less than on his unhappy love affair with Fanny Brawne. It is clear that he was both attracted and repelled by the notion of the poet as teacher or prophet. Though profoundly aware of the suffering in life, he preferred to think of himself as of Shakespeare, that is as the 'chameleon poet' who enters with equal delight into all states, good and evil. He distrusted the utopianism of his liberal friends, but 'the burden of the mystery' oppressed him. Like Wordsworth and Coleridge he made imagination the supreme gift so that 'what the Imagination seizes as beauty must be truth'. In other words, 'Beauty is truth, truth beauty.' Valid or not for the philosopher, this was valid for Keats's poetry. Having prepared the 1820 volume for the press, Keats, now seriously ill with consumption, sailed for Italy in September 1820, reached Rome and died there attended only by his artist friend Severn. Shelley lamented him in *Adonais* and his grave in the Protestant cemetery is a place of pilgrimage to this day. Except for his sister Fanny, the family, his loyalty to which is witnessed in the letters, was extinct in England, his brother George, to whom some of the most important letters are addressed, having emigrated to America in 1818. Modern editions are by E. de Selincourt (1921), M. B. Forman (1931), Garrod (1956), and H. E. Rollins, 2 vols. (1959). See Lives by Houghton (1848), Colvin (1886, 1917), Amy Lowell (1925), Dorothy Hewlett (1937), Murchie (1955), Middleton Murry (4th ed. 1955), Bate (1964), Gittings (1968), and essays ed. by K. Muir (1959).

KEBLE, John (1792–1866), English churchman, was born at Fairford, Gloucestershire, near his father's living of Coln St Aldwins. At fifteen he was elected a scholar at Corpus, Oxford, and in 1810 took a double first. In 1811 he was elected a fellow of Oriel and in 1812 won the Latin and English prize essays. In 1815 he was ordained deacon, beginning active work as curate of East Leach, while still continuing to reside in Oxford, where he was college tutor 1818–23. In 1827 he published *The Christian Year*. His theory of poetry, explained in the *British Critic* in 1838, was worked out at length in his Latin lectures delivered as Oxford professor of Poetry (1831–41). Meanwhile Keble had gathered round him a small band of pupils of whom the most striking was Hurrell Froude, and in this circle originated the Tractarian movement. In his sermon on National Apostasy (1833) Keble gave the signal for action, and for the next eight years was engaged with Newman, Pusey, I. Williams and others in the issue of *Tracts for the Times*, brought to an end by Tract No. 90 in 1841. Keble had in 1835 married, and had removed to the Hampshire living of Hursley, where he remained until his death. With Dr Pusey he was the steadying influence which supported the party under the shock caused by Newman's secession to Rome. Other works are a Life of Bishop Wilson, an edition of Hooker, the *Lyra Innocentium* (1846), a poetical translation of the Psalter, *Letters of Spiritual Counsel*, twelve volumes of parochial sermons, *Studia Sacra*, &c. Keble College, Oxford, was erected as a memorial of him (1870). See *Memoir* by Sir J. Coleridge (1869), J. C. Shairp's *Essay* and *Studies* (1872),

a collection of memorials by J. F. Moor (1866), Lives by Locke (1893), Wood (1909), and study by Battiscombe (1963).

KEELER, James Edward (1857–1900), American astronomer, born at La Salle, Ill., and educated at The Johns Hopkins University, Heidelberg and Berlin. Director of the Lick Observatory from 1898, he discovered the composition of Saturn's rings, and carried out important spectroscopic work on nebulae, discovering 120,000 of them.

KEELEY, Robert (1793–1869), English comedian, was born and died in London. He married Miss Mary Goward (1806–99), who, born at Ipswich, made her début at the Lyceum in 1825. Their daughters were both actresses. See W. Goodman's *The Keeleys on the Stage and at Home* (1895).

KEENE, Charles Samuel (1823–91), English illustrator, born at Hornsey, having tried both law and architecture, was apprenticed to a wood engraver. He worked for the *Illustrated London News* and for *Punch* from 1851 to within five months of his death at Hammersmith. He also illustrated books, including *Robinson Crusoe* and *The Cloister and the Hearth*. See Lives by Layard (1893) and D. Hudson (1947), and work by Pennell and Chesson (1897).

KEIGHTLEY, Thomas, *kīt'li* (1789–1872), Irish writer, born in Dublin, in 1824 settled in London. His histories of Rome, Greece, and England long held their place as school manuals and his *Fairy Mythology* (1850) and his Life and annotated edition of Milton (1855–59) are still remembered.

KEITEL, Wilhelm, *kī'tel* (1882–1946), German field-marshal, joined the army in 1901 and was an artillery staff officer in World War I. In the 'thirties he became an ardent Nazi, his faith being rewarded in 1938 by the post of chief of the supreme command of the armed forces. In 1940 he signed the Compiègne armistice with France and in 1945 he was one of the German signatories of unconditional surrender to Russia and the Allies in Berlin. He was executed in October 1946 for war crimes.

KEITH, (1) Viscount. See ELPHINSTONE (1).

(2) Sir Arthur (1866–1955), Scottish anthropologist, born at Aberdeen, wrote *Introduction to the Study of Anthropoid Apes* (1896), *Human Embryology and Morphology* (1901) and works on ancient man, including *Concerning Man's Origin* (1927) and *New Theory of Human Evolution* (1948). He was knighted in 1921.

(3) Arthur Berriedale (1879–1944), professor of Sanskrit at Edinburgh University from 1914, wrote on Sanskrit literature, and Dominion constitutions.

(4) James (1696–1758), Scottish soldier and Prussian field-marshal, was born at the castle of Inverugie near Peterhead. He came of a family, represented now by the Earl of Kintore, which from the 12th century had held the hereditary office of Great Marischal of Scotland. Sir William Keith was created Earl Marischal in 1458; and George, the fifth Earl (*c.* 1553–1623), in 1593 founded Marischal College in Aberdeen. William, ninth Earl (d. 1712), was the father of Marshal Keith and of his elder brother,

Georg, tenth Earl Marischal (1693–1778). James was destined for the law, but in 1715 he engaged with his brother in the Jacobite rising, and in 1719 in Alberoni's expedition to the West Highlands, which ended in the 'battle' of Glenshiel. Both times the brothers escaped to the Continent. James held for nine years a Spanish colonelcy and took part in the siege of Gibraltar (1726–27). But his creed, the Episcopal, was against him and in 1728 he entered the Russian service as a major-general. He distinguished himself in the wars with Turkey and Sweden, particularly at the siege of Otchakoff (1737) and the reduction of the Åland Islands (1743). He next visited Paris and London, where he made his peace with the Hanoverian government. In 1747, finding the Russian service disagreeable, he exchanged it for that of Prussia, and Frederick the Great gave him at once the rank of field-marshal. From this time his name is associated with that of Frederick, who relied as much on Keith's military genius as he did on the diplomatic ability of his brother, the Earl Marischal. Keith's talents became still more conspicuous upon the breaking out of the Seven Years' War (1756). He shared Frederick's doubtful fortunes before Prague, was present at the victories of Lobositz and Rossbach, and conducted the masterly retreat from Olmütz. At Hochkirch he was shot dead while for the third time charging the enemy. Keith died poor and unmarried, but he left children by his mistress, the Swede, Eva Merthens (d. 1811). See his own *Memoir, 1714–34* (Spalding Club, 1843); *Memoir of Marshal Keith* (Peterhead 1869); Carlyle's *Frederick*; Cuthell's *Last Earl Marischall* (1915); German *Lives* by Varnhagen von Ense (1844; new ed. 1888) and Lieut. von Paczynski-Tenczyn (1889).

(5) **Robert** (1681–1757), from 1727 an Episcopal bishop, was born at Uras, Kincardineshire, and lived in Edinburgh and Leith. His *History of the Scottish Reformation* (1734) was republished by the Spottiswoode Society in 1844–45.

KEITH-FALCONER. See FALCONER (2).
KEKULÉ VON STRADONITZ, Friedrich August, *kay'koo-lay* (1829–96), German chemist, born at Darmstadt, became professor at Ghent and at Bonn (1867). He made a major contribution to organic chemistry by developing structural theories, including the cyclic structure of benzene.
KELLER, (1) **Gottfried** (1819–90), Swiss poet and novelist, born near Zürich, studied landscape painting at Munich 1840–42, but took to literature. From 1861 to 1876 he was state secretary of his native canton. His chief works are *Der grüne Heinrich* (1854), *Die Leute von Seldwyla* (1856; includes *A Village Romeo and Juliet*), *Sieben Legenden* (1872), *Züricher Novellen* (1878), and *Martin Salander* (1886). It was as a writer of short stories rather than as a poet or novelist that he excelled and his powers of characterization and description and his sense of humour are best illustrated in his volumes of *Novellen*. See studies by Huch (1904), Maync (1925), Hauch (1916), M Hay (1920) and H. W. Reichert (1949).

(2) **Helen Adams** (1880–1968), born at Tuscumbia, Ala., became deaf and blind at nineteen months, but, educated by Miss Anne M. Sullivan (Mrs Macy), she later learnt to speak, graduated B.A. 1904, and attained high distinction as a lecturer, writer and scholar. See *Autobiography and Letters* (1946), and study by Tibble (1957).
KELLERMANN, François Étienne Christophe, Duke of Valmy (1735–1820), born at Wolfsbuchweiler in Alsace, entered the French army and was major-general at the Revolution. In 1792 he repelled the Duke of Brunswick, and delivered France by the famous 'cannonade of Valmy'. Yet on allegation of treason he was imprisoned by Robespierre. He afterwards served in Italy, and under the Empire was made a marshal and duke. In 1809 and 1812 he commanded the reserves on the Rhine. At the Restoration he attached himself to the Bourbons. His son, **François Étienne** (1770–1835), by a charge turned Marengo into a victory.
KELLGREN, Johan Henrik (1751–95), Swedish poet, born at Floby. From satire and didactic poems he turned to pure lyrics, in which he excelled. He was first director of the Swedish Academy. See studies by Atterbom (1863) and O. Sylwan (1912).
KELLOGG, Frank Billings (1856–1937), American statesman, born at Potsdam, N.Y., was senator (1917–23), ambassador in London (1923–25), secretary of state (1925–1929). He drew up the Briand-Kellogg Pact (1928) outlawing war, which became the legal basis for the Nuremberg trials (1945–46), and was a judge of the Permanent Court of Justice at the Hague (1930–35). In 1929 he was awarded the Nobel peace prize.
KELLY, or Kelley, Edward. See DEE, JOHN.
KELLY, (1) **Sir Gerald Festus** (1879–1972), English painter, born in London. He was educated at Eton and Trinity Hall, Cambridge, and studied art in Paris. He was elected an A.R.A. in 1922, an R.A. in 1930 and was P.R.A. (1949–54). In 1945 he painted state portraits of King George VI and Queen Elizabeth. He was knighted in 1945 and made a K.C.V.O. in 1955.
(2) **Ned** (1855–80), horse-thief and from 1878 bushranger in Victoria and New South Wales, was hanged at Melbourne. See *Life* by M. Brown (1948).
KELVIN, William Thomson, 1st Baron (1824–1907), Scottish mathematician and physicist, was born in Belfast, and at eleven entered Glasgow University, where his father had become professor of Mathematics. At Cambridge he highly distinguished himself as an original thinker even in his undergraduate days. He was second wrangler and first Smith's prizeman of 1845, and was elected a fellow of Peterhouse. In 1846 he became professor of Natural Philosophy in the University of Glasgow. In an early paper (1842) he solved important problems in electrostatics. It was largely owing to his refined researches in the transmission of electric currents in submarine cables that the Atlantic cable was successful (for which in 1866 he was knighted). In 1892 he was created a peer with the title of Lord Kelvin. His electrometers of various design—absolute,

portable, quadrant, &c.—embody the perfection of mechanical and geometrical adjustment. He constructed ampère-meters, voltmeters and watt-meters, suitable alike for the electrical workshop and laboratory. His sounding apparatus and compass were adopted by the Admiralty and the principal mercantile lines. In pure science Lord Kelvin did incomparable work. Specially may be mentioned his thermodynamic researches from 1848 onwards, including the doctrine of the dissipation or degradation of energy; his magnetic and electric discoveries, including general theorems of great value and the beautiful method of electric images; and his work in hydrodynamics, more especially in wave-motion and in vortex-motion. Basing upon the phenomena of gyrostatic motion, he imagined a kinetic theory of inertia of high interest; and his dynamical theory of dispersion, and indeed all his views on the nature of the ether, are full of significance. In 1872 his electrostatic and magnetic papers were reprinted in collected form (2nd ed. 1884); and his other papers have been similarly published under the title *Mathematical and Physical Papers* (6 vols. 1882–1911), besides *Popular Lectures* (3 vols. 1889–94), *Molecular Tactics of a Crystal* (1894), &c. He was joint-author with Professor Tait of *A Treatise on Natural Philosophy* (vol. i 1867; 2nd ed. 1879). He was president of the British Association (1871), repeatedly president of the Royal Society of Edinburgh, and (1890) president of the Royal Society of London. He died December 17. See the Life by Silvanus Thompson (1910), and books by Mrs King (1910), Miss A. G. King (1925) and A. Russell (1938).

KEMAL PASHA. See MUSTAFA KEMAL.

KEMBLE, family of actors:

(1) **Adelaide** (1816–79), daughter of (2), operatic singer, retired in 1842 on her marriage with F. Sartoris. Author of *A Week in a French Country House* (1867), *Medusa and Other Tales* (1868), and *Past Hours* (1880).

(2) **Charles** (1775–1854), actor, brother of (5), born at Brecon, made his first appearance at Sheffield in 1792 and in 1794 played Malcolm to John Kemble's Macbeth. He retired from the stage in 1840, when he was appointed examiner of plays. He chiefly excelled in characters of the second rank, and in comedy he specially distinguished himself.

(3) **Frances Anne,** ' Fanny Kemble ' (1809–1893), daughter of (2), made her début at Covent Garden on October 5, 1829, when her ' Juliet ' created a great sensation. For three years she played leading parts in London, then in 1832 went with her father to America, where in 1834 she married Pierce Butler, a Southern planter. They were divorced in 1848 and, resuming her maiden name, she gave Shakespearian readings for twenty years. She published dramas, poems, eight volumes of autobiography, &c. See Lives by Bobbé (1932) and L. S. Driver (1933).

(4) **John Mitchell** (1807–57), Anglo-Saxon scholar, son of (2), attended Trinity, Cambridge, and studied at Göttingen under Jakob Grimm. His edition of *Beowulf* (1833–37) and *Codex Diplomaticus Aevi Saxonici*

(1839–48) were valuable, but less important than his unfinished *History of the Saxons in England* (1849; new ed. by Birch, 1876). He edited the *British and Foreign Review* (1835–1844) and in 1840 succeeded his father as examiner of plays. See Study by B. Dickens (1940).

(5) **John Philip** (1757–1823), eldest son of (6), was born at Prescot. His father intended him for the Catholic priesthood, and sent him to a seminary at Sedgley Park, Staffordshire, and to the English college at Douai. But the stage mania was on him, and he became an actor. His first appearance was at Wolverhampton, January 8, 1776. He joined the York circuit under Tate Wilkinson and he played in Ireland. The success of his sister, Mrs Siddons, gave him his opportunity, and on September 30, 1783, he played Hamlet at Drury Lane, and aroused the keenest interest. He continued to play leading tragic characters at Drury Lane for many years, and in 1788 became Sheridan's manager. In 1802 he purchased a share in Covent Garden Theatre, became manager, and made his first appearance there in 1803 as Hamlet. In 1808 the theatre was burned, and on the opening of the new building (1809) the notorious O. P. (i.e., ' Old Price ') Riots broke out. Kemble retired in 1817, and afterwards settled at Lausanne, where he died. Handsome, stately, and of remarkable intellectual power, he probably has had no superior as a tragedian. See Life by Borden (1925).

(6) **Roger** (1721–1802), a travelling manager, father of (2), (5) and (7).

(7) **Stephen** (1758–1822), brother of (5), born at Kington, Herefordshire, was chiefly remarkable for his enormous bulk, which enabled him to play Falstaff without stuffing. He was (1792–1800) manager of the Edinburgh theatre, where he was in continual hot water through lawsuits and other troubles.

KEMP, (1) **George Mickle** (or **Meikle**) (1795–1844), Scottish draughtsman, born at Hillriggs near Biggar, until fourteen assisted his shepherd father. Becoming a carpenter and millwright, he sought work in England and France, settling where he could study Gothic architecture. He returned to Scotland in 1826, and became a draughtsman in Edinburgh. In 1838 his second design for the Scott Monument at Edinburgh was accepted, but before its completion he was accidentally drowned in the canal at Edinburgh. See Life by T. Bonnar (1892).

(2) **John** (c. 1380–1454), born at Olantigh near Ashford, Kent, became a fellow of Merton College, Oxford, Bishop of Rochester (1419), and of Chichester and London (1421), chancellor and Archbishop of York (1426), a cardinal (1439), and Archbishop of Canterbury (1452). See Hook's *Lives of the Archbishops*, vol. v.

(3) **William** (d. 1603), a comedian who in 1599 danced from London to Norwich. See his *Nine Daies Wonder* (ed. by Dyce, Camden Society).

KEMPE, Margery (b. 1364), mystic, daughter of a mayor of Lynn, wife of a burgess there, mother of fourteen children. Her spiritual autobiography, *The Book of Margery Kempe* (printed in part by Wynkyn de Worde, *c.* 1501), recounts her persecution by devils and men, repeated accusations of Lollardy, her copious weepings, her journeys to Jerusalem and to Germany, and has been hailed as a classic. See *The Book of Margery Kempe* (modernized text) by W. Butler-Bowdon (1936), the original text ed. by Neech and Hope Allen (1940), and study by K. Cholmley (1947).

KEMPIS, Thomas à (1379–1471), German religious writer, so called from his birthplace, Kempen. In 1400 entered the Augustinian convent of Agnetenberg near Zwolle, took Holy Orders in 1413, was chosen subprior in 1429, and died as superior. Wrote sermons, ascetical treatises, pious biographies, letters and hymns, the only one of special note the treatise *On the Following (or Imitation) of Christ*. In its pages, says Dean Milman, ' is gathered and concentred all that is elevating, passionate, profoundly pious in all the older mystics '. Translated into English about 1440 and again (by Atkinson and the Lady Margaret) about 1502, the *Imitation* has been ascribed to the celebrated Jean Gerson (q.v.), and, from the 17th century, to Gersen, abbot of Vercelli, whose very existence has not been proved. Most authorities, however, assign it to Kempis. Its theology is almost purely ascetical, and (excepting the 4th book, which is based on the doctrine of the real presence) the work has been used by Christians of all denominations. Probably completed between 1415 and 1424, the first edition (Augsburg 1471 or 1472) was reprinted by Dr Adrian Fortescue. See study by S. Kettlewell (1883).

KEMSLEY, James Gomer Berry, 1st Viscount (1883–1968), British newspaper proprietor, born at Merthyr Tydfil, became chairman of Kemsley Newspapers Ltd in 1937, controlling the *Sunday Times* and other newspapers. Created a baronet in 1928, raised to the peerage in 1936, he received a viscountcy in 1945. In 1950 published *The Kemsley Manual of Journalism*. His brothers, **Henry Seymour, Lord Buckland** (1877–1928), and **William Ewert, 1st Viscount Camrose** (q.v.), also owned newspapers. See Camrose's *British Newspapers and Their Controllers* (1947).

KEN, Thomas (1637–1711), born at Little Berkhampstead, Herts, held several livings and in 1666 was elected a fellow of Winchester where he prepared his *Manual of Prayers for Scholars of Winchester College* (1674), and wrote his morning, evening, and midnight hymns, the first two of which, ' Awake, my soul ', and ' Glory to Thee, my God, this night ', are among the best-known hymns. In 1679 he was appointed by Charles II chaplain to Princess Mary, wife of William of Orange, but offended William, and returned home in 1680, when he became a royal chaplain. In 1683, on the king's visit to Winchester, Ken refused to give up his house for the accommodation of Nell Gwynne. In 1683 too he went to Tangiers as a chaplain, and in 1685 was consecrated Bishop of Bath and Wells. The chief event of his bishopric was his trial and acquittal among the ' Seven Bishops ' in 1688, for refusing to read the *Declaration of Indulgence*. At the Revolution he refused to take the oath to William, and was deprived

of his bishopric in 1691. See Lives by Bowles (1831), Anderdon (1851–54), Plumptre (2 vols. 1888), and Clarke (1896).

KENDAL, Madge, stage name of **Margaret Brunton Grimston,** *née* Margaret Shafto Robertson (1849–1935), English actress, born at Cleethorpes, sister of T. W. Robertson (q.v.). Appeared in Shakespearean rôles and by the 1870s was leading lady at the Haymarket Theatre. In 1869 she married **William Hunter Kendal,** properly **Grimston** (1843–1917), actor, with whom she appeared in many productions, particularly Shakespearean. She was created a D.B.E. in 1926.

KENDALL, Edward Calvin (1886–1972), American chemist, born at S. Norwalk, Conn., known for his isolation of thyroxin (1915), and for his research on adrenal hormones, for which, with P. S. Hench and T. Reichstein (qq.v.), he won the Nobel prize for medicine in 1950. See his autobiography (1971).

KENDREW, John Cowdery (1917–), British scientist, born at Oxford, educated at Clifton and Trinity College, Cambridge. With Perutz (q.v.) he carried out researches in the chemistry of the blood and discovered the structure of myoglobin, and shared the Nobel chemistry prize for 1962.

KENNEDY, (1) **Benjamin Hall** (1804–89), English classical scholar, born at Summerhill, Birmingham. After teaching at Harrow (1830–36), and Shrewsbury (1836–67), he became professor of Greek at Cambridge. The most celebrated of his many classical writings is *Sabrinae Corolla* (1850).

(2) **James** (*c.* 1408–65), Scottish bishop, grandson of Robert III and nephew of James I, was a graduate of St Andrews University, becoming Bishop of Dunkeld in 1437. Later, as Bishop of St Andrews and advisor to James II, he opposed the growing dominance of the Douglases in Scotland. During the minority of James III, he led the ' old lords ' party in support of the Lancastrians. He founded St Salvator's College at St Andrews. See book by Dowden (1912).

(3) **John Fitzgerald** (1917–63), 35th president of the U.S., son of (4), born at Brookline, Mass., studied at Harvard and under Laski (q.v.) in London, and after service at the embassy there (1938), wrote a thesis on Britain's unpreparedness for war. His *Profiles of Courage* (1956) won the Pulitzer prize. As a torpedo boat commander in the Pacific, he was awarded the Navy medal and the Purple Heart. Elected Democrat representative (1947) and senator (1952) for Massachusetts, in 1960 he was the first Catholic, and the youngest person, to be elected president, on the smallest majority of the popular vote. The conservatism of Congress stalled his bid for a 'new frontier ' in social legislation. Through his brother (6) he supported federal desegregation policy in schools and universities, and prepared further civil rights legislation. He displayed firmness and moderation in foreign policy, and in October 1962 at the risk of nuclear war induced Russia to withdraw its missiles from Cuba, and achieved a partial nuclear test ban treaty with Russia in 1963. On Nov. 22, 1963, he was assassinated by rifle fire while

being driven in an open car through Dallas, Texas. The alleged assassin, **Lee Oswald**, was himself shot and killed at point blank range two days later while under heavy police escort on a jail transfer. See Schlesinger, *A Thousand Days* (1965), Sorensen, *Kennedy* (1965), W. Manchester, *The Death of a President* (1967), *The Official Warren Commission Report* (1964) on the assassination, and M. Lane, *Rush to Judgement* (1966), criticizing the latter.—In 1953 Kennedy had married **Jacqueline Lee Bouvier** (b. 1929), who in 1968 married Aristotle Onassis (q.v.).

(4) **Joseph Patrick** (1888–1969), American multi-millionaire, born in Boston, grandson of an Irish Catholic immigrant, son of a Boston publican, educated at Harvard, made a large fortune in the 1920s, and during the 1930s was a strong supporter of Roosevelt and the 'New Deal', being rewarded with minor administrative posts, and the ambassadorship to Britain (1938–40). After World War II he concentrated on fulfilling his ambitions of a political dynasty through his sons. He had married in 1914 **Rose Fitzgerald**, daughter of a local politician, John F. Fitzgerald, also of Irish immigrant descent. They had nine children, including four sons, at whose political disposal he placed his fortune. The eldest, **Joseph Patrick** (1915–44), was killed in a flying accident while on naval service in World War II. For the careers of **John** and **Robert**, see (3) and (6). The youngest and only surviving son, **Edward Moore** (1932–), was born at Brookline, Mass., educated at Harvard and Virginia University Law School, admitted to the Massachusetts bar in 1959, and was elected as Democratic senator for his brother John's Massachusetts seat in 1962. In 1969 he became the youngest-ever majority whip in the U.S. senate. See McCarthy, *The Remarkable Kennedys* (1962), and R. J. Whalen, *The Founding Father* (1965).

(5) **Margaret** (1896–1967), English novelist, journalist, and playwright, born in London. Her many light novels all gained a fair measure of success, particularly her second, *The Constant Nymph* (1924). In 1934 her play, *Escape Me Never*, was published. In 1925 she married David Davies, knighted 1952, died 1964.

(6) **Robert Francis** (1925–68), American politician, third son of (4), born at Brookline, Mass., educated at Harvard and Virginia University Law School, served at sea (1944–1946) in World War II, was admitted to the Massachusetts bar (1951) and served on the Select Committee on Improper Activities (1957–59), when he prosecuted several top union leaders. An efficient manager of his brother's (3) presidential campaign, he was an energetic attorney-general (1961–64) under the latter's administration, notable in his dealings with civil rights problems. Senator for New York from 1965, his tardy decision to stand as a Democratic presidential candidate in 1968 branded him as an opportunist to some, as an idealistic reformer, closely identified with the struggles of America's underprivileged minorities, to others. On June 5, 1968, after winning the Californian primary election, he was shot, and died the following day. His assassin, **Sirhan Bishara**

Sirhan, a 24-year-old Jordanian-born immigrant, was sentenced to the gas chamber in 1969. See his *To Seek a Newer World* (1968), and Life by M. Laing (1968).

KENNELLY, Arthur Edwin (1861–1939), American engineer, born in Bombay, became a professor at Harvard in 1902, and in the same year discovered, almost simultaneously with Oliver Heaviside (q.v.), the ionized layer in the atmosphere known sometimes as the Kennelly-Heaviside layer, more often as the Heaviside layer.

KENNETH I, called **Macalpine**, seems to have succeeded his father Alpin as king of the remnant of the Dalriada Scots in 834, and to have repelled a Danish invasion and completely conquered the Picts in 846. He was connected by blood with the Pictish royal family. He became king of a united Alban extending to the Firths of Clyde and Forth.

KENNICOTT, Benjamin (1718–83), biblical scholar, born at Totnes, educated at Wadham College, Oxford, known for his edition of the Hebrew Old Testament (1776–80), for which 615 Hebrew MSS and 16 MSS of the Samaritan Pentateuch were collated.

KENNINGTON, Eric Henri, A.R.A. (1888–1960), English painter and sculptor, born in London. He was an official war artist in both world wars, and in the field of sculpture, designed many memorials, etc., e.g., his head of T. E. Lawrence in St. Paul's Cathedral. His books include *Drawing the R.A.F.* (1942) and *The British Home Guard* (1945).

KENNY, Elizabeth (1886–1954) Australian nursing sister, renowned for her method of treating poliomyelitis.

KENT, Dukes of:

(1) **Edward** (1767–1820), 4th son of George III, born at Buckingham Palace. At Gibraltar, first (1790–91) as colonel, and then (1802) as governor, his martinet discipline caused continual mutinies. These culminated in an encounter in which blood was shed, after which he was recalled. In 1818 he married Victoria Mary Louisa (1786–1861), daughter of the Duke of Saxe-Saalfeld-Coburg, and widow of the Prince of Leiningen. For the sake of economy they lived at Leiningen, and came to England for the birth (May 24, 1819) of their child the Princess Victoria. The duke died 8 months later. Owing to the deaths of his three elder brothers, George IV, the Duke of York, and William IV, without issue, the crown came to the Princess Victoria.

(2) **George Edward Alexander Edmund** (1902–42), 4th son of King George V and Queen Mary, passed out of Dartmouth Naval College in 1920, but because of delicate health, served in the Foreign Office and inspected factories for the Home Office, the first member of the royal family to work in the Civil Service. In 1934 he was created duke and married **Princess Marina** of Greece and Denmark (1906–68), a first cousin of King George I of Greece and a great-niece of Queen Alexandra. He was killed on active service, as chief welfare officer of the R.A.F. Home Command, when his Sunderland flying-boat on its way to Iceland crashed in the north of Scotland. Their three children are: (1) **Edward** (b. 1935), Duke of Kent, who

KENT

734

KER

married in 1961 Katharine Worsley (b. 1933); their son is George Philip Nicholas (b. 1962), Earl of St Andrews, and daughter Helen Marina Lucy (b. 1964).—(2) **Alexandra** (b. 1936), who married in 1963 the Hon. Angus James Bruce Ogilvy (b. 1928); their son is James Robert Bruce (b. 1964), and daughter Marina Victoria Alexandra (b. 1966).—(3) **Michael** (b. 1942).

KENT, (1) **James** (1763–1847), American lawyer, born at Fredericksburgh, N.Y., after serving in the New York legislature was professor of Law in Columbia College 1794–98, and then a justice of the supreme court of New York. In 1804 he became chief justice, and in 1814–23 was state chancellor. Kent's *Commentaries on American Law* (1826–30) is a standard work.

(2) **William** (1684–1748), painter, landscape gardener, and Palladian architect, was a native of Yorkshire, and died at Burlington House. His best-known work is the Horse Guards block in Whitehall. See Life by M. Jourdain (1948).

KENTIGERN, St (c. 518–603), the apostle of Cumbria, according to legend son of a Princess Thenew, who was cast from Traprain Law, then exposed on the Firth of Forth in a coracle. It carried her to Culross, where she bore a son (about 518). Mother and child were baptized by St Serf (an anachronism), who reared the boy in his monastery, where he was so beloved that his name Kentigern (' chief lord ') was often exchanged for Mungo (' dear friend '). He founded a monastery at Cathures (now Glasgow), and in 543 was consecrated Bishop of Cumbria. In 553 he was driven to seek refuge in Wales, where he visited St David, and where he founded another monastery and a bishopric, which still bears the name of his disciple, St Asaph. In 573 he was recalled by a new king, Rederech Hael, and about 584 was visited by Columba. He was buried in Glasgow Cathedral. A fragment of a Life and the *Vita Kentigerni* by Joceline of Furness both belong to the 12th century. See Bishop Forbes's *Lives of SS. Ninian and Kentigern* (1874), Skene's *Celtic Scotland* (vol. ii, 1877), and Beveridge's *Culross* and *Tulliallan* (1885).

KENYATTA, Jomo (c. 1889–), Kenyan politician, born an orphan at Mitumi, Kenya, educated at a Scots mission school and began as a herd boy. Joined the Kikuyu Central Association (1922), and became its president. Visited Britain in 1929 and from 1931 to 1944. Studied for a year at London University under Malinowski, who wrote the preface to his book *Facing Mount Kenya* (1938). Visited Russia thrice, and was president of the Pan African Federation with Nkrumah (q.v.) as secretary. Worked on the land during the war and married an Englishwoman in 1942. On returning to Kenya in 1946 his Kenya African Union advocated extreme nationalism, and he led the *Mau Mau* terrorist society. Sentenced to 7 years' hard labour in 1952, he was released in 1958, but exiled first to a remote northern area, then to his native village. Elected president of the dominant K.A.N.U. party, and M.P. in 1961, he became prime minister in June 1963, retaining the post after Kenya's independence in Dec. 1963,

and president of the republic of Kenya in Dec. 1964. See Life by G. Delf (1961).

KENYON, (1) **Sir Frederic George** (1863–1952), English classical scholar, born in London, director and chief librarian of the British Museum (1909–30). He edited Bacchylides' poems and was responsible for a number of editions of classical and biblical texts.

(2) **John** (1784–1856), British philanthropist, the wealthy acquaintance of Coleridge, Lamb, Landor, Crabb Robinson, Ticknor, &c., was born in Jamaica, and died at Cowes. A lifelong friend of Browning, he was responsible for introducing the poet to Elizabeth Barrett. He published some poetry.

KEPLER, or **Keppler, Johann** (1571–1630), German astronomer, was born at Weil der Stadt in Württemberg. He studied at Tübingen, in 1593 was appointed professor of Mathematics at Graz, about 1596 commenced a correspondence with Tycho Brahe, and in 1600 went to Prague to aid him in his work. After Tycho's death (1601) Kepler was astronomer, often unpaid, to the Emperor Rudolf II. In 1612 he became a mathematics teacher at Linz, and in 1628 astrologer to Wallenstein. In his *Mysterium* (1596), he proclaimed that 5 kinds of regular polyhedral bodies govern the 5 planetary orbits; and in his *Harmonice Mundi*, 1619, Kepler's Third Law, that the ' square of a planet's periodic time is proportional to the cube of its mean distance from the sun ', appeared. He tried to find a law for the movements of Mars, and in 1609 published his First and Second Laws, which formed the groundwork of Newton's discoveries, and are the starting-point of modern astronomy. He also made many discoveries in optics, general physics, and geometry. See studies by Donsky (1880), Herz (1895), Bryant (1921), C. Baumgardt (1952), M. Caspar (trans. 1960), and an opera on his life by Hindemith, *Die Harmonie der Welt* (1957).

KEPPEL, (1) **Augustus, 1st Viscount** (1725–1786), admiral, son of the second Earl of Albemarle, served under Hawke in 1757, captured Goree in 1758, took part in the battle of Quiberon Bay in 1759, and in the capture of Belleisle in 1761, and commanded at the capture of Havana in 1762. In 1778 he encountered the French fleet off Ushant on July 27. Owing to a disagreement with Palliser, his second in command, the French escaped. Both admirals were tried by court martial, but acquitted. In 1782 created Viscount Keppel, he became first lord of the Admiralty. See Life by T. Keppel (1842).

(2) **Sir Henry** (1809–1904), successively vice-admiral (1867), admiral (1869), and admiral of the fleet (1877), was a son of the fourth Earl of Albemarle. He saw service during the war against China in 1842, and in a campaign against pirates, and commanded the naval brigade before Sebastopol. In 1857 he took part in the destruction of the Chinese fleet. G.C.B. (1871), O.M. (1902), he wrote on Borneo, &c. See his *A Sailor's Life under Four Sovereigns* (3 vols. 1899), and memoir by West (1905).

KER, (1) **John** (1673–1726), of Kersland, Dalry parish, Ayrshire, a Cameronian who intrigued with the Jacobites, but was really a government spy. See his shameless Memoirs (1726).

(2) **William Paton** (1855–1923), Scottish scholar, born in Glasgow, educated there and at Balliol, was professor of English at Cardiff (1883), London (1889), and of Poetry at Oxford (1920). Talker, lecturer, and writer of prodigious learning and vitality, he wrote *Epic and Romance* (1897), *The Art of Poetry* (1923), &c.

KERENSKY, Alexander (1881–1970), Russian revolutionary, born at Simbirsk (now Ulyanovsk), son of a high school principal, studied law in Leningrad. He took a leading part in the revolution of 1917, becoming minister of justice (March), for war (May), and premier (July). He crushed Kornilov's military revolt (September), but was deposed (November) by the Bolsheviks and fled to France. In 1940 he went to Australia and in 1946 to America. His writings include *The Prelude to Bolshevism* (1919), *The Catastrophe* (1927), *The Road to Tragedy* (1935), and *The Kerensky Memoirs* (1966).

KERGUÉLEN-TRÉMAREC, Yves (1745–97), a French naval officer, born at Quimper in Brittany, who in 1772 discovered Kerguelen's Land.

KERN, Jerome (1885–1945), American composer, born in New York, wrote a vast quantity of music for musical comedy and films. His scores include *The Red Petticoat*, which first brought a 'western' setting to Broadway in 1912, *Sally, Roberta*, and *Very Warm for May*, and contain such evergreen songs as 'Look for the Silver Lining' and 'Smoke Gets in your Eyes'. His greatest success came with the operetta *Show Boat* (1927), a work which has had a lasting influence upon American light entertainment.

KERNER, Andreas Justinus (1786–1862), German poet, born in Ludwigsburg in Württemberg, became a physician at Wildbad, and settled finally at Weinsberg in 1818. He published several volumes of poetry between 1811 and 1852, studied animal magnetism, believed in occultism, and wrote *Die Seherin von Prevorst* (1829). See A. Watts, *Life and works of Kerner* (1884); English Goethe Society, *Letters of J. Kerner to Graf A. von Württemberg* (1938).

KEROUAC, Jack (officially **John**) (1922–69), American author born in Lowell, Mass., won a scholarship to Columbia University, while wandering through the country doing odd jobs. His first novel *The Town and the City* (1950) was written in the orthodox manner which he abandoned in *On the Road* (1957), a spontaneous work in 'beatnik' idiom, expressing the youthful discontent of the 'beat' generation. Later works include *The Dharma Bums, The Subterraneans* (1958) and *Big Sur* (1962).

KERR, or Ker, an Anglo-Norman family, found in Scotland at the end of the 12th century. Sir Andrew Ker of Cessford (d. 1526), whose younger brother, George, was ancestor of the Kers of Faudonside, had two sons—Sir Walter, whose grandson, Robert Ker, was created Earl of Roxburghe 1616, and Mark, commendator of Newbattle, whose son, Mark Kerr, was created Earl of

Lothian 1606. The second Earl of Roxburghe was only a Ker by his mother. His grandson, fifth Earl, was created duke in 1707. John, third Duke (1740–1804), was the famous book-collector. Robert Carre (see OVERBURY) belonged to the Fernihirst line.

KERR, John (1824–1907), Scottish physicist, born at Ardrossan, educated at Glasgow in theology, became a lecturer in mathematics and was later elected F.R.S. In 1876 he discovered the magneto-optic effect which was then named after him. He was the author of *An Elementary Treatise on Rational Mechanics* (1867).

KERVYN DE LETTENHOVE, Joseph, *let-en-hō′vé* (1817–91), Belgian historian, died at Brussels. Works include *Froissart* (1857), and series of chronicles.

KESSELRING, Albert (1885–1960), German air commander in World War II, led the Luftwaffe attacks on France and (unsuccessfully) on Britain. In 1943 he was made c.-in-c. in Italy and in 1945 in the West. Condemned to death as a war criminal in 1947, he had his sentence commuted to life imprisonment but was released in 1952. See his Memoirs (1953).

KETCH, Jack (d. 1686), hangman and headsman from about 1663.

KETT, Robert (d. 1549), a landowner of Wymondham in Norfolk, who in July 1549 headed 16,000 insurgents, enclosures being their principal grievance. Norwich was twice captured by the rebels; on the second occasion they held it until they were driven out by the Earl of Warwick, Kett being captured and hanged, December 7. See books by F. W. Russell (1860), Joseph Clayton (1912), and S. T. Bindoff (1949).

KETTELER, Wilhelm (1811–77), German ecclesiastic, from 1850 Ultramontane bishop of Mainz. He was principal opponent of Bismarck's *Kulturkampf*.

KEULEN, L. van. See CEULEN, L. VAN.

KEY, (1) Ellen (1849–1926), Swedish author, born at Sundsholm, Småland, took to teaching (1880) when her father lost his fortune, and made her name as a writer and lecturer on the feminist movement, child welfare, &c. See Life by Hamilton (1913).

(2) **Francis Scott** (1780–1843), American lawyer, attorney for the District of Columbia, during the British attack on Baltimore (1814), which he witnessed from a British man-of-war, wrote 'The Star-spangled Banner'. See O. G. T. Sonneck, *The Star-spangled Banner* (1914).

(3) **Thomas Hewitt** (1799–1875), English scholar, headmaster of University College School, professor of Comparative Grammar in University College London, author of a *Latin Grammar* and of a *Latin-English Dictionary*. See Life by J. P. Hicks (1893).

KEYES, (1) Roger John Brownlow, 1st Baron Keyes (1872–1945), British admiral, entered the Royal Navy in 1885, served at Witu (1890) and in the Boxer Rebellion (1900), in World War I was chief of staff Eastern Mediterranean (1915) and in 1918 commanded the Dover Patrol, leading the raid on Zeebrugge. He was created K.C.B. in 1918. Recalled in 1940, he was appointed director of amphibious warfare, subsequently becoming liaison officer to the

Belgians. See his *Naval Memoirs* (2 vols. 1934–35), *Adventures Ashore and Afloat* (1939) and *Amphibious Warfare and Combined Operations* (1943). His son, Lieut-Col. Geoffrey Keyes, M.C. and posthumous V.C., was killed in the historic commando raid on Rommel's H.Q. in 1941.

(2) Sydney (1922–43), English poet, born at Dartford, Kent, was killed in Tunisia in April 1943. His first book of poems, *The Iron Laurel*, was published in 1942, and his second, *The Cruel Solstice*, in 1944, in which year he was posthumously awarded the Hawthornden prize. See his *Collected Poems*, edited with memoir and notes by M. Meyer (1945).

KEYNES, John Maynard, 1st Baron (1883–1946), English economist, pioneer of the theory of full employment, son of **John Neville** (1852–1949) the Cambridge logician and political economist, born at Cambridge and educated at Eton and King's College, Cambridge, where he became one of the ' Bloomsbury group ' and where off and on from 1908 he lectured in economics. He was at the India Office (1906–08) and in 1913 as a member of the Royal Commission on Indian finance and currency, published his first book on this subject. In both world wars he was an adviser to the Treasury, which he represented at the Versailles Peace Conference but resigned in strong opposition to the terms of the draft treaty, set out in his *Economic Consequences of the Peace* (1919) written with the encouragement of Smuts. In 1921 *Treatise of Probability* appeared, in which he explored the logical relationships between calling something ' highly probable ' and a ' justifiable induction '. In 1923 he became chairman of the Liberal periodical, *Nation*, and pamphleteered his controversial views on European reconstruction, strongly attacking Churchill's restoration of the gold standard (1925). The unemployment crises inspired his two great works, *A Treatise on Money* (1930) and the revolutionary *General Theory of Employment, Interest and Money* (1936). He argued that full employment was not an automatic condition, expounded a new theory of the rate of interest, and set out the principles underlying the flows of income and expenditure, and fought the Treasury view that unemployment was incurable. His views on a planned economy influenced Roosevelt's ' New Deal ' administration. He married a Diaghilev ballerina, Lydia Lopokova and with her helped to found the Vic-Wells ballet. He financed the establishment of the Arts Theatre, Cambridge. In 1943 he proposed the international clearing union, played a leading part (1944–46) in the formulation of the Bretton Woods agreements, the establishment of the International Monetary Fund, and the troublesome, abortive negotiations for a continuation of American Lend-lease. Created C.B. (1917), elected F.B.A. (1929), he died just prior to being awarded the O.M. See his *Essays in Persuasion* (1931), *Essays in Biography* (1933), studies by Dillard (1948), Pigou (1950), Memoirs, ed. at Cambridge (1949), F. A. Keynes (1950), and Life by Harrod (1951).

KEYSERLING, Hermann Graf, *kī′ser-ling* (1880–1946), German philosopher, born at Koenno in Livonia, travelled widely, founded a ' School of Wisdom ' at Darmstadt and attempted a synthesis of western and eastern thought. See his *Travel Diary of a Philosopher* (1919; trans. 1925), and M. G. Parks, *Introduction to Keyserling* (1934).

KHAMA, (1) (1835–1923), a reforming chief of the Bamangwato in the Bechuanaland Protectorate. See Life by J. Mockford (1931).

(2) Sir Seretse (1921–), African politician, born at Serowe, Bechuanaland (now Botswana), nephew of Tshekedi Khama (1905–59), who was chief regent of the Bamangwato from 1925. Seretse was educated in Africa and Balliol College, Oxford. While a student at the Inner Temple in 1948 he married an English woman, and in 1950, with his uncle, was banned from the chieftainship and the territory of the Bamangwato. Allowed to return in 1956, he became active in politics, and was restored to the chieftainship in 1963. He became first prime minister of Bechuanaland in 1965 and president of Botswana in 1966, having received a knighthood.

KHAN, (Mohammed) Ayub (?–), Pakistani statesman, born Abbottabad, educated Aligarh Moslem University and Sandhurst, served in World War II, became first C.-in-C. of Pakistan's army (1951) and field-marshal (1959). He became president of Pakistan in 1958 after a bloodless army *coup*, and established a stable economy and political autocracy. In March 1969, after widespread civil disorder and violent opposition from both right and left wings, Ayub Khan relinquished power and martial law was re-established. See his *Friends, Not Masters* (1967).

KHATCHATURIAN, Aram (1903–), Russian composer, student of folksongs, and authority on oriental music, born at Tiflis in 1903. His compositions include two symphonies, concertos, ballets, film and instrumental music. See Lives by Martinov (Moscow 1947) and Shneerson (trans. 1960).

KHAYYÁM, Omar. See OMAR.

KHRUSHCHEV, Nikita Sergeyevich, *kroosh′-chof* (1894–1971), Soviet politician, born at Kalinovka near Kursk, was a shepherd boy and a locksmith and is said to have been almost illiterate until the age of 25. Joining the Communist Party in 1918, he fought in the Civil War and rose rapidly in the party organization. In 1939 he was made a full member of the Politburo and of the Presidium of the Supreme Soviet. In World War II he organized guerrilla warfare against the invading Germans and took charge of the reconstruction of devastated territory. In 1949 he launched a drastic reorganization of Soviet agriculture. In 1953 on the death of Stalin he became first secretary of the All Union Party and three years later, at the 20th Congress of the Communist Party, denounced Stalinism and the ' personality cult '. The following year he demoted Molotov, Kaganovich and Malenkov—all possible rivals. Khrushchev, who did much to enhance the ambitions and status of the Soviet Union abroad, was nevertheless deposed in 1964 and forced into retirement. He was at his peak the greatest power behind the Iron Curtain, and a decisive voice in world politics and strategy. See Lives by V. Alexandrov (1957), and G. Paloczi-Horvath (1960), and studies by E. Crankshaw (1966) and M. Frankland (1966).

KIDD, (1) John (1775–1851), English chemist and physician, born in London, studied medicine at Guy's Hospital, and became professor of Chemistry at Oxford (1803), and fellow of the Royal Society. In 1819, with Garden, he discovered naphthalene in coal tar.

(2) William (*c.* 1645–1701), Scottish privateer and pirate, born probably at Greenock, son, it is thought, of a Covenanting minister who died in 1679, went early to sea, saw much privateering service, and gained a high reputation for courage, and in 1691 a reward of £150 from New York City. In 1696 he was given a ship of 30 guns to act against the French and to seize pirates. In 1697 he reached Madagascar, the pirates' chief rendezvous, but turned pirate himself. After a two years' cruise he returned to the West Indies, and venturing to Boston, was arrested, sent to England and hanged May 23, 1701. See the *Trial* (ed. Brooks, 1930), C. N. Dalton, *The real Captain Kidd: a vindication* (1911); H. T. Wilkins, *Captain Kidd and his Skeleton Island* (1935).

KIELLAND, Alexander, *kel'ahn* (1849–1906), Norwegian novelist, was born at Stavanger, where in 1891 he became burgomaster. His works include *Garman and Worse* (1884), *Skipper Worse* (1885), *Tales of Two Countries* (1891).

KIENZL, Wilhelm, *keen'tsl'* (1857–1941), Austrian composer, born at Waizenkirchen, Austria, became *kapellmeister* at Amsterdam, Krefeld, Graz, Hamburg and Munich. His third opera, *Der Evangelimann* (Berlin 1895; London 1897), was his first success. See his *Richard Wagner* (Munich 1904).

KIEPERT, Heinrich, *kee'pert* (1818–99), German geographer, born at Berlin, conducted the Geographical Institute at Weimar (1845–52), in 1859 became professor of Geography at Berlin, and wrote on ancient geography. Published works include *Atlas antiquus, 12 maps of the ancient world* (7th ed. 1882).

KIERKEGAARD, Sören Aaby, *keer'kė-gawr* (1813–55), Danish philosopher and theologian, progenitor of modern existentialism, was born deformed at Copenhagen, where he read theology (in which he graduated in 1840 but without taking orders), philosophy and literature. Obsessed by some mysterious guilt of his father's, he broke off, after much heart-searching, his engagement to Regine Olsen. Such deliberate, significant choosing of one's future self became the basis of his philosophizing. It is something that has to be lived through and experienced, purely speculative systems of thought such as Hegel's being irrelevant to existence-making choices, because existence on account of its multiplicity can never be incorporated into a system. For Hegel's synthesis, Kierkegaard substituted the disjunction *Either/Or* (1843), the basis of choice. In *Philosophical Fragments* (1844; tr. Princeton 1936) and especially in *Concluding Unscientific Postscript* (1846; tr. Princeton 1941) he attacked all philosophical system building and formulated

the thesis that subjectivity is truth. He also attacked organized dogmatic Christianity in nine issues of the journal, *The Instant*, because it failed to make sufficiently clear the absolute moral isolation of the individual, the necessity for really choosing Christ, instead of just adhering to prescribed dogma and ritual. Forerunner of the existentialism of Sartre, Heidegger, Jaspers, Barth and Buber. See his *Samlede Voerker* (1920–31; tr. W. Lowrie 1938 ff.), biographical *Glimpses and Impressions*, ed. T. H. Croxall (1959) and studies by E. Hirsch (1933), T. Haecker (tr. A. Dru 1936), L. Shestov (1936), R. Jolivet (1951), J. D. Collins (1954) and H. Diem (1959).

KILIAN, St. See CILIAN.

KILLIGREW, (1) Thomas (1612–83), English dramatist, brother of (2), page in the household of Charles I, and afterwards a companion of Charles II in exile and his groom of the bedchamber after the Restoration. He published in 1664 nine indifferent plays, written, he tells us, in nine different cities. He was for some time manager of the king's company, and obtained permission to give female parts to women.

(2) Sir William (1606–95), English dramatist, brother of (1), fought in the Civil War, and wrote a comedy, *Pandora*, and tragicomedies, *Selindra*, *Ormasdes*, and *The Siege of Urbin*. See book by Harbage (Philadelphia 1930).

KILMUIR, 1st Earl of (1900–67), formerly **Sir David Patrick Maxwell Fyfe,** British lawyer and Conservative politician, born in Aberdeen and educated at George Watson's College, Edinburgh, and at Balliol College, Oxford. He took silk in 1934, the youngest K.C. since the time of Charles II. He was M.P. for West Derby (Liverpool) (1935–54) when he became lord high chancellor. He was deputy chief prosecutor at the Nuremberg trial of the principal Nazi war criminals. Home secretary and minister for Welsh affairs in the 1951 Government, he advised on a heavy programme of controversial legislation. Knighted 1942, created Viscount 1954, and Earl and Baron Fyfe of Dornoch in 1962. He wrote *Monopoly* (1948) and *Political Adventure* (1964).

KILVERT, Francis (1840–79), English clergyman, whose *Diary (1870–79)* (discovered 1937, ed. by W. Plomer in 3 vols. 1938, 1939, 1940, n.e. 1961; in 1 vol. 1944) describing his life as curate and vicar, is an important social historical document of his period, if not quite on a par with Pepys and Evelyn.

KILWARDBY, Robert (d. 1279), a Dominican, was in 1273 made Archbishop of Canterbury, and in 1278 a cardinal. He died at Viterbo. See study by E. Sommer-Seckendorff (Rome 1937).

KIMBERLEY, John Wodehouse, 1st Earl of (1826–1902), Liberal statesman, was lord privy-seal 1868–70, colonial secretary 1870–74 and 1880–82, secretary for India 1882–85 and 1886, secretary for India and lord president of the Council 1892–94, and then foreign secretary till 1895. Kimberley in South Africa was named after him.

KIMHI, or Kimchi, David, *kim'κHi* (*c.* 1160–1235), Jewish grammarian, lived and died at Narbonne. Subsequent Hebrew grammars and lexicons are based on his. See his *Hebrew grammar systematically presented and critically annotated* by W. Chomsky (New York 1952).

KINCK, Hans Ernst (1865–1926), Norwegian novelist and dramatist, born at Öksfjord. His works illustrate his deep love of nature and his interest in the lives of peasants and include *Sneskaulenbrast* (1918–19) and *Driftekaren* (1908), a verse play. He died at Oslo.

KING, (1) Edward (1612–37), Milton's fellow-student, whose drowning off the Welsh coast is commemorated in *Lycidas*.

(2) **Edward** (1829–1910), English bishop, son of the Archdeacon of Rochester, graduated from Oriel College, Oxford in 1851, and was principal of Cuddesdon 1863–73, and regius professor of Pastoral Theology 1873–1885, and then bishop of Lincoln. Tried in 1890 for ritualistic practices, he was condemned on only two charges. See his *Sermons and addresses* (1911), and study by Randolph and Townroe (1918).

(3) **Martin Luther** (1929–68), American Negro minister, born at Atlanta, Ga., son of a Baptist pastor, studied systematic theology at Boston University, and set up first ministry at Montgomery, Ala. Became a leader of a civil rights movement, based on principle of non-violence. In 1964 he received an honorary doctorate from Yale, the Kennedy peace prize, and the Nobel peace prize. He was assassinated in Memphis, Tenn., while on a civil rights mission. His white assassin, **James Earl Ray**, was apprehended in London, and in 1969 was sentenced in Memphis to 99 years.

(4) **William Lyon Mackenzie** (1874–1950), Canadian Liberal statesman, born at Kitchener, Ontario, studied law at Toronto, won a fellowship in political science at Ontario and accepted the newly created post of deputy minister of labour (1900–08), when he left the civil service and became an M.P., being appointed minister of labour (1909–14). In 1914 he became director of industrial relations in the Rockefeller Foundation for industrial problems, publishing an important study on the subject, *Industry and Humanity* in 1918. In 1919 he became Liberal leader and was prime minister 1921–26, 1926–30, and 1935–48. His view that the dominions should be autonomous communities within the British Empire and not form a single entity as Smuts advocated, materialized in the famous Statute of Westminster (1931). He opposed sanctions against Italy over Ethiopia and on the eve of World War II wrote to Hitler, Mussolini and President Mosicki of Poland urging them to preserve the peace, but promptly declared war on Germany with the other dominions once Poland was attacked. He opposed conscription, except eventually for overseas service, and signed agreements with Roosevelt (1940–41) integrating the economies of the two countries and represented Canada at the London and San Francisco foundation conferences of the United Nations (1945). He was awarded the O.M. in 1947. See study by Ferns and Ostry (1955) and Lives by Hutchison (1952), Dawson, Vol. I (1958) and Neatby, Vol. II (1963).

(5) **William Rufus** (1786–1853), American statesman, born in N. Carolina, member of the state legislature for 3 years, entered congress in 1810, senator for Alabama 1820–1844, minister to France 1844–46, senator again 1846–53, and, just before his death, vice president of the U.S.

KINGDON - WARD, Frank (1885–1958), English botanist, plant explorer and writer, son of the botanist **Harry Marshall Ward** (1854–1906), made important botanical journeys in China, Tibet, Burma, Thailand, &c., and wrote on his travels and on his associated plant discoveries. His publications include *The Land of the Blue Poppy* (1913), *In Farthest Burma* (1921), &c.

KINGLAKE, Alexander William (1809–91), English historian, born at Wilton House, near Taunton, from Eton passed in 1828 to Trinity College, Cambridge. He was called to the bar in 1837, and made a fair practice, but retired in 1856 to devote himself to literature and politics. A tour about 1835 had already given birth to *Eōthen* (1844), one of the most brilliant and popular books of Eastern travel. In 1854 he went out to the Crimea. He was returned for Bridgwater as a Liberal in 1857, took a prominent part against Lord Palmerston's Conspiracy Bill, and denounced the French annexation of Savoy. His *History of the War in the Crimea* (8 vols. 1863–87) is on the literary side one of the finest historical works of its century. See a study by Tuckwell (1902).

KINGO, Thomas Hansen, *keeng'ō* (1634–1703), Danish religious poet, born in Slangerup. He was of Scottish descent, and became Bishop of Fyn in 1677. He wrote several collections of hymns and much religious and secular poetry.

KINGSFORD, Anna, *née* **Bonus** (1846–88), English doctor and writer, born at Stratford, Essex. In 1867 she married a Shropshire clergyman, and thereafter became a convert to Catholicism (1870), an antivivisectionist, M.D. of Paris (1880), a vegetarian, a Theosophist, &c. See Life by E. Maitland (1895).

KINGSLEY, (1) Charles (1819–75), English author, born at Holne vicarage, Dartmoor. In 1838 entered Magdalene College, Cambridge, and took a classical first in 1842. As curate and then (1844) rector, he spent the rest of his life at Eversley in Hampshire. His dramatic poem, *The Saint's Tragedy, or The True Story of Elizabeth of Hungary* (1848), was followed by *Alton Locke* (1850) and *Yeast* (1851), brilliant social novels which had enormous influence at the time. He had thrown himself into various schemes for the improvement of the working classes, and like Maurice was a 'Christian Socialist'. As 'Parson Lot' he published an immense number of articles on current topics, especially in the *Christian Socialist* and *Politics for the People*. *Hypatia* (1853) is a brilliant picture of early Christianity in conflict with Greek philosophy at Alexandria. *Westward Ho!* (1855) is a lifelike presentment of Elizabethan England and the Spanish Main. *Two Years Ago* (1857) and *Hereward the Wake* (1866) were his later novels. In 1860 he was appointed professor of Modern History at Cambridge, *The Roman and the Teuton* (1864) being based on his Cambridge lectures. In

1869 he resigned his professorship and was appointed canon of Chester. In 1869–70 he made a voyage to the West Indies, and on his return issued the charming record *At Last*. In 1873 he was appointed canon of Westminster and chaplain to the Queen. The collected works of this combative, enthusiastic and sympathetic apostle of what was called (*not* by him) 'muscular Christianity' fill 28 volumes (1879–81), and include *Glaucus* (1855), *The Heroes* (1856), *The Water Babies* (1863), *Town Geology* (1872), *Prose Idylls* (1873) and *Health and Education* (1874). See *Life by his widow* (2 vols. 1877), G. Kendall, *Charles Kingsley and his Ideas* (1947), U. Pope-Hennessy, *Canon Charles Kingsley* (1948).

(2) **George Henry** (1827–92), brother of (1), studied medicine, travelled much, and wrote many books of sport and travel, including *South Sea Bubbles* (1872).

(3) **Henry** (1830–76), brother of (1), was educated at King's College School, London, and Worcester College, Oxford. From 1853 to 1858 he resided in Australia, and on his return published a vigorous picture of colonial life in *Geoffry Hamlyn* (1859). To this succeeded *Ravenshoe* (1861), his masterpiece; *Austin Elliot* (1863); *The Hillyars and the Burtons*, another novel of Australian life (1865), &c. In 1869–70 he edited the *Edinburgh Daily Review*. See S. M. Ellis, *Henry Kingsley*.

(4) **Mary** (1862–1900), daughter of (2), was an enterprising traveller in West Africa, wrote admirably, and died a nurse in a South African hospital during the Boer war. See *Lives* by Gwynne (1932), C. Howard (1957) and Olwen Campbell (1957). H. Simpson, *A Woman Among Wild Men* (1938), I. M. Holmes, *In Africa's Service* (1949) and R. Glynn, *Mary Kingsley in Africa* (1956).

(5) **Mary St Leger** (1852–1931), daughter of (1), married in 1876 the Rev. W. Harrison, rector of Clovelly, and as 'Lucas Malet' completed her father's *Tutor's Story* (1916) and wrote powerful novels—*Mrs Lorimer* (1882), *Colonel Enderby's Wife* (1885), *The Wages of Sin* (1890), *The Carissima* (1896), *Sir Richard Calmady* (1901), &c. She became a Roman Catholic in 1899.

KINGSTON, William Henry Giles (1814–80), English author, son of a merchant in Oporto, where he spent much of his youth. He wrote over 150 boys' adventure stories including such favourites as *Peter the Whaler* (1851) and *The Three Midshipmen* (1862).

KINKEL, (1) **Gottfried** (1815–82), German poet, born at Oberkassel near Bonn, lectured at Bonn on theology, poetry and the history of art. Involved in the revolutionary movement of 1848, he was imprisoned in Spandau (1850), from where he escaped. He taught German in London until 1866, when he was appointed professor of Archaeology and Art at Zürich. As a poet his fame rests upon *Otto der Schütz* (1846; 73rd ed. 1894), *Der Grobschmied von Antwerpen* (1872), *Tanagra* (1883), *Gedichte* (1843–68) and a drama, *Nimrod* (1857). He also wrote a history of art (1845) and monographs on Freiligrath (1867), Rubens (1874), &c. See *Lives* by Strodtmann (1850), Henne-Am Rhyn (1883), and Lübke (1893), also E. Bebler, *Conrad F.*

Meyer und Gottfried Kinkel (Zürich 1949). His first wife, **Johanna** (1810–58), a distinguished musician, wrote a novel, *Hans Ibeles in London* (1860), and, with her husband, *Erzählungen* (1849), a collection of tales.

KINMONT WILLIE. See ARMSTRONG (8).

KIPLING, Rudyard (1865–1936), English writer, was born at Bombay, the son of John Lockwood Kipling, C.I.E. (1837–1911), principal in 1875–93 of the School of Art at Lahore, and author of *Beast and Man in India* (1891). Rudyard was educated in England, but returned in 1880 to India, where he worked as a journalist on the Lahore *Civil and Military Gazette*. His mildly satirical verses *Departmental Ditties* (1886), and the short stories *Plain Tales from the Hills* (1888) and *Soldiers Three* (1889), won him a reputation in England, whither he returned in 1889 and settled in London, where *The Light that Failed* (1890), his first attempt at a full-length novel—a genre in which he was never too happy—was not altogether successful. In London he met Wolcott Balestier the American author-publisher, with whom he collaborated in *The Naulakha* (1892), and whose sister Caroline he married (1892). A spell of residence in his wife's native state of Vermont ended abruptly in 1899 through incompatibility with in-laws and locals, and the remainder of Kipling's career was spent in England. Meanwhile he had written the brilliantly successful *Barrack Room Ballads* (1892) and *The Seven Seas* (1896), both collections of verse, and further short stories published as *Many Inventions* (1893) and *The Day's Work* (1899). The two *Jungle Books* (1894–95) have won a place among the classic animal stories, and *Stalky and Co* (1899) presents semi-autobiographical but delightfully uninhibited episodes based on the author's schooldays at the United Services College at Westward Ho!. *Kim* appeared in 1901, and the children's classic *Just So Stories* in 1902. The verse collection *The Five Nations* (1903) included the highly successful, though now somewhat démodé, 'Recessional' written for Queen Victoria's diamond jubilee. Later works include *Puck of Pook's Hill* (1906), *Rewards and Fairies* (1910), *Debits and Credits* (1926), and the autobiographical *Something of Myself* (1937). Kipling's real merit as a writer has tended to become obscured in recent years by the decline in his popularity brought about by the current fashion of denigrating Britain's period of colonial greatness; but those who condemn his forthright patriotism as 'jingoistic' and 'imperialistic' ignore not only the great body of his work which was far removed from this sphere, but also his own criticisms and satire on some of the less admirable aspects of colonialism. It must not be forgotten that he was awarded the Nobel prize for literature in 1907. See bibliography by F. V. Livingston (N.Y. 1927) with Supplement (Cambridge, Mass. 1938); also *Lives* by B. Dobrée (1951) and C. E. Carrington (1955), and study by J. M. S. Tompkins (1959).

KIPP, Petrus Jacobus (1808–64), Dutch chemist, was born in Utrecht, Holland, and started a business in laboratory apparatus in Delft in 1830. He invented the apparatus called after him for the continuous and automatic production of gases such as carbon dioxide, hydrogen and hydrogen sulphide. A representation of it appears in the arms of the Dutch Chemical Society. He also invested a method of fixing carbon and pastel drawings.

KIPPING, Frederick Stanley (1863–1949), British chemist, F.R.S. (1897), professor of Chemistry at Nottingham, investigated silicon compounds and was responsible for their development and use in the production of plastics capable of resisting higher temperatures. See Perkin and Kipping: *Organic Chemistry* (1894; new edition 1949).

KIRBY, William (1759–1850), English entomologist, born at Witnesham Hall, Suffolk, author of *Monographia Apum Angliae* (1802), *Introduction to Entomology* (1815–26), written with James Spence, and *Habits and Instincts of Animals* (Bridgewater Treatise, 1835). See Life by Freeman (1852).

KIRCHHOFF, Gustav Robert, *keerKH'hōf* (1824–87), German physicist, born at Königsberg, became professor at Berlin in 1874. He distinguished himself in elasticity, heat, optics and especially spectrum analysis. See Life by Boltzmann (1888).

KIRCHNER, Ernst Ludwig, *kirHK-nėr* (1880–1938), German artist, born at Aschaffenburg. He studied architecture at Dresden, but he became the leading spirit in the formation, with Erich Heckel and Karl Schmidt-Rottluff, of ' Die Brücke ' (1905–13), the first group of German expressionists, whose work was much influenced by primitive German woodcuts. Many of his works were confiscated as degenerate in 1937, and he committed suicide in 1938. See monograph by W. Grohmann (1926).

KIRK, Robert (c. 1641–92), Scottish author, turned the metrical Psalms into Gaelic, and was the author of *The Secret Commonwealth of Elves, Fauns, and Fairies* (1691), latest ed. (1933) with introduction by R. B. Cunninghame Graham.

KIRKCALDY, Sir William, of Grange (c. 1520–73), Scottish politician, as one of Beaton's murderers (1546) was imprisoned at Mont St Michel (1547–50). He took service with France, but in 1559 was opposing the French cause in Scotland. He figured at Carberry Hill, was made governor of Edinburgh Castle, and did much to win Langside; but going over to Queen Mary's party, held Edinburgh Castle for her till May 1573. He was hanged on August 3. See Lives by James Grant (1849) and Barbé (1897).

KIRKE, (1) **Edward** (1553–1613), Spenser's friend, author of the preface and commentary of his *Shepheardes Calender* (1579), and from 1580 rector of Risby, Bury St Edmunds.

(2) **Percy** (c. 1646–91), English Army colonel who had served 1681–84 in Tangiers, and whose men (' Kirke's Lambs ') committed after Sedgemoor (1685) fearful atrocities. He early deserted to William, and helped to raise the siege of Londonderry.

KIRKUP, Seymour Stocker (1788–1880), English artist, Dante scholar, and spiritualist, the friend of Haydon, Landor, Trelawny, the Brownings, &c., was born in London, and from 1816 lived in Italy, chiefly at Florence,

where in 1840 he discovered Giotto's portrait of Dante.

KIRKWOOD, Daniel (1814–95), American astronomer, born at Harford, Maryland, became professor of Mathematics at Delaware (1851) and at Indiana (1856). He explained the unequal distribution of asteroids in the ring system of Saturn in terms of the ' Kirkwood gaps ' and subjected La Place's theories to penetrating criticism. His works include *Comets and Meteors* (1873) and *The Asteroids* (1887).

KIRWAN, Richard (1733–1812), Irish chemist, born in Galway, published (1784) the first systematic English treatise on mineralogy, and was a leading exponent of the phlogiston theory.

KISFALUDY, *kish'fė-loo-di,* (1) **Karoly** (1788–1830), Hungarian dramatist, brother of (2), regenerator of the national drama, became famous by his *Tartars in Hungary* (1819).

(2) **Sandor** (1772–1844), Hungarian poet, brother of (1), served in the Austrian army, 1793–1801, and again in 1809. The rest of his life was devoted to literature and farming.

KITAIBEL, Paul (1757–1817), Hungarian chemist, in 1789 discovered tellurium independently of Müller, and in 1794 became professor of Botany and Chemistry at Pest.

KITASATO, Shibasaburo (1856–1931), Japanese bacteriologist, studied in Germany under Koch and later founded in Japan an Institute for Infectious Diseases. He discovered the bacillus of bubonic plague (1894), isolated the bacilli of symptomatic anthrax, dysentery and tetanus, and prepared a diphtheria antitoxin.

KITCHENER, Horatio Herbert, 1st Earl, Kitchener of Khartoum (1850–1916), English soldier and statesman, was born near Ballylongford, Kerry, and entered the Engineers in 1871. On the Palestine survey, 1874–78, and then on that of Cyprus till 1882, he served in the Sudan campaign 1883–85. Sirdar of the Egyptian army from 1890, he by the final rout of the Khalifa at Omdurman, September 2, 1898, won back the Sudan for Egypt, and was made a peer. Successively chief of the staff and commander-in-chief in South Africa (1900–02), he finished the Boer war, received a grant of £50,000, was made viscount, O.M., commander-in-chief in India (1092–09), and agent and consul-general in Egypt (1911). Made secretary for war August 7, 1914, he organized a great army before he was lost with H.M.S. *Hampshire* (mined off Orkney), June 5, 1916. See Life by Arthur (1920); R. B. Esher, *The Tragedy of Lord Kitchener* (1921); V. W. Germains, *The Truth about Kitchener* (1925); C. R. Ballard, *Kitchener* (1930); P. Magnus, *Kitchener: Portrait of an Imperialist* (1958).

KITTO, John (1804–54), English biblical scholar, born at Plymouth, author of *The Pictorial Bible* (1838; new ed. 1855), *Pictorial History of Palestine* (1839–40), *Daily Bible Illustrations* (1849–53; new ed. by Dr Porter, 1867), &c. See Lives by Ryland (1856) and Eadie (1857).

KIVI, Aleksis, real name **Steuvall** (1834–72), Finnish dramatist and novelist, born at Nurmijärvi, wrote penetratingly of Finnish peasant life, and is now recognized as one of his country's greatest writers, but died insane, poverty-stricken and unrecognized. See Life by Tarkainen (1916).

KJELDAHL, Johan Gustav Christoffer Thorsager, *kel'dahl* (1849–1900), Danish chemist, was noted for his analytical methods of determination, and specially so for the method of nitrogen determination named after him.

KJELLAND. See KIELLAND.

KJERULF, Halfdan, *ke'roolf* (1815–68), Norwegian composer, best known for his charming songs, was born and died in Christiania.

KLAPKA, George (1820–92), Hungarian soldier and patriot, born at Temesvár, became lieut.-gen. in the Austrian army, but in the revolution fought valiantly against the Austrians, holding Komorn for eight weeks after the rest of Hungary had submitted. The amnesty of 1867 let him return from exile, and he died at Budapest. He wrote a history of the war (1851) and *Memoirs* (1850–87).

KLAPROTH, *klap'rōt,* (1) **Heinrich Julius von** (1783–1835), German orientalist, son of (2), born at Berlin, in 1805 was appointed interpreter to a Russian embassy to China. It was stopped on the frontier, when Klaproth explored Siberia, as afterwards (in 1807–08) the Caucasus and Georgia. In 1816 he was appointed professor of Asiatic Languages by the king of Prussia, with permission to work in Paris.

(2) **Martin Heinrich** (1743–1817), German chemist, born at Wernigerode, father of (1), became the first professor of Chemistry at Berlin University, devised new analytical methods, discovered zirconium and uranium, and named tellurium.

KLÉBER, Jean Baptiste (1753–1800), French soldier, born at Strasbourg, in 1776 obtained a commission in the Austrian army. Inspector for a time of public buildings at Belfort, in 1792 he enlisted as a volunteer, and by 1793 had risen to a general of brigade. As such he commanded in the Vendean war, but was recalled for leniency. In 1794 he led the left wing at Fleurus, and captured Maastricht; in June 1796 he gained the victory of Altenkirchen. He accompanied Bonaparte to Egypt, was wounded at Alexandria, and won the battle of Mount Tabor (1799). When Bonaparte left Egypt he entrusted the chief command to Kléber, who concluded a convention with Sir Sidney Smith for its evacuation; but on Admiral Keith's refusal to ratify it Kléber resolved to reconquer Egypt, and destroyed the Turkish army at Heliopolis. In the course of an attempt to conclude a treaty with the Turks, he was assassinated by a Turkish fanatic at Cairo in 1800. See G. Lecomte, *Au chant de la Marseillaise . . . Merceau et Kléber* (Paris 1929).

KLEE, Paul, *klay* (1879–1940), Swiss artist, born at Münchenbuchsee near Bern. He studied at Munich and settled there, being associated with Marc and Kandinsky in the Blaue Reiter group (1911–12). From 1920 to 1932 he taught at the Bauhaus, his *Pädagogisches Skizzenbuch* being published in 1925. After he had returned to Bern in 1933, many of his works were confiscated in Germany as degenerate. Klee's work has been called

surrealist, but in his fantastic, small-scale, mainly abstract pictures he created, with supreme technical skill in many media, a very personal world of free fancy, expressed with a sly wit and subtle colouring and giving the effect of inspired doodling, e.g., the well-known *Twittering Machine* in the Museum of Modern Art, New York. See the monographs by D. Cooper (1949), W. Grohmann (1954), and Schmidt (1958), and study by G. di San Lazzaro (1957).

KLEIBER, Erich, *klī'-ber* (1890–1956), Austrian conductor, born in Vienna, at the age of 33 became director of the Berlin State Opera, which post he held for 12 years until forced by the Nazis to leave Germany. In 1938 he became a citizen of the Argentine. After the war he was again appointed director of the Berlin State Opera until his resignation in 1955. He gave the first performance of Berg's *Wozzeck.*

KLEIST, *klīst,* (1) **Ewald Christian von** (1715–1759), German poet, born at Zeblin, Pomerania. He was killed at the battle of Kunersdorf. See Life by Einbeck (1861).

(2) **Heinrich von** (1777–1811), German dramatist and poet, born at Frankfurt-on-Oder, October 18, left the army in 1799 to study, and soon devoted himself to literature. His best plays are still popular, notably *Prinz Friedrich von Homburg* (1811). His finest tale is *Michael Kohlhaas.* He shot himself November 21, 1811. See Lives by E. and G. Romien (1931), R. March (1954), and E. L. Stahl, *H. von Kleist's Dramas* (1949).

KLEMPERER, Otto (1885–1973), German conductor, born in Breslau, studied at Frankfurt and Berlin and first appeared as a conductor in 1907. He made a name as a champion of modern music and in 1927 he was appointed director of the Kroll Opera in Berlin until it was closed down in 1931. Naziism drove him to the United States (in 1933) where he was director of the Los Angeles Symphony Orchestra till 1939. In spite of continuing ill-health, he was musical director of Budapest opera from 1947 to 1950. In his later years he concentrated mainly on the German classical and romantic composers, and was particularly known for his interpretation of Beethoven. He has composed a mass and lieder.

KLINGER, (1) **Friedrich Maximilian von** (1752–1831), German playwright and romance writer, was born at Frankfurt-am-Main, died at Dorpat. The ' Sturm-und-Drang ' school was named after one of his tragedies. See works by Erdmann (1877) and Rieger (1880).

(2) **Max** (1857–1920), German artist, born at Leipzig, studied at Karlsruhe, Brussels and Paris, and excited hostility as well as admiration by his pen drawings and etchings, which were audaciously original in concept and often imbued with macabre realism. Later, he turned to painting, and did much work in coloured sculpture, including Beethoven (1902). See study by M. Schmid (1926).

KLOPSTOCK, Friedrich Gottlieb (1724–1803), German poet, was born at Quedlinburg. Inspired by Virgil and Milton, he began *The Messiah* as a student at Jena (1745), continued it at Leipzig (1748), and completed it in 1773. He settled in Hamburg in 1771 with a sinecure appointment, and pensions from Frederick V of Denmark (from 1751) and the Margrave of Baden. Regarded in his own time as a great religious poet, he helped to inaugurate the golden age of German literature, especially by his lyrics and odes. See Life by Muncker (1888).

KLUCK, Alexander von (1846–1934), Prussian general, born at Münster, in August 1914 drove the Anglo-French forces almost to Paris, but defeated at the Marne (September 6), had to retreat. Wounded 1915, he retired in 1916. See his *Der Marsch auf Paris . . .* (1920).

KLUGE, Günther von, *kloo'gě* (1882–1944), German general who carried out the Nazi occupation (1939) of the Polish corridor, commanded the German armies on the Central Russian front (1942) and in July 1944 replaced Rundstedt as commander-in-chief of the Nazi armies in France confronting the Allied invasion, but was himself replaced after the Falaise gap débâcle.

KNELLER, Sir Godfrey (1646–1723), portrait painter, born at Lübeck, studied at Amsterdam and in Italy, in 1676 came to London, and in 1680 was appointed court painter. In 1691 William III knighted him, and in 1715 George I made him a baronet. He died at Twickenham. His best-known works are the *Beauties of Hampton Court* (painted for William III), his forty-eight portraits of the 'Kit-Cat Club,' and of nine sovereigns (Charles II to George I, Louis XIV, Peter the Great, and the Emperor Charles VI). See C. H. C. Baker, *Lely and Kneller* (1922); M. M. Killanin, *Sir Godfrey Kneller and his Times* (1948). His brother, **John Zacharias** (1644–1702), architectural and portrait painter, also settled in England.

KNICKERBOCKER, Harmen Jansen (*c.* 1650–*c.* 1716), of Friesland, was one of the earliest settlers of New Amsterdam (New York). A descendant, **Johannes** (1749–1827), was a friend of Washington Irving, who immortalized the name through his *History of New York* by ' Diedrich Knickerbocker ' (1809).

KNIGHT, (1) Charles (1791–1873), English author and publisher, born in Windsor. From journalism, as proprietor of the *Windsor and Eton Express* (1811–21) he turned to publishing popular editions of serious literature (*Pictorial Shakespeare,* 1838–41, *Popular History of England,* 1862, &c.) and reference books (*Penny Cyclopaedia,* 1838, &c.). From 1860 he published the *London Gazette.* See his *Passages of a Working Life* (1863–65), and Life by A. Clowes (1892).

(2) **Harold** (1874–1961), English portrait painter, husband of (3). He studied at Nottingham and in Paris, and worked in Yorkshire, Cornwall and Holland. Knight painted a large number of commissioned portraits, including those of *Sir Laurence Olivier* and *Lord Iliffe.* He was elected R.A. in 1937.

(3) **Dame Laura** (1877–1970), English artist, wife of (2), born at Long Eaton. She studied at Nottingham, married her fellow-student, Harold Knight, in 1903, and travelled in many parts of the world. She

produced a long series of oil paintings of the ballet, the circus and gipsy life, in a lively and forceful style, and also executed a number of watercolour landscapes. She was created D.B.E. in 1929 and elected R.A. in 1936. See her autobiography *Oil Paint and Grease Paint* (1936).

(4) **Richard Payne** (1750–1824), English numismatist, a London connoisseur, who left his coins, bronzes, gems, &c. to the British Museum. He was M.P. for Leominster (1780), and Ludlow (1784–1806).

KNIPPERDOLLING, Bernhard (*c.* 1490–1536), German reformer, a noted leader (1527–36) of the fanatical Münster Anabaptists. See E. B. Bax, *Rise and Fall of the Anabaptists* (1903).

KNOBLOCK, Edward (1874–1945), British playwright and novelist, born in New York. Educated at Harvard, he came to Britain to write a series of successful plays, Among these are *The Faun* (1911), *My Lady's Dress* (1914) which some consider to be his best, *Tiger, Tiger* (1918), *The Mulberry Bush* (1930). He collaborated with Arnold Bennett in two plays, *Milestones* (1912), *London Life* (1924). He also produced stage versions of Vicki Baum's *Grand Hotel* (1931) and J. B. Priestley's *Good Companions* (1931) with the author. *The Ant Heap* (1929), *The Man with Two Mirrors* (1931) *Love Lady* (1933) and *Inexperience* (1941) are some of his novels. He became a naturalized British subject in 1916.

KNOLLES, *nōlz,* (1) **Richard** (*c.* 1550–1610), English historian, a schoolmaster at Sandwich, wrote a *Generall Historie of the Turkes* (1603).

(2) **Sir Robert** (*c.* 1317–1407), English soldier, a leader of free companies in France, who some time followed the Black Prince and opposed Du Guesclin. He died at his Norfolk seat, Sculthorpe.

KNOLLYS, Sir Francis, *nōlz* (*c.* 1514–96), English statesman, from 1572 treasurer of Queen Elizabeth's household. In 1568–69 he had charge of Mary, Queen of Scots.

KNOWLES, (1) Herbert (1798–1817), English poet, born at Gomersal, Leeds, and remembered by his ' Stanzas in Richmond Churchyard '.

(2) **Sir James** (1831–1908), English architect and editor, born in London, educated at University College, designed many important churches and edifices. Early a contributor to literature, he in 1869 founded the Metaphysical Society, became editor of the *Contemporary Review* in 1870, and in 1877 founded the *Nineteenth Century.*

(3) **James Sheridan** (1784–1862), Irish dramatist, born at Cork, was a cousin of Richard Brinsley Sheridan (q.v.). After serving in the militia and studying medicine, he appeared on the stage first at Bath and then at Dublin. But he never attained much eminence, and subsequently he became a teacher in Belfast and (1816–28) in Glasgow. His *Caius Gracchus* (1815) was first performed at Belfast. *Virginius,* his most effective play, had been a success in Glasgow before Macready in 1820 produced it at Covent Garden. Besides *William Tell,* in which Macready achieved one of his greatest triumphs.

Knowles's other best plays are *Love, The Hunchback, The Love Chase*, and *The Wife*. Knowles appeared with fair success in many of his own pieces. About 1844 he became a Baptist preacher, drew large audiences to Exeter Hall, and published two anti-Roman Catholic works. From 1849 he had a civil list pension of £200 a year. He died at Torquay. Of a Life (1872) by his son only twenty-five copies were printed. See L. H. Meeks, *Sheridan Knowles and the Theatre of his Time* (1933).

KNOX, (1) **Edmund George Valpy**, pen-name 'Evoe' (1881–1971), English humorous writer and parodist, brother of (4), who joined the staff of *Punch* in 1921 and became editor from 1932 to 1949, contributing articles under his pen-name. His best work was republished in book form and includes *Parodies Regained, Fiction as She is Wrote, It Occurs to Me, Awful Occasions, Here's Misery* and *Folly Calling*.

(2) **John** (c. 1513–72), Scottish reformer, born at or near Haddington, was educated there and probably at the University of Glasgow. From 1540 to 1543 he acted as notary in Haddington, and must till the latter year have been in Catholic orders. In 1544 he was acting as tutor to the sons of two families, by whom he was brought into contact with George Wishart (q.v.), now full of zeal for the Lutheran reformation; and with him Knox thenceforward identified himself. Wishart was burned in March 1546, and Beaton was murdered in May. The cardinal's murderers held the castle of St Andrews; and here Knox joined them with his pupils (1547). Here he was formally called to the ministry, and preached with acceptance. A few months later the castle surrendered to the French and for eighteen months Knox remained a prisoner on the French galleys. In February 1549, on the intercession of Edward VI, Knox regained his liberty, and for four years made his home in England. In 1551 he was appointed one of six chaplains to Edward VI, and in 1552 was offered but refused the bishopric of Rochester. Knox, with five others, was consulted by Cranmer regarding his forty-two articles, and largely on Knox's representation the thirty-eighth article was so couched as to commit the Church of England to the Genevan doctrine of the eucharist. On Mary's accession Knox fled to Dieppe, and thence early in 1554 went to Geneva. In the autumn he accepted a call from the English congregation at Frankfurt-am-Main, where he remained only a few months. At Geneva he found a congregation of his own way of thinking, but ventured into Scotland in September 1555, making preaching journeys to Kyle, Castle Campbell, &c., and returned to Geneva in July 1556. For the next two years he remained chiefly in Geneva, and was much influenced by Calvin. To 1558 belongs his *First Blast of the Trumpet against the Monstrous Regiment of Women*. In 1557 the advocates of reform in Scotland bound themselves to religous revolution by the *First Covenant*; and by 1558 they felt themselves strong enough to summon Knox to their aid. From May 1559 Knox, again

in Scotland, was preaching at Perth and St Andrews. He gained these important towns to his cause, and by his labours in Edinburgh he also won a strong party. But the Reformers could not hold their ground against the regent, Mary of Guise, subsidized by France with money and soldiers. Mainly through the efforts of Knox, the assistance of England was obtained against the French invasion; and by the treaty of Leith and the death of the regent (1560) the insurgent party became masters of the country. Parliament ordered the ministers to draw up a Confession of Faith and Protestantism was established. Now the ministers drew up the first *Book of Discipline*, with its suggestions for the religious and educational organization of the country. The return of the young queen to Scotland (August 1561) introduced new elements into the strife of parties; and during the six years of her reign Knox's attitude towards her was that of uncompromising antagonism. The celebration of mass in Holyrood Chapel first roused his wrath; and a sermon delivered by him in St Giles led to the first of his famous interviews with Mary. He went so far as to alienate the most powerful noble of his own party—Lord James Stuart, afterwards the Regent Moray; but the marriage of Mary with Darnley (1565) brought them together again. After the murder of Rizzio he withdrew to Ayrshire, where he wrote part of his *History of the Reformation in Scotland*. The murder of Darnley, Mary's marriage with Bothwell, and her flight into England again threw the management of affairs into the hands of the Protestant party; and under Moray as regent the acts of 1560 in favour of the Reformed religion were duly ratified by the Estates. The assassination of Moray in 1570, and the formation of a strong party in favour of Mary, once more endangered the cause, and Knox removed to St Andrews for safety. On November 9, 1572, at the induction of his successor, he made his last public appearance at St Giles. He died on the 24th, and was buried in the churchyard attached to St Giles. His first wife, Marjory Bowes, died in 1560, leaving him two sons. By his second wife, Margaret Stewart, daughter of Lord Ochiltree, whom (then not above sixteen) he married in 1564, he had three daughters. Knox is the pre-eminent type of the religious Reformer—dominated by his one transcendent idea, indifferent to or hostile to every interest of life that did not subserve its realization. The term fanatic is hardly applicable to one who combined in such degree the shrewdest worldly sense with ever-ready wit and native humour. The impress of his individuality, stamped on every page of his *History of the Reformation in Scotland*, renders his work unique. See E. Muir, *John Knox, Portrait of a Calvinist* (1929); Lord E. Percy, *John Knox* (1937); H. Watt, *John Knox in Controversy* (1950); G. MacGregor, *The Thundering Scot* (1958); A new edition of *The History of the Reformation in Scotland* appeared in 1950.

(3) **Robert** (1791–1862), Scottish anatomist, born in Edinburgh, became conservator of the newly-established museum of Edinburgh

College of Surgeons in 1824, and from 1826–1840 ran an anatomy school. He won fame as a teacher but attracted considerable odium through having obtained subjects for dissection from Burke (q.v.) and Hare. He is the subject of Bridie's play *The Anatomist*.

(4) **Ronald Arbuthnott** (1888–1957), English theologian and essayist, brother of (1), was born in Birmingham. Educated at Eton and Balliol College, Oxford, he became a fellow and lecturer at Trinity College, Oxford, in 1910, but resigned in 1917 on his reception into the Church of Rome. From 1926 to 1939 he was Catholic chaplain at the University. Author of numerous works of apologetics, his translation of the Bible, widely used by Roman Catholics, is specially noteworthy. His essays are distinguished by their satirical wit and trenchant criticism of some contemporary modes and manners. See *Life* by E. Waugh (1959).

KNUT. See CANUTE.

KOCH, *koкн*, (1) **Karl** (1809–79), German botanist, born near Weimar, in 1836 visited southern Russia, and in 1843–44 Armenia, Transcaucasia, &c. He became extraordinary professor of Botany at Jena in 1836, and in 1848 at Berlin. His chief work is *Dendrologie* (1869–72); with books of travel, *Flora des Orients* (1848–54), &c.

(2) **Ludwig** (1881–   ), German naturalist, author, and lecturer. He followed a musical career in Paris and Milan, first as a violinist, then as a lieder and oratorio singer. He organized the ' Music in the Life of the Nations ' exhibition (1927), and in 1928 joined the staff of a recording company. He made the first out-door recordings of songs of wild birds, and, coming to England in 1936, became known, particularly through his broadcasts, for his unique collection of bird and animal sounds. His joint publications include *Songs of Wild Birds* (1936) and *Animal Language* (1938): see also his *Memoirs of a Birdman* (1955). Became an M.B.E. (1960).

(3) **Robert** (1843–1910), German bacteriologist, born at Klausthal in the Harz, practised medicine at Hanover and elsewhere. His work on wounds, septicaemia and splenic fever gained him a seat on the imperial board of health in 1880. Further researches in microscopy and bacteriology led to his discovery in 1882 of the *Bacillus tuberculosis*. In 1883 he was leader of the German expedition sent to Egypt and India in quest of the cholera germ. For his discovery of the cholera bacillus he received a gift of £5000 from the government. His discovery in 1890 of the phthisis bacillus and his lymph-inoculation cure (tuberculin) raised higher hopes than were realized. Professor at Berlin (1885), and director of the hygienic institute, in 1891 he became director of the new institute for infectious diseases. In 1896 and 1903 he was summoned to S. Africa to study rinderpest and other cattle plagues. He won a Nobel prize in 1905. See *Lives* by C. Wezel (Berlin 1912), Heymann (Leipzig 1932).

KOCHANOWSKI, Jan, *koкн-an-of'ski*(1530–1584), Polish poet, knew Ronsard in Paris, and was secretary to King Sigismund Augustus. He wrote elegies, epigrams, Latin poems, and translated the Psalms. See his poems trans. by D. P. Radin (California 1928).

KOCHBAS. See BAR COCHBA.

KÖCHEL, Ludwig Ritter von, *kæ-кнél* (1800–1877), Austrian musicologist, born at Stein, compiler of the famous catalogue of Mozart's works, which he arranged in chronological order, giving them the numbers commonly used to identify them today.

KOCHER, Emil Theodor, *koкн'ér* (1841–1917), Swiss surgeon, born and educated in Berne where he became a professor in 1872, was noted for his work on the physiology, pathology and surgery of the thyroid gland. In 1909 he was awarded the Nobel prize for physiology and medicine. See R. A. Leonard *History of Surgery* (1943).

KOCK, Paul de (1794–1871), French novelist, born at Passy, produced an endless series of novels, vivacious, piquant and very readable. His son, **Henri** (1819–92), followed with a far weaker series of works.

KODÁLY, Zoltán, *kŏ'dal-y'* (1882–1967), Hungarian composer, born at Kecskemét, studied in Budapest Conservatoire where he became professor. Among his best known works are his *Háry János* suite, *Dances of Galanta* and his many choral compositions, especially his *Psalmus Hungaricus* and *Te Deum*. In 1913 he and Bartok drafted a plan for a Hungarian folk-music collection, but the first volume was not published until 1951. For bibliography see Janos Bartok's article in *Magyar Zenei Szemle* (Budapest 1943).

KOENIG, Karl Rudolph, *kæ'neeg* (1832–1901), German physicist who settled in Paris and became an authority on acoustics. One of his inventions was a clock fork for the determination of absolute pitch.

KOESTLER, Arthur (1905–   ), Hungarian-born author and journalist, the best known political refugee and prisoner of his time, born in Budapest, studied pure science at Vienna and embracing the cause of Zionism as described in *Promise and Fulfilment* (1949) worked on a collective farm in Palestine (1926), but his idealism modified by his experiences, he became a political correspondent and later scientific editor for a German newspaper group. Dismissed as a Communist, he travelled in Russia (1932–33), but became disillusioned, breaking with the party finally in 1938 as described in *The Gods that Failed* (1950). He reported the Spanish Civil War (1936–37) for the London *News Chronicle*, was imprisoned under death-sentence by Franco, as retold in *Spanish Testament* (1938) and *Dialogue with Death* (1942) and again by the French (1940), escaped from German-occupied France via the French Foreign Legion, and, after a short imprisonment in London, joined the Pioneer Corps. These experiences, described in *Scum of the Earth* (1941), provided the background of his first novel in English, *Arrival and Departure* (1943). The degeneration of revolutionary idealism in Roman times under Spartacus he portrayed in *The Gladiators* (1939) which was followed in 1940 by the striking modern equivalent, *Darkness at Noon*, Koestler's masterpiece and one of the great political novels of the century. Intelligent humanism and anti-Communism provide the themes for such essays as *The Yogi and the Commissar* (1945), *The Trail of the Dinosaur* (1955), *Reflections on Hanging* (1956) and *The Sleepwalkers*, intro. H. Butterfield (1959), on the theories, lives and struggles with religious orthodoxy of Copernicus, Kepler and Galileo. *The Act of Creation* (1964) and *The Ghost in the Machine* (1967) are among his recent works. See his autobiography (1954) and *Arthur Koestler* by J. Atkins (1956).

KOFFKA, Kurt (1886–1941), German psychologist, held posts in U.S.A. and at Oxford. With Wertheimer and Köhler he founded the *Gestalt* school of psychology. See his *Principles of Gestalt Psychology* (1935).

KÖHLER, Wolfgang, *kœ'lèr* (1887–1967), German psychologist, born in Estonia, an authority on *Gestalt* psychology, specially noted also for research in animal psychology.

KOHLRAUSCH, Friedrich Wilhelm Georg, *kōl-rowsh* (1840–1910), German physicist, professor of physics at Berlin, noted for his researches on magnetism and electricity. See his handbook, *Leitfaden der praktischen Physik* (1870).

KOKOSCHKA, Oskar, *-kosh'-* (1886–), British artist, born at Pöchlarn, Austria. He studied from 1904–08 at Vienna and taught at the Dresden Academy of Art (1919–24); from this time he travelled widely, and painted many Expressionist landscapes in Spain, France, England, &c. In 1938 he fled to England for political reasons, becoming naturalized in 1947, and painted a number of politically symbolic works, as well as portraits and landscapes. In the 'twenties he also wrote a number of Expressionist dramas, including *Orpheus und Eurydike*. In 1959 he was awarded the C.B.E. See biography by E. Hoffmann (1947) and monograph by H. M. Wingler (1958).

KOLBE, Hermann (1818–84), German scientist, born near Göttingen, was professor at Leipzig (1865). He did much in the development of chemical theory.

KOLCHAK, Aleksandr Vasilievich (1874–1920), Russian admiral (1916), who rose in World War I to command the Black Sea Fleet. After the revolution of November 1917, he became the chief hope of the anti-Bolsheviks, and till 1919 had much military success, but in 1920 yielded place to Denikin, and coming into the hands of the Bolsheviks, was shot (February 7).

KOLLÁR, Jan (1793–1852), Czech poet and Slavonic scholar, a Hungarian Slovak, Protestant pastor at Pest, and then, from 1849, professor of Archaeology at Vienna. See Autobiography in his *Collected Works* (2nd ed. 1868).

KÖLLIKER, Rudolph Albert von (1817–1905), Swiss anatomist and embryologist, famous for his microscopic work, was born at Zürich, and became professor there (1845) and at Würzburg (1847). His chief works include: *Manual of Human Histology* (1852; trans. 1854) and *Entwicklungsgeschichte des Menschen* (1861). See his *Erinnerungen* (1899).

KOLTSOV, Alexei Vasilievich (1809–42), Russian lyric poet, was born and died at Voronezh.

KOMENSKÝ. See COMENIUS.

KOMOROWSKI, Tadeusz Bór, *kom-or-ov'-skee* (1895–1966), Polish soldier, born at Lwów, as ' General Bór ' led the heroic but unsuccessful Warsaw rising against the occupying Germans (1944), and settled in England after World War II.

KÖNIG, Friedrich (1774–1833), German printer, inventor of the steam-press, born at Eisleben, obtained in 1810 through the support of Bensley, a printer in London, a patent for a press. A second patent was obtained in 1811 for a cylinder-press, improved and in 1814 adopted by *The Times.* He also made steam printing-presses near Würzburg. See Goebel's monograph (1883).

KÖNIGSMARK, (1) Marie Aurora, Countess of Königsmark (1668?–1728), sister of (2), became in 1694 mistress of Augustus II of Saxony, and by him mother of Marshal Saxe; she died prioress at Quedlinburg. See German books by Corvin-Wiersbitzky (2nd ed. 1890), Burg (1925).

(2) **Count Philipp Christoph von** (1665–*c.* 1694), a Swede, entered the service of Hanover, was accused of an intrigue with Sophia Dorothea (1666–1726), wife of the future George I (q.v.) of England, and suddenly disappeared (probably murdered) in 1694. See Wilkins, *The Love of an Uncrowned Queen* (1900).

KONRAD. See CONRAD.

KOO, Vi Kyuin Wellington (1888–), Chinese statesman, was educated at Columbia University, U.S.A. He was Chinese ambassador to Britain 1941–46, to U.S. 1946–56. In 1964 he became vice president of the international court of justice.

KOPP, Hermann Franz Moritz (1817–92), German chemist, professor of Chemistry at Giessen and Heidelberg, was one of the founders of physical chemistry and a historian of the subject.

KORDA, Sir Alexander (1893–1956), Hungarian film producer, born at Turkeÿe, Hungary. First a newspaperman in Budapest, he became a film producer there, then in Vienna, Berlin, Hollywood, where he was director of United Artists Corporations of America and Paris. He came to Britain and in 1932 founded London Film Productions and Denham studios. His films include *The Private Life of Henry VIII, Rembrandt, The Third Man* and *The Red Shoes.* He was knighted in 1942. See Life by Tabori (1959).

KORNBERG, Arthur (1918–), American biochemist, born in Brooklyn, became professor of Biochemistry at Stanford in 1959, the year in which he was awarded, with Ochoa (q.v.), the Nobel prize for medicine for his work on the biological synthesis of nucleic acids.

KÖRNER, Karl Theodor (1791–1813), German lyric poet, born at Dresden, wrote fiery patriotic songs (*Leier und Schwert*, 1814). The *Schwert-Lied* was written shortly before his death in battle. See Life by his father Christian G. Körner, a friend of Schiller and correspondent of Goethe.

KORNILOV, Lavr Georgyevich (1870–1918), Russian commander-in-chief (August 1917), a Cossack born in W. Siberia, marched on St Petersburg, 8 September, to set up a military directory, but was forced to surrender by Kerensky. Next year he fell in battle.

KOROLENKO, Vladimir (1853-1921), Russian novelist, was born at Zhitomir. Returning from exile in Siberia (1885), he published *Makar's Dream*, and made a name by stories and articles.

KOSCIUSKO (Kosciuszko), Tadeusz, *koshchyoosh'ko* (1746-1817), Polish patriot, born near Slonim in Lithuania, chose the career of arms, and was trained in France. In 1777 he went to the United States, where he fought for the colonists and became brigadier-general. When Russia attacked his country in 1792, with 4000 men he held Dubienka for five days against 18,000. In 1794, after the second partition of Poland, he headed the national movement in Cracow, and was appointed dictator and commander-in-chief. His defeat of a greatly superior force of Russians at Raclawice was followed by a rising in Warsaw. He established a provisional government and took the field, but, defeated, fell back upon Warsaw and maintained himself there, until overpowered by superior numbers in the battle of Maciejowice, October 10, 1794, and wounded, he was taken prisoner. Two years later the Emperor Paul restored him to liberty. He went first to England, then in 1797 to America, and finally in 1798 to France, where he farmed near Fontainebleau. In 1806 he refused to support Napoleon's plan for the restoration of Poland. He settled at Soleure in Switzerland in 1816, and died by the fall of his horse over a precipice. See Lives by Michelet (1863), Cholonievski (1902) and Gardner (1920).

KOSSEL, (1) Albrecht (1853-1927), German physiological chemist, father of (2), professor at Heidelberg (1901-23), Nobel prizewinner for medicine (1910), investigated the chemistry of cells and of proteins.

(2) **Walther** (1888-1956), physicist, son of (1), professor of Physics at Kiel (1921) and Danzig (1932), did much research on atomic physics, especially on Röntgen spectra, and was known for his physical theory of chemical valency.

KOSSUTH, Louis, *kos'ooth* (1802-94), leader of the Hungarian revolution, was born at Monok near Zemplin of poor but noble family. He practised law for a time, in 1832 was a deputy at the diet of Pressburg, and edited a journal which, owing to the law, was not printed, but transcribed. The issue of a lithographed paper led, in 1837, to imprisonment. Liberated in 1840, he became editor of the *Pesti Hirlap*, advocating extreme Liberal views. In 1847, sent by Pest to the diet, he became leader of the opposition; and after the French Revolution of 1848 he demanded an independent government for Hungary. In September 1848, at the head of the Committee of National Defence, he prosecuted with extraordinary energy the measures necessary for carrying on war; and in April 1849 he induced the National Assembly at Debrecen to declare that the Hapsburg dynasty had forfeited the throne. Appointed provisional governor of Hungary, he sought in vain to secure the intervention of the Western Powers; and finding that the

dissensions between himself and Görgei (q.v.) were damaging the national cause, he resigned his dictatorship in favour of Görgei. After the defeat at Temesvár on August 9, 1849 he fled to Turkey, where he was made a prisoner, but not extradited. In September 1851, liberated by British and American influence, he came to England, where, as subsequently in the United States, he was received with respect and sympathy. From 1852 he resided mainly in England till, on the Franco-Italian war with Austria in 1859, he proposed to Napoleon to arrange a Hungarian rising against Austria. The peace of Villafranca bitterly disappointed Kossuth; and in 1861 and in 1866 he tried in vain to bring about a rising against Austria. When in 1867 Deák effected the reconciliation of Hungary with the dynasty, Kossuth retired from active political life, and afterwards lived mostly in Turin. In 1867 he refused to avail himself of the general amnesty. In 1880-82 he published three volumes of *Memories of my Exile* (Eng. ed. vol. i, 1880); others followed in 1890; and at his death he had completed a work on Hungarian history.

KOSTER. See JANSZOON.

KOSYGIN, Alexei Nikolayevich (1904-), Russian politician, born and educated in Leningrad. Elected to the Supreme Soviet (1938), he held a variety of industrial posts, being a member of the Central Committee (1939-60) and of the *Politburo* (1946-52). Chairman of state economic planning commission (1959-60) and first deputy prime minister (with Mikoyan) from 1960 he in 1964 succeeded Khruschev as chairman of the Council of Ministers.

KOTELAWALA, Sir John, *kot-ė-lah'wė-la* (1896-), Sinhalese statesman, educated at Colombo and Cambridge University, became leader of the House of Representatives in 1952, and was prime minister of Ceylon (1953-56). He was created K.B.E. in 1948.

KOTZEBUE, *kot'-*, **(1) August Friedrich Ferdinand von** (1761-1819), German dramatist, born at Weimar, filled various offices in the service of Russia, and was a facile writer of plays, tales, satires, historical works, &c.; he was stabbed, March 23, 1819, by Sand, a Jena student, because he had ridiculed the *Burschenschaft* movement. Besides quarrelling with Goethe, Kotzebue satirized the leaders of the Romantic school. Among his two hundred lively but superficial dramas are *Menschenhass und Reue* (known on the English stage as *The Stranger*), *Die Hussiten vor Naumburg, Die beiden Klingsberge,* &c. See French Life by Rabany (1893).

(2) **Otto** (1787-1846), son of (1), born at Reval, accompanied Krusenstern round the world in 1803-06, and afterwards made two voyages of exploration in the Pacific. He died at Reval. His two books on his voyages were translated into English (1821 and 1830).

KOVALEVSKY, (1) Alexander (1840-1901), Russian embryologist, was born at Dünaburg, and became professor at St Petersburg. He is known for his researches on the embryology of invertebrates, which led to Haeckel's Gastraea theory; for his discovery of the life history and true position of the Ascidians; and for investigations of the development of the Amphioxus, Balanoglossus, Sagitta, and Brachiopods.

(2) **Sonia** or **Sophie** (1850–91), sister-in-law of (1), daughter of a Moscow artillery officer, made a distinguished name for herself throughout Europe as a mathematician. In 1884 she became professor of Mathematics at Stockholm, and left a brilliant series of novels, of which *Vera Barantzova* was translated in 1895. See Leffier's monograph (trans. 1895).

KOZLOV, (1) **Ivan Ivanovich** (1779–1840), Russian poet, translated Byron and Moore. He turned to poetry after going blind at the age of thirty.

(2) **Peter** (1863–1935), Russian traveller and archaeologist, explored the Altai, the Gobi desert, and the head-waters of the great Chinese rivers. In 1909 he discovered the ancient city of Khara Khoto in the Gobi, with library, &c.

KRAEPELIN, Emil (1856–1926), German psychiatrist, professor at Munich, a pioneer in the psychological study of mental diseases, which he divided into two groups, manic-depressive and dementia-praecox. He did research on brain fatigue and on the mental effects of alcohol.

KRAFFT-EBING, Richard, Freiherr von (1840–1902), German specialist in nervous diseases, born at Mannheim, in 1889 accepted a chair at Vienna.

KRAPOTKIN. See KROPOTKIN.

KRASIŃSKI, Zygmunt, Count (1812–59), Polish poet, was born and died in Paris. One of his principal works is the strange poem *Nieboska Komedya* ('The Undivine Comedy,' 1834). See M. Gardner's *The Anonymous Poet of Poland* (1919).

KRASZEWSKI, Józef Ignacy, *krash-ef'skee* (1812–87), Polish historical novelist and poet, born in Warsaw, was one of the most prolific of all Polish authors, his works exceeding 300. His best-known novel is *Jermola the Potter* (1857). In 1884 he was imprisoned at Magdeburg for treason.

KRAUSE, Karl Christian Friedrich, *krow'ze* (1781–1832), German philosopher, born at Eisenberg, studied at Jena, lived at Dresden 1805–13, lectured at Göttingen 1823–30, and died at Munich. His *Ideal of Humanity* was translated in 1890.

KREBS, Sir Hans Adolf (1900–), German-British physiologist, born at Hildesheim, winner (with Lipmann) of the Nobel prize for physiology and medicine in 1953 for researches into metabolic processes. He was knighted in 1958.

KREISLER, Fritz, *krīs'-* (1875–1962), Austrian violinist, born in Vienna, studied medicine and was an Uhlan officer. He composed violin pieces, a string quartet and an operetta, *Apple Blossoms* (1919), which was a Broadway success. He became a U.S. citizen in 1943 and died in New York.

KŘENEK, Ernst, *kêr-zhe'-nek* (1900–), Czech-Jewish composer born in Vienna, became eventually professor · at Vassar College, New York. He has written operas and symphonies, and his style ranges from austere counterpoint to jazz (as in his famous opera *Jonny spielt auf,* Leipzig 1927). He has written *Über neue Musik* (1937), &c.

KRETZER, Marx, *kret'sêr* (1854–1941), German novelist, born at Posen. Essentially a writer on social problems and working people, he has, on account of his realism, been called the German Zola. His books include *Die Betrogenen* (1882), on poverty and prostitution, *Die Verkommenen* (1883), *Meister Timpe* (1888), and *Das Gesicht Christi* (1897).

KREUGER, Ivar, *krü'gêr* (1880–1932), Swedish financier, was born at Kalmar. Trained as a civil engineer, he emigrated to America where he worked as real-estate salesman and building contractor. He went to South Africa before returning to Sweden in 1907. In 1913 he founded the United Swedish Match Company and began the series of acquisitions and combinations which brought him control of three-quarters of the world's match trade. He lent large sums to governments in return for monopolistic concessions. In 1931 he was in difficulties and in March 1932, unable to meet a bank demand, he committed suicide. Irregularities over seven years were revealed after his death.

KRILOF. See KRYLOV.

KRISHNA MENON, Vengalil Krishnán (1896–), Indian politician, born at Calicut, Malabar, and educated at the Presidency College, Madras, and at London University. He came to Britain in 1924 and became a history teacher and a London barrister. In 1929 he became secretary of the India League and the mouthpiece of Indian nationalism in Britain. When India became a Dominion in 1947 he became India's high commissioner in London. In 1952 he became leader of the Indian delegation to the United Nations, bringing Pandit Nehru's influence to bear on international problems as leader of the Asian 'uncommitted' and 'neutralist' bloc. During the first 1956 Suez crisis on the nationalization of the Canal he formulated a plan to deal with it. As defence minister (1957–62), he came into conflict at the United Nations with Britain over Kashmir. He was minister of defence production for a short time in 1962.

KRISHNAMURTI (1891–), Indian theosophist, born in Madras, was educated in England by Dr Annie Besant, who in 1925 proclaimed him the Messiah. Later he dissolved *The Order of the Star in the East* (founded by Dr Besant), and retired.

KROGH, (Schack) August (Steenberg), *krawg* (1874–1949), Danish physiologist, professor at Copenhagen. He was Nobel prizewinner for medicine (1920) for his discovery of the regulation of the motor mechanism of capillaries.

KROPOTKIN, Prince Peter (1842–1921), Russian geographer, savant, revolutionary, Nihilist, was born at Moscow, and in 1857 entered the Corps of Pages. After five years' service and exploration in Siberia, he returned to the capital in 1867 to study mathematics, whilst acting as secretary to the Geographical Society. In 1871 he explored the glacial deposits of Finland and Sweden; in 1872 he associated himself with the extremest section of the International. Arrested (March 1874) and imprisoned in Russia, in July 1876 he effected his escape to England. At Lyons he was condemned in 1883 to five years' imprisonment for anarchism. Released in 1886, he settled in England till the Revolution of 1917 took him back to Russia. He wrote on anarchism, the French Revolution, Russian literature, Asia, mutual aid in evolution; and *Memoirs of a Revolutionist* (1900). See *The Anarchic Prince* by S. Woodcock and Avakumovic (1950).

KRÜDENER, Barbara Juliana von (1764–1824), religious enthusiast, daughter of Baron von Vietinghoff, was born at Riga. Married in 1782 to Baron von Krüdener, Russian ambassador at Venice, she from 1789 lived mostly apart from him, in Riga, St Petersburg and Paris. In 1803 she published a remarkable novel, *Valérie*, supposed to be autobiographical, and presently gave herself up to an exaggerated mysticism. Expelled in 1817–18 from Switzerland and Germany, and repulsed by her former worshipper, the Emperor Alexander, she retired to her paternal estates near Riga, where she entered into relations with the Moravian Brethren. She died at Karasu-Bazar in the Crimea. See Krug's *Conversations with Mme von Krüdener* (1818), and books by Eynard (1849) and Knapton (1939).

KRUGER, Stephanus Johannes Paulus (1825–1904), born at Colesberg in Cape Colony, with his fellow-Boers trekked to Natal, the Orange Free State, and the Transvaal, and won such a reputation for cleverness, coolness, and courage that in the war against Britain (1881), he was appointed head of the provisional government. In 1883 he was elected president of the Transvaal or South African Republic, and again in 1888, 1893 and 1898. 'Oom Paul' was the soul of the policy that issued in the war of 1899–1902, showed consummate 'slimness', resolution, and energy, but after the tide had fairly turned against the Boers, came to Europe to seek (in vain) alliances against Britain. He made his headquarters at Utrecht, and thence issued *The Memoirs of Paul Kruger, told by Himself* (1902). See M. Nathan's *Paul Kruger, his Life and Times* (3rd ed. 1942).

KRUPP, *kroop*, name of a German family of armament manufacturers and industrialists, of whom the most noteworthy in chronological order were:—

(1) **Alfred** (1812–87), born at Essen, succeeded his father Friedrich (1787–1826), who had founded a small iron forge there in 1810. At the Crystal Palace Great Exhibition (1851) he exhibited a solid flawless ingot of cast steel weighing 4000 kg, established the first Bessemer steel plant and became the foremost arms supplier not only to Germany but to any country in the world, his first steel gun being manufactured in 1847. He acquired large mines, collieries, docks, and became a dominating force in the development of the Ruhr territories. See Life by W. Berdow (1926).

(2) **Friedrich Alfred** (1854–1902), son of (1), incorporated shipbuilding, armour-plate manufacture (1890) and chrome nickel steel production into the Krupp empire and became a personal friend of the Prussian emperor. See Life by W. Berdow (1915).

(3) **Bertha** (1886–1957), daughter of (2),

married in 1906 **Gustav von Bohlen und Halbach**. By special imperial edict he was allowed to adopt the name ' Krupp ' (inserted before the ' von '). He took over the firm, gained the monopoly of German arms manufacture during World War I and manufactured the long range gun for the shelling of Paris, nicknamed ' Big Bertha '. He turned to agricultural machinery and steam engines after the war, backed first Hindenburg against Hitler, but then supported the latter's party financially and connived in secret rearmament, contrary to the Versailles Treaty, after the latter's rise to power in 1933. Hitler's *Lex-Krupp* (1943) confirmed exclusive family ownership for the firm. After World War II, the Krupp empire was split up by the Allies, but Gustav was too senile to stand trial as war criminal at Nuremberg.

(4) **Alfred Alwin Felix** (1907–67), son of (3), graduated at Aachen Technical College, became deputy director (1934), an honorary member of Hitler's S.S., and in 1943 succeeded his father to the Krupp empire. He was arrested (1945) and convicted (1947) with eleven fellow-directors by an American Military Tribunal for plunder in Nazi-occupied territories and for employment under inhuman conditions of concentration camp victims and non-German slave labour. He was sentenced to 12 years' imprisonment and his property was to be confiscated. By an amnesty (1951) he was released, his property restored with the proviso under the Mehlem agreement (1953) negotiated with the three allied powers and incorporated in the Federal German Constitution, that he should sell for a reasonable offer within five years his iron and steel assets, this period being extended yearly from 1958 with diminishing prospect of fulfilment. Meanwhile he actually increased these assets by the acquisition of the Bochumer Verein (1958). Krupps played a prominent part in the West German ' economic miracle ', building entire factories in Turkey, Pakistan, India and the Soviet Union. In 1959 he belatedly agreed to pay some compensation to former forced labour, but of Jewish origin only. His son **Arndt** succeeded him. See Life by G. Young (1960), family study by B. Menn (1939) and of the firm by G. von Klass (trans. 1954).

KRUSENSTERN, Adam Johann, Baron von (1770–1846), Russian admiral, born at Haggud in Estonia, served (1793–99) in the British navy, and was put in command of a Russian exploring expedition in the North Pacific, which ultimately became a voyage round the world (1803–06).

KRYLOV, Ivan Andreevich, *kree'lof* (1768–1844), Russian fabulist, born in Moscow, was a writer from his twentieth year. Secretary to a prince, and then aimless traveller through Russia, he obtained a government post in 1806, and, settling down, wrote the fables for which he is famous. Collections appeared in 1809 and 1811. See also translation into English verse by B. Pares (1927).

KUBELIK, (1) Jan (1880–1940), Czech violin virtuoso and composer, born near Prague, studied there, and becoming a Hungarian citizen took the name of Polgar.

(2) **Jeronym Rafael** (1914–), Czech conductor, son of (1), born at Bychory, studied at Prague Conservatory, and first conducted the Czech Philharmonic Orchestra before he was twenty. By 1939 he had established an international reputation, and in 1948 settled in England. He was conductor of the Chicago Symphony Orchestra (1950–1953), at Covent Garden (1955–58) and from 1961 with the Bavarian Radio Orchestra. He has composed an opera, *Veronika*, 2 symphonies, concertos, and other works.

KUBIN, Alfred, *koo'bin* (1877–1959), Austrian painter and engraver, born at Leitmeritz. He exhibited in Munich with the Blaue Reiter group in 1911. He was also influenced by Goya and Odilon Redon in his drawings and engravings of dreamlike subjects, and he illustrated many books in this vein.

KUBLAI KHAN, *koo'blī kahn* (1214–94), Mongol khan, emperor of China, grandson of Genghis Khan, completed the conquest of northern China. An energetic prince, he suppressed his rivals, adopted the Chinese mode of civilization, encouraged men of letters, and made Buddhism the state religion. An attempt to invade Japan ended in disaster. He established himself at Cambaluc (the modern Peking), the first foreigner ever to rule in China. His dominions extended from the Arctic Ocean to the Strait of Malacca, and from Korea to Asia Minor and the confines of Hungary. The splendour of his court inspired the graphic pages of Marco Polo, who spent seventeen years in the service of Kublai—and at a later date fired the imagination of Coleridge. See Yule's *Marco Polo* (1875), and Cordier's (1920); Howorth's *History of the Mongols* (part i, 1876).

KUENEN, Abraham, *kü'nen* (1828–91), Dutch theologian, was born at Haarlem, and became, in 1855, professor at Leyden. His *Historisch-Critisch Onderzoek* (1861–65) embodied modern theories on the history of Israel, developed further in *De Godsdienst van Israel* (1869–70; trans. 1873–75), and in the 2nd edition of his *Onderzoek* (1885–1889).

KUGLER, Franz, *koog'ter* (1808–58), born at Stettin, in 1833 became professor in the Academy of Art and *docent* at the University of Berlin. Part of his history of painting from the time of Constantine the Great (1837) was translated by the Eastlakes (6th ed. 1891) and others.

KUHLAU, Friedrich, *koo'low* (1786–1832), German composer of operas, chamber music, and piano sonatinas much used as teaching pieces, was born at Ülzen.

KUHN, kün, (1) **Franz Felix Adalbert** (1812–1881), German philologist and folklorist, born at Königsberg, died in Berlin.

(2) **Richard** (1900–67), Austrian chemist, known for his work on the structure and synthesis of vitamins and carotenoids. He refused the Nobel prize under Nazi pressure in 1938.

KÜHNE, Wilhelm, *kü'ne* (1837–1900), German physiologist, professor at Heidelberg from 1871, noted for his study of the chemistry of digestive processes. He introduced the term *enzyme* to describe organic substances which activate chemical changes.

KUN, Béla (1886–c. 1937), communist leader, born in Transylvania, was a journalist, soldier and prisoner in Russia, and in March 1919 set up in Hungary a Soviet republic which lasted till August. He then returned to Russia.

KUNIGUNDE, St (d. 1030), who vindicated her chastity by walking barefoot over hot ploughshares, was the daughter of Count Siegfried of Luxemburg, and wife of Duke Henry of Bavaria, chosen emperor in 1014. After his death in 1024 she retired into the convent of Kaufungen near Cassel, and died there. She was canonized in 1200.

KUPRIN, Alexander (1870–1938), Russian novelist, gave up the army for literature. As a teller of short tales he ranks next to Chekhov. *The Duel*, *The River of Life*, *A Slav Soul*, *The Bracelet of Garnets*, *Sasha*, &c., have been translated.

KURCHATOV, Igor Vasilevich (1903–60), Russian physicist, born in Eastern Russia, was appointed director of nuclear physics at the Leningrad Institute (1938) and, before the end of World War II, of the Soviet Atomic Energy Institute. He carried out important studies of neutron reactions and was the leading figure in the building of Russia's first atomic (1949) and thermonuclear (1953) bombs. He became a member of the Supreme Soviet in 1949 and was awarded the Stalin prize and the Order of Lenin.

KUROKI, Tamasada, Count (1844–1923), Japanese general, born in Satsuma, defeated the Russians in Manchuria, at Yalu, Kiu-lienling, &c. (1904–05).

KUROPATKIN, Alexei Nikolaievich (1848–1925), born a noble of Pskov, was Russian chief of staff under Skobeleff in the Turkish war 1877–78, commander-in-chief in Caucasia 1897, minister of war 1898, commander-in-chief in Manchuria (1904–05) against the victorious Japanese. He commanded the Russian armies on the northern front Feb.–Aug. 1916, and then was governor of Turkestan till the Revolution in 1917.

KUROSAWA, Akira (1910–), Japanese film director who brilliantly adapted the techniques of the *No* theatre to film-making in such films as *Rashomon* (1951), which won the Venice Film Festival prize, *The Seven Samurai* and *Living.* Also characteristic are his adaptations of Shakespeare's *Macbeth* and Dostoevsky's *The Idiot.*

KUSCH, Polykarp (1911–), American physicist, born at Blankenburg, Germany, professor of Physics at Columbia (1949), shared the 1955 Nobel award for physics for his precision determination of the magnetic movement of the electron.

KUTS, Vladimir, *koots* (1927–), Russian and world champion athlete. He broke the 10,000 metre record in Moscow in 1956 in 28 minutes 30·4 seconds, and the 5000 metre record at Rome in 1957 in 13 minutes 35 seconds. He was voted the best athlete at the 1956 Olympic Games.

KUTUZOV, Mikhail Ilarionovich, Prince of Smolensk, *koo-too'zof* (1745–1813), Russian field-marshal, distinguished himself in the

Turkish war, and in 1805 commanded against the French. In 1812, as commander-in-chief, he fought Napoleon obstinately at Borodino, obtained a great victory over Davout and Ney at Smolensk.

KUYP. See CUYP.

KUZNETSOV, Pavel, *koos-nyi-tsof'* (1878–), Russian artist, born at Saratov. He studied in Moscow and produced mainly realistic landscapes and scenes of Kirghiz life, his work being represented in the Tretiakov Gallery in Moscow.

KYAN, John Howard (1774–1850), inventor 1812–36 of the 'kyanizing' process for preserving wood. Born in Dublin, he died in New York.

KYD, Thomas (1558–94), English dramatist, born in London and probably educated at Merchant Taylors' School, was most likely brought up as a scrivener under his father. His tragedies early brought him reputation, specially *The Spanish Tragedy.* Kyd trans-lated from the French (1594) a tedious tragedy on Pompey's daughter Cornelia, perhaps produced *Solyman and Perseda* (1592) and *Arden of Feversham.* He has been credited with a share in other plays, and probably wrote the lost original *Hamlet.* In 1590–93 he was in the service of an unknown lord. Imprisoned in 1593 on a charge of atheism (Unitarianism), which he tried to shift on to Marlowe's shoulders, Jonson's ' sporting Kyd ' died in poverty. An edition of his plays by Boas was published in 1901.

KYNEWULF. See CYNEWULF.

KYRLE, John (1637–1724), English philan-thropist, styled the ' Man of Ross ' by Pope, having passed most of his life at Ross in Herefordshire. He spent his time and fortune in building churches and hospitals on an income of £600 a year. Pope sang his praises in his third *Moral Epistle,* and Warton said that he deserved to be celebrated beyond any of the heroes of Pindar.

L

LAAR, Pieter van, known as **Il Bamboccio,** (*c.* 1590–*c.* 1658), Dutch painter of pastoral scenes, fairs, &c., was born and died at Haarlem, but worked much in Rome.

LABADIE, Jean de (1610–74), French ex-Jesuit Protestant pietist, was born at Bourg near Bordeaux, and died at Altona.

LA BALUE, Jean de (1421–91), French cardinal, Bishop of Evreux and Angers, a minister of Louis XI, who imprisoned him, but not in an iron cage, 1469–80. He was born in Poitou, and died in Rome.

LABANOFF, Prince Alexander (1788–1866), a Russian general, the chivalrous defender of Mary, Queen of Scots, whose Letters he edited (7 vols. London 1844).

LABÉ, or Charlieu, Louise (*c.* 1520–66), a beautiful French poetess, born at Parcieux, Ain, who in 1542 fought disguised as a knight at the siege of Perpignan, and afterwards married a wealthy rope manufacturer, Perrin, at Lyons; hence she was called ' la Belle Cordière '. See works by Gonon (1844) and Laur (1873).

LABÉDOYÈRE, Charles, Comte de, *la-bed-wah-yayr* (1786–1815), a Napoleonic field-marshal, born in Paris, was shot after the second Bourbon restoration.

LABICHE, Eugène, *la-beesh* (1815–88), French author of over a hundred comedies, farces and vaudevilles, was born and died in Paris, and in 1880 was elected to the Academy. His *Frisette* (1846) was the original of Mor-ton's ' Box and Cox ' and *Le Voyage de M. Perrichon* (1860) is a perennial classroom favourite. See Augier's introduction to the *Théâtre de Labiche* (10 vols. 1879), P. Sou-pault, *Eugène Labiche, sa vie, son œuvre* (1945).

LABLACHE, Luigi (1794–1858), operatic singer, was born and died in Naples. His father was a French émigré, his mother an Irishwoman. He sang at La Scala, Milan (1817), and elsewhere. He taught singing to Queen Victoria. His voice was a magnificent deep bass and his acting was almost as remarkable as his singing.

LABOUCHÈRE, *la-boo-shayr,* (1) **Henry, Baron Taunton** (1798–1869), English states-man, of Huguenot ancestry, was educated at Winchester and Christ Church, Oxford. In 1826 he became a Whig M.P., from 1830 for Taunton; and, having been president of the Board of Trade and colonial secretary, was in 1859 raised to the peerage.

(2) **Henry** (1831–1912), nephew of (1), was educated at Eton, and from 1854 to 1864 was attaché or secretary at Washington, Munich, Stockholm, St Petersburg, Dresden, Constantinople, &c. A Liberal M.P. 1866–1906, he founded (1877), edited, and till 1910 owned *Truth.* See Lives by Thorold (1913), Pearson (1936).

LABOULAYE, Edouard René de, *la-boo-lay* (1811–83), French jurist and politician, was born and died in Paris, and in 1849 became professor of Comparative Jurisprudence in the Collège de France. His chief works are on French law, and a *Histoire politique des États-Unis* (1855–66). He edited a historical review and some of his tales, including *Paris en Amérique,* have been translated. He entered the National Assembly in 1871, and in 1876 became a life senator. See Life by Wallon (1889).

LA BOURDONNAIS, Bertrand François Mahé de, *la boor-don-nay* (1699–1753), French sailor, born at St-Malo, by 1723 had distinguished himself as captain in the naval service of the French Indies. In 1734 he became governor of Île de France and Bourbon and as such he lives for ever in *Paul et Virginie* by J. H. Bernardin de Saint-Pierre. In 1740 he inflicted great loss upon England; in 1746 compelled Madras to capitulate, but granted terms on payment of 9,000,000 livres. Accused by Dupleix of betraying the company's interests, he returned to Paris in 1748, and he languished in the Bastille until 1752, when he was declared guiltless.

LA BRUYÈRE, Jean de, *brü-yayr* (1645–96), French writer, born at Paris, and educated by the Oratorians, was chosen to aid Bossuet in educating the dauphin. For a time he was treasurer at Caen. He became tutor to the Duc de Bourbon, grandson of the Great Condé, and received a pension from the Condés until his death. His *Caractères* (1688), which gained him a host of implacable enemies as well as an immense reputation, consists of two parts, the one a translation of Theophrastus, the other a collection of maxims, reflections and character portraits of men and women of the time. He found a powerful protectress in the Duchesse de Bourbon, a daughter of Louis XIV. In 1693 he was elected to the Academy. His *Dialogues sur le quiétisme* (1699) were directed against Fénelon. A great writer rather than a great thinker, his insight into character is shrewd rather than profound. See the edition by Servois (3 vols. 1864–82); the translation of the *Caractères* by Helen Stott (1890); Sainte-Beuve's *Portraits littéraires*; and works by Morillot (1904), Lange (1909) and Magne (1914).

LACAILLE, Nicolas Louis de, *la-kah'y'* (1713–62), a French astronomer, who in 1751 visited the Cape. He was the first to measure a South African arc of the meridian.

LA CALPRENÈDE. See CALPRENÈDE.

LACÉPÈDE, Bernard de Laville, Comte de, *la-se-ped* (1756–1825), French writer and naturalist, born at Agen, became curator in the Royal Gardens at Paris in 1785, and at the Revolution professor of Natural History in the Jardin des Plantes. He was made senator in 1799, minister of state in 1809, and in 1814 peer of France. Besides continuing Buffon's *Natural History*, he wrote *Histoire naturelle des poissons* (1803), *Les Âges de la nature* (1830), &c. An edition of his works appeared in 1876.

LACHAISE, François d'Aix (1624–1709), French Jesuit, born at the castle of Aix in Forez. Louis XIV selected him for his confessor in 1675—a post he retained till his death in spite of the difficulties of his position. The cemetery *Père Lachaise* was called after him. See Life by Chantelauze (1859).

LA CHAUSSÉE, Pierre Claude Nivelle de, *la shö-say* (1692–1754), French playwright, born in Paris, began writing plays after he was forty and produced several of a sentimental nature, which enjoyed great popularity. *La Comédie larmoyante,* as his work was named by critics, did however have a certain influence on later writers, including Voltaire. Among his plays were *Préjuge à la mode* (1735), *Mélanide* (1741), and *L'École des mères* (1744). See G. Lanson, *Nivelle de la Chaussée* (1887).

LACHMANN, Karl Konrad Friedrich Wilhelm, *laкн'man* (1793–1851), German critic and philologist, born at Brunswick, was professor successively at Königsberg and Berlin, and

a member of the Academy. He edited the *Nibelungenlied,* Walter von der Vogelweide, Propertius, Lucretius, &c. In his *Betrachtungen* he maintained that the *Iliad* consisted of sixteen independent lays enlarged and interpolated. The smaller edition of his New Testament appeared in 1831; the larger in 1842–50—both based mainly on uncial MSS. See Life by Hertz (1851).

LACLOS, Pierre Ambroise François Choderlos de, *-klö* (1741–1803), French novelist and politician, born in Amiens. Romantic and frustrated, he spent nearly all his life in the army but saw no active service until he was sixty and ended his career as a general. He is remembered by his one masterpiece, *Les Liaisons dangereuses* (1782). This novel in letters reveals the influence of Rousseau and Richardson and is a cynical, detached analysis of personal and sexual relationships. A translation by R. Aldington, under the title of *Dangerous Acquaintances,* appeared in 1924, and a modern film version by R. Vadim in 1960.

LACOMBE, Louis Trouillon, *-köb* (1818–84), French composer, born at Bourges. His best-known work is the cantata *Sappho* (1878). His opera *Winkelried* was produced at Geneva in 1892. See Life by Boyer (Paris 1888).

LACONDAMINE, Charles Marie de (1701–1774), French geographer, was born and died in Paris, served in the army, travelled extensively, and was sent to Peru (1735–43) to measure a degree of the meridian. He explored the Amazon, brought back curare and definite information as to india rubber, and wrote in favour of inoculation.

LACORDAIRE, Jean Baptiste Henri (1802–1861), French theologian, born at Recey-sur-Ource, studied law in Paris. A convert from Deism, he was ordained in 1827. He attracted attention by his *Conférences* at Notre Dame (1835–36) but withdrew to Rome at the height of his fame, entering the Dominican order in 1839. Next year he reappeared at Notre Dame, where he renewed his success, and in 1854 he delivered his last and most eloquent *Conférences* at Toulouse, thereafter becoming director of the Collège de Sorèze. He was a member of the Academy. See his letters, his *Testament* (1870), and Lives by Montalembert (trans. 1863), Chocarne (trans. 1867), De Broglie (1889), Honnef (1924).

LACOSTE, Robert (1898–), French Socialist politician, was born at Azerat, S.W. France, and began his career as a tax-collector. Later he became editor of the civil servants' journal and a member of the administrative committee of the C.G.T. In World War II, he began the first trade union Resistance group. In 1944 he was minister of industrial production and minister for industry and commerce in 1946–47 and again in 1948. In 1956–57 he was resident minister in Algeria, and his at times ruthless campaign against the rebels there served to underline one controversial aspect of French postwar politics.

LACRETELLE, (1) Jean Charles Dominique de (1766–1855), French journalist and historian, born at Metz, was attracted to

Paris on the outbreak of the Revolution. He helped to edit the *Débats* and the *Journal de Paris*, was a member of the French Academy from 1811 and its president in 1816. Of his works the best-known are *Histoire du dix-huitième siècle* (1808), *Précis historique de la Révolution* (1801–06), and *Histoire de France pendant les guerres de religion* (1814–16). See Life by Alden (1959).

(2) **Pierre Louis** (1751–1824), brother of (1), was an advocate and journalist, and wrote on law. He was a member of the Paris Commune and was elected to the States-General and Legislative Assembly.

LACROIX, la-krwah, (1) **Paul** (1806–84), French scholar, better known as **P. L. Jacob, Bibliophile,** was born and died in Paris. While still at school he began to edit the old French classics, as Marot, Rabelais, &c. He wrote an immense number of romances, plays, histories, biographies, and a great series on the manners, customs, costumes, arts and sciences of France from the middle ages. He also wrote two elaborate works on the *History of Prostitution* under the name 'Pierre Dufour'. From 1855 he was keeper of the Arsenal library.

(2) **Silvestre François** (1765–1843), French mathematician, was born and died in Paris. His works on the Calculus (1797–1800) are famous. They were translated into English in 1816.

LACTANTIUS, Lucius Caelius (or Caecilius) Firmianus (4th cent.), Christian apologist, was brought up in Africa, and settled as a teacher of rhetoric in Nicomedia in Bithynia, where he was converted probably by witnessing the constancy of the Christian martyrs under the persecution of Diocletian. About 313 he was invited to Gaul by Constantine, to act as tutor to his son Crispus. His principal work is his *Divinarum Institutionum libri vii.* See editions by Migne (vol. vi, 1844) and Brandt and Laubmann (Vienna 1890–97).

LACY, Peter, Count (1678–1751), Russian field-marshal, was born in Limerick, and had fought as an Irish Jacobite and in the French service, when about 1698 he entered that of Russia.

LAËNNEC, René Théophile Hyacinthe (1781–1826), French physician, born at Quimper in Brittany, from 1799 an army doctor, in 1814 became editor of the *Journal de Médecine* and physician to the Salpêtrière and in 1816 chief physician to the Hôpital Necker, where he invented the stethoscope. His work on tuberculosis, peritonitis and chest diseases was valuable. In 1819 he published his *Traité de l'auscultation médiate.* See Lives by Lallour (1868), Du Chatellier (1885), Webb (1928).

LA FARGE, John (1835–1910), American landscape and ecclesiastical painter, born in New York, is best known by his mural and stained-glass work. He wrote *Lectures on Art, Letters from Japan,* &c.

LA FARINA, Giuseppe (1815–63), Italian historian and statesman, was born at Messina. He died in Turin. He was an early advocate of Italian unity and wrote a history of Italy.

LAFAYETTE, Marie Joseph Paul Yves Roch Gilbert Motier, Marquis de (1757–1834), French reformer, was born in the castle of Chavagnac in Auvergne. He entered the

army, sailed for America in 1777 to aid the colonist, and by Washington was given a division. He was home for a few months in 1779, crossed the Atlantic again, was charged with the defence of Virginia, and shared in the battle of Yorktown. On a third visit to America in 1784, he had an enthusiastic reception. Now a pronounced reformer, he was called to the Assembly of Notables in 1787, sat in the States-General, and in the National Assembly of 1789. He laid on its table a declaration of rights based on the American Declaration of Independence and, appointed to command the armed citizens, formed the National Guard. He struggled incessantly for order and humanity, but the Jacobins hated his moderation, and the court abhorred his reforming zeal. He supported the abolition of title and all class privileges. He won the first victories at Philippeville, Maubeuge and Florennes, but the hatred of the Jacobins increased, and at length he rode over the frontier to Liège and was imprisoned by the Austrians till Bonaparte obtained his liberation in 1797. He sat in the Chamber of Deputies in 1818–24 as one of the extreme Left, and in 1825–30 was again a leader of the Opposition. In 1830 he took part in the Revolution, and commanded the National Guards. In 1824 he revisited America, by invitation of Congress, who voted him 200,000 dollars and a township. He died at Paris. See *Mémoires, Correspondance, et Manuscrits* (1837–40); studies by Warin (1824), Sarrans (1832), Tuckerman (1889), Bardoux (1892–93), Tower (1895), Crow (1916), Delteil (1928), Kayser (1928), Whitlock (1929), De la Bedoyère (1933), Gottschalk (1942).

LA FAYETTE, Marie Madeleine Pioche de Lavergne, Comtesse de (1634–93). French novelist and reformer of French romance-writing, was born in Paris, her father being marshal and governor of Le Havre. She married the Comte de La Fayette in 1655, and in her thirty-third year formed a liaison with La Rochefoucauld, which lasted until his death in 1680. Down to her own death she still played a leading part at the French court, as was proved by her *Lettere inedite* (Turin 1880); prior to their publication it was believed that her last years were given to devotion. Her novels are *Zaïde* (1670) and *La Princesse de Clèves* (1678) which is a vivid picture of the court-life of her day and led to a reaction against the long-winded romances of Calprenède and Scudéry. See *Mémoires* (ed. by Asse 1890), books by Ashton (1922), Magne (1922), Styger (1944), and Sainte-Beuve's *Portraits de Femmes.*

LAFERTÉ, Victor. See DOLGORUKOVA.

LAFFITTE, (1) Jacques (1767–1844), French financier and statesman, born at Bayonne, acquired great wealth as a Paris banker, and in 1814 became governor of the Bank of France. He was elected to the Chamber of Deputies in 1817. In 1830 his house was the headquarters of the Revolution, and he supplied a great part of the funds needed. In November he formed a cabinet, but he only held power until March. From the ruins of his fortune he founded a Discount Bank in 1837. In 1843 he was elected president of the Chamber of Deputies. See his *Souvenirs* (1844), as recorded by Marchal.

(2) **Pierre** (1823–1903), French philosopher, born at Beguey (Gironde), was friend and disciple of Comte.

LA FOLLETTE, Robert Marion (1855–1925), American politician, born at Primrose, Wis., was a senator from 1905, and as ' Progressive ' candidate for the presidency was defeated in 1924, having gained nearly 5 million votes.

LA FONTAINE, Jean de (1621–95), French poet, born at Château-Thierry in Champagne, assisted his father, a superintendent of woods and forests. He early devoted himself to the study of the old writers and to verse writing. In 1654 he published a verse translation of the *Eunuchus* of Terence, and then went to Paris, where Fouquet became his patron. His *Contes et nouvelles en vers* appeared in 1665, his *Fables choises mises en vers* in 1668, and his *Amours de Psyché et de Cupidon* in 1669. For nearly twenty years he was maintained in the household of Mme de la Sablière. In 1684 he read an admirable *Discours en vers* on his reception by the Academy. He was one of the most frivolous and dissipated of men, but he was likewise one of the most charming and gifted. La Fontaine was a great and brilliant writer and his verse, especially as found in the *Contes* and *Fables*, lively and original. The best edition is by Regnier (11 vols. 1883–92). See Sainte-Beuve's *Portraits*, vol. i; works by Girardin (2nd ed. 1876), Taine (1882), Faguet (1900), F. Hamel (1912), Gohin (1931); English verse translation by E. Marsh (1933).

LAGERKVIST, Pär (1891–   ), Swedish writer, studied at Uppsala, began his literary career as an expressionist poem with *Angest* (1916) and *Kaos* (1918), emphasizing the catastrophe of war, but later, in the face of extremist creeds and slogans, adopted a critical humanism in such plays as *Bödeln* (1934) and *Dvärgen* (1944), which expose the political and social destroyer. He was awarded the Nobel prize in 1951 for the novel *Barabbas* (1951), the thief in whose place Christ was crucified. The ideological play *Lat människan Leva*, ' Let Man Live ' (1949), is a study of political terrorism in which Christ, Socrates, Bruno, Joan of Arc and an American negro appear as victims. He was elected a Swedish Academician in 1940.

LAGERLÖF, Selma (1858–1940), Swedish novelist, born in Värmland, became a schoolteacher, and sprang to fame with *Gösta Berling's Saga* (1891). Her fairy tales and romances earned her a Nobel prize (1909), and a seat in the Swedish Academy (1914).

LAGRANGE, Joseph Louis, Comte, -*grãzh* (1736–1813), mathematician, was born of French ancestry at Turin. In 1766 he was appointed director of the Berlin Academy, having gained a European reputation by his completion of the Calculus of Variations, investigations of sound, harmonics, &c. While in Prussia (1766–87), Lagrange read before the Berlin Academy about sixty dissertations on the application of the higher analysis to mechanics and dynamics;

one of these was his principal work, the *Mécanique analytique* (1788), its central theory the principle of virtual velocities, which he had established in 1764. In Paris he was welcomed by the court and lodged in the Louvre with a pension of 6000 francs. After the Revolution he was appointed professor in the Normal and Polytechnic Schools and a member of the Bureau des longitudes. Napoleon made him a member of the senate and a Count, and gave him the Grand Cross of the Legion of Honour. Other important works are *Théorie des fonctions*, *Leçons sur le calcul des fonctions*, and *Résolution des équations numériques*. Lagrange died at Paris, and was buried in the Panthéon. His works have been edited by Serret and Darboux (14 vols. 1866–92).

LA GUARDIA, Fiorello Henry (1882–1947), American lawyer and politician, born in New York of Italian-Jewish origin, became deputy attorney-general of New York (1915–17), served with the American air force in Italy and sat in congress (1917–21, 1923–33) as a Republican. As a popular mayor of New York (thrice re-elected, 1933–45) he initiated housing and labour safeguards schemes, was one of the early opponents of Hitler's anti-Semitic policies—he had his ears boxed in public by enraged American fascists—and was civil defence director (1941–42). He became civil administrator of allied-occupied Italy, and in 1946 was appointed director-general of U.N.R.R.A. New York's airport is named after him. See his autobiography (1948), and Life by E. Cuneo (1955).

LAGUERRE, Louis (1663–1721), French artist, born in Paris. In 1683 he came to London, where he carried out schemes of elaborate, allegorical decoration at Chatsworth, Petworth, Blenheim, &c.

LAHARPE, Frédéric César (1754–1838), Swiss politician, born at Rolle in Vaud, president of the Helvetic Republic in 1798–1800, lived a good deal in Russia as tutor and guest of Alexander I. He died at Lausanne.

LA HARPE, Jean François de (1739–1803), French poet and critic, born at Paris, in 1763 produced a successful tragedy, *Warwick*. His best-known works are, however, his critical lectures, *Lycée, ou Cours de littérature* (1799–1805). His *Correspondance littéraire* (1801) by the bitterness of its criticisms rekindled fierce controversies. He supported the Revolution at first, but after five months' imprisonment (1794) became a firm supporter of church and crown.

LAIDLAW, William (1780–1845), Scottish friend and amanuensis of Sir Walter Scott, and himself a writer of lyrics, was born at Blackhouse in Selkirkshire. After farming with little success at Traquair and Liberton, he settled in 1817 as a kind of factor on the Abbotsford estate, and was Scott's trusted counsellor in all his schemes of improvement. Here, with the exception of three years after the disaster in Scott's affairs, he lived till Scott's death in 1832. Afterwards he was factor successively on two Ross-shire estates.

LAING, (1) Alexander Gordon (1793–1826), Scottish explorer, born at Edinburgh, served seven years as an officer in the West Indies. He was sent to explore the Niger's source which he found, but was murdered after leaving Timbuktu.

(2) **David** (1793–1878), Scottish antiquary, the son of an Edinburgh bookseller, for thirty years followed his father's trade, and from 1837 till his death was librarian of the Signet Library. He was honorary secretary of the Bannatyne Club, and edited many of its issues. An LL.D. of Edinburgh, he left behind him a private library of unusual value, and bequeathed many rare MSS. to Edinburgh University. His more important works were his editions of Baillie's *Letters and Journals* (1841–42), of John Knox (1846–64), Sir David Lyndsay, Dunbar and Henryson. See Life by G. Goudie (1914).

(3) **John.** See HALKETT, SAMUEL.

(4) **Malcolm** (1762–1818), Scottish historian, was born in Orkney, educated at Kirkwall and Edinburgh University, and called to the bar in 1785, but never became a successful advocate. He completed Henry's *History of Great Britain* (1793), and in 1802 published his own *History of Scotland, 1603–1707*. His *Poems of Ossian* is an onslaught on Macpherson.

(5) **Samuel** (1780–1868), brother of (4), travelled and wrote on Norway, Sweden, Russia, France, &c., and translated the *Heimskringla*.

(6) **Samuel** (1812–97), son of (5), chairman of the Brighton railway, Liberal M.P. for Wick, wrote on the conflict of scince with religion.

LAIRD, (1) **John** (1805–74), a Birkenhead shipbuilder and M.P., born at Greenock, one of the earliest constructors of iron vessels.

(2) **John** (1887–1946), Scottish philosopher, born at Durris, Kincardineshire, studied at Edinburgh, Heidelberg and Cambridge, and was professor at Dalhousie, Nova Scotia (1912), Belfast (1913–24) and at Aberdeen (1924–46). His *Study in Realism* (1920) defined his own metaphysical standpoint. He is best known, however, for his studies of Hume (1932) and Hobbes (1934) and his edition of Samuel Alexander's works (1939). He was Gifford lecturer at Glasgow (1939) and was elected F.B.A. in 1933.

(3) **Macgregor** (1808–61), brother of (1), also born at Greenock, shared Lander's last expedition to the Niger.

LAIRESSE, Gérard de (1641–1711), Dutch painter and etcher, the author, after he became blind in 1690, of *Art of Painting* (trans. 1738).

LAÏS, the name of two Corinthian courtesans, famous for their beauty. The elder flourished during the Peloponnesian war; the younger, born in Sicily, came as a child to Corinth, and sat as a model to Apelles.

LAKE, Gerard, Viscount (1744–1808), British general, served in Germany 1760–62, America 1781, and the Low Countries 1793–94, his most brilliant exploit being the capture of some forts near Lille. In 1798 he routed the rebels at Vinegar Hill, and received the surrender of the French near Cloone. In N.W. India (1801–07), against Sindia and Holkar he won several battles and took Aligarh, Delhi and Agra. See Memoir by Pearce (1908).

LALANDE, Joseph Jérôme Le Français de

(1732–1807), French astronomer, born at Bourg-en-Bresse, was sent to Berlin in 1751 to determine the moon's parallax. He was from 1762 professor of Astronomy in the Collège de France, from 1795 director of the Paris Observatory. His chief work is *Traité d'astronomie* (1764; 3rd ed. 1792).

LALIQUE, René, *la-leek* (1860–1945), French jeweller, born at Ay. He was also an artist-craftsman in glass which he decorated with relief figures, animals and flowers.

LALLY, (1) **Thomas Arthur, Comte de, Baron de Tollendal** (1702–66), French general, born at Romans in Dauphiné, son of Sir Gerard O'Lally, an Irish Jacobite in the French service. Lally distinguished himself in Flanders, accompanied Prince Charles Edward to Scotland in 1745, and in 1756 became commander-in-chief in the French East Indies. He commenced vigorous hostilities against the British, and besieged Madras; but being defeated, retreated to Pondicherry, which was attacked in March 1760 by a superior British force. Lally capitulated in January 1761, and was conveyed to England. Accused of cowardice, he returned to France, and was thrown into the Bastille. The parliament of Paris at last condemned him, and he was executed May 7, 1766. But his son, supported by Voltaire, procured a royal decree in 1778, declaring the condemnation unjust, and restoring all the forfeited honours. See Malleson's *French in India*.

(2) **Trophime Gérard, Marquis de Lally-Tollendal** (1751–1830), son of (1), was one of those nobles who acted in the States-General in 1789 with the Third Estate, but soon allied himself with the court. He advocated a constitution with two chambers, and sought to protect the king, but had to flee to England. Louis XVIII made him a peer. He wrote *Defence of the French Emigrants* (1794), and *Life of Wentworth, Earl of Strafford* (2nd ed. 1814).

LALO, (Victor Antoine) Édouard (1823–92), French composer and viola player, born at Lille of a military family. His musical compositions include *Symphonie espagnole* and other violin works, and operas, the best known being *Le Roi d'Ys*, and the ballet *Namouna*.

LAMARCK, Jean Baptiste Pierre Antoine de Monet, Chevalier de (1744–1829), French naturalist and pre-Darwinian evolutionist, was born at Bazentin, and at seventeen joined the French army in Germany. Stationed as an officer at Toulon and Monaco, he became interested in the Mediterranean flora; and resigning after an injury, he held a post in a Paris bank, and meanwhile worked at botany. In 1773 he published a *Flore française*. In 1774 he became a member of the French Academy and keeper of the royal garden (afterwards the nucleus of *Jardin des plantes*), and here he lectured for twenty-five years on Invertebrate Zoology. About 1801 he had begun to think about the relations and origin of species, expressing his conclusions in his famous *Philosophie zoologique* (1809). His *Histoire des animaux sans vertèbres* appeared in 1815–22. Hard work and illness enfeebled his sight and left him blind and poor. Lamarck broke with the old notion of species, expressly denied the unchangeableness of species, sought to explain their transformation and the evolution of the animal world, and prepared the way for the now accepted theory of descent. See Cuvier's *Éloge* of him (1832); C. Claus, *Lamarck als Begründer der Descendenztheorie* (1888); Haeckel, *Darwin, Goethe, und Lamarck* (1882), Packard, *Lamarck the Founder of Evolution* (1902), E. Perrier, *Lamarck* (1925), and H. G. Cannon, *Lamarck and Modern Genetics* (1960).

LA MÁRMORA, Alfonso Ferrero, Marquis de (1804-78), Italian soldier, born at Turin, distinguished himself in the national war of 1848, and in 1849 was appointed minister of war. He commanded the Sardinian troops in the Crimea (1855), took part in the war of 1859, was commander-in-chief in 1861, and in 1864 prime minister. In the campaign against Austria in 1866 he lost the battle of Custozza. His publication (1873) of the secret negotiations between Prussia and Italy incurred the censure of Bismarck. See monograph by Massari (1880).

LAMARTINE, Alphonse Marie Louis de (1790-1869), French poet, statesman and historian, born at Mâcon, was brought up on ultraroyalist principles, spent much of his youth in Italy, and on the fall of Napoleon entered the gardeｌ royale. His first volume of poems, probably his best known and most successful, the *Méditations*, was published in 1820. He was successively secretary of legation at Naples and *chargé d'affaires* at Florence. In 1829 he declined the post of foreign secretary in the Polignac ministry, and by another series of poems, *Harmonies poétiques et religieuses*, achieved his unanimous election to the Academy. Lamartine, still a royalist, disapproved of the Revolution of 1830. A tour to the East produced his *Souvenirs d'Orient*. Recalled to France in 1833, he became deputy for Mâcon. Between 1834 and 1848 he published his poems, *Jocelyn* and *La Chute d'un ange*, and the celebrated *Histoire des Girondins*. The Orleanist *régime* was repugnant to him; and he became a member of the Provisional Government (1848), and, as minister of foreign affairs, the ruling spirit. After two risings of the extreme party of Louis Blanc and Ledru Rollin, the executive committee resigned, and conferred the command of the forces on Cavaignac. After a terrible conflict the insurrection was suppressed. When Napoleon came to power Lamartine devoted himself to literature, publishing *Confidences, Raphaël* (both autobiographical), *Geneviève*, the *Tailleur de pierres de St-Point* (a prose tale), and *Histoire de la restauration*. He wrote on Joan of Arc, Cromwell, Madame de Sévigné, &c., and issued monthly *Entretiens familiers*. He died at Passy, February 28. See monographs by Lady M. Domville (1888), Reyssié (1892), Rod (1892), Deschanel (1893), Quentin-Bauchart (1903-07), Doumic (1912), Lanson (1915), Barthou (1916), Whitehouse (1919); and Baillon and Harris: *L'État présent des études lamartiniennes* (1933).

LAMB, (1) Lady Caroline. See MELBOURNE.

(2) **Charles** (1775-1834), English essayist, was born in the Temple, London, where his father was clerk to Samuel Salt, a wealthy bencher. At Christ's Hospital 1782-89, he soon afterwards obtained a situation in the South Sea House, but in 1792 procured promotion to the India House, where he remained for more than thirty years. In 1792 also, Samuel Salt died, and with a legacy from him, Charles's salary, and whatever his elder sister Mary (1764-1847) could earn by needlework, the family retired to humble lodgings. In 1796 the terrible disaster occurred which was destined to mould the future life of Charles Lamb. The strain of insanity inherited from the mother, began to show itself in Mary and in an attack of mania she stabbed her mother. Her brother's guardianship was accepted by the authorities and to this trust Charles Lamb from that moment devoted his life. In the meantime Charles had fallen in love, but renounced all hope of marriage when the duty of tending his sister appeared to him paramount. Lamb's earliest poems (1795), first printed with Coleridge's in 1796-97, were prompted by this deep attachment. In 1798 Lamb and Charles Lloyd made a venture in a slight volume of their own (*Blank Verse*); and here for the first time Lamb's individuality made itself felt in the ' Old Familiar Faces '. In 1797 he also published his little prose romance, *The Tale of Rosamund Gray and Old Blind Margaret*; and in 1801 *John Woodvil*—the fruit of that study of the dramatic poetry of the Elizabethan period, in whose revival he was to bear so large a part. Meantime, Lamb and his sister were wandering from lodging to lodging, and in 1801 they removed to Lamb's old familiar neighbourhood, where they continued for sixteen years. Charles's experiments in literature had as yet brought him neither money nor reputation and, to raise a few pounds, he wrote a farce, *Mr H.*, produced at Drury Lane in December 1806, and famous only for its failure. For William Godwin's ' Juvenile Library ', Charles and Mary wrote in 1807 their *Tales from Shakespeare*—Mary Lamb taking the comedies, Charles the tragedies. This was Lamb's first success. The brother and sister next composed jointly *Mrs Leicester's School* (1807) and *Poetry for Children* (1809). Charles also made a prose version of the *Adventures of Ulysses*; and a volume of selections from the Elizabethan dramatists exhibited him as one of the most subtle and original of poetical critics. Three years later his unsigned articles in Leigh Hunt's *Reflector* on Hogarth and the tragedies of Shakespeare proved him a prose writer of new and unique quality. In 1818 Lamb collected his scattered verse and prose in two volumes as the *Works of Charles Lamb*, and this paved the way for his being invited to join the staff of the new *London Magazine*. His first essay, in August 1820, ' Recollections of the old South Sea House ', was signed *Elia*, the name of a foreigner who had been a fellow-clerk. *The Last Essays of Elia* were collected in 1833. In 1825 Lamb, who had been failing in health, resigned his

post in the India House, with a pension of £441. The brother and sister were now free to wander; finally they removed to Edmonton. The absence of settled occupation had not brought Lamb the comfort he had looked for: the separation from his friends and the now almost continuous mental alienation of his sister left him companionless, and with the death of Coleridge in 1834 the chief attractions of his life were gone. In December of that year, he too died. He was buried in Edmonton churchyard. His sister survived him nearly thirteen years, and was buried by his side. Lamb's place in literature is unique and unchallengeable. As a personality he is more intimately known to us than any other figure in literature, unless it be Samuel Johnson. He is familiar to us through his works, which are composed in the form of personal confidences; through his many friends who have made known his every mood and trait; and through his letters, the most fascinating correspondence in our language. The profound and imaginative character of his criticism, and with it the reckless humour of the Bohemian and the *farceur*; his loyalty and generosity to his friends; his wild fun alternating with tenderness or profound philosophic musings —it is this wonderful blending of opposites that has made Lamb the most dearly loved of English men of letters. The chief authorities for Lamb are his own writings, and the *Life and Letters* (1837) and *Final Memorials* (1848) by Talfourd. See monographs by B. W. Procter (1866), Ainger (1882), Derocquigny (Paris 1904); Life of Mary Lamb by Mrs Gilchrist (1883); *The Lambs* by Hazlitt (1897); Edmund Blunden, *Charles Lamb and his Contemporaries* (1933), and *Charles Lamb: His Life Recorded by his Contemporaries* (1934); the editions by Ainger (1883–88), W. Macdonald (12 vols. 1903), and E. V. Lucas (in 7 vols., together with the Life in 2 vols., 1903–05; revised 1921; Letters, 3 vols., 1935).

(3) **William.** See MELBOURNE.

(4) **Willis Eugene** (1913–), American physicist, professor of Physics at Columbia (1948), Stanford (1951), Oxford (1956), Yale (1962). In 1955 he shared with Kusch the Nobel prize for physics for his researches into the hydrogen spectrum.

LAMBALLE, Marie Thérèse Louise de Savoie-Carignan, Princess de (1749–92), born at Turin, daughter of the Prince of Carignan, in 1767 married Louis of Bourbon, Prince of Lamballe, but next year was left a widow. Beautiful and charming, she was made by Marie Antoinette superintendent of the household (1774), and her own intimate companion. She escaped to England in 1791, but returned to share the queen's imprisonment in the Temple, and refused the oath of detestation of the king, queen and monarchy (September 3, 1792). As she stepped out of the courtroom she was cut down, amid barbarities that have since been exaggerated. See Lives by Lescure (1865), Bertin (2nd ed. 1894), Sir F. Montefiore (1896) and B. C. Hardy (1908).

LAMBE, John (d. 1628), an astrologer, patronized by Buckingham, and mobbed to death.

LAMBERT, (1) Constant (1905–51), English composer, conductor and critic, the son of George Washington Lambert, A.R.A. (1873–1930), portrait painter, was born in London. His first success came when, as a student at the Royal College of Music, he was commissioned by Diaghilev to write a ballet, *Romeo and Juliet*, first performed in 1926. For several years Lambert worked as conductor for the Camargo Society and later of Sadler's Wells Ballet, upon which company his outstanding musicianship and understanding of the problems of ballet had a lasting influence; he was also active as a concert conductor and music critic. His book *Music Ho!* (1934) is enlivened by his understanding of painting, his appreciation of jazz, his devotion to Elizabethan music and the works of such debatable composers as Liszt and Berlioz, and by its acidly witty, polished style. Of his compositions, *The Rio Grande* (1929), one of the most successful concert works in jazz idiom, is perhaps the most famous, but his lyrical gifts show themselves in the ballets *Pomona* (1927) and *Horoscope* (1938) as well as the cantata *Summer's Last Will and Testament* (1936). His concerto for piano and chamber orchestra was composed in memory of Philip Heseltine.

(2) **Johann Heinrich** (1728–77), German mathematician, was born at Mülhausen in Alsace, and died in Berlin. From 1764 he was a member of the Academy of Sciences. He first showed how to measure scientifically the intensity of light, in his *Photometria* (1760). A work of his on analytical logic (1764) was greatly valued by Kant. Among his other works are *Kosmologische Briefe* (1761) and *Anlage zur Architektonik* (1771). See Life by Huber (1829) and Baensch's monograph on his philosophy (1902).

(3) **John** (1619–84), English soldier, born at Calton near Settle, Yorkshire, studied at the Inns of Court, but on the outbreak of the Great Rebellion became a captain under Fairfax, and at Marston Moor led Fairfax's cavalry. Commissary-general of the army in the north (1645), and major-general of the northern counties (1647), he helped Cromwell to crush Hamilton at Preston, and captured Pontefract Castle in March 1649. In 1650 he went with Cromwell to Scotland as major-general, led the van at Dunbar, won the victory of Inverkeithing, followed Charles to Worcester, and at the battle commanded the troops on the eastern bank of the Severn. He helped to instal Oliver as protector, but opposed the proposition to declare him king. He headed the cabal which overthrew Richard Cromwell; was now looked upon as the leader of the Fifth Monarchy or extreme republican party; suppressed the royalist insurrection in Cheshire, August 1659 and virtually governed the country with his officers as the 'committee of safety'. Monk's counter-plot frustrated his designs. He was sent to the Tower, tried in 1662, and kept prisoner on Drake's Island till his death. See W. H. Dawson, *Cromwell's Understudy* (1938).

LAMBTON, John George. See DURHAM.

LAMÉ, Gabriel (1795–1870), French mathematician and engineer worked in Russia as an engineer before becoming professor of Physics at the École polytechnique in Paris. He investigated problems of elasticity and heat.

LAMENNAIS, Félicité Robert de, *la-mě-nay* (1782–1854), French writer, born at St-Malo, retired with his brother, a priest, to their estate at La Chesnaie near Dinan, where he wrote *Réflexions sur l'état de l'église* (1808) which was suppressed by Napoleon. On returning from London, whither he had fled during the Hundred Days, he was ordained priest, and began in 1816 his famous *Essai sur l'indifférence en matière de religion* (1818–24), a magnificent, if paradoxical denunciation of private judgment and toleration, which was favourably received at Rome. But notions of popular liberty, fanned by the revolution of 1830, began to change his outlook, and *L'Avenir,* a journal founded by him in 1830 with Montalembert and others, was suspended in 1831 and officially condemned by the pope in 1832. The *Paroles d'un croyant* (1834) brought about complete rupture with the church, and revolutionary doctrines in his later work got him a year's imprisonment. Active in the 1848 revolution, he sat in the Assembly until the *coup d'état.* At his death he refused to make peace with the church. His works include the remarkable *Esquisse d'une philosophie* (1840–46). See works by Roussel (1892), Gibson (1896), Marechal (1907–13) and Duine (1922).

LAMETTRIE, Julien Offray de (1709–51), French philosopher, born at St-Malo, became a French army surgeon in 1742; but the publication in 1745 of a materialistic work, *L'Histoire naturelle de l'âme,* roused such odium that he sought refuge in Leyden (1746). He published *L'Homme machine* (1748), and escaped arrest by accepting an invitation from Frederick the Great. In Berlin he continued his materialistic studies in *L'Homme plante* (1748), *L'Art de jouir* (1751), *La Volupté,* &c. He also wrote satirical books against doctors. See a memoir by Frederick prefixed to his works (1774), and monographs by Quépat (1873), Du Bois-Reymond (1875) and Poritzky (1900).

LAMOND, Frederic (1868–1948), Scottish pianist and composer, born in Glasgow. A pupil of Bülow and Liszt, he made his début at Berlin in 1885. He excelled in playing Beethoven. Among his compositions are an overture *Aus dem schottischen Hochlande,* a symphony and several piano works.

LAMONT, Johann von (1805–79), Scottish-German astronomer, born in Braemar, went in 1817 to the Scottish seminary at Ratisbon, and became in 1835 director of Bogenhausen Observatory. In 1852 he became professor of Astronomy at Munich. He wrote *Handbuch des Erdmagnetismus.*

LAMORICIÈRE, Christophe Léon Louis Juchault de, *la-mor-ees-yayr* (1806–65), French general, born at Nantes, entered the army in 1826, and served in Algeria 1833–47. Through his energy chiefly the war was brought to an end by the capture of Abd-el-Kader in 1847. In June 1848 he carried the Paris barricades and quelled the Socialists. He was war minister under Cavaignac, but

was banished at the *coup d'état* of 1851. He went to Rome in 1860, commanded the papal troops, but, defeated by Cialdini (September 18), capitulated at Ancona. He died near Amiens. See *Lives* by Keller (3rd ed. 1891) and Rastoul (1894).

LA MOTTE, (1) Antoine Houdar de (1672–1731), French poet and playwright, was born and died in Paris. He was translator of the *Iliad* into French verse. Of his other writings, perhaps the best known is the play *Inès de Castro.*

(2) **Jeanne de Valois, Comtesse de** (1756–1791), French adventuress who duped the Cardinal de Rohan over the Diamond Necklace, and was branded and imprisoned (1786), but escaped (1787) to London, where she was killed by falling drunk from a three-story window. See her autobiography (1793), and Carlyle's *Essays* (1837).

LA MOTTE FOUQUÉ. See FOUQUÉ.

LANCASTER, (1) Sir James (1554 or 1555–1618), English navigator, was a soldier and merchant in Portugal, visited the East Indies in 1591–94, and in 1595 captured Pernambuco. In 1600–03 he commanded the first fleet of the East India Company that visited the East Indies, and on his return was knighted. He promoted the voyages of Hudson, Baffin, &c., in search of the Northwest Passage. See Markham's *Voyages of Sir James Lancaster* (1877), and *The Voyages of Sir James Lancaster,* ed. Sir W. Foster (1940).

(2) **Joseph** (1778–1838), English educationist, opened a school in London in 1798 based on a monitorial system which was taken up by the Nonconformists, Andrew Bell and his rival system being supported by the Church of England. The Lancasterian schools were undenominational, and the Bible formed a large part of the teaching. The Royal Lancasterian Society, afterwards known as the British and Foreign School Society, was formed in 1808. Thriftless and unmethodical, Lancaster quitted the Society in anger, emigrated in 1818 to the U.S., and died at New York. See *Life* by Salmon (1904).

LANCRET, Nicolas, *lā-kray* (1690–1743), French painter, born in Paris, who imitated the style of Watteau. His fête-galante paintings have charm, are cleverly executed but fall short of Watteau's in depth.

LAND, Edwin Herbert (1909–), American inventor and physicist, born at Bridgeport, Conn., known especially for his discoveries relating to light polarization, for his invention of the ' Polaroid ' camera, which takes and processes photographs on the spot, and for research on the nature of colour vision.

LANDAU, Lev Davidovich (1908–68), Russian scientist, born at Baku, graduated at Leningrad, became professor of Physics at Moscow. Known for his important quantum theory researches, he received the Nobel prize for physics in 1962 for work on theories of condensed matter, particularly helium.

LANDELLS, (1) Ebenezer (1808–60), English wood-engraver, born at Newcastle-on-Tyne, the originator in 1841 of *Punch,* worked under Bewick, and in 1829 settled in London. He contributed wood engravings to both *Punch* and the *Illustrated London News.*

(2) **Robert Thomas** (1833–77), eldest son

of (1), was a war artist for the *Illustrated London News* in the Crimean and Franco-Prussian wars.

LANDER, Richard (1804–34), British traveller, born at Truro, in 1825 accompanied Clapperton as his servant to Sokoto. There Clapperton died, and Lander published an account of the expedition. The British government sent him and his brother John (1807–39) to make further researches along the lower Niger. In 1830 they proved that the Niger falls by many mouths into the Bight of Benin, as described in their *Journal* (1832). During a third expedition, Richard Lander was wounded by Niger natives, and died at Fernando Pó. See Laird and Oldfield's *Narrative* of this journey (1837).

LANDESMANN, Heinrich, pseud. Hieronymus Lorm (1821–1902), German deaf and blind poet and prose-writer, born at Nikolsburg in Moravia.

LANDOR, Walter Savage (1775–1864), English writer, was born at Warwick, the son of an ex-doctor. At ten he was sent to Rugby, but was removed for insubordination; and from Trinity College, Oxford, which he entered in 1793, he was rusticated next year. Soon after publishing *Poems* in 1795, he quarrelled with his father, but was reconciled, and retired to South Wales on an allowance of £150 a year. *Gebir* (1798), a poem showing the influence of Milton and Pindar, was the occasion of his lifelong friendship with Southey; but it was a failure. On his father's death in 1805 Landor had a considerable income, but much of it went in equipping volunteers to fight Napoleon in Spain (1808). Next year he purchased Llanthony Abbey, but soon quarrelled with neighbours and tenantry alike, and had ruin staring him in the face. In 1811 he married unhappily Miss Julia Thuillier, and in 1814 he left her in Jersey and crossed to France. Rejoined by his wife at Tours, he went in 1815 to Italy, where he remained at Como, Pisa and Florence till 1835, with the exception of a short visit to England. *Count Julian*, lacking in all the qualities of a successful tragedy, had appeared in 1812; and to this period belongs his best-known work, *Imaginary Conversations* (i and ii, 1824–29). A second quarrel with his wife in 1835 led to his return to Bath till 1858. During these years he wrote the *Examination of Shakespeare* (1834), *Pericles and Aspasia* (1836), *Pentameron* (1837), *Hellenics* (1847), and *Poemata et Inscriptiones* (1847). In 1858 an unhappy scandal (see his *Dry Sticks Fagoted*), which involved him in an action for libel, again drove him to Italy; and at Florence he lived till his death. Physically imposing, strong-willed, and intelligent, Landor is ranked, by a narrow circle of admirers, with the great names of English literature. But many readers find his work artificial. See Forster, *Life and Works* (2 vols, 1869; new ed. 1895); Sidney Colvin, *Landor* (1881); S. Wheeler's *Letters of Landor* (1897–99); Minch in *Last Days, Letters, and Conversation* (1934); M. Elwin, *Savage Landor* (1942) and *Landor, a Replevin* (1958); the *Complete Works*, ed. Welby and Wheeler (1927–33); the *Letters* (1897) and the *Poetical Works* (1937), ed. Wheeler.

LANDOWSKA, Wanda, *lan-dof'ska* (1879–1959), Polish pianist, harpsichordist, and musical scholar, born in Warsaw. In 1900 went to Paris, and in 1912 became professor of the Harpsichord at the Berlin Hochschule. After World War I, in which she was detained, she undertook many extensive concert tours. At Saint-Leu-la-Forêt near Paris she established in 1927 her École de musique ancienne, where she gave specialized training in the performance of old works. In 1940 she had to flee first to the south of France, then to Switzerland, and finally in 1941 to the U.S. She excelled as a player in the music of Bach and Handel. She renewed interest in the harpsichord and Falla wrote for her his concerto for this instrument. She herself composed songs and piano and orchestral pieces. She made a profound study of old music and on this subject wrote *La Musique ancienne* (1908, trans. 1927). Among her other writings were *Bach et ses Interprètes* (1906) and many articles.

LANDRU, Henri Desiré, *lã-drü* (1869–1922), French murderer, born in Paris, served in the army, then worked in garages or was employed in the furniture trade. Between 1904 and 1915 he was imprisoned four times for swindling, &c. His career as a mass murderer began in 1915 and lasted for four years, and he was convicted of the murders of ten women and a boy. He was arrested in 1919, tried in 1921 and executed.

LANDSEER, Sir Edwin Henry (1802–73), English animal painter, born in London, son of the engraver, John Landseer, A.E.R.A. (1769–1852). Trained by his father to sketch animals from life, he began exhibiting at the Royal Academy when only thirteen. His animal pieces were generally made subservient to some sentiment or idea, without, however, losing their correctness and force of draughtsmanship. Dogs and deer were his favourite and best subjects; the scene of several fine pictures is laid in the highlands of Scotland, which he first visited in 1824. In 1826 he was elected an A.R.A., in 1830 an R.A., and in 1850 was knighted. His *Monarch of the Glen*, which in 1892 fetched 6900 guineas, was exhibited in 1851; the bronze lions at the foot of Nelson's Monument in Trafalgar Square were modelled by him (1859–66). Elected P.R.A. in 1866, he declined the honour. He was buried in St Paul's. Most of Landseer's pictures are well known from the excellent engravings of them by his elder brother Thomas (1796–1880). See works by Stephens (1880), Loftie (1891), Manson (1902).

LANDSTEINER, Karl (1868–1943), Austrian pathologist, born in Vienna, was professor of Pathological Anatomy there from 1909. In the United States he was a member of the Rockefeller Institute for Medical Research (1922–39) and won the Nobel prize in 1930 for physiology and medicine, especially for his valuable discovery of the four different types of human blood and of the Rh factor.

LANE, (1) (William) Arbuthnot (1856–1943), Scottish surgeon, born at Fort George, Inverness-shire. He was one of the most outstanding surgeons of his day, being the first to join fractures with metal plates instead of wires. Other important contributions to medicine were his treatment of the cleft palate and of 'chronic intestinal stasis'. In 1925 he founded the New Health Society.

(2) **Edward William** (1801–76), English Arabic scholar, born at Hereford, began life as an engraver; but the need of a warmer climate took him to Egypt (1825–28, 1833–1835), and with Egypt the whole of his subsequent work was connected. The result was his *Manners and Customs of the Modern Egyptians* (1836). This was followed by the annotated translation of the *Thousand and One Nights* (1838–40), which was the first accurate rendering, and by *Selections from the Koran* (1843). Lane's third visit to Egypt (1842–49) was devoted to laborious preparation for the great work of his life, the *Arabic Lexicon* (5 vols. 1863–74), completed (1876–90) by his grand-nephew, Stanley Lane-Poole (q.v.), who also wrote his Life (1877). See also POOLE.

(3) **Sir Hugh Percy** (1875–1915), Irish art collector, was born at Ballybrack, Cork. He was responsible for founding a gallery of modern art in Dublin at the beginning of the 20th century by his encouragement of contemporary artists, such as John B. Yeats and William Orpen, and by his own gifts of pictures. Director of the National Gallery of Ireland in 1914, he was drowned the following year when the *Lusitania*, on which he was a passenger, was torpedoed. He bequeathed to Dublin in a codicil to his will, his collection of thirty-nine French impressionist pictures; but as this was not witnessed they were held by the National Gallery in London until in 1959 a compromise was arranged whereby each half of the collection was to go to Dublin's municipal art gallery for five years successively over a period of twenty years.

(4) **Richard James** (1800–72), brother of (2), born at Berkeley Castle, associate-engraver of the R.A. (1827), turned to lithography, reproducing with unsurpassed delicacy and precision works by Lawrence, Gainsborough, Leslie, Landseer and G. Richmond. He was also no mean sculptor.

LANE-POOLE, (1) Reginald (1857–1939), English historian, born in London, was keeper of the Bodleian (1914–26) and an authority on Wyclif. His many and scholarly writings include *The Huguenots of the Dispersion* (1880), *Illustrations of Medieval Thought* (1884) and *The Exchequer in the Twelfth Century* (1912).

(2) **Stanley** (1854–1931), English archaeologist, brother of (1), was born in London and graduated from Corpus Christi College, Oxford, in 1878. He went, for the government, as archaeologist to Egypt and Russia and wrote on Mohammedan history, Oriental numismatics, Egyptian life, &c. He was the author of a Life of his grand-uncle Edward William Lane (q.v.), whose *Arabic Lexicon* he also completed. He was professor of Arabic at Trinity College, Dublin (1898–1904).

LANFRANC (*c.* 1005–89), Archbishop of Canterbury, was born at Pavia, and educated for the law. About 1039 he founded a school at Avranches, in 1041 became a Benedictine

at Bec, and in 1046 was chosen prior. He contended against Berengarius in the controversy as to the real presence. He at first condemned the marriage of William of Normandy with his cousin, but in 1059 went to Rome to procure the papal dispensation; and in 1062 William made him prior of St Stephen's Abbey at Caen, and in 1070 Archbishop of Canterbury. His chief writings are Commentaries on the Epistles of St Paul, a Treatise against Berengar, and Sermons. See Life by A. J. Macdonald (1926), Hook's *Lives of the Archbishops of Canterbury*, vol. ii, Freeman's *Norman Conquest*, vols. ii-v, and Z. N. Brooke, *The English Church and the Papacy* (1935).

LANFRANCO, Giovanni (*c.* 1581–1647), religious painter, born at Parma, was one of the first Italian baroque painters. His work, the best of which can be seen on the dome of S. Andrea della Valle in Rome and in his paintings for the cathedral at Naples, was widely copied by later painters. He died in Rome. See E. K. Waterhouse, *Baroque Painting in Rome* (1937).

LANFREY, Pierre, *lã-fray* (1828–77), French historian and republican politician, was born at Chambéry, and died at Pau. His great work was his (hostile) *Histoire de Napoléon I* (5 vols. 1867–75).

LANG, (1) Andrew (1844–1912), Scottish man of letters, born at Selkirk, was educated at Edinburgh Academy, St Andrews University and Balliol College, Oxford. He was elected a fellow of Merton in 1868. Soon he became one of the busiest and most versatile writers in the world of London journalism. He took a leading part in the controversy with Max Müller and his school about the interpretation of mythology and folk tales. LL.D. of St Andrews (1885), in 1888 he was first Gifford lecturer there. *Ballads and Lyrics of Old France* (1872), *Ballades in Blue China* (1880), *Helen of Troy* (1882), *Rhymes à la Mode* (1884), *Grass of Parnassus* (1888), and *Ballades of Books* (1888) are volumes of graceful verse. *Custom and Myth* (1884), *Myth, Ritual, and Religion* (1887; 2nd ed. 1899), *Modern Mythology* (1897), and *The Making of Religion* (1898) are solid contributions to the study of the philosophy and religion of primitive man. Other works are *The Library* (1881), *Books and Bookmen* (1886), *Letters to Dead Authors* (1886), *Lost Leaders* (1889), a history of St Andrews (1894), a novel, *The Monk of Fife* (1895), a *History of Scotland* (3 vols. 1899–1904), a *History of English Literature* (1912), *Magic and Religion* (1901), many fairy books, and volumes on Homer, Joan of Arc, Scott, Lockhart, Mary Stuart, John Knox, Prince Charlie, Pickle the Spy, Tennyson, Gowrie Conspiracy, &c. He translated Theocritus and Homer (*Iliad* with W. Leaf and E. Myers; *Odyssey* with S. H. Butcher). See M. Beerbohm's *Andrew Lang* (1929) and studies by Green (1946 and 1962).

(2) **Cosmo Gordon** (1864–1945), Anglican prelate, born at Fyvie, Aberdeenshire, third son of **John Marshall Lang** (1834–1909), principal of Aberdeen University. Entering the Church of England in 1890, he was a curate at Leeds, became Dean of Divinity at Magdalen

College, Oxford, Bishop of Stepney (1901–08) and Canon of St Paul's. In 1908 he was appointed Archbishop of York and in 1928 Archbishop of Canterbury until he retired in 1942. He was created Baron Lang of Lambeth in 1942. A man of wide interests, he was accepted by all parties in the Church of England and was both counsellor and friend to the royal family. See Charles Herbert's *Twenty Years as Archbishop of York* (1928) and J. G. Lockhart's *Cosmo Gordon Lang* (1949).

LANGE, (1) **Carl Georg** (1834–1900), Danish physician and psychologist, with William James advanced the James-Lange theory of emotion. He also wrote a history of materialism, but his main work was *Über Gemütsbewegungen* (1887).

(2) **Johann Peter** (1802–84), German theologian, born at Sonnborn near Elberfeld, in 1841 became professor of Theology at Zürich, and in 1854 at Bonn. His best-known works are a *Life of Jesus Christ* (1839; Eng. trans. by Marcus Dods), and his great *Bibelwerk* (1857 *et seq.*).

LANGER, Susanne (1895–), American aesthetic philosopher, disciple of Ernst Cassirer, whose influence permeates her first work, *Philosophy in a New Key* (1942). Her formalist theory of art is set out in *Feeling and Form* (1953) and *Problems of Art* (1957), and her edited *Reflections on Art* (1958) examine the considerations, facts and views which form the basis of her theory. She is the leading aesthetic philosopher of her time.

LANGEVIN, *lāzh-vĭ*, (1) **Sir Hector Louis** (1826–1906), Canadian statesman, born in Quebec, was called to the bar in 1850 and became mayor of Quebec (1858–60). Thereafter he held many government posts, including solicitor-general (1864–66), postmaster-general (1860–67) and secretary of state (1867–69).

(2) **Paul** (1872–1946), French physicist, professor at the Sorbonne (1909), noted for his work on the molecular structure of gases, and for his theory of magnetism. Imprisoned by the Nazis after the occupation of France, he was later released, and though kept under surveillance at Troyes managed to escape to Switzerland. After the liberation he returned to Paris, where he died.

LANGHAM, Simon (d. 1376), born at Langham in Rutland, became prior and abbot of Westminster (1349), treasurer of England (1360), Bishop of Ely (1362), chancellor (1363), Archbishop of Canterbury (1366) and a cardinal (1368). He died at Avignon. See vol. iv of Hook's *Lives of the Archbishops of Canterbury*.

LANGHORNE, John (1735–79), English poet, born at Winton, Kirkby Stephen, from 1766 was rector of Blagdon, Somerset. He wrote poems and, with his brother, the Rev. William Langhorne (1721–72), translated Plutarch's *Lives* (6 vols. 1770).

LANGLAND, or **Langley, William** (*c.* 1332– *c.* 1400), English poet, born probably at Ledbury in Herefordshire; became a clerk, but, having married early, could not take more than minor orders, and possibly earned a poor living by singing in a chantry and by copying legal documents. He lived many

years in London in poverty. His famous *Vision of William concerning Piers the Plowman* has great defects as a work of art, but the moral earnestness and energy of the author sometimes glow into really noble poetry brightened by vivid glimpses of the life of the poorer classes. The conception of the Plowman grows as the poem proceeds from a mere honest labourer into Christ. The verse is alliterative. The earlier editions were superseded by Prof. Skeat's for the Early English Text Society (1867–84). See Jusserand, *La Poésie mystique de William Langland* (1893; trans. 1894), a book by Bright (1929), and modern versions by K. E. Warren (1895) and H. W. Wells (1895). A theory of multiple authorship was advanced by Prof. Manly in the *Cambridge English Literature*, vol. ii (1908); see also R. W. Chambers, *Man's Unconquerable Mind* (1939).

LANGLEY, (1) **John Newport** (1852–1925), British physiologist, professor at Cambridge from 1903, was noted for his research on the sympathetic nervous system. He owned and edited the *Journal of Physiology*.

(2) **Samuel Pierpont** (1834–1906), American astronomer and aeronautics pioneer, born at Roxbury, Mass., was in 1867 appointed professor of Astronomy at Western University of Pennsylvania and director of the Allegheny Observatory. He became from 1887 secretary of the Smithsonian Institution. He greatly advanced solar physics, invented the bolometer for measuring radiant heat, and built an aeroplane that failed to launch in 1903 but flew until 1914. He is recognized as a pioneer of flying machines. See F. Cajori, *History of Physics* (1899) and M. J. B. Davy, *Interpretive History of Flight* (1937).

LANGMUIR, Irving (1881–1957), American chemist, born in Brooklyn, N.Y., educated at Columbia and Göttingen, was associated with the General Electric Company (1909– 1950), being from 1932 associate director of the research laboratory. He won the Nobel prize in 1932 for work on surface chemistry. His many inventions include the gas-filled tungsten lamp, and atomic hydrogen welding.

LANGTON, (1) **Bennet** (1737–1801), a Lincolnshire gentleman and militia officer, one of Johnson's greatest friends. Also a scholar, he was professor of Ancient Literature at the Academy. See Birkbeck Hill, *Dr Johnson, his Friends and his Critics* (1878).

(2) **Stephen** (*c.* 1150–1228), English theologian, whose birthplace is unknown, educated at the University of Paris. His friend and fellow-student Pope Innocent III in 1206 gave him a post in his household and made him a cardinal. On the disputed election to the see of Canterbury in 1205–07, Langton was recommended by the pope, and, having been elected, was consecrated by Innocent himself at Viterbo, June 27, 1207. His appointment was resisted by King John, and Langton was kept out of the see until 1213, living mostly at Pontigny. He sided warmly with the barons against John, and his name is the first of the subscribing witnesses of Magna Carta. Although the pope excommunicated the barons, Langton refused to publish the excommunication, and was

suspended from his functions in 1215. He was reinstated in 1218. See Hook's *Archbishops* (1861), and studies by Leeming (1915), Powicke (1928).

LANGTRY, Lillie, properly **Emilie Charlotte,** *née* Le Breton (1853–1929), British actress, born in Jersey, daughter of the dean of the island, one of the most noted beauties of her time. She married Edward Langtry in 1874, and made her first important stage appearance in 1881. Her sobriquet, *The Jersey Lily,* originated in the title of Millais's portrait of her. She managed the Imperial theatre which was never successful and which had to be taken down. Widowed in 1897, she married in 1899 (later Sir) Hugo Gerald de Bathe (Bt.), and became well-known as a racehorse owner. She died in Monte Carlo. She wrote *All at Sea* (as Lillie de Bathe) in 1909, and her reminiscences *The Days I Knew* (1925). See Life by E. Dudley (1958), and novel by P. Sichel (1958).

LANIER, Sidney, *lan-eer'* (1842–81), American poet, born at Macon, Ga., Confederate private in Virginia, advocate at Macon, flute player at Baltimore, and lecturer in English Literature at Johns Hopkins University. Among his writings are a novel, *Tiger Lilies* (1867), *The Science of English Verse* (1880), *The English Novel* (1883), as well as poetry. He believed in a scientific approach towards poetry-writing, breaking away from the traditional metrical techniques and making it more akin to musical composition, illustrated in later poems, such as ' Corn ' and ' The Symphony '. See Works (Centennial Edition in 10 volumes in 1945) and Life by Starke (1933).

LANJUINAIS, Jean Denis, *lã-zhwee-nay* (1753–1827), French statesman, born at Rennes, a Girondist, made a count by Napoleon, and a peer by Louis XVIII. See Life by his son, prefixed to his *Oeuvres complètes* (4 vols. 1832).

LANKESTER, Sir Edwin Ray (1847–1929), English zoologist, born in London, the son of Dr Edwin Lankester (1814–74), scientific writer. Was fellow and tutor of Exeter College, professor in London and in Oxford, and 1898–1907 director of the British Museum (Natural History). His contributions to zoology were many and varied and included important work in embryology and protozoology. Largely responsible for the founding of the Marine Biological Association in 1884, he became president of it in 1892. Among his many books are *Comparative Longevity* (1871), *Degeneration* (1880), *Advancement of Science* (1890), *Science from an Easy Chair* (1910–12), and he edited a great *Treatise on Zoology* (1900–09).

LANNES, Jean, Duke de Montebello, *lan* (1769–1809), French marshal, born at Lectoure (Gers), son of a livery stable keeper, entered the army in 1792, and by his conspicuous bravery in the Italian campaign fought his way up to be general of brigade by 1796. He rendered Napoleon important service on the 18th Brumaire. In 1800, he won the battle of Montebello, and had a distinguished share at Marengo, Austerlitz, Jena, Eylau and Friedland, and took Saragossa. In 1809 he commanded the centre at Aspern, where he was mortally wounded, and died at Vienna. See Life by Thoumas (Paris 1891).

LANSBURY, George (1859–1940), British politician, born near Lowestoft, for many years before entering parliament worked for the reform of the conditions of the poor. He was first elected Labour member of parliament for Bow and Bromely in 1910, resigning in 1912 to stand again as a supporter of women's suffrage. He was defeated and was not re-elected until 1922. Meanwhile he founded the *Daily Herald*, which he edited until 1922, when it became the official paper of the Labour Party. In 1929 he became first commissioner of works and a very able leader of the Labour party (1931–35). Besides his help to the poor, he opened up London's parks for games and provided a bathing place on the Serpentine. See his *My Life* (1928) and Life by Postgate (1951).

LANSDOWNE, (1) Henry Petty-Fitzmaurice, 3rd Marquis of (1780–1863), son of the first marquis, better known as the Earl of Shelburne (q.v.). Graduated at Cambridge in 1801, and was returned for Calne next year. He led in the attack on Lord Melville (1805), and succeeded Pitt as member for Cambridge University (1806), and also as chancellor of the Exchequer in the Grenville administration. In 1809, by the death of his half-brother, he became marquis. A cautious Liberal, he in 1826 entered the Canning cabinet, and in the Goderich administration (1827–28) presided at the Foreign Office. Under Lord Grey (1830) Lansdowne became president of the council, and helped to pass the Reform Bill of 1832. He held office, with a short interval, till 1841. In 1846, under Russell, he resumed his post, taking with it the leadership of the Lords. Requested to form an administration in 1852, he preferred to serve without office in the Aberdeen coalition and in 1855 again declined the premiership. He formed a great library and art collection. See A. Aspinall, *Formation of Canning's Ministry* (1937); *Greville Memoirs,* ed. P. W. Wilson (1927) and G. P. Gooch, *Later Correspondence of Lord John Russell* (1925).

(2) Henry Charles Keith Petty-Fitzmaurice, 5th Marquis of (1845–1927), became marquis in 1866, from 1868 held minor offices in the Liberal administration. In 1872–74 under-secretary for war, in 1880 for India, joining the Liberal Unionists. Governor-general of Canada (1883–88), of India (1888–94), war secretary in 1895–1900. In 1900–05 as foreign secretary promoted arbitration treaties (with U.S.A., &c.), the *Entente Cordiale,* and the Japanese alliance. Unionist leader in the Lords from 1903, he sat (without portfolio) in Asquith's coalition cabinet 1915–16, advocating peace by negotiation in 1917. See Life by Newton (1929).

LANSING, Robert (1864–1928), American lawyer and statesman, born at Watertown, N.Y., became a barrister 1889, and made a name as U.S. counsel in arbitration cases (Behring Sea, N. Atlantic coast fisheries, &c.). An authority on international law, became counsellor for the department of state in 1914, succeeded Bryan as Woodrow Wilson's secretary of state in June 1915, supported the

President during the Great War, attended the Peace Conference in Paris, 1919, and resigned in 1920. He was author of *The Peace Negotiations* (1921) and *The Big Four and others of the Peace Conference* (1921).

LANSON, Gustave, *là-sõ* (1857–1934), French critic and historian, born at Orleans, became professor of French Literature at the Sorbonne in 1900, and director of the École normale supérieure 1919–27. Among his scholarly works are a standard history of French literature (1894), *Manuel bibliographique de la littérature française moderne* (1913), and critical studies of French authors and their works, including Voltaire, Corneille and Lamartine.

LANSTON, Tolbert (1844–1913), American inventor, born in Troy, Ohio, patented his Monotype, ' a type-forming and composing machine ', in 1887. It was first used commercially in 1897 and revolutionized printing processes.

LANZI, Luigi, *lan'tzee* (1732–1810), Italian antiquary, held Etruscan to be akin to Latin, Oscan, Umbrian and Greek. His *History of Painting in Italy* (1792–1806) was translated by Roscoe (1828). See Life by Cappi (1840).

LÃO-TSZE (' Old Philosopher ') (*c.* 604 B.C.–?), is said to have been the founder of Tâoism, which shares the allegiance of the Chinese with Confucianism and Buddhism. He was for some time a curator of the royal library at Loh in Ho-nan. The treatise called the *Tâo Teh King* is our sole record of his teaching of the way in which things came into being, and in which the phenomena of nature go on quietly without striving. The secret of good government is to let men alone. Tâoism as a religion is dated much later.

LA PÉROUSE, Jean François de Galaup, Comte de, *pay-rooz* (1741–88), French navigator, born at Guo near Albi, distinguished himself in the naval war against Britain (1778–83), by destroying the forts of the Hudson's Bay Company. In 1785, in command of an expedition of discovery, he visited the north-west coast of America, explored the north-eastern coasts of Asia, and sailed through La Pérouse Strait between Sakhalin and Yezo. In 1788 he sailed from Botany Bay, and his two ships were wrecked north of the New Hebrides. Part of his journals had been sent home and was published as *Voyage autour du monde* (1797). See Life by Marcel (1888).

LAPLACE, Pierre Simon, Marquis de (1749–1827), French mathematician and astronomer born at Beaumont-en-Auge, near Trouville, the son of a poor farmer. He studied at Caen, and, after teaching mathematics, went to Paris and, as professor in the Royal Military School, became famous for his mastery of the whole range of mathematical science and its application to practical astronomy. He was chosen an associate of the Academy of Sciences in 1773 and member in 1785. His great generalization that our whole planetary system is stable bestowed upon astronomy the ' Three Laws of Laplace '. He explained the ' secular inequalities ' in the motions of Jupiter and Saturn. He was the first to construct a complete theory of

the satellites of Jupiter, and his investigation of the tidal theory was one of his greatest achievements. He helped to establish the Polytechnic and Normal Schools in Paris, and was president of the Bureau des Longitudes. Bonaparte made him minister of the interior, but superseded him in six weeks. In 1799 Laplace entered the senate; in 1803 he was appointed its chancellor. A count under the empire, he was created in 1815 a peer, in 1817 a marquis, by Louis XVIII. Elected to the Academy in 1816, he was next year appointed president. He published many treatises on lunar and planetary problems, molecular physics, electricity and magnetism. *Mécanique céleste* (1799–1825) stands alone amongst works on mathematical astronomy. The *Système du monde* (1796), written for non-mathematicians, is a clear statement of all the leading astronomical facts and theories. In a note at the end of the later editions occurs the famous Nebular Hypothesis. In 1784 Laplace issued his *Théorie des planètes*, and in 1812–14–20 his *Théorie analytique des probabilités*. The last remains a classic to algebraists. His *Oeuvres complètes* were issued by the Academy (14 vols. 1878–1912).

LAPPENBERG, Johann Martin (1794–1865), German historian, born in Hamburg, was keeper of the archives there for forty years, wrote histories of England, the Hanse towns, Heligoland, the Steelyard in London, &c. See Memoir by Meyer (1867).

LAPWORTH, Charles (1842–1920), British geologist, born at Farringdon, was a schoolteacher at Galashiels and did important work in elucidating the geology of the south of Scotland and also of the northwest Highlands. He was professor of Geology at Birmingham 1881–1913 and wrote especially on graptolites. The term Ordovician was introduced by him. He became a fellow of the Royal Society in 1888.

LA RAMÉE. See OUIDA.

LARDNER, (1) **Dionysius** (1793–1859), Irish scientific writer, born in Dublin, attracted attention by works on algebraic geometry (1823) and the calculus (1825), but is best known as the originator and editor of *Lardner's Cyclopaedia* (132 vols. 1830–44), followed by the historical *Cabinet Library* (12 vols. 1830–32), and *Museum of Science and Art* (12 vols. 1854–56). In 1840 he went to the United States and gave lectures there until in 1845 he went to Paris. He died in Naples.

(2) **Nathaniel** (1684–1768), English Nonconformist (ultimately Unitarian) divine and biblical scholar, was born and died at Hawkhurst in Kent. See Life by Kippis prefixed to his works (11 vols. 1788).

LARGILLIÈRE, Nicolas, *lar-zheel-yer* (1656–1746), French portrait painter, was born and died in Paris, having lived for some years in England where he was Lely's assistant. He was one of the most popular portraitists of his day.

LARIVEY, Pierre (*c.* 1550–1612), French dramatist of Italian descent, as the introducer of Italian-style comedy to the French stage foreshadowed Molière and Regnard. His licentious *Comédies facétieuses* (2 vols.;

1579, 1611) were adaptations of existing Italian pieces.

LARKIN, (1) **James** (1876–1947), Irish Labour leader, born in Liverpool, was organizer of the Irish Transport and General Workers' Union. Deported from U.S.A. in 1923 for his anarchistic activities, he continued at the head of the I.T. and G.W.U., organizing strikes and fostering strife until expelled in 1924. He was Ireland's representative at the Third International, but later gave up Communism, continuing as an extreme Labour leader.

(2) **Philip** (1922–), English poet and novelist, librarian of Hull University. His collections of poems include *The North Ship* (1945), *The Less Deceived* (1955), *The Whitsun Weddings* (1964). In 1965 he won the Queen's Gold Medal for Poetry.

LA ROCHEFOUCAULD, François, 6th Duc de, *rosh-foo-kō* (1613–80), French writer, born at Paris, devoted himself to the cause of the queen in opposition to Richelieu, and became entangled in a series of love adventures and political intrigues, the result being that he was forced to live in exile from 1639 to 1642. About 1645 he formed a liaison with Mme de Longueville. He then joined the Frondeurs and was wounded at the siege of Paris. In 1652, wounded again, he retired to the country. On Mazarin's death in 1661 he repaired to the court of Louis XIV, and about the same time began his liaison with Mme de Sablé. A surreptitious edition of his *Mémoires*, written in retirement, was published in 1662; as it gave wide offence he disavowed its authorship. His *Réflexions, ou sentences et maximes morales*, appeared in 1665. His last years were brightened by his friendship with Mme de La Fayette, which lasted until he died. For brevity, clearness and finish of style the *Maxims* could hardly be excelled. Their author was a remorseless analyst of man's character, tracks out self-love in its most elusive forms and under its cunningest disguises, and forgets that self-love is not the sole motive by which men are impelled. The best edition of La Rochefoucauld's works is that by D. L. Gilbert and J. Gourdault (1868–84). See work in German by Rahstede (Brunswick 1888) and French by Bourdeau (1895), and *Les Maximes*, ed. F. C. Green (1945).

LAROCHEJAQUELEIN, Du Verger de, *la-rosh-zhak-lĩ*, an old noble family named from a place in Poitou:

(1) **Henri, Comte de** (1772–94), after August 10, 1792, headed the insurgent royalists in La Vendée. He for a time successfully repelled the republican forces, but was defeated on December 21, 1793. He raised a new body of troops, but was killed at Nouaillé.

(2) **Louis du Verger, Marquis de** (1777–1815), brother of (1), emigrated at the Revolution, returned to France in 1801, and in 1813 headed the royalists in La Vendée. Louis XVIII gave him in 1814 the command of the army of La Vendée, where, during the Hundred Days, he maintained the royalist cause, supported by the British. He fell at Pont-des-Mathis.

(3) **Marie Louise Victoire** (1772–1857),

wife of (2), published valuable *Mémoires* of the war (1815). See her Life by Mrs Maxwell Scott (1911).

LAROUSSE, Pierre Athanase (1817–75), French lexicographer, born at Toucy in Yonne, edited the *Grand dictionnaire universel* (15 vols. 1864–76).

LARRA, Mariano José de (1809–37), Spanish poet, satirist and political writer, was born at Madrid. As a journalist he was unequalled and he published two periodicals between 1828 and 1833, but it was as a satirist that he became well known. His prose writings are masterly and include *El Doncel de Don Enrique el Doliente* (1834), a novel, *Macias* (1834), a play and adaptations of French plays. See Life by I. S. Estevan (1934).

LARREY, Jean Dominique, Baron, *la-ray* (1766–1842), French surgeon, born at Beaudéan near Bagnères-de-Bigorre, served as a naval surgeon, and in 1793 joining the army, introduced the 'flying ambulance' service. From 1797 he accompanied Napoleon in his campaigns, became head of the army medical department, and a baron. He wrote on army surgery and the treatment of wounds. See German memoir by Werner (1885).

LARSSON, Lars Erik (1908–), Swedish composer, he was a student in Stockholm and in Vienna, where Alban Berg was his master. He has written three symphonies, an opera *The Princess of Cyprus*, a cantata *The Disguised God*, a saxophone concerto and music for the stage and films.

LA SALLE, (1) **Antoine de** (*c.* 1398–1470), French writer, born in Burgundy or Touraine, lived at the courts of Provence and Flanders, and wrote *Chronique du petit Jehan de Saintré*, a knightly romance *Quinze joyes de mariage*, and was the reputed author of *Cent nouvelles nouvelles*.

(2) **Jean Baptiste, Abbé de** (1651–1719), French educational reformer, born at Rheims, set up schools for the poor, training colleges for teachers, and reformatories, and was the founder in 1684 of the Brothers of Christian Schools. He was canonized in 1900. See W. J. Battersby, *De la Salle Education* (1948).

(3) **Robert Cavelier, Sieur de** (1643–87), French explorer was born at Rouen, and, having settled in Canada at twenty-three, descended the Ohio and Mississippi to the sea (1682). Two years later an expedition was fitted out to establish a French settlement on the Gulf of Mexico. But La Salle spent two years in fruitless journeys, while his harshness embittered his followers, and he was assassinated. See works by Parkman (q.v.), and Life by R. Syme (1953).

LASCARIS, (1) **Constantine** (d. 1493 or 1501), Greek grammarian who, after the capture of Constantinople by the Turks, fled to Italy, and revived the study of Greek at Rome, Naples and Messina, where he died. His Greek grammar (1476) was the first Greek book printed in Italy. His library is now in the Escorial. See A. F. Villemain, *Lascaris ou les Grecs du 15e siècle* (1825).

(2) **John** or **Janus,** called **Rhyndacenus** (*c.* 1445–1535) collected MSS. for Lorenzo dei Medici, taught Greek, and on Lorenzo's

death went to Paris, and finally was employed in literary work and diplomatic missions to France and Venice by Leo X. He died at Rome. He edited Greek classics, and wrote grammars, letters and epigrams. See works by Villemain (1825), Vast (1878) and P. de Nolhac (1886), and J. E. Sandys, *History of Classical Scholarship* (1902–08).

LAS CASAS, Bartolomé de (1474–1566), the ' Apostle of the Indians ', was born at Seville. He sailed in the third voyage of Columbus, and in 1502 went to Hispaniola. Eight years later he was ordained to the priesthood. In 1511 he accompanied Diego Velázquez to Cuba, assisted in the pacification of the island, and was rewarded by a commandery of Indians. But soon love for, and a desire to protect and defend the natives, made him give up his own slaves, and he went to Spain, where he prevailed on Cardinal Ximenes to send a commission of inquiry to the West Indies. He revisited Spain to secure stronger measures; and finally, to prevent the extirpation of the natives, he proposed that the colonists should be permitted to import negro slaves—a proposal only too readily acceded to. He also attempted to carry out Castilian peasants as colonists, but failed, and spent eight years (1522–30) in a convent in Hispaniola. In 1530 he again visited Spain, and, after missionary travels in Mexico, Nicaragua, Peru and Guatemala, returned to devote four years to the cause of the Indians, writing his *Veynte Razones* and *Brevísima Relación*. Appointed Bishop of Chiapa, he was received (1544) with hostility by the colonists, returned to Spain, and resigned his see (1547). He still contended with the authorities in favour of the Indians until his death in Madrid. His most important work is the unfinished *Historia de las Indias* (1875–76). See Life by Sir A. Helps (1868) and study by F. A. MacNutt (1909).

LAS CASES, Emmanuel Dieudonné, Comte de, *kahz* (1766–1842), French historian, born at Las Cases, Haute Garonne, was a lieutenant in the navy, but fled to England at the Revolution. His *Atlas historique* (1803–04) gave him a European reputation. Though a royalist by birth, he was so fascinated by Napoleon's genius that he insisted on sharing his exile. Deported to the Cape by Sir Hudson Lowe in 1816, he returned to Europe, and published (1821–23) the *Mémorial de Sainte-Hélène*, which caused an immense sensation.

LASCO, Johannes a, or **Jan Łaski** (*c.* 1499–1560), Polish reformer, was highly born at Łask, Piotrkow. He was ordained priest in 1521, and in 1523 at Basel came in contact with Erasmus and Farel. Caught in the current of the Reformation, he left home in 1538 and about 1540 moved to East Friesland, where he established a presbyterian form of church government as superintendent at Emden. In 1550, on Cranmer's invitation, he became head of a congregation of Protestant refugees in London. Mary's accession in 1553 drove him back to Emden, and he finally returned to Poland in 1556. See Dalton's unfinished *John a Lasco* (Eng. trans. from the German, 1886), and Pascal's *Jean de Lasco* (Paris 1894).

LASHLEY, Karl Spencer (1890–1958), American psychologist, born at Davis, Virginia, research professor of neuropsychology at Harvard (1937). In 1942 he became director of Yerkes laboratories of primate biology at Orange Park, Florida. A specialist in genetic psychology, he made valuable contributions to the study of localization of brain function. His writings include *Brain Mechanisms and Intelligence* (1929).

LASKER, (1) **Eduard** (1829–84), Prussian Liberal politician, was born of Jewish parentage in Posen. He was one of the founders of the National Liberal party and is important chiefly for the codification of the laws of Germany, for which he was largely responsible. He died at New York on a visit to America.

(2) **Emanuel** (1868–1941), German chessplayer and mathematician, born at Berlinchen, Prussia, held the world's championship 1894–1921, 1924–25. See Life by Hannak (1959).

LASKI, (1) **Harold Joseph** (1893–1950), English political scientist and socialist, born, a Jew, at Manchester. He was educated at Manchester Grammar School and New College, Oxford, and lectured at McGill University (1914–16), Harvard (1916–20), Amherst (1917) and Yale (1919–20, 1931). In 1920 he joined the staff of the London School of Economics, and became professor of Political Science in 1926. He was chairman of the Labour party (1945–46). Laski was a brilliant talker and as lecturer at the London School of Economics had a great influence over his students, who revered him. His political philosophy was a modified Marxism. He had a strong belief in individual freedom, but the downfall of the Labour government in 1931 forced him to feel that some revolution in Britain was necessary. His works include *Authority in the Modern State* (1919), *A Grammar of Politics* (1925), *Liberty in the Modern State* (1930) and *The American Presidency* (1940). See *Holmes-Laski Letters*, ed. M. de Wolfe Howe (2 vols. 1953) and Life by Kingsley Martin (1953).

(2) **Jan.** See Lasco.

(3) **Marghanita** (1915–), English-Jewish novelist and critic, born in Manchester and educated at Oxford. Her first novel, *Love on the Supertax*, appeared in 1944, and she has written extensively for newspapers and reviews. Her later novels include *Little Boy Lost* (1949) and *The Victorian Chaiselongue* (1953). In 1959 she wrote a play *The Offshore Island*. She married John E. Howard in 1937.

LASSALLE, Ferdinand (1825–64), German social democrat, was born, the son of a rich Jewish merchant, at Breslau. A disciple of Hegel, he wrote a work on Heraclitus (published 1858), and in Paris made the acquaintance of Heine. On his return to Berlin he met in 1844–45 the Countess Sophie Hatzfeld (1805–81), a lady at variance with her husband, prosecuted her cause before thirty-six tribunals, and after eight years of litigation forced the husband to a compromise favourable to the countess. He took part in the revolution of 1848, and for an inflammatory speech got six months in prison. He lived in the Rhine country till 1857, when he returned to Berlin, and wrote his *System der erworbenen Rechte* (1861). At Leipzig he founded the Universal German Working-men's Association to agitate for universal suffrage. In 1863-64 he tried to win the Rhineland and Berlin to his cause; in his *Bastiat-Schulze, or Capital and Labour*, he attacked Schulze-Delitzsch, the representative of Liberalism. In 1864 Lassalle met Helene von Dönniges, and they resolved to marry in spite of the strongest opposition from her parents. Under pressure from them she renounced Lassalle in favour of the Wallachian Count Racowitza. Lassalle sent to both father and lover a challenge, which was accepted by the latter and at Geneva he fell mortally wounded, and died two days afterwards. He taught that Europe's historical development is to culminate in a democracy of labour, in which political interests shall be subservient to social—the social democracy. See the Memoirs (1879) and *Autobiography* (trans. 1910) of Helene von Racowitza (who committed suicide in 1911); works by Brandes (trans. 1911), W. H. Dawson (1888), Bernstein (trans. 1893), Seillière (1897), Oncken (1904), Rosenbaum (1911), Mayer (1921-25), Footman (1946); Meredith's *Tragic Comedians* (ed. with Lassalle bibliography by C. K. Shorter, 1891); Lassalle's Diary (Breslau 1891).

LASSELL, William (1799-1880), British astronomer, born at Bolton, built an observatory at Starfield near Liverpool, where he constructed and mounted equatorial reflecting telescopes. He discovered several planetary satellites, including Triton and Hyperion (at the same time as W. C. Bond of Harvard). At Malta with a larger reflecting telescope he made observations (1861-65); and then settled near Maidenhead.

LASSEN, Christian (1800-76), Norwegian orientalist, born at Bergen, assisted Schlegel and Eugène Burnouf, and was professor of Ancient Indian Languages at Bonn from 1830 till he became blind in 1864. Amongst his most important books are works on Persian cuneiforms (1836-45), the Greek Kings in Bactria (1838), Prakrit (1837), and Indian civilization (1844-61).

LASSUS, Orlandus, or **Orlando di Lasso** (c. 1532-94), Netherlands musician, born at Mons, composer of many masses, motets, &c. He died at Munich, having visited Italy, England and France, and been ennobled by Maximilian II in 1570. Unlike Palestrina, his contemporary, he wrote not only church music but also a vast number of secular works, and ranks as one of the greatest composers of early times. See Lives by Declève (Mons 1894), Destouches (Munich 1894), Schnitz (1915) and Van den Borren (3rd ed. 1930).

LÁSZLÓ, Sir Philip, properly **Philip Alexius László de Lombos,** *lahs'lō* (1869-1937), portrait painter, born at Budapest. He studied at Budapest, Munich and Paris, and came to England in 1907, being naturalized in 1914. During his lifetime he gained an international reputation as a painter of royalty and heads of states, e.g., Edward VII, Theodore Roosevelt and Lord Roberts.

LATHAM, (1) John, M.D. (1740-1837), English ornithologist, one of the founders of the Linnaean Society, born at Eltham, lived from 1796 at Romsey.

(2) **Robert Gordon** (1812-88), English ethnologist and philologist, was born at Billingborough vicarage, Lincolnshire. From Eton he passed in 1829 to King's College, Cambridge, of which he was elected fellow. From 1842 (when he took his M.D.) to 1849 he held appointments in London hospitals; in 1839 he became professor of English in University College London, a tour six years before in Denmark and Norway having directed his attention to Scandinavian philology. The author of textbooks on English language, philology and etymology, he revised Johnson's Dictionary (1870), and wrote also on the ethnology of the British Isles and Europe. In *Elements of Comparative Philology* (1862) he advanced the view that the Aryan race originated in Europe. In 1863 he received a government pension of £100. He died at Putney.

LATIMER, Hugh (c. 1485-1555), English Protestant martyr, was born, a yeoman's son, at Thurcaston, near Leicester. He was sent to Cambridge, in 1510 was elected a fellow of Clare, and was in 1522 appointed a university preacher. In 1524 for his B.D. thesis he delivered a philippic against Melanchthon, for he was, in his own words, ' as obstinate a papist as any in England '. Next year, however, through Bilney (q.v.), he ' began to smell the Word of God, forsaking the school doctors and such fooleries ', and soon becoming noted as a zealous preacher of the reformed doctrines. One of the Cambridge divines appointed to examine the lawfulness of Henry's marriage, he declared on the king's side; and he was made chaplain to Anne Boleyn and rector of West Kington in Wiltshire. In 1535 he was consecrated Bishop of Worcester and at the opening of Convocation in June 1536 he preached two powerful sermons urging on the Reformation. As that work rather retrograded him, out of favour at court he retired to his diocese, and laboured there in a continual round of ' teaching, preaching, exhorting, writing, correcting and reforming '. Twice during Henry's reign he was sent to the Tower, in 1539 and 1546, on the former occasion resigning his bishopric. At Edward VI's accession he declined to resume his episcopal functions, but devoted himself to preaching and practical works of benevolence. Under Mary he was (1554) examined at Oxford, and committed to jail. In September 1555, with Ridley and Cranmer, he was found guilty of heresy, and on October 16 was burned with Ridley opposite Balliol College. His powerful, homely, humorous sermons, letters, &c., were edited, with a memoir, by Corrie (2 vols. 1844-45). See Lives by Gilpin (1755), Demaus (1869; new ed. 1922), R. M. and A. J. Carlyle (1899), and works by Darby (1953) and Chester (1954).

LATINI, Brunetto, *la-tee'nee* (c. 1210-c. 1295), a Florentine statesman, author during his banishment to France of the encyclopaedic *Livres dou Trésor*, as also of an Italian poem.

LA TOUCHE, Gaston, *la-toosh* (1854–1913), French painter and engraver, born at St Cloud, was a pupil of Manet.

LATOUR, Maurice Quentin de, *la-toor* (1704–1788), French pastellist and portrait painter, was born and died at St Quentin. His best works include portraits of Madame de Pompadour, Voltaire and Rousseau.

LA TOUR, Georges de, *la toor* (1593–1652), French artist, born at Vic-sur-Seille. He was identified about 1915, some of his works having been previously attributed to Le Nain and followers of Caravaggio. His works are mainly dramatically-lighted religious paintings, for example, the *St Jerome* and *St Joseph* in the Louvre. Only fourteen of his works are known. See study by P. Jamot (Paris 1942).

LA TOUR D'AUVERGNE, Théophile Malo Corret de, *la toor dō-vern'y'* (1743–1800), French soldier, born at Carhaix in Finistère, enlisted in 1767, distinguished himself at Port Mahon in 1782, steadily refused advancement and was killed, a simple captain, at Oberhausen in Bavaria. His remains were interred in the Panthéon in 1889. French biographies are full of instances of his valour, Spartan simplicity and chivalrous affection. He was known as the ' First Grenadier of France '. He wrote a book on the Breton language and antiquities.

LATREILLE, Pierre André, *la-tray* (1762–1833), French entomologist, was born at Brives in Corrèze, and died professor of Natural History at Paris. He is best known for his work on the classification of insects and crustaceans.

LATTRE DE TASSIGNY, Jean de, *tas-seen-yee* (1889–1952), French general, was born at Mouilleron-en-Pareds, was educated at the Jesuit College at Poitiers and St Cyr, and commanded an infantry battalion during World War I, was wounded four times and decorated with the Croix de Guerre. By 1940 he commanded the 14th division in rearguard actions against the advancing Germans, was sent by the Vichy government to command in Tunisia, recalled for sympathy with the Allies and arrested in 1942 for resisting the German occupation of the neutral zone. He escaped from Rion prison in 1943, was secretly flown by an R.A.F. plane to London, and later he took a brilliant part in the Allied liberation of France 1944–45, signing the German surrender. He was responsible for the reorganization of the French army and was appointed c.-in-c. of Western Union Land Forces under Montgomery in 1948. In 1950 he successfully turned the tide against the Vietminh rebels, by introducing novel tactics as c.-in-c. in French Indo-China. He was posthumously made a Marshal of France in 1952.

LATUDE, Henri Masers de (1725–1805), French artillery officer who sought to secure Madame de Pompadour's favour by revealing a plot to poison her. The plot was of his own contriving, and he was sent without trial to the Bastille in 1749. He made three daring but futile escapes from prison, and was at last released in 1777, on condition that he lived in his native village of Montagnac in Languedoc. Lingering in Paris,

he was reimprisoned till 1784. At the Revolution he was treated as a victim of despotism and voted a pension. See monograph by Thiéry (1792; re-edited by Bertin 1889).

LAUBE, Heinrich, *low'bě* (1806–84), German playwright and manager, was born at Sprottau in Silesia and died in Vienna. He was one of the leaders of the ' Young Germany ' movement and editor of *Die elegante Welt*, its literary organ. He was director of Vienna's Burgtheater, 1850–67, and among his writings are works on the theatre, on historical themes, novels such as *Das junge Europa* (1833–37), *Die Karlsschüler* (1847), a drama of the young Schiller, and a biography of Grillparzer. See *Gesammelte Werke*, ed. H. H. Houben (50 vols., 1908–10), J. Proelss, *Das junge Deutschland* (1892), H. H. Houben, *Laubes Leben und Schriften* (1906), M. Krammer, *H. Laube* (1926).

LAUD, William (1573–1645), Archbishop of Canterbury, was born at Reading, a well-to-do clothier's son. From Reading free school he passed at sixteen to St John's College, Oxford, of which four years later he became a fellow. Ordained in 1601, he made himself obnoxious to the university authorities by his open antipathy to the dominant Puritanism; but his solid learning, his amazing industry, his administrative capacity, his sincere and unselfish churchmanship, soon won him friends and patrons. One of these was Charles Blount, Earl of Devonshire, whom in 1605 Laud married to the divorced Lady Rich (an offence that always was heavy on his conscience); another was Buckingham, to whom he became confessor in 1622, having a month previously disputed before him and the countess his mother with Fisher the Jesuit. Meanwhile he rose steadily from preferment to preferment—incumbent of five livings (1607–10), D.D. (1608), president of his old college and king's chaplain (1611), prebendary of Lincoln (1614), Archdeacon of Huntingdon (1615), Dean of Gloucester (1616), prebendary of Westminster and Bishop of St Davids (1621), Bishop of Bath and Wells, Dean of the Chapel Royal, and a privy councillor (1626), Bishop of London (1628), Chancellor of Oxford (1630), and finally Archbishop of Canterbury (1633), in the very week that he received two offers of a cardinal's hat. Already, after Buckingham's assassination, he had virtually become the first minister of the crown, one with Strafford and Charles I in the triumvirate whose aim was absolutism in church and state. Laud's task was to raise the Church of England to its rightful position of a branch of the Church Catholic, to root out Calvinism in England and Presbyterianism in Scotland. In the former country he drew up a list of ' Orthodox ' and ' Puritan ' ministers, whom he proceeded to separate by scolding, suspending, depriving. Freedom of worship was withdrawn from Walloon and French refugees; Englishmen abroad were forbidden to attend Calvinistic services; and at home ' gospel preaching ', justification by faith, and Sabbatarianism were to be superseded by an elaborate ritual, by the doctrine of the real presence, celibacy and confession, and by the Book of Sports—changes rigorously enforced by the court of High Commission and the Star Chamber. In Scotland Laud's attempt (1635–37) to Anglicize the Scottish Church gave birth to the riot in St Giles', Edinburgh, that riot to the Covenant, the Covenant to the ' Bishops' war ', and this to the meeting of the Long Parliament, which on December 18, 1640, impeached the archbishop of treason, and ten weeks later sent him to the Tower. He would not escape (Grotius urged him to do so); and at last, after a tedious and complicated trial before a handful of peers, on December 17, 1644, he was voted ' guilty of endeavouring to subvert the laws, to overthrow the Protestant religion, and to act as an enemy to Parliament '. The judges declared that this was not treason; but under an unconstitutional ordinance of attainder, he was beheaded on Tower Hill. Of Laud's works (7 vols. Anglo-Catholic Library, 1847–60) the most interesting is his Diary, published in 1694. Peter Heylin, Laud's chaplain, first wrote his biography, *Cyprianus Anglicanus* (1668); and there are also Lives by Le Bas (1836), Mozley (1845; republished in *Essays*, 1878), Hook (*Archbishops*, 1875), A. C. Benson (1887), Simpkinson (1894), W. H. Hutton (1895), Duncan-Jones (1927) and H. R. Trevor-Roper (1940).

LAUDER, (1) Sir Harry (1870–1950), Scottish comic singer, born at Portobello, started his career on the music hall stage as an Irish comedian, but made his name as a singer of Scots songs, made famous of his own composition, e.g., *Roamin' in the Gloamin'*. He was knighted in 1919 for his work in organizing entertainments for the troops during the 1914–18 war. His appeal was by no means confined to Scottish audiences; almost his biggest successes were on the stages of London's famous music halls and his popularity abroad was immense, especially in the United States and the Commonwealth countries, which he toured almost every year after 1907. He wrote volumes of memoirs, the best known of which is *Roamin' in the Gloamin'* (1928).

(2) **Robert Scott** (1803–69), Scottish painter, born at Silvermills, Edinburgh, in 1829 became R.S.A. He lived in Italy and at Munich in 1833–38, then in London till 1849, when he returned to Edinburgh. Sir Walter Scott's novels provided him with subjects for his most successful paintings.

(3) **Sir Thomas Dick** (1784–1848), Scottish writer, eldest son of Sir Andrew Lauder of Fountainhall, served in the Cameron Highlanders, married in 1808 the heiress of Relugas in Morayshire, succeeded to the baronetcy in 1820, and lived at the Grange, Edinburgh, from 1832 until his death. He was secretary to the Board of Scottish Manufactures (1839–1848). Lauder wrote two romances, *Lochandhu* (1825) and *The Wolfe of Badenoch* (1827), but his best works are his *Morayshire Floods* (1830) and unfinished *Scottish Rivers*, which appeared in *Tait's Magazine*, 1847–49. His *Legendary Tales of the Highlands* (1841) may also be mentioned. He was a Liberal, and of unwearying public spirit. See Dr John Brown's preface to the reprint of *Scottish Rivers* (1874).

(4) **William** (*c.* 1680–1771), Scottish one-legged scholar, who sought in 1747–50 by impudent forgeries to prove Milton a plagiarist. He died poor in Barbados.

LAUDERDALE, John Maitland, Duke of (1616–82), Scottish statesman, was born at Lethington (now Lennoxlove) near Haddington. He displayed ardent zeal for the Covenant, and in 1643 was a Scottish commissioner at the Westminster Assembly. He succeeded his father as second Earl of Lauderdale in 1645, was taken prisoner at Worcester in 1651, and lay nine years in the Tower, at Windsor and at Portland. At the Restoration he became Scottish secretary of state, and for the first seven years he was engaged in an incessant struggle to maintain his place against rivals. His main object was to bring about the absolute power of the crown in church and state, and for this end he laboured with unceasing persistence. He formed a militia of 20,000 men, and drilled the Episcopal Church into complete subservience. A member of the privy council, he had a seat in the Cabal ministry, and was created duke in 1672. Fresh intrigues against him (1674) were foiled by his own ability and the king's regard for him. In May 1678 a vote was carried in the Commons praying for Lauderdale's removal from the royal presence for ever; but through corrupt practices, it was thrown out by a single vote. Another short struggle with Hamilton in the Convention of Estates left him again triumphant for two years more. It seems probable that many of Lauderdale's harsher measures, especially towards Scotland, were due not so much to personal ambition but to his inability to suffer gladly the follies and indiscretions of his much less astute contemporaries. His dukedom died with him in 1682, while the earldom passed to his brother. See Airy's selection (Camden Society 1884–85) from Lauderdale MSS., and Life (1923) by Mackenzie.

LAUE, Max von, *low'é* (1879–1960), German physicist, born near Koblenz, was professor at Zürich, Frankfurt and Berlin. He did good work in relativity and X-rays, and was a Nobel prizeman in physics (1914). He was later appointed director of the Kaiser Wilhelm Institute for Theoretical Physics.

LAUGHTON, *law'tên*, (1) Charles (1899–1962), English actor, born at Scarborough, became U.S. citizen in 1950. He first appeared on the stage in 1926 and his parts included Ephikhodov in *The Cherry Orchard*, Mr Crispin in *A Man with Red Hair*, Poirot in *Alibi* and William Marble in *Payment Deferred*. He appeared with the Old Vic Company, played in and produced Shaw's *Don Juan in Hell* and *Major Barbara*, and as a Shakespearean actor gave fine performances in, among others, *Macbeth*, *Measure for Measure* and *King Lear*. He began to act in films in 1932 and his great dramatic sense and technique made memorable such rôles as Henry VIII in *The Private Life of Henry VIII*, Mr Barrett in *The Barretts of Wimpole Street* and Bligh in *Mutiny on the Bounty*.

(2) **Sir John Knox** (1830–1915), English naval historian, born in Liverpool, became professor of Modern History at King's

College in 1883. His books include *Studies in Naval History* (1887), *Defeat of the Spanish Armada* (1894) and *Nelson* (1895).

LAURENCIN, Marie, *lō-rā-sī* (1885–1957), French artist, born in Paris. She exhibited in the Salon des Indépendents in 1907. Best known for her portraits of women in misty pastel colours, she also illustrated many books with water colours and lithographs.

LAURENS, *lō-rās*, (1) **Henri** (1885–1954), French painter and sculptor, born in Paris, a leading exponent of three-dimensional Cubism.

(2) **Jean Paul** (1838–1921), French historical painter, was born at Fourquevaux. A painter of scenes and subjects from church history, he was called the Benedictine.

LAURENT, Auguste (1807–53), French chemist, born at La Folie, Haute Marne, spent most of his life in poverty and died of tuberculosis. After eight years as professor in Bordeaux he went to Paris to work with Gerhardt (q.v.). Ignored by his fellow-scientists, he was forced by financial difficulties to become assayer at the Mint. He propounded the nucleus theory of organic radicals, discovered anthracine, worked on the classification of organic compounds and gave his name to ' Laurent's Acid '. His very valuable *Méthode de chimie* was published posthumously in 1854.

LAURIER, Sir Wilfrid (1841–1919), Canadian statesman, born at St Lin, Quebec, shone at the Canadian bar and in 1877 was minister of inland revenue in the Liberal ministry. In 1891 he became leader of the Liberal party and prime minister in 1896. He was the first French-Canadian and also the first Roman Catholic to be premier of Canada. In 1911 his government was defeated on the question of commercial reciprocity with the United States, but he remained Liberal leader. Though he had a strong feeling for Empire, Laurier was a firm supporter of self-government for Canada. During World War I his party was divided on the conscription question, Laurier being against conscription though entirely in agreement with Canada's entering the war. In his home policy he was an advocate of free trade, passed many reforms to benefit the working classes and helped to plan a transcontinental railway, the Grand Trunk. See O. D. Skelton, *Life and Letters of Sir Wilfrid Laurier* (2 vols. 1921).

LAURISTON, Alexandre Jacques Bernard Law, Marquis de, *lō-rees-tō* (1768–1828), French soldier, born at Pondicherry, was a grand-nephew of John Law (q.v.), the financier. He was Napoleon's comrade at the Artillery School, filled diplomatic appointments at Copenhagen and London, held high commands at Wagram (1809) and in the retreat from Moscow (1812), fought at Bautzen (1813) and Katzbach, and was taken prisoner at Leipzig. Already ennobled, he was made a peer by Louis XVIII, became marquis in 1817 and marshal in 1821.

LAUZUN, Antonin Nompar de Caumont, Duc de, *lō-zæ* (1633–1723), Gascon soldier, who in 1688 conducted Mary of Modena on her flight from London to Paris. He was imprisoned by Louis XIV for his affair with Mme de Montpensier, whom he may have wed secretly. See Lives by Duc de la Force (1913) and M. F. Sandars (1908), and V. Sackville-West, *Daughter of France* (1959). Armand Louis de Gontaut, Duc de Biron (q.v.), also bore the title of Duc de Lauzun.

LAVAL, (1) **Carl Gustaf Patrik de** (1845–1913), Swedish engineer, born at Orsa, invented a steam turbine and a centrifugal cream separator. He died at Stockholm.

(2) **Pierre** (1883–1945), French politician, born at Châteldon (Puy-de-Dôme), became an advocate, deputy (1914), senator (1926), premier (1931–32, 1935–36). From Socialism he moved to the Right, and in the Vichy government was Pétain's deputy (1940), rival and prime minister (1942–44), when he openly collaborated with the Germans. Fleeing after the liberation, from France to Germany and Spain, he was brought back, condemned to death as a collaborationist and executed in 1945. See study by Thomson (1951).

LAVALETTE, Antoine Marie Chamans, Comte de (1769–1830), French politician and Napoleonic general, who served in the Alps, was aide-de-camp to Napoleon and, after the war, French minister to Saxony, postmaster general and a councillor of state. After the second Bourbon restoration (1815) he was condemned to death, but escaped by changing clothes with his wife, a niece of the Empress Josephine.

LA VALLIÈRE, Louise Françoise de Labaume Leblanc, Duchesse de, *la val-yayr* (1644–1710), born at Tours, was brought to court by her mother, became Louis XIV's mistress in 1661 and bore him four children. When Madame de Montespan superseded her she retired to a Carmelite nunnery in Paris (1674). *Réflexions sur la miséricorde de Dieu par une dame pénitente* (1680) is attributed to her. See her Letters; Lives by Lair (trans. 1908), Trouncer (1936), and J. Sanders, *The Devoted Mistress* (1959).

LAVAL-MONTMORENCY, François Xavier, *-mō-mō-rā-see* (1622–1708), French missionary, was sent as Vicar Apostolic to Quebec in 1659. Laval University was named after him.

LAVATER, Johann Kaspar (1741–1801), Swiss physiognomist, theologian and poet, born at Zürich, in 1769 received Protestant orders. He made himself known by a volume of poems, *Schweizerlieder* (1767). His *Aussichten in die Ewigkeit* (1768–78) is characterized by religious enthusiasm and mysticism. He attempted to elevate physiognomy into a science in his *Physiognomische Fragmente* (1775–78; trans. by Holcroft 1793). Whilst tending the wounded at the capture of Zürich by Masséna (September 1799) he received a wound, of which he later died.

LAVELEYE, Émile Louis Victor de, *lav-lay* (1822–92), Belgian economist, born at Bruges, in 1864 became professor of Political Economy at Liège. His works include *De la propriété* (1874; trans. 1878); *Le Socialisme contemporain* (1881; trans. 1885); *Éléments d'économie politique* (1882); &c. He was made a baron just before his death. See Life by Count Goblet d'Alviella (1894).

LAVER, James (1899–   ), English writer and art critic, born in Liverpool, in 1921 was awarded the Newdigate prize for verse at Oxford, and later books of verse include *His Last Sebastian* (1922) and *Ladies' Mistakes* (1933). In 1922 he was appointed an assistant keeper at the Victoria and Albert Museum and in 1927 a keeper, retiring in 1959. He has written several books of art criticism, e.g., *French Painting and the 19th century* (1937) and *Fragonard* (1956), and has made a substantial contribution to the history of English costume with such books as *Taste and Fashion* (1937), *Fashions and Fashion Plates* (1943), *Children's Costume in the 19th Century* (1951), &c.

LAVERAN, Charles Louis Alphonse, *lav-rã* (1845–1922), French physician and parasitologist, born and educated at Paris, became professor of Military Medicine and Epidemic Diseases at the military college of Val de Grâce (1874–78) and again (1884–94). He studied malaria in Algeria (1878–83), discovering in 1880 the blood parasite which caused the disease. He also did important work on other diseases including sleeping-sickness and kala-azar. From 1896 until his death he was at the Pasteur Institute at Paris. In 1907 he was awarded the Nobel prize for physiology and medicine.

LAVERY, Sir John (1856–1941), Irish painter, born at Belfast, studied in Glasgow, London and Paris. He was a portrait painter of the Glasgow school and his work enjoyed great popularity, especially his paintings of women. Elected R.S.A. in 1896, R.A. in 1921, he was knighted in 1918. He wrote a lively auto-biography, *The Life of a Painter* (1940). See W. Shaw-Sparrow, *John Lavery and his Work* (1912).

LAVIGERIE, Charles Martial Allemand, Cardinal, *la-veezh-ree* (1825–92), born at Bayonne, in 1863 was made Bishop of Nancy, in 1867 Archbishop of Algiers. He became well-known for his missionary work in Africa and he founded the order of the White Fathers. See Clarke's *Cardinal Lavigerie and the African Slave-trade* (1890), and French Lives by Préville (1894) and Lavigerie (1896).

LAVISSE, Ernest, *la-vees* (1842–1922), French historian, born at Nouvion-en-Thiérache, Aisne. He taught history to the son of Napoleon III and was professor of History at the Sorbonne, where he completely changed the teaching methods. In 1892 he was elected to the Academy, edited the *Revue de Paris* (1894) and became director of the École normale supérieure (1902–20). He wrote works on Prussian history after visiting Germany, but is perhaps best known for the immense history which he published in collaboration with Rambaud, *Histoire générale du IVe siècle à nos jours* (1893–1900). Then came *Histoire de France depuis les origines jusqu'à la Revolution* (9 vols. 1903–11) and *Histoire contemporaine* (10 vols. completed 1922).

LAVOISIER, Antoine Laurent, *la-vwaz-yay* (1743–94), French chemist, born at Paris. To obtain means for his investigations, he accepted in 1768 the office of farmer general of taxes and in that year was also made an Academician. As director of the government

powder mills, he (1775) greatly improved gunpowder, its supply and manufacture, and successfully applied chemistry to agriculture. Regarded as the founder of modern chemistry, he discovered oxygen, by rightly interpreting Priestley's facts, its importance in respiration, combustion and as a compound with metals. His *Traité elémentaire de chimie* (1789) was a master-piece. Politically Liberal, he saw the great necessity for reform in France but was against revolutionary methods. But despite a lifetime of work for the state, inquiring into the problems of taxation, which he helped to reform, hospitals and prisons, he was guillotined as a farmer of taxes. See Lives by Grimaux (1888), Berthelot (1890), Cochrane (1931) and McKie (1952).

LA VOISIN, *vwa-zĩ* (?–1680), French poisoner, whose real name was **Catherine Monvoison**. She amassed riches by con-cocting potions and selling them to the ladies at the court of Louis XIV. When the poison plots were discovered in 1679 involving such well-known figures as the Duchess Mancini and Mme de Montespan, La Voisin was found to be responsible after an examination by a secret tribunal. She was burned in 1680.

LAW, (1) Andrew Bonar (1858–1923), British statesman, born in New Brunswick, was an iron merchant in Glasgow. Unionist M.P. from 1900, in 1911 he succeeded Balfour as Unionist leader in the House of Commons, was colonial secretary in 1915–16, then a member of the War Cabinet, chancellor of the exchequer (1916–18), lord privy seal (1919), and from 1916 leader of the House of Commons. He retired in March 1921, but despite ill-health was premier October 1922 to May 1923.

(2) **Edward.** See ELLENBOROUGH.

(3) **John** (1671–1729), Scottish financier, born at Edinburgh, son of a goldsmith and banker, who was proprietor of the estate of Lauriston. In 1694 he had to flee from London for having killed ' Beau ' Wilson in a duel. At Amsterdam he made a study of the credit operations of the bank. In 1700 he returned to Edinburgh, a zealous advocate of a paper currency; but his proposals to the Scottish parliament on this subject were unfavourably received. Back on the Con-tinent, he won and lost vast sums in gambling and speculation, but at last settling in Paris, he and his brother William (1675–1752) set up in 1716 a private bank. This prospered so that the Regent Orleans adopted in 1718 Law's plan of a national bank. In 1719 Law originated a joint-stock company for reclaim-ing and settling lands in the Mississippi valley, called the *Mississippi scheme*, and next year he was made comptroller-general of finances. When the bubble burst he became an object of popular hatred, quitted France, and spent four years in England. He finally settled in Venice, where he died poor and forgotten. See Lives by Levasseur (1854), Alexi (Berlin 1885), Wiston-Glynn (1908), Oudard (1927), H. M. Hyde (1948).

(4) **William** (1686–1761), English divine, born at Kingscliffe, Northamptonshire, son of a grocer, entered Emmanuel College,

Cambridge, in 1705, becoming a fellow in 1711. He was unable to subscribe the oath of allegiance to George I, and forfeited his fellowship. About 1727 he became tutor to the father of Edward Gibbon, and for ten years was 'the much-honoured friend and spiritual director of the whole family'. The elder Gibbon died in 1737, and three years later Law retired to Kingscliffe, and was joined by his disciples, Miss Hester Gibbon, sister of his pupil, and Mrs Hutcheson. The two ladies had a united income of about £3000 a year, and most of this they spent in works of charity. About 1733 Law had begun to study Jacob Boehme, and most of his later books are expositions of his mysticism. Law won his first triumphs against Bishop Hoadly in the famous Bangorian controversy with his *Three Letters* (1717). His *Remarks on Mandeville's Fable of the Bees* (1723) is a masterpiece of caustic wit and vigorous English. Only less admirable is the *Case of Reason* (1732), in answer to Tindal the Deist. But his most famous work remains the *Serious Call to a Devout and Holy Life* (1729), which profoundly influenced Dr Johnson and the Wesleys. See Walton's *Notes and Materials for a Complete Biography* (1854), Overton's *William Law, Nonjuror and Mystic* (1881), and books by A. Whyte (1892), S. Hobhouse (1927) and Talon (1948).

LAWES, (1) Henry (1596–1662), English composer, born at Dinton, Wiltshire, set Milton's *Comus* to music and also the verses of Herrick. Highly regarded by Milton, who sang his praises in a sonnet, his adaptation of music to verse and rhythm was masterly. His half-brother, **William** (d. 1645), was also a composer, one of Charles I's court musicians; he was killed at Chester during the Civil War. See Life by Lefkowitz (1960).

(2) Sir John Bennet (1814–1900), English agriculturist, born at Rothamsted, St Albans, carried out a long series of experiments with plants and then with crops on his estate there and from these grew the artificial fertilizer industry. For the manufacture of his superphosphates he set up a factory at Deptford Creek in 1842. Even more important than this commercial enterprise were his purely scientific researches into agriculture. With him, aided by his partner J. H. Gilbert (q.v.), agriculture became a science and the Rothamsted Experimental Station which he founded in 1843, now controlled largely by the government, has become famous throughout the world. Elected F.R.S. in 1854 he received with Gilbert the gold medal of the Society in 1867.

LAWLER, Ray (1911–), Australian playwright, born in Melbourne, was a factory-hand at the age of thirteen but soon gravitated to the stage. His *Summer of the Seventeenth Doll*, a play of the 'outback', with its down-to-earth realism and with Lawler himself in a leading rôle, brought him fame outside Australia.

LAWRENCE, St (martyred 258), said to have been born at Huesca in Spain, became a deacon at Rome. In the persecution of Valerian he was condemned to be broiled.

LAWRENCE, (1) David Herbert (1885–1930), English poet and novelist, born in Eastwood,

Notts, the son of a miner. With tuberculous tendencies, of which he eventually died, he became, through his mother's devotion, a schoolmaster and began to write, encouraged by the notice taken of his work by Ford Madox Hueffer and Edward Garnett. In 1911, after the success of his first novel, *The White Peacock*, he decided to live by writing. He travelled in Germany, Austria and Italy during 1912 and 1913, and in 1914, after her divorce from Professor Ernest Weekley, married Frieda von Richthofen, a cousin of the German air ace, Baron von Richthofen (q.v.). They returned to England at the outbreak of war and lived in an atmosphere of suspicion and persecution in a cottage in Cornwall. In 1915 he published *The Rainbow* and was horrified to find himself prosecuted for obscenity. He left England in 1919, and after three years' residence in Italy, left for America, settling in Mexico until the progress of his disease drove him in 1921 back to Italy where his last years were spent. His sensitive spirit was again shocked by his further prosecutions for obscenity over the publication in Florence of *Lady Chatterley's Lover* in 1928 and over an exhibition of his paintings in London the same year. Opinion is still divided over Lawrence's worth as a writer; but there can be no doubt about his effect on the younger intellectuals of his period. He challenged them by his attempt to interpret human emotion on a deeper level of consciousness than that handled by his contemporaries. This provoked either sharp criticism or an almost idolatrous respect. Now that his strong but ambiguous personality is removed, it is possible to agree with T. S. Eliot, who said that he was 'a writer who had to write often badly in order to write sometimes well'. His descriptive passages are sometimes superb, but he had little humour, and this occasionally produced unintentionally comic effects. His burning idealism—and it is entirely wrong to imagine that Lawrence was ever deliberately erotic—glows through all his work. His finest writing occurs in his poems, where all but essentials have been pared away; but the larger proportion of his novels have an enduring strength. These include *Sons and Lovers* (1913), *Women in Love* (1921), *Aaron's Rod* (1922), *Kangaroo* (1923) and *The Plumed Serpent* (1926). His collected poems were published in 1928. See J. Middleton Murry, *Son of Woman* (1931), R. Aldington, *Portrait of a Genius, But . . .* (1950), a composite biography (ed. by Nehls in 3 vols., 1957–59), his *Collected Letters* (ed. by Moore in 2 vols., 1962), and studies by Leavis (1955), Rees (1958), and Moore and Roberts (1966).

(2) Ernest Orlando (1901–58), American physicist, born at Canton, South Dakota, studied there, at Minnesota and at Yale, became assistant professor at Berkeley, California, in 1927, where in 1936 he was appointed director of the radiation laboratory, having constructed the first cyclotron for the production of artificial radioactivity, fundamental to the development of the atomic bomb. He was awarded the Hughes Medal of the Royal Society (1937), the Comstock Prize (1937), and the Nobel prize (1939), becoming an officer of the Légion d'Honneur in 1948.

(3) **Geoffrey, 3rd Baron Trevithin and 1st Baron Oaksey** (1880–   ), English lawyer, a son of Lord Trevithin (succeeding his brother to the title in 1959), lord chief justice of England, graduated at Oxford and was called to the bar in 1906. He became a judge of the high court of justice (King's Bench Division) in 1932, a lord justice of appeal in 1944 and was a lord of appeal in ordinary between 1947 and 1957. He was president of the International Tribunal for the trial of war criminals at Nuremberg in 1945 and was distinguished for his fair and impartial conduct of the proceedings. He was knighted in 1932, created baron in 1947.

(4) **Sir Henry Montgomery** (1806–57), British soldier and administrator, born at Matara, Ceylon, was educated at Derry, Bristol and Addiscombe, and in 1823 joined the Bengal Artillery. He took part in the first Burmese war (1828), in the first Afghan war (1838), and in the Sikh wars (1845 and 1848). In 1856 he pointed out the danger of reducing the British army, and the latent germs of rebellion. In 1857 he was appointed to Lucknow, and did all he could to restore contentment there, but the mutiny broke out in May. It was owing to his foresight that it was made possible for a thousand Europeans and eight hundred Indians to defend the Residency for nearly four months against 7000 rebels. He was mortally injured by a shell. 'Here lies Henry Lawrence, who tried to do his duty', is his self-chosen epitaph. See Lives by Edwardes and Merivale (1872–1873), Innes (1898), Morison (1934).

(5) **John Laird Mair, 1st Baron** (1811–79), British administrator, brother of (4), was born at Richmond, Yorkshire. In 1827 he obtained a presentation to Haileybury College. His first years in the Indian civil service were spent at Delhi. Successively commissioner and lieutenant-governor of the Punjab, he used every effort to curb the oppression of the people by their chiefs, devised a system of land tenure, and devoted his whole energy to restoring peace and prosperity. The once restless Sikhs had become so attached to his rule that Lawrence was enabled to disarm the mutineers in the Punjab, to raise an army of 59,000 men, and to capture Delhi from the rebels after a siege of over three months. In 1863 he succeeded Lord Elgin as governor-general of India. He did not believe in British interference in Asia beyond the frontier of India, and was especially opposed to intriguing in Afghanistan. Created Baron Lawrence on his return home in 1869, he was chairman of the London School-board 1870–73. He devoted the last days of his life in parliament (1878) to an exposure of the policy which led up to the disastrous Afghan war. See Lives by Bosworth Smith (1883), Temple (1889) and Aitchison (1892) and study by Pal (1952).

(6) **Sir Thomas** (1769–1830), English painter, son of a Bristol innkeeper, was famed as a child for his portraits. At twelve he had his studio at Bath, at eighteen he entered as a student of the Royal Academy, having a year before given up crayons for oils. His full-length portrait of Queen Charlotte, now in the National Gallery, which he painted at the age of twenty, was remarkable for its maturity and is one of his best works. In 1791 he was elected A.R.A., and in 1794 R.A., in 1792 was appointed limner to the king, in 1815 was knighted by the Prince Regent, and in 1820 succeeded West as P.R.A. He died in London, and was buried in St Paul's. Lawrence was the favourite portrait painter of his time, and had an immense practice, but many of his paintings are now deemed over-facile, lacking in dignity, and his colouring blatant. He was perhaps most sincere in his fine portraits of Frederick William III of Prussia and Archduke Charles of Austria. See Life by Goldring (1951).

(7) **Thomas Edward** (1888–1935), British soldier, was a junior member of the British Museum archaeological team at Carchemish, on the Euphrates, and thus made his first intimate acquaintance with the desert dwellers. With the war of 1914–18 his ability to penetrate the 'closed shop' of nomadic tribal life enabled him to reanimate the wilting Arab revolt against the Turk. Operating in command of the Emir Feisal's levies, his co-operation with General Allenby's triumphal advance demonstrated his outstanding abilities as a partisan leader. As a delegate to the Peace Conference and, later, as adviser on Arab affairs to the Colonial Office, his inability to secure all he had set out to achieve for the Arab cause he had espoused led to his withdrawal from what he termed 'the shallow grave of public duty', and to his obscure but valuable service, under the name of Aircraftsman Shaw, in the R.A.F. He was killed in a motor-cycling accident in May 1935. Publications: *The Seven Pillars of Wisdom* (for private circulation, 1926), *Revolt in the Desert* (1927), *Crusader Castles* (1936), *Oriental Assembly* (ed. A. W. Lawrence, 1929) and *The Mint* (1955). See Lives by R. Graves (1927), Lowell Thomas (1958), Aldington (1955) and Villars (1958), his *Letters* (ed. by Garnett, 1964), and Rattigan's play *Ross* (1960).

LAWSON, (1) **Cecil Gordon** (1851–82), English landscape painter, was born at Wellington, Shropshire, but brought up in London. He exhibited at the Academy in 1870, but remained obscure, many of his pictures being rejected, till 1878, when his *Minister's Garden* at the Grosvenor made him famous. The short remainder of his life was a brilliant success. See Memoir by Gosse (1883).

(2) **Henry Hertzberg** (1867–1922), Australian writer, born in New South Wales of Scandinavian ancestry, published short stories and narrative verse of the Australian scene, collected in *Short Stories in Prose and Verse* (1894), *While the Billy Boils* (1896), &c.

LAXNESS, Haldór Kiljan, *lahks'-* (1902–   ), Icelandic writer, born in Reykjavik, travelled in Europe and America after the first World War and became a Catholic. A Christian communism is a favourite theme in his works, which include *Salka Valka* (1934), a story of Icelandic fishing folk, the epic *Sjalfstaet folk* (1934–35), *Islands Klukkan* (1943), which describes 18th-century Iceland under Danish rule, *Gerpla* (1952), &c. A master of the narrative, he rejuvenated his native tongue and was awarded the Nobel prize in 1955.

LAYAMON (fl. early 13th cent.), English priest at Ernley (now Areley), on the Severn near Bewdley. He produced an amplified imitation of Wace's *Brut d'Angleterre*, important in the history of English versification as the first poem written in Middle English. See Madden's edition (1847); *Layamon's Brut Selections*, ed. Hall (1924); E. K. Chambers's *Arthur of Britain* (1927).

LAYARD, Sir Austin Henry (1817–94), English archaeologist and politician, was born in Paris, a son of a Dean of Bristol, and passed his boyhood in Italy. In 1845–47 he carried on excavations at the ruins of Nimrud, the supposed site of Nineveh, finding the remains of four palaces. He published *Nineveh and its Remains* (1848), *Monuments of Nineveh* (1850), &c. He was appointed M.P. for Aylesbury 1852–57, for Southwark 1860–69, foreign under-secretary 1861–66, chief commissioner of Works 1868–69. In 1869 he went as British ambassador to Spain, in 1877 to Constantinople (where he showed strong philo-Turkish sympathies). See his *Early Adventures* (1878) and his *Autobiography and Letters* (ed. Bruce, 1903).

LAZARUS, Emma (1849–87), a New York Jewess who from 1866 published five striking volumes of poems and translations. See her *Poems* (2 vols. 1888).

LEACOCK, Stephen Butler (1869–1944), Canadian economist and humorist, educated at the University of Toronto, became first a teacher, later a lecturer at McGill University, and in 1908 head of the Economics department there. He wrote several books on his subject, including *Elements of Political Science* (1906), *Practical Political Economy* (1910) and *The Economic Prosperity of the British Empire* (1931). It is, however, as a humorist that he became widely known. Among his popular short stories, essays and parodies are *Literary Lapses* (1910), *Nonsense Novels* (1911), *Behind the Beyond* (1913), *Winsome Winnie* (1920) and *The Garden of Folly* (1924). He wrote also biographies of Twain (1932) and Dickens (1933). *The Boy I Left Behind Me*, an autobiography, appeared in 1946. See P. McArthur, *Stephen Leacock* (1923).

LEADE, Jane, *née* Ward. See BOEHME.

LEAKE, William Martin (1777–1860), English topographer of Greece and antiquarian, born in London. In the army from 1794, he served in Turkey and other parts of the Levant. He helped in the survey of the valley of the Nile and retired from the army with the rank of lieutenant-colonel in 1823. He wrote learned works on Greece and Greek antiquities, including *Topography of Athens* (1821) and *Numismata Hellenica* (1854). See *Memoir* by Marsden (1864).

LEAKEY, Louis Seymour Bazett (1903–72). British anthropologist, born at Kabete, Kenya, educated at Weymouth College and St. John's College, Cambridge, took part in several archaeological expeditions in East Africa, made a study of the Kikuyu and wrote much on African anthropology. He was curator of the Coryndon Memorial Museum at Nairobi (1945–61). His great discoveries took place in East Africa, where in 1959 he unearthed the skull of *Zinjanthropus*, nicknamed ' nutcracker man ', a primitive species 1¾ million years old; in 1964 remains of *Homo habilis*, a smaller species some 2 million years old (postulating the simultaneous evolution of two different species, of which *Homo habilis* was the true ancestor of man, while *Zinjanthropus* became extinct); and in 1967 *Kenyapithecus Africanus*, fossilized remains of ' pre-man ', *c.* 14 million years old.

LEAR, Edward (1812–88), English artist and author, born in London, had a passion for painting, and was sent by the Earl of Derby to Italy and Greece, where he painted many landscapes. He exhibited at the Royal Academy from 1850 to 1873. His later years were spent in Italy, and he died at San Remo. Lear is less known by his paintings than by his illustrated books of travels—*Sketches of Rome* (1842) *Illustrated Excursions in Italy* (1846), &c. But it is by his *Book of Nonsense* (1846), written for the Earl of Derby's grandchildren, that he is now remembered. *Nonsense Songs, Stories and Botany* followed in 1870, *More Nonsense Rhymes* in 1871, *Laughable Lyrics* in 1876. See Life by A. Davidson (1938).

LEARMONT. See THOMAS THE RHYMER.

LEAVIS, Frank Raymond (1895–), English critic, from 1936 to 1962 fellow of Downing College, Cambridge, fought against mere literary dilettantism in the quarterly, *Scrutiny* (1932–53), which he edited, as well as in *New Bearings in English Poetry* (1932). His sociological study, *Culture and Environment* (1933; with D. Thomson), deploring their separation in modern times and stressing the importance of inculcating critical standards in the young, has become a classic. Other works include *Revaluation* (1936), *The Great Tradition* (1948), *The Common Pursuit* (1952), *D. H. Lawrence* (1955), *Two Cultures?* (1962), in which he challenged the theories of C. P. Snow (q.v.) on literature and science, and *Anna Karenina and Other Essays* (1967).

LEBEDEV, Pëtr Nikolajevich (1866–1912), Russian physicist, born in Moscow, studied at Strasbourg under' Kundt and became professor of Physics at Moscow (1912). He proved that light exerts a pressure on bodies, and investigated the earth's magnetism.

LEBRUN, Albert, *lĕ-brœ̈* (1871–1950), French statesman, was born at Mercy-le-Haut (Meurthe-et-Moselle), studied mining engineering, became a deputy (Left Republican) in 1900, was minister for the colonies 1911–14, for blockade and liberated regions 1917–19, senator 1920, and president of the Senate 1931. The last president of the Third Republic, he surrendered his powers to Pétain in 1940, and went into retirement from which he did not re-emerge, although consulted by General de Gaulle in 1944. His health was affected by a period of internment after arrest by the Gestapo in 1943.

LE BRUN, (1) Charles (1619–90), French historical painter, born in Paris, studied four years in Rome, and for nearly forty years (1647–83) exercised a despotic influence over French art and artists, being usually considered the founder of the French school of painting. He helped to found the Academy of Painting and Sculpture in 1648 and was the first director of the Gobelins tapestry works (1662). From 1668 to 1683 he was employed by Louis XIV in the decoration of Versailles. See works by Genevay (1885), Jouin (1889) and Marcel (1909).

(2) **Marie Élisabeth Louise** (1755–1842), French painter, born in Paris, a daughter of one Vigée, a painter, in 1776 married J. B. P. Le Brun, picture dealer and grand-nephew of Charles Le Brun. Her great beauty and the charm of her painting speedily made her work fashionable. Her portrait of Marie Antoinette (1779) led to a lasting friendship with the queen and she painted numerous portraits of the royal family. She left Paris for Italy at the outbreak of the Revolution, and after a kind of triumphal progress through Europe, arrived in London in 1802. There she painted portraits of the Prince of Wales, Lord Byron, &c. In 1805 she returned to Paris. See her *Souvenirs* (1837; trans. 1904), *Memoirs* (1926) and a study by Helm (1915).

LE CARON, Major Henri, *ka-rõ* (1840–94), assumed name of **Thomas Beach,** of Colchester, whose spying on Irish-American Fenians is described in his *Twenty-five Years in the Secret Service* (1892).

LE CHATELIER. See CHATELIER.

LECKY, William Edward Hartpole (1838–1903), Irish historian and philosopher, born near Dublin, graduated B.A. in 1859 at Trinity College. In 1861 he published anonymously *The Leaders of Public Opinion in Ireland*, four brilliant essays on Swift, Flood, Grattan and O'Connell. One of the greatest and most unbiased historians, his works include *History of England in the 18th Century* (1878–90). A decided Unionist but having a real sympathy with Irish problems, he became M.P. for Dublin University in 1895, a privy councillor in 1897 and O.M. (1902). See Life by his wife (1909), and *A Victorian Historian* (Private Letters 1859–78), ed. Hyde (1947).

LECLAIR, Jean Marie (1697–1764), French composer and violinist, wrote many fine sonatas for the instrument, also the opera *Scylla et Glaucis* (1746).

LECLANCHÉ, Georges, *le-klã-shay* (1839–82), French chemist, born in Paris, remembered for the galvanic cell invented by him and given his name.

LE CLERC, Jean, *lè-kler,* or **Johannes Clericus** (1657–1736), Arminian theologian and Biblical scholar, born at Geneva, became in 1684 professor of Philosophy in the Remonstrant seminary at Amsterdam. His works number over seventy, and revealed what were then startling opinions on the authorship of the Pentateuch and on inspiration generally. His Bible commentaries were completed in 1731. Serial publications were *Bibliothèque universelle et historique* (25 vols. 1686–93), *Bibliothèque choisie* (28 vols. 1703–13), and *Bibliothèque ancienne et moderne* (29 vols. 1714–26).

LÉCLUSE, Charles de, *lay-klüz* (1525–1609), the botanist 'Clusius', was born at Arras, travelled in Spain, England, Hungary, &c., and from 1593 was a professor at Leyden.

LECOCQ, Alexandre Charles (1832–1918), French composer of comic operas, was born at Paris. His many Offenbachian operettas include *Le Docteur Miracle* (1857), *Giroflé-Girofla* (1874) and *L'Égyptienne* (1890).

LECONTE DE LISLE, Charles Marie, *lè-kõt dè leel* (1818–94), French poet, was born in Réunion, and after some years of travel settled to a literary life in Paris. He exercised a profound influence on all the younger poets, headed the school called *Parnassiens*, and succeeded to Victor Hugo's chair at the Academy in 1886. His early poems appeared as *Poésies complètes* (1858). Other volumes are *Poèmes barbares* (1862) and *Poèmes tragiques* (1884); and he translated many classics. His verse is marked by regularity and faultlessness of form. See monographs, Dornis (1895), Leblond (1906), Flottes (1939) and A. Fairlie, *Leconte de Lisle's Poems on the Barbarian Races* (1947).

LE CORBUSIER. See CORBUSIER.

LECOUVREUR, Adrienne, *le-koov-rœr* (1692–1730), French actress, born near Chalons, made her début at the Comédie Française in 1717, and soon became famous for her acting, her fascinations, and her admirers, amongst whom were Marshal Saxe, Voltaire and Lord Peterborough. Her death was by some ascribed to poisoning by a rival, the Duchesse de Bouillon. This is the plot of the play by Scribe and Legouvé. See Monval's *Lettres d'Adrienne Lecouvreur* (1892), and study by Rivollet (1925).

LEDRU-ROLLIN, Alexandre Auguste, *-lï* (1807–74), French politician, was born at Fontenay. Admitted to the bar in 1830, he made a name as defender of Republicans and as a democratic agitator. In 1841 he was elected deputy for Le Mans, and visited Ireland during O'Connell's agitation. His *Appel aux travailleurs* (1846) declared universal suffrage the panacea for the miseries of the working classes. At the Revolution of 1848 he became minister of the interior in the Provisional Government, and in May was elected one of the interim government. But he gave offence by his arbitrary conduct, and resigned June 28. As candidate for the presidency against Louis Napoleon he was beaten and an unsuccessful attempt to provoke an insurrection in June 1849 drove him to England. He was amnestied in 1870, and after his return was elected to the Assembly. See his *Discours politiques et écrits divers* (1879), and Calman's *Ledru-Rollin and the Second French Republic* (1922).

LEE, (1) Ann (1736–84), English mystic, the illiterate daughter of a Manchester blacksmith, married in 1762 Abraham Stanley, also a blacksmith. Imprisoned in 1770 for street-preaching, she emigrated to America in 1774, and in 1776 founded at Niskayuna, 7 miles northwest of Albany, N.Y., the parent Shaker settlement. See *The Shakers*, by F. W. Evans (N.Y. 1859), and short Life by Axon (1876).

(2) **Charles** (1731–82), a cantankerous American general in the War of Independence, was born in Cheshire, and had served several years as a British officer in America. *Junius's Letters* have been ascribed to him.

(3) **Harriet** (1757–1851), English novelist, born in London, wrote with her sister *The Canterbury Tales*, one of which was dramatized by Byron and called *Werner, or, The Inheritance.*

(4) **James Paris** (1831–1904), American inventor, born at Hawick, Scotland. He emigrated with his parents to Canada, later going from Ontario to Hartford, Connecticut. The Lee-Enfield and Lee-Metford rifles are based in part on his designs. See METFORD, W. E.

(5) **Nathaniel** (1649–92), English dramatist, from Westminster passed to Trinity College, Cambridge, failed as an actor through nervousness (1672), produced nine or ten tragedies between 1675 and 1682, spent five years in Bedlam (1684–89). His best play is *The Rival Queens* (1677). He wrote with Dryden two plays, *Oedipus* and *The Duke of Guise.* See Hann, *Otway and Lee* (1931).

(6) **Richard Henry.** See LEE, ROBERT EDWARD.

(7) **Robert, D.D.** (1804–68), Scots divine, was born at Tweedmouth, and educated at Berwick (where he was also for a time a boat-builder) and St Andrews. In 1843 he became minister at Old Greyfriars, Edinburgh, and in 1846 he was appointed professor of Biblical Criticism in Edinburgh University and a Queen's chaplain. In 1857 he began his reform of the Presbyterian church-service. He restored the reading of prayers, kneeling at prayer and standing during the singing and in 1863 he introduced a harmonium, in 1865 an organ, into his church. These ' innovations ' brought down upon him bitter attacks. His works include a *Handbook of Devotion* (1845), *Prayers for Public Worship* (1857), &c. See Life by R. H. Story (1870).

(8) **Robert Edward** (1807–70), American soldier, was fifth in descent from Richard Lee of Shropshire, who emigrated to Virginia in the reign of Charles I, received large grants of land between the Potomac and Rappahannock rivers, and built the original Stratford House. In a later house, erected by his grandson, Thomas Lee, were born the distinguished brothers, **Richard Henry** (1732–1794), mover of the resolution in favour of American Independence and a signer of the Declaration; **Francis Lightfoot** (1734–1797), a signer of the Declaration; and **William** (1737–95) and **Arthur** (1740–92), diplomatists. There also was born Robert Edward, the son of General Henry Lee. At eighteen he entered West Point, graduated second in his class in 1829, and received a commission in the engineers. In the Mexican war (1846) he was chief engineer of the central army in Mexico, and at the storming of Chapultepec was severely wounded. In 1852–55 he commanded the U.S. Military Academy, and greatly improved its efficiency. His next service was as a cavalry officer on the Texan border 1855–59. At the John Brown raid he was ordered to Harper's Ferry to capture the insurgents. He was in command in Texas in 1860, but was recalled to Washington in March 1861 when seven states had formed the Southern Confederacy. Virginia seceded on April 17, and Colonel Lee, believing that his allegiance was due to

his state, sent in his resignation. Within two days he was made commander-in-chief of the forces of Virginia. At Richmond he super-intended the defences of the city till the autumn, when he was sent to oppose General Rosecrans in West Virginia. In the spring of 1862 he was working at the coast defences of Georgia and South Carolina, but on McClellan's advance was summoned to the capital. General J. E. Johnston, chief in command, was wounded at Seven Pines in May, and Lee was put in command of the army around Richmond. His masterly strategy in the seven days' battles around Richmond defeated McClellan's purpose; his battles and strategy in opposing General Pope, his invasion of Maryland and Pennsylvania, and other achievements are cardinal to the history of the war. The increasing resources of the North and the decreasing resources of the South could only result in the final success of the former. On April 9, 1865, Lee surrendered his army of 28,231 men to General Grant at Appomattox Courthouse, Virginia, and the war was practically ended. After the close of the war he frankly accepted the result, and although deprived of his former property at Arlington on the Potomac, and the White House on the Pamunky, he declined offers of pecuniary aid, and accepted the presidency of what came to be called the Washington and Lee University at Lexington, Virginia. He married in 1832 Mary Randolph Custis (1806–73). Their eldest son, George Washington Custis Lee, resigned as first-lieutenant in the U.S. army in 1861, was aide-de-camp to Jefferson Davis 1861–63, major-general of a division in 1864, and successor of his father as president of the Washington and Lee University.. William Henry Fitzhugh Lee, second son, was major-general of Confederate cavalry, and was elected to congress. Captain Robert E. Lee of the Confederate cavalry was the third son. See *Lee's Dispatches* (1915); studies by Long (1886), F. Lee (1894), White (1897), Trent (1899), R. E. Lee (1904), Bradford (1912), Freeman (1934), Burne (1939).

(9) **Samuel** (1783–1852), English orientalist, born at Longnor, Shropshire, was the author of *Hebrew, Chaldaic and English Lexicon* (1840).

(10) **Sir Sidney** (1859–1926), English critic, born in London, became assistant editor of the *Dictionary of National Biography* in 1883, editor in 1891, and professor of English, East London College, 1913. He wrote a standard *Life of Shakespeare* (1898; new ed. 1915); *Lives of Queen Victoria* (1902), *Edward VII* (1925–27), &c. He was knighted in 1911. See Life by C. H. Firth (1931).

(11) **Sophia** (1750–1824), English writer, sister of (3), wrote plays and novels, including *The Chapter of Accidents* (1780), the success of which enabled her to open a girls' school at Bath.

(12) **Tsung-Dao** (1926–   ), Chinese physicist, born in Shanghai, educated at Kiangsi and at Chekiang University, won a scholarship to Chicago in 1946, became a lecturer at the University of California, and from 1956 was professor at Columbia University, as well as a member of the Institute for Advanced Study (1960–63). With Yang

(q.v.) he disproved the parity principle, till then considered a fundamental physical law, and they were awarded the Nobel prize for 1957.

(13) **Vernon**, pen-name of **Violet Paget** (1856–1935), English aesthetic philosopher, critic and novelist, born in Boulogne of English parentage, travelled widely in her youth and settled in Florence. Her studies of Italian and Renaissance art, *Euphorion* (1884), and *Renaissance Fancies and Studies* (1895), were followed by her philosophical study, *The Beautiful* (1913), one of the best expositions of the empathy theory of art. She also wrote two novels and a dramatic trilogy *Satan the Waster* (1920) giving full rein to her pacifism. See study by P. Gunn (1964).

LEECH, John (1817–64), English artist of Irish descent, born in London, the son of a coffee-house proprietor, went to the Charter-house with Thackeray, studied medicine, but at eighteen published *Etchings and Sketchings, by A. Pen, Esq.* In 1836 he was contributing to *Bell's Life* and sent his first contribution to *Punch* in 1841. His *Punch* cartoons are full of high qualities; but even more delightful are the smaller woodcuts. In the intervals of work for *Punch* Leech contributed much to other journals and publications, including woodcuts in *Once a Week* (1859–62) and the *Illustrated London News* (1856), in *The Comic English* and *Latin Grammars* (1840), Hood's *Comic Annual* (1842), Smith's *Wassail Bowl* (1843), and *A Little Tour in Ireland* (1859); etchings in *Bentley's Miscellany*, *Jerrold's Magazine*, the Christmas books of Dickens, the *Comic History of England* (1847–48), *Comic History of Rome* (1852), and the *Handley Cross* sporting novels. He also drew several lithographed series, of which *Portraits of the Children of the Mobility* (1841) is the most important. Leech was buried close to Thackeray at Kensal Green. See Brown's *John Leech* (1882), Kitton's *Biographical Sketch* (1883) and Life by Frith (1891).

LEEDS, Thomas Osborne, Duke of (1632–1712), English statesman, better known as Earl of Danby, was the son of a Yorkshire baronet. He entered parliament for York in 1661, and in 1667 became a treasury auditor, in 1671 treasurer of the Navy, in 1673 Viscount Latimer and Baron Danby, and in 1674 lord high treasurer and Earl of Danby. He sought to enforce the laws against Roman Catholics and Dissenters, used his influence to get Princess Mary married to William of Orange in 1677, and negotiated with Louis XIV for bribes to Charles. Louis, however, intrigued for Danby's downfall, and the Commons impeached him in 1678 for treating with foreign powers, aiming at the introduction of arbitrary power and squandering public money. He was kept in the Tower until 1684, although Charles at once gave him a full pardon, as the Commons persisted in the impeachment. When James began to threaten the Established Church Danby signed the invitation to William of Orange. His reward was the marquisate of Carmarthen and the presidency of the council, and he resumed his old methods of government. He was created Duke of Leeds in 1694. In 1695, again impeached for accepting 5000 guineas from the East India Company, he staved off condemnation. But his power was gone, and in 1699 he retired, though he spoke in defence of Sacheverell in 1710. He died at Easton, Northants. See books by Courtenay (1838), A. Browning (1913, 1945, &c.).

LEESE, Sir Oliver William Hargreaves, Bart. (1894–), English general, won the D.S.O. in World War I and in 1939 became deputy chief of staff of the British Expeditionary Force in France. In 1942 he was promoted lieutenant-general and commanded an army corps from El Alamein to Sicily, where he succeeded Montgomery to the command of the Eighth Army during the Italian campaign. In November 1944 he commanded an army group in Burma. He was created K.C.B. in 1943 and was appointed lieutenant of the Tower of London in 1954.

LEEUWENHOEK, Anton van, *lay'ven-hook* (1632–1723), Dutch scientist, born at Delft, was a clerk in an Amsterdam cloth warehouse till 1654, and after that became at Delft the most famous microscopist, conducting a series of epoch-making discoveries in support of the circulation of the blood, and in connection with blood corpuscles, spermatozoa, &c. He first detected the fibres of the crystalline lens, the fibrils and striping of muscle, the structure of ivory and hair, the scales of the epidermis, and the distinctive characters of rotifers. His *Opera* appeared at Leyden in 1719–22; an English selection at London in 1798–1801. See a monograph by C. Dobell (1932).

LE FANU, Joseph Sheridan, *lef'ĕ-nyoo* (1814–1873), Irish novelist, was born and died in Dublin. He was a grand-nephew of Richard Sheridan. He began writing for the *Dublin University Magazine*, of which he was editor and later, proprietor. His novels include *The House by the Churchyard* (1863), *Uncle Silas* (1864), probably his best known, *In a Glass Darkly* (1872), and fourteen other works. A leading feature in them is their weird uncanniness. His *Poems* were edited by A. P. Graves (1896). See Memoir prefixed to his *Purcell Papers* (1880), *Seventy Years of Irish Life*, by his brother, W. R. Le Fanu (1893), S. M. Ellis, *Wilkie Collins, Le Fanu and others* (1931), and N. Browne, *Le Fanu* (1951).

LEFEBVRE, François Joseph, Duke of Danzig, *lĕ-fay'vr'* (1755–1820), marshal of France, was born at Ruffach in Alsace, and was a sergeant in the Guards at the Revolution. He fought at Fleurus, Altenkirchen and Stockach, in 1799 took part with Bonaparte in the overthrow of the Directory, and in 1804 was made a marshal. He took Danzig, and was created Duke of Danzig (1807), distinguished himself in the early part of the Peninsular war, and suppressed the insurrection in the Tyrol. During the Russian campaign he had the command of the Imperial Guard, and in 1814 of the left wing of the French army. Submitting to the Bourbons, he was made a peer, a dignity restored to him in 1819, though he had sided with his old master during the Hundred Days.

LEFORT, François Jacob, *lĕ-for* (1653–99), Swiss diplomat, born at Geneva of Scottish extraction, served in the Swiss Guard at

Paris, but entered the Russian service in 1675. Heading the intrigues which made Peter sole ruler, he became his first favourite. An able diplomat and administrator, he backed up the tsar's reforms, and in 1694 was made admiral and generalissimo. See German Lives by Posselt (1866) and Blum (1867).

LEFROY, Sir John Henry (1817–90), British soldier, born at Ashe, Hants, he became an artillery officer, director-general of ordnance and governor of Bermuda (1870–77). He was made K.C.M.G. in 1877 and was appointed governor of Tasmania in 1880. He wrote on the Bermudas, antiquities and on ordnance, his *Handbook of Field Ordnance* (1854) being the first of this type of text-book.

LE GALLIENNE, (1) **Eva** (1899–), English actress on American stage, daughter of (2), founder (1926) and director of the Civic Repertory Theater of New York.

(2) **Richard** (1866–1947), English writer, born of Guernsey ancestry at Liverpool, in 1891 became a London journalist but later lived in New York. He published many volumes of prose and verse from 1887. His style, that of the later 19th century, is outmoded and mannered, but his best books are *Quest of the Golden Girl* (1896), *The Romantic Nineties* (1926) and *From a Paris Garret* (1936). See study by Egan and Smerdon (1960).

LEGENDRE, Adrien Marie, *lė-zhä'dr'* (1752–1833), French mathematician, was born at Toulouse, studied at Paris, and became professor of Mathematics at the Military School, and (1783) member of the Academy of Sciences. Appointed in 1787 one of the commissioners to connect Greenwich and Paris by triangulation, he was elected an F.R.S. In his report Legendre first enunciated the ' proposition of spherical excess ', just as in 1806 he made the first proposal to use the ' method of least squares '. In 1827 appeared his famous *Traité des fonctions elliptiques*; in 1830 his *Théorie des nombres*. Carlyle translated his *Éléments de géométrie* (1794).

LÉGER, Fernand, *lay-zhay* (1881–1955), French painter, born in Argentan, helped to form the cubist movement, but later developed his own ' aesthetic of the machine '. He worked in New York and Paris. See monograph by D. Cooper (1950).

LEGGE, James (1815–97), Scottish Chinese scholar, born at Huntly, graduated at Aberdeen in 1835. He took charge of the Anglo-Chinese college in Malacca; next worked for thirty years at Hong Kong, and in 1876 became professor of Chinese at Oxford. His greatest work was the *Chinese Classics*, with text, translation, notes, &c. (1861–86).

LEGOUIS, Émile, *lė-gwee* (1861–1937), French scholar, born at Honfleur, became professor of English at the Sorbonne, 1904–1932. He wrote books on Wordsworth, Chaucer and Spenser, and *Histoire de la littérature anglaise* (1924) (trans. 1926).

LEGOUVÉ, Ernest, *lė-goo-vay* (1807–1903), French playwright and prose writer, born in Paris. He was Scribe's collaborateur in *Adrienne Lecouvreur* (1849). He was elected to the Academy in 1855. See his *Soixante Ans de souvenirs* (1886–87).

LEGRENZI, Giovanni (1625–90), Venetian composer, born at Clusone near Bergamo, wrote church music for St Mark's, much chamber music, and 18 operas.

LEGROS, lė-grõ, (1) **Alphonse** (1837–1911), French painter and etcher, born at Dijon, was apprenticed to a house painter. Attracting attention in the Salon between 1859 and 1866, he settled in London, and, becoming naturalized, was in 1876 appointed Slade Professor in University College, London.

(2) **Pierre** (1656–1719), French sculptor, born in Paris, lived and died in Rome.

LEHÁR, Franz (1870–1948), Hungarian composer, born at Komárom, was a conductor in Vienna and wrote a violin concerto. He is best known for his operettas which include his most popular *The Merry Widow* (1905), *The Count of Luxembourg, Frederica* and *The Land of Smiles*. See Life by Pope and Murray (1953).

LEHMANN, (1) **Beatrix** (1903–), English actress, daughter of (6) and sister of (2) and (4), was born at Bourne End, Bucks. She first appeared on the stage in 1924 at the Lyric, Hammersmith, and since then has appeared in many successful plays, including, in recent years, *Family Reunion*, Ustinov's *No Sign of the Dove*, and *Waltz of the Toreadors*. In 1946 she became director-producer of the Arts Council Midland Theatre company. She has also appeared in films and written two novels and several short stories.

(2) **John Frederick** (1907–), English poet and man-of-letters, born at Bourne End, Buckinghamshire, was educated at Eton and Trinity College, Cambridge, founded the periodical in book format, *New Writing*, in 1936. He was managing director of the Hogarth Press (1938–46), and ran his own firm with his sister, Rosamond, as codirector from 1946 to 1953. In 1954 he inaugurated *The London Magazine*, which he edited until 1961. He has published, among many works, a *Garden Revisited* (1931), *Forty Poems* (1942), and a study *Edith Sitwell* (1952), and has conducted a literary radio-magazine on the B.B.C. See his autobiography (3 vols., 1955, 1960 and 1966), and *Ancestors and Friends* (1962). He was made C.B.E. in 1964.

(3) **Liza,** properly **Elizabeth Nina Mary Frederika** (1862–1918), English soprano and composer, daughter of (5), was born in London. Very popular as a concert singer, she also composed ballads, a light opera *The Vicar of Wakefield* (1906) and a song-cycle *In a Persian Garden* (1896).

(4) **Rosamond Nina** (1903–), English novelist, sister of (1) and (2), born in London, educated at Cambridge. Her novels show a fine sensitive insight into character and her women especially are brilliantly drawn. Among her books are *Dusty Answer* (1927), *A Note in Music* (1930), and *The Echoing Grove* (1953). She has also written a play *No More Music* (1939), and a volume of short stories *The Gypsy's Baby* (1946). See her *The Swan in the Evening* (1967).

(5) **Rudolf** (1819–1905), German painter, born near Hamburg, in 1866 settled in London and became a naturalized British subject. He married a daughter of Dr Robert Chambers. See his *An Artist's Reminiscences* (1894).

(6) **Rudolph Chambers** (1856–1929), English journalist, nephew of (5) and father of (1), (2) and (4), was born at Sheffield. He was a journalist on *Punch* (1890–1919), editor of the *Daily News* (1901), Liberal M.P. for Harborough (1906–10). A well-known oarsman and coach, he published *The Complete Oarsman* in 1908.

LEHMBRUCK, Wilhelm, *laym-brook* (1881–1919), German sculptor and illustrator, was born in Meidensich near Duisberg, and committed suicide in Berlin. He was early influenced by Maillol, and later produced expressionist sculpture, specializing in elongated and exaggerated female torsos.

LEIBL, Wilhelm, *lī'bl'* (1844–1900), German artist, born at Cologne. He studied in Paris, being much influenced by Courbet's realism, and later worked in Munich. Most of his paintings are genre scenes of Bavaria and the lower Alps, although he painted a number of portraits. See the monograph by W. L. Waldmann (1921).

LEIBNIZ, Gottfried Wilhelm, *līb'nits* (1646–1716), German philosopher and mathematician, one of the world's great intellects, born July 6 in Leipzig, where his father was professor of Moral Philosophy. Refused a doctorate there in 1666 on account of his youth, he was granted one by the University of Altdorf and, preferring a less secluded life, turned down the accompanying offer of a professorship. Through a fellow-member of a Rosicrucian circle in Nuremberg, the diplomat Baron von Boineburg, he obtained a position at the court of the powerful Elector of Mainz, partly on the strength of an essay on legal education. To divert Louis XIV from his designs on Germany, Leibniz was dispatched by the German princes to Paris with a master plan, devised by him for a French invasion of Egypt, said to have been consulted more than a century later by Napoleon. In Paris Leibniz met Malebranche, Arnauld and Huygens, studied Cartesianism and mathematics and invented a calculating machine, for which he was elected F.R.S. on his visit to London in 1673. There he met English mathematicians acquainted with Newton's work and this led to the undignified controversy later as to whether he or Newton was the inventor of the infinitesimal calculus. Leibniz certainly invented a system, the basis of that employed today, with a more advanced notation than that of Newton, in Paris in 1675–76, which he published in 1684, whereas Newton did not publish until 1687, although his system of 'fluxions' dates back to 1665. Clarke defended Newton's claims, but Leibniz was forced to conduct his own defence through an imaginary protagonist author of his *Historia et Origo Calculi Differentialis*. The controversy was never really settled, despite the Royal Society's formal declaration for Newton in 1711. On his way to take up his last post as librarian to the duke of Brunswick at Hanover in 1676, Leibniz met Spinoza in Amsterdam and discussed parts of the latter's *Ethics* with him. He improved the drainage of mines and the coinage, arranged the library at Wolfenbüttel, and in Austria and Italy gathered materials for a history of the house of Brunswick. He

worked for a reconciliation of Protestant and Roman Catholic churches and induced Frederick I to found (1700) the Academy of Sciences in Berlin, of which he became first president. Unpopular with George of Hanover, he was left behind when the court moved to London and was allowed to die without recognition, November 14, 1716. Leibniz left a vast corpus of writings, only a fraction of which was published in his lifetime. Bertrand Russell, in his brilliant study of Leibniz's philosophy (1900), distinguished between the popular works, written with an eye to popular and princely favour (such as the *Théodicée* (1710; trans. E. M. Huggard 1952), a perversion of which, summed up by its optimistic doctrine of 'all is for the best in this best of all possible worlds', Voltaire brilliantly satirized in *Candide*) and the *Monadologie* (1714; trans. R. Latta 1898) of which esoteric philosophical doctrines of which seem less so when read in conjunction with the profoundly logical, but theologically controversial arguments, prudently left unpublished, such as the *Discours de metaphysique* (1846; trans. P. Lucas and L. Grant 1953) and the correspondence with Arnauld (trans. G. R. Montgomery, Chicago 1902) and Clarke (trans. H. G. Alexander 1956). Leibniz defined substance as an infinite number of indivisible, therefore nonmaterial mutually isolated *monads*, each one reflecting the world from its own point of view. These monads form a hierarchy, the very highest of which is God, and they constitute a dualism with material phenomena, synchronized, as when a human being lifts his arm, by a preestablished harmony. Each monad is the sum of its predicates throughout its existence. Human choice is still subject in a special way to this determinism, for by the principle of sufficient reason there are always ' inclining reasons ' for one action rather than another, although ' not necessitating '. Leibniz's mathematical preoccupations led him to conceive of a universal linguistic calculus, incorporating all existing knowledge, which would render argument obsolete and displace it by a process of calculation. His great influence, not least upon Russell, was primarily as a mathematician and as a pioneer of modern symbolic logic. The complete edition of his works was published by the Berlin Academy (1923 ff.). See also his *Nouveaux Essais* (1765) criticizing Locke, Lives in German by G. E. Guhrauer (1846), K. Fischer (1920), and in English by J. T. Herz (1884), also W. H. Barber, *Leibniz in France* (1953), studies by B. Russell (1900, n.e. 1937), confirmed by L. Couturat's (Paris 1901) comprising freshly discovered logical fragments, H. W. B. Joseph, *Lectures*, ed. J. L. Austin (1949) and R. L. Saw (1954).

LEICESTER, Robert Dudley, Earl of, *les'ter* (c. 1532–88), was fifth son of John Dudley, Duke of Northumberland, and grandson of the notorious Edmund Dudley (q.v.) beheaded by Henry VIII. His father was executed for his support of Lady Jane Grey (q.v.). He too was sentenced to death, but, liberated in 1554, was by Elizabeth made master of the horse, Knight of the Garter, a privy councillor, high steward of the

University of Cambridge, Baron Dudley, and finally in 1564, Earl of Leicester. In 1550 he had married Amy, daughter of Sir John Robsart. On September 8, 1560, at Cumnor Place, Berkshire, the house of Anthony Forster, a creature of her husband's, she was found dead, as some think by suicide; but it was generally believed that she was murdered, and that Dudley, if not Elizabeth herself, was an accessory to the crime; and the archives at Simancas indicate that there had been a plot to poison her. Elizabeth continued to favour Leicester in spite of his unpopularity and of his secret marriage in 1573 to the Dowager Lady Sheffield. In 1563 she had suggested him as a husband for Mary, Queen of Scots, and in 1575 she was magnificently entertained by him at his castle of Kenilworth. In 1578 he bigamously married the widow of Walter, Earl of Essex; yet Elizabeth was only temporarily greatly offended. In 1585 he commanded the expedition to the Low Countries in which Sir Philip Sidney, his nephew, met with his death at Zutphen. In 1587 he again showed his military incapacity in the same field, and had to be recalled. In 1588 he was appointed to command the forces assembled at Tilbury against the Spanish Armada. He died suddenly on September 4 of the same year at Cornbury, in Oxfordshire, of poison, said rumour, intended for his wife. See Milton Waldman, *Elizabeth and Leicester* (1944).

LEICESTER OF HOLKHAM, Thomas William Coke, Earl of, *les'ter of hōk'em* (1752–1842), was a descendant of the famous lawyer Coke. He was one of the first agriculturists of England; by his efforts northwest Norfolk was converted from a rye-growing into a wheat-growing district, and more stock and better breeds were kept on the farms. Coke represented Norfolk as a Whig most of the period 1776–1833, and in 1837 he was created Earl of Leicester of Holkham, to distinguish the title from the Townshend earldom of Leicester. He died at Longford Hall, Derbyshire.

LEICHHARDT, Ludwig, *līкн'-hart* (1813–48), German explorer, born at Trebatsch near Frankfort-on-Oder, in 1841 went to Australia, and led an expedition (1843–48) from Moreton Bay to the Gulf of Carpentaria. In 1846 he failed to cross Cape York Peninsula. In December 1847 he again started from Moreton Bay to cross the continent, but was last heard of on April 3, 1848. See *Journal of an Overland Expedition in Australia* (1847) and Life by Mrs C. D. Cotton (1938).

LEIF ERIKSSON, *layv,* born in Iceland, the son of Eric the Red, christianized Greenland and discovered land (*c.* 1000),which he named Vinland after the vines he found growing there. It is still uncertain where Vinland actually is, some saying Labrador or Newfoundland, others Massachusetts. See E. Haughen, *Voyages to Vinland* (1942).

LEIGHTON, *lay'tĕn,* (1) **Frederic, 1st Baron Leighton** (1830–96), English painter, was born at Scarborough, a doctor's son. He early showed a gift for painting, visited Rome, Florence, Frankfurt, Berlin, Paris and Brussels, and everywhere received instruction from the most distinguished masters. He

exhibited at the Royal Academy in 1855 his *Cimabue's Madonna carried in Procession through Florence*—a picture purchased by Queen Victoria. Among his later works were *Paolo and Francesca* (1861), *The Daphnephoria* (1876; sold in 1893 for £3700), and *The Bath of Psyche* (1890). Lord Leighton also won distinction as a sculptor, and in 1877 his *Athlete struggling with a Python* was purchased out of the Chantrey Bequest. Several of his paintings, as for example *Wedded* (1882), became mass bestsellers in photogravure reproduction. In 1864 he was elected A.R.A., in 1869 R.A., and in 1878 president and knighted. His *Addresses* were published in 1896. He was created a baronet in 1886, and Lord Leighton of Stretton in January 1896. He died unmarried, and was buried in St Paul's. His *Academy Addresses* appeared in 1897. See a study by Ernest Rhys (new ed. 1900), and his *Life and Letters* by Mrs Russell Barrington (1906).

(2) **Robert** (1611–84), Scottish archbishop, born probably in London, was the second son of Alexander Leighton, M.D. (*c.* 1568–*c.* 1649), Presbyterian minister in London and Utrecht, author of *Sion's Plea against the Prelacie* (1628), which earned him from Laud scourging, the pillory, branding and mutilation, heavy fine and imprisonment. Robert studied at Edinburgh University and spent some years in France. He was ordained minister of Newbattle in 1641, signed the Covenant two years later, and took part in all the Presbyterian policy of the time; most of the *Sermons* and the *Commentary on the First Epistle of Peter* were the work of the Newbattle period. In 1653 he was appointed principal of Edinburgh University. Soon after the Restoration Leighton was induced by the king himself to become one of the new bishops, chose Dunblane, the poorest of all the dioceses, and for the next ten years he laboured to build up the shattered walls of the church. His aim was to preserve what was best in Episcopacy and Presbytery as a basis for comprehensive union; but he succeeded only in being misunderstood by both sides. The continued persecution of the Covenanters drove him to London in 1665 to resign his see, but Charles persuaded him to return. Again in 1669 he went to London to advocate his scheme of 'accommodation' and became Archbishop of Glasgow in the same year. Next followed his fruitless conferences at Edinburgh (1670–71) with leading Presbyterians. In despair of success he was allowed to retire in 1674. His last ten years he spent at Broadhurst Manor, Sussex often preaching in the church of Horsted Keynes, where he lies. He died in a London inn. There have been several editions of his works—all of which reveal a deep spirituality, a heavenly exaltation and devotion—since that by his friend Fall (1692–1708). There are *Selections* (1883) by Blair; *Life and Letters* by Rev. D. Butler (1903); a Life by Bp. E. A. Knox (1930).

LEININGEN. See KENT, DUKE OF.

LEISHMAN, Sir William Boog (1865–1926), Scottish bacteriologist, born in Glasgow, became professor of Pathology in the Army Medical College, and director-general,

Army Medical Service (1923). He discovered an effective vaccine for inoculation against typhoid and was first to discover the parasite of the disease kala-azar. He was knighted in 1909. See H. H. Scott's *History of Tropical Medicine* (ii) (1939).

LELAND, (1) **Charles Godfrey**, pseud. **Hans Breitmann** (1825–1903), American author, born in Philadelphia, graduated at Princeton in 1845, and afterwards studied at Heidelberg, Munich and Paris. He was admitted to the Philadelphia bar in 1851, but turned to journalism. From 1869 he resided chiefly in England and Italy, and investigated the Gypsies, a subject on which between 1873 and 1891 he published four valuable works. He is best known for his poems in ' Pennsylvania Dutch ', the famous *Hans Breitmann Ballads* (1871; continued in 1895). Other similar volumes gained him great popularity during his lifetime. He also translated the works of Heine. See his *Memoirs* (1893), and his *Life and Letters* by Mrs Pennell (1906).

(2) **John** (c. 1506–52), English antiquary, born in London, was educated at St Paul's School under William Lily, then at Christ's College, Cambridge, and All Souls, Oxford. After a residence in Paris he became chaplain to Henry VIII, who in 1533 made him ' king's antiquary ', with power to search for records of antiquity in the cathedrals, colleges, abbeys and priories of England. In six years he collected ' a whole world of things very memorable '. His church preferments were the rectories of Peuplingues near Calais and Haseley in Oxfordshire, a canonry of King's College (now Christ Church), Oxford, and a prebend of Salisbury. Most of his papers are in the Bodleian and British Museum. Besides his *Commentarii de Scriptoribus Britannicis* (ed. by Hall, 1709), his chief works are *The Itinerary* (ed. by L. T. Smith, 1905–10) and *De Rebus Britannicis Collectanea* (ed. by Hearne, 1715). See Huddesford's *Lives of Leland, Hearne, and Wood* (1772).

(3) **John** (1691–1766), English Presbyterian minister, born at Wigan, was educated at Dublin, where from 1716 he was minister. He wrote against Tindal (1733) and Morgan (1739–40). His chief work is *A View of the Principal Deistical Writers* (1754–56). See Life prefixed to his *Discourses* (1768–89).

LELY, **Sir Peter** (1618–80), Dutch painter, originally Pieter van der Faes, was born probably at Soest, Westphalia. He settled in London in 1641 as a portrait painter. He was employed by Charles I, Cromwell, and Charles II, for whom he changed his style of painting. The last nominated him court-painter, and in 1679 knighted him. His *Beauties* are collected at Hampton Court. The 13 Greenwich portraits are among his best works; these, the English admirals who fought in the second Dutch war, are outstanding for depth and sincerity of characterization. They present a marked contrast to his very popular and often highly sensuous court portraits which have often a hasty, superficial appearance. See C. H. Collins Baker, *Lely and the Stuart Portrait Painters* (1912).

LEMAIRE, **Philippe Honoré** (1798–1880), French sculptor, was born at Valenciennes,

and died in Paris. Among his works is a statue of Hoche at Versailles and one of Napoleon at Lille.

LE MAIRE DE BELGES, **Jean** (c. 1473–1524), the first French humanist poet, served the Duc de Bourbon, Margaret of Austria, to whom he dedicated his *Épîtres de l'amant vert*, and Louis XII. See studies by P. Spaax (1926) and K. M. Munn (1936).

LEMAÎTRE, (1) **François Élie Jules** (1853–1914), French playwright and critic, was born at Vennecy, Loiret, and in 1895 was elected to the Academy. His articles written first for the *Journal des débats* were issued in book form as *Impressions de théâtre* (1888–1898), and those written for *Revue bleue* on modern French literature became *Les Contemporains* (1886–99). A masterly critic with a charming, lucid style, he wrote also *Rousseau* (1907), *Racine* (1908), *Fénelon* (1910) and *Chateaubriand* (1912). See studies by Morice (1924), Durrière (1934) and Seillière (1935).

(2) **Frédérick** (1800–76), French actor, born at Le Havre. His first success was in *Richard Darlington*, a play based on Scott's *The Surgeon's Daughter*, and this was followed by a succession of triumphs including *Hamlet*, *Kean ou Désordre et Genie*, *Ruy Blas*, and the greatest of all, *L'Auberge des Adrets*. This last was in reality Lemaître's own play. Based on an inferior melodrama, he made the character Robert Macaire a villain of genius. Writers of the day acclaimed him; Dumas called him the French Kean, Flaubert called his Macaire the greatest symbol of the age and Hugo wrote *Ruy Blas* for him. He visited London four times and on one occasion shocked Queen Victoria by his Ruy Blas. He suffered ill health in his later years and died in great poverty. See Lives by Lecomte (2 vols. 1888) and Baldick (1959).

(3) **Georges Henri** (1894–1966), Belgian astrophysicist, professor of the Theory of Relativity at Louvain, internationally known for his work on that subject and on its application to the theory of the expanding universe.

LEMAN, **Gérard Mathieu**, *lĕ-mǎ* (1851–1920), Belgian general, born at Liège, was also a director of studies, engineer and mathematician. He was wounded and captured at Liège, whose forts, as military governor, he gallantly held against the Germans, August 4–7, 1914.

LEMNIUS (c. 1505–50), German humanist and Latin poet, was a student of Melanchthon at Wittenberg. Antagonistic to Luther and his teaching, he wrote against him in two books of epigrams (1538). His other works included *Monachopornomachia*, a satirical poem, love poems, *Amores* (1542) and a Latin translation of the Odyssey (1549). He died at Chur.

LEMOINE, **Sir James MacPherson**, *lĕ-mwan* (1825–1912), born in Quebec, became superintendent of inland revenue at Quebec in 1858. He studied archaeology, ornithology and other sciences, wrote on Canadian history and was the first Canadian author to receive a knighthood.

LEMON, **Mark** (1809–70), English author and journalist, born in London, in 1835 wrote a farce, followed by melodramas, operettas, novels (the best, perhaps, *Falkner Lyle*, 1866), children's stories, a *Jest Book* (1864) and essays. In 1841 he helped to establish *Punch*, becoming first joint editor, then sole editor from 1843 to his death. See J. Hatton, *Reminiscences of Mark Lemon* (1871).

LEMONNIER, *lė-mon-yay*, (1) **Antoine Louis Camille** (1844–1913), Belgian writer, born at Ixelles near Brussels, took to art criticism in 1863, and by his novels *Un Mâle* (1881), *Happe-Chair* (1888) and other works, in French, but full of strong Flemish realism and mysticism, won fame as one of Belgium's leading prose writers. He wrote books on art, including *Gustave Courbet* (1878), *Alfred Stevens et son œuvre* (1906) and *L'École Belge de la peinture* (1906).

(2) **Pierre Charles** (1715–99), French astronomer, born in Paris, was a member of the Academy of Sciences at the age of twenty because of his lunar map. He greatly advanced astronomical measurement in France, and made twelve observations of Uranus before it was recognized as a planet.

LE MOYNE, *lė-mwan*, (1) **Charles** (1626–83), French pioneer, born at Dieppe, sailed for Canada in 1641, lived among the Hurons, and fought with the Iroquois. In 1668 Louis XIV made him Seigneur de Longueuil. He was long captain of Montreal.

(2) **Charles** (1656–1729), eldest son of (1), served in the French army, was governor of Montreal and commandant-general of the colony, and was made a baron in 1700. His descendant, Charles Colmor Grant, had his Canadian title of seventh Baron de Longueuil recognized by Queen Victoria in 1880.

(3) **François** (1688–1737), French painter of mythological subjects, e.g., the Salon d'Hercule at Versailles, was born and committed suicide at Paris. Boucher was his pupil. See examples in the Wallace Collection.

(4) **Joseph** (1668–1734), son of (1), served in the French navy, and in 1719 captured Pensacola. In 1723 he became governor of Rochefort.

LEMPRIÈRE, **John**, *lā-pryayr* (c. 1765–1824), British scholar, born in Jersey, was headmaster of Abingdon and Exeter grammar schools, and rector of Meeth and Newton-Petrock in Devon. His *Classical Dictionary* (1788) was long a standard work. Another book was *Universal Biography* (1808).

LENARD, **Philipp Eduard Anton** (1862–1947), German physicist, born at Pozsony (Bratislava), professor of Physics at Heidelberg (1896–98 and 1907–31), was awarded the Nobel prize in 1905. His main research concerned cathode rays, upon which subject he wrote several books. He was an enthusiastic believer in Nazi doctrines.

LENAU, **Nikolaus** (**Nikolaus Niembsch von Strehlenau**), *lay'nau* (1802–50), German poet, born at Czatad in Hungary, studied law and medicine at Vienna. His life was rendered unhappy by his morbid poetic discontent; and in 1844 he became insane, dying in an asylum near Vienna. His poetic power is best shown in his short lyrics; his longer pieces include *Faust* (1836), *Savonarola* (1837) and *Die Albigenser* (1842). See Lives

by Schurz (1855), Frankl (1885–92) and Roustan (1899).

LENBACH, **Franz**, *len-ba*KH (1836–1904), German portrait painter, born at Schrobenhausen, Bavaria, worked mostly in Munich. For some time he copied the great masters, including Titian, Rubens and Velasquez, before becoming one of the greatest 19th-century German portrait painters. His portraits of Bismarck are specially famous.

LENCLOS, **Anne**, called **Ninon de**, *lā-klō* (1616–1706), born of good family at Paris, commenced at sixteen her long career of gallantry. Among her lovers were two marquises, two marshals, the great Condé, the Duc de Larochefoucauld, and an abbé or two. She had two sons, but never showed the slightest maternal feeling. One of them, brought up in ignorance of his mother, conceived a passion for her. Informed of their relationship, he blew out his brains. Ninon was nearly as celebrated for her manners as for her beauty. The most respectable women sent their children to her to acquire taste, style, politeness. Mirecourt's *Mémoires* is a romance; the letters attributed to her are mostly spurious. See books by Hayes (1908), Rowsell, Magne 1925), Day (1958).

LENGLEN, **Suzanne**, *lā-lā* (1899–1938), French lawn tennis player, born at Compiègne. Trained by her father, she became famous in 1914 by winning the women's world hard-court singles championship at Paris. She was the woman champion of France (1919–1923, 1925–26), and her Wimbledon championships were the women's singles and doubles (1919–23, 1925), and the mixed doubles (1920, 1922, 1925). In 1921 she was Olympic champion. She became a professional in 1926, toured the U.S., and retired in 1927 to found the Lenglen School of Tennis in Paris. Perhaps the greatest woman player of all time, she set a new fashion in female tennis dress. She published *Lawn Tennis, the Game of Nations* (1925) and a novel, *The Love-Game* (1925). See Olliff's *The Romance of Wimbledon* (1949).

LENIN (formerly **Ulyanov**), **Vladimir Ilyich** (1870–1924), Russian revolutionary, was born into a family of the minor intelligentsia at Simbirsk (Ulyanov). He was educated at Kazan University and in 1892 began to practise law in Samara (Kuibyshev). In 1894, after five years' intensive study of Marx, he moved to St Petersburg (Leningrad), organizing the illegal ' Union for the Liberation of the Working Class '. Arrested for his opinions, he was exiled to Siberia for three years. His Western exile began in 1900 in Switzerland, where with Plekhanov he developed an underground Social Democratic Party, to assume leadership of the working classes in a revolution against Tsarism. In 1903 he became leader of the Bolshevik wing whose Marxism was opposed to the ' bourgeois reformism ' of the Mensheviks. Lenin returned to Russia in 1905, ascribing the failure of the rising of that year to lack of support for his own programme. He determined that when the time came Soviets (councils of workers, soldiers and peasants) should be the instruments of total revolution.

Lenin left Russia in 1907 and spent the next decade strengthening the Bolsheviks against the Mensheviks, interpreting the gospel of Marx and Engels and organizing underground work in Russia. In April 1917, a few days after the deposition of the tsar Nicholas II, Lenin made with German connivance his fateful journey in a sealed train from Switzerland to Petrograd. He told his followers to prepare for the overthrow of the shaky Provisional Government and the remaking of Russia on a Soviet basis. In the October Revolution the Provisional Government collapsed and the dominating Bolshevik 'rump' in the second Congress of Soviets declared that supreme power rested in them. Lenin inaugurated the 'dictatorship of the proletariat' with the formal dissolution of the Constituent Assembly. For three years he grappled with war and anarchy. In 1922 he began his 'new economic policy' of limited free enterprise to give Russia a breathing space before entering the era of giant state planning. He died on January 21, 1924, and his body was embalmed for veneration in a crystal casket in a mausoleum in the Red Square, Moscow. He left a testament in which he proposed the removal of the ambitious Stalin as secretary of the Communist Party. Shrewd, dynamic, implacable, pedantic, opportunist, as ice-cold in his economic reasoning as in his impersonal political hatreds that could encompass millions, Lenin lived only for the furtherance of Marxism. He inspired in the name of democracy a despotism boundless in the power of its ambition and sense of destiny. For years after his death Lenin was looked upon in the Soviet Union as a demi-god. Publications include: *Workers of the World Unite* (Geneva 1897) and *Imperialism the Last Stage of Capitalism* (1917). See Selected Works (English trans. 1936–39), and Lives and studies of Lenin by L. Trotsky (1925), V. Marcu (1928), D. S. Mirsky (1931), G. Vernadsky (1931), R. Fox (1933), P. Kerzhensev (1937), C. Hill (1947), D. Shrub (1948).

LENNEP, Jacob van (1802–62), Dutch writer and lawyer, born at Amsterdam, achieved a great reputation for legal knowledge. He has been called the Walter Scott of Holland. His most popular works were comedies, *Het Dorp aan die Grenzen* and *Het Dorp over die Grenzen.* Of his novels, several (e.g., *The Rose of Dekama* and *The Adopted Son*) have been translated.

LENO, Dan, *lee'nō,* stage name of George Galvin (1860–1904), English comedian. He began his career at the age of four, singing and dancing in public houses, and by eighteen became a champion clog-dancer and was invited to appear in the Surrey pantomime. Ten years later he joined the Augustus Harris management at Drury Lane, where he appeared for many years in the annual pantomime. Leno was a thin, small man and his foil was the huge, bulky Herbert Campbell. When Campbell died in 1904 as the result of an accident, Leno pined and died six months later, insane from overwork and loneliness. He will be remembered for his realistic 'dames' with their inimitable blend of Cockney humour and sentiment. See Hickory Wood, *Dan Leno* (1905) and M. W. Disher, *Winkles and Champagne* (1938).

LENOIR, Jean Joseph Étienne (1822–1900), French inventor who constructed an internal combustion engine (*c.* 1859) and later a small car (1860).

LENORMAND, Henri René, *lĕ-nor-mã* (1882–1951), French dramatist, born in Paris, the author of *Les Possédés* (1909), *Le Mangeur de rêves* (1922), a modern equivalent of *Oedipus Rex, L'Homme et ses fantômes* (1924), and other plays in which Freud's theory of subconscious motivation is adapted to dramatic purposes. See study by P. Blanchard (1947).

LENORMANT, François, *lĕ-nor-mã* (1837–1883), French archaeologist, was born in Paris, the son of Charles Lenormant (1802–1859), himself profoundly learned in Egyptology, numismatics and archaeology generally. At twenty he carried off the prize in numismatics of the Académie des Inscriptions, at twenty-three was digging at Eleusis; and he continued his explorations, in the intervals of his work as sub-librarian at the Institute (1862–72), and professor of Archaeology at the Bibliothèque Nationale (1874–83), until his health broke down from overwork and a wound received during the siege of Paris. Just before his death he was converted to Catholicism from scepticism. His chief work was *Les Origines de l'histoire d'après la Bible* (1880–84).

LENÔTRE, André (1613–1700), the creator of French landscape-gardening, was born and died in Paris. He designed the gardens at Versailles, and laid out St James's Park in London. See monograph by J. Guiffrey (1912).

LENTHALL, William (1591–1662), English barrister, born at Henley, was Speaker of the Long Parliament 1640–53, and master of the Rolls from 1643. He was again made Speaker in 1654, and in 1657 became one of Cromwell's peers.

LENZ, (1) **Heinrich Friedrich Emil** (1804–65), German physicist, was born at Dorpat and died at Rome. He first studied theology, but became professor of Physics at St Petersburg and a member of the Russian Academy of Sciences. He was the first to state Lenz's law governing induced current, and is credited with discovering the dependence of electrical resistance on temperature (Joule's law).

(2) **Jakob Michael Reinhold** (1751–92), German author, born in Livonia, was one of the young authors who surrounded Goethe in Strasbourg. He first wrote two plays which were well received, *Der Hofmeister* (1774) and *Die Soldaten* (1776). Like all the 'Sturm und Drang' poets he was a fervent admirer of Shakespeare, and this was expressed in his *Anmerkungen übers Theater* (1774). He was a gifted writer of lyrics, some of them being at first attributed to Goethe. He suffered a mental breakdown while still young and died in poverty at Moscow. See studies by Waldmann (1894), Rosanow (1909).

LEO, the name of thirteen popes, whose tenures of the papacy were as follows: I

(440–61); II (682–83); III (795–816); IV (847–55); V (903); VI (928–29); VII (936–39); VIII (963–65); IX (1049–54); X (1513–21); XI (1605); XII (1823–29); XIII (1878–1903).

Leo I (*c.* 390–461), ' the Great ', a saint, and one of the most eminent of the Latin Fathers, was of good Roman family. In a council held at Rome in 449 he set aside the proceedings of the Council of Ephesus, which had pronounced in favour of Eutyches, and summoned a new council at Chalcedon, in which Leo's celebrated ' Dogmatical Letter ' was accepted ' as the voice of Peter '. He interposed with Attila (q.v.) in defence of Rome, and with Gaiseric (q.v.). See the Rev. C. L. Feltoe (Library of Fathers, vol. xii 1896) and T. G. Jalland's *Life of St Leo the Great* (1941).

Leo III (*c.* 750–816), saw during his pontificate the formal establishment of the Empire of the West. In the 8th century the popes, through the practical withdrawal of the Eastern emperors, had exercised a temporal supremacy in Rome, under the protectorate of the Frankish sovereigns. Leo was in 799 obliged to flee to Spoleto, whence he repaired to Paderborn to confer with Charlemagne. On his return to Rome he was received with honour. In 800 Charlemagne, having come to Rome, was crowned emperor by the pope, and the temporal sovereignty of the pope over the Roman city and state was formally established, under the suzerainty of the emperor.

Leo X, Giovanni de' Medici (1475–1521), second son of Lorenzo the Magnificent, was created cardinal at the age of thirteen. In the expulsion of the Medici from Florence the young cardinal was included. He was employed as legate by Julius II, at whose death in 1513 he was chosen pope as Leo X. He brought to a successful conclusion the fifth Lateran Council. He concluded a concordat with Francis I of France; he consolidated and extended the reconquests of his warlike predecessor, Julius II. His desertion of Francis I for Charles V was dictated by the interests of Italy. But it is as a patron of learning and art that the reputation of Leo has lived. He founded a Greek college in Rome and established a Greek press. His vast project for the rebuilding of St Peter's, and his permitting the preaching of an indulgence in order to raise funds, provoked Luther's Reformation. He regarded the movement as of little importance; and though he condemned the propositions of Luther, his measures were not marked by severity. In his moral conduct he maintained a strict propriety, and, although not free from nepotism, he was an enlightened prince. See works on him by Ranke; Creighton; Vaughan's *Medici Popes* (1908); Symonds's *Renaissance* (1875–86) and G. B. Picotti, *La Giovinezza di Leone X* (1928).

Leo XIII (1810–1903), 258th Roman pontiff, was born at Carpineto, son of Count Ludovico Pecci. Having become Doctor of Laws, he was appointed by Gregory XVI a domestic prelate in 1837, received the title of prothonotary apostolic, and was a vigorous apostolic delegate at Benevento, Perugia and Spoleto. He was made Archbishop of Damietta *in partibus* and sent to Belgium as nuncio in 1843, nominated Archbishop of Perugia in 1846, and in 1853 created a cardinal by Pius IX, soon holding the important office of camerlengo. Upon the death of Pius IX in 1878 Vincenzo Gioacchino Cardinal Pecci was elected to the papacy under the title of Leo XIII. He restored the hierarchy in Scotland and composed the difficulty with Germany. In 1888 he denounced the Irish Plan of Campaign. He manifested enlightened views, but on questions affecting the church and his own status held staunchly to his rights. He regarded himself as the despoiled sovereign of Rome, and as a prisoner at the Vatican; and persistently declined to recognize the law of guarantees. He protested against heresy and ' godless ' schools, and in his encyclicals affirmed that the only solution to the socialistic problem is the influence of the papacy. In 1894 he constrained the French clergy and the monarchists to accept the republic. In 1883 he opened the archives of the Vatican for historical investigations, and he made himself known as a poet, chiefly in the Latin tongue. The jubilee of his episcopate in 1893 was marked by pilgrimages, addresses and gifts, as was that of his priesthood in 1887. In 1896 he issued an encyclical pronouncing Anglican orders invalid. See Lives by O'Reilly (1887), T'serclaes (Paris 1894, 1907), Boyer d'Agen (*Jeunesse de Léon XIII*, 1896), McCarthy (1896), and in German by W. Goetz (1923), Walterbay (6th ed. 1931), also his addresses, &c., in *The Pope and the People* (new ed. 1913).

LEO III (*c.* 680–741), called the Isaurian from being born in Isauria in Asia Minor, raised the Byzantine Empire from a very low condition, having, as a general in the East, seized the crown in 716. He reorganized the army and financial system, and in 718 repelled a formidable attack of the Saracens. In 726 he by an edict prohibited the use of images (i.e., pictures or mosaics; statues were hardly known as yet in churches) in public worship. In Italy, however, the appearance of the Image-breakers or Iconoclasts roused an enthusiastic resistance on the part of the people, and the controversy raised by the edict rent the empire for over a century. In 728 the exarchate of Ravenna was lost, and the eastern provinces became the prey of the Saracens, over whom, however, Leo won a great victory in Phrygia. See J. B. Bury, *The Later Roman Empire* (vol. 2, 1889) and *Histoire du moyen âge*, ed. Glotz (vol. 3 1944).

LEO AFRICANUS (properly **Alhassan ibn Mohammed Alwazzan** or **Alwezaz**) (1494–1552), a Cordovan Moor, who from *c.* 1512 travelled in northern Africa and Asia Minor. Falling into the hands of Venetian corsairs, he was sent to Leo X at Rome, where he lived twenty years, and accepted Christianity, but returned to Africa and (perhaps) his old faith, and died at Tunis. He wrote *Africae Descriptio* (1526) an account of his African travels in Italian (first printed 1550), long the chief source of information about the Sudan. Dr R. Brown re-edited John Pory's translation of 1600 (Hakluyt Society 1896).

LEOCHARES, *lee-ok'a-reez* (*c.* 370 B.C.), an Athenian sculptor who, with his master Scopas (q.v.), decorated the Mausoleum of Halicarnassus.

LEÓN, Ponce de. See PONCE DE LEÓN.

LEONARDO DA VINCI (1452–1519), Italian painter, sculptor, architect and engineer, was born at Vinci, between Pisa and Florence, the natural son of a Florentine notary. About 1470 he entered the studio of Andrea del Verrocchio. In 1482 he settled in Milan, and attached himself to Lodovico Sforza. His famous *Last Supper* (1498), commissioned jointly by Lodovico and the monks of Santa Maria delle Grazie, was painted on a wall of the refectory of the convent. Owing to dampness, and to the method of tempera painting—not oil, nor fresco—upon plaster, it soon showed signs of deterioration, and it has been often 'restored'; yet still it is one of the world's masterpieces. Among other paintings in Milan were portraits of two mistresses of the duke—one of them perhaps *La Belle Ferronnière* of the Louvre. Leonardo also devised a system of hydraulic irrigation of the plains of Lombardy and directed the court pageants. After the fall of Duke Lodovico in 1500 Leonardo retired to Florence, and entered the service of Cesare Borgia, then Duke of Romagna, as architect and engineer. In 1503 he returned to Florence, and commenced a *Madonna and Child with St Anne*, of which only the cartoon now in the Royal Academy, London, was completed. Both he and Michelangelo received commissions to decorate the Sala del Consiglio in the Palazzo della Signoria with historical compositions. Leonardo dealt with *The Battle of Anghiari*, a Florentine victory over Milan, and finished his cartoon; but, having employed a method of painting upon the plaster which proved a failure, he in 1506 abandoned the work. About 1504 he completed his most celebrated easel picture, *Mona Lisa* (stolen from the Louvre 1911; recovered 1913). Another work, now lost, portrayed the celebrated beauty Ginevra Benci; and Pacioli's *De divina Proportione* (1509) contained sixty geometrical figures from Leonardo's hand. In 1506 he was employed by Louis XII of France. Francis I bestowed on him in 1516 a yearly allowance, and assigned to his use the Château Cloux, near Amboise; hither he came that same year, and here he died May 2, 1519. Among his later works are *The Virgin of the Rocks*, now in the National Gallery, London (a replica in the Louvre), a figure of *St John the Baptist*, and a *Saint Anne*. There is in existence no sculpture which can positively be attributed to him, but he may well have designed or been closely associated with three works—the three figures over the north door of the Baptistery at Florence, a bronze statuette of horse and rider in the Budapest Museum and the wax bust of Flora. In his art Leonardo was hardly at all influenced by the antique; his practice was founded upon the most patient and searching study of nature and in particular the study of light and shade. He occupies a supreme place as an artist, but so few in number are the works by his hand that have reached us that he may be most fully studied in his drawings, of which there are rich collections at Milan, Paris, Florence and Vienna, as well as in the British Museum and at Windsor. His celebrated *Trattato della Pittura* was published in 1651; but a more complete manuscript, discovered by Manzi in the Vatican, was published in 1817. Voluminous MSS by him in Milan (*Codice-Atlantico*), Paris, Windsor, &c. have been reproduced in facsimile (1881–1901). Leonardo had a wide knowledge and understanding far beyond his times of most of the sciences, including biology, physiology, hydrodynamics, aeronautics, and his notebooks contain original remarks on all of these. See his *Literary Works*, ed. by Richter (1883; rev. and enl. 1939); his *Note-books*, trans. by MacCurdy (1938); monographs by Richter (1880), Séailles (new ed. 1906), Müntz (trans. 1899), MacCurdy (1904, 1933), Von Seidlitz (1909), Thiis (1913), Sirén (trans. 1916), Mrs Annand Taylor (1927), C. Bax (1932), Uzielli (2nd ed. 1896), Merezhkovsky (1931), K. M. Clark (1939), Goldscheider (1959); A. E. Popham, *The Drawings of Leonardo da Vinci* (1946).

LEONCAVALLO, Ruggiero (1858–1919), Italian composer, born at Naples, produced *I Pagliacci* (1892), followed by other less successful operas including *La Bohème* which failed where Puccini's on the same theme was a success.

LEONI, Leone, *lay-ō'nee* (1509–90), Italian goldsmith, medallist and sculptor, was born at Arezzo, worked at Milan, Genoa, Brussels and Madrid, and was the rival of Benvenuto Cellini in talent, vice and violence. His fine medals often depicted well-known artists, as Titian and Michelangelo, and his sculpture which was mostly in bronze included busts of Charles V and Philip II, both of whom he served for some time. See French monograph by Plon (1887).

LEONIDAS, *-on'-* (d. 480 B.C.), king of Sparta, succeeded his half-brother, Cleomenes, 491 B.C. When the Persian king Xerxes approached with an immense army Leonidas opposed him at the narrow pass of Thermopylae (480 B.C.) with his 300 Spartans; there all of them found a heroic death.

LEOPARDI, Giacomo, *lay-ō-pahr'dee* (1798–1837), Italian poet, was born of poor but noble parentage at Recanati. At sixteen he had read all the Latin and Greek classics, could write with accuracy French, Spanish, English and Hebrew, and wrote a commentary on Plotinus. After a short sojourn in Rome, he devoted himself at home to literature, but finding his home increasingly unbearable he began to travel and now a confirmed invalid, he lived successively in Bologna, Florence, Milan and Pisa. In 1833 he accompanied his friend Ranieri to Naples, and there in constant bodily anguish and hopeless despondency he lived till his death. His pessimism was unquestionably the genuine expression of Leopardi's deepest nature as well as of his reasoned conviction. Ranieri edited his works (1845). He was specially gifted as a writer of lyrics, which were collected under the title *I Canti* and are among the most beautiful in Italian literature. His prose works include the Dialogues and

Essays classed as *Operette Morali*, and his *Pensieri* and letters. His Essays and Dial-logues were trans. by Edwardes (1882), his Poems by G. Bickersteth (with critical introduction and bibliography, 1923). See Gladstone's *Gleanings*, vol. ii; and works by Carducci (1898), De Sanctis (1921), Origo (1953) and J. H. Whitfield (1954).

LEOPOLD, name of two Holy Roman emperors:

Leopold I (1640–1705), in 1658 succeeded his father, the Emperor Ferdinand III. He provoked the Hungarians to rebellion by his severity. Tekeli received aid from the Porte, and Kara Mustapha besieged Vienna (1683), which was rescued only by an army of Poles and Germans under John Sobieski. The power of the Turks now declined. In 1686 they lost Buda, after occupying it for nearly 150 years; and by the treaty of Carlowitz (1699) they were almost entirely cleared out of Hungary. The struggle between Leopold and Louis XIV of France for the heirship to the king of Spain led to the war of the Spanish Succession. Leopold was of sluggish and phlegmatic character, wholly under Jesuit influences. See German *Life* of him by Baumstark (1873).

Leopold II (1747–92), third son of Francis I and Maria Theresa, succeeded his father as Grand-duke of Tuscany in 1765, and his brother, Joseph I, as emperor in 1790. He succeeded in pacifying the Netherlands and Hungary; was led by the downfall of his sister, Marie Antoinette, to form an alliance with Prussia against France; but died before the war broke out.

LEOPOLD, name of three kings of Belgium:

Leopold I (1790–1865), king of the Belgians, son of Francis, Duke of Saxe-Coburg, and uncle of Queen Victoria, was a general in the Russian army, and served at Lützen, Bautzen and Leipzig. He married in 1816 the Princess Charlotte (q.v.); in 1829 (morganatically and unhappily) Caroline Bauer (q.v.); in 1832 Louise, daughter of Louis-Philippe. After hesitation he declined the crown of Greece (1830) and in June 1831 he was elected king of the Belgians. He conducted himself with prudence and moderation, with constant regard to the principles of the Belgian con-stitution and by his policy did much to prevent Belgium becoming too involved in the revolutions which were raging in other European countries in 1848. See L. de Lichtervilde, *Leopold I et la formation de la Belgique contemporaine* (1928).

Leopold II (1835–1909), born in Brussels, son of Leopold I, his chief interest was the expansion of Belgium abroad. He became king in 1885 of the independent state of the Congo, which was annexed to Belgium in 1908. At home he strengthened his country by military reforms and established a system of fortifications. He was not popular as a king, but under him Belgium flourished, develop-ing commercially and industrially, especially during the later years of his reign. He was succeeded by his nephew, Albert (q.v). See N. Ascherson's *The King Incorporated* (1963).

Leopold III (1901–), son of Albert, king from 1934, on his own authority ordered the capitulation of the army to the Nazis (May 28,

1940), thus opening the way to Dunkirk, and remained a prisoner in his own palace at Laeken. He refused to abdicate until July 16, 1951, in favour of his son Baudouin (q.v.).

LEOPOLD V (1157–94), Duke of Austria, crusader in 1182 and 1190–92, and the captor of Richard I (q.v.) of England.

LEOPOLD, Prince. See ALBANY (DUKE OF).

LEPAGE. See BASTIEN-LEPAGE.

LEPIDUS, Marcus Aemilius (d. 13 B.C.), Roman politician, declared for Caesar against Pompey (49 B.C.), and was by Caesar made dictator of Rome and his colleague in the consulate (46 B.C.). He supported Anthony, and became one of the triumvirate with Octavian and Antony, with Africa for his province (40–39 B.C.). He thought he could maintain himself in Sicily against Octavian, but his soldiers deserted him.

LE PLAY, Pierre Guillaume Frédéric (1806–1882), French political economist and engineer, was born at Honfleur, and lived in Paris, where he was professor in the School of Mines. He was one of the first to realize the importance of sociology and its effect on economics; he stressed the need for coopera-tion between employer and employee without intervention from government. See his *Les Œuvriers européens* (1855) and *Reforme sociale en France* (1864).

LEPSIUS, Karl Richard (1810–84), German Egyptologist, was born at Naumburg. His first work on palaeography as an instrument of philology (1834) obtained the Volney prize of the French Institute. In 1836 at Rome he studied Egyptology, Nubian, Etruscan, and Oscan, writing numerous treat-ises. In 1842–45 he was at the head of an antiquarian expedition sent to Egypt by the king of Prussia, and in 1846 was appointed professor in Berlin. His *Denkmäler aus Aegypten und Aethiopien* (12 vols. 1849–60) remains a masterpiece ; his *Chronologie der Aegypter* laid the foundation for a scientific treatment of early Egyptian history. Other works are his letters from Egypt, Ethiopia and Sinai (1852), the *Königsbuch* (1858), the *Todtenbuch* (1867), the Egyptian Book of the Dead. He wrote on Chinese, Arabic and Assyrian philology; and was a member of the Royal Academy, director of the Egyptian section of the Royal Museum, and chief-librarian of the Royal Library at Berlin. See Life by Ebers (1885, trans. New York 1887).

LERINS, Vincent of. See VINCENTIUS.

LERMONTOV, Mikhail Yurevich (1814–41), Russian poet, was born, of Scottish extraction (Learmont), in Moscow. He attended the Moscow University for a short time and then the military cavalry school of St Petersburg, where he received a commission in the Guards. A poem which he wrote in 1837 on the death of Pushkin caused his arrest and he was sent to the Caucasus. Reinstated, he was again banished following a duel with the son of the French ambassador. Another duel was the cause of his death in 1841. He started writing at an early age, but much of his work was not published until the last years of his short life and his fame was posthumous. The sublime scenery of the Caucasus inspired his best poetic pieces, such as ' The Novice ', ' The Demon ', ' Ismail

Bey', &c. His novel, *A Hero of our Time* (1839; trans. 1912, 1928, 1940), was a masterpiece of prose writing. He wrote also a romantic verse play, *Masquerade.* See *Poems*, ed. by E. N. Steinhart, with trans., biography, &c. (1917), and *Lermontov in English* by Heifetz (N.Y. 1942), and studies by Laurin (1959) and Mersereau (1962).

LEROUX, Pierre, *lĕ-roo* (1797–1871), French Humanitarian, born near Paris, influenced George Sand and with her founded *Revue Indépendente* (1841). A member of the Constituent Assembly and the Legislative Assembly he was exiled from 1851 to 1869 after opposing Louis Napoleon's *coup d'état.* He wrote *De l'Humanité* (1840) and *De l'Egalité* (1848).

LE SAGE, Alain René, *lĕ-sazh* (1668–1747), French novelist and dramatist, born at Sarzeau in Brittany, in 1692 went to Paris to study law, but an early marriage drove him to seek a less tardy livelihood in literature. The Abbé de Lionne, who had a good Spanish library, made Le Sage free of it, with a pension of 600 livres. The first fruit was a volume (1700) containing two plays imitated from Rojas and Lope de Vega. In 1702 *Le Point d'honneur*, from Rojas, failed on the stage. His next venture (1704) was a rifacimento of Avellaneda's *Don Quixote.* In 1707 *Don César Ursin*, from Calderón, was played with success at court, and *Crispin rival de son maître* in the city; more successful was the *Diable boiteux* (largely from Luis Velez de Guevara). In 1708 the Théâtre-Français accepted but shelved one play and rejected another, afterwards altered into his famous *Turcaret.* In 1715 *Gil Blas* (vols. i and ii) came out, followed in 1717–21 by an attempt at an Orlando. In 1724 came vol. iii of *Gil Blas*; in 1726 a largely extended *Diable boiteux*; in 1732 *Guzman de Alfarache* and *Robert Chevalier de Beauchêne*; in 1734 *Estebanillo Gonzalez*; in 1735 vol. iv of *Gil Blas* and the *Journée des Parques*; in 1736–38 the *Bachelier de Salamanque*; in 1739 his plays, in two vols.; in 1740 *La Valise trouvée*, a volume of letters; and in 1743 the *Mélange amusant*, a collection of facetiae. The death of his son (1743), a promising actor, and his own increasing infirmities, made him abandon Paris and literary life, and retreat with his wife and daughter to Boulogne, where his second son held a canonry; and there he died in his eightieth year. Le Sage's reputation as a dramatist and as a novelist rests in each case on one work. The author of *Turcaret* might have become, but did not, almost a second Molière; the author of *Gil Blas* stands in the front rank of the novelists. Some deny originality to one who borrowed ideas, incidents and tales from others as Le Sage did; but he was the first to perceive the capabilities of the picaresque novel. His delightful style makes him the prince of raconteurs, and the final effect of his work is all his own. See works by Barberet (1887), Claretie (1890–94) and Lintilhac (1893), and F. C. Green, *French Novels, Manners and Ideas* (1928).

LESCOT, Pierre, *les-kō* (c. 1510–78), French Renaissance architect, born in Paris. One of the greatest architects of his time, among

his works are the screen of St G l'Auxerrois, the Fontaine des Innocer the Hôtel de Ligneris. His masterpie the Louvre, one wing of which he com rebuilt.

LESKIEN, August, *les-keen'* (1840- German Slavonic philologist, born a became one of the 'Young Gramma at Leipzig, where he was a professor 1870. Of his writings on Slavonic lan most important are his *Handbuc Altbulgarischen* (1871) and *Deklinati Slavisch-Litauischen und Germanischen (*

LESLIE, Lesly, or Lesley, the Family first found between 1171 and 1199 in p sion of the pastoral parish of Lesslyn or in Aberdeenshire, and was ennobled in when George Leslie of Rothes was Earl of Rothes and Lord Leslie. The f earl was father of Norman Leslie, Mas Rothes, chief actor in the murder of Ca Beaton. John, sixth earl (1600–41), wa of the ablest of the Covenanting leaders. son John (1630–81) became lord chan of Scotland in 1667, and in 1680 was cr Duke of Rothes, &c. These honours be extinct upon his death without male iss 1681. The earldom of Rothes went t elder daughter, in whose family the titl continued. The Balquhain branch gave to several men of mark, such as the le John Leslie (q.v.), Bishop of Ross, champion of Mary, Queen of Scots; Alexander Leslie of Auchintoul, a ge in the Muscovite service (died 1663); Charles Leslie. Other distinguished men of the family were:

(1) **Alexander** (c. 1580–1661), who be field-marshal of Sweden under Gust Adolphus. Recalled to Scotland in 1 he took command of the Covenanting a and in 1641 was made Earl of Leven Lord Balgony. His honours and l eventually passed to his great-gran David Melville, third Earl of Leven second Earl of Melville. See *Life Campaigns*, by Sanford Terry (1899).

(2) **David** (1601–82), fifth son of the Lord Lindores (a son of the fifth Ea Rothes), served under Gustavus Adol and, returning to Scotland in 1640, act lieutenant-general to the Earl of Leven was present at Marston Moor, and def Montrose at Philiphaugh. Route Cromwell at Dunbar in 1650, and prisoner by him at Worcester in 165 was imprisoned in the Tower till the Re tion. He was made Lord Newark in 1

(3) **Walter** (1606–67), a cadet of the quhain line, distinguished himself i Austrian army, and in 1637 was cre count, as a reward for his services i murder of Wallenstein. He was succ (1667) by his nephew, James, Austrian marshal. The title became extinct in 1

LESLIE, (1) **Charles** (1650–1722), nor born at Dublin, became chancellor cathedral of Connor in 1687. Depri the Revolution for declining the o allegiance, he retired to England and against Papists, Deists, Socinians, Jew Quakers, as well as in support of th juring interests. He was mostly wi

Pretender in France and Italy (1713–21), and then returning to Ireland, died at Glaslough. His *Short and Easy Method with the Jews* appeared in 1684; his *Short and Easy Method with the Deists* in 1697; he issued a collected edition of his *Theological Works* in 1721 (new ed. 1832). See Life by R. J. Leslie (1885).

(2) **Charles Robert** (1794–1859), genre painter, was born in London of American parentage. Educated from 1800 at Philadelphia, in 1811 he returned to England and entered as a student in the Royal Academy. His paintings were mostly scenes from famous plays and novels. He was elected R.A. in 1824. In 1833 he was for one year professor of Drawing at West Point, New York, and from 1848 to 1852 he was professor of Painting at the Royal Academy. His lectures were published in the *Handbook for Young Painters* (1855). He wrote a Life of Constable (1843), and began one of Reynolds, completed by Tom Taylor, who edited his *Autobiographical Recollections* (1860). His son, **George Dunlop** (1835–1921), born in London, aimed ' to paint pictures from the sunny side of English domestic life ', was elected R.A. in 1876. He wrote *Letters to Marco* (1893), *Riverside Letters*, and *Inner Life of the Royal Academy* (1914).

(3) **Frank**, the name adopted by **Henry Carter** (1821–80), English illustrator and journalist, who was born at Ipswich. At seventeen he entered a London mercantile house and the success of sketches sent by him to the *Illustrated London News* led him to join its staff. In 1848 he went to the United States, assumed the name Frank Leslie, and in 1854 founded the *Gazette of Fashion* and the *New York Journal*. *Frank Leslie's Illustrated Newspaper* began in 1855 (German and Spanish editions later), the *Chimney Corner* in 1865; he also started the *Boys' and Girls' Weekly*, the *Lady's Journal*, &c.

(4) **John** (1527–96), Scottish prelate, son of the rector of Kingussie, studied at King's College, Aberdeen, at Paris, and at Poitiers, and in 1566 became Bishop of Ross. A zealous partisan of Queen Mary, he joined her at Tutbury in 1569, suffered imprisonment, and in 1574 went to France. He died in a monastery near Brussels. His Latin history of Scotland *De Origine, Moribus, et Rebus Gestis Scotorum* (Rome, 1578) was rendered into Scots in 1596 by a Scottish Benedictine of Ratisbon, Father James Dalrymple (ed. by Father Cody, Scottish Text Society 1884–91).

(5) **Sir John** (1766–1832), Scottish natural philosopher, born at Largo, studied at St Andrews and Edinburgh, and travelled as tutor in America and on the Continent, meanwhile engaging in experimental research. The fruits of his labours were a translation of Buffon's *Birds* (1793), the invention of a differential thermometer, a hygrometer and a photometer, and *Inquiry into Heat* (1804). In 1805 he obtained the chair of Mathematics at Edinburgh, though keenly opposed by the ministers as a follower of Hume. In 1810 he succeeded in freezing water under the air pump. Transferred to the chair of Natural Philosophy (1819), he invented the pyroscope,

atmometer and aethrioscope. He was knighted in 1832. See Memoir by Macvey Napier (1838).

(6) **Thomas Edward Cliffe** (1827–82), Irish political economist, born in Co. Wexford, qualified for the bar, but in 1853 became professor of Economics and Jurisprudence at Belfast. His writings were published as *The Land Systems* (1870), studies on the land question in Ireland, Belgium, and France, and *Essays in Political and Moral Philosophy* (1879). He was one of the founders of the historic method of political economy.

(7) **Walter, Count**. See LESLIE Family (3).

LESPINASSE, Claire Françoise, or Jeanne Julie Eléonore de (1732–76), was born at Lyons, an illegitimate daughter of the Countess d'Albon. At first a teacher, she became in 1754 companion to Madame du Deffand, whose friends, especially d'Alembert, she quickly attached to herself, and after the inevitable rupture, she was enabled to maintain a salon of her own which became a centre for the literary figures of her day. The charm she exercised was in no way due to beauty. Her passion for the Marquis de Mora, and later for M. de Guibert, cost her the deepest pangs, when the first died and the second married. Many of her letters (aglow with fire and passion) to her two lovers have been published since 1809. See also her *Lettres inédites* (1887; mostly to Condorcet); *Letters* (trans. 1902); *Love Letters to and from the Comte de Guibert* (1929); books by C. Jebb (1908), Marquis de Ségur (new Eng. ed. 1913), and N. Royde-Smith (1931).

LESSEPS, Ferdinand, Vicomte de (1805–94), French engineer, born at Versailles, a cousin of the Empress Eugénie, from 1825 held diplomatic posts at Lisbon, Tunis, Cairo, &c. In 1854 he conceived his scheme for a Suez Canal, and in 1856 obtained a concession from the viceroy. The works were begun in 1860, and completed in August 1869. He received the Grand Cross of the Legion of Honour, an English knighthood, election to the Academy, &c. In 1881 work began on his stupendous scheme for a Panamá Canal; but in 1892–93 the management was charged with breach of trust, and five directors were condemned—Lesseps, now a broken old man, to five years' imprisonment and a fine, as was also his son Charles. Charles was released in June 1893; his father, who had been too ill to be taken from his house, died December 7, 1894. Lesseps wrote an *Histoire du canal de Suez* (1875–79; trans. 1876) and *Souvenirs de quarante ans* (1887; trans. 1887). See Lives by Bertrand and Ferrier (Paris 1887), Barnett Smith (2nd ed. 1895) and C. Beatty (1956).

LESSING, Gotthold Ephraim (1729–81), German man of letters, was born, a pastor's son, at Kamenz in Saxony, and in 1746 entered as a theological student at Leipzig. Soon he was writing plays in the French style, and leaving Leipzig in debt, at Berlin joined the unorthodox Mylius in publishing *Beiträge zur Historie des Theaters* (1750), and independently wrote plays, translated and did literary hack-work; his chief support was the *Vossische Zeitung*, to which he contributed criticisms. In 1751 he withdrew

to Wittenberg, took his master's degree, and produced a series of *Vindications* of unjustly maligned or forgotten writers, such as Cardan, Lemnius, &c. Again at Berlin he in *Ein Vademecum für Herrn S. G. Lange* (1754) displayed unrelenting hostility to pretentious ignorance; with Moses Mendelssohn he wrote an essay on *Pope, ein Metaphysiker* (1755). His successful tragedy *Miss Sara Sampson* (1755) is after English models. In 1758 he was assisting Mendelssohn and Nicolai with a new critical Berlin journal, in which he revolted from the dictatorship of French taste, combated the inflated pedantry of the Gottsched school, and extolled Shakespeare. While secretary to the governor of Breslau he wrote his famous *Laokoon* (1766), a critical treatise defining the limits of poetry and the plastic arts. The comedy *Minna von Barnhelm* (1767) is the first German comedy on the grand scale. Appointed playwright to a new theatre at Hamburg in 1767, he wrote the *Hamburgische Dramaturgie* (1769), in which he finally overthrew the dictatorship of the French drama. The Hamburg theatre failed, and Lessing was soon in the thick of a controversy, this time with Klotz, a Halle professor, producing the *Briefe antiquarischen Inhalts* (1769) and *Wie die Alten den Tod gebildet* (1769). In 1769 the Duke of Brunswick appointed Lessing Wolfenbüttel librarian; and he at once began to publish some of the less-known treasures of the library in *Zur Geschichte und Litteratur* (1773–81). In 1772 he wrote the great tragedy *Emilia Galotti*. Shortly before his marriage he spent eight months in Italy as companion to the young Prince Leopold of Brunswick. In 1774–78 he published the *Wolfenbüttelsche Fragmente*, a rationalist attack on orthodox Christianity from the pen of Reimarus (q.v.), which, universally attributed to Lessing, provoked a storm of refutations. The best of Lessing's counter-attacks were *Anti-Goeze* (1778) and the fine dramatic poem, *Nathan der Weise* (1779), one of the noblest pleas for toleration ever penned. Later works were *Erziehung des Menschengeschlechts* (1780) and *Ernst und Falk* (1778–80), five dialogues on free-masonry. Lessing died at Brunswick. His *Sämmtliche Schriften*, ed. by Lachmann, were reissued by Muncker in 1886–1907. His chief works have been translated into English. See Lives by Danzel and Guhrauer (2nd ed. 1880), Düntzer (1882), Stahr (10th ed. 1900), Erich Schmidt (4th ed. 1923), Borinski (1900), Sime (1877), Helen Zimmern (1878), and Rolleston (1889)—the last three in English. See also J. G. Robertson, *Lessing's Dramatic Theory* (1939).

L'ESTRANGE, Sir Roger (1616–1704), English journalist, born at Hunstanton, narrowly escaped hanging as a royalist spy for a plot to seize Lynn in 1644, and was imprisoned in Newgate, whence he escaped after four years. Pardoned by Cromwell in 1653, he lived quietly till the Restoration made him licenser of the press. He fought in all the quarrels of the time with a shower of pamphlets, vigorous and not coarser than those of his antagonists; and he holds a place in the history of journalism by his papers, *The Public Intelligencer*

(1663–66) and *The Observator* (1681–87). He translated Aesop's *Fables*, Seneca's *Morals*, Cicero's *Offices*, the *Colloquies* of Erasmus, Quevedo's *Visions*, and Josephus. He was knighted in 1685. See Life by G. Kitchin (1913).

LE SUEUR, lě sü-œr, (1) **Eustache** (1617–55), French painter, pupil of Vouet, whose style he imitated until, about 1645, he came under the influence of Nicolas Poussin's classical style. In his early style his most important work was the decoration of two rooms in the Hôtel Lambert in Paris and in his later manner paintings of the life of St Bruno for the Charterhouse of Paris. The Louvre possesses 36 religious pictures by him, and 13 mytho-logical.
   (2) **Hubert** (*c.* 1580–*c.* 1670), French sculptor, born in Paris, came to England about 1628. His most important work was the equestrian statue of Charles I at Charing Cross (1633).

LESZCZYŃSKI. See STANISLAUS.

LETHINGTON. See MAITLAND.

LETTS, Thomas (1803–73), English book-binder, born at Stockwell, London, began after his father's death in 1803 to manufacture diaries and by 1839 was producing twenty-eight varieties.

LEUCHTENBERG. See BEAUHARNAIS.

LEUCIPPUS (fl. *c.* 400 B.C.), Greek philo-sopher, born at Miletus (not Abdera), was the founder of the Atomic school of Greek philosophy and forerunner of Democritus. He wrote *The Great World System* and *On Mind*.

LEUCKART, Karl Georg Friedrich Rudolf, *loy'-kart* (1822–98), German zoologist, born at Helmstedt, studied at Göttingen, and in 1850 became professor of Zoology at Giessen, in 1869 at Leipzig. His work on classi-fication is important and especially note-worthy was his division of the Radiata into Coelenterata and Echinodermata. He dis-tinguished himself by his study of the Entozoa, writing his great work *Parasites of Man* from 1879–94 (trans. 1886).

LEUTZE, Emanuel, *loy'tzě* (1816–68), Ger-man painter, born at Gmünd in Württemberg, was brought up in America, studied in Europe 1841–59, then settled in New York in 1859. His paintings were mainly scenes from American history, the best known of which was *Washington crossing the Delaware*.

LEVAILLANT, François, *lě-vī-yã* (1753–1824), French traveller and ornithologist, was born at Paramaribo, Dutch Guiana, and studied in Paris. He explored in South Africa 1781–84, and wrote of his expeditions in *Voyage dans l'intérieur de l'Afrique* (1790), &c., and published books on birds.

LEVEN, Earl of. See LESLIE.

LEVER, (1) **Charles** (1806–72), Irish novelist, was born of purely English parentage in Dublin, graduated at Trinity College in 1827, and then went to Göttingen to study medicine. His most popular work, *Charles O'Malley,* is a reflex of his own college life in Dublin. About 1829 he spent some time in the backwoods of Canada and North America, and embodied his experiences in *Con Cregan* and *Arthur O'Leary*. He practised medicine at various Irish country towns, and in 1840 at Brussels. Returning to Dublin, he published *Jack Hinton* in 1843, and from 1842 to 1845 acted as editor of the *Dublin University Magazine*, and wrote further novels. In 1845 he again went to Brussels, Bonn, Karlsruhe, where he published the *Knight of Gwynne*, and to Florence, where he wrote *Roland Cashel*. At Spezia *Luttrel of Arran* and three other novels were produced in rapid succession. Then, completely changing his style, he wrote the *Fortunes of Glencore*, followed by *The Martins of Cro-Martin* and *The Daltons*. Lever was in 1858 appointed British vice-consul at Spezia, and continued to write, his work including some racy essays in *Blackwood's* by ' Cornelius O'Dowd '. In 1867 he was promoted to the consulship at Trieste, where he died. Lever's work contained brilliant, rollicking sketches of a phase of Irish life which was passing away, though no doubt his caricatures created a false idea of Irish society and character. His daughter edited his novels (37 vols. 1897–99). See *Life and Letters* by Downey (1906), and L. Stevenson, *Dr Quicksilver* (1939).

(2) **William Hesketh, 1st Viscount Leverhulme** (1851–1925), British soapmaker and philanthropist, born at Bolton. Beginning in his father's grocery business, he opened new shops and in 1886 with his brother, James, started the manufacture of soap from vegetable oils instead of tallow and the new town of Port Sunlight was founded. Among his many benefits, he endowed at Liverpool University a school of tropical medicine and gave Lancaster House to the nation. He was made a Baron in 1917 and a Viscount in 1922. See W. H. L. Leverhulme, *Viscount Leverhulme, by his Son* (1927).

LEVERRIER, Urbain Jean Joseph, *lê-ver-yay* (1811–77), French astronomer, born at St Lô, Normandy, in 1836 became teacher of astronomy at the Polytechnique. His *Tables de Mercure* and several memoirs gained him admission to the Academy in 1846. From disturbances in the motions of planets he inferred the existence of an undiscovered planet, and calculated the point in the heavens where, a few days afterwards, Neptune was actually discovered by Galle at Berlin. For this he received the Grand Cross of the Legion of Honour and a chair of Astronomy in the Faculty of Sciences. Elected in 1849 to the Legislative Assembly, he became counter-revolutionary. In 1852 Louis Napoleon made him a senator and in 1854 he succeeded Arago as director of the Observatory of Paris. See ADAMS (JOHN COUCH).

LEVESON-GOWER, George, 2nd Earl Granville, *loo'sèn gōr'* (1815–91), English statesman, was educated at Eton and Oxford, in 1836 became M.P. for Morpeth, in 1840 for Lichfield, and was for a brief period undersecretary for foreign affairs. He was a consistent Liberal and a freetrader. He succeeded to the peerage in 1846, and became foreign secretary in 1851, president of the council in 1853, and leader of the House of Lords in 1855. Having failed to form a ministry in 1859, he joined Lord Palmerston's second administration. He retired with Earl Russell in 1866, having been made lord warden of the Cinque Ports in 1865. In December, 1868 he became colonial secretary in

Gladstone's first ministry, and in 1870 foreign secretary, as again in 1880–85, when he had to face the troubles in Egypt and the Sudan, differences with Germany and France, and the threatened rupture with Russia over the Afghan boundary question. He returned once more for a few months to office as colonial secretary in 1886 and supported Gladstone's home-rule policy. See Life by E. Fitzmaurice (1905).

LEVI. See MATTHEW, SAINT.

LEVI CIVITA, Tullio, *lay'vee chee-vee'ta* (1873–1942), Italian mathematician, noteworthy for his studies on differential geometry and relativity. Professor of Mechanics at Padua and at Rome from 1918 to 1938, he was a member of the Royal Society in 1930. Among his works are *Lezioni di meccanica rationali* (1922) in collaboration with U. Amaldi, *Questioni di meccanica classica et relativisti* (1924) and *The Absolute Differential Calculus* (1937).

LEVITA, Elias, *lê-vee'ta* (1465–1549), Jewish grammarian and exegete, was born at Neustadt near Nuremberg. An expulsion of Jews forced him to Italy, where he taught successively in Padua (1504), Venice, Rome (1514), and finally (1527) Venice again. He wrote on Job, the Psalms, Proverbs, Amos, and the vowel points; a Hebrew grammar; and a Talmudic and Targumic Dictionary. See Life by J. Leir (Breslau 1888).

LEWALD, Fanny, *lay'valt* (1811–89), German novelist, born at Königsberg, in 1855 married Adolf Stahr (1805–76), a Berlin critic. She was an enthusiastic champion of women's rights. Her best book is perhaps *Von Geschlecht zu Geschlecht* (1863–65). An English translation of *Stella* (1884) appeared in the same year. She wrote records of travel in Italy (1847) and Great Britain (1852), and published an autobiography, *Meine Lebensgeschichte* (1861–63). See K. Frenzel, *Erinnerungen und Strömungen* (1890).

LEWES, George Henry (1817–78), English littérateur, was born in London, a grandson of the comedian, **Charles Lee Lewes** (1740–1803). Educated partly at Greenwich under Dr Burney, and partly in Jersey and Brittany, he left school early to enter first a notary's office, and then the house of a Russian merchant. He next tried walking the hospitals, but could not stand the operating room. In 1838 he went to Germany for nearly two years, studying the life, language and literature of the country. On his return to London he fell to work writing about anything and everything as a Penny Encyclopaedist and Morning Chronicler, as a contributor afterwards to a dozen more journals, reviews and magazines, and as editor of the *Leader* (1851–54), and of the *Fortnightly* (1865–66), which he himself founded. He was unhappily married and had children when his connection with George Eliot (q.v.) began in July 1854; it ended only with his death at their house in Regent's Park. His works, besides a tragedy and two novels (1841–48), include *The Spanish Drama* (1846); a *Life of Robespierre* (1848); *Comte's Philosophy of the Sciences* (1853), which is more than a translation; the admirable *Life and Works of Goethe* (1855);

Studies in Animal Life (1862); *Aristotle* (1864); *On Actors and the Art of Acting* (1875); and *Problems of Life and Mind* (1874–79). See A. T. Kitahel, *George Lewes and George Eliot* (1934).

LEWIS, (1) **Alun** (1915–44), Welsh poet, born in S. Wales, was killed in Arakan. His poetry is contained in *Raiders' Dawn* (1942) and *Ha! Ha! the Trumpets* (1944).

(2) **Clive Staples** (1898–1963), British medievalist and Christian apologist, born at Belfast, professor of Medieval and Renaissance English at Cambridge from 1954, published his first book *Dymer* (1926) under the name of Clive Hamilton. It is a narrative poem in rhyme royal, at once satirical and idealistic, a flavour which characterizes most of his work. His *Allegory of Love* was awarded the Hawthornden Prize (1936). His widest-known book is *The Screwtape Letters* (1942). Other titles include *The Problem of Pain* (1940), *Beyond Personality* (1944), works of scientific fiction including *Out of the Silent Planet* (1938) and *Perelandra* (1943), and books for children of which *The Last Battle* was awarded the Carnegie Prize in 1957. See Life by C. Walsh (1949).

(3) **Sir George Cornewall** (1806–63), English statesman and author, born in London, was educated at Eton and Christ Church, Oxford. Called to the bar in 1831, he became a Poor-Law commissioner in 1839. Liberal M.P. for Herefordshire 1847–52, for the Radnor Boroughs from 1855, he was chancellor of the exchequer 1855–58, home secretary 1859–61, and then war secretary. He edited the *Edinburgh Review* from 1852 to 1855 and succeeded to a baronetcy in 1855. He wrote *Origin of the Romance Languages* (1835), *Inquiry into the Credibility of Ancient Roman History* (1855–against Niebuhr), *Astronomy of the Ancients* (1859), *Dialogue on the Best Form of Government* (1859), &c. See his *Letters* (1870) and Bagehot's *Literary Studies* (1879).

(4) **Sir George Henry** (1833–1911), English criminal solicitor, was born at Holborn. His cases included the Hatton Garden diamond robbery, and he was solicitor for Parnell and other Irish nationalists (1888–89). He was knighted in 1893 and made a baronet in 1902.

(5) **John Llewellyn** (1880–1969), American labour leader, born in Iowa, was president of the United Mine Workers' Union from 1920 to 1960. In 1935 he formed a combination of unions, the Congress of Industrial Organizations, of which he was president till 1940. A skilful negotiator, he has made the miners' union one of the most powerful in the United States.

(6) **Matthew Gregory**, nicknamed **Monk** (1775–1818), English novelist, born in London, was educated at Westminster, Christ Church, Oxford, and Weimar, where he was introduced to Goethe. In 1794 he went as an attaché to The Hague, and there, inspired by Glanvill and the *Mysteries of Udolpho*, wrote *Ambrosio, or the Monk* (1795), the gruesome, unclean romance which made him so famous that in 1798 his invitation to dine at an Edinburgh hotel could elate Scott as nothing before or afterwards. A musical drama, *The Castle Spectre* (1798),

The Bravo of Venice (1804) and a host more of blood-and-thunder plays, novels and tales are mostly forgotten. In 1796 he entered parliament as a silent member, and in 1812 he inherited from his father two large estates in Jamaica. So, to better the condition of his slaves there, he made the two voyages, in 1815–17, which furnished materials for his one really valuable work, the posthumous *Journal of a West India Proprietor* (1834; ed. by M. Wilson, 1929). On his way home he died of yellow fever. See his *Life and Correspondence* (1839), Birkhead's *The Tale of Terror* (1921) and A. M. Killen, *Le Roman terrifiant* (1923).

(7) **(Harry) Sinclair** (1885–1951), American novelist, born in Sauk Center, Minnesota. The son of a doctor, educated at Yale, he became a journalist and wrote several minor works before *Main Street* (1920), the first of a series of best-selling novels satirizing the arid materialism and intolerance of American small-town life. *Babbitt* (1922) still lends its title as a synonym for middle-class American philistinism. Other titles of this period are *Martin Arrowsmith* (1925), *Elmer Gantry* (1927) and *Dodsworth* (1929). Thereafter he tended to exonerate the ideologies and self-sufficiency he had previously pilloried, though he continued to be eagerly read. His later novels include *Cass Timberlane* (1945) and *Kingsblood Royal* (1947). He refused the Pulitzer prize for *Arrowsmith*, but accepted the Nobel prize for literature in 1930, being the first American writer to receive it. See Lives by C. Van Doren (N.Y., 1933) and M. Schorer (1963).

(8) **(Percy) Wyndham** (1884–1957), English artist, writer and critic, born in Bay of Fundy, Maine. He studied at the Slade School of Art, and with Ezra Pound founded *Blast*, the magazine of the Vorticist school. His writings are satirical, and include the novels *Tarr* (1918), *Childermass* (1928), *Men Without Art* (1934), and two autobiographical books *Blasting and Bombardiering* (1937) and *Rude Assignment* (1950). His paintings include works of abstract art, a series of war pictures, imaginative works and portraits, notably those of Eliot and Edith Sitwell. Five works of his are in the Tate Gallery, London. See studies by Porteous (1933), Kenner (1954), Tomlin (1955), *The Art of Wyndham Lewis* (ed. Read, 1951), and his *Letters* (ed. by Rose, 1963).

LEYDEN, **John** (1775–1811), Scottish poet and orientalist, was born, a shepherd's son, at Denholm, Roxburghshire. He studied medicine, &c., at Edinburgh University, and was licensed as a preacher in 1798. He helped Scott to gather materials for his *Border Minstrelsy*, and his translations and poems in the *Edinburgh Magazine* attracted attention. In 1803 he sailed for India as assistant surgeon at Madras, travelled widely in the East, acquired 34 languages, and translated the gospels into five of them. He accompanied Lord Minto as interpreter to Java, and died of fever at Batavia. His ballads have taken a higher place than his longer poems, especially *Scenes of Infancy* (1803); his dissertation on Indo-Chinese languages is also well known. See Lives by Scott (1811), Reith (1908) and Seshadri (1913).

L'HÔPITAL, Michel de, *lō-pee-tal* (1507–73), French statesman, born at Aigueperse in Auvergne, studied law at Toulouse and Padua and settled as an advocate in Paris at thirty. In 1547–48 he represented Henry II at the Council of Trent, and then was in the household of the Duchess of Berri. In 1554 he became superintendent of finances, in 1560 chancellor of France. He strove to pacify the religious quarrel by staying the hand of the Catholic persecutors. After 1563 he lost ground and in 1568 resigned and retired to his estate near Étampes. His Latin poems, speeches, &c., appeared in 1824–25. See Lives by C. T. Atkinson (1900), A. E. Shaw (1905), R. Anchel (1937).

LHOTE, André, *lōt* (1885–1962), French artist, teacher, and writer on art, born at Bordeaux. He associated with the Cubists and in his painting he combined classic precision of composition and a free, sensitive use of colour, but his greatest influence was exerted through his writings, e.g., *Treatise on Landscape* (1939) and *Treatise on the Figure* (1950), and his teaching in Paris. See the monograph by P. Courthion (Paris 1936).

LIADOV, Anatol Konstantinovich, *lya'dof* (1855–1914), Russian composer, born at St Petersburg, where he studied under Rimsky-Korsakov. His works include music for the piano and the vivid nationalist symphonic poems *Baba-Yaga, Kikimora* and *The Enchanted Lake.* He also made collections of Russian folksongs, conducted and was professor at St Petersburg.

LIAQUAT ALI KHAN (1895–1951), Pakistani statesman, after leaving Oxford became a member of the Inner Temple. He joined the Moslem League in 1923, and became prime minister of Pakistan in 1947. He was assassinated in 1951.

LIBANIUS (A.D. 314–393), Greek sophist, born at Antioch, taught at Athens, Constantinople and Antioch. A pagan, he yet was the instructor and friend of St Chrysostom and St Basil. See Lives by Petit (1866) and Sievers (1868).

LIBBY, Willard Frank (1908–), American scientist, born at Grand Valley, Colorado, studied and lectured at Berkeley, Cal., where he became associate professor in 1945. He did atom-bomb research (1941–45) on the separation of the isotopes of uranium at Columbia, and from 1945–54 was professor of Chemistry at Chicago. From 1954–59 he served on the U.S. Atomic Energy Commission. He was awarded the Nobel prize in chemistry (1960) for his part in the invention of the Carbon-14 method of determining the age of an object. From 1959 he has been professor of Chemistry at California University, and from 1962 director of the Institute of Geophysics.

LIBERIUS (d. 366), born in Rome, became pope in 352, but was banished in 355 for refusing to confirm the decree against Athanasius (q.v.). In 358 he regained the papal throne.

LICHTENBERG, Georg Christoph (1742–99), German physicist and satirist, born near Darmstadt, in 1770 became professor of Mathematics at Göttingen. He visited England, admired Garrick, and wrote a witty Commentary on Hogarth's plates (1794). See

works by Grisebach (1871), Meyer (1886), Lauchert (1893), Bouillier (1915).

LICK, James (1796–1876), a Californian millionaire, born at Fredericksburg, Pa., the founder of the Lick Observatory on Mount Hamilton.

LIDDELL, Henry George (1811–98), English scholar, from Charterhouse passed to Christ Church, Oxford, and took a double first in 1833. He became tutor of his college, and in 1845 professor of Moral Philosophy. Headmaster of Westminster 1846–55, he returned to Christ Church as dean, was vice-chancellor 1870–74, and resigned the deanship in 1891. The great *Greek Lexicon* (1843), based on Passow, was a joint work by him and Robert Scott, D.D. (1811–87), master of Balliol (1854–70), and then Dean of Rochester. Liddell also wrote a *History of Rome* (1855; abridged as *The Student's Rome*). See Life by Thompson (1899).

LIDDELL HART, Basil Henry (1895–1970), English military journalist and historian, born in Paris, educated at St Paul's and Cambridge, served in the 1914–18 war and retired from the army in 1927. He was responsible for various tactical developments during the war, and wrote the postwar official manual of Infantry Training (1920). He was military correspondent to the *Daily Telegraph* (1925–1935) and to *The Times* (1935–39). In 1937 he relinquished his position as personal adviser to the minister of war to publicize the need for immediate development of air power and mechanized warfare. He wrote more than thirty books on warfare, as well as biographies of Scipio, T. E. Lawrence, &c. See his *Memoirs* (2 vols., 1965).

LIDDON, Henry Parry (1829–90), English divine, born at North Stoneham, Hampshire, graduated at Oxford in 1850. Ordained in 1852, from 1854 to 1859 he was vice-principal of Cuddesdon Theological College, and in 1864 became a prebendary of Salisbury, in 1870 a canon of St Paul's, and Ireland professor of Exegesis at Oxford (till 1882). In 1866 he delivered his Bampton Lectures on the *Divinity of Our Lord.* He strongly opposed the Church Discipline Act of 1874, and as warmly supported Mr Gladstone's crusade against the Bulgarian atrocities in 1876. Canon Liddon was the most able and eloquent exponent of Liberal High Church principles. He died suddenly at Weston-super-Mare. An *Analysis of the Epistle to the Romans* was published in 1893; his Life of Pusey was edited by Johnston and Wilson. See his own Life by Johnston (1904).

LIE, lee, (1) **Jonas** (1833–1908), Norwegian novelist and poet, was born at Eker near Drammen and abandoned law for literature. His novels, which give realistic pictures of fisher-life in Norway, include *The Visionary* (1870; trans. 1894), *One of Life's Slaves* (1883; trans. 1896), &c. He also wrote *Weird Tales* (trans. 1893) and comedies.

(2) **Marius Sophus** (1842–99), Norwegian mathematician, was educated at Christiania (Oslo) University, where he became an assistant tutor and in 1872 professor of Mathematics. In 1886 was appointed professor at Leipzig but returned to Christiania in 1898. He is specially noted for his

theory of tangential transformations. See his *Theorie der Transformationsgruppen* (1893).

(3) **Trygve Halvdan** (1896–1968), Norwegian lawyer, born in Oslo, was a Labour member of the Norwegian parliament and held several posts, including minister of justice and minister of supply and shipping, before having to flee in 1940 with the government to Britain, where he acted as its foreign minister until 1945. He was elected secretary-general of the U.N. in 1946, but resigned in 1952. He was minister of industry (1963–1964) and of commerce and shipping from 1964. See his *In the Cause of Peace* (1954).

LIEBER, Francis, *lee'ber* (1800–72), German writer on law, government, &c., was born in Berlin, but in 1827 went to America for political reasons and became a naturalized American and professor of History and Political Economy at South Carolina College, Columbia and Columbia Law School. See Life by T. Sergeant Perry (Boston 1882).

LIEBERMANN, Max, *lee'ber-man* (1847–1935), German painter and etcher, born in Berlin, studied at Weimar and in Paris, where he first won fame. In Germany from 1878 he painted open-air studies and scenes of humble life which were often sentimental. Later, however, his work became more colourful and romantic, and, influenced by the French impressionists, he became the leading painter of that school in his own country.

LIEBIG, Justus, Freiherr von, *lee'biKH* (1803–1873), German chemist, born at Darmstadt, studied at Bonn and Erlangen, and in 1822 went to Paris, where Gay-Lussac took him into his laboratory. In 1824 he became professor of Chemistry at Giessen, and in 1852 at Munich. In 1845 he was created Baron. Liebig was one of the most illustrious chemists of his age; equally great in method and in practical application, he made his mark in organic chemistry, animal chemistry, the doctrine of alcohols, &c. He was the founder of agricultural chemistry, a discoverer of chloroform and chloral and with Wohler (q.v.) of the benzoyl radical. By him an admirable chemical laboratory, practically the first, was established at Giessen. He vastly extended the method of organic analysis, and invented appliances for analysis by combustion and Liebig's condenser. His most important treatises were on the analysis of organic bodies (1837), *Animal Chemistry* (1842), *Organic Chemistry* (1843), and *Agricultural Chemistry* (1855), &c., and numerous papers in scientific journals (317 in the Royal Society's *Transactions*). See four volumes of his Correspondence (1884–92), and books by A. W. Hofmann (1876), W. A. Shenstone (1895), Vollhard (1909) and Benrath (1921).

LIEBKNECHT, *leeb'kneKHt*, (1) **Karl** (1871–1919), German barrister and politician, son of (2), was a member of the Reichstag from 1912 to 1916. During the 1914–18 war he was imprisoned as an independent, anti-militarist, social democrat. He took part in the Revolution (1918) and was murdered.

(2) **Wilhelm** (1826–1900), German social democrat, born at Giessen, for his part in the Baden insurrection of 1848–49 had to take refuge in Switzerland and England. He returned to Germany in 1862 and during a two-years' imprisonment was elected to the Reichstag (1874). With Bebel (q.v.) he edited *Vorwärts*.

LIEBRECHT, Felix, *leeb'reKHt* (1812–90), German writer, born at Namslau in Silesia, was professor of German at Liège 1849–67. He early made himself known by articles on the origin and diffusion of folk tales, and by translations enriched with annotations. Among these are Basile's *Pentamerone* (1846), *Barlaam und Josaphat* (1847), and Dunlop's *Geschichte der Prosadichtungen* (1851).

LIEVEN, Dorothea, Princess, *née* von Benkendorf (1784–1857), early married the Russian diplomatist Prince Lieven (1774–1857), and from 1837 lived mostly in Paris, where her salon was much visited by diplomats. See her Correspondence with Earl Grey (1891), letters from London (1902), *Unpublished Diary* (1925), and Parry's *The Correspondence of Lord Aberdeen and Princess Lieven* (1939).

LIEVENSZ (Lievens), Jan (1607–74), Dutch historical painter and etcher, born at Leyden. A friend of Rembrandt, he shared a studio with him in Leyden. He visited England and lived in Antwerp before returning to Holland, where his paintings of allegorical subjects and his portraits became very successful.

LIFAR, Serge, *li-far'y* (1905–), Russian dancer and choreographer, born in Kiev, became a student and friend of Diaghilev, whose company he joined at the age of eighteen. Since his first important appearance in *La Boutique fantasque*, he has danced with Pavlova, Karsavina and Spessirtzeva, and his many successes include *Le Pas d'Acier*, *Apollon* and *L'Après-Midi d'un faune*. He scored his first triumph as a choreographer in Paris in 1929 with *Créatures de Promethée* and since then he has been the force and the genius behind the Paris Opéra. He has written a biography of Diaghilev (1940) and *The Three Graces* (trans. 1959).

LIGHTFOOT, (1) Hannah. See GEORGE III.

(2) **John** (1602–75), Hebraist, born at Stoke-upon-Trent, studied at Christ's College, Cambridge, and in 1630 became rector of Ashley, Staffordshire, in 1643 of St Bartholomew's, London, and in 1644 of Great Munden, Herts. He was one of the most influential members of the Westminster Assembly, but, as an ' Erastian ', often stood alone. In 1650 he was appointed master of Catharine Hall, Cambridge, in 1654–55 vice-chancellor, and in 1668 a prebendary of Ely, where he died. Lightfoot's works include the unfinished *Harmony of the Four Evangelists* (1644–50), *Commentary upon the Acts of the Apostles* (1645), and *Horae Hebraicae et Talmudicae* (1658–74), the great labour of his life. The best edition of his works is by Pitman, with Life (1822–25).

(3) **Joseph Barber** (1828–89), Bishop of Durham, was born at Liverpool, and from King Edward's School, Birmingham, passed in 1847 to Trinity College, Cambridge, where he graduated in 1851. Elected fellow in 1852, and ordained in 1854, he became tutor of Trinity in 1857, Hulsean professor of divinity in 1861, canon of St Paul's in 1871, Lady Margaret professor of Divinity at Cambridge

in 1875, and Bishop of Durham in 1879. A supreme grammarian and textual critic, he wrote admirable commentaries on the Pauline epistles, *Galatians* (1860), *Philippians* (1868), *Colossians and Philemon* (1875). His many other works include *On a Fresh Revision of the English New Testament* (1871), *Biblical Essays* (1893), and several volumes of sermons. The work of the Church Temperance Society and the White Cross Army was furthered by his exertions. He died at Bournemouth, and was buried at Durham. See short *Life* by Westcott (1894) and *Lightfoot of Durham*, by Eden and Macdonald (1932).

LIGNE, Charles Joseph, Prince de, *leen'y'* (1735–1814), Austrian soldier, born at Brussels, son of an imperial field-marshal whose seat was at Ligne near Tournai. He served at Kolin, Leuthen, Hochkirch and the siege of Belgrade (1789). A skilful diplomatist, the favourite of Maria Theresa and Catharine of Russia, and the friend of Frederick the Great, Voltaire and Rousseau, he wrote *Mélanges* (34 vols. 1795–1811), *Oeuvres posthumes* (1817), a Life of Prince Eugene (1809), and *Lettres et Pensées* (1809).

LIGONIER, John, 1st Earl, *lig-ō-neer'* (1680–1770), British soldier, born at Castres of Huguenot parentage, escaped to Dublin in 1697, and from 1702 served with high distinction under Marlborough. Colonel from 1720 of a splendid Irish regiment of dragoons, he commanded the foot at Fontenoy (1745), was taken prisoner at Val (1747), was made commander-in-chief and a viscount (1757), an earl and field-marshal (1766). He was buried in Westminster Abbey. See Life by R. Whitworth (1958).

LIGUORI, St Alfonso Maria de, *lee-gwō'ree* (1696–1787), Italian bishop, born at Naples, forsook law to take orders, and in 1732 with twelve companions founded the order of Liguorians or Redemptorists. In 1762 he became Bishop of Sant' Agata de' Goti, and proved an ideal bishop; but he resigned in 1775, and returned to his order. He was canonized in 1839. His works, edited by Monza in 70 vols., embrace divinity, casuistry, exegesis, history, canon law, hagiography, asceticism, even poetry. See Lives by Berthe (trans. 1906) and Baron Angot des Rotours (trans. 1916).

LI HUNG-CHANG, *lee-hoong-jang* (1823–1901), Chinese statesman, born at Hofei in Nganhui, took the Hanlin degree in 1849. In 1853, in the Taiping rebellion, he joined the Imperial army as secretary, was appointed a provincial judge, and in 1862 governor of Kiangsu, out of which, in conjunction with ' Chinese Gordon ', he drove the rebels in 1863. Made an hereditary noble of the third class, in 1864 he was appointed governor-general of the Kiang provinces, and in 1872 of Chih-li and senior grand secretary. He founded the Chinese navy and promoted a native mercantile marine. On the outbreak of the war with Japan (1894), Li, in supreme command in Korea, was thwarted by the incompetence, dishonesty and cowardice of inferior officers. The Chinese were swept out of Korea, and Li, whose policy was that of peace, was deprived of his honours and

summoned to Peking. He refused to comply, and the disastrous course of events soon compelled the emperor to restore him to honour. Through his efforts the war was brought to a termination in 1895, China ceding Formosa and paying a war indemnity of £35,000,000. Well aware of the value of Western culture and industry, he visited Europe and America in 1896. Intriguing with Russia, he fell in 1898. See his *Memoirs* (1913) and Life by J. O. P. Bland (1917).

LILBURNE, John (*c.* 1614–57), English Leveller or ultra-republican, born at Greenwich, and whipped and imprisoned by the Star Chamber in 1638, rose in the Parliamentary army to the rank of lieutenant-colonel. He became an indefatigable agitator, thought Cromwell's republic too aristocratic, and demanded greater liberty of conscience and numerous reforms. Repeatedly imprisoned for his treasonable pamphlets, he died at Eltham. See Life by P. Gregg (1961).

LILIENCRON, Detlev von, *lee'lee-en-krōn* (1844–1909), German poet and novelist, born at Kiel, fought in the Prussian army 1866 and 1870. He went to America but returned to Holstein in 1882, where for a time he held a civil service post. He is best known for his lyrics, which are fresh, lively and musical; his first volume *Adjutantenritte* appeared in 1883. Other volumes of verse were *Der Heidegänger* (1890), *Neue Gedichte* (1893) and *Gute Nacht* (1909). He also wrote, but not so successfully, novels and an epic poem *Poggfred* (1896). See Life by H. Spiero (Berlin 1913).

LILIENTHAL, Otto, *leel'yen-tahl* (1849–96), German aeronautical inventor, born at Anklam, studied bird-flight in order to build heavier-than-air flying machines resembling the birdman designs of Leonardo da Vinci. He made many short flights in his machines, but crashed to his death near Berlin in 1896. His brother, **Gustav** (1849–1933), continued his experiments and also invented a weather-proofing material. See Otto's *Der Vogelflug als Grundlage der Fliegerkunst* (1889) on the theory of flying machines.

LILLIE, Beatrice, by marriage **Lady Peel** (1898–   ), Canadian revue singer, born in Toronto, after an unsuccessful start as a drawing-room ballad singer found her true bent in 1914 in music hall and the new vogue of ' intimate revue ' which Charlot had brought over from Paris. An unrivalled comic singer, she made famous Noel Coward's ' Mad Dogs and Englishmen '. During World War II she played to the troops and was decorated by General de Gaulle. She married Sir Robert Peel, 5th Bart., in 1920.

LILLO, George (1693–1739), English dramatist and jeweller, born in London of mixed Dutch and English Dissenting parentage, wrote seven plays, including *George Barnwell* (1731) and *Fatal Curiosity* (1736), both tragedies edited by Sir A. W. Ward (1906). His *Arden of Feversham* (brought out 1759) is a weak version of the anonymous play of that title (1592). Among the first to put middle-class characters on the English stage he had a considerable influence on European drama. See Life by T. Davies prefixed to his

Dramatic Works (1810) and W. H. Hudson, *A Quiet Corner in a Library* (1915).

LILLY, William (1602–81), English astrologer, born at Diseworth, Leicestershire, in 1620 went to London, where for seven years he served an ancient citizen, married his widow, and on her death in 1633 inherited £1000. He took up astrology, and soon acquired a considerable fame and large profits. In 1634 he obtained permission to search for hidden treasure in the cloisters of Westminster, but was driven from his midnight work by a storm, which he ascribed to demons. From 1644 till his death he annually issued his *Merlinus Anglicus, Junior*, containing vaticinations. In the Civil War he attached himself to the Parliamentary party as soon as it promised to be successful, and was rewarded with a pension. After the Restoration he was imprisoned for a little, and was reapprehended on suspicion of knowing something about the great fire of London in 1666. He died at Hersham. He wrote nearly a score of works on astrology. See his *History of his Life and Times* (1715).

LILLYWHITE, Frederick (1792–1854), English cricketer, was born near Goodwood, and started as a bricklayer. Famous as a roundarm bowler, he did not become a professional cricketer until middle age. ' Me bowling, Pilch batting, and Box keeping wicket ' was his definition of cricket.

LILY, John. See LYLY.

LILYE, or Lily, William (*c*. 1466–1522), English classical grammarian, was born at Odiham, Hampshire, studied at Magdalen College, Oxford. He visited Jerusalem, Rhodes and Italy, and learned Greek from refugees from Constantinople. After teaching for a while in London he was appointed (1512) by Dean Colet first headmaster of his new school of St Paul's; this post he held till he was carried off by the plague. Lilye, who has good claims to be considered the first who taught Greek in London, had a hand in Colet's *Brevissima Institutio*, which, as corrected by Erasmus, and redacted by Lilye himself, was known as the *Eton Latin Grammar*. Besides this he wrote Latin poems (Basel 1518) and a volume of Latin verse against a rival schoolmaster (1521).

LIMBORCH, Philip van, *lim'bor*KH (1633–1712), Dutch theologian, was preacher at Gouda and Amsterdam, and became in 1668 professor in the Remonstrant or Arminian college at Amsterdam. Of his numerous works the most valuable are *Institutiones Theologiae Christianae* (1686, trans. 1702) and *History of the Inquisition* (trans. 1731).

LIMBURG, Pol, Henneguin and Hermann de, *lim'-bær*KH (fl. early 15th cent.), three brothers, Flemish miniaturists, of whom comparatively little is known. Taken prisoner as youths in Brussels in time of war, on their way home from Paris they were released by the Duke of Burgundy and attached to his household as painters. In 1411 they became court painters to the Duke of Berry and produced 39 illustrations for his celebrated manuscript *Très Riches Heures du Duc de Berri*. Other works have been attributed to Pol de Limbourg, including

Heures d'Ailly, two pages of the Turin-Milan Hours and several in a book of Terence. It is now believed that the three brothers were all dead by 1416. See P. Durieu, *Les Très Riches Heures de Jean, Duc de Berry* (1904).

LIMOUSIN, or Limosin, Léonard, *lim-oo-zi* (*c*. 1505–77), French painter in enamel, flourished from 1532 to 1574 at the French court and was appointed by Francis I head of the royal factory at Limoges.

LINACRE, Thomas (*c*. 1460–1524), English humanist and physician, born at Canterbury, studied at Oxford, was elected fellow of All Souls in 1484, and went to Italy, where he learned Greek, and took his M.D. at Padua. Erasmus and Sir Thomas More were both taught Greek by him. About 1501 Henry VII made him tutor to Prince Arthur. As king's physician to Henry VII and Henry VIII he practised in London; he also founded the Royal College of Physicians. Late in life he took orders. Linacre was one of the earliest champions of the New Learning. He translated several of Galen's works into Latin, and wrote grammatical treatises. See Lives by Johnson (1835) and Osler (1908).

LINCOLN, (1) Abraham (1809–65), sixteenth president of the United States, was born near Hodgenville, Ky., the son of a restless pioneer. After several moves, the family settled in southwest Indiana in 1816. In 1818 Abraham's mother died and his father remarried shortly. His stepmother encouraged Abraham's education although there was little schooling in that backwoods country. In 1830 the Lincolns moved on to Illinois and Abraham went to work as a clerk in a store at New Salem, Illinois. Defeated as a candidate for the legislature, he purchased a small store, whose failure left him in debt; but, being made village postmaster and deputy county surveyor, he studied law and grammar. Elected to the legislature in 1834, he served until 1842, being leader of the Whigs. He began the practice of law in 1836. At Springfield, in 1842, he married Mary Todd (1818–82). In 1846 he sat in congress; but professional work was drawing him from politics when in 1854 Stephen A. Douglas repealed the Missouri Compromise of 1820, and reopened the question of slavery in the territories. The bill roused intense feeling throughout the North, and Douglas defended his position in a speech at Springfield in October. Lincoln delivered in reply a speech which first fully revealed his power as a debater. He was then elected to the legislature. When the Republican party was organized in 1856 to oppose the extension of slavery Lincoln was its most prominent leader in Illinois, and the delegates of his state presented him for the vice-presidency. In 1858 Douglas, seeking re-election to the senate, began a canvass of Illinois in advocacy of his views of ' popular sovereignty '. Lincoln was also a candidate, and the contest, which gave Douglas the election, attracted the attention of the whole country. In May 1860 the Republican convention on the third ballot nominated Lincoln for the presidency. The Democratic party was divided between Douglas and Breckinridge. After an exciting campaign Lincoln received a popular vote of 1,866,462; Douglas, 1,375,157; Breckinridge, 847,953; and Bell, 590,631. Of the electors Lincoln had 180; Breckinridge, 72; Bell, 39; and Douglas, 12. South Carolina now seceded from the Union, and with the six Gulf states formed, in February 1861, the Confederate States of America. Lincoln, at his inaugural address on March 4, declared the Union perpetual, argued the futility of secession, and expressed his determination that the laws should be faithfully executed in all the states. On April 12, 1861, the Confederates began the Civil War by attacking Fort Sumter in Charleston harbour. Lincoln called a special session of congress, summoned 75,000 militia, ordered the enlistment of 65,000 regulars, and proclaimed a blockade of the southern ports. The Confederacy soon had control of eleven states, and put in the field 100,000 men. The first important battle was fought at Bull Run, Virginia, July 21, 1861, and resulted in the rout of the Union army. On September 22, 1862, just after McClellan's victory at Antietam, Lincoln proclaimed that on and after January 1, 1863, all slaves in states or parts of states then in rebellion should be free. On the following New Year's Day the final proclamation of emancipation was made. This greatest achievement of his administration, wrung from him by the exigencies of Civil War, was completed by the passage (1865) of the Thirteenth Amendment of the Constitution, which he planned and urged. In July 1863 Grant's capture of Vicksburg restored to the Union full control of the Mississippi River, while Meade's defeat of Lee at Gettysburg destroyed the last hope of the Confederates to transfer the seat of war north of the Potomac. General Grant, called to the chief command in March 1864, entered upon that policy of persistent attrition of the Confederate forces which finally brought peace. In the Republican Convention in June Lincoln was unanimously nominated for a second term. The Democrats nominated General McClellan. In November Lincoln received of the popular vote 2,216,000, and McClellan 1,800,000; of the electoral votes Lincoln had 212, McClellan 21. In his second inaugural address, in March 1865, Lincoln set forth the profound moral significance of the war. On Good Friday, April 14, at Ford's Theatre, Washington, he was shot by J. Wilkes Booth, an actor, and died next morning. Lincoln was fair and direct in speech and action, steadfast in principle, sympathetic and charitable, a man of strict morality, abstemious and familiar with the Bible, though not a professed member of any church. His fame is established as the saviour of his country and the liberator of a race. His Collected Works are to be found in several editions. These include his eloquent speeches— Emancipation Proclamation of 1862, the Gettysburg Address of 1863 when first were heard these words, ' government of the people, by the people, for the people ', and the Inaugural Address of 1865. See Lives by Arnold (1885), Herndon and Weik (1889), Nicolay and Hay (10 vols. 1890), Morse (1893), Binns (1907), Strunsky (1914), Charnwood (1916), Barton (1925), Sandburg (1926, 1939), Beveridge (1928), Ludwig (trans. 1932), and the synthetic autobiography compiled by Stephenson (1927).

(2) **Benjamin** (1733–1810), American soldier, born at Hingham, Mass., in 1776 reinforced Washington after the defeat on Long Island and in 1777 was appointed major-general, in August receiving command of the southern department. In 1780 besieged by Clinton in Charleston, he was compelled to capitulate. He took part in the siege of Yorktown, and was secretary of war 1781–84.

LIND, (1) **James** (1716–94), Scottish physician, born in Edinburgh, first served in the Navy as a surgeon's mate, then, after qualifying in medicine at Edinburgh, became physician to the naval hospital at Haslar. His work towards the cure and prevention of scurvy induced the Admiralty in 1795 at last to issue the order that the Navy should be supplied with lemon juice. His A Treatise of the Scurvy (1753) was and is a classic of medical literature and won him an international reputation. See R. S. Allison, Sea Diseases (1943), M. E. M. Walker, Pioneers of Public Health (1930) and Lind's Treatise on Scurvy contained in a ' Bicentenary Volume with Additional Notes ' issued by the Edinburgh University Press (1953).

(2) **Jenny** (1820–87), Swedish soprano, born of humble family at Stockholm, at nine entered the court theatre school of singing, and after lessons in Paris attained great popularity everywhere. Her earnings were largely devoted to founding and endowing musical scholarships and charities in Sweden and England. In 1852 the ' Swedish Nightingale ' married Otto Goldschmidt (1829–1907). In 1883–86 she was professor of Singing at the Royal College of Music. See Life by Bulman (1956).

(3) **Samuel Colville** (1879–1965), American chemist, director of the School of Chemistry, Minnesota (1926), and dean of the Institute of Technology there (1935), invented an electroscope for radium measurements and advanced the ionization theory of the chemical effects of radium rays.

LINDAU, lin'dow, (1) **Paul** (1839–1919), German writer, born at Magdeburg, founded Die Gegenwart and Nord und Süd, and wrote books of travel and works of criticism. He is better known as a writer of plays and novels; the most successful of the former was perhaps Maria und Magdalena. The novels include Herr und Frau Bewer (1882), and Berlin (1886–87).

(2) **Rudolf** (1829–1910), brother of (1), author and diplomatist, wrote travel books, novels, &c., and was an editor of Revue des deux mondes and Journal des débats.

LINDBERGH, Charles Augustus (1902–), American aviator, born in Detroit, made the first solo nonstop transatlantic flight (New York-Paris, 1927), in the monoplane The Spirit of St Louis. His book of that name (1953) gained the Pulitzer prize (1954). See Life by K. S. Davis (1960). His wife, **Anne Morrow Lindbergh** (1906–), has written North to the Orient (1935), Listen, the Wind (1938), &c.

LINDEMANN. See CHERWELL.

LINDLEY, John (1799–1865), English botanist, was born at Catton near Norwich, the son of a nursery-gardener, author of *Orchard and Kitchen Gardens*. Appointed assistant-secretary to the Horticultural Society in 1822, he from 1829 to 1860 was professor of Botany in University College, London. Of his writings, *The Vegetable Kingdom* (1846) was the most important.

LINDSAY, (1) see CRAWFORD.

(2) **Alexander Dunlop, 1st Baron Lindsay of Birker** (1879–1952), Scottish scholar, born in Glasgow and educated at Glasgow University and University College, Oxford. A lecturer at Victoria University, he became in 1906 fellow of Balliol and Jowett lecturer in 1911. From 1922 to 1924 he was professor of Moral Philosophy at Glasgow, becoming in the latter year Master of Balliol. In 1949 he was appointed head of the new University College of North Staffordshire. His philosophical writings include *The Essentials of Democracy* (1929), &c., but he is best known for his excellent translation of Plato's *Republic* (1907).

(3) **Sir David.** See LYNDSAY.

(4) **Nicholas Vachel** (1879–1931), American poet, born at Springfield, Ill., tramped in America, trading and reciting his very popular ragtime rhymes for hospitality. His irrepressible spirits appear in *General Booth enters Heaven* (1913) and *The Congo* (1914). His later volumes of verse were less successful, and having lost his zest for life he returned to Springfield and committed suicide.

(5) **Robert.** See PITSCOTTIE.

LINGARD, John (1771–1851), English historian, born at Winchester of Catholic parents, was sent in 1782 to the English College of Douai, where he remained till the Revolution. In 1795 he received priest's orders, and in 1811 accepted the mission of Hornby, near Lancaster, declining the offer of a chair at Maynooth, as fourteen years later of a cardinal's hat. In 1821 he obtained his doctorate from Pius VII and in 1839 received a crown pension of £300. His *Antiquity of the Anglo-Saxon Church* (1806) was the pioneer of what became the labour of his life—a *History of England to 1688* (1819–30). This was fiercely assailed in the *Edinburgh Review*, but Lingard increased his reputation as a candid Catholic scholar. See his *Life and Letters* by Haile and Bonney (1911).

LINKLATER, Eric (1899–), Scottish novelist, born at Dounby in Orkney, was educated at Aberdeen, where he studied first medicine, then English. After serving in World War I he became a journalist in Bombay, an assistant lecturer in English at Aberdeen University and while in the United States (1928–30) wrote *Poet's Pub* (1929), the first of a series of clever satirical novels. His books include *Laxdale Hall* (1951), filmed in 1953, *Juan in America* (1931), *Private Angelo* (1946), filmed in 1949, and *The Merry Muse* (1959). *The Man on my Back* (1941) is autobiographical.

LINLEY, Thomas (1732–95), English composer, born at Wells, taught singing and conducted concerts at Bath. In 1775 his son-in-law Sheridan induced him to set his comic opera *The Duenna* to music. In 1776 they and Ford bought Garrick's share of Drury Lane Theatre. During the next fifteen years Linley was its musical director, composing songs, operas, &c. Of his sons, Thomas (1756–78), a friend of Mozart, possessed real musical genius, and William (1767–1835) composed glees, songs, &c. Of his gifted daughters, Elizabeth Ann (1754–92), singer, married Sheridan (q.v.). See C. Black's *Linleys of Bath* (1911; new ed. 1926).

LINNAEUS, or **Linné, Carl** (1707–78), Swedish botanist, founder of modern botany, was born the son of the parish clergyman of Råshult in South Sweden, and studied at Lund and Uppsala. In 1730 he was appointed assistant to the professor of Botany in Uppsala. An exploring trip through Swedish Lapland produced his *Flora Lapponica* (1737). Then followed a journey of scientific exploration through Dalecarlia; and in 1735–38 he was in Holland, mainly at Leyden, working at botany and arranging gardens. Meanwhile he had visited England and Paris, and published *Systema Naturae Fundamenta Botanica, Genera Plantarum, Critica Botanica*, in which he expounded his system of classification, based on sexual characteristics, long the dominant system. He practised as a physician in Stockholm, and in 1742 became professor of Botany at Uppsala. In 1745–46 he published *Flora Suecica* and *Fauna Suecica*; in 1751 *Philosophia Botanica*; and in 1753 *Species Plantarum*. He was ennobled in 1757. See Life by Fries (Eng. adaptation by Jackson, 1923), who also edited his *Correspondence*, and N. Gourlie, *Prince of Botanists* (1953).

LINNELL, John (1792–1882), English artist, a disciple and patron of Blake, was born in London, and studied at the Royal Academy. He painted portraits of Blake, Malthus, Whately, Peel, Carlyle, &c. His landscapes were mostly Surrey scenes. He is also known for his sculpture and engraving. See Life by A. T. Story (1892).

LIN PIAO (1908–), Chinese soldier and politician, son of a factory owner, educated at Whampoo military academy, joined the Communists against the Kuomintang in 1927, and was commander of the Northeast People's Liberation Army in 1945. He became defence minister and a vice chairman in 1959, and emerged from the 'cultural revolution' of 1966 as second-in-command to Mao Tse Tung, whose most likely successor he is at present.

LINSCHOTEN, Jan Huygen van (c. 1563–1611), Dutch traveller, born at Haarlem, wrote *Voyages into the East and West Indies* (trans. 1598).

LINTON, (1) Sir James Dromgole (1840–1916), English painter, born in London, laboured with success to elevate the status of painting in watercolours and reorganized the Royal Institute of Painters in Watercolours. Its first president in 1884–99, he was re-appointed in 1909. In 1885 he was knighted.

(2) **William James** (1812–98), English wood-engraver born in London, did some of his finest work for the *Illustrated London News*. In 1867 he went to the United States, and settled at New Haven, Conn. A zealous Chartist, he wrote *The Plaint of Free-*

dom (1852), *Life of Thomas Paine* (1879), &c. See his *Memories* (1895). His wife, **Eliza Lynn** (1822–98), born at Keswick, was also a writer, first as a novelist and later as a journalist. With her husband she prepared a volume on *The Lake Country* (1864), he furnishing the illustrations. In 1867 they separated. Her ' Girl of the Period ' articles in the *Saturday* were collected in 1883. See her *My Literary Life* (1899) and Life by Layard (1901).

LINTOT, Barnaby Bernard (1675–1736), English publisher, born at Horsham in Sussex, was associated with many of the celebrated writers of his day. Among the works which he published were Pope's translation of the *Iliad* in 6 volumes (1715–1720), and his *Odyssey* (1725–56), the first complete edition of Steele's *Dramatic Works* in collaboration with his rival publisher Jacob Tonson, and works by Gay, Cibber, Parnell and Rowe.

LIN YUTANG, *lin'yü-* (1895–   ), Chinese author, born at Changchow, Amoy, studied at Shanghai, Harvard and Leipzig, became professor of English at Peking (1923–26), secretary of the Ministry of Foreign Affairs (1927) and was chancellor of Singapore University (1954–55). He is best known for his numerous essays on, and anthologies of, Chinese wisdom and culture, and as co-author of the official romanization plan for the Chinese alphabet. See A. A. Lin, *Our Family* (1941).

LIPCHITZ, Jacques (1891–   ), Lithuanian-born sculptor, worked in Paris and, from 1941, in the U.S.A. At first an exponent of Cubism, he developed in the 'thirties a more dynamic style which he applied with telling effect to bronze figure and animal compositions.

LIPMANN, Fritz Albert (1899–   ), German-American biochemist, born at Königsberg, professor of Biochemistry at Harvard 1949–1957. He has done notable work on the vitamin-B complex. His discovery of ' coenzyme A ' brought him a Nobel prize for physiology and medicine (jointly with Krebs) in 1953.

LI PO, *lee-pō* (*c.* 700–762), Chinese poet, born in the province of Szechwan, led a gay dissipated life at the Emperor's court and later, as one of a wandering band calling themselves ' The Eight Immortals of the Wine Cup '. Regarded as the greatest poet of China, he wrote colourful verse of wine, women and nature. It is believed that he was drowned while attempting to kiss the moon's reflection. See Waley, *Poetry and Career of Li Po* (1951).

LIPPI, (1) Filippino (*c.* 1458–1504), Italian painter, son of (2), was a contemporary and associate of Botticelli, who almost certainly was a pupil of his father. He completed *c.* 1484 the frescoes in the Brancacci Chapel in the Carmine, Florence, left unfinished by Masaccio. Other celebrated series of frescoes were painted by him between 1487 and 1502, one in the Strozzi Chapel in Sta Maria Novella and one in the Caraffa Chapel, S. Maria sopra Minerva in Rome. Easel pictures painted by him are *The Virgin and Saints, The Adoration of the Magi* and *The Vision of St Bernard*.

His predilection for antiquity led him to over-introduce it into his later works. See works by Konody (1911), and J. B. Supino's *Les Deux Lippi* (2nd ed. 1904).

(2) **Fra Filippo,** called **Lippo** (*c.* 1406–69), Italian religious painter, was born in Florence. An orphan, he was sent to the Carmine in Florence, where the Brancacci Chapel was painted by Masaccio whose pupil Lippi became. The style of his master can be seen in his early work, for example in the frescoes, *The Relaxation of the Carmelite Rule* (*c.* 1432). Of his stay in Padua, *c.* 1434, no artistic record has survived. The *Tarquinia Madonna* (1437), his first dated painting, shows the Flemish influence. His greatest work was on the choir walls of Prato cathedral begun in 1452. Between 1452 and 1464 he abducted and later was allowed to marry the nun Lucrezia, who was the model for many of his fine Madonnas. She was the mother of his son Filippino (1). His later works are deeply religious and include the series of *Nativities*. He was working in the cathedral at Spoleto when he died. See books by Strutt (1901), Konody (1911), Oertel (1942).

LIPPINCOTT, Joshua Ballinger (1813–86), American publisher, born in Burlington, N.J., had charge of a bookseller's business in Philadelphia 1834–36, and then founded his well-known publishing firm. *Lippincott's Magazine* dates from 1868.

LIPPMANN, (1) Gabriel (1845–1921), French physicist, professor of Mathematical and Experimental Physics at the Sorbonne (1886), was a Nobel prizewinner in 1908, when he was also elected F.R.S. He invented a capillary electrometer, and produced the first coloured photograph of the spectrum.

(2) **Walter** (1889–   ), American journalist, born in New York, educated at Harvard, on the editorial staff of the *New York World* until 1931, then a special writer for the *Herald Tribune*. His daily columns became internationally famous, and he won many awards, including the Pulitzer prize for International Reporting (1962). Among his best known books are *The Cold War* (1947), *Western Unity and the Common Market* (1962), &c.

LIPPS, Theodor (1851–1914), German aesthetic philosopher and psychologist, born at Wallhaben, was professor at Bonn, Breslau and Munich, and is best known as an early exponent of the psychological and aesthetic theory of empathy, i.e., self-projection into an experienced object, especially in his book *Ästhetik* (1903–06), which influenced Vernon Lee (q.v.).

LIPSIUS, (1) Justus, or **Joest Lips** (1547–1606), Flemish humanist, born at Issche, near Brussels, a great classical scholar of Louvain, who was successively Catholic, Lutheran, Calvinist and once more Catholic. Professor at Louvain, Jena and Leyden, his writings include editions of Tacitus and Seneca. See French Lives of him by Galesloot (1877) and Amiel (1884), and J. E. Sandys, *History of Classical Scholarship* (1903–08).

(2) **Richard Adelbert** (1830–92), German theologian, born at Gera, became professor at Vienna in 1861, at Kiel in 1865, and at Jena in 1871. A pioneer of the evangelical

movement, he wrote on dogmatics. His brother, **Justus Hermann** (1834–1920), in 1869 became professor of Classical Philology at Leipzig, and edited the *De Corona* of Demosthenes (1876), &c. Their sister **Marie** (1837–1927) made valuable contributions to music and its history.

LIPTON, Sir Thomas Johnstone (1850–1931), Scottish business man and philanthropist, born in Glasgow. When nine years old he began work as an errand-boy, and in 1865 went to America, where he worked successively on a tobacco plantation, in the rice-fields and in a grocer's shop. Returning to Glasgow, in 1871 he opened there his first grocer's shop, which was rapidly followed by many others. They prospered, due to high-quality goods at low prices and astute advertising, to the extent of making him a millionaire at the age of thirty. His munificent gifts to various charities brought him a knighthood in 1898 and a baronetcy in 1902. In 1899 he made his first challenge for the America's Cup with his yacht *Shamrock I*, this being followed at intervals by four other attempts, all of them unsuccessful. See *The Lipton Story* by A. Waugh (1951).

LISLE, *lîl*, (1) Alicia (*c.* 1614–85), the widow of one of Cromwell's lords, was beheaded at Winchester by order of Judge Jeffreys for sheltering a rebel fugitive from Sedgemoor. At Charles I's execution she had said that her 'blood leaped within her to see the tyrant fall'.

(2) See ROUGET DE LISLE.

LISSAJOUS, Jules Antoine, *lee-sa-zhoo* (1822–80), French physicist, professor at the Collège St Louis, Paris, in 1857 invented the vibration microscope which showed visually the 'Lissajous figures' obtained as the resultant of two simple harmonic motions at right angles to one another. His researches extended to acoustics and optics. His system of optical telegraphy was used during the siege of Paris (1871).

LISSAUER, Ernst, *lis'ow-er* (1882–1937), German poet and dramatist, born in Berlin, much of whose writings had a strong nationalist flavour. *1813* (1913), a poem cycle, is a eulogy on the Prussian people in their fight to remove Napoleon from their land, as is the successful drama *Yorck* (1921) about the Prussian general. The poem *Hassgesang gegen England* (1914) achieved tremendous popularity in wartime Germany with its well-known refrain 'Gott strafe England'. Other works include a play about Goethe called *Eckermann* (1921), poems on Bruckner, *Gloria Anton Bruckners* (1921) a critical work, *Von der Sendung des Dichters* (1922), and some volumes of verse.

LIST, Friedrich (1789–1846), German political economist, born at Reutlingen, Württemberg, was a disciple of Adam Smith. Charged with sedition in 1824, he went to the U.S.A. and became a naturalized citizen. He was U.S. consul at Baden, Leipzig and Stuttgart successively. A strong advocate of protection for new industries, he did much by his writings to form German economic practice. His main work was *National System of Political Economy*, published in Germany in 1841. See Lives by Goldschmidt (Berlin 1878), Jentsch (1901), M. E. Hirst (1909).

LISTER, Joseph, Lord (1827–1912), English surgeon, was the second son of the microscopist, Joseph Jackson Lister, F.R.S. (1786–1869), of Upton, Essex. He graduated at London University in arts (1847) and medicine (1852), and became F.R.C.S. (1852) and F.R.C.S.E. (1855), after being house surgeon to James Syme (q.v.), whose daughter he married in 1856. He was successively lecturer on Surgery, Edinburgh; regius professor of Surgery, Glasgow; professor of Clinical Surgery, Edinburgh (1869), of Clinical Surgery, King's College Hospital, London (1877–93); president of the Royal Society (1895–1900). In addition to important observations on the coagulation of the blood, inflammation, &c., his great work was the introduction (1860) of the antiseptic system, which revolutionized modern surgery. He was president of the British Association in 1896. He was made a baronet in 1883, a baron in 1897, O.M. in 1902. See Lives by R. J. Godlee (1917; rev. 1924), Thompson (1934), H. C. Cameron (1948), K. Walker (1956).

LISTON, (1) John (1776–1846), English low comedian, born in London, played from 1805 to 1837 at the Haymarket, Drury Lane, and the Olympic. 'Paul Pry' (1825) was his best creation.

(2) **Robert** (1794–1847), Scottish surgeon, born at Ecclesmachan manse, Linlithgow, studied at Edinburgh and London, and settled in Edinburgh in 1818 as lecturer on Surgery and Anatomy. His surgical skill soon won him a European reputation. In 1835 he became professor of Clinical Surgery at University College, London. It was he who first used a general anaesthetic in a public operation at University College Hospital on December 21, 1846. His chief works are *Elements of Surgery* (1831) and *Practical Surgery* (1837).

LISZT, Franz (1811–86), Hungarian composer and pianist, was born at Raiding near Oedenburg. At nine he played in public, and was sent to study at Vienna. He afterwards went to Paris, studied and played there. He next made a tour to Vienna, Munich, Stuttgart and Strasburg; visited England thrice (1824–1827); in 1831 heard Paganini, and was fired by the resolve to become the Paganini of the piano. He became intimate with most of the great *littérateurs* then in Paris, and from 1835 to 1839 lived with the Comtesse d'Agoult (q.v.), by whom he had three children, one of whom, Cosima, married Wagner. Between 1839 and 1847 he was at the height of his brilliance, giving concerts throughout Europe. He met Princess Carolyne zu Sayn-Wittgenstein in 1847 with whom he lived till his death. In 1849, at the height of popularity, he retired to Weimar to direct the opera and concerts, to compose and teach. Here he brought out Wagner's *Lohengrin* and Berlioz's *Benvenuto Cellini*, and Weimar became the musical centre of Germany. In 1861 he resigned his appointment, and his life was subsequently divided mainly between Weimar, Rome and Budapest. In 1865 he received minor orders in the Church of Rome, and was known as Abbé. His visit to London in 1886 was a triumphal progress. He died at Bayreuth, where he is buried. As a pianist Liszt was unapproachable. His supreme command of technique was forgotten by hearers in admiration of the poetic qualities of his playing. His literary works on music include monographs on Chopin and Franz, and the music of the Gypsies. All his original compositions have a very distinct, sometimes a very strange, individuality. In his twelve symphonic poems he created a new form of orchestral music. One or two masses, the *Legend of St Elizabeth*, and a few other works, embody his religious aspirations. See his *Letters* (trans. 1894); Lives by Ramann (1880–94; trans. 1882), Nohl (trans. 1884), Martin (1886), Beaufort (1886), Göllerich (1888), Vogel (1888), Kapp (1909), Huneker (N.Y. 1911); Janka Wohl, *Recollections* (1888); and books by Hervey (1911), by his daughter, Cosima Wagner (1911), F. Corder (1925), S. Sitwell (1955), W. Beckett (1956).

LI T'AI PO. See LI Po.

LITHGOW, William (1582–c. 1645), Scottish traveller, born at Lanark, had already visited the Shetlands, Bohemia, Switzerland, &c., when, in 1610, he set out on foot from Paris to Palestine and Egypt. His second tramp led him through North Africa from Tunis to Fez, and home by way of Hungary and Poland. In his last journey (1619–21) to Spain via Ireland he was seized as a spy at Malaga and tortured. At London Gondomar, the Spanish ambassador, promised him reparation, but contented himself with promising. So Lithgow assaulted, or by another account was assaulted by, him in the king's ante-room, for which he was placed in the Marshalsea. He died at Lanark. His interesting *Rare Adventures and Paineful Peregrinations* was published in a complete form in 1632, incompletely in 1614. Besides he wrote *The Siege of Breda* (1637), *Siege of Newcastle* (1645), *Poems* (ed. by Maidment, 1863), &c.

LITTLETON, or Lyttleton, Sir Thomas (1402–81), English jurist, born at Frankley House, Bromsgrove, was recorder of Coventry in 1450, king's sergeant in 1455, in 1466 judge of common pleas, and in 1475 a knight of the Bath. His reputation rests on his treatise on *Tenures*, written in law French, first printed at London (? 1481), translated into English about 1500. It was the text that E. Coke (q.v.) commented on in his *Coke upon Littleton* (1826).

LITTRÉ, Maximilien Paul Émile, *lee-tray* (1801–81), French lexicographer and philosopher, born in Paris, from medicine turned to philology. His translation of Hippocrates (q.v.) procured his election in 1839 to the Academy of Inscriptions. He fought on the barricades in 1830, was one of the principal editors of the *National* down to 1851, and became an enthusiastic Comtist. *La Poésie homérique et l'Ancienne Poésie française* (1847) was an attempt to render book i of the *Iliad* in the style of the trouvères. In 1854 Littré became editor of the *Journal des savants*. His splendid *Dictionnaire de la langue française* (1863–72; supplement, 1878) did not prevent the Academy in 1863 from rejecting its author, whom Bishop Dupanloup denounced as holding impious

doctrines. In 1871 Gambetta appointed him professor of History and Geography at the École polytechnique; he was chosen representative of the Seine department in the National Assembly; and in December 1871 the Academy at last admitted him. See Sainte-Beuve's *Notice* (1863), and *Nouveaux Lundis* (vol. v); Caro, *Littré et le Positivisme* (1883); and Pasteur's discourse (1882).

LITVINOV, Maxim (1876–1951), Soviet politician born, a Polish Jew, at Bielostok, in Russian Poland. He early joined in revolutionary activities and was exiled to Siberia, but escaped. In 1917–18 he was Bolshevist ambassador in London. He became in 1921 deputy people's commissar for foreign affairs and commissar from 1930 to 1939. From 1941 to 1942 he was ambassador to the U.S.A., and from 1942 to 1946 vice-minister of foreign affairs. By his efforts at international conferences, &c., he furthered acceptance of the Soviet Union abroad, and his skill in diplomacy was recognized more by America and Britain than in his own country.

LIUTPRAND, or Luitprand, *lyoot-prant* (c. 922–72), Italian prelate and historian, was born of a Longobard family in Pavia, passed from the service of Berengar, king of Italy, to that of the Emperor Otto I. Otto made him Bishop of Cremona, and sent him on an embassy to Constantinople. His *Antapodosis* treats of history from 886 to 950. *De Rebus Gestis Ottonis* covers 960–964, and *De Legatione Constantinopolitanâ* is a satire on the Greek court. See his works, ed. Becker (1915); trans. Wright (1930), and books by Köpke (1842) and Baldeschi (1889).

LIVENS. See LIEVENSZ.

LIVERPOOL, Robert Banks Jenkinson, Earl of (1770–1828), British statesman, son of the first Earl (1727–1808), was educated at the Charterhouse and Christ Church, Oxford, and entered parliament in 1791 as member for Rye. A Tory with Liberal ideas on trade and finance, in 1794 he became a member of the India Board, and in 1801 as foreign secretary negotiated the unpopular Treaty of Amiens. In 1803 he was created Lord Hawkesbury, and on Pitt's return to power he went to the Home Office. On the death of Pitt he declined to form an administration. In 1807 he again took the Home Office, and next year succeeded his father as Earl of Liverpool. In Perceval's ministry of 1809 he was secretary for war and the colonies. In 1812 he formed an administration which lasted for nearly fifteen years. The attitude of the government to Poland, Austria, Italy and Naples, coercive measures at home, and an increase in the duty on corn were regarded as reactionary. Lord Liverpool himself was a Free Trader, and ultimately sought to liberalize the tariff. Notwithstanding the blunder of the sinking fund, his financial policy generally was sound, enlightened and economical. He united the old and the new Tories at a critical period. In February 1827 he was struck with apoplexy, and died the following year. See Life by C. D. Yonge (3 vols. 1868), and studies by W. R. Brock (1941) and Petrie (1954).

LIVINGSTON, an American family, descended from the fifth Lord Livingstone, guardian of Mary, Queen of Scots, and from his grandson, John Livingstone (1603–72), minister of Ancrum, banished for refusing the oath of allegiance to Charles II, and from 1663 pastor of the Scots kirk at Rotterdam. His son Robert (1654–1728) went to America in 1673, settled at Albany, and received land. See *Life* by L. H. Ledler (1961). Of his grandsons, Philip (1716–78) signed the Declaration of Independence; and William (1723–90), was the first and able governor of New Jersey 1776–90. **Robert R.** Livingston (1746–1813), great-grandson of the first Robert, was born in New York, and admitted to the bar in 1773. Sent to congress in 1775, he was one of the five charged with drawing up the Declaration of Independence, and till 1801 was chancellor of New York state. As minister plenipotentiary at Paris he negotiated the cession of Louisiana. He enabled Fulton to construct his first steamer, and introduced in America the use of sulphate of lime as a manure, and the merino sheep. See *Life* by F. De Peyster (1876). **Edward Livingston** (1764–1836), also a great-grandson of the first Robert, was born at Clermont, N.Y., and called to the bar in 1785. He sat in congress from 1795 to 1801, when he became U.S. district attorney for New York, and mayor of New York; but in 1803, owing to a subordinate's misappropriations, he found himself in debt to the federal government. He handed over his property to his creditors, and in 1804 settled in New Orleans, where he obtained lucrative practice at the bar. During the second war with England he was aide-de-camp to General Jackson; and 1822–29 he represented New Orleans in congress. In 1823–24 he systematized the civil code of Louisiana. His criminal code was completed, but not directly adopted. Livingston was elected in 1829 to the senate, and in 1831 appointed secretary of state. In 1833 he went to France as plenipotentiary. He died at Rhinebeck, N.Y. See *Life* by C. H. Hunt (1864).

LIVINGSTONE, David (1813–73), Scottish missionary and traveller, was born at Low Blantyre, Lanarkshire, and from ten till twenty-four years of age was a worker in a cotton factory there. A pamphlet by Karl Gutzlaff kindled the desire to become a missionary; and he resolved to apply himself to medicine. Having completed his studies in London, prevented by war from carrying out his wish to work in China, he was attracted to Africa by Dr Moffat, and, ordained under the London Missionary Society in November 1840, reached Simon's Bay March 11, 1841, Kuruman July 31, and for several years laboured in Bechuanaland. Repulsed by the Boers in an effort to plant native missionaries in the Transvaal, he travelled northward, discovered Lake Ngami, and determined to open trade routes east and west. The journey occupied from June 1852 to May 1856, when he arrived at Quilimane. It was accomplished with a mere handful of followers, amid sicknesses, perils and difficulties without number. But a vast amount of valuable information was gathered respecting the country, its products and the native tribes. Not the least among his discoveries was the Victoria Falls of the Zambezi. He was welcomed home with extraordinary enthusiasm. During the fifteen months spent in England and Scotland he published his *Missionary Travels* (1857), and having severed his connection with the London Missionary Society in order to be free to undertake future explorations, was appointed by the government chief of an expedition for exploring the Zambezi. Setting out in March 1858, he explored the Zambezi, Shiré and Rovuma; discovered Lakes Shirwa and Nyasa, and came to the conclusion that Lake Nyasa and its neighbourhood was the best field for commercial and missionary operations, though he was hampered by the Portuguese authorities, and by the discovery that the slave trade was extending in the district. His wife Mary, Moffat's daughter, whom he had married in 1844, died in 1862, and was buried at Shupanga. The expedition was recalled in July 1863. At his own cost he now journeyed a hundred miles westward from Lake Nyasa; then himself navigated his little steamer to Bombay; and returned to England in 1864. His second book, *The Zambesi and its Tributaries* (1865), was designed to expose the Portuguese slave traders, and to find means of establishing a settlement for missions and commerce near the head of the Rovuma. A proposal was made to him by the Royal Geographical Society to return to Africa and settle a disputed question regarding the watershed of central Africa and the sources of the Nile. In March 1866 he started from Zanzibar, pressed westward amid innumerable hardships, and in 1867–68 discovered Lakes Mweru and Bangweulu. Obliged to return for rest to Ujiji, he struck westward again as far as the river Lualaba, thinking it might be the Nile, but far from certain that it was not, what it proved afterwards to be, the Congo. On his return after severe illness to Ujiji, Livingstone was found there by Stanley (q.v.), sent to look for him by the *New York Herald*. Determined to solve the problem, he returned to Bangweulu, but fell into wretched health, and in Old Chitambo (now in Zambia), on the morning of May 1, 1873, he was found by his attendants, dead. His faithful people embalmed his body, and carried it to the coast. It was conveyed to England, and was buried in Westminster Abbey. Livingstone's *Last Journals*, brought down to within a few days of his death, were published in 1874; the family letters in 1959; the *Private Journals* (1851–53) in 1960. See Blaikie's *Personal Life of David Livingstone* (1880), Lives by Thomas Hughes (1889), R. J. Campbell (1929), Macnair (1940), Seaver (1957), Sir H. H. Johnston's *Livingstone and the Exploration of Central Africa* (1891), and Sir R. Coupland's *Livingstone's Last Journey* (1945).

LIVIUS. See LIVY.

LIVIUS ANDRONICUS (fl. 3rd cent. B.C.), the father of Roman dramatic and epic poetry, was a Greek by birth, probably a native of Tarentum, was carried as a slave to Rome in 272 B.C., but was afterwards freed by his master. He translated the *Odyssey* into Latin Saturnian verse, and wrot ᴐ tragedies, comedies, and hymns after Greek models. Only fragments are extant (ed. by L. Müller, 1885).

LIVY, properly **Titus Livius** (59 B.C.–A.D. 17), Roman historian, was born at Padua, of a noble and wealthy family, and on coming to Rome was admitted to the court of Augustus. He never flattered the emperor, but avowed his preference for a republic. He praised Brutus and Cassius, sympathized with Pompey, and stigmatized Cicero, an accessory to the murder of Caesar, as having got from Antony's bravoes only his deserts. Of the great Caesar himself he doubted whether he was more of a curse or a blessing to the commonwealth. Such friendship as they had for each other Livy and Augustus never lost. Livy died at his native Patavium. His history of Rome from her foundation to the death of Drusus, 9 B.C., comprised 142 books, of which those from the 11th to the 20th, and from the 46th to the 142nd, have been lost. Of the 35 that remain, the 41st and 43rd are imperfect. The ' periochae ', or summaries of the contents of each book, composed in the wane of Roman literature, to catalogue names and events for rhetorical purposes, have all, however, come down to us, except those of books 136 and 137. But what has been spared is more than enough to confirm in modern days the judgment of antiquity which places Livy in the forefront of Latin writers. His impartiality is not less a note of his work than his veneration for the good, the generous, the heroic in man. His style is as nearly perfect as is compatible with his ideal of the historian. For investigation of facts he did not go far afield. Accepting history as fine art rather than as science, he was content to take his authorities as he found them, and where they differed was guided by taste or predilection. Gronovius, Drakenborch, Ruddiman, Madvig, Alschefski, Weissenborn, Luchs, Müller, and Zingerle purified Livy's text, also critically edited by Conway and Walters (1914 *et seq.*). See edition with trans. by Foster (1919 *et seq.*), and Philemon Holland's fine Elizabethan English trans. (1600).

LLEWELLYN, Richard, *hloo-el'lin,* pseud. of **Richard Doyle Vivian Llewellyn Lloyd** (1907–), Welsh author, born at St David's, Pembrokeshire, established himself, after service with the regular army and a short spell as a film director, as a best-selling novelist with *How Green was my Valley* (1939), a good example of the Welsh genius for blending realism and humour with sympathetic understanding of the human condition. Later works include *None but the Lonely Heart* (1943), and *The Flame of Hercules* (1957).

LLORENTE, Juan Antonio, *lyō-rayn'tay* (1756–1823), Spanish priest and historian, born at Rincón del Soto, rose to be secretary to the Inquisition in 1789 and was made canon of Toledo in 1806. In 1809, when the Inquisition was suppressed, Joseph Bonaparte placed all its archives in his hands and he went to Paris, where the *Histoire critique de l'inquisition d'Espagne* came out in 1817–18. Its value was recognized at once, but it provoked

bitter feeling, and Llorente was ordered to quit France. See his *Autobiography.*

LLOYD, (1) **Charles** (1775–1839), English poet, the friend of Coleridge and Lamb, born of Quaker parentage at Birmingham, about 1811 began to become deranged, and died in an asylum near Versailles.

(2) **Edward** (d. *c.* 1730), the London coffee-house keeper in 1688–1726, after whom is named ' Lloyd's ', the London society of underwriters. The coffee house became a haunt of merchants and ship-owners and for them Lloyd started his *Lloyd's News,* later to become *Lloyd's List.*

(3) **Humphrey** (1800–81), Irish scientist, born and educated in Dublin, where he became provost of Trinity College, was president of the British Association in 1857. He is best known for his researches in optics and his experiments on internal conical refraction

(4) **(John) Selwyn Brooke** (1904–), English politician, born in Liverpool of Anglo-Welsh parentage, was educated at Fettes and Cambridge. He studied law and became a barrister in 1930 with a practice in Liverpool. He stood unsuccessfully as Liberal candidate for Macclesfield and in 1931 transferred his allegiance to the Conservative party. Meantime he entered local government, becoming in 1936 chairman of the Hoylake Urban District Council. During World War II, he was a staff officer rising to the rank of colonel general staff, Second Army. In parliament in 1945 as Conservative member for Wirral, he continued to practise law, becoming a K.C. in 1947. In 1951 he was appointed minister of state, and in 1954 became successively minister of supply and minister of defence. As foreign secretary in 1955, he defended Eden's policy on Suez, and was retained in this post until 1960 when he became chancellor of the Exchequer, resigning in Macmillan's ' purge ' in 1962. Refusing a peerage, he was given the task of investigating the Conservative Party organization. He was lord privy seal and leader of the House (1963–64).

LLOYD-GEORGE OF DWYFOR, (1) **David Lloyd George, 1st Earl** (1863–1945), Liberal statesman of Welsh parentage, was born in Manchester. At the age of two when his father died his family were taken to Wales to Llanystumdwy near Criccieth, the home of his uncle Richard Lloyd, and it was he who, seeing the latent brilliance in the young Lloyd George, took his education in hand. It was from his uncle that he acquired his religion, his industry, his vivid oratory, his radical views and his Welsh nationalism. He became a solicitor and in 1890 his career as a politician began when he was elected as an advanced Liberal for Carnarvon Boroughs. From 1905 to 1908 he was president of the Board of Trade and was responsible for the passing of three important Acts—the Merchant Shipping Act in 1906, and the Census of Production Act in 1906, and the Patents Act of 1907. As chancellor of the Exchequer from 1908 to 1915, he reached the heights as a social reformer with his Old Age Pensions Act in 1908, the National Insurance Act in 1911, and the momentous budget of 1909–10, whose rejection by the Lords led to the onstitutional crisis and the Parliament Act of 1911. Up to the outbreak of the war in 1914 he had been regarded as a pacifist. As a strong upholder of the national rights of a smaller country he saw the parallel between the Welsh and the Boers and his condemnation of the Boer War had been loud. The threat of invasion of Belgium by Germany dispelled all pacifist tendencies. In 1915 he was appointed minister of munitions, and in 1916 became war secretary and superseded Asquith as coalition prime minister, holding office from 1916 to 1922. By his forceful policy he was, as Hitler later said of him, ' the man who won the war '. He was one of the ' big three ' at the peace negotiations, which he handled brilliantly although he was inclined to pay too much attention to the demands of the small countries. This later, as with Greece, led Britain into difficulties. At home there was a split in the Liberal party which never completely healed. In 1921 he treated with the Sinn Feiners and conceded the Irish Free State. This was very unpopular with the Conservatives in the government and led to his downfall and the downfall of the Liberals as a party at the election of 1922. He retained his seat until the year of his death, in which year he was made an earl. He wrote his *War Memoirs* (1933–36) and *The Truth about the Peace Treaties* (1938). See Lives by A. J. Sylvester (1947), M. Thomson (1949), Earl Lloyd George (1960), and W. George, *My Brother and I* (1958).

(2) **Gwilym, 1st Viscount Tenby** (1894–1967), politician, second son of (1), was born at Criccieth and entered parliament as Liberal member for Pembrokeshire in 1922, again from 1929 to 1950 during which term he was parliamentary secretary to the Board of Trade (1939–41) and minister of fuel and power (1942–45). In 1951 he was returned as Liberal-Conservative member for Newcastle North and was minister of food until 1954. He was minister for Welsh affairs until 1957, when he was created Viscount Tenby of Bulford.

(3) **Lady Megan** (1902–66), politician, born at Criccieth, younger daughter of (1), was elected Liberal member of parliament for Anglesey in 1929 and Independent Liberal between 1931 and 1945. Defeated in the election of 1951, she in 1955 joined the Labour party and was M.P. for Carmarthen from 1957. She was awarded the C.H. posthumously.

LLYWARCH HÊN, Welsh poet, flourished about 700.

LLYWELYN, the name of two Welsh princes, *hloo-el'in*, (1) **ab Iorwerth**, called **the Great** (d. 1240), successfully maintained his independence against King John and Henry III. He died, a Cistercian, at Aberconway.

(2) **ab Gruffydd** (d. 1282), grandson of (1), the opponent of Edward I, was slain near Builth and with him Wales lost her political independence.

LOBACHEVSKI, Nikolai (1793–1856), Russian mathematician, born at Makariev, founder of non-Euclidean geometry. He became professor at Kazan in 1814. His ideas were published in *Über die Principien der Geometrie* (1829–30).

L'OBEL or **Lobel, Matthias de** (1538–1616), Flemish naturalist, born at Lille, became botanist and physician to James VI and I, and gave his name to the *Lobelia*. He died at Highgate.

LÔBO, (1) Francisco Rodrigues (c. 1580–1622), Portuguese writer, born at Leiria, wrote *Primavera* (1601) and other remarkable prose pastorals and verse. He was drowned in the Tagus. His lyrics are of great beauty and his work holds a valuable place in the literature of his country. See A. F. G. Bell, *Portuguese Literature* (1922).

(2) **Jeronimo** (1593–1678), Portuguese Jesuit traveller, born at Lisbon, went to India in 1621, and was superintendent of missions in Abyssinia, 1625–34. He wrote of his travels in *Voyage historique d'Abissinie*, translated and published in French in 1728.

LOCHIEL. See CAMERON OF LOCHIEL.

LOCHNER, Stefan, *loKH'ner* (c. 1400–51), German painter, born at Meersburg on Lake Constance, and the principal master of the Cologne school, marking the transition from the Gothic style to naturalism. His best-known work is the great triptych in Cologne Cathedral. His use of a varnish medium, as in his *Three Saints* in the National Gallery, London, gives him an important place in the early development of oil painting.

LOCKE, (1) Alain LeRoy (1886–1954), American Negro educationist, born at Philadelphia, was a Rhodes scholar at Oxford (1907–10), and from 1917 professor of Philosophy at Howard University. He wrote *The New Negro* (1925), *Negro Art* (1937), &c.

(2) **John** (1632–1704), English philosopher, the principal founder of philosophical Liberalism and with Bacon, of English Empiricism, born August 29 at Wrington, Somerset, was educated at Westminster School under Richard Busby (q.v.) and at Christ Church, Oxford, where he found the prevailing Aristotelianism ' perplexed with obscure terms and useless questions '. He was elected to a life studentship there, which was withdrawn in 1684 by order of the king. His dislike of the Puritan intolerance of the College divines prevented him from taking orders. Instead, he dabbled in medicine and scientific experimentation and discussion and became known as ' Doctor Locke '. In 1667 he entered as physician the household of Anthony Ashley Cooper, later first Earl of Shaftesbury (q.v.). After successfully operating upon the latter for an abscess in the chest (1668) he became Ashley's close confidential adviser in political and scientific matters and was elected F.R.S. The latter directed Locke's interests towards philosophy. A small club for discussion of theological and philosophical questions was founded by Locke, and at such a gathering in the winter (1670–1671) the group welcomed Locke's suggestion, which was to be key to his famous *Essay*, that before attempting to solve any such questions, they should first of all discover what the human understanding was fitted to deal with. In 1672, Ashley became first Earl of Shaftesbury and lord chancellor, and Locke secretary of the Board of Trade. For health reasons he spent the politically

troublesome years (1675–79) in Montpelier and Paris, where he made contact with the brilliant circle of Gassendi and Arnauld. Shaftesbury, after a short spell in the Tower, was restored to favour and Locke re-entered his service. In 1683, however, he found it prudent to follow his late master to Holland. How far Locke was involved in Shaftesbury's secret plotting for Monmouth is not certain. But Locke settled under the name of Dr Van der Linden in Amsterdam, where he struck up an intimate friendship with the liberal theologians Limborch and Le Clerc. In 1687 he removed to Rotterdam and joined the English supporters of William of Orange. His famous *Treatises on Government* (1689), published anonymously, were not, as is commonly supposed, written to justify the 'Glorious Revolution' (1688). There is evidence that they may have been written as early as 1681 and they constitute Locke's reply to the patriarchal Divine Right Theory of Sir Robert Filmer and *a fortiori* the political philosophy of Hobbes. Locke also built up his political theory from the shortcomings of an imagined pre-civil society, which for Hobbes was simply war of everyman with everyman. Locke, however, insisted on the natural morality of pre-social man. Hence, contracting into civil society by surrendering personal power to a ruler and magistrates is for Locke a method of securing natural morality more efficiently. The ruling body if it offends against natural law must be deposed. This sanctioning of rebellion, together with Locke's curious doctrine of property, became for the American colonists and the French revolutionaries in the next century, in the words of Oakeshott, 'a brilliant abridgement of the political habits of Englishmen'. It was enshrined in the American Constitution. On his return to England, he declined an ambassadorship and became a commissioner of appeals. His last years were spent at Oates, Essex, at the home of Sir Francis and Lady Masham, an admirer, the daughter of Cudworth (q.v.). His *Essay Concerning Human Understanding* (1690), in its acceptance of the possibility of rational demonstration of moral principles and the existence of God, its scholastic doctrine of substance, is still caught up in Cartesian rationalism, but its denial of innate ideas, its demonstration that 'all knowledge is founded on and ultimately derives itself from sense . . . or sensation' was the real starting-point of British empiricist epistemology. Locke's *Thoughts on Education* (1693), the four *Letters on Toleration* (1689, 1690, 1692, and posthumous fragment), his *Reasonableness of Christianity* (1695) in which he aimed at a reunion of the churches, as well as his several defences of his doctrines against Norris, Stillingfleet, Leibniz, Proast, are also important. He died October 28, 1704, and was buried in the churchyard of High Laver. As a philosopher Locke had his betters. But as a champion and codifier of liberal principles in an intolerant age and as a pioneer of new ways of thought, he has few equals. See Life by M. Cranston (1957), *Correspondence with Clarke*, ed. B. Rand (1927), Leibniz's criticisms in the latter's

Nouveaux Essais (1765), and studies by ▴ Alexander (1908), J. Gibson (1917), R. I. Aaron (1937), D. J. O'Connor (1952), J. W. Yolton (1956), M. Salvadori (1960).

(3) **Matthew** (*c.* 1630–77), English composer, born in Exeter. He collaborated with Shirley on the masque *Cupid and Death*, winning a reputation as a theatre composer. After composing the music for Charles II's coronation procession, Locke became composer-in-ordinary to the king. His works include much incidental music for plays (though that for *Macbeth* long attributed to him is of doubtful authenticity), Latin church music, songs and chamber works. Locke was a champion of the 'modern' French style of composition.

(4) **William John** (1863–1930), English novelist, born at Demerara, British Guiana (Guyana), educated in Trinidad and at Cambridge. He taught between 1890 and 1897 at Clifton and Glenalmond. Disliking teaching, he then became secretary of the Royal Institute of British Architects until 1907. In 1895 appeared the first of a long series of novels and plays which with their charmingly written sentimental themes had such a success during his life in both Britain and America. *The Morals of Marcus Ordeyne* (1905) and *The Beloved Vagabond* (1906) assured his reputation. Others of his popular romances included *Simon the Jester* (1910), *The Joyous Adventures of Aristide Pujol* (1912) and *The Wonderful Fear* (1916). His plays, some of which were dramatized versions of his novels, were all produced with success on the London Stage.

LOCKER-LAMPSON, Frederick (1821–95), English writer, born in London, came of naval ancestry, and from Mincing Lane and Somerset House passed to the Admiralty, where he became the trusted confidant of three first lords. *London Lyrics* (1857) revealed him as a writer of bright and clever *vers de société*; later books were *Lyra Elegantiarum* (1867) and *Patchwork* (1879). In 1850 he married Charlotte (d. 1872), daughter of the seventh Earl of Elgin; and in 1874 Hannah (d. 1915), only daughter of Sir Curtis Lampson, whose name he added to his own. See his *My Confidences* (1896), and Life by A. Birrell (1920).

LOCKHART, (1) **George** (1673–1731), of Carnwath, Lanarkshire, from 1702 a Jacobite M.P., was killed in a duel. See the *Lockhart Papers* (1817).

(2) **John Gibson** (1794–1854), Scottish biographer and critic, born near Wishaw, spent his boyhood in Glasgow, where at eleven he passed from the high school to the college. At thirteen, with a Balliol Snell exhibition, he went up to Oxford. In 1813 he took his classics; then, after a visit to the Continent (to Goethe at Weimar), studied law at Edinburgh, and in 1816 was called to the Scottish bar. But he was no speaker; and having while still at Oxford written the article 'Heraldry' for the *Edinburgh Encyclopaedia*, and translated Schlegel's *Lectures on the History of Literature*, from 1817 he took more and more to letters, and with Wilson became the chief mainstay of *Blackwood's*. In its pages he

first exhibited the caustic wit that made him the terror of his Whig opponents. *Peter's Letters to His Kinsfolk* (' 2nd ed.' 1819), a clever skit on Scottish society, was followed by four novels—*Valerius* (1821), *Adam Blair* (1822), *Reginald Dalton* (1823) and *Matthew Wald* (1824). *Ancient Spanish Ballads* appeared in 1823; Lives of Burns and Napoleon in 1828 and 1829; and the Life of Scott, Lockhart's masterpiece, in 1837–38. He had met Scott in May 1818, and in April 1820 married his eldest daughter, Sophia. In 1825 he removed to London to become editor until 1853 of the *Quarterly Review*. In 1843 he also became auditor of the duchy of Cornwall. But his closing years were clouded by illness and deep depression; by the secession to Rome of his only daughter, with her husband, J. R. Hope-Scott; and by the loss of his wife in 1837, of his two boys in 1831 and 1853. The elder was the ' Hugh Littlejohn ' of Scott's *Tales of a Grandfather*; the younger, Walter, was a scapegrace in the army. Like Scott, Lockhart visited Italy in search of health; like Scott, he came back to Abbotsford to die. He is buried in Dryburgh at Sir Walter's feet. See Life by Andrew Lang (2 vols. 1896), and study by G. Macbeth (1935).

(3) **William Ewart** (1846–1900), Scottish subject painter, born at Annan in Dumfriesshire, was elected an A.R.S.A. in 1870, an R.S.A. in 1878. He painted the Jubilee Celebration in Westminster (1887) and was popular as a portrait painter.

(4) **Sir William Stephen Alexander** (1841–1900), K.C.B. (1887), K.C.S.I. (1895), British officer saw service in Abyssinia, Afghanistan, Burma, &c. In 1897 he commanded the expedition against the Afridis. He was c.-in-c. in India from 1898.

LOCKYER, Sir Joseph Norman (1836–1920), English astronomer, born at Rugby, became a clerk in the War Office (1857) and in the Science and Art Department (1875). In 1868 (26 years before Ramsay) he detected helium in the sun's chromosphere by daylight. In 1869 he was made F.R.S., and in 1870 lecturer on Astronomy at South Kensington. He headed many eclipse expeditions, started (1869) and edited *Nature*, and wrote much on solar chemistry and physics, on the meteoritic hypothesis, and on the orientation of stone circles.

LODGE, (1) **Edmund** (1756–1839), English biographer and writer on heraldry, is best known by his *Portraits of Illustrious Personages* (1821–34) and *The Genealogy of the Existing British Peerage* (1832, enlarged 1859).

(2) **Henry Cabot** (1850–1924), American Republican senator, historian and biographer, was born in Boston. He was assistant editor of the *North American Review*, but from 1878 his career was mainly political and he became a senator in 1893. See his *Early Memories* (1914). His grandson, **Henry Cabot** (1902–), became a Republican senator in 1936, was American U.N. delegate (1953–60), and ambassador to South Vietnam 1963–64, and from 1965.

(3) **Sir Oliver Joseph** (1851–1940), English physicist, born at Penkhull, studied at the Royal College of Science and at University College, London, and became in 1881 professor of Physics at Liverpool. In 1900 he was appointed first principal of the new university at Birmingham and was knighted in 1902. Specially distinguished in electricity, he was a pioneer of wireless telegraphy. He was made a fellow of the Royal Society in 1887. His scientific writings include *Signalling across Space without Wires* (1897), *Talks about Wireless* (1925) and *Advancing Science* (1931). He gave much time to psychical research and on this subject wrote *Raymond* (1916) and *My Philosophy* (1933). *Past Years: An Autobiography*, appeared in 1931. His brother, **Sir Richard** (1855–1936), was the first professor of Modern History at Glasgow University (1894–99) and thereafter at Edinburgh University (1899–1933). Among his works are *A History of Modern Europe* (1885) and *The Close of the Middle Ages, 1273–1494* (1901).

(4) **Thomas** (*c.* 1558–1625), English dramatist, romance writer, and poet, was born at West Ham. From Merchant Taylors' he passed to Trinity College, Oxford, and thence in 1578 to Lincoln's Inn, but led a wild and rollicking life. About 1588 and in 1591 he took part in two sea expeditions and wrote a euphuistic romance, *Rosalynde* (1590), his best-known work, which supplied Shakespeare with many of the chief incidents in *As You Like It*, besides two second-rate dramas, *The Wounds of the Civil War* (1594) and *A Looking-glass for London and England* (with Greene, 1594). He turned Catholic and is believed to have taken a medical degree at Avignon (1600), and to have written a *History of the Plague* (1603). He died in London. Among his remaining writings are *A Fig for Momus* (1595); translations of Seneca (1614) and Josephus (1602); *Life of William Longbeard* (1593); *Robin the Divell*, *Wits Miserie*, and *Glaucus and Silla*, a collection of poems (1589). See his *Works* (4 vols. ed. Gosse, 1884); Gosse's *Seventeenth Century Studies* (1883); Life by Paradise (1931), and *Thomas Lodge and Other Elizabethans*, ed. Sisson (1933).

LOEB, *lœb*, (1) **Jacques** (1859–1924), German-American biologist, born in Mayen and educated at Berlin, Munich and Strasbourg, emigrated to U.S.A. (1891) and after various university appointments became head of the general physiology division at the Rockefeller Institute for Medical Research (1910–24). He did pioneer work on artificial parthenogenesis and also carried out research in comparative physiology and psychology. His writings include *Dynamics of Living Matter* (1906) and *Artificial Parthenogenesis and Fertilisation* (1913).

(2) **James** (1867–1933), American banker with the firm of Kuhn Loeb & Co., was born in New York City. With his fortune he founded the Institute of Musical Art in New York, a mental clinic in Munich and, himself a classical scholar, provided funds for the publication of the famous Loeb Classical Library of Latin and Greek texts with English translations.

LOEWE, Johann Karl Gottfried, *lœ'vě* (1796–1869), German composer, was born near Halle, studied music and theology at Halle, and in 1822 became a musical teacher at Stettin. In 1847 he sang and played before the court in London. He composed operas (of which only one, *The Three Wishes*, was performed), oratorios, symphonies, concertos, duets, and other works for piano, but his ballads, his most notable bequest, are (including the *Erlkönig*) remarkable dramatic poems. See A. Bach, *The Art Ballad* (1890); Loewe's Autobiography (1870); and German Lives by Runze (1884–1888), Wellmer (1886) and Wossidlo (1894).

LOEWI, Otto, *læ'vee* (1873–1961), German pharmacologist, born at Frankfurt-am-Main, educated at Strasbourg and Munich, was professor of Pharmacology at Graz (1909–38) and research professor at New York Univ. College of Medicine from 1940. In 1936 he shared with Sir Henry Hallet Dale (q.v.) the Nobel prize for medicine, for investigations on nerve impulses and their chemical transmission.

LÖFFLER, Friedrich August Johann (1852–(1915), German bacteriologist, born at Frankfurt an der Oder, was a military surgeon, professor at Greifswald (1883) and from 1913 director of the Koch Institute in Berlin. He first cultured the diphtheria bacillus (1884) discovered by Klebs and called the ' Klebs-Löffler bacillus ', discovered the causal organism of glanders and swine erysipelas (1886), isolated an organism causing food poisoning and prepared a vaccine against foot-and-mouth disease (1899). He wrote an unfinished history of bacteriology (1887).

LOFFT, Capell (1751–1824), English writer and lawyer, born in London, the patron of Bloomfield, was a Whig barrister with a taste for letters, especially poetry. His best work was a translation of Spanish, Italian and other foreign verse under the title of *Laura, an Anthology of Sonnets* (5 vols. 1814). His fourth son, Capell (1806–73), who died at Millmead, Va., wrote poetry and an autobiography called *Self-Formation* (1837).

LOFTUS, Cissie. See McCARTHY, JUSTIN.

LOGAN, (1) **James** (*c*. 1794–1872), Celtic antiquary, author in 1831 of *the Scottish Gael*, was born in Aberdeen, and lived and died in London.

(2) **John** (1748–88), Scottish poet, was born a farmer's son, at Soutra, Midlothian. In 1773 was chosen minister of South Leith; but in 1786, owing to intemperance and other matters of scandal, he had to resign his charge, and took to literary work in London. Besides two posthumous volumes of sermons, he wrote a tragedy, *Runnamede* (1783), withdrawn after a single performance at Edinburgh. His *Poems* (1781) included the ' Ode to the Cuckoo ' and others that he had already published as the work of Michael Bruce (q.v.). Logan's authorship of the exquisite ' Braes of Yarrow ' is not disputed, though its best lines are justifiably reminiscent.

(3) **John Alexander** (1826–86), American soldier and legislator, born in Illinois, served in the Mexican war, was called to the bar in 1852, and was elected to congress as a Democrat in 1858. He raised an Illinois regiment in the civil war, and retired at its close as major-general. Returned to congress as a Republican in 1866, he was repeatedly

chosen a U.S. senator. See Life by G. F. Dawson (1887).

(4) **Sir William Edmund** (1798–1875), Scottish geologist, born, a baker's son, at Montreal, was sent over in 1814 to Edinburgh High School and University. After ten years in a London counting house, he became (1828) book-keeper at Swansea to a copper-smelting company. There he made a map of the coal basin, which was incorporated into the geological survey. In 1842–71 he directed the Canadian Geological Survey. Knighted in 1856, he died in Wales. See Life by Harrington (1883).

LOISY, Alfred Firmin, *lwa'zee* (1857–1940), French theologian, born at Ambrières, Haute-Marne, ordained priest in 1879 and in 1881 became professor of Holy Scripture at the Institut Catholique, where by his lectures and writings he incurred the disfavour of the church and was dismissed. In 1900 he was appointed lecturer at the Sorbonne, but resigned after his works on Biblical criticism were condemned by Pope Pius X in 1903 as too advanced. These books, which proved him to be the founder of the modernist movement, were, *L'Évangile et l'Église* (1902), *Quatrième Évangile* (1903) *and Autour d'un petit livre* (1903). For subsequent works of the same kind he was excommunicated in 1908. He was professor of History of Religion in the Collège de France in 1909–32. See his *Choses passées* (1913), and study by Petre (1944).

LOMBARD, Peter (*c*. 1100–64), Italian theologian, born near Novara in Lombardy, studied at Bologna, at Reims, and (under Abelard) at Paris, and, after holding a chair of Theology there, in 1159 became Bishop of Paris. He was generally styled *Magister Sententiarum*, or the ' Master of Sentences ', from his collection of sentences from Augustine and other Fathers on points of Christian doctrine, with objections and replies. The theological doctors of Paris in 1300 denounced some of his teachings as heretical; but his work was the standard textbook of Catholic Theology down to the Reformation.

LOMBROSO, Cesare (1836–1909), Italian founder of the science of criminology, was born of Jewish stock at Verona, and after acting as an army surgeon, professor of Mental Diseases at Pavia, and director of an asylum at Pesaro, became professor of Forensic Medicine and Psychiatry at Turin. His theory postulated the existence of a criminal type distinguishable from the normal man. His great work is *L'uomo delinquente* (1875). See Life by H. Kurella (trans. 1911).

LOMONOSOV, Mikhail Vasilievich, *-nō'sof* (1711–65), Russian philologist, poet, writer and scientist, born at Denisovka, near Archangel. The son of a fisherman, he ran away to Moscow in search of education, and later studied at St Petersburg and at Marburg under Christian Wolff; he returned to St Petersburg and became professor of Chemistry there. In his poetry he introduced a new form of versification, and his greatest contribution to Russian culture was his systemization of the grammar and orthography. His writings include works on rhetoric (1748), grammar (1755), and ancient

Russian history (1766). See *History of Russian Literature* by D. S. Mirsky (1927) and study by A. Martel (Paris 1933).

LONDON, Jack (1876–1916), American novelist, born at San Francisco, was successively sailor, tramp and gold miner before he took to writing. He used his knowledge of the Klondyke in the highly successful *Call of the Wild* (1903) and *White Fang* (1907), and of the sea in *Sea-Wolf* (1904) and *The Mutiny of the 'Elsinore'* (1914), and, as well as pure adventure tales, wrote the more serious political novel *The Iron Heel* (1907), and his autobiographical tale of alcoholism *John Barleycorn* (1913). His wife, **Charmian**, wrote his biography (1921), &c. See also *The Bodley Head Jack London* (ed. by Calder-Marshall), *Jack London, American Rebel* (ed. by Foner, 1947), and studies by O'Connor (1965) and Walcutt (1966).

LONDONDERRY. See PITT and CASTLE-REAGH.

LONG, (1) **Crawford Williamson** (1815–78), American physician, was born at Danielsville, Ga. In 1842, operating on a neck tumour, he was the first to use ether as an anaesthetic, but did not reveal his discovery until 1849.

(2) **Earl Kemp** (1895–1960), brother of (4), continued his brother's methods of corrupt administration coupled with sound social legislation, as lieutenant-governor (1936–38) and governor (1939–40, 1948–52, 1956–60) of Louisiana. Suffering from paranoiac schizophrenia, he was at his wife's request placed in a mental hospital in May 1959 and forcibly detained there with police help, until, using his powers as governor, he dismissed the mental hospitals superintendent and appointed politically favourable medical officers. See Life by A. J. Liebling (1962).

(3) **George** (1800–79), English scholar, born at Poulton, Lancashire, a fellow (1823) of Trinity College, Cambridge, professor at the universities of Virginia (1824–28) and London (1828–46), a founder of the Royal Geographical Society (1830), published *Decline of the Roman Republic* (1864–74), translated the classics, and edited the *Penny Encyclopaedia* (1833–46).

(4) **Huey Pierce** (1893–1935), American politician, brother of (2), born at Winnfield, La., was a lawyer and became governor of Louisiana (1928–31). Notorious for corruption and demagoguery, he won the support of the poor by his intensive social service and public works programmes. He was murdered.

LONGCHAMP, William de, *lõ-shā* (d. 1197), English prelate, a low-born favourite of Richard I, who in 1189–90 made him chancellor, Bishop of Ely, and joint justiciar of England; in 1191 he was likewise made papal legate, but for his heated arrogance he had to withdraw to Normandy. He regained Richard's favour by raising his ransom, and was made chancellor again. He died at Poitiers. See French monograph by L. Boivin Champeaux (1885).

LONGFELLOW, Henry Wadsworth (1807–1882), American poet, born at Portland, Me., graduated at Bowdoin College in Brunswick, Me. In 1826 the college trustees sent him to Europe to qualify for the chair of Foreign Languages, and he spent three years abroad.

He married in 1831, but his wife died in 1835. *Outre Mer*, an account of his first European tour, appeared in 1835; and *Hyperion*, which is a journal of the second, in 1839. In 1836 he became professor of Modern Languages and Literature in Harvard, and held the chair nearly eighteen years. *Voices of the Night* (1839), his first book of verse, made a favourable impression, which was deepened by *Ballads* (1841), including ' The Skeleton in Armour ', ' The Wreck of the Hesperus '. ' The Village Blacksmith ', and ' Excelsior '. *Poems on Slavery* appeared in 1842. Longfellow made a third visit to Europe in 1842, and next year married his second wife, who was burned to death in 1861. *The Belfry of Bruges and other Poems* appeared in 1846. One of his most popular poems is *Evangeline* (1847), a tale (in hexameters) of the French exiles of Acadia. *The Golden Legend* (1851) is based on *Der arme Heinrich* of Hartmann von Aue; *Hiawatha* (1855), on legends of the Redskins. *The Courtship of Miles Standish* (1858) is a story in hexameters of the early days of the Plymouth colony in Massachusetts. His translation of Dante (1867–70) has added little and his plays less to his reputation. *Flower-de-Luce* (1867) has had its admirers. He paid a last visit to Europe in 1868–69. As a poet he was extremely popular during his lifetime and although his work lacks the real depth of great poetry, his gift of simple, romantic story-telling in verse makes it still read widely and with pleasure. He died in his home at Cambridge, Mass. See Lives by his brother, the Rev. Samuel Longfellow (1891), Higginson (1902) and Gorman (1927).

LONGHI or **Falca, Pietro**, *long'gee* (1702–85), Venetian painter. He was a pupil of Balestra, and excelled in small-scale satiric pictures of Venetian life. Most of his work is in Venetian public collections, but the National Gallery, London, has three, of which the best known is *Rhinoceros in an Arena*. His son **Alessandro** (1733–1813) was a pupil of Nogari. Some of Alessandro's portraits are now attributed to his father. See A. Ravà, *Pietro Longhi* (1923).

LONGINUS, Dionysius Cassius (*c.* A.D. 213–273), Neoplatonic philosopher, taught rhetoric in Athens, but settling at Palmyra, became chief counsellor to Queen Zenobia. For this Aurelian beheaded him. It is now very doubtful that the treatise *On the Sublime* was written by him. This has been edited by (among others) Rhys Roberts (1899), Prickard (1906) and W. Hamilton Fyfe (1932).

LONGLEY, Charles Thomas (1794–1868), English prelate, born near Rochester, from Westminster passed to Christ Church, Oxford; was headmaster of Harrow 1829–1836, and became Bishop of Ripon (1836), Archbishop of York (1860) and Archbishop of Canterbury (1862).

LONGMAN, Thomas (1699–1755), founder of the publishing firm which bears his name, son of a Bristol merchant, bought a bookselling business in Paternoster Row in 1724, and shared in publishing Boyle's *Works*, Ainsworth's *Latin Dictionary*, Ephraim Chambers's *Cyclopaedia*, and Johnson's *Dictionary*. His nephew, Thomas Longman (1730–97), brought out a new edition of Chambers's *Cyclopaedia*. Under Thomas Norton Longman (1771–1842) the firm had relations with Wordsworth, Southey, Coleridge, Scott, Moore, Sydney Smith, &c. After Constable's failure in 1826 the *Edinburgh Review* became the property of the firm, who also published Lardner's *Cabinet Cyclopaedia* (1829–46). Thomas Longman (1804–79), eldest son of T. N. Longman, issued under his special care a beautifully illustrated New Testament. His brother, William (1813–77), wrote *Lectures on ihe History of England* (1859), *History of Edward III* (1869), &c. The event of this generation was the publication of Macaulay's *Lays* (1842), *Essays* (1843) and *History* (1848–61). See Cox and Chandler *The House of Longman* (1925).

LONGOMONTANUS, Christian Sörensen (1562–1647), Danish astronomer, born at Longberg, Jutland, in 1589 became an assistant of Tycho Brahe (q.v.), whom he accompanied to Germany. Returning to Denmark he became a professor at Copenhagen, where he inaugurated the building of the observatory.

LONGSTREET, James (1821–1904), American general, born in South Carolina, fought in the Mexican war, and, as a Confederate, in both battles of Bull Run, at Williamsburg, Richmond, Fredericksburg, Gettysburg, Chickamauga and the Wilderness. He was minister to Turkey in 1880–81.

LONGUEVILLE, Anne, Duchesse de, *lō-veel* (1619–79), born at Vincennes, the 'soul of the Fronde', was the only daughter of the Prince of Condé, and in 1639 was married to the Duc de Longueville. She exerted a considerable influence on politics in which she first began to interest herself as the mistress of the Duc de la Rochefoucauld. In the first war of the Fronde (1648) she sought in vain to gain over her brother, the Great Condé. In the second she won over both him and Turenne. After the death of her husband and her desertion by la Rochefoucauld, she entered a convent but continued to have influence at court. See Lives by Cousin (1891–97) and Williams (1907).

LONGUS, wrote the Greek prose romance *Daphnis and Chloe*, possibly in the 3rd century A.D.

LÖNNROT, Elias, *læn'rot* (1802–84), Finnish scholar, born at Sammatti in Nyland, practised medicine for twenty years in Kajana, and was professor of Finnish at Helsingfors 1853–62. He published collections of Finnish folksongs, notably the *Kalevala* which by his hand became a long, connected epic poem, proverbs, riddles, and a great Finnish-Swedish Dictionary (1866–1880) which helped to further his aim of establishing a literary Finnish language. See Life by Ahlqvist (Helsingfors 1885).

LONSDALE, (1) Frederick (1881–1954), British playwright, born in Jersey, Frederick Leonard, son of a tobacconist, known for his witty and sophisticated society comedies, among them *The Last of Mrs Cheyney* (1925), *On Approval* (1927) and *Canaries Sometimes Sing* (1929). He collaborated in operettas, including *Maid of the Mountains* (1916). See Life by F. Donaldson (1957).

(2) **Hugh Cecil Lowther, 5th Earl of** (1857–1944), was a noted sportsman and Cumberland landowner. He founded the Lonsdale belt for boxing. See *The Yellow Earl* by D. Sutherland (1965).

(3) **William** (1794–1871), English geologist, born at Bath, served in the army but left it in 1815 and took up geology. He made a study of the fossils in north and south Devon, in 1837 placing them between the Silurian and the Carboniferous. This led to the establishment of the Devonian System by Murchison and Sedgwick (1839).

LOOMIS, Elias (1811–89), American writer on mathematics, astronomy, meteorology, &c., born at Willington, Conn., graduated at Yale, was tutor there (1833–36), professor at Cleveland (1837–44), New York (1844–60) and Yale (from 1860).

LOPE (DE VEGA). See VEGA CARPIO.

LOPES, Francisco Higino Craveiro (1894–1964), Portuguese politician, born in Lisbon of a distinguished military family. Educated at the Military School, Lisbon, he fought in the Expeditionary Force in Mozambique in the first World War. As a full colonel in 1942 he entered negotiations for co-operation with the Allies and was responsible for the modernization of the Portuguese air force. In 1944 he entered parliament, in 1949 he was promoted to general, and was president of Portugal from 1951 to 1958.

LÓPEZ, Francisco Solano (1827–70), born in Asunción, a grand-nephew of Francia, succeeded his father as president of Paraguay in 1862. In 1864 he provoked war with Brazil and was faced with an alliance of Brazil, Uruguay and Argentina. The war lasted for five years during which Paraguay was completely devastated and López himself having fled was shot by a soldier.

LÓPEZ DE AYALA. See AYALA.

LOPOKOVA, Lydia. See KEYNES.

LORCA, Federigo García (1899–1936), Spanish poet, was born in Fuente Vaqueros, and was killed, by design or misunderstanding, early in the Spanish Civil War at Granada. His gypsy songs—*Canciones* (1927) and *Romancero Gitano* (1928 and 1935), probably his best and most widely-read work, reveal a classical control of imagery, rhythm and emotion. He wrote, also, several successful plays, including *Bodas de Sangre* (1933), *Yerma* and *La Casa de Bernarda Alba*. See study by R. Campbell (1952).

LORD, Thomas (1755–1832), English sportsman, born in Thirsk, Yorkshire, founder of the Lord's Cricket Ground, home of the Marylebone Cricket Club since 1787.

LOREBURN, Robert Threshie Reid, 1st Earl of (1846–1923), lawyer, born of Scottish parents at Corfu, studied at Balliol, was called to the bar in 1871, and became M.P. in 1880, solicitor-general and attorney-general in 1894, and in 1905 lord chancellor and a baron, in 1911 an earl. He resigned in 1912.

LORENTZ, Hendrik Antoon (1853–1928), Dutch physicist, born at Arnhem, studied at Leiden, became professor of Mathematical Physics there in 1878. He also directed research at Haarlem from 1923. He worked out the explanation by the 'Fitzgerald-Lorentz Contraction' of the Michelson-

Morley experiment, and prepared the way for Einstein. In 1902 he was awarded, with Zeeman, the Nobel prize for physics.

LORENZETTI, (1) **Ambrogio** (?1300–?48), Sienese artist, younger brother of (2). He worked at Cortona and Florence, but is best known for his allegorical frescoes in the Palazzo Pubblico at Siena, symbolizing the effects of good and bad government. An *Annunciation* is also at Siena. See studies by G. Sinibaldi (1933) and G. Rowley (1959).

(2) **Pietro,** also called **Pietro Laurati** (?1280–?1348), Sienese artist, elder brother of (1), probably the pupil of Duccio. He was one of the liveliest of the early Sienese painters, and he also worked at Arezzo (the polyptych in S. Maria della Pieve) and Assisi, where he painted dramatic frescoes of the *Passion* in the Lower Church of S. Francis. A *Madonna* (1340) is in the Uffizi Gallery. See studies by E. T. De Wald (Cambridge, Mass., 1930) and G. Sinibaldi (1933).

LORENZO, called **il Monaco** (*c.* 1370–*c.* 1425), Italian painter, born at Siena. He worked in Florence, and was the master of Fra Angelico. His charming pictures, usually on a small scale, are represented in both the Uffizi and the Louvre galleries. See studies by O. Siren (1905) and V. Golzio (1931).

LORIMER, (1) **James** (1818–90), Scottish jurist, born at Aberdalgie, Perthshire, was an eminent authority on international law, and from 1862 professor at Edinburgh. *The Institutes of the Law of Nations* was his best-known book.

(2) **Sir Robert Stodart** (1864–1929), Scottish architect and younger son of (1), did much to further the national domestic style. Among the buildings so restored are Earlshall, Balmanno, Dunblane Cathedral and Paisley Abbey. He was the architect of the Scottish War Memorial at Edinburgh Castle and the Thistle Chapel in St Giles', which brought him international recognition. See C. Hussey, *The Architecture of Sir Robert Lorimer* (1931).

LORJOU, Bernard, *-zhoo* (1908–), French artist, born at Blois. He was the founder of L'Homme Témoin group in 1949 and among a number of large satirical paintings is his *Atomic Age* (1951).

LORM. See LANDESMANN.

LORNE, Marquis of. See ARGYLL.

LORRAINE, (1) **Charles, Cardinal de.** See GUISE.

(2) **Claude.** See CLAUDE LORRAINE.

(3) **Ducal House of.** See GUISE.

LORRIS, Guillaume de, *lor-ees* (fl. 13th cent.), French poet, wrote, before 1260, the first part (*c.* 4000 lines) of the *Roman de la Rose*, continued by Jean de Meung.

LORTZING, Gustav Albert (1801–51) German musician, born in Berlin, went early on the stage, sang in opera, conducted and composed *Zar und Zimmermann* (1837) and other operas with librettos by himself.

LOSINGA, Herbert de (*c.* 1054–1119), Bishop of Thetford from 1091, and from 1094 first Bishop of Norwich, was probably a native of Lorraine. See Life by Goulburn and Symonds (1878).

LOTHROP, Amy. See WARNER (4).

LOTI, Pierre. See VIAUD.

LOTTI, Antonio (*c.* 1665–1740), Italian church and operatic composer, was born and died in Venice. He was organist of St Mark's from 1704.

LOTTO, Lorenzo (*c.* 1480–1556), Italian religious painter, was born at Venice. A masterly portrait painter, his subjects are alive and full of character. He worked in Treviso, Bergamo, Venice and Rome, finally becoming a lay brother in the Loreto monastery, where he died. See monograph by Berenson (1956).

LOTZE, Rudolf Hermann (1817–81), German idealist philosopher, born at Bautzen, studied medicine and philosophy at Leipzig, and became professor of Philosophy there in 1842, at Göttingen in 1844. It was as a physiologist that he first attracted notice, combating the then accepted doctrine of vitalism. His *General Physiology of Bodily Life* (1851) led many to rank him with the materialists, though his real views were expressed in his *Metaphysik* (1841). The most comprehensive statement of his teleological idealism is in his *Microcosmus* (1856–1864). Books on *Logic* (1874) and on *Metaphysics* (1879) were part of an unfinished comprehensive system. See works by H. Jones (1895), Falckenberg (1901 *et seq.*), Schoen (1902), E. E. Thomas (1922).

LOUBET, Émile, *loo-bay* (1838–1929), French statesman, born at Marsanne (Drôme), was seventh president of the Republic (1899–1906).

LOUCHEUR, Raymond, *loo-shœr* (1899–), French composer, born at Tourcoing, who studied at the Paris Conservatoire under Gédalge and D'Indy. Winner of the *grand prix de Rome* in 1928 and the Georges Bizet prize in 1935, he has composed two symphonies, songs, chamber music, the *Rapsodie malgache* and the ballet *Hop Frog* based on the tale by Edgar Allan Poe. This was a tremendous success when presented at the Paris Opera House in 1953. In 1956 he became director of the Conservatoire.

LOUDON, (1) **Gideon Ernst, Freiherr von** (1717–90), Austrian generalissimo, born at Tootzen, Livonia, whither his ancestor had migrated from Ayrshire in the 14th century. In 1732 he entered the Russian service, but ten years later exchanged into that of Austria. In the Seven Years' War he won the battle of Kunersdorf (1759); and his loss of the battle of Liegnitz (1760) was due mainly to Lacy and Daun. As field-marshal he commanded in the war of the Bavarian succession (1778), and against the Turks (1788–89), capturing Belgrade and Semendria. See Life by Malleson (1884).

(2) **John Claudius** (1783–1843), Scottish horticulturist, born at Cambuslang, studied landscape gardening from an early age, working in England and travelling in Europe. The results of his studies are to be found in many works on horticulture including his *Encyclopaedia of Gardening* (1822).

LOUGHBOROUGH. See WEDDERBURN.

LOUIS. The name of eighteen French kings.

Louis I (778–840), ' the Debonair ' of

France, was also emperor, and was a son of Charlemagne. **Louis II** (846–879), ' the Stammerer ', was the son of Charles the Bold. and began to reign over France in 877. **Louis III** (d. 881), was his eldest son. **Louis IV** (921–954), grandson of Louis II, began to reign in 936. **Louis V**, ' le Fainéant ' (966–987), son of Lothair III, was the last of the Carolingians. **Louis VI**, ' the Fat ' (1078–1137), was son of Philip I, and succeeded in 1108. **Louis VII**, his son (1120–80), came to the crown 1137, launched the disastrous second crusade (1147–49), divorced his wife Eleanor of Aquitaine, who afterwards married Henry II of England, and so gave rise to long wars for the possession of that territory. **Louis VIII** (1187–1226), son of Philip Augustus, came to the throne 1223, led the Albigensian crusade, and acquired Languedoc for the crown.

Louis IX, or St Louis (1215–70), king of France, born at Poissy, succeeded his father, Louis VIII, in 1226, and by his victories compelled Henry III of England to acknowledge French suzerainty in Guienne. During a dangerous illness he made a vow to go as a crusader. Having appointed his mother (the pious Blanche of Castile) regent, he landed with 40,000 men in Egypt in 1249. He captured Damietta, but was afterwards defeated, taken prisoner, and ransomed for 100,000 marks in 1250. He proceeded to Acre with the remnant of his army, and remained in Palestine till his mother's death (1252) compelled his return to France. He did much to strengthen loyalty to his house, determined by the Pragmatic Sanction the relation of the French Church to the pope, countenanced the Sorbonne, set up in the provinces royal courts of justice or parliaments, and authorized a new code of laws. He embarked on a new crusade in 1270, and died of plague at Tunis. Pope Boniface VIII canonized him in 1297. See *Vie de St Louis* by his friend Joinville (q.v.), and *Cambridge Medieval History*, VI (1929).

Louis X (1289–1316), ' the Quarrelsome ', was the son of Philip IV and reigned for only two years, 1314–16, during which time he was guided in his policy by Charles of Valois.

Louis XI (1423–83), eldest son of Charles VII, born at Bourges, made unsuccessful attempts against his father's throne, and had to flee to Burgundy. In 1461 he succeeded to the crown. The severe measures which he adopted against the great vassals led to a coalition against him, headed by Burgundy and Brittany. Louis owed his success more to cunning than to arms. His agents stirred up Liège to revolt against Charles the Bold, Duke of Burgundy, and Charles seized Louis, and compelled him to assist in the punishment of Liège. Louis now stirred up against Charles the Flemish towns and the Swiss republics; and the Swiss defeated Charles twice, and killed him (1477). Louis then claimed Burgundy as a vacant fief, but failed, as Mary, the rightful heir, was married to Maximilian of Austria. The latter defeated the French at Guinegate (1479), but after a new war and the death of Mary, a treaty (1482) gave Burgundy and Artois to France. Louis also annexed Provence. In

order to weaken his feudal vassals he increased the power and number of parliaments. He spent his later years in great misery, in superstitious terrors and excessive horror of death; his chief advisers the barber Olivier le Dain, Tristan l'Hermite and Cardinal Balue. He died at Plessis-lez-Tours. He cherished art and sciences, and founded three universities. See his *Lettres* (1883–1909); Comines's *Mémoires*; works by Legeay (1874), Willert (1876), Buet (2nd ed. 1886), Vaesen and Charavay (1885–90), Sée (1892), Hare (1907), Champion (1927); and *Quentin Durward*.

Louis XII (1462–1515), succeeded Charles VIII in 1498, and by his just and kindly rule became known as the ' Father of the People '. He overran Milan, and helped the Spaniards to conquer Naples. He humbled the Venetians in 1509, was driven out of Italy in 1513, and defeated at the ' Battle of the Spurs ' (1513) by the emperor and Henry VIII of England. He was married to a daughter of Louis XI, to Anne of Brittany, and to a sister of Henry VIII, and was succeeded by his son-in-law Francis I. See works by Seyssel (1558), Maulde-La Clavière (1890–95) and Bridge (1929–36).

Louis XIII (1601–43), son of Henry IV and Marie de' Medici, born at Fontainebleau, succeeded on his father's assassination (1610), his mother being regent. She entered into alliance with Spain and the pope, and betrothed the king to Anne of Austria, daughter of Philip III of Spain, upon which the Huguenots took up arms; but peace was concluded in 1614.· The king, now declared of age, confirmed the Edict of Nantes, and the French States-General were summoned for the last time till the reign of Louis XVI. The restoration of Catholic church rights in Béarn led to the religious war which ended in 1622. After the death of De Luynes, in 1624, Richelieu became chief minister. He obtained complete control over the weak king, and greatly increased monarchical power. The overthrow of the Huguenots was completed by the capture of Rochelle in 1628. Richelieu now led Louis to take part in the Thirty Years' War, supporting Gustavus Adolphus and the Dutch against the Spaniards and Austrians. His eldest son was Louis XIV; his second, Philip, Duke of Orleans, ancestor of the present House of Orleans. See MARIE DE' MEDICI, RICHELIEU; and works by Bazin (new ed. 1846), Topin (1876), Zeller (1879–92), Batiffol (1907–10), Patmore (1909), Romain (1934), Vaunois (1936), Champigneule (1958).

Louis XIV (1638–1715), born at St Germain-en-Laye, succeeded Louis XIII in 1643. His mother, Anne of Austria, became regent, and Mazarin (q.v.) her minister. In 1648 certain of the nobles, aggrieved at being excluded from high offices, rose in rebellion, and began the civil wars of the *Fronde*, so called from *frondeur*, a slinger; metaphorically, a grumbler. Peace was concluded in 1659; and in the following year Louis married the Infanta Maria Theresa. On Mazarin's death in 1661 Louis assumed the reins of government, and from that time forth exercised with rare energy a pure despotism. He had a cool and clear head, much dignity and amenity of manners, and indomitable perseverance. He was ably supported by his ministers, and manufactures began to flourish. Colbert restored prosperity to the ruined finances, and provided the means for war, while Louvois raised admirably equipped armies. On the death of Philip IV of Spain Louis, as his son-in-law, claimed part of the Spanish Netherlands; in 1667, with Turenne, he crossed the frontier, and made himself master of French Flanders and Franche Comté. The *triple alliance*— between England, Holland and Sweden— arrested his conquests; and the treaty of Aix-la-Chapelle (1668) surrendered Franche Comté. He now made German alliances, purchased the friendship of Charles II of England, seized Lorraine in 1670, and in 1672 again entered the Netherlands with Condé and Turenne, and conquered half the country in six weeks. The States-General formed an alliance with Spain and the emperor, but Louis made himself master of ten cities of the empire in Alsace, in 1674 took the field with three great armies, and, notwithstanding the death of Turenne and the retirement of Condé, continued to extend his conquests in the Netherlands. The peace of Nijmegen in 1678 left him fortresses in the Spanish Netherlands and Franche Comté. He now established in Metz and elsewhere packed courts of law, which confiscated to him territories belonging to the Elector Palatine, the Elector of Trier, and others, and in 1681 made a sudden and successful descent on Strasburg, a free and powerful German city, which he finally secured by treaty in 1684. Louis had now reached the zenith of his career. All Europe feared him; France regarded him with Asiatic humility; all remnants of political independence had been swept away. Even the courts of justice yielded to the absolute sway of the monarch, who interfered at pleasure with the course of law by commissions, or withdrew offenders by *lettres de cachet*, of which he issued about 9000. The court was the heart of the national life of France, and there the utmost splendour was maintained. In 1685 Louis married his mistress, Madame de Maintenon, who was herself governed by the Jesuits— hence the revocation of the Edict of Nantes (1685) and a bloody persecution of Protestants, which drove half a million of the best and most industrious inhabitants of France to other lands. Yet Louis convened a council of French clergy, which declared the papal power to extend only to matters of faith. The Elector Palatine dying in 1685, Louis claimed part of the territory for the Duchess of Orleans. A French army invaded the Palatinate, Baden, Württemberg and Trier in 1688, and in 1689 the Lower Palatinate was laid waste by fire and sword. Success for a time attended the French arms, but reverses ensued, and the war continued for years with varying success. After the French had gained the battle of Neerwinden (1693), the means of waging war were almost exhausted, and Louis concluded the peace of Ryswick (1697) amid universal distress and discontent. Charles II of Spain at his death (1700) left all

his dominions to a grandson of his sister, Louis's queen. Louis supported the claim of his grandson (Philip V) while the Emperor Leopold supported that of his son, afterwards the Emperor Charles VI. The ' War of the Spanish Succession ' had to be maintained both in the Netherlands and in Italy. One defeat followed another; Marlborough was victorious in the Low Countries, and Prince Eugene in Italy. In April 1713 peace was concluded at Utrecht, the French prince obtaining the Spanish throne, but at a sacrifice to France of valuable colonies. France, indeed, now was almost completely ruined; but the monarch maintained to the last an unbending despotism. He was succeeded by his great-grandson, Louis XV, his son and his eldest grandson having both died in 1711. The reign of Louis XIV, ' le Roi Soleil ', is regarded as the Augustan age of French literature and art, producing such writers as Corneille, Racine, Molière and Boileau, and divines like Bossuet, Fénelon, Bourdaloue and Massillon. See Voltaire's *Siècle de Louis XIV* (1740); Saint-Simon (1788); works by Chotard (1890), Gérin (1894), Chérot (1894), Hassall (Eng. 1895), Perkins (Eng. 1897), Lavisse's *Histoire de France* (vii–viii, 1908), the *Cambridge Mod. Hist.* (v, 1908), de St Leger and Sagnac (1935), Gaxotte (1944), Bailly (1946), Lewis (1959).

Louis XV (1710–74), great-grandson of Louis XIV, born at Versailles, succeeded September 1, 1715. The Duke of Orleans was regent, and became infatuated with the financial schemes of the Scotsman, Law. All available capital was pocketed by the financial cliques, the court, and the state. At fifteen Louis married Maria Leszczyńska, daughter of Stanislas, the dethroned king of Poland. At the death of the regent Louis reigned personally, under the advice of his wise teacher, Cardinal Fleury. In the war of the Polish Succession the duchy of Lorraine was obtained for Louis's father-in-law, and for the French crown after him. In 1740 commenced the war of the Austrian Succession, in which France supported the claims of the Elector of Bavaria to the imperial crown, against those of Maria Theresa, Queen of Hungary. After a course of easy conquest in 1741, the French were badly beaten in 1742: regret and worry brought Fleury to the grave next year. But presently France, in alliance with Frederick the Great of Prussia, was repeatedly victorious on land, as at Fontenoy (1745), over English, Austrians and Dutch, though the English put an end to the French navy and sea trade. After the peace of Aix-la-Chapelle the king sank under the control of Madame de Pompadour, to whom he gave notes on the treasury for enormous sums. War broke out again with Britain concerning the boundaries of Nova Scotia. In 1756 began the Seven Years' War, and an alliance was formed between France and Austria against Prussia and Britain. In spite of disaster, financial embarrassment, and the misery of the people, the king, governed by his mistress, obstinately persevered in war, even after the terrible defeat of Minden in 1759; while the British conquered almost all the French colonies both in the East and West Indies, with Canada. A humiliating peace was concluded in 1763. The Paris parliament secured, after a contest, the suppression of the Jesuits in 1764, and now attempted, ineffectively, to limit the power of the crown by refusing to register edicts of taxation. The Duc de Choiseul was dismissed, a new mistress, Madame du Barry, having taken the place of Madame de Pompadour. The councillors of the parliament of Paris were banished, and a dutiful parliament appointed (1771). The gifts to Madame du Barry in five years amounted to 180 millions of livres. Louis, whose constitution was ruined by a life of vice, was seized with smallpox, and ' le bien aimé ' died unwept. See Voltaire's *Siècle de Louis XV* (1768–70), and works by Tocqueville (2nd ed. 1847), Bonhomme (1873), Broglie (Eng. trans. 1879), Pajol (1881–92), Vandal (1882), Carré (1891), Soulange-Bodin (1894), Haggard (1906), Imbert de Saint-Amand (1887–95), Gaxotte (1933), Leroy (1938), Mazé (1944).

Louis XVI (1754–93), was the third son of the dauphin, Louis, only son of Louis XV, and became dauphin by the death of his father and his elder brothers. He was married in 1770 to Marie Antoinette, youngest daughter of the Empress Maria Theresa. When he ascended the throne (1774) the public treasury was empty, the state was burdened with a debt of 4000 millions of livres, and the people were crushed under the taxes. By advice of Maurepas the king restored to the Paris and provincial parliaments their semi-political rights. Malesherbes and Turgot proposed thoroughgoing reforms, accepted by the king, but rejected by the court, aristocracy, parliaments, and church. Turgot resigned. Yet Louis remitted some of the most odious taxes, made a few inconsiderable reforms, and was for a time extremely popular, being handsome, healthy, and moral, fond of manly exercises, and of working as a locksmith. In 1777 Necker was made director-general, and succeeded in bringing the finances to a more tolerable condition; but through France's outlay in the American War of Independence he was obliged to propose the taxation of the privileged classes, and their resistance compelled him to resign. The lavish Calonne (1783) renewed for a while the splendour of the court, and advised the calling together of an Assembly of Notables. The noblemen, clergymen, state officials, councillors of parliaments, and municipal officers thus collected compelled him to fly to London. His successor, Brienne, obtained some new taxes, but the parliament of Paris refused to register the edict. The convening of the States-General was universally demanded. The king registered the edicts and banished the councillors of parliament, but had to recall them. In May 1788 he dissolved all the parliaments and established a *Cour plénière*. Matters became still worse when in August appeared the edict that the treasury should cease all cash payments except to the troops. Brienne resigned, and Necker again became minister. An assembly of the States of the kingdom, in abeyance since 1614, was

resolved upon; and by the advice of Necker the Third Estate was called in double number. The States-General met in May 1789 at Versailles. The *tiers-état*, taking matters into their own hands, formed themselves into a National Assembly, thereby commencing the Revolution; and undertaking to make a new constitution, they called themselves the Constituent Assembly. The resistance of Louis to the demands of the deputies for political independence, equal rights and universal freedom, led to their declaration of inviolability. The king retaliated by ordering troops under arms, dissolving the ministry, and banishing Necker. The consequence was revolutionary outbreaks in Paris on July 12, 1789. Next day the National Guard of Paris was called out, and on the 14th the people stormed the Bastille. Meanwhile the provinces repeated the acts of Paris. On August 4 feudal and manorial rights were abrogated by the Assembly, which declared the equality of human rights. The royal princes and all the nobles who could escape sought safety in flight. The royal family, having in vain attempted to follow their example, tried to conciliate the people by the feigned assumption of republican sentiments, but on October 5 the rabble attacked Versailles and compelled Louis and his family to return to Paris, whither the Assembly also moved. The next two years witnessed the inauguration and the subsequent withdrawal of various constitutional schemes. Louis alternately made concessions to the republicans, and devised schemes for escaping from their surveillance (in June 1791 the king and queen had got as far as Varennes, whence they were brought back), and each month added to his humiliation and to the audacity of those surrounding him. The Constituent Assembly was succeeded in 1791 by the Legislative Assembly. The king was compelled by the Girondists to a war with Austria in April 1792, and the early defeats of the French were visited on Louis, who was confined, in August, with his family in the Temple. The advance of the Prussians under the Duke of Brunswick into Champagne threw Paris into the wildest excitement. The Assembly dissolved itself in September; the National Convention took its place, and the Republic was proclaimed. In December the king was brought to trial, and called upon to answer for repeated acts of treason against the Republic. On January 20, 1793, sentence of death was passed, and next day he was guillotined in the Place de la Révolution. See MARIE ANTOINETTE, NECKER, TURGOT MIRABEAU; and works by Beaucourt (1892), Souriau (1893), Haggard (1909), Ségur (1909–13), Webster (1936–37), Mazé (1941–1943), de la Fuye (1943), Faÿ (trans. 1968).

Louis XVII, Charles (1785–95), second son of Louis XVI, became dauphin on the death of his brother in 1789. After the death of his father he continued in prison under the charge of a Jacobin shoemaker named Simon. He died, so it was reported, June 8, 1795— rumour said by poison. Several persons subsequently claimed to be the dauphin—one of them a half-caste Indian, another a Potsdam watchmaker, Karl Wilhelm Naundorf, who, with a striking resemblance to the Bourbons, found his way to France in 1833, but was expelled in 1836, lived a while in England, and died at Delft, August 10, 1845. His children in 1851 and 1874 raised fruitless actions against the Comte de Chambord. See books by C. Welch (1908), Turquan (1908), Allen (1912), Buckley (1927), A. Castelot (1948).

Louis XVIII, Stanislas Xavier (1755–1824), younger brother of Louis XVI, in his brother's reign opposed every salutary measure of the government. He fled from Paris to Belgium, and assumed the royal title in 1795. The victories of the republic and Napoleon's enmity compelled him frequently to change his place of abode, till in 1807 he found a refuge in England (at Hartwell, Bucks). On the fall of Napoleon (April 1814) he landed at Calais; and then began the ascendency of the ' legitimist ' party. The Napoleonic constitution was set aside, and though a new constitution, with two chambers, was granted, in every essential the king resumed the baneful traditions of the ancient monarchy. The nobles and priests moved him to severe treatment of Imperialists, Republicans and Protestants. This opened the way for Napoleon's return from Elba, when the royal family fled from Paris, and remained at Ghent till after Waterloo. Louis issued from Cambrai a proclamation in which he acknowledged former errors, and promised an amnesty to all but traitors. But the Chamber of Deputies was so reactionary that the king dissolved it; whereupon arose royalist plots for his dethronement. Assassins slew hundreds of adherents of the Revolution and of Protestants. Driven by royalist fanatics, the king dismissed his too moderate prime minister Decazes, and sent an army to Spain to maintain absolutism. See works by Petit (1885), Imbert de Saint-Amand (1891), M. F. Sandars (1910).

LOUIS, Ger. Ludwig. Name of three Bavarian kings, of the family of Wittelsbach.

Louis I (1786–1868), born in Strasbourg, came to the throne in 1825, and by his lavish expenditure on pictures, public buildings and favourites, and by taxes and reactionary policy, provoked active discontent in 1830, and again in 1848, when he abdicated in favour of his son, Maximilian II. See MONTEZ (LOLA).

Louis II (1845–86), Maximilian's son, was born in Nymphenburg, and succeeded in 1864. He devoted himself to patronage of Wagner and his music. In 1870 he decidedly threw Bavaria on the side of Prussia, and offered the imperial crown to William I, though he took no part in the war, and lived the life of a recluse. He was almost constantly at feud with his ministers and family, mainly on account of his insensate outlays on superfluous palaces, and was declared insane in 1886. A few days later he accidentally or intentionally drowned himself (and his physician) in the Starnberger Lake near his castle of Berg. See books by Pourtalès (1929) and Mayr-Ofen (trans. 1937).

Louis III (1854–1921), the son of the Prince Regent Luitpold, was born in Munich and reigned for only five years, from 1913 to 1918,

when he abdicated. He was the last of the Wittelsbach family to be on the throne.

LOUIS, Joe, *loo'is* (1914–), professional name of **Joseph Louis Barrow,** American Negro boxer, ' the Brown Bomber ', born in Lafayette. In 1934 he won the amateur light-heavyweight title and turned professional, becoming world heavyweight champion when he beat Braddock in 1936. He held the title for twelve years, defending it twenty-five times. He retired in 1948, but returned in 1950 and lost his title to Ezzard Charles. He then won eight more fights before being knocked out by Marciano in 1951. In all, he won sixty-eight out of seventy-one fights. See his autobiography (1947) and study by Diamond (1956).

LOUIS NAPOLEON. See NAPOLEON.

LOUIS-PHILIPPE (1773–1850), king of the French, born in Paris, was the eldest son of the Duke of Orleans, and was brought up by Madame de Genlis. He entered the National Guard, and, along with his father, renounced his titles, and assumed the surname Égalité. He fought in the wars of the republic, but was included in the order for arrest issued against Dumouriez, and escaped with him into Austrian territory. For a time he supported himself as a teacher in Switzerland; he went in 1796 to the United States, and in 1800 took up his abode at Twickenham near London. In 1809 he married Marie Amélie, daughter of Ferdinand I of the Two Sicilies. On the Restoration he recovered his estates, and though disliked by the court, was very popular in Paris. After the Revolution of 1830 he was first appointed lieutenant-general, and then accepted the crown as the elect of the sovereign people. The country prospered under the rule of the ' citizen king ', and the middle classes amassed riches. The parliamentary franchise was limited to the aristocracy of wealth and their hangers-on. The political corruption of the *bourgeoisie*, and its wholesale bribery by the king, united all extremists in a cry for electoral reform. A man of great ability but of little character, Louis-Philippe was by fear carried into paths of reactionary violence. The newspapers were muzzled, and trial by jury was tampered with. Prince Louis Napoleon seized this opportunity of acting twice the part of a pretender (1836, 1840). After the Duke of Orleans's death in 1842, republicans, socialists, communists, became more and more threatening. In vain did Louis-Philippe provide, by campaigning in Algeria, an outlet for the military spirit of his subjects. ' Reform banquets ' began to be held. Their repression led to violent debates in the Chamber. The Paris mob rose in February 1848, with the complicity of the regulars, national guards, and municipal police. Louis-Philippe dismissed Guizot (q.v.), and promised reforms; but it was too late. He had to abdicate, and escaped to England as ' Mr Smith '. He died at Claremont. See P. de La Gorce, *La Restoration* (1931); J. Lucas-Dubreton, *Louis-Philippe* (1938), an account of his early years in V. Wyndham's *Life of Madame de Genlis* (1958), and Howarth (1961).

LOUISA (1776–1810), queen of Prussia, was born at Hanover, where her father, Duke

Karl of Mecklenburg-Strelitz, was commandant. Married to the Crown Prince of Prussia, afterwards Frederick-William III, in 1793, she was the mother of Frederick-William IV and William I, afterwards emperor. She endeared herself to her people by her spirit and energy during the period of national calamity that followed the battle of Jena, and especially by her patriotic and self-denying efforts to obtain concessions at Tilsit from Napoleon, though he had shamelessly slandered her.

LOUVEL, Pierre Louis. See BERRI.

L'OUVERTURE. See TOUSSAINT L'OUVERTURE.

LOUVOIS, François Michel le Tellier, Marquis de, *loo-vwah* (1641–91), war minister of Louis XIV, born in Paris. His father was chancellor and secretary of state in the war department; the son joined him as assistant secretary in 1662, and became an energetic war minister in 1668, reforming and strengthening the army. His labours bore fruit in the great war that ended with the peace of Nijmegen (1678). He took a leading part in the capture of Strasburg (1681) and in the persecution of Protestants. See Lives by C. Rousset (6th ed. 1879) and L. André (1942).

LOUŸS, Pierre, *lwee* (1870–1925), French poet and novelist, born at Ghent, came to Paris, where in 1891 he founded a review called *La Conque* to which Régnier, Gide and Valéry were contributors. In this were printed his first poems, most of which later appeared in *Astarté* (1891). His lyrics, based on the Greek form which he so much admired, are masterpieces of style. Other volumes are *Poésies de Méléagre de Gédara* (1893), *Scènes de la vie des courtisanes de Lucien* (1894) and *Les Chansons de Bilitis* (1894). In 1896 his novel *Aphrodite* was published with great success and a psychological novel *La Femme et le pantin* appeared in 1898.

LOVAT, Simon Fraser, Lord (*c.* 1667–1747), Scottish chief, was born at Tomich in Ross-shire. In the 14th century his ancestor had migrated from Tweeddale to Inverness-shire, and Hugh, his grandson, had been made Lord Lovat in 1431. Simon took his M.A. at Aberdeen in 1695, having the year before accepted a commission in a regiment raised for King William. In 1696 his father, on the death of his grand-nephew, Lord Lovat, assumed that title, and Simon next year attempted to abduct the late lord's daughter and heiress, a child nine years of age. Baffled in this, he seized and forcibly married her mother, a lady of the Atholl family—a crime for which he was found guilty of high treason and outlawed. After four years of petty rebellion (during which, in 1699, he succeeded his father as twelfth Lord Lovat), in 1702, when the Atholl family became all powerful, he fled to France, but a year later returned to Scotland as a Jacobite agent. He was at the bottom of the ' Queensberry plot ', in which he professed to reveal the policy of the exiled court and a plan for a Highland rising; but the discovery of his duplicity obliged him once more to escape to France. He was still the darling of his clan, and in 1714 they called him over. Next year Simon took the

government side; his clan at once left the insurgents; and for this service he obtained a full pardon, with possession of the Lovat territory. In the '45 Lovat sent forth the clan under his son to fight for the Pretender, whilst he was protesting his loyalty. Culloden lost, he fled, but was captured and brought up to London, being sketched at St Albans by Hogarth. At his impeachment he defended himself with ability and dignity, and he met death (by beheading) gallantly. A finished courtier, a good scholar, an elegant letter-writer, he was also a ruffian, a liar, a traitor and a hypocrite. During the lifetime of the lady he had ravished he twice more married. See Lives by Hill Burton (1847), Mackenzie (1908); Sir W. Fraser's *Chiefs of Grant* (1883), *Major Fraser's Manuscript* (ed. Fergusson, 1889), the *Fraser Papers* (1924; Scot. Hist. Soc.) and M. McLaren, *Lovat of the '45* (1957).

LOVELACE, Richard (1618–57), Cavalier lyrist, was born at Woolwich, or perhaps in Holland, in 1618, the eldest son of a Kentish knight. He was educated at Charterhouse and Gloucester Hall, Oxford, found his way to court and went on the Scottish expedition in 1639. In 1642 he was imprisoned for presenting to the House of Commons a petition from the royalists of Kent ' for the restoring the king to his rights ', and was released on bail. He spent his estate in the king's cause, assisted the French in 1646 to capture Dunkirk from the Spaniards, and was flung into jail on returning to England in 1648. In jail he revised his poems, and in 1649 published *Lucasta*. He was set free at the end of 1649. In 1659 his brother collected his poems. Most of Lovelace's work does not reach the heights he attained in the faultless lyrics, ' To Althea from Prison ' and ' To Lucasta on going to the Wars ', but many others have been set to music. See C. H. Wilkinson's edition of his Poems (1925; abbrev. 1930).

LOVELL, Sir Alfred Charles Bernard (1913–), English astronomer, a graduate of Bristol University, in 1951 became professor of Radio Astronomy at Manchester University and director of Jodrell Bank experimental station. Elected a fellow of the Royal Society in 1955, he gave the Reith Lectures in 1958, taking for his subject *The Individual and the Universe*. He has written several books on radio astronomy and on its relevance to life and civilization today. His works include *Science and Civilisation* (1939), *World Power Resources and Social Development* (1945) *Radio Astronomy* (1951) *The Story of Jodrell Bank* (1968). He was knighted in 1961.

LOVER, Samuel (1797–1868), Irish artist, novelist, songwriter and dramatist, born in Dublin, in 1818 established himself there as a marine painter and miniaturist. He published *Legends and Stories of Ireland* (1831), *Rory O'More* (1836) and *Handy Andy* (1842), having in 1835 settled in London, where he wrote for the periodicals, and in 1844 started an entertainment, called ' Irish Evenings ', which was a hit both at home and in America (1846–48). See Lives by Bernard (1874) and Symington (1880).

LOW, (1) Sir David (1891–1963), British political cartoonist, born in Dunedin, N.Z., worked for several newspapers in New Zealand and for the *Bulletin* of Sydney, before coming in 1919 to the *Star* in London. In 1927 he joined the staff of the *Evening Standard*, for which he drew some of his most successful cartoons. His art ridiculed all political parties, and some of his creations will never die, notably Colonel Blimp, who has been incorporated into the English language. From 1953 he worked with *The (Manchester) Guardian*, and was knighted in 1962. He produced volumes of collected cartoons, including *Lloyd George and Co.* (1922), *Low and I* (1923), *A Cartoon History of the War* (1941), *Low's Company* (1952), *Low's Autobiography* (1956) and many more.

(2) Sampson (1797–1886), English publisher born in London, began business in 1819 as a bookseller and stationer. In 1848 he opened a publishing office at Red Lion Court, Fleet Street.

LOWE, (1) Sir Hudson (1769–1844), British soldier, born at Galway, in 1809 helped to conquer Zante and Cephalonia, and for nearly two years was governor of Santa Maura, Ithaca and Cephalonia. He was afterwards attached to the Prussian army of Blücher. In April 1816 he arrived as governor at St Helena, where his strict guard over Napoleon brought rancorous attacks, especially from O'Meara (q.v.). In 1825–31 he had an appointment in Ceylon.

(2) **Robert.** See SHERBROOKE.

LÖWE, Karl. See LOEWE.

LOWELL, (1) Amy (1874–1925), American imagist poet, born at Brookline, Mass. She wrote volumes of vers libre which she named 'unrhymed cadence' and also polyphonic prose. Her works, apart from her own verse, include *Six French Poets* (1915), *Tendencies in Modern American Poetry* (1917) and a biography of Keats (1925).

(2) **James Russell** (1819–91), American poet, essayist and diplomat, was born in Cambridge, Massachusetts, the son of a minister, and graduated at Harvard in 1838. In 1841–44 he published two volumes of poetry, in 1845 *Conversations on the Old Poets*; and in 1843 he helped to edit *The Pioneer*, with Hawthorne, Poe and Whittier for contributors. In 1846, at the outbreak of the war with Mexico, he wrote a satiric poem in the Yankee dialect denouncing the pro-slavery party and the conduct of the government; and out of this grew the *Biglow Papers*. A great many serious poems were written about 1848, and formed a third volume. *A Fable for Critics* (1848) is a series of witty and dashing sketches of American authors. In 1851–52 he visited Europe. In 1855 he was appointed professor of Modern Languages and Literature at Harvard and went to Europe to prosecute his studies. He also edited the *Atlantic Monthly* from 1857, and with C. E. Norton the *North American Review* 1863–67. His prose writings —*My Study Windows* and *Among my Books*— have high qualities. The second series of *Biglow Papers* appeared during the civil war. Lowell was an ardent abolitionist, and from the first gave himself unreservedly to the cause of freedom. Though he had never been a politician, he was appointed in 1877 U.S. minister to Spain, and was transferred in 1880 to Great Britain, where he remained until 1885. His *Collected Writings* were published in 1890–91. See his Letters (1893, 1934), and Lives by Underwood (1893), Scudder (1900), Greenslet (1906).

(3) **Percival** (1855–1916), American astronomer, born at Boston, educated at Harvard, established the Flagstaff Observatory in Arizona (1894). He is best known for his observations of Mars and for his prediction of the existence of the planet Pluto. He was the author of works on astronomy and on Japan.

LOWNDES, William Thomas (c. 1798–1843), English bookseller and bibliographer, born in London, to whom we owe *The Bibliographer's Manual of English Literature* (1834) and *The British Librarian* (1839).

LOWRY, (Laurence) Stephen (1887–), English artist, born and trained in Manchester, becoming A.R.A. in 1955, and R.A. in 1962. He has produced many pictures of the Lancashire industrial scene, mainly in brilliant whites and greys, peopled with scurrying antlike men and women. See *Drawings of L. S. Lowry* by M. Levy (1963).

LOWTH, Robert (1710–87), English bishop and scholar, born at Winchester, in 1741 became professor of Poetry at Oxford, in 1766 Bishop of St Davids and of Oxford, and in 1777 of London. He published *De Sacra Poesi Hebraeorum* (1753), *Life of William of Wykeham* (1758) and a new translation of Isaiah. He was one of the first to treat the Bible poetry as literature.

LOWTHER, (1) Hugh Cecil. See LONSDALE.

(2) **James William, 1st Viscount Ullswater** (1855–1949), was Conservative M.P. for Penrith 1886–1921, and Speaker of the House of Commons 1905–21.

LOYOLA, Ignatius de, *loy-ō'la* (1491–1556), is the name by which history knows Iñigo López de Recalde, Spanish soldier and ecclesiastic, born at his ancestral castle of Loyola in the Basque province of Guipúzcoa. A page in the court of Ferdinand, he then embraced the profession of arms. In the defence of Pampeluna he was severely wounded in the leg, which he had to have re-broken in order to be re-set. After this operation his convalescence was slow; and, his stock of romances exhausted, he turned to the lives of Christ and of the saints. The result was a spiritual enthusiasm as intense as that by which he had hitherto been drawn to chivalry. Renouncing the pursuit of arms, he resolved to begin his new life by a pilgrimage to Jerusalem. In 1522 he set out on his pilgrimage, the first step of which was a voluntary engagement to serve the poor and sick in the hospital of Manresa. There his zeal and devotion attracted such notice that he withdrew to a cavern in the vicinity, where he pursued alone his course of self-prescribed austerity, until, utterly exhausted, he was carried back to the hospital. From Manresa he repaired to Rome, whence he proceeded on foot to Venice and there embarked for Cyprus and the Holy Land. He returned ot Venice and Barcelona in 1524. He now resolved to prepare himself for the work of religious teaching, and at thirty-three returned to the rudiments of grammar, followed up by a course at Alcalá, Salamanca and Paris. In 1534 he founded with five associates the Society of Jesus. The original aim was limited to a pilgrimage to the Holy Land, and the conversion of the Infidels, but as access to the Holy Land was cut off by war with the Turks, the associates sought to meet the new wants engendered by the Reformation. Loyola went to Rome in 1539, and submitted to Pope Paul III the rule of the proposed order, and the vow by which the members bound themselves to go as missionaries to any country the pope might choose. The rule was approved in 1540, and next year the association elected Loyola as its first general. From this time he resided in Rome. At Manresa he wrote the first draft of the *Spiritual Exercises*, so important for the training of the Jesuits. He died July 31, 1556; was beatified in 1609; and was canonized in 1622. See books by Ribadaneira (1572), Maffei (1585), Bouhours (1679), Denis (1885), Rose (1891), Gothein (1896), Thompson (1909), Sedgwick (1923), Van Dyke (1926), Astrain (trans. 1928) and J. Brodrick (1956).

LOYSON, Charles. See HYACINTHE, PÈRE.

LUBBOCK, (1) **Sir John, 1st Baron Avebury** (1834–1913), born in London, the son of the astronomer, Sir J. W. Lubbock (1803–65). From Eton he went at fourteen into his father's banking house; in 1856 became a partner; served on several educational and currency commissions; and in 1870 was returned for Maidstone in the Liberal interest, in 1880 for London University—from 1886 till 1900 as a Liberal-Unionist. He succeeded in passing more than a dozen important measures, including the Bank Holidays Act (1871), the Bills of Exchange Act, the Ancient Monuments Act (1882), and the Shop Hours Act (1889). He was vice-chancellor of London University 1872–80, president of the British Association (1881), V.P.R.S., president of the London Chamber of Commerce, chairman of the London County Council 1890–92, &c. Best known for his researches on primitive man and on the habits of bees and ants, he published *Prehistoric Times* (1865; revised 1913), *Origin of Civilisation* (1870) and many books on natural history. See Life by Horace Hutchinson (1914), and *The Life-work of Lord Avebury* by A. Grant Duff (1924).

(2) **Percy** (1879–1965), English critic and essayist, born in London, the grandson of (1). He was librarian of Magdalene College from 1906 to 1908, and among his writings are *The Craft of Fiction* (1921), *Earlham* (1922), a book of personal childhood memories, and studies of Pepys (1909) and Edith Wharton (1947). In 1952 he was made a C.B.E.

LÜBKE, Wilhelm (1826–93), German writer on art, was born at Dortmund, and died at Karlsruhe. His most important work was *Grundriss der Kunstgeschichte* (1860).

LUCA DELLA ROBBIA. See ROBBIA (3).

LUCAN, George Charles Bingham, Earl of (1800–88), British soldier, accompanied the Russians as a volunteer against the Turks in 1828 ,succeeded as third earl in 1839, and as commander of cavalry in the Crimea fought at the Alma, Balaklava and Inkermann. Made G.Ç.B. in 1869, he became field-marshal in 1887.

LUCANUS, Marcus Annaeus (A.D. 39–65), Latin poet, was born at Corduba (Córdoba) in Spain. Annaeus Seneca, the rhetorician, had three sons—M. Annaeus Seneca, the Gallio of the Acts of the Apostles; L. Annaeus Seneca, the philosopher; and M. Annaeus Mela, father of Lucan. Rome's attraction had already drawn thither Seneca, the philosopher; and Mela, with his wife, followed, to place their son under his uncle's charge. Young Lucan became proficient in rhetoric and philosophy; and his aptitude for prose and verse was ominous of the fatal fluency which evolved the first three books of the *Pharsalia* while yet in his teens. At first the young emperor and the young poet were friends, and Nero's favour had conferred on Lucan the quaestorship. But when, in a great public contest, the palm went over Nero's head to Lucan, the emperor's marked discourtesies were returned by his successful rival with satire and with redoubled efforts to outshine him, till Nero was stung into forbidding Lucan either to publish poems or to recite them. Lucan became a ringleader of the Pisonian conspiracy; it was discovered and he himself betrayed. He was ordered to die, and, having had his veins opened, bled to death in a bath. Except a few fragments, we now have nothing of Lucan's many writings but the *Pharsalia*, recounting the mighty duel of Pompey and Caesar for the empire of the world. It is frequently bombastic, careless and inaccurate historically, but his descriptions are powerful, his use of language vivid and at its best his rhetoric is brilliant. See editions by Oudendorp (1728), Haskins (1887), Hosius (1905), Francken (1895–98), Housman (1926). There are translations by Marlowe (1st book), Sir F. Gorges, T. May (who continued the poem in Latin verse), Rowe (1718), Ridley (1897), and in prose by Riley (1853), Duff (1928).

LUCARIS, or Lukaris, Cyril (1572–1638), Greek theologian, born in Crete, studied at Venice, Padua and Geneva, where he was influenced by Calvinism. He rose by 1621 to be Patriarch of Constantinople. He opened negotiations with the Calvinists of England and Holland with a view to union and the reform of the Greek Church; he corresponded with Gustavus Adolphus, Archbishop Abbot and Laud; he presented the Alexandrian Codex to Charles I. The *Eastern Confession of the Orthodox Church*, of strong Calvinistic tendency, issued in 1629, it is now thought may not have been written by him. The Jesuits five times brought about his deposition, and are supposed to have instigated his murder by the Turks. In June 1637 he was seized, and believed to have been strangled.

LUCAS, *loo'kas*, (1) **Colin Anderson** (1906–   ), English architect, born in London. He studied at Cambridge, and in 1930 designed a house at Bourne End which was the first English example of the domestic use of monolithic reinforced concrete. Subsequent designs (1933–39), in partnership with A. D.

Connell and Basil Ward, played an important part in the development in England of the ideas of the European modern movement in architecture. He is a founder member of the MARS group of architects.

(2) **Edward Verrall** (1868–1938), English essayist and biographer, born at Eltham, Kent, became a bookseller's assistant, a reporter, contributor to and assistant editor of *Punch* and finally a publisher. He compiled anthologies, wrote novels, the best of which was *Over Bemerton's* (1908), books of travel and about 30 volumes of essays in a light, charming vein. An authority on Lamb, he wrote a Life in 1905.

(3) **Frank Lawrence** (1894–1967), English critic and poet, born at Hipperholme, Yorkshire. A fellow of and former reader in English at King's Coll., Cambridge, he wrote many scholarly works of criticism, including *Seneca and Elizabethan Tragedy* (1922), and *Eight Victorian Poets* (1930). Among his volumes of poetry are *Time and Memory* (1929) and *Ariadne* (1932). His plays include *Land's End* (1938). He also wrote novels and popular translations of Greek drama and poetry.

(4) **James** (1813–74), Dickens's 'Mr Mopes', from 1849 lived as an unwashed hermit on buns and gin at Elmwood, Hertfordshire.

(5) **John Seymour** (1849–1923), English historical painter, born in London, became A.R.A. in 1886, R.A. in 1897. Among his works is a fresco at the Royal Exchange depicting William the Conqueror's granting of London's first charter.

LUCAS VAN LEYDEN or **Lucas Jacobsz** (1494–1533), Dutch painter and engraver, was born and died at Leyden. He practised almost every branch of painting, and as an engraver ranks but little below Albrecht Dürer, whom he knew and by whom he was much influenced. See French work by Evrard (1883) and German ones by Volbehr (1888) and M. Friedlaender (1924).

LUCE, Henry Robinson (1898–1967), American magazine publisher and editor, born in Shantung, China, founded *Time* (1923), *Fortune* (1930) and *Life* (1936). He also in the 1930s inaugurated the radio programme 'March of Time', which became a film feature. He married in 1935 Clare Boothe (q.v.).

LUCIAN (*c.* A.D. 117–180), Greek writer, was born at Samosata in Syria. Having learned Greek and studied rhetoric, he practised as an advocate in Antioch, and wrote and recited show speeches for a living, travelling through Asia Minor, Greece, Italy and Gaul. Having thus made a fortune and a name, he settled in Athens, and there devoted himself to philosophy. There, too, he produced a new form of literature—humorous dialogue. In his old age he accepted a good appointment in Egypt, where he died. Lucian lived when the old faiths, the old philosophy, the old literature, were all rapidly dissolving. Never was there a fairer field for satire; and Lucian revelled in it. The absurdity of retaining the old deities without the old belief is brought out in the *Dialogues of the Gods*, *Dialogues of the Dead*, *Charon*, &c. Whether philosophy was more disgraced by the shallowness or the vices of those who now professed it, it would be hard to tell from his *Symposium, Halieus, Biōn Prasis, Drapetæ* &c. The old literature had been displaced by novels or romances of adventure of the most fantastic kind, which Lucian parodies in his *True Histories*. Apart from the purity of his Greek, his style is simple, sparkling, delightful. See editions by Hemsterhuis and Reitz (1730–45), Lehmann (1822–29), Bekker (1853), Sommerbrodt (1888), Nilén (1906); translations by Fowler and Harmon.

LUCILIUS, Gaius (*c.* 180–102 B.C.), Roman satirist, was born at Suessa Aurunca in Campania, and died at Naples. He wrote thirty books of *Satires*, of which only fragments remain. Written in hexameters, they give a critical insight into his times. See the editions by Lachmann (1876), L. Müller (1872), F. Marx (1904–05), Terzaghi (1934).

LUCRETIA, wife of L. Tarquinius Collatinus, when outraged by Sextus Tarquinius, summoned her husband and friends, and, making them take oath to drive out the Tarquins, plunged a knife into her heart. The tale has formed the basis of several works, notably Shakespeare's *Rape of Lucrece* and the opera *The Rape of Lucretia* by Benjamin Britten. See BRUTUS.

LUCRETIUS (Titus Lucretius Carus) (*c.* 99–55 B.C.), Roman poet, was said to have died mad from the effects of a love potion given to him by his wife Lucilia (so in Tennyson's poem). The great work of Lucretius is his hexameter poem *De Natura Rerum*, in six books. Lucretius aspired to popularize the philosophical theories of Democritus and Epicurus on the origin of the universe, with the special purpose of eradicating anything like religious belief, which he savagely denounces as the one great source of man's wickedness and misery. A calm and tranquil mind was his *summum bonum*, and the only way to it lay through a materialistic philosophy. His poem abounds in strikingly picturesque phrases; up and down are episodes of exquisite pathos and vivid description, perhaps hardly equalled in Latin poetry; and when he allegorizes myths into moral truths, he is one of the sublimest of poets. Lachmann's text (1850) was improved by Munro (1860), who added (1864) a commentary and translation. See Creech's (1714) and Trevelyan's (1937) verse trans., Bailey's (1910) and Jackson's (1929) prose trans.; also Sellar's *Roman Poets* (1863); books by Veitch (1875), Masson (1907–09), Thomson (1915), Sikes (1936).

LUCULLUS, Lucius Licinius (*c.* 110–57 B.C.), Roman general, commanded the fleet in the first Mithridatic war, as consul in 74 defeated Mithridates, and introduced admirable reforms into Asia Minor. He twice defeated Tigranes of Armenia (69 and 68). But his legions became mutinous, and he was superseded by Pompey (66). He attempted to check Pompey's power, and was one of the first triumvirate, but soon withdrew from politics. He had acquired prodigious wealth and spent the rest of his life in luxury. See J. M. Cobban, *Senate and Provinces* 79–49 B.C. (1935).

LUCY, St (d. 303), the patron of the blind

was a virgin martyred under Diocletian at Syracuse. Her feast is kept on December 13.

LUCY, (1) Sir Henry William (1845–1924), English journalist, born at Crosby near Liverpool, worked as reporter on the *Shrewsbury Chronicle*, the *Pall Mall Gazette* and the *Exeter Gazette* (of which he became assistant editor), before being appointed *Daily News* parliamentary reporter. The 'Toby, M.P.' of *Punch* from 1881 to 1916, he was also a novelist and a writer of books on parliamentary process. See his autobiography, *Fifty Years in the Wilderness* (1909).

(2) **Sir Thomas** (1532–1600), Warwickshire squire and Justice of the Peace, said to have prosecuted Shakespeare for stealing deer from Charlecote Park, and to have been the original of Justice Shallow.

LUDD, Ned (fl. 1779), a Leicestershire idiot, destroyed some stocking frames about 1782. From him the Luddite rioters (1812–18) took their name.

LUDENDORFF, Erich von (1865–1937), German general, born near Posen, was a staff-officer 1904–13. In 1914 as quartermaster-general in East Prussia he defeated Samsonov at Tannenberg. When Hindenburg superseded Falkenhayn in 1916, Ludendorff as his first quartermaster sent Mackensen to the Dobruja, and, in general, conducted the war to the end, having been transferred to the Western front, where he conducted a series of defensive campaigns. In 1923 he was a leader in the Hitler putsch at Munich, but he was acquitted of treason. As a candidate for the presidency of the Reich in 1925 he polled few votes. Strongly opposed to Jews, Jesuits and freemasons, he was for a time a member of the National Socialist party, but from 1925 led a minority party of his own. See his *War Memories* (trans. 1919) and study by D. J. Goodspeed (1966).

LUDLOW, (1) Edmund (c. 1617–92), English regicide, born at Maiden Bradley, Wilts, served under Waller and Fairfax, was returned for Wilts in 1646, sat among the king's judges, and was elected to the council of state. In 1651 he was sent to Ireland as lieutenant-general of horse, but refused to recognize Cromwell's protectorate. Member for Hindon in 1659, he urged the restoration of the Rump, commanded again a while in Ireland, was nominated by Lambert to the committee of safety, and strove in vain to reunite the republican party. After the Restoration he made his way to Vevey. In 1689 he came back, but, the House of Commons demanding his arrest, he returned to Vevey. See his valuable *Memoirs* (ed. Firth (1894).

(2) **John Malcolm Forbes** (1821–1911), British social reformer, and founder of the Christian socialists. He was chief registrar of Friendly Societies.

LUDMILLA, St (d. 921), Bohemia's patroness, the wife of its first Christian duke, was murdered by her heathen daughter-in-law, Drahomira.

LUDWIG, *lood′veeKH*, (1) see LOUIS.

(2) originally **Cohn, Emil** (1861–1948), German author, born at Breslau, long resident in Switzerland, wrote some plays, but made his name as a biographer of

the intuitive school, with lives of Goethe, Napoleon, William II, Bismarck, Christ, Lincoln, &c.

(3) **Karl Friedrich Wilhelm** (1816–95), German physiologist, born at Witzenhausen, professor at Leipzig (1865–95), did pioneer research on glandular secretions, and his invention of the mercurial blood-gas pump revealed the rôle of oxygen and other gases in the bloodstream.

LU HSUN or **Lu Hsin,** *shoon* (1881–1936), Chinese writer, born at Shaohsin in Chekiang, of a family of scholars, became in 1909 dean of studies at the Shaohsin Middle School and later its principal. By 1913 he was professor of Chinese Literature at the National Peking University and National Normal University for Women. In 1926 he went as professor to Amoy University and later was appointed dean of the College of Arts and Letters at Sun Yat-Sen University, Canton. His career as an author began with a short story, *Diary of a Madman* (1918). In 1921 appeared *The True Story of Ah Q*. Considered his most successful book, it has been translated into many languages. Between 1918 and 1925 he wrote 26 short stories and these appear in two volumes entitled *Cry* and *Hesitation*.

LUINI, or **Lovino, Bernardino,** *loo-ee′nee* (c. 1481–1532), Lombard painter, born at Luino on Lago Maggiore, was trained in the school of Leonardo da Vinci, to whom many of his works have been attributed. He painted much at Milan. He is one of the five whose 'supremacy' Ruskin affirmed. See Life by G. C. Williamson (1899) and monograph by L. Beltrami (1911).

LUITPRAND. See LIUTPRAND.

LUKE, (1) (*Loukas,* i.e., *Lucanus*), a companion of St Paul, mentioned in Col. iv. 14 as 'the beloved physician'; his name is suggestive of an Italian origin. Church tradition made him a native of Antioch in Syria, one of 'the seventy' mentioned in Luke x, a painter by profession, and a martyr. He is first named as author of the third gospel in the Muratorian canon (2nd century); and tradition has ever since ascribed to him both that work and the Acts of the Apostles. See A. Harnack, *Luke the Physician* (1907) and *Acts of the Apostles* (1909); J. M. Creed, *Gospel according to St Luke* (1930).

(2) **Sir Samuel.** See BUTLER, SAMUEL.

LULL, Ramón. See LULLY (2).

LULLY, (1) Giovanni Battista, *loo′lee* (1632–1687), French composer of Italian parentage, born in Florence, came as a boy to Paris, and was finally, after much ambitious intriguing, made operatic director by Louis XIV (1672). With Quinault as librettist, he composed many operas, in which he made the ballet an essential part; the favourites (till Gluck's time) were *Thésée, Armide, Phaéton, Atys, Isis,* and *Acis et Galatée.* He also wrote church music, dance music and pastorals. See books by Radet (1891), Prunières (1910).

(2) **Raymond** (sometimes **Lull**) (c. 1232–1315), Spanish theologian and philosopher, 'the enlightened doctor', born at Palma in Majorca, in his youth served as a soldier and led a dissolute life, but from 1266 gave himself up to asceticism and resolved on a

spiritual crusade for the conversion of the Mussulmans. To this end, after some years of study, he produced his *Ars Magna*, the 'Lullian method'; a mechanical aid to the acquisition of knowledge and the solution of all possible problems by a systematic manipulation of certain fundamental notions (the Aristotelian categories, &c.). He also wrote a book against the Averroists, and in 1291 went to Tunis to confute and convert the Mohammedans, but was imprisoned and banished. After visiting Naples, Rome, Majorca, Cyprus and Armenia, he again sailed (1305) for Bugia (Bougie) in Algeria, and was again banished; at Paris lectured against the principles of Averroes; and once more at Bugia, was stoned and died a few days afterwards. The Lullists combined religious mysticism with alchemy, but it has been disproved that Lully himself ever dabbled in alchemy. Apart from his *Ars Magna*, of his works *Llibre de Contemplació* is masterly and he was the first to use a vernacular language for religious or philosophical writings. He also wrote impressive poetry. See Life by Allison Peers (1929).

LUMIÈRE, *lüm-yayr,* **Auguste Marie Louis Nicolas** (1862–1954), and **Louis Jean** (1864–1948), French chemists, brothers, manufacturers of photographic materials, invented a cine camera (1893) and a process of colour photography.

LUMUMBA, Patrice Emergy (1925–61), Congolese politician, born in Katako Kombe, became leader of the Congolese national movement and when the Congo became an independent republic in 1960 was made premier. Almost immediately the country was plunged into chaos by warring factions, and after being deposed in 1960, Lumumba was assassinated in 1961.

LUNARDI, Vincenzo (1759–1806), Italian aeronaut, born at Lucca, made from Moorfields, on September 15, 1784, the first hydrogen balloon ascent in England.

LUPTON, Thomas Goff (1791–1873), English mezzotint engraver, was born and died in London. He was one of the first to use steel in engraving. Among his works are Turner's *Ports* and *Rivers*.

LUSIGNAN. See GUY DE LUSIGNAN.

LUTHARDT, Christoph Ernst, *loo-tart* (1823–1902), Lutheran theologian, became professor at Marburg (1854) and at Leipzig (1856). He wrote a Commentary on John's Gospel (1852–1853; 2nd ed. 1876), *St John the Author of the Fourth Gospel*, works on ethics, dogmatics, &c. See his *Reminiscences* (2nd ed. 1891).

LUTHER, Martin (1483–1546), German religious reformer, was born at Eisleben, the son of a miner, and went to school at Magdeburg and Eisenach. In 1501 he entered the University of Erfurt, and took his degree in 1505. Before this, however, he was led to the study of the Scriptures, and spent three years in the Augustinian monastery at Erfurt. In 1507 he was ordained a priest, in 1508 lectured on philosophy in the University of Wittenberg, in 1509 on the Scriptures, and as a preacher produced a still more powerful influence. In 1511 he was sent to Rome, and after his return his career as a Reformer commenced. Money was greatly needed at

Rome; and its emissaries s to raise funds by the sal Luther's indignation at the carried on by the Domini (1517) became irrepressible ninety-five theses on indulg the pope all right to forgive on October 31 he nailed on at Wittenberg. Tetzel retrea to Frankfurt an der Oder, lished a set of counter-th Luther's. The Wittenberg st by burning Tetzel's. In 1 joined by Melanchthon. Th at first took little heed of but in 1518 summoned Lutl answer for his theses. His u elector interfered, and ineffect were undertaken by Cardin by Miltitz, envoy of the pop court. Eck and Luther hel disputation at Leipzig (1519). time attacked the papal syst more boldly. Erasmus and joined in the conflict. In 152 published his famous address tian Nobles of Germany ', treatise *On the Babylonish C Church*, which works attac doctrinal system of the Chu The papal bull, containing fo issued against him he bur multitude of doctors, student in Wittenberg. Germany was excitement. Charles V had co diet at Worms in 1521; an or for the destruction of Luther he was summoned to appear b Ultimately he was put under Empire, on his return from seized, at the instigation of Saxony, and lodged (really for in the Wartburg. During the here he translated the Script posed various treatises. Dis Luther to Wittenberg in 152 the unruly spirits, and made lawlessness on the one hand the other. In this year he acrimonious reply to Henry V sacraments. Estrangement sprung up between Erasmus a there was an open breach Erasmus published *De Liber* Luther followed with *De Ser* that year Luther married Kath (q.v.), one of nine nuns who from conventual life. In 15 in his famous conference at Zwingli and other Swiss divi maintaining his views as to substantial) Presence in the drawing up of the Augsbu Melanchthon representing Lu culmination of the Germa (1530). Luther died at Eis buried at Wittenberg. Endo human sympathies, massive and affectionate simplicity, sometimes coarse, humour, edly a spiritual genius. H divine truth were bold, vivid if not philosophical and com

ossessed the power of kindling other souls the fire of his own convictions. His minous works include *Table-talk, Letters Sermons.* His Commentaries on Gala- and the Psalms are still read; and he one of the great leaders of sacred song, hymns having an enduring power. The t editions of his works are those of enberg (12 vols. German; 7 vols. Latin, –58); Halle, ed. by Walch (German, ols. 1740–53); Erlangen and Frankfort vols. German; 33 vols. Latin, 1826–73); Weimar (1883 *et seq.*). See Lives by lin (1875; 5th ed. 1903), Kolde (1884–), H. Grisar (trans. 1913–17; Catholic), hmer (1925, trans. 1957), and in English Mackinnon (4 vols. 1925–30), Aubigne 8), Bainton (1952), and Osborne's play *er* (1961).

HULI, Albert John (1899?–1967), Afri- resistance leader, son of a Zulu Christian ionary, was educated at an American ion school near Durban and spent 15 s as a teacher before being elected tribal f of Groutville, Natal. Deposed for -apartheid activities, he became president- eral of the African National Congress, which capacity he dedicated himself to a paign of non-violent resistance and was efendant in the notorious Johannesburg son trial (1956–59). In 1961 he was rded the Nobel Peace prize for his werving opposition to racial violence in face of repressive measures by the South ican government and impatience from emist Africans. He was elected rector of sgow University (1962) but severe rictions imposed by the South African ernment (in 1961, and for another five rs in 1964), prevented him from leaving al. See his *Let My People Go* (1962).

TEREL or Luttrell, Edward (fl. 1670– 0), English engraver who probably came n Dublin to London, where he was a lent of law. But abandoning this for art became a crayon painter and one of the : mezzotint engravers. He executed traits of Samuel Butler, Bishop Morley Archbishop Sancroft.

YENS, Sir Edwin Landseer (1869–1944), lish architect, born in London, has been ed the greatest architect since Christopher en. His designs ranged from the pictur- ue of his early country houses, including rsh Court, Stockbridge and Lindisfarne tle to those in the Renaissance style as athcote, Ilkley and Salutation, Sandwich, finally he evolved a classical style ibited in the Cenotaph, Whitehall, and ich reached its height in his design for erpool R.C. Cathedral. Other prominent rks were his magnificent Viceroy's House, w Delhi, a masterpiece in classical design, British Pavilion at the Rome Exhibition of 0, &c. He became president of the Royal ademy in 1938 and in 1942 received the Order Merit. See Life by C. Hussey (1951).

ZOW, Ludwig Adolf Wilhelm, Freiherr , *lüt'zō* (1782–1834), Prussian soldier, rn in Berlin, gave name to a renowned ps of volunteers, 'the Black Jäger', sed by him during the war of liberation in 3. See work by von Jagwitz (1892).

LUXEMBOURG, Duc de, François Henri de Montmorency-Bouteville (1628–95), born in Paris, was trained by his aunt, mother of the Great Condé, and adhered to Condé through the wars of the Fronde. After 1659 he was pardoned by Louis XIV, who created him Duc de Luxembourg (1661)—he had just married the heiress of Luxembourg-Piney. In 1667 he served under Condé in Franche- Comté; in 1672 he himself successfully invaded the Netherlands, and, driven back in 1673, conducted a masterly retreat. During the war he stormed Valenciennes and twice defeated the Prince of Orange. Made a marshal in 1675, soon after the peace (1678) he quarrelled with Louvois (q.v.), and was not employed for twelve years. In 1690 he commanded in Flanders, and defeated the allies at Fleurus, and later twice more routed his old opponent, now William III, at Steinkirk and Neerwinden. He died in Paris.

LUXEMBURG, Rosa (1871–1919), German revolutionary of the extreme left, born at Zamość in Poland, was with Karl Liebknecht leader of the Spartakusbund, and with him was murdered in Berlin. She wrote *Die Akkumulation des Kapitals* (1913).

LUYNES, Charles d'Albert, Duc de, *lü-een* (1578–1621), the unworthy favourite of Louis XIII of France, became in 1619 a peer of France, and in 1621 chancellor. See Life by Zeller (Paris 1879).

LVOV, Prince Georgi Evgenievich (1861– 1925), Russian liberal politician, head of the provisional government in the revolution of 1917. Succeeded by Kerensky, he left Russia.

LWOFF, André (1902–), French scientist, of Russo-Polish origin, born in Allier dept., professor of Microbiology at the Sorbonne. He was awarded Nobel prize for medicine in 1965 with Jacob (3) and Monod.

LYALL, Sir Alfred Comyn (1835–1911), English administrator and author, born at Coulsdon, Surrey, educated at Eton and Haileybury, was lieutenant-governor of the northwest Provinces of India (1882–87). He wrote on India and on literature, &c. See Life by H. M. Durand (1913).

LYAUTEY, Louis Hubert Gonzalve, *lee-ō-tay* (1854–1934), French marshal (1921), born at Nancy, held administrative posts in Algeria, Tongking and Madagascar (under Galliéni); but his most brilliant work was done in Morocco, where he was resident commissary- general in 1912–16, 1917–25. See Life by Maurois (trans. 1931).

LYCURGUS *lī-kur'goos*, (1) traditional, possibly mythological, law-giver of Sparta, assigned to the 9th century B.C.

(2) (c. 396–324 B.C.), Attic orator, sup- ported Demosthenes, and as manager of the public revenue distinguished himself by his integrity and love of splendid architecture. One speech and a fragment have survived.

LYDEKKER, Richard, *-dek'-* (1849–1915), English naturalist and geologist, born in London, was an authority on mammals. He studied at Trinity, Cambridge, and worked on the Indian Geological Survey (1874–82). His works include *Phases of Animal Life* (1892), &c.

LYDGATE, John (c. 1370–c. 1451), an imitator of Chaucer, was born at Lydgate,

near Newmarket, and became a Benedictine monk at Bury St Edmunds. He may have studied at Oxford and Cambridge; he travelled in France and perhaps Italy, and became prior of Hatfield Broadoak in 1423. A court poet, he received a pension in 1439, but died in poverty. Lydgate's longer works are the *Troy Book*, the *Siege of Thebes* and the *Fall of Princes*. The *Siege of Thebes* is represented as a new Canterbury tale, and was based on a French verse romance. The versification is rough, and the poem dull and prolix. The *Troy Book* was founded on Colonna's Latin prose *Historia Trojana*, and the *Fall of Princes* on Boccaccio. Other works include the *Daunce of Machabre*, from the French, and *Temple of Glas*, a copy of Chaucer's *House of Fame*. See E.E.T.S. editions (esp. *Temple of Glas* by Schick and *Minor Poems* by H. N. MacCracken, who attempts to establish the Lydgate canon).

LYELL, Sir Charles (1797–1875), Scottish geologist, born at Kinnordy, Forfarshire, the eldest son of the mycologist and Dante student, Charles Lyell (1767–1849). Brought up in the New Forest, and educated at Ringwood, Salisbury, and Midhurst, in 1816 he entered Exeter College, Oxford, and took his B.A. in 1819. At Oxford in 1819 he attended the lectures of Buckland, and acquired his taste for geology. He studied law, and was called to the bar; but devoting himself to geology, made European tours in 1824 and 1828–30, and published the results in the *Transactions of the Geological Society* and elsewhere. His *Principles of Geology* (1830–33) may be ranked next after Darwin's *Origin of Species* among the books which exercised the most powerful influence on scientific thought in the 19th century. It denied the necessity of stupendous convulsions, and taught that the greatest geological changes might have been produced by forces still at work. The *Elements of Geology* (1838) was a supplement. The *Geological Evidences of the Antiquity of Man* (1863) startled the public by its unbiased attitude towards Darwin. Lyell also published *Travels in North America* (1845) and *A Second Visit to the United States* (1849). In 1832–33 he was professor of Geology at King's College, London. Repeatedly president of the Geological Society, and in 1864 president of the British Association, he was knighted in 1848, and created a baron in 1864. See *Life, Letters, and Journals* (1881), a work by Bonney (1895), and Life by Bailey (1963).

LYLY, John, *lil'i* (c. 1554–1606), English dramatist and novelist, ' the Euphuist ', was born in the Weald of Kent. He took his B.A. from Magdalen College, Oxford, in 1573, and studied also at Cambridge. Lord Burghley gave him some post of trust in his household, and he became vice-master of the St Paul's choristers. Having in 1589 taken part in the Marprelate controversy, he was returned to parliament for Aylesbury and Appleby, 1597–1601. His *Euphues*, a romance in two parts—*Euphues, the Anatomie of Wit* (1579), and *Euphues and his England* (1580)—was received with great applause. One peculiarity of his ' new English ' is the constant employment of similes drawn from fabulous stories

about the properties of animals, plants and minerals; another is the excessive indulgence in antithesis. Lyly's earliest comedy was *The Woman in the Moone*, produced in or before 1583. *Campaspe* and *Sapho and Phao* were published in 1584, *Endimion* in 1591, *Gallathea* and *Midas* in 1592, *Mother Bombie* in 1594, and *Love's Metamorphosis* in 1601. The delightful songs (of doubtful authorship) were first printed in the edition of 1632. Lyly's *Complete Works* were edited by R. Warwick Bond in 1902. See books by C. G. Child (Leipzig 1894), Feuillerat (1910), V. M. Jeffery (1929), G. K. Hunter (1962).

LYND, Robert (1879–1949), Irish essayist and critic, born in Belfast. He was for many years literary editor of the *News Chronicle* and also contributed to the *New Statesman*, signing himself Y. Y. His essays, of which he wrote numerous volumes, are on a wide variety of topics. Of an intimate, witty and charming nature rather reminiscent of Lamb, some titles are *The Art of Letters* (1920), *The Blue Lion* (1923), and *In Defence of Pink* (1939).

LYNDHURST, John Singleton Copley, Baron (1772–1863), Anglo-American lawyer, son of J. S. Copley, R.A. (q.v.), was born at Boston, Mass. At three, with his mother, he followed the painter to London, and in 1790 entered Trinity College, Cambridge, graduating in 1794. Next year he got a fellowship, and in 1796 paid a visit to the States. On his return he studied for the bar, and was called in 1804. Success was slow till 1812, when he made a hit by his ingenious defence of a Luddite rioter. In 1817 he obtained the acquittal of Thistlewood and Watson on their trial for high treason; but for the next state prosecution the government secured him on their side, and in 1818 he entered parliament as member for Yarmouth. Henceforward he continued a fairly consistent Tory. In 1819, as Sir John Copley, he became solicitor-general, in 1824 attorney-general, and in 1826 master of the rolls. As Baron Lyndhurst he was lord chancellor under three administrations from 1827 to 1830, when his Whig opponents made him chief baron of the Exchequer; that office he exchanged for the woolsack under Peel (1834–35). In 1841–46 he was for the third time lord chancellor. Lyndhurst's judgments have never been excelled for lucidity, method and legal acumen. See Atlay, *Victorian Chancellors* (1906).

LYNDSAY, or Lindsay, Sir David, of the Mount (c. 1486–1555), Scottish poet, was born probably at one of his father's seats— the Mount near Cupar, Garmylton (now Garleton), near Haddington. In 1512 he was appointed ' usher ' of the newborn prince who became James V. In 1522 or earlier Lyndsay married Janet Douglas, the king's sempstress; in 1524 (probably), under the Douglases, he lost (or changed) his place; in 1538 he seems to have been Lyon King-of-Arms; by 1542 he had been knighted. He went on embassies to the Netherlands, France, England and Denmark. He or another David Lyndsay represented Cupar in the parliaments of 1540–46. For two centuries he was the poet of the Scottish people. His poems, often coarse, are full of humour, good sense and knowledge of the world, and were said to have done more for the Reformation in Scotland than all the sermons of Knox. The earliest and most poetic of his writings is *The Dreme*; the most ambitious, *The Monarche*; the most remarkable, *The Satyre of the Thrie Estaitis* (a dramatic work first performed at Linlithgow in 1540, and revived with great success at the Edinburgh Festivals of 1948 and 1959); the most amusing, *The Historie of Squyer Meldrum*. There are editions by Chalmers (1806), Laing (1879), Small, Hall, and Murray (E.E.T.S. 1865–71), Hamer (S.T.S. 1931–36). See also Murison, *Sir David Lyndsay* (1938).

LYNDSAY OF PITSCOTTIE. See PITS-COTTIE.

LYNEDOCH, Thomas Graham, 1st Baron, *lin'do*KH (1748–1843), son of the laird of Balgowan in Perthshire, raised in 1793 the 99th Regiment of foot, and served at Quiberon and in Minorca (1798). He besieged Valetta in 1800, was at Coruña and in Walcheren (1809), at Barrosa defeated the French (1811), fought at Ciudad Rodrigo (1812), Badajoz, and Salamanca, commanded the left wing at Vitoria (1813), captured Tolosa and San Sebastián and in Holland conquered at Merxem, but failed to storm Bergen-op-Zoom (1814). He was created Baron Lynedoch of Balgowan (1814). He founded the Senior United Service Club (1817). See Lives by Graham (2nd ed. 1877) and Delavoye (1880).

LYNEN, Feodor (1911–), German biochemist, head of Biochemistry at Munich Univ., and director of Max Planck Inst. für Zelichemie. He was awarded the Nobel prize for Medicine with Bloch (5) in 1964 for his work in lipid biochemistry on the formation of the cholesterol molecule, discovering the biochemistry of the vitamin biotin.

LYON, John (d. 1592), English yeoman, in 1571 founded the great public school of Harrow.

LYONS, (1) **Edmund, 1st Baron** (1790–1858), English admiral, born at Burton, Hants, commanded in the Dutch West Indies (1810–1811) and in Crimean waters, and was made a peer in 1856.

(2) **Sir Joseph** (1848–1917), English business man, born in London, first studied art and invented a stereoscope before joining with three friends, Isidore and Montague Gluckstein and Barnett Salmon, to establish what was to become J. Lyons and Co. Ltd. Starting in Piccadilly with a teashop, he became head of one of the largest catering businesses in Britain. He was knighted in 1911.

(3) **Joseph Aloysius** (1879–1939), Australian statesman, born at Stanley, Tasmania, educated at Tasmania University, became a teacher but entered politics in 1909 as Labour member in the Tasmanian House of Assembly. He held the post of minister of education and railways (1914–16) and was premier (1923–29). In the federal parliament, he was in turn postmaster-general, minister of public works and treasurer. In 1931 he broke away as a protest against the government's financial policy and led an opposition party, the United Australian Party, which he himself founded. In 1932 he became

prime minister, which position he held until his death.

(4) **Richard Bickerton Pemell, 1st Earl** (1817–87), born at Lymington, son of (1), English diplomat, was ambassador to the United States, Turkey and France, was made a viscount in 1881, an earl in 1887. See Life by Lord Newton (1913).

LYRA, Nicolaus de (1270?–1340), born at Lyre near Évreux, was a lecturer at Paris, provincial of the Franciscans, and author of very famous *Postillae* or commentaries on scripture, in which he insisted on the literal meanings and protested against the traditional allegorizing method.

LYSANDER (d. 395 B.C.), Spartan admiral, as commander of the fleet defeated the Athenians at Aegospotami (405), and in 404 took Athens, thus ending the Peloponnesian war.

LYSENKO, Trofim Denisovich (1898–), the *enfant terrible* of Soviet genetics, born in Karlovka, Ukraine, gained a considerable reputation as an instiller of good crop husbandry into the Russian peasantry during the famines of the early 'thirties. On the basis of a borrowed discovery that the phases of plant growth can be accelerated by short doses of low temperature, he built up a quasi-scientific creed, compounded of Darwinism and the Michurinian thesis, that heredity can be changed by good husbandry, but otherwise more in line with Marxism than with genuine scientific theorizing. Failing to obtain scientific pre-eminence in the usual manner, he in 1948 with the approval of the Communist Party, declared the accepted Mendelian theory erroneous and banished many outstanding Soviet scientists. With the rise of Khrushchev and his agricultural policies, Lysenko faded from the limelight but was reinstated in 1958. He finally resigned from the presidency of the Academy of Agricultural Sciences, of which he was in charge (1938–56; 1958–62), on grounds of ill-health, and after Khrushchev's downfall was relieved of his post as head of the Institute of Genetics (1965). He was awarded the Order of Lenin in 1949 and the Stalin prize in 1949 for his book *Agrobiology* (1948).

LYSIAS (c. 450–380 B.C.), Greek orator, was the son of a rich Syracusan, who settled in Athens about 440. He was educated at Thurii in Italy. The Thirty Tyrants in 404 stripped him and his brother Polemarchus of their wealth, and killed Polemarchus. The first use to which Lysias put his eloquence was, on the fall of the Thirty (403), to prosecute Eratosthenes, the tyrant chiefly to blame for his brother's murder. He then practised with success as a writer of speeches for litigants. From his surviving speeches we see that Lysias is delightfully lucid in thought and expression, and strong in character-drawing.

LYSIMACHUS, *li-sim'a-koos* (d. 281 B.C.), Macedonian general of Alexander, afterwards King of Thrace, to which he later added northwest Asia Minor and Macedonia. He was defeated and killed at Koroupedion by Seleucus.

LYSIPPUS, *-sip'-* (fl. c. 360–316 B.C.), of

Sicyon, a prolific Greek sculptor, made several portrait busts of Alexander the Great. See Gardner's *Six Greek Sculptors* (1910).

LYTE, Henry Francis (1793–1847), Scottish hymnwriter, born at Ednam, near Kelso, entered Trinity College, Dublin. He took orders in 1815, and was for twenty-five years incumbent of Lower Brixham. His *Poems, chiefly Religious* (1833; reprinted as *Miscellaneous Poems*, 1868), are nearly forgotten; but 'Abide with me', 'Pleasant are thy courts', and other hymns have endured. See Life prefixed to the *Remains* (1850) and J. Julian, *A Dictionary of Hymnology* (1892).

LYTTLETON, (1) **George, 1st Baron** (1709–1773), English politician and author son of Sir Thomas Lyttleton of Hagley in Worcestershire, entered parliament in 1730, soon acquired eminence as a speaker, held several high political offices, and was raised to the peerage in 1759. His poetry gained him a place in Johnson's *Lives of the Poets*; his prose works include *The Conversion and Apostleship of St Paul* (1747), *Dialogues of the Dead* (1750), &c. See *Memoirs and Correspondence* (1845), and Rao, *A Minor Augustan* (1934).

(2) **George William, 4th Baron,** second creation (1817–76), as chairman of the Canterbury Association sent Anglican colonists to New Zealand and so founded Canterbury, N.Z., the port of which bears his name. He was under-secretary for the Colonies (1846).

(3) **Oliver.** See CHANDOS.

(4) **Thomas, Lord Lyttleton** (1744–79), son of (1), the 'wicked Lord Lyttelton', died three days after a death-warning dream. The *Poems by a Young Nobleman* (1780) may partly have been his, but the *Letters of the late Lord Lyttelton* (1780–82) were probably by W. Combe. See Lives by Frost (1876), Blunt (1936), Lang, *Valet's Tragedy* (1903).

(5) **Sir Thomas.** See LITTLETON.

LYTTON, (1) **Edward George Lytton Bulwer-, 1st Baron** (1803–73), English novelist, playwright, essayist, poet and politician, was born in London, youngest son of General Earle Bulwer (1776–1807) by Elizabeth Barbara Lytton (1773–1843), the heiress of Knebworth in Hertfordshire. He took early to poetry and in 1820 he published *Ismael and other Poems*. At Trinity Hall, Cambridge (1822–25), he won the Chancellor's gold medal for a poem upon 'Sculpture', but left with only a pass degree. His unhappy marriage (1827), against his mother's wishes,

to the Irish beauty, Rosina Wheeler, ended in separation (1836), but called forth a marvellous literary activity, for the temporary estrangement from his mother threw him almost wholly on his own resources. His enormous output, vastly popular during his lifetime, but now forgotten, includes *Eugene Aram* (1832), *The Last Days of Pompeii* (1834), and *Harold* (1843). Some of his plays are *The Lady of Lyons* (1838), *Richelieu* (1839), *Money* (1840), and his poetry includes an epic, *King Arthur* (1848–49). M.P. for St Ives (1831–41), he was created a baronet in 1838, and in 1843 he succeeded to the Knebworth estate and assumed the surname of Lytton. He re-entered parliament as member for Hertfordshire in 1852, and in the Derby government (1858–59) as colonial secretary he called into existence the colonies of British Columbia and Queensland and in 1866 he was raised to the peerage. See his *Life, Letters, and Literary Remains* (vols. i–ii, 1883) by his son (down to 1832), Memoir (1913) by his grandson, 2nd Earl of Lytton. See also Life by Escott (1910), and the 'panorama' by Sadleir (i, 1931).

(2) **Edward Robert Bulwer, 1st Earl of** (1831–91), poet, diplomatist and statesman, son of (1), was born in London, and educated at Harrow and at Bonn. In 1849 he went to Washington as attaché and private secretary to his uncle, Sir Henry Bulwer (q.v.); and subsequently he was appointed attaché, secretary of legation, consul or *chargé d'affaires* at Florence (1852), Paris (1854). The Hague (1856), St Petersburg and Constantinople (1858), Vienna (1859), Belgrade (1860), Constantinople again (1863), Athens (1864), Lisbon (1865), Madrid (1868), Vienna again (1869) and Paris (1873). In the last year he succeeded his father as second Lord Lytton, and in 1874 became minister at Lisbon, in 1876–80 was Viceroy of India, and in 1880 was made Earl of Lytton; in 1887 he was sent as ambassador to Paris, and there he died. His works, published mostly under the pseudonym of 'Owen Meredith', include novels, poems, and translations from Serbian. See his *Indian Administration* (1899) and his *Letters* (1906), both edited by his daughter, Lady Betty Balfour.

(3) **Sir Henry Alfred** (1867–1936), English actor, born in London, first appeared on the stage in the D'Oyly Carte Opera Company in Glasgow in 1884. Till 1932 he played leading parts in Gilbert and Sullivan opera. He wrote *Secrets of a Savoyard* (1927), *A Wandering Minstrel* (1933).

M

MAARTENS, Maarten, pen-name of **Jost Marius Willem van der Poorten Schwart** (1858–1915), who, born at Amsterdam, spent part of his boyhood in England, went to school in Germany, and studied and taught law at Utrecht University. He wrote power-

ful novels in nervous English, including *The Sin of Joost Avelingh* (1889), *God's Fool* (1893), &c. See his *Letters*, ed. his daughter (1930), and a study by Maanen (1928).

MABILLON, Jean, *mab-ee-yõ* (1632–1707), French Benedictine monk, born at St

Pierremont in Champagne, from 1664 worked in St Germain-des-Prés at Paris, where he died. He edited St Bernard's works (1667), wrote a history of his order (1668–1702), &c.

MABLY, Gabriel Bonnot de, *ma-blee* (1709–1785), French historian, born at Grenoble, the elder brother of Condillac, for a time was secretary to the minister Cardinal Tencin, his uncle, and wrote *Entretiens de Phocion* (1763), *Parallèle des Romains et des Français* (1740) and *Observations sur l'histoire de la Grèce* (1766). His *De la manière d'écrire l'histoire* (1783) contains severe strictures on Hume, Robertson, Gibbon and Voltaire. See books by Guerrier (1886) and Whitfield (1930).

MABUSE, Jan, real name Gossart, *ma-büz* (c. 1470–1532), Flemish painter, was born at Maubeuge (Mabuse), in 1503 entered the painters' guild of St Luke at Antwerp, and was influenced by Memlinc and Quentin Matsys. In 1508–09 he accompanied Philip of Burgundy to Italy, and returned with his style greatly modified by the Italian masters. Drunken but sumptuous, he lived latterly at Middelburg, and died at Antwerp.

McADAM, John Loudon (1756–1836), inventor of the 'macadamizing' system of road-making, was born at Ayr, September 21, 1756. He went to New York in 1770, became a successful merchant, and on his return to Scotland in 1783 bought the estate of Sauchrie, Ayrshire. Surveyor (1816) to the Bristol Turnpike Trust, he re-made the roads there cheaply and well. His advice was sought in all directions. Impoverished through his labours, he petitioned parliament in 1820, and in 1825 was voted £2000, in 1827 made surveyor-general of metropolitan roads. He died November 26. He wrote three books on road-making (1819–22). See *Life* by M. R. R. M. Pember-Devereux (1940).

MACALPINE, John. See MACHABEUS.

MacARTHUR, Douglas (1880–1964), American soldier, born at Little Rock, Arkansas, and educated at West Point. Commissioned in the Corps of Engineers in 1903, he went to Tokyo in 1905 as aide to his father, then chief U.S. observer at the Russo-Japanese war. In the first World War he served with distinction in France, was decorated thirteen times and cited seven additional times for bravery. Promoted brigadier in August 1918, he became in November the youngest divisional commander in France. In 1919 he became the youngest-ever superintendent of West Point and in 1930 was made a general and chief of staff of the U.S. Army. In 1935 he became head of the U.S. military mission to the Philippines and in 1941 commanding general of the U.S. armed forces in the Far East. In March 1942, after a skilful but unsuccessful defence of the Bataan peninsula, he was ordered to evacuate from the Philippines to Australia, where he set up H.Q. as supreme commander of the SW. Pacific Area. As the war developed he carried out a brilliant 'leap-frogging' strategy which enabled him to recapture the Philippine Archipelago from the Japanese. In 1944 he was appointed a general of the Army, and completed the liberation of the Philippines in July 1945. Then, formally accepting as supreme commander of the Allied Powers the surrender of

Japan, he exercised in the occupied Empire almost unlimited authority. He gave Japan a new constitution and carried out a programme of sweeping reform. When war broke out in Korea in June 1950 President Truman ordered him to support the South Koreans in accordance with the appeal of the U.N. Security Council. In July he became c.-in-c. of the U.N. forces. After initial setbacks he pressed the war far into North Korea, but after the Chinese entered the war in November, MacArthur demanded powers to blockade the Chinese coast, bomb Manchurian bases and to use Chinese Nationalist troops from Formosa against the Communists. This led to acute differences with the U.S. Democratic Administration and on April 11, 1951, President Truman relieved him of his commands. He failed to be nominated for the presidency in 1952. A brilliant military leader and a ruler of Japan imbued with a deep moral sense, MacArthur was almost a legend in his lifetime. Equally he inspired criticism for his imperious belief in his own mission, his strong sense of self-dramatization. See *The General and the President*, by Rovere and Schlesinger (1952), and his own *Reminiscences* (1965).

MACARTNEY, George, 1st Earl (1737–1806), British diplomat, born at Lissanoure near Belfast, and educated at Trinity College, Dublin, in 1764 was sent as an envoy to Russia, in 1769–72 was chief-secretary of Ireland, and in 1775 was governor of Grenada. There (an Irish baron from 1776) he was taken prisoner by the French in 1779. Governor of Madras 1781–85, in 1792 he was made an earl and headed the first diplomatic mission to China. After a mission to Louis XVIII at Verona (1795–96), he went out as governor to the Cape (1796), but returned in ill health in 1798. See *Life* by Mrs Robbins (1908), *Private correspondence* ed. by Davies (1950).

MACAULAY, (1) Rose (1889–1958), English novelist, essayist and poet. Her father, G. C. Macaulay, was a Cambridge lecturer and translator of Herodotus and Froissart, and having imbibed from this background a taste for literature she began writing at an early age, her first book, *Abbots Verney*, appearing in 1906, followed by *Views and Vagabonds* (1912) and *The Lee Shore* (1913), which won a publisher's £1000 prize. Among her many witty and erudite subsequent books were *Dangerous Ages* (1921), which was awarded the Femina Vie Heureuse Prize, *Told by an Idiot* (1923), *They were Defeated* (1932), *Fabled Shore* (1949), *The Pleasure of Ruins* (1953), and *The Towers of Trebizond* (1956), which won The Tait Black Memorial Prize. She was renowned for her enormous vigour and zest for life, which she retained even in her old age. Despite her apparent physical frailty she was an indefatigable traveller and an all-the-year-round swimmer. She was made a D.B.E. in 1958.

(2) **Thomas Babington, 1st Baron Macaulay** (1800–59), British author, son of (3), was born at Rothley Temple, Leics., on October 25. In 1812 young Macaulay was sent to a private school at Little Shelford near Cambridge, moved in 1814 to Aspenden Hall in Hertfordshire, whence, an exceptionally

precocious boy, he entered Trinity College, Cambridge, in 1818. He detested mathematics, but twice won the Chancellor's medal for English verse, and obtained a prize for Latin declamation. In 1821 he carried off the Craven, in 1822 took his B.A., and in 1824 was elected to a fellowship. He was one of the most brilliant disputants in the Union. Called to the bar in 1826, he had no liking for his profession—literature had irresistible attractions for him. In 1823 he became a contributor to *Knight's Quarterly Magazine*, in which appeared some of his best verses— *Ivry*, *The Spanish Armada* and *Naseby*. In 1825 he was discovered by Jeffrey, and his famous article on Milton in the August number of the *Edinburgh Review* secured him a position in literature. For nearly twenty years he was one of the most prolific and popular of the writers to the *Edinburgh*. In 1830 he entered parliament for the pocket borough of Calne, and in the Reform Bill debates his great powers as an orator were established. Commissioner, and then secretary, to the Board of Control, he still wrote steadily for the *Edinburgh*, and made a great reputation as a conversationalist in society. Mainly for the sake of his family, impoverished by the father's devotion to philanthropy, he accepted the office of legal adviser to the Supreme Council of India, with a salary of £10,000, and sailed for Bengal in 1834, returning to England in 1838. In 1839 he was elected member of parliament for Edinburgh, and entered Lord Melbourne's Cabinet as secretary at war. The *Lays of Ancient Rome* (1842) won an immense popularity; so too did his collected *Essays* (3 vols. 1843). His connection with the *Edinburgh* ceased in 1845; he had now commenced his *History of England from the Accession of James II*. In 1846 he was re-elected for Edinburgh; but defeated at the general election of 1847. In 1852 he was again returned for Edinburgh; in 1856 he retired. The first two volumes of his *History* appeared in 1848, and at once attained greater popularity than had ever fallen to a purely historical work; the next two followed in 1855, and an unfinished fifth volume was published in 1861. In 1849 he was elected lord rector of Glasgow University. In 1857 he was raised to the peerage as Baron Macaulay of Rothley. He died in his armchair at Holly Lodge, Kensington, December 28, 1859, and was buried in Westminster Abbey. Macaulay's reputation is not what once it was—he has been convicted of historical inaccuracy, of sacrificing truth for the sake of epigram, of allowing personal dislike and Whig bias to distort his views of men and incidents. But as a picturesque narrator he has no rival. See his *Life and Letters* by his nephew, G. O. Trevelyan (1876), Morison's *Monograph* (1882), an essay by Morley (*Critical Miscellanies*, 1886), and studies by Bryant (1932), Giles St Aubyn (1953) and M. Thomson (1959).

(3) **Zachary** (1768–1838), father of (2), had a somewhat chequered career as a West India merchant, but was best known as an abolitionist and a member of the ' Clapham sect '. See Lives by Knutsford (1900), Booth (1934).

McAULEY, Catherine (1787–1841), Irish religious foundress born in Dublin. She founded the Order of Sisters of Mercy in 1831. See Life by R. B. Savage (1949).

MACBETH (*d.* 1057), Mormaer of Moray, married Gruoch, granddaughter of Kenneth Dubh, King of Alban, and became commander of the forces of Scotland. In 1040 he slew King Duncan, and succeeded him. He seems to have represented a Celtic reaction against English influence; and his seventeen years' reign is commemorated in the chronicles as a time of plenty. Malcolm Canmore, Duncan's son, ultimately defeated and killed him at Lumphanan, August 15, 1057. Shakespeare got his story from Holinshed, who drew on Boece. See Skene's *Celtic Scotland* (1876).

MacBRIDE, Maud, *née* Gonne (1865–1953), Irish nationalist, the daughter of an English colonel, became an agitator for the cause of Irish independence, edited a nationalist newspaper, *L'Irlande libre*, in Paris, and married Major John MacBride, who fought against the British in the Boer War and was executed as a rebel in 1916. After his death she became an active Sinn Feiner in Ireland. W. B. Yeats dedicated poems to her. Her son Sean (b. 1904) was foreign minister of the Irish Republic from 1948 to 1951.

MacBRYDE, Robert (1913–), Scottish artist, born in Ayrshire. He worked in industry for five years before studying at the Glasgow School of Art and later worked with Robert Colquhoun, painting brilliantly-coloured cubist still lifes, and later, brooding expressionist figures.

MACCABEES, a celebrated Jewish family. The founder of the dynasty, Mattathias, a priest, was the first to make a stand against the persecutions of the Jewish nation and creed by Antiochus Epiphanes. He was the great-great-grandson of Hasmon and the family is often known as the ' Hasmoneans '. Mattathias and his five sons, Jochanan, Simon, Jehudah, Eleazer and Jonathan, together with a handful of faithful men, rose against the national foe, destroyed heathen worship, and fled into the wilderness of Judah. Their number soon increased; they were able to make descents into the villages and cities, where they restored the ancient worship of Jehovah. At the death of Mattathias (166 B.C.) his son Jehudah or Judas, now called Makkabi (*Makkab*, ' hammerer ') or Maccabaeus, took the command of the patriots, and repulsed the enemy, reconquered Jerusalem, purified the Temple, and re-inaugurated the holy service (164). Having concluded an alliance with the Romans, he fell in battle (160). His brother Jonathan renewed the Roman alliance, acquired the dignity of high priest, but was treacherously slain by the Syrians. Simon, the second brother, completely re-established the independence of the nation (141), and ' Judah prospered as of old '. But he was foully murdered (135) by his son-in-law, Ptolemy. See the articles HYRCANUS, HEROD; the Apocryphal books of the Maccabees; and histories of the period by De Saulcy (1880), Ewald, and Schürer.

MacCAIG, Norman Alexander (1910–), Scottish poet, born at Edinburgh, and educated at the University there. His poetry collections include *Far Cry* (1943), *Riding Lights* (1955), *A Common Grace* (1960), *A Round of Applause* (1962), and *Surroundings* (1966). Though he writes in English his topics and temperament are unmistakably Scots. A metaphysical approach to ideas with the speculation subtly expressed, is the hallmark of his work, which is deliberately quiet in tone. He edited *Honour'd Shade* (1959), an anthology of the most modern and significant in Scottish poetry commemorating the bicentenary of Burns.

MacCARTHY, (1) Denis Florence (1817-82), Irish author, born in Dublin, was prepared for the priesthood, but wrote poetry, translated Calderón, and published *Shelley's Early Life* (1872).

(2) **Sir Desmond** (1878-1952), writer and critic, born at Plymouth. Educated at Eton and Trinity College, Cambridge, he entered journalism and was successively editor of *New Quarterly* and *Eye Witness* (later *New Witness*). By 1913 he was writing for *The New Statesman*, of which he became literary editor in 1920, and later dramatic critic. He became editor of *Life and Letters*, book reviewer for *The Sunday Times*, and a broadcaster of repute. He was knighted in 1951. His criticism, collected in book form, is represented by *Portraits* (1931), *Experience* (1935), *Drama* (1940), *Humanities* (1954) and *Theatre* (1955). See *A Number of People* by Marsh (1939), the preface to *Humanities* by MacCarthy's son-in-law, David Cecil, and his autobiographical *Memories* (1953).

McCARTHY, (1) Joseph Raymond (1909-57), American politician and inquisitor, born at Grand Chute, Wisconsin, studied at Marquette University, Milwaukee, and in 1939 was a state circuit judge. After war services in the Marines and as an air-gunner, he was elected senator in 1945, although as a serving judge his election was contrary to the Constitution. Defying a Supreme Court ruling, he took his seat in the senate and in 1950 was re-elected by a huge majority, having exploited the general uneasiness felt after the treason trials of Nunn May, Fuchs and Alger Hiss, by accusing the State Department of harbouring 205 prominent Communists, a charge that he was later incapable of substantiating, before a special subcommittee on foreign relations. Undaunted, he accused the Truman administration of being 'soft on Communism' and the Democratic party of a record of 'twenty years of treason'. After the Eisenhower victory, McCarthy, in January 1953, became chairman of the powerful Permanent Subcommittee on Investigations and by hectoring cross-examination, damaging innuendo, and 'guilt by association' arraigned a great number of mostly innocent citizens and officials, often with full television publicity, overreaching himself when he came into direct conflict with the army, which he accused of 'coddling Communists'. Formally condemned by the Senate, again controlled by the Democrats in 1954, for financial irregularities, he was stung into attacking President Eisenhower and so lost most of his remaining Republican support. Truman rightly described him as a 'pathological character assassin'. See *Life*

by J. Anderson and R. W. May (1953), and critical study by R. H. Rovere (1960).

(2) **Justin** (1830-1912), Irish politician, novelist and historian, born in Cork, joined the staff of the *Northern Times*, Liverpool, in 1853, and in 1860 entered the reporters' gallery for the *Morning Star*, becoming its chief editor in 1864. He resigned in 1868, and devoted the next three years to a tour of the United States. Soon after his return he became connected with the *Daily News*, and he contributed to the *London*, *Westminster* and *Fortnightly Reviews*. He entered parliament in 1879 for Longford. He is better known, however, as a novelist than as a politician. His novels include *Dear Lady Disdain* (1875) and *Miss Misanthrope* (1877). Other works are *A History of our Own Times* (7 vols. 1879-1905), *The Four Georges and William IV* (4 vols. 1889-1901), &c. See his *Reminiscences* (1899-1911).

(3) **Justin Huntly** (1860-1936), son of (2), was a Nationalist M.P. 1884-92; in 1894 he married the clever impersonator and actress, Cissie Loftus (1876-1943; born in Glasgow), who divorced him in 1899. He wrote stories, plays, verse, *England under Gladstone* (1884), *Ireland since the Union* (1887), *The French Revolution* (4 vols. 1890-97), &c.

(4) **Mary** (1912-), American novelist and critic, born at Seattle. Orphaned in 1918, she was brought up in Minneapolis, and educated at Vassar Coll. She has worked as publisher's editor, theatre critic and teacher, as well as publishing novels, including *The Company She Keeps* (1942), *The Oasis* (1949), *The Groves of Academe* (1952), a book of short stories, and *The Group* (1963). Other works include *Sights and Spectacles* (1956), *Vietnam* (1967), and her autobiographical *Memories of a Catholic Girlhood* (1957).

MACCHABEUS. See MACHABEUS.
MACCHIAEVLLI. See MACHIAVELLI.
McCLELLAN, George Brinton (1826-85), American general, was born at Philadelphia. At the Civil War in 1861, as major-general in the U.S. army, he drove the enemy out of West Virginia, and was called to Washington to reorganize the Army of the Potomac. In November he was made commander-in-chief, but held the honour only five months. His Virginian campaign ended disastrously. He advanced near to Richmond, but was compelled to retreat, fighting the 'seven days' battles' (June 25 to July 1, 1862). After the disastrous second battle of Bull Run (August 29-30), followed by a Confederate invasion of Maryland, he reorganized the army at Washington, marched north, met Lee at Antietam, and compelled him to recross the Potomac. He followed the Confederates into Virginia, but too slow and cautious, he was superseded by Burnside. In 1864 he opposed Lincoln for the presidency, and in 1877 was elected governor of New Jersey. See *McClellan's Own Story* (1886), and vindication by J. H. Campbell (1917).

McCLINTOCK, Admiral Sir Francis Leopold (1819-1907), British polar explorer, born at Dundalk, entered the navy in 1831, and was knighted in 1860 for discovering the fate of the Franklin (q.v.) expedition. In 1891 he was created a K.C.B.

McCLURE, Sir Robert John le Mesurier (1807–73), was born at Wexford, January 28, entered the navy in 1824, and served in Back's Arctic Expedition in 1836, and Ross's Franklin Expedition in 1848. As commander of a ship in another Franklin Expedition (1850–54) he penetrated eastwards to the north coast of Banks Land. Having been icebound there for nearly two years, he was rescued by Captain Kellett, who had come westwards. The rescuing ship was in turn abandoned after another winter. Thus in three ships, with two ice journeys, McClure accomplished the Northwest Passage. After serving in Chinese waters he died, an admiral. See his *Voyages* (2 vols. 1884).

MacCOLL, Dugald Sutherland (1859–1948), Scottish painter and art historian, born in Glasgow, graduated at London University and at Oxford, where he won the Newdigate Prize in 1882. After travelling Europe studying works of art he established a reputation as a critic and brought out his *Nineteenth Century Art* in 1902. As keeper of the Tate Gallery (1906–11) and of the Wallace Collection (1911–24) he instituted many reforms and improvements, and he also published poems and a noteworthy biography of Wilson Steer (1945; Tait Black Memorial Prize). See his *Confessions of a Keeper* (1931).

McCORMACK, John (1884–1945), Irish tenor singer, born in Athlone. He studied in Milan, made his London début in 1905, and was engaged for Covent Garden opera for the 1905–06 season, appearing also in oratorio and as a lieder singer. As an Irish nationalist, he did not appear in England during World War I, but took American citizenship in 1917, and turned to popular sentimental songs. He was raised to the papal peerage as a count in 1928. See Lives by Strong (1949) and Foxall (1963).

McCOSH, James (1811–94), Scottish philosopher, born at Carskeoch, Ayrshire, became a minister of the Church of Scotland and later of the Free Church. In 1851 he became professor of Logic at Belfast and in 1868 president of Princeton. His *Intuitions of the Mind* (1860) brought the natural realism of the Scottish school back from Hamilton's Kantian superstructure to the 'common sense' positions of Reid and Stewart. In his *Examination of Mr J. S. Mill's Philosophy* (1866) he attempted a vindication of the Scottish school against the mortal blow dealt it by Mill. See his *The Scottish Philosophy* (1875). See Life by W. M. Sloane.

McCRACKEN, Esther Helen, *née* **Armstrong** (1901–), English playwright and actress, born in Newcastle-on-Tyne. From 1924 to 1937 she acted with the Newcastle Repertory Company. Her first play, *The Willing Spirit*, was produced in 1936, but it was with *Quiet Wedding* (1938) that her reputation was made as a writer of domestic comedy. Other successes were *Quiet Weekend* (1941) and *No Medals* (1944). Her first husband, Lt.-Col. Angus McCracken, died of wounds in 1943, and the following year she married Mungo Campbell.

McCRIE, Thomas (1772–1835), Scottish historian and divine, born at Duns, author of lives of Knox (1812) and Melville (1819) and of

History of the Reformation in Spain (1829). See Life (1840) by his son, **Thomas** (1798–1875), professor in the Presbyterian college at London, and himself author of *Sketches of Scottish Church History* (1841) and *Annals of English Presbytery* (1872).

MacCRIMMON, a Skye family, hereditary pipers to Macleod of Dunvegan, the greatest Patrick Mór (fl. 1650). See book by F. T. Macleod (1933).

McCULLERS, Carson, *née* **Smith** (1917–67), American author, born in Columbus, Ga., educated Columbia and New York Universities. Her novels, set in the deep south, are both realistic, often tragic, and symbolic. They include *The Heart is a Lonely Hunter* (1940), *Reflections in a Golden Eye* (1941), a violent melodrama set on a peacetime army camp, *The Member of the Wedding* (1946, which she turned into a play, 1950 (New York Critics Award), filmed 1952), a sympathetic study of unhappy adolescence, and *Clock Without Hands* (1961). She also wrote a novella, *The Ballad of the Sad Café* (1951), another play and short stories.

MACCULLOCH, John (1773–1835), Scottish geologist, born in Guernsey, noted for his geological studies of the Western Isles.

McCULLOCH, John Ramsay (1789–1864), political economist, born at Whithorn, March 1, 1789, edited the *Scotsman* 1818–19, and for twenty years provided most of the articles on economics in the *Edinburgh Review*. He lectured in London; in 1828 became professor of Political Economy in University College, and in 1838 comptroller of H.M. Stationery Office. He wrote books on economics and commerce.

MacCUNN, Hamish (1868–1916), Scottish composer, born in Greenock, March 22, 1868, studied at the Royal College of Music, and in 1888–94 was professor of Harmony at the Royal Academy of Music. His works, largely Scottish in character and subject, include the overtures *Cior Mhor* (1887), *Land of the Mountain and the Flood*, and *The Dowie Dens of Yarrow*, choral works, such as *The Lay of the Last Minstrel*, the operas *Jeanie Deans* (1894) and *Diarmid* (1897), and songs.

MacDIARMID, Hugh, *mak-dir'mid*, pen-name of Christopher Murray Grieve (1892–), Scottish poet, pioneer of the Scottish literary renaissance, born at Langholm, Dumfries, served with the medical corps in Greece during World War I and was a munitions worker in World War II. A journalist in Montrose in the 'twenties, he took to poetry, fostering his own work in the *Scottish Chapbook*, a monthly review which he edited. Beginning with such outstanding early lyrical verse as 'Watergaw', he established himself as the new prophetic voice of Scotland by *A Drunk Man Looks at the Thistle* (1926), bursting with political, metaphysical and nationalistic reflections on the Scottish predicament. In his later works, however, this master of polemic, or 'flyting' increasingly allowed his poetical genius to be overburdened by philosophical gleanings, in the service of a highly personal form of Communism. Nevertheless items such as 'The Seamless Garment', 'Cattle Shaw', 'At Lenin's Tomb' raise these later works to a very high level. They are *To Circumjack Cencrastus* (1930), the two *Hymns to Lenin* (1930; 1935), *Scots Unbound* (1932), *Stony Limits* (1934), *A Kist o' Whistles* (1947) and *In Memoriam James Joyce* (1955). His numerous essays such as *Albyn* (1927), *The Islands of Scotland* (1939) suffer from the same intellectual scrapbook tendency. Foundermember of the Scottish National Party, off and on an active Communist, he stood against Sir Alec Douglas-Home as a Communist candidate in 1963. He dedicated his life to the regeneration of the Scottish literary language, repudiated by his fellow Scottish poet, Edwin Muir, in 1936. He brilliantly succeeded by employing a vocabulary drawn from all regions and periods, intellectualizing a previously parochial tradition. He received an honorary Edinburgh doctorate in 1957. See his autobiography, *Lucky Poet* (1943), and *The Company I've Kept* (1966), Wittig, *The Scottish Tradition in Literature* (1958), and studies by Buthley (1964) and Glen (1964).

MacDONALD, (1) James Ramsay (1866–1937), British politician, born at Lossiemouth (Morayshire), and educated at a Board school, wrote on Socialism and other problems. He was a leading member of the I.L.P. (1893–1930) and was secretary (1900–11) and leader (1911–14, 1922–31) of the Labour Party. A member of the L.C.C. (1901–04) and of parliament from 1906, he became leader of the Opposition in 1922, and from January to November 1924 was prime minister and foreign secretary of the first Labour government in Britain—a minority government at the mercy of the Liberals. The election of 1924 put him out of office; that of 1929 brought him in again; but he met the financial crisis of 1931 by forming a predominantly Conservative ' National ' government, the bulk of his party opposing; and in 1931 reconstructed it after a general election. In 1935–37 he was lord president. See Lives by G. E. Elton (1939), L. M. Weir (1938).

(2) **Malcolm** (1901–   ), British administrator, son of (1), born at Lossiemouth, studied at Oxford, was National Government M.P. (1936–45) and held several ministerial appointments, including those of colonial secretary (1935; 1938–40) and minister of Health (1940–41). He has held positions as high commissioner in Canada (1941–46), governor-general of Malaya and Borneo (1946–48), commissioner-general in South East Asia (1948–55), high commissioner in India (1955–60), governor-general (1963–64), and high commissioner (1964–65) in Kenya, and special representative in east and central Africa from 1965. His books include *Borneo People* (1956) and *Angkor* (1958), and several on ornithology.

MACDONALD, (1) Fr. *mak-do-nahl,* **Jacques Étienne Joseph Alexandre** (1765–1840), marshal of France, was born at Sedan, the son of a Scottish Jacobite schoolmaster. He entered the army in 1785, distinguished himself in the cause of the Revolution, and rapidly rose to high rank. In 1798 he was made governor of Rome, and subjugated Naples. Suvoroff defeated him after a bloody contest on the Trebbia (1799). In 1805 he lost the favour of Bonaparte; but,

restored to command in 1809, he took Laibach, distinguished himself at Wagram, and was created marshal and Duke of Taranto. He held a command in Spain in 1810, and in the Russian campaign; and in 1813 he contributed to the successes of Lützen and Bautzen, but was routed by Blücher at the Katzbach. After Leipzig he helped to cover the French retreat. The Bourbons made him a peer, and from 1816 he was chancellor of the Legion of Honour. See his *Souvenirs* (2nd ed. 1892; Eng. trans. 1892).

(2) **Flora** (1722–90), Scottish heroine, born in South Uist, lost her father, a tacksman, at two; and at thirteen was adopted by Lady Clanranald, wife of the chief of the clan. When the rebellion of the '45 broke down she is said to have conducted the Pretender (June 1746), disguised as ' Betty Burke ', from Benbecula to Portree. Flora was not a Jacobite; but those three short perilous days endeared her to more than Jacobites, and she was much fêted during her year's captivity on the troopship in Leith Roads and at London. In 1750 she married the son of Macdonald of Kingsburgh, where in 1773 she entertained Dr Johnson. In 1774 her husband emigrated to North Carolina, and in 1776 in the War of Independence became a brigadier-general. He was made prisoner and Flora returned to Scotland in 1779. After two years she was rejoined by her husband, and they settled again at Kingsburgh. The *Autobiography of Flora Macdonald* (1869) is a forgery; but see works by Macgregor (1882) and Jolly (1886).

(3) **George** (1824–1905), Scottish poet and novelist, born at Huntly, was educated at Aberdeen and the Congregationalist College at Highbury. He became pastor at Arundel and at Manchester, but ill-health drove him to literature. He wrote poetry and novels, but is now best known for his children's books. In 1877 he received a Civil List pension of £100. See a Life by his son (1924).

(4) **Sir George** (1862–1940), born at Elgin, educated at Ayr Academy, Edinburgh University and Balliol, Oxford, became secretary of the Scottish Education Department and a great authority on Roman Britain. See Memoir by A. O. Curle (1940).

(5) **Sir John Alexander** (1815–91), Canadian statesman, born in Glasgow, emigrated with his parents in 1820. He was called to the bar in 1836 and ʳappointed Q.C. Entering politics he became leader of the Conservatives and premier in 1856, and in 1867 formed the first government for the new Dominion, minister of Justice and attorney-general of Canada until 1873, he was again in power from 1878 till his death at Ottawa. He was mainly instrumental in bringing about the confederation of Canada and in securing the construction of the intercolonial and Pacific railways. His widow was made a peeress. See Lives by Collins (1892), Pope (1894), Parkin (1906).

MACDONELL, Alastair Ruadh (c. 1724–61), Scottish Jacobite, was a captain in the French Scots brigade, lay in the Tower of London 1745–47, succeeded his father in 1754 as thirteenth chief of Glengarry, and died with the character of ' one of the best men in the Highlands '. Andrew Lang proved him to have been a spy on his fellow Jacobites. See *Pickle the Spy* (1897) and *Companions of Pickle* (1899).

McDOUGALL, William (1871–1938), Anglo-American psychologist, born in Lancashire. After studying at Weimar, Manchester and Cambridge, he trained in medicine at St Thomas's, and in 1898 accompanied an anthropological expedition to the Torres Strait. He held academic posts in both Oxford and Cambridge, served in the R.A.M.C. in World War I, and in 1920 went to Harvard as professor of Psychology. In 1927 he transferred to Duke University, North Carolina. He preached purposive psychology as opposed to behaviourism. His chief works are *Physiological Psychology* (1905), *Body and Mind* (1911), *Outlines of Psychology* (1923) and *The Energies of Man* (1933).

MacDOWELL, Edward Alexander, *mak-dow'él* (1861–1908), American composer and pianist, born in New York. He studied in Paris, Wiesbaden and Frankfurt, and in 1881 was appointed head teacher of pianoforte at Darmstadt conservatoire. At the invitation of Liszt, he played his First Piano Concerto in Zürich in 1882. He returned to the United States in 1888, and was head of the newly-organized department of music at Columbia University from 1896 until 1904, when he suffered a mental breakdown. He composed extensively for orchestra, voices and piano, and is best remembered for some of his small-scale piano pieces, as *Woodland Sketches* and *Sea Pieces*. See Life by his wife (1950).

McEVOY, Ambrose, *mak'-* (1878–1927), English painter, known especially for his portraits and genre paintings. His *The Earring* is in the Tate Gallery. He was elected A.R.A. in 1924.

McEWEN, Sir John Blackwood (1868–1948), Scottish composer, born at Hawick, taught music in Glasgow, and was principal of the Royal College of Music in London, 1924–36.

MACFARREN, Sir George Alexander (1813–1887), born in London, studied at the Royal Academy of Music. In 1837 he became a professor there, in 1875 principal, and professor of Music at Cambridge. He was knighted in 1883. In 1865 he became blind. Among his works are operas, cantatas, oratorios and books on musical theory and history. See Life by Banister (1891).

McGILL, James (1744–1813), born in Glasgow, emigrated to Canada, and made a fortune in the northwest fur trade and at Montreal. He bequeathed land and money to found McGill College, Montreal, which became McGill University in 1821.

McGONAGALL, William (b. 1830), Scottish doggerel poet, son of an Irish weaver, came from Dundee to Edinburgh, where he gave readings in public houses, published broadsheets of topical verse, and was lionized by the legal and student fraternity. His poems are uniformly bad, but possess a disarming naïveté and a calypso-like disregard for metre which still never fail to entertain. See *Poetic Gems* (1934) and *More Poetic Gems* (1963).

MacGREGOR, John (1825–92), British writer and traveller, born at Gravesend, graduated at Trinity College, Cambridge, travelled widely in Europe, the Middle East and Russia, but is best remembered as the pioneer and popularizer of canoeing in Britain and designer of the Rob Roy type canoe. His travel books include *A Thousand Miles in a Rob Roy Canoe* (1866), &c.

McGREGOR, Robert. See ROB ROY.

MACGREGOR, Sir William, P.C., G.C.M.G., M.D. (1847–1919), was governor of New Guinea, Lagos, Newfoundland, and (1909–1914) Queensland.

MACH, Ernst, *mahκH* (1838–1916), Austrian physicist and philosopher, born in Turas, Moravia, studied at Vienna University, and became professor of Mathematics at Graz in 1864, of Physics at Prague in 1867, and of Physics also at Vienna in 1895. He carried out much experimental work on supersonic projectiles and on the flow of gases, obtaining some remarkable early photographs of shock waves and gas jets. His findings have proved of great importance in aeronautical design and the science of projectiles, and his name has been given to the ratio of the speed of flow of a gas to the speed of sound (Mach number) and to the angle of a shock wave to the direction of motion (Mach angle). In the field of epistemology he was determined to abolish idle metaphysical speculation. His writings greatly influenced Einstein and laid the foundations of logical positivism. See his *Mechanik in ihrer Entwickelung* (1883, trans. 1902) and *Beiträge zur Analyse der Empfindung*,' Contributions to the Analysis of Sensation ' (1897).

MACHABEUS, Johannes (d. 1557), a Scottish reformer, one of the clan Macalpine, was Dominican Prior at Perth 1532–34, fled then as a heretic to England, married, went on to Germany, and from 1542 was professor of Theology at Copenhagen till his death.

MACHADO, Antonio, *ma-chah'THŏ* (1875–1939), Spanish writer, born at Seville, wrote lyrics characterized by a nostalgic melancholy, among them *Soledades, Galerías y otros poemas* (1907) and *Campos de Castilla* (1912). See study by Trend (1953). His brother **Manuel** (1874–1947), also a poet, collaborated with him in several plays. See study by Brotherston (1968).

MACHAR, Josef Svatopluk, *maκH'ar* (1864–1942), Czech poet, author of satirical and political verse, known for the trilogy *Confiteor* (1887), the verse romance *Magdalena* (1893), the epic *Warriors of God* (1897), &c. See study by Martinek (1912).

MACHAUT, Guillaume de. See GUILLAUME DE MACHAUT.

MACHIAVELLI, Niccolo di Bernardo dei, *mak-ee-a-vel'lee* (1469–1527), Italian statesman, born at Florence, May 3, 1469, saw the troubles of the French invasion (1493), when the Medici fled, and in 1498 became secretary of the Ten, a post he held until the fall of the republic in 1512. He was employed in a great variety of missions, including one to Cesare Borgia in 1502, of which an account is preserved in fifty-two letters, one to the Emperor Maximilian, and four to France. His dispatches during these journeys, and his treatises on the 'Affairs of France and Germany', are full of a far-reaching insight. On the restoration of the Medici, Machiavelli was involved in the downfall of his patron, the Gonfaloniere Soderini. Arrested on a charge of conspiracy in 1513, and put to the torture, he disclaimed all knowledge of the alleged conspiracy; but although pardoned, he was obliged to withdraw from public life, and devoted himself to literature. It was not till 1519 that he was commissioned by Leo X to draw up his report on a reform of the state of Florence; in 1521–25 he was employed in diplomatic services and as historiographer. After the defeat of the French at Pavia (1525), Italy lay helpless before the advancing forces of the Emperor Charles V, and Machiavelli strove to avert from Florence the invading army on its way to Rome. In May 1527 the Florentines again drove out the Medici and proclaimed the republic; but Machiavelli, bitterly disappointed that he was to be allowed no part in the movement for liberty, and already in feeble health, died on June 22. Through misrepresentation and misunderstanding his writings were spoken of as almost diabolical, his most violent assailants being the clergy. The first great edition of his works was not issued until 1782. From that period his fame as the founder of political science has steadily increased. Besides his letters and state papers, Machiavelli's historical writings comprise *Florentine Histories*, *Discourses on the First Decade of Titus Livius*, a *Life of Castruccio Castracani* (unfinished), and *History of the Affairs of Lucca*. His literary works comprise an imitation of the *Golden Ass* of Apuleius, an essay on the Italian language, and several minor compositions. He also wrote *Seven Books on the Art of War*. But the great source of his reputation, for good or for evil, is *De Principatibus* or *Il Principe* (Rome 1532). The main theme of the book is that all means may be resorted to for the establishment and maintenance of authority and that the worst and most treacherous acts of the ruler are justified by the wickedness and treachery of the governed. *The Prince* was condemned by Pope Clement VIII. The comedies of Machiavelli form an epoch in the history of the Italian theatre; *La Mandragola*, full of biting humour and shameless indecency, is a masterpiece of art. See books by Villari (1877–82; 3rd ed. 1912; trans. 1892), Tommasini (1883–1911), Prezzolini (trans. 1928), Macaulay's essay, Ranke's study, Morley's lecture (1897), Butterfield (revised ed. 1955) and Chabod (1956).

MACÍA, Francisco, *ma-thee'a* (1859–1933), leader of the Catalan movement and first president of Catalonia.

MacINDOE, Sir Archibald (1900–60), British plastic surgeon, born in Dunedin, N.Z., was educated at Otago, the Mayo Clinic, and St Bartholomew's Hospital. The most eminent pupil of Sir Harold Gillies (q.v.), he won fame during World War II as surgeon-in-charge at the Queen Victoria Hospital, East Grinstead, where the faces and limbs of injured airmen were remodelled with unsurpassed skill. He was knighted in 1947,

and was vice-president of the Royal College of Surgeons (1957–59). See Lives by McLeave (1961) and Mosley (1962).

MACINTOSH, Charles (1766–1843), a Glasgow manufacturing chemist, patented (1823) and gave name to Syme's (q.v.) method of waterproofing.

McINTYRE, Duncan Ban (1724–1812), the Gaelic poet-gamekeeper of Beinndòrain, was born in Glenorchy, fought as a Hanoverian at Falkirk in 1746, and in 1799–1806 was one of the City Guard of Edinburgh. See his *Poems* ed. and trans. by A. Macleod (1952).

MACK, Karl, Freiherr von (1752–1828), Austrian general, born at Nennslingen in Franconia, in 1770 entered the Austrian service, and, after fighting the Turks and the French republicans, was in 1797 created field-marshal. For the king of Naples he occupied Rome, but had to conclude an armistice with the French, and was driven to seek safety with them by riots in Naples. He was carried prisoner to Paris, but escaped in 1800. Having surrendered with his army to the French at Ulm in 1805, he was tried by court martial and condemned to death, but the sentence was commuted to twenty years' imprisonment. In 1808 he was liberated, in 1819 fully pardoned.

MACKAIL, John William (1859–1945), Scottish classical scholar, born at Kingarth, Bute, after a brilliant career at Oxford was elected a fellow of Balliol in 1882, left university life for the civil service and became assistant secretary to the Board of Education, but resigned in 1919 to give his full time to scholarship and criticism. His reputation rests on his studies on Virgil, on his *Latin Literature* (1895), his lectures on classical subjects and on the English poets, and his biographies of William Morris (1899) and George Wyndham (1925). He was elected professor of Poetry at Oxford in 1906 and was awarded the O.M. in 1935. He married the daughter of the artist Burne-Jones (q.v.), and his son **Denis** (1892–1971) and his daughter **Angela Thirkell** (1890–1961) are both well-known as novelists.

MACKAY, *mě-ki'*, (1) Alexander Murdoch (1849–90), pioneer missionary to Uganda 1878–87, was born at Rhynie in Aberdeenshire, trained as an engineer, but during a residence at Berlin in 1873 was led by the court preacher Baur to turn to missionary work. See Lives by his sister (1891) and A. R. Evans (1956).

(2) **Charles** (1814–89), Scottish songwriter, born at Perth, was editor of the *Glasgow Argus* 1844–47, of the *Illustrated London News* 1848–59 and New York correspondent of the *Times* during the civil war (1862–65). Two of his songs, 'There's a Good Time Coming' and 'Cheer, Boys, Cheer', had an extraordinary vogue. His prose works included *Popular Delusions* (1841), *Forty Years' Recollections* (1877), &c. His daughter was Marie Corelli (q.v.) and his son Eric (1851–98) achieved a reputation as a poet.

(3) **Robert** (1714–78), the Reay country Gaelic poet 'Rob Donn' ('brown'), was a Sutherland herd. See Life with his *Poems* (1898).

MACKENSEN, August von (1849–1945),

German field-marshal, born at Leipnitz, swept the Russians from Galicia 1915, the Rumanians from Dobrudja 1916. See Life by M. Luyken (1920).

MACKENZIE, (1) Sir Alexander (c. 1755–1820), Canadian fur-trader, born at Stornoway, in 1789 discovered the Mackenzie River, and in 1792–93 crossed the Rockies to the Pacific. See Life by Wade (1927).

(2) **Alexander** (1822–92), Canadian statesman, born at Logierait, Perthshire, removed to Canada in 1842, and was a mason and contractor. In 1852 he became editor of a Reform paper, from 1867 led the opposition in the Dominion parliament, and in 1873–78 was premier. He thrice declined knighthood, and died at Toronto.

(3) **Sir Alexander Campbell** (1847–1935), Scottish composer, born in Edinburgh, studied music at Sondershausen, and from 1862 at the Royal Academy, London. In 1865–79 he was teacher, violinist and conductor in Edinburgh, and in 1887–1924 was principal of the Royal Academy of Music. *The Rose of Sharon* (1884), an oratorio, contains some of his best work. He wrote operas; cantatas; Scottish rhapsodies; a concerto and a *pibroch* for violin; chamber music, songs, &c. See his *A Musician's Narrative* (1927).

(4) **Sir (Edward Montague) Compton** (1883–1972), British writer, born in West Hartlepool. His first novel, *The Passionate Elopement*, was published in 1911. There followed, *Carnival* (1912), *Sinister Street* (two volumes, 1913–14), *Guy and Pauline* (1915). In 1917 he became director of the Aegean Intelligence Service in Syria. Thereafter, from his considerable output, may be mentioned: *Sylvia Scarlett* (1918), *Poor Relations* (1919), *Rich Relatives* (1921), *Vestal Fire* (1927), *The Four Winds of Love* (4 volumes, 1937–45), *Aegean Memories* (1940), *Whisky Galore* (1947), *Eastern Epic*, vol. I (1951), and *Rockets Galore* (1957). He was awarded the O.B.E. in 1919, knighted in 1952 and was made a C.Lit. in 1968. See his monumental autobiography *My Life and Times* (1963–71) in ten *Octaves*, and book by Urquhart (1956).

(5) **Sir George** (1636–91), Scottish lawyer, born at Dundee, studied at St Andrews, Aberdeen and Bourges; in 1656 was called to the bar at Edinburgh; and in 1661 defended the Marquis of Argyll. He was knighted, entered parliament for Ross-shire in 1669, and in 1677 was named king's advocate. His career up to this point had been patriotic; unhappily in the popular mind he lives as 'Bluidy Mackenzie', the criminal prosecutor in the days of the persecution. He cultivated literature, was one of the first Scots to write English with purity, and in 1682 founded the Advocates Library at Edinburgh. He retired at the Revolution to Oxford, and dying in London, May 8, 1691, was buried at Edinburgh in Greyfriars Churchyard. His works were collected by Ruddiman (1716–22). See his *Memoirs of the Affairs of Scotland*, edited by T. Thomson (1821); and Andrew Lang's *Sir George Mackenzie* (1909).

(6) **Henry** (1745–1831), Scottish author, the 'Man of Feeling', born in Edinburgh,

became crown attorney in the Scottish Court of Exchequer, and in 1804 comptroller of taxes. For upwards of half a century he was 'one of the most illustrious names connected with polite literature in Edinburgh', where he died. His *Man of Feeling* was published in 1771 (ed. H. Miles 1928); *The Man of the World* followed in 1773, and *Julia de Roubigné* in 1777. He deserves remembrance for his recognition of Burns, and as an early admirer of Lessing and of Schiller. See *A Scottish Man of Feeling* (1931) by H. W. Thompson, who edited his *Anecdotes and Egotisms* (1928).

(7) **Sir James** (1853–1925), British physician, elected F.R.S. (1915), an authority on the heart, invented the polygraph to record graphically the heart's action. See his *Diseases of the Heart* (1908). See Life by R. M. Wilson (1945).

(8) **Sir Morell** (1837–92), British throat specialist, born at Leytonstone, was knighted in 1887 after attending the German Crown Prince (later Frederick III), whose throat condition proved ultimately to be malignant and fatal, contrary to Mackenzie's diagnosis. Mackenzie's apologia provoked much resentment in German medical circles and earned him the censure of the Royal College of Surgeons. See Life by Haweis (1893).

(9) **William Forbie** (1801–62), Scottish politician, born at Portmore, Peeblesshire, M.P. for Peeblesshire 1837–52, introduced a liquor Act for Scotland, passed in 1853, providing for Sunday closing and other controls.

(10) **William Lyon** (1795–1861), Canadian politician, born in Dundee, emigrated to Canada in 1820, and in 1824 established the *Colonial Advocate*. In 1828 he was elected to the provincial parliament for York, but was expelled in 1830 for libel on the Assembly. In 1837 he published in his paper a declaration of independence, headed a band of insurgents, and after a skirmish with a superior force, for a time maintained a camp on an island. Having fled to New York, he was sentenced by the U.S. authorities to twelve months' imprisonment. He returned to Canada in 1849, was a member of parliament 1850–58, and died at Toronto. He was the grandfather of W. L. Mackenzie King (q.v.). See Life by his son-in-law Charles Lindsey (1862), also M. Bellasis, *Rise, Canadians* (1955).

MACKENZIE KING. See KING (3).

McKINLEY, William (1843–1901), twenty-fourth president of the United States, was born January 29, 1843, at Niles in Ohio, and served in the Civil War, retiring in 1867 as major to Canton, where he practised law. He was elected to congress in 1877, and repeatedly re-elected. In 1891 he was made governor of Ohio, his name being identified with the high protective tariff carried in the McKinley Bill of 1890, though subsequently modified by the Democrats in 1894. Chosen Republican candidate for the presidency in 1896 and 1900, he conducted exciting contests with W. J. Bryan, who advocated the cause of free silver, denounced trusts, high tariffs, and imperialism, and was understood to favour labour at the expense of capital. Some Democrats, 'Gold Democrats' or 'Sound Money

Democrats', in spite of their dislike of McKinley's policy on many points, supported him. In November 1900, as in 1896, he secured a large majority in the electoral college, as the representative of a gold standard and of capital. In his first term the war with Spain (1898) took place, with the conquest of Cuba and the Philippines. He was shot by an anarchist September 6, and died September 14, 1901. See studies by M. Leech (1959) and H. Wayne Morgan (1963).

MACKINTOSH (1) **Charles Rennie** (1868–1928), Scottish architect, was born in Glasgow. He exercised considerable influence on European design, his chief work being Glasgow School of Art. See Pevsner's *Pioneers of the Modern Movement* (1936), and study by Howarth (1952).

(2) **Elizabeth** (? –1952), British novelist and playwright, born in Inverness. Under the pseudonym of **Gordon Daviot** she wrote her best known novel, *Kif* (1929), and her more serious works, including the historical drama, *Richard of Bordeaux* (1932)—the work for which she is most remembered—and a biography of Claverhouse (1937). *The Daughter of Time* (1951), a detective story, was one of several which she wrote as **Josephine Tey.**

(3) **Sir James** (1765–1832), Scottish writer, born at Aldourie in Inverness-shire, studied medicine but settled in London as a journalist. His *Vindiciae Gallicae* (1791) was written in reply to Burke's *Reflections on the French Revolution*; and he became secretary of the 'Friends of the People'. He was called to the bar in 1795. In 1799 he delivered a brilliant series of lectures on the law of nature and of nations at Lincoln's Inn; and his defence of Peltier (1803), charged with a libel on Bonaparte, was a splendid triumph. In 1804 he was knighted, and appointed recorder of Bombay, and in 1806 judge of its Admiralty Court; he spent seven years at Bombay, entering parliament after his return as Whig member for Nairn (1813). He wrote on history and philosophy. See the *Memoirs* by his son (1835), and the essays of Macaulay and De Quincey.

(4) **William** (1662–1743), Scottish Jacobite, of Borlum, Inverness-shire, was 'out' in 1715 and 1719, and the first time escaped from Newgate, but died after long captivity in Edinburgh Castle. He was an early arboriculturist.

MACKLIN, Charles (c. 1697–1797), actor, born in the North of Ireland, the son of William McLaughlin, after a wild, unsettled youth, played in Bristol and Bath, and in 1733 was engaged at Drury Lane. He steadily rose in public favour, till in 1741 he appeared in his great character, Shylock. From this time he was accounted one of the best actors whether in tragedy or comedy. His last performance was at Covent Garden in 1789; but he survived, with an annuity of £200, till July 11, 1797. He was generous, high-spirited, but irascible: in 1735 he killed a brother-actor in a quarrel over a wig, and was tried for murder. He wrote a tragedy and several farces and comedies; of these *Love à la Mode* (1759) and *The Man of the World* (1781) were printed. See *Lives* by Congreve (1798) and Parry (1891).

MACLAREN, (1) **Charles** (1782–1866), Scottish writer and editor, born at Ormiston, East Lothian, was the first editor of *The Scotsman*, editor of *The Encyclopaedia Britannica* (6th edition), and wrote *Geology of Fife and the Lothians* (1839).

(2) **Ian,** pen name of John Watson (1850–1907), a Liverpool Presbyterian minister, born of Scottish parentage at Manningtree in Essex, whose amazing success with his *Beside the Bonnie Brier Bush* (1894), &c., gave rise to the name ' Kailyard School'.

MACLAURIN, Colin (1698–1746), Scottish mathematician, born at Kilmodan, Argyll, graduated at Glasgow in 1713, and in 1717 became professor of Mathematics at Aberdeen, in 1725 at Edinburgh. In 1719 he was made F.R.S. and published *Geometrica Organica*. His *Treatise on Fluxions* (1742) was of great importance.

MACLEAN, Sir Fitzroy Hew (1911–), British diplomat and soldier, educated at Eton and Cambridge, served with the Foreign Office from 1933, and in World War II distinguished himself as commander of the British military mission to the Jugoslav partisans (1943–45). M.P. for Lancaster from 1941, and for Bute and N. Ayrshire from 1959, he was under-secretary for war from 1954 to 1957. His *Eastern Approaches* (1949), *Disputed Barricade* (1957), *A Person from England* (1958), and *Back from Bokhara* (1959) have gained for him a considerable reputation. He was created a baronet in 1957.

MACLEHOSE, Agnes, née **Craig** (1759–1841), Scottish surgeon's daughter, married in 1776 a Glasgow lawyer, from whom she separated in 1780, and who went to Jamaica in 1784. She met Burns at a party in 1787, and subsequently carried on with him the well-known correspondence under the name ' Clarinda '. A number of Burns's poems and songs were dedicated to her.

MacLEISH, Archibald (1892–), American poet, born at Glencoe, Ill., started out as a lawyer, was librarian of Congress 1939–44, and professor of Rhetoric at Harvard 1949–62. His first volume of poetry *Tower of Ivory* appeared in 1917, and he won Pulitzer prizes for *Conquistador* (1932), a long poem on Cortez, for *Collected Poems 1917-52* (1953), and for one of his several social dramas in modern verse, *J.B.* (1959), based on the story of Job, affirming modern man's nobler qualities.

McLENNAN, John Cunningham (1867–1935), Canadian physicist, professor at Toronto (1907–31), did much research on electricity and the superconductivity of metals. In 1932 he succeeded in liquefying helium.

MacLEOD, George Fielden, *-lowd'* (1895–), Scottish presbyterian divine, second son of Sir John MacLeod, 1st Bart, a Glasgow M.P., was educated at Winchester and Oriel College, Oxford, won the M.C. and Croix de Guerre in World War I, and subsequently studied theology at Edinburgh, becoming a minister of St Cuthbert's there (1926–30) and at Govan (1930–38). He founded the Iona Community, which set about restoring the ruined abbey on that historic island. The original dozen ministers and helpers soon grew in number and, working there every summer, renovated most of the monastic buildings. As moderator of the General Assembly (1957–58) he created controversy by supporting the unpopular scheme to introduce bishops into the kirk in the interests of church unity. Well known as a writer and broadcaster, he is strongly left-wing, as his *Only One Way Left* (1956) testifies. He succeeded to the baronetcy in 1924, but prefers not to use the title. In 1967 he was created a life peer, as Baron Macleod of Fuinary.

MACLEOD, (1) Fiona. See SHARP (6).

(2) **John James Rickard** (1876–1935), Scottish physiologist, educated at Aberdeen, Leipzig and Cambridge, professor of Physiology at Cleveland, Ohio (1903), Toronto (1918) and Aberdeen (1928), in 1922 along with Banting and Best discovered insulin. He was elected F.R.S. in 1923, in which year also he shared the Nobel prize with Banting.

(3) **Norman** (1812–72), Scottish divine, was born, a minister's son, at Campbeltown, Argyll. He attended Glasgow University, and was minister of Loudon 1838–43, Dalkeith 1843–45 and the Barony Church, Glasgow, from 1851 till his death. He was made a Queen's Chaplain in 1857, and in 1869 was moderator of the General Assembly. From 1860 till 1872 he edited and contributed to *Good Words*, and wrote several books. See *Memoir* by Macleod (1876).

MACLISE, Daniel (1806–70), British painter, son of a Highland soldier named McLeish, born at Cork, entered the school of the Royal Academy, London, in 1828. His frescoes in the Royal Gallery of the House of Lords, *The Meeting of Wellington and Blücher* (1861) and *The Death of Nelson* (1864) are his most notable works. His sketches of contemporaries in *Fraser's Magazine* (1830–38) were republished in 1874 and 1883. See the Memoir by O'Driscoll (1871).

MACMAHON, Marie Edmé Patrice Maurice de, *mĕk-mahn'* (1808–93), descended from an Irish Jacobite family, was born at Sully near Autun. Entering the army, he served in Algeria, and distinguished himself at Constantine (1837), commanded at the Malakoff (1855), was again conspicuous in Algeria (1857–58), and for his services in the Italian campaign (1859) was made marshal and Duke of Magenta. He became governorgeneral of Algeria in 1864. In the Franco-German war (1870–71) he commanded the first army corps, but was defeated at Wörth, and captured at Sedan. After the war, as commander of the army of Versailles, he suppressed the Commune. In 1873 he was elected president of the Republic for seven years, and was suspected, not unjustly, of reactionary and monarchical leanings. He resigned in 1879. See Lives by Grandin (1893) and Montbrillant (1894).

MacMASTER, John Bach (1852–1932), American historian, born at Brooklyn, studied civil engineering, but in 1883–1920 was professor of American History in Pennsylvania University. He wrote a *History of the People of the U.S.* (8 vols. 1883–1913), *Franklin as a Man of Letters* (1887), and other works.

MACMILLAN, (1) Alexander (1818–96). See (2).

(2) **Daniel** (1813–57), Scottish bookseller and publisher, was born at Upper Corrie, Arran. Apprenticed to booksellers in Scotland and Cambridge, in 1843 he and his brother Alexander opened a bookshop in London, and in the same year moved to Cambridge. By 1844 he had branched out into publishing, first educational and religious works and by 1855 English classics such as Kingsley's *Westward Ho!* and *Tom Brown's Schooldays* in 1857. In the year after his death (1858) the firm opened a branch in London and by 1893 had become a limited liability company with Daniel's son, Frederick (1851–1936), as chairman. His other son, Maurice, father of (3) was also a partner. See a memoir by Hughes (1882), a life of Alexander by C. L. Graves (1910) and Morgan, *House of Macmillan* (1943).

(3) **Maurice Harold** (1894–   ), British statesman, educated at Eton, took a first class in classical Moderations at Balliol College, Oxford, his studies having been interrupted by service with the Grenadier Guards during World War I, in which he was seriously wounded. In 1919–20 he was in Canada as A.D.C. to the governor-general, the Duke of Devonshire, whose daughter Lady Dorothy (d. 1966) he married. Returning to Britain, he partnered his brother Daniel in the family publishing firm, but preserved his interest in politics and stood successfully as Conservative M.P. for Stockton-on-Tees in 1924, was defeated in 1929, but was re-elected in 1931. Partly because he was not always willing to conform with the party line, and partly, no doubt, because his air of intellectual superiority irked his more senior colleagues, he remained a backbencher until 1940, when Churchill made him parliamentary secretary to the Ministry of Supply. After a brief spell as colonial under-secretary in 1942 he was sent to North Africa to fill the new Cabinet post of minister resident at Allied Headquarters where he achieved distinction by his foresight and acumen and by his ability as a mediator in the many clashes of factions and personalities which bedevilled his term of office. Defeated in the Socialist landslide of 1945, he was returned later the same year for Bromley, which he held until his retiral in 1964. He was minister of housing (1951–54), silencing general doubts by achieving his promised target of 300,000 houses in a year. He was minister of defence from autumn to spring 1954–55, and thereafter foreign minister to the end of 1955, when he was appointed chancellor of the Exchequer. On Eden's resignation in 1957 he emerged, in Butler's words, as 'the best prime minister we have', his appointment being received without enthusiasm, for as an intellectual and a dyed-in-the-wool aristocrat he was regarded with suspicion by many. Nevertheless, his economic expansionism at home, his resolution in foreign affairs, his integrity, and his infectious optimism inspired unforeseen confidence, and his popularity soared. Having piloted the Conservatives to victory in the General Election, he embarked upon a

new term as prime minister in 1959. His ' wind of change ' speech at Cape Town (1960) acknowledged the inevitability of African independence. In 1962, after some electoral setbacks, he carried out a drastic ' purge ' of his government, involving seven cabinet ministers. Further setbacks followed, however, with the Vassall spy case (1962) and the Profumo scandal (1963), and a prostate gland operation brought about his reluctant resignation on October 10, 1963. See his autobiographical *Winds of Change, 1914–39* (1966) and *The Blast of War, 1939–1945* (1967) and study by A. Sampson (1967).

(4) **John** (1670–1753), founder of the Reformed Presbyterians, was born in Minnigaff, Kirkcudbrightshire, and died at Bothwell.

MacMILLAN, Donald Baxter (1874–1970), American Arctic explorer, carried out anthropological research among the Eskimos of Labrador, and important exploration in Greenland (1913–17). He also led expeditions to Baffin Land (1921–22), North Greenland (1923–24), the Pole (1925), &c. See his *Four Years in the White North* (1926) and *Etah and Beyond* (1927).

McMILLAN, (1) **Edwin Mattison** (1907–), American physical chemist, born in California, professor of Physics at the University of California from 1946, was awarded (with Seaborg) the 1951 Nobel prize for chemistry for his part in the discovery of the transuranic elements.

(2) **Margaret** (1860–1931), British educational reformer, born in New York and brought up near Inverness. She agitated ceaselessly in the industrial north for medical inspection and school clinics, and in 1902 she joined her sister **Rachel** (1859–1917) in London, where they opened the first school clinic in 1908, and the first open-air nursery school in 1914. After Rachel's death, the Rachel McMillan Training College for nursery and infant teachers was established as a memorial. Margaret received the C.B.E. in 1917 and became a C.H. in 1930. See studies by D'Arcy Cresswell (1948), Stevinson (1954), and Life by Lowndes (1960).

McNAUGHTON, Daniel, *mĕk-naw'tĕn*, was tried in 1843 for the murder of Edward Drummond, private secretary to Sir Robert Peel. The question arose whether he knew the nature of his act. The House of Lords took the opinion of the judges, and the law of England as to the criminal responsibility of the insane was now embodied in the judges' ' answers ', known as the McNaughton Rules: (*a*) Every man is presumed sane until the contrary is proved. (*b*) It must be clearly proved that at the time of committing the act, the accused was labouring under such a defect of reason as not to know the nature of the act, or that he was doing wrong.

MACNEE, Sir Daniel (1806–82), Scottish portrait painter, born at Fintry, Stirlingshire, became P.R.S.A. in 1876, knighted in 1877.

MacNEICE, Louis (1907–63), British writer, born in Belfast. Primarily a poet, he was the author of several memorable verse plays for radio, as well as translations of Aeschylus and of Goethe's *Faust*. He also produced several volumes of literary criticism. His *Collected Poems* were published in 1949.

MACPHERSON, James (1736–96), ' translator ' of the Ossianic poems, was born at Ruthven in Inverness-shire, where he became a schoolmaster. He published a poem, the *Highlander* (1758), and at Moffat in 1759 showed ' Jupiter ' Carlyle and John Home some fragments of Gaelic verse, with ' translations ', published in 1760. The Faculty of Advocates now sent Macpherson on a tour through the Highlands to collect more; but his unsatisfactory statements about his originals excited grave suspicions. The result of his labours was the appearance at London in 1762, of *Fingal, an Epic Poem, in Six Books*, and, in 1763, *Temora, an Epic Poem, in Eight Books*. A storm of controversy soon arose in regard to their genuineness. The general verdict is that though Macpherson probably based some of the work on truly Gaelic originals, the poems of Ossian as he published them are largely his own invention. Macpherson was appointed in 1764 surveyor-general of the Floridas, in 1779 agent to the Nabob of Arcot, and sat in parliament for Camelford from 1780. He was buried at his own cost in Westminster Abbey. He wrote a poor prose translation of the *Iliad*, &c. See Lives by Smart (1905), and Thomson, *The Gaelic Sources of Macpherson's ' Ossian '* (1952).

MACQUARIE, Lachlan, *mĕ-kwor'ee* (1761–1824), Scottish soldier and colonial administrator, born on the isle of Ulva, off Mull, joined the Black Watch, and after service in North America, India and Egypt, was appointed governor of New South Wales following the deposition of Bligh (q.v.). The colony, depressed and demoralized, populated largely by convicts, and exploited by influential land-grabbers and monopolists, was raised by his energetic administration and firm rule to a state of prosperity; its population trebled, extensive surveys were carried out, and many miles of road were built. In 1821 political chicanery by the monopolists and his own ill health compelled him to return to Britain. Known as the ' Father of Australia ' he has given name to the Lachlan and Macquarie rivers, and to Macquarie Island. See Life by M. H. Ellis (1947).

MACQUER, Pierre Joseph, *ma-kayr* (1718–1784), French chemist, one of the first to study platinum, discovered the arsenates of potassium and sodium. He was the compiler of a chemical dictionary (1766).

MACREADY, William Charles (1793–1873), English actor, son of W. McCready, actor and provincial manager, was born in London, March 3, 1793, and sent to Rugby. He was intended for the bar, but his father failing, he made his début at Birmingham in 1810; in 1816 he appeared at Covent Garden; but not till 1837 did he take his position as leading English actor. In 1837 he inaugurated his famous Covent Garden management, during which he produced Shakespeare worthily. After two seasons he took Drury Lane (1841–1843), then played in the provinces, Paris and America. His last visit to the U.S. was marked by terrible riots (May 10, 1849) arising out of the ill-feeling borne by the American actor Forrest to Macready. In 1851 Macready took his farewell of the stage at Drury Lane. See his *Reminiscences and Diaries* (1875), *Diaries* (ed. by W. Toynbee, 1912), memoirs by Pollock (2nd ed. 1885), Archer (1890), Price (1895) and Life by Trewin (1955).

MACROBIUS, Ambrosius Theodosius, a 5th-century neo-Platonist who wrote a commentary on Cicero's *Somnium Scipionis*, and *Saturnaliorum Conviviorum Libri Septem*, a series of historical, mythological and critical dialogues. See study by Whittaker (1923).

McTAGGART, John McTaggart Ellis (1866–1925), British philosopher, born in London, was educated at Clifton College and, under Sidgwick and Ward, at Trinity College, Cambridge, where he lectured (1897–1923). His brilliant commentaries and studies on Hegel's dialectic (1896), cosmology (1901) and logic (1910) in which he clarified and consolidated Hegel's system, although rejecting many of the latter's arguments and in particular Hegelian ethics and political philosophy, were preliminaries to his own constructive system-building in *Nature of Existence* (vol. I, 1921; vols II and III, posthumously, 1927). In this he argued for Hegelian conclusions but from novel starting-points which owed more to Leibniz than to Hegel. His arguments for the unreality of time bewitched Russell and drove Moore to philosophizing in protest. An atheist yet a member of the Church of England, he set out his arguments for human immortality in *Some Dogmas of Religion* (1906). He was elected F.B.A. in 1906. See memoir by C. D. Broad in 2nd edition of the above (1930), Life by G. Lowes Dickinson (1931) and an exhaustive *Examination* by C. D. Broad (1933–38). A summary of his system appeared, *Contemporary British Philosophy*, vol. I, ed. J. H. Muirhead (1924).

MacTAGGART, William (1835–1910), Scottish artist, born in Kintyre, studied painting with Macnee and Scott Lauder, and lived in and near Edinburgh, painting genre and landscape with imaginative insight. See Life by Caw (1917). His grandson **Sir William** (1903–), also a painter, is a prominent representative of the modern Scottish school. He was elected R.S.A. in 1948, P.R.S.A. in 1959, was knighted in 1962 and received the *Légion d'honneur* in 1968.

MacWHIRTER, John (1839–1911), Scottish artist, born at Edinburgh, was apprenticed to a bookseller, but turned to painting, specializing in Highland scenery. He was elected R.S.A. in 1867 and R.A. in 1893. See Life by Spielmann.

MADARIAGA, Salvador de, *ma-THa-ryah'ga* (1886–), Spanish writer, was born at Coruña, was educated at the Instituto del Cardenal Cisneros, Madrid, and at the École Polytechnique, Paris. He was a London journalist from 1916 to 1921 and director of the disarmament section of the League of Nations Secretariat from 1922 to 1927. From 1928 to 1931 he was professor of Spanish Studies at Oxford and was Spanish ambassador to the U.S.A. in 1931 and to France from 1932 to 1934. A Liberal opponent of the Franco régime, he has lived in exile since. Publications include: *The Genius of Spain* (1923), *Theory and Practice*

of International Relations (1938), *Portrait of Europe* (1952) and *Democracy v. Liberty?* (1958), *Latin America between the Eagle and the Bear* (1962).

MADDEN, Sir Frederick (1801–73), English antiquary, born at Portsmouth, and knighted in 1832, was keeper of MSS. in the British Museum (1837–66). He wrote in *Archaeologia*, and edited *Havelok the Dane* (1833), *William and the Werwolf* (1832), the early English versions of the *Gesta Romanorum* (1838), *The Wycliffite Versions of the Bible* (1850), Layamon's *Brut* (1847), and Matthew Paris (1858).

MADERO, Francisco Indalecio, *ma-THay'rō* (1873–1913), Mexican politician, born at San Pedro, Coahuila State, and educated at the university of California. After some years' exile in France, he entered Radical politics in Mexico in 1903 and in 1910 became leader in the successful revolutionary war against the government of Díaz. He was elected president in 1911 and assassinated in 1913. See studies by S. R. Ross (1955) and J. C. Valadés (1959).

MADISON, James (1751–1836), fourth president of the United States, born at Port Conway, Va., March 16, 1751, in 1776 was a member of the Virginia Convention, in 1780 of the Continental Congress, and in 1784 of the legislature of Virginia. In the Convention of 1787, which framed the Federal constitution, he acted with Jay and Hamilton, and with them wrote the *Federalist*. He was the chief author of the ' Virginia plan ', and suggested the compromise by which, for taxation, representation, &c., slaves were regarded as population and not chattels, five being reckoned as three persons, and which secured the adoption of the constitution by South Carolina and the other slave-holding states. Madison was elected to the first national congress, now showed himself anxious to limit the powers of the central government, and became a leader of the Jeffersonian Republican party. In 1801, Jefferson having been elected president, Madison was made secretary of state. In 1809 he was elected president. The European wars of that period, with their blockades, &c., were destructive of American commerce, and brought on a war with Britain (1812). In 1817, at the close of his second term, Madison retired. He died at Montpelier, Va., June 28, 1836. See Lives (1902) by G. Hunt, who edited his *Writings* (9 vols. 1900–10), and I. Brant (5 vols. 1941–56).

MÄDLER, Johann Heinrich von, *may'dler* (1794–1874), astronomer, born at Berlin, became director of Tartu Observatory, produced a map of the moon and carried out research on double stars. He died at Hanover.

MADOC, a Welsh prince; long believed by his countrymen to have discovered America in 1170. The story is in Lloyd and Powell's *Cambria* (1584), and in Southey's poem; the essay by Thomas Stephens written in 1858 for the Eisteddfod, and published in 1893, proves it to be baseless.

MADVIG, Johan Nicolai (1804–86), Danish classical scholar, in 1829 became professor of Latin at Copenhagen, in 1848 inspector of higher schools. He was one of the chief speakers of the national Liberal party, was minister of religion and education (1848–51), and was repeatedly president of the Danish parliament. Among his works were *Opuscula Academica* (1834–42), the great *Latin Grammar* (1841), *Greek Syntax* (1846) and an *Autobiography* (1887).

MAECENAS, Gaius Cilnius (d. 8 B.C.), Roman statesman and trusted counsellor of Augustus, whose name has become a synonym for a patron of letters. See J. W. Duff, *Minor Latin Poets* (1934).

MAELZEL, Johann Nepomuk (1770–1838), German patentee of the metronome. See BEETHOVEN.

MAERLANT, Jacob van (c. 1235–c. 1300), Flemish didactic poet, author of verse translations of French and Latin originals, including the *Roman de Troie* (c. 1264) and de Beauvais' *Speculum Majas* (1284).

MAETERLINCK, Count Maurice, *may'tèr-lingk* (1862–1949), Belgian dramatist, born at Ghent. He studied law at Ghent University, but became a disciple of the Symbolist movement, and in 1889 produced his first volume of poetry, *Les Serres chaudes.* In the same year came his prose play, *La Princesse Maleine,* and in 1892 *Pelléas et Mélisande,* on which Debussy based his opera; other plays include *Joyzelle* (1903) and *Mary Magdalene* (1910). *La Vie des abeilles* (1901) is one of his many popular expositions of scientific subjects, and he also wrote several philosophical works. He was awarded the Nobel prize for literature in 1911, made a count of Belgium in 1932, and a member of the French Academy of Moral and Political Sciences in 1937. See Lives by A. Bailey (1931) and W. Halls (1960).

MAFFEI, Francesco Scipione, Marchese di, *maf-fay'ee* (1675–1755), Italian dramatist, born at Verona, served 1703–04 under his brother Alessandro, a field-marshal. His tragedy *Merope* (1714) ran through seventy editions; the comedy *Le Ceremonie* (1728) was also successful; and *Verona illustrata* (1731–32) was an important work. See Life by N. Ivanoff (Padova 1942).

MAGELLAN, Port. **Magalhães, Ferdinand** (c. 1480–1521), Portuguese navigator, born near Villa Real in Tras os Montes, served in the East Indies, and was lamed for life in action in Morocco. Offering his services to Spain, he laid before Charles V a scheme for reaching the Moluccas by the west, and sailed from Seville, August 10, 1519, with five ships of from 130 to 60 tons. Having coasted Patagonia, he threaded the strait which bears his name (October 21–November 28, 1520), and reached the ocean which he named the Pacific. He fell in an expedition in the Philippine Isles; but his ship, brought safely to Spain, September 6, 1522, completed the first circumnavigation of the world. See books by E. F. Benson (1929), S. Zweig (1938), and J. A. Robertson's translation (1906) of Pigafetta's contemporary account.

MAGENDIE, François, *ma-zhã-dee* (1783–1855), French physiologist and physician, was born at Bordeaux, became prosector in Anatomy (1804), physician to the Hôtel-Dieu in Paris, and professor of Anatomy in the Collège de France (1831). He made important additions to our knowledge of nerve physiology, the veins and the physiology of food, and wrote numerous works, including the *Elements of Physiology.* In his *Journal de la physiologie expérimentale* are recorded the experiments on living animals which gained for him the character of an unscrupulous vivisector.

MAGINN, William (1794–1842), Irish writer, born at Cork, and educated at Trinity College, Dublin; took his LL.D. at an early age, taught in Cork for ten years, and in 1823 removed to London. He was a prolific contributor to *Blackwood's Magazine,* the *Standard* and *Fraser's Magazine.* A collection of his tales was edited by Partridge (1933). See study by M. Thrale (N.Y. 1934).

MAGINOT, André, *ma-zhee-nõ* (1877–1932), French politician, born in Paris, was first elected to the Chamber in 1910. As minister of war (1922–24; 1926–31) he pursued a policy of military preparedness and began the system of frontier fortifications which was named the ' Maginot Line ' after him. See Life by P. Belpenon (Paris 1940).

MAGLIABECHI, Antonio, *mal-ya-bek'ee* (1633–1714), Italian bibliophile, born at Florence, was till his fortieth year a goldsmith, but gradually entombed himself among books. His learning and his memory were prodigious and precise. In 1673 he was appointed court-librarian by the Grand-duke of Tuscany; his vanity and intolerance involved him in bitter literary squabbles. His library of 30,000 vols. he bequeathed to the Grand-duke; it is now a free library, and bears its collector's name. See Hill Burton's *Book-Hunter* (1862).

MAGNUS, St, (1) a Scandinavian Earl of Orkney, assassinated 1114 in Egilsay by his cousin Hakon. See study by J. Mooney.
(2) A monk of St Gall, traditionally brought the gospel to the Allgäu, and founded the monastery of Füssen, where he died c. 750.

MAGNUS. The name of seven kings of Norway.
Magnus I, called **The Good** (reigned 1024–47), made a succession treaty (1038) with Hardicanute of Denmark, of which country he became ruler on the latter's death in 1042. He also inherited Hardicanute's title to the English throne but could not enforce it owing to internal strife.
Magnus V, called **Lageböter,** ' improver of the laws ' (1238–80), ascended the throne in 1263, gave up the Western Isles and the Isle of Man to Scotland, and evolved a new legal code, introducing the principle that crime was an offence against the state rather than against the individual.

MAGNUS, or Magni, Olaus (1490–1558), Swedish historian, became secretary to his brother Johannes, Archbishop of Uppsala. After the Reformation they settled in Rome. On Johannes' death Olaus became titular archbishop. Both wrote on Swedish history; Olaus' famous work is his *Historia de Gentibus Septentrionalibus* (1555).

MAHAN, Alfred Thayer, *ma-han'* (1840–1914), American naval historian, born at West Point, N.Y., served in the U.S. navy (1854–1896), and in 1906 was given the rank of rear-admiral retired. He wrote *Influence of Sea Power upon History, 1660–1812* (3 vols. 1890–92), Lives of Farragut, Nelson, &c. See life by W. D. Puleston (1939) and bibliography (N.Y. 1925).

MAHDI. See MOHAMMED ALI.

MAHLER, Gustav (1860–1911), Czech-Austrian composer, born in Kalist. In 1875 he went to Vienna Conservatory, where he studied composition and conducting. Unsuccessful in an opera composition with the work which he later turned into the cantata *Das klagende Lied*, he turned to conducting, rapidly reaching important positions at Prague, Leipzig, Budapest and Hamburg, and in 1897 he became conductor and artistic director at Vienna State Opera House, where he established the high standards for which that theatre has since become famous. Disliking the intrigues of theatrical life and the frequent personal attacks upon him due to his Jewish birth (though he had become a convert to Roman Catholicism), he resigned after ten years to devote himself to composition and the concert platform, and from 1908 to 1911 he was conductor of the New York Philharmonic Society, spending his summers composing in Austria. His mature works consist entirely of songs and symphonies, in which latter form he composed nine works on a large scale, five of them requiring voices, and he is best known by the song-symphony *Das Lied von der Erde*, which is not included in the nine; he left a Tenth Symphony unfinished. One of the greatest masters of the orchestra, his work, gaining popularity in Britain and already accepted in America and on the Continent, is the bridge between the late romantic 19th-century style and the revolutionary works of Schoenberg and his followers. See *Gustav Mahler, Memories and Letters*, by A. Mahler (trans. B. Creighton, 1946), and biographies by B. Walter (1937) and D. Mitchell (1958).

MAHMUD II (1785–1839), Sultan of Turkey from 1808. His reign was marked by the cession of Bessarabia to Russia (1812), Greece's successful struggle for independence (1820–28), a disastrous war with Russia (1828–29), and by the triumphs of Mehemet Ali (q.v.). He shattered the power of the janissaries by a massacre in 1826. He introduced many domestic reforms such as compulsory primary education and did much to westernize Turkey.

MAHMUD OF GHAZNI (971–1030), sovereign from 997 of Khorasan and Ghazni, repeatedly invaded India, and carried his conquering arms to Kurdistan on the west, to Samarkand on the north. See Life by M. Nāzim (1931).

MAHOMET. See MOHAMMED.

MAHON, Lord. See STANHOPE (5).

MAHONY, Francis (1804–66), Irish priest, known as ' Father Prout ', born at Cork in 1804, became a Jesuit priest, but forsook his calling for journalism and poetry, and is remembered as author of the poems ' The Bells of Shandon ' and ' The Lady of Lee '. See his works ed. Charles Kent (1881).

MAI, Angelo, *mah'ee* (1782–1854), Italian cardinal, born at Schilpario in Lombardy, was educated to be a Jesuit, but became a

secular priest at Milan, and keeper of the Ambrosian Library, where he discovered and edited MSS. or fragments of several long-lost works. Transferred to the Vatican, he edited a number of important ancient texts, and left an edition of the *Codex Vaticanus* unfinished at his death. See Life by Prina (1882).

MAIDMENT, James (1794–1879), Scottish lawyer and editor, born in London, was called to the Scottish bar in 1817, and became a great authority on genealogical law cases. His most ambitious work was *The Dramatists of the Restoration* (14 vols. 1872–79), edited with W. H. Logan. See bibliography by T. G. Stevenson (1883).

MAILLOL, Aristide Joseph Bonaventure, *ma-yol* (1861–1944), French sculptor, born at Banyuls-sur-mer. He studied at the École des Beaux-Arts, and spent some years designing tapestries. The latter half of his life was devoted to the representation of the nude female figure (e.g., the *Three Graces* in the Tate Gallery, London) in a style of monumental simplicity and classical serenity. See the monograph by Bouvier (1945).

MAIMBOURG, Louis, *mī-boor* (1610–86), French Jesuit church-historian, born at Nancy, was expelled in 1685 from the order for his defence of Gallicanism, but became a pensioner of Louis XIV. He wrote histories of Arianism, Lutheranism, Calvinism, and the prerogatives of the Church of Rome.

MAIMON, Solomon, *mī'mon* (c. 1754–1800), German philosopher, born of Jewish parents in Lithuania, married at the age of twelve and studied medicine in Berlin. He wrote a critical commentary on the philosophy of Maimonides and was one of the earliest critics of the Kantian system in *Versuch über die Transzendentalphilosophie* (1790) which Kant acknowledged.

MAIMONIDES, *mī-mon'i-deez*, or **Rabbi Moses ben Maimon** (1135–1204), Jewish philosopher, was born at Córdoba, March 30, 1135, and studied the Aristotelian philosophy and Greek medicine under the best Arab teachers. His family had to conform to Mohammedanism, and migrated to Egypt, where he became physician to Saladin, and died at Cairo, December 13, 1204. He has been reckoned next to Moses himself for his influence on Jewish thought. Among his works are a commentary on the Mishna, and the *Book of the Precepts*, written first in Arabic; the *Mishne Torah* or ' Second Law ' (in Hebrew); and his greatest achievement, *Guide for the Perplexed* (see edition by Roth 1948). See bibliography by J. I. Gorfinkle (N.Y. 1932) and Lives by S. Zertlin (1935), A. Heschel (1935) and L. Roth (1948).

MAINE, Sir Henry James Sumner (1822–88), English historian, born August 15, 1822, from Christ's Hospital passed in 1840 to Pembroke College, Cambridge. After various teaching posts in England, and administrative appointments in India, he was elected master of Trinity Hall at Cambridge in 1877, and in 1887 Whewell professor of International Law. He died at Cannes, February 3, 1888. It is by his work on the origin and growth of legal and social institutions that Maine will be best remembered. His books include *Ancient Law* (1861), *Early Law and Custom*

(1883), and *International Law* (1888). See Memoir by Sir M. E. Grant Duff (1892).

MAINTENON, Françoise d'Aubigné, Marquise de, *mĭ-tĕ-nŏ* (1635–1719), second wife of Louis XIV, granddaughter of the Huguenot Théodore Agrippa d'Aubigné (q.v.), was born near the conciergerie of Niort where her father was a prisoner, November 27, 1635. At four years old she was carried to Martinique, whence she returned to France after her father's death (1645), and became a Catholic; her mother's death left her at fifteen in penury. She married the crippled poet Scarron (1652), and on his death (1660) again was reduced to poverty; but her husband's pension was continued to her. In 1669 she was given the charge of the king's two sons by Madame de Montespan. By 1674 the king's presents enabled her to purchase the estate of Maintenon, and in 1678 she had it made a marquisate. She had firmly established her ascendency over Louis, who, after the queen's death (1683), married her privately in 1685. Her morals were severe, for her heart was cold. Her political influence was supreme in all but important questions of policy; she was a liberal patroness of letters. Often unhappy, she turned for solace to the home for poor girls of good family she had established at St Cyr. Hither she retired when the king died (1715); and here she died, April 15, 1719. Her pretended *Mémoires* (1755) are spurious, but her delightful *Lettres* (1756; ed. Lavallée, 1856; ed. Geffroy, 1887) are genuine. See works by M. Cruttwell (1930), M. Langlois (1932) and H. C. Barnard (1934).

MAIR, John. See MAJOR.

MAISTRE, mes'tr', (1) Joseph Marie, Comte de (1753–1821), French diplomat and political philosopher, born at Chambéry, on the occupation of Savoy in 1792 by the French, went into exile; in 1803–17 he was the king of Sardinia's ambassador to St Petersburg. In his writings de Maistre maintained the pope as the source and centre of all earthly authority, and an ordered theocracy as the only protection from social and religious anarchy. See study by F. Bayle (Paris 1945).

(2) **Xavier, Comte de** (1763–1852), brother of (1), born at Chambéry, joined the Russian army and became a general. He was an accomplished landscape and portrait artist, and wrote several charming novels. He died at St Petersburg. See books by Rey (1865), Maystre and Perrin (1895).

MAITLAND, (1) Frederick William (1850–1906), English historian, grandson of the historian **Samuel Roffey Maitland** (1792–1866), educated at Eton and Trinity, Cambridge, was a barrister (1876), reader in English Law at Cambridge (1884) and Downing professor (1888). He wrote a *History of English Law* (1895, with Sir F. Pollock, q.v.), *Domesday Book and Beyond* (1897), and other brilliant works on legal antiquities and history. See A. L. Smith, *F. W. Maitland, two Lectures and a bibliography* (1908), and Life by H. A. L. Fisher (1910).

(2) **Sir Richard** (1496–1586), of Lethington, Scottish lawyer and poet, father of (3),

became a lord of session in 1551, lord privy seal in 1562, and was conspicuous for his moderation and integrity. His poems—mostly lamentations for the distracted state of his country—were published in 1830 by the Maitland Club. He made a collection of early Scottish poetry, now forming two MS. vols., which are in the Pepysian collection at Cambridge. He wrote also a *Historie of the Hous of Seytoun*.

(3) **William** (*c.* 1528–73), son of (2), ' Secretary Lethington ', who in 1558 became secretary of state to the queen-regent, and in 1559 joined the lords of the congregation, then in arms against her. In August 1560 he acted as speaker in the Convention of Estates, and was sent to the English court to represent the interests of the Protestants. On the arrival of Queen Mary in 1561, Maitland associated himself with Moray in opposing the extreme proposals of Knox. He represented Mary more than once at the court of Elizabeth; but made her his enemy by his connivance at Rizzio's murder (1566), again, however, to become her counsellor. At first he favoured Bothwell, and was privy to the murder of Darnley, yet on Bothwell's marriage with Mary he acted with the insurgents. Nevertheless, after the queen's flight to England, while seeming to side with the new government, he secretly favoured the exiled queen. One of the commissioners who accompanied Moray to present to Elizabeth their indictment against Mary (1568), he was plotting against his colleagues; and the formation of a party in favour of Mary was mainly his work. Shut up in Edinburgh Castle, Maitland and Kirkcaldy of Grange surrendered, May 29, 1573. Maitland died in prison in Leith on June 9. See Buchanan's *Chamaeleon*; studies by J. Skelton (1887–88), E. Russell (1912). See also LAUDERDALE.

MAJOR, or Mair, John (*c.* 1470–1550), Scottish theologian and historian, born near North Berwick, studied at Oxford, Cambridge and Paris, lectured on Scholastic Logic and Philosophy. He also wrote commentaries on Peter Lombard, and a history of England and Scotland. He was provost of St Salvator's College, St Andrews, from 1533 until his death. See Arch. Constable's translation of his *History* (Scottish Hist. Soc. 1892).

MAKARIOS III, properly **Mihail Christodoulou Mouskos** (1913–), Archbishop and Primate of the Orthodox Church of Cyprus, born in Ano Panciyia near Paphos. He was ordained priest in 1946, elected Bishop of Kition in 1948 and Archbishop in 1950. He reorganized the Enosis Movement and in so doing revealed himself as a very shrewd politician and publicist. Implicated by the ' Grivas Diaries ' in the affairs of Eoka terrorism, he was arrested and detained for a time in the Seychelles, but returned to a tumultuous welcome in March 1959 to become chief Greek-Cypriot minister in the new Greek-Turkish provisional government. In December 1959 he was elected president of Cyprus, an office which he has held ever since.

MAKART, Hans, *mah'kart* (1840–84), Austrian painter, born at Salzburg, studied at Munich and in Italy, settled in Vienna in

1869, and in 1879 became professor at the academy there. He painted spectacular and historical pictures, of bold colour and of gigantic size. See the Life of him by Von Lützow (1886).

MAKEHAM, William Matthew, *mayk'em* (d. 1892), British statistician, who formulated about 1860 the law of human mortality which bears his name. It was recognized by the Institute of Actuaries in 1887, but was later superseded in actuarial practice.

MAKKARI, Ahmed el-, *mak'-* (c. 1585–1631) Moorish historian, born at Makkara in Algeria. He wrote a *History of the Mohammedan Dynasties of Spain.*

MALACHY, St (c. 1094–1148), born at Armagh, became Abbot of Bangor (1121), Bishop of Connor (1125) and Archbishop of Armagh (1134). In 1140 he journeyed to Rome, visiting St Bernard at Clairvaux. On his return (1142) he introduced the Cistercian Order into Ireland. In 1148 he once more went to France, and died at Clairvaux in St Bernard's arms. The curious so-called 'Prophecies of St Malachy' first published in *Lignum Vitae* (1595) by the Flemish Benedictine, Arnold Wion, are erroneously ascribed to him. See St Bernard's *Vita Malachiae* (in Migne's *Patr.* clxxi) and Life by Luddy (1930).

MALAN, Daniel François, *ma-lahn'* (1874–1959), South African politician, born at Riebeek West, Cape Province, and educated at Victoria College, Stellenbosch, and Utrecht University. On his return to South Africa in 1905 he became a predikant of the Dutch Reformed Church and after ten years abandoned his clerical career to become editor of *Die Burger,* the Nationalist newspaper. He became an M.P. in 1918 and in 1924 in the Nationalist-Labour government he held the portfolios of the interior, of education and of public health. He introduced measures strengthening the Nationalist position—in particular, that making Afrikaans an official language. He was leader of the Opposition from 1934 to 1939 and from 1940 to 1948 when, becoming prime minister and minister for external affairs, he embarked on the hotly controversial policies of *apartheid* with the aim of re-aligning South Africa's multi-racial society. He described as the kernel of his segregation policies the Group Areas Act, dividing the country into white, black and coloured zones. The *apartheid* legislation, which involved strongly-contested constitutional changes, was met by non-violent civil disobedience at home and vigorous criticism abroad. Dr Malan resigned from the premiership in 1954. Crusty, austere, a scholar of profound convictions and an uncompromising manner, Dr Malan was a back-veldt Moses to the Boers. He never wavered in his pulpiteering belief in a strict white supremacy, in a Heaven-sent Afrikaner mission and a rigidly hierarchical society. He died at his home at Stellenbosch on Feb. 7, 1959.

MALCOLM, name of four kings of Scotland.

Malcolm I, son of Donald, king of Alban 942-954.

Malcolm II, son of Kenneth, king of Scotia 1005-34.

Malcolm III, called **Canmore** (Gael. *Ceann-mor,* 'great head'), was a child when his father, King Duncan, was slain by Macbeth (1040). He spent his youth in Northumbria with his uncle, Earl Siward, who in 1054 established him in Cumbria and Lothian. In 1057, after Macbeth was slain, he became king of all Scotland. His first wife, Ingibiorg, widow of Thorfinn of Orkney, had died; and in 1069 Malcolm wedded Margaret (q.v.), sister of Edgar the Atheling, whose cause he made his own. Five times he harried Northumbria (1069, 1070, 1079, 1091, 1093); and there were counter invasions by William the Conqueror and Prince Robert, in 1072 and 1080. In 1092 Rufus wrested from Scotland all Cumbria south of the Solway; and next year Malcolm marched into England, but was entrapped and slain at Alnwick, November 13, 1093. He left five sons, of whom four succeeded him, Duncan, Edgar, Alexander and David.

Malcolm IV (1141-65), Malcolm the Maiden, king of Scotland from 1153.

MALCOLM, Sir John (1769–1833), British soldier and diplomat, born at Burnfoot near Langholm, at thirteen entered the Madras army; was thrice ambassador to Persia (1800, 1807, 1810), governor of Bombay (1827–30) and was knighted in 1812. He entered parliament in 1831, opposing the Reform Bill. He published works on India and Persia. See Life by Kaye (1856).

MALEBRANCHE, Nicolas, *mal-brāsh* (1638–1715), French philosopher, born at Paris, joined the Oratorians (1660), and studied theology till Descartes's works drew him to philosophy. His famous *De la recherche de la vérité* (1674; 6th ed. 1712) combines a psychological investigation of the causes of error with a mystic idealism—' the vision of all things in God', the intervention of God being necessary to bridge over the gulf between things so unlike as the human soul and the body. Other works are *Traité de la nature et de la grâce* (1680), *Méditations chrétiennes et métaphysiques* (1683) and *Traité de morale* (1684). He died October 13, 1715. For bibliography see E. A. Blampignon (1882). See studies by R. W. Church (1931), A. A. Luce (1934).

MALENKOV, Georgi Maksimilianovich, *mahl'yen-kof* (1902–), Soviet politician, born at Orenburg, became a deputy prime minister of the U.S.S.R. in 1946, and succeeded Stalin in 1953. In February 1955 Malenkov suddenly resigned, pleading inadequate experience and admitting responsibility for the failure of Soviet agricultural policy. He was succeeded by Marshal Bulganin (q.v.) and relegated to the office of minister for electrical power stations, but in July 1957, having been accused, with Molotov and Kaganovich, of setting up an ' anti-party group ', he was dismissed not only from the government but from the party Presidium and Central Committee, and was rusticated to remotest Kazakhstan as manager of a hydroelectric plant.

MALESHERBES, Chrétien Guillaume de Lamoignon de, *mal-zerb* (1721–94), French statesman, born at Paris, December 6, became in 1750 president of the *cour des* *aides*. He was a determined opponent of government rapacity and tyranny; as censor of the press he showed himself tolerant, and to him we may ascribe the publication of the *Encyclopédie*. In 1771 his remonstrances against royal abuses of law led to his banishment to his country-seat of Ste Lucie; at Louis XVI's accession (1774) he was recalled, and took office, but retired on the dismissal of Turgot, and, save a short spell in office in 1787, spent his time in travel or in the improvement of his estates. Under the Convention he came to Paris to defend the king, and from that day himself was doomed. He was arrested in December 1793, and guillotined, April 22, 1794, along with his daughter and her husband. Malesherbes was a member of the Academy, and brought an able pen to the discussion of agriculture and botany as well as political and financial questions. His *Oeuvres choisies* (1809) contains his most interesting writings. See Lives by Boissy d'Anglas (1818), Rozet (1831), Dupin (1841) and Vignaux (1874), and studies by H. Robert (1927) and J. Allison (1938).

MALET, (1) David. See MALLET.

(2) Lucas. See KINGSLEY (5).

MALHERBE, François de (1555–1628), French poet, born at Caen, ingratiated himself with Henry IV, and received a pension. He was an industrious writer, producing odes, songs, epigrams, epistles, translations, criticisms, &c. His own poetry is colourless and insipid, but he founded a literary tradition—'Enfin Malherbe vint'; he led his countrymen to disdain the richly-coloured and full-sounding verses of Ronsard, and to adopt a style clear, correct and refined, but cold and prosaic. See Tilley's *From Montaigne to Molière* (1908); and study by J. de Celles (Paris 1937).

MALIBRAN, Marie Felicita, *mal-ee-brã* (1808–36), Spanish mezzo-soprano singer, born at Paris, March 24, 1808, was the daughter of the Spanish singer Manuel García (q.v.). See Life by A. Flauent (Paris 1937).

MALIK, Jacob Alexandrovich (1906–), Soviet politician, was born in the Ukraine. Said to be one of Stalin's favourite 'juniors', he was ambassador to Japan from 1942 to 1945 and deputy foreign minister in 1946. In 1948 he succeeded Andrei Gromyko as Soviet spokesman at UNO and was ambassador to Britain 1953–60. Since 1960 he has again been deputy foreign minister.

MALINOVSKY, Rodion Yakovlevich, *-nof'-* (1898–1967), Russian general, born in Odessa, was a corporal in the first World War, when, after the Russian collapse, he escaped via Siberia and Singapore to fight in a Russian brigade in France, joined the Red Army after the revolution and was major-general at the time of the Nazi invasion in 1941. He commanded the forces which liberated Rostov, Kharkov and the Dnieper basin and led the Russian advance into Budapest and into Austria (1944–45). When Russia declared war on Japan, he took a leading part in the Manchurian campaign. In October 1957 he succeeded Zhukov as Khrushchev's minister of defence and appeared to be the latter's *éminence grise* at the abortive

East-West 'Summit' meeting in Paris in May 1960.

MALINOWSKI, Bronislaw (1884–1942), Polish anthropologist, born in Cracow, professor at London University and Yale, took part in expeditions to New Guinea and Melanesia, after which he wrote *Argonauts of the Western Pacific* (1922), *Sex and Repression in Savage Society* (1927), &c. He died in New Haven, Conn., on May 16, 1942. See H. M. Gluckman, *Analysis of Sociological Theories of Malinowski* (1949).

MALIPIERO, Francesco, *'mal-i-pyav'rō* (1882–), Italian composer born at Venice, studied under Bossi and later went to Paris. He has written much symphonic music in a highly characteristic style and has edited Monteverdi and Vivaldi. He is the author of *Claudio Monteverdi* (Milan 1930), *Igor Stravinsky* (Venice 1945) and the autobiographical *Cosi va lo mondo, 1922-45* (Milan 1946). See also book by M. Bontempelli (Milan 1942*)*.

MALLARMÉ, Stéphane (1842–98), French Symbolistic poet, born at Paris, taught English in various schools in Paris and elsewhere and visited England on several occasions. He translated Poe's 'The Raven' (1875) and other poems. In prose and verse he was a leader of the Symbolist school, revelling in allegory, obscurity, bizarre words and constructions, *vers libre* and word-music. *L'Après-midi d'un faune*, illustrated by Manet (1876) is his best-known poem and made the wilful obscurity of his style famous. His *Les Dieux antiques* (1880), *Poésies* (1899), and *Vers et prose* (1893) were other works admired by the 'decadents'. See works by H. Cooperman (1933) and H. Mondor (Paris 1941–42), and bibliography by M. Mondor and F. Monkel (1927).

MALLET, David (*c*. 1705–65), Scottish poet, was born near Crieff, the son of a farmer. Janitor at Edinburgh High School in 1717–18, he then studied at the university; in 1720 became a tutor, from 1723 to 1731 in the family of the Duke of Montrose, living mostly in London, and changed his name 'from Scots Malloch to English Mallet'. *William and Margaret* gained him a reputation as a poet, which he enhanced by *The Excursion* (1728). He also tried his hand at play-writing. *Mustapha* pleased for a while in 1739; *Eurydice* (1731) and *Elvira* (1763), tragedies, were failures. *Alfred, a Masque* (1740), was written in conjunction with Thomson, and one of its songs, 'Rule Britannia', was claimed for both. See memoir by Dinsdale prefixed to his *Ballads and Songs* (1857).

MALLOCK, William Hurrell (1849–1923), English political philosopher and satirist, a nephew of the Froudes, born at Cockington Court, Devon, won the Newdigate in 1871 while at Balliol, Oxford. He made a hit with *The New Republic* (1877) and *The New Paul and Virginia* (1878).

MALMESBURY, Earls of:

(1) **James Harris, 1st Earl** (1746–1820), English diplomat, grandfather of (2), son of 'Hermes' Harris (q.v.), held posts at Madrid (1768), Berlin, St Petersburg, The Hague (1784), and was made K.C.B. (1778), baron (1788) and Earl of Malmesbury (1800). In

1793 he had seceded from Fox to Pitt, and in 1795 had married by proxy and conducted to England the Princess Caroline. See *Diaries and Correspondence* (1844) and *Lord Malmesbury and his Friends* (1870).

(2) **James Howard Harris, 3rd Earl** (1807–1889), English statesman, grandson of (1), who succeeded in 1841, and in 1852 and 1858–59 was foreign secretary; in 1866–68 and 1874–76, privy seal. See his *Memoirs of an Ex-Minister* (1884).

MALMESBURY, William of. See WILLIAM OF MALMESBURY.

MALONE, Edmund (1741–1812), Irish editor of Shakespeare, born in Dublin, graduated at Trinity College, was called to the Irish bar in 1767, but from 1777 devoted himself to literary work in London, his first work being a ' supplement ' to Steevens's edition of Shakespeare (1778). Malone's own edition of the great dramatist (1790) was warmly received. He had been one of the first to express his disbelief in Chatterton's Rowley poems, and in 1796 he denounced the Shakespeare forgeries of Ireland (q.v.). He left behind a large mass of materials for ' The Variorum Shakespeare ', edited in 1821 by James Boswell the younger. See Life by J. Prior (1860).

MALORY, Sir Thomas (d. 1471), English writer, immortal in his work, the *Morte d'Arthur*. We learn from Caxton's preface that Malory was a knight, that he finished his work in the ninth year of the reign of Edward IV (1469–70), and that he ' reduced ' it from some French book. Probably he was the Sir Thomas Malory (d. 1471) of Newbold Revel, Warwickshire, whose quarrels with a neighbouring priory and (probably) Lancastrian politics brought him imprisonment. Of Caxton's black-letter folio but two copies now exist (reprinted by Oskar Sommer with essay by A. Lang, 1889–91). An independent manuscript was discovered at Winchester in 1934. *Morte d'Arthur* ' is indisputably ', says Scott, ' the best prose romance the English language can boast of ', and was a happy attempt to give epic unity to the whole mass of French Arthurian romance. Tennyson, Swinburne and many others are debtors to Malory. See his Works edited by E. Vinaver (3 vols. 1947), and Lives by E. Hicks (1928), E. Vinaver (1929).

MALPIGHI, Marcello, *mal-pee'gee* (1628–94), Italian physiologist, was born March 10, 1628, near Bologna, where he studied medicine. He was professor at Pisa, Messina and Bologna, and from 1691 chief physician to Pope Innocent XII. A pioneer in microscopic anatomy, animal and vegetable, he wrote a series of works on his discoveries. See Italian essays on him by Virchow, Haeckel, &c. (1897), and bibliography by C. Frati (Milan 1897).

MALRAUX, André, *mal-rō* (1901–), French writer, born in Paris, studied oriental languages and spent much time in China, where he worked for the Kuomintang and was active in the 1927 revolution. He also fought as a pilot in the Spanish Civil War, and in World War II he escaped from a prisoner-of-war camp to join the French resistance movement. He was minister of information in de

Gaulle's government (1945–46), minister delegate from 1958 and minister of cultural afairs (1960–69). He is known for his novels, which constitute a dramatic meditation on human destiny and are highly coloured by his personal experience of war, revolution and resistance to tyranny. Among them are *Les Conquérants* (1928), *La Condition humaine* (1933, winner of Goncourt prize) and *L'Espoir* (1937). He also wrote *La Psychologie de l'art* (1947). See studies by Mauriac (Paris 1946), Savane (Paris 1946), Hartmann (1960) and his *Anti-mémoires* (1967).

MALTHUS, Thomas Robert (1766–1834), English economist, was born at The Rookery near Dorking, February 17, 1766. He was ninth wrangler at Cambridge in 1788, was elected fellow of his college (Jesus) in 1793, and in 1797 became curate at Albury, Surrey. In 1798 he published anonymously his *Essay on the Principle of Population*, of which in 1803 he brought out a greatly enlarged and altered edition. In it he maintained that the optimistic hopes of Rousseau and Godwin are rendered baseless by the natural tendency of population to increase faster than the means of subsistence. Malthus gives no sanction to the theories and practices currently known as Malthusianism. An amiable and benevolent man, he suffered much misrepresentation and abuse at the hands of both revolutionaries and conservatives. The problem had been handled by Franklin, Hume and many other writers, but Malthus crystallized the views of those writers, and presented them in systematic form with elaborate proofs derived from history. Darwin saw ' on reading Malthus *On Population* that natural selection was the inevitable result of the rapid increase of all organic beings ', for such rapid increase necessarily leads to the struggle for existence. In 1804 Malthus married happily, and next year was appointed professor of Political Economy in the East India College at Haileybury. He wrote *An Inquiry into the Nature and Progress of Rent* (1815), largely anticipating Ricardo, and *Principles of Political Economy* (1820); and died near Bath, December 23, 1834. See Bonar's *Malthus and his Work* (1885).

MALUS, Étienne Louis (1775–1812), French physicist, born in Paris, carried out research in optics and discovered the polarization of light by reflection. His paper explaining the theory of double refraction in crystals won him the Institute's prize in 1810. His death in Paris at an early age was due to the hardships of campaigning—he was an army instructor engineer.

MALVERN. See HUGGINS (1).

MAMAEA, mother of Alexander Severus (q.v.).

MAMELI, Goffredo (1827–49), Italian poet and patriot, born at Genoa, wrote the fine war song *Fratelli d'Italia*, and died in defence of Rome. See Life by M. Marchini (Milan 1928).

MANASSEH (1), eldest son of Joseph, and founder of a tribe.

(2) Son of pious Hezekiah, succeeded him as king of Judah (697–642 B.C.), but earned an evil name for idolatry and wickedness till, a

captive in Babylon, he repented. *The Prayer of Manasseh* is apocryphal.

MANASSEH BEN ISRAEL (1604–57), Jewish scholar, born at Lisbon and taken early to Amsterdam, at eighteen became chief rabbi of the synagogue there. In 1655–57 he was in England, securing from Cromwell the readmission of the Jews. He wrote works in Hebrew, Spanish and Latin, and in English a *Humble Address* to Cromwell, *A Declaration*, and *Vindiciae Judaeorum* (1656). See Life by C. Roth (1934).

MANBY, George William (1765–1854), English inventor, barrack-master at Yarmouth from 1803, showed in 1807 how to save shipwrecked persons by firing a rope to the ship from a mortar on shore. He wrote on this method, on lifeboats, criminal law and other subjects. He was elected F.R.S. in 1831.

MANCHESTER, Edward Montagu, 2nd Earl of (1602–71), after leaving Sidney Sussex College, Cambridge, accompanied Prince Charles to Spain (1623), and in 1626 was raised to the House of Lords as Baron Montagu of Kimbolton, but was better known by his courtesy title of Viscount Mandeville. Siding with the popular party, and an acknowledged leader of the Puritans in the Upper House, he was charged by the king (January 3, 1642) with entertaining traitorous designs, along with the five members of the House of Commons. He succeeded his father as second earl in the same year. On the outbreak of hostilities he of course fought for the parliament. He served under Essex at Edgehill, then held the associated (eastern) counties against Newcastle, took Lincoln (1644), and routed Prince Rupert at Marston Moor—that is to say, he nominally commanded; the real fighting was done by Cromwell and his Ironsides. He then marched to oppose the royalists in the southwest, and defeated them at Newbury (the second battle). But after this battle he again showed slackness in following up the victory, a fault that had been noticed after Marston Moor. In consequence Cromwell accused him of military incompetency in the House of Commons, and the two had a downright quarrel. The Self-denying Ordinance deprived Manchester of his command (1645), and this did not allay his bitterness against Cromwell. He opposed the trial of the king, and protested against the Commonwealth. Afterwards, having been active in promoting the Restoration, he was made lord chamberlain, a step designed to conciliate the Presbyterians.

MANCINI, *man-chee'nee*, a Roman family famous for five sisters, daughters of Michele Lorenzo Mancini and Jeronima, sister of Cardinal Mazarin:

(1) **Hortense, Duchesse de Mazarin** (1646–1699), was married off by Mazarin to Armand Charles de la Porte, who assumed the Mazarin title, but she separated from him and became famous for her beauty at the court of Charles II of England. She died at Chelsea.

(2) **Laura, Duchesse de Mercoeur** (1636–57), came to the French court and was married to Louis de Vendôme. The famous Duc de Vendôme (q.v.) was their son.

(3) **Marie, Princesse de Colonna** (1640–1715), was a favourite of Louis XIV, who was prevented from marrying her only by the machinations of Mazarin. She lived in Spain for most of her life.

(4) **Marie Anne, Duchesse de Bouillon** (1649–1714), became renowned for her literary salon and for her patronage of La Fontaine. She was banished in 1680, having been involved in the *cause celèbre* of the notorious sorceress La Voisin (q.v.).

(5) **Olympe, Comtesse de Soissons** (1639–1708), also a court favourite, was involved with her sister in the La Voisin intrigues and, accused of poisoning her husband and the Queen of Spain, fled to the Netherlands. Her son was Prince Eugene of Savoy.

MANDER, Karel van (1548–1606), Flemish painter of portraits, born at Meulebeke, lived mostly in Haarlem, and is chiefly remembered for his *Schilderbouck* (1604), a collection of biographical profiles of painters, important as a source for the art history of the Low Countries.

MANDEVILLE, (1) Bernard (1670–1733), English satirist, born at Dort in Holland, took his M.D. at Leyden in 1691, immediately settled in London in medical practice, and died there. He is known as the author of a short work in doggerel verse originally entitled *The Grumbling Hive* (1705), and finally *The Fable of the Bees* (1723). Writing in a vein of acute paradox, he affirms that 'private vices are public benefits', and that every species of virtue is at bottom some form of gross selfishness, more or less modified. The book was condemned by the grand jury of Middlesex, and was attacked by Law the nonjuror, by Berkeley, Brown, Warburton, Hutcheson and others. Other works in an unpleasant tone are *The Virgin Unmasked*, *Free Thoughts on Religion*, &c. See J. M. Robertson's *Pioneer Humanists* (1907).

(2) **Geoffrey de, Earl of Essex** (d. 1144), succeeded his father as constable of the Tower about 1130, proved a traitor alternately to King Stephen and the Empress Matilda, and taking finally to open brigandage, was besieged in the Cambridgeshire fens and slain. See monograph by J. H. Round (1892).

(3) **Jehan de, or Sir John,** the name assigned to the compiler of a famous book of travels, published apparently in 1366, and soon translated from the French into all European tongues. It seems to have been written by a physician, Jehan de Bourgogne, otherwise Jehan à la Barbe, who died at Liège in 1372, and who is said to have revealed on his death-bed his real name of Mandeville (or Maundevylle), explaining that he had had to flee from his native England for a homicide. Some scholars, however, attribute it to Jean d'Outremeuse, a Frenchman. Mandeville claims to have travelled through Turkey, Persia, Syria, Arabia, North Africa and India, but much of his book is a compilation from various literary sources. See Hamelius's edition (E.E.T.S. 1919–23) and studies by M. Letts (1949) and J. W. Bennett (1954).

MÁNES, Josef, *mah'-* (1820–71), Czech artist, born in Prague. He was the pupil of his father, the landscape artist **Antonín** (1784–

1843), and he was well known for his genre and historical paintings and portraits, many of which are in the Prague museums. See study by M. Lamač (Prague 1952).

MANET, Édouard, *ma-nay* (1832–83), French painter. Intended for a legal career, he was sent on a voyage to Rio to distract his thoughts from art, but this proved ineffectual, and having studied for a while under Couture he exhibited at the Salon in 1861. His *Déjeuner sur l'herbe* (1863), which scandalized the traditional classicists, was rejected, and, although the equally provocative *Olympia* was accepted in 1865, the Salon remained hostile and Manet's genius was not recognized until after his death. With Monet, Renoir and other rebels against tradition, he exhibited in the *Salon des Refusés* and helped to form the group out of which the Impressionist movement arose. Manet's works are all characterized by a masterly understanding of the effects of light, but it is in his later canvases, such as *Bar at the Folies Bergères* (1882), that he is seen in the more truly Impressionistic vein. See a Life by Tabarant (1947).

MANETHO, Egyptian historian, was highpriest of Heliopolis in the 3rd century B.C. Only epitomes of his history of the 30 dynasties are given by Julius Africanus (A.D. 300), Eusebius, and George Syncellus (A.D. 800).

MANFRED (1232–66), King of Sicily, was a natural son of the Emperor Frederick II, and was made Prince of Tarentum. For his halfbrother, Conrad IV, he acted as regent in Italy (especially Apulia), and subsequently for his nephew Conradin (q.v.) bravely defended the interests of the empire against the aggression of Pope Innocent IV, who, however, compelled Manfred to flee for shelter to the Saracens. With their aid he defeated the papal troops, and became, in 1257, master of the whole kingdom of Naples and Sicily. On the (false) rumour of Conradin's death (1258) he was crowned king at Palermo, and, in spite of excommunication by Pope Alexander VI, occupied Tuscany. His brief government was mild and vigorous; but Pope Urban IV renewed the excommunication, and bestowed his dominions on Charles of Anjou, brother of Louis IX of France. Manfred fell in battle at Benevento.

MANGAN, James Clarence (1803–49), Irish poet and attorney's clerk, whose life was a tragedy of hapless love, poverty and intemperance, till his death in a Dublin hospital. There is fine quality in his original verse, as well as in his translations from old Irish and German. See editions of his Poems (1903), Prose Writings (1904), Lives by D. J. O'Donoghue (1897) and J. D. Sheridan (1937). For bibliography see P. S. O'Hegarty (1941).

MANGNALL, Richmal (1769–1820), English teacher, born probably in Manchester, was the headmistress of a ladies' school near Wakefield, where she died. Her redoubtable *Questions*, the pride and terror of generations of schoolgirls, reached an 84th edition in 1857, and was even reprinted in 1892.

MANICHAEUS, or **Mani,** *man-i-kee'us* (c. A.D. 215–276), the founder of the heretical

Manichaeans, was born at Ecbatana, and about 245 began to proclaim his new religion at the court of the Persian king, Sapor (Shahpur) I. Bahram I abandoned him to his enemies, who crucified him. See study by E. Rochat (Geneva 1897).

MANIN, Daniele (1804–57), Venetian statesman, born of Jewish ancestry at Venice, practised at the bar, and became a leader of liberal opinion; made president of the Venetian republic (1848), he was the soul of the heroic five months' defence against the Austrians. When Venice capitulated (August 24, 1849), Manin, with thirty-nine others, was excluded from the amnesty, but escaped to Paris, where he taught Italian, and died of heart disease. His bones were brought to free Venice in 1868. See Lives by R. Errera (1923) and G. M. Trevelyan (1923).

MANKOWITZ, (Cyril) Wolf, *man'kō-vits* (1924–   ), British author, playwright and antique dealer, was born at Bethnal Green, London. An authority on Wedgwood, he published *Wedgwood* (1953), *The Portland Vase* (1953), and is an editor of *The Concise Encyclopedia of English Pottery and Porcelain* (1957). Other publications include the novels *Make Me an Offer* (1952) and *A Kid for Two Farthings* (1953), and a collection of short stories, *The Mendelman Fire* (1957). Among his plays is *The Bespoke Overcoat* (1954).

MANLEY, Mary de la Rivière (c. 1672–1724), English author of plays, and of the scandalous anti-Whig *New Atalantis* (1709), and Swift's successor as editor of *The Examiner* (1711), was born in Jersey, about 1688 married bigamously a cousin, John Manley of Truro, M.P., and died at Lambeth.

MANN, (1) **Heinrich** (1871–1950), German novelist, brother of (4), born at Lübeck, began to be described as the German Zola for his ruthless exposure of pre-1914 German society in *Im Schlaraffenland* (1901), translated as *Berlin, the Land of Cockaigne* (1925), and the trilogy describing the three classes of Kaiser Wilhelm II's empire, *Die Armen* (1917) the proletariat, *Der Untertan* (1918) the underling or bourgeois, and *Der Kopf* (1929) the head or governing class. He is best known for the macabre, expressionist novel, *Professor Unrat* (1904), describing the moral degradation of a once outwardly respectable schoolmaster, which was translated and filmed as *The Blue Angel* (1932). He lived in France (1933–40) and then escaped to the United States. Other works include *Die kleine Stadt* (1901), set in a small Italian town, and a remarkable autobiography, *Ein Zeitalter wird besichtigt* (1945–46). His influence is noticeable in Wassermann and Feuchtwanger. See studies by W. Schröder (1931), K. Lemke (1946) and H. Thieme (1951).

(2) **Sir Horace** (1701–86), Horace Walpole's lifelong correspondent, from 1740 was British plenipotentiary at Florence. See Doran's *Mann and Manners* (1876), and Sieveking's memoir (1912).

(3) **Horace** (1796–1859), American educationist, born at Franklin, Mass., entered the Massachusetts legislature in 1827, and was president of the state senate. He was for eleven years secretary of the Board of

Education. From 1853 he was president of Antioch College in Ohio. See *Life and Works* (1891) and books by G. A. Hubbell (Phila-delphia 1910) and E. I. F. Williams (N.Y. 1937).

(4) **Thomas** (1875–1955), the greatest modern German novelist, brother of (1), born June 6 into a patrician family of merchants and senators of the Hanseatic city of Lübeck, his mother being a talented musician of mixed German and Portuguese West Indian blood. The opposition between a conservative business outlook and artistic inclinations, the clash between Nordic and Latin tempera-ments inherent in his own personality, and the Schopenhauerian doctrine of art, being the self-abnegation of the will as the end product of decay, were to form his subject-matter. At nineteen, without completing school, he settled with his mother in Munich, and after dabbling at the university, he joined his brother in Italy, where he wrote his early masterpiece, *Buddenbrooks* (1901; trans. 1924), the saga of a family like his own, trac-ing its decline through four generations, as business acumen gives way to artistic sensi-bilities. At twenty-five Mann thus became a leading German writer. On his return to Munich, he became reader for the satirical literary magazine, *Simplicissimus*, which pub-lished many of his early, remarkable short stories. The novelettes *Tonio Kröger* (1902), *Tristan* (1903) and *Der Tod in Venedig*, ' Death in Venice ' (1913; trans. 1916), all deal with the problem of the artist's salvation, positively in the case of the first, who resembles Goethe's Werther, negatively in the last in which a successful writer dies on the brink of perverted eroticism. World War I pre-cipitated a quarrel between the two novel-ist brothers, Thomas's *Betrachtungen eines Unpolitischen*, ' Meditations of an Unpolitical Person ' (1918), revealing his militant Ger-man patriotism, already a feature of his essay on Frederick the Great (1915) and a distrust of political ideologies, including the radical-ism of his brother. *Der Zauberberg*, ' The Magic Mountain ' (1924; trans. 1927), won him the Nobel prize in 1929. It was inspired by a visit to his wife at a sanatorium for consumptives at Davos in 1913 and tells the story of such a patient, Hans Castorp, the sanatorium representing Europe in its moral and intellectual disintegration. The same year, Mann delivered a speech against the rising Nazis and in 1930 exposed Italian fascism in *Mario und der Zauberer*, ' Mario and the Magician ' (1930; trans. 1934). He left Germany for Switzerland after 1933 and in 1936 delivered an address for Freud's eightieth birthday. Both shared an enthusi-asm for Joseph, and Mann wrote a tetralogy on the life of that biblical figure (1933–43; trans. 1934–44). He settled in the United States in 1936 and wrote a novel on a visit to Goethe by an old love, Charlotte Buff, *Lotte in Weimar* (1939). His anti-Hitler broadcasts to Germany were collected under the titles *Achtung Europa!* and *Deutsche Hörer* (1945). In 1947 he returned to Switzerland and was the only returning exile to be fêted by both West and East Germany. His greatest work, a modern version of the medieval legend,

Doktor Faustus (1947; trans. 1948), runs together art and politics in the simultaneous treatment of the life and catastrophic end of an atonality-pioneering composer, Adrian Leverkühn, and German disintegration in two world wars. His last unfinished work, hailed as Germany's greatest comic novel, *Bekenntnisse des Hochstapler's Felix Krull*, Part I (1954), ' Confessions of the Confidence Trickster Felix Krull ' (trans. 1955), written with astonishing wit, irony and humour and without the tortuous stylistic complexities of the *Bildungsroman*, commended itself most to English translators. Mann died August 12, 1955. Essentially a 19th-century German conservative, whose cultural landmarks vanished in the first World War, he was compelled towards a critique of the artistic. Ambivalently the artist and the bourgeois fearer of Bohemianism, the unpolitical man with political duties, he was the brilliant story-teller in the classical German tradition, whose subject-matter was paradoxically the end of that tradition. Other later works include *Der Erwählte* (1951), on the life of the incestuous Pope Gregory, *Die Betrogene* (1953) and *Last Essays* (trans. 1959), on Schiller, Goethe, Nietzsche and Chehov. See bibliography, ed. K. W. Jonas (Minnesota 1955), Mann's *Sketch of My Life* (trans. 1961), biographical studies by J. Cleugh (1933) and J. G. Brennan (1942), and critical studies by H. Hatfield (1952), J. M. Lindsay (1954), R. H. Thomas (1956) and especially E. Heller, *The Ironic German* (1958).

(5) **Tom** (1856–1941), English Labour leader, by profession an engineer, was born in Warwickshire. See his *Memoirs* (1923).

MANNERHEIM, Carl Gustav Emil, Freiherr von, *man'ér-hīm* (1867–1951), Finnish soldier and statesman, was born at Villnäs and became an officer in the Russian Army in 1889. He fought in the Russo-Japanese War of 1904–05 and in World War I. When Finland declared her independence in 1918 (after the Russian Revolution), he became supreme commander and regent. Defeated in the presidential election of 1919, he retired into private life, but returned as commander-in-chief against the Russians in the Winter War of 1939–40. He continued to command the Finnish forces until 1944, when he became president of the Finnish Republic until 1946. See book by T. Borenius (1940).

MANNERS. See RUTLAND and GRANBY.

MANNING, (1) **Henry Edward** (1808–92), English Roman Catholic cardinal, born at Totteridge, Hertfordshire, from Harrow passed in 1827 to Balliol College, Oxford, and, after taking a classical first in 1830, was in 1832 elected a fellow of Merton. An eloquent preacher and a High Churchman, in 1833 he became rector of Woollavington and Graffham, Sussex, and in 1840 Archdeacon of Chichester. On April 6, 1851, he joined the Church of Rome, and in 1865 succeeded Cardinal Wiseman as Archbishop of West-minster. At the Oecumenical Council of 1870 Manning was one of the most zealous supporters of the infallibility dogma; and, named cardinal in 1875, he continued a leader of the Ultramontanes. He was a member of the royal commissions on the housing of the poor (1885) and on education (1886), and took a prominent part in temperance and benevolent movements. He died January 14, 1892. See Lives by E. S. Purcell (2 vols. 1896), V. A. McLelland (1962) and E. E. Reynolds, *Three Cardinals* (1958).

(2) **Robert.** See ROBERT DE BRUNNE.

(3) **Thomas** (1772–1840), English traveller, born at Broome rectory, Suffolk, in 1790 entered Caius College, Cambridge; stayed there some years, studying Chinese; in 1799 formed his friendship with Lamb; in 1806 went out as a doctor to Canton; in 1811–12 visited Lhasa in Tibet, the first Englishman ever there; returned in 1817 to England; visited Italy 1827–29; and died at Bath. See Memoir by C. R. Markham (1876).

MANNS, Sir August (1825–1907), German musician, born in Prussia, in 1855 became musical director at the Crystal Palace, and in 1883–1902 conducted the Handel Festivals. He was knighted in 1903. See study by H. S. Wyndham (1909).

MANNY, Sir Walter de (d. 1372), English knight, born in Hainault, followed Queen Philippa to England in 1327, and fought splendidly for Edward III by land and sea against the Scots, Flemings and French. He was knighted and made Lord de Manny, received large grants of land, founded the Charterhouse monastery, and died in London.

MANNYNG, Robert. See ROBERT DE BRUNNE.

MANOEL I. See EMANUEL I.

MANOEL II. See MANUEL II.

MANRIQUE, Jorge, *-ree′kay* (1440–79), Spanish poet, born at Paredes de la Nava, is remembered for his fine elegy on his father's death, *Coplas por la muerte de su padre.*

MANSARD, or **MANSART,** *mä-sahr,* (1) **François** (1598–1666), French architect, brought a simplified adaptation of the Baroque style into use in France, designed Ste Marie de la Visitation (1632) and other Paris churches, the Château de Blois, Château de Maisons-Lafitte, &c., and made fashionable the high pitched type of roof which bears his name. See studies by Sir R. Blomfield (1935) and A. Blunt (1941).

(2) **Jules Hardouin** (1645–1708), French architect, great nephew of (1), born in Paris, became chief architect to Louis XIV and designed part of the palace of Versailles, including the Grand Trianon.

MANSBRIDGE, Albert (1878–1952), C.H. (1931), English educationist, born at Gloucester, founded the Workers' Educational Association (1903). See his *Trodden Road* (1940).

MANSEL, Henry Longueville (1820–71), English philosopher, Dean of St Paul's, was born at Cosgrove rectory, Northamptonshire. Educated at Merchant Taylors' and St John's College, Oxford, he became Waynflete professor in 1859, professor of Ecclesiastical History and Canon of Christ Church in 1867, and Dean of St Paul's in 1869. The pupil and part-editor of Hamilton (q.v.), he went beyond his master in emphasizing the relativity of knowledge—alleging that we have no positive conception of the attributes of God. His works include *Prolegomena Logica* (1851), *Metaphysics* (1860), *The Limits of Religious Thought* (Bampton Lectures,

1858), *The Philosophy of the Conditioned* (1866) and *The Gnostic Heresies* (with Life, 1874). See study by Matthews (1956).

MANSFELD, Counts of, a noble German family (founded *c.* 1060), whose castle stood near the Harz Mountains, 14 miles NW. of Halle.

(1) **Count Peter Ernst I** (1517–1604), afterwards prince, took part in Charles V's expedition against Tunis, and was made governor of Luxembourg. He fought against the French, made a name as one of the most brilliant Spanish generals in the Low Countries, was sent by Alva to the assistance of the French king against the Protestants (1569), and acted as governor of the Spanish Low Countries.

(2) **Count Ernst** (1580–1626), natural son of (1), was a soldier of fortune in the Thirty Years' War. Refused his father's possessions, the promised reward for his brilliant services in Hungary and elsewhere, he went over to the Protestant princes. After defending the Count-Palatine Frederick for a time (1618–20), he was driven by the disaster of the Weissenberg to retreat to the Palatinate, from which he carried on for two years a predatory war on the imperialists, defeating Tilly in 1622. He afterwards took service with the United Netherlands, beating the Spaniards at Fleurus (1622). At Richelieu's solicitation he raised an army of 12,000 men (mostly in England), but in 1626 he was crushed by Wallenstein at Dessau. Later, when marching to join Bethlen Gabor of Transylvania, he died near Sarajevo in Bosnia.

MANSFIELD, Earls of:

(1) **William Murray, 1st Earl** (1705–93), British judge, born at Perth, the fourth son of Viscount Stormont, from Westminster passed to Christ Church, Oxford, graduating B.A. in 1727. Called to the bar, he soon acquired an extensive practice; was appointed solicitor-general in 1742; entered the House of Commons as member for Boroughbridge; was appointed attorney-general in 1754; and became chief-justice of the King's Bench in 1756, a member of the cabinet, and Baron Mansfield. He was impartial as a judge, but his opinions were unpopular; Junius bitterly attacked him, and during the Gordon riots of 1780 his house was burned. Made earl in 1776, he resigned office in 1788. See Lives by Holliday (1797), Fifoot (1936).

(2) **David Murray, 2nd Earl** (1727–96), British statesman, held various diplomatic posts abroad, became a privy councillor in 1763, a secretary of state in 1779–82, and president of the council in 1783 and 1794–96.

MANSFIELD, Katherine, pen name of Kathleen Middleton Murry, *née* Beauchamp (1888–1923), English short-story writer, born in Wellington, New Zealand, in 1908 settled in Europe. She married John Middleton Murry (q.v.) in 1918, and died of tuberculosis at the Gurdiev settlement at Fontainebleau. Her sensitive style, which owed much to Chehov, has had a powerful influence on subsequent writers in the same genre. Her chief works are: *Bliss* (1920), *The Garden Party* (1922) and *Something Childish* (1924). Other publications are her

Journal (1927), *Letters* (1930), *Collected Short Stories* (1945) and *Letters to John Middleton Murry* (1951). See studies by A. Alpers (1954) and J. Middleton Murry (1959).

MANSON, (1) **George** (1850–76), Scottish watercolour painter, born in Edinburgh, in 1866 became a wood-engraver with Messrs W. & R. Chambers. In 1871 he devoted himself wholly to painting. See Memoir by J. M. Gray (1880).

(2) **Sir Patrick** (1844–1922), Scottish doctor, known as 'Mosquito Manson'—from his pioneer work with Ross in malaria research—was born in Aberdeenshire, practised medicine in the East, became medical adviser to the Colonial Office, and helped to found the London School of Tropical Medicine. See Life by P. Manson-Bahr (1962).

MANSTEIN, Fritz Erich von, *man'shtīn* (1887–   ), German general, became at the outset of World War II chief of staff to Rundstedt in the Polish campaign and later in France, where he was architect of Hitler's *Blitzkreig* invasion plan. In 1941 he was given command of an army corps on the eastern front and though not trained in armoured warfare handled his panzers with great resource in the Crimea. Given the unenviable task of pulling the chestnuts out of the fire after the disaster of Stalingrad, he contrived with slender resources to extricate the right wing in sufficient strength to stage a successful counter-attack at Kharkov, though he failed to relieve the sixth army, beleaguered through Paulus's blind obedience to Hitler's imbecilic 'stand fast' orders. After being captured in 1945 he was imprisoned as a war criminal but released in 1953. A strong advocate of fluid defence for preventing the enemy from exploiting an advantage, he embodied his theories and an account of his military career in his *Lost Victories* (Eng. trans. 1959).

MANSUR. See ALMANSUR.

MANTEGAZZA, Paolo, *man-te-gat'za* (1831–1910), Italian physiologist, born at Monza, practised medicine in Argentina and at Milan, and became professor in 1860 of Pathology at Pavia, in 1870 of Anthropology at Florence. He wrote largely on the physiology of pleasure, pain and love, on spontaneous generation, and on physiognomy, as well as books of travel and novels. See Memoir by Raynaudi (Milan 1894).

MANTEGNA, Andrea, *man-tayn'ya* (1431–1506), Italian painter, born in Vicenza in 1431, was the favourite pupil and adopted son of Squarcione, the tailor-painter; a precocious genius, he set up a studio of his own when only seventeen. Having married a sister of the Bellinis and quarrelled with Squarcione, he was in 1460 induced by Lodovico Gonzaga, Duke of Mantua, to settle in his city. There he remained, with the exception of a visit to Rome (1488–90) to paint a series of frescoes (now destroyed) for Pope Innocent VIII's private chapel in the Vatican, until his death. His greatest works at Mantua were nine tempera pictures representing the *Triumph of Caesar* (1482–92), acquired by Charles I, and now at Hampton Court. Mantegna was also engraver, architect, sculptor and poet. He did not aim at

grace and beauty in his pictures—some of them are ugly; but his technical excellences greatly influenced Italian art. See books by Julia Cartwright (1881), Maud Cruttwell (1901), Kristeller (trans. Armstrong, 1901), W. G. Constable (1937) and E. Tietze-Conrat (1955).

MANTELL, Gideon Algernon (1790–1852), English palaeontologist, born at Lewes, practised as a doctor there and at Brighton, Clapham and London, wrote popular books, and did important work on Wealden fossils.

MANTEUFFEL, Edwin Hans Karl Freiherr von, *man'toy-fel* (1809–85), Russian field-marshal, born at Dresden of old Pomeranian family, was colonel of the Prussian guards by 1854. As commander of the Prussian troops in Sleswick he began the war with Austria in 1866, helped to reduce the Hanoverians to capitulation, and defeated the Bavarians in four battles. In 1870–71 he first commanded the army of the north, then in command of the army of the south drove Bourbaki and 80,000 men into Switzerland. As viceroy of Alsace-Lorraine (from 1879) he was very unpopular. See Life by Keck (1889).

MANUCCI, A. See ALDUS MANUTIUS.

MANUEL, name of two Byzantine emperors:

Manuel I, Comnenus (*c.* 1120–80), son of John II, during his reign (1143–80), attempted to restore the fortunes of the East Roman Empire, and was successful against the Turks until his defeat at Myriokephalon in 1176, which invalidated all his earlier successes and marked the beginning of the downfall of the empire.

Manuel II, Palaeologus (1350–1423), son of Johannes V, for much of his reign, which extended from 1391 to 1423, was besieged in Constantinople by the Turks. At one point he was relieved by Tamur the Tartar advancing into Asia Minor, but, being a scholar rather than a statesman, he failed to profit from this diversion and was overwhelmed.

MANUEL, *man'yoo-el*, kings of Portugal:

Manuel I, more often known as **Emanuel** (q.v.).

Manuel II, also **Manoel** (1889–1932), King of Portugal, born at Lisbon, on the assassination of his father King Carlos I and the Crown Prince Luis on February 1, 1908, became king, but was forced to abdicate at the revolution of October 3, 1910. He settled in England at Fulwell Park, Twickenham, where he died.

MANUEL, (1) **Nikolaus**, called **Deutsch** (1484–1530), Swiss poet, painter and reformer, was born and died at Bern. Beginning as a painter of stained glass, he changed over to orthodox media and produced biblical and mythological pictures in the Renaissance style, often showing the influence of Baldung in his tendency toward the macabre. He held several government offices, was a member of the Great Council, and wrote satirical verse. See works by Handeke (1889) and Mandach and Kögler (1940). His son, **Hans Rudolf** (1525–71), was also a painter.

(2) **Peter** (1931–58), Scottish criminal, perpetrator of at least eight of the most callous murders in the history of crime. Between September 1956 and January 1958,

in addition to committing a number of burglaries, he broke into the house of a Mr William Watt in Rutherglen and shot the three occupants dead, strangled and robbed a girl at Mount Vernon, robbed the house at Uddingston of a family named Smart, all three members of which he killed, and he shot dead a Newcastle taxi driver. He was also accused of battering to death Ann Kneilands at East Kilbride, but was acquitted through lack of evidence. His trial at Glasgow High Court was one of the most sensational in legal history. Having already successfully defended himself against a former charge, he clearly considered himself more than a match for the conventional forces of law and order, and arrogantly dismissed the eminent counsel appearing on his behalf. Conducting his case with considerable skill, he brought in a special defence plea giving alibis and attributing the Rutherglen murders to Watt, who had already suffered 67 days of imprisonment as a suspect. But he overreached himself, was found guilty of seven of the murders, and was hanged on June 19, 1958. The Newcastle shooting was later officially attributed to him by an inquest jury. See J. G. Wilson, *The Trial of Peter Manuel* (1959).

MANUZIO. See ALDUS MANUTIUS.

MANZONI, Alessandro (1785–1873), Italian novelist and poet, was nobly born at Milan, where he died. He published his first poems in 1806, married happily in 1810, and spent the next few years in writing sacred lyrics and a treatise on the religious basis of morality. But the work which gave Manzoni European fame is his historical novel, *I Promessi Sposi*, a Milanese story of the 17th century (1825–27), the most notable novel in Italian literature. Despite his Catholic devoutness, he was a strong advocate for a united Italy. His last years were darkened by the frequent shadow of death within his household. See Hoepli's edition of his complete works, including his letters (Milan 1913), and books on him by Graf (1898), De Sanctis (1922), B. Reynolds (1950) and A. Colquhoun (1954).

MAO TSE-TUNG, *mow'dze-doong'* (1893–), Chinese Communist leader, first chairman (1949) of the People's Republic of China, was born in Hunan, the son of a peasant farmer. Educated at Changsha, he went in 1918 to the university of Peking, where as a library assistant he studied the works of Marx and others and helped to found the Chinese Communist party. Thereafter he set up a Chinese Soviet Republic in S.E. China, defying the attacks of Chiang Kai-shek's forces until 1934, when he and his followers were obliged to uproot themselves and undertake an arduous and circuitous ' long march ' to NW. China. From his headquarters in Yenan he resisted the Japanese, and on their collapse issued forth to shatter the Nationalist régime of Chiang Kai-shek and proclaim the People's Republic of China in Peking in September 1949. He resigned the chairmanship of the republic in January 1959, but continued as chairman of the party Politburo. He was conspicuously absent from the Moscow conference of Communist leaders (1960).

Ideological differences over Khruschev's policy of peaceful coexistence became apparent. The Chinese were bitter over Khruschev's *volte face* over missiles on Cuba (1962) and Moscow gave no support to the Chinese in their border war (1962) with India. Chinese-Soviet talks in Moscow in 1963 proved in vain, each power canvassing support among other Communist parties. The Communism of Mao Tse-tung, with its emphasis on the peasants, though allied with that of Russia, is neither modelled on it nor dominated by it: it is set forth in his *New Democracy* (1940). His personal power was greatly reinforced by the Red Guard ' cultural revolution ' in 1967 which eliminated the more liberal forces. See Life by R. Payne (1951), and studies by Schwartz (1951), J. Ch'ên (1965), and S. Schram (1967 ed.).

MAO-TUN, pseud. of **Shen Yen-ping** (1896–), Chinese author, born in Chekiang province, became a leading literary figure in Peking, where he was a founder member of the Literary Research Society. His military experiences in Chiang Kai-shek's Northern Expedition of 1926 provide colour for his famous trilogy *Shih* (1927–28). In Britain he is better known for his short stories, several of which have appeared in translation.

MAP, or Mapes, Walter (*c*. 1137–1209), Welsh poet and ecclesiastic, was born, of Welsh family, apparently in Herefordshire, studied at Paris, became a clerk of the royal household, went on a mission to Rome, and became canon of St Paul's and archdeacon of Oxford. He was certainly the author of the *De Nugis Curialium* (ed. M. R. James, 1915); probably reduced the Arthurian romances to their existing shape; and may have written some part of the Latin poems (see Wright's edition, 1841), in connection with which his name is best known. The *Confessio Goliae* is also attributed to him. See studies by Foster (1913) and Pauphilet (1921).

MAR, John Erskine, 6th or 11th Earl of (1675– 1732), Scottish Jacobite, born at Alloa, began life as a Whig, and by his frequent change of sides earned the nickname of ' Bobbing Joan '. He headed the Jacobite rebellion of 1715, was defeated at Sheriffmuir, and died in exile at Aix-la-Chapelle. See his *Legacy*, published by the Scottish History Society in 1896. See the Earl of Crawford's *Earldom of Mar in Sunshine and Shade* (1882), and study by W. D. Simpson (1949).

MARAIS, Marin, *ma-ray* (1656–1728), French composer and viol player, was born and died in Paris. As a boy he was in the Sainte Chapelle choir, later becoming a bass violist in the Royal Band and in the orchestra of the Opera, of which he later became joint conductor. A pupil of Lully, he wrote several operas, the most famous of which was *Alcyone* (1705), but his posthumous and ever-increasing reputation is based on his music for the viol.

MARAT, Jean Paul, *ma-ra* (1743–93), French revolutionary politician, was born at Boudry near Neuchâtel. He studied medicine at Bordeaux, next went to Paris, Holland and London, and practised there with success. He was made brevet-physician to his guards by the Comte d'Artois, afterwards Charles X—

an office which he held till 1786. Meantime he continued work in optics and electricity, and wrote several scientific works. But now revolution was in the air, and Marat became a member of the Cordelier Club, and established his infamous paper, *L'ami du peuple.* His virulence provoked hatred; but it made him the darling of the scum of Paris, and placed great power in his hands. Twice at least he had to flee to London, and once he was forced to hide in the sewers of Paris. His misadventures increased his hatred of constituted authority, and on his head rests in great measure the guilt of the infamous September massacres. He was elected to the Convention as one of the deputies for Paris, but was one of the least influential and most unpopular men in the House. After the king's death his last energies were spent in a mortal struggle with the Girondins. But he was dying fast of a disease contracted in the sewers, and could only write sitting in his bath. There his destiny reached him through the knife of Charlotte Corday (q.v.), on the evening of July 13, 1793. His body was committed to the Panthéon with the greatest public honours, to be cast out fifteen months later amid popular execration. See Ch. Simond's *Autobiographie de Marat* (1909); his *Correspondance,* ed. by Vellay (1908); Bax's *Marat* (1900), Phipson's (1924); Lives by Chèvremont (1881), Cabanès (1890, 1911), L. Gottschalk (N.Y. 1927) and J. Shearing's *Angel of the Assassination* (1935).

MARATTI, Carlo (1625–1713), Italian painter, was born at Camerano, a leader of the 17th-century Baroque school. His chief works are in Rome, but the British Royal Collection contains a number of his drawings.

MARBECK, or **Merbecke, John** (d. *c.* 1585), English musician and theologian, organist of St George's Chapel, Windsor, was condemned to the stake in 1544 as a Reformer, but pardoned by Bishop Gardiner. In 1550 he published his famous *Boke of Common Praier Noted,* an adaptation of the plain chant to the first Prayer-book of Edward VI. He prepared the earliest concordance to the whole English Bible, and wrote several theological works.

MARC, Franz (1880–1916), German artist, born at Munich, studied at Munich and in Italy and France; with Kandinsky he founded the Blaue Reiter expressionist group in Munich in 1911. Most of his paintings were of animals (e.g. the famous *Tower of the Blue Horses*) portrayed in forceful colours, with a well-defined pictorial rhythm. He was killed at Verdun. See the monograph by A. J. Schardt (1936).

MARCANTONIO, or in full **Marcantonio Raimondi** (*c.* 1488–1534), Italian engraver, born at Bologna, was at first a goldsmith. At Rome, where he worked from 1510, he was chiefly engaged in engraving Raphael's works; and he is reckoned the best amongst the engravers of the great painter. The capture of Rome by the Constable Bourbon in 1527 drove him back to Bologna, where he seems to have died. See A. M. Hind's monograph (1912).

MARCEAU, François Séverin Desgraviers, mar-sō (1769–96), French general, born at

Chartres, helped in 1792 to defend Verdun with a body of volunteers, and for his services with the republican army in La Vendée was made general of division. He commanded the right wing at Fleurus, and in 1796 the first division of Jourdan's army, investing Mainz, Mannheim and Coblenz. But while covering the French retreat at Altenkirchen he was shot, September 19, and died of his wound. His body was brought to the Panthéon in 1889. See *Lives* by Maze, Parfait, T. G. Johnson (1896), Chuquet's *Quatre Généraux de la Révolution* (1911–12) and study by G. Lecomte (Paris 1929).

MARCEL, Gabriel (1889–   ), French Christian Existentialist philosopher and author, born in Paris, lectured and taught from 1912, served in the Red Cross during World War I, and in his *Journal metaphysique* (1927; trans. 1947) and in the essay *Existence et Objectivité* (appended 1952) struggled to break from idealism to a closer understanding of actual 'existence'. Even the empiricist explanation of the universe through sensations is to obscure actual existence by treating one's own body as a 'third person'. Philosophical reflection should not abstract but get as close as possible to actual existence. Even God's existence cannot be arrived at intellectually but is bound up with our own ontological nature. *Être et Avoir* (1935), 'Being and Having' (trans. 1950), *The Philosophy of Existence* (trans. 1948), in which he criticizes the more undisciplined ethics of Sartre's Existentialism, and *Le Mystère de l'être* (1951), his Gifford Lectures at Aberdeen (1949–50), take his Existentialism further. In 1929 he became a Roman Catholic. See also his plays, *Un Homme de Dieu* (1929), *Le Chemin de Crête* (1936), *La Soif* (1938), *Croissez et multipliez* (1955), &c. He was awarded the Grand Prix de l'Académie française (1948). See also studies by E. Gilson (1947) and R. Troisfontaines, *De l'Existence à l'Être* (2 vols., Paris 1953).

MARCELLO, Benedetto (1686–1739), Italian composer, was a judge of the Venetian republic, and a member of the Council of Forty, and afterwards held offices at Pola and Brescia. As a composer he is remembered for his *Estro poetico armonico* (1724–27), an 8-volume collection of settings for 50 of the Psalms of David, for his oratorio *Le Quattro Stagioni* (1731), and for his keyboard and instrumental sonatas. He wrote the satirical *Il Teatro alla moda* (1720). See *Lives* by Busi (1884) and D'Angeli (Milan 1940). His brother **Alessandro** (*c.* 1684–*c.* 1750), philosopher and mathematician as well as composer, published a number of cantatas, sonatas and concertos under the pseudonym 'Eterico Stinfalico'.

MARCELLUS, (1) the name of two popes, the first martyred in 310; the second as Cardinal Marcello Cervini presided over the Council of Trent, was elected pope in 1555, but survived his elevation only three weeks. See study by G. B. Manucci (Siena 1921).

(2) **M. Claudius** (*c.* 268 B.C.–208 B.C.), Roman general, who, in his first consulship (222 B.C.) defeated the Insubrian Gauls, and slew their king, Britomartus or Virido-

marus, whose spoils he dedicated as *spolia opima*—the third and last time in Roman history. In the second Punic war he checked Hannibal at Nola (216). Again consul in 214, he conducted the siege of Syracuse, which yielded only in 212. In his fifth consulship, 208, he fell in a skirmish against Hannibal.

MARCH, *mark,* (1) **Auziàs** (1397–1459), Catalan poet, born in Valencia, was pioneer of the trend away from the lyricism of the troubadours towards a more metaphysical approach. Influenced by Italian models, he wrote chiefly on the themes of love and death. See study by Pagès (Paris 1912).

(2) **Francis Andrew,** LL.D. (1825–1911), American philologist, born at Millbury, Mass., graduated at Amherst 1845, and became known for his historical researches in English grammar. See book by R. N. Hart (Easton, Pa. 1907).

MARCHAND, Jean Baptiste, *mar-shã* (1863–1934), French soldier, joined the army at twenty, explored the White Nile, and caused a Franco-British crisis by hoisting the tricolor at Fashoda in 1898. As a general he distinguished himself in World War I. See Life by J. Delebecque (Paris 1936).

MARCHMONT. See HUME (6).

MARCION (*c.* 100–*c.* 165), early Christian heretic, a wealthy shipowner of Sinope in Pontus, about 140 repaired to Rome, and founded the semi-Gnostic Marcionites (144). See studies by A. Harnack (Leipzig 1924), E. S. Blackman (1948).

MARCONI, Guglielmo, Marchese (1874–1937), Italian inventor, was born at Bologna in 1874, his mother being Irish. He successfully experimented with wireless telegraphy in Italy and England and succeeded in sending signals across the Atlantic in 1901. He was awarded the Nobel prize in 1909 and took some part in Italian foreign affairs. See Lives by O. E. Dunlap (N.Y. 1937), S. Epstein and B. Williams (N.Y. 1943).

MARCO POLO. See POLO.

MARCUS AURELIUS ANTONINUS (121–180). See AURELIUS.

MARCUS AURELIUS ANTONINUS (176–217). See CARACALLA.

MARE, De La. See DE LA MARE.

MARENZIO, Luca (1560–99), Italian composer, born at Coccaglio near Brescia, court musician to Sigismund III of Poland, was a prolific writer of madrigals.

MAREY, Étienne Jules (1830–1903), French physiologist, born at Beaune, pioneered scientific cinematography with his studies (1887–1900) of animal movement. In the course of his researches he invented a number of improvements in camera design and succeeded in reducing exposure time to the region of 1/25,000 of a second for the purpose of photographing the flight of insects.

MARGARET, Saint (*c.* 1045–93), Scottish queen, born in Hungary, later came to England, but after the Norman Conquest with her mother, sister and her boy brother, Edgar the Atheling (q.v.), she fled from Northumberland to Scotland. Young, lovely, learned and pious, she won the heart of the Scottish king, Malcolm Canmore (q.v.), who next year wedded her at Dun-

fermline. She did much to civilize the northern realm, and still more to assimilate the old Celtic Church to the rest of Christendom. She built, too, a stately church at Dunfermline, and re-founded Iona. Innocent IV canonized her in 1251. See the Latin Life ascribed to her confessor Turgot (trans. by Forbes-Leith, 3rd ed. 1896), Samuel Cowan's *The Princess Margaret* (1911), Lucy Menzies's *St Margaret* (1925), and Life by A. Henderson-Howat (1948).

MARGARET (1353–1412), Queen of Denmark, Norway and Sweden, was the daughter of Waldemar IV of Denmark, and wife of Haakon VI of Norway and on the death of her father without male heirs in 1375, the Danish nobles offered her the crown in trust for her infant son Olaf (who died 1387). By Haakon's death in 1380 Margaret became ruler of Norway; and in 1388 the Swedish nobles, disgusted with their king, Albert of Mecklenburg, offered her his crown, whereupon she invaded Sweden, and took Albert prisoner. She got her grand-nephew Eric of Pomerania crowned king of the three Scandinavian kingdoms (1396), the power remaining in her own hands. In 1397 the Union of Calmar stipulated that the three kingdoms should remain for ever under one king, each retaining its laws. See Life by M. Hill (1899).

MARGARET OF ANJOU (1429–82), Queen of England, daughter of René of Anjou, in 1445 was married to Henry VI (q.v.) of England. Owing to his weak intellect she was the virtual sovereign; and the war of 1449, in which Normandy was lost, was laid by the English to her charge. In the Wars of the Roses, Margaret, after a brave struggle of nearly twenty years, was finally defeated at Tewkesbury (1471), and lay in the Tower four years, till ransomed by Louis XI. She then retired to France, and died at the castle of Dampierre near Saumur. See Lives by Mrs Hookham (1872) and J. J. Bagley (1948).

MARGARET OF AUSTRIA (1480–1530), regent of the Netherlands, daughter of Maximilian I, she married first the Infante Juan, then Philibert II of Savoy. From 1507 she proved a wise regent of the Netherlands. See works by C. Hare (1907), Tremayne (1908), M. Brucher (Lille 1927), H. Carton de Wiart (Paris 1935).

MARGARET OF NAVARRE (1492–1549), Queen of Navarre, in her youth known as Marguerite d'Angoulême, was the sister of Francis I of France. In 1509 she was married to the Duke of Alençon, who died in 1525; and in 1527 to Henri d'Albret, titular King of Navarre, to whom she bore Jeanne d'Albret, mother of the great Henry IV. She encouraged agriculture, the arts and learning, and sheltered religious reformers like Marot. Her writings include Letters (ed. by Génin, 1843), poems entitled *Les Marguerites de la marguerite des princesses* (1547; ed. by Frank, 1873), and especially the famous *Heptaméron* (1558; ed. by Leroux de Lincy, 5 vols. 1855; trans., with critical essay by Saintsbury, 1894) and modelled on Boccaccio. In 1895 were discovered two dramas, letters, dialogues, and *Le Navire* and *Les Prisons*, written in the last four years of her life, many of them in mental anguish (*Les Dernières poésies*, ed. by A. Lefranc, 1896). See the scholarly study by Pierre Jourda (Paris 1931); also *The Pearl of Princesses* by Williams (1916), and works by S. Putnam (1936), L. Febvre (1944) and Iongh (1954).

MARGARET OF PARMA (1522–86), regent of the Netherlands, natural daughter of Charles V, married in 1536 Alessandro de' Medici, and in 1538 Ottavio Farnese, Duke of Parma and Piacenza, to whom she bore Alessandro Farnese. From 1559 to 1567 she was regent of the Netherlands, masterful, able, a staunch Catholic. Her correspondence with Philip II was edited by Reiffenburg (1842) and also by Gachard (1867–1881). See Life by F. Rachfal (Monaco 1898).

MARGARET OF SCOTLAND (1424–44), Queen of France, a poetess, and the eldest daughter of James I, in 1436 married at Tours the Dauphin Louis (Louis XI), who hated and neglected her. See Jusserand's *English Essays* (1895) and a study by Barbé (1917).

MARGARET OF VALOIS (1553–1615), Queen of Navarre, daughter of Henry II and Catharine de' Medici, in 1572 became the first wife of Henry IV (q.v.) of France—a childless marriage, dissolved in 1599. See her *Mémoires* (trans. by Violet Fane, 1892) and Lives by Saint-Poncy (1887), J. H. Mariéjol (Paris 1928; Eng. trans. 1930) and M. Donnay (Paris 1946).

MARGARET ROSE, Princess (1930–), only sister of Queen Elizabeth II, was born at Glamis Castle, Scotland, on August 21, 1930, the second daughter of King George VI and Queen Elizabeth and the first scion of the Royal House in the direct line of succession to be born in Scotland for more than three centuries. A girl of great beauty and charm, her name was often linked in the newspapers with those of possible suitors. In 1955 she denied rumours of her possible marriage to Group-Captain Peter Townsend, whose previous marriage had been dissolved. In April 1958, as the representative of Queen Elizabeth, she officially inaugurated the first Parliament of the West Indian Federation. In May 1960 she married **Antony Armstrong-Jones** (1930–), a photographer, who was created Viscount Linley and Earl of Snowdon in October 1961. The former title devolved upon Princess Margaret's son, David Albert Charles, born on November 3, 1961. A second child, Sarah Frances Elizabeth, was born on May 1, 1964.

MARGARET TUDOR (1489–1541), Queen of Scotland, the eldest daughter of Henry VII, in 1503 married James IV (q.v.) of Scotland, in 1514 Archibald Douglas, Earl of Angus, and, having divorced him, in 1527 Henry Stewart, Lord Methven. She spent most of her life in a series of political intrigues. See vol. iv of 'Mrs Green's *Princesses of England*, and Life by M. Glenne (1952).

MARGGRAF, Andreas Sigismund (1709–82), German chemist, studied at Berlin, Strasbourg, Halle and Freiberg. In 1747 he discovered the sugar in sugar-beet and so prepared the way for the sugar-beet industry.

MARGUERITE D'ANGOULÊME. See MARGARET OF NAVARRE.

MARGUERITTE, Paul (1860–1918), and his brother **Victor** (1866–1942), born in Algeria, wrote in collaboration or separately ↓novels, histories, &c., many dealing with the Franco-German war period, as the series *Une Époque* (1898–1904). See works by E. Pilon (Paris 1905), J. Guiree (Paris 1927, 1929).

MARHEINEKE, Philipp Konrad, *mahr-hī'nĕ-kĕ* (1780–1846), German Protestant theologian, born at Hildesheim, was professor of Theology at Berlin (1811–46) and represented orthodox Hegelianism. He wrote on dogmatics, Christian ethics, and the Reformation. See study by A. Weber (Strasbourg 1857).

MARIA CHRISTINA (1806–78), Queen of Spain, the daughter of Francis I, king of the Two Sicilies, and fourth wife of Ferdinand VII of Spain, was left by Ferdinand at his death regent for their daughter Isabella II. A Carlist war broke out, and in 1836 she was forced to grant a constitution; in 1840 she was driven to France, whence she returned in 1843. Her share in the schemes of Louis-Philippe as to the marriage of her daughters in 1846, and her reactionary policy, made her unpopular. In 1854 a revolution again drove her to France, where, except in 1864–68 (when she was in Spain), she afterwards lived. See E. B. D'Auvergne's *A Queen at Bay* (1910).

MARIA THERESA (1717–80), empress, daughter of the Emperor Charles VI, was born at Vienna, May 13, 1717. By the ' Pragmatic Sanction ', for which the principal European powers became sureties, her father appointed her heir to his hereditary thrones. In 1736 she married Francis of Lorraine, afterwards Grand-duke of Tuscany; and at her father's death in 1740 she became Queen of Hungary and of Bohemia, and Archduchess of Austria. At her accession the chief European powers put forward claims to her dominions. The young queen was saved by the chivalrous fidelity of the Hungarians, supported by Britain. The War of the Austrian Succession (1741–48) was terminated by the Peace of Aix-la-Chapelle. She lost Silesia to Prussia, and some lands in Italy, but her rights were admitted and her husband was recognized as emperor. Maria Theresa instituted financial reforms, fostered agriculture, manufactures and commerce, and nearly doubled the national revenues, while decreasing taxation. Marshal Daun reorganized her armies; Kaunitz (q.v.) took charge of foreign affairs. But the loss of Silesia rankled in her mind; and, with France as an ally, she renewed the contest with the Prussian king. But the issue of the Seven Years' War (1756–1763) was to confirm Frederick in the possession of Silesia. After the peace she carried out a series of reforms; her son Joseph, after the death of her husband (1765), being associated with her in the government. She joined with Russia and Prussia in the first partition of Poland (1772), securing Galicia and Lodomeria; while from the Porte she obtained Bukovina (1777), and from Bavaria several districts. She died November 29, 1780. A woman of majestic figure and an undaunted spirit, she combined feminine tact with masculine energy; and not merely won the affection and even enthusiastic admiration of her subjects, but raised Austria from a wretched condition to a position of assured power. Although a zealous Roman Catholic, she sought to correct some of the worst abuses in the church. Of her ten surviving children, the eldest son, Joseph II, succeeded her; Leopold, Grand-duke of Tuscany, succeeded him as Leopold II; Ferdinand became Duke of Modena; and Marie Antoinette was married to Louis XVI of France. See Lives by Arneth (Vienna, 10 vols. 1863–79), J. F. Bright (1910), Mary M. Moffat (1911), C. L. Morris (1938); *Frederick the Great and Maria Theresa*, by the Duc de Broglie (trans. 1883); study by G. P. Gooch (1951); and other works under FREDERICK II.

MARIANA, Juan de (1536–1624), Spanish Jesuit historian, born at Talavera, taught in Jesuit colleges in Rome, Sicily and Paris. His last years of ill-health he spent in literary labour at Toledo. His invaluable *Historiae de Rebus Hispaniae* (1592) he afterwards continued down to the accession of Charles V in 1605; and his own Spanish translation (1601–1609) is a classic. His *Tractatus VII Theologici et Historici* (1609) roused the suspicion of the Inquisition. But his most celebrated work is the *De Rege et Regis Institutione* (1599), which answers affirmatively the question whether it be lawful to overthrow a tyrant, even if he is a lawful king. See study by J. Laurès (N.Y. 1928).

MARIANUS SCOTUS, (1) (*c.* 1028–83), Irish chronicler, was a Benedictine monk at Cologne (1052–58) and then a recluse at Fulda and at Mainz. His *Chronicon Universale*, from the creation to 1082, was printed in 1559, 1601 and 1706, but first correctly by Waitz in *Monumenta Germaniae*.

(2) (d. *c.* 1088), Irish abbot and calligrapher, came to Bamberg in 1067, became a Benedictine, was founder and abbot of the monastery of St Peter's at Ratisbon. He was a great calligraphist, copied the whole Bible repeatedly, and left commentaries on Paul's Epistles and on the Psalms.

MARIE AMÉLIE (1782–1866), queen of Louis-Philippe (q.v.), born at Caserta, the daughter of Ferdinand IV of Naples, she married Louis-Philippe in 1809. After the revolution of 1848 she lived with her husband at Claremont. See books by Imbert de St Amand (1891–94).

MARIE ANTOINETTE, Josephe Jeanne (1755–93), Queen of France, was born November 2, 1755, the fourth daughter of Maria Theresa and the Emperor Francis I; and was married to the Dauphin, afterwards Louis XVI, on May 16, 1770. Young and inexperienced, she aroused criticism by her extravagance and disregard for conventions, and on becoming queen (1774) she soon deepened the dislike of her subjects by her devotion to the interests of Austria, as well as by her opposition to all the measures devised by Turgot and Necker for relieving the financial distress of the country. The miseries of France became identified with her extravagance, and in the affair of the Diamond Necklace (1784–86) her guilt was taken for granted. She made herself a centre of opposition to all new ideas, and prompted

the poor vacillating king into a retrograde policy to his own undoing. She was capable of strength rising to the heroic, and she possessed the power of inspiring enthusiasm. Amid the horrors of the march of women on Versailles (1789) she alone maintained her courage. But to the last she failed to understand the troublous times; and the indecision of Louis and his dread of civil war hampered her plans. She had an instinctive abhorrence of the liberal nobles like Lafayette and Mirabeau, but was at length prevailed on to make terms with Mirabeau (July 1790). But she was too independent frankly to follow his advice, and his death in April 1791 removed the last hope of saving the monarchy. Less than three months later occurred the fatal flight to the frontier, intercepted at Varennes. The storming of the Tuileries and slaughter of the brave Swiss guards, the trial and execution of the king (January 21, 1793), quickly followed, and soon she herself was sent to the Conciergerie like a common criminal (August 2, 1793). After eight weeks more of insult and brutality, the ' Widow Capet ' was herself arraigned before the Revolutionary Tribunal. She bore herself with dignity and resignation. Her answers were short with the simplicity of truth. After two days and nights of questioning came the inevitable sentence, and on the same day, October 16, 1793, she died by the guillotine. See the Histories of the French Revolution, letters ed. by A. von Arneth and others (Paris 1865–91), Heidenstam (1913), Söderhjolm (1934). Among many lives the following are some of the most recent: S. Zweig (1933), C. Kunstler (Eng. trans. 1940), H. Belloc (7th ed. 1951), F. W. Kenyon (1956), A. Castelot (Eng. trans. 1957).

MARIE DE FRANCE (fl. *c.* 1160–90) , French poetess, was born in Normandy but spent much of her life in England, where she wrote her *Lais* sometime before 1167 and her *Fables* sometime after 1170. She translated into French the *Tractatus de Purgatorio Sancti Patricii* (c. 1190) and her works contain many classical allusions. The *Lais*, her most important work, dedicated to ' a noble king ', probably Henry II, comprise 14 romantic narratives in octosyllabic verse based on Celtic material. A landmark in French literature, they influenced a number of later writers. See edition with introduction by Ewert (1944), and study by Hoepffner (1935).

MARIE DE' MEDICI (1573–1642), daughter of Francis I, Grand-duke of Tuscany, was married to Henry IV of France in 1600, and gave birth to a son, afterwards Louis XIII, in 1601. She was an obstinate and passionate woman, greatly under the influence of favourites; and the murder of her husband (1610) did not greatly grieve her. She proved as worthless a regent (1610–17) as she had been a wife; and when (1617) young Louis XIII assumed royal power the queen-mother was confined to her own house. She made her submission to her son in 1619. Failing to win over Richelieu, she tried to undermine his influence with the king, failed, was imprisoned, but escaped to Brussels in 1631. Her last years were spent in utter destitution.

MARIE LOUISE (1791–1847), Empress of France, daughter of Francis I of Austria, was married to Napoleon in 1810 (after the divorce of Josephine), and in 1811 bore him a son, who was created King of Rome and who became Napoleon II. On Napoleon's abdication she returned to Austria, and was awarded the Duchy of Parma. In 1822 she contracted a morganatic marriage with Count von Neipperg. See Mrs Cuthell's *An Imperial Victim* (1911); works by Imbert de Saint-Amand (trans. 1886–91), Billard (trans. 1910), Méneval (1911); her *Correspondance* (1887); the *Mémoires* of Mme Durand (1885); Life by E. M. Oddie (1931).

MARIE LOUISE, full name **Francisca Josepha Louise Augusta Marie Helene Christina, Princess** (1872–1956), granddaughter of Queen Victoria, daughter of Prince Christian of Schleswig-Holstein and great-aunt of Queen Elizabeth II. In 1891 she married Prince Aribert of Anhalt, but the marriage was dissolved in 1900 by her father-in-law and the Princess returned to England, where she dedicated herself to social and charitable work. See *My Memories of Six Reigns* (1956).

MARIETTE PASHA, Auguste Édouard (1821–1881), Egyptian explorer, was born at Boulogne, where he was made professor in 1841. In 1849 he entered the Louvre, and in 1850 was dispatched to Egypt, where he brought to light important monuments and inscriptions in Memphis, Sakkara and Gizeh. In 1858 he was appointed keeper of monuments to the Egyptian government, and excavated the Sphinx, the temples of Dendera and Edfu, and made many other discoveries. He wrote various works and his *Itinéraire de la haute Égypte* was translated by his brother (*Monuments of Upper Egypt*, 1877). He was made a pasha in 1879. See his *Oeuvres diverses* (1904) with Life by Maspero.

MARIN, John (1872–1953), American artist, born in New Jersey, trained and worked as an architect before studying art in Pennsylvania, New York and Paris. Famous for his brilliant watercolour sketches of the New York and Maine regions and for his unusual seascapes, he exhibited annually in New York from 1909. His paintings are to be found in many European and American galleries.

MARINETTI, Emilio Filippo Tommaso (1876–1944), Italian poet and writer, born in Alexandria, studied in Paris and Genoa, and published the original Futurist manifesto in *Figaro* in 1909. In his writings he glorified war, the machine age, speed and ' dynamism ', and in 1919 he became a Fascist. His publications include *Le Futurisme* (1911), *Teatro sintetico futurista* (1916) and *Manifesti del Futurismo* (4 vols. 1920). He condemned all traditional forms of literature and art, and his ideas were applied to painting by Boccioni, Balla and others. See *Il Potea Marinetti e il Futurismo* by A. Viviani (Turin 1940).

MARINI, Giambattista (1569–1625), an Italian poet who was born and died at Naples, was ducal secretary at Turin, and wrote his best work, the *Adone* (1622) at the court of France. His florid hyperbole and overstrained imagery were copied by the Marinist school. See study by J. V. Mirollo (1965).

MARIO, Guiseppe (1810–83), Italian tenor, by birth **Don Giovanni de Candia** and son of a general, born at Cagliari, achieved a long series of operatic triumphs in Paris, London, St Petersburg and America. His wife was the famous singer Giulia Grisi. After his retirement he lost his fortune through disastrous speculations. See Pearse and Hird's *Romance of a Great Singer* (1910).

MARIOTTE, Edme (1620–84), French physicist, born in Burgundy, was prior of St Martin-sous-Beaune, and died at Paris. One of the earliest members of the Academy of Sciences, he wrote on percussion, air and its pressure, the movements of fluid bodies and of pendulums, colours, &c. What was for a long time on the Continent called Mariotte's Law was rather Boyle's Law.

MARIS, Dutch family of three brothers, all painters. (1) **Jakob** (1837–99), painter of landscape and genre, was born at The Hague, and studied there, at Antwerp, and 1866–71 in Paris, coming under the influence of Diaz, Corot and Millet. (2) **Matthijs** (1839–1917) and (3) **Willem** (1843–1910), were also famous See D. C. Thomson, *The Brothers Maris* (' Studio ', 1907).

MARISCHAL. See KEITH (4).

MARITAIN, Jacques, *ma-ree-ti* (1882–), French Catholic philosopher, was professor at the Institut Catholique in Paris (1913–40) and subsequently at Toronto, and from 1948 at Princeton. He early abandoned Bergsonism for orthodox neo-Thomism and was converted to Roman Catholicism. His most thorough-going philosophical work is *Distinguer pour unir, ou Les degrés du savoir* (1932, trans. 1938), He is best known outside France for his numerous writings on art, politics and history, including *Creative Intuition in Art and Poetry* (1953) and *On the Philosophy of History* (1957), &c. He was French ambassador to the Holy See (1945–1948). See study by C. A. Fecher (1953).

MARIUS, (1) **Gaius** (157–86 B.C.), Roman general, served at Numantia (134), and in 119 was tribune. He served in Africa during the war against Jugurtha, and as consul ended it in 106. Meanwhile an immense horde of Cimbri and Teutons had burst into Gaul, and repeatedly defeated the Roman forces. Marius, consul for the second, third, fourth and fifth times (104–101), annihilated them after two years' fighting in a terrible two days' battle near Aix, in Provence, where 100,000 Teutons were slain; and turning to the Cimbri in north Italy, crushed them also near Vercellae (101). Marius was declared the saviour of the state, the third founder of Rome, and was made consul for the sixth time in 100. When Sulla as consul was entrusted with the conduct of the Mithridatic war, Marius, insanely jealous of his patrician rival, attempted to deprive him of the command, and a civil war began (88). Marius was soon forced to flee, and after frightful hardships and hairbreadth escapes made his way to Africa. Here he remained until a rising of his friends took place under Cinna. He then hurried back to Italy, and, with Cinna marched against Rome, which had to yield. Marius was delirious in his revenge upon the aristocracy; 4000 slaves carried on the work of murder for five days and nights. Marius and Cinna were elected consuls for the year 86, but Marius died a fortnight afterwards.

(2) (Ger. Mayr), Simon (1570–1624), German astronomer, a pupil of Tycho Brahe, in 1609 claimed to have discovered the four satellites of Jupiter independently of Galileo. He named them Io, Europa, Ganymede and Callisto, but other astronomers would not follow his example and merely numbered them, as they did not recognize his claim to discovery. He was one of the earliest users of a telescope and the first to observe by this means the Andromeda nebula (1612).

MARIVAUX, Pierre Carlet de Chamblain de, *ma-ree-vō* (1688–1763), born at Paris of a good Norman family, published *L'Homère travesti*, a burlesque of the *Iliad*, in 1716, and brought out his best comedy, *Le Jeu de l'amour et du hasard* in 1730. His famous romance, *La Vie de Marianne* (1731–41), he never concluded; it is marked by an affected ' precious ' style—' Marivaudage '. His numerous comedies are the work of a clever analyst rather than a dramatist. His other romances, *Pharamond* and *Le Paysan parvenu*, are greatly inferior to *Marianne*. See works by Fleury (1881), Deschamps (1897), Green (1928), McKee (1959).

MARK, more fully, ' John, whose surname was Mark ' (Acts, xii. 12, 25), is named by the oldest tradition as the author of the second canonical gospel. Mark accompanied Paul and Barnabas on their first missionary journey, but quitted them at Perga, was later reconciled with Paul, and, according to tradition, was the ' disciple and interpreter ' of Peter in Rome. He is also said to have gone to Alexandria as preacher. In medieval art Mark is symbolized by the lion.

MARK ANTONY. See ANTONIUS.

MARKHAM, (1) Mrs. See PENROSE.

(2) **Sir Clements Robert** (1830–1916), English geographer, born at Stillingfleet near York, educated at Westminster, was in the navy 1844–51, and served in the Franklin search. He explored (1852–54) Peru, introduced (1860) cinchona culture from South America into India, and was geographer (1867–68) to the Abyssinian expedition. He wrote travel books and biographies, and edited the *Geographical Magazine* (1872–1878). He was made K.C.B. (1896). See Life (1917) by his brother, Sir Albert H. Markham (1841–1918), well-known Arctic voyager.

MARKIEVICZ, Constance Georgine, Countess, *mahr-kyay'vich* (1868–1927), Irish nationalist, daughter of Sir Henry Gore-Booth of County Sligo, married Count Casimir Markievicz, fought in the Easter Rebellion (1916) and was sentenced to death but reprieved. Elected the first British woman M.P. in 1918, she did not take her seat, but was a member of the Dail from 1923. See Life by S. O'Faoláin (1934).

MARKOVA, Dame Alicia, professional name of Lilian Alivia Marks, *mar-ko'fa* (1910–), English prima ballerina, born in London, after studying under Seraphine Astafieva, joined the Diaghilev company in 1924, and appeared for the Sadlers Wells Ballet

company from 1933 to 1935. There followed a period of partnership with Anton Dolin, after which she joined the Ballet Russe de Monte Carlo and (1941–45) the Opera Ballet of New York Metropolitan Opera; then, after further collaboration with Dolin, she was from 1950 to 1952 prima ballerina of the Festival Ballet Company. She was created C.B.E. in 1958 and D.B.E. in 1963. See biography by H. Fisher (1964).

MARLBOROUGH, John Churchill, 1st Duke of (1650–1722), English general, born either May 26 or June 24 (according to different sources), the son of Sir Winston Churchill, an impoverished Devonshire Royalist. Young Churchill's first post was as page to the Duke of York. Handsome and attractive, the favour of the voluptuous Duchess of Cleveland enriched him with a *douceur* of £5000, and secured him an ensigncy in the Guards. Meritorious service in Tangier and with the British contingent under the Duke of Monmouth and Marshal Turenne in Holland, together with the influence of his cousin Arabella as York's mistress, combined to bring Churchill promotion to colonel. His prospects were even further enhanced by his clandestine marriage, in 1677, to the beautiful termagant, Sarah Jennings. In 1678 his discreet handling of a confidential mission to William of Orange led to his ennoblement as Baron Churchill of Eyemouth in Scotland (1682). In 1685 he faithfully completed the task of quelling the rebellion raised by his old comrade-in-arms, Monmouth; his reward being an English barony. But with the landing of the Prince of Orange his lingering fealty to an obviously moribund cause was not proof against the call of ambition, and he pledged his support to the cause of ' Dutch Billy '. The value of his defection was recognized by his elevation to the earldom of Marlborough. Yet by 1692, despite his brilliant service in William's Irish campaign, the suspicion that he was still sympathetic to the Jacobites brought him into temporary disfavour. It was not until the War of the Spanish Succession that the supreme command of the British forces was conferred on him by Queen Anne, with an annual stipend of £10,000. Marlborough's earlier activities were gravely hampered by the reluctance of the Dutch field deputies to commit their troops to action. But as the British Army gained in strength, the Duke could operate with greater impact and freedom. His splendidly organized march to the Danube brought him the invaluable co-operation of Prince Eugène of Savoy, and led to the victory of Donauworth and the costly but unequivocal triumph of Blenheim. Made a prince of the Holy Roman Empire, additional honours were showered upon the victor—the Garter, a dukedom, the mastergeneralship of the ordnance, and an estate and palatial residence at Woodstock, while Duchess Sarah flaunted it as groom of the stole, mistress of the robes, keeper of the privy purse, and the Queen's bosom friend. In the campaign of 1706 the military pretensions of Louis XIV were sharply rebuffed at Ramillies; while in 1708 Vendôme's attempt to recover Flanders led to his shattering defeat at Oudenarde and the surrender of Lille and Ghent. With superior man-power to call upon, the French recovered from their failure at Malplaquet of 1709; but in 1711 the manoeuvre by which Marlborough forced Villars' 'impregnable' *ne plus ultra* lines and went on to capture Bouchain, exhibited the hallmark of consummate generalship. But in England Harley and the Tories had been conspiring for a compromise peace—the Treaty of Utrecht, which sacrificed virtually all the objects for which the war had been fought—and for Marlborough's public overthrow. In this design Harley was inadvertently aided by the folly with which Sarah still sought to domineer over a queen who, wearying of being hectored, had transferred her favour to the Duchess's cousin, the subtle intriguante Abigail Masham. Charges were preferred against the Duke of having illicitly received some £63,000 in regular payments from the Army's bread contractors, and a deduction of 2½ per cent. from the pay of the foreign auxiliaries. Despite the fact that Marlborough proved conclusively that this was a perquisite regularly allowed to the commander-in-chief in Flanders to maintain his secret service fund, on December 31, 1711, the Duke was dismissed from all public employment. In appointing the Duke of Ormond as his successor, the Ministry proceeded to confirm him in the very perquisites it had previously declared to be illegal. Publicly reviled in England, for a time Marlborough sojourned in honoured retirement abroad. With the accession of George I the Duke was restored to his honours; his advice being freely sought at the time of the Jacobite uprising of 1715. He died on June 16, 1722; his obsequies in Westminster Abbey being attended by many loyal but humble veterans of his campaigns. Singularly sweet tempered and serene, Marlborough was a devoted husband and fond parent. His concern for the welfare of his troops was deep-rooted and unfailing; and having restored mobility to warfare, he exploited it with a skill amounting to genius. If, on occasion, he employed somewhat dubious means to secure his advancement, that was no more than the common practice of the times in which he lived. See Lives by Coxe (1819), Lord Wolseley (1894), Fortescue (1932), Belloc (1933) and W. S. Churchill (1933). **Sarah Jennings**, who was born in 1660, survived till October 1744. See studies by S. J. Reid (1914), Dobrée (1927), F. Chancellor (1932) and L. Kronenberger (1958).

For 3rd Duke, see SUNDERLAND (3).

MARLOWE, Christopher (1564–93), the greatest of Shakespeare's predecessors in English drama, was born, a shoemaker's son, at Canterbury. From the King's School there he was sent to Benet (now Corpus) College, Cambridge; proceeded B.A. in 1583; and commenced M.A. in 1587. His *Tamburlaine the Great*, in two parts, was first printed in 1590, and probably produced in 1587. In spite of its bombast and violence it is infinitely superior to any tragedy that had yet appeared on the English stage. Earlier dramatists had employed blank verse, but it had been stiff and ungainly, and Marlowe was the first to discover its strength and variety. The *Tragical History of Dr Faustus* was probably produced soon after *Tamburlaine*; the earliest edition is dated 1604. *Faustus* is rather a series of detached scenes than a finished drama; some of these scenes are evidently not by Marlowe; but the nobler scenes are marvellously impressive. *The Jew of Malta*, produced after 1588 and first published in 1633, is a very unequal play. The first two acts are conducted with masterly skill and vigour; but the last three are absurdly extravagant, degenerating into vulgar caricature. *Edward II*, produced about 1590, is the most mature of Marlowe's plays. It has not the magnificent poetry that we find in *Faustus* and in the first two acts of *The Jew of Malta*, but it is planned and executed with more firmness and solidity. The various characters are skilfully discriminated, and the action is never allowed to flag. Many critics have preferred it to Shakespeare's *Richard II*; it is certainly no whit inferior. *The Massacre at Paris*, the weakest of Marlowe's plays, has descended in a mutilated state. It was written after the assassination of Henry III of France (August 2, 1589), and was probably one of the latest plays. *The Tragedy of Dido* (1594), left probably in a fragmentary state by Marlowe and finished by Nash, is of slight value. Marlowe had doubtless a hand in the three parts of *Henry VI*, and probably in *Titus Andronicus*. A wild, shapeless tragedy, *Lust's Dominion* (1657), may have been adapted from one of Marlowe's lost plays. The unfinished poem, *Hero and Leander*, composed in heroic couplets of consummate beauty, was first published in 1598; a second edition, with Chapman's continuation, followed the same year. Shakespeare quoted in *As You Like It* the line, 'Who ever loved that loved not at first sight?' and feelingly apostrophized the poet as 'Dead Shepherd'. Marlowe's translations of Ovid's *Amores* and of the first book of Lucan's *Pharsalia* add nothing to his fame. The pastoral ditty, 'Come, live with me and be my love,' to which Sir Walter Raleigh wrote an Answer, was imitated, but not equalled, by Herrick, Donne and others. It was first printed in *The Passionate Pilgrim* (1599), without the fourth and sixth stanzas, with the author's name, 'C. Marlowe', subscribed. Another anthology, Allot's *England's Parnassus* (1600), preserves a fragment by Marlowe, beginning 'I walked along a stream for pureness rare'. Marlowe led an irregular life, mingled with the *canaille*, and was on the point of being arrested for disseminating atheistic opinions when, in May 1593, at the age of twenty-nine, he was fatally stabbed at Deptford in a tavern brawl. In tragedy he prepared the way for Shakespeare, on whose early work his influence is firmly stamped. See the editions by Dyce (1850 and 1858), Cunningham (1872), Havelock Ellis (best plays; 1887), Bullen (1888), Tucker-Brooke (1910) and Case (1930). See books by Ingram (1904), Hotson (1925), Ellis-Fermor (1927), Boas (1929, 1940), Eccles (1934), Bakeless (1938, 1942), Norman (1948), Steane (1964).

MARMION, (1) of Scrivelsby, the family

which long provided the hereditary champions at English coronations, came in with the Conqueror, but became extinct under Edward I.

(2) **Shackerley** (1603–39), minor dramatist, born at Aynho, Northants, squandered a fortune, and fought in the Low Countries. He left behind an epic, *Cupid and Psyche*, and three comedies, *Holland's Leaguer*, *A Fine Companion* and *The Antiquary*.

(3) **Simon** (1425–89), French miniaturist, born probably at Amiens, whose illuminations are the finest in 15th-century manuscript art.

MARMONT, Auguste Frédéric Louis Viesse de (1774–1852), Marshal of France, was born at Châtillon-sur-Seine, went with Napoleon to Italy, and fought at Lodi, in Egypt, and at Marengo. He was sent to Dalmatia in 1805, defeated the Russians there, and was made Duke of Ragusa. In 1809 he was entrusted at Wagram with the pursuit of the enemy, won the battle of Znaim, and earned a marshal's baton. He was next governor of the Illyrian provinces, and in 1811 succeeded Massena in Portugal. A severe wound at Salamanca compelled him to retire to France. In 1813 he fought at Lützen, Bautzen and Dresden, and maintained the contest in France in 1814 till further resistance was hopeless, when he concluded a truce with the Russians, which compelled Napoleon to abdicate, and earned Marmont from the Bonapartists the title of the traitor. The Bourbons loaded him with honours. At the Revolution of 1830 he endeavoured to reduce Paris to submission, and finally retreating with a few faithful battalions, conducted Charles X across the frontier. Thenceforward he resided chiefly in Vienna or in Venice, where he died. See his *Esprit des institutions militaires* (1845) and his *Mémoires* (9 vols. 1856–57).

MARMONTEL, Jean François (1723–99), French author, was born at Bort in the Limousin, and studied in a Jesuit college. Settling in Paris in 1745 by advice of Voltaire, he wrote successful tragedies and operas, and in 1753 got a secretaryship at Versailles through Madame de Pompadour. In the official journal, *Le Mercure*, now under his charge, he began his oft-translated *Contes moraux* (1761). Elected to the Academy in 1763, he became its secretary in 1783, as well as historiographer of France. His most celebrated work was *Bélisaire*, a dull and wordy political romance, containing a chapter on toleration which excited furious hostility. His uncritical *Éléments de littérature* (1787) consists of his contributions to the *Encyclopédie*. See his *Mémoires* (1805), Saintsbury's edition of the *Moral Tales* (1895) and study by Knauer (1936).

MARMORA, La. See LA MARMORA.

MARNIX, Philippe de, Baron de St Aldegonde (1538–98), Flemish statesman, born at Brussels, studied under Calvin and Beza at Geneva, and at home was active in the Reformation, and in 1566 in the revolt against Spain. An intimate friend of William of Orange, he represented him at the first meeting of the Estates of the United Provinces, held at Dort in 1572, and was sent on special missions to the courts of France and England. As burgomaster of Antwerp, he defended the city thirteen months against the Spaniards; but having then capitulated, he incurred so much ill-will that he retired from public life. He wrote the patriotic *Wilhelmus* song; the prose satire, *The Roman Beehive* (1569); a metrical translation of the Psalms (1580); and part of a prose translation of the Bible. See Lives in Dutch by Broes (1840), Frédéricq (1882), von Schelven (1939), and in French by Juste (1858).

MARO. See VIRGIL.

MAROCHETTI, Carlo, Baron, *ma-ro-ket'tee* (1805–67), sculptor, born at Turin and trained at Paris and in Rome, settled at Paris, and at the revolution of 1848 came to London, where he produced many fine statues (Queen Victoria, Coeur-de-Lion, &c.). He died at Passy.

MAROT, Clément, *ma-rō* (c. 1497–1544), French poet, born at Cahors, entered the service of the Princess Margaret, afterwards Queen of Navarre. He was wounded at the battle of Pavia in 1525, and soon after imprisoned on a charge of heresy, but liberated next spring. He made many enemies by his witty satires, and in 1535 fled first to the court of the Queen of Navarre, and later to that of the Duchess of Ferrara. He returned to Paris in 1536, and in 1538 began to translate the Psalms into French, which when sung to secular airs, helped to make the new views fashionable; but the part published in 1541 having been condemned by the Sorbonne, he had again to flee in 1543. He made his way to Geneva, but, finding Calvin's company uncongenial, went on to Turin, where he died. His poems consist of elegies, epistles, rondeaux, ballads, sonnets, madrigals, epigrams, nonsense verses and longer pieces; his special gift lay in badinage and graceful satire. Probably, like many of his friends, he had no very definite theological beliefs. See Life by Vitet (1868); Douen's *Clément Marot et le Psautier Huguenot* (1879), Plattard's *Marot, sa carrière poétique, son oeuvre* (1938), and Kinch, *La Poésie satirique de Clément Marot*.

MAROZIA (d. 938), a Roman lady of noble birth, but of infamous reputation, was thrice married, the mistress of Pope Sergius III, and mother of Pope John XI and grandmother of Pope John XII. She had influence enough to secure the deposition of Pope John X, her mother's lover, and the election of her own son, John XI. She died in prison at Rome.

MARQUAND, John Phillips (1893–1960), American writer, born at Wilmington, Del., known for his detective stories and social satires, some with an oriental background. His *The Late George Apley* (1937) won him the Pulitzer prize. See study by Hamburger (1953).

MARQUET, (Pierre) Albert, *mar-kay* (1875–1947), French artist, born at Bordeaux, studied under Gustave Moreau and was one of the original Fauves. After initial hardships, he became primarily an Impressionist landscape painter and travelled widely, painting many pictures of the Seine (e.g., the *Pont neuf*), Le Havre and Algiers in a cool restrained style. In his swift sketches he showed himself a master of line.

MARQUETTE, Jacques (1637–75), French Jesuit missionary, born at Laon, was sent in 1666 to North America, where he brought Christianity to the Ottawa Indians around Lake Superior and accompanied Jolliet on the expedition which discovered and explored the Mississippi (1673). See his account of the journey, and a *Life* by A. Repplier (1929).

MARQUIS, Don, properly **Donald Robert** (1878–1937), American writer, was a New York columnist, creator of comic characters (the Old Soak, Archy the cockroach, Mehitabel the cat, &c.) which he used as vehicles for social and political satire.

MARRIOTT, (1) Charles (1811–58), English divine who was associated with the Tractarian and Oxford movements, joint editor of *The Library of the Fathers*. See J. W. Burgon's *Twelve Good Men* (1888); B. C. Boulter's *Anglican Reformers* (1933).

(2) **Sir John Arthur Ransome** (1859–1945), English historian and educationist, was educated at Oxford, where he later administered successfully for twenty-five years the University Extension delegacy. From 1917 to 1929 he was a member of parliament, and was knighted in 1924. He was an expert on the Eastern Question, modern European history and the British Empire, on which subjects he wrote extensively.

MARRYAT, (1) Florence (1838–99), English novelist, daughter of (2), was successively Mrs Ross Church and Mrs Lean, was born at Brighton, and from 1865 published about eighty novels, besides a drama and many articles in periodicals. She edited *London Society* (1872–76). See H. C. Black's *Notable Women Authors* (1893).

(2) **Frederick** (1792–1848), English naval officer and novelist, father of (1), the son of an M.P., in 1806 sailed as midshipman under Lord Cochrane. After service in the West Indies, he had command of a sloop cruising off St Helena to guard against the escape of Napoleon (1820–21); he also did good work in suppressing the Channel smugglers, and some hard fighting in Burmese rivers. On his return to England (1826) he was made C.B., and was given the command of the *Ariadne* (1828). He resigned in 1830, and thenceforth led the life of a man of letters. He was the author of a series of novels on sea life of which the best known are *Frank Mildmay* (1829), *Peter Simple* (1833), *Jacob Faithful* (1834) and *Mr Midshipman Easy* (1834). In 1837 Marryat set out for a tour through the United States, where he wrote *The Phantom Ship* (1839) and a drama, *The Ocean Waif*. He received £1200 for *Mr Midshipman Easy* and £1600 for his *Diary in America* (1839), but was extravagant and unlucky in his speculations, and at last was financially embarrassed. *Poor Jack, Masterman Ready, The Poacher* and *Percival Keene* appeared before he settled (1843) on his small farm of Langham, Norfolk, where he spent his days in farming and in writing stories for children. He died at Langham, August 9, 1848. For improvements in signalling, &c., he had been made F.R.S. (1819) and a

member of the Legion of Honour (1833). As a writer of sea stories Marryat has no superior; his sea fights, his chases and cutting-out expeditions, are told with irresistible gusto. See *Collected Novels* (26 vols. 1929–30), the *Life and Letters* by his daughter (1872) and Lives by D. Hannay (1889), C. Lloyd (1939), O. Warner (1953).

MARS, Anne Françoise Boutet Monvel (1779–1847), was a leading French actress at the Comédie-Française from 1799, excelling in the plays of Molière and Beaumarchais. She retired in 1841. See *Mémoires* (2 vols. 1849) and *Confidences* (3 vols. 1855).

MARSCHNER, Heinrich (1795–1861), German operatic composer, born at Zittau, successively music director at Dresden, Leipzig and Hanover, is remembered mainly for his opera *Hans Heiling*. See Lives by G. Fischer (Hanover 1918) and G. Hausswald (Dresden 1938).

MARSH, (1) George Perkins (1801–82), American diplomatist and philologist, was born in 1801 at Woodstock, Vermont; studied law; was elected to congress in 1842; and was U.S. minister to Turkey (1849–53) and Italy (1861–82). He was made LL.D. of Harvard in 1859. He died at Vallombrosa in Italy, July 23, 1882. He wrote *Lectures on the English Language* (1861), *Origin and History of English* (1862), *Man and Nature* (1864; largely recast, 1874), &c. See Life by his widow (1888).

(2) **James** (1789–1846), English chemist, expert on poisons, worked at the Royal Arsenal, Woolwich, and assisted Faraday at the Military Academy for a payment of thirty shillings a week, thereby leaving his widow and family in straitened circumstances. He invented the standard test for arsenic which has been given his name.

(3) **Othniel Charles** (1831–99), American palaeontologist, born at Lockport, N.Y., October 29, 1831, studied at Yale, at New Haven, and in Germany, and became first professor of Palaeontology at Yale 1866. He discovered (mainly in the Rocky Mountains) over a thousand species of extinct American vertebrates, and described them in monographs (published by government) on *Odontornithes* (1880), *Dinocerata* (1884), *Sauropoda* (1888), &c. He died March 18, 1899. See Life by C. M. Le Vene (1940).

MARSHAL, William, 1st Earl of Pembroke and Strigul (c. 1146–1219), English knight, regent of England (1216–19), a nephew of the Earl of Salisbury, won a military reputation fighting the French and in 1170 was appointed tutor to the young prince Henry. After displaying his knightly prowess in Europe, he supported Henry against Richard Coeur de Lion and at his dying behest went on a crusade to the Holy Land. Pardoned by Richard, who recognized his worth, he was given in 1189 the hand of the heiress of Strongbow (q.v.), which brought him his earldom. He was appointed a justiciar and shared the marshalcy of England with his brother John until the latter's death gave him full office. He saw further fighting in Normandy in 1196–99, and after Richard had been mortally wounded he supported the new king, John, but was shabbily treated by him and spent the years 1207–12 in Ireland. When John's troubles with the pope and with his barons began to mount, however, his loyalty asserted itself, and he returned to become the king's chief adviser. After John's death in 1216 he was by common consent appointed regent for the nine-year-old Henry III, and as such concluded a peace treaty with the French. He died at Caversham, having served in the reigns of four monarchs with unswerving fidelity.

MARSHALL, (1) Alfred (1842–1924), English economist, born in London, and educated at Merchant Taylors' and St John's, Cambridge, became a fellow (1865), principal of University College, Bristol (1877), lecturer on Political Economy at Balliol (1883) and professor of Political Economy at Cambridge (1885–1908). Of his works, his *Principles of Economics* (1890) is still a standard text-book, containing his concept of ' time analysis ' and other contributions to the science. See Pigou's study (1926), and his wife's autobiography, *What I remember* (1951).

(2) **General George Catlett** (1880–1959), American soldier and statesman, born at Uniontown, Pa., was educated at the Virginia Military Institute, and commissioned in 1901. He rose to the highest rank and as chief of staff (1939–45) he directed the U.S. Army throughout the second World War. After two years in China as special representative of the president he became secretary of state (1947–49) and originated the Marshall Aid plan for the post-war reconstruction of Europe (E.R.P.). He was awarded the Nobel Peace Prize in 1953. See *Speeches* ed. H. A. De Weerd (1945).

(3) **John** (1755–1835), American judge, born in Virginia, studied law, but served 1775–79 in the army. He rose in his profession, in 1788 was elected to the state convention and in 1799 to Congress. In 1800–01 he was secretary of state; and from 1801 he was chief-justice of the United States. His decisions are a standard authority on constitutional law; a selection was published at Boston in 1839. He wrote a Life of Washington (1807; new ed. 1892). See monograph by Magruder (1885) and Lives by A. J. Beveridge (1916), D. Loth (1949).

(4) **William Calder** (1813–94), Scottish sculptor, was born in Edinburgh, and trained under Chantrey. He exhibited at the Royal Academy, becoming A.R.S.A. 1842 and R.A. 1852. As well as memorial statues, busts, &c., he did the group *Agriculture* on the Albert Memorial.

MARSHMAN, Joshua (1768–1837), English missionary and orientalist, born at Westbury, Leigh, Wilts, had been a bookseller's apprentice, a weaver and a schoolmaster, when in 1799 he went as a Baptist missionary to Serampur, where he founded a college and translated the Bible into various dialects.— His son, John Clark (1794–1877), assisted his father in his work and later made much by publishing, and spent much on native education, returning to England in 1852. He wrote *History of India* (1842; 5th ed. 1860), *Life and Times of the Serampore Missionaries* (1859), &c.

MARSTON, (1) John (1576–1634), English dramatist and satirist, a son of John Marston of Gayton in Salop, by his wife, daughter of an Italian surgeon, was born at Wardington, Oxfordshire, and studied at Brasenose, Oxford. Except *The Insatiate Countess* (which is of doubtful authorship), all his plays were published between 1602 and 1607. He then gave up play-writing, took orders in 1609, and in 1616–31 held the living of Christ Church, Hampshire. He died in London. His first work was *The Metamorphosis of Pygmalion's Image: and Certain Satires* (1598). The licentious poem was condemned by Archbishop Whitgift. Another series of uncouth and obscure satires, *The Scourge of Villany*, appeared in the same year. Two gloomy and ill-constructed tragedies, *Antonio and Mellida* and *Antonio's Revenge*, were published in 1602; in them passages of striking power stand out above the general mediocrity. *The Malcontent* (1604), more skilfully constructed, was dedicated to Ben Jonson, between whom and Marston there were many quarrels and reconciliations. *Eastward Ho* (1605), written in conjunction with Chapman and Jonson, is far more genial than any comedy that Marston wrote single-handed. For some reflections on the Scots the authors were imprisoned (1604). Other plays include *Parasitaster, or the Fawn* (1606), *Sophonisba* (1606) and *What You Will* (1607). The rich and graceful poetry scattered through *The Insatiate Countess* (1613) is unlike anything that we find in Marston's undoubted works. Probably Marston left the play unfinished when he took orders, and William Barksteed took it in hand. See editions by Halliwell-Phillipps (1856), Bullen (1887) and Harvey Wood (1934 *et seq*.), and works by M. S. Allen (Columbus 1920) and T. S. Eliot (in *Elizabethan Essays* 1934).

(2) **John Westland** (1819–90), English dramatic poet, father of (3), born at Boston, gave up law for literature; and in 1842 his *Patrician's Daughter* was brought out at Drury Lane by Macready. It was the most successful of more than a dozen plays, all Sheridan-Knowlesian, and all forgotten. He wrote a novel (1860), a good book on *Our Recent Actors* (1888), and a mass of poetic criticism. He died in London, January 5. See his Collected Works (2 vols. 1876).

(3) **Philip Bourke** (1850–87), English poet, son of (2), was born in London, became blind at the age of three. He was grief-stricken at the death of his fiancée and then of his sisters, and his friends, Oliver Madox Brown and Rossetti. He is remembered for his friendship with Rossetti, Watts-Dunton and Swinburne rather than for his sonnets and lyrics—although a few of these are exquisite. *Songtide, All in All* and *Wind Voices* were the three volumes of poetry he published between 1870 and 1883; to a posthumous collection of his short stories (1887) is prefixed a memoir by W. Sharp. See Life by C. C. Osborne (1926).

MARTEL, (1) Charles. See CHARLES MARTEL.

(2) **Sir Giffard Le Quesne** (1889–1958), British soldier, during World War I aided in the development of the first tanks, and in 1925 was responsible for the construction of the first one-man tank. In 1940 he com-

manded the Royal Armoured Corps and in 1943 headed the British military mission in Moscow.

MARTEL DE JANVILLE, Comtesse de. See GYP.

MARTEN, Harry (1602–80), English regicide, elder son of the civilian, Sir Henry Marten (c. 1562–1641), was born and educated at Oxford. He was a prominent member of the Long Parliament, but was expelled from it 1643–46 as an extremist, and fought meantime in the great Rebellion. He sat on Charles I's trial, led an immoral life and fell into debt, had his life spared at the Restoration, but died still a prisoner at Chepstow. See Forster's *Lives of British Statesmen* (vol. iv, 1837).

MARTENSEN, Hans Lassen (1808–84), Danish theologian, Metropolitan of Denmark, became professor of Philosophy at Copenhagen, and in 1845 court-preacher also. In 1840 he published a monograph on *Meister Eckhart*, and in 1849 the conservative Lutheran *Christian Dogmatics* (trans. 1866). This gained him in 1854 the primacy, but provoked a powerful attack by Kierkegaard. His *Christian Ethics* (1871–78; trans. 1873–1892) made his influence more dominant than ever. See his *Autobiography* (1883), and Life by S. Arildsen (Copenhagen 1932).

MARTIAL, Marcus Valerius Martialis (c. 40–c. A.D. 104), Latin poet and epigrammatist, born in Spain, came to Rome in A.D. 64 and became a client of the influential Spanish house of the Senecas, through which he found a patron in L. Calpurnius Piso. The tragic failure of the Pisonian plot lost Martial his warmest friends—Lucan and Seneca. He courted imperial and senatorial patronage by his *vers de circonstance*. When (A.D. 80) Titus dedicated the Colosseum, Martial's epigrams brought him equestrian rank; this flattery of Domitian was gross and venal. Advancing years having bereft him of Domitian and his friends of the palace, in a fit of home-sickness he borrowed from his admirer, the younger Pliny, the means of returning to Bilbilis, where he spent the rest of his life. Much of his best work is his least pure. If, however, we excise 150 epigrams from the 1172 of the first twelve books, his writings are free from licentiousness. His genius and skill in verse are hard to over-estimate. See the editions of Martial by Friedländer (1886), Lindsay (1902) and Ker (with trans. 1919–20).

MARTIN, St (c. 316–c. 400), Bishop of Tours, was born, a military tribune's son, at Sabaria in Pannonia, was educated at Pavia, and served in the army under Constantine and Julian. He became a disciple of Hilary of Poitiers, and, returning to Pannonia, was so persecuted by the Arian party that he removed first to Italy, then to Gaul, where about 360 he founded a monastery near Poitiers; but in 371–72 he was drawn by force from his retreat, and made Bishop of Tours. The fame of his sanctity and his repute as a worker of miracles attracted crowds of visitants; and to avoid distraction he established the monastery of Marmoutier near Tours, in which he himself resided. His Life by his contemporary, Sulpicius Severus,

teems with miraculous legends. See Cazenove's *St Hilary and St Martin* (1883), Scullard's *Martin of Tours* (1891); Life by P. Monceaux (Paris 1926, Eng. trans. 1928).

MARTIN, the name of five popes.

St Martin I, a Tuscan, became pope in 649, held the first Lateran Council (against the Monothelites), and was banished by Constans II in 654 to the Crimea, where he died in 655.

Martin II, properly Marinus I, born at Gallese, was pope 883–884.

Martin III, properly Marinus II, was pope in 942–946.

Martin IV, Simon de Brie (c. 1210–85), born at Montpensier in Touraine, elected pope in 1281, was a mere tool of Charles of Anjou.

Martin V, Oddone Colonna (1368–1431), in the pontiff in whose election the Western Schism was finally extinguished, was elected in 1417 during the Council of Constance, over whose remaining sessions he presided. He died suddenly in 1431, just after the opening of the Council of Basel. See work by K. A. Finke (Berlin 1938).

MARTIN, (1) **Archer John Porter** (1910–   ), British biochemist, with R. L. M. Synge developed the technique of paper chromatography now widely used in chemistry for purposes of analysis and shared the Nobel prize for chemistry (1952).

(2) **Bon Louis Henri,** *mar-tĭ* (1810–83), French historian, was born at St Quentin, February 20, 1810, and educated as a notary. He joined Paul Lacroix, the 'Bibliophile Jacob', in his vast project for a History of France in 48 vols. of extracts from old histories and chronicles, published the first volume in 1833, and henceforward toiled alone at the work, which was completed on a reduced scale in 1836, as the great *Histoire de France* (15 vols.). Martin was chosen deputy for Aisne in 1871, senator in 1876 and a member of the Academy in 1878. See Life by Hanotaux (1885), Mulot's *Souvenirs intimes* (1885), and Jules Simon's *Mignet, Michelet, Henri Martin* (1889).

(3) **Frank,** *mar-tĭ* (1890–   ), Swiss composer and pianist, born in Geneva, studied at Geneva Conservatoire and in 1928 was appointed professor at the Jacques-Dalcroze Institute in Geneva. His works are marked by refinement and precision of style, and include the oratorios *Golgotha* and *In Terra Pax,* a Mass and the cantata *Le Vin herbé*, based upon the legend of Tristan and Isolde, as well as incidental music and works for orchestra and chamber combinations.

(4) **John** (1789–1854), English painter, brother of (5), was born at Haydon Bridge near Hexham. After a struggling youth in London (from 1806) as an heraldic and enamel painter, he in 1812 exhibited at the Royal Academy the first of his sixteen 'sublime' works, displaying 'immeasurable spaces, innumerable multitudes, and gorgeous prodigies of architecture and landscape'. Their memory is kept lurid by the coloured engravings of the *Fall of Babylon* (1819), *Belshazzar's Feast* (1821), *The Deluge* (1826), &c. See Lives by M. L. Hendered (1923) and

T. Balston (1948), and study by J. Seznec (1964).

(5) **Jonathan** (1782–1838), brother of (4), after serving in the Navy became mentally deranged, developed extremist religious ideas and eventually fired York Minster in 1829. The rest of his life was spent in an asylum. See his *Autobiography* (1826 and later edns.).

(6) **Martin** (d. 1719), Scottish author and traveller, was a Skye factor, who took his M.D. at Leyden, and died in London in 1719. He wrote *Voyage to St Kilda* (1698) and *A Description of the Western Isles of Scotland* (1703) which aroused Dr Johnson's interest in the country.

(7) **Richard** (1754–1834), Irish lawyer and humanitarian, dubbed ' Humanity Martin ' by George IV, who was his friend, was born at Dublin and educated at Harrow and Trinity, Cambridge. As M.P. for Galway (1801–26) he sponsored in 1822 a bill to make illegal the cruel treatment of cattle, the first legislation of its kind. Through his efforts the R.S.P.C.A. was formed. See Life by W. Pain (1925).

(8) **Sir Theodore** (1816–1909), Scottish man of letters, born in Edinburgh and educated there, in 1846 settled in London, and became a parliamentary solicitor. The well-known *Bon Gaultier Ballads* (1855), written in conjunction with Aytoun, were followed by verse translations from Goethe, Horace, Catullus, Dante and Heine. He was requested by Queen Victoria to write the life of Prince Albert (5 vols. 1874–80) and also wrote Lives of Aytoun (1867), and Lord Lyndhurst (1883), and the Princess Alice (1885). His wife, **Helen Faucit** (1820–98), was a well-known actress, noted for her interpretations of Shakespeare's heroines. See Life by her husband (1900).

(9) **Violet Florence,** pseud. **Martin Ross** (1862–1915), Irish writer, born in County Galway, is known chiefly for a series of novels written in collaboration with her cousin **Edith Oenone Somerville** (1858–1949), including *An Irish Cousin* (1889), *Some Experiences of an Irish R.M.* (1908); also travel books about the Irish countryside.

MARTIN DU GARD, Roger, *mar-tĭ dü gahr* (1881–1958), French novelist, born at Neuilly, known for his eight-novel series *Les Thibault* (1922–40) dealing with family life during the first decades of the present century. Author also of several plays, he was awarded the Nobel prize in 1937. See study by H. C. Rice (1941).

MARTINEAU, (1) Harriet (1802–76), English writer, sister of (2), born at Norwich, June 12, in 1821 wrote her first article for the (Unitarian) *Monthly Repository*, and next produced *Devotional Exercises* and short stories about machinery and wages. In 1829 the failure of the house in which she, her mother and sisters had placed their money obliged her to earn her living. In 1832 she became a successful authoress through *Illustrations of Political Economy* (repeatedly refused by publishers), and settled in London. After a visit to America (1834–36) she published *Society in America* and a novel, *Deerbrook*, in 1839. From 1839 to 1844 she was an invalid at Tynemouth but recovered

through mesmerism (her subsequent belief in which alienated many friends), and fixed her abode at Ambleside in 1845, the year of *Forest and Game-law Tales*; after visiting Egypt and Palestine she issued *Eastern Life* (1848). In 1851, in conjunction with Mr H. G. Atkinson, she published *Letters on the Laws of Man's Social Nature* (so agnostic as to give much offence); and in 1853 she translated and condensed Comte's *Philosophie positive*. She also wrote much for the daily and weekly press and the larger reviews. Always delicate, and after 1820 very deaf, she died June 27, 1876, and was buried at Birmingham. See her *Autobiography* (1877), and Lives by T. Bosanquet (1927), J. C. Nevill (1943) and R. K. Webb (1960).

(2) **James** (1805–1900), English theologian, brother of (1), was born at Norwich, April 21. He was educated at the grammar-school there and under Dr Lant Carpenter at Bristol, and had been a Unitarian minister at Dublin and Liverpool, when in 1841 he was appointed professor of Mental and Moral Philosophy at Manchester New College. He removed to London in 1857, after that institution had been transferred thither, becoming also a pastor in Little Portland Street Chapel. He was principal of the college 1869–85. One of the profoundest thinkers and most effective writers of his day, he wrote *Endeavours after the Christian Life* (1843–47), *A Study of Spinoza* (1882), *Types of Ethical Theory* (1885), *A Study of Religion* (1888), *The Seat of Authority in Religion* (1890), &c. He died January 11, 1900. See his *Life and Letters* by Drummond and Upton (1902), and Carpenter's study (1905).

MARTINET, Jean (d. 1672), French officer, won renown as a military engineer and tactician (he devised forms of battle manœuvre, pontoon bridges, and a type of copper assault boat used in Louis XIV's Dutch campaign), but notoriety for his stringent and brutal forms of discipline.

MARTÍNEZ DE CAMPOS, Arsenio, *mar-tee'nayth* (1831–1900), Spanish general, put down one Cuban rebellion in 1877, but failing to end another, was recalled (1896).

MARTÍNEZ RUIZ, José. See AZORÍN.

MARTÍNEZ SIERRA, Gregorio (1881–1947), Spanish novelist and dramatist. A theatre manager and an original and creative producer as well as publisher, he was also a prolific writer. His plays *The Cradle Song* (Eng. trans. 1917), *The Kingdom of God* (Eng. trans. 1923) and *The Romantic Young Lady* (Eng. trans. 1923) were popular in England and America. Much of his writing was done in collaboration with his wife Maria, whose feminist opinions find expression in some of the plays.

MARTINI, (1) Frederick (1832–97), Swiss engineer, a Hungarian by birth and Swiss by adoption, served as engineer officer in the Austrian army in the Italian war of 1859, and establishing machine-works at Frauenfeld in Switzerland, invented the breech-action, which, with the Henry barrel, constituted the Martini-Henry rifle (1871).

(2), or **Memmi, Simone** (c. 1284–1344), Italian painter, born at Siena, was a pupil of Duccio and the most important artist of the

14th-century Sienese school, notable for his grace of line and exquisite colour. He worked at Assisi from 1333 to 1339 and at the Papal court at Avignon from then until 1344. His *Annunciation* is in the Uffizi Gallery. See *Simone Martini et les peintures de son école* (1920) by V. R. S. van Marle, and study by G. Paccagnini (trans. 1957).

MARTINU, Bohuslav, *mahr'ti-noo* (1890–1959), Czech composer, born at Polička. The son of a cobbler, Martinu began to compose at the age of ten, and in 1906 he was sent by a group of fellow-townsmen to Prague Conservatoire, where disciplinary regulations and the routine course of studies irritated him. Expelled from the Conservatoire, he played the violin in the Czech Philharmonic Orchestra, and in 1920 attracted attention with his ballet *Ishtar*. Readmitted to the Conservatoire, he studied under Suk until interest in the French Impressionist composers led him to work in Paris until 1941, when he escaped from Occupied France to America, where he produced a number of important works, including his first symphony, commissioned by Koussevitsky for the Boston Symphony Orchestra in 1942. In 1945 he ʼreturned to Prague as professor of Composition at the Conservatoire. A prolific composer, he ranges from orchestral works in 18th-century style, including a harpsichord concerto, to modern programme pieces evoked by unusual stimuli such as football (*Half Time*) or aeroplanes (*Thunderbolt P. 47*). His operas include the miniature *Comedy on a Bridge*, written for radio and successfully adapted for television and stage.

MARTIUS, Carl Friedrich Philipp von, *mahr'-tsee-oos* (1794–1868), German naturalist, born at Erlangen, studied medicine there, and in 1817–20 made important researches in Brazil, described in books on the journey and on the plants, aborigines and languages of the country. He was professor of Botany (1826–64) at Munich, where he died. See Lives by Schramm (2 vols. Leipzig 1869) and Meissner (Munich 1869).

MARTYN, Henry (1781–1812), English missionary, born at Truro, February 18, graduated from St John's College, Cambridge, as senior wrangler and first Smith's prizeman in 1801, and in 1802 became a fellow. Through the influence of Charles Simeon he sailed in 1805 for India as a chaplain under the Company. He translated the New Testament into Hindustani, Hindi and Persian, as well as the Prayer-book into Hindustani and the Psalms into Persian. After a missionary journey in Persia, he died of fever at Tokat in Asia Minor, October 16, 1812. See *Journals and Letters* (1837), and Lives by Sargent (1819; new ed. 1885), G. Smith (1892), and C. E. Padwick (1922).

MARTYR, Peter. See PETER.

MARVELL, Andrew (1621–78), English poet, born March 31, 1621, at Winestead rectory, S.E. Yorkshire, and educated at Hull and Trinity College, Cambridge, travelled (1642–1646) in Holland, France, Italy and Spain. After a period as tutor to Lord Fairfax's daughter, when he wrote his pastoral and garden poems, he was appointed tutor to Cromwell's ward, William Dutton; and in 1657 he became Milton's assistant. In January 1659 he took his seat in Richard Cromwell's parliament as member for Hull, for which he was returned again in 1660 and 1661. In 1663–65 he accompanied Lord Carlisle as secretary to the embassy to Muscovy, Sweden and Denmark, but the rest of his life was devoted to his parliamentary duties, doing battle against intolerance and arbitrary government. His republicanism was less the outcome of abstract theory than of experience. He accepted the Restoration without ceasing to praise Cromwell. His writings show him willing to give Charles II a fair chance, but convinced at last that the Stewarts must go. His last satires are a call to arms against monarchy. Though circulated in manuscript only, they were believed to endanger his life. He died in August 1678 through the stubborn ignorance of his physician—a baseless rumour suggested poison. Marvell's works are divided by the Restoration into two very distinct groups. After 1660 his pen was given up to politics, except when his friendship for Milton drew from him the lines prefixed to the second edition of *Paradise Lost*. In 1672–73 he wrote *The Rehearsal Transprosʼd* against religious intolerance; and in 1677 his most important tractate, the *Account of the Growth of Popery and Arbitrary Government*, was published anonymously. As a poet Marvell belongs to the pre-Restoration period. ʻA witty delicacyʼ, in Lamb's phrase, and a genuine enjoyment of nature and of gardens mark his poetry; Birrell recognizes his ʻglorious momentsʼ and ʻlovely stanzasʼ. He is perhaps the greatest master in English of the eight-syllable couplet. See books by Birrell (1905), Pierre Legouis (Paris 1928), Bradbrook and Thomas (1940).

MARX, (1) Julius (Groucho) (1895–   ), American comedian, born in New York. With his brothers **Leonard (Chico)** (1891–1961), **Arthur (Harpo)** (1893–1964) and **Herbert (Zeppo)** (1901–   ), he began his stage career in vaudeville in a team called the Six Musical Mascots that included his mother, Minnie (d. 1929), and an aunt. Later, the brothers appeared as The Four Nightingales and finally as the Marx Brothers. They appeared in musical comedy, but their main reputation was made in a series of films including *Animal Crackers*, *Monkey Business* (both 1932), *Horse Feathers* and *Duck Soup* (both 1933). Herbert retired from films in 1935 and the remaining trio scored further successes in *A Night at the Opera*, *A Day at the Races*, *A Day at the Circus*, *Go West* and *The Big Store*. The team then broke up and the brothers led individual careers. Each had a well-defined stencil: Groucho with his wisecracks, Chico, the pianist with his technique, and Harpo, the dumb clown and harp maestro. Julius Marx is the author of *Many Happy Returns* and a serious study of American Income Tax. See biography by Kyle Crichton (1951) and autobiography, *Groucho and Me* (1959).

(2) Karl (1818–83), German founder of modern international Communism, born at Trier, May 5, the son of a Jewish lawyer, studied law at Bonn and Berlin but took up history, Hegelian philosophy and Feuerbach's materialism. In 1842 he became editor of the democratic *Rheinische Zeitung* but his virulent attacks upon the government brought about its closure. He married, moved to Paris in 1843, and there wrote *Deutsch-französische Jahrbücher* (1843) and edited *Vorwärts* (1844). Expelled from Paris in 1845, he settled in Brussels, where he attacked Proudhon's socialist *Philosophie de la misère* with *Misère de la philosophie* (1847). With Engels (q.v.) as his closest collaborator and disciple, he reorganized the Communist League, which met in London in 1847. Engels having written a first draft, Marx rewrote the famous *Communist Manifesto* (1848), a masterpiece of political propaganda and intellectual brow-beating, ending with the celebrated watchwords: ' The workers have nothing to lose but their chains. They have a world to win. Workers of all lands, unite!' In it the state is attacked as a mere instrument of oppression, religion and culture are mere ideologies of the capitalist class, overproduction the latter's inevitable downfall. Utopian Socialism is dismissed as a feeble *petit-bourgeois* attempt to avoid the crash. The immediate result was Marx's expulsion from Brussels, and after participating in the revolutionary upheavals in the Rhineland, in 1849 he settled with his family in London. Often reduced to poverty, he was supported by Engels and Lassalle, and three of his children died young. At the British Museum reading room, where he was the first to make use of government blue books, he acquired a vast knowledge of economics, supplemented by Engels' first-hand experience of British industry. *Zur Kritik der politischen Oekonomie* (1859) was followed by his *magnum opus*, Vol. I of *Das Kapital* (1867). Here he argues that capitalist expansion depends on surplus value, the difference between the mere subsistence wage paid to labour and the considerably greater value produced by it. Capitalist competition however is only successful at the expense of the worker, who becomes poorer, more desperate and self-conscious. The antagonisms must inevitably lead to revolution. Here we have the Hegelian dialectic, but inverted, not in terms of spiritual abstraction but materialism. The synthesis which results from the extinction of the capitalist class is, after a short dictatorship of the proletariat, the classless society, in which the state has ' withered away '. The rôle of the Communist is to alleviate the birth pangs of the new era, by making the proletariat conscious of its historic rôle. ' Philosophers have previously offered various interpretations of the world. Our business is to change it.' Marx was among the founders of the First International (Working-men's Association) which broke up in 1873 into Marxist and Bakunin's anarchist factions, the former surviving until 1876. With *Das Kapital* unfinished, Marx died March 14, 1883, and was buried in Highgate cemetery. Marx provided an original and compelling analysis of the underlying social tensions of his time, which revolutionized the manner in which

economic history and sociology were to be conducted. The defects of his dialectical approach are endemic to all forms of historicism. He failed to provide a political programme because on his thesis politics come to an end with the classless society. He did not foresee the future decisive rôle of the managerial class, which has no place in his system. But as the propounder of a political creed he exerted a powerful influence which a century after the publication of the *Manifesto* showed no signs of abating. See also his *Civil War in France* (1850; trans. Postgate 1921), *Der 18te Brumaire des Louis Bonaparte* (1852), Vols. 2 and 3 of *Das Kapital*, ed. F. Engels (1885–95), their joint work, published posthumously, *German Ideology*, written (1845–46) and Collected Works, ed. Marx-Engels Institute (1927 ff.). See also biographical studies by M. Beer (1925), R. W. Postgate (1933), E. H. Carr (1934), F. Mehring (trans. E. Fitzgerald 1935), S. Hook (1936), H. J. Laski, C. J. Sprigge (1939), I. Berlin (1939), studies by B. Croce (1914), V. I. Lenin (1919), K. Kautsky (1919), A. D. Lindsay (1925), G. D. H. Cole (1934 and 1948), L. Schwarzschild (1948), H. Marcuse (1959), and K. R. Popper, *The Open Society*, Vol. 2 (1945), H. B. Acton, *The Illusion of an Epoch* (1955), and G. A. Wetter, *Dialectical Materialism* (Freiburg 1952, trans. P. Heath 1959).

MARY (Heb. *Miriam*, Gr. *Mariam*), the Blessed Virgin, the mother of Jesus Christ. The genealogy of Jesus in St Matthew is traced through Joseph; and it is assumed that Mary was of the same family. The incidents in her personal history will be found in Matt. i, ii, xii; Luke i, ii; John ii, xix; and Acts i. The date of her death is often given as A.D. 63; the tradition of her having been assumed into heaven is celebrated in the festival of the Assumption. See works by F. M. William (1938), C. C. Martindale (1940).

MARY I (1516–58), Queen of England, daughter of Henry VIII by his first wife, Catharine of Aragon, was born at Greenwich, February 18, 1516. She was well educated, a good linguist, fond of music, devoted to her mother, and devoted to her church. With the divorce of her mother her troubles began. Henry forced her to sign a declaration that her mother's marriage had been unlawful. During the reign of her half-brother Edward she lived in retirement, and no threats could induce her to conform to the new religion. On his death (1553) she became entitled to the crown by her father's testament and the parliamentary settlement. The Duke of Northumberland had, however, induced Edward and his council to set Henry's will aside in favour of his daughter-in-law Lady Jane Grey (q.v.), but the whole country favoured Mary, who without bloodshed entered London on August 3 in triumph. Northumberland and two others were executed, but Lady Jane and her husband were, for the present, spared. The queen proceeded very cautiously to bring back the old religion. She reinstated the Catholic bishops and imprisoned some of the leading Reformers, but dared not restore the pope's supremacy. The question upon which all turned was the queen's marriage; and she, in spite of the protests of the nation, obstinately set her heart on Philip of Spain. The unpopularity of the proposal brought about the rebellion of Wyatt, quelled mainly through the courage and coolness of the queen. Lady Jane was now, with her husband and father, brought to the block; the Princess Elizabeth, suspected of complicity, was committed to the Tower. Injunctions were sent to the bishops to restore ecclesiastical laws to their state under Henry VIII. In July 1554 Philip was married to Mary, remaining in England for over a year. In November Pole entered England as papal legate, parliament petitioned for reconciliation to the Holy See, and the realm was solemnly absolved from the papal censures. Soon after, the persecution which gave the queen the name of ' Bloody Mary ' began. In 1555 Ridley and Latimer were brought to the stake; Cranmer followed in March 1556; and Pole, now Archbishop of Canterbury, was left supreme in the councils of the queen. How far Mary herself was responsible for the cruelties practised is doubtful; but during the last three years of her reign 300 victims perished in the flames. Broken down with sickness, with grief at her husband's heartlessness, with disappointment at her childlessness, and with sorrow for the loss of Calais to the French, Mary died November 17, 1558. See *England under Edward VI and Mary*, by Tytler, M. Hume's *Two English Queens and Philip* (1908), a study by J. M. Stone (1901), Life by F. H. M. Prescott (1953).

MARY II (1662–94). See WILLIAM III.

MARY, Queen, formerly Princess of Teck. See GEORGE V.

MARY OF GUELDRES. See JAMES II (Scotland).

MARY OF GUISE. See GUISE (6).

MARY OF MEDICI. See MARIE DE' MEDICI.

MARY OF MODENA (1658–1718), Queen of James II, only daughter of the Duke of Modena, in 1673 became the second wife of the Duke of York, who in 1685 succeeded as James II (q.v.). Five daughters and one son had all died in infancy, when on June 10, 1688, she gave birth to Prince James Francis Edward, and six months later escaped with him to France. She bore a daughter in 1692, and spent her last days at St Germain. See Lives by M. Haile (1905) and C. Oman (1962).

MARY, Queen of Scots (1542–87), was the daughter of James V of Scotland by his second wife, Mary of Guise, and was born at Linlithgow, December 7 or 8, 1542, while her father lay on his deathbed at Falkland. A queen when she was a week old, she was promised in marriage by the regent Arran to Prince Edward of England, but the Scottish parliament declared the promise null. War with England followed, and the disastrous defeat of Pinkie (1547); but Mary was offered in marriage to the eldest son of Henry II of France and Catharine de' Medici. The offer was accepted; and in 1548 Mary sailed from Dumbarton to Roscoff, and was affianced to the Dauphin at St Germain. Her next ten years were passed at the French court, where she was carefully educated; and in 1558 she was married to the Dauphin, who

was a year younger than herself. Mary was induced to sign a secret deed, by which, if she died childless, both her Scottish realm and her right of succession to the English crown (she was the great-granddaughter of Henry VII) were conveyed to France. In 1559 the death of the French king called her husband to the throne as Francis II, and the government passed into the hands of the Guises; but the sickly king died in 1560, when the reins of power were grasped by Catharine de' Medici as regent for her next son, Charles IX. The young queen's presence was already urgently needed in Scotland, which the death of her mother had left without a government, while convulsed by the throes of the Reformation; and she sailed from Calais on the 14th, and arrived at Leith on August 19, 1561. Her government began auspiciously. The Reformation claimed to have received the sanction of the Scottish parliament, and Mary was content to leave affairs as she found them, stipulating only for liberty to use her own religion. Her chief minister was a Protestant, her illegitimate brother, James Stuart, whom she created Earl of Moray. Under his guidance, in the autumn of 1562, she made a progress to the north, which ended in the defeat and death of the Earl of Huntly, the powerful chief of the Roman Catholic party in Scotland. Meanwhile the kings of Sweden, Denmark and France, the Archduke Charles of Austria, Don Carlos of Spain, the Dukes of Ferrara, Nemours and Anjou, the Earl of Arran, and the Earl of Leicester were proposed as candidates for her hand. Her own preference was for Don Carlos, and only after all hopes of obtaining him were quenched, her choice fell, somewhat suddenly (1565), on her cousin, Henry Stewart, Lord Darnley, son of the Earl of Lennox. By his marriage with a granddaughter of Henry VII of England. He was thus among the nearest heirs to the English crown; and this and his good looks were his sole recommendation. He was weak, needy, insolent and vicious; he was a Roman Catholic; and he was three years younger than Mary. The marriage was the signal for an easily quelled insurrection by Moray and the Hamiltons. But Mary almost at once was disgusted by Darnley's debauchery, and alarmed by his arrogance. She had given him the title of king, but she hesitated to grant his demand that the crown should be secured to him for life, and that, if she died without issue, it should descend to his heirs. Her chief adviser since Moray's rebellion had been her Italian secretary David Rizzio (q.v.). The king had been his sworn friend, but now suspected in him the real obstacle to his designs upon the crown. In this belief, he entered into a formal compact with Moray, Ruthven, Morton and other Protestant chiefs, and himself led the way into the queen's cabinet and held her while the others killed the Italian in an antechamber (March 9, 1566). Dissembling her indignation, Mary succeeded in detaching her husband from his allies, and escaped with him from Holyrood to Dunbar; Ruthven and Morton fled to England; Moray was received by the queen; and Darnley, who had betrayed both sides, became an object of mingled abhorrence and contempt. A little before the birth (June 19, 1566) of the prince who became James VI, the queen's affection for her husband seemed to revive; but the change was only momentary; and before the boy's baptism, in December, her estrangement was greater than ever. Divorce was openly discussed, and Darnley spoke of leaving the country, but fell ill of the smallpox at Glasgow about January 9, 1567. On the 25th Mary went to see him, and brought him to Edinburgh on the 31st. He was lodged in a small mansion beside the Kirk o' Field, just outside the southern walls. There Mary visited him daily, slept for two nights in a room below his bedchamber, and passed the evening of Sunday, February 9, by his bedside in kindly conversation. She left him between ten and eleven o'clock to take part in a masque at Holyrood, at the marriage of a favourite valet; and about two hours after midnight the house in which the king slept was blown up by gunpowder, and his lifeless body was found in the garden. The chief actor in this tragedy was undoubtedly the Earl of Bothwell (q.v.), who had of late enjoyed the queen's favour; but there were suspicions that the queen herself was not wholly ignorant of the plot. On April 12 Bothwell was brought to a mock-trial, and acquitted; on the 24th he intercepted the queen on her way from Linlithgow to Edinburgh, and carried her, with scarcely a show of resistance, to Dunbar. On May 7 he was divorced from his comely and newly-married wife; on the 12th Mary publicly pardoned his seizure of her person, and created him Duke of Orkney; and on the 15th, three months after her husband's murder, she married the man every one regarded as his murderer. This fatal step at once arrayed her nobles in arms against her. Her army melted away without striking a blow on the field of Carberry (June 15), when nothing was left but to surrender to the confederate lords. They led her to Edinburgh, where the insults of the rabble drove her well-nigh frantic. Hurried next to Lochleven, she was constrained (July 24) to sign an act of abdication in favour of her son, who, five days afterwards, was crowned at Stirling. Escaping from her island-prison (May 2, 1568), she found herself in a few days at the head of an army of 6000 men, which was defeated (May 13) by the regent Moray at Langside near Glasgow. Three days afterwards Mary crossed the Solway, and threw herself on the protection of Queen Elizabeth, only to find herself a prisoner for life—first at Carlisle, then at Bolton, Tutbury, Wingfield, Coventry, Chatsworth, Sheffield, Buxton, Chartley and Fotheringay. The presence of Mary in England was a constant source of uneasiness to Elizabeth and her advisers. A large Catholic minority naturally looked to Mary as the likely restorer of the old faith. Plot followed plot; and that of Antony Babington had for its object the assassination of Elizabeth and the deliverance of Mary. It was discovered; letters from Mary approving the death of Elizabeth fell into Walsingham's hands; and, mainly on the evidence of

copies of these letters, Mary was brought to trial in September 1586. Sentence of death was pronounced against her on October 25 but it was not until February 1, 1587, that Elizabeth took courage to sign the warrant of execution. It was carried into effect on the 8th, when Mary laid her head upon the block with the dignity of a queen and the resignation of a martyr, evincing to the last her devotion to the church of her fathers. Her body, buried at Peterborough, was in 1612 removed to Henry VII's Chapel at Westminster, where it still lies in a sumptuous tomb erected by James VI. The statue there and the contemporary portraits by Clouet (q.v.) are the best representations of Mary. Her beauty and accomplishments have never been disputed. The charm of her soft, sweet voice is described as irresistible; and she sang well, accompanying herself on the harp, the virginal and the lute. She spoke three or four languages, conversed admirably, and wrote in both prose and verse. Of six extant pieces of her poetry (less than 300 lines) the best is the poem of eleven stanzas on the death of her first husband. The longest is a *Meditation* of a hundred lines, written in 1572. All are in French, except one sonnet in Italian. The sweet lines beginning ' Adieu, plaisant pays de France ', are not hers. A volume of French verse on the *Institution of a Prince* has been lost since 1627, along with a Latin speech in vindication of learned women, delivered in the Louvre. See works by Philippson (1891–92), Skelton (1893), Hay Fleming (1897), S. Cowan (1901, 1907), Stoddart (1908), Shelley (1913), Mumby (1914, 1921), Mahon (1924, 1930), N. B. Morrison (1960); Lang's *Mystery of Mary Stuart* (1901), her *Trial* (ed. Steuart, 1951), and *Papal Negotiations* (Scot. Hist. Soc., 1901); Rait and Cameron, *King James's Secret* (1927); Willcocks (1939); and Tannenbaum's bibliography (3 vols. 1944–46).

MASACCIO, *maz-at'chō,* (1) real name **Tomasso Guidi** (1401–28?), Italian painter, a pioneer of Italian renaissance painting, influenced such great masters as Michelangelo and Raphael. See works by Somaré (1924), H. Lindberg (1931), Salmi (1935).

(2) real name **Maso di Bartolommeo** (1406–1457), Italian sculptor, a Florentine, assisted Donatello and worked in Florence Cathedral and other N. Italian churches.

MASANIELLO, properly **Tommaso Aniello,** *ma-zan-ee-el'lō* (1623–47), Neapolitan patriot, a fisherman of Amalfi, led the successful revolt of the Neapolitans against their Spanish oppressors on July 7, 1647. He was assassinated by agents of the Spanish viceroy on July 16. See Lives by M. Schipa (Bari 1925), A. Rosso (Naples 1952).

MASARYK, *ma-sa-rik',* (1) **Jan** (1886–1948), Czech diplomat and statesman, son of (2), served in Czech diplomatic service after 1918, being minister in London 1925–38. He became foreign minister in the Czech government set up in London in 1940 and continued in that post after 1945 in Prague. In 1948 the Communists took control of the government and he is thought to have committed suicide. See Life by Lockhart (1956).

(2) **Thomas Garrigue** (1850–1937), first

president of the Czechoslovak Republic (1918–35), father of (1), was born at Hodonin, Moravia. An ardent Slovak, while in exile during World War I he organized the Czechoslovak independence movement. See Lives by Seton-Watson (1943) and Birley (1951).

MASCAGNI, Pietro, *mas-kan'yee* (1863–1945), Italian composer, born a baker's son at Leghorn, produced in 1890 the brilliantly successful one-act opera, *Cavalleria Rusticana.* His many later operas failed to repeat this success, though arias and intermezzi from them are still performed. They include *L'Amico Fritz* (1891), *Guglielmo Ratcliffe* (1895), *Le Maschere* (1901) and *Londoletta* (1917). See the autobiographical *Mascagni parla* (Rome 1945), Lives by C. Cogo (Venice 1931) and E. Mascagni (1936).

MASCALL, Eric Lionel (1905–), Anglo-Catholic theologian, author, and since 1962 professor of Historical Theology at King's College, London. He read mathematics for four years at Cambridge with the intention of making his career as an applied mathematician. An interest in philosophy led to another in theology, however, and he was ordained priest in 1932. After a few years in parish work he became sub-warden of Lincoln Theological College where he remained for eight years. From 1946 to 1962 he was tutor in Theology and university lecturer in the Philosophy of Religion at Christ Church, Oxford. Apart from his academic work, he has shown a considerable interest in the life of the religious communities of the Church of England and in the ecumenical field. See his books *He Who Is* (1943) and *Existence and Analogy* (1949) which have acquired more or less the character of text-books on Natural Theology, *Christian Theology and Natural Science* (Oxford Bampton Lectures, 1956) on the relations of theology and science, and the ecumenical *The Recovery of Unity* (1958).

MASEFIELD, John (1878–1967), English poet and novelist, was born at Ledbury. Schooled for the merchant service, he served his apprenticeship on a windjammer and acquired that intimate knowledge of the sea which gives atmosphere and authenticity to his work. Ill-health drove him ashore, and after three years in New York he returned to England to become a writer in 1897, first making his mark as a journalist. His earliest poetical work, *Salt Water Ballads*, appeared in 1902; *Dauber* (1913) confirmed his reputation as a poet of the sea. *Nan* (1909) is a tragedy of merit. His ability to tell a story in verse is reminiscent of Chaucer. This is specially noticeable in his finest narrative poem *Reynard the Fox* (1919). Other works are *The Everlasting Mercy* (1911); *The Widow in the Bye-Street* (1912); *Shakespeare* (1911); *Gallipoli* (1916); the novels *Sard Harker* (1924), *Odtaa* (1926) and *The Hawbucks* (1929); and the plays *The Trial of Jesus* (1925) and *The Coming of Christ* (1928). He became poet laureate in 1930 and was awarded the O.M. in 1935. See his autobiographical *In the Mill* (1941) and *So Long to Learn* (1952), and studies by Hamilton (1922) and Thomas (1932).

MASHAM, Abigail, Lady, *née* **Hill** (d. 1734), cousin to the Duchess of Marlborough (q.v.), whom she superseded as Queen Anne's favourite. She married in 1707, and died December 6, 1734.

MASINISSA (*c.* 238–149 B.C.), King of the Eastern Numidians, helped the Carthaginians to subdue the Massylii or Western Numidians, accompanied his allies to Spain, and fought valiantly against the Romans. But going over to them (*c.* 210 B.C.), he received as his reward Western Numidia and large portions of Carthaginian territory.

MASKELYNE, *mas'ke-lin,* (1) **John Nevil** (1839–1917), English illusionist, born in Wiltshire. Of farming stock, he became a watchmaker, which directed his interest towards the automata which he used so effectively in his entertainments. As a young man he joined forces with a Mr Cooke and they appeared together, first at Cheltenham and then at the Crystal Palace, in 1865. In 1873 they leased the Egyptian Hall for three months, but their tenancy lasted for thirty-one years. Maskelyne then moved his ' Home of Magic ' to the St George's Hall in 1905, where his particular brand of spectacular conjuring continued to flourish under his son's management. He devoted much energy to exposing spiritualistic frauds. His grandson, **Jasper** (1903–), first appeared in his grandfather's show at the age of eleven, and has continued as a conjuror on his own. He utilized his peculiar knowledge to confound the enemy during World War II and wrote an account of the family in *White Magic* (1936).

(2) **Mervyn Herbert Nevil Story-** (1823–1911), English mineralogist, grandson of (3), advocated the study of natural science at Oxford, where he became Waynflete professor of Mineralogy and also reorganized the mineralogy department of the British Museum. He was also F.R.S. and M.P.

(3) **Nevil** (1732–1811), English astronomer, grandfather of (2), educated at Westminster and Trinity College, Cambridge, in 1758 was elected F.R.S., went to Barbadoes to test the chronometers (1763), and in 1765 was appointed astronomer-royal. During the forty-six years that he held this office he improved methods and instruments of observation, invented the prismatic micrometer, and made important observations. In 1774 he measured the earth's density from the deflection of the plumb-line at Schiehallion in Perthshire. His numerous publications include the *British Mariner's Guide* (1763), the *Nautical Almanac* (1765–67), *Tables for computing the Places of the Fixed Stars &c.,* and the first volume of the Greenwich *Astronomical Observations.* He was rector from 1775 of Shrawardine, Salop, and from 1782 of North Runcton, Norfolk, and died February 9, 1811. See *Royal Observatory Greenwich* (1900) for account of his life and work.

MASOLINO DA PANICALE (1383–1447), Florentine artist, identified with **Tomasso Fini.** A distinguished early Renaissance painter, he was the master of Masaccio (q.v.), with whom he collaborated in the Brancacci chapel. His frescoes in Castiglione d'Olona were only discovered in 1843. He also worked in Hungary and Rome. See works by Layard (1868) and Toesca (1958).

MASON, (1) **Alfred Edward Woodley** (1865–1948), English novelist, born at Dulwich, educated at Oxford, became a successful actor, subsequently combined writing with politics, being Liberal M.P. for Coventry in 1906–10. His first published novel was *A Romance of Wastdale* (1895). *Four Feathers* (1902) captured the popular imagination and *The Broken Road* (1907) cemented his success. With *At the Villa Rose* (1910) Mason embarked on the novel of detection and introduced his ingenious Inspector Hanaud; thereafter he alternated historical adventure and detective fiction. Several of his books have been filmed. Representative titles are: *The House of the Arrow* (1924); *No other Tiger* (1927); *The Prisoner in the Opal* (1929); *Fire over England* (1936); *Königsmark* (1938); *Life of Francis Drake* (1941).

(2) **Charles** (1730–87), British astronomer, employed at Greenwich, with **Jeremiah Dixon** (of whom little is known except that he is reputed to have been born in a coal-mine) he observed the transit of Venus at the Cape of Good Hope in 1761. From 1763 to 1767 Mason and Dixon were engaged by Lord Baltimore and Mr Penn to survey the boundary between Maryland and Pennsylvania and end an eighty-year-old dispute. They reached a point 224 miles west of the Delaware River, but were prevented from further work by Indians. The survey was completed by others, but the boundary was given the name Mason-Dixon Line.

(3) **Daniel Gregory** (1873–1953), grandson of (5), American composer, born in Brookline, Mass., studied under D'Indy in Paris, and became a leading exponent of neo-classical composition in America. He wrote books on American musical conditions and a study of Beethoven's String Quartets. Mason composed three symphonies, the last of which is a study of Abraham Lincoln, and a considerable amount of chamber music.

(4) **Sir Josiah** (1795–1881), English philanthropist and pen manufacturer, born at Kidderminster, began life as a hawker, after 1822 manufactured split-rings, and in 1829 began to make pens for Perry & Co., and soon became the greatest pen-maker in the world. He was partner with Elkington in electroplating (1842–65), and had smelting-works for copper and nickel. He endowed almshouses and an orphanage at Erdington at a cost of £260,000, and gave £180,000 to found the Mason College (now Birmingham University). See Memoir by Bunce (1890).

(5) **Lowell** (1792–1872), American musician, born in Medfield, Mass., as organist of a Presbyterian church in Savannah, compiled a book of hymns, taking melodies from the works of Handel, Mozart and Beethoven. The success of this work led him to produce similar volumes for school use, and additional hymn books. In 1832 he founded the Boston Academy of Music, to give free instruction to children, and was compelled by its success to organize classes for adults. The most famous of his compositions is probably the

hymn tune 'From Greenland's icy mountains'.

(6) **William** (1725–97), English poet, was a friend of Gray, who had been attracted to him by his *Musaeus* (1747), a lament for Pope in imitation of Milton's *Lyctdas*. He published two poor tragedies, *Elfrida* and *Caractacus*; the *English Garden* (1772–82), a tedious poem in blank verse; and, as Gray's executor, the *Memoirs of Gray* in 1775. He became vicar of Aston, Yorkshire, in 1754, canon of York in 1762. See his *Correspondence with Walpole* (1851), *with Gray* (1853), and Life by Draper (1929).

(7) **William** (1829–1908), son of (5), studied the piano under Liszt and, in the course of a successful concert career, organized influential chamber music concerts in Boston.

MASPERO, **Sir Gaston**, Hon. K.C.M.G. (1846–1916), French Egyptologist, born at Paris of Italian parents, in 1874 became professor of Egyptology at the Collège de France, and was in 1881–86, 1899–1914 keeper of the Bulak Museum and director of explorations in Egypt, making valuable discoveries at Sakkara, Dahshûr, Ekhmim, &c. He wrote many works on Egyptology.

MASSÉNA, **André**, *mas-say'na* (1758–1817), French soldier, the greatest of Napoleon's marshals, served fourteen years in the Sardinian army, and in the French Revolution rose rapidly in rank, becoming in 1793 a general of division. He distinguished himself greatly in the campaigns in Upper Italy, gained his crushing victory over Suvorov's Russians at Zürich (1799), and became marshal of the empire in 1804. In Italy he kept the Archduke Charles in check, crushed him at Caldiero, and overran Naples. In 1807, after Eylau, he commanded the right wing, and was created Duke of Rivoli. In the campaign of 1809 against Austria he covered himself with glory and earned the title of Prince of Essling. In 1810 he compelled Wellington to fall back upon his impregnable lines at Torres Vedras, was forced after five months, by total lack of supplies, to make a masterly retreat, but was recalled with ignominy by his imperious master. At the Restoration he adhered to the Bourbons and on Napoleon's return from Elba Masséna refused to follow him; he died April 4, 1817. See his *Mémoires* (7 vols. 1849–50), and books by Toselli (1869), Gachot (5 vols. 1901–13) and Sabor (1926).

MASSENET, **Jules**, *mas-ė-nay* (1842–1912), French composer, born near St Étienne, studied at the Paris Conservatoire, where in 1878–96 he was professor. He made his fame by the comic opera *Don César de Bazan* in 1872. Other operas are *Hérodiade* (1884), *Manon* (1885), *Le Cid* (1885), *Werther* (1892) and *Thaïs* (1894), and among his works are oratorios, orchestral suites, music for piano and songs. See his autobiographical *Mes Souvenirs* (Paris 1912, Eng. trans. Boston 1919), Life by Bruneau (Paris 1935).

MASSEY, (1) **Gerald** (1828–1907), English poet and mystic, born near Tring, became a Christian Socialist, edited a journal, lectured, and between 1851 and 1869 published eight or nine volumes of poetry (*Babe Christabel and other Poems*, *Craigcrook Castle*, &c.), mostly collected in *My Lyrical Life* (1890). He wrote also mystical and speculative theological or cosmogonic works, and discovered a ' Secret Drama ' in Shakespeare's sonnets. See book by Flower (1895), and Collins's *Studies* (1905).

(2) **Vincent** (1887–1967), Canadian statesman and diplomat, born in Toronto, joined the Canadian cabinet after World War I, became Canadian minister in Washington (1926–30), high commissioner in London (1935–46), and governor-general of Canada (1952–59). His brother **Raymond** (1896–   ), is a well-known actor of stage (début in 1922 in *In the Zone*, played Lincoln in *Abe Lincoln* (1938–39)), screen (played leading parts in *Things to come*, *49th Parallel*, &c.), and television (in the rôle of ' Dr Gillespie ' in the long-running *Dr Kildare* series during the 1960s).

(3) **William Ferguson** (1856–1925), New Zealand statesman, born in Ireland, went to New Zealand and became a farmer. Elected to the house of representatives he became opposition leader and in 1912 prime minister, which office he held until his death. See Life by H. J. Constable (1925).

MASSILLON, Jean Baptiste, *mas-see-yŏ* (1663–1742), French preacher, born at Hyères in Provence, was trained for the church in the Oratory. He preached before Louis XIV, became Bishop of Clermont, and next year preached before Louis XV his celebrated *Petit Carême*—a series of ten short Lenten sermons. In 1719 he was elected to the Academy; in 1723 he preached the funeral oration of the Duchess of Orleans, his last public discourse in Paris. From this time he lived almost entirely for his diocese, where his charity and gentleness gained him the love of all. He died of apoplexy. See Blampignon's monograph (1884), Sainte-Beuve's *Causeries du Lundi* (vol. ix) and works by Ingold (1880) and Pauthe (1908).

MASSINE, Léonide, *ma-seen'* (1896–   ), Russo-American dancer and choreographer, born in Moscow. He was principal dancer and choreographer with Diaghilev and the Ballet Russe de Monte Carlo, and has produced and danced in ballets in Europe and America, among his best known works being *La Boutique fantasque* and *Le Sacré du printemps*. See study by Anthony (1939).

MASSINGER, Philip (1583–1640), English dramatist, baptized at St Thomas's, Salisbury, November 24, was a son of a retainer of the Earl of Pembroke. After leaving Oxford without a degree he became a playwright and was associated with Henslowe, who died in 1616. In later years he wrote many plays single-handed, but much of his work is mixed up with that of other men, particularly Fletcher. Fletcher was buried in St Saviour's Church, Southwark, August 29, 1625; and Massinger was laid in the same grave, March 18, 1640. Probably the earliest of Massinger's extant plays is *The Unnatural Combat*, a repulsive tragedy, printed in 1639. The first in order of publication is *The Virgin Martyr* (1622), partly written by Dekker. In 1623 was published *The Duke of Milan*, a

fine tragedy, but too rhetorical. Other plays include *The Bondman*, *The Roman Actor* (1626), *The Great Duke of Florence* (1627), and *The Emperor of the East* (1631), &c. Nathaniel Field joined Massinger in writing the fine tragedy *The Fatal Dowry*, printed in 1632. *The City Madam*, licensed in 1632, and *A New Way to Pay Old Debts*, printed in 1633, are Massinger's most masterly comedies —brilliant satirical studies, though without warmth or geniality. Some of Massinger's plays are (as Coleridge said) as interesting as a novel; others are as solid as a treatise on political philosophy. His verse, though fluent and flexible, lacks the music and magic of Shakespeare's. No writer repeats himself more frequently. It is difficult to say how far Massinger was concerned in the authorship of plays that pass under the name of ' Beaumont and Fletcher '. There are editions (none complete) by Gifford (1805, 1813), Coleridge (1840), Cunningham (1867), and Symons (1887–89, 1904); studies by Cruickshank (1920), Maxwell (1939) and Dunn (1958).

MASSON, David (1822–1907), Scottish scholar and literary critic, the biographer of Milton, was born at Aberdeen, and educated at Marischal College there and the University of Edinburgh. In 1847 he settled in London, writing for reviews, encyclopaedias, &c. In 1852 he became professor of English Literature in University College London, and in 1865 in Edinburgh University; he resigned in 1895. His *Essays, Biographical and Critical* (1856), were extended in 1874–76. His *Life of John Milton* (6 vols. 1859–80) is the most complete biography of any Englishman. Other works include editions of Milton's poems and De Quincey's works (14 vols. 1889–91). See his autobiographical *Memories of London in the Forties* (1908) and *Letters* (1908).

MASSYS. See MATSYS.

MASTERS, Edgar Lee (1869–1950), American author, wrote the satirical *Spoon River Anthology* (1915), dealing with the lives of people in the midwest. See his autobiography *Across Spoon River* (1936).

MASÛDI, Abul Hassan Ali, *ma-soo'dee* (d. 957), Arab traveller, born at Bagdad, visited Egypt, Palestine, the Caspian, India, Ceylon, Madagascar, perhaps even China. His chief works are the *Annals*, *Meadows of Gold* (printed with French trans. 1861–77, and at Boulak in 1867), and *Indicator*.

MATA HARI, stage name of **Margarete Gertrude Zelle** (1876–1917), Dutch spy, born at Leeuwarden, who became a dancer in France and, found guilty of espionage for the Germans, was shot in Paris. See book by Newman (1956).

MATEJKO, Jan Alois, *ma-te'y'-kō* (1838–93), Polish painter, born at Cracow, noted for his paintings of scenes from Polish history.

MATHER, (1) Cotton (1663–1728), American divine, son of (2), after graduating at Harvard became colleague to his father at Boston. He published as many as 382 books, and his *Memorable Providences relating to Witchcraft and Possessions* (1685) did much to fan the cruel fury of the New Englanders. During the Salem witchcraft mania Mather wrote his *Wonders of the Invisible World* (1692), and on his head must rest a heavy burden of bloodguiltiness. His *Magnalia Christi Americana* (1702) is an undigested mass of materials for the church history of New England. The *Essays to do Good* (1710) are feeble. He died February 13, 1728. See his Life by his son (1729); Upham, *The Salem Delusion* (1831); and Lives by Marvin (1892), and R. and L. Boas (1929).

(2) **Increase** (1639–1723), American divine, father of (1), was the eldest son of an English Nonconformist minister who emigrated in 1635. He was born at Dorchester, Mass., June 21, 1639, and graduated at Harvard in 1656, and again at Trinity College, Dublin, in 1658. His first charge was Great Torrington in Devon; but in 1661, finding it impossible to conform, he returned to America, and from 1664 till his death, August 23, 1723, was pastor of the North Church, Boston, and from 1681 also president of Harvard. He published no less than 136 separate works, including *Remarkable Providences* (1684) and a *History of the War with the Indians* (1676). Sent to England in 1689 to lay colonial grievances before the king, he obtained a new charter from William III. He was far less an alarmist about witchcraft than his son, and his *Causes of Conscience concerning Witchcraft* (1693) helped to cool the heated imaginations of the colonists. See Life by K. B. Murdock (1925).

MATHEW, Theobald, called ' Father Mathew ' (1790–1856), Irish temperance reformer, was born at Thomastown in Tipperary, October 10, 1790. He took priest's orders in the Capuchin order in 1814; and in his ceaseless labours at Cork, seeing how much of the degradation of his people was due to drink, became (1838) an ardent advocate of total abstinence. His crusade extended to England, Scotland and America. He achieved great success, and everywhere roused enthusiasm and secured warm affection. Ill health followed, and he was only saved from serious pecuniary distresses by a Civil List pension and a private subscription. Worn out by his labours, he died at Queenstown. See Lives by Maguire (1863), Matthew (1890), Tynan (1908) and Rogers (1943).

MATHEWS, (1) Charles (1776–1835), English comedian, father of (2), made his début as an actor at Richmond in 1793, but forsook the legitimate stage in 1818 and achieved great success as an entertainer, visiting America twice. See his Memoirs by his wife (4 vols. 1839).

(2) **Charles James** (1803–78), English comedian, son of (1), was a delightful light comedian of charming grace and delicacy. In 1838 he married Madame Vestris (q.v.). See his *Life*, edited by the younger Dickens (1879).

MATHIAS CORVINUS. See MATTHIAS.

MATHIEU, Georges, *ma-tyœ* (1921–   ), French painter, born at Boulogne, took a degree in literature, but began to paint in 1942; he settled in Paris in 1947, and exhibited there and in New York. With Bryen and others, he has perfected a form of lyric, nongeometrical abstraction, in close sympathy with the American neo-Expressionists. See his *Au-delà du Tachisme* (1963).

MATHILDA (d. 1115), countess of Tuscany, a daughter of the count of Tuscany, supported (with money and men) Pope Gregory VII in his long struggle with the Empire, and married first Godfrey, Duke of Lorraine, and then the young Welf of Bavaria. In 1077 she made a gift of all her vast possessions to the Church. It was at her castle of Canossa that Henry IV did penance to Gregory. See Lives by N. Duff (1909) and N. Grimaldi (Florence 1928).

MATHIS. See GRÜNEWALD (2).

MATILDA, called ' the Empress Maud,' (1102–67), who carried on the Civil War in England with Stephen (q.v.), was the only daughter of Henry I. In 1114 she was married to the Emperor Henry V, and in 1128 to Geoffrey of Anjou, by whom she became the mother of Henry II. See Life by O. Rössler (Berlin 1897).

MATISSE, Henri, *ma-tees* (1869–1954), French artist, born at Le Cateau, studied at the Académie Julian and at the École des Beaux-Arts under Gustave Moreau. From 1904 he became the leader of the Fauves (Derain, Vlaminck, Dufy, Rouault and others). Although he painted several pictures influenced by the Cubists, the Impressionists and by Cézanne, his most characteristic paintings display a bold use of brilliant, luminous areas of primary colour, organized within a rhythmic two-dimensional design, which has affinities with the art of Gauguin and oriental work. The purity of his line-drawing is seen in his many sketches, book illustrations, and etchings, and in many of his paintings. During the early 1930s he travelled in Europe and the U.S.A., and in 1949 he decorated a Dominican chapel at Venice. He was working right up to his death, his style fundamentally unchanged, producing pictures more sophisticated than his early work, but with exquisite sense of design and balance of colour. His works are represented in the Tate Gallery, London, and the Museums of Modern Art in Paris and New York. See monographs by R. Fry (1935), G. Diehl (1954), J. Lassaigne (trans. 1959) and R. Escholier (trans. 1960).

MATSYS, or **Massys, (1) Jan** (1509–75), son of (2), was an imitator of his father and worked in Antwerp.

(2) **Quentin** (c. 1466–c. 1531), Flemish painter, father of (1), born at Louvain, was, according to legend, a blacksmith. In 1491 he joined the painters' guild of St Luke in Antwerp. His pictures are mostly religious, treated with a reverent spirit, but with decided touches of realism, and of exquisite finish. He ranks high as a portrait painter. See works by M. J. Friedländer (1929) and study by Sir M. Conway, *The Van Eycks and their followers* (1921).

MATTEOTTI, Giacomo, *-ot'-* (1885–1924), Italian politician. A member of the Italian Chamber of Deputies, in 1921 he began to organize the United Socialist Party on a constitutional basis in opposition to Mussolini's Fascists. Matteotti's protests against Fascist outrages led to his murder in 1924, which caused a crisis and nearly brought the Fascist régime to an end.

MATTHAY, Tobias, *ma-tay* (1858–1945), English pianist and teacher, of German descent, born in London, was professor of Pianoforte at the Royal Academy of Music from 1880 to 1925, when he resigned to devote himself to his own school, which he had founded in 1900. His method of piano playing was enunciated in *The Act of Touch* (1903) and subsequent publications.

MATTHESON, Johann (1681–1764), German composer, born at Hamburg, was a singer and orchestral player before beginning to compose operas and many choral and instrumental pieces, and was also the author of manuals on continuo playing. See study by H. Schmidt (1897).

MATTHEW, Saint (1st cent. A.D.), one of the twelve apostles, was a tax gatherer before becoming a disciple of Jesus, and is identified with Levi in Mark (ii, 14) and Luke (v, 27). According to tradition he was the author of the first gospel, was a missionary to the Hebrews, and suffered martyrdom, but nothing is known with certainty about his life.

MATTHEW OF WESTMINSTER, long the supposed author of the *Flores Historiarum* (first printed by Archbishop Parker in 1567; ed. by Luard in 1890; trans. by Yonge, 1853), is of doubtful existence, the work being perhaps merely an abridgment of Matthew Paris (q.v.) or of Roger of Wendover, named from a copy at Westminster.

MATTHEW PARIS. See PARIS (3).

MATTHEWS, (1) Alfred Edward (1869-1960), English actor, born at Bridlington, began his career in 1887, filled innumerable comedy rôles from *Charley's Aunt* to *Quiet Weekend* and was still a popular favourite at ninety. See his *Autobiography* (1952).

(2) **Sir Stanley** (1915–), English footballer, born in Hanley. The son of Jack Matthews, 'the fighting barber of Hanley', a notable pugilist in his day, he started his athletic career as a sprinter. He soon concentrated on football and was picked to play for England at twenty. He played for Blackpool from 1947 to 1961, received fifty-six international caps, and celebrated his silver jubilee in association football in 1956. He was created C.B.E. in 1957, knighted in 1965, and became Port Vale club manager in 1965. See his Autobiography (1960).

MATTHIAS CORVINUS (c. 1443–90), king of Hungary, the second son of John Hunyady (q.v.), was elected in 1458. But it cost him a six years' hard struggle against Turks, Bohemians, the Emperor Frederick III and disaffected magnates before he could have himself crowned. He drove the Turks back across the frontiers; made himself master of Bosnia (1462) and of Moldavia and Wallachia (1467); and in 1478 concluded peace with Ladislaus of Bohemia, obtaining Moravia, Silesia, and Lusatia. Out of this war grew another with Frederick III, in which Matthias besieged and captured Vienna (1485), and took possession of a large part of Austria proper. He greatly encouraged arts and letters: he founded the University of Buda, built an observatory, adorned his capital with the works of renowned sculptors, employed literary men in Italy to copy MSS., and so

founded a magnificent library. Finances were brought into order, industry and commerce promoted, and justice administered strictly. But his rule was arbitrary and his taxes heavy. See Life by Fraknoi (German trans. 1891).

MATURIN, (1) Basil William (1847–1915), Irish Catholic preacher and writer, son of (3), one of the Cowley brotherhood, and a wellknown pulpit orator, when in 1897 he 'went over' to Rome. He was on the torpedoed *Lusitania*. See *Memoir* by M. Ward (1920).

(2) **Charles Robert** (1782–1824), Irish dramatist and romancer, father of (3), a curate of St Peter's, Dublin, made his name with a series of extravagant novels in macabre vein that rivalled those of Mrs Radcliffe. These included *The Fatal Revenge*, *Melmoth* (1820), and *The Albigenses*. His tragedy, *Bertram*, had a success at Drury Lane in 1816; its successors, *Manuel* and *Fredolpho*, were failures. See memoir prefixed to new edition of *Melmoth* (1892) and *Letters* (1927).

(3) **William** (1803–87), Irish divine, son of (2), father of (1), a High Churchman, whose views kept him from preferment. He was perpetual curate of Grangegorman from 1844.

MAUD. See MATILDA.

MAUDE, (1) Cyril (1862–1951), English actormanager, made his name in *The Second Mrs Tanqueray* and *The Little Minister*, was associate-manager of the Haymarket Theatre (1896–1905) and in 1907–15 directed his own company at the Playhouse. He was famous as Andrew Bullivant in *Grumpy* (1915). His son, **John Cyril** (1901–), an eminent judge and Q.C., sat in parliament for Exeter (1945–51).

(2) **Sir Frederick Stanley** (1864–1917), major-general, served in the Sudan and South Africa. In World War I he took part in the Dardanelles evacuation, and in command in Mesopotamia turned a British failure to a success, but died of cholera. See Life by Callwell (1920).

MAUDLING, Reginald (1917–), British Conservative minister, born in London, was educated at Merchant Taylors' and Merton College, Oxford, was called to the bar, served in the air force during World War II and in 1945 became one of Mr Butler's 'backroom boys' in the Conservative Central Office. He entered parliament in 1950 and after two junior ministerial posts, became minister of supply (1953–57), paymaster-general (1957–1959), president of the Board of Trade (1959–61), colonial secretary (1961), chancellor of the Exchequer (1962–64), and deputy leader of the Opposition in 1964.

MAUDSLAY, Henry (1771–1831), English engineer, learned his job as apprentice to Joseph Bramah (q.v.), set up on his own in 1797 and invented various types of machinery, including a screw-cutting lathe. With **Joshua Field** (1757–1863) he began producing marine engines and started the famous firm of Maudslay, Sons and Field (1810).

MAUDSLEY, Henry (1835–1918), English mental pathologist, born near Giggleswick, was physician to the Manchester Asylum, and professor of Medical Jurisprudence at University College, 1869–79. He was one of the first to consider mental illness as curable in some cases, and the Maudsley Hospital, Denmark Hill, London, is named after him.

MAUGHAM, William Somerset, *mawm* (1874–1965), British writer, a modern master of the short story, born January 25, in Paris, of Irish origin, was educated at King's School, Canterbury, read philosophy and literature at Heidelberg and qualified as a surgeon at St Thomas's Hospital, London. Afflicted by a bad stammer, he turned to writing in his student days and a year's medical practice in the London slums gave him the material for his first novel, the lurid *Liza of Lambeth* (1897), and the magnificent autobiographical novel, *Of Human Bondage*, eventually published in 1915. Attempts to have his plays accepted having failed, he settled in Paris and with Laurence Housman (q.v.) revived a 19th-century annual, *The Venture* (1903–04). With the success of *Lady Frederick* (1907), four of his plays ran in London in 1908. In 1914 he served first with a Red Cross unit in France, then as a secret agent in Geneva and finally in Petrograd, attempting to prevent the outbreak of the Russian Revolution. *Ashenden* (1928) is based on these experiences. He voyaged in the South Seas, visiting Tahiti, which inspired *The Moon and Sixpence* (1919), in which an English Gauguin, Strickland, leaves wife and stockbroking to end his life in a leper's hut. Maugham spent two years in a Scottish tuberculosis sanatorium and this again finds expression in several excellent short stories. He then visited the Far East, writing such plays as *East of Suez* (1922) and *Our Betters* (1923). In 1928 he settled in the South of France, where he wrote his astringent, satirical masterpiece, *Cakes and Ale* (1930). A British agent again in World War II, he fled from France in 1940 with only a suitcase, and lived until 1946 in the U.S., where he ventured into mysticism with *The Razor's Edge* (1945). But Maugham is best known for his short stories, several of which were filmed under the titles *Quartet* (1949), *Trio* (1950) and *Encore* (1951). The best of them, *Rain*, originally published in the collection, *The Trembling of a Leaf* (1921), an early, if unconscious piece of Freudian literature, exposes the tragic flaw of unhealthy asceticism in a devout missionary who falls from divine grace for a fellow-passenger, a prostitute, and commits suicide. His sparse, careful prose has sometimes unjustly been mistaken for superficiality. He refused to do more than tell a story; all else is propaganda, which seriously impairs a work of art. He was made C.H. in 1954. Other works include *Catalina* (1948), *The Complete Short Stories* (3 vols., 1951), *A Writer's Notebook* (1949) and essays on Goethe, Chehov, James, Mansfield in *Points of View* (1958). See bibliography (Mass. 1950) and studies by Aldington (1939), Stott (1950), Brophy (1952), Jonas (1954), Pfeiffer (1959), Cordell (1961), and R. Maugham, *Somerset and All the Maughams* (1966).

MAUNDEVILLE. See MANDEVILLE.

MAUPASSANT, Guy de, *mō-pas-ā* (1850–93), French novelist, born on August 5, at the Norman château of Miromesnil, was educated at Rouen and spent his life in Normandy.

After a short spell as a soldier in the Franco-German war he became a government clerk, but encouraged by Flaubert, who was a friend of his mother, he took to writing and mingled with Zola and other disciples of Naturalism. His stories range from the short tale of one or two pages to the full-length novel. Free from sentimentality or idealism, they lay bare with minute and merciless observation the pretentiousness and vulgarity of the middle class of the period and the animal cunning and traditional meanness of the Norman peasant. His first success, *Boule de suif* (1880), which could be called either a short novel or a long short story, exposes the hypocrisy, prudery and ingratitude of the bourgeois in the face of a heroic gesture by a woman of the streets, while *La Maison Tellier* (1881) tells with penetrating satire and humour the tale of an outing for the inmates of a provincial house of ill-fame. At the other end of the scale *Le Horla* and *La Peur* describe madness and fear with a horrifying accuracy which foreshadows the insanity which beset de Maupassant in 1892 and finally caused his death. His short stories number nearly 300, and he wrote several full-length novels, including *Une Vie* (1883) and *Bel Ami* (1885). See Life by R. Dumesnil (1948) and studies by E.D. Sullivan (1954) and A. M. Vial (1954).

MAUPEOU, Nicolas Augustin de, *mō-poo* (1714–92), succeeded his father as chancellor of France in 1768, and incurred great unpopularity by suppressing the *parlements* and establishing new courts. On Louis XV's death (1774) he was banished. See *Remontrances du Parlement de Paris au 18ᵉ siècle* by J. G. Flammermont (1888).

MAUPERTUIS, Pierre Louis Moreau de, *mō-per-twee* (1698–1759), mathematician, was born at St Malo, served in the army, and as a strenuous supporter of Newton's physical theories was made a member of the Royal Society of London in 1728. In 1736–37 he was at the head of the French Academicians sent to Lapland to measure a degree of longitude. Frederick the Great made him president of the Berlin Academy. But his temper provoked general dislike and the special enmity of Voltaire, who satirized him in *Micromégas*, &c., driving him to Basel, where he died. See Lives by La Beaumelle (1856) and Lesueur (1897).

MAUREPAS, Jean Frédéric Phélippeux, Comte de, *mō-rė-pah* (1701–81), French statesman, and later minister of marine, rendered services to his department by promoting the French expedition to the North Pole and the Equator in 1736–37, but he displeased the all-powerful Pompadour, and was banished from court in 1749. Recalled and made first minister in 1774, he sought to humiliate England by recognizing the United States. See his *Mémoires* (4 vols. 1792).

MAURIAC, François, *mō-ryak* (1885–1970), French novelist, born at Bordeaux of Roman Catholic parentage, being regarded as the leading novelist of that faith. His treatment of the themes of temptation. sin and redemption, set in the brooding Bordeaux countryside, showed his art as cathartic, exploring the universal problems of sinful, yet aspiring, man. His principal novels, all translated into English, are: *Le Baiser au Lépreux* (1922); *Génitrix* (1923); the *Thérèse* novels; and *Nœud de Vipères* (1932). Also important is his play *Asmodée* (1938). He was awarded the 1952 Nobel prize for literature. See his *Mémoires politiques* (1968); and studies by E. Rideau (Paris 1945; with bibliography) and M. Jarret-Kerr (1954).

MAURICE, Prince of Orange and **Count of Nassau** (1567–1625), son of William the Silent, on whose assassination (1584) he was chosen stadhouder. A great part of the Netherlands was still in the hands of the Spaniards; but Maurice, aided by an English contingent under Leicester and Sidney, rapidly wrested from them the cities and fortresses. In 1597 he defeated the Spaniards at Turnhout, and in 1600 at Nieuwpoort; and for more than three years baffled all the power of Spain by his defence of Ostend. Finally, in 1609, Spain was compelled to acknowledge the United Provinces as a free republic. From this time keen religious dissension grew up between the Orange party, who favoured the orthodox Gomarists, and the liberal Remonstrants or Arminians (see BARNEVELDT, ARMINIUS), and the former triumphed. See Groen van Prinsterer, *Maurice et Barneveldt* (1875).

MAURICE, Prince (1620–52). See RUPERT.

MAURICE, Duke of Saxony. See AUGUSTUS II OF POLAND, CHARLES V, HOLY ROMAN EMPEROR.

MAURICE, (1) John Frederick Denison (1805–1872), English theologian, son of a Unitarian minister, was born at Normanston near Lowestoft, and studied at Trinity College and Trinity Hall, Cambridge, but as a Dissenter, left in 1827 without a degree, and commenced a literary career in London. He wrote a novel, *Eustace Conway*, and for a time edited the *Athenaeum*. Influenced by Coleridge, he took orders in the Church of England, became chaplain to Guy's Hospital (1837) and to Lincoln's Inn (1841–60); in 1840 he became professor of Literature at King's College, London, where he was professor of Theology 1846–53, and from 1866 till his death was professor of Moral Philosophy at Cambridge. The publication in 1853 of his *Theological Essays*, dealing with the atonement and eternal life, lost him his professorship of Theology. His books include *Moral and Metaphysical Philosophy*, *The Conscience*, and *Social Morality*. Maurice strenuously controverted Mansel's views on our knowledge of God, and denounced as false any political economy founded on selfishness and not on the universe. He was the mainspring of the movement known as Christian Socialism; and was the founder of the Working Man's College and of the Queen's College for Women, in both of which he taught. See Life by H. G. Wood (1950).

(2) **Sir John Frederick** (1841–1912), son of (1), professor (1885–92) of Military History at the Staff College, was author of *Life of Frederick Denison Maurice* (1884), a *System of Field Manœuvres* (1872), *The Ashantee War* (1874), *War* (1891), &c.

MAURIER. See DU MAURIER.

MAUROIS, André, pseud. of **Emile Herzog,** *mōr-wa* (1885–1967), French novelist and biographer, born in Elbeuf of a family of Jewish industrialists from Alsace who settled in Normandy after 1870. He was a pupil of Alain and took a degree in philosophy. During World War I he was a liaison officer with the British army and began his literary career with two books of shrewd and affectionate observation of British character, *Les Silences du Colonel Bramble* (1918) and *Les Discours du Docteur O'Grady* (1920). His large output includes *Ariel*, a life of Shelley (1923), *Disraeli* (1927), *Voltaire* (1935), *A la recherche de Marcel Proust* (1949), and *The Life of Sir Alexander Fleming* (trans. 1959). See studies by G. Lemaître (1940) and V. Dupin (Lausanne, 1945).

MAURRAS, Charles, *mō-rah* (1868–1952), French journalist and critic, born at Martigues (Bouches-du-Rhône). A student of philosophy at Paris, he was early influenced by the ideas of Auguste Comte, and this influence, combined with discipleship to the *Félibrige* movement, fostered in him a spirit critical of the contemporary scene, but by 1894 he had outgrown the association and was established as an *avant-garde* journalist. A trip to Greece made him a pronounced philhellene, and influenced by the Dreyfus case, he moved away from republicanism to a belief in the efficacy of monarchy. *Trois idées politiques* . . . (1898) and *Enquête sur la monarchie* (1901) state his views with clarity and vigour. From 1908, in *Action française*, his articles wielded a powerful influence on the youth of the country and this was reinforced by such studies as *Les Conditions de la victoire* (1916–18). *Action française* was finally discredited and in 1936 Maurras was imprisoned for violent attacks on the government of the day, the culmination of his bitter campaign in *Figaro*, *Gazette de France*, and other newspapers, against democratic ideals. His election to the Académie Française in 1938 accordingly caused much controversy and feeling ran very high when, at the fall of France in 1940, he supported the Vichy government. When the country was liberated in 1945, he was brought to trial and sentenced to life imprisonment. He was released, on medical grounds, in March 1952, and later that year died, a man whose considerable talent for dialectics and capacity for uninhibited expression of his strongly-held views had finally availed him nothing, since he had sponsored an unworthy cause.

MAURY, *mō-ree*, (1) **Jean Siffrein** (1746–1817), French prelate, was born at Valréas (dep. Vaucluse). Eloquent *éloges* on the dauphin, &c., gained him in 1784 admission to the Academy. In 1789 he was sent to the States General, where as an orator he rivalled Mirabeau and was one of the chief supporters of the crown. At the dissolution of the Constituent Assembly he withdrew to Rome, and was made an archbishop *in partibus*, and cardinal (1794); but he made his submission in 1804 to Napoleon, who appointed him in 1810 Archbishop of Paris. See Lives by his nephew (1827), Poujoulat (1835), and Ricard (1887).

(2) Matthew Fontaine (1806–73), American hydrographer, born at Spotsylvania, Va., entered the U.S. navy in 1825, and during a voyage round the world commenced his well-known *Navigation* (1834). Lamed for life in 1839, he was appointed superintendent in 1842 of the Hydrographical Office at Washington, and in 1844 of the Observatory. Here he wrote his *Physical Geography of the Sea* (1856), and his works on the Gulf Stream, Ocean Currents, and Great Circle Sailing. He became an officer of the Confederate navy, and later professor of Physics at Lexington. See Life by his daughter (1888).

MAUSER, Paul von, *mow'zėr,* (1838–1914), German fire-arm inventor, born in Oberndorf, Neckar, with his brother **Wilhelm** (1834–82) was responsible for the improved needle-gun (adopted by the German army in 1871) and for the improved breech-loading cannon. Paul produced the first magazine-rifle in 1897.

MAUSOLUS. See ARTEMISIA.

MAUVE, Anton, *mow'vė* (1838–88), Dutch painter, born at Zaandam, one of the greatest landscapists of his time, was influenced by Corot and Millet and painted country scenes. From 1878 he lived at Laren, gathering other painters round him in a kind of Dutch Barbizon school.

MAVOR, (1) O. H. See BRIDIE.

(2) William Fordyce (1758–1837), an Oxfordshire clergyman and schoolmaster, born at New Deer, compiled a commonplace book in his own system of shorthand, c. 1810.

MAWSON, Sir Douglas (1882–1958), English explorer and geologist, born at Bradford, Yorks, was ' educated at Sydney University, and in 1907 was appointed to the scientific staff of Shackleton's Antarctic expedition. In 1911 he was appointed leader of the Australasian Antarctic expedition, which charted 2000 miles of coast; he was knighted on his return. He was awarded the O.B.E. in 1920, and led the joint British-Australian-New Zealand expedition to the Antarctic in 1929–31. See F. Hurley, *Argonauts of the South* (1925).

MAX, Adolphe, *maks* (1869–1939), Belgian politician and patriot, born in Brussels. First a journalist, then an accountant, he became burgomaster of Brussels in 1909. When the German troops approached Brussels in August 1914, he boldly drove to meet them and opened negotiations. He defended the rights of the Belgian population against the invaders, and in September was imprisoned by the Germans, later refusing an offer of freedom on condition that he went to Switzerland and desisted from anti-German agitation. In November 1918 he returned to Belgium, was elected to the house of representatives, and became a minister of state.

MAXIM, Sir Hiram Stevens (1840–1916), born at Sangersville, Maine, U.S., became a coachbuilder. From 1867 he took out patents for gas apparatus, electric lamps, &c. His machine gun was perfected in London in 1883; he also invented a pneumatic gun, a smokeless powder, and a flying machine

(1894). He was knighted in 1901. See *My Life* (1915), and Life by Mottelay (1920).

MAXIMILIAN I (1459–1519), German emperor, the son of Frederick III. By his marriage with Mary, heiress of Charles the Bold, he acquired Burgundy and Flanders; but this involved him in war with Louis XI of France, and in 1482 he was forced to give Artois and Burgundy to Louis. In 1486 he was elected King of the Romans. In 1490 he drove out the Hungarians who, under Matthias Corvinus, had seized (1487) much of the Austrian territories. At Villach in 1492 he routed the Turks, and in 1493 he became emperor. Having next married a daughter of the Duke of Milan, he turned his ambition towards Italy. But after years of war he was compelled (1515) to give up Milan to France and Verona to the Venetians; and in 1499 the Swiss completely separated themselves from the German Empire. The hereditary dominions of his house, however, were increased by the peaceful acquisition of Tirol; the marriage of his son Philip with the Infanta Joanna united the Houses of Spain and Hapsburg; while the marriage in 1521 of his grandson Ferdinand with the daughter of Ladislaus of Hungary and Bohemia brought both these kingdoms to Austria. He also improved the administration of justice, greatly encouraged the arts and learning, and caused to be written *Theuerdank* in verse and *Weisskunig* in prose, of both of which he himself is the hero, and probably part-author. He was called ' the foremost knight of the age '. See Lives by Klüpfel (1864) Ulmann (1884–91), ' Christopher Hare ' (1913) and study by Waas (1941).

MAXIMILIAN, Ferdinand-Joseph, Emperor of Mexico (1832–67), the younger brother of Francis-Joseph I, became an Austrian admiral. In 1863 the French called together a Mexican assembly, which offered the crown of Mexico to Maximilian; he accepted it, and in June 1864 entered Mexico. But Juarez (q.v.) again raised the standard of independence, and Napoleon III had to withdraw his troops. In vain the Empress Charlotte (1840–1927), a daughter of Leopold I of Belgium, went to Europe to enlist support; her reason gave way under grief and excitement. Maximilian felt bound to remain and share the fate of his followers. With 8000 men he made a brave defence of Querétaro, but in May 1867 was betrayed, and on June 19 shot. He has been called a ' marionette Emperor '. Seven volumes of his sketches of travel, essays, &c. (*Aus meinem Leben*) were published in 1867. See books by Martin (1914), Corti (1928), Blasio (1944) and Hyde (1946).

MAX-MÜLLER. See MÜLLER (3).

MAXTON, James (1885–1946), Scottish politician, born in Glasgow, was educated at the university there and became a teacher. A supporter of the Independent Labour Party, he became its chairman in 1926 and he sat as M.P. for Bridgeton from 1922 until his death. A man of strong convictions, he was a staunch pacificist, and suffered imprisonment for attempting to foment a strike of shipyard workers during World War I, in which he was a conscientious objector. His extreme views claimed few supporters, but his sincerity won the respect of all. See Life by McNair (1955).

MAXWELL, (1) James Clark. See CLERK-MAXWELL.

(2) Sir William Stirling. See STIRLING-MAXWELL.

MAY, (1) Phil (1864–1903), English caricaturist, born at Wortley near Leeds, was left an orphan at nine, after years of poverty became poster artist and cartoonist of the *St Stephen's Review*, went to Australia and on his return in 1890 established himself by his *Annual* and contributions to *Punch*, &c. He excelled in depicting East London types. See Life by J. Thorpe (1948).

(2) Thomas (1594–1650), English dramatist and historian, was educated at Cambridge, and became a member of Gray's Inn and a courtier. He wrote dramas, comedies, poems and translations of the Georgics and Lucan. As secretary and historiographer to parliament he produced a *History of the Parliament 1640–1643* (1647), and a *Breviary* (1650). See Life by Chester (1932).

(3) Sir Thomas Erskine, 1st Baron Farnborough (1815–86), English constitutional jurist, educated at Bedford School, became assistant librarian of the House of Commons in 1831, clerk-assistant in 1856, and clerk of the House in 1871. He was created a baron in 1881 on his retirement. His *Treatise on the Law, Privileges, Proceedings, and Usage of Parliament* (1844) has been translated into various languages and remains a standard work; his *Constitutional History of England 1760–1860* (1861–63; edited and continued by F. Holland, 1912) is a continuation of Hallam.

MAYAKOVSKY, Vladimir (1894–1930), Soviet poet, began writing at an early age, became interested in new techniques, and was regarded as the leader of the futurist school. During the 1917 Revolution he emerged as the propaganda mouthpiece of the Bolsheviks. Among his revolutionary pieces are *150 million* (1920) and *Mystery Bouffe* (1918). He also wrote satirical plays. He died by his own hand. See study with translations by H. Marshall (1945).

MAYER, mi'er, Julius Robert von (1814–78), German physicist, was born at Heilbronn, and settled as physician there in 1841. In 1842 he announced from physiological considerations, the equivalence of heat and work and the law of the conservation of energy, independently of Joule (q.v.), and his mental health suffered on account of the dispute over priority. See studies by Dühring (1893) and Weyrauch (1889).

MAYHEW, Henry (1812–87), English author and joint editor of *Punch* with Mark Lemon (q.v.), was born in London, ran away from Westminster School and collaborated with his brother **Augustus** (1826–75) in writing numerous successful novels such as *The Good Genius that turns everything to Gold* (1847), *Whom to Marry* (1848), &c. He also wrote on many subjects, his best-known work being the classic social survey, *London Labour and the London Poor* (1851–62). Another brother, **Horace** (1816–72), also collaborated with Henry and was a contributor to *Punch*. See R. G. G. Price, *History of 'Punch'* (1957).

MAYO, (1) Charles Horace (1865–1939), American surgeon, made a special study of goitre, and with his brother organized the Mayo Clinic within what is now St Mary's Hospital, Rochester, Minn.

(2) Katherine (1868–1940), American journalist, born at Ridgeway, Pa., is remembered for her books exposing social evils, especially *Isles of Fear* (1925), condemning American administration of the Philippines, and *Mother India* (1927), a forthright indictment of child marriage and other customs.

(3) Richard Southwell Bourke, Earl of (1822–72), Indian statesman, was born in Dublin, and was educated at Trinity College, Dublin. He entered the House of Commons as a Conservative in 1847, and was appointed chief-secretary of Ireland by Lord Derby in 1852, 1858, and 1866. Sent out in 1868 to succeed Lord Lawrence, he was eminently successful as viceroy of India, but was fatally stabbed by a convict while inspecting the settlement at Port Blair on the Andaman Islands. See Life by Hunter (2 vols. 1875).

(4) William James (1861–1939), American surgeon, brother of (1), specialist in stomach surgery, established the Mayo Clinic and along with (1) set up the Mayo Foundation for Medical Education and Research (1915).

MAYOW, John (1640–79), English chemist, fellow of All Souls, Oxford, and of the Royal Society, preceded Priestley and Lavoisier by a century with his discoveries relating to respiration and the chemistry of combustion.

MAZARIN, ma-za-rî, Jules, orig. Giulio Mazarini (1602–61), cardinal and minister of France, was born July 14 at Pescina in the Abruzzi, studied under the Jesuits at Rome and at Alcalá in Spain. He accompanied a papal legate to the court of France, was papal nuncio there (1634–36), entered the service of Louis XIII as a naturalized Frenchman (1639), and two years later became cardinal through the influence of Richelieu, who before his death in 1642 recommended Mazarin to the king as his successor. Louis died in 1643, but Mazarin knew how to retain his power under the queen-regent, Anne of Austria; she certainly loved him, even if it cannot be proved that there was a private marriage between them (the cardinal had never taken more than the minor orders). He ruled more efficiently than Richelieu, and was almost as powerful. The parliament resisted the registration of edicts of taxation; but Mazarin caused the leaders of the opposition to be arrested (August 1648), upon which the disturbances of the Fronde began. The court retired to St Germain, but at length triumphed by the aid of Condé. The hatred against Mazarin, however, blazed out anew in the provinces, when at his instigation the queen-regent arrested Condé, Conti and Longueville in January 1650. Mazarin triumphed at Réthel, but soon had to succumb and retire to Brühl. Meantime the press teemed with pamphlets and satires against him—the *Mazarinades*. The cardinal used all his influence to form a new royal party, won the support of Turenne, and in February 1653 returned to Paris, regaining all his power and popularity. He acquired the alliance of Cromwell at the price of Dunkirk; and by the marriage of Louis XIV with the Infanta Maria Theresa (1659), brought the succession to the throne of Spain nearer. Mazarin died at Vincennes, March 9, leaving an immense fortune. His magnificent library was bequeathed to the Collège Mazarin, and his name lives in the rare 'Mazarin Bible'. His seven nieces whom he brought from Italy to the French court varied in character and ultimate fate, but all married counts, dukes or princes, though more than one died in poverty or obscurity. See Chéruel's Histories of France (1879–82), his edition of Mazarin's Letters (1879–91) and works by Renée (1856), Masson (1886), Hassall (1903), Roca (1908), Bailly (1935).

MAZEPPA, Ivan Stepanovich, *ma-zyay'pa* (*c.* 1644–1709), hetman of the Cossacks, was born of a noble family, and became a page at the court of Poland. A nobleman, having surprised him in an intrigue with his wife, had him bound naked upon his horse, which, let loose, carried him, torn and bleeding, to its native wilds of the Ukraine—or, in another story, to his own home. Mazeppa now joined the Cossacks, and in 1687 was elected hetman. He won the confidence of Peter the Great, who made him Prince of the Ukraine; but when Peter curtailed the freedom of the Cossacks, Mazeppa entered into negotiations with Charles XII of Sweden. His hopes of an independent crown perished in the disaster of Pultowa (1709), and he fled with Charles to Bender, where he died. His story is the theme of poems, notably that by Byron, plays, novels, opera, paintings, &c., and of a history by Kostomaroff (1882).

MAZZINI, *mat-zee'nee*, Giuseppe (1805–72), Italian patriot, was born at Genoa, June 22, studied at the university there, and at nineteen was practising as an advocate. In 1821 his heart was stirred by the sight of refugees from the unsuccessful rising in Piedmont. He wrote in favour of romanticism, became a more and more ardent champion of liberalism, and joining the Carbonari in 1829, was betrayed (1830) to the Sardinian police, and imprisoned in Savona. Released next year, he organized at Marseilles the Young Italy Association, which sought to create a free and united nation of Italians—republican from the nature of the case—and to work for the governance of the world by the moral law of progress. In 1831 he addressed to Charles Albert of Piedmont an appeal, urging him to put himself at the head of the struggle for Italian independence; the answer, under Metternich's influence, was a sentence of perpetual banishment, and in 1832 the French authorities expelled him from France. Henceforward he was the most untiring political agitator in Europe. He wrote incessantly with fervid eloquence and intense conviction. In 1834 he organized an abortive invasion of Savoy. The next two years Mazzini spent in Switzerland scattering, by means of his journal *Young Italy*, the seeds of republican revolt through Europe. Banished from Switzerland, he found a refuge in London in 1837; and, struggling with poverty, contrived to teach and civilize many of his poorer countrymen, the organboys of London. In 1844 he proved his

charge against the British government of opening his letters and communicating their contents to the rulers in Italy—a charge which raised a storm of indignation throughout the country. He threw himself into the thick of the Lombard revolt in 1848. After Milan capitulated he tried with Garibaldi to keep the war alive in the valleys of the Alps. Leghorn received him with wild enthusiasm in February 1849, just before the republic was proclaimed at Rome, where in March Mazzini, Saffi, and Armellini were appointed a triumvirate with dictatorial powers. In April the French arrived; after a struggle the republic fell; and the triumvirs indignantly resigned (June). From London Mazzini planned the attempted risings at Mantua (1852), Milan (1853), Genoa (1857), and Leghorn (1857). Here also he founded, along with Kossuth and Ledru-Rollin, the republican European Association, and organized the Society of the Friends of Italy. In 1859 Mazzini condemned the alliance between Piedmont and Napoleon III. He supported Garibaldi in his expedition against Sicily and Naples; and when Piedmont defeated and took him prisoner at Aspromonte (1862), Mazzini broke finally with the monarchical party. In 1866–67 Messina in protest elected him its deputy to the Italian parliament four times in succession. Again expelled from Switzerland, he was (1870) arrested at sea and imprisoned for two months at Gaeta. He settled at Lugano, but died at Pisa, March 10, 1872. Utopian idealist, political dreamer, apostle of the democratic evangel, and restless conspirator, Mazzini was also a man of great organizing power; thoroughly sincere and disinterested, he felt only impatience and scorn for moderates and opportunists. It was inevitable that he and Cavour should dislike and distrust one another. Yet it was Mazzini who prepared the ground for Italian unity, Garibaldi who did most of the harvesting, and Cavour who entered into their labours. Mazzini's writings are mostly political. *On the Duties of Man* (new ed. 1955) contains an outline of ethical theory; *Thoughts upon Democracy in Europe* is a discussion of economics and socialism. See the collected edition of his *Scritti, editi ed inediti* (16 vols. 1861); the English *Life and Writings* (1864–70); the *Selected Essays* (edited by Clarke, 1887); the selections by Stubbs (1891); *Memoir* by Venturi (1874); and Lives by B. King (1938), C. O. Griffith (1932), D. Silone (1939), C. Sforza (1926), and G. Salvemini (1956).

MBOYA, Tom (1930–1969), African nationalist leader, born on a sisal estate in the white highlands of Kenya, educated at Holy Ghost College, Mangu, became a sanitary inspector (1951) but soon came under the influence of Kenyatta (q.v.) and joined his Kenya African Union, of which he was P.R.O. and later (1953) treasurer. On the suppression of the party, he turned to trade union activity, becoming secretary of the Kenya Federation of Labour. The unsatisfactory new Constitution of 1954 drove him to passive resistance and campaigning for independence. At the round-table conference in London (1960), he obtained important constitutional concessions for Africans, especially on land reform. After the resurgence of Kenyatta's party as the Kenya African National Union in 1960 he became its general secretary; he was Kenyan minister of labour (1962–63), minister of justice (1963–64), and minister of economic development and planning from 1964. He was assassinated in Nairobi in 1969.

MEAD, (1) Margaret (1901–   ), American anthropologist, born in Philadelphia, was appointed assistant curator of ethnology at the American Museum of Natural History in 1926, associate curator from 1942, and curator from 1964. After expeditions to Samoa and New Guinea she wrote *Coming of Age in Samoa* (1928) and *Growing up in New Guinea* (1930). Her works combine authority with the ability to make anthropology intelligible to the layman. Later publications include *Male and Female* (1949) and *Growth and Culture* (1951).

(2) **Richard** (1673–1754), fashionable London physician, succeeded Radcliffe as leader of his profession and published on poisons and infections. Physician to Queen Anne, he was consulted by the consumptive French painter Watteau, who visited London specially for the purpose. See Memoirs by Maty (1755) and Winslow, *Conquest of Epidemic Disease* (1944).

MEADE, George Gordon (1815–72), American general, born at Cadiz in Spain, graduated at West Point in 1835, and served against the Seminoles and in the Mexican War. In 1861 he distinguished himself at Antietam and Fredericksburg, and in 1863 he commanded the Army of the Potomac and defeated Lee at Gettysburg. See Lives by his son (New York 1913) and Pennypacker (1901); also T. Lyman *Meade's Headquarters, 1863–65* (Boston 1922).

MEADOWS-TAYLOR, Philip. See TAYLOR.

MEAGHER, *mah'ér,* **Thomas Francis** (1822–1867), Irish patriot, was born in Waterford. He became a prominent member of the Young Ireland party and in 1848 was transported for life to Van Diemen's Land. He made his escape in 1852, studied law in the United States, in 1861 organized the 'Irish brigade' for the Federals, and distinguished himself at Richmond and elsewhere. While secretary of Montana territory, and keeping the Indians in check, he was drowned in the Missouri. See Cavanaugh, *Memoirs of General Thomas Francis Meagher* (1892).

MECHNIKOV, Ilya (1845–1916), Russian biologist, was born at Ivanovka near Kharkov and in 1870 became professor at Odessa. In 1888 he joined Pasteur in Paris and shared the Nobel prize with Ehrlich in 1908 for his work on immunology. He discovered that phagocytes, cells which devour infective organisms. See Life by his widow (1921).

MEDAWAR, Sir Peter Brian (1915–   ), Brazilian-born British zoologist, professor of Zoology at Birmingham (1947–51), Jodrell professor of Comparative Anatomy at London University (1951–62), director of National Inst. for Medical Research, Mill Hill, from 1962. He shared the Nobel prize in 1960 with Burnet (3) for experiments on immunological intolerance. He gave the brilliant Reith Lectures (1959) on *The Future of Man*, became

C.B.E. in 1958, was knighted in 1965, and was created C.H. in 1971.

MEDHURST, George (1759–1827), English engineer who first suggested a pneumatic dispatch (1810), was born at Shoreham.

MEDICI, *may'dee-chee,* a Florentine family which amassed great wealth by the efforts of Giovanni (1360–1429), the banker of Cafaggiolo in the Mugello, and which exerted a great political and cultural influence from the 14th century onwards. See works on the Medici Family by Smeaton (1902), Schevill (1909), G. F. Young (1909), Pieraccini (1925), Neale (1943). Noteworthy members were:

(1) **Catharine.** See CATHARINE DE' MEDICI.

(2) **Cosimo** (1389–1464), ' Pater Patriae ', son of the banker Giovanni, and father of (7), began the glorious epoch of the family. He procured for Florence (nominally still republican) security abroad and peace from civil dissensions. He employed his wealth in encouraging art and literature. He made Florence the centre of the revival of learning, and enriched her with splendid buildings and great libraries. See works on him by Armstrong (1900) and Gutkind (1938).

(3) **Cosimo I** (1519–74), ' the great ', was descended on his mother's side from (6). He possessed the astuteness of character, the love of art and literature of his greater predecessors, but was cruel and relentless in his enmities, though one of the ablest rulers of his century. He was created grand-duke of Tuscany in 1569 and thus became the founder of a dynasty which lasted until the 18th century. The later Medici grand-dukes were not of outstanding ability but managed to preserve the character of the Florentine state during the years of foreign domination. See Life by Booth (1921).

(4) **Giovanni** (1475–1521), cardinal, son of (6), became Pope Leo X (q.v.).

(5) **Giulio** (1478–1534), grandson of (7), became Pope Clement VII (q.v.).

(6) **Lorenzo** (1449–92), ' the magnificent ', son of (7) and father of (4) and (8), became at twenty joint-ruler with his brother **Giuliano** (1453–78). The growing power of the Medici had roused much envy; and in 1478 the malcontents, headed by the Pazzi and in league with the pope, Sixtus IV, formed a plot to overthrow them. Giuliano fell a victim to the assassins; Lorenzo increased his popularity by the courage and judgment that he showed in this crisis. He was a just and magnanimous ruler, one of the most distinguished lyric poets of the day, an enthusiastic member of the Platonic Academy, the friend of artists and scholars, a promoter of the art of printing. His many-sided gifts combined to make the Laurentian Age (1469–1492) the most glorious period in Florentine history. Yet he sapped the existing forms of government, and by seeking the advancement of his family, left Florence a ready prey to her enemies. See Lives by E. Rho (1926), Fiori (1938), and Ady (1955).

(7) **Piero I** (1414–69), ' the gouty ', son of (2), father of (6), ruled for five troubled years.

(8) **Piero II** (1471–1503), son of (6), allied himself with the king of Naples against Lodovico Sforza of Milan; and when the latter in 1492 called to his aid Charles VIII of

France, Piero surrendered Pisa and Leghorn to the French. The magistrates and people, incensed at his cowardice, drove him from Florence and declared the Medici traitors and rebels. All efforts of the Medici to regain their power were vain until in 1512 a Spanish papal army invaded Tuscany, Prato was taken and sacked, and the Florentines, helpless and terrified, recalled the Medici, headed by Giuliano II (1478–1516). In 1513 the elevation of (4) to the papal chair completed the restoration of the family to all their former splendour and made Florence into a papal dependency.

MEDTNER, Nikolai (1879–1951), Russian composer and pianist of German descent, born in Moscow, lived in the West from 1922. His classical-romantic compositions included two piano concertos and much piano music. See R. Holt, *Nicholas Medtner* (1955).

MEDWALL, Henry (1462–c. 1505), English dramatist, wrote *Fulgens and Lucres*, the earliest English secular play extant written before 1500.

MEE, Arthur (1875–1943), English journalist, editor and writer, born at Stapleford, Nottingham, most widely known for his *Children's Encyclopaedia* (1908) and for his *Children's Newspaper*. He also produced a *Self-Educator* (1906), a *History of the World* (1907), both with Sir John Hammerton, a *Popular Science* (1912), a *Children's Shakespeare* (1926), and *The King's England* (1936–1953), a series of topographical books describing the English counties.

MEEGEREN, Van. See VAN MEEGEREN.

MEGASTHENES, *me-gas'the-neez* (fl. 300 B.C.), a Greek ambassador (306–298 B.C.) at the Indian court of Sandrocottus or Chandra Gupta. Here he gathered materials for his *Indica*, from which Arrian, Strabo, &c. borrowed. The fragments were edited by Schwanebeck (1846) and Müller (1848).

MEGERLE, Ulrich. See ABRAHAM-A-SANTA-CLARA.

MEHEMET 'ALI (c. 1769–1849), better Mohammed 'Ali, viceroy of Egypt, an Albanian officer of militia, was sent to Egypt with a Turkish-Albanian force on the French invasion in 1798. After the departure of the French he, at the head of his Albanians, supported the Egyptian rulers in their struggles with the Mamelukes. Having become the chief power in Egypt, he in 1805 had himself proclaimed viceroy by his Albanians, and was confirmed in this post by the sultan. He secured for Egypt a galvanic prosperity by the massacre of the Mamelukes in the citadel of Cairo (1811), the formation of a regular army, the improvement of irrigation, and the introduction of the elements of European civilization. In 1816 he reduced part of Arabia by the generalship of his adopted son Ibrahim; in 1820 he annexed Nubia and part of the Sudan; and from 1821 to 1828 his troops, under Ibrahim, occupied various points in the Morea and Crete, to aid the Turks in their war with the insurgent Greeks. The Egyptian fleet was annihilated at Navarino, and Ibrahim remained in the Morea till forced to evacuate by the French in 1828. In 1831 Ibrahim began the conquest of Syria, and in 1832 totally routed the Ottoman army at Koniya, after which the Porte ceded Syria to Mehemet Ali on condition of tribute. The victory at Nezib in 1839 might have elevated him to the throne of Constantinople; but the quadruple alliance in 1840, the fall of Acre to the British, and the consequent evacuation of Syria compelled him to limit his ambition to Egypt. In 1848 he became insane and was succeeded by Ibrahim. See works by Mouriez (1857), Sabry (1930), Dodwell (1931).

MEHRING, Franz (1846–1919), German left-wing writer, born in Schlawe, Pomerania, was a founder of the German Communist Party and author of historical studies of the workers' movement, including *Geschichte der deutsche Sozialdemocratie* (1898) and a life of Marx (1919).

MÉHUL, Étienne Nicolas, *may-ül* (1763–1817), French operatic composer, born at Givet, became in 1795 professor of the Paris Conservatoire. Of his numerous operas, *Joseph* (1807) is his masterpiece. See Lives by Pougin (1889) and Brancour (Paris 1912).

MEILHAC, *may-yak*, Henri (1831–97), French playwright, born in Paris, from 1855 produced a long series of light comedies—some in conjunction with Halévy, and some, including *La Belle Hélène*, well known through Offenbach's music. His *chef-d'œuvre* is *Frou-Frou* (1869). He also collaborated with Halévy and Gille respectively in the libretti of the operas *Carmen* and *Manon*.

MEILLET, Antoine, *may-yay* (1866–1936), French philologist, born at Moulins, a great authority on Indo-European languages, was professor at the Collège de France from 1906, and wrote standard works on Old Slav, Greek, Armenian, Old Persian, &c.

MEINHOLD, Johann Wilhelm, *mīn-holt* (1797–1815), born on the island of Usedom, Lutheran pastor there and at Krummin and Rehwinkel, published poems and dramas, but is best known for his *Amber Witch* (trans. 1894).

MEINONG, Alexius von, *mī'-* (1853–1930), Austrian philosopher, born at Lemberg, *privatdozent* at Vienna (1878), was appointed professor at Graz (1882). A disciple of Brentano (q.v.), he wrote *Humestudien* (1877–92) and, in his *Untersuchungen zur Gegenstandstheorie und Psychologie*, 'Investigations into the theory of objects and psychology' (1904), attempted to preserve an objectivity for all kinds of entities. Bertrand Russell brilliantly attacked this on the principle of Occam's razor, that entities ought not to be multiplied except of necessity, differentiating sharply between grammatical and logical objects. See study by J. N. Findlay (1933) and RUSSELL.

MEI SHENG (d. 140 B.C.), Chinese poet to whom is given the credit of introducing the five-character line. For this he is sometimes called the father of modern Chinese poetry.

MEISSONIER, Jean Louis Ernest, *may-son-yay* (1813–91), French painter, mostly of genre and military scenes, was born at Lyons. See Lives by Mollet (1882), Gréard (1897) and Formentin (1901).

MEITNER, Lise, *mīt'nèr* (1878–1968), Austrian physicist, born in Vienna, professor in Berlin and member (1917–38) of the Kaiser

MELA

Wilhelm Institute for Chemistry, in 1917 shared with Hahn the discovery of the radioactive element protactinium. She is known for her work on nuclear physics. In 1938 she went to Sweden, to the Nobel Physical Institute, and in 1947 to the Royal Swedish Academy of Engineering Sciences, Stockholm, retiring to England in 1960.

MELA, Pomponius (fl. A.D. 40), the first Latin writer who was strictly a geographer, was born in S. Spain, and lived under the Emperor Claudius. His work, an unsystematic compendium, is entitled *De Situ Orbis*. The text is very corrupt. See work by H. Zimmermann (1895).

MELANCHTHON (Gk. for original surname Schwarzerd, 'black earth'), **Philip**, *melank'thon* (1497–1560), German religious reformer, born at Bretten in the Palatinate, was appointed professor of Greek at Wittenberg in 1516 and became Luther's fellow-worker. His *Loci Communes* (1521) is the first great Protestant work on dogmatic theology. The Augsburg Confession (1530) was composed by him. After Luther's death he lost the confidence of some Protestants by concessions to the Catholics; while the zealous Lutherans were displeased at his approximation to the doctrine of Calvin on the Lord's Supper. His conditional consent to the introduction of the stringent Augsburg Interim (1549) in Saxony led to painful controversies. See Life by C. J. Manschreck (1957), studies by C. L. Hill (1944) and Hildebrandt (1946), and works by Harnack (1897), Ellinger (1902) and Engelland (1931).

MELBA, Dame Nellie, *née* **Mitchell** (1861–1931), Australian prima donna, born at Melbourne, appeared at Covent Garden in 1888. The wonderful purity of her soprano voice won her worldwide fame. She was created D.B.E. (1927). See her autobiographical *Melodies and Memories* (1925) and P. Colson, *Melba* (1931).

MELBOURNE, William Lamb, 2nd Viscount (1779–1848), English statesman, born in London, March 15, and educated at Eton, Trinity, Cambridge and Glasgow, became Whig M.P. for Leominster in 1805, but accepted in 1827 the chief-secretaryship of Ireland in Canning's government, and retained it under Goderich and Wellington. Succeeding as second viscount (1828), he returned to the Whigs, became home secretary in 1830, for a few months of 1834 was premier, and, premier again in 1835, was still in office at the accession of Queen Victoria (1837), when he showed remarkable tact in introducing her to her duties. In 1841 he passed the seals of office to Peel, and after that took little part in public affairs. His wife (1785–1828), a daughter of the Earl of Bessborough, wrote novels as Lady Caroline Lamb, and was notorious for her nine month's devotion (1812–13) to Lord Byron. The charge brought against Melbourne in 1836 of seducing the Hon. Mrs Norton (q.v.) was thrown out at once. See Lives by Torrens (1878), Dunckley (1880) and Lord David Cecil (1965). See also A Cecil, *Queen Victoria and her Prime Ministers* (1952).

MELCHETT. See MOND (1).
MELCOMBE, Lord. See DODINGTON.

MELEAGER, *mel-ee-ah'jĕr* (fl. 80 B.C.), of Gadara, Palestine, was author of 128 exquisite epigrams. See translations by Headlam (1891) and Aldington (1920).

MELÉNDEZ VALDÉS, Juan (1754–1817), Spanish poet, born near Badajoz, became a professor of Classics at the University of Salamanca and fought for Napoleon in the War of Independence. Reckoned the greatest lyric poet of his time, he is known for his odes, ballads and romantic verses. See study by W. E. Colford (1942).

MELLON, (1) Andrew William (1855–1937), American politician, born in Pittsburgh, inherited a fortune from his father, which he used to establish himself as a banker and industrial magnate. Entering politics, he became secretary of the treasury in 1921 and made controversial fiscal reforms. He was ambassador to the U.K. in 1932–33. He endowed the National Gallery of Art at Washington.

(2) **Harriot** (c. 1777–1837), English actress, born in London, appeared at Drury Lane in 1795. She married her elderly protector, Thomas Coutts (q.v.), who left her all his money, in 1815; and in 1827 the Duke of St Albans. See her Memoirs (2 vols. 1886) and book by Pearce (1915).

MELLONI, Macedonio (1798–1854), Italian physicist, born at Parma, where later he was professor of Physics (1824–31), had to flee to France on account of political activities. Returning to Naples in 1839, he directed the Vesuvius Observatory till 1848. He is specially noted for his work on radiant heat. He introduced the term diathermancy to denote the capacity of transmitting infrared radiation.

MELO, Francisco Manuel de (1608–66), Portuguese writer, born at Lisbon, had an arduous and hazardous life as soldier, political prisoner, and exile in Brazil, whence he returned in 1657. He wrote in both Spanish and Portuguese, and is better remembered for his critical works and his history of the Catalan wars than for his voluminous poetry.

MELVILL, Thomas (1726–53), Scottish scientist, educated at Glasgow for the church, was the first (1752) to study the spectra of luminous gases. His early death at Geneva obscured the importance of his experiments.

MELVILLE, (1) Andrew (1545 – c. 1622), Scottish Presbyterian theologian, uncle of (6), was born at Baldowie, Montrose, and educated at St Andrews and Paris, became in 1568 professor at Geneva. On his return to Scotland (1574) he rendered eminent service as principal of Glasgow University. He had a very important share in drawing up the Presbyterian Second Book of Discipline. Chosen principal of St Mary's College, St Andrews (1580), besides lecturing on theology, he taught Hebrew, Chaldee and Syriac. In 1582 he preached boldly against absolute authority before the General Assembly; in 1584, to escape imprisonment, he went to London. He was repeatedly moderator of the General Assembly. In 1596 he headed a deputation to 'remonstrate' with James VI; and in 1606, with seven other ministers, was called to England to confer with him.

Having ridiculed the service in the Chapel Royal in a Latin epigram, he was summoned before the English privy council, and sent to the Tower. In 1611 he was released through the intercession of the Duke of Bouillon, who wanted his services as a professor in his university at Sedan. See Lives by McCrie (1819) and Morison (1899).

(2) **George John Whyte.** See WHYTE-MELVILLE.

(3) **Henry Dundas, 1st Viscount.** See DUNDAS Family (1).

(4) **Herman** (1819–91), American novelist, born in New York, became a bank clerk, but in search of adventure, joined a whaling ship bound for the South Seas. He deserted at the Marquesas and spent some weeks with a savage tribe in the Typee valley, an episode which inspired his first book, *Typee* (1846). Having been taken off by an Australian whaler, he was jailed at Tahiti as a member of a mutinous crew, but escaped and spent some time on the island. This adventure was the basis of his second book, *Omoo* (1847). *Mardi* (1849) also dealt with the South Seas, but entered the realm of satire not too successfully, so that Melville returned to adventure fiction with *Redburn* (1849) and *White Jacket* (1850), in which he drew on his experiences as a seaman on the man-of-war which brought him home from Tahiti. In 1847 he had married, and after three years in New York he took a farm near Pittsfield, Mass., where Nathaniel Hawthorne (q.v.) was his neighbour and friend. It was during this period that he wrote his masterpiece, *Moby Dick* (1851), a novel of the whaling industry, whose extraordinary vigour and colour and whose philosophical and allegorical undertones reflecting on the nature of evil have given it a place among the classic sea stories. Later novels include *Pierre* (1852), in a symbolic vein which was not appreciated by his readers, the satirical *Confidence Man* (1857), and *Billy Budd*, published posthumously in 1924 and used as the subject of an opera by Benjamin Britten in 1950. Now regarded as one of America's greatest novelists, Melville was not so successful during his life, even *Moby Dick* being unappreciated. After 1857, disillusioned and now a New York customs official, he wrote only some poetry. Recognition did not come until some thirty years after his death. See his *Letters* (1960), and studies by Weaver (1922), Mumford (1929), Anderson (1939), Sedgwick (1944), Arvin (1940), and Humphreys (1962).

(5) **Sir James,** of Halhill (1535–1617), Scottish soldier and diplomat, went to France as page to the young Queen Mary, and subsequently undertook missions to the courts of England and the Palatinate. See his *Memoirs* (Bannatyne Club, 1827).

(6) **James** (1556–1614), Scottish Reformer and diarist, nephew of (1), was born near Montrose, professor of Oriental Languages at St Andrews and minister in 1586 of Kilrenny, Fife. He took a leading part with his uncle in ecclesiastical politics and went to London in 1606. He was moderator of the general assembly in 1589. He is best known for his *Diary* (1556–1601), written in a racy, vigorous and idiomatic Scots.

MEMLINC, or **Memling, Hans** (c. 1440–94), Flemish religious painter, was born at Seligenstadt of Dutch parents, and lived mostly at Bruges. A pupil of Roger van der Weyden (q.v.), he repeated the types of his master. The triptych of the *Madonna Enthroned* at Chatsworth (1468), the *Marriage of St Catherine* (1479) and the *Shrine of St Ursula* (1489), both at Bruges, are among his best works. He was also an original and creative portrait painter. See Lives by Weale (1901), and K. Voll (New York 1913), also M. Conway, *The Van Eycks and their Followers* (1921).

MEMMI, Simone. See MARTINI (2).

MENAECHMUS (375–325 B.C.), Greek mathematician, one of the tutors of Alexander the Great, was the first to investigate conics as sections of a cone.

MÉNAGE, *may-nahzh*, **Giles** (1613–92), French lexicographer, born at Angers, gave up the bar for the church, but chiefly spent his time in literary pursuits. He founded, in opposition to the Academy, a salon, the Mercuriales, which gained him European fame and Molière's ridicule as Vadius in *Femmes savantes*. His chief work is his *Dictionnaire étymologique* (1650). See Lives by Baret (1859) and Ashton (Ottawa 1920).

MENANDER (c. 343–291 B.C.), the greatest Greek poet of the New Comedy, was born at Athens, and was drowned at the Piraeus. His comedies were more successful with cultured than with popular audiences; but Quintilian praised him without reserve, and Terence imitated him closely. Only a few fragments of his work were known till 1906, when Lefebvre discovered in Egypt a papyrus containing 1328 lines from four different plays. In 1957, however, the complete text of the comedy *Dyskolos* (' The Bad-tempered Man') was brought to light in Geneva. See G. Norwood, *Greek Comedy* (1931), and Webster, *Studies n Menander* (1950).

MENCHIKOV. See MENSHIKOV.

MENCIUS, properly **Meng-tse** (372–289 B.C.), a Chinese sage, born in Shantung, founded a school on the model of that of his great predecessor Confucius. When forty years of age he travelled from one princely court to another for more than twenty years, seeking a ruler who would put into practice his system of social and political order. But, finding none, he retired. After his death his disciples collected his sayings and published them as the *Book of Meng-tse*. The aim of his teaching was practical: how men, especially rulers, shall best regulate their conduct. His system is based on belief in the ethical goodness of man's nature, from which follow the cardinal virtues of benevolence, righteousness, moral wisdom, and propriety of conduct. He advocated free trade, the deposition of bad rulers, division of labour, inspection of work by government, maintenance of good roads and bridges, poor laws, education and the abolition of war. See Legge's *Life* (1875) and studies by Richards (1932) and Giles (1942).

MENCKEN, Henry Louis (1880–1956), American philologist, editor and satirist, born at Baltimore, became a journalist and literary critic. Satirical, individual and iconoclastic, he greatly influenced the American literary scene in the 'twenties. In 1924 he founded the *American Mercury*, and his great work, *The American Language*, was first published in 1918. See his autobiographical *Days of H. L. Mencken* (3 vols. in 1, N.Y. 1947), Life by Manchester (1952), and studies by Goldberg (1925) and Kemler (Boston 1950).

MENDEL, (1) **Gregor Johann** (1822–84), Austrian biologist, was born, son of a peasant proprietor, near Odrau in Austrian Silesia. Entering an Augustinian cloister in Brünn, he was ordained a priest in 1847. After studying science at Vienna (1851–53) he returned to Brünn, and in 1868 became abbot there. Meanwhile he had been pursuing remarkable researches on hybridity in plants, and eventually established the Mendelian Law of dominant and recessive characters. His principle of factorial inheritance and the quantitative investigation of single characters have become the basis of modern genetics. See works by Bateson (1913), Iltis (trans. 1932) and Ford (1931).

(2) **Lafayette Benedict** (1872–1935), American chemist, professor at Yale, did much original work on nutrition, discovering Vitamin A (1913) and the function of Vitamin C.

MENDELEYEV, Dmitri Ivanovich, *myen-dye-lyay'ef* (1834–1907), Russian chemist, born at Tobolsk, professor of Chemistry at St Petersburg from 1866, formulated the periodic law by which he predicted the existence of several elements which were subsequently discovered. Element No 101 is named mendelevium after him. See *Essays* by Thorpe (1923).

MENDELSOHN, Erich (1887–1953), German architect (from 1933 in England and from 1941 in America), was born in Allenstein. A leading exponent of functionalism, his most famous works include the Einstein Tower at Potsdam and the Hebrew University at Jerusalem. See study by Whittick (1940).

MENDELSSOHN, Moses (1729–86), German philosopher, grandfather of the composer, Mendelssohn-Bartholdy (q.v.), was born at Dessau. His father, whose name was Mendel, was a Jewish schoolmaster and scribe. He went to study in Berlin at thirteen and eventually became the partner of a rich silk manufacturer. He was a diligent student of Locke, Shaftesbury and Pope; and as a zealous defender of enlightened Monotheism, was an apostle of Deism, and the prototype of Lessing's *Nathan*. His principal works are on Pope as a philosopher (conjointly with Lessing, 1755), on the Sensations (1755), on Evidence in Metaphysics (1763); and *Jerusalem* (1783). See Lives by Kayserling (2nd ed. 1887) and F. Bamberger (1923).

MENDELSSOHN - BARTHOLDY, Felix (1809–47), German composer, the grandson of Moses Mendelssohn (q.v.), was born the son of a Hamburg banker who added the name Bartholdy. Felix was carefully educated, especially in music, and at ten made his first public appearance as pianist. Within the next few years he formed the acquaintance of Goethe, Weber and Moscheles, and composed his Symphony in C minor and the B minor Quartet. The August of 1825 saw the completion of his opera, *Camacho's Wedding*. With the

Midsummer Night's Dream overture (1826) Mendelssohn may be said to have attained his musical majority. In London in 1829 he conducted his *Symphony in C Minor*. A tour of Scotland in the summer inspired him with the *Hebrides* overture and the *Scotch Symphony*. He conducted the Lower Rhine festival at Düsseldorf in 1833 and 1834 and in 1835 the Gewandhaus concerts at Leipzig. He settled in Berlin in 1841 when the king of Prussia asked his assistance in the founding of an Academy of Arts. In 1843 the new music school at Leipzig was opened for him with Schumann and David among his associates. He produced his *Elijah* in Birmingham in 1846. He had scarcely returned from his tenth and last visit to England, in May 1847, when the news of his sister Fanny's death reached him. Periods of illness and depression followed rapidly; and he died at Leipzig on November 4. He was eminent as pianist and organist. His music, however, suffers from lack of emotional range, often deteriorates into fairylike prestos and sugary sentimental andantes. His violin concerto (1844) characterizes this criticism, yet its charm almost defies it. See Lives by Benedict (1850), Moscheles (1873), Stratton (1901), Petitpierre (1948), Radcliffe (1954), his *Letters* (ed. Selden-Gott, 1947) and Jacob's *Mendelssohn and his Times* (1963).

MENDERES, Adnan, *men'de-rez* (1899–1961), Turkish statesman, born near Aydin. Though educated for the law, he became a farmer, entered politics in 1932, at first in opposition, then with the party in power under Kemal Ataturk. In 1945 he became one of the leaders of the new Democratic party and was made prime minister when it came to power in 1950. Re-elected in 1954 and 1957, in May 1960 he was deposed and superseded by General Cemal Gursel after an army *coup*. He appeared as defendant with over 500 officials of his former Democratic Party administration at the Yassiada trials (1960–61), was sentenced to death and hanged on Sept. 17, 1961, at Imrali.

MENDÈS, Catulle (1841–1909), French writer, born at Bordeaux of Jewish parentage, passed from the Parnassians to the Romantics, and wrote poems, novels, dramas and libretti as well as journalistic articles and criticisms. See critical biography (French) by A. Bertrand (1908).

MENDÈS-FRANCE, Pierre, *mã-dez-frãs* (1907–), French statesman, entered parliament in 1932 as a Radical. In 1941 he made a daring escape from imprisonment in Vichy France and came to England to join the Free French forces. After a short time as minister for national economy under de Gaulle in 1945, he became prominent on the opposition side, and in June 1954 succeeded M. Laniel as prime minister. At a troubled period he handled France's foreign affairs with firmness and decision, but his government was defeated on its North African policy, and he resigned in 1955. A firm critic of de Gaulle, he lost his seat in the 1958 election. See study by A. Werth (1956).

MENDOZA, distinguished family of Basque origin:
(1) **Diego Hurtado de** (1503–75), great-

grandson of (2). He was entrusted by Charles V with the conduct of his Italian policy and the representation of his views at the Council of Trent. He inherited his ancestor's gifts as a statesman and man of letters. His *War of Granada* is a masterpiece of prose.

(2) **Inigo Lopez de** (fl. 1450), Spanish statesman and poet, father of (3) and great-grandfather of (1), created Marquis of Santillana by John II of Castile in 1445 for his services on the field, was a wise statesman, a sturdy patriot, and an admired poet. He left an excellent account of the Provençal, Catalan and Valencian poets, and was an early folklorist and collector of popular proverbs.

(3) **Pedro Gonzalez de** (1428–95), Spanish prelate and son of (2), was Cardinal Archbishop of Toledo and trusted prime minister of Ferdinand and Isabella.

MENÉNDEZ PIDAL, Ramon, *pee-THahl'* (1869–), Spanish philologist and critic, born at Coruña, a pupil of Menéndez Pelayo (q.v.), became professor at the University of Madrid in 1899, founded the Madrid Centre of Historical Studies, and carried on the tradition of exact scholarship. His *La España del Cid* (1929) is the finest Spanish modern historical study. He published critical works on Spanish ballads and chronicles.

MENÉNDEZ Y PELAYO, Marcelino, *may-nen'dayth ee pay-lah'yō* (1856–1912), Spanish scholar, critic and poet, regarded as the founder of modern Spanish literary history. His writings, all exemplifying his traditionalism and Catholicism, include the *History of Aesthetic Ideas in Spain* (1844–91) and history of Spanish heterodoxies (1880–81). His verse includes *Odes* (1883) and anthologies. See studies by M. Artigas (Madrid 1927) and A. Sandoval (Madrid 1944).

MENGER, Karl (1840–1921), a founder of the ' Austrian school ' of economics, was a native of Galicia, and from 1873 professor in Vienna. See J. A. Schumpeter, *Ten Great Economists* (1952).

MENGS, Anton Raphael (1728–79), German painter, was born, the son of a Danish artist, at Aussig in Bohemia. Having eventually settled at Rome, he turned Catholic, married, and directed a school of painting. In Madrid (1761–70 and 1773–76) he decorated the dome of the grand salon in the royal palace with the *Apotheosis of the Emperor Trajan.*

MENG-TSE. See MENCIUS.

MENIER, Émile Justin, *men-yay* (1826–81), French industrialist, established at Noisiel a great chocolate factory.

MENKEN, Adah Isaacs, originally (probably) **Adah Bertha Theodore** (1835?–68), Jewish actress, born near New Orleans, appeared as Mazeppa with immense success in London (1864) and elsewhere. She had many husbands (Heenan, the ' Benicia Boy ', illegally as she discovered), and many literary friends. Her posthumous poems, *Infelicia*, were dedicated to Dickens. See B. Falk, *The Naked Lady* (1952).

MENNIN, Peter (1923–), American composer, born in Erie, Pennsylvania, studied at the Eastman College of Music and rapidly established himself as a composer of large-scale works. He has composed 7 symphonies, including *The Cycle*, a choral work to his own text, as well as concertos, choral and chamber music.

MENOTTI, Gian-Carlo (1911–), American composer, born in Milan, settled in America at the age of seventeen. Instinctively imbued with the Italian operatic tradition, Menotti has achieved international fame with a series of operas that began with *Amelia goes to the Ball*, produced in 1937 at Philadelphia, where he was a student. Menotti writes his own libretti, and his later works, *The Medium* (1946), *The Consul* (1950; Pulitzer prize), *Amahl and the Night Visitors* (1951) composed for television performance, *The Saint of Bleecker Street* (1954; Pulitzer prize), *Maria Golovin* (1958), &c., have great theatrical effectiveness although their musical style is derived from a wide variety of models.

MENSHIKOV, (1) **Alexander Danilovich** (*c.* 1660–1729), Russian field-marshal and statesman, was born of poor parents in Moscow, but entering the army, distinguished himself at the siege of Azov, and afterwards accompanied Peter the Great in his travels to Holland and England. During the war with Sweden (1702–13) he played an important part at Pultowa—Peter made him a field-marshal there—Riga, Stettin, &c. At the capture of Marienburg the girl who became Catharine I fell into Menshikov's hands, and was through him introduced to the tsar. Towards the end of Peter's reign Menshikov lost favour owing to extortions and suspected duplicities. But when Peter died he secured the succession of Catharine, and during her reign and that of her young successor, Peter II, he governed Russia with almost absolute authority. He was about to marry his daughter to the young tsar when the jealousy of the old nobility led to his banishment to Siberia and the confiscation of his estates.

(2) **Alexander Sergeievich** (1789–1869), great-grandson of (1), rose to the rank of general in the campaigns of 1812–15, was severely wounded at Varna in the Turkish campaign of 1828, and was made head of the Russian navy. His overbearing behaviour as ambassador at Constantinople brought about the Crimean war. He commanded at Alma and Inkermann, and defended Sebastopol, but in 1855 was recalled because of illness.

MENTEITH, Sir John de, *men-teeth'*, Scottish knight who captured Wallace (q.v.) at Glasgow and took him to London (1305).

MENUHIN, Yehudi, *men'yoo-in* (1916–), American violinist, born in New York, at the age of seven appeared as soloist with the San Francisco Symphony Orchestra. This was followed by appearances all over the world as a prodigy, and after eighteen months' retirement for study, he continued his career as a virtuoso, winning international renown. His sister *Hephzibah* (b. 1920) is a gifted pianist. See Life by Magidoff (1956).

MENZEL, *men'tsel,* (1) **Adolf** (1815–1905), German painter, illustrator and engraver, born at Breslau, is known for his drawings illustrating the times of Frederick the Great and William I. See works by Jordan (1905) and Waldmann (1941).

(2) **Wolfgang** (1798–1873), German critic

and historian, born at Waldenburg in Silesia, studied at Jena and Bonn, but from 1825 lived mainly in Stuttgart. He edited magazines, and wrote poems, novels, histories of German literature, poetry, &c., a history of the world, literary criticism and polemics. See his autobiographical *Denkwürdigkeiten* (1876).

MENZIES, Sir Robert Gordon (1894–), Australian statesman, born at Jeparit, Victoria, practised as a barrister before entering politics, becoming member of the Victoria parliament in 1928. Six years later, in 1934, he went to the Federal House of Representatives, sitting as the member for Kooyang. He was Commonwealth attorney-general for the years 1935 to 1939, prime minister from 1939 to 1941, and leader of the opposition from 1943 to 1949, when he again took office as premier of the coalition government. He had been appointed a privy councillor in 1937; and his qualities of high purpose and warm humanity were displayed during the war and the succeeding years. In 1956 he headed the Five Nations Committee which sought to come to a settlement with Nasser on the question of Suez. He was knighted in 1963 (K.T.) and retired in 1966.

MERCATOR, (1) Gerhardus, Latinized form of **Gerhard Kremer** (1512–94), a Flemish mathematician, geographer and map-maker, of German extraction. The projection which has since borne his name was used in his map of 1568. See L. A. Brown, *The Story of Maps* (Boston 1950).

(2) (Ger. **Kaufmann**), **Nicolaus** (c. 1620–87), German mathematician and astronomer, as engineer was responsible for the construction of the fountains at Versailles, as mathematician is credited with the discovery of a series for log $(1+x)$. From 1660 he lived in England.

MERCER, (1) Cecil William. See YATES (1).

(2) **John,** *mėr'sėr* (1791–1866), English dye chemist, born near Blackburn, Lancs., is chiefly known for his invention of mercerization—a process by which cotton is given a silky lustre resembling silk. Almost entirely self-educated, he made many important discoveries connected with dyeing and calico printing, and became F.R.S. in 1852.

MEREDITH, (1) George (1828–1909), English novelist, was born at Portsmouth, the grandson of a famous tailor (the ' great Mel ' of *Evan Harrington*), and was educated privately and in Germany. He was thus able to view the English class system with detachment. In London after being articled to a solicitor he turned to journalism and letters, his first venture appearing in *Chambers's Journal* in 1849, the year in which he married Mary Ellen Nicolls, a widowed daughter of Thomas Love Peacock. No doubt this disastrous marriage gave him an insight into sex relations, which bulk as largely in his work as his other great interest, viz., natural selection as Nature's way of perfecting man. His works did not bring him much financial reward; he had to rely on his articles in *The Fortnightly* and his work as a reader in the publishing house of Chapman and Hall. His prose works started with a burlesque Oriental fantasy, *The*

Shaving of Shagpat (1855), to be succeeded in 1859 by *The Ordeal of Richard Feverel*, which turns on parental tyranny and a false system of private education. The mawkish love affairs make it barely readable today. He did not achieve general popularity as a novelist till the delightful *Diana of the Crossways* appeared in 1885. Intermediately we may write off his two novels on the Italian revolt of 1848, *Sandra Belloni* (1864) and *Vittoria* (1866); but not *Evan Harrington* (1860), for the light it throws on Meredith's origins; *Harry Richmond* (1871); and least of all *Beauchamp's Career*, which poses the question of class and party and is well constructed and clearly written. This last cannot be said of Meredith's later major novels, *The Egoist* (1879), a study of refined selfishness, and *The Amazing Marriage* (1895). These two powerful works are marred by the artificiality and forced wit which fatigues in so much of his poetry. His first volume of verse (1851) is quite unremarkable, but *Poems and Lyrics of the Joy of Earth* (1883) displays his new cryptic manner and discusses the two master themes —the ' reading of earth ' and the sex duel. His masterpiece on the latter theme had appeared in 1862 when he consorted with the pre-Raphaelite poets and painters. This is *Modern Love*, a novelette in pseudo-sonnet sequence form in which the novelist in him plays powerfully on incompatibility of temper. His reading of earth is expressed cryptically in the magnificent *Woods of Westermain*, intelligibly in *The Thrush in February* and thrillingly in *The Lark Ascending*. The volume called *A Reading of Life* (1901) adds little to the record. The modern revaluation of the Victorians has enhanced the fame of this very cerebral poet. See studies by G. M. Trevelyan (1906), R. Galland (1923), M. S. Gretton (1926), L. Stevenson (1953), J. Lindsay (1956) and P. Bartlett (1963).

(2) **Owen.** See LYTTON (2).

MEREZHKOVSKI, Dmitri Sergeyevich (1865–1941), Russian novelist, critic and poet, born at St Petersburg, wrote a historical trilogy, *Christ and Antichrist* (*The Death of the Gods, The Forerunner, Peter and Alexis*), books on Tolstoy, Ibsen, &c. His wife, **Zinaida Nikolayevna Hippius** (1870–1945), was also a poet, novelist and critic.

MERGENTHALER, Ottmar, *mer'gen-tahl-ėr* (1854–99), German-American inventor, born at Hachtel in Germany, became an American citizen in 1878 and invented the linotype machine (patented in 1884).

MÉRIMÉE, Prosper, *me-ree-may* (1803–70), French novelist, born at Paris, son of a painter, studied law, visited Spain in 1830, and held posts under the ministries of the navy, commerce and the interior. Admitted to the Academy in 1844, he became a senator in 1853. His last years were clouded by ill-health and melancholy, and the downfall of the empire hastened his death, at Cannes. He wrote novels and short stories, archaeological and historical dissertations, and travels, all of which display exact learning, keen observation, strong intellectual grasp, real humour, and an exquisite style. Among his novels are *Colomba, Mateo Falcone, Carmen, La Vénus d'Ille, Lokis, Arsène Guillot, La Chambre bleue* and *L'Abbé Aubain.* His letters include the famous *Lettres à une inconnue* (1873), the *Lettres à une autre inconnue* (1875) and the Letters to Panizzi (1881). See works by D'Haussonville (1888), Filon (1894–98), W. H. Pater (1900), Pinvert (1906, 1911), Trahard (1925) and Johnstone (1926).

MERIVALE, Charles (1803–93), English historian, son of **John Herman** (1779–1844), Greek scholar, and brother of **Herman** (1806–1874), English economist, was educated at Harrow and St John's College, Cambridge, where he became fellow and tutor. His *History of the Romans under the Empire* (1850–62) is too generous to imperialism. See his autobiography (1899). His son, **Herman Charles** (1839–1906), wrote some successful plays and novels. See his autobiography (1902).

MERLE D'AUBIGNÉ. See D'AUBIGNÉ (1).

MERLIN, an ancient British prophet and magician, supposed to have flourished during the decline of the native British power in its contest with the Saxons, and a hero of the Arthurian legend. There may have been two real Merlins—a 5th-century Welsh Merlin and a Caledonian 6th-century duplicate. See W. E. Mead, *Outline of the History of Merlin* (1889), and E. K. Chambers, *Arthur of Britain* (1927).

MERRICK, orig. **Miller, Leonard** (1864–1939), English novelist, born in London, wrote a number of sentimental novels, mostly with a Paris setting, such as *The Actor Manager* (1898), *A Chair on the Boulevard* (1908), *While Paris Laughed* (1918), &c.

MERRILL, Stuart (1863–1915), American symbolist poet, born at Hempstead, Long Island, New York, and educated in Paris. His French poems *Les Gammes* (1895), *Les Quatre Saisons* (1900), &c., developed the musical conception of poetry, often with alliteration's artful aid. See study by Henry (1927).

MERRIMAN, (1) **Henry Seton,** pseud. of **Hugh Stowell Scott** (1862–1903), English novelist, born at Newcastle-upon-Tyne, wrote *The Sowers* (1896), *The Velvet Glove* (1901) and many other novels in the Dumas tradition.

(2) **John Xavier** (1841–1926), South African statesman, born at Street, Somerset, went early to South Africa—his father was Bishop of Grahamstown—was a member of various Cape ministries from 1875, and premier (South African party) 1908–10. See Life by P. Laurence (1930).

MERSENNE, Marin (1588–1648), French mathematician and musician and a friend of Descartes, took the habit of a Minim Friar in 1611, and spent his life in study, teaching in convent schools, and travel. He stoutly defended the orthodoxy of the Cartesian philosophy.

MERTENS, Eva. See KEITH (4).

MERTON, (1) **John Ralph** (1913–), English artist, was born in London. He studied at Oxford and in Italy, and painted many portraits in tempera, including a notable one of the Countess of Dalkeith (1958).

(2) **Walter de** (d. 1277), founder in 1264 of Merton College, Oxford, the prototype of the collegiate system in English universities, was probably born at Merton in Surrey, and was Bishop of Rochester from 1274.

MERYON, Charles (1821–68), French etcher, was born in Paris, the son of an Englishman. After serving for a short time as a naval officer, he worked in poverty in Paris, and is known by his sombre and imaginative etchings of Paris streets and buildings. He was colour blind, and became insane. See monographs by Burty (1879), Wedmore (new ed. 1892), L. Delteil (trans. 1928) and C. Dodgson (1921).

MESDAG, Hendrik Willem (1831–1915), Dutch marine painter, born at Groningen, settled at The Hague, where his personal collection is housed in the Mesdag Museum. See H. Zilcken, *Mesdag, Painter of the North Sea* (trans. 1896).

MESMER, Friedrich Anton or **Franz** (1734–1815), Austrian physician and founder of mesmerism, born near Constance, studied medicine at Vienna, and about 1772 took up the opinion that there exists a power which he called animal magnetism. In 1778 he went to Paris, where he created a sensation. He refused 20,000 livres for his secret; but in 1785, a learned commission reporting unfavourably, he retired into obscurity in Switzerland. See books by Graham (1890) and F. A. Goldsmith (1934); also S. Zweig, *Mental Healers* (1933).

MESSAGER, André Charles Prosper, -sa-zhay (1853–1929), French composer, mostly of operettas, was born at Montlugon. *La Basoche* (1890), a comic opera, was his best. See study by M. Auge-Laribe (Paris 1951).

MESSALINA, Valeria (d. A.D. 48), the wife of the emperor Claudius, a woman infamous for avarice, lust and cruelty. Among her victims were the daughters of Germanicus and Drusus, Valerius Asiaticus, and her confederate Polybius. In the emperor's absence she publicly married one of her favourites. The emperor at last had her executed. See study by Stadelmann (1924).

MESSERSCHMITT, Wilhelm (1898–), German aviation designer and production chief, in 1923 established the Messer-schmitt aircraft manufacturing works, of which he was the chairman and director. During World War II he supplied the Luft-waffe with its foremost types of combat aircraft. From 1955 he continued his activities with the revived Lufthansa and later also entered the automobile industry.

MESSIAEN, Olivier Eugène Prosper Charles, mes-i-ã (1908–), French composer and organist, son of the poetess Cécile Sauvage, was born in Avignon. He studied under Duprès and Dukas, and was appointed professor at the Schola Cantorum. In 1941, he became professor of Harmony at the Paris Conservatoire. Messiaen has composed extensively for organ, orchestra, voice and piano, and made frequent use of new instruments such as the 'Ondes Martenot'. His music, which has evolved intricate mathematical rhythmic systems, is motivated by religious mysticism, and is best known outside France by the two-and-a-half-hour piano work, *Vingt regards sur l'enfant Jésus,* and the mammoth *Turangalila* Symphony, which makes use of Indian themes and rhythms. See the *Technique de mon language musicale* (2 vols. 1944, trans. 1957).

MESTROVIĆ, Ivan, *mesh'tro-vich* (1883–1962), Yugoslav sculptor, was born at Vrpolje in Dalmatia; a shepherd boy, he was taught woodcarving by his father, eventually studying in Vienna and Paris, where he became a friend of Rodin (q.v.). He designed the national temple at Kossovo (1907–12). He lived in England during World War II and executed many portrait busts, including that of Sir Thomas Beecham. After the war he designed several war memorials. His work is naturalistic, emotionally intense and is characterized by an impressive simplicity. See *Life* by M. Curcin (trans. 1935). His self-portrait bust is in the Tate.

METASTASIO, the Grecized name of **Pietro Trapassi** (1698–1782), Italian poet, who was born at Rome. A precocious gift for improvising verses gained him a patron in Gravina, a lawyer, who educated him, and left him (1718) his fortune. He gained his reputation by his masque, *The Garden of Hesperides* (1722), wrote the libretti for 27 operas, including Mozart's *Clemenza di Tito*, and became court poet at Vienna in 1729. See his *Letters*, edited by Carducci (1883); Vernon Lee's *Studies* (1886); and Lives by Burney (1796) and L. Russo (1921).

METAXAS, **Yanni**, *me-taks'as* (1870–1941), Greek politician, born in Ithaka, graduated from the Military College in 1890, fought in the Thessalian campaign against the Turks in 1897, and later studied military science in Germany. He took a leading part in reorganizing the Greek army before the 1912–13 Balkan Wars and in 1913 became chief of the general staff. A Royalist rival of the Republican Venizelos, he opposed Greek intervention in World War I. On King Constantine's fall he fled to Italy, but returned with him in 1921. In 1923 he founded the Party of Free Opinion. In 1935 he became deputy prime minister after the failure of the Venizelist coup, and in April 1936 became prime minister, in August establishing an authoritarian government with a cabinet of specialist and retired service officers. His work of reorganizing Greece economically and militarily bore fruit in the tenacious Greek resistance to the Italian invasion of 1940–41.

METCALF, **John**, *met'kahf* (1717–1810), ' Blind Jack of Knaresborough ', lost his eyesight at six, but, tall and vigorous, fought at Falkirk and Culloden, smuggled, drove a stagecoach, and from 1765 constructed 185 miles of road and numerous bridges in Lancashire and Yorkshire.

METCHNIKOFF. See MECHNIKOV.

METELLUS, a Roman plebeian family which rose to front rank in the nobility. One member of it twice defeated Jugurtha (109 B.C.); another conquered Crete (97 B.C.).

METFORD, **William Ellis** (1824–99), English engineer and inventor, born at Taunton. He was appointed in 1857 to the East India Railway, where his experiences during the Mutiny impaired his health, and he returned to England. His work on an explosive rifle

bullet was frustrated by the condemnation of the St Petersburg Convention, and he turned to the design of breech-loading rifles. In 1888 the Lee-Metford rifle was adopted by the British War Office. See LEE (4).

METHODIUS. See CYRIL.

METHUEN, until 1899 **Stedman**, **Sir Algernon Methuen Marshall**, **Bart.**, *meth'yoo-in* (1856–1924), English publisher, born in London. He was a teacher of Classics and French (1880–95), and began publishing as a sideline in 1889 to market his own textbooks. His first publishing success was Kipling's *Barrack-Room Ballads* (1892), and, amongst others, he published works of Belloc, Chesterton, Conrad, Masefield, R. L. Stevenson and Oscar Wilde. He was created a baronet in 1916.

METSU, **Gabriel**, *met-sü'* (1630–67), Dutch genre painter, born at Leyden, settled in Amsterdam.

METTERNICH, **Prince Clemens Lothar Wenzel** (1773–1859), Austrian statesman, born at Coblenz, May 15, the son of an Austrian diplomat, studied at Strasburg and Mainz, was attached to the Austrian embassy at The Hague, and at twenty-eight was Austrian minister at Dresden, two years later at Berlin, and in 1805 (after Austerlitz) at Paris. In 1807 he concluded the treaty of Fontainebleau; in 1809 was appointed Austrian foreign minister, and as such negotiated the marriage between Napoleon and Marie Louise. In 1812–13 he maintained at first a temporizing policy, but at last declared war against France; the Grand Alliance was signed at Teplitz; and Metternich was made a prince of the empire. He took a very prominent part in the Congress of Vienna, rearranging a German confederation (while disfavouring German unity under Prussian influence), and guarding Austria's interests in Italy. From 1815 he was the most active representative of reaction all over Europe, persistently striving to repress all popular and constitutional aspirations. As the main supporter of autocracy and police despotism at home and abroad he is largely responsible for the tension that led to the upheaval of 1848. The French Revolution of that year, which overturned for a time half the thrones of Europe, was felt at Vienna, and the government fell. Metternich fled to England, and in 1851 retired to his castle of Johannesberg on the Rhine. He died at Vienna, June 11. A brilliant diplomat, a man of iron nerve and will, though personally kind, he had few deep convictions, no warm sympathies, and no deep insight into the lessons of history. See his not too trustworthy *Autobiography* (trans. 1880–83), and works by Sandeman (1911), F. de Reichenberg (1938), A. Cecil (3rd ed., 1947), C. de Grunwald (trans. 1953), G. de Bertier de Sauvigny (1962), and H. A. Kissinger, *A World restored* (1957).

METTRIE. See LAMETTRIE.

MEULEN, *mœ'len*, **Adam François van der** (1632–90), Flemish painter, born at Brussels, was from 1666 battle painter to Louis XIV.

MEUNG, **Jean de**, *mœ̃*, or **Jean Clopinel** (c. 1250–1305), satirist, flourished at Paris under Philip the Fair. He translated many books into French, and left a witty *Testament*. But his great work is his lengthy continuation (18,000 lines) of the *Roman de la Rose*, which substituted for tender allegorizing satirical pictures of actual life and an encyclopaedic discussion of every aspect of contemporary learning, which inspired many later authors to write in support of or in opposition to his views.

MEURSIUS, Lat. form of **De Meurs**, (1) **Johannes** or **Jan** (1579–1639), Dutch classical scholar, father of (2), born at Loozduinen near The Hague, became in 1610 professor of History, and in 1611 of Greek, at Leyden, historiographer to the States-General, and in 1625 professor of History at Sorö in Denmark, where he died. He edited Cato's *De Re Rustica*, Plato's *Timaeus*, Theophrastus's *Characters*, and a long series of the later Greek writers; he also wrote on Greek antiquities and Dutch and Danish history.

(2) **Johannes** (1613–54), son of (1), also wrote antiquarian works of value, but his name has wrongly been connected with the filthy *Elegantiae linguae Latinae* (probably by Chorier of Vienne, 1609–92).

MEUSNIER, Jean Baptiste Marie, *mœ-nyay* (1754–93), French general and scientist, made ascents in a balloon, stated the theorem which bears his name, relating to the centre of curvature of any plane section, and in the military field defended the fort of Königstein against the Prussians (1793).

MEYER, *mī'ér*, (1) **Conrad Ferdinand** (1825–1898), Swiss poet and novelist, was born at Zürich. After a period during which he concentrated mainly on ballads and verse romances, he composed the epic poem *Huttens Letzte Tage* (1871) and a number of historical novels such as *Jürg Jenatsch* (1876), *Der Heilige* (1880), &c., in which he excels in subtle and intricate psychological situations and complex characters. See works on him by Mayne (1925), Burkhardt (1932), and Williams (1963).

(2) **Joseph** (1796–1856), German publisher, was born at Gotha, and issued many important serial works, editions of German classics, the encyclopaedia known as *Konversations-lexikon*, historical libraries, &c. His business, the ' Bibliographical Institute ', was in 1828 transferred from Gotha to Hildburghausen, in 1874 (by his son) to Leipzig.

(3) **Julius Lothar von** (1830–95), German chemist, born at Varel, Oldenburg, became the first professor of Chemistry at Tübingen in 1876. He discovered the Periodic Law independently of Mendeleyev (q.v.) in 1869 and showed that atomic volumes were functions of atomic weights.

(4) **Viktor** (1848–97), German chemist who studied under Bunsen in Heidelberg, became professor at Zürich, Göttingen, and finally at Heidelberg (1889). He discovered and investigated thiophene and the oximes. The nature of his work undermined his health and he died by his own hand.

MEYERBEER, Giacomo, *mī'ér-bayr* (1791–1864), German operatic composer, was born at Berlin. Originally Jakob Beer, son of a Jewish banker, he adopted the name Meyer from a benefactor, and reconstructed and Italianized the whole. At seven he played in public Mozart's D-minor concerto, and at fifteen was received into the house of Abt Vogler at Darmstadt, where Weber was his fellow-pupil. His earlier works were unsuccessful, but in Vienna he obtained fame as a pianist. After three years' study in Italy he produced operas in the new (Rossini's) style, which at once gained a cordial reception. From 1824 to 1831 he lived mostly in Berlin. He next applied himself to a minute study of French opera. The result of this was seen in the production at Paris in 1831 of *Robert le Diable* (libretto by Scribe), whose totally new style secured unparalleled success over all Europe. It was followed in 1836 by the even more successful *Huguenots*. Appointed *kapellmeister* at Berlin, he wrote the opera *Ein Feldlager in Schlesien*. His first comic opera, *L'Étoile du nord* (1854), was a success, as was *L'Africaine*, produced after his death at Paris. Praised extravagantly by Fétis and others, Meyerbeer was severely condemned by Schumann and Wagner on the ground that he made everything subsidiary to theatrical effect. His successive adoption of widely-different styles bears this out. But even opponents concede the power and beauty of some of his pieces. See Lives by Hervey (1913), Dauriac (1930) and Kapp (1932).

MEYERHOF, Otto Fritz, *mī'ér-hŏf* (1884–1951), German physiologist, professor at Kiel (1918–24), director of the physiology department at the Kaiser Wilhelm Institute for Biology (1924–29), professor at Heidelberg (1930–38), is best known for his work on the metabolism of muscles. Forced to leave Germany in 1938, he continued his work in France and later in America. In 1922 he shared with A. V. Hill the Nobel prize for medicine. He died in Philadelphia.

MEYNELL, Alice Christiana Gertrude, *née* Thompson, *men'él* (1847–1922), English essayist and poet, was born in Surrey. Her volumes of essays include *The Rhythm of Life* (1893), *The Colour of Life* (1896) and *Hearts of Controversy* (1917). She published several collections of her own poems, and anthologies of Patmore, of lyric poetry, and of poems for children. With her husband, Wilfrid Meynell (1852–1948), author and journalist, she edited several periodicals. See the memoir by her daughter, V. Meynell (1929).

MEYRINK, Gustav, *mī'-* (1868–1932), German writer, born in Vienna, translated Dickens and wrote satirical novels with a strong element of the fantastic and grotesque. Among the best known are *Der Golem* (1915), *Das grüne Gesicht* (1916) and *Walpurgisnacht* (1917).

MIALL, Edward (1809–81), English divine, born at Portsmouth, was an Independent minister at Ware and Leicester. In 1840 he founded the *Nonconformist* newspaper in which he led the campaign for the disestablishment of the Church of England. He was M.P. from 1852. See *Life* by Miall (1884).

MICAH (fl. *c.* 700 B.C.), the sixth of the twelve minor Old Testament prophets, was a native of Moresheth Gath in SW. Judah, and prophesied during the reigns of Jotham, Ahaz and Hezekiah, being a younger contemporary of Isaiah, Hosea and Amos. On the book of Micah, see works by Caspar (1852) and Ryssel (1889) in German; and commentaries in English by Robinson (1926) and Wade (1932).

MICHAEL (1921–), king of Rumania 1927–30, 1940–47, son of Carol II, first succeeded to the throne on the death of his grandfather Ferdinand I, his father having renounced his own claims in 1925. In 1930 he was supplanted by Carol, but again made king in 1940 when the Germans gained control of Rumania. In 1944 he played a considerable part in the overthrow of the dictatorship of Antonescu. He announced the acceptance of the Allied peace terms, and declared war on Germany. His attempts after the war to establish a broader system of government were foiled by the progressive Communization of Rumania. In 1947 he was forced to abdicate and has since lived in exile.

MICHAEL VIII PALAEOLOGUS (1234–82), Eastern Roman emperor from 1259, distinguished himself as a soldier and was made regent for John Lascaris, whom he ultimately deposed and banished. His army took Constantinople in 1261 and defeated the Greeks in 1263–64. Involved in hostilities with Charles of Sicily, he was obliged to acknowledge papal supremacy in 1274, a policy which provoked discontent among his subjects, precipitated Charles's unsuccessful attempt on Constantinople (1281), and was a contributory cause of the revolt and massacre known as the Sicilian Vespers (1282). See study by Geanakoplos (1960).

MICHAELIS, Johann David, *mee-kay'lis* (1717–91), German Protestant theologian, was born at Halle, professor of Philosophy (1746) and Oriental Languages (1750) at Göttingen, pioneered historical criticism in biblical interpretation. See his *Introduction to the New Testament* (trans. 1801), &c., and *Autobiography* (1793).

MICHEL, *mee-shel,* (1) **Francisque** (1809–87), French antiquary, born at Lyons, from 1839 a professor at Bordeaux, earned a reputation by researches in Norman history, French chansons, argot and the Basques, and wrote *Les Écossais en France et les français en Écosse* (1862) and *A Critical Inquiry into the Scottish Language* (1882).

(2) **Louise** (1830–1905), French anarchist, born at Vroncourt, spent many years preaching revolution, and suffered imprisonment. She resided for ten years in London. See her *Mémoires* (Paris 1886) and Life by Boyer (Paris 1927).

MICHELANGELO, properly **Michelagniolo di Lodovico Buonarroti** (1475–1564), Italian sculptor, painter and poet, born 6 March at Caprese in Tuscany, where Lodovico his father was mayor. A few weeks after his birth the family returned to Florence. The boy was placed in the care of a stonemason and his wife at Settignano where Lodovico owned a small farm and marble quarry. At school the boy devoted his energies more to drawing than to his studies. Despite his father's opposition, in 1488 Michelangelo was bound to Domenico Ghirlandaio for 3 years. By this master he was recommended to Lorenzo de' Medici and entered the school for which the ' Magnifico ' had gathered together

a priceless collection of antiques. Lorenzo was not long in noting his talents, and to the beneficence of his patron Michelangelo owed the acquaintanceship of Poliziano, poet and tutor of the Medici children, and many of the most learned men of his time. To this period belong two interesting reliefs. In the *Battle of the Centaurs* the classical influence of Lorenzo's garden is strikingly apparent, though the straining muscles and contorted limbs, which mark the artist's mature work, are already visible. A marvellous contrast to the *Centaurs* is the *Madonna*, conceived and executed in the spirit of Donatello, which though not consciously antique, is far more classical. After Lorenzo's death in 1492, Piero, his son and successor, is said to have treated the artist with scant courtesy; and Michelangelo fled to Bologna for a time, but in 1495 he returned to Florence. During this sojourn to his native city he fashioned the marble *Cupid*. An acquaintance persuaded him to bury the work to give it an antique look and then send it to Rome to be sold. The *Cupid* was bought by Cardinal San Giorgio who discovered the fraud but recognized the talent of the sculptor and summoned him to Rome in 1496. The influence of Rome and the antique is easily discernible in the *Bacchus*, now in the National Museum in Florence. To the same period belongs the exquisite *Cupid* of the South Kensington Museum in London. The *Pieta* (1497), now in St Peter's, shows a realism wholly at variance with the antique ideal. For four years the sculptor remained in Rome and then, returning to Florence, fashioned the *David* out of a colossal block of marble. *David* is the Gothic treatment of a classical theme; in pose and composition there is a stately grandeur, a dignified solemnity. The *Holy Family of the Tribune* and the *Madonna* in the National Gallery in London belong to the same time, and, like a cartoon (now existing only as a copy) for a fresco never completed in the Great Hall of the Council, prove that Michelangelo had not wholly neglected the art of painting. His genius, however, was essentially plastic; he had far more interest in form than in colour. In 1503 Julius II, succeeding to the pontificate, summoned the painter-sculptor back to Rome. Michelangelo could as little brook opposition as the pope, and their dealings were continually interrupted by bitter quarrels and recriminations. The pope commissioned the sculptor to design his tomb, and for forty years Michelangelo clung to the hope that he would yet complete the great monument; but intrigue and spite were too strong for him. Other demands were continually made upon his energy, and the sublime statue of Moses is the best fragment that is left to us of the tomb of Julius. Bramante, if Vasari's account be true, poisoned the pope's mind against the sculptor; instead of being allowed to devote himself to the monument, he was ordered to decorate the ceiling of the Sistine Chapel with paintings. In vain he protested that sculpture was his profession, in vain he urged Raphael's higher qualifications for the task; the pope was obdurate, and in 1508–1512 Michelangelo achieved a masterpiece of decorative design.

Almost superhuman invention, miraculous variety of attitude and gesture, place this marvellous work among the greatest achievements of human energy. No sooner had he finished his work in the Sistine Chapel than he returned with eagerness to the tomb. But in 1513 Pope Julius II died, and the cardinals, his executors, demanded a more modest design. Then Pope Leo X, of the Medici family, commissioned Michelangelo to rebuild the façade of the church of San Lorenzo at Florence and enrich it with sculptured figures. The master reluctantly complied, and set out for Carrara to quarry marble; from 1514 to 1522 his artistic record is a blank, as the elaborate scheme was ultimately given up, though the sculptor remained in Florence. But in 1528 danger to his native city forced him to the science of fortification, and when in 1529 Florence was besieged Michelangelo was foremost in its defence. After the surrender he completed the monuments to Giuliano and Lorenzo de' Medici, which are among the greatest of his works. In 1533 yet another compact was entered into concerning Pope Julius's ill-fated sepulchre; whereupon he was once again commissioned to adorn the Sistine Chapel with frescoes. After some years he began in 1537 to paint *The Last Judgment*, which was his last pictorial achievement. Next year he was appointed architect of St Peter's, and devoted himself to the work with loyalty until his death, on February 18, 1564. Michelangelo is by far the most brilliant representative of the Italian Renaissance. He was not only supreme in the arts of sculpture and painting—in which grandeur and sublimity rather than beauty was his aim—but was versed in all the learning of his age, a poet, architect and military engineer. See bibliography by Steinmann and Wittkower (1927), studies by C. Tolnay (1945–64) and A. Allan (1956) and Milanesi's *Lettere di Michelangelo* (1873).

MICHELET, Jules, *meesh-lay* (1798–1874), French historian, born in Paris, lectured on history at the École Normale, assisted Guizot at the Sorbonne, worked at the Record Office, and was ultimately elected to the Academy in 1838 and appointed professor of History at the Collège de France. The greatest of many historical works are his monumental *Histoire de France* (24 vols. 1833–67) and his *Histoire de la Révolution* (7 vols. 1847–53). By refusing to swear allegiance to Louis Napoleon he lost his appointments, and henceforth worked mostly in Brittany and the Riviera. His second wife, Adèle Mialaret, is believed to have collaborated in several nature books, including *L'Oiseau* (1856), *L'Insecte* (1857) and *La Mer* (1861). In his last years he set himself to complete his great *Histoire*, but lived to finish only 3 volumes (1872–75). See books by G. Monod (1875 and 1905), Corréard (1886), J. Simon (1889) and Mme Quinet (1900).

MICHELL, John (1724–93), English geologist, born in Nottinghamshire, fellow of Queen's College, Cambridge, and professor of Geology (1769), described a method of magnetization, founded seismology, and is credited with the invention of the torsion balance. In 1767 he became rector of Thornhill, Yorkshire.

MICHELOZZI, Michelozzo di Bartolommeo, *mee-ke-lot'see* (1396–1472), Italian architect and sculptor, born at Florence, was associated with Ghiberti (q.v.) on his famous bronze doors for the baptistery there, and collaborated with Donatello (q.v.) in several major sculpture groups, including monuments to Pope John XXIII and Cardinal Brancacci (1427). He was court architect to Cosimo de' Medici, with whom he was in exile at Venice, where he designed a number of buildings. One of his finest works is the Ricardi Palace in Florence. See study by Wolff (1900).

MICHELSON, Albert Abraham (1852–1931), American physicist, born at Strelno in Germany, professor of Physics at Chicago from 1892, became in 1907 the first American scientist to win a Nobel prize. He invented an interferometer and an echelon grating, and did important work on the spectrum, but is chiefly remembered for the Michelson-Morley experiment to determine ether drift, the negative result of which set Einstein on the road to the theory of relativity.

MICKIEWICZ, Adam, *mits-kyay'vich* (1798–1855), Polish poet, was born near Novogrodek in Lithuania (Minsk), December 24, and educated at Vilna. He published his first poems in 1822, and as founder of a students' secret society was banished to Russia (1824–1829); there he produced three epic poems, glowing with patriotism. After a journey in Germany, France and Italy appeared (1834) his masterpiece, the epic *Pan Tadeusz* ('Thaddeus'; Eng. trans. 1886)—a brilliant delineation of Lithuanian scenery, manners and beliefs. After teaching at Lausanne, he was appointed Slavonic professor at Paris in 1840, but deprived in 1843 for political utterances. He went to Italy to organize the Polish legion, but in 1852 Louis Napoleon appointed him a librarian in the Paris Arsenal. He died November 28, 1855, at Constantinople, where the emperor had sent him to raise a Polish legion for service against Russia. His body, first buried at Montmorency in France, was in 1890 laid beside Kosciusko's in Cracow cathedral. Mickiewicz, the national poet of the Poles, is after Pushkin the greatest of all Slav poets. See Lives by his son (1888), M. M. Gardner (1911) and M. Jastrun (1949).

MICKLE, William Julius (1735–88), Scottish poet, born in Langholm manse, and educated at Edinburgh High School, failed as a brewer, and turned author in London. In 1765 he published a poem, *The Concubine* (or *Syr Martyn*), and in 1771–75 his version rather than translation of the *Lusiad* of Camoens. In 1779 he went to Lisbon as secretary to Commodore Johnstone, but his last years were spent in London. His ballad of *Cumnor Hall* (which suggested *Kenilworth* to Scott) is poor poetry, but 'There's nae luck aboot the hoose' is assured of immortality. See Life by Sim prefixed to Mickle's *Poems* (1806), and ADAM (4).

MIDDLETON, (1) Conyers (1683–1750), English controversialist, born at Richmond in Yorkshire, became a fellow of Trinity College, Cambridge, librarian to the university, and rector of Hascombe in Surrey. He died at his seat at Hildersham in Cambridgeshire. His *Letter from Rome, showing an exact Conformity between Popery and Paganism* (1729) was an attack on the Catholic ritual. He next assailed the orthodox Waterland, giving up literal inspiration and the historical truth of the Old Testament. He professed to be answering Tindal and other Deists, but it is none too certain that he was not himself a freethinker. In 1747–48 he published his *Introductory Discourse* and the *Free Inquiry* into the miraculous powers claimed for the post-Apostolic church. His famous *Life of Cicero* (1741) was largely borrowed from Bellenden (q.v.).

(2) **Sir Hugh** (*c.* 1560–1631), a London goldsmith, born at Galch Hill near Denbigh, in 1609–13 constructed the New River, a canal bringing water from springs in Hertfordshire to the New River Head at Clerkenwell to augment London's supply. He represented Denbigh from 1603, and was made a baronet in 1622.

(3) **Thomas** (*c.* 1570–1627), English dramatist, is first mentioned in Henslowe's *Diary* in 1602, when he was engaged with Munday, Drayton and Webster on a lost play, *Cæsar's Fall*. First on the list of his printed plays is *Blurt, Master Constable* (1602), a light, fanciful comedy. Two interesting tracts, *Father Hubbard's Tale* and *The Black Book*, exposing London rogues, were published in 1604, to which year belongs the first part of *The Honest Whore* (mainly written by Dekker, partly by Middleton). *The Phœnix* and *Michaelmas Term* (1607) are lively comedies; even more diverting is *A Trick to Catch the Old One* (1608); and *A Mad World, My Masters*, from which Aphra Behn pilfered freely in *The City Heiress*, is singularly adroit. *The Roaring Girl* (1611; written with Dekker) idealizes the character of a noted cutpurse and virago. Middleton was repeatedly employed to write the Lord Mayor's pageant. *A Chaste Maid in Cheapside* was probably produced in 1613, as was *No Wit, No Help like a Woman's*. *A Fair Quarrel* (1617) and *The World Lost at Tennis* (1620) were written in conjunction with Rowley, as were probably *More Dissemblers Besides Women* (1622?) and *The Mayor of Quinborough*. In 1620 Middleton was appointed city chronologer, and a MS. Chronicle by him was extant in the 18th century. The delightful comedy, *The Old Law*, first published in 1656, is mainly the work of Rowley, with something by Middleton, all revised by Massinger. In the three posthumously-published plays, *The Changeling*, *The Spanish Gypsy* and *Women Beware Women*, Middleton's genius is seen at its highest. Rowley had a share in the first two and probably in the third. A very curious and skilful play is *A Game at Chess*, acted in 1624. *The Widow*, published in 1652, was mainly by Middleton. *Anything for a Quiet Life* (*c.* 1619) may have been revised by Shirley. Middleton was concerned in the authorship of some of the plays included in the works of Beaumont and Fletcher. See study by R. H. Barker (1959).

MIERIS, Frans van, *meer'ees* (1635–81), Dutch painter, born at Leyden, excelled in small-scale, exquisitely finished genre paintings in the style of Dou and Ter Borch. His sons **Jan** (1660–90) and **Willem** (1662–1747) followed his example. Willem's son **Frans** (1689–1773) was less successful as a painter, but made his name as a writer of antiquarian works.

MIES VAN DER ROHE, Ludwig, *mees* (1886–1969), German-born American architect, born at Aachen, was a director of the famous Bauhaus at Dessau (1929–33), then emigrated to the U.S. where he was from 1938–58 professor of Architecture at the Chicago Technical Institute (later called the Illinois) for which he built new premises on characteristically functional lines. Other notable designs include the German pavilion at Barcelona (1929) and flats in Berlin (1926) and Chicago (1948–49). See study by P. C. Johnson (N.Y. 1947).

MIGNE, Jacques Paul, *meen'y'* (1800–75), French theologian, born at St Flour, was ordained in 1824. A difference with his bishop drove him to Paris in 1833, where he started the Catholic *L'Univers*. In 1836 he sold the paper, and soon after set up a great publishing house at Petit Montrouge near Paris, which gave to the world *Scripturae Sacrae Cursus* and *Theologiae Cursus* (each 28 vols. 1840–45), *Collection des orateurs sacrés* (100 vols. 1846–48), *Patrologiae Cursus* (383 vols. 1844 *et seq.*), and *Encyclopédie théologique* (171 vols. 1844–66). None of these possesses critical value. The Archbishop of Paris, thinking that the undertaking had become a commercial speculation, forbade it to be continued, and when Migne resisted, suspended him. A great fire put an end to the work in February 1868.

MIGNET, François Auguste Marie, *meen-yay* (1796–1884), French historian, was born at Aix in Provence, and there studied law with Thiers. In 1821 he went to Paris, wrote for the *Courrier français*, and lectured on Modern History. His *Histoire de la révolution française* (1824) was the first, a sane and luminous summary. With Thiers he signed the famous protest of the journalists in 1830, and after the Revolution became keeper of the archives at the Foreign Office (till 1848). In 1833 he explored the famous Simancas Archives. Elected to the Academy of Moral Sciences at its foundation in 1832, he succeeded Comte as its perpetual secretary in 1837, and was elected to fill Raynouard's chair among the Forty in 1836. His works include *La Succession d'Espagne sous Louis XIV* (1836–42), *Antonio Perez et Philippe II* (1845), *Franklin* (1848), *Marie Stuart* (1851), *Charles-Quint* (1854), *Éloges historiques* (1843–64–77), and *François I et Charles V* (1875). See works by Trefort (Budapest 1885), E. Petit (Paris 1889), J. Simon (1889).

MIGUEL, Maria Evarist (1802–66), king of Portugal, born at Lisbon, the third son of King John VI, plotted (1824) to overthrow the constitutional form of government granted by his father; but with his mother, his chief abettor, was banished. At John's death in 1826 the throne devolved upon Miguel's elder brother, Pedro, emperor of Brazil; he, however, resigned it in favour of his daughter, Maria, making Miguel regent; but Miguel summoned a Cortes, which proclaimed him king in 1828. In 1832 Pedro captured Oporto and Lisbon, and Charles Napier destroyed Miguel's fleet off Cape St Vincent (1833). Next year Maria was restored, and Miguel withdrew to Italy. He died at Bronnbach in Baden.

MIHAILOVICH, Dragoljub or **Drazha,** me-hīl′o-vich (1893–1946), Serbian soldier, was a regular officer in World War I, after which he rose to the rank of colonel in the Yugoslav army. In 1941 he remained in Yugoslavia, after the German occupation, and from the mountains organized resistance, forming groups called Chetniks to wage guerrilla warfare. When Tito's Communist Partisans' resistance developed, Mihailovich allied himself with the Germans and then with the Italians in order to fight the Communists. He was executed by the Tito government for collaboration with the occupying powers.

MIKLOSICH, Franz von (1813–91), Slavonic scholar, born at Luttenberg, studied at Graz, worked in the Imperial library at Vienna, and was professor of Slavonic at the University of Vienna (1850–85), being elected to the Academy in 1851, and knighted in 1869. His thirty works include *Lexicon Linguae Palaeoslovenicae* (1850), *Vergleichende slawische Grammatik* (1852–74), works on the Gypsies (1872–80) and the great *Etymologica Slav Dictionary* (1886).

MIKOLAJCIK, Stanislaw, -lī′chik (1901–67), Polish politician, born, a miner's son, in Westphalia, became leader of the Peasant Party in Poland in 1937. In 1940–43 he held office in the exiled Polish government in London, and in 1943–44 was prime minister. After the German defeat he became deputy premier in the new coalition government in Warsaw, but fled to the U.S.A. when the Communists seized power in 1947.

MIKOYAN, Anastas Ivanovich (1895–1970), Soviet politician, born in Armenia, of poor parents, studied theology and became a fanatical revolutionary. Taken prisoner in the fighting at Baku, he escaped and made his way to Moscow, where he met Lenin and Stalin. A member of the Central Committee in 1922, he helped Stalin against Trotsky, and in 1926 became minister of trade, in which capacity he did much to improve Soviet standards of living. He showed himself willing to learn from the West, e.g., in the manufacture of canned goods and throughout the food industry generally. While other politicians came and went, Mikoyan's genius for survival enabled him to become a first vice-chairman of the council of ministers (1955–64), and president of the presidium of the Supreme Soviet from 1964.

MILFORD, Robin Humphrey (1903–), English composer, studied under Vaughan Williams, wrote much choral music, a violin concerto and other instrumental works, and the oratorio *A Prophet in the Land* (1931).

MILHAUD, Darius, mee-yō (1892–), French composer, born at Aix-en-Provence, studied under Widor and D'Indy, and from 1917 to 1918 was attached to the French Embassy at Rio de Janeiro, where he met the

playwright Paul Claudel, with whom he frequently collaborated, e.g., on the opera *Christopher Columbus.* For a time he was a member of *Les Six.* In 1940 he went to the U.S., where he was professor of Music at Mills Coll., Calif. (1940–47), and since then has lived in both France and America. Milhaud is one of the most prolific of modern composers, having written several operas, much incidental music for plays, ballets (including the jazz ballet *La Création du monde*), symphonies and orchestral, choral and chamber works.

MILL, (1) James (1773–1836), Scottish philosopher, father of (3), born, a shoemaker's son, near Montrose, studied for the ministry at Edinburgh, but in 1802 settled in London as a literary man. He edited and wrote for various periodicals, and in 1806 commenced his *History of British India* (1817–18). In 1819 the directors of the East India Company made him (though a Radical) assistant-examiner with charge of the revenue department, and in 1832 head of the examiner's office, where he held control of all the departments of Indian administration. Many of his articles (on government, jurisprudence, colonies, &c.) for the *Encyclopaedia Britannica* were reprinted. In 1821–22 he published *Elements of Political Economy*, in 1829 *Analysis of the Human Mind* and in 1835 the *Fragment on Mackintosh.* He was no mere disciple of Bentham, but a man of profound and original thought, as well as of great learning. His conversation gave a powerful stimulus to many young men like his own son and Grote. He took a leading part in founding University College London. See J. S. Mill's *Autobiography* and A. Bain (1882) and bibliography under (3).

(2) **John** (1645–1707), English New Testament critic, born at Shap in Westmorland, entered Queen's College, Oxford, as servitor in 1661, and was fellow and tutor, rector of Blechingdon, Oxfordshire (1681), principal of St Edmund's Hall (1685), and prebendary of Canterbury (1704). His *Novum Testamentum Graecum*, the labour of thirty years, sponsored by Dr Fell (q.v.), appeared a fortnight before his death.

(3) **John Stuart** (1806–73), English philosopher and radical reformer, born May 20 in London, the son of (1), who made himself responsible for John's unique education. He was taught Greek at the age of three, Latin and arithmetic at eight, logic at twelve, and political economy at thirteen, his only recreation being a daily walk with his father, who conducted all the while oral examinations. In 1820 he visited France, and on his return read history, law and philosophy. His first published writings appeared in the newspaper *The Traveller* (1822). In 1823 he began a career under his father at the India Office, from which he retired in 1858 as head of his department, declining a seat on the new India Council. His father moulded him into a future leader of the Benthamite movement and in 1823 he became a member of a small Utilitarian society which met in Bentham's house, the adjective 'utilitarian' having been taken to describe its doctrines from one of Galt's novels. He also became a frequent orator in

the London Debating Society, met Maurice and Sterling, 'the Coleridge Liberals', corresponded with Carlyle, and often contributed to the *Westminster Review*. A devout Malthusian, he was arrested in 1824 for helping to distribute birth control literature among London's poor. In 1826 he underwent an intellectual crisis which modified his attitude to Benthamism, which stressed reason to the exclusion of emotion. He realized that happiness was best achieved not by making it a direct aim but indirectly by enthusiastically following some ideal or cultural pursuit. His reviews on Tennyson (1835), Carlyle (1837) and particularly on Bentham (1838) indicate his newly-found divergencies from the creed he still professed to serve. In 1830 he met Harriet Taylor, the blue-stocking wife of a wealthy London merchant, and their long romance culminated in marriage in 1851, two years' after her tolerant husband's death, and she prevented Mill's modifications of Utilitarianism from going too far. In 1843 he published his great *System of Logic* with its four celebrated canons of inductive method which function effectively, provided that causality or Mill's 'Law of the Uniformity of Nature' is assumed. His treatment of induction influenced Jevons, Venn, Johnson and Keynes, and its rejection formed the basis of the mathematical logic systems of Frege, Meinong and Russell. In 1848 he published *Principles of Political Economy*, which foreshadowed the marginal utility theory and remained long a standard work. But he is best remembered for his brilliant essay *On Liberty* (1859), revised with great care in collaboration with Harriet, shortly before her death. It argues not only for political freedom but for social freedom, not only against the tyranny of the majority but also against the social tyranny of prevailing conventions and opinions. Essays on *Representative Government* and *Utilitarianism* (both 1861) followed, the latter making explicit Mill's modification of Benthamism, admitting qualitative differences in pleasures and providing proofs of the two chief Utilitarian principles that happiness alone is intrinsically good and that a right action is one which makes for the happiness of the greatest number. In proving the first he commits the celebrated howler of equating 'desired' with 'desirable'. His *Examination of Sir W. Hamilton's Philosophy* (1865) effectively criticized that philosopher's mixture of Scottish school and Kantian philosophy. Standing as a working-man's candidate for Westminster in 1865, he was surprisingly elected and also became lord rector of St Andrews University. His three years in parliament were devoted to women's suffrage, supporting the Advanced Liberals and campaigning against the governor of Jamaica's handling of a mutiny. Inspired by his late wife's views on the marriage contract and the inequalities suffered by women, he wrote *The Subjection of Women* (1869), an essay which provoked great antagonism. In 1872 he became godfather ' in a secular sense' to Lord Amberley's second son, Bertrand Russell, who was later to outrival

him in terms of pure philosophical achievement. But Mill, like Locke, changed the intellectual climate and exerted a profound and abiding influence on the political reformers of his day. He died May 8, 1873, and was buried at Avignon. Other works include an important preface to his father's *Analysis of the Phenomena of the Human Mind* (1869), *Auguste Comte and Positivism* (1865), *Three Essays on Religion* (1874), *Dissertations and Discussions* (1859–75), *Letters*, ed. H. S. R. Elliot (1910), *Autobiography* (1873; new ed. H. J. Laski 1924). See Lives by A. Bain (1882), F. A. Hayek (1951), R. Borchard (1957), M. St J. Packe (1957), M. Cranston (1958), and studies by J. McCosh (1866), A. Bain (1884), T. Whittaker (1908), K. Jackson (1941), R. P. Anschotz (1953), K. Britton (1953), B. Russell (1955), J. C. Rees (1956), J. Plamenatz, *The English Utilitarians* (1950) and *British Empirical Philosophers*, ed. A. J. Ayer and P. Winch (1951).

MILLAIS, Sir John Everett, *mil-ay* (1829–96), English painter, born at Southampton, June 8, of an old Jersey family, studied in the schools of the Royal Academy, and at seventeen exhibited his *Pizarro seizing the Inca of Peru*. He now became associated with the pre-Raphaelite Brotherhood, especially with Dante Gabriel Rossetti and Holman Hunt, and was markedly influenced by them and by Ruskin. His first pre-Raphaelite picture, a scene from the *Isabella* of Keats, figured in the Academy in 1849, where it was followed in 1850 by *Christ in the House of His Parents*, which met the full force of the anti-pre-Raphaelite reaction. The pre-Raphaelite style is also apparent in the well-known *Ophelia* and *The Order of Release* (1853), but *Autumn Leaves* and *The Blind Girl* (1856) embody more sincerity and depth of feeling. The exquisite *Gambler's Wife* (1869) and *The Boyhood of Raleigh* (1870) mark the transition of his art into its final phase, displaying brilliant and effective colouring, effortless power of brushwork, and delicacy of flesh-painting. The interest and value of his later works lie mainly in their splendid technical qualities. In great part they are portraits (Bright, Beaconsfield, Newman, Gladstone, &c.), varied by a few such important landscapes as *Chill October* (1871), and by such an occasional figure piece as *The Northwest Passage* (1873). Millais executed a few etchings, and his illustrations in *Good Words*, *Once a Week*, *The Cornhill*, &c. (1857–64) place him in the very first rank of woodcut designers. He became a baronet in 1885, P.R.A. in February 1896; and, dying on August 13, was buried in St Paul's. See Ruskin's *Notes* on his Grosvenor Exhibition in 1886, Spielmann's *Millais and his Works* (1898), and Lives by Armstrong (new ed. 1896) and (1899) Sir John's fourth son, **John Guille** (1865–1931), animal painter, naturalist and big-game hunter.

MILLAY, Edna St Vincent (1892–1950), American poet, born at Rockland, Me., won the Pulitzer prize with her *The Harp-Weaver* (1922). Her published work includes *A Few Figs from Thistles* (1920), *Conversation at Midnight* (1937) and *The Murder of Lidice* (1942), as well as collections of lyrics and sonnets. See study by E. Atkins (1936).

MILLE, DE. See DE MILLE.

MILLER, (1) Arthur (1915–), American playwright, was born in New York City. His *Death of a Salesman* (1949) won the Pulitzer prize and brought him international recognition, though *All My Sons* (1947) had already placed him in the front rank of American dramatists. *The Crucible* (1953) is probably, to date, his most lasting work, since its theme, the persecution of the Salem witches equated with contemporary political persecution, stands out of time. Other works include *A View from the Bridge* (1955), the filmscript of *The Misfits* (1960) and *After the Fall* (1963). His marriage to Marilyn Monroe (d. 1962), the film actress, from whom he was divorced in 1961, and his brush with the authorities over early Communist sympathies brought him considerable publicity.

(2) Henry (1891–), American author, born in New York, is known for his satires and reminiscences coloured by the wanderings of an adventurous early life and by antagonism to various facets of modern society. His early books, published in Paris, were originally banned in Britain and America. His works include *Tropic of Cancer* (1934), *Tropic of Capricorn* (1938), *Air-Conditioned Nightmare* (1945) and *Selected Prose* (2 vols., 1965). See study by Perlès (1956).

(3) Hugh (1802–56), Scottish geologist and writer, born at Cromarty, from sixteen to thirty-three worked as a common stonemason, devoting the winter months to writing, reading and natural history. In 1829 he published *Poems written in the Leisure Hours of a Journeyman Mason*, followed by *Scenes and Legends of the North of Scotland* (1835). His *Letter to Lord Brougham* on the 'Auchterarder Case' brought him into notice. In 1834–39 he acted as bank accountant; in 1839 was invited to Edinburgh to edit the Non-intrusion *Witness*; and in 1840 published in its columns the geological articles afterwards collected as *The Old Red Sandstone* (1841). At the British Association of 1840 he was warmly praised by Murchison and Buckland; and Agassiz proposed that a fossil discovered by him in a formation thought to be nonfossiliferous should be named *Pterichthys Milleri*. Miller's editorial labours during the heat of the Disruption struggle were immense; he used the term 'Free Church' before 1843. Worn out by overwork, he shot himself. Miller contributed to Wilson's *Tales of the Borders* (1835) and to *Chambers's Journal*. His *First Impressions of England* (1847) is the record of a journey in 1845; in *Footprints of the Creator* (1850) he combated the evolution theory; *My Schools and Schoolmasters* (1854) is the story of his youth; and *Testimony of the Rocks* (1857) is an attempt to reconcile the 'days' of Genesis with geology. Posthumous works include *The Cruise of the Betsey* (1858), geological investigations among the islands of Scotland, *Sketch Book of Popular Geology* (1859), &c. See Lives by Bayne (1871), Leask (1896), and Geikie's address (1902).

(4) Joaquin, pen-name of **Cincinnatus Heine Miller** (1839–1913), American poet. Born in Indiana, he became a miner in California, fought in the Indian wars, was an express messenger, practised law in Oregon, edited a paper suppressed for disloyalty, in 1866–70 was a county judge in Oregon, was a Washington journalist, and in 1887 settled in California as a fruitgrower. His poems include *Songs of the Sierras* (1871); his prose works, *The Danites in the Sierras* (1881). He also wrote a successful play, *The Danites*. See his *My Life among the Modocs* (1873) and *My Own Story* (new ed. 1891), Life by Peterson (1937), and M. M. Marbury's *Splendid Poseur* (1954).

(5) Patrick (1731–1815), Scottish inventor of an early experimental steamboat with an engine by William Symington (q.v.), which he launched on the loch at his estate, Dalswinton, near Dumfries, in 1788.

(6) William (1781–1849), a New York farmer, founded the religious sect of Second Adventists or Millerites. See Lives by S. Bliss (1853) and J. White (1875).

(7) William (1810–72), Scottish poet, born in Glasgow, was a woodturner by profession, having relinquished a medical career through ill-health. He is now remembered only as the author of *Wee Willie Winkie*, one of his numerous dialect poems about children and childhood. A collection, *Scottish Nursery Songs and Other Poems*, appeared in 1863.

MILLERAND, Alexandre, *-rã* (1859–1943), French statesman, born in Paris, edited socialist papers, entered parliament 1885, was minister of commerce 1899–1902, of works 1909–10, of war 1912–13, when he resigned over a personal incident but was reinstated until 1915, when he resigned on complaints of deficiency of supplies. His chief critic, Clemenceau, later appointed him commissaire général in Alsace Lorraine 1919. As prime minister, 1920, he formed a coalition (Bloc National) and gave support to the Poles during the Russian invasion 1920. He became president 1920 and resigned in 1924 in face of opposition from *cartel des gauches* under M. Herriot. He later entered the senate and organized the opposition to the *cartel*.

MILLES, Carl Vilhelm Emil (1875–1955), Swedish sculptor, born near Uppsala, was especially renowned as a designer of fountains. Much of his work is in Sweden and the U.S.A., noteworthy examples being *Wedding of the Rivers* (1940) at St Louis, and *St Martin of Tours* (1955) at Kansas City, his last work. See Life by C. G. Laurin (Stockholm 1936).

MILLET, Jean François, *mee-lay* (1814–75), French painter, born at Grouchy near Gréville, worked on the farm with his father, a peasant, but, showing a talent for art, he was in 1832 placed under a painter at Cherbourg, who induced the municipality to grant his pupil an annuity. In 1837 Millet came to Paris, worked under Delaroche, studied the great masters, and eked out a living by producing fashionable potboilers after Boucher and Watteau. In 1840 and 1842 his entries for the Salon were rejected, but in 1844 his *Milkwomen* and *Riding Lesson* were hung. The 1848 Revolution and dire need drove him from Paris, and he settled with his wife and children at Barbizon, near the forest of Fontainebleau, living much like the peasants around him, and painting the rustic life of France with sympathetic power. His famous *Sower* was completed in 1850. His *Peasants Grafting* (1855) was followed by *The Gleaners* (1857), *The Angelus* (1859) and other masterpieces He also produced many charcoal drawings of high quality, and etched a few plates. He received little public notice, and was never well off, but after the Great Exhibition of 1867 at Paris, in which nine of his best works were on show, his merit came to be recognized, and he was awarded the *Légion d'honneur*. After 1870, too late for him to benefit, his pictures began to realize high prices. See works by Roger-Milès (1895), Rolland (1902), Gurney (1954), and D. C. Thomson, *Barbizon School* (1890). Two minor French landscape painters were also named **Jean François Millet**, father (1642–79) and son (1666–1732).

MILLIKAN, Robert Andrews (1868–1954), American physicist, born in Illinois, studied at Oberlin College, Berlin, and Göttingen, taught physics in Chicago University from 1896 (as professor from 1910) till 1921 when he became head of Pasadena Institute of Technology. He determined the charge on the electron, gained a Nobel prize (1923), and discovered cosmic rays (1925) which he explained as due to atom-building. See his *Autobiography* (1951).

MILLS, Percy Herbert, 1st Viscount Mills (1896–1968), English politician and industrialist, born at Thornaby-on-Tees, won recognition in the drive to step up war production in 1939–45, and as one of the leaders of the Allied Control Commission played a leading part in fixing the level of Germany's postwar steel production. He was adviser to the government on housing (1951–52), chairman of the National Research and Development Association (1950–55), from 1957–59 held the newly-created office of minister of power, from 1959–61 was paymaster-general, and from 1961–62 minister without portfolio. He was created baronet in 1953, baron in 1957, and viscount in 1962.

MILMAN, (1) Henry Hart (1791–1868), English poet and church historian, was born in London, son of Sir Francis Milman (1746–1821), physician to George III. He was educated at Eton and Oxford, where he won the Newdigate Prize (1812). In 1816 he became vicar at Reading; in 1821–31 professor of Poetry at Oxford and in 1849 Dean of St Paul's. His *Poems and dramatic works* (3 vols. 1839) are almost forgotten except a few hymns. His principal historical work is *The History of Latin Christianity* (1854–55). See Life by his son (1900).
(2) **Robert** (1816–76), poet and theologian, nephew of (1), became Bishop of Calcutta in 1867. He published poems and theological works. See Life by his sister (1879).

MILN, James (1819–81), Scottish antiquary, made excavations on a Roman site at Carnac, Brittany (1872–80). Miln Museum, Carnac, contains his collection. Results published: *Excavations at Carnac* 1877 and 1881.

MILNE, (1) Alan Alexander (1882–1956), English author, born at St John's Wood, London, educated at Westminster and Trinity College, Cambridge, where he edited the undergraduate magazine *Granta*. He joined the staff of *Punch*, and became well known for his light essays and his comedies, notably *Wurzel-Flummery* (1917), *Mr Pim Passes By* (1919) and *The Dover Road* (1922). In 1924 he achieved world fame with his book of children's verse, *When We were Very Young*, written for his own son, Christopher Robin; further children's classics include *Winnie-the-Pooh* (1926), *Now We are Six* (1927) and *The House at Pooh Corner* (1928). See his autobiographical *It's Too Late Now* (1939).
(2) **Edward Arthur** (1896–1950), British astrophysicist, assistant director of the Cambridge Solar Physics Observatory (1920–1924), professor of Mathematics at Oxford (1928), president of the Royal Astronomical Society (1943–45), made notable contributions to the study of cosmic dynamics. He estimated the age of the universe to be *c.* 2,000,000,000 years.
(3) **John** (1859–1913), British seismologist, was born at Liverpool, worked in Newfoundland as a mining engineer, and was for twenty years mining engineer and geologist to the Japanese government, married a Japanese wife, became a supreme authority on earthquakes, travelled widely, and finally established a private seismological observatory at Newport, Isle of Wight. He published important works on earthquakes, seismology and crystallography.

MILNE-EDWARDS, (1) Alphonse (1835–1900), French naturalist, son of (3), whom he assisted in his later work.
(2) **Frederick William** (1777–1842), physiologist, elder brother of (3).
(3) **Henri** (1800–85), naturalist, was born at Bruges, his father being English, studied medicine at Paris, became professor at the Jardin des plantes, and wrote a famous *Cours élémentaire de zoologie* (1834; rewritten 1851; trans. 1863), works on the crustacea, the corals, physiology and anatomy, researches on the natural history of the French coasts (1832–45) and the coasts of Sicily, and on the natural history of the mammalia (1871).

MILNER, (1) Alfred, 1st Viscount Milner (1854–1925), British statesman, born at Bonn, son of the university lecturer on English at Tübingen, had a brilliant career at Oxford, winning a New College fellowship. For a time he was assistant editor of the *Pall Mall Gazette*, and then private secretary to Goschen, who recommended him (1889) for the under-secretaryship of Finance in Egypt, where he wrote *England in Egypt* (1892; 12th ed. 1915). In 1892–97 he was chairman of the Board of Inland Revenue, in 1897–1901 governor of the Cape Colony, governor of the Transvaal and Orange River Colony 1901–05, and high commissioner for S. Africa 1897–1905, receiving a barony (1901) and a viscountcy (1902) for his services before and during the Boer War. In December 1916 he entered the War Cabinet; in 1918–19 he was secretary for war; in 1919–21 colonial secretary. K.G. in 1921, he recommended virtual independence for Egypt. See *Milner Papers, South Africa, 1897–1899* (1931) and *1899–1905* (1933); studies by E. A. Walker (1943), L. Curtis (1951), V. Halperin (1952), and Life by J. E. Wrench (1958).

(2) **Isaac** (1750–1820), English mathematician, Dean of Carlisle and Lucasian professor at Cambridge, wrote the life and edited works of his brother (4), besides works on scientific and theological subjects.

(3) **John** (1752–1826), English divine, called by Newman ' the English Athanasius ', was born in London. Catholic priest at Winchester from 1779, in 1803 he was made a bishop *in partibus* and vicar-apostolic of the Midlands. He wrote a great history of Winchester (1798–1801) and much polemical theology. See Life by Husenbeth (1862).

(4) **Joseph** (1744–97), English church historian, born at Leeds and educated at Cambridge, was headmaster of Hull grammar school, and in 1797 vicar of Holy Trinity, Hull. His principal work, *History of the Church of Christ* (1794–1908), was completed by his brother Isaac (2). See Life by his niece (1842).

MILNER-GIBSON. See GIBSON (7).

MILNES, Richard Monckton, 1st Baron Houghton (1809–85), English politician, was born in London (not at Pontefract). His father, ' single-speech Milnes ' (1784–1858), declined the chancellorship of the Exchequer and a peerage; his mother was a daughter of the fourth Lord Galway. At Cambridge he was a leader in the Union, and one of the famous ' Apostles ', and he was M.P. for Pontefract from 1837 until he entered the House of Lords in 1863. A Maecenas of poets, he got Lord Tennyson the laureateship, soothed the dying hours of poor David Gray, and was one of the first to recognize Swinburne's genius. Besides this, Lord Houghton—the ' Mr Vavasour ' of Beaconsfield's *Tancred*—was a traveller, a philanthropist, an unrivalled after-dinner speaker, and Rogers' successor in the art of breakfast-giving. He went up in a balloon and down in a diving-bell; he was the first publishing Englishman who gained access to the harems of the East; he championed oppressed nationalities, liberty of conscience, fugitive slaves, the rights of women; and carried a bill for establishing reformatories (1846). As well as his poetry and essays, he published *Life, Letters and Remains of Keats* (1848). See Life by Wemyss-Reid (1890). His son, **Robert Offley Ashburton Crewe Milnes** (1858–1945), viceroy of Ireland 1892–95, Earl of Crewe (1895), marquis (1911), married Lord Rosebery's daughter and wrote his Life (1931), held cabinet rank 1905–16, 1931, was British ambassador in Paris 1922–28.

MILO, of Crotona in Magna Graecia, twelve times victor for wrestling at the Olympic and Pythian games, commanded the army which defeated the Sybarites (511 B.C.). He carried a live ox upon his shoulders through the stadium of Olympia, and afterwards, it was said, ate the whole of it in one day. In old age he attempted to split up a tree, which closed upon his hands, and held him fast until he was devoured by wolves.

MILTIADES, *mil-tī′a-deez* (d. *c.* 488 B.C.), Greek general, won the victory of Marathon against the Persians. He also attacked the island of Paros to gratify a private enmity, but, failing in the attempt, was on his return to Athens condemned to pay a fine of fifty talents, but died in prison of a wound received in Paros before paying it.

MILTON, John (1608–74), English poet, was born at Bread Street, Cheapside, the son of a London scrivener, a composer of some distinction who early discerned the boy's genius. From St Paul's School he went up to Christchurch, Cambridge, where he spent seven not altogether blameless years, followed by six years of studious leisure at Horton which he regarded as preparation for his life's work as a poet. His prentice work at Cambridge—apart from some poems of elegant Latinity written there or at Horton—includes the splendid Nativity Ode, the brilliant epitaph on Shakespeare and 'At a Solemn Music '. The poems he wrote at Horton—*L'Allegro* and *Il Penseroso, Comus* and *Lycidas*—he also regarded as preparatory for the great poem or drama which was to be ' doctrinal and exemplary for a nation '. *L'Allegro* and *Il Penseroso* are indeed set studies, but to eye and ear the alternative delights, gay and reflective of country life, are communicated with consummate art. *Comus* (1634) was the libretto of a masque which depends for its effect on the outside setting and on dance and song. The ' Doric delicacy ' of the numbers offset the somewhat priggish Puritanism of the dialogue, which, however, is cast in a smooth early Shakespearean blank verse. *Lycidas* (1637) is our finest pastoral elegy, though it was censured for its outburst against the Laudian clergy by critics who were ignorant of the Renaissance pastoral convention. No doubt the acrimony of the outburst is prophetic of the struggle ahead. With this note struck so ominously Milton concluded his formal education with a visit to Italy (1638–39). The fame of his Latin poems had preceded him and he was received in the academies with distinction. His Italian tour was interrupted by news of the imminent outbreak of Civil War. This event, into which he threw himself with revolutionary ardour, silenced his muse for twenty years except for occasional sonnets, most of which were published in the volume of 1645. They range from civilities to friends to trumpet-blasts against his and the Commonwealth's detractors. Two stand out—the noble ' On His Blindness ' and ' On the Late Massacre in Piedmont '. The reading of Milton's sonnets made Wordsworth a sonneteer on the Petrarchian model and in the same lofty vein. On his return to London in 1639 Milton undertook the education of his two nephews, but in 1641, the year when ' the dykes gave way ', he emerged as the polemical champion of the revolution in a series of pamphlets against episcopacy, including an *Apology for Smectymnuus* (1642), Smectymnuus (q.v.) being an attack on episcopacy by five Presbyterians. He was now launched on his second series of controversial pamphlets—the divorce pamphlets which were occasioned by the refusal of his wife, Mary Powell, daughter of a Royalist, whom he married in 1642, to return to him after a visit to her people. The first of these, *The Doctrine and Discipline of Divorce* (1643), involved him in three supplementary pamphlets against the opponents of his views on divorce, and these occasioned a threat of prosecution by a parliamentary committee dominated by the Presbyterians who were now to be reckoned his chief enemies with episcopacy. *Areopagitica, A Speech for the Liberty of Unlicensed Printing* (1644) was the famous vindication which is still quoted when the press is in danger. The contemporary *Tractate on Education*, a brilliant exposition of the Renaissance ideals of education, has much less appeal to moderns. Meanwhile his wife returned to him in 1645 accompanied by her whole family as refugees after the 'crowning mercy' of Naseby, and two years later, his father having left him a competence, he was able to give up schoolmastering. The execution of King Charles launched him on his third public controversy, now addressed however to the conscience of Europe. As Latin secretary to the new council of state to which he was appointed immediately after his defence of the regicides, *The Tenure of Kings and Magistrates* (1649), he became official apologist for the Commonwealth and as such wrote *Eikonoklastes* and two *Defensiones*, the first *Pro Populo Anglicano Defensio* (1650), addressed to the celebrated humanist Salmasius; the second, also in Latin, *Defensio Secunda* (1654), which contains autobiographical matter and so supplements the personal matter in the *Apology for Smectymnuus*. Meanwhile, his wife having died in 1652, leaving three daughters, he married Catherine Woodcock, whose death two years later is the theme of his beautiful and pathetic sonnet ' Methought I saw my late espoused Saint '. Although blind from 1652 onwards, he retained his Latin secretaryship till the Restoration, which he roused himself to resist in his last despairing effort as pamphleteer. But the fire had gone out of him, and *The Readie and Easie Way*, which pointed to dictatorship, became the target of the Royalist wits. After the Restoration Milton went into hiding for a short period, and then after the Act of Oblivion (August 1660) he devoted himself wholly to poetry with the exception of his prose *De Doctrina Christiana*, which did not see the light till 1823. He married a third wife, Elizabeth Minshull, in 1662 and spent his last days in what is now Bunhill Row. His wife survived him. The theme of *Paradise Lost* had been in Milton's mind since 1641. It was to be a sacred drama then; but when in 1658 his official duties were lightened so as to allow him to write, he chose the epical form. The first three books reflect the triumph of the godly—so soon to be reversed; the last books, written in 1663, are tinged with despair. God's kingdom is not of this world. Man's intractable nature frustrates the planning of the wise. The heterodox theology of the poem which is made clear in his late *De Doctrina Christiana* did not trouble Protestant readers till modern

critics examined it with hostile intent; at the same time they made him responsible for that ' dissociation of sensibility ' in the language of poetry which had fatal effects on his 18th-century imitators. T. S. Eliot's recantation of the latter charge does not go very far. *Paradise Regained* ought to have appeased these critics, for its manner is quiet and grave, though not without grand rhetorical passages. The theme here is the triumph of reason over passion; Christ is more the elevated stoic than the redeemer. The disparagement of ancient poetry and philosophy may mean that, as Grierson says, ' The Humanist in Milton has succumbed to the Puritan '. Resignation is the note of *Paradise Regained* but *Samson Agonistes*, published along with it in 1674, shows the reviving spirit of rebellion, due no doubt to the rise of Whig opposition about 1670. The parallel of his own fortunes, both in the private and the public sphere, with those of Samson made Milton pour out his great spirit into this Greek play, the only one which in itself or as the libretto of Handel's oratorio has succeeded in English. Samson's reviving powers following on repentance are a sign of God's grace and their exercise in public may herald a new triumph of the ' good old cause ' in England. The public cause and the vituperation of woman are the twin themes of this great poem, but it also plumbs the depths of questioning and despair. H. Darbishire's *Early Lives of Milton* (1932) includes the near-contemporary Lives by Milton's nephews, John and Edward Philips, and Toland. See also Lives by Symmons, Mitford, Todd, and Masson's great Life (7 vols. 1859–94) which is a too compendious history of the times. Dr Johnson's Life in *Lives of the Poets* is a fascinating study of honest but often misguided criticism struggling with distaste for Milton and all he stood for. Later and more discriminating studies are by R. Bridges (1893), Sir W. Raleigh (1900), D. Saurat (1924), E. M. Tillyard (1930), T. S. Eliot (1947), D. Daiches (1958) and R. Tuve (1958).

MINDSZENTY, Jozsef, Cardinal (1892–), Roman Catholic primate of Hungary, born at Mindszent, Vas, Hungary, son of Janos Pehm, became internationally known in 1948 when charged with treason by the Communist government in Budapest. He was sentenced to life imprisonment in 1949, but in 1955 was released on condition that he did not leave Hungary. In 1956 he was granted asylum in the American legation at Budapest. See S. K. Swift's *The Cardinal's Story* (1950), and book by Shuster (1956).

MINGHETTI, Marco, *min-get'tee* (1818–86), Italian statesman, Cavour's successor, was born in Bologna, studied there, and travelled in Europe and Britain. Pope Pius IX in 1846 made him, now a journalist, minister of public works. The pope's reforming zeal was short-lived, and Minghetti entered the Sardinian army, and at Custozza earned a knighthood. After Novara he settled at Turin, an ardent student of economics, a free-trader and a devoted friend of Cavour. Premier in 1863, he concluded with the Emperor Napoleon the ' September Convention' in 1864. At Rome in 1873–76 he was prime minister for the second time. He wrote on Raphael and Dante, *Economia pubblica* (1859), and *La Chiesa e lo Stato* (1878). See his *Ricordi* (1888).

MINIÉ, Claude Étienne, *meen-yay* (1804–79), French improver of firearms, born in Paris, from a private became colonel, and in 1849 invented the Minié rifle, and also perfected the expanding bullet. He was for a time at Cairo in the Khedive's service.

MINKOWSKI, Hermann, *min-kof'ski* (1864–1909), Russian-German mathematician, born near Kovno, was professor at Königsberg (1895), Zürich (1896), where he taught Einstein, and Göttingen (1902). He wrote on the theory of numbers and on space and time (1909), preparing the way for Einstein.

MINOT, George Richards (1885–1950), American physician, professor of Medicine at Harvard (1928–48), first suggested, with Murphy (2), the importance of a liver diet in the treatment of pernicious anaemia. In 1934 they shared the Nobel prize for medicine.

MINSHEU, John, *min'shoo* (fl. 1617), English lexicographer, taught languages in London. His dictionary, *Guide into Tongues* (1617), in eleven languages, is of great value for the study of Elizabethan English.

MINTO, Earls of, (1) **Sir Gilbert Elliot-Murray-Kynynmound, 1st Earl** (1751–1814), British statesman, born in Edinburgh, educated in France, Edinburgh and Oxford, was called to the bar in 1774. Elected M.P. in 1776, he supported Burke against Warren Hastings. He was later viceroy of Corsica (1794–96), and as governor-general of India (1806–13) he established order and security. See Life by his greatniece, Countess of Minto (1874–80).

(2) **Gilbert John Elliot-Murray-Kynynmound, 4th Earl** (1847–1914), colonial administrator, great-grandson of (1), served in many wars 1870–82. He was governor-general of Canada (1898–1904), and as viceroy of India (1905–10) was associated with Morley in the constitutional reforms. See Life by J. Buchan (1924); correspondence in Mary, Countess of Minto's *India, Minto and Morley* (1934), and study by Wasti (1964).

MINTO, William (1845–93), Scottish man of letters and critic, born near Alford, Aberdeenshire, became, after a spell of journalism, professor of Logic and English at Aberdeen. He wrote *Manual of English Prose Literature* (1872) and *Characteristics of English Poets* (1874). See Wright's *Some 19th Century Scotsmen* (1902).

MINTOFF, Dominic (1916–   ), Malta Labour politician, was educated at Malta and Oxford Universities, afterwards becoming a civil engineer. In 1947 he joined the Malta Labour Party and in the first Malta Labour government that year he became minister of works and deputy prime minister. He became prime minister in 1955 and in 1956–57 undertook negotiations with Britain to integrate Malta more closely with the former. These broke down in 1958, when his demands for independence and irresponsible political agitation over the transfer of the naval dockyard to a commercial concern, led directly to the suspension of Malta's constitution in January 1959. Having resigned in 1958 to lead the Malta Liberation Movement, he became opposition leader in 1962.

MINTON, (1) (Francis) John (1917–57), English artist, born at Cambridge. He studied in London and Paris, and from 1943 to 1956 taught at various London art schools. He was noted for his book illustrations and his brilliant watercolours, and also as a designer of textiles and wallpaper.

(2) **Thomas** (1765–1836), English pottery and china manufacturer, born at Shrewsbury, founded the firm which bears his name. Originally trained as a transfer-print engraver, he worked for Spode for a time, but in 1789 he set up his own business at Stoke-on-Trent, producing copper plates for transfer-printing in blue underglaze. He is reputed to have invented the willow pattern (for which an original copperplate engraved by him is in the British Museum). In 1793 he built a pottery works at Stoke, but he very soon produced a fine bone china (approximating to hard paste) for which the best period is 1798–1810. Much of it was tableware, decorated with finely painted flowers and fruit. His son, **Herbert** (his partner from 1817 to 1836), took over the firm at his death.

MINUCIUS FELIX (*c.* 2nd cent.), early Christian apologist, author of *Octavius,* a dialogue between a pagan and a Christian. See Rendall's edition (Loeb Library, 1931), Kühn's monograph (1882), Freese's trans. (1918) and Account by H. J. Baylis (1928).

MIRABEAU, *mee-ra-bō,* (1) **André Boniface Riqueti, Vicomte de** (1754–92), French soldier and politician, son of (3), brother of (2), fought in the American army (1780–1785) and at the outbreak of the French Revolution was returned to the States General. He raised a legion of *emigrés* against the republic but was accidentally killed at Freiburg-im-Breisgau. Notorious for his thirst and his corpulence, he was nicknamed *tonneau*—i.e., barrel. See Lives by Sarrazin (Leipzig 1893) and E. Berger (1904).

(2) **Honoré Gabriel Riqueti, Comte de** (1749–91), French orator and revolutionary, son of (3), brother of (1), was born at Bignon, in Loiret, March 9, 1749. At seventeen he entered a cavalry regiment, and lived so recklessly that his father imprisoned him in 1768 on the Île de Rhé, and next sent him with the army to Corsica. But his father refusing to purchase him a company, he left the service in 1770. He married (1772), but lived extravagantly and unhappily; and on account of his debts his father confined him (1773–75) at Manosque, and the Château d'If, and the castle of Joux near Pontarlier. Hence he fled with the young wife of the grey-haired Marquis de Monnier to Amsterdam, where for eight months he earned his bread by laborious hack work for the book-sellers. His *Essai sur le despotisme* made a sensation by its audacity. Meantime the *parlement* of Besançon sentenced him to death; and in May 1777 he was handed over by the States-General and flung into the castle of Vincennes, where, in close imprisonment of three and a half years, he wrote *Erotica*

biblion, Ma conversion, and his famous *Essai sur les lettres de cachet* (2 vols. 1782). In 1780 he was released, and in 1782 he got his sentence annulled. Drowned in debt, he made for some years a shifty living by writing. In England he was intimate with the Earl of Minto, Lord Lansdowne and Romilly, and his close observation of English politics taught him the good of moderation, compromise and opportunism. In 1786 he was sent on a secret mission to Berlin, and there obtained the materials for his work, *Sur la monarchie prussienne sous Frédéric le Grand* (4 vols. 1787). Rejected by the nobles of Provence as candidate for the States-General, he turned to the *tiers état,* and was elected by both Marseilles and Aix. When the *tiers état* constituted itself the National Assembly, Mirabeau's political sagacity made him a great force, while his audacity and volcanic eloquence endeared him to the mob. It was he who proposed the establishment of a citizen-guard, but he trembled at the revolutionary legislation of August 4, 1789. In conjunction with the Count de la Marck, a friend of Marie Antoinette, he drew up a memoir, setting forth the necessity for a new constitution, with a responsible ministry after the English pattern. But the queen detested the great tribune, and the Assembly passed a self-denying ordinance that no member should take office under the crown. Mirabeau surrounded himself with a group of friends who provided him with his facts, and even wrote his speeches and articles; he fused the materials so prepared for him in the alembic of his own genius. In the spring of 1790 communication opened anew with the court; Mirabeau was mortified to find himself mistrusted; but the court provided money to pay his debts and promised a monthly allowance. He risked all his popularity by successfully opposing Barnave's motion that the right of peace and war should rest not with the king but the Assembly. The queen gave him an interview in the gardens at Saint-Cloud, and Mirabeau assured her that the monarchy was saved. But as the popular movement progressed his dream of placing the king at the head of the Revolution became hopeless, and he found that the court did not grant him its full confidence, though he showed himself a really great financier in his measures to avert national bankruptcy. His secret aim was now to undermine the Assembly and compel it to dissolve, hoping that he might guide a new Assembly to wise concessions. But the queen would not commit herself to his guidance. In 1790 he was president of the Jacobin Club; on January 30, 1791, he was elected president of the Assembly for the fortnight. He defeated the proposed law against emigration, and successfully resisted Sieyès' motion that in the event of the king's death the regent should be elected by the Assembly. But his health had been sinking, though he refused to abate his giant labours; and he died April 2, 1791. His writings were collected by Blanchard (10 vols. 1822). See *Mémoires de Mirabeau écrits par lui-même, par son père, son oncle, et son fils adoptif* (8 vols. 1834); Loménie, *Les Mirabeau* (5 vols.

1878–91); French books by Rousse (1891) Mézières (2nd ed. 1908), Barthou (1913, 1926), Meunier (1926), Caste (1942), Vallentin (1948, Eng. trans. 1949); German by Stern (1889), Erdmannsdörffer (1900); English by Willert (1898), Warwick (1905), Trowbridge (1907), Fling (1908), Tallentyre (1908).

(3) **Victor Riqueti, Marquis de** (1715–89), French soldier and economist, father of (1) and (2), expounded physiocratic political philosophy in *Ami des hommes* (1756) and *La Philosophie rurale* (1763). See Loménie, *Les Mirabeau* (1879), Oncten (Berne 1886), Ripert (1901).

MIRANDA. See SÁ DE MIRANDA.

MIRANDOLA. See PICO.

MIRBEAU, Octave, *meer-bō* (1850–1917), dramatist, novelist, journalist, was born at Trevières (Calvados). A radical, he attracted attention by the violence of his writings. His *Les Affaires sont les affaires* (1903) was adapted by Sidney Grundy (1905). See *Œuvres complètes* (9 vols. 1934–36), study by M. Renon (Paris 1924).

MIRÓ, Joán, *mee-rō'* (1893–), Spanish artist, born at Montroig, studied in Paris and Barcelona, and exhibited in Paris with the Surrealists. He lived in Spain from 1940 to 1944, but has mainly worked in France. His paintings are predominantly abstract, and his humorous fantasy makes play with a restricted range of pure colours and dancing shapes, for example, *Catalan Landscape (The Hunter)* of 1923–24 in the Museum of Modern Art, New York. See monograph by S. Hunter (1959).

MISES, Richard von, *mee'zes* (1883–1953), German mathematician and philosopher, was professor at Dresden (1919), Berlin (1920–33), and from 1933 at Istanbul. An authority in aerodynamics and hydrodynamics, he set out in *Wahrscheinlichkeit, Statistik und Wahrheit,* ' Probability, Statistics and Truth ' (1928), a frequency theory of probability which he claimed to be empirical, although his requirement of ' randomness ' or ' principle of impossibility of gambling systems ' together with his reliance on convergence in an infinite series, raised the question whether his frequency-assertions could be confirmed or falsified by empirical investigations, which are confined to finite series. See W. Kneale, *Probability and Induction* (1949).

MISTINGUETT, stage name of **Jeanne Marie Bourgeois,** *mees-ti-get* (1874–1956), French dancer and actress, born at Pointe de Raquet, made her début in 1895 and became the most popular French music hall artiste of the first three decades of the century, reaching the height of success with Maurice Chevalier at the Folies Bergère. She also distinguished herself as a straight actress in *Madame Sans-Gêne, Les Misérables,* &c. See her *Toute ma vie* (1954).

MISTRAL, (1) **Frédéric** (1830–1914), Provençal poet, was born, lived and died at Maillane near Avignon. After studying law at Avignon, he went home to work on the land and write poetry; and he helped to found the Provençal renaissance movement (Félibrige school). In 1859 his epic *Miréio* (trans. 1890) gained him the poet's prize of the French academy and the *Légion d'honneur.* He was awarded a Nobel prize in 1904. Other works are *Calendau* (epic, 1861), *Lis Isclo d'or* (poems, 1876), *La Reino Jano* (tragedy, 1890), and a Provençal-French dictionary (1878–86). See his *Mémoires* (trans. 1907), and books by Downer (N.Y. 1901), Coulon (1930), Girdlestone (1937) and Leonard (Paris 1945).

(2) **Gabriela**, pseud. of **Lucila Godoy de Alcayaga** (1889–1957), Chilean educationalist, diplomatist and writer, born in Vicuña, as a teacher won a poetry prize with her *Sonetos de la muerte* at Santiago in 1915. She taught at Columbia University, Vassar and in Puerto Rico, and was formerly consul at Madrid and elsewhere. The cost of publication of her first book, *Desolación* (1922), was defrayed by the teachers of New York. Her work is inspired by her vocation as a teacher, by religious sentiments and a romantic preoccupation with sorrow and death, infused with an intense lyricism. She was awarded the Nobel prize for literature in 1945.

MITCHEL, John (1815–75), Irish patriot, born, a Presbyterian minister's son, near Dungiven, Co. Derry, studied at T.C.D., practised as an attorney, and became assistant editor of the *Nation*. Starting the *United Irishman* (1848), he was tried for his articles on a charge of ' treason-felony ' and sentenced to fourteen years' transportation; but in 1853 he escaped from Van Diemen's Land to the United States, and published his *Jail Journal* (1854). Returning in 1874 to Ireland, he was next year elected to parliament for Tipperary, declared ineligible and re-elected, but died the same month. He published a *Life of Hugh O'Neill* (1845) and a *History of Ireland from the Treaty of Limerick* (1868). See studies by W. Dillon (1888), E. Montégut (trans. 1915), O'Hegarty (1917).

MITCHELL, (1) Donald Grant, pseud. **Ik Marvel** (1822–1908), American author, born in Norwich, Conn., was in 1853 appointed U.S. consul at Venice. He wrote *Reveries of a Bachelor* and *Dream Life* (1850–51; new eds. 1889); a novel, *Dr Johns* (1866); and *English Lands, Letters, and Kings* (4 vols. 1889–97). See Life by Dunn (N.Y. 1922).

(2) **James Leslie.** See GIBBON, LEWIS GRASSIC.

(3) **Margaret** (1900–49), American novelist, was born at Atlanta, Georgia, and studied for a medical career. She turned to journalism, but after her marriage to J. R. Marsh in 1925, began the ten-year task of writing her only novel, *Gone with the Wind* (1936). This book sold eight million copies, was translated into thirty languages and filmed.

(4) **Sir Peter Chalmers** (1864–1945), Scottish zoologist and journalist, started his career as a lecturer at Oxford and London, and in 1903 was elected secretary of the Zoological Society. He inaugurated a period of prosperity at the London Zoo and was responsible for the Mappin terraces, Whipsnade, the Aquarium and other improvements. He was scientific correspondent to *The Times* from 1922 to 1934, and wrote a number of books on zoological subjects. He retired to Spain, but was forced to return by the Civil War. He was created C.B.E.

in 1918, and knighted in 1929. See his autobiographical *My Fill of Days* (1937).

(5) **Reginald Joseph** (1895–1937), English aircraft designer. Trained as an engineer, he was led by his interest in aircraft to join in 1916 an aviation firm, where he soon became chief designer. He designed seaplanes for the Schneider trophy races (1922–1931) and later the famous Spitfire, the triumph of which he did not live to see.

(6) **Silas Weir** (1829–1914), American physician and author, was born at Philadelphia. He specialized in nervous diseases and pioneered in the application of psychology to medicine. As well as historical novels and poems he wrote medical texts, including *Injuries of Nerves* (1872) and *Fat and Blood* (1877). See his *Works* (16 vols., N.Y. 1913–14), and Lives by Burr (N.Y. 1929), Mumey (1934) and Earnest (1950).

(7) **Sir Thomas Livingstone** (1792–1855), Scottish explorer, born at Craigend, Stirlingshire, served in the Peninsular War, and from 1828 was surveyor-general of New South Wales. In four expeditions (1831, 1835, 1836, 1845–47) he did much to explore Eastern Australia (' Australia Felix ') and Tropical Australia, especially the Murray, Glenelg and Barcoo rivers. He wrote on his travels, and was knighted in 1839.

(8) **William** (1879–1936), American aviation pioneer, beginning his army career in the signal service, he became an early enthusiast for flying and commanded the American air forces in World War I. He foresaw the development and importance of air power in warfare, but his outspoken criticism of those who did not share his convictions resulted in a court martial which suspended him from duty. His resignation followed and he spent the rest of his life lecturing and writing in support of his ideas. His vindication came with World War II and he was posthumously promoted and decorated. See Lives by E. Garreau (N.Y. 1942), I. D. Levine (N.Y. 1943), R. Mitchell (N.Y. 1953).

MITCHISON, Naomi Margaret (1897–   ), British writer, born in Edinburgh, daughter of J. S. Haldane (q.v.), won instant attention with her brilliant and personal evocations of Greece and Sparta in a series of novels: *The Conquered* (1923), *When the Bough Breaks* (1924), *Cloud Cuckoo Land* (1925), *Black Sparta* (1928), &c. In 1931 came the erudite *Corn King and Spring Queen*, which brought to life the civilizations of ancient Egypt, Scythia and the Middle East. She married Gilbert Richard Mitchison (b. 1890; created life peer, 1964) in 1916. He was a Labour M.P. (1945–64), and joint parliamentary secretary, ministry of land (1964–66).

MITFORD, (1) Diana. See MOSLEY.

(2) **John** (1781–1859), miscellaneous writer, was born at Richmond, Surrey, ordained and was a pluralist in Suffolk. Much of his time was devoted to literary pursuits, collecting and gardening. He edited the *Gentleman's Magazine* from 1834 to 1850 and also volumes for the *Aldine Poets* including Gray, Cowper and Milton. See his *Letters* by Houstoun (new ed. 1891).

(3) **John Freeman, 1st Baron Redesdale**

(1748–1830), English lawyer, brother of (7), M.P. 1788. He became successively solicitor-general, attorney-general, speaker of the House of Commons and lord chancellor of Ireland. He opposed Catholic emancipation in Ireland, which made him unpopular.

(4) **Mary Russell** (1787–1855), English novelist and dramatist, daughter of a spend-thrift physician, at the age of ten drew £20,000 in a lottery and went to school at Chelsea. As the family became more and more impoverished she had to write to earn money. Several plays were produced successfully but failed to keep the stage. Her gift was for charming sketches of country manners, scenery and character, which after appearing in magazines were collected as *Our Village* (5 vols. 1824–32). She received a civil list pension in 1837 which was aug-mented on her father's death from subscrip-tions raised to pay his debts. In 1852 she published *Recollections of a Literary Life*. See *Letters* (ed. A. G. L'Estrange, 3 vols. 1870, ed. H. F. Chorley, 2 vols. 1872), *Friendships* (ed. A. G. L'Estrange, 2 vols. 1872), *Corres-pondence with Boner and Ruskin* (ed. E. Lee, 1914), Lives by W. J. Roberts (1913), C. Hill (1920), M. Astin (1930), V. G. Watson (1949).

(5) **Nancy** (1904–73), English author, sister of (1) and (6), and daughter of the 2nd Baron Redesdale, established a reputation with her witty novels such as *Pursuit of Love* (1945) and *Love in a Cold Climate* (1949). Her bio-graphical books, *Madame de Pompadour* (1953), *Voltaire in Love* (1957), *The Sun King* (1966), are also popular. As one of the essayists in *Noblesse Oblige*, edited by herself (1956), she helped to originate the famous ' U ', or upper-class, and ' non-U ' classifica-tion of linguistic usage and behaviour. Her marriage (1933) to the Hon. Peter Rodd was dissolved in 1958. A fourth sister, **Jessica** (b. 1917), wrote *Hons and Rebels* (1960), her autobiography and story of the unconven-tional Mitford childhood.

(6) **Unity Valkyrie** (1914–48), sister of (1) and (5), was notorious for her associations with leading Nazis in Germany but returned to Britain during World War II in January 1940, suffering from a gunshot wound.

(7) **William** (1744–1827), English historian, brother of (3), born in London, studied at Queen's College, Oxford, in 1761 succeeded to the family estate of Exbury, and in 1769 became a captain in the South Hampshire Militia, of which Gibbon was major. On Gibbon's advice he undertook his pugnacious anti-democratic *History of Greece* (5 vols. 1784–1818), which, in virtue of careful research, held the highest place in the opinion of scholars until the appearance of Thirlwall and Grote. He sat in parliament 1785–1818. See Memoir prefixed to 7th edition of his *History* (1838), by his brother (3).

MITHRADATES, *mith-ra-day'teez* (Grecized from the Persian, ' gift of Mithras '), the name of several kings of Pontus, Armenia, Commagene and Parthia.

Mithradates VI, surnamed **Eupator,** called **the Great,** king of Pontus, succeeded to the throne about 120 B.C., a boy of barely thirteen, soon subdued the tribes who

bordered on the Euxine as far as the Crimea, and made an incursion into Cappadocia and Bithynia, then Roman. In the *First Mithra-datic War*, commenced by the Romans (88), Mithradates' generals repeatedly defeated the Asiatic levies of the Romans, and he himself occupied the Roman possessions in Asia Minor. But in 85 he was defeated by Flavius Fimbria, and compelled to make peace with Sulla, relinquishing all his conquests in Asia, giving up 70 war galleys, and paying 2000 talents. The wanton aggressions of the Roman legate gave rise to the *Second Mithradatic War* (83–81), in which Mithradates was wholly successful. In the *Third Mithradatic War* (74) he obtained the services of Roman officers of the Marian party, and at first prospered; but Lucullus compelled him to take refuge with Tigranes of Armenia (72), and defeated both of them at Artaxata (68). In 66 Pompey defeated Mithradates on the Euphrates, and compelled him to flee to his territories on the Cimmerian Bosporus. Here his new schemes of vengeance were frustrated by his son's rebellion, and he killed himself (63 B.C.). He had received a Greek education, spoke twenty-two languages, and made a great collection of pictures and statues. See study by Reinach (Paris 1890) and Life by Duggan (1958).

MITSCHERLICH, Eilhard, *mi'-cher-liKH* (1794–1863), German chemist, born at Neuende near Jeve, professor of Chemistry at Berlin from 1822, studied Persian at Heidel-berg and Paris, medicine at Göttingen, and geology, mineralogy, chemistry and physics at Berlin and Stockholm. His name is identified with the laws of isomorphism and dimorphism, and with artificial minerals, benzene and ether. His *Lehrbuch der Chemie* (1829) went through several editions. See memoir by his son (1894).

MIVART, St George (1827–1900), English biologist, was educated for the bar, but devoted himself to the biological sciences, and before his death was by Cardinal Vaughan debarred from the sacraments for his liberal-ism. In 1874–84 he was professor of Zoology and Biology at the Roman Catholic Univer-sity College in Kensington, and in 1890 accepted a chair of the Philosophy of Natural History at Louvain. An evolutionist save as regards the origin of mind, he was yet an opponent of the ' Natural Selection ' theory. Among his works are *The Genesis of Species* (1871), *Nature and Thought* (1883), *The Origin of Human Reason* (1889). See account in Murray's *Science and Scientists* (1925).

MODIGLIANI, Amedeo, *mō-deel-yah'nee* (1884–1920), Italian painter and sculptor of the modern school of Paris, was born in Leghorn. His early work was influenced by the painters of the Italian Renaissance, particularly the primitives, and in 1906 he went to Paris, where he was further influenced by Toulouse-Lautrec and ' les Fauves '. In 1909, impressed by the Rumanian sculptor Brancuşi, he took to sculpture and produced a number of elongated stone heads in African style, a style he continued to use when he later resumed painting, with a series of richly-coloured, elongated portraits—a feature characterizing all his later work. In 1918 in Paris he held virtually his first one-man show, which included some very frank nudes; the exhibition was closed for indecency on the first day. It was only after his death from tuberculosis that Modigliani obtained recognition and the prices of his paintings soared. See study by C. Roy (1958), and Lives by his daughter Jeanne (trans. E. R. Clifford, 1959) and A. Salmon (1961).

MODJESKA, Helena (1844–1909), Polish actress, born in Cracow, began to act in 1861, made a great name at Cracow in 1865, and 1868–76 was the first actress of Warsaw. After learning English, however, she achieved her greatest triumphs in the United States and in Great Britain, in such rôles as Juliet, Rosalind, Beatrice, and in *La Dame aux camélias*. See her *Memories and Impressions* (N.Y. 1910) and Lives by M. Collins (1883) and A. Gronowicz (1959).

MOE, Jörgen (1813–82). See ASBJÖRNSEN.

MOERAN, Edward James (1895–1950), English composer, born in Middlesex, studied at the Royal College of Music and, after service in World War I, under John Ireland. He first emerged as a composer in 1923, but left London to live in Herefordshire, where he worked prolifically in all forms. As well as a large number of songs, Moeran composed a symphony and concertos for violin, piano and cello.

MOFFAT, Robert (1795–1883), Scottish missionary, born at Ormiston, East Lothian, turned from gardening to the mission field in 1815. Arriving at Capetown in January 1817, he began his labours (1818) in Great Namaqualand. He finally settled at Kuruman (1826–70) in Bechuanaland, which soon became, through his efforts, a centre of Christianity and civilization. He printed both New (1840) and Old (1857) Testaments in Sechwana and published *Labours and Scenes in South Africa* (1842). Livingstone married his daughter. See Lives by J. S. Moffat (1885), E. W. Smith (1925), J. C. W. Holt (1955).

MOFFATT, James (1870–1944), Scottish theologian, was born in Glasgow and ordained a minister of the United Free Church of Scotland in 1896. He held professorships at Mansfield College, Oxford (1911–14), at the United Free Church College, Glasgow, (1914–27) and at the Union Theological Seminary New York (1927–39). His most famous work is the translation of the Bible into modern English. His New Testament was published in 1913 and his Old Testament in 1924. He also wrote theological works, including *Presbyterianism* (1928).

MOGRIDGE, George (1787–1854), English miscellaneous writer, born at Ashted near Birmingham, failed in business and took to writing. Author of many children's books, religious tracts and ballads, he wrote under various pseudonyms including ' Old Humphrey ' and ' Peter Parley ' (also used by other writers). See Life by C. Williams (1856), A. R. Buckland (in *John Strong* 1904).

MOHAMMED or **Mahomet**, western forms of Arabic **Muhammad**, ' praised ' (570–632), born at Mecca, the son of Abdallâh, a poor merchant (though of the powerful tribe of the Koreish), who died soon after the child's birth; the mother died when he was six years old, and the boy was brought up by his uncle, Abu Tâlib. For a time he gained a scanty livelihood by tending sheep; but in his twenty-fifth year he entered the service of a rich widow, named Khadîja, who, fifteen years his senior, by-and-by offered him her hand, and, a faithful wife, bore him two sons (who died early) and four daughters. Mohammed continued his merchant's trade at Mecca, but spent most of his time in solitary contemplations. Just before Mohammed's time some earnest men in the Hedjaz denounced the futility of the ancient pagan creed, and preached the unity of God; and many, roused by their words, turned either to Judaism or to Christianity. Mohammed felt moved to teach a new faith, which should dispense equally with idolatry, narrow Judaism and corrupt Christianity. He was forty years of age when, at the mountain Hirâ near Mecca, Gabriel appeared to him, and in the name of God commanded him to preach the true religion. His poetical mind had been profoundly impressed with the doctrine of the unity of God and the moral teaching of the Old Testament, as well as with the legends of the Midrash. His whole knowledge of Christianity was confined to a few apocryphal books, and with all his deep reverence for Jesus, whom he calls the greatest prophet next to himself, his notions of the Christian religion were vague. His first revelation he communicated to no one but his wife, daughters, stepson and one friend, Abu Bekr. In the fourth year of his mission, however, he had made forty proselytes, chiefly slaves and very humble people; and now some verses were revealed to him, commanding him to come forward publicly as a preacher. He inveighed against the superstition of the Meccans, and exhorted them to a pious and moral life, and to the belief in an all-mighty, all-wise, everlasting, indivisible, all-just but merciful God, who had chosen him as he had chosen the prophets of the Bible before him, so to teach mankind that they should escape the punishments of hell and inherit everlasting life. God's mercy was principally to be obtained by prayer, fasting and almsgiving. The Káaba and the pilgrimage were recognized by the new creed. The prohibition of certain kinds of food belongs to this first period, when Mohammed was under the influence of Judaism; the prohibition of gambling, usury and wine came after the Hegira. His earliest Koranic dicta, written down by amanuenses, consisted of brief, rhymed sentences, and for a time the Meccans considered him a common ' poet ' or ' soothsayer ', perhaps not in his right senses. Gradually, however, fearing for the sacredness of Mecca, they rose in fierce opposition against the new prophet and his growing adherents. Mohammed's faithful wife Khadîja died, and his uncle and protector, Abu Tâlib; and he was reduced to utter poverty. An emigration to Taîf proved a failure; he barely escaped with his life. About this time he converted some pilgrims from Medina. The next pilgrimage brought twelve, and the third more than seventy adherents to the new faith from Medina; and now he resolved to seek refuge in their friendly city, and about June A.D. 622 (the date of the Mohammedan Era, the Hegira) fled thither. A hundred families of his faithful followers had preceded him. Heretofore a despised ' madman or impostor ', he now assumed at once the position of highest judge, lawgiver, and ruler of the city and two powerful tribes. He failed in securing the support of the Jews in the city, and became their bitter adversary. The most important act in the first year of the Hegira was his permission to go to war with the enemies of Islam—especially the Meccans—in the name of God. The first battle, between 314 Moslems and 600 Meccans, was fought at Badr, in December 623; the former gained the victory and made many prisoners. A great number of adventurers now flocked to Mohammed, and he successfully continued his expeditions against the Koreish and the Jewish colonies. In January 625 the Meccans defeated him at Ohod, where he was dangerously wounded. The siege of Medina by the Meccans in 627 was frustrated by Mohammed's ditch and earthworks. In 628 he made peace with the Meccans, and was allowed to send his missionaries all over Arabia. Some Meccans having taken part in a war against a tribe in Mohammed's alliance, he marched at the head of 10,000 men against Mecca; it surrendered, and Mohammed was recognized as chief and prophet. With this the victory of the new religion was secured in Arabia (630). In March 632 he undertook his last pilgrimage to Mecca, and there on Mount Arafat fixed for all time the ceremonies of the pilgrimage (Hajj). He fell ill soon after his return, and when too weak to visit the houses of his nine wives, chose as his last sojourn that of Ayeshah, his best-beloved, the daughter of Abu Bekr. He took part in the public prayers as long as he could, and died in Ayeshah's lap about noon of Monday the 12th (11th) of the third month in the year 11 of the Hegira (June 8, 632). See Sir W. Muir's *Life of Mahomet* (4 vols. 1858–61, new ed. 1912, abr. ed. 1923) and *Mahomet and Islam* (1887); also books by Syed Ameer Ali (1890), A. N. Wollaston (1904), D. S. Margoliouth (N.Y. 1905), J. T. Andrae (Stockholm 1917, Ger. trans. 1932, Eng. trans. 1936 and N.Y. 1957), R. V. C. Bodley (1946), W. M. Watt (1953, 1956), Mohammed Ibn Ishak (Eng. trans. 1955), Emile Dermenghem (trans. J. M. Watt, 1959).

MOHAMMED, the name of six sultans of Turkey, of whom

Mohammed I (*c.* 1387–1421), sultan 1413–1421, led recovery from conquests of Tamburlaine.

Mohammed II (1430–81), born at Adrianople, succeeded his father, Murad II, in 1451, and took Constantinople in 1453—thus extinguishing the Byzantine Empire and giving the Turks their commanding position on the Bosphorus. Checked by Hunyady at Belgrade, he yet annexed most of Serbia, all Greece, and most of the Aegean Islands, threatened Venetian territory, was repelled from Rhodes by the Knights of St John (1479), took Otranto in 1480 and died in a

campaign against Persia. See Kritoboulos, *History of Mehmed the Conqueror* (1955).

Mohammed III (1566–1603), sultan 1595–1603, son of Murad III.

Mohammed IV (*c.* 1641–91), sultan 1648–1687, son of Ibrahim; deposed 1687.

Mohammed V (1844–1918), sultan 1909–18.

Mohammed VI (1861–1926), sultan 1918–1922, brother of V, unsuccessful in suppressing the Nationalists led by Mustafa Kemal; died in exile.

MOHAMMED AHMED (1848–85), the Mahdi (or Moslem Messiah), born in Dongola, was for a time in the Egyptian Civil Service, then a slave trader, and finally a relentless and successful rebel against Egyptian rule in the Eastern Sudan. He made El Obeid his capital in 1883, and on November 5 defeated Hicks Pasha and an Egyptian army. On January 26, 1885, Khartum was taken, and General Gordon (q.v.) killed. The Mahdi died June 22, 1885. See books by F. R. Wingate, *Mahdism* (1891), R. Bermann, *Mahdi of Allah* (1931), and A. B. Theobald, *The Mahdiya: history of Anglo-Egyptian Sudan 1881–99* (1951).

MOHAMMED 'ALI. See MEHEMET 'ALI.

MOHAMMED BEN YOUSEF. See SIDI MOHAMMED.

MOHL, (1) Hugo von (1805–72), German botanist, professor of Botany at Tübingen, carried out researches on the anatomy and physiology of vegetable cells. In 1846 he discovered and named protoplasm.

(2) **Julius von** (1800–76), German orientalist, born at Stuttgart, became professor of Persian at the Collège de France in 1847. His great edition of the *Shâh Námeh* was published in 1838–78. The salon of his accomplished wife, *née* Mary Clarke (1793–1883), was a popular centre for Parisian intellectuals. See studies by K. O'Meara (1885), M. C. M. Simpson (1887) and M. E. Smith (Paris 1927).

MÖHLER, Johann Adam (1796–1838), German theologian, born at Igersheim, professor of Roman Catholic theology at Tübingen and Munich, wrote *Symbolik* (1832), on the doctrinal differences of Catholics and Protestants. See J. Friedrich, *J. A. Möhler* (Munich 1894).

MOHN, Henrik (1835–1916), Norwegian meteorologist, was born at Bergen, studied at Oslo, and became keeper of the university observatory and director of the meteorological institute 1866–1913. He superintended a scientific expedition off the northern coasts of Norway in 1876–78, wrote on meteorology, on the climate of Norway, on the Arctic Ocean, and first worked out the theory of Arctic drift and currents that Nansen utilized.

MOHS, Friedrich (1773–1839), German mineralogist, born Gernrode, was successively professor at Graz, Freiburg and Vienna. His scale of hardness is still in use. He died at Agordo in Italy. Author of *The Natural History System of Mineralogy* (1821), and *Treatise on Mineralogy* (3 vols. 1825).

MOHUN, Charles, 4th Baron Mohun, *moon* (*c.* 1675–1712), notorious rake, involved in frequent duels and brawls, was twice tried by House of Lords for murder and acquitted

In 1701 he was involved in lawsuit with James Douglas, 4th Duke of Hamilton, which ended in a duel in which both were killed. This duel figures in Thackeray's *Henry Esmond*. See also R. S. Forsythe, *A Noble Rake: Life of Charles, 4th Lord Mohun* (Mass. 1928).

MOINAUX. See COURTELINE.

MOIR, David Macbeth (1798–1851), Scottish physician and writer, born at Musselburgh, practised there as a physician from 1817 till his death. Under his pen-name of *Delta* (Δ) he contributed verses to *Blackwood's Magazine* (coll. 1852), and is remembered for his humorous *The Life of Mansie Wauch* (1828).

MOISEIWITSCH, Benno, *moy-zay'vich* (1890–1963), Russian-born British pianist, born in Odessa, studied at the Imperial Academy of Music, Odessa, where he won the Rubinstein prize at the age of nine, and subsequently worked in Vienna under Leschetizky. Rapidly winning recognition as an exponent of the music of the romantic composers, he first appeared in Britain in 1908, and took British nationality in 1937.

MOISSAN, Henri, *mwa-sã* (1852–1907), French chemist, was born in Paris. A noted experimenter and teacher, he held various posts in Paris, including the professorships of Toxicology at the School of Pharmacy (1886) and Inorganic Chemistry at the Sorbonne (1900). He was awarded the Lacase prize (1887) and the Nobel prize for chemistry (1906). He is chiefly known for his work on fluorine and the electric furnace, which he developed to further his researches with the carbides, silicides and borides. He discovered carborundum and was able to produce tiny artificial diamonds in his laboratory. For a bibliography see *Notice sur les travaux scientifiques de M. Henri Moissan* (1891).

MOIVRE, Abraham de. See DEMOIVRE.

MOKANNA, al (Arab. 'The Veiled '), properly **Hakim ben Atta** (d. 780), was the founder of a sect in the Persian province of Khurasan. Ostensibly to protect onlookers from the dazzling rays from his divine countenance, but actually to conceal the loss of an eye, he wore a veil. Setting himself up as a reincarnation of God he gathered enough followers to seize several fortified places, but the khalif Almahdi, after a long siege, took his stronghold of Kash (A.D. 780), when, with the remnant of his army, Mokanna took poison. His story is the subject of one of Thomas Moore's poems in *Lalla Rookh*.

MOLÉ, Louis Matthieu, Comte (1781–1855), French politician, whose father was guillotined during the Terror. In his *Essai de morale et de politique* (1806) he vindicated Napoleon's government on the ground of necessity, and was made a count. Louis XVIII made him a peer and minister for the navy; and Louis-Philippe foreign minister and, in 1836, prime minister, but his régime was unpopular. He left politics after the *coup d'état* of 1851. See Helie de Noailles, *Le Comte Molé, sa vie, ses mémoires* (6 vols. 1922–30).

MOLESWORTH, (1) John Edward Nassau (1790–1877), English clergyman and writer, father of (4), born in London, and educated at Greenwich and Trinity College, Oxford, from 1840 was vicar of Rochdale. He edited *Penny Sunday Reader*, sermons, pamphlets and a novel, *The Rick-Burners*, popular at the time of the Chartist movement.

(2) **Mary Louisa,** *née* **Stewart** (1839–1921), novelist and writer of children's stories, born, of Scottish parentage, at Rotterdam, May 29, passed her childhood in Manchester, Scotland and Switzerland. She began writing as a novelist under the pseudonym 'Ennis Graham', but she is best known as a writer of stories for children, some of which, such as *The Carved Lion* and *Cuckoo Clock*, are still published today. See R. L. Green's *Mrs Molesworth* (1961).

(3) **Sir William, Bt.** (1810–55), English politician, born in London, studied at Edinburgh (1824–27) and Cambridge (1827–1828), and was M.P. for East Cornwall (1832–37), Leeds (1837–41) and Southwark (1845–55). He held office under Aberdeen and Palmerston. Spokesman with Grote for the ' philosophical radicals ', he founded the *London Review* (1835) and merged it with the *Westminster Review* (1836), transferring ownership to J. S. Mill (1837). He edited Hobbes (16 vols. 1839–45), denounced transportation, and promoted colonial self-government. See M. G. Fawcett, *Life of Sir William Molesworth* (1903).

(4) **William Nassau** (1816–90), historian, eldest son of (1), born at Millbrook, educated at Canterbury and Cambridge, held a living near Rochdale (1844–89). Friend of Bright and Cobden, he was an early supporter of the Co-operative Movement which he became acquainted with through the Rochdale Pioneers. Works include *History of the Reform Bill of 1832* (1864), *History of England from 1830* (1871–73), *History of the Church of England from 1660* (1882), &c.

MOLIÈRE, stage name of **Jean Baptiste Poquelin** (1622–73), French playwright, was born in Paris, January 15, the son of a well-to-do upholsterer. He studied under the Jesuits at the Collège de Clermont, under Gassendi, the philosopher, and under the regular teachers of law. He may have been called to the bar. His mother, who had some property, died when he was ten years old, and thus when he came of age he received his share of her fortune at once. He declined to follow his father's business, hired a tennis-court, and embarked on a theatrical venture (1643) with the Béjart family and others, under the style of *L'Illustre Théâtre*, which lasted for over three years in Paris and failed. The company then proceeded to the provinces (from Lyons to Rouen), and had sufficient success to keep going from 1646 to 1658. The Prince de Conti took it under his protection for a time; and when he took to Catholic Methodism, Molière obtained the patronage of the king's brother, Philippe d'Orléans, so that his troupe became the servants of Monsieur. He played before the king on October 24, 1658, and organized a regular theatre, first in the Petit Bourbon, then, on its demolition, in the Palais Royal. In the provinces Molière had acquired experience as a comic writer, mostly in the style of the old farces. But he had also written *L'Étourdi* and *Le Dépit amoureux*. As a theatre manager he had to give tragedy as well as comedy. Corneille's *Nicomède*, with which he opened, was not a success; and though the other great tragedian of the day, Racine, was a personal friend of Molière's, their connection as manager and author was brief and unfortunate. But Molière soon realized his own immense resources as a comic writer. *Les Précieuses ridicules* was published in November 1659, and from that time to his death no year passed without at least one of the greatest achievements in their own line that the world has seen. In the spring of 1662 Molière married Armande Béjart, an actress in his own company, probably about nineteen, and the youngest member of the Béjart family, of which two other sisters, Madeleine and Geneviève, and one brother, Joseph, had been members of the Illustre Théâtre. It has been asserted, in the face of such evidence as exists, that Madeleine Béjart and Molière were lovers, that Armande was Madeleine's daughter, even that Molière was the father of his own wife! It is also said that Armande was unfaithful to her husband. In August 1665 the king adopted Molière's troupe as his own servants. In 1667 symptoms of lung disease showed themselves; on February 17, 1673, the night after having acted as the *Malade* in the seventh representation of his last play, Molière died in his own house in the Rue de Richelieu of haemorrhage from the bursting of a blood vessel. His character would appear to have been generous and amiable; and there are insufficient grounds for the accusations of irreligion brought against him. The dates and titles of Molière's plays are: *L'Étourdi, Le Dépit amoureux* (1658; in the provinces 1656); *Les Précieuses ridicules* (1659); *Sganarelle* (1660); *Don Garcie de Navarre* (1661); *L'École des maris, Les Fâcheux, L'École des femmes* (1662); *La Critique de l'école des femmes, Impromptu de Versailles* (1663); *Le Mariage forcé, La Princesse d'Élide, Tartuffe* (partially, 1664); *Le Festin de Pierre* [*Don Juan*], *L'Amour médecin* (1665); *Le Misanthrope, Le Médecin malgré lui, Mélicerte, Le Sicilien* (1666); *Tartuffe* (1667); *Amphitryon, George Dandin, L'Avare* (1668); *Monsieur de Pourceaugnac* (1669); *Les Amants magnifiques, Le Bourgeois gentilhomme* (1671); *Les Fourberies de Scapin* (1671); *La Comtesse d'Escarbagnas, Les Femmes savantes* (1672); *Le Malade imaginaire* (1673). To this must be added part of *Psyché* (1671), in collaboration with Quinault and Corneille, two farces, a few court masques, and some miscellaneous poems. In France he is called a poet; but, though he could manage verse well enough, he is best almost always in prose. It is as a comic dramatist of manners, satirizing folly and vice, yet without sacrificing the art to the purpose, that he is absolutely unrivalled. Romantic or poetical comedy he hardly ever tried. It is instructive to compare *Les Précieuses ridicules*, almost his first play, with *Les Femmes savantes*, almost his last. Amusing as *Les Précieuses ridicules* is, it is not much more than farce of the very best

sort; *Les Femmes savantes* is comedy of the highest kind. It is not till *L'École des femmes*, perhaps not till *Le Misanthrope*, that the full genius of the author appears; and these two, with *Tartuffe, Le Festin de Pierre, Les Femmes savantes, Le Malade imaginaire*, and perhaps the admirable *Le Bourgeois gentilhomme* as an example of the lower kind, may be said to be Molière's masterpieces. But from *Le Dépit amoureux* onward no play of his, not even the slightest, is without touches of his admirable wit, his astonishing observation, his supreme power over his own language, his masterly satire. Of all French writers he is the one whose reputation stands highest by the combined suffrage of his own countrymen and of foreigners, and even after three hundred years, his best plays still hold the stage. The first complete edition of Molière's works was that in 1682 by La Grange and Vinot; by far the best as to text, life, lexicon, &c., is that of Despois and Mesnard (' Les Grands Écrivains français '; 13 vols. 1873–1900). Other editions are by Anatole France (' Collection Lemerre '; 7 vols. 1876–91), and with notes by G. Monval (' Librairie des bibliophiles '; 8 vols. 1882). A bibliography which supplements that in vol. xi of the Despois edition is Saintonge and Christ's *Fifty Years of Molière Studies: A Bibliography 1892-1941* (Baltimore 1942). See also M. Turnell, *The Classical Moment* (1947), W. G. Moore, *Molière: A New Criticism* (1949), and Life by D. B. Wyndham Lewis (1959).

MOLINA, Luis (1535–1600), Spanish Jesuit theologian, was born at Cuenca, studied at Coimbra, was professor of Theology at Evora for twenty years, and died at Madrid. His principal writings are a commentary on the *Summa* of Aquinas (1593); a treatise, *De Justitia et Jure* (1592); and the celebrated treatise on grace and free will, *Concordia Liberi Arbitrii cum Gratiae Donis* (1588). Molina asserts that predestination to eternal happiness or punishment is consequent on God's foreknowledge of the free determination of man's will. This view was assailed as a revival of Pelagianism, and hence arose the dispute between Molinists and Thomists. A papal decree in 1607 permitted both opinions; and Molinism has been taught by the Jesuits. For bibliography see L. R. *Molina, antecedentes, titulos y trabajos* (Buenos Aires 1942). See also TÉLLEZ.

MOLINOS, Miguel de (1640–97), Spanish divine, was born, of noble parentage, near Saragossa, December 21. He was arrested for his views, which embodied an exaggerated form of Quietism, and after a public retraction, condemned to life imprisonment. See his *Spiritual Guide*, ed. by K. Lyttelton (6th ed. 1950), and study by Dudon, *Le Quiétiste espagnol Miguel de Molinos* (1921). His ideas are used by Shorthouse in his *John Inglesant*.

MÖLLER, Poul Martin (1794–1838), Danish literary figure, born at Uldum, graduated in theology at Copenhagen and later became a professor of Philosophy, first in Oslo, and then in Copenhagen. His chief work, *A Danish Student's Tale*, which he finished in 1824, but which was published posthumously, is a charming, light-hearted account of student life in Copenhagen. During a journey to China he wrote in verse nostalgically of his homeland. *Leaves from Death's Diary* is a representative work, showing how he eschews the abstract and metaphysical, for his credo was ' all poetry that does not come from life is a lie '. He made the first Danish translation of *The Odyssey*, wrote philosophical essays and coined brilliant aphorisms. His early death was a loss to Danish letters. See study by T. Rönning (1911).

MOLLET, Guy Alcide, *mol-ay* (1905–), French Socialist politician, born at Flers, Normandy, of working-class parentage, joined the Socialist party in 1923 and shortly afterwards became English master at the Arras Grammar School—a post which he occupied till World War II, from which he emerged as a captain in the secret resistance army. In 1946 he became mayor of Arras, an M.P., secretary-general of the Socialist party and a cabinet minister in the Léon Blum government. A keen supporter of a Western European Federation, he became in 1949 a delegate to the Consultative Assembly of the Council of Europe and was its president in 1955. He became prime minister in February 1956. He survived the international crisis over the Anglo-French intervention in Suez in November, but fell from office in May 1957 after staying in power longer than any French premier since the war. In 1959 he was elected a senator of the French Community.

MOLLISON, James Allan (1905–59), Scottish airman, born in Glasgow, a consultant engineer who was commissioned into the R.A.F. in 1923, won fame for his record flight, Australia-England in July-August 1931 in 8 days 19 hours 28 mins. In 1932 he married his female rival, Amy Johnson (q.v.), made the first east-west crossing of the North Atlantic and in February 1933 the first England-South America flight. With his wife, he flew Britain-U.S.A. (1933) and Britain-India (1934). He was awarded the Britannia Trophy (1933). His marriage was dissolved in 1938.

MOLNÁR, Ferenc (1878–1952), Hungarian novelist and dramatist, born in Budapest, is best known for his novel *The Paul Street Boys* (1907), and his plays *The Devil* (1907), *Liliom* (1909) and *The Good Fairy* (1930), all of which have achieved success in English translation.

MOLOTOV, orig. **Skriabin, Vyacheslav Mikhailovich,** *-mol'-* (1890–), Russian politician, born at Kukaida, Vyatka, was educated at Kazan High School and Polytechnic. In the 1905 revolution he joined the Bolshevik section of Lenin's Social Democratic Workers' party and in 1912 became the staunch disciple of Stalin when *Pravda* was launched. During the March 1917 Revolution he headed the Russian bureau of the central committee of the Bolshevik party and in October was a member of the military revolutionary committee which directed the coup against Kerensky. In 1921 he became secretary of the central committee of the Russian Communist party and the youngest candidate-member of the Politburo. In 1928

his appointment to the key position of secretary of the Moscow committee of the all-Union Party marked the launching of the first Five-year Plan. Molotov, who was chairman of the council of people's commissars from 1930 to 1941, became an international figure in May 1939 when he took on the extra post of commissar for foreign affairs, shaping the policy which led to the nonaggression pact with Nazi Germany. In 1942 he signed in London the 20 years' Treaty of Alliance with Britain. He was Marshal Stalin's chief adviser at Teheran and Yalta and represented the Soviet Union at the 1945 founding conference of the United Nations at San Francisco and at the Potsdam Conference. After the war Molotov, who negotiated the pacts binding the satellite states to the Soviet Union, emerged as the uncompromising champion of world Sovietism. His ' no ' at meetings of the United Nations and in the councils of foreign ministers became a byword. His attitude led to the prolongation of the ' cold war ' and the division of Germany into two conflicting States. In 1949 he was released from his duties as foreign minister but retained his post as deputy prime minister. He was re-appointed foreign minister in the 1953 Malenkov government and switched to the ' peace offensive '. He resigned in 1956 and was appointed minister of state control. In 1957 Mr Khrushchev called him a ' saboteur of peace ', accused him of policy failures and appointed him ambassador to Outer Mongolia (until 1960). This prim revolutionary stood at the centre of the Soviet Union's executive machine for quarter of a century. His unwearied diplomacy was backed by a fanatical Slavophilism and an intense devotion to the Revolution and Marshal Stalin. See *Both Sides of the Curtain* by Sir Maurice Peterson (1950), and study by B. Bromage (1956).

MOLTKE, (1) Helmuth, Count von (1800–91), Prussian field-marshal, was born October 26. In 1819 he became lieutenant in a Danish regiment, but in 1822 entered the Prussian service. In 1832 he was appointed to the staff, and in 1835 obtained leave to travel. Asked by the sultan to remodel the Turkish army, he did not return to Berlin till 1839. From 1858 to 1888 he was chief of the general staff in Berlin, and reorganized the Prussian army. His wonderful strategical power was displayed in the successful wars with Denmark in 1863–64, with Austria in 1866, and with France in 1870–71. He married in 1841 his stepsister's daughter by an English father, Marie von Burt (1825–68). Known as ' The Silent ', he was a man of great modesty and simplicity of character. He died in Berlin. His Military Works were issued (1892 *et seq.*) by the general staff, for whom he prepared histories of the campaigns against Denmark, Austria and France. See his *Letters* (trans. 1878–96), *Essays, Speeches, and Memoirs* (trans. 1893), Life by M. Jähns (1894–1900), *Moltke, His Life and Character* (trans. M. Herms, 1892), F. E. Whitton, *Moltke* (1921), and study by E. Kessel (Stuttgart 1959).

(2) **Helmuth** (1848–1916), nephew of (1), likewise rose to be chief of the general staff in

1906, but was superseded by Falkenhayn early in Great War 1 (December 1914).

MOMMSEN, Theodor (1817–1903), German historian, was born, the son of a pastor, at Garding in Schleswig, November 30. He studied at Kiel for three years, examined Roman inscriptions in France and Italy for the Berlin Academy (1844–47), and in 1848 was appointed to a chair of Law at Leipzig, of which he was deprived two years later for the part he took in politics. In 1852 he became professor of Roman Law at Zürich, and in 1854 at Breslau, in 1858 of Ancient History at Berlin. He edited the monumental *Corpus Inscriptionum Latinarum*, helped to edit the *Monumenta Germaniae Historica*, and from 1873 to 1895 was perpetual secretary of the Academy. In 1882 he was tried and acquitted on a charge of slandering Bismarck in an election speech. His greatest works remain his *History of Rome* (3 vols. 1854–55) and *The Roman Provinces* (1885). He was awarded a Nobel prize for literature in 1902, and died November 1, 1903. Amongst his 920 separate publications were works on the Italic dialects (1845, 1850), Neapolitan inscriptions (1857), Roman coins (1850), Roman constitutional law (1871), and an edition of the Pandects (1866–70). For bibliography see K. Zangemeister, *Theodore Mommsen als Schriftsteller* (Heidelberg 1887), and supplement by E. Jacobs (Berlin 1905). See also studies by C. Bardt (1903), Hartmann (1908) and Heuss (1956).

MOMPESSON, William (1639–1709), rector of Eyam, Derbyshire, when in 1665–66 the plague (brought from London in a box of infected cloths) carried off 267 of his 350 parishioners. He persuaded his people to confine themselves entirely to the parish, and the disease was not spread. In 1669 he became rector of Eakring, Notts, and in 1676 was made a prebendary of Southwell. See Wood's *History of Eyam* (4th ed. 1865) and C. Daniel, *The Plague Village : A History of Eyam* (new ed. 1938).

MONBODDO, James Burnett, Lord (1714–1799), Scottish judge and anthropologist, born at Monboddo House, Kincardineshire, was educated at Aberdeen, Edinburgh and Gröningen, in 1737 was called to the Scottish bar, and in 1767 was raised to the bench as Lord Monboddo. His *Origin and Progress of Language* (6 vols. 1773–92) is a learned but eccentric production, whose theory of human affinity with monkeys seems less laughable now; and in his study of man as one of the animals he anticipated the modern science of anthropology. He further published, also anonymously, *Ancient Metaphysics* (6 vols. 1779–99). See study by W. Knight (1900).

MONCK. See MONK (1).

MONCKTON, (1) Lionel (1861–1924), English composer, was born in London. Prominent as an amateur actor while at Oxford, he turned to composition and contributed songs to many of the shows of George Edwardes, at the Gaiety Theatre and elsewhere in London. He was composer of several musical comedies, of which *The Quaker Girl* and *The Country Girl* remain popular.

(2) **Walter Turner, 1st Viscount Monckton**

of Brenchley (1891–1965), British lawyer and Conservative minister, born at Plaxtol, Kent, was educated at Harrow and Balliol, called to the bar in 1919, and became attorney-general to the Prince of Wales in 1932, in which capacity he was adviser to him (as Edward VIII) in the abdication crisis of 1936. He held many legal offices, and in World War II was director-general of the Ministry of Information; in the 1945 caretaker government he was solicitor-general. M.P. for Bristol West from 1951 until his elevation to the peerage in 1957, he was minister of labour (1951–55), of defence (1955–56) and paymaster-general (1956–57).

MONCRIEFF, *mon-kreef'*, Colonel Sir Alexander, K.C.B. (1829–1906), Scottish soldier and engineer, born in Edinburgh, invented the Moncrieff Pits and disappearing carriages for siege and fortress guns.

MOND, (1) Alfred Moritz, 1st Baron Melchett (1868–1930), British industrialist and politician, son of (2), after some years in industry became Liberal M.P. in 1906, was first commissioner of works (1916–21) and minister of health (1922). He helped to form the I.C.I., of which he became chairman and a conference he organized in 1928 with the T.U.C. suggested the formation of a national industrial council. He was raised to the peerage in 1928. See life by H. H. Bolitho (1932).

(2) **Ludwig** (1839–1909), German-English chemist and industrialist, father of (1), was born at Cassel, and settling in England in 1864, perfected at Widnes his sulphur recovery process. He founded in 1873 great alkali-works at Winnington, Cheshire, made discoveries in nickel manufacture, &c., and in 1896 gave to the Royal Institution for the nation a physico-chemical laboratory costing £100,000. See lives by F. G. Donnan (1939) and J. M. Cohen (1955).

MONDRIAN or Mondriaan, Piet, *mon'dree-an* (1872–1944), Dutch artist, born at Amersfoort, was associated with his compatriot, van Doesburg (1883–1931), in founding the De Stijl movement in architecture and painting. From 1919 until 1938 he worked in Paris, subsequently going to London and thence in 1940 to New York. His rectilinear abstracts in black, white and primary colours have had considerable influence and he is considered the leader of neo-Plasticism. See his collected essays, *Plastic Art and Pure Plastic Art* (1951), and the monograph by M. Seuphor (1956).

MONET, Claude, *mon-ay* (1840–1926), French Impressionist painter, born in Paris, spent his youth in Le Havre, where he met Boudin (q.v.), who encouraged him to work in the open air. Moving to Paris, he associated with Renoir, Pissarro and Sisley, and exhibited with them at the first Impressionist Exhibition in 1874: one of his works at this exhibition, *Impression: soleil levant*, gave name to the movement. Later he worked much at Argenteuil. With Pissarro, Monet is recognized as being one of the creators of Impressionism, and he was one of its most consistent exponents. He visited England, Holland and Venice, and he spent his life in expressing his instinctive way of seeing the most subtle nuances of colour, atmosphere and light in landscape. Apart from many sea and river scenes, he also executed several series of paintings of subjects under different aspects of light—e.g., *Haystacks* (1890–91), *Rouen Cathedral* (1892–95) and the almost abstract *Waterlilies* (at the Orangerie, Paris). The last years of his life were spent as a recluse at Giverny. He is represented in the Tate Gallery, the Louvre, and in many other galleries in Europe and in the United States. See the monographs by G. Besson (1951) and D. Rouart (1958).

MONGE, Gaspard, *mōzh* (1746–1818), French mathematician, physicist and inventor of descriptive geometry, born at Beaune, became professor of Mathematics at Mézières in 1768, and in 1780 was elected to the French Academy, in the same year becoming professor of Hydraulics at the Lycée in Paris. While there he discovered (1783), independently of Watt or Cavendish, that water resulted from an electrical explosion of oxygen and hydrogen. During the Revolution he was minister for the navy, but soon took charge of the national manufacture of arms and gunpowder. He helped to found (1794) the École polytechnique, and became professor of Mathematics there. The following year there appeared his *Leçons de géométrie descriptive*, in which he stated his principles regarding the general application of geometry to the arts of construction (descriptive geometry). He was sent by the Directory to Italy, from where he followed Napoleon to Egypt. In 1805 he was made a senator and Count of Pelusium, but lost both dignities on the restoration of the Bourbons. See Lives by L. de Launay (1933), R. Taton (Paris 1951) and P. Aubry (1954).

MONICA. See AUGUSTINE.

MONIER-WILLIAMS. See WILLIAMS (5).

MONIZ, Antonio Egas (1874–1955), Portuguese neurosurgeon and diplomat, introduced the operation of prefrontal lobotomy for relief of schizophrenia. He was awarded the Nobel prize for medicine in 1949. He also led the Portuguese delegation to the Paris Peace conference (1919).

MONK, (1) George, 1st Duke of Albemarle (1608–70), English general, the second son of a Devonshire baronet of loyalist sympathies, was a ' volunteer ' in the *Île de Rhé* expedition of 1628. Ten years active campaigning in the Low Countries preceded his service with the Royalists in Scotland. Captured at the battle of Nantwich, after two years' imprisonment in the Tower he was persuaded to support the Commonwealth cause. His successful activities in Ireland brought him to the notice of Cromwell. Conspicuous at Dunbar in 1650, and successful in pacifying Scotland, with the first Dutch War he speedily adapted his talents to sea fighting, playing a major part in the 1653 victory over the Hollanders off the Gabbard. Returning to his command in Scotland, with the Lord Protector's death Monk's intensely practical nature revolted at the turmoil and confusion that characterized Richard Cromwell's faction-torn régime. Convinced that the catalyst required to heal the nation's health was a revival of monarchal rule, he was instrumental in bringing about the restoration of Charles II. He was rewarded with the Dukedom of Albemarle, an annual pension of £7000, and the appointment of lieutenant-general of the forces. In the second Dutch War Monk played a conspicuous and useful part, defeating the Dutch at St James's Fight on July 25, 1666. Throughout the Great Plague he exercised a wise and enheartening rule over stricken London. In 1667, with De Ruyter raiding the Medway virtually unopposed, Monk hastened to Gillingham to take command of the defences. Thereafter canny, taciturn ' Old George ' retired more and more into private life. He died and was buried in Westminster Abbey in 1670. See Lives by Gumble (1671), Skinner (1723), Corbett (1889), O. Warner (1936), and the *Regimental History of Cromwell's Army*, Firth and Davies (1940).

(2) **Maria** (c. 1817–50), Canadian impostor who pretended in 1835 to have escaped from a nunnery at Montreal, and published *Awful Disclosures*. See works by W. L. Stone (1836, 1837).

(3) **William Henry** (1823–89), English organist and composer, professor of Music and organist at several London churches, is best known as musical editor of *Hymns Ancient and Modern* and composer of the tune to ' Abide with me ' and to other hymns.

MONKHOUSE, William Cosmo (1840–1901), English poet and art critic, a Board of Trade official by occupation, published several books of poetry and did important work as art critic and historian. See article by Sir E. Gosse in *Art Journal* (1902).

MONMOUTH, James, Duke of (1649–85), natural son of Charles II, was born at Rotterdam, April 9, 1649, the son of Lucy Walter by Charles II (q.v.), she said, but more likely by Colonel Robert Sidney. Charles committed the boy to the care of Lord Crofts; and in 1662 ' Mr James Crofts ' came to England with the queen-dowager. In 1663 he was created Duke of Monmouth, wedded to a rich heiress, Anne, Countess of Buccleuch (1651–1732), and also made Duke of Buccleuch; in 1670 he succeeded Monk as captain-general. A weak, pretty, affable libertine, he became the idol of the populace, thanks to his humanity at Bothwell Bridge (1679), to the Popish Plot and the Exclusion Bill, and to his two semi-royal progresses (1680–82). Shaftesbury pitted the ' Protestant Duke ' against the popish heir-presumptive, and enmeshed him in the Rye House Plot (1683), on whose discovery Monmouth fled to the Low Countries. At Charles's death, in concert with Argyll's Scottish expedition, he landed (June 11, 1685) at Lyme Regis with eighty-two followers, branded James as a popish usurper, and asserted his own legitimacy and right to the crown. At Taunton he was proclaimed King James II; and on July 6 he attempted with 2600 foot and 600 horse (peasants mostly and miners) to surprise the king's forces, 2700 strong, encamped on Sedgemoor near Bridgwater. His men were mowed down by the artillery. Monmouth fled, but on the 8th was taken in a ditch near Ringwood. Brought before James, he wept and crawled, and even offered to turn Catholic; but on July 15 he was beheaded upon Tower Hill. For the 'Bloody Assize', see JEFFREYS. See Lives by Elizabeth D'Oyley (1938), D. J. Porrit (1953), and studies by W. R. Emerson (1951), B. Little (1956).

MONNET, Jean, *mon-ay* (1888–   ), French statesman, born at Cognac, was educated locally, and in 1914 entered the ministry of commerce. A distinguished economist and expert in financial affairs, he became in 1947 commissioner-general for the 'Plan de modernisation et d'équipement de la France' (Monnet Plan). He was awarded the Prix Wateler de la Paix (1951), and he was president of the European Coal and Steel High Authority (1952–55). In 1956 he became president of the Action Committee for the United States of Europe.

MONNIER, Marc, *mon-yay* (1829–85), French writer of novels, comedies, historical works, &c., was born at Florence and died at Geneva, where he was professor of Comparative Literary History from 1870. See studies by Godet (Paris 1888) and Baridon (1942).

MONOD, *mon-ō,* (1) **Adolphe** (1802–56), French Protestant pastor, brother of (2), born of Swiss parentage at Copenhagen, laboured as a preacher or professor at Naples, Lyons, Montauban and Paris, and published sermons, &c. See his Life and Letters (Eng. trans. 1885), works by Bossuet (1898), F. Dahlbohm (1923).

(2) **Frédéric** (1794–1863), French Protestant pastor, brother of (1), was thirty years a prominent pastor in Paris, and helped (1849) to found the Free Reformed Church of France.

(3) **Jacques** (1910–   ), French scientist, born in Paris, head of the Cellular Biochemistry department at the Pasteur Institute, Paris, since 1954, professor of Molecular Biology at the Collège de France since 1967. He was awarded the Nobel prize for medicine with Jacob and Lwoff in 1965.

(4) **Théodore** (1902–   ), French ethnographer and archaeologist, born at Rouen, founded the Institut Français d'Afrique Noire in Dakar (1938), and wrote on the Cameroons and on the archaeology of the Sahara.

MONRO, *mĕn-rō',* (1) **Alexander** (1697–1767), Scottish anatomist, was born in London, and studied at London, Paris, and Leyden under Boerhaave. From 1719 he lectured at Edinburgh on anatomy and surgery, and was professor of these subjects 1725–59. He helped to found the Infirmary, and gave clinical lectures there. He wrote *Osteology* (1726), *Essay on Comparative Anatomy* (1744), *Observations Anatomical and Physiological* (1758), and *Account of the Success of Inoculation of Smallpox in Scotland*. See Life by A. Duncan (1780), D. Monro (in *Works* 1781).

(2) **Alexander** (1733–1817), Scottish anatomist, son of (1), father of (3), studied at Edinburgh, Berlin and Leyden, succeeded to his father's chair, and wrote on the nervous system (1783), the physiology of fishes (1785), and the brain, eye and ear (1797). See Life by A. Duncan (1818), Memoir by A. Monro (Edinburgh 1840).

(3) **Alexander** (1773–1859), Scottish anatomist, son of (2), succeeded his father and wrote on hernia, the stomach and human anatomy.

(4) **Edward** (1815–66), English divine and author, born in London and educated at Harrow and Oriel, from 1842 was incumbent of Harrow Weald, where he established a college for poor boys, and from 1860 of St John's, Leeds. His stories and allegories were popular and influential.

MONROE, (1) **Harriet** (1860–1936), American poet and critic, born in Chicago, founded in 1912 the magazine *Poetry*, which was influential in publicizing the work of Lindsay, Eliot, Pound and Frost, among others. She wrote the 'Columbian Ode' on the 400th anniversary of the discovery of America.

(2) **James** (1758–1831), fifth president of the United States, was born in Westmoreland County, Va., April 28. After serving in the War of Independence he was elected to the assembly of Virginia and in 1783 to congress, where he sat for three years. He was chairman of the committee (1785) that prepared the way for framing the constitution, which, however, as a States' Rights man, he disapproved. As a member of the United States senate 1790–94, he opposed Washington and the Federalists; the government recalled him in 1796 from the post of minister to France. He was governor of Virginia 1799–1802, and in 1803 he helped to negotiate the Louisiana purchase. The next four years were spent in less successful diplomacy at London and Madrid. In 1811 he was again governor of Virginia, in 1811–17 secretary of state, and in 1814–15 also secretary of war. In 1816 he was elected president of the United States, and in 1820 re-elected almost unanimously. His most popular acts were the recognition of the Spanish American republics, and the promulgation in a message to congress (1823) of the 'Monroe Doctrine', embodying the principle 'that the American continents . . . are henceforth not to be considered as subjects for future colonization by any European power', though existing colonies were not to be interfered with. In 1825 Monroe retired to his seat at Oak Hill, Va., till, deep in debt, he found refuge with relatives in New York. See his *Writings* (1898–1903); *Autobiography*, ed. S. G. Brown (1960); Lives by Adams (1850), Cresson (1947); books by Kraus (1913), Hart (1916), Perkins (1927).

(3) **Marilyn.** See MILLER (1).

MONSARRAT, Nicholas John Turney (1910–   ), English novelist, born at Liverpool, was educated at Winchester and at Trinity College, Cambridge, abandoned law for literature and wrote three novels, passably successful, and a play, *The Visitors*, which reached the London stage. During the war Monsarrat served in the Navy. Out of his experiences emerged his extremely successful, bestselling novel *The Cruel Sea* (1951), which was filmed. *The Story of Esther Costello* (1953) repeated the pattern of success. He settled in Ottawa, Canada, as director of the U.K. Information Office (1953–56) after holding a similar post in South Africa (1946–52). See his autobiography, *Life is a Four-Letter Word* (vol. 1, 1966).

MONSON, Sir William, *mun'sĕn* (1569–1643), English admiral, born at South Carlton, Lincs fought the Spaniards (1585–1602), was a prisoner (1591–93) on Spanish galleys, and was admiral of the narrow seas (1604–16). He wrote *Naval Tracts* which are partly autobiographical (5 vols. 1902–14, ed. M. Oppenheim).

MONSTRELET, Enguerrand de, *mõstrĕ-lay* (*c.* 1390–1453), French chronicler, born near Boulogne, was provost of Cambrai. His *Chronicle*, 1400–44, written from the Burgundian standpoint, was edited by Douet d'Arcq (1857–62); and a continuation by Mathieu d'Escouchy to 1461 by Beaucourt (1863).

MONTAGNA, Bartolomeo, *mon-ta'nya* (*c.* 1450–1523), Italian painter, a native of Brescia, probably studied at Venice under Giovanni Bellini and Carpaccio. He founded a school of painting at Vicenza and also worked at Verona and other places. See works by A. Foratti (Padua 1908), and *Painters of Vicenza* by T. Borenius (1909).

MONTAGU, (1) *mon'ta-gyoo.* See HALIFAX, MANCHESTER and SANDWICH.

(2) Elizabeth, *née* Robinson (1720–1800), English writer and society leader, first of the 'blue-stockings', with £10,000 a year, who entertained everyone from king to chimney-sweep, and wrote an *Essay on Shakespeare.* See books by E. J. Climenson (1903), R. Huchon (1907), R. Blunt (1923) and J. Busse (1928).

(3) Lady Mary Wortley (1689–1762), English writer, eldest daughter of the Earl (later Duke) of Kingston, who, losing his wife in 1694, made his clever daughter preside at his table at a very early age. She married Edward Wortley Montagu in 1712, and lived in London, where she gained a brilliant reputation, and was the intimate of Addison, Pope and others. In 1716 Montagu was appointed ambassador at Constantinople, and there till 1718 he and his wife remained. There she wrote her entertaining *Letters* describing Eastern life, and thence she introduced inoculation for smallpox into England. For the next twenty years her abode was at Twickenham. In 1739, for reasons unknown, she left England and her husband, parting from him, however, on very good terms, though they never met again. She lived till 1761 in Italy, where Horace Walpole, meeting her in Florence in 1740 referred to her as an 'old, foul, tawdry, painted, plastered personage'. She died August 21. See her works, ed. with Life by her great-grandson, Lord Wharncliffe (3rd ed. 1887); books by I. Barry (1928), V. S. Wortley (1948), L. Gibbs (1949), R. Halsband (1956); and her *Letters*, (2 vols. 1966, ed. Halsband).

(4) Richard (1577–1641), English bishop. As an opponent of Puritanism he was the centre of controversy, but with Laud's influence he became successively Bishop of Chichester (1628) and Norwich (1638).

MONTAGUE, Charles Edward (1867–1928), English novelist and essayist, of Irish parentage, was on the staff of the *Manchester Guardian* in 1890–1925. His writings include *A Hind Let Loose, Disenchantment* (1922), *Rough Justice* (1926). See memoir by O. Elton (1929).

MONTAIGNE, Michel Eyquem de, *mõ-ten'y'* (1533–92), French essayist, third son of the

Seigneur de Montaigne, was born at the Château de Montaigne in Périgord, February 28. Till the age of six the boy spoke no language but Latin; and at the Collège de Guienne in Bordeaux he remained for seven years, boarding in the rooms of his famous teachers, George Buchanan and Muretus. He subsequently studied law; but from the age of thirteen to twenty-four little is known of him, though it is certain that he was frequently in Paris, knew something of court life, and took his full share of its pleasures. By-and-by he obtained a post in connection with the *parlement* of Bordeaux, and for thirteen years was a city counsellor. He formed a close friendship with Étienne de la Boëtie (1530–63). He married (September 27, 1565) Françoise de la Chassaigne, daughter of a fellow counsellor. A translation (1569) of the *Natural History* of a 15th-century professor at Toulouse was his first effort in literature, and supplied the text for his *Apologie de Raymond Sebond*, in which he exhibited the full scope of his own sceptical philosophy. In 1571, his two elder brothers being dead, Montaigne succeeded to the family estate, and here till his death on September 13, 1592, he lived the life of a country gentleman, varied only by visits to Paris and a tour in Germany, Switzerland and Italy; here, too, he began those *Essais* which were to give him a place among the first names in literary history. The record of his journey (1580–81) in French and Italian was first published in 1774. Unanimously elected mayor of Bordeaux (against his wish), he performed his duties to the satisfaction of the citizens, and was re-elected. Notwithstanding the free expression of scepticism in his writings, he devoutly received the last offices of the church. From the very first, men like Pascal, profoundly separated from him on all the fundamental problems of life (as in his inconclusive philosophy, his easy moral opinions, his imperfect sense of duty), have acknowledged their debt to his fearless and all-questioning criticism, expounded mainly in haphazard remarks, seemingly inspired by the mere caprice of the moment, but showing the highest originality, the very broadest sympathies, and a nature capable of embracing and realizing the largest experience of life. There are translations by Florio (q.v.), by Charles Cotton (q.v.), by G. B. Ives (1926) and D. M. Frame (1958); and of the *Journals* by Waters (1903–04). See books by M. E. Lowndes (1898), G. Norton (1905), F. Strowski (Paris 1906), G. Lanson (Paris 1930), P. Villey (Paris 1933), A. Gide (1948) and A. Thibaudet (1963); bibliography by S. A. Tannenbaum (N.Y. 1942).

MONTALE, Eugenio, *mon-tah'lay* (1896–), Italian poet, was born in Genoa. He is the leading poet of the modern Italian 'Hermetic' school, and his primary concern is with language and meaning. His works include *Ossi di seppia* (1925), *Le occasioni* (1939), *La bufera* (1956). See study by R. Lunardi (1948).

MONTALEMBERT, Charles René Forbes de, *mõ-ta-lã-ber* (1810–70), French historian and politician. He was born in London, May 15, the eldest son of a noble French *émigré* and his English wife, was educated at Fulham and the Collège Ste Barbe. In 1830 he eagerly joined the Abbé Lamennais and Lacordaire in the *Avenir*, a High Church Liberal newspaper. In 1831 Montalembert and Lacordaire opened a free school in Paris, which was immediately closed by the police. Montalembert, who had succeeded to his father's peerage, pleaded with great eloquence the cause of religious liberty, and when the *Avenir*, being condemned by the pope (1831), was given up, Montalembert lived for a time in Germany, where he wrote the *Histoire de Ste Élizabeth*. In 1835 again in Paris, he spoke in the Chamber in defence of the liberty of the press, and a famous protest against tyranny was his great speech in January 1848 upon Switzerland. After the Revolution he was elected a member of the National Assembly; and he supported Louis Napoleon till the confiscation of the Orleans property, when he became a determined opponent of the imperial régime. He was elected to the Academy in 1851, visited England in 1855, and wrote *L'Avenir politique de l'Angleterre*. In 1858 an article in the *Correspondant* made such exasperating allusions to the imperial government that he was sentenced to six months' imprisonment and a fine of 3000 francs—a sentence remitted by the emperor. Besides his great work, *Les Moines d'occident* (7 vols. 1860–77; 5th ed. 1893), he wrote *Une Nation en deuil: la Pologne* (1861), *L'Église libre dans l'état libre* (1863), *Le Pape et la Pologne* (1864), &c. He died in Paris, March 13, 1870, sixteen days after writing a celebrated letter on papal infallibility. See Memoir by Mrs Oliphant (1872), and French works by Foisset (1877), L. R. P. Lecanuet (3 vols. 1897–1901), the Vicomte de Meaux (1897), P. de Lallemand (Paris 1927), A. Trannoy (Paris 1947).

MONTANO. See ARIAS.

MONTCALM, Louis Joseph, Marquis de Montcalm Gezan de Saint Véran, *mō-kalm* (1712–59), French general, born near Nîmes. A soldier at fifteen, in 1746 he was severely wounded and made prisoner at the battle of Piacenza. In 1756 he assumed command of the French troops in Canada, and captured the British post of Oswego, and also Fort William Henry, where the prisoners (men, women and children) were massacred by the Indian allies. In 1758 he, with a small force, successfully defended Ticonderoga and after the loss to the French of Louisburg and Fort Duquesne, removed to Quebec, and with 16,000 troops prepared to defend it against a British attack. In 1759 General Wolfe (q.v.) ascended the St Lawrence with about 8000 troops and a naval force under Admiral Saunders. After repeated attempts to scale the heights of Montmorency, he, before dawn on September 13, with 5000 men, gained the plateau, and in a battle on the Plains of Abraham drove the French in disorder on the city. Montcalm tried in vain to rally his force, was borne back by the rush, and, mortally wounded, died next morning (September 14). See Parkman's *Montcalm and Wolfe* (1884), H. R. Casgrain's *Wolfe and Montcalm* (1906, rev. 1926), and Life by G. Robitaille (Montreal 1936).

MONTECUCCULI, Raimondo, Count, *-koo'-koo-lee* (1608–81), Italo-Austrian general, born near Modena, entered the Austrian service in 1625, and distinguished himself during the Thirty Years' War, against the Turks (1664), and against the French on the Rhine (1672–75). He was made a Prince and Duke of Melfi. See his *Opere Complete* (new ed. 1821), and the Lives by Campori (1876), Grossmann (1878), I. Senesi (Turin 1933).

MONTEFIORE, Sir Moses Haim, *-fyō'ray* (1784–1885), Anglo-Jewish philanthropist, was born in Leghorn, retired with a fortune from stockbroking in 1824, and from 1829 was prominent in the struggle for removing Jewish disabilities. After long exclusion and repeated re-election, he was admitted sheriff of London in 1837, being knighted the same year, and made a baronet in 1846. Between 1827 and 1875 he made seven journeys in the interests of his oppressed countrymen in Poland, Russia, Rumania and Damascus. He endowed a Jewish college at Ramsgate in 1865. See the *Diaries of Sir Moses and Lady Montefiore* (1890), Lives by L. Wolf (1884), E. Wolbe (1909), P. Goodman (Philadelphia 1925).

MONTELIUS, Oscar (1843–1921), Swedish archaeologist, born at Stockholm, became director of archaeology there, wrote on early Swedish culture and developed the typological method. See *Memoir* (Stockholm 1922).

MONTEMAYOR, Jorge de, *-mah'yor* (*c.* 1515–61), Spanish novelist and poet of Portuguese descent, wrote *Diana* (pastoral romance), &c., in Castilian, and influenced Sir Philip Sidney and others. See Life by G. Schönherr (Halle 1886), and H. A. Rennert, *Spanish Pastoral Romances* (1892).

MONTESI, Wilma, *mon-tay'zee* (1932–53), Italian model, the daughter of a Roman middle-class carpenter. The finding of her body on the beach near Ostia in April 1953 led to prolonged investigations involving sensational allegations of drug and sex orgies in Roman society. After four years of debate, scandal, arrests, re-arrests and libel suits, the Venice trial in 1957 of the son of a former Italian foreign minister, a self-styled marquis and a former Rome police chief for complicity in her death ended in their acquittal after many conflicts of evidence. The trial left the mystery unsolved, but exposed corruption in high public places and helped to bring about the downfall of the Scelba Government in 1955. See W. Young, *The Montesi Scandal*, and M. S. Davis, *All Rome Trembled* (both 1957).

MONTESPAN, Françoise Athénais, Marquise de, *mō-tès-pã* (1641–1707), French favourite of Louis XIV, daughter of the Duc de Mortemart, married in 1663 the Marquis de Montespan, and became attached to the household of the queen. Her beauty and wit captivated the heart of Louis XIV, and about 1668 she became his mistress. The marquis was flung into the Bastille, and in 1676 his marriage was annulled. Montespan reigned till 1682, and bore the king seven children, who were legitimized, but was supplanted by Madame de Maintenon, the governess of her children. In 1687 she left the court, and retired to a convent. See her *Mémoires* (trans. 1895); studies by H. N. Williams (1903), G. Truc (1936), H. Carré (1939).

MONTESQUIEU, Charles de Secondat, Baron de la Brède et de, *mŏ-tĕs-kyœ* (1689–1755), French philosopher and jurist, was born January 18 at the Château La Brède near Bordeaux, became counsellor of the *parlement* of Bordeaux in 1714, and its president in 1716. He discharged the duties of his office faithfully, but, till defective eyesight hindered him, by preference devoted himself to scientific researches. His first great literary success was the *Lettres persanes* (1721), containing a satirical description, put in the mouths of two Persian visitors to Paris, of French society. Weary of routine work, he sold his office in 1726, and then settled in Paris. He travelled for three years to study political and social institutions, visiting, among other places, England, where he remained for two years (1729–31), mixing with its best society, frequenting the Houses of Parliament, studying the political writings of Locke, and analysing the English constitution. *Causes de la grandeur des Romains et de leur décadence* (1734) is perhaps the ablest of his works. His monumental *De l'esprit des lois* (1748) was published anonymously and put on the Index, but passed through twenty-two editions in less than two years. By the spirit of laws he means their *raison d'être*, and the conditions determining their origin, development and forms; the discussion of the influence of climate was novel. The work, which held up the free English constitution to the admiration of Europe, had an immense influence. In 1750 he published a *Défense de l'esprit des lois*, followed afterwards by *Lysimaque* (1748), a dialogue on despotism, *Arsace et Isménie*, a romance, and an essay on taste in the *Encyclopédie*. A member of the French Academy since 1728, he died, totally blind, at Paris, February 10. See books by Sorel (trans. 1887), C. P. Ilbert (1904), Barckhausen (1907), Churton Collins (1908), J. Dedieu (1913), G. Lanson (1932), F. T. H. Fletcher (1939), P. Barrière (1946).

MONTESSORI, Maria (1870–1952), Italian doctor and educationalist, born at Rome, studied feeble-minded children, and developed (*c.* 1909), a system of education for children of three to six based on spontaneity and freedom from restraint. The system was later worked out for older children. See her *The Montessori Method* (rev. ed. 1919). See Lives by A. M. Maccheroni (Edinburgh 1947), E. M. Standing (1958).

MONTEVERDI, Claudio (1567–1643), Italian composer, born at Cremona, was the eldest son of a doctor. As a pupil of Ingegneri at Cremona cathedral between 1580 and 1590 he became a proficient violist and learnt the art of composition, publishing a set of three-part choral pieces, *Cantiunculae Sacrae*, at the age of fifteen. About 1590 he was appointed court musician to the Duke of Mantua, with whose retinue he travelled in Switzerland and the Netherlands, and whose *maestro di capella* he became in 1602. In 1612 the duke died and his successor dismissed Monteverdi, who returned to Cremona in straitened circumstances with arrears of salary unpaid.

Luckily the post of *maestro di capella* at St Mark's, Venice, fell vacant in 1613 and he was appointed, remaining there until his death. By his efforts the musical reputation of that church, sadly declined since the great days of the Gabrielis (q.v.), was restored to its former high position. Monteverdi left no purely instrumental compositions. His 8 books of madrigals, which appeared at regular intervals between 1587 and 1638, embody in the later examples some audaciously experimental harmonies which brought much criticism from academic quarters but underlined the composer's originality and pioneering spirit, while his first opera, *Orfeo* (1607), with its programmatic use of orchestral sonorities, its dramatic continuity and the obbligato character of the accompaniment, marked a considerable advance in the evolution of the *genre*. The two surviving operas of his later period, *Il Ritorno d'Ulisse* (1641) and *L'Incoronazione di Poppea* (1642), both written when he was well past seventy, show further development towards the Baroque style and foreshadow the use of the *leitmotif*. Monteverdi's greatest contribution to church music is the magnificent Mass and Vespers of the Virgin (1610), the excellence of which was a deciding factor in his appointment to St Mark's, and which contained tone colours and harmonies well in advance of its time. Among other new features introduced by Monteverdi were the orchestral ritornello, and the use of tremolo and pizzicato. Monteverdi has been called the 'last madrigalist and first opera composer', an inaccurate designation which, even if it were entirely true, would not be the reason for the immense importance of his rôle, which is that of a great innovator at one of the most formative periods in the history of musical style. See works by H. Prunières (trans. 1926), G. F. Malipiero (Milan 1930), Schrade (1951) and Redlich (1952).

MONTEZ, Lola (1818–61), Irish dancer and adventuress, born at Limerick, after an unsuccessful marriage turned dancer at Her Majesty's Theatre, and while touring Europe, came to Munich (1846), where she soon won an ascendency over the eccentric artist-king, Louis I, who created her Countess of Landsfeld. For a whole year she exercised enormous influence in favour of Liberalism and against the Jesuits; but the revolution of 1848 sent her adrift. She died, a penitent, at Astoria, Long Island. See her *Autobiography* (1858); books by H. Wyndham (1935), I. Goldberg (1936), H. Holdredge (1957).

MONTEZUMA, the name of two Mexican emperors:

Montezuma I (*c.*1390–1464), ascended the throne about 1437, annexed Chalco, and crushed the Tlascalans.

Montezuma II (1466–1520), last Mexican emperor, succeeded in 1502, was a distinguished warrior and legislator and died during the Spanish conquest. (See CORTÉS.) One of his descendants was viceroy of Mexico 1697–1701. The last, banished from Spain for Liberalism, died at New Orleans 1836. See study by M. Collis (1954).

MONTFORT, (1) Simon IV de, Earl of

Leicester (*c.* 1160–1218), Norman crusader, father of (2), undertook in 1208 the crusade against the Albigenses and fell at the siege of Toulon. See study by H. J. Warner, *Albigensian Heresy* (1928).

(2) **Simon de, Earl of Leicester** (*c.* 1208–65), English statesman and soldier, son of (1). Young Simon was well received by Henry III of England in 1230, was confirmed in his title and estates in 1232, and in 1238 married the king's youngest sister, Eleanor. In 1239 he quarrelled with the king and crossed to France, but, soon nominally reconciled, was again in England by 1242. In 1248, sent as king's deputy to Gascony, Simon put down disaffection with a heavy hand. But his jealous master listened eagerly to complaints against his rule, and arraigned him. Earl Simon, acquitted, resigned his post in 1253, and returned to England. Bad harvests, famine, fresh exactions of Rome and the rapacity of foreign favourites had exhausted the endurance of the country, and in 1258, at Oxford, the parliament drew up the Provisions of Oxford, which the king swore solemnly to observe. Prince Edward intrigued with the subtenants, and the barons quarrelled among themselves; and in 1261 the king announced that the pope had declared the Provisions null and void. All men now looked to Earl Simon as leader of the barons and the whole nation, and he at once took up arms. After some varying success, both sides sought an arbitrator in Louis IX of France, who decided in the *Mise* of Amiens for surrender to the royal authority. London and the Cinque Ports repudiated the agreement, and Simon, collecting his forces, surprised the king's army at Lewes, and captured Prince Edward (1264). The *Mise* of Lewes arranged that there were to be three electors, Earl Simon, the Earl of Gloucester, and the Bishop of Hereford, who were to appoint nine councillors to nominate the ministers of state. To aid these councillors in their task a parliament was called, in which, together with the barons, bishops and abbots, there sat four chosen knights from each shire, and for the first time two representatives from certain towns. This, the Model Parliament, held the germ of our modern parliament. But the great earl's constitution was premature; the barons soon grew dissatisfied with the rule of Simon the Righteous; and his sons' arrogance injured his influence. Prince Edward, escaping, combined with Gloucester, and defeated Simon at Evesham, August 4, 1265. See Stubbs's *Constitutional History*; and Lives by Pauli (1867; trans. 1876), C. Bémont (1884; trans. 1930), M. Creighton (1876), G. W. Prothero (1877), S. Bateman (1923), B. C. Boulter (1939) and M. W. Labarge (1962).

MONTGOLFIER, Joseph Michel, *mõ-gol-fyay* (1740–1810), and **Jacques Étienne** (1745–99), French aeronauts, sons of a paper manufacturer of Annonay, became intensely interested in the aeronautical theories propounded by the 14th-century Augustine monk, Albert of Saxony, and the 17th-century Jesuit priest, Francesco de Luna. In 1782 they constructed a balloon whose bag was lifted by lighting a cauldron of paper beneath it, thus heating and rarefying the air

it contained. A flight of six miles, at 300 feet, was achieved; but additional experiments were frustrated by the outbreak of the French Revolution, Étienne being proscribed, and his brother returning to his paper factory. Joseph was subsequently elected to the Académie des sciences and created a *Chevalier de la légion d'honneur* by Napoleon.

MONTGOMERIE, (1). See EGLINTON.

(2) **Alexander** (*c.* 1545–*c.* 1611), Scottish poet, born probably at Hessilhead Castle near Beith, was ' maister poet ' to James VI. He was detained in a Continental prison, and embittered by the failure of a law-suit involving loss of a pension. Implicated in Barclay of Ladyland's Catholic plot, he was denounced as a rebel in 1597. His fame rests on the *Cherrie and the Slae* (ed. Harvey Wood, 1937), which, partly a love-piece, partly didactic, has real descriptive power, with dexterous mastery of rhyme. See his works, ed. by Cranstoun (Scot. Text Soc. 1886–87; supplement by Stevenson, 1910). See works by D. Hoffman (Altenburg 1894), C. M. Maclean (1915).

MONTGOMERY, (1) Bernard Law, 1st Viscount Montgomery of Alamein (1887–), British field-marshal, was born November 17, the son of the late Bishop Montgomery, and educated at St Paul's School and R.M.C. Sandhurst. He served with the Royal Warwickshire Regiment in World War I. Thereafter, a succession of staff and command appointments brought him to the head of the 3rd Division, with which he shared the retreat to Dunkirk. In North Africa in 1941 the 8th Army had only partially recovered from its rough handling by the Axis forces when Montgomery was appointed to its command. His quality of bravura and supreme ability in ' putting himself over ' proved invaluable in dealing with ' Hostilities Only ' formations, and he speedily restored bruised confidence and the will to win. Conforming to General Alexander's sound strategic plans, Montgomery launched the successful battle of Alamein (October 1942). This was energetically followed up by a series of hard-fought engagements that eventually drove the Axis forces back to Tunis. Montgomery's subsequent activities in Sicily and Italy were solid if somewhat pedestrian. Appointed commander for the ground forces for the Normandy invasion, his strategy was characterized by wariness and unflagging tenacity. By deliberately attracting the main weight of the German counter-offensive to the British flank, he freed the American armoured formations to inaugurate the joint drive across France and Belgium. His attempt to roll up the German right flank by way of Arnhem lacked co-ordination and the deployment of the proper means to ensure success; but his timely intervention helped materially to frustrate Rundstedt's surprise offensive of December 1944. Accepting the German capitulation on Lüneburg Heath, his command of the Occupation Forces was followed by his appointment as deputy supreme commander to the representative contingents serving under NATO. He retired in 1958. Montgomery's forte was the set-battle, launched after careful planning and never willingly undertaken with anything but the most comprehensive resources in men and material. He became field-marshal 1944, K.C.B. 1942, K.G. 1946, viscount 1946. His publications include *Normandy to the Baltic* (1947), his controversial *Memoirs* (1958), *The Path to Leadership* (1961) and *History of Warfare* (1968). See de Guingand, *Operation Victory* (1947), and Lives by Moorhead (1946), Peacock (1951) and Clark (1960).

(2) **Gabriel, Comte de** (*c.* 1530–74), French soldier, an officer in the French king's Scottish Guard, at a tournament in 1559 wounded Henry II, who died eleven days after. He retired to Normandy and England, turned Protestant, and returned to become a leader of the Huguenot cause. Narrowly escaping to Jersey and England from the massacre of St Bartholomew, he later landed in Normandy, but was compelled to surrender, taken to Paris, and beheaded. See Life by L. Marlet (Paris 1890).

(3) **James** (1771–1854), Scottish poet, was born at Irvine. The son of a Moravian pastor, he settled down, after various occupations, as a journalist in Sheffield, where in 1794 he started the *Sheffield Iris*, which he edited till 1825. In 1795 he was fined £20, and got three months in York Castle for printing a 'seditious' ballad; in 1796 it was £30 and six months for describing a riot. Yet by 1832 he had become a moderate Conservative, and in 1835 accepted from Peel a pension of £150. He died at Sheffield. His poems (4 vols. 1849) are 'bland and deeply religious'. See *Memoirs* by J. Holland and J. Everett (1856–58) and W. Odem, *Sheffield Poets* (1929).

(4) **Robert** (1807–55), English preacher and poet, was born at Bath, natural son of Gomery, a clown. He studied at Lincoln College, Oxford; and from 1843, after some years in Glasgow, was minister of Percy Chapel, London. *The Omnipresence of the Deity* (1828; 29th ed. 1855) and *Satan* (1830) are remembered by Macaulay's onslaught in the *Edinburgh Review* for April 1830. See study by E. Clarkson (1830).

MONTHERLANT, Henri Millon de, *mō-ter-lā* (1896–1972), French novelist and playwright, was born in Neuilly-sur-Seine. He was severely wounded in the first World War, after which he travelled in Spain, Africa and Italy. Himself a man of athletic interests, in his novels, as in his plays, he advocates the overcoming of the conflicts of life by vigorous action, disdaining the consolation of bourgeois sentiment. His novels, all showing his mastery of style, include the largely autobiographical *La Relève du matin* (1920), *Le Songe* (1922), *Les Bestiaires* (trans. 1927, *The Bullfighters*), *Les Jeunes filles* (1935–39) and *L'Histoire d'amour de la rose de sable* (1954). His plays include *La Reine morte* (1942), *Malatesta* (1946), *Don Juan* (1958) and *Le Cardinal d'Espagne* (1960). See studies by M. Saint-Pierre (1949) and Perruchot (1959).

MONTHOLON, Charles Tristan, Marquis de, *mō-to-lō* (1783–1853), French general and diplomat, born at Paris, served in the navy and cavalry, was wounded at Wagram, and

in 1809 was made Napoleon's chamberlain. He accompanied him to St Helena, and with Gourgaud published *Mémoires pour servir à l'histoire de France sous Napoléon, écrits sous sa dictée* (8 vols. 1822–25). Condemned in 1840 to twenty years' imprisonment as Louis Napoleon's proposed chief of the staff, he was liberated in 1848, having published in 1846 *Récits de la captivité de Napoléon.* See *Letters,* ed. Connard (1906), J. T. Tussaud, *The Chosen Four* (1928).

MONTI, Vincenzo (1754–1828), Italian poet, born at Alfonsine, remarkable for his political tergiversation, was professor at Pavia and historiographer to Napoleon. He wrote epics and tragedies and translated Homer. See *Collected Works* (Milan 1939–42) and books by C. Cantu (Milan 1879), E. Bevilagua (Florence 1928), U. Fraccia (1947), G. Bustico, *Bibliography of M.* (Florence 1924).

MONTICELLI, Adolphe Joseph Thomas (1824–86), French painter, born at Marseilles, studied at Paris, where he lived mainly till 1870, returned to Marseilles, and died there in poverty. His most characteristic paintings are notable for masses of warm and luxurious colour, and vague, almost invisible figures, in Impressionistic style, though he is placed with the Barbizon group. See works by G. Arnaud d'Agnel and E. Isnard (Paris 1926), L. Guinard (1931), L. Venturi in *Burlington Magazine* (1938).

MONTLUC, Blaise de, *mō-lük* (1502–77), French marshal, fought in Italy, and as governor of Guienne treated the Huguenots with great severity. His *Mémoires* (best ed. 1865–72) were called 'la bible du soldat' by Henry IV. See Lives by J. J. de Broqua (Paris 1924) and J. Le Gras (Paris 1927).

MONTMORENCY, *mō-mor-ā-see*, (1) **Anne, Duc de** (1493–1567), Marshal and Constable of France, grandfather of (2), distinguished himself at Marignano (1515), Mézières and Bicocca, was taken prisoner along with Francis I at Pavia (1525), defeated Charles V at Susa (1536) and became constable (1538). Suspected by the king of siding with the Dauphin, he was banished from court in 1541. He was restored to his dignities by Henry II (1547), commanded at the disaster of St Quentin (1557), and was taken prisoner by the Spaniards. He opposed the influence of Catharine de' Medici, commanded against the Huguenots at Dreux (1562), and was taken prisoner a third time. In 1563 he drove the English out of Havre. He again engaged Condé at St Denis (1567), but received his death-wound. See Life by Decrue (1885–89).

(2) **Henri, Duc de** (1595–1632), French marshal, grandson of (1), commanded the Catholics of the south in the religious wars (1621–30), took Ré and Oléron (1625), and penetrated into Piedmont (1630). But provoked into rebellion by Richelieu, he was defeated at Castelnaudary and beheaded at Toulouse. See Life by Hartmann (1928).

MONTPENSIER, Anne Marie Louise d'Orleans, Duchesse de, *mō-pā-syay* (1627–1693), known as 'La Grande Mademoiselle', a niece of Louis XIII, she supported her father and Condé in the Fronde, where she commanded an army and later the Bastille. After a period in disgrace she returned to the court and wished to marry M. de Lauzun, but the king refused his consent for many years. Her marriage in the end was not successful and her last years were spent in religious duties. See her *Mémoires* (1729 and later edns.), Lives by B. N. de C. La Force (Paris 1927), A. Ducasse (1937), F. Steegmüller (1955) and V. Sackville-West (1959).

MONTROSE, James Graham, Marquis of (1612–50), Scottish general, was educated at St Andrews and travelled in Italy, France and the Low Countries. He returned in the very year (1637) of the ' Service-book tumults ' in Edinburgh, and he was one of the four noblemen who drew up the National Covenant. In 1638 he was dispatched to Aberdeen, which he occupied for the Covenanters. When Charles invited several Covenanting nobles to meet him at Berwick, Montrose was one of those who went; and the Presbyterians dated his ' apostasy ' from that interview. In the General Assembly of 1639 he showed disaffection towards the Covenant. In the second Bishops' War Montrose was the first of the Scottish army to ford the Tweed (August 20, 1640); but that very month he had entered into a secret engagement against Argyll. It leaked out that he had been communicating with the king; he was cited before a committee of the Scottish parliament, and next year was confined five months in Edinburgh Castle. In 1644 he quitted his forced inaction at Oxford, and, disguised, made his way into Perthshire as lieutenant-general and Marquis of Montrose. At Blair Atholl he met 1200 Scoto-Irish auxiliaries under Macdonell (' Colkitto '), and the clans quickly rallied round him. On September 1 he routed the Covenanters under Lord Elcho at Tippermuir near Perth. He next gained a victory at Aberdeen (September 13), and took the city, which was this time abandoned for four days to the horrors of war. The approach of Argyll with 4000 men compelled Montrose to retreat; but he suddenly appeared in Angus, where he laid waste the estates of the Covenanting nobles. Later, receiving large accessions from the clans, he marched into the Campbell country, devastated it, drove Argyll himself from his castle at Inveraray, and then wheeled north towards Inverness. The ' Estates ' placed a fresh army under Baillie, who was to take Montrose in front, while Argyll should fall on his rear; but Montrose instead surprised and utterly routed Argyll at Inverlochy, February 2, 1645. He then passed with fire and sword through Moray and Aberdeenshire, eluded Baillie at Brechin, captured and pillaged Dundee (April 3), and escaped into the Grampians. On May 4 he defeated Baillie's lieutenant at Auldearn near Nairn, and on July 2 routed Baillie himself at Alford; towards the end of the month he marched southward with over 5000 men. Baillie, following, was defeated with a loss of 6000 at Kilsyth (August 15); this, the most notable of Montrose's six victories, seemed to lay Scotland at his feet, but the clansmen slipped away home to secure their booty. Still, with 500 horse and

1000 infantry, he had entered the Border country, when, on September 13, he was surprised and routed by 6000 troopers under David Leslie at Philiphaugh near Selkirk. Escaping to Athole, he endeavoured, vainly, to raise the Highlands; on September 3, 1646, he sailed for Norway, and so passed to Paris, Germany and the Low Countries. When news of Charles's execution reached him, he swore to avenge the death of the martyr, and, undertaking a fresh invasion of Scotland, lost most of his little army by shipwreck in the passage from Orkney to Caithness, but pushed on to the borders of Ross-shire, where, at Invercharron, his dispirited remnant was cut to pieces, April 27, 1650. He was nearly starved to death in the wilds of Sutherland, when he fell into the hands of Macleod of Assynt, who delivered him to Leslie, and, conveyed with all contumely to Edinburgh, he was hanged in the High Street, May 21, 1650. Eleven years afterwards his mangled remains were collected from the four airts, and buried in St Giles', where a stately monument was reared to him in 1888. Montrose's few passionately loyal poems are little known, save the one stanza, ' He either fears his fate too much ', &c.; even its ascription to Montrose (first made in 1711) is doubtful. See Latin Memoirs by his chaplain, Dr Wishart (Amsterdam 1647; Eng. trans. 1893); Mark Napier's *Memoirs of Montrose* (1838; 4th ed. 1856); Lives by J. Buchan (1913; new ed., 1957), C. V. Wedgwood (1952) and M. Irwin, *Proud Servant* (a novel, 1934).

MONTUCLA, Jean Étienne, mõ-tük-la (1725–1799), French mathematician, born at Lyons, wrote the first history of mathematics worthy of the name.

MONTYON, Jean Baptiste Auget, Baron de, mõ-tyõ (1733–1820), French lawyer and philanthropist, is best known for the prizes he established for scientific and literary achievements. He also wrote on economics from a philanthropic point of view. See Life by L. Guimbaud (1909).

MOODY, (1) Dwight Lyman (1837–99), American evangelist, born at Northfield, Mass., February 5, was a shopman in Boston, and in 1856 went to Chicago, where he engaged in missionary work. In 1870 he was joined by Ira David Sankey (1840–1908), who was born at Edinburgh, Pennsylvania. In 1873 and 1883 they visited Great Britain as evangelists, Moody preaching and Sankey singing; afterwards they worked together in America. See Lives by his sons W. R. Moody (1930), P. D. Moody (1938) and by G. Bradford (1927). See also Sankey's *Autobiography* (1906).

(2) **William Vaughn** (1869–1910), American poet and dramatist, wrote *The Mask of Judgment* (1900), *The Death of Eve, The Firebringer*, &c., as well as prose plays and dramas, of which the best known were *The Great Divide* (1906) and *The Faith Healer* (1909). See *Collected Works* (1912), *Letters*, ed. D. G. Mason (1913), and Lives by E. H. Lewis (1914), D. C. Henry (Boston 1934).

MOON, William (1818–94), English inventor of type for the blind, was born in Kent. Partially blind from the age of four, Moon became totally blind in 1840 and began to teach blind children. Dissatisfied with existing systems of embossed type, he invented a system based on Roman capitals, and he later invented a stereotype plate for use with his type. Although requiring more space, his type is easier to learn and is still widely used. See Life by J. Rutherford (1898).

MOORE, (1) **Albert Joseph** (1841–93), English painter, son of (14), brother of (8), is best known for his Hellenic decorative paintings. See Life by A. H. Baldry (1894).

(2) **Anne**, *née* **Pegg** (1761–1813), English impostor, from 1807 to 1813 the 'fasting woman of Tutbury', then proved a fraud. See Life by E. Anderson, and various accounts (1809–13).

(3) **Edward** (1712–57), English dramatist, was a London linen-draper, born at Abingdon, who, going bankrupt, took to writing plays. *The Gamester* (1753) is his best-known production. He also edited *The World* (1753–57). See Life by J. H. Caskey (New Haven 1927).

(4) **Francis** (1657–1715), English astrologer, born at Bridgnorth, practised physic in London, and in 1700 started ' Old Moore's ' astrological almanac.

(5) **George** (1852–1933), Irish writer, was the son of a landed gentleman in southwest Ireland who was an M.P. and bred horses for racing. Moore's youth was spent partly there and partly in London. He early became an agnostic, abandoned the military career proposed for him by his family, and lived a bohemian life in London before his father's death in 1870 left him free to follow his bent as a dilettante artist and writer in Paris. After ten years of this life Zola's example revealed to him his true métier as a novelist of the realist school. His importance as a writer is that in the years of relative poverty in London, that is from 1880 to 1892, he introduced this type of fiction into England. Arnold Bennett confessed his debt to Moore's *A Mummer's Wife* (1884), and it is not difficult to see the same influence on Somerset Maugham and others. *Esther Waters* (1894), the last of his novels in this vein, was regarded as rather offensive, but these novels of low life, drawn from Moore's own experience of racing touts and shabby lodgings, introduced the public to a wider world than the fashionable novel of the day. The Boer war saw Moore self-exiled to Ireland—such was his hatred of England's wars—and this had the double effect of raising his interests, as in *Evelyn Innes* (1898), and *Sister Teresa* (1901), to love, theology and the arts, and encouraging his preoccupation with the texture of his prose which more and more engaged his attention. The Irish scene also helped to woo him from sordid realism as in *A Drama in Muslin* (1886), and the stories in *An Untilled Field* (1903). Moore returned to England early in the century and eventually occupied the flat in Ebury Street whence emanated dialogues, conversations (*Conversations in Ebury Street*) and confessions—a sure sign that he had exhausted his experience for novel writing. He had already written *Confessions of a Young Man* (1888), but now we have *Memoirs of My Dead Life* (1906) and the belated (and

inferior) *In Single Strictness* (1926). The most famous of his works of this sort is *Hail and Farewell* in three parts, *Ave* (1911), *Salve* (1912) and *Vale* (1914). The malicious element in this trilogy in which he wrote about his friends and his associates in setting up the Abbey Theatre in Dublin, particularly W. B. Yeats, does not detract from his claim to be one of the great memoirists. With his prose style now perfected, Moore turned in his last phase to romanticize history, beginning with the masterpiece *The Brook Kerith* (1916), which relates an apocryphal story of Paul and Jesus among the Essenes. The slightly archaic English in this novel enhances the limpid purity of his diction. *Héloïse and Abelard* (1921) tells the famous love-story with distinction and compassion. In the mythical *Aphrodite in Aulis* (1930), the manner begins to pall on us, as all contrived manners must in the end. See studies by John Freeman (1922) and Humbert Wolfe (1931). Also Nancy Cunard, *Memories of George Moore* (1956), and short study in F. Swinnerton's, *The Georgian Literary Scene* (1935).

(6) **George Edward** (1873–1958), English Empiricist philosopher, leader of the philosophical revolution against idealism, brother of (13), born November 4, in London, was educated at Dulwich College and read classics at Trinity College, Cambridge, until he was persuaded by a senior fellow-student, Bertrand Russell, to change over to philosophy. With the latter, he suffered a brief infatuation with Hegelian idealism, brilliantly represented at Cambridge by McTaggart (q.v.), but it was the singularity of such philosophers' claims, as for example, that time is unreal, that drove Moore to philosophizing in protest. Awarded a prize fellowship in 1898, he struck the first blow for philosophical ' common sense ' in an article in the periodical *Mind* (1899) entitled ' The Nature of Judgment '. This effected Russell's ' emancipation from idealism ' and in 1903, that red letter year in modern British philosophy, three great works appeared by the two friends. Russell's *Principles of Mathematics*, Moore's famous *Mind* article, *The Refutation of Idealism*, and his *Principia Ethica*, a restatement of which appeared as a famous monograph, *Ethics* (1916), written while he was living in Edinburgh and Richmond (1904–11). Moore made the important discovery, overlooked by almost all moral philosophers, particularly the Utilitarians, that the word ' good ' cannot be defined in terms of natural qualities, because whichever of them are chosen for this special rôle, it will always make sense to ask whether anything possessing them is good. His further classification of goodness as a simple, non-natural quality is controversial, but nevertheless his teaching and outlook dominated what later became known as the ' Bloomsbury circle ', Leonard Woolf, Lowes Dickinson, Keynes and Forster included. In 1911 he returned to Cambridge as university lecturer in Moral Science and became professor of Mental Philosophy and Logic (1925–39). He also followed Stout as editor (1921–47) of the periodical *Mind* and made it the outstanding

philosophical journal of the English-speaking world. In 1925 he published his important essay entitled *A Defence of Common Sense* in *Contemporary British Philosophy*, vol. i (1925), and emerged as a disciple of Reid in his British Academy Lecture, ' The Proof of an External World ' (1939). Moore showed that philosophy must not undermine common-sense matters of fact, but rather provide an analysis of them. This Socratic analytical quest, he pursued with supreme honesty. In *Reply to My Critics* in *The Philosophy of G. E. Moore*, ed. P. A. Schilpp (2nd edn. 1952), he characteristically admitted that in the case of the two major problems with which he had wrestled all his life, the objectivity of goodness and the problem of perception, he was still unable to make up his mind between two incompatible views. He also paid a truly self-effacing tribute to a former student and later colleague, Wittgenstein, whose lectures (1930–33) he attended and recorded in *Philosophical Papers* (1959). Moore lectured in America (1940–44), was elected F.B.A. in 1918 and awarded the O.M. in 1951. See also *Philosophical Studies* (1922), *Some More Problems in Philosophy* (1954), study by A. R. White (1958), and G. J. Warnock, *English Philosophy since 1900* (1958).

(7) **Gerald** (1899–   ), English pianoforte accompanist, born at Watford, studied music at Toronto and established himself as an outstanding accompanist of the world's leading singers and instrumentalists, a constant performer at international music festivals and a notable lecturer and TV broadcaster on music. See his engaging and instructive account of his art and experiences in *The Unashamed Accompanist* (1943; n.e. 1959).

(8) **Henry** (1831–95), English painter, son of (14), brother of (1), starting as a landscape painter, later achieved great success as a sea painter and became A.R.A. (1886) and R.A. (1893).

(9) **Henry Spencer** (1898–   ), English sculptor, born at Castleford, Yorkshire, the son of a coal miner, studied at Leeds and at the Royal College of Art, London, where he taught sculpture from 1924 to 1931, and from 1931 to 1939 he taught at the Chelsea School of Art. He travelled in France, Italy, Spain, U.S.A. and Greece, and was an official war artist from 1940 to 1942. During this time he produced a famous series of drawings of air-raid shelter scenes. In 1948 he won the International Sculpture Prize at the Venice Biennale. He is recognized as one of the most original and powerful modern sculptors, producing mainly figures and groups in a semi-abstract style based on the organic forms and rhythms found in landscape and natural rocks. His interest lies in the spatial, three-dimensional quality of sculpture, an effect he achieves by the piercing of his figures. His principal commissions include the well-known *Madonna and Child* in St Matthew's Church, Northampton (1943–44), and the decorative frieze (1952) on the Time-Life building, London. Examples of his work may be seen in the Tate Gallery, the Victoria and Albert Museum, the

Museum of Modern Art, New York, and in many other public galleries. He was awarded the O.M. in 1963. See the Life by G. C. Argan, the monographs edited by Herbert Read (1949 and 1955), and study by E. Neumann (trans. 1960).

(10) **John** (1729–1802), Scottish physician and writer, father of (11), after studying medicine and practising in Glasgow, travelled with the young Duke of Hamilton 1772–78, and then settled in London. His *View of Society in France, Switzerland, Germany, and Italy* (1779–81) was well received; but it is for the novel *Zeluco* (1789), which suggested Byron's *Childe Harold*, that he is best remembered today. Moore died at Richmond. See Memoir by Anderson prefixed to his Works (7 vols. 1820).

(11) **Sir John** (1761–1809), British general, son of (10), born at Glasgow, distinguished himself in the descent upon Corsica (1794) and served in the West Indies (1796), in Ireland (1798), and in Holland (1799). He was in Egypt in 1801, obtaining the Order of the Bath; and in 1802 served in Sicily and Sweden. In 1808 he was sent with a corps of 10,000 men to strengthen the English army in Spain, and in August assumed the chief command. In October he received instructions to co-operate with the Spanish forces in the expulsion of the French from the Peninsula, and moved his army from Lisbon towards Valladolid. But Spanish apathy, French successes elsewhere, and the intrigues of his own countrymen soon placed him in a critical position. When the news reached him that Madrid had fallen, and that Napoleon was marching to crush him with 70,000 men, Moore, with only 25,000, was forced to retreat. In December he began a disastrous march from Astorga to Coruña, nearly 250 miles, through a mountainous country, made almost impassable by snow and rain, and harassed by the enemy. They reached Coruña in a lamentable state; and Soult was waiting to attack as soon as the embarkation should begin. In a desperate battle on January 16, 1809, the French were defeated with the loss of 2,000 men. Moore was mortally wounded by a grape-shot in the moment of victory, and was buried early next morning (as in Wolfe's poem). See Lives by his brother (1835) and Gen. Maurice (1817), and Maurice's reply in his edition of Moore's *Diary* (1904) to strictures in Oman's *Peninsular War* (1902). See also Lives by B. Brownrigg (1923), C. Oman (1953), and study by J. F. C. Fuller (1925).

(12) **Thomas** (1779–1852), Irish poet, born at Dublin, May 28, the son of a Catholic grocer, was educated at Trinity College, Dublin, and the Middle Temple. His translation of Anacreon (1800) proved a great hit, and, with his musical talent, procured him admission to the best society. In 1803 appointed registrar of the admiralty court at Bermuda, he arranged for a deputy and returned after a tour of the States and Canada. In 1811 he married an actress, Bessy Dyke, and later settled in Wiltshire. Meanwhile Moore had published the earlier of the *Irish Melodies* (1807–34) and *The Twopenny Post-bag* (1812). In 1817 the long-

expected *Lalla Rookh* appeared, dazzling as a firefly, for which Longmans paid him 3000 guineas; the *Irish Melodies* brought in £500 a year. Moore had 'a generous contempt for money', his Bermuda deputy embezzled £6000, and in 1819, to avoid arrest, he went to Italy and then to Paris. He returned in 1822 to Wiltshire, where he passed his last thirty years, during which he wrote lives of Sheridan and Byron and other works. In 1835 he received a pension of £300, but his last days were clouded by the loss of his two sons. Moore in his lifetime was as popular as Byron. His poetry was light, airy, graceful, but soulless. He is best in his lyrics. See his *Memoirs*, 'edited' by Lord John Russell (8 vols. 1852–56), and studies by Stephen Gwynn (1905), L. A. G. Strong (1937), H. M. Jones (N.Y. 1937).

(13) **Thomas Sturge** (1870–1944), English poet, critic and wood-engraver, brother of (6), born in Sussex, is known as the author of polished verse of classical style, works on Dürer and other artists and as a distinguished designer of book-plates. See Life by F. L. Gwynn (1952).

(14) **William** (1790–1851), English painter, father of (1) and (8), a well-known portrait painter in York, he was the father of thirteen sons, several of whom also became well-known artists.

MOR, More or **Moro, Anthonis** (1519–75), Dutch portrait-painter, born at Utrecht, in 1547 entered the Antwerp guild of St Luke; in 1550–51 visited Italy, in 1552 Spain, and in 1553 England, where he was knighted (Sir Anthony More), and painted Queen Mary. From about 1568 he lived at Antwerp. See Life by V. Hymans (Brussels 1910).

MORAND, Paul, *mo-rã* (1889–   ), French diplomat and writer, born in Paris. In the French diplomatic service from 1912 until 1944, his early posts included the secretaryship of the French embassies in London—where he was also minister plenipotentiary in 1940—Rome and Madrid. In 1939 he was head of the French mission of economic warfare in England, in 1943 minister at Bucharest and in 1944 ambassador at Berne. He turned to writing in 1920, beginning with poetry, then publishing short stories and novels, with a background of cosmopolitan life in postwar Europe. These include *Ouvert l anuit* (1922), *Fermé la nuit* (1923) and *Lewis et Irène* (1924). He has also written travel books, studies of cities, and political and biographical works. Among his later works are *Vie de Maupassant* (1942), *Journal d'un attaché d'ambassade* (1948), *Fouquet* (1961) and *Tais-toi* (1965).

MORANT, Philip (1700–70), English antiquary and historian, an Essex clergyman, he wrote *The History of Essex* (2 vols. 1760–1768), other historical and theological works, and also edited some of the ancient records of parliament.

MORATA, Olympia (1526–55), Italian scholar and poetess, daughter of the poet Morato, she gave public lectures when fifteen; but, having in 1548 married the German physician Andreas Grundler, she followed him to Germany, became a Protestant, and, reduced to penury, died at Heidelberg, leaving

numerous Latin and Greek poems, a treatise on Cicero, dialogues, letters, &c. See the monograph by Bonnet (4th ed. Paris 1865).

MORATIN, Leandro de (1760–1828), Spanish dramatist and poet, born at Madrid, wrote a number of successful comedies influenced by French ideas and especially by Molière. His acceptance of the post of librarian to Joseph Bonaparte resulted in his exile to Paris in 1814. See works by J. M. Rubio (Valencia 1893), F. Venizer (Paris 1909).

MORAY, James Stuart, Earl of (1531–70), regent of Scotland, the natural son of James V of Scotland, by a daughter of Lord Erskine, in 1538 was made prior *in commendam* of St Andrews, in 1556 joined the Reformers. In 1561 he was dispatched to France, to invite his half-sister, Queen Mary, to return to her kingdom; and on her arrival he acted as her prime minister. In 1562 she created him Earl of Moray, and also of Mar; and he put down for her the Border banditti, and defeated Huntly at Corrichie. On her marriage to Darnley (1565) he appealed to arms, but was forced to take refuge in England. He did not return to Edinburgh till the day after Rizzio's murder (in 1566), to which he was privy. In April 1567 he withdrew to France, but next August was recalled by the nobles in arms against Mary, to find her a prisoner at Lochleven, and himself appointed regent of the kingdom. On Mary's escape he defeated her forces at Langside (May 13, 1568), and was one of the commissioners sent to England to conduct the negotiations against her. After his return to Scotland, by his vigour and prudence he succeeded in securing the peace of the realm and settling the affairs of the church. But on January 20, 1570, he was shot at Linlithgow by James Hamilton of Bothwellhaugh. See RANDOLPH, SIR THOMAS, and study by M. Lee (1953).

MORDAUNT. See PETERBOROUGH.

MORE, (1) Hannah (1745–1833), English writer, was born at Stapleton near Bristol, February 2. She wrote verses at an early age, and in 1762 published *The Search after Happiness*, a pastoral drama. In 1774 she was introduced to the best literary society of London. During this period she wrote two tales in verse, and two tragedies, *Percy* and *The Fatal Secret*, both of which were acted. Led by her religious views to withdraw from society, she retired to Cowslip Green near Bristol, where she did much to improve the condition of the poor. Her essays on *The Manners of the Great* and *The Religion of the Fashionable World*, her novel *Coelebs in Search of a Wife* (1809), and a tract called *The Shepherd of Salisbury Plain* were her most popular works. See Lives by Harland (1901), Meakin (1911), M. A. Hopkins (1947), M. G. Jones (1952) and her *Letters*, ed. R. B. Johnson (1925).

(2) **Henry** (1614–87), English philosopher, known as the 'Cambridge Platonist', was educated at Eton and Christ's College, Cambridge, where he became fellow in 1639, and remained all his life. He gave himself entirely to philosophy, especially to Plato and the Neoplatonists; and his earlier

rationality gradually gave place to hopeless mysticism and theosophy. His *Divine Dialogues* (1668) is a work of unusual interest; his *Philosophicall Poems* were edited by Dr Grosart (' Chertsey Library ' 1878), and by Bullough (1931). See Lives by Ward (1710; new ed. 1911), P. R. Anderson (N.Y. 1933), and F. J. Powicke, *Cambridge Platonists* (1926).

(3) **Sir Thomas** (1478–1535), English statesman, born in London, February 7, the son of a judge, was educated at Oxford under Colet and Linacre. Having completed his legal studies at New Inn and Lincoln's Inn, he was for three years reader in Furnival's Inn, and spent the next four years in the Charterhouse in ' devotion and prayer '. During the last years of Henry VII he became under-sheriff of London and member of parliament. Introduced to Henry VIII through Wolsey, he became master of requests (1514), treasurer of the exchequer (1521), and chancellor of the Duchy of Lancaster (1525). He was speaker of the House of Commons, and was sent on missions to Francis I and Charles V. On the fall of Wolsey in 1529, More, against his own strongest wish, was appointed lord chancellor. In the discharge of his office he displayed a primitive virtue and simplicity. The one stain on his character as judge is the harshness of his sentences for religious opinions. He sympathized with Colet and Erasmus in their desire for a more rational theology and for radical reform in the manners of the clergy, but like them also he had no promptings to break with the historic church. He saw with displeasure the successive steps which led Henry to the final schism from Rome. In 1532 he resigned the chancellorship. In 1534 Henry was declared head of the English Church; and More's steadfast refusal to recognize any other head of the church than the pope led to his sentence for high treason after a harsh imprisonment of over a year. Still refusing to recant he was beheaded on July 7, 1535. More was twice married; his daughter Margaret, the wife of his biographer William Roper, was distinguished for her high character, her accomplishments, and her pious devotion to her father. By his Latin *Utopia* (1516; Eng. trans. 1556) More takes his place with the most eminent humanists of the Renaissance. His *History of King Richard III* (1513) ' begins modern English historical writing of distinction '. From Erasmus we realize the virtues and attractions of a winning rather than an imposing figure. In 1935 he was canonized. See Lives by Roper (ed. Hitchcock 1935), Harpsfield (ed. with Rastell's fragments, 1932), Bridgett (1891), C. Hollis (1934), A. Cecil (1936), L. Pane (1953), E. E. Reynolds (1953), J. Farrow (1954); also Campbell on *Utopia* (1930), his edition of the *English Works* (1931), Chambers and others, *Fame of Blessed Thomas More* (1930), Routh, *More and his Friends* (1934), and *Correspondence* ed. E. F. Rogers (1947).

MORÉAS, Jean, orig. **Yannis Papadiamantopoulos** (1856–1910), French poet, born at Athens, wrote first in Greek, then settled in Paris (1879) and became a leader of the

Symbolist school, to which he gave its name, though his later work shows a return to classical and traditional forms. His works include *Les Syrtes* (1884), *Cantilènes* (1886), *Le Pèlerin passioné* (1891) and *Les Stances* (1905), the masterpiece of his classical period. See studies by M. Barrès (Paris 1910) and R. Niklaus (Paris 1936).

MOREAU, Jean Victor, *mor-ō* (1761–1813), French general, born at Morlaix, August 11, the son of an advocate, he studied law, but at the Revolution commanded the volunteers from Rennes, served under Dumouriez in 1793, and in 1794 was made a general of division; he took part, under Pichegru, in reducing Belgium and Holland. In command on the Rhine and Moselle, he drove the Austrians back to the Danube, was forced to retreat and later deprived of his command. In 1798 he took command in Italy and skilfully conducted the defeated troops to France. The party of Sieyès, which overthrew the Directory, offered him the dictatorship; he declined it, but lent his assistance to Bonaparte on 18th Brumaire. In command of the army of the Rhine, he gained victory after victory over the Austrians in 1800, drove them back behind the Inn, and at last won the decisive battle of Hohenlinden. Napoleon, grown very jealous of Moreau, accused him of sharing in the plot of Cadoudal (q.v.); and, a sentence to two years' imprisonment (1804) being commuted to banishment, Moreau settled in New Jersey. In 1813 he accompanied the Emperor of Russia in the march against Dresden, where (August 27) a French cannon-ball broke both his legs. Amputation was performed, but he died at Laun in Bohemia, September 2. He was buried in St Petersburg. See works by Beauchamp (trans. 1814), E. Picard (Paris 1905) and Daudet (1909).

MORERI, Louis, *mor-ay-ree* (1643–80), French scholar, born in Provence, took orders, and was a noted preacher at Lyons, where he published his *Grand dictionnaire historique* (1674; 20th ed. 1759; Eng. trans. 1694). In 1675 he went to Paris, and laboured at the dictionary's expansion till his death.

MORESBY, John (1830–1922), English admiral and explorer, born at Allerton, Somerset, known for his exploration and survey work in New Guinea, where he discovered the fine natural harbour now fronted by Port Moresby, which was named after him.

MORETTO DA BRESCIA, properly **Alessandro Bonvicino** (1498–1554), Italian painter, was born in Brescia, where he painted for several churches and also became a fine portrait painter. See Pater's *Miscellaneous Studies* (1895), and study by G. Gombosi (Basel 1943).

MORGAGNI, Giovanni Battista, *mor-gan'yee* (1682–1771), Italian physician, born at Forlì, became professor of Medicine at Padua and founded the science of pathological anatomy. See book by G. Bilancioni (Rome 1922), and H. E. Sigerist, *Great Doctors* (1933).

MORGAN, (1) Augustus De. See DE MORGAN (1).

(2) **Charles Langbridge** (1894–1958), English author, was born in Kent, son of

Sir Charles Morgan, civil engineer. He served in Atlantic and China waters as a midshipman, 1911–13, but finding the life uncongenial (*vide* his *Gunroom*, 1919), resigned. He rejoined the navy, however, in 1914 and was later interned in Holland until 1917. On repatriation, he went to Oxford University, where he became a well-known personality. In 1921, on leaving Oxford, he joined the editorial staff of *The Times*, and was their principal dramatic critic from 1926 until 1939. Under the pen-name of 'Menander' he also wrote for *The Times Literary Supplement* critical essays of a mellow, meditative sort, called *Reflections in a Mirror*, which were later (1944–45) collected in two series. In *Liberties of the Mind* (1951) the urbanity has disappeared and Morgan reveals himself as deeply disturbed by the age's loss of liberty in mental and moral judgments and choices. His novels and plays show high professional competence, but lack vividness and urgency. *Portrait in a Mirror* (1929), which won the Femina Vie Heureuse prize in 1930, is Morgan's most satisfying novel. Later works show too much preoccupation with values of the heart to the detriment of narrative sweep, and his earnestness seems unduly solemn, pompous and vaguely sentimental. None the less, *The Fountain* (1932) won the Hawthornden prize and *The Voyage* (1940) won the James Tait Black Memorial prize. His plays are *The Flashing Stream* (1938), *The River Line* (1952) and *The Burning Glass* (1953). See study by Duffin (1959) and *Selected Letters*, ed. by E. Lewis, with Memoir (1967).

(3) **Sir Henry** (*c.* 1635–88), British buccaneer, born in Glamorganshire of good family, seems to have been kidnapped at Bristol, and shipped to Barbadoes. Joining the buccaneers, he conducted triumphant, unbridled expeditions against Spanish possessions (Porto Bello, Maracaibo, Panama, &c.). He died lieutenant-governor of Jamaica. See Haring's *Buccaneers in the West Indies* (1910), and Lives by C. Hutcheson (1890) and W. A. Roberts (1933).

(4) **John Pierpont** (1837–1913), American financier, was born at Hartford, Conn., the son of **Junius Spencer Morgan** (1813–90), founder of the international banking firm of J. S. Morgan and Company. His house organized the Steel Trust, formed an Atlantic shipping combine, controlled railways, &c. Philanthropist and art collector, he left over £15,000,000. His like-named only son (1867–1943) placed contracts, raised loans, &c., for the British government during the first World War. See Lives by H. L. Satterlee (1939) and F. L. Allen (1949).

(5) **Lady**, *née* **Sydney Owenson** (1780–1859), Irish novelist, was born in Dublin. Her father, a theatrical manager, falling into difficulties, she supported the family, first as governess, next as author. In 1812 she married Thomas Charles Morgan, M.D. (1783–1843), afterwards knighted. Her works—lively novels, verse, travels, &c.— include *St Clair* (1804), *The Wild Irish Girl* (1806), *O'Donnel* (1814) and *Memoirs* (1862).

(6) **Lewis Henry** (1818–81), American archaeologist, was born at Aurora, N.Y.,

became a lawyer at Rochester, and served in the state assembly (1861) and senate (1868). An authority on American-Indian tribal culture, he wrote *The League of the Iroquois* (1851), *The American Beaver* (1868), *Consanguinity and Affinity* (1869), *Ancient Society* (1877), *House-life of the American Aborigines* (1881), &c.

(7) **William De.** See DE MORGAN (2).

MORGHEN, Raphael (1758–1833), Italian engraver, born at Naples, known for his plates after Raphael, Leonardo (notably *The Last Supper*) and others, under the patronage of the Grand Duke of Tuscany. See work by Fred. R. Halsey (New York 1885).

MORIER, James Justinian (1780–1849), English novelist, son of the consul at Smyrna, turned to literature after a diplomatic career. His great work is that inimitable picture of Persian life, *The Adventures of Hajji Baba of Ispahan* (1824), with the less brilliant *Hajji Baba in England* (1828).

MÖRIKE, Eduard, *mœ'ri-kĕ* (1804–75), German poet and novelist, born in Ludwigsburg, entered the theological seminary at Tübingen in 1822 and became vicar of Kleversulzbach in 1834, retiring in 1843. He was weak, hypochondriacal, unhappily married and lazy, yet he produced a minor masterpiece in *Mozart auf der Reise nach Prag* (1856) and many poems of delicacy and beauty with something of the deceptive simplicity of Heine. These were collectively published in 1838. Three volumes of his collected letters, edited by H. Mayne, appeared between 1909 and 1914.

MORIN, or **Morinus, Jean** (1591–1659), French theologian, a founder of biblical criticism, wrote on ecclesiastical antiquities.

MORISON, (1) **James** (1816–93), Scottish divine, a Kilmarnock United Secession minister, born at Bathgate, in 1843, with three other ministers, founded the Evangelical Union, its system a modified Independency.

(2) **Robert** (1620–83), Scottish botanist, a native of Aberdeen, having borne arms as a royalist, retired to France, took his M.D. at Angers (1648), and had charge of the garden of the Duke of Orleans. Charles II made him one of his physicians, 'botanist royal', and professor of Botany at Oxford. His chief work is *Plantarum Historia Universalis Oxoniensis* (1680).

(3) **Stanley** (1889–1967), English typographer, typographical adviser to Cambridge University Press (1923–44 and 1947–59) and to the Monotype Corporation, from 1923 designed the Times New Roman type, introduced in 1932, edited *The Times Literary Supplement* (1945–47) and was the author of many works on typography and calligraphy. He also edited the history of *The Times* (1935–52). In 1961 he was appointed to the editorial board of the *Encylopaedia Britannica*.

MORISOT, Berthe Marie Pauline, *mo-ree-sō* (1841–95), French painter, a great-granddaughter of Fragonard, was the leading female exponent of Impressionism. Her early work shows the influence of Corot, who was her friend and mentor, but her later style owes more to Renoir. She herself exercised an influence on Manet, whose brother

Eugène she married. See her *Correspondance*, ed. Rouart, trans. B. W. Hubbard (1957).

MORITZ, Karl Philipp, *mō-rits'* (1756–93), German writer, born at Hameln, was in turn hat-maker's apprentice, actor, teacher and professor. Self-educated, he travelled in England and Italy and wrote *Reisen eines Deutschen in England* (1783), and *Reisen eines Deutschen in Italien* (1792–93). His autobiographical novel, *Anton Reiser* (1785–90), influenced Goethe. Moritz was a precursor of the German Romantic movement, delved into the past, and wrote *Versuch einer deutschen Prosodie* (1786), which he dedicated to Frederick the Great. See studies by M. Dessoir (Berlin 1889) and H. Henning (1908).

MORLAND, George (1763–1804), English painter, was born in London, June 26, the eldest son of the crayonist Henry Morland (1712–97), who brought him up with extreme rigour. From the time he was his own master, his life was a downward course of drunkenness and debt. Yet in the last eight years of his life he turned out nearly nine hundred paintings and over a thousand drawings, many of them hastily completed to bring in money and inferior in quality. His strength lay in country subjects (pigs, gypsies, and stable interiors). He died of brain-fever in a Holborn sponging-house. See works by Dawe (1807), Ralph Richardson (1895), J. T. Nettleship (1899), G. C. Williamson (1904), Sir W. Gilbey (1907).

MORLEY, (1) Christopher Darlington (1890–1957), American novelist and essayist, born in Haverford, Pa., was a Rhodes scholar at Oxford. His style is distinguished by its whimsical urbanity and an occasional flight into satiric fantasy. His work includes *Parnassus on Wheels* (1917), *Thunder on the Left* (1925), *Swiss Family Manhattan* (1932), *Human Being* (1932), *Streamlines* (1937), *Kitty Foyle* (1939), *The Ironing Board* (1949) and a book of poems, *The Middle Kingdom* (1944).

(2) Henry (1822–94), English writer and editor, born in London, became a lecturer (1857–65) and professor of English (1865–89) at London University, wrote biographical and critical works, and edited ' Morley's Universal Library ' of English classics. See *Life* by Solly (1899).

(3) John, 1st Viscount Morley (1838–1923), English journalist, biographer, philosophical critic, Radical politician and statesman, was born at Blackburn, December 24. Educated at Cheltenham and Lincoln College, Oxford, he was called to the bar, but chose literature as a profession. His works (collected 1921 *et seq*.) include *Edmund Burke* (1867), *Critical Miscellanies* (1871–77), *Voltaire* (1872), *On Compromise* (1874), *Rousseau* (1876), *Diderot and the Encyclopaedists* (1878), *Richard Cobden* (1881; new ed. 1896) and *Studies in Literature* (1891). From 1867 till 1882 he edited the *Fortnightly Review*; and he was editor of the ' English Men of Letters ' series, writing the volume on Burke, while for the ' English Statesmen ' he wrote *Walpole* (1889). From 1880 to 1883 he edited the *Pall Mall Gazette*. His articles and speeches in favour of Home Rule made him Gladstone's most conspicuous supporter. In 1886 he was a successful Irish Secretary,

and again in 1892–95. He sat for Newcastle 1883–95, for Montrose Burghs from 1896 until his elevation to the peerage in 1908, was secretary for India in 1905–10 (repressing sedition and making the government more representative), and lord president of the council from 1910 till Britain entered the war, August 1914. O.M. (1902), he wrote a great life of Gladstone (4 vols. 1903), and *Recollections* (1917). See studies by Morgan (1924), Ali Khan, Braybrooke (1924), F. W. Hirst (1927).

(4) Samuel (1809–86), English woollen manufacturer, politician and philanthropist, born in Homerton, the son of a hosier. By 1860 he had greatly extended his father's business with mills in Nottingham, Leicester and Derbyshire. Deeply religious, he was a conscientious employer, a supporter of the temperance movement and was a Liberal M.P. (1865–85). See *Life* by E. Hodder (1887). His son, Arnold (1849–1916), was chief Liberal whip and P.M.G. (1892–95).

(5) Thomas (1557–1603), English composer, was a pupil of William Byrd (q.v.). He became organist at St Paul's cathedral, and from 1592 was a Gentleman of the Chapel Royal. He is best known for his *A Plaine and Easie Introduction to Practicall Musicke* (1597), written in entertaining dialogue with the purpose of encouraging part-singing for pleasure; also for his volumes of madrigals and canzonets, which include such evergreen favourites as ' Now is the month of maying ', ' My bonny lass she smileth ' and ' It was a lover and his lass '. He was compiler of the collection called, in honour of Queen Elizabeth, *The Triumphes of Oriana* (1603).

MORNAY, Philippe de, Seigneur du Plessis-Marly (1549–1623), a French statesman, converted to Protestantism in 1560, and nicknamed the ' Pope of the Huguenots '. His treatise on Christianity was translated into English in 1589 at the request of his dead friend, Sir Philip Sidney.

MORNY, Charles Auguste Louis Joseph, Duc de (1811–65), was believed to be the son of Queen Hortense and the Comte de Flahault, and so half-brother of Louis Napoleon. Born in Paris, and adopted by the Comte de Morny, he served in Algeria; but soon he left the army, and in 1838 became a manufacturer of beet sugar. From that time he was mixed up in all sorts of speculations. Chosen a deputy in 1842, he quickly became prominent in financial questions. After 1848 he supported his half-brother, took a prominent part in the *coup d'état*, and became minister of the interior. In 1854–65 he was president of the *corps législatif*, and was ambassador to Russia in 1856–57. He is the ' Duc de Mora ' in Daudet's *Nabab*. See Loliée's *Frère d'empereur* (1909) and Life by M. Chapman (1931).

MORONI, Giovanni Battista (1525–78), Italian portrait and religious painter, was born at Bondo near Albino. A splendid example of his style is *The Tailor* in the National Gallery, London. See study by Lendorff (Bologna 1939).

MORPHY, Paul (1837–84), American advocate and chess champion, was born at New Orleans.

MORRIS, (1) **George Pope** (1802–64), American poet, author of ' Woodman, spare that Tree ', was born in Philadelphia, founded and edited the *New York Mirror* (1823), and died in New York.

(2) **Gouverneur** (1752–1816), American statesman, born in Morrisania, N.Y., January 31, was admitted to the bar in 1771. In 1780 he lost a leg by an accident. Assistant in the finance department 1781–84, in 1787 he took his seat in the convention that framed the U.S. constitution, and in 1788 sailed for Paris. The greater part of 1791 he spent in England as Washington's agent, and then till 1794 was U.S. minister to France. Returning to America in 1798, he sat in the Senate 1800–03, and died November 6. See *Memoirs* by Jared Sparks (1832), monograph by Roosevelt (1888), and Morris's *Diary and Letters* (1889).

(3) **Sir Lewis** (1833–1907), Welsh poet, born in Carmarthen, January 23, was educated at Sherborne and Jesus College, Oxford. *Songs of Two Worlds* (3 vols. 1871–75) by ' A New Writer ' was followed in 1876 by *The Epic of Hades*, which ran into several series, and more verse and drama. In 1895 he was made a knight-bachelor.

(4) **Reginald Owen** (1886–1948), English composer and writer on music, was born in York. He taught at the Royal College of Music, London, and at the Curtis Institute, Philadelphia, and published *Contrapuntal Technique in the 16th Century* (1922).

(5) **Robert** (1734–1806), the ' Financier of the American Revolution ', went early from Lancashire to Philadelphia, was a signatory of the Declaration of Independence, and in old age was a prisoner for debt. See Life by W. G. Sumner (1892).

(6) **Tom** (1821–1908), ' the Nestor of golf ', was born in St Andrews, and served an apprenticeship as golf-ball maker with the celebrated Allan Robertson. He went to Prestwick as green-keeper in 1851, won the championship belt in 1861–62, 1864, 1866, having returned to St Andrews as green-keeper in 1863. His son ' Tommy ' (1851–75) was the best player of his time, and carried off the champion belt by winning it three times in succession (1868–70).

(7) **William** (1834–96), English craftsman and poet, was educated at Marlborough and Exeter College, Oxford. He meant to take orders, but his friendship with members of the pre-Raphaelite brotherhood, particularly Burne-Jones, made him realize that his interest in theology was limited to an ardent love of Gothic architecture. From architecture he turned, on Rossetti's advice, to painting, which he practised professionally from 1857 to 1862, when he discovered his true métier and also his social gospel, the revival of the handicrafts and finally the revolutionizing of the art of house decoration and furnishing in England. To this end he founded, with the help of his pre-Raphaelite associates, the firm of Morris, Marshall, Faulkner and Company. Morris decoration and furnishing have, like other fashions, passed out and even become slightly ridiculous, but his experience as a masterworkman added to his enthusiasm for the

Gothic persuaded him that the excellence of mediaeval arts and crafts came from the joy of the free craftsman which was destroyed by mass-production and capitalism. In 1883 he joined the Social Democratic Federation and a year later on its disruption he organized the Socialist League. English Socialism has far less to do with Continental Marxism than with the Utopia imagined for it by Morris. His two prose romances, *The Dream of John Ball* (1888) and *News from Nowhere* (1891), were romances of Socialist propaganda, charming but a little fatiguing too, owing to the sense of unreality. His other prose romances being inspired by his late enthusiasm for the Icelandic sagas do not suffer in this way—these include *The House of the Wolfings* (1889), *The Roots of the Mountains* (1890) and *The Story of the Glittering Plain* (1891). These all show that trait which appeared in his first volume of poetry, *The Defence of Guinevere* (1858), that is, a primitivism in which the brutalities of chivalrous life are blended with soft romance. Tennyson had not dared to show that side of the age of chivalry. The long narrative poems, *The Life and Death of Jason* (1867) and *The Earthly Paradise* (1868–70), are perhaps too prolix for modern taste and they suffer from Morris's idea of the epic as anything a ' singer ' could extemporize as he wove at the loom. Chaucer is his model in *The Earthly Paradise* and his framework allows for alternate Greek and mediaeval tales with beautiful seasonal intercalations. Norse inspiration, however, gave his muse a decided lift—*Sigurd the Volsung* (1876), with its savagery and sense of doom expressed in something like Homeric dactyllics, is his best narrative poem. Later, as we have seen, the prose romance almost exclusively occupied his leisure, but *Poems by the Way* (1891) praised revolutionary Socialism. His Virgil's *Aeneid* (1875) and Homer's *Odyssey* cannot rank high as translation, for he has gothicized them out of recognition, but passages in them have a bizarre charm. The translation of many of the Icelandic sagas in which he collaborated with Magnusson are more faithful to the text. His exuberant energy and love of beautiful craft caused him in 1890 to set up the Kelmscott Press at Hammersmith, whence issued his own works and reprints of classics. A brief notice of Morris hardly does justice to his influence in the waning Victorian era—his resistance to technology and mass production and to high finance was no doubt vain and perhaps his nostalgic mediaevalism was not the best way of resisting them, but his career was a symbol of the revolt of man against the machine and of the love of beautiful things in the home and in public places. See *Collected Works* (24 vols., edited by May Morris, 1910–15); Lives by J. W. Mackail (1899), May Morris (1936) and E. P. Thomson (1955); also Margaret Grennan, *W. Morris, Mediaevalist and Revolutionary* (1945) and R. Page Arnot, *W. Morris, The Man and the Myth* (1964).

MORRISON, (1) **Arthur** (1863–1945), English novelist, born in Kent, became a clerk, then a journalist. His reputation rests on his powerfully realistic novels of London life such as *A Child of the Jago* (1896).

(2) **Herbert Stanley, Baron Morrison of Lambeth** (1888-1965), British politician, born at Lambeth, London, was educated at an elementary school and by intensive private reading. After being an errand-boy and a shop-assistant, he helped to found the London Labour Party, and became its secretary in 1915. Mayor of Hackney from 1920 to 1921, he entered the L.C.C. in 1922, becoming its leader in 1934; he grouped together London's passenger transport system, and much of the credit for the ' Green Belt ' was due to him. He was M.P. for South Hackney three times between 1923 and 1945, when he was elected for East Lewisham. In Winston Churchill's Cabinet he was home secretary and minister of home security. He was a powerful figure in the postwar social revolution, uniting the positions of deputy prime-minister, lord president of the Council, and leader of a Commons which enacted the most formidable body of legislation ever entrusted to it. For seven months in 1951 he was, less felicitously, foreign secretary. In 1951 he became deputy leader of the opposition and a Companion of Honour, and in 1955 was defeated by Hugh Gaitskell in the contest for the leadership of the labour party. He was created a life peer in 1959. He wrote *How London is Governed* (1949) and *Government and Parliament* (1954). See *Autobiography* (1960).

(3) **Richard James.** See ZADKIEL.

(4) **Robert** (1782-1834), Scottish missionary. He was born near Morpeth or Jedburgh, and after studying theology in his spare time, in 1807 was sent to Canton by the London Missionary Society. In 1809-14 he translated and printed the New Testament. By 1819, with some help, he had done the same with the Old Testament; and in 1823 he completed his great *Chinese Dictionary*. In 1818 he established an Anglo-Chinese College at Malacca. After a visit to Europe (1824-26) he returned to China, where he spent the rest of his life. See Lives by his widow (1839), Townsend (1888), M. Broomhall (1924), L. Ride (Hong Kong 1957).

MORRITT, John Bacon Sawrey (1772-1843), English traveller and scholar, who, after travelling in the East and surveying the site of Troy, returned to England and was an M.P. for many years. He is best remembered as a friend of Sir Walter Scott, who dedicated *Rokeby* to him.

MORROW, Dwight Whitney (1873-1931), American diplomat and finance expert, born at Huntington, W. Va., became a leading member of the banking firm of J. P. Morgan, and in 1927 was appointed ambassador to Mexico. See *Life* by Nicolson (1935).

MORSE, Samuel Finley Breese (1791-1872), American artist and inventor, the eldest son of Rev. Dr Jedidiah Morse, geographer, was born at Charlestown, Mass. He graduated at Yale in 1810, went to England to study painting, and was a founder and first president of the National Academy of Design at New York. He studied chemistry and electricity, and in 1832 conceived the idea of a magnetic telegraph, which he exhibited to congress in 1837, and vainly attempted to

patent in Europe. He struggled on heroically against scanty means until 1843, when congress appropriated 30,000 dollars for a telegraph line between Washington and Baltimore. His system, widely adopted, at last brought him honours and rewards. The well-known Morse code was evolved by him for use with his telegraph. See his *Letters and Journals*, ed. by his son (1915) ; Lives by Mabee (1943), O. W. Larkin (Boston 1954), J. L. Latham (N.Y. 1954)

MORTARA, Edgar (1852-1940), Italian Jew, principal in the ' Mortara ' case, was in 1858 carried off from his parents by the Archbishop of Bologna, on the plea that he had been baptized, when an infant, by a Catholic maid servant. The refusal of the authorities to give him up to his parents excited great indignation in England. He became an Augustinian monk, and retained his Christian faith.

MORTIER, Édouard Adolphe Casimir Joseph, Duke of Treviso, *mor-tyay* (1768-1835), French soldier, marshal of Napoleon, campaigned brilliantly in Germany, Russia and Spain. He held high office under Louis-Philippe, at whose side he was killed by a bomb.

MORTIMER, Favell Lee, *née* **Bevan** (1802-1878), English writer, a keen educationalist, wrote many books for children, the most popular being *Peep of Day*. After the death of her husband, a clergyman, she devoted herself to the care of the destitute.

MORTIMER, Earls of March. See EDWARD II and III.

MORTON, Earls of, a branch of the family of Douglas (q.v.):

James Douglas, 4th Earl (*c.* 1525-81), regent of Scotland, the younger son of Sir George Douglas of Pittendriech near Edinburgh, became Earl of Morton in right of his wife, and in 1563 was made lord high chancellor. Conspicuous in Rizzio's assassination (1566), he fled to England, but obtained his pardon from the queen. He was privy to the plan for Darnley's murder, but purposely absented himself from Edinburgh (1567); and, on Bothwell's abduction of Mary, he joined the confederacy of the nobles against them. He figured prominently at Carberry Hill; discovered the ' Casket Letters '; led the van at Langside (1568); and, after the brief regencies of Moray, Lennox, and Mar, in November 1572 was himself elected regent. His policy was in favour of Elizabeth, from whom in 1571 he was receiving bribes; and his high-handed treatment alike of the nobles and of the Presbyterian clergy, his attempts to restore episcopacy, and the rapacity imputed to him swelled the number of his enemies. He seemed to have retrieved his temporary downfall by the seizure two months later of Stirling Castle (May 1578); but Esmé Stuart in 1580 completely supplanted him in young King James's favour; and on June 2, 1581, as ' art and part ' in Darnley's murder, he was beheaded by means of the ' Maiden ' in the Edinburgh Grassmarket.

MORTON, (1) Henry Vollam (1892-), English author and journalist who began his career on the staff of the *Birmingham Gazette* in 1910 and became assistant editor in 1912. He is the author of many informative and informal travel books, including *The Heart of London* (1925), *In the Steps of the Master* (1934), *Middle East* (1941), *In Search of London* (1951), others in the *In Search of . . .* series, and *A Wanderer in Rome* (1957).

(2) **John** (*c*. 1420–1500), English cardinal and statesman, born at Milborne St Andrew in Dorsetshire, practised as an advocate in the Court of Arches. He adhered with great fidelity to Henry VI, but after the battle of Tewkesbury he made his peace with Edward IV and was made master of the rolls and Bishop of Ely. Richard III imprisoned him, but he escaped, and joining Henry VII, was made Archbishop of Canterbury and chancellor (1486). In 1493 he became a cardinal. See Gairdner's *Henry VII* (1889), and a Life of Morton by Woodhouse (1895).

(3) **John Cameron Andrieu Bingham Michael** (1893–   ), English author and journalist, after serving through World War I he took up writing and has published many books of humour, fantasy and satire, as well as a number of historical works including several on the French Revolution. Since 1924 he has contributed a regular humorous column to the *Daily Express* under the name of ' Beachcomber '.

(4) **John Maddison** (1811–91), English dramatist, son of (6), born at Pangbourne, became a prolific writer of farces (mostly from the French), but is best remembered as the author of *Cox and Box* (1847). The rise of burlesque was his ruin and he became a ' poor brother ' of the Charterhouse. See the memoir by Clement Scott prefixed to *Plays for Home Performance* (1889).

(5) **Levi Parsons** (1824–1920), American banker and politician, born at Shoreham, Vt., began as a country storekeeper's assistant, and in 1863 founded banking-houses in New York and London. In 1878–80 he was returned to congress as a Republican, in 1881–85 was minister to France, vice-president of the U.S. (1889–93), governor of New York State (1895–96). See Life by McElroy (1930).

(6) **Thomas** (1764–1838), English dramatist, father of (4), born in Durham, quitted Lincoln's Inn for play writing, and produced *Speed the Plough* (1798, with its invisible ' Mrs. Grundy '), *The Blind Girl* (1801), *Town and Country* (1807), *School for Grown Children* (1826), and other popular plays. For thirty-five years he lived at Pangbourne near Reading, till in 1828 he removed to London. See study by R. A. L. Mortvedt in *Summaries of Harvard Theses* (Cambridge, Mass., 1935).

(7) **Thomas** (1781–1832), Scottish ship-builder, inventor about 1822 of the patent slip, which provides a cheap substitute for a dry dock.

(8) **William Thomas Green** (1819–68), American dentist, born at Charlton, Mass., in 1846 was the first to employ in opera-tions anaesthesia produced by sulphuric ether. See Life by R. M. Baker (N.Y. 1946).

MORYSON, Fynes (1566–1630), English traveller, was born at Cadeby, Lincs, and after becoming a fellow of Peterhouse,

Cambridge, he travelled over Europe and the Levant, and published his *Itinerary* (1617; complete ed. 4 vols Glasgow 1907–08).

MOSCHELES, Ignaz, *mōˈshe-les* (1794–1870), Bohemian pianist and composer, born at Prague of Jewish parents, was by 1808 the favourite musician and music-master of Vienna. He taught in London from 1825, and from 1844 in Leipzig. He edited in English Schindler's *Life of Beethoven* (1841). See Life by his wife, his Corres-pondence with Mendelssohn (trans. 1888) and *Fragments of an Autobiography* (1899).

MOSCHUS, *mosˈkus* (fl. 150 B.C.), Greek poet of Syracuse, was author of a short epic *Europa*. His works are generally printed along with those of Theocritus and Bion, and there is a fine prose translation of the three by Andrew Lang (1889).

MOSCICKI, Ignacy, *mosh-cheetsˈkee* (1867–1946), president of Poland, was born at Mier-zanow. An ardent patriot, he spent many years in Switzerland, where he became a chemist. He later returned to Poland, where he was a professor of Chemistry until 1926, when his friend Pilsudski made him president. In 1939 he fled to Rumania and then retired to Switzerland where he died.

MOSELEY, Henry Gwyn Jeffreys (1887–1915), English physicist, a lecturer under Rutherford at Manchester and later at Oxford, began research in radioactivity and determined by means of X-ray spectra the atomic numbers of the elements. His brilliant career was cut short at Gallipoli.

MOSER, (1) George Michael (1704–83), Swiss gold chaser and enameller, father of (2), coming early to London, became the head of his profession. A founder member of the Royal Academy, was elected the first keeper.

(2) **Mary** (?1744–1819), English flower painter, daughter of (1), was one of the founder members of the Royal Academy, and an intimate friend of the royal family.

MOSES (Heb. *Môsheh*) (15th–13th cent. B.C.), Hebrew prophet and lawgiver, according to the Pentateuch led the people of Israel out of Egypt by way of Sinai, Kadesh and Moab (where he died) towards the Holy Land. The Pentateuch used to be regarded as his work; but most modern critics agree that its historical portions, as well as most of the legislative documents, belong to a much later time. See Gressman, *Mose und seine Zeit* (1913), study by M. Buber (1946), and M. Noth, *A History of Israel* (1960).

MOSES, Anna Mary, known as **Grandma Moses** (1860–1961), American primitive artist, born in Washington County, N.Y. She began to paint at about the age of seventy-five, mainly country scenes remem-bered from her childhood—' old timey things . . . all from memory '. From her first show in New York in 1940, she had great popular success in the United States. See her *My Life's History* (1952).

MOSHEIM, Johann Lorenz von, *mōsˈhīm* (1694–1755), German theologian, born at Lübeck, in 1723 became professor of Theology at Helmstedt, and in 1747 at Göttingen. His *Institutiones Historiae Ecclesiasticae* (1726; new ed. 1755) proved him, in Gibbon's phrase, ' full, rational correct, and moderate', and was translated into English. See Life by K. Heussi (1960).

MOSLEY, Sir Oswald Ernald, 6th Bart. (1896–), English politician, successively Conservative, Independent and Labour M.P., was a member of the 1929 Labour government. He later resigned and became leader of the British Union of Fascists. Detained under the Defence Regulations during World War II, he founded a new 'Union' Movement in 1948. His vision of a politically and economically united Europe is embodied in his *Europe: Faith and Plan* (1958). He married the Hon. Diana Mitford in 1936. See study by J. Drennan (1934).

MOSSADEGH, Mohammed (1881–1967), Persian statesman, born in Tehran, held office in Persia in the 1920's, returned to politics in 1944, and directed his attack on the Anglo-Iranian Oil Co., which, by his Oil Nationalization Act of 1951 (in which year he became prime minister), he claimed to have expropriated. His government was overthrown by a Royalist uprising in 1953, and he was imprisoned. He was released in 1956.

MÖSSBAUER, Rudolf (1929–), American physicist, born in Munich, discovered the 'Mössbauer effect' concerning gamma radiation in crystals, and shared the 1961 Nobel prize with Hofstadter for research into atomic structure. Mössbauer has been professor of Experimental Physics at the Technische Hochschule, Munich, and visiting professor of physics at the Californian Institute of Technology since 1964.

MOSZKOWSKI, Moritz, *mosh-kof'skee* (1854–1925), Polish composer and pianist, born at Breslau, taught at the Kullak Academy, Berlin, and later lived in Paris. A prolific composer for piano and orchestra, he is now remembered almost solely for his lively *Spanish Dances.*

MOTHERWELL, William (1797–1835), Scottish journalist and poet, a native of Glasgow, from 1819 to 1829 sheriff-clerk depute of Renfrewshire, published *Minstrelsy, Ancient and Modern* (1819) and other verse collections. See Memoir prefixed to his *Poetical Remains* (1848).

MOTLEY, John Lothrop (1814–77), American historian and diplomat, was born in Dorchester, Mass., studied at Harvard and several German universities, and began a diplomatic career. He soon turned to literature, however, and ten years were spent on his *Rise of the Dutch Republic* (1856), which established his fame. This was continued in the *History of the United Netherlands* which appeared in 1860–69. In 1861–67 he was minister to Austria, in 1869–70 to Great Britain. His last work was *The Life and Death of John Barneveld*, a biography which is virtually a part of his main theme. See his Correspondence edited by G. W. Curtis (1888 and 1910); short Life by Prof. Jameson (1897); and study by C. Lynch (Washington, D.C., 1944).

MOTT, John R. (1865–1955), American Y.M.C.A. leader, born at Livingston Manor, New York, became known the world over by his work for the Young Men's Christian Associations, Student Volunteer Movement and World Missionary Conference. See

Lives by Matthews (1934) and Fisher (N.Y. 1953).

MOTTE, William de la (1775–1863), English painter, of Huguenot ancestry, was born at Weymouth. He became well-known for his watercolour landscapes and exhibited at the Royal Academy for many years.

MOTTEUX, Peter Anthony, *mo-tœ* (1660–1718), English playwright and translator, left Rouen for London after the revocation of the Edict of Nantes (1685) and after a time took up journalism. He is best known for his translations of Rabelais and *Don Quixote.* See Lives by Van Laun (1880), R. N. Cunningham (1933); bibliography by R. N. Cunningham (1933).

MOTTRAM, Ralph Hale (1883–1971), English novelist, born in Norwich, began his working life as a banker. Galsworthy is the main influence in his work, as is clearly seen in his first book, *Spanish Farm* (1924). See his autobiographical *Window Seat, or Life Observed* (1954).

MOULINS, Master of, *moo-li* (c. 1460–c. 1529), French artist whose principal work was the triptych in Moulins Cathedral of the *Virgin and Child*, and he is regarded as the most accomplished French artist of the time. The influence of Hugo van der Goes can be seen in his vividly coloured and realistic paintings, and some authorities identify him with Jean Perreal or Jean de Paris, court painter to Charles VIII.

MOUNTBATTEN, surname assumed in 1917 by (1) and members of the Battenberg family (q.v.) in Britain:

(1) **Prince Louis Alexander** (1854–1921), father of (2), married in 1884 the eldest daughter of the Princess Alice of Hesse and became Marquess of Milford Haven in 1917, having relinquished his German titles and taken the surname, Mountbatten. He was first sea lord (1912–14) and admiral of the Fleet (1921).

(2) **Louis (Francis Albert Victor Nicholas), 1st Earl Mountbatten of Burma** (1900–), British sea lord, the younger son of (1), educated at Osborne and Cambridge, entering the Royal Navy in 1913. He was commander of the 5th destroyer flotilla in 1939 and in 1942 was made chief of combined operations. Appointed C.-in-C. S.E. Asia, he saw Burma reconquered before presiding over the transfer of power in India as viceroy and governor-general. Service afloat in 1952 was followed by his appointment as first sea lord in 1955 and he was chief of the defence staff from 1959–65, when he became governor of the Isle of Wight. He was created an earl in 1947. See R. Murphy, *The Last Viceroy* (1948). He married in 1922 the Hon. **Edwina Cynthia Annette Ashley** (1901–1960), who rendered distinguished service particularly during the London 'Blitz' (1940–42) to the Red Cross and St John's Ambulance Brigade, of which she became superintendent-in-chief in 1942. As vicereine of India (1947) her work in social welfare brought her the friendship of Gandhi. She died suddenly while on an official tour in Borneo. See M. Masson, *Edwina* (1958).

(3) **Prince Philip.** See EDINBURGH, DUKE OF.

MOUNTEVANS, Edward Ratcliffe Garth

Russell Evans, 1st Baron (1881–1957), British admiral, educated at Merchant Taylors' School, entered the Royal Navy in 1897. In 1900–04 he was second-in-command to Scott's Antarctic expedition. In the 1914–18 war he fought at Jutland, and in command of H.M.S. *Broke*—in company with Commander Peck—he scored an outstanding victory over four German destroyers. In 1929 he was appointed rear admiral commanding the Royal Australian Navy, subsequently serving as C.-in-C. Africa Station. Recalled in 1939, he assumed the post of London regional commissioner. He was made a baron in 1945. See his *Keeping the Seas* (1920) and *South with Scott* (1921).

MOUSSORGSKY, Modest Petrovich (1835–1881), Russian composer, born at Karevo (Pskov), was educated for the army but resigned his commission in 1858 after the onset of a nervous disorder and began the serious study of music under Balakirev. A member of the Glinka-inspired nationalist group in St Petersburg, which included Dargomizhsky and Rimsky-Korsakov, Moussorgsky first made a name with his songs, among them the well-known setting of Goethe's satirical ' Song of the Flea ' (1879); but his great masterpiece is the opera *Boris Godunov*, first performed at St Petersburg in 1874; his piano suite *Pictures from an Exhibition* (1874) has also kept a firm place in the concert repertoire. Other operas and large-scale works remained uncompleted as the composer sank into the chronic alcoholism which hastened his early death. His friend Rimsky-Korsakov undertook the task of musical executor, arranged or completed many of his unfinished works and rearranged some of the finished ones, sometimes to the detriment of their robust individuality. See studies by von Riesemann (1935) and Calvacoressi (1946).

MOYNIHAN, (1) Berkeley George Andrew, 1st Baron Moynihan of Leeds (1865–1936), an outstandingly skilful and bold English operating surgeon, was born in Malta. He held various posts at the Leeds General Infirmary, specializing in the techniques of abdominal, gastric and pancreatic operations. The driving impulse of his life was the promotion of scientific surgery, and he set out his doctrine in his *Abdominal Operations* (1905). He formed the Moynihan Chirurgical Club, was active in starting the Association of Surgeons of Great Britain and Ireland, and was also a leader of the movement to found the *British Journal of Surgery*. He was president of the Royal College of Surgeons from 1926 to 1932. Knighted in 1912, he was created a baronet in 1922, and raised to the peerage in 1929.

(2) **Rodrigo** (1910–), English painter, studied at the Slade School, and joined the London Group in 1933. From 1943 to 1944 he was an official war artist, and was professor of Painting at the Royal College of Art 1948–57. Most of his works are of an Impressionist nature, with soft tones (e.g., his portrait of Queen Elizabeth II as *Princess Elizabeth*), but he has now changed to non-figurative painting—of equal sensitivity. Elected R.A. in 1954, he resigned in 1957.

MOZART, Wolfgang Amadeus Chrysostom, *mō′tsahrt* (1756–91), Austrian composer, the younger child of Leopold Mozart, *kapellmeister* to the Archbishop of Salzburg, where he was born. He made his first professional tour through Europe when he was six years old. Other tours followed and a period of study in Italy, and in 1781 Mozart settled in Vienna as *konzertmeister* to the Archbishop, who had moved thither from Salzburg. He was badly treated, however, and resigned when his employer left the city. He married Constanze Weber, cousin of the composer, who was a charming wife but a wretched manager; and debts and difficulties increased. The lively opera *Die Entführung aus dem Serail* paved the way for the *Marriage of Figaro* (1786), which created a furore. The extraordinary success of *Don Giovanni* (1787) made it impossible for the court still to overlook the composer, and he was appointed chamber musician to Joseph II, at a salary of £80 a year. The emperor ordered a new opera, *Così fan tutte*, but owing to his death and the indifference to art of Leopold II, the composer reaped no pecuniary benefit. His carelessness, improvidence, and senseless generosity overwhelmed him with endless embarrassments. In 1791 Schikaneder, a theatre manager, begged of him a new opera on an incoherent subject of his own, *The Magic Flute*, which, at first coldly received, ended by making Schikaneder's fortune. In writing the noble Requiem Mass commissioned for Count Walsegg, he felt he was writing his own requiem; and he caught typhus and died before it was finished. He was buried in the common ground of St Mark's Churchyard. Mozart wrote more than 600 compositions; he left no branch of the art unenriched by his genius. Gifted with an inexhaustible vein of the richest, purest melody, he is at once the glory and the reproach of the Italian school; for, while he surpasses all Italians on their own chosen ground, his strict training in the German school placed at his service wonderful resources of harmony and instrumentation. Of forty-one symphonies three hold preeminence—the C major (called the ' Jupiter '), G minor and E flat. The quartets are very beautiful and exceedingly original. His pianoforte sonatas and those for the violin and piano are few of them of great importance except in the development of musical form, but his piano concertos are brilliant. The complete works were indexed in 1862–64 by Ludwig Köchel (q.v.) (3rd ed. 1937) and individual compositions are often referred to by their ' Köchel number ' to avoid confusion. See Lives by Otto Jahn (1856–59; trans. 1882), Nohl (trans. 1877), Meinardus (1882), Holmes (2nd ed. 1878), Wyzewa and G. de Saint-Foix (5 vols. Paris 1912–46); books by Dent (2nd ed. 1947), Hussey (1927), W. J. Turner (1938), A. Einstein (1956 ed.); the Correspondence edited by Nohl (2nd ed. 1877), *Letters of Mozart and his Family*, ed. and trans. Emily Anderson (1938).

MOZLEY, (1) James Bowling (1813–78), English theologian, brother of (2), born at Gainsborough, became a fellow of Magdalen. He took an active part in the Oxford Movement and was appointed in 1871 regius professor of Divinity at Oxford. He wrote on predestination, baptism and miracles, and published volumes of sermons. See his *Letters* (1884), and Liddon's *Pusey* (1893–1894).

(2) **Thomas** (1806–93), English divine and journalist brother of (1), an enthusiastic tractarian, wrote much in support of the movement, and later became a leader writer for *The Times*. See his *Reminiscences of Oriel College* (1882) and *Reminiscences Chiefly of Towns* (1885).

MUDIE, Charles Edward (1816–90), English bookseller, was born at Chelsea, and after some experience as a bookseller, established in 1842 his library, which became a well-known institution.

MUFTI OF JERUSALEM. See HUSSEINI.

MUGGLETON, Lodowick (1609–98), English Sectarian, a London Puritan tailor, who, with his cousin, John Reeve (1608–58), founded about 1651 the sect of Muggletonians. See Jessopp's *Coming of the Friars* (1888).

MUIR, (1) **Edwin** (1887–1959), Scottish poet, was born in Orkney, the son of crofter folk who, when he was fourteen, migrated to Glasgow, where he suffered the period of drab existence described in his *The Story and the Fable* (1940), revised as *An Autobiography* in 1954. He moved from job to job, but spent much time reading Nietzsche, Shaw, Ibsen, Heine and Blatchford, and he interested himself in left-wing politics. In course of time his material circumstances improved; in 1919 he married Willa Anderson, with whom he migrated to Prague, where the couple collaborated in translations of Kafka and Feuchtwanger, and where he published his first volume of verse in 1925. Returning to Scotland on the outbreak of World War II, he joined the staff of the British Council in 1942, and in 1945 returned to Prague as first director of the British Institute there, which was closed after the Communist coup of 1948. He then took over the British Institute in Rome until 1950, when he was appointed warden of the adult education college at Newbattle Abbey, Midlothian. After a year as Eliot Norton Professor of Poetry at Harvard (1955–56), he retired to Swaffham Prior near Cambridge, where he died. His verses appeared in eight slim volumes—*First Poems* (1925), *Chorus of the Newly Dead* (1926, omitted from *Collected Poems*), *Variations on a Time Theme* (1934), *Journeys and Places* (1937), *The Narrow Place* (1943), *The Voyage* (1946), *The Labyrinth* (1949), *New Poems* (1949–51) and finally *Collected Poems* (1952). Other poems appeared in *The Listener* and other periodicals later. Muir's poetry springs organically from the archetypal world, but the landscape of his vision is that of his native Orkney which quickened in his mind the belief that our life is lived on two planes, the actual and the fabulous. Without obvious virtuosity as a poet (his early poetry has no distinction of language or metre) he is able to depict this double vision in a singularly vivid manner. His later poetry shows a considerable advance in virtuosity without ever compromising his native simplicity, so that he was able to

employ successfully various lyrical and elegiac forms in such a way as to suggest the 17th rather than the 20th century. Muir's critical work includes a controversial study of John Knox, *Scott and Scotland*, *Essays on Literature and Society* and *Structure of the Novel*. See J. C. Hall's introduction to *Collected Poems* (1952), and *Belonging* (1968), a memoir by Willa Muir.

(2) **John** (1810–82), Scottish Sanskrit scholar, brother of (4), was born in Glasgow, and after spending twenty-five years in the East India Company's Civil Service in Bengal, settled in Edinburgh, where he founded a chair of Sanskrit. His great work was his *Original Sanskrit Texts* (5 vols. 1858–70; 2nd ed. 1868–73). Another book is *Metrical Translations from Sanskrit Writers* (1878).

(3) **Thomas** (1765–99), Scottish politician, born in Glasgow, advocated parliamentary reform, was transported for sedition to Botany Bay, escaped in 1796, but died in France of a wound received (1796) on a Spanish frigate in a fight with British vessels. See Life by G. Pratt-Insh (1949).

(4) **Sir William** (1819–1905), Anglo-Indian administrator and scholar, brother of (2), joined the Bengal Civil Service, and became foreign secretary to the Indian government in 1865. He held other high offices in India and from 1885 to 1902 was principal of Edinburgh University. His works include a *Life of Mahomet* (4 vols. 1858–61), *The Caliphate* (new ed. 1915), *The Corân* (1878).

MUIRHEAD, (1) **John Henry** (1855–1940), Scottish Idealist philosopher, born in Glasgow, editor of the well-known *Library of Philosophy* from 1890, and professor of Mersey College, Birmingham (1897–1921), wrote *The Platonic Tradition in Anglo-Saxon Philosophy* (1931), a Life and study of Caird, with Sir H. Jones (1921), *Bernard Bosanquet and his Friends* (1935) and other works from a neo-Platonist standpoint. See Autobiography, ed. J. W. Harvey (1942).

(2) **(Litellus) Russell** (1896–   ), British editor and traveller, educated at University College School and Christ's College, Cambridge, in 1930 became editor of the ' Blue Guides ' to Europe, his other editorial work including scientific journals and the *Penguin* guides to England and Wales (1938–49). The author of numerous travel books and articles, he has broadcast on topographical subjects.

MUKADDASI (fl. 967–985), Arab geographer, born at Jerusalem, travelled much and described Moslem lands in a work published in A.D. 985. His works were edited by G. S. A Ranking and R. F. Azoo (Calcutta 1897–1901).

MULCASTER, Richard (c. 1530–1611), English educationist, a native of Cumberland and a brilliant Greek and Oriental scholar, was one of the great Elizabethan schoolmasters, his ideas on education being well in advance of his time. His *Positions* (1581) was re-edited by Quick in 1888, with a biography. See Life by T. Klahr (1893) and *Educational Writings* ed. J. Oliphant (1903).

MULHALL, Michael George (1836–1900), Irish writer on statistics, was born in Dublin, and went to Buenos Aires, where he founded an English newspaper. His *Dictionary of Statistics* was published in 1883 (4th ed. 1899).

MULLER, Hermann Joseph (1890–1967), American biologist, born in New York, held academic appointments in Moscow (1933–37), Edinburgh (1938–40) and Indiana (from 1945), and was one of the great authorities on genes. He was awarded the Nobel prize for physiology in 1946.

MÜLLER, (1) Sir Ferdinand (1825–96), German-Australian botanist, born at Rostock, emigrated to Australia in 1847, and was director of Melbourne Botanic Gardens 1857–73. He introduced the blue gum tree into America, Europe and Africa. See Life by M. Willis (Sydney 1949).

(2) **Franz Joseph, Baron von Reichenstein** (1740–1825), Austrian chemist and mineralogist, in 1783 discovered a new metal which Klaproth (q.v.) named tellurium.

(3) **Friedrich Max** (1823–1900), Anglo-German philologist and orientalist, was born at Dessau, where his father, Wilhelm Müller (1794–1827), lyric poet, was ducal librarian. He studied at Dessau, Leipzig and Berlin, and took up the then novel subject of Sanskrit and its kindred sciences of philology and religion. In Paris he began (1845) to prepare an edition of the Rig-Veda, coming to England in 1846 to examine the MSS. and the East India Company commissioned him (1847) to edit it at their expense (1849–74). For a time Taylorian professor of Modern Languages at Oxford, he was in 1866 appointed professor there of Comparative Philology, a study he did more than any one else to promote in England. He became a naturalized British subject. Among his most popular works were *Lectures on the Science of Language* (1861–64), *Auld Lang Syne* (1898), *My Indian Friends* (1898), and he edited the *Sacred Books of the East* (51 vols. 1875 onwards). A foreign member of the French Institute, he was a knight of the *Ordre pour le mérite*, commander of the *Légion d'honneur* (1896), LL.D. of various universities, and P.C. (1896). His widow edited his *Life and Letters* (1902).

(4) **Fritz** (1821–97), German zoologist, brother of (6), Darwin's ' prince of observers ', born near Erfurt, went with Blumenau to Brazil, studied butterflies, and advanced Darwinism with his *Für Darwin* (1864). See work by A. Möller (Jena 1915–31).

(5) **Georg** (1805–98), German-English preacher and philanthropist, was born at Kroppenstedt, studied at Halle, and came to London in 1829. Called to a Nonconformist chapel in Teignmouth, he abolished collections and depended on voluntary gifts. In 1836 he founded an Orphan House at Ashleydown, Bristol. See *Autobiography* (1905); *The Lord's Dealings with George Müller* (1837–56); Lives by A. T. Pierson (1899), and K. G. Sabiers (Los Angeles 1943); also his Diary (ed. Short, 1954).

(6) **Hermann** (1829–83), German botanist, brother of (4), born at Mühlberg, studied at Halle and Berlin, and wrote a classical book on insect pollination of flowers (1873).

(7) **Johann.** See REGIOMONTANUS.

(8) **Johannes** (1801–58), German physiologist, the founder of modern physiology, born at Coblenz, was professor of Physiology and Anatomy at Bonn and from 1833 at Berlin. His *Handbuch der Physiologie des Menschen* (1833–40; Eng. trans. 1840–49) exercised a great influence. He studied the nervous system and comparative anatomy. See Life by W. Haberling (Leipzig 1924).

(9) **Johannes von** (1752–1809), Swiss historian, was born at Schaffhausen, and studied at Göttingen. In 1774–80 he taught in Geneva, wrote his *Allgemeine Geschichte* (3 vols. 1810), and commenced his *Geschichte der schweizerischen Eidgenossenschaft* (5 vols. 1786–1808; new ed. 1826). He held posts at Cassel, Mainz and Vienna. At Berlin in 1804 he was installed as royal historiographer; and Napoleon appointed him (1807) secretary of state for Westphalia. See Lives by Monnard (French 1839), Thiersch (1881) and R. Henking (Stuttgart, 2 vols. 1910–18).

(10) **Julius** (1801–78), German theologian, brother of (11), was professor of Theology at Halle from 1839 and wrote *Der christliche Lehre von der Sünde* (1839; 7th ed. 1889; trans. 1868). See Life by Kähler (1878) and study by L. Schültze (Bremen 1879).

(11) **Karl Otfried** (1797–1840), German archaeologist, brother of (10), born at Brieg, in Silesia, became professor of Archaeology at Göttingen in 1819, and made valuable contributions to the scientific study of archaeology and mythology. His great work is *Geschichte hellenischer Stämme und Städte* (new ed. 1844); and other valuable works are *System of Mythology* (1825, trans. 1844), *Ancient Art* (1830; new ed. 1878; trans. 1847), and *History of the Literature of Ancient Greece* (1841; new ed. 1884; trans. 1846). See Memoirs by Lücke (1841), F. Ranke (1870), O. and E. Kern (1908).

(12) **Otto Frederick** (1730–84), Danish biologist, born in Copenhagen, was the first to describe diatoms and bring to notice the animal kingdom of *Infusoria*. He was the inventor of the naturalist's dredge.

(13) **Paul** (1899–1965), Swiss chemist, who in 1939 synthesized D.D.T. and demonstrated its insecticidal properties. He gained the Nobel prize for medicine for 1948.

(14) **William James** (1812–45) English painter, born at Bristol. His early landscapes dealt mainly with Gloucestershire and Wales. He later travelled abroad and produced many masterly sketches. See Life by N. Neal Solly (1875) and study by G. E. Bunt (1948).

MULLIKEN, Robert Sanderson (1896–   ), U.S. scientist, professor at Chicago University, won the Nobel prize for chemistry, 1966, for work on chemical bonds and the electronic structure of molecules.

MULOCK, Miss. See CRAIK (2).

MULREADY, William (1786–1863), Irish painter, a native of Ennis, studied at the Royal Academy, painting such subjects as *A Roadside Inn, Barber's Shop, Boys Fishing* (1813), &c. He was elected A.R.A. in 1815, and R.A. in 1816. He also worked at portrait painting and book illustration, and designed the ' Mulready envelope '. See Life by Stephens (1890).

MULTATULI. See DEKKER (1).

MUMFORD, Lewis (1895–   ), American author, editor and critic, a lecturer on social problems, was born at Flushing, Long Island. He wrote *The Story of Utopias* (1922), *The Brown Decades* (1931), *Faith for Living* (1940), *The Human Prospect* (1955), &c.

MUNCH, Edvard, *moongk* (1863–1944), Norwegian painter, born at Löten, studied at Oslo, travelled in Europe and finally settled in Norway in 1908. While in Paris, he came under the influence of Gauguin. He was obsessed by subjects such as death and love, and illustrated them in his characteristic Expressionist Symbolic style, using bright colours and a tortuously curved design, e.g., *The Scream* (1893). His engraved work was also important and influenced Die Brücke in Germany. See Life by F. B. Deknatel (1950), and studies by Moen (1956) and O. Benesch (1960).

MÜNCHHAUSEN, Karl Friedrich Hieronymus, Baron von (1720–97), German soldier, born at Bodenwerder, a member of an ancient Hanoverian house, proverbial as narrator of ridiculously exaggerated exploits, served in Russian campaigns against the Turks. A collection of marvellous stories attributed to him was first published in English as *Baron Munchausen's Narrative of his Marvellous Travels and Campaigns in Russia* (London 1785; final form, 1792). The best of it was written by **Rudolf Erich Raspe** (1737–94), a scholarly and versatile author who became professor of Archaeology and keeper of the gems and medals at Cassel. Found to be stealing and selling the medals, he fled to England, held a post in a Cornish mine, catalogued Tassie's collections in Edinburgh, as a mining expert swindled Sir John Sinclair (suggesting to Scott his Dousterswivel), and died of fever, skulking in Donegal. *Munchausen* is based partly on 16th-century German jokes, partly on hits at Bruce and other travellers. See Seccombe's edition (1895) and Life of Raspe by Carswell (1950).

MUNDAY, Anthony (1553–1633), English poet and playwright, was born in London. A stationer and actor, he wrote many poems and pamphlets and plays in collaboration. He reported on the activities of English Catholics in France and Italy and was pageant writer for London. See bibliography by S. A. Tannenbaum (N.Y. 1942) and Life by C. Turner (Berkeley, Cal., 1928).

MUNGO, St. See KENTIGERN.

MUNK, Kaj, born **Kaj Petersen,** *moongk* (1898–1944), Danish dramatist, priest and patriot, born in Maribo, Laaland, studied at Copenhagen, and as vicar of a small parish in Jutland, wrote essays, poems and notably plays, displaying his sincere faith and ardent patriotism. His first play was *En Idealist* (1928), and there followed *Ordet* (1932; ' The Word ') and *Han sidder ved smeltediglen* (1938; ' He sits by the melting-pot '). He became one of the spiritual leaders of the Danish resistance movement during the German occupation, and, taken away from home by German officers on the night of January 4, 1944, he was found murdered in a ditch near Silkeborg the following morning.

MUNKÁCSY or Lieb, Michael, *moon'kah-chi*

(1846–1900), Hungarian painter, born at Munkács, went as apprentice to Vienna, studied painting, and in 1872 settled in Paris. His best known pictures include *Christ before Pilate* (1881) and *Death of Mozart* (1884). See study by Waller (Los Angeles 1947).

MUNNINGS, Sir Alfred (1878–1959), English painter, was born in Suffolk, the son—like Constable—of a miller. A specialist in the painting of horses and sporting pictures, he became president of the Royal Academy (1944–49). His work is in many public galleries and he is well known for forthright criticism of modern art. See his *Autobiography* (3 vols. 1950–52), and studies by L. Lindsay (1942) and R. Pound (1962).

MUNRO, (1) Sir Hector, of Novar (1726–1805), Anglo-Indian general, was victor at the decisive battle of Buxar in Bihar, and in other hard-won Indian battles.

(2) **Hector Hugh,** pseud. Saki (1870–1916), British novelist and short-story writer, was born in Burma and came to London about 1900, becoming a successful journalist. He is best known for his short stories, humorous and macabre, which are highly individual, full of eccentric wit and unconventional situations. Collections of his stories are *Reginald* (1904), *The Chronicles of Clovis* (1911) and *Beasts and Superbeasts* (1914). His novels *The Unbearable Bassington* (1912) and *When William Came* (1913) show his gifts as a social satirist of his contemporary upper-class Edwardian world. Munro was killed on the French front during the war. See the biography by his sister in his *The Square Egg* (1924).

(3) **Hugh Andrew Johnstone** (1819–85), Scottish classical scholar, a native of Elgin, professor of Latin at Cambridge (1869–1872), his greatest achievement was an edition of Lucretius. See memoir by J. D. Duff in his translation of Lucretius (1908).

(4) **Neil** (1864–1930), Scottish novelist and journalist, was born at Inveraray and wrote *The Lost Pibroch* (1896), *John Splendid* (1898) and other romances, and edited the *Glasgow Evening News.* See his autobiography, *Brave Days* (1931).

(5) **Robert** (1835–1920), Scottish archaeologist, who, after practising as a doctor, retired and founded (1911) at Edinburgh a lectureship in Anthropology and Prehistoric Archaeology. He wrote *Lake-Dwellings of Scotland* (1882), *Lake-Dwellings of Europe* (1890), *Bosnia* (1896), *Prehistoric Problems* (1897), *Prehistoric Britain* (1914). See his *Autobiographic Sketch* (1921).

(6) **Sir Thomas** (1761–1827), Anglo-Indian general, born at Glasgow, served from 1780 as soldier and administrator in Madras and was governor from 1819. He promoted the education of the natives and championed their rights. See Lives by Gleig (1830), Bradshaw (1894) and P. R. Krishnaswami (Madras 1947).

MÜNSTER, Sebastian (1489–1552), German theologian and cosmographer, born at Ingelheim, became a Franciscan monk, but after the Reformation taught Hebrew and theology at Heidelberg, and from 1536 mathematics at Basel. He brought out a Hebrew Bible (1534–35), Hebrew and

Chaldee grammars, &c., and wrote a famous *Cosmographia* (1544). See Life by V. Hautsch (Leipzig 1898).

MUNTHE, Axel, *mun'té* (1857–1949), Swedish physician and writer, was born at Oskarshamn. He practised as a physician and psychiatrist in France and Italy, was Swedish court physician and retired to Capri, where he wrote his best-selling autobiography, *The Story of San Michele* (1929). See Life by G. L. Munthe (1953).

MÜNZER, Thomas, *mün'tsèr* (c. 1489–1525), German preacher and Anabaptist, born at Stolberg, studied theology, and in 1520 began to preach at Zwickau. His socialism and mystical doctrines soon brought him into collision with the authorities. After preaching widely he was in 1525 elected pastor of the Anabaptists of Mühlhausen, where his communistic ideas soon roused the whole country. But in May 1525 he was defeated at Frankenhausen, and executed a few days after. See Life and Letters, ed. D. H. Brandt (Jena 1933).

MURASAKI, Shikibu (978–c. 1031), Japanese authoress, wrote a remarkable novel, *Genji Monagatari, or The Tale of Genji* (trans. A. Waley, 1925–33). See A. S. Omori and D. Kochi, *Diaries of Court Ladies of Old Japan* (Tokyo 1935).

MURAT, *mü-rah*, (1) **Joachim** (1767–1815), French marshal and king of Naples, father of (2) and (3), born, an innkeeper's son, at La Bastide-Fortunière near Cahors, March 25, at the Revolution entered the army, and soon rose to be colonel. He served under Bonaparte in Italy and in Egypt, rose to be general of division (1799), returned with Bonaparte to France, and on 18th Brumaire dispersed the Council of Five Hundred at St Cloud. Bonaparte gave him his sister, Caroline, in marriage. In command of the cavalry at Marengo he covered himself with glory, and in 1801 was nominated governor of the Cisalpine Republic. He contributed not a little to the victories of Austerlitz (1805), Jena and Eylau. In 1806 the grand-duchy of Berg was bestowed upon him, and in 1808 he was proclaimed king of the Two Sicilies as Joachim Napoleon. He took possession of Naples, though the Bourbons, supported by Britain, retained Sicily, and won the hearts of his subjects. In the Russian expedition he commanded the cavalry, and indeed the army after Napoleon left it. He crushed the Austrians at Dresden (1813), fought at Leipzig, and concluded a treaty with Austria and a truce with the British admiral; but, on Napoleon's escape from Elba, he commenced war against Austria, and was twice defeated. With a few horsemen he fled to Naples, and thence to France. After Napoleon's final overthrow, he proceeded with a few followers to the coast of Calabria, and proclaimed himself king; but was taken, court-martialled, and shot, October 13, 1815. See books by Gallois (1828), Coletta (1821), Helfert (1878), Hilliard-Atteridge (1911), M. Dupont (Paris 1934) and J. Lucas-Dubreton (1944).

(2) **Napoléon Achille** (1801–47), French-American author, son of (1), settled in Florida, married a niece of Washington, and published a work on American government

(1833). See Life by A. H. Hanna (Norman Okla., 1946).

(3) **Napoléon Lucien Charles** (1803–78), French senator, son of (1), suffered reverses in fortune, but, returning to France after 1848, attached himself to Louis Napoleon, who in 1849 sent him as ambassador to Turin, and in 1852 made him a senator.

MURATORI, Lodovico Antonio, *moo-ra-tō'ree* (1672–1750), Italian historian, born near Modena, in 1695 was appointed Ambrosian librarian at Milan, and ducal librarian and archivist at Modena in 1700. He published *Rerum Italicarum Scriptores* (29 vols. fol. 1723–51), *Annali d'Italia* (12 vols. 1744–1749), and *Antiquitates Italica* (6 vols. 1738–42, containing the 'Muratorian Fragment', a canon of the New Testament books, apparently written by a contemporary of Irenaeus). In later years he was attacked by the Jesuits for teaching heresies, but found a protector in Pope Benedict XIV. See Lives by his nephew (1756), G. Bertoni (Rome 1926) and G. Cavazzutti (Turin 1939).

MURCHISON, Sir Roderick Impey (1792–1871), Scottish geologist, born at Tarradale, Ross-shire, served in Spain and Portugal, and, quitting the army in 1816, devoted himself to geology. His establishment of the Silurian system won him the Copley Medal and European fame, increased by his exposition of the Devonian, Permian and Laurentian systems. He explored parts of Germany, Poland and the Carpathians; and in 1840–45, with others, carried out a geological survey of the Russian empire. Struck with the resemblance between the Ural Mountains and Australian chains, Murchison in 1844 foreshadowed the discovery of gold in Australia. He was president of the British Association in 1846, and for many years of the Royal Geographical Society. In 1855 he was made director-general of the Geological Survey and director of the Royal School of Mines. His principal works were *The Silurian System* (1839) and *The Geology of Russia in Europe and the Urals* (1845; 2nd ed. 1853). See Life by Geikie (1875).

MURDOCH, Iris, *mœr'dok* (1919–), Irish novelist and philosopher, born in Dublin, was educated at Badminton School, Bristol, and Somerville College, Oxford, was an assistant-principal at the Treasury (1938–42) and served with U.N.R.R.A. (1944–46). In 1948 she was appointed fellow and tutor at St Anne's College, Oxford. A professional philosopher in the Moore-Wittgenstein tradition, which has no point of contact with French existentialism, she yet wrote an excellent study of Sartre (1953) and as a hobby took to novelwriting. *Under the Net* (1954), *Flight from the Enchanter* (1955), *The Sandcastle* (1957) combine philosophical speculations with fanciful, ironical and even shocking situations in which rootless intellectuals, amorous outsiders of postwar disillusionment, are depicted objectively, but with compassion. *The Bell* (1958), describing the tangle of human relationships within a small Anglican lay community, established her as an outstanding novelist, who without disturbing the genuine logical achievements of anti-metaphysical philosophizing, yet learnt to appreciate the value of a metaphysical basis for a self-discovered personal morality. Later works include *An Unofficial Rose* (1962), *The Red and the Green* (1965), *The Time of the Angels* (1966) and *The Nice and the Good* (1968). See her essay ' Metaphysics and Ethics ' in *Nature of Metaphysics*, ed. Pears (1957).

MURDOCK, William (1754–1839), Scottish engineer and inventor of coal gas, was born near Auchinleck. He worked with his father, a millwright, and then with Boulton & Watt of Birmingham, by whom he was sent to Cornwall to erect mining engines. At Redruth he constructed in 1784 the model of a high-pressure engine to run on wheels. He introduced labour-saving machinery, a new method of wheel rotation, an oscillating engine (1785), a steam-gun, &c.; and he also improved Watt's engine. His distillation of coal gas began at Redruth in 1792; successful experiments were made at Neath Abbey in 1796; but it was not till 1803 that the premises at Soho were lighted with gas. See *Life* by A. Murdoch (1892).

MURE, Sir William (1594–1657), Scottish poet, of Rowallan in Ayrshire, was wounded at Marston Moor, and wrote *The True Crucifixe for True Catholikes* (1629), a fine version of the Psalms (1639), &c. See his *Works*, ed. by W. Tough (2 vols. 1898).

MURET, Marc Antoine, *mü-ray* (1526–85), French humanist, born at Muret near Limoges, lectured on civil law in France, but later settled in Italy, edited Latin authors and wrote orations, poems, &c. See monograph by Dejob (Paris 1881).

MURFREE, Mary. See CRADDOCK.

MURGER, Henri, *mür-zhay* (1822–61), French writer, born in Paris, began life as a notary's clerk, and, giving himself to literature, led the life of privation and adventure described in his first and best novel, *Scènes de la vie de Bohème* (1845), the basis of Puccini's opera. During his later years he wrote slowly and fitfully in the intervals of dissipation. *Le Manchon de Francine* is one of the saddest short stories ever penned. Other prose works are *La Vie de jeunesse, Le Pays Latin*, &c. His poems, *Les Nuits d'hiver*, are graceful and often deeply pathetic; several were translated by Andrew Lang in his *Lays of old France*. See Lives by Montorgueil (1929), Moss and Marvel (1948).

MURILLO, Bartolomé Esteban, *moo-ree'lyō* (1618–82), Spanish painter, was born, of humble parentage, at Seville, where he learned to paint, and produced stiff and rough religious pictures for the fairs of Seville and for exportation to South America. At Madrid (1641), by favour of his townsman Velázquez, he was enabled to study the *chefs d'oeuvre* of Italian and Flemish art in the royal collections. In 1645 he returned to Seville and painted eleven remarkable pictures for the convent of San Francisco, became famous, and was soon the head of the school there. In 1648 he married a lady of fortune, and maintained a handsome establishment. He now passed from his first or ' cold ' style—dark with decided outlines— to his second or ' warm ' style, in which the drawing is softer and the colour improved. In 1656 he produced the first examples of his third or ' vaporous ' manner, the outlines vanishing in a misty blending of light and shade. The Academy of Seville was founded by him in 1660. After this came Murillo's most brilliant period; eight of the eleven pictures painted in 1661–74 for the almshouse of St Jorge are accounted his masterpieces. He executed some twenty pieces for the Capuchin Convent after 1675. He frequently chose the Immaculate Conception or Assumption of the Virgin as a subject, and treated them much alike; the *Conception* in the Louvre was bought (1852) at the sale of Marshal Soult's pictures for £24,000. In 1681 he fell from a scaffold when painting an altarpiece at Cadiz, and died at Seville, April 3. His pictures naturally fall into two great groups—scenes from low life, as gypsies and beggar children (mostly executed early in his life), and religious works. See books by E. E. Minor (1882), C. B. Curtis (1883), G. C. Williamson (1902), P. Lafond (Paris 1930).

MURPHY, (1) Arthur (1727–1805), Irish actor and playwright, born at Clomquin, Roscommon, was educated at St Omer. In 1752–74 he published the weekly *Gray's Inn Journal*, and so got to know Dr Johnson. By going on the stage he paid his debts, and entered Lincoln's Inn in 1757. In 1758 he produced *The Upholsterer*, a successful farce; in 1762 he was called to the bar, but continued to write for the stage. His translation of Tacitus (1793) is excellent; not so his *Essay on Johnson* and *Life of Garrick*. See Lives by Jesse Foot (1811) and H. H. Dunbar (N.Y. 1946).

(2) **William Parry** (1892–), American physician, taught for some years at Harvard and then in 1923 took up private practice in Boston. He made a special study of anaemia and with Minot (q.v.) first suggested the liver diet. They shared the Nobel prize for medicine (1934).

MURRAY, (1) Alexander (1775–1813), Scottish philologist, born, a shepherd's son, in Minnigaff parish, Kirkcudbright, acquired, while a shepherd, a mastery of the classics, the chief European tongues and Hebrew, and after 1794 studied at Edinburgh. In 1806 he became minister of Urr, in 1812 professor of Oriental Languages at Edinburgh. He left a *History of the European Languages* (with Life by Sir H. W. Moncrieff, 1823).

(2) **Charles** (1754–1821), Scottish actor and dramatist, son of (9), father of (13), trained as a surgeon, later took to the stage, where he was commended for the parts of old men. He is credited with one or two poor plays.

(3) **Charles** (1864–1941), Scottish poet, born in Aberdeenshire, trained as an engineer and had a successful career in South Africa, where in 1917 he was director of defence. His poems were written in the Aberdeenshire dialect and admirably portrayed country life and character at the turn of the century. His first collection, *Hamewith* (1900), was his best and most characteristic. It was followed by *A Sough o' War* (1917) and *In Country Places* (1920). See a memoir by C. Christie (Pretoria 1943).

(4) Sir David (1849–1933), Scottish painter, was born at Glasgow and educated for commerce, but instead became a painter noted for landscapes of Scotland, the Italian lakes, &c. He was elected R.A. in 1905 and knighted in 1918.

(5) Lord George (*c.* 1700–60), Scottish Jacobite general, son of the Duke of Atholl, took part in the Jacobite risings of 1715 and 1719 and was later pardoned. In 1745 he joined the Young Pretender, and was one of his generals. After Culloden he escaped abroad and died in Holland. See books by W. Duke (1927) and K. Tommason (1958).

(6) George Gilbert Aimé (1866–1957), classical scholar, author and lifelong Liberal, was born in Sydney, N.S.W. Arriving in England aged eleven, he went to the Merchant Taylors' School and Oxford. He was appointed professor of Greek at Glasgow University (1889) and regius professor of Greek at Oxford (1908). His work as a classical historian and translator of Greek dramatists brought him acclamation as ' the foremost Greek scholar of our time '. His celebrated verse translations of Greek plays, including *The Trojan Women, Bacchae, Medea* and *Electra*, were performed at London's Court Theatre from 1902. Many works on classics include *History of Ancient Greek Literature* (1897), *The Rise of the Greek Epic* (1907), *Five Stages of Greek Religion* (1913). He stood for parliament, unsuccessfully, six times. President of the League of Nations Union (1923–38), and first president of the United Nations Association General Council, he was awarded the O.M. in 1941. See his *Unfinished Autobiography* (1960), and Life by J. A. K. Thomson (1958).

(7) Sir James Augustus Henry (1837–1915), Scottish philologist and lexicographer, born at Denholm, was for many years master at Mill Hill school. His *Dialects of the Southern Counties of Scotland* (1873) established his reputation. The great work of his life, the editing of the Philological Society's New English Dictionary, was begun at Mill Hill (1879), and (barring supplements) completed (1928) at Oxford. Murray himself edited about half the work, but he created the organization and the inspiration for completing it. See Memoir by H. Bradley, *Proc. Brit. Acad.* (viii, 1917–18).

(8) Sir John (1841–1914), British marine zoologist, was born at Cobourg, Ontario, studied in Canada and at Edinburgh University, and after a voyage on a whaler, was appointed one of the naturalists to the *Challenger* Expedition (1872–76), and successively assistant editor and editor-in-chief (1882) of the *Reports*. He wrote a *Narrative* of the expedition and a report on deep-sea deposits, and published innumerable papers on oceanography and biology, fresh-water lakes, &c.

(9) Sir John (1715–77), Scottish Jacobite, father of (2), of Broughton, Peeblesshire, was Prince Charles Edward's secretary during the '45, but, captured after Culloden, saved his life by betraying his fellow Jacobites. He succeeded as baronet in 1770. See his *Memorials*, edited by Fitzroy Bell (Scot. Hist. Soc. 1898).

(10) John (1745–93), British publisher, originally McMurray, was born in Edinburgh, became an officer in the Royal Marines in 1762, but in 1768 bought Sandby's bookselling business in London, and published the *English Review*, Disraeli's *Curiosities of Literature*, &c. His son, John (1778–1843), who carried the business from Fleet Street to Albemarle Street, projected the *Quarterly Review* of which the first issue appeared in 1809. Byron received £20,000 for his works, Crabbe, Moore, Campbell and Irving being treated generously. His ' Family Library ' was begun in 1829, and he issued the travels of Mungo Park, Belzoni, Parry, Franklin, &c. His son, John Murray the third (1808–92), issued the works of Livingstone, Borrow, Darwin, Smiles, Smith's dictionaries, and *Handbooks for Travellers* (begun 1836). See Memoir (1919) by his son and successor, Sir John Murray (1851–1928; K.C.V.O. 1926), who absorbed Smith, Elder & Co., 1917, edited Gibbon's *Autobiography* and Byron's letters and began publication of the *Letters of Queen Victoria*. Sir John (1884–1967), his son, completed the publication of Queen Victoria's letters. See a history of the firm (1930), book by G. Paston (1932), and Smiles, *A Publisher and his Friends* (1891).

(11) John (1741–1815), Anglo-American divine, born in England, went to America and preached the doctrine of universal salvation and became known as the ' Father of American Universalism '. See his Autobiography (1816).

(12) Lindley (1745–1826), Anglo-American grammarian, born at Swatara, Pa., practised law, made a fortune during the War of Independence and then, for health reasons, retired to England and bought an estate near York. His *English Grammar*, long a standard (1795), was followed by *English Exercises*, the *English Reader*, and religious works. See his *Memoirs* (1826), and Life by W. H. Egle (N.Y. 1885).

(13) William Henry (1790–1852), Scottish actor-manager, son of (2), born at Bath, went to Edinburgh (1809), where he remained for over forty years as actor and manager. He was particularly associated with dramatizations of the Waverley novels.

MURRY, John Middleton (1889–1957), British writer and critic, born in Peckham, wrote some poetry and many volumes of essays and criticism which had a strong influence on the young intellectuals of the 'twenties. He was the husband of Katherine Mansfield and introduced her work in *The Adelphi*, of which he was editor from 1923 to 1948. He also produced posthumous selections from her letters and diaries, and a biography in 1932. He became a pacifist and was editor of *Peace News* from 1940 to 1946. Towards the end of his life he became interested in agriculture, and started a community farm in Norfolk. See Life by F. A. Lea (1959).

MUSAEUS, *moo-zee'us*, (1) Greek poet, reputed author of oracles, hymns, &c., of which we possess but a few doubtful fragments.

(2) (5th–6th cent. A.D.), Greek poet, wrote a beautiful little Greek poem *Hero and Leander*, which has been translated into many lan-

guages. See trans. by E. H. Blakeney (1935), F. L. Lucas (1949).

MUSA IBN NOSAIR (640–717), Arab general, conquered northern Africa in 699–709 and Spain in 712, fell under the displeasure of the Khalif of Damascus, and died in poverty in the Hejaz.

MUSÄUS, Johann Karl August, *moo-zay'oos* (1735–87), German writer, born at Jena, studied theology there, and in 1770 became professor at the Weimar gymnasium. His first book (1760) was a parody of Richardson's *Sir Charles Grandison*; in 1798 he satirized Lavater in *Physiognomische Reisen*. But his fame rests on his German popular tales, which professed, falsely, to be a collection taken down from the lips of old people. Their chief note is artificial naïveté, but they are a blending of satirical humour, quaint fancy and graceful writing. See Life by M. Müller (1867) and study by A. Ohlmer (Munich 1912).

MUSORGSKI. See MOUSSORGSKY.

MUSPRATT, James (1793–1886), British chemist, took part in the Peninsular War and then returned to his trade of druggist. He began manufacturing acids, &c., and greatly improved the methods of so doing. With Josias Gamble he was the founder of the chemical industry in St Helens.

MUSSCHENBROEK, Pieter van, *mœ'sěn-brook* (1692–1761), Dutch physicist, born at Leyden, where he studied and later became professor of Physics, invented the pyrometer and in 1746 discovered the principle of the Leyden jar.

MUSSET, Alfred de, *mü-say* (1810–57), French poet and dramatist, was born in Paris, December 11. After tentative study first at the law, then at medicine, he found he had a talent for writing and at eighteen published a translation of De Quincey's *Opium Eater*. His first collection of poems, *Contes d'Espagne et d'Italie* (1830), largely Byronic in outlook, won the approval of Victor Hugo (q.v.) who accepted him into his *Cénacle*, the inner shrine of militant Romanticism. But Musset had no real desire to commit himself to any particular cult; indeed he had already begun to poke gentle fun at the Movement, and had indicated that he wished to ' se débugotiser '. His first excursion into drama, *La Nuit vénitienne*, failed at the Odéon in 1830, and thenceforward he conceived an ' armchair theatre ' with plays intended for reading only. The first of these, *La Coupe et les lèvres* and *À quoi rêvent les jeunes filles*, together with the narrative poem *Namouna*, were published as *Spectacle dans un fauteuil* in 1832, and next year the tragi-comedies *André del Sarto* and *Les Caprices de Marianne* appeared in the *Revue des deux mondes*. Also among his *Comédies et proverbes*, as these pieces were called, are *Lorenzaccio* (1834), *On ne badine pas avec l'amour* (1836) and *Il ne faut jurer de rien* (1836). *Un Caprice*, published in 1837, and several of his other ' armchair ' plays were staged successfully more than ten years later, and thus reassured he wrote *On ne saurait penser de tout* (1849), *Carmosine* (1850) and *Bettine* (1851) for actual performance. Musset's dramatic work, much of

which is devoted to dissecting the anatomy of love between the sexes, is unique for originality, intensity, wit and variety. In 1833 Musset had met George Sand (q.v.), and there began the stormy love affair which coloured much of his work after that date. The pair set out to spend the winter together at Venice, but Musset became ill, George became capricious, and in April the poet returned alone, broken in health and sunk in depression. His *Nuits*, from *Nuit de mai* (1835) through *Nuit de décembre* (1835) and *Nuit d'août* (1836) to *Nuit d'octobre* (1837), trace the emotional upheaval of his love for George Sand from despair to final resignation. His autobiographical poem *Confessions d'un enfant du siècle* (1835) is a study of the prevalent attitude of mind—the *mal du siècle* —resulting from the aftermath of revolution and the unrest of the early years of the century; much of his work is tinged with this outlook, and his heroes, who are often amoral and charming at the same time, portray the consequent blend of hedonism and pessimism as seen in *Namouna*, *Rolla* and elsewhere. *L'Espoir en Dieu*, an expression of the soul's longing for certainty, is perhaps not altogether convincing. In 1838 Musset was appointed Home Office librarian; in 1852 he was elected to the Academy. He died of heart failure, probably exacerbated by high living. See Lives by Oliphant (1890), Séché (1907), Donnay (1915), Villiers (Paris 1939), van Tieghem (1945); for both sides of the love affair with George Sand see her *Elle et lui*, and his brother Paul's *Lui et elle*.

MUSSOLINI, Benito (1883–1945), Italian dictator, born a blacksmith's son, at Predappio, near Forlì, Romagna, edited the Socialist *Avanti*, but after serving in the First World War, founded the *Popolo d'Italia*, and organized the Fascisti as militant nationalists to defeat socialism. In October 1922 his black-shirts marched on Rome; and ' II Duce ' established himself as dictator by melodramatic means, including murder. He ruled forcefully and intolerantly, not without efficiency. Greece was bullied, the League of Nations flouted. The Vatican State was set up by the Lateran Treaty (1929). The Axis with Germany was formed. Franco was aided in Spain. With the annexation of Abyssinia (1936) and Albania (1939) to the Italian crown Mussolini's dream of a new Roman empire seemed to be coming true. At the most favourable moment (1940) he entered the second World War, and met with disaster everywhere. In 1943 his followers fell away and he resigned (July 25), was arrested, was rescued by German parachutists, and sought to regain what he had lost. On April 28, 1945, he and other Fascists were caught by Italians at Dongo on the Lake of Como, and, after some form of trial, shot, their bodies being exposed to insult in Como and in Milan, the old headquarters of Fascism. See his Autobiography (trans. 1928) and works by M. H. H. Macartney (1944), P. Saporiti (1947), R. Dabrowski (1956); I. Kirkpatrick (1964); and Rachele Mussolini, *My Life with Mussolini* (1959).

MUSSORGSKY. See MOUSSORGSKY.

MUSTAFA KEMAL ATATÜRK (1881–1938), Turkish general and statesman, born in Salonika, led the Turkish nationalist movement from 1909 and was a general in World War I. Elected president (1923–38), he was responsible for many reforms and for the modernization of Turkey. See Lives by H. C. Armstrong (1932), R. Brock (N.Y. 1954) and Kinross (1964).

MYERS, (1) Ernest James (1844–1921), English poet and translator, brother of (2), published several volumes of verse, translated Pindar, and collaborated in a translation of the *Iliad*.

(2) Frederic William Henry (1843–1901), English poet and essayist, the son of the Rev. Frederic Myers of Keswick (author of four series of *Catholic Thoughts*), was from 1872 a school inspector. He wrote poems (collected 1921), essays, *Wordsworth* (1881), and *Human Personality and its Survival of Bodily Death* (1903). He was one of the founders of the Society for Psychical Research. See memoir by Oliver Lodge and others (1901), A. C. Benson's *The Leaves of the Tree* (1911), and book by G. D. Cummings (1948).

MYLNE, (1) Robert (1734–1811), Scottish architect, born in Edinburgh, designed Blackfriars' Bridge (erected in 1769 and pulled down in 1868) and planned the Gloucester and Berkeley Ship Canal and the Eau Brink Cut for fen drainage at King's Lynn. His buildings, for example St Cecilia's Hall, Edinburgh (1763–65), show an elegance typical of the best late 18th-century work. Mylne was elected F.R.S. in 1767. See the monograph by A. E. Richardson (1955).

(2) or MILN, Walter (d. 1558), last Scottish Protestant martyr, while on a visit to Germany became imbued with the doctrines of the Reformation, and later as priest of Lunan in Angus was denounced for heresy. Condemned by Cardinal Beaton to be burnt wherever he might be found, he fled the country, but after the cardinal's death he mistakenly thought it safe to return. Taken prisoner at Dysart, he was tried at St Andrews and although by this time over eighty years old was condemned to the stake.

MYRON (fl. 450 B.C.), Greek sculptor. A contemporary of Phidias, he worked in bronze and is known for the celebrated *Discobolos*. See study by P. E. Arias (Florence 1940).

MYTENS, Daniel, mī'tens (c. 1590–1642), Flemish portrait-painter, born at The Hague, he worked for James I and Charles I, who made him 'King's painter'. He painted portraits of many notable persons of the time. See work by C. H. Collins (1912).

N

NABOKOV, Vladimir (1899–), Russian-born American author, was born and educated in St Petersburg, studied at Trinity College, Cambridge, and in 1940 settled in the United States, where he became a research fellow in entomology at Harvard, and in 1948 professor of Russian Literature at Cornell. A considerable Russian author, he established himself also as a novelist in English with *The Real Life of Sebastian Knight* (1941), *Bend Sinister* (1947), *Pnin* (1957) and a collection of his best short stories, *Nabokov's Dozen* (1959). But he is best known by his controversial novel *Lolita* (1955; in Britain 1959), which concerns the attachment of a middle-aged intellectual for a twelve-year-old girl. Nabokov coined the word 'nymphet' for a fledgling charmer of this type. See his autobiographical *Conclusive Evidence* (1950) and *Speak Memory* (1967); and study by A. Field (1968).

NACHTIGAL, Gustav, naкн'ti-gahl (1834–1885), German traveller, was born at Eichstedt, studied medicine, served as army surgeon, and in 1863 went to North Africa. He travelled across the Sahara from Tripoli to Cairo (1869–74) and in 1884 he went to annex Togoland, Cameroons and Angra Pequena for Germany, and died on the return journey off Cape Palmas. See his *Sahara and Sudan* (1879–89), and works by D. Berlin (1887), J. Weise (1914), H. Heuer (1927).

NADIR SHAH, the Conqueror (1688–1747), king of Persia, was born in Khorasan of a Turkish tribe, expelled the Afghan rulers of Persia and restored Tamasp to the throne. He defeated the Turks in 1731, imprisoned Tamasp, and elevated his infant son, Abbas III, to the throne in 1732. The death of this puppet in 1736 opened the way for Nadir himself, who resumed the war with the Turks, and ultimately was victorious. He also conquered Afghanistan and drove back the Uzbegs. Difficulties arose with the Great Mogul, and Nadir ravaged the north-west of India and took Delhi, with rich booty, including the Koh-i-nûr. He next reduced Bokhara and Khiva; but he was assassinated June 20. See Maynard's *Nadir Shah* (1885), and Lives by L. Lockhart (1938) and J. D. Fraser (Calcutta 1954).

NAEVIUS, Gnaeus (c. 264–194 B.C.), Roman poet and dramatist, was born, probably in Campania, about 264 B.C., and served in the first Punic war. A plebeian, he for thirty years satirized and lampooned the Roman nobles in his plays, and was compelled to withdraw from Rome, ultimately retiring to Utica in Africa, where he died in 194 B.C. Fragments of an epic, *De Bello Punico*, are extant. See Warmington (ed. and trans.) *Remains of Old Latin* (ii, 1936), and W. Beare, *The Roman Stage* (1950).

NÄGELI, Karl Wilhelm von, nay'gel-ee (1817–1891), Swiss botanist and physicist, professor at Munich (1858), was one of the early writers on evolution. He investigated the growth of cells and originated the micellar theory relating to the structure of starch grains, cell walls, &c. He died at Munich.

NAGY, Imre, *nod'y'* (1895–1958), Hungarian politician, born at Kaposvar, Hungary, was captured in the Austrian Army in the first World War, and sent to Siberia. At the Revolution he escaped, joined the Bolshevik forces and became a Soviet citizen in 1918. Back in Hungary in 1919 he had a minor post in the Béla Kun revolutionary government, but later fled to Russia, where he remained throughout the second World War. Returning with the Red Army, he became minister of agriculture in the provisional government, enforcing Communist land reforms. In 1947 he became speaker of the Hungarian Parliament, and in 1953 prime minister, introducing a 'new course' of milder political and economic control. In February 1955 the Rakosi régime removed him from office as a 'right deviationist'. He returned to the premiership in 1956 on Rakosi's downfall. When the revolution broke out in October 1956 he promised free elections and a Russian military withdrawal. When, in November, Soviet forces began to put down the revolution he appealed to the world for help, but was displaced by the Soviet puppet Janos Kadar and was later executed.

NAHUM (7th cent. B.C.), one of the twelve minor Hebrew prophets, who seems to have been an Israelite or Judaean who had been a captive in Nineveh, and wrote his prophecy between 663 and 612 B.C.

NAIDU, Sarojini, *née* Chattopadhyay, *nah'i-doo* (1879–1949), Indian poet and feminist, born at Hyderabad, was educated at Madras, London and Cambridge. Her verse (1905–1917) showed her mastery of the lyric form in English and was translated into many Indian languages. She then turned to national and feminist affairs. Associated with Gandhi, she was the first Indian woman to be chairman of the National Congress (1925), and with Gandhi took part in the Round Table Conference (1931). She was imprisoned for her part in the civil disobedience movement and later took part in the negotiations leading to independence. In 1947 she became governor of the United Provinces. As leader of the women's movement in India she did much to remove the barrier of purdah. See *Life* by R. R. Bhatnagar (Allahabad 1946).

NAIRNE, Carolina Oliphant, Baroness (1766–1845), Scottish song writer, was born at the 'auld hoose' of Gask in Perthshire, third daughter of its Jacobite laird. In 1806 she married her second cousin, Major William (1757–1830), who became sixth Lord Nairne. She lived at Edinburgh and, after her husband's death, in Ireland, then on the Continent. Her eighty-seven songs appeared first in *The Scottish Minstrel* (1821–24), and posthumously as *Lays from Strathearn*. Some of them are mere bowdlerizations of 'indelicate' favourites; but four at least are immortal—the 'Land o' the Leal' (*c.* 1798), 'Caller Herrin',' 'The Laird o' Cockpen', and 'The Auld Hoose'. See *Lives* by Rogers (1869), G. Henderson (1900); and Kington Oliphant's *Jacobite Lairds of Gask* (1870).

NAMIER, Sir Lewis Bernstein, *nay'mee-èr* (1888–1960), British historian, of Russian origin, was educated at Balliol College, and had a long and distinguished career, crowned with the professorship of Modern History at the University of Manchester from 1931 to 1952. His influence created a Namier School of history, in which the emphasis was on microscopic analysis of events and institutions, particularly Parliament, so as to reveal the entire motivation of the individuals involved in them. He compelled a 're-thinking' of history through his *Structure of Politics at the Accession of George III* (1929) and *England in the Age of the American Revolution*, Vol. I (1930). His followers have been thought by some critics, perhaps unjustly, to be making more ado about the trees than the wood, but there was no detracting from Namier's achievement. For a critical appraisal of the Namier school, see H. Butterfield, *George III and the Historians* (1957); for an appreciation, *Essays*, ed. Pares and Taylor (1956).

NANAK, *na'-* (1469–1538), founder of Sikhism, was born near Lahore. A Hindu by birth and belief, he fell under Moslem influence and denounced many Hindu practices as idolatrous. His doctrine, set out later in the *Adi-Granth*, sought a fusion of Brahmanism and Islam on the grounds that both were monotheistic, although Nanak's own ideas leaned rather towards pantheism.

NANA SAHIB, *nom de guerre* of Brahmin Dundhu Panth (*c.* 1820–*c.* 1859), Indian rebel, adopted son of the ex-peshwa of the Mahrattas, became known as the leader of the Indian Mutiny in 1857. He was disappointed that the peshwa's pension was not continued to himself, on the outbreak of the Mutiny was proclaimed peshwa, and perpetrated the massacres at Cawnpore. After the collapse of the rebellion he escaped into Nepal. He died probably after 1859.

NANSEN, Fridtjof (1861–1930), Norwegian explorer, was born near Oslo, and studied at the university there, as well as later at Naples. In 1882 he made a voyage into the Arctic regions in the sealer *Viking*, and on his return was made keeper of the natural history department of the museum at Bergen. In the summer of 1888 he made an adventurous journey across Greenland from east to west. He described it in *The First Crossing of Greenland* (trans. 1890). But his great achievement was the partial accomplishment of his scheme for reaching the North Pole by letting his ship get frozen into the ice north of Siberia and drift with a current setting towards Greenland. He started in the *Fram*, built for the purpose, in August 1893, reached the New Siberian islands in September, made fast to an ice floe, and drifted north to 84° 4' on March 3, 1895. There, accompanied by Johansen, he left the *Fram* and pushed across the ice, reaching the highest latitude till then attained, 86° 14' N., on April 7. The two wintered in Franz Josef Land. *Farthest North* (2 vols. 1897) recounts his adventures. Professor of Zoology (1897) and of Oceanography (1908) at Oslo, Nansen furthered the separation of Norway and Sweden, and was Norwegian ambassador in London (1906–08). He published *In Northern Mists* (1911), *Through Siberia* (1914), &c. In 1922 he got a

Nobel peace prize for Russian relief work and he did much for the League of Nations. See books by Sörenson (trans. 1933), Ristelhueber (Montreal 1944), Reynolds (1956) and Höyer (1958).

NAOROJI, Dadhabai, *now-rō'jee* (1825–1917), Indian politician, born at Bombay, became professor of Mathematics in Elphinstone College there, and a member of the Legislative Council; and in 1892–95 represented Finsbury in the House of Commons —the first Indian M.P., and was also president of the Indian National Congress. See Life by R. P. Masani (1939).

NAPIER, (1) Sir Charles (1786–1860), British admiral, born at Merchiston Hall near Falkirk, a cousin to the hero of Sind, went to sea at thirteen, received his first command in 1808, and later served as a volunteer in the Peninsular army. Commanding the *Thames* in 1811, he inflicted incredible damage upon the enemy in the Mediterranean. In 1814 he led the way in the ascent of the Potomac, and he took part in the operations against Baltimore. In command of the fleet of the young queen of Portugal, he defeated the Miguelite fleet and placed Donna Maria on the throne. In the war between the Porte and Mehemet Ali he stormed Sidon, defeated Ibrahim Pasha in Lebanon, attacked Acre, blockaded Alexandria, and concluded a convention with Mehemet Ali. A K.C.B., he commanded the Baltic fleet in the Russian war; but the capture of Bomarsund failed to realize expectations, and he was superseded. He twice sat in parliament, and until his death he laboured to reform the naval administration. See Lives by E. Napier (1862), Noel Williams (1917).

(2) Sir Charles James (1782–1853), British general, brother of (7), conqueror of Sind, was a descendant of Napier of Merchiston. He was born at Westminster, served in Ireland during the rebellion, in Portugal (1810), against the United States (1813), and in the storming of Cambrai (1815). In 1838 he was made K.C.B., and in 1841 was ordered to India to command in the war with Sind, and at the battle of Meeanee (1843) broke the power of the amirs. After another battle at Hyderabad, Napier was made governor. He gained the respect of the inhabitants, but was soon engaged in an acrimonious war of dispatches with the home authorities. In 1847 he returned to England, but was back in India before the close of the Sikh war. As commander-in-chief of the army in India, he quarrelled with Lord Dalhousie about military reform, and bade a final adieu to the East in 1851. See Lives by his brother (1857), W. Napier Bruce (1885), W. Butler (1890), R. N. Lawrence (1952) and H. T. Lambrick (1952).

(3) John (1550–1617), Scottish mathematician, the inventor of logarithms, was born at Merchiston Castle, Edinburgh, matriculated at St Andrews in 1563, travelled on the Continent, and settled down to a life of literary and scientific study. In 1593 he published his *Plaine Discouery of the whole Reuelation of Saint John*, which was translated into Dutch, French and German. He made a contract with Logan of Restalrig for the

discovery of treasure in Fast Castle (1594), devised warlike machines for defence against Philip of Spain, and recommended salt as a fertilizer of land. A strict Presbyterian, he was also a believer in astrology and divination. He described his famous invention of logarithms in *Mirifici Logarithmorum Canonis Descriptio* (1614), and the calculating apparatus called ' Napier's Bones ' in *Rabdologiae seu Numerationis per Virgulas libri duo* (1617); and two years later a second work on logarithms was published by his son Robert (new ed. by W. R. Macdonald, 1889). Napier's eldest son was raised to the peerage as Lord Napier in 1627, and the ninth Baron Napier in 1872 became Baron Ettrick also. See Lives by the Earl of Buchan (1787) and Mark Napier (1834), who also edited Napier's *Ars Logistica*, a system of arithmetic and algebra (1839); and the *Tercentenary Memorial Volume* (1916).

(4) Macvey (1776–1847), Scottish lawyer and editor, born at Glasgow, in 1799 became a writer to the signet in Edinburgh, in 1805 signet librarian (till 1837), and in 1824 first professor of Conveyancing. He edited the supplement to the fifth edition of the *Encyclopaedia Britannica* (1816–24), the seventh edition (1830–42) and from 1829 the *Edinburgh Review*. See *Correspondence* (1879).

(5) Robert (1791–1876), Scottish shipbuilder and engineer, born at Dumbarton, built the first four Cunard steamships and some of the earliest ironclad warships and helped to make the Clyde a great shipbuilding centre. See Life by J. Napier (1904).

(6) Robert Cornelis, 1st Baron Napier of Magdala (1810–90), British soldier, born at Colombo, Ceylon, was educated at Addiscombe, and entered the Bengal Engineers in 1826. He served in campaigns in India, and during the Indian Mutiny he distinguished himself at the siege of Lucknow, and was made K.C.B. He received the thanks of parliament for his services in the Chinese war of 1860 and for his brilliant conduct of the expedition in Abyssinia in 1868. In 1870 he became commander-in-chief in India and a member of the Indian Council, and was subsequently governor of Gibraltar, field-marshal, and constable of the Tower. See Life by his son (1927).

(7) Sir William Francis Patrick, K.C.B. (1785–1860), British soldier and military historian, brother of (2), served through the Peninsular campaign and retired from the army in 1819. He began writing and published his *History of the War in the Peninsula* (1828–40), *The Conquest of Scinde* (1845) and the Life of his brother (1857). See Lives by H. A. Bruce (1864), W. F. Butler (1890).

NAPOLEON I or **Napoleon Bonaparte** (1769–1821), second son of **Charles Bonaparte** (q.v.), assessor to the royal tribunal of Corsica, was born at Ajaccio, August 15. Granted free military education in France, he studied French at Autun before entering the military schools at Brienne (1779) and Paris (1784). In 1785 he was commissioned second-lieutenant of artillery in the regiment of la Fère, garrisoned at Valence. At Auxonne he saw the beginnings of the French Revolution, but, more concerned with Corsica than France, he went home on leave to organize a revolution and was temporarily struck off the army list for returning to his regiment late (1792). He was given command of the artillery at the siege of Toulon (1793) and was promoted general of brigade. On the fall of Robespierre Napoleon was arrested on a charge of conspiracy because of his friendship with the younger Robespierre, but the charges were not proven and he was released. In 1795 he helped to defeat supporters of the counter-Revolution in Paris and was then appointed commander of the Army of Italy (1796), in which rôle he was able to demonstrate his great military genius. Two days before his departure for Italy he married Joséphine, widow of General Vicomte de Beauharnais, who had been executed during the Reign of Terror. On arrival at Nice he was appalled by the poverty and indiscipline of the French army. Since his army was outnumbered by the combined Piedmontese-Austrian forces he determined to separate them. He finally routed the Piedmontese at Mondovi, after which Sardinia sued for peace, and the Austrians at Lodi, after which he entered Milan. He next broke through the Austrian centre and occupied the line of the Adige, taking Verona and Legnago from the neutral republic of Venice. Austria made attempts to recover Lombardy, but she was defeated at Arcola and Rivoli. When Napoleon's position in Italy was secured he advanced on Vienna, and reached Leoben in April 1797. Negotiations for a peace settlement with Austria commenced but progressed slowly as Austria hoped to benefit from the political crisis in France, where the moderates and royalists were gaining power on the legislative councils. Napoleon, however, despatched General Augerau to assist the Directory in disposing of their opponents by force. In October 1797 Austria signed the Treaty of Campo Formio, by which France obtained Belgium, the Ionian Islands and Lombardy, while Austria got Istria, Dalmatia and Venetia and engaged to try to get the left bank of the Rhine for France. The Directory, fearing Napoleon's power and ambition, hoped to keep him away from Paris by giving him command of the Army of England. But, realizing the folly of invading England while her fleet was supreme, he set out on an expedition to Egypt in the hope of damaging Britain's trade with India. He set sail in May 1798, captured Malta, and escaping the British fleet, arrived at Alexandria on June 30. He then twice defeated the Mamelukes and entered Cairo on July 24, but his position was endangered by the destruction of the French fleet on August 1 by Nelson at the battle of the Nile. He defeated the Turks at Mount Tabour but failed to capture St Jean d'Acre, defended by the British squadron under Sir Sidney Smith, and was obliged to return to Egypt. He defeated a Turkish army which had landed at Aboukir, but learning of French reverses in Italy and on the Rhine, he secretly embarked for France on August 22, 1799. Sieyès, one of the Directors, realizing the unpopularity and weakness of the government, was considering a *coup d'état* when Napoleon arrived. They coalesced, despite their distrust of each other, and the Revolution of 18th Brumaire followed (November 9, 1799), when Sieyès, Roger Ducos and Napoleon drew up a new constitution. Under it the executive was vested in three consuls, Napoleon, Cambacérès and Lebrun, of whom Napoleon was nominated first consul for ten years. Before embarking on military campaigns Napoleon had to improve the perilous state of the French treasury. He made plans to found the Bank of France, stabilize the franc and regulate the collection of taxes by employing paid officials. He also tried to improve the system of local government and the judicial system which had become very lax. Offers of peace negotiations were made to England and Austria but he was not surprised when these were rejected. While Masséna occupied the attention of the Austrian general Mélas in Piedmont Napoleon secretly collected an army, reached the plains of Italy, and occupied Milan. In June 1800 the Austrians were routed at Marengo. Napoleon returned to Paris to disprove the rumours about his defeat and death. Moreau's victory at Hohenlinden (1800) led to the signing of the Treaty of Luneville (February 1801) by which the French gains of the Campo Formio treaty were reaffirmed and increased. France's power in Europe was further consolidated by the Concordat with Rome by which Pope Pius VII recognized the French Republic and by the peace of Amiens with war-weary England (1802). By this treaty England was allowed to retain Ceylon and Trinidad but relinquished Egypt, Malta and the Cape of Good Hope; France agreed to evacuate Naples; the independence of Portugal and the Ionian Islands was recognized. Napoleon then continued his domestic reforms: he restored the church, realizing that many people, especially the peasants, felt the need of religion; he made an effort to improve secondary education; and he instituted the *Légion d'honneur*. He was elected first consul for life. Peace between England and France did not last long because Napoleon annexed Piedmont, occupied Parma and interfered in Swiss internal affairs and because Britain refused to give up Malta. Napoleon made vast preparations for the invasion of England, at the same time seizing Hanover. England sent help to the royalist conspirators led by Cadoudal, who were plotting against Napoleon's life, but Napoleon arrested the conspirators and rid himself of Moreau, his most dangerous rival, by accusing him of conspiring with the royalists. He also executed the Duc d'Enghien, a young Bourbon prince, although his connection with the conspirators was not proved. He assumed the hereditary title of emperor, May 18, 1804, because France did not want to be left without a rightful leader in the event of his death. In 1805 he found himself at war with Russia and Austria, as well as with England. Forced by England's naval supremacy to abandon the notion of invasion, he suddenly, in August 1805, led his armies from Boulogne to the Danube, leaving Villeneuve to face the English fleet. He succeeded in surprising the Austrians under Mack at Ulm and they surrendered (October 19), leaving him free to enter Vienna on November 13. On December 2 he inflicted a disastrous defeat on the Russians and Austrians at Austerlitz. The Holy Roman Empire came to an end, the Confederation of the Rhine was formed under French protection, and Napoleon then entered into negotiations for peace with Russia and England. Prussia, afraid that an Anglo-French alliance would mean the loss of Hanover to England, mobilized her army in August 1806; but Napoleon crushed her at Jena and Auerstadt on October 14. Russia, who had intervened, was defeated at Friedland, June 14, 1807. By the peace of Tilsit Prussia lost half her territory and Napoleon was now the arbiter of Europe. Knowing England's reliance on her trade he tried to cripple her by the Continental System, by which he ordered the European states under his control to boycott British goods. He sent an army under Junot to Portugal, who refused to adhere to the Continental System, another under Murat to Spain because he was uncertain of her loyalty. When he placed his brother Joseph on the throne many of the nobles and clergy rebelled against the French, while a British army, under Wellesley, landed in Portugal, defeated Junot at Vimeiro (1808) and forced him to evacuate Portugal under the terms of the Convention of Cintra. So began the Peninsular war which was to occupy a large part of the French army until 1813 when Wellington routed the French and forced them out of Spain. Meanwhile the Prussian reformer Stein was trying to rouse the Prussians to rebel against the French domination but Napoleon forced the government to dismiss him (1808). In 1809 Austria took advantage of the French troubles in Spain to declare war on France. Napoleon drove the Austrians out of Ratisbon, and entered Vienna, May 13, and won the battle of Wagram on July 5 and 6. Although resistance was kept up for a time in Tirol by the patriot Hofer, by the treaty of Schönbrunn (October 20, 1809) France obtained from Austria the Illyrian provinces, and a heavy money indemnity. In December Napoleon, desirous of an heir, divorced Joséphine, who was childless, and married, April 1, 1810, the Archduchess Marie Louise of Austria. A son was born on March 20, 1811. Still bent on the humiliation of England, he soon increased the stringency of the Continental System, and he annexed Holland and Westphalia. Russia opened its ports to neutral shipping and convinced Napoleon that the tsar was contemplating alliance with England. He decided to invade Russia and teach her a lesson. He narrowly defeated the Russians at Borodino (September 6) leaving him free to enter Moscow, which he found deserted and which was destroyed by the fires which broke out the next night. He was then forced to retreat from Moscow, his army hungry, encumbered by the sick and wounded and suffering from the effects of the Russian winter which he had underestimated. Only a mere fraction of the Grand Army that had set out for Russia reached Vilna. Napoleon hurried to Paris to raise new levies, stem the rising panic and belie rumours of his death.

Meanwhile the Prussian and Austrian contingents withdrew from the Grand Army. Prussia and Saxony allied with Russia, but Austria and the middle states doubted the ability of the allies to defeat Napoleon and disliked the idea of an alliance with Russia. Napoleon left Paris on April 15, 1813, moved on Leipzig, and won the battle of Lützen on May 2. He then followed the allies, beat them at Bautzen, May 20 and 21, and forced them to retire into Silesia. Austria then asked for concessions of territory; but he merely offered to concede Illyria to them and Austria joined the allies. Napoleon inflicted a crushing defeat on the Austrians near Dresden but part of the French army under Vandamme were forced to surrender at Kulm. In October he was defeated at Leipzig and led back the remnant of his army across the Rhine. The invasion of France followed the rejection of peace terms which deprived France of much of her territorial conquests. Napoleon won four battles in four days at Champaubert, Montmirail, Vauchamps and Montereau but benefited little from the battles of Craonne and Laon which followed. On March 30, 1814, the allies attacked Paris, and Marmont signed the capitulation of Paris. Napoleon fell back to Fontainebleau; but his position was desperate and Wellington had now led his army across the Pyrenees into France. The French marshals forced him to abdicate, first in favour of his son, then unconditionally (April 11). By the treaty of Fontainbleau he was given the sovereignty of Elba, allowed to retain the title of emperor, and awarded a revenue from the French government. The Bourbons in the person of Louis XVIII were restored to the throne of France, but their return was unpopular. The army was disgusted at their treatment by the king and also at the appointment to commands of émigrés who had fought against France, and alarm was caused by proposals to return national lands to the émigrés and the church. The coalition, too, broke up because of quarrels over territorial settlement, especially over Prussia. Napoleon hoped to take advantage of the situation and landed on the French coast on March 1, 1815. On the 20th he entered Paris, having been joined by the army. Europe had declared war against him but only a mixed force under Wellington in Belgium and a Prussian army under Blücher in the Rhine provinces were in the field. Napoleon's aim being to strike suddenly and then defeat each force separately, he occupied Charleroi and on June 16 defeated Blücher at Ligny. But not till next day did he send Grouchy to follow the retreating Prussians, thus enabling Blücher to move on to Wavre to join Wellington who had retired to Mont St Jean, while Grouchy was engaged with the Prussian rearguard only. After his defeat by Wellington and Blücher at Waterloo, Napoleon fled to Paris, abdicated on June 22, decided to throw himself on the mercy of England, and surrendered to Captain Maitland of the *Bellerophon* at Rochefort on July 15. He was banished by the British government to St Helena, where he died on May 5, 1821, of either liver disease or cancer of the stomach. The bibliography falls into three categories: firstly, books dealing with his career by writers more or less contemporary with him, such as Thiers and Jomini, and his generals, such as Masséna; secondly, books concerning his private life by contemporaries, such as Bourrienne (Eng. trans. 4 vols. 1893), Las Cases, and O'Meara; thirdly, modern works in a more critical spirit, such as Lanfrey's *Histoire de Napoléon I* (5 vols. 1867-75), Jung's *Bonaparte et son Temps* (1880-81), and books on him by Seeley (1885), Wolseley (1895), Sloane (1896-1897), Lavisse and Rambaud (1897), Rose (1902 *et seq.*), Fournier (trans. 1911), F. Masson (1893 *et seq.*), H. A. L. Fisher (1913), N. Young (1914-15), W. H. Hudson (1915), Dirault (1910-27, 1928, 1930), Bainville (1932), Lefebvre (1935), Geyl (1949), Savant (1958), Markham (1963). See, too, his *Correspondance* (33 vols. 1858-87); *Lettres inédites* (1898, 1903); and bibliographies by G. Davois (1909-12), F. M. N. Kircheisen (1908 *et seq.*).

NAPOLEON II (1811-32), king of Rome, Duke of Reichstadt, was Napoleon I's son by Marie Louise. See Lives by Bourgoing (Paris 1933), Derville (1934), Bibl (1935).

NAPOLEON III, Charles Louis Napoléon Bonaparte (1808-73), born at Paris, April 20, the third son of Louis Bonaparte (q.v.), King of Holland, was brought up at Geneva, Augsburg, and his mother's residence, the Swiss castle of Arenenberg on the Lake of Constance. He hastened with his elder brother Louis into Italy in 1831 to assist the Romagna in its revolt against pontifical rule, an expedition in which Louis perished of fever. On the death of the Duke of Reichstadt, only son of Napoleon I, in 1832, he became the head of the Napoleonic dynasty. He published in 1832-36 his *Rêveries politiques, Projet de constitution,* and *Considérations politiques et militaires sur la Suisse.* In 1836 he put his chances to a premature test by appearing among the military at Strasburg, was easily overpowered, and conveyed to America. He was recalled to Europe by his mother's last illness (1837); and when the French government demanded of Switzerland his expulsion he settled in London. In 1838 he published his *Idées napoléoniennes.* In 1840 he made at Boulogne a second and equally abortive attempt on the throne of France, and was condemned to perpetual imprisonment in the fortress of Ham. Here he continued his Bonapartist propaganda by writing *Aux mânes de l'empereur,* &c., and actually helped to edit the *Dictionnaire de la conversation.* After an imprisonment of more than five years he made his escape (May 25, 1846), and returned to England. The Revolution of February 1848 was a victory of the working-men, to whom some of his political theories were especially addressed; he hurried back to France as a virtual nominee of the *Fourth Estate,* or working-classes. Elected deputy for Paris and three other departments, he took his seat in the Constituent Assembly, June 13, 1848. On the 15th he resigned and left France. His quintuple election recalled him in September, and he commenced his candidature for the presidency; 5,562,834 votes were recorded for him, only 1,469,166

for General Cavaignac, his genuinely Republican competitor. On December 20 he took the oath of allegiance to the Republic. For a few days concord seemed established between the different political parties in the Assembly; but the beginning of 1849 witnessed the commencement of a struggle between the president and the majority of the Assembly. Then he committed the command of the army to those devoted to him, and established his supporters in posts of influence. He paraded as a protector of popular rights and of national prosperity; but, hampered by the National Assembly in his efforts to make his power perpetual, he threw off the mask of a constitutional president. On December 2, 1851, he, with the help of the military, dissolved the Constitution. Imprisonment, deportation, the bloody repression of popular rebellion, marked this black day's work. France appeared to acquiesce; for when the vote was taken on it in December, he was re-elected for ten years by 7,000,000 votes. The imperial title was assumed a year after the *coup d'état,* in accordance with another plebiscite. Political parties were either demoralized or broken. Napoleon III gagged the press, awed the *bourgeoisie,* and courted the clergy to win the peasantry. On January 29, 1853, he married Eugénie de Montijo (1826-1920), a Spanish countess, born at Granada. The Emperor now proclaimed the right of peoples to choose their own masters, availing himself of it in the annexation (1860) of Savoy and Nice to France, in his Mexican intervention, and in his handling of the Italian question. At home the price of bread was regulated, public works enriched the working-men, while others were undertaken to enhance in value the property of the peasantry. The complete remodelling of Paris under the direction of Baron Haussmann raised the value of house property. International exhibitions and treaties of commerce were a further inducement to internal peace. A brilliant foreign policy seemed to dawn on the Crimean war (1854-56); the campaign in Lombardy against Austria (1859), to which Napoleon was somewhat paradoxically encouraged by the murderous attack of Orsini on his person; and the expeditions to China (1857-60). In all those undertakings Napoleon had the support if not the co-operation of Great Britain. With Prussia his relations were very different. At the death of Morny in 1865 the controlling power of Napoleon's measures was almost spent. His *Vie de César,* written to extol his own methods of government, met with loud protests. Forewarned, Napoleon reorganized his army, set himself up more proudly as an arbiter in Europe, and took a more conciliatory attitude to liberalism. In 1869 his prime minister Rouher, an advocate of absolutism, was dismissed, and new men were called into power to liberalize the constitution. By another plebiscite the new parliamentary scheme was sanctioned by 7½ million votes (May 8, 1870). But 50,000 dissentient votes given by the army revealed an unsuspected source of danger. Anxious to rekindle its ardour, and ignorant of the corruption that existed in his ministry of war, he availed himself of a pretext—the scheme to place Leopold of Hohenzollern on the Spanish throne—to declare war against Prussia, July 15, 1870. By July 30, Prussia had 500,000 men in the field, while the French had with great exertion collected 270,000 by the beginning of August. The emperor assumed the command, but never got across the Rhine, and had to fight at a disadvantage within Alsace and Lorraine. The campaign opened with a small success at Saarbrücken (August 2), followed by the defeats of Weissenburg (August 4), Wörth and Spicheren (August 6). Napoleon had retired to Metz, and abandoned the chief command to Marshal Bazaine, whose escape from Metz was prevented by the defeats of Mars-la-Tour (August 16) and Gravelotte (August 18). Metz surrendered on October 27. Meanwhile a hastily organized force of 120,000 men under Marshal Macmahon was moved to the assistance of Bazaine. On reaching Sedan Macmahon found himself surrounded by the Germans, and on September 1 suffered a crushing defeat. Next day the emperor surrendered with 83,000 men. On September 4 the Second Empire was ended. Till the conclusion of peace he was confined at Wilhelmshöhe. In March 1871 he joined the ex-empress at Chislehurst, Kent, and resided there in exile till his death. His son, **Eugène Louis Jean Joseph** (1856–79), Prince Imperial, born March 16, was in the field with his father in 1870, but escaped to England, where he entered Woolwich Academy. He was killed (June 1) in the Zulu campaign of 1879. See Lives and studies of Napoleon III by B. Jerrold (4 vols. 1874–82), F. A. Simpson (1925), Baron d'Ambès (trans. 1912), Aubry (1933), Sencourt (1933), and Zeldin (1958); De la Gorce, *Histoire du Second Empire* (1894–1905); Ollivier, *L'Empire libéral* (1894–1913); Lives of the Prince Imperial by Hérisson (1890), Martinet (1895), Filon (1912), F. A. Simpson (1958); books on the Empress, her son, and the Court by E. Legge (1910–16), and studies by T. Zeldin (1958) and G. P. Gooch (1960).

NAPOLEON, Prince. See BONAPARTE.

NARES, Sir George Strong, *nayrz* (1831–1915), Scottish vice-admiral and explorer, born at Aberdeen, commanded the *Challenger* (1872–74) and the *Alert-Discovery* expedition (1875–76). See his *Voyage to the Polar Sea* (2 vols. 1878).

NARSES (*c.* A.D. 478–573), Byzantine statesman and Persian general, born in Armenia, rose in the imperial household at Constantinople to be keeper of the privy purse to Justinian. In 538 he was sent to Italy, but recalled the next year. In 552 Belisarius was recalled from Italy and Narses succeeded him, defeated the Ostrogoths, took possession of Rome, and completely extinguished the Gothic power in Italy. Justinian appointed him prefect of Italy in 554, and he administered its affairs with vigour and ability. But he was charged with avarice; and on Justinian's death the Romans complained to Justin, who deprived him in 567 of his office. See Diehl, *Justinian* (1901).

NARVÁEZ, Ramón María, *nahr-vah'ayth* (1800–68), Spanish general and statesman, born at Loja, defeated the Carlists in 1836, and took part in the insurrection against Espartero in 1840, but that failing, fled to France, where he was joined by Queen Christina, and set about those plots which overthrew Espartero in 1843. In 1844 he was made president of council and Duke of Valencia. His ministry was reactionary, but was overthrown in 1846. After a brief exile as special ambassador to France he was premier again several times, **NASH, (1) John** (1752–1835), English architect, born in London or Cardigan, trained as an architect, but after coming into a legacy retired to Wales. Having lost heavily by speculations in 1792, he resumed practice and gained a reputation by his country house designs. He came to the notice of the Prince of Wales, later the Prince Regent, and was engaged (1811–25) to plan the layout of the new Regent's Park and its approaches. He re-created Buckingham Palace from old Buckingham House, designed the Marble Arch which originally stood in front of it, and rebuilt Brighton Pavilion in oriental style. On the strength of a patent (1797) for improvements to the arches and piers of bridges he claimed much of the credit for introducing steel girders. The skilful use of terrain and landscape features in his layouts marks him as one of the greatest town planners. See Life by Summerson (2nd ed. 1950) and study by Davis (1960).

(2) **Paul** (1899–1946), English painter, born in London, was educated at St Paul's and the Slade School. He became an official war artist in 1917, and as such is remembered for his poignant *Menin Road* (1919). Developing a style which reduced form to bare essentials without losing the identity of the subject, he won renown as a landscape painter and also practised scene painting, commercial design, and book illustration. For a while he taught at the Royal College of Art. Experiments in a near abstract manner were followed by a phase of surrealism until, in 1939, he again filled the rôle of war artist, this time for the Air Ministry and the Ministry of Information, producing such pictures as *Battle of Britain* and *Totes Meer*. Shortly before his death he turned to a very individual style of flower painting. See his autobiography, *Outline* (1949), *Memorial Volume* (ed. Eates, 1948), and books by A. Bertram (1955) and G. F. W. Digby (1955).

(3) **Richard** (1674–1762), 'Beau Nash', English dandy, born at Swansea, educated at Carmarthen and Oxford, held a commission in the army, and in 1693 entered the Middle Temple. He then made a shifty living by gambling, but in 1704 became master of the ceremonies at Bath, where he conducted the public balls with a splendour never before witnessed. His reforms in manners, his influence in improving the streets and buildings and his leadership in fashion helped to transform Bath into a fashionable holiday centre. See Life by Goldsmith (1762), Gosse's *Gossip in a Library* (1891), study by L. Melville (1907) and Life by W. Connely (1955).

NASHE, Thomas (1567–1601), English dramatist and satirist, born at Lowestoft, studied for seven years at St John's College, Cambridge, travelled in France and Italy, and then went to London to earn a precarious living by his pen. His first work was the *Anatomie of Absurditie* (1589), perhaps written at Cambridge. He plunged into the Martin Marprelate controversy, giving expression to a talent for vituperation which never left him. *Pierce Penilesse, his Supplication to the Divell* (1592) began the series of attacks on the Harveys (Richard Harvey had criticized Nashe's preface to Greene's *Menaphon*) which culminated in *Have with you to Saffron Walden* (1596), against Gabriel Harvey who had by then assailed Greene's memory in *Foure Letters*. In 1599 the controversy was suppressed by the Archbishop of Canterbury. Nashe's satirical masque *Summer's Last Will and Testament* (1592) contains the well-known song ' Spring the sweet Spring is the year's pleasant king '. *The Unfortunate Traveller* (1594) is a picaresque tale, one of the earliest of its kind. After Marlowe's death, Nashe prepared his unfinished tragedy *Dido* (1596) for the stage. His own play *The Isle of Dogs* (1597), now lost, drew such attention to abuses in the state that it was suppressed, the theatre closed, and the writer himself thrown into the Fleet prison. His last work was *Lenten Stuffe* (1599). See McKerrow's edition of works (1904–07, revised by F. P. Wilson, 1958) and study by E. G. Harman (1923).

NASMITH, David (1799–1839). Scottish philanthropist, born in Glasgow, founded the city missions in various cities in Europe and America, and other benevolent associations. See memoir by J. Campbell.

NASMYTH, *nay'smith*, (1) **Alexander** (1758–1840), Scottish painter, father of (2) and (3), born in Edinburgh, was a pupil of Allan Ramsay and became a well-known portrait painter in Edinburgh, his portrait of Burns in the Scottish National Gallery being particularly famous. He later confined himself to landscape painting.

(2) **James** (1808–90), Scottish engineer, son of (1), born in Edinburgh, from boyhood he evinced a bent for mechanics; and in 1834 he started in business at Manchester, and in 1836 established at Patricroft the Bridgewater Foundry. His steam hammer was devised in 1839 for forging an enormous wrought-iron paddle-shaft, and in 1842 he found it at work at Le Creusot in France; it had been adapted from his own scheme-book. Nasmyth patented his invention, and it was adopted by the Admiralty in 1843. Among other of his inventions was a steam pile-driver. He published *Remarks on Tools and Machinery* (1858) and *The Moon* (1874). He died in London, May 7, 1890. See Autobiography, edited by Smiles (1883).

(3) **Patrick** (1787–1831), Scottish landscape painter, son of (1), born in Edinburgh, settled in England, painted many English scenes and became known as the ' English Hobbema '.

NASO. See OVID.

NASR-ED-DIN (1829–96), shah of Persia from 1848, visited England in 1873 and 1889, introduced European ideas into Persia, granted trade concessions to Britain and Russia, and was shot near Teheran by an assassin. He was succeeded by his second son, Muzzaffar-ed-Din. See selections from his *Diary*, ed. Hadiqa-i-Fasahar (1905).

NASSER, Gamal Abdel (1918–70), Egyptian political leader, president of the United Arab Republic, born in Alexandria, as an army officer with bitter experience of the mismanaged Palestine campaign of 1948, he became dissatisfied with the inefficiency and corruption of the Farouk régime, and founded the military Junta which encompassed its downfall. Chief power behind the *coup* in 1952, he was mainly responsible for the rise to power of General Neguib (q.v.), but tension between the two, as a result of Neguib's suspected dictatorial ambitions, culminated in Nasser's assumption of the premiership in April 1954 and of presidential powers in November 1954, when Neguib was deposed. Nasser was officially elected president in June 1956, and his almost immediate action in expropriating the Suez Canal led to a state of tension in the Middle East which culminated in Israel's invasion of the Sinai Peninsula. When Anglo-French forces intervened, widespread differences of opinion in Britain and elsewhere, coupled with veiled Russian threats, enabled Nasser to turn an abject military débâcle into a political victory. His aim was clearly now to build an Arab empire stretching across North Africa, the first step being the creation, by federation with Syria, of the United Arab Republic in February 1958. In March 1958 the Yemen and the U.A.R. formed the United Arab States. This was followed by a sustained effort to break up the Baghdad Pact and liquidate the remaining sovereign states in the Middle East, a policy which succeeded in Iraq, but was thwarted in Jordan and the Lebanon by the deployment of American and British forces. His plans for unity among the Arab states received a setback when Syria withdrew from the U.A.R. and when the union with the Yemen was dissolved (1961). In 1964, however, the U.A.R. formed joint Presidency Councils with Iraq and the Yemen. After the six-day Arab-Israeli war in June 1967, heavy losses on the Arab side led to Nasser's resignation but he was persuaded to withdraw it almost immediately.

NATION, Mrs Carry (1846–1911), American temperance agitator, after 1890 pursued a career of saloon wrecking (her weapon and emblem a hatchet) in Kansas and elsewhere, and suffered repeated imprisonments. See Asbury's *Life* (1930), Autobiography (1904).

NATTA, Guilio (1903–), Italian chemist, was a professor at Pavia, Rome and Turin, and from 1939 held the chair of Industrial Chemistry at Milan Institute of Technology. With Karl Ziegler, he was awarded the Nobel prize for chemistry in 1963 for his researches on polymers which led to important developments in plastics and other industrial chemicals.

NATTIER, Jean Marc, *nat-yay* (1685–1766), French artist, was born and died in Paris. His father was a portrait painter, his mother the miniaturist Marie Courtois, and as the result of parental tuition he won the Academy prize at the age of fifteen. He executed historical pictures and portraits, including those of Peter the Great and the Empress Catherine, but after losing his money in the John Law (q.v.) financial crisis he took up the fashionable stereotyped style of court portraiture now labelled ' le portrait Nattier '.

NAUNDORF, Karl W. See LOUIS XVII.

NAUNTON, Sir Robert (1563–1635), English statesman and writer, born at Alderton, Suffolk, became public orator at Cambridge in 1594, travelled, entered parliament, and was secretary of state 1618–23. He wrote *Fragmenta Regalia* (1641), a sketch of Elizabeth's courtiers. See Memoirs (1814).

NAVARRO, Mme de. See ANDERSON (8).

NAVILLE, Henri Edouard, *na-veel* (.1844–1926), Swiss Egyptologist, born at Geneva, became professor of Egyptology there, excavated in Egypt for many years, edited the Book of the Dead, and wrote a number of books on Egypt.

NAYLER, James (c. 1617–60), English Quaker minister, born at Ardsley near Wakefield, served in the parliamentary army. Later he became a Quaker, gathered a band of disciples and was persecuted and imprisoned for blasphemy. See Lives by M. R. Brailsford (1927) and E. Fogelklou (Eng. trans. 1931).

NAZIANZEN. See GREGORY.

NAZIMOVA, Alla, *na-zim'ō-va* (1879–1945), Russian actress, born in the Crimea, she made her début in St Petersburg in 1904, and in 1905 appeared in New York as Hedda Gabler. In 1910 she took the 39th Street Theatre, rechristening it ' The Nazimova ', and became one of the most popular emotional actresses of her day. She had a successful period in films, her films including *The Brat, Camille, A Doll's House, The Red Lantern* and her own *Salome*, based on the Beardsley illustrations to Wilde's play. She specialized in the plays of Ibsen, Turgenev, Chehov and O'Neill.

NAZOR, Vladimir, *nas'or* (1876–1949), Croatian poet, born at Postire on the island of Brač, wrote lyrics and ballads as well as epic poems and dramatic works in a style approaching that of the Symbolists. His works include *Slav Legends* (1900), *Lirika* (1910), *Carmen Vitae,* an anthology (1922), and a diary of his experiences with the Yugoslav partisans in World War II.

NEAL, (1) Daniel (1678–1743), English clergyman and historian, born in London, in 1706 became an Independent minister there. He wrote a *History of New England* (1720) and the laborious and accurate *History of the Puritans* (1732–38; new ed., with Life by J. Toulmin, 1793).

(2) **John** (1793–1876), American writer, born of Quaker parentage at Falmouth (now Portland, Maine), in 1816 failed in business, and turned to law, supporting himself by his pen. He was one of the first Americans to write in the greater English magazines, and lived in England 1823–27. After his return he practised law, edited newspapers and lectured. See his autobiographical *Wandering Recollections of a* *Somewhat Busy Life* (1869), and Life by W. P. Daggett (1920).

NEALE, (1) Edward Vansittart (1810–92), English social reformer, born at Bath, graduated at Oxford, became a barrister, and from 1851 he was a pioneer Christian Socialist and an advocate of co-operation, devoting much time and money to the movement. See *Memorial* by H. Pitman (Manchester 1894).

(2) **John Mason, D.D.** (1818–66), English hymnologist, born in London, January 24, was a scholar of Trinity College, Cambridge, and from 1846 warden of Sackville College, East Grinstead, where he died, August 6. An advanced High Churchman, he was inhibited by his bishop 1849–63. He wrote many books on Church history, &c., but is remembered chiefly for his hymns, and many of his translations are cherished by all English-speaking Christendom. Among his best-known pieces are 'Jerusalem the Golden ' and ' O happy band of pilgrims '. See his *Collected Hymns* (1914); Life by E. A. Towle (1906).

NEANDER, Johann August Wilhelm, orig. **David Mendel,** *ne-an'der* (1789–1850), German church historian, born at Göttingen of Jewish parentage, in 1806 he renounced Judaism and changed his name. In 1813 he became professor of Church History at Berlin. Profoundly devotional, sympathetic, glad-hearted, profusely benevolent, he inspired universal reverence, and attracted students from all countries. He probably contributed more than any other to overthrow antihistorical Rationalism and dead Lutheran formalism. He wrote many books on church history, of which the best known is his *General History of the Christian Religion and Church* (Eng. trans. 9 vols. 1847–55). See studies by Schaff (1886), Wiegand (with bibliography, 1889), Schneider (1894).

NEARCHUS, *nee-ar'kus* (4th cent. B.C.), Macedonian general, was a native of Crete, who settled in Amphipolis during the reign of Philip, and became the companion of the young Alexander the Great. In 330 B.C. he was governor of Lycia; in 329 he joined Alexander in Bactria with a body of Greek mercenaries, and took part in the Indian campaigns. Having built a fleet on the Hydaspes (mod. Jhelum), Alexander gave Nearchus the command. He left the Indus in November 325, and, skirting the coast, reached Susa in February 324. His narrative is preserved in the *Indica* of Arrian.

NEBUCHADREZZAR II (d. 562 B.C.), king of Babylon, succeeded his father Nabopolassar in 605 B.C. During his reign of forty-three years he recovered the long-lost provinces of the kingdom, and once more made Babylon queen of nations. He not only restored the empire and rebuilt Babylon, but almost every temple throughout the land underwent restoration at his hands. Not a mound has been opened by explorers which has not contained bricks, cylinders or tablets inscribed with his name. In 597 he captured Jerusalem; and in 586 he destroyed the city, and removed most of the inhabitants to Chaldea.

NECKAM or Nequam, Alexander (1157–1217),

English scholar, born at St Albans on the same night as Richard I, was nursed by his mother along with the future king. Educated at St Albans and Paris (where he lectured), he returned to England to be schoolmaster at Dunstable. In 1213 he became Abbot of Cirencester. In his *De naturis rerum* and *De utensilibus* he was the first in Europe to describe the use of a magnetic needle by sailors.

NECKER, Jacques (1732–1804), French statesman and financier, born at Geneva, at fifteen went to Paris as a banker's clerk, and in 1762 established the London and Paris bank of Thellusson and Necker. In 1776 he was made director of the Treasury, and next year director-general of Finance. Some of his remedial measures were a boon to suffering France, but his most ambitious scheme—the establishment of provincial assemblies, one of whose functions should be the apportionment of taxes—proved a disastrous failure. His retrenchments were hateful to the queen, and his famous *Compte rendu* (1781) occasioned his dismissal. He retired to Geneva, but in 1787 returned to Paris; and when M. de Calonne cast doubt on the *Compte rendu*, he published a justification which drew upon him his banishment from Paris. Recalled to office in September 1788, he quickly made himself the popular hero by recommending the summoning of the States-General. But the successful banker quickly proved himself unfit to steer the ship of state amid the storms of revolution. On July 11 he received the royal command to leave France at once, but the fall of the Bastille three days later frightened the king into recalling him amid the wildest popular enthusiasm. But after spurning the help of Lafayette and Mirabeau, and leading the king to surrender his suspensive veto, he finally resigned, September 1790. He retired to his estate near Geneva where he died. His works were edited by his grandson (with Life prefixed, 1820–21). See also *Manuscrits de M. Necker*, published by his famous daughter, Mme de Staël (q.v.), in 1804; her *Vie privée de M. Necker* (1804); the *Mélanges* from his wife's papers (1798–1802), D'Haussonville's *Salon de Mme Necker* (trans. 1882), and Gambier-Parry's *Mme Necker* (1913); and Lives by E. Lavaquery (Paris 1933) and E. Chapuisat (1938).

NEFERTITI, -*tee'tee* (14th cent. B.C.), Egyptian queen, the consort of Akhnaton (q.v.), immortalized in the beautiful sculptured head found at Amarna in 1912, now in the Berlin museum.

NEGRETTI, Henry (1817–79), Italian-English optician, born at Como, came to London in 1829, and was partner with Joseph Warren Zambra from 1850.

NEGRI, Ada, *nay'gree* (1870–1945), Italian poet, born at Milan, became a teacher, wrote socialistic verse and short stories. See study by N. Podenanzi (Milan 1930).

NÉGUIB, Mohammed, *ne-geeb'* (1901–), Egyptian leader, was general of an army division when in July 1952 he carried out a *coup d'état* in Cairo which banished King Farouk and initiated the 'Egyptian Revolution'. Taking first the offices of commander-

in-chief and prime minister, he abolished the monarchy in 1953 and became president of the republic, but was deposed in 1954 and succeeded by Colonel Abdel Nasser (q.v.).

NEGUS, Francis (d. 1732), English soldier, a colonel who had served under Marlborough, he is reputed to have invented the drink 'negus' called after him.

NEHEMIAH (5th cent. B.C.), Jewish prophet, cupbearer to Artaxerxes Longimanus, who in 444 B.C. obtained full powers to act as governor-extraordinary of Judaea. He had the walls of Jerusalem rebuilt, and repopulated the city by drafts from the surrounding districts. We read of a second visit of Nehemiah to Jerusalem, twelve years afterwards, on which occasion he either initiated or renewed and completed certain reforms which henceforth were among the most characteristic features of post-exilic Judaism. The canonical Book of Nehemiah originally formed the closing chapters of the undivided work, Chronicles-Ezra-Nehemiah. Compare Sayce, *Introduction to Ezra, Nehemiah, and Esther* (3rd ed. 1889); the commentary of Bertheau-Ryssel (1887), and those of Keil (Eng. trans. 1873), and Rawlinson (*Speaker's Commentary*). See study by L. W. Batten (Edinburgh 1913).

NEHRU, *nay'roo*, family of distinguished Indian political leaders:

(1) **Jawaharlal** (1889–1964), Indian statesman, son of (2), was born at Allahabad. After an undistinguished career at Harrow School and Trinity College, Cambridge, where he took the natural sciences tripos, he read for the bar (Inner Temple 1912), returned home and served in the high court of Allahabad. A persistent vision of himself as an Indian Garibaldi made him become a member of the Indian Congress Committee in 1918 and brought him, if with scientific reservations, under the spell of Mahatma Gandhi. He was imprisoned in 1921 and spent 18 of the next 25 years in gaol. In 1928 he was elected president of the Indian National Congress, an office he often held afterwards. Although sympathetic to the Allied Cause in World War II, he, in common with other Congress Party leaders, did not cooperate and turned down the Cripps offer of dominion status for India made in 1942. But in 1947 when India achieved independence, Nehru became her first prime minister and minister of external affairs. As democratic leader of the first republic within the Commonwealth, he followed a policy of neutralism and peace-making during the Cold War, often acting as a go-between between the Great Powers. He committed India to a policy of industrialization, to a reorganization of its states on a linguistic basis and, although championing his people's claim to Kashmir, acted with restraint to bring this outstanding dispute with Pakistan to a peaceful solution. His many works include *Soviet Russia* (1929), *India and the World* (1936), *Independence and After* (1950) and an *Autobiography* (1936). See also a Life by F. Moraes (1956) and studies by D. E. Smith (1959) and V. Sheean (1960).

(2) **Motilal** (1861–1931), Indian nationalist

leader, lawyer and journalist, father of (1), became a follower of Gandhi in 1919, founded the *Independent* of Allahabad and became the first president of the reconstructed Indian National Congress. See J. Nehru's *Autobiography* (1936).

NEILSON, (1) **James Beaumont** (1792–1865), Scottish inventor, born at Shettleston, invented the hot-blast in iron manufacture and was foreman and manager of Glasgow gasworks 1817–47. See *Life* by T. B. Mackenzie (1928).

(2) **Julia** (1868–1957), English actress, was born in London. After a brilliant career at the Royal Academy of Music, she made her début at the Lyceum in 1888; her greatest success was as Rosalind in the record-breaking run of *As You Like It* (1896–98). She married Ellen Terry's brother **Fred** (1863–1933), who often appeared with her and who partnered her in management from 1900. Their children **Dennis** (1895–1932) and **Phyllis** (1892–   ) Neilson-Terry also became famous for their acting, the latter especially in the title rôle of *Trilby*, and for their productions.

NEKRASOV, **Nikolai Alexeievich** (1821–78), Russian lyrical poet of the Realistic school, was born near Vinitza, Podolia, and suffered great poverty before making his name as a singer of the social wrongs of the humble. His epic, *Who can be Happy and Free in Russia?*, was translated in 1917. See studies by N. L. Stepanov (1947), C. Corbet (1948).

NELSON, (1) **Horatio, Viscount Nelson** (1758–1805), born September 29 at Burnham Thorpe rectory, Norfolk, entered the navy in 1770. He made a voyage to the West Indies, served in the Arctic expedition of 1773, and afterwards in the East Indies, whence he returned invalided in September 1776. As lieutenant of the *Lowestoft* frigate (1777) he went to Jamaica, and in 1779 was posted to the *Hinchingbrook* frigate. In January 1780 he commanded the naval force in the expedition against San Juan; on the pestilential river his health again broke down. In 1781 he commissioned the *Albemarle*, and joined the squadron under Lord Hood in America. In 1784 he was appointed to the *Boreas* frigate for service in the West Indies, where he enforced the Navigation Act against the Americans. Here he married the widow of Dr Nisbet of Nevis; and in December 1787 he retired with his wife to Burnham Thorpe for five years. Appointed to the *Agamemnon* in 1793, he accompanied Lord Hood to the Mediterranean. When Toulon was given up to the allies Nelson was ordered to Naples. He was employed in the blockade of Corsica, and next year com-manded the naval brigade at the reduction of Bastia and of Calvi; here a blow from a bit of gravel, scattered by a shot, destroyed his right eye. In 1795 he was in Hotham's two victories outside Toulon. During 1796 with a small squadron in the Gulf of Genoa he commanded the road along the shore. When Spain concluded a treaty with France, and sent her fleet into the Mediterranean, Jervis found himself opposed by very superior forces, and retired ultimately to Lisbon. He

was determined that the Spanish fleet should not pass, and inflicted a signal defeat on it off Cape St Vincent, February 14, 1797. Nelson, now commodore, was in the rear of the line. In thwarting an attempt to reunite the two divisions of the Spanish fleet, he for nearly half an hour withstood the whole Spanish van. When the Spaniards fled, Nelson let his ship fall foul of the Spanish *San Nicolas*, which he boarded, and, leading his men across her deck to the *San Josef*, took possession of her also. Nelson was rewarded with the Cross of the Bath; and, promoted rear-admiral in July, was sent with an inadequate squadron to seize a richly-laden Spanish ship at Santa Cruz. The attack was made on the night of July 21; but the boats were repulsed with severe loss, and Nelson had his right elbow shattered by a grapeshot, and amputated. In March 1798 he hoisted his flag on the *Vanguard*, and was sent into the Mediterranean with a small squadron to watch the French. But the *Vanguard*, dismasted in a gale, was obliged to put into San Pietro to refit, while the French expedi-tion sailed to Egypt. On June 7 Nelson was reinforced by ten sail of the line; but his frigates had all parted company, and after a fruitless search he put into Syracuse, when he learned at last that they had gone to Egypt. Thither he followed, and on August 1 found them at anchor in Aboukir Bay. His fleet was numerically inferior, but the wind was blowing along the French line, so he concentrated his attack on the weather end. He thus captured or destroyed the whole fleet, with the exception of the two rearmost ships and two of the frigates, which fled. Nelson returned in triumph to Naples, the queen welcomed him with ardour, and Lady Hamilton (q.v.), the wife of the English ambassador, fell on his breast in a paroxysm of rapture. A woman of extreme beauty, winning manners and shady ante-cedents, she enslaved Nelson by her charms, and the two became bound by a liaison which only death severed. Nelson was raised to the peerage as Baron Nelson of the Nile, parlia-ment voted him a pension of £2000 a year, the East India Company awarded him £10,000 and the king of Naples conferred on him the title of Duke of Bronte, in Sicily. After subduing the Jacobin uprising in Naples, in July 1799 Nelson received an order from Lord Keith, commander-in-chief in the Mediterranean, to bring the greater part of his force to defend Minorca. Nelson refused to obey the order; and when it was repeated, sent Sir John Duckworth, his second in command, while he himself remained at Naples or Palermo, and controlled the blockade of Malta. The Admiralty censured him for his disobedience, and, resigning his command, he made his way home overland with Lady Hamilton and her husband, arriving in November 1800. His meeting with his wife was not a happy one, and after an angry interview they parted for good. In January 1801 Nelson was promoted to be vice-admiral, and was appointed second in command of the expedition to the Baltic, under Sir Hyde Parker. The whole conduct of the attack on Copenhagen and the Danish fleet was entrusted to Nelson. After three to four hours of furious combat, the enemy's ships were subdued. A suspension of hostilities led to an armistice, which the news of the tsar's death converted into a peace. Nelson, created a viscount, succeeded Parker as commander-in-chief; but, his health having given way, he returned to England. He was ordered to undertake the defence of the coast, in prospect of a French invasion; and though he failed in an attempt to destroy the flotilla at Boulogne, his watch was so vigilant that the boats never ventured from under the protection of their batteries. On the renewal of the war Nelson cruised for eighteen months off Toulon. During a temporary absence, in March 1805, the French fleet put to sea under Villeneuve, and got away to Martinique, where they expected to be joined by the fleet from Brest. Nelson, though delayed for six weeks by his ignorance of Villeneuve's movements, was only twenty days behind him; and Villeneuve hastily returned to Europe. Nelson again followed, and arrived off Cadiz some days before the French approached the shores of Europe. Conceiving that Villeneuve's aim might be to overpower the fleet off Brest, he reinforced it with most of his ships, returning himself to England. Within a fortnight it was known that Villeneuve had gone to Cadiz, and Nelson resumed the command in September. Villeneuve was meantime urged by positive orders to put to sea, and on October 20 he reluctantly came out. Of French and Spanish ships there were thirty-three; Nelson had twenty-seven. At daybreak on the 21st the two fleets were in presence of each other off Cape Trafalgar. At noon the lee division of the British fleet, under Collingwood in the *Royal Sovereign*, broke through the rear of the Franco-Spanish line. Nelson, with the other division, threw himself on the centre of the van. As the *Victory* passed astern of Villeneuve's flagship she fell foul of the *Redoutable* of seventy-four guns, and her quarter-deck became exposed to the musketry fire from the *Redoutable*'s tops. Nelson, while speaking to Captain Hardy, fell mortally wounded by a shot on the left shoulder. He was carried below, and died some three hours later, just as the battle ended in victory. The enemy's fleet was annihilated. Nelson's body was brought home and buried in St Paul's. See Lives by Clarke and McArthur (2 vols. 1809; 2nd ed. 1840), Southey (1813), Laughton (1895), Mahan (2 vols. 1897), Wilkinson (1931), Oman (1947), Warner (1958); Nelson's *Dispatches and Letters*, edited by N.· H. Nicolas (1844–46); his *Last Diary* (1917); his *Letters to his Wife*, ed. Naish (1958); J. C. Jeaffreson's *Lady Hamilton and Nelson* (1888) and *The Queen of Naples and Nelson* (1889); and E. H. Moorhouse's *Nelson in England* (1913).

(2) **Robert** (1656–1714), born in London, son of a rich Turkish merchant, went with his widowed mother to Dryfield in Gloucestershire, where he was brought up by Dr George Bull. In 1680, elected an F.R.S., he travelled with Halley in France and Italy, returning with Lady Theophila Lucy (1654–7105), a

widow and daughter to the Earl of Berkeley, who in 1683 became his wife, and soon after was converted to Catholicism by Cardinal Howard and Bossuet. Her ill-health had taken them again to Italy at the Revolution; but Nelson was from the first a (passive) Jacobite, and on his return in 1691 he joined the Nonjurors. He was received back into the Established Church in 1710, though he still would not pray for Queen Anne. He died at Kensington. One of the earliest members of the S.P.C.K. and S.P.G., Nelson was the author of five devotional works, of which *Festivals and Fasts* (1703) sold 10,000 copies in four and a half years. See Lives by Teale (1840–46) and Secretan (1860).

(3) **Thomas** (1780–1861), an Edinburgh publisher, who left two sons, **William** (1816–1887) and **Thomas** (1822–92), the former the restorer of the old Parliament Hall.

NEMOURS, Duc de, *ne-moor* (1814–96), the second son of Louis Philippe, after the fall of the monarchy played an inconspicuous part. See Life by R. Bazin (1907).

NENNI, Pietro, *nen'nee* (1891–   ), Italian Socialist politician, born at Faenza, Romagna. An agitator at seventeen, as editor of *Avanti* he was exiled by the Fascists in 1926. In the Spanish War he was political commissar of the Garibaldi Brigade. He became secretary-general of the Italian Socialist party in 1944, vice-premier in the De Gasperi coalition cabinet (1945–46), and foreign minister (1946–47). His pro-Soviet party did not break finally with the Communists till 1956. In 1963 Nenni became deputy prime minister in the new central-left four-party coalition government, including Social Democrats and Socialists. In 1966 he succeeded in his longstanding aim of uniting the two groups as the United Socialist party. In the 1968 elections, the coalition had overall gains, but the Socialists lost ground, mainly to the Communist party, and against Nenni's advice, withdrew from the coalition in June 1968. He was foreign minister in a new coalition government from December 1968 but resigned July 1969.

NENNIUS (fl. 796), Welsh writer, the reputed author of a *Historia Britonum*. His book gives the mythical account of the origin of the Britons, the Roman occupation, the settlement of the Saxons, and closes with King Arthur's twelve victories. See works by W. F. Skene (1868), H. Zimmer (Berlin 1893) and F. Lot (Paris 1934).

NEOT, St, *neet* (d. 877), Saxon hermit, according to legend a monk of Glastonbury, lived in Cornwall. His relics were brought to Crowland about 1003. See work by W. A. Axworthy (1894).

NEPOMUK, St John of. See JOHN OF NEPOMUK, ST.

NEPOS, Cornelius (*c.* 99–25 B.C.), Roman historian, a native of Pavia or Hostilia, was the contemporary of Cicero, Atticus and Catullus. Of his *De Viris Illustribus* only twenty-five biographies of warriors and statesmen, mostly Greeks, survive—untrustworthy, but written in a clear and elegant style. See Freudenberg, *Quaestiones historicae in C. Nepotis vitas* (1839), and Eng. trans. by Rolfe (*Loeb Library*) 1929).

NERI, St Philip (1515–95), Italian founder of the Oratory, was born at Florence. He went to Rome at the age of eighteen, and for many years spent most of his time in works of charity and instruction, and in solitary prayer. In 1551 he became a priest, and gathered around him a following of disciples which in 1564 became the Congregation of the Oratory and later received the approbation of the pope. The community was finally established at Vallicella, where Philip built a new church (Chiesa Nuova) on the site of Sta Maria. He was canonized with Ignatius Loyola and others in 1622. Philip's literary remains consist of a few letters (1751) and some sonnets. The best Life was by Bacci (1622; trans. ed. by F. W. Faber, 1849; new ed. 1902). See also Life by Archbishop Capecelatro (trans. 2nd ed. 1894), and works by L. Ponnelle and L. Bordet (Eng. trans. 1932), V. J. Matthews (1934) and T. Maynard (Milwaukee 1946).

NERNST, Walther Hermann (1864–1941), German physical chemist, was born in Briesen in W. Prussia and died in Berlin. Nernst became professor of Chemistry in Göttingen (1891) and in Berlin (1905). In 1925 he became director of the Berlin Physical Institute. In 1906 he proposed the heat theorem (third law of thermodynamics). He also investigated the specific heat of solids at low temperature in connection with quantum theory, and proposed the atom chain-reaction theory in photochemistry. He won the Nobel prize for chemistry in 1920.

NERO (A.D. 37–68), Roman emperor from A.D. 54 to 68, was born at Antium, son of Cneius Domitius Ahenobarbus and of the younger Agrippina, daughter of Germanicus. His mother became the wife of the Emperor Claudius, who adopted him (50). After the death of Claudius (54) the Praetorian Guards declared him emperor. His reign began with much promise, but owing to the baleful influence of his mother and his own moral weakness and sensuality, he soon plunged headlong into debauchery, extravagance and tyranny. He caused Britannicus, the son of Claudius, to be poisoned, and afterwards murdered his mother and his wife Octavia. In July 64 occurred a great conflagration in Rome, by which two-thirds of the city was burned. Nero is stated to have been the incendiary; and we are told that he admired the spectacle from a distance, reciting verses about the burning of Troy. But he found a scapegoat in the Christians, many of whom were put to death with unheard-of cruelties. He rebuilt the city with great magnificence, and reared on the Palatine Hill a splendid palace; but in order to provide for his expenditure Italy and the provinces were plundered. A conspiracy against Nero in 65 failed, and Seneca and the poet Lucan fell victims to his vengeance. In a fit of passion he murdered his wife Poppaea, by kicking her when she was pregnant. He then offered his hand to Antonia, daughter of Claudius, but was refused; whereupon he caused her to be put to death, and married Statilia Messallina, after murdering her husband. He also executed or banished many persons distinguished for integrity and

virtue. His vanity led him to seek distinction as poet, philosopher, actor, musician and charioteer. In 68 the Gallic and Spanish legions, and after them the Praetorian Guards rose against him to make Galba emperor. Nero fled to the house of a freedman, four miles from Rome, and saved himself from execution by suicide, June 11, 68. See W. Wolfe Capes, *Early Roman Empire*, Merivale's *Romans under the Empire*, the Life by B. W. Henderson (1903), and works by M. P. Charlesworth (1939), C. M. Franzero (1954), G. Walter (1957).

NERUDA, (1) Jan (1834–91), Czech writer, born in Prague, began as a disciple of Romanticism but developed into the foremost classical poet in modern Czech literature. He is also known for some excellent prose and drama.
(2) Madame. See HALLÉ.

NERVA, M. Cocceius (c. 32–98), Roman emperor, was elected in A.D. 96. He introduced liberal reforms and died in 98. See B. W. Henderson, *Five Roman Emperors* (1927).

NERVAL, Gérard de, properly Gérard Labrunie (1808–55), French writer, was born at Paris. He published at twenty a translation of *Faust*. Desultory work, a love affair, fits of restless travel, of dissipation, of gloom and of insanity, and death by his own hand, sum up the story of his life. Nerval wrote admirably alike in prose and verse. But his travels, criticism, plays and poems are less interesting than his fantastic short tales, the *Contes et facéties* (1852), the semi-autobiographic series of *Filles du feu* (1856) and *La Bohème galante*. See works by Arvède Barine (1897), Gauthier Ferrières (1906), Aristide Marie (1914), R. Bizet (1928), A. Béguin (1936), L. H. Sébillotte (1948), S. A. Rhodes (1951), and the *Fortnightly*, December 1897.

NERVI, Pier Luigi (1891–), Italian architect, graduated as an engineer and set up as a building contractor. His works include a complex of exhibition halls at Turin (1948–50) and he achieved an international reputation by his designs for the Olympic stadii in Rome (1960), in which a bold and imaginative use is made of concrete in roofing in the large areas. In 1960 he was awarded the gold medal of the R.I.B.A.

NESBIT, Edith, maiden and pen name of Mrs Hubert Bland, from 1917 Mrs Thomas Tucker (1858–1924), English writer, born in London, educated at a French convent, who began her literary career by writing poetry but is perhaps best remembered for her children's stories, which reacted against the namby-pamby moralizing then prevalent and have remained popular to the present day. Among them are *The Story of the Treasure Seekers* (1899), *The Wouldbegoods* (1901), *Five Children and It* (1902) and *The Railway Children* (1906). See life by D. L. Moore (1933, rev. 1967), study by N. Streatfield (1958) and monograph by A. Bell (1960).

NESSELRODE, Karl Robert, Count, -rō'dĕ (1780–1862), Russian diplomatist, was born at Lisbon, son of the Russian ambassador. He gained the confidence of the Emperor Alexander, took a principal part in the negotiations which ended in the Peace of Paris, and in the Congress of Vienna, and was one of the most active diplomatists of the Holy Alliance. He dealt a deadly blow to the revolutionary cause in Hungary in 1849. He exerted himself to preserve peace with the Western Powers, and in 1854 strove for the re-establishment of peace. See his autobiography (1866), *Lettres et Papiers* (1904–12).

NESTORIUS (d. A.D. 451), Syrian ecclesiastic, was a native of Germanicia in northern Syria, and as priest became so eminent for his zeal, ascetic life, and eloquence that he was selected as patriarch of Constantinople (428). The presbyter Anastasius having denied that the Virgin Mary could be truly called the Mother of God, Nestorius warmly defended him; and so emphasized the distinction of the divine and human natures that antagonists accused him—falsely—of holding that there were two persons in Christ. A controversy ensued, and at a general council at Ephesus in 431 Nestorius was deposed. He was confined in a monastery near Constantinople, was banished to Petra in Arabia, and died (*c.* 451) after confinement in the Greater Oasis in Upper Egypt and elsewhere. There are still a few Nestorians in Kurdistan and Iraq, and a small body of Christians in India are nominally Nestorian. See books by Bethune-Baker (1908) and Loofs (1914).

NESTROY, Johann (1801–62), Austrian dramatist, born in Vienna, began life as an operatic singer, turned playwright and was director of the Vienna Carl-Theater (1854–60). His sixty-odd plays, which include *Der böse Geist lumpazivagabundus* (1833), *Einen Jux will er sich machen* (1842), *Der Unbedeu tende* (1846), *Judith und Holofernes* (1849), are mostly elaborate jibes at theatrical sentimentality characterized by a deft play on words, thoughts and afterthoughts. They revolutionized the Viennese theatre and influenced Wittgenstein (q.v.).

NETTLESHIP, (1) Henry (1839–93), English classical scholar, brother of (2), from 1878 Corpus Latin professor at Oxford, he was born at Kettering, and educated at Lancing, Durham, Charterhouse and Corpus, taking only a second, but winning the Hertford, Gaisford and Craven. He was elected a fellow of Lincoln, was a master at Harrow 1868–73, completed Conington's *Virgil*, and published *Contributions to Latin Lexicography* (1889), &c. See his *Literary Remains* by A. Bradley (1897).

(2) **Richard Lewis** (1846–92), English philosopher, brother of (1), took the place of T. H. Green as a tutor at Balliol. He was lost on Mont Blanc. The Nettleship scholarship at Balliol was founded in his honour. See his *Philosophical Lectures and Remains*, edited, with memoir, by Bradley and Benson (2 vols. 1897).

NEUMANN, noy'man, (1) Balthasar (1687–1753), German architect, born at Eger, was at first a military engineer in the service of the Archbishop of Würzburg, but soon found his true *métier*, and after visiting Paris and absorbing new ideas, he became professor of Architecture at Würzburg. Many out-

standing examples of the Baroque style were designed by him, the finest being probably Würzburg Palace and Schloss Bruchsal. See studies by Sedlmaier and Pfister (1923) and F. Knapp (1937).

(2) **Johann von** (1903–57), Hungarian American mathematician, born in Budapest, escaped from Hungary during the Communist régime (1919), studied chemistry at Berlin, chemical engineering at Zürich, mathematics at Budapest and on a Rockefeller fellowship at Göttingen became acquainted with Oppenheimer (q.v.). In 1931 he became professor at Princeton and in 1933 research professor at the Institute for Advanced Study there. His classic work on quantum mechanics (1932) proved rigorously that cause-and-effect operates for large-scale physical phenomena only and not for sub-atomic events. He worked on the atomic bomb project at Los Alamos during World War II and his mathematical treatment of shock waves helped to determine the height of the explosions over Hiroshima and Nagasaki in August 1945. He made important contributions to point-set theory, theory of continuous groups, operator theory and mathematical logic, such giant computers as M.A.N.I.A.C. (his own ironical label) having been constructed on the basis of his mathematical work for high-speed calculations for H-bomb development. In *Theory of Games and Economic Behaviour* (1944), written with O. Morgenstern, he distinguishes between the more complex games, requiring strategy, and nonstrategic games. R. B. Braithwaite utilized this theory as *A Tool for the Moral Philosopher* (1955). He differed with Oppenheimer on the advisability of advancing the H-Bomb projects, but testified to the latter's loyalty and integrity (1954). He died of cancer.

NEURATH, Baron Konstantin von, *noy'raht* (1873–1956), Nazi ' Protector of Bohemia and Moravia ', was born at Klein-Glattbach, Württemberg, in 1873. After consular service, he joined the German Embassy in Istanbul and in 1921 became ambassador to Italy and in 1930 to Britain. He was foreign minister from 1932 to 1938. From 1939 to 1943 he was the Reich protector of the Czech territories. At the Nuremberg Trial he was sentenced to 15 years' imprisonment for war crimes, but released in 1954.

NEUVILLE, Alphonse Marie de, *næ-veel* (1836–85), French painter of pictures of French military exploits in the Crimea, Italy and Mexico, and against Germany. He excelled as an illustrator of books.

NEVILLE, Richard. See WARWICK.

NEVINSON, (1) Christopher Richard Wynne (1889–1946), English artist, son of (2), born at Hampstead, studied at the Slade School and in Paris, and painted a number of Futurist pictures about 1912. He achieved fame as an official war artist (1914–15), his war pictures being exhibited in London in 1916. He also achieved note as an etcher and lithographer. See his autobiographical *Paint and Prejudice* (1937).

(2) **Henry Woodd** (1856–1941), English war correspondent and journalist, father of (1), born in Leicester, was correspondent

for various papers in, among many other campaigns, the Boer War, the Balkans and the Dardanelles. In 1904 he exposed the Portuguese slave trade in Angola. His publications include *Lines of Life* (verse, 1920), *Essays in Freedom and Rebellion* (1921) and a study of Goethe (1931). See his autobiographical series, *Changes and Chances* (1925–28).

NEVISON, John (1639–84), English highwayman, born at Pontefract, after a long career of robbery and murder was hanged at York.

NEWALL, (1) **Hugh Frank** (1857–1944), British astronomer, son of (2), born near Gateshead, educated at Rugby and Trinity College, Cambridge, worked at the Cavendish Laboratory under Thomson, and in 1909 became first professor of Astrophysics. In 1913 he was appointed first director of the Solar Physics Observatory, a position which he held for the rest of his life, carrying out important research on solar phenomena.

(2) **Robert Stirling** (1812–89), British engineer and astronomer, father of (1), was born at Dundee. In 1940 he patented a new type of wire rope and founded a business to manufacture it at Gateshead. Turning his inventive genius to the submarine cable, he devised improvements both to the cable itself and to methods of laying it, and his firm was responsible for many of the early undersea cables in different parts of the world.

NEWBERY, John (1713–67), English publisher and bookseller, born a Berkshire farmer's son, settled about 1744 in London as a vendor of books and patent medicines. He was the first to publish little books for children, and he was himself—perhaps with Goldsmith—part author of some of the best of them, notably *Goody Two-Shoes*. In 1758 he started the *Universal Chronicle, or Weekly Gazette*, in which the *Idler* appeared. In the *Public Ledger* (1760) appeared Goldsmith's *Citizen of the World*. See a book on him by C. Welsh (1885). Since 1922 the Newbery medal has been awarded annually for the best American children's book.

NEWBOLT, Sir Henry John (1862–1938), English poet, born at Bilston, Staffs., studied at Oxford, went to the bar, and in 1895 published *Mordred*, a drama. He is best known, however, for his sea songs—*Admirals All, The Island Race, Drake's Drum*, &c. He was knighted in 1915. See his autobiography (1932) and *Later Life and Letters*, ed. by his wife (1942).

NEWCASTLE. See CAVENDISH and PELHAM.

NEWCOMB, Simon (1835–1909), American astronomer, born at Wallace, Nova Scotia, graduated at Harvard, in 1861–97 was professor of Mathematics in the U.S. navy, had charge of the naval observatory at Washington, and edited the American *Nautical Almanac*. In 1894–1901 he was professor in the Johns Hopkins University. He made many astronomical discoveries, and wrote, besides innumerable memoirs, a long series of works, including *Elements of Astronomy, The Stars*, and his own Reminiscences (1903).

NEWCOMEN, Thomas (1663–1729), English inventor, born at Dartmouth, by 1698 had invented the atmospheric steam engine, an improvement on one by Capt. Savery, with whom he became associated. From 1712 his invention was used for pumping water out of mines. See work by R. Jenkins (1913).

NEWDIGATE, Sir Roger (1719–1806), English antiquary, was born and died at Arbury, Warwickshire, having sat for thirty-six years as member for Middlesex and Oxford University. He built up a famous collection of antiquities and endowed the Newdigate prize poem at Oxford, winners of which have included Heber, Ruskin, M. Arnold, Laurence Binyon and John Buchan. See Lady Newdigate-Newdegate's *Cheverels of Cheverel Manor* (1898), and work by R. Churton (1881).

NEWLANDS, John Alexander Reina (1837–1898), English chemist, worked in a sugar refinery at the Victoria Docks. He was the first to arrange the elements in order of atomic number and to see the connection between every eighth. This 'Law of Octaves' brought him ridicule at the time (1864), but it was the first idea of a periodic law and in 1887 the Royal Society awarded him its Davy medal in recognition of his work. He was the author of a handbook on sugar (1888).

NEWMAN, (1) **Ernest** (1868–1959), English music critic, born in Liverpool, was successively music critic of the *Manchester Guardian*, the *Birmingham Post* and the *Sunday Times* (from 1920). His writings are noted for their wit and elegance, and for their strict factual accuracy. His works include studies of Gluck and Hugo Wolf, and of opera (e.g., *Opera Nights* and *Wagner Nights*); but it is for his far-reaching studies and deep understanding of Wagner that he is best known—his four-volume biography of that composer (1933–37) is the most complete and authoritative account of the composer in existence. In *A Musical Critic's Holiday* Newman vindicates music criticism as a valuable study.

(2) **Francis William** (1805–97), English scholar, brother of (3), was born in London. In 1826 he obtained a double first at Oxford and resigned a Balliol fellowship. He withdrew from the university in 1830, declining subscription to the Thirty-nine Articles. After a three years' stay in the East, he became classical tutor in Bristol College in 1834, in 1840 professor in Manchester New College, and in 1846–63 professor of Latin in University College, London. In religion he took a part directly opposite to his brother's, being eager for a religion including whatever is best in all the historical religions. *Phases of Faith* (1853), the best known of his works, was preceded by *The Soul* (1849), and other works include a small book on his brother (1891). See *Memoir and Letters*, by I. G. Sieveking (1909).

(3) **John Henry, Cardinal** (1801–90), English theologian, brother of (2), was born in London, February 21, 1801. His father was a banker; his mother, a moderate Calvinist, deeply influenced his early religious views. He went up to Trinity College, Oxford, in 1817, and in 1822, in spite of his second-class, he was elected a fellow of

Oriel, and here he formed his close intimacy with Pusey and Hurrell Froude. In 1824 he was ordained, in 1828 became vicar of St Mary's, in 1830 broke definitely with Evangelicalism. His first book, *The Arians of the Fourth Century* (1833), argued that Arianism was a Judaizing heresy which sprang up in Antioch. In 1832–33 Newman accompanied Hurrell Froude and his father on a Mediterranean tour, when many of the poems in *Lyra Apostolica* (1834) were written and also ' Lead, kindly Light '. He was present at Keble's Oxford assize sermon on National Apostasy (July 1833), which he regarded as the beginning of the Tractarian movement. Into the *Tracts for the Times* Newman threw himself with energy, and he himself composed a number of them. Tract 90 (1841) was the most famous of the tracts. Newman contended that the intention of the Thirty-nine Articles was Catholic in spirit, and that they were aimed at the supremacy of the pope and the popular abuses of Catholic practice, and not at Catholic doctrine. But Tract 90 provoked an explosion which was the end of the Tractarian movement, and brought on the conversion to Rome of those of the Tractarians who were most logical as well as most in earnest. Newman struggled for two years longer to think his position tenable, but in 1843 resigned the vicarage of St Mary's, which he had held since 1828, and retired to Littlemore. The magnificent sermon on ' Development in Christian Doctrine ' was the last which he preached in the university pulpit, February 2, 1843. In October 1845 he invited the Passionist Father Dominic to his house at Littlemore in order that he might be received into the Roman Catholic Church. He went to Rome for a year and a half, and on his return in 1848 he established a branch of the brotherhood of St Philip Neri in England at Edgbaston, a suburb of Birmingham; and here he did a great deal of hard work, devoting himself to the sufferers from cholera in 1849 with the utmost zeal. The lectures on *Anglican Difficulties* (1850) drew public attention to Newman's great power of irony and the singular delicacy of his literary style, and were followed by his lectures on *Catholicism in England* (1851). His long series of Oxford sermons contain some of the finest ever preached from an Anglican pulpit, and his Roman Catholic volumes— *Sermons addressed to Mixed Congregations* (1849) and *Sermons on Various Occasions* (1857)—though less remarkable for their pathos, are even fuller of fine rhetoric, and show the rarest finish. In 1864 a casual remark by Canon Kingsley in *Macmillan's Magazine* on the indifference of the Roman Church to the virtue of truthfulness, an indifference which he asserted that Dr Newman approved, led to a correspondence which resulted in the publication of the remarkable *Apologia pro Vita Sua*. In 1865 he wrote a poem of singular beauty, *The Dream of Gerontius*, republished in *Verses on Various Occasions* (1874). In 1870 he published his *Grammar of Assent*, on the philosophy of faith. In the controversies which led to the Vatican Council Newman sided

with the Inopportunists. He was at this time in vehement opposition to the Ultramontanes under Manning and William George Ward, and the bitterness between the two parties ran very high. Leo XIII, anxious to show his sympathy with the moderates, in 1879 summoned Newman to Rome to receive the cardinal's hat. He died at Edgbaston, August 11, 1890. See the Life by Wilfred Ward (1912, 3rd ed. 1927); books by Waller and Burrow (1902), Barry (1904), Brémond (1905–12), Whyte (1901), Sarolea (1908), Bellasis (1916), Dark (1934), Houghton (1945), Ward (1948), Harrold (1955), Bouyer (1958) and Trevor (2 vols. 1962); *Newman's Letters*, ed. by Miss Mozley (1891), *Autobiographical Writings*, ed. Tristram (1957) and *Letters and Diaries*, definitive edition by Dessain, from 1961.

NEWNES, Sir George (1851–1910), English publisher, the son of a Matlock Congregational minister, was educated at Shireland Hall, Warwickshire, and the City of London School. He founded *Tit-Bits* (1881), *The Strand Magazine* (1891), *The Wide World Magazine* (1898), &c.; was Gladstonian M.P. for the Newmarket division 1885–95; and then was created a baronet. See Life by H. Friederichs (1911).

NEWTON, (1) **Alfred** (1829–1907), English zoologist, born at Geneva, was in 1866 appointed professor of Zoology at Cambridge, and wrote valuable works on ornithology. See Life by A. F. R. Wollaston (1921).

(2) **Sir Charles Thomas** (1816–94), English archaeologist, born at Bredwardine, held a British Museum post 1840–52, as vice-consul at Mitylene made important finds (*Discoveries in the Levant*, 1865), and was British Museum keeper of antiquities 1861–1885.

(3) **Eric** (1893–1965), English writer and art critic, born at Marple Bridge, near Glossop, Derbyshire, worked as a mosaic designer and craftsman, and was art critic to the *Manchester Guardian* from 1930 to 1947, and to the *Sunday Times* from 1937 to 1951. His publications include *European Painting and Sculpture* (1941), *Tintoretto* (1952) and *The Romantic Rebellion* (1962).

(4) **Sir Isaac** (1642–1727), English scientist and mathematician, was born at Woolsthorpe, Lincolnshire, near Grantham, at whose grammar school he got his education. In 1661 he entered Trinity College, Cambridge. In 1665, when he took his B.A., he committed to writing his first discovery on fluxions; and in 1665 or 1666 the fall of an apple suggested the train of thought that led to the law of gravitation. But on his first attempt so to explain lunar motions, it is commonly said that an erroneous estimate of the radius of the earth produced such discrepancies that he dropped the investigation for the time, though better estimates seem to have been available. Be this as it may, he turned to study the nature of light and the construction of telescopes. By a variety of experiments upon sunlight refracted through a prism, he concluded that rays of light which differ in colour differ also in refrangibility—a discovery which suggested that the indistinctness of the image formed

by the object-glass of telescopes was due to the different coloured rays of light being brought to a focus at different distances. He concluded (rightly for an object-glass consisting of a single lens) that it was impossible to produce a distinct image, and was led to the construction of reflecting telescopes; and the form devised by him is that which reached such perfection in the hands of Herschel and Rosse. Newton became a fellow of Trinity in 1667, and Lucasian professor of Mathematics in 1669, and in 1671–72 he was elected a member of the Royal Society. He resumed his calculations about gravitation, and by 1684 had demonstrated the whole theory, which, on the solicitation of Halley, he expounded first in *De Motu Corporum*, and more completely in *Philosophiae Naturalis Principia Mathematica* (1687). The part he took in defending the rights of the university against the illegal encroachments of James II procured him a seat in the Convention Parliament (1689–90). A crisis of some sort in 1693 seems to have left his suspicious, quarrelsome temper worse than ever. In 1696 he was appointed warden of the Mint, and was master of the Mint from 1699 till the end of his life. He again sat in parliament in 1701 for his university. He solved two celebrated problems proposed in June 1696 by John Bernoulli, as a challenge to the mathematicians of Europe; and performed a similar feat in 1716, by solving a problem proposed by Leibniz. Newton was president of the Royal Society from 1703 till his death. He superintended the publication of Flamsteed's *Greenwich Observations*, which he required for the working out of his lunar theory—not without much disputing between himself and Flamsteed. In the controversy between Newton and Leibniz as to priority of discovery of the differential calculus or the method of fluxions, Newton acted secretly through his friends. The verdict of science is that the methods were invented independently, and that although Newton was the first inventor, a greater debt is owing to Leibniz for the superior facility and completeness of his method. In 1699 Newton was elected foreign associate of the Academy of Sciences, and in 1705 he was knighted by Queen Anne. He died March 20, 1727, and was buried in Westminster Abbey. An admirable reprint of the *Principia* is that by Lord Kelvin and Professor Blackburn (1871). Clarke's Latin translation of the *Optics* appeared in 1706, the *Optical Lectures* in 1728, the *Fluxions* in 1736, and Horsley edited an edition of his Collected Works (1779–85). Newton was a student of alchemy; and he left a remarkable MS. on the prophecies of Daniel and on the Apocalypse, a history of Creation, and some tracts. See Lives by Brewster (1855), de Morgan (1885), More (1934), Sullivan (1938), Andrade (1950), Sootin (N.Y. 1955), and his *Correspondence* (vols. 1–3 ed. by Turnbull, 1959–61, and vol. 4 ed. by Scott, 1967).

(5) **John** (1725–1807), English divine and writer, was born in London, son of a shipmaster, sailed with his father for six years, and for ten years engaged in the African slave trade. In 1748 he was converted, but still went on slave trading; in 1755 he became tide surveyor at Liverpool; and in 1764 he was offered the curacy of Olney in Bucks, and took orders. To Olney the poet Cowper came four years later, and an extraordinary friendship sprang up. In 1779 Newton became rector of St Mary Woolnoth, London. Newton's prose works are little read, save the *Remarkable Particulars in his own Life*. But some of his *Olney Hymns* have been taken to the heart by the English world, including ' Approach, my soul, the mercy-seat ', ' How sweet the name of Jesus sounds ' and ' One there is above all others '. See Lives by Cecil (1808), R. Bickersteth (1865) and B. Martin (1950); Collected Works (1816); and books cited at COWPER.

NEXÖ, Martin Andersen, *nik'sœ* (1869–1954), Danish novelist, was born in a poor quarter of Copenhagen, and spent his boyhood in Bornholm near Nexö (whence his name). From shoemaking and bricklaying he turned to books and teaching, and in 1906 won European fame with *Pelle the Conqueror* (trans. 1915–17; 4 parts), describing poor life from within and the growth of the labour movement. See his Reminiscences (Copenhagen 4 vols. 1932–39) and work by W. A. Berendsohn (Copenhagen 1948).

NEY, Michel (1769–1815), French marshal, was born, a cooper's son, at Saarlouis, and rose to be adjutant-general (1794) and general of brigade (1796). For the capture of Mannheim he was made general of division in 1799. Under the empire he was made marshal. In 1805 he stormed the entrenchments of Elchingen, and was created Duke of Elchingen. He distinguished himself at Jena and Eylau, and his conduct at Friedland earned him the grand eagle of the *Légion d'honneur*. Serving in Spain, he quarrelled with Masséna and returned to France. In command of the third corps (1813) he covered himself with glory at Smolensk and Borodino, received the title of Prince of the Moskwa, and led the rear-guard in the disastrous retreat. In 1813 he was present at Lützen and Bautzen, but was defeated by Bülow at Dennewitz. He fought heroically at Leipzig, but submitted to Louis XVIII, who loaded him with favours. On Napoleon's return from Elba Ney, sent against him, went over to his old master's side. He opposed Brunswick at Quatrebras, and led the centre at Waterloo. After the capitulation of Paris he was condemned for high treason, and shot. See his *Mémoires* (1833), and books by Bonnal (1910–14), A. H. Atteridge (1913), L. Blythe (1937) and J. B. Morton (1958).

NIARCHOS, Stavros Spyros, *ni–ahr'kos* (1909–), Greek ship-owner, controller of one of the largest independent fleets in the world, served during World War II in the Royal Hellenic Navy, then pioneered the construction of super-tankers, as did his brother-in-law Aristotle Onassis (q.v.).

NICCOLA PISANO. See PISANO (3).

NICCOLO DI FOLIGNO, or Di Liberatore. See ALUNNO.

NICHOL, (1) John (1833–94), Scottish writer, son of (2), Glasgow professor of

English Literature 1861–89, he wrote poems and books on Byron, Bacon, Burns, *American Literature* (1882), &c. See Life by Knight (1896).

(2) **John Pringle** (1804–59), Scottish astronomer, father of (1), after several years teaching he became professor of Astronomy at Glasgow and was well known for his public lectures.

NICHOLAS, St (4th cent.), patron saint of Russia, Bishop of Myra in Lycia, was imprisoned under Diocletian and released under Constantine, and his supposed relics were conveyed to Bari in 1087. St Nicholas is the patron of youth, particularly of scholars (*Santa Claus* is an American corruption of the name), merchants, sailors, travellers, thieves. See books by L'Abbé Marin (1917), E. Crozier (1949).

NICHOLAS, the name of five popes and an antipope:

Nicholas I, St (pope, 858–867), asserted the supremacy of the Church and forbade the divorce of Lothair, King of Lorraine. See Life by J. Roy (1899), studies by E. Perels (Berlin 1920) and J. Haller (1937).

Nicholas II (pope, 1058–61), enacted regulations for papal elections. See study by P. Brand and J. Garin (Chambéry 1925).

Nicholas V (1397–1455), pope from 1447, prevailed on the antipope, Felix V, to abdicate and thus restored the peace of the Church. A liberal patron of scholars, he may almost be said to have founded the Vatican Library. He vainly endeavoured to arouse Europe to the duty of succouring the Greek empire. See studies by G. Sforza (Lucca 1884) and K. Pleyer (Stuttgart 1927).

Nicholas V (antipope, 1328–30), set up in opposition to John XXII.

NICHOLAS, the name of two emperors of Russia:

Nicholas I (1796–1855), third son of Paul I, on July 13, 1817, married the daughter of Frederick-William III of Prussia. On the death of his brother, Alexander I (1825), owing to the resignation of Constantine, he succeeded to the throne, and suppressed a military conspiracy with vigour and cruelty. After a brief ebullition of reforming zeal, he reverted to the ancient policy of the tsars—absolute despotism, supported by military power. Wars with Persia and Turkey resulted in giving Russia increase of territory. The movement of 1830 in the west of Europe was followed by a rising of the Poles, which was suppressed after a severe contest of nine months; and Nicholas, converting Poland into a Russian province, strove to extinguish the Polish nationality. In Russia intellectual activity was kept under official guidance. The tsar's Panslavism also prompted him to Russianize all the inhabitants of the empire, and to convert Roman Catholics and Protestants to the Russian Greek Church. During the political storm of 1848–49 he assisted the emperor of Austria in quelling the Hungarian insurrection, and drew closer the alliance with Prussia. The re-establishment of the French empire confirmed these alliances, and led Nicholas to think that the time had come for absorbing Turkey; but the opposition of Britain and France brought

on the Crimean war, during which he died, March 2, 1855. See Lacroix, *Histoire de Nicolas I* (1864–73); works by J. Schiemann (Berlin 1904–08), C. de Grunwald (Eng. trans. 1954).

Nicholas II (1868–1918), in 1894 succeeded his father, Alexander III, married a princess of Hesse, and initiated (1898) The Hague Peace Conference. His reign was marked by the alliance with France, *entente* with Britain, disastrous war with Japan (1904–05), and the establishment of the Duma (1906). He took command of the Russian armies against the Central Powers in 1915. Forced to abdicate at the Revolution, he was shot with his family by the Red Guards. See Lives by P. Gilliard (Eng. trans. 1921), C. Radziwill (1931).

NICHOLAS, Grand-Duke (1856–1929), Russian general, a nephew of Alexander II, was Russian commander-in-chief against Germany and Austria, August 1914 to September 1915, and commander-in-chief in the Caucasus 1915–17. After 1919 he lived quietly in France. See Life by J. Daniloff (Berlin 1930).

NICHOLAS OF CUSA. See NICOLAUS.

NICHOLS, (1) John (1745–1826), father of (2), editor of the *Gentleman's Magazine* (1797–1826), edited and published literary and historical works, including *Literary Anecdotes of the Eighteenth Century*. See his Memoirs (1804).

(2) **John Bowyer** (1779–1863), son of (1), father of (3), succeeded his father as editor of the *Gentleman's Magazine* for a time and published many important county histories. See memoir by J. G. Nichols (1864).

(3) **John Gough** (1806–73), son of (2). He too edited the *Gentleman's Magazine* and also made valuable contributions to the materials of English history and genealogy. See memoir by R. C. Nichols (1874).

NICHOLSON, (1) Ben (1894–   ), English artist, son of (8), born at Denham, exhibited with the Paris Abstraction-Création group in 1933–34 and at the Venice Biennale in 1954, designed a mural panel for the Festival of Britain (1951) and in 1952 executed another for the Time-Life building in London. As one of the leading abstract artists, he has an international reputation and won the first Guggenheim award in 1957 against competition from 13 countries. Although he has produced a number of purely geometrical paintings and reliefs, in general he uses conventional still-life objects as a starting point for his finely drawn and subtly balanced and coloured variations. Three times married, his second wife was Barbara Hepworth (q.v.). See monograph by Read (2 vols. 1948, 1956) and study by Hodin (1958).

(2) **John** (1822–57), British soldier and administrator, was born at Lisburn (or possibly in Dublin), in 1839 joined the East India Company's service, and in 1842 was captured at Ghazni in Afghanistan. During the Sikh rebellion of 1848 he saved the fortress of Attock, and at Chillianwalla and Gujrat earned the special approval of Lord Gough. Nicholson was appointed deputy-commissioner (1851) of the Punjab, and in 1857 he perhaps did more than any other

man to hold the province. As brigadier-general, on September 14 he led the storming party at the siege of Delhi, and was mortally wounded. See Lives by Captain Trotter (1897) and H. Pearson (1939).

(3) **Joseph Shield** (1850–1927), English economist, was born at Wrawby near Brigg, and in 1880–1925 was professor of Political Economy at Edinburgh. He wrote on *Money* (1888), *Principles of Political Economy* (3 vols. 1893–1901), and other works on economics advocating the ideas of Adam Smith. See Life by W. R. Scott (1928).

(4) **Seth Barnes** (1891–1963), American astronomer, born at Springfield, Ill., notable as the discoverer of the 9th, 10th and 11th satellites of Jupiter.

(5) **William** (1753–1815), English physicist, waterworks engineer for Portsmouth and Gosport, invented the hydrometer named after him, and also a machine for printing on linen. With Carlisle he constructed the first voltaic pile in England, and in so doing discovered that water could be dissociated by electricity. He compiled a *Dictionary of Practical and Theoretical Chemistry* (1808).

(6) **William** (1781–1844), Scottish portrait painter and etcher, born in Ovingham-on-Tyne, about 1814 settled in Edinburgh, was the first secretary of the Royal Scottish Academy, and was noted for his portraits of Sir Walter Scott and other famous contemporaries.

(7) **William** (1816–64), Australian statesman, born near Whitehaven, emigrated as a grocer to Melbourne in 1841, became mayor 1850, and premier of Victoria 1859. He had the ballot adopted in 1855.

(8) **Sir William Newzam Prior** (1872–1949), English artist, father of (1), born at Newark, studied in Paris and was influenced by Whistler and Manet. He became a fashionable portrait painter, but is principally remembered for the posters produced (with his brother-in-law, James Pryde) under the name of **J. and W. Beggarstaff**, for his woodcut book illustrations, and for his glowing still-life paintings (e.g., the *Mushrooms* in the Tate Gallery). He was knighted in 1936. See studies by M. Steen (1943) and L. Browse (1956); also a Life of J. Pryde by D. Hudson (1949).

NICIAS (d. 413 B.C.), Athenian statesman and general, belonged to the aristocratic party, and opposed Cleon and Alcibiades. In 427–426 B.C. he defeated the Spartans and the Corinthians. In 424 he ravaged Laconia, but in 421 made peace between Sparta and Athens. In the naval expedition against Sicily (418) he was one of the commanders. In 415 he laid siege to Syracuse, and was at first successful, but subsequently experienced a series of disasters; his troops were forced to surrender, and he was put to death. See Plutarch's *Life of Nikias* (ed. by H. A. Holden, 1887).

NICOL, (1) **Erskine** (1825–1904), Scottish painter, was born at Leith, lived in Dublin 1843–46, and settled in London in 1862. He was R.S.A. and A.R.A. and painted homely incidents in Irish and Scottish life.

(2) **William** (c. 1744–97), Scottish schoolmaster, a classics master in the High School of Edinburgh, was the too convivial intimate of Robert Burns.

NICOLAI, (1) **Christoph Friedrich** (1733–1811), German author, bookseller and publisher, born at Berlin, early distinguished himself by a series of critical letters (1756) contributed to many literary journals, and for many years edited the *Allgemeine deutsche Bibliothek* (106 vols. 1765–92). He wrote topographical works, satires, anecdotes of Frederick the Great, and an autobiography (recording strange apparitions and hallucinations of his own). See studies by M. Sommerfeld (Halle 1921) and W. Strauss (Stuttgart 1927).

(2) **Otto** (1810–49), German composer, born at Königsberg, in 1847 became *kapellmeister* at Berlin, where his opera *The Merry Wives of Windsor* was produced just before he died. See Life by G. R. Kruse (Berlin 1911).

NICOLAS, Sir Nicholas Harris (1799–1848), English antiquary, born at Dartmouth, served in the navy 1808–16, and was called to the bar in 1825. He devoted himself chiefly to genealogical and historical studies, as in his *History of British Orders of Knighthood* (1841–42), *Synopsis of the Peerage* (1825), &c.

NICOLAUS OF CUSA (1400–64), German cardinal and philosopher, born at Cusa or Cues on the Moselle, studied at Heidelberg and at Padua. As Archdeacon of Liège he took a prominent part in the Council of Basel, insisting in *De Concordantia Catholica* that the pope was subordinate to Councils; but ultimately he sided with the pope, and was made cardinal. As papal legate he visited Constantinople to promote the union of the Eastern and Western churches. He exposed the false Isidorian decretals, was in advance of his time in science, denounced perverted scholasticism in an *Apologia Doctae Ignorantia* and taught that the earth went round the sun. See German monographs by Düx (1848), Scharpff (1871), Glossner (1891) and Jaspers (1964).

NICOLE, Pierre (1625–95), French Jansenist, born at Chartres, was one of the most distinguished of the Port Royalists, the friend of Arnauld and Pascal, and author of *Essais de morale* (1671 *et seq*). See works by E. Thouverex (Paris 1926) and Le Breton-Grandmaison (Paris 1945). See JANSEN.

NICOLINI. See PATTI (1).

NICOLL, Sir William Robertson (1851–1923), Scottish man of letters, was born at Lumsden, studied at Aberdeen, was Free Church minister at Dufftown 1874–77 and Kelso 1877–85. He then addressed himself to literary work in London, becoming editor of the *Expositor*, the *British Weekly* (1886) and the *Bookman*. He wrote books on theology and literature, and was knighted in 1909. See Life by T. H. Darlow (1925).

NICOLLE, Charles Jules Henri (1866–1936), French physician and bacteriologist, a pupil of Pasteur, was director of the Pasteur Institute at Tunis (1903), and professor at the Collège de France (1932). He discovered that the body louse is a transmitter of typhus fever, and in 1928 was awarded the Nobel prize for medicine.

NICOLSON, (1) **Adela Florence.** See HOPE (2).

(2) **Sir Harold George** (1886–1968), English diplomat, author and critic, was born in Teheran, where his father, later 1st Baron Carnock, was British chargé-d'affaires. Educated at Wellington College and Balliol College, Oxford, Nicolson had a distinguished career as a diplomat, entering the service in 1909, and holding posts in Madrid, Constantinople, Tehran and Berlin until his resignation in 1929, when he turned to journalism. From 1935 to 1945 he was National Liberal M.P. for West Leicester. He wrote several biographies, including those of Tennyson, Swinburne and the official one of George V, as well as books on history, politics and, in *Good Behaviour* (1955), manners. He was highly regarded as a literary critic. In 1913 he married Victoria Sackville-West (q.v.), and he was knighted in 1953. See his *Diaries and Letters* (2 vols., ed. by his son, 1966, 1967).

(3) **William** (1655–1727), English divine and antiquary, born at Plumbland, became successively Bishop of Carlisle and Derry, published the *Historical Library* (English, Scottish and Irish) and other important works and collections. See Life by F. G. James (1957) and *Letters*, ed. J. Nichols (1809).

NICOT, Jean, *nee-kō* (1530–1600), French diplomat and scholar, born at Nîmes, became French ambassador at Lisbon, and in 1561 introduced into France the tobacco plant, called after him *Nicotiana*. He compiled one of the first French dictionaries (1606). See his *Correspondance*, ed. E. Falgairolle (Paris 1897).

NIEBUHR, (1) **Barthold Georg** (1776–1831), German historian, son of (2), he was born at Copenhagen, and studied at Kiel, London and Edinburgh (1798–99). In 1800 he entered the Danish state service, and in 1806 the Prussian civil service. The opening of Berlin University in 1810 introduced a new era in his life. He gave (1810–12) a course of lectures on Roman History, which established his position as one of the most original and philosophical of modern historians. In 1816 he was appointed Prussian ambassador at the papal court, and on his return in 1823 he took up his residence at Bonn, where his lectures gave a powerful impetus to historical learning. Niebuhr possessed great intuitive sagacity in sifting true from false historic evidence; and though his scepticism as to the credibility of early history goes too far, the bulk of his contribution to history still stands substantially unshaken. His *Römische Geschichte* and other important works were translated into English. See Madame Hensler's *Lebensnachrichten* (1838; trans. 1852), and studies by Classen (1876), C. Seitz (1909) and F. Schnabel (1931).

(2) **Carsten** (1733–1815), German traveller, father of (1), born at Lauenburg, joined a Danish expedition and travelled in Africa, Arabia and India. He then settled in Denmark and wrote about his travels. See Life by his son (1817).

(3) **Reinhold** (1892–1971), American theo-

logian, born in Wright City, Mo., educated at Yale, professor of Christian Ethics in the Union Theological Seminary, New York, from 1928. He wrote *Nature and Destiny of Man* (1941–43). See study by Davis (1945).

NIEL, Adolphe (1802–69), French marshal, was born at Muret (Upper Garonne), and entered the army as an engineer officer. He took part in the storming of Constantine in Algeria (1836), the siege of Rome (1849), the bombardment of Bomarsund (1854), the fall of Sebastopol (1856), and the battles of Magenta and Solferino (1859) and became minister of war in 1867. See Life by J. J. de la Tour (Paris 1912).

NIELSEN, Carl August, *neel'sén* (1865–1931), Danish composer, was born at Nørre-Lyndelse, near Odense, Fünen, the son of a house-painter who was also a village fiddler, became a bandsman at Odense, and in 1883 entered Copenhagen Conservatoire. His compositions of this time—including the G minor quartet and oboe fantasias—are not revolutionary, being rather in the tradition of Gade (q.v.), but with his first symphony (1894) his new tendencies of progressive tonality and rhythmic audacity become apparent, though still within a classical structure. In his second symphony (' The Four Temperaments ', 1901–02) polytonality is first used in Danish music, along with the contrapuntal style which was to become characteristic of Nielsen. His other works include four further symphonies (1912, 1916, 1922 and 1925), the tragic opera *Saul and David* (1902), the comic opera *Masquerade* (1906), chamber music, concertos for flute, clarinet and violin, and a huge organ work, *Commotio* (1931). In 1915 he was appointed director of Copenhagen Conservatoire. As Denmark's greatest twentieth-century composer, striving through new harmonies, rhythms and melodic ideas of truly Nordic character to divest Danish music of its prevalent romanticism, and as a conductor of note, Nielsen exerted a tremendous influence on the musical development of Denmark. See Life by R. W. L. Simpson (1952), and his early autobiography, translated as *My Childhood* (1953).

NIEMBSCH. See LENAU.

NIEMÖLLER, Martin, *nee'-* (1892–   ), German Lutheran pastor and defier of Hitler, born at Lippstadt, Westphalia, rose from midshipman to one of Germany's ace submarine commanders in World War I, studied theology, was ordained in 1924 and became pastor at Berlin-Dahlem in 1931. Summoned with other Protestant church leaders to Hitler, who wished to get their co-operation for the Nazi régime, Niemöller declared that he, like Hitler, had also a responsibility for the German people, given by God, which he could not permit Hitler to take away from him. His house was ransacked by the Gestapo and, continuing openly to preach against the *Führer*, he was arrested and confined from 1937 to 1945 in Sachsenhausen and Dachau concentration camps. Acclaimed by the Allies as one of the few ' good Germans ' at the end of the war, he caused great astonishment when it was discovered that he had in 1941 volunteered in vain to serve again in the German navy, despite his opposition to Hitler. His explanation was that he had a duty to ' give unto Caesar what is Caesar's '. In 1945 he was responsible for the ' Declaration of Guilt' by the German churches for not opposing Hitler more strenuously. On the other hand he loudly condemned the abuses of the de-Nazification courts. He vigorously opposed German rearmament and the nuclear arms race. Federal Germany he described as ' begotten in Rome and born in Washington '. In 1947–64 he was church president of the Evangelical Church in Hesse and Nassau. In 1961 he became president of the World Council of Churches. See his *Vom U-Boot zur Kanzel*, ' From U-Boat to the Pulpit ' (Berlin 1934), and collections of his sermons (1935, 1939, 1946, 1956), particularly *Six Dachau Sermons* (Munich 1946), also Life by D. Schmidt (trans. 1959).

NIEPCE, *nee-eps,* (1) **de St Victor, Claude Marie François** (1805–70), French photographer, nephew of (2), further developed photography as invented by his uncle and Daguerre and wrote a treatise on the subject (1856). See Life by R. Colson (Paris 1898).

(2) **Joseph Nicéphore** (1765–1833), French chemist, uncle of (1), one of the inventors of photography, was born at Chalon-sur-Saône, served in the army, and in 1795 became administrator of Nice. At Chalon in 1801 he devoted himself to chemistry, and at length succeeded in producing a photograph on metal. He co-operated with Daguerre in further research. See Life by Fouqué (1867), and H. and A. Gernsheim's *Daguerre* (1956).

NIETZSCHE, Friedrich Wilhelm, *neetz'shé* (1844–1900), German philosopher and critic, born at Röcken, Saxony, the son of a Lutheran pastor, was passionately religious as a boy and so brilliant an undergraduate at Bonn and Leipzig that he was offered and accepted the professorship of Classical Philology at Basel (1869–79) before graduating. A disciple of Schopenhauer, he dedicated his first book, *Die Geburt der Tragödie* (1872), ' The Birth of Tragedy ' (trans. 1909), to his friend Wagner, whose operas he regarded as the true successors to Greek tragedy. In four brilliant critical essays, *Unzeitgemässige Betrachtungen,* ' Untimely Contemplations ' (1873–76), he first expressed his enthusiasm for the aristocratic ideal and his contempt for the masses in history. Convinced that Christianity was bankrupt, he determined to give his age new values, Schopenhauer's ' will to power ' serving as the basic principle, but turned from a pessimistic to a zestful ' Yea-saying ' affirmation of life by the warrior-aristocrat. Only the strong ought to survive. Human sympathy only perpetuates the unfit and the mediocre. These egotistical evolutionary ethical doctrines begin to appear in his *Menschliches, Allzumenschliches,* ' Human, all too Human ' (1878), *Fröhliche Wissenschaft* (1882), ' Joyous Wisdom ' (trans. 1910), of his positivist period beginning with his breach with Wagner (1876) whose *Parsifal* he thought Christian-inspired. His major work, *Also sprach Zarathustra* (1883–1885), ' Thus spake Zarathustra ' (trans. 1933), develops the idea of the superman;

Jenseits von Gut und Böse, ' Beyond Good and Evil ' (1886), the twin moralities for the master on the principle ' Nothing is true; everything is allowed ' and slaves whose suffering is insignificant for ' almost everything we call higher culture is based upon the spiritualizing and intensifying of cruelty '. Etymological justification for his transformation of moral terms is presented in *Genealogie der Moral* (1887). Much of his esoteric doctrine appealed to the Nazis, but intensely individualistic, he was no nationalist and not anti-Semitic. With Kierkegaard whom he despised, he greatly influenced Existentialism. He died after twelve years of insanity at Weimar. See Collected Works, ed. Nietzsche Archiv (Weimar 1922), Life by his sister, E. Förster-Nietzsche (1895–1904), who also wrote three biographical studies (trans. 1912, 1915, 1924), and *Letters* (1909–26) to Wagner (trans. 1922), Lives by D. Halévy (1909), and C. Andler (1920–31) ; and studies by K. Jaspers (1936), F. C. Copleston (1942), J. Laurin (1948), W. A. Kaufmann (1950), E. Heller, *The Disinherited Mind* (1952) and F. A. Lea (1957).

NIEUWLAND, Julius Arthur (1878–1936), American chemist, born in Belgium, took holy orders (1903) and became professor of Chemistry at Notre Dame University (1923). His researches led to the production of artificial rubber (duprene) and he played an important part in the discovery of lewisite.

NIGHTINGALE, Florence (1820–1910), English hospital reformer, daughter of William Edward Nightingale of Embly Park, Hants, was born at Florence. She went into training as a nurse at Kaiserswerth (1851) and Paris. In 1854 war was declared with Russia; after the battle of the Alma Miss Nightingale offered to go out and organize a nursing department at Scutari, and in October she departed with thirty-eight nurses. She arrived in time to receive the wounded from Inkermann (November 5) into overcrowded wards; soon she had 10,000 sick men under her care. But she saw in the bad sanitary arrangements of the hospitals the causes of their frightful mortality, and devoted herself to the removal of these causes. She returned to England in 1856 and a fund of £50,000 was subscribed to enable her to form an institution for the training of nurses at St Thomas's and at King's College Hospital. She devoted many years to the question of Army sanitary reform, to the improvement of nursing and to public health in India. Her main work, *Notes on Nursing* (1859), went through many editions. She received the Order of Merit in 1907. See books by E. Cook (1913), D. E. Muir (1946), C. Woodham-Smith (1950) and Z. Pope (1958), and *Selected Writings,* ed. L. R. Seymer (1954).

NIJINSKY, Vaslav, *ni-zhin'ski* (1890–1950), Russian dancer, born in Kiev, was trained at the Imperial School, St Petersburg, and first appeared in ballet at the Maryinski Theatre. As the leading dancer in a company taken to Paris in 1909 by Diaghilev, Nijinsky became enormously popular, and in 1911 he appeared as Petrouchka in the first performance of Stravinsky's ballet. His work as a choreographer, except for the controversial *L'Après-midi d'un faune*, was not successful. Nijinsky was interned in Hungary during the early part of World War I, rejoined Diaghilev for a world tour, but became insane in 1917 in Switzerland. See Life by R. Nijinsky.

NIKISCH, Arthur (1855–1922), Hungarian conductor, was conductor of the Boston Symphony Orchestra 1889–93, Gewandhaus Concerts, Leipzig, from 1895, and Berlin Philharmonic Orchestra. See Life by F. Pfohl (Hamburg 1925).

NILAND, D'Arcy, *ni'-* (? -), Australian writer, contributed over five hundred short stories to magazines and established himself as a leading Australian novelist with his natural and vivid descriptions of life in the ' outback ' in *The Shiralee* (1955), which was filmed, *Call me when the Cross turns over* (1958), *Big Smoke* (1959), and *The Ballad of the Fat Bushranger* (1961).

NILSSON, Christine (1843–1921), Swedish operatic singer, born at Wexiö, Sweden, made her début at Paris in 1864, and became a leading prima donna in Europe and the United States. She retired in 1888. See Lives by H. Headland (Rock Island, Ill., 1943) and M. L. Löfgren (Stockholm 1944).

NIMITZ, Chester William, *nim'its* (1885–1966), American admiral, born at Fredericksburg, Texas, graduated from the U.S. Naval Academy in 1905, served mainly in submarines, and by 1938 had risen to the rank of rear-admiral. Chief of the bureau of navigation during 1939–41, in 1941–45 he commanded the U.S. Pacific Fleet and Pacific Ocean areas, contributing largely to the defeat of Japan. He was made a fleet admiral in 1944, and became chief of naval operations in 1945–47, signing the Japanese surrender documents for the U.S. Special assistant to the secretary of the Navy (1947–49), he led the U.N. mediation commission in the Kashmir dispute in 1949. He was created G.C.B. in 1945. See S. E. Morison's *History of U.S. Naval Operations in World War II* (1947–54).

NIMROD. See APPERLEY, C. J.

NINIAN, St, Lowland Scots, **Ringan** (*c.* 360–*c.* 432), the first known missionary in Scotland, was born on the shores of the Solway Firth. He made a pilgrimage to Rome, was consecrated bishop (394) by the pope, visited St Martin at Tours, and he founded the church of Whithorn (397). He laboured successfully for the evangelization of the Britons and Southern Picts. See his Life by St Ailred (1109–66), edited by Bishop Forbes (1874), and studies by A. B. Scott (1916) and W. D. Simpson (1940).

NIPKOW, Paul, *nip'kof* (1860–1940), German engineer, born at Lauenburg, one of the pioneers of television, became interested in the electrical transmission of visual images and invented in 1884 the Nipkow disc, a mechanical scanning device consisting of a revolving disc with a spiral pattern of apertures. In use until 1932, it was superseded by electronic scanning.

NITHARDT, M. See GRÜNEWALD, M.

NITHSDALE, William Maxwell, 5th Earl of (1676–1744), Scottish Jacobite, at seven succeeded his father, in 1699 married Lady

Winifred Herbert (*c.* 1679–1749), youngest daughter of the Marquis of Powis, and lived at his Kirkcudbrightshire seat, Terregles. A Catholic in 1715 he joined the English Jacobites and was taken prisoner at Preston. He was tried for high treason in London, and sentenced to death; but on February 23, 1716—the night before the day fixed for his execution—he escaped from the Tower in woman's apparel, through the heroism of his countess. They settled at Rome, where the earl died. See W. Fraser's *Book of Carlaverock* (1873) and H. Taylor, *Lady Nithsdale* (1939).

NITZSCH, (1) **Gregor Wilhelm** (1790–1861), German philologist, son of (3), father of (4), brother of (2), fought as a volunteer at Leipzig and from 1827 devoted himself to defending the unity of the Homeric poems. See study by Lübker (Jena 1864).

(2) **Karl Immanuel** (1787–1868), German Lutheran theologian, son of (3), brother of (1), became professor at Bonn in 1822, and in 1847 at Berlin. He subordinated dogma to ethics, and was one of the leaders of the broad evangelical school. His chief books are *System der christlichen Lehre* (1829; Eng. trans. 1849), *Praktische Theologie* (1847–67), *Christliche Glaubenslehre* (1858), several volumes of sermons and essays. See studies by Beyschlag (2nd ed. 1882) and Hermens (1886).

(3) **Karl Ludwig** (1751–1831), German Protestant theologian, father of (1) and (2), in 1790 became professor at Wittenburg. See study by Hoppe (Halle 1832).

(4) **Karl Wilhelm** (1818–80), German historian, son of (1), a pupil of Niebuhr, he was professor at Kiel, Königsberg and Berlin. His writings embrace historical studies on Polybius (1842) and the Gracchi (1847), *Die römische Annalistik* (1873), *Deutsche Studien* (1879), German history to the peace of Augsburg (1883–85), and a history of the Roman republic (1884–85).

NIVELLE, Robert (1857–1924), French general, born at Tulle, was artillery colonel in August 1914, and made his name when in command of the army of Verdun by recapturing Douaumont and other forts (October–December 1916). He was commander-in-chief, December 1916 to May 1917, when his Aisne offensive failed and he was superseded by Pétain. See study by Hellot (1917).

NIXON, Richard Milhous (1913–), American politician, born in Yorba Linda, California, after five years in practice as a lawyer, he served in the U.S. Navy, prior to his election to the House of Representatives in 1946. He became a senator in 1950, and vice-president in 1952. His swift climb in political circles was a result of fearless outspokenness and brilliant political tactics, and he was particularly prominent as a member of the Committee on Un-American Activities, working on the Alger Hiss (q.v.) case. In May 1958 he and his wife were subjected to violent anti-American demonstrations in Peru and Venezuela, during a goodwill tour of Latin America, and in 1959 on a visit to Moscow he achieved notoriety by his outspoken exchanges with Mr Khruschev. As the Republican candidate, he lost the presidential election (1960) to Kennedy by a tiny margin. Standing for the governorship of California in 1962, he was again defeated. See his autobiography, *Six Crises* (1962). He won the presidential election in 1968 by a small margin, and was re-elected in 1972 by a large majority. During an official investigation into a break-in attempt at the Democratic National Committee's headquarters at Watergate, Washington, Nixon lost credibility with the American people by at first claiming executive privilege for senior White House officials to prevent them being questioned, and by refusing to hand over tapes of relevant conversations. He resigned in August 1974 under threat of impeachment after several leading members of his government had been found guilty of being involved in the Watergate scandal. In September 1974 he was given a full pardon by President Gerald Ford.

NKRUMAH, Kwame (1909–72), Ghanaian politician, was born at Ankroful and was educated at Achimota College, Lincoln University, Penn., and London School of Economics. He returned to Africa and in 1949 formed the nationalist Convention People's party with the slogan ' self-government now '. In 1950 he was imprisoned for his part in calling strikes and was elected to parliament while still in jail. A year later he was released, and became virtual prime minister with the title of Leader of Business in the Assembly. He was confirmed in power at the 1956 election and in 1957 became the first prime minister of the independent Commonwealth State of Ghana. Called the 'Gandhi of Africa' he was a significant leader first of the movement against white domination and then of Pan-African feeling. Ghana became a republic in 1960. Nkrumah was the moving spirit behind the Charter of African States (1961). Economic reforms sparked off political opposition and several attempts on his life. Legal imprisonment of political opponents for five years and more without trial, and interference with the judiciary in the treason trial (1963), when he dismissed the chief justice, heralded the successful referendum for a one-party state in 1964 in which the secrecy of the ballot was called in question. In 1966 his regime was overthrown by military *coup* during his absence in China. He returned to Guinea where he was appointed head of state. Publications include *Towards Colonial Freedom* (1946), his Autobiography (1957), *Consciencism* (1964). See Life by Timothy (1955).

NOAILLES, *nō-ah'y*, famous French family:
(1) **Adrien Maurice, 3rd Duke of** (1678–1766), son of (3), grandfather of (9), won his marshal's baton in Louis XV's wars. See his *Mémoires* (1839).
(2) **Anna-Elisabeth, Comtesse de** (1876–1933), poet and novelist, wrote many poems and novels and was acclaimed 'Princesse des lettres'. See books by J. Larnac (Paris 1931) and C. Fournet (Geneva 1950).
(3) **Anne Jules, 2nd Duke of** (1650–1708), father of (1), brother of (8), commanded against the Huguenots and in Spain and became marshal.

(4) **Antoine de** (1504–62), admiral and ambassador to England 1553–56.
(5) **Emanuel Henri Victurnien de** (1830–1909), diplomat, son of (10), brother of (7), was ambassador in Italy, Constantinople and Berlin, and wrote on Poland.
(6) **Emanuel Marie Louis de** (1743–1822), diplomat, brother of (11), grandfather of (10), was ambassador at Amsterdam, London and Vienna.
(7) **Jules, 7th Duke of** (1826–95), economist and writer, son of (10), brother of (5).
(8) **Louis Antoine de** (1651–1729), ecclesiastic, brother of (3), Archbishop of Paris (1695), he became cardinal in 1700 and was a reformer of clerical practice. See book by E. de Barthelemy (Paris 1886).
(9) **Louis Marie de** (1756–1804), soldier, grandson of (1), served in America under Lafayette, supported the French Revolution for a time, then returned to America and defended San Domingo against the English.
(10) **Paul, 6th duke of** (1802–85), historian, grandson of (6), grandnephew of (11), was a member of the Academy (1849) and ambassador to St Petersburg (1871).
(11) **Paul François, 5th duke of** (1739–1824), chemist, brother of (6), granduncle of (10), was a soldier before becoming a chemist.

NOBEL, Alfred (1833–96), Swedish inventor and manufacturer, was born at Stockholm, discovered how to make a safe and manageable explosive—dynamite. He also invented blasting-jelly and several kinds of smokeless powder. Ultimately he had manufactories at Bofors in Sweden, and experimented on mild steel for armour-plates, &c. He left a fortune of over £2,000,000, most of which he destined to go for annual prizes in the fields of physics, chemistry, physiology or medicine, literature and peace. See Lives by Pauli (1947), Halasz (1960) and Bergengren (1962).

NOBILE, Umberto, *nŏ'bee-lay* (1885–), Italian airman, born at Lauro, became an aeronautical engineer and built the airships *Norge* and *Italia*. Wrecked in the airship *Italia* when returning from the North Pole (May 1928), he was adjudged (1929) responsible for the disaster. In the U.S.A. 1939–42, he later returned to Italy and was re-instated. See AMUNDSEN.

NOBILI, Leopoldo (1784–1835), Italian physicist, professor of Physics at Florence, invented the thermopile used in measuring radiant heat, and the astatic galvanometer.

NOCARD, Edmond Isidore Étienne (1850–1903), French biologist, made important discoveries in veterinary science, and showed that meat and milk from tubercular cattle could transmit the disease to man.

NODDACK, Ida Eva (1896–), and **Walter Karl Friedrich** (1893–1960), German chemists, husband and wife, in 1925 discovered the elements *masurium* and *rhenium*.

NODIER, Charles, *nod-yay* (1780–1844), French writer, deeply influenced the Romanticists of 1830, but only his short stories and fairy tales are remembered. See studies by Wey (1844), Magnin (1911), and Henri-Rosier (1931).

NOEL-BAKER, Philip (1889–), British Labour politician, after a brilliant athletic and academic career at Cambridge, captained the British Olympic team (1912), and in the war commanded a Friends' ambulance unit. He served on the secretariat of the peace conference (1919) and of the League of Nations (1919–22), was M.P. for Coventry (1929–31) and for Derby from 1936. He was Cassel professor of International Relations at London (1924–29) and Dodge Lecturer at Yale (1934), where he was awarded the Howland prize. He has written a number of books on international problems, including *Disarmament* (1926), and a standard work, *The Arms Race* (1958). During and after World War II he held several junior ministerial posts and was Labour secretary of state for Air (1946–47), of commonwealth relations (1947–50) and minister of fuel and power (1950–51). He was awarded the Nobel peace prize in 1959. His son, Francis (1920–), was a Labour M.P. 1945–50 and from 1955.

NOGUCHI, Hideyo (1876–1928), Japanese bacteriologist, born in Japan, worked in the U.S. from 1899, and made important discoveries in the cause and treatment of syphilis and also of yellow fever from which he died. See Life by G. Eckstein (1931).

NOLDE, Emil, pseud. of Emil Hansen (1867–1956), German artist, born at Nolde, was one of the most important Expressionist painters, his powerful style being summed up by the phrase 'blood and soil'. He was a member of Die Brücke (1906–07) and produced a large number of etchings, lithographs and woodcuts. See his *My Own Life* (2 vols. 1931–34).

NOLLEKENS, Joseph, R.A. (1737–1823), English sculptor, born in London, executed likenesses of most of his famous contemporaries—Garrick, Sterne, Goldsmith, Johnson, Fox, Pitt, George III, &c. See J. T. Smith's *Nollekens and his Times* (1828, new ed. 1949) and P. Colson, *Their Ruling Passions* (1950).

NOLLET, Jean Antoine, *nol-ay* (1700–70), French abbé and physicist, discovered osmosis (1748), invented an electroscope, and improved the Leyden jar.

NONIUS MARCELLUS (4th cent. A.D.), Latin grammarian, was the author of a poor treatise, *De Compendiosa Doctrina*, precious as preserving many words in forgotten senses, and passages from ancient Latin authors now lost. See ed. by W. M. Ramey (1903).

NONNUS (5th cent. A.D.), Greek poet of Panopolis (Egypt), wrote a long Bacchus epic (*Dionysiaca*, trans. Rouse, 1940) and a verse paraphrase of St John's Gospel. See study by J. Golega (1930).

NORDAU, Max Simon (1849–1923), Jewish-Hungarian author, born of Jewish descent at Budapest, he studied medicine and established himself as physician, first at his birthplace (1878), and then at Paris (1886). He wrote several books of travel, but became known as the author of works on moral and social questions, including *Conventional Lies of Society* (1883; 15th ed. 1890; Eng. trans. 1895), and as a novelist. He was also an active Zionist leader in Europe. See books by A. and M. Nordau (N.Y. 1943) and M. Ben-Horin (N.Y. 1957).

NORDEN, John (1548–1625?), English cartographer, born in Somerset, became an attorney, but about 1580 began to make surveys of the English counties. He published descriptions of several counties and maps which were the first printed English maps to show roads and a scale. Several of his maps were used for Camden's *Britannia*. He made surveys of Crown lands, and other works include a travel guide (1625).

NORDENSKJÖLD, (1) Baron Nils Adolf Erik, *nor'dén-shæl* (1832–1901), Swedish Arctic navigator, was born at Helsingfors, November 18, 1832, naturalized himself in Sweden, and made several expeditions to Spitsbergen, mapping the south of the island. After two preliminary trips proving the navigability of the Kara Sea, he accomplished (June 1878–September 1879) the navigation of the Northeast Passage, from the Atlantic to the Pacific along the north coast of Asia. He later made two expeditions to Greenland. See his *Voyage of the Vega* (Eng. trans. 1881), *Scientific Results of the Vega Expedition* (1883), &c.; and works by A. Leslie (1879) and S. Hedin (1928).

(2) **Nils Otto Gustav** (1869–1928), Swedish Antarctic explorer, nephew of (1), after travels in S. America led an expedition to the Antarctic (1901–03) and explored the Andes (1920–21). See Life by H. Munthe (Stockholm 1928).

NORFOLK, Dukes of. See HOWARD.

NORMAN, Montagu, 1st Baron (1871–1950), English banker, after serving in the South African war entered banking and became associated with the Bank of England. He was elected governor of the Bank in 1920 and held this post until 1944. During this time he wielded great influence on national and international monetary affairs. See Lives by Clay (1957) and Boyle (1967).

NORRIS, (1) Frank (1870–1902), American novelist, born in Chicago, first studied art but later turned to journalism, and while a reporter was involved in the Jameson raid in South Africa. He was influenced by Zola and was one of the first American naturalist writers, his major novel being *McTeague* (1899). See Life by F. Walker (1932) and study by E. Marchand (1942).

(2) **Kathleen** (1880–1966), American novelist, born in San Francisco, began writing stories and published her first novel, *Mother,* in 1911. After that she wrote many popular novels and short stories, including *Certain People of Importance* (1922) and *Over at the Crowleys* (1946).

NORTH, (1) Brownlow (1810–75), English evangelist, after living a life of pleasure for many years, became an evangelist preaching mainly in Scotland. See Life by K. Moody-Stuart (1929).

(2) **Sir Dudley** (1641–91), economist, brother of (5), (7), (9), a Turkey merchant, lived for a time in Constantinople, became a sheriff of London and a commissioner of customs. He was a keen-eyed observer, and had great mechanical genius, and his *Discourses upon Trade* (1691) anticipated Adam Smith. See Life by R. North (1744).

(3) **Sir Dudley Burton Napier** (1881–1961), British admiral, entered the navy in 1895 and was commander of the cruiser *New Zealand* at Heligoland and Jutland. He was chief of

staff of the home fleet from 1932 to 1933 and commanded the North Atlantic station in 1939–40. He was relieved of his command after six Vichy French warships had been allowed to pass through the Gibraltar Straits to oppose the Dakar landing. In 1957 the prime minister, while exonerating him from charges of negligence, refused to open an inquiry into his case.

(4) **Sir Edward, 1st Baron** (1496–1564), lawyer, father of (10), a privy councillor, held important posts during the reigns of Henry VIII, Edward VI, Mary and Elizabeth. See work by Lady F. Bushby (1911).

(5) **Francis, 1st Baron Guilford** (1637–85), lawyer, brother of (2), (7), (9), educated at Cambridge and called to the bar in 1655, was successively solicitor-general, attorney-general, lord chief-justice of the court of common pleas, privy councillor, lord chancellor (1682), and Baron Guilford (1683). See Life by R. North (1742).

(6) **Frederick, 8th Lord North and 2nd Earl of Guilford** (1732–92), statesman, entered parliament at the age of twenty-two, became a lord of the treasury, chancellor of the exchequer and in 1770 prime minister. He was largely responsible for the measures that brought about the loss of America, being too ready to surrender his judgment to the king's. In 1782 he resigned and later entered into a coalition with Fox, hitherto his opponent, and served with him under the Duke of Portland in 1783. See Lives by R. Lucas (1913), W. B. Pemberton (1938) and study by H. Butterfield (1949).

(7) **John** (1645–83), scholar, brother of (2), (5), (9), a fellow of Jesus College, Cambridge, succeeded Barrow as master of Trinity College in 1677, and became clerk of the closet to Charles II. See Life by R. North (1744).

(8) **Marianne** (1830–90), flower painter, a descendant of (9), painted flowers in many countries and gave her valuable collection to Kew Gardens. See her Autobiography (2 vols. 1892–93).

(9) **Roger** (1653–1734), lawyer and writer, brother of (2), (5), (7), was educated at Jesus College, Cambridge, entered the Middle Temple and rose to a lucrative practice at the bar. A Nonjuror, he retired after the Revolution. His three hypereulogistic biographies, his autobiography (all collected by Jessop in 1890) and his *Examen* (1740) give him a place in English literature.

(10) **Sir Thomas** (?1535–?1601), translator, son of (4), is known for his translation of Plutarch (1579), a noble monument of English from which Shakespeare drew his knowledge of ancient history (ed. by Wyndham 6 vols. 1895 *et seq.*). See work by F. Bushby (1911).

NORTHBROOK. See BARING (4).
NORTHCLIFFE, Lord. See HARMSWORTH (1).
NORTHCOTE, (1) James (1746–1831), English painter, the son of a Plymouth watchmaker, painted portraits and historical pictures, among them the well-known *Princes in the Tower* and *Prince Arthur and Hubert*, but is also remembered by Hazlitt's *Conversations with Northcote* (ed. by Gosse,

1894) and his own with Ward (1901). He was elected R.A. in 1787. See Life by Gwynn (1898).

(2) **Sir Stafford.** See IDDESLEIGH.
NORTHROP, John Howard (1891–), American biochemist, born at New York, educated at Columbia University, became professor of Bacteriology at California in 1949. He discovered the fermentation process for the manufacture of acetone, worked on enzymes and published *Crystalline Enzymes* (1939). In 1946 he shared the Nobel prize for chemistry with Stanley and Sumner for their study of ways of producing purified enzymes and virus products.

NORTHUMBERLAND, Dukes of. See PERCY.

NORTON, (1) Andrews (1786–1853), American Unitarian theologian, father of (3), studied at Harvard, became professor there, and wrote *Reasons for not believing the Doctrines of Trinitarians* (1833), and two works on *The Genuineness of the Gospels*.

(2) **Caroline Elizabeth Sarah** (1808–77), Irish poet and novelist, was born in London, second of the three beautiful grand-daughters of Richard Brinsley Sheridan. In 1827 she married a barrister, the Hon. George Chapple Norton (1800–75). She bore him three sons, of whom the second succeeded as fourth Lord Grantley; but the marriage proved most unhappy, and her friendship with Lord Melbourne (q.v.) led her husband to institute a groundless and unsuccessful action of divorce (1836). She supported her family by her writings, and her experiences and publications helped to improve the legal status of women. In March 1877 she married Sir William Stirling Maxwell (q.v.), but died June 15. See Lives by J. G. Perkins (1909) and A. Acland (1948).

(3) **Charles Eliot** (1827–1908), American author, son of (1), joint editor with Lowell of the *North American Review*, was professor of Art at Harvard from 1875 and personal friend of Carlyle, Lowell, Emerson, Ruskin and Clough, whose letters he edited. See his *Letters* (N.Y. 1913), study by E. W. Emerson and W. F. Harris (N.Y. 1912), and Life by K. Vanderbilt (1960).

(4) **Thomas** (1532–84), English lawyer, M.P., and poet, with Sackville (q.v.) joint author of *Gorboduc*, was born in London.
NORWAY, N. S. See SHUTE (2).
NORWICH. See COOPER (2).
NOSTRADAMUS, or Michel de Notredame (1503–66), French astrologer, born at St Remi in Provence, December 14, 1503, became doctor of medicine in 1529, and practised at Agen, Lyons, &c. He set himself up as a prophet about 1547. His *Centuries* of predictions in rhymed quatrains (two collections, 1555–58), expressed generally in obscure and enigmatical terms, brought their author a great reputation. Charles IX on his accession appointed him physician-in-ordinary. See books on him by Jaubert (1656) and C. A. Ward (1891); *Complete prophecies*, ed. H. C. Roberts (1947).
NOTTINGHAM, Earls of. See FINCH (2) and HOWARD Family (6).
NOVÁK, Viteslav (1870–1949), Czech composer, born at Kamenitz, studied then

taught at Prague. His many compositions bear the impress of his native folk melody.

NOVALIS, the pen-name of **Friedrich von Hardenberg** (1772–1801), German Romantic poet, who was called the ' Prophet of Romanticism '. At Weissenfels (1795) he fell in love with a beautiful girl, whose early death left a lasting impression upon him. He died of consumption. He left two philosophical romances, both incomplete, *Heinrich von Ofterdingen* and *Lehrlinge zu Sais*. His *Hymnen an die Nacht* and his *Poems* and *Sacred Songs* are completed works. See Carlyle's *Miscellaneous Essays* (vol. ii), the Life published at Gotha (2nd ed. 1883), and the correspondence with the Schlegels (1880).

NOVATIAN (fl. 3rd cent. A.D.), a Roman Stoic, was converted to Christianity and ordained a priest. In A.D. 251, soon after the Decian persecution, a controversy arose about those who fell away during persecution. Pope Cornelius (251–53) defended indulgence towards the lapsed; Novatian was chosen by a small party and ordained bishop in opposition to Cornelius. The Novatians denied the lawfulness of readmitting the lapsed to communion. The sect, in spite of persecution, survived into the 6th century.

NOVELLO, (1) **Ivor,** in full **Ivor Novello Davies** (1893–1951), Welsh actor, composer, songwriter and dramatist, son of the singer Dame Clara Novello Davies, was born in Cardiff and educated at Magdalen College School, Oxford, where he was a chorister. His song ' Keep the Home Fires Burning' was one of the most successful of World War I. He first appeared on the regular stage in London in 1921. He enjoyed great popularity, his most successful and characteristic works being his ' Ruritanian ' musical plays such as *Glamorous Night* (1935), *The Dancing Years* (1939), *King's Rhapsody* (1949). See Life by P. Noble (1951).

(2) **Vincent** (1781–1861), English organist, composer and music publisher, born in London of an Italian father and English mother, was a founder of the Philharmonic (1813), and its pianist and conductor. His compositions improved church music, and he was a painstaking editor of unpublished works. His son, **Joseph Vincent** (1810–96), also organist and music publisher, from 1857 lived at Nice and at Genoa with his sister, Mrs Cowden Clarke (q.v.). Another sister, **Clara Anastasia** (1818–1908), vocalist, born in London, won triumphs all over Europe; but in 1843 married Count Gigliucci; returned to the stage 1850–60.

NOYES, (1) **Alfred** (1880–1958), English poet, born in Staffordshire, began writing verse as an undergraduate at Oxford, and on the strength of getting a volume published in his final year he left without taking a degree. This book, *The Loom of Years* (1902), which gained a word of praise from George Meredith, was followed by *The Flower of Old Japan* (1903) and *The Forest of Wild Thyme* (1905), both of which attracted some notice. Noyes now turned to the subject of some of his most successful work—the sea, and in particular the Elizabethan tradition. *Forty Singing Seamen* (1908) and the epic *Drake* (1908) were in this vein. Having married an American, he travelled in the U.S.A. lecturing and receiving many academic honours, culminating in the visiting professorship of Poetry at Princeton (1914). In 1922 appeared *The Torchbearers*, a panegyric in blank verse on the hitherto comparatively unsung men of science. Noyes' verse shows great craftsmanship, and has rhythm, melody and lyric quality; he has however been criticized for conservatism and unwillingness to experiment. That he had no affection whatsoever for modern trends is apparent in his *Some Aspects of Modern Poetry* (1924), which is a defence of traditionalism. He also wrote essays, plays, and studies of William Morris and Voltaire. The latter, published shortly after his conversion to Roman Catholicism, involved him in a mild controversy with the clergy. See his autobiographical *Two Worlds for Memory* (1953).

(2) **John Humphrey** (1811–86), American Perfectionist, born at Brattleboro, Vermont, as a theological student thought that the prevailing theology was wrong. He founded a ' Perfectionist ' church at Putney, Vermont, and he and his converts put their property into a common stock. In 1848 the communists removed to Oneida, N.Y. See his several works, Hepworth Dixon's *New America*, &c.; Nordhoff, *Communistic Societies of the United States* (1875).

NUFFIELD, William Richard Morris, 1st Viscount (1877–1963), British motor magnate and philanthropist, started in the cycle business and by 1910 was manufacturing prototypes of Morris Oxford cars. He was the first British manufacturer to develop the mass production of cheap cars. He received a baronetcy in 1929 and was raised to the peerage in 1934. He used part of his vast fortune to benefit hospitals, charities and Oxford University. In 1943 he established the Nuffield Foundation for medical, scientific and social research.

NUNCOMAR. See HASTINGS (4).

NÚÑEZ DE ARCE, Gaspar, *noo'nyeth* THay *ar'thay* (1834–1903), Spanish poet, dramatist and statesman, born at Valladolid, held office in the government in 1883 and 1888, and in 1894 received a national ovation at Toledo. As a lyric poet he may be styled the ' Spanish Tennyson ', and among his poems are *Gritos del Combate* (1875), *Última Lamentación de Lord Byron* (1879), *El Vértigo* (1879), *La Pesca* (1884) and *La Maruja* (1886). His plays include *La Cuenta del Zapatero* (1859) and *El Haz de Leña* (1872).

NUR ED-DIN MAHMŪD, Malek al-Adel (1117–73), born at Damascus, succeeded his father as ruler of Northern Syria in 1145, and from this time his life was one long duel with the Christians. Count Joscelin's great defeat at Edessa gave occasion to the second Crusade; and the Crusaders were foiled by Nur ed-Din before Damascus. The emir next conquered Tripolis, Antioch and Damascus (1153). His nephew, Saladin, completed the conquest of Egypt from the Fatimes. Nur ed-Din, created by the khalif of Baghdad sultan of Syria and Egypt, became jealous of Saladin, and was preparing to march into Egypt when he died.

NUREYEV, Rudolf (1939–), Russian ballet-dancer, born in Siberia, obtained political asylum in Paris in 1961 and became a member of Le Grand Ballet du Marquis de Cuevas. Since then he has played many different rôles in various countries of the world, often appearing with Margot Fonteyn (q.v.), with whom he made his Covent Garden début in 1962. Films in which he has appeared include *Swan Lake* (1966). See his Autobiography (1962).

NURI ES-SA'ID. See Es-Sa'id.

NYERERE, Julius Kambarage, *nĭ-reer'-ee* (1922?–), Tanzanian politician, born at Butiama village, Lake Victoria, qualified as teacher at Makerere College and, after a spell of teaching, took a degree in history and economics at Edinburgh. On his return, he reorganized the nationalists into the Tanganyika African National Union (1954) of which he became president, entered the Legislative Council (1958) and in 1960 became chief minister. In 1961, Tanganyika was granted internal self-government and Nyerere became premier. During 1962 he retired for a while to reorganize his party, but was elected president in December when Tanganyika became a republic. In 1964 he negotiated the union of Tanganyika and Zanzibar (which became Tanzania in October of the same year).

O

OAKSEY. See Lawrence, Geoffrey.

OASTLER, Richard (1789–1861), English reformer, advocate of a ten-hours' working day and the factory laws, by his opposition to the Poor Law irritated his employer, Thomas Thornhill, who dismissed him from his stewardship of Fixby estate, near Huddersfield, and had him jailed (1840–44) for a debt of £2000, ultimately paid by subscription. See *Life* by C. Driver (1947).

OATES, (1) Lawrence Edward Grace (1880–1912), English explorer, was born in Putney in 1880, and educated at Eton, which he left to serve in the South African War with the Inniskilling Dragoons. In 1910 he set out with Scott's Antarctic Expedition, and was one of the party of five to reach the South Pole (January 17, 1912). On the return journey the explorers suffered dangerous delay and became weatherbound. Lamed by severe frostbite, Oates, convinced that his crippled condition would fatally handicap his companions' prospect of winning through, walked out into the blizzard, deliberately sacrificing his life to enhance his comrades' chances of survival. See L. C. Bernacchi, *A Very Gallant Gentleman* (1933).

(2) **Titus** (1649–1705), English conspirator and perjurer, born at Oakham, the son of an Anabaptist preacher, attended Cambridge University. Next taking orders, he held curacies and a naval chaplaincy, from all of which he was expelled for infamous practices. With the Rev. Dr Tonge he resolved to concoct the ' narrative of a horrid plot ', and, feigning conversion to Catholicism, was admitted to the Jesuit seminaries of Valladolid and St Omer. From both in a few months he was expelled for misconduct; but, returning to London in June 1678, he forthwith communicated to the authorities his pretended plot, the main features of which were a rising of the Catholics, a general massacre of Protestants, the burning of London, and the assassination of the king, his brother James being placed on the throne. He swore to the truth of it before a magistrate, Sir Edmund Berry Godfrey, who on October 17 was found dead in a ditch—murdered possibly by Titus and his confederates. All London straightway went wild with fear and rage, and Oates became the hero of the day. Many other wretches came forward to back or emulate his charges; the queen herself was assailed; and many Catholics were cast into prison. He was directly or indirectly the cause of thirty-five judicial murders; but after two years a reaction set in. In May 1683 Oates was fined £100,000 for calling the Duke of York a traitor, and being unable to pay, was imprisoned; in May 1685 he was found guilty of perjury, and sentenced to be stripped of his canonicals, pilloried, flogged and imprisoned for life. The Revolution of 1688 set him at liberty, and he was even granted a pension. See Seccombe's *Lives of Twelve Bad Men* (1894), and Pollock's *The Popish Plot* (new ed. 1944).

OBEL, Matthias de l'. See L'Obel.

OBERLIN, Johann Friedrich, *ö'bĕr-leen* (1740–1826), Alsatian clergyman, was born at Strasburg, and in 1767 became Protestant pastor of Waldbach, in the Ban de la Roche, which had suffered in the Thirty Years' War. Oberlin introduced better methods of cultivation and manufacture, made roads and bridges, founded a library and schools. See Lives by Bodemann (1868) and Butler (1882), and study by Scheuermann (1941).

O'BRIEN, (1) William (1852–1928), Irish journalist and Nationalist, born at Mallow, became a journalist, founded *United Ireland*, sat in parliament as a Nationalist (1883–95), was nine times prosecuted and imprisoned for two years. He retired in 1895 owing to dissensions in the party, headed the Independent Nationalists, but returned to parliament (1900–18) for Cork, and founded the (anti-Redmondite) United Irish League. He wrote *Recollections* (1905), *Evening Memories* (1920), *An Olive Branch* (on ' All-for-Ireland ', 1910), *The Irish Revolution* (1923), &c.

(2) **William Smith** (1803–64), Irish insur-

gent, son of Sir Edward O'Brien, born in County Clare, entered parliament in 1826, and though a Protestant, supported the Catholic claims as a Whig. In October 1843 he joined O'Connell's Repeal Association. But O'Connell's aversion to physical force made a wide gulf between him and the fiery ' Young Ireland ' party. After many disputes O'Brien in 1846 withdrew from the Associ-ation, and the Young Irelanders set up a Repeal League under his leadership. The sentence of John Mitchel for ' treason-felony ' in 1848 hastened the projected rising, which ended ludicrously in an almost bloodless battle in a cabbage-garden at Ballingarry. Smith O'Brien was arrested, tried and sentenced to death; but the sentence was commuted to transportation for life. In 1854 he was released on condition of not returning to Ireland, and in 1856 he received a free pardon. He died at Bangor (N. Wales).

O'BRYAN, William (1778–1868), English Nonconformist, son of a Cornish yeoman, quarrelled with the Methodists and founded a new Methodist communion, the (Arminian) Bible Christians or Bryanites.

O'CASEY, Sean (1884–1964), Irish playwright, born in a poor part of Dublin, picked up what education he could and worked as a labourer and for nationalist organizations before beginning his career as a dramatist. His early plays, dealing with low life in Dublin—*Shadow of a Gunman* (1923) and *Juno and the Paycock* (1924)—were written for the Abbey Theatre. Later he became more experimental and impressionistic. Other works include *The Silver Tassie* (1929), *Cockadoodle Dandy* (1949) and *The Bishop's Bonfire* (1955). He also wrote essays, such as *The Flying Wasp* (1936). He was awarded the Hawthornden Prize in 1926. See his autobiography, begun in 1939 with *I Knock at the Door* and continuing through several volumes to *Sunset and Evening Star* (1954). See study by Krause (1960).

OCCAM, William. See Ockham.

OCCLEVE, Thomas. See Hoccleve.

OCHINO, Bernardino, ō-kee'nō (1487–1564), Italian Protestant reformer, born at Siena, joined the Franciscans, but in 1534 changed to the Capuchins. In four years' time he was vicar-general of the order. In 1542 he was summoned to Rome to answer for evangelical tendencies, but fled to Calvin at Geneva. In 1545 he became preacher to the Italians in Augsburg. Cranmer invited him to England, where he was pastor to the Italian exiles and a prebend in Canterbury. At Mary's accession (1553) he fled to Switzerland, and ministered to the Italian exiles in Zürich for ten years. The publication of *Thirty Dialogues,* one of which the Calvinists said contained a defence of polygamy, led to his being banished. Ochino fled to Poland, but was not permitted to stay there and died at Slavkow in Moravia. See Lives by Benrath (Eng. trans. 1876) and Bainton (1940).

OCHOA, Severo (1905–), American bio-chemist, born in Spain, studied medicine in Madrid and emigrated to the U.S.A. in 1940, joining the staff of the New York College of Medicine two years later. He was awarded, with Kornberg, the 1959 Nobel prize for medicine for work on the biological synthesis of nucleic acids.

OCHTERLONY, Sir David, -lō'- (1758–1825), British general, born of Scottish descent at Boston, Mass., went to India as a cadet, and was made lieutenant-colonel in 1803. His greatest services were rendered against the Gurkhas of Nepal in 1814 and 1815, with whom a treaty was made in 1816. The same year Ochterlony was made a baronet. He also held a command in the Pindari and Mahratta wars of 1817 and 1818.

OCKHAM, or Occam, William of (c. 1300– c. 1349), English Nominalist philosopher, was born at Ockham, Surrey. He entered the Franciscan order, studied at Oxford and Paris, and headed the Franciscans' revolt against Pope John XXII's denunciation of Evangelical poverty (1322). After four months' imprisonment at Avignon he fled to Munich, and found there a defender in the Emperor Louis of Bavaria, whom he in his turn defended stoutly against the temporal pretensions of the pope. In 1342 he seems to have become general of the Franciscans. Besides insisting on the independent divine right of temporal rulers, Ockham won fame as the reviver of Nominalism (the doctrine that universal ideas are merely names), for which he won a final victory over the rival Realism. To some of the arguments of theologians he applied the dictum that beings ought not to be multiplied except out of necessity—known as ' Occam's razor '. His views on civil government are expounded in *Super Potestate Papali* and his *Dialogues,* his philosophical views in *Summa Logices* (1488), commentaries on Porphyry and Aristotle, and the commentary on the *Sentences* of Peter the Lombard, and his theological in this last and the *Tractatus de Sacramento Altaris* (1516).

OCKLEY, Simon (1678–1720), English orien-talist, in 1711 became Arabic professor at Oxford. His *History of the Saracens* (1708– 1718) was long a standard, though not based on the best authorities.

O'CONNELL, Daniel (1775–1847), Irish political leader, called ' the Liberator ', was born near Cahirciveen, Co. Kerry, August 6. Called to the Irish bar in 1798 he built up a highly successful practice. Leader of the agitation for the rights of Catholics, he formed in 1823 the Catholic Association, which successfully fought elections against the landlords. Elected M.P. for Clare in 1828, he was prevented as a Catholic from taking his seat, but was re-elected in 1830, the Catholic Emancipation Bill having been passed in the meantime. He formed a new society for Repeal of the union, revived as often as suppressed by others under new names. He denounced the ministry of Wellington and Peel, but in the face of a threatened prosecution (1831) he temporized, saved himself, and was made King's Counsel. In 1830 the potato crop had been very poor, and under O'Connell's advice the people declined to pay tithes, and that winter disorder was rampant everywhere. He had sat last for Kerry, when at the general election of 1832 he was returned for Dublin. At this time he nominated about half of the candidates returned, while three of his sons and two of his sons-in-law composed his 'household brigade'. Of the 105 Irish members 45—his famous 'tail'—were declared Repealers. He fought fiercely against the Coercion Act of 1833. By Feargus O'Connor, the *Freeman's Journal*, and his more ardent followers he was forced to bring the Repeal movement prematurely into parliament; a motion for inquiry was defeated by 523 to 38. For the next five years (1835–40) he gave the Whigs a steady support. Mulgrave and Drummond governed Ireland so mildly that O'Connell was prepared to abandon the Repeal agitation. In 1836 he was unseated on petition for Dublin, and he was returned for Kilkenny. In 1837 the mastership of the rolls was offered to him but declined. In August he founded his 'Precursor Society', and in April 1840 his famous Repeal Association. Yet the agitation languished till the appearance of the *Nation* in 1842 brought him the aid of Dillon, Duffy, Davis, Mangan and Daunt. In 1841 O'Connell lost his seat at Dublin, but found another at Cork, and in November he was elected lord mayor of Dublin. In 1843 he brought up Repeal in the Dublin corporation, and carried it by 41 to 15. The agitation now leaped into prominence, but the Young Ireland party began to grow impatient of the old chief's tactics, and O'Connell allowed himself to outrun his better judgment. Wellington poured 35,000 men into Ireland. A great meeting was fixed at Clontarf for Sunday, October 8, 1843, but it was proclaimed the day before, and O'Connell issued a counter-proclamation abandoning the meeting. Early in 1844, with his son and five of his chief supporters, he was imprisoned and fined for a conspiracy to raise sedition. The House of Lords set aside the verdict on September 4; but for fourteen weeks the Tribune lay in prison. He opposed Peel's provincial 'godless colleges', and it soon came to an open split between him and Young Ireland (1846). Next followed the potato famine. A broken man, he left Ireland for the last time in January 1847, and died at Genoa. Of O'Connell's writings the most characteristic is the *Letter to the Earl of Shrewsbury* (1842). His *Memoir of Ireland* (1843) is poor and inaccurate. There are Lives by his son John (1846), MacDonagh (1903), Gwynn (1929), O'Faolain (1938) and Tierney (1949); also *Correspondence*, ed. Fitzpatrick (1888).

O'CONNOR, (1) **Feargus Edward** (1794–1855), Irish Chartist, studied at Trinity College, Dublin, was called to the Irish bar, and entered parliament for Cork Co. in 1832. Estranged from O'Connell, he devoted himself to the cause of the working classes in England. His eloquence and enthusiasm gave him vast popularity, and his Leeds *Northern Star* (1837) did much to advance Chartism. Elected for Nottingham 1847, he presented the monster petition in April 1848. In 1852 he became hopelessly insane.

(2) **Frank**, pseud. of **Michael O'Donovan** (1903–66), Irish writer, born at Cork. Although he wrote plays and some excellent literary criticism—*Art of the Theatre* (1947),

The Modern Novel (1956), *The Mirror in the Roadway* (1957)—his best medium was almost exclusively the short story. Yeats said of him that he was 'doing for Ireland what Chehov did for Russia'. Representative titles are: *Guests of the Nation* (1931), *Bones of Contention* (1936), *Crab Apple Jelly* (1944), *Travellers' Samples* (1956), and collections of short stories (1946, 1953, 1954 and 1956). He also wrote a memoir, *An Only Child* (1961), and critical studies, *The Lonely Voice* (1963) and *Shakespeare's Progress* (1960). See his autobiography (1968).

(3) **Thomas Power** (1848–1929), P.C. (1924), born at Athlone, was educated at Queen's College, Galway, became a journalist. Elected M.P. for Galway in 1880, he sat for Liverpool 1885, and was a conspicuous Irish Nationalist. He wrote *Memoirs of an Old Parliamentarian* (1928), &c. See *Life* by Hamilton Fyfe (1934).

OCTAVIA (d. 11 B.C.), sister of the Emperor Augustus, distinguished for beauty and womanly virtues. On the death of her first husband, Marcellus, she consented in 40 B.C. to marry Antony, to reconcile him and her brother; but in a few years Antony forsook her for Cleopatra.

OCTAVIAN. See AUGUSTUS.

ODESCALCHI. See INNOCENT XI.

ODETS, **Clifford**, *o-dets'* (1906–63), American playwright and actor, born in Philadelphia, in 1931 joined the Group Theatre, New York, under whose auspices his early plays were produced. The most important American playwright of the 1930s, his works are marked by a strong social conscience and grow largely from the conditions of the Great Depression of that time. They include *Waiting for Lefty*, *Awake and Sing* and *Till the Day I Die*, all produced in 1935, and *Golden Boy* (1937). He was responsible for a number of film scenarios, including *The General Died at Dawn*, *None but the Lonely Heart* (which he directed), *Deadline at Dawn*, *The Big Knife*.

ODLING, **William** (1829–1921), British chemist, Waynflete professor of Chemistry at Oxford, F.R.S. (1859), classified the silicates and advanced suggestions with regard to atomic weights which made $O = 16$ instead of 8.

ODO (*c.* 1036–97), Bishop of Bayeux and Earl of Kent, was half-brother to William the Conqueror (q.v.), and played under him a conspicuous part in English history. He rebuilt Bayeux cathedral and may have commissioned the Bayeux tapestry.

ODOACER, or **Odovacar**, *ō-dō-ay'sèr* (d. 493), barbarian warrior, son of a Germanic captain in the service of the Western Roman empire, took part in the revolution which (475) drove Julius Nepos from the throne and conferred on Orestes's son Romulus the title of Augustus, scoffingly turned to Augustulus. With the Herulians and other Germanic mercenaries he marched against Pavia, and stormed the city (476). Romulus abdicated, and thus perished the Roman empire. Odoacer was a politic ruler; but his increasing power excited the alarm of the Byzantine Emperor Zeno, who encouraged Theoderic, King of the Ostrogoths, to undertake an expedition against Italy (489). Odoacer, defeated in three great battles, shut himself up in Ravenna, which he defended for three years. Compelled by famine, he capitulated (493); a fortnight later he was assassinated by Theoderic himself. See Hodgkin's *Italy and her Invaders*.

O'DONNELL, (1) Hugh Roe (?1571–1602), Lord of Tyrconnel, fought against the English in Ireland, and fled to Spain in 1602, leaving his power to his brother, **Rory** (1575–1608), who kissed the king's hand, and was made Earl of Tyrconnel (1603); but having plotted to seize Dublin Castle (1607), fled, and died at Rome.

(2) **Leopold** (1809–67), marshal of Spain, born at Tenerife, was descended from an Irish family. He supported the infant Isabella against Don Carlos, and emigrated with the queen-mother to France. In 1843 his intrigues against Espartero were successful; and as governor-general of Cuba he amassed a fortune. He returned to Spain in 1846; was made war minister by Espartero in 1854, but in 1856 supplanted him by a *coup d'état*. He was in three months' time succeeded by Narváez, but in 1858 he returned to power; in 1859 he commanded in Morocco, took the Moorish camp, and was made Duke of Tetuan. In 1866 his cabinet was upset by Narváez.

O'DONOVAN, Michael. See O'CONNOR, FRANK.

OECOLAMPADIUS, Joannes, Latinized Greek for Hüssgen or Hausschein (1482–1531), was born at Weinsberg in Swabia. He studied at Heidelberg, became tutor to the sons of the Elector Palatine, and subsequently preacher at Basel, where Erasmus employed him. In 1516 he entered a convent at Augsburg, but under Luther's influence commenced reformer at Basel in 1522 as preacher and professor of Theology. On the Lord's Supper he gradually adopted the views of Zwingli, disputed with Luther at Marburg in 1529, and wrote treatises. See Lives by Herzog (1843) and Hagenbach (1859).

OEHLENSCHLÄGER, Adam Gottlob, *œ'lẽn-shlay-gẽr* (1779–1850), born in Copenhagen, was by 1805 foremost of Danish poets. *Hakon Jarl* was his first tragedy (1807; trans. by Lascelles, 1875); *Correggio* (trans. by Theod. Martin, 1854) dates from 1809. In 1810 he was made professor of Aesthetics in Copenhagen University. His fame rests principally on his twenty-four tragedies. See his Autobiography (1830–31) and Reminiscences (1850).

OERSTED, Hans Christian (1777–1851), Danish physicist, professor at the University of Copenhagen, discovered electromagnetism.

OETINGER, Christoph Friedrich, *œh'-ting-er* (1702–82), German theosophic theologian, leader of the Pietists and a disciple of Swedenborg.

O'FAOLAIN, Sean, *ō-fay'lẽn* (1900–), Irish writer, born in Dublin, was educated at the National University of Ireland, and took his M.A. at Harvard. He lectured for a period (1929) at Boston College, then took a post as a teacher at Strawberry Hill, Middlesex. In 1933 he returned to Ireland to teach. His first writing was in the Gaelic, and he produced an edition of translations from the Gaelic—*The Silver Branch*—in 1938. Before this, however, he had attracted attention with a novel, *A Nest of Simple Folk* (1933). He never quite repeated its success with later novels, and thereafter wrote many biographies, including *Daniel O'Connell* (1938), *De Valera* (1939), and *The Great O'Neill* (1942), this last being a life of the 2nd Earl of Tyrone. He edited the autobiography of Wolfe Tone (1937). His *Stories of Sean O'Faolain* (1958) cover thirty years of writing and progress from the lilting ' Irishry ' of his youth to the deeper and wider artistry of his maturity, showing him as a master of this most exacting literary form.

OFFA (d. 796), king of Mercia from 757, contended successfully against Wessex and the Welsh, and made Mercia the principal state in England. He was probably the most powerful English monarch before the tenth century, and is reputed to have founded the abbeys of Bath and StputAlbans.

OFFENBACH, Jacques (1819–80), German-Jewish composer of *opéra bouffe*, born at Cologne, came to Paris in 1833, becoming *chef d'orchestre* in the Théâtre-Français in 1848, and manager of the *Bouffes parisiens* in 1855. He composed a vast number of light, lively operettas, *Le Mariage aux lanternes*, &c., but is best known as inventor of modern *opéra bouffe*, represented by *Orphée aux enfers* (1858), *La Belle Hélène*, *La Barbe bleu*, *La Grande Duchesse*, *Geneviève de Brabant*, *Roi Carotte*, and *Madame Favart*. The well-known *Contes d'Hoffmann* was not produced till after his death. See the diary of his American tour, trans. MacClintock (1948) and study by Kracauer (Eng. trans. 1937).

O'FLAHERTY, Liam, *ō-flah'-* (1897–), Irish writer, born in the Aran Islands, Galway. He fought in the British army during World War I and on the Republican side in the Irish civil war. *The Informer* (1926) won the James Tait Black prize and was a popular success. Other books, reflecting the intensity of his feeling and style, include *Spring Sowing* (1926), *The Assassin* (1928), *The Puritan* (1932), *Famine* (1937) and *Land* (1946). See his autobiographical *Two Years* (1930) and *Shame the Devil* (1934).

OFTERDINGEN, Heinrich von (12th–13th cent.), one of the famous minnesinger or lyric poets of Germany, who flourished between the years 1170 and 1250.

OGDEN, Charles Kay (1889–1957), English linguistic reformer, educated at Rossall School, took a first class in classics at Cambridge, where he was first editor of the *Cambridge Magazine* (1912–22) and founder in 1917 of the Orthological Institute. In the 1920s he conceived the idea of Basic English, which he developed, with the help of Ivor Armstrong Richards (1893–), another eminent Cambridge scholar, into a practical, easily learnt language with a vocabulary of only 850 words.

OGIER LE DANOIS, a vassal noble of Charlemagne, whose revolt against the emperor is the theme of a *chanson de geste*, written by Raimbert of Paris before 1150.

OGILBY, John (1600–76), Edinburgh-born topographer, printer and map-maker, became a dancing teacher in London and a tutor in Strafford's household, lost all in the Civil War, but after the Restoration obtained court recognition and became a London publisher. The great fire of 1666 destroyed his stock but got him the job, with William Morgan, of surveying the gutted sites in the city. With the proceeds he established a thriving printing house and was appointed 'king's cosmographer and geographic printer'. His early productions include his own translations of Vergil and Homer (sneered at by Pope), but his most important publications were the maps and atlases engraved in the last decade of his life, including Africa (1670), America (1671) and Asia (1673); also a road atlas of Britain (1675) unfinished at his death. His map of London, completed by Morgan (1677), is also important.

OGLETHORPE, James Edward (1696–1785), English general, born in London, the son of Sir Theophilus Oglethorpe, served with Prince Eugene, and in 1722–54 sat in parliament. Meanwhile he projected a colony in America for debtors from English jails and persecuted Austrian Protestants. Parliament contributed £10,000; George II gave a grant of land, after him called Georgia; and in 1732 Oglethorpe went out with 120 persons and founded Savannah. In 1735 he took out 300 more, including the two Wesleys; and in 1738 he was back again with 600 men. War with Spain was declared in 1739; in 1740 Oglethorpe invaded Florida, and in 1742 repulsed a Spanish invasion of Georgia. In 1743 he left the colony to repel malicious charges. He was tried and acquitted after the '45 for failing as major-general to overtake Prince Charles's army. He died at Cranham Hall, Essex. See Lives by Harris (1841), Cooper (1904), Ettinger (1936).

O'HIGGINS, Bernardo (1778–1842), Chilean revolutionary, natural son of Ambrosio O'Higgins (c. 1720–1801), the Irish-born viceroy of Chile (1789) and of Peru (1795), was born at Chillán, played a great part in the Chilean revolt of 1810, and in 1817–23 was the new republic's first president.

OHM, Georg Simon (1787–1854), German physicist, became in 1849 professor at Munich. Ohm's Law was a result of his researches in electricity, and the measure of resistance is called the *ohm*.

OHNET, Georges, ō-*nay* (1848–1918), French novelist, was born in Paris. Under the general title of *Les Batailles de la vie*, he published a series of novels, some of which went beyond a hundredth edition.

OHTHERE (9th cent.), a Norse sailor, made two exploring voyages for King Alfred between 880 and 900—one round the North Cape to the White Sea.

OKEGHEM, Joannes, *o'keg-em* (1430–95), Flemish composer, born probably at Termonde, E. Flanders, in 1452 became a court musician to Charles VII of France, and was in 1459 treasurer of the abbey of St Martin at Tours. He was also *kapellmeister* to Louis XI. He played an important part in the stylistic development of church music in the 15th century and was renowned as a teacher; Josquin des Prés (q.v.) was among his

pupils. See studies by de Marcy (Termonde 1895) and Brenet (Paris 1911).

O'KELLY, Sean Thomas (1882–1966), Irish statesman, born in Dublin, a pioneer in the Sinn Fein movement and the Gaelic league, fought in the Easter Rising (1916) and was imprisoned. Elected to the first Dail in 1918, he became Speaker (1919–21), minister for local government (1932–39) and for finance and education (1939–45). He was president of the Irish Republic in 1945–52, and again in 1952–59.

OKEN, Lorenz (1779–1851), German naturalist and nature philosopher, became professor of Medicine at Jena in 1807. In 1816 he issued a journal called *Iris*, which led to government interference and his resignation. In 1828 he obtained a professorship at Munich, and in 1832 at Zürich. His theory that the skull is a modified vertebra is exploded.

OLAF, the name of five kings of Norway, of whom the following are noteworthy:
Olaf I Tryggvesson (c. 965–1000), grandson of Harald Haarfagr, was an exile in his youth, but took part in Viking expeditions against Britain and came to the throne of Norway after overthrowing King Haakon in 995. Having turned Christian, he attempted the conversion of Norway with limited success. He was killed in a naval battle against the Danes and Swedes.
Olaf II Haraldsson, St (c. 995–1030), fought as a young man in England for Ethelred against the Danes, became a Christian and completed successfully the work of conversion which Olaf I had begun, but his reforms provoked internal dissension and he was defeated and killed by a rebel army at the battle of Stiklestad. He was later recognized as the patron saint of Norway.
Olav V (1903–), only child of Haakon VII (q.v.) and Maud, daughter of Edward VII born in England, educated in Norway and, at Balliol College, Oxford, succeeded his father to the Norwegian throne in 1957. An outstanding sportsman in his youth, Olav was appointed head of the Norwegian Armed Forces in 1944, and later that year escaped with his father to England on the Nazi occupation, returning in 1945. In 1929 he married Princess Martha (1901–54) of Sweden and had two daughters and a son, **Harald** (1937–), heir to the throne.

OLAUS. See MAGNUS and PETRI (2).

OLBERS, Heinrich Wilhelm Matthäus (1758–1840), German physician and astronomer, practised medicine at Bremen. He calculated the orbit of the comet of 1779; discovered the minor planets Pallas (1802) and Vesta (1807); discovered five comets (all but one already observed at Paris); and invented a method for calculating the velocity of falling stars. See the Life prefixed to his works by Schilling (3 vols. 1894–97).

OLCOTT, Colonel Henry Steel (c. 1830–1907), American theosophist, was by 1856 distinguished in the United States as an agriculturist, fought in the Civil War, and held posts in the accounts department of the army and navy. After the war he devoted himself to theosophy.

OLDCASTLE, Sir John (c. 1378–1417),

Lollard leader and rebel, the ' good Lord Cobham ', is first heard of as serving Henry IV on the Welsh marches. He acquired the title of Lord Cobham by marrying the heiress, and presented a remonstrance to the Commons on the corruptions of the church. He had Wycliffe's works transcribed and distributed, and paid preachers to propagate his views. In 1411 he commanded an English army in France, and forced the Duke of Orléans to raise the siege of Paris; but in 1413, after the accession of Henry V, he was examined, and condemned as a heretic. He escaped from the Tower into Wales; a Lollard conspiracy in his favour was stamped out; after four years' hiding he was captured, brought to London, and was ' hanged and burnt hanging '. Halliwell-Phillipps first proved in 1841 that Shakespeare's Sir John Falstaff was based on a popular tradition of dislike for the heretic Oldcastle. Though he stood high in the favour of Prince Hal, there is no historical ground for representing him as his ' boon companion '.

OLDENBARNEVELDT. See BARNEVELDT.

OLDFIELD, Anne (1683–1730), English actress, was born in London, made her début in 1700, stood high in public favour by 1705, and played till the last year of her life. See Edward Robins, *The Palmy Days of Nance Oldfield* (1898).

OLDHAM, John (1653–83), English poet, born near Tetbury, graduated at Oxford. His Juvenalian satires against the Jesuits won the praise of Dryden.

OLDMIXON, John (1673–1742), English author of dull, partisan histories of England, Scotland, Ireland and America, and of works on logic and rhetoric. He is one of the heroes of Pope's *Dunciad*.

OLD MORTALITY. See PATERSON (3).

OLDYS, William, *olds* (1696–1761), English bibliographer, natural son of Dr Oldys, chancellor of Lincoln, for about ten years was librarian to the Earl of Oxford, whose valuable collections of books and MSS. he arranged and catalogued, and by the Duke of Norfolk he was appointed Norroy king-of-arms. His chief works are a *Life of Sir Walter Raleigh*, prefixed to Raleigh's *History of the World* (1736); *The British Librarian* (1737); *The Harleian Miscellany* (1753), besides many miscellaneous articles.

OLE-LUK-OIE. See SWINTON.

OLGA, St (d. 968), a Russian saint, wife of the Duke of Kiev, who governed during the minority of her son, till 955. Thereafter she was baptized at Constantinople, and returning to Russia, laboured for the new creed.

OLIPHANT, (1) Laurence (1829–88), English travel writer and mystic, was born at Capetown, son of the attorney-general there. His first work, *A Journey to Khatmandu* (1852), was followed by *The Russian Shores of the Black Sea* (1853). As secretary to the Earl of Elgin he travelled to China, thus finding material for further books. In 1861, while acting as *chargé d'affaires* in Japan, he was severely wounded by assassins. From 1865 to 1868 he sat for the Stirling burghs. His *Piccadilly* (1870) was a book of exceptional promise, bright with wit and delicate

irony. He joined the religious community of T. L. Harris (q.v.) in America, and later settled at Haifa in Palestine. His mystical views he published in *Sympneumata* (1886) and *Scientific Religion* (1888). See Memoir by M. Oliphant (1891).

(2) **Marcus Laurence Elwin** (1901–   ), Australian nuclear physicist, born in Adelaide, studied there and at Trinity College and Cavendish Laboratory, Cambridge, where he did valuable work on the nuclear disintegration of lithium. Professor at Birmingham (1937), he designed and built a sixty-inch cyclotron, completed after World War II. He worked on the atomic bomb project at Los Alamos (1943–45), but at the end of hostilities strongly argued against the American monopoly of atomic secrets. In 1946 he became Australian representative of the U.N. Atomic Energy Commission, designed a proton-synchroton for the Australian government and in 1950 became research professor at Canberra. Elected F.R.S. in 1937, he was awarded the Hughes Medal (1943) and was made K.B.E. (1959).

(3) **Margaret,** *née* Wilson (1828–97), Scottish novelist, born at Wallyford near Musselburgh, in 1849 her *Passages in the Life of Mrs Margaret Maitland* instantly won approval. This was followed by a rapid succession of novels, including the *Chronicles of Carlingford* with which she made her name. Her contributions to general literature, mostly historical and biographical, were numerous. See her *Autobiography and Letters* (1899).

OLIVARES, Gaspar de Guzmán, Count of (1587–1645), Duke of San Lúcar, born at Rome where his father was ambassador, was the favourite of Philip IV of Spain, and his prime minister for twenty-two years. He wrung money from the country to carry on foreign wars. His attempts to rob the people of their privileges provoked insurrections and roused the Portuguese to shake off the Spanish yoke in 1640, and the king was obliged to dismiss him in 1643.

OLIVE, Princess, assumed title of **Mrs Olivia Serres,** *née* Wilmot (1772–1834), English impostor, was born at Warwick, the daughter of a house painter, Robert Wilmot, and married in 1791 John Thomas Serres (1759–1825), a marine painter, from whom she separated in 1804. In 1817 she claimed to be an illegitimate daughter of the Duke of Cumberland, brother of George III, then in 1821 had herself rechristened as Princess Olive, legitimate daughter of the Duke and his first wife, Olive. The same year, arrested for debt, she produced an alleged will of George III, leaving £15,000 to her as his brother's daughter, but in 1823 her claims were found to be baseless, and she died within the rules of the King's Bench. Her elder daughter, Mrs Lavinia Ryves (1797–1871), took up her mother's claim of legitimacy, which a jury finally repudiated in 1866.

OLIVER, Isaac (c. 1560–1617), miniature painter, probably of Huguenot origin, but usually regarded as English, was the pupil and later the rival of Nicholas Hilliard, and executed portraits of Sir Philip Sidney, Anne of Denmark, &c. His son and pupil,

Peter (1594–1648), continued his work, and was employed by Charles I to copy old master paintings in miniature. See G. Reynolds, *Nicholas Hilliard and Isaac Oliver* (1947).

OLIVIER, (1) Sir **Laurence Kerr** (1907–), English actor, producer and director, born in Dorking. His first professional appearance was as the Suliot officer in *Byron* in 1924, since when he has played all the great Shakespearean rôles, including a memorable Titus, while his versatility was underlined by his virtuoso display in *The Entertainer* (1957) as a broken-down low comedian. After war service he became in 1944 codirector of the Old Vic Company. He produced, directed and played in films of *Henry V*, *Hamlet* and, notably, *Richard III*. He was knighted in 1947. He was divorced from his first wife, Jill Esmond, in 1940 and in the same year married **Vivien Leigh** (1913–1967), English actress, who first appeared professionally in *The Green Sash*. Her beauty, charm and ability were exhibited in *The Doctor's Dilemma*, *The Skin of our Teeth*, and other plays, and in film rôles such as Scarlett O'Hara in *Gone With the Wind* and Blanche in *A Streetcar Named Desire*. See F. Barker, *The Oliviers* (1953). They were divorced in 1960, and Miss Leigh died of T.B. in 1967. In 1961 Olivier married **Joan Plowright** (b. 1929), the English stage actress. In 1962 he succeeded brilliantly as director of a new venture, the Chichester Theatre Festival and later the same year was appointed director of the National Theatre, where among many successes he directed and acted a controversial but outstanding *Othello* (1964).

(2) **Sidney, 1st Baron Olivier of Ramsden** (1859–1943), British colonial administrator and writer, was governor of Jamaica (1907–1913), secretary to the Board of Agriculture (1913–17) and in the Labour government of 1924 he was secretary for India, being raised to the peerage in the same year. A founder of the Fabian Society, of which he was secretary (1886–90), he contributed to *Fabian Essays* (1889) and wrote several authoritative books on colonial questions.

OLLIVIER, Olivier Émile, *ol-leev-yay* (1825–1913), French politician, born at Marseilles, established a reputation at the Parisian bar, and after 1864 acquired influence as a member of the Legislative Assembly. In 1865 the viceroy of Egypt appointed him to a judicial office. In January 1870 Napoleon III charged him to form a constitutional ministry. But ' with a light heart ' he rushed his country into war with Germany. He was overthrown on August 9 and withdrew to Italy for a time. He was the author of numerous works, including *L'Empire libéral*, a defence of his policy (16 vols. 1894–1912). See study by T. Zeldih (1963).

OLMSTED, Frederick Law (1822–1903), American landscape architect and travel writer, born at Hartford, Conn., was co-designer of Central Park, New York, and of other famous parks, and planned the layout of the Chicago World's Fair of 1893.

OLNEY, Richard (1835–1917), American Democratic statesman, was born at Oxford, Mass. He was educated at Harvard, and called to the bar. In 1893 he became attorney-general under Cleveland, in June 1895 secretary of state, and within six months caused a crisis by his interference, in virtue of the Monroe Doctrine, in the boundary question between British Guiana and Venezuela. In 1897 he returned to the bar at Boston. In 1913 he declined the ambassadorship to London.

OLYMPIAS (d. 316 B.C.), wife of Philip of Macedon, and mother of Alexander the Great, was the daughter of the king of Epirus. When Philip left her and married Cleopatra, niece of Attalus, she instigated (337 B.C.) his assassination, and subsequently brought about the murder of Cleopatra. After Alexander's death she secured the death of his half-brother and successor. Cassander besieged her in Pydna, and on its surrender put her to death.

OLYMPIODORUS, name of several Greek authors: (1) (6th cent. A.D.), an Alexandrian Neoplatonist, left a *Life of Plato*, with commentaries on several of his dialogues; (2) (5th cent.), a Peripatetic, also at Alexandria; (3) (5th cent.), from Thebes in Egypt, wrote in Greek a history of the Western empire.

O'MAHONY, *ō-mah'nee*, (1) **Daniel** (d. 1714), Irish soldier, went to France in 1692, held commands under Villeroy and Vendôme, and did prodigies with his Irish dragoons at Almanza in the Spanish service.

(2) **John** (1816–77), Fenian head-centre (leader), was born at Kilbeheny, Co. Limerick, studied at Trinity College, Dublin, translated Keating's *History of Ireland*, joined in 1848 in Smith O'Brien's rebellion, and after Stephens played the most prominent part in organizing Fenianism.

OMAN, Sir Charles William Chadwick (1860–1946), English historian, born at Muzaffarpur in India, was educated at Winchester and New College, Oxford, and was made a fellow of All Souls in 1883, establishing his reputation with brilliant studies on Warwick the Kingmaker (1891), Byzantine history (1892), and the art of war in the Middle Ages (1898). The appearance in 1902 of the first part of his great 7-volume history of the Peninsular war, which took him 28 years to complete, gave an indication of the immense scholarship and meticulous research which became the hallmark of his many authoritative works on mediaeval and modern history. In 1905 he was elected Chichele professor of Modern History, and from 1919 to 1935 sat in parliament for the university. He was knighted in 1920 in recognition of his services to the Foreign Office during the war. See his *Things I have Seen* (1933) and *Memories of Victorian Oxford* (1941).

OMAR, or '**Umar** (c. 581–64), the second khalif, was father of one of Mohammed's wives, and succeeded Abu-bekr in 634. By his generals he built up an empire comprising Persia, Syria and all North Africa. He was assassinated.

OMAR KHAYYÁM, or '**Umar Khayyám** (c. 1050–c. 1123), the astronomer-poet of Persia, was born (a tent-maker's son) and died at Nishapur. Summoned to Merv by the sultan, he reformed the Moslem calendar.

Of his Arabic mathematical treatises, one on algebra was edited and translated by Woepke (1851); and it was as a mathematician that he was known to the western world, until in 1859 Edward FitzGerald published his 'translation' of seventy-five of his *Rubáiyát* or quatrains. Omar was the poet of Agnosticism, though some see nothing in his poetry save the wine-cup and roses, and others read into it that Sufi mysticism with which it was largely adulterated long after Omar's death. FitzGerald's translation is far finer than the original. The *Rubáiyát* is now regarded as an anthology of which little or nothing may be by Omar. There are editions of the *Rubáiyát* by Nicolas (464 quatrains, 1867), Sadik Ali (nearly 800 quatrains, 1878), Whinfield (1883), Dole (1896), Heron Allen (1912). Other translations are by Whinfield (1882), J. H. McCarthy (prose, 1889), J. Payne (1898), E. Heron Allen (prose, 1898), Pollen (1915). See Life by Shirazi (1905), works cited at FITZGERALD, and Potter's *Bibliography of the Rubáiyát of Omar Khayyám.*

OMAR PASHA, properly **Michael Latas** (1806–71), Ottoman general, was born at Plasky in Croatia, and served in the Austrian army. In 1828 he deserted, fled to Bosnia, and, embracing Mohammedanism, became writing-master to Abdul-Medjid, on whose accession to the Ottoman throne in 1839 Omar Pasha was made colonel, and in 1842 governor of Lebanon. In 1843–47 he suppressed insurrections in Albania, Bosnia and Kurdistan. On the invasion of the Danubian Principalities by the Russians in 1853 he defeated the Russians in two battles. In February 1855 he repulsed the Russians at Eupatoria in the Crimea. He was sent too late to relieve Kars. In 1861 he again pacified Bosnia and Herzegovina, and overran Montenegro in 1862.

O'MEARA, Barry Edward (1786–1836), Irish physician, served as surgeon in the army, but was dismissed in 1808 for his share in a duel. He was on the *Bellerophon* when Napoleon came on board, and accompanied him as private physician to St Helena, took part in his squabbles with Sir Hudson Lowe, and was compelled to resign in 1818. Asserting in a letter to the Admiralty that Sir Hudson Lowe had dark designs against his captive's life, he was dismissed from the service. His *Napoleon in Exile* (1822) made a great sensation.

OMNIUM, Jacob. See HIGGINS (1).

ONASSIS, Aristotle Socrates (1906–), millionaire ship-owner, born in Smyrna, now an Argentinian subject. At sixteen he left Smyrna for Greece as a refugee, and from there he went to Buenos Aires where later he was Greek consul for a time. Since the purchase of his first ships (1932–33) he has built up one of the world's largest independent fleets, and is a pioneer in the construction of super-tankers. He married (1) Athina, daughter of Stavros Livanos, a Greek ship-owner, and (2) Jacqueline Kennedy, widow of John F. Kennedy (q.v.).

O'NEILL, (1) Eugene Gladstone (1888–1953), American playwright, born in New York, the son of the actor James O'Neill (1847–1920).

After a fragmentary education and a year at Princeton, he took various clerical and journalistic jobs and signed on as a sailor on voyages to Australia, South Africa and elsewhere. Then he contracted tuberculosis and spent six months in a sanatorium where he felt the urge to write plays, the first being *The Web.* He joined the Provincetown Players in 1915, for whom *Beyond the Horizon* (1920; Pulitzer prize) was written. This was followed, during the next two years, by *Exorcism, Diff'rent, The Emperor Jones, Anna Christie* (1922; Pulitzer prize) and *The Hairy Ape. Desire Under the Elms,* his most mature play to date, appeared in 1924. He then began experimenting in new dramatic techniques. In *The Great God Brown* (1926) he used masks to emphasize the differing relationships between a man, his family and his soul. *Marco Millions* (1931) is a satire on tycoonery. *Strange Interlude* (1928; Pulitzer prize), a marathon nine-acter, lasting five hours, uses asides, soliloquies and ' streams of consciousness '. In the same year he wrote *Lazarus Laughed,* a humanistic affirmation of his belief in the conquest of death. *Mourning Becomes Electra* (1931) is a re-statement of the Orestean tragedy in terms of biological and psychological cause and effect. *Ah, Wilderness,* a nostalgic comedy, appeared in 1933 and *Days Without End* in 1934. Then, for twelve years he released no more plays but worked on *The Iceman Cometh* (New York 1946, London 1958) and *A Moon for the Misbegotten* (1947). The former is a gargantuan, broken-backed, repetitive parable about the dangers of shattering illusions. It is impressive by its sheer weight and redeemed by O'Neill's never-failing sense of the theatre. *Long Day's Journey into Night* (1957; Pulitzer prize), probably his masterpiece, whose tragic Tyrone family is closely based on O'Neill's early life, *Hughie* and *A Touch of the Poet* were published posthumously. He was awarded the Nobel prize for literature in 1936, the first American dramatist to be thus honoured. See Life by A. and B. Gelb (1962), studies by B. H. Clark (rev. ed. 1947), C. Leech (1963) and J. H. Raleigh (1965), and, by his second wife, A. Boulton, *Part of a Long Story* (1958).

(2) **Hugh,** Earl of Tyrone, and ' archrebel ', was the son of an illegitimate son of Con O'Neill (?1484–?1559), a warlike Irish chieftain who was made Earl of Tyrone on his submission to Henry VIII in 1542. His grandson, Hugh (born about 1540), was invested with the title and estates in 1587, but soon plunged into intrigues with the Irish rebels and the Spaniards against Elizabeth, as ' the O'Neill ' spread insurrection in 1597 all over Ulster, Connaught and Leinster, and in spite of Spanish support was defeated by Mountjoy at Kinsale and badly wounded. He made submission, but intrigued with Spain against James I, and in 1607 fled, dying at Rome in 1616. His nephew, **Owen Roe** (?1590–1649), won a distinguished place in the Spanish military service, came to Ireland in 1642, fought for a time with great success against Scots and English for an independent Ireland, but died suddenly when

about to measure himself against Cromwell. See a monograph by J. F. Taylor (1896). A kinsman, **Sir Phelim**, was the leader of the insurrection, not so much against the English government as against the English and Scots settlers in Ulster, in which occurred the massacre of 1641. **Shane** (?1530–67), eldest legitimate son of Con O'Neill, was second Earl of Tyrone, nominally acknowledged Elizabeth, but was always at war with the Scots and the O'Donnells.
(3) **Peggy**. See EATON.

ONKELOS (?2nd cent. A.D.), the reputed author of an Aramaic Targum of the Pentateuch, produced by the scholars of R. Akiba between A.D. 150 and 200 in Palestine. ' Onkelos ' is a corruption of Akylas (Greek for Aquila), the name of the actual translator of the Old Testament into Greek, c. A.D. 130.

ONNES, Heike Kamerlingh, *o'nes* (1853–1926), born at Groningen, became professor of Physics at Leyden. He obtained liquid helium, and discovered that the electrical resistance of metals cooled to near absolute zero all but disappears. In 1913 he was awarded the Nobel prize for physics.

ONSLOW, Arthur (1691–1768), son of a commissioner of excise, was trained a barrister, entered parliament in 1720, and for thirty-three years was a dignified and blameless speaker of the House of Commons.

OPIE, (1) Amelia (1769–1853), wife of (2), the daughter of a Norwich physician, Dr Alderson, while very young wrote songs and tragedies. She was married to Opie in 1798. In 1801 her first novel, *Father and Daughter*, appeared; next year a volume of poems. On her husband's death she published his lectures, with a memoir. Mrs Opie became a Quaker in 1825, and afterwards published moral tracts and articles, but no more novels. See *Memoirs* by Miss Brightwell (1854), Lady Richmond Ritchie's *Book of Sibyls* (1883), and works by Macgregor (1933), Menzies-Wilson and Lloyd (1937).
(2) **John** (1761–1807), English portrait and historical painter, was born, a carpenter's son, near St Agnes, Cornwall. His attempts at portrait painting interested Dr Wolcot (' Peter Pindar '), by whom in 1780 he was taken to London to become the ' Cornish Wonder '. His works include the well-known *Murder of Rizzio*, *Jephtha's Vow* and *Juliet in the Garden*. He wrote a Life of Reynolds and a discourse on Art, and lectured on Art at the Royal Institution.

OPITZ, Martin (1597–1639), German poet, born at Bunzlau in Silesia. He earned an inflated reputation by toadying to the German princes. In 1620 he fled to Holland to escape war and the plague; but of the plague he died in Danzig. His poems have no imagination and little feeling, and are cold, formal, didactic, pedantic. His works include translations from classic authors (Sophocles and Seneca), the Dutchmen Heinsius and Grotius, and from the Bible. See books by Palm (1862), Borinski (1883), Berghöfer (1888), Stössel (1922) and Gundolf (1923).

OPPENHEIM, Edward Phillips (1866–1946), English novelist, born in London, had his first book published in 1887 and went on to become a pioneer of the novel of espionage

and diplomatic intrigue. Among his best are *Mr Grex of Monte Carlo* (1915), *Kingdom of the Blind* (1917), *The Great Impersonation* (1920) and *Envoy Extraordinary* (1937). See his autobiography, *The Pool of Memory* (1941).

OPPENHEIMER, (1) Sir Ernest (1880–1957), South African mining magnate, politician and philanthropist, was born at Friedberg, Germany, the son of a Jewish cigar merchant. At the age of seventeen he worked for a London firm of diamond merchants and, sent out to Kimberley as their representative, soon became one of the leaders of the diamond industry. In 1917 he formed the Anglo-American Corporation of South Africa and at the time of his death his interests extended over 95 per cent. of the world's supply of diamonds. He was mayor of Kimberley (1912–15), raised the Kimberley Regiment and, a friend of Smuts, was M.P. for Kimberley (1924–38). He endowed university chairs and slum clearance schemes in Johannesburg. He was knighted in 1921. His son, **Harry Frederick** (b. 1908), succeeded him in 1957 and in 1960 criticized the South African government's *apartheid* policy.
(2) **J. Robert** (1904–67), American nuclear physicist, born in New York, studied at Harvard, Cambridge (England), Göttingen, Leyden and Zürich, became assistant professor of Physics at the California Institute of Technology (1929), studied electron-positron pairs, cosmic ray theory and worked on deuteron reactions. In 1942 he joined the atom bomb project and in 1943 became director of the Los Alamos laboratory, resigning in 1945. He argued for joint control with the Soviet Union of atomic energy. He was chairman of the advisory committee to the U.S. Atomic Energy Commission (1946–1952) and in 1947 became director and professor of Physics at the Institute for Advanced Study, Princeton. In 1953 he was suspended from secret nuclear research by a security review board, although many people disagreed with the charges brought against him. He delivered the B.B.C. Reith Lectures (1953), and received the Enrico Fermi award in 1963.

ORANGE, Princes of. See WILLIAM III, WILLIAM THE SILENT.

ORCAGNA, Andrea, *or-kan'ya* (c. 1308–68), a nickname, corrupted from *Arcagnuolo*, ' Archangel ', of **Andrea di Cione**, who, the son of a Florentine silversmith, distinguished himself as sculptor, painter, architect and poet. The tabernacle in Or San Michele at Florence is a triumph in sculpture. His greatest paintings are frescoes, an altarpiece in Santa Maria Novella, and *Coronation of the Virgin* in the National Gallery. He is considered by many to be second in the 14th century only to Giotto, who influenced him.

ORCHARDSON, Sir William Quiller (1832–1910), Scottish painter, born in Edinburgh, came to London in 1862, and was elected R.A. in 1877. He painted portraits, but is best known for historical and social subject paintings. Most famous is the scene of Napoleon on board the *Bellerophon* (1880) in the Tate Gallery; among other well-known subjects are *Queen of the Swords* (1877), *Mariage de convenance* (1884) and *Her*

Mother's Voice (1888). He was knighted in 1907. See Life by his daughter, Mrs Gray (1930).

ORCZY, Baroness Emmuska, *or'tsi* (1865–1947), British novelist and playwright, born, the daughter of a musician, in Tarnaörs, Hungary. *The Scarlet Pimpernel* (1905) was the first success in the Baroness's long writing career. It was followed by many popular adventure romances, including *The Elusive Pimpernel* (1908) and *Mam'zelle Guillotine* (1940), which never quite attained the success of her early work. See her autobiographical *Links in the Chain of Life* (1947).

ORDERICUS VITALIS (1075–1143), mediaeval historian, born, the son of a French priest and an Englishwoman, at Atcham near Shrewsbury, and educated in the Norman abbey of St Evroul, where he spent his life, although he visited England to collect materials for his *Historia Ecclesiastica* (1123–41), a history mainly of Normandy and England—a singular mixture of important history and trivial gossip. See Dean Church's *St Anselm* (1870) and Freeman's *Norman Conquest.*

O'REILLY, John Boyle (1844–90), the son of a schoolmaster near Drogheda, was bred a compositor, but becoming a hussar in 1863, was in 1866 sentenced to twenty years' penal servitude for spreading Fenianism in the army. He escaped in 1867 from Western Australia, and settled as a journalist in Boston, U.S., where he became known as an author of songs and novels.

O'RELL, Max. See BLOUET.

ORELLANA, Francisco de (*c.* 1500–*c.* 49), Spanish explorer, born at Trujillo, went with Pizarro to Peru and, crossing the Andes, descended the Amazon to its mouth (1541). See study by F. Markham (Hakluyt Soc. 1859).

ORFF, Carl (1895–), German composer, born in Munich, studied under Kaminski and in 1925 helped to found the Günter School in Munich and subsequently taught there. His aim, to which his didactic composition *Schulwerk* (1930–54) testifies, was to educate in the creative aspects of music. The influence of Stravinsky is apparent in his compositions, which include three realizations of Monteverdi's *Orfeo* (1925, 1931, 1941), an operatic setting of a 13th-century poem entitled *Carmina burana* (1936), *Die Kluge*, ' The Prudent Woman ' (1943), an operatic version of Hölderlin's translation of *Antigone* (Salzburg Festival, 1949) and *Astutuli* (1953).

ORFILA, Mathieu Joseph Bonaventure (1787–1853), French chemist, founder of toxicology, born at Mahón in Minorca, studied at Valencia, Barcelona and Paris. In 1811 he lectured on chemistry, botany and anatomy. In 1813 appeared his celebrated *Traité de toxicologie générale.* In 1819 he became professor of Medical Jurisprudence, and in 1823 of Chemistry.

ORFORD. See WALPOLE.

ORIGEN (185–254), the most learned and original of the early church fathers, was born probably at Alexandria, and was the son of the Christian martyr Leonidas. He studied in the catechetical school of Clement, and soon acted as master. He made a thorough study of Plato, the later Platonists and Pythagoreans, and the Stoics, under the Neoplatonist Ammonius Saccas. At Alexandria he taught for twenty-eight years (204–232), composed the chief of his dogmatic treatises, and commenced his great works of textual and exegetical criticism. During his visit to Palestine in 216 the bishops of Jerusalem and Caesarea employed him to lecture in the churches, and in 230 they consecrated him presbyter without referring to his own bishop. An Alexandrian synod deprived him of the office of presbyter. The churches of Palestine, Phoenicia, Arabia and Achaea declined to concur in this sentence; and Origen, settling at Caesarea in Palestine, founded a school of literature, philosophy and theology. In the last twenty years of his life he made many journeys. In the Decian persecution at Tyre he was cruelly tortured, and there he died in 254. His exegetical writings extended over nearly the whole of the old and New Testaments, and included *Scholia, Homilies* and *Commentaries.* Of the Homilies only a small part has been preserved in the original, much, however, in the Latin translations by Rufinus and Jerome; but the translators tampered with them. Of the Commentaries a number of books on Matthew and John are extant in Greek. His gigantic *Hexapla*, the foundation of the textual criticism of the Scriptures, is mostly lost. His *Eight Books against Celsus*, preserved entire in Greek, constitute the greatest of early Christian apologies. The speculative theology of the *Peri Archon* is extant mostly in the garbled translation of Rufinus. Two books on *The Resurrection* and ten books of *Stromata* are lost. The eclectic philosophy of Origen bears a Neoplatonist and Stoical stamp. The idea of the proceeding of all spirits from God, their fall, redemption and return to God, is the key to the development of the world, at the centre of which is the incarnation of the Logos. All scripture admits of a threefold interpretation—literal, psychical or ethical, and pneumatic or allegorical. See Harnack's *Dogmengeschichte*, Farrar's *Lives of the Fathers* (1889); German works on Origen by Thomasius (1837), Redepenning (1846) and Lieske (1938); French by Joly (1860), Freppel (1868), Denis (1884), de Faye (3 vols. 1923–28), Cadion (1932); English by J. Patrick (1892), Fairweather (1901).

ORKHAN, Turkish sultan (1326–59), son of Othman, took Brusa in his father's time, and afterwards reduced Nicaea and Mysia. He organized the state and founded the Janissaries.

ORLÉANS (Eng. *Orleans*), a ducal title conferred thrice by French kings on brothers—in 1392 by Charles VI, in 1626 by Louis XIII, and in 1660 by Louis XIV on Philippe (1640–1701). His son was the regent, Philippe (1674–1723), and his great-grandson was ' Égalité ' (see 4). Égalité's son was King Louis Philippe (q.v.). His eldest son (1810–1842) took the title, but it was not borne by that duke's son, the Comte de Paris (q.v.), who settled in England in 1883, became head of the Bourbon house, and died in

1894. His son (see (5)) resumed the old ducal title. (Louis Philippe's younger sons were the Dukes of Aumale, Nemours, Montpensier, and the Prince de Joinville.)

(1) **Charles** (1391–1465), married in 1406 his cousin Isabella, widow of Richard II of England. In alliance with the infamous Bernard d'Armagnac, he did his best to avenge on the Duke of Burgundy his father's murder. He commanded at Agincourt (October 1415), and was taken prisoner and carried to England, where he spent over a quarter of a century. composing ballades, rondels, &c., in French and English, conventional, musical and graceful. He was ransomed in 1440, and during the last third of his life he maintained a kind of literary court at Blois. His son became Louis XII. See his *English Poems*, ed. Steele (E.E.T.S. 1941), and R. L. Stevenson, in *Familiar Studies* (1882).

(2) **Jean Baptiste Gaston** (1608–60), third son of Henry IV of France, troubled his country with bloody but fruitless intrigues against Richelieu. He was lieutenant-general of the kingdom during the minority of Louis XIV, was at the head of the Fronde, but soon made terms with Mazarin. See his *Mémoires* (1683).

(3) **Philippe** (1674–1723), regent of France during the minority of Louis XV, son of the first Duke Philippe, and grandson of Louis XIII, possessed excellent talents, but was early demoralized. He showed courage at Steenkirk and Neerwinden, and commanded with success in Italy and Spain. For some years he lived in exile from the court, spending his time by turns in profligacy, the fine arts and chemistry. Louis XIV at his death appointed (1715) the Duke of Orléans sole regent. (Orléans had married Mlle de Blois, daughter of Louis XIV and Mme de Montespan.) He was popular, but his adoption of Law's schemes led to disaster. His alliance with England and Holland (1717) was joined by the emperor, and overthrew Alberoni. He expelled the Pretender from France, debarred the parliament of Paris from meddling with political affairs, and to appease the Jesuits sacrificed the Jansenists. See works by Piossens (1749), Capefigue (1838), Leclerq (1921), Saint-André (1928), Soulié (1933), d'Erlanger (1938).

(4) **Louis Philippe Joseph** (1747–93), famous **Égalité**, succeeded to the title on his father's death in 1785. He early fell into debauchery, and was looked upon coldly at court, especially after the accession of Louis XVI (1774). He visited London frequently, became an intimate friend of the Prince of Wales, afterwards George IV, infected young France with Anglomania in the form of horse-racing and hard drinking, and made himself popular by profuse charity. In 1787 he showed his liberalism boldly against the king, and was sent by a *lettre-de-cachet* to his château of Villers-Cotterets. As the States-General drew near he lavished his wealth in disseminating throughout France books and papers by Sieyès and other Liberals. In 1788 he promulgated his *Délibérations*, written by Laclos, to the effect that the *tiers état* was the nation, and in June 1789

he led the forty-seven nobles who seceded from their own order to join it. He dreamed of becoming constitutional king of France, or at least regent. He gradually lost influence, felt hopeless of the Revolution, and thought of going to America. In 1792, all hereditary titles being swept away, he adopted the name of Philippe Égalité, was twentieth deputy for Paris to the Convention, and voted for the death of the king. His eldest son, afterwards King Louis-Philippe, rode with Dumouriez, his commander, into the Austrian camp. Égalité was at once arrested, with all the Bourbons still in France, and, after six months' durance, was found guilty of conspiracy and guillotined. See works by Baschet, by Tournois (1840–43), by Britsch (1926), and Elliot's *Journal* (1859).

(5) **Louis Philippe Robert** (1869–1926), eldest son of the Comte de Paris, went to France in 1890, and was imprisoned for contravening the law banishing the heirs of families that have reigned.

(6) **Jean, Duc de Guise** (1874–1940), his brother-in-law, son of the Duc de Chartres, succeeded as head of the house. His brother, **Prince Henri of Orleans** (1867–1901), traveller (his *Tonkin and Siam* was translated 1893), fought a duel with the Count of Turin in 1897.

ORLEY, Bernard, or **Barend van** (*c.* 1491–1542), Flemish painter, was born and died at Brussels, became court painter to the regent, Margaret of Austria, and was one of the first Flemish painters to adopt the Italian Renaissance style. He executed a number of altarpieces and tryptyches of biblical subjects to be seen in Brussels, at the Louvre, the Prado, the Metropolitan Museum at New York and elsewhere, and in his later years he designed tapestries and stained glass. See Friedlander on Flemish painting (1930).

ORLOV, a Russian family that rose to eminence, when one of its members, Gregory (1734–83), succeeded Poniatowski as the favourite of Catharine II. It was he who planned the murder of Peter III, and his brother Alexis (1737–1808) who committed the deed (1762). The legitimate line of Orlov became extinct; but Feodor, a brother of Gregory and Alexis, left four illegitimate sons, one of whom, Alexis (1787–1862), distinguished himself in the French wars and in Turkey, represented Russia at the London conference of 1832, in 1844 was at the head of the secret police, stood high in favour with the Emperor Nicholas, in 1856 was Russian representative at the congress of Paris, and was made president of the grand council of the empire.

ORM, or **Ormin** (fl. *c.* 1200), versifier and spelling reformer, born probably in Lincolnshire, was an Augustinian monk, author of the ' Ormulum ' named after him, a series of homilies in verse on the gospel history.

ORMEROD, Eleanor Anne (1828–1901), LL.D. (Edin. 1900), entomologist, daughter of George Ormerod (1785–1873), the historian of Cheshire, in 1882–92 was consulting entomologist to the Royal Agricultural Society. She was the author of *Manual of Injurious Insects* (1881), *Guide to Methods of Insect Life* (1884), and *Agricultural Entomol-*

ogy (2nd ed. 1892). See her *Autobiography* (1904).

ORMONDE, (1) **James Butler, Duke of** (1610–1688), of the ancient Anglo-Irish family of Butler, was born in London, and in 1632 succeeded to the earldom and estates of Ormonde. During the Strafford administration he greatly distinguished himself, and in the rebellion of 1640 was appointed to the chief command of the army; but when, in 1643, he concluded an armistice, his policy was condemned by both great parties. In the last crisis of the king's fortunes he retired to France, returned again to Ireland with the all but desperate design of restoring the royal authority, but after a gallant struggle was compelled (1650) to return to France. At the Restoration he was rewarded by the ducal title of Ormonde. He twice again returned to the government of Ireland. In 1679 an attempt was made on his life by the notorious Colonel Blood, supposed to have been instigated by the Duke of Buckingham. He escaped uninjured, and lived until 1688. See Lives by Carte (1736) and Lady Burghclere (1912).

(2) **James Butler, 2nd Duke** (1665–1746), grandson of (1), was born in Dublin. As Earl of Ossory he served in the army against Monmouth. After his accession to the dukedom in 1688, he took his share in the Revolution conflict. He headed William's lifeguards at the battle of the Boyne. In 1702 he commanded the troops in Rooke's expedition against Cadiz; in 1703 he was appointed lord-lieutenant of Ireland, and in 1711 commander-in-chief against France and Spain. Under George I he fell into disgrace, and was impeached in 1715 of high treason, his estates being attainted; he retired to France, spent years in the intrigues of the Pretender, and died abroad. Letters written by him in organizing the attempt by Spain to invade England and Scotland in 1719 were in 1890 brought to light, and in 1896 published by the Scottish History Society.

ORNSTEIN, **Leo,** *orn'stîn* (1895–), American composer, born in Russia, had appeared as a child prodigy at the piano in Russia before his parents settled in the U.S.A. in 1906, and he made his American début at sixteen. In the years following 1915, Ornstein composed much music that placed him among the *avant-garde* and has had considerable influence upon younger American composers, but his later works, which include a symphony and various pieces of piano music, are more traditional in style.

OROSIUS, **Paulus** (5th cent. A.D.), a Spanish presbyter and historian, visited Augustine in 415, and went to study under Jerome at Bethlehem. His uncritical compilation, *Historiarum adversus Paganos Libri vii* (ed. by Zangemeister, Vienna 1882), from the Creation to A.D. 417, a favourite textbook during the Middle Ages, was translated into English by King Alfred (ed. Sweet, 1883). There is a modern English version by I. W. Raymond (1936).

O'ROURKE, **Sir Brian-na-Murtha** (d. 1591), Irish chieftain in Galway, Sligo, and the west of Ulster, was in frequent collision with the English authorities, sheltered the Spaniards

of the Armada wrecked on Irish coasts, and in 1591 went to Scotland to seek support from James VI, who handed him over to the English. He was tried and executed at Tyburn in 1591.

ORPEN, **Sir William** (1878–1931), British painter, born at Stillorgan, Co. Dublin, studied at the Metropolitan School of Art at Dublin and at the Slade School. He did many sketches and paintings at the front in World War I, and was present at the Paris peace conference as official painter. The results may be seen at the Imperial War Museum. He is also known for Irish genre subjects, but is most famous for his portraits, whose vitality and feeling for character place them among the finest of the century. He was knighted in 1918 and elected R.A. in 1919.

ORR, **Boyd.** See BOYD ORR.

ORRERY. See BOYLE.

ORSINI, **Felice** (1819–58), Italian conspirator, born at Meldola, in the States of the Church, of an ancient and distinguished family, was, as the son of a conspirator, early initiated into secret societies, and in 1844 was sentenced at Rome to the galleys, amnestied, and again imprisoned for political plots. In 1848 he was elected to the Roman Constituent Assembly. He took part in the defence of Rome and Venice, agitated in Genoa and Modena, and in 1853 was shipped by the Sardinian government to England, where he formed close relations with Mazzini. Next year he was at Parma, Milan, Trieste, Vienna, until arrested and confined at Mantua. In 1856 he escaped to England, where he supported himself by public lecturing, and wrote *Austrian Dungeons in Italy* (1856). In 1857 he went to Paris to assassinate Napoleon III as an obstacle to revolution in Italy. Orsini and three others threw three bombs under Napoleon's carriage (January 14, 1858); 10 persons were killed, 156 wounded, but Napoleon and the empress remained unhurt. Orsini and another were guillotined March 13. See his *Memoirs*, written by himself (Eng. trans. 1857), his *Letters* (1861), and a work by Montazio (1862).

ORTEGA Y GASSET, **José,** *or-tay'ga ee gah-set'* (1883–1955), Spanish humanist, born in Madrid, was professor there from 1911. His introduction of such writers as Proust and Joyce to Spain and his critical writings made him there the most influential author of his time. *Meditaciones del Quijote* (1914) outlines national symbols in Spanish literature and compares them with those of others. In *Tema de nuestro tiempo* (1923) he argues that great philosophies demarcate the cultural horizons of their epochs. *La Rebelión de Las Masas* (1930) foreshadowed the Civil War. He lived in South America and Portugal (1931–46). *Man of Crisis* (1959) is a collection of lectures, posthumously translated, also *On Love*, trans. T. Talbot (1959).

ORTELIUS (1527–98), the Latinized name of the geographer Abraham Ortel, born of German parents at Antwerp, where he died. His *Theatrum Orbis Terrarum* (1570) was the first great atlas.

ORTON, **Arthur.** See TICHBORNE.

ORWELL, **George,** pseud. of **Eric Arthur Blair** (1903–50), English novelist and essayist, born at Motihari in Bengal, was educated at Eton College, served in Burma in the Indian Imperial Police from 1922 until 1927 (later recalled in the novel *Burmese Days* (1935)) and then was literally *Down and Out in Paris and London* (1933), making an occasional living as tutor or bookshop assistant. *Coming Up for Air* (1939) is a plea for the small man against big business. He fought and was wounded in the Spanish Civil War and he developed his own brand of socialism in *The Road to Wigan Pier* (1937), *Homage to Catalonia* (1938) and *The Lion and the Unicorn* (1941). During World War II, he was war correspondent for the B.B.C. and *The Observer* and wrote for *Tribune*. His intellectual honesty motivated his biting satire of Communist ideology in *Animal Farm* (1945) which was made into a cartoon film, and the hair-raising prophecy for mankind in *Nineteen Eighty-Four* (1949), the triumph of the scientifically perfected servile state, the extirpation of political freedom by thought-control and an ideologically delimited basic language or *new-speak* in which 'thought crime is death'. Other penetrating collections of essays include *Inside the Whale* (1940) and *Shooting an Elephant* (1950). See *Collected Essays, Journalism and Letters* (4 vols.) ed. by S. Orwell and I. Angus (1968) and studies by Atkins (1954), Brander (1954), Hopkinson (1955), Hollis (1956), and Thomas (1965).

OSBORN, (1) **Henry Fairfield** (1857–1935), American zoologist, born at Fairfield, Conn., studied at Princeton, was assistant professor there 1881–90, professor of Zoology at Columbia University 1891–1910, and thereafter research professor. His work especially on fossil vertebrates is important, and as director he made the American Museum of Natural History famous. He wrote also on evolution, education, a Life of Cope, &c.

(2) **Sherard** (1822–75), British naval officer, born at Madras, entered the navy in 1837. He took part in the Chinese war of 1841–42, commanded vessels in two expeditions (1849 and 1852–55) in search of Sir John Franklin, was head of the British squadron in the Sea of Azov during the Crimean war, and took a leading share in the Chinese war of 1857–59. He helped to lay a cable between Great Britain and Australia, was made rear-admiral in 1873, and helped to fit out the Arctic expedition of Nares and Markham (1875). He published his *Arctic Journal* (1852), *Journals of McClure* (1856) and *Fate of Sir John Franklin* (1860).

OSBORNE, (1) **Dorothy**. See TEMPLE (3).

(2) **John James** (1929–   ), British playwright and actor, son of a Welsh commercial artist, left Belmont College, Devon, at sixteen and became a copywriter for trade journals. Hating it, he turned actor (1948) and by 1955 was playing leading rôles in new plays at the Royal Court Theatre. There his fourth play, *Look Back in Anger* (1956; filmed 1958), and *The Entertainer* (1957; filmed 1960), with Sir Laurence Olivier playing Archie Rice, established Osborne as the leading younger exponent of British social drama. The 'hero' of the first, Jimmy Porter, the prototype 'Angry Young Man',

as well as the pathetic, mediocre music hall joker of the latter, both echo the author's uncompromising hatred of outworn social and political institutions and attitudes. An earlier play, *Epitaph for George Dillon*, written in collaboration with A. Creighton and exploring the moral problems of a would-be literary genius, was also staged in 1957. Among other works are *Luther* (1960), *Inadmissible Evidence* (1965), *Time Present* and *The Hotel in Amsterdam* (1968), and the filmscript of *Tom Jones*. See his *Credo* in *Declaration*, ed. T. Maschler (1957).

(3) **Thomas**, See LEEDS.

OSBOURNE, Lloyd (1868–1947), American author, stepson and collaborator of R. L. Stevenson (q.v.), born in San Francisco, was U.S. vice-consul in Samoa, and wrote *Love the Fiddler*, stories and dramas.

OSCAR I (1799–1859), king of Sweden and Norway, ascended the throne in 1844, carried out social and economic reforms and pursued a policy of Scandinavian unity and Swedish neutrality.

OSCAR II (1829–1907), king of Sweden (1872–1907), and of Norway (1872–1905), a great-grandson of Charles XIV (q.v.), translated *Faust*, wrote a Life of Charles XII and poems.

O'SHAUGHNESSY, Arthur (1844–81), British poet, born in London, in 1861 entered the British Museum (the natural history department in 1863), and wrote *Epic of Women* (1870), *Lays of France* (1872), *Music and Moonlight* (1874) and *Songs of a Worker* (1881). His best-known poem is *The Music-Makers*. See Life by L. C. Moulton (1894).

OSIANDER, Andreas (1498–1552), German reformer, born at Gunzenhausen, a preacher at Nürnberg (1522), persuaded that city to declare for Luther. Deprived for refusing to agree to the Augsburg Interim (1548), he was made professor of Theology at Königsberg, but soon became entangled in bitter theological strife, disputing the imputation of Christ's righteousness in favour of an infusion doctrine. See Lives by Wilken (1844), Möller (1870) and Hase (1879).

OSLER, Sir William (1849–1919), British physician, born in Canada, became professor of Medicine at McGill (1875–84), Pennsylvania (1884–88), Johns Hopkins (1889–1905), and finally Oxford (1905–11). He became a baronet in 1911. His special study was angina pectoris, and he wrote also on the history of medicine. His *Principles and Practice of Medicine* (1892) became a standard work. See Life by Cushing (1940).

OSMAN. See OTHMAN.

OSMAN DIGNA, *né* George Nisbet (1836–1926), born at Rouen, a slave-dealer and from 1881 a Mahdist leader on the Red Sea coast and the Abyssinian frontier, was defeated and taken at Tokar (1900). See Life by H. C. Jackson (1926).

OSMAN NURI PASHA (1837–1900), Turkish general, born at Amasia or at Tokat, held Plevna against the Russians in 1877. See work by Levaux (1891).

OSMUND, St (d. 1099), coming from Normandy with the Conqueror, became chancellor (1072) and Bishop of Salisbury (1078). He established the 'Use of Sarum'.

OSSIAN, heroic poet of the Gael, and son of the 3rd-century hero Fingal or Fionn MacCumhail, whose poems James Macpherson (q.v.) professed to have collected and translated. See *Ossian*, with introduction by W. Sharp (1897).

OSSOLI. See FULLER (4).

OSTADE, Adriaan van, *os-tah'dě* (1610–85), Dutch painter and engraver, born probably at Haarlem, was a pupil of Frans Hals, and his use of chiaroscuro shows the influence of Rembrandt. His subjects are taken mostly from everyday life—tavern scenes, farmyards, markets, village greens, &c. His *Alchemist* is in the National Gallery. His brother Isaac (1621–49) treated similar subjects, but excelled at winter scenes and landscapes. See a study by Van der Wiele (Paris 1893) on both brothers, and one by Godefroy (Paris 1930) on Adriaan's engraved work.

OSTROVSKY, Alexander (1823–85), Russian dramatist, born at Moscow, whose best known play is *The Storm* (1860; trans. C. Garnett, 1899).

OSTWALD, Wilhelm, -*valt* (1853–1932), German chemist, born at Riga, was professor at Leipzig 1887–1906, and was awarded a Nobel prize (1909). He discovered the dilution law which bears his name, and invented a process for making nitric acid by the oxidation of ammonia. He also developed a new theory of colour.

OSWALD, St (*c.* 605–642), son of Ethelfrith of Bernicia, fought his way to the Northumbrian crown by the defeat (635) of Caedwalla the Welsh king. He had been converted to Christianity at Iona, and established Christianity in Northumbria with St Aidan's help. He fell in battle with Penda.

OTHMAN, or Osman I (1259–1326), founder of the Ottoman (Turkish) power, was born in Bithynia, and, on the overthrow of the Seljuk sultanate of Iconium in 1299 by the Mongols, gradually subdued a great part of Asia Minor. From his name are derived the terms Ottoman and Osmanli.

OTHMAN (d. 656), third caliph, was Mohammed's secretary and son-in-law, and was chosen in 644. His weak government raised complaints and insurrections on all sides. But Persia was finally subdued, and Herat, Merv and Balkh captured. He was besieged in Medina, and murdered.

OTHO, Marcus Salvius (32–69), joined Galba in his revolt against Nero (68), but, not being proclaimed Galba's successor, rose against the new emperor, who was slain. Otho was recognized as emperor everywhere save in Germany, whence Vitellius marched on Italy, and completely defeated Otho's forces. Next day Otho, who had worn the purple only three months, stabbed himself.

OTIS, James (1725–83), American statesman, born at West Barnstable, Mass., became a leader of the Boston bar. He was advocategeneral in 1760, when the revenue officers demanded his assistance in obtaining from the superior court general search warrants allowing them to enter any man's house in quest of smuggled goods. Otis refused, resigned, and appeared in defence of popular rights. In 1761, elected to the Massachusetts assembly, he was prominent in resistance to the revenue acts. In 1769 he was savagely beaten by revenue officers and others, and lost his reason. He was killed by lightning. His fame chiefly rests on *The Rights of the Colonies Asserted* (1764). See Life by W. Tudor (1823).

OTTO, the name of four Holy Roman Emperors:

Otto I (912–973), son of Henry I, in 936 crowned king of the Germans, in 962 emperor, subdued many turbulent tribes, maintained almost supreme power in Italy, and established Christianity in Scandinavian and Slavonic lands. See study by Holtzmann (1936).

Otto II (955–983), son of Otto I, became emperor in 973, successfully fought the Danes and Bohemians, and subdued insurgent Bavaria which he reduced in size by splitting it up. He invaded France, but overreached himself in attempts on the Eastern Empire.

Otto III (980–1002), son of Otto II, came to the throne as a child of three. His mother held the regency until her death (991), despite attempts to seize power by the Duke of Bavaria, and was succeeded by his grandmother Adelaide. Having engineered first his cousin then his tutor into the papacy, he lived most of his short life in Rome, whence he was driven by the hostility of the people to Paterno, where he died.

Otto IV (*c.* 1174–1218), son of Henry the Lion, elected emperor in 1198, was immediately involved in rivalry for the throne with Philip of Swabia, after whose murder in 1208 a new election was held in which Otto's claim was re-established, and he was crowned in 1209. Excommunicated for attacking Tuscany, Apulia and Sicily, he was supplanted on the German throne by Frederick of Sicily. Civil war followed, and he was defeated by Philip of France at Bouvines (1214). He fled to Saxony and Frederick replaced him as emperor (see FREDERICK II) in 1215.

OTTO, Nikolaus August (1832–91), German engineer, born near Schlangenbad, invented in 1876 the four-stroke internal combustion engine, the sequence of operation of which is named the Otto cycle after him.

OTWAY, Thomas (1652–85), English dramatist, was born at Trotton in Sussex, and from Winchester passed in 1669 to Christ Church College, Oxford. He quitted the university without a degree in 1672, failed utterly as an actor, but made a fair hit with his tragedy *Alcibiades* (1675). In it beautiful Mrs Barry made her first appearance, and with her Otway is said to have fallen in love. In 1676 Betterton accepted his *Don Carlos*, a good tragedy in rhyme. In 1677 Otway translated Racine's *Titus and Berenice*, as well as Molière's *Cheats of Scapin*. In 1678–79 he was in Flanders as a soldier; in the May of the former year appeared his coarse but diverting comedy, *Friendship in Fashion*. The year 1680 yielded two tragedies, *The Orphan* and *Caius Marius*, and his one important poem, *The Poet's Complaint of his Muse*; to 1681 belongs *The Soldier's Fortune*. His greatest work, *Venice Preserved, or a Plot Discovered* (1682), is a masterpiece of tragic passion. For a time he sinks out of sight, to reappear again in 1684 with *The Atheist*, a feeble comedy, and in February 1685 with *Windsor Castle*, a poem addressed to the new king, James II. He died in poverty. In 1719 a badly edited tragedy, *Heroick Friendship*, was published as his. The best edition of his works is by Ghosh (1932). See R. G. Ham's *Otway and Lee* (1931).

OUD, Jacobus Johann Pieter, *owd* (1890–), Dutch architect, born at Purmerend, collaborated with Mondrian (q.v.) and others in launching the review *de Stijl* and became a pioneer of the modern architectural style based on simplified forms and pure planes. Appointed city architect at Rotterdam in 1918, he designed a number of striking buildings, including municipal housing blocks. See study by Hitchcock (1931).

OUDINOT, *oo-dee-nō*, (1) **Nicolas Charles** (1767–1847), marshal of France, born at Bar-le-Duc, served in the revolutionary wars. In 1805 he obtained the Grand Cross of the Legion of Honour and the command of ten reserve battalions, the ' grenadiers Oudinot '. He fought at Austerlitz and Jena, gained the battle of Ostrolenka (1807), and helped at Friedland. Conspicuous in the Austrian campaign of 1809, he was created Marshal of France and Duke of Reggio. In 1810 he was charged with the occupation of Holland, and took part in the Russian campaign and in the battles of 1813 with the Russians and Austrians. He was one of the last to abandon Napoleon. At the second restoration he became a minister of state, commander-in-chief of the royal and national guards, peer of France, &c. In 1823 he commanded in Spain. See Lives by Nollet (1850) and Stiegler (1894), and *Memoirs of Marshal Oudinot* (trans. 1896).

(2) **Nicolas Charles Victor,** Duke of Reggio (1791–1863), son of (1), fought in Algeria, and commanded the expedition to Rome in 1849.

OUGHTRED, William, *aw'tred* (1575–1660), English mathematician, educated at Eton (where he was born) and Cambridge, wrote much on mathematics, notably *Clavis Mathematica* (1631), a textbook on arithmetic in which he introduced multiplication and proportion signs. He invented the trigonometric abbreviations *sin*, *cos*, &c. Another invention was a slide rule. He died at Albury, Surrey.

OUIDA, *wee'da*, pseud. of **Louise Ramé** or **de la Ramée** (1839–1908), English novelist. Born at Bury St Edmunds, she lived long in London, from 1874 made her home in Italy, and died in poverty at Lucca. She wrote *Strathmore* (1865), *Under Two Flags* (her best, 1868), and many other romantic novels as well as children's stories. See Lives by Elizabeth Lee (1914), Y. ffrench (1938).

OUSELEY, (1) **Sir Frederick Arthur Gore, 2nd Bart.** (1825–89), English musician, son of (2), born in London, graduated at Oxford, where he became professor of Music in 1855. He was founder and benefactor of St Michael's College, Tenbury, to which he bequeathed his music library.

(2) **Sir Gore, 1st Bart.** (1770–1844), English diplomat and Orientalist, father of (1), was ambassador in Persia (1810–15).

(3) **Sir William** (1767–1842), Orientalist, brother of (2), wrote on Persian history, language and literature, and on his travels in the East. His son, **Sir William Gore** (1797–1866), held important diplomatic offices in South America.

OUTRAM, Sir James (1803–63), British soldier, the ' Bayard of India ', was born at Butterley Hall, Derbyshire, the residence of his father, Benjamin Outram (1764–1805), engineer, and was educated in Aberdeen. In 1819 he joined the Bombay native infantry, organized a corps of wild Bhils (1825–35), and was political agent in Gujrat (1835–38). In 1839 he attended Sir John Keane as aide-de-camp into Afghanistan, and did good service; and his eight days' ride of 355 miles from Kelat through the Bolan Pass to the sea is famous. Political agent in Sind (1840), he defended the residency at Hyderabad against 8000 Beluchis (1843), and opposed Sir Charles Napier's aggressive policy towards the Amir. He was afterwards resident at Satara and Baroda, and in 1854, on the eve of the annexation of Oudh, was made resident at Lucknow. In 1857 he commanded the brief and brilliant Persian expedition, and he returned to India a G.C.B. when the Mutiny was raging. Lord Canning tendered him the command of the forces advancing to the relief of Lucknow, but he chivalrously waived the honour in favour of his old lieutenant, Havelock, and accompanied him as a volunteer and as chief-commissioner of Oudh. Lucknow was relieved, and Outram took command, only to be in turn himself besieged. He held the Alum-bagh against overwhelming odds, until Sir Colin Campbell relieved him; and his skilful movement up the Gumti led to a complete victory. For his services he was in 1858 made lieutenant-general, thanked by parliament, and created a baronet. He took his seat as a member of the Supreme Council at Calcutta, but in 1860 had to return to England. He spent a winter in Egypt, died at Pau, and was buried in Westminster Abbey. See Lives by Goldsmid (1880) and Trotter (1903).

OVERBECK, Johann Friedrich (1789–1869), German painter, born at Lübeck, studied art at Vienna (1806–10), and settled in Rome, where he allied himself with the like minded Cornelius, Schadow, Schnorr and Veit, who, from the stress they laid on religion and moral significance, were nicknamed the Nazarenes, and scoffed at as Church Romanticists, pre-Raphaelites, &c. A Madonna (1811) brought Overbeck into notice; and Bartholdy, the Prussian consul, employed him to adorn his house with Scripture subjects. He next painted in fresco, in the villa of the Marchese Massimo, five compositions from Tasso's *Jerusalem Delivered*. In 1813 he became a Roman Catholic. His oil pictures are inferior to his frescoes. See Life by Atkinson (1882) and study by Heise (1928).

OVERBURY, Sir Thomas (1581–1613), English courtier and poet, was born at Compton-Scorpion, Warwickshire. After three years at Oxford (1595–98), he studied at the Middle Temple, then travelled on the Continent.

In 1601 at Edinburgh he met Robert Carr, afterwards minion of James I, who in 1611 made him Viscount Rochester. The two became inseparable friends, and Overbury was, through Carr's influence, knighted by James I in 1608. Meanwhile, in 1606, the lovely but profligate Frances Howard (1592–1632) had married the third Earl of Essex, and had intrigued with more than one lover—Carr the most favoured. Overbury had played pander; but when Carr proposed to get Lady Essex divorced, and marry her, he declared she might do for a mistress but not for a wife. Lady Essex offered Sir Davy Wood £1000 to assassinate him. On April 26, 1613, Overbury, on a trivial and illegal pretext—his refusal to go on an embassy—was thrown into the Tower, where on September 15 he was poisoned. Three months later Carr (now Earl of Somerset) and his paramour were married. But in 1615 an inquiry was instituted, and four of the humbler instruments were hanged. In May 1616 the countess pleaded guilty, and the earl was found guilty; but by a stretch of the royal prerogative they were pardoned. In 1622 they were released from the Tower; and Somerset survived till 1645. Overbury's works, posthumous and partly spurious, include *The Wife* (1614), a didactic poem; *Characters* (1614; partly his); and *Crumms fal'n from King James's Table* (1715; doubtful). Rimbault collected them in 1856. See Amos's *The Great Oyer of Poisoning* (1846), Whibley's *Essays in Biography* (1913) and Parry's *Overbury Mystery* (1925).

OVERLAND, Arnulf (1889–), Norwegian lyric poet, born at Kristiansund, wrote patriotic lyrics and from 1940 was prominent in the resistance movement. He was interned in a concentration camp in 1941–45.

OVERSTONE, Samuel Jones Loyd, Baron (1796–1883), English economist, born in London, entered his father's banking house, later merged in the London and Westminster Bank, and established himself as a leading authority on banking and currency by his famous series of tracts (1837–57). Whig M.P. for Hythe in 1819–26, he was made a peer in 1850.

OVID, in full **Publius Ovidius Naso** (43 B.C.–A.D. 17), Latin poet, born at Sulmo (Solmona), in the Abruzzi, son of a well-to-do *eques*, was trained for the bar; but in spite of extraordinary forensic aptitude, he gave his whole energies to poetry, and visited Athens. His first literary success was his tragedy *Medea*. Then came his *Epistolae* or *Heroides*, imaginary love letters from ladies of the heroic days to their lords, and his *Amores*, short poems about his mistress, Corinna. His *Medicamina Faciei* (a practical poem on artificial aids to personal beauty) seems to have been preliminary to his true masterwork, the *Ars Amandi*, or *Ars Amatoria*, in three books, which appeared about 1 B.C., followed by a subsidiary book entitled *Remedia Amoris*. His second period of poetic activity opens with the *Metamorphoses*, in fifteen books, and with the *Fasti*, designed to be in twelve, of which six only were completed. Midway in composition he was banished (A.D. 8), for some reason unknown,

to Tomi on the Black Sea. There he died in A.D. 17. On his way from Rome he began his third period with the elegies which he published in five books, the *Tristia*. Similar in tone and theme are the four books of the *Epistolae ex Ponto*. His *Ibis*, written in imitation of Callimachus, and his *Halieutica*, a poem extant only in fragments, complete the list of his remains. A master of metrical form, Ovid is the most voluminous of Latin poets. See the monograph by Zingerle (1869–71), and books by A. Church (1876), Rand (1926), Wright (1938).

OVIEDO Y VALDÉS, Gonzalo Hernández de, *ov-yay'THŌ ee val-days'* (1478–1557), Spanish historian, born at Madrid, was sent to San Domingo in 1514 as inspector-general of goldmines, and, as historiographer of the Indies, wrote after his return a history thereof (1526; trans. by Eden, 1555).

OWEN, (1) John (*c.* 1560–1622), Welsh epigrammatist, born at Llanarmon, Pwllheli, became a fellow of New College, Oxford, in 1584, and about 1594 a schoolmaster at Warwick. His Latin *Epigrammata* (1606–13; best ed. by Renouard, Paris 1794) have been five times translated into English since 1619.

(2) **John** (1616–83), English Puritan, born at Stadhampton vicarage, Oxfordshire, took his B.A. in 1632 from Queen's College, Oxford, and in 1637 was driven from Oxford by dislike of Laud's statutes. He spent some years as private chaplain; then in 1642 he removed to London, and published *The Display of Arminianism* (1643), for which he was rewarded with the living of Fordham in Essex. In 1646 he removed to Coggeshall, and showed his preference for Independency over Presbyterianism. Cromwell took him in 1649 as his chaplain to Ireland, where he regulated the affairs of Trinity College. Next year (1650) he went with Cromwell to Scotland. In 1651–52 he became dean of Christ Church and vice-chancellor of Oxford University. Here he wrote a number of theological works. He was one of the Triers appointed to purge the church of scandalous ministers. He opposed the giving the crown to the Protector, and the year after Cromwell's death he was ejected from his deanery. He bought an estate at Stadhampton, and formed a congregation. In 1673 he became pastor in Leadenhall Street. To the end he preached and wrote incessantly. See Orme's *Memoirs* (1820), and *Life* by Thomason, prefixed to Goold's edition of Owen's works (1850–1855).

(3) **Sir Richard** (1804–92), English zoologist, born at Lancaster, studied medicine at Edinburgh and at St Bartholomew's; became curator in the museum of the Royal College of Surgeons, where he produced a marvellous series of descriptive catalogues; and in 1834–55 he lectured as professor of Comparative Anatomy, for two years at Bartholomew's, and afterwards at the College of Surgeons. He was a commissioner of health (1843–46), and for the Great Exhibition of 1851. In 1856 he became superintendent of the natural history department of the British Museum, but continued to teach at the Royal Institution and elsewhere. F.R.S. (1834), president of the British Association

(1857), associate of the French Institute (1859), C.B. (1873), K.C.B. (1883), he also received many scientific medals, degrees and honorary titles from many nations. His essay on *Parthenogenesis* was a pioneer work. A pre-Darwinian, he maintained a cautious attitude to detailed evolutionist theories. See Life by his grandson (1894).

(4) **Robert** (1771–1858), Welsh social reformer, was born, a saddler's son, at Newtown, Montgomeryshire. At ten he was put into a draper's shop at Stamford, and by nineteen had risen to be manager of a cotton-mill. In 1799 he married the daughter of David Dale (q.v.), the philanthropic owner of the New Lanark cotton mills, where next year he settled as manager and part owner. He laboured to teach his workpeople the advantages of thrift, cleanliness, and good order, and established infant education. He began social propagandism in *A New View of Society* (1813), and finally adopted socialism; he lost much of his influence by his utterances on religion. His socialistic theories were put to the test in experimental communities at Orbiston near Bothwell, and later at New Harmony in Indiana, in County Clare, and in Hampshire, but all were unsuccessful. In 1828 his connection with New Lanark ceased; and, his means having been exhausted, the remainder of his days were spent in secularist, socialistic and spiritualistic propagandism. See Holyoake, *Co-operation in England* (1875); Owen's Autobiography (1857–58); also Lives by Booth (1869), Jones (1890), Podmore (1906), Cole (1925).

(5) **Robert Dale** (1801–77), son of (4), went in Glasgow, went to America in 1825 to help in the New Harmony colony. He settled in America in 1827, edited the *Free Inquirer* in New York, was a member of the Indiana legislature, and entered congress in 1843. Later he helped to remodel the constitution of Indiana; acted first as *chargé d'affaires*, next as minister at Naples (1853–58); and was an abolitionist and spiritualist. See his autobiography (1874). Two other sons of (4), **David Dale** (1807–60) and **Richard** (1810–1890), were notable geologists.

(6) **Wilfred** (1893–1918), English poet of World War I, killed in action on the Western Front. His poems were edited by his friend Siegfried Sassoon (1920). They were distinguished by the use of assonance in place of rhyme. See study by Welland (1960) and *Memoirs* by his brother, H. Owen (3 vols. 1963–65).

OWEN AP GRUFFYDD (d. 1169), prince of Gwynedd or North Wales, fiercely resisted Henry II, but ultimately submitted.

OWEN GLENDOWER. See GLENDOWER.

OWENS, (1) **James Cleveland (Jesse)** (1913–), American athlete, born in Decatur, Alabama, won three gold medals, and was a member of a winning U.S. relay team at the

1936 Olympic Games at Berlin. Snubbed on that occasion by Hitler, who refused to shake hands with him as a gold medallist because he was coloured, at the 1956 Games he was President Eisenhower's personal representative.

(2) **John** (1790–1846), a Manchester cotton merchant, who left £96,655 for the foundation of an nonsectarian college there, now a university.

(3) **Robert Bowie** (1870–1940), American chemist and engineer, professor at Nebraska, McGill and Philadelphia, invented a differentiation machine, an electric accelerometer and an electromagnetic system for guiding ships and aeroplanes. He is sometimes credited with the discovery of alpha-rays.

OWENSON, Sydney. See MORGAN (5).

OXENSTJERNA, or **Oxenstern, Count Axel** (1583–1654), Swedish statesman, was trained for the church, but entered the public service in 1602, and from 1612 till his death was chancellor. He negotiated peace with Denmark, with Russia, with Poland; and though he sought to prevent Gustavus Adolphus from plunging into the Thirty Years' War, he supported him in it loyally throughout, and on his death kept the Swedish armies together and sustained the Protestant cause. His eldest son, **Johan** (1611–57), was a diplomatist; another, **Erik** (1624–56), succeeded his father as chancellor.

OXFORD, Earl of. See ASQUITH, HARLEY, VERE.

OYAMA, Iwao, Prince (1842–1916), Japanese field-marshal (Hon. O.M. 1906), born in Satsuma, took Port Arthur and Wei-hei-Wei from China (1894–95), and commanded against Russia (1904–05).

OZANAM, Antoine Frédéric (1813–53), French literary historian, a Neo-Catholic of the school of Lacordaire, and one of the founders of the Society of St Vincent de Paul, born at Milan, became in 1841 professor of Foreign Literature at the Sorbonne. He wrote *Dante et la philosophie catholique* (1839), *Histoire de la civilisation au Vᵉ siècle* (1845; trans. 1868), and *Études germaniques* (1847–49). See Lives by O'Meara (1876), Baunard (1912); and Letters (trans. 1886).

OZENFANT, Amédée, *o-zã-fã* (1886–1966), French artist, born at St Quentin, was the leader of the Purist movement in Paris and published a manifesto of Purism with Le Corbusier in 1919. From 1921 to 1925 they published an *avant-garde* magazine, *Esprit nouveau*, and in 1925 the book *La Peinture moderne*. His still-lifes based on this theory reduce vases and jugs to a static counterpoint of two-dimensional shapes. He founded art schools in London (1935) and New York (1938); his publications include *Art* (1928) and his diaries for the years 1931–34. See the monograph by K. Nierendorf (1931).

P

PAASIKIVI, Juo Kusti, *pah'-* (1870–1956), Finnish statesman, born in Tampere, became conservative prime minister after the civil war in 1918. He recognized the need for friendly relations with Russia, and took part in all Finnish-Soviet negotiations. He sought to avoid war in September 1939, conducted the armistice negotiations and became prime minister again in 1944. He succeeded Mannerheim as president (1946–56).

PACHECO, Francisco, *pa-chay'kō* (1571–1654), Spanish painter, was born and died at Seville. Influenced by Raphael, he painted portraits and historical subjects, and he opened a school of art at Seville, where Velasquez was his pupil and became his son-in-law. He wrote a notable technical treatise *Arte de la pintura* (1639).

PACHELBEL, Johann, *paKH'el-bel* (*c.* 1653–1706), German composer and organist, born in Nuremberg, held a variety of organist's posts before, in 1695, he returned to Nuremberg as organist of St Sebalds' Church. His works profoundly influenced J. S. Bach.

PACHMANN, Vladimir de, *paKH'-* (1848–1933), pianist, born at Odessa, studied at Vienna, and won fame as an interpreter of Chopin.

PACHOMIUS (4th cent.), an Egyptian, superseded the system of solitary recluse life by founding (*c.* A.D. 318), the first monastery on an island in the Nile.

PADEREWSKI, Ignace Jan, *pad-ê-ref'skee* (1860–1941), Polish pianist, composer and patriot, born at Kurylowka in Podolia, began to play as an infant of three. He studied at Warsaw, becoming professor in the Conservatoire there in 1878. In 1884 he taught in the Strasbourg Conservatoire, but thereafter became a virtuoso, appearing with prodigious success in Europe and America. He became director of Warsaw Conservatoire in 1909. In 1919 he was one of the first premiers of Poland, for whose freedom he had striven. Very soon, however, he retired from politics and went to live in Switzerland. He resumed concert work for some years, but when Poland's provisional parliament was established in Paris in 1940, he was elected president. He died in Switzerland.

PADILLA, Juan de, *pa-deel'ya* (1490–1521), a Spanish popular hero, was commandant of Saragossa under Charles V, headed an insurrection against the intolerable taxation, and after some successes was defeated (April 23, 1521) and beheaded. His wife held Toledo against the royal forces.

PAGANINI, Nicolo (1782–1840), Italian violin virtuoso, was born, a porter's son, at Genoa. He gave his first concert in 1793 (when his father reduced his age by two years in advertisements); began his professional tours in Italy in 1805; in 1828–31 made a great sensation in Austria and Germany, Paris and London. His dexterity and technical brilliance acquired an almost legendary reputation and it was said that he was in league with the devil. He revolutionized violin technique, among his innovations being the use of stopped harmonics. See study by G. I. C. de Courcy (1958).

PAGE, (1) Sir Frederick Handley (1885–1962), English pioneer aircraft designer and engineer, in 1909 founded the firm of aeronautical engineers which bears his name. His twin-engined 0/400 (1918) was one of the earliest heavy bombers, and his Hampden and Halifax bombers were used in the second World War; his civil aircraft include the Hannibal, Hermes and Herald transports. He was knighted in 1942.

(2) **Thomas Nelson** (1853–1922), American diplomat, born at Oakland, Va., practised law at Richmond, wrote many stories, some in Negro dialect, and became U.S. ambassador to Italy in 1913.

(3) **Walter Hines** (1855–1918), American diplomat, born in N. Carolina, edited the *Forum* (1890–95), *Atlantic Monthly* (1896–99), *World's Work* (1900–13), and became U.S. ambassador in London in 1913. See his *Life and Letters* by Hendrick (1922).

PAGÈS. See GARNIER-PAGÈS.

PAGET, (1) Sir George Edward (1809–92), born at Yarmouth, studied at Cambridge, and in 1872 became regius professor of Physics there. See his *Lectures*, with memoir by C. E. Paget (1893).

(2) **Sir James** (1814–99), brother of (1), born at Yarmouth, wrote standard *Lectures on Surgical Pathology* and *Clinical Lectures*. See *Memoirs* (1901) by his son.

(3) **Violet.** See LEE, VERNON.

PAHLAVI, Mohammad Reza (1919–), Shah of Persia, succeeded on the abdication of his father, Reza Shah, in 1941. His first two marriages, to Princess Fawzia, sister of Farouk, and to Soraya Esfandiari, ended in divorce after the failure of either to produce a male heir. By his third wife Farah Diba, daughter of an army officer, he has had two sons, Crown Prince Reza (1960), Ali Reza (1966), and a daughter, Princess Farahnaz (1963). His reign has been marked by social reforms and a movement away from the old-fashioned despotic concept of the monarchy.

PAIN, Barry Eric Odell (1867–1928), English humorous novelist and parodist, born in Cambridge, wrote *Eliza* (1900), &c.

PAINE, Thomas (1737–1809), English deist and radical, was born at Thetford, the son of an ex-Quaker stay-maker, had by turns been stay-maker and marine, schoolmaster, exciseman, and tobacconist, when in 1774 he sailed for Philadelphia. In 1776 his pamphlet *Common Sense* argued for complete independence; his *Crisis* came a year later; and Paine, then serving with the American army, was made secretary to the committee of foreign affairs. He lost that post in 1779 for divulging state secrets, but was appointed clerk of the Pennsylvania legislature, and in 1785 received from congress $3000 and a farm. In 1787 he returned to England, where in 1791–92 he published *The Rights of Man*, most famous of the replies to Burke's *Reflections*, which involved many in heavy penalties. Paine had slipped off to Paris, having been elected by Pas-de-Calais deputy to the National Convention. He voted with the Girondists, proposed to offer the king an asylum in America, and so offending the Robespierre faction, in 1794 was imprisoned. Just before his arrest he wrote part i of *The Age of Reason*, in favour of Deism. Part ii appeared in 1795, and a portion of part iii in 1807. The book alienated Washington and most of his old friends. After an imprisonment of eleven months he was released and restored to his seat in the Convention, but became disgusted with French politics. In 1802 he returned to America, and he died in New York. There are editions of his works by Mendum (1850) and Moncure Conway (4 vols. 1895–96); among biographies are those by ' Francis Oldys ' (i.e., George Chalmers, 1791), Cheetham (1809), Rickman (1819), Sherwin (1819), Vale (1841), Blanchard (1860), Conway (1892), E. Sedgwick (1899), Gould (1925), Best (1927), Pearson (1937), C. Cohen (1945), W. E. Woodward (N.Y. 1945), H. M. Fast (N.Y. 1946).

PAINLEVÉ, Paul, *pī-lė-vay* (1863–1933), French mathematician and statesman, born in Paris, was professor at Lille, the Sorbonne, and the École polytechnique, repeatedly minister for war, twice air minister, and twice (1917, 1925) premier.

PAINTER, William (?1540–94), English translator, studied at Cambridge, was master of Sevenoaks school, but in 1561 became clerk of ordnance in the Tower. His *Palace of Pleasure* (1566–67; ed. Miles, 1930), largely composed of stories from Boccaccio, Bandello, and Margaret of Navarre, became popular, and was the main source whence many dramatists drew their plots, Shakespeare among them.

PAISIELLO, Giovanni (1740–1816), Italian composer, born at Taranto, studied at Naples, wrote at first only church music, but turned successfully to opera, and in 1776–84 was court musician to the Empress Catharine at St Petersburg. In 1799 he was appointed director of national music by the republican government of France and later enjoyed the patronage of Napoleon. He returned to Naples in 1804. Paisiello was the most successful Neapolitan opera composer of his time: his *Barbiere di Seviglia* was so popular that Rossini's use of the same libretto met with considerable hostility, but his ninety-odd pieces are seldom if ever staged today, possibly because of their comparative superficiality, though they contain a wealth of delightful tunes, one of which, *Nel cor più non mi sento*, was used by both Beethoven and Paganini as a theme for variations.

PALACIO VALDÉS. See VALDÉS (1).

PALACKÝ, František, *pa'lat-ski* (1798–1876), was a Czech publicist and politician in Prague, and the most distinguished historian of Bohemia.

PALAFOX Y MELZI, José de, *-foKH'* (1780–

1847), Spanish patriot, nominally head of the heroic defence of Saragossa (July 1808 to February 1809), was carried prisoner to France, and not released until 1813. He was made Duke of Saragossa (1836) and grandee of Spain (1837).

PALESTRINA, Giovanni Pierluigi da (1525–1594), Italian composer, born at Palestrina, was sent at the age of ten to the choir school of Sta Maria Maggiore at Rome, where he learnt composition and organ playing. In 1544 he became organist and *maestro di canto* at the cathedral of St Agapit in his native town, and at the age of twenty-two married the heiress of a well-to-do citizen. The new pope, Julius III, had been bishop of Palestrina and aware of the talent possessed by his late organist, appointed him master of the Julian choir at St Peter's, for which he composed many fine masses. In 1555 Julius engineered him into the exclusive and highly privileged Pontifical Choir without an entrance examination or the customary election by existing members, but Paul IV, coming to the papal throne in the same year, tightened up the regulations and Palestrina was compulsorily retired. He now became choirmaster at the Lateran, but walked out without notice in 1560, probably owing to his disagreement with economy cuts imposed by the impoverished canons. In 1561 he returned to Sta Maria Maggiore as choirmaster, remaining until 1567, though only on a part-time basis after 1565, when he was appointed music master at the new Roman Seminary set up by the Council of Trent. The years between 1572 and 1580 were tragic ones for Palestrina, who during this time lost his wife and three sons in the terrible epidemics which intermittently ravaged Rome. Eight months after his wife's death he was married again, this time to a wealthy widow who had come into a furrier's business, which he took over, apparently with success. A great task entrusted to him at this time was the revision of the Gradual, ordained in 1577 by the Council of Trent, a monumental labour which was abandoned after a few years. He continued to live in Rome, composing and working at St Peter's, refusing an offer from the Duke of Mantua, an old friend of his, to become his musical director. He died in Rome, February 2, 1594, and was buried in St Peter's. Palestrina's place as the most distinguished composer of the Renaissance is unchallenged, as is his status as one of the greatest figures in musical history, to whom generations of later composers, including Bach, Mozart, Wagner, Liszt and Debussy, have acknowledged their debt. His works include over 90 masses and a large number of motets, hymns and other liturgical pieces as well as some excellent madrigals. Apart from a few organ *ricercari* of doubtful authenticity, no instrumental music has been ascribed to him. His compositions, free from sentimentality yet with an extraordinary depth of feeling, are characterized by an uncanny skill in the handling of contrapuntal texture, but also contain examples of homophony and subtle dissonances which are immensely effective chorally. Having in its original form no division into bars, his music is free-flowing and unhampered by rhythmic conventions. See Life by Pyne (1922), and studies by Coates (1938) and Jeppesen (1946); also H. K. Andrews, *An Introduction to the Technique of Palestrina* (1958).

PALEY, William (1743–1805), English theologian, born at Peterborough, fellow and tutor of Christ's College, Cambridge (1768–1776), published *Principles of Moral and Political Philosophy* (1785), expounding a form of utilitarianism. In 1790 appeared his most original work, *Horae Paulinae*, the aim of which is to prove the great improbability of the hypothesis that the New Testament is a cunningly devised fable. It was followed in 1794 by his famous *Evidences of Christianity*. In 1802 he published perhaps the most widely popular of all his works, *Natural Theology, or Evidences of the Existence and Attributes of the Deity*. See the Life by G. W. Meadley (1809).

PALGRAVE, (1) **Sir Francis** (1788–1861), English historian, was born in London, the son of Meyer Cohen, a Jewish stockbroker, but on his marriage (1823) he assumed his mother-in-law's maiden name. He was called to the bar in 1827; and, knighted in 1832, was in 1838 appointed deputy-keeper of Records. Among his works are *The English Commonwealth* (1832), *The Merchant and the Friar*, and a *History of Normandy and of England* (1851–64 incomplete). He also edited *Parliamentary Writs* (1830–34), *Rotuli Curiae Regis* (1835), *Ancient Kalendars of the Treasury of the Exchequer* (1836), and *Documents illustrating the History of Scotland* (1837). A collected edition of his historical works (1919–22) was started by his third son, **Sir Robert Harry Inglis** (1827–1919), political economist.

(2) **Francis Turner** (1824–97), eldest son of (1), poet and critic, born in London, became scholar of Balliol, Oxford, and fellow of Exeter, was successively vice-principal of a training college, private secretary to Earl Granville, an official in the education department, and professor of Poetry at Oxford (1886–95). His works include *Idylls and Songs* (1854), *Essays on Art* (1866), *Hymns* (1867), *Lyrical Poems* (1871), *Visions of England* (1881), and *Landscape in Poetry* (1897). He is best known as the editor of the *Golden Treasury of English Lyrics* (1861, re-edited 1896; poor 2nd series, 1897); *Children's Treasury of Lyrical Poetry* (1875); *Sonnets and Songs of Shakespeare* (1877); selections from Herrick (1877) and Keats (1885); and *Treasury of Sacred Song* (1889). See Life (1899) by G. F. Palgrave, his daughter.

(3) **Sir Reginald Francis Douce** (1829–1904), K.C.B. (1892), fourth son of (1), was in 1886 appointed clerk to the House of Commons, and wrote on parliamentary practice and history.

(4) **William Gifford** (1826–88), second son of (1), graduated at Oxford in 1846. He joined the Bombay Native Infantry, but becoming a Jesuit, studied at Rome, and was sent as a missionary to Syria. For Napoleon III he went disguised as a physician on a daring expedition through Arabia (1862–63), described in his (untrustworthy) *Narrative of a Year's Journey through Central and Eastern Arabia* (1865). Quitting the Jesuits in 1864, he was sent by the British government in 1865 to treat for the release of the captives in Abyssinia. He became consul at Trebizond, St Thomas and Manila; consul-general in Bulgaria 1878, and Siam 1880; and British minister to Uruguay 1884. There he married, was reconciled to the church, and died.

PALISSY, Bernard (c. 1509–89), French potter, was born in Agen, and, after wandering for ten years over France as a glass-painter, about 1538 married and settled at Saintes. Resolved to discover how to make enamels, he neglected all else and experimented for sixteen years, exhausting all his resources, but was at length rewarded with success (1557). His ware bearing in high relief plants and animals coloured to represent nature, soon made him famous; and, though as a Huguenot he was in 1562 imprisoned, he was speedily released and taken into royal favour. In 1564 he established his workshop at the Tuileries, and was specially exempted from the massacre of St Bartholomew (1572). During 1575–84 he lectured on natural history, physics and agriculture. In 1588 he was again arrested as a Huguenot and was thrown into the Bastille of Bucy, where he died. Palissy's writings, with an account of his experiences, were edited by A. France (1880). See Life by H. Morley (1852), and French ones by Audiat (1868), Burty (1886), Dupuy (1902) and Levoux (1928).

PALLADIO, Andrea (1518–80), Italian architect, was born and died at Vicenza. He founded modern Italian architecture, as distinguished from the earlier Italian Renaissance. The Palladian style is modelled on the ancient Roman as apprehended by Vitruvius. His *Quattro Libri dell' Architettura* (1570) greatly influenced his successors, especially Inigo Jones, whose notes are given in Leoni's Eng. trans. (1715), and Christopher Wren. See Lives by B. F. Fletcher (1902), Zanella (1880), Barichella (1880).

PALLADIUS, (1) **St**, is said to have been sent 'in Scotiam', in 430, by Pope Celestine; but the Scotia here meant was certainly Ireland. Skene doubts if Palladius was ever in Scotland till after his death, when St Ternan brought his relics to Fordoun in Kincardineshire.

(2) **Rutilius Taurus Aemilianus** (4th cent. A.D.), Roman author, who wrote *De Re Rustica* (On Agriculture), in fourteen books.

PALLAS, Peter Simon (1741–1811), born at Berlin, was in 1768 invited to St Petersburg by the Empress Catharine as an eminent naturalist. He spent six years (1768–74) exploring the Urals, the Kirghiz Steppes, the Altai range, part of Siberia, and the steppes of the Volga, returning with an extraordinary treasure of specimens; and he wrote a series of works on the geography, ethnography, flora and fauna of the regions visited. He settled in the Crimea.

PALLAVICINO, Sforza, -*vi-chee'nō* (1607–1667), Italian historian, became in 1638 a Jesuit, and a cardinal in 1659. His best-known work is *Istoria del Concilio di Trento* (1656–57), a reply to the work of Sarpi,

PALMA, Jacopo, called **Palma Vecchio** (' Old Palma ') (c. 1480–1528), stands at the head of the second class of great Venetian artists. His pictures are sacred subjects or portrait groups. See work by Locatelli (1890). His brother's grandson, **Jacopo** (1544–1628), called **Il Giovane** (' the Younger '), painted poorish religious pictures.

PALMER, (1) **Daniel David** (1845–1913), American osteopath and founder of chiropractic, born at Toronto, settled at Davenport, Iowa, where he first practised spinal adjustment and founded the Palmer School of Chiropractic in 1898. Later he established a college of chiropractic at Portland, Oregon.

(2) **Edward Henry** (1840–82), English orientalist, was born at Cambridge, and at the university he devoted himself to oriental studies. In 1871 he was appointed Lord Almoner's professor of Arabic at Cambridge, and in 1874 he was called to the bar. In 1881 he turned journalist, writing principally for the *Standard*. In 1882, on the eve of Arabi's Egyptian rebellion, sent by government to win over the Sinai tribes, he, Capt. Gill, R.E., and Lieut. Charrington, R.N., were murdered in the ravine of Wady Sadr. Among Palmer's works are the *Desert of the Exodus* (1871) and a translation of the *Koran* (1880). See Life by Besant (1883), and Haynes, *Man-hunting in the Desert* (1894).

(3) **Roundell** and **William.** See SELBORNE.

(4) **Samuel** (1805–81), English landscape painter and etcher, born in London, produced chiefly watercolours in a mystical and imaginative style derived from Blake, who was his friend. His work, outmoded during his lifetime by the Victorian demand for realistic sentimentality, is now assessed at its true value.

PALMERSTON, Henry John Temple, 3rd Viscount (1784–1865), was born at 20 Queen Anne's Gate, Westminster, of the Irish branch of the ancient English family of Temple. In 1800 he went to Edinburgh University, in 1802 succeeded his father, and was at Cambridge University (1803–06). As Tory candidate for the university he was rejected in 1806, elected in 1807 for Newport (Wight); but from 1811 he represented his *alma mater* for twenty years, and only lost his seat when he supported the Reform Bill. Afterwards he was returned for South Hampshire, lost his seat in 1835, but found a seat for Tiverton. He was junior lord of the Admiralty and secretary at war under Perceval, the Earl of Liverpool, Canning, Goderich and the Duke of Wellington (1809–28). His official connection with the Tory party ceased in 1828. The Duke's government was swept away in 1830, and Earl Grey offered the seals of the foreign office to Palmerston. For the first time on record England and France acted in concert. Palmerston took a leading part in securing the independence of Belgium, in establishing the thrones of Isabella of Spain and Maria of Portugal, and in endeavouring, in alliance with Austria and Turkey, to check Russian influence in the East. In 1841 Palmerston went out of office with the Whigs on the question of free trade in corn, and under Lord John Russell in 1846 resumed the seals of the Foreign Office. His second term was embarrassed by the Spanish marriages (see GUIZOT), the revolutions in 1848, the rupture between Spain and Great Britain, the affair of Don Pacifico (a Gibraltar Jew living in Athens, who claimed the privileges of a British subject), and the consequent quarrel with Greece. His self-asserting character, his brusque speech, his interferences in foreign affairs, were little calculated to conciliate opponents at home, and secured for ' Firebrand Palmerston ' many enemies abroad. A vote of censure on the foreign policy was in 1850 carried in the House of Lords, but defeated in the Lower House. In December 1851 Palmerston expressed to the French ambassador his approbation of the *coup d'état* of Louis Napoleon, without consulting either the premier or the Queen, and Lord John Russell advised his resignation. Next February he shattered the Russell administration on a Militia Bill. He refused office under the Earl of Derby, but was home secretary in Aberdeen's coalition (1852), whose fall (1855) brought Palmerston the premiership. He vigorously prosecuted the Russian war. Defeated in 1857 on Cobden's motion condemning the Chinese war, he appealed to the country, and met the House of Commons with a largely increased majority, but fell in February 1858, over the Conspiracy Bill. In June 1859 he again became prime minister, remaining in office till his death, the chief events the American Civil War, Napoleon's war with Austria, and the Austro-Prussian war with Denmark. It was his ambition to be the minister of a nation rather than of a political party, and his opponents admitted that he held office with more general acceptance than any minister since Chatham. He is buried in Westminster Abbey. See Lives by Dalling and Ashley (5 vols. 1870–76), Trollope (1882), the Duke of Argyll (1892), Bell (1936), Webster (1951), and Martin (1963); also *Regina v. Palmerston* (ed. Connell, 1962).

PALMIERI, Luigi (1807–96), Italian meteorologist, became in 1847 professor at Naples, and in 1854 director of the Vesuvius observatory. He invented a rain gauge and other meteorological instruments.

PALTOCK, Robert (1697–1767), English writer, born in London, and bred to the law, wrote *Peter Wilkins* (1751); its authorship remained a mystery till 1835. See Bullen's edition (1884) and *Athenaeum* (1884–85).

PALUDAN-MÜLLER, Frederik (1809–76), Danish poet, wrote poems, dramas and romances. But his fame rests on *Adam Homo* (1841–49), a humorous, satiric, didactic poem. See Brandes, *Eminent Authors* (1886), and a study by F. Lange (1899).

PANCRAS, St (d. 304), Christian martyr, son of a heathen noble of Phrygia, was baptised at Rome, but immediately afterwards was slain in the Diocletian persecution, being only fourteen years old.

PANDER, Christian Heinrich (1794–1865), Russian scientist, was born at Riga. At Würzburg he did valuable research on chick development in the egg, with particular regard to the embryonic layers now called by his name. Having published his findings in 1817, in 1820 he accompanied as a naturalist a Russian mission to Bokhara, and was elected a member of the St Petersburg Academy of Sciences in 1826.

PANDULF, Cardinal (d. 1226), Italian prelate, the commissioner sent (1213) by Innocent III to King John, who returned to England as legate (1218-21), and in 1218 was made Bishop of Norwich.

PANHARD, René (1841-1908), French engineer and inventor, born at Paris, a pioneer of the motor industry. With Émile Levassor, his partner from 1886, he was the first to mount an internal combustion engine on a chassis (1891). He founded the Panhard Company.

PANIZZI, Sir Anthony (1797-1879), Italian bibliographer, born at Brescello in Modena, was an advocate, but, sharing in the revolution of 1821, fled to Liverpool, and in 1828 became Italian professor in University College London, in 1831 assistant librarian, and in 1856 chief librarian of the British Museum, where he showed great administrative ability, undertook a new catalogue, and designed the reading room, politically active the while for the Italian cause. See Lives by Brooks (1931), Miller (1967).

PANKHURST, Emmeline (1857-1928), English suffragette, born (Goulden) at Manchester, organized (1905) the Women's Social and Political Union, and fought for women's suffrage by violent means. Of her daughters and fellow workers, Dame Christabel (1880-1958), turned later to preaching Christ's Second Coming; and Sylvia (1882-1960) diverged to pacificism, internationalism and Labour politics, and wrote a Life of her mother (1935). See Christabel's Unshackled (1959), and Mitchell, The Fighting Pankhursts (1967).

PANZINI, Alfredo (1863-1939), Italian writer of short stories, novels and criticisms, born at Senigallia, educated at Bologna, taught in Milan and Rome, and was an original academician.

PAOLI, Pasquale de (1725-1807), Corsican patriot, born at Stretta in Corsica, son of a patriot driven in exile to Naples in 1739. Thence Pasquale returned to take part in the heroic struggle against the Genoese, and in 1755 was appointed to the chief command. The Genoese sold the island (1768) to France. For a year he held out against a French army, but was overpowered, and escaped to England, where he was welcomed. Boswell, who had visited him in Corsica, introduced him to Dr Johnson. On the French Revolution he became governor of Corsica, but he organized a fresh insurrection against the Convention, favouring union with England. He returned to England in 1796. See Life by Ravenna (Florence 1927).

PAOLO, Fra. See SARPI.

PAPAGOS, Field-Marshal Alexander (1883-1956), Greek statesman, a distinguished soldier who, after a brilliant military career, became in 1952 prime minister of Greece at the head of an exclusively Greek Rally government.

PAPEN, Franz von, pah'pėn . (1879-), German politician, born at Werl, Westphalia,

was military attaché at Mexico and Washington, chief of staff with a Turkish army, and took to Centre party politics. As Hindenburg's chancellor (1932) he suppressed the Prussian Socialist government, as Hitler's vice-chancellor (1933-34) signed a concordat with Rome. He was ambassador to Austria (1936-38) and Turkey (1939-44) and was taken prisoner in 1945. He stood trial at Nuremberg in 1946 but was acquitted.

PAPIAS (2nd cent. A.D.), bishop at Hierapolis in Phrygia, a 'companion of Polycarp'. Irenaeus, Eusebius, &c., preserve fragments of his lost ' Exposition of Oracles of the Lord '.

PAPIN, Denis, pa-pi (1647-?1712), French physicist, born at Blois, helped Huygens and Boyle in their experiments, invented the condensing pump and the steam digester (1681), and was made a member of the Royal Society (1680). For four years he was at Venice, was back in London in 1684, in 1687 became professor of Mathematics at Marburg but from 1696 to 1707 worked in Cassel, after which he returned to England.

PAPINEAU, Louis Joseph (1789-1871), French-Canadian party leader, speaker of the House of Assembly for Lower Canada (1815-37), opposed the union with Upper Canada, and agitated against the imperial government. At the rebellion of 1837 a warrant was issued against him for high-treason. He escaped to Paris; but returned to Canada, amnestied, in 1847.

PAPINI, Giovanni, -pee'nee (1881-1956), Italian author and philosopher, born at Florence and educated there, wrote Un Uomo finito (1913), Storia di Cristo (1921), Sant' Agostino (1929), &c.

PAPINIANUS, Aemilius (c. A.D. 140-212), Roman jurist, held offices at Rome under Septimius Severus, but was put to death by Caracalla. Nearly 600 excerpts from his legal works were incorporated in Justinian's Pandects.

PAPPENHEIM, Gottfried Heinrich Graf zu (1594-1632), imperial general in the Thirty Years' War, was born at Pappenheim in Franconia, of an ancient Swabian family. At twenty he went over to the Roman Catholic Church, served the king of Poland, joined the army of the Catholic League, and decided the battle of Prague (1620). In 1625 he became general of the Spanish horse in Lombardy; but in 1626 re-entered the Austrian service, and after suppressing a peasant revolt cooperated with Tilly against Danes, Swedes and Saxons. On his head rests in great measure the guilt of the ferocious massacres at Magdeburg. He involved Tilly in the disastrous battle of Breitenfeld, but made heroic efforts to protect the retreat. After Tilly's death he served under Wallenstein. He arrived at Lützen when Wallenstein's army was on the point of being routed by Gustavus Adolphus, and charged the Swedes' left wing with such fury as to throw it into confusion. He was mortally wounded in the last charge, and died next day.

PAPPUS OF ALEXANDRIA (fl. late 3rd-early 4th cent. A.D.), Greek mathematician, whose ' Mathematical Collection ' is extant in an incomplete form. See Hultsch's edition (1876-78).

PARACELSUS, a name coined for himself by Theophrastus Bombastus von Hohenheim (1493–1541), son of a physician at Einsiedeln (Schwyz). He went to Basel University at sixteen, studied alchemy and chemistry with Trithemius, Bishop of Würzburg, and then learned the properties of metals and minerals at the mines in Tirol. In subsequent wanderings he amassed a vast store of facts, learned the actual practice of medicine, but lost all faith in scholastic disquisitions and disputations. He acquired fame as a medical practitioner (1526), was made town physician at Basel, and lectured on medicine at the university, but flouted at Galen and Avicenna, and justified the furious enmities that pursued him by his own vanity, arrogance, aggressiveness and intemperate habits. A dispute with the magistrates in 1528 drove him from Basel; he wandered for a dozen years, and settled in 1541 at Salzburg. His works are mainly written in Swiss-German. The earliest printed work was *Practica D. Theophrasti Paracelsi* (1529). Collected German editions appeared at Basel in 1589–1591 and again in 1603–05 (reissued 1618), Latin editions in 1603–05 and 1658. In spite of his attraction to alchemy and mysticism, he made new chemical compounds, and improved pharmacy and therapeutics, encouraged research and experiment, and, in an empirical fashion, revolutionized hidebound medical methods. See books by M. B. Lessing (1839), Marx (1842), Mook (1876), Kahlbaum (1894), Stoddart (1915), Stillman (1920), Gundolf (1928), W. Pagel (Basel 1959) and Browning's poem.

PARDO BAZÁN, Emilia, Condesa de, *ba-*THahn' (1851–1921), Spanish novelist, reckoned the best of her time, born near Coruña, passed from romanticism to naturalism. Her greatest works are *La Cuestión palpante* (1883), *Los Pazos de Ulloa* (1886), *La Madre naturaleza* (1887), *La Piedra Angular* (1891), *Dulce Dueño* (1911). She also wrote plays, and was an ardent feminist.

PARÉ, Ambroise (1517–90), French surgeon, ' the father of modern surgery ', was born near Laval, in 1537 as surgeon joined the army starting for Italy, and was surgeon to Henry II, Charles IX and Henry III. He died in Paris. Paré improved the treatment of gunshot wounds, and substituted ligature of the arteries for cauterization with a red-hot iron after amputation. His *Cinq Livres de chirurgie* (1562) and other writings exercised a great influence on surgery. See Lives by Paulmier (1884), Stephen Paget (1898), F. R. Packard (1922), and H. E. Sigerist, *Great Doctors* (1933).

PARES, Sir Bernard (1867–1949), English historian, educated at Harrow and Cambridge, was professor of Russian History, Language and Literature at Liverpool University (1908–17) and at London University (1919–36). Among his many authoritative books on Russian subjects are *A History of Russia* (1926), *Fall of the Russian Monarchy* (1939) and *Russia and the Peace* (1944). He also contributed the chapters on Russia in the *Cambridge Modern History*.

PARETO, Vilfredo (1848–1923), Italian economist and sociologist, born in Paris, was professor of Political Economy at Lausanne, writing well-known textbooks on the subject in which he demonstrated a mathematical approach. In Sociology his *Trattato di sociologica generale* (1916; trans. *The Mind and Society*) anticipated some of the principles of Fascism.

PARINI, Giuseppe (1729–99), Italian poet, born near Milan became a priest in 1754. He made his name as a poet by the sequence of poems called collectively *Il Giorno* (1763–1803).

PARIS, (1) Gaston (1839–1903), French scholar, born at Paris, in 1872 became professor of Old French at the Collège de France in succession to his father, Paulin Paris (1800–81). He edited mediaeval poems, wrote a long series of valuable works on mediaeval French literature, founded *Romanio* (1872), a review of Romance Philology, and was in 1896 elected to the Academy.

(2) **Louis Philippe, Comte de** (1834–94), grandson of King Louis-Philippe, served in the American war (of which he wrote a history), lived mainly in England, and on the death of the Comte de Chambord (q.v.) became head of the Bourbon house. See BOURBON, ORLEANS.

(3) **Matthew** (c. 1200–59), the best Latin chronicler of the 13th century, was born in England, entered the Benedictine monastery of St Albans in 1217, and later went on a mission to Norway. His principal work is his *Historia Major*, or *Chronica Majora*, a history from the creation down to 1259, the first part compiled from Roger of Wendover and others, from 1235 his own work. It was published in 1571 by Archbishop Parker. The *Historia Anglorum* is abridged from the greater work. Other works are lives of abbots and a book of *Additamenta*. See Jessopp, *Studies by a Recluse* (1892), and study by R. Vaughan (1958).

PARK, Mungo (1771–1806), Scottish explorer of Africa, was born at Foulshiels on the Yarrow, and studied medicine in Edinburgh (1789–91). Through Sir Joseph Banks, he was named assistant surgeon on the *Worcester* bound for Sumatra (1792); and in 1795 his services were accepted · by the African Association. He learnt Mandingo at an English factory on the Gambia, started inland in December, was imprisoned by a chief, but escaping, reached the Niger at Sego in July 1796. He pursued his way westward along its banks to Bammaku, and then crossing a mountainous country, fell ill, but was ultimately brought back by a slave trader to the factory again, after an absence of nineteen months. He told his adventures in *Travels in the Interior of Africa* (1799). He married (1799), and settled as a surgeon at Peebles; but the life was repugnant to him, and in 1805 he undertook another journey to Africa at government expense. Again he started from Pisania on the Gambia, with a company of forty-five; but when he reached the Niger he had only seven followers. From Sansanding he sent back his journals and letters in November 1805 and embarked in a canoe with four European companions. Through many perils and difficulties they reached Boussa, where they were attacked by the natives, and drowned in the fight. See Life by Wishaw prefixed to his later *Journal* (1815), and works by Joseph Thomson (1890), Maclachlan (1898) and S. Gwynn (1934).

PARKER, (1) **Dorothy,** *née* Rothschild (1893–1967), American writer, noted for her satiric humour as shown in her collections of verse *Enough Rope* (1926), *Not so Deep as a Well* (1936), &c., and of short stories *Laments for the Living* (1930), *Here Lies* (1939), &c.

(2) **Sir Gilbert** (1862–1932), British author, born in Canada, became lecturer in English at a college in Toronto, edited a paper in Sydney, and wrote novels, including *When Valmond came to Pontiac* (1895), *The Battle of the Strong* (1898), &c. He was M.P. (Unionist) for Gravesend in 1900–18, and was made a knight in 1902, baronet in 1915, P.C. in 1916.

(3) **Sir Hyde** (1739–1807), British admiral, son of vice-admiral Sir Hyde Parker (1714–1782), in 1801 was appointed to command the fleet sent to the Baltic to act against the armed coalition of Russia, Sweden and Denmark. He had no share in the battle of Copenhagen, which was directed by Nelson.

(4) **Joseph** (1830–1902), English Congregationalist preacher and author, the son of a stonecutter, born at Hexham, studied at Moorfields Tabernacle and University College London (1852), and became pastor of Congregational chapels at Banbury, Manchester, and, in 1869, of what became in 1874 the City Temple in London. He was noted as a pulpit orator, and as the author of many religious works. See Life by W. Adamson (1902).

(5) **Matthew** (1504–75), second Protestant Archbishop of Canterbury, born at Norwich, became chaplain to Queen Anne Boleyn (1535), dean of a college at Stoke in Suffolk, a royal chaplain, canon of Ely, master of Corpus Christi (1544), vice-chancellor (1545) and dean of Lincoln. He married, and by Mary was deprived of his preferments. Under Elizabeth he was consecrated Archbishop of Canterbury (1559). The ritual was not the Roman one; but the scandalous fable that he was informally consecrated in an inn called the Nag's Head originated in Catholic circles forty years later. The new primate strove to bring about more general conformity. The Thirty-nine Articles were passed by convocation in 1562; and his ' Advertisements ' for the regulation of service, and measures of repression perhaps forced upon him by the queen, provoked great opposition in the growing Puritan party. Parker originated the revised translation of the Scriptures known as the Bishops' Bible. He edited works by Aelfric, Matthew Paris, Walsingham and Giraldus Cambrensis, was an indefatigable collector of books, and maintained printers, transcribers, engravers. *De Antiquitate Britannicae Ecclesiae* (1572) was an original work. His letters fill a volume (Parker Soc. 1853). See Lives by Strype (1824), Kennedy (1908); Hook's *Archbishops*, vol. ix.

(6) **Richard** (*c.* 1767–97), English seaman, born at Exeter, volunteered into the navy in 1797, and from May 10 till June 13 that year was ringleader of the mutiny at the Nore,

having for a time thirteen ships of the line, besides frigates, under his orders. He was hanged on June 30.

(7) **Theodore** (1810–60), American preacher, was born at Lexington, Mass., graduated at Harvard in 1836, and settled as Unitarian minister at West Roxbury, now in Boston. The rationalistic views which separated him from conservative Unitarians were expounded in *A Discourse of Matters pertaining to Religion* (1841), followed by *Sermons for the Times*. From then on he wrote incessantly. He lectured throughout the States, and plunged into the antislavery agitation. His health broke down, and he died in Florence. See Lives by Weiss (1864), Dean (1877), Chadwick (1900) and Commager (1936).

PARKES, (1) **Alexander** (1813–90), British chemist and inventor, born in Birmingham, noted for his inventions in connection with electroplating, in the course of which he even electroplated a spider's web. He invented xylonite (celluloid; first patented 1855).

(2) **Sir Harry Smith** (1828–85), British diplomat, born near Walsall, went to China in 1841, served as consul at Canton, Amoy and Foochow, figured prominently in the *Arrow* episode, and in 1858 was appointed a commissioner after the capture of Canton. His treacherous seizure by the Chinese while acting as Lord Elgin's envoy in 1860 led to the burning of the Summer Palace at Pekin. He was British minister in China from 1883.

(3) **Sir Henry** (1815–96), Australian statesman, was born, the son of a yeoman, at Stoneleigh, Warwickshire, emigrated to New South Wales in 1839, and at Sydney became eminent as a journalist. A member of the colonial parliament in 1854, he held various offices, from 1872 was repeatedly prime minister, and was identified with free trade. He was made K.C.M.G. in 1877. See his autobiography (1892) and Lives by Charles E. Lyne (1897) and Sir T. Bavin (1941).

PARKINSON, (1) **Cyril Northcote** (1909–   ), English political scientist, graduated from Emmanuel College, Cambridge, of which he became a fellow in 1935. Professor of History at the University of Malaya (1950–58), and visiting professor at Harvard and Illinois, he has written many works on historical, political and economic subjects, but achieved wider renown by his seriocomic tilt at bureaucratic malpractices *Parkinson's Law, the Pursuit of Progress* (1958). Parkinson's Law '—that work expands to fill the time available for its completion, and subordinates multiply at a fixed rate, regardless of the amount of work produced—has passed into the language.

(2) **James** (1755–1824), British physician, in 1817 gave the first description of paralysis agitans, or Parkinson's disease as it has been called. He had already (1812) described appendicitis and perforation, and was the first to recognize the latter condition as a cause of death.

(3) **John** (1567–1650), a London herbalist, a native probably of Nottinghamshire, was apothecary to James I and author of *Paradisus Terrestris* (1629) and *Theatrum Botanicum* (1640), long the most comprehensive English herbal.

PARKMAN, Francis (1823–93), American historian, graduated at Harvard in 1844, studied law, and became the authoritative writer on the rise and fall of the French dominion in America. His works included *The California and Oregon Trail* (1849), *The Pioneers of France in the New World* (1865), *La Salle and the Great West* (1869), *Frontenac and New France* (1877), *A Half-Century of Conflict* (1893), *Montcalm and Wolfe* (1884). See Lives by Farnham (1900) and Sedgwick (1904), and D. Leon, *History as a Romantic Art* (1960).

PARLEY, Peter. See GOODRICH.

PARMENIDES, *pahr-men'i-dees* (fl. 5th cent. B.C.), with Heraclitus (q.v.), whose doctrines he opposed, the greatest of the Greek Presocratic philosophers, was a native of the Greek settlement of Elea in southern Italy and became the greatest of the Eleatic school, which derived its doctrines from the Pythagoreans. Parmenides held that nothing changes. All that one is logically entitled to do is to affirm existence, say ' it is ', since it is impossible to know what is not, for ' it is the same thing that can be thought and can be '. His doctrines are set out in a didactic poem, *On Nature*, divided into two parts ' the way of truth ' and ' the way of opinion ', foreshadowing Plato's metaphysics. He is not so much the founder of logic, but the pioneer of certain perennial metalogical arguments concerning the category of substance. His great disciple was Zeno (q.v.). See fragments, ed. Diehls (1897), J. Burnet, *Early Greek Philosophy* (4th ed. 1952), and G. S. Kirk and J. E. Raven, *The Presocratic Philosophers* (1957).

PARMIGIANO, or **Parmigianino,** properly **Girolamo Francesco Maria Mazzola,** -*jah'no* (1503–40), Italian painter of the Lombard school, born at Parma, at first painted there, but after 1523 worked at Rome, whence he fled to Bologna when the city was sacked in 1527. At Bologna he painted his famous Madonna altarpiece for the nuns of St Margaret before returning to Parma in 1531. He shows the influence of Correggio and Raphael. His *Vision of St Jerome* is in the National Gallery, London. See monograph by Freedberg (1950).

PARNELL, (1) Charles Stewart (1846–91), Irish politician, was born at Avondale, Co. Wicklow. His father belonged to an old Cheshire family which purchased an estate in Ireland under Charles II. His great-grandfather, Sir John Parnell (1744–1801), was chancellor of the Irish Exchequer. Thomas Parnell (q.v.), the poet, belonged to the same family. Charles, whose mother was the daughter of an American admiral, studied four years at Magdalen College, Cambridge, but took no degree. In 1874 he became high sheriff of County Wicklow; that same year he contested County Dublin without success, but in April 1875 was returned as a Home Ruler for County Meath. In 1877–78 he gained great popularity in Ireland by his audacity in the use of deliberate obstruction in parliamentary tactics. In 1878 he threw himself into agrarian agitation, and was elected president of the Irish National Land League. From the United States he brought home £70,000 for the cause. In 1880 he was returned for Meath and Mayo and for the city of Cork, sat for the last, and was chairman of the Irish parliamentary party. In 1880 too he formulated the method of ' boycotting '. Mr Gladstone's government put Parnell and other leading members of the Land League on trial, but the jury failed to agree. In opposing the government's Coercion Bill, Parnell was ejected from the House, with thirty-four of his followers (February 3, 1881). He refused to accept Mr Gladstone's Land Bill as a final settlement. In October Mr Gladstone sent him to Kilmainham jail; he was released on May 2, 1882. Parnell in the House of Commons expressed his detestation of the tragedy of Phoenix Park. The Crimes Act was now hurried through parliament in spite of the Irish party. The Land League, proclaimed illegal after the issue of the ' No Rent ' manifesto, was revived in 1884 as the National League, Parnell being president. The year before the sum of £35,000, mostly raised in America, had been presented to him by his admirers. After an unsuccessful attempt to make terms with the Conservatives, Parnell flung his vote—now eighty-six strong —into the Liberal scale, and brought about the fall of the short-lived first Salisbury government. Mr Gladstone's Home Rule Bill was defeated owing to the defection of Liberal members. The consequent appeal to the country (July 1886) gave Lord Salisbury a Unionist majority of over a hundred, and threw Parnell into a close alliance with Mr Gladstone. Now it was that *The Times* published ' Parnellism and Crime '—with letters as by Parnell, expressing approval of Mr Burke's murder. A Special Commission sat 128 days, and, after the flight and suicide at Madrid of Pigott (q.v.), who had imposed upon *The Times* with forgeries, cleared Parnell (November 1889) of the charge of having been personally guilty of organizing outrages; but his party were declared guilty of incitements to intimidation, out of which had grown crimes which they had failed to denounce. Parnell now raised an action against *The Times*, settled by a payment of £5000. The ' uncrowned king ' of Ireland was presented with the freedom of Edinburgh in July 1889. His frequent mysterious absences from his parliamentary duties were explained by his appearance as co-respondent in a divorce case brought by Captain O'Shea against his wife, and decree was granted with costs against Parnell (November 17, 1890). The Gladstonian party now demanded his retirement from leadership; and though the Irish members had reappointed him chairman, they met to reconsider the position a week later, and, after five days of wrangling, the majority elected Justin McCarthy chairman. Parnell, with the remnants of his party. carried the warfare into Ireland; but his condemnation by the church and the emphatic defeat of his nominees at by-elections foretokened the collapse of his party at the general election of 1892, when seventy-two anti-Parnellites were returned against nine of his supporters. Before this, Parnell had died suddenly at Brighton, five months after his marriage to Mrs O'Shea; he is buried in

Glasnevin cemetery, Dublin. His sister, Fanny Parnell (1854–82), wrote fiery poems and articles in aid of the cause. There are Lives by T. P. O'Connor (1891), R. F. Walsh (N.Y. 1892), Barry O'Brien (1899), his widow (1914), his brother John (1916). See also T. P. O'Connor's *Parnell Movement* (1886), and *Gladstone, Parnell, and the Great Irish Struggle* (1891); Justin McCarthy, *A History of Our Own Times* (vol. v 1897); and studies by St John Ervine (1925), W. O'Brien (1926) and Harrison (1931).

(2) **Thomas** (1679–1718), English poet, born in Dublin, was educated at Trinity College, took orders, and received the archdeaconry of Clogher, a prebend, and the vicarage of Finglass. The head of an English family settled in Ireland, with property both there and in Cheshire, he lived mostly in London, where his wit procured him the friendship of Harley, Swift and Pope. After his wife's death he took to drinking, and died at Chester, while on his way to Ireland. Next year Pope published a selection of his poems, the best-known of which is the *Hermit*. The *Nightpiece* and the *Hymn to Contentment* are better poetry. See Mitford's edition of the poems, with Life, &c., re-edited by G. A. Aitken (1894).

PARR, (1) **Catharine** (1512–48), sixth wife of Henry VIII, daughter of Sir Thomas Parr of Kendal, married first Edward Borough, and next Lord Latimer, and on July 12, 1543, became queen of England by marriage with Henry VIII. She was distinguished for her learning and knowledge of religious subjects, her discussion of which with the king well-nigh brought her to the block. She persuaded Henry to restore the succession to his daughters. Very soon after Henry's death (1547) she married a former lover, Lord Thomas Seymour of Sudeley, and died in childbirth next year at Sudeley Castle near Cheltenham.

(2) **Thomas** ('Old Parr') (?1483–1635), was born, according to the tradition, in 1483. He was a Shropshire farm-servant, and when 120 years old married his second wife, and till his 130th year performed all his usual work. In his 152nd year his fame had reached London, and he was induced to journey thither to see Charles I. But he was treated at court so royally that he died, November 14, 1635. Taylor, the Water-poet, wrote his Life, and the great Harvey in his postmortem report repeats the popular hearsay. There is no sound evidence.

PARRHASIUS (4th cent. B.C.), according to tradition the greatest painter of ancient Greece, and reputedly the first to use shading, worked at Athens.

PARRISH, Edward (1822–72), American pharmacist of Philadelphia, introduced ' Parrish's Chemical Food ', the *Compound Syrup of Phosphate of Iron.*

PARRY, (1) **Sir Charles Hubert Hastings** (1848–1918), composer, was born at Bournemouth, the son of *Thomas Gambier Parry* (1816–88) of Highnam Court, Gloucester, inventor of the spirit-fresco process. Educated at Eton and Oxford, in 1883 he became professor in the Royal College of Music, and in 1895 its director. He composed the

oratorios *Judith, Job* and *King Saul*; an opera on *Lancelot and Guinevere*; symphonies, quartets, cantatas, &c.; and wrote *Evolution of the Art of Music* (1896), a Life of Bach, *The Oxford History of Music*, vol. iii (1907). See Life by C. L. Graves (1926).

(2) **Joseph** (1841–1903), Welsh musician, was born at Merthyr Tydfil, studied at the Royal Academy of Music, and became professor at Cardiff College. He composed oratorios and operas, songs and hymns.

(3) **Sir William Edward** (1790–1855), Arctic navigator, was born at Bath, son of *Caleb Hillier Parry* (1755–1822), an eminent physician. Entering the navy as midshipman, he served against the Danes in 1808, and in 1810 was sent to the Arctic regions to protect the whale fisheries. He took command in five expeditions to the Arctic regions—in 1818 (under Ross), 1819, 1821–23, 1824–25, and 1827—the last an attempt to reach the Pole on sledges from Spitsbergen. In 1829 he was knighted, and in 1837 was made comptroller of a department of the navy. He was subsequently superintendent of Haslar (1846), made rear-admiral (1852), and governor of Greenwich Hospital (1853). See the collected edition of his voyages (1833), and the Life by his son (1857).

PARSONS, (1) **Alfred William** (1847–1920), English painter and book illustrator, known especially for his watercolour landscapes. Elected R.A. in 1911, he was president of the Royal Society of Painters in Watercolour (1914–20).

(2) **Sir Charles Algernon** (1854–1931), British engineer, the fourth son of the third Earl of Rosse, educated at Cambridge, developed the steam turbine, and built the first turbine-driven steamship (1897). He was knighted in 1911.

(3) **Robert** (1546–1610), English Jesuit, born at Nether Stowey, Somerset, passed from Taunton to Oxford, and became a fellow and tutor of Balliol. His enemies secured his forced retirement from Oxford in 1574. He now turned Catholic, and at Rome entered the Society of Jesus (1575), becoming a priest in 1578. With Campion (q.v.), Parsons landed at Dover in 1580, disguised as a merchant of jewels, amazed Catholics and Protestants by his activity and success, and for twelve months baffled all the attempts of government to catch him. In 1581 he escaped to the Continent. In 1582 he was at Paris conferring with the Provincial of the French Jesuits, the Archbishop of Glasgow, the papal nuncio, and the agent of the king of Spain, concerning his own project for the invasion of England; and this plan he himself carried to King Philip at Madrid. Now began his influence with the Spanish king, and the series of political enterprises which culminated in the Armada of 1588. At Rouen in 1582 he had finished his *Christian Directory*; in 1588 he was rector of the college at Rome, and he founded a number of Jesuit seminaries. In *The Conference on the next Succession to the Crown* he insists on the right of the people to set aside, on religious grounds, the natural heir to the throne.

PARTON, James (1822–91), American writer, was born at Canterbury, but taken when a child to America, where he became a journalist, wrote biographies of Greeley, Butler, Franklin, Voltaire and others, and did much miscellaneous work. He married in 1856 Sara, a sister of N. P. Willis (q.v.), who, as ' Fanny Fern ', wrote many children's books.

PARTRIDGE, (1) **Sir Bernard** (1861-1945), English artist, born in London, began as a stained-glass designer but made his name as staff cartoonist for *Punch* (from 1891). He was knighted in 1925.

(2) **Eric Honeywood** (1894-   ), British lexicographer, born near Gisborne, N.Z., educated at Queensland and Oxford Universities, became, after fighting in World War I, Queensland travelling fellow at Oxford. He was a lecturer at Manchester and London Universities in 1925-27 and wrote on French and English literature, but later, and especially after World War II, in which he served in the R.A.F., he made a specialized study of slang and colloquial language. His works in this field include the standard *Dictionary of Slang and Unconventional English* (1937, 3rd ed. 1949), *Usage and Abusage* (1947), *Dictionary of Forces Slang* (with W. Granville and F. Roberts, 1948), and *A Dictionary of the Underworld, British and American* (1950).

(3) **John** (1644-1715), English astrologer and almanac-maker, was originally a shoe maker at East Sheen, but contrived to learn Latin, Greek, Hebrew, medicine and astrology, and published a number of astrological books. The manifold quackery of his prophetic almanac, *Merlinus Liberatus*, led Swift (under the name of Bickerstaff) to ridicule and expose him.

PASCAL, Blaise, *-kahl* (1623-62), French mathematician, physicist, theologian and man-of-letters, was born June 19 at Clermont-Ferrand, the son of the local president of the court of exchequer. The mother having died, the family in 1630 moved to Paris, where the father, a considerable mathematician, personally undertook his children's education. Unlike John Stuart Mill, Blaise was not allowed to begin a subject until his father thought he could easily master it. Consequently it was discovered that the eleven-year-old boy had worked out for himself in secret the first twenty-three propositions of Euclid, calling straight lines ' bars ' and circles ' rounds '. At sixteen he published a paper on solid geometry which Descartes refused to believe was the handiwork of a youth. Father and son collaborated in experiments to confirm Torricelli's theory, unpalatable to the schoolmen, that nature does, after all, not abhor a vacuum. These experiments carried out by Blaise's brother-in-law, Florin Périer, consisted in carrying up the Puy de Dôme two glass tubes containing mercury, inverted in a bath of mercury and noting the fall of the mercury columns with increased altitude. Again Descartes surprisingly disbelieved the principle, which Blaise fully described in three papers on the void published in 1647, when he also patented a calculating machine, later simplified by Leibniz, which Blaise had built to assist his father in his accounts. The former led on to the invention of the barometer, the hydraulic

press and the syringe. In 1648 Richelieu appointed Pascal senior to a post at Rouen, but the latter died in 1651. Pascal's sister, Jacqueline, entered the Jansenist convent at Port-Royal, but Blaise divided his time between mathematics and the social round in Paris until November 23, 1654, approaching midnight when he had the first of two revelations, according to a note found sewn into his clothes, and he came to see that his religious attitude had been too intellectual and remote. Promptly he joined his sister in her retreat at Port-Royal, gave up mathematics and social life almost completely and joined battle for the Jansenists against the Jesuits of the Sorbonne who had publicly denounced Arnauld (q.v.), the Jansenist mathematician, as a heretic. In eighteen brilliant anonymous pamphlets, the *Lettres provinciales* (1656-57), Pascal attacked in superb prose, novel in its directness, the Jesuits' meaningless jargon, casuistry and moral laxity. This early prose masterpiece in the French language, the model for Voltaire, failed to save Arnauld, but undermined for ever Jesuit authority and prestige. Pascal's papers on the area of the cycloid (1661) heralded the invention of the differential calculus. Fragments jotted down for a case book of Christian truths were discovered after his death, August 19, 1662, and published as the *Pensées* in 1669 in order of completeness, but this arbitrariness was exposed by Cousin in 1842. No edition of these fragments is entirely satisfactory. The groundwork for Pascal's intended Christian apology, they contain the most profound insight into religious truths coupled, however, with scepticism of rationalist thought and theology. Their style owes much to Montaigne, Charron and the 13th-century Spaniard, Raimundo Marti. For Jacqueline Pascal, see works by Cousin (1845) and Weizel (New York 1880). See Life by his sister, Mme Périer, prefacing the *Pensées* (1687), biographical studies by C. A. Sainte Beuve, Port-Royal, vols. i-iii, 6th ed. (1901), E. Mortimer (1959), and studies by F. Strowski (1907-13), H. F. Stewart (1915, 1940, 1942 and 1945), J. Chevalier (1922, 1944), L. C. Brunschvicg (1924, 1945), C. C. J. Webb (1929), J. Lhermet (1931), F. Mauriac (1941), D. G. M. Patrick (1947), J. Mesnard, intro. R. A. Knox (trans. 1952).

PASCHAL was the name of two popes (817-824 and 1099-1118), and of an antipope (died 1168).

PASCOLI, Giovanni, *pas'kō-lee* (1855-1912), Italian poet and writer, born at San Mauro di Romagna, was professor of Latin at Bologna from 1907. Much of his poetry set in the background of native Romagna is of a tragic nature and his volumes of verse include *Myricae* (1891), *In Or San Michele* (1903) and *Canti di Castelvecchio* (1903). *Sotto il Velame* (1900) and *La Mirabile Visione* (1902) are critical studies of Dante's *Divine Comedy*. See *Giovanni Pascoli* by Croce (1920).

PAŠIĆ, Nikola, *pash'eet-y'* (c. 1846-1926), Serb ' Old Radical ' leader, born at Zaječar, condemned to death 1883 for his part in the ' Revolution of Zaitchar ', a plot against King Milan, but he survived on the accession of King Peter to be prime minister of Serbia and later of Yugoslavia 1891-92, 1906, and from 1908 almost continuously until his death.

PASKEVICH, Ivan Feodorovich, *pus-kyay'vich* (1782-1856), Russian field-marshal, was born at Poltava, served against the French in 1805, and against the Turks, and took a prominent part in the campaign of 1812. In 1826, conquering Persian Armenia and taking Erivan, he was made Count of Erivan; in 1828-29 he made two campaigns against the Turks in Asia, taking Kars and Erzerûm. In 1831 he suppressed the rising in Poland, and was made Prince of Warsaw. Under his governorship Poland was (1832) incorporated with Russia. In 1848, sent to the support of Austria, he defeated the insurgent Hungarians. In 1854 he commanded the Russian army on the Danube, was wounded at Silistria and retired to Warsaw, where later he died. See French Lives by Tolstoi (1835) and Stcherbatoff (1888).

PASMORE, Edwin John Victor (1908–), English artist, born at Chelsham, began painting without academic training. One of the founders of the London ' Euston Road School ' (1937), he became an art teacher and after World War II began to paint in a highly abstract style, in which colour is often primarily used to suggest relief. His works include *Rectangular Motif* (1949), *Inland Sea* (1950, Tate, London) and *Relief Construction in White, Black, Red and Maroon* (1957). He was created C.B.E. in 1959.

PASQUIER, Étienne Denis, Duc de, *pa-kyay* (1767-1862), French statesman under Napoleon, the Bourbons and Louis-Philippe, was chancellor of France in 1837-48. See his *History of my Time* (trans. 1894).

PASSAGLIA, Carlo, *pas-sahl'ya* (1812-87), Italian theologian, born at Lucca, in 1827 entered the Society of Jesus, and in 1844 became professor in the Collegio Romano. In 1849-51 he taught in England. In 1855 he wrote on the Immaculate Conception, then, leaving the Jesuits, against the temporal power, *Pro Causo Italica* (1859). He withdrew to Turin, where he was professor of Moral Philosophy.

PASSFIELD, Baron. See WEBB (6).

PASSOW, Franz, *pah'sō* (1786-1833), German scholar, born at Ludwigslust in Mecklenburg, in 1815 became professor of Greek at Weimar gymnasium and of Ancient Literature at Breslau. His *Handwörterbuch der griechischen Sprache* (1819-24; 5th ed. 1841-57) formed the basis of Liddell and Scott's *Greek Lexicon.* Other works include *Grundzüge der griechischen and römischen Literatur—und Kunstgeschichte* (2nd ed. 1829) and editions of classical authors. See Life by Wachler (1839).

PASSY, *pa-see,* (1) **Frederic** (1822-1912), French economist and author, father of (2), born at Paris, became a member (1881-1889) of the Chamber of Deputies, was a founder member of the International Peace League in 1867, and a member of the International Peace Bureau in Bern in 1892. In 1901 he shared the Nobel peace prize with Jean Dunant. His writings include *Mélanges économiques* (1857), *L'Histoire du travail* (1873) and *Vérités et paradoxes* (1894).

(2) **Paul Édouard** (1859-1940), French philologist and phonetician, son of (1), was born at Versailles. An advocate of phonetic selling, he founded the International Phonetic Association in 1894, and was assistant professor of Phonetics at the Sorbonne. His publications include *Le Français parlé* (1886) and *Etudes sur les changements phonétiques* (1890).

PASTERNAK, Boris Leonidovich (1890-1960), Russian lyric poet, novelist and translator of Shakespeare, son of Leonid (1862-1945), the painter and illustrator of Tolstoy's works, was born in Moscow, studied law at the university, then musical composition under Scriabin, abandoning both for philosophy at Marburg. A factory worker in the Urals during the first World War, he was employed in the library of the education ministry, Moscow, after the revolution. His early collections of verse written between 1912 and 1916 were published under the title *Above the Barriers* (1931), followed by *My Sister, Life* (1922), *Themes and Variations* (1923). Under the influence of his friend Mayakovsky (q.v.) he wrote the political poems *The Year 1905* (1927), on the Bolshevik uprising, and *Lieutenant Schmidt* (1927), on the *Potemkin* mutiny. *Spectorsky* and *Second Birth* (both 1932) are autobiographical. Among his outstanding short stories are the collection *Aerial Ways* (1933) and particularly *The Childhood of Lyuvers* (1924), a delicate presentation of a girl's first impressions of womanhood, and *A Tale* (1934) translated as ' The Last Summer ' (1959), in which Pasternak's imagery is at its freshest and most unexpected. The long years of Stalin turned Pasternak into the official translator into Russian of Shakespeare, Verlaine, Goethe and Kleist, but he did compose incidental verse such as *In Early Trains* (1936-41) and *The Sapper's Death* (1943). With Khrushchev's misleading political ' thaw ' Pasternak abortively ventured into verse (1954) and caused a political earthquake with his first novel, *Dr Zhivago* (trans. M. Hayward and M. Harari, 1958), banned in the Soviet Union. A fragmentary, poet's novel, it describes with intense feeling the Russian revolution as it impinged upon one individual, both doctor and poet. But the vast array of characters fail to live, they are creatures of poetic necessity. Yet despite its technical shortcomings, it has a sublime moral grandeur. Its strictures on the post-revolutionary events are those not of an anti-Marxist but of a Communist who is disappointed that history has not conformed to his vision. Expelled by the Soviet Writers' Union in October 1958, Pasternak had to take the unprecedented step of refusing the Nobel prize and in a thoroughly self-critical letter to Khrushchev, echoed Ovid by his plea that exile would for him be the equivalent of death. See the autobiographical *Safe Conduct* (1931; trans. A. Brown and L. Pasternak-Slater, 1959), *Essay in Autobiography* (1954; trans. M. Harari and intro. E. Crankshaw, 1959), *Letters to Georgian Friends* (1968), and *Prose and Poems*, ed. Schimanski, trans. B. Scott and intro. J. M. Cohen (1959).

PASTEUR, Louis, *pas-tœr* (1822–95), French chemist, born at Dôle, studied at Besançon and Paris, and held academic posts at Strasbourg, Lille and Paris, where in 1867 he became professor of Chemistry at the Sorbonne. His work was at first chemical, as on tartrate crystals and ' left-handed ' tartrates. He discovered a living ferment, a microorganism comparable in its powers to the yeast plant, which would, in a solution of ammonia, select for food the ' right-handed ' tartrates alone, leaving the ' left-handed '. He next showed that other fermentations, lactic, butyric, acetic, are essentially due to organisms, greatly extended Schwann's researches on putrefaction, gave valuable rules for making vinegar and preventing wine disease, and refuted supposed proofs of spontaneous generation. On his findings the modern study of bacteriology was based. After 1865 he tackled, with brilliant success, silkworm disease, injurious growths in beer, splenic fever, and fowl cholera. He showed that it was possible to attenuate the virulence of injurious microorganisms by exposure to air, by variety of culture, or by transmission through various animals. He thus demonstrated by a memorable experiment that sheep and cows ' vaccinated ' with the attenuated bacilli of anthrax were protected from the evil results of subsequent inoculation with the virulent virus; and, by the culture of antitoxic reagents, prophylactic treatment of diphtheria, tubercular disease, cholera, yellow fever and plague has been found effective. His treatment of hydrophobia depends on similar proofs and in 1888 the Institut Pasteur was founded for the treatment by inoculation of this disease. Here Pasteur worked until his death. See studies by Frankland (1898), Vallery-Radot (1919), Descours (1922), Holmes (1925), and Life by Cuny (1965).

PASTON, a Norfolk family, named from the village of Paston, whose letters and papers, published in 1787–1789–1823 as the *Paston Letters,* shed a vivid light on domestic life in the 15th century. Gairdner edited them with more fullness in 1872–75, and again completely in 1904, after the recovery of two long lost volumes. See also a selection edited by N. Davis (1958). The chief members of the family were William Paston (1378–1444), justice of common pleas; his son John (1421–66); Clement (c. 1515–97), a sailor; and Sir Robert (1631–83), Earl of Yarmouth. See *The Pastons and their England* by H. S. Bennett (1922).

PATER, (1) Jean Baptiste Joseph, *pa-tayr* (1695–1736), French genre painter, born at Valenciennes, was a talented pupil and follower of Watteau.

(2) **Walter,** *pay'tèr* (1839–94), English critic, born in London, was educated at King's School, Canterbury, and Queen's College, Oxford, became a fellow of Brasenose and thenceforth lived the retired life of the scholar. His *Studies in the History of the Renaissance* (1873), which first brought him to the notice of the scholarly public, shows the influence of the pre-Raphaelites with whom he associated. His philosophic romance *Marius the Epicurean* (1885) appealed to a wider audience for it

dealt in an extremely seductive manner with the spread of Christianity in the days of the catacombs. His *Imaginary Portraits* (1887) and *Appreciations* (1889), followed by *Plato and Platonism* (1893), established his position as a critic, but already people were beginning to talk of his influence as being unhealthy, in the sense that he advocated a cultivated hedonism. That his neo-Cyrenaism, as it might be called, involved strenuous self-discipline, hardly occurred to his critics, who found in his style alone an enervating quality. His influence on Oxford, however, was profound. He died at Oxford, having left unfinished another romance, *Gaston de Latour* (1896), dealing with the France of Charles IX and containing portraits of Montaigne and Ronsard with whom his philosophy of charm and the cultivation of beauty had much in common. See studies by A. C. Benson (1904), T. Wright (1907), Edward Thomas (1913) and A. Symonds (1932).

PATERCULUS, Marcus Velleius (*c.* 19 B.C.–*c.* A.D. 30), Roman historian, served under Tiberius, was alive in A.D. 30, and may have perished next year as a friend of Sejanus. His *Historiae Romanae,* a compendium of universal, but more particularly of Roman history, is not complete, and is superficial and rhetorical.

PATERSON, (1) Andrew Barton, nicknamed ' Banjo ' (1864–1941), Australian journalist and poet, was a first World War correspondent and the author of several books of light verse including *The Animals Noah Forgot* (1933). He is best known however as the author of ' Waltzing Matilda ', adapted from a traditional ditty, which became Australia's premier national song.

(2) **Helen.** See ALLINGHAM (2).

(3) **Robert** (1715–1801), Scottish stonecutter, the original ' Old Mortality ', born, a farmer's son, near Hawick, was apprenticed to a stone mason, and rented a quarry in Morton parish. From about 1758 he neglected to return to his wife and five children, and for over forty years devoted himself to the task of repairing or erecting headstones to Covenanting martyrs. He died at Bankhill, and was buried at Caerlaverock, where a monument was erected to him by Messrs A. & C. Black in 1869. See Introduction to Scott's *Old Mortality* and Ramage's *Drumlanrig Castle* (1876).

(4) **William** (1658–1719), Scottish financier founder of the Bank of England, was born at Skipmyre farm, in Tinwald parish, Dumfriesshire, and spent some years in the West Indies. Returning to Europe, he promoted his Darien Scheme in London, Hamburg, Amsterdam (where he worked for the Revolution of 1688) and Berlin, made a fortune by commerce in London, founded the Hampstead Water Company in 1690, projected the Bank of England, and was one of its first directors in 1694. At Edinburgh, as a strong advocate of free trade, he talked the whole nation into his Darien Scheme. He sailed with the expedition in a private capacity, shared all its troubles, and returned with its survivors a broken man in December 1699. But his energy remained unabated,

He had a considerable share in promoting the Scottish union, and was elected to the first united parliament by the Dumfries burghs. In 1715 he was awarded £18,000 as indemnity for his Darien losses. See the Life by S.Bannister (1858), editor of his *Works* (1859); and that by J. S. Barbour (1907). See also G. P. Insh, *The Company Scotland* (1932), and J. Clapham, *The Bank of England*, vol. i (1944).

PATHÉ, Charles, *pa-tay* (1863–1957), French film pioneer, the inaugurator of the newsreel in France in 1909 and in America in 1910. In 1911 the company of Pathé Frères was established which gave Britain her first newsreel and the screen magazine Pathé Pictorial. In 1949 the Company became Associated British Pathé Ltd.

PATMORE, Coventry Kersey Dighton (1823–1896), English poet, born at Woodford, was an assistant in the library of the British Museum and was associated with the pre-Raphaelite brotherhood. His magnum opus, *The Angel in the House*, which delighted the respectable Victorian public till Swinburne flaunted his less respectable muse, described with domestic, often ludicrous, detail the intimacies of a rectory courtship. The poem lives not by its narrative part but by its Preludes, which display profound knowledge of a lover's moods and felicitous expression. Only in the Preludes do we have a hint of the Patmore who can be acclaimed as a major poet—the poet of *The Unknown Eros*. We should associate the change from the Victorian domesticity of *The Angel in the House* to the erotic mysticism of *The Unknown Eros* (1877), with the death of his first wife in 1862 and his conversion to the Roman Catholic faith in 1864. Four of the odes which compose the book—' The Azalea ', ' Departure ', ' The Toys ' and ' If I were dead '— are about his dead wife and his motherless children. Others show his rabid Toryism which ascribed the decline of England to ' the disfranchisement (in 1867) of the upper and middle class by the false English nobles and their Jew '. The rest are in a vein of lofty mysticism in which the myth of Eros and Psyche is used to symbolize the marriage of earthly and heavenly love. Apparently the ' Song of Solomon ' justified him in applying this erotic language to sacred mysteries, but churchmen—Newman and Hopkins—were offended. Nevertheless, the metaphysical reaction of the last generation finds in them and in less mystical poems like the early *Tamerton Church Tower* and *Amelia* (1878), ' true poetry of the rarest and perhaps highest kind '. Nor is Sir Herbert Read singular in this verdict. On the other hand, his arrogance and Biblical eroticism will always repel average taste. Patmore would not have his odes called Pindarics—they are extremely loose but are not uncontrolled. His prosodic innovation was to discard the metrical foot and substitute the musical ' bar ' measured from stress to stress. He explained his metrics in an Appendix to his *Collected Poetical Works* in 1886. See Derek Patmore, *Portrait of My Family* (1933), expanded as *Life and Times of Coventry Patmore* (1949); also *The Memoirs and Correspondence of Coventry Patmore* ed. Basil Champneys

(1900); and studies by Burdett (1921) Herbert Read in *The Great Victorians* (1932), F. Page (1933) and E. J. Oliver (1956).

PATON, (1) Alan (1903–), South African writer and educator, National President of the South African Liberal Party, born in Pietermaritzburg, spent ten years as a schoolteacher, first in a native school and later at Pietermaritzburg College. In 1935 he was appointed principal of the Diepkloof Reformatory, where he became known for the success of his enlightened concern with the racial problem in South Africa sprang the novel *Cry the Beloved Country* (1948). Later books include *Too Late the Phalarope* (1953), *Hope for South Africa* (1958), a political study written from the Liberal standpoint, and *Debbie Go Home* (1961), short stories.

(2) John (d. 1684), Scottish Covenanter, was the son of a farmer at Fenwick in Ayrshire, became a captain in the army of Gustavus Adolphus, fought at Rullion Green and Bothwell Brig (1679), and, apprehended in 1684, was hanged May 9.

(3) John Gibson (1824–1907), Scottish missionary, the son of a stocking-maker, was born in Kirkmahoe parish, Dumfriesshire. In 1858 he went as a missionary of the Reformed Presbyterian Church to the cannibals of the New Hebrides. His brother published and edited his missionary narratives (1889). See also A. K. Langridge and F. H. L. Paton, *John G. Paton: Later Years* (1910).

(4) Sir Joseph Noel (1821–1901), Scottish painter, was born in Dunfermline, and studied at the Royal Academy, London. A painter of historical, fairy, allegorical and religious subjects, notable early pictures are the two on *Oberon and Titania*, both in the National Gallery at Edinburgh. He illustrated Aytoun's *Lays of the Scottish Cavaliers* and the *Ancient Mariner*. R.S.A., Queen's Limner for Scotland from 1865, knighted (1867), he published two volumes of poems. See *Art Journal* for April 1895.

PATRICK, St (*c.* 385–*c.* 461), the Apostle of Ireland, must have been born late in the 4th century, perhaps in South Wales, less probably at Boulogne-sur-Mer, or Kilpatrick near Dumbarton. His father was a deacon named Calpurnius. His own Celtic name or nickname was Succat. In his sixteenth year he was seized by pirates, carried to Ireland and sold to an Antrim chief called Milchu. After six years he escaped, and, probably after a second captivity, went to France, where he became a monk, first at Tours and afterwards at Lérins. He was ordained a bishop at forty-five, and in 432 it is thought went as a missionary to Ireland, Palladius, sent thither by Pope Celestine a short time before, having died. Patrick landed at Wicklow; thence he sailed north to convert his old master Milchu. In Down he converted another chief, Dichu. At Tara in Meath he preached to the king of Tara, Laoghaire. Thence he proceeded to Croagh-Patrick in Mayo, to Ulster, and as far as Cashel in the south. He addressed himself first to the chiefs, and made use of the spirit of clanship. After twenty years spent in missionary labours, he fixed his see at Armagh (454). He died at Saul (Saul-patrick; *Sabhal*, 'barn'), the spot which Dichu had given him on his arrival, and was very probably buried at Armagh. Ussher, followed by Todd, fixes his death at 493—a date that would make Patrick's age quite 120 years; but the true date seems to be *c.* 461. The only certainly authentic literary remains of the Saint (both in very rude Latin) are his 'Confession' and a letter addressed to Coroticus, a British chieftain who had carried off some Irish Christians as slaves. See the Lives by J. H. Todd (1863), Newell (1890), Zimmer (1904, disputing his historical existence), J. B. Bury (1905, reaffirming it), Ardill (1931), E. Macneill (1934), P. Gallico (1958); the *Tripartite Life*, ed. Stokes (1887).

PATTERSON-BONAPARTE. See BONA-PARTE (1).

PATTESON, John Coleridge (1827–71), English martyr-bishop, was born in London, the son of Sir John Patteson, judge in the King's Bench, and of a niece of Coleridge. He passed through Eton and Balliol, and was a fellow of Merton, and curate of Alfington in Devonshire. From 1855 he spent sixteen years in missionary work in the New Hebrides, Banks, Solomon and Loyalty Islands; and in 1861 he was consecrated Bishop of Melanesia. He was killed by the natives of the Santa Cruz group. See Life by C. M. Yonge (2 vols. 1874).

PATTI, *paht'tee*, (1) Adelina (1843–1919), Italian singer, was born at Madrid, the daughter of a Sicilian tenor. At seven she sang in New York, and there she made her début as 'Lucia' in 1859. In London she appeared in 1861, when her success was as splendid as it afterwards was wherever she sang. Her voice was an unusually high, rich, ringing soprano. She married in 1866 the Marquis de Caux, and, on her divorce in 1886, the Breton tenor Ernesto Nicolini (1834–98), and in 1899 the Swedish Baron Cederström. Her home was Craig-y-nos Castle near Swansea. In 1898 she was naturalized. See Life by Klein (1920).

(2) **Carlotta** (1840–89), sister of (1), also a great soprano, was born at Florence, made her début at New York in 1861 as a concert singer (being debarred by lameness from opera), and married in 1879 the 'cellist Ernst de Munck.

PATTISON, (1) Dorothy Wyndlow (1832–78), English philanthropist, sister of (2), was born at Hauxwell. In 1861 she started a life of labour for others as schoolmistress at Little Woolston near Bletchley. In 1864 she joined a sisterhood at Coatham near Redcar, and in 1865 she began as 'Sister Dora' her devoted labours as nurse at Walsall. In 1877 she took charge of the municipal epidemic hospital (mainly for smallpox). She was indefatigable in all good works. See Margaret Lonsdale's *Sister Dora* (1880).

(2) **Mark** (1813–84), English scholar and critic, brother of (1), born at Hornby in Yorkshire, graduated from Oriel, Oxford (1837), and was elected fellow of Lincoln (1839). Under Newman's influence he forsook Evangelicalism and almost followed his master into Catholicism. Then came a reaction towards liberalism, and he soon became a tutor of exceptional influence. An attempt to deprive him of his fellowship failed; but for ten years he took little share in Oxford life. He published an article on education in the *Oxford Essays*, went with a commission on education to Germany, and served for three months of 1858 as *Times* correspondent at Berlin. In 1861, he was elected rector of his college, and in 1862 he married Emilia Frances Strong (afterwards Lady Dilke, q.v.). His standard of perfection in scholarship was so high that his actual achievement is only suggestive of his powers, and the greatest project of his life—the study of Scaliger—remains a fragment, printed by Prof. Nettleship in vol. i of Pattison's collected *Essays* (1889). He did publish *Suggestions on Academical Organisation* (1868); admirably annotated editions of Pope's *Essay on Man* (1869) and *Satires and Epistles* (1872); *Isaac Casaubon* (1875); *Milton*, in the 'Men of Letters' (1879); the *Sonnets* of Milton (1883); and *Sermons* (1885). See his frank posthumous *Memoirs* (1885) and Lionel Tollemache's *Recollections of Pattison* (1895).

PATTON, George Smith (1885–1945), American general, was born at San Gabriel, California, and graduated from West Point in 1909. In the first World War he commanded an armoured brigade on the Western Front. In 1941 he commanded the 1st Armoured Corps and later led the first U.S. troops to fight in North Africa. In 1943 he commanded the 7th Army in the Sicilian campaign. At the head of the 3rd Army he swept across France in 1944 and in the following year reached the Czech frontier. See his *War As I Knew It* (1948), and Ayer, *Before the Colours Fade* (1965).

PAUL, (1) Charles Kegan (1828–1902), English author and publisher, born at White Laekington in Somerset, was a graduate of Oxford and entered the Church, becoming in 1852 a chaplain at Eton and in 1862 vicar at Sturminster Hall. During this time he wrote religious works and edited the *New Quarterly Magazine*. In 1874 he left the Church to settle in London, where he wrote *William Godwin, his Friends and Contemporaries* (1876). In 1877 he took over the publishing firm of H. S. King, which became C. Kegan Paul & Co. Among his first publications were the monthly *Nineteenth Century*, and the works of G. W. Cox, Tennyson, Meredith and Stevenson. Joined by Alfred Trench in 1881, the firm became Kegan Paul, Trench & Co., in 1889 a limited company, Kegan Paul, Trench, Trübner & Co. Ltd., and finally incorporated in the publishing house George Routledge & Sons, Ltd. Paul became a Roman Catholic and among his many works were *Biographical Sketches* (1883), *Maria Drummond* (1891), works on religion and translations from Goethe and Pascal.

(2) **Jean.** See RICHTER (4).

(3) **Lewis** (d. 1759), English inventor of French descent, a ward of Lord Shaftesbury, who invented a roller-spinning machine and with the mechanic John Wyatt opened two mills, one at Birmingham and one at Northampton. This machine was a failure commercially, although the idea was later utilized by Arkwright. In 1738 he invented a

carding machine which was used in Lancashire after his death and in 1758 patented another type of spinning machine. He was befriended by Samuel Johnson, who took a lively interest in his enterprises.

(4) Vincent de. See VINCENT DE PAUL.

PAUL (fl. 1st cent. A.D.), the Apostle of the Gentiles, was born of Jewish parents at Tarsus in Cilicia. At the age of about fourteen, he trained as a rabbi under Gamaliel at Jerusalem, acquiring also the trade of tent-maker. A strenuous Pharisee, he assisted in persecuting the Christians. He was on his way to Damascus on this mission when a vision of the Crucified converted him into a fervent adherent of the new faith. After three years spent mainly at Damascus, but partly in Arabia, he visited Jerusalem again, and after the apostles had been persuaded by Barnabas of his conversion, he began to preach: but opposition to him was strong and for ten years he lived in retirement at Tarsus. Brought to Antioch by Barnabas, he was there for a year before undertaking with him and John Mark his first mission-tour in Cyprus, Pisidia, Pamphylia and Lycaonia. Returning to Antioch, he found the controversy raised as to the condition under which Gentiles and Jews respectively were to be admitted to the Christian Church, a controversy which led to the first apostolic council in Jerusalem c. A.D. 49 or 50. Paul opposed Peter during the debate and when the question was finally settled by a compromise, he addressed himself thereafter mainly to the Gentiles. His second mission-journey led him, with Silas, again to Asia Minor and through Galatia and Phrygia to Macedonia and Achaia, where in Corinth he was especially successful. A year and a half later he was again at Jerusalem and Antioch, and then undertook a third mission-tour—to Galatia and Phrygia. Driven from Ephesus, he visited Achaia and Macedonia again, and by way of Miletus returned by sea to Jerusalem. There the fanaticism of the Jews against him led to disturbances, whereupon he was brought to Caesarea to be tried before Felix the procurator, and after two years' imprisonment, before Felix's successor M. Porcius Festus. Now using his right as a Roman citizen, Paul appealed to Caesar, and in the spring of A.D. 62 arrived in Rome, where he spent two years a prisoner, but in his own hired house. He was executed under Nero—probably at the end of the two years' captivity, though tradition makes him visit Spain and other countries. The ancient church recognized thirteen of the New Testament Epistles as Paul's, but did not unanimously regard Hebrews as his. All but the most destructive modern critics accept unhesitatingly as Paul's the Epistles to the Galatians, Romans and Corinthians (1st and 2nd). But a considerable body of scholars dispute the Pauline authorship of the Pastoral Epistles, 2nd Thessalonians and Ephesians, and some also Colossians and Philippians. The order of the Epistles is certainly not chronological, though it is difficult to fix the succession. See the works on Paul by Deissmann (1912), Schweitzer (1912), Smith (1919), Foakes-Jackson (1927), Scott (1927),

Nock (1938), W. Barclay (1959) and C. Tresmontant, trans. D. Attwater (1958).

PAUL, name of six popes:

Paul I (757–67) and **Paul II** (1464–71) were unimportant.

Paul III, named **Alessandro Farnese** (1468–1549), a Tuscan, created cardinal-deacon in 1493, was pope from 1534. One of his first acts was to give cardinal's hats to two of his boy grandsons, and throughout his reign he laboured to advance his bastard sons. Yet he surrounded his throne with good cardinals like Contarini, Pole and Sadolet. He convoked a general council in 1542, but it did not actually assemble (in Trent) until 1545. In 1538 he issued the bull of excommunication and deposition against Henry VIII of England, and also the bull instituting the order of the Jesuits in 1540.

Paul IV, named **Giovanni Pietro Caraffa** (1476–1559), was born in Naples. As Bishop of Chieti he laboured for the reformation of abuses and for the revival of religion and morality. A rigorous enemy of heresy, under his influence Paul III organized the Inquisition in Rome. Elected pope in 1555, he enforced upon the clergy the observance of all the clerical duties, and enacted laws for the maintenance of public morality. He established a censorship, issued a full *Index librorum prohibitorum*, completed the organization of the Roman Inquisition, and helped the poor. He was embroiled with the Emperor Ferdinand, with Philip II of Spain, and with Cosmo, Grand-duke of Tuscany.

Paul V, named **Camillo Borghese** (1552–1621), born in Rome, became nuncio in Spain, and cardinal, and on the death of Leo XI in 1605 was elected pope. In his time took place the great conflict with the republic of Venice, as to the immunity of the clergy from the jurisdiction of civil tribunals, and other questions. Paul issued a denouncing excommunication against the doge and senate, placing the republic under an interdict. By the intervention of Henry IV of France the dispute was settled in 1607, after the pope had abandoned his claims. Paul promoted charities and useful public works.

Paul VI, named **Giovanni Battista Montini** (1897–), born at Concesio, son of the editor of a Catholic daily paper, graduated at the Gregorian University of Rome, was ordained in 1920, and entered the Vatican diplomatic service, where he remained until 1944. He was then appointed Archbishop of Milan, in which important diocese he became known for his liberal views and support of social reform. Made a cardinal in 1958, he was elected pope on the death of John XXIII, many of whose opinions he shared, in 1963.

PAUL (1754–1801), emperor of Russia, second son of Peter III and Catharine II, succeeded his mother in 1796. His father's murder and his mother's neglect had exerted a baneful influence on his character. His earliest measures were the exile of the murderers and the pardon of Polish prisoners, including Kosciusko. But he soon revealed his violent temper and lack of capacity, and irritated all his subjects by vexatious regulations. He suddenly declared for the allies against France, and sent an army of 56,000 men under Suvorov into Italy; sent a second to cooperate with the Austrians, retired from the alliance, quarrelled with England, and entered into close alliance with Bonaparte. After his convention with Sweden and Denmark, England sent a fleet into the Baltic under Nelson to dissolve the coalition (1801). His own officers conspired to compel Paul to abdicate, and in a scuffle he was strangled.

PAUL I, King of the Hellenes (1901–64), was born in Athens and educated at the Naval Academy. In 1922 he served with the Greek Navy in the campaign against the Turks, but in 1924 when a Republic was proclaimed went into exile with his elder brother George II. In 1935 he returned to Greece as crown prince. In World War II he served with the Greek General Staff in the Albanian campaign. In exile in London from 1941 until 1946, he succeeded his brother in 1947.

PAUL OF SAMOSATA (fl. 3rd cent. A.D.), was born at Samosata on the Euphrates, and in 260 became bishop or patriarch of Antioch, and so was practically the viceregent of Queen Zenobia of Palmyra; but in 272 was deposed for monarchianism—the doctrine that the Son is rather an attribute of the Father than a person.

PAULA. See FRANCIS, SAINT (2).

PAULDING, James Kirke, *pol′ding* (1778–1860), American writer, born in Putnam Co., N.Y., was a friend of Washington Irving. He wrote part of *Salmagundi*, and during the 1812 war published the *Diverting History of John Bull and Brother Jonathan*. In 1814 a more serious work, *The United States and England*, gained him an appointment on the Board of Naval Commissioners. He also wrote *The Dutchman's Fireside* (1831), *Westward Ho!* (1832), a *Life of Washington* (1835), and a defence of *Slavery in the United States* (1836). In 1837 he became secretary of the navy. See *Literary Life* by his son (1867) and Life by his A. L. Herold (1926).

PAULET, or Poulet, Sir Amyas, *paw′let* (c. 1536–88), succeeded his father as governor of Jersey, was ambassador to France (1576–1579), and was keeper of Mary, Queen of Scots from 1585 till her death (1587). See his *Letter-book* (ed. Morris, 1874).

PAULI, *pow′lee*, (1) **Reinhold** (1823–82), German historian, was born in Berlin, studied at Bonn and at Oxford, and in 1849–1852 was private secretary to Bunsen. He was successively professor of History at Rostock, Tübingen, Marburg and Göttingen. Pauli's lifelong studies were devoted to English history, on which he wrote several books.

(2) **Wolfgang** (1900–58), Austrian-Swiss theoretical physicist, born in Vienna, the son of the professor of Chemistry, studied under Sommerfeld at Munich and Niels Bohr in Copenhagen. He formulated the ' exclusion principle ' (1924), that no two electrons can be in the same energy state, of great importance in the application of the quantum theory to the periodic table of chemical elements, and postulated (1931) the existence of an electrically neutral particle in subatomic physics, later confirmed by Fermi, and in 1957 carried out experiments confirming the nonparity theory of Yang and Lee (qq.v.)

in nuclear interactions. He was visiting professor at Princeton in 1935 and at Einstein's invitation again (1939–46). A Nobel prizewinner in 1945, he was a foreign member of the Royal Society.

PAULING, Linus Carl (1901–), American biochemist, born at Portland, Oregon, professor of Chemistry at the California Institute of Technology (1961–63), at the University of California at San Diego from 1967, applied the quantum theory to chemistry and was awarded the Nobel prize (1954) for his contributions to the electrochemical theory of valency, and with Campbell and Pressman, prepared artificial antibodies. An official inspector of defence projects in World War II, he became a controversial figure from 1955, as the leading professionally scientific critic of the American nuclear deterrent policy, forcibly setting out his views in *No More War* (1958). He was elected a foreign member of the Royal Society, and was awarded the Nobel peace prize in 1963.

PAULINUS, (1) St, of Nola **(Pontius Meropius Anicius Paulinus)** (353–431), born in Bordeaux, accepted Christian baptism (c. 389) and settled at Nola in Italy, where he became known for his charity and his rigid asceticism. He was consecrated Bishop of Nola (c. 409). He is remembered for his *Carmina* and for his epistles to Augustine, Jerome, Sulpicius Severus, and Ausonius.

(2) (d. 644), first Archbishop of York, was a Roman sent with Augustine to Kent by Pope Gregory in 601. Ordained bishop by Justus, fourth archbishop, in 625, he accompanied Ethelburga on her marriage to the heathen Edwin of Northumbria, who was baptized at York in 627. Edwin's death in battle drove him back to Kent, where, having in 633 received the *pallium* as Archbishop of York, he remained till his death.

PAULUS, (1). See AEMILIUS and SCIPIO AFRICANUS.

(2) **Friedrich,** *pow′loos* (1890–1957), German field-marshal and tank specialist, capitulated to the Russians with the remnants of his army at the siege of Stalingrad in 1943. Released from captivity in 1953, he became a lecturer on military affairs under the East German Communist government.

(3) **Heinrich Eberhard Gottlob** (1761–1851), German pioneer of rationalism, was born at Leonberg near Stuttgart, studied at Tübingen and, as professor at Jena (1789–1803), produced a New Testament commentary (1800–04), one on the Psalms (1791), and one on Isaiah (1793). He was afterwards professor at Würzburg and at Heidelberg, where he died. In his theological works he asserted the impossibility of the supernatural, and explained the miracles as due to mistaken opinions and errors. See his Autobiography (1839) and study by Meldegg (1853).

PAULUS AEGINETA (fl. 7th cent.), Greek physician, was born in Aegina. His *Synopsis of the Medical Art* went through many editions and translations.

PAULUS DIACONUS (fl. 8th cent.), ' Paul the Deacon ', Lombard historian, was born at Friuli, and probably resided at the court of the Duke of Beneventum. He became a monk about 774, but spent some years at the court of Charlemagne, and retired to Monte Cassino in 787. His *Historia Romana* is based on Eutropius. The *Historia Langobardorum* comes down to 744. Other works are a *Life of Gregory the Great*; *Gesta Episcoporum Mettensium*; a *Book of Homilies*, selected from Augustine, Chrysostom, &c.; and poems and letters.

PAUL VERONESE. See VERONESE.

PAUSANIAS, (1) Spartan regent and general, a nephew of Leonidas, commanded the Greeks at Plataea (479 B.C.), where the Persians were routed. He then compelled the Thebans to give up the chiefs of the Persian party, and haughtily treated the Athenians and other Greeks. Capturing the Cyprian cities and Byzantium, he negotiated with Xerxes in the hope of becoming ruler under him of all Greece and was twice recalled for treachery. He tried to stir up the helots, was betrayed, and fled to a temple of Athena, where he was built up and only taken out to die of hunger.

(2) (fl. 2nd cent. A.D.), Greek geographer and historian, born probably in Lydia, travelled through almost all Greece, Macedonia and Italy, and also through part of Asia and Africa, and composed from his observations and researches an *Itinerary* of Greece, describing the different parts of that country and the monuments of art. His style is unpretentious and easy, and his *Itinerary* possesses the rare merit of being the work of an accurate eye-witness, one of the earliest examples of the antiquary: bare and meagre as it is, it remains one of the most precious records of antiquity. There are translations by Shilleto and Frazer. See M. Verrall's *Ancient Athens* (1890), and books by Kalkmann (1886), Gurlitt (1890), Bencker (1890), Heberdey (1896), Frazer (1900) and Robert (1909).

PAVLOV, Ivan Petrovich (1849–1936), Russian physiologist, born near Ryazan, a village priest's son, studied medicine at St Petersburg, conducted research in Breslau and Leipzig, and returned to St Petersburg, where he became professor (1891) and director of the Institute of Experimental Medicine (1913). He worked at the physiology of circulation and digestion, but is most famous for his study of 'conditioned' or acquired reflexes, associated each with some part of the brain cortex—the brain's only function being in his view the coupling of neurones to produce reflexes. He was awarded the Nobel prize for medicine in 1904. See Life by B. P. Babkin (1951).

PAVLOVA, Anna, *pav'lo-va* (1885–1931), Russian ballerina, born at St Petersburg, became world famous, forming her own company in 1909, and some of her most successful performances were in *Giselle*, *The Dying Swan*, *Don Quixote* and her own ballet *Autumn Leaves*. See Life by her husband, V. Dandré (1932).

PAXTON, Sir Joseph (1801–65), English gardener and architect, born at Milton-Bryant near Woburn, was a working gardener to the Duke of Devonshire, at Chiswick and Chatsworth; he remodelled the gardens, and managed the duke's Derbyshire estates. He designed a building for the Great Exhibition of 1851, which he re-erected as the Crystal

Palace (destroyed by fire 1936). He wrote on gardening, and sat as Liberal for Coventry from 1854. See Life by V. Markham (1935).

PAYER, Julius von (1842–1915), born at Teplitz, went with Weyprecht on an Arctic expedition, and discovered and explored Franz-Josef Land (1872). Afterwards he went to Munich and became a painter.

PAYN, James (1830–98), English novelist, was born at Cheltenham, and educated at Eton, Woolwich Academy, and Trinity, Cambridge. In 1855 he published a volume of poems, in 1859–74 was Leitch Ritchie's successor as editor of *Chambers's Journal*, and in 1882–96 edited the *Cornhill*. He wrote a hundred novels. See his *Some Literary Recollections* (1886) and *Gleams of Memory* (1894).

PAYNE, (1) Henry Neville (d. *c.* 1710), wrote tragedies and comedies, intrigued in Scotland for James II after the Revolution, was tortured in Edinburgh with ' the boot ' in 1690, and was imprisoned till 1700.

(2) John Howard (1791–1852), American actor and playwright, born in New York, made his début there in February 1809, and in 1813 appeared in London. For thirty years he had a successful career as actor and author of plays, chiefly adaptations; that called *Clari* contains the song *Home, Sweet Home*, the music being by Sir Henry Bishop. Payne was appointed American consul at Tunis in 1841, and died there.

(3) Peter (*c.* 1380–1455), English Wycliffite, was born near Grantham, studied at Oxford, and became in 1410 principal of St Edmund Hall. Charged with heresy, he fled about 1416 to Bohemia, where, till his death in 1455, he played a conspicuous part as a controversialist amongst the Hussites, taking the Taborite or extreme view. See Baker's *A Forgotten Great Englishman* (1894).

(4) Roger (1739–97), English bookbinder, born at Windsor, became famous, after 1766, as the most artistic bookbinder in London. See *Roger Payne* by C. J. Davenport (1929).

PAYNE-SMITH, Robert (1819–95), English theologian, was born at Chipping Camden, studied at Pembroke College, Oxford, and, as sub-librarian of the Bodleian (1857–65), began his great *Thesaurus Syriacus* (1870–93). Sermons on *Isaiah* (1862) led to his appointment as regius professor of Theology at Oxford (1865–70), whence he removed to the deanery of Canterbury.

PEABODY, George (1795–1869), American philanthropist, born at South Danvers, Mass., now called Peabody, became a partner in a Baltimore dry-goods store in 1829. He established himself in London in 1837 as a merchant and banker, and in his lifetime gave away a million and a half for philanthropic purposes—Kane's Arctic expedition, education (at Harvard, &c.), industrial homes in London. He died in London. See Life by P. A. Hanaford (1882).

PEACE, Charles (1832–79), English criminal and murderer, born in Sheffield. First imprisoned for robbery at the age of eighteen, he subsequently divided his time between picture-frame making by day and burglary by night. In August 1876 he shot a policeman in Whalley Range, Manchester, and after escaping attended the trial of William and

John Habron for his crime. John was found not guilty, and William was, on account of his youth, sentenced to life imprisonment for the crime. In November 1876 Peace murdered Arthur Dyson, whose wife he had been annoying, in Sheffield, but again escaped. He made his way to London, where he lived a life of seeming respectability, and was, two years later, arrested for attempted murder, having fired upon a policeman while attempting a burglary in Blackheath. In the following January, while serving sentence for the latter crime, he was accused of the murder of Dyson and found guilty. Shortly before his execution, he confessed to the Whalley Range murder. See his *Trials*, ed. N. Teignmouth Shore (1926).

PEACH, Benjamin Neeve (1842–1926), British geologist, born at Gorran Haven, Cornwall, educated at Peterhead and Wick academies and London School of Mines, worked along with Dr John Horne on the Geological Survey. Their brilliant collaboration elucidated the very intricate geology of the north-west Highlands. Their joint works include the *Silurian Rocks of Scotland* (1899) and *Chapters on the Geology of Scotland* (1930).

PEACOCK, Thomas Love (1785–1866), English novelist and poet, born at Weymouth, was the son of a London merchant and friend of Shelley. He entered the service of the East India Company in 1819 after producing three satirical romances, *Headlong Hall* (1816), *Melincourt* (1817) and *Nightmare Abbey* (1818). *Crotchet Castle* (1831) concluded this series of satires, but in 1860 the veteran returned to the stage with *Gryll Grange*, which shows signs of hardening. He also published two romances properly so-called, *Maid Marian* (1822) and *The Misfortunes of Elphin* (1829). The framework of his satirical fictions is always the same—a company of humorists meet in a country house and display their crotchets or prejudices which are the things Peacock, the reasonable man, most disliked, that is, morbid romance, the mechanical sort of political economy, the 'march of science' and transcendental philosophy. The satire is relieved by some excellent songs and the eccentrics by one or two less unbalanced men and some gay natural young women. Otherwise the characters are stock types as in Ben Jonson's comedies. Exception should be made for the mellow divine who first appears as Dr Gaster in *Headlong Hall*, becomes three-dimensional in Dr Folliott in *Crotchet Castle* and re-appears as Dr Opimian in *Gryll Grange*. To add to the piquancy of the fictions the poets of the Romantic school, Wordsworth, Coleridge, Shelley, Byron, Southey, are caricatured along with the Edinburgh Reviewers, who offer the extra target of being Scots. His two romances vary in tone from genuine love of romance to boisterous fun or Rabelaisian comedy. Peacock was poised between the Voltairian and the romantic view of life—hence the 'sauce piquant' of his admirable satires. See *The Novels of Thomas Love Peacock*, ed. D. Garnett (1949); the Life by Van Doren (1911); studies by A. M. Freeman (1911) and J. B. Priestley (1927).

PEANO, Giuseppe, *pay-ah'nō* (1858–1932), Italian mathematician, born at Cuneo, taught at the University of Turin, was known for his work on mathematical logic and for his promotion of a universal language based on uninflected Latin.

PEARS, Peter, *peerz* (1910–), English tenor, born in Farnham, after being organ scholar of Hertford College, Oxford, studied singing (1933–34) at the Royal College of Music. He toured the U.S.A. and Europe with Benjamin Britten, and in 1943 joined Sadler's Wells. After the success of *Peter Grimes* (1945) he joined Britten in the English Opera Group, and was co-founder with him, in 1948, of the Aldeburgh Festival. He is noted for his sympathy with and understanding of modern works. He was created C.B.E. in 1957.

PEARSE, Patrick (or Padraic) Henry (1879–1916), Irish writer and nationalist, was a leader of the Gaelic revival and editor of its journal. Having commanded the insurgents in the Easter rising of 1916 he was proclaimed president of the provisional government, but, after the revolt had been quelled, was arrested, court-martialled and shot. He wrote poems, short stories and plays. See Life by Ryan (1919).

PEARSON, (1) Sir Cyril Arthur (1866–1921), English newspaper and periodical proprietor, born at Wookey, Somerset, educated at Winchester, became a journalist, founded *Pearson's Weekly* in 1890 and various other periodicals. In 1900 he became associated with newspapers, founding the *Daily Express*, and amalgamating the *St James Gazette* with the *Evening Standard*. Turning blind, he founded St Dunstan's home for blinded soldiers and was president of the National Institution for the Blind.

(2) **Hesketh** (1887–1964), English biographer, born at Hawford in Worcestershire, worked in a shipping office before beginning a successful stage career in 1911. In 1931 he emerged as a writer of popular and racy biographies. Among these are *Gilbert and Sullivan* (1935), *Shaw* (1942), *Conan Doyle* (1943), *Oscar Wilde* (1946), whose *Works* and *Essays* he edited, *Dizzy* (1951), *Sir Walter Scott* (1955), and *Charles II* (1960). He also wrote *Common Misquotations* (1937) and a play *Writ for Libel* (1950) with Colin Hurry.

(3) **John** (1613–86), English divine, was born at Great Snoring, Norfolk, son of the Archdeacon of Suffolk. He was educated at Eton and at Queen's and King's Colleges, Cambridge, and in 1640 appointed chaplain to the lord-keeper Finch, and later presented to the rectory of Thorington in Suffolk. In 1659 he published his learned *Exposition of the Creed*, and edited the remains of John Hales of Eton. In 1660 he was presented to the rectory of St Christopher's in London, and made prebendary of Ely, archdeacon of Surrey, and master of Jesus College, Cambridge. In 1661 he was the principal antagonist of Baxter in the Savoy Conference, and became Margaret professor of Divinity; in 1662 he was made master of Trinity, Cambridge, and in 1673 bishop of Chester. He defended the genuineness of the Ignatian epistles (1672), and in 1684 published his *Annales Cyprianici*.

(4) **Karl** (1857–1936), British scientist, born in London, turned from the law to mathematics, becoming professor of Applied Mathematics in University College London, and Galton professor of Eugenics. He published *The Grammar of Science* (1892), and works on eugenics, mathematics, biometrics. In his *Life of Galton* (1914–30) the head of the Eugenics Laboratory applies the methods of his science to the study of its founder. See Life by his son, E. S. Pearson (1938).

(5) **Lester Bowles** (1897–1972), Canadian politician, was born in Newtonbrook, Ontario, educated at Toronto and Oxford Universities. He became successively first secretary at the London office of the Canadian high commissioner (1935–39), assistant under-secretary of state for external affairs (1941), ambassador in Washington (1945–46). He was a senior adviser at the Charter Conference of the U.N. in 1945 and was later leader of Canadian U.N. delegations. In 1952–53 he was president of the U.N. General Assembly, and in 1957 was awarded the Nobel peace prize. Secretary of state for external affairs (1948–57), and leader of the Opposition party from 1958, he became prime minister in 1963, retaining power with a minority government in 1965. He resigned as party leader and as prime minister in 1968. He was awarded the O.M. in 1971.

PEARY, Robert Edwin (1856–1920), American admiral and explorer, born at Cresson Springs, Penn., made eight Arctic voyages by the Greenland coast, in 1891–92 arriving on the east coast by crossing the ice. In 1906 he reached 87° 6′ N. lat., and on April 6, 1909, attained the North Pole. See accounts of his travels by himself in *Northward over the Great Ice* (1898), *The North Pole* (1910), &c., his wife, Heilprin, and Hobbs (1936).

PEASE, (1) **Edward** (1767–1858), English industrialist, born at Darlington, carried on till 1817 his father's woollen mill there. He later promoted railways, and was George Stephenson's supporter in his famous Stockton to Darlington project of 1825. The family were Quakers and worked for the Peace and Antislavery Societies; two of Edward's sons entered zealously into their father's schemes, and were in parliament.

(2) **Francis Gladheim** (1881–1938), American astronomer and designer of optical instruments, was born at Cambridge, Mass. He was observer and optician at Yerkes Observatory, Wis. (1901–04), and instrument-maker (1908–13) at the Mount Wilson Observatory, Pasadena, where he designed the 100-inch telescope, and the 50-foot interferometer telescope by means of which he gained direct measurements of star diameters. He was also associated in the design of the 200-inch Palomar telescope.

PECOCK, Reginald, *pee'kok* (*c.* 1395–*c.* 1460), Welsh theologian, was a fellow of Oriel, Oxford, and received priest's orders in 1422. He was master of Whittington College, London, and rector of its church (1431); bishop of St Asaph's (1444); and of Chichester (1450). He plunged into the Lollard and other controversies, and compiled many treatises including *The Reule of Crysten Religioun* (*c.* 1443; ed. Greet, E.E.T.S.,

1927), *The Book of Feith* (ed. Morison, 1909) and *The Repressor of Over Much Blaming of the Clergy* (*c.* 1455; ed. Babington, Rolls Series, 1860). His philosophic breadth and independence of judgment brought upon him the suspicions of the church. In 1457 he was denounced for having written in English, and for making reason paramount to the authority of the old doctors. He was summoned before Archbishop Bourchier, condemned as a heretic, and given the alternative of abjuring or being burned. He elected to abjure, gave up fourteen of his books, resigned his bishopric, and retired to Thorney Abbey. See study by V. H. H. Green (1945).

PECQUET, Jean, *pek-ay* (1622–74), French anatomist, born in Dieppe, worked at Montpellier, where in 1647 he was the first to see clearly the thoracic duct. He described his findings in *Experimenta nova anatomica* (1651). He became a dipsomaniac and died in Paris.

PEDEN, Alexander (*c.* 1626–86), Scottish Covenanter, studied at Glasgow, was ejected in 1662 from his ministry at New Luce in Galloway, and subsequently wandered preaching at conventicles and hiding in caves. He was repeatedly in Ireland, and in 1673–77 was imprisoned on the Bass Rock. Many of his utterances were regarded as prophecies.

PEDERSEN, Christiern (1480–1554), Danish writer, born probably at Elsinore, a leader of the Reformation in Denmark, is remembered for his Danish-Latin dictionary, and his translations of the New Testament (1521) and the Psalms (1531). He also worked on the famous ' Christian III ' version of the Bible, which appeared in 1550.

PEDRELL, Felipe (1841–1922), Spanish composer, born at Tortosa, was self-taught. He wrote operas, choral works, songs, &c. He became professor at Madrid, and lived later at Barcelona. He was the author of critical and historical works on music.

PEDRO, name of two emperors of Brazil:

Pedro I (1798–1834), second son of John VI of Portugal, fled to Brazil with his parents on Napoleon's invasion, and became prince-regent of Brazil on his father's return to Portugal (1821). A Liberal in outlook, he declared for Brazilian independence in 1822, and was crowned as Pedro I. The new empire did not start smoothly, and Pedro in 1831 abdicated and withdrew to Portugal. He was Pedro IV of Portugal on the death of his father, but abdicated in favour of his daughter.

Pedro II (1825–91), son of Pedro I, succeeded on his father's abdication, and, distinguished by his love of learning and scholarly tastes, reigned in peace until the 1889 revolution drove him to Europe. He died in Paris. See Life by M. W. Williams (1938).

PEDRO THE CRUEL (1334–69), king of Castile and León, succeeded his father, Alfonso XI, in 1350, and assuming full power in 1353, became exceedingly popular with the people for his justice, but alienated the nobles and clergy. When he had marched to suppress a revolt in Estremadura, he was betrayed by his brother Henry and taken prisoner. Escaping, despite the excommunication of the pope, he speedily crushed the rebels. But now he became suspicious of everyone; and the rest of his reign was devoted to the establishment of his own authority on the ruins of the feudal tyranny of the great vassals, and to long-continued and bloody wars with Aragon and Granada. He owes the epithet Cruel mainly to the murder of his brother Don Fadrique in 1358. The people were in general well and justly governed, but heavy taxes dissipated his popularity. Henry returned from France (1366) at the head of a body of exiles, backed by Du Guesclin, and aided by Aragon, France and the pope. Edward the Black Prince, persuaded to espouse Pedro's cause in 1367, defeated Henry and Du Guesclin at Navarrete (April 13). But, disgusted by his ally's nonfulfilment of his promises, the English prince repassed the Pyrenees and left Pedro to his fate. The whole kingdom groaned under his cruelties; rebellions broke out everywhere; and when, in 1367, Henry returned, Pedro was routed at Montiel (1369), and in single combat with Henry, developing into a mêlée, was slain. See studies by Prosper Mérimée (1848) and Storer (1910).

PEEL, Sir Robert (1788–1850), English statesman, was born near Bury in Lancashire. His father, **Sir Robert Peel** (1750–1830) (M.P. from 1790, created baronet in 1800), was a wealthy cotton manufacturer and calico printer, and from him he inherited a great fortune. He had three years at Harrow, took a double first from Christ Church, Oxford, in 1808, and entered parliament in 1809 as Tory member for Cashel. In 1811 he was appointed under-secretary for the colonies, and in 1812–18 secretary for Ireland. In this capacity 'Orange Peel' displayed a strong anti-Catholic spirit, and was so fiercely attacked by O'Connell (q.v.) that he challenged him to a duel. From 1818 till 1822 Peel remained out of office, but sat for the University of Oxford. In 1819 he was chairman of the Bank Committee, and moved the resolutions which led to the resumption of cash payments. In 1822 he re-entered the ministry as home secretary, and he and Canning as foreign secretary worked together pretty well, Peel devoting himself to the currency. But on 'Roman Catholic emancipation' Canning was in advance of Peel, and when Canning formed a Whig-Tory ministry, Peel, along with the Duke of Wellington and others, withdrew from office (1827). Yet, when the death of Canning led to the Wellington-Peel government, its great measure was that for the relief of the Roman Catholics (1829). As home secretary he reorganized the London police force ('Peelers' or 'Bobbies'). Peel opposed parliamentary reform, and in 1830 the Wellington-Peel ministry was succeeded by a Whig ministry under Earl Grey, which, in 1832, carried the Reform Bill. Peel shrank from factious obstruction of the measure, but as leader of the 'Conservative' opposition, sought by vigilant criticism of Whig measures to retard the too rapid strides of Liberalism. Rejected by Oxford in 1829, but returned for Westbury, Peel represented Tamworth from 1833 till his death. In November 1834 he accepted office as prime minister but gave place to Lord Melbourne in April 1835. The general election of 1841 was virtually a contest between Free Trade and Protection, and Protection won. The Conservative party, headed by Peel, now came into office. The Whigs were bent upon a fixed but moderate duty on foreign corn; the Anti-Corn-Law League would hear of nothing short of repeal; while Sir Robert carried (1842) a modification of the sliding-scale. The deficit in the revenue led him to impose (1842) an 'income tax' of 7d. in the pound, to be levied for three years. To alleviate the new burden Peel revised the general tariff, and either abolished or lowered the duties on several very important articles of commerce. He resolutely repressed the malcontents of Ireland, and O'Connell's influence was broken. In 1845 the allowance to Maynooth was changed into a permanent endowment, and the Irish unsectarian colleges were founded. But the potato rot in Ireland, followed by a frightful famine, rendered 'cheap corn' a necessity. Cobden and the League redoubled their exertions. Peel again yielded, telling his colleagues that the corn laws were doomed. Lord Stanley (afterwards Earl of Derby) seceded, and, with Lord George Bentinck, Disraeli and others, formed a 'no-surrender' Tory party; but the Duke of Wellington, Graham, Aberdeen, Gladstone and other eminent Conservatives stood by him, and repeal was carried. Defeated on an Irish Protection of Life Bill, he retired in June 1846, giving place to a Whig administration under Lord John Russell to which he gave independent but general support. In the critical times of 1847–48 he was one of the most important props of the government, whose free trade principles he had now accepted. He had a keen English interest in sport, and a cultivated taste in matters literary and artistic. On June 29, 1850, he was thrown from his horse, and was so much injured that he died July 2. See his (non-biographical) *Memoirs*, edited by Earl Stanhope and Viscount Cardwell (1857), *Speeches* (1835 and 1853), his *Private Letters* (ed. G. Peel, 1920), and C. S. Parker's *Peel Papers* (3 vols. 1891–99); his *Life and Times* by Sir T. Lever; books by Guizot (1851), Laurence Peel, Lord Dalling, Barnett Smith, F. C. Montague, Justin McCarthy, J. R. Thursfield, A. A. W. Ramsay (1928), G. K. Clark (1929); Shaw Lefevre, *Peel and O'Connell* (1887). Peel's eldest son, **Sir Robert** (1822–95), and the second, **Sir Frederick** (1823–1906), held office as ministers; **Arthur Wellesley**, the fifth and youngest (1829–1912), was speaker of the House of Commons 1884–95, and then was created Viscount Peel.

PEELE, George (c. 1558–98), English Elizabethan dramatist, born in London, went up to Oxford in 1571. He took his bachelor's degree in 1577, his master's in 1579. By 1581 he had removed to London, where for seventeen years he lived a roistering Bohemian life as actor, poet and playwright. He was one of those warned to repentance by Greene in his *Groatsworth of Wit* (1592). *The Arraignment of Paris* (1584), is a dramatic pastoral containing ingenious flatteries of Elizabeth.

Other works include his *Farewell to Sir John Norris* on his expedition to Portugal (1589, eked out by *A Tale of Troy*), *Eclogue Gratulatory* (1589) to the Earl of Essex, *Polyhymnia* (1590), *Speeches* for the reception of Queen Elizabeth (1591), and *Honour of the Garter* (1593). The historical play of *Edward I* (1593) is marred by its slanders against Queen Eleanor. His play, *The Old Wives' Tale* (1595), probably gave Milton the subject for his *Comus*. *David and Bethsabe* was published in 1599. Peele's works were first collected by Dyce (1828–39; reissue, with Greene, in 1861). A later edition is by A. H. Bullen (1888). See Symonds's *Shakspere's Predecessors* (1884).

PÉGUY, Charles Pierre, *pay-gee* (1873–1914), French nationalist, publisher, and neo-Catholic poet, born of peasant stock at Orléans, he was educated at the École Normale and the Sorbonne, after which he opened a bookshop. In 1900 he founded the *Cahiers de la quinzaine* in which were first published his own works as well as those of such writers as Romain Rolland, who later became famous. Deeply patriotic, he combined sincere Catholicism with Socialism and his writings reflect his intense desire for justice and truth. His most important works include *Le Mystère de la charité de Jeanne d'Arc* (1910), *Victor Marie, Comte Hugo* (1910), *L'Argent* (1912) and *La Tapisserie de Notre Dame* (1913). He was killed in World War I. See studies by Halévy (1918; trans. 1947), A. Rousseaux (1947), Dru (1956), and B. Guyon (1961).

PEIRCE, *purse*, (1) **Benjamin** (1809–80), American mathematician, father of (2), in 1833 became professor at Harvard, in 1849 astronomer to the American Nautical Almanac, and in 1867–74 was superintendent of the Coast Survey. His papers on the discovery of Neptune (1848), on Saturn's rings (1851–55) and his *Treatise on Analytic Mechanics* (1857) attracted great attention.

(2) **Charles Sanders** (1839–1914), American philosopher, pioneer of pragmatism, son of (1), born at Cambridge, Mass., through his father became associated with the Coastal and Geodesic Survey (1861–91), but devoted most of his leisure time to philosophy and spent the rest of his life in almost complete seclusion, apart from private tutoring at Milford, subsisting on the generosity of William James, whose version of pragmatism so repelled Peirce, however, that he relabelled himself ' pragmaticist '. For Peirce, truth is the opinion which is fated to be ultimately agreed by all who investigate. A profoundly original mathematical logician, he modified Booleian logical algebra to accommodate De Morgan's logic, distinguished a threefold division of predicates and elaborated a triadic theory of meaning. See his *Studies in Logic* (1883), *Collected Papers*, vols. i–vi, ed. C. Hartshorne and P. Weiss (1931–35), vols. vii–viii, ed. A. W. Burks (1958), and studies by J. Buchler (1940), T. A. Goudge (1950), ed. P. P. Wiener and F. H. Young (1952) and W. B. Gallie (1952).

PEIRSON, Francis (1757–81), major, commanding the troops at St Helier in Jersey, after the governor had been captured by a French force, was killed in victoriously repelling the invaders. His death is the subject of Copley's famous picture in the National Gallery.

PEISISTRATOS. See PISISTRATUS.

PELAGIUS (*c*. 360–*c*. 420), heretic, was born a Briton or an Irishman, his name being a Greek translation of the Celtic *Morgan* (' sea-born '). He was a monk, but never took orders, and settled in Rome about 400. Here he wrote *On the Trinity*, *On Testimonies* and *On the Pauline Epistles*, and attached Celestius, an Irish Scot, to his views. About 409 the two withdrew to Africa, and Pelagius made a pilgrimage to Jerusalem. Celestius having sought ordination at Carthage, his doctrines were examined and condemned; and in 415 Pelagius too was accused of heresy before the synod of Jerusalem. The Pelagian heresy was held to deny original sin; the will is equally free to choose to do good and to do evil. The impeachment failed, but a new synod of Carthage in 416 condemned Pelagius and Celestius; and ultimately Pope Zosimus adopted the canons of the African Council, and Pelagius was banished from Rome in 418. The Pelagian sect was soon extinguished, but Pelagianism and Semi-Pelagianism often troubled the church.

PELAYO (fl. 8th cent.), said to have been the first Christian king in Spain, seems to have made headway against the Arabs in Asturias. His deeds are obscured by legend.

PELHAM, name of an English land-owning family:

(1) **Sir Thomas** (*c*. 1650–1712), in 1706 was created Baron Pelham.

(2) **Thomas Pelham Holles** (1693–1768), son and successor of (1), succeeded in 1711 to the estates of his maternal uncle, John Holles, Duke of Newcastle. George I created him Earl of Clare (1714) and Duke of Newcastle (1715). A Whig and a supporter of Walpole, in 1724 he became secretary of state, and held the office for thirty years. In 1754 he succeeded his brother, Henry Pelham, as premier, but retired in 1756. In July 1757 he was again premier, and compelled to take the first William Pitt into his ministry and to give him the lead in the House of Commons and the supreme direction of the war and of foreign affairs—Newcastle, an incapable minister, but strong in courtcraft and intrigue, being a mere figurehead. On the accession of George III Bute superseded Newcastle (1762). In the Rockingham ministry (1765), he was for a few months lord privy seal.

(3) **Henry Pelham** (*c*. 1695–1754), younger brother of (2), took an active part in suppressing the rebellion of 1715, became secretary for war in 1724, and was a zealous supporter of Walpole. In 1743 he took office. Events during his ministry (reconstructed in 1744 as the ' Broad-bottom administration ') were the Austrian Succession war, the '45, the financial bill of 1750, the reform of the calendar, and Hardwicke's Marriage Act.

(4) **Henry Pelham-Clinton** (1811–64), fifth Duke of Newcastle and twelfth Earl of Lincoln, represented South Notts from 1832 to 1846, when he was ousted for supporting Peel's free trade measures. He was a lord

of the treasury in 1834–35, first commissioner of woods and forests in 1841–46, and then Irish secretary. He succeeded to the dukedom in 1851, and returned to office in 1852, being colonial secretary in the Aberdeen government. At the Crimean war he was made secretary of state for war—the first to hold that office. But the sufferings of the British army in the winter of 1854 raised a storm, and he resigned. He was colonial secretary under Palmerston, 1859–64. See Life by Martineau (1908).

PÉLISSIER, Aimable Jean Jacques, Duc de Malakoff, *pay-lees-yay* (1794–1864), French military leader, born near Rouen, served in Spain in 1823, in the Morea in 1828, in Algeria in 1830 and 1839. In 1845 he acquired notoriety by suffocating 500 fugitive Arabs in caves in the Dahna. In the Crimean war (1854) he commanded the first corps, and succeeded Canrobert in the chief command before Sebastopol. For storming the Malakoff he was made Marshal and Duc de Malakoff. In 1858–59 he was French ambassador in London and thereafter governor of Algeria.

PELL, John (1610–85), English mathematician and clergyman, born at Southwick in Sussex, a brilliant student at Cambridge, was appointed professor of Mathematics at Amsterdam in 1643 and lecturer at the New College at Breda in 1646. Employed by Cromwell, first as a mathematician and later in 1654 as his agent, he went to Switzerland in an attempt to persuade Swiss Protestants to join a Continental Protestant league led by England. In 1661 he became rector at Fobbing in Essex and in 1663 vicar of Laindon. His published mathematical writings are relatively few, but a large collection of unpublished papers is in the British Museum. He is remembered chiefly for his equation called the Pell equation and for introducing the division sign $\div$ into England. He was one of the early fellows of the Royal Society.

PELLEGRINI, Carlo, *pel-leg-ree'nee* (1839–1889), Italian caricaturist, born at Capua, came to London in 1864, and from 1869 till his death was the cartoonist, 'Ape', of *Vanity Fair*.

PELLETIER, Pierre Joseph, *pel-tyay* (1788–1842), French chemist, born in Paris, professor and later assistant director at the School of Pharmacy there, with J. B. Caventou discovered strychnine, quinine, brucine and other alkaloids. He was responsible for the naming of chlorophyll.

PELLICO , Silvio (1788–1854), Italian writer and patriot, born at Saluzzo in Piedmont, spent four years at Lyons, and at Milan (1810) was French tutor in the military school. His tragedies of *Laodamia* and *Francesca da Rimini* gained him a name, and he translated Byron's *Manfred*. In 1820 he was arrested and imprisoned for two years at Venice. He was then, on a charge of Carbonarism, condemned to death, but had his sentence commuted to fifteen years' imprisonment in the Spielberg near Brünn, and was liberated in 1830. During this time he wrote two other dramas. He published an account of his imprisonment, *Le mie Prigioni* (1833), and subsequently numerous

tragedies, poems and a catechism on the duties of man. See Lives by Chiala (Italian, 1852), Bourdon (8th ed. Paris 1885), Rivieri (1899–1901) and Barbiera (1936).

PELLISSON-FONTANIER, Paul, *pel-lee-sŏ-fŏ-tan-yay* (1624–93), French writer of a history of the French Academy, and was a member of it. Sainte Beuve ranks him as a classic.

PELOPIDAS (d. 364 B.C.), Theban general, in 382 B.C. was driven from Thebes by the oligarchic party, who were supported by the Spartans, and sought refuge at Athens, whence he returned with a few associates in 379, and recovered possession of the citadel. His ' sacred band ' of Theban youth largely contributed to Epaminondas's victory at Leuctra (371). In the expedition against Alexander of Pherae (368) he was treacherously taken prisoner, but rescued by Epaminondas next year. He was then ambassador to the Persian court. In 364, in command of a third expedition against Alexander of Pherae, he marched into Thessaly, and won the battle of Cynoscephalae, but was himself slain.

PELTIER, Jean Charles Athanase, *pel-tyay* (1785–1845), French physicist, born at Hain, Somme, originally a watchmaker, discovered the thermoelectric reduction of temperature known as the Peltier effect and later used by Lenz as a method of freezing water. He died in Paris.

PEMBERTON, Sir Max (1863–1950), English reviewer and novelist, born at Birmingham, educated at Merchant Taylors' School and Caius College, Cambridge, made writing his career. He was editor of *Chums* (1892–93) and from 1894 to 1906 editor of *Cassell's Magazine*. He produced a succession of readable novels, many of them historical adventure stories, and also wrote plays. Successful titles were: *Impregnable City* (1895), *Queen of the Jesters* (1897), *The Show Girl* (1909), *Captain Black* (1911), *The Mad King Dies* (1928). He founded the London School of Journalism and in 1920 became a director of Northcliffe newspapers, two years later publishing a biography of Lord Northcliffe. He was knighted in 1928.

PEMBROKE. See HERBERT, MARSHAL, STRONGBOW.

PENDA (c. 577–655), heathen king of Mercia, constantly at war with Northumbria, defeated Edwin at Heathfield (633), Oswald at Maserfelth (642), but was himself defeated and slain by Oswy on the Winwaed, either in Lothian or in Yorkshire.

PENDEREL, the name of five Shropshire Catholic yeomen who aided Charles II (q.v.) at Boscobel. See Allan Fea's *Flight of the King* (1897).

PENGELLY, William (1812–94), English geologist, born at Looe, a schoolmaster and tutor at Torquay, was eminent as a geologist, especially in connection with the exploration of the Brixham Cave and Kent's Cavern. See the Life by his daughter (1897).

PENG TEH-HUAI (1899–   ), Chinese Communist general, born in Hunan, fought in the Sino-Japanese War (1937–45), became second-in-command to Chu Teh (q.v.), and led the Chinese ' volunteer ' forces in the Korean war.

PENIAKOFF, Vladimir, nicknamed **Popski** (1897–1951), soldier and author, of Russian parentage, born in Belgium and educated in England, joined the British army and from 1940 to 1942 served with the Long Range Desert Group and the Libyan Arab Force. In October 1942, with the sanction of the army, he formed his own force, the famous Popski's Private Army which carried out spectacular raids behind the German lines. He rose to the rank of lieutenant-colonel and was decorated for bravery by Britain, France and Belgium. His book *Private Army* was published in 1950. See Willett's *Popski* (1954) and Yunnie's *Warriors on Wheels* (1959).

PENN, William (1644–1718), English Quaker and founder of Pennsylvania, the son of Admiral William Penn, was born in London. He was sent down from Christ Church, Oxford, for having become a zealous Quaker; and his father sent him to the Continent, in the hope that the gaiety of French life would alter the bent of his mind. He returned a polished man of the world, having served for a little in the Dutch war. In 1666 the admiral dispatched him to look after his estates in Cork, but he was imprisoned for attending a Quaker meeting in Cork. He returned to England a thoroughgoing Quaker. In 1668 he was thrown into the Tower for his *Sandy Foundation Shaken*, in which he attacked the ordinary doctrines of the Trinity. While in prison he wrote the most popular of his books, *No Cross, no Crown*, and *Innocency with her Open Face*, a vindication of himself that contributed to his liberation, obtained through the intervention of his father's friend, the Duke of York. In September 1670 Admiral Penn died, leaving his son an estate of £1500 a year. In the same month he was again imprisoned for preaching; and in 1671 he was sent to Newgate for six months. He took advantage of the Indulgence for making preaching tours, and he visited Holland and Germany for the advancement of Quakerism. In 1681 he obtained from the crown, in lieu of his father's claim upon it, a grant of territory in North America, called Pensilvania in honour of the old admiral; his desire being to establish a home for his co-religionists. Penn with his emigrants sailed for the Delaware in 1682, and in November held his famous interview with the Indians on the site of Philadelphia. He planned the city of Philadelphia, and for two years governed the colony wisely, with full tolerance for all that was not regarded as wicked by Puritanism (card-playing, play-going, &c., being strictly forbidden as 'evil sports and games'). Penn returned to England to exert himself in favour of his persecuted brethren at home. His influence with James II and his belief in his good intentions were curiously strong. The suspicion that Penn allowed himself to be used as a tool is not justified by any known facts. Through his exertions, in 1686 all persons imprisoned on account of their religious opinions (including 1200 Quakers) were released. After the accession of William III Penn was repeatedly accused of treasonable adherence to the deposed king, but was finally acquitted in 1693. In 1699 he paid a second visit to Pennsylvania, where his

constitution had proved unworkable, and had to be much altered. He did something to mitigate the evils of slavery, but held Negro slaves himself. He departed for England in 1701. His last years were embittered by disputes about boundaries, &c.; he was even, in financial embarrassment, thrown for nine months into the Fleet in 1708. He was twice married, and wrote over forty works and pamphlets. See Lives by Dixon (1856), Dobrée (1932), Vulliamy (1934), Monastier (1944) and Peare (1960).

PENNANT, Thomas (1726–98), Welsh traveller, was born at Downing near Holywell, Flintshire. In 1744 he went to Oxford, but left without a degree. His many tours included visits to Ireland (1754), the Continent (1765), Scotland (1769 and 1772), and the Isle of Man (1774), besides rambles through England and Wales. He was F.R.S. and D.C.L. From boyhood a naturalist, for years a correspondent of Linnaeus, Pennant published *British Zoology* (1765–77), *British Quadrupeds* (1771), *Arctic Zoology* (1785), *History of London* (1790), &c. He is remembered by his *Tours in Scotland* (1771–75) and Wales (1778–81). See his *Literary Life* by himself (1793), and the memoir in Rhys's edition of the *Tours in Wales* (1883).

PENNELL, Joseph (1860–1926), American etcher and book illustrator, born at Philadelphia, lived much in England. He wrote on book illustration and produced illustrated tours on the Thames, in Provence, in Hungary and elsewhere, and a Life of Whistler (1908). His wife, **Elizabeth Robins** (1855–1936), an authoress, many of whose books he illustrated, wrote, among others, biographies of *Mary Wollstonecraft* (1884), and *Charles Godfrey Leland* (1906).

PENNEY, Baron William George (1909–   ), British physicist, born in Gibraltar, became professor of Mathematics at the Imperial College of Science in South Kensington, where he had been a student before going to the Universities of Wisconsin and Cambridge. He became well known for his research work on nuclear weapons and was an observer when the atomic bomb was dropped on Nagasaki. In 1947 he was appointed chief superintendent of armament research at the Ministry of Supply, made a K.B.E. in 1952, and became director of the Atomic Weapons Research Establishment at Aldermaston (1953–59). In 1959 he headed the British team of scientists in the 'technical working group' set up by the Geneva three-power conference, and was deputy chairman (1961), and then chairman (1964–67), of the U.K. Atomic Energy Authority. He was created a life peer in 1967 and became rector of Imperial College.

PENNY, Thomas (d. 1589), English clergyman and botanist, educated at Cambridge, was a prebendary of St Paul's. His interest in botany and entomology was such that he assisted Gesner (q.v.) in his work. After his death his drawings passed into the possession of Moffet, who made use of them in his *Insectorum Theatrum* (1634).

PENRY, John (1559–93), Welsh Puritan pamphleteer, born in Brecknockshire, graduated at both Cambridge and Oxford, and set

up (c. 1588) a printing press which turned out anti-Episcopal tracts under the name Martin Marprelate. Hounded from place to place, the press was ultimately discovered, but Penry escaped to Edinburgh (1590). Venturing to London in 1592, he was arrested and hanged.

PENTREATH, Dolly (1685–1777), reputed to be the last person to speak Cornish (others say Bernard Victor, d. 1875), an itinerant fishwife and fortune-teller, and wife of a man called Jeffery. She was born and died at Mousehole on Mount's Bay. See Jago's *Ancient Language of Cornwall* (1882).

PÉPIN, or **Pippin,** *pay-pi* or *pi-peen,* the name of a Frankish family of which the following became rulers: (1) **of Héristal** (d. 714), was mayor of the palace in Austrasia, to which he added after 687 the similar vice-royalties of Neustria and Burgundy, and called himself ' Duke and Prince of the Franks '. He was their real ruler during several reigns. He was father of Charles Martel. (2) (c. 715–68), surnamed ' the Short ', king of the Franks, younger son of Charles Martel (q.v.) and father of Charlemagne (q.v.), founded the Frankish dynasty of the Carlovingians. Childeric, the last of the Merovingians, having been deposed, Pépin was chosen king in his stead (751). When Pope Stephen III was hard pressed by the Longobards, Pépin led an army into Italy (754), compelled the Longobard Aistulf to become his vassal, and laid the foundation of the temporal sovereignty of the popes (756). The rest of his life was spent in semicrusading wars against Saxons and Saracens. (3) (777–810), son of Charlemagne, was crowned king of Italy in 781, and fought against the Avars, Slavs, Saxons and Saracens.

PEPLOE, Samuel John (1871–1935), Scottish artist, was born in Edinburgh. As a mature and established painter, he went to Paris in 1911 and returned to Edinburgh to remodel his style in accordance with Fauve colouring and Cézannesque analysis of form. His later still-life paintings brought him fame as a colourist. See the study by S. Cursiter (1947).

PEPPER, John Henry (1821–1900), English inventor, born in Westminster, became in 1848 analytical chemist at the Royal Polytechnic, and wrote several handbooks of popular science. He is best known as the improver and exhibitor of ' Pepper's Ghost ' (see DIRCKS). Pepper travelled with this show in America and Australia, and became public analyst at Brisbane.

PEPUSCH, Johann Christoph (John Christopher), *pe'poosh* (1667–1752), German composer and musical theorist, born in Berlin, was appointed to the Prussian court at the age of fourteen, but subsequently emigrated to Holland and settled in London in his early thirties. Best known as the arranger of the music for Gay's *The Beggar's Opera* from popular and traditional sources, Pepusch was a prolific composer of music for the theatre and church as well as of instrumental works.

PEPYS, Samuel (1633–1703), English Admiralty official and diarist, son of a London tailor, was educated at St Paul's School and Magdalene College, Cambridge. In Com-

monwealth times he lived poorly with his young wife whom he married in 1655, but after the Restoration, through the patronage of the Earl of Sandwich, his father's cousin, he rose rapidly in the naval service and became secretary to the Admiralty in 1672. He lost his office on account of his alleged complicity in the Popish Plot, 1679, but was reappointed in 1684 and in that same year became president of the Royal Society. At the Revolution he was again ' outed '. Probably he did not feather his nest at the Admiralty more than was customary in those times, and his famous Diary attests his punctilious regard for the efficiency of the service. The Diary, which ran from January 1, 1660, to May 31, 1669, the year his wife died and his eyesight failed him, is of extraordinary interest, both as the personal record (and confessions) of a man of abounding love of life, and for the vivid picture it gives of contemporary life, including naval administration and Court intrigue. The highlights are probably the accounts of the three disasters of the decade—the great plague, the burning of London and the sailing up the Thames by the Dutch fleet (1665–67). The veracity of the Diary has been accepted. It was written in cipher, in which form it remained at Magdalene College till 1825, when it was deciphered by John Smith and edited by Lord Braybrooke. The complete edition was edited by Henry B. Wheatley in 4 vols. (1893–99). See, among others, J. B. Tanner, *Mr Pepys: an Introduction to the Diary* (1925), and studies by Arthur Bryant (1947–49).

PERCEVAL, Spencer (1762–1812), British statesman, second son of the second Earl of Egmont, was educated at Harrow and Trinity, Cambridge, and called to the bar in 1786. He soon obtained a reputation as a diligent lawyer, in 1796 entered parliament for Northampton, and became a strong supporter of Pitt. In the Addington administration he became solicitor-general in 1801 and attorney-general in 1802, and in the Portland administration of 1807 chancellor of the Exchequer, and was even then the real head of the government, being trusted by George III for his opposition to Catholic claims. At Portland's death in 1809 Perceval became premier also, and retained office till his tragic death, when he was shot while entering the lobby of the House of Commons by a bankrupt Liverpool broker, John Bellingham, who was later hanged for the murder. See Lives by Spencer Walpole (1874) and P. Treherne (1909).

PERCIER, Charles, *per-syay* (1764–1838), French architect, born in Paris, who, with his friend and partner, Pierre Fontaine (1762–1853), was among the first to create buildings in the Empire style. For Napoleon they remodelled the Malmaison, worked on the Rue de Rivoli, the palace of St Cloud, the Louvre and the Tuileries, and in the gardens there erected the Arc du Carrousel in 1807. See M. Fouché, *Percier et Fontaine* (1905).

PERCIVAL, (1) James Gates (1795–1856), American poet, born at Berlin, Conn., graduated at Yale in 1815, studied botany and medicine, and became professor of Chemistry at West Point in 1824, geologist of Wisconsin in 1854. His poems *Prometheus* and *Clio* appeared in 1822–27; and *The Dream of a Day* in 1843. See Life by J. H. Ward (1866), and a study in M. Rukeyser's *Willard Gibbs* (1942).

(2) **John** (1834–1918), English schoolmaster, born **a grocer's son**, became headmaster of Clifton in 1862, president of Trinity, Oxford, in 1878, headmaster of Rugby in 1887, and Bishop of Hereford in 1895.

PERCY, (1) a noble north of England family, whose founder, **William de Percy** (*c*. 1030–96), came with the Conqueror, and received lands in Yorkshire, Lincolnshire, Hampshire and Essex. **Richard** (*c*. 1170–1244) was one of the barons who extorted Magna Carta. **Henry** (*c*. 1272–1315) aided Edward I in subduing Scotland, was governor of Galloway; driven out of Turnberry Castle by Robert Bruce, he received from Edward II a grant of Bruce's forfeited earldom of Carrick and the wardenship of Bamburgh and Scarborough Castles. In 1309 he purchased from Bishop Antony Bek the barony of Alnwick, the chief seat of the family ever since. His son defeated and captured David II of Scotland at Neville's Cross (1346); his grandson fought at Crécy; his great-grandson, **Henry** (1342–1408), fourth Lord Percy of Alnwick, in 1377 was made marshal of England and Earl of Northumberland. His eldest son, **Henry** (1364–1403), was the famous Hotspur whom Douglas defeated at Otterburn (1388), and who himself fell fighting against Henry IV at Shrewsbury, where his uncle, **Sir Thomas, Earl of Worcester** (q.v.), was captured and soon after executed. The father, who had helped Henry of Lancaster to the throne, was dissatisfied with Henry's gratitude, and with his sons plotted the insurrection. Later he joined Archbishop Scrope's plot, and fell at Bramham Moor (1408), when his honours were forfeited, but restored (1414) to his grandson, who became High Constable of England, and fell in the first battle of St Albans (1455). His son, the third earl, fell at Towton (1461). The title and estates were now given to a brother of Warwick, the kingmaker, but in 1469 Henry, son of the third earl, was restored by Edward IV. The sixth earl, who had in youth been the lover of Anne Boleyn, died childless in 1537, and as his brother, Sir Thomas Percy, had been attainted and executed for his share in the Pilgrimage of Grace, the title of Duke of Northumberland was conferred by Edward VI upon John Dudley, Earl of Warwick, who in turn was attainted and executed under Mary in 1553. In 1557 Mary granted the earldom to **Thomas Percy** (1528–72), son of the attainted Sir Thomas. A devoted Catholic, he took part in the Rising of the North, and was beheaded at York. His brother **Henry**, eighth earl, became involved in Throgmorton's conspiracy in favour of Mary Stuart, and was committed to the Tower, where he was found dead in bed (1585). His son, ninth earl, was imprisoned for fifteen years in the Tower, and fined £30,000 on a baseless suspicion of being privy to the Gunpowder Plot. His son, tenth earl, fought for parliament in the Civil War; on

the death of his son (1670), eleventh earl, the male line of the family became extinct. Charles II created his third bastard by the Duchess of Cleveland Earl, and afterwards Duke of Northumberland, but he died childless in 1716. The eleventh earl's daughter, Baroness Percy, married Charles Seymour, Duke of Somerset; their son was created in 1749 Baron Warkworth and Earl of Northumberland, with remainder to his son-in-law, Sir Hugh Smithson (1715–86), who assumed the name of Percy, and in 1766 was created Duke of Northumberland. See E. B. de Fonblanque's *House of Percy* (privately printed, 1887), and Brenan's *House of Percy* (1902).

(2) **Eustace, 1st Baron of Newcastle** (1887–1958), English statesman, seventh son of the Duke of Northumberland, entered the diplomatic service and was for several years in Washington. Member of parliament for Hastings from 1921 to 1937, he became president of the Board of Education (1924–1929) and minister without portfolio (1935–1936). His books include *The Responsibilities of the League* (1920), *Education at the Crossroads* (1930), *Democracy on Trial* (1931) and *The Heresy of Democracy* (1954). *Some Memories* was published in the year of his death.

(3) and (4) **Reuben** and **Sholto**, were the names under which Thomas Byerley (d. 1826) and Joseph Clinton Robertson (d. 1852) published *The Percy Anecdotes* (1820–23).

(5) **Thomas** (1729–1811), English antiquary, poet and churchman, born, a grocer's son, at Bridgnorth, in 1746 entered Christ Church, Oxford, and in 1753 became vicar of Easton Maudit, Northamptonshire, and in 1756 also rector of Wilby. He produced *Hau Kiou Choaun* (1761), a Chinese novel translated from the Portuguese, and *Miscellaneous Pieces relating to the Chinese* (1762), as well as anonymously *Runic Poetry translated from Icelandic* (1763), prompted by the success of Macpherson, and *A New Translation of the Song of Solomon* (1764). In 1764 his friend Dr Johnson paid him a visit. In 1765 Percy published the *Reliques of Ancient English Poetry*. He had long been engaged in collecting old ballads from every quarter, and a large folio MS. of ballads had fallen accidentally into his hands. Of the 176 pieces in the first edition, only 45 (a good deal touched up) were taken from the MS., which was only printed in full by Dr Furnivall (1867–68), with Introductions by Professor Hales and himself. Made chaplain to the Duke of Northumberland and George III, Percy in 1770 published his translation of the *Northern Antiquities* of Paul Henri Mallet (q.v.). In 1771 Percy wrote the 'Hermit of Warkworth'. In 1778 he was appointed Dean of Carlisle, in 1782 Bishop of Dromore. See the Life by Pickford in Hales and Furnivall, and that by A. C. C. Gaussen (1908).

PERDICCAS (d. 321 B.C.), Macedonian general under Alexander the Great and virtually regent for his successors, was murdered by mutineers from his own army.

PEREDA, José María de, *pay-ray'*THa (1833–1906), Spanish novelist, 'the modern Cervantes', was born at Polanco near Santander.

His novels give a realistic picture of the people and scenery of the region where he was born and where much of his life was spent, an outstanding example being *Sotileza* (1885). Other novels are *Del Tal palo tal astilla* (1880), *Pedro Sanchez* (1883), and perhaps his finest, *Peñas arriba* (1895).

PEREGRINUS, Petrus (Peter the Pilgrim, Peter de Maricourt) (fl. 13th cent.), French scientist and soldier, a native of Picardy, a Crusader, was the first to mark the ends of a round natural magnet and to call them poles. He also invented a compass with a graduated scale.

PEREIRA, Jonathan, *pay-ray'ra* (1804–53), English pharmacologist, born in London, was lecturer on chemistry and physician to the London Hospital (1841), author of *Elements of Materia Medica* (1839–40), *Diet*, and *Polarised Light* (1843).

PEREIRE, orig. Pereira, Giacobbo Rodriguez, *pay-rayr'* (1715–80), Spanish-born inventor of a sign language for deaf-mutes, gave up business at Bordeaux to devote himself to his humanitarian work with such success that in 1749 he presented a pupil before the Paris Academy of Sciences and in 1759 was made a member of the Royal Society.

PERETZ, David (1906–), Bulgarian artist, born at Plovdiv, studied in Sofia, and worked in Paris under André Lhote. His paintings, of still life and Provençal landscape, are of thick impasto and vigorous colour.

PÉREZ, Antonio, *pay'rayth* (c. 1540–1611), Spanish statesman, secretary to Philip II. Don John of Austria having become an object of suspicion, Pérez procured, with the king's consent, the assassination of Escovedo, Don John's secretary and abettor (1578), who had threatened to tell the king of Pérez's love for the Princess Éboli. The family of Escovedo denounced Pérez, and though the king sought to shield him, he was arrested in July 1579, and ultimately forced to confess. Condemned to imprisonment for embezzlement, he escaped to Aragon, where he put himself under protection of its *fueros*. The king next got the Inquisition to apprehend him, but the people rose in tumult; at last (1591) Philip entered Aragon with an army and abolished the old constitutional privileges. Pérez escaped to Paris and to London, where he was the intimate of Bacon and the Earl of Essex. He spent his later years in Paris, and died there, in great poverty. See his own *Relaciones*, books by Mignet (5th ed. 1881) and J. Fitzmaurice-Kelly (1922).

PÉREZ DE AYALA, Ramón, *a-yah'la* (1881–1962), Spanish novelist, poet and critic, born at Oviedo, first attracted attention with his poetry when *La Paz der sendero* was published in 1904. A sequel volume appeared in 1916 under the title *El Sendero innumerable*. As a novelist he combines realism with beauty, best shown in the philosophical *Belarmino y Apolonio* (1921). Other novels include the humorous and satirical *Troteras y Danzaderas* (1913), the anti-Jesuit *A.M.D.G.* (1910), and perhaps his best, *Tigre Juan* (1924), which with *El Curandero de ru honra* appeared in English as *Tiger Juan* (1933).

Among his works of criticism are *Máscaras* and *Política y Toros*. He was ambassador to London from 1931 to 1936.

PÉREZ DE HITA, Ginés, *ee'ta* (1544–1619), Spanish writer and soldier who fought in the Moorish war in 1569–70 and wrote a semi-romantic history entitled *Historia de los bandos de los Zegríes y Abencérajes* in two parts (1595 and 1604). Known as *Las Guerras civiles de Granada*, it was republished in Madrid (1913–15).

PÉREZ GALDÓS, Benito (1843–1920), Spanish novelist and dramatist, born in the Canary Islands, was brought up in Madrid. Regarded as Spain's greatest novelist after Cervantes, he was deeply interested in his own country and its history. His short *Episodios nacionales*, of which there are forty-six, gives a vivid picture of 19th-century Spain from the viewpoint of the people. The longer novels included in the *Novelas españolas contemporáneas* number thirty-one, and in these the conflicts and ideas of the Europe of his day are recorded forcefully but often with humour. Some of these, including *Trafalgar*, *Gloria*, *Doña Perfecta*, *León Roch*, have been translated. His plays, many of them based on his novels, also achieved success. See L. B. Walton, *Pérez Galdós and the Spanish Novel of the 19th Century* (1928), and a study by H. C. Berkowitz (1948).

PERGOLESI, Giovanni Battista, *per-go-lay'zee* (1710–36), Italian musician, was born at Jesi near Ancona, and died at Naples. His first great works were the oratorio *San Guglielmo* (1731) and the operetta *La Serva Padrona* (1732). His last works were the cantata *Orfeo* and his great *Stabat Mater*. He also composed operas, oratorios, &c.

PERI, Jacopo, *pay'ree* (1561–1633), Italian composer, born in Rome, as a student became attached to the Medici family in Florence, and became the leading composer in a group of artists whose aim was to restore what they believed to be the true principles of Greek tragic declamation. Experimenting in instrumentally-accompanied declamatory style, they hit upon the principles of modern opera, a form which Peri exploited in a series of works, beginning with *Dafne* and *Euridice*, with libretti by the poet Rinuccini, historically accepted as the first genuine operas.

PERIANDER, Gr. Periandros (c. 665–585 B.C.), one of the Seven Wise Men of Greece, succeeded his father Cypselus as tyrant of Corinth (c. 625 B.C.). He conquered Epidaurus and Corcyra (Corfu).

PERICLES, *per'i-kleez* (c. 490–429 B.C.), Athenian statesman, born of distinguished parents, was carefully educated, and rapidly rose to the highest power as leader of the dominant democracy. About 463 he struck a great blow at the oligarchy by depriving the Areopagus of its most important political powers. His successful expeditions to the Thracian Chersonese and to Sinope, together with his numerous colonies, increased the naval supremacy of Athens. His greatest project was to form a grand Hellenic confederation to put an end to mutually destructive wars; but the Spartan aristocrats brought the scheme to nothing. Athens and Sparta were already in the mood which rendered the Peloponnesian war ineviable; but the first troubles were allayed by a thirty years' peace with Sparta (445). Cimon was now dead, and the next leaders of the aristocratic party sought in vain (in 444 B.C.) to overthrow the supremacy of Pericles by attacking him in the popular assembly for squandering the public money on buildings and in festivals and amusements. Thereafter Pericles reigned undisputed master in the city of Aeschylus, Sophocles, Euripides, Anaxagoras, Zeno, Protagoras, Socrates, as well as Myron and Phidias. In the Samian war (439) Pericles gained high renown as a naval commander. His enemies, who dared not attack himself, struck at him in the persons of his friends—Aspasia, Phidias, Anaxagoras. Greek architecture and sculpture under the patronage of Pericles reached perfection. To him Athens owed the Parthenon, the Erechtheum, the Propylaea, the Odeum and numberless other public and sacred edifices; he liberally encouraged music and the drama; and during his rule industry and commerce flourished. At length in 431 the inevitable Peloponnesian war broke out between Athens and Sparta. The plague ravaged the city in 430, and in the autumn of 429 Pericles himself died after a lingering fever. See Thucydides and Plutarch; the histories of Greece by Thirlwall, Grote, and Curtius; Watkiss Lloyd's *Age of Pericles* (1875); A. J. Grant's *Greece in the Age of Pericles* (1893); *Cambr. Anc. Hist.* v (1927); studies by Abbott (1891), Mackenzie (1937), de Sanctis (1944), Burn (1948).

PÉRIER, Casimir, *payr-yay* (1777–1832), French statesman, born at Grenoble, founded a Paris bank with his brother Antoine Scipion (1776–1821). He secured a seat in the Chamber of Deputies in 1817, was minister of finance in 1828, president of the council in 1830, and premier in 1831. For his son, see CASIMIR-PÉRIER.

PERKIN, Sir William Henry (1838–1907), English chemist, born in London and knighted in 1906, was assistant to Hofmann, and in 1856 made the discovery of mauve, which led to the foundation of the aniline dye industry. His son and namesake (1860–1929) became in 1892 professor of Chemistry at Manchester, in 1912 at Oxford.

PERMEKE, Constant, *per'may-kè* (1886–1951), Belgian painter and sculptor, born at Antwerp, studied at Bruges and Ghent, and later settled in Laethem-Saint-Martin, where he became the leader of the modern Belgian Expressionist school. After 1936, he concentrated on sculpture.

PERÓN, (1) Juan Domingo (1895–   ), Argentine soldier and statesman, born in Lobos, took a leading part in the army revolt of 1943, achieved power and great popularity among the masses (because of social reforms), and became (1946) president of a virtually totalitarian régime. In 1955, having antagonized the Church, the armed forces and many of his former supporters among the labour movements, he was deposed and exiled. See T. Owen, *Perón: His Rise and Fall* (1957).

(2) **Maria Eva Duarte De** (1919–52), wife of (1), born at Los Toldos, Buenos Aires, was an actress before her marriage in 1945.

She became a powerful political influence, agitating for women's suffrage, and acquiring control of newspapers and business companies. She founded the Eva Perón Foundation for the promotion of social welfare.

PEROSI, Lorenzo (1872–1956), Italian priest and composer, the son of a musician at Tortona in Piedmont, was ordained priest, and is author of *The Resurrection of Lazarus*, *The Passion of Christ* and other oratorios.

PÉROUSE. See LA PÉROUSE.

PEROWNE, John James Stewart (1823–1904), English prelate, the son of a missionary in Bengal, educated at Corpus, Cambridge, held office at King's College (London), Lampeter, Trinity College (Cambridge), became Dean of Peterborough in 1878. From 1875 he had been also Hulsean professor of Divinity at Cambridge. In 1891–1901 he was Bishop of Worcester. Perowne sat on the committee for the revision of the Old Testament. His works include a Commentary on the Psalms (1864–68), Hulsean Lectures on *Immortality* (1869) and *Remains* of Thirlwall (1878).

PERRAULT, Charles, *per-ō* (1628–1703), French writer, was born at Paris, studied law, and filled from 1654 till 1664 an easy post under his brother, the receiver-general of Paris. In 1663 he became a secretary or assistant to Colbert, through whom he was admitted to the Academy in 1671. His poem, *Le Siècle de Louis XIV*, read to the Academy, and Boileau's outspoken criticisms of it, opened up the dispute about the relative merits of the ancients and moderns; to the modern cause Perrault contributed his poor *Parallèle des anciens et des modernes* (1688–1696), and his *Hommes illustres du siècle de Louis XIV* (1696–1700). His *Mémoires* appeared in 1769. All his writings would have been forgotten but for his eight inimitable fairy-tales, the *Histoires ou Contes du temps passé* (1697), including ' The Sleeping Beauty ', ' Red Riding Hood ' and ' Bluebeard '. There are editions by Giraud (1865), Lefèvre (1875), Paul Lacroix (1876) and Andrew Lang (1888). See Deschanel's *Boileau, Perrault* (1888).

PERRET, Auguste, *per-ay* (1874–1954), French architect, born in Brussels, spent most of his life in Paris, where he pioneered the use of reinforced concrete in a number of buildings, mainly in the neo-classical style, including the Théâtre des Champs Élysées and the Musée des travaux publics. He also designed churches at le Raincy and Montmagny. See study by P. Jamot (Paris 1927).

PERRIN, Jean Baptiste, *pe-rî* (1870–1942), French physicist, born at Lille, educated at Paris, was from 1910 professor of Physical Chemistry at the University of Paris. For important researches in molecular physics and radioactivity, and for his discovery of the equilibrium of sedimentation he was awarded the Nobel prize in 1926.

PERRON, General (really **Pierre Aullier**) (1755–1834), French military adventurer, was born in Sarthe, went as a soldier to the Île-de-France, served for a time in the navy, deserted and took service with various native Indian princes. In 1790 he obtained an appointment under his countryman De Boigne, then commanding Sindia's forces.

He succeeded De Boigne, and exercised enormous military and political influence in India, but was crushed in 1803 by Lake at Laswari, and by Wellesley at Assaye. He returned the same year to France. See H. Compton's *European Military Adventurers of Hindustan* (1892).

PERRONNEAU, Jean Baptiste, *per-on-nō* (c. 1715–83), French pastellist painter, best known for his *Girl with a Kitten* painted in 1745 and now in the National Gallery, London. He travelled widely in Europe and died in Amsterdam.

PERROT, (1) Georges, *per-ō* (1832–1914), French archaeologist, travelled in Greece and Asia Minor, in 1877 became professor of Archaeology in the University of Paris and in 1833 director of the École normale. He wrote on Crete (1866) and archaeology, especially, with Charles Chipiez, a *History of Art in Antiquity* (in Egypt, Chaldaea, Primitive Greece, &c.; 1882 *et seq.*).

(2) **Sir John,** *-ot* (c. 1527–92), commonly reputed to be a son of Henry VIII, was lord deputy of Ireland during the troublous time there of Queen Elizabeth, and died in the Tower, under trial for treason with Spain.

PERRY, Oliver Hazard (1785–1819), American sailor, born at South Kingston, Rhode Island, defeated a British squadron on Lake Erie in 1813. See Lives by Mackenzie (1843) and Lyman (1905).

PERSE. See ST JOHN PERSE.

PERSHING, John Joseph (1860–1948), American soldier, born in Linn County, Mo., was first a schoolteacher, went to West Point, and became military instructor there and at Nebraska University. He served in the Cuban War in 1898, in the Japanese army during the Russo-Japanese War (1904–05) and was in Mexico during World War I. In 1917 he was appointed c.-in-c. of the American Expeditionary Force in Europe and chief of staff, U.S. Army, 1921–24.

PERSIGNY, Jean Gilbert Victor Fialin, Duc de, *per-seen-yee* (1808–72), French politician, born at Saint-Germain Lespinasse, expelled from the army in 1831, secured the favour of Louis Napoleon, and had the chief hand in the affairs of Strasbourg (1836) and Boulogne (1840), where he was captured, and condemned to twenty years' imprisonment. Released in 1848, he strongly supported his patron then and in 1851, in 1852–55 and 1860–63 was minister of the Interior, in 1855–60 ambassador to England, and a senator until the fall of the empire. See his *Mémoires* (1896), and study by Chrétien (1943).

PERSIUS (Aulus Persius Flaccus) (A.D. 34–62), Roman satirist, born of a distinguished equestrian family at Volaterrae in Etruria, was educated in Rome, where he came under Stoic influence. But he died before completing his twenty-eighth year. He wrote fastidiously and sparingly, leaving at his death six admirable satires, the whole not exceeding 650 hexameter lines. These were published by his friend Caesius Bassus after his death. Dryden and others have translated them into verse.

PERTHES, family of German publishers:
(1) **Friedrich Christoph** (1772–1843), nephew of (2), started business in Hamburg in 1796,

and soon was in the front rank of publishers. An ardent patriot, he in 1810 started the *National Museum*, and resisted the establishment of French authority in Germany. After the peace, he removed in 1821 to Gotha. See Life (7th ed. 1892; trans. 1878) by his son Clemens Theodor.

(2) **Johann Georg Justus** (1749–1816), established a publishing-house at Gotha in 1785, which acquired, in the hands of his sons, a great reputation as a geographical institute; it issued *Petermann's Mitteilungen,* Stieler's *Atlas,* books of travel and geography, and the *Almanach de Gotha.*

PERTINAX, Publius Helvius (A.D. 126–193), Roman emperor, born at Alba-Pompeia in Liguria. When the assassins of Commodus forced him to accept the purple, his accession was hailed with delight; but he was slain by rebellious praetorians three months after.

PERUGINO ('The Perugian'), *per-oo-jee'nō* (c. 1450–1523), the usual name of the painter Pietro Vannucci, born at Città della Pieve in Umbria, who established himself in Perugia. He executed works, no longer extant, at Florence, Perugia (1475) and Cerqueto (1478). At Rome, where he went about 1483, Sixtus IV employed him in the Sistine Chapel; his fresco of *Christ giving the Keys to Peter* is the best of those still visible, others being destroyed to make way for Michelangelo's *Last Judgment.* At Florence (1486–1499) he had Raphael for his pupil. At Perugia (1499–1504) he adorned the Hall of the Cambio; after 1500 his art visibly declined. In his second Roman sojourn (1507–12) he also, along with other painters, decorated the Stanze of the Vatican; and one of his works there, the Stanza del Incendio, was the only fresco spared when Raphael was commissioned to repaint the walls and ceilings. He died of the plague near Perugia. See also BARTOLI (2) and F. Canuti's *Il Perugino* (2 vols. 1931).

PERUTZ, Max Ferdinand (1914–), Austrian-born British scientist, graduated at Vienna, came to Cambridge in 1936 to carry on research at the Cavendish Laboratory, where he began work on the structure of haemoglobin and became director of the Medical Research Council's unit for Molecular Biology. Twenty-five years' work in this field resulted in the joint award to Perutz and Kendrew (q.v.) of the Nobel chemistry prize for 1962.

PERUZZI, Baldassare Tommaso, *pay-root'see* (1481–1536), Italian architect, was born at Ancajano near Volterra. In 1503 he went to Rome, where he designed the Villa Farnesina, and painted frescoes in the Church of S. Maria della Pace in 1516. After a short period as city architect in Siena, he returned to Rome in 1535 and designed the Palazzo Massimo. He was influenced by Bramante and ancient Italian architecture; drawings and designs by him are in the Uffizi Gallery.

PESTALOZZI, Johann Heinrich, *-lot'see* (1746–1827), Swiss educationalist, born at Zürich, devoted himself to the children of the very poor. Believing in the moralizing virtue of agricultural occupations and rural environment, he chose a farm in the canton Aargau upon which to live with his collected waifs and strays; but owing to faulty domestic organization it had to be abandoned after a five years' struggle (1780). He then for a time withdrew from practical life, to think out the educational problem, and wrote his *Evening Hours of a Hermit* (1780). Then came a social novel, *Leonard and Gertrude* (1781). In 1798 he opened his orphan school at Stanz, but at the end of eight months it was broken up. He next took a post in the people's school at Berthoud (Burgdorf), in canton Bern, only to be ejected from it by the jealous senior master. In partnership with others, and under the patronage of the Swiss government, he opened a school of his own at Berthoud. While there he published *How Gertrude Educates her Children* (1801), the recognized exposition of the Pestalozzian method, setting forth that the development of human nature should be in dependence upon natural laws, with which it is the business of education to comply, observation being the method by which all objects of knowledge are brought home to us. In 1805 Pestalozzi moved his school to Yverdon, and applied his method in a large secondary school. His incapacity in practical affairs brought the school down step by step till it was closed in 1825. Pestalozzi addressed to mankind the *Song of the Swan*, a last educational prayer, and withdrew to Brugg, where he died. See books by Green (1913), Anderson (1932), Reinhart (1945) and Silber (1960).

PÉTAIN, Henri Philippe Omer, *pay-tl* (1856–1951), Marshal of France, born at Cauchyà-la-Tour, passed through St Cyr to a commission in the *chasseurs alpins*. As a junior officer, his confidential report was marked, ' If this officer rises above the rank of major it will be a disaster for France '; but seniority brought him the military governorship of Paris and appointments on the instructional staff. A temporary brigadier in 1914, by 1916 he was in command of an army corps and entrusted with the defence of Verdun. Succeeding as commander-in-chief in 1917, his measures of appeasement, while ' puttying-up ' the widespread mutinies that had followed on General Nivelle's disastrous offensive, ended by virtually removing the French army as a fighting force from the war. Minister for war in 1934, his eager sponsorship of the useless Maginot Line defence system only too faithfully reflected the defeatist spirit of contemporary France. With the French collapse in early 1940, he succeeded M. Reynaud as the head of the government and immediately sought terms from the Germans. Convinced that France could ' only be regenerated through suffering ', his administration at Vichy was the tool of such outright collaborationists as Laval and Deat. With the liberation of France Pétain was brought to trial, his death sentence for treason being commuted to life imprisonment on the Île de Yeu. He died in captivity in 1951. See ' Pertinax ', *The Gravediggers of France* (1944), and Life by G. Bolton (1957).

PETAVIUS, Dionysius, or **Denys Petau** (1583–1652), French theologian, born at Orleans, became in 1621 professor of Theology in Paris. In 1646 he retired and

devoted himself to the completion of about fifty works in philology, history and theology. An ardent Jesuit, among his learned writings are *Rationarium Temporum* (1634) and *De Theologicis Dogmatibus* (1644–50).

PETER, St, apostle, named originally **Symeon** or **Simon,** was of Bethsaida, but during the public ministry of Jesus had his house at Capernaum. Originally a fisherman, he soon became leader amongst the twelve apostles, regarded by Jesus with particular favour and affection. He was the spokesman of the rest on the day of Pentecost, he was the first to baptise a Gentile convert, and he took a prominent part in the council at Jerusalem. At Antioch he for a time worked in harmony with Paul, but ultimately the famous dispute arose (Gal. ii. 11–21) which, with other causes, led to the termination of Paul's ministry in that city. Bauer regarded him as the head of the Judaic party in opposition to the wider Pauline school. Peter's missionary activity seems to have extended to Pontus, Cappadocia, Galatia, Asia and Bithynia. That he suffered martyrdom is clear from John xxi. 18, 19, and is confirmed by ecclesiastical tradition: Eusebius says he was impaled or crucified with his head downward; as to the place, tradition from the end of the 2nd century mentions Rome. But the comparatively late tradition which assigns him a continuous bishopric of twenty-five years in Rome from A.D. 42 to A.D. 67 is unhistorical. Many distinguished scholars (Protestant) deny that Peter ever was in Rome. The first Epistle of Peter is usually accepted as genuine, but not the second. Holtzmann's *Einleitung* (1886), Salmon (*Introduction*) and Weiss defend the genuineness of both. See Littledale's *Petrine Claims* (1889); Lightfoot's *Apostolic Fathers*; Döllinger's *First Age of the Church*; Schmid's *Petrus in Rom*; Lipsius, *Die apokryphen Apostelgeschichten* (1883–90); Foakes-Jackson's monograph (1927); Selwyn's commentary (1946); Beare (1947).

PETER THE CRUEL. See PEDRO.

PETER, the name of 3 emperors of Russia:

Peter I, the Great (1672–1725), emperor of Russia, was the son of the Tzar Alexei, and was born at Moscow. His father died in 1676, leaving the throne to his eldest son, Feodor, Peter's half-brother, who, dying in 1682, named Peter as his successor, to the exclusion of his own full brother, Ivan, who was weakminded. This step provoked an insurrection of the ' streltzi ' or militia, fomented by Ivan's sister, the grand-duchess Sophia, who secured the coronation (July 1682) of Ivan and Peter as joint rulers, and her own appointment as regent; and Peter was put under the charge of a capable tutor, Lefort, a Genevese. In 1689, on his marriage to Eudoxia, Peter called upon his sister to resign. At first worsted in the struggle, he was soon joined by the foreigners in the Russian service, with Patrick Gordon (q.v.) and Lefort at their head; and the streltzi flocking to his standard, Sophia resigned the contest, and was shut up in a convent, where she died in 1704. Peter gave Ivan nominal supremacy and precedence, reserving the power for himself. Ivan died in 1696. Peter's first care was to organize an army on

European principles. He also laboured to create a navy, both armed and mercantile. But at this time Russia had only one port, Archangel being shut out from the Baltic by Sweden and Poland; so, for his fleet's sake, Peter declared war against Turkey, and took (1696) the city of Azov. Peter was eager to see for himself the countries for which civilization had done so much; and, after repressing a revolt of the streltzi, he left Russia in April 1697, in the train of an embassy of which Lefort was the head. He visited the three Baltic provinces, Prussia and Hanover, reaching Amsterdam, where, and at Zaandam, he worked as a common shipwright; he also studied astronomy, natural philosophy, geography, and even anatomy and surgery. For three months at London and Deptford, he amassed information, and from England he carried (1698) English engineers, artificers, surgeons, artisans, artillerymen, &c., to the number of 500. From Vienna a formidable rebellion of the streltzi recalled him to Russia. General Gordon had already crushed the revolt, and Peter finally broke up the institution that had given him so much trouble. The Empress Eudoxia, as associated with the conspiracy, which had been the work of the anti-reform party, was divorced and shut up in a convent. Peter put the press on a proper footing, published translations of famous foreign books, and established naval and other schools. Trade with foreign countries was permitted, or even insisted upon. Many changes in dress, manners and etiquette were introduced and enforced and the national church was reorganized. In 1700 Peter, with Poland and Denmark, attacked Sweden, but was defeated at Narva; yet he quietly appropriated a portion of Ingria, in which he laid the foundation of the new capital, St Petersburg (1703), which soon became the Russian commercial depot for the Baltic. In the long contest with Sweden the Russians were almost always defeated; but at last the Swedish king, Charles XII, was totally routed at Pultowa in 1709. Peter seized the whole of the Baltic provinces and a portion of Finland in 1710. He now prepared for strife with the Turks, who, at the instigation of Charles XII, had declared war against him. In this contest Peter was reduced to great straits, but a treaty was concluded (1711) by which Peter lost only Azov and the territory belonging to it. The war against Sweden in Pomerania was pushed on with the greater vigour. In 1712 he married his mistress, Catharine (see CATHARINE I), and the government was transferred to St Petersburg. In 1716–17, in company with the tsarina, he made another tour of Europe. Soon after this his son Alexis, who had opposed some of his father's reforms, was condemned to death, and died in prison. Many nobles implicated in his plans were punished with savage barbarity. In 1721 peace was made with Sweden, which definitely ceded the Baltic provinces, Ingria and part of Finland. In 1722 Peter commenced a war with Persia, and secured three Caspian provinces. During his last years he was chiefly engaged in beautifying and improving

his new capital and carrying out plans for the diffusion of knowledge and education. In the autumn of 1724 he was seized with a serious illness and died soon after. Catharine succeeded him. See Russian Lives by Golikov (1797) and Ustjalov (1858–63), French by Waliszewski (trans. 1897), and English by Graham (1929), Schuyler (1944), Klynchevsky (trans. 1959) and Grey (1962).

Peter II (1715–30), grandson of Peter the Great and son of Alexis, succeeded Catharine I (1727), but died of smallpox.

Peter III (1728–62), grandson of Peter the Great (son of his eldest daughter Anna, wife of the Duke of Holstein-Gottorp), was born at Kiel. In 1742 he was declared by the Tsarina Elizabeth (q.v.) her successor, and married Sophia-Augusta, a princess of Anhalt-Zerbst, who assumed the name of Catharina Alexeievna. Peter succeeded Elizabeth on her death in 1762 and his first act was to restore East Prussia to Frederick the Great, and to send to his aid 15,000 men. In 1762 a formidable conspiracy, headed by his wife, broke out, originating in the general discontent at the tsar's liberal innovations, the preference he showed for Germans, his indifference to the national religion, and his servility to Frederick the Great. He was declared to have forfeited his crown; his wife was proclaimed as Catharine II; and Peter was strangled by Orlov and some of the conspirators.

PETER II, king of Yugoslavia (1923–70). A grandson of Peter I, he succeeded his father, Alexander I, in 1934 with his uncle Prince Paul as regent. He assumed sovereignty in 1941 at the time of the German invasion, and lost his throne in 1945 when his country became a republic. His memoirs, *A King's Heritage*, appeared in 1955.

PETER LOMBARD. See LOMBARD.

PETER THE HERMIT (c. 1050–c. 1115), French monk, a preacher of the First Crusade, was born about the middle of the 11th century at Amiens. He served some time as a soldier, became a monk, and is said to have made a pilgrimage to Palestine before 1095. Legends have gathered round his name, and his importance has been exaggerated. The scheme of a crusade originated with the pope, Urban II, to whom Alexius Comnenus had appeared. At a council at Clermont in France (1096) it was definitely resolved upon. After Urban's famous sermon there many preachers, of whom Peter was one of the most notable, traversed Europe, preaching everywhere, and producing extraordinary enthusiasm by impassioned descriptions of the cruelties of the Turks towards pilgrims, and their desecration of the holy places. When the feelings of Europe had been sufficiently heated, four armies, amounting to 275,000 disorderly persons, started for Palestine. The first was cut to pieces in Bulgaria. The second, led by Peter in person, reached Asia Minor, but was utterly defeated by the Turks at Nicaea. The other two were exterminated by the Hungarians. A fifth crusading army, 600,000 strong, under renowned leaders, set out in 1096, and was joined by Peter the Hermit. During the siege of Antioch, which lasted seven months, the besiegers' ranks were fearfully thinned by famine and disease. Many lost heart, and among the deserters was Peter, who was several miles on his way home when he was brought back to undergo a public reprimand. He founded a monastery in France or the Low Countries.

PETER MARTYR, (1) (d. 1252), patron saint of the Inquisition, a Dominican of Verona, who, for the severity with which he exercised his inquisitorial functions, was slain at Como by the populace. He was canonized in 1253.

(2) Ital. **Pietro Martire Vermigli** (1500–62), reformer, born in Florence; became a canon of St Augustine and abbot at Spoleto and Naples. As visitor-general of his order in 1541 his rigour made him hateful to the dissolute monks, and he was sent to Lucca as prior, but soon fell under the suspicions of the Inquisition, and fled to Zürich (1542). At Strasbourg he was made Old Testament professor. In 1547 he came to England, and lectured at Oxford. Mary's accession drove him back to Strasbourg, and in 1555 to Zürich, where he died. His *Loci Communes* was printed at London in 1575. See C. Schmidt's *Leben der Väter der reformirten Kirche* (1858).

PETER MARTYR ANGLERIUS (1459–1525), Italian historian, born at Arona on Lago Maggiore, from 1487 rose to high ecclesiastical preferment in Spain, and was named Bishop of Jamaica. He wrote *De Orbe Novo* (1516), giving the first account of the discovery of America, *De Legatione Babylonica* (1516), and *Opus Epistolarum* (1530).

PETER THE WILD BOY (d. 1785), was found in July 1725 in a wood near Hameln in Hanover; ' he was walking on his hands and feet, climbing up trees like a squirrel, and feeding upon grass and moss of trees '. Brought to England in 1726 by George I, he could never be taught to articulate more than a few syllables, and was apparently an idiot. From 1737 till his death he lived on a Hertfordshire farm near Berkhampstead.

PETERBOROUGH, Charles Mordaunt, 3rd Earl of (c. 1658–1735), seems to have gone to Oxford in 1674, but by 1680 had been in (perhaps three) naval expeditions to the Barbary coast. In that year he began to take an active part in politics, identifying himself with the extreme Whig party; and on the accession of James II he was one of the earliest intriguers for his overthrow. After the Revolution he rose into high favour with the new king, being made first commissioner of the treasury and Earl of Monmouth. On William's departure for Ireland, he was one of the Queen's council of regency. He became hostile to the king and his measures, and was embroiled in plots that resulted (January 1697) in his committal to the Tower for three months. In 1705, in the war of the Spanish Succession, Monmouth, now Earl of Peterborough (by his uncle's death), was appointed to the command of an army of 4000 Dutch and English soldiers, with which he proceeded to Barcelona, captured the strong fort of Montjuich, and so reduced the city. Gerona,

Tarragona, Tolosa and Lérida opened their gates; and he reached Valencia early in February 1706. Meanwhile an army under the Duke of Anjou, the French claimant to the throne, and Marshal Tessé was closely investing Barcelona, which was at the same time blockaded by a fleet under the Count of Toulouse. Hurrying back, Peterborough himself took command of the English squadron, and drove Toulouse and his fleet from before the port. This success was followed by the raising of the siege. Now came a series of disputes with his colleagues and allies, recriminations and futile schemes and expeditions hither and thither. His imperious temper seems to have made him unfit for anything but supreme command, and led to his recall in March 1707. He was an intimate friend of Pope. The famous singer Anastasia Robinson (d. 1755), whom he married secretly, it is said, in 1722, was not publicly acknowledged as his countess till shortly before his death. See Lives by Russell (2 vols. 1887), Stebbing (1890), Ballard (1929).

PETERMANN, August (1822–78), Gotha cartographer and geographer. See PERTHES.

PETERS, (1) **Hugh** (1598–1660), English Independent divine, born in Cornwall, emigrated to Holland, then to New England, but returning in 1641, became army chaplain, and was active in parliamentarian politics. He published numerous pamphlets, and was executed for assumed complicity in the death of Charles I.

(2) **Karl** (1856–1918), German traveller and administrator, born at Neuhaus in Hanover, helped to establish German East Africa as a colony by his negotiations with native chiefs in 1884. In the same year he had formed the Gesellschaft für deutsche Kolonisation. Without the sanction of Bismarck, he claimed Uganda for Germany, was made commissioner of Kilimanjaro (1891–93), but his harsh treatment of the natives caused his recall. He returned to Africa in 1906 when gold was discovered in the Zambesi district.

PETERSEN, Nis (1897–1943), Danish poet and novelist, cousin of Kaj Munk (q.v.), born in South Jutland, rebelled against a strict upbringing, was a journalist, casual labourer and vagabond until he became famous for his novel of Rome in the time of Marcus Aurelius, *Sandalmagernes Gade* (trans. 1932 as *The Street of the Sandal-makers*). His later poetry has given him a high place among modern Danish writers.

PÉTION DE VILLENEUVE, Jérôme, *paytyõ dè veel-nœv* (c. 1756–94), French revolutionary, born at Chartres, in 1789 was elected deputy to the *Tiers État*. He was a prominent member of the Jacobin Club, and became a great ally of Robespierre. He was one of those who brought back the royal family from Varennes, advocated the deposition of the king, was elected mayor of Paris, and was the first president of the Convention. On the triumph of the Terrorists, he cast in his lot with the Girondists. He voted at the king's trial for death, but headed the unsuccessful attack on Robespierre. Proscribed on June 2, 1793, he escaped to Caen, and thence, on the failure of the attempt to make armed opposition against the Convention, to the Gironde, where his and Buzot's bodies were found in a cornfield, partly devoured by wolves. His *Oeuvres* fill 3 vols. (1792). See works by Regnault-Warin (1792) and Dauban (1866).

PETIT, *pé-tee*, (1) Alexis Thérèse (1791–1820), French physicist, born at Vesoul, H.-S., professor at the Lycée Bonaparte, enunciated with Dulong the 'law of Dulong and Petit' that for all elements the product of the specific heat and the atomic weight is the same. He died in Paris.

(2) Jean Louis (1674–1750), French surgeon, gained experience with the army and then lectured in Paris on anatomy and surgery. He was the inventor of the screw tourniquet and the first to operate with success for mastoiditis. He died in Paris.

(3) Roland (1924–), French choreographer and dancer, born in Paris, at nine began his studies at the Ballet de l'Opéra under Ricaux and Lifar and was its *premier danseur* (1943–44). Equally ambitious as a choreographer, he founded his own *troupe* in 1945 and in 1948 the world-famous company which bears his name. He has created a whole repertory of new ballet including *Le Rossignol et la Rose* (1944), a story by Oscar Wilde set to Schumann's music ; *Les Forains* (1945) with Cocteau ; *Le Jeune Homme et la Mort* (1946) which the latter had rehearsed strictly to jazz until the opening night when Bach was substituted ; and Anouilh's *Les Desmoiselles de la Nuit* (1948). He was also responsible for the ballet sequences in the film *Hans Christian Andersen* (1952).

PETIT DE JULLEVILLE, Louis (1841–1900), French critic, born in Paris, became professor at the École normale supérieure and the Sorbonne. He wrote an *Histoire du théâtre en France* and edited a monumental *Histoire de la langue et de la littérature française*.

PETITOT, Jean, *pet-ee-tō* (1607–91), Swiss painter in enamel, born in Geneva, after some years in Italy went to England and obtained the patronage of Charles I. After the king's execution he moved to Paris, where Louis XIV gave him lodgings in the Louvre and a share in his patronage. As a Protestant, he fled back to Geneva after the revocation of the Edict of Nantes (1685). Examples of his work may be seen in the South Kensington Museum.

PETO, Sir Samuel Morton (1809–89), English civil engineer and contractor, born at Woking, Surrey, attained great wealth as a contractor, laying railways in England, Russia, Norway, Algiers and Australia. He was a Liberal M.P. (1847–68), and was created a baronet in 1855. See *Memorial Sketch* (1893).

PETÖFI, Sandor, *pet'œ-fee* (1823–49), Hungarian poet, born at Kiskörös, was successively actor, soldier and literary hack, but by 1844 had secured his fame as a poet. In 1848 he threw himself into the revolutionary cause, writing numerous war-songs. He fell in battle at Segesvár. His poetry broke completely with the old pedantic style, and, warm with human and national feeling, began a new epoch in Hungarian literature. Selections have been translated by Bowring and others. He also wrote a novel, *The Hangman's Rope*, and translated Shakespeare's *Coriolanus*. See Lives by Opitz (1868), Fischer (1888) and Ferenczi (Budapest 1897).

PETRARCH, Francesco Petrarca (1304–74), Italian poet and scholar, one of the earliest and greatest of modern lyric poets, was the son of a Florentine notary, who, exiled (1302) along with Dante, settled in Arezzo, where Francesco was born. In 1312 his father went to Avignon, to the then seat of the papal court; and there and at Bologna the boy devoted himself with enthusiasm to the study of the classics. After his father's death Petrarch returned to Avignon (1326). Being without means, he became a churchman, though perhaps never a priest, and lived on the small benefices conferred by his many patrons. It was at this period (1327) that he first saw Laura (possibly Laure de Noves, married in 1325 to Hugo de Sade; she died, the mother of eleven children, in 1348). She inspired him with a passion which has become proverbial for its constancy and purity. Now began also his friendship with the powerful Roman family of the Colonnas. As the fame of Petrarch's learning and genius grew, his position became one of unprecedented consideration. His presence at their courts was competed for by the most powerful sovereigns of the day. He travelled repeatedly in France, Germany and Flanders, searching for MSS. In Liège he found two new orations of Cicero, in Verona a collection of his letters, in Florence an unknown portion of Quintilian. Invited by the senate of Rome on Easter Sunday, 1341, he ascended the capitol clad in the robes of his friend and admirer, King Robert of Naples, and there, after delivering an oration, he was crowned poet laureate. In 1353, after the death of Laura and his friend Cardinal Colonna, he left Avignon (and his country house at Vaucluse) for ever, disgusted with the corruption of the papal court. His remaining years were passed in various towns of Northern Italy, and at Arquà near Padua he died. Petrarch may be considered as the earliest of the great humanists of the Renaissance. He himself chiefly founded his claim to fame on his epic poem *Africa*, the hero of which is Scipio Africanus, and his historical work in prose, *De Viris Illustribus*, a series of biographies of classical celebrities. Other Latin works are the eclogues and epistles in verse; and in prose the dialogues, *De Contemptu Mundi* (or *Secretum*), the treatises *De Otio Religiosorum* and *De Vita Solitaria*, and his letters—he was in constant correspondence with Boccaccio. Great as were his merits as patriot or student, it is by his lyrics alone that his fame has lasted for over five centuries. His title deeds to fame are in his *Canzoniere*, in the Italian sonnets, madrigals, and songs, almost all inspired by his unrequited passion for Laura. The *Opera Omnia* appeared at Basel in 1554. His Italian lyrics were published in 1470, and have since gone through innumerable editions—a notable one that of Marsand (1819), used by Leopardi for his edition and commentary (1826). See the Abbé de Sade, *Mémoires de Pétrarque* (1764); Mézières, *Pétrarque* (1868; new ed.

1896); Koerting, *Petrarcas Leben* (1878); Eppelsheimer, *Petrarca* (Bonn 1926); works by Henry Reeve (1878), De Sanctis (1869), Zumbini (1878), Nolhac (Paris 1892), Robinson and Rolfe (1894), Hollway-Calthorp (1907), Maud Jerrold (1909), Tatham (1925-26), Tonelli (1930), Whitfield (1943).

PETRE, Edward, *pee'tèr* (1631-99), born in London of an old Catholic house, studied at St Omer, but was not admitted a Jesuit until 1671. His influence as confessor of James II made him extremely unpopular. In 1693 he became rector of St Omer.

PETRI, *pay'tree*, (1) **Laurentius** (1499-1573), Swedish reformer, studied under Luther at Wittenberg, was made professor at Uppsala, and in 1531 first Protestant Archbishop of Uppsala. He and his brother Claus did most to convert Sweden to the Reformed doctrines, and superintended the translation of the Bible into Swedish (1541).

(2) **Olaus** (1493-1552), brother of (1), gained, after his return (1519) from Wittenberg, the ear of Gustavus Vasa, who made him (1531) chancellor of the kingdom—a post he resigned in 1539 to spend the rest of his life as first pastor of Stockholm. His works include memoirs, a mystery-play, hymns and controversial tracts.

PETRIE, *pee'tree*, (1) **George** (1789-1866), Irish archaeologist, born at Dublin, was trained to be a landscape-painter, but was early attracted by the old buildings of Ireland. In 1833-46 he was attached to the Ordnance Survey of Ireland, and from 1832 he contributed much to the *Dublin Penny Journal*. He wrote on Tara, Irish music, &c.; and his famous *Essay on Round Towers* proved that they were Christian ecclesiastical buildings.

(2) **Sir William Matthew Flinders** (1853-1942), English Egyptologist, was born at Charlton, Kent. His earliest studies bore fruit in his *Stonehenge* (1880), and he next turned his attention to the pyramids and temples of Gizeh, to the mounds of Said and Naukratis. Year after year, even in old age, he excavated in Egypt and Palestine, and published a long succession of books mainly on his own diggings and methods, besides occupying (1892-1933) the chair of Egyptology in University College London. See his *Seventy Years of Archaeology* (1931), &c.

PETRONIUS ARBITER (fl. 1st cent. A.D.), Latin writer, supposed to be the Gaius Petronius whom Tacitus calls 'arbiter elegantiae' at the court of Nero, is generally believed to be the author of *Satirae*, the satirical romance in prose and verse, of which the 15th and 16th books have, in a fragmentary state, come down to us. The work depicts with wit, humour and realism the licentious life in Southern Italy of the upper or moneyed class. The favour Petronius enjoyed as aider and abettor of Nero and the *jeunesse dorée* in every form of sensual indulgence aroused the jealousy of another confidant, Tigellinus, who procured his disgrace and banishment. Ordered to commit suicide, he opened his veins.

PETROVITCH. See ALEXEI (2).

PETTENKOFER, Max von (1818-1901), German chemist, born near Neuburg, in 1847-94 was professor of Chemistry at Munich. He made valuable contributions to science on gold refining, gas-making, ventilation, clothing, epidemics and hygiene. He shot himself. Of his works, the best known is his *Handbuch der Hygiene* (1882 *et seq.*).

PETTIE, John (1839-93), Scottish painter, born in Edinburgh, joined Orchardson in London in 1862. He was elected A.R.A. in 1866 and R.A. in 1873. His works, apart from his portraits, were mainly of historical and literary subjects and had considerable popularity. Examples of these are *Juliet and Friar Lawrence* (1874) and *The Vigil* (1884).

PETTIT, Edison (1890-1962), American astronomer, famous for research on the sun and on ultra-violet light with reference to biology, in 1920 was appointed astronomer at the Mount Wilson observatory. See his *Forms and Motions of the Solar Prominences* (1925).

PETTY, Sir William (1623-87), English economist, was born at Romsey, Hants, the son of a clothier. He went to sea, and then studied at a Jesuit college in Caen, at Utrecht, Amsterdam, Leyden, Paris and Oxford, where he taught anatomy. Appointed physician to the army in Ireland (1652), he executed a fresh survey of the Irish lands forfeited in 1641 and started ironworks, lead-mines, sea-fisheries and other industries on estates he bought in southwest Ireland. He was made surveyor-general of Ireland by Charles II, who knighted him. Inventor of a copying machine (1647), and a double-keeled sea-boat (1663), he was one of the first members of the Royal Society. In political economy he was a precursor of Adam Smith, and wrote a *Treatise on Taxes* (1662) and *Political Arithmetic* (1691), the latter a discussion of the value of comparative statistics. He married the Baroness Shelburne, and his sons were successively Lord Shelburne (q.v.). His *Economic Writings* were edited by C. H. Hull (2 vols. 1899). See Life by Lord Edmond Fitzmaurice (1895).

PEUTINGER, Conrad, *poy'ting-èr* (1465-1547), German scholar, a keeper of the archives of Augsburg, who published a series of Roman inscriptions. His *Tabula Peutingeriana*, now at Vienna, is a copy, made in 1264, of an itinerary or a Roman map of the military roads of the 4th century A.D.

PEVSNER, (1) **Antoine** (1886-1962), French constructivist sculptor, was born in Russia. In Moscow he helped to form the Suprematist Group, with Malevitch, Tatlin and his brother Naum Gabo (q.v.). In 1920 he broke away from the Suprematists and issued the *Realist Manifesto* with his brother: this ultimately caused their exile from Russia, and he migrated to Paris. Several of his completely nonfigurative constructions (mainly in copper and bronze) are in the Museum of Modern Art, New York.

(2) **Nikolaus** (1903-), German art historian, born in Leipzig, lost his post at Göttingen University on the advent of Hitler and came to Britain, where he has become an authority on architecture and especially on English architecture. On the editorial board of *The Architectural Review*, art editor

of Penguin Books, he was from 1949 to 1955 Slade professor of Fine Art at Cambridge and in 1955 gave the Reith lecture on the Englishness of English art. Since the appearance of his *Pioneers of Modern Design* (1936), which made a strong impression in architectural circles, his scholarly but lucid works have stimulated a wide popular interest in art and architecture. Outstanding among these was *An Outline of European Architecture* (1942) in the Pelican series. Of his many other writings the monumental and unique work, as yet unfinished is *The Buildings of England* in 50 volumes for Penguin Books.

PFEFFER, Wilhelm (1845–1920), German botanist, born near Cassel, a specialist in plant physiology, professor successively at Bonn, Basel, Tübingen and Leipzig, was noted particularly for his researches on osmotic pressure. His *Handbuch der Pflanzenphysiologie* (1881) was a standard work.

PFEIFFER, *pfī'fèr,* (1) **Ida,** *née* **Reyer** (1797–1858), Austrian traveller, born at Vienna, made two journeys round the world (1846–1848, 1851–54). In 1856 she went on an expedition to Madagascar, endured terrible hardships, and came home to die. She wrote accounts of all her journeys; that of the last, edited by her son, contains a Life.

(2) **Richard Friedrich Johannes** (1858–?1945), German bacteriologist, was born near Posen (now Poznań, Poland), studied under Koch (q.v.), and became professor at Berlin (1894), Königsberg (1899) and Breslau (1901). He worked on the immunization of man against typhoid, on the influenza bacillus, discovered a serum against cholera, and published books on hygiene and microbiology. He was presumed dead in 1945.

PFITZNER, Hans Erich (1869–1949), German musician, born in Moscow, taught in various German conservatoria, and conducted in Berlin, Munich and Strasbourg. He composed *Palestrina* (1917) and other operas, choral and orchestral music (*Von deutscher Seele*, 1921) and chamber music. A romantic, he went his own way, refusing to follow passing fashions.

PFLEIDERER, *pflī'der-èr,* (1) **Edmund** (1842–1902), German philosopher, became professor of Philosophy at Kiel in 1873, and in 1878 at Tübingen. His writings include studies on Leibniz (1870), Hume (1874), Kantian criticism and English philosophy (1881), &c.

(2) **Otto** (1839–1908), German philosophic theologian, brother of (1), was born at Stetten in Württemberg, studied at Tübingen (1857–61), became pastor at Heilbronn in 1868, in 1870 professor of Theology at Jena, and in 1875 at Berlin. In New Testament criticism Pfleiderer belonged to the critical school which grew out of the impulse given by Baur, and was an independent thinker, suggestive and profoundly learned. His works include *Primitive Christianity* (14 vols. trans. 1906–11), *The Influence of the Apostle Paul on Christianity* (Hibbert Lectures, 1885) and *The Philosophy of Religion* (Gifford Lectures, 1894).

PFLÜGER, Eduard Friedrich Wilhelm (1829–1910), German physiologist, born at Hanau, professor at Bonn (1859), did important work on the sensory function of the spinal cord and on the digestive and metabolic systems. He helped in the construction of the mercurial blood pump. He died at Bonn.

PHAEDRUS, or **Phaeder** (1st cent. A.D.), translator of Aesop's fables into Latin verse, was a Graecized Macedonian, who came young to Italy. From a slave he became the freedman of Augustus or Tiberius. Under Tiberius he published the first two books of his fables, but his biting though veiled allusions to the tyranny of the emperor and his minister Sejanus caused him to be accused and condemned—to what punishment is unknown. On the death of Sejanus he published his third book. The fourth and fifth books belong to his last years. He died probably at an advanced age. Phaedrus was more than a reproducer of Aesop; he invented fables of his own, and it seems certain that the five books contain many fables that are not from his pen. See the editions of Bentley, Dressel, Orelli, Müller, Ramorino (1884), Havet (1895), Postgate (1922).

PHALARIS (6th cent. B.C.), Greek tyrant of Agrigentum in Sicily, was an adventurer from Asia Minor, who greatly embellished the city, and extended his sway over large districts in Sicily. After holding power for sixteen years he was overthrown for his cruelties, and roasted alive in his own invention, the brazen bull. The 148 letters bearing his name were proved by Bentley in 1697 and 1699 to be spurious.

PHELPS, Samuel (1804–78), English actor-manager, born in Devonport, became quite early a reader on the *Globe* and *Sun* newspapers, but by 1826 his interest in acting led him to his stage career. By 1837 he was a success, especially with his performance as Shylock, but his genius did not get full scope until he became manager of Sadler's Wells. For eighteen years with an excellent company of actors he produced legitimate plays, appearing himself equally successfully in comic and tragic rôles. See Life by W. M. Phelps and J. Forbes-Robertson (1886).

PHIDIAS (Gr. *Pheidias*), *fi'di-as* (5th cent. B.C.), the greatest sculptor of Greece, was born at Athens c. 500 B.C., and received from Pericles a magnificent commission to execute the chief statues with which he proposed to adorn the city, and was superintendent of all public works. He had under him architects, statuaries, bronze-workers, stone-cutters, &c. He constructed the Propylaea and the Parthenon, and the gold and ivory Athena there and the Zeus at Olympia were accounted the masterpieces of his own chisel. Charged with appropriating gold from the statue and carving his own head on an ornament, he was accused of impiety, and disappeared from Athens.

PHILARET (1782–1867), Russian prelate, the greatest preacher and the most influential Russian churchman of his day, became in 1817 Bishop of Reval, in 1819 Archbishop of Tver, and in 1821 of Moscow.

PHILIDOR, François André Danican (1726–1795), French chess player and operatic composer, was born at Dreux, and died in London.

PHILIP II (382-336 B.C.), king of Macedonia, father of Alexander the Great, was born at Pella, the youngest son of Amyntas II. The assassination of his eldest brother (367), and the death in battle of his second (359), left him guardian to his infant nephew Amyntas, but in a few months he made himself king. Dangers beset him from without and within, but in a year he had secured the safety of his kingdom, and gained for himself a dreaded name; henceforward his policy was one of aggression. The Greek towns on the coast of Macedonia were the first objects of attack. In Thrace he captured Crenides, which as Philippi soon acquired wealth. The gold-mines of the surrounding district supplied him with the means of paying his armies and of bribing traitorous Greeks. He advanced into Thessaly, but Thermopylae he found strongly guarded by the Athenians. He therefore directed his arms against the Thracians, and captured all the towns of Chalcidice, including Olynthus. Requested by the Thebans to interfere in the ' Sacred War ' raging between them and the Phocians, he marched into Phocis, destroyed its cities, and sent many of the inhabitants as colonists to Thrace (346). He next secured a footing in the Peloponnese, by espousing the cause of the Argives, Messenians and others against the Spartans. In 339 the Amphictyonic Council declared war against the Locrians of Amphissa, and in 338 appointed Philip commander-in-chief of their forces. The Athenians, alarmed, formed a league with the Thebans against him; but their army was utterly defeated at Chaeronea (338), and all Greece lay at the feet of the conqueror. He was now in a position to enter on the dream of his later years—the invasion of the Persian empire. Preparations for it were in progress when he was assassinated by Pausanias (336). See David G. Hogarth's *Philip and Alexander of Macedon* (1897) and A. Momigliano's *Filippo il Macedone* (1934).

PHILIP. Name of six kings of France:

Philip I (1052-1108), son of Henry I, reigned from 1067 without glory or credit.

Philip II (1165-1223), better known as **Philip-Augustus**, son of Louis VII, was crowned joint king in 1179, succeeded his father in 1180, and married Isabella of Hainault, the last direct descendant of the Carlovingians. His first war, against the Count of Flanders, gave him Amiens. He punished heretics and despoiled the Jews, and reduced the Duke of Burgundy. He supported the sons of Henry II of England against their father. Richard (Coeur de Lion) and he set out on the Third Crusade, but they quarrelled in Sicily. After three months in Syria he returned to France, having sworn not to molest Richard's dominions; but no sooner had he returned than he made a bargain with John for the partition of Richard's French territories. Richard's sudden return occasioned an exhausting war till 1199. On Richard's death Philip supported Arthur against his uncle John in the French domains of the English crown, but was for a while fully occupied by his quarrel with the pope. He had put away his second wife Ingeborg of Denmark, in order to marry Agnes of Meran, but the anger of the Vatican forced him to replace Ingeborg upon her throne. The murder of Arthur again gave him the excuse he sought. The fortress of Château Gaillard surrendered to him in 1204, and that same year he added to his dominions Normandy, Maine, Anjou and Touraine, with part of Poitou, as well as the overlordship of Brittany. The victory of Bouvines (August 29, 1214) over the Flemish, the English, and the Emperor Otho established his throne securely, and the rest of his reign he devoted to reforms of justice and to the building and fortifying of Paris—Notre Dame remaining a lasting monument of this great king. He died at Nantes. See works by Mazabran (1878), Davidsohn (Stuttgart 1888), Luchaire (Paris 2nd ed. 1909), W. H. Hutton (1896), Cambridge Medieval History, vol. 6 (1929).

Philip III, ' le Hardi ' (1245-85), was with his father St Louis at his death in Tunis (1270), fought several unlucky campaigns in Spain, the last of which, the attack on Aragon, caused his death. See Life by Langlois (1887).

Philip IV, ' the Fair ' (1268-1314), succeeded his father, Philip III, in 1285. By his marriage with Queen Joanna of Navarre he obtained Navarre, Champagne and Brie. He overran Flanders, but a Flemish revolt broke out at Bruges, and at Courtrai on the ' Day of Spurs ' he was disastrously defeated. His great struggle with Pope Boniface VIII grew out of his attempt to levy taxes from the clergy. In 1296 Boniface forbade the clergy to pay taxes; Philip replied by forbidding the export of money or valuables. A temporary reconciliation in 1297 was ended by a fresh quarrel in 1300. Philip imprisoned the papal legate, and summoned the Estates. Boniface issued the bull *Unam Sanctam.* Philip publicly burned the bull, and confiscated the property of those prelates who had sided with the pope. Boniface now excommunicated him, and threatened to lay the kingdom under interdict, but the king sent to Rome William de Nogaret, who seized and imprisoned the pope, with the aid of the Colonnas. Boniface soon afterwards died. In 1305 Philip obtained the elevation of one of his own creatures as Clement V, and placed him at Avignon, the beginning of the seventy years' ' captivity '. He compelled the pope to condemn the Templars (1310) and abolish the order (1312); they were condemned and burned by scores, and Philip appropriated their wealth. Under him the taxes were greatly increased, the Jews persecuted and their property confiscated.

Philip V, ' the Tall ' (1293-1322), second son of the preceding, succeeded his brother, Louis X, in 1316. He ended the war with Flanders (1320), and tried to unify the coinage.

Philip VI, of Valois (1293-1350), son of Charles of Valois, younger brother of Philip IV, succeeded to the throne of France on the death of Charles IV in 1328. His right was denied by Edward III of England, son of the daughter of Philip IV, who declared that females, though excluded by the Salic law, could transmit their rights to their children.

Marching into Flanders to support the count against his rebellious subjects, he vanquished them at Cassel (August 23, 1328). He gave up Navarre, but retained Champagne and Brie. The Hundred Years' War with England began in 1337. The French fleet was destroyed off Sluys (1340). In 1346 Edward III landed in Normandy, ravaged to the environs of Paris, and defeated Philip at Crécy. A truce was concluded just as destruction threatened France in the ' Black Death '.

PHILIP. Name of five kings of Spain, of whom the following are noteworthy:

Philip I (1478-1506), son of the Emperor Maximilian, reigned only for a few months.

Philip II (1527-98), only son of the Emperor Charles V, was born at Valladolid. In 1543 he married Mary of Portugal, who died in 1546, after bearing the ill-fated Don Carlos. He spent three years with his father at Brussels. In 1554 he made a marriage of policy with Mary Tudor, Queen of England. During his fourteen months' stay in England he laboured unsuccessfully to ingratiate himself with his wife's subjects. In 1555 he became by the abdication of his father the most powerful prince in Europe, having under his sway Spain, the Two Sicilies, the Milanese, the Low Countries, Franche Comté, Mexico and Peru. But the treasury was deficient, drained by the expenditure of his father's wars. His first danger was a league formed between Henry II of France and Pope Paul IV. Alva overran the papal territories, while Philip's troops defeated the French at St Quentin (1557) and Gravelines (1558), and Henry made peace (1559). In January 1558 the French had captured Calais, and Mary Tudor died eleven months later. Philip failed to secure the hand of Elizabeth, and in 1559 married Isabella of France. Seeking to concentrate all power in himself, he laboured to destroy free institutions in all his dominions, while putting himself at the head of the Catholic party in Europe. He found the Inquisition the best engine of his tyranny in Spain, but in the Low Countries it caused a formidable revolt, which ended in 1579 with the independence of the Seven United Provinces. To replenish his treasury Philip exacted enormous contributions. His son, Don Carlos (q.v.), whom he hated, died in prison in 1568. Philip did not disdain the aid of murder in the pursuit of his policy, and the death of William the Silent (1584) and the persecution of Antonio Pérez (q.v.) show how pitiless and persistent was his hatred. He married in 1570 his niece, Anne of Austria, whose son by him became Philip III. His one great triumph was the naval victory of Lepanto (1571), won by his half-brother, Don John of Austria, over the Turks. In 1580, the direct male line of Portugal having become extinct, Philip claimed the throne, and dispatched Alva to occupy the kingdom. His attempt to conquer England resulted in hopeless disaster, as the Armada was swept to destruction (1588). His intrigues against Henry of Navarre were foiled (1592). The stubborn heroism of the Netherlanders and the ravages of the English on the Spanish Main, added to financial distress at home, embittered Philip's last years. He possessed great abilities but little

political wisdom, and he engaged in so many vast enterprises at once as to overtask his resources without leading to any profitable result. He dealt a fatal blow to Spain by crushing its chivalrous spirit, and destroyed its commerce by oppressive exactions and by a bitter persecution of the industrious Moriscos. The good points of Philip, who was a tender husband and very affectionate to his daughters, are brought out in Froude's *Spanish Story of the Armada* (1892), Martin Hume's *Philip II of Spain* (1897), and *Two English Queens and Philip* (1908). See also the histories of Prescott, Motley and Froude; Forneron's *Histoire de Philippe II* (3rd ed. 1887); and books by Gachard, Mignet, Rubis, Tomas and Petrie (1963).

Philip V (1683-1746), first Bourbon king of Spain, second son of the Dauphin Louis (son of Louis XIV and Maria Theresa of Spain), was born at Versailles. In 1700, when Duke of Anjou, he was bequeathed the crown of Spain by Charles II. He entered Madrid in February 1701, and after a long struggle against his rival, the Archduke Charles, was left in possession of the throne by the peace of Utrecht in 1713. Next year died the queen, Maria Louisa, daughter of the Duke of Savoy, whom Philip had married in 1702; and soon after he married ' the termagant ' Elizabeth Farnese (q.v.). By her influence the government was committed to Alberoni, but Philip was obliged by the Quadruple Alliance to dismiss him in 1719. He abdicated in favour of his son Don Louis in 1724, but resumed the crown on Louis' death eight months later. The queen's dearest wish was to drive the Hapsburgs out of Italy in the interests of her sons by a former marriage, but she only secured the Two Sicilies for Don Carlos. Spain joined the coalition against Maria Theresa, and her younger son Don Philip was at first successful in conquering the Milanese; but as soon as the Silesian war was closed the Austrian queen drove the Spaniards out of Italy. At the crisis Philip died. See Baudrillart's *Philippe V et la cour de France, 1700-15* (1890-91).

PHILIP. Name of two Dukes of Burgundy:

Philip the Bold (' le Hardi ') (1342-1404), founder of the second and last ducal House of Burgundy, was the fourth son of John the Good, king of France. At Poitiers (1356) he displayed heroic courage, shared his father's captivity in England, and was made Duke of Burgundy in 1363. He married Margaret, heiress of Flanders, in 1369. In 1372 he commanded with success against the English, and in 1380 helped to suppress the sedition of the Flemish towns against his father-in-law; but the rebels, especially the burghers of Ghent, were finally subdued only after the defeat of Rosbeck (1382), where 26,000 Flemings were slain. Flanders fell to him by the death of the count in 1384, and his wise government won the esteem of his new subjects. He encouraged arts, manufactures and commerce, and his territory was one of the best governed in Europe. For his imbecile nephew, Charles VI of France, he was obliged to take the helm of affairs. See study by R. Vaughan (1963).

Philip the Good (1396-1467), son of John

the Fearless and grandson of Philip the Bold, bent on avenging his father's murder by the dauphin, entered into an alliance with Henry V of England in 1419, recognizing him as heir to the French crown. This agreement was sanctioned by the French king and States-General (1420), but the dauphin (Charles VII after 1422) took to arms, and was twice defeated. Disputes with the English prompted Philip to conclude a treaty with Charles in 1429. But by ceding to him Champagne and paying a large sum, the English regained his alliance. At this time, by falling heir to Brabant, Holland and Zeeland, he was at the head of the most powerful realm in Europe. Smarting under fresh insults of the English viceroy, he made final peace (1435) with Charles. When the English committed great havoc on Flemish ships, Philip declared war against them, and, with the king of France, gradually expelled them from their French possessions. The imposition of taxes excited a rebellion, headed by Ghent; but the duke inflicted a terrible defeat (July 1454) upon the rebels, of whom 20,000 fell. The later part of his reign was troubled by the quarrels between Charles VII and his son (afterwards Louis XI) who sought shelter with Philip. Under him Burgundy was the most wealthy, prosperous and tranquil state in Europe. He was founder of the order of the Golden Fleece.

PHILIP, Prince. See EDINBURGH, DUKE OF.

PHILIP, an American-Indian chief (d. 1676), son of a staunch ally of the Pilgrim settlers of Plymouth, became the leader of a confederation of nearly 10,000 warriors, and in King Philip's War (1675) against the whites thirteen towns were destroyed and 600 colonists slain. After reprisals and retaliations Philip's supporters fell away, and he was surprised and shot by Captain Benjamin Church. See Drake's edition of *King Philip's War* by Church (1825).

PHILIP NERI, St. See NERI.

PHILIPPA OF HAINAULT (*c.* 1314–69), in 1328 married Edward III at York. In 1347 she obtained mercy for the Calais burgesses. See B. C. Hardy's *Philippa and her Times* (1900).

PHILIPS, (1) **Ambrose** (1674–1749), English poet, born at Shrewsbury, was educated at St John's College, Cambridge. A friend of Addison and Steele, he did hack work for Tonson, and gained a reputation by the *Winter-piece* in the *Tatler* and six Pastorals in Tonson's *Miscellany* (1709). Pope's jealousy started a bitter feud. He was dubbed ' Namby Pamby ' by either Carey or Swift for the over-sentimentality of some of his poetry. Of his plays only *The Distrest Mother*, based on Racine's *Andromaque*, found favour with his contemporaries. Philips sat for Armagh, was secretary to the Archbishop of Armagh, purse-bearer to the Irish lord chancellor, and registrar of the Prerogative Court. See *The Poems of Ambrose Philips*, ed. Segar (1937).

(2) **John** (1676–1709), English poet, was born at Bampton, Oxfordshire, the son of the Archdeacon of Shropshire, and educated at Winchester and Christ Church, Oxford. He wrote three very popular poems, *The Splendid*

Shilling (1701), a Miltonic burlesque; *Blenheim* (1705), a Tory celebration of Marlborough's great victory; and *Cyder* (1708), an imitation of Virgil's *Georgics*. He died at Hereford of consumption and was buried in the cathedral there. He has a monument in Westminster Abbey. Lloyd Thomas edited his *Poems* (1927).

(3) **Katherine** (1631–64), *née* Fowler, English poetess, called ' the matchless Orinda ', was born in London, the daughter of a London merchant, and at sixteen married James Philips of Cardigan Priory. Orinda is the earliest English sentimental writer (her first printed poem was an address to Vaughan the Silurist). She received a dedication from Jeremy Taylor (*Discourse on the Nature, Offices and Measures of Friendship*, 1659). On a visit to London she caught smallpox, and died. She translated Corneille's *Pompée* and the greater part of his *Horace*. Her poems, surreptitiously printed in 1663, were issued in 1667. See Saintsbury's *Minor Poets of the Caroline Period* (1905), Gosse's *Seventeenth Century Studies* (2nd ed. 1885), P. W. Souers's study (Harvard 1931) and her own letters, *From Orinda to Poliarchus*.

PHILLIMORE, Sir Robert Joseph (1810–85), English judge, educated at Westminster and Christ Church, after serving in the Board of Control had a brilliant career at the bar. He sat in parliament as a Whig 1853–57; and became advocate-general (1862, when he was knighted), judge advocate-general (1871), judge of the Arches Court (1867–75), and of the High Court of Admiralty (1867–83). He was made a baronet in 1881. He wrote *Commentaries upon International Law* (1854–1861) and *Ecclesiastical Law* (1873–76).

PHILLIP, (1) **Arthur** (1738–1814), first governor of New South Wales, born in London, trained at Greenwich and joined the navy in 1755. He saw service in the Mediterranean war with Byng, was at the taking of Havana, and in 1787 as captain led the ' First Fleet ' to Botany Bay. Finding that site unsuitable, he founded his settlement at Sydney (1788). He explored the Hawkesbury River, piloted his colony through difficulties and predicted its future importance. He left in 1792, being made vice-admiral in 1809. See Lives by G. Mackaness (1937) and M. B. Eldershaw (1938).

(2) **John** (1817–67), Scottish painter, was born, an old soldier's son, at Aberdeen. He was apprenticed to a painter and glazier, but in 1836 was sent by Lord Panmure to London, where in 1838 he began to exhibit in the Academy. Most of his early subjects were Scottish, but after a visit to Spain (1851), for health, his main triumphs were in Spanish themes. He became an R.A. in 1859.

PHILLIPPS. See HALLIWELL-PHILLIPPS.

PHILLIPS, (1) **Edward** (1630–*c.* 1696), English writer, son of Milton's sister Ann, was brought up and educated by his uncle. He went to Oxford in 1650, but left next year without taking a degree. In 1663 he was tutor to the son of John Evelyn, and is mentioned in Evelyn's Diary as ' not at all infected by Milton's principles ', yet he not only extolled his uncle in his *Theatrum Poetarum*, but has left us a short Life of the poet. Among his numerous works are a complete edition (the first) of the Poems of Drummond of Hawthornden (1656); *New World of English Words* (1658), a kind of dictionary; the *Continuation* of Baker's *Chronicle of the Kings of England* (1665); *Theatrum Poetarum, or a Complete Collection of the Poets* (1675).

(2) **John** (1631–1706), English writer, brother of (1), also educated by his uncle, replied to Salmasius's attack on him, and acted as his amanuensis. His *Satyr against Hypocrites* (1655) was a bitter attack on the Presbyterian ministers, *Speculum Crape Gownorum* on the High Churchmen. *Maronides* travesties Virgil. An anonymous Life of Milton is attributed to him by Helen Darbishire.

(3) **John** (1800–74), English geologist, born at Marden in Wiltshire, worked with his uncle William Smith, the father of English geology, and was professor of Geology at London, Dublin and Oxford. He was keeper of the Ashmolean Museum (1854–70) and president of the Geological Society of London (1859–60). His writings include *Geology of Yorkshire* (1829–36), and *Life on the Earth: Its Origin and Succession* (1860).

(4) **Stephen** (1868–1915), English poet, was born, son of the precentor of Peterborough Cathedral, at Somertown, near Oxford. For six years he acted in Benson's company, next taught history, then took to literature, and from 1913 edited the *Poetry Review*. He wrote *Christ in Hades* (1896), *Poems* (1897), which enjoyed a transitory success, and blank verse plays, the best *Paolo and Francesca* (1899).

(5) **Wendell** (1811–84), abolitionist, born at Boston, Mass., graduated at Harvard 1831, and was called to the bar 1834. But by 1837 he was the chief orator of the antislavery party. He also championed the causes of temperance and women, and advocated the rights of the Indians. His speeches and letters were collected in 1863. See Life by Austin (1888).

PHILLPOTTS, (1) **Eden** (1862–1960), English novelist, dramatist and poet, born at Mount Aboo, India, studied for the stage in London, but took to literature instead (1893), and made his name by realistic novels chiefly dealing with Devonshire. Of his plays, *The Farmer's Wife* (1917: staged 1924) and *Yellow Sands* (1926), which he wrote with his daughter Adelaide, were perhaps the most successful. In all he wrote more than 250 books.

(2) **Henry** (1778–1869), Bishop of Exeter, born at Bridgwater, was elected fellow of Magdalen in 1795, and became Dean of Chester in 1828, and Bishop of Exeter in 1831. A zealous Tory, a High Churchman, a keen controversialist, he refused to institute Gorham (q.v.).

PHILO (*c*. 2nd cent. B.C.), Byzantine scientist, wrote a treatise on military engineering of which some fragments remain. He was probably the first to record the contraction of air in a globe over water when a candle is burnt in it.

PHILO JUDAEUS (fl. 1st cent. A.D.), Hellenistic Jewish philosopher, born at Alexandria of a wealthy family, was nurtured in Greek culture but remained faithful to the Jewish religion. When over fifty he went to Rome to plead for certain Alexandrians who had refused to worship the insane Caligula, described in his *De Legatione*. His importance to Jews and Christians alike is his fusion of Platonic philosophy with the doctrines of the Hebrew scriptures. Most of his writings have been lost, but three works on the Pentateuch are still extant. See translations (1929 ff.) and studies by Drummond (1888), H. E. Ryle (1895), Moore (1927) and Woolfson (1947).

PHILO OF BYBLIUS (fl. late 1st and 2nd cents. A.D.), a Hellenized Phoenician grammarian of Byblus in Phoenicia, wrote a distorted and misleading account of the religion and history of the Phoenicians, much of it professedly translated from Sanchoniathon.

PHILOPOEMEN, *fil-ō-pee'men* (*c*. 252–183 B.C.), Greek general, born at Megalopolis, as commander-in-chief of the Achaean League crushed the Spartans at Mantinea (208), sought to unite Greece against the Romans, and was poisoned by the Messenians.

PHILOSTRATUS, *fi-los'-* (*c*. 170–245 A.D.), Greek sophist, studied at Athens, and established himself at Rome, where he wrote an idealized Life of Apollonius of Tyana, the bright *Lives of the Sophists*, and the amatory *Epistles*. The *Heroicon* and the *Imagines*, a description of thirty-four pictures supposed to be hung in a villa near Naples, are now ascribed to his nephew; and further *Imagines* to a third and related Philostratus. See texts by Kayser (1844) and Westermann (1849), and translations by Conybeare (1912) and Phillimore (1912).

PHIPPS, Sir William (1651–95), American colonial governor, born at Pemmaquid (Bristol), Maine, was successively shepherd, carpenter and trader, and in 1687 recovered £300,000 from a wrecked Spanish ship off the Bahamas. This gained him a knighthood and the appointment of provost-marshal of New England. In 1690 he captured Port Royal (now Annapolis) in Nova Scotia, but failed in 1691 in a naval attack upon Quebec. In 1692 he became governor of Massachusetts. He died in London. See Life by Bowen in Sparks's *American Biography* (1834–37), and that by H. O. Thayer (1927).

PHIZ. See BROWNE (5).

PHOCAS (d. 610), emperor of Constantinople, overthrew his predecessor Maurice in 602. Through his monstrous vices, tyranny and incapacity the empire sank into utter anarchy, and he was overthrown in 610 by Heraclius (q.v.).

PHOCION, *fō'shi-on* (*c*. 402–317 B.C.), Athenian general, commanded a division of the Athenian fleet at Naxos in 376, and helped to conquer Cyprus in 351 for Artaxerxes III. In 341 he crushed the Macedonian party in Euboea, and in 340 forced Philip to evacuate the Chersonesus, but advised Athens to make friends with him. The advice was not taken; but the fatal battle of Chaeronea proved its soundness. After the murder of Philip (336) he struggled at Athens to repress the reckless desire for war, and again on the death of Alexander in

323 vainly endeavoured to hinder the Athenians from going to war with Antipater. Ultimately regarded as a traitor, he fled to Phocis, was in the intrigues of Cassander, the rival of Polyperchon, who delivered him up to the Athenians, and was condemned to drink hemlock.

PHOTIUS (*c.* 820–91), ex-soldier and secretary, on the deposition of Ignatius from the patriarchate of Constantinople for correcting the vices of the Emperor Michael, was hurried through all the stages of Holy Orders, and installed in his stead. In 862, however, Pope Nicholas I called a council at Rome, which declared Photius's election invalid, excommunicated him, and reinstated Ignatius. Supported by the emperor, Photius assembled a council at Constantinople in 867, which condemned many points of doctrine and discipline of the Western Church as heretical, excommunicated Nicholas, and withdrew from the communion of Rome. Under the Emperor Basilius in 867 Photius was banished to Cyprus, and Ignatius reinstated. In 869 the eighth general council, at which Pope Adrian II's legates presided, assembled at Constantinople; Photius was again excommunicated, and the intercommunion of the churches restored. Yet, on the death of Ignatius, Photius was reappointed. In 879 he assembled a new council at Constantinople, renewed the charges against the Western Church, and erased the *filioque* from the creed. Photius was finally deprived, and exiled to Armenia by Leo, son of Basilius, in 886. His chief remains are *Myriobiblon* or *Bibliotheca*, a summary review of 280 works which Photius had read, and many of which are lost; a *Lexicon*; the *Nomocanon*, a collection of the acts and decrees of the councils and ecclesiastical laws of the emperors; and a collection of letters. See F. Dvornik's *The Photian Schism* (1948).

PHRYNE, *frī'nee* (4th cent. B.C.), a beautiful Greek courtesan of antiquity, born at Thespiae in Boeotia, became enormously rich through her many lovers. Accused of profaning the Eleusinian mysteries, she was defended by the orator Hyperides (q.v.), who threw off her robe, showing her loveliness and so gained the verdict.

PIAGET, Jean (1896–), Swiss psychologist, born at Neuchâtel, professor of Psychology at Geneva University, director of the Centre d'Epistémologie génétique and a director of the Institut des Sciences de l'Education. He is best known for his research on the development of cognitive functions (perception, intelligence, logic) and for his intensive case study methods of research. His many publications include *La Gènese du nombre chez l'enfant* (1941, trans. 1952), *Le Développement de la notion de temps chez l'enfant* (1946), *La Réprésentation de l'espace chez l'enfant* (with Inhelder, 1947, trans. 1956) and *Logic and Psychology* (1957).

PIAZZI, Giuseppe, *pya'tsee* (1746–1826), Italian astronomer, professor of Mathematics in Palermo; he set up an observatory there (1789) and published a catalogue of the stars (1803, 1814).

PICABIA, Francis (1879–1953), French *Dadaist* painter, born in Paris, took part in the Parisian artistic revolutions from neo-Impressionism, Cubism with Marcel Duchamp, whom he met in 1910, to Futurism, and finally to *Dadaism* (see DUCHAMP), which they introduced to New York in 1915. His anti-art productions, often portraying senseless machinery, include *Parade Amoureuse* (1917), *Infant Carburettor*, and many of the cover designs for the American anti-art magazine *291* which he edited. See study by M. Sanouillet (Paris, 1964).

PICARD, *pee-kar*, (1) **Charles Émile** (1856–1941), French mathematician, professor at the Sorbonne (1886–97), president of the French Academy of Science (1910), was specially noted for his work on the theory of functions and on differential equations, published in his *Théorie des fonctions algébriques de deux variables indépendantes* (1897–1906) and *Traité d'analyse* (1891–96).

(2) **Jean** (1620–82), French astronomer, born at La Flèche, Anjou. In 1645 he became professor in the Collège de France and helped to found the Paris observatory. He made the first accurate measurement of a degree of a meridian and thus arrived at an estimate of the radius of the earth. He visited Tycho Brahe's observatory on the island of Hven, and determined its latitude and longitude. He died in Paris.

PICASSO, Pablo, *pee-kas'sō* (1881–1973), Spanish-born painter, the dominating figure of early 20th-century French art and, with Braque, a pioneer of Cubism, was born October 25 at Malaga, Andalusia, of which his mother, Maria Picasso, was a native. His father, José Ruiz Blasco, painter and art teacher, came from the Basque country. At the age of fourteen Pablo entered the academy at Barcelona and painted *Barefoot Girl* (1895) and two years later transferred to Madrid for advanced training. In 1898 he won a gold medal for *Customs of Aragon*, which was exhibited in his native town. In 1901 he set up in a studio at 13 Rue de Ravignon (now Place Émile-Goudeau), Montmartre. By now a master of the traditional forms of art, to which such works as his *Gipsy Girl on the Beach* (1898) abundantly testify, Picasso quickly absorbed the neo-Impressionist influences of the Paris school of Toulouse-Lautrec, Dégas and Vuillard, exemplified by such works as *Longchamp* (1901), *The Blue Room* (1901; Washington), but soon began to develop his own idiom. The blue period (1902–04), a series of striking studies of the poor in haunting attitudes of despair and gloom, gave way to the gay, life-affirming pink period (1904–06), in which Picasso achieved for harlequins, acrobats and the incidents of circus life what Dégas had previously done for the ballet. Pink turned to brown in *La Coiffure* (1905–1906; Modern Art, N.Y.) and the remarkable portrait of Gertrude Stein (1906). His first dabblings in sculpture and his new enthusiasm for Negro art are fully reflected in the transitional *Two Nudes* (1906), which heralded his epoch-making break with tradition in *Les Demoiselles d'Avignon* (1906–07; Modern Art, N.Y.), the first full-blown exemplar of analytical Cubism, an attempt to render the three-dimensional on the flat picture surface without resorting to perspective. Nature was no longer to be copied, decorated or idealized, but exploited for creative ends. Its exclusive emphasis on formal, geometric criteria contrasted sharply with the cult of colour of the *Fauvists*, to whom Braque for a time belonged, before joining forces with Picasso in 1909 for their exploration of Cubism through its various phases; analytic, synthetic, hermetic and rococo, in which *collage*, i.e., pieces of wood, wire, newspaper and string became mediums side by side with paint. The *Ma Jolie* series of pictures, after the music-hall song score which appears in them (1911–14), are examples of the last phase. Braque broke with Picasso in 1914. From 1917 Picasso, through Jean Cocteau, became associated with Diaghilev's Russian Ballet, designing costumes and sets for *Parade* (1917), *Le Tricorne* (1919), *Pulcinella* (1920), *Le Train bleu* (1924), in both Cubist and neo-Classical styles, and thus made the former acceptable to a wider public. The grotesque facial and bodily distortions of the *Three Dancers* (1925; Modern Art, N.Y.) foreshadows the immense canvas of *Guernica* (1937; Modern Art, N.Y. and filmed 1949), which expressed in synthetic Cubism Picasso's horror of the bombing of this Basque town during the Civil War, of war in general and compassion and hope for its victims. The canvas was exhibited in the Spanish Pavilion in the Paris World Fair (1937) and Picasso became director of the Prado Gallery, Madrid (1936–39). During World War II he was mostly in Paris, and after the liberation joined the Communists. Neither *Guernica* nor his portrait of Stalin (1953) commended him to the party. Only the ' Picasso Peace Dove ' had some propagandist value. He designed stage sets for Cocteau and Petit, illustrated translations of classical texts, experimented in sculpture, ceramics and lithography, allowed his canvas to be filmed while at work and wrote a play. He is above all the great innovator. See studies by Gertrude Stein (1938), W. Boeck and J. Sabarté (1955), Elgar (1955), F. Wittgens (1957) and R. Penrose (1958), who also edited the catalogue of the exhibition at the Tate, London (1960).

PICCARD, (1) Auguste, *pee-kar* (1884–1962), Swiss physicist, born at Basel, became professor at Brussels in 1922 and held posts at Lausanne, Chicago and Minnesota Universities. He ascended 16–17 km. by balloon (1931–32) into the stratosphere. In 1948 he explored the ocean depths off W. Africa in a bathyscaphe constructed from his own design. His son **Jacques**, together with an American naval officer **Donald Walsh**, established a world record by diving more than seven miles in the U.S. bathyscaphe *Trieste* into the Marianas Trench of the Pacific Ocean in January 1960. See the father's *In Balloon and Bathyscaphe* (1956).

(2) **Jean Felix** (1884–1963), Swiss scientist, twin brother of (1), took a Chemical Engineering degree at the Swiss Institute of Technology in 1907. Subsequently held a chair at New York, and became professor emeritus of Aeronautical Engineering at Minnesota University. His chief interest was in explor-

ation of the stratosphere and he designed and ascended (with his wife) in a balloon from Dearborn, Detroit, in 1934, to a height of 57,579 ft, collecting valuable data concerning cosmic rays.

PICCINNI, Niccola, *pee-chee'nee* (1728–1800), Italian composer, born at Bari, wrote over a hundred operas as well as oratorios and church music. In 1766 he was summoned to Paris, and became the representative of the party opposed to Gluck (q.v.). See E. Demoiresterres, *Gluck et Piccinni* (1872).

PICCOLOMINI, an old Italian family, who obtained possession of the duchy of Amalfi. It produced numerous *littérateurs* and warriors, one pope (**Pius II**) and several cardinals. **Ottavio**, Duke of Amalfi (1599–1656), entered the Spanish service, and, sent to aid the Emperor Ferdinand II, fought against the Bohemians (1620), in the Netherlands, and in Wallenstein's army at Lützen (1632), and contributed to the fall of Wallenstein. He won great distinction at Nördlingen (1634), and next year was sent to aid the Spaniards in the Netherlands to drive out the French. In 1640 he stopped the advance of the Swedes for a time, but he was worsted by them in Silesia. In 1643 he commanded the Spanish armies in the Netherlands, and after the peace of Westphalia (1648) was created field-marshal. His son Max, who figures in Schiller's *Wallenstein*, is a poetical fiction. See German works by Weyhe-Eimke (1870–71), and Elster (1911).

PICHEGRU, Charles, *peesh-grü* (1761–1804), French soldier, born, a labourer's son, at Arbois, enlisted in 1783, and by 1793 was a general of division. With Hoche, he drove back the Austrians and overran the Palatinate; then defeating the Austrians at Fleurus in 1794, he continued the struggle into the winter, and entered Amsterdam in 1795. Recalled by the Thermidorians, Pichegru crushed an insurrection in Paris, and next took Mannheim. But at the height of his fame he sold himself to the Bourbons, and by deliberately remaining inactive, allowed Jourdan to be defeated. The Directory superseded him by Moreau. In 1797 he became president of the council of Five Hundred, and continued his Bourbon intrigues, but was arrested and deported to Cayenne. Escaping next year, he made his way to London, and thereafter lived in Germany and England until the Bourbon conspiracy of Cadoudal (q.v.) for the assassination of the first consul. The pair reached Paris, but were betrayed, and Pichegru was lodged in the Temple, where he was found strangled in bed. See works by Sir John Hall (1915) and Caudrillier (1908).

PICHON, Stéphen Jean Marie, *pee-shõ* (1857–1933), French statesman and journalist, born at Arnay-le-Duc in Burgundy, served on Clemenceau's paper *La Justice* before entering in 1885 the Chamber of Deputies. Sent in turn as minister to Port-au-Prince, San Domingo, Rio de Janeiro, Peking and Tunis, he represented the powers in negotiations with China during the Boxer Rebellion. He became minister of foreign affairs twice, in 1906 and again from 1917 to 1920, when he joined *Le Petit Journal* as its political editor.

PICKEN, (1) Andrew (1788–1833), Scottish

author, was born in Paisley and died in London, having published a series of novels, including *The Sectarian* (1829), *The Dominie's Legacy* (1830) and *Waltham* (1833).

(2) **Ebenezer** (1769-1816), Scottish poet, born at Paisley, died a teacher in Edinburgh. He published several volumes of Scots poems and a *Pocket Dictionary of the Scottish Dialect* (1818).

PICKERING, (1) **Edward Charles** (1846-1919), American astronomer, born at Boston, educated at Harvard, became professor of Physics at the Massachusetts Institute of Technology. In 1876 he was appointed professor of Astronomy and director of the observatory at Harvard, where his work was concerned with stellar photometry and classification of spectra of the stars. He invented the meridian photometer.

(2) **William** (1796-1854), English publisher, set up for himself in 1820, and became known by his ' Diamond Classics ' (1821-31), his ' Aldine ' edition of the poets, &c.

(3) **William Henry** (1858-1938), American astronomer, brother of (1), born at Boston, discovered Phoebe, the 9th satellite of Saturn. He was in charge of an observation station at Arequipa and from 1900 director of a station at Mandeville, Jamaica.

PICKFORD, Mary, *née* **Gladys Mary Smith** (1893-), American actress, born in Toronto, first appeared on the stage at the age of five, and in 1913 made her first film, *The Violin Maker of Cremona*, directed by D. W. Griffith. Her beauty and ingenuous charm soon won her the title of ' The World's Sweetheart '. Her many successful films included *Rebecca of Sunnybrook Farm, Poor Little Rich Girl* and *The Taming of the Shrew*.

PICKLE THE SPY. See MACDONELL.

PICO DELLA MIRANDOLA (1463-94), Italian philosopher, the son of the Count of Mirandola, in his youth visited the chief universities of Italy and France. In 1486 he issued a challenge to all comers to debate on any of nine hundred theses at Rome, but the debate was forbidden by the pope on the score of the heretical tendency of some of the theses, and Pico suffered persecution until Alexander VI in 1493 absolved him of heresy. He was the last of the schoolmen; and his works are a bewildering compound of mysticism and recondite knowledge. A humanist as well as a theologian, he wrote various Latin epistles and elegies and a series of florid Italian sonnets. His philosophical writings include *Heptaplus* and *De Hominis Dignitate*, the theme of which is free will. See the Life by his nephew (trans. by Sir Thomas More; best ed. by J. M. Rigg, 1890) and A. Dulles, *Princeps Concordiae* (1941).

PICTET, *peek-tay*. Name of a Swiss family to which belonged:

(1) **Adolphe** (1799-1875), a native of Geneva, and writer on the Celts and primitive Aryans.

(2) **François Jules** (1809-72), zoologist and palaeontologist.

(3) **Marcus Auguste** (1752-1825), physicist.

(4) **Raoul** (1846-1929). chemist and physicist at Geneva and Berlin, known from his liquefaction of oxygen, hydrogen and carbonic acid.

PICTON, Sir Thomas (1758-1815), British soldier, born at Poyston, Pembrokeshire, entered the army in 1771. In 1794 he went out to the West Indies, took part in the conquest of several of the islands, and was appointed (1797) governor of Trinidad, in 1801 becoming general. In 1803 he was superseded, but immediately after appointed commandant of Tobago. He returned, however, to England to take his trial for having permitted, under the old Spanish laws, a female prisoner to be tortured. He was found technically guilty (1806), but on appeal was acquitted. He saw active service again in the Walcheren expedition (1809), and was made governor of Flushing. In 1810 he went to Spain, and in command of the ' Fighting Division ' rendered brilliant service at Busaco, Fuentes de Oñoro, Ciudad Rodrigo, Badajoz, Vitoria, the battles of the Pyrenees, Orthez and Toulouse. Created a G.C.B., he was seriously wounded at Quatre Bras, and fell leading his men to the charge at Waterloo. See Memoirs by H. B. Robinson (1835).

PIERCE, Franklin (1804-69), American politician, fourteenth president of the United States, born at Hillsborough, N.H., studied law, and was admitted to the bar in 1827. From 1829 to 1833 he was a member of the state legislature, and for two years speaker; he was then elected to congress as a Democrat, and in 1837 to the U.S. Senate. As a leader of his party, he advocated the annexation of Texas with or without slavery, and, after his opponents, the Whigs and Freesoilers, had been victorious in 1846, volunteered for the Mexican war and was made brigadier-general. In 1852 Pierce was nominated as a compromise candidate for the presidency against General Scott, the Whig nominee, and elected. He defended slavery and the fugitive slave law. The events of his administration were the treaty for reciprocity of trade with the British American colonies, the treaty with Japan, the filibustering expeditions of Walker to Nicaragua and of others to Cuba, and, especially, the repeal of the Missouri Compromise and the passing of the Kansas-Nebraska Act, which kindled a flame that ultimately led to the Civil War. The unpopularity of this act led to his enforced retirement from politics in 1857.

PIERO DELLA FRANCESCA, *fran-chays'ka* (*c.* 1420-92), a Florentine religious painter, was born and died at Borgo San Sepolcro. He is known especially for his frescoes, long neglected, the *Story of the True Cross* in the choir of San Francesca, Arezzo. He also wrote a treatise on geometry and a manual on perspective. See studies by K. Clark (1951), Venturi (1953) and Berenson (1954).

PIERO DI COSIMO, properly **Piero di Lorenzo** (1462-1521), Florentine painter, took the name of his master, Cosimo Rosselli. His later style was influenced by Signorelli and Leonardo da Vinci and among his best-known works are *Perseus and Andromeda* (Uffizi) and *Death of Procris* (Nat. Gallery, London). See monograph by R. Langton Douglas (1946).

PIERRE, Abbé, properly **Grouès, Henri Antoine** (1912–), French priest, born in Lyon, served with distinction during World War II and became a member of the resistance movement in 1942. Elected deputy in the constituent assembly after the war, he resigned in 1951 to concentrate on helping the homeless of Paris. Forming his band of Companions of Emmaus, he provided, with little monetary assistance, at least a minimum of shelter for hundreds of families and finally secured the aid of the French government in dealing with this problem.

PIERSON, originally **Pearson, Henry Hugo** (1815–73), English composer, born at Oxford, the son of the Dean of Salisbury, was educated at Harrow and Trinity College, Cambridge. In 1844–45 he was Reid professor of Music in Edinburgh, and from 1846 lived in Germany. He composed the music for the second part of Goethe's *Faust*, the operas *Leila* and *Contarini*, the oratorios *Jerusalem* and *Hezekiah*, and many songs.

PIETRO. See PETER.

PIGAFETTA, Francesco Antonio (1491–1535), Italian traveller, born at Vicenza, sailed with Magellan (q.v.), and wrote the account of the voyage (trans. with introd. by Robertson, 1906).

PIGALLE, Jean Baptiste, *pee-gal* (1714–85), French sculptor, born and died in Paris, was extremely popular in his day. His works include a statue of Voltaire and the tomb of Marshal Maurice de Saxe at Strasbourg. His *Vénus, l'Amour et l'Amitié* is in the Louvre.

PIGNON, Edouard, *peen-yõ* (1905–), French painter, born at Marles-les-Mines, was a Sunday painter until 1943. His works are rich in colour, and his treatment of forms was influenced by the Cubists and by Villon. Many of his pictures are studies of miners— e.g., the *Mineur mort* (1952)—and of harvest scenes and peasants.

PIGOTT, Richard (*c.* 1828–89), Irish journalist, born in County Meath, became editor and proprietor of *The Irishman* and two other papers of Fenian or extreme Nationalist type, which he disposed of in 1881 to Parnell and others. Already suspected by his party, he sold in 1886 to a 'Loyal and Patriotic Union' papers incriminating Parnell in the Phoenix Park tragedy, on which were based *The Times* articles 'Parnellism and Crime'. Convicted of falsehood, he confessed that he had forged the more important papers, fled, and shot himself in Madrid. See his *Reminiscences* (2nd ed. 1883).

PIJPER, Willem, *pī'per* (1894–1947), Dutch composer, born at Zeist, one of the foremost of modern composers of the Netherlands, taught at Amsterdam Conservatoire. He wrote symphonies and other orchestral pieces and an opera, *Halewijn*.

PILATE, Pontius, fifth Roman procurator of Judaea and Samaria, from A.D. 26 to 36, in whose time Jesus suffered. Under his rule there were many outbreaks, and at length Vitellius sent him to Rome to answer to Caesar (A.D. 36) on charges of rapacity and cruelty. Eusebius tells us that Pilate made away with himself; others say he was banished to Vienna Allobrogum (*Vienne*),

or beheaded under Nero. Tradition makes him (or his wife) accept Christianity, and associates him with Pilatus in Switzerland. The so-called *Acts of Pilate* are utterly unauthentic. See Lipsius, *Die Pilatus-Acten* (1871).

PILE, Sir Frederick Alfred, 2nd Bart. (1884–), British general, won the D.S.O. and the M.C. in the first World War and throughout the second commanded Britain's anti-aircraft defences. In 1945 he was appointed director-general of the Ministry of Works.

PILNYAK, Boris (1894–?1938), Russian author whose real name was Boris Andreyevich Vogau, wrote novels and short stories including *The Naked Year* (1922) and *The Volga Flows Down to the Caspian Sea* (1930; English trans. 1932). His main theme was the effect of the revolution on the middle classes in Russia. He was arrested in 1938 and may now be dead. See G. Struve, *Twenty-five Years of Soviet Russian Literature* (1944).

PILON, Germain, *pee-lõ* (1537–90), French sculptor, born in Paris, is recognized as one of the leading Renaissance artists Among his works are the statues of Henry II and Catherine de' Medici at St Denis, the 'Virgin' in St Paul de Louis in Paris and the bronze Cardinal René de Biraque in the Louvre. In these, in contrast with his earlier more conventional work, such as 'The Three Graces', his keen feeling for and observation of nature have produced figures which are both more realistic and more emotional. He also produced skilful medals, especially of the French royal family. See study by J. Babelon (1927).

PILOTY, Karl von (1826–86), German painter, born at Munich, became head of a new Munich school of painters, in 1856 professor of Painting at the Munich Academy, and in 1874 director. Piloty was a pronounced realist. His finest pictures belong to the class of historical genre. Most have melancholy subjects.

PILPAY. See BIDPAI.

PIŁSUDSKI, Józef (1867–1935), Polish marshal and statesman, born at Zulów (Wilno), suffered frequent imprisonment in the cause of Polish independence. In 1887 he was sent to Siberia for five years, on his return becoming leader of the Polish Socialist party and from 1894 editor of the unauthorized *Workman*. After further terms of imprisonment in Warsaw and St Petersburg, he escaped to Cracow and began to form a band of troops which at the beginning of the 1914–18 war fought on the side of Austria. In 1917, realizing that Poland's situation was not to be bettered by a change from Russian to Austro-German domination, he disbanded his fighting force and was imprisoned in Magdeburg by the Germans. In 1918 a republic was set up in Poland with Piłsudski as its provisional president. In 1919, now a marshal, he led an army in a struggle to establish Poland's frontiers, but was driven back in 1920 by the Bolshevik army. In 1921 he went into retirement owing to disagreement with the government which he returned to overthrow in 1926, becoming minister of war and later premier. His reforms in the constitution produced in Poland a dictatorship which prevailed until his death. Although he had resigned the premiership in 1928, he remained the real ruler of the country in his capacity of minister of war. See Life by R. Landau (English trans. 1931).

PINAY, Antoine, *pee-nay* (1891–   ), French politician, born in the Rhône department. Primarily an industrialist and very successful mayor of the town of St Chamond, he entered politics in 1936 as deputy, becoming senator in 1938. He has been minister of transport and public works and of tourism; in 1952 became prime minister from March to December; and was minister of foreign affairs (1955–56), and of finance and economic affairs (1958–60).

PINCHBECK, (1) Christopher (*c.* 1670–1732), a London clockmaker and constructor of automata, invented the alloy of copper and zinc called by his name.

(2) **Christopher** (*c.* 1710–83), 2nd son of (1), invented astronomical clocks, automatic pneumatic brakes, patent candle snuffers, &c.

PINCKNEY, Charles Cotesworth (1746–1825), American statesman, born at Charleston, S.C., was sent to England and educated at Oxford, read law, and studied at Caen Military Academy. He afterwards settled as barrister at Charleston. He was Washington's aide-de-camp at Brandywine and Germantown, but was taken prisoner at the surrender of Charleston (1780). A member of the convention that framed the U.S. constitution (1787), he introduced the clause forbidding religious tests. In 1796 the Directory refused to receive him as minister to France. In 1804–08 he was twice Federalist candidate for the presidency.

PINDAR, (1) Gr. Pindaros (*c.* 522 B.C.–*c.* 440 B.C.), the chief lyric poet of Greece, born of an old and illustrious family, at Cynoscephalae near Thebes, the capital of Boeotia. He commenced his career as a composer of choral odes at twenty with a song of victory still extant (*Pyth.* X, written in 502). He soon reached the highest rank in his profession, and composed odes for persons in all parts of the Greek world—for the tyrants of Syracuse and Macedon, as well as for the free cities of Greece. In his poems he gives advice and reproof as well as praise to his patrons. Pindar was in the prime of life when Salamis and Thermopylae were fought, when Greek poetry and philosophy were at their greatest. He wrote hymns to the gods, paeans, dithyrambs, odes for processions, mimic dancing songs, convivial songs, dirges, and odes in praise of princes. Of all these poems we possess fragments only, but his *Epinikia* or Triumphal Odes have come down to us entire. They are divided into four books, celebrating the victories won in the Olympian, Pythian, Nemean and Isthmian games. They show the intense admiration of the Greeks for bodily prowess and beauty; such gifts come from the gods and are sacred. The groundwork of Pindar's poems consists of those legends which form the Greek religious literature, and his protest against myths dishonouring to the gods shows his pious nature. See works by Tycho Mommsen

(1845), L. Schmidt (1862), Friederichs (1863), Norwood (1945) and Bowra (1964).

(2) **Peter.** See WOLCOT.

PINEL, Philippe (1745–1826), French physician, born in Languedoc, graduated at Toulouse, worked in Montpellier and in 1793 became head of the Bicêtre and later worked at the Salpêtrière. His humanitarian methods, emphasizing the psychological approach, reformed the old barbarous treatment of the insane and are contained in his great *Traité médico-philosophique sur l'aliénation mentale* (1801).

PINERO, Sir Arthur Wing, *pi-nay'rō* (1855–1934), English playwright, born in London, studied law, but in 1874 made his début on the stage at Edinburgh, and in 1875 joined the Lyceum company. His first play, *£200 a Year*, appeared in 1877, followed by a series of comedies. In 1893, with *The Second Mrs Tanqueray*, generally reckoned his best, he began a period of realistic tragedies which were received with enthusiastic acclamation and made him the most successful playwright of his day. The author of some fifty plays which included *The Squire* (1881) and *The Profligate* (1889) from his earlier works and from his later *The Gay Lord Quex* (1899), *His House in Order* (1906), and *Mid-Channel* (1909), he was knighted in 1909.

PINKERTON, (1) Allan (1819–84), American detective, born in Glasgow, was a cooper and a Chartist who in 1842 settled at Dundee, Ill. He became a detective and deputy-sheriff and in 1861 guarded Abraham Lincoln. He was head of the American secret service, and founder at Chicago of a great detective agency, the first in the U.S.

(2) **John** (1758–1826), Scottish man of letters, born at Edinburgh, in 1780 settled in London, and in 1802 in Paris. His 24 books include *Essay on Medals* (1784), *Origin of the Scythians or Goths* (1787), in which he first fell foul of the Celts against whom he was strongly prejudiced, *Iconographia Scotica* (1795–97) and *Walpoliana* (1799). See his *Literary Correspondence* (1830).

PINTER, Harold (1930–   ), British dramatist, born the son of a London East End tailor of Portuguese-Jewish ancestry (da Pinta), became a repertory actor and wrote poetry and later plays. His first London production was trounced by the critics unused to his highly personal dramatic idiom. A superb verbal acrobat, he exposes and utilizes the illogical and inconsequential in everyday talk, not to illustrate some general idea (as does Ionesco), but to induce an atmosphere of menace in *The Birthday Party* (1957), or of claustrophobic isolation in *The Caretaker* (1958; filmed 1963). His TV play *The Lover* (1963) won the Italia prize. Other plays include *The Collection* (TV 1961; stage 1962), *The Dwarfs* (radio 1960; stage 1963), and *The Homecoming* (1965). Filmscripts: *The Servant* (1963), *The Pumpkin Eaters* (1964), &c.

PINTO, Fernão Mendez (*c.* 1510–83), Portuguese adventurer, born near Coimbra, at twenty-seven made his way to India, and remained for 21 years in southeast Asia, leading a life of adventure, fighting pirates, trading and going on special missions to Japan or elsewhere. He returned in 1558, and wrote an extravagant account of his adventures, *Peregrinaçam* (1614; Eng. trans. by F. Cogan, 1663; abridged ed. 1891).

PINTURICCHIO, the name given to the painter **Bernardino di Betto Vagio**, *peen-too-reek'yō* (1454–1513), was born at Perugia. An assistant to Perugino, he helped him with the frescoes in the Sistine Chapel at Rome, and he himself painted frescoes in several Roman churches and in the Vatican library, also at Orvieto, Siena, &c. See two works by Schmarsow (1880–82), and one by Ricci (trans. 1902).

PINWELL, **George John** (1842–75), English artist, born in London, known for his wood engravings and illustrations for Goldsmith, Jean Ingelow, *The Arabian Nights*, &c., and for exquisite watercolour subject paintings, few in number because of his early death.

PINZÓN, **Vicente Yáñez**, *peen-thon'* (*c.* 1460–*c.* 1524), Spanish discoverer of Brazil, belonged to a wealthy Andalusian family. He commanded the *Nina* in the first expedition of Columbus (1492), and, unlike his brother, Martin, who commanded another vessel, remained loyal to his chief. In 1499 he sailed on his own account, and on January 26, 1500, landed near Pernambuco, on the Brazil coast, which he followed north to the Orinoco. He was made governor of Brazil by Ferdinand and Isabella. See J. R. McClymont's *Vicente Añez Pinçon* (1916).

PIOMBO, **Sebastian del**, *pyom'bō* (1485–1547), painter, was of the family of Luciani, and was called Del Piombo (' of the Seal ') from his becoming in 1523 sealer of briefs to Pope Clement VII. He studied under Giovanni Bellini and Giorgione; went to Rome about 1510, where he worked in conjunction with Michelangelo. In 1519 he painted his masterpiece, the *Raising of Lazarus* (now in the National Gallery, London); and was an excellent portrait painter. See Milanesi, *Les Correspondants de Michel Ange* (Fr. trans. 1890).

PIOZZI or THRALE, **Mrs**, *née* Hester Lynch Salusbury, *pyot'see* (1741–1821), was born at Bodvel in Caernarvonshire, and in 1763 married Henry Thrale, a prosperous Southwark brewer. Dr Samuel Johnson in 1765 conceived an extraordinary affection for her, was domesticated in her house at Streatham Place for over sixteen years, and for her sake learned to soften many of his eccentricities. Thrale also esteemed Johnson, carried him to Brighton, to Wales in 1774, and to France in 1775, and made him one of his four executors. Thrale died in April 1781, after his wife had borne him twelve children, and in 1784 the brewery was sold for £135,000. Dr Johnson began to feel himself slighted as the widow became attached to the Italian musician Piozzi, whom she married in 1784. After extensive travels in Europe, the couple returned to England in 1787, to Streatham in 1790; but soon after Mrs Piozzi built Brynbella on the Clwyd, where Piozzi died in 1809. She wrote poems and published *Anecdotes of Dr Johnson* (1786) and *Letters to and from Dr Johnson* (1788). See her *Autobiography* (reprinted 1861), her *Thraliana* (notebook; ed. by Hughes, 1913), her letters to Penelope Pennington (1913),

French Journals of Mrs Thrale and Dr Johnson (1932), the *Queeney Letters* (ed. Lord Lansdowne, 1934—Queeney was her eldest daughter), Mangin's *Piozziana* (1833), books by Clifford (1941), and Scott,*The Blue-stocking Ladies* (1947).

PIPER, **John** (1903–), English artist, born at Epsom. In 1933 he met Braque, and experiments in many media, including collage, led to a representational style which grew naturally from his abstract discipline. He designed sets for the theatre and painted a series of topographical pictures, e.g., the watercolours of *Windsor Castle* commissioned by H.M. the Queen in 1941–42, and dramatic pictures of war damage. His publications include *Brighton Aquatints* (1939) and *Buildings and Prospects* (1949). See the study edited by S. J. Woods (1955).

PIPPI. See GIULIO ROMANO.
PIPPIN. See PÉPIN.
PIRANDELLO, **Luigi** (1867–1936),. Italian dramatist, novelist and short story writer, was born at Girgenti (Agrigento). He studied at Rome and Bonn, becoming a lecturer in literature at Rome (1897–1922). After writing powerful and realistic novels and short stories, including *Il Fu Mattia Pascal* (1903) and *Si Gira* (1916), he turned to the theatre and became a leading exponent of the ' grotesque ' school of contemporary drama. Among his plays are *Six Characters in Search of an Author* (1920), *Enrico IV* (1922) and *Come Tu Mi Vuoi* (1930). In 1925 he established a theatre of his own in Rome and his company took his plays all over Europe. Many of his later plays have been filmed. In 1934 he was awarded the Nobel prize for literature. See study by W. Starkie (1927).

PIRANESI, **Giambattista**, *pee-ra-nay'zee* (1720–78), Italian architect and copperengraver of Roman antiquities, was born at Venice. He worked in Rome producing innumerable etchings of the city both in ancient times and in his own day. See studies by Mayor (1952) and H. Thomas (1954).

PIRE, **Georges**, *peer* (1910–69), Belgian priest, born at Dinant, lectured in moral philosophy at Louvain (1937–47) and was awarded the Croix de Guerre for resistance work as priest and intelligence officer in the second World War and in 1958 the Nobel Peace prize for his scheme of ' European villages ', including ' Anne Frank village ', in Germany, for elderly refugees and destitute children. See his Autobiography (trans. 1960).

PIRON, **Alexis**, *pee-rō* (1689–1773), French poet, playwright and wit, born at Dijon, who, according to his own epitaph, ' was nothing, not even an Academician '. See Saintsbury's *Miscellaneous Essays* (1892).

PISANO, (1) **Andrea** (*c.* 1270–1349), Italian sculptor, born at Pontedera, became famous as a worker in bronze and a sculptor in marble, settling in Florence. In 1347 he worked in the cathedral at Orvieto on reliefs and statues.

(2) **Giovanni** (*c.* 1250–*c.* 1320), Italian sculptor, assisted his father (3). He built the fine pulpit in Pisa cathedral and for several years worked on Siena cathedral.

(3) **Niccola** (*c.* 1225–*c.* 1284), Italian

sculptor of Pisa, father of (2), executed three works still admired for their excellence—the pulpit of the baptistery at Pisa (1260), the shrine of St Dominic for a church at Bologna (1267) and the pulpit of Siena cathedral (1268). He was also an architect and engineer.

(4) **Vittore, or Antonio Pisanello** (c. 1395–c. 1455), born at San Visilio, was both frescopainter and medallist and also was noted for his drawings of animals.

PISISTRATUS, Gr. Peisistratos, *pī-sis'trė-tus* (c. 600–527 B.C.), ' tyrant ' of Athens, acted at first with his kinsman Solon, but soon became leader of a people's party in Attica, eager for equality of political privileges. In 560, with a band of personal followers, he seized the Acropolis. The leaders of the aristocratic party fled, but returned in 554 and drove Pisistratus into exile (552). Supported by Thebes and Argos, he in 541 landed at Marathon, and marched on the capital. At Pallene he completely defeated his opponents, and thenceforward lived in undisturbed possession of power, transmitting at his death his supremacy to his sons, Hippias and Hipparchus, the *Pisistratidae.* He enforced obedience to the laws of Solon, emptied the city of its poorest citizens, making them agriculturists, and secured provision for old and disabled soldiers.

PISSARRO, *pee-sa-rō,* (1) **Camille** (1830–1903), French Impressionist artist, born at St Thomas, West Indies, went in 1855 to Paris, where he was much influenced by Corot's landscapes. In 1870 he lived in England for a short time, this being the first of several visits. Most of his works were painted in the countryside round Paris, and he lived at Pontoise from 1872 to 1884. In the next year he met Signac and Seurat and for the next five years adopted their divisionist style. Pissarro was the leader of the original Impressionists, and the only one to exhibit at all eight of the Group exhibitions in Paris from 1874 to 1886. He had considerable influence on Cézanne and Gauguin at the beginning of their artistic careers. His famous painting of the *Boulevard Montmartre* by night (1897) is in the National Gallery, London. See his *Letters to his son Lucien,* edited in 1943 by J. Rewald.

(2) **Lucien** (1863–1944), French painter, designer, wood-engraver and printer, son of (1), came to England in 1890, founded (1894) the Eragny press, designed types, and painted landscapes, showing the divisionist touch.

PISTON, Walter (1894–), American composer of Italian descent, born in Rockland, Me., trained as an artist, first took a serious interest in music as a student at Harvard. He later studied in Paris under Nadia Boulanger and returned to Harvard as professor of Music. He has produced books on harmony, counterpoint and orchestration. His compositions are in a modern, neoclassical style that includes elements from jazz and popular music.

PITCAIRN, Robert (1793–1855), Scottish writer and antiquary, born in Edinburgh, was editor of *Criminal Trials in Scotland, 1484–1624* (1830–33). He held a post in the Register House at Edinburgh.

PITCAIRNE, Archibald (1652–1713), Scottish

physician and satirist, born in Edinburgh, practised medicine there before being appointed in 1692 professor at Leyden. Returning to Edinburgh in 1693, he was notorious as a Jacobite, an Episcopalian and satirist of Presbyterianism. He founded the medical faculty at Edinburgh and his medical writings appeared in 1701 under the title of *Dissertationes medicae.* See Life by Webster (1781).

PITMAN, Sir Isaac (1813–97), English inventor of a shorthand system, was born at Trowbridge, Wiltshire. First a clerk, he became a schoolmaster at Barton-on-Humber (1832–36) and at Wotton-under-Edge, where he issued his *Stenographic Sound Hand* (1837). Dismissed from Wotton because he had joined the New (Swedenborgian) Church, he conducted a school at Bath (1839–43). Henceforward his career is the history of the development of shorthand and spelling reform. In 1842 he brought out the *Phonetic Journal,* and in 1845 opened premises in London. He was knighted in 1894. See Life by A. Baker (1908).

PITSCOTTIE, Robert Lindsay of (c. 1500–65), Scottish historian, born at Pitscottie near Cupar, was the author of *The Chronicles of Scotland, 1436–1565.* His style is quaint and graphic, and his facts trustworthy, except where he deals in marvels. The best edition is Mackay's (1899–1911).

PITT, (1) **Thomas** (1653–1726), son of the rector of Blandford, became a wealthy East India merchant, governor of Madras, and purchaser for £20,400 of the Pitt Diamond, which he sold in 1717 to the French regent to become one of the state jewels of France. In 1791 it was valued at £480,000. His eldest son, Robert, was father of the Earl of Chatham (q.v.); his second, Thomas (c. 1688–1729), was first Earl of Londonderry.

(2) **William, the Elder.** See CHATHAM.

(3) **William** (1759–1806), English statesman, second son of the Earl of Chatham, was born at Hayes near Bromley. He was never sent to school, but entered Pembroke Hall, Cambridge, at fourteen. From his youth he was trained for political life. He became an excellent classical scholar, but he valued the classical writers mainly as a school of language and of taste. He was called to the bar in June 1780, but in September parliament was dissolved, and he stood for Cambridge University, but was rejected. Sir James Lowther, however, gave him a seat for Appleby, and Pitt entered the House of Commons in January 1781. The Tory ministry of Lord North was then tottering under the disasters in America, and confronted by the Old Whigs who followed Rockingham, among them Fox and Burke, and by a smaller body who had been attached to the fortunes of Chatham, such as Shelburne, Camden, and Barré. Pitt threw himself into the fray, and on several occasions assailed the falling ministry, but refused to cast in his lot with the opposition. Upon North's resignation in March 1782 a ministry was formed under Rockingham, but Pitt declined several offers of position. He gave general support to the new ministers, but brought forward the question of parliamen-

tary reform. On July 1, 1782, Rockingham died, and while Fox insisted on the leadership of the Duke of Portland, the king made Shelburne first lord. Fox resigned, and Pitt became chancellor of the Exchequer. Peace negotiations between England and the United States were signed in November and with France and Spain in January 1783, while a truce was established with Holland, and the first steps were taken towards a liberal commercial treaty with the United States. While Pitt's reputation steadily rose, the Shelburne ministry was weak and divided; but Pitt stood loyally by his chief. Two votes of censure directed against the peace were carried through the Commons, and on February 24, 1783, Shelburne resigned. The king implored Pitt, who had displayed splendid parliamentary talents, to accept the leadership, and gave him an absolute authority to name his colleagues. It was a dazzling offer, but he saw clearly that the hour of triumph had not yet come. After a long struggle the king was obliged to yield, and on April 2 a coalition ministry was formed under the Duke of Portland, with Fox and North as joint secretaries of state. Pitt refused his old post of chancellor of the Excheuqer, and as leader of the Opposition brought forward an elaborate scheme of parliamentary reform. He was defeated by 293 to 149, but he succeeded in bringing Fox and North into direct collision. His other measure for the reform of abuses in the public offices passed the Commons, but was rejected in the Lords. A government bill modifying the charter of the East India Company shared a like fate; the ministry refused to resign, and the Commons supported them by large majorities; but the king dismissed them in December 1783, and Pitt took office as chancellor of the Exchequer and first lord of the Treasury. His position seemed hopeless; there was a majority of more than a hundred against him in the Commons, in which Pitt was the only Cabinet minister, while Dundas was the only considerable debater who supported him against the attacks of North, Fox, Burke and Sheridan. But Pitt fought his battle with a skill and resolution never surpassed in parliamentary history. A long succession of hostile votes was carried, but failed to drive him from office, and soon signs appeared that the country was with him. The magnanimity he showed in refusing a great sinecure office added greatly to his popularity. The majorities against him grew steadily smaller. At last, on March 25, 1784, parliament was dissolved, and the ensuing election made Pitt one of the most powerful ministers in all English history, and prepared the way for a ministry which lasted, almost unbroken, for twenty years. Now the House of Commons acquired a new importance in the constitution, the people a new control over its proceedings, and the first lord of the Treasury complete ascendency in the government. The regency question established parliamentary rights. Direct parliamentary corruption was finally put down. Great numbers of sinecure places were abolished, reforms were introduced into revenue methods, and the whole system

of taxation and of trade duties was thoroughly revised. The finances of the country, disorganized by the American war, became once more flourishing. An enlightened commercial treaty was negotiated with France. In foreign politics Pitt was for some years equally successful. His love of peace was sincere, but the influence of England in European councils rose greatly, and he showed much tact in extricating England from the ambitious designs of Prussia. But he cast aside too lightly on the first serious opposition parliamentary reform and the abolition of the slave trade. His attempt to establish free trade between England and Ireland failed through an explosion of manufacturing jealousy in England. More real blame attaches to his opposition to reforming the enormous abuses in the Irish parliament and to his uncertain policy towards the Irish Catholics. He created peerages with extreme lavishness. When the French Revolution broke out his policy was one of absolute neutrality. Reluctantly he drew the sword believing that a struggle with France would be both short and easy. His early military enterprises were badly planned and badly executed but the navy, fostered by him in peace time, was much stronger than that of France. Through fear of the revolutionary spirit, he was led into stern domestic measures. Corn had risen to famine price and great distress prevailed, and the government attempted to meet it by very ill-conceived relaxations of the poor laws. In Ireland Pitt tried first to win the Catholics by measures of conciliation. He then, after the rebellion, suggested a legislative union which, was to be followed by Catholic emancipation, the payment of the priests and a commutation of tithes. The first measure was carried by very corrupt means, but the king declared himself inexorably opposed to Catholic emancipation. Pitt resigned his office into the hands of his follower Addington in February 1801; but a month later he declared that he would abandon Catholic claims and resumed office in May 1804 on this understanding. The war, suspended by the peace of Amiens, had broken out with renewed vehemence. There was danger of invasion, and Pitt desired to combine the most eminent men of all parties in the ministry; but the king's animosity towards Fox lost him Fox's supporters and he was not aided by an alliance with the weak Addington. But with little help from his colleagues Pitt was hailed as the saviour of Europe after the great victory of Trafalgar in 1805. His health was now broken, however, and he died at Putney, and was buried in Westminster Abbey. Pitt was never married, and he never mixed much in general society. Few men possessed to a higher degree the power of commanding, directing and controlling, and he inspired the nation with unbounded confidence. He was one of the first statesmen to adopt the teaching of Adam Smith. His political Life was written by Gifford (1809) and Bishop Tomline (1822); the standard biography is by Lord Stanhope (4th ed. 1879). See Macaulay's essay, books by Sergeant (1882), Walford (1890), Lord

Rosebery (1891), Lord Ashbourne (1899), Whibley (1906), Holland Rose (1911–12, 1926), Sir Charles Petrie (1935).

PITTACUS OF MITYLENE (*c.* 650–570 B.C.), Greek ruler, one of the ' Seven Wise Men ' of Greece, whose experience, according to the ancients, was embodied in ' Know thine opportunity ' and other aphorisms.

PITTER, Ruth (1897–), English poetess, born at Ilford, Essex, wrote verse from a very early age and later was encouraged by Hilaire Belloc. Her writing belongs to no particular school and for inspiration she has drawn mainly upon the beauty of natural things. In 1955 she was awarded the Queen's Gold Medal for Poetry, having already won the Hawthornden Prize in 1936 with *A Trophy of Arms.* Other volumes include *First and Second Poems* (1927), *A Mad Lady's Garland* (1934), *Urania* (1951) and *The Ermine* (1953).

PITT-RIVERS, Augustus Henry Lane-Fox (1827–1900), English soldier and archaeologist, born in Yorkshire, educated at Sandhurst, worked to improve army small arms training and was a promoter of the Hythe school of musketry, ultimately becoming a lieutenant-general (1882). Having in 1880 inherited Wiltshire estates, rich in Romano-British and Saxon remains, from his great-uncle, Lord Rivers, he devoted himself to archaeology, evolving a new scientific approach to excavation which became a model for later workers. His collections were presented to Oxford museum. He became F.R.S. in 1876, first inspector of ancient monuments in 1882.

PIUS, the name of twelve Roman pontiffs.

Pius I was Bishop of Rome 140–155.

Pius II, named **Enea Silvio de Piccolomini** (1405–64), in youth wrote poems, letters and a novel. At twenty-six he was secretary to the Bishop of Fermo at the Council of Basel, and in 1432–35 was employed on missions to Scotland, England and Germany. He took an office under the Emperor Frederick III, regulated his life, took orders, was made Bishop of Trieste, and after returning to Italy (1456) a cardinal. On the death of Callistus III in 1458 he was elected pope, and took the name of Pius II. His reign is memorable for his efforts to organize an armed confederation of Christian princes to resist the Turkish arms. Aeneas Sylvius was one of the most eminent scholars of his age. His works (Basel 1551) are chiefly historical; his letters throw a vivid light upon their age. See Lives by Voigt (1856–63), Weiss (1897), Boulting (1909), Ady (1913), Creighton's *History of the Papacy* (vol. ii 1882), and Pastor's *History of the Popes* (vol. iii 1895).

Pius IV, named **Giovanni Angelo Medici** (1499–1565), born at Milan, became cardinal in 1549, and pope in 1559. He brought to a close the deliberations of the Council of Trent, and issued (1564) the Creed of Pius IV, or Tridentine Creed.

Pius V, named **Michele Ghislieri** (1504–72), born near Alessandria, became a bishop in 1556, and a cardinal in 1557. As inquisitor-general for Lombardy he rigorously repressed the Reformed doctrines. Pope from 1566, he laboured to restore discipline and morality, and reduced the expenditure of his court. The bull *In Coena Domini* (1568) applies to the 16th century the principles and the legislation of Hildebrand. His bull releasing Queen Elizabeth's subjects from their allegiance (1570) was ineffectual. The most momentous event of his pontificate was the expedition which he organised, with Spain and Venice, against the Turks, resulting in the naval engagement of Lepanto (1571). He was canonized in 1712.

Pius VI, named **Giovanni Angelo Braschi** (1717–99), was born at Cesena, became cardinal in 1773, pope in 1775. To him Rome owes the drainage of the Pontine Marsh, the improvement of the port of Ancona, the completion of St Peter's, the foundation of the New Museum of the Vatican, and the embellishment of the city. The pope repaired to Vienna, but failed to restrain the reforming Emperor Joseph from further curtailing his privileges. Soon after came the French Revolution and the confiscation of church property in France. The pope launched his thunders in vain, and then the murder of the French agent at Rome (1793) gave the Directory an excuse for the attack. Bonaparte took possession of the Legations, and afterwards of the March of Ancona, and extorted (1797) the surrender of these provinces from Pius. The murder of a member of the French embassy in December was avenged by Berthier taking possession of Rome. Pius was called on to renounce his temporal sovereignty, and on his refusal was seized, carried to Siena, the Certosa, Grenoble and finally Valence, where he died.

Pius VII, named **Luigi Barnaba Chiaramonti** (1742–1823), was born at Cesena. He became Bishop of Tivoli, and, already a cardinal, succeeded Pius VI in 1800. Rome was now restored to the papal authority, and next year the French troops were withdrawn from most of the papal territory. Pius restored order in his states, and in 1801 concluded a concordat with Napoleon, which the latter altered by autocratic *Articles organiques.* In 1804 Napoleon compelled Pius to come to Paris to consecrate him as emperor. He failed to get any modification of the articles, and soon after his return to Rome the French seized Ancona and entered Rome. This was followed by the annexation (May 1809) of the papal states to the French empire. The pope in June retaliated by excommunicating the robbers of the Holy See. He was next removed to Grenoble, and finally to Fontainebleau, where he was forced to sign a new concordat and sanction the annexation. The fall of Napoleon (1814) allowed him to return to Rome, and the Congress of Vienna restored him his territory. Brigandage was suppressed, as well as secret societies; while the Jesuits were restored. See Life by Mary H. Allies (1872 and 1897).

Pius IX, named **Giovanni Maria Mastai Ferretti** (1792–1878) born at Sinigaglia, took deacon's orders in 1818, in 1827 was made Archbishop of Spoleto, and in 1832 Bishop of Imola. In 1840 he became a cardinal, and on the death of Gregory XVI in 1846 was elected pope. He entered at once on a course of reforms. He granted an amnesty to all political prisoners and exiles, removed most of the disabilities of the Jews, authorized railways, projected a council of state, and in March 1848 published his *Statuto Fonda-mentale*, a scheme for the temporal government of the papal states by two chambers, one nominated by the pope, the other (with the power of taxation) elected by the people. At first the new pope was the idol of the populace. But the revolutionary fever of 1848 spread too fast for a reforming pope, and his refusal to make war upon the Austrians finally forfeited the affections of the Romans. On November 15, 1848, his first minister, Count Rossi, was murdered, and two days later a mob assembled in the square of the Quirinal. On the 24th the pope escaped to Gaeta, and a republic was proclaimed in Rome. In April 1849 a French expedition was sent to Civita Vecchia; in July General Oudinot took Rome, after a siege of thirty days; and henceforward the papal government was re-established. Pio Nono proved an unyielding Conservative and ultramontane, closely allied with the Jesuits. The war of the French and Sardinians against Austria in 1859 and the popular vote of 1860 incorporated a great part of papal territory with the Sardinian (Italian) kingdom; but Pius always refused to recognize the fact. He re-established the hierarchy in England, sanctioned a Catholic university in Ireland, and condemned the Queen's Colleges. He concluded a reactionary concordat with Austria. By the bull ' Ineffabilis Deus ' (1854) he decreed the Immaculate Conception; his famous encyclical ' Quanta Cura ' and the Syllabus of errors appeared in 1864. The Vatican Council (1869–70) proclaimed the infallibility of the pope. For the last ten years the pope's temporal power had been only maintained by the French garrison; on its withdrawal in 1870 the soldiers of Victor Emmanuel entered Rome. For the rest of his days the pope lived a voluntary ' prisoner ' within the Vatican.

Pius X, named **Giuseppe Sarto** (1835–1914), born at Riese near Venice, and ordained in 1858, became Bishop of Mantua in 1884, in 1893 Cardinal and Patriarch of Venice and in 1903 was elected pope. The separation of church and state in France and Portugal, toleration in Spain, and Pius's attacks on modernism led to strained relations and embarrassments.

Pius XI, named **Achille Ratti** (1857–1939), born at Desio near Milan, was ordained in 1879. Linguist, scholar, alpinist, he was librarian of the Ambrosian (Milan) and Vatican libraries, papal nuncio to Poland, Archbishop of Lepanto, Cardinal Archbishop of Milan in 1921 and pope in 1922. He became sovereign of the Vatican State in 1929.

Pius XII, named **Eugenio Pacelli** (1876–1958), born in Rome, distinguished himself in the Papal diplomatic service and as secretary of state to the Holy See before succeeding Pius XI. He was elected pope in 1939 and during World War II under his leadership the Vatican did much humanitarian work, notably for prisoners of war and refugees. There has been continuing controversy, however, over his attitude to the treatment of the Jews in Nazi Germany, critics arguing that he could have used his influence with Catholic Germany to prevent the massacres, others that any attempt to do so would have proved futile and might possibly have worsened the situation. In the postwar years the plight of the persecuted churchmen in the Communist countries, and the fate of Catholicism there, became the Pope's personal concern. Pius XII was widely respected both in the Catholic and non-Catholic world as a distinguished scholar and as a man of immense moral authority.

PIZARRO, *pee-thar'ō*, (1) **Francisco** (*c.* 1478–1541), born at Trujillo, served under Gonsalvo di Cordova in Italy. In 1509 he was at Darien, and he served under Balboa when he discovered the Pacific. In 1526 Pizarro and Almagro sailed for Peru; and, after many misadventures and delays, they reached its port of Tumbes, and collected full information respecting the empire of the Incas. Pizarro repaired to Spain for authority to undertake the conquest, which he got in 1529, he being made captain-general and Almagro marshal. He sailed again from Panamá in December 1531, with 183 men and 37 horses; Almagro was to follow with reinforcements. Landing at Tumbes, the Spaniards commenced the march inland in May 1532, and in November entered Cajamarca. Near this Pizarro captured the Inca Atahualpa by treachery, and [after extorting an enormous ransom, amounting to £3,500,000, put him to death, August 29, 1533. Pizarro then marched to Cuzco, set up the young Inca Manco as nominal sovereign, and was himself created a marquis by the Emperor Charles V. Almagro undertook the conquest of Chile, Pizarro was busy founding Lima and other cities on the coast, and his brothers were at Cuzco, when an Indian insurrection broke out. Both Cuzco and Lima were besieged, and Juan Pizarro was killed, but in the spring of 1537 Almagro returned from Chile, raised the siege of Cuzco, and took possession of the city. Pizarro had no intention of allowing his rival to retain Cuzco. Too old to take the field himself, he entrusted the command of his forces to his brothers, who defeated Almagro, April 26, 1538, and beheaded him soon afterwards. One of Almagro's followers, named Juan de Rada, matured a conspiracy for the assassination of Pizarro. The conspirators attacked his house in Lima, and murdered the old conqueror. His brother, Hernando Pizarro, for having beheaded Almagro at Cuzco, was imprisoned until 1560 on his return to Spain. He died in 1578. See Lives by A. Helps (1869) and Towle (1878).

(2) **Gonzalo** (*c.* 1506–48), half-brother of (1), whom he accompanied in the conquest of Peru, and did good service when the Indians besieged Cuzco, and in the conquest of Charcas. In 1539 he undertook an expedition to the eastward of Quito, and endured fearful hardships. One of his lieutenants, Francisco de Orellana, sent in advance for supplies, deserted his starving comrades, discovered the whole course of the Amazon, and returned to Spain. Only 90 out of 350

Spaniards returned with Gonzalo in June 1542. On his brother's assassination Gonzalo retired to Charcas. In 1544 the new viceroy, Vela, arrived in Peru to enforce the ' New Laws '. The Spaniards, dismayed, entreated Gonzalo to protect their interests. He mustered 400 men, entered Lima in October 1544, and was declared governor of Peru; the viceroy Vela was defeated and killed in battle (1546). When news of this revolt reached Spain, Pedro de la Gasca, an able ecclesiastic, was sent to Peru as president to restore order, and landed at Tumbes in June 1547. Gonzalo Pizarro defeated a force sent against him, and met Gasca near Cuzco in April 1548. But his forces deserting him, he gave himself up, and was beheaded at the age of forty-two. See C. R. Markham's *History of Peru* (1892).

PIZZETTI, Ildebrando, *pits-et'ee* (1880–1968), Italian composer, born in Parma. The son of a piano teacher, he studied at Parma Conservatoire, and in 1908 became professor of Harmony and Counterpoint at the Instituto Musicale, Florence. He was director there from 1917 to 1924, when he became director of the Guiseppe Verdi Conservatory, Milan. He won a high reputation as an opera composer with *Fedra* (1912) and *Debora e Jaele* (1923), and in 1936 he succeeded Respighi as professor of Composition at the Accademia di Sancta Cecilia, Rome. He composed extensively in all forms. See Life by G. M. Gatti (1951).

PLACE, Francis (1771–1854), English reformer, born in London, a self-educated London tailor, champion of radicalism and the right of combination, he contrived the repeal of the Combination Laws in 1824 and was a leading figure in the agitation which brought about the passing of the Reform Bill in 1832. Drafter of the People's Charter, and a pioneer of birth-control study, he wrote *The Principle of Population* (1822; ed. Himes, 1930). See Life by Wallas (1898; n.e. 1918).

PLANCHÉ, James Robinson, *plä-shay* (1796–1880), English playwright, antiquary and herald, born, of Huguenot descent, in London. He wrote books on the history of dress, *Regal Records* (1838), *The Pursuivant of Arms* (1852; 3rd ed. 1874), innumerable dramas, burlesques and extravaganzas and his *Recollections and Reflections* (2 vols. 1872). He was made Rouge Croix in 1845 and Somerset herald in 1866.

PLANCK, Max Karl Ernst (1858–1947), German theoretical physicist, the formulator of the quantum theory which revolutionized physics, born April 23 at Kiel, studied at Munich and under Kirchhoff and Helmholtz at Berlin where he succeeded the former in the professorship (1889–1926) and became secretary of the Prussian Academy of Sciences (1912–43) and president of the Kaiser Wilhelm Society (1930–37). His work on the law of thermodynamics and black body radiation led him to abandon classical dynamical principles and formulate the quantum theory (1900), which assumed energy changes to take place in violently abrupt instalments or quanta. This successfully accounted for and predicted certain phenomena inexplicable in the Newtonian theory. Einstein's application of the quantum theory to light (1905) led to

the theories of relativity and in 1913 Niels Bohr successfully applied it to the problems of sub-atomic physics. He was awarded the Nobel prize (1918) and in 1926 was elected a foreign member of the Royal Society. One of Planck's sons, **Erwin,** was executed in 1944 for plotting against Hitler.

PLANQUETTE, Robert, *plä-ket* (1850–1903), French composer, born in Paris, and educated at the Conservatoire there, composed *Paul Jones* (1889), and other light operas.

PLANTAGENET, a surname applied to the Angevin family which in 1154 succeeded to the throne of England in the person of Henry II and reigned till Richard III's death. *Plante-geneste* was the nickname of Geoffrey, Count of Anjou, husband of Matilda, daughter of Henry I—possibly from the sprig of broom (*planta genista*) which he wore in his cap, possibly because he used a broom-switch in penance, possibly from the village of Le Genest in Maine. The first to use *Plantaginet* (sic) as his family name, was Richard, Duke of York, in 1460, in laying claim to the crown. But the sovereigns called Plantagenet kings are Henry II, Richard I, John, Henry III, Edward I–III, Richard II, Henry IV–VI, Edward IV–V and Richard III. See study by J. Harvey (1948).

PLANTÉ, Gaston, *plä-tay* (1834–89), French physicist, born at Orthy, followed up Ritter's discovery of the secondary cell and constructed the first practical storage battery (1860).

PLANTIN, Christophe, *plä-ti* (1514–89), French printer, born at St Avertin near Tours, settled as bookbinder at Antwerp in 1549; six years later he began to print. His *Biblia Polyglotta* (1569–73), his Latin, Hebrew and Dutch Bibles, and his editions of the classics are all famous. His printing-houses in Antwerp, Leyden and Paris were carried on by his sons-in-law. His office in Antwerp, bought by the city in 1876, is now the ' Musée Plantin '. See French works by M. Rooses (2nd ed. 1892), A. de Backer and C. Ruelens (1866), L. Degeorge (3rd ed. 1886), C. Clair (1960), and Plantin's *Correspondence* (1884–86).

PLANUDES, Maximus, *pla-nyoo'deez* (*c.* 1260–1310), a monk of Constantinople, sent as ambassador to Venice in 1296. His tasteless Anthology of poetry (Florence 1494), from that of Cephalas (10th century), was the only one known in the West until 1606. See his Letters, edited by Treu (Breslau 1890).

PLASKETT, John Stanley (1865–1941), Canadian astronomer, born at Woodstock, Ontario, was a graduate of Toronto University. At the Dominion Observatory, Ottawa, his work included research in spectroscopy and improvements in the design of the spectrograph. In 1918 the Dominion astrophysical observatory was built at Victoria to accommodate a huge telescope with a 72-inch reflector which he had designed. He was director here until he retired in 1935. During these years important investigations were carried out into motion and matter in interstellar space and results included the discovery of the largest known star which was named Plaskett's star.

PLATEAU, Joseph Antoine Ferdinand, *plah-tō* (1801–83), Belgian physicist, born in Brussels, became professor of Physics at Ghent (1835). In his study of optics he damaged his own eyesight by looking into the sun for twenty seconds in order to find out the effect on the eye. By 1840 he was blind, but continued his scientific work with the help of others. He was the discoverer of the tiny second drop, named after him, which always follows the main drop of a liquid falling from a surface.

PLATO (*c.* 427–*c.* 347 B.C.), Athenian philosopher, one of the supremely great philosophical geniuses of all time, born possibly in Athens, of an aristocratic family, but little is known of his early life. He saw military service in the Peloponnesian war, became a disciple of Socrates (q.v.), attended the latter's trial at the hands of the Democrats (399) and immortalized the latter's attitude and manner of death in three of his dialogues: *Apology*, or defence of his tutor; *Crito* on Socrates' willingness to die; and *Phaedo* on immortality. Socrates appears in most of Plato's 35 dialogues, but increasingly he becomes the spokesman not of Socratic but of Platonic doctrines. Plato spent some time at Megara in company with the Eleatic philosopher, Euclides, and from 390 possibly visited Egypt, was certainly at Cyrene with Theodorus, the mathematician, toured the Greek cities in Southern Italy, where he imbibed Pythagorean doctrines and at Syracuse converted Dion, son-in-law of the tyrant Dionysus I, to his ideology of the philosopher-king. In 388 Plato founded his own school, the original 'Academy' in the western suburbs of Athens in which mathematical and political studies were carried on. In 368 he returned to Syracuse at Dion's request to convert the fickle Dionysus II, but they soon quarrelled and Plato, after a second visit, gave it up. He died, in his eighty-first year, at a wedding feast. The chronology of the dialogues is a vexed subject, but stylistic considerations allow the following approximate groupings: (1) The early, truly Socratic ('what is it?') dialogues in which the main interest is definition as, for example, of self-knowledge in *Charmides*, courage in *Laches*, piety in *Euthyphro*, virtue equated with knowledge in *Protagoras* and which include the above mentioned. (2) The middle dialogues in which Plato increasingly outlines his own characteristic doctrines, including the *Meno*, possibly the *Timaeus*, outlining Plato's Pythagorean cosmology with time as 'the moving image of eternity' and the celebrated *Republic*. This, the first blueprint Utopia in history, examines the nature of justice, which eludes the tripartite division of the soul (wisdom, spiritedness or courage, and restrained passions) and which Plato's Socrates hopes to find 'in the larger letters of the state'. For, to this division conveniently correspond the three principal classes of the ideal state, the guardians, the military and the workers. Justice results when all these work in harmony. Plato's ideal state is static, a closed society without class mobility achieved by the propagation of convenient myths. The guardians, however, must be carefully trained and brought up to live in a Spartan communism, in which women share all the men's tasks for which they are fitted, marriages take place on certain festival days and are arranged ostensibly by lot, but rigged on eugenic principles, the offspring brought up anonymously by the state. This aristocracy may decline, first, into timocracy or government of honour by the military, then oligarchy or government of wealth, followed inevitably after the revolution of the poverty-stricken masses by democracy, the least desirable form of government barring tyranny, which necessarily follows. The education of the guardians brings Plato to his famous theory of ideas, or forms. He distinguishes sharply between the sphere of transient, finite, fickle particulars or objects of sense impressions, fit data only for opinion and belief, and that of the timeless, unchanging universal exemplars of the former, the forms, which are the true objects of knowledge. The unphilosophical man, at the mercy only of his sense-impressions is like a prisoner in a cave, who mistakes the shadows on the wall for reality. True knowledge is the apprehension of the universal forms. There is, for example, a universal form, 'table', which subsumes all the particular tables to be found in the world of sense impressions. Since art is essentially imitation of particulars it is therefore twice removed from reality and therefore doubly misleading. Artists are to be given applause but must be instantly deported from the Republic. (3) The later dialogues are remarkable for Plato's rigorously philosophical self-criticism unequalled among philosophers with the possible exception of Wittgenstein. The theory of forms, except in the *Phaedrus* on sexual love, becomes less prominent and undergoes devastating criticism in the *Parmenides*. It is modified to a theory of types, the relationship of 'participation' between forms and particulars is examined, but the logical problem of predication inherent in all this and unsuccessfully attempted in the *Sophist* awaits Aristotle. The *Theaetetus* examines perception, the *Laws*, considerably modify the political doctrines of the *Republic*, and the *Symposium* on love, reveals Plato, the poet. But all the dialogues are equally works of literature and philosophy. From the former standpoint, the translations by B. Jowett (new ed. 1925) are best, from the latter, F. M. Cornford's translations of *Theaetetus* and *Sophist* entitled *Plato's Theory of Knowledge* (1933), of *Timaeus*, entitled *Plato's Cosmology* (1937), of *Parmenides*, entitled *Plato and Parmenides* (1939), and the *Republic* (trans. 1941), are preferable. Of the *Epistles*, 6th, 7th, 8th are now generally regarded as authentic. Plato's influence is universal. It extends first through his great disciple and critic Aristotle, through the Stoics into Christian theology via Philo Judaeus (q.v.), was repeatedly revived beginning with the rediscovery of Plato's works (except for the *Timaeus* never lost) at the Renaissance when Aristotelian scholasticism was under attack, and by various Platonist and Neo-Platonist movements since. Rationalist and Idealist schools owe much to Plato, who successfully merged two opposing strands of Greek philosophy, the logical ' one ' of Parmenides and the ' flux ' (' the many ') of Heraclitus into one comprehensive metaphysical thesis. See biographical studies by A. E. Taylor (1929) and G. C. Field (1930), studies of the *Republic* by N. R. Murphy (1951), R. L. Nettleship, ed. Benson (1955), on the *Phaedrus* by R. Hackforth (1952), on the *Phaedo*, by R. S. Bluck (1955), on the theory of ideas by Sir W. D. Ross (1951), ethics (1928), education (1947), art (1953), by R. C. Lodge, and general studies by E. Zeller (trans. 1888), J. Burnet, *Greek Philosophy* (1914), G. M. A. Grube (1935), W. W. Jaeger, *Paideia* (trans. 1944), D. J. Allan (1952), W. L. Robinson (1953), R. B. Levinson (1953), R. C. Lodge (1956), R. E. Cushman (1958), P. Friedländer (trans. 1958), also critical works, Cherniss, *Aristotle's Criticisms of the Academy*, K. R. Popper, vol. i, *The Open Society and Its Enemies* (1945), and R. H. S. Crossman, *Plato Today* (new ed. 1959).

PLATOV, Matvei Ivanovich, Count (1757–1818), born at Azov, served in the Turkish campaign of 1770–71, and in 1801 was named by Alexander I ' Hetman of the Cossacks of the Don '. He took part in the campaigns against the French (1805–07), and hung on their retreat from Moscow with pitiless pertinacity (1813), defeating Lefebvre at Altenburg, gaining a victory at Laon, and making his name memorable by the devastations of his hordes of semi-savages.

PLAUTUS, Titus Maccius (wrongly *M. Accius*) (*c.* 250–184 B.C.), the chief comic poet of Rome, was born at Sarsina in Umbria. It is probable that he went to Rome while still young, and acquired there his mastery of the most idiomatic Latin. At Rome he found employment in connection with the stage, and saved money enough to enable him to leave Rome and start in business on his own account in foreign trade. His plays evince close familiarity with seafaring life and adventure, and an intimate knowledge of all the details of buying and selling and book-keeping. He failed, however, in business, and returned to Rome in such poverty that he had to earn his livelihood in the service of a baker by turning a handmill. While in this humble calling he wrote three plays which he sold to the managers of the public games. The price paid him enabled him to leave the mill, and he spent the rest of his life at Rome. Probably he commenced to write about 224 B.C., and, until his death, he continued to produce comedies with wonderful fecundity. His plays appear to have been left in the hands of the actors, who probably interpolated and omitted passages to suit them for the stage. Almost all the prologues were written after his death. About 130 plays were attributed to him in the time of Gellius, who held most of them to be the work of earlier dramatists revised and improved by Plautus. Roman critics considered most of them spurious. Varro limited the genuine comedies to twenty-one; and these so-called ' Varronian comedies ' are the same which we now possess, the *Vidularia* being fragmentary. Plautus's plays were immensely popular, and were acted, as Arnobius tells us,

in the time of Diocletian, five centuries later. Plautus borrowed his plots to a large extent from the New Attic Comedy, which dealt with social life to the exclusion of politics. But he infused a new and robuster life, which was typically Roman. His perfect spontaneity, vivacity and vigour of language, and the comic power of his dialogues, are his own. The charm of Plautus, lying in his genuine humour and powerful grasp of character, goes deep down to the roots of human nature. Shakespeare adapted the *Menaechmi* as *The Comedy of Errors*. Molière's *L'Avare* is borrowed from the *Aulularia*. English translations are by Thornton and Warner (1767–74), H. T. Riley (1880), Sugden (1895), Sir R. Allison (5 plays, 1914). Ritschl restored the very corrupt text (2nd ed. 1871); Goetz and Schoell completed his work (1892–96). The Loeb Library edition (5 vols. 1916 *et seq.*) has a trans. by Nixon.

PLAYFAIR, (1) **John** (1748–1819), Scottish mathematician and geologist, born at Benvie near Dundee, studied at St Andrews, and in 1773 became minister of Liff and Benvie. In 1785 he became joint professor of Mathematics at Edinburgh, but he exchanged his chair for that of Natural Philosophy in 1805. He was a strenuous supporter of the Huttonian theory in geology, and travelled much to make observations. Besides his famous *Illustrations of the Huttonian Theory* (1802), he wrote *Elements of Geometry* (1795) and *Outlines of Natural Philosophy* (1812–16).

(2) **Lyon, 1st Baron Playfair** (1819–98), British scientist, born at Meerut, studied at St Andrews, Glasgow, London and Giessen, was manager of textile-printing works at Clitheroe 1840–43, Edinburgh Chemistry professor 1858–68, Liberal M.P. from 1868, postmaster-general 1873–74, vice-president of council 1886. He was created a peer in 1829. He wrote on chemistry and political economy.

(3) **Sir Nigel Ross** (1874–1934), English actor-manager and producer, was born in London. First a barrister, he went on the stage and from 1902 to 1918 was a successful character actor. Becoming in 1919 manager of the Lyric Theatre, Hammersmith, he was responsible for a long series of successful productions, many of which were drawn from 18th-century comedy. Outstanding of these was *The Beggar's Opera*, produced with an original artistry, and others included *The Duenna* and *The Rivals*. He wrote *The Story of the Lyric Theatre, Hammersmith* (1925) and *Hammersmith Hoy* (1930). See G. Playfair, *My Father's Son* (1937).

(4) **William Henry** (1789–1857), Scottish architect, born in London, nephew of (1), designed Donaldson's Hospital, the National Monument, National Gallery, and many other Edinburgh buildings.

PLEKHANOV, Georgi Valentinovich, *plekah'nof* (1857–1918), Russian Marxist revolutionary, born in Tambov province, joined the Narodnist Populist movement as a student and in 1876 led the first popular demonstration in St Petersburg. In 1883 he helped to found the League for the Emancipation of Labour and spent the years 1883–1917 in exile in Geneva. From 1889 to 1904 he was Russian delegate to the Second International.

With Lenin, whose revolutionary mentor he was, he edited the journal *Spark* (1900). After the Bolshevik-Menshevik break, he supported the latter faction, returning to Russia in 1917, where he edited a paper. He died in Finland. His commentaries on Marxist theory fill 26 volumes.

PLETHON, Georgios Gemistos, *plee'thon* (*c.* 1355–1450), Greek scholar, probably a native of Constantinople, was counsellor in the Peloponnesus to Manuel and Theodore Palaeologus, and was sent to the Council of Florence in 1439. Here, if he did little for the union of the Churches, he did much to spread a taste for Plato.

PLEVEN, René Jean, *ple-vã* (1901–), French statesman, born in Brittany, studied law and became managing director of the International Cable Company. During World War II he served with the Free French air force and in the French National Committee in London. In French governments after 1944 he was successively minister of finances, minister of defence and he was prime minister July 1950-Feb. 1951 and Aug. 1951-Jan. 1952.

PLEYEL, Ignaz Joseph, *plī'el* (1757–1831), Austrian composer, born near Vienna, in 1783 became *kapellmeister* of Strasbourg Cathedral. In 1791 he visited London, in 1795 opened a music shop in Paris and in 1807 added a pianoforte manufactory. His forgotten compositions include quartets, concertos and sonatas.

PLIMSOLL, Samuel (1824–98), English social reformer, known as 'the sailors' friend', was born at Bristol, and in 1854 started business in the coal trade in London. Shortly afterwards he began to interest himself in the dangers affecting the mercantile marine. He accumulated a mass of facts proving that the gravest evils resulted from the employment of unseaworthy ships, from overloading, undermanning, bad stowage and over-insurance. He entered parliament for Derby in 1868; but it was not until he had published *Our Seamen* (1873) and had made an appeal to the public that the Merchant Shipping Act (1876) was passed, by which, *inter alia*, every owner was ordered to mark upon his ship a circular disc (the 'Plimsoll Mark'), with a horizontal line drawn through its centre, down to which the vessel might be loaded. He retired from parliamentary life in 1880. In 1890 he published *Cattle-ships*, exposing the cruelties and dangers of cattle-shipping. See Japp, *Good Men and True* (1890).

PLINY, (1) Gaius Plinius Secundus (A.D. 23–79), the Elder, came of a North Italian stock possessing estates at Novum Comum (*Como*), where he was born. He was educated in Rome, and when about twenty-three entered the army and served in Germany. He became colonel of his regiment (a cavalry one), and while attentive enough to his military duties to write a treatise on the throwing of missiles from horseback and to compile a history of the Germanic wars, he made a series of scientific tours in the region between the Ems, Elbe and Weser, and the sources of the Danube. Returning to Rome in 52, he studied for the bar, but withdrew to Como, and devoted himself to readnig and author-

ship. Apparently for the guidance of his nephew, he wrote his *Studiosus*, a treatise defining the culture necessary for the orator, and the grammatical work, *Dubius Sermo*. By Nero he was appointed procurator in Spain, and through his brother-in-law's death (71) he became guardian of his sister's son, Pliny the Younger, whom he adopted. Vespasian, whom he had known in Germany, was now emperor, and was henceforth his most intimate friend; but court favour did not wean him from study, and he brought down to his own time the history of Rome by Aufidius Bassus. A model student, amid metropolitan distraction he worked assiduously, and by lifelong application filled the 160 volumes of manuscript which, after using them for his *Historia Naturalis* (77), he bequeathed to his nephew. In 79 he was in command of the Roman fleet stationed off Misenum when the great eruption of Vesuvius was at its height. Eager to witness the phenomenon as closely as possible, he landed at Stabiae (*Castellamare*), but had not gone far when he succumbed to the stifling vapours rolling down the hill. His *Historia Naturalis* alone of his many writings survives. Under that title the ancients classified everything of natural or non-artificial origin. Pliny adds digressions on human inventions and institutions, devoting two books to a history of fine art, and dedicates the whole to Titus. His observations, made at second-hand, show no discrimination between the true and the false, between the probable and the marvellous, and his style is inartistic, sometimes obscure. But he supplies us with information on an immense variety of subjects as to which, but for him, we should have remained in the dark.

(2) **Gaius Plinius Caecilius Secundus** (A.D. 62–*c.* 114), the Younger, was born at Novum Comum. He wrote a Greek tragedy in his fourteenth year, and made such progress under Quintilian that he became noted as one of the most accomplished men of his time. His proficiency as an orator enabled him at eighteen to plead in the Forum, and brought him much practice. Then he served as military tribune in Syria, where he frequented the schools of the Stoic Euphrates and of Artemidorus; at twenty-five, the earliest possible age, he was *quaestor Caesaris*, then praetor, and afterwards consul in 100 A.D., in which year he wrote his laboured panegyric of Trajan. In 103-5 he was propraetor of the Provincia Pontica, and, among other offices, held that of curator of the Tiber, chiefly for the prevention of floods. He married twice; his second wife, Calpurnia, is fondly referred to in one of his most charming letters for the many gifts and accomplishments with which she sweetened his rather invalid life. He died without issue about 114. It is to his letters that Pliny owes his assured place in literature as a master of the epistolatory style. His meaning, though never obscure, is generally fuller than his expression; and, reading between the lines, we discern the features of a truly lovable man, much given to hospitality, and always pleased to help a less favoured brother, such as Suetonius or Martial. We derive from

him many of our most distinct impressions of the life of the upper class in the 1st century; above all, it is from his correspondence with Trajan that we get our clearest knowledge of how even the most enlightened Romans regarded the then obscure sect of the Christians and their 'depraved and extravagant superstition'. Keil's text of the *Epistles* and *Panegyricus* (1853) is the best; a useful selection with a good commentary was published by Church and Brodribb (1871). Melmoth's translation of the Letters (1746), revised by W. M. L. Hutchinson, is given with the text in the Loeb Classical Library (1915).

PLOMER, William Charles Franklin (1903–), British writer, born at Pietersburg, Transvaal, educated at Rugby, was a farmer and trader in South Africa before turning author, and also lived a while in Greece and Japan. With Roy Campbell (q.v.) he ran a South African literary review, and in World War II he served at the Admiralty. His works include the novels *Turbott Wolfe* (1926), *Sado* (1931) and *Ali the Lion* (1936); collections of short stories *I Speak of Africa* (1928) and *Paper Houses* (1929); and *Collected Poems* (1960). He edited the diaries of Francis Kilvert (q.v.). See his autobiographical *Double Lives* (1943).

PLOTINUS, *plo-tī'-* (205–270), one of the first and most original of Neoplatonic philosophers, born possibly at Lycopolis in Egypt, in 242 joined Gordianus's expedition to Persia, in order to study philosophy there and in India, but after the emperor's assassination in Mesopotamia, barely escaped to Antioch. In 244 he settled in Rome and became a popular lecturer in Neopythagorean and Neoplatonic doctrines, advocating asceticism and the charms of a contemplative life. Many of his wealthy patrons gave away their wealth to the poor, and freed slaves in response to his appeal of ascetic piety. When sixty years old, he attempted to found with the help of the emperor Gallienus a platonic 'Republic' in Campania, but died at Minturnae. His fifty-four works were edited by his pupil Porphyry, or Malchus, who arranged them in six groups of nine books or *Enneads*. Plotinus's system combines the various pre-Socratic schools of Greek philosophy, Aristotelian metaphysics, Platonism and Stoicism with an oriental theory of Emanation. He postulates a trinity, with The One, or God at the top, Spirit or intellectual principle second and lastly the soul, or author of all living things. The last is subdivided into an inner and an outer, the first intent upwards on spirit, the second facing down to the degenerate world of matter. He greatly influenced early Christian theology and some German Idealist schools of philosophy. See translations by S. MacKenna (1917), study by W. R. Inge (1918) and F. Copleston's *History of Philosophy*, vol. i (1947).

PLOWDEN, Edmund (1518–85), English Catholic lawyer, was born in Shropshire and educated at Cambridge. He sat in parliament in the reign of Queen Mary, retiring with thirty-nine other members over the question of heresy laws. One of the ablest lawyers of his day, from 1561 to 1571 he was treasurer of the Middle Temple. His excellent

commentaries were first published in 1571. A fine monument was erected to him in Temple church.

PLÜCKER, Julius (1801–68), German mathematical physicist, born at Elberfeld, was professor of Mathematics at Bonn (1836) and of Physics (1847). He investigated diamagnetism, originated the idea of spectrum analysis, and in 1859 discovered cathode rays, produced by electrical discharges in gases at low pressures.

PLUME, Thomas (1630–1704), English divine, born at Maldon, educated at Chelmsford and Christ's College, Cambridge, was vicar of Greenwich from 1658 and Archdeacon of Rochester from 1679. He endowed an observatory and the Plumian chair of astronomy and experimental philosophy at Cambridge, and bequeathed his extensive library to the town of Maldon, where it still exists intact. See Deed and Francis, *Catalogue of the Plume Library* (1959).

PLUMER, Herbert Charles Onslow, 1st Baron (1857–1932), British soldier and administrator, served in Sudan (1884), led the Rhodesian relief force to Mafeking (1900), and greatly distinguished himself as commander of the 2nd army, B.E.F. (1915–18), notably at the great attack on Messines, and G.O.C. Italian Expeditionary Force (1917–1918). He was made a field-marshal in 1919, was governor of Malta 1919–24, and high commissioner for Palestine 1925–28. See Life by C. Harington (1935).

PLUMPTRE, Edward Hayes, D.D. (1821–91), English divine, born in London, took a double first in 1844 from University College, Oxford, and was elected a fellow of Brasenose. He became a professor at King's College, London (1853), a prebendary of St Paul's (1863), principal of Queen's College, Harley Street (1875), and Dean of Wells (1881). He wrote on theology, and made verse translations of Sophocles, Aeschylus and Dante, as well as original verse.

PLUNKET, William Conyngham, 1st Baron Plunket (1764–1854), Irish lawyer, born at Enniskillen, opposed the Union (1798), prosecuted Emmett (1803), and rose to be lord chancellor of Ireland (1830–41).

PLUNKETT, Sir Horace Curzon (1854–1932), Irish agricultural reformer, third son of Lord Dunsany, after Eton and Oxford was for ten years on a cattle ranch, and from 1889 promoted agricultural cooperation in Ireland, being the founder in 1894 of the Irish Agricultural Organization Society. He was M.P. for Dublin Co. (S.) 1892–1900, vice-president of the Irish Department of Agriculture 1899–1907, and chairman of the Irish Convention 1917–18. He was a senator of the Irish Free State 1922–23. See Life by Digby (1950).

PLUTARCH, Gr. Ploutarchos (c. A.D. 46–c. 120), Greek historian, biographer and philosopher, was born at Chaeroneia in Boeotia. His higher education was commenced at Athens in 66. He paid more than one visit to Rome—once as *chargé d'affaires* of his native town—and there gave public lectures in philosophy. He spent all his mature life at his native place. His extant writings comprise his historical works, and those which are grouped under the general head of *Opera Moralia*. To the former belong his *Parallel Lives*—the work by which he is best known. These contain a gallery of forty-six portraits of the great characters of the ages preceding his own. They were published in successive books, each pair forming one book, and a Greek and Roman, with some resemblance between their respective careers, being chosen for the subject of each. The sequels which come after most of the Lives, giving a detailed comparison of each warrior, statesman, legislator or hero, are regarded as spurious by some critics. Plutarch's *Biographies* are monuments of great literary value for the precious materials which they contain, based as they are on lost records. The author adheres throughout to his professed purpose —portraiture of character; he either omits or briefly touches upon the most famous actions or events which distinguish the career of each subject of his biography, holding that these do not show a man's virtues or failings so well as some trifling incident, word or jest. The other and less known half of his writings —the *Morals*—are a collection of short treatises, sixty or more (though certainly not all from Plutarch's hand), upon various subjects—*Ethics, Politics, History, Health, Facetiae, Love-stories, Philosophy* and *Isis and Osiris*. Some of the essays breathe quite a Christian spirit, although the writer probably never heard of Christianity. The nine books of his *Symposiaca* or Table-talk exhibit him as the most amiable and genial of boon companions; while his dialogue *Gryllus* reveals a remarkable sense of humour. Though not a profound thinker, Plutarch was a man of rare gifts, and occupies a unique place in literature as the encyclopaedist of antiquity. There are translations of the *Lives* by the brothers Langhorne and one sponsored by Dryden (re-ed. Clough, 1859)— neither so scholarly as the French of Jacques Amyot (1559), from which Sir Thomas North (q.v.) made his version (1579). See Oakesmith's *Religion of Plutarch* (1902), Dill's *Roman Society* (1905), Mahaffy's *Silver Age of the Greek World* (1911).

POBEDONOSTSEV, Constantin Petrovich, *-nost'sef* (1827–1907), Russian jurist, son of a Moscow professor, became himself a professor of Civil Law there in 1858 and favoured liberal reforms in the law. Later he reacted against this, becoming strongly opposed to any westernization of Russia, and as procurator of the Holy Synod (from 1880) was the most uncompromising champion of the autocracy and of the supremacy of the orthodox church.

POCAHONTAS (1595–1617), Indian princess, daughter of an Indian chief, Powhatan, twice saved the life of Captain John Smith (q.v.). Cajoled to Jamestown in 1612, she embraced Christianity, was baptised Rebecca, married an Englishman, John Rolfe (1585–1622), in 1613, and came to England with him in 1616. Having embarked for Virginia, she died off Gravesend in March 1617. She left one son, and several Virginia families claim descent from her. See John Smith, *Travels and Works* (2 vols. 1910).

PO CHÜ-I, *paw-jü-ee* (772–846), Chinese poet

under the T'ang dynasty, was born in Honan, of which he became governor in 831. He was so noted as a lyric poet that his poems were collected by imperial order and engraved on stone tablets.

POCOCKE, (1) **Edward** (1604–91), English orientalist, born at Oxford, was elected a fellow of Corpus in 1628. He sailed for Aleppo in 1630 as chaplain to the English factory, but in 1636 became Oxford professor of Arabic, and in 1643 rector of Childrey. He was appointed to the chair of Hebrew in 1648. His main writings were *Specimen Historiae Arabum* (1649) and an edition of Abulfaraj's History (1663).

(2) **Richard** (1704–65), English traveller, born at Southampton, studied at Corpus, Oxford. Precentor successively of Lismore and Waterford, then Archdeacon of Dublin (1745), in 1756 he became Bishop of Ossory, and had just been translated to Meath when he died. His travels, which took up nearly nine years of his life, are described in two folios, dealing with his four years' wanderings in Syria, Egypt and Mesopotamia (1743–45), in a volume on his tours in Scotland (Scot. Hist. Soc., 1887), in two on England (Camden Soc., 1888–89) and in one on Ireland (ed. 1891)—books that are as dull as they are valuable. Pococke was the pioneer of Alpine travel; in 1741 he led a dozen Englishmen to the valley of Chamonix.

PODIEBRAD, George of, *pod'ye-brat* (1420–1471), Bohemian king, born at Podiebrad, became an adherent of the moderate Hussites. When the Catholic barons (1438) carried the election of the Emperor Albert II to the Bohemian crown, Podiebrad allied himself with the Utraquists in Tabor, who offered it to Casimir, king of Poland. After forcing Albert to raise the siege of Tabor and retire to Prague, Podiebrad became leader of the Utraquists, seized Prague (1448), and had himself made regent (1453–57) for the young King Ladislaus. On Ladislaus's death, Podiebrad was crowned his successor in 1458. He succeeded for a while in allaying the bitternesses of religious zeal. In 1462 he decided to uphold the terms of the *compactata* of Prague (1433); this angered Pius II, but the emperor restrained him from excommunicating Podiebrad. The next pope, however, Paul II, excommunicated him in 1466. Matthias Corvinus of Hungary took the field to enforce the ban; but Podiebrad forced him into a truce at Wilamow (1469). Nevertheless Matthias was crowned king by the Catholic barons. Podiebrad left the succession to Bohemia to a Polish prince. See German works by Jordan (1861) and Bachmann (1878), and a French one by Denis (1891).

POE, Edgar Allan (1809–49), American poet and story writer, born at Boston, Mass., and orphaned in his third year, was adopted by John Allan, a wealthy and childless merchant. In 1815–20 the family were in England, and the boy went to school at Stoke Newington. The year 1826 was spent at the University of Virginia; but, offended by his dissipation and gambling debts, his patron removed him to the counting-room, whence he absconded to Boston. He published *Tamerlane and other*

Poems (1827), enlisted that same year, and rose to be sergeant-major in 1829. Mr Allan procured his discharge and after a year's delay his admission to West Point Military Academy (July 1830), but the next March he was dismissed for deliberate neglect of duty. Now he was thrown on his own resources. A third edition of his *Poems* (1831) contained ' Israfel ', his earliest poem of value, and ' To Helen '. Of his life in Baltimore during the next two years few records remain. Nearly the first earnings of his pen was the $100 prize won in 1833 by ' A MS. found in a Bottle '. From this time he lived with his aunt, Mrs Clemm, and wrote for the *Saturday Visitor*. His connection with the *Southern Literary Messenger* began with his tale *Berenice* in March 1835; a few months later he went to Richmond as its assistant editor. In May 1836 he married his cousin Virginia. For more than a year he worked hard on the *Messenger*. But he was ' irregular, eccentric and querulous '. He left Richmond in 1837, and after a year or less in New York, of which the chief fruit was *The Narrative of Arthur Gordon Pym*, in 1838 established himself in Philadelphia. Here he published *Tales of the Grotesque and Arabesque* (1840), was connected with Burton's *Gentleman's Magazine* (1839), and for a year (1842–43) edited *Graham's Magazine*. A second prize of $100 was won in 1843 by his wonderful story ' The Gold Bug '. In 1844 he removed to New York, and in *The Evening Mirror* (January 29, 1845) published ' The Raven ', which won immediate fame. On January 30, 1847, his wife died. ' The Bells ', ' The Domain of Arnheim ', the wild ' prose poem ' *Eureka* (1848), and a few minor pieces, belong to the brief remainder of his life. He attempted suicide in November 1848, and had an attack of *delirium tremens* in June 1849. Recovering, he spent over two months in Richmond, lecturing there and at Norfolk. He became engaged to a lady of means, and in September went to wind up his affairs in the north. On October 3 he was found in a wretched condition in Baltimore, and died in the hospital. Weird, wild, fantastic, dwelling by choice on the horrible, Poe's genius was yet great and genuine. His short stories show great originality, and from some of them, e.g. ' The Murders in the Rue Morgue ', Poe emerges as a pioneer of the modern detective story. The chief charm of his poems is exquisite melody. He deeply impressed Baudelaire and the ' Decadents '. See studies by Lauvrière (Paris 1911), Ransome (1915), Mauclair (1925), Pope-Hennessy (1934), Quinn (1941), Lindsay (1953), Bittner (1963), and Wagenknecht (1963).

POERIO, *pō-ay'ree-ō,* name of two Italian patriots:

(1) **Carlo** (1803–67), born in Naples, in 1848 became director of police, minister of public instruction and deputy for Naples. In July 1849 Ferdinand II had him arrested, and sentenced to twenty-four years in irons; but in 1858 shipped him with other prisoners to America. They persuaded the captain to land them at Cork, and Poerio returned to Turin, where he became a member of parliament, and in 1861 its vice-president.

(2) **Alessandro** (1802–48), brother of (1), devoted himself to poetry, and fell in battle for the liberation of Venice. He was the author of the patriotic poem *Il Risorgimento*.

POGGENDORFF, Johann Christian (1796–1877), German physicist and chemist, became professor of Chemistry at Berlin from 1834. He made discoveries in connection with electricity and galvanism, and invented a multiplying galvanometer. He was the founder of the journal *Annalen der Physik und Chemie* in 1824 and its editor until 1874.

POGGIO, later self-styled **Bracciolini,** *pod-jō* (1380–1459), Florentine humanist, in 1403 became a secretary to the Roman curia. At the Council of Constance (1414–18) he explored the Swiss and Swabian convents for MSS. He recovered MSS. of Quintilian, Ammianus Marcellinus, Lucretius, Silius Italicus, Vitruvius and others. In 1453 he retired to Florence, and became chancellor and historiographer to the republic. His writings include letters, moral essays, a rhetorical Latin *History of Florence*, a series of invectives against contemporaries, and—his most famous book—the *Liber Facetiarum*, a collection of humorous stories, mainly against monks and secular clergy. See *Life and Letters* by E. Walser (Leipzig 1916), J. A. Symonds, *Renaissance in Italy* (1875), and J. E. Sandys, *History of Classical Scholarship* (1908).

POINCARÉ, *pwĭ-kar-ay,* (1) **Jules Henri** (1854–1912), French mathematician, born at Nancy, Academician (1908), was a savant eminent in mathematics, physics, mechanics and astronomy. His special study was of the theory of functions in which he made important advances. As a philosopher he wrote *Science et hypothèse* (1903) and *Science et méthode* (1908), both of which have English translations. See study by Dantzig (1954).

(2) **Raymond Nicolas Landry** (1860–1934), French statesman, cousin of (1), born at Bar-le-Duc, studied law, became a deputy in 1887, senator 1903, minister of public instruction 1893, 1895, of finance 1894, 1906, premier 1911–13, 1922–24 and 1926–29. He was elected president of the Republic in 1913, remaining in office until 1920. He occupied the Ruhr 1923, and his National Union ministry averted ruin in 1926. Member of the Académie française (1909), he wrote on literature and politics, *Memoirs* (trans. 1925), and *How France is Governed* (1913).

POINSOT, Louis, *pwĭ-sō* (1777–1859), French mathematician, born in Paris, in 1804 became professor of Mathematics at the Lycée Bonaparte. From 1813 an Academician, he wrote *Éléments de la statique* (1803), which was an account of his work on the theory of couples.

POISSON, Siméon Denis, *pwa-sō* (1781–1840), French mathematician, born at Pithiviers, studied medicine but turned to applied mathematics and became first professor of Mechanics at the Sorbonne. Famous for his researches in mathematical physics, he was made a peer of France in 1837.

POITIERS. See Diane de Poitiers.
POLANYI, Michael (1891–), Hungarian

physical chemist and social philosopher born in Budapest, studied there and at Karlsruhe, lectured at Berlin, but emigrated to Britain after Hitler's rise to power and was professor of Physical Chemistry (1933–1948) and of Social Studies (1948–58) at Manchester. He did notable work on reaction kinetics and crystal structure, published *Atomic Reactions* (1932) and wrote much on the freedom of scientific thought, philosophy of science and latterly social science, including *Personal Knowledge* (1958) and *The Study of Man* (1959). He was elected F.R.S. in 1944, awarded the du Nouy award (1959) American Le.s on the compatibility of science for his book.

and rel de la, a family descended from a Hull **POLE** merchant, whose son Michael (*c.* 1330-89) in 1383 became chancellor, in 1385 was made Earl of Suffolk, and died an exile in France. His grandson, William (1396–1450), was in 1449 raised to be Duke of Suffolk, having since 1445 been practically prime minister. His administration was disastrous; and he was on his way to a five years' banishment in Flanders when he was intercepted off Dover and beheaded. John de la Pole, second Duke (1442–91), married Elizabeth, sister to Edward IV and Richard III and from this marriage sprang John, Earl of Lincoln (*c.* 1464–87), Edmund, Earl of Suffolk (*c.* 1472–1513, executed by Henry VIII), two churchmen, four daughters, and Richard, on whose death at the battle of Pavia (1525) the line became extinct.

POLE, (1) Reginald (1500–58), Archbishop of Canterbury, born at Stourton Castle near Stourbridge, was the son of Sir Richard Pole and Margaret, Countess of Salisbury (1473–1541), daughter of the Duke of Clarence and niece of Edward IV. At nineteen he went to Italy to finish his studies. He returned in 1527, and was then high in Henry VIII's favour. When the question of the divorce was raised, Pole seemed at first disposed to take the king's side; but later expressed disapproval, refused the archbishopric of York, and, going to Italy in 1532, formed intimate friendships with many eminent men eager for an internal reformation of the church. In 1535 he entered into a political correspondence with Charles V, and was now compelled by Henry to declare himself, which he did in a violent letter to the king, afterwards expanded into the treatise *Pro Unitatis Ecclesiasticæ Defensione*. The king withdrew Pole's pension and preferments. Paul III made him a cardinal (1536), and sent him as legate to the Low Countries to confer with the English malcontents. Henry retaliated by setting a price on his head and beheading his mother and other relatives. Pole's several attempts to procure the invasion of England were not successful. In 1541–42 he was governor of the ' Patrimony of St Peter '; and at the Council of Trent (1545) he was one of the presidents. In 1549 he was on the point of being elected pope; after the election of Julius III he lived in retirement until the death of Edward VI, when he was commissioned to Queen Mary as legate *a latere*. Pole was still only in deacon's orders, and cherished

the idea of marrying the queen; but Charles V carried the match with his son, Philip of Spain. Pole arrived in London in November 1554, with powers to allow the owners of confiscated church property to retain their possessions. He absolved parliament and country from their schism, and reconciled the Church of England to Rome. As long as Cranmer lived, Pole would not accept the archbishopric of Canterbury, but Pole was ordained priest March 1556, and consecrated archbishop after Cranmer was burnt. Pope Paul IV, indignant at the concession made by authority of his predecessor to the holders of church property, revived the accusations of heresy formerly brought against Pole. Paul IV was, moreover, now at war with Spain, and could not tolerate Pole as his ambassador at the court of Mary. So his legation was cancelled, and he was summoned before the Inquisition. Mary angrily protested, and the pope relented, but would not reinstate Pole. When the queen died, November 17, 1558, Pole was dangerously ill; he died on the same day. It has been disputed how far he was responsible for Mary's persecution of Protestants; certainly when Pole became the queen's supreme adviser the persecution increased in violence. See his letters, with Life (1744), and other Lives by Beccatelli (trans. 1690 and 1766), Phillipps (1764–67), Hook (*Archbishops of Canterbury*), Zimmermann (1893), Haile (1910), Schenk (1950).

(2) **William** (1814–1900), English engineer and musician, was born at Birmingham. He became professor of Engineering at Bombay (1844–47), at University College, London (1859–67), and (1871–83) was consulting engineer in London for the imperial railways in Japan. He was a high authority on music and whist.

POLIGNAC, -leen-yak, an ancient French family to which belonged **Cardinal Melchior de Polignac** (1661–1742), plenipotentiary of Louis XIV at Utrecht (1712) and French minister at Rome. A **Duchesse de Polignac** (1749–93) who died at Vienna, and her husband (died at St Petersburg, 1817), grand-nephew of the cardinal, were among the worst, but unhappily most favoured, advisers of Marie Antoinette, and were largely responsible for the shameful extravagance of the court. Their son, **Auguste Jules Armand Marie, Prince de Polignac** (1780–1847), born at Versailles, at the Restoration returned to France and became intimate with the Comte d'Artois, afterwards Charles X. In 1820 he was made a prince by the pope, appointed ambassador at the English court in 1823, and in 1829 became head of the last Bourbon ministry, which promulgated the fatal ordinances that cost Charles X his throne. He was condemned to imprisonment for life in the castle of Ham, but was set at liberty by the amnesty of 1836. He took up residence in England, but died in Paris.

POLITIAN, Angelo Ambrogini (1454–94), Italian humanist, born at Montepulciano in Tuscany, and called *Poliziano* from the Italian name of his birthplace, at ten was sent to Florence, and made incredible progress in the ancient languages. By his sixteenth year he had written brilliant Latin and Greek epigrams, at seventeen he began the translation of the *Iliad* into Latin hexameters and, having secured the friendship of the all-powerful Lorenzo de' Medici (whose sons he taught), he was soon recognized as the prince of Italian scholars. At thirty he became professor of Greek and Latin at Florence. Lorenzo's death in 1492 was a serious blow, and he mourned his death in a remarkable Latin elegy. He himself died in Florence, during a temporary supremacy of Savonarola, whose religious zeal was directed against every principle of that pagan revival which it had been the life work of Lorenzo and Politian to forward. Politian was vicious in life, but was a scholar of the first rank and a poet of high merit. Among his works were Latin translations of a long series of Greek authors, and an excellent edition of the *Pandects* of Justinian. His original works in Latin fill a thick quarto, half of which is made up of letters; the rest with miscellanies in prose and verse. His *Orfeo* was the first secular drama in Italian. See J. A. Symonds's *Renaissance in Italy*.

POLK, (1) James Knox (1795–1849), eleventh President of the United States, was born in Mecklenburg county, N.C. He was admitted to the bar in 1820, and in 1823 was elected a member of the legislature of Tennessee, and in 1825 returned to congress as a Democrat. For five years he was Speaker of the House of Representatives. He was in 1839 elected governor of Tennessee, and in 1844 elected president over Henry Clay, mainly because of his ' firm ' attitude with regard to the annexation of Texas. In December 1845 Texas was admitted to the Union, and jurisdiction was extended to the disputed territory. The president next forced on hostilities by advancing the American army to the Rio Grande; the capital was taken in September; and by the terms of peace the United States acquired California and New Mexico. The Oregon boundary was settled by a compromise with England. Polk condemned the antislavery agitation, and he was devoted to the Democratic principles of Jefferson and Jackson—state rights, a revenue tariff, independent treasury, and strict construction of the constitution. See Life by Jenkins (1850) and Chase's History of his administration (1850).

(2) Leonidas (1806–64), American soldier, was born at Raleigh, N.C. Graduating at West Point in 1827, he held a commission in the artillery, but in 1831 received Holy Orders in the Episcopal Church. In 1838 he was consecrated a missionary bishop of Arkansas, and from 1841 till his death was Bishop of Louisiana, even when at the head of an army corps. In the Civil War he was made major-general by Jefferson Davis. At Belmont, in November 1861, he was driven from his camp by Grant, but finally forced him to retire. At Shiloh and Corinth he commanded the first corps; promoted lieutenant-general, he conducted the retreat from Kentucky. After Chickamauga, where he commanded the right wing, he was relieved of his command; reappointed (December 1863), he opposed Sherman's march. He

was killed reconnoitring on Pine Mountain (1915 ed.).

See W. M. Polk's *L. Polk, Bishop and General*

POLLAIUOLO, Antonio, *pol-lī-wo'lō* (1429–1498), Florentine goldsmith, medallist, metal-caster and painter, cast sepulchral monuments in St Peter's at Rome for Popes Sixtus IV and Innocent VIII. His pictures are distinguished for life and vigour. He was one of the first painters to study anatomy and apply it to his art, and was skilled in suggesting movement. His brother, **Pietro** (1443–1496), was associated with him in his work.

POLLARD, (1) Albert Frederick (1869–1948), English historian, born at Ryde, graduating at Oxford, was assistant editor, after of *The Dictionary of National Biography*, becoming professor of Constitutional History, at London University from 1903 to 1931, founding in 1920 its Institute of Historical Research. From 1908 to 1936 he was a fellow of All Souls, Oxford. Among his many historical works are lives of *Henry VIII* (1902), *Thomas Cranmer* (1904) and *Wolsey* (1929), *A Short History of the Great War* (1920) and *Factors in American History* (1925). The Historical Association was founded by him in 1906 and he was editor of *History* from 1916 to 1922.

(2) Alfred William (1859–1944), English scholar and bibliographer, born in London, a graduate of Oxford, was an assistant in the department of printed books at the British Museum and keeper from 1919 to 1924. In 1915 he was appointed reader in Bibliography at Cambridge and professor of English Bibliography at London from 1919 to 1932. An authority on Chaucer and Shakespeare, his contributions to Shakespearean criticism have been invaluable in such scholarly studies as his *Shakespeare Folios and Quartos* (1909) and *Shakespeare's Fight with the Pirates* (1917). Important earlier work on Chaucer had produced *A Chaucer Primer* (1893) and his edition of the Globe Chaucer (1898). In 1926 was completed the *Short Title Catalogue of English Books, 1475–1640*, for which he was largely responsible.

POLLIO, Gaius Asinius (76 B.C.–A.D. 4), Roman orator, poet and soldier, sided with Caesar in the civil war, commanded in Spain, and, appointed by Antony to settle the veterans on the lands assigned them, saved Virgil's property from confiscation. He founded the first public library at Rome, and was the patron of Virgil and Horace. His orations, tragedies and history have perished save for a few fragments.

POLLITT, Harry (1890–1960), British Communist politician, was born at Droylesden, Lancs, entered a cotton mill at twelve and joined the I.L.P. at sixteen. Later he became a boilermaker and was a shop steward by the age of twenty-one. He was secretary of the National Minority Movement from 1924 to 1929, when he became secretary of the Communist party of Great Britain. A stormy demagogue, he frequently clashed with authority, being imprisoned for seditious libel in 1925 and being deported from Belfast in 1933. During the Spanish War he helped to found the British battalion of the International Brigade. In 1956 he resigned the secretaryship of the party and became its chairman. See his autobiographical *Serving My Time* (1940).

POLLOCK, (1) an illustrious English family descended from David Pollock, saddler to George III, of which the following, arranged chronologically, were distinguished members.—(1) **Sir David** (1780–1847), eldest son of the saddler, chief-justice of Bombay. (2) **Sir Jonathan Frederick** (1783–1870), brother of (1), passed from St Paul's to Trinity College, Cambridge, and graduated in 1806 as senior wrangler. Next year he was elected a fellow and called to the bar. In 1827 he became K.C.; in 1831 was returned as a Tory for Huntingdon; and was successively attorney-general and chief baron of the Exchequer. He was knighted in 1834, and in 1866 made a baronet. See *Life* by Lord Hanworth (1929). (3) **Sir George** (1786–1872), field-marshal, third son of the saddler, entered the East India Company's army in 1803. He was engaged at the siege of Bhartpur (1805) and in other operations against Holkar, saw service in the Nepal (Gurkha) campaigns of 1814–16, and in the first Burmese war (1824–26) won his colonelcy. In 1838 he became major-general. After the massacre of General Elphinstone in Afghanistan the Indian government sent him to the relief of Sir Robert Sale in Jelalabad. In April 1842 he forced the Khyber Pass and reached Sir Robert Sale, pushed on to Kabul, defeated Akbar Khan, and recovered 135 British prisoners. Then, joined by Nott, he conducted the united armies back to India, and was rewarded with a G.C.B. and a political appointment at Lucknow. He returned to England in 1846, was director of the East India Company 1854–56, was created a field-marshal in 1870 and a baronet in 1872, and in 1871 was appointed constable of the Tower. See *Life* by Low (1873). (4) **Sir William Frederick** (1815–88), eldest son of (2), educated at St Paul's and Trinity, in 1838 was called to the bar. He was appointed a master of the Court of Exchequer (1846) and Queen's Remembrancer (1874); in 1876 became senior master of the Supreme Court of Judicature; in 1886 resigned his offices. He published a blank verse translation of Dante (1854) and *Personal Remembrances* (1887). (5) **Sir Charles Edward** (1823–97), fourth son of the first baronet, was a baron of Exchequer, and from 1875 justice of the High Court. (6) **Sir Frederick, P.C., K.C.** (1845–1937), eldest son of (4), third baronet, born in London, was educated at Eton and Trinity, and in 1868 obtained a fellowship. He was called to the bar in 1871, became professor of Jurisprudence at University College, London (1882), Corpus professor of Jurisprudence at Oxford (1883), professor of Common Law in the Inns of Court (1884–90), editor of the Law Reports (1895), judge of Admiralty Court of Cinque Ports (1914). Besides his *Spinoza* (1880), he published *Principles of Contract* (1875), *Digest of the Law of Partnership* (1877), *Law of Torts* (1887), all of which had many editions, *Oxford Lectures* (1891), *History of English Law before Edward I* (with Dr. F. W. Mait-

land, 1895), *The Etchingham Letters* (with Mrs Fuller-Maitland, 1899), and reminiscences, *For My Grandson* (1933). (7) **Walter Herries** (1850–1926), younger son of (4), was called to the bar in 1874, edited the *Saturday Review* 1884–94, and published *Lectures on French Poets, Verses of Two Tongues, A Nine Men's Morrice, King Zub,* &c. (7) **Sir Charles Edward** (1823–97), fourth son of the first baronet, was a baron of Exchequer, and from 1875 justice of the High Court.

(2) **Jackson** (1912–56), American artist, born in Cody, Wyoming, was the first exponent of tachism or action painting in America. His art developed from surrealism to abstract art and the first drip paintings of 1947. This technique he continued with increasing violence and often on huge canvases as in *One* which is seventeen feet long. Other striking works include *No. 32,* the black and white *Echo* and *Blue Poles.* He was killed in a motor accident.

POLLOK, Robert (1798–1827), Scottish poet, born at Muirhouse, Eaglesham, Renfrewshire, studied at Glasgow for the Secession Church, and in 1824–25 wrote feeble *Tales of the Covenanters,* in 1827 *The Course of Time,* a poetical description of the spiritual life of man. Meantime, seized with consumption, he set out for Italy, but died near Southampton. See *Memoir* (1843).

POLO, Marco (1254–1324), Venetian traveller, was born of a noble family at Venice, while his father and uncle had gone on a mercantile expedition by Constantinople and the Crimea to Bokhara and to Cathay (China), where they were well received by the great Kublai Khan. The Mongol prince commissioned them as envoys to the pope, requesting him to send 100 Europeans learned in the sciences and arts—a commission they tried in vain to carry out in Italy (1269). The Polos started again in 1271, taking with them young Marco, and arrived at the court of Kublai Khan in 1275, after travelling by Mosul, Baghdad, Khorassan, the Pamír, Kashgar, Yarkand and Khotan, Lob Nor, and across the desert of Gobi, to Tangut and Shangtu. The khan took special notice of Marco, and soon sent him as envoy to Yunnan, northern Burma, Karakorum, Cochin-China and Southern India. For three years he served as governor of Yang Chow, and helped to reduce the city of Saianfu. The khan long refused to think of the Polos leaving his court; but at length, in the train of a Mongol princess, they sailed by Sumatra and Southern India to Persia, finally reaching Venice in 1295. They brought with them great wealth in precious stones. In 1298 Marco was in command of a galley at the battle of Curzola, where the Venetians were defeated by the Genoese, and he was a prisoner for a year at Genoa. Here it was once thought that he dictated to another captive, one Rusticiano of Pisa, an account of his travels. It is now believed that he had his notes which he had written for Kublai sent to him from Venice and that Rusticiano helped to make a record from them. After his liberation he returned to Venice, where he died. Marco Polo's book consists of: (1) a Prologue the only part containing persona narrative; and (2) a long series of chapters descriptive of notable sights, manners of different states of Asia, especially that of Kublai Khan, ending with a dull chronicle of the internecine wars of the house of Genghis during the second half of the 13th century. Nothing disturbs the even tenor of his narrative. His invaluable work contains not a few too marvellous tales (such as those of the Land of Darkness, the Great Roc, &c.). Ramusio (1485–1557) assumed that it was written in Latin, Marsden supposed in the Venetian dialect, Baldelli-Boni showed (1827) that it was French. There exists an old French text, published in 1824, which Yule believed the nearest approach to Marco's own oral narrative. See Yule's edition (1871; new ed. 1921), containing a faithful English translation from an eclectic text, an exhaustive introduction, and notes; also Latham's *Travels of Marco Polo* (Penguin 1958).

POLYBIUS, *-lib'* (*c*. 205–*c*. 123 B.C.), Greek historian, born at Megalopolis, was one of the 1000 noble Achaeans who, after the conquest of Macedonia in 168, were sent to Rome and detained in honourable captivity. Polybius was the guest of Aemilius Paulus himself, and became the close friend of his son, Scipio Aemilianus, who helped him to collect materials for his great historical work. In 151 the exiles were permitted to return to Greece; Polybius, however, soon rejoined Scipio, followed him in his African campaign, and was present at the destruction of Carthage in 146. The war between the Achaeans and Romans called him back to Greece, and, after the taking of Corinth, he used all his influence to procure favourable terms for the vanquished. In furtherance of his historical labours he undertook journeys to Asia Minor, Egypt, upper Italy, southern France and even Spain. His history, the design of which was to show how and why it was that all the civilized countries of the world fell under the dominion of Rome, covers the period 221–146 B.C. The greater part has perished; of forty books only the first five are preserved complete, but the plan of the whole is fully known. The merits of Polybius are the care with which he collected his materials, his love of truth, his breadth of view, and his sound judgment; but his tone is didactic and dull. See Mahaffy, *The Greek World under Roman Sway* (1890), Laqueur's *Polybius* (1913), and commentary by Walbank (1956).

POLYCARP (*c*. 69–*c*. 155), one of the ' Apostolic Fathers ', was Bishop of Smyrna during the earlier half of the 2nd century. He bridges the little-known period between the age of his master the Apostle John and that of his own disciple Irenaeus. His parentage was probably Christian. Ephesus had become the new home of the faith, and there Polycarp was ' taught by apostles ', John above all, and ' lived in familiar intercourse with many who had seen Christ '. He was intimate with Papias and Ignatius. At the close of his life Polycarp visited Rome to discuss the vexed question of the time or keeping the Easter festival; and he returned to Smyrna, only to win the martyr's crown in a persecution which broke out during

a great pagan festival. The fire, it was said, arched itself about the martyr, and he had to be dispatched with a dagger (A.D. 155 or 156). The graphic *Letter of the Smyrnaeans* tells the story of the martyrdom. The only writing of Polycarp extant is the *Epistle to the Philippians*, incomplete in the original Greek, but complete in a Latin translation. Somewhat commonplace in itself, it is of great value for questions of the canon, the origin of the Roman Church, and the Ignatian epistles. See Gebhardt's *Patrum Apostol. Opera* (1876) and Lightfoot's *Apostolic Fathers*, part ii (2nd ed. 1889).

POLYCLITUS, *-klī'* (5th cent. B.C.), Greek sculptor from Samos, contemporary with Phidias. He was highly thought of by Pliny, especially for his bronze *Doryphorus*, which he deemed perfect sculpture. See Gardner's *Six Greek Sculptors* (1910).

POLYCRATES, *po-lik'ra-teez*, ' tyrant ' of Samos *c*. 536–522 B.C., conquered several islands and towns on the Asiatic mainland and made alliance with Amasis, king of Egypt. According to Herodotus, Amasis, thinking him too fortunate, wrote advising him to throw away his most valuable possession, and so avert the spleen of the gods. Polycrates cast a precious signet-ring into the sea, but next day a fisherman brought him a fish with the ring in its belly. It was quite clear to Amasis now that Polycrates was a doomed man, and he broke off the alliance. Polycrates yet successfully defied an attack from Spartans, Corinthians, and disaffected Samians, but was enticed to Magnesia by a Persian satrap, seized, and crucified.

POLYDORE VERGIL. See VERGIL.

POLYGNOTUS (5th cent. B.C.), a Greek painter born in the isle of Thasos, was the first to give life and character to painting. His principal works were at Athens, Delphi and Plataea.

POMBAL, Sebastião José de Carvalho e Mello, Marquês de (1699–1782), Portuguese statesman, was born near Coimbra. In 1739 he was sent as ambassador to London and to Vienna. Appointed secretary for foreign affairs (1750), he reattached many crown domains unjustly alienated; at the great Lisbon earthquake (1755) he showed great calmness and resource, and next year was made prime minister. He sought to subvert the tyranny of the church, opposed the intrigues of nobles and Jesuits, and in 1759 banished the Jesuits. He established elementary schools, reorganized the army, introduced fresh colonists into the Portuguese settlements and established East India and Brazil companies. The tyranny of the Inquisition was broken. Agriculture, commerce and finance were improved. In 1758 he was made Count of Oeyras, in 1770 Marquis of Pombal. On the accession of Maria I (1777), who was under clerical influence, the ' Great Marquis ' lost his offices. See books by G. Moore (1819), John Smith (1843), Carnota (trans. 1871) and M. Cheke (1938).

POMPADOUR, Jeanne Antoinette Poisson, Marquise de (1721–64), mistress of Louis XV, was born in Paris, and was supposed to be the child of Le Normant de Tournehem, a wealthy *fermier-général*. She grew up a woman of remarkable grace, beauty and wit. In 1741 she was married to Le Normant's nephew, Le Normant d'Étoiles, became a queen of fashion, attracted the eye of the king at a ball, was installed at Versailles, and ennobled as Marquise de Pompadour. She assumed the entire control of public affairs, for twenty years swayed the whole policy of the state, and lavished its treasures on her own ambitions. She reversed the traditional policy of France because Frederick the Great lampooned her, filled all public offices with her nominees, and made her own creatures ministers of France. Her policy was disastrous, her wars unfortunate—the ministry of Choiseul was the only fairly creditable portion of the reign. She founded the École Militaire and the royal factory at Sèvres. A lavish patroness of the arts, she heaped her bounty upon poets and painters. She held her difficult position to the end, and retained the king's favour by relieving him of all business, by diverting him with private theatricals, and at last by countenancing his debaucheries. The *Mémoires* (1766) are not genuine. See Studies by Capefigue (1858), Campardon (1867), Goncourt (new ed. 1927), H. N. Williams (1902), P. de Nolhac (1904, 1913), Tinayre (1925), Trouncer (1937), N. Mitford (1958); Beaujoint's *Secret Memoirs* (1885); but esp. her *Correspondance*, ed. Malassis (1878), and Bonhomme (1880).

POMPEY, Gnaeus Pompeius Magnus (106–48 B.C.), at seventeen fought in the Social War against Marius and Cinna. He supported Sulla, and destroyed the remains of the Marian faction in Africa and Sicily. He next drove the followers of Lepidus out of Italy, extinguished the Marian party in Spain under Sertorius (76–71), and annihilated the remnants of the army of Spartacus. He was now the idol of the people, and was elected consul for the year 70. Hitherto Pompey had belonged to the aristocratic party, but latterly he had been looked upon with suspicion, and he now espoused the people's cause and carried a law restoring the tribunician power to the people. He cleared the Mediterranean of pirates; conquered Mithridates of Pontus, Tigranes of Armenia, and Antiochus of Syria, subdued the Jews and captured Jerusalem, and entered Rome in triumph for the third time in 61. But now his star began to wane. Henceforward he was distrusted by the aristocracy, and second to Caesar in popular favour. When the senate declined to accede to his wish that his acts in Asia should be ratified he formed a close intimacy with Caesar, and the pair, with the plutocrat Crassus, formed the all-powerful ' First Triumvirate '. Pompey's acts in Asia were ratified, and his promises to his troops fulfilled; Caesar's designs were gained; and Caesar's daughter, Julia, was given in marriage to Pompey. Next year Caesar repaired to Gaul, and for nine years carried on a career of conquest, while Pompey was wasting his time at Rome. Jealousies arose between the two, and Julia died in 54. Pompey now returned to the aristocratic party. Caesar was ordered to lay down his office,

which he consented to do if Pompey would do the same. The senate insisted on unconditional resignation, otherwise he would be declared a public enemy. But crossing the Rubicon, Caesar defied the senate and its armies. The story of the war is recorded at CAESAR. After his final defeat at Pharsalia in 48, Pompey fled to Egypt, where he was murdered. His younger son, Sextus, secured a fleet, manned largely by slaves and exiles, and, occupying Sicily, ravaged the coasts of Italy. But in 36 he was defeated at sea by Agrippa, and in 37 slain at Mitylene.

PONCE DE LEÓN, *pon'thay* THAY *lay-on'*, (1) **Juan** (1460–1521), Spanish explorer, born at San Servas in Spain, was a court page, served against the Moors, and became governor, first of part of Hispaniola, then (1510–12) of Porto Rico. On a quest for the fountain of perpetual youth, he discovered Florida in March 1512, and was made governor, but failed to conquer his new subjects, retired to Cuba, and died there from the wound of a poisoned arrow. See Life by A. Bell (1925).

(2) **Luis** (1527–91), Spanish monk, scholar and poet, born at Granada, in 1544 entered the Augustinian order, and became professor of Theology at Salamanca in 1561. In 1572–76 he was imprisoned by the Inquisition for his translation and interpretation of the Song of Solomon; but shortly before his death he became general of his order. His poetical remains, published in 1631, comprise translations from Virgil, Horace and the Psalms; his few original poems are lyrical masterpieces. See German monographs by Wilkens (1866) and Reusch (1873); also a Spanish Life by Blanco García (1904).

PONCELET, Jean Victor, *pō-sè-lay* (1788–1867), French engineer-officer and geometrician, was born at Metz. His *Traité des propriétés projectives des figures* (1822) gives him an important place in the development of projective geometry. He became professor of Mechanics at Metz and Paris.

PONCHIELLI, Amilcare, *pon-kyel'lee* (1834–1886), Italian composer, born at Paderno Fasolare near Cremona, wrote *La Gioconda* (1876) and other operas.

POND, John (1767–1836), English astronomer-royal from 1811, improved methods and instruments of observation at Greenwich. His work was notable for its extreme accuracy.

PONIATOWSKI, *pon-ya-tof'skee*, name of a princely family of Poland:

(1) **Joseph Antony** (1762–1813), nephew of (3), was born in Warsaw and trained in the Austrian army. In 1789 the Polish Assembly appointed him commander of the army of the south, with which he gained brilliant victories over the Russians (1792); and he commanded under Kosciusko (1794). When the duchy of Warsaw was constituted (1807), he was appointed minister of war and commander-in-chief. In 1809, during the war between Austria and France, he invaded Galicia. Three years later with a large body of Poles he joined Napoleon in his invasion of Russia, and distinguished himself at Smolensk at Borodino, and at Leipzig, where, in covering the French retreat, he was drowned in the Elster.

(2) **Stanislas** (1677–1762), father of (3), joined Charles XII of Sweden in supporting Stanislas Leszczynski and later under Augustus II and III was appointed to several administrative posts in Lithuania and Poland.

(3) **Stanislas Augustus** (1732–98), son of (2), last king of Poland, in St Petersburg in 1755 while in the suite of the British ambassador became much favoured by the Empress Catherine. Largely through her influence he was elected king in 1764, though not fitted to rule the country at such a crisis. Frederick the Great, who had gained the consent of Austria to a partition of Poland, made a like proposal to Russia, and the first partition was effected in 1772. The diet tried, too late, to introduce reforms. The intrigues of discontented nobles led again to Russian and Prussian intervention, and a second fruitless resistance was followed in 1793 by a second partition. The Poles now became desperate; a general rising took place (1794), the Prussians were driven out, and the Russians were several times routed. But Austria now appeared on the scene, Kosciusko was defeated, Warsaw was taken, and the Polish monarchy was at an end. Stanislas resigned his crown (1795), and died at St Petersburg.

PONSONBY, Sarah. See BUTLER (3).

PONT, Timothy (*c.* 1560–1630), Scottish cartographer, graduated at St Andrews in 1584, became minister of Dunnet (1601), and in 1609 subscribed for 2000 acres of forfeited lands in Ulster. He first projected a Scottish atlas, and surveyed all the counties and isles of the kingdom. His collections were rescued from destruction by Sir John Scot of Scotstarvet, and his maps, revised by Robert Gordon of Straloch, appeared in Blaeu's *Theatrum Orbis Terrarum* (1654). See Dobie's *Cunninghame Topographised by Pont* (1876).

PONTIAC (*c.* 1720?–69), Chief of the Ottawa Indians, in 1763 organized a conspiracy against the English garrisons, and for five months besieged Detroit. He was murdered by an Illinois Indian in 1769. See F. Parkman, *History of the Conspiracy of Pontiac* (1851).

PONTOPPIDAN, (1) **Erik** (1698–1764), Danish theologian, born at Aarhus, professor of Theology at Copenhagen (1738), Bishop of Bergen (1747), wrote *Annales Ecclesiae Danicae Diplomaticae*, a Danish topography, a Norwegian glossary, and *Norges Naturlige Historie* (trans. 1755), describing the Kraken (sea-serpent), &c.

(2) **Henrik** (1857–1944), Danish novelist, born a pastor's son at Fredericia, trained as an engineer but turned to writing. Among his novels were *Land of Promise* (1891–95), *Lykke-Per* (1898–1904) and *The Realm of the Dead* (1912–16). He was a Nobel prizeman (1917). See his memoirs *Back to Myself* (1941).

PONTORMO, Jacopo da (1494–1552), Florentine painter, whose family name was Carucci. He was a pupil of Leonardo da Vinci, Piero di Cosimo and Andrea del Sarto. His works included frescoes, notably of the Passion (1522–25), in the Certosa near Florence. The *Deposition* (*c.* 1525), which forms the altarpiece in a chapel in Sta Felicità, Florence, is possibly his masterpiece. This and much of his later work shows the influence of Michelangelo. He also painted portraits and the Medici villa at Poggio a Caiano was partly decorated by him.

POOLE, (1) **Paul Falconer** (1807–79), English painter, born at Bristol, was self-taught and his work, mainly of historical subjects, was very popular during his life. He was elected an A.R.A. in 1846, and R.A. in 1861.

(2) **Reginald Stuart** (1832–95), English archaeologist, born in London, lived in Cairo from 1842 to 1849, becoming an eminent Egyptologist. He was keeper of coins at the British Museum from 1870. He was a nephew of E. W. Lane (q.v.).

(3) **William Frederick** (1821–94), American librarian, born at Salem, Mass., graduated at Yale in 1849. There in 1848 he published an *Index of Periodical Literature*, to which supplements were later added. In 1856–69 he was librarian of the Boston Athenaeum, and from 1888 of the Newberry Library at Chicago.

POPE, (1) **Alexander** (1688–1744), English poet, was the son of a London linen-draper who retired in the year the poet was born and finally settled at Binfield in Windsor Forest, which is as much associated with the poet's name as Twickenham in later years. The family was Catholic, which meant that Pope was denied a formal education. He made up for it by his reading, chiefly of the English poets, but he also insisted on going to London at fifteen to be taught Italian and French and was therefore fairly well equipped for his literary career. In London, he was patronized by the elderly wits Wycherley and Walsh, who passed on his precocious verse, chiefly pastorals and modernizations of Chaucer, after the example of Dryden's *Fables*, to the fashionable wits Congreve, Garth and ' Granville the polite ', so that when his first fruits appeared in Tonson's *Miscellany* (1709), that is, his four pastorals and one of his Chaucer adaptations, there was a friendly audience of ' the great ' to welcome them. Here at the very entrance to his career begins the literary vendetta which poisoned his existence. The *Miscellany* also contained Ambrose Philips' much inferior pastorals which Addison or one of his whiggish henchmen was to praise in the *Guardian* at the expense of Pope. Politics bedevilled everything then, especially when the question of the succession loomed ahead. Meanwhile Pope moved between London, where he cut a dash, and the Forest, where he was familiar with the Catholic gentry, above all with the Blounts, Teresa and Martha. His spirits then can be judged by the lovely poem he wrote for Teresa on her leaving London after George I's coronation, though Martha turned out to be his ' real flame ' and life-long companion. Pope's next publication was *An Essay on Criticism* (1711), in which he contrived to express the dull matter of neoclassic art in witty and quotable couplets. Unfortunately he introduced a sneer at the formidable old critic and playwright John Dennis, and this started a new vendetta in which Pope could not hope to be victor for Dennis stooped to abuse of his deformed person—a mortal blow to the poet. Addison's appreciation of the *Essay on Criticism*, conveyed in a paper in *The Spectator*, despite his disapproval of the attack on Dennis, was no doubt balm to Pope's hurt mind, but politics were soon to bedevil what was a genuine regard on both sides when Pope embarked on his friendship with the Tories, Swift, Oxford and Bolingbroke. *Windsor Forest* (1713) is a fine descriptive poem perhaps marred by its periphrastic jargon. *The Rape of the Lock*, satirizing the quarrel between two eminent families over the stealing of a lock of hair, appeared in Tonson's *Miscellanies* in 1712. This first version of the poem, in two cantos, was enlarged into mock-epical form in the five-canto version of 1714. Wit and gaiety never shone brighter and the susceptibilities aroused by it in the lady were much exaggerated. Pope now turned to translation to settle his finances. In 1715 he started on the *Iliad* and followed up by the inferior *Odyssey*, much of it the work of hacks. Altogether he made nine thousand pounds by his labours which assisted him to build and lay out his villa at Twickenham (1718). Thanks to Homer, he ' could thrive/Indebted to no prince or peer alive '. The translation, however, was the cause of more hostility between Pope and Addison because the latter openly preferred the translation of the Whig, Thomas Tickle, which appeared two days after the first book of Pope's Iliad. This was the last straw. Pope now intermittently worked at the great satirical lines on ' Atticus ', to which he gave final and deadly form in the *Epistle to Doctor Arbuthnot*, first published in 1734. If any of his poems could persuade us that Pope was a romantic diverted to satire by the rage of enemies it is the *Epistle of Eloisa to Abelard* and the *Elegy to the Memory of an Unfortunate Lady* which appeared in his *Works* (1717), which also contained the final form of *The Rape of the Lock*, with the added speech of Clarissa. The romantic setting of *Eloisa to Abelard* and the genuine expression of passion are less successfully repeated in *The Elegy*, the close of which is neoclassic poetizing, but the poem is moving too, though the actual occasion on which it was based misled the author. In 1717 his father died and Pope moved with his mother to Twickenham, where his new villa engaged him, on a miniature scale, in all the delights of 18th-century artificial gardening. It was destined to become an occasional meeting place for the Tory lords who now began to revive in spirit after their defeat in 1714. The wits also frequented the poet; though Swift was in Ireland, there were still Dr Arbuthnot and Gay. Whilst he was working on his translations he ignored the attacks of the Grub Street critics. Thereafter he was free to settle accounts with those who concentrated on his lack of Greek when they were not abusing his person. He then published an edition of Shakespeare (1725), but the noted Shakespearian scholar, Lewis Theobald, exposed Pope's errors in a pamphlet, *Shakespeare Restored* (1726), and so qualified for the place of hero in the first version of *The*

Dunciad, a satire on dullness in which he mocked such critics as Dennis, Colley Cibber, &c. The latter, then poet laureate, replaced Theobald as hero in the final version because of his attempts at retaliation. Beside personal pique there was the awareness, which he shared with Swift, of a catastrophic decline in standards. Both these great writers were humanists of the older type who regarded the new science and talk about progress and enlightenment as barbarous. *The Dunciad* (1726) is indeed a devastating attack on scientific humanism. The fourth part of it, which was added in 1742, is one of the most brilliant satires on pedantry and social fads ever written. It is also capital fun, though the splendid close is no laughing matter. In 1732 appeared the first part of the philosophical *Essay on Man* together with the first of his four moral essays, viz. *Of the Knowledge and Characters of Men*; *Of the Characters of Women*; and two *Of the Uses of Riches*. The *Essay on Man* has been rather unfairly censured for its second-hand philosophy, but Pope only did what Tennyson did for his day; he popularized learned notions and attitudes and gave to them brilliant expression. The two poems *Of the Uses of Riches* are concerned with contemporary taste in laying out great seats. *Of the Characters of Women* contains the terrible attacks on the Duchess of Marlborough and Lady Mary Wortley Montagu who willingly joined with Lord Hervey in the sport of Pope-baiting. He now gathered himself together for his supreme work which makes nonsense of the view that he was a romantic at heart. Bolingbroke is said to have directed him to the adaptation of the Satires and Epistles of Horace, whose situation vis-à-vis the dunces resembled Pope's own. In 1733 he modernized the first epistle of the second book, then he proceeded to the second of the same book and finished his imitations of Horace with two of the satires. Later, to make a book of it, he added two of Donne's satires (unfortunately not the splendid third) and for a prologue chose the glorious *Epistle to Arbuthnot*, which is at once an apologia and a summing-up of themes in the satires. For an epilogue he employed two political dialogues, *One Thousand Seven Hundred & Thirty Eight*, which reflected the growing hopes of the Tory party with its patriotic slogans. *The Satires and Epistles of Horace Imitated* in its final form is the greatest work of our greatest verse satirist. Pope had much to depress him in these years—ill-health, rancorous abuse, the death or absence of his friends. His beloved Gay died in 1732, his mother and his intimate Arbuthnot the following year. Bolingbroke left England for a second exile in 1735, Swift was in Ireland. The affection he expresses for these and other friends relieves the acrimony of his personal satire. The story of his publication of his Letters is both comic and scandalous. He employed the usual complaint of piracy (Curll had produced an edition in 1735) to excuse the unusual course of publishing his own letters in 1737, collected from all his correspondents for shamefully manipulated. Two years later he completed the work by including the letters to Swift which he secured by the usual subterfuges. It is clear that he wanted to present himself to posterity in the most favourable light, as he had done in the *Epistle to Arbuthnot*. The standard edition of the poems was that by Elwin and Courthope (1887–89) but now superseded by the Twickenham edition, general editor John Butt, six vols. (1932 *et seq.*), *Prose Works*, ed. Norman Ault (1936 *et seq.*). The Elwin and Courthope edition provided a Life, but much more understanding and detailed is Professor G. Sherburn's *The Early Career of Alexander Pope* (1934) and his later work on the poet. Dame Edith Sitwell's study is more intuitive than critical. G. Tillotson attempted a revaluation of Pope (1938), and has written several other studies. See also works by Ault (1949), Rogers (1955), Brower (1959), Edwards (1963). Dobrée's *Alexander Pope* (1951) is the best short study of Pope.

(2) **John** (1822–92), American army commander, born in Louisville, Ky., graduated at West Point in 1842, and served with the engineers in Florida (1842–44) and in the Mexican war. He was exploring and surveying in the west till the Civil War, when as brigadier-general in 1861 he drove the guerillas out of Missouri. As major-general he commanded the Army of the Mississippi (1862) and then that of Virginia, but was defeated at the second battle of Bull Run. He was transferred to Minnesota, where he kept the Indians in check, and held commands until 1886, when he retired.

POPHAM, Sir John (*c.* 1531–1607), English lawyer, born at Huntworth near Bridgwater, became speaker in 1580 and lord chief-justice in 1592. He presided at the trial of Guy Fawkes.

POPOV, Aleksandr Stepanovich (1859–1905), Russian physicist, claimed by his countrymen to be the inventor of wireless telegraphy, was the first to use a suspended wire as an aerial.

POPPER, Sir Karl Raimund (1902–), Austrian philosopher, born in Vienna, studied at the university there and published for the 'Vienna Circle' of logical positivists, of which he was not a member, even in some ways an opponent, the greatest modern work in scientific methodology, *Die Logik der Forschung* (1934) 'The Logic of Scientific Discovery' (trans. with postscript, 1958), in which he refuted the long-established Baconian principles of scientific method and argued that testing hypotheses by selective experimentation rather than proof was the essence of scientific induction. For Popper, to be scientific, a theory must in principle be falsifiable, not verifiable in the logical positivist sense, and this criterion marks off a genuine science, such as physics, from what he calls the 'pseudo-sciences', such as Marxian economics and Freudian psychology which instead of challenging falsification impose a rigid finality from the outset. Popper left Vienna shortly before Hitler's *Anschluss*, lectured at Canterbury College, New Zealand (1937–45), when he became first reader in Logic (1945–48) then professor of Logic and Scientific Method at the London School of Economics. Philosophical attempts

to reduce history to a predetermined pattern he exposed in articles in *Economica* (1945–48), republished under the title *The Poverty of Historicism* (1957), and in the brilliant philosophical polemic, *The Open Society and Its Enemies* (1945), written in the heat of the second World War, in which he ruthlessly examines all the great philosophical systems with totalitarian implications in political theory from Plato to Karl Marx. More recent publications include *The Logic of Scientific Discovery* (1959) and *Conjectures and Refutations* (1963). He was knighted in 1965. See his philosophical autobiography in *British Philosophy in the Mid-Century*, ed. C. A. Mace (1957).

POPSKI. See PENIAKOFF.

PORDAGE, John. See BOEHME.

PORDENONE, Il, *por-day-nō'nay* (1483–1539), the name given to the Italian religious painter, Giovanni Antonio Licinio, who was born at Corticelli near Pordenone. In 1535 he settled at Venice, and in 1538 was summoned by the duke to Ferrara. He painted frescoes in the cathedral at Cremona and in Sta Maria da Campagna at Piacenza.

PORPHYRY (*c.* A.D. 233–304), Neoplatonist, born at Tyre or Batanea, is said, improbably, to have been originally a Christian. He studied at Athens under Longinus, and about 263 at Rome under Plotinus. In Sicily he wrote his once celebrated treatise against the Christians, now lost. He then returned to Rome to teach. His philosophy keeps close to life and practical duties, its object the salvation of the soul, to be effected by the extinction of impure desires through strict asceticism and knowledge of God. His chief writings are the Lives of Plotinus and Pythagoras, *Sententiae*, *De Abstinentia*, and the *Epistola ad Marcellam*, addressed to his wife. See monograph by Bouillet (1864) and Alice Zimmern's translation of *Porphyry to his Wife Marcella* (1896).

PORPORA, Niccola Antonio (1686–1766), Italian composer and teacher of singing, born in Naples, established a school for singing, from which came many famous singers. During 1725–55 he was in Dresden, Venice, London (1734–36) and Vienna (where he taught Haydn), composing operas and teaching. He figures in George Sand's *Consuelo*.

PORSCHE, Ferdinand (1875–1951), German automobile designer, born at Hafersdorf, Bohemia, designed cars for Daimler and Auto Union, but set up his own independent studio in 1931 and in 1934 produced the plans for a revolutionary type of cheap car with engine in the rear, to which the Nazis gave the name *Volkswagen* ('People's car') and which they promised to mass-produce for the German worker. After World War II it proved a record-breaking commodity in the export market.

PORSON, Richard (1759–1808), English scholar, was born at East Ruston in Norfolk, son of the parish clerk, in 1778 entered Trinity College, Cambridge, was elected a scholar, won the Craven Scholarship and the first chancellor's medal, and in 1782 was elected a fellow. He now began to contribute to reviews; his *Notae breves ad Toupii*

Emendationes in Suidam (1790) carried his name beyond England. In 1787 appeared in the *Gentleman's Magazine* his three sarcastic letters on Hawkins's *Life of Johnson*; and during 1788–89 his far more famous letters on the Spurious Verse 1 John v, 7, which brought him no little odium. In 1792 his fellowship ceased to be tenable by a layman, and friends raised for him a fund of £100 a year; he was also appointed to the regius professorship of Greek at Cambridge, an office worth £40 a year. In 1795 he edited Aeschylus, and in 1797–1801 four plays of Euripides. He married in 1796, but his wife died five months later. In 1806 he was appointed librarian of the London Institution, but neglected his duties. Two years later he died of apoplexy. Porson possessed a stupendous memory, unwearied industry, great acuteness, fearless honesty, and masculine sense, but was hindered all his life by poverty, ill-health, dilatoriness and fits of intemperance. He achieved little, besides the works already named, but a few *bons mots*, some brilliant emendations, and the posthumous *Adversaria* (1812), notes on Aristophanes (1820), the lexicon of Photius (1822), Pausanias (1820) and Suidas (1834). His *Tracts and Criticisms* were collected by Kidd (1815). See Lives by Watson (1861), Clarke (1937), and his *Correspondence* edited by Luard (1867).

PORTA, (1) **Baccio della.** See BARTOLOMMEO.

(2) **Carlo** (1776–1821), Italian poet, was born in Milan. Writing in the dialect of Milan, he showed his insight into human character in narrative poems which are satirical and grimly realistic. These include *La Nomina del Capellan, La Guerra di Pret* and *I Disgrazzi di Giovannin Bongee*.

(3) **Giacomo della** (1541–1604), Italian architect, a pupil of Vignola, is best known for the cupola of St Peter's and his work on the Palazzo Farnese, left unfinished by Michelangelo. He was also responsible for some of the fountains of Rome.

(4) **Giovanni Battista della** (1543–1615), Neapolitan physicist and philosopher, wrote on physiognomy, natural magic, gardening, &c., besides several comedies.

(5) **Guglielmo della** (*c.* 1510–77), Italian sculptor, whose main work was the tomb of Pope Paul III in the choir of St Peter's.

PORTALIS, Jean Étienne Marie (1745–1807), French jurist and statesman, practised law in Paris, was imprisoned during the Revolution, but under Napoleon compiled the *Code Civil*. See Life by Lavollée (1869).

PORTEOUS, John (d. 1736), Scottish soldier, the ne'er-do-well son of an Edinburgh tailor, enlisted and served in Holland, and soon after 1715 became captain of the Edinburgh town guard. On April 14, 1736, he was in charge at the execution of one Wilson, a smuggler who had robbed the Pittenweem custom-house. There was some stone-throwing; whereupon Porteous made his men fire on the mob, wounding twenty persons and killing five or six. For this he was tried and condemned to death (July 20), but reprieved by Queen Caroline. But on the night of September 7 an orderly mob burst open the Tolbooth, dragged Porteous to the

Grassmarket, and hanged him from a dyer's pole. See Scott's notes to *The Heart of Midlothian* and the *Trial of Capt. Porteous*, ed. by W. Roughead (1909).

PORTER, (1) **Anna Maria** (1780–1832), English novelist, younger sister of (8), born in Durham, blossomed precociously into *Artless Tales* (1793–95), followed by a long series of works, among which were *Octavia* (1798), *The Lake of Killarney* (1804), *The Hungarian Brothers* (1807), *The Recluse of Norway* (1814), *The Fast of St Magdalen* (1818) and *Honor O'Hara* (1826).

(2) **Cole** (1891?–1964), American composer, born at Peru, Indiana, studied law at Harvard before deciding upon a musical career and entering the Schola Cantorum in Paris. Attracted to musical comedy, he composed lyrics and music for many stage successes, culminating, in 1948, in *Kiss me Kate* and, in 1953, with *Can-Can*. His highly personal style and dramatic sense is illustrated by such popular songs as ' Night and Day ' and ' Begin the Beguine '. See Life by G. Eells (1967).

(3) **David** (1780–1843), American sailor, born at Boston, Mass., son of a naval officer, entered the navy in 1798, became captain in 1812 and captured the first British war ship taken in the war. In 1813 he nearly destroyed the English whale fishery in the Pacific, and took possession of the Marquesas Islands; but in March 1814 his frigate was destroyed by the British at Valparaiso. He afterwards commanded an expedition against pirates in the West Indies. He resigned in 1826, and for a time commanded the Mexican navy. In 1829 the United States appointed him consul-general to the Barbary States, and then minister at Constantinople, where he died. See the Life (1875) by his son.

(4) **David Dixon** (1813–91), son of (3), born at Chester, Penn., accompanied his father against the pirates and in the Mexican service. In the Civil War, as commander of the mortar flotilla, in April 1862 he bombarded the New Orleans forts. In September, with the Mississippi squadron, he passed the batteries of Vicksburg, and bombarded the city; in December 1864 he silenced Fort Fisher, taken next month. Superintendent till 1869 of Annapolis naval academy, he was in 1870 made admiral of the navy. He wrote three romances, *Incidents of the Civil War* (1885), and *History of the Navy During the War of the Rebellion* (1887).

(5) **Eleanor Hodgman** (1868–1920), American novelist, was born at Littleton, New Hampshire, and studied music at the New England Conservatory. Her first novels included *Cross Currents* (1907) and *Miss Billy* (1911). In 1913 *Pollyanna* appeared; this was an immediate success and has retained its popularity ever since. A sequel, *Pollyanna Grows Up*, was published in 1915 and two volumes of short stories, *The Tangled Threads* and *Across the Years* appeared posthumously in 1924.

(6) **Endymion** (1587–1649), English royalist, servant to James VI and I, was groom of the bedchamber to Charles I, and fought for him in the Great Rebellion. He wrote verses and was painted by Van Dyck. See *Life and*

Letters by D. Townshend (1897) and study by G. Huxley (1959).

(7) **Gene**, *née* **Stratton** (1868–1924), American novelist, was born on a farm in Wabash Co., Ind., married in 1886 Charles D. Porter, and as Gene Stratton Porter attained great popularity by *A Girl of the Limberlost* (1909) and other stories full of sentiment and nature study.

(8) **Jane** (1776–1850), English writer, born at Durham, the daughter of an army surgeon, made a great reputation in 1803 by her high-flown romance, *Thaddeus of Warsaw*, and had even more success in 1810 with *The Scottish Chiefs*, its hero a most stilted and preposterous Wallace. Other books were *The Pastors' Fireside* (1815), *Duke Christian of Lüneburg* (1824), *Tales Round a Winter's Hearth* (with her sister Anna Maria, 1824), and *The Field of Forty Footsteps* (1828); *Sir Edward Seaward's Shipwreck* (1831), a clever fiction, edited by her, was almost certainly written by her eldest brother, Dr William Ogilvie Porter (1774–1850).

(9) **Katherine Anne** (1894–   ), American writer of short stories, was born at Indian Creek, Texas. She started writing at a very early age but allowed nothing to be published until she was thirty. Among her collections of stories is *Pale Horse, Pale Rider* (1939). *Ships of Fools* (1962) is an immense allegorical novel analysing the German state of mind in the 1930s. A volume of essays, *The Days Before*, appeared in 1952.

(10) **Noah** (1811–92), American clergyman, born at Farmington, Conn., studied at Yale, was a Congregational pastor 1836–46, then became professor of Moral Philosophy at Yale, and in 1871–86 was president of the college. Among his numerous works are *The Human Intellect* (1868), *Books and Reading* (1870), *Moral Science* (1885). See *Memorial*, ed. by Merriam (1893).

(11) **Robert Ker** (1775–1842), English painter, brother of (8), a clever battle painter, visited Russia in 1804, where he was historical painter to the tsar. He accompanied Sir John Moore's expedition in 1808, becoming K.C.H. in 1832. He was afterwards British consul in Venezuela, and published books of travel in Russia, Sweden, Spain, Portugal, Georgia, Persia and Armenia.

(12) **William S.** See HENRY, O.

PORTLAND, Duke of. See BENTINCK.

PORTO-RICHE, Georges de, *por-tō-reesh* (1849–1930), French dramatist, was born at Bordeaux. He wrote several successful psychological plays, including *L'Amoureuse* (1891), *Le Vieil homme* (1911) and *Le Marchand d'Estampes* (1917).

PORTSMOUTH, Louise de Kéroualle, Duchess of (1649–1734), mistress of Charles II of England, born in Brittany, came to England in 1670 in the train of Henrietta, Charles II's cherished sister, ostensibly as a lady in waiting, but secretly charged to influence the king in favour of the French alliance. The political influence wielded by the ' baby-faced Breton ' was negligible, but Charles was sufficiently responsive to her charms to make her his mistress and ennoble her (1673) and her son, who became Duke of Richmond. Rapacious and haughty, ' Madame Carwell '

was universally detested. See *inter alia* works by Bryant (1931) and Drinkwater (1936).

PORUS. See ALEXANDER THE GREAT.

POSIDONIUS (*c.* 135–51 B.C.), stoic philosopher, born at Apamea in Syria, studied at Athens, and settled at Rhodes, whence in 86 he was sent as envoy to Rome; there, the friend of Cicero and Pompey, he died, leaving works on philosophy, astronomy and history, of which only fragments are extant.

POTEMKIN, properly **Potyomkin, Grigori Aleksandrovich**, *pot-yom'kin* (1739–91), was born near Smolensk, of a noble but impoverished Polish family. He entered the Russian army, attracted the notice of Catharine II by his handsome face and figure, in 1774 became her recognized favourite, and directed Russian policy. There is good reason to believe they were secretly married. In charge of the new lands in the south acquired by conquest, he made an able administrator. In 1787 Catharine paid a visit to his government in the south, but the story of his setting her route with stage villages and hired villagers is not now believed. In the war with the Turks Potemkin was placed at the head of the army, and reaped the credit of Suvorov's victories (1791). He died in the same year. Licentious, astute and unscrupulous, in spite of his lavish extravagance he heaped up an immense fortune. He gained for Russia the Crimea and the north coast of the Black Sea, and he founded Sevastopol, Nikolaev and Ekaterinoslav (Dnepropetrovsk). See *Memoirs* (1812), Lives by his secretary Saint-Jean (German; new ed. 1888), and Soloveytchik (English 1938).

POTT, (1) August Friedrich (1802–87), German philologist, born at Nettelrede in Hanover, became in 1833 professor of the Science of Language at Halle. The foundation of Pott's reputation was laid by his *Etymologische Forschungen* (1833–36); and his article on the Indo-Germanic stock in Ersch and Gruber's *Encyklopädie* is a masterpiece.

(2) **Percival(l)** (1714–88), English surgeon, born in London, who became, after a period of training under Edward Nourse, assistant and then senior surgeon at St Bartholomew's Hospital, where his lectures became very popular with both students and visitors. His writings were many, the most important being *Fractures and Dislocations* (1765), in which he described a compound leg fracture suffered by himself and which is now known as ' Pott's fracture ', and his account of a disease of the spine, ' Pott's disease ', in *Remarks on That Kind of Palsy of the Lower Limbs which is Frequently Found to Accompany a Curvature of the Spine* (1779). He became a fellow of the Royal Society in 1764.

POTTER, (1) Beatrix (1866–1943), English authoress, born in London, lived in Kensington and the Lake District and wrote many books for children which she illustrated herself. The best known are the stories of *Peter Rabbit, Jemima Puddleduck, Mrs Tiggy-Winkle* and *Squirrel Nutkin*. She married William Heelis in 1913. See *The Tale of Beatrix Potter* by M. Lane (1946).

(2) **John** (*c.* 1674–1747), Eniglish scholar

and divine, born at Wakefield, became regius professor of Divinity at Oxford in 1707, Bishop of Oxford in 1715, and in 1737 Archbishop of Canterbury. He published *Archaeologia Graeca, or Antiquities of Greece* (1697–99), &c.

(3) **Paul** (1625–54), Dutch painter and etcher, was born a painter's son at Enkhuizen, and died at Amsterdam. His best pictures are small pastoral scenes with animal figures. He also painted large pictures, the life size *Young Bull* (1647, at The Hague) being especially celebrated. The Rijksmuseum at Amsterdam possesses the *Bear-hunt*. See Cundall's *Landscape Painters of Holland* (1891).

(4) **Stephen** (1900–69), English writer and radio producer, joined the B.B.C. in 1938, and is best known in radio as co-author with Joyce Grenfell of the *How* series. His books include a novel, *The Young Man* (1929), an educational study, *The Muse in Chains* (1937), the comic *Gamesmanship* (1947), *Lifemanship* (1950) and *One-Upmanship* (1952), in which he humorously delineated the gentle art of demoralizing opposition, *Potter on America* (1956) and *Supermanship* (1958). See his *Steps to Immaturity* (1959).

POUISHNOFF, Leff Nicholas (1891–1959), Russian pianist, born in Odessa, left Russia at the outbreak of the revolution. Settling in Britain in 1920, he gave concerts and soon was hailed as one of the greatest modern pianists. He excelled in playing Chopin, Liszt and the Russian composers.

POUJADE, Pierre, *poo-zhad* (1920–), French political leader, born in Saint Céré. After serving in World War II, he became a publisher and bookseller. In 1951 he was elected a member of the Saint Céré municipal council, and in 1954 he organized his Poujadist movement (union for the defence of tradesmen and artisans) as a protest against the French tax system. His party had successes in the 1956 elections to the National Assembly. He published his manifesto, *J'ai choisi le combat*, in 1956.

POULENC, Francis, *poo-lãk* (1899–1963), French composer, born in Paris, fought in World War I, studied composition under Koechlin, came under the influence of Satie (q.v.), and as a member of ' Les Six ' was prominent in the reaction against Debussyesque impressionism. He wrote a good deal of chamber music in a cool, limpid style, often for unusual combinations of instruments, and is also known for some excellent ballet and *opera bouffe*, especially *Les Biches* and *Les Mamelles de Tirésias*. His cantata *Figure humaine* (1945) has as its theme the occupation of France. But perhaps his major contribution to music is his considerable output of songs, more romantic in outlook than his other compositions; they include *Poèmes de Ronsard* (1924), *Fêtes Galantes* (1943), &c.

POULSEN, Valdemar, *powl'sen* (1869–1942), Danish electrical engineer, born in Copenhagen, became associated with the Telephone Company there. He invented an arc generator for use in wireless telegraphy.

POUND, (1) (Alfred) Dudley Pickman Rogers (1877–1943), British sailor, became a captain in 1914, commanded with distinction the battleship *Colossus* at the battle of Jutland (1916) and for the remaining two years of World War I directed operations at the Admiralty. Promoted to the rank of rear-admiral, he from 1936 to 1939 was commander-in-chief, Mediterranean fleet, becoming in 1939 admiral of the fleet. In the same year he was appointed first sea lord and this post he held through the most difficult years of the war. He was awarded the Order of Merit in 1943, the year of his death.

(2) **Ezra Loomis** (1885–1972), American poet, was born at Hailey, Idaho. Graduating M.A. at Pennsylvania University in 1906, he became an instructor in Wabash College, but after four months left for Europe, travelling widely in Spain, Italy and Provence. He was co-editor of *Blast* (1914–15), and London editor of the Chicago *Little Review* (1917–19), and in 1920 became Paris correspondent for *The Dial*. From 1924 he made his home in Italy. He became infected with fascist ideas and stirred up much resentment by antidemocracy broadcasts in the early stages of the war. In 1945 he was escorted back to the U.S. and indicted for treason. The trial did not proceed, however, as he was adjudged insane, and placed in an asylum. In 1958 he was certified sane and released. Throughout his career he was a stormy petrel, and critical opinion is sharply divided on his merits as a writer. In addition to his poetry he wrote books on literature, music, art and economics, and translated much from Italian, French, Chinese and Japanese. As a poet, of the Imagist school at the outset of his career, he was a thoroughgoing experimenter, deploying much curious learning in his illustrative imagery and in the development of his themes. T. S. Eliot regarded him as the motivating force behind ' modern ' poetry, the poet who created a climate in which English and American poets could understand and appreciate each other. *Homage to Sextus Propertius* (1919) and *Hugh Selwyn Mauberley* (1920) are among his most important early poems. His *Cantos*, a loosely-knit series of poems, appeared first in 1917, continuing in many instalments, via the *Pisan Cantos* (1948) to *Thrones: Cantos 96–109* (1959). His work in the Classics and Chinese poetry are discernible in their form. Apart from his life work in poetry, significant collections are *Translations of Ezra Pound* (1933) and *Literary Essays* (1954). See T. S. Eliot, *Ezra Pound* (1917), studies of his poetry by H. Kenner (1951), G. S. Fraser (1960), D. Davie (1965), his *Letters* (ed. D. Page, 1951), Life by N. Stock (1970), *Discretions* (1971) by his daughter, M. de Rachewiltz, and further details in the *Autobiography* of W. C. Williams (1951).

(3) **Roscoe** (1870–1964), American jurist, born at Lincoln, Nebraska, was educated at Nebraska University and the Harvard Law School. Among his appointments were those as commissioner of appeals of the supreme court of Nebraska (1901–03), assistant professor of Law at Nebraska University (1899–1903), and successively professor of Law at Northwestern University, Chicago University, Harvard Law School,

and in 1936 at the University of Harvard. An able and influential teacher, especially of jurisprudence, his theories, with the emphasis on the importance of social interests in connection with the law, have had a universal effect. His legal writings were many and include *Readings on the History and System of the Common Law* (1904), *Introduction to the Philosophy of Law* (1922), *Law and Morals* (1924) and *Criminal Justice in America* (1930). An authority also on botany, he was largely responsible for the botanical survey of Nebraska, and on this subject, in collaboration with Dr F. E. Clements, wrote *Phytogeography of Nebraska* (1898).

POUNDS, John (1766–1839), English cripple shoemaker, born at Portsmouth, became unpaid teacher of poor children, regarded as the founder of ragged schools.

POUSSIN, *poo-si*, (1) **Gaspar** (1613–75), French painter, whose real name was Gaspar Dughet, was the brother-in-law and pupil of (2). He worked in Rome and became well known as a landscapist. His popularity in the 18th century was high, though many paintings attributed to him may not have been his work.

(2) **Nicolas** (1594–1665), French painter, born at Les Andelys in Normandy, went at eighteen to Paris to study, and by 1623 had attained the means of visiting Rome. He received important commissions from Cardinal Barberini, and soon acquired fame and fortune. Among the masterpieces of this period was the *Golden Calf*, now in the National Gallery. After sixteen years he returned to Paris and was introduced by Richelieu to Louis XIII, who appointed him painter-in-ordinary. But the altar pieces and mural decorations which he was required to paint were unsuited to his genius, and for this reason, and being annoyed by intrigues, he in 1643 returned to Rome. There, besides classical and religious works which became increasingly geometric in design, he began to paint landscapes on classical lines. His style is a combination of classical ideals and Renaissance tendencies. See works by Bouchitte (1858), Poillon (2nd ed. 1875), Magne (1914) and Friedlaender (1914).

POWELL, (1) Baden. See BADEN-POWELL.

(2) **Cecil Frank** (1903–69), English physicist, born at Tonbridge, Kent, professor of Physics at Bristol (1948–63), director of the Wills Physics Laboratory, Bristol, from 1964, known for his work on the photography of nuclear processes. He received the Nobel physics prize for 1950.

(3) **Frederick York** (1850–1904), English historian and Icelandic scholar, born in London, was educated at Rugby and Christ Church, Oxford. In 1894 with Professor Vígfússon he worked on the records and ancient poetry of Scandinavia and compiled with him *Icelandic Prose Reader* (1879). He became at Oxford regius professor of Modern History. He helped to found the *English Historical Review* (1885).

(4) **John Wesley** (1834–1902), American geologist, born at Mount Morris, New York, lost his right arm in the Civil War, and became a professor of Geology, surveyor

(1868–72) of the Colorado River and its tributaries, and director of the Bureau of Ethnology and of the U.S. Geological Survey. He wrote on the arid region, the Uinta Mountains, the Colorado River and its canyons, and on Indian languages.

(5) **Mary.** See MILTON.

POWERS, Hiram (1805–73), American sculptor, was born a farmer's son at Woodstock, Vermont, became apprentice to a clockmaker in Cincinnati, and was taught to model in clay by a German sculptor. Employed for seven years making wax figures for the Cincinnati museum, in 1835 he went to Washington, where he executed busts, and in 1837 to Florence in Italy, where he resided till his death. There he produced his *Eve*, and in 1843 the still more popular *Greek Slave*. Among his other works were busts of Washington, Calhoun and Daniel Webster.

POWHATTAN. See POCAHONTAS.

POWYS, *pō-is*, name of three brothers, English writers, of Welsh descent:

(1) **John Cowper** (1872–1964), poet, essayist, novelist, born in Shirley, Derbyshire, best known of the three. For a time he taught German at Brighton, and later lectured. Books of verse include *Mandragora* (1917) and *Samphire* (1922). His novels are *A Glastonbury Romance* (1932), *Owen Glendower* (1940), *Porius* (1951), *All or Nothing* (1960), &c. Essays are concerned with questions of philosophy and literary criticism. See his *Autobiography* (1934).

(2) **Llewelyn** (1884–1939), essayist and novelist, brother of (1), born in Dorchester, suffered from recurrent tuberculosis which caused him to spend some years in Switzerland and in Kenya, and from which he finally died. From 1920 to 1925 he was a journalist in New York. Works include *Ebony and Ivory* (1922), *Apples be Ripe* (1930) and the biographical *Confessions of Two Brothers* (with (1), 1916), *Skin for Skin* (1925) and *The Verdict of Bridlegoose* (1926). See Life by Elwin (1953).

(3) **Theodore Francis** (1875–1953), novelist and short story writer, brother of (1) and (2), born in Shirley, lived in seclusion and wrote original and eccentric novels of which the best known is *Mr Weston's Good Wine* (1927). See also *Mr Tasker's Gods* (1925), *Captain Patch* (1935) and *Goat Green* (1937). See study by H. Coombes (1960).

POYNINGS, Sir Edward (1459–1521), English soldier and diplomat, took part in a rebellion against Richard III, escaped to the Continent and joined the Earl of Richmond (Henry VII), with whom he later returned to England. In 1493 he was governor of Calais, and in 1494 went to Ireland as deputy-governor for Prince Henry (Henry VIII). His aim was to anglicize the government of Ireland. This he accomplished by means of the Statutes of Drogheda, known as Poynings' Law, to the effect that all Irish legislature had to be confirmed by the English privy council. This was not repealed until 1782. He was often abroad on diplomatic missions. In 1520 he was present at the Field of the Cloth of Gold, which he had taken an active part in arranging.

POYNTER, Sir Edward John (1836–1919), English painter, was born of Huguenot ancestry in Paris, the son of the architect, Ambrose Poynter (1796–1886). Educated at Westminster and Ipswich, he studied 1853–1854 at Rome and 1856–60 in Paris and elsewhere. He made designs for stained glass, and drawings on wood for *Once a Week* and other periodicals, and for Dalziel's projected illustrated Bible. This led to studies in Egyptian art, which resulted in his *Israel in Egypt* (1867). His watercolours are numerous. He was elected R.A. in 1876. In 1871 he became Slade professor in University College, London, in 1876–81 director for art at South Kensington, in 1894–1905 director of the National Gallery and in 1896 was made president of the Royal Academy. Among his works are *The Ides of March* (1883), *The Visit of the Queen of Sheba to Solomon* (1891), and *Nausicaa and her Maidens*, painted (1872–79) for the Earl of Wharncliffe at Wortley Hall. In 1869–70 he designed the cartoons for a mosaic of St George in the Houses of Parliament.

POYNTING, John Henry (1852–1914), English physicist, born at Monton, Lancs, educated at Manchester and Cambridge, became professor of Physics at Birmingham (1880) and F.R.S. (1888). He wrote on electrical phenomena and on radiation, and determined the constant of gravitation by a torsion experiment. He also did important work on the measurement of the earth's density and on this subject wrote *On the Mean Density of the Earth* (1893) and *The Earth* (1913). With J. J. Thomson he wrote a *Textbook of Physics* (1899–1914).

POZZO, Andrea, *pot'sō* (1642–1709), Italian Jesuit artist, was born in the north of Italy, becoming a Jesuit lay brother in 1665. In Rome from 1681, his main work was the decoration of the church of S. Ignazio, the ceiling of which he painted in the perspective style known as *sotto in sù*. In Vienna from 1702, his work in the Liechtenstein palace is all that survives. His treatise *Perspectiva pictorum* . . . (1693–98, English trans. 1693) had considerable influence on 18th century artists.

POZZO DI BORGO, Carlo Andrea, Count, *pot'sō dee bor'gō* (1764–1842), Corsican-born Russian diplomatist, born at Alala, practised as an advocate in Ajaccio, in 1790 joined the party of Paoli, who made him president of the Corsican council and secretary of state, but in 1796 was obliged to seek safety from the Bonapartes in London. In 1798 he went to Vienna and effected an alliance of Austria and Russia against France. In 1803 he entered the Russian diplomatic service. He laboured strenuously to unite Napoleon's enemies against him, seduced Bernadotte (q.v.) from the Napoleonic cause and urged the allies to march on Paris. He represented Russia at Paris, the Congress of Vienna, the Congress of Verona, and was ambassador to London from 1834 to 1839, when he settled in Paris, where he died. See his Correspondence (Paris 1890) and a French monograph by Maggiolo (1890).

PRAED, Winthrop Mackworth, *prayd* (1802–1839), English man of letters, born in London,

at Eton was one of the most brilliant contributors to the *Etonian*. In 1821 he entered Trinity College, Cambridge, distinguishing himself in Greek and Latin verse, and cultivating the lighter letters in Charles Knight's *Quarterly Magazine*. In 1829 he was called to the bar, in 1830 entered parliament as a Conservative, and in 1834–35 was secretary to the Board of Control. Praed excelled in *vers de société*—his note individual, his rhythm brilliant, and his wit bright. But he is also admirable in a kind of metrical genre painting—e.g., 'The Vicar'; while in 'The Red Fisherman' and 'Sir Nicholas' he not unskilfully emulates Hood. His Poems appeared in 1864, with a memoir by Derwent Coleridge; in 1887 his prose essays; in 1888 his political poems. See Saintsbury's *Essays in English Literature* (1890) and study by D. Hudson (1939).

PRASAD, Rajendra (1884–1963), Indian statesman, left legal practice to become a follower of Gandhi. A member of the Working Committee of the All-India Congress in 1922, he was president of the Congress several times between 1934 and 1948. In 1946 he was appointed minister for food and agriculture in the government of India and president of the Indian Constituent Assembly. He was the first president of the Republic of India from 1950 to 1962. He wrote several books, including *India Divided At the Feet of Mahatma Gandhi* and an autobiography *Atma Katha* (1958).

PRATI, Giovanni (1815–84), Italian lyric and narrative poet, was born near Trento, and died in Rome. Court poet to the House of Savoy, he became a deputy to the Italian parliament (1862) and a senator (1876). His lyrics, which fill several volumes, were published as *Canti lirici*, *Canti del popolo*, &c. See A. Ottolini, *Giovanni Prati* (1911).

PRAXITELES, *prax-it'ē-leez* (fl. 4th cent. B.C.), one of the greatest of Greek sculptors, was a citizen of Athens. His works have almost all perished, though his *Hermes carrying the boy Dionysus* was found at Olympia in 1877.

PREECE, Sir William Henry (1834–1913), British electrical engineer, born of Welsh parents in Carnarvon, was instructed in electrical engineering by Michael Faraday (q.v.) at the Royal Institution. With the Electric and International Telegraph Company from 1853 and the Channel Islands Telegraph Company from 1858 to 1862, he in 1870 was attached to the Post Office, of which he became electrician-in-chief, engineer-in-chief and finally consulting engineer. A pioneer of wireless telegraphy and telephony, he also improved the system of railway signalling and introduced the first telephone receivers. He wrote several books, including *Telegraphy* (1876) with J. Sivewright and *A Manual of Telephony* (1893) with A. J. Stubbs.

PREGL, Fritz, *prayg'l'* (1869–1930), Austrian chemist, born in Laibach, Yugoslavia, became professor of Applied Medical Chemistry at Innsbruck and later at Graz. He was specially noted for the microchemical methods of analysis which gained him a Nobel prize in 1923.

PREMPEH (d. 1931), last King (1888–96) of Ashanti, was deposed by the British, imprisoned at Elmina, and exiled to the Seychelles. He was allowed to return in 1924, with chief's rank from 1926.

PRÉS. See DES PRÉS.

PRESCOTT, William Hickling (1796–1859), American historian, was born at Salem, Mass., the son of a lawyer. He studied at Harvard (where a piece of bread playfully thrown blinded his left eye, and greatly weakened his right one), travelled in England, France and Italy, married in 1820, and, abandoning law for literature, devoted himself to severe study, and, in spite of his grievous disabilities, formed splendid literary projects. His first studies were in Italian literature, but by 1826 he had found his life's work in Spanish history. His *History of Ferdinand and Isabella* (1838) quickly carried his name to the Old World, and was translated into French, Spanish and German. The *History of the Conquest of Mexico* (1843), followed by the *Conquest of Peru* (1847), confirmed his reputation; he was chosen a corresponding member of the French Institute. In 1855–58 he published three volumes of his *History of Philip II*, but died in New York before completing it. Prescott's scholarly but vivid style alone would have assured him popularity. See Life by George Ticknor (1864), and D. Levin, *History as a Romantic Art* (1960).

PRESSENSÉ, *pres-sā-say,* (1) **Edmond Dehaut de** (1824–91), French Protestant theologian, studied at Paris, Lausanne, Berlin and Halle, and in 1847 became a pastor at Paris. He was deputy to the National Assembly for the Seine (1871–76), and elected a life senator in 1883. He was made D.D. by Breslau in 1869 and Edinburgh in 1884. A vigorous writer as well as eloquent preacher, Pressensé took a leading part in the great theological and ecclesiastical controversies of the day. Among his works are *L'Église et la Révolution* (1864; trans. 1869) and *Les Origines* (1882; trans. 1883). See Life by Rousset (1894).

(2) **Francis de** (1853–1914), born in Paris, son of (1), was a notable Socialist and journalist, and a defender of Dreyfus.

PRESTWICH, Sir Joseph (1812–96), English geologist, born at Pensbury, Clapham, was a wine merchant till sixty, but in 1874 became Oxford professor of Geology, and in 1896 was knighted. His work on the water-bearing strata round London (1851) was a standard authority. See Life by his wife (1899).

PRETORIUS, *pre-tō'ri-us,* (1) **Andries Wilhelmus Jacobus** (1799–1853), Boer leader, was born in the Cape Colony. A prosperous farmer, he joined the Great Trek of 1835 into Natal, where he was chosen commandant-general. He took revenge on the Zulus for earlier atrocities, and at first resisting, later accepted British rule, but, after differences with the governor, he trekked again, this time across the Vaal. Eventually the British recognized the Transvaal Republic, later the South African Republic, whose new capital was named Pretoria after him.

(2) **Marthinus Wessels** (1819–1901), son of (1), whom he succeeded as commandant-general in 1853, in 1854 led a punitive expedition against the Kaffirs. He was elected president of the South African Republic in 1857, and of the Orange Free State in 1859. Failing in his ambition to unite the two republics, he resigned the presidency of the Orange Free State in 1863. The discovery of gold in Bechuanaland and diamonds in the Vaal led to difficulties with the *Volksraad,* and he resigned the presidency of the South African Republic in 1871. He fought against the British again in 1877, until the independence of the Republic was recognized. He lived to see it extinguished in 1901.

PRÉVOST, *pray-vō,* (1) **Abbé (Antoine François Prévost d'Exiles)** (1697–1763), French novelist, born in Artois, was educated by the Jesuits. At sixteen he enlisted, but soon returned to the Jesuits, and had almost joined the order when he was again tempted to the soldier's life. In 1720, following an unhappy love affair, he joined the Benedictines of St Maur, and spent the next seven years in religious duties and in study. But about 1727 he fled for six years, first to London, where he started to write *Histoire de Cleveland,* and then to Holland (1729–31). He issued vols. i–iv of *Mémoires d'un homme de qualité* in 1728, vols. v–vii in 1731, *Manon Lescaut* forming vol. vii. He employed himself in additional novels—*Cleveland; Le Doyen de Killerine* and in translations. In London again after another affair, he started *Le Pour et contre* (1733–40), a periodical review of life and letters, modelled on the *Spectator.* In France by 1735, he was appointed honorary chaplain to the Prince de Conti, and compiled over a hundred volumes more. He died suddenly at Chantilly. Prévost lives securely by *Manon Lescaut.* It remains fresh, charming and perennial, from its perfect simplicity, the stamp of reality and truth throughout, and a style so flowing and natural that the reader forgets it altogether in the pathetic interest of the story. See French monographs by Harrisse (1896), Schroeder (1899).

(2) **Eugène Marcel** (1862–1941), French novelist, born in Paris, till 1891 was engineer in a tobacco factory. From the age of twenty-five he wrote in his leisure hours, and in 1909 was elected to the Académie. Of his clever novels and plays many have been translated—*Cousin Laura, Frédérique, Léa,* &c.

(3) **Pierre** (1751–1839), Swiss physician, classicist and philosopher, born at Geneva, occupied chairs of philosophy and physics at Berlin and Geneva. He formulated the theory of exchanges in connection with the laws of radiation. His writings and translations covered many subjects.

PRÉVOST-PARADOL, Lucien Anatole (1829–70), French journalist and diplomat, born in Paris, after a year at Aix as professor of French Literature became in 1856 a journalist in Paris, and from time to time published collections of essays, the best his *Essais sur les moralistes français* (1864). In 1865 he was elected to the Academy, in 1868 visited England. Opposed as a moderate Liberal to the empire, he accepted the post of envoy to the United States under Ollivier

January 1870. His mind unhinged by republican attacks and the struggle with Germany, he committed suicide at Washington just after the outbreak of the Franco-Prussian War.

PRICE, Richard (1723–91), Welsh moral and political philosopher, born at Tynton, Glamorganshire, went to a Dissenting academy in London, was preacher at Newington Green and Hackney, and established a reputation by his *Review of the Principal Questions in Morals* (1758) and *Importance of Christianity* (1766). In 1769 he was made D.D. by Glasgow, and published the celebrated *Northampton Mortality Tables*, &c. In 1771 appeared his *Appeal on the National Debt*; in 1776 his *Observations on Civil Liberty and the War with America*, which brought him an invitation from congress to assist in regulating its finances. In his great treatise on morals he held that right and wrong are simple ideas incapable of analysis, and received immediately by the intuitive power of the reason. In 1791 he became an original member of the Unitarian Society. See Lives by W. Morgan (1815), and R. Thomas (1924) and book by Cone (1952).

PRICHARD, James Cowles (1786–1848), English ethnologist, born in Herefordshire, son of a Quaker merchant, studied medicine, and from 1810 practised in Bristol. In 1813 appeared his *Researches into the Physical History of Mankind* (4th ed. 1841–51), which secured him a high standing. In *The Eastern Origin of the Celtic Nations* (1831) he established the close affinity of the Celtic with the Sanskrit, Greek, Latin and Teutonic languages. Besides several medical works, he published an *Analysis of Egyptian Mythology* (1819) and *The Natural History of Man* (1843). He was president of the Ethnological Society, and in 1845 became a commissioner of lunacy. He died in London.

PRIDE, Thomas (d. 1658), Parliamentarian, born perhaps near Glastonbury, had been a London drayman or brewer, when at the beginning of the Civil War he became parliamentary captain, and quickly rose to be colonel. He commanded a brigade in Scotland, and when the House of Commons betrayed a disposition to effect a settlement with the king, was appointed to expel its Presbyterian royalist members. By 'Pride's Purge' over a hundred were excluded, and the House, reduced to about eighty members, proceeded to bring Charles to justice. Pride sat among his judges, and signed the death warrant. He was present at the battles of Dunbar (1650) and Worcester (1651); opposed to Cromwell becoming 'king', he played little additional part in protectorate politics.

PRIDEAUX, Humphrey, pri'dō (1648–1724), English Orientalist, born at Padstow, from Westminster passed to Christ Church, Oxford. His *Marmora Oxoniensia* (1676), an account of the Arundel Marbles, procured for him the friendship of Heneage Finch (q.v.) and ecclesiastical appointments. His chief work, *The Old and New Testament connected in the History of the Jews* (1715–17) ran to many editions. See his ▸ *Letters to John Ellis* (Camden Soc. 1875).

PRIESTLEY, (1) John Boynton (1894–), English novelist, playwright and critic, born at Bradford, was educated there and at Trinity Hall, Cambridge. He had already made a reputation by critical writings such as *The English Comic Characters* (1925), *The English Novel* (1927), *English Humour* (1928), and books on Meredith (1926) and Peacock (1927) in 'The English Men of Letters' series when the geniality of his novel *The Good Companions* (1929) gained him a wide popularity. It was followed by other humorous novels, though not all of equal merit, including *Angel Pavement* (1930), *Let the People Sing* (1939), *Jenny Villiers* (1947), *The Magicians* (1954). His reputation as a dramatist was established by *Dangerous Corner* (1932), *Time and the Conways* (1937), and other plays on space-time themes, as well as popular comedies, such as *Laburnum Grove* (1933). Best known as a writer of novels, Priestley is also master of the essay form. He is an astute, original and controversial commentator on contemporary society—*Journey Down the Rainbow* (1955), written with his wife Jacquetta Hawkes (b. 1910; younger daughter of Sir Frederick Gowland Hopkins and a noted archaeologist and writer), is a jovial indictment of American life; in serious vein, his collected essays *Thoughts in the Wilderness* (1957) deal with both present and future social problems. See studies by Hughes (1958) and Evans (1964).

(2) **Joseph** (1733–1804), English Presbyterian minister and chemist, was born, a clothdresser's son, at Fieldhead in Birstall Parish, Leeds. After four years at a Dissenting academy at Daventry, in 1755 he became minister at Needham Market, and wrote *The Scripture Doctrine of Remission*. In 1758 he went to Nantwich, and in 1761 became a tutor at Warrington Academy. In visits to London he met Franklin, who supplied him with books for his *History of Electricity* (1767). In 1764 he was made LL.D. of Edinburgh, and in 1766 F.R.S. In 1767 he became minister of a chapel at Mill Hill, Leeds, where he took up the study of chemistry. In 1774, as literary companion, he accompanied Lord Shelburne on a continental tour and published *Letters to a Philosophical Unbeliever*. But at home he was branded as an atheist in spite of his *Disquisition relating to Matter and Spirit* (1777), affirming from revelation our hope of resurrection. He was elected to the French Academy of Sciences in 1772 and to the St Petersburg Academy in 1780. He became in that year minister of a chapel in Birmingham. His *History of Early Opinions concerning Jesus Christ* (1786) occasioned renewed controversy. His reply to Burke's *Reflections on the French Revolution* led a Birmingham mob to break into his house and destroy its contents (1791). He now settled at Hackney, and in 1794 removed to America, where he was well received; at Northumberland, Pa., he died, believing himself to hold the doctrines of the primitive Christians, and looking for the second coming of Christ. Priestley was a pioneer in the chemistry of gases, and one of the discoverers of oxygen (see Scheele).

See his *Works*, ed. Ruff (1831–32), including Autobiographical Memoir; and Life by Anne Holt (1931).

PRIM (Y PRATS), Juan, *preem* (1814–70), Spanish general, born at Reus, so distinguished himself in war and statesmanship as to be made general, marshal and marquis. As progressist he opposed Espartero. Failing in an insurrectionary attempt in 1866, he fled to England and Brussels, but here he guided the movement that in 1868 overthrew Isabella. He was war minister under Serrano, but soon became virtually dictator. Prim secured the election of Amadeus (q.v.) as king, and was later shot by an assassin.

PRIMATICCIO, Francesco, *pree-ma-teet'chō* (1504–*c*. 1570), Italian painter, born at Bologna, came to France in 1531 at the invitation of Francis I, to help in the decoration of the palace of Fontainebleau. A collection of drawings is in the Louvre.

PRIMO DE RIVERA, Miguel, Marqués de Estella (1870–1930), Spanish general, born at Jerez de la Frontera, during the Spanish-American war served in Cuba and the Philippines and from 1909 to 1913 he was in Morocco, in 1915 becoming military governor of Cadiz and in 1922 of Barcelona. He effected a military *coup d'état* in 1923, and ruled Spain as dictator until he retired in 1929.

PRINCE, (1) Henry James (1811–99), English divine, born at Bath, studied medicine, but took Anglican orders, and in 1849 at Spaxton near Bridgwater founded the ' Agapemone ', a community of religious visionaries. See Hepworth Dixon's *Spiritual Wives* (1868).

(2) **John** (1643–1723), a Devon clergyman, author of *The Worthies of Devon* (1701).

PRINGLE, Thomas (1789–1834), Scottish writer, born at Blakelaw, Roxburghshire, studied at Edinburgh University, and in 1817 started the *Edinburgh Monthly Magazine*, the parent of *Blackwood*. In 1820 he sailed for Cape Colony, and for three years was government librarian at Capetown. He started a Whig paper, but it was suppressed by the governor, and returning to London in 1826, he became secretary of the Anti-Slavery Society. His *Ephemerides* (1828) is a collection of graceful verse. See Life and Works by W. Hay (1912).

PRINGSHEIM, -hīm, (1) Ernst (1859–1917), German physicist, noted for his work with Otto Lummer on black-body radiation. His results influenced Planck (q.v.) in his development of the quantum theory.

(2) **Nathanael** (1823–94), German biologist, born in Wziesko in Silesia, noted for his research on the fertilization of plants, was professor at Jena for a short time but for the most part worked privately. He was the first scientist to observe and demonstrate sexual reproduction in algae. He died in Berlin.

PRINSEP, (1) Henry Thoby (1793–1878), English civil servant in India, born at Thoby Priory, Essex, was a member 1858–74 of the Indian Council, and wrote a history of India under the Marquis of Hastings (1823).

(2) **Valentine Cameron** (1838–1904), second son of (1), born at Calcutta, painted many Indian pictures, including one of Lord Lytton's Indian durbar at Delhi, and wrote *Imperial India, an Artist's Journal* (1879), and novels. In 1894 he was elected R.A.

PRINTEMPS, Yvonne, *prĭ-tä* (1894–   ), French actress, born in Ermont, Seine-et-Oise, made her first appearance at the Théâtre Cigale, Paris in 1908, and appeared regularly in revue and musical comedy until 1916, when she began to work with Sacha Guitry, whom she subsequently married. She appeared in London and New York, but did not undertake English parts until 1934, when she played in Noel Coward's *Conversation Piece*. In 1937 she returned to Paris as manager of the Théâtre de la Michodière.

PRIOR, Matthew (1664–1721), English diplomatist and poet, was the son of a joiner of Wimborne, Dorset, but under the patronage of Lord Dorset he was sent to Westminster School and thence with a scholarship from the Duchess of Somerset to St John's College, Cambridge. He was first employed as secretary to the ambassador to The Hague. In Queen Anne's time he turned Tory and was instrumental in bringing about the treaty of Utrecht (1713), for which dubious service he was imprisoned for two years, after the queen's death. His Tory friends recouped his fortunes by subscribing handsomely to a folio edition of his works (1719). He also received a gift of £4000 from Lord Harley to purchase Down Hall in Essex. Prior was a master of what Addison called ' the easie way of writing ', that is neat, colloquial and epigrammatic verse. His first work, in collaboration with Charles Montagu (Lord Halifax), was *The Hind and the Panther Transvers'd*, a witty satire on Dryden's *Hind and the Panther*. His long poem, *Alma or The Progress of the Mind* (1718), written in the manner of *Hudibras*, despite its surface glitter, tends to pall. The long soliloquy in couplet form *Solomon on the Vanity of the World* is definitely tedious. His political verse, with the exception of his brilliant burlesque of Boileau's *Épître au roi—An English Ballad on the Taking of Namur*, is now of historical interest only. The Prior who survives and is the delight of the anthologist is the poet of light occasional verse—mock-lyrics such as *A Better Answer* (*to Chloe Jealous*) or charming addresses to noble children (*A Letter to the Lady Margaret Cavendish when a Child*) and, in serious vein, *Lines Written in the Beginning of Mézeray's History of France*, a favourite with Scott. His most witty trifle is *The Secretary*, but perhaps the poet who comes closest to our affections is the author of *Jinny the Just*. The folio of 1719 was by no means inclusive. A. R. Waller's 2-vol. edition (1905–07) added greatly to it and included the four prose *Dialogues of the Dead*. See study by L. G. Wickham Legg (1921) and *The Literary Works of Matthew Prior*, ed. H. B. Wright and M. K. Spears, 2 vols. (1959).

PRISCIAN, Lat. Priscianus (fl. *c*. A.D. 500) of Caesarea, first of Latin grammarians, in the beginning of the 6th century taught Latin at Constantinople. Besides his *Institutiones Grammaticae*, which was very highly thought of in the middle ages, he wrote six smaller grammatical treatises and two hexameter poems.

PRISCILLIAN (*c.* 340–385), Bishop of Ávila, was excommunicated by a synod at Saragossa in 380, then tolerated, but ultimately executed —the first case of capital punishment for heresy in the history of the Church. His doctrine, said to have been brought to Spain from Egypt, contained Gnostic and Manichaean elements, and was based on dualism. The Priscillianists were ascetics, eschewed marriage and animal food, and were said to hold strict truth obligatory only between themselves. See *Priscillian et le Priscillianisme*, by E. C. Babut (Paris 1909).

PRITCHARD, Charles (1808–93), English schoolmaster, clergyman and astronomer, was from 1870 Savilian professor at Oxford, where he established an observatory. He wrote on stellar photometry in *Uranometria Nova Oxoniensis* (1885). See Memoirs (1896).

PROBUS, (1) Marcus Aurelius (d. 282), Roman emperor, born at Sirmium in Pannonia, greatly distinguished himself under Valerian on the Danube and in Africa, Egypt, Asia, Germany and Gaul, was by Tacitus appointed governor of Asia, and by his soldiers, on Tacitus's death, was forced to assume the purple (A.D. 276). The Germans were driven out of Gaul and the Barbarians from the frontier, while Persia was forced to a humiliating peace. Probus next devoted himself to developing the internal resources of the empire. But fearing that the army would deteriorate with inactivity, he employed the soldiers on public works. Such occupations, deemed degrading, excited discontent; and a body of troops engaged in draining the swamps about Sirmium murdered him in 282.

(2) Marcus Valerius (fl. late 1st cent. A.D.), Latin grammarian from Syria, wrote a biography of Persius and prepared annotated editions of classical authors, including Horace, Terence and Lucretius.

PROCLUS (*c.* A.D. 412–485), Greek Neoplatonist philosopher, born in Constantinople, studied at Alexandria and Athens. His vivid imagination convinced him, when all the influences of the mysteries were brought to bear upon him, of his direct intercommunion with the gods. The Orphic Poems, the writings of Hermes, and all the mystical literature of that occult age were to him the only source of true philosophy. Of an impulsive piety, and eager to win disciples from Christianity itself, he made himself obnoxious to the Christian authorities in Athens, who banished him. Allowed to return, he acted with more prudence. His Neoplatonism based on Plotinus combined all the most important strands of Greek philosophy, the traditions of the Roman, Syrian and Alexandrian schools into one comprehensive theological metaphysic. Euclid, Plato and Pythagoras are all grist to his mill. Hegel's dialectic originated in Proclus' triadic law of development. See edition of some of his works by V. Cousin (1820–25), *Elements of Theology* (trans. E. R. Dodds 1932), W. B. Frankland, *The First Book of Euclid's Elements based upon that of Proclus* (1933).

PROCOP, Andrew (*c.* 1380–1434), Bohemian Hussite leader, from a monk became one of Žižka's followers, and on Žižka's death commander of the Taborites. Under him the fearful raids into Silesia, Saxony and Franconia were carried out, and he repeatedly defeated German armies. He and his colleague, Procop the Younger, headed the internal conflict of the Taborites with the more moderate Calixtines; both fell at Lipan near Böhmischbrod.

PROCOPIUS (*c.* A.D. 499–565), Byzantine historian, born at Caesarea in Palestine, studied law, and accompanied Belisarius against the Persians (526), the Vandals in Africa (533) and the Ostrogoths in Italy (536). He was highly honoured by Justinian, and seems to have been appointed prefect of Constantinople in 562. His principal works are his *Historiae* (on the Persian, Vandal and Gothic wars), *De Aedificiis*, and *Anecdota* or *Historia Arcana*, a sort of *chronique scandaleuse* of the court of Justinian. There are editions by Haury (1905 *et seq.*), and in the Loeb Lib. with trans. by H. B. Dewing (1914–40). See THEODORA; and works by Dahn (1865) and Haury (1891).

PROCTER, (1) Adelaide Ann (1825–64), English minor poet, daughter of (2), was born and died in London and in 1851 turned Roman Catholic. By her *Legends and Lyrics* (1858–60), some of which were written for *Household Words*, she won poetical renown. Her verse includes *The Lost Chord*, which was set to music by Sir Arthur Sullivan.

(2) Bryan Waller, pseud. **Barry Cornwall** (1787–1874), born at Leeds, and educated at Harrow with Byron and Peel for schoolfellows, became a solicitor, came to London and in 1815 began to contribute poetry to the *Literary Gazette*. In 1823 he married Basil Montagu's step-daughter, Anne Benson Skepper (1799–1888). He had meanwhile published poems and produced a tragedy at Covent Garden, whose success was largely due to the acting of Macready and Kemble. He was called to the bar in 1831, and in 1832–61 was a metropolitan commissioner of lunacy. His works comprise *Dramatic Scenes* (1819), *Marcian Colonna* (1820), *The Flood of Thessaly* (1823), and *English Songs* (1832), besides memoirs of Kean (1835) and Charles Lamb (1866). The last is always worth reading; but his poems are rarely more than studied if graceful exercises. Yet 'Barry Cornwall' was a man beloved by many of the greatest of his time. See *Autobiographical Fragment*, ed. by Coventry Patmore (1877).

PROCTOR, Richard Anthony (1837–88), English astronomer, born at Chelsea, graduated from St John's, Cambridge, in 1860. Devoting himself from 1863 to astronomy, in 1866 he was elected F.R.A.S. His name is associated with the determination of the rotation of Mars, the theory of the solar corona, and stellar distribution. He charted the 324,198 stars contained in Argelander's great catalogue. Very popular as a lecturer and writer, he founded his magazine *Knowledge* in 1881, in which year he settled in the States.

PRODICUS (fl. 5th cent. B.C.), born at Iulis

in Ceos, a Greek sophist of the time of Socrates, was author of the story, ' The Choice of Hercules '.

PROKHOROV, Alexander (1916–), Russian physicist, professor at Lebedev Physics Inst., Moscow. He won the Nobel prize for physics in 1964 with Basov and Townes for work on development of laser beams.

PROKOFIEV, Sergei Sergeevitch, *pro-kof'yef* (1891–1955), Russian composer, was born at Sontsovka, Ukraine. Taught the piano by his mother, he began to compose at five and had started his first opera at the age of nine. He studied at the St Petersburg Conservatory under Rimsky-Korsakov and Liadov, composing prolifically and winning a reputation as a virtuoso pianist. During World War I Prokofiev lived in London, and at its close he moved to the United States until in 1934 he returned to Russia. Induced to do so by the Soviet Government, he simplified his style, producing a large number of occasional works for official celebrations in addition to his later Symphonies and popular pieces like *Peter and the Wolf.* His works range from the glittering romanticism of his early days to the mellow lyricism of his second Russian period, and in all spheres from opera to film music he was a consummate artist combining acute imagination with a precise technique. See *Autobiography* (1960).

PROKOP. See PROCOP.

PROKOPOVICH, Feofan, *-pŏ'-* (1681–1736), Russian prelate, educated at Kiev Orthodox Academy, where in 1711 he was appointed rector, and Rome. In St Petersburg in 1716 his sermons and theories for church reforms brought him to the notice of Peter the Great, who made him his adviser, Bishop of Pskov and in 1724 Archbishop of Novgorod. He was responsible for setting up a Holy Synod instead of the existing patriarchate, whereby the respective powers of church and state were established.

PROPERTIUS, Sextus (*c.* 48–*c.* 15 B.C.), the most impassioned of the Roman elegiac poets, was born probably at Asisium (the modern Assisi). He had a portion of his patrimony confiscated after Philippi by the Triumvirs, to reward their veterans, but retained means enough to proceed to Rome for education and to make poetry the business of his life. He won the favour of Maecenas, to whom he dedicated a book of his poems, and even ingratiated himself with Augustus, whose achievements he duly celebrated. But the central figure of his inspiration was his mistress Cynthia. Propertius left Rome apparently only once, on a visit to Athens. Of his poems only the first book, devoted to Cynthia, was published during his lifetime; certainly the last of the four was given to the light by his friends. Later criticism shows increasing admiration for his native force, his eye for dramatic situation, and his power over the reader's sympathies. But he is often rough to harshness and obscure from defect of finish. There are texts by Postgate, Phillimore, Richmond (1928), Butler and Barber (1933). There are translations by Phillimore (1906) and Butler (1913).

PROSPER OF AQUITAINE (*c.* 390–*c.* 463), the champion of Augustinian doctrine against the Semi-Pelagians, born in Aquitaine, was a prominent theologian in southern Gaul in 428–434, and then settled in Rome. Besides letters, *Responsiones* and pamphlets on grace and freewill, he wrote a chronicle, coming down to 455, a hexameter poem against the Pelagians, and *Epigrammata ex sententiis Sancti Augustini,* compiled from Augustine.

PROTAGORAS, *-tag'-* (*c.* 485–411 B.C.), the earliest Greek sophist, born at Abdera, taught in Athens, Sicily, &c. a system of practical wisdom fitted to train men for citizens' duties, and based on the doctrine that ' man is the measure of all things '. All his works are lost except a fragment of his *On the Gods.* He perished at sea.

PROTHERO. See ERNLE.

PROTOGENES, *-toj'ĕ-neez* (fl. late 4th cent. B.C.), Greek painter, born at Caunus in Caria, lived in Rhodes, where he worked steadily on through the siege of 305–304 B.C.

PROUDHON, Pierre Joseph, *proo-dõ* (1809–1865), French socialist, born at Besançon, contrived as a compositor to complete and extend his education. He became partner (1837) in the development of a new typographical process, contributed to an edition of the Bible notes on the Hebrew language, and in 1838 published an *Essai de grammaire générale.* He subsequently contributed to an *Encyclopédie catholique.* In 1840 he issued *Qu'est-ce que la propriété?* affirming the bold paradox ' Property is Theft ', as appropriating the labour of others in the form of rent. In 1842 he was tried for his revolutionary opinions, but acquitted. In 1846 he published his greatest work, the *Système des contradictions économiques.* During the Revolution of 1848 he was elected for the Seine department, and published several newspapers advocating the most advanced theories. He attempted also to establish a bank which should pave the way for a socialist transformation by giving gratuitous credit, but failed utterly. The violence of his utterances at last resulted in a sentence of three years' imprisonment, and in March 1849 he fled to Geneva, but returned to Paris in June and gave himself up. While in prison he published *Confessions d'un révolutionnaire* (1849), *Actes de la Révolution* (1849), *Gratuité du crédit* (1850) and *La Révolution sociale démontrée par le coup d'état* (1852). In June 1852 he was liberated, but in 1858 was again condemned to three years' imprisonment, and retired to Belgium. Amnestied in 1860, he died near Paris. A forerunner of Marx, his theories emphasized liberty, equality and justice, and one of his main themes was that as man becomes morally mature the artificial restrictions of law and government can be dispensed with. See *Lives* by Sainte-Beuve (1872) and Woodcock (1956); and A. Gray, *The Socialist Tradition* (1946).

PROUST, *proost,* (1) **Joseph Louis** (1754–1826), French chemist, born at Angers, was director of the royal laboratory in Madrid (1789–1808). He returned to France after the fall of Charles IV, his patron, and the destruction of the laboratory by the French. He stated the law of constant proportion, known as *Proust's Law,* in a controversy with Berthollet lasting about eight years and was the first to isolate and identify grape sugar. He died at Angers.

(2) **Marcel** (1871–1922), French novelist, born at Auteuil, Paris, was a semi-invalid all his life. He was cosseted by his mother, and her death in 1905, when he was thirty-four years old, robbed him of desire to continue his hitherto ' social butterfly ' existence. Instead he withdrew from society, immured himself in a sound-proof flat and gave himself over entirely to introspection. Out of this delving into the self below the levels of superficial consciousness, he set himself to transform into art the realities of experience as known to the inner emotional life. Despite the seemingly dilettante approach to life prior to his start on his novel, *A la recherche du temps perdu* (13 vols.), it is evident from the various volumes that make up this title that no detail ever escaped the amazingly observant eye of this artist in transcription, who subjected experience to searching analysis to divine in it beauties and complexities that escape the superficial response of ordinary intelligence. Thinking around the philosophy of Henri Bergson on the subconscious, his distinctions between the various aspects of time, and insistence on the truths perceived by involuntary memory, Proust evolved a mode of communication by image, evocation and analogy for displaying his characters—not as a realist would see them, superficially, from the outside—but in terms of their concealed emotional life, evolving on a plane that has nothing to do with temporal limitations. Consequently he comes incredibly close to the mainsprings of human action. *The Quest* started off with *Du côté de chez Swann* (1913), and, after delay caused by the war, *A l'ombre des jeunes filles en fleur*, which won the Prix Goncourt in 1919. *Le Côté de Guermantes* (1920–21; 2 vols.) followed and *Sodome et Gomorrhe* (1922; 3 vols.). These achieved an international reputation for Proust and an eager public awaited the posthumously-published titles, *La Prisonnière*, *Albertine disparue*, and *Le Temps retrouvé*, each of two volumes. Apart from his masterpiece, there has also been posthumous publication of an early novel, *Jean Santeuil* (1957) and a book of critical credo—*Contre Sainte-Beuve*, trans. by S. Townsend Warner (1958). See *Comment travaillait Proust*, with bibliography, by L. Pierre-Quint (Paris 1928), and studies by E. Seillière (Paris 1931), H. March (1948), F. C. Green (1949), Maurois (1950), G. Painter vol. i (1959), R. Barker (1959) and Moss (1963).

PROUT (1) **Ebenezer** (1835–1909), English composer and writer on musical theory, edited Handel's Messiah, for which he provided additional accompaniments. In 1894 he became professor of Music at Dublin.

(2) **Father**. See MAHONY.

(3) **Samuel** (1783–1852), English watercolourist, born at Plymouth, in 1815 was elected to the Watercolour Society, and in 1818 went to Rouen. Architecture thenceforward was the feature of his works. Prout's numerous elementary drawing-books influenced many. See Memoir by Ruskin in *Art Journal* (1852), and his *Notes on the Drawings by Prout and Hunt* (1879–80).

(4) **William** (1785–1850), English chemist and physiologist, was born at Horton near Chipping Sodbury. A graduate of Edinburgh, he practised in London from 1812. He is noteworthy for his discovery of the presence of hydrochloric acid in the stomach and for his ' Hypothesis ' (1815), which, rejected at first, is now looked upon as a modification of the Atomic Theory.

PRUDENTIUS, Marcus Aurelius Clemens (348–c. 410), a Latin Christian poet, was born in the north of Spain. He practised as a pleader, acted as civil and criminal judge and afterwards received a high office at the imperial court. A Christian all his life, he devoted himself in his later years to the composition of religious poetry. The year of his death is uncertain. Of his poems the chief are *Cathemerinon Liber*, a series of twelve hortatory hymns (Eng. trans. 1845); *Peristephanon*, fourteen lyrical poems in honour of martyrs; *Apotheosis*, a defence of the Trinity; *Hamartigeneia*, on the Origin of Evil; *Psychomachia*, on the Christian Graces; *Contra Symmachum*, against the heathen gods; *Diptychon*, on scriptural incidents. He is the best of the early Christian versemakers. His works have been edited by J. Bergman (1936). See F. St John Thackeray's *Translations from Prudentius* (1890).

PRUD'HON, Pierre Paul, *prü-dõ* (1758–1823), French painter, born at Cluny, studied in Dijon, trained with engravers in Paris and having won the Rome prize, went to Italy. He did little work there, returning to Paris to draw and paint in a refined style not in accord with revolutionary Paris. Patronized, however, by the empresses of Napoleon, he was made court painter, and among his best work is a portrait of the empress Josephine. Many of his paintings had mythological and allegorical subjects and were commissioned for public buildings. He also designed furniture and interiors on classical lines. Unhappily married at the age of nineteen, he formed a liaison with his pupil, Constance Mayer, which ended tragically with her suicide in 1821. See works by Clément (3rd ed. 1880), Gauthiez (1886), Guiffrey (1924).

PRUS, Boleslaw, pseud. of **Aleksander Głowacki**, *proos* (1847–1912), Polish novelist, born at Hrubieszów, who belonged to the period of realism in literature which followed the unsuccessful revolt against Russian domination in 1863–64. His novels and short stories are written mainly about the people, the social novel being characteristic of the writing of this time, and include *The Blunder*, *The Outpost* (1884), *The Doll* (1887), considered to be his masterpiece, a vivid and sympathetic picture of Warsaw, and *Emancipated Women* (1893).

PRYDE, James. See NICHOLSON (8).

PRYNNE, William (1600–69), English pamphleteer, born at Swanswick near Bath, graduated from Oriel College, Oxford, in 1621. He was called to the bar, but was early drawn into controversy, and during 1627–30 published *The Unloveliness of Love-lockes*, *Healthes Sicknesse* (against drinking of healths), and three other Puritan diatribes. In 1633 appeared his *Histrio-Mastix : the*

Players Scourge, for which, on account of a supposed reflection on the virtue of Henrietta Maria, he was in 1634 sentenced to have his book burnt by the hangman, pay a fine of £5000, be expelled from Oxford and Lincoln's Inn, lose both ears in the pillory, and suffer perpetual imprisonment. Three years later, for assailing Laud and the hierarchy in two more pamphlets, a fresh fine of £5000 was imposed; he was again pilloried, and was branded on both cheeks with *S. L.* (' seditious libeller '; rather ' stigmata Laudis ' by Prynne's own interpretation). He remained a prisoner till in 1640 he was released by a warrant of the House of Commons. He acted as Laud's bitter prosecutor (1644), and in 1647 became recorder of Bath, in 1648 member for Newport in Cornwall. But, opposing the Independents and Charles I's execution, he was one of those of whom the House was ' purged ', and was even imprisoned 1650–52. On Cromwell's death he returned to parliament as a royalist; and after the Restoration Charles II made him keeper of the Tower records. Prynne was a great compiler of constitutional history, his best works the *Calendar of Parliamentary Writs* and his *Records.* See *Documents relating to Prynne*, ed. Gardiner (1877); Life by Kirby (1931).

PRZHEVALSKI, Nikolai Mikhailovich (1839–1888), Russian traveller, born near Smolensk, from 1867 to his death at Karakol (Przhevalsk) made important journeys in Mongolia, Turkestan and Tibet, reaching to within 160 miles of Lhasa. He explored the upper Hwang-ho, reaching as far as Kiachta. He amassed a valuable collection of plants and animals, including a wild camel and a wild horse.

PRZYBYSZEWSKI, Stanisław, *pshi-bi-shef'-ski* (1868–1927), Polish novelist, dramatist and critic, educated in Germany, lived from 1898 in Cracow, where he became editor of *Life* and a leader of the new literary ' Young Poland ' movement. His work, reflecting his ' naturalist ' ideas, includes *Homo Sapiens* (1901), *Matka* (1903) and the drama *Śnieg (Snow)*, which was translated into English in 1920.

PSALMANAZAR, George (*c.* 1679–1763), ' the Formosan ', real name unknown, was born probably in Languedoc. Educated by monks and Jesuits, he at sixteen turned vagabond, and wandered through France, Germany and the Low Countries, by turns an ' Irish pilgrim ', a ' Japanese convert ', a waiter, a ' heathen Formosan ' and a soldier. At Sluys in 1703 he found an accomplice in one Innes, chaplain to a Scottish regiment, who baptized him ' George Lauder ', and brought him to London. For Bishop Compton he translated the Church Catechism into the ' Formosan ' language; and to him he dedicated his *Historical and Geographical Description of Formosa* (1704), which found many believers in spite of its patent absurdities. Later he was the alleged importer of a white ' Formosan ' enamel, a tutor, a regimental clerk (1715–17), a fan-painter and, lastly, for years a diligent hack-writer. The *Universal History* was largely of his compiling; and his, too, a popular *Essay on*

Miracles. But in all his strange life there is nothing stranger than the esteem expressed for him by Samuel Johnson as ' the best man he ever knew '. See his autobiographical *Memoirs* (1764) and Farrer's *Literary Forgeries* (1907).

PSELLUS, Michael (11th cent.), a Byzantine politician and teacher of philosophy, wrote *Synopsis in Aristotelis logicam* and *Chronographia*, valuable both historically and autobiographically. He had considerable influence during the reigns of Constantine Monomachus (who appointed him head of the new faculty of philosophy at the university of Constantinople), Isaac Comnenus and Constantine Ducas, whose son was his pupil.

PTOLEMY, name of the Macedonian kings who ruled Egypt for three hundred years. **Ptolemy (I) Soter** (d. 283 B.C.), a son of Lagos, was one of the greatest of the generals of Alexander the Great, upon whose death he obtained Egypt (323 B.C.). Nominally subject to Macedonia, Ptolemy occupied the first half of his reign in warding off outside attacks and consolidating his government. In 306 he was defeated by Demetrius in a sea-fight off Salamis in Cyprus. Notwithstanding this, he assumed the title of king of Egypt, and defended his dominions against Antigonus and Demetrius. In 305 he defended the Rhodians against Demetrius, and received from them his title Soter (Saviour). Alexandria, his capital, became the centre of commerce and Greek culture. He abdicated in 285 and was succeeded by his son **Ptolemy (II) Philadelphus** (d. 247), under whom the power of Egypt attained its greatest height. He was successful in his external wars, founded the Museum and Library of Alexandria, purchased the most valuable manuscripts, engaged the most celebrated professors, and had made for him the Septuagint translation of the Hebrew Scriptures and the Egyptian history of Manetho. **Ptolemy (III) Euergetes**, his son, pushed the southern limits of the empire to Axum. **Ptolemy (IV) Philopator** (221–204), his son, began his reign by murdering his mother, Berenice. He abandoned himself to luxury, and the decadence of the Egyptian empire set in. He warred with Antiochus, persecuted the Jews, and encouraged learning. He was succeeded by his infant son **Ptolemy (V) Epiphanes** (204–180). The kings of Syria and Macedonia wrested from Egypt her provinces, and the king's ministers called in the aid of Rome, whose influence in Egypt after this was supreme. The successors of Epiphanes were worthless as rulers down to the time of the celebrated Cleopatra (q.v.), after which Egypt became a Roman province. See Mahaffy, *Empire of the Ptolemies* (1896) and Bevan, *Egypt under the Ptolemies* (1927).

PTOLEMY, or Claudius Ptolemaeus (*c.* A.D. 90–168), astronomer and geographer, was a native of Egypt, and flourished in Alexandria. His ' great compendium of astronomy ' seems to have been denominated by the Greeks *megistē*, ' the greatest ', whence was derived the Arab name *Almagest*, by which it is generally known. With his *Tetrabiblos Syntaxis* is combined another work called *Karpos* or *Centiloquium*, because it contains a hundred aphorisms—both treat of astrological subjects, so have been held by some to be of doubtful genuineness. Then there is a treatise on the fixed stars or a species of almanac, the *Geographia*, with other works dealing with map making, the musical scale and chronology. Ptolemy, as astronomer and geographer, held supreme sway over the minds of scientific men down to the 16th–17th century; but he seems to have been not so much an independent investigator as a corrector and improver of the work of his predecessors. In astronomy he depended almost entirely on Hipparchus. But, as his works form the only remaining authority in ancient astronomy, the system they expound is called the *Ptolemaic System*, which, the system of Plato and Aristotle, was an attempt to reduce to scientific form the common notions of the motions of the heavenly bodies. The Ptolemaic astronomy, handed on by Byzantines and Arabs, assumed that the earth is the centre of the universe, and that the heavenly bodies revolve round it. Beyond and in the ether surrounding the earth's atmosphere were eight concentric spherical shells, to seven of which one heavenly body was attached, the fixed stars occupying the eighth. The apparent irregularity of their motions was explained by a complicated theory of epicycles. As a geographer Ptolemy is the corrector of a predecessor, Marinus of Tyre. His geography (ed. by Müller, Paris 1883) contains a catalogue of places, with latitude and longitude; general descriptions; details regarding his mode of noting the position of places—by latitude and longitude, with the calculation of the size of the earth. He constructed a map of the world and other maps. See works edited by Heiberg (1898–1907).

PUBLIUS SYRUS. See SYRUS.

PUCCINI, Giacomo Antonio Domenico Michele Secondo Maria, *poo-chee'nee* (1858–1924), Italian composer, born in Lucca, where, at nineteen, he was an organist and choirmaster, his first extant compositions being written for use in the church. Poverty prevented his undertaking regular studies until a grant from the queen in 1880 enabled him to attend the Milan Conservatory. His first opera, *Le Villi*, failed to secure a prize in the competition for which it was composed, but impressed Ricordi, the publisher, sufficiently to induce him to commission a second work, *Edgar*, which failed at its first performance in 1889. *Manon Lescaut* (1893) was his first great success, but it was eclipsed by *La Bohème* (1896). *Tosca* and *Madame Butterfly* (both 1900) have also remained popular favourites. His last opera, *Turandot*, was left unfinished at his death, and was completed by his friend Alfano. Puccini was, perhaps, the last great representative of the Italian operatic tradition, which absorbed almost all his energies throughout his mature working life. See *Letters*, ed. Adami (1931), Life by R. Specht (1933) and a study by M. Carner (1958).

PÜCKLER-MUSKAU, Hermann Ludwig, Fürst von, *pük'ler-moos'cow* (1785–1871), German traveller, author and horticulturalist.

See Life by Assing (1873), and *Regency Visitor* (1957), ed. Butler.

PUFFENDORF, or **Pufendorf, Samuel, Freiherr von** (1632–94), German writer on jurisprudence, born near Chemnitz, studied at Leipzig and at Jena. He was tutor to the sons of the Swedish ambassador at Copenhagen when war broke out between Denmark and Sweden, and he was imprisoned. There he thought out his *Elementa Jurisprudentiae Universalis*, dedicated to the Elector Palatine, who made him professor of the Law of Nations at Heidelberg (1661). As ' Severinus de Monzambano ' he exposed absurdities of the constitution of the Germanic empire in *De Statu Imperii Germanici* (1667). In 1670 he became professor at Lund, and wrote his great *De Jure Naturae et Gentium* (1672), based upon Grotius (q.v.), with features from Hobbes. Appointed Swedish historiographer, he published a history of Sweden from the wars of Gustavus Adolphus to the death of Queen Christina. In 1688 the Elector of Brandenburg invited him to Berlin to write the history of the Great Elector.

PUGACHEV, Emelian, *poo-ga-chof'* (*c.* 1744–1775), Russian Cossack soldier and pretender, fought in the Seven Years' War and in the war against Turkey (1769–74), before retiring to a lawless life in the south of Russia. In 1773 proclaiming himself Peter III, Catharine II's dead husband, he began a reign of organized rebellion in the south, gathering to him the discontented masses out of which he created a military force. Promising to his followers freedom and possessions, he besieged fortresses and towns and his power by 1774 had spread alarmingly. Catharine made half-hearted attempts to curb Pugachev with a weak and badly led force, but finally sent her general Mikhelson against him, and in a battle near Tsaritsyn he was defeated, captured and conveyed in an iron cage to Moscow, where he was executed. There was not another rebellion of this magnitude in Russia until the beginning of the 20th-century revolution.

PUGET, Pierre, *pü-zhay* (1622–94), French sculptor and painter, born in Marseilles, where later he did most of his work. Examples of his sculpture may be seen in the Louvre (Hercules, Milo of Crotona, Alexander and Diogenes, &c.). See Life by Ginoux (1894).

PUGIN, *pü-zhī*, (1) **Augustus Welby** (1812–52), English architect, was born in London, the son of a French architect, Auguste Pugin (1762–1832), in whose office, after schooling at Christ's Hospital, he was trained, chiefly by making drawings for his father's books on Gothic buildings. While working with Sir C. Barry he designed and modelled a large part of the decorations and sculpture for the new Houses of Parliament (1836–37). He became about 1833 a convert to Catholicism; and most of his plans were made for churches within that faith, for example the Roman Catholic cathedral at Birmingham. He did much to revive Gothic architecture in England. He died insane at Ramsgate. He wrote *Contrasts between the Architecture of the 15th and 19th Centuries* (1836), *Chancel Screens* (1851) and *True Principles of Christian Architecture* (1841). See Ferrey's *Recollec-*

tions of Pugin and his Father (1861) and M. Trappes-Lomax, *Pugin: a Mediaeval Victorian* (1932).

(2) **Edward Welby** (1834–75), son of (1), completed much of his father's work and designed many Catholic churches, including the cathedral at Cóbh, Eire.

PUŁASKI, Kazimierz (1748–79), Polish count and military leader, fought against Russia, and was outlawed at the partition of Poland (1772). In 1777 he went to America, and for his conduct at Brandywine was given a brigade of cavalry. In 1778 he organized ' Pulaski's legion ', in May 1779 entered Charleston, and held it until it was relieved. He was mortally wounded at the siege of Savannah.

PULCI, *pool'chee,* the name of two Florentine poets, brothers:

(1) **Bernardo** (1438–88), wrote an elegy on the death of Simonetta, mistress of Julian de' Medici, and the first translation of Virgil's *Eclogues.*

(2) **Luigi** (1432–84), wrote *Il Morgante Maggiore* (' Morgante the Giant ', 1481), a burlesque epic with Roland for hero, one of the most valuable specimens of the early Tuscan dialect. He also produced a comic novel and several humorous sonnets.

PULITZER, Joseph (1847–1911), American newspaper proprietor was born at Makó, Hungary, of Magyar-Jewish and Austro-German parentage, but emigrated to join the American army. Discharged in 1865, he came penniless to St Louis. He became a reporter, was elected to the State legislature and began to acquire and revitalize old newspapers. The *New York World* (1883), sealed his success. He endowed the Columbia University School of Journalism, and in his will established annual Pulitzer prizes for literature, drama, music and journalism. See *Life* by D. C. Seitz (1924), and study by A. Ireland (1914).

PULLMAN, George Mortimer (1831–97), American inventor, born at Brocton, in New York state, in 1859 made his first sleeping-cars, and in 1863 the first on the present lines. He also introduced dining-cars. The Pullman Palace Car Company was formed in 1867. In 1880 he founded ' Pullman City ', since absorbed by Chicago.

PULSZKY, Francis Aurelius, *pool'ski* (1814–1897), Hungarian politician and author, born at Eperies, studied law, travelled and published (1837) a successful book on England. In 1848 he became Esterházy's factotum, but, having joined the revolution, fled to London, where he became a journalist. When Kossuth came to England Pulszky became his companion, and went with him to America. His wife, **Theresa** (1815–66), wrote *Memoirs of a Hungarian Lady* (1850) and *Tales and Traditions of Hungary* (1851). Pulszky was condemned to death in 1852, but after living in Italy 1852–66, and being imprisoned in Naples as a Garibaldian, was pardoned in 1867. He returned to Hungary, sat in parliament, and was director of museums. See his Autobiography (1879–82; Ger. trans. 1883), and F. W. Newman's *Reminiscences of Two Exiles* (1889).

PULTENEY, William, Earl of Bath (1684–

1764), English politician, the son of a London knight, was educated at Westminster and Christ Church, Oxford. He became Whig member for Heydon in 1705, and was an eloquent speaker. Disgusted with Walpole's indifference to his claims, in 1728 he headed a group of malcontent ' patriots ', and was henceforth Walpole's bitterest opponent. He was Bolingbroke's chief assistant in the *Craftsman,* which involved him in many political controversies, and called forth some of his finest pamphlets. On Walpole's resignation Pulteney was sworn into the privy council, and in 1742 created Earl of Bath. Horace Walpole places him amongst his *Royal and Noble Authors.*

PURBACH, or Peuerbach, Georg von, *poor'-*baᴋн (1423–61), Austrian astronomer and mathematician, the first great modern astronomer, Regiomontanus's master, was a professor at Vienna. Thought to be the first to introduce sines into trigonometry, he compiled a sines table. See German monograph by Schubert (1828).

PURCELL, (1) Edward Mills (1912–), American physicist, born at Taylorville, Ill., has held posts at Massachusetts Institute of Technology and Harvard University, where he was appointed professor of Physics in 1949 and Gerhard Gade professor in 1960. He was Nobel prize-winner in 1952 (with Bloch, q.v.) for his work on the magnetic moments of atomic particles.

(2) **Henry** (1659–95), English composer, born probably in Westminster, the son of Thomas Purcell, a court musician and Chapel Royal chorister, was himself one of the ' children of the chapel ' from about 1669 until 1673, when, his voice having broken, he was apprenticed to the keeper of the king's keyboard and wind instruments, whom he ultimately succeeded in 1683. In the meantime he had followed Locke (q.v.) as ' composer for the king's violins ' (1677), and had been appointed organist of Westminster Abbey (1679) and of the Chapel Royal (1682). It is known that he began to compose when very young, though some early pieces ascribed to him are probably the work of his uncle Henry, also a professional musician. About 1680 he began writing incidental music for the Duke of York's Theatre, and thenceforward until his early death his output was prolific. Though his harpsichord pieces and his well-known set of trio-sonatas for violins and continuo have retained their popularity, his greatest masterpieces are among his vocal and choral works. In his official capacity he produced a number of fine ' odes ' in celebration of royal birthdays, St Cecilia's Day, and other occasions, also many anthems and services, but had he never written these, his incidental songs such as ' Nymphs and Shepherds ' (Shadwell's *The Libertine*), ' I Attempt from Love's Sickness ' (*The Indian Queen*), and ' Arise, ye Subterranean Winds ' (*The Tempest*), would ensure his immortality. Purcell is credited with six operas, but of these only the first, *Dido and Aeneas* written to a libretto by Nahum Tate (q.v.) in 1689 for performance at a Chelsea girls' school, is opera in the true sense. The others—

Dioclesian (1690; adapted from Beaumont and Fletcher), *King Arthur* (1691; Dryden), *The Fairy Queen* (1692; adapted from *A Midsummer Night's Dream*), *The Tempest* (1695; Shadwell's adaptation) and *The Indian Queen* (1695; Dryden and Howard) consist essentially of spoken dialogue between the main characters interspersed with masques and other musical items supplied by nymphs, shepherds, allegorical figures and the like. Purcell was writing at the time when the new Italian influence was first beginning to be felt in England, and his music includes superb examples in both this and the traditional English style, as well as in the French style exemplified by Lully (q.v.). John Blow's fine ode on his untimely end and tributes by other contemporary musicians show that he was recognized in his own time, as now, as the greatest English composer of the age. His brother Daniel (*c.* 1663–1718) was also a distinguished composer, for some time organist of Magdalen College, Oxford. See Lives by J. F. Runciman (1909), Arundell (1928), Holland (1932), Westrup (1937), essays, *Henry Purcell (1659–1695)*, ed. Holst (1959) and an analytical catalogue of his music by Zimmerman (1963).

PURCHAS, Samuel (1577–1626), English compiler of travel books, born at Thaxted, studied at St John's College, Cambridge, and became vicar of Eastwood in 1604, and in 1614 rector of St Martin's, Ludgate. His great works were *Purchas his Pilgrimage, or Relations of the World in all Ages* (1613; 4th ed. enlarged,1626), and *Hakluytus Posthumus, or Purchas his Pilgrimes* (1625), based on the papers of Hakluyt (q.v.) and archives of the East India Company. Another work is *Purchas his Pilgrim: Microcosmus, or the History of Man* (1619).

PURKINJE, Jan Evangelista (also Purkyne), *poor'kin-yay* (1787–1869), Czech physiologist, born at Libochowitz, was professor at Breslau (1823) and Prague (1850). He did research on the eye, the brain, muscles, embryology, digestion and sweat glands. ' Purkinje's figure ' is an effect by which one can see in one's own eye the shadows of the retinal blood vessels. ' Purkinje's cells ' are situated in the middle layer of the cerebellar cortex.

PUSEY, Edward Bouverie (1800–82), English theologian, was born at Pusey in Berkshire. His father, the youngest son of the first Viscount Folkestone, had assumed the name Pusey when he inherited the Pusey estates. He was educated at Eton and Christ Church, Oxford, in 1823 was elected a fellow of Oriel, and in 1825–27 in Germany made himself acquainted with German theological teaching. In 1828 he was ordained deacon and priest and appointed regius professor of Hebrew at Oxford, a position which he retained until his death. His first work was an essay on the causes of Rationalism in recent German theology, which was criticized as being itself rationalistic. The aim of his life was to prevent the spread of Rationalism in England. Hence, when in 1833 Newman began the issue of the *Tracts for the Times*, Pusey very soon joined him; and they, with Keble, were the leaders of the movement.

They endeavoured to make the church live again before the eyes and minds of men as it had lived in times past. With this aim Pusey wrote his contributions to the *Tracts*, especially those on Baptism and the Holy Eucharist; and commenced in 1836 the *Oxford Library of the Fathers*, to which his chief contributions were translations of Augustine's Confessions and works of Tertullian. But Newman's celebrated Tract 90 was condemned in 1841, and in 1843 Pusey was suspended for two years from preaching in Oxford for a university sermon on the Holy Eucharist; at the first opportunity he reiterated his teaching, and was left unmolested. But before his suspension was over Newman, with several of his leading disciples, had joined the Roman communion. With Keble, Pusey at once set himself to reassure those who were distressed by this development. But soon another band of distinguished men, including Archdeacon (Cardinal) Manning and Archdeacon Wilberforce, departed to the Roman Church. Still Pusey loyally laboured on. His numerous writings during this period included a letter on the practice of confession (1850), a general defence of his own position in *A Letter to the Bishop of London* (1851), *The Doctrine of the Real Presence* (1856–57), and the series of three *Eirenicons* (1865–69), clear the way for reunion between the Church of England and that of Rome. The reform of Oxford University, which destroyed the intimate bond between the university and the church, greatly occupied Pusey's mind. His evidence before the commission, his remarkable pamphlet on *Collegiate and Professorial Teaching*, and his assiduous work on the Hebdomadal Council are proofs of the interest he took in the university. By 1860 the tide had turned. The teaching for which the Tractarians had laboured was beginning to be recognized. But the fruits of the intolerance and persecution of which Oxford had been the scene were also ripening into religious indifference and Rationalism. Against such teaching Pusey contended for the rest of his life. In private life Pusey was an ascetic, deeply religious man of warm affection, widely known for his gentleness, sincerity and humility, and was constantly sought as a spiritual guide by persons of every station. He spent large sums in helping to provide churches in East London and Leeds, and in founding sisterhoods. He married in 1828 Maria Catherine Barker, who died of consumption in 1839; his only son, Philip Edward (1830–80), also predeceased him. He himself died at Ascot Priory, Berks, and was buried in Oxford Cathedral. See Life by Canon Liddon and the Revs. J. O. Johnston and R. J. Wilson (4 vols. 1893–97, with vol. v, *Spiritual Letters*, 1898) and Prestige (1933).

PUSHKIN, Alexandr Sergeevich, *poosh'kin* (1799–1837), Russian poet, was born at Moscow. In 1817 he entered the service of the government, but for his Liberalism was in 1820 exiled to Southern Russia, and 1824 dismissed and confined to his estate near Pskov, not returning to Moscow until after the accession of Nicholas I. His marriage to Natalia Goncharova proved unhappy and led to his early death in a duel. Hailed in Russia as her greatest poet, his first success was the romantic poem, *Ruslan and Lyudmila* (1820), followed by the *Prisoner of the Caucasus* (1822), *Fountain of Bakhchisarai* (1826), *Tzigani* (1827) and the masterly *Eugene Onegin* (1828), a novel in verse somewhat after the style of Byron's *Beppo*; *Poltava* (1829) has Mazeppa for its hero. *Boris Godunov* is his finest tragedy. He wrote also many graceful lyrical poems, a *History of the Revolt of Pugachev*, several tales and essays, and was appointed Russian historiographer. His *Eugene Onegin* was translated in verse by Spalding (1881), and by O. Elton (1938); and there are translations of his *Daughter of the Commandant* (1891), *Prose Tales* (1894) and *Poems*, with introduction and notes by Panin (N.Y. 1889). Later translations are by Morison (poems) (1945), V. de S. Pinto and H. W. Marshall (tragedies) (1946). See Lives by Mirsky (1926), Simmons (1937) and Magarshack (1967).

PUTNAM, (1) **George Palmer** (1814–72), American publisher, born in Brunswick, Maine, grand-nephew of (2), went to London and in 1840 became partner in a New York book firm. In 1848 he started business alone, establishing in 1866 the firm of G. P. Putnam & Sons (now G. P. Putnam's Sons). In 1852 he founded *Putnam's Magazine*. See Life (1912) by his son, **George Haven Putnam** (1844–1930), who also wrote *Memories of a Publisher* (1913), &c.

(2) **Israel** (1718–90), American general, born at Danvers, Mass., became a farmer, but in 1755 helped as a captain to repel a French invasion of New York, and was present at the battle of Lake George. In 1758 he was captured by the savages, tortured and about to be burnt when a French officer rescued him. In 1759 he was given command of a regiment, in 1762 went on the West India campaign, and in 1764 helped to relieve Detroit, then besieged by Pontiac (q.v.). In 1775, after Concord, he was given command of the forces of Connecticut, was at Bunker Hill, and held the command at New York and in August 1776 at Brooklyn Heights, where he was defeated by Howe. In 1777 he was appointed to the defence of the Highlands of the Hudson. See Life by Tarbox (1876).

(3) **Rufus** (1738–1824), cousin of (2), served against the French in 1757–60, and then settled as a farmer and millwright. In the war he rendered good service as an engineer, commanded a regiment, and in 1783 became brigadier-general. In 1788 he founded Marietta, Ohio; in 1789 he was appointed a judge of the supreme court of the Northwest Territory; and in 1793–1803 was surveyor-general of the United States.

PUVIS DE CHAVANNES, Pierre, *pü-vee dè shav-an* (1824–98), French decorative, symbolic painter, born at Lyons. Murals by him of the life of St Geneviève may be seen in the Panthéon, Paris, and large allegorical works such as 'Work' and 'Peace' on the staircase of the Musée de Picardie, Amiens. See works by Vachon (1895) Michel (1913), Mauclair (1928).

PU-YI, personal name of **Hsuan T'ung** (1906–1967), last emperor of China (1908–12) and the first of Manchukuo (from 1934 until it ceased to exist in 1945). After the revolution of 1912 the young emperor was given a pension and a summer palace near Peking. He became known as Henry Pu-yi, but in 1932 he was called from private life to be provincial dictator of Manchukuo and from 1934 to 1945 he was emperor under the name of **Kang Teh**. After then he lived as a private citizen in Peking until his death. See his *From Emperor to Citizen* (1964).

PYAT, Félix, *pyah* (1810–89), French journalist and communist, in 1831 was admitted to the bar, but chiefly wrote articles, feuilletons and plays. He signed Ledru-Rollin's appeal to the masses to arm in 1849, escaped to Switzerland, Brussels and London, and was a member of the 'European revolutionary committee'. Returning to Paris on amnesty in 1870, he was a leader of the communards, and again escaped to London. He was condemned to death, in absence, in 1873, but pardoned in 1880.

PYE, Henry James (1745–1813), English poet, born in London, studied at Magdalen College, Oxford. He held a commission in the Berkshire militia, in 1784 became member for that county, in 1790 succeeded Warton as laureate, and in 1792 was appointed a London police magistrate. He died at Pinner near Harrow. The works of 'poetical Pye' number nearly twenty, and include *Alfred: an Epic* (1801), with numerous birthday and New-Year odes, all extremely loyal and extremely dull.

PYM, John, *pim* (1584–1643), English politician, born at Brymore near Bridgwater, entered Broadgates Hall (now Pembroke College), Oxford, in 1599, as a gentleman-commoner, but left in 1602 without taking a degree, and then became a student of the Middle Temple. In 1614 he was returned to parliament for Calne, exchanging that seat in 1625 for Tavistock. He attached himself to the Country party, and made war against monopolies, papistry, the Spanish match and absolutism with a vigour that brought him 3 months' imprisonment. In 1626 he took a prominent part in the impeachment of Buckingham. In the parliament of 1628 he stood second only to Sir John Eliot in supporting the Petition of Right, but he opposed him on tonnage and poundage. In the Short Parliament (1640) he 'brake the ice by a two hours' discourse, in which he summed up shortly and sharply all that most reflected upon the prudence and justice of the government, that they might see how much work they had to do to satisfy their country'. And in the Long Parliament, having meanwhile joined with the Scots, and ridden with Hampden through England, urging the voters to their duty, Pym on November 11 named Strafford, twelve years earlier his friend and ally, as the 'principal author and promoter of all those counsels which had exposed the kingdom to so much ruin'. In the impeachment of Strafford which followed, resulting in his execution, Pym took the leading part. In the proceedings against Laud, Pym was also conspicuous, as in the carrying of the Grand Remonstrance and in every other crisis up to the time when

war became inevitable; he was the one of the 'Five Members' whom Charles singled out by name. On the breaking out of hostilities he remained in London, and there in the executive rendered services to the cause not less essential than those of a general in the field. He died a month after being appointed Lieutenant of the Ordnance. 'The most popular man', says Clarendon, 'and the most able to do hurt that hath lived in any time.' He was neither revolutionist nor precisian; his intellect was 'intensely conservative', in Gardiner's phrase; he was a champion of what he believed to be the ancient constitution. See Forster's *Eminent British Statesmen* (1837), Goldwin Smith's *Three English Statesmen* (1867), C. E. Wade's *John Pym* (1912), and works cited at CHARLES I, ELIOT and STRAFFORD.

PYNE, William Henry, *pīn* (1769–1843), English artist, born in London, became popular for his landscapes filled with humorous characters. Some of these were 'Travelling Comedians', 'Bartholomew Fair' and 'Anglers'. He was one of the early members of the Old Watercolour Society. Later he concentrated on writing on art, and his books include *Microcosm, or a Picturesque Delineation of the Arts, Agriculture and Manufactures of Great Britain . . .* (1806), *The Costume of Great Britain* (1808), *The History of the Royal Residences of Windsor Castle, St James's Palace . . .* (1829), and under the pseudonym 'Ephraim Hardcastle', *Wine and Walnuts, or After-dinner Chit-chat* (1823), a series of art anecdotes.

PYNSON, Richard (d. 1530), printer of Norman birth, studied at the University of Paris, learned printing in Normandy, and practised his trade in England. In 1497 appeared his edition of Terence, the first classic to be printed in London. He became printer to King Henry VIII (1508), and introduced roman type in England (1509).

PYRRHO, *pir'ō* (c. 360–270 B.C.), Greek philosopher, born at Elis, whose opinions we know not from his own writings but from his pupil Timon. He taught that we can know nothing of the nature of things, but that the best attitude of mind is suspense of judgment, which brings with it calmness of mind. Pyrrhonism is often regarded as the *ne plus ultra* of (philosophical) scepticism: consistent Pyrrhonists were said even to doubt that they doubted.

PYRRHUS (c. 318–272 B.C.), became king of Epirus when Cassander lost it (307), was driven out again, but restored by help of Ptolemy Soter, and extended his dominions by the addition of western Macedonia. In 281 the Tarentines, a Greek colony in Lower Italy, invited him to help them against the Romans, and in 280 he sailed for Tarentum with 25,000 men and a number of elephants. The first battle, on the river Siris, was long and bloody, but Pyrrhus won it by help of his elephants, till then unknown to the Romans. 'Another such victory,' he said (now or after Asculum), 'and I must return to Epirus alone'—hence the proverbial expression 'a Pyrrhic victory'. Many of the Italian nations now joined Pyrrhus, and he marched northward, came dangerously near Rome, but found it too well prepared, and withdrew to Tarentum, where he wintered. In 279 the Romans were again defeated (at Asculum); but Pyrrhus himself lost so heavily that he had again to withdraw to Tarentum. Here a truce was agreed to, and Pyrrhus crossed over to Sicily to assist the Sicilian Greeks against the Carthaginians in 278. His first exploits in that island were brilliant; but his repulse at Lilybaeum broke the spell; he became involved in misunderstandings with the Greeks, and in 275 quitted the island to renew his war with Rome. While he was crossing over, the Carthaginians attacked him and destroyed seventy of his ships. In 274 he was utterly defeated by the Roman consul Curius Dentatus near Beneventum. He was now forced to abandon Italy and return to Epirus, where he engaged in war with Antigonus Gonatas, king of Macedonia. His success was complete; but in less than a year he was at war with the Spartans, by whom he was repulsed in all his attempts on their city. He then marched against Argos, where he was killed by a tile hurled at him from a roof by a woman. The principal ancient authority for the life of Pyrrhus is Plutarch. See also German *Life* by R. Schubert (1894).

PYTHAGORAS, *pī-thag'o-ras* (fl. 6th cent. B.C.), Greek philosopher and mathematician, born in Samos, became acquainted with the teachings of the early Ionic philosophers, and, through his travels, with those of the Egyptian priests and other foreigners. About 530 he settled at Crotona in Magna Graecia, where he founded a moral and religious school. Pythagoreanism was first a way of life, not a philosophy, a life of moral abstinence and purification, reactionary against the popular and poetic religions, but yet sympathetic towards the old (Doric) aristocratic forms and institutions. All that can be certainly attributed to Pythagoras is the doctrine of the transmigration of souls, the institution of certain religious and ethical regulations, the beginning of those investigations into the relations of numbers which made the school famous, and astronomical attainments beyond their contemporaries. How much of the mysticism called Neopythagorean (and akin to Neoplatonism) was directly derived from him is hard to say. The Pythagoreans as an aristocratic party became unpopular after the defeat of the Sybarites by the Crotoniates in 510, and at first were instrumental in putting down the democratic party in Lower Italy; but the tables were afterwards turned, and they had to flee from persecution. See a German monograph by Rothenbücher (1867), a French one by Chaignet (2nd ed. 1875), and B. Russell, *History of Western Philosophy* (1946).

PYTHEAS (fl. 4th cent. B.C.), of Massilia (Marseilles), a Greek mariner, about 330 B.C. sailed to Thule (?Iceland), past Spain, Gaul and the east coast of Britain.

PYTHIAS. See DAMON.

Q

Q. See COUCH (QUILLER); QUEENSBERRY.

QUAIN, (1) **Sir John Richard** (1817–76), English lawyer, born at Mallow, became judge of the Queen's Bench in 1871, and justice of the High Court of Judicature in 1875. Along with H. Holroyd he published *New System of Common Law Procedure* (1852).

(2) **Jones** (1796–1865), half-brother of (1), born at Mallow, studied medicine at Dublin and Paris, and in 1831–35 was professor of Anatomy in London University. He wrote the text book, Quain's *Elements of Anatomy* (1828, 10th ed. 1890–96).

(3) **Richard**, F.R.S. (1800–87), brother of (2), born at Fermoy, was professor of Clinical Surgery in University College, London (1848–1866), surgeon-extraordinary to the Queen, and president of the College of Surgeons (1868). He left £75,000 to University College for 'education in modern languages (especially English) and natural science '.

(4) **Sir Richard** (1816–98), cousin of (2), born at Mallow, was the Lumleian lecturer at the College of Physicians in 1872, and Harveian orator in 1885, and was made physician-extraordinary to the Queen, LL.D. of Edinburgh in 1889, president of the General Medical Council in 1891, and a baronet in 1891. He edited the *Dictionary of Medicine* (1882; 2nd ed. 1894).

QUANTZ, Johann Joachim, *kvants* (1697–1773), German flautist and composer, born near Göttingen, spent many years in the service of the King of Saxony, toured extensively in Italy, France and England, and became teacher of Frederick the Great and later his court composer. Author of a treatise on flute-playing, Quantz composed some three hundred concertos for one or two flutes as well as a vast quantity of other music for this instrument.

QUARLES, Francis (1592–1644), English poet, was born at the manor house of Stewards near Romford. He studied at Christ's College, Cambridge, and at Lincoln's Inn, and was successively cup-bearer to the Princess Elizabeth (1613), secretary to Archbishop Ussher (*c.* 1629), and chronologer to the City of London (1639). He married in 1618 a wife who bore him eighteen children and prefixed a touching memoir to his *Solomon's Recantation* (1645). Quarles was a royalist and churchman who suffered in the cause by having his books and manuscripts destroyed. He wrote abundantly in prose and verse. His *Emblems*, in spite of many imperfections, shows wealth of fancy, excellent sense, felicity of expression, and occasionally a flash of poetic fire. Other poetical works include *A Feast of Wormes* (1620), *Argalus and Parthenia* (1629), *Divine Poems* (1630), *The Historie of Samson* (1631), *Divine Fancies* (1632). The prose includes *Enchyridion* (1640) and *The Profest Royalist* (1645). See *Works* edited by Grosart (3 vols. 1880–81) and M. Praz, *Studies in Seventeenth-Century Imagery* (1939).

QUASIMODO, Salvatore (1901–68), Italian poet, born in Syracuse, Sicily, a student of engineering, became a travelling inspector for the Italian state power board before taking up a career in literature and music. A professor of Literature at the Conservatory of Music in Milan, he has written since 1942 five volumes of spirited poetry. These reflect above all his deep interest in the fate of Italy, and his language is made particularly striking by the use simultaneously of both Christian and mythological allusions. In 1959, for his lyrical poetry, he received the Nobel prize for literature, becoming the fourth Italian to gain this award. His works include *Ed e Subito Sera*, 'And suddenly it is Evening' (1942), *La Vita non e sogno*, 'Life is not a Dream' (1949) and *La Terra impareggiabile*, 'The Matchless Earth' (1958).

QUATREFAGES DE BRÉAU, Jean Louis Armand de, *kahtr-fahzh-dè-bray-ō* (1810–92), French naturalist and ethnologist, born at Berthezème (Gard), in 1850 was elected professor in the *Lycée Napoléon* and in 1855 at the Natural History Museum. His chief works are *Souvenirs d'un naturaliste* (1854; trans. 1857), *L'Espèce humaine* (1877; Eng. trans. 1879), *Crania Ethnica* (1875–82), *Les Pygmées* (1887; trans. 1895) and *Darwin et ses précurseurs français* (1892).

QUATREMÈRE, (1) **Antoine Chrysostome,** *kahtr'-mayr* (1755–1849), French archaeologist and politician, was condemned to death during the Terror but later acquitted. He was a member of the Council of Five Hundred. He edited a dictionary of architecture.

(2) **Étienne Marc** (1782–1857), French orientalist, born in Paris, in 1807 entered the MS. department of the Imperial Library, and in 1809 became professor of Greek at Rouen, in 1819 of Ancient Oriental Languages at Paris, in 1827 of Persian. Although a man of vast knowledge, he had little critical insight or originality. He wrote on the language of ancient Egypt, the Mameluke sultans and the Mongols of Persia, &c.

QUEEN, Ellery, pseud. of **Frederic Dannay** (1905–) and his cousin **Manfred B. Lee** (1905–71), American writers of crime fiction, both born in Brooklyn. As business men they entered for and won with *The Roman Hat Mystery* (1929) a detective-story competition and thereafter concentrated on detective fiction, using Ellery Queen both as pseudonym and as the name of their detective. Others of their very popular stories are *The French Powder Mystery* (1930), *The Greek Coffin Mystery* (1932), *The Tragedy of X* (1940), *Double, Double* (1950) and *The Glass Village* (1954). They have also written under the pseudonym Barnaby Ross.

QUEENSBERRY, (1) William Douglas, Duke of (1724–1810), ' Old Q ', succeeded his father as Earl of March, his mother as Earl of Ruglen, and his cousin in 1778 as fourth Duke of Queensberry. From 1760 to 1789 he was lord of the bedchamber to George III.

He was famous as a patron of the turf, and infamous for his shameless debaucheries. He died unmarried, worth over a million sterling. See Lives by Robinson (1895) and Melville (1927).

(2) Sir John Sholto Douglas, 8th Marquis of (1844–1900), an enthusiastic supporter of Bradlaugh and a keen patron of boxing, supervised the formulation in 1867 of new rules to govern that sport, since known as the ' Queensberry rules '. In 1895 he was tried and acquitted for publishing a defamatory libel on Oscar Wilde (q.v.) of whose friendship with his son, Lord Alfred Douglas (q.v.), he disapproved. This led to the trial and imprisonment of Wilde.

QUEIPO DE LLANO, Gonzalo, Marquis of Queipo de Llano y Sevilla, *kay'i-pō* THay *lyah'nō*, (1875–1951), Spanish general, born at Valladolid. After military service in Cuba and Morocco, he was promoted to the rank of major-general in the Republican Army, but went over to the rebel side at the beginning of the Spanish Civil War. In July 1936 he led the forces which captured Seville, and became commander-in-chief of the Southern Army. In one of his many propaganda broadcasts from Seville he originated the phrase ' fifth column ', using it to describe the rebel supporters inside Madrid, who were expected to add their strength to that of the four columns attacking from outside. In April 1950 he was given the title of Marquis.

QUENNELL, Peter Courtney (1905–), English biographer, son of Marjorie Quennell (1884–1972), the illustrator, was born in London and educated at Berkhamsted and Balliol College, Oxford. Professor of English at Tokyo in 1930, he wrote *A Superficial Journey through Tokio and Pekin* (1932). Author of several books of verse and prose and editor of *The Cornhill Magazine* (1944–51), he is best known for his biographical studies of Byron (1935; 1941), Queen Caroline (1939), John Ruskin (1949), Shakespeare (1963), as well as those of Boswell, Gibbon, Sterne and Wilkes in *Four Portraits* (1945) and *Hogarth's Progress* (1955).

QUENTAL, Anthero de, *kän-tahl'* (1842–91), Portuguese poet, born in Ponta Delgada, in the Azores. He studied at Lisbon and Coimbra, publishing his first collection of sonnets in 1861 and his *Odes Modernas* in 1865; he followed the latter with a pamphlet, *Good Sense and Good Taste*, which propounded the view that poetry depends upon richness and vitality of ideas rather than upon technical skill with words. Quental lived in Paris and America from 1866 to 1871, and on his return to Portugal became a leading socialist until, after a severe nervous illness, he committed suicide.

QUERCIA, Jacopo Della, *kwer'cha* (*c.* 1367– 1438), Italian sculptor, born in Quercia Grossa, Sienna, went to Lucca, where one fine example of his work is the beautiful tomb of Ilaria del Carretto in the cathedral. In direct contrast are the strongly dramatic reliefs for the doorway of the church of San Petronio at Bologna which he left unfinished at his death.

QUEROUAILLE or Kéroualle. See PORTSMOUTH.

QUESADA, Gonzalo Jiménez de, *kay-sah'*THa (*c.* 1497–1579), Spanish conqueror, was born at Córdoba or Granada. Appointed magistrate at Santa Marta in what is now Colombia, he in 1536 headed an expedition and after many hardships and loss of men conquered the rich territory of the Chibchas in the east. This he called New Granada and its chief town Santa Fé de Bogotá. In 1569, during a later expedition in search of El Dorado, he reached the river Guaviare not far from the point where it meets the Orinoco. His history *Los tres ratos de Suesca* has been lost. See *The Conquest of New Granada* by Sir C. Markham (1912) and by R. B. Cunningham Graham (1922).

QUESNAY, François, *ke-nay* (1694–1774), French physician and economist, born at Mérey, Seine-et-Oise, studied medicine at Paris, and at his death was first physician to the king. But the fame of the ' European Confucius ' depends on his essays in political economy. Around him and his friend, M. de Gournay, gathered the famous group of the *Économistes*, also called the Physiocratic School. Quesnay's views were set forth in *Tableaux économiques*. Only a few copies were printed (1758), and these are lost; yet Quesnay's principles are well known from his contributions to the *Encyclopédie*, and from his *Maximes du gouvernement économique*, *Le Droit naturel*, &c.—collected in Oncken's edition of his *Oeuvres* (1888). See H. Higgs, *The Physiocrats* (1897).

QUESNEL, Pasquier, *ke-nel* (1634–1719), French Jansenist theologian, born in Paris, studied at the Sorbonne, became in 1662 director of the Paris Oratory, and here wrote *Réflexions morales sur le Nouveau Testament*. In 1675 he published the works of Leo the Great, which, for Gallicanism in the notes, was placed on the *Index*. Having refused to condemn Jansenism in 1684, he fled to Brussels, where his *Réflexions* were published (1687–94). The Jesuits were unceasing in their hostility, and Quesnel was flung into prison (1703), but escaped to Amsterdam. His book was condemned in the bull *Unigenitus* (1713). See his Letters (1721–23).

QUESNOY, François du, *ke-nwa* (1594–1646), sculptor, was born at Brussels, lived much at Rome, and died at Leghorn, poisoned perhaps by his jealous brother, Jérome (1612–1654), a sculptor too, who was burnt for unnatural crimes.

QUÉTELET, Lambert Adolphe Jacques, *kayt-lay* (1796–1874), Belgian statistician and astronomer, born at Ghent, became in 1819 professor of Mathematics at the Brussels Athenaeum, in 1828 director of the new Royal Observatory, in 1836 professor of Astronomy at the Military School, and in 1834 perpetual secretary of the Belgian Royal Academy. In his greatest book, *Sur l'homme* (1835), as in *L'Anthropométrie* (1871), &c., he shows the use that may be made of the theory of probabilities, as applied to the ' average man '.

QUEVEDO Y VILLEGAS, Francisco Gómez de, *ke-vay'*THō ee *veel-yay'gas* (1580–1645), Spanish writer, was born at Madrid. His father was secretary to the queen, and his mother a lady-in-waiting. He quitted the

University of Alcalá with a reputation for varied scholarship. The fatal issue of a duel drove him in 1611 to the court of the Duke of Ossuna, viceroy of Sicily; he made him his right-hand man, and, when promoted to the viceroyalty of Naples, chose him for minister of finance. Quevedo was involved in Ossuna's fall in 1619, and put in prison, but allowed to retire to the Sierra Morena. He returned to Madrid in 1623 and became *persona grata* at the court of Philip IV. In his *Política de Dios* (1626) he appealed to the king to be a king, not in name only, but in fact; in 1628 he followed up this attack on government by favourites with an apologue, *Hell Reformed.* He remained, however, on friendly terms with Olivares and accepted the honorary title of royal secretary. In 1639 a memorial in verse to the king, imploring him to look to the miserable condition of his kingdom, was one day placed in Philip's napkin. Quevedo was denounced as the author, arrested and imprisoned in a convent at Leon, where he was struck down by an illness, from which he never recovered. In 1643 Olivares fell from power, and Quevedo was free to return to Madrid. He died two years later. Quevedo was one of the most prolific Spanish poets, but his verses were all written for his friends or for himself, and, except those in the *Flores* of Espinosa (1605), the few pieces published in his lifetime were printed without his consent. His poetry is therefore for the most part of an occasional character; sonnets, serious and satirical, form a large portion of it, and light humorous ballads and songs a still larger. About a dozen of his interludes are extant, but of his comedies almost nothing is known. His prose is even more multifarious than his verse. His first book (1620) was a Life of St Thomas de Villanueva, and his last (1644) one of St Paul; and most of his prose is devotional. Of his political works the *Política de Dios* is the chief. His brilliant picaresque novel, the *Vida del Buscón Pablos* (1626), or, as it was called after his death, the *Gran Tacaño*, at once took its place beside *Guzmán de Alfarache.* His five *Visions* were printed in 1627; to obtain a licence they were barbarously mutilated; and it is in this mangled shape that they have been printed since 1631. The fullest edition of his works is that in the *Biblioteca de Autores Españoles.* The earliest translations from Quevedo were into French, and from them most of the English versions have been made—e.g.: *Visions; or Hel's Kingdome*, by R. Croshawe (1640); *Hell Reformed*, by E. M. (1641); *Buscon, the Witty Spaniard*, by J. Davies (1657); and the *Visions*, by Sir R. L'Estrange (1667). Captain John Stevens in 1697–1707 produced a translation from the original of *Fortuna con Seso*, the *Vida del Buscón*, &c.; his translations, with L'Estrange's *Visions*, were published in 1798 as *Quevedo's Works.* See Eng. trans. by Duff (1926); also work by E. Mérimée (1886).

QUEZON, Manuel Luis, *kay'son* (1878–1944), first Philippine president, born at Baler, Luzon, studied at Manila, served with Aguinaldo during the insurrection of 1898 and in 1905 became governor of Tayabas.

In 1909 he went to Washington as one of the resident Philippine commissioners and began to work for his country's independence. President of the Philippine senate (1916–35), he was elected first president of the Philippine Commonwealth (1935). He established a highly centralized government verging on 'one-man' rule and displayed great courage during the Japanese onslaught on General MacArthur's defences in December 1941, refusing to evacuate to the United States until appealed to by President Roosevelt. He died at Saranac, U.S.A. The new capital of the Philippines on the island of Luzon is named after him.

QUICK, Robert Hebert (1831–91), English educationist, born in London, and educated at Harrow and Trinity College, Cambridge, was a curate in Whitechapel and Marylebone, a schoolmaster, and vicar of Sedbergh 1883–87. The great interest of his life was education. To the discussion of its theories he brought wide study, independent thought, and ripe wisdom. His main work was *Essays on Educational Reformers* (1868).

QUILLER-COUCH. See COUCH.

QUILTER, Roger (1877–1953), English composer, born in Brighton. He studied in Germany and lived entirely by composition, holding no official posts and making few public appearances. His works include an opera, *Julia*, a radio opera, *The Blue Boar*, and the *Children's Overture*, based on nursery tunes, but he is best known for his songs.

QUIN, (1) James (1693–1766), Irish actor, born in London, made his début at Dublin in 1714. At Drury Lane in 1716 the sudden illness of a leading actor led to Quin's being called on to play Bajazet in *Tamerlane*. His success was marked. At Lincoln's Inn Fields (1718–32) and at Drury Lane (1734–41) he was by universal consent the first actor in England; then Garrick largely eclipsed him. Retiring in 1751, Quin died at Bath. See anonymous Lives (1766, 1887).

(2) Wyndham-. See DUNRAVEN, EARL OF.

QUINAULT, Philippe, *kee-nō* (1635–88), French poet and dramatist, born in Paris, was valet to the poet Tristan L'Hermite, qualified as an *avocat*, and wrote comedies and libretti for the operas of Lully (q.v.).

QUINCEY. See DE QUINCEY.

QUINCY, Josiah (1772–1864), American statesman, was born at Boston, Mass., the son of the lawyer, Josiah Quincy (1744–75). He graduated at Harvard, was called to the bar in 1793, was a leading member of the Federal party, and elected in 1804 to congress, distinguished himself as an orator. He denounced slavery, and in one most remarkable speech declared that the admission of Louisiana would be a sufficient cause for the dissolution of the union. Disgusted with the triumph of the Democrats and the war of 1812, he declined re-election to congress, and devoted his attention to agriculture; but he was a member of the Massachusetts legislature, served as mayor of Boston 1823–28, and in 1829–45 was president of Harvard. He died at Quincy, Mass. Among his works are Memoirs of his father (1825) and J. Q. Adams (1858), histories of Harvard (1840), the Boston Athenaeum (1851), and Boston (1852).

His *Speeches* were edited (1874) by his son, Edmund Quincy (1808–77), who was secretary of the American Anti-Slavery Society.

QUINE, Willard Van Orman (1908–), American mathematical logician, born at Akron, Ohio, from 1948 professor of Philosophy at Harvard, carried on Russellian studies in symbolic logic, and with Carnap and Tarski held that modal logic is a branch of semantics. He adapted Russell's Theory of Descriptions as a means of determining what on purely logical grounds is entitled to ' existence '. See his *Mathematical Logic* (1940), *Methods of Logic* (1950), *From a Logical Point of View* (1953) and *Set Theory and its Logic* (1963).

QUINET, Edgar, *kee-nay* (1803–75), French writer and politician, born at Bourg, studied at Strasbourg, Geneva, Paris and Heidelberg. The remarkable Introduction to his translation of Herder's *Philosophy of History* (1825) won him the friendship of Cousin and Michelet; a government mission to Greece bore fruit in *La Grèce moderne* (1830). *Ahasvérus* (1833), a kind of spiritual imitation of the ancient mysteries, was followed by the less successful poems, ' Napoléon ' (1836) and ' Prométhée ' (1838); in his *Examen de la vie de Jésus* (1838) he shows that Strauss is too analytic, and that religion is the very substance of humanity. Appointed in 1839 professor of Foreign Literature at Lyons, he began those lectures which formed his brilliant *Du génie des religions* (1842); then recalled to the Collège de France at Paris, he joined Michelet in attacking the Jesuits. His lectures caused so much excitement that the government suppressed them in 1846. At the Revolution Quinet took his place on the barricades, and in the National Assembly voted in the Extreme Left. After the *coup d'état* he was exiled to Brussels, whence in 1857 he emigrated to Switzerland. At Brussels he produced *Les Esclaves* (1853), and in Switzerland *Merlin l'Enchanteur* (1860). Other works were *La Révolution religieuse au XIXᵉ siècle* (1857), *Histoire de mes idées* (1858), *Histoire de la campagne de 1815* (1862), and *La Révolution* (1865). After the downfall of Napoleon III he returned to Paris, and during the siege strove to keep patriotism aglow. He sat in the National Assemblies at Bordeaux and Versailles, and aroused great enthusiasm by his orations. Quinet's latest books were *La Création* (1870), *La République* (1872), *L'Esprit nouveau* (1874), and *Le Livre de l'exilé* (1875). His wife published in 1870 *Mémoires d'exil*; his *Correspondance inédite* followed in 1877, *Lettres d'exil à Michelet* in 1884–86. His *Oeuvres complètes* (30 vols. 1857–79) include

a Life by Chassin. See also *Edgar Quinet avant et depuis l'exil* (1887–89) and *Cinquante ans d'amitié* (1900), by his second wife; books by Heath (1881), and Tronchon (1937).

QUINTANA, Manuel José, *keen-tah'-na* (1772–1857), Spanish poet and advocate, born in Madrid, whose house became a resort of advanced Liberals. Besides his classic *Vidas de los Españoles célebres* (1807–1834), he published tragedies and poetry written in a classical style, the best of which are his odes, ardently patriotic but yet restrained. On the restoration of Ferdinand VII he was imprisoned 1814–20; but he recanted, and by 1833 had become tutor to Queen Isabella. In 1835 he was nominated senator.

QUINTERO, Serafín Álvarez, *keen-tay'rō* (1871–1938) and **Joaquín Álvarez** (1873–1944), brothers, born at Utrera, Seville, wrote many plays in collaboration, usually depicting Andalusian life. These include comedies and shorter pieces such as *El Patio, Las de Caín* and *Malvaloca* all written with delightful insight into Spanish life and character. Translations have been made by H. and H. Granville-Barker, e.g. *Pueblo de las mujeres* (The Women have their Way), *El Centenario* (A Hundred Years Old).

QUINTILIAN, Marcus Fabius Quintilianus (*c.* A.D. 35–100) was born at Calagurris (*Calahorra*) in Spain, studied oratory at Rome, returned there in 68 in the train of Galba, and became eminent as a pleader and still more as a teacher of the oratorical art. His pupils included Pliny the Younger and the two grand-nephews of Domitian. The emperor named him consul and gave him a pension. His reputation rests securely on his great work, *De Institutione Oratoria*, a complete system of rhetoric, remarkable for its sound critical judgments, purity of taste, admirable form and the perfect familiarity it exhibits with the literature of oratory. Quintilian's own style is excellent, though not free from the florid ornament and poetic metaphor characteristic of his age.

QUINTUS CURTIUS. See CURTIUS (4).

QUISLING, Vidkun, *kwiz'-* (1887–1945), Norwegian diplomat and Fascist leader, born in Fyresdal, was an army major, League of Nations official, had the care of British interests in Russia 1927–29, was defence minister in Norway 1931–33, and in 1933 founded the *Nasjonal Samling* (National Party) in imitation of the German National Socialist Party. As puppet prime minister in occupied Norway he has given his name to all who play a like traitorous part. He gave himself up in May 1945, was tried and executed. See study by Hewins (1965).

R

RAAB, Julius (1891–1964), Austrian politician, born at St Pölten, became an engineer and was a Christian Socialist member of the Austrian Diet (1927–34), federal minister of Trade and Transport (1938), retired from politics during the Nazi régime and in 1945 was one of the founders of the People's party, chairman of the party (1951–60), minister of economic reconstruction and in 1953 was elected chancellor of Austria.

RAABE, Wilhelm, pseud. **Jakob Corvinus,** *rah'bĕ* (1831–1910), German novelist, was born at Eschershausen in Brunswick, and in 1870 settled in Brunswick. Reacting against 19th-century progress, he wrote novels which were often grim, tragic and pessimistic. Some of these are *Der Hungerpastor* (1864), *Des Reiches Krone* (1870) and *Meister Autor* (1871), &c.

RABANUS MAURUS. See HRABANUS MAURUS.

RABELAIS, François, *rab-ĕ-lay* (1494?–1553?), French satirist, said to have been born at a farmhouse near Chinon, or possibly in the town of Chinon, where his father was an advocate. At nine he was sent to the Benedictine abbey of Seuilly, and thence to the Franciscan house of La Baumette near Angers. He became a novice of the Franciscan order, and entered the monastery of Fontenay le Comte, where he had access to a large library, learned Greek, Hebrew and Arabic, and studied all the Latin and old French authors within his reach, medicine, astronomy, botany and mathematics. In Fontenay Rabelais found a friend, André Tiraqueau, lawyer and scholar; his patron, the Bishop of Maillezais, lived close by; and he corresponded with Budaeus. But Franciscan jealousy of the old learning was transformed into jealousy of the new. His books were taken from Rabelais; he conceived a loathing for the convent, and he fled to a Benedictine house near Orleans. He seems to have sought the protection of his friend the bishop, and through him obtained the pope's permission (1524) to pass from the Franciscan to the Benedictine order; but he remained with the bishop for at least three years. In September 1530 he entered the university of Montpellier as a student of medicine. He left the university in 1532, went to Lyons, where he remained as physician to the hospital. At this time Lyons was a great intellectual centre, and round its great printer Gryphius was gathered a company of scholars and poets, men of broad thought and advanced opinions. It was at Lyons that Rabelais began the famous series of books by which he will for ever be remembered. In 1532 there appeared at Lyons fair a popular book, *The Great and Inestimable Chronicles of the Grand and Enormous Giant Gargantua.* It was almost certainly not by Rabelais, but to this book he wrote, in the same year, a sequel, *Pantagruel,* in which serious ideas are set forth side by side with

overwhelming nonsense. In 1534 he supplied a first book of his own, a new *Gargantua,* fuller of sense and wisdom than *Pantagruel.* Both books (published under the name of Alcofri bas Nasier, an anagram of François Rabelais) had a prodigious success. Meanwhile he had begun his almanacs or *Pantagrueline Prognostications,* which he continued for a number of years; few of them survive. In 1533 he accompanied Jean du Bellay, Bishop of Paris, to Rome; in 1536 he was in Italy again with Du Bellay, the latter now a cardinal. There he amused himself with collecting plants and curiosities—to Rabelais France owes the melon, artichoke and carnation. He also received permission to go into any Benedictine house which would receive him, and was enabled to hold ecclesiastical offices and to practise medicine. From 1537 (when he took his doctorate) to 1538 he taught at Montpellier. From 1540 to 1543 he was in the service of the cardinal's brother, Guillaume du Bellay, sometimes in Turin (where Guillaume was governor), sometimes in France. Guillaume died in 1543, in which year Rabelais was appointed one of the *maîtres des requêtes.* For some years his movements are uncertain, but in 1546 he published his third book, this time under his own name. The Sorbonne condemned it—as it had done its predecessors—and Rabelais fled to Metz, where he practised medicine. In 1547 Francis I died; Henry II sent the French cardinals to Rome; and thither Du Bellay summoned Rabelais as his physician (1548). In Rome till 1549, he thereafter stayed near Paris; he received two livings from the Cardinal in January 1551–52, and resigned them two years later. He is said to have died April 9, 1553, certainly before May 1, 1554. A ' partial edition ' of a fourth book had appeared in 1548, the complete book in January 1552–53 (to be banned by the theologians); and a professed fifth book, *L'Isle sonante,* perhaps founded on scraps and notes by Rabelais, in 1562. The riotous licence of his mirth has made Rabelais as many enemies as his wisdom has made him friends, yet his works remain the most astonishing treasury of wit, wisdom, commonsense and satire that the world has ever seen. Of the many modern editions of Rabelais may be named those by Ch. Marty-Laveaux (6 vols. 1868–1902), Plattard (5 vols. 1929), and Abel Lefranc (director; 5 vols. 1912–31). See Eng. trans. by Urquhart and Motteux (1653–94; often reprinted), and W. F. Smith (1893); also works by Fleury (1877), W. Besant (1879, 1881), Stapfer (1889), Heulhard, Millet (1891), Bertrand (1894), A. Tilley (1907), Brémond (1877–1901), W. F. Smith (1917), Plattard (1910, 1927, 1929), Anatole France (trans. 1929), Putnam (1930), Powys (1948), Screech (1958).

RABI, Isidor Isaac (1898–   ), American physicist, born in Rymanow, Austria, which he left in childhood, was a graduate of

Cornell and Columbia University, where he became professor of Physics in 1937. An authority on nuclear physics and quantum mechanics, in 1944 he was awarded a Nobel prize for his precision work on neutrons.

RABUTIN. See BUSSY-RABUTIN.

RACAN, Honorat de Bueil, Marquis de, *ra-kã* (1589–1670), French poet, a disciple of Malherbe, wrote *Bergeries* (a pastoral play) and other verse, and was an original member of the Académie. See Life by Arnould (1901).

RACHEL, Élisa, properly Élisa Félix, *rah-shel* (1821–58), tragic actress, was born at Mumpf in Aargau, the daughter of Alsatian-Jewish pedlars. Brought to Paris about 1830, she received lessons in singing and declamation, made her début in *La Vendéenne* in 1837 with moderate success, but in June 1838 appeared as Camille in *Horace* at the Théâtre Français. From this time she shone without a rival in classical rôles, scoring her greatest triumph as Phèdre. In *Adrienne Lecouvreur*, written for her by Legouvé and Scribe, she had immense success. She visited London (Charlotte Brontë saw her there), Brussels, Berlin and St Petersburg, everywhere meeting with enthusiastic applause. In 1855, in America, her health gave way. She died of consumption at Cannet. As an artist Rachel has left a tradition never quite equalled. See Lives by F. Gribble (1911), J. Agate (1928) and J. Lucas Dubreton (1936).

RACHMANINOV or Rakhmaninov, Sergius Vassilievich, *-man'-* (1873–1943), Russian composer and pianist, born at Nijni-Novgorod, studied at St Petersburg Conservatoire and later at Moscow, where he won the gold medal for composition. A brilliant performer, he travelled all over Europe on concert tours, visiting London in 1899. Having fled from the Russian revolution he settled in the U.S.A. in 1918 and died in California. An accomplished composer, he wrote with ease operas, orchestral works and songs, but is best known for his piano music, which includes four concertos, the first three of which achieved enormous popularity, and the inveterate *Prelude in C Sharp Minor*, the demand for which at his own concerts nauseated even the composer himself. His style, devoid of national characteristics, epitomizes the lush romanticism of the later 19th century, which is still manifest in his last major composition, *Rhapsody on a Theme of Paganini* (1934) for piano and orchestra, a work of great craftsmanship which has remained a concert favourite. See Lives by W. Lyle (1939) and J. Culshaw (1949).

RACINE, Jean, *ra-seen* (1639–99), French dramatic poet, was born, a solicitor's son, at La Ferté-Milon (dep. Aisne), and was sent to the college of Beauvais, whence he went to Port Royal in 1655. Here he studied hard, and early discovered a faculty for verse-making and a liking for romance that caused his teachers no little uneasiness. At nineteen when he went to study philosophy at the Collège d'Harcourt, he appears to some extent to have exchanged the severity of his Jansenist upbringing for libertinism and the life of letters. He wrote an ode, *La Nymphe de la Seine*, on the marriage of Louis XIV, finished one piece and began another for the theatre, made the acquaintance of La Fontaine, Chapelain and other men of letters, and assisted a cousin who was a secretary to the Duc de Luynes. In 1661 he went to Uzès in Languedoc, hoping in vain to get a benefice from his uncle, the vicar-general of the diocese. Again in Paris, he obtained in 1664 a gift from the king for a congratulatory ode. Another ode, *La Renommée aux muses*, gained him the lifelong friendship of Boileau; and now began the famous friendship of ' the four '—Boileau, La Fontaine, Molière and Racine. His earliest play, *La Thébaïde ou Les Frères ennemis*, was acted by Molière's company at the Palais Royal (1664); his second, *Alexandre le grand* (1665), was after its sixth performance played by the rival actors at the Hotel de Bourgogne, which led to a rupture with Molière. Racine showed himself as hostile to Corneille. Stung by one of Nicole's *Lettres visionnaires* (1666) condemning in accordance with Port Royal ethics the romancer or dramatist as an ' empoisonneur public ', he published a clever letter to the author, full of indecent personalities. During the following ten years Racine produced his greatest works—*Andromaque* (1667); *Les Plaideurs* (1668), satirizing lawyers; *Britannicus* (1669); *Bérénice* (1670); *Bajazet* (1672); *Mithridate* (1673), produced almost at the moment of his admission to the Academy; *Iphigénie* (1675), a masterpiece of pathos; and *Phèdre* (1677), a marvellous representation of human agony. Now the *troupe du roi* introduced an opposition *Phèdre*, by Pradon, which was supported by a powerful party. Whether from mortification or from alleged conversion, Racine turned from dramatic work, made his peace with Port Royal, married in June 1677, and settled down to twenty years of domestic happiness. His wife brought him money (as well as two sons and five daughters); and he had found ample profit in the drama, besides enjoying an annual *gratification* that grew to 2000 livres, at least one benefice, and from 1677, jointly with Boileau, the office of historiographer-royal. In 1689 he wrote *Esther* for Madame de Maintenon's schoolgirls at Saint-Cyr; *Athalie* followed in 1691. Four *cantiques spirituelles* and an admirable *Histoire abrégée de Port Royal* make up Racine's literary work. In his later years he somehow lost the favour of the king. In France Racine is regarded as the greatest of all masters of tragic pathos; this estimate does not greatly exceed the truth. He took the conventional French tragedy from the stronger hands of Corneille, and added to it all the grace of which it was capable, perfecting exquisitely its versification, and harmoniously subordinating the whole action to the central idea of the one dominant passion. But he was a far greater poet even than dramatist, fascinating by the tender sweetness of his rhythm, the finished perfection and flexibility of his cadence. A biography was written by his son Louis (1692–1763), also a poet. The *Distressed Mother* was translated by Ambrose Philips (1712); *Phaedra* by Edmund Smith (staged 1707); and there is a complete metrical version by Boswell (1889–90). See works by Lemaître (1908), Mauriac (1930), Giraudoux (1930), Jasinski (1958), Mauran (1958); in English: Duclaux (1925), Clark (1940), Orgel (1948), Turnell (1948) and E. Vinaver (trans. P. Mansell Jones, 1955).

RACKHAM, Arthur (1867–1939), English artist, studied at Lambeth School of Art. A fellow of the Royal Society of Painters in Watercolours, he excelled in illustrating fairy tales and the like. See Life by Derek Hudson (1960).

RACOCZY. See Rákóczi.

RADCLIFFE, (1) *née* **Ward, Ann** (1764–1823), English romantic novelist, was born in London. At twenty-three, at Bath, she married William Radcliffe, a graduate of Oxford and student of law, who became proprietor and editor of the weekly *English Chronicle*. In 1789 she published *The Castles of Athlin and Dunbayne*, followed by *A Sicilian Romance* (1790), *The Romance of the Forest* (1791), *The Mysteries of Udolpho* (1794), and *The Italian* (1797). For the last she received £800; for its predecessor, £500. She travelled much, and her journal shows how keen an eye she had for natural scenery and ruins. A sixth romance, *Gaston de Blondeville*, with a metrical tale, ' St Alban's Abbey ', and a short Life, was published in 1826. Her contemporary reputation was considerable. She was praised by Scott, and influenced writers such as Byron, Shelley and Charlotte Brontë. Her particular brand of ' gothick romance ' found many imitators, most of them unfortunately inferior to herself. Their work drew forth Jane Austen's satire *Northanger Abbey*. See studies by C. F. McIntyre (1921) and J. M. S. Tompkins (1932).

(2) **Cyril John, Viscount** (1899–   ), British lawyer, was educated at Haileybury and New College, Oxford. From 1941 to 1945 he was director-general of the Ministry of Information. In 1949 he was created a lord-of-appeal-in-ordinary and a life peer and in 1962 he was created Viscount. In 1956, as Constitutional Commissioner, Cyprus, he drew up a constitution for the future of the island.

(3 **Sir George** (1593–1657), English politician, born at Thornhill near Dewsbury, studied at University College, Oxford, was called to the bar, from 1627 managed the affairs of Strafford (q.v.), shared his imprisonment, and died in exile at Flushing. See Whitaker's edition of his Correspondence (1810).

(4) **John** (1650–1714), English physician, born at Wakefield, studied at University College, Oxford, became a fellow of Lincoln, took his M.B. in 1675 and his M.D. in 1682. In 1684 he removed to London, where he soon became the most popular physician of his time, original, capricious, not too temperate. A Jacobite, he yet attended William III and Queen Mary; in 1713 he was elected M.P. for Buckingham. He bequeathed the bulk of his large property to the Radcliffe Library, Infirmary and Observatory, and University College at Oxford, and St Bartholomew's Hospital, London. See Life by Hone (1950).

RADCLIFFE - BROWN, Alfred Reginald

(1881–1955), British anthropologist, studied at Cambridge and was professor at Kapstadt, Sydney, Chicago and from 1937 at Oxford. By his field studies of *The Andaman Islanders* (1922), which served as a basis for his more theoretical *Structures and Function in Primitive Society* (1952), he established himself with Malinowski (q.v.) as one of the founders of modern social anthropology. He stressed the need for comparative rather than merely descriptive studies of primitive institutions and distinguished the concept of social structure from that of culture.

RADCLYFFE, James. See Derwentwater.

RADEK, Karl, *rah'-*, originally **Sobelsohn** (1885–?1939), Russian politician, born of Jewish parentage in Lwów, studied at Cracow and Bern. A member of the Polish Social Democratic party, he wrote for Polish and German newspapers and during World War I published propaganda literature from Switzerland. He crossed Germany with Lenin after the outbreak of the Russian revolution (1917) and took part in the Brest-Litovsk peace negotiations. He organized the German Communists during their revolution (1918) and was imprisoned (1919). Returning to the Soviet Union, he became a leading member of the Communist International, but lost standing with his growing distrust of extremist tactics. Nevertheless he became editor of *Pravda* and rector of the Sun Yat-Sen Chinese university in Moscow. He was charged as a Trotsky supporter and expelled from the party (1927–30) but readmitted only to fall victim to one of Stalin's ' trials ' in 1937 when he was sentenced to ten years' imprisonment but probably soon died.

RADETZKY, Johann Joseph, Count (1766–1858), Austrian soldier, born at Trebnitz near Tabor in Bohemia, fought against the Turks in 1788–89 and in nearly all the wars between the Austrians and the French. Commander-in-chief in Lombardy from 1831, in 1848 Field-marshal Radetzky was driven out of Milan by the insurgents, but held Verona and Mantua for the Hapsburgs. Defeated at Goito, he won a victory at Custozza, and re-entered Milan. In March 1849 he almost destroyed the Sardinian army at Novara, forced Venice to surrender, and till 1857 again ruled the Lombardo-Venetian territories with an iron hand. He died at Milan. See his *Denkwürdigkeiten* (1887) and *Briefe an seine Tochter* (1892). See also work by E. Schmahl (1938).

RADHAKRISHNAN, Sir Sarvepalli (1888–   ), Indian philosopher and statesman, born in Tiruttani, Madras, was educated at Madras Christian College. He has been professor at the universities of Mysore, Calcutta and Oxford, where he gave the Upton lectures at Manchester College in 1926 and 1929, and in 1936 he became Spalding professor of Eastern Religions and Ethics at Oxford. He also lectured abroad, in America in 1926 and 1944 and in China in 1944. He was knighted in 1931. From 1931 to 1939 he attended the League of Nations at Geneva as a member of the Committee of Intellectual Cooperation. In 1946 he was chief Indian delegate to Unesco, becoming chairman of Unesco in 1949. A member of the Indian Assembly in 1947, he was appointed first Indian ambassador to Russia in 1949 and in 1952 became vice-president of India. He was awarded the O.M. in 1963. He has written many scholarly philosophic works including *Indian Philosophy* (1927), his Hibbert lectures of 1929 published as *An Idealist View of Life* (1932), which is often thought to be his greatest work, and *Eastern Religion and Western Thought* (2nd ed. 1939).

RADOWITZ, Joseph von (1797–1853), Prussian general, born at Blankenburg in the Harz, in 1813 entered the Westphalian army, in 1823 the Prussian, and in 1830 became chief of the artillery staff. Connected by marriage with the Prussian aristocracy, he headed the anti-revolutionary party, and was Frederick-William IV's adviser. After 1848 the Prussian scheme of a German constitution by means of the alliance of the three kings was largely his work. He wrote political treatises.

RAE, John (1813–93), Arctic traveller, born near Stromness in Orkney, studied medicine at Edinburgh, and in 1833 became doctor to the Hudson Bay Company. In 1846–47 he made two exploring expeditions, and in 1848 he accompanied Richardson on a Franklin search voyage. In 1853–54 he commanded an expedition to King William's Land. It was on this journey that he met the Eskimos who gave him definite news of Franklin's expedition and its probable fate. In 1860 he surveyed a telegraph line to America by the Faroes and Iceland, and visited Greenland, and in 1864 made a telegraph survey from Winnipeg over the Rockies. He died in London.

RAEBURN, Sir Henry (1756–1823), Scottish portrait painter, born at Stockbridge, Edinburgh, was apprenticed to a goldsmith, but took to art, producing first watercolour miniatures and then oils. At twenty-two he married the widow of Count Leslie, a lady of means, studied two years in Rome (1785–87), then settled in Edinburgh, and soon attained pre-eminence among Scottish artists. In 1814 he was elected A.R.A., in 1815 R.A.; he was knighted by George IV in 1822, and appointed king's limner for Scotland a few days before his death. His style was to some extent founded on that of Reynolds, to which a positiveness was added by his bold brushwork and use of contrasting colours. Among his sitters were Scott, Hume, Boswell, 'Christopher North', Lord Melville, Sir David Baird, Henry Mackenzie, Principal Robertson, Lord Jeffrey and Lord Cockburn. *The Macnab*, considered his best work, fetched £25,400 in 1917. See Life by his great-grandson, W. R. Andrew (1886); and studies by W. E. Henley (1890), Sir W. Armstrong (1901), J. Greig (1911).

RAEDER, Erich, *ray'der* (1876–1960), former German grand admiral, entered the Navy in 1894 and during World War I was chief of staff to Admiral von Hipper. In 1928 he was promoted admiral and became C.-in-C. of the Navy. In 1939 Hitler made him a grand admiral, and in 1943 he became head of an anti-invasion force. At the Nuremberg Trials in 1946 he was sentenced to life imprisonment for having helped to prepare a war of aggression. He was released in September 1955. See his Memoirs, translated by E. Fitzgerald (1959).

RAEMAEKERS, Louis, *rah'mah-kers* (1869–1956), Dutch artist, born at Roermond, attained worldwide fame in 1915 by his striking anti-German war cartoons.

RAFF, Joachim (1822–82), Swiss composer, born at Lachen on the Lake of Zürich, in 1850–56 lived near Liszt in Weimar, taught music at Wiesbaden until 1877, and then was director of the conservatory at Frankfurt-am-Main. Among his compositions are the symphonies *Lenore* and *Im Walde* and violin and piano works. In support of Wagner he wrote *Die Wagner-Frage* (1854).

RAFFAELLO. See RAPHAEL.

RAFFLES, Sir Thomas Stamford (1781–1826), English colonial administrator, was born a sea-captain's son, off Port Morant in Jamaica. In 1795 he was appointed to a clerkship in the East India House, and in 1805 secretary to an establishment at Penang. In 1811 he accompanied the expedition against Java as secretary to Lord Minto; and on its capture, as lieutenant-governor, completely reformed the internal administration. In 1816 ill-health brought him home to England, where he wrote his *History of Java* (1817), and was knighted. Lieutenant-governor of Benkoelen (1818), he formed, without authority, a settlement at Singapore, but in 1824 had again to return to England. His ship took fire off Sumatra, and his natural history collections, East Indian vocabularies, &c., were lost. He founded the London Zoo and was its first president. See Lives by his widow (1830), R. Coupland (1934), C. Wurtzburg (1954), N. Epton (1956).

RAFN, Karl Christian (1795–1864), Danish philologist, became sub-librarian of Copenhagen University in 1821, a professor in 1826, and founded (1825) the Northern Antiquities Society. His works include a Danish translation of Norse sagas (1821–26) and *Antiquitates Americanae* (1837), on the Norse discovery of America in the 10th century.

RAGLAN, Fitzroy James Henry Somerset, 1st Baron (1788–1855), British general, the youngest son of the fifth Duke of Beaufort, entered the army in 1804, graduating from regimental duty to service on Wellington's staff. He was present at Waterloo, losing his sword arm. Thereafter, he sat in parliament as M.P. for Truro, and spent many years at the War Office, being appointed master-general of the ordnance and elevated to the peerage in 1852. In 1854 he was promoted field-marshal and nominated to head a grossly ill-prepared expeditionary force against the Russians, in the Crimea, in alliance with the French. Swift pursuit after Raglan's victory at the Alma might well have ended the campaign by Sevastopol's immediate capture. But the French ' dragged their feet ', as they continued to do, unreproached, throughout the ensuing weary months of siege warfare. In effect, Raglan's intended conduct of operations was sacrificed to the preservation of a queasy alliance, with the commander-in-chief an unprotesting scapegoat for cabinet unpreparedness and inefficiency. He died in harness on June 28, 1855, and ' never was there a nobler or more self-denying public servant' (Fortescue). See Fortescue, *A Gallant Company* (1927), and Vulliamy, *Crimea* (*passim*) (1939).

RAHBEK, Knud Lyne (1760–1830), Danish poet, critic and editor, was born in Copenhagen. He became professor of Aesthetics at Copenhagen University, edited several literary journals, notably *Den Danske Tilskuer* (the Danish *Spectator*). Besides poetry, he wrote many plays and songs and works on the drama.

RAHEL (Rahel Antonie Frederike Levin) (1771–1833), born a Jewess at Berlin, in 1814 turned Christian and married Varnhagen von Ense (q.v.). Her house in Berlin was a gathering-place for philosophers, poets and artists, and she encouraged the genius of Jean Paul, Tieck, Fouqué, Fichte, Hegel, Heine, Thiers, Benjamin Constant, and especially the Romanticists. Into the patriotic struggle against Napoleon she threw herself heart and soul. See her *Correspondence* (11 vols. 1833–75), and works by Jennings (1876), Ellen Key (trans. 1913), L. Feist (1927).

RAHERE (d. 1144), English churchman of Frankish descent who on a pilgrimage to Rome suffered an attack of malarial fever. During his convalescence, he made a vow to build a hospital and on his return to London he was granted the site at Smithfield by Henry I. In 1123 the building of St Bartholomew's hospital and St Bartholomew's Church was begun. In charge of the hospital until 1137, he retired in that year to the priory.

RAHN, Johann Heinrich (d. 1676), Swiss mathematician, town treasurer of Zürich (where he was born), in 1659 was the first to use the division sign ÷. His book *Teutsche Algebra* was translated into English.

RAIBOLINI, Francesco. See FRANCIA.

RAIKES, Robert (1735–1811), English philanthropist, born at Gloucester, in 1757 succeeded his father as proprietor of the *Gloucester Journal*. His pity for the misery and ignorance of many children in his native city led him in 1780 to start a Sunday School where they might learn to read and to repeat the Catechism. He lived to see such schools spread over England. See *Lives* by Gregory (1877), Eastman (1880), and study by Kendall (1939).

RAIMONDI. See MARCANTONIO.

RAINIER III, properly **Rainier Louis Henri Maxence Bertrand de Grimaldi,** *ray-nyay* (1923–), prince of Monaco, born at Monaco, succeeded his grandfather, Louis II, in 1950, as 26th ruling prince of the,House of Grimaldi, which dates from 1297. In 1956 he married Grace Patricia Kelly, an American film actress, and now has two daughters, the Princesses Caroline Louise Marguerite, born 1957, and Stephanie Marie Elisabeth, born 1965, and a son, Prince Albert Alexander Louis Pierre, born in 1958, heir-presumptive to the throne.

RAINY, Robert (1826–1906), Scottish divine, studied at Glasgow and at New College in Edinburgh, and after being minister of the Free Church in Huntly and Edinburgh, was from 1862 to 1900 professor of Church History in the New (Free Church) College in Edinburgh, becoming its principal (1874). Rainy carried the union (1900) of the Free and United Presbyterian Churches as the United Free Church, of which he became the first moderator. See *Life* by P. C. Simpson (1909).

RAIT, Sir Robert Sangster (1874–1936), Scottish historian, born in Narborough, Leicestershire, was professor of Scottish History at Glasgow University (1913–29), its principal and vice-chancellor from 1929, and was historiographer-royal for Scotland (1919–29). He was knighted in 1933.

RÁKÓCZI, *ra-kŏ'tsi,* a princely family of Hungary and Transylvania that became extinct in 1780. The most important member was the popular **Francis II** (1676–1735), who in 1703 led a Hungarian revolt against Austria. He had little success but was hailed by his countrymen as a patriot and a hero. His later years were spent as a Carmelite monk first in France and then in Turkey, where he died.

RALEIGH, (1) Sir Walter (1552–1618), English courtier, navigator and author, was born of an ancient but decayed family at the Devon manor house of Hayes Barton near Sidmouth. He entered Oriel College, Oxford, in 1566, but left, probably in 1569, to volunteer in the Huguenot cause in France, and fought at Jarnac and Moncontour. In 1578 he joined the profitless expedition of his half-brother, Sir Humphrey Gilbert; in 1580 he went to Ireland with one hundred foot to act against the rebels, and quickly attracted notice by his dash and daring. Returning to England in 1581, he now entered the court as a protégé of Leicester, whom in 1582 he accompanied to the Netherlands; and after his return he became prime favourite of the queen. She heaped favours upon him—estates, the 'farm of wines', and a licence to export woollen broadcloths. In 1584 he was knighted, in 1585 appointed lord warden of the Stannaries and vice-admiral of Devon and Cornwall; that same year he entered parliament for Devon. A fleet sent out by him in 1584 to explore the American coast north of Florida took possession of a district to which Elizabeth gave the name Virginia. In 1585–87 he fitted out two more expeditions, but the colonists either returned or perished; the only results were the introduction of potatoes and tobacco into England. It is supposed that Raleigh spent £40,000 over these attempts to colonize Virginia. In 1587 the appearance at court of the handsome young Earl of Essex endangered Raleigh's place in the queen's favour, and repairing to Ireland, where he had received 42,000 acres in Munster, he set about repeopling this tract with English settlers. He became a close friend of the poet Spenser, visiting him at his estate at Kilcolman,and reading him his poem of *The Ocean's Love to Cynthia* (Elizabeth). In his Youghal garden ·Raleigh planted tobacco and potatoes. He quickly recovered his influence at court, and busied himself with further schemes for reprisals on the Spaniards. His famous tract on the fight of the *Revenge*, which inspired Tennyson's noblest ballad, appeared anonymously in 1591. Early in

1592 Raleigh prepared a new expedition to seize the Spanish treasure ships, but his doting mistress forbade him to sail with the fleet, which he entrusted to Frobisher and Burgh. Hardly had he got back to London when Elizabeth discovered his intrigue with Bessy Throckmorton, one of her maids-of-honour. In July he was committed to the Tower, and for more than four years after this was excluded from the queen's presence. Meantime Burgh had captured the *Madre de Dios*, and brought her into Dartmouth. So great was the excitement that none but Raleigh could control the tumult, and he was sent down to Dartmouth with a keeper. He now married Bessy Throckmorton and for the next two years lived with her in quiet happiness at Sherborne. About 1593 his imagination was fired by the descriptions of Guiana, with its vast city of Manoa and its El Dorado; and in 1595, with five ships, he explored the coasts of Trinidad, and sailed up the Orinoco. Early in 1596 he published *The Discovery of Guiana* (Hakluyt Soc. 1848, 1929). In June he sailed with Howard and Essex to Cadiz, and it was his advice that governed that splendid triumph; his *Relation of Cadiz Action* remains the best history of the exploit. It was 1597 before Raleigh was allowed to resume his place as Captain of the Guard. Essex was glad of his support in a new expedition against Spain, which, in July 1597, sailed from Plymouth. A desperate storm compelled many of the ships to put back, but Raleigh met Essex off the island of Flores. They agreed to attack Fayal, but Raleigh reached the harbour first, and carried the town by storm, to the great mortification of Essex. In 1600 Raleigh became governor of Jersey, and in three years did much to foster its trade. In the dark intrigues at the close of Elizabeth's reign he took little part, while Cecil and others got the ear of James, and poisoned his mind against Raleigh. Before long the latter was stripped of all his offices. Possibly he may have in haste spoken, or at least listened to, words expressing a preference for Arabella Stuart. But the only witness against him was the miserable Lord Cobham, and he made and retracted eight separate charges with facility. Raleigh was arrested on July 17, 1603, and in his first despair tried to kill himself. His defence on his trial at Winchester was splendid; all his popularity came back to him from that hour. Yet he was condemned to death, and only on the scaffold was his sentence commuted to perpetual imprisonment. Within the Tower Raleigh employed himself with study and chemical experiments and with writing his excellent *History of the World* (1614), whose first and only volume (in 1300 folio pages) comes down to the second Roman war with Macedon. It was at first suppressed as 'too saucy in censuring the acts of kings', but its merit was quickly realized and many editions appeared within the century. Other writings of Raleigh's captivity were *The Prerogative of Parliaments* (written 1615, published in 1628); *The Cabinet Council*, published by Milton in 1658; and *A Discourse of War*, one of his most perfect pieces of writing. On January 30, 1616, Raleigh

was released from the Tower to make an expedition to the Orinoco in search of a gold-mine. He engaged not to molest the dominions of the king of Spain. In April 1617 he sailed; but storms, desertion, disease and death followed the expedition from the first, and before they reached the mouth of the river Raleigh himself was stricken down by sickness and compelled to stay behind with the ships, and to entrust the command to Keymis. The adventurers burned a new Spanish town, San Thomé, but never reached the mine. In the fight young Walter Raleigh was struck down; Keymis killed himself; and Raleigh in June 1618, arrived at Plymouth with his ship, the *Destiny*, alone and utterly cast down. Arrested by his false cousin, Sir Lewis Stukeley, at Salisbury he penned his touching *Apology for the Voyage to Guiana*; but he was beheaded at Whitehall, under the old Winchester sentence. See Lives by Cayley (1805), Tytler (1833), Kingsley (*Miscellanies*, 1859), Edwards (1868), Gosse (1886), Stebbing (1892), Hume (1897), De Sélincourt (1908), Waldman (1928), Strathmann (1951), Wallace (1960); Harlow, *Raleghs Last Voyage* (1932) and Irwin, *That Great Lucifer* (1960); also Brushfield's Bibliography (1908).

(2) **Sir Walter Alexander** (1861–1922), English scholar, critic and essayist, born in London, was professor of English Literature at Liverpool, Glasgow and at Oxford from 1904. Among his writings are *The English Novel* (1894), *Milton* (1900), *Wordsworth* (1903) and *Shakespeare* (1907). Chosen to compile the official history of the war in the air (1914–18), he died while collecting material for it. His *Letters* were edited by his wife in 1926.

RALSTON, William Ralston Shedden (1828–1889), Russian scholar and folklorist, surname originally Shedden, was born in London. He was trained for the bar but in 1853–75 held a post in the British Museum library. He wrote on Russian folksongs and tales, besides a translation of Turgenev's *Liza* (1869), and *Kriloff and his Fables* (1869).

RAMAN, Sir Chandrasekhara Venkata (1888–1970), Indian physicist, born at Trichinopoly and educated at Madras University, became professor of Physics at Calcutta (1917–33) and then director of the Indian Institute of Science at Bangalore. In 1929 he was knighted, and in 1930 awarded the Nobel prize for physics, for important discoveries in connection with the diffusion of light (the Raman effect). He also worked on the theory of musical instruments.

RAMBAUD, Alfred Nicolas, *rã-bō* (1842–1905), French historian, born at Besançon, in 1896–98 was minister of public instruction. From 1870 he wrote on Russia, French civilization, colonial France, &c., and edited the *Histoire générale, du IV* *siècle à nos jours* (12 vols. 1892–99).

RAMBOUILLET, Catherine de Vivonne, Marquise de, *rã-boo-yay* (1588–1665), French noblewoman, born at Rome, the daughter of Jean de Vivonne, Marquis of Pisani, at twelve was married to the son of the Marquis de Rambouillet, who succeeded to the title in 1611. From the beginning she disliked both the morals and manners of the French court. Virtuous and spirituelle, she gathered together in the famous Hôtel Rambouillet for fifty years the talent and wit of France culled from both the nobility and the literary world. See Livet's *Précieux et Précieuses* (4th ed. 1896) and Brunetière's *Nouvelles Études* (2nd ed. 1886).

RAMEAU, Jean Philippe, *rah-mō* (1683–1764), French composer, born at Dijon, had been organist, when he settled in Paris (1721) and wrote his *Traité de l'harmonie* (1722), a work of fundamental importance in the history of musical style. In 1732 he produced his first opera, *Hippolyte et Aricie,* which created a great sensation; his best was *Castor et Pollux* (1737). By 1760 he had composed twenty-one operas and ballets, besides harpsichord pieces. Louis XV ennobled him. See studies by Pougin (1876), La Laurencie (1908), Laloy (1908), Masson (1927) and Girdlestone (1957). Rameau's nephew, who gave the title to a singular work by Diderot (q.v.), was Louis Sébastien Mercier (1740–1814), author of the *Tableau de Paris.*

RAMÉE, De la. See RAMUS and OUIDA.

RAMENGHI. See BAGNACAVALLO.

RAMESES, *ram'seez,* the name of twelve monarchs of the 19th Egyptian dynasty (c. 1350–1115 B.C.). Only the second and third of the name were of importance.

Rameses II, usually called the Great, defeated the Hittites at Kadesh, then formed a peace with them, and married a Hittite princess. During his long reign (1292–1225 B.C.) he built magnificent monuments, temples, &c., completing the mortuary temple of Seti I at Luxor and the colonnaded hall of the Karnak temple, and building the rock temple of Abu Simbel.

Rameses III (1198–1167 B.C.), warred with the Philistines and maritime tribes of Greece and Asia Minor, and repeated the conquest of Ethiopia. Tradition identifies the warrior king Rameses II with the Pharaoh of the oppression, and Merenptah or Rameses III with the Pharaoh of the Exodus; the identification is doubtful. The mummy of Rameses II was found at Deir-el-Bahari in 1881, that of Rameses III at Bulak in 1886.

RAMMOHUN ROY, or **Rájá Rám Mohán Rái** (1774–1833), Indian religious reformer, born at Burdwan in Bengal of high Brahman ancestry, came early to question his ancestral faith, and studied Buddhism in Tibet. Revenue collector for some years in Rangpur, in 1811 he succeeded to affluence on his brother's death. He published various works in Persian, Arabic and Sanskrit, with the aim of uprooting idolatry; and he helped in the abolition of suttee. He issued an English abridgment of the *Vedanta,* giving a digest of the Vedas. In 1820 he published *The Precepts of Jesus,* accepting the morality preached by Christ, but rejecting His deity and miracles; and he wrote other pamphlets hostile both to Hinduism and to Christian Trinitarianism. In 1828 he began the Brahma Samaj association, and in 1830 the emperor of Delhi bestowed on him the title of raja. In 1831 he visited England, where he gave valuable evidence before the Board of Control on the condition of India, and died at Bristol. His English works were edited by Jogendra Chunder Ghose (1888).

RAMÓN Y CAJAL, Santiago, *ra-mon' ee ka-hal'* (1852–1934), Spanish histologist, born at Petilla de Aragon, a graduate of Saragossa University, he was professor of Anatomy at Valencia (1881–86), of Histology at Barcelona (1886–92) and at Madrid (1892–1922). In 1906 he shared with Golgi (q.v.) the Nobel prize for medicine. He was specially noted for his work on the brain and nerves. He wrote much on medical subjects, and also published his *Recollections* (trans. Craigie, 1937).

RAMSAY, (1). See DALHOUSIE.

(2) **Sir Alexander** (d. 1342), a Scottish patriot, famed for his deeds of bravery, who was captured and starved to death at Hermitage Castle in 1342 by William Douglas, the 'flower of chivalry'.

(3) **Allan** (c. 1685–1758), Scottish poet, was born at Leadhills, Lanarkshire. His father was manager of Lord Hopetoun's mines there, and his mother, Alice Bower, was the daughter of a Derbyshire mining expert. In 1704 he was apprenticed for five years to a wigmaker in Edinburgh. By 1718 he had become known as a poet, having issued several short humorous satires printed as broadsides; he had also written (1716–18) two additional cantos to the old Scots poem of *Christ's Kirk on the Green,* felicitous pictures of rustic life and broad humour. Ramsay now commenced business as bookseller, later adding a circulating library—apparently the first in Great Britain. ' Honest Allan's ' career was eminently prosperous though the theatre he built in Edinburgh at his own expense (1736) was soon shut up by the magistrates. In 1740 he built himself a quaint house (the ' goose-pie ') on the Castle Hill where he spent his last years in retirement. Among his works are: *Tartana, or the Plaid* (1718); *Poems,* collected edition published by subscription in 1721, by which it is said he realised 400 guineas—other editions, 1720, 1727, 1728; *Fables and Tales* (1722); *Fair Assembly* (1723); *Health, a Poem* (1724); *The Tea-table Miscellany,* a collection of songs (4 vols. 1724–37); *The Evergreen,* ' being a collection of Scots Poems wrote by the Ingenious before 1660 ' (1724); *The Gentle Shepherd, a Pastoral Comedy* (1725), his best and most popular work; and *Thirty Fables* (1730). See Mackail in *Essays and Studies,* x (Engl. Assoc. 1924); Gibson, *New Light on Allan Ramsay* (1927); Martin, *Allan Ramsay* (1931), and *Bibliography of Allan Ramsay* (1932).

(4) **Allan** (1713–84), eldest son of (3), was a distinguished portrait painter, who trained in Italy, worked first in Edinburgh, but in 1762 settled in London, and in 1767 was appointed portrait painter to George III. In his best works his painting is simple and delicate and he excels in portraits of women, notably that of his wife. He delighted in convers on and was acquainted with many of the writers of his day, including Samuel Johnson; he also corresponded with such men as Rousseau and Voltaire. See study by Smart (1952).

(5) **Sir Andrew Crombie** (1814–91), Scottish geologist, was born at Glasgow. In 1841 he joined the geological survey and in 1871 became director-general, retiring in 1881 with a knighthood. He died at Beaumaris. See *Life* by Sir Archibald Geikie (1895).

(6) **Andrew Michael (André Michel)** (1686–1743), the 'Chevalier de Ramsay', French writer, of Scottish parentage, was born at Ayr, the son of a baker. He served in the Low Countries, in 1710 was converted by Fénelon to Catholicism, and lived with him for five years. In 1724–25 he was tutor to Prince Charles Edward in Rome and in 1730 he visited England, and was made F.R.S. and D.C.L. of Oxford. He died at St Germain. He wrote *Vie de Fénelon* (1723), *Les Voyages de Cyrus* (1727), &c.

(7) **Edward Bannerman Burnett** (1793–1872), Scottish divine, was born in Aberdeen, the son of Alexander Burnett, sheriff of Kincardineshire, who in 1806 succeeded to his uncle Sir Alexander Ramsay's estates, took the surname Ramsay, and was created a baronet. Young Ramsay was educated at Durham and St John's College, Cambridge, held two Somerset curacies 1816–24, and then removed to Edinburgh. In 1830 he became incumbent of St John's, and in 1846 also dean of the diocese. He wrote various religious works, and the delightful *Reminiscences of Scottish Life and Character* (1857; 22nd ed. with Memoir by Cosmo Innes, 1874).

(8) **Sir William** (1852–1916), Scottish chemist, was born at Glasgow. Professor of Chemistry at Bristol (1880–87), at University College, London (1887–1912), in conjunction with Lord Rayleigh he discovered argon in 1894. Later he obtained helium, neon, krypton and xenon, and won a Nobel prize (1904). His writings on his subject include *The Gases of the Atmosphere* and *Elements and Electrons*. See *Life* by M. Travers (1956).

(9) **Sir William Mitchell** (1851–1939), Scottish archaeologist, born in Glasgow, was professor of Humanities at Aberdeen, 1886–1911. An authority on Asia Minor, he wrote a *Historical Geography of Asia Minor* (1890), and on the history of early Christian times published several works, the best known being *The Church in the Roman Empire before A.D. 170* (1893).

RAMSDEN, Jesse (1735–1800), F.R.S. (1786), English instrument-maker, born near Halifax, improved optical and survey instruments and devised the mural circle.

RAMSEY, (1) Arthur Michael (1904–), Archbishop of Canterbury from 1961, educated at Repton and Cambridge, where he was president of the Union (1926) and regius professor of Divinity (1950–52), became Bishop of Durham in 1952 and Archbishop of York in 1956.

(2) **Frank Plumpton** (1903–30), English philosopher, was a colleague of Wittgenstein at Cambridge and an early critic of his *Tractatus*. He maintained, in opposition to Wittgenstein, that the propositions of mathematics are tautologies, not equations, continued the Russellian quest of deriving mathematics exclusively from non-empirical propositions and in inductive logic veered towards pragmatism. He rejected the suggestion that there may be metaphysical truths inaccessible to the limitations of language by the famous remark: 'What we can't say we can't say and we can't whistle it either'. His early death prevented a major philosophical work, but his brilliant philosophical papers were published under the title, *The Foundation of Mathematics*, ed. R. B. Braithwaite (1931).

RAMUS, Petrus, or **Pierre de la Ramée,** *ra-mü* (1515–72), French humanist, born at Cuth near Soissons, became servant to a rich scholar at the Collège de Navarre, and by studying at night made rapid progress in learning. The dominant philosophy dissatisfied him, and he put higher value on 'reason' than on 'authority'. Graduating at twenty-three, he had great success as lecturer on the Greek and Latin authors, and undertook to reform the science of logic. His attempts excited much hostility among the Aristotelians and his *Dialectic* (1543) was fiercely assailed by the doctors of the Sorbonne, who had it suppressed. But Cardinals de Bourbon and Lorraine in 1545 had him appointed principal of the Collège de Presles; and Lorraine in 1551 instituted a chair for him at the Collège Royal. He mingled largely in the literary and scholastic disputes of the time, and ultimately turned Protestant. He had to flee from Paris, and travelled in Germany and Switzerland; but returning to France in 1571, he perished in the massacre of St Bartholomew. He wrote treatises on arithmetic, geometry and algebra, and was an early adherent of the Copernican system. His theories had no small influence after his death, and all over Europe the Ramist system of logic was adopted and taught. See studies by Waddington-Kastus (1855), Desmaze (1864), Lobstein (1878), Graus (1912).

RAMUZ, Charles Ferdinand, *ra-müz* (1878–1947), Swiss writer, was born at Cully near Lausanne. He wrote in French, mainly about life in his native canton of Vaud. His first book, *Le Petit Village*, appeared in 1903, and thereafter he wrote prolifically. His pure prose style and fine descriptive power won him wide admiration and repute, his European popularity being somewhat tempered in Britain, though he has been translated into English—*Beauté sur la terre* (1927; trans. *Beauty on Earth*) and *Présence de la mort* (1922; trans. The*Triumph of Death*). Other writings include *Jean Luc persécuté* (1909), *La Guérison de maladies* (1917), *Adam et Ève* (1932) and *Besoin de grandeur* (1937). See studies by P. Claudel (1947), A. Tissot (1948) and W. Günther (1948).

RANCÉ, Armand Jean le Bouthillier de, *rã-say* (1626–1700), French monk, founder of the Trappists, was an accomplished but worldly priest, to whom fell the Cistercian abbey of La Trappe (dep. Orne). Affected by the tragic deaths of two of his friends, he underwent a conversion, in 1662 undertook a reform of his monastery (becoming abbot), and finally established what was practically a new religious order, its principles perpetual prayer and austere self-denial. Intellectual work was forbidden; only manual labour was allowed to the monks. He wrote of his order in *Traité de la sainteté et des devoirs de* *la vie monastique* (1683), a book the contents of which caused much controversy on the place of study in monastic life. See Bremond's *L'Abbé Tempête* (1929) and its answer, Luddy's *The Real Rancé* (1931).

RANDALL, (1) **James Ryder** (1839–1908), American poet, born in Baltimore, was first a teacher, then a journalist. His lyrics, which in the Civil War gave powerful aid to the Southern cause, include ' Maryland, my Maryland ' (1861), ' Stonewall Jackson ' and ' There's life in the old land yet '.

(2) **Sir John Turton** (1905–   ), English physicist, professor at King's College, University of London, in 1940 along with Boot designed a cavity magnetron valve for use in radar. For this he received a government award of £12,000 (1949). He was knighted in 1962.

(3) **Samuel Jackson** (1828–90), American Democratic statesman, born in Philadelphia, was a member of the House of Representatives (1863–90). As speaker (1876–81), he codified the rules of the House and considerably strengthened the speaker's power.

RANDEGGER, **Cavaliere Alberto** (1832–1911), Italian composer, conductor and singing master, born at Trieste. He settled in London in 1854, and became in 1868 professor of Singing at the Royal Academy of Music, and afterwards a conductor of the Carl Rosa Opera Company (1879–85).

RANDOLPH, (1) **Edmund Jennings** (1753–1813), American statesman, born at Williamsburg, Va., studied at William and Mary College, and in 1786–88 was governor of Virginia, in 1787 a member of the convention which framed the U.S. constitution. He was working at a codification of the state laws of Virginia when Washington appointed him attorney-general (1789). In 1794 he was made secretary of state, but, falsely charged with bribery, resigned (1795), and was practically ruined. He resumed law practice at Richmond, Va., and was chief counsel for Aaron Burr (q.v.) at his treason trial. See Life by M. D. Conway (1888).

(2) **John** (1773–1833), ' of Roanoke ', American statesman, born at Cawsons, Va., a second cousin of (1), in 1799 entered congress, where he became distinguished for his eloquence, wit, sarcasm and eccentricity. He was the Democratic leader of the House of Representatives, but quarrelled with Jefferson and opposed the war of 1812; he opposed also the Missouri Compromise and Nullification. In 1825–27 he sat in the senate, in 1830 was appointed minister to Russia. By his will he manumitted his slaves. See Lives by Garland (1850), Adams (1882), Bruce (1922).

(3) **Sir Thomas** (d. 1332), Scottish soldier and statesman, the nephew and from 1308 the comrade of Bruce, who created him Earl of Moray. He recaptured Edinburgh Castle from the English (1314), commanded a division at Bannockburn, took Berwick (1318), won the victory of Mitton (1319), reinvaded England (1320, 1327), and was regent from Bruce's death (1329) till his own at Musselburgh.

(4) **Sir Thomas** (1523–90), English political agent and ambassador, a zealous Protestant, lived abroad during Mary's reign, and by Elizabeth was employed on diplomatic missions in Germany, Russia, France and specially Scotland, where off and on during 1559–86 he played his mistress's cards. He was twice shot at there, and in 1581 had to flee for his life. From 1585 he was chancellor of the Exchequer in England.

(5) **Thomas** (1605–35), English poet and dramatist, born at Newnham near Daventry, and educated at Westminster and Trinity College, Cambridge, was elected a fellow, began early to write, gained the friendship of Ben Jonson, and led a boisterous life. He died and was buried at Blatherwick near Oundle. Randolph left a number of bright, fanciful, sometimes too glowing poems, and six plays: *Aristippus, or the Jovial Philosopher*; *The Conceited Peddler*; *The Jealous Lovers*; *The Muses' Looking-glass*; *Amyntas, or the Impossible Dowry*; and *Hey for Honesty*. See editions by W. Carew Hazlitt (1875) and Thorn-Drury (1929).

RANJIT SINGH (1780–1839), the ' Lion of the Punjab ', at twelve succeeded his father, a Sikh chief, as ruler of Lahore, and directed all his energies to founding a kingdom which should unite all the Sikh provinces. With the help of an army trained by Western soldiers, including Generals Ventura and Allard, he became the most powerful ruler in India. He was a firm ally of the British, the boundary between their territories having been amicably fixed at the river Sutlej. In 1813 he procured from an Afghan prince, as the price of assistance in war, the Koh-i-noor diamond. See Life by Sir L. Griffin (1892).

RANJITSINHJI, **Prince** (1872–1933), the ' Black Prince of Cricketers ', born in Kathiawar state, studied at Cambridge, succeeded as Jam Sahib of Nawanagar in 1906, and was made a maharaja in 1918. He wrote a book on cricket (1897). For a description of him as a cricketer see Neville Cardus, *The Summer Game* (1929).

RANK, **Joseph Arthur, 1st Baron Rank** (1888–1972), British film magnate, born in Hull, chairman of many film companies, including Gaumont-British and Cinema-Television. He did much to promote the British film industry at a time when Hollywood and American companies seemed to have the monopoly. A staunch and active supporter of the Methodist church, he was keenly interested in social problems. He was raised to the peerage in 1957.

RANKE, **Leopold von** (1795–1886), German historian, was born at Wiehe in Thuringia, studied at Halle and Berlin, and in 1818 became a schoolmaster at Frankfurt an der Oder, but his heart was set on the study of history. A work on the Romance and Teutonic peoples in the Reformation period, and another criticizing contemporary historians, procured his call to Berlin as professor of History (1825–72). In 1827–31 he was sent to examine the archives of Vienna, Venice, Rome and Florence. The fruits of his labours were a work on South Europe in the 16th and 17th centuries (1827), books on Serbia and Venice, and *History of the Popes in the 16th and 17th Centuries* (1834–37; trans. by Sarah Austin, 1846), perhaps his greatest achievement. Then he turned his attention to central and northern Europe, and wrote on German Reformation history, Prussian history (1847–48), French history in the 16th and 17th centuries (1852–61), and English history in the 17th century (1859–67; trans. 1875). Other books were on the origin of the Seven Years' War (1871), the German Powers and the Confederation (1871), the revolutionary wars of 1791–92 (1875), Venetian history (1878), a universal history (1881–88), and the history of Germany and France in the 19th century (1887), besides monographs on Wallenstein (1869), Hardenberg (1877–78), and Frederick the Great and Frederick-William IV (1878). Ranke was ennobled in 1865, and died in Berlin. His standpoint was that of the statesman; and he fails to give due prominence to the social side of national development. See his autobiographical *Zur eigenen Lebensgeschichte* (1890), and monographs by Winckler (1885), Von Giesebrecht, Guglia, Ritter (1895), Oncken (1922).

RANKINE, William John Macquorn (1820–1872), Scottish engineer and scientist, born at Edinburgh, was appointed in 1855 to the chair of Engineering at Glasgow. Elected a fellow of the Royal Society in 1853, his works on the steam engine, machinery, shipbuilding, applied mechanics, &c., became standard textbooks; and he did much for the new science of thermodynamics and the theories of elasticity and of waves. He wrote humorous and patriotic *Songs and Fables* (1874). See Life by Tait prefixed to his *Miscellaneous Papers* (1880).

RANSOME, (1) Arthur Mitchell (1884–1967), English writer, born in Leeds, wrote studies of Edgar Allan Poe (1910), Oscar Wilde (1912), and impressions of Russia, before making his name with books for young readers. His works for them are carefully written and rank high among their kind. They include *Swallows and Amazons* (1931), *We didn't mean to go to Sea* (1938), *The Big Six* (1940) and *Great Northern?* (1947).

(2) **Robert** (1753–1830), English agricultural implement maker, born at Wells in Norfolk, in 1789 founded at Ipswich the great Orwell Works for agricultural implements.

RAOULT, François Marie, *ra-ool* (1830–1901), French chemist, born at Fournes (Nord), was educated at Paris and in 1870 became professor of Chemistry at Grenoble. He discovered the law (named after him) which relates the vapour pressure of a solution to the number of molecules of solute dissolved in it.

RAPHAEL, properly **Raffaello Santi** or **Sanzio**, *raf'a-el*, *raf-a-el'lō* (1483–1520), Italian painter, was born at Urbino, the son of the poet-painter, Giovanni Santi (d. 1494). He seems to have studied under Timoteo Viti, and then from about 1500 at Perugia under Perugino, becoming such a clever imitator of his style that to this day the early pictures of the disciple are confounded with those of his master. Among his earliest paintings were the *Crucifixion* (1502–03, Dudley collection), an *Assumption of the Virgin* (Vatican), and a *Marriage of the Virgin* (1504, Milan). Probably about 1504 Raphael began to discern the advantage of greater independence, yet for some time longer he showed Peruginesque influence. In 1505 he went to Siena, where he assisted Pinturicchio, and next to Florence; but before starting he probably took commissions, which produced the *Madonna Ansidei* (National Gallery), the *Madonna of Sant' Antonio* and the *Madonna of Terranuova* (Berlin Museum). Raphael, who now had painting-rooms at Florence and at Perugia, resolved to acquire and assimilate some of the boldness of Michelangelo and the sweetness of Leonardo. In portraiture more than elsewhere da Vinci's influence is visible, and the likeness of *Maddalena Doni* (Florence) is inspired by the *Mona Lisa*. Of special interest is the *St George*, sent by the Duke of Urbino to Henry VII of England; while attractive in other ways are the painter's own likeness (Uffizi) and the *Madonnas* of Orleans, of the Palm, of St Petersburg and of Canigiani in which Raphael finally appears as a pure Tuscan. The Borghese *Entombment* (1507) is an embodiment of all the new principles which Raphael acquired at Florence and of colour such as only Raphael could give. He became attracted by the style of Fra Bartolommeo; and, under the influence of that master, finished the *Madonna del Baldacchino* at Florence. Some of the best work of his Florentine period was now produced—the small *Holy Family* (Madrid), the *St Catharine* (Louvre), the *Bridgewater* and *Colonna Madonnas*, the *Virgin and Sleeping Infant* (Milan), the large *Cowper Madonna*, the *Belle Jardinière*, and the *Esterhazy Madonna*. In 1508 Raphael went to Rome at the instigation of his relative Bramante, then in high favour with Julius II, who had laid the foundation of the new cathedral of St Peter, and who caused the papal chambers to be decorated afresh because he disliked the frescoes of the older masters. The date of Raphael's engagement to paint the *Camere* of the Vatican is now fixed as 1509. In the ceiling of the chamber ' of the Signature ' the space is divided into fields, in which the Temptation, the Judgment of Solomon, the Creation of the Planets, and Marsyas and Apollo were inserted side by side with medallions enclosing allegories of Theology, Philosophy, Justice and Poetry. On the walls of the *camera* Raphael began the *Disputa*, in which he represented the Eternal, Christ, Mary and the apostles and angels presiding in heaven over the Trinitarian controversy. The *School of Athens*, the Parnassus, and the allegory of Prudence followed. Subordinate pictures are the pope accepting the Decretals (1511), Justinian receiving the Pandects, and Augustus saving the manuscripts of Virgil. Raphael divided his time between the labours of the Vatican and easel pictures. The portraits of Julius II and the Virgin of the Popolo were now executed, drawings were furnished to the copperplate-engraver Marcantonio for the Massacre of the Innocents, and Madonnas and Holy Families were composed; while on the ceiling of the chamber of Heliodorus at the Vatican he finished the picture in which the Eternal appears to Noah, Abraham's Sacrifice, Jacob's Dream and the Burning Bush. The pontiff is introduced into the Expulsion of Heliodorus and the Mass of Bolsena. The death of Julius in 1513 but slightly interrupted the labours of the painter, who gave a noble rendering of Leo X and his suite in the *Defeat of Attila*. The *Deliverance of Peter* completed the decorations. The constant employment of disciples enabled Raphael in the three years 1511–14 also to finish the *Madonna di Foligno*, the *Isaiah of St Agostino*, the *Galatea of the Farnesina*, the *Sibyls of the Pace*, and the mosaics of the Popolo ordered by Agostino Chigi. He painted, too, the *Madonna of the Fish* (Madrid) and *Madonna della Sedia* (Florence), while in portraits such as *Altoviti* (Munich) and *Inghirami* (Florence) he rises to the perfect rendering of features and expression which finds its greatest triumph in the *Leo X* (Florence). Leo selected Raphael to succeed Bramante as architect of St Peter's in 1514, and secured from him for the Vatican chambers the frescoes of the Camera dell' Incendio, which all illustrate scenes from the lives of Leonine popes. But much of Raphael's attention was taken up with the cartoons (Kensington) executed, with help from assistants, for the tapestries of the Sistine Chapel. The first was completed in December 1516, the second woven at Brussels in 1519. His portraits of the Duke of Urbino, Castiglione, Bembo and Navagero, and his decoration of Cardinal Bibiena's rooms at the Vatican, tell of the company which Raphael now frequented. When Leo X succumbed to Francis I, Raphael followed the pontiff there to Florence and Bologna, and found there new patrons for whom he executed the *Sistine Madonna*, the *St Cecilia* of Bologna, and the *Ezechiel* of the Pitti. The labours subsequently completed were immense, including the *Spasimo* (Madrid), the *Holy Family* and *St Michael*, which the pope sent to the king of France in 1518, the likeness of the vice-queen of Aragon, and the *Violin-player* (Sciarra collection at Rome). In wall-painting he produced, with help, the cycle of the Psyche legend at the Farnesina, the gospel scenes of the Loggie of the Vatican, and the frescoes of the Hall of Constantine. His last work, the *Transfiguration*, was nearly finished when Raphael died. See the great work on him by Crowe and Cavalcaselle (1882); H. Strachey's monograph (1900), Oppé's (1909), Holmes's (1933), Pittaluga's (1956); French works by Passavant (1860; trans. 1872), Gruyer (1863–81), Müntz (1881–96); German by Grimm (trans. 1889), Springer (3rd ed. 1896), Lübke (1881), Von Lützow (1890), Von Seidlitz (1891), Knackfuss (trans. 1899).

RAPIN, Paul de, *ra-pī* (1661–1725), French historian, born at Castres in Languedoc, the son of the Seigneur de Thoyras, studied at the Protestant college of Saumur, and passed as advocate in 1679. After the revocation of the Edict of Nantes (1685) he went to Holland, enlisted in a Huguenot volunteer corps, followed the Prince of Orange to England in 1688, was made ensign in 1689, and distinguished himself at the Boyne and at Limerick. For some years he travelled as tutor with the Earl of Portland's son, then settled at Wesel where he devoted his

remaining years to the composition of his great *Histoire d'Angleterre* (1724), undoubtedly the best work on English history that had until then appeared. It was continued from William III's accession to his death by David Durant (1734), and was translated into English by Tindal (1726–31).

RAPP, (1) George (1770–1847), religious leader, founder of the Harmonists, was born in Württemberg, and emigrated with his followers to Western Pennsylvania in 1803, establishing a settlement named Harmony. After migrating to New Harmony in Indiana (1815), they returned in 1824 to Pennsylvania and built Economy on the Ohio, 15 miles NW of Pittsburgh. Looking for the speedy second coming of Christ, the community sought to amass wealth for the Lord's use, practised rigid economy, self-denial and celibacy, all things being held in common, and, diminished in number, owned farms, dairies and vineyards, and railway and bank shares worth millions of dollars. See German monograph by Knortz (1892).

(2) **Jean, Comte de** (1772–1821), French soldier, born at Colmar, entered the French army in 1788, distinguished himself in Germany and Egypt, and became aide-de-camp to Napoleon. For his brilliant charge at Austerlitz he was made general of division (1805); in 1809 he became a Count of the Empire. He accompanied the emperor on the Russian expedition, defended Danzig for nearly a year, on its surrender was sent prisoner to Russia, and did not return till 1814. During the Hundred Days he supported Napoleon, but after the Restoration he was made a peer. See his *Memoirs* (1823; new ed. 1895).

RASCHIG, Friedrich August, *rash-iKH* (1863–1928), German chemist and industrialist, born in Brandenburg, discovered nitramide and chloramine, and new production methods for hydrazine and phenol. He died at Duisburg.

RASHDALL, Hastings (1858–1924), English moral philosopher and theologian, born in London, was educated at Harrow and Oxford. He was elected a fellow of Hertford College, Oxford, in 1888, divinity tutor and chaplain at Balliol, and from 1895 to 1917 was tutor in philosophy at New College. Given a canonry at Hereford in 1909, he in 1917 became dean of Carlisle. Among his writings are the scholarly *Universities of Europe in the Middle Ages* (3 vols., new ed. 1936), and *Theory of Good and Evil* (2 vols. 1917), containing his nonhedonistic 'ideal utilitarian' system of ethics in which right and wrong are judged by the ideal and which may, but not of necessity, be pleasurable. *Idea of Atonement in Christian Theology* (1919) includes his Bampton lectures given in 1915. See *Life* by P. E. Matheson (1928).

RASK, Rasmus Christian (1787–1832), Danish philologist, born in Fünen, in 1819–23 travelled to India and Ceylon. He returned to Copenhagen, and in 1825 became professor of Literary History, in 1828 of Oriental Languages, and in 1831 of Icelandic. His study of Icelandic (1818), with Bopp's and Grimm's works opened up the science of comparative philology. See Lives by Rönning and Wimmer (1887), 'and study by Jespersen (1918).

RASMUSSEN, Knud Johan Victor (1879–1933), Danish explorer and ethnologist, was born at Jacobshavn, Greenland, of Danish and Eskimo parents. From 1902 onwards he directed several expeditions to Greenland in support of the theory that the Eskimos and the North American Indians were both descended from migratory tribes from Asia. In 1910 he established Thule base on Cape York, and in 1921–24 crossed from Greenland to the Bering Strait. English translations of his books include *Greenland by the Polar Sea* (1921), *Myths and Legends from Greenland* (1921–25), and *Across Arctic America* (1927).

RASPAIL, François Vincent, *ras-pah'y'* (1794–1878), French chemist, doctor, deputy, and advocate of universal suffrage, as a revolutionist was banished from France in 1848 but allowed to return in 1859. His camphor system (1845) was a forerunner of antiseptic surgery. See monograph by Saint-Martin (1877).

RASPE. See MÜNCHHAUSEN.

RASPUTIN, Grigoriy Efimovich (1871?–1916), Russian peasant monk, born at Pokrovskoye in Tobolsk province, wielded a malign, magnetic and mystic power over the Tsarina and others at the Russian court, causing the dismissal of ministers, including the prime minister Kokovtsev. He was assassinated at the Yusupov Palace by a party of noblemen led by the Grand-Duke Dimitry Pavlovich and Prince Yusupov. See studies by M. Rodzyanko (1927) and R. Fülop-Miller (1928).

RASSAM, Hormuzd (1826–1910), Turkish Assyriologist, born at Mosul, the son of Chaldaean Christians. He assisted Layard at Nineveh in 1845–47 and 1849–51, and succeeded him, until 1854, as British agent for Assyrian excavations, finding the palace of Assurbani-Pal (Sardanapalus). After holding political offices at Aden and Muscat, he was sent (1864) to Abyssinia, where King Theodore cast him into prison till 1868, when he was released by Sir Robert Napier. In 1876–82 he made explorations in Mesopotamia for the British Museum. He wrote on his Abyssinian experiences (1869), and did much work for the *Academy*, &c.

RASTELL, (1) **John** (1475–1536), English printer, lawyer and dramatist, born in Coventry, was called to the bar and in 1510 set up his own printing press. Married to the sister of Sir Thomas More (q.v.), he printed More's *Life of Pico*, a grammar by Linacre, the only copy of Medwall's play *Fulgens and Lucres* and many law books. Himself a dramatist, his plays, printed on his own press, include *Nature of the Four Elements* (1519), *Of Gentylness and Nobylyte . . . (c.* 1527) and *Calisto and Meleboea* (*c.* 1527). An ingenious deviser of pageants, he presented several of them at court. His expedition to found a settlement in the ' New Found Lands ' in 1517 came to nothing through mutiny on his ship.

(2) **William** (1508–65), English printer and lawyer, son of (1) and nephew of Sir Thomas More (q.v.), worked until 1529 with his father. He then set up his own printing press and during the next five years printed many of More's works, Fabyan's *Chronicle*, Henry Medwall's *Nature*, plays by his brother-in-law, John Heywood, as well as many law books. Abandoning printing for law when More fell from favour with the king, he was by 1549 treasurer of Lincoln's Inn. His kinship with More and his relationship through marriage with a daughter of More's protégé, John Clement, drove him with the Clements into exile at Louvain. With him went letters and other works written by More in the Tower. These, edited and printed by him, were to appear in More's *English Works* (1557). Exiled again during the reign of Elizabeth, he died abroad.

RATHAUS, Karol, *rat'hows* (1895–1954), Polish composer, who came to England in 1934 after studying in Vienna and teaching in Berlin. He later settled in the United States. His main works are a piano concerto, three symphonies and string quartets.

RATHENAU, Walther, *rah'tènow* (1867–1922), German electrotechnician and industrialist, born in Berlin of Jewish family, organized the Allgemeine Elektrizitäts Gesellschaft, founded by his father, and German war industries during World War I. In 1921 as minister of reconstruction he dealt with reparations. He wrote *Von kommenden Dingen, &c.* He was murdered soon after becoming foreign minister. See study by H. Graf Kessler (1928).

RATHKE, Martin Heinrich, *raht'kè* (1793–1860), German biologist, born in Danzig, became professor of Physiology at Dorpat (1829) and Königsberg (1835), in 1829 discovered gill-slits and gill-arches in embryo birds and mammals. ' Rathke's pocket ' is the name given to the small pit on the dorsal side of the oral cavity of developing Vertebrates.

RATICH, or Ratke, Wolfgang, *rah'tiкн* (1571–1635), German educationist, born in Holstein, based a new system of education on Bacon's *Advancement*, which he put into practice at Köthen in 1618. A second trial at Magdeburg in 1620 also ended in failure, and after some years of ineffectual wanderings he died at Erfurt. Though his ideas on education and methods of teaching were unsuccessful and unpopular in his lifetime, they had some influence on later reformers, especially Comenius. See monographs by Krause (1872), Störl (1876), Schumann (1876), Vogt (1894), and Seiler (1931); and Quick's *Essays on Educational Reformers* (1868; new ed. 1890).

RATTAZZI, Urbano, *rat-tat'see* (1808–73), Italian statesman, born at Alessandria, practised as advocate at Casale, and in 1848 entered the Second Chamber at Turin, becoming minister of the interior and later of justice till after Novara. In 1853 he took the portfolio of justice under Cavour; but, accused of weakness in suppressing the Mazzinian movement, retired in 1858. In 1859 he was minister of the interior, but retired because of the cession of Savoy and Nice (1860). Twice prime minister for a few months (1862, 1867), he twice had to resign because of his opposition to Garibaldi. See

Life by Morelli (1874) and his widow's *Rattazzi et son temps* (1881–87).

RATTIGAN, Terence Mervyn (1911–), English playwright, born in London, educated at Harrow and Oxford, scored a considerable success with his comedy *French Without Tears* (1936). Since then, most of his works, with the possible exception of *Adventure Story* (1949), a play about Alexander the Great, have been internationally acclaimed; and reveal not only a wide range of imagination but a deepening psychological knowledge. Best known are *The Winslow Boy* (1946), based on the Archer Shee case, *The Browning Version* (1948), *The Deep Blue Sea* (1952), *Separate Tables* (1954) and *Ross* (1960), a fictional treatment of T. E. Lawrence. He has been responsible for several successful films made from his own and other works.

RAUCH, Christian Daniel, *row*KH (1777–1857), German sculptor, born at Arolsen, practised sculpture while still valet to Frederick-William of Prussia, and in 1804 went to Rome. In 1811–15 he chiselled the recumbent effigy for the tomb of Queen Louisa at Charlottenburg. His works included statues of Blücher, Dürer, Goethe, Schiller and Schleiermacher; his masterpiece was the Frederick the Great (1851) in Berlin. See Life by Eggers (1873–90; Eng. trans. Boston 1893).

RAUMER, *row'mèr,* (1) **Friedrich Ludwig Georg von** (1781–1873), German historian, born at Wörlitz near Dessau, entered the Prussian state service in 1801; in 1811 became professor of History at Breslau; in 1819–53 filled the chair of Political Science at Berlin; and was secretary of the Berlin Academy. In 1848 he went to Paris as German ambassador. His chief works are a history of the Hohenstaufen emperors (1823–1825) and a history of Europe from the 16th century (1832–50). See his *Autobiography and Correspondence* (1861).

(2) **Karl Georg** (1783–1865), brother of (1), born at Wörlitz, became professor of Mineralogy at Breslau in 1811, and at Halle in 1819, of Natural History in 1827 at Erlangen. He wrote books on physiography, geography, Palestine, geognosy and crystallography, a great history of pedagogics (1843–1851), and an Autobiography (1866).

(3) **Rudolf** (1815–76), son of (2), Teutonic philologist, from 1846 was a professor at Erlangen and wrote, among other works, *Geschichte des germanischen Philologie* (1870).

RAUSCHER, Joseph Othmar von, *row'shèr* (1797–1875), Austrian cardinal, from 1853 prince-archbishop of Vienna, opposed, but ended by accepting, the infallibility dogma.

RAVAILLAC, François, *rav-ī-yak* (1578–1610), French bankrupt schoolmaster, who, after long imprisonment and a brief service in the Order of Feuillants, was moved by Catholic fanaticism to stab Henry IV (q.v.) of France. He was torn to pieces by horses. See works by Loiseleur (1873), Tharaud (1913).

RAVEL, Maurice (1875–1937), French composer, born at Ciboure in the Basque country, entered the Paris Conservatoire as a piano student in 1889. He eschewed the formal type of study and practice, and was some-

thing of a rebel; his early compositions met with considerable disapproval from the authorities, but after joining Gabriel Fauré's composition class in 1898 he developed considerably, though his first orchestral piece, the overture to *Schéhérazade,* an opera which never saw the light of day, had a hostile reception on its first performance in 1899. In the same year, however, he won recognition with his *Pavane pour une infante défunte,* slender compared with later work, but strongly redolent of his Basque background. In 1901 he was runner-up for the Prix de Rome with his cantata *Myrrha,* and his *Jeux d'eau* for piano won a popular success. He made two more fruitless attempts at the Prix de Rome and was intending to try a fourth time, but was barred from entering. He himself was indifferent, but the case was seized upon by the press as an example of personal prejudice in high quarters. Significantly, all Ravel's successful rivals were consigned to oblivion by posterity within a half-century. Now at the height of his powers, Ravel wrote his *Sonatina* (1905), *Miroirs* (1905), *Ma Mère l'Oye* (1908) and *Gaspard de la nuit* (1908) for piano; and in 1909 he began the music for the Diaghilev ballet *Daphnis et Chloé,* which was first performed in 1912. His comic opera *L'Heure espagnole* was completed in 1907 and produced in 1911. When war broke out he was forty, but he joined the army and saw active service; his *Tombeau de Couperin* (1917), a piano suite on the 18th-century pattern, which he later orchestrated, was dedicated to friends killed in action. The opera *L'Enfant et les sortilèges,* written to a libretto by Colette, was performed with great success in 1925, and the ' choreographic poem ' *La Valse,* epitomizing the spirit of Vienna, had been staged in 1920. These two works, both begun in 1917, were Ravel's last major contributions. The *Boléro* (1928), despite its popularity in Promenade concerts and elsewhere, is of smaller stature and was intended as a miniature ballet. The composer visited England in 1928 and received an honorary doctorate at Oxford. In 1933 his mental faculties began to fail, and it was found that he had a tumour on the brain. He composed no more but remained fairly active physically, and was able to tour Spain before he died, December 27, 1937. Ravel's music is scintillating and dynamic; he defied the established rules of harmony with his unresolved sevenths and ninths and other devices, his syncopation and strange sonorities, and he made the piano sound as it had never sounded before. His orchestrations are brilliant, especially in their masterly use of wind instruments and unusual percussion effects, often characteristically French, sometimes with a Spanish flavour stemming from his Basque background. It is interesting to note that his only work written purely for orchestra is *Rapsodie espagnole* (1907); everything else orchestral is either opera, ballet, or orchestrated piano pieces. See Lives by Demuth (1948), Myers (1960).

RAVENSCROFT, Thomas (1592–1640), English composer and author of *Pammelia* (1609), *Melismata* (1611) and *The Whole Book* *of Psalms* (1621). *Pammelia,* a collection of rounds and catches, was the first book of its kind in England. Some well-known tunes, such as St Davids and Bangor, are by him.

RAWLINSON, (1) **George** (1812–1902), English orientalist, brother of (2), born at Chadlington, Chipping Norton, in 1861 became Camden professor of Ancient History, in 1872 a canon of Canterbury, and in 1888 rector of All Hallows, Lombard Street. His annotated translation of Herodotus (1858–60) was followed by *The Five Great Eastern Monarchies* (1862–67), *History of Ancient Egypt* (1881), and theological works.

(2) **Sir Henry Creswicke** (1810–95), English diplomat and Assyriologist, brother of (1), born at Chadlington, entered the East India Company's army in 1827. In 1833–39 he helped to reorganize the Persian army, studying the while the cuneiform inscriptions, and translating Darius's Behistun inscription. He was political agent at Kandahar 1840–42, at Baghdad from 1843, later consul also, and made excavations and collections. A director of the East India Company in 1856, in 1859–60 he was British minister in Persia, in 1858, 1865–68, a Conservative M.P., and in 1858–59, 1868–95 a member of the Council of India. He wrote books on cuneiform inscriptions, the Russian question, *History of Assyria* (1852), &c. See Life by his brother, G. Rawlinson (1898).

(3) **Henry Seymour, 1st Baron Rawlinson** (1864–1925), eldest son of (2), served in Burma, Sudan and S. Africa, commanded the 4th Army in France in 1918, and broke the Hindenburg line, winning fame, a peerage in 1919 and a grant of £30,000. He was commander-in-chief in India (1920). See Life by Maurice (1928).

RAWSTHORNE, Alan (1905–71), English composer, born in Haslingden, Lancs, first studied dentistry, but turned to music at the age of twenty and studied at the Royal Manchester College of Music. From 1932 to 1934 he taught at Dartington Hall, but settled in London in 1935. His works, forthright, and polished in style, include symphonies, *Symphonic Studies,* for orchestra, concertos for piano and for violin, and various pieces of choral and chamber music.

RAY, (1) **John** (1627–1705), English naturalist, born, a blacksmith's son, at Black-Notley near Braintree, in 1649 became a fellow of Trinity College, Cambridge. At the Restoration he accepted Episcopal ordination, but was ejected by the 'Bartholomew Act' (1662). With a pupil, Francis Willughby (q.v.), Ray travelled (1662–66) over England and Wales, the Low Countries, Germany, Italy and France, studying botany and zoology. In 1667 he was elected F.R.S., and he contributed valuable papers to the *Transactions.* Ray's classification of plants was the foundation of the 'Natural System'; his zoological works were called by Cuvier the basis of all modern zoology. He wrote *Methodus Plantarum Nova* (1682), *Catalogus Plantarum Angliae* (1670), *Historia Plantarum* (1686–1704), and *Synopsis Methodica Animalium* (1693), besides three volumes on Birds, Fishes and Insects, &c. Lankester

edited *Memorials of Ray* (1846) and his *Correspondence* (1848) for the Ray Society, founded in 1844, and Gunther edited *Further Correspondence* (1928). See Life by Raven (1942). (2) **Martha.** See HACKMAN.

RAYLEIGH, (1) **John William Strutt, 3rd Baron** (1842–1919), English physicist, born near Maldon in Essex, graduated in 1865 from Trinity College, Cambridge, as senior wrangler and Smith's prizeman, and was elected a fellow (1866). He succeeded his father as third baron in 1873; was Cambridge professor of Experimental Physics 1879–84, in 1888–1905 of Natural Philosophy at the Royal Institution; and president of the Royal Society (1905–08). He became chancellor of Cambridge University (1908), O.M. (1902), and Nobel prizewinner (1904). His work included valuable studies and research on vibratory motion, the theory of sound and the wave theory of light. With Sir W. Ramsay he was the discoverer of argon (1894). Interested in psychical problems, he was a member, and president in 1901, of the Society for Psychical Research. His writings include *The Theory of Sound* (1877–1878; 2nd ed. 1894–96) and *Scientific Papers* (1899–1900). See study by his son (1924). (2) **Robert John Strutt, 4th Baron** (1875–1947), English physicist, son of (1), born at Terling Place, Essex, became professor of Physics at the Imperial College of Science from 1908 to 1919. Notable for his work on rock radioactivity, he became a fellow of the Royal Society in 1905 and a Rumford medallist. His writings include two excellent biographies, one of his father, the other of Sir J. J. Thomson (q.v.).

RAYNOUARD, François Juste Marie, *raynwar* (1761–1836), French poet and philologist, born at Brignoles in Provence, was a prosperous Paris advocate, in 1791 entered the legislative assembly, joined the Girondins, and was imprisoned. His poems and tragedies were successful, and in 1807 he was elected to the Academy, of which he became perpetual secretary in 1817. He was elected to the imperial legislative body in 1806 and 1811. After 1816 he wrote on the Provençal language and literature, notably his *Lexique Roman* (1838–44).

READ, Sir Herbert (1893–1968), English poet and art critic, born near Kirby Moorside, Yorkshire. He was an assistant keeper at the Victoria and Albert Museum, London, and from 1931 to 1933 was professor of Fine Art at Edinburgh University. He was editor of the *Burlington Magazine* from 1933 to 1939, and held academic posts at Cambridge, Liverpool, London and Harvard Universities, having achieved fame as a poet and a writer on aesthetics. His publications include *The Meaning of Art* (1931), *Art Now* (1933), *Collected Poems* (1946), the autobiographical *Annals of Innocence and Experience* (1940), &c. He was knighted in 1953, and received the Dutch Erasmus prize in 1966 for contributions to European culture.

READE, Charles (1814–84), English novelist and playwright, was born at Ipsden House, Oxfordshire, the youngest of eleven. After five years (all flogging) at Iffley, and six under two milder private tutors, in 1831 he gained a demyship at Magdalen College, Oxford, and in 1835, having taken third-class honours, was duly elected to a lay fellowship. Next year he entered Lincoln's Inn, and in 1843 was called to the bar. In 1850 he first put pen seriously to paper, 'writing first for the stage —about thirteen dramas, which nobody would play'. Through one of these dramas he formed his platonic friendship with Mrs Seymour, a warmhearted actress, who from 1854 till her death (1879) kept house for him. His life after 1852 is a succession of plays, by which he lost money, and novels that won profit and fame. These novels illustrate social injustice and cruelty in one form or another and his writing is realistic and vivid. They include *Peg Woffington* (1852), *Hard Cash* (1863), *Foul Play* (1869, with Dion Boucicault), *A Terrible Temptation* (1871), and *A Woman-hater* (1877). His masterpiece was his long, historical novel of the 15th century, *The Cloister and the Hearth* (1861). He was not one of the great novelists of the century, but of the second order he is perhaps the best. *Charles Reade* (1887), by his brother and a nephew, is a poor biography. See Swinburne's *Miscellanies* (1886), and studies by Coleman (1903) and Elwin (1931).

READING, Rufus Daniel Isaacs, 1st Marquess of (1860–1935), English lawyer and statesman, born in London, was educated there and in Brussels and Hanover. In parliament as Liberal member for Reading in 1904, he also began to gain a reputation as an eminent advocate. In 1910 he was appointed solicitor-general and later attorney-general and as such in 1912 was the first to become a member of the cabinet. Lord chief justice in 1913, during World War I he was special envoy to the United States in negotiating financial plans. He was British ambassador in Washington from 1918 to 1921, and thereafter viceroy of India until 1926. Created marquess on his return, he took charge of many business concerns, including the chairmanship of United Newspapers Ltd. and the presidency of Imperial Chemical Industries. In 1931 he was for a short time foreign secretary in the National government.

RÉAUMUR, René Antoine Ferchault de, *ray-ō-mür* (1683–1757), French physicist, born at La Rochelle, became in 1708 a member of the Academy of Sciences, and superintended an official *Description des arts et métiers*. He made researches in natural history, as to woods, rivers and mines, and in metallurgy and glassmaking. His thermometer (with spirit instead of mercury) has eighty degrees between the freezing- and boiling-points.

RÉCAMIER, Madame (*née* **Jeanne Françoise Julie Adélaïde Bernard**), *ray-kam-yay* (1777–1849), French beauty, born at Lyons, in 1793 married a rich banker thrice her own age. Her salon was soon filled with the brightest wits of the day, but her temperament prevented any hint of scandal. When her husband was financially ruined she visited Madame de Staël at Coppet (1806). Here she met Prince August of Prussia. A marriage was arranged, provided M. Récamier would consent to a divorce. He consented to this, but Madame could not desert him in adversity. The most distinguished friend of her later

years was Chateaubriand. See her *Souvenirs et correspondence* (1859), and Lives by E. Herriot (trans. 1906) and Trouncer (1949).

RECLUS, Jean Jacques Élisée, *ré-klü* (1830–1905), French geographer, born at Ste-Foix-la-Grande (Gironde), was educated at Montauban and Berlin. An extreme Democrat, he left France after the *coup d'état* of 1851, and spent seven years in England, Ireland and America. He returned in 1858, and published *Voyage à la Sierra Nevada de Ste Marthe* (1861), &c. For his share in the Commune (1871) he was banished. In Switzerland he began his masterpiece, *Nouvelle Géographie universelle* (19 vols. 1876–94; Eng. trans. by Ravenstein and A. H. Keane). He also wrote a physical geography, *La Terre* (1867–68; trans. 1871 and 1887), *Histoire d'une montagne* (1880; trans. 1881), &c. In 1893 he became a professor at Brussels.

RECORDE, Robert (*c.* 1510–58), English mathematician, born at Tenby, studied at Oxford, in 1545 took his M.D. at Cambridge, became physician to Edward VI and Queen Mary, but died in debtors' prison. His works include *The Grounde of Artes* (1540), on arithmetic; *Pathwaye to Knowledge* (1551), an abridged Euclid; *Castle of Knowledge* (1551), on astronomy; and *Whetstone of Wit* (1557), an important treatise on algebra. He was first to use the sign =.

REDGRAVE, (1) Sir Michael Scudamore (1908–), British stage and film actor, born at Bristol, son of actor parents and grandfather, educated at Clifton College and Magdalene College, Cambridge, was first a modern-language teacher at Cranleigh school, began his acting career with Liverpool Repertory Company (1934–36). His sensitive, intellectual approach to acting has been most successful in classical rôles, such as the title parts of *Hamlet* (Old Vic and Elsinore, 1949–50) and *Uncle Vanya* (Chichester and National Theatre, 1963–64). Modern plays in which he has appeared include *Tiger at the Gates* (1955) and his own adaptation of *The Aspern Papers* (1959), &c. He has also acted in many films since his début in *The Lady Vanishes* (1938), including *The Way to the Stars* (1945) and the outstanding *The Browning Version* (1951). Created C.B.E. (1952) and knighted (1959), he became director of the Yvonne Arnaud Theatre at Guildford in 1962. See *Life* by Findlater (1956). He married the actress Rachel Kempson (1910–) in 1935, and their three children are all actors: **Vanessa** (1937–), won acclaim with the Royal Shakespeare Company, particularly as 'Rosalind' in *As You Like It* (1961), and has also appeared successfully in films; **Corin** (1939–) acts on stage and television; and **Lynn** (1944–) is also a stage and film actress, gaining particular notice in the film *Georgy Girl* (1967).

(2) **Richard** (1804–88), English subject painter, A.R.A. (1840), R.A. (1851), from 1857 was inspector-general of art schools. He wrote, with his brother, **Samuel** (1802–76), *A Century of English Painters* (1866) and *Dictionary of Artists of the English School* (1874).

REDI, Francesco, *ray'dee* (1626–97), Italian

physician and poet, born at Arezzo, studied at Florence and at Pisa, and became physician to the dukes of Tuscany. He wrote a book on animal parasites and proved by a series of experiments that maggots cannot form on meat which has been covered. He also wrote the dithyrambic *Bacco in Toscana* (1685).

REDMOND, John Edward (1856–1918), Irish politician, born in Dublin, the son of a Wexford M.P., was called to the bar at Gray's Inn 1886, and entered parliament 1881. A champion of Home Rule, he became chairman of the Nationalist party in 1900. He declined a seat in Asquith's coalition ministry (1915), but supported the war, deplored the Irish rebellion, and opposed Sinn Fein. See Life by D. Gwynn (1932).

REDON, Odilon, *rė-dõ* (1840–1916), French artist, born at Bordeaux, is usually regarded as a pioneer surrealist, owing to his use of dream images in his work. He made many charcoal drawings and lithographs of extraordinary imaginative power, but after 19 00 he painted, especially in pastel, pictures of flowers and portraits in intense colour. He was also a brilliant writer; his diaries (1867–1915) were published as *À soi-même* (1922), and his *Lettres* in 1923. See also Life by M. and A. Leblond (1941).

REDPATH, Anne (1895–1965), Scottish painter, born at Galashiels, was one of the most important modern Scottish artists, her paintings in oil and watercolour showing great richness of colour and vigorous technique. She was elected to the R.S.A. in 1952, and was awarded the O.B.E. in 1955. Examples of her work have been acquired for the permanent collections of Edinburgh, Manchester, Vancouver, &c.

REED, (1) Sir Carol (1906–), English film director, born at Putney, educated at King's School, Canterbury, took to the stage (1924) and acted and produced for Edgar Wallace until 1930. He produced or directed such memorable films as *Kipps* (1941), *The Young Mr Pitt* (1942), *The Way Ahead* (1944), the Allied War Documentary *The True Glory* (1945), *The Fallen Idol* (1948), but is best remembered for his Cannes Film Prize-winning version of Graham Greene's novel, *The Third Man* (1949), depicting the sinister underworld of postwar, partitioned Vienna. *Outcasts of the Islands* (1952) based on a Conrad novel, was another triumph of location work in the East, and *Our Man in Havana* (1959) marked a return to his postwar brilliance. He was knighted in 1952.

(2) **Sir Edward James** (1830–1906), English naval engineer, born at Sheerness, was chief constructor of the navy (1863–70) and designed battleships for both the British and foreign navies. Created K.C.B. in 1880, he was Liberal M.P. for Cardiff until 1895, becoming lord of the Treasury in 1886. He wrote *The Stability of Ships* (1884), &c.

(3) **Isaac** (1742–1807), English editor of Shakespeare, born in London, was an unenthusiastic conveyancer with considerable interest in archaeology and literature. A meticulous commentator and editor, he is best known for his revisions of Dr Johnson's and George Steevens' 'variorum' edition of Shakespeare.

(4) **Talbot Baines** (1852–93), English author of books for boys, was born in London, the son of Sir Charles Reed (1819–81), chairman of the London School Board. He became head of his father's firm of typefounders and wrote books on the history of printing (see his *History of the Old English Letter-foundries* (1887)). His robust, moral, but entertaining school stories first appeared in the *Boy's Own Paper*. They include *The Fifth Form at St Dominic's* (1881), *The Master of the Shell* (1887), and *Cockhouse at Fellsgarth* (1891).

(5) **Walter** (1851–1902), American army doctor, born in Belroi, Virginia, was in the medical corps from 1875 and was appointed professor of Bacteriology in the Army Medical College, Washington, in 1893. Investigations carried out by him in 1900 proved that transmission of yellow fever was by mosquitoes and his researches led to the eventual eradication of this disease from Cuba.

REEVE, Clara (1729–1807), English novelist of the 'Gothic' school, born at Ipswich, the daughter of the rector of Freston, translated Barclay's *Argenis* (1772), and wrote *The Champion of Virtue, a Gothic Story* (1777), renamed *The Old English Baron*, which was avowedly an imitation of Walpole's *Castle of Otranto*. She wrote four other novels and *The Progress of Romance* (1785).

REEVES, John Sims (1818–1900), English singer, born at Shooter's Hill, appeared as a baritone at Newcastle in 1839, and acquired fresh fame as a tenor. He studied at Paris (1843), sang at Milan, and was recognized as the first English tenor. Leaving the stage in 1860, he sang at concerts and in oratorio. See Life by Sutherland Edwards (1881) and his own *My Jubilee* (1889).

REGENER, Erich, *ray′gen-er* (1881–1955), German physicist, professor of Physics at Berlin and Stuttgart, was dismissed for political reasons in 1937, and reinstated in 1946. He is known for his pioneer work on cosmic rays and for his researches on the stratosphere.

REGER, Max, *ray′ger* (1873–1916), German composer, born at Brand, Bavaria, taught music at Wiesbaden and Munich, became director of Music in Leipzig University (1907), and professor (1908). He composed organ music, piano concertos, choral works and songs.

REGIOMONTANUS (1436–76), the name given to **Johannes Müller**, German mathematician and astronomer, from his Franconian birthplace, Königsberg (*Mons Regius*). He studied at Vienna, and in 1461 accompanied Cardinal Bessarion to Italy to learn Greek. In 1471 he settled in Nuremberg, where the patrician Bernhard Walther subsidized him. The two laboured at the *Alphonsine Tables*, and published *Ephemerides 1475-1506* (1473), of which Columbus made much use. He established the study of algebra and trigonometry in Germany, and wrote on waterworks, burning-glasses, weights and measures, the quadrature of the circle, &c. He was summoned to Rome in 1474 by Sixtus IV to help to reform the calendar, and died there.

REGNARD, Jean François, *rė-nyahr* (1655–1709), French comic dramatist, born in

Paris, a rich shopkeeper's son, found himself at twenty master of a considerable fortune, and set out on his travels. In his autobiographical romance, *La Provençale*, we read of his and his Provençal mistress's capture and sale as slaves by Algerian corsairs, their bondage at Constantinople, and their ransom. After wanderings as far as Lapland, he found his vocation in the success of *Le Divorce* at the Théâtre-Italien in 1688. *Le Joueur* (1696), a hit at the Théâtre-Français, was followed by *Le Distrait* (1697), *Le Retour imprévu* (1700), *Les Folies amoureuses* (1704), and his masterpiece *Le Légataire universel* (1708). There are editions by Didot (1820), Michiels (1854), Fournier (1875) and Moland (1893). See studies by Mahrenholtz (1887), Hallays (1929), and *Bibliographie* by Marcheville (1877).

REGNAULT, *rĕ-nyō,* **(1) Alexandre Georges Henri** (1843–71), French painter of mythological, Spanish and Moorish subjects, was born in Paris, and gained the Prix de Rome in 1866. In 1869 he painted his equestrian portrait of Prim, in 1870 his *Salome* and *Moorish Execution*. In the Franco-Prussian war he volunteered as a private soldier, and fell at Buzenval. See Lives by Cazalis (1872) and Marx (1887), and his *Correspondance* (1873).

(2) Henri Victor (1810–78), French chemist and physicist, father of (1), born at Aix-la-Chapelle, was a shop assistant in Paris and a professor at Lyons, whence, in 1840, he was recalled to Paris as a member of the Academy of Sciences. Having filled chairs in the École Polytechnique and the Collège de France, he became in 1854 director of the Sèvres porcelain factory. He investigated gases, latent heat, steam-engines, &c., and published a *Cours élémentaire de chimie* (14th ed. 1871). See *Éloge* by Dumas (1881).

RÉGNIER, *ray-nyay,* **(1) Henri François Joseph de** (1864–1936), French Symbolist poet, novelist and critic, born at Honfleur, studied law in Paris, turned to letters, and was elected to the Academy in 1911. His *Poèmes anciens et romanesques* (1890) revealed him as a Symbolist, though later he returned to more traditional versification. In both poetry and prose his style and mood were admirably suited to evocation of the past, and expressive of a melancholy disillusion induced by the passage of time. Poetical works include *La Sandale ailée* (1906), *Vestigia flammae* (1921) and *Flamma tenax* (1928). His novels were mainly concerned with France and Italy in the 17th and 18th centuries. Two of these are *La Double Maîtresse* (1900) and *Le Bon Plaisir* (1902). See studies in French by Berton (1910), Honnert (1923) and Parmée (1939).

(2) Mathurin (1573–1613), French satirist, born at Chartres, was tonsured at nine, but grew up dissipated and idle, obtained a canonry at Chartres, and enjoyed the favour of Henry IV. His whole work hardly exceeds 7000 lines—sixteen satires, three epistles, five elegies, and some odes, songs and epigrams, yet it places him high among French poets. He is greatest in his satires, admirably polished, but vigorous and original and giving a lively picture of the

Paris of his day. Editions are by Poitevin (1860), Barthélemy (1862), and Courbet (1875). See Cherrier's *Bibliographie* (1889), and Life by Vianey (1896).

REGULUS, Marcus Atilius (d. *c.* 250 B.C.), obtained a triumph as Roman consul in 267 B.C. Consul again (256), he defeated the Carthaginian fleet, then landed in Africa, and, at first victorious, at last suffered a total defeat and was taken prisoner (255). He remained five years in captivity, until, reverses inducing the Carthaginians to sue for peace, he was released on parole and sent to Rome with the Punic envoys. He successfully dissuaded the senate from agreeing to their proposals, then, according to legend, returned to Carthage, and was put to death with horrible tortures.

REGULUS, or Rule, St (4th cent. A.D.), according to legend a monk of Constantinople or bishop of Patras, who in A.D. 347 came to Muckross or Kilrimont (afterwards St Andrews), bringing relics of St Andrew from the East. For the possible identification of him with an Irish St Riagail of the 6th century, see Skene's *Celtic Scotland* (1877).

REICH, Ferdinand (1799–1882), German physicist, professor at the Freiberg School of Mines, codiscoverer with Richter of the element indium (1863).

REICHENBACH, *rī'кнĕn-baкн,* **(1) Hans** (1891–1953), German philosopher, born in Hamburg, was professor at Berlin (1926–33), Istanbul (1933–38) and from 1938 at California. An early associate of the 'Vienna Circle' of logical positivists, he was best known for his frequencies probability logic, in which the two truth values are replaced by the multivalued concept 'weight', set out in *Warscheinlichkeitslehre,* 'Theory of Probability' (1935; trans. 1949). Other works include *Experience and Prediction* (1938) and the posthumous papers, *Modern Philosophy of Science,* ed. M. Reichenbach (1959).

(2) Heinrich Gottlieb Ludwig (1793–1879), German botanist and zoologist, from 1820 professor at Dresden. His writings include *Iconographia Botanica seu Plantae Criticae* (1823–32) and *Handbuch des Natürlichen Pflanzensystems* (1837).

(3) Heinrich Gustav (1824–89), German botanist, son of (2), was a Hamburg professor from 1862. He wrote on orchids, and in 1864 was director of the Hamburg botanical gardens.

(4) Karl, Baron von (1788–1869), German natural philosopher and industrialist, born at Stuttgart, in 1821–34 made a fortune as a manufacturer at Blansko in Moravia. He worked at the compound products of the distillation of organic substances, and discovered paraffin (1830) and creosote (1833). Studying animal magnetism, he discovered, as he thought, a new force, which he called Od, intermediate between electricity, magnetism, heat and light, and recognizable only by the nerves of sensitive persons. He wrote on the geology of Moravia, on magnetism and several works on 'odic force' (1852–58). See Lives by Schrötter (1869) and Fechner (1876).

REICHSTADT, Duke of. See NAPOLEON II

REICHSTEIN, Tadeusz, rīKH'shtīn (1897–), Swiss chemist, born in Poland, has done outstanding work on the adrenal hormones and received (with Kendall and Hench) the Nobel award for medicine in 1950.

REID, (1) Sir George (1841–1913), Scottish painter, born at Aberdeen, A.R.S.A. (1870), R.S.A. (1877), from 1891 (when he was knighted) to 1902 was P.R.S.A. Best known by his portraits, he also produced admirable landscapes and book illustrations.

(2) or Robertson, John (1721–1807), Scottish soldier and musician, of Perthshire stock, entered the army in 1745, rose to be general, was a flute-player and composer, and left £50,000 to found a chair of music at Edinburgh.

(3) Sir Robert Threshie. See LOREBURN.

(4) Thomas (1710–96), head of the Scottish school of Philosophy, was born at Strachan manse, Kincardineshire, took his M.A. at Marischal College, Aberdeen, in 1726, and was college librarian 1733–36. He then visited Oxford, Cambridge and London, and in 1737 became minister of New Machar in Aberdeenshire. In 1739 appeared Hume's Treatise on Human Nature, which determined Reid to seek a new foundation for the common notions as to a material world; and he became the chief of a school whose aim was to deliver philosophy from scepticism, by resting finally on principles of intuitive or a priori origin. In 1752 he became professor of Philosophy in King's College, Aberdeen, in 1763 of Moral Philosophy at Glasgow; and in 1764 he published his Inquiry into the Human Mind. He retired from the duties of his chair in 1780. In 1785 the Philosophy of the Intellectual Powers appeared, in 1788 the Active Powers. See Life by Dugald Stewart in Reid's works (1803), the edition by Sir W. Hamilton (1853), sketch by A. C. Fraser (1899), and study by O. M. Jones (1927).

(5) Thomas Mayne (1818–83), Irish writer of boys' stories, born at Ballyroney, Co. Down, in 1840 emigrated to New Orleans, and served in the U.S. army during the Mexican war (1847). Returning to England in 1849, he settled down to a literary life in London, Bucks and Herefordshire. His vigorous style and profusion of hairbreadth escapes delighted his readers. Among his books were the Rifle Rangers (1850), Scalp Hunters (1851), Boy Hunters (1853), War Trail (1857), Boy Tar (1859), and Headless Horseman (1866). See Captain Mayne Reid by his widow, E. Reid (1900).

(6) Sir Thomas Wemyss (1842–1905), Scottish journalist and biographer, born at Newcastle, edited the Leeds Mercury 1870–87, then was manager of Messrs Cassell, and in 1890–99 editor of the Speaker. He was knighted in 1894. He wrote Lives of Charlotte Brontë and Lord Houghton, a book about Tunis and several novels.

(7) Sir William (1791–1858), Scottish meteorologist, soldier and administrator, writer on winds and storms, born at Kinglassie, Fife, served with high distinction in the Peninsular war, and was governor of Bermuda, the Windwards and Malta.

REIMARUS, Hermann Samuel, rī-mah'roos (1694–1768), German philosopher, born in Hamburg, from 1728 held an Oriental chair in his native city. His famous Wolfenbüttelsche Fragmente eines Ungenannten, first published by Lessing in 1774–78, denied the supernatural origin of Christianity. He wrote also on natural religion in his Vornehmste Wahrheiten der natürlichen Religion. See studies by Strauss (trans. 1879), Engert (1908 and 1916).

REINECKE, Karl, rī'nekė (1824–1910), German pianist and composer, born at Altona, from 1860 to 1895 was leader of the Leipzig Gewandhaus orchestra. In his day he was considered unrivalled as an interpreter of Mozart.

REINHARDT, Max, rīn'hart (1873–1943), Austrian theatre manager, born at Baden near Vienna, did much to reorganize the art and technique of production. His most notable success was The Miracle (London 1911). Other productions were Everyman and Faust for the Salzburg festivals of 1920 ff. He left Hitler's Germany in 1933 and died in New York.

REITH, John Charles Walsham, 1st Baron Reith of Stonehaven, reeth (1889–1971), British statesman and engineer, born in Stonehaven. He was educated at Glasgow Academy and Gresham's School, Holt, and served an engineering apprenticeship in Glasgow. Later entering the field of radio communication, he became the first general manager of the British Broadcasting Corporation in 1922 and its director-general from 1927 to 1938. He was M.P. for Southampton in 1940, and minister of works and buildings from 1940 to 1942. Created baron in 1940, he was chairman of the Commonwealth Telecommunications Board from 1946 to 1950. See his autobiographical Into the Wind (1949) and Wearing Spurs (1966). The B.B.C. inaugurated the Reith Lectures in 1948 in honour of his influence on broadcasting.

REIZENSTEIN, Franz, rī'zėn-shtīn (1911–), German composer and pianist, studied under Hindemith and in 1934 came to England, where he was a pupil of Vaughan Williams. Among his compositions are cello, piano and violin concertos, the cantata Voices by Night, two radio operas, and chamber and piano music.

RÉJANE, Gabrielle, ray-zhan (1856–1920), French actress, born in Paris, was noted for her playing of such parts as 'Zaza' and 'Madame Sans-Gêne'. Equally gifted in both tragic and comic rôles, she was regarded in France almost as highly as Bernhardt and was also popular in England and the U.S.A.

REMAK, Robert (1815–65), German physician, born in Posen, from 1859 a Berlin professor, studied pathology, embryology, and was a pioneer in electrotherapy.

REMARQUE, Erich Maria, re-mahrk' (1898– 1970), German novelist, born in Osnabrück, went to the United States in 1939 and became a naturalized American. He wrote All Quiet on the Western Front (1929), The Road Back (1931), The Black Obelisk (1957), &c.

REMBRANDT, in full Rembrandt Harmensz van Rijn (1606–69), Dutch painter, born at Leyden, the son of a prosperous miller called Harmen Gerritsz van Rijn. From his twelfth or thirteenth year he studied painting under various masters, particularly Pieter Lastmann in Amsterdam, who possibly influenced his early work by introducing him to Italian art and especially the art of Caravaggio. He began his career as an etcher early, and etched beggars and picturesque heads, including his own; also *Christ presented in the Temple*. Other works of this early period include his *Philosopher* (National Gallery) and *Supper at Emmaus* (Paris). In 1631 he settled in Amsterdam, where he set up a studio and took pupils, still finding time to paint portraits and biblical subjects and to etch forty plates in the same year. *The Anatomical Lesson* dates from 1632, and with it his reputation as a portrait painter was assured. In 1634 he married Saskia van Ulenburgh (1613–42), whom we know by the portraits her husband made of her. The year of her death produced the famous *Night Watch*. Commissioned by an officers' guild, Rembrandt produced his artistic masterpiece at the expense of his popularity. His subjects, but for two in the foreground, are in shadow and this first flouting of the conventions was followed by other financial failures. He was bankrupt now and unfashionable, but he did not relax his diligence. He continued to work with undiminished energy and power. His portraits, no longer of the wealthy burghers, became less elaborate, more arresting and displayed a deep insight into the characters of his sitters. He reached the height of his greatness with his self-portrait (National Gallery) and with the portraits of Hendrickje Stoffels (with whom he lived after the death of his wife). In his landscapes his use of light, as in all his work, was effective and often dramatic. To religious painting he brought a simplicity without detracting from the mystical significance of the subjects. His works (preserved) total over 650 oil paintings, 2000 drawings and studies, and 300 etchings. He was not blind to the merits of Italian art, but his own practice was founded on the direct study of nature, both in human life and landscape. His chiaroscuro is always conducive to his purpose. No artist ever combined more delicate skill with more energy and power. His treatment of mankind is full of human sympathy; his special study was old age. See Lives by Vosmaer (2nd ed. 1877), Michel (trans. 1893), Rosenburg (1949), de Beaufort (1959); books by M. Bell (1907), Baldwin Brown (1907), Bode (1897–1908); on the etchings by Hamerton (1894), A. M. Hind (1912); C. H. de Groot's *Catalogue raisonné* of 17th-century Dutch painters (vol. vi; trans. 1916). See also *Drawings*, ed. Benesch (6 vols. 1958).

REMIGIUS, St. See REMY.

REMINGTON, Philo (1816–89), American inventor, born at Litchfield, N.Y., entered his father's small-arms factory, and for twenty-five years superintended the mechanical department. The perfecting of the Remington breech-loading rifles and the Remington typewriter was largely due to him.

REMIZOV, Alexei Mikhailovich (1877–1957), Russian writer, born in Moscow, lived in St Petersburg, but left Russia at the revolution,

going first to Berlin and finally settling in Paris. His writing is full of national pride and a deep love of old Russian traditions and folklore; it contains realism, fantasy and humour. His main works are the novels, *The Pond*, *The Clock*, *Fifth Pestilence* and *Sisters of the Cross*, legends, plays and short stories.

RÉMUSAT, *ray-mü-za*, (1) **Charles François Marie, Comte de** (1797–1875), was born at Paris, son of the Comte de Rémusat (1762–1823), who was chamberlain to Napoleon. He early developed liberal ideas, and took to journalism. He signed the journalists' protest which brought about the July Revolution, was elected deputy for Toulouse, in 1836 became under-secretary of state for the Interior and in 1840 minister of the Interior. Exiled after the *coup d'état*, he devoted himself to literary and philosophical studies, till, in 1871, Thiers called him to the portfolio of Foreign Affairs, which he retained until 1873. Among his writings are *Essais de philosophie* (1842); *Abélard* (1845); *L'Angleterre au XVIIIᵉ siècle* (1856); studies on *St Anselm* (1853), *Bacon* (1857), *Channing* (1857), *John Wesley* (1870) and *Lord Herbert of Cherbury* (1874); *Histoire de la philosophie en Angleterre de Bacon à Locke* (1875); and two philosophical dramas, *Abélard* (1877) and *La Saint Barthélemy* (1878). See his *Correspondance* (1883–86). The *Mémoires* (1879–80) and *Lettres* (1881) of his mother, **Claire, Comtesse de Rémusat** (1780–1821), *dame du palais* to Josephine, both translated into English, throw a flood of light on the society of the First Empire and the character of Napoleon.

(2) **Jean Pierre Abel** (1788–1832), French physician and Chinese scholar, born at Paris, took his diploma in medicine in 1813, but in 1811 had published an essay on Chinese literature. In 1814 he was made professor of Chinese in the Collège de France. Among his numerous works are one on the Tartar tongues (1820) and his great *Grammaire chinoise* (1822). He wrote also on Chinese writing (1827), medicine, topography and history, and *Mélanges* (1843). In 1822 he founded the Société Asiatique, and in 1824 became curator of the oriental department in the Bibliothèque Royale.

REMY, St (*c*. 438–533), Bishop of Rheims, according to Gregory of Tours baptized Clovis, king of the Franks, in the Christian faith. He was known as the Apostle of the Franks.

RENAN, Ernest, *rė-nã* (1823–92), French philologist and historian, born at Tréguier in Brittany, till his sixteenth year was trained for the church there, wholly under clerical influences. He was one of the youths chosen in 1836 by the Abbé Dupanloup for the Catholic seminary of St Nicolas du Chardonnet in Paris, whence, after three years, he was transferred to St Sulpice and its branch at Issy. As the result of the study of Hebrew and of German criticism, traditional Christianity became impossible for him; in 1845 he quitted St Sulpice and abandoned all thoughts of the church as a profession. With his elder sister Henriette's assistance and counsel he was enabled to follow out his purpose, a life of study untrammelled by creeds or formularies. In 1850 he obtained a post in the Bibliothèque Nationale, and having become known through *mémoires* on Oriental studies, in 1860 he was one of a commission sent by the government to study the remains of Phoenician civilization. In 1861 he was chosen professor of Hebrew in the Collège de France; but the emperor, inspired by the clerical party, refused to ratify the appointment; and it was not until 1870 that he was established in the chair. In 1878 he was elected to the Academy. His work as author began with a paper (1847), collected into his *Histoire générale des langues sémitiques* (1854). *Averroès et l'Averroïsme* (1852) proved his familiarity with the life and thought of the Middle Ages. And he wrote frequent essays, afterwards collected in his *Études d'histoire religieuse* (1856) and *Essais de morale et de critique* (1859). But his European reputation dates from the publication of the *Vie de Jésus* (1863), first in the series which its author regarded as his special work, the *Histoire des origines du Christianisme*. In the *Vie de Jésus* the combined weakness and strength of Renan's method were exaggerated to caricature. Of the volumes that followed, those on St Paul (1869) and Marcus Aurelius (1882) are specially noteworthy. In completion of his life's task Renan undertook a history of the people of Israel (5 vols. 1887–94). Other works include books on Job (1858), the Song of Solomon (1860), Ecclesiastes (1882), *Questions contemporaines, Dialogues philosophiques, Drames philosophiques, Souvenirs d'enfance* (1883), *L'Abesse de Jouarre* (1888), and *Ma Soeur Henriette* (1895; trans. as *Brother and Sister*, 1896). Madame Renan (1838–94), whom he married in 1856, was a niece of Ary Scheffer. In London he delivered the Hibbert Lectures (1880), *The Influence of Rome on Christianity*. See Life by Mme Darmesteter (1897), and books by Monod (1893), Barry (1905), Guérard (1913), Mott (1921), Pommier (1923); Girard and Moncel, *Bibliographie* (1923), J. Psichari (1925), H. Psichari (1947) and J. H. Chadbourne (1958).

RENAUDOT, Théophraste, *rĕ-nō-dō* (1586–1653), French Protestant doctor, born at Loudun, settled in Paris in 1624. In 1631 he founded the first French newspaper, the *Gazette de France,* also started the earliest Mont-de-Piété (1637), and advocated gratis dispensaries. See Life by Bonnefont (1893).

RENÉ I, 'the Good' (1409–80), Duke of Anjou, Count of Provence and Piedmont, failed in his efforts (1438–42) to make good his claim to the crown of Naples, married his daughter to Henry VI of England (1445), and ultimately devoted himself to Provençal poetry and agriculture at Aix. See Life by Lecoy de la Marche (Paris 1875).

RENI, GUIDO, *ray'nee* (1575–1642), Italian painter, born near Bologna, studied under Calvaert and Ludovico Caracci, and went to Rome in 1599 and again in 1605. *Aurora and the Hours* there is usually regarded as his masterpiece, but some critics rank even higher the unfinished *Nativity* in San Martino at Naples. Because of a quarrel with Cardinal Spinola regarding an altar piece for St Peter's

he left Rome and settled at Bologna, where he died. He was a prolific painter, and his works are in all the chief European galleries. He also produced some vigorous etchings. See study by M. v. Boehn (1925).

RENNELL, (1) **James** (1742–1830), English geographer, served in the navy, became a major in the East India Company's army, and surveyor-general of Bengal. His *Bengal Atlas* was published in 1779 and in 1781 he was elected a fellow of the Royal Society. Interested in hydrography, ancient geography and oceanography, he was the author of a *Treatise on the Comparative Geography of Western Asia* (posthumously 1831). See Life by C. R. Markham (1895).

(2) **James Rennell Rodd, 1st Baron** (1858–1941), English poet, historian, diplomatist, born in London, was educated at Haileybury and Balliol. His principal diplomatic service was in Italy, where he was ambassador (1908–19). He wrote many books, including the volume of poetry *Ballads of the Fleet* (1897), and the scholarly works *Rome of the Renaissance and Today* (1932) and *Homer's Ithaca* (1927). His *Social and Diplomatic Memories* were published in 3 vols. (1922–25).

RENNER, Karl (1870–1950), Austrian statesman who became first chancellor of the Austrian republic (1918–20), was imprisoned as a Socialist leader in 1934, and was chancellor again (1945). He wrote political works, and a national song. From 1946 until his death he was president of Austria.

RENNIE, (1) **George** (1791–1866), Scottish engineer, eldest son of (2), born in London, was superintendent of the machinery of the Mint, and aided his father. With his brother John he carried on an immense business—shipbuilding, railways, bridges, harbours, docks, machinery and marine engines.

(2) **John** (1761–1821), Scottish civil engineer, born at Phantassie farm, East Linton, after working as a millwright with Andrew Meikle studied at Edinburgh University (1780–83). In 1784 he entered the employment of Messrs Boulton & Watt; in 1791 he set up in London as an engineer, and soon became famous as a bridge-builder—building Kelso (1803), Leeds, Musselburgh, Newton-Stewart, Boston, New Galloway, and the old Southwark and Waterloo Bridges, and planning London Bridge. He made many important canals; drained fens; designed the London Docks, and others at Blackwall, Hull, Liverpool, Dublin, Greenock and Leith; and improved harbours and dockyards at Portsmouth, Chatham, Sheerness and Plymouth, where he constructed the celebrated breakwater (1811–41). See Smiles's *Lives of the Engineers* (1874).

(3) **John** (1794–1874), Scottish engineer, second son of (2), born in London, was knighted in 1831 on his completion of London Bridge. He was engineer to the Admiralty and wrote on harbours. See his *Autobiography* (1875).

RENOIR, (1) **Jean,** *rĕ-nwahr* (1894–), French film director, son of (2), born in Paris, won the Croix de Guerre in World War I, and from script-writing turned to film-making. His version of Zola's *Nana* (1926) his anti-war masterpiece, *La Grande Illusion*

(1937), *La Bête humaine* (1939), *The Golden Coach* (1953) and *Le Déjeuner sur l'herbe* (1959) are among the masterpieces of the cinema. He left France in 1941 during the invasion and became a naturalized American.

(2) **Pierre Auguste** (1841–1919), French Impressionist artist, father of (1), was born at Limoges. He began as a painter on porcelain; in this trade, and then as a painter of fans, he made his first acquaintance with the work of Watteau and Boucher which was to influence his choice of subject matter as deeply as Impressionism was to influence his style. He entered the studio of Gleyre in 1862 and began to paint in the open air about 1864. From the year 1870 onwards he obtained a number of commissions for portraits. In the years 1874–79 and in 1882 he exhibited with the Impressionists, his important, controversial picture of sunlight filtering through leaves—the *Moulin de la Galette* (in the Louvre) dating from 1876. He visited Italy in 1880 and during the next few years painted a series of *Bathers* in a more cold and classical style influenced by Ingres and Raphael. He then returned to hot reds, orange, and gold to portray nudes in sunlight, a style which he continued to develop to the end, although his hands were crippled by arthritis in later years. He is represented in the Louvre, the Tate Gallery, and in many public galleries in the United States. See monographs by G. Besson (1932) and M. Drucker (1944), and *Renoir, My Father* (1962) by (1).

RENOUF, Sir Peter Le Page, *rĕ-noof* (1822–1897), British Egyptologist, born in Guernsey, studied at Oxford and turned Catholic in 1842. He was professor of Ancient History and Oriental Languages in Dublin 1855–64, a school inspector 1864–85, and keeper of Egyptian and Assyrian antiquities at the British Museum 1885–91. He wrote on ancient Egypt, notably a translation of *The Book of the Dead*, and gave the Hibbert Lectures on Egyptian religion in 1879.

RENOUVIER, Charles Bernard, *rĕ-noo-vyay* (1815–1903), French idealist philosopher, born at Montpellier, was a modified Kantian and founder of the movement known as Neocriticism. His works include *Essai de critique générale* (4 vols. 1859–64), *Psychologie rationelle* (3 vols. 1875), *Histoire et solutions des problèmes métaphysiques* (1901) and *Le Personnalisme* (1903). See books by Séailles (1905) and Arnal (1908).

RENWICK, *ren'ik,* (1) **James** (1662–88), Scottish Covenanter, born at Moniaive, studied at Edinburgh University, joined the Cameronians, proclaimed the Lanark Declaration (1682), and was sent to complete his studies in Holland. In 1683 he preached his first sermon at Darmead Moss near Cambusnethan; in 1684 he was outlawed for his *Apologetic Declaration.* On James VII's accession he published at Sanquhar a declaration rejecting him. A reward was offered for his capture; and at last he was taken in Edinburgh, and executed. See Life by Simpson (1843).

(2) **James** (1790–1863), physicist, born at Liverpool of Scottish-American parents, was professor at Columbia College, N.Y., and wrote books on mechanics. His son **James**

(1818–95) designed Grace Church and St Patrick's Cathedral, New York, the Smithsonian Institution and the Bank of the State of New York.

REPSOLD, Johann Georg (1770–1830), German instrument-maker, designed a special pendulum, named after him, for the accurate determination of ' g '. Chief of the Hamburg fire brigade, he was killed when a wall collapsed during a fire.

REPTON, Humphrey (1752–1818), English landscape-gardener, was born at Bury St Edmunds. He completed the change from the formal gardens of the early 18th century to the ' picturesque ' types favoured later.

RESNAIS, Alain (1922–), French film director, born at Vannes, Brittany, studied at l'Institut des hautes études cinématographiques in Paris, made a series of outstanding and prizewinning short documentaries, e.g., *Van Gogh* (1948, Oscar award), *Guernica* (1950) and *Nuit et Bruillard* (1955), a haunting evocation of the horror of Nazi concentration camps. His first feature film, *Hiroshima mon amour* (1959), intermingles the nightmare World War II past of its heroine with her unhappy love for a Japanese against the tragic background of present-day Hiroshima. His next film, *L'Année dernière à Marienbad* (1961), illustrates his interest in the merging of past, present and future to the point of ambiguity, being hailed as a surrealistic and dreamlike masterpiece by some, as a confused and tedious failure by others. *Muriel* (1963) and *La Guerre est finie* (1967) had similarly mixed receptions.

RESPIGHI, Ottorino, *res-pee'gee* (1879–1936), Italian composer, was born at Bologna. A pupil of Bruch and of Rimski-Korsakov, his works include nine operas, the symphonic poems, *Fontane di Roma* and *Pini di Roma*, and the ballet *La Boutique fantasque*.

RESTIF (Rétif) de la Bretonne, Nicolas Edme, *res-teef* or *ray-teef* (1734–1806), French writer, was born at Sacy, Yonne. His many voluminous and licentious novels, such as *Le Pied de Fanchette, Le Paysan perverti* and *Mémoires d'un homme de qualité*, give a vividly truthful picture of 18th-century French life, and entitle him to be considered as a forerunner of realism. His own not unsullied life he described in the 16-volume *Monsieur Nicolas* (1794–97). He also wrote on social reform.

RESZKE, *resh'kĕ,* Polish family of singers, born in Warsaw:

(1) **Edouard de** (1856–1917), operatic bass, successful throughout Europe in a wide range of parts. He and his brother Jean frequently appeared together.

(2) **Jean de** (1850–1925), operatic tenor, brother of (1), began his career as a baritone, and after his début as a tenor in 1879, he succeeded in most of the leading French and Italian operatic rôles, adding Wagnerian parts after 1885. Originally criticised for his acting, he developed into an artist of convincing authority. See study by C. Leiser (1933).

(3) **Joséphine de** (1855–91), operatic soprano, sister of (1) and (2), sang at the Paris Opéra but withdrew from the stage on her marriage with Baron von Kronenburg.

RETHEL, Alfred, *ray'tel* (1816–59), German historical painter, born at Diepenbend near Aachen, decorated the imperial hall of the Römer, Frankfurt-am-Main, the Council House of Aachen with frescoes of the Life of Charlemagne, and executed a series of fantastic designs (1842–44; Dresden) on the theme of Hannibal's crossing of the Alps. His later drawings and woodcuts bear witness to his advancing mental derangement.

RETZ, (1) Rais, or Raiz, Gilles de Laval, Baron de (1404–40), a Breton of high rank who fought by the side of the Maid at Orleans, became marshal of France at twenty-five, but soon retired to his estates, where for over ten years he is alleged to have indulged in the most infamous orgies, kidnapping 150 children, who were sacrificed to his lusts or sorceries. He was hanged and burned at Nantes, after a trial closed by his own confession. See works by Bossard (1886), Baring-Gould (1865), Vizetelly (1902), Vincent and Binns (1926).

(2) Jean Paul de Gondi, Cardinal de (1614–1679), French churchman, born at Montmirail, was bred for the church in spite of amours, duels and political intrigues. He became in 1643 coadjutor to his uncle, the Archbishop of Paris, plotted against Mazarin, and instigated the outbreak of the Fronde in 1648. He received a cardinal's hat, but in 1652 was flung into prison. After two years he made his escape, wandered in Spain and England, appeared at Rome, and in 1662 made his peace with Louis XIV by resigning his claim to the archbishopric in exchange for the abbacy of St Denis and restoration to his other benefices. His debts (four million francs!) he provided for in 1675 by making over to his creditors his entire income save 20,000 livres. Retz figures pleasingly in the letters of Madame de Sévigné. His own masterly *Mémoires* (1655; best ed. in ' Les Grands Écrivains ', 10 vols. 1872–90) throw much light on the Fronde. See works by Curnier (1863), Topin (3rd ed. 1872), Chantelauze (1878–79), Gazier (1876), Ogg (1912), Batiffol (1927, 1930), Dyssard (1938).

RETZSCH, Friedrich August Moritz (1779–1857), German painter and engraver, born in Dresden, became a professor there in 1824. He acquired great celebrity by his etchings in outline after Schiller, Goethe, Fouqué and Shakespeare. His masterpiece is ' The Chessplayers '.

REUCHLIN, Johann, *royкн'lin* (1455–1522), German humanist and Hebraist, born at Pforzheim, as travelling companion to a prince of Baden visited Paris, where he studied Greek, at Basel wrote his Latin dictionary (1476), made a second sojourn in France, and in 1481 set up as lecturer at Tübingen. In 1482, 1490 and 1498 he was in Italy on state business; in 1492 we find him studying Hebrew under a learned Jewish court physician. In 1496 Reuchlin went to Heidelberg, where he became the main promoter of Greek studies in Germany; in 1500 he received a judicial appointment at Stuttgart. In 1506 appeared his *Rudimenta Linguae Hebraicae*. In 1510 Pfefferkorn, a Jewish renegade, urged the emperor to burn all Jewish books except the Old Testament; and Reuchlin's contention that no Jewish books should be destroyed except those directly written against Christianity drew on him the enmity of the Dominicans of Cologne, especially of the inquisitor Hoogstraten; but all the independent thinkers in Germany (see HUTTEN) were on his side; and the Duke of Bavaria appointed him in 1519 professor at Ingolstadt. Reuchlin edited various Greek texts, published a Greek grammar, a whole series of polemical pamphlets, and a satirical drama (against the Obscurantists), and in *De Verbo Mirifico* and *De Arte Cabbalistica* shows a theosophico-cabbalistic tendency. See books on him by Geiger (1871), Horawitz (1877) and Holstein (1888).

REUTER, *roy'tér*, (1) Fritz (1810–74), Plattdeutsch humorist, born at Stavenhagen in Mecklenburg-Schwerin, studied law at Rostock and Jena. In 1833 he was condemned to death—with other Jena students he had indulged in wild talk about the fatherland—a sentence commuted to thirty years' imprisonment. Released in 1840, with his career spoilt and his health ruined, he tried to resume his legal studies, learned farming, and taught pupils. His rough Plattdeutsch verse setting of the jokes and merry tales of the countryside, *Läuschen un Rimels* (1853), became at once a great favourite; another humorous poem, *Reis' nah Belligen* (1855), was equally successful, followed by a second volume of *Läuschen un Rimels* (1858) and the tragic poem *Kein Hüsung* (1858). The rest of his best works, except the poem *Hanne Nüte* (1860), were all written in Low German prose. *Ut de Franzosentid* (1860; Eng. trans. as *The Year '13*, 1870), *Ut mine Festungstid* (1862), and *Ut mine Stromtid* (1862–64) made him famous throughout all Germany. He lived at Eisenach from 1863, and there he died. See Wilbrandt's biography in the *Werke* (15 vols. 1863–75), and works by Glagau (2nd ed. 1875), Ebert (1874), Gaedertz (1890 and 1900), Römer (1895), Raatz (1895), Brandes (1899), Dohse (1910).

(2) Paul Julius, Freiherr von (1816–99), born at Cassel, in 1849 formed at Aachen an organization for transmitting commercial news by telegraph. In 1851 he fixed his headquarters in London; and gradually his system spread to the remotest regions. In 1865 he converted his business into a limited liability company, and in 1871 was made a baron by the Duke of Saxe-Coburg-Gotha. See G. Storey, *Reuters' Century* (1951) and R. Jones, *A Life in Reuters* (1951).

REUTHER, Walter Philip, *roy'tér* (1907–70), American trade-union leader, president of the American Auto Workers' Union, in 1935 began to organize the automobile workers into what later became the largest union in the world, and fought against Communist influence in trade unionism.

REVERE, Paul, *ré-veer'* (1735–1818), American patriot, hero of a poem by Longfellow, was born in Boston, Mass., and after serving as lieutenant of artillery (1756), followed the trade of goldsmith and copperplate printer. He was one of the party that destroyed the tea in Boston harbour, and he was at the head of a secret society formed to watch the British. On April 18, 1775, the night before

Lexington and Concord, he rode from Charleston to Lexington and Lincoln, rousing the minutemen as he went. In the war he became lieutenant-colonel of artillery. In 1801 he founded the Revere Copper Company at Canton, Mass. See Lives by Goss (2 vols. 1892) and Taylor (1930).

RÉVILLE, Albert, ray-veel (1826–1906), French Protestant theologian of the advanced school, born at Dieppe, was pastor of the Walloon Church at Rotterdam 1851–72, lectured at Leyden, and in 1880 became professor of the History of Religions in the Collège de France. His works include a comparative history of philosophy and religion (1859; trans. 1864).

REYBAUD, Louis, ray-bō (1799–1879), French journalist and politician, born at Marseilles, travelled in the Levant and India, and returning to Paris in 1829, wrote for the Radical papers and edited a history of the French expedition to Egypt (1830–36), &c. His Réformateurs ou Socialistes modernes (1840–43) popularized the word ' Socialism '. He also wrote satirical novels, ridiculing the manners and institutions of his time.

REYMONT, Władysław Stanislaw, ray'mont (1867–1925), Polish novelist, born at Kobiele Wielke, author of the tetralogy, The Peasants (1904–09), was awarded a Nobel prize in 1924. Other books are The Comédienne (1896; trans. 1920) and The Year 1794 (1913–18).

REYNAUD, Paul, ray-nō (1878–1966), French statesman, born at Barcelonnette, originally a barrister, held many French government posts, being premier during the fall of France in 1940. He was imprisoned by the Germans during World War II. Afterwards he re-entered politics, until losing his seat in 1962, and was a delegate to the Council of Europe (1949). Among several works are La France a sauvé l'Europe (1947), Au Coeur de la mêlée 1930–45 (trans. 1955), and his Mémoires (1960, 1963).

REYNOLDS, (1) George William MacArthur (1814–79), English journalist, Chartist, and blood-and-thunder novelist, born at Sandwich. In 1850 he started Reynolds's Weekly.

(2) John Fulton (1820–63), American army officer, born at Lancaster, Pa., was commandant at West Point in 1859, fought at Mechanicsville and Gaines's Mills, and was taken prisoner at Glendale, but exchanged in August 1862. At the second battle of Bull Run his brigade prevented a total rout. In 1863 he commanded a corps at Fredericksburg, and fell at Gettysburg.

(3) John Hamilton (1794–1852), English minor poet and lawyer, born at Shrewsbury and educated at Christ's Hospital, friend of Leigh Hunt, Keats and Hood.

(4) Sir Joshua (1723–92), English portrait painter, was born at Plympton Earls near Plymouth, the seventh son of a clergyman and schoolmaster. Sent in 1740 to London to study art, in 1747 he settled at Plymouth Dock, now Devonport. At Rome (1749–52) he studied Raphael and Michelangelo, and in the Vatican caught a chill which permanently affected his hearing. He then established himself in London, and by 1760 was at the height of his fame. In 1764 he

founded the literary club of which Dr Johnson, Garrick, Burke, Goldsmith, Boswell and Sheridan were members. He was one of the earliest members of the Incorporated Society of Artists, and on the establishment of the Royal Academy (1768) was elected its first president; in 1769 he was knighted. In that year he delivered the first of his Discourses to the students of the Academy, which, along with his papers on art in the Idler, his annotations to Du Fresnoy's Art of Painting, and his Notes on the Art of the Low Countries (the result of a visit in 1781), show a cultivated literary style. In 1784 he became painter to the king, and finished his Mrs Siddons as the Tragic Muse, a work existing in several versions. In 1789 his sight became affected, and he ceased to paint. The following year was embittered by a dispute with the Academy, which led to his resignation of the presidency, a resolution he afterwards rescinded. He was buried in St Paul's. It is in virtue of his portraits that Reynolds ranks as the head of the English school. They are notable for the power and expressiveness of their handling, and the beauty of their colouring. His pictures of children have an especial tenderness and beauty as in The Strawberry Girl, Simplicity, &c. His works number from two to three thousand; and from these 700 engravings have been executed. See Memoirs by Northcote (1813), The Literary Works (with memoir, &c., by Beechy, 1835), Life by Leslie and Tom Taylor (1865), Catalogue raisonné of the engravings by E. Hamilton (2nd ed. 1884), Reynolds and Gainsborough by Sir W. M. Conway (1885), and Lives by C. Phillips (1894), Graves and Cronin (1900) and D. Hudson (1958).

(5) Osborne (1842–1912), British engineer, born in Belfast, became the first professor of Engineering at Manchester (1868) and a Royal Society gold medallist (1888). He greatly improved centrifugal pumps. The ' Reynolds number ', a dimensionless ratio characterizing the dynamic state of a fluid, takes its name from him.

(6) Samuel William (1773–1835), English engineer, born in London, was an accomplished mezzotinter, and produced many engravings after portraits of Sir Joshua Reynolds, Turner, Lawrence and Opie.

(7) Walter (d. 1327), English churchman, the son of a Windsor baker, was made by Edward II treasurer (1307) and Bishop of Worcester (1308), chancellor (1310), and Archbishop of Canterbury (1314). He later declared for Edward III, whom he crowned.

RHAZES, or Räzi, ray'zeez (fl. 925), Persian physician and alchemist of Baghdad. He wrote many medical works, some of which were translated into Latin and had considerable influence on medical science in the Middle Ages. See A. Castiglioni, History of Medicine (1947).

RHEE, Syngman (1875–1965), Korean statesman, was born near Kaesong. Imprisoned from 1897 to 1904 for campaigning for reform and a constitutional monarchy, he went soon after his release to America, where he was influenced by Wilson, the apostle of self-determination. In 1910 he returned to Japanese-annexed Korea, and after the unsuccesful rising of 1919 he became president of the exiled Korean Provisional Government. On Japan's surrender in 1945 he returned to Korea, and in 1948 was elected president of the Republic of South Korea. He opposed the Korean truce of 1953, calling Korea's continued partition 'appeasement of the Communists'. Reelected for a fourth term as president in March 1960, he was obliged to resign in April after large-scale riots and the resignation of his cabinet. A man of inflexible and often bellicose patriotism, his immense personal authority was derived from a lifetime of resistance and exile. His publications include *Japan Inside Out* (1941).

RHEGIUS, Urbanus (1489–1541), German reformer, preached Lutheran doctrines at Augsburg and later lived at Celle.

RHEINBERGER, Joseph, *rīn'berg-ėr* (1839–1901), German composer, born at Vaduz in Liechtenstein, held musical posts at Munich (1855–94). His works include operas and organ sonatas.

RHETICUS, real name **Georg Joachim von Lauchen** (1514–76), German astronomer and mathematician, born at Feldkirch in Austria, became professor of Mathematics at Wittenberg (1537). He is noted for his trigonometrical tables (1596) and his table of sines to fifteen decimal places (1613). For a time he worked with Copernicus, whose *De Revolutionibus Orbium Coelestium* he was instrumental in publishing. His own *Narratio prima de libris revolutionum Copernici* (1540) was the first account of the Copernican theory. He died at Cassovia in Hungary.

RHIGAS, Konstantinos, *ree'gas* (1760–98), Greek poet, organized the anti-Turkish revolutionary movement at Vienna, but was betrayed and shot.

RHIJN, Pieter Johannes van, *rīn* (1886–1960), Dutch astrophysicist, born at Gouda, educated at Groningen, became the assistant, collaborator and successor of Kapteyn (q.v.).

RHIND, Alexander Henry (1833–63), Scottish antiquary, born at Wick, founded the Rhind Lectures in archaeology, delivered at Edinburgh.

RHINE, Joseph Banks (1895–   ), American psychologist, pioneer of parapsychology, born at Waterloo, Pennsylvania, studied at Chicago and Harvard and in 1937 became professor of Psychology at Duke University. His laboratory-devised experiments involving packs of specially designed cards established the phenomena of extrasensory perception and of telepathy on a statistical basis, since some guessers achieved considerably better results than the average chance successes. See his respectably scientific works *New Frontiers of the Mind* (1937), *Extrasensory Perception* (1940), *Reach of Mind* (1948) and with J. G. Pratt, *Parapsychology* (1958).

RHODES, Cecil John (1853–1902), South African statesman, was born at Bishop's Stortford, where his father was vicar. He was sent for his health to Natal, and subsequently made a fortune at the Kimberley diamond diggings and succeeded in amalgamating the several diamond companies to form the De Beers Consolidated Mines Company in 1888. (In that year he sent £10,000 to Parnell to forward the cause of Irish Home Rule.) He came back to England, entered Oriel College, Oxford, and although his residence was cut short by ill-health, he ultimately took his degree. He entered the Cape House of Assembly as member for Barkly. In 1884 General Gordon asked him to go with him to Khartoum as secretary; but Rhodes declined, having just taken office in the Cape ministry. In 1890 he became prime minister of Cape Colony; but even before this he had become a ruling spirit in the extension of British territory in securing first Bechuanaland as a protectorate (1884) and later (1889) the charter for the British South Africa Co., of which till 1896 he was managing director, and whose territory was later to be known as Rhodesia. His policy was the ultimate establishment of a federal South African dominion under the British flag. In 1895 he was made a member of the privy council. In 1896 he resigned the Cape premiership in consequence of complications arising from the 'unauthorized' raid into the Transvaal of Dr Jameson (q.v.), the Chartered Company's administrator, in aid of the Uitlanders' claims. His action was condemned by the South Africa Commission and by the British government. In the same year he succeeded in quelling the Matabele rebellion by personal negotiations with the chiefs. In 1899 he was capped D.C.L. at Oxford. He was a conspicuous figure during the war of 1899–1902, when he organized the defences of Kimberley during the siege. He left a remarkable will which, besides making great benefactions to Cape Colony, founded scholarships at Oxford for Americans, Germans and colonials. See Lives by Williams (1921), McDonald (1927), Millin (1933) and Gross (1956), and study by Lockhart and Woodhouse (1963).

RHYS, *rees*, (1) **Ernest Percival** (1859–1946), Anglo-Welsh editor and poet, born in London, spent much of his youth in Carmarthen and became a mining engineer. Abandoning this for a writing career in 1886, he was first a freelance, then on the staff of Walter Scott's publishing house, for whom he edited the Camelot Classics series. He is perhaps best known as editor of the Everyman Library of classics. He wrote volumes of romantic verse including *A London Rose* (1891), *Rhymes for Everyman* (1933) and *Song of the Sun* (1937). Also a notable literary critic, he wrote *English Lyric Poetry* (1913). *Everyman Remembers* (1931) and *Wales England Wed* (1941) are volumes of reminiscences.

(2) **Sir John** (1840–1915), Welsh philologist, born in Cardiganshire, taught in Anglesea until 1865, when he entered Jesus College, Oxford, and continued his studies in France and Germany. From 1871 an inspector of schools in Wales, in 1877 he became professor of Celtic at Oxford, in 1881 a fellow of Jesus, and in 1895 its principal. He was a distinguished authority on Celtic philology, author of *Celtic Britain* (1882), *Celtic Heathendom* (Hibbert Lectures, 1888), &c.

RHYS-DAVIDS. See DAVIDS.

RIBALTA, Francisco de (1550–1628), Spanish

painter, born in Castellón de la Plana, studied at Rome, and settled at Valencia. Noted as a painter of historical subjects and for his use of chiaroscuro, his works include *The Last Supper* and his *Christ* in Madrid. His sons, José (1588–1656) and Juan (1597–1628), were also Valencian painters.

RIBBENTROP, Joachim von (1893–1946), German politician, was a wine merchant who became a member of the National Socialist party in 1932. Finally Hitler's adviser in foreign affairs, he was responsible in 1935 for the Anglo-German naval pact, becoming the following year ambassador to Britain and foreign minister (1938–45). He was taken by the British in 1945 and condemned to death and executed at Nuremberg.

RIBERA, Jusepe de (1588–1656), called Lo Spagnoletto (' The Little Spaniard '), Spanish painter and etcher, born at Játiva, settled in Naples, and became court painter. He delighted in the horrible, choosing often such subjects as the martyrdom of the saints and painting them with a bold, unsympathetic power. Later works were calmer and more subtle and include *The Immaculate Conception* and paintings of the Passion.

RIBOT, ree-bō, (1) Alexandre (1842–1923), French statesman, was born at St Omer and became premier in 1892, 1895, 1917, foreign minister 1890–93, finance minister 1914–17. An academician in 1906, he wrote *Letters to a Friend*, which were translated in 1925.

(2) **Théodule Armand** (1839–1916), French psychologist, born at Guingamp, was from 1888 a Collège de France professor. A pioneer in experimental psychology, he wrote many works including *English Psychology* (1873), *Heredity* (1875) and *Diseases of the Will* (1884).

RICARDO, David (1772–1823), English political economist, born in London, was brought up by his father, a Jewish stockbroker, to the same business. In 1793 he married Priscilla Ann Wilkinson, a Quakeress, and turned Christian; then, starting for himself, he made a large fortune by 1814. In 1799 his interest in political economy was awakened by Smith's *Wealth of Nations*. His pamphlet, *The High Price of Bullion, a Proof of the Depreciation of Banknotes* (1809), was an argument in favour of a metallic basis. In 1817 appeared the work on which his reputation chiefly rests, *Principles of Political Economy and Taxation*, a discussion of value, wages, rent, &c. In 1819 he became Radical M.P. for Portarlington. He died at his Gloucestershire seat, Gatcombe Park. His collected works were edited, with a Life, by McCulloch (1846); his letters to Malthus, to McCulloch, and to H. Trower and others were edited by Bonar and Hollander (1887–1899). See study by Hollander (1910).

RICASOLI, Baron Bettino (1809–80), Italian statesman, born at Florence, was a leading agriculturist, and for ten years worked successfully at draining the Tuscan Maremma. In 1859 he opposed the grand-duke, on whose flight he was made dictator of Tuscany. A strong advocate of the unification of Italy, he supported Cavour (q.v.) in the struggle to join Piedmont with Tuscany. He was head of the ministry in 1861–62 and 1866–67. See

his *Lettere e documenti* (1886–94), and Lives by Gotti (1894) and Hancock (1926).

RICCI, Matteo, reet'chee (1552–1610), Italian missionary, founder of the Jesuit missions in China, was born at Macerata, studied at Rome, and lived at Nanking and at Peking. He so mastered Chinese as to write dialogues, &c., which received much commendation from the Chinese literati, and he met with extraordinary success as a missionary although his methods aroused much controversy.

RICCIO. See Rizzio.

RICE, (1) Edmund Ignatius (1762–1844), Irish philanthropist, born near Callan, was originally a Waterford provision merchant. In 1802–20 he founded the Irish Christian Brothers for the education of the poor. He was superior-general of the order till 1838.

(2) **Elmer** (1892–1967), American dramatist, born Elmer Reizenstein in New York, studied law and took to writing plays. His prolific output includes *The Adding Machine* (1923), *Street Scene* (1929), which won a Pulitzer prize, *The Left Bank* (1931), *Two on an Island* (1940), *Cue for Passion* (1958), &c.

(3) **James** (1843–82), English novelist, from 1872 *collaborateur* with Sir Walter Besant (q.v.), was born at Northampton, studied at Queen's College, Cambridge, drifted from law into literature, and was proprietor and editor of *Once a Week* 1868–72.

RICH, (1) Barnabe (c. 1540–1620), English pamphleteer and romance writer, was born in Essex, and under the patronage of Sir Christopher Hatton served as a soldier in France, the Low Countries and Ireland. His *Apolonius and Silla* (contained in *Riche, his Farewell to the Military Profession*, 1581) was used by Shakespeare as a source for the plot of *Twelfth Night*.

(2) **Edmund.** See Edmund (St).

(3) **Penelope.** See Sidney, Sir Philip.

RICHARD, name of three kings of England:

Richard I (1157–99), Coeur de Lion, third son of Henry II, was born at Oxford, and while still a child was invested with the duchy of Aquitaine, his mother Eleanor's patrimony. Richard did not spend in all his life a full year in England; it may reasonably be doubted whether he could speak English. He was induced by his mother to join his brothers Henry and Geoffrey in their rebellion (1173) against their father (see Henry II); and in 1189 he was again in arms against his father and in league with Philip Augustus of France. Richard became King of England, Duke of Normandy and Count of Anjou on July 5, 1189. But he had already taken the crusader's vows; and to raise the necessary funds he sold whatever he could. In 1190 he and Philip set out for Palestine. Both spent the winter in Sicily, whose throne had just been seized by the Norman Tancred. The latter made his peace by giving up to Richard his sister Johanna, the widowed queen, and her possessions, and by betrothing his daughter to Arthur, Richard's nephew and heir. In 1191 part of Richard's fleet was wrecked on Cyprus, and the crews were most inhospitably treated by the sovereign, Isaac Comnenus. Richard sailed back from Rhodes, routed Isaac, deposed him, and gave his crown to Guy de Lusignan. In Cyprus he married Berengaria of Navarre, and on June 8 landed near Acre, which surrendered. Richard's exploits—his march to Joppa, his two advances on Jerusalem (the city he never beheld), his capture of the fortresses in the south of Palestine, and his relief of Joppa—excited the admiration of Christendom. In September he concluded a three years' peace with Saladin, and started off home alone. He was shipwrecked in the Adriatic, and in disguise made his way through the dominions of his bitter enemy, Leopold, Duke of Austria, but was recognized, seized and handed over to the Emperor Henry VI (1193), who demanded a heavy ransom. Richard's loyal subjects raised the money, and he returned home (March 1194). Although his brother John used his utmost endeavours to prevent his return, Richard generously forgave him; and, proceeding to France, spent the rest of his life warring against Philip. He was killed while besieging the castle of Chaluz, and was buried at Fontevrault. See BLONDEL; Stubbs's *Const. Hist.* (vol. i), and books by K. Norgate (1903, 1924), Ramsay (1903) and P. Henderson (1958).

Richard II (1367–1400), son of Edward the Black Prince, was born at Bordeaux, and succeeded his grandfather, Edward III, June 21, 1377. The government was entrusted to a council of twelve, but John of Gaunt (q.v.) gained control of it. The war going on with France and the extravagance of the court cost money; and more was wasted by the government, for which John of Gaunt was held to be mainly responsible. The poll tax of 1380 provoked popular risings; the men of Essex and Kent, 100,000 strong, marched upon London. The Essex men consented to return home when Richard at Mile End (June 14, 1381) assured them he would liberate the villeins and commute their personal service into money rent. The men of Kent, after destroying the Savoy (Gaunt's palace), burning Temple Bar, opening the prisons, breaking into the Tower, and slaying the Archbishop of Canterbury, met the king at Smithfield (15th), where, during the negotiations, William Walworth, mayor of London, struck down Wat Tyler, their leader. The king at once rode amongst them, exclaiming he would be their leader, and granted them the concessions demanded. From this time John of Gaunt kept much in the background, until in 1386 he retired to the Continent. In 1385 Richard invaded Scotland and burned Edinburgh. About the same time another coalition of the baronial party, headed by the Duke of Gloucester, began to oppose the king. They impeached several of his friends in 1388, and secured convictions and executions. But on May 3, 1389, Richard suddenly declared himself of age; for eight years he ruled as a moderate constitutional monarch, and the country was fairly prosperous. But in 1394 Richard's first wife, Anne of Bohemia, died; in 1396 he married Isabella (1389–1409), daughter o. Charles VI of France, and seems to have adopted French tastes, manners, and ideas, and to have asserted the pretensions of an absolute monarch. He had Gloucester,

Arundel and Warwick arrested for conspiracy. Arundel was beheaded; Gloucester was sent a prisoner to Calais, and died in prison, probably murdered; Warwick was banished, and so was the Archbishop of Canterbury. In 1398 the Duke of Norfolk and the Duke of Hereford (Henry, John of Gaunt's son) were accused of treason; Norfolk was banished for life and Hereford for ten years. In 1399 John of Gaunt died, and Hereford succeeded him as Duke of Lancaster. Richard in May went over to Ireland, and Henry of Lancaster landed on July 4. Richard hurried back, submitted to his cousin at Flint (August 19), and was put in the Tower. On September 29 he resigned the crown, and next day was deposed by parliament, which chose Henry as his successor. Richard seems to have been murdered at Pontefract Castle early in 1400. See study by A. Steel (1941).

Richard III (1452–85), youngest brother of Edward IV, was born at Fotheringhay Castle. After the defeat and death of his father, the Duke of York, in 1460, he was sent to Utrecht for safety, but returned to England after Edward had won the crown (1461), and was created Duke of Gloucester. In the final struggle between York and Lancaster he took an active share, and is believed to have had a hand in the murder of Prince Edward, Henry VI's son, after Tewkesbury, and of Henry himself. In 1472 he married Anne, younger daughter of Warwick the Kingmaker. This alliance was resented by his brother, the Duke of Clarence, who had married the elder sister, and wished to keep Warwick's vast possessions to himself. Clarence was impeached and put to death in the Tower, February 18, 1478. Of this judicial murder Gloucester is likewise accused; but the evidence is slight. In 1482 he commanded the army that invaded Scotland and captured Berwick. In 1483, while still in Yorkshire, he heard of King Edward's death (April 9), and learned that he himself was guardian of his son and heir, Edward V, then thirteen. On his way south the Protector arrested Earl Rivers and Lord Richard Grey, the uncle and stepbrother of the young king, and rallied to himself the old nobility. On June 13 he suddenly accused Lord Hastings, a leading member of the council, of treason, and had him beheaded. On June 16 the queen-dowager was induced to give up her other son, the little Duke of York, and he was put into the Tower to keep his brother, the king, company. The parliament desired Richard to assume the crown, and on July 6 he was crowned, Rivers and Grey having been executed on June 25. Richard's principal supporter all through had been the Duke of Buckingham; but he soon after Richard's coronation entered into a plot with the friends of Henry Tudor, Earl of Richmond (afterwards Henry VII), the chief representative of the House of Lancaster, to effect Richard's overthrow and proclaim Henry king. The attempted rising collapsed, and Buckingham was executed on November 2. It seems to have been shortly before this that Richard is believed to have had his nephews murdered in the Tower. The deed was done so secretly that the nation did not know of it until some time after, and Richard has never been conclusively proved guilty. Henry landed at Milford Haven on August 7, 1485; Richard met him at Bosworth on the 22nd, and there lost his kingdom and his life. Had Richard succeeded to the throne peacefully, he would probably have been a great king, for he was a very capable ruler. See Sir T. More's *History of King Richard III* (1513), H. Walpole's *Historic Doubts* (1768), Jesse's *Memoirs of Richard III* (1862), Legge's *The Unpopular King* (1885), Gairdner's *Life and Reign of Richard III* (3rd ed. 1898), Markham (1907), and Life by Kendall (1955, and ed. by him, *The Great Debate* (1965)).

RICHARD, (1) of Bury. See AUNGERVILLE.

(2) **of Cirencester** (*c.* 1335–1401), English chronicler, was in 1355 a Benedictine monk at Westminster. His only extant work is a poor compilation, the *Speculum Historiale de Gestis Regum Angliae 447–1066*, edited by Prof. Mayor (Rolls series, 1863–69). But Richard's name is best known as the alleged author of the *De Situ Britanniae*, long accepted as an authoritative work on Roman Britain, and first printed in 1758 by its ingenious compiler, Charles Julius Bertram (1723–65), English teacher at Copenhagen, who professed to have discovered it in the Royal Library there. An English translation forms one of the ' Six Old English Chronicles' in Bohn's ' Antiquarian Library' (1848). Stukeley, Gibbon and Lingard cited it with respect; but its authenticity received its deathblow from Mr B. B. Woodward in the *Gentleman's Magazine* (1866–67). See Prof. Mayor's preface.

(3) **of Cornwall** (1209–72), born at Winchester, second son of King John, in 1225–26 with his uncle, William of Salisbury, commanded an expedition which recovered Gascony. Married to a daughter of the Earl of Pembroke, he for some years acted with the English barons. But in 1240–41 he was away on a crusade; in 1244 he married Sanchia of Provence, sister of Queen Eleanor; and in 1257 he was elected titular king of the Romans, and crowned at Aix-la-Chapelle. In the struggle between Henry III and the barons Richard at first acted as peacemaker, but soon he sided with his brother against Simon de Montfort. He was taken prisoner at Lewes (1264), and imprisoned until Evesham (1265) set him free.

(4) **of Wallingford** (1292–1335), studied mathematics and astronomy, and in 1326 became abbot of St Albans. He is regarded as the father of English trigonometry.

RICHARDS, (1) Dickinson W. (1895–), American surgeon, born at Orange, N.J., educated at Yale, specialized in cardiac surgery, which he taught at Columbia University (1928–61), becoming professor of Medicine there in 1947. He was awarded jointly with Cournand and Forssmann the Nobel prize for medicine and physiology in 1956 for developing operational techniques.

(2) **Frank**, properly **Charles Hamilton** (1875–1961), English author of the ' Tom Merry', ' Billy Bunter' and other school-story series, wrote for boys' papers, and particularly for *The Gem* (1906–39) and *The Magnet* (1908–40).

After World War II he published school stories in book and play form, and his *Autobiography* (1952).

(3) **Sir Gordon** (1904–), English jockey, born at Oakengates, Shropshire, the son of a miner, was champion jockey many times from 1925, and by 1952 had established the world record of winning rides (over 4500). He was knighted in 1953, and retired in 1954. thereafter concentrating on training.

(4) **Henry Brinley** (1819–85), Welsh pianist and composer, born at Carmarthen, the son of an organist, composed songs, piano pieces and choruses, among them ' God Bless the Prince of Wales'.

(5) **Ivor A.** See OGDEN.

(6) **Theodore William** (1868–1928), American chemist, born in Germantown, Pennsylvania, became professor at Harvard in 1901 and won the Nobel prize in 1914. Best known for his work on atomic weights, he also carried out important investigations in thermochemistry and thermodynamics.

RICHARDSON, (1) Sir Albert Edward (1880–1964), English architect, born in London. He studied at London University, was professor of Architecture there from 1919 to 1946, and in 1947 became professor in the Royal Academy Schools. He was president of the Royal Academy from 1954 to 1956. His publications include *Design in Civil Architecture* (1948) and *Georgian Architecture* (1949). He was elected to the Royal Academy in 1944 and was knighted in 1956.

(2) **Charles** (1775–1865), English lexicographer, born at Tulse Hill, Norwood, studied law, kept school till 1827 at Clapham, published *Illustrations of English Philology* (1815), but is remembered for his *New English Dictionary* (2 vols. 1835–37). A later work was *On the Study of Language* (1854).

(3) **Dorothy Miller** (1873–1957), English novelist, born at Abingdon, was an early exponent of the ' stream of consciousness' style. She wrote a dozen novels of this type, collected under the title *Pilgrimage*.

(4) **Henry Handel**, pen-name of **Ethel Florence Lindesay** (1870–1946), Australian novelist, was born in Melbourne, travelled and studied on the Continent, and after her marriage in 1895 lived in Strasbourg, in 1904 settling in England. Her first novel was *Maurice Guest* (1908), but she attained distinction only with the third part of the somewhat ponderous trilogy *The Fortunes of Richard Mahony* in 1929. See her unfinished posthumous autobiography *Myself When Young* (1948), study ed. Purdie and Roncoroni (1958) and Life by Buckley (1962).

(5) **Henry Hobson** (1838–86), an American architect, whose specialty was Romanesque, and his chief work Trinity Church, Boston (1877).

(6) **Sir John** (1787–1865), Scottish naturalist, born at Dumfries, in 1807 became a navy-surgeon, served in the Artic expeditions of Parry and Franklin (1819–22, 1825–27), and the Franklin search expedition of 1848–1849. Knighted in 1846, he wrote *Fauna Boreali-Americana* (1829–37), *Ichthyology of the Voyage of H.M.S. Erebus and Terror* (1844–48), &c. See Life by McIlraith (1868).

(7) **Jonathan** (1665–1745), a London portrait painter and writer on art.

(8) **Sir Owen Willans** (1879–1959), English physicist, was born in Dewsbury, Yorks, and educated at Cambridge, where at the Cavendish Laboratory he began his famous work on *thermionics*, a term he himself coined to describe the phenomena of the emission of electricity from hot bodies; for this work he was awarded the 1928 Nobel prize for physics. He was appointed professor of Physics at Princeton in 1906, at King's College, London, in 1914, and from 1924 to 1944 was Yarrow research professor of the Royal Society. Elected F.R.S. in 1913, he was knighted in 1939.

(9) **Sir Ralph** (1902–   ), English actor, was born in Cheltenham. He made his London début in 1926 at the Haymarket, and played leading parts (including the title rôles of Maugham's *Sheppey* and Priestley's *Johnson over Jordan*) with the Old Vic Company (1930–32 and 1938). After war service he became codirector of the Old Vic, played with the Stratford-on-Avon company in 1952, and toured Australia and New Zealand in 1955. Other stage appearances include *Home at Seven*, *The White Carnation* and *A Day at the Sea*, and his films include *The Shape of Things to Come*, *Anna Karenina* and *The Heiress*. He was knighted in 1947. See biography by H. Hobson (1958).

(10) **Samuel** (1689–1761), English novelist, was born in Derbyshire, where his father, a London joiner, had apparently taken refuge after the Monmouth rebellion. He may have gone to Merchant Taylors' School. He was apprenticed to a printer, married his master's daughter and set up in business for himself in Salisbury Court, where in the heyday of his fame (and in much enlarged premises) he received Dr. Johnson, Young and the bluestockings. His wife does not seem to have elevated herself for such company. He was represented as the model parent and champion of women, but his three daughters seem to have had a repressed upbringing. In an autobiographic letter he says that as a boy he wrote their love letters for a group of young women and that this may have been the origin of his epistolary novels. In (1741) he published *Letters Written to and for Particular Friends*, generally referred to as *Familiar Letters*, which gave advice on ' How to think and act justly and prudently in the common concerns of human life '. *Pamela* (1741), his first novel, is also ' a series of familiar letters now first published in order to cultivate the Principles of Virtue and Religion ', and this was the aim of all his works. The virtue taught was of the prudential sort and the manners mean and bourgeois and, as is well known, Fielding started his career with his parody, *Joseph Andrews*, in reaction against the printer's stuffy moralism. After holding out for conditions against her brutal employer, Pamela, in the sequel, plays the Lady Bountiful and mingles easily in genteel life. Whether we dislike more Richardson's morality or his obsequiousness to ' the quality ' is a moot point. In his second novel, *Clarissa, Or the History of a Young Lady*, we are in high life, of which Richardson confessed he knew little. Clarissa Harlowe in the toils of Lovelace is the main theme but

parental repression is also to be corrected. With all her charm Clarissa is too much the victim of her pride for her tragedy to be truly moving and Lovelace is too ambiguous a character to be credible. Nevertheless, our ancestors wallowed through the seven volumes issued in 1748. Richardson was now famous, flattered by society as he took the cure at Tunbridge Wells or was visited at his fine new house, Northend. He corresponded with several society women, including Lady Bradshaigh, Mrs Chapone, &c. Fine ladies and gentlemen like Lady Mary Wortley Montagu, Horace Walpole and Lord Chesterfield might ' hesitate dislike ', the middle orders were enthusiastic. Richardson's third novel, *Sir Charles Grandison*, 1754, designed to portray the perfect gentleman, turns on the question of divided love; Sir Charles having engaged himself to an aristocratic Italian girl is not free to marry Harriet, whom he had rescued from the vicious Sir Hargrave Pollexfen. Love finds a way and in the end Clementina Porretta decides that she cannot marry a heretic. The Italian scene is quite beyond Richardson's experience and Sir Charles has always been voted a prig. Even Lady Bradshaigh protested. Still, if one can find time to get through one or other of these ' large still books ' one may understand why not only English bluestockings but Continental writers raved about them. Diderot's eulogy in *Le Journal étranger*, though extravagant, is sincere—his *La Religieuse* is modelled on Richardson—and Rousseau's *La Nouvelle Héloïse* confesses his discipleship. Apart from its technical advantages (and disadvantages), the epistolary method was a means to suggest authenticity at a time when mere fiction was frowned upon. Thus Richardson called himself the editor not author of his works. He was a redoubtable correspondent. Mrs Barbauld's edition of the correspondence, with biography, did not exhaust it, nor has it been finally collected. See studies by Clara Thomson (1900) based on Mrs Barbauld but with use of the Forster collection of letters. More recent studies are by A. D. McKillop and W. M. Sale, both 1936. Saintsbury's *Letters from Sir Charles Grandison* (1895) is useful to the student as it interweaves a synopsis of the narrative with the letters selected.

RICHELIEU, Armand Jean Duplessis, Cardinal, Duc de, *ree-shě-lyæ* (1585–1642), was born into a noble but impoverished family, of Richelieu near Chinon, and was baptized in Paris. He abandoned the military profession for the clerical in order to keep in the family the bishopric of Luçon, to which he was consecrated at twenty-two. In 1616 he rose to be secretary at war and for foreign affairs, but next year was sent back to his diocese. In 1622 he was named cardinal, in 1624 minister of state to Louis XIII. His first important measure was the blow to Spain of an alliance with England, cemented by the marriage (1625) of the king's sister Henrietta with Charles I. His next great task was to destroy the political power of the Huguenots. La Rochelle was starved into submission (1628); and he destroyed

Montauban, the last refuge of Huguenot independence. From 1629 he was chief minister and actual ruler of France. In 1630 he entered Italy with a splendid army, and reduced Savoy. Meanwhile he plunged into tortuous intrigues with the Italian princes, the pope and the Protestants of the North against the House of Austria. He promised a large subsidy to Gustavus Adolphus, and succeeded in persuading Ferdinand to dismiss Wallenstein. The first treaty of Cherasco (April 1631) ended the Italian war; the second gave France the strategic position of Pinerolo. Just before this final triumph Richelieu successfully surmounted a great combination formed for his downfall by the queen-mother, the House of Guise and others. He now was made duke, and governor of Brittany. Further intrigues and attempted rebellions were crushed with merciless severity. In July 1632 Richelieu had seized the duchy of Lorraine. He continued his intrigues with the Protestants against Ferdinand, subsidizing them with his gold, but till 1635 took no open part in the war. In that year, after completing his preparations and concluding an alliance with Victor Amadeus of Savoy, Bernard of Saxe-Weimar and the Dutch, he declared war on Spain. His first efforts were unsuccessful; Piccolomini entered Picardy and threatened Paris. But Richelieu rose to the height of his genius; with 30,000 foot and 12,000 horse he swept the enemy out of Picardy while Bernard drove them across the Rhine, and in 1638 destroyed the imperial army at Rheinfelden. His policy soon led to the disorganization of the power of Spain, the victories of Wolfenbüttel and Kempten over the Imperialist forces in Germany, and at length in 1641 in Savoy, also the ascendency of the French party. But the hatred of the great French nobles continued, and his safety lay in the king's helplessness without him. The last conspiracy against him was that of Cinq-Mars (q.v.), whose intrigues with the Duke of Bouillon and the Spanish court were soon revealed to the cardinal, the centre of a network of espionage which covered the whole of France. Cinq-Mars and De Thou were arrested and executed. But the great minister died December 4, 1642. While overwhelming the citizens with taxation, he had built up the power of the French crown, achieved for France a preponderance in Europe, destroyed the local liberties of France, and crushed every element of constitutional government. He never sacrificed to personal ambition what he thought the interests of his country, but he often forgot in his methods the laws of morality and humanity. The weakest point in Richelieu's character was his literary ambition. His plays sleep in safe oblivion, but his *Mémoires* are still read with interest. Other works include *Instruction du chrétien* (1619) and *Traité de la perfection du chrétien* (1646). He founded the French Academy. See his Correspondence and State Papers (8 vols. 1853–77), and books by Dussieux (1885), D'Avenel (1884–90), Fagniez (1893–94), Lodge (1896), Belloc (1937), Burckhardt (Eng. trans. 1940) and C. V. Wedgwood 1949).

RICHEPIN, Jean, *reesh-pī* (1849–1926), French poet, playwright and novelist, was

humbly born at Medeah, Algeria, and prior to the appearance of his first romance in 1872 had been franc-tireur, sailor, actor. His revolutionary book of poems, *La Chanson des Gueux* (1876), led to a fine and his imprisonment.

RICHET, Charles Robert, *ree-shay* (1850–1935), French physiologist, was born and educated in Paris, where he was professor from 1887 to 1927. For his work on the phenomenon of anaphylaxis he was awarded the 1913 Nobel prize for medicine. He also did research on serum therapy.

RICHMOND, (1) **George** (1809–96), English portrait painter, was born, a miniaturist's son, at Brompton; came under Blake's influence; made a Gretna Green marriage (1831); studied in Paris, Italy, and Germany; was made A.R.A. 1857 and R.A. 1866.

(2) **Legh** (1772–1827), English clergyman, born at Liverpool. He wrote the *Dairyman's Daughter, Negro Servant,* and *Young Cottager,* three famous evangelical tracts, collected as *Annals of the Poor* (1814). See Mundy and Wright's *Turvey and Legh Richmond* (2nd ed. 1894).

(3) **Sir William Blake** (1843–1921), English portrait and mythological painter, son of (1), born in London, studied in Italy, was Oxford Slade professor 1878–83, and was made A.R.A. 1888, R.A. 1896, K.C.B. 1897. The St Paul's mosaics are his work.

RICHTER, (1) **Hans** (1843–1916), Hungarian conductor, born at Raab, had conducted in Munich, Budapest and Vienna, when in 1879 he began the Orchestral Concerts in London. In 1893 he became first court *kapellmeister* at Vienna, in 1900–11 was conductor of the Hallé orchestra. He was an authority on the music of Wagner, with whom he was closely associated in the Bayreuth festival.

(2) **Hieronymus Theodor** (1824–98), German chemist, born in Dresden, at the age of nineteen, with Reich, discovered by spectroscopic analysis the element *indium* in zincblende. He became director of the Freiburg School of Mines.

(3) **Jeremias Benjamin** (1762–1807), German chemist, was born in Silesia, studied under Kant at Königsberg, and discovered the law of equivalent proportions.

(4) **Johann Paul Friedrich,** often known as **Jean Paul** (1763–1825), German novelist and humorist, was born at Wunsiedel in N. Bavaria, and was sent in 1781 to Leipzig to study theology; but literature had stronger charm for him. He got into debt, and in 1784 fled from Leipzig, to hide in the poverty-stricken home of his widowed mother at Hof. His first literary 'children' were satires which no one would publish, until in 1783 Voss of Berlin gave him forty louis d'or for *The Greenland Law-suits.* The book was a failure, and for three years Jean Paul struggled on at home. In 1787 he began to teach, and during his nine years of tutorship produced the satirical *Extracts from the Devil's Papers* (1789), &c., the beautiful idylls *Dominie Wuz* (1793), *Quintus Fixlein* (1796; trans. by Carlyle, 1827), and the *Parson's Jubilee* (1797); grand romances, e.g., *The Invisible Lodge* (1793), *Campanerthal* (1797) on the immor-

tality of the soul; and the prose idyll, *My Prospective Autobiography* (1799). The *Invisible Lodge* was his first literary success; *Hesperus* (1795) made him famous. For a few years Jean Paul was the object of extravagant idolatry on the part of the women of Germany. In 1801 he married and three years later settled at Bayreuth, where he died. The principal works of his married life were the romances, *Titan* (1800–03) and *Wild Oats* (1804–05), the former accounted by himself his masterpiece; *Schmeltzle's Journey to Flätz* (1809; trans. by Carlyle, 1827) and *Dr. Katzenberger's Trip to the Spa* (1809), the best of his satirico-humorous writings; the idyll *Fibel's Life* (1812); the fragment of another grand romance, *Nicholas Markgraf*, or *The Comet* (1820–22); reflections on literature (*Vorschule der Aesthetik*; improved ed. 1812); another series on education (*Levana*, 1807), a book that ranks with Rousseau's *Émile*; various patriotic writings (1808–12); and an unfinished *Autobiography* (1826). Jean Paul stands by himself in German literature. All his great qualities of imagination and intellect were made ministers to his humour, which had the widest range, moving from the petty follies of individual men and the absurdities of social custom up to the paradoxes rooted in the universe. But of all great writers he is one of the most difficult to understand. See Lives by Nerrlich (1889), Harich (1925), Burschell (1926); Carlyle's *Miscellaneous Essays*; an English Life, with Autobiography (1845); and Lady Chatterton's translated extracts (1859).

(5) **Sviatoslav Teofilovitch** (1914–), Russian pianist, born at Zhitomir, studied at the Moscow Conservatoire (1942–47). He has made extensive concert tours, with a repertoire ranging from Bach to 20th-century composers. He was awarded the Stalin prize in 1949.

RICHTHOFEN, *riкHt'hŏf-en*, (1) **Ferdinand, Baron von** (1833–1905), German geographer and traveller, born at Karlsruhe in Silesia, in 1860 accompanied a Prussian expedition to eastern Asia, then during the next twelve years travelled in Java, Siam, Burma, California, the Sierra Nevada, and China and Japan (1868–72). After his return (1872) he became president of the Berlin Geographical Society (1873–78), professor of Geology at Bonn (1875), and of Geography at Leipzig (1883), at Berlin (1886). His reputation rests upon his great work on *China* (1877–1912), *Aufgaben der Geographie* (1883), &c.

(2) **Manfred, Baron von** (1882–1918), German airman, born in Schweidnitz. At first in the cavalry, he later joined the German air force, and during World War I, as commander of the 11th Chasing Squadron (' Richthofen's Flying Circus '), was noted for his high number (80) of aerial victories. He was shot down behind the British lines. See Life by Gibbons (1930) and Nowarra and Brown, *The Flying Circus* (1959).

RICKMAN, Thomas (1776–1841), English architect, born at Maidenhead, was in succession chemist, grocer, doctor, corn-factor, insurance agent at Liverpool, before becoming in 1820 architect at Birmingham. He designed a number of churches in the revived Gothic style; also the New Court at St John's College, Cambridge. He wrote *Styles of Architecture in England* (1817).

RIDDELL, (1) **George Allardice Riddell, 1st Baron** (1865–1934), British lawyer and newspaper proprietor, born at Duns, Berwickshire. Educated in London, he rose from boy clerk to solicitor, and through one of his clients, the Cardiff *Western Mail*, became further involved in the newspaper world, at first as legal adviser to the *News of the World*, later as its chairman; he became chairman also of George Newnes, Ltd. Knighted in 1909, he represented the British press at the Paris peace conference in 1919, and the following year was raised to the peerage. See his *Diaries* (1933) from 1908 to 1923.

(2) **Henry Scott** (1798–1870), minor Scottish poet, born, a shepherd's son, at Ewes, Dumfriesshire, from 1831 was a minister at Teviothead. See memoir by Dr Brydon prefixed to *Poems* (1871).

RIDDING, George (1828–1905), born at Winchester, and educated there and at Balliol, became a fellow of Exeter in 1851, head of Winchester in 1868, as such making widespread improvements in the amenities and standard of education of the school. He became first Bishop of Southwell in 1884.

RIDEAL, Sir Eric Keightley, *ri-deel'* (1890–), English chemist, educated at Cambridge and Bonn, held chairs at Cambridge (1930–46), the Royal Institution, London (1946–49), and London University (1950–55). He worked on colloids and catalysis, and devised the Rideal-Walker test for the germicidal power of a disinfectant. He was elected F.R.S. in 1930 and knighted in 1951.

RIDGE, William Pett (1857–1930), English writer, born at Chartham, Kent, is best known as an exponent of cockney humour (*A Clever Wife, Mord Em'ly*, &c.).

RIDGWAY, (1) **Matthew Bunker** (1895–), American general, commanded airborne troops in World War II, headed the U.N. Command in the Far East 1951–52, succeeded Eisenhower as supreme allied commander in Europe, was army chief of staff from 1953 until 1955, in which year he was awarded the Hon. K.C.B.

(2) **Robert** (1850–1929), American ornithologist, born in Mount Carmel, Illinois, wrote *The Birds of Middle and North America* (8 vols. 1901–19), &c.

RIDING, Laura (1901–), American poet and critic, born in New York, came to England in 1925 and remained in Europe until the outbreak of World War II. Her works include *A Survey of Modernist Poetry* (with Robert Graves, 1927), *Contemporaries and Snobs* (1928), *Collected Poems* (1938).

RIDLEY, Nicholas (*c.* 1500–55), English Protestant martyr, born at Unthank Hall near Haltwhistle, was elected in 1524 a fellow of Pembroke, Cambridge, studied at Paris and Louvain 1527–30, and became proctor at Cambridge in 1534, domestic chaplain to Cranmer and Henry VIII, master of Pembroke in 1540, canon, first of Canterbury, then of Westminster, rector of Soham, and in 1547 Bishop of Rochester. An ardent and outspoken Reformer, he was in 1550, on the deprivation of Bonner, Bishop of London, made his successor. In this high position he distinguished himself by his moderation, learning and munificence, and assisted Cranmer in the preparation of the Articles. On the death of Edward VI he espoused the cause of Lady Jane Grey, and was stripped of his dignities and sent to the Tower. In 1554 he was tried at Oxford, with Latimer and Cranmer, by a committee of Convocation; all three were adjudged obstinate heretics and condemned. Ridley lay in jail for eighteen months, and after a second trial was burnt, along with Latimer, in front of Balliol College. His writings were collected in the Parker Society series (1841). See Foxe's *Actes*, the memoir prefixed to Moule's edition of Ridley's *Declaration of the Lord's Supper* (1895) and *Life* by Ridley (1957).

RIDPATH, George (*c.* 1717–72), Scottish historian, born at Ladykirk manse in Berwickshire, and minister from 1742 of Stitchell, wrote a *Border History* (1776).

RIEGGER, Wallingford, *ree'gĕr* (1885–1961), American composer, born in Albany, Georgia, studied at Cornell University, the Institute of Musical Art, New York, and in Berlin, returning to America when the United States entered the first World War. He held posts at Drake University and Ithaca Conservatory, New York. His works, which show the influence of Schoenberg's ' twelve note ' system and his German training, received little attention until the performance of his third Symphony in 1948, since when his work has been increasingly recognized. He wrote extensively for orchestra and for chamber music combinations.

RIEL, Louis, *ree-el'* (1844–85), Canadian insurgent, born at St Boniface, Manitoba, succeeded his father as a leader of the Métis or French half-breeds, and headed the Red River rebellion in 1869–70. In 1885 he again established a rebel government in Manitoba, and on November 16, the rising having been quelled, he was executed.

RIEMANN, *ree'*-, (1) Georg Friedrich Bernhard (1826–66), German mathematician, born September 17 at Breselenz, Hanover, studied at Göttingen under Gauss and at Berlin and in 1851 became professor at the former. His early work was an outstanding contribution to the theory of functions, but he is best remembered for his development of the conceptions of Bolyai and Lobachevsky which resulted in a fully-fledged non-Euclidian geometry, dealing with ' manifolds ' and curvatures on the assumption of polydimensional, finite and unbounded space. This was set out in a paper (1854; trans. *Nature*, vol. 8) ' On the hypotheses which form the foundation of Geometry '. He was elected F.R.S. in 1866.

(2) Hugo (1849–1919), German musicologist, author of many works on history and theory of music, was born at Sondershausen and died at Leipzig, where he was professor from 1901.

RIEMENSCHNEIDER, Tilman, *ree'mĕn-shnī-dĕr* (1460–1531), German sculptor, born at Osterode, spent his life after 1483 at Würzburg, where he rose to become burgomaster, but was imprisoned for participating in the peasants' revolt of 1525. The greatest carver

of his period, he executed many fine sepulchral monuments and church decorations. See studies by Knapp (1935), Demmler (1939) and K. H. Stein (1944).

RIENZI, or Rienzo, Cola di, *ryent'see* (*c.* 1313–1354), Italian patriot, born humbly at Rome, was in 1343 spokesman of a deputation sent in vain to Avignon to beseech Clement VI to return to Rome. In May 1347 he incited the citizens to rise against the rule of the nobles. The senators were driven out, and Rienzi was invested with practically dictatorial power. At his request the Italian states sent deputies to Rome to devise measures for unification and common good, and Rienzi was crowned tribune. But the nobles were still bitterly hostile. The papal authority was turned against him; and, his seven months' reign over, he fled to Naples. After two years of religious meditation Rienzi resumed his life as political reformer, but was taken prisoner by the emperor and sent to Clement VI at Avignon. A new pope, Innocent VI, sent him to Rome to crush the power of the nobles, but after accomplishing this Rienzi aimed at re-establishing himself in supreme authority. In August 1354, having raised a small body of soldiers, he made a sort of triumphal entry into Rome. But his conduct now was such that the Romans murdered him, October 8. Wagner's opera on his story was produced in 1842. See books by Rodocanachi (1888), Cosenza (1913), Origo (1938), and *Life* (ed. Ghisalberti 1928).

RIESENER, Jean Paul, *ree'zĕ-ner*; Fr. *reez-nayr* (1734–1806), cabinetmaker, born in München-Gladbach, Prussia, worked in Paris, was a master, favoured by Louis XVI's court, of marquetry and ebony work.

RIETSCHEL, Ernst, *ree'chĕl* (1804–61), German sculptor, of the Dresden school, executed the Goethe and Schiller monument at Weimar, the Luther memorial at Worms and many other monuments and portrait busts. There is a Rietschel museum at Dresden.

RIGAUD, Hyacinthe, *ree-gō* (1659–1743), French portrait painter, born at Perpignan, settled in Paris in 1681. His portrait of Louis XIV (1701) is in the Louvre.

RIISAGER, Knudåge (1897–   ), Danish composer, was born at Port Kunda, Russia, and by 1900 had returned with his parents to Denmark. He took a political economy degree at Copenhagen University, then went to Paris, where, giving rein to his early musical ambitions, he studied under Paul le Flem and Albert Roussel, and was also influenced by other French composers of the time. On his return to Denmark he shocked conventional musical circles there by his revolutionary compositions and writings. Polytonality, polyrhythm and unique syncopations abound in his works, which include the overtures *Erasmus Montanus* and *Klods Hans*, four symphonies, ballets, including the well-known *Quarrtsiluni*, and a piano sonata (1931).

RILEY, James Whitcomb (1849–1916), American poet, known as the ' Hoosier poet ', born at Greenfield, Indiana. His poems about children, including ' Little Orfant Annie ' are well known. See Life by M. Dickey (1922).

RILKE, Rainer Maria, -kè (1875–1926), Austrian lyric poet, born at Prague, deserted a military academy to study art history at Prague, Munich and Berlin. The spiritual melancholy of his early verse turns into a mystical quest for the deity in such works as *Geschichten vom lieben Gott* (1900) and *Das Stundenbuch* (1905), written after two journeys to Russia (1899–1900), where he met Tolstoy and was deeply influenced by Russian pietism. In 1901 he married Klara Westhoff, a pupil of Rodin, whose secretary Rilke became in Paris, publishing *Das Rodin-Buch* (1907). Mysticism was abandoned for the aesthetic ideal in *Gedichte* (1907, 1908). *Die Aufzeichnungen des Malte Laurids Brigge* (1910) portrays the anxious loneliness of an imaginary poet. In 1923 he wrote two masterpieces, *Die Sonnette an Orpheus* and *Duineser Elegien*, in which he exalts the poet as the mediator between crude nature and pure form. His work greatly extended the range of expression and subtlety of the German language. See *Poems 1906 to 1926* trans. and intro. J. B. Leishman (1957), *Ewald Tragy* (trans. 1958), *Letters* (trans. 1958), Selected Works (trans. by Leishman, 2 vols., 1960–61), E. Heller, *The Disinherited Mind* (1952), and studies by E. M. Butler (1941), Heerikhuizen (trans. 1951), Holthusen (1952), Belmore (1954) and F. Wood (1958).

RIMBAUD, (Jean Nicolas) Arthur, rĭ-bō (1854–91), Belgian poet, was born at Charleville, Ardennes, the son of an army captain and his stern, disciplinarian wife. After a brilliant academic career at the Collège de Charleville, he published in 1870 his first book of poems, and the same year ran away to Paris, the first stage in his life of wandering. He soon returned to Charleville, where he wrote, while leading a life of idling, drinking and bawdy conversation, *Le Bateau ivre*, which, with its verbal eccentricities, daring imagery and evocative language, is perhaps his most popular work. Soon after its publication in August 1871 Verlaine invited Rimbaud to Paris, where they began together a life of debauchery and ill-repute, with periods in London. In Brussels in July 1873 Rimbaud threatened to terminate the friendship, and was thereupon shot at and wounded by Verlaine, who was imprisoned for attempted murder. The relationship had, however, given Rimbaud some measure of stability, and from its height, the summer of 1872, date many of *Les Illuminations*, the work which most clearly states his poetic doctrine. These prose and verse poems, as it were flashes of sensation, show Rimbaud as a precursor of symbolism, with his use of childhood, dream and mystical images to express dissatisfaction with the material world and a longing for the spiritual. In 1873 Rimbaud published the prose volume *Une Saison en enfer*, which symbolized his struggle to break with his past—his ' enfer ', was bitterly disappointed at its cold reception by the literary critics, burned all his manuscripts, and at the age of nineteen bade a farewell to literature. Then began years of varied and colourful wandering in Europe

and the East—in Germany, Sweden, Aden, Cyprus and Harar, as soldier, trader, explorer and gun-runner. During these years, in 1886, Verlaine published *Les Illuminations* as by the ' late Arthur Rimbaud ', but the author ignored, rather than was ignorant of, the sensation they caused and the reputation they were making for him. In April 1891 troubled by a leg infection, he left Harar and sailed to Marseilles, where his leg was amputated, and where, after a brief return to Belgium, he died, November 10, 1891. See studies by E. Starkie (1937, 1947), Fowlie (1946, 1966) and Hackett (1957).

RIMINI. See FRANCESCA DA RIMINI.

RIMSKY-KORSAKOV, Nikolai Andreievich (1844–1908), Russian composer, was born at Tikhvin, Novgorod. His early musical education was perfunctory until 1859, when he took some lessons from the pianist Canille, a musician of some repute but no method, and developed a taste for composition, making arrangements of the operatic tunes of Glinka (q.v.), whom he greatly admired. In 1861 he was introduced to Balakirev (q.v.), who became his friend and mentor, and to Moussorgsky (q.v.), then young and struggling. Encouraged by his new companions, he started a callow symphony, said to be the first by a Russian, in E♭ minor (later transposed, not surprisingly, into the more manageable key of E minor). Following a family tradition, he was destined for the sea, and his musical activities were interrupted when he became a naval cadet, passed out in 1862, and went on a routine cruise which took in England and America. His interest in music had meantime subsided, but was revived when he met Balakirev again and became a member of his circle, which included Moussorgsky and Borodin (q.v.). He finished his symphony, which was performed with some local success, wrote some songs, and became interested in folk music. His knowledge of the tools of the composer's trade was still extremely limited when, in 1867, he wrote his first version of the fairytale fantasy *Sadko* and began his opera *The Maid of Pskov* in 1868. In 1871 he was offered a professorship at the St Petersburg Conservatoire which, conscious of his technical shortcomings, he hesitated to accept, but eventually he took the plunge and by assiduous study caught up on his academic deficiencies, though his music went through a temporary phase of stuffiness on this account. He was helped much at this time by Nadezhda Purgold, a brilliant musician and a composer in her own right, who became his wife in 1872. In 1877 he published a collection of Russian folk songs, and he spent a good deal of time studying instrumentation with his friend Borodin, after whose death he and Glazunov (q.v.) completed the unfinished *Prince Igor*. In 1887–88 he produced his three great orchestral masterpieces—*Capriccio Espagnol*, *Easter Festival* and *Scheherazade*—but thereafter turned to opera, which occupied his attention, apart from revisions of earlier works, for the rest of his life. Among his best in this genre are *The Snow Maiden* (1882), *The Tsar Saltan* (1900), *The Invisible City of Kitesh* (1906) and

The Golden Cockerel, begun in 1906, his last work, based on a satire against autocracy by Pushkin and therefore banned at first from the Russian stage. A revised version of *Sadko* appeared in 1898, and *The Maid of Pskov* reappeared, staged by Diaghilev as *Ivan the Terrible*, in 1908. Since 1892 Rimsky-Korsakov had suffered with cerebrospinal neurasthenia, and his life was saddened by the loss of two children in 1891 and 1893. He died at Lyubensk on June 21, 1908. His music is notable for its brilliance and native vitality, and for the colour engendered by his great flair for orchestration. Ever conscious of his bygone technical shortcomings, he rewrote almost all his early work. Stravinsky (q.v.) was his pupil. See his *My Musical Life* (trans. Joffe 1942), and Lives by Montagu-Nathan (1916) and G. Abraham (1945).

RINGAN, St. See NINIAN.

RINUCCINI, Ottavio, *ree-noot-chee'nee* (1562–1621), Italian poet, wrote *Dafne* (1594), the first Italian melodrama, based on the Greek recitative. See PERI.

RIOPELLE, Jean Paul, *ree-ō-pel* (1924–), Canadian painter, born in Montreal, one of the leading colourists among the abstract ' action painters '.

RIPLEY, George (1802–80), American social reformer and literary critic, born at Greenfield, Mass., graduated at Harvard, and until 1841 was pastor in Boston. He joined in the Transcendental movement, and on leaving the pulpit he started the Brook Farm experiment. In 1849 he engaged in literary work at New York. He was joint-editor of Appleton's *New American Cyclopaedia*. See Life by Frothingham (1882).

RIPON, (1) Frederick John Robinson, Earl of (1782–1859), English statesman, second son of the second Lord Grantham, was educated at Harrow and St John's College, Cambridge. In 1806 he entered parliament as a moderate Tory, and had successively been undersecretary for the colonies, vice-president of the Board of Trade, and chancellor of the Exchequer, when, as Viscount Goderich, in 1827 he became head of a brief administration. He was later colonial secretary, lord privy seal, and president of the Board of Trade, and in 1833 was created Earl of Ripon. See Jones, *Prosperity Robinson* (1968).

(2) **George Frederick Samuel Robinson, Marquis of** (1827–1900), son of (1), English statesman, succeeded his father as Earl of Ripon and his uncle as Earl de Grey. Since 1852 he had sat in parliament as a Liberal, and he became successively under-secretary for war (1859), under-secretary for India (1861), secretary for war (1863), secretary for India (1866), lord president of the Council (1868), grand master of the Freemasons (1870, which office he resigned in 1874 on his conversion to Catholicism), Marquis of Ripon (1871), and viceroy of India (1880–84). He was first lord of the Admiralty in 1886, colonial secretary in 1892–95, and lord privy seal in 1905–08. See book on his viceroyalty, by S. Gopal (1953).

RIPPERDA, Johann Wilhelm, Baron de, *rip'-* (1680–1737), Dutch political adventurer who, born at Groningen, played an amazing part at the Spanish court, turned first Catholic and

then Moslem, and died at Tetuan, after commanding against Spain. See French monograph by Syveton (1896).

RISHANGER, William (*c.* 1250–1312), a monk of St Albans, who wrote a number of short contemporary chronicles in continuation of the historical work of Matthew Paris, but probably did not write the *Chronica Wilhelmi Rishanger* (1259–1306).

RISTORI, Adelaide, *ree-stō'ree* (1822–1906), Italian tragédienne, born at Cividale in Friuli, rapidly became the leading Italian actress. In 1847 her marriage with the Marquis del Grillo (died 1861) temporarily interrupted her dramatic career. She won a complete triumph before a French audience in 1855, when Rachel was at the height of her fame; and gained fresh laurels in nearly every country of Europe, in the United States (1866, 1875, 1884–85), and in South America. See her *Memoirs and Artistic Studies* (trans. 1907).

RITCHIE, Anne Isabella, Lady (1837–1919), English writer, the daughter of William Makepeace Thackeray, was born in London. A close companion of her father, and well acquainted with his friends of literary and artistic note, she contributed valuable personal reminiscences to an 1898–99 edition of his works, and also wrote memoirs of their contemporaries, such as Tennyson and Ruskin. Her novels include *The Village on the Cliff* (1867) and *Old Kensington* (1873).

RITSCHL, *rich'ĕl,* (1) Albrecht (1822–89), Protestant theologian, born at Berlin, became professor of Theology at Bonn (1851), Göttingen (1864). His principal work is on the doctrine of justification and reconciliation (1870–74; 4th ed. 1896). Other works were on Christian perfection (1874), conscience (1876), Pietism (1880–86), theology and metaphysics (1881), &c. The distinguishing feature of the Ritschlian theology is the prominence it gives to the practical, ethical, social side of Christianity. See Life by his son, Otto (2 vols. 1892–96); and works on Ritschlianism by Pfleiderer (1891), Garvie (1899), Swing (1901), Orr (1903), Edghill (1910) and Mackintosh (1915).

(2) **Friedrich Wilhelm** (1806–76), German scholar, born near Erfurt, received classical chairs at Breslau (1834), Bonn (1839) and Leipzig (1865). His great edition of Plautus (1848–54; new ed. 1881–87) was preceded by *Parerga Plautina et Terentiana* (1845). His *Priscae Latinitatis Monumenta Epigraphica* (1864) was the forerunner of the *Corpus Inscriptionum*. See Life by Ribbeck (1879–81).

RITSON, Joseph (1752–1803), English antiquary, born at Stockton-on-Tees, came to London in 1775, and practised as a conveyancer, but was enabled to give most of his time to antiquarian studies. He was notorious for his vegetarianism, whimsical spelling and irreverence as for his attacks on bigger men than himself. His first important work was an onslaught on Warton's *History of English Poetry* (1782). He assailed (1783) Johnson and Steevens for their text of Shakespeare, and Bishop Percy in *Ancient Songs* (1790); in 1792 appeared his *Cursory Criticisms* on Malone's Shakespeare. Other works were *English Songs* (1783); *Ancient Popular Poetry* (1791); *Scottish Songs* (1794); *Poems . . . by*

Laurence Minot (1795); *Robin Hood Ballads* (1795); and *Ancient English Metrical Romances* (1802). See his Letters edited, with Life, by Sir H. Nicolas (1833), and the studies by Burd (1916) and Bronson (1938).

RITTER, (1) **Johann Wilhelm** (1776–1810), German physicist, was born in Silesia, and while working in Jena discovered in 1802 the ultraviolet rays in the spectrum (see W. H. WOLLASTON). He also worked on electricity.

(2) **Karl** (1779–1859), German geographer, born at Quedlinburg, became professor of Geography at Berlin (1829), academician, and director of studies of the Military School. He laid the foundations of modern scientific geography, his most important work, *Die Erkunde* . . . (1817), stressing the relation between man and his natural environment. He also wrote a comparative geography (Eng. ed. 1865). See Life by Gage (1867).

RIVAROL, Antoine, *ree-va-rol* (1753–1801), French writer, born at Bagnols in Languedoc, came to Paris in 1780, and in 1788 set the whole city laughing at the sarcasms in his *Petit Almanach de nos grands hommes.* Emigrating in 1792, and supported by royalist pensions, he wrote pamphlets in Brussels, London, Hamburg and Berlin. See Lives by Le Breton (1895) and L. Latzarus (1926).

RIVAS, Angel de Saavedra, Duque de, *ree'vas* (1791–1865), Spanish politician and writer, was born in Córdoba and educated in Madrid. He served in the Civil War, lived in exile (1823–1834), became minister of the interior in 1835, and was soon exiled again. In 1837 he returned, became prime minister, and later was ambassador in Naples, Paris (1856) and Florence (1860). Alongside his political life, Rivas led his literary one, as an early exponent of Spanish romanticism. His works include the epics *Florinda* (1826) and *El Moro expósito* (1834), the dramatic poems, *Romances históricos* (1841), and several dramas, including *Don Alvaro* or *La Fuerza del Sino* (1835), on which Verdi based his opera *La Forza del Destino.* See study by Peers (1923).

RIVERA, Diego, *ri-vay'ra* (1886–1957), Mexican painter, born at Guanajuato, in 1921 began a series of murals in public buildings depicting the life and history (particularly the popular uprisings) of the Mexican people. From 1930 to 1934 he executed a number of frescoes in the U.S., mainly of industrial life. His art is a curious blend of the rhetorical realism of folk art and revolutionary propaganda, with overtones of Byzantine and Aztec symbolism. See his books *Portrait of America* (1934) and *Portrait of Mexico* (1938), and Life by Wolfe (1939).

RIVERS, (1) **Anthony Woodville, 2nd Earl** (1442?–83), son of (3), stuck closely to Edward IV, who made him captain-general of the forces. After Edward's death he was put to death by Richard III.

(2) **Augustus Pitt-.** See PITT-RIVERS.

(3) **Richard Woodville, 1st Earl** (d. 1469), English soldier, was esquire to Henry V, and during his son's reign was made governor of the Tower (1424) and knighted (1425). He fought in France and for the Lancastrians in the Wars of the Roses. He married Jacquetta of Luxembourg, widow of the Duke of Bedford, and it was their daughter

Elizabeth whom Edward IV married. This led him to go over to the Yorkists, and Edward made him Constable of England, Baron Rivers (1448) and Earl Rivers (1466). But the favour shown to the Rivers family offended the old nobility, and their avarice aroused popular enmity, and in 1469 Earl Rivers was beheaded at Northampton.

(4) **William Halse Rivers** (1864–1922), English anthropologist and psychologist, lectured at Cambridge, applied his genealogical method in the Torres Straits and among the Todas, wrote important books on *Kinship* (1914) and on *The History of Melanesian Society* (1915), drawing the story of a long-past migration from the linkage of elements in a culture. In *Instinct and the Unconscious* (1920) and *Conflict and Dream* (1923) he is a modified Freudian.

RIVIÈRE, (1) **Briton,** *rė-veer'* (1840–1920), English artist, born of Huguenot ancestry in London, the son of a drawing-master, graduated at Oxford in 1867, was elected R.A. in 1881, and excelled in paintings of wild animals.

(2) **Jacques,** *ree-vyayr* (1886–1925), French writer and critic, born in Bordeaux, in 1919 became first editor of the *Nouvelle revue française,* as such playing a prominent part in the cultural life of postwar France. His writings include novels, essays and a justification of the Christian conception of God, *A la trace de Dieu* (1925). See his correspondence with Claudel (1925) and Fournier (1926–28), and the Life by B. Cook (1958).

RIVINGTON, Charles (1688–1742), English publisher, born at Chesterfield, Derbyshire, went to London, where he founded in 1711 the Rivington publishing firm which remained under family direction until absorbed by Longmans in 1890. In 1889 Septimus Rivington was a cofounder of the firm of Percival and Co., which in 1893 became Rivington, Percival and Co., and, after 1897, Rivington & Co. See S. Rivington, *The House of Rivington* (1894).

RIZAL, José, *ree-sal'* (1861–96), Filipino patriot and writer, born at Calamba, Luzon, studied medicine at Madrid, and on his return to the Philippines published a political novel, *Noli me tangere* (1886), whose anti-Spanish tone led to his exile. He practised in Hong Kong, where he wrote *El Filibusterismo* (1891), a continuation of his first novel. Returning to the Philippines, he arrived simultaneously with an anti-Spanish revolt, which he was accused of instigating, and was shot. See study by C. E. Russell and E. B. Rodriguez (1923).

RIZZIO, or **Riccio, David,** *rit'si-o, reech'-* (1533?–66), Italian courtier and musician, entered the service of Mary, Queen of Scots in 1561, and rapidly becoming her favourite, was appointed private foreign secretary in 1564. He negotiated Mary's marriage (1565) with Darnley, with whom he was at first on friendly terms, but the queen's husband soon became jealous of his influence over Mary and of his strong political power, and entered with other nobles into a plot to kill him. Rizzio was dragged from the queen's presence and brutally murdered at the palace of Holyrood, March 9, 1566.

ROBBE-GRILLET, Alain (1922–), French novelist, born in Brest and educated in Paris, worked for some time as an agronomist and then in a publishing house. His first novel, *Les Gommes* (*The Erasers*, 1953), aroused much controversy and with the appearance of his later ones (*Dans le labyrinthe*, 1959, &c.) he emerged as a leader of the *nouveau roman* group. He uses an unorthodox narrative structure and concentrates on external reality, believing this to be the only one. He has also written film scenarios, e.g., *L'Année dernière à Marienbad* and essays, *Pour un nouveau roman* (1963).

ROBBIA, DELLA, the name of a family of Florentine sculptors, including:

(1) **Andrea** (1435–1525), nephew of (3), who worked at reliefs and whose bambini medallions are on the Ospedale degli Innocenti, Florence.

(2) **Giovanni** (1469–1529?), son of (1), whose frieze *Seven Works of Mercy* is at Pistoia.

(3) **Luca** (*c*. 1400–82), who executed between 1431 and 1440 ten unequalled panels of angels and dancing boys for the cathedral, for whose sacristy he also made (1448–67) a bronze door with ten panels of figures in relief. In marble he sculptured, in 1457–58, the tomb of the Bishop of Fiesole. He is almost equally famous for his figures in terra-cotta, including medallions and reliefs, white or coloured. See works by Cruttwell (1902) and Marquand (various, 1912–28).

ROBERT. Name of three kings of Scotland:

(1) **Robert I**. See Bruce Family (7).

(2) **Robert II** (1316–90), born March 2, was the son of Walter Stewart (q.v.) and of Marjory, only daughter of Robert the Bruce. Throughout the disastrous reign of his uncle, David II, he was one of the most prominent nobles of Scotland, and twice acted as regent. On David's death (1371) he obtained the crown, founding the Stewart dynasty. His powerful and intractable barons shaped the policy of the country very much according to their pleasure. The misery inflicted by their raids and the reprisals of the English wardens was frightful; the great events were the invasions of Scotland by English forces in 1384 and in 1385, and the retaliatory expedition of the Scots in 1388, ending with Otterburn. He married (1384) his mistress, Elizabeth Mure of Rowallan, and (1355) a daughter of the Earl of Ross; he had over a dozen children.

(3) **Robert III** (*c*. 1340–1406), son of (2), was originally called John. His incapacity threw the government into the hands of his ambitious brother, in 1398 created Duke of Albany. In 1400 Henry IV of England invaded Scotland and penetrated as far as Edinburgh; the Scots retaliated in 1402 by the expedition which ended in the disaster at Homildon Hill. Robert had two sons, the elder of whom was David, Duke of Rothesay (1378–1402), a clever but very licentious youth. Albany received orders from the king to act as his guardian, and after a short time starved him to death at Falkland. Robert, anxious for the safety of his younger son, James, sent him to France; and died when news came that the vessel in which James sailed had been captured by an English ship.

ROBERT, Duke of Normandy. See Henry I, of England.

ROBERT-FLEURY, *ro-bayr-flœ-ree*, (1) **Joseph Nicolas** (1797–1890), French historical painter, born in Cologne, was a pupil of Gros. He is notable for his historical accuracy of subject matter and use of contemporaneous techniques.

(2) **Tony** (1837–1911), French historical painter, son of (1), born in Paris, was a pupil of Delaroche.

ROBERT OF ANJOU, *ã-zhoo* (1275–1343), king of Naples and Sicily, succeeded his father, Charles II, in 1309. He supported the Guelph cause, and was a notable patron of literature and the arts. See Baddeley's *Robert the Wise* (1897).

ROBERT OF BRUNNE, the name by which Robert Manning, or Mannyng, is usually designated from his birthplace Bourn, in Lincolnshire, 6 miles from the Gilbertine monastery of Sempringham that he entered in 1288. He died about 1338. His chief work is his *Handlyng Synne* (1303), a free and amplified translation into English verse of William of Wadington's *Manuel des Pechiez*, with such judicious omissions and additions as made his version much more entertaining than the original. It is one of the best landmarks in the transition from early to later Middle English. He also made a new version in octosyllabic rhyme of Wace's *Brut d'Angleterre*, and added to it a translation of the French rhyming chronicle of Peter Langtoft.

ROBERT OF GLOUCESTER (fl. 1260–1300), author of a metrical English chronicle to 1135, edited by Wright (Rolls series, 1887).

ROBERT OF JUMIÈGES (fl. 1037–52), a Norman abbot of Jumièges from 1037, came to England in 1043 with Edward the Confessor, who made him Bishop of London (1044) and Archbishop of Canterbury (1050). He was the head of the anti-English party which in 1051 banished Earl Godwin and his sons. Their return next year drove him to Normandy. The Witan stripped him of his archbishopric, and he died at Jumièges.

ROBERT OF MELUN, *me-lã* (d. 1167), English theologian, taught in Paris and Melun, and was elected Bishop of Hereford in 1163. He acted as a mediator between Becket and Henry II, latterly, however, giving his support to Becket.

ROBERTI, Ercole de' (*c*. 1455–96), Italian painter, born in Ferrara. His *Madonna* in the Brera Gallery, Milan, and *Pietà*, in the Walker Art Gallery, Liverpool, are characteristic of his work, which is less austere than that of Cossa and Tura (qq.v.), his contemporaries of the Ferrarese school. See B. Nicolson, *The Painters of Ferrara* (1950).

ROBERTS, (1) **Sir Charles George Douglas** (1860–1943), Canadian naturalist, writer and poet, born in New Brunswick, graduated at Fredericton in 1879, was professor in King's College, Nova Scotia (1885–95), and settled in New York as an author, joining the Canadian army at the outbreak of World War I. He wrote *Orion, In Divers Tones*, and other verse, a history of Canada, *Canada in Flanders* (1918), and nature studies, in which he particularly excelled, including *The Feet of the Furtive* (1912) and *Eyes of the Wilderness* (1933). He was knighted in 1935.

(2) **David** (1796–1864), Scottish painter, born at Edinburgh, October 24, as a scenepainter at Drury Lane attracted attention with pictures of Rouen and Amiens cathedrals at the Royal Academy. Among his pictures, the fruit of his wide travels, were *Departure of the Israelites from Egypt* (1829), *Jerusalem* (1845), *Rome* (1855) and *Grand Canal at Venice* (1856). He was elected R.A. in 1841. See Life by J. Ballantine (1866).

(3) **Frederick Sleigh Roberts, Earl, of Kandahar, Pretoria, and Waterford** (1832–1914), was born at Cawnpore. He was educated at Clifton, Eton, Sandhurst and Addiscombe; entered the Bengal Artillery in 1851; was at the siege of Delhi; and took an active part in the subsequent operations down to the relief of Lucknow, winning the V.C. in 1858. He was assistant quartermaster general in the Abyssinian (1868) and Lushai (1871–72) expeditions. In the Afghan war in 1878, now major-general, he forced the Afghan position on Peiwar Kotul, and was made K.C.B. (1879). After the murder of Cavagnari and his escort at Kabul, he defeated the Afghans at Charásia, took possession of Kabul, and assumed the government. Yákúb Khan was sent a prisoner to India, but Abdul Rahman was proclaimed amir, General Burrows was crushingly defeated at Maiwand, and the British Kandahar garrison was besieged. On August 9, 1880, he set out with 10,000 men on his memorable march through Afghanistan to the relief of Kandahar; three weeks later he reached it, and routed Ayub Khan. In 1881, now a baronet, he was appointed commander-in-chief of the Madras army, and in 1885–93 he was commander-in-chief in India. Created Lord Roberts of Kandahar and Waterford in 1892, he became field marshal and commander-in-chief in Ireland in 1895. He published *The Rise of Wellington* (1895) and *Forty-One Years in India* (1895). After the first checks of the Boer war he was sent out to assume the chief command, relieved Kimberley and made the great advance to Pretoria, and came home in 1901 to be commander-in-chief. Created earl in 1901, he retired in 1904, and died while visiting troops in the field in France. See Lives by Forest (1914), de Watteville (1938) and James (1954).

(4) **Morley** (1857–1942), English writer, born in London, was educated at Bedford and Owens College, served before the mast, on Australian sheep-runs, on Texan ranches, on Californian railways, and British Columbian sawmills, and multiplied his experiences in the South Seas, the Transvaal, Rhodesia and Corsica. From 1887 onwards he published a long series of works, mostly novels, including *The Purification of Dolores Silva* (1894), *The Colossus, A Son of Empire, Immortal Youth, Lady Penelope* (1904) and *Sea Dogs* (1910). See Life by Jameson (1961).

(5) **William Patrick** (1895–), English artist, born in London, was associated with Roger Fry, Wyndham Lewis (as a Vorticist) and with the London Group, and in both World Wars was an official war artist. His art is now devoted to the portrayal of Cockney characters in a very formal cubist, or rather cylindrical, style, with a certain satirical emphasis. He is represented in the Tate Gallery and became an A.R.A. in 1958

ROBERTS-AUSTEN, Sir William Chandler (1843–1902), English metallurgist, was born at Kennington, London. Elected F.R.S. In 1875, he was in 1880 appointed professor at the Royal School of Mines, two years later becoming chemist and assayer at the Mint. A pioneer of alloy research, he demonstrated the possibility of diffusion occurring between a sheet of gold and a block of lead.

ROBERTSON, (1) Brain Hubert, 1st Baron of Oakridge (1896–), British general, won the D.S.O. and M.C. in World War I and, retiring from the army, became managing director of the South African section of Dunlop (1935). In World War II he was General Alexander's administrative officer during the Italian campaign (1944–45), was deputy (1945), then military governor (1947), and finally high commissioner (1949–50) of the British Zone in Germany. From 1953–61 he was chairman of the British Transport Commission. He succeeded his father as 2nd baronet of Welbourn in 1919, and became a peer in 1961.

(2) **Frederick William** (1816–53), English clergyman, born in London, was educated for the army at Tours and Edinburgh, but devoting himself to the church, studied at Oxford (1837–40), and in 1847 became incumbent of Trinity Chapel, Brighton, where his earnestness, originality and sympathies for revolutionary ideals arrested attention, but provoked suspicion. He resigned in June 1853 because his vicar had refused to confirm his nomination of a curate. He published but one sermon—the five series (1855, 1855, 1857, 1859–63, 1880) so well known over the English-speaking world are really recollections, sometimes dictated and sometimes written out. See his *Life and Letters*, by the Rev. Brooke (1865).

(3) **George Croom** (1842–92), Scottish philosopher, born at Aberdeen, in 1866 became professor of Mental Philosophy and Logic at University College, London. He wrote on Hobbes, founded (1876) and edited *Mind*. See memoir by Prof. Bain prefixed to his *Philosophical Remains* (1894).

(4) **James Logie.** See HALIBURTON (1).

(5) **Joseph** (1810–66), Scottish antiquary, born and educated at Aberdeen, became historical curator at the Edinburgh Register House. He was an originator of the Aberdeen Spalding Club (1839–70), and contributed much to Chambers's *Encyclopaedia*. Among his works are *The Book of Bon-Accord* (1839) and *Concilia Scotiae: Ecclesiae Scoticanae Statuta, 1225–1559* (1866).

(6) **Madge.** See KENDAL.

(7) **Thomas William** (1829–71), English dramatist, brother of (6), was born at Newark-on-Trent, of an old actor family. Coming up to London in 1848, he was actor, prompter and stage manager, wrote unsuccessful plays, contributed to newspapers and magazines, translated French plays, &c. His first notable success as a dramatist was with

David Garrick (1864) and *Society* (1865), and his next comedy, *Ours* (1866), established his fame. *Caste* (1867), *Play* (1868), *School* (1869), *M.P.* (1870)—all brought out by the Bancrofts at the Prince of Wales Theatre—and *Home* (1869) and *Dreams* (1869) were all equally successful. See his *Principal Dramatic Works*, with memoir by his son (1889), and Life by Pemberton (1893).

(8) **William** (1721–93), Scottish historian, born at the manse of Borthwick in Midlothian, studied at Edinburgh, and at twenty-two was ordained minister of Gladsmuir. He volunteered for the defence of Edinburgh against the rebels in 1745, from 1751 took a prominent part in the General Assembly, and soon became leader of the ' Moderates '. From 1761 till his death he was joint minister with Dr Erskine of Greyfriars, Edinburgh. In 1761 he became a royal chaplain, in 1762 principal of Edinburgh University, and in 1764 king's historiographer. His *History of Scotland 1542–1603* (1759) was a splendid success. Next followed the *History of Charles V* (1769), his most valuable work, highly praised by Voltaire and Gibbon. The *History of America* appeared in 1777, and a disquisition on *The Knowledge which the Ancients had of India* in 1791. See Lives by Stewart (1801) and Gleig (1812).

(9) **Sir William Robert** (1860–1933), English soldier, enlisted as private in 1877 and rose to be field-marshal in 1920. Chief of the Imperial General Staff from 1915 to 1918, he became a baronet in 1919. See his autobiographical *From Private to Field-Marshal* (1921).

ROBERVAL, Gilles Personne de (1602–75), French mathematician, was born at Roberval near Beauvais, and in 1632 was appointed professor of Mathematics at the Collège de France. He devised a method of drawing tangents and invented the balance now called after him.

ROBESON, Paul Le Roy, *rōb'sėn* (1898–), American Negro singer and actor, born in Princeton, N.J., was admitted to the American bar before embarking on a stage career in New York in 1921, appearing in Britain in 1922. Success as an actor was matched by popularity as a singer, and he appeared in works ranging from *Show Boat* to plays by O'Neill and Shakespeare's *Othello*, a part which he first played in London in 1930 and in which he scored a triumphant American success ten years later. He gave song recitals, notably of Negro spirituals, throughout the world, and appeared in numerous films. From the end of World War II his racial and political sympathies somewhat embittered his relationship with the United States, and from 1958 to 1963, when he retired and returned to the U.S., he lived in England. See his autobiographical *Here I Stand* (1958) and Life by Seton (1958).

ROBESPIERRE, Maximilien Marie Isidore de, *rō-bės-pyayr* (1758–94), French revolutionary, was born, of Irish origin, at Arras, May 6, 1758. He was admitted *avocat* in 1781, and was elected to the States General in 1789 by Artois. He attached himself to the extreme Left, and soon commanded attention.

His influence grew daily, and the mob frantically admired his earnest cant and his boasted incorruptibility. In 1791 he carried the motion that no member of the present Assembly should be eligible for the next, and was appointed public accuser. Next followed the flight to Varennes (June 21), Lafayette's last effort to control the right of insurrection on the Champ-de-Mars (July 17), the abject terror of Robespierre, his hysterical appeal to the Club, the theatrical oath taken by every member to defend his life, and his conduct home in triumph by the mob at the close of the Constituent Assembly (September 30). The Girondist leaders in the new Legislative Assembly were eager for war. Robespierre offered a strenuous opposition in the Jacobin Club. In April 1792 he resigned his post of public accuser. In August he presented to the Legislative Assembly a petition for a Revolutionary Tribunal and a new Convention. It does not appear that he was responsible for the September massacres. He was elected first deputy for Paris to the National Convention, where the bitter attacks upon him by the Girondists threw him into closer union with Danton. Robespierre vigorously opposed the Girondist idea of a special appeal to the people on the king's death, and Louis's execution (January 21, 1793) opened up the final stage of the struggle, which ended in a complete triumph for the Jacobins on June 2. The first Committee of Public Safety was decreed in April 1793, and Robespierre, elected in July, was now one of the actual rulers of France; but it is doubtful whether henceforth he was not merely the stalking-horse for the more resolute party within the Twelve. Next came the dark intrigues and desperate struggles that sent Hébert and his friends to the scaffold in March 1794, and Danton and Camille Desmoulins in April. The next three months Robespierre reigned supreme. He nominated all the members of the Government Committees, placed his creatures in all places of influence in the commune of Paris, and assumed complete control of the Revolutionary Tribunal. But as his power increased his popularity waned. On May 7 Robespierre, who had previously condemned the cult of Reason, advocated a new state religion and recommended the Convention to acknowledge the existence of God; on June 8 the inaugural festival of the Supreme Being took place. Meantime the pace of the guillotine grew faster; public finance and government generally drifted to ruin, and Saint-Just demanded the creation of a dictatorship in the person of Robespierre. On July 26 the dictator delivered a long harangue complaining that he was being accused of crimes unjustly. The Convention, after at first obediently passing his decrees, next rescinded them and referred his proposals to the committees. That night at the Jacobin Club his party again triumphed. Next day at the Convention Saint-Just could not obtain a hearing, and Robespierre was vehemently attacked. A deputy proposed his arrest; at the fatal word Robespierre's power crumbled to ruin. He flew to the Common Hall, whereupon the Convention declared him an outlaw. The National Guard under Barras turned out to protect the Convention, and Robespierre had his lower jaw broken by a shot fired by a gendarme. Next day (July 28; 10th Thermidor 1794) he was sent to the guillotine with Saint-Just, Couthon, and nineteen others. See histories of the Revolution by Lamartine, Michelet, Blanc, Carlyle, Von Sybel, Morse Stephens, Taine, de Tocqueville, and Machar; the Lives by G. H. Lewes (1849) and Thompson (1939); Hamel's eulogistic *Vie de Robespierre* (1865-1867), also his *Thermidor* (1891); works by Hilaire Belloc (1902), Mathiez (trans. 1927) and J. Eagan (1938).

ROBEY, Sir George (1869-1954), English comedian, born at Herne Hill, first appeared on the stage in 1891, changed his name from Wade to Robey, made a name for himself in musical shows such as *The Bing Boys* (1916), and later emerged as a Shakespearean actor in the part of Falstaff. Dubbed the 'Prime Minister of Mirth', he was famous for his robust, often Rabelaisian humour, his bowler hat, long black collarless frockcoat, hooked stick and thickly painted eyebrows. He was knighted in 1954. See his *Looking Back on Life* (1933), and A. E. Wilson's *Prime Minister of Mirth* (1956).

ROBIN HOOD, the hero of a group of old English ballads, the gallant and generous outlaw of Sherwood Forest, where he spent his time gaily under the greenwood tree with Little John, Scarlet, Friar Tuck, and his merry men all. Unrivalled with bow and quarter-staff, he waged war on proud abbots and rich knights, helping himself to riches but giving generously to the poor and needy. The 'rymes of Robyn Hood' are named in *Piers Plowman* (c. 1377) and the plays of Robin Hood in the *Paston Letters* (1473). Tradition made the outlaw into a political personage, a dispossessed Earl of Huntingdon and other characters, and in Scott's *Ivanhoe* he is a Saxon holding out against the Normans. But there is no evidence that he was anything but the creation of popular imagination, a yeoman counterpart to the knightly King Arthur. There are about forty Robin Hood ballads, some eight of them of the first rank. See Gutch, *Lytell Geste of Robin Hode* (1847), Hales's Introduction to the *Percy Folio* (1867), especially Child's *Ballads* (part v. 1888), and the Bibliography by J. H. Gable (1939).

ROBINS, Benjamin (1707-51), English mathematician and father of the art of gunnery, was born, of Quaker family, at Bath. He set up as teacher of mathematics in London, published several treatises, commenced his experiments on the resisting force of the air to projectiles, studied fortification, and invented the ballistic pendulum. In 1735 he demolished, in a treatise on *Newton's Methods of Fluxions*, Berkeley's objections. His *New Principles of Gunnery* appeared in 1742. Engineer to the East India Company (1749), he died at Madras. His works were collected in 1761.

ROBINSON, (1) Anastasia. See PETER-BOROUGH.

(2) **Edward** (1794-1863), American scholar, born at Southington, Conn., studied in Germany, and in 1830 became a professor of Theology at Andover, in 1837 at New York.

His survey of Palestine (1838) resulted in *Biblical Researches in Palestine and Adjacent Countries* (1841); and a second visit in 1852 produced a second edition (1856). See Life by Smith and Hitchcock (1863). He married in 1828 **Therese Albertine Louise von Jakob** (1797-1869), daughter of a Halle professor; under the acronym of her initials, 'Talvj', she wrote *Psyche* (1825), and translated Scott's *Black Dwarf* and *Old Mortality*, and *Volkslieder der Serben* (1825-26).

(3) **Edwin Arlington** (1869-1935), American poet, of the traditional school, was born at Head Tide, Maine, and educated at Harvard. His publications include *Captain Craig* (1902), *The Town down the River* (1910), *The Man against the Sky*, which made his name, and *King Jasper* (1935) and he was three times a Pulitzer prizewinner, for his *Collected Poems* (1922), *The Man Who Died Twice* (1925) and *Tristram* (1928), one of his several modern renderings of Arthurian legends. See studies by E. Neff (1949) and E. Barnard (1952).

(4) **(Esmé Stuart) Lennox** (1886-1958), Irish dramatist, born at Douglas, Co. Cork. His first play, *The Clancy Game*, was produced in 1908 at the Abbey Theatre, Dublin, of which he was appointed manager in 1910 and then director from 1923 to 1956. Other plays include *The Cross Roads* (1909), *The Dreamers* (1915) and *The White-Headed Boy* (1920); he also compiled volumes of Irish verse, including the Irish *Golden Treasury* (1925), and edited Lady Gregory's *Journals* (1946). See his autobiographical *Three Homes* (1938) and *Curtain Up* (1941).

(5) **Frederick John.** See RIPON (1).

(6) **George Frederick Samuel.** See RIPON (2).

(7) **Henry Crabb** (1775-1867), English lawyer and diarist, born at Bury St Edmunds, was articled to a Colchester attorney 1790-95. From 1800 he studied for five years at German universities, making friends of the great German writers of the day, and during 1807-1809 was engaged on *The Times* in Spain—the first war correspondent. In 1813 he was called to the bar, from which he retired in 1828. A Dissenter and a Liberal, he was one of the founders of London University (1828). See the selections edited by Sadler (1869) and by Edith Morley (1922-29). See Life by Edith Morley (1935).

(8) **Hercules George Robert, Lord Rosmead** (1824-97), English colonial governor, brother of (13), second son of Admiral Hercules Robinson (1789-1864), became governor of Hong Kong (1859, with a knighthood), Ceylon (1865), New South Wales (1872), New Zealand (1878), and Cape Colony, perhaps the scene of his ablest administration (1880 and again 1895); he retired in 1897. In 1859 he was created a G.C.M.G., in 1890 a baronet, and in 1896 Lord Rosmead.

(9) **John** (c. 1576-1625), English clergyman, pastor of the Pilgrim Fathers, was born in Lincolnshire, studied at Cambridge, held a curacy at Norwich, became a Puritan and in 1608 escaped to Leyden, where he established a church in 1609. In 1620, after a memorable sermon, he saw part of his flock set sail in the *Speedwell* for Plymouth where they joined the *Mayflower*. He died at

Leyden. See Lives by Davis (1903), Ashton (in the *Works*, 1851), Powicke (1920), and Dr J. Brown's *Pilgrim Fathers* (1895).

(10) **Mary**, known as ' Perdita ' (1758–1800), English actress, born at Bristol, played Perdita and other Shakespearian parts at Drury Lane 1776–80, and became mistress in 1779 to the future George IV, who gave her a bond (never paid) for £20,000. She wrote poems, plays and novels; in 1783 she received a pension of £500, but died poor and ill. See her Memoirs, edited by her daughter (1801; 2nd ed. 1895).

(11) **Mary**. See DARMESTETER.

(12) **Sir Robert** (1886–   ), English chemist, was born in Chesterfield and educated at Manchester University. He held chairs at Sydney, Liverpool, St Andrews, Manchester, London and Oxford, where he was Waynflete professor from 1930 to 1955. He is particularly noted for his work on plant pigments, alkaloids and other natural products, and aided in the development of penicillin. From 1945 to 1950 he was president of the Royal Society, and was Nobel prizewinner for Chemistry in 1947. He was knighted in 1939, and awarded the O.M. in 1949.

(13) **Sir William Cleaver Francis** (1834–97), brother of (8), from 1874 was three times governor of Western Australia, and was created G.C.M.G. in 1887.

(14) **William Heath** (1872–1944), English artist, cartoonist and book-illustrator, was born in Hornsey Rise, London. He attended the Islington School of Art and the Royal Academy Schools, and in 1897 appeared an edition of *Don Quixote*, the first of many works to be illustrated by him; others include editions of *Arabian Nights* (1899), *Twelfth Night* (1908) and *Water Babies* (1915). But his fame, rests mainly on his humorous drawings—in his ability to poke fun, in colour and in black and white of superb draughtsmanship, at the machine age with countless ' Heath Robinson contraptions ' of absurd and complicated design and with highly practical and simple aims, such as the raising of one's hat, the shuffling and dealing of cards, or the recovering of a collar-stud which has slipped down the back. See his autobiographical *My Line of Life* (1938) and the study by L. Day (1947).

ROB ROY, Gaelic for ' Red Robert ' (1671–1734), Scottish freebooter, was the second son of Lieut.-Col. Donald Macgregor of Glengyle. Till 1661 the ' wicked clan Gregor' had for a century been pursued with fire and sword; the very name was proscribed. But from that year until the Revolution the severe laws against them were somewhat relaxed, and Rob Roy lived quietly enough as a grazier at Balquhidder. His herds were so often plundered by the outlaws from the north that he had to maintain a band of armed followers to protect both himself and such of his neighbours as paid him blackmail. And so with those followers espousing in 1691 the Jacobite cause, he did a little plundering for himself, and, two or three years later having purchased from his nephew the lands of Craigroyston and Inversnaid, laid claim to be chief of the clan. Suffering losses (1712)

in cattle speculations, for which he had borrowed money from the Duke of Montrose, his lands were seized, his houses plundered, and his wife turned adrift with her children in midwinter. Rob now gathered his clansmen and made open war on the duke. This was in 1716, the year after the Jacobite rebellion, in which at Sheriffmuir, Rob Roy had stood watch for the booty. Marvellous stories were current round Loch Katrine and Loch Lomond of his hairbreadth escapes, of his evasions when captured, and of his generosity to the poor, whose wants he supplied at the expense of the rich. They in return warned him of the designs of his arch-foes, the Dukes of Montrose and Atholl, and of the redcoats; besides, Rob enjoyed the protection of the Duke of Argyll, having assumed his mother's name—Campbell. Late in life he is said to have turned Catholic, but in the list of subscribers to the Episcopalian church history of Bishop Keith (1734) occurs the name ' Robert Macgregor *alias* Rob Roy '. On December 28, 1734, Rob Roy died in his own house at Balquhidder. He left five sons, two of whom died in 1754—James, the notorious outlaw James Mohr, in Paris; and Robin, the youngest, on the gallows at Edinburgh for abduction. See the introduction and notes to Scott's *Rob Roy* (1817); Dorothy Wordsworth's *Tour in Scotland in 1803*, with her brother's poem; and the Lives of Rob Roy by K. Macleay (1818; new ed. 1881) and A. H. Millar (1883).

ROBSART, Amy. See LEICESTER, EARL OF.

ROBSON, Dame Flora (1902–   ), English actress, born at South Shields, first appeared in 1921 and gained fame mainly in historical rôles in plays and films, as Queen Elizabeth in *Fire over England* (1931), Thérèse Raquin in *Guilty* (1944), &c. She was made D.B.E. in 1960. See Life by Dunbar (1960).

ROCHAMBEAU, Jean Baptiste Donatien de Vimeur, Comte de, *ro-shã-bō* (1725–1807), French soldier, born at Vendôme, entered the French army in 1742, was at the siege of Maestricht, and distinguished himself at Minorca in 1756. In 1780 he was sent out with 6000 men to support the Americans, and in 1781 rendered effective help at Yorktown. He became marshal in 1791, and in 1804 Napoleon made him a grand officer of the Legion of Honour. See his *Mémoires* (1809; Eng. trans. 1838).

ROCHE, St (*c.* 1295–1327), patron of the plague-smitten, was born at Montpellier. His festival is celebrated on August 16.

ROCHEFORT, Victor Henri, Marquis de Rochefort-Luçay, *rosh-for* (1832–1913), French journalist and politician, born in Paris, became a clerk in the hôtel-de-ville, but was dismissed in 1859 for neglecting his duties. He took to journalism, in 1868 starting *La Lanterne*, which was quickly suppressed. He fled to Brussels, but returning in 1869 on his election to the Chamber of Deputies, started the *Marseillaise*, in which he renewed his attacks on the imperial régime. On the cowardly murder of his contributor, Victor Noir, by Prince Pierre Bonaparte, the paper was suppressed and its editor imprisoned. The fall of the empire opened up a rôle for him. In 1871 he was elected to the National Assembly, and soon sided with the Communards in *Le Mot d'ordre*. He escaped from Paris, but the Prussians caught him and sent him to Versailles; sentenced to life imprisonment, he escaped from New Caledonia in 1874, and returned to France after the amnesty of 1880. His *L'Intransigeant* showed him intractable as ever. He sat in the National Assembly (1885–86), buried his influence in Boulangism, fled in 1889 to London, returned to Paris in 1895, and was an active anti-Dreyfusard. See his *Adventures of my Life* (trans. 1896).

ROCHEFOUCAULD. See LA ROCHEFOU-CAULD.

ROCHEJACQUELEIN. See LAROCHE-JACQUELEIN.

ROCHESTER, John Wilmot, Earl of (1647–1680), English courtier and poet, was born at Ditchley, Oxfordshire, and was educated at Burford school and Wadham College, Oxford. He travelled in France and Italy, and then repaired to court, where his handsome person and lively wit made him a prominent figure. In 1665 he showed conspicuous courage against the Dutch. He is said to have been a patron of the actress Elizabeth Barry (q.v.), and of several poets. With his friend Windham, he had engaged that, ' if either of them died, he should appear and give the other notice of the future state, if there was any '. Windham was killed, but did not disturb the rest of his friend, who now plunged into a life of the grossest debauchery and buffoonery, yet wrote excellent letters, satires and bacchanalian and amatory songs and verses. At the last he was moved to repentance by Bishop Burnet (see Burnet's *Passages of the Life and Death of John, Earl of Rochester,* 1680). Among the best of his poems are imitations of Horace and Boileau, *Verses to Lord Mulgrave,* and *Verses upon Nothing.* See Hayward's edition of his *Works* (1926), and studies by Prinz (Leipzig, 1927) and Williams (1935), and *The Rochester-Saville Letters* (ed. Wilson 1941).

ROCHESTER, Viscount. See OVERBURY.

ROCKEFELLER, John Davison (1839–1937), American millionaire monopolist and philanthropist, born at Richford, New York, in 1857 was clerk in a commission house and then in a small oil refinery at Cleveland, Ohio, and after 1875, by his Standard Oil Company founded with his brother **William** (1841–1922), secured control of the oil trade of America. He gave over 500 million dollars in aid of medical research, universities, Baptist churches, the Rockefeller Foundation being established in 1913 ' to promote the well-being of mankind. See study by W. H. Allen (1930). His son **John Davison, 2nd** (1874–1960), was chairman of the Rockefeller Institute of Medical Research. Of his sons, **John Davison, 3rd** (1906–), became chairman of the Rockefeller Foundation in 1952; **Nelson Aldrich** (1908–), elected Republican governor of New York State in 1958, was re-elected in 1962, and again in 1966; and **Winthrop** (1912–73), a racial moderate, became Republican governor of Arkansas in 1966. See book by J. Abels (1967).

ROCKINGHAM, Charles Watson Wentworth,

Marquis of (1730–82), English statesman, in 1750 was created Earl of Malton and succeeded his father as second Marquis. In 1751 he was made K.G.; but, opposing the policy of Bute, was dismissed from his appointments in 1762. As leader of the Whig Opposition, he was in 1765 called on to form his first ministry. He repealed the Stamp Act, and would have done more for progress but for court intrigues and the defection of the Duke of Grafton. He resigned in 1766, and opposed Lord North and his ruinous American policy. He again became premier in March 1782, but died four months later. See *Memoirs* by the Earl of Albemarle (1852).

ROCKSTRO, William Smith (1823–95), English organist, composer and authority on old music, was born at North Cheam, Surrey. He composed songs, madrigals and piano works, and wrote a Life of Handel, histories of music, and textbooks on harmony and counterpoint.

ROD, Édouard, *rod* (1857–1910), Swiss writer, born at Nyon in Vaud, studied at Lausanne, Bonn and Berlin, was professor at Geneva, and settled in Paris. Among his thirty works are *La Chute de Miss Topsy* (1882), *La Course à la mort* (1885), *Le Sens de la vie* (1889), *Le Dernier Refuge* (1896) and *Les Unis* (1909).

RODBERTUS, Johann Karl (1805–75), German economist, founder of scientific socialism, was the son of a Greifswald professor, held law appointments under the Prussian government, but in 1836 settled down on his estate. In 1848 he entered the Prussian National Assembly, and for a fortnight was minister of education; in 1849 he carried the Frankfurt constitution. He held that the socialistic ideal will work itself out gradually according to the natural laws of change and progress. The state will then own all land and capital, and superintend the distribution of all products of labour. See studies by E. Gonner (1899) and Thier, Lassalle and Wagner (1930).

RODD, Sir James Rennell. See RENNELL OF RODD.

RODERIC, the last Visigoth king of Spain, was defeated by the Moors beside the Guadalete, July 711, was killed in or drowned after the battle (if there was such a battle), or escaped and survived till 713.

RODGERS, (1) John (1771–1838), American sailor, born in Maryland, in 1798 entered the U.S. navy, and in 1805 he extorted treaties from Tripoli and Tunis, and in the war with Britain took twenty-three prizes.

(2) **John** (1812–82), American sailor, son of (1), in 1863 captured the Confederate ironclad *Atlanta,* and became rear-admiral and (1877) superintendent of the U.S. naval observatory. See Memoir by Prof. J. Russell (1882).

(3) **Richard.** See HAMMERSTEIN (2).

RODIN, (François) Auguste (René), *rō-dĭ* (1840–1917), French sculptor, was born in Paris, November 12, 1840, the son of a clerk. After three unsuccessful attempts to enter the École des Beaux-Arts, from 1864 (the year in which he produced his first great work, *L'Homme au nez cassé*) until 1875 he worked in Paris and Brussels under the sculptors Barye, Carrier-Belleuse and Van Rasbourg, collaborating with the latter in some of the decorations for the Brussels Bourse. In 1875 he travelled in Italy, studying the work of Donatello, Michelangelo and others, and in 1877 made a tour of the French cathedrals; much later, in 1914, he published *Les Cathédrales de la France*. The Italian masters and the Gothic cathedrals both influenced Rodin's work considerably, as did his interest in the ancient Greeks, but the greatest influence on him was the current trend of Romanticism. This prolific Impressionist sculptor, who said of his work that it glorified ' the latent heroism of all natural movement ', found his expression in the varying surfaces and degree of finish of his works, thus producing in sculpture of the most dramatic and imaginative conception the Impressionist painter's effects of light and shade. In 1877 Rodin exhibited anonymously at the Paris Salon the highly controversial *L'Âge d'airain*, the sculptor of which was accused of taking the cast from a living man, and in 1879 he exhibited the more highly developed *Saint Jean Baptiste*. The great *Porte de l'enfer*, inspired by Dante's *Inferno*, was commissioned for the Musée des arts décoratifs in 1880, and during the next thirty years Rodin was primarily engaged on the 186 figures for these bronze doors. Many of his works were originally conceived as part of the design of the doors, among them *Le Baiser* (1898) and *Ugolin*, both in the Luxembourg, and *Le Penseur* (1904), in front of the Panthéon in Paris. From 1886 to 1895 he worked on *Les Bourgeois de Calais*, there being replicas in London, at the Victoria Tower Gardens and in Paris of the original monument in Calais. His statues include those of Victor Hugo (1897) and Balzac (1898), the latter being refused recognition by the Societé des gens de lettres who had commissioned it; and among his portrait busts are those of Madame Rodin, Bastien-Lepage, Puvis de Chavannes, Victor Hugo and Bernard Shaw. His works are represented in the Musée Rodin, Paris, in the Rodin Museum, Philadelphia, and in the Victoria and Albert Museum, London, where there is a collection of his bronzes which he presented to the British nation in 1914. He died at Meudon near Paris, November 17, 1917. See works by Bourdelle (1937), S. Story (new ed. 1951) J. Cladel (new ed. 1953), Elsen (1964).

RODNEY, George Brydges Rodney, 1st Baron (1719–92), English sailor, born in London of an old Somersetshire family, entered the navy in 1732, was made lieutenant in 1739, in 1742 post-captain, and in 1747 had a brilliant share in Hawke's victory of October 14. Governor of Newfoundland 1748–52, in 1757 he served under Hawke in the futile expedition against Rochefort, and in 1758 under Boscawen at Louisburg. In 1759 as rear-admiral he commanded the squadron which bombarded Havre and destroyed the flotilla for the invasion of England. In 1761 he was appointed commander-in-chief on the Leeward Islands station, where in 1762 he captured Martinique, St Lucia and Grenada. A vice-admiral (1763) and baronet (1764), he was in 1765 appointed governor of

Greenwich Hospital, but in 1771 was recalled to active service, and sent out as commander-in-chief at Jamaica. In 1774 he returned to England, and was on half-pay till 1779, when, again commander-in-chief at the Leeward Islands, he put to sea with a powerful squadron for the relief of Gibraltar. In January 1780 he captured a Spanish convoy off Cape Finisterre. Passing Cape St Vincent on the 16th he met the Spanish squadron, and took seven ships out of eleven. In February he sailed for the West Indies, and in April and May fought three indecisive engagements with a French fleet. Now a K.B., in January 1781 he seized the Dutch settlements. In December he again sailed for the West Indies, off Dominica sighted the French fleet under de Grasse, and on April 12, 1782, captured seven ships and de Grasse himself, a victory of which the full extent was not realized by the new administration in England until after Admiral Pigot had been sent out to supersede Rodney. On his return to England, however, Rodney was raised to the peerage and received the thanks of parliament and a pension of £2000. He thereafter lived in retirement until his death in Hanover Square, May 24, 1792. See *Lives* by Mundy (1830) and Hannay (1891).

RODÓ, José Enrique, ro-THŌ' (1872–1917), Uruguayan writer and critic, born at Montevideo, wrote in Spanish *Ariel*, in which he stresses the importance of spiritual as compared with materialistic values, and other philosophical essays, such as *Motivos de Proteo* and *El Mirador del Prospero*.

ROE, (1) Edward Payson (1838–88), American clergyman and novelist, born in New Windsor, N.Y., became chaplain in the volunteer service (1862–65), and afterwards pastor of a Presbyterian church at Highland Falls. The Chicago fire of 1871 furnished him with a subject for his first novel, *Barriers Burned Away* (1872), whose success led him to resign his pastorate in 1874. See memoirs and reminiscences by his sister (1899).

(2) **Sir Thomas** (c. 1580–1644), English diplomat, born at Low Leyton, near Wanstead, studied at Magdalen, Oxford, and, after holding court appointments, was knighted in 1605, and sent as a political agent to the West Indies, Guiana and Brazil. M.P. for Tamworth (1614), in 1615–19 he was ambassador to the Great Mogul Jahangir at Agra, to the Porte in 1621–28, and afterwards to Germany. See the journal of his mission to Agra (new ed. 1921).

ROEBUCK, (1) John (1718–94), English inventor, grandfather of (2), was born in Sheffield, studied at Edinburgh, and graduated M.D. at Leyden. He gave up his practice in Birmingham to return to chemistry research, which led to improvements in methods of refining precious metals and in the production of chemicals. In 1759 he founded in Stirlingshire the Carron ironworks, and later was a friend and patron of James Watt (q.v.).

(2) **John Arthur** (1802–79), British politician, grandson of (1), was born at Madras but brought up in Canada. Coming to England in 1824, and called to the bar in 1831, in 1832 he became Radical member for Bath. He

represented Sheffield 1849–68, and again from 1874 till his death at Westminster. His motion for inquiring into the state of the army before Sebastopol overthrew the Aberdeen administration (1855). He supported Beaconsfield's policy during the Eastern crisis in 1877–78, and in 1879 was made a privy councillor. He wrote *Colonies of England* (1849) and *History of the Whig Ministry of 1830* (1852). See Leader's edition of his *Life and Letters* (1897).

ROEMER, Olaus, *rœ'mer* (1644–1710), Danish astronomer, was born at Aarhus, Jutland, and became professor of Astronomy at Copenhagen. He discovered the finite velocity of light, which he measured by observing the time variations in the eclipses of Jupiter's satellites. He erected the earliest practical transit instrument.

ROGER, *ro'jėr,* Fr. *ro-zhay,* name of two Norman counts of Sicily, one of whom became king:

Roger I (1031–1101), joined his famous brother, Robert Guiscard (q.v.), in South Italy, and helped him to conquer Calabria. In 1060 he was invited to Sicily to fight against the Saracens, and took Messina. Everywhere the Normans were welcomed as deliverers from the Moslem yoke; in 1071 the Saracen capital, Palermo, was captured, and Robert made Roger Count of Sicily. After Robert's death (1085) Roger succeeded to his Italian possessions, and became the head of the Norman power in southern Europe.

Roger II (1095–1154), second son of (1), became Count of Sicily, his mother at first acting as regent. On the death (1127) of the Duke of Apulia, grandson of Robert Guiscard, his duchy passed to Roger, who thereupon welded Sicily and South Italy into a strong Norman kingdom, of which he was crowned king by Anacletus the antipope in 1130. He next added to his dominions Capua (1136), Naples and the Abruzzi (1140). In 1139 he took prisoner Pope Innocent II, with whom he concluded a bargain, Innocent recognizing him as King of Sicily, whilst Roger acknowledged Innocent and held his kingdom as a fief of the Holy See. The Byzantine Emperor Manuel having insulted his ambassador, Roger's admiral, George of Antioch, ravaged the coasts of Dalmatia and Epirus, took Corfu, and plundered Corinth and Athens (1146). He carried off silk-workers, and introduced that industry into Sicily. Finally (1147), Roger won Tripoli, Tunis and Algeria. His court was one of the most magnificent in Europe, and his government was firm and enlightened.

ROGER-DUCASSE, Jean Jules Aimable, *ro-zhay-dü-kas* (1873–1954), French composer, was born and died in Bordeaux. He studied under Fauré, in 1909 was appointed inspector of singing to Paris schools, and in 1935 succeeded Dukas at the Paris Conservatoire. His works include piano pieces, an opera, *Cantegril* (1931), choral works, and orchestral pieces. See French study by L. Ceillier (Paris 1920).

ROGER OF HOVEDON, English chronicler, was probably born at Howden in Yorkshire, and died about 1201, with which year his Latin *Chronicle* ends. It was edited by

Stubbs (Rolls Series, 1868–71) and translated by Riley (1853).

ROGER OF WENDOVER (d. 1236), prior of the Benedictine monastery of St Albans, revised and carried on the abbey chronicle, enlarged later by Matthew Paris (q.v.).

ROGERS, (1) Bernard (1893–), American composer, born in New York. He studied under Ernest Bloch and Nadia Boulanger, and lived for a time in England, before becoming a professor of Composition at the Eastman School of Music. An amateur painter, much of his music is pictorial in intention, and he composes mainly for orchestra in classical forms. His works include operas, symphonies, an oratorio, *The Passion* (1941–42), and cantatas on Biblical subjects.

(2) **Claude** (1907–), English artist, born in London, studied and lectured at the Slade School, professor of Fine Art at Reading Univ. from 1963, and president of the London group from 1952 until 1965. With Victor Pasmore and William Coldstream he founded the Euston Road School in 1937. His work is represented in the Tate Gallery, Ashmolean Museum, &c.

(3) **James Edwin Thorold** (1823–90), English economist, born at West Meon, Hampshire, became professor of Political Economy at Oxford 1862–67, but made so many enemies by his outspoken zeal for reforms that he was not re-elected till 1888. An advanced Liberal, he represented Southwark 1880–85, and Bermondsey 1885–86. He wrote many works on economics.

(4) **John** (*c.* 1500–55), English Marian protomartyr, born near Birmingham, was a London rector 1532–34, and at Antwerp and Wittenberg embraced the Reformed doctrines. He helped to prepare the revised translation called ' Matthew's Bible ' in 1537, and, having married and returned to England in 1548, preached at St Paul's Cross in 1553, just after Mary's accession, against Romanism, and was burned. See Life by J. L. Chester (1861).

(5) **Randolph** (1825–92), U.S. sculptor, lived in Rome, was born at Waterloo, N.Y. His statues include *Ruth* (Metropolitan Museum, N.Y.) and *Lincoln* (Philadelphia).

(6) **Samuel** (1763–1855), English poet, born at Stoke-Newington, at sixteen or seventeen entered his father's bank, in 1784 was taken into partnership, and in 1793 became head of the firm. In 1781 he contributed essays to the *Gentleman's Magazine*, next year wrote a comic opera, and in 1786 published *An Ode to Superstition.* In 1792 appeared *The Pleasures of Memory,* on which his poetical fame was chiefly based (19th ed. 1816). There followed *An Epistle to a Friend* (Richard Sharp, 1798), the fragmentary *Voyage of Columbus* (1812), *Jacqueline* (1814, bound up with Byron's *Lara*), and the inimitable *Italy* (1822–28). The last, in blank verse, proved a monetary failure; but the loss was recouped by the splendid edition of it and his earlier poems, brought out at a cost of £15,000 (1830–34), with 114 illustrations by Turner and Stothard. In 1803, with £5000 a year, he withdrew from the bank as a sleeping partner, and settled down to bachelor life at 22 St James's Place, to cultivate his muse and

caustic wit, to raise breakfast-giving to a fine art, to make little tours at home and on the Continent, and to gather an art collection which sold at his death for £50,000. He made a good use of his riches, for he was quietly generous to Moore and Campbell, as well as to some unknown writers. But with the kindest heart he had so unkind a tongue that ' melodious Rogers ' is better remembered today by a few ill-natured sayings than by his poetry. See Dyce's *Table-talk of Samuel Rogers* (1856); *Recollections by Rogers*, edited by his nephew William Sharpe (1859); works by Clayden (1887, 1889) and Roberts (1910); the *Reminiscences and Table-talk*, ed. Powell (1903) and C. P. Barbier, *Samuel Rogers and William Gilpin* (1959).

(7) **Woodes** (d. 1732), English navigator, led a privateering expedition against the Spanish (1708–11) which took off Alexander Selkirk (q.v.) from Juan Fernández island and on his successful return wrote *Voyage round the World* (1712). As governor of the Bahamas (1718–21, 1729–32) he suppressed piracy, founded a House of Assembly and resisted Spanish attacks.

ROGET, Peter Mark, *ro-zhay* (1779–1869), English scholar and physician, son of a Huguenot minister, became physician to the Manchester Infirmary in 1804; physician to the Northern Dispensary, London, in 1808, F.R.S. (1815), and its secretary 1827–49; Fullerian professor of Physiology at the Royal Institution 1833–36; and an original member of senate of London University. He wrote *On Animal and Vegetable Physiology* (Bridgewater Treatise, 1834); and his *Thesaurus of English Words and Phrases* (1852) reached a 28th edition in his lifetime.

ROGIER VAN DER WEYDEN. See WEYDEN.

ROHAN-GIÉ, Henri, Duc de, *rō-ä-zhee-ay* (1579–1638), Prince of Léon, born at the Château of Blain in Brittany, was a favourite of Henry IV, and in 1605 married the daughter of Sully. After the king's murder he became a Huguenot leader. On the surrender of La Rochelle (1628) a price was set on his head, and he made his way to Venice, but soon after was summoned by Richelieu to serve his king in the Valtelline, out of which he drove Imperialists and Spaniards. He next served under Bernard of Saxe-Weimar, but died in 1638 of a wound received at Rheinfelden. See his *Mémoires* (1630 and 1738), and works by Fauvelet du Toc (1667), Schybergson (1880), Lagarde (1884), Laugel (1889), and Veraguth (German, 1894), and the *Edinburgh Review* for April 1890.

ROHAN-GUÉMÉNÉE, Louis René Édouard, Prince de, *rō-ä-gay-may-nay* (1734–1803), French cardinal, embraced the clerical life in spite of dissolute morals, and became coadjutor to his uncle the Bishop of Strasbourg. In 1772 he was sent as minister to Vienna, but injured himself at the French court by slanderous gossip about Marie Antoinette, and was recalled in 1774. In 1778 he received a cardinal's hat, and in 1779 became Bishop of Strasbourg. His eagerness to recover his footing at court made him an easy prey to Cagliostro and the Comtesse de La Motte, who tricked him into believing that the queen knew nothing of the affair, wished him to stand security for her purchase by instalments of a priceless diamond necklace. The adventurers collected the necklace from the jewellers supposedly to give it to the queen, but left Paris in order to sell the diamonds for their own gain. When the plot was discovered Rohan Guéménée was sent to the Bastille, but was acquitted by the *parlement* of Paris, 1786. He was elected to the States-General in 1789, but refused to take the oath to the constitution in 1791, retiring to the German part of his diocese, where he died. See works cited at LA MOTTE (2).

ROHLFS, Gerhard, *rōlfs* (1831–96), German explorer, born at Vegesack near Bremen, studied medicine, and joined (1855) the Foreign Legion in Algeria. He travelled through Morocco (1861–62), and was plundered and left for dead in the Sahara. From 1864 he travelled widely in North Africa, the Sahara and Nigeria, and, commissioned by the German emperor, undertook expeditions to Wadai (1878) and Abyssinia (1885). He wrote books about his travels, including *Drei Monate in der Libyschen Wüste* (1875) and *Quid novi ex Africa?* (1886).

RÖHM, Ernst, *rœm* (1887–1934), German soldier, politician and Nazi leader, early a supporter of Hitler, was organizer and commander of the stormtroopers, and as such was executed on Hitler's orders in June 1934. See his Memoirs (1934).

ROHMER, Sax, pseud. of **Arthur Sarsfield Ward,** *rō'mėr* (1886–1959), English author of mystery stories, was born in Birmingham. Early interested in things Egyptian, he found literary fame with his sinister, sardonic, Oriental villain, Fu Manchu, whose doings were told in many spine-chilling tales of the East, including *Dr Fu Manchu* (1913), *The Yellow Claw* (1915), *Moon of Madness* (1927) and *Re-enter Fu Manchu* (1957).

ROKITANSKY, Karl, Baron von (1804–78), Austrian physician, born in Königgrätz, professor 1834–75 of Pathological Anatomy at Vienna, wrote the great *Handbuch der pathologischen Anatomie* (1842–46; trans. 1849–52).

ROKOSSOVSKY, Konstantin, *-sof'ski* (1896–1968), Russian soldier, born in Warsaw of Polish descent, served in the first World War in the tsarist army, and joined the Red Guards in 1917. In the second World War he was one of the defenders of Moscow, played a leading part in the battle of Stalingrad, recaptured Orel and Warsaw, and led the Russian race for Berlin. In 1944 he was promoted marshal of the Soviet Union, and at the end of the war Field-Marshal Montgomery presented him with the Order of the Bath (K.C.B.). In 1949 he was appointed Polish minister of defence, a post he was made to resign when Gomulka became premier in November 1956. He then became a deputy-minister of defence of the Soviet Union, and in 1957 he was appointed to a military command in Transcaucasia.

ROLAND, *ro-lä* (acc. to tradition d. 778), hero of the *Chanson de Roland* (11th century) and most celebrated of the Paladins of Charlemagne, was the nephew of Charlemagne, and the ideal of a Christian knight. The only evidence for his historical existence is one (doubtfully genuine) passage in Einhard's *Life of Charlemagne*, which refers to Roland as having fallen at Roncesvalles. Boiardo's *Orlando Innamorato* and Ariosto's *Orlando Furioso* depart widely from the old traditions.

ROLAND DE LA PLATIÈRE, Jean Marie, *ro-lā dĕ la pla-tyayr* (1734–93), French statesman, born near Villefranche-sur-Saône, February 18, 1734, had risen to be inspector of manufactures at Amiens, when in 1775 he made the acquaintance of **Marie Jeanne Phlipon** (1754–93), the daughter of an engraver, whom he married in February 1780. In 1791 Roland was sent to Paris by Lyons to watch the interests of the municipality; and there Madame Roland became the queen of a coterie of young and eloquent enthusiasts that included all the leaders of the Gironde, such as Brissot, Pétion and François Buzot (1760–94). In March 1792 Roland became minister of the interior, but was dismissed three months later for a remonstrance to the king. He was recalled after the king's removal to the Temple, made himself hateful to the Jacobins by his protests against the September massacres, and took part in the last struggle of the Girondists. It was then that the friendship between Madame Roland and Buzot grew into love, but she sacrificed passion to duty. On May 31, 1793, the Twenty-two were proscribed. Roland had been arrested, but escaped and fled to Rouen; Buzot and others fled to Caen to organize insurrection, but in vain; next day Madame Roland was carried to the Abbaye. Set at liberty two days later, she was arrested anew and taken to Sainte-Pélagie. During her five months in prison she wrote her unfinished *Mémoires*, in which we have a serene and delightful revelation of her youth, though she is best and most natural in her letters. On November 8, 1793, she was guillotined. Two days later her husband committed suicide by his sword near Rouen. See book by U. Pope-Hennessy (1917).

ROLLAND, Romain, *ro-lā* (1866–1944), French author, born in Clamecy, Nièvre, studied in Paris and at the French School in Rome, and in 1895 gained his doctorate of letters with a thesis on early opera, *L'Histoire de l'opéra en Europe avant Lulli et Scarlatti*; a number of dramatic works written at this time won comparatively little success. In 1910 he became professor of the History of Music at the Sorbonne, and in the same year published *Beethoven,* the first of many biographical works including lives of Michelangelo (1906), Handel (1910), Tolstoy (1911) and Gandhi (1924). His ten-volume novel *Jean-Christophe,* the hero of which is a musician, was written between 1904 and 1912, and in 1915 he was awarded the Nobel prize for literature. During the first World War he aroused unpopularity by his writings, out of Switzerland, showing a pacifist attitude; these were published in 1915 as *Au dessus de la mêlée.* He lived in Switzerland until 1938, completing a series of plays upon the French Revolution, several novels, and a further study of Beethoven, as well as numerous pieces of music criticism. On his return to France he became a mouthpiece of

the opposition to Fascism and Naziism, and his later works contain much political and social writing. See books by S. Zweig (1921), M. Descotes (Paris 1948) and R. Arcos (Paris 1950).

ROLLE, Richard. See HAMPOLE.

ROLLESTON, George, *rōl'stĕn* (1829–81), English physician, born near Rotherham, elected Linacre professor of Anatomy and Physiology at Oxford in 1860, is known for his *Forms of Animal Life* (1876) and for his dissertation on craniology in Greenwell's *British Barrows* (1877).

ROLLIN, (1) Charles (1661–1741), French historian, born in Paris, was author of *Traité des études* (1726–31), *Histoire ancienne* (1730–38) and *Histoire romaine* (1738–48). He lost the rectorship of Paris University (1720) and other academic posts because of his Jansenist sympathies.

(2) **Ledru.** See LEDRU-ROLLIN.

ROLLO, or Rou (*c.* 860–*c.* 932), leader of a band of Northmen, secured from Charles the Simple in 912 a large district on condition of being baptized and becoming Charles's vassal. This grant was the nucleus of the duchy of Normandy. William the Conqueror's ancestor, Rollo is probably the same as Rólf the Ganger, a Norwegian chief outlawed by Harold Haarfager about 872.

ROLLOCK, Robert, *rol'ĕk* (*c.* 1555–99), born at Powis near Stirling, in 1583 became first regent, in 1585 first principal, of Edinburgh University. He wrote Latin commentaries. See Masson's *Edinburgh Sketches* (1892).

ROLLS, Charles Stewart, *rōlz* (1877–1910), automobilist and aeronaut, was born in London, the third son of the 1st Baron Llangattock. Educated at Eton and Cambridge, from 1895 he experimented with the earliest motor cars and combined with F. H. Royce (q.v.) for their production. In 1906 he crossed the English Channel by balloon, and in 1910 made a double crossing by aeroplane. He lost his life in a crash soon afterwards. See H. F. Morriss, *Two Brave Brothers* (1929), and study by L. Meynell (1955).

RÖLVAAG, Ole Edvart, *rol'vahg* (1876–1931), American author, born at Dönna, Norway, emigrated to America, becoming an American citizen in 1910. Writing in Norwegian, he published in 1912 his *Letters from America,* and his best-known novel, translated as *Giants in the Earth* (1927), dealing with the life of Norwegian settlers in South Dakota in the 1870s, was followed by *Peder Victorious* (1929) and *Their Fathers' God* (1931). See biography by Jorgenson and Solum (1939).

ROMAINS, Jules, *ro-mi,* pseud. of **Louis Farigoule** (1885–1972), French writer, born at Saint-Julien Chapteuil, after graduating in both science and literature at the École normale supérieure, taught in various lycées. In 1908 his poems, *La Vie unanime,* established his name and, along with his *Manuel de déification* (1910), the Unanimist school. He remained prominent in French literature, and was from 1936 to 1941 president of the International P.E.N. Club. His works include the books of poems *Odes et prières* (1913), *Chants des dix années 1914–1924* (1928), *L'Homme blanc* (1937), the dramas

L'Armée dans la ville (1911), Knock ou le triomphe de la médecine (1923), his most successful play, and the novels Mort de quelqu'un (1910), Les Copains (1913), and the great cycle Les Hommes de bonne volonté in 27 volumes (1932–46), covering the early 20th-century era of French life. See his autobiographical Souvenirs et confidences d'un écrivain (1958).

ROMAN, Johan Helmich, roo'man (1694–1758), Swedish composer of the baroque era, twice visited England, where he met Handel, Geminiani and other leading figures in contemporary music, travelled in France and Italy, and in 1745 was appointed intendent of music to the Swedish court. His compositions, which include symphonies, concerti grossi, trio sonatas, a Swedish Mass, settings in the vernacular of the Psalms, and occasional music, show the influence of the Italian style and, less markedly, of Handel and the French and North German schools.

ROMANES, George John, rō-mah'neez (1848–1894), British naturalist, born at Kingston, Canada. While at Cambridge University he formed a friendship with Darwin, and he powerfully reinforced his master's arguments in his Croonian, Fullerian and other lectures, and in his various works—Animal Intelligence (1881), Scientific Evidences of Organic Evolution (1881), &c. He was elected an F.R.S. in 1879, married in that year, removed in 1890 to Oxford, and died there in 1894. Originally a defiant agnostic or sceptic, he was latterly a devout, if not wholly orthodox, Christian. See Life by his wife (1896).

ROMANINO, Girolamo (1485–1566), Italian religious painter, was born and died at Brescia, and worked in Padua, Venice and Cremona. See Pater's Miscellaneous Studies (1895).

ROMANO, Giulio. See GIULIO.

ROMANOV, ro-ma'nof, a family that originally emigrated from (Slavonic) Prussia to the principality of Moscow. Its head, Michael, was elected tsar by the other Russian boyars in 1613, and the tsardom became hereditary in his house till in 1762, on the death of the Tsaritsa Elizabeth, the Duke of Holstein-Gottorp, son of Peter the Great's daughter, succeeded as Peter III. Later tsars (till the 1917 revolution) were descended from him and his wife, Catharine II.

ROMILLY, Sir Samuel (1757–1818), English lawyer and law reformer, was born in London, the son of a watchmaker of Huguenot descent. At twenty-one he entered Gray's Inn, and found his chief employment in Chancery practice. In 1790 he published an able pamphlet on the French Revolution. Appointed solicitor-general in 1806, and knighted, he entered parliament and pertinaciously set himself to mitigate the severity of the criminal law. He shared in the anti-slavery agitation, and opposed the suspension of the Habeas Corpus Act and the spy system. He committed suicide three days after his wife's death. See his Speeches (1820), Memoirs (1840), and a book by C. G. Oakes (1935). His second son, John, Baron Romilly (1802–74), was solicitor-general in 1848, attorney-general in 1850, master of the rolls in 1851, and a baron in 1866.

ROMMEL, Erwin (1891–1944), German field-marshal, born at Heidenheim, educated at Tübingen, distinguished himself in World War I. An instructor at the Dresden Military Academy, Rommel was an early Nazi sympathizer. He commanded Hitler's headquarters guard during the Austrian, Sudeten-land and Czech occupations and throughout the Polish campaign. Leading a Panzer Division during the 1940 invasion of France, he displayed such drive and initiative that he was promoted to command the Afrika Korps, where his spectacular successes against the attenuated 8th Army earned him the sobriquet of the 'Desert Fox' and the unstinted admiration of his opponents. Rusé and brilliantly opportunist, and with a talent for improvisation extremely rare in the German, his chief defect was a tendency to desert his headquarters in action for 'up forward', and thus lose control of the battle. Eventually driven into retreat by a strongly reinforced 8th Army, he was withdrawn—a sick man—from North Africa at Mussolini's insistence, the Duce believing that 'the Italian generals do better' (Goebbels Diaries). Hitler consoled him with the award of the Knight's Cross with diamonds, subsequently appointing him to an Army Corps command in France. Returning home wounded in 1944, his condoning of the plot against the Fuehrer's life brought him the choice between court martial and the firing squad, and suicide. He chose to die by self-administered poison, thus preserving his estate for his family. See Rommel, Young (1950), The Rommel Papers (1953).

ROMNEY, George, rom'ni or rum'ni (1734–1802), English painter, born at Dalton-in-Furness, Lancashire, worked for ten years at his father's trade of cabinetmaker. In 1755 he was articled to a 'Count' Steele at Kendal to be taught 'the art or science of a painter'; in 1756 married Mary Abbot of Kirkland; in 1757 set up as a portrait painter; and in 1762 came up to London, leaving behind wife, boy and baby girl, because, it is said, Sir Joshua Reynolds had told him that art and marriage do not mix. Of Romney's next thirty-five years there is little to record beyond his two visits to France (1764; 1790) and his two years' residence in Italy (1773–75), after which, for twenty-two years, he lived in Cavendish Square, and slaved at his art, which so far rewarded him that in 1786 he made by portrait painting 3500 guineas. Lady Hamilton (q.v.) he painted in fully thirty characters. Sensibility, Miss Sneyd as Serena, and The Parson's Daughter are also well known. In 1799, nearly mad and quite desolate, Romney returned to Kendal to his wife, who received him charitably and nursed him with devotion until his death in 1802. See, besides the Memoirs by Hayley (1809) and his son, the Rev. John Romney (1830), the Lives by Ward and Roberts (1904), and Henderson (1922); also works by Gower (1882, 1904), Chamberlain (1911) and Lloyd (1917).

ROMULUS, rom'yoo-lus, legendary founder and first king of Rome, according to tradition the son by Mars of Rhea Silvia, the daughter of King Numitor of Alba Longa, with his twin brother Remus exposed by a usurping uncle, but suckled by a she-wolf. In 753 B.C. he founded his city on the Tiber, and in 716 was said to have been carried up to heaven in a chariot of fire.

ROMULUS AUGUSTUS. See AUGUSTULUS.

RONALD, orig. **Russell, Sir Landon** (1873–1938), English conductor, composer and pianist, was a son of Henry Russell, the songwriter. He toured with Melba, conducted the New Symphony Orchestra, notably in Elgar, Strauss and Tchaikovsky, was principal of the Guildhall School of Music (1910–37), wrote many songs, including ' Down in the Forest Something Stirred ', and was knighted in 1922. See his autobiographical *Variations on a Personal Theme* (1922) and *Myself and Others* (1931).

RONALDS, Sir Francis (1788–1873), English inventor, a London merchant's son, in 1816 fitted up in his garden at Hammersmith an electric telegraph. His offer of the invention to the Admiralty was refused; he published a description of it in 1823. He also invented (1845) a system of automatic photographic registration for meteorological instruments. He was made superintendent of the Meteorological Observatory at Kew in 1843, F.R.S. in 1844, and knighted in 1871.

RONDELET, Guillaume, *rŏ-dė-lay* (1507–66), French naturalist and physician, was born at Montpellier, where he became in 1545 professor of Medicine, and published two important works (1544 and 1555) on aquatic animals of the Mediterranean.

RONSARD, Pierre de, *rŏ-sahr* (1524–85), French poet, born at the Château de la Possonnière in Vendôme, September 11, served the dauphin and the Duc d'Orléans as page, and accompanied James V with his bride, Marie de Lorraine, to Scotland, where he stayed three years. Becoming deaf, he abandoned arms for letters, and studied under the great humanist Jean Dorat, at first with his future fellow member of the Pléiade, Jean Antoine de Baïf, at the house of his father the scholar and diplomat Lazare de Baïf, and later at the Collège de Coqueret, where du Bellay and Belleau (qq.v.) joined them. His seven years of study bore its first fruit in the *Odes* (1550), which excited violent opposition from the older national school. In 1552 appeared his *Amours,* a collection of Petrarchian sonnets, followed by his *Bocage* (1554), his *Hymnes* (1555), the conclusion of his *Amours* (1556), and the first collected edition of his poetry (1560). He subsequently wrote two bitter reflections on the political and economic state of the country—*Discours des misères de ce temps* (1560–69) and *Remonstrance au peuple de France* (1563), and in 1572, following the massacre of St Bartholomew, *La Françiade,* an unfinished epic. Charles IX, like his predecessors, heaped favours on the poet, who, despite recurrent illness, spent his later years in comfort at the abbey of Croix-Val in Vendôme. He died at his priory of St Cosme-les-Tours. The most important poet of 16th-century France, Ronsard was the chief exemplar of the doctrines of the Pléiade, which aimed at raising the status of French as a literary language and ousting the formal classicism

inherited from the Middle Ages. Despite the great success of Ronsard's poems in his lifetime, the classicists regained the upper hand after his death, and his fame suffered an eclipse until the 19th century, when the Romantic movement brought recognition of his true worth. See Lives by Binet (1586) and Bishop (1940), and studies by Franchet (1922), Cohen (1923), Gadoffre (1960), and Desonay (3 vols., 1952, 1954, 1961).

RÖNTGEN, Wilhelm Konrad von, *rænt'gėn* (1845–1923), German physicist, was born at Lennep in Prussia, studied at Zürich, and was professor at Strasbourg, Giessen, Würzburg, and (1899–1919) Munich. At Würzburg in 1895 he discovered the electric-magnetic rays which he called X-rays (known also as Röntgen rays), and for his work on them he was awarded in 1896, jointly with Lenard (q.v.), the Rumford medal, and in 1901 the Nobel prize for physics. He also did important work on the heat conductivity of crystals, the specific heat of gases, and the electromagnetic rotation of polarized light. See study by O. Glasser (new ed. 1958).

ROOKE, Sir George (1650–1709), English admiral, born near Canterbury, became at thirty post-captain, and in 1689 rear-admiral. In 1692 he did splendid service at Cape La Hogue, and was knighted. In 1702 he commanded the expedition against Cadiz, and destroyed the plate-fleet at Vigo. With Sir Cloudesley Shovel he captured Gibraltar (1704), and then engaged off Málaga a much heavier French fleet. See his *Journal* (1897).

ROON, Albrecht Theodor Emil, Graf von, *rōn* (1803–79), Prussian war minister from 1859, effectively reorganized the army and wrote on military subjects.

ROOSEVELT, *rōz'ė-velt,* (1) **Anna Eleanor** (1884–1962), niece of (3), wife of (2), whom she married in 1905, took up extensive political work during her husband's eight years' illness and proved herself an invaluable social adviser to him when he became president. In 1941 she became assistant director of the office of civilian defence; after her husband's death in 1945 she extended the scope of her activities, and was a delegate to the U.N. Assembly in 1946, chairman of the U.N. Human Rights Commission (1947–51) and U.S. representative at the General Assembly (1946–52). She was also chairman of the American U.N. Association. Her publications include *The Lady of the White House* (1938), *India and the Awakening East* (1953), *On My Own* (1959), and her Autobiography (1962).

(2) **Franklin Delano** (1884–1945), thirty-second president of the United States, a distant cousin of (3), was born near Poughkeepsie, N.Y. He became a barrister (1907), a New York state senator (1910–13), assistant secretary of the navy (1913–20), and was Democratic candidate for the vice-presidency in 1920. Stricken (1921–24) by paralysis, he was governor of New York (1928–32). In the presidential election of 1932 he defeated Hoover, repeal of prohibition being a vital party issue, and at once in 1933 met an economic crisis with his ' New Deal ' for national recovery. He was elected for a second term in 1936, a third (a new thing in American

history) in 1940, a fourth in 1944. He strove in vain to ward off war, modified America's neutrality to favour the Allies (as by the Lend-Lease plan), and was brought in by Japan's action at Pearl Harbour (1941). A conference with Churchill at sea produced the ' Atlantic Charter ', a statement of peace aims; and there were other notable meetings, as with Churchill and Stalin at Tehran and Yalta. He died at Warm Springs, Georgia, where he had long gone for treatment, three weeks before the Nazi surrender. See studies by Lindley (1932, 1933 and 1937), Perkins (1947), Sherwood, *Roosevelt and Hopkins*, Schlesinger, *The Age of Roosevelt* (3 vols., 1957, 1959, 1961), and Leuchtenburg, *F.D.R. and the New Deal* (1963).

(3) **Theodore** (1858–1919), twenty-sixth president of the United States, was born, of Dutch and Scottish descent, in New York, studied at Harvard, was leader of the New York legislature in 1884, and president of the New York police board in 1895–97. He was assistant secretary of the navy when in 1898 he raised and commanded ' Roosevelt's Roughriders ' in the Cuban war, and came back to be governor of New York State (1898–1900). Appointed (Republican) vice-president (1901), he became president on the death (by assassination) of McKinley (1901), and was re-elected in 1905. An ' expansionist ', he insisted on a strong navy, the purification of the civil service, and the regulation of trusts and monopolies. He returned from a great hunting tour in Central Africa in time to take active part in the elections of 1910, and helped to split the Republican party, those with whom he acted forming the ' progressive ' section. As Progressive candidate for the presidency in 1912 he was defeated by Wilson. After exploring the Rio Duvida, or Teodoro, in Brazil (1914), he worked vigorously during World War I. He wrote on American ideals, ranching, hunting, zoology. See his *Autobiography* (1913), G. E. Mowry, *The Era of Theodore Roosevelt* (1958), and Lives by Pringle (1932) and Putnam (1959).

ROOT, Elihu (1845–1937), American statesman, born at Clinton, N.Y., was U.S. secretary of war 1899–1904, of state 1905–09, and was awarded a Nobel peace prize in 1912 for his promotion of international arbitration.

ROOZEBOOM, Hendrik Willem Bakhuis, *rō'zĕ-bōm* (1854–1907), Dutch physical chemist, born at Alkmaar, became professor of Chemistry at Amsterdam. He demonstrated the practical application of Gibbs's phase rule.

ROPER, Margaret. See MORE (3).

ROPS, Felicien (1833–98), Belgian artist, born at Namur, known for his lithographs and etchings, which often had satirical or social significance, and for his illustrations of the works of Baudelaire.

RORSCHACH, Hermann (1884–1922), Swiss psychiatrist and neurologist, born at Zürich, devised a diagnostic procedure for mental disorders based upon the patients' interpretation of a series of standardized ink blots. See Klopfer and Kelly, *Rorschach Technique* (1946).

ROSA, *rō'za*, (1) orig. **Rose, Carl August**

Nicolas (1842–89), German impresario and violinist, born at Hamburg, became *konzertmeister* there in 1863, appeared in London as a soloist in 1866, and in 1873 founded the Carl Rosa Opera Company, giving a great impulse to ' English opera '—opera sung in English, and also operas by English composers.

(2) **Salvator** (1615–73), Italian painter, was born near Naples. At Rome his talents as painter, improvisatore, actor and poet brought him fame, but he made powerful enemies by his satires, and withdrew to Florence for nine years. After that he returned to Rome, where he died. Salvator owes his reputation mainly to his landscapes of wild and savage scenes. He executed numerous etchings. His *Satires* were published in 1719. A theory that he was also a composer has now been disproved. See Lives by Baldinucci (new ed. 1830), Cantu (1844) and Cattaneo (1929).

ROSAMOND. See ALBOIN; CLIFFORD Family.

ROSAS, Juan Manuel de (1793–1877), Argentine dictator, born in Buenos Aires, became commander-in-chief in 1826, and was governor of the province in 1829–32. Disappointed of re-election, he headed a revolt, and from 1835 to 1852 governed as dictator. His rule was one of terror and bloodshed. In 1849 Rosas secured for Buenos Aires the entire navigation of the Plate, the Uruguay and the Paraná. This roused the other river provinces, and Urquiza, governor of Entre Ríos, supported by Brazil, in February 1852 routed him at Monte Caseros near Buenos Aires. Rosas escaped to England, where he lived till his death.

ROSCELLINUS, Johannes, *ros-ĕ-lī'nus* (c. 1050–after 1120), French scholar, born probably at Compiègne and studied at Soissons. He defended Nominalism, of which he is considered the founder, against attacks by Abelard. In 1092 the council of Soissons condemned his teaching as implicitly involving the negation of the doctrine of the Trinity.

ROSCIUS, Quintus (c. 134–62 B.C.), a slave by birth, became the greatest comic actor in Rome, reckoned the dictator Sulla and Cicero among his patrons, and gave Cicero lessons in elocution. He wrote a treatise on eloquence and acting. On his being sued at law for 50,000 sesterces, Cicero defended him in his extant oration, *Pro Q. Roscio Comoedo*.
—For the ' Young Roscius ', see BETTY.

ROSCOE, (1) Sir Henry Enfield (1833–1915), English chemist, grandson of (2), was born in London and educated at Liverpool High School, University College, London, and Heidelberg, where with Bunsen he did research on quantitative photochemistry. From 1857 to 1886 he was professor of Chemistry at Manchester, and worked on the preparation and properties of pure vanadium. Elected F.R.S. in 1863 and knighted in 1884, he was Liberal M.P. for South Manchester 1885–95, vice-chancellor of London University 1896–1902. His works include *Spectrum Analysis* (1868), the great *Treatise on Chemistry* (with Schorlemmer; 6 vols. 1878–89), a book on Dalton, and his own *Life and Experiences* (1906). See short Life by Thorpe (1916).

(2) **William** (1753–1831), English historian, grandfather of (1), born at Liverpool, in 1769 was articled to an attorney, and began to practise in 1774. In 1777 he published a poem, *Mount Pleasant*, and in 1787 *The Wrongs of Africa*, a protest against the slave trade. But it was his *Life of Lorenzo de' Medici* (1796) that established his literary reputation. His second great book, *Life of Leo X* (1805), like the former, was translated into German, French and Italian. He had retired from business in 1796, but in 1799 became partner in a Liverpool bank, which involved him (1816–20) in pecuniary embarrassment. He also wrote poems, of which the best known is the *Butterfly's Ball* (1807); an edition of Pope; and a monograph on Monandrian plants. See Life by his son, Henry (1833), and Espinasse's *Lancashire Worthies* (2nd series, 1877).

ROSE, (1) George (1744–1818), English statesman, father of (5), a supporter of Pitt, born near Brechin, died near Lyndhurst. See his *Diaries* (1859).

(2) **Hugh.** See STRATHNAIRN.

(3) **Hugh James** (1795–1838), English theologian, born at Little Horsted, Sussex, studied at Trinity, Cambridge. At his Suffolk rectory was held in 1833 the ' Hadleigh conference ' that preceded the Tractarian movement. See Burgon's *Twelve Good Men* (1888).

(4) **John Holland** (1855–1942), English historian, born at Bedford, was professor of Naval History at Cambridge (1919–33) and an authority on Napoleon.

(5) **William Stewart** (1775–1843), English poet and translator, son of (1), rendered Casti's *Animali Parlanti* (1819) and the *Orlando Furioso* of Ariosto (8 vols. 1823–31) into English verse.

ROSEBERY, Archibald Philip Primrose, 5th Earl of (1847–1929), British statesman, born in London, and educated at Eton and Christ Church, succeeded his grandfather in 1868. In 1874 he was president of the Social Science Congress, and in 1878 lord rector of Aberdeen University, in 1880 of Edinburgh, in 1899 of Glasgow, in 1881–83 under-secretary of the Home Department, and in 1884 became first commissioner of works. In July 1886, and again in 1892–94, he was secretary for foreign affairs in the Gladstone administration. Cambridge gave him the degree of LL.D. in 1888. In 1889–90 and 1892 he was chairman of the London County Council. On the retirement of Gladstone he became Liberal premier (March 1894); and after his government had been defeated at the general election (1895) remained leader of the Liberal Opposition till 1896, when he resigned the leadership. A spokesman for imperial federation, he was imperialist during the Boer war, and as head of the Liberal League from 1902 represented a policy, first set forth in a famous speech at Chesterfield, but not accepted by official Liberals. His attitude in 1909–10 was Independent or Conservative. In 1911 he was created Earl of Midlothian. He died May 21, 1929. Lord Rosebery published books on Pitt (1891), Peel (1899),

the ' last phase ' of Napoleon's career (1900), Chatham (1910), and *Miscellanies* (2 vols. 1921). In 1878 he married Hannah (1851–90), the only daughter of Baron Meyer de Rothschild. He won the Derby thrice (1894, 1895, 1905). See Lives by the Marquis of Crewe (1931) and James (1963).

ROSECRANS, William Starke, *rōz'krans* (1819–98), American general, born at Kingston, Ohio, in 1861 became aide to McClellan, whom he succeeded, and kept Lee out of Western Virginia. In 1862 he commanded a division at the siege of Corinth, and after its capture commanded the army of the Mississippi; in September he defeated Price at Iuka, and in October defended Corinth against Price and Van Dorn. In the battles at Stone River (December 1862 and January 1863), against Bragg, he converted what had nearly been a defeat into a victory; but at Chickamauga, September 19–20, 1863, he was defeated by Bragg, although he held Chattanooga. He was superseded by Grant, but in 1864 repelled Price's invasion of Missouri. In 1868–69 he was minister to Mexico, in 1881–85 congressman, and then registrar of the U.S. treasury (1885–93).

ROSEGGER, Peter, known until 1894 as **P. K. (Petri Kettenfeier),** *rōz'eg-gėr* (1843–1918), Austrian poet and novelist, was born of peasant parents near Krieglach, Styria. In 1870 he published *Zither und Hackbrett*, a volume of poems in his native dialect, and followed this with autobiographical works such as *Waldheimat* (1897) and later *Mein Himmelreich* (1901), and novels, including *Die Schriften des Waldschulmeisters* (1875), *Der Gottsucher* (1883) and *Jakob der Letzte* (1888), vividly portraying his native district and its people. See study by F. Pock (1943) and his biography and letters by O. Janda (1948).

ROSENBERG, *rō'-*, (1) **Alfred** (1893–1946), German politician, was born in Estonia. An avid supporter of National Socialism, he joined the party in 1920, edited Nazi journals, for a time (1933) directed the Party's foreign policy, and in 1934 was given control of its cultural and political education policy. In his *The Myth of the 20th Century* (1930) he expounded the extreme Nazi doctrines which he later put into practice in eastern Europe, for which crime he was hanged at Nuremberg in 1946.

(2) **Julius** (1917–53), and his wife **Ethel** (1916–53), American Communists, were part of a transatlantic spy ring uncovered after the trial of Klaus Fuchs (q.v.) in Britain. The husband was employed by the American army, and the wife's brother, David Greenglass, at the nuclear research station at Los Alamos. They were convicted of passing on atomic secrets through an intermediary to the Soviet vice-consul. Greenglass turned witness for the prosecution and saved his life. The Rosenbergs were sentenced to death in April 1951 and, despite numerous appeals from many West European countries and three stays of execution, were executed on June 19, 1953, at Sing Sing prison, New York.

ROSENFELD. See KAMENEV.

ROSENKRANZ, Karl (1805–79), German

philosopher, born at Magdeburg, in 1833 became professor of Philosophy at Königsberg. His works include an encyclopaedia of theology, criticisms of Schleiermacher and Strauss, and books on poetry, education, Diderot and Goethe; but he is best known by his works on the Hegelian system (1840–1856) and his Life of Hegel (1844). See his unfinished autobiography (1873) and Life by Quäbicker (1879).

ROSENKREUTZ, Christian, *rō'zẽn-kroyts,* the alleged founder in 1459 of the Rosicrucians. See ANDREÄ, and Waite's *Real History of the Rosicrucians* (1887).

ROSMEAD, Lord. See ROBINSON (8).

ROSMINI (-SERBATI), Antonio, *roz-mee'nee* (1797–1855), Italian philosopher, was born at Rovereto in the Italian Tirol, studied for the priesthood at Padua and was ordained in 1821. Master of an ample fortune, he worked out a philosophical system for the truths of revelation, while he planned a new institution for the training of teachers and priests. In 1826–28 he lived mostly in Milan, thought out the rule of his new order, visited Rome, gained the approval of Pius VIII, and published his *New Essay on the Origin of Ideas* (1830), his most important work. After a few years he had settled in 1837 at Stresa on Lago Maggiore, and in 1839 received from Gregory XVI the formal approval of his Institute but incurred the hostility of the Jesuits. His dream in politics, as expressed in his *Constitution according to Social Justice* (1848), was a confederation of the states of Italy under the pope as perpetual president. For seven weeks he was envoy of Piedmont at the papal court, and followed Pius IX to Gaeta, but found his mind poisoned against him by Antonelli and the reactionary party. When his *Constitution* and *The Five Wounds* of *Holy Church* (1848) were prohibited by the Congregation of the Index, he returned to Stresa to spend the rest of his life in devotion and the development of his philosophy. After a scrutiny (1851–54) the Congregation had declared Rosmini's writings to be entirely free from censure, when he died July 1, 1855. In 1888 forty propositions from his posthumous works were condemned by the Holy Office. The 'Institute of the Fathers of Charity' survived. Other works are *Psychology* (1846–48, trans. 1884–88), *Maxims of Christian Perfection* (trans. 1949) and *Theosophy* (1859–74), left unfinished at his death. His *Sketch of Modern Philosophies* was translated by Father Lockhart (1882; 3rd ed. 1891). A Bibliography, with a Life is prefixed by Thomas Davidson to his trans. (1882) of the *Sistema Filosofico* (1845). See Lives by Paoli (1880–84), Lockhart (2nd ed. 1886).

ROSNY, *rō-nee,* **Joseph Henri,** joint pseudonym of the brothers **Joseph Henri** (1856–1940) and **Séraphin Justin François** (1859–1948) **Boëx,** *bō-eks',* French novelists, born in Brussels. Their vast output of social novels, naturalistic in character, includes *L'Immolation* (1887) and *L'Impérieuse Bonté* (1905), signed jointly, and after 1908, when they separated, Rosny aîné's *L'Appel au bonheur* (1919) and *La Vie amoureuse de Balzac* (1930), and *La Courtesane passionée* (1925) and *La*

Pantine (1929) by Rosny jeune. See study by Poinsot (1907).

ROSS, (1) Alexander (1590/1–1654), a voluminous Scottish author, remembered solely from a couplet on *Hudibras,* was born at Aberdeen, and became a schoolmaster and clergyman at Southampton.

(2) Sir James Clark (1800–62), English explorer, nephew of (3), accompanied Sir John on his first and second polar voyages, and in the interval between was with Parry on his expeditions. He discovered the north magnetic pole in 1831. After being employed in a magnetic survey of the British Isles, he commanded the *Erebus* and *Terror* in an expedition to the Antarctic seas (1839). He was knighted in 1843, and in 1847 published his *Voyage of Discovery.* In 1848–49 he made a voyage to Baffin Bay in search of Franklin. He died at Aylesbury. Ross Barrier, Sea and Island are named after him.

(3) Sir John (1777–1856), Scottish Arctic explorer, born at Inch manse in Wigtownshire, served with distinction in the French wars. In 1818 he went to explore Baffin Bay and attempt a Northwest Passage. Another expedition (1829–33), fitted out by Sir Felix Booth, discovered the peninsula of ' Boothia Felix '. He made an unsuccessful attempt to find Sir John Franklin in 1850. He wrote on his voyages (1819, 1835) and a Life of Lord de Saumarez (1838).

(4) Martin. See MARTIN (9).

(5) Sir Ronald (1857–1932), British physician, discoverer (1895–98) of the malaria parasite and of its life history, was born at Almora in India. He studied medicine at St Bartholomew's. In 1881–99 he was in the Indian Medical Service and later was professor of Tropical Medicine at Liverpool. Nobel prizewinner for medicine (1902), he was the author of poems, romances and *Memoirs* (1923), besides writings on malaria. See Life by Mégroz (1931).

ROSSE, William Parsons, 3rd Earl of (1800–1867), Irish astronomer, born in York, graduated from Magdalen College, Oxford, with a first in Mathematics (1822). During his father's lifetime he sat in parliament for King's County as Lord Oxmantown from 1821 to 1834; in 1841 he succeeded as third earl. He experimented in fluid lenses, and made great improvements in casting specula for the reflecting telescope. In 1842–45 he constructed his great reflecting telescope, 58 feet long, in the park at Birr Castle, his Irish home, at a cost of £30,000; in 1848–54 he was P.R.S. Sir Charles Parsons (1854–1931), the inventor and engineer, was his son.

ROSSETER, Philip, *ros'e-tẽr* (1568–1623), English lutenist and composer, was a musician at the court of James I when he published his *Ayres* (1601). His *Lessons for Consort* appeared in 1609, and thereafter he was active in court theatricals.

ROSSETTI, (1) Christina (1830–94), English poet, was born in London, the daughter of (3) and sister of (2), to whose early poetry she owed much. A devout Anglican, she denied herself the fulfilment of marriage and exercised her genuine talent on religious poetry. Her estrangement from her fiancé accounts in part for the melancholy and unhappiness in much of her poetry. In her verse, which is characterized by depth of feeling and simplicity of theme and style, she displayed to perfection the pre-Raphaelite manner from which she never deviated. Submission to God's will as in ' Passing Away ' and ' Arise, Come Away, My Love, My Sister, My Spouse ' strikes the devotional note, while ' Spring Quiet ', ' Winter Rain ' and ' Child's Talk in April ' illustrate her vein of pure lyricism. See her *Goblin Market and Other Poems* (1862), *The Prince's Progress* (1866), *A Pageant and Other Poems* (1881), and *New Poems* (1896), also, in prose, *Commonplace and Other Stories* (1870), and Lives by Bell (1898) and Stuart (1930).

(2) **Dante Gabriel** (1828–82), English poet and painter, was born in London and in 1846 entered the Antique School of the Royal Academy. About 1850 he formed with Millais, Holman Hunt, Thomas Woolner and others, the pre-Raphaelite Brotherhood, whose object, as explained in *The Germ*—four numbers, 1850—was to resist modern art conventions by a return to pre-Renaissance art forms involving vivid colour and detail. Without religious belief he exploited religious feeling in paintings such as *The Girlhood of Mary Virgin* (1849), *The Annunciation* (1850) and the triptych in Llandaff Cathedral, *The Infant Christ adored by a Shepherd and a King*. His later manner became more pagan as the sense of human beauty, divorced from religion, grew in him. In both painting and poetry his development was from religious simplicity based on significant detail to a more complicated and ornate manner. *The Blessed Damozel* and the painting he made of it illustrate the earlier manner and therefore can be quoted as typical of pre-Raphaelite art. *My Sister's Sleep* and *The Portrait* are also typical of the manner but with a greater infusion of thought. In 1860 Rossetti married Elizabeth Siddal, the model in so many of his pictures, but her tragic death two years later from an overdose of laudanum affected him so strongly that he enclosed the MSS. of his poems in her coffin. They were retrieved seven years later and published in 1870. Robert Buchanan's attack on the poems, *The Fleshly School of Poetry* (1871), following upon his wife's tragedy and his enslavement to chloral turned the poet into a moody recluse. His next published work, *Ballads and Sonnets* (1881), however, includes some of his most outstanding work. He had attempted the artificial ballad in his previous volume—' Stratton Water ' is his only imitation of the simple mediaeval ballad—and in ' Sister Helen ' had achieved something of a masterpiece. Perhaps ' The Bride's Tragedy ', and ' Rose Mary ' of the later volume should be called rather mediaeval romances and ' The White Ship ' and ' The King's Tragedy ' historical lays. The sonnet sequence, *The House of Life*, the sumptuous expression of Rossetti's cult of love and beauty, describes love's pilgrimage from birth to death. Passion is restrained by the dialectic of love which he had learned from the early Italian poets (see his *Early Italian Poets*, 1861).

See the *Family Letters*, with Memoir of the poet, by W. M. Rossetti (1895–1905), R. D. Waller's *The Rosetti Family* (1932), G. Pedrick's *Life with Rosetti* (1964), and studies by Hall Caine (1882, 1928), Hueffer (1902), Marillier (3rd ed., 1904), Waugh (1928), Gaunt (1942), Doughty (new ed., 1960).

(3) **Gabriele** (1783–1854), Italian poet and writer, father of (1), (2) and (4), sometime curator of ancient bronzes in the Museum of Bronzes at Naples, was a member of the provisional government set up by Murat in Rome, 1813. After the restoration of Ferdinand to Naples, he joined the Carbonari and saluted the constitution extorted by the patriots in 1820 in a famous ode. On the overthrow of the constitution he withdrew to London (1824), where he became professor of Italian at the new University of London. Besides writing poetry he was a close student of Dante whose *Inferno* he maintained was chiefly political and anti-papal. See book by Vincent (1936).

(4) **William Michael** (1829–1919), son of (3) and brother of (1) and (2), was an Inland Revenue official as well as a man of letters and one of the seven pre-Raphaelite ' brothers ', editor of their manifesto *The Germ* (1850). Like all his family he was devoted to the study of Dante, whose *Inferno* he translated. He was equally devoted to his family, as his memoirs of his brother (1895) and his sister Christina (1904) witness.

ROSSI, *rōs'see*, (1) **Bruno** (1905–), Italian-American physicist, born in Venice, became professor of Physics at Cornell University in 1940. He has done much work, including the identification of photons, on cosmic rays.

(2) **Giovanni Battista de** (1494–1541), Italian religious painter, born in Florence, and summoned to France in 1530, committed suicide.

(3) **Giovanni Battista de** (1822–94), Italian archaeologist, born at Rome, known for his researches on the Christian catacombs there.

(4) **Pellegrino, Count** (1787–1848), Italian statesman and economist, born at Carrara, became professor of Law at Bologna at twenty-five. Exiled after the fall of Murat, he obtained a chair at Geneva, and there wrote his *Traité de droit pénal*. In 1833 Louis-Philippe made him professor of Political Economy at the Collège de France. He was sent to Rome as French ambassador in 1845. Called to the ministry by Pius IX, Rossi, by opposing the Savoy party and striving for an Italian confederation with the pope as president, roused the hatred of the Romans, and was assassinated.

ROSSINI, Gioacchino Antonio, *ros-see'nee* (1792–1868), Italian composer, was born at Pesaro, the son of a strolling horn player and a baker's daughter turned singer. He was taught to sing and play at an early age in order to help the family, and in 1806 began to study composition at the Liceo in Bologna, where in 1808 he won the prize for counterpoint with a cantata. Tiring of the stern academic routine he wrote several slender comic operas, among them *La Scala di seta* (1812), whose lively overture is popular today although the opera itself was a failure. At Milan in the same year *La Pietra del Paragone* made a great impression; in 1813 at Venice *Tancredi* and *L'Italiana in Algeri* were a success, though *Sigismondo* (1815) failed, possibly because it was an *opera seria* and Rossini's talents were more scintillating in the lighter vein; *Elisabetta*, a version of the Amy Robsart story, succeeded at Naples in the same year but gained little favour elsewhere. The name part in the latter was taken by the beautiful Spanish singer, Isabella Colbran, who became Rossini's wife in 1821. In 1816 his masterpiece, *Il Barbiere di Seviglia*, was received in Rome with enthusiasm despite a disastrous opening night. *Otello* (1816) marked an advance, but the libretto was weakened by pandering to the whims of the audience and it has justly been eclipsed by Verdi's masterpiece. *La Cenerentola* was favourably received at Rome, *La Gazza Ladra* (*The Thieving Magpie*) at Milan in 1817, and these were followed at Naples by *Armida* and *Mosè in Egitto* (1818), *La Donna del Lago* (1819) and *Maometto Secondo* (1820). *Semiramide* (1823), the most advanced of his works, had only a lukewarm reception from the Venetians. Meantime Rossini and his wife had won fresh laurels at Vienna and in London, and he was invited to become director of the Italian Theatre in Paris, where he adapted several of his works to French taste: *Maometto* (as *Le Siège de Corinth*), *Moïse* and *Le Comte Ory*. Here appeared in August 1829 his greatest work *Guillaume Tell*, conceived and written in a much nobler style than his Italian operas; its success was immense but not lasting. In 1837 he separated from La Colbran, whose extravagance and selfishness had become insupportable, and in 1847 he married Olympe Pelissier, who had been nurse to his children. From this period he produced little but the *Stabat Mater* (1841), which, despite its popularity, is too baroque for some tastes. In 1836 he retired to Bologna and took charge of the Liceo, which he raised from an almost moribund state to a high position in the world of music. The revolutionary disturbances in 1847 drove him to Florence in a condition of deep depression, but he recovered and returned to Paris in 1855, where he died. Rossini has been criticized for immoderate use of long crescendos and other devices in his overtures but he was in this a superb craftsman using the tools of his trade quite legitimately to create an atmosphere of excitement and expectancy in his audience, and the sheer sparkle and vivacity of his music, enlivened as it is by flashes of the puckish sense of humour for which he was renowned, is sufficient to ensure its immortality. See Stendhal's fascinating but innaccurate contemporary Memoir (1824); also books by Toye (1834) and Lord Derwent (1934).

ROSTAND, Edmond, *ro-stä* (1868–1918), French poet and dramatist, born at Marseilles, published *Les Musardises*, a volume of verse, in 1890, rose to fame in 1897 with *Cyrano de Bergerac* (1897), *L'Aiglon* (1900), *Chantecler* (1910), and other plays in verse, in 1902 being elected to the Académie française. See studies by Grieve (1931) and Gérard (1935).

ROSTOPCHINE, Feodor Vassilievich, Count, *ros-top-cheen'* (1763–1826), Russian general,

won great influence over the Emperor Paul, and in 1812 became, under Alexander, governor of Moscow. It was he who planned, or at least had a share in, the burning of Moscow. His works include historical memoirs and two comedies, &c., in Russian and French. See Life by Ségur (1872).

ROSTROPOVICH, Mstislav Leopoldovitch (1927–), Russian cellist and composer, born at Baku, studied at the Moscow Conservatoire (1937–48), where he has been professor since 1960. He was awarded the Lenin prize in 1964.

ROSWITHA. See HROSWITHA.

ROTHENSTEIN, *rō'then-stīn,* (1) **Sir John Knewstub Maurice** (1901–), English art historian, was born in London, the son of (2), and studied at Worcester College, Oxford, and University College, London. From 1927 to 1929 he taught in the United States, and was director of Leeds and Sheffield city art galleries between 1932 and 1938, when he was appointed director and keeper of the Tate Gallery, retiring in 1964. He was knighted in 1952. His many works on art include *Modern English Painters* (1952–56), and his Autobiography (2 vols., 1965, 1966). See study by R. Speaight (1962).
(2) **Sir William** (1872–1945), English artist, born at Bradford, studied at the Slade School and in Paris, won fame as a portrait painter, and was principal of the Royal College of Art, South Kensington (1920–35). See his *Men and Memories* (1931–32), *Since Fifty* (1939).

ROTHERMERE, Viscount. See HARMSWORTH (3).

ROTHSCHILD, Meyer Amschel, Ger. *rōt' shilt*; Eng. *roths'child* (1743–1812), German financier, named from the 'Red Shield', signboard of his father's house, born at Frankfurt, was educated as a Jewish rabbi, but founded a business as a moneylender and became the financial adviser of the Landgrave of Hesse. The house got a heavy commission for transmitting money from the English government to Wellington in Spain, paid the British subsidies to Continental princes, and negotiated loans for Denmark between 1804 and 1812. At his death, the founder left five sons, all of whom were made barons of the Austrian empire in 1822. **Anselm Meyer** (1773–1855), eldest son, succeeded as head of the firm at Frankfurt; **Solomon** (1774–1855) established a branch at Vienna; **Nathan Meyer** (1777–1836), one in 1798 at London; **Charles** (1788–1855), one at Naples (discontinued about 1861); and **James** (1792–1868), one at Paris. They negotiated many of the great government loans of the 19th century, and Nathan raised the house to be first amongst the banking houses of the world. He staked his fortunes on the success of Britain in her duel with Napoleon, and, receiving the first news of Waterloo, sold and bought stock which brought him a million of profit. His son **Lionel** (1808–79) did much for the civil and political emancipation of the Jews in Great Britain. Lionel's son, **Nathan** (1840–1915), succeeded (1876) to his uncle Anthony's baronetcy (1846), and was made Baron Rothschild in 1885. His son, **Lionel** (1868–1937), second Baron set up a valuable zoological museum at Tring. See books by Reeves (1887), Balla (1913), Corti (trans. 1928), Roth (1939) and Morton (1962).

ROTHWELL, Evelyn. See BARBIROLLI.

ROTROU, Jean de, *ro-troo* (1609–50), French playwright, born at Dreux, went early to Paris, qualified as a lawyer, and turned to writing plays, as well as becoming one of the five poets who worked into dramatic form the ideas of Richelieu. His first pieces were in the Spanish romantic style. Next followed a classical period, culminating in three masterpieces, *Saint-Genest*, a tragedy of Christian martyrdom, *Don Bertrand* and *Venceslas*. He died of the plague. Thirty-five of his plays are still extant. A complete edition was edited by Viollet-le-Duc (1820–1822). See works by Jarry (1868), Steffens (1891), and Stiefel (1891).

ROU. See ROLLO.

ROUAULT, Georges, *roo-ō* (1871–1958), French painter and engraver, was born in Paris. He was apprenticed to a stained-glass designer in 1885, and in all his work he retained the characteristic glowing colours, outlined with black, to achieve a concise statement of his feelings about the clowns, prostitutes and Biblical characters whom he chose as his subjects. He studied under Gustave Moreau, and in 1898 was made curator of the Moreau Museum. About 1904 he joined the Fauves (Matisse, Derain and others), and in 1910 held his first one-man show. Many of his works were acquired by Vollard, who commissioned the series of large religious engravings, finally published after Vollard's death as *Miserere* (Eng. ed. 1951). See also Lives by Venturi (N.Y. 1940, new ed. 1959) and Soby (N.Y. 1947).

ROUBILLAC, Louis François, *roo-bee-yak* (1702 or 1705–62), sculptor, born at Lyons, studied at Paris, and before 1738 settled in London, where he spelt his name Roubiliac. His statue of Handel for Vauxhall Gardens in 1738 first made him popular. His other most famous statues are those of Newton (1755) at Cambridge, of Shakespeare (1758), now in the British Museum, and another of Handel in Westminster Abbey. See *Life and Works* by Esdaile (1929), Dobson's *Eighteenth Century Vignettes* (1894).

ROUGET DE LISLE, Claude Joseph, *roo-zhay dё leel* (1760–1836), French army officer, born at Lons-le-Saunier, wrote and composed the *Marseillaise* when stationed in 1792 as captain of engineers at Strasbourg. Wounded at Quiberon (1795), he quitted the army, and published in 1796 a volume of *Essais en vers et en prose*. The *Marseillaise*, by its author called *Chant de l'armée du Rhin*, was made known in Paris by troops from Marseilles. See Life by Tiersot (1892, 1915).

ROUHER, Eugène, *roo-ayr* (1814–84), French statesman, born at Riom, in 1848 was returned to the Constituent Assembly, and until 1869 held various offices in the government. He negotiated the treaty of commerce with England in 1860 and with Italy in 1863. In 1870 he was appointed president of the Senate. A staunch Napoleonist, after the fall of the empire he fled abroad. Later he represented Corsica in the National Assembly.

ROUMANILLE, Joseph, *roo-ma-nee'y'* (1818–1891), French writer, was born at Saint-Rémy, Bouches-du-Rhône. He taught at Avignon, his pupils including Frédéric Mistral (q.v.), and in 1847 he published *Li Margarideto*, a book of his own poems, in 1852 a volume of Provençal poems, and thereafter many volumes of verse and prose in Provençal dialect. With Mistral and others he founded the 'Soci dou Félibrige' for the revival of Provençal literature. See biography by Mariéton (1903).

ROUS, (1) Francis, *rows* (1579–1659), English Presbyterian, born at Dittisham, Devon, and educated at Oxford, was a member of the Long Parliament, sat in the Westminster Assembly of Divines, and in 1644 was made provost of Eton. His writings were collected in 1657. His metrical version of the Psalms was recommended by the House of Commons to the Westminster Assembly, and is still substantially the Presbyterian psalter.

(2) **Francis Peyton** (1879–1970), U.S. scientist, born in Baltimore, educated at Johns Hopkins University and Medical School. He became assistant 1909–10, associate 1910–12, associate member 1912–20 and member 1920–45 of the Rockefeller Institute for Medical Research. In 1910 he discovered a virus to induce malignant tumours in hens, the outstanding importance of which has become apparent over the years. In 1962 he received the U.N. prize for cancer research, and in 1966 shared the Nobel prize for medicine with Huggins (1).

ROUSSEAU, (1) Henri, known as **Le Douanier** *roo-sō, lё dwa-nyay* (1844–1910), French primitive painter, born at Laval, joined the army at about eighteen, but most of his life was spent as a minor customs official, hence his nickname. He retired in 1885 and spent his time painting and copying at the Louvre. From 1886 to 1898 he exhibited at the Salon des Indépendants and again from 1901 to 1910. He met Gauguin, Pissarro and later Picasso, but his painting remained unaffected. Despite its denial of conventional perspective and colour, it has a fierce reality more surrealist than primitive. He produced painstaking portraits, and painted dreams, e.g., the *Sleeping Gipsy* (1897) in the Museum of Modern Art, N.Y., and exotic, imaginary landscapes with trees and plants which he had seen in the Jardin des Plantes. See studies by A. Basler (Paris 1927) and G. F. Hartlaub (1956).

(2) **Jean Baptiste** (1671–1741), French poet, born in Paris, a shoemaker's son, wrote for the theatre, and by lampoons on the literary frequenters of the Café Laurent raised feuds which led to recriminations, lawsuits and a sentence of banishment (1712). Henceforth he lived abroad, in Switzerland, Vienna (with Prince Eugene) and Brussels, where he died. Rousseau's sacred odes and *cantates* are splendidly elaborate, frigid and artificial; his epigrams are bright, vigorous and unerring in their aim. See his *Life and Works* by H. A. Grubbs (1941).

(3) **Jean Jacques,** *roo-sō* (1712–78), Genevan political philosopher, educationist and essayist, was born June 28 at Geneva, his mother dying at his birth. In 1722 his father,

involved in a brawl, left him to the care of his relations. Without any formal education except his own reading of Plutarch's *Lives* and a collection of Calvinist sermons, he was employed first by a notary who found him incompetent and then by an engraver who maltreated him so that in 1728 he ran away. Feigning enthusiasm for Catholicism, he was sent to Madame de Warens who, separated from her husband, became a convert to Catholicism and assisted other converts. She sent him to Turin to be baptized and there he eventually found employment with a shopkeeper's wife, whose lover he became until her husband's return. After short spells as footman and secretary, he returned to Annecy, to Madame de Warens. He became her general factotum and lover, joined the local choir school to complete his education and picked up a fair knowledge of Italian music. On an unauthorized visit to Lyons with the music master, he meanly deserted the latter during an epileptic fit. Eventually supplanted in his mistress's affections by a wigmaker, he made for Paris in 1741 with a new musical notation, which the Academy of Sciences pronounced 'neither useful nor original'. With secretarial work and musical copying for a livelihood, he began his association, which was to be lifelong, with a maid at his hostelry, Thérèse Le Vasseur, who was neither good-looking nor literate and by whom he boasted he had five children, whom, despite his much-vaunted sensibility and regard for the innocence of childhood, he consigned, in turn, to the foundling hospital. He composed an opera *Les Muses galantes* which led to a correspondence with Voltaire and eventually acquaintance with Diderot and the *encyclopédistes*. On a visit to Diderot in prison, he discovered in a periodical the prize essay competition by the academy of Dijon on whether the arts and sciences had a purifying effect upon morals. This he won in 1750 by maintaining that they did not, having seduced man from his natural and noble estate, decreasing his freedom. He was lionized by the Parisians and further triumphed with his opera *Le Devin du village* (1752). In 1754 he wrote *Discours sur l'origine de l'inégalité parmi les hommes* (1755), which re-emphasized the natural goodness of man and the corrupting influences of institutionalized life. He returned to Geneva and Calvinism, where he began his novel in letter form, *La Nouvelle Héloïse* (1761). In *Lettre sur les spectacles* (1758) he argued against the establishment of a theatre at Geneva on puritan grounds. Back in Paris, a reformed man, who was trying hard to live up to his newly-found natural estate, he accepted a cottage for himself, Thérèse and her mother at Montmorency from an admirer, Mme d'Épinay, but quarrelling with her over her sister, he set up in 1757 in Luxembourg. The year 1762 saw his masterpiece, *Contrat social*, 'Social Contract' which attempted to solve the problem posed by its opening sentence: 'Man is born free; and everywhere he is in chains', by postulating a social contract by which the citizen surrenders his rights and possessions to the 'general will' which, thus undivided by

sectarian and private interests, must necessarily aim at the impartial good. Thus if a man acts against the 'general will' or sovereign, he must in Rousseau's curious phrase 'be forced to be free'. With its slogan 'Liberty, Equality, Fraternity', it became the bible of the French revolution. Its doctrines, favourably interpreted, greatly influenced Kant, but they were easily perverted by Hegel into his philosophy of right, which gave birth to the modern totalitarian theories of the state. The same year he published his great work on education, *Émile*, in novel form, which greatly influenced such educationists as Froebel and Pestalozzi. Its views on monarchy and governmental institutions outraged the powers that be and those on natural religion, unorthodox to both Catholics and Protestants, which he placed into the mouth of the confessing Savoyard Vicar, forced him to flee to Môtiers in Neuchâtel under the protection of Frederick the Great. There he botanized, wrote *Lettres de la montagne* and accepted David Hume's generous invitation to settle in England, at Wootton Hall near Ashbourne (1766–67), where he wrote most of his *Confessions* (1781), a work remarkable for a frankness unsurpassed at that time. Persecution mania and hypersensitivity soured his relations with his English friends and a cruel practical joke by Horace Walpole who published a forged letter, convinced Rousseau that the British government through Hume were seeking his life. He fled, unjustly accusing Hume, and took shelter with the Marquis de Mirabeau and the Prince de Conti. In 1770 he was back in Paris, eking out a living as a copyist, and wrote the half-insane dialogues, justifying to himself his past actions, *Rousseau, juge de Jean Jacques*, followed by the contrastingly calm, sane *Rêveries* (1782), in parts beautifully composed as a continuation to the *Confessions*. Seeking shelter in a hospital, he eventually died insane in a cottage at Ermenonville, July 2, 1778, from a sudden attack of thrombosis, which long aroused suspicions of suicide. He was buried there until in 1794 his remains were placed with Voltaire's in the Panthéon, Paris. His writings ushered in the age of romanticism and found their echo in German and English idealism. See Lives by J. H. Fuessli (1767), de Staël (trans. 1789), J. Morley (1873), *Annales de la société Jean Jacques Rousseau* (1905) and studies by Collins (1908), Ducros (1908–12), Babbitt (1919), Wright (1929), C. E. Vulliamy (1931), Cobban (1934), Mowat (1938), Osborne (1940), Cassirer (trans. 1945), Green (1950).

(4) **Theodore** (1812–67), French landscape painter, born in Paris, studied the old masters in the Louvre, and by 1833 had begun sketching in the Forest of Fontainebleau. He first exhibited in the Salon of 1831; and in 1834 his *Forest of Compiègne* was bought by the Duc d'Orléans. Some twelve years of discouragement followed, but in 1849 he resumed exhibiting, and was thenceforward prominent. He was an exceedingly prolific, if a somewhat unequal, painter. See study by Sensier (1872); and D. C. Thomson, *The Barbizon School* (1890). His brother,

Philippe (1816–87), animal and still-life painter, was born and died in Acquigny (Eure).

ROUSSEL, *roo-sel*, (1) **Albert** (1869–1937), French composer, born in Tourcoing, educated for the navy, at the age of twenty-five resigned his commission to study with Gigout, in 1896 joining the Schola Cantorum under Vincent d'Indy. His works, after his period of study, are adventurous in harmony and texture, reconciling modern experimental styles with the conservative tradition of his teachers. A voyage to India and the Far East gave him an interest in Oriental music which inspired the choral *Évocations* (1912) and the opera *Padmâvatî*, begun in 1914 and completed after World War I. Service in the war ruined Roussel's health, and after his demobilization he largely retired into seclusion, devoting his time entirely to composition. His works include ballets (the best-known of which are *Bacchus and Ariane* and *Le Festin de l'araignée*), four symphonies and numerous choral and orchestral works. See studies by Norman Demuth (1947), Robert Bernard (Paris 1948) and M. Pincherle (1957).

(2) **Ker Xavier** (1867–1944), French artist, born at Lorry-les-Metz, was a member of the Nabis, and associated with Bonnard, Vuillard and Denis. He is best known for his classical subjects portrayed in typical French landscapes, using the Impressionist palette.

ROUTH, *rowth*, (1) **Edward John** (1831–1907), British mathematician, born at Quebec, and educated at University College, London, and Peterhouse, Cambridge, became a mathematical coach, and by 1888, when he retired, had turned out twenty-seven senior wranglers. He wrote on dynamics and analytical statics.

(2) **Martin Joseph** (1755–1854), English patristic scholar, born at St Margaret's, South Elmham, Suffolk, from Beccles went up in 1770 to Queen's College, Oxford. In 1771 he was elected a demy, in 1775 a fellow, and in 1791 president of Magdalen; in 1810 he became rector of Tylehurst near Reading. He died at Magdalen, December 22, 1854, in his hundredth year. A little shrunken figure, with 'such a wig as one only sees in old pictures', he had grown very deaf, but till well after ninety retained his eyesight and marvellous memory and capacity for work. Newman and Bancroft were among his later friends; the earlier had included Dr Parr, Samuel Johnson and Porson. He was a great patristic scholar when patristic scholars were few, a Caroline churchman, a liberal Tory, a lover of animals, fond of jokes, a mighty book-buyer—his 16,000 volumes he bequeathed to Durham University. Throughout seventy years he published only six works; two of these are editions of Burnet (' I know the man to be a liar, and I am determined to prove him so '). He will be remembered by his *Reliquiae Sacrae* (1814–48) a collection of fragments of early Christian writings, but still more for his sage advice, ' Always verify your references, sir '. See *Life* by R. D. Middleton (1938).

ROUTLEDGE, **George**, *rut'lej* (1812–88), English publisher, born at Brampton, Cumberland, went to London in 1833, and started up as a bookseller in 1836, and as a publisher in 1843. In 1848, the year in which he founded both ' Railway Library ' of cheap reprints, and 1851 respectively he took his two brothers-in-law, W. H. and Frederick Warne into partnership. In 1947 the firm acquired the undertaking of Kegan Paul, Trench, Trubner and Co. Ltd. See Mumby's *The House of Routledge, 1834-1934* (1934).

ROUX, *roo*, (1) **Pierre Émile** (1853–1933), French bacteriologist, born at Confolens (Charente), studied at Clermont-Ferrand, and became assistant to Pasteur, and in 1905–18 was his successor. With Yersin he discovered (1894) the antitoxic method of treating diphtheria, and he also worked on cholera and tuberculosis.

(2) **Wilhelm** (1850–1924), German anatomist and physiologist, born at Jena, became a professor at Innsbruck in 1889, at Halle in 1895. On his extensive practical and theoretical work on experimental embryology (his *Entwicklungsmechanik*, or developmental mechanics) he wrote many books, including *Entwicklungsmechanik der Organismen* (2 vols. 1895).

ROW, *roo*, (1) **John** (*c.* 1525–80), Scottish Reformer, educated at Stirling and St Andrews, in 1550 was sent by the archbishop to Rome. In 1558 he returned to Scotland, and next year turned Protestant. He aided in compiling the *Confession of Faith* (1560) and *First Book of Discipline* (1561), became minister of Perth, and sat in the first General Assembly. He was four times moderator and took a share in preparing the *Second Book of Discipline*.

(2) **John** (1568–1646), eldest son of (1), minister from 1592 of Carnock near Dunfermline, wrote a prolix but reliable *History of the Kirk of Scotland* from 1558 to 1637, continued to 1639 by his second son (edited for the Wodrow and Maitland Clubs by David Laing, 1842). He was strongly opposed to the introduction of episcopacy into Scotland.

(3) **John** (*c.* 1598–1672), son of (2), successively rector of Perth grammar school, minister at Aberdeen, moderator of the Assembly there in 1644, and principal of King's College in 1651. Like his father and grandfather he was a learned Hebraist.

ROWAN, **Archibald Hamilton**, *rō'an* (1751–1834), Irish nationalist, was born in London, the son of Gawin Hamilton and on his maternal grandfather's death took his name of Rowan. Educated at Cambridge, he went to Ireland in 1784, in 1791 joined the United Irishmen, and three years later was imprisoned for sedition. He escaped to France, went to America, obtained pardon and returned to Ireland, where he supported the cause of Catholic emancipation.

ROWE, **Nicholas**, *rō* (1674–1718), English poet and dramatist, born at Little Barford, Bedfordshire, and educated at Westminster, was called to the bar, but from 1692 devoted himself to literature. Between 1700 and 1715 he produced eight plays of which three (ed. Sutherland, 1929) were long popular—*Tamerlane* (1702), *The Fair Penitent* (1703) and *Jane Shore* (1714). Lothario in *The Fair Penitent* was the prototype of Lovelace in

Richardson's *Clarissa* and the name is still the synonym for a fashionable rake. Rowe translated Lucan's *Pharsalia*, and his work, says Dr Johnson, ' deserves more notice than it obtains '. His edition of Shakespeare (1709–10) at least contributed to the popularity of his author. In 1709–11 Rowe was under-secretary to the Duke of Queensberry; in 1715 he was appointed poet laureate and a surveyor of customs to the port of London; the Prince of Wales made him clerk of his Council, and Lord Chancellor Parker clerk of presentations in chancery.

ROWLAND, Henry Augustus, *rō'land* (1848–1901), American physicist, born at Honesdale, Pennsylvania, from 1875 to 1901 was first professor of Physics at Johns Hopkins University. He invented the concave diffraction grating used in spectroscopy, discovered the magnetic effect of electric convection, and improved on Joule's work on the mechanical equivalent of heat.

ROWLANDSON, Thomas, *rō'land-sėn* (1756–1827), English caricaturist, born in London, and sent at fifteen to Paris, there studied art and gained a taste for the pleasures of the town. The £7000 left him by a French aunt he gambled away, yet he hated debt, and maintained his uprightness of character. He travelled over England and Wales, and enjoyed to the full tavern life and the company of friends like Morland, Gillray and Bunbury. Rowlandson possessed rare dexterity of touch and fertility of imagination; and his work, though even for his time often crude and vulgar, is alive and vigorous. He was a relentless hater of Napoleon, belittling his greatness by countless travesties. Some of his best-known works are his *Imitations of Modern Drawings* (1784–88), and his illustrations to *Syntax's Three Tours*, the *Dance of Death*, Sterne's *Sentimental Journey*, *Peter Pindar*, the *Bath Guide*, *Munchausen*, &c. See studies by Oppé (1923), Wolf (1946) and Roe (1947).

ROWLEY, *rō-li*, (1) **Thomas.** See CHATTERTON.

(2) **William** (c. 1585–c. 1642), English actor and playwright, of whose life little is known, save that he collaborated with Dekker, Middleton, Heywood, Webster, Massinger and Ford. Four plays published with his name are extant: *A New Wonder, a Woman Never Vext* (1632); *All's Lost by Lust*, a tragedy (1633); *A Match at Midnight* (1633); and *A Shoomaker a Gentleman* (1638).

ROWNTREE, *rown'tree*, (1) **(Benjamin)** Seebohm (1871–1954), English manufacturer and philanthropist, son of (2), born at York, was chairman of the family firm (1925–41), devoted his life to the study of social problems and welfare and wrote many books, including the austere factual study of *Poverty* (1900), *Poverty and Progress, English Life and Leisure*, &c. See study by A. Briggs (1961).

(2) **Joseph** (1836–1925) Quaker industrialist, social and industrial reformer, father of (1), born at York, promoted with his brother, **Henry Isaac** (d. 1883), the cocoa-manufacturing business acquired by the latter in 1862.

ROWSE, Alfred Leslie (1903–), English historian, born at St Austell, educated at

Oxford, became a Fellow of All Souls and wrote many works on English history including *Tudor Cornwall* (1941), *The Use of History* (1946), *The England of Elizabeth* (1950). He has also written some poetry, much of it on Cornwall, several works on aspects of Shakespeare, a Life of Marlowe (1964), and his own autobiography *A Cornishman at Oxford* (1965).

ROWTON, Montagu William Lowry-Corry, **1st Baron,** *row'-* (1838–1903), English politician and philanthropist, born in London. Called to the bar in 1863, he became private secretary to Disraeli (1866–1868, 1874–80). He was created baron in 1880. Later he devoted his time and money to the provision of decent cheap accommodation for working men, and six Rowton houses were built in London, with total accommodation for five thousand. Although Rowton's motives were entirely philanthropic, his houses in fact made a profit.

ROXBURGHE, Duke of. See KERR.

ROY. See RAMMOHUN ROY.

ROY, William (1726–90), British military surveyor, born at Miltonhead, Carluke, Lanarkshire, in 1747 was engaged on the survey of Scotland, in 1755 held an army commission, was elected F.R.S. in 1767, and rose to be major-general in 1781. In 1784, in connection with the triangulation of the southeastern counties, he measured with great accuracy a base line of 5¼ miles on Hounslow Heath. For this he received the Royal Society's Copley medal. In 1764 Roy studied the Roman remains in Scotland, and his *Military Antiquities of the Romans in Britain* was published in 1793 by the Society of Antiquaries. See G. Macdonald, *Roy and his Military Antiquities* (1917).

ROYCE, (1) **Sir (Frederick) Henry** (1863–1933), English engineer, born near Peterborough. He was apprenticed to the G.N.R., but, becoming interested in electricity and motor engineering, he founded (1884) at Manchester the firm of Royce, Ltd., mechanical and electrical engineers. He made his first car in 1904, and his meeting with C. S. Rolls (q.v.) in that year led to the formation (1906) of the famous business of Rolls-Royce, Ltd., motor-car and aero-engine builders, of Derby and London. He was created a baronet in 1930. See Life by M. Pemberton (1935).

(2) **Josiah** (1855–1916), American philosopher, born in Grass Valley, California, was professor at Harvard from 1892. Much influenced by Hegel, he developed a philosophy of idealism, avoiding the pitfalls of both realism and mysticism, and stressed the importance of the individual in his loyalty to the community. He published *The Spirit of Modern Philosophy* (1892), *Essays upon Problems of Philosophy and of Life* (1898), *The World and the Individual* (Gifford Lectures, 1900–01) and *The Problem of Christianity* (1913).

ROYDEN, Agnes Maud (1876–1956), English social worker and preacher, was born in Liverpool, educated at Lady Margaret Hall, Oxford, was prominent in the women's suffrage movement, from 1917 to 1920 was assistant at the City Temple, and published

Woman and the Sovereign State, The Church and Woman, Modern Sex Ideals, &c. She was made C.H. in 1930.

ROYER-COLLARD, Pierre Paul, *rwa-yay ko-lar* (1763–1845), French philosopher and politician, born at Sompuis in Champagne, began as an advocate, on the outbreak of the Revolution was elected member of the municipality of Paris. In 1792 he fled from the Jacobins to his birthplace, and in 1797 served for a few months on the Council of Five Hundred. Professor of Philosophy in Paris from 1810, he exercised an immense influence on French philosophy, rejecting the purely sensuous system of Condillac, and giving special prominence to the principles of the Scottish School of Reid and Stewart. Strongly ' spiritualist ' as opposed to materialist, he originated the ' Doctrinaire ' school of Jouffroy and Cousin. In 1815–20 he was president of the Commission of Public Instruction, in 1815 was returned as deputy for Marne, and in 1827 entered the French Academy. He became president in 1828 of the Chamber of Representatives, and presented the address of March 1830, which the king refused to hear read.

ROZANOV, Vasili Vasilievich, *roz'-* (1856–1919), Russian writer, thinker and critic, was born at Vetluga, Kostroma, and became a teacher in provincial schools. His literary studies include that of Dostoievsky's *Grand Inquisitor*, which, published in 1894, first brought him into prominence. Though a Christian, in his prolific writings he criticized from a Nietzschian standpoint the contemporary standards in morals, religion, education, and particularly the too-strict attitude towards sex, which was for him the very soul of man. Much of his work is highly introspective and his literary reputation is firmly grounded on the two books of fragments and essays, *Solitaria* (1912; trans. 1927) and *Fallen Leaves* (1913, 1915; trans. 1929).

RUBBRA, Edmund (1901–), English composer and music critic, was born in Northampton. While working as a railway clerk, he had piano lessons from Cyril Scott, and in 1919 won a composition scholarship to Reading University. There he studied under Howard Jones and Holst, and won a scholarship to the Royal College of Music, where he was a pupil of Vaughan Williams and, most influentially, of R. O. Morris (q.v.). An interest in the polyphonic music of the 16th and 17th centuries is reflected in Rubbra's characteristic contrapuntal style of composition, which he uses not only in works such as his Spenser sonnets (1935), his madrigals and his Masses (1945 and 1949), but also in his larger symphonic canvases. In these he has progressed from a relentless prosecution of polyphonic principles in the first two to a more flexible interpretation of them in his later symphonies. As well as his seven symphonies he has written chamber, choral and orchestral music, songs and works for various solo instruments. In 1947 he was appointed lecturer in Music at Oxford, and fellow of Worcester College in 1963.

RUBENS, Peter Paul, *roo'benz* (1577–1640), Flemish painter, was born June 29, 1577, at Siegen in Westphalia, where his father, an Antwerp lawyer and religious exile in Cologne, was then imprisoned for a liaison with the wife of William the Silent. On the death of her husband at Cologne in 1587, his mother returned to Antwerp, where the boy was educated in the Jesuits' college. He was for a short time in the service of Margaret de Ligne, widow of the Count of Lanaing, and was intended for the law; but at thirteen he began to study art. In 1600 he went to Italy, and in Venice studied the works of Titian and Veronese. He next entered the service of Vincenzo Gonzaga, Duke of Mantua; and in 1605 was dispatched on a mission to Philip III of Spain, thus beginning the career as a diplomatist, for which his keen intellect, polished urbanity and linguistic attainments qualified him. While at Madrid he executed many portraits, as well as several historical subjects. On his return from Spain he travelled in Italy, copying celebrated works for the Duke of Mantua. His paintings of this Italian period are much influenced by the Italian Renaissance, and already show the Rubens characteristics of vigorous composition and brilliant colouring—for example, the altarpieces for the church of Santa Croce in Gerusalemme (now in Grasse), the *Baptism of Christ* (Antwerp) and the *Circumcision* (Genoa). In 1608 he returned home, and, settling in Antwerp, was appointed in 1609 court painter to the Archduke Albert, and soon afterwards married his first wife, Isabella Brant, whom he often portrayed; a famous full-length portrait of her and her husband is in the Old Pinakothek, Munich. Through the less successful *Adoration of the Kings* (Prado) and the *Elevation of the Cross* (Antwerp Cathedral) Rubens was now approaching his artistic maturity, and his triptych *Descent from the Cross* (1611–14) in Antwerp Cathedral is usually regarded as his masterpiece. By this time he was famous, and pupils and commissions came in a steady stream to the master's studio, from which issued vast numbers of works, witnesses to the extraordinary energy and ability of the prolific Rubens. In 1620 he was invited to France by Marie de' Medici, the queen mother, who was then engaged in decorating the palace of the Luxembourg; and he undertook for her twenty-one large subjects on her life and regency—works, exemplifying the typical collaboration of Rubens and his pupils, which were completed in 1625 and are now in the Louvre. To this period also belong an *Adoration of the Magi* (Madrid), one of many Rubens painted on this subject, a St Ildefonso triptych in the Vienna Museum, and *The Assumption of the Virgin* (Antwerp Cathedral). In 1628 he was dispatched by the Infanta Isabella on a diplomatic mission to Philip IV of Spain. In Madrid he made the acquaintance of Velazquez, and executed some forty works, including five portraits of the Spanish monarch. In 1629 he was appointed envoy to Charles I of England, to treat for peace; and, while he conducted a delicate negotiation with tact and success, he painted the *Peace and War* (National Gallery) and the portrait of the king and his queen in the *St George* at Buckingham Palace, and also made sketches for the Apotheosis of James I for the banqueting hall at Whitehall, completing the pictures on his return to Antwerp. He was knighted by Charles I, and received a similar honour from Philip IV. His first wife having died in 1626, Rubens married in 1630 Helena Fourment, and retired to his estate at Steen, where his landscape painting, direct from nature, attained the high standard of his other works. In 1635 he designed the decorations which celebrated the entry of the Cardinal Infant Ferdinand into Antwerp as governor of the Netherlands; and, having completed *The Crucifixion o St Peter* for the church of that saint in Cologne, he died at Antwerp, May 30, 1640. A successful diplomat, a distinguished humanist, a man of wide erudition and culture, Rubens was outstanding for versatility even in his time, and the main characteristics of his productions—their power, spirit and vivacity, their sense of energy, of exuberant life—may be largely attributed to the comprehensive qualities of the man himself. He produced more than twelve hundred works, many of his finest being at Antwerp; the Old Pinakothek at Munich contains many examples of his work, including the *Battle of the Amazons*, and he is well represented in the Prado, Madrid, and the Vienna Kunsthistorisches Museum. Among his works in the National Gallery, London, are *The Rape of the Sabines* (1635), *The Birth of Venus, The Castle of Steen*, and a painting of the Holy Family. See *The Letters of Peter Paul Rubens*, trans. and ed. by R. S. Magurn (1955), and works by Sainsbury (1859), Bertram (1928), Cammaerts (1932), H. G. Evers (1943), Leo van Puyvelde (trans. 1947 by E. Winkworth), E. Larsen (Antwerp 1952) and J. S. Held (1954 and 1959).

RUBINSTEIN, *roo'bin-stīn,* (1) **Anton** (1829–1894), Russian pianist and composer, born in Moldavia, studied in Berlin and Vienna, and in 1848 settled in St Petersburg, where he taught music and took a part in founding the conservatoire, of which he was for a time director. He made concert tours in Europe and, in 1872–73, the United States, gaining widespread acclaim and lasting distinction for his mastery of technique and musical sensitivity. Once also highly esteemed were his compositions, including operas, oratorios and piano concertos, but, apart from some songs and melodious piano pieces, they have not stood the test of time. His brother **Nikolai** (1835–81) founded Moscow Conservatoire. See Anton's *Autobiography* (trans. 1891).

(2) **Artur** (1888–   ), American pianist, born in Łódź, Poland. At the age of twelve he appeared successfully in Berlin, and after further study with Paderewski, began his career as a virtuoso, appearing in Paris and London in 1905 and visiting the United States in 1906. After the second World War he lived in America, making frequent extensive concert tours. See study by B. Gavoty (1956).

RUBRUQUIS, William de, *rü-brü-kee'* (fl. 13th cent.), French traveller, born probably at Rubrouck near St Omer, entered the Franciscan order, and was sent from Acre in 1253 by Louis IX to Sartak, the son of the Mongol

prince, Batû Khan, a supposed Christian. Friar William travelled across the Black Sea and the Crimea to the Volga, by Sartak was referred to his father, and by him was sent forward to the Mongol emperor, Mangû Khan, whom he found on December 27, about ten days' journey south of Karakorum in Mongolia. With him he remained until July 1254, then returned to the Volga, and by way of the Caucasus, Armenia, Persia and Asia Minor, arrived at Tripoli in August 1255. Louis had returned to France, and Friar William wrote him an account of his journey, edited by D'Avezac in *Recueil de voyages* (Paris Geog. Soc. 1839). He was still living in 1293, when Marco Polo was returning from the East.

RUCCELLAI, *roo-chel-lah'ee,* (1) **Bernardo** (1449–1514), Florentine scholar and diplomatist, father of (2).

(2) **Giovanni** (1475–1525), Italian poet, who lived much in Rome and took orders. His works, including *Le Api*, an instructive poem based on book 4 of Virgil's *Georgics*, were edited by Mazzoni, with Life (1887).

RÜCKERT, Friedrich (1788–1866), German poet, born at Schweinfurt, studied law, philology and philosophy at Würzburg, and during the Napoleonic wars stirred up German patriotism with his *Deutsche Gedichte* (1814). After the wars he studied Oriental languages, of which he became professor at Erlangen (1826–41) and Berlin (1841–48), and recast in German verse many famous books of countries of the Orient. His original work includes the lyrical *Liebesfrühling* (1923), the reflective poems *Die Weisheit des Brahmanen* (1836–39), and the personal *Kindertotenlieder*, posthumously published in 1872 and set to music by Mahler in 1902. See studies by Reuter (1891), Magon (1914) and Golfing (1935).

RUDBECK, Olof, *rood'bek* (1630–1702), Swedish zoologist and botanist, discoverer of the lymphatic glands. His name was given to the botanical genus *Rudbeckia*, and he published (1675–98) *Atlantikan.*

RUDDIMAN, Thomas (1674–1757), Scottish classical grammarian and philologist, born at Boyndie, Banffshire, studied at Aberdeen University, in 1700 was appointed assistant keeper of the Advocates' Library, Edinburgh, in 1707 starting up business also as a book auctioneer and in 1715 as a printer, and became in 1730 principal keeper of the Advocates' Library. He edited Latin works of Volusenus and Arthur Johnston (qq.v.), published in 1715 his great edition of Buchanan's works, with its controversial introduction, and produced his own *Rudiments of the Latin Tongue* (1714) and the impressive *Grammaticae Latinae Institutiones* (1725–32) on which his philological reputation mainly rests. He was an ardent Jacobite. See Life by Chalmers (1794).

RUDE, François (1784–1855), French sculptor, originally a smith, was born at Dijon, and died in Paris. His most famous work is the relief group *Le Départ* (1836) on the Arc de Triomphe in Paris. See Life by Calmette (1920).

RUDOLF. Name of three kings of Burgundy:
Rudolf I (d. 912), was king of Transjuranic Burgundy from 888.

Rudolf II (d. 937), son of the above, whom he succeeded.

Rudolf III (d. 1032), grandson of the above, ruled from 993 to 1032.

RUDOLF. Name of two German rulers:

Rudolf I (1218–91), founder of the Hapsburg imperial dynasty, was born at Schloss Limburg in the Breisgau, and, becoming a warm partisan of Frederick II, increased his possessions by inheritance and marriage, until he was the most powerful prince in Swabia. In 1273 the electors chose him German king; never having been crowned by the pope, he was not entitled to be called kaiser or emperor. Ottocar of Bohemia refused to tender his allegiance, and in 1278 was defeated and slain at Marchfeld. Rudolf did much to suppress the robber knights. He died at Speyer. His son Albert, to whom (and his brother Rudolf) Austria, Styria and Carniola had been given in 1278, succeeded him as German king. See works by Hirn (1874), Kaltenbrunner (1890) and Redlich (1903).

Rudolf II (1552–1612), born at Vienna, eldest son of the emperor Maximilian II, became King of Hungary in 1572; King of Bohemia, with the title King of the Romans, in 1575; and emperor on his father's death in 1576. Gloomy, taciturn, bigoted and indolent, he put himself in the hands of the Jesuits and low favourites, and left the empire to govern itself. His taste for astrology and the occult sciences made him extend his patronage to Kepler and Tycho Brahe; and their *Rudolphine Tables* were called after him. Meanwhile the Protestants were bitterly persecuted; the Turks invaded Hungary and defeated the Archduke Maximilian (1596); Transylvania and Hungary revolted; and at last Rudolf's brother Matthias wrested from him Hungary, Bohemia, Austria and Moravia. See works by Gindely (1865), von Bezold (1885) and Moritz (1895).

RUDOLF, Prince. See FRANCIS-JOSEPH.

RUDOLF VON EMS (d. 1254), Middle High German poet, of noble family, wrote in the style of Hartmann von Aue and Gottfried (qq.v.) the religious *Der gute Gerhard* and *Barlaam und Josaphat* and an incomplete *Weltchronik*. See study by G. Ehrismann (1919).

RUE. See DE LA RUE.

RUEDA, Lope de, *rway'THa* (c. 1510–65), Spanish dramatist, born in Seville, became manager of a group of strolling players. A pioneer of Spanish drama, he wrote comedies in the Italian style, short humorous pastoral dialogues, and ten burlesques (forerunners of interludes). See study by G. Salazar (Santiago de Cuba 1911).

RUFF, William (1801–56), London sporting reporter, in 1842 started his *Guide to the Turf*.

RUFFINI, Giovanni Domenico, *roof-fee'nee* (1807–81), Italian writer, born at Genoa, in 1833 joined Young Italy, and in 1836 had to flee to England. From 1875 he lived at Taggia in the Riviera. He wrote *Lorenzo Benoni: Passages in the Life of an Italian* (1853), *Dr Antonio* (1855), *Vincenzo* (1863), &c.

RUFINUS, *roo-fi'nus* (c. 345–410), Italian theologian, was the friend and later the

opponent of St Jerome, the orthodoxy of Origen being their subject of dispute.

RUGE, Arnold, *roo'gĕ* (1802–80), German writer and political thinker, born at Bergen in Rügen, in 1837 helped to found the *Hallesche* (later *Deutsche*) *Jahrbücher*, the organ of Young Germany. Its liberal tendencies were condemned, and Ruge withdrew to Paris and Switzerland. He published in 1848 the democratic *Reform*, entered the Frankfurt parliament for Breslau, and took part in the disturbances at Leipzig in 1849. In 1850 he fled to England, where with Mazzini and Ledru-Rollin he organized the Democratic Committee. He settled at Brighton, and lived by teaching, writing and translating.

RUGGLES-BRISE, Sir Evelyn John, *-brĭs* (1857–1935), British penal reformer, was born at Finchingfield, Essex. A civil servant, he was in 1895 appointed chairman of the Prison Commission, a position which he held for twenty-six years. Amongst the many reforms by which he humanized penal treatment, the Borstal system, introduced under the Children Act, 1908, is the best known. He was knighted in 1902. See the memoir by S. Leslie (1938).

RUHMKORFF, Heinrich Daniel, *room'korf* (1803–77), German instrument-maker, born at Hanover, settled (1839) in Paris, and invented (1855) his induction coil.

RUÏSDAEL. See RUYSDAEL.

RULE, St. See REGULUS, ST.

RUMFORD, Benjamin Thompson, Count (1753–1814), Anglo-American administrator and scientist, born at Woburn, Mass., March 26, 1753, was assistant in a store and a school teacher, but in 1771 married a wealthy Mrs Rolfe (1739–92). He was made major in a New Hampshire regiment, but left wife and baby daughter, and fled to England (1776), possibly because he was politically suspect. He gave valuable information to the government as to the state of America, and received an appointment in the Colonial Office. In England he experimented largely with gunpowder, and was elected F.R.S. (1779). In 1782 he was back in America, with a lieutenant-colonel's commission. After the peace he was knighted, and in 1784 entered the service of Bavaria. In this new sphere he reformed the army, drained the marshes round Mannheim, established a cannon foundry and military academy, and planned a poor-law system, spread the cultivation of the potato, disseminated a knowledge of nutrition and domestic economy, improved the breeds of horses and cattle, and laid out the English Garden in Munich. For these services he was made head of the Bavarian war department and count of the Holy Roman Empire. During a visit to England (1795–96) he endowed the two Rumford medals of the Royal Society, and also two of the American Academy, for researches in light and heat. Back in Munich, he found it threatened by both French and Austrians. The Elector fled, leaving Count Rumford president of the Council of Regency and generalissimo. Out of his supervision of the arsenal at Munich, where he was impressed by the amount of heat generated in cannon boring, arose his experiments proving the motion, as opposed to the caloric, theory of heat. In 1799 he quitted the Bavarian service, returned to London, and founded the Royal Institution; in 1802 he removed to Paris, and, marrying Lavoisier's widow in 1804, lived at her villa at Auteuil, where he died. He also invented the Rumford shadow photometer. See Memoir by Ellis accompanying his *Works*, Life by Renwick (Boston 1845), German one by Bauernfeind (1889), Prof. Tyndall's *New Fragments* (1892), and E. Larsen, *An American in Europe* (1953).

RUMSEY, James (1743–92), American engineer whose steamboat, propelled by the ejection of water from the stern and exhibited on the Potomac in 1787, was one of the earliest constructed. He died in London while preparing a second version for exhibition on the Thames.

RUNDSTEDT, Karl Rudolf Gero von, *roont' shtet* (1875–1953), German field-marshal, was born in the Old Mark of Brandenburg. He served in World War I, rising to chief of staff of the First Army Corps. In the early 'thirties he was military commander of Berlin and in 1938 commanded occupation troops in the Sudetenland, but was ' purged ' for his outspokenness about Hitler. Recalled in 1939, he directed the *Blitzkriege* in Poland and France. Checked in the Ukraine in 1941, he was relieved of his command, but in 1942 was appointed to a command stretching from Holland to the Italian frontier. On the success of the Allied invasion of France in 1944 he was again relieved of his command, but returned as c.-in-c. in September, his last great action being the Ardennes offensive. Once more he lost his command and in May 1945 was captured by the Americans in Munich. War crimes proceedings against him were dropped on the grounds of his ill-health and he was a prisoner in Britain (1946–1948). See study by Blumentritt (1952).

RUNEBERG, Johan Ludvig, *roo'nĕ-ber-y'* (1804–77), Finnish poet, writing in Swedish, was born at Jakobstad in Finland, taught at Helsingfors from 1830, and at Borga 1837–57. Among his works are *Lyric Poems* (1830), *The Elk Hunters* (1832), *Nadeschda* (1841), a third volume of *Poems* (1843), *King Fjala* (1844), narrative poems, one of which, ' Our Land', became Finland's national anthem, a comedy *Can't* (1862), and *The Kings in Salamis* (1863), a tragedy. In 1857 Runeberg edited for the Lutheran Church of Finland a *Psalm Book*, in which were included above sixty pieces of his own. See Söderhjelm's study (1904–07); Gosse's criticism and translations in *Studies in the Literature of Northern Europe* (1879); also Magnússon and Palmer's translation (1878).

RUNGE, Friedlieb Ferdinand, *roong'ĕ* (1795–1867), German chemist, born at Hamburg, discovered carbolic acid and aniline in coal tar (1834).

RUNYON, (Alfred) Damon, *run'-* (1884–1946), American author and journalist, was born in Manhattan, Kansas, and after service in the Spanish-American war (1898) turned to newspaper reporting, then to feature-writing. His first publications were volumes of verse, *Tents of Trouble* (1911) and *Rhymes of the*

Firing Line (1912), but it was his short stories, written in a characteristic racy, present-tense style, with liberal use of American slang and jargon, and depicting life in underworld New York and on Broadway, which won for him his great popularity. One collection, *Guys and Dolls* (1932), was adopted for a musical revue (1950); other books include *Blue Plate Special* (1934) and *Take it Easy* (1939), and the play, with Howard Lindsay, *A Slight Case of Murder* (1935). From 1941 he worked as a film producer.

RUPERT, Prince (1619–82), third son of the Elector Palatine Frederick V and Elizabeth, daughter of James I of England, was born at Prague, December 18, 1619. After a year and a half at the English court, he served in 1637–38, during the Thirty Years' War, against the Imperialists, until at Lemgo he was taken prisoner, and confined for nearly three years at Linz. In 1642 he returned to England, and for the next three years the ' Mad Cavalier ' was the life and soul of the Royalist cause, winning many a battle by his resistless charges, to lose it as often by a too headlong pursuit. He had fought at Worcester, Edgehill, Brentford, Chalgrove, Newbury, Bolton, Marston Moor, Newbury again, and Naseby, when in August 1645 his surrender of Bristol so irritated Charles, who in 1644 had created him Duke of Cumberland and generalissimo, that he dismissed him. A court martial, however, cleared him, and he resumed his duties, only to surrender at Oxford to Fairfax in June 1646. He now took service with France, but in 1648 accepting the command of that portion of the English fleet which had espoused the king's cause, acquitted himself with all his old daring and somewhat more caution. But in 1650 Blake attacked his squadron, and burned or sank most of his vessels. With the remnant the prince escaped to the West Indies, where with his brother, Prince Maurice (1620–52), till the loss of the latter in a hurricane, he maintained himself by seizing English and other merchantmen. In 1653 he was back in France, where and in Germany he chiefly resided till the Restoration. Thereafter he served under the Duke of York, and in concert with the Duke of Albemarle, in naval operations against the Dutch. He took part in founding the Hudson's Bay Company, which was granted its charter in 1670. He held various offices and dignities being a privy councillor, governor of Windsor, F.R.S., &c. His last years were spent in chemical, physical and mechanical researches. Though he was not the inventor of mezzotint, he improved the processes of the art, which he described to the Royal Society in 1662; and he invented an improved gunpowder and ' Prince's metal '. See Lives by Warburton (1849), Gower (1890), Scott (1899) and Erskine (1910).

RUSH, (1) Benjamin (1745–1813), American politician and physician, born at Byberry, Pa., studied medicine at Edinburgh and Paris, and, in 1769 became professor of Chemistry at Philadelphia. Elected a member of the Continental Congress, he signed the Declaration of Independence (1776). In 1777 he was appointed surgeon-general, and later physician-general, of the Continental army. In 1778 he resigned his post because he could not prevent frauds upon soldiers in the hospital stores, and resumed his professorship. In 1799 he became treasurer of the U.S. Mint. He wrote *Medical Inquiries* (1789–93), *Diseases of the Mind* (1821), &c. See Life by Goodman (1934).

(2) **Richard** (1780–1859), American lawyer and statesman, son of (1), was minister to England (1817–25), where he negotiated the Fisheries and Northeastern Boundary Treaties, and was secretary of the Treasury (1825–29).

RUSHWORTH, John (c. 1612–90), English historian, born at Acklington Park, Warkworth, studied at Oxford, and settled in London as a barrister. When the Long Parliament met in 1640 he was appointed clerk-assistant to the House of Commons; he represented Berwick 1657–60, 1679, and 1681; and he was secretary to Fairfax 1645–1650, and in 1677 to the lord keeper. In 1684 he was flung into the King's Bench for debt, and there he died. Rushworth's *Historical Collections* (8 vols. 1659–1701) cover the period 1618–48, and are valuable on the Great Rebellion.

RUSK, Dean (1909–), American politician, born in Cherokee County, Ga., educated at Davidson College, N.C., and at Oxford, and in 1934 was appointed associate professor of Government and dean of the Faculty in Mills College. After service in the army in World War II, he held various governmental posts, including that of special assistant to the secretary of war (1946–47), assistant secretary of state for U.N. affairs, deputy undersecretary of state and assistant secretary for Far Eastern Affairs (1950–51). In 1952 he was appointed president of the Rockefeller Foundation and from 1961 was secretary of state, in which capacity he played a major role in handling the Cuban crisis of 1962. He retained the post under the Johnson administration.

RUSKIN, John (1819–1900), English author and art critic, was the son of a prosperous wine merchant in London who was interested in the arts though, like his wife, narrowly evangelical. Private tutoring took the place of schooling so that when he went up to Christ Church, Oxford, in 1836, he was not versed in the ways of men and this lack clung to him throughout life. At Oxford he won the Newdigate prize and fancied himself as a poet till shortly after graduating he met Turner and discovered that his immediate task was to rescue the great painter from obscurity and neglect. *Modern Painters* (1843–60) was the result of this championship which may well have embarrassed the painter. It was more than that, of course, as it developed into a spiritual history of Europe with sidelooks into every phase of morals and taste. For this task he had the advantage of frequent visits to the Continent in company with his parents. His marriage in 1848 to the lady who afterwards became Millais' wife was legally annulled about the time he began his crusade on behalf of a new set of obscure or vilified painters, the pre-Raphaelite brotherhood, with which Millais was associated.

Modern Painters and the outlying splinters of that great work, viz., *The Seven Lamps of Architecture* (1848) and *The Stones of Venice* (1851–53), with its great chapter 3 'On the Nature of the Gothic', made him the critic of the day and something more than that, for the moral and social criticism in those works erected him into a moral guide or prophet. Oxford made him its first Slade professor of Fine Art in 1870, an office he held, with one interruption, till 1884, though latterly his crotchets and eccentricities drew more curious than interested hearers. Following on the publication of the completed *Modern Painters* he transferred his interest in art to the social question which had been implicit in much pre-Raphaelite painting. Carlyle's attacks on utilitarianism no doubt helped, but Ruskin's resentment against the social injustice and squalor resulting from unbridled capitalism led him to a sort of Christian Communism for which he was denigrated. *Unto This Last* (1860), a protest against the law of supply and demand, was discontinued on its first appearance in *Cornhill Magazine* by Thackeray and as it approved the mediaeval injunction against interest we can understand the outcry, but most of the specific reforms proposed have been carried out. The contemptuous rejection of his social economics in this work and in *Munera Pulveris* which followed was almost mortal to Ruskin; in *Sesame and Lilies* (1864–69), addressed to privileged young ladies and admonishing them on their duties, he likened his temper to that of Dean Swift. His appointment to the Slade professorship temporarily reassured him and now his incomparable vitality showed in the publication of various Slade lectures but more memorably in *Fors Clavigera*, a series of papers addressed 'To the Workmen and Labourers of Great Britain' (1871–84), in which his social philosophy is fully discussed. The announcement 'I simply cannot paint nor read . . . because of the misery that I know of' links him with Tolstoy, and though he did not, like Tolstoy, denounce middle-class culture he postponed it till the social misery was a thing of the past. The response from the workers and labourers was nil. Meanwhile he began to divest himself of his fortune in such individual enterprises as the St George's Guild, a non-profit-making shop in Paddington Street, the John Ruskin school at Camberwell, and the Whitelands College at Chelsea. His last regret was that he had not, like St Francis, denuded himself of all wealth. In his last work, the singularly beautiful *Praeterita*, also published in numbers (1886–88), he discoursed quietly on his memories, all passion spent save for a final jab at the railways which disturbed rural beauty. His last years were spent at Brantwood, Coniston, his solitude being consoled by the affection of his cousin Mrs Arthur Severn and her family. We do not take our bearings in art from *Modern Painters*—the moralism is too intrusive and 'Select nothing and neglect nothing' cannot apply to Turner's brilliant impressionism. Nor do we take our bearings in economics from *Unto This Last*, which assumes a primitive society. But apart from his splendid descriptive writing, we value Ruskin as one of the great Victorians who roused England to a sense of responsibility for the squalor in which commercial competition had involved the country. See his *Letters from Venice* (ed. Bradley, 1955); *Diaries* (ed. Evans and Whitehead, 1956–58) and studies by Wilenski (1955) and Quennell (1956).

RUSSEL, Alexander (1814–76), Scottish journalist, editor of *The Scotsman* from 1848, was born and died in Edinburgh. A Liberal and an antagonist of the Corn Laws, he was a caustic wit and great angler.

RUSSELL, a great Whig house whose origin has been traced back to Thor. Less fancifully, it goes back to one Henry Russell, a Weymouth M.P. and merchant in the Bordeaux wine trade, who lived at the beginning of the 15th century. Among his descendants have been the Earls and Dukes of Bedford, the Earls Russell, Sir William, Baron Russell of Thornhaugh, Edward, Earl of Orford, and William, Lord Russell, described hereafter in that order. See J. H. Wiffen, *Historical Memoirs of the House of Russell* (1833); Froude, *Cheneys and the House of Russell* (1884); G. Scott-Thomson, *Two Centuries of Family History* (1930), *Life in a Noble Household* (1937), *The Russells of Bloomsbury* (1940), and *Family Background* (1947); also *Silver-plated Spoon* (1959) by the Duke of Bedford.

John, 1st Earl of Bedford (*c.* 1486–1555), great-grandson of the above-mentioned Henry, became a gentleman usher to the king, was entrusted with several diplomatic missions and later held many court appointments, including those of comptroller of the household and lord privy seal. Among the rich possessions which he amassed were the abbeys of Woburn and Tavistock, and the London properties of Covent Garden and Long Acre. Created earl in 1550, he led the mission to Spain in 1554 which escorted back Philip to marry Mary Tudor.

Francis, 2nd Earl (1527–85), son of the above, was involved in the Lady Jane Grey affair and fled the country until Elizabeth's accession, when he returned and held several offices, among them that of lord president of Wales.

Francis, 4th Earl (1593–1641), son of Sir William, Baron Russell (see below), with the help of Inigo Jones (q.v.) developed Covent Garden and built the mansion of Woburn; he also continued the fen drainage scheme initiated by his father and known as the Bedford Level.

William, 5th Earl and 1st Duke (1613–1700), was created Marquess of Tavistock and 1st Duke in 1694. He fought with Cromwell at Edgehill (1642), turned royalist in the following year, but after the battle of Newbury changed his coat yet again for parliament. He completed the Bedford Level.

John, 4th Duke (1710–71), a member of the anti-Walpole group, was first lord of the admiralty under Pelham; lord-lieutenant of Ireland (1755–61) and ambassador to France (1762–63).

Francis, 5th Duke (1765–1802), a friend of ' Prinny ', built Russell and Tavistock Squares in London and employed Henry Holland (q.v.) to make additions to Woburn.

Herbrand, 11th Duke (1858–1940), declined political office, preferring to preside autocratically over his landed estates. Elected F.R.S. for his services to zoology, president of the Zoological Society from 1899, he established the collections of rare animals at Woburn, including the Prjevalsky wild horses and the Père David deer. His duchess, **Mary du Caurroy** (1865–1937), from 1898 kept a model hospital at Woburn, in which she later worked as a radiographer, took up flying at the age of sixty and participated in record-breaking flights to India and Africa before being lost off the east coast of England while flying solo in 1937.

William, 12th Duke (1888–1953), son of the above, acquired a reputation for his collection of parrots and homing budgerigars and for his adherence to pacifism, Buchmanism and near-fascism which nearly landed him in difficulties during World War II. He was killed in a shooting accident.

John Robert, 13th Duke (1917–   ), was estranged from his family at an early age and lived for a while on a slender pittance in a Bloomsbury boarding house until, having been invalided out of the Coldstream Guards in 1940, he became in turn house agent, journalist and South African farmer. After succeeding to the title he became famous for his energetic and successful efforts to keep Woburn Abbey for the family by running it commercially as a show place with popular amenities and amusements.

John, 1st Earl Russell (1792–1878), British statesman, born in London, August 18, 1792, the third son of the sixth Duke of Bedford, studied at the University of Edinburgh, and in 1813 was returned for Tavistock. His strenuous efforts in favour of reform won many seats for the Liberals at the 1830 election; the ' Great Duke ' was driven from office; and in Earl Grey's ministry Lord John became paymaster of the forces. He was one of the four members of the government entrusted with the task of framing the first Reform Bill (1832), and on him devolved the honour of proposing it. In November 1834 Lord John left office with Melbourne; the carrying of his motion (1835) for applying the surplus revenues of the Irish Church to education caused the downfall of Peel and the return of Melbourne to power, with Lord John as home (from 1839 colonial) secretary and leader of the Lower House. In the general election of 1841 he was returned for the City, which he represented until his elevation to the Upper House. In November 1845 he wrote a letter to his constituents announcing his conversion to the repeal of the Corn Laws. This led to Peel's resignation; and Lord John was commissioned to form an administration. He failed, owing to Lord Grey's antipathy to Palmerston, so Peel was forced back to office, and carried the repeal. On the very day the bill passed the Lords Peel was defeated by a coalition of Whigs and Protectionists; whereupon a Whig ministry succeeded, with Lord John as prime minister (1846–52). In Lord Aberdeen's Coalition of 1852 he was foreign secretary and leader in the Commons. His inopportune Reform Bill (1854), the Crimean mismanagement, his resignation (January 1855) and his bungling at the Vienna Conference, all combined to render him unpopular; and for four years he remained out of office. But in June 1859, in the second Palmerston administration, he became foreign secretary, in 1861 was created Earl Russell, and K.G. in 1862. Though he did much for Italian unity, non-intervention was his leading principle, e.g., during the American Civil War and the Schleswig-Holstein difficulty. On Palmerston's death in 1865 Earl Russell again became prime minister, but was defeated in June on his new Reform Bill and resigned. He continued busy with tongue and pen till his death at his residence, Pembroke Lodge, Richmond Park, May 28, 1878. Earl Russell was twice married, and by his second wife, daughter of the Earl of Minto, was the father of John, Viscount Amberley (1842–76), author of the posthumous *Analysis of Religious Belief.* His sons succeeded as second and third earl respectively. Earl Russell's works include a tale and two tragedies, a *Life of William Lord Russell* (1819), *Memoirs of the Affairs of Europe* (1824), *The Correspondence of John, fourth Duke of Bedford* (1842–46), and Memoirs of Fox and Moore. See his *Speeches and Despatches* (1870), his *Recollections and Suggestions* (1875), *Early Correspondence* (1913), and Lives by Walpole (1889), Reid (1893), and Tilby (1930). His nephew, George William Erskine Russell (1853–1919), was a Liberal under-secretary and miscellaneous author.

John Francis Stanley, 2nd Earl Russell (1865–1931), brother of the 3rd Earl, held secretaryships in the second Labour administration. An American divorce and marriage led to three months' imprisonment for bigamy (1901). For his third wife, see ARNIM (1).

Bertrand Arthur William, 3rd Earl Russell (1872–1970), English philosopher, mathematician and controversialist, one of the greatest logicians of all time, was born May 18 at Ravenscroft near Trelleck, Monmouthshire, son of Viscount Amberley and brother of the 2nd Earl, was educated privately and at Trinity College, Cambridge, where he graduated with first-class honours in mathematics (1893) and moral sciences (1894). After a few months as a British Embassy attaché in Paris, he went to Berlin to study economics, wrote his first book, *German Social Democracy* (1896), and married Alys Pearsall Smith. Elected fellow of Trinity (1895), his early infatuation with the Hegelian idealism of McTaggart was dispelled by his researches into the symbolic logic of Peano and Frege, his own brilliant study of Leibniz (1900) and the antimetaphysical common sense of a junior colleague, G. E. Moore (q.v.). The problem he posed himself was that first raised by Kant—how to defend the objectivity of mathematics. Frege and Peano had already attempted to derive, by means of symbolic logic, the whole of mathematics from certain logical constants. Russell wrote to the former (1902), pointing out a contradiction in his system, the famous antinomy

of the class of all classes which is not a member of itself. This Frege with immense disappointment courageously acknowledged in a postscript to his work. Meanwhile Russell published his own bold *Principles of Mathematics* (1903) and with A. N. Whitehead (q.v.) carried on the Fregeian endeavour to its conclusion in the monumental *Principia Mathematica* (1910–13). In this he made strenuous attempts to resolve Frege's contradictions by the famous Russellian theory of types, or classes. Another epochmaking philosophical achievement was his famous theory of descriptions set out in an article in *Mind* (1905), ' On Denoting ', which first differentiated between the ' logical and grammatical subject of a proposition. This successfully countered Meinong's extraordinary theory of objects which had it that every subject of a proposition, be it fictitious or otherwise, must be credited with some sort of ' existence '. Russell dissected this inflated ontology, using Occam's razor, preserving meaningfulness, if falseness, of propositions containing fictitious entities such as ' round square ', ' the present king of France ' as subjects. On this account ' Socrates ', for example, is a disguised description and not a logically proper name. The theory of descriptions provided a masterly solution of longstanding logical problems and if it later came under attack from linguistic considerations that does not detract from Russell's permanent achievement. Russellian methods were fully deployed by his brilliant student Wittgenstein, who was at Cambridge (1912–13), in a rigorously logical and ostensibly ' antimetaphysical ' system, which eventually matured into the famous *Tractatus* (1922) for the English version of which Russell wrote the introduction. Wittgenstein's earliest views Russell entitled ' logical atomism ', and believing Wittgenstein to have been killed in the war, lectured on them with generous acknowledgments in the United States and published them in *The Monist* (1919). His own last great work on the subject *Introduction to Mathematical Philosophy* (1919) was written in prison. His approach, frequently modified in later works, to general philosophical problems is set out in such works as *Some Problems in Philosophy* (1912), a minor classic, *Our Knowledge of the External World* (1914), *The Analysis of Mind* (1927), *An Enquiry into Meaning and Truth* (1940), with an excellent account of probability, and *Human Knowledge* (1948). Russell, like his ' secular ' godfather, John Stuart Mill, an ardent feminist, in 1907 offered himself as a Liberal candidate but was turned down for his ' free-thinking '. In 1916 his pacifism deprived him of his Trinity fellowship and in 1918 he was imprisoned. Henceforth the controversialist, who had to make a living by lecturing and journalism took charge of Russell, the philosopher. A visit to the Soviet Union, where he met Lenin, Trotsky and Gorky, sobered his early enthusiasm and resulted in the critical *Theory and Practice of Bolshevism* (1919). He was professor at Peking (1920–21), was divorced by his wife and married Dora Winifred

Black, a fellow of Girton College, Cambridge. With her he ran a progressive school near Petersfield (1927) and set out his educationist theories in *On Education* (1926) and *Education and the Social Order* (1932). His second divorce (1934) made his book *Marriage and Morals* (1932) highly controversial, although much of its advocacy was no more startling than the matrimonial reforms in More's *Utopia*. Nevertheless, his lectureship at the City College of New York was terminated in 1940 after protests from clergy and ratepayers against this ' enemy of religion and morality '. But he won an action against the Barnes Foundation which broke a lecture contract. In 1936 he married Helen Patricia Spence, his research assistant for *Freedom and Organisation, 1814-1914* (1934). The evils of fascism analysed in *In Praise of Idleness* (1936), he renounced pacifism in 1939 and went so far in the early postwar period as to advocate atomic bombardment of Russia, while the United States still had the nuclear monopoly. After 1949 he became a champion of nuclear disarmament, engaging in unprecedented correspondence with various world leaders, as at the time of the Cuban crisis in 1963, and protesting against U.S. involvement in Vietnam. In 1952, having divorced his third wife, he married an American fellow-novelist, Edith Finch. His fellowship at Trinity was restored in 1944 and he gave the first B.B.C. Reith Lectures, *Authority and the Individual* (1949). A controversial public figure, an 18th-century rationalist who had strayed into the 20th, who wrote his own jesting obituary notice for *The Times*, he will be remembered as the greatest logician since Aristotle. He succeeded to his brother's title in 1931, was elected F.R.S. (1908), awarded its Sylvester medal (1934), O.M. (1949) and Nobel prize for literature (1950). See also his popular expositions, *ABC of Atoms* (1923), *ABC of Relativity* (1925; revised 1958), *Why I am not a Christian* (1957), collections of his best philosophical papers, *Mysticism and Logic* (1910), *Logic and Knowledge*, ed. R. C. Marsh (1956), his edition of his parents' letters and diaries, *The Amberley Papers* (1937), his biting literary outlines of leading contemporaries, *Portraits from Memory* (1956), the autobiographical note and critical studies by fellow-philosophers in *The Philosophy of B. Russell*, ed. P. A. Schilpp (1944), *My Philosophical Development* (1959), and his *Autobiography* (Vol. 1, 1967, Vol. 2, 1968); also studies by Fritz (1952) on his satire, ed. Egner (1958), and Lives by Leggett (1949) and Wood, *The Passionate Sceptic* (1957).

Sir William, Baron Russell (cr. 1603) **of Thornhaugh** (c. 1558-1613), son of the 2nd Earl of Bedford, was governor of Flushing (1587-88) and lord deputy of Ireland (1594-1597). His experience of lowland drainage methods while in the former post led him to initiate reclamation work in the Cambridgeshire fens.

Edward, Earl of Orford (1683-1727), nephew of the 1st Duke of Bedford, English admiral, was a supporter of William of Orange, and is remembered as the commander of a combined British and Dutch fleet in the victory over the French at La Hogue (1692). He was created an earl in the same year.

William, Lord Russell (1639-83), born September 29, 1639, third son of the fifth Earl of Bedford, studied at Cambridge, made the Grand Tour, and at the Restoration was elected M.P. for Tavistock. He was ' drawn by the court into some disorders ' (debts and duelling), from which he was rescued by his marriage (1669) with Lady Rachel Wriothesley (1636-1723), second daughter and co-heiress of the Earl of Southampton and widow of Lord Vaughan. In 1674 he spoke against the actions of the Cabal, and thenceforth was an active adherent of the Country Party. He dallied unwisely with France, but took no bribe; he shared honestly in the delusion of the Popish Plot; he presented the Duke of York as a recusant; and he carried the Exclusion Bill up to the House of Lords. He was arrested with Essex and Sidney for participation in the Ryehouse Plot, was arraigned of high treason, and, infamous witnesses easily satisfying a packed jury, was found guilty, and beheaded on July 21, 1683. The pity of his judicial murder, the pathos of Burnet's story of his end, and the exquisite letters of his noble wife, who at his trial appeared in court as his secretary, have secured him a place in history. See Life by Lord John Russell (1819; 4th ed. 1853); *Letters of Lady Russell* (1773; 14th ed. 1853); and Lives of her by Miss Berry (1819), Lord John Russell (1820), Guizot (Eng. trans. 1855) and Lady Stepney (1899).

RUSSELL, (1) **Anna,** stage name of **Claudia Anna Russell-Brown** (1911-), English singer and musical satirist, born in London, studied singing, and began an orthodox operatic career before realizing the possibilities of satire offered by opera and concert singing, and appearing as a concert debunker of musical fads in New York in 1948, since when she has achieved universal fame in this medium.

(2) **Bertrand.** See RUSSELL, 3RD EARL, under RUSSELL Family.

(3) **Charles Taze** (1852-1916), ' Pastor Russell ', born at Pittsburgh, was a travelling preacher, and founded the International Bible Students' Association (Jehovah's Witnesses), a sect with peculiar views of prophecy and eschatology.

(4) **George** (1857-1951), English horticulturist, born at Stillington, Yorkshire. After twenty-five years of research and experiment he succeeded in producing lupins of greatly improved strains and of over sixty different colours. For this achievement he was awarded a Veitch Memorial Medal by the Royal Horticultural Society in 1937 and the M.B.E. in 1951.

(5) **George William,** pseud. Æ (1867-1935), Irish poet, writer and economist, was born at Lurgan, Co. Armagh. In 1877 the family went to Dublin, where at the Metropolitan School of Art Russell met W. B. Yeats, and, already something of a mystic, through him became interested in theosophy; this led him to give up painting, except as a hobby. Having worked first in a brewery, then as a draper's clerk, Russell published in 1894 his first book, *Homeward: Songs by the Way,*

and thereafter became a recognized figure in the Irish literary renaissance. Of nationalistic sympathies, he was editor of the *Irish Homestead* from 1906 to 1923, when it amalgamated with the *Irish Statesman*, and as editor of the latter from 1923 to 1930, he aimed at expressing balanced Irish opinion of the 1920's. His writings include books on economics, *The Candle of Vision* (1918), which is an expression of his religious philosophy, books of essays, many volumes of verse, all expressing his mysticism, among them *The Divine Vision* (1903) and *Midsummer Eve* (1928), and a play, *Deirdre* (1907). See Memoir by John Eglinton (1937).

(6) **Henry.** See (11).

(7) **Henry Norris** (1877–1957), American astronomer, was born at Oyster Bay, N.Y., was educated at Princeton and Cambridge, and became professor of Astronomy at Princeton in 1911. He developed a theory of stellar evolution, from dwarf to giant stars, which has now been superseded.

(8) **Jack,** properly **John** (1795–1883), English ' sporting parson ', born at Dartmouth, and educated at Oxford, was perpetual curate of Swymbridge near Barnstaple (1832–1880), and withal master of foxhounds and sportsman generally. A breed of terrier found in the West Country was named after him. See Memoir (new ed. 1883).

(9) **John** (1745–1806), English portrait painter and Methodist enthusiast, was born at Guildford, and elected R.A. in 1788. See Life by Williamson (1894).

(10) **John Scott** (1808–82), Scottish engineer, inventor of the ' wave system ' of shipbuilding, was born near Glasgow, and died at Ventnor.

(11) **William Clark** (1844–1911), born in New York, was son of the vocalist Henry Russell (1812–1900), who, born at Sheerness, was composer of ' Cheer, Boys, Cheer ', ' A Life on the Ocean Wave ' and other popular songs. Clark Russell served an apprenticeship at sea, and from 1874 devoted himself to writing a long succession of sea stories. See also RONALD.

(12) **Sir William Howard** (1821–1907), British special correspondent, born near Tallaght, County Dublin, joined *The Times* in 1843, and was called to the bar in 1850. From the Crimea he wrote those famous letters (published in book form 1856) which opened the eyes of Englishmen to the sufferings of the soldiers during the winter of 1854–55. He next witnessed the events of the Indian Mutiny. He established the *Army and Navy Gazette* in 1860; and in 1861 the Civil War drew him to America, which he soon made too hot for him by a candid account of the Federal defeat at Bull Run. He accompanied the Austrians during the war with Prussia (1866), and the Prussians during the war with France (1870–71); visited Egypt and the East (1874) and India (1877) as private secretary to the Prince of Wales; and went with Wolseley to South Africa in 1879. He was knighted in 1895. Among his books are a novel, *The Adventures of Dr Brady* (1868), *Hesperothen* (1882) and *A Visit to Chile* (1890). See R. Furneaux, *The First War Correspondent* (1945).

RUSSELL OF KILLOWEN, Charles Russell, 1st Baron (1832–1900), British lawyer, born at Newry, studied at Trinity College, Dublin, was called to the English bar in 1859. He became a Q.C. (1872), a Liberal M.P. (1880), attorney-general (1886, 1892–94), a knight (1886), lord chief justice (1894), and a life peer. A supporter of Irish home rule, he was leading counsel for Parnell in the tribunal of 1888–89. See Life by O'Brien (1901).

RUTEBEUF (*c.* 1230–86), French trouvère, Champenois in origin but Parisian by adoption, was author of the semi-liturgical drama *Miracle de Théophile* (*c.* 1260, a prototype of the Faust story), the *Dit de l'Herberie*, a monologue by a quack doctor, full of comic charlatanesque rhetoric, and also several typical *fabliaux*. See studies by Clédat (1891) and Leo (1922).

RUTH, George Herman (Babe) (1895–1948), U.S. baseball player, born in Baltimore, began his career with the Baltimore Orioles before joining the Boston Red Sox, then the New York Yankees, with whom he played till his retirement in 1934. He was the holder of innumerable records and took part in more World series matches than any other player. *The Babe Ruth Story* was filmed in 1948.

RUTHERFORD, ruTH'-, (1) **Alison.** See COCKBURN (2).

(2) **Daniel** (1749–1819), Scottish physician and botanist, stepbrother of Sir Walter Scott's mother, was born in Edinburgh, where he became professor of Botany in 1786. In 1772 he published his discovery of the distinction between ' noxious air ' (nitrogen) and carbon dioxide.

(3) **Ernest Rutherford, 1st Baron Rutherford of Nelson** (1871–1937), New Zealand-born British physicist, one of the greatest pioneers of subatomic physics, was born August 30 at Spring Grove (later Brightwater) near Nelson, New Zealand, the fourth of twelve children of a wheelwright and flaxmiller. Educated at local state schools, he won scholarships to Nelson College and Canterbury College, Christchurch. His first research projects were on magnetization of iron by high-frequency discharges (1894) and magnetic viscosity (1896). In 1895 he was admitted to the Cavendish Laboratory and Trinity College, Cambridge, on an 1851 Exhibition scholarship. There he made the first successful wireless transmissions over two miles. Under the brilliant direction of J. J. Thomson (q.v.), Rutherford discovered the three types of uranium radiations. In 1898 he became professor of Physics at McGill university, Canada, where, with Soddy, he formulated the theory of atomic disintegration to account for the tremendous heat energy radiated by uranium, thus overthrowing the classical law of conservation of matter. In 1907 he became professor at Manchester and there established that alpha particles were doubly ionized helium ions by counting the number given off with a Geiger counter. This led to a revolutionary conception of the atom as a miniature universe in which the mass is concentrated in the nucleus surrounded by planetary electrons. His assistant, Niels Bohr (q.v.), applied to this the quantum theory (1913) and the concept of the ' Rutherford-Bohr atom ' of nuclear

physics was born. During World War I, Rutherford did research on submarine detection for the admiralty. In 1919, in a series of brilliant experiments, he discovered that alpha-ray bombardments induced atomic transformation in atmospheric nitrogen, liberating hydrogen nuclei. The same year he succeeded J. J. Thomson to the Cavendish professorship at Cambridge and reorganized the laboratory, the world's centre for the study of *The Newer Alchemy* (1937). In 1920 he predicted the existence of the neutron, later discovered by his colleague, Chadwick, in 1932. He was elected F.R.S. in 1903, was awarded its Rumford (1904) and Copley (1922) medals, the Nobel prize for chemistry (1908) and the O.M. (1925), was knighted (1914) and made a peer (1931), was president of the British Association (1923), of the Royal Society (1925–30) and was chairman of the advisory council of D.S.I.R. (1930–37). He published nearly 150 original papers, and his books include *Radioactivity* (1904), *Radioactive Transformations* (1906) and *Radioactive Substances* (1930). He died at Cambridge, October 19, 1937, and was buried in Westminster Abbey. See biographical studies by A. S. Eve (1939), N. Feather (1940) and J. Rowland (1955).

(4) **Dame Margaret** (1892–1972), British theatre and film actress, born in London, made her first stage appearance in 1925 at the Old Vic theatre, and her film début in 1936. She gradually gained fame as a character actress and comedienne, her gallery of eccentrics including such notable rôles as ' Miss Prism ' in *The Importance of Being Earnest* (stage 1939, film 1952), ' Madame Arcati ' in *Blithe Spirit* (stage 1941, film 1945), and ' Miss Whitchurch ' in *The Happiest Days of Your Life* (stage 1948, film 1950). She also scored a success as Agatha Christie's ' Miss Marple ' in a series of films from 1962, appearing with her husband, the actor **Stringer Davis** (1899–   ), whom she married in 1945. She was created O.B.E. in 1961, D.B.E. in 1967, and won an Oscar as Best Supporting Actress for her part in *The V.I.P.s* in 1964.

(5) **Mark.** See WHITE (9).

(6) **Samuel** (*c.* 1600–61), Scottish theologian and preacher, born at Nisbet near Jedburgh, took his M.A. at Edinburgh in 1621. In 1623 he was appointed professor of Humanity; he was dismissed in 1626, having ' fallen in fornication '; but next year he was settled as minister of Anwoth. Here he began that correspondence with his godly friends which has been called ' the most seraphic book in our literature '. *Exercitationes pro divina Gratia* (1636) was against the Arminians, and brought him an invitation to a Divinity chair in Holland and a summons before the High Commission Court in July 1636, when he was forbidden to preach, and banished to Aberdeen (till 1638). He became professor of Divinity at St Andrews in 1639, and in 1647 principal of the New College; in 1643 he was sent to the Westminster Assembly. His *Due Right of Presbyteries* (1644), *Lex Rex* (1644), &c., belong to this period. *Lex Rex* was burned by the hangman in Edinburgh in 1661, and its author deposed and summoned

for high treason; but he received the citation when on his deathbed. See Lives by Murray (1828) and Thomson (1884), Bonar's edition of the *Letters*, and Dr A. Whyte's *Samuel Rutherford and his Correspondents* (1894).

RUTHVEN, *riv'ĕn*, (1) **John** (*c.* 1578–1600), second son of (2), succeeded a brother as 3rd Earl in 1588, and travelled in Italy, Switzerland and France. Soon after his arrival back in Scotland he was killed with a brother in his house at Perth in the ' Gowrie Conspiracy '—controversially an alleged attempt to murder or kidnap James VI. See Barbé's *Tragedy of Gowrie House* (1887) and Roughead's *The Riddle of the Ruthvens* (1919).

(2) **William** (*c.* 1541–84), created Earl of Gowrie in 1581, carried off the boy king, James VI, to Castle Ruthven near Perth—the ' Raid of Ruthven '—was first pardoned, then ordered to leave the country, but was beheaded at Stirling for his part in a conspiracy to take Stirling Castle.

RUTLAND, John James Robert Manners, 7th Duke of (1818–1906), English politician, born at Belvoir Castle, entered parliament in 1841, succeeded to the dukedom in 1888, and held office in the various Conservative ministries between 1852 and 1892. A member of the Young England party (1842–45), he wrote poems, descriptions of tours and a yachting cruise, ballads, &c. See study by C. Whibley (1925).

RUYSBROEK, Johannes, *roys'brook* (1293–1381), Flemish mystic, born at Ruysbroek near Brussels, was vicar of St Gudule's in Brussels, but in 1353 withdrew to the Augustinian monastery of Groenendael near Waterloo, of which he became prior. His mysticism is expressed in his *Book of Supreme Truth*, &c. See Lives of the *Doctor ecstaticus* by Engelhardt (1838) and Otterloo (1874), and books by Maeterlinck (Eng. trans. 1894) and Evelyn Underhill (1915).

RUYSDAEL, or Ruïsdael, Jacob van, *roys'dahl* (*c.* 1628–82), one of the greatest landscape painters of the Dutch school, was born in Haarlem. Perhaps a pupil of his uncle **Salomon van Ruysdael** (*c.* 1600–70), a Haarlem landscape painter, he became a member of the Haarlem painters' guild in 1648, about 1655 moved to Amsterdam, thereafter travelling in Holland and Germany. He died in an almshouse in Haarlem. His best works are country landscapes, and he also excelled in cloud effects, particularly in his seascapes. He was not highly regarded by his contemporaries, but modern appreciation of him has prevailed in spite of an unpleasant darkening through time of the green of his landscapes. He is represented in the National Gallery, London (*Holland's Deep* and *Landscape with Ruins*), Glasgow Art Gallery (*View of Katwijk*), the Louvre (*Le Coup de Soleil*), &c. See study by Rosenberg (1928).

RUYTER, Michiel Adrianszoon de, *roy'tĕr* (1607–76), Dutch sailor, born at Flushing, went to sea as a cabin boy, but by 1635 had become a captain in the Dutch navy. In the war with England in 1652 he repelled an attack off the Lizard, and with de Witt had to retire after attacking Blake off the mouth of the Thames; but two months later they defeated Blake off Dover. In 1653 he repeatedly fought with Blake, Monk and Deane, and was at the battle off the Texel (July 29), where his superior, Tromp, was killed and the Dutch fleet defeated. After 1654 he blockaded the coasts of Portugal, and then those of Sweden; and after the Dano-Swedish war was ennobled by the king of Denmark. The years 1661–63 were principally occupied with the Barbary corsairs. In the next English war (1664) he took Gorée and some Guinea forts; in 1665 he preyed upon English merchant vessels in the West Indies; in 1666, now admiral-in-chief, he held his own for four days (June 1–4) against Monk and Prince Rupert off Dunkirk; in July he was driven back to Holland by Monk. In 1667 he sailed up the Medway to Rochester, burned some of the English ships, and next sailed up the Thames to Gravesend, besides attacking Harwich. In a third war (1672) against England and France combined, he attacked the English and French fleets under the Duke of York, the Earl of Sandwich, and Count d'Estrées in Solebay (May 28, 1672); and defeated Prince Rupert and d'Estrées in June 1673, and again in August. In 1675 de Ruyter sailed for the Mediterranean to help the Spaniards against the French. He encountered the French fleet near the Lipari Islands about the New Year, and again in the Bay of Catania. In the second fight the Dutch-Spanish fleet was routed and de Ruyter wounded. He died April 29, in Syracuse. See Lives by Brandt (1698), Richer (1783) and Blok (trans. 1933).

RUŽIČKA, Leopold, roo'zheech-ka (1887–), Swiss chemist, born at Vukovar, Yugoslavia, became professor of Chemistry at Utrecht in 1926 and at Zürich in 1929. He made the earliest synthesis of musk, worked on higher terpenes and steroids, and was the first to synthesize sex hormones, for which he was awarded with Butenandt the 1939 Nobel prize for chemistry.

RUZZANTE, real name Angelo Beolco, root-tsan'tay (1502–42), Italian dramatist and actor, born in Padua, wrote mainly comedies of rural life. See study by Cataldo (1933).

RYDBERG, rüd'ber-y', (1) Abraham Viktor (1828–95),Swedish author, born in Jönköping, was on the staff of a Göteborg newspaper, later a professor in Stockholm. Among his works are several novels of the highest merit, including Fribrytaren på Östersjön (1857). He also wrote Biblical criticism.
(2) Johannes Robert (1854–1919), Swedish physicist, born at Halmstad, was professor at Lund from 1901 to 1919, developed a formula for spectral lines, incorporating the constant known by his name.

RYDER, rī'dèr, (1) Albert Pinkham (1847–1917), American painter, born in New Bedford, Mass., excelled in figures and landscapes, executed in a romantic style.
(2) Samuel (1859–1936), English businessman, donor (1927) of the Ryder Cup, competed for by British and American professional golfers. Ryder, the son of a Cheshire nurseryman, built up, mainly by his scheme of selling penny packets of seeds, a prosperous business at St Albans.

RYLANDS, John, rī'lèndz (1801–88), English textile manufacturer and merchant, born at St Helens. In 1899 his widow established the John Rylands Library in Manchester.

RYLE, rīl, (1) Gilbert (1900–), English philosopher, educated at Brighton College and Queen's College, Oxford, served in the Welsh Guards from 1939 until 1945, when he became Waynflete professor of Metaphysical Philosophy at Oxford. In 1931 he became a convert to the view that 'philosophy is the detection of the sources of linguistic idioms of recurrent misconstructions and absurd theories'. His Concept of Mind (1949) displays brilliant linguistic detective work in exorcizing 'the ghost in the machine' or the philosophical remains of Cartesian dualism. In 1947 he became editor of Mind. Other works include Dilemmas (1954) and Plato's Progress (1966). He edited Revolution in Philosophy (1957).
(2) Herbert Edward (1856–1925), second son of (3), born in London, Bishop of Exeter (1900–03), Bishop of Winchester (1903–10), Dean of Westminster (1910), K.C.V.O. (1921), wrote on the Old Testament canon, Genesis, Philo, &c. See Fitzgerald's Memoir (1928).
(3) John Charles (1816–1900), Bishop of Liverpool (1880–1900), was born at Macclesfield. A prominent Evangelical, he wrote countless popular tracts and books. See Life by M. L. Loane (1953).
(4) Martin (1918–), English radio-astronomer, educated at Bradfield and Christ Church, Oxford, worked at the Cavendish Laboratory, Cambridge (1945–48), and subsequently became a fellow of Trinity, lecturer in Physics (1948–59) and professor of Radio-astronomy from 1959. Using the Cambridge radio-telescope to plot the intensity-distribution curve of stars up to 3000 million and more light years distant, he obtained controversial data which led him in 1961 to throw doubt on the generally accepted 'steady state' theory of the universe.

RYMER, Thomas, rī'mèr (1641–1713), English critic and historian, born at Yafforth Hall, Northallerton, Yorks, the son of a Roundhead gentleman who was hanged at York in 1664, studied at Sidney Sussex, Cambridge, and entered Gray's Inn in 1666. He published translations, critical discussions on poetry, dramas and works on history, and in 1692 was appointed historiographer royal. His principal critical work is The Tragedies of the Last Age Considered (1678); but he is chiefly remembered as the compiler of the collection of historical materials known as the Foedera (1704–35). Hardy's Syllabus of the whole was published in 1869–85.

RYMOUR. See THOMAS THE RHYMER.

RYSBRACK, (John) Michael, rīs'brak (c. 1693–1770), Flemish sculptor, born perhaps at Antwerp, settled in London in 1720. Among his works are the monument to Sir Isaac Newton in Westminster Abbey (1731), statues of William III, Queen Anne, George III, and busts of Gay, Rowe, Pope, Sir R. Walpole, &c. See study by Webb (1954).

RYVES, Mrs. See OLIVE, PRINCESS.

S

SAADI. See SÁDI.

SAARINEN, Eero (1910–61), Finnish-American architect, born in Finland, accompanied his father, Gottlieb Eliel Saarinen (1873–1950), to the U.S. in 1923. After studying sculpture in Paris and architecture at Yale University he worked with his father, designing many public buildings in U.S.A. and in Europe, including the Columbia Broadcasting System H.Q., N.Y., and the U.S. chancelleries in Oslo and London. He claimed an almost religious rôle for architecture. See *Eero Saarinen on his Work* (1963).

SABATIER, sa-ba-tyay, (1) **Louis Auguste** (1839–1901), French Protestant theologian, born at Vallon (Ardèche), wrote the very influential *Esquisse d'une philosophie de la religion* (1897, trans. 1897).

(2) **Paul** (1858–1928), French Protestant theologian, brother of (1), was a vicar in Strasbourg until expelled by the Germans in 1889, became professor at Strasbourg in 1919, and after a *Life* in 1893 wrote much on St Francis of Assisi.

(3) **Paul** (1854–1941), French chemist, was born at Carcassonne, and in 1882 became professor at Toulouse. He did notable work in catalysis, discovering with Senderens (q.v.) a process for the catalytic hydrogenation of oils, and shared with Grignard (q.v.) the 1912 Nobel prize for chemistry.

SABATINI, Rafael, sa-ba-tee'nee (1875–1950), novelist, was born of Italian and British parentage at Jesi, Italy. Writing in English, he first made his name as an author of historical romances with *The Tavern Knight* (1904), which he followed after he settled in England in 1905 with many other such tales, including *The Sea Hawk* (1915) and *Scaramouche* (1921), historical biographies, and a study of *Torquemada* (1913).

SABBATAI Z'VI, sa-bat'ay-ī tsè-vee' (1626–1675), a messiah, who, born in Smyrna, gained a great following, but latterly embraced Islam. See Life by Kastein (1931).

SABINE, Sir Edward, sa'bin (1788–1883), British astronomer, physicist and soldier, born in Dublin, accompanied Ross and Parry as astronomer in 1818–20. But his reputation rests on his valuable pendulum experiments and labours in terrestrial magnetism. He was elected F.R.S. in 1818, was P.R.S. 1861–71, was knighted in 1869 and became a general in 1870.

SACCHETTI, Franco, sak-ket'tee (c. 1330–1400), Italian novelist, a follower of Boccaccio, was born in Florence, and held several diplomatic offices. Of his 258 *Novelle*, first printed in 1724, ten are translated in Roscoe's *Italian Novelists* (1825). Gigli edited his *Opere* (1857–61) and *Novelle* (1886); Morpurgo his *Rime* (1892), with a Life.

SACCHI, Andrea, sak'kee (c. 1599–1661), Italian painter, was born at Netturo near Rome. He upheld the classical tradition in Roman painting, and is represented by the *Vision of St Romuald* and *Miracle of Saint Gregory*, painted for Pope Urban VIII, and by religious works in many Roman churches.

SACCHINI, Antonio Maria Gasparo, sak-kee'nee (1734–86), Italian composer, born at Pozzuoli, travelled in Italy and Germany, lived in London (1772–82). He wrote operas and church and chamber music.

SACCO, Nicola (1891–1927), and **Vanzetti Bartolomeo** (1888–1927), chief figures in an American *cause célèbre* which had worldwide reverberations. Accused of a payroll murder and robbery in 1920, they were found guilty, and seven years later were executed in spite of conflicting and circumstantial evidence, and the confession of another man to the crime. Both had been extreme left-wing labour agitators, and the suspicion that this had provoked deliberate injustice aroused an outcry in all parts of the world.

SACHARISSA. See WALLER (2).

SACHER-MASOCH, Leopold von, zahKH'èr-mah'zoKH (1836–95), Austrian lawyer and writer, born in Lemberg, wrote many short stories and novels, including *Der Don Juan von Kolomea* (1866), depicting the life of smalltown Polish Jews. The term ' masochism ' has been coined to describe the form of eroticism detailed in his later works.

SACHEVERELL, sa-shev'èr-èl, (1) **Henry** (c. 1674–1724), English political preacher, was born at Marlborough, the son of a High Church rector, and went in 1689 to Magdalen College, Oxford, where he shared rooms with Addison, who dedicated to his ' dearest Henry ' *An Account of the Greatest English Poets* (1694). Gaining his doctorate in 1708, he had held the Staffordshire vicarage of Cannock, when in 1709 he delivered the two sermons—one at Derby assizes, the other at St Paul's—which have given him a place in history. The rancour with which he assailed the Revolution Settlement and the Act of Toleration, while asserting the doctrine of nonresistance, roused the wrath of the Whig government, and he was impeached (1710) before the House of Lords. Ardent crowds, shouting ' High Church and Sacheverell! ' and now and then wrecking a meeting house, attended him to Westminster. He was found guilty, and suspended from preaching for three years. The Godolphin ministry fell that same summer, and in 1713 Sacheverell was selected by the House of Commons to preach the Restoration sermon. He was presented to the rich rectory of St Andrew's, Holborn, after which little is heard of him save that he squabbled with his parishioners, and was suspected of complicity in a Jacobite plot. See F. Madan's *Bibliography of Dr Sacheverell* (1887).

(2) **William** (1638–91), English politician, sometimes called the ' First Whig ', studied law, entered the House of Commons as member for Derbyshire in 1670, and rapidly became one of the leaders of the anti-Court party, instrumental in framing the Test Act, which overthrew Charles II's ' cabal '

ministry. He was prominent amongst those later demanding the resignation of Lord Danby and a keen supporter of the Exclusion Bill. Fined by Judge Jeffreys in 1682 for opposing the king's remodelled charter for Nottingham, and defeated in the 1685 election, he sat in the Convention parliament of 1689 which offered the throne to William. Throughout his career of 'opposition' Sacheverell was distinguished for his powers of parliamentary oratory.

SACHS, *zahks,* (1) **Hans** (1494–1576), German poet and dramatist, born November 5, 1494, at Nuremberg, the son of a tailor, was bred a shoemaker, and early learnt verse-making from a weaver. On finishing his apprenticeship in 1511 he travelled through Germany, practising his craft in various cities, and frequenting the schools of the *Meistersinger*. On his return to Nuremberg in 1516 he commenced business as a shoemaker, becoming a master of his guild in the following year; and, after a long and prosperous life, died January 19 (or 25), 1576. Sachs' literary career, which resulted in the tremendous output of more than 6300 pieces, falls into two periods. In the first he celebrated the Reformation and sang Luther's praises in an allegorical tale (1523) entitled *Die Wittenbergisch Nachtigall,* while his poetical flysheets, numbering about 200, furthered in no small measure the Protestant cause. In his second period his poetry deals more with common life and manners, and is distinguished by its vigorous language, good sense, homely morality and fresh humour. It is, however, deficient in high imagination and brilliant fancy, and contains much prosaic and insipid verse. His best works are *Schwänke,* or Merry Tales, the humour of which is sometimes unsurpassable; serious tales; allegorical and spiritual songs; and Lenten dramas. His *Complete Works* were edited by Goetze and Von Keller (1870–1908). See the studies by Genée (1902), Geiger (1904), Landau (1924) and Röttinger (1927).

(2) **Julius von** (1832–97), German botanist, born at Breslau, in 1867 became professor of Botany at Freiburg, in 1868 at Würzburg. There he carried on important experiments, especially on the influence of light and heat upon plants, and the organic activities of vegetable growth. See study by E. C. Pringsheim (1932).

(3) **Nelly** (1891–1970), Swedish writer, born in Berlin of Jewish descent, fled from Germany in 1940, settled in Stockholm and took Swedish nationality. Her first book *Legends and Tales* (1921) was followed by numerous lyrical and dramatic works and anthologies. She was awarded the Nobel prize for literature in 1966, jointly with Agnon.

SACKVILLE, (1) **Charles, 6th Earl of Dorset** (1638–1706), succeeded to the earldom in 1677, having two years before been made Earl of Middlesex. He was returned by East Grinstead to the first parliament of Charles II, and became an especial favourite of the king, and notorious for his boisterous and indecorous frolics. He served under the Duke of York at sea, but could not endure the tyranny of James II and ardently supported the cause of William. His later years were

honoured by a generous patronage of Prior, Wycherley, Dryden. He died at Bath, January 19, 1706. He wrote lyrics (as 'To all you Ladies now at Land') and satirical pieces.

(2) **Lord George** (1716–85), youngest son of the first Duke of Dorset, was wounded at Fontenoy (1745), and dismissed the service for not charging at Minden (1759). Colonial secretary 1775–82, in 1770 he took the surname Germain, and in 1782 was created Viscount Sackville. See L. Marlowe, *Sackville of Drayton* (1948).

(3) **Thomas, 1st Earl of Dorset** (1536–1608), English poet and statesman, was born at Buckhurst in Sussex, the only son of Sir Richard Sackville, chancellor of the Exchequer. In 1555 he married, and in 1558 was in parliament. With Thomas Norton he produced the blank-verse tragedy of *Ferrex and Porrex* (afterwards called *Gorboduc*) which in 1560–61 was acted before Queen Elizabeth, Sackville's second cousin. This work, after the style of Seneca, claims notice as the earliest tragedy in English. Dramatic energy it has none, but the style is pure and stately, evincing eloquence and power of thought. *The Induction* and *Buckingham,* contributed to *A Myrrovre for Magistrates* (1563), are noble poetry. His prodigality brought Sackville into disgrace, and he travelled in France and Italy (c. 1563–66), was imprisoned in Rome as a suspected spy, received Knole as a gift from the queen (1566), and in 1567 was knighted and created Lord Buckhurst. He was then employed as a diplomatist in France and the Low Countries, in 1586 announced her death sentence to Mary, Queen of Scots, and in 1589 was made K.G., in 1599 lord high treasurer, and in 1604 Earl of Dorset. He died April 19, 1608. See Works, ed. Sackville-West (1859), *Induction* and *Buckingham,* ed. M. Hearsey (1936, from the author's MS., with Life); Sackville-West, *Knole and the Sackvilles* (1947).

SACKVILLE-WEST, Victoria Mary (1892–1962), English poet and novelist, born at Knole House, Kent, the daughter of the 3rd Baron Sackville. In her *Orchard and Vineyard* (1921) and her long poem *The Land,* which won the 1927 Hawthornden prize, her close sympathy with the life of the soil of her native county is expressed. Her prose works include the novels *The Edwardians* (1930), *All Passion Spent* (1931), *Knole and the Sackvilles* (1947) and studies of Andrew Marvell and Joan of Arc. In 1913 she married Harold Nicolson (q.v.). *Passenger to Teheran* (1926) records their years in Persia. She was made C.H. in 1948.

SACROBOSCO, Johannes de (or **John Holywood**), English mathematician, seems to have been born at Halifax, to have studied at Oxford, and to have been professor of Mathematics at Paris, where he died in 1244 or 1256. He was one of the first to use the astronomical writings of the Arabians. His treatise, *De Sphaera Mundi,* a paraphrase of part of Ptolemy's *Almagest,* passed during 1472–1647 through forty editions.

SACY, *sa-see,* (1) **Antoine Isaac, Baron Silvestre de** (1758–1838), French Arabist, born in Paris, became in 1795 professor of Arabic in the Institute of Oriental Languages, in 1806 also of Persian. He was perpetual secretary of the Academy of Inscriptions, founder and member of the Asiatic Society, and member of the Chamber of Peers.

(2) **Samuel Ustazade Silvestre de** (1801–79), son of (1), long one of the leading writers on the *Journal des débats* from 1855 a member of the Academy, edited (1861–64) the letters of Madame de Sévigné.

SADE, Donatien Alphonse François, Marquis de, *sahd* (1740–1814), French writer, born in Paris, fought in the Seven Years' War, and was in 1772 condemned to death at Aix for his cruel sexual vices. He made his escape, but was afterwards imprisoned at Vincennes and in the Bastille, where he wrote his fantastically scandalous romances, *Justine* (1791), *La Philosophie dans le boudoir* (1793), *Juliette* (1798) and *Les Crimes de l'amour* (1800). He died mad at Charenton. The word 'sadism', derived from his name, is used to describe the type of unnatural sexual perversion from which he suffered. See study by Gorer (1934).

SÁ DE MIRANDA, Francisco, *sa-*TH*è-mee-rãn'da* (c. 1485–1558), Portuguese poet, founder of the Petrarchan school, born at Coimbra, spent some years in Italy, wrote sonnets, eclogues, prose comedies and interesting verse epistles.

SÁDI, Saadi, or **Sa'adi,** the assumed name of **Sheikh Muslih Addin** (c. 1184–?1292), Persian poet, highly regarded in his native land, was a descendant of Ali, Mohammed's son-in-law. He studied at Bagdad, travelled much, and near Jerusalem was taken prisoner by the Crusaders, but was ransomed by a merchant of Aleppo, who gave him his daughter in marriage. The catalogue of his works comprises twenty-two different kinds of writings in prose and verse, in Arabic and Persian, of which odes and dirges form the predominant part. The most celebrated of his works, however, is the *Gulistan*, or Flower Garden, a kind of moral work in prose and verse, intermixed with stories, maxims, philosophical sentences, puns and the like. Next comes the *Bostan*, or Tree Garden, in verse, and more religious than the *Gulistan*. Third stands the *Pend-Nameh*, or Book of Instructions. The *Gulistan* has been translated into English by Gladwin, Ross, Eastwick and Platts. The *Bostan* was translated by H. W. Clarke (1879). See the French essay by H. Massi (1919).

SADLEIR, Michael, *sad'lèr* (1888–1957), English author and publisher, born at Oxford, a son of **Sir Michael Ernest Sadler** (1861–1943), educationist and great-grand-nephew of M. T. Sadler (q.v.), he reverted to an older form of the name to avoid confusion. Educated at Rugby and Oxford, he joined the publishing firm of Constable, becoming a director in 1920. As well as numerous bibliographical works—he was Sandars reader in Bibliography at Cambridge in 1937 —he published novels, including *Hyssop* (1915), *These Foolish Things* (1937) and *Fanny by Gaslight* (1940), and biographies, of which *Michael Ernest Sadler: a memoir by his son* (1949) and *Anthony Trollope* (1927) are noteworthy.

SADLER, (1) **Sir Michael Ernest.** See Sadleir.

(2) **Michael Thomas** (1780–1835), English social reformer, born at Snelston, Derbyshire, became a linen manufacturer, sat in parliament (1829–32), wrote on Irish social questions, and did much to reduce the monstrous hours of children in factories, introducing in 1831 the first Ten-hour Bill. He died at Belfast. See memoir by Seeley (1842).

(3) **Sir Ralph** (1507–87), English diplomat, born at Hackney, from 1537 was employed in diplomacy with Scotland. He was left one of the twelve councillors of Edward VI's minority, fought at Pinkie, sat in the commission on Queen Mary at York, was her jailer at Tutbury, and was perhaps sent with the news of her execution to her son. His *Papers,* valuable for Border and Scottish history, were edited by Arthur Clifford, with historical notes by Sir Walter Scott (1809).

SADOLETO, Jacopo, *sa-dō-lay'tō* (1477–1547), Italian churchman, born at Modena, went to Rome in 1502, and took orders. Leo X made him apostolical secretary, an appointment he retained under Clement VII and Paul III. By Leo he was made Bishop of Carpentras in 1517, and by Paul in 1536 a cardinal. In 1544 he was legate to Francis I. Sadoleto ranks as one of the great churchmen of his age. He corresponded with many Protestant leaders, and sought to find a basis for reunion. There is a French study by Joly (1856).

ŠAFAŘÍK, Pavel Josef, *sha'far-zheek* (1795–1861), Czech author of important works on Slavonic literature and antiquities, was in 1848 professor at Prague University.

SAGAN, Françoise, *sah-gã,* pen-name of **Françoise Quoirez** (1936–), French novelist, born in Paris and educated at a convent and private schools, at eighteen wrote the best-selling *Bonjour tristesse* (1954; filmed 1958), followed by *Un Certain Sourire* (1956; filmed 1958), both remarkably direct testaments of wealthy adolescence, written with the economy of a remarkable literary style. Irony creeps into her third, *Dans un mois, dans un an* (1957), but moral consciousness takes over in her later novels, such as *Aimez-vous Brahms . . .* (1959; filmed 1961 as *Goodbye Again*), *La Chamade* (1966). A ballet to which she gave the central idea, *Le Rendez-vous manqué,* enjoyed a temporary *succès de scandale* in Paris and London in 1958. Her later work, including several plays, e.g., *Château en Suède* (1960) and *Les Violons, parfois . . .* (1961), has had a mixed critical reception.

SAGASTA, Práxedes Mateo, *-gas'-* (1827–1903), Spanish Liberal leader from 1875, born at Torrecilla, took part in insurrections in 1856 and 1866, and had twice to flee to France. Several times premier, he introduced universal male suffrage and trial by jury.

SA'ID, Nuri Es. See Es-Sa'id.

SA'ID PASHA, *sa-eed'* (1822–63), viceroy of Egypt from 1854, gave the concession for the Suez Canal.

SAINT AMANT, Antoine Girard de, *sĩt a-mã* (1594–1661), French poet, was born in Rouen. An early exponent of French burlesque poetry, he also wrote the heroic idyll, *Moyse sauvé,* and an ode, *À la solitude.*

SAINT ARNAUD, Jacques Leroy de, *sĭt ar-nõ* (1796–1854), French soldier, born at Bordeaux, fought for the Greeks (1822–26), but made his reputation in Algeria, and in 1851 carried on a bloody but successful warfare with the Kabyles. Louis Napoleon recalled him; and as war minister he took an active part in the *coup d'état* of December 2. He was rewarded with the marshal's baton. In the Crimean war he commanded the French forces, and co-operated with Lord Raglan at the Alma, but nine days afterwards died on his way home to France. See his *Lettres* (1864) and work by Cabrol (1895).

SAINTE-BEUVE, Charles Augustin, *sĭt-bœv* (1804–69), French writer, the greatest literary critic of his time, was born at Boulogne-sur-Mer, December 23, 1804, son of a commissioner of taxes, who died three months before the birth of his son, leaving his wife in straitened circumstances. Till his fourteenth year Sainte-Beuve attended school in Boulogne, then went to the Collège Charlemagne in Paris, and next (1824–27) followed a course of medical study. M. Dubois, one of his teachers at the Collège Charlemagne, founded a literary and political paper called the *Globe*, and to it, along with Jouffroy, Rémusat, Ampère and Mérimée, Sainte-Beuve became a contributor. For three years he wrote the short articles collected as *Premiers Lundis*. In 1827 a eulogistic review of the *Odes et Ballades* of Victor Hugo led to the closest relations between the poet and his critic, which lasted until broken in 1834 by Sainte-Beuve's liaison with Madame Hugo. For a time Sainte-Beuve was the zealous advocate of the romantic movement. In 1828 he published *Tableau de la poésie française au seizième siècle*; in 1829 and 1830 *Vie et Poésies de Joseph Delorme* and *Les Consolations*, poems fraught with morbid feeling. In 1829 in the *Revue de Paris* he began the *Causeries* or longer critical articles on French literature. After the Revolution of July 1830 he again wrote for the *Globe*, now in the hands of the Saint-Simoniens; but his new colleagues soon passed the limits of his sympathy, and for the next three years he was on the staff of Carrel's *National*, the organ of extreme republicanism. In 1830–36 he became a sympathetic listener of Lamennais; but with the ultra-democratic opinions of Lamennais after his breach with Rome he had no sympathy. His solitary novel, *Volupté* (1835), belongs to this period. In 1837 he lectured on the history of Port Royal at Lausanne; in book form these lectures contain some of his finest work. At Lausanne he produced his last volume of poetry, *Pensées d'août*. A journey into Italy closes the first period of his life. In 1840 he was appointed keeper of the Mazarin Library. During the next eight years he wrote mainly for the *Revue des deux mondes*, in 1845 he was elected to the French Academy. The political confusions of 1848 led him to become professor of French Literature at Liège, where he lectured on *Chateaubriand et son groupe*. In 1849 he returned to Paris, and began to write for the *Constitutionnel* an article on some literary subject, to appear on the Monday of every week. In 1861 these *Causeries du lundi* were transferred to the *Moniteur*, in 1867 back to the *Constitutionnel*, and finally in 1869 to the *Temps*. In 1854, on his appointment by the emperor as professor of Latin Poetry at the Collège de France, the students refused to listen to his lectures, and he was forced to demit the office; the undelivered lectures contained his critical estimate of Virgil. Nominated a senator in 1865, he regained popularity by his spirited speeches in favour of that liberty of thought which the government was doing its utmost to suppress. He died in Paris, October 13, 1869. It was his special instruction that he should be buried without religious ceremony. It is by the amount and variety of his work, and the ranges of qualities it displays, that Sainte-Beuve holds such a place among literary critics. He is unapproachable in his faculty of educing the interest and significance of the most various types of human character and the most various forms of creative effort. His work marks an epoch in the intellectual history of Europe. By its delicacy, subtlety and precision it extended the limits of the study of human character and of the products of human intelligence. Besides the writings mentioned above he published many other literary works, including *Critiques et portraits littéraires* (1836–39), *Portraits de femmes* (1844), and, posthumously, *M. de Talleyrand* and *Souvenirs et indiscrétions*. See Sainte-Beuve's own 'Ma Biographie' in *Nouveaux Lundis*, vol. xiii; the strongly prejudiced book of the Vicomte d'Haussonville, *C. A. Sainte-Beuve, sa vie et ses oeuvres* (1875); and the *Souvenirs* of his last secretary, M. Troubat (1890). See works by Levallois (1872), Morand (1895), Michaut (1921), Mott (1925) and Bellesort (1927).

SAINTE-CLAIRE DEVILLE, Henri Étienne, *sĭt-klayr dĕ-veel* (1818–81), born in St Thomas, West Indies, in 1851 became professor of Chemistry in the École normale at Paris, and shortly afterwards in the Sorbonne. It was he who first produced aluminium (1855) and platinum in commercial quantities, and demonstrated the general theory of the dissociation of chemical compounds at a high temperature. He also examined the forms of boron and silicon, and produced artificially sapphire, aluminium, &c. Besides many papers, he published *De l'aluminium* (1859) and *Métallurgie du platine* (1863). See *French Life* by Gay (1889).

SAINT-ÉVREMOND, Charles Marguetel de Saint Denis, Seigneur de, *sĭt-ay-vrĕ-mõ* (1610–1703), French writer and wit, born at St Denis le Guast near Coutances, fought at Rocroi, Freiburg and Nördlingen, was steadily loyal throughout the Fronde, but in 1661 fled by way of Holland to England on the discovery of his witty and sarcastic letter to Créqui on the Peace of the Pyrenees. He was warmly received by Charles II, and in London he spent almost all the rest of his days, delighting the world with his wit. His satire, *La Comédie des académistes* (1644), is masterly, and his letters to and from Ninon de Lenclos charming. Des Maizeaux collected his writings with *Life* (1705). See studies by W. M. Daniels (1907) and K. Spalatin (1934).

SAINT-EXUPÉRY, Antoine de, *sit-eg-zü-pay-ree* (1900–44), French airman and author, was born in Lyon, and became a commercial airline pilot and wartime reconnaissance pilot. His philosophy of 'heroic action', based on the framework of his experiences as a pilot, is expressed in his sensitive and imaginative *Courier sud* (1929), *Vol de nuit* (1931) and *Pilote de guerre* (1942). He was declared missing after a flight in the second World War. See studies by A. Gide (1951) and J. Bruce (1953), and M. A. Smith's *Knight of the Air* (1959).

SAINT-GAUDENS, Augustus, *saynt-gawd'ēnz* (1848–1907), born in Dublin, a French shoemaker's son, was taken to America as a baby, trained as a cameo-cutter, studied sculpture in Paris and in Rome, where he was influenced by the Italian renaissance and returned to America, where he became the foremost sculptor of his time. See his *Reminiscences* (1913) and study by Hind (1908).

SAINT-GELAIS, Mellin de, *sī-zhé-lay* (1491–1558), French poet, a contemporary and imitator of Clement Marot (q.v.).

SAINT-HILAIRE. See BARTHÉLEMY and GEOFFROY.

SAINTINE, or Boniface, Joseph Xavier, *sī-teen* (1798–1865), a Frenchman, the author of plays, poems and tales without number, the best known being the sentimental *Picciola, the Story of a Prison Flower* (1836).

ST JOHN, Henry. See BOLINGBROKE (2).

SAINT-JOHN PERSE, pen-name of Marie René Auguste Alexis Saint-Léger Léger (1887–), French poet and diplomat, born at St Léger des Feuilles, an island near Guadeloupe, studied at Bordeaux and after adventurous travels in New Guinea and a voyage in a skiff along the China coast, entered in 1904 the French foreign ministry. Secretary-general in 1933, he was dismissed in 1940 and fled to the United States, where he became an adviser to Roosevelt on French affairs. The Vichy government burnt his writings and deprived him of French citizenship, restored in 1945. His blank verse utilizes an exotic vocabulary of little-used words. The panoramic sweep of his landscape imagery, heightened by liturgical metres, gives his poetry a visionary quality. The best known of his earlier works, which include *Images à Crusoë* (1909), *Éloges* (1910), *Amitié du prince* (1924), is the long poem *Anabase* (1924; trans. T. S. Eliot, 1930). Later works include *Exil* (1942), *Pluies* (1944), *Amers* (1957) and *Chroniques* (1960). Hammarskjöld (q.v.) was his Swedish translator. He was awarded the Nobel prize in 1960. See study by R. Caillois (1954).

SAINT-JUST, Louis Antoine Léon Florelle de, *sī-zhüst* (1767–94), French revolutionary, was born at Decize near Nevers, and educated by the Oratorians at Soissons, studied law at Rheims, but early gave himself to letters. At nineteen he set off for Paris, with some of his mother's valuables, and was, at her request, imprisoned for selling them. He published (1789) a poor poem, *L'Organt*, and in 1791 an essay of a different promise, *L'Esprit de la révolution*. Returned for Aisne to the Convention (1792) he attracted notice by his fierce tirades against the king; and as a devoted follower of Robespierre was sent on missions to the armies of the Rhine and the Moselle. He made bombastic speeches before the Convention, and began the attacks on Hébert which sent him and Danton to their doom. In 1794 he laid before the Convention a comprehensive report on the police, and soon after proposed, along with other fanciful schemes of like Spartan character, Robespierre's preposterous civil institutions, by which boys were to be taken from their parents at seven and brought up for the state. Saint-Just fell with Robespierre by the guillotine, July 28, 1794. See Fleury, *Saint-Just et la Terreur* (1851), and studies by D. C. Bineau (1936) and R. Korngold (1937).

ST LAURENT, Louis Stephen, *sī-lō-rā* (1882–1973), Canadian politician, was born in Compton, Quebec, trained as a lawyer in Quebec, and entered the Dominion parliament in 1941 as a Liberal. He was minister of justice and attorney-general (1941–46) and minister of external affairs (1946–48), and in 1948 became leader of the Liberal party and prime minister of Canada. He resigned the latter office on the defeat of his party in the 1957 General Election, and in 1958 was succeeded as leader of the party by Lester Pearson (q.v.).

ST LEGER, *sel'in-jèr* or (the race always) *saynt lej'èr*, (1) Sir Anthony (*c.* 1496–1559), English statesman, was in 1540 appointed lord deputy of Ireland, where he was at first highly successful in his treatment of the fractious clans, who, however, later rebelled. Accused of fraud, he died during the investigation.

(2) Barry (1737–89), British army colonel, fought in the American revolution, and founded in 1776 his horse-racing stakes at Doncaster.

SAINT-LÉGER, Alexis. See SAINT-JOHN PERSE.

SAINT-MARC GIRARDIN. See GIRARDIN (3).

SAINT-MARTIN, Louis Claude de, *sī-mar-tī* (1743–1803), French philosopher ('le Philosophe inconnu'), a vigorous opponent of sensationalism and materialism, was born at Amboise. See Life by Waite (1901 and 1922).

SAINT-PIERRE, *sī-pyayr*, (1) Charles Irénée Castel, Abbé de (1658–1743), French writer, published an optimistic *Projet de la paix perpétuelle* (1713), for his *Discours sur la polysynodie* and in 1718 for his *Discours sur la polysynodie*, and wrote on political economy and philosophy, in which his principles were those of the physiocratic school. See study by Drouet (1912).

(2) Jacques Henri Bernardin de (1737–1814), French author, was born at Havre, January 19, 1737, and after a voyage to Martinique served some time in the Engineers, but quarrelled with his chiefs and was dismissed, and next year was sent to Malta, with the same result. His head was turned by the writings of Rousseau, and he made public employment impossible by the innumerable utopian criticisms with which he deluged the ministers. With dreams of a new state to be founded on the shores of the Sea of Aral, he

travelled to Russia, and returned in dejection to Warsaw. He abandoned a government expedition to Madagascar at the Île de France (Mauritius), to spend there almost three years of melancholy and observation. His *Voyage à l'Île de France* (1778) gave a distinctly new element to literature in its close portraiture of nature. His *Études de la nature* (3 vols. 1784) showed the strong influence of Rousseau; a fourth volume (1788) contained the popular *Paul et Virginie*, the story, to modern readers over-sentimental and over-didactic, of the growth of love between two young people, untainted by civilization, in the natural surroundings of Mauritius. His next works were *Voeux d'un solitaire* (1789) and the novel, *La Chaumière indienne* (1791). His *Harmonies de la nature* (1796) was but a pale repetition of the *Études*. Besides these *Le Café de Surate* and the *Essai sur J.-J. Rousseau* alone merit mention. A member of the Institute from its foundation in 1795, he was admitted to the Academy in 1803. Napoleon heaped favours upon him, and he lived comfortably till his death at Eragny near Pontoise, January 21, 1814. His *Oeuvres complètes* (1813–20) and *Correspondance* (1826) were edited by Aimé Martin. See the extravagant Life by the latter (1820), with others works by Mornet (1907), Roule (1930) and d'Alméras (1937).

SAINT-RÉAL, César Vichard, Abbé de, *si-ray-al* (1631–92) French historian, born at Chambéry, visited London, and in 1679 returned to his birthplace as historiographer to the Duke of Savoy. He wrote *Dom Carlos* (1672) and *La Conjuration que les Espagnols formèrent en 1618 contre Venise* (1674), early examples of the serious French historical novel. See study by Dulong (1921).

SAINT-SAËNS, (Charles) Camille, *si-sās* (1835–1921), French composer and music critic, was born in Paris on October 9, 1835. He entered the Paris Conservatoire in 1848, was a pupil of Benoist and Halévy, and at the age of sixteen had begun his long and prolific career of composition with his prizewinning *Ode à Sainte Cécile* (1852), followed shortly afterwards by his first symphony (performed 1853, published 1855). He was a distinguished pianist, and from 1858 to 1877 won considerable renown as organist of the Madeleine in Paris, giving recitals also in London, Russia and Austria. Although himself conservative as a composer, he was a founder in 1871 of the Société Nationale de Musique, and as such was influential in encouraging the performance of works by young contemporary French composers, for whose style he was also an impeccable model of directness, clarity and technical skill. He wrote four further symphonies, thirteen operas, including his best-known, *Samson et Dalila* (1877), four symphonic poems, *Le Rouet d'Omphale* (1871), *Phaëton* (1873), *Danse macabre* (1874) and *La Jeunesse d'Hercule* (1877), five piano, three violin and two cello concertos, *Carnaval des animaux* (1886) for two pianos and orchestra, church music, including his *Messe solennelle* (1856), and chamber music and songs. He was a sound music critic, although latterly somewhat prejudiced, because of his own temporarily

declining reputation against his younger contemporaries; his writings include *Harmonie et mélodie* (1885), *Portraits et souvenirs* (1899) and *Au courant de la vie* (1914). Saint-Saëns died at Algiers. See studies by A. Hervey (1921), W. Lyle (1923), A. Dandelot (1930) and J. Chantavoine (1947).

SAINTSBURY, George Edward Bateman (1845–1933), English literary critic, was born at Southampton and educated at King's College School, London, and Merton College, Oxford. In 1868–76 he was a schoolmaster at Manchester, Guernsey and Elgin, but soon after established himself as one of the most active critics of the day; in 1895–1915 he was professor of English Literature at Edinburgh. All his work is characterized by clearness of thought, fullness of knowledge and force, if not always grace of style. He contributed to the greater magazines (he edited *Macmillan's*), and to encyclopaedias. Among his books are histories of literature, both French and English; books on Dryden, Marlborough, Scott, Matthew Arnold, Thackeray, the early renaissance, minor Caroline poets; histories of criticism (3 vols. 1900–04), English prosody (1906–10), prose rhythm (1912), and a novel (1912); and after his retirement came *The Peace of the Augustans* (1916), *A History of the French Novel* (1917–19), *Notes on a Cellar-book* (1920) and *Scrapbooks* (1922–1924).

SAINT-SIMON, *si-see-mõ,* (1) **Claude Henri, Comte de** (1760–1825), founder of French socialism, was born of the ducal line in Paris, October 17. He served in the American War of Independence; during the French Revolution he was imprisoned as an aristocrat, but made a small fortune by speculating in confiscated lands. His marriage (1801) was terminated by a divorce; and his lavish expenditure reduced him to utter poverty. Beginning to be in straits, he published his *Lettres d'un habitant de Genève à ses contemporains* (1803); but the first enunciations of socialism occurred in *L'Industrie* (1817), followed by *L'Organisateur* (1819), *Du système industriel* (1821), *Catéchisme des industriels* (1823), and his last and most important work, *Nouveau christianisme* (1825). But for the kindness of friends and a small pension allowed him by his family in 1812 he would have died of starvation. In 1823 he tried to shoot himself, and lost an eye in the attempt; he died in Paris May 19, 1825. Saint-Simon's works are wanting in judgment and system; but notwithstanding all his vagaries, the man who originated Comtism and French socialism must be regarded as a seminal thinker of high rank. In opposition to the destructive spirit of the Revolution, he sought after a positive reorganization of society. He desired that the feudal and military system should be superseded by an industrial order controlled by industrial chiefs, and that the spiritual direction of society should pass from the church to the men of science. See monographs by A. J. Booth (1871), Charléty (1896), Bouglé (1925), Butler (1926) and N. Mitford (1958).

(2) **Louis de Rouvroy, Duc de** (1675–1755), was born at Paris, January 16, son of a page and favourite of Louis XII] who became

duke in 1636, but soon after fell from favour. He entered the army at sixteen but left dissatisfied in 1702, and repaired to Versailles, without for some years enjoying any measure of the royal favour. He embroiled himself in endless disputes about precedence and privilege, but recovered the king's favour by his efforts to bring his friend Orleans to a more reputable life. The king's death in 1714 opened up a bitter struggle between Orleans and the Duc de Maine, eldest of the king's bastards, in which Saint-Simon supported his friend with warmth and boldness. His influence decreased as that of Dubois rose; but he was sent to Spain in 1721 to demand the hand of the Infanta for the young king, Louis XV. After the death of Orleans in 1723, he retired to his château of La Ferté Vidame near Chartres. He died, utterly bankrupt, March 2, 1755. He seems to have begun his journal before 1699, and to have prepared the *Mémoires* (1752) in their final form. This precious manuscript, with his impressions and descriptions, sometimes lively, sometimes cumbersome, but always diverse, imaginative and convincingly detailed of court life as he saw and experienced it between 1695 and 1723, was impounded in 1761 by the Duc de Choiseul for the French foreign office. A volume of garbled extracts appeared in 1780; in 1830 the first authentic edition appeared. The first adequate edition was by Chéruel in 1856–58. But the final edition is that in *Les Grands Écrivains*, by M. A. de Boislisle (43 vols. 1879–1930). There is an abridged English translation by F. Arkwright (1915 *et seq.*), and selections by L. Norton, *Saint-Simon at Versailles*, were published in 1958. See monographs by Chéruel (1865), Collins (1880), Cannan (1885), Pilastre (1905, 1909) and Doumic (1919).

ST VINCENT, John Jervis, Earl (1735–1823), English admiral, born at Meaford Hall, Stone, Staffordshire, January 9, entered the navy in 1749, became a lieutenant in 1755, and so distinguished himself in the Quebec expedition in 1759 that he was made commander. In 1778 he fought in the action of Brest, and in 1782 captured the *Pégase* of 74 guns, whereupon he was made a K.B. In 1793 he commanded the naval part of the successful expedition against the French West India Islands. In 1795, now admiral, he received the command of the Mediterranean fleet. On February 14, 1797, with fifteen sail, he fell in, off Cape St Vincent, with the Spanish fleet of twenty-seven. Jervis completely defeated the enemy, and captured four ships. The genius of Nelson contributed greatly to the success of the day. Jervis was created Earl St Vincent, and parliament granted him a pension of £3000. After repressing a mutiny off Cadiz, he was compelled by ill-health to return home. As commander of the Channel fleet he subdued the spirit of sedition, and as first lord of the Admiralty in 1801–04 reformed innumerable abuses. He resumed the Channel command 1806–07, and died March 13, 1823. See poor Life by Brenton (1838), good ones by Tucker (1844) and Anson (1913); and *Letters*, *1801–04* (1927).

SAKI. See MUNRO (2).

SALA, George Augustus Henry (1828–95), English journalist and novelist, born in London of Italian ancestry, studied art and did book illustrations, but in 1851 became a contributor to *Household Words*, as afterwards to the *Welcome Guest*, *Temple Bar* (which he founded and edited 1860–66), the *Illustrated London News* and *Cornhill*. As special correspondent of the *Daily Telegraph* he was in the United States during the Civil War, in Italy with Garibaldi, in France in 1870–71, in Russia in 1876, and in Australia in 1885. *Twice Round the Clock* (1859) is a social satire, and he also wrote novels, many books of travel and the autobiographical *Life and Adventures* (1895).

SALADIN, in full **Salah-ed-din Yussuf ibn Ayub, sal'-** (1137–93), sultan of Egypt and Syria and founder of a dynasty, was born at Tekrit, on the Tigris, of which his father Ayub, a Kurd, was governor under the Seljuks. He entered the service of Nur-eddin, emir of Syria, held command in the expeditions to Egypt (1167–68), and was made grand vizier of the Fatimite calif, whom in 1171 he overthrew, constituting himself sovereign of Egypt. On Nur-eddin's death (1174) he further proclaimed himself sultan of Egypt and Syria, reduced Mesopotamia, and received the homage of the Seljuk princes of Asia Minor. His remaining years were occupied in wars with the Christians and in the consolidation of his extensive dominions. In 1187 the Christian army suffered a terrible defeat near Tiberias; then Jerusalem was stormed (October 3), and almost every fortified place on the Syrian coast was taken. Thereupon a great army of crusaders, headed by the kings of France and England, captured Acre in 1191; Richard Cœur-de-Lion defeated Saladin, took Caesarea and Jaffa, and obtained a three years' treaty. Saladin died at Damascus. His wise administration left traces for centuries in citadels, roads and canals. His opponents recognized his chivalry, good faith, piety, justice and greatness of soul. See Lives by Reinaud (1874) and Stanley Lane-Poole (1926).

SALANDRA, Antonio (1853–1931), Italian statesman, professor of Administrative Science at Rome, was premier (1914–16) when Italy entered the first World War. Though at first an opponent of Fascism, he became a senator under Mussolini in 1928.

SALAZAR, António de Oliviera, -*zahr'* (1889–1970), Portuguese dictator, born near Coimbra, studied and became professor of Economics there. In 1928 he was made minister of finance by Carmona with extensive powers to deal with the widespread economic chaos. Having been elected prime minister in 1932, he gradually converted Portugal into a corporate state by virtue of his considerable financial skill. His tenure of the ministries of war (1936–44) and of foreign affairs (1936–47) included the delicate period of the Spanish Civil War. He further curtailed political opposition, which in any case was only permitted during the brief election periods, after his opponent polled relatively well in 1959. He retired in 1968.

SALDANHA, João Carlos, Duke of, *sal-dan'ya* (1790–1876), Portuguese statesman and marshal, born at Arinhaga, fought at Busaco (1810), helped Brazil against Montevideo (1817–22), sided with Dom Pedro against Dom Miguel as a moderate constitutionalist, and during 1846–56 was alternately head of the government and in armed opposition. Created a duke in 1846, he was twice ambassador at Rome, prime minister in 1870, and ambassador at London from 1871.

SALE, (1) George (*c.* 1697–1736), English oriental scholar, was born in Kent, educated at King's School Canterbury, and bred to the law. He is best known by his translation of the Koran (1734; new ed. 1882–86).

(2) **Sir Robert Henry** (1782–1845), British soldier, was commissioned in 1795, fought at Seringapatam (1799), the capture of Mauritius (1810), and throughout the Burmese war (1824–25). In the Afghan war of 1838 he distinguished himself at Ghazni. In Jalalabad he was besieged for six months (1841–42), until relieved by Pollock. He was killed at Mudki, fighting against the Sikhs, December 18, 1845. See Gleig, *Sale's Brigade in Afghanistan* (1846). Lady Sale, whom he married in 1809, and who was captured by the Afghans and kept prisoner until Pollock's arrival, wrote a *Journal of the Disasters in Afghanistan* (1843).

SALES, Francis of. See FRANCIS (SAINTS) (3).

SALIERI, Antonio, *sa-lyay'ree* (1750–1825), Italian composer, was born in Verona and died in Vienna, having worked there for fifty years. A teacher of Beethoven and Schubert, he was bitterly antipathetic towards Mozart, whom he did not, however, contrary to a once prevalent tale, poison. He wrote over forty operas, an oratorio and masses.

SALINGER, Jerome David (1919–   ), American author, born in New York, educated there at Pennsylvania military academy, served with the army in World War II. He began writing at an early age but his fame rests mainly on his novel *Catcher in the Rye* (1951), written in the first person in the idiom of a New York 16-year-old and portraying with acute observation and sympathetic insight the motivation of a ' mixed-up ' teenager who has run away from school. Other books, generally made up of stories of novella length, include *For Esmé, with Love and Squalor* (1953) and *Franny and Zooey* (1962); many of the stories portray his highly intelligent and temperamental Glass family. See *Personal Portrait*, ed. Grunwald (1964).

SALISBURY, Earls and Marquises of. See CECIL.

SALISBURY, *sawlz'bêr-i*, **(1) Frank Owen** (1874–1962), British artist, executed a large number of pictures, many of them official, and portraits of members of the British royal family and of notable Americans. See his book *Sarum Chase* (1953). He was created C.V.O. in 1938.

(2) **John of.** See JOHN OF SALISBURY.

(3) **William** (*c.* 1520–*c.* 1600), Welsh lexicographer, published a Welsh and English Dictionary (1547), and translated the New Testament into Welsh (1567).

SALK, Jonas Edward (1914–   ), American virologist, discoverer of the anti-poliomyelitis vaccine in 1953, was born of Polish-Jewish immigrant parents in New York. He worked as a research fellow on an influenza vaccine at Michigan (1942–44), where he was appointed assistant professor and transferred to Pittsburgh as director of virus research (1947–49) and research professor (1949–54). There in 1953–54 he prepared the vaccine which, after stringest tests, he tried out successfully on his family. A huge publicity campaign (1955) in which, unknown to him, vaccine was used which had not been as stringently tested, resulted in over 200 cases of polio, 11 of them fatal. But an improved vaccine has fully vindicated his achievement. He has since been engaged on cancer research.

SALLUST, Lat. **Gaius Sallustius Crispus,** *sal'ust* (86–34 B.C.), Roman historian, was born of Plebeian family at Amiternum in the Sabine country. He had risen to be tribune in 52 when he helped to avenge the murder of Clodius upon Milo and his party. Such was the scandal of his licentious life that he was expelled in 50 from the senate—though his attachment to Caesar's party doubtless strengthened the reasons for his expulsion. In 47 he was made praetor and restored to senatorial rank. He served in the African campaign, and was left as governor of Numidia. His administration was sullied by oppression and extortion, but the charges brought against him failed before the partial tribunal of Caesar. With the fruit of his extortion he laid out famous gardens on the Quirinal and the splendid mansion which became an imperial residence of Nerva, Vespasian and Aurelian. In this retirement he wrote his famous histories, the *Catilina*, the *Jugurtha* and the *Historiarum Libri Quinque* (78–67 B.C.), of which latter but a few fragments survive. He was one of the first Roman writers to look directly for a model to Greek literature. There are translations by Pollard (1882) and Rolfe (1921).

SALMASIUS, Claudius, or **Claude de Saumaise** (1588–1653), French scholar, born at Semur in Burgundy, studied philosophy at Paris and law at Heidelberg (1606), where he professed Protestantism. In 1629 appeared his chief work, *Plinianae Exercitationes in Solinum* (1629), after whose publication he mastered Hebrew, Arabic and Coptic. In 1631 he was called to Leyden to occupy Joseph Scaliger's chair. Unavailing efforts were made (1635–40) to induce him to return to France. He was probably the most famous scholar of his day in Europe. In England Salmasius is best known through his controversy with Milton. At the request of Charles II, Salmasius published (1649) his *Defensio Regio pro Carolo I,* answered in 1651 by Milton in his *Pro Populo Anglicano Defensio.* See the *Vita* prefixed to his letters (1656).

SALOME, *sa-lō'may* (*c.* A.D. 14–before A.D. 62), traditional name of the daughter of Herodias—see HEROD (2). She danced before Herod and, at her mother's instigation, asked for as a reward, and received, the head of John the Baptist.

SALOMON, Johann Peter (1745–1815), German violinist, impresario and composer, born at Bonn served Prince Henry of Prussia

1765–80, and then settled in London. At his philharmonic concerts (1791–94) were produced the twelve 'Salomon' or 'London' symphonies commissioned from Haydn.

SALOTE, *sa-lō'tay* (1900–65), Queen of Tonga, educated in New Zealand, succeeded her father, King George Tupou II, in 1918. Her prosperous and happy reign saw in 1924 the reunion, for which she was mainly responsible, of the Tongan Free Church majority with the Wesleyan Church. Queen Salote is remembered in Britain for her colourful and engaging presence during her visit in 1953 for the coronation of Queen Elizabeth.

SALT, Sir Titus (1803–76), English manufacturer and benefactor, born at Morley near Leeds, was a wool stapler at Bradford, started wool-spinning in 1834, and was the first to manufacture alpaca fabrics in England. Round his factories in a pleasant valley, 3 miles from Bradford, on the Aire, rose the model village of Saltaire (1853). Mayor of Bradford in 1848, and its Liberal M.P. in 1859–61, he was created a baronet in 1869. See Life by Balgarnie (1877).

SALTEN, Felix (1869–1945), Austrian novelist and essayist, born at Budapest, known especially for his animal stories, including *Bambi* (1929), and *Bambi's Children* (1940), which, in translation, achieved great popularity in America and Britain.

SALTYKOV, Michail Evgrafovich, pseud. of **N. Shchedrin**, *sal-ti-kof'* (1826–89), Russian writer, born in Tver, was exiled (1848–56) because of his satirical story *Contradictions* (1847), but later became a provincial vice-governor. He edited with Nekrasov the radical *Notes of the Fatherland*, and of his many, mainly melancholy, books *The Golovlyov Family* and the *Fables* are among those translated.

SALVATOR ROSA. See ROSA (2).

SALVIATI, Antonio (1816–90), born at Vicenza, and died at Venice, revived in 1860 the glass factories of Murano and the art of mosaic.

SALVINI, Tommaso, *sal-vee'nee* (1830–1915), Italian actor, born at Milan, first became well known as a member of Ristori's company. In Paris he played in Racine and in London he enjoyed immense popularity in Shakespearean rôles, especially as Othello and Hamlet. He played also in comedies such as those of Goldoni, but won fame mainly as a tragedian. The part which he played in fighting in the revolutionary war of 1848 added to his popularity. In 1884 he retired. See his *Autobiography* (1893) and *Ricordi* (1895).

SAMAIN, Albert Victor, *sa-mi* (1858–1900), French poet, born at Lille, was a clerk in the Prefecture of the Seine. His symbolist poetry, though not original in subject, is delicate, fresh and musical and was well received in his lifetime. Among his collections of verse are *Au jardin de l'infante* (1893), *Aux flancs de la vase* (1898) and *Le Chariot d'or*, published posthumously. See L. Bocquet, *Albert Samain* (1905), and E. Gosse, *French Profiles* (1905).

SAMBOURNE, Edward Linley (1844–1910), English cartoonist, born in London, was at sixteen apprenticed to marine engineer works at Greenwich, but in April 1867 began his lifelong connection with *Punch*. He illustrated Kingsley's *Water Babies*, Andersen's *Fairy Tales*, &c.

SAMSON, (1) the last of the twelve judges in the Book of Judges. His life as recounted in the Bible, however, represents him not as a leader but as an individual whose deeds on behalf of Israel made him a popular hero. His exploits suggested to Goldziher (*Hebrew Mythology*, Eng. trans. 1877) the improbable idea that elements of solar mythology may have come into his story.
(2) (*c.* 480–565), a Welsh saint, who died Bishop of Dol in Brittany.
(3) (1135–1211), in 1182 became abbot of Bury St Edmunds. See JOCELIN.

SAMUEL (Heb. *Shemū'el*, probably 'name of God ', 11th cent. B.C.), last of the judges, first of the prophets, and next to Moses the greatest personality in the early history of Israel, was an Ephraimite, native of Ramathaim or Ramah in Mount Ephraim. As a child he was dedicated to the priesthood. The story of 1 Sam. vii–xvi combines two widely different accounts of his career. According to one of these, Israel lay under the Philistine yoke for twenty years, when a national convention was summoned to Mizpah by Samuel. The Philistines came upon them, but only to sustain a decisive repulse. The prophet thenceforward ruled peacefully and prosperously as judge over Israel till age compelled him to associate his sons with him in the government. Dissatisfaction with their ways gave the elders a pretext for asking for a king such as every other nation had. Although seeing the folly of this, equivalent to a rejection of Yahweh, he after some remonstrance, granted their prayer, and at Mizpah Saul was chosen. The older account makes him a 'man of God ', a man 'held in honour ', and a seer whose every word 'cometh surely to pass ', but occupying a position hardly so prominent as that of judge of Israel. Saul was divinely made known to him as God's instrument to deliver Israel, and the seer secretly annointed him. A month later Saul's relief of Jabesh-Gilead resulted in his being chosen king. The accounts of Samuel's conduct during Saul's reign are discrepant.

SAMUEL, Herbert Louis, 1st Viscount Samuel (1870–1963), British Liberal statesman and philosophical writer, born into a Jewish banking family, was educated at University College School and Balliol, Oxford. Entering parliament in 1902, he held various offices, including that of chancellor of the Duchy of Lancaster (1909), postmaster-general (1910 and 1915), home secretary (1916; 1931–32) and was high commissioner for Palestine (1920–25). His philosophical works include *Practical Ethics* (1935), *Belief and Action* (1937) and *In Search of Reality* (1957). He was president of the Royal Statistical Society (1918–20), was created viscount (1937) and was awarded the O.M. (1958). See Life by J. Bowle (1957).

SANCHEZ, Thomas, *san-cheth* (1550–1610), Jesuit moral theologian and casuist, became master of novices at Granada. His *Disputationes de Sancto Matrimonii Sacramento*

(1592) deals with the legal, moral and religious questions that arise out of marriage.

SANCROFT, William (1617–93), Archbishop of Canterbury, born at Fressingfield, Suffolk, was elected fellow of Emmanuel, Cambridge, in 1642, but in 1651 was expelled from his fellowship or refusing to take the 'Engagement', and in 1657 crossed over to Holland. After the Restoration his advancement was rapid—king's chaplain and rector of Houghton-le-Spring (1661), prebendary of Durham and master of Emmanuel (1662), Dean first of York and next of St Paul's (1664), as such having a principal hand in the rebuilding of the cathedral, Archdeacon of Canterbury (1668), and Archbishop (1678). A Tory and High Churchman, Sancroft refused to sit in James II's Ecclesiastical Commission (1686), and in 1688 was sent to the Tower as one of the Seven Bishops. But after the Revolution, having taken the oath of allegiance to James, he would not take it to William and Mary, so was suspended (1689), and retired to his native village where he died. The *Fur Praedestinatus* (1651), an attack on Calvinism by an unknown author, has been ascribed to him. See Life by D'Oyly (1821) and Miss Strickland's *Lives of the Seven Bishops* (1866).

SANCTORIUS (Santorio Santorio) (1561–1636), Italian physician, born in Capodistria, studied at Padua and in 1611 became professor of Theoretical Medicine there. He invented the clinical thermometer, a pulsimeter, a hygrometer and other instruments. But he is best known for his investigations into the fluctuations in the body's weight under different conditions due to 'insensible perspiration'. His experiments were conducted on a balance made by himself. See A. Castiglioni, *History of Medicine* (1947).

SAND, (1) **George**, the pseud. of **Amandine Aurore Lucie Dupin, 'Baronne' Dudevant, sā** (1804–76), French novelist, born in Paris. Aurore's father died when she was very young, and she lived principally at Nohant in Berri with her grandmother, Madame Dupin, on whose death the property descended to her. At eighteen she was married to Casimir, Baron Dudevant, and had two children, and after nine years left her husband and went to Paris to make her living by literature in the Bohemian society of the period (1831). For the best part of twenty years her life was spent in the company and partly under the influence of various more or less distinguished men. At first her interests were with poets and artists, the most famous being Alfred de Musset (q.v.), with whom she travelled in Italy, and Chopin (q.v.), who was her companion for several years. In the second decade her attention shifted to philosophers and politicians, such as Lamennais, the socialist Pierre Leroux (qq.v.), and the republican Michel de Bourges. After 1848 she settled down as the quiet 'châtelaine of Nohant', where she spent the rest of her life in outstanding literary activity, varied by travel. In her work some have marked three, others four periods. When she first went to Paris, and with her companion Jules Sandeau (q.v.), from the first half of whose name her pseudonym was taken, settled to novel-writing, her

books—*Indiana* (1832), *Valentine* (1832), *Lelia* (1833) and *Jacques*—partook of the Romantic extravagance of the time, informed by a polemic against marriage. In the next her philosophical and political teachers engendered the socialistic rhapsodies of *Spiridion* (1838), *Consuelo* (1842–44) and the *Comtesse de Rudolstadt* (1843–45). Between the two groups came the fine novel *Mauprat* (1837). Then she began to turn towards the studies of rustic life—*La Petite Fadette, François le Champi, La Mare au diable* (1846)—which some constitute a third division and are, by modern standards, her best works. A fourth group would comprise the miscellaneous works of her last twenty years—some of them, such as *Les Beaux Messieurs de Bois Doré, Le Marquis de Villemer, Mlle la Quintinie*, of high merit. Her complete works (over 100 vols.), besides novels, plays, &c., include the charming *Histoire de ma vie, Hiver à Majorque, Elle et lui* (on her relations with de Musset), and delightful letters, published after her death. See monographs by Rocheblave (1905), Gribble (1907), Séché and Bertaut (1909), R. Doumic (trans. 1910), Karénine (1899–1927); Maurras, *Les Amants de Venise* (new ed. 1917); M. L'Hôpital, *La Notion d'artiste chez George Sand* (1946); M. Toesca, *The Other George Sand* (1947).

(2) **Karl Ludwig** (1795–1820), Jena theological student and member of the Burschenschaft, was beheaded for stabbing Kotzebue (q.v.).

SANDAY, William (1843–1920), English biblical critic, born at Holme Pierrepont, Nottingham, was principal of Hatfield's Hall, Durham (1876–82), Ireland professor of Exegesis at Oxford (1882–95), and then Lady Margaret professor of Divinity and canon of Christ Church. He wrote many critical works, including *The Authorship and Historical Character of the Fourth Gospel* (1872), *The Early History and Origin of the Doctrine of Biblical Inspiration* (1893) and perhaps the most important, in collaboration with A. C. Headlam, *Commentary on the Epistle to the Romans* (1895). He did much to promote modern methods of biblical study.

SANDBURG, Carl (1878–1967), American poet, born at Galesburg, Ill., of Swedish stock, after trying various jobs, fighting in the Spanish-American war and studying at Lombard College, became a journalist and started to write for *Poetry*. His verse, realistic and robust but often also delicately sensitive, reflects industrial America. Among his volumes of poetry are *Cornhuskers* (1918), *Smoke and Steel* (1920), *Slabs of the Sunburnt West* (1922) and *Good Morning, America* (1928). His *Complete Poems* gained him the Pulitzer prize in 1950. Interested in American folksongs and ballads, he published a collection in *The American Songbag* (1927). He also wrote a vast *Life of Abraham Lincoln*. See *Selected Poems*, ed. Rebecca West (1926), and F. B. Millett, *Contemporary American Authors* (1940).

SANDBY, (1) **Paul** (1725–1809), English painter born in Nottingham, has been called the father of the watercolour school His career began as a draughtsman, but later, living at Windsor with his brother, he made seventy-six drawings of Windsor and Eton. His watercolours, outlined with the pen, and only finished with colour, take, however, the purely monochrome drawing of this school one step forward. He was an original member of the Royal Academy.

(2) **Thomas** (1721–98), deputy-ranger of Windsor Park from 1746, was brother of (1). He also became an R.A. and first professor of Architecture to the Royal Academy. See W. Sandby, *Thomas and Paul Sandby* (1892), and A. R. Oppé, *The Drawings of Paul and Thomas Sandby at Windsor Castle* (1947).

SANDEAU, Jules, *să-dō* (1811–83), French author, born at Aubusson, went early to Paris to study law, but soon gave himself to letters. He was associated with George Sand in *Rose et Blanche* (1831). His first independent novel was *Madame de Sommerville* (1834) and his first hit *Marianna* (1840). His books give an accurate picture of the social conflicts of the France of his day and he was a master of the *roman de mœurs*. He became keeper of the Mazarin Library in 1853, an Academician in 1858, and librarian at St Cloud in 1859. See *Life* by Claretie (1883), and Saintsbury's *Essays on French Novelists* (1891).

SANDEMAN, Robert. See GLAS (2).

SANDERS, or Saunder, Nicholas (c. 1530–81), Roman Catholic historian and controversialist, born near Reigate, was educated at Winchester and New College, Oxford. A fellow in 1548, he lectured on Canon Law in 1558, in 1559 he went abroad; at Rome was created D.D. and ordained priest, and in 1561 accompanied Cardinal Hosius to the Council of Trent. He had been theological professor at Louvain for thirteen years, and had twice visited Spain (1573–77). As a papal agent in 1579 he landed in Ireland where he later died. His best known works are *De Visibili Monarchia Ecclesiae* (1571) and *De Origine ac Progressu Schismatis Anglicani* (completed by Rishton, 1585; trans. 1877).

SANDERSON, Robert (1587–1663), greatest of English casuists, born in Yorkshire, graduated at Lincoln College, Oxford, of which he became a fellow (1606–19), reader of logic (1608) and thrice subrector (1613–16). Regius professor of Divinity (1642–48), he was deprived of his professorship during the Civil War but was reinstated and became Bishop of Lincoln in 1660. To him are due the second preface to the Prayer Book and perhaps the General Thanksgiving, as well as works on casuistry. See *Life* by Izaak Walton (1678).

SANDOW, Eugene, *san'dō* (1867–1925), German 'strong man' and exponent of physical culture, was born in Königsberg of Russian parents. After a successful career as a strong man and as an artist's model, he opened an Institute of Health in St James's Street.

SANDRART, Joachim von (1606–88), German painter, copper-engraver and historian of art, was born at Frankfurt, and died at Nuremberg.

SANDWICH, (1) Edward Montagu, 1st Earl of (1625–72), English admiral, fought for the parliament at Marston Moor, sat in parliament 1645–48, shared the command of the fleet with Blake from 1653. For helping to

forward the Restoration, he was given an earldom. Ambassador to Spain 1666–69, he was blown up in a sea-fight with the Dutch. See *Life* by Harris (1912).

(2) **John Montagu, 4th Earl of** (1718–92), corrupt politician, remembered as the inventor of *sandwiches*, to eat at the gaming-table.

SANDYS, sands, (1) Duncan (1908–), British Conservative politician, educated at Eton and Oxford, in the Diplomatic Service from 1930 to 1933, he became in 1935 M.P. for Norwood, London. In 1951 he was made minister of supply in the Churchill government, in 1954 became minister of housing, and as minister of defence (1957) inaugurated a controversial programme of cutting costs and streamlining the Forces. When the Conservatives were returned in 1959 he was minister of aviation (1959–60), secretary of state for commonwealth relations (1960-64), and for the colonies (1962–64). In opposition after 1964 his strongly right-wing views made him a controversial figure. In 1935 he married Diana, daughter of Winston Churchill (q.v.).

(2) **George** (1578–1644), English traveller and translator, born at Bishopthorpe, Yorkshire, son of the Archbishop of York, wrote *Relation of a Journey Begun An. Dom. 1610*, an account of his travels in Europe and the Near East. In America (1621–31) he acted as treasurer of the colony of Virginia and made a verse translation of Ovid's *Metamorphoses*. He was much admired by Dryden as a versifier. He also wrote poetic versions of the Psalms and the Song of Solomon and a tragedy, *Christ's Passion* (1640). See study by R. B. Davies (1955).

SANGER, (1) John (1816–89), and his brother **George** (1825–1911), English showmen, both calling themselves ' Lord ', became famous first with their travelling circuses in the provinces and then in London. See George Sanger's *Seventy Years a Showman*.

(2) **Margaret** (1883–1966), American leader of the birth control movement, was born in New York and educated at Claverack College. Her interest in contraception being excited by the tragedies which she encountered as a nurse, she risked charges of obscenity by stressing the need for birth control in her magazine *Woman Rebel*. In 1914 she left the U.S., having been charged for founding the National Birth Control League, and visited the Jacobs Birth Control Clinics in Holland. In 1916 she was imprisoned for starting such a clinic in Brooklyn but gradually she overcame prejudice. She visited many other countries and launched the birth control movement in India.

SANKEY, Ira David. See MOODY (1).

SAN MARTÍN, José de (1778–1850), S. American patriot, born at Yapeyu, Argentina, played a great part in winning independence for his native land, Chile and Peru. In January 1817 he led an army across the Andes into Chile. In 1821 he became protector of Peru but resigned in 1822 and died an exile in Boulogne. See book by Schoelkopf (1924), and Pilling, *The Emancipation of South America* (1893).

SANNAZARO, Jacopo, *-zah'rō* (c. 1458–1530), Italian poet, born at Naples, attached himself to the court there. His *Arcadia* (1485), a medley of prose and verse, is full of beauty and had a direct influence on Sydney's *Arcadia*. It went through many editions. Other works are *Sonetti e Canzoni* and *De Partu Virginis*. See *Arcadia*, ed. E. Carrara (1926).

SANSON, a family of Paris executioners. ' M. de Paris ', Charles Henri Sanson, executed Louis XVI. See *Memoirs of the Sansons* (1875).

SANSOVINO, *san-sō-vee'nō*, (1) or properly **Andrea Contucci** (1460–1529), Italian religious sculptor, born at Monte Sansovino, from which he took his name. He worked in Florence, Portugal, at the court of John II and in Rome. Some of his work survives, including, at S. Maria del Popolo, a monument of Cardinal Sforza.

(2) properly **Jacopo Tatti** (1486–1570), sculptor and architect, born at Florence, was a pupil of (1) and took his name. He lived from 1527 in Venice, where he did his best work. As an architect his most noteworthy works are the Libreria Vecchia, the Palazzo della Zecca and the Palazzo Corner, and as a sculptor, the two giants on the steps of the ducal palace. See L. Pittoni, *I Sansovino* (1909).

SANT, James (1820–1916), English subject and portrait painter (R.A. 1870, painter-in-ordinary to Queen Victoria 1871, C.V.O. 1914), was born at Croydon.

SANTA ANNA, Antonio López de (1797–1876), Mexican president, born at Jalapa, in 1821 joined Iturbide, but in 1822 overthrew him, and in 1833 himself became president of Mexico. His reactionary policy in 1836 cost the country Texas. He invaded the revolted province, but was routed by Houston, and imprisoned for eight months. In 1838 he lost a leg in the gallant defence of Vera Cruz against the French. From 1841 to 1844 he was either president or the president's master, and was recalled from exile in 1846 to be president during the unlucky war with the United States, in which he was twice defeated in the field. He was recalled from Jamaica by a revolution in 1853, and appointed president for life, but in 1855 he was driven from the country. Under Maximilian he intrigued industriously, and ultimately had to flee. In 1867, after the emperor's death, he tried to effect a landing, was captured, and sentenced to death, but allowed to retire to New York. He returned at the amnesty in 1872. See Lives by F. C. Hanighen (1934), W. H. Calcott (1936) and R. F. Muñoz (1936).

SANTAYANA, George (1863–1952), Spanish-born American philosopher, poet and novelist, was born in Madrid and educated in America. He became professor at Harvard (1907–12) but retained his Spanish nationality. His writing career began as a poet with *Sonnets and other Verses* (1894), but later philosophy became his chief interest. His reputation as a stylist, however, rather than his importance as a philosopher proved the more lasting. He held that the given was no more than appearance and that ' animal faith ' alone led to the belief in substance. His major philosophical works were *The Life*

of Reason (1905–06), *Scepticism and Animal Faith* (1923), &c.; *The Last Puritan* (1935) was a witty and very successful novel. See studies of his work edited by P. A. Schilpp (1940) and of his aesthetics, I. Singer (1957).

SANTERRE, Antoine Joseph, *sã-ter* (1752–1809), wealthy French brewer, received a command in the National Guard in 1789, took part in the storming of the Bastille and was in charge at the king's execution. Appointed general of division (1793), he marched against the Vendéan royalists, but, miserably beaten, was recalled and imprisoned. See Life by Carro (1847).

SANTILLANA, Iñigo López de Mendoza, Marqués de (1398–1458), Spanish scholar and poet, influenced by the poetry of Dante and Petrarch, introduced their style and methods into Spanish literature. His shorter poems, especially his *serranillas*, are among his best work and he was the first Spanish poet to write sonnets. His principal prose work, *Carta Proemio*, is a discourse on European literature of his day.

SANTLEY, Sir Charles (1834–1922), English baritone singer, was born in Liverpool and trained partly in Milan (1855–57). He made his début in Haydn's *Creation* in 1857, and from 1862 devoted himself to Italian opera. Latterly he again became better known at concerts and in oratorio. He was knighted in 1907. See his *Reminiscences* (1909).

SANTOS-DUMONT, Alberto (1873–1932), Brazilian aeronaut, born in São Paolo, in 1898 built and flew a cylindrical balloon having a gasoline engine. In 1901 he did the same with an airship in which he made the first flight from St Cloud round the Eiffel Tower and back. Two years later he built the first airship station, at Neuilly. He then experimented with heavier-than-air machines, and eventually flew 715 feet in a plane constructed on the principle of the box-kite. In 1909 he succeeded in building a light monoplane, a forerunner of modern light aircraft. See study by Wykeham (1962).

SAPPHO (born *c.* 650 B.C.), Greek poetess, born in Lesbos, fled about 596 B.C. from Mitylene to Sicily, but after some years was again at Mitylene. Her famous plunge into the sea from the Leucadian rock, because Phaon did not return her love, seems to have no historical foundation. Tradition represents her as exceptionally immoral, a view first disputed by Welcker (1816). The greatest poetess of antiquity, she wrote lyrics unsurpassed for depth of feeling, passion and grace. Only two of her odes are extant in full, but many fragments have been found in Egypt. See H. T. Wharton's edition, with Life, translation, bibliography, &c. (4th ed. 1898), and H. J. Rose, *Handbook of Greek Literature* (1934).

SARASATE, Martin Meliton, *sah-ra-sah'tay* (1844–1908), Spanish violinist, born of Basque parentage at Pampeluna, studied at Paris, and in 1857 began to give concerts. A skilled performer in concertos, he perhaps played best the Spanish dance music he composed himself.

SARDANAPALUS (669–640 B.C.), the Greek form of **Assur-bani-pal**, king of Assyria, eldest son of Esar-Haddon, and grandson of Sennacherib, with all the ambition but without the genius of his father, was a generous patron of art and letters, and his reign marks the zenith of Assyrian splendour. He extended his sway from Elam to Egypt, but the revolt of Babylon shook the empire.

SARDOU, Victorien (1831–1908), French dramatist, was born at Paris. His first efforts were failures, but through his marriage with the actress Brécourt, who nursed him when sick and in want, he became acquainted with Déjazet, for whom he wrote successfully *Monsieur Garat* and *Les Prés Saint-Gervais* (1860). Soon he had amassed a fortune and had become the most successful playwright of his day, not only in France but in Europe, and his popularity was immense in America. Pieces like *Les Pattes de monde* (1860), *Nos intimes* (1861), *La Famille Benoîton* (1865), *Divorçons* (1880), *Odette* (1882), and *Marquise* (1889) are fair samples of his work. For Sarah Bernhardt he wrote *Fédora* (1883), *La Tosca* (1887), &c., and with Moreau *Madame Sans-Gene*; for Irving, *Robespierre* (1899), *Dante* (1903). He attempted the higher historical play in *La Patrie* (1869). Today his plays appear overtechnical and over-theatrical and the plots and characters shallow and rather obvious. Sardou was elected to the Academy in 1877. See study by J. Hart (1913).

SARGENT, (1) **Sir (Harold) Malcolm (Watts)** (1895–1967), English conductor, born at Stamford, trained originally as an organist. He first appeared as a conductor when his *Rhapsody on a Windy Day* was performed at a Promenade Concert in 1921. He was conductor of the Royal Choral Society from 1928, was in charge of the Liverpool Philharmonic Orchestra (1942–48), and of the B.B.C. Symphony Orchestra (1950–57). Sargent's outstanding skill in choral music, his sense of occasion and unfailing panache won him enormous popularity at home and abroad. He was knighted in 1947.
(2) **John Singer** (1856–1925), American painter, born at Florence, the son of a physician, studied painting there and in Paris, where he first gained recognition. Most of his work was, however, done in England, where he became the most fashionable portrait painter of his age. He was elected an R.A. in 1897. His early painting shows the influence of France, but Spain had a more lasting effect and *Carmencita* is perhaps the best example of this. He travelled much to America, where as well as portraits he worked on series of decorative paintings for public buildings, including the *Evolution of Religion* for Boston library. He also, especially in later life, painted landscapes, often in watercolour, but it was as a painter of elegant and lively portraits that he will always be best known.

SARMIENTO. See DARÍO.

SAROYAN, William, *-roy'-* (1908–), American playwright and novelist, was born in Fresno, California. His first work, *The Daring Young Man on the Flying Trapeze* (1934), a volume of short stories, was followed by a number of highly original novels and plays. One of his plays, *The Time of Your Life* (1939), was awarded the Pulitzer prize. A later work was an autobiography, *The Bicycle Rider in Beverley Hills* (1952).

SARPI, Pietro, or **Fra Paolo** (1552–1623), born at Venice, from 1575 was professor of Philosophy in the Servite monastery there. He studied Oriental languages, mathematics, astronomy, medical and physiological sciences, &c. In the dispute between Venice and Paul V about clerical immunities Sarpi became the champion of the republic and of freedom of thought. On the repeal (1607) of the edict of excommunication launched against Venice, he was summoned to Rome to account for his conduct. He refused to obey, was excommunicated and was seriously wounded by assassins. He afterwards busied himself with writing his great *Istoria del Concilio Tridentino* (London 1619). He tended to favour the Protestants and was also interested in the new developments in Science. His collected works were published at Naples (24 vols. 1789–90). See Lives by Campbell (1869), Bianchi-Giovini (1836), Pascolato (1893) and A. Robertson (1894), and T. A. Trollope's *Paul the Pope and Paul the Friar* (1861). A new edition of the *Istoria* (3 vols.) by G. Gambarin appeared in 1935.

SARRAIL, Maurice Paul Emmanuel, *sar-rah'y'* (1856–1929), French general, born at Carcassonne, led the 3rd army at the battle of the Marne in 1914, commanded the Allied forces in the East (Salonica) 1915–17, and as high commissioner in Syria (1924–25) was recalled after the bombardment of Damascus during a rising.

SARSFIELD, Patrick, Earl of Lucan (1645?–1693), Irish soldier, born at Lucan near Dublin, had fought abroad under Monmouth, and at Sedgemoor against him, when in 1688 he was defeated at Wincanton, and crossed over to Ireland. Created Earl of Lucan by James II, he drove the English out of Sligo, was present at the Boyne and Aghrim, defended Limerick, and on its capitulation (1691) entered the French service. He fought at Steenkirk (1692), and was mortally wounded at Neerwinden. See Life by Todhunter (1895).

SARTI, Guiseppe (1729–1802), composer, born at Faenza, held posts at Copenhagen, Venice, Milan and St Petersburg, and died at Berlin. He composed a dozen operas, masses, sonatas, &c. Cherubini was one of his pupils.

SARTO, Andrea del (1486–1531), Florentine painter, whose real name was **Vannucchi,** ' del Sarto ' being an allusion to his father's trade of tailor. In 1509–14 he was engaged by the Servites in Florence to paint for their church of the Annunciation a series of frescoes and a second series was next painted for the Recollets. In 1518, on the invitation of Francis I, he went to Paris, returned next year to Italy, with a commission to purchase works of art, but squandered the money and dared not return to France. He died of the plague at Florence. Many of Andrea's most celebrated pictures are at Florence. He was a rapid worker and accurate draughtsman, displaying a refined feeling for harmonies of colour, but lacked the elevation and spiritual imagination of the greatest masters. See studies by H. Guinness (1899), F. Knapp (1908) and A. J. Rucconi (1935).

SARTORIS, Adelaide. See KEMBLE (1).

SARTRE, Jean-Paul, *sahr'tr'* (1905–), French philosopher, dramatist and novelist, with Heidegger the most prominent exponent of atheistic existentialism, born in Paris, taught philosophy at Le Havre, Paris and Berlin (1934–35), joined the French army in 1939, was a prisoner in Germany (1941), and after his release became an active member of the resistance in Paris. In 1945 he emerged as the leading light of the left-wing, left-bank intellectual life of Paris, with the Café de Flore as its hub, but he eventually broke with the Communists. In 1946 he became editor of the avant-garde monthly *Les Temps modernes.* A disciple of Heidegger, he developed his own characteristic existentialist doctrines, derived from an early anarchistic tendency, which found full expression in his autobiographical novel *La Nausée* (1938) and in *Le Mur* (1938), a collection of short stories. The Nazi occupation provided the grim background to such plays as *Les Mouches,* a modern version of the Orestes theme, and *Huis clos,* ' Vicious Circle ' (both 1943). *Les Mains sales* (1952), the inept title of the film and English version of which was *Crime passionel,* movingly portrayed the tragic consequences of a choice to join an extremist party. Choice is at the core of Sartre's existentialism. Existence is prior to essence. Man is nothing at birth and throughout his life he is no more than the sum of his past commitments. To believe in anything outside his own will is to be guilty of ' bad faith '. Existentialist despair and anguish is the acknowledgment that man is condemned to freedom. There is no God, so man must rely upon his own fallible will and moral insight. He cannot escape choosing. His doctrines are outlined in *L'Existentialisme est un humanisme* (1946; trans. and intro. P. Mairet 1948) and fully worked out in *L'Être et le néant* (1943), 'Being and Nothingness' (trans. and intro. H. E. Barnes, 1957). Its cumbersome Hegelian terminology defies analysis, except on its own terms. Other notable works include *Les Chemins de la liberté* (1945), and the play *Les Séquestrés d'Altona* (1959). In 1964 he was awarded, but declined to accept, the Nobel prize for literature. See works by his disciple, Simone de Beauvoir, and studies in French by R. Troisfontaines (1945), G. Varet (1948), and in English by P. Dempsey (1950), I. Murdoch (1953), W. Desani (1954), A. Ussher (1955), P. Thody (1960) and M. Cranston (1962).

SASSOFERRATO, or Giovanni Battista Salvi (1605–85), Italian religious painter, was born at Sassoferrato in the March of Ancona, and worked at Rome. Very popular in the 19th century, his paintings are now regarded as over-sentimental though very fine in colouring. See E. K. Waterhouse, *Baroque Painting in Rome* (1937).

SASSOON, Siegfried Lorraine, *-soon'* (1886–1967), English poet and novelist, was born in Kent. World War I, in which he served, engendered in him a hatred of war, fiercely expressed in his *Counterattack* (1918) and *Satirical Poems* (1926). A semifictitious autobiography, *The Complete Memoirs of George Sherston* (1937), was begun with *Memoirs of a Fox-Hunting Man* (1928; Hawthornden prize 1929), and continued in *Memoirs of an Infantry Officer* (1930) and *Sherston's Progress* (1936). Truly autobiographical are *The Old Century* (1938), *The Weald of Youth* (1942) and *Siegfried's Journey 1916–20* (1945). He was created C.B.E. in 1951 and became a Roman Catholic in 1957. See study by M. Thorpe (1966) and S. Jackson *The Sassoons* (1968).

SATIE, Erik Alfred Leslie, *sa-tee* (1866–1925), composer, born at Honfleur of French-Scottish parents, after work as a café composer studied under D'Indy and Roussel. In his own work (ballets, lyric dramas, whimsical pieces) he was in violent revolt against Wagnerism and orthodoxy in general, and had some influence on Debussy, Ravel and others. See study by Myers (1948).

SAUD IBN. See IBN SAUD.

SAUL, *sawl* (11th cent. B.C.), son of Kish, the first king elected by the Israelites, conquered the Philistines, Ammonites and Amalekites, became madly jealous of David, his son-in-law, and was ultimately at feud with the priestly class. At length Samuel secretly anointed David king. Saul fell in battle with the Philistines on Mount Gilboa.

SAUMAREZ, James, 1st Baron de, *sô'ma-rez* (1757–1836), British naval commander, born in Guernsey, served in the navy during the American war (1774–82). Now a commander, he distinguished himself in the fight between Rodney and De Grasse (April 12, 1782), and for his capture (1793) of the frigate *La Réunion* was knighted. He fought at L'Orient (1795) and Cape St Vincent (1797), and was second in command at the Nile. In 1801, a baronet and vice-admiral, he fought his greatest action, off Cadiz (July 12), defeating fourteen French-Spanish ships with six, and was made K.C.B. He commanded the British Baltic fleet sent (1809) to assist the Swedes. He was promoted to the rank of admiral in 1814 and created a peer in 1831. See Sir John Ross, *Memoirs and Correspondence of Admiral Lord de Saumarez* (1838), and Mahan, *Types of Naval Officers* (1902).

SAUNDER, Nicholas. See SANDERS.

SAUNDERSON, Nicholas (1682–1739), English blind mathematician, born at Thurlstone near Penistone, lost his eyesight from small-pox when a year old. At Cambridge he lectured on the Newtonian philosophy, optics, &c., and in 1711 became Lucasian professor of Mathematics. A Life is prefixed to his *Algebra* (1740); another treatise by him is on *Fluxions* (1756).

SAUSSURE, *sô-sür,* (1) Horace Bénédict de (1740–99), Swiss physicist and geologist, born at Conches near Geneva, was professor of Physics and Philosophy at Geneva (1762–1788). He travelled in Germany, Italy and England, and traversed the Alps by several routes. He was the first traveller (not a guide) to ascend Mont Blanc (1787). A pioneer in the study of mineralogy, botany, geology and meteorology, his invaluable observations are recorded in his *Voyages dans les Alpes* (1779–96). He devised the hair hygrometer and other instruments and published an *Essai sur l'hygrométrie* (1783).

The mineral saussurite is named after him and it was he who introduced the word *geology* into scientific nomenclature. See Lives by Senebier (1801) and D. W. Freshfield (1920).

(2) **Nicolas Théodore** (1767–1845), son of (1), botanist, wrote *Recherches chimiques sur la végétation* (1804), which contains valuable discoveries about the growth of plants.

SAUVAGE, Frédéric, *sō-vahzh* (1785–1857), Boulogne shipbuilder, is by the French regarded as the inventor of the screw-propeller, in virtue of his having in 1832 improved the pattern in use.

SAVAGE, Richard (1697?–1743), English poet, claimed to be the illegitimate child of Richard Savage, fourth and last Earl Rivers, and the Countess of Macclesfield. In the dedication to his comedy *Love in a Veil* (1718) he asserted the parentage, but in Curll's *Poetical Register* (1719) the story is for the first time fully given. Aaron Hill befriended him, and in 1724 published in *The Plain Dealer* an outline of his story which brought subscribers for his *Miscellanies* (1726). In 1727 he killed a gentleman in a tavern brawl, and narrowly escaped the gallows. His attacks upon his alleged mother (now Mrs Brett), became louder and more bitter in his poem *The Bastard* (1728). *The Wanderer* (1729) was dedicated to Lord Tyrconnel, nephew of Mrs Brett, who had befriended him. Savage's disreputable habits brought misery and hunger, and the queen's pension (1732) of £50 for a birthday ode was dissipated in a week's debauchery. On Queen Caroline's death (1737) Pope tried to help him, but after about a year he went to Bristol, was flung into jail for debt, and died there. Savage owes his reputation solely to Samuel Johnson, who knew him in his own years of hunger in London, and, moved by pity to partiality, wrote what is perhaps the most perfect shorter Life in English literature. That the story contains improbabilities and falsehoods was proved by Moy Thomas in *N. & Q.* (1858). See Makower, *Richard Savage: A Mystery in Biography* (1909).

SAVARIN. See BRILLAT-SAVARIN.

SAVART, Felix, *sa-vahr* (1791–1841), French physician and physicist, was born at Mézières in Ardennes. He taught physics in Paris, and invented *Savart's wheel* for measuring tonal vibrations, and the *Savart quartz plate* for studying the polarization of light. With Biot he discovered the law (named after them) governing the force in a magnetic field round a long straight current. He died in Paris.

SAVARY, Anne Jean Marie René, Duc de Rovigo, *sav-a-ree* (1774–1833), French soldier, born at Marcq in Ardennes. Napoleon employed him in diplomatic affairs. In 1804 he presided at the execution of the Duc d'Enghien, and in the wars of 1806–08 acquired high reputation. Now Duke of Rovigo (1808), he was sent to Spain, and negotiated the kidnapping of the Spanish king and his son. In 1810 he became minister of police. After Napoleon's fall he wished to accompany him to St Helena, but was confined at Malta. He escaped and (1819) was reinstated in his honours. In 1831–33 he was commander-in-chief in Algeria. His *Mémoires* (1828) are unreliable.

SAVIGNY, Friedrich Karl von, *sa-veen-yee* (1779–1861), German jurist, born of Alsatian family at Frankfurt, in 1803 became a Law professor at Marburg, and published a treatise on the Roman law of property (Eng. trans. 1849) that won him European fame. In 1808 he was called to Landshut and in 1810 to Berlin, where he was also in 1810–42 member of the commission for revising the code of Prussia, &c. He resigned office in 1848. His greatest books were his *Roman Law in the Middle Ages* (1815–31; trans. 1829) and *System of Roman Law* (1840–49), with its continuation on *Obligations* (1851–1853). See books by Arndt (1861), Rudorff (1862), Bethmann-Hollweg (1867) and Landsberg (1890).

SAVILE, (1). See HALIFAX (4).

(2) **Sir Henry,** *sav'il* (1549–1622), scholar, born at Bradley near Halifax, became fellow of Merton College, Oxford, travelled on the Continent (1578), was Queen Elizabeth's tutor in Greek and mathematics, became warden of Merton in 1585, and provost of Eton in 1596, and was knighted in 1604. In 1619 he founded chairs of Geometry and Astronomy at Oxford. His principal works are *Rerum Anglicarum Scriptores* (1596), containing the works of William of Malmesbury, Henry of Huntingdon, Roger Hoveden, and 'Ingulph' (q.v.); *Commentaries concerning Roman Warfare* (1598); *Fower Bookes of the Histories* and the *Agricola* of Tacitus (1581); and a magnificent edition of St Chrysostom (1610–13).

SAVONAROLA, Girolamo (1452–98), Italian religious and political reformer, was born of noble family at Ferrara and in 1474 entered the Dominican order at Bologna. He seems to have preached in 1482 at Florence; but his first trial was a failure. In a convent at Brescia his zeal won attention, and in 1489 he was recalled to Florence. His second appearance in the pulpit of San Marco—on the sinfulness and apostasy of the time—was a great popular triumph; and by some he was hailed as an inspired prophet. Under Lorenzo the Magnificent art and literature had felt the humanist revival of the 15th century, whose spirit was utterly at variance with Savonarola's conception of spirituality and Christian morality. To the adherents of the Medici therefore, Savonarola early became an object of suspicion but till the death of Lorenzo (1492) his relations with the church were at least not antagonistic and when, in 1493, a reform of the Dominican order in Tuscany was proposed under his auspices, it was approved by the pope, and Savonarola was named the first vicar-general. But now his preaching began to point plainly to a political revolution as the divinely-ordained means for the regeneration of religion and morality, and he predicted the advent of the French under Charles VIII, whom soon after he welcomed to Florence. Soon, however, the French were compelled to leave Florence, and a republic was established, of which Savonarola became the guiding spirit, his party ('the Weepers') being completely in the ascendant. Now the Puritan of Catholicism displayed to the full his extraordinary genius and the extravagance of his theories. The republic of Florence was to be a Christian commonwealth, of which God was the sole sovereign, and His Gospel the law; the most stringent enactments were made for the repression of vice and frivolity; gambling was prohibited; the vanities of dress were restrained by sumptuary laws. Even the women flocked to the public square to fling down their costliest ornaments, and Savonarola's followers made a huge 'bonfire of vanities'. Meanwhile his rigorism and his claim to the gift of prophecy led to his being cited in 1495 to answer a charge of heresy at Rome and on his failing to appear he was forbidden to preach. Savonarola disregarded the order, but his difficulties at home increased. The new system proved impracticable and although the conspiracy for the recall of the Medici failed, and five of the conspirators were executed, yet this very rigour hastened the reaction. In 1497 came a sentence of excommunication from Rome; and thus precluded from administering the sacred offices, Savonarola zealously tended the sick monks during the plague. A second 'bonfire of vanities' in 1498 led to riots; and at the new elections the Medici party came into power. Savonarola was again ordered to desist from preaching, and was fiercely denounced by a Franciscan preacher, Francesco da Puglia. Dominicans and Franciscans appealed to the interposition of divine providence by the ordeal of fire. But when the trial was to have come off (April 1498) difficulties and debates arose, destroying Savonarola's prestige and producing a complete revulsion of public feeling. He was brought to trial for falsely claiming to have seen visions and uttered prophecies, for religious error, and for sedition. Under torture he made avowals which he afterwards withdrew. He was declared guilty and the sentence was confirmed by Rome. On May 23, 1498, this extraordinary man and two Dominican disciples were hanged and burned, still professing their adherence to the Catholic Church. In morals and religion, not in theology, Savonarola may be regarded as a forerunner of the Reformation. His works are mainly sermons, theological treatises, the chief *The Triumph of the Cross*, an apology of orthodox Catholicism, some poems, and a discourse on the government of Florence. An edition appeared in 1633–40; Ferrari edited *Prediche e Scritti* (1930), Ridolfi his *Lettere* (1933). The great Life of him is by Prof. Villari (2 vols. 1859–61; Eng. trans. 1863). See English works by R. Madden (1853), W. R. Clark (1878), Herbert Lucas, S.J. (1899), P. Villari (1918) and R. Ridolfi (trans. 1959); Mrs Oliphant, *Makers of Florence*; George Eliot, *Romola* and M. de la Bedoyère, *The Meddlesome Friar* (1958).

SAWTREY, William (?–1401), a Lollard burnt at Smithfield, February 26, 1401, the first victim in England.

SAXE, (1) John Godfrey (1816–87), American poet, born at Highgate, Vt., was by turns lawyer, journalist, politician, lecturer and journalist again. His numerous poems are mostly humorous and satirical.

(2) **Maurice, Comte de** (1696–1750), usually called **Marshal de Saxe**, natural son of Augustus II, Elector of Saxony and king of Poland, and Countess Aurora von Königsmark, was born at Goslar. At twelve he ran off to join the army of Marlborough in Flanders, and next the Russo-Polish army before Stralsund (1711). He fought against the Turks in Hungary under Prince Eugene, and studied the art of war in France. In 1726, elected Duke of Courland, he maintained himself against Russians and Poles, but was compelled to retire in 1729. He took a brilliant part in the siege of Philippsburg (1734); and in the war of the Austrian succession he invaded Bohemia and took Prague by storm. In 1744, now marshal of France, he commanded the French army in Flanders, showed splendid tactical skill, and took several fortresses. In 1745 he defeated the Duke of Cumberland at Fontenoy. In 1746 he gained the victory of Raucoux, and was made marshal-general. For the third time, at Laffeld (July 2, 1747), he defeated Cumberland and captured Bergen-op-Zoom. He then retired to his estate of Chambord, and died November 30, 1750. His work on the art of war, *Mes Rêveries*, was published in 1751. See Carlyle's *Frederick the Great*, Lives by Karl von Weber (2nd ed. 1870), Saint-René Taillandier (1865), Vitzthum von Eckstädt (1867), the Duc de Broglie (1891), Brandenburg (1897), J. M. White (1962) and J. Colin, *Les Campagnes du Maréchal de Saxe* (3 vols. 1901–06).

SAXE-COBURG-GOTHA, Alfred Ernest Albert, Prince of (1844–1900), second son of Queen Victoria, was born at Windsor Castle and studied at Bonn and Edinburgh before entering the royal navy in 1858. He was elected King of Greece in 1862, but declined the dignity. In 1866 he was created Duke of Edinburgh and in 1874 married the Russian Grand Duchess Marie Alexandrovna (1853–1920). In 1893 he succeeded his uncle as reigning Duke of Saxe-Coburg-Gotha.

SAXO GRAMMATICUS, ' the Scholar' (c. 1140–1206), Danish chronicler and a Zealander by birth, was secretary to Archbishop Absalom of Roskilde, at whose request he wrote the *Gesta Danorum* in 16 books. This fine example of medieval literature, partly legendary (bks. i–ix) and partly historical, is written after the style of Valerius Maximus. He is said to have died at Roskilde. See O. Elton's translation of Books i–ix (1894) and Weibull, *Saxo* (1915).

SAY, Jean Baptiste (1767–1832), French political economist, born at Lyons, passed part of his youth in England. On the outbreak of the Revolution he worked for Mirabeau on the *Courrier de Provence*, and was secretary to the minister of finance. In 1794–1800 he edited *La Décade*, and in it expounded the views of Adam Smith. A member of the tribunate in 1799, as a protest against the arbitrary tendencies of the consular government he resigned (1804). In 1803 he issued his *Traité d'économie politique* (8th ed. 1876). In 1814 the government sent him to England to study its economics; he laid down the results in *De l'Angleterre et des Anglais* (1816). From 1819 he lectured on political economy, and in 1831 became professor at the Collège de France. He also wrote *Catéchisme d'économie politique* (1815) and *Mélanges et correspondance* (1833). As a disciple of Adam Smith and through his own writings his influence on French economics of the first half of the 19th century was of the greatest importance. His grandson, **Léon** (1826–96), was a journalist, statesman and political economist.

SAYCE, Archibald Henry (1845–1933), English philologist, born at Shirehampton near Bristol, took a classical first from Oxford in 1869, and became a professor of Assyriology (1891–1919). A member of the Old Testament Revision Company, he wrote on biblical criticism and Assyriology.

SAYERS, (1) **Dorothy Leigh** (1893–1957), English writer, born in Oxford. Perhaps the most celebrated detective-story writer since Conan Doyle. Her novels are distinguished by a taste and style unequalled at the time when they were written. Beginning with *Clouds of Witness* (1926), she related the adventures of her hero Lord Peter Wimsey in various accurately observed milieux—such as advertising in *Murder Must Advertise* (1933) or campanology in *The Nine Tailors* (1934)—until, in *Gaudy Night* (1935) and *Busman's Honeymoon* (1937), her characters started to walk out of their frames and she wrote no more about them. She next earned a reputation as a leading Christian apologist with two successful plays, *The Zeal of Thy House* (1937) and *The Devil to Pay* (1939), a cycle for broadcasting, *The Man Born to be King* (1943) and a closely reasoned essay *The Mind of the Maker* (1941). A translation of Dante's *Inferno* appeared in 1949 and of *Purgatorio* in 1955. The *Paradiso* was left unfinished at her death.

(2) **James** (1912–), British physicist, a member of the British team associated with the atomic bomb project, became professor of Electron Physics at Birmingham (1946). In 1949 he was given a government award for his work on the cavity magnetron valve, of much importance in the development of radar.

(3) **Tom** (1826–65), pugilist, was born in Pimlico, and became a bricklayer. From 1849, his first fight, he was beaten only once, though under the average of middleweight champions. His last and most famous contest with Heenan, the Benicia Boy, in 1860, lasted for 2 hours and 6 minutes and ended after 37 rounds in a draw. A subscription of £3000 was raised for Sayers. See account of the Sayers-Heenan fight in *My Confidences* by F. Locker-Lampson (1896).

SCALA, Della. See SCALIGER.

SCALIGER, *skal'i-jėr*, (1) **Joseph Justus** (1540–1609), third son of (2), was born at Agen. After studying at Bordeaux, with his father and in Paris, acquired a surpassing mastery of the classics and eventually boasted that he spoke 13 languages, ancient and modern. While in Paris he became a Calvinist and later visited Italy, England and Scotland, only the last of which seems to have appealed to him, especially through the beauty of its ballads. In 1570 Scaliger settled at Valence and for two years studied under the jurist Cujacius. From 1572 to 1574 he was professor in Calvin's College at Geneva. He then spent twenty years in France and there produced works which placed him at the head of European scholars. Among them are his editions of Catullus, Tibullus, Propertius and Eusebius. By his edition of Manilius and his *De Emendatione Temporum* (1583) he founded modern chronology. From 1593 he held a chair at Leyden and to his inspiration Holland owes her long line of scholars. His last years were embittered by controversy, especially with the Jesuits, who charged him with atheism and profligacy. By his combined knowledge, sagacity and actual achievement he holds the first place among the scholars of his time. See his *Autobiography* (trans. 1927), Life by Bernays (1855), works by Nizard (1852) and Tamizey de Larroque (1881), and Mark Pattison's *Essays* (1889).

(2) **Julius Caesar** (1484–1558), father of (1), according to the highly doubtful story of his famous son, was the second son of Benedetto della Scala, descendant of a princely family of Verona and was brought up a soldier under his kinsman the Emperor Maximilian, gaining marvellous distinction in the French armies attempting the conquest of Italy. Despite these activities, he is said to have gained a knowledge of medicine and Greek. But it seems more probable that he was the son of a signpainter, Benedetto Bordone, and that he graduated in medicine at Padua. He became a French citizen in 1528 and settled at Agen, where he produced learned works on the Latin cases, on Theophrastus, Aristotle and Hippocrates. His poems of invective, as in his attack on Erasmus, were considerable. See books by Nisard (1860) and Magen (1880).

SCANDERBEG. See SKANDERBEG.

SCARLATTI, (1) **Alessandro** (1659–1725), Italian composer, born at Palermo, Sicily. His musical career began in Rome, where in 1680 he produced his first opera. This gained him the patronage of Queen Christina of Sweden, whose *maestro di cappella* he became. A few years later he went to Naples, where he was musical director at the court (1693–1703) and conducted the conservatoire there. He was the founder of the Neapolitan school of opera. He wrote nearly 120 operas; 35 of these survive, the most famous being *Tigrane* (1715). He also wrote 200 masses, 10 oratorios, 500 cantatas and many motets and madrigals. See study by E. J. Dent (new ed. 1960).

(2) **Guiseppe Domenico** (1685–1757), son of (1), also a musician, born at Naples, held many court appointments. In Rome (1709) he was official composer to the Queen of Poland, for whom he composed several operas. In Lisbon (1720) he served the king, taught the Infanta Barbara, and in 1729 went to the Spanish Court in Madrid. He was also (1714–19) choirmaster of St Peter's, Rome, and wrote much church music. He was a skilled performer on the harpsichord and it is as a writer of brilliant sonatas for this instrument that he is best remembered. He wrote over 600, and his work had an important effect on the development of the sonata form. See S. Sitwell,

A Background for Domenico Scarlatti (1935).

SCARLETT, (1) **James, Baron Abinger** (1769–1844), born in Jamaica, studied at Trinity, Cambridge, took silk in 1816, and in 1819 became Whig M.P. for Peterborough. Canning made him attorney-general, with a knighthood, in 1827; and in 1834, now lord chief baron of the Exchequer, he was created Baron Abinger.

(2) **Sir James Yorke** (1799–1871), British general, second son of (1), was educated at Eton and Trinity. He commanded the 5th Dragoon Guards (1840–53), and on October 25, 1854, led the heavy-cavalry charge at Balaclava. He subsequently commanded all the cavalry in the Crimea, and in 1865–70 commanded at Aldershot.

(3) **Robert** (*c.* 1499–1594), the Peterborough sexton who buried Catharine of Aragon and Mary, Queen of Scots.

SCARRON, Paul, *ska-rõ* (1610–60), French writer, born at Paris, the son of a lawyer, became an *abbé*, and gave himself up to pleasure. About 1634 he paid a long visit to Italy, and in 1638 began to suffer from a malady which ultimately left him paralysed. He obtained a prebend in Mans (1643), tried physicians in vain, and, giving up all hope of remedy, returned to Paris in 1646 to depend upon letters for a living. From this time he began to pour forth endless sonnets, madrigals, songs, epistles and satires. In 1644 he published *Typhon, ou la gigantomachie*; and made a still greater hit with his metrical comedy, *Jodelet, ou le maître valet* (1645), followed by *Les Trois Dorothées* and *Les Boutades du Capitan Matamore* (the plots taken from the Spanish). In 1648 appeared his *Virgile travesti* (part i) and the popular comedy, *L'Héritier ridicule*. One of the bitterest satires against Mazarin which he wrote for the *Fronde* probably lost him his pensions. The burlesque predominates in most of his writing, but it is as the creator of the realistic novel that he will always be remembered. *Le Roman comique* (1651–57) was a reaction against the euphuistic and interminable novels of Mlle de Scudéry and Honoré d'Urfé. The work of Le Sage, Defoe, Fielding and Smollett owes much to him. In 1652 he married Françoise d'Aubigné, afterwards Madame de Maintenon (q.v.), who brought an unknown decorum into his household and writings. See books by Christian (1841), Morillot (1888), Boislisle (1894), Chardon (1904); Magne, *Scarron et son milieu* (1924), *Roman comique*, ed. Magne (1938); and Jusserand's introduction to Tom Brown's *Comical Works of Scarron* (1892).

SCÈVE, Maurice, *sayv* (1510–64), French renaissance poet, born at Lyons, a leader of the *école lyonnaise*, which paved the way for the *Pléiade* (see RONSARD).

SCHACHT, Hjalmar Horace Greely, *shah*KHt (1877–1970), German financier, born of Danish descent at Tinglev, North Schleswig, in 1923 became president of the Reichsbank, and founded a new currency which ended the inflation of the mark. He resigned in 1929, was called back by the Nazis in 1933, and the following year, as minister of econo-mics, he restored the German trade balance by unorthodox methods and by undertaking an expansionist credit policy. He resigned his post as minister of economics in 1937, and in 1939 was dismissed from his office as president of the Reichsbank because of his disagreement with Hitler over the latter's rearmament expenditure. Charged with high treason and interned by the Nazis, in 1945 he was acquitted by the Allies at Nuremberg of crimes against humanity, and was finally cleared by the German de-Nazification courts in 1948. In 1952 he advised Dr Mossadeq on Persia's economic problems, and in 1953 set up his own bank in Düsseldorf. Schacht, while deploring the excesses of the Nazi régime, helped to give it in its formative years financial stability and efficiency. See his autobiographical *My First Seventy-six Years* (1955).

SCHADOW, *shah'dõ*, name of a family of Prussian artists:

(1) **Friedrich Wilhelm,** changed surname to **Schadow-Godenhaus** (1789–1862), son of (2), was a painter of the Overbeck school, from 1819 professor at Berlin, and in 1826–59 head of the Düsseldorf Academy. See Hübner, *Schadow und seine Schule* (1869).

(2) **Johann Gottfried** (1764–1850), father of (1) and (3), born at Berlin, became court sculptor and director of the Academy of Arts.

(3) **Rudolf** (1786–1822), son of (2), also a sculptor, executed *Spinning Girl* and the *Daughters of Leucippos* at Chatsworth. His works include the quadriga on the Brandenburg Gate at Berlin.

SCHAFER, Sir Edward Sharpey-. See SHARPEY-SCHAFER.

SCHAFF, Philip, *shaf* (1819–93), Swiss-born American Presbyterian theologian, born at Coire in Switzerland, was *privat-dozent* in Berlin, when in 1844 he was called to a chair at the German Reformed seminary at Mercersburg, Penn. In 1870 he became professor in the Union Seminary, New York. A founder of the American branch of the Evangelical Alliance, he was president of the American Old Testament Revision Committee. Among his works are a *History of the Christian Church* (1883–93), *The Creeds of Christendom* (1877), &c.

SCHALL, Johann Adam von (1591–1669), German Jesuit, born at Cologne, was sent out to China as a missionary in 1622, and at Pekin was entrusted with the reformation of the calendar and the direction of the mathematical school. By favour of the Manchu emperor the Jesuits obtained liberty to build churches (1644), and in fourteen years they are said to have made 100,000 converts. But in the next reign Schall was thrown into prison, and died there. A large MS. collection of his Chinese writings is preserved in the Vatican. In Latin he wrote a history of the China Mission (1655).

SCHAMYL. See SHAMYL.

SCHARF, Sir George, *shahrf* (1820–95), British illustrator, son of a Bavarian lithographer, George Scharf (1788–1860), who settled in London in 1816, became a draughtsman, painted a few oil pictures, travelled in Lycia, lectured on art, and was the first secretary of the National Portrait Gallery (from 1857).

SCHARNHORST, Gerhard Johann David von, *shahrn'horst* (1755–1813), German general, son of a Hanoverian farmer, fought in Flanders (1793–95). He directed the training-school for Prussian officers (1801). Wounded at Auerstädt and taken prisoner at Lübeck, he was present at Eylau; from 1807 he reorganized the Prussian army, introduced the short-service system, restored the morale of the Prussian army, so making it possible to defeat Napoleon at Leipzig (1813). But before that he died at Prague of a wound received at Grossgörschen. See Lives by Klippel (1869–71) and Lehmann (1886–87).

SCHARWENKA, Xaver, *shahr-veng'ka* (1850–1924), German-Polish pianist and composer, born at Samter near Posen, in 1881 started a music school in Berlin, and in 1891–98 was in New York. He composed symphonies, piano concertos and Polish dances. See his autobiography (1922).

SCHAUDINN, Fritz Richard, *show'din* (1871–1906), German zoologist, born at Rösening-ken, in East Prussia, became director of the department of protozoological research, Institute for Tropical Diseases, Hamburg. He demonstrated the amoebic nature of tropical dysentery, and with Hoffmann discovered the *spirochaeta pallida* which causes syphilis (1905).

SCHAUKAL, Richard, *show'kahl* (1874–1942), Austrian symbolist poet, born at Brünn in 1874, was in the Austrian civil service, and like Hofmannsthal turned away from the decadence of the declining Austrian empire to seek perfection in lyrical expression of poetic dreams in *Verse* (1896), *Tage und Träume* (1899), *Sehnsucht* (1900), &c., and *Spätlese* (1943).

SCHEELE, Carl Wilhelm, *skay'lė* (1742–86), Swedish chemist, born at Stralsund (then Swedish), was apprenticed to a chemist at Gothenburg, and was afterwards chemist at Malmö, Stockholm, Uppsala and Köping. He discovered hydrofluoric, tartaric, benzoic, arsenious, molybdic, lactic, critic, malic, oxalic, gallic, and other acids, and separated chlorine (1774), baryta, oxygen, glycerine (1783), and sulphuretted hydrogen. He first described the pigment called Scheele's green, or arsenite of copper, and scheelite or tungsten. He showed in 1777, independently of Priestley, that the atmosphere consists chiefly of two gases, one supporting combustion, the other preventing it. In 1783 he described prussic acid. His papers were translated by Dobbin (1931). See Life by O. Zekert (1931).

SCHEEMAKERS, Pieter, *skay'mah-kėrs* (1691–1770), Belgian sculptor, Nollekens' master, was born and died at Antwerp, lived in London (1735–69), and executed several monuments and portrait busts, including those of Mead and Dryden in Westminster Abbey.

SCHEER, Reinhard (1863–1928), German admiral, born in Hesse-Nassau, commanded the German High Seas Fleet in 1916–18 and was in charge at the battle of Jutland.

SCHEFFEL, Joseph Viktor von, *shef'fel* (1826–86), German poet and novelist, born at Karlsruhe, was bred for the law at Heidel-berg, Munich and Berlin, but in 1852 went to Italy to write. His best book is *Der Trompeter von Säckingen* (1854), a romantic and humorous tale in verse. Other works include a novel, *Ekkehard* (1857), a collection of songs, *Gaudeamus* (1867), the romances, *Hugideo* (1884) and *Juniperus* (1863) and poems. He settled at Karlsruhe in 1864. See Lives by Prölss (1902), Sallwürk (1920).

SCHEFFER, Ary (1795–1858), French painter, born at Dordrecht, Holland, of a German father, studied under Guérin, and became known for his subject pictures and portraits in the romantic style. Puvis de Chavannes (q.v.) was his pupil.

SCHEFFLER, Johann. See ANGELUS.

SCHEIDEMANN, Philipp, *shi'dė-* (1865–1939), German socialist political leader, was minister of finance and colonies in the provisional government of 1918, and first chancellor of the republic in 1919.

SCHELLING, Friedrich Wilhelm Joseph von (1775–1854), German philosopher, born at Leonberg in Württemberg, studied at Tübingen and Leipzig, and from 1798 lectured on philosophy at Jena as successor to Fichte. In 1803–08 he was professor at Würzburg; then until 1820 secretary of the Royal Academy of Arts at Munich; again professor at Erlangen until 1827, when he returned to Munich; and finally from 1841 at Berlin. His works may be grouped into three periods, in the first of which (1797–1800), embracing the *Philosophy of Nature* (1799) and *Transcendental Philosophy* (1800), he was under the influence of Fichte; the second (1801–03) culminates in the ' Philosophy of Identity ', Schelling's lights being Spinoza and Boehme; the third and least valuable represents the growth of his Positive (in opposition to the previous Critical or Negative) Philosophy. He began as an adherent of Fichte's principle of the Ego as the supreme principle of philosophy, and developed the pantheism characteristic of the idealism of Fichte and Hegel. In the *Philosophy of Nature* writings and in *The World-Soul* (1797–99) he supplements the Fichtian Ego or Absolute Ego by showing that the whole of Nature may be regarded as an embodiment of a process by which Spirit tends to rise to a consciousness of itself. The *Transcendental Idealism* (1800) speaks of the two fundamental and complementary sciences, Transcendental Philosophy and Speculative Physics. The promised Positive Philosophy which was to advance beyond merely negative or critical philosophy came to be simply the philosophy of Mythology and Revelation. His son edited his works (1856–1861; new ed. 1927–28). See books by Noack (1859), Plitt (Life, 1870), Becker (1875), Watson (1883), Groos (1889), Metzger (1911), H. Knittermeyer (1929).

SCHENKEL, Daniel, *shen-kel* (1813–85), German Protestant theologian, born at Dägerlen in Zürich, was professor of Theology at Heidelberg from 1851. His *Charakter-bild Jesu* (1864) is an attempt to construct the human character of Jesus and entirely eliminate the supernatural.

SCHIAPARELLI, Giovanni Virginio, *skyah' pah-rel'li* (1835–1910), Italian astronomer, born at Savigliano, Piedmont, worked under F. G. W. Struve (q.v.) at Pulkova, was head of Brera observatory, Milan, studied meteors and double stars, and discovered the ' canals ' of Mars (1877) and the asteroid Hesperia (1861).

SCHICKELE, René, *shik'e-lė* (1883–1940), German Alsatian writer, born at Oberehnheim, wrote poems, novels, including the trilogy *Das Erbe am Rhein* (1925–31), and plays.

SCHIEFNER, Franz Anton von, sнee- (1817–1879), Russian philologist of Ostiak and other Siberian tongues.

SCHILLER, (1) Ferdinand Canning Scott (1864–1937), British pragmatist philosopher, tutor at Corpus Christi College, Oxford, and professor of Philosophy (1929) at Los Angeles, wrote *Humanism* (1903), his name for pragmatism, *Logic for Use* (1929), &c. See study by Abel (1955).

(2) **Johann Christoph Friedrich von** (1759–1805), German master of the historical drama, poet and historian, was born November 10, the son of an army surgeon, in the service of the Duke of Württemberg at Marbach on the Neckar. He was educated at the grammar school at Ludwigsburg, and intended for the church, but at thirteen, at the personal behest of the duke, was obliged to attend the latter's military academy, studying the law instead of theology, but finally qualified as a surgeon (1780) and was posted to a regiment in Stuttgart. Although outwardly conforming well, he found an outlet for his true feelings in the reading and eventually writing of *Sturm und Drang* verse and plays. His first play, *Die Räuber* (1781), published at his own expense, was, on account of its seemingly anarchical and revolutionary appeal, an instant success when it reached the stage at Mannheim the following year. But its noble revolutionary hero, Karl Moor, does finally recognize the social order in the memorable words ' Two such men as I would destroy the entire moral structure of the world '. Schiller played truant from his regiment to attend the performance, was arrested but, forbidden to write anything but medical works in the future, fled and, in hiding at Bauerbach, finished the plays, *Fiesko* and *Kabale und Liebe* (1783). For a few months he was dramatist to the Mannheim theatre. He next issued a theatrical journal, *Die rheinische Thalia*, begun in 1784, in which were first printed most of his *Don Carlos*, many of his best poems, and the stories *Verbrecher aus verlorener Ehre* and *Der Geisterseher*. In 1785 he went by invitation to Leipzig; and at Dresden, where Körner was living, he found rest from emotional excitement and pecuniary worries. Here he finished *Don Carlos* (1787), written in blank verse, not prose, his first mature play, though it suffers artistically from excessive length and lack of unity. Amongst the finest fruits of his discussions with Körner and his circle are the poems *An die Freude*, later magnificently set to music by Beethoven in his choral symphony, and *Die Künstler*. After two years in Dresden and an unhappy

love affair (not the first) he went to Weimar, where he studied Kant, met his future wife, Charlotte von Lengefeld, and began his history of the revolt of the Netherlands. In 1788 he was appointed honorary professor of History at Jena, and married, but his health broke down with overwork from writing a history of the Thirty Years' War, the letters on aesthetic education (1795) and the famous *Über naive und sentimentalische Dichtung* (1795–96), in which he differentiates ancient from modern poetry by their different approaches to nature. His short-lived literary magazine, *Die Horen* (1795–97), was followed by the celebrated *Xenien* (1797), a collection of satirical epigrams against philistinism and mediocrity in the arts, in which the newly found friendship between Goethe and Schiller found mutual expression. This inspired the great ballads (1797–98), *Der Taucher, Der Ring des Polykrates, Die Kranische des Ibykus*, the famous *Lied von der Glocke*, ' Song of the Bell ', completed in 1799 and, under Shakespeare's spell, the dramatic trilogy, *Wallenstein* (1796–99), comprising *Wallensteins Lager, Die Piccolomini*, and *Wallensteins Tod*, the greatest historical drama in the German language. This was followed by *Maria Stuart* (1800; trans. S. Spender 1957), a remarkable psychological study of the two queens, Elizabeth and Mary, in which the latter by her death gains a moral victory. Schiller the historian is here at odds with Schiller the dramatist. Again, in *Die Jungfrau von Orleans* (1801) St Joan dies on the battlefield and is resurrected; no doubt in the interests of drama. *Die Braut von Messina* (1803) portrays the relentless feud between two hostile brothers and the half-legend of *Wilhelm Tell* (1804) is made by Schiller a dramatic manifesto for political freedom. There is a fragment of *Demetrius*, his unfinished work. He was ennobled (1802), fell ill (1804) and died May 9, 1805, at Weimar. See collected works, intro. C. G. Körner (1812–15), Lives by Thomas Carlyle (1825), R. Weltrich (1855–99), J. Sime (1882), H. W. Nevinson (1889), K. Berger (1905–09), F. Strich (1927), H. Cysarz (1934), E. Tonnelat (1934), A. Buchenwald (1937), and studies by L. Bettermann (3rd ed. 1905), J. G. Robertson (1905), T. Rea (1906), V. Basch (1911), K. Berger (1939), H. Hefele (1940), E. Spranger (1941), E. L. Stahl (1954).

SCHILLING, Johannes (1828–1910), German sculptor, born at Mittweida in Saxony, professor of Art at Dresden (1868–1906), executed the four groups of the *Seasons* for Dresden; the Niederwald monument of Germania (1883) opposite Bingen; and he also executed monuments of Schiller for Vienna, the Emperor Maximilian for Trieste, &c.

SCHIMMELPENNINCK, née Galton, Mary Anne (1778–1856), English author, born at Birmingham, a Quaker, in 1818 joined the Moravian communion. Her nine works (1813–60) include two on Port Royal, a *Theory of Beauty, Sacred Musings*, and an *Autobiography*.

SCHIMPER, Andreas Franz Wilhelm (1856–1901), German botanist, son of Wilhelm Philipp (1808–80), the authority on mosses, born at Strasbourg, became an extraordinary professor at Bonn. He prepared the first map of plant distribution (1898), studied the development of starch grains and introduced the term *chloroplast*. His father's uncle, **Karl Friedrich** (1803–67), made important contributions to plant morphology.

SCHINKEL, Karl Friedrich (1781–1841), German architect, born at Neuruppin in Brandenburg, in 1820 became professor at the Berlin Royal Academy, designed military buildings, Berlin, in classical style, museums, churches, &c. He also attained distinction as a painter and illustrator. See monograph by F. Stahl (1912).

SCHIRACH, Baldur von, *sheer'a*KH (1907–), German Nazi politician, born in Berlin, became a party member in 1925, a member of the Reichstag in 1932, and in 1933 founded and organized the Hitler Youth, of which he was leader until his appointment as Gauleiter of Vienna in 1940. Captured in Austria in 1945 and tried before the Nuremberg Tribunal, he was found guilty of participating in the mass deportation of Jews, and was sentenced to 20 years' imprisonment. He was released from Spandau prison in 1966. See *The Price of Glory* by his wife (1960).

SCHLAF, Johannes, *shlahf* (1862–1941), German novelist and dramatist, born at Querfurt, studied at Berlin and with Holz wrote *Papa Hamlet* (1889), a volume of short-stories, *Die Familie Selicke* (1890), a social drama, *Peter Boies Freite* (1902), &c.

SCHLAGINTWEIT, *shlah'gint-vit,* the name of five brothers, born in Munich, distinguished as travellers and scientific writers on geography:

(1) **Adolf von** (1829–57), worked closely together with **Hermann** (1826–82) and **Robert** (1833–85). Hermann and Adolf published two books (1850–54) on the physical geography of the Alps (1850, 1854). Wilhelm von Humboldt then had them recommended to the British East India Company, which sent the three brothers to India to make observations on terrestrial magnetism, altitudes in the Deccan, the Himalayas, Tibet, Assam, &c. Hermann was the first European to cross the Kunlun mountains. Adolf was put to death by the emir of East Turkestan. Robert became professor of Geography at Giessen in 1863, travelled to the United States and wrote on the Pacific railway (1870), California (1871) and the Mormons (1874). See their *Results of a Scientific Mission to India and High Asia* (1860–69).

(2) **Eduard von** (1831–66), a fourth brother, took part in the Spanish invasion of Morocco (1859–60), wrote an account of it and fell at Kissingen fighting for Bavaria against the Prussians.

(3) **Emil von** (1835–1904), the fifth brother, became a lawyer, but wrote *Buddhism in Tibet* (London 1860), *Die Könige von Tibet* (1865), *Indien in Wort und Bild* (1880–81), &c.

(4) **Hermann von.** See under (1).

(5) **Robert von.** See under (1).

SCHLEGEL, *shlay-gel,* (1) **August Wilhelm von** (1767–1845), German poet and critic, brother of (2), born at Hanover, studied theology at Göttingen, but soon turned to literature. In 1795 he settled in Jena, and in 1796 married a widow, Caroline Böhmer (1763–1809), who separated from him in 1803 and married Schelling. In 1798 he became professor of Literature and Fine Art at Jena, and in 1801–04 he lectured at Berlin. Most of the next fourteen years he spent in the house of Madame de Staël at Coppet, though he lectured on *Dramatic Art and Literature* (Eng. trans. 1815) at Vienna in 1808, and was secretary to the crown prince of Sweden, 1813–14. From 1818 till his death (May 12, 1845) he was professor of Literature at Bonn. He is famous for his translations of 17 plays of Shakespeare, revised, and the remaining plays translated by D. Tieck and W. Baudissin, which versions are still regarded as the best. He also translated works by Dante, Calderón, Cervantes and Camoens, and edited the *Bhagavad-Gita* and the *Ramayana*. A leading figure of the romantic movement, he severely criticized Schiller, Wieland and Kotzebue, although his own poetry was lifeless. His lectures, essays and history of fine arts are still valued. See A. Sidgwick, *Caroline Schlegel and her Friends* (1889), and study by O. Brandt (1919).

(2) **Karl Wilhelm Friedrich von** (1772–1829), the greatest critic produced by the German romantic movement, brother of (1), was born at Hanover, March 10, and educated at Göttingen and Leipzig. He abducted in 1798 Dorothea (1763–1839), daughter of Moses Mendelssohn, wife of the Jewish merchant Veit, and mother of Veit the religious painter, and next year utilized his experiences in a notorious romance, *Lucinde*. He then joined his brother at Jena, and with him wrote and edited the journal *Das Athenaeum*, in the interests of Romanticism. The *Charakteristiken und Kritiken* (1801) contain some of both brothers' best writing. From 1808 down to his death at Dresden, Friedrich, who had become a devout Roman Catholic, was employed in the public service of Austria; it was he who penned the Austrian proclamations against Napoleon in 1809. His best-known books are lectures on the *Philosophy of History* (Eng. trans. 1835) and *History of Literature* (trans. 1859). There are also English versions of his *Philosophy of Life* (1847) and *Lectures on Modern History* (1849). *Über die Sprache und Weisheit der Indier* (1808) was a pioneer for the study of Sanskrit in Europe. See his Letters to his brother (1890), and studies by C. Enders (1913), F. Imle (1927) and B. von Wiese (1927).

SCHLEICHER, *shlī'*KHer, (1) **August** (1821–1868), German philologist, in 1850 became professor of Slavonic Languages at Prague, and in 1857 honorary professor at Jena, compiled the *Comparative Grammar of the Indo-Germanic Languages* (4th ed. 1876; Eng. trans. 1874–77). See Memoir by Lefmann (1870).

(2) **Kurt von** (1882–1934), German general and politician, born at Brandenburg, was on the general staff during World War I. Minister of war in von Papen's government of 1932, he succeeded him as chancellor, but his failure to obtain dictatorial control provided Hitler with his opportunity to seize power in 1933. Schleicher and his wife were

executed by the Nazis on a trumped-up charge of treason. See study by K. von (Reibnitz (1932).

SCHLEIDEN, Matthias Jakob, *shlī′den* (1804–1881), German botanist, born at Hamburg, in 1839 became professor of Botany at Jena, and in 1863 at Dorpat. He did much to establish the cell theory.

SCHLEIERMACHER, Friedrich Ernst Daniel, *shlī′ĕr-mah-*ĸʜer (1768–1834), German theologian and philosopher, born at Breslau, having broken from the dogmatic narrowness of the Moravians, studied philosophy and theology at Halle. From 1796, then a preacher in Berlin, he was closely allied with the devotees of Romanticism. In his *Reden über die Religion* (1799), *Monologen* (1800), and *Grundlinien einer Kritik der bisherigen Sittenlehre* (1803) he expounded that hostility to the traditional moral philosophy and the Kantian ethic to which he had already (1801) given expression in the ' Confidential Letters on Schlegel's *Lucinde* '. The translation of Plato, begun by him and Schlegel, was carried through in 1804–10 by Schleiermacher alone. He was professor at Halle (1804–06) and Berlin (1810). He was equally eminent as a preacher, and was the soul of the movement which led to the union in 1817 of the Lutheran and Reformed Churches in Prussia. He produced *Die Weihnachtsfeier* (1806; Eng trans. *Christmas Eve*, 1889); a critical treatise on the first epistle to Timothy (1807); and his most important work, *Der christliche Glaube* (1821–22; 6th ed. 1884). Afterwards appeared a work on Christian ethics, a Life of Jesus, sermons and letters (partly trans. by Frederica Rowan, 1860). He taught that religion, philosophy and science do not contradict one another, but that religion needed to be purged of metaphysical and dogmatic reflections. See his Correspondence (1852–87); Lives by Schenkel (1868), Dilthey (1870; new ed. 1922); essays by K. Barth in *From Rousseau to Ritschl* (trans. 1959) and *Theology and Church* (trans. 1962); R. R. Niebuhr, *Schleiermacher: On Christ and Religion* (1965).

SCHLICK, Moritz (1882–1936), German philosopher, one of the leaders of the ' Vienna Circle ' of logical positivists, born in Berlin, was professor in Rostock, Kiel and from 1922 in Vienna. He was an early exponent of Einstein's relativity theories and in *Allgemeine Erkenntnislehre* (1918) foreshadowed some of the doctrines of Wittgenstein's *Tractatus*. Other important works include *Problems of Ethics* (1930; trans. 1939) and the collected essays (1938). He was shot down on the steps of the university by a student whose thesis he had rejected. See A. J. Ayer, *Logical Positivism* (1960).

SCHLIEFFEN, Alfred, Count von, *shleef′ĕn* (1833–1913), Prussian field-marshal, born in Berlin, who advocated the plan which bears his name (1895) on which German tactics were unsuccessfully based in World War I. In the event of a German war on two fronts, he envisaged a German breakthrough in Belgium and the defeat of France within six weeks by a colossal right-wheel flanking movement through Holland and then southwards, cutting off Paris from the sea, holding off the Russians meanwhile with secondary forces. See study by Ritter (trans. 1958).

SCHLIEMANN, Heinrich, *shlee′mahn*)1822–1890), German archaeologist, the excavator of the sites of Mycenae and with Dörpfeld (q.v.) of Troy, born at Neubuckow, went into business at home, in Amsterdam (1842–46) and in St Petersburg (1846–63), acquiring a large fortune and a knowledge of the principal modern and ancient European languages. He retired early in order to realize his ambition, set out in his *Ithaka, der Peloponnes und Troja* (1869), of vindicating Homer by excavating the mound of Hissarlik, the traditional site of Troy, which city current Homeric criticism held to be part of the Homeric myth. Official delays overcome, excavations were begun in 1872 and his first publication *Trojanische Althertümer* (1874) sceptically received. Assisted by the professional Dörpfeld, he discovered nine superimposed city sites, one of which contained a considerable treasure, which he overhastily identified as Priam's, although part of an earlier pre-Homeric site. The Trojan findings he presented to the German nation in violation of his agreement with the Turkish government, and after compensation was paid, they were housed in the Ethnological Museum in Berlin (1882). He also excavated the site of Mycenae (1876), the treasure of which is in the Athens Polytechnic, in Ithaca (1869 and 1878), at Orchomenos (1881–82) and at Tiryns (1884–85), and his reports were published and translated under these names. An amateur who had the courage to keep his own counsel in the face of expert opinion, he was responsible for some of the most spectacular archaeological discoveries of modern times. See his autobiography (1891), study by Schuchhardt (trans. 1891), Lives by Emil Ludwig (1931), L. and G. Poole (1967), Cottrell, *The Bull of Minos* (1953) and R. Payne *The Gold of Troy* (1960).

SCHMELZER, Johann Heinrich (1623–80), Austrian composer, son of a soldier, was trained as a musician in the emperor's service and won fame throughout Europe as a violinist. In 1679 he became *kapellmeister* to Leopold I, but next year died of the plague in Prague, whence the court had fled from the great epidemic in Vienna. The first to adapt the tunes of the Viennese street musicians and Tyrolean peasants to the more sophisticated instrumental styles of the court, he is often regarded as the true father of the Viennese waltz.

SCHMIDT, (1) Bernhard (1879–1935), German astronomer of Swedish-German origin, born at Nargen, Estonia, studied optics in Sweden and made a precarious living grinding reflectors at Jena with his left hand, as his right had been lost in early youth. In 1926 he became associated with the Bergedorf observatory near Hamburg. In 1932 he devised a method to overcome aberration of the image in spherical mirrors and lenses, by the introduction of a correcting plate at the centre of curvature. This was utilized in the Palomar Schmidt telescope.

(2) **Johann Friedrich Julius** (1825–84), German astronomer, born at Eutin, became in 1858 director of the national observatory

in Athens. An eminent selenographer, he suggested that the moon's surface is still changing slightly. He also published a map of the moon (1875).

(3) **Johannes** (1877–1933), Danish biologist, born at Jägerspris, solved the problem of the European eel's life history, by his discovery of the breeding-ground on the ocean bed near Bermuda in 1904.

SCHNABEL, Artur, *shnah'běl* (1882–1951), Austrian pianist and composer, born in Lipnik, studied under Leschetizky and made his début at the age of eight. He taught in Berlin, making frequent concert appearances throughout Europe and America, and with the advent of the Nazi government, settled first in Switzerland, then in America from 1939. He was an authoritative player of a small range of German classics—notably Beethoven, Mozart and Schubert; his compositions include a piano concerto, chamber music and piano works. See Life by C. Saerchinger (1957).

SCHNITZER, Eduard. See EMIN PASHA.

SCHNITZLER, Arthur (1862–1931), Austrian dramatist and novelist of Jewish origin, born in Vienna, was a physician before he turned playwright. His highly psychological, often strongly erotic short plays and novels, executed with great technical skill, frequently underline some social problem, mostly against the familiar easy-going Viennese background, as in *Anatol* (1893) and *Reigen* (1900), which are cycles of one-act plays linked with one another by the overlapping of one of the characters until the chain is completed by a character of the last meeting one from the first, as in the film *La Ronde* (1950). Other notable works include *Der grüne Kakadu* (1899), *Liebelei* (1895), *Der Weg ins Freie* (1908), *Professor Bernhardi* (1912), on anti-Semitism, and *Flucht in die Finsternis* (1931). Several have been translated into English.

SCHNORR VON CAROLSFELD, Baron Julius (1794–1872), German historical and landscape painter, born at Leipzig, became associated with the school of Cornelius and Overbeck, who went back for their inspiration to Raphael's predecessors. He was professor of Historical Painting at Munich (1827), and painted frescoes of the *Nibelungenlied*, Charlemagne, Barbarossa, &c. In 1846 he became professor at Dresden and director of the gallery. He illustrated the *Nibelungen*, designed stained-glass windows, &c.

SCHÖFFER, Peter (*c.* 1425–1502), German printer in Mainz, the partner of Gutenberg and Fust, whose son-in-law he was and with whom he printed most probably the Mazarin Bible before 1456, although this work is also claimed for Gutenberg, by whose name it is also known. In 1457 they issued the *Mainz Psalter*, the first work on which the name of the printer and date of publication appears. After the death of Gutenberg and Fust, Schöffer claimed to be the inventor of printing. See work by Roth (1892).

SCHOFIELD, John McAllister, *skō'-* (1831–1906), American general, born in Chautauqua county, New York, in the Civil War distinguished himself at Franklin (1864) and Wilmington (1865), was secretary of war

1868–69, and was commander-in-chief 1888–1895.

SCHOLES, Percy Alfred, *skōlz* (1877–1958), English musicologist, born at Leeds, graduated at Oxford in 1908, and as university extension lecturer there, at Manchester, London and Cambridge, as music critic to the *Observer* (1920–25), as the first music adviser to the B.B.C., and as the editor of *The Oxford Companion to Music* (1938), widely fostered musical appreciation and knowledge. But it is as the author of *The Puritans and Music* (1934) and *The Life of Dr Burney* (1948) that his reputation as musicologist rests. He was awarded the O.B.E. in 1957.

SCHOMBERG, (1) Frederick Hermann, 1st Duke of (1615–90), general in French and British service, born at Heidelberg of a German father and English mother, fought against the Imperialists in the Thirty Years' War. He was captain in the Scottish Guards in the French army (1652–54), fought at the battle of the Dunes (1658), and, though a Protestant, obtained a marshal's baton in 1675. After the revocation of the Edict of Nantes (1685), he retired to Portugal and afterwards took service under the Elector of Brandenburg. He commanded under William of Orange in the English expedition (1688), was made K.G. and created Duke of Schomberg (1689) and was commander-in-chief in Ireland. He conducted the Ulster campaign, but was killed at the Boyne.

(2) **Meinhard, 1st Duke of Leinster and 3rd Duke of Schomberg** (1641–1719), British soldier, son of (1), after serving under the French and the Elector of Brandenburg, commanded the right wing in the battle of the Boyne (1690) and fought in the Spanish Succession War.

SCHOMBURGK, Sir Robert Hermann, *-boork* (1804–65), Prussian-born British traveller and official, surveyed (1831) in the Virgin Islands, where he was a merchant, and was sent by the Royal Geographical Society to explore British Guiana (1831–35). In ascending the Berbice River he discovered the magnificent Victoria Regia lily, described in his *British Guiana* (London 1840) and magnificent *Views in the Interior of Guiana* (folio, 1841). In 1841–43 he was employed by government in Guiana to draw the long-controverted 'Schomburgk-line' as a provisional boundary with Venezuela and Brazil, and in 1844 was knighted. He was accompanied by his brother **Richard** (1811–90), who wrote *Reisen in Britisch Guiana, 1840–44* (Leipzig 1847–48). In 1848 Sir Robert published a *History of Barbadoes*. In 1848–57 he was British consul in San Domingo, in 1857–64 in Siam.

SCHÖNBEIN, Christian Friedrich, *shæn'bīn* (1799–1868), German chemist, born at Metzingen, Württemberg, from 1828 professor at Basel, discovered ozone, gun-cotton and collodion, and experimented on oxygen. See Life by Hagenbach (1869).

SCHÖNBERG, Arnold, *shæn'-* (1874–1951), Austrian composer, born in Vienna, learned the violin as a boy, but, apart from lessons in counterpoint, he was entirely self-taught. In his twenties he earned his living by orchestrating operettas while composing such early works as the string sextet *Verklärt*

Nacht (1899) and the mammoth *Gurrelieder* (1900), and from 1901 until 1903, when he returned to Vienna, he was in Berlin as conductor of a cabaret orchestra and teacher. His search for a personal musical style began to show in such works as his first *Chamber Symphony*, which caused a riot at its first performance in 1907 through its abandonment of the traditional concept of tonality, and Schönberg's works up to the time of his military service in the first World War were written in the style that has come to be known as ' atonal '. From this position, he evolved the discipline known today as ' twelve-note ' or ' serial ' music. At the end of the first World War he taught in Vienna, visited Amsterdam, and then became a professor at the Prussian Academy of Arts until he was exiled by the Nazi government in 1933 and settled in America. A teacher of unusual authority and integrity, Schönberg avoided any sort of propaganda for his own music and theories both in the lecture hall and in his textbooks, and his later works such as the Third String Quartet have shown that despite the originality and complexity of his style, it can become a vehicle for deeply moving and profound works. See books by Wellesz (1925), Leibowitz (1949), Stuckenschmidt (1960), and *Letters* (ed. Stein; trans. 1964).

SCHONGAUER, or **Schön, Martin**, *shōn'-gow-ėr* (1450–91), German painter and engraver, was born at Colmar. His famous *Madonna of the Rose Garden* altar piece at Colmar, one of the most exquisite of early representations of the Virgin, shows Flemish influence, probably that of Rogier van der Weyden. Other religious paintings attributed to Schongauer have not been authenticated, but well over 100 of his engraved plates have survived, including *The Passion, The Wise and Foolish Virgins, Adoration of the Magi*, and other religious subjects, executed with a delicacy of line and a feeling for modelling and composition unequalled among 15th-century German engravers. See studies by H. Wendland (1907) and E. Buchner (1941).

SCHOOLCRAFT, Henry Rowe (1793–1864), American ethnologist, born in Albany county, N.Y., in 1820 went with General Cass to Lake Superior as geologist. In 1822 he became Indian agent for the tribes round the lakes, and in 1823 married a wife of Indian blood. In 1832 he commanded an expedition which discovered the sources of the Mississippi (*Narrative*, 1834). While superintendent for the Indians, he negotiated treaties by which the government acquired 16,000,000 acres. In 1845 he collected the statistics of the Six Nations (*Notes on the Iroquois*, 1848). For the government he prepared his *Information respecting the Indian Tribes of the U.S.* (6 vols. 1851–57).

SCHOPENHAUER, Artur, *shō'pen-how-er* (1788–1860), German pessimist philosopher, born February 22 at Danzig. His father was a banker, his mother a novelist who in her later life kept a literary salon at Weimar. He was educated at Gotha, Weimar, Göttingen and Berlin, graduated from Jena with his first book, *On the Fourfold Root of the Principle of Sufficient Reason* (trans. 1888), and in 1819

became *privat-dozent* in Berlin. He boldly held his lectures at the same times as Hegel, but without success. In 1821 he finally retired to Frankfurt-am-Main, a lonely, violent and unbefriended man, who shared his bachelor's existence with a poodle, named ' Atma ', or ' world soul '. In him feeling and reason were in perpetual conflict; his disposition was severe, distrustful and suspicious. Lastly, he believed that he had founded a philosophy which made him the successor of Socrates, yet saw himself and his thinking passed over, and what he regarded as the fatuous ravings of Hegel, Schelling and Fichte praised as the highest wisdom. The cardinal articles of his philosophical creed were: first, Subjective Idealism—i.e., that the world is my idea, a mere phantasmagoria of my brain, and therefore in itself nothing; secondly, that the possibility of knowledge of the ' thing-in-itself ' was demolished for ever by Kant; and thirdly, that to the intuition of genius the ideas of Art are accessible—the only knowledge not subservient to the Will and to the needs of practical life. Finally, Will, the active side of our nature, or Impulse, is the key to the one thing we know directly from the inside—i.e., the self, and therefore the key to the understanding of all things. Will is the creative, primary, while Idea is the secondary, receptive factor in things. His chief work, *The World as Will and Idea* (1819; trans. Haldane and Kemp, 8th ed. 1937) expounds the logic, metaphysics, aesthetics and ethics of this view. *Seeing and Colours* (1816) contains practically Goethe's entire theory of colour, and *Parerga and Paralipomena* (1851) Schopenhauer's occasional papers. The doctrine of the will reappears in the philosophies of Nietzsche, Bergson, James and Dewey, but his influence has been greater in the world of literature, not least upon Thomas Mann. Frauenstädt edited his complete works (1876). See also *Selected Essays* by E. B. Bax (1891) and W. Jekyll, *The Wisdom of Schopenhauer* (1911), German Lives by W. von Gwinner (1862) and J. Volkelt (5th ed. 1923), English Lives by H. Zimmern (1876); rev. ed. 1932), E. Wallace (1890) and T. Whittaker (1909), and studies by G. Simmel (1907), C. Gebhardt (1913), H. Masse (1926), K. Pfeiffer (1932), Thomas Mann (1938; trans. 1939) and F. Copleston (1946).

SCHOUVALOFF. See SHUVALOV.

SCHRADER, Eberhard, *shrah'dėr* (1836–1908), German oriental scholar, born at Brunswick, professor of Theology at Zürich, Giessen, and Jena, and of Oriental Languages at Berlin (1875), pioneered the study of Assyriology in Germany.

SCHREIBER, *née* **Bertie, Lady Charlotte Elizabeth**, *shrī'bėr* (1812–95), Welsh scholar, born at Stamford, a daughter of the Earl of Lindsey, married in 1833 Sir Josiah John Guest, and in 1855 Charles Schreiber, M.P. She is best known for her translation (1838–1849) of the *Mabinogion*, but was also an authority on fans and playing-cards. She bequeathed her collections of these to the British Museum.

SCHREINER, Olive, *shrī'ner* (1855–1920), South African author, born in Basutoland, the daughter of a Methodist missionary of German origin, grew up largely self-educated and became a governess. She lived in England (1881–89), where her novel, *The Story of a South African Farm* (1883), the first sustained, imaginative work to come from Africa, was published under the pseudonym Ralph Iron. The manuscript had been rejected by three publishers but was accepted by the fourth, whose reader was George Meredith. She had a fiery, rebellious temperament, a lifelong hatred of her mother and in her later works the creative artist gave way to the passionate propagandist for women's rights, pro-Boer loyalty and pacificism. These include *Trooper Peter Halket* (1897), *Woman and Labour* (1911), *From Man to Man* (1926). In 1894 she married S. P. Cronwright, who took her name, wrote a Life of her (1924) and edited her letters (1926). See also A. Le B. Chapin, *Their Trackless Way* (1931), and books by O. L. Hobman (1955) and L. Gregg (1957). Her brother, William Philip (1857–1919), was prime minister of the Cape Colony (1898–1900) and high commissioner for South Africa from 1914.

SCHRÖDINGER, Erwin, *shræ'-* (1887–1961), Austrian physicist, born and educated in Vienna, became professor at Stuttgart, Breslau, Zürich, Berlin, fellow of Magdalen College, Oxford (1933–38), professor at the Dublin Institute for Advanced Studies (1940) and returned to Vienna as professor in 1956. He originated the study of wave mechanics as part of the quantum theory with his celebrated wave equation for which he shared with Dirac the Nobel prize in 1933, and also made contributions to the field theory. In 1949 he became a foreign member of the Royal Society and was awarded the German O.M. See his *Collected Papers* (1928), *What is Life?* (1946) and *Science and Man* (1958), &c.

SCHRÖTER, Johann Hieronymus (1745–1816), German astronomer, born at Erfurt, studied at Göttingen and in 1778 became chief magistrate of Lilienthal near Bremen, where he built an observatory and studied the surface of the moon, measuring the heights of many of its mountains.

SCHUBART, Christian Friedrich Daniel (1739–91), German poet, born at Obersontheim in Swabia, wrote satirical and religious poems. He was imprisoned at Hohenasperg (1777–87) by the Duke of Württemberg, whom he had irritated by an epigram. He is largely remembered for his influence on Schiller (q.v.). See his Autobiography (1791–93), and monographs by D. F. Strauss (1849), Hauff (1885) and Nagele (1888).

SCHUBERT, (1) Franz (1808–78), German violinist and composer of Dresden, who felt insulted when the publishers attributed to him works by his great Viennese contemporary (2).

(2) **Franz Peter** (1797–1828), Austrian composer, born January 31 in Vienna, the son of a schoolmaster, received early instruction in the violin and piano, at eleven entered the *Stadtkonvikt*, a choristers' school attached to the court chapel. During the five austere years he spent there, he tried his hand at almost every kind of musical composition, including a symphony in D (1813). In 1814 he became assistant master at his father's school, composed an opera, the Mass in F and that masterpiece of song, *Gretchen am Spinnrade*, from Goethe's *Faust*. Another, equally famous, the *Erlkönig*, followed in 1815, but was not performed until 1819. From 1817 he lived on his wits and on his Bohemian friends, who included amateur artists and poets and the operatic baritone, Vogl, with whom he was to found the new Viennese entertainment, the 'Schubertiads', private and public accompanied recitals of his songs, which made them known throughout Vienna. In 1818, and again in 1824, he stayed at Zseliz as the tutor of Count Esterházy's three daughters. The famous 'Trout' piano quintet in A major was written after a walking tour with Vogl in 1819. Schubert's veneration of Beethoven made him frequent the same coffee house, but he was too awestruck ever to approach the great man, except when the latter was sick, when he sent him his compositions; in 1822 a set of variations for a piano duet dedicated to Beethoven, and in 1827 a collection of his songs, which the dying Beethoven greatly admired. The year 1822 saw the Unfinished Symphony (No. 8), the 'Wanderer' fantasia for piano and the spiritual conflicts in the composer that came with the knowledge that he had contracted syphilis. The song cycle, *Die schöne Müllerin*, which includes the well-known refrain, *Das Wandern*, and the incidental music to *Rosamunde* followed in 1823, the string Quartets in A and D minor in 1824. Schubert sent Goethe in 1825 a number of settings of his poems, but the latter returned them ungraciously without acknowledgment. In 1826 Schubert applied unsuccessfully for the post of assistant musical director to the court, wrote the *Winterreise* cycle of songs, the string quartets in G major and D minor and the songs *Who is Sylvia?* and *Hark, Hark the Lark*, which, however, contrary to popular belief, he did not hurriedly scribble on the back of a menu or bill. Before he died of typhus on November 19, 1828, he had written the great C major symphony (No. 9), the fantasy in F minor for four hands and the posthumously published songs, the *Schwanengesang*, or 'Swan-song'. He was buried as near as possible to Beethoven's grave under Grillparzer's well-meant but unjust epitaph: 'Music has here entombed a rich treasure, but still fairer hopes'. For Schubert's works are sufficient to preserve his place among the great masters, not least for his infectiously lyrical spontaneity, his lavish musical inventiveness and as the originator and greatest exponent of the art of the German Lieder See Schubert's *Letters and Other Writings* (1928), study by R. Capell (1928) and *Symposium*, ed. G. Abraham (1947), and Lives by N. Flower (1928), A. Hutchings (1945), O. E. Deutsch (1946), M. J. E. Brown (1958), and *Memoirs by his Friends*, ed. O. E. Deutsch (1958).

SCHUCHARDT, Hugo, *shooкн'-* (1842–1927), German philologist, born at Gotha, professor of Philology at Halle and Gotha, chiefly known for his studies in Romance philology which concentrated on linguistic rather than social or historical phenomena, and which include *Der Vokalismus des Vulgär-lateins* (1866–68) and *Baskische Studien* (1893). See Life by L. Spitzer (2nd ed. 1928).

SCHULENBURG, Countess Ehrengard Melusina von der (1667–1743), German mistress of George I, nicknamed 'the Maypole' because of her lean figure, was created Duchess of Kendal in 1719.

SCHULZE-DELITZSCH, Hermann, *shoolt´ze day´leech* (1808–83), German cooperative politician and economist, born at Delitzsch in Prussian Saxony, advocated constitutional and social reform on the basis of self-help in the National Assembly in Berlin. He started the first ' people's bank ' at Delitzsch, on a cooperative basis. Other branches were founded and joined in 1864 under one organization which eventually spread over middle Europe. He wrote on banks and cooperation. See Life by Bernstein (1879).

SCHUMACHER, Kurt Ernst Karl, *shoo´maKH-er* (1895–1952), German statesman, born at Kulm, Prussia, studied law and political science at the universities of Leipzig and Berlin, and from 1930 to 1933 was a member of the Reichstag and of the executive of the Social Democratic parliamentary group. An outspoken opponent of National Socialism, he spent ten years from 1933 in Nazi concentration camps, where he showed outstanding courage. He became in 1946 chairman of the Social Democratic party and of the parliamentary group of the Bundestag, Bonn. He strongly opposed the German government's policy of armed integration with Western Europe.

SCHUMAN, (1) Robert (1886–1963), French statesman, born in Luxemburg, a member of the Resistance during World War II, prime minister in 1947 and 1948, propounded (1950), the ' Schuman plan ' for pooling the coal and steel resources of Western Europe, was elected president of the Strasbourg European Assembly in 1958 and awarded the Charlemagne prize. He survived de Gaulle's electoral reforms, being re-elected to the National Assembly in November 1958.

(2) **William Howard** (1910–   ), American composer, born in New York, studied under Roy Harris and at Salzburg, winning in 1943 the first Pulitzer prize to be awarded to a composer. In 1945 he became president of the Juilliard School of Music in New York. His work ranges from the gay (e.g., his opera, *The Mighty Casey*) to the austere and grim. He composed eight symphonies, concertos for piano and violin and several ballets as well as choral and orchestral works.

SCHUMANN, (1) Clara Josephine, *née* **Wieck** (1819–96), German pianist and composer, wife of (3) and daughter of the Leipzig pianoforte teacher, Wieck, who turned her into one of the most brilliant concert pianists of her day. She gave her first *Gewandhaus* concert when only eleven and the following year four of her Polonaises were published. After their marriage in 1840, the Schumanns made concert tours to Hamburg and she alone to Copenhagen (1842) and to Russia. From 1856 she very often played for the

Philharmonic Society in London, fostering her husband's work wherever she went. Her own compositions include a Trio in G minor, a set of three Preludes and fugues and lighter pieces such as the *Soirées musicales*, many of which were taken over by her husband for his Impromptus, the ' Davids-bundlertänze ' &c. From 1878 she was principal pianoforte teacher in the Frankfurt-am-Main Conservatoire. See Life by B. Litzmann (trans. 1913) and under (3).

(2) **Elisabeth** (1889–1952), German-born operatic soprano and lieder singer, born at Merseburg, was in 1919 engaged by Richard Strauss for the Vienna State Opera and sang in his and Mozart's operas all over the world, making her London début in 1924. Latterly she concentrated more on Lieder by such composers as Schubert, Wolf and Richard Strauss. She left Austria in 1936 and in 1938 became a citizen of the United States. See Puritz, *The Teaching of Elisabeth Schumann* (1956).

(3) **Robert Alexander** (1810–56), German composer, husband of (1), born at Zwickau, spent his boyhood browsing in his father's bookshop, and began at twenty-one a desultory course of legal studies at Leipzig and Heidelberg. After hearing Rossini's operas performed in Italy and Paganini playing at Frankfurt-am-Main, he persuaded his parents to allow him to change over to the pianoforte, under the formidable teacher Wieck of Leipzig. The latter, however, was mostly away on his daughter's concert tours and Schumann, left to his own devices, studied Bach's *Well-tempered Clavier*, wrote a prophetic newspaper article on the talents of the young Chopin, and broke a finger of his right hand on a finger-strengthening contraption (1832), thus ruining for good his prospects as a performer. The deaths of a brother and a sister-in-law and an obsessive fear of insanity drove him to attempt suicide. Fortunately, his first compositions, the Toccata, Paganini studies, and Intermezzi, were published in 1833 and in 1834 he founded and edited (for ten years) the biweekly *Neue Leipzige Zeitschrift für Musik*, his best contributions to which were translated under the title, *Music and Musicians* (1877–80). In these, he championed romanticism, and in 1853 contributed another prescient essay, this time on the young Brahms. In 1835 he met Chopin, Moscheles and Mendelssohn, who had become director of the Leipzig *Gewandhaus*. The F sharp minor sonata was begun and another in C major, written posthaste for the Beethoven commemorations, but not published until 1839. His attachment to Clara Wieck did not escape the disapproving father, who whisked her away on concert tours as much as possible. That they were secretly engaged, however, he did not know. Clara dutifully repudiated Schumann, who retaliated by a brief encounter with the Scottish pianist, Robina Laidlaw, to whom he dedicated his *Fantasiestücke*. In 1839, the former lovers were reconciled and after a long legal wrangle to obtain permission to marry without her father's consent, they married in September 1840, after Schumann had written his first songs, the Fool's Song in

Twelfth Night, and aptly, the Chamisso songs *Frauenliebe und Leben*, or ' Woman's Love and Life '. Clara immediately brought pressure on her bridegroom to attempt some major orchestral composition, and her efforts were rewarded by the first symphony in B flat major, which was performed under Mendelssohn's direction at the *Gewandhaus*. Then followed the A Minor piano concerto the Piano Quintet, the choral *Paradise and the Peri*, and his best work in that medium, the scenes from *Faust*, completed in 1848, the ' Spring ' Symphony in B flat, &c. In 1843 he was appointed professor of the new Leipzig Conservatoire. The Schumanns' Russian concert tour, during which Clara played before Nicholas I (1844), inspired Robert to write five poems on the Kremlin. Recurring symptoms of mental illness prompted the move from Leipzig to the less exciting Dresden. The Symphony in C major was completed in 1847 and the death of his great friend prompted him to write *Reminiscences of Mendelssohn-Bartholdy*, first published in 1947. Revolution broke out in Dresden in 1849 when Prussian troops confronted republican revolutionaries, among them Wagner. The Schumanns fled, but Robert wrote some stirring marches. His mental state allowed him one final productive phase in which he composed pianoforte pieces, many songs and the incidental music to Byron's *Manfred*. His appointment as musical director at Düsseldorf in 1850 only worsened his condition, of which he was fully aware. He heard alternatively sublime and hellish music, took to table-turning, and in 1854 threw himself into the Rhine, only to be rescued by fishermen. He died in an asylum two years later. Schumann was primarily the composer for the pianoforte. His early works show a tremendous fertility of musical and extra-musical ideas, to which the names of many of them, ' Abegg ' variations (after a dancing partner), *Carnaval*, *Kreisleriana*, *Papillons*, &c., testify. His operatic and many of his orchestral compositions were not successful because of their repetitive character. But his music comprises the best in German romanticism. See Lives by J. W. von Wasielewski (1858; trans. 1878), H. Bedford (1925), F. Niecks (1925), A. W. Patterson (1934), J. Chissell (1948; new ed. 1956), O. Wheeler (1949), P. M. Young (1961) and *A Symposium*, ed. G. Abraham (1952).

SCHURZ, Carl, *shoorts* (1829–1906), German-American statesman and journalist, born near Cologne, joined the revolutionary movement of 1849. In America from 1852 he was politician, lawyer, major-general in the Civil War, journalist, senator 1869–75, secretary of the interior 1877–1881. He wrote Lives of Henry Clay and Lincoln, and *Reminiscences* (1909).

SCHUSCHNIGG, Kurt von (1897–), Austrian statesman, born at Riva, South Tirol, served and was decorated in the first World War and then practised law. He was elected a Christian Socialist deputy in 1927, became minister of justice (1932) and education (1933). After the murder of Dollfuss in 1934, he succeeded as chancellor until March 1938, when Hitler occupied

Austria. Imprisoned by the Nazis, he was liberated by American troops in 1945. He was professor of Political Science at St Louis in the United States (1948–67). See his *Farewell Austria* (1938) and *Austrian Requiem* (trans. 1947).

SCHUSTER, Sir Arthur (1851–1934), British physicist, born in Frankfurt of Jewish parents, studied at Heidelberg and Cambridge and became professor of Applied Mathematics (1881) and Physics (1888–1907) at Manchester. He carried out important pioneer work in spectroscopy and terrestrial magnetism. The Schuster-Smith magnetometer is the standard instrument for measuring the earth's magnetic force. He led the eclipse expedition to Siam in 1875, was president of the British Association in 1915 and was knighted in 1920.

SCHÜTZ, Heinrich, also known by the Latin form **Sagittarius** (1585–1672), German composer, was born at Köstritz near Gera, and in 1608 went to Marburg to study law. Going in 1609 to Venice to study music, he became a pupil of Gabrieli (q.v.), and published in 1611 a book of five-part madrigals, showing the Italian influence. He returned to Germany in 1613, continued his law studies at Leipzig, and in 1617 was appointed *Hofkapellmeister* in Dresden, where he introduced Italian-type music and styles of performance—madrigals, the use of continuo, and instrumentally-accompanied choral compositions, for example his *Psalms of David* (1619)—and he may thus be regarded as the founder of the Baroque school of German music. A visit to Italy in 1628 acquainted him with the more recent developments effected by Monteverdi in Italian music, and from 1633 until his return to Dresden in 1641 he travelled between various courts, including those at Copenhagen and Hanover, everywhere preaching his gospel of Italianism. Creatively Schütz lies between the polyphony of Palestrina and the more elaborate orchestration of such composers as Bach and Handel, his compositions including much church music—psalms, motets, passions (' The Seven Words on the Cross ' and ' The Resurrection '), a German requiem, and the first German opera, *Dafne*, produced in Torgau in 1627. See studies by A. Einstein (1928), H. Hoffmann (1940) and H. J. Moser (1959).

SCHUYLER, Philip John, *skī'ler* (1733–1804), a leader of the American Revolution, born at Albany, raised a company and fought at Lake George in 1755. He was a member of the colonial assembly from 1768, and delegate to the Continental congress of 1775, which appointed him one of the first four major-generals. Washington gave him the northern department of New York, and he was preparing to invade Canada when ill-health compelled him to tender his resignation. He still retained a general direction of affairs from Albany, but jealousies rendered his work both hard and disagreeable, and in 1779 he finally resigned. Besides acting as commissioner for Indian affairs and making treaties with the Six Nations, he sat in congress 1777–81, and was state senator thirteen years between 1780 and 1797, U.S. senator 1789–91 and 1797–98, and surveyor-general of the state from 1782. With Hamilton and John Jay he shared the leadership of the Federal party in New York; and he aided in preparing the state's code of laws. See Lives by Lossing (enlarged ed. 1872), G. W. Schuyler (1888), B. Tuckerman (1905).

SCHWABE, Heinrich Samuel, *shvah'bĕ* (1789–1875), German astronomer, born at Dessau, discovered (1843) a ten-year sunspot cycle (later found to be rather more than eleven years).

SCHWANN, Theodor, *shvahn* (1810–82) German physiologist, born at Neuss, in 1838 became professor at Louvain, in 1848 at Liège. He discovered the enzyme pepsin, investigated muscle contraction, demonstrated the rôle of micro-organisms in putrefaction and brilliantly extended the cell theory, previously applied to plants, to animal tissues. See Life by Henle (1882).

SCHWANTHALER, Ludwig von, *shvahn'tah-lĕr* (1802–48), Munich sculptor, executed for King Louis of Bavaria bas-reliefs and figures for public buildings, and in 1835 became professor at Munich Academy. Among his works are the colossal statue of Bavaria, statues of Goethe, Jean Paul Richter, Mozart, &c.

SCHWARZ, Berthold, *shvahrts* (fl. 1320), German Franciscan monk of Freiburg (or Dortmund), whose real name was Konstantin Anklitzen, Schwarz ('black') being a nickname due to his chemical experiments. He it was who about 1320 brought gunpowder (or guns) into practical use. See monograph by Hansjakob (1891).

SCHWARZENBERG, *shvarts'ĕn-*, (1) **Adam, Count von** (1584–1641), was (1619) prime minister of George William, Elector of Brandenburg, and was all-powerful during the Thirty Years' War.

(2) **Felix Ludwig Johann Friedrich** (1800–1852), Austrian statesman, nephew of (3), sent on a mission to London in 1826, became involved in the Ellenborough divorce suit, was Austrian ambassador at Naples 1846–48, then distinguished himself in the Italian campaign, as prime minister called in the aid of the Russians against Hungary, and pursued a bold absolutist policy. See Lives by Berger (1853), E. Heller (1932) and A. Schwarzenberg (1946).

(3) **Karl Philipp, Prince of** (1771–1820), Austrian field-marshal, uncle of (2), served against the Turks and the French republic. He was ambassador to Russia in 1808, fought at Wagram (1809), conducted the negotiations for the marriage between Napoleon and Maria Louisa, and as ambassador at Paris gained the esteem of Napoleon, who demanded him as general of the Austrian contingent in the invasion of Russia in 1812. In 1813 he was generalissimo of the united armies which won the battles of Dresden and Leipzig. In 1814 he helped to occupy Paris. See Life by Kerchnawe and Veltze (1913).

SCHWARZKOPF, Elisabeth, *shvahrts'-* (1915–), German soprano, born at Jarotschin, studied at the Berlin High School for Music and sang in the Vienna State Opera (1944–48) and Royal Opera, Covent Garden (1949–52), at first specializing in coloratura rôles and

only later appearing as a lyric soprano. See monograph by B. Gavoty (1958).

SCHWATKA, Frederick (1849–92), American Arctic explorer, born at Galena, Ill., was lieutenant of cavalry on the frontier till 1877, meanwhile being admitted to the Nebraska bar and taking a medical degree in New York. In 1878–80 he commanded an expedition which discovered the skeletons of several of Franklin's party, and filled up all gaps in the narratives of Rae and M'Clintock, besides performing a sledge-journey of 3251 miles. In 1883 he explored the course of the Yukon, in 1886 led the *New York Times* Alaskan expedition, and in Alaska in 1891 opened up 700 miles of new country. See his *Along Alaska's Great River* (1885), and book by W. H. Gilder (1881).

SCHWEIGGER, Johann Salomo Christoph, *shvī'gĕr* (1779–1857), German physicist, born at Erlangen, invented the string galvanometer.

SCHWEINFURTH, Georg August, *shvīn'-foort* (1836–1925), German explorer, born at Riga, in 1864 made a journey up the Nile and along the Red Sea to Abyssinia. In 1869 from Khartoum he passed through the country of the Dinka, Niam-Niam and Monbuttu, and discovered the Welle. Between 1874 and 1883 he made botanical expeditions in Egypt and Arabia, and in Eritrea (1891–94). See his *Heart of Africa* (new ed. 1918).

SCHWEITZER, Albert, *shvī'-* (1875–1965), Alsatian medical missionary, theologian, musician and philosopher, in terms of intellectual achievement and practical morality the noblest figure of the 20th century, born January 14 at Kaysersberg in Alsace and brought up at Günsbach in the Münster valley, where he attended the local *realgymnasium*, learnt the organ eventually under Widor in Paris, studied theology and philosophy at Strasbourg, Paris and Berlin, and in 1896 made his famous decision that he would live for science and art until he was thirty and then devote his life to serving humanity. In 1899 he obtained his doctorate on Kant's philosophy of religion, became curate at St Nicholas Church, Strasbourg, in 1902 *privat-dozent* at the university, and in 1903 principal of the theological college. In 1905 he published his authoritative study, *J. S. Bach, le musicien-poète* (1905), translated by Ernest Newman (1911), followed in 1906 by a notable essay on organ-design. Schweitzer was all for the preservation of old organs, many of which he considered had a better tone than modern factory-built ones. The same year appeared the enlargement of his theological thesis (1901), *Von Reimarus zu Wrede*, re-issued in 1913 as *Geschichte der Leben-Jesu Forschung*, 'The Quest of the Historical Jesus' (trans. 1910), a thoroughgoing demolition of Liberal theology which had emphasized the rôle of Christ as ethical teacher, in favour of an eschatological interpretation, i.e., Christ as the herald of God's Kingdom at hand, in which the ethical teaching, which would only serve a short interim period, is correspondingly devalued. It marked a revolution in New Testament criticism. To these his Pauline studies *Geschichte der Paulinischen Forschung* (1911; trans. 1912) and *Die Mystik des Apostels*

Paulus (1930; trans. 1931) were intended as companion volumes. True to his vow, despite his international reputation as musicologist, theologian and organist, he began to study medicine (1905), resigned as principal of the theological college (1906) and, duly qualified (1913), set out with his newly-married wife to set up a hospital to fight leprosy and sleeping sickness at Lambaréné, a deserted mission station on the Ogowe river in the heart of French Equatorial Africa. Except for his internment by the French (1917–18) as a German and periodic visits to Europe to raise funds for his mission by organ recitals, he made his self-built hospital the centre of his paternalistic service to Africans, in a spirit ' not of benevolence but of atonement '. His newly discovered ethical principle ' reverence for Life ' was fully worked out in relation to the defects of European civilization in *Verfall und Wiederaufbau der Kultur* (1923), ' The Decay and Restoration of Civilization ', (trans. 1923) and philosophically in *Kultur und Ethik* (1923; trans. 1923). He was Hibbert lecturer at Oxford and London (1934) and Gifford Lecturer at Edinburgh (1934–35). He was awarded the Nobel peace prize (1952) and an honorary O.M. (1955). See his *On the Edge of the Primeval Forest* (trans. 1922), *More from the Primeval Forest* (trans. 1931), *Out of My Life and Thought* (1931; postscript 1949), *From My African Notebook* (1938), theological studies by E. N. Mozley (1950) and G. Seaver (rev. ed. 1955), musical studies, ed. C. R. Joy (1953), philosophical study by J. M. Murry (1948), biographical studies by C. E. B. Russell (1944), O. Kraus (1944), G. Seaver (1948), H. Hagedorn (1954), F. Franck (1959), McKnight (1964), and pictorial study (1955) and film (1957) by Anderson.

SCHWENKFELD, Kaspar von, *shvengk'-* (*c.* 1490–1561), German reformer, founder of a Protestant sect, born at Ossig near Liegnitz, served at various German courts, and about 1525 turned Protestant, though he differed widely from Luther. His doctrines resembled those of the Quakers, and brought him banishment and persecution; but he everywhere gained disciples. He died at Ulm. Most of his ninety works were burned by both Protestants and Catholics. Some of his persecuted followers (most numerous in Silesia and Swabia) emigrated to Holland. In 1734 forty families emigrated to England, and thence to Pennsylvania, where, as Schwenkfeldians, they maintained a distinct existence, numbering some 300 members. See monographs by Kadelbach (1861), F. Hoffmann (1897), Hartrauft, Ellsworth and Johnson (1907 ff.).

SCHWINGER, Julian (1918–), American scientist, professor at Harvard, shared the 1965 Nobel prize for physics with Feynman and Tomonaga, for work in quantum electrodynamics.

SCIOPPIUS, or Schoppe, Kaspar (1576–1649), German classical scholar controversialist, born at Neumarkt, at Prague in 1598 abjured Protestantism and attacked his former coreligionists, together with Scaliger and James I of England. He devoted himself at Milan to philological studies and theological

warfare (1617–30), and died at Padua. A great scholar, he wrote *Grammatica Philosophica* (1628); *Verisimilium Libri Quatuor* (1596), *Suspectae Lectiones* (1597), &c.

SCIPIO, Publius Cornelius, Africanus Major (237–183 B.C.), Roman general, fought against the Carthaginians at the Trebia and at Cannae. In 210 he was sent as a general extraordinary to Spain. By a sudden march he captured (209) Nova Carthago, stronghold of the Carthaginians, checked Hasdrubal, and soon held the whole of Spain. He was consul in 205, and in 204 sailed with 30,000 men to carry on the war in Africa. His successes compelled the Carthaginians to recall Hannibal from Italy, and the great struggle between Rome and Carthage was terminated by the Roman victory at Zama in 202. Peace was concluded in 201. The surname of Africanus was conferred on Scipio, and popular gratitude proposed to make him consul and dictator for life— honours Scipio refused. In 190 he served as legate under his brother Lucius in the war with Antiochus, whose power they crushed in the victory of Magnesia. But on their return the brothers were charged with having been bribed by Antiochus, the excuse being the too lenient terms granted. Popular enthusiasm supported Scipio against the ill-will of the senatorial oligarchy; but he soon retired to his country-seat at Liternum in Campania. He daughter was Cornelia, mother of the Gracchi. He is regarded as the greatest Roman general before Julius Caesar. See B. H. L. Hart, *A Greater than Napoleon* (1926), and study by Scullard (1930).

SCIPIO ÆMILIANUS, Publius Cornelius, Africanus Minor (185–129 B.C.), Roman statesman and general, was a younger son of Lucius Aemilius Paulus who conquered Macedon, but was adopted by his kinsman Publius Scipio, son of the great Scipio Africanus. He accompanied his father against Macedon, and fought at Pydna (168). In 151 he went to Spain under Lucius Lucullus, and in 149 the third and last Punic war began. The incapacity of the consuls, Manilius and Calpurnius Piso (149–148), and the brilliant manner in which their subordinate rectified their blunders, drew all eyes to him. In 147 he was elected consul and invested with supreme command. The story of the siege of Carthage, the despairing heroism of its inhabitants, the determined resolution of Scipio, belongs to history. The city was finally taken in the spring of 146, and by orders of the senate levelled to the ground. Scipio was now sent to Egypt and Asia on a special embassy; but affairs meanwhile were going badly in Spain, where the Roman armies had suffered the most shameful defeats. At last in 134 Scipio, re-elected consul, went to Spain, and after an eight months' siege forced the Numantines to surrender, and utterly destroyed their city. He then returned to Rome, where he took part in political affairs as one of the leaders of the aristocratic party, and although a brother-in-law of Tiberius Gracchus (q.v.), disclaimed any sympathy with his aims. The Latins, whose lands were being seized under the Sempronian law, appealed to

Scipio, and he succeeded (129) in getting the execution suspended. But his action caused the most furious indignation, and shortly after Scipio was found dead in his bed, doubtless murdered by an adherent of the Gracchi.

SCOGAN, John (fl. 1480–1500), English jester at the court of Edward IV whose *Jests* are said to have been compiled by Andrew Boorde (q.v.).

SCOPAS (fl. 395–350 B.C.), Greek sculptor, founder, with Praxiteles, of the later Attic school, was a native of Paros, and settled in Athens. See Gardner, *Six Greek Sculptors* (1910).

SCORESBY, William (1789–1857), English Arctic explorer, born near Whitby, went as a boy with his father, a whaling captain, to the Greenland seas, and himself made several voyages to the whaling grounds. He attended Edinburgh University, and published *The Arctic Regions* (1820), the first scientific accounts of the Arctic seas and lands. In 1822 he surveyed 400 miles of the east coast of Greenland. Having studied at Cambridge, and been ordained (1825), he held various charges at Exeter, and Bradford. He was elected F.R.S. in 1824. See Life by his nephew (1861).

SCOT, (1) Michael. See SCOTT (18).

(2) or **Scott, Reginald** (c. 1538–99), English author, was a younger son of Sir John Scot of Smeeth in Kent. He studied at Hart Hall, Oxford, was collector of subsidies for the lathe of Shepway in 1586–87 and was M.P. (1588–89). He is credited with the introduction of hop-growing into England, and his *Perfect Platform of a Hop-garden* (1574) was the first manual on hop culture in the country. His famous *Discoverie of Witchcraft* (1584), is an admirable exposure of the childish absurdities which formed the basis of the witchcraft craze, and excited the antipathy of King James, who wrote his *Daemonologie* (1597) 'chiefly against the damnable opinions of Wierus and Scot', and had Scot's book burnt by the hangman. Answers and refutations were also written by Meric Casaubon and other divines.

SCOTT, name of a great Scottish Border family which has been traced back, somewhat dubiously, to one Uchtred Filius Scoti, or Fitz-Scot, a witness to David I's charter to Holyrood Abbey (1128), and thereafter to Richard Scot of Murthockston in Lanarkshire (1294), the cradle, however, of the race having been Scotstoun and Kirkurd in Peeblesshire. We find them possessors of Buccleuch in Selkirkshire in 1415, and of Branxholm near Hawick, from 1420–46 onwards. The then Sir Walter Scott fought for James II at Arkinholm against the Douglases (1455), and received a large share of the forfeited Douglas estates; his descendants acquired Liddesdale, Eskdale, Dalkeith, &c., with the titles Lord Scott of Buccleuch (1606) and Earl of Buccleuch (1619). Among them were two Sir Walters, one of whom (c. 1490–1552) fought at Flodden (1513), Melrose (1526), Ancrum (1544) and Pinkie (1547), and in 1552 was slain in a street fray at Edinburgh by Kerr of Cessford, while the other Sir Walter, 1st Baron Scott of Buccleuch (1565–1611), was the rescuer of Kinmont Willie

from Carlisle Castle (1596). Francis, second earl (1626—51), left two daughters—Mary (1647—61), who married the future Earl of Tarras, and Anna (1651–1732), who married James, Duke of Monmouth, who took the surname Scott and was created Duke of Buccleuch. After his execution (1685) his duchess, who had borne him four sons and two daughters, retained her title and estates, and in 1688 married Lord Cornwallis. Her grandson Francis succeeded her as second duke, and through his marriage in 1720 with a daughter of the Duke of Queensberry that title and estates in Dumfriesshire devolved in 1810 on Henry, third Duke of Buccleuch (1746–1812), a great agriculturist. Walter Francis, fifth duke (1806–84), was the builder of the pier and breakwater at Granton. The Harden branch (represented by Lord Polwarth) separated from the main stem in 1346; and from this sprang the Scotts of Raeburn, ancestors of Sir Walter. See works by Sir William Fraser (1879), J. R. Oliver (1887), K. S. M. Scott (1923) and Jean Dunlop (1957).

SCOTT, (1) Alexander (c. 1525–84), a Scottish lyrical poet of the school of Dunbar, who lived near Edinburgh, wrote thirty-six short poems (Scot. Text Soc. 1895) rather in the style of the love lyrics in *Tottel's Miscellany*, though more terse and strong. He was essentially of the pre-Reformation period in Scottish literature.

(2) **Charles Prestwich** (1846–1932), one of the great modern English newspaper editors, born in Bath, was educated at Corpus Christi College, Oxford, became at twenty-six editor of the *Manchester Guardian*, which he raised into a serious Liberal rival of *The Times* by highly independent and often controversial editorial policies, such as opposition to the Boer war, and by his high literary standards. He was Liberal M.P. (1895–1906). See Life by J. L. Hammond (1934). He was succeeded in 1929 by his son, **Edward Taylor** (1883–1932), who was accidentally drowned in Lake Windermere the year his father died.

(3) **Cyril Meir** (1879–1970), English composer, born in Oxton, Cheshire, as a child studied the piano in Frankfurt-am-Main, returning there to study composition in early manhood. His works won a hearing in London at the turn of the century, and in 1913 he was able to introduce his works to Vienna; his opera, *The Alchemist*, had its first performance in Essen in 1925. Scott has composed three symphonies, piano, violin and cello concertos, and numerous choral and orchestral works, but is best known for his piano pieces and songs. He has also written poems, studies of music and occultism, &c. See his *My Years of Indiscretion* (1924).

(4) **David** (1806–49), Scottish historical painter, born in Edinburgh, was apprenticed to his father as a line-engraver, and in 1829 was admitted R.S.A. In 1831 he designed his twenty-five 'Illustrations to the *Ancient Mariner*' (1837). In 1832–33 he visited Italy, and painted *The Vintager*, now in the National Gallery; many historical paintings followed. The main value of his works lies in their Blake-like power and originality. See Memoir (1850) by his brother, **William Bell**

(1811–90), also a painter, and monograph by J. M. Gray (1884).

(5) **Dred** (1795?–1858), American Negro slave whose claim (1852–57) to be free as having long lived in the free state of Illinois was negatived by the Supreme Court. The case was of great importance in the slavery controversy as it involved constitutional issues. See book by Hopkins (1951).

(6) **Duncan Campbell** (1862–1947), Canadian poet, born at Ottawa, rose in the Canadian civil service to deputy superintendent-general for Indian affairs, wrote *The Magic House* (1893), *Labour and the Angel* (1898), *New World Lyrics and Ballads* (1905) and other collections of verse reflecting romantically his love for the Canadian Rockies and Prairies. His prose sketches include *In the Village of Viger* (1896).

(7) **Dukinfield Henry** (1854–1934), British botanist, son of (9), studied at Oxford, became assistant professor at the Royal College of Science and in 1892 keeper of Jodrell Laboratory, Kew. He collaborated with W. E. Williamson in a number of brilliant studies of fossil plants and established in 1904 the class Pteridospermeae.

(8) **Francis George** (1880–1958), Scottish composer, born in Hawick, studied at the universities of Edinburgh and Durham, and in Paris under Roger-Ducasse. From 1925 until 1946 he was lecturer in Music at Jordanhill Training College for Teachers, Glasgow. His *Scottish Lyrics* (five vols. 1921–39) comprise original settings of songs by Dunbar, Burns and other poets, and exemplify Scott's aim of embodying in music the true spirit of Scotland. Primarily a song composer, Scott also wrote the orchestral suite *The Seven Deadly Sins* (after Dunbar's poem) and other orchestral works. See essay by Hugh McDiarmid (1955).

(9) **Sir George Gilbert** (1811–78), English architect, grandson of (24), grandfather of (10) and father of (7), was born, July 13, at Gawcott, Bucks. Aroused by the Cambridge Camden Society and an article of Pugin's (1840–41), he became the leading practical architect in the Gothic revival, and, as such, the building or restoration of most of the public buildings, ecclesiastical or civil, was in his hands. The Martyrs Memorial at Oxford (1841), St Nicholas at Hamburg (1844), St George's at Doncaster, the new India office (exceptionally, owing to pressure by Lord Palmerston, in the style of the Italian Renaissance), the Home and Colonial Offices (from 1858), the somewhat notorious Albert Memorial (1862–63), St Pancras Station and hotel in London (1865), Glasgow University (1865), the chapels of Exeter and St John's Colleges, Oxford, and the Episcopal Cathedral at Edinburgh are examples of his work. He was elected A.R.A. (1855), R.A. (1861), P.R.I.B.A. (1873–76); he was professor of Architecture at the Royal Academy (1868); and he was knighted (1872). The establishment of the Society for Protection of Ancient Buildings (1877) was due to his inspiration. He died March 27, 1878, and was buried in Westminster Abbey. He wrote works on English mediaeval Church architecture. See his *Recollections* (1879).

(10) **Sir Giles Gilbert** (1880–1960), English architect, grandson of (9), was educated at Beaumont College, Old Windsor. He was the architect, pre-eminently, of the great Anglican Cathedral at Liverpool, and also designed, among many other public buildings, the new nave at Downside Abbey, the new buildings at Clare College and the new library at Cambridge. He planned the new Waterloo bridge and was responsible for the rebuilding of the House of Commons after World War II. Elected R.A. (1922), he was knighted (1924) and received the O.M. (1944).

(11) **Hew** (1791–1872), Scottish divine, born at Haddington and educated at Aberdeen, was, from 1839, minister of Wester Anstruther, compiled *Fasti Ecclesiae Scoticanae* (1866–71; new ed. 1915–28).

(12) **Hugh Stowell.** See MERRIMAN (1).

(13) **John.** See ELDON.

(14) **John** (1783–1821), Scottish journalist, born and educated at Aberdeen, became first editor of the *London Magazine* in 1820, and was shot in a duel with Jonathan Christie, whose friend, Lockhart, he had attacked in the magazine.

(15) **John** (1794–1871), English horse-trainer, born at Chippenham and brought up in West Australia, trained six Derby winners, including West Australian, which won the three great racing events in 1853, the Two Thousand Guineas, the Derby and the St Leger.

(16) **Lady John.** See SPOTTISWOODE (1).

(17) **Michael** (*c.* 1175–*c.* 1230), Scottish scholar and astrologer, the 'wondrous wizard', who studied at Oxford and on the Continent, was tutor and astrologer at Palermo to Frederick II, settled at Toledo 1209–20 and translated Arabic versions of Aristotle's works and Averrhoës' commentaries. Returning to the Imperial court at Palermo, he refused the proffered archbishopric of Cashel (1223). His translation of Aristotle was seemingly used by Albertus Magnus, and was one of the two familiar to Dante. Dante alludes to him in the *Inferno* (canto xx, 115–117) in a way which proves that his fame as a magician had already spread over Europe; and he is also referred to by Albertus Magnus and Vincent of Beauvais. In Border folklore he is credited with having 'cleft the Eildon Hills in three and bridled the Tweed with a curb of stone'; and his grave is shown in Melrose Abbey. See Life by J. Wood Brown (1897).

(18) **Michael** (1789–1835), Scottish author, born at Cowlairs, Glasgow, after four years (1801–06) at the university went to seek his fortune in Jamaica. He spent a few years in the W. Indies, but in 1822 settled in Glasgow. His vivid, amusing stories, *Tom Cringle's Log* (1829–33), *The Cruise of the Midge* (1834–35), &c., first appeared in *Blackwood's*.

(19) **Michael** (1902–   ), English Anglican missionary and agitator, was educated at King's College, Taunton, and St Paul's College, Grahamstown, served in a London East End parish and as chaplain in India (1935–39), where he collaborated with the Communists. Invalided out of the R.A.F. in 1941, he served (1943–50) in various

missions in South Africa. No longer associating with Communists, he exposed the atrocities in the Bethal farming area and in the Transvaal, defended the Basutos against wrongful arrest, and brought the case of the dispossessed Herero tribe before the United Nations. He became *persona non grata* in the Union and in the Central African Federation. He founded the London Africa Bureau in 1952. In 1958 he suffered a short imprisonment for his part in nuclear disarmament demonstrations. He was expelled from Nagaland in 1966. See his autobiography, *A Time to Speak* (1958).

(20) **Sir Percy Moreton, 1st bart.** (1853–1924), English sailor and gunnery expert, was born in London, entered the Navy and served (1873–1900) in Ashanti, Egypt, S. Africa and China. Retiring in 1909, he returned to active service as gunnery adviser to the fleet; and in September 1915 was placed in charge of the anti-aircraft gun defences of London. See his *Fifty Years in the Royal Navy* (1919).

(21) **Sir Peter Markham** (1909–), English artist, ornithologist and broadcaster, born in London, the son of (23), began to exhibit his characteristic paintings of bird scenes and his portraits in 1933. He represented Britain (single-handed dinghy sailing) at the 1936 Olympic Games, served with distinction with the Royal Navy in World War II, founded the Severn Wild Fowl Trust in 1948, explored in the Canadian Arctic in 1949, and was leader of several ornithological expeditions (Iceland, 1951 and 1953; Australasia and the Pacific, 1956–57). Through television he has helped to popularize natural history, and his writings include *Morning Flight* (1935), *Wild Chorus* (1938), *The Battle of the Narrow Seas* (1945) and *Wild Geese and Eskimos* (1951). He was created C.B.E. in 1953, and was rector of Aberdeen University, 1960–63. He was knighted 1973. See his autobiographical *The Eye of the Wind* (1961).

(22) **Robert.** See LIDDELL.

(23) **Robert Falcon** (1868–1912), English Antarctic explorer, father of (21), born near Devonport, entered the navy in 1881 and in the *Discovery* commanded the National Antarctic Expedition (1900–04) which explored the Ross Sea area, and discovered King Edward VII Land. Scott was promoted captain in 1906, and in 1910 embarked upon his second expedition in the *Terra Nova* and with a sledge party which consisted of Wilson, Oates, Bowers, Evans and himself reached the South Pole on January 17, 1912, only to discover that the Norwegian expedition under Amundsen had beaten them by a month. Delayed by blizzards and the sickness of Evans, who died, and Oates, who gallantly left the tent in a blizzard, the remainder eventually perished in the tantalizing vicinity of One Ton Depot at the end of March, where their bodies and diaries were found by a search party eight months later. Scott was posthumously knighted and the statue of him by his wife, Kathleen, Lady Scott, the sculptress, stands in Waterloo Place, London. The Scott Polar Research Institute at Cambridge was founded in his memory. See his *Voyage of the Discovery* (1905) and

diary published as *Scott's Last Expedition*, ed. L. Huxley (1913), accounts of the expeditions by A. B. Armitage (1905), G. Taylor (1916), E. R. Evans (1921), A. Cherry-Garrard (1922), and Lives by S. Gwynn (1929) and G. Seaver (1940).

(24) **Thomas** (1747–1821), English divine, grandfather of (9), born at Braytoft, Lincolnshire, began as a surgeon but is best remembered by his *Bible, with Explanatory Notes* (1788–92). See Life (1822) by his son.

(25) **Walter** (c. 1614–94), of Satchells, Scottish soldier and genealogist, served in Holland and at home 1629–86, and then wrote his doggerel *History of the Scotts* (1688; 5th ed. 1894).

(26) **Sir Walter** (1771–1832), Scottish novelist and poet, was born at Edinburgh, son of a writer to the Signet and of Anne Rutherford, a daughter of the professor of Medicine at the University. When young he was sent to his grandfather's farm at Sandyknowe and thus early came to know the Border country which is perhaps the main scene in his creative work. Neither at the High School, Edinburgh, nor at the University did he show much promise. His real education came from people and from books—Fielding and Smollett, Walpole's *Castle of Otranto*, Spenser and Ariosto and, above all, Percy's *Reliques* and German ballad poetry. He did better in his father's office as a law clerk and was admitted advocate in 1792. His first incursion into the Highlands, which were to be second only to the Borders as an inspiration for his work, occurred when, as a law clerk, he was directing an eviction. The young advocate made his first raid in Liddesdale, which also was to figure in his novels, in 1792. His first publication was rhymed versions of ballads by Bürger, 1796. The year following we find him an ardent volunteer in the yeomanry and on one of his 'raids' he met at Gilsland spa a Mlle Charpentier, daughter of a French émigré, whom he married at Carlisle on Christmas Eve, 1797. Two years later he was appointed sheriff of Selkirkshire. The ballad meanwhile absorbed all his literary interest. *Glenfinlas* and *The Eve of St John* were followed by a translation of Goethe's *Goetz von Berlichingen*. His prenticeship in the ballad led to the publication by James Ballantyne, a printer in Kelso, of Scott's first major work, *The Border Minstrelsy* (vols. 1 & 2, 1802, vol. 3, 1803). The *Lay of the Last Minstrel* (1805) made him the most popular author of the day. The other romances which followed, *Marmion* (1808), and *The Lady of the Lake* (1810), enhanced his fame, but the lukewarm reception of *Rokeby* (1811), despite its superior human interest, and of *Lord of the Isles* (1815) warned him that this vein was exhausted. The calculation was fortunate, for modern taste rejects a great deal of this verse romance outpouring, while the novel which replaces it is permanent in the affections of readers everywhere. The business troubles which darkened his later career began with the setting up of James Ballantyne and his brother John as publishers in the Canongate. All went well at first, but with expanding business came

expanding ambitions, and when Constable with his London connections entered the scene, Scott lost all control over the financial side of the vast programme of publication, much of it hack publication, on which he now embarked. Hence the bankruptcy in midstream of his great career as a novelist (1826). The Waverley novels fall into three groups—first from *Waverley* (1814) to *Bride of Lammermoor* and *Legend of Montrose* (1819); next from *Ivanhoe* to *The Talisman* (1825), the year before his bankruptcy; *Woodstock* opens the last period, which closes with *Castle Dangerous* and *Count Robert of Paris* (1832), in the year of his death. The first period established the historical novel based, in Scott's case, on religious dissension and the clash of races English and Scottish, Highland and Lowland, his aim being to illustrate manners but also to soften animosities. In *Guy Mannering* first appear his great character creations of the humorous sort, but *Heart of Midlothian* and *Old Mortality* divide the honours. The *Bride of Lammermoor* has the stark outlines of the ballad. His Scottish vein exhausted, he turned to the Middle Ages in *Ivanhoe*, the scene of which is now England. With *The Monastery* and *The Abbot* he moved to Reformation times, where he showed a respect for what was venerable in the ancient church which might have been predicted from his harshness to the covenanters in *Old Mortality*. This group is distinguished by its portrait gallery of queens and princes. The highlights in the last period are *Woodstock* (1826), not quite successful, and *The Fair Maid of Perth* (1828), where again the ballad motif appears. Modern taste may reject much in the verse romances (not however the introductions to *Marmion* with their playful charm or patriotic ardour), but it does not reject the fine lyrics scattered throughout the novels. Here also he worked best on a traditional or ballad theme, as in *Proud Maisie*, but Highland themes, as in *The Pibroch* and *The Coronach*, equally called forth his lyric powers. There are also his immense labours for the publishers, much of which was simply hack work—the editions of Dryden (1808); of Swift (1814); the *Life of Napoleon* (1827), &c. The *Tales of a Grandfather* (1828-30), however, keeps its charm, and his three letters ' from Malachi Malagrowther ' (1826), are remembered for their patriotic assertion of Scottish interests. Scott has been criticized on the grounds of style and also for his lack of ideas. The language of his verse romances is often trite, due partly to haste of composition, and the more romantic or manufactured material in his novels is too often tinged with tushery. In dialogue his gentlefolk (especially in love scenes) tend to be affected, but there are many shades here—nobody, for example, would charge the talk in the noble last scenes of *Redgauntlet* with affectation, and all are agreed that the talk of his more humble characters is in character. As for lack of ideas (E. M. Forster's complaint), Scott's acceptance of his world and its conventions ruled that out. The charge that he patronized his peasants and fisherfolk hardly holds.

Cuddie Headrigg may be too much of a bumpkin and his mother Mause too strident, but the episode of the Mucklebakkits in *The Antiquary* shows a rare sympathy with working folk. Having regard to the esteem in which Scott as man and writer has been held we may take as his epitaph ' Scott is greater than anything he wrote '. Lockhart's great Life (1837-38) is a classic, but as the publication of the *Letters* by Grierson (1932-1937) showed, dealt too tenderly with certain episodes. Grierson's own *Life* (1938) puts these in better perspective. This had been preceded by John Buchan's admirable Life (1932). See also Scott's *Journal*, ed. Tait (1939, &c.). O. Elton's study, *A Survey of English Literature, 1780-1830*, chap. xi, is excellent. Georg Brandes, *Main Currents in 19th-Century Literature* (trans. 1905) started a school of denigration (which E. M. Forster encouraged).

(27) **William**. See STOWELL.

(28) **William Bell**. See SCOTT (4).

(29) **Winfield** (1786-1866), American soldier, born near Petersburg, Virginia, was admitted to the bar in 1807, but obtained a commission as artillery captain in 1808. As major-general, he framed the ' General Regulations ' and introduced French tactics and helped (1839) to settle the disputed boundary line of Maine and New Brunswick. He succeeded to the chief command of the army in 1841. He took Vera Cruz, March 26, 1847, put Santa Anna to flight, and entered the Mexican capital in triumph, September 14. Unsuccessful Whig candidate for the presidency (1852), he retained nominal command of the army until October 1861. See his Memoirs (1864) and the Life by M. J. Wright (1894).

SCOTT-MONCRIEFF, (1) **Charles Kenneth Michael** (1889-1930), British translator into English of Proust, Stendhal, Pirandello, &c., was educated at Winchester and Edinburgh University, and was on the staff of *The Times* (1921-23).

(2) **Sir Colin Campbell**, K.C.S.I., K.C.M.G. (1836-1916), Scottish engineer and administrator, had a great hand in Egyptian irrigation, and in 1892-1902 was under-secretary for Scotland. See Life by M. A. Hollings (1917).

SCOTUS. See DUNS, ERIGENA, MARIANUS.

SCRIABIN, **Alexander**, *skryah'byin* (1872-1915), Russian composer and pianist, born at Moscow, studied at the conservatoire with Rachmaninov and Medtner and was professor of the Pianoforte (1898-1904). His compositions include three symphonies, two tone poems, ten sonatas, studies and preludes. His piano music is technically highly original, but he increasingly relied on extramusical factors and applied religion, occultism (and even light) in *Prometheus* and other tone poems. See study by A. E. Hull (1916).

SCRIBE, **Augustin Eugène**, *skreeb* (1791-1861), French dramatist, born in Paris, was intended for the law. After 1816 his productions became so popular that he established a type of theatre workshop in which numerous *collaborateurs* worked under his supervision turning out plays by ' mass-production ' methods. His plots are interesting and his dialogue light and sparkling, if in modern eyes highly artificial. The best known are *Le Verre d'eau* (1840), *Adrienne Lecouvreur* (1848), *Bataille des dames* (1851), &c. Scribe also wrote novels and composed the *libretti* for sixty operas, including *Masaniello, Fra Diavolo, Robert le Diable, Les Huguenots, Le Prophète*, &c. See Life by Legouvé (1874), and study by N. C. Arvin (1924).

SCRIBLERUS. See ARBUTHNOT.

SCRIBNER, Charles (1821–71), American publisher, born in New York, graduated at Princeton in 1840, and in 1846 founded with Isaac Baker the New York publishing firm bearing his name. *Scribner's Magazine* dates from 1887. His three sons continued the business.

SCRIPPS. Family of American newspaper publishers: **James Edmund** (1835–1906), born in London, was the founder of the *Detroit Evening News*. He was associated with his half-brother, **Edward Wyllis** (1854–1926), in the foundation of many newspapers, notably at St Louis and Cleveland. His sister, **Ellen Browning** (1836–1932), born in London, served on many of the family newspapers. The family interest passed to **Robert Paine** (1895–1938), Edward's son. The Scripps were first in the field of syndicated material with the Newspaper Enterprises Association (1902).

SCROGGS, Sir William (1623–83), English judge, born at Deddington, Oxfordshire, chief justice of the King's Bench from 1678, was notorious for cruelty and partiality during the ' Popish Plot ' trials (see OATES). In 1680 he was impeached, but removed from office by the king on a pension.

SCROPE, *skroop,* a north of England family that produced Richard le Scrope, chancellor in 1378 and 1381–82; Richard le Scrope (*c.* 1350–1405), Archbishop of York, beheaded for conspiracy against Henry IV; and Henry Lord Scrope, warden of the West Marches under Queen Elizabeth.

SCUDDER, (1) Horace Elisha (1862–1902), American storyteller, biographer, historian, editor, &c., was born at Boston, Mass.

(2) **Janet** (1875–1968), American sculptor, known for her statues of children and her sculptured fountains.

(3) **Samuel Hubbard** (1837–1911), American entomologist, an authority on fossil insects, also wrote on the Orthoptera and Lepidoptera.

SCUDÉRY, *skü-day-ree,* (1) **Georges de** (1601–1667), French writer, brother of (2), born at Le Havre, after a brief military career wrote a number of plays, which achieved some success. In 1637 his *Observations sur le Cid* led to a controversy with Corneille. He later wrote novels and had some small share in his sister's works, which first appeared under his name.

(2) **Madeleine de** (1608–1701), French novelist, sister of (1), was left an orphan at six, came to Paris *c.* 1630 and with her brother was accepted into the literary society of Mme de Rambouillet's *salon.* From 1644 to 1647 she was in Marseilles with her brother. She had begun her literary career with the romance *Ibrahim ou l'illustre Bassa* (1641), but her most famous work was the ten-volume *Artamène ou le Grand Cyrus* (1649–

1659), followed by *Clélie* (1654–60). These highly artificial, ill-constructed pieces, overladen with pointless dialogue, were popular at the court because of their sketches of and skits on public personages. See Lives by MacDougall (1938) and Mongrédien (1946).

SEABORG, Glenn Theodore (1912–), American nuclear chemist and physicist, professor of Chemistry at Berkeley, California, since 1945, helped to discover the transuranic elements plutonium (1940), americium and curium (1944). By bombarding the last two with alpha rays he produced the elements berkelium and californium in 1950. He was awarded the Nobel prize in 1951.

SEABURY, Samuel (1729–96), American divine, born at Groton, Conn., graduated at Yale in 1748, studied medicine at Edinburgh, and received orders in England in 1753. Three years a missionary of the S.P.G., in 1757 he became rector of Jamaica, Long Island, and in 1767 of Westchester, New York. Despite imprisonment for his loyalty to Britain which he maintained through the War of American Independence as a royalist army chaplain, he was elected first bishop of Connecticut in 1783. The Church of England refusing to consecrate him because he could not take the Oath of Allegiance, three bishops of the Scottish Episcopal Church performed the ceremony at Aberdeen (1784). See *Memoir* by W. J. Seabury (1909).

SEAMAN, Sir Owen, 1st Bart. (1861–1936), was educated at Shrewsbury and Clare College, Cambridge, became professor of Literature at Newcastle (1890), was *Punch* editor (1906–32). His parodies and *vers de société*, which include *Paulopostprandials* (1883), *In Cap and Bells* (1889), *From the Home Front* (1918), &c., rank him with Calverley.

SEARLE, serl, (1) Humphrey (1915–), English composer, born in Oxford, studied at the Royal College of Music and in Vienna, became musical adviser to Sadler's Wells Ballet in 1951. He has written *Twentieth Century Counterpoint*, and a study of the music of Liszt. An exponent of the ' twelve note system ', he has composed several symphonies, a piano concerto and a trilogy of works for speaker and orchestra to words by Edith Sitwell and James Joyce.

(2) **Ronald William Fordham** (1920–), English artist, born in Cambridge. He served in World War II with the Royal Engineers and the drawings he made during his three years' imprisonment by the Japanese helped to establish his reputation as a serious artist. After the war he soon became widely known as the creator of the macabre schoolgirls of ' St Trinians '. He joined the staff of *Punch* in 1956.

SEBASTIAN, St (d. 288), was a native of Narbonne, a captain of the praetorian guard, and secretly a Christian. Diocletian, hearing that he favoured Christians, ordered him to be slain. But the archers did not quite kill him: a woman named Irene nursed him back to life. When he upbraided the tyrant for his cruelty, Diocletian had him beaten to death with rods.

SEBASTIAN (1554–78), king of Portugal, a grandson of the Emperor Charles V, fell in battle against the Moors at Alcazar in Algeria; but soon doubt was thrown upon his death, and impostors began to crop up—first in 1584 a son of a potter; then Matheus Alvares, a sort of brigand-insurgent; in 1594 a Spanish cook; then one Catizzone, a Calabrian, hanged in 1603. The popular belief that Sebastian would come again revived in 1807–08 during the French occupation, and again in 1838 in Brazil. See Life by A. Figueiredo (1925).

SÉBASTIANI, François Horace Bastien, Count, *say-bast-ya-nee* (1772–1851), French soldier and diplomat, born near Bastia in Corsica, became one of Napoleon's most devoted partisans. He fought at Marengo, was wounded at Austerlitz, twice undertook missions to Turkey (1802–06), commanded an army corps in Spain, and distinguished himself in the Russian campaign (1812) and at Leipzig. He joined Napoleon on his return from Elba, but after 1830 was twice in the ministry, and was ambassador at Naples and London. He was made marshal of France in 1840.

SEBASTIANO DEL PIOMBO. See PIOMBO.

SÉBILLOT, Paul, *say-bee-yō* (1843–1918), French folklorist, born at Matignon, Côtes-du-Nord, abandoned law for painting, and from 1870 to 1883 exhibited in the Salon. He then held a post in the ministry of public works, became Chevalier of the *Légion d'honneur* 1889, and devoting himself to the study of Breton folk tales, published the standard work *Le Folklore de France* (1907), &c.

SECCHI, Angelo, *sek-kee* (1818–78), Italian astronomer, born at Reggio and trained as a Jesuit, became professor of Physics at Washington, U.S., and in 1849 director of the observatory at the Collegio Romano. He originated classification of stars by spectrum analysis.

SECKENDORFF, (1) Friedrich Heinrich (1673–1763), Austrian soldier and diplomat, nephew of (2), defeated the French at Klausen (1735) and fought in the Bavarian army during the War of the Austrian Succession.

(2) **Veit Ludwig von** (1626–92), German statesman, uncle of (1), served the princes of Saxony and Brandenburg, was chancellor of the University of Halle, and wrote a Latin compendium of church history (1664) and a work *De Lutheranismo* (1688).

SEDGWICK, (1) Adam (1785–1873), English geologist, born at Dent, fifth wrangler at Trinity College, Cambridge, in 1808, became a fellow in 1810, Woodwardian professor of Geology in 1818, a canon of Norwich in 1834, and vice-regent of Trinity in 1847. His best work was on *British Palaeozoic Fossils* (1854); with Murchison he studied the Alps and the Lake District. He strongly opposed Darwin's *Origin of Species*. See his *Life and Letters* by Clark and Hughes (1890).

(2) **Anne Douglas** (1873–1935), American novelist, born at Englewood, New Jersey, studied painting in Paris and, influenced by Henry James, wrote *Tante* (1911), *The Encounter* (1914), *Dark Hester* (1929), &c., and volumes of short stories. See her autobiographical *Portrait in Letters*, ed. by her husband, B. de Selincourt (1936).

SEDLEY, Sir Charles (1639–1701), English courtier and poet, born probably in London, was notorious at court for debauchery and wit. He joined William III at the Revolution, out of *gratitude* to James, who had seduced his daughter and made her Countess of Dorchester. ' Since his Majesty has made my daughter a countess ' said he, ' it is fit I should do all I can to make his daughter a queen.' He is remembered less for his plays—*The Mulberry Garden, Antony and Cleopatra, Bellamira*—than for a few songs and *vers de société*. See study (1927) by V. de Sola Pinto, who also edited the *Works* (1928).

SEEBOHM, Frederic (1833–1912), English historian, was called to the bar in 1856, but became partner in a bank at Hitchin. He was author of *The Oxford Reformers of 1498* (1867), *The English Village Community* (1883), &c. His brother, **Henry** (1832–95), was ornithologist and traveller in Greece, Asia Minor, Norway, Siberia, &c.

SEEFRIED, Irmgard, *zay'freet* (1919–), Austrian soprano, born in Köngetried, Germany, famed for her performances with Vienna State Opera, especially in the operas of Mozart and Richard Strauss.

SEELEY, Sir John Robert (1834–95), English historian, third son of the publisher, Robert Benton Seeley (1798–1886). He was educated at City of London School and at Cambridge. In 1863 he became professor of Latin in University College, London, in 1869 of Modern History at Cambridge. His *Ecce Homo* (1865), a popular Life of Christ, caused much controversy in religious circles. Other works include the authoritative *Life and Times of Stein* (1874) and *The Expansion of England* (1883). He was knighted in 1894. See memoir by Prothero prefixed to Seeley's *Growth of British Policy* (1895).

SEELIGER, Hugo, *zay'-* (1849–1924), German astronomer, born at Bielitz, professor of Astronomy at Munich, is best known for his work on star distribution and for his theory for the birth of a nova.

SEFERIADES, George (pseud. Seferis) (1900–1971), Greek poet and diplomat, born in Smyrna, educated at Athens and the Sorbonne. Ambassador to the Lebanon (1953–1957) and the U.K. (1957–62), he wrote lyrical poetry, collected in *The Turning Point* (1931), *Mythistorema* (1935), &c. He translated T. S. Eliot's *Waste Land* into Greek. In 1963 he was awarded the Nobel prize for literature.

SEFSTRÖM, Nils Gabriel (1787–1854), Swedish physician and chemist, in 1831 discovered the element vanadium in a specimen of soft iron.

SEGONZAC, André Dunoyer de, *sé-gõ-zac* (1884–), French painter and engraver, born at Boussy-Saint-Antoine. He was influenced by Courbet and Corot, and produced many delicate watercolour landscapes, etchings and illustrations. His series of engravings of *Beaches* was published in 1935, and his work is represented in the Musée d'art moderne, Paris.

SEGOVIA, Andres, *se-gō'vee-a* (1894–), Spanish guitarist, born in Limares. Influenced by the Spanish nationalist composers, he has evolved a revolutionary guitar technique permitting the performance of a wide range of music, and many modern composers have composed works for him. See monograph by Gavoty (1956).

SEGRAVE, Sir Henry O'Neal de Hane, *see'-* (1896–1930), British racing driver, born of Irish parentage at Baltimore, U.S.A., was educated at Eton and Sandhurst, served in the Royal Flying Corps and was wounded in 1916, when he became technical secretary to the air minister. A leading postwar racing driver, he helped to design the Sunbeam car, in which he broke the land speed record with a speed of 203·9 m.p.h., raising this to 231 in 1929, when he was knighted. He was killed in his boat *Miss England* on Lake Windermere, June 13, 1930, when on a trial run, during which he had surpassed the world motorboat speed record.

SEGRÈ, Emilio, *seg'ray* (1905–), Italian-American physicist, a pupil of Fermi (q.v.), fled from the Mussolini régime to the U.S.A. and took American nationality in 1944, having already been on the staff of the University of California for several years. He shared the 1959 Nobel prize with Owen Chamberlain for researches on the antiproton.

SEGUIER, William, *seg-yay* (1771–1843), English artist, born in London of Huguenot descent, studied under George Morland, but abandoned painting for the art of the restorer and connoisseur, and helped George IV to gather together the Royal Collection. When the National Gallery was inaugurated, he became its first keeper. As superintendent of the British Institution, he was succeeded at his death by his brother **John** (1785–1856), also a painter and his partner in the picture-restoring business.

SÉGUR, *say-gür,* a French family, distinguished in arms and letters, some of whose members were Huguenots.

(1) **Henri François,** Comte de Ségur (1689–1751), was a general in the War of the Austrian Succession.

(2) **Philippe Henri,** Marquis de Ségur-Ponchat (1724–1801), son of (1), fought in the Seven Years' War, and became marshal in 1783.

(3) **Louis Philippe,** Comte de Ségur d'Aguesseau (1753–1820), son of (2), ambassador at St Petersburg, was a great favourite with Catharine II, served in the American War of Independence, and hailed the French revolution. Among his writings (33 vols.) are *La Politique de tous les cabinets de l'Europe* (1793), &c.

(4) **Philippe Paul** (1780–1873), son of (3), was a general of the first empire, and wrote a history (1824) of the Russian campaign of 1812, *Histoire de Russie et de Pierre le Grand* (1829), &c. See Life by Taillandier (1875) and his Reminiscences (Eng. trans. 1895).

(5) **Pierre** (1853–1916), French historian.

(6) **Sophie Rostopchine,** Comtesse de Ségur (1799–1874), author of *Les Mémoires d'un âne* and many other writings for the young.

SEIBER, Mátyás, *zī'-* (1905–60), Hungarian-born British composer, born at Budapest, studied there under Kodály, and was a private music teacher (1925) and professor of Jazz (1928–33) at Hoch's Conservatory at Frankfurt-am-Main. He settled in Britain in 1935 and in 1942 became a tutor at Morley College, London. He gained only belated recognition as a composer, with strong musical affinities to Bartok and Schönberg. His compositions include three string quartets, of which the second (1935) is the best known, other chamber works, piano music and songs and the *Ulysses* cantata (1946–47) based on Joyce's novel. He was killed in a motor accident in South Africa.

SEJANUS. See TIBERIUS.

SELBORNE, (1) Roundell Palmer, 1st Earl of (1812–95), English jurist and hymnologist, father of (2), born at Mixbury, Oxfordshire, was solicitor-general (1861), attorney-general (1863–66), but his dislike of Gladstone's Irish Church policy delayed his promotion to lord chancellor (1872–74, 1880–85). He reformed the judicators and wrote hymnological and liturgical studies. See his *Memorials* (1898).

(2) **William Waldegrave Palmer, 2nd Earl of** (1859–1942), English politician, son of (1), was under-secretary for the Colonies (1895–1900) first lord of the Admiralty (1900–05), high commissioner for S. Africa (1905–10), president of the Board of Agriculture (1915–1916), warden of Winchester (1920–25).

(3) **Roundell Cecil Palmer, 3rd Earl of** (1887–), son of (2), was minister of works (1940–42) and minister of economic warfare (1942–45).

SELBY-BIGGE, Sir John. See BIGGE.

SELDEN, John (1584–1654), English historian and antiquary, born near Worthing, studied at Oxford and London, where he acquired wealth, yet found time for profound and wide study. In 1610 appeared his *Duello,* or *Single Combat*; his *Titles of Honour* (1614) is still an authority. *Analecton Anglo-Britann-icon* (1615) dealt with the civil government of Britain previous to the Norman Conquest. In 1617 appeared his erudite work on the Syrian gods, *De Diis Syriis.* His *History of Tithes* (1618), demolishing their divine right, brought upon his head the fulminations of the clergy, and was suppressed by the privy council. In 1621 Selden was imprisoned for advising the parliament to repudiate King James's doctrine that their privileges were originally royal grants, in 1623 he was elected member for Lancaster. In 1628 he helped to draw up the Petition of Right, and the year after he was committed to the Tower with Eliot, Holles and the rest. In 1635 he dedicated to the king his *Mare Clausum* (an answer to the *Mare Liberum* of Grotius). In 1640 he entered the Long Parliament for Oxford University, and opposed the policy that led to the expulsion of the bishops from the House of Lords and finally to the abolition of Episcopacy. He took no direct part in the impeachment of Strafford and voted against the Attainder Bill, and had no share in Laud's prosecution. He sat as a lay member in the Westminster Assembly (1643), and was appointed keeper of the records in the Tower and (1644) an Admiralty commissioner. In 1646 he subscribed the Covenant. In 1647 he was appointed a university visitor, and sought to moderate the fanaticism of his colleagues. After the execution of Charles I, of which he disapproved, he took little share in public matters. He was buried in the Temple Church. He had also written in Latin books on the Arundel Marbles (1624) and on Hebrew law (1634–50), besides posthumous tracts and treatises, of which the most valuable is his *Table Talk* (1689). See Singer's biographical preface to his works (1726), Aikin's *Lives of Selden and Usher* (1811), G. W. Johnson's *Memoir* (1835), and S. H. Reynolds's introduction to his edition of the *Table Talk* (Oxford 1892).

SELEUCUS, the name of six kings of the Seleucidae, the dynasty to whom fell that portion of Alexander the Great's Asiatic conquests which included Syria, part of Asia Minor, Persia, Bactria, &c. See ANTIOCHUS.

Seleucus I, surnamed Nicator (*c.* 358–280 B.C.), Macedonian general under Alexander the Great, obtained Babylonia, to which he added Susiana, Media and Asia Minor, but was assassinated in 280 B.C. He founded Greek and Macedonian colonies, and also built Antioch, Seleucia on the Tigris, &c.

Seleucus II, surnamed Callinicus (*c.* 247–226 B.C.), son of Antiochus II, was beset by Ptolemy of Egypt, his own half-brother, and the Parthians, and lost Asia Minor and Parthia.

SELFRIDGE, Harry Gordon (1858?–1947), British merchant, born at Ripon, Wisconsin. Educated privately, he joined a trading firm in Chicago, brought into the business new ideas and great organizing ability, and in 1892 was made a junior partner. While visiting London in 1906 he bought a site in Oxford Street, and built upon it the large store, opened in March 1909, which bears his name. He took British nationality in 1937. See Life by R. Pound (1960).

SELIM. The name of three sultans of Turkey:

Selim I (1467–1520), in 1512 dethroned his father, Bajazet II, and caused him, his own brothers, and nephews to be put to death. In 1514 he declared war against Persia, and took Diarbekir and Kurdistan. He conquered in 1517 Egypt, Syria and the Hejaz, with Medina and Mecca; won from the Abbasid calif at Cairo the headship of the Mohammedan world; chastized the insolence of the Janizaries; sought to improve the condition of the peoples he had conquered; and cultivated the poetic art. He was succeeded by his son, Soliman the Magnificent.

Selim II (1524–74), a degraded sot, succeeded his father, Soliman, in 1566; he owed whatever renown belongs to his reign to his father's old statesmen and generals. Arabia was conquered in 1570, Cyprus in 1571, but the Turkish fleet was annihilated by Don John of Austria in 1571 off Lepanto. During this reign occurred the first collision of Turks with Russians; three-fourths of the Turkish army were lost in the Astrakhan expedition.

Selim III (1761–1807), succeeding his brother in 1789, prosecuted the war with Russia; but the Austrians joined the Russians, and Belgrade surrendered to them, while the Russians took Bucharest, Bender, Akerman and Ismail. Numerous reforms

were projected; but the people were hardly prepared for them, and Selim's projects cost him his throne and life.

SELKIRK, (1) Alexander or Alexander Selcraig (1676–1721), Scottish sailor, whose story is supposed to have suggested the Robinson Crusoe of Defoe, was a native of Largo in Fife. After getting into several scrapes at home, in his twenty-eighth year he joined the South Sea buccaneers. In 1704 he quarrelled with his captain, and at his own request was put ashore on Juan Fernández. Having lived alone here four years and four months, he was at last taken off by Thomas Dover (q.v.). He returned to Largo in 1712, and at his death was a lieutenant on a man-of-war. See Life by Howell (1829).

(2) **J. B.**, pseud. of **James Brown** (1832–1904), Scottish poet, born in Galashiels but a lifelong dweller in Selkirk. Besides poems (1869, &c.) he published two prose volumes.

(3) **Thomas Douglas, 5th Earl of** (1771–1820), Scottish colonizer, settled emigrants from the Scottish Highlands in Prince Edward Island (1803) and in the Red River Valley, Manitoba, although twice evicted by the Northwest Fur Company (1815–16). See his *Diary*, 1803–04 (Toronto 1958), and account of his work by C. Martin (1916).

SELLAR, William Young (1825–90), born near Golspie, was educated at Edinburgh Academy, Glasgow University and Balliol, graduating with a classical first. He filled for four years (1859–63) the Greek chair at St Andrews, and was then elected to the Latin chair at Edinburgh. He made his name widely known by his brilliant *Roman Poets of the Republic* (1863; enlarged 1881), which was followed by *The Roman Poets of the Augustan Age—Virgil* (1877) and *Horace and the Elegiac Poets* (1892), the latter edited by his nephew, Andrew Lang, with memoir.

SELLON, Priscilla Lydia (1821–76), English founder in 1849 at Plymouth of the second Anglican sisterhood, its spiritual director Dr Pusey. See Life by T. J. Williams (1950).

SELOUS, Frederick Courtenay, *se-loos'* (1851–1917), English explorer and big-game hunter, born in London, first visited South Africa in 1871. He wrote *A Hunter's Wanderings in Africa* (1881), *Travel and Adventure in Southeast Africa*, &c., fought in Matabeleland (1893, 1895), and in 1916 won the D.S.O. and fell in action in East Africa. See Life by J. G. Millais (1918).

SELWYN, (1) George (1719–91), English wit, was educated at Eton and Hertford College, Oxford, whence, after making the Grand Tour, he was expelled (1745) for a blasphemous travesty of the Eucharist. He entered parliament in 1747, and sided generally with the Court party. At Paris he had the *entrée* of the best society, while among his intimates were the Duke of Queensberry, Horace Walpole and 'Gilly' Williams. He died penitent. See Lives by H. J. Jesse (1843) and S. P. Kerr (1909).

(2) **George Augustus** (1809–78), English divine, born at Hampstead, was educated at Eton and St John's College, Cambridge, where he rowed in the first university boat-race (1829), and graduated in 1831. In 1841,

he was consecrated first and only Bishop of New Zealand and Melanesia of whose church he played a large part in settling the constitution. In 1867 he was appointed Bishop of Lichfield, where upon his initiative the first Diocesan Conference in which the laity were duly represented met in 1868. Selwyn College, Cambridge, was founded (1882) in his memory. See Lives by Tucker (2 vols. 1879) and Creighton (1923). His son, **John Richardson** (1844–98), was Bishop of Melanesia 1877, and master of Selwyn College, Cambridge.

SEMENOV, Nikolai, *sem-yo'nof* (1896–), Russian scientist, born at Saratov, graduated at Petrograd in 1917 and after a spell on the staff of Leningrad Physical Technical Institute (1920–31) joined the Institute of Chemical Physics of the Soviet Academy of Sciences, later being made its director. An expert in molecular physics, he carried out important research on chain-reactions, for which he was awarded the Nobel prize, jointly with Hinshelwood, in 1956.

SEMIRAMIS, *-mir'-* (9th cent. B.C.), wife of Ninus, with whom she is supposed to have founded Nineveh. The historical germ of the story seems to be the three years' regency of Sammu-ramat (811–808 B.C.), widow of Shamshi-Adad V, but the details are legendary, derived from Ctesias and the Greek historians, with elements of the Astarte myth. See Lenormant, *La Légende de Sémiramis* (1873).

SEMLER, Johann Salomo (1725–91), German theologian, born at Saalfeld, in 1753 became professor of Theology at Halle. He exercised a profound influence as pioneer of the historical method in biblical criticism. He was distinctively a rationalist, but he sincerely believed in revelation. In insisting on the distinction of the Jewish and Pauline types of Christianity he anticipated the Tübingen school. See his Autobiography (1781–82) and W. Nigg, *Die Kirchengeschichtsschreibung* (1934).

SEMMELWEISS, Ignaz Philipp, *zem'ĕl-vīs* (1818–65), Hungarian obstetrician, born at Budapest, studied there and at Vienna. Appalled by the heavy death-rate in the Vienna maternity hospital where he worked, he introduced antiseptics. The death-rate fell from 12% to 1½%, but his superiors would not accept his conclusions and he was compelled to leave Vienna and return to Pest. He contracted septicaemia in a finger and died in a mental hospital near Vienna from the disease he had spent his life in combating. See Life by W. J. Sinclair (1909), and F. G. Slaughter, *Immortal Magyar* (1950).

SEMMES, Raphael, *sems* (1809–77), American sailor, commander of the Confederate States cruiser *Alabama*, entered the U.S. navy in 1826, but was called to the bar. He served again during the Mexican war, and in 1858 was made secretary of the Lighthouse Board. On the outbreak of the Civil War he first commanded the *Sumter*; then, taking over the *Alabama* at the Azores (August 24, 1862), proceeded to capture 65 vessels, nearly all of which were sunk or burned, and to destroy property estimated at $6,000,000. But it was by the heavy insurance for war risks, and still more by the difficulty in getting freights, that the *Alabama's* career caused almost

incalculable injury to the U.S. marine. On June 19, 1864, the *Alabama* was sunk in action off Cherbourg by the U.S. cruiser *Kearsarge*; but its commander escaped. Later he edited a paper, was a professor, and practised law in Mobile. He wrote several books on service afloat. See Arthur Sinclair, *Two Years on the Alabama* (1896).

SEMPER, (1) Gottfried (1803–73), German architect, born in Hamburg, deserted law for architecture and travelled in France, Italy and Greece. In 1834 he was appointed professor at Dresden, but his part in the revolution of 1848 compelled him to flee to England, where he designed the Victoria and Albert Museum. He eventually settled in Vienna, where the Burgtheater, the imperial palace and two museums, as well as the art gallery and railway station at Dresden, testify to his adaptation of the Italian renaissance style. See *Monograph* by C. Lipsius (1880).

(2) **Karl** (1832–93), German naturalist, born at Altona, studied at Kiel, Hanover and Würzburg, and, after travelling in the Philippines and South Sea Islands, became in 1868 professor of Zoology at Würzburg. He wrote on the Philippines, on several problems of comparative anatomy, and *The Natural Conditions of Existence as they affect Animal Life* (trans. 1880).

SEMPILL, (1) Francis (1616?–1682), Scottish minor poet, son of (3), author of *The Banishment of Povertie*.

(2) **Robert** (1530?–1595), Scottish author of witty ballads full of coarse vigour, e.g., *The Legend of a Lymaris Life* and *Sege of the Castel of Edinburgh*. He was an enemy of Queen Mary and wrote satirical Reformation broadsides, such as the *Life of the Tulchene Bishop of St Andrews*.

(3) **Robert** (1595?–1665?), father of (1). He revived the methods of the Scottish *Makaris* and set the fashion for future vernacular elegies. He wrote *Habbie Simson, The Blythesome Bridal* (also attributed to (1)), and, possibly, *Maggie Lauder*.

SEN, Keshub Chunder (1838–84), Indian religious reformer, a native of Bengal, about 1858 was attracted by the Brahma Samâj (see RAMMOHUN ROY), and in 1866 founded the more liberal ' Brahma Samâj of India '. He visited England in 1870. In 1878 a schism broke out in his church, caused largely by his autocratic temper; and his last years brought disappointment. See Max-Müller's *Biographical Essays* (1884).

SÉNANCOUR, Étienne Pivert de, *say-nã-koor* (1770–1846), French author, born in Paris. After nine years in Switzerland, he returned to Paris about 1798. His fame rests securely on three books: *Rêveries sur la nature primitive de l'homme* (1799), *Obermann* (1804) and *Libres Méditations d'un solitaire inconnu*. In the first we see the student of Rousseau weighed down by the dogma of necessity. In *Obermann* the atheism and dogmatic fatalism of the *Rêveries* have given place to universal doubt no less overwhelming. Nowhere is the desolating ' mal du siècle ' more effectively expressed than in this book, which is yet completely original in its delicate feeling for nature, and its melancholy eloquence. The influence of Goethe's

Werther is persistent in his work. Sénancour, neglected in his day, found fit audience in George Sand, Sainte-Beuve and Matthew Arnold.

SENDERENS, Jean Baptiste (1856–1937), French chemist, born at Barbachen, Hautes-Pyrénées, with Sabatier discovered the hydrogenation of oils by catalysis in 1899.

SENEBIER, Jean, *sě-ně-byay* (1742–1809), Swiss pastor, chemist and librarian in Geneva, in 1782 first demonstrated the basic principle of photosynthesis.

SENECA, *sen'e-ka,* (1) **Lucius** (or **Marcus**) **Annaeus,** called ' **the Elder** ' (*c.* 55 B.C.–*c.* A.D. 40), Roman rhetorician, father of (2), born at Cordova, Spain. Besides a history of Rome, now lost, he wrote *Oratorum et Rhetorum Sententiae, Divisiones, Colores Controversiae* (partly lost) and *Suasoriae*. His other sons were M. Annaeus Novatus and by adoption L. Iunius Gallio (of the Acts xviii. 12); also M. Annaeus Mela, father of Lucan, the poet.

(2) **Lucius Annaeus,** called ' **the Younger** ' (*c.* 5 B.C.–A.D. 65), Roman philosopher and statesman, son of (1), born in Cordova, Spain, and educated for the bar in Rome. After years of devotion to philosophy and rhetoric, he entered the Curia, but in A.D. 41 lost the favour he had won with Claudius by getting involved in a state trial and was banished to Corsica, whence he returned after eight years. Entrusted by Agrippina with the education of her son Nero, he acquired over the youth a strong and salutary influence, and by Nero (now emperor) was made consul in A.D. 57. His high moral aims gradually incurred the aversion of the emperor, and he withdrew from public life. An attempt by Nero to poison him having failed, he was drawn into the Pisonian conspiracy, accused, and condemned. Left free to choose his mode of death, he elected to open his veins, A.D. 65. In philosophy he inclined to the Stoic system, with Epicurean modifications. He employed an epigrammatic style, which despite his moralizing lacked depth. His writings include *De Ira, De Consolatione, De Providentia, De Animi Tranquillitate, De Constantia Sapientis, De Clementia, De Brevitate Vitae, De Vita Beata, De Otio aut Secessu Sapientis, De Beneficiis, Epistolae ad Lucilium, Apocolocyntosis* (a scathing satire on the Emperor Claudius) and *Quaestiones Naturales*. Seneca was also a poet, if we may accept as his the epigrams and the eight tragedies (*Hercules Furens, Thyestes, Phaedra, Oedipus, Troades, Medea, Agamemnon, Hercules Oetaeus,* and part of a *Thebais*) usually comprised among his *opera omnia*. The publication of the *Tenne Tragedies* in 1581 was important in the evolution of Elizabethan drama, which took from it the five-act division, as well as the horrors and the rhetoric. See C. M. Barlow, *Seneca's Correspondence with St Paul* (1938) and T. S. Eliot, *Selected Essays* (1932).

SENEFELDER, Aloys, *zay'ně-fel-der* (1771–1834), Bavarian inventor, born in Prague, and successively actor, author and printer, about 1796 invented lithography, and after various trials in 1806 opened an establishment of his own in Munich, where he died.

SENIOR, Nassau William (1790–1864), English economist and ' prince of interviewers ', born at Compton Beauchamp, Berks, was educated at Eton and Magdalen College, Oxford. In 1819 he was called to the bar; in 1825–30, and again in 1847–62, was professor of Political Economy at Oxford; in 1832 was appointed a Poor-law commissioner; and in 1836–53 was a master in chancery. He stressed the importance of the last hour's work in the cotton factories and opposed the trade unions. His publications include *On the Cost of Obtaining Money* (1830), *Value of Money* (1840), as well as many biographical and critical essays. See study by S. L. Levy (1928).

SENNACHERIB, *-nak'-* (d. 681 B.C.), king of Assyria, succeeded his father, Sargon, in 705 B.C. He invaded Judaea and besieged Hezekiah in Jerusalem. His great achievement was the rebuilding of Nineveh, and the making of the embankment of the Tigris, canals, water-courses, &c. He was slain by one of his sons.

SENUSRIT. See SESOSTRIS.

SEPÚLVEDA, Juan Ginés de (1490–1574), Spanish historian, born near Córdoba, became historiographer to Charles V, preceptor to the future Philip II, and a canon of Salamanca. He was a champion of humanism. His Latin works include histories of Charles V and Philip II, a Life of Albornoz, and a History of Spain in the New World.

SÉQUARD. See BROWN-SÉQUARD.

SEQUOYAH, *se-kwoy'ě* or **George Guess** (*c.* 1770–1843), American half-Cherokee scholar, who in 1826 invented a Cherokee syllabary of eighty-five characters. His name was given to a genus of giant coniferous trees (*Sequoia*) and to a national park. See Life by G. E. Foster (1886).

SERAO, Matilde, *say-rah'ō* (1856–1927), Italian novelist, was born at Patras in Greece, the daughter of an Italian political refugee and a Greek, and in 1880 she married Edoardo Scarfoglio, editor of a Neapolitan paper. Her tales, mostly of Neapolitan life, include *Cuore Infermo, Fantasia, Le Leggende Napolitane, Riccardo Joanna, All' Erta Sentinella, Il Paese di Cuccagna*. See Life by R. Garzia (1916).

SERF, St, a Scottish saint who founded the church of Culross between 697 and 706, but who yet figures in the legend of St Kentigern (q.v.).

SERGEYEV-TSENSKY, Sergey (1875–1958), Russian novelist, born in Tambov province, from a Dostoevskian passion for morbid characterization, as in *The Tundra* (1902), developed greater simplicity of style and social sense in the massive ten-volume novel sequence, *Transfiguration* (1914–40), which won him the Stalin prize in 1942.

SERRANO, Francisco, Duke de la Torre, *ser-rah'nō* (1810–85), Spanish statesman, fought against the Carlists and, nominally a liberal, favoured by Isabella, played a conspicuous part in various ministries. Banished in 1866, he in 1868 drove out the queen, and was regent until the accession of Amadeus of Savoy (1870). He waged successful war against the Carlists in 1872 and 1874; and again regent (1874), resigned the power into the hands of Alfonso XII. See Life by Marqués de Villa-Urrutia (1932).

SERRES, Olivia. See OLIVE (PRINCESS).

SERTORIUS, Quintus (123–72 B.C.), Roman soldier, born in Nursia in the Sabine country, fought with Marius in Gaul (102 B.C.), supported him against Sulla, then led an adventurous life in Spain, where he headed a successful rising of natives and Roman refugees, holding out against Sulla's commanders for eight years till he was assassinated. See Life by A. Schulten (1926).

SERTÜRNER, Friedrich Wilhelm Adam (1783–1841), German chemist, born at Neuhaus near Paderborn, in 1805 isolated morphine from opium and proved that organic bases contained nitrogen.

SERVETUS, Michael, *-vay'-* (1511–53), Spanish theologian and physician, born at Tudela, worked largely in France and Switzerland. In *De Trinitatis Erroribus* (1531) and *Christianismi Restitutio* (1553) he denied the Trinity and the divinity of Christ; he escaped the Inquisition but was burnt by Calvin at Geneva for heresy. He studied medicine at Paris and discovered the pulmonary circulation of the blood. See Life by W. Osler (1910), and E. M. Wilson, *A History of Unitarianism* (1945).

SERVICE, Robert William (1874–1958), English-born Canadian poet, born at Preston, went to Canada, travelled as a reporter for the *Toronto Star*, served as ambulance driver in World War I and wrote popular verse, such as *Rhymes of a Rolling Stone* (1912) and *The Shooting of Dangerous Dan McGrew*. He also wrote novels, of which *Ploughman of the Moon* (1945) and *Harper of Heaven* (1948) are autobiographical.

SERVIUS TULLIUS (578–534 B.C.), 6th king of Rome, distributed all freeholders (for military purposes primarily) into tribes, classes and centuries, making property, not birth, the standard of citizenship. His reforms provoked patrician jealousy, and he was assassinated.

SESOSTRIS, or **Senusrit,** according to Greek legend an Egyptian monarch who invaded Libya, Arabia, Thrace and Scythia, subdued Ethiopia, placed a fleet on the Red Sea, and extended his dominions to India, but was possibly Sesostris I (*c.* 1980–1935 B.C.), II (*c.* 1906–1887 B.C.) and III (*c.* 1887–1849 B.C.) compounded into one heroic figure.

SESSIONS, Roger (1896–   ), American composer, born in Brooklyn, New York, studied under Ernest Bloch. From 1925 to 1933 he was in Europe, but later taught in the United States, becoming professor of Music at California University in 1945 and professor at Princeton University (1953–65). His compositions include five symphonies, a violin concerto, piano and chamber music, a one-act opera of Brecht's *The Trial of Lucellus* and a three-act opera, *Montezuma* (1959–63).

SETTLE, Elkanah (1648–1724), English dramatist, born at Dunstable, went from Oxford to London to make a living by his pen. In 1671 he made a hit by his tragedy of *Cambyses*. To annoy Dryden, Rochester got his *Empress of Morocco* played at Whitehall by the court lords and ladies. In *Absalam and Achitophel* Dryden scourged ' Doeg '

with his scorn, and Settle speedily relapsed into obscurity.

SEURAT, Georges Pierre, *sœ-rah* (1859–91), French artist, born in Paris. He studied at the École des Beaux-Arts. In 1883 he painted *Une Baignade* (in the Tate Gallery, London) and in 1885–86 the famous *Un Dimanche d'été à la Grande Jatte* (at Chicago). All his works were painted according to his divisionist method, called by the critics pointillist, the entire picture being composed of tiny rectangles of pure colour, which merge together when viewed from a distance. The composition was also constructed architecturally according to scientific principles. His colour theories influenced Signac, Pissarro, Degas and Renoir, but his principal achievement was the marrying of an impressionist palette to classical composition. See studies by G. Seligmann (1947) and J. Rewald (1947), his *Paintings and Drawings*, edited by D. C. Rich (1958), and C. M. de Hauke: *Seurat et son œuvre* (1963).

SEVERINI, Gino, *say-vě-ree'nee* (1883–1966), Italian artist, born at Cortona. He studied in Rome and Paris and signed the first Futurist manifesto in 1910, associating with Balla and Boccioni, with whom he exhibited in Paris and London. After 1914 he reverted to a more representational style, which he used in fresco and mosaic work, particularly in a number of Swiss and Italian churches. From 1940 onwards he adopted a decorative cubist manner. His many publications include *Du cubisme au classicisme* (1921) and an autobiography *Tutta la vita di un pittore* (1946). See the monographs by J. Maritain (1930) and P. Courthion (1941).

SEVERN, Joseph (1793–1879), portrait and subject painter, the son of a Hoxton music master, about 1816 befriended Keats, whom he accompanied on his last journey to Rome in 1820. He was British consul in Rome (1861–1872). See books by William Sharp (1892), Lady Birkenhead (1943). His son, **Joseph Arthur Palliser** (1841–1931), who married Ruskin's cousin, was also an artist.

SEVERUS, (1) Lucius Septimius (146–211), Roman emperor, born near Leptis Magna in Africa, rose to be praetor in 178, and commander of the army in Pannonia and Illyria. After the murder of Pertinax (193) he was proclaimed emperor, marched upon Rome, utterly defeated his two rivals in 195 and 197, and between these dates made a glorious campaign in the East, and took Byzantium. In 198 he met with the most brilliant success in his campaign against the Parthians. He replaced the praetorian guard by a new guard drawn from the legions. At Rome in 202 he gave shows of unparalleled magnificence, and distributed extravagant largess. A rebellion in Britain drew him thither in 208, when he marched, it is said, to the extreme north of the island. To shield south Britain from the Meatae and Caledonians, he repaired Hadrian's wall and died soon after at Eboracum (York), February 4, 211. See also ALEXANDER SEVERUS.

(2) **Sulpicius.** See SULPICIUS.

SÉVIGNÉ, Madame de, *née* **Marie de Rabutin-Chantal,** *say-veen-yay* (1626–96), French writer, born at Paris, was early left an orphan and was carefully brought up by an uncle, the Abbé de Coulanges. She married the dissolute Marquis Henri de Sévigné (1644); but he was killed in a duel (1651). Henceforward, in the most brilliant court in the world, her thoughts were centred on her children Françoise Marguerite (b. 1646) and Charles (b. 1648). On the marriage of the former to the Comte de Grignan in 1669, she began the series of letters to her daughter which grew sadder as friend after friend passed away. She died at Grignan of smallpox, after nursing her daughter through a tedious illness. Madame de Sévigné's twenty-five years of letters reveal the inner history of the time in wonderful detail, but the most interesting thing in the whole 1600 (one-third letters to her from others) remains herself. She was religious without superstition; she had read widely and gained much from conversation. She possessed a solid understanding and strong good sense. But it needed the warm touch of affection to give her letters the freedom, the rapidity, the life of spoken words. See edition of her *Letters* ed. Hammersley (1955), and Lives by Miss Thackeray (1881), G. Boissier (1887; trans. 1882), E. Faguet (1910), M. Duclaux (1914), A. Hallays (1920), A. Tilley (1936).

SEWARD, (1) Anna (1747–1809), English poet, known as the ' Swan of Lichfield ', born at Eyam Rectory, Derby, lived from ten at Lichfield, where her father, himself a poet, became a canon. He died in 1790, but she lived on in the bishop's palace, and wrote romantic poetry. Her ' Elegy on Captain Cook ' (1780) was commended by Dr Johnson. Scott edited her works (1810). See Lives of ' the Swan ' by E. V. Lucas (1909), M. Ashmun (1931) and H. Pearson (1936).

(2) **William Henry** (1801–72), American statesman, born at Florida, N.Y., May 16, graduated at Union College in 1820, and was admitted to the bar at Utica in 1822. In 1830 he was elected to the state senate, where he led the Whig opposition to the dominant democratic party. In 1838 and 1840 he was governor of New York State; in 1849 he was elected to the U.S. senate, and re-elected in 1855. In 1850, while urging the admission of California to the Union, he declared that the national domain was devoted to liberty by ' a higher law than the constitution '. He opposed the Compromise Bill of 1850, separated himself from those Whigs who followed President Fillmore in his proslavery policy, and on the formation of the Republican party became one of its leaders. In 1860 he was a candidate for the presidential nomination, but, failing, became Lincoln's secretary of state (1861–69). The Civil War rendered the foreign relations of the United States unusually delicate, especially in view of the attitude of France and Britain. In the ' *Trent* affair ' during the Civil War he advised that the Confederate envoys should be given up to England. He protested against the fitting out of the *Alabama* and similar vessels in British ports, and declared that the United States would claim indemnities. He supported President Johnson's reconstruction policy, thereby incurring much censure from

his own party. In 1870–71 he made a tour round the world. See his Autobiography (1877), Life by his son (1895), Memoir by Baker in his *Works* (5 vols. 1853–84), and Welles, *Lincoln and Seward* (N.Y. 1874).

SEWELL, Anna (1820–78), British novelist, born in Yarmouth, was an invalid for most of her life. Her *Black Beauty* (1877), the story of a horse, written as a plea for the more humane treatment of animals, is perhaps the most famous fictional work about horses. See study by M. J. Baker (1956).

SEXTUS EMPIRICUS (fl. A.D. 200–250), Greek physician and philosophical sceptic, who lived at Alexandria and Athens, as physician was a representative of the Empirics, as philosopher the chief exponent of scepticism. In his two extant works—the *Hypotyposes* and *Adversus Mathematicos*—he left a prodigious battery of arguments against dogmatism in grammar, rhetoric, geometry, arithmetic, music, astrology, logic, physics, ethics. See Loeb Library edition, trans. R. G. Bury (1933–36).

SEYDLITZ, Friedrich Wilhelm, Baron von, *zīd'-* (1721–73), Prussian cavalry general, born at Kalkar, Cleve, served in the Silesian wars and so distinguished himself at Kolin (1757) that at Rossbach (1757) Frederick the Great promoted him over the heads of two generals to take charge of the cavalry, which under Seydlitz's brilliant charges won the battle practically without infantry. Seydlitz was wounded but won another victory at Zorndorf (1758) and covered the Prussian retreat at Hochkirch. Severely wounded at the defeat of Kunersdorf (1758), he did not return to the front until 1761, when, in command of both cavalry and infantry groups, he won the battle of Freyburg (1762).

SEYMOUR, an historic family, originally from St Maur in Normandy (hence the name), who obtained lands in Monmouthshire in the 13th century, and in the 14th at Hatch Beauchamp, Somerset, by marriage with an heiress of the Beauchamps. Important members are:

(1) **Algernon, 7th Duke of Somerset** (1684–1750), son of (2), who, in 1749, was created Earl of Northumberland, with remainder to his son-in-law, Sir Hugh Smithson, the ancestor of the present Percy line.

(2) **Charles, 6th Duke of Somerset** (1662–1748), known as the ' proud Duke of Somerset ', held high posts under Charles II, William III and Anne. He married the heiress of the Percies.

(3) **Edward** (c. 1506–52), eldest son of (10), was successively created Viscount Beauchamp, Earl of Hertford, and Duke of Somerset, and, as Protector, played the leading part in the first half of the reign of Edward VI (q.v.). He defeated a Scottish army at Pinkie 1547, but was indicted by Warwick (Northumberland) and executed.

(4) **Edward** (1539–1621), son of (3), by a second marriage, created Earl of Hertford by Elizabeth, married the Lady Catherine Grey, sister of Lady Jane Grey—a marriage which cost him nine years' imprisonment and a fine of £15,000.

(5) **Sir Edward** (1695–1757), became 8th

Duke of Somerset on the death of (1); he was a descendant of (3) by his first marriage.

(6) **Francis, 3rd Marquis of Hertford** (1777–1842), grandson of (7), was the prototype of Thackeray's Marquis of Steyne.

(7) **Francis Seymour-Conway** (1719–94), cousin of (5), was, when the earldom became extinct, created Earl of Hertford in 1750, Marquis in 1793.

(8) **Frederick Beauchamp Paget.** See ALCESTER.

(9) **Jane** (*c.* 1509–37), became the third queen of Henry VIII and mother of Edward VI. Holbein painted her picture. She was daughter of (10).

(10) **Sir John** (*c.* 1476–1536), father of Jane Seymour, helped to suppress the Cornish insurrection in 1497, and accompanied Henry VIII to France.

(11) **Thomas** (*c.* 1508–49), fourth son of (10), created Lord Seymour of Sudeley, became lord high admiral of England and the second husband of Henry's widow (Catherine Parr). On her death, he wished to marry the Princess Elizabeth, but was arrested and executed for treason.

(12) **William** (1588–1660), grandson of (4), in 1621 became Earl of Hertford, secretly married Lady Arabella Stuart (1610), a cousin of James I; and subsequently played a conspicuous part in the Royalist cause (he defeated Waller at Lansdown and took Bristol in 1643), obtained a reversal of the Protector's attainder, and at the Restoration took his seat in the House of Lords as 3rd Duke of Somerset.

SEYSS-INQUART, Artur von, *sīs-* (1892–1946), Austrian ' Quisling ', was born in the Sudetenland, practised as a lawyer in Vienna and saw much of Schuschnigg. When the latter became chancellor in 1938, he took office under him, informing Hitler of every detail in Schuschnigg's life, in the hope of becoming Nazi chancellor of Austria after the ' Anschluss '. Instead, he was appointed commissioner for the Netherlands in 1940, where he ruthlessly recruited slave labour. In 1945, he was captured by the Canadians, tried at Nuremberg and executed for war crimes.

SFORZA, name of a celebrated Italian family founded by a peasant of the Romagna called Muzio Attendolo (1369–1424), who became a great *condottiere* or soldier of fortune, and received the name of Sforza (' Stormer '—i.e., of cities). Its most noteworthy members were:

(1) **Francesco** (1401–66), natural son of the above and father of (2) and (3), sold his sword to the highest bidder, fighting for or against the pope, Milan, Venice and Florence. From the Duke of Milan he obtained his daughter's hand; and before his death had extended his power over Ancona, Pesaro, all Lombardy and Genoa. See C. M. Ady, *History of Milan under the Sforza* (1907).

(2) **Galeazzo Maria** (1444–76), son of (1), a competent ruler, although notorious for his debauchery and prodigality, was assassinated.

(3) **Ludovico,** called Il Moro, ' the Moor ' (1451–1508), from 1480 became the real ruler of Milan, his nephew **Gian Galeazzo** (1476–1494), the rightful ruler, being reduced to a constitutional puppet. But, fearing an insurrection from the latter's friends, Ludovico called in the aid of the French (1494), who in 1499 drove him out, and he died a prisoner in France. He was a sound administrator and is best remembered as the patron of Leonardo da Vinci. See F. Malaguzzi-Valeri, *La Corte di Lodovico Il Moro* (1913–1923).

SFORZA, **Carlo,** Count (1873–1952), Italian statesman, born at Lucca, became minister of foreign affairs (1920–21) and negotiated the Rapallo treaty. A senator (1919–26) he became leader of the anti-Fascist opposition and from 1922 lived in Belgium and the United States (1940). See his *European Dictatorships* (1931), &c.

SGAMBATI, Giovanni (1841–1914), Italian composer and pianist, born in Rome, was a friend of Liszt. His compositions include two symphonies, a requiem and chamber and piano music.

SHACKLETON, Sir Ernest Henry (1874–1922), British explorer, born at Kilkee, Ireland. He was educated at Dulwich College, apprenticed in the Merchant Navy, and became a junior officer under Captain Robert Scott, on the *Discovery*, in the National Antarctic Expedition, 1901–03. In 1909, in command of another expedition, reached a point 97 miles from the South Pole —at that time a southern record. While on another expedition, in 1915, his ship *Endeavour* was crushed in the ice. By sledges and boats Shackleton and his men reached Elephant Island, from where Shackleton and five others made a perilous voyage of 800 miles to South Georgia and organized relief for those on Elephant Island. He died at South Georgia while on a fourth Antarctic expedition, begun in 1920. He was knighted in 1909. See his own *The Heart of the Antarctic* (1909) and *South* (1919), and the biography by M. and J. Fisher (1957).

SHADWELL, Thomas (*c.* 1642–92), English dramatist, born at Broomhill House, Brandon, made a hit with the first of his thirteen comedies, *The Sullen Lovers* (1668). He also wrote three tragedies. Dryden, grossly assailed by him in the *Medal of John Bayes*, heaped deathless ridicule upon him in *MacFlecknoe* (' Shadwell never deviates into sense '), and as ' Og ' in the second part of *Absalom and Achitophel*. His works (ed. in 5 vols. by Montague Summers, 1927) exhibit talent and comic force. He succeeded Dryden as laureate in 1689. See *Works*, ed. M. Summers (1927), and study by A. S. Borgman (1930).

SHAFTESBURY, (1) **Anthony Ashley Cooper, 1st Earl of** (1621–83), was born July 22, 1621, at Wimborne St Giles, Dorset, the seat of his mother's father, Sir Anthony Ashley (1551–1628), a clerk of the privy council. He was the elder son of John Cooper of Rockborne in Hampshire, who next year (1622) was created a baronet. As a gentleman commoner at Exeter College, Oxford, he ' not only obtained the good-will of the wiser and elder sort, but became the leader even of all the rough young men '. He left without a degree, and in 1639 married Margaret, daughter of the lord keeper Coventry. She died in 1649; and nine months later he married Lady Frances Cecil, the Earl of Exeter's sister, who died in 1654. In 1655 he married the pious Margaret Spencer, the Earl of Sunderland's sister, who survived him till 1693. By all three marriages he largely strengthened his family connections. Meanwhile in 1640 he had entered the Short Parliament for Tewkesbury, but he had not a seat in the Long. A Royalist colonel (1643) after ten months' service he went over to the parliament, and commanded their forces in Dorsetshire, then from 1645 to 1652 lived as a great country gentleman. In 1653 he entered the Barebones Parliament, and was appointed one of Cromwell's council of state, but from 1655 he was in opposition. He was one of the twelve commissioners sent to Breda to invite Charles II home, and a carriage accident on the way thither caused him that chronic internal abscess which in 1666 secured him a lifelong attendant and friend in Locke. He was made a privy councillor (1660), and next year Baron Ashley and chancellor of the Exchequer. He served on the trial of the regicides; supported the war with Holland; and after Clarendon's fall (1667) sided with Buckingham, with whom he formed one of the infamous Cabal, and like whom he was fooled as to the Catholic clauses in the secret treaty of Dover (1669–70). He seems to have opposed the 'stop of the exchequer' (1672), which yet he justified; that same year was made Earl of Shaftesbury and lord chancellor (he proved a most upright judge); but in 1673, espousing the popular Protestantism, supported the Test Bill, which broke up the Cabal. In October the Great Seal was demanded of him, and he ranged himself as a champion of toleration (for Dissenters only) and of national liberties. He opposed Danby's nonresistance Test Bill (1675), and in 1677, for his protest against a fifteen months' prorogation, was sent to the Tower, whence he was only released a year later on making a full submission. Though the 'Popish Plot' was not of his forging, he used that two years' terror (1678–80) with ruthless dexterity. Not even the Habeas Corpus Act, long known as Shaftesbury's Act, is a set-off against the judicial murder of Lord Stafford, his personal enemy. The fall of Danby was followed by his appointment as president of Temple's new privy council of thirty members (1679), and an attempt to exclude James from the succession, in favour of Shaftesbury's puppet, the bastard Monmouth. Shaftesbury now received his congé from the king, and driven to more extreme opposition, indicted James as a recusant (1680), and brought armed followers to the Oxford parliament (1681). In July 1681 he was again sent to the Tower for high treason, but the Middlesex Whig grand jury threw out the bill. Monmouth and Russell hung back from the open rebellion to which he urged them, and he fled to Holland in December 1682. On January 22, 1683, he died at Amsterdam. Transcendently clever, eloquent and winning, he yet stands condemned by the many talents committed to him; self was the dominant principle to which alone he was

true. He was the author of party government, ever ready to make capital out of religious animosities, 'atrocities', perjuries, forgeries, anything. It is doubtful whether he was the pure, highminded and great statesman that Christie would make him, or, what Charles pronounced him, 'the wickedest dog in England'. See Dryden's *Absalom and Achitophel* and *Medal* (1681), part iii of Butler's *Hudibras* (1678), Life by L. F. Brown (1933) and other works cited at Locke and Charles II.

(2) **Anthony Ashley Cooper, 3rd Earl of** (1671–1713), English philosopher, grandson of (1), was born in London. Locke superintended his early education at Clapham; he spent three years at Winchester and three more in travel. He sat as a Whig for Poole in 1695–98, but ill-health drove him from politics to literature. On his two visits to Holland (1698–99 and 1703–04) he formed friendships with Beyle and Le Clerc. He succeeded to the earldom in 1699 and in 1711 removed to Naples, where he died. His somewhat overfine writings were all, with one exception, published after 1708, and were collected as *Characteristics of Men, Manners, Opinions, Times* (1711, enlarged 1714). Here he expounded the system immortalized in the *Essay on Man*, and argued that ridicule is the test of truth, that man possesses a moral sense, and that everything in the world is for the best. He found a follower in Hutcheson (q.v.). While at home he was attacked as a deist; abroad he attracted the attention of Leibnitz, Voltaire, Diderot, Lessing and Herder. See Lives by Rand (1900) and R. L. Brett (1951), study by T. Fowler (1882), and J. Bonar, *Moral Sense* (1930); also his *Letters*.

(3) **Anthony Ashley Cooper, 7th Earl of** (1801–85), English factory reformer and philanthropist, born in London, educated at Harrow and Christ Church, Oxford, entered parliament in 1826. He succeeded to the peerage in 1851. As Lord Ashley, he undertook the leadership of the factory reform movement in 1832 and piloted successive factory acts (1847, 1850) through the House, regulating conditions in the coalmines and the provision of lodging-houses for the poor (1851). His Coal Mines Act (1842) prohibited underground employment of women and of children under thirteen. He was chairman of the Ragged Schools Union for 40 years, assisted Florence Nightingale in her schemes for army welfare and took an interest in missionary work. Strongly evangelical, he opposed radicalism although he worked with the trade unions for factory reforms. See study by J. L. and L. B. Hammond (1939).

SHAGALL. See CHAGALL.

SHAH JAHAN (1592–1666), 5th of the Mogul Emperors of Delhi, was from 1624 in revolt against his father, Jehangir, but on his death (1627) succeeded him. The chief events of his reign were a war in the Deccan, ending in the destruction of the kingdom of Ahmadnagar (1636) and the subjugation (1636) of Bijapur and Golconda; an attack on the Uzbegs of Balkh (1645–47); unsuccessful attempts to recover Kandahar from the Persians (1637, 1647–53); and a second successful war in the Deccan (1655). In 1658 the emperor fell ill, and was held prisoner by his son Aurungzebe till his death. He was a just and an able ruler; the magnificence of his court was unequalled; and he left buildings such as the Taj Mahal, the tomb of his beloved Mumtaz Mahal and the ' pearl mosque ' in the Red Fort at Agra and the palace and great mosque at Delhi. See Life by B. P. Sakasena (1932).

SHAHN, Ben (1898–1969), American painter, born in Kaunas, Lithuania, emigrated with his parents to New York, and studied painting in night school. In 1922 he visited the European art centres and came under the influence of Rouault. His didactic pictorial commentaries on contemporary events such as his 23 satirical gouache paintings on the trial of Sacco and Vanzetti (1932) and the 15 paintings on Tom Mooney, the Labour leader (1933), *Death of a Miner* (1947) and the precarious world situation caught in the frightening confidence of a team of trick cyclists in *Epoch* (1950; Philadelphia) earned him the title of ' American Hogarth '. He was the first painter to deliver the Charles Eliot Norton Lectures at Harvard, published as *The Shape of Content* (1958). See study by Soby (1947).

SHAIRP, John Campbell (1819–85), Scottish poet, born at Houston House, West Lothian. He became deputy professor (1857), professor of Latin (1861) and principal (1868) of St Andrews, and in 1877 and 1882 he was appointed professor of Poetry at Oxford. Strong poetic instincts and a keen and kindly critical faculty appear in his writings, which include *Kilmahoe and Other Poems* (1864), *Studies in Poetry and Philosophy* (1868) and *Burns* (1879). See Knight's *Shairp and his Friends* (1888).

SHAKESPEARE, William (1564–1616), English dramatist and poet, was born at Stratford-on-Avon in April 1564, the son of John Shakespeare, a glover, and of his wife, Mary Arden, who came of prosperous farming stock. William was the eldest of three sons; there were four daughters, only one of whom survived the poet. Modern scholarship has uncovered a good deal more about his upbringing and life than was known even to so late a biographer as Sidney Lee, whose revised Life of Shakespeare appeared in 1915. The first *Life*, by Nicholas Rowe, was prefixed to his edition of the works (1709); this was followed by Aubrey's account of Shakespeare in his *Brief Lives* (written in the 17th century, but not printed till 1813). Between them Rowe and Aubrey gave currency to various rumours somewhat damaging to Shakespeare's start in life. Rowe was the more culpable for he underrated the position of John Shakespeare in Stratford—he was really a man of some civic consequence and not a butcher—set going the legend that the boy was removed from the ' Free-school ' at a tender age and so ' had no knowledge of the writings of the ancient poets ' (which then meant total ignorance) and that after an early marriage he ' fell into ill company '. The deer-stealing episode follows, with Shakespeare's flight to London to avoid prosecution. Aubrey repeated some of this, but corrected the story in one important point, viz., he had heard from a Mr Beeston that the poet had enough education to become a schoolmaster. The classical allusions and quotations in the early plays would seem to support this notion, which was developed by Dr J. S. Smart in his *Shakespeare Truth and Tradition* (1928) and has since then been regarded as at least plausible. Aubrey's guess that Shakespeare came to London in 1585 is also plausible. His wife, Anne Hathaway, of good farming stock, had borne him a daughter, Susanna, in 1583, and the twins Hamnet and Judith two years later. The poet may well have sought the city for a livelihood. Since the first published reference to him (Greene's attack in *A Groat's-worth of Witte*) is in 1592, there is a gap variously filled in by scholars, the most conjectural view being that of Professor Peter Alexander (*A Shakespeare Primer*, 1951), viz., that having certainly written the third part of *Henry VI*, Shakespeare may be credited with having written also the first two parts of that trilogy and perhaps the early comedies, *Two Gentlemen of Verona* and the *Comedy of Errors*. *Love's Labour's Lost*, however, cannot be earlier than 1592. The traditional view that 1591 is the start of his dramatic career is, however, still held by critics of the standing of E. K. Chambers, Dover Wilson and others. During the years 1592–94, when the theatres were closed for the plague, Shakespeare wrote his erotic poems ' Venus and Adonis ' and ' The Rape of Lucrece ', 1593 and 1594 respectively, both dedicated to the Earl of Southampton, the ideal Renaissance man, soldier and scholar, who may figure as the friend in the ' drama ' of the sonnets. They illustrate the pagan side of the Renaissance with its sensual mythological imagery. The sonnets present an intractable problem. They were not published till 1609, but were known by 1598, when Francis Meres talks of ' his sugred sonnets among his private friends '. There are two main groups of sonnets—1 to 126 addressed to a fair young man, and 127 to 154 addressed to a ' dark lady ' who holds both the young man and the poet in thrall. The young man's suit is preferred (there is also a rival poet), hence self-loathing on the part of the poet. Who these people are—we cannot dismiss them as fictitious—has provided an exercise in detection for numerous critics. The favourite guess is that the young man (' Mr W. H.' in the dedication) is Henry Wriothesley, Earl of Southampton, to whom the poems were dedicated; but it may be William Herbert, Earl of Pembroke, the lover of Mary Fitton who is not the ' Dark Lady ' of the Sonnets ', since she was fair. It is the poetry of the sequence which enchants us, the eloquent discourse and unfailing verbal melody, the amazing variety of tone from serene acceptance to towering passion, and the lovely imagery. The themes are those current at the Renaissance—the idea of Beauty, the eternizing power of the poet, the theme of Identity. But Shakespeare makes them his own. The first evidence of Shakespeare's association with the stage is the Treasurer's order to pay three leading members of the Chamberlain's company of players—William Kemp, William Shakespeare and Richard Burbage—for two performances in the Christmas week, 1594. The Chamberlain's men had previously acted as the servants of Lord Strange. Shakespeare had apparently been associated with a rival company, Lord Pembroke's men, for four of his early plays, printed in garbled versions in 1594–95, profess to have been acted by that company. On the failure of Pembroke's men (owing to the enforced idleness of the plague years) he transferred to the Chamberlain's company, later ' the King's men ', taking with him the doubtful *Titus Andronicus*, *The Taming of the Shrew* and an early reputed version of *Hamlet*. Their playhouse was the Theatre (built and owned by the father of the tragic actor Richard Burbage) down to 1597, when the expiry of the lease forced them to seek new quarters. The expense of building the new structure on the south bank of the river, the famous Globe, probably induced the Burbages to take in as partners five of the company, of whom Shakespeare was one. He was now on the way not only to fame but to the financial rewards which do not always go with fame. He lived modestly at the house of a Huguenot refugee in Silver Street from about 1602 to 1606 and then shifted to the south side near the Globe. Dr Leslie Hotson disclosed two facts which enhance our view of the poet in London society—the Thos. Russell, Esq., who acted as executor to his will was familiar with the great world, and William Johnson who witnessed a mortgage for Shakespeare was the host of the Mermaid. Slender facts to build on, but they indicate what we expect on other grounds—that he was known to scholars and soldiers and was equally at home among the wits of the Mermaid. His preparations for retirement to Stratford— purchasing arable land and buying up tithes— show that he was the successful manager anxious to figure as a man of consequence in his native place. Russell was near him there and the well-known physician, Dr Hall, married his elder daughter Susanna. It is interesting to note that he entertained Ben Jonson and Drayton at New Place, his Stratford house. Families could not count then on generations. Susanna, the poet's heir, had a daughter, Elizabeth, who survived to 1670, but Judith's three daughters died childless. The only living descendants must trace their lineage through Joan Hart, the poet's married sister. The only reference to his wife, Anne Hathaway, after the christening of the twins in 1595, is as a beneficiary of his will (' my second-best bed with the furniture ') which good Shakespearians will not take as derisory. An enormous amount of investigation on the authorship, text and chronology of the plays marks the modern era of Shakespeare scholarship. In addition, works like Dover Wilson's *Life in Shakespeare's England* (1911) and the tercentenary *Shakespeare's England* (1916) greatly extend our knowledge of the age or of particular aspects of it. Intimate study of the Elizabethan stage, including audience reaction, the players' companies, &c., has also yielded valuable

results. Authorship is still a controversial subject in respect of certain plays such as *Titus Andronicus*, *Two Noble Kinsmen*, *Henry VI*, part I, and of Shakespeare's part in *Timan of Athens*, *Pericles* and *Henry VIII* The question of text is one of great difficulty, involving, for example, such differences as exist between the first and second Quarto editions of *Hamlet* and between these and the Folio version of 1623. This has entailed among other things an examination of the complicated business of publication in that era. In a series of studies from 1909 onwards A. W. Pollard, employing the test of ' good ' and ' bad ' quartos, assigned prior authority to the quartos. His *Shakespeare's Fight with the Pirates* (1917) became a classic. His example was followed by Dover Wilson in his editing of the New Cambridge Shakespeare. The authority of the Folio of 1623 was thus weakened because its editors, Heminge and Condell, had inveighed against ' diverse stolne and surreptitious copies ', claiming that they had direct access to Shakespeare's MSS., whereas they retained the text of certain ' good ' quartos unchanged. They also included plays which Shakespeare certainly did not write. The whole matter is too complicated for discussion here, but we can say that to the pioneers of ' scientific ' textual criticism—to W. W. Greg (*Principles of Emendation*, 1918); to A. W. Pollard for the work referred to above and for the series which he edited with Dover Wilson, *Shakespeare Problems*; to Professor Peter Alexander for the third volume of that series in which he proved Shakespeare's authorship of 2 and 3 *Henry VI*, we owe a vastly improved text. The most outstanding disciple of these pioneers is Prof. George Duthie in *The Bad Quarto of Hamlet* (1941) and his *King Lear* (1949). With regard to appreciations of Shakespeare's work, Dr Johnson's famous preface, Morgann's essay on Falstaff, Coleridge's lectures on Shakespeare and A.C. Bradley's *Shakespearian Tragedy* were early highlights. But of more modern interpretation there has been a great deal, most of it controversial. The main difference is between the idealists or traditionalists who write as if Shakespeare could not go wrong and who gloss over his contradictions, and the realists who explain his inconsistencies of fact and characterization by the conditions in which he worked. The American critic Prof. Stoll and the German Prof. Lewin Schücking were the disruptive influences here, but their work was a salutary check to the ' idealism ' of which Alexander's admirable *A Shakespeare Primer* is not free and of which Dover Wilson's *What Happened in Hamlet*—a best seller in literary detective work—is a notable example. Another important method of interpretation, of which G. Wilson Knight's *Wheel of Fire* and *The Imperial Theme* (1931) are eloquent examples, proceeds by an examination of the imagery and symbolism of the plays. This method gives rather much scope for fancy, but Knight's work adds another dimension to Shakespearean study. A word on the chronology of the plays. We have long since rejected Dowden's sentimental categories (*Shakespeare's Mind and Art*, 1883), but we recognize phases in Shakespeare's development. His earliest period closes in 1594 when we may assume he had written the *Henry VI* trilogy, *Titus Andronicus* (if it was his), *The Taming of the Shrew*, and perhaps an early *Hamlet*. Garbled versions of these (except for *Titus Andronicus* which is a 'good' text) appeared in the Stationers' registers (1594–95). We may also conjecture that to this period belong the comedies *Two Gentlemen of Verona*, *Comedy of Errors* and *Love's Labour's Lost*. Francis Mere's *Palladis Tamia* (1598) lists six comedies and six tragedies and gives a clue (apart from other evidence) to the plays of the second period, that is 1594–99. In default of genuine tragedies (*Romeo and Juliet* is here however), Meres ekes out with four histories, Richard II, Richard III, Henry IV and King John. For comedy he lists '*Gentlemen of Verona*, his *Errors*, his *Love's Labour's Lost*, his *Midsummer's Night Dreame* and his *Merchant of Venice*'. We may assign *Richard II* and *Merchant of Venice* to 1595; *Romeo and Juliet* and *Midsummer Night's Dream* to 1596 and the two parts of *Henry IV* and *Merry Wives of Windsor* to 1597; *Much Ado About Nothing* and *As You Like it* to 1598 and *Henry V* to 1599. The third period, 1599–1608, opens with *Julius Caesar* (1599), and includes a final *Hamlet*, *Othello*, *Lear*, *Macbeth*, *Antony and Cleopatra*, *Timon of Athens* and the 'dark' comedies— *All's Well that Ends Well*, *Measure for Measure* and *Troilus and Cressida*. *Cymbeline*, *A Winter's Tale* and *The Tempest* and his part in *Henry VIII* are the work of his last period, 1609–13. If we did not realize that these plays represent the highest flight of genius, we might think the list tedious. To give some slight idea of their contents—the histories were his prentice work in tragedy. The earlier cycle, *Henry VI* to *Richard III* followed the line of history which is rarely conclusive in the way tragedy should be. These histories are therefore episodic and relieved only by the patriotism and comic matter which his audience came to expect. They are, however, a textbook of political, often cynical, wisdom. In the second cycle, from *Richard II* onward, history begins to provide a background for the conflict in the mind of the 'hero', but the two Richards being weak or vicious characters, those plays resemble more the 'falls of princes' than true tragedies. The theme of 'This England', however, appears in Gaunt's speech in *Richard II*, culminates in *Henry V*, and has its final echo in Cranmer's speech over Elizabeth's cradle in *Henry VIII*, which is almost Shakespeare's last word to the world. In the *Henry IV-Henry V* trilogy he often displays a ruthlessness to certain characters—the rejection of Falstaff is the classic instance—which also appears in the comedies along with a complacency towards evil-doers at the close and this is not altogether to be excused by the story he worked on. The early comedies show a tiro's preference for symmetry in character and situation resulting in a certain lifelessness. *Midsummer Night's Dream* is a beautiful fantasy relieved by the fun of the rustics and enchantingly lyrical in tone. Equally lyrical and pictorial, *As You Like It*

has a deeper vein of thought—the theme being the contrast between the corrupt court and country innocence—not so innocent after all. In Jaques we have the type (fashionable just then) Malcontent of which Hamlet is the splendid realization. The 'dark' comedies—*All's Well*, *Measure for Measure* and *Troilus*—prepare us for the great tragedies but with this difference that the ugly cynicism of the former gives place to the serenity of high tragedy which plumbs the depths but also purges the soul. We should resist the temptation to explain the sombre nature of these comedies by reference to personal loss or frustration on Shakespeare's part, the collapse of Essex's party to which the poet may have been sympathetic, or the supposed betrayal of his passion in the drama of the sonnets. Better, perhaps, refer it to the *zeitgeist* and the example of his contemporaries Ben Jonson and Middleton. In the great tragedies every stop of the mighty organ is out. All the passions which destroy men and empires are explored. Stoll thought it a mistake to impose the Aristotelian formula for tragedy on Shakespeare—that is the grave flaw in a hero having tragic consequences. The formula fits Othello well enough, but Hamlet leaves us puzzled; no explanation of his conduct is convincing—hence T. S. Eliot's denigration. The 'flaw' in *Lear*, as shown in the first two scenes, is ludicrously insufficient to bear the tremendous passion which develops. In the Roman plays—*Julius Caesar*, *Antony and Cleopatra*, *Coriolanus*—the human passions are involved in the ruin of the world. The first two are panoramic in the scope of the scene. Perhaps the strict adherence to the unities of time and place in *The Tempest* is Shakespeare's reply to Jonson's ridicule of such romantic extravagance. That he returned to Romance in his last period has been taken as a sign of world weariness, which calls for forgiveness and reconciliation. That is too simple. Prospero's breaking of his magic wand and the ensuing reconciliations do not dispose of evil in the heart of man. On the contrary, *The Tempest* has inspired such meditations on the human situation as Browning's 'Caliban upon Setebos' and W. H. Auden's 'The Sea and the Mirror'. But one must not think of Shakespeare after 1600 as having quite divested himself of his native gaiety. *Twelfth Night* belongs to the same year as *Hamlet*, that is 1601. For Bacon and other anti-Stratford theories see R. C. Churchill, *Shakespeare and His Betters* (1958). If Shakespeare took little interest in the publication of his plays, posterity has made up for it. Curiously the 17th century contented itself with reprints of the great Folio of 1623 (1632, 1663–64 and 1685). The 18th century has nine new editions to its credit and scholarship begins to appear with Rowe's edition (with a Life) in 1709. Between that and Malone's critical edition (1790), which first discussed the chronology on modern lines, we have Pope's edition (1726), with its happy guesses at difficult passages; Theobald's improved text; and Dr Johnson's edition (1765), with its monumental preface. Variorum editions, involving a closer scrutiny of the text, culminated in Furness's great Variorum edition from 1871 onwards. Various one-volume and school texts heralded a new era of publication—Sir Sidney Lee's Caxton Shakespeare and the old Arden Shakespeare, with its agreeable format, were gradually ousted by the New (Cambridge) edition edited by Quiller-Couch and J. Dover Wilson (begun 1921) and this, now completed, has a friendly rival in the new Arden edition begun after the war and edited by Ellis-Fermor. The standard Life is by E. K. Chambers (1930, revised 1951); but see also Dr J. S. Smart's *Shakespeare Truth and Tradition* (1928), and P. Alexander's *Shakespeare's Life and Art* (1939). For sources see *Narrative and Dramatic Sources* (ed. Bullough, 1957). For criticism Nichol Smith, *Eighteenth Century Essays on Shakespeare*; Granville-Barker, *Prefaces to Shakespeare's Plays*; and C. H. Herford's *A Sketch of Recent Shakespearian Investigation* (1923). For the stage see Chambers, *Elizabethan Stage* (1923). See also other works by the above-mentioned authors, as well as various books on aspects of Shakespeare by F. S. Boas, Ivor Brown, J. R. Brown, L. B. Campbell, L. C. Knights, K. Muir, A. L. Rowse, E. M. Tillyard and P. A. Traversi.

SHALIAPIN. See CHALIAPIN.

SHAMYL, i.e., **Samuel** (1797-1871), leader of the tribes in the Caucasus in their thirty years' struggle against Russia, became a Sufi mullah or priest, and strove to end the tribal feuds. He was one of the foremost in the defence of Himry against the Russians in 1831, in 1834 was chosen head of the Leshians, and by abandoning open warfare for surprises, ambuscades, &c., secured numerous successes for the mountaineers. In 1839, and again in 1849, he escaped from the stronghold of Achulgo after the Russians had made themselves masters of it, to continue preaching a holy war against the infidels. The Russians were completely baffled, their armies sometimes disastrously beaten, though Shamyl began to lose ground. During the Crimean war the allies supplied him with money and arms, but after peace was signed the Russians compelled the submission of the Caucasus. On April 12, 1859, Shamyl's chief stronghold, Weden, was taken. For several months he was hunted till surprised, and after a desperate resistance captured.

SHAPLEY, Harlow (1885-1972), American astrophysicist, born at Nashville, Tenn., worked at the Mount Wilson observatory from 1914 and was director of Harvard Univ. Observatory (1921–52). He demonstrated that the Milky Way is much larger than had been supposed, and that the Solar System is located on the Galaxy's edge, not at its centre. He has done notable work on photometry and spectroscopy and his writings include *Star Clusters* (1930), *Galaxies* (1943), *Climatic Changes* (1954) and *The Vew from a Distant Star* (1963).

SHARP, (1) Abraham (1653-1742), English astronomer, in 1684–91 assisted Flamsteed at Greenwich Observatory in constructing the large mural arc, &c. He published tables of logarithms and *Geometry Improved* (1717). See life by Ludworth (1889).

(2) Cecil James (1859-1924), English collector of folk songs (of which he published numerous collections) and folk dances, was born in London, and was principal of the Hampstead Conservatoire in 1896-1905. His work is commemorated by Cecil Sharp House, the headquarters of the English Folk Dance (founded by him in 1911) and Song Societies. See Life by A. H. Fox-Strangways (1933).

(3) Granville (1735-1813), English abolitionist, born at Durham, was apprenticed to a London linen-draper, in 1758 got a post in the Ordnance department, but resigned in 1776 through sympathy with America. He wrote many philological, legal, political and theological pamphlets; but his principal labours were for the Negro. He defended the Negro James Sommersett or Somerset, securing the decision (1772) that as soon as a slave touches English soil he becomes free; and worked with Clarkson for the abolition of Negro slavery. His idea of a colony for freed slaves at Sierra Leone was put into practice in 1787. He was also active in many religious associations, including the British and Foreign Bible Society (1804), and wrote on New Testament scholarship. See Memoirs by P. Hoare (1820), and study by E. C. P. Lascelles (1928).

(4) James (1613-79), Scottish divine, born at Banff, May 4, studied for the church at King's College, Aberdeen (1633-1637). In 1651-52 he was taken prisoner to London with some other ministers; and in 1657 he was chosen by the more moderate party in the church to plead their cause before Cromwell. Sent by Monk to Breda, he had several interviews with Charles II (1660). His correspondence for some months after his return from Holland is full of apprehensions of Prelacy; but its perfidy stands revealed in his letter of May 21, 1661, to Middleton, which proves that he was then in hearty co-operation with Clarendon and the English bishops for the re-establishment of Episcopacy in Scotland. The bribe was a great one, for in December he was consecrated Archbishop of St Andrews. The dexterous tool of Middleton or Lauderdale, an oppressor of those he had betrayed, he soon became an object of popular detestation and of contempt to his employers. On May 3, 1679, twelve Covenanters (see JOHN BALFOUR and HACKSTON) dragged him from his coach on Magus Muir and hacked him to death. See Life by T. Stephen and O. Airy, Lauderdale Papers (1884).

(5) William (1749-1824), English engraver, born in London, a businessman in the City, executed plates after Guido, West, Trumbull and Reynolds. He was a friend of Thomas Paine and Horne Tooke. See Life by W. S. Baker (1875).

(6) William (1855-1905), Scottish writer, born at Paisley, settled in London 1879, and published *Earth's Voices* (1884). He wrote books on contemporary English, French and German poets, but is chiefly remembered as the author of the remarkable series of Celtic —or neo-Celtic—tales and romances by ' Fiona Macleod '—a pseudonym he systematically refused to acknowledge. They include

Pharais (1894), *The Mountain Lovers* and *The Sin-Eater* (1895), *The Immortal Hour* (1900), &c. The latter, a verse play set to music, had a great success in London during the 1920s. See Memoir by his wife (1910).

SHARPE, Charles Kirkpatrick (1781–1851), Scottish antiquarian, born at Hoddam Castle, Dumfries, contributed two original ballads to Scott's *Minstrelsy*, and edited club books, but is chiefly remembered by his correspondence (2 vols. 1888).

SHARPEY-SCHAFER, Sir Edward (1850–1935), English physiologist, born at Hornsey, educated at University College, London, was professor there (1883–99) and at Edinburgh (1899–1933). Known especially for his researches on muscular contraction, he devised the prone-pressure method of artificial respiration.

SHASTRI, Lal Bahadour (1904–66), Indian politician, born in Benares, the son of a clerk in Nehru's father's law office, joined Gandhi's independence movement at 16 and was seven times imprisoned by the British. He excelled as a Congress Party official and politician in the United Provinces and joined Nehru's cabinet in 1952 as minister for the railways, becoming minister of transport (1957) and of commerce (1958) and home secretary (1960). Under the Kamaraj plan to invigorate the Congress Party at grass roots' level he resigned with other cabinet ministers in 1963 but was recalled by Nehru in 1964, after the latter's stroke, as minister without portfolio, and succeeded him as prime minister in 1964. He died suddenly of a heart attack in 1966 while in Tashkent, U.S.S.R., for discussions on the India-Pakistan dispute.

SHAW, (1) George Bernard (1856–1950), Irish dramatist, essayist, critic and pamphleteer, was born of Irish Protestant parents in Dublin. His mother established herself as a singing-teacher both in Dublin and later in London, and from her he inherited strength of character and the great love and knowledge of music so influential in his life and work. After short and unhappy periods at various schools, he entered in 1871 a firm of land-agents, disliked office routine, and left Ireland for good to follow his mother and sister Lucy, a musical-comedy actress, to London. His literary life had already begun in 1875 with a letter to the press (henceforth one of his favourite means of expression), shrewdly analysing the effect on individuals of sudden conversion by the American evangelists, Moody and Sankey. In London his early years were a long period of struggle and impoverishment, and of the five novels he wrote between 1879 and 1883, the best of which are probably *Love Among the Artists* and *Cashel Byron's Profession*, all were rejected by the more reputable publishers. But in them is already to be found, besides some striking character studies and much originality of thought, glimmerings of the supple and virile Shavian style to be more fully developed after several years of experience. An encounter (1882) with Henry George and the reading of Karl Marx turned his thoughts towards Socialism, and while any direct propagation of it is absent from his plays, his faith in it and a 'kindly dislike'

(if not dread) of capitalist society form the backbone of all his work. Political and economic understanding stood him in good stead as a local government councillor in Saint Pancras (1897–1903) and also on the executive committee of the small but influential Fabian Society, to which he devoted himself selflessly for many years (1884–1911) and for which he edited *Fabian Essays* (1889) and wrote many well-known socialist tracts. Journalism provided another lively platform for him, and it was as 'Corno di Bassetto', music critic for the new *Star* newspaper (1888–90), that he made his first indelible impact on the intellectual and social consciousness of his time. In this and in his later music criticism for *The World* (1890–94) and, above all, in his dramatic criticism for Frank Harris's *Saturday Review* (1895–98), he was in fact attempting, as De Quincey said of Wordsworth, to create the taste by which he was to be appreciated. To this period also belong *The Quintessence of Ibsenism* (1891) and *The Perfect Wagnerite* (1898), tributes to fellow 'artist-philosophers' who, together with Bunyan, Dickens, Samuel Butler and Mozart, had acknowledged influence on his work. The rest of Shaw's life, especially after his marriage (1898) to the Irish heiress Charlotte Payne-Townshend, is mainly the history of his plays. His first, *Widowers' Houses*, was begun in 1885 in collaboration with his friend William Archer, but was finished independently in 1892 as the result of the challenge he felt to produce the newer drama of ideas he had been advocating. Into the earliest plays, which also include *Mrs Warren's Profession, Arms and the Man* and *Candida* (one of the first in a long series of remarkable female portraiture), comes already the favourite Shavian theme of conversion—from dead system and outworn morality towards a more creatively vital approach to life—and this is further developed in *Three Plays for Puritans*: *The Devil's Disciple, Caesar and Cleopatra*, and *Captain Brassbound's Conversion*. His long correspondence with the famous Lyceum actress, Ellen Terry, was also at its peak during these years. At last Shaw was becoming more widely known, first of all in the United States and on the Continent, and then, with the important advent of the playwright-producer-actor, Harley Granville-Barker, in England itself, especially after the epoch-making Vedrenne-Barker Court Theatre season of 1904–07. This had been preceded by one of Shaw's greatest philosophical comedies, *Man and Superman* (1902), in which, in quest of a purer religious approach to life, Shaw advocated through his Don Juan the importance of man's unceasing creative evolutionary urge for world-betterment as well as for his own self-improvement. Other notable plays from the early part of the century are *John Bull's Other Island* (1904), *Major Barbara* (1905), *The Doctor's Dilemma* (1906), and two uniquely Shavian discussion plays, *Getting Married* (1908) and *Misalliance* (1910). They further display Shaw's increasing control of his medium and the wide range of his subject matter (from politics and statecraft to family life, prostitution and vaccination). Before the Joint Committee on Stage Censorship in 1909 he proudly proclaimed himself as 'immoralist and heretic', and insisted on the civilized necessity for toleration and complete freedom of thought. Just before World War I came two of his most delightful plays: *Androcles and the Lion*, a 'religious pantomime', and *Pygmalion*, an 'anti-romantic' comedy of phonetics (adapted as a highly successful musical play, *My Fair Lady* (1956), filmed in 1964). During the war, though he later toured the Front at official invitation, he called forth controversy and recrimination with his *Common Sense About the War*, one of the most provocative and fearless documents ever written. After the war followed three of his very greatest dramas in near succession: *Heartbreak House* (1919), an attempt to analyse in an English Chehovian social environment the causes of present moral and political discontents; *Back to Methuselah* (1921), five plays in one, in which Shaw conducted a not altogether successful dramatic excursion from the Garden of Eden to 'As Far as Thought Can Reach'; and *Saint Joan* (1923), in which Shaw's essentially religious nature, his genius for characterization (above all of saintly but very human women), and his powers of dramatic argument are most abundantly revealed. In 1925 Shaw was awarded the Nobel prize for literature, but donated the money to inaugurate the Anglo-Swedish Literary Foundation. In 1931 he visited Russia, and during the 30's made other long tours, including a world one with Mrs Shaw in 1932, during which he gave a memorable address on Political Economy in the Metropolitan Opera House, New York. Greater perhaps than any of the plays written during the last years of his life are the two prose works: *The Intelligent Woman's Guide to Socialism and Capitalism* (1928), one of the most lucid introductions to its subjects, and *The Black Girl in Search of God* (1932), a modern *Pilgrim's Progress*. The later plays, except for *The Apple Cart* (1929), have scarcely received adequate public stage presentation, but they continue to preach the stern yet invigorating Shavian morality of individual responsibility, self-discipline, heroic effort without thought of reward or 'atonement', and the utmost integrity. Plays such as *Too True to Be Good* (1932) and *The Simpleton of the Unexpected Isles* (1934) also show signs of sounding a newer and even more experimental dramatic note altogether. Shaw died at the age of 94 on November 2, 1950. In spite of some decline in his personal popularity in Britain after his death, the interest in his work now seems to be increasing and universal. His plays, prefaces and essays, as published in the Standard Edition of his work (Constable & Co. Ltd.), take up 35 substantial volumes, and the number of books about him is considerable—see those by G. K. Chesterton (1910, new ed. 1935), A. Henderson (1911), H. Pearson (1942), E. R. Bentley (1947, new ed. 1967), C. E. M. Joad (1949), D. McCarthy (1951) and St John Ervine (1956).

(2) **Henry Wheeler.** See BILLINGS (1).

(3) **Jack** (1780–1815), English pugilist of prodigious strength who, serving in the Life Guards, fell at Waterloo, first killing ten cuirassiers.

(4) **Martin** (1876–1958), English composer, born in London, studied under Stanford at the Royal College of Music, composed the ballad opera, *Mr Pepys* (1926), with Clifford Bax, set T. S. Eliot's poems to music, but is best known for his songs and as co-editor with his brother, **Geoffrey Turton** (1879–1943), the church musician, of national songbooks, and with Vaughan Williams of *Songs of Praise* and the *Oxford Carol Book*. See his autobiography, *Up to Now* (1929).

(5) **Richard Norman** (1831–1912), English architect in London, born in Edinburgh, was a leader of the trend away from Victorian styles back to traditional Georgian designs, as in Swan House, Chelsea, New Scotland Yard (1888), the Gaiety Theatre, Aldwych (1902; now demolished), and the Piccadilly Hotel (1905). See *Life* by R. Blomfield (1940).

(6) **Sir William Napier** (1854–1945), English meteorologist, born in Birmingham, was 16th wrangler at Cambridge in 1876 and in 1877 was elected fellow of Emmanuel College and became assistant director of the Cavendish Laboratory. He was director of the Meteorological office, London (1907–20), and from 1918 scientific adviser to the government. He became professor of the Royal College of Science in 1920. In his *Life History of Surface Air Currents* (1906) he established with Lempfert the 'polar front' theory of cyclones propounded by Bjerknes (q.v.). In 1915 he was knighted and received the Royal Medal of the Royal Society (1923). His *Manual of Meteorology* (1919–31) became a standard work.

SHAW-LEFEVRE, -*le-fee'ver*, (1) **Charles, 1st Viscount Eversley** (1794–1888), English Liberal politician, was called to the bar in 1819, in 1830 entered parliament, and was speaker 1839–57, being then made a peer.

(2) **George John, Baron Eversley** (1832–1928), English Liberal politician, born in London, served in Liberal ministries (1881–1884, 1892–95), formed with Grote, Stephen and John Stuart Mill in 1866 the Commons Preservation Society to protect common lands from the encroaching builder, as P.M.G. (1883–84) introduced sixpenny telegrams, as commissioner of works (1880–83, 1892–94) threw open Hampton Court park and Kew Palace, served on the London County Council from 1897 and in 1906 was created baron.

SHAWCROSS, Sir Hartley William, Baron Shawcross (1902–), English lawyer, born in Giessen, Germany, was educated at Dulwich College, called to the bar at Gray's Inn in 1925 and was senior lecturer in Law at Liverpool (1927–34). After service in World War II, he was attorney-general (1945–51) and president of the Board of Trade (1951) in the Labour government. He established an international legal reputation for himself as chief British prosecutor at the Nuremberg Trials (1945–46), led the investigations of the Lynskey Tribunal (1948) and prosecuted in the Fuchs atom spy case

(1950). Finding the narrow opposition tactics of the Labour Party irksome, he resigned his parliamentary seat in 1958. He was knighted in 1945 and created a life peer in 1959.

SHAYS, Daniel (1747–1825), American leader of the rebellion in Western Massachusetts (1786–87) which bears his name, served against the British at Bunker's Hill, Ticonderoga, &c., and was commissioned. He led the insurrection by the farmers against the U.S. government, which was imposing heavy taxation and mortgages. After raiding the arsenal at Springfield, Mass., the insurrectionists were routed at Petersham (1787) and Shays was condemned to death, but pardoned (1788).

SHEE, Sir Martin Archer (1769–1850), Anglo-Irish painter, born in Dublin, in 1788 settled in London, and became R.A. in 1800 and P.R.A. 1830, when he was knighted. His *Captain John Wolmore* at Trinity House shows the influence of Lawrence. He also dabbled in literature. See Life by his son (1860).

SHEEPSHANKS, (1) **John** (1787–1863), English art-collector, born in Leeds, who in 1857 presented his collection (233 oil paintings and 103 drawings) to the nation. They are now at South Kensington.

(2) **Richard** (1794–1855), English astronomer, brother of (1), instrumental in the adoption of a standard of length (1855).

SHEFFIELD, John, 1st Duke of Buckingham and Normanby (1648–1721), English political leader and poet, succeeded his father as third Earl of Mulgrave in 1658, served in both navy and army, and was lord chamberlain to James II and a cabinet councillor under William III, who in 1694 made him Marquis of Normanby. Anne made him Duke of (the county of) Buckingham (1703); but for his opposition to Godolphin and Marlborough he was deprived of the Seal (1705). After 1710, under the Tories, he was lord steward and lord president till the death of Anne, when he lost all power, and intrigued for the restoration of the Stuarts. Patron of Dryden and friend of Pope, he wrote two tragedies, a metrical *Essay on Satire*, an *Essay on Poetry*, &c.

SHEIL, Richard Lalor, *sheel* (1791–1851), Irish dramatist and politician, born at Drumdowney, Kilkenny, wrote a series of plays, aided O'Connell in forming the New Catholic Association (1825), and supported the cause by impassioned speeches. He was M.P. and in 1839 under Melbourne became vice-president of the Board of Trade, and a privy councillor—the first Catholic to gain that honour. In 1846 he was appointed master of the Mint. See *Memoir* by McCullagh (1855) and his *Speeches* (1845–55).

SHELBURNE, William Petty, 2nd Earl of (1737–1805), English statesman, great-grandson of Sir William Petty (q.v.), was born in Dublin, studied at Christ Church, Oxford, served in the army, entered parliament, succeeded his father to the earldom in 1761, and in 1763 was appointed president of the Board of Trade, and in Chatham's second administration (1766) secretary of state. Upon the fall of Lord North's ministry in

1782 Shelburne declined to form a government, but became secretary of state under Rockingham. Upon the latter's death the same year, the king offered Shelburne the Treasury. Fox resigned, and Shelburne introduced William Pitt into office as his chancellor of the Exchequer. This ministry resigned when outvoted by the coalition between Fox and North (February 1783). Shelburne was in 1784 made Marquis of Lansdowne, and at Lansdowne House and Bowood, Wilts, he collected a splendid gallery of pictures and a fine library. See Lives by Lord Edmond Fitzmaurice (1912) and C. W. Alvord (1925).

SHELDON, Gilbert (1598–1677), English prelate, chaplain to Charles I, warden of All Souls College, Oxford, and from 1663 Archbishop of Canterbury, built the Sheldonian Theatre at Oxford (1669).

SHELLEY, (1) **Mary Wollstonecraft** (1797–1851), English writer, was the daughter of William Godwin and Mary Wollstonecraft (qq.v.). Her life from 1814 to 1822 was bound up with that of Shelley. Her first and most impressive novel was *Frankenstein* (1818), her second *Valperga* (1823). In 1823 she returned to England with her son. Her husband's father, in granting her an allowance, insisted on the suppression of the volume of Shelley's *Posthumous Poems*, edited by her. *The Last Man* (1826), a romance of the ruin of human society by pestilence, fails to attain sublimity. In *Lodore* (1835) the story is told of Shelley's alienation from his first wife. Her last novel, *Falkner*, appeared in 1837. Of her occasional pieces of verse the most remarkable is *The Choice*. Her *Journal of a Six Weeks' Tour* (partly by Shelley) tells of the excursion to Switzerland in 1814; *Rambles in Germany and Italy* (1844) describes tours in 1840–43; Garnett collected her *Tales* in 1890. Koszul edited two unpublished mythological dramas, *Proserpine* and *Midas*, in 1922. See Lives by F. A. Marshall (1889), R. Church (1928), R. G. Grylls (1938), and H. N. Brailsford, *Shelley, Godwin and their Circle* (2nd ed. 1951).

(2) **Percy Bysshe** (1792–1822), was born at Field Place, Horsham, Sussex. After two years at Sion House School, Isleworth, where he acquired a taste for natural science, but where he was bullied, he entered Eton in 1804. Here, besides the classics, he imbibed sceptical and revolutionary ideas. In 1810 he became an undergraduate at University College, Oxford. His chief friend there, Thomas Jefferson Hogg, has described his career at Oxford, which was terminated after only a year by expulsion for issuing a pamphlet, *The Necessity of Atheism*. Hogg shared in this undergraduate revolt and was sent down at the same time. Left to himself in London the poet formed a connection with Harriet Westbrook, daughter af a retired coffee-house keeper, whose unhappy home circumstances induced Shelley to make a runaway marriage at Edinburgh (August 1811). The rights and wrongs of this unfortunate union have never been satisfactorily decided—Shelley never reproached himself for Harriet's tragedy—but no doubt the aim

he now set himself of 'reforming the world' under the direction of the teaching of the philosopher, William Godwin, explains almost everything. This aim led for a time to an itinerant mission to, among other places, Dublin and Lynmouth where he commenced his long poem *Queen Mab*—the first of his poems, which might be called 'Godwin versified'. Of Harriet's unhappy life during the three years (1811–14) they more or less lived together, little is known. Possibly her insistence on a Church remarriage in 1814 led to the final breach and left Shelley free to cultivate the friendship of Godwin's daughter Mary. Such was his notion of marital fidelity—free love was part of the Godwinian ideology—we find him after the breach inviting Harriet to join him and Mary Godwin in a visit to Switzerland. The year before, Harriet had borne him a daughter Ianthe and now, January 1816, Mary bore him a son, William, out of wedlock. A few months later Harriet was found drowned in the Serpentine. By arrangement with his father Shelley now had settled on him out of his grandfather's estate £1000 a year and so was free to marry Mary Godwin and travel abroad. A lawsuit over the custody of Harriet's children Ianthe and Charles (1814–26) was decided by Lord Eldon against him on the ground of his atheistic opinions, a verdict which further embittered him against the 'Establishment'. In 1818 he set out for Italy accompanied by Mary, his son William and daughter Clara, and Miss Clairmont, Mary's half-sister, and her daughter Allegra, child of an amour with Byron. This family of free-lovers was now to travel round Italy from Venice (where Shelley met Byron) to Rome, to Naples, back to Rome (where he wrote the last two acts of *Prometheus Unbound*), to Leghorn and Florence and finally to the lonely house on the bay of Spezia where 'The Triumph of Life' was written and whence he set out for Leghorn to meet Leigh Hunt and his family, a journey from which he was not to return, his small boat having foundered in a storm on the way home. The seriousness with which Shelley (unlike the libertine Byron) held his heretical doctrines is best indicated by the immense liberation the Italian scene effected on his spirits and his poetry. Hitherto, apart from the doctrinal poems, *Queen Mab* and *The Revolt of Islam*, he had only *Alastor* (1816), a study of the egocentric romantic, himself, which has been much overpraised, the *Hymn to Intellectual Beauty* and *Mont Blanc* to his credit. Now in *Lines Written in the Euganean Hills* the theme of Italian liberty is worked out in octosyllables of striking force and brevity of diction. In *Julian and Maddalo* also, which belongs to his 'Venetian' period he found another medium for his conversation with Byron, who is Maddalo, viz., a finely modulated conversational form of the heroic couplet, which he later used for both humorous and romantic purposes in his *Letter to Maria Gisborne* (1820). These two poems along with his satire on Wordsworth, *Peter Bell the Third*, are the answer to those critics who think of him as a poet of moonshine and cloud shapes.

He further displayed technical versatility in his esoteric drama *The Cenci* which owes something to the Jacobean school of Webster and Tourneur. It is a study of absolute evil and he had a story to work on, in which the dreadful and the heroic mingle. The poetry is kept to a minimum here and there is no humour. If we are to think of the 'uncommitted' Shelley, reference must also be made to that brilliant poem, the finest of all his fantasies, *The Witch of Atlas*, which gathers up all the gaieties of classical mythology—a rainbow fabric of pure vision, which recalls Renaissance virtuosity at its best. *Prometheus Unbound*, completed at Rome, 1820, a study of the revolt of man against law and custom which oppress him. This is Godwinian doctrine removed to the realm of mythology, but now quickened by the more genial spirit of Plato, whose Symposium he had translated in 1818. Christianity is dethroned, but it is by the spirit of Christ. The assertion of the Godwinian doctrine of free love, modified by the Platonic notion of intellectual love, appears in *Epipsychidion* (1821) in the most seductive guise. To the same year belongs *Adonais*, which fittingly celebrates Keats and crowns his own career as poet and 'legislator'. He had the machinery of classical pastoral elegy to work on, but he etherealizes it and performs the feat of employing the Spenserian stanza for a heroic purpose. It is enshrined in the hearts of all lovers of the two poets. In 1822 he returned to the theme of liberty. *Hellas* sings prophetically of the delivery of Greece from the Turk. It contains his greatest impersonal lyric 'The world's great age begins anew'. His last (unfinished) poem, *The Triumph of Life*, is a Petrarchian pageant, a vision of the world to be, marred only by the intrusion of Rousseau. He has not quite mastered Dante's terza rima, but the strict form imposes some restraint on him. The theme is again that of *The Revolt of Islam*—the true conquerors are those who resist 'royal anarchs'. Shelley is still the rebel and the anarchist, as he was when he wrote *The Masque of Anarchy* to denounce 'Peterloo'. Saintsbury remarked on his immediate mastery of every poetical form he attempted. This is certainly true of his lyrics, which are as perfect in his early as in his latest period. This lyricism, effortless as breathing, pervades all his poetry. Of the longer sort of lyric or ode 'To a Skylark', 'Ode to the West Wind', 'The Cloud' and 'The Sensitive Plant' register with consummate artistry the whole range of his feeling. The shorter love lyrics—'I arise from dreams of thee', 'To Constantia singing', 'Rarely, rarely comest thou', 'Swifter far than summer's flight', &c., rank with the greatest of their kind. Shelley was also a skilful master of the art of prose writing. His prose work includes the uncompleted *A Defence of Poetry* (1822), stating the eternal problem of art in its bearing on conduct. He asserts the Platonic notion that the poet is divinely inspired and therefore may be, in some sense, a 'legislator' to mankind. The modern edition of the *Collected Works* is by Ingpen and Peck (10 vols. 1926–30), but H. Buxton Forman, whose *Complete Works* (8 vols.

1876–80) it displaced, did invaluable work for the text and bibliography. The two-volume edition of the *Poems* by C. D. Locock (1911) has a valuable introduction by A. Clutton Brock, who also wrote *Shelley, the Man and the Poet* (1909). *The Letters*, ed. R. Ingpen (1909) are indispensible. Peck's Life (1927), followed by R. Bailey's study (1934) and E. Blunden's *Shelley, a Life Story* (1946), displaced Dowden's standard Life (1886). Other studies are Brailsford's *Shelley, Godwin and their Circle* (2nd ed. 1951), *Shelley and his Circle* (ed. by K. N. Cameron, 1961); Campbells' *Shelley and the Unromantics* (1924), Maurois' *Ariel* (1924, trans. 1961), and King-Hele's *Shelley, his Thought and Work* (1960). See also Life of Harriet by L. S. Boas (1962).

SHENSTONE, William (1714–63), English poet, born at Halesowen, studied at Pembroke College, Oxford, published in 1741 *The Judgment of Hercules* and the following year *The Schoolmistress*, which, written in imitation of Spenser, foreshadowed the mood of Gray's *Elegy*. *Pastoral Ballad* (1755) was commended by Gray and Johnson. In later life he suffered many financial embarrassments due to his elegant mode of life on his estate of the Leasowes. See *Letters*, ed. Williams (1939), and Lives by E. M. Purkis (1931), M. Williams (1935) and A. R. Humphreys (1937).

SHEPILOV, Dmitri Trofimovitch (1905–), Soviet politician, was born at Ashkhabad and was educated at Moscow University. From 1926 to 1931 he was a public prosecutor in Siberia and later became a lecturer in political economy. In 1952 he became chief editor of *Pravda*; in 1954 a member of the Supreme Soviet; and in 1956 foreign minister. He was 'purged' by the party leadership in 1957 and banished to a distant teaching post.

SHEPPARD, (1) Hugh Richard Lawrie, known as '**Dick**' (1880–1937), Anglican divine and pacifist, born at Windsor, a popular preacher with distinctly modern views on the Christian life and a pioneer of religious broadcasting, was vicar of London's St Martin-in-the-Fields (1914–27), published *The Human Parson* (1924) and *The Impatience of a Parson* (1927), became dean of Canterbury (1929–31) and canon of St Paul's Cathedral (1934–37). He was an ardent pacifist and founded the Peace Pledge Union in 1936. He was appointed C.H. in 1927. See Lives by R. E. Roberts (1941) and Matthews (1948).

(2) **Jack** (1702–24), English robber, born at Stepney, committed the first of many robberies in July 1720, and in 1724 was five times caught, and four times escaped. He was hanged at Tyburn in the presence of 200,000 spectators. He was the subject of many plays and ballads, tracts by Defoe and a novel by Ainsworth. See book ed. Bleakley and Ellis (1933).

SHERATON, Thomas (1751–1806), English cabinetmaker, born at Stockton-on-Tees, settled in London about 1790, wrote a *Cabinetmaker's Book* (1794). His neoclassical designs had a wide influence on contemporary taste in furniture. See studies, ed. R. Edwards (1945).

SHERBROOKE, Robert Lowe, 1st Viscount (1811–92), English politician, born at Bingham, Notts, from Winchester went in 1829 to University College, Oxford. Called to the bar in 1842, he emigrated the same year to Australia, soon attained a lucrative practice, and also took a leading part in politics. Home again in 1850, and returned to parliament (1852), he took office under Aberdeen and Palmerston. During 1859–64 he was vice-president of the Education Board, and introduced the Revised Code of 1862 with its ' payment by results '. In 1868 his feud with the Liberals was forgotten in his strenuous aid towards disestablishing the Irish Church, and Gladstone made him chancellor of the Exchequer. In 1873 he became home secretary; in 1880 went to the Upper House as Viscount Sherbrooke. He opposed the exclusive study of the classics. See Life by A. Patchett Martin (1893).

SHERE ALI, *shayr ah'lee* (1825–79), Amir of Afghanistan, a younger son of Dost Mohammed, succeeded as amir in 1863. Disagreements with his half-brothers soon arose, which kept Afghanistan in anarchy; Shere Ali fled to Kandahar; but in 1868 regained possession of Kabul, with assistance from the viceroy of India, Sir John Lawrence. In 1870 his eldest son, Yakub Khan, rebelled, but was captured and imprisoned. Shere Ali's refusal to receive a British mission (1878) led to war; and, after severe fighting, he fled to Turkestan, there to die. Yakub Khan succeeded.

SHERIDAN, (1) Philip Henry (1831–88), American soldier, born in Albany, N.Y., March 6, of Irish parentage, in 1848 entered West Point, and graduated in 1853. In 1861 he was an infantry captain, but in 1862 was given a cavalry regiment, and rose rapidly to command a division. He distinguished himself at Perryville and at Stone River, fought at Chickamauga, and was engaged in all the subsequent operations of the Civil War, gaining credit for the gallantry with which his division drove the enemy over Missionary Ridge. In 1864 he was given command of the cavalry of the Army of the Potomac, took part in the Battle of the Wilderness, made a notable raid on Confederate communications with Richmond, and led the advance to Cold Harbor. In August Grant placed him in command of the Army of the Shenandoah with instructions to make the valley ' a barren waste '. In September he attacked the enemy under Early, drove him beyond Winchester, again dislodged him from Fisher's Hill, and pursued him through Harrisonburg and Staunton, but Early, reinforced by Lee, again appeared in the Shenandoah Valley, and on October 19 surprised the Northern army and drove it back in confusion. Sheridan, who was at Winchester, twenty miles away, galloped to the field and turned defeat into victory. He was promoted major-general and received the thanks of congress. Defeating the enemy at Five Forks on April 1, he had an active share in the final battles which led to Lee's surrender at Appomattox Court-house, April 9, 1865. A lieutenant-general in 1870, he was with Moltke at Gravelotte and other battles. In 1883 he succeeded Sherman as general-in-chief. He died at Nonquitt, Mass., August 5. Sheridan never lost a battle. Among the Northern generals he ranks next to Grant and Sherman. See his *Personal Memoirs* (1888) and *Life* by Davies (1895).

(2) **Richard Brinsley** (1751–1816), British dramatist, born in Dublin, October 30, was grandson of Swift's friend, Thomas Sheridan, D.D. (1687–1738), and son of Thomas Sheridan (1719–88), a teacher of elocution, actor and author of a *Life of Swift*. His mother, Frances Sheridan, *née* Chamberlaine (1724–66), was the author of a novel called *Sidney Biddulph* and of one or two plays. Richard Sheridan was educated at Harrow, and after leaving school, with a schoolfriend named Halhed wrote a three-act farce called *Jupiter* and tried a verse translation of the *Epistles of Aristoenetus*. After a romantic courtship, Richard married Elizabeth Linley in 1773. The young couple settled in London to a life much beyond their means. Sheridan now made more serious efforts at dramatic composition. On January 17, 1775, *The Rivals* was produced at Covent Garden, and after a slight alteration in the cast met with universal approval. In the same year appeared the poor farce called *St Patrick's Day* and also *The Duenna*. In 1776 Sheridan, with the aid of Linley and another friend, bought half the patent of Drury Lane Theatre for £35,000 from Garrick, and in 1778 the remaining share for £45,000. His first production was a purified edition of Vanbrugh's *Relapse*, under the title of *A Trip to Scarborough*. Three months later (1777) appeared his greatest work, *The School for Scandal*. *The Critic* (1779), teeming with sparkling wit, was Sheridan's last dramatic effort, with the exception of a poor tragedy, *Pizarro*. On the dissolution of parliament in 1780 Sheridan was elected for Stafford, and in 1782 became under-secretary for foreign affairs under Rockingham, afterwards secretary to the treasury in the coalition ministry (1783). His parliamentary reputation dates from his great speeches in the impeachment of Warren Hastings. In 1794 he again electrified the House by a magnificent oration in reply to Lord Mornington's denunciation of the French Revolution. He remained the devoted friend and adherent of Fox till Fox's death, and was also the defender and mouthpiece of the prince regent. In 1806 he was appointed receiver of the Duchy of Cornwall, and in 1806 treasurer to the navy. In 1812 he was defeated at Westminster, and his parliamentary career came to an end. In 1792 his first wife died, and three years later he married Esther Ogle, the silly and extravagant daughter of the Dean of Winchester, who survived him. The affairs of the theatre had gone badly. The old building had to be closed as unfit to hold large audiences, and a new one, opened in 1794, was burned in 1809. This last calamity put the finishing touch to Sheridan's pecuniary difficulties, which had long been serious. He died July 7, 1816, in great poverty, but was given a magnificent funeral in Westminster Abbey. See Memoirs in editions of his works by Leigh Hunt (1840), and Rhodes (1928); *Memoirs of Mrs Frances Sheridan*, by her granddaughter, Alicia Le Fanu (1824); Lives by Fraser Rae (2 vols. 1896) and W. Sichel (2 vols. 1909), Rhodes (1933), Darlington (1933); also the articles DUFFERIN and NORTON.

SHERIFF, Lawrence (d. 1567), London grocer, born at Rugby, founded its great public school (1567).

SHERLOCK, (1) Thomas (1678–1761), English prelate, son of (2), bishop successively of Bangor (1728), Salisbury (1734) and London (1748), opposed Bishop Hoadly (q.v.) in the Bangorian controversy and temporarily lost influence at court. See Life by E. F. Carpenter (1936).

(2) **William** (1641–1707), English prelate, father of (1), born at Southwark, became master of the Temple in 1685 and Dean of St Paul's in 1691. He was a nonjuror, but took the oaths in 1690. The most controversial of his 60 works were *Vindication of the Doctrines of the Trinity and of the Incarnation* (1690), which made South charge him with Tritheism, and *Case of Allegiance* (1691).

SHERMAN, (1) Henry Clapp (1875–1955), American biochemist. Educated at Maryland and Columbia, Sherman became professor of Organic Chemistry (1907), of Nutritional Chemistry (1911) and of Chemistry (1924) at the latter university. He did important quantitative work on vitamins.

(2) **John** (1823–1900), American statesman, brother of (4), born at Lancaster, Ohio, was in turn chairman of financial committees in both houses of Congress. He was largely author of the bills for the reconstruction of the seceded states and for the resumption of specie payment in 1879. He was appointed in 1877 secretary of the Treasury, and in 1878 had prepared a redemption fund in gold that raised the legal tender notes to par value. In 1881 and 1887 he was again returned to the senate, was its president, and afterwards chairman of the committee on foreign relations. In 1897 he was made secretary of state, but retired on the war with Spain in 1898. The Sherman Act (1890; repealed 1893) sanctioned large purchases of silver by the Treasury. See Life by Bronson (2nd ed. 1888), *Selected Speeches* (1879), *Sherman Letters*, between the brothers (1894), his *Recollections of Forty Years* (N.Y. 1896).

(3) **Roger** (1721–93), American statesman and patriot, born at Newton, Mass., lived in Connecticut from 1743. First elected to the state assembly in 1755, he became a judge of the superior court (1766–89) and mayor of New Haven (1784–93). A signatory of the Declaration of Independence, as a delegate to the Convention of 1787 he took a prominent part in the debates on the Constitution. See Life by Boutell (1896).

(4) **William Tecumseh** (1820–91), American soldier, brother of (2), born at Lancaster, Ohio, graduated at West Point in 1840. After serving in Florida and California, he became a banker in San Francisco. In May 1861 he was commissioned colonel of the Thirteenth Infantry; at Bull Run he won his promotion to brigadier-general of volunteers. In August he was sent to Kentucky, at first under Anderson, but when he asked for 200,000 men to put an end to the war there, he was deprived of his command. But soon

in command of a division, he took a distinguished part in the battle of Shiloh (April 1862) and was made major-general. In Grant's various movements against Vicksburg Sherman was most active. In July 1863, promoted brigadier, he drove General Johnston out of Jackson, Miss. In November he joined Grant at Chattanooga, and rendered excellent service in the victory of the 25th; soon after, he relieved Burnside, besieged at Knoxville. In March 1864 he was appointed by Grant to the command of the southwest. In April he commenced his campaign against Atlanta. He first encountered Johnston at Dalton, May 14, and drove him beyond the Eaowah, and finally to Atlanta, which was evacuated on September 1. After giving his army a rest Sherman commenced his famous march to the sea, with 65,000 men. Meeting with little serious opposition, he reached Savannah on December 10. The works were soon carried, and on the 20th the city was evacuated. In February he left Savannah for the north, and by the 17th, compelling the evacuation of Charleston, had reached Columbia. Thence he moved on Goldsboro', fighting two battles on the way. On April 9 Lee surrendered, and Johnston made terms with Sherman (disapproved as too lenient by Secretary Stanton). For four years Sherman commanded the Mississippi division; when Grant became president he was made head of the army. In 1874, at his own request, to make room for Sheridan, he was retired on full pay. He died in New York, February 14. See his own Memoirs (1875; revised 1891), his Letters, ed. Thorndike (1894), and Lives by E. Robins (1905), B. Liddell Hart (1930) and A. H. Burne (1939).

SHERRIFF, Robert Cedric (1896–), British playwright, novelist and scriptwriter, born at Kingston-upon-Thames, achieved an international reputation with his first play, *Journey's End* (1929), based on his experiences in the trenches during the first World War. In 1931 he turned student at Oxford and in 1933 went to Hollywood. His later plays did not match up to his first, but he wrote the scripts for such films as *The Invisible Man* (1933), *Goodbye Mr Chips* (1936), *The Four Feathers* (1938), *Lady Hamilton* (1941) and *The Dambusters* (1955).

SHERRINGTON, Sir Charles Scott (1857–1952), English physiologist, born in London, passed through Caius College, Cambridge, was professor of Physiology at Liverpool (1895–1913) and Oxford (1913–35). His researches on reflex action and especially on *The Integrative Action of the Nervous System* (1906) constitute a landmark in modern physiology. His poetry is worthy of note. In 1920–25 he was P.R.S., in 1922 president of the British Association; he was awarded the O.M. in 1924, and a Nobel prize for medicine in 1932. See Life by Lord Cohen (1958).

SHERWOOD, (1) **Mary Martha** (1775–1851), English writer of children's books, daughter of Dr Butt, chaplain to George III, was born at Stanford, Worcs. In 1803 she sailed for India. Her 77 works include *Little Henry and his Bearer*, and the long-popular *History of*

the Fairchild Family. See her own Life (ed. Darton, 1910), and one by her daughter, Mrs Kelly (1854).
(2) **Robert Emmet** (1896–1955), American playwright and author, born in New Rochelle, New York. He wrote his first play, *Barnum Was Right*, while at Harvard, and after service in the first World War became editor (1924–28) of *Life*. He won four Pulitzer prizes, the first three for drama (*Idiot's Delight*, 1936; *Abe Lincoln in Illinois*, 1939; and *There Shall be No Night*, 1941), and the last (1949) for his biographical *Roosevelt and Hopkins*.

SHEVCHENKO, Taras (1814–61), Ukrainian poet and prose writer, born a serf at Kirilovka (Kiev), was freed and became professor at Kiev (1845), founded an organization for radical social reforms, was exiled to Siberia for ten years, and published collections of poems in the Ukrainian language.

SHIELD, William (1748–1829), English viola player and composer, born at Swalwell in Durham, was apprenticed to a boatbuilder, and, encouraged by Giardini, studied music, composed anthems that were sung in Durham cathedral, and conducted at Scarborough. He published a comic opera, *The Flitch of Bacon*, in 1778, and, as composer to Covent Garden (1778–97), produced others. Some of his songs are still known. In 1792 he travelled in Italy. From 1817 he was master of the King's Musicians. See *Memorial* (1891).

SHIH HUANG TI (259–210 B.C.), Chinese emperor from 246, and 4th monarch of the Chin dynasty. Assuming the title of 'the first emperor', he greatly extended the empire and built the Great Wall, completed in 204, to keep out barbarians. He had all historical documents burnt in 212 to maintain himself and his successors in power.

SHILLABER, Benjamin Penhallow (1814–90), American humorist, author of *Sayings of Mrs Partington* (1854).

SHILLIBEER, George (1797–1866), British pioneer of London omnibuses, born in London, established a coachbuilding business in Paris and from 1829 ran the first London omnibus coach service from the City to Paddington.

SHINWELL, Emanuel (1884–), British Labour politician, born in Spitalfields, London, began work as an errand boy in Glasgow at the age of twelve. An early student of public library and street-corner Socialism, he was elected to Glasgow Trades Council in 1911 and, one of the ' wild men of Clydeside ', served a five months' prison sentence for incitement to riot in 1921. M.P. in 1931 and secretary to the Department of Mines (1924, 1930–31), in 1935 he defeated Ramsay MacDonald at Seaham Harbour, Durham, in one of the most bitterly contested election battles of modern times. From 1942 he was chairman of the Labour Party committee which drafted the manifesto ' Let Us face the Future ', on which Labour won the 1945 election. As minister of fuel and power he nationalized the mines (1946), and the following year, when he was said to be a scapegoat for the February fuel crisis, he became secretary of state for war.

From 1950 to 1951 he was minister of defence. In these last two offices, 'Manny's' considerable administrative ability outshone his prickly party political belligerence and earned him the respect of such discerning critics in defence matters as Churchill and Montgomery. In his later years he mellowed into a back-bench 'elder statesman'. He became Labour Party chairman in 1964, was created C.H. in 1965 and awarded a life peerage in 1970. See his autobiographical *Conflict without Malice* (1955).

SHIPTON, (1) Eric Earle (1907–), British mountaineer. He gained his early mountaineering experience during five expeditions to the mountains of East and Central Africa, climbing Kamet (25,447 ft.) in 1931. He obtained much of his knowledge of the East during his terms as consul-general in Kashgar (1940–42 and 1946–48) and in Kunming (1949–51). Between 1933 and 1951 he either led or was member of five expeditions to Mount Everest. He probably did more than any other man to pave the way for the successful Hunt-Hillary expedition of 1953. He was made a C.B.E. in 1955. See his *Upon that Mountain* (1948), *Mount Everest Reconnaissance Expedition* (1951).

(2) Mother (1488–c. 1560), English witch, born near Knaresborough, and baptized as Ursula Southiel, at twenty-four married Tony Shipton, a builder, and died at over seventy years of age—according to S. Baker, who edited her 'prophecies' (1797). A book (1684) by Richard Head tells how she was carried off by the devil, bore him an imp, &c. A small British moth, with wing-markings, resembling a witch's face, is named after her. See book by W. H. Harrison (1881).

SHIRLEY, (1) Sir Anthony (1565–c. 1635), English adventurer. After following Essex from 1597, he was knighted by the king of France without the assent of Queen Elizabeth, who had him imprisoned until he renounced the title, which is therefore nominal only. His voyage to America and Jamaica (1595) is recorded by Hakluyt. In 1599 he went to Persia on a trade mission, and returned as the Shah's envoy in an unsuccessful attempt to form an alliance against the Turks. His account of this adventure was published in 1613. Proscribed from entering Britain, he wandered in Europe and died at Madrid.

(2) James (1596–1666), English late Elizabethan dramatist, born in London, September 18, from Merchant Taylors' passed in 1612 to St John's, Oxford, but migrated to Catharine Hall, Cambridge. He took orders, and held a living at St Albans. Turning Catholic, he taught (1623–24) in the grammar school there, but soon went to London and became playwright. The suppression of stage plays in 1642 ended his livelihood, and he took to teaching again. The Restoration revived his plays, but brought him no better fortunes. His death was a result of the Great Fire of London. Beaumont and Fletcher and Ben Jonson were his models, but he has little of the grand Elizabethan manner. Most of his plays are tragi-comedies. His chief works are *Eccho* (1618), a poem on the Narcissus subject; comedies, *The Witty Fair One* (1628); *The*

Wedding (1628); *The Grateful Servant* (1629); *The Example* (1634); *The Opportunity* (1634); *The Lady of Pleasure*, the most brilliant of his comedies (1635); tragedies, *The Cardinal*, to the author himself 'the best of his flock' (1641); *The Traytor* (1631), a great drama. As a masque writer he is second only to Jonson; among his best masques are *The Triumph of Peace* (1633) and *The Contention of Ajax and Ulysses* (1659, including 'The glories of our blood and state'). His thirty-five plays were edited by Gifford and Dyce (1833), his *Poems* by R. L. Armstrong (1941). See studies by Schipper (1911), Forsythe (1915) and Nason (1915).

(3) John (1366?–1456), English traveller and transcriber of Chaucer and Lydgate.

(4) Lawrence. See FERRERS.

(5) Robert (1581?–1628), brother of (1), accompanied him to Persia and remained there. He made two journeys to European courts as envoy of the Shah of Persia (1608, 1615), being accepted by James I of England for three years (1624–27), when he returned to Persia and died out of favour.

SHIRREFF, (1) Emily Anne Eliza (1814–97), English pioneer of women's education, was mistress of Girton College from 1870. She published works on Kindergartens and the Fröbel system.

(2) Patrick (1791–1876), Scottish farmer in East Lothian, born near Haddington, was the pioneer of cereal hybridizing, and produced many varieties of wheat and oats.

SHOLOKHOV, Mikhail (1905–), Russian novelist, born near Veshenskaya, wrote *Quiet Flows the Don* (trans. 1935) and other novels of Cossack life, *The Upturned Soil* (1940) on the effects of the new régime on farm life, and short stories. He won the Stalin prize in 1941, and the Nobel prize for literature in 1965.

SHORE, (1) Jane (d. c. 1527), born in London, early married William Shore, a goldsmith. After her intrigue with Edward IV began, about 1470, her husband abandoned her, but she lived till Edward's death in luxury, enjoying great power, yet 'never abusing it', as More tells us, 'to any man's hurt, but to many a man's comfort and relief'. After the king's death she lived under the protection of Hastings, and on his death, it is said, of the Marquis of Dorset; but Richard III, to make his brother's life odious, relieved her of over two thousand marks, and caused the Bishop of London to make her walk in open penance, taper in hand, dressed only in her kirtle. She forms the subject of a tragedy by Rowe (1714).

(2) John, 1st Baron Teignmouth (1751–1834), English governor-general of India (1793–98), originated the Bengal *zamindari* system and many of Cornwallis's reforms. He supported Hastings at the latter's trial (1797) and settled the Oude succession. He was first president of the British and Foreign Bible Society and was created an Irish peer (1798).

SHORT, Sir Frank (1857–1945), English engraver, known especially for etchings and mezzotints, including the plates for Turner's *Liber Studiorum*.

SHORTER, Clement King (1858–1926),

English journalist and critic, born in London, edited the *Illustrated London News* (1891–1900), founded and edited the *Sketch*, and from 1900 was editor of the *Sphere*. He wrote on the Brontës, on Victorian literature, on Borrow and Boswell. His first wife was **Dora Sigerson** (d. 1918), Irish author of *Verses* (1894), *The Fairy Changeling* (1897), &c.

SHORTHOUSE, Joseph Henry (1834–1903), English novelist, born at Birmingham, became a chemical manufacturer there. In 1881 his romance, *John Inglesant*, revealed a subtle and sympathetic insight into old-world phases of the spiritual mind. It was followed by *The Little Schoolmaster Mark* (1883–84), *Sir Percival* (1886), *A Teacher of the Violin* (1888), *The Countess Eve* (1888), and *Blanche, Lady Falaise* (1891). See his Life by his wife (1905).

SHOSTAKOVICH, Dmitri, -ko'- (1906–), Russian composer, was born in St Petersburg (now Leningrad), where he entered the Conservatoire in 1919. His First Symphony, composed in 1925, the year his studies ended, attracted considerable attention. His music, in which he attempted to support Soviet principles, was at first highly successful, but the development of a more conservative attitude on the part of the Soviet Government, coinciding with his own development of a more experimental outlook, led to official criticism of his opera *The Nose*, his Second ('October') Symphony, and a second opera, *A Lady Macbeth of Mtensk*, which had to be withdrawn after violent press attacks on its decadence and its failure to observe the principles of 'Soviet realism'. Shostakovich was reinstated by his Fifth Symphony (1938). He has composed prolifically in all forms, and his Seventh ('Leningrad') Symphony, his Tenth Symphony, and his Violin Concerto have won considerable popularity outside Russia. His Eleventh Symphony, for which he was awarded a Lenin prize in 1958, is based upon the events of the October Revolution of 1905. See study by Rabinovich (1960).

SHOVEL, Sir Cloudesley (1650–1707), English sailor, served against the Dutch and in the Mediterranean, burned four corsair galleys at Tripoli (1676), commanded a ship at the battle in Bantry Bay (1689), and was knighted. In 1690 he took part in the battle off Beachy Head; in 1692 he supported Russell at La Hogue, and burned twenty of the enemy's ships. He served under Rooke in the Mediterranean, and with him took Gibraltar in 1704. In 1705 he was made rear-admiral of England. That year he took part with Peterborough in the capture of Barcelona, but failed in his attack on Toulon in 1707. On the voyage home his ship (and others) struck a rock off the Scilly Isles on the foggy night of October 22, 1707, and went down. His body was washed up, and buried in Westminster Abbey.

SHRAPNEL, Henry (1761–1842), English artillery officer, retired from active service as a lieutenant-general in 1825. In about 1793 he invented the shrapnel shell.

SHREWSBURY. See TALBOT Family.

SHUTE, (1) **John.** See BARRINGTON (3).
(2) **Nevil,** pen-name of **Nevil Shute Norway**

(1899–1960), English writer, born in Ealing, emigrated to Australia. He served in the 1914–18 war and immediately afterwards began an aeronautical career. He was chief calculator to the Airship Guarantee Company during the construction of the airship R100 and flew the Atlantic twice in her. He founded Airspeed Ltd., aircraft constructors, and became its managing director. His novels include *The Pied Piper* (1942), *Most Secret* (1945), *The Chequerboard* (1947), *No Highway* (1948), *A Town Like Alice* (1949), *Round the Bend* (1951), *Requiem for a Wren* (1955), *Beyond the Black Stump* (1956) and *On the Beach* (1957). His success was largely due to his brisk style and his ability to make technical language and procedure understandable to a lay public.

SHUVALOV, shoo-vah'lof, (1) **Count Paul** (1830–1908), Russian general, brother of (2), fought at Sebastopol and Inkermann, and helped to organize the liberation of the Russian serfs (1861). He fought in Turkey (1878), was ambassador to Germany (1885) and governor of Warsaw (1895).
(2) **Count Petr Andreyevich** (1827–89), Russian diplomatist, brother of (1), became head of the secret police in 1866; in 1873, sent on a secret mission to London, he arranged the marriage between the Duke of Edinburgh and the only daughter of Alexander II. In 1878 he was one of the Russian representatives at the Congress of Berlin.

SIBBALD, Sir Robert (1641–1722), Scottish naturalist and physician, born at Edinburgh, became a physician there, but gave much time to botany and zoology. He helped to establish a botanic garden, and was virtual founder of the Royal College of Physicians of Edinburgh. He was knighted in 1682 and appointed professor of Medicine and Scottish geographer royal. He wrote *History of Fife* (1710), pamphlets on medical subjects, natural history and antiquities, and *Autobiography* (1833; 1932).

SIBELIUS, Jean, si-bay'li-oos (1865–1957), Finnish composer, born in Tavastehus. The son of a surgeon, he studied the piano as a child, but was sent to Helsinki University to study law. He abandoned a legal career for full-time musical study in 1885, leaving Helsinki Conservatory in 1889 with a state grant which enabled him to continue his studies in Berlin and Vienna. A passionate nationalist, on his return to Finland he began the series of symphonic poems (including the well-known *Swan of Tuonela*) based on episodes in the Finnish epic *Kalevala*, and his first great success came with *En Saga* (1892). From 1897 until his death a state grant enabled him to devote himself entirely to composition, and his symphonies, symphonic poems—notably *Finlandia* (1899)—and violin concerto won great popularity, in Britain and America as well as in Finland, for their originality of form and idiom. After his Seventh Symphony (1924–25) and *Tapiola* (1926), he released no more music for performance or publication. See studies by C. Gray (1935), Neville Cardus (1945), H. E. Johnson (1960), and of his symphonies by S. Parmet (trans. 1959).

SIBLEY, Henry Hastings (1811–91), American statesman, first governor and 'Father of Minnesota', born at Detroit, put down the Sioux outbreak of 1862.

SIBOUR, Marie Dominique Auguste (1792–1857), French prelate, from 1848 Archbishop of Paris, was murdered during mass by an excommunicated priest. See *Life* by Poujoulat (2nd ed. 1863).

SICKERT, Walter Richard (1860–1942), British artist, was born at Munich. After three years on the English stage (an interest reflected in many pictures of music halls) he studied at the Slade School, and under Whistler. While working in Paris, he was much influenced by Degas. He had many studios in London, paying regular visits to France, and he used Degas' technique to illustrate London low life. Sickert was a member of the New English Art Club, and about 1910 the Camden Town Group (later the London Group) was formed under his leadership. His famous interior *Ennui* (in the Tate Gallery) belongs to this period. Both his painting and his writings on art have had great influence on later English painters; see his autobiography *A Free House!* (1947), the *Life and Opinions* edited by R. Emmons (1941), and study by L. Browse (1960).

SICKINGEN, Franz von, *zik'-* (1481–1523), German knight, born at Ebernburg near Kreuznach, fought in 1508 against the Venetians for the Emperor Maximilian, but in peace led the life of a freelance. During 1513–19 he warred against Worms, Metz, Philip of Hesse and Württemberg. Ulrich von Hutten from 1520 was his constant guest, and won him over to the cause of the Reformation. In 1521 he assisted the emperor in his French campaign; in 1522 he opened a Protestant war against the Archbishop of Trier. That war miscarried; and, put to the ban of the empire and besieged in his castle of Landstuhl, he was killed.

SIDDAL, Elizabeth Eleanor. See ROSSETTI (2).

SIDDONS, Sarah (1755–1831), English actress, was born at Brecon, July 5, the eldest child of Roger Kemble (q.v.), manager of a small travelling theatrical company, of which Sarah was a member from her earliest childhood. In 1773 she married at Coventry her fellow-actor, William Siddons. Her first appearance at Drury Lane in December 1775 as Portia met with no great success. But her reputation grew so fast in the provinces that in 1782 she returned to Drury Lane, and made her reappearance in October as Isabella in Garrick's adaptation of Southerne's *Fatal Marriage*. Her success was immediate, and from this time she was the unquestioned queen of the stage. In 1803 she followed her brother, John Philip Kemble, to Covent Garden, where she continued till her formal farewell to the stage as Lady Macbeth, June 29, 1812. Thereafter she appeared occasionally, but only for special benefits, and she sometimes gave public readings. Endowed with a gloriously expressive and beautiful face, a queenly figure, and a voice of richest power and flexibility, she worked assiduously to cultivate

her gifts until as a tragic actress she reached a height of perfection probably unsurpassed by any player of any age or country. In comedy she was less successful. See *Lives* by Boaden (1827; new ed. 1893), Thomas Campbell (1834), N. H. Kennard (1886), F. M. Parsons (1909), A. Maurois (1927) and N. G. R. Smith (1933).

SIDGWICK, (1) Henry (1838–1900), English moral philosopher, born at Skipton, was educated at Rugby and Trinity College, Cambridge, of which he was fellow (1859–69), praelector of Moral Philosophy (1875–83) and then Knightsbridge professor. He is best known for his analytical examination of the various schools in moral philosophy in *Methods of Ethics* (1874), in which he attempts to restate the philosophically unsatisfactory arguments of J. S. Mill's *Utilitarianism* by relating it to intuitionism. Other works include *Outlines of the History of Ethics* (1886), the *Principles of Political Economy* (1883) and *Practical Ethics* (1898). He was an active member of the Psychical Research Society. See *Life* (1906) by his brother, the Greek scholar, **Arthur Sidgwick** (1840–1920) and his widow, **Eleanor Mildred Balfour** (1845–1936), sister of A. J. Balfour and principal of Newnham College (1892–1910). See also C. D. Broad, *Ethics and the History of Philosophy* (1952).

(2) **Nevil Vincent** (1873–1952), English chemist, professor at Oxford, known for his work on molecular structure and his formulation of a theory of valency. See his *The Electronic Theory of Valency* (1927). He was elected F.R.S. in 1922 and awarded the Royal Society's Royal Medal in 1937.

SIDI MOHAMMED BEN YOUSSEF (1911–61), sultan of Morocco from 1927, was born in Meknès, a scion of the Alouite dynasty. Exercising both spiritual and temporal power, he privily supported the nationalist Istaqlal party and constantly obstructed French hegemony. Tribal hostility to him gave the French the chance to depose him in 1953, but he was restored in 1955, and when Morocco attained independence in 1957 he became King Mohammed V. He died suddenly after a minor operation and was succeeded by his eldest son, **Prince Moulay Hassan,** who had already emerged as the spokesman of chauvinistic Moroccan youth. His eldest daughter, **Princess Lalla Ayesha** repudiated the *yasmak* and became a leader of the women's emancipation movement.

SIDMOUTH, Henry Addington, 1st Viscount (1757–1844), English statesman, the son of Lord Chatham's physician, **Anthony** (1713–1790), was educated at Winchester and Brasenose College, Oxford, quitted the bar for politics, and in 1783 was returned for Devizes. He was speaker 1789–1801, when, upon Pitt's resignation, he was invited to form a ministry. His undistinguished administration, whose one great event was the Peace of Amiens (1802), came to an end in 1804. Next year he was created Viscount Sidmouth, and thereafter was thrice president of the Council, once lord privy seal, and from 1812 to 1821 home secretary, as such being unpopular for his coercive measures.

He retired from the Cabinet in 1824. He was a sincere Tory. See *Life* by L. G. Pellew (1847) and E. M. G. Belfield, *Annals of the Addington Family* (1960).

SIDNEY, (1) **Algernon** (1622?–83), English politician, grandnephew of Sir Philip, and second son of the second Earl of Leicester, was born probably at Penshurst, Kent, and in 1622. He accompanied his father on his embassy in 1632 to Denmark, and in 1636 to France. In 1641–43 he commanded a troop of horse in Ireland, of which country his father was (nominally) lord-lieutenant. Declaring for the parliament, he was wounded at Marston Moor (1644); in 1645 was appointed governor of Chichester, and returned by Cardiff to parliament; in 1646 attended his brother, Viscount Lisle, now lord-lieutenant, to Ireland as lieutenant-general of horse and governor of Dublin; and in 1647, after receiving the thanks of the House of Commons, was appointed governor of Dover. In 1649, though nominated a commissioner, he took no part in the king's trial, which however he justified on abstract grounds. An extreme republican, he resented Cromwell's usurpation of power, and retired to Penshurst (1653–59). Then, made one of the Council of State, he undertook a political mission to Denmark and Sweden. After the Restoration he lived on the Continent, but in 1677 was pardoned and returned to England. In 1679 he twice stood unsuccessfully for parliament, and an attempt was made to involve him in the sham Meal-tub Plot. The attempt miscarried; still, he deemed it prudent to retire to France; and, to detach Louis XIV from Charles, entered into negotiations with him through Barillon. That prior to this he had taken monies from the French ambassador, either for himself or (more likely) for the republican cause, is admitted by Hallam and Macaulay, but disputed by Ewald. The next year he was back in England, and possibly helped Penn with the Pennsylvanian constitution, features of which were the ballot, universal suffrage, the abolition of a property qualification, religious equality, prison reform, and the abolition of capital punishment save for murder and treason. In June 1683, when the Rye House Plot was announced, the chance was seized to get rid of men felt to be dangerous, and, with Lords Russell, Essex and Howard, Sidney was sent to the Tower. In November he was tried for high treason before Jeffreys, and, on no evidence but the traitor Lord Howard's and his own unpublished *Discourses concerning Government* (1698), was beheaded December 7. His attainder was reversed in 1689. See R. C. Sidney's *Brief Memoir* of the trial (1685), Blencowe's *Sidney Papers* (1813), and *Lives* by Meadley (1813) and Ewald (1873).

(2) **Dorothea.** See WALLER (2).

(3) **Sir Henry** (1529–86), English administrator, father of (4), lord deputy of Ireland (1565–71; 1575–78), crushed Shane O'Neill in Ulster (1566–67), failed to establish English settlers, but organized a system of presidency councils. He served also as president of the council of Wales (1559–86).

(4) **Sir Philip** (1554–86), English poet, son of (3), born November 30 at Penshurst, Kent. Philip went up about 1568 from Shrewsbury to Christ Church, Oxford, and in 1572–75 travelled in France, Germany and Italy. At first a favourite of the queen, he was sent in 1577 as ambassador to the Emperor Rudolf and then to the Prince of Orange. Elizabeth displayed her ingratitude towards his father for his exertions as lord deputy in Ireland, and Philip wrote in his defence; he also addressed the queen against her projected match with the Duke of Anjou. Elizabeth was displeased; and his mother's brother, the once-powerful Leicester, fell into disfavour. Sidney retired (1580) to his sister Mary, now Lady Pembroke, at Wilton, where, probably, most of his *Arcadia* was written. In 1583 he was knighted, and married Frances, daughter of Sir F. Walsingham. His arrangement (1585) to accompany Drake on one of his buccaneer expeditions was defeated by Elizabeth's caprice and Drake's treachery. It was poor amends that Sidney was ordered to accompany Leicester, chosen by the queen to carry her half-hearted support to the Netherlanders in their struggle against Spain. After one small brilliant exploit, he received, September 22, 1586, his death wound under the walls of Zutphen, dying like a hero and a Christian on October 17. His work in literature we may place between 1578 and 1582. Widely celebrated as it was in his lifetime, nothing was published till after his death. His brilliant character, his connections, his generous patronage of men of letters, with the report of those to whom his writings were communicated, united to give him his pre-eminent contemporary fame. This was, however, amply supported when the *Arcadia* (written probably 1578–80, but never finished) appeared, imperfectly in 1590, completely in 1598. This book long retained a vast popularity, though it is almost unread. It is a pastoral romance, founded upon the *Arcadia* (1504) of Sannazaro, being an intricate love story, intermixed with poems and written in melodious but elaborate prose, not free from the artificial 'conceits', the euphuism, of that age. But here Englishmen found their earliest model for sweet, continuous, rhythmical prose. To about 1580 may be assigned Sidney's *Apologie for Poetrie* (1591, afterwards named *Defence of Poesie*), written in clear, manly English in reply to an abusive Puritan pamphlet. In 1575 Sidney had met Penelope Devereux (c. 1562–1607), daughter of the first Earl of Essex; but it was only in 1581, the year following her marriage to the Puritan Lord Rich, who afterwards divorced her, that Sidney awoke too late to love for her, and to find also that she might have loved him. The 108 sonnets and 11 songs of *Astrophel and Stella* (1591) offer a marvellous picture of passionate love. That Sidney's fame falls far below his deserts is due in part to that inequality of his workmanship which he shares with other supreme writers of sonnet sequences; nor did life allow him to acquire their finished art. See the *Complete Works*, ed. by Feuillerat (4 vols. 1912–26); *Lives* by Fulke Greville (1652; 1907), Symonds (1886), Wallace (1915), M. Wilson

(1931); and studies by S. Goldman (1934), Myrick (1935), Boas (1955), Howell (1968).

SIDONIUS APOLLINARIS (*c.* 430–*c.* 483), French Latin author, born at Lyons, held high civil offices at Rome, and in 472 became Bishop of Clermont. His letters are modelled on Pliny's; his poems comprise panegyrics on three emperors, and two epithalamia. See study by Stevens (1933).

SIEBOLD, *zee'bolt*, (1) **Karl Theodor Ernst** (1804–65), German anatomist, brother of (2), was professor at Munich, and wrote on the Invertebrata (trans. 1857), parthenogenesis, salamanders, and the freshwater fish of central Europe. See Life by Siebold (1896).

(2) **Philipp Franz von** (1796–1866), German physician and botanist, brother of (1), born at Würzburg, became sanitary officer to the Dutch in Batavia, and, accompanying the Dutch embassy to Japan, made Japan known to the Western world by his writings.

SIEGBAHN, Karl Manne Georg (1886–   ), Swedish physicist, born at Örebro, professor at Lund (1920), at Uppsala (1923) and professor of the Royal Academy of Sciences and director of the Nobel Institute for Physics at Stockholm from 1937, discovered the M series in X-ray spectroscopy for which he was awarded the Nobel prize for 1924. He also constructed a vacuum spectrograph.

SIEGEN, Ludwig von, *zee'gen* (1609–*c.* 1675), German engraver, in 1642 invented the mezzotint process, which he disclosed to Prince Rupert at Brussels in 1654.

SIEGFRIED, André, *zeeg'freed* (1875–1959), French economist, historian and Academician, was specially noted for his studies of Canada, the States and Latin America. See his *Les États-unis d'aujourd'hui* (1927, trans. *America comes of Age*), *Le Canada, Puissance internationale* (1937), *Suez and Panama* (trans. 1940) and *America in Mid-century* (1955).

SIEGMUND. See SIGISMUND.

SIELMANN, Heinz, *zeel'-* (1917–   ), German naturalist and photographer specializing in nature films; born at Königsberg. Interested in animal photography from boyhood, he started making films in 1938 and won the German Oscar for documentary films three years running (1953–55). He evolved techniques enabling him to take films of happenings inside the lairs of animals and inaccessible types of birds' nests (e.g., the woodpecker), which have revolutionized the study of animal behaviour. See his *My Year with the Woodpeckers* (trans. 1959).

SIEMENS, *zee'-*, name of a German family of electrical engineers and industrialists, of whom the following are especially noteworthy:

(1) **Ernst Werner von** (1816–92), German engineer and founder of the firm, brother of (2), born at Lenthe, Hanover, in 1834 entered the Prussian artillery, and in 1844 took charge of the artillery workshops at Berlin. He developed the telegraphic system in Prussia, discovered the insulating property of gutta-percha, and devoted himself to making telegraphic and electrical apparatus. In 1847 was established at Berlin the firm since 1867 called Siemens Brothers, with branches elsewhere. Besides devising numerous forms of galvanometer and other electrical instruments, Siemens was one of the discoverers of the self-acting dynamo. He determined the electrical resistance of different substances, the Siemens Unit being called after him. In 1886 he endowed a technological institute; in 1888 he was ennobled. See his *Personal Recollections* (trans. 1893), and Life by J. O. Scott (1958). One of his sons, Wilhelm (1855–1919), was one of the pioneers of the incandescent lamp.

(2) **Sir William (Karl Wilhelm)** (1823–83) German-born British electrical engineer, brother of (1), born at Lenthe, in 1843 visited England, introduced a process for electro-gilding invented by Werner and himself, in 1844 patented his differential governor, and was naturalized in 1859. F.R.S. from 1862, he received many distinctions for his inventions in metallurgy, was president of the British Association (1882), was knighted in April 1883, and died in London. As manager in England of the firm of Siemens Brothers, he was actively engaged in the construction of telegraphs, designed the steamship *Faraday* for cable-laying, promoted electric lighting, and constructed the Portrush Electric Tramway (1883). The principle of his regenerative furnace was largely utilized, notably by himself in the manufacture of steel. Other inventions were a water-meter, pyrometer and bathometer. See Lives by Pole (1888) and J. D. Scott (1958). He was assisted in England by another brother, **Friedrich** (1826–1904), who invented a regenerative smelting oven (1856) extensively used in glassmaking.

SIENKIEWICZ, Henryk, *sheng-kyay'vich* (1846–1916), Polish novelist, born near Łuków, lived in America from 1876 to 1878, and after a hunting expedition in East Africa (1892) wrote the children's story *Desert and Wilderness*. Most of his works, however, are strongly realistic; many have been translated, among them *With Fire and Sword* (1884), *The Deluge* (1886), *Children of the Soil* (1893) and *Quo Vadis* (1896). He was awarded the Nobel prize in 1905. See *Letters*, ed. C. Morley (1960).

SIERRA. See MARTÍNEZ SIERRA.

SIEYÈS, Emmanuel Joseph Comte, *syay-yes* (1748–1836), French statesman, generally called the Abbé Sieyès, born at Fréjus, May 3, studied theology and became canon at Tréguier (1775), then chancellor and vicar-general of Chartres, and as such was sent to the assembly of the clergy of France. His three pamphlets carried his name over France: *Vues sur les moyens d'exécution* (1788), *Essai sur les privilèges* (1788), and, the most famous of all, *Qu'est-ce que le tiers-état?* (1789). He was elected deputy for Paris, and had much to do with the formation of the National Assembly. He gained great influence, and the division of France into departments was mainly his work. He took part in the declaration of the Rights of Man (August 26, 1789), and opposed the royal veto. He was elected to the Legislative Assembly, sat in the centre, and also voted for the king's death; but as the Revolution grew, he lapsed into ' philosophic silence '. He opposed the new constitution of Year III

(1795), and declined a seat on the Directory named by the new *corps législatif*, but had a share in the *coup d'état* of September 3, 1797. In 1798 he went on a mission to Berlin, in 1799 was elected to the Directory. Bonaparte returned from Egypt in October, and together they plotted the Revolution of 18th Brumaire (November 9, 1799), the result of which was the institution of the Consulate of Sieyès, Bonaparte and Roger Ducos. Sieyès drew up a constitution, a masterpiece of complexity, its aim to break the force of democracy by dividing it. Finding himself deceived by Bonaparte, he threw up his consulship, but received the title of count, 600,000 francs, and the estate of Crosne. Exiled at the Restoration, he lived in Belgium for fifteen years, returned in 1830, and died June 20, 1836. See works by Mignet (1836), Beauverger (1858), Bigeon (1894), Clapham (1912), Van Deusen (1932) and P. Bastid (1939).

SIGISMUND (1368–1437), Holy Roman emperor (1411–37), son of Charles IV, in 1396 as king of Hungary was heavily defeated by the Turks at Nicopolis, but later conquered Bosnia, Herzegovina and Serbia. As Holy Roman emperor, he induced Pope John XXIII to summon the Council of Constance to end the Hussite schism, supported the party of reform, but made no effort to uphold the safe conduct he had granted to Huss, and permitted him to be burned. In consequence his succession to the throne of Bohemia was opposed by the Hussites. See a book by Main (1903).

SIGISMUND, the name of three kings of Poland:

Sigismund I (1466–1548), king from 1506, father of (II). His court was filled with factions fomented by his wife, the daughter of the Duke of Milan, and the Reformation raised new troubles. In a war with Russia he lost Smolensk, but was partly compensated with the overlordship of Moldavia. In 1537 occurred the first rebellion of the nobility against the kingly authority, and Sigismund was obliged to make concessions.

Sigismund II (1520–72), king from 1548, son of (I), uncle of (III). During his reign the Reformation spread rapidly. In 1569 Lithuania was joined to Poland, and Poland acquired Livonia.

Sigismund III, Sigismund Vasa (1566–1632), elected king of Poland in 1587, from 1592 to 1604 was also at least nominal king of Sweden. Constant disputes took place between him and the Diet, and he was a great persecutor of the Protestants. He supported the false Demetrius (q.v.). The Poles took Moscow and caused his son, Ladislaus, to be crowned tsar, but in 1618 he finally resigned his claims.

SIGNAC, Paul, *see-nyak* (1863–1935), French artist, born in Paris. He exhibited in 1884 with the Impressionists and was later associated with Henri Edmond Cross (1856–1910), and Seurat (q.v.) in the neo-Impressionist movement. Signac, however, used mosaiclike patches of pure colour (as compared with Seurat's pointillist dots), mainly in seascapes, for he sailed to most French ports and was particularly fond of

St Tropez. He published *D'Eugène Delacroix à néo-impressionisme*, in which he sought to establish a scientific basis for his 'divisionist' theories (1899), and a study of *Jongkind* (1927).

SIGNORELLI, Luca, *seen-yo-rel'lee* (c. 1441–1523), Italian painter, born at Cortona, worked, especially in frescoes, at Loreto, Rome, Florence, Siena, Cortona and Orvieto, where the cathedral contains his greatest work, the frescoes of *The Preaching of Anti-Christ* and *Last Judgment* (1500–04) which display his great technical skill in the drawing of male nudes. He was one of the painters summoned by Pope Julius II in 1508 to adorn the Vatican, and dismissed to make way for Raphael. See studies by M. Crutwell (1899), G. Mancini (1903) and A. Venturi (1922).

SIGURDSSON, Jón, *si'gurths-son* (1811–79), Icelandic scholar and politician, was educated at Copenhagen University. He published editions of the Icelandic classics as well as authoritative works on the history and laws of Iceland. He became the revered leader of the movement to secure greater political autonomy and freedom of trade for Iceland—a movement which culminated in 1874 in the grant of a constitution by Denmark.

SIKORSKI, Władysław (1881–1943), Polish statesman and soldier, born in Galicia, studied engineering at Cracow and Łwów universities, joined the underground movement for Polish freedom from Tsarist rule, served under General Piłsudski as head of the war department, but after the treaty of Brest-Litovsk was imprisoned by the Austrians. In 1919 he commanded a Polish Infantry Division at Vilna during the Russian-Polish war and in 1920 defended Warsaw. In 1921 he became commander-in-chief and in 1922 was elected premier. After Piłsudski's *coup d'état* (1926) he retired and wrote military history in Paris. He returned to Poland in 1938, advocated a strong alliance with Britain and France, but was treated with suspicion and refused a command when Poland was invaded. He fled, fought in France, became c.-in-c. of the Free Polish forces and premier of the Polish government in exile from June 1940 in London. He signed a treaty with the Soviet Union in 1941 which annulled the Russo-German partition of Poland in 1939. But the discovery of Polish officers' graves at Katyn (1943) led to the breaking off of diplomatic relations between the two countries. He was killed in an aircrash over Gibraltar, July 4, 1943.

SIKORSKY, Igor Ivan, *-kor'-* (1889–1972), Russian-born American aeronautical engineer, born in Kiev, built and flew the first four-engined aeroplane (1913), emigrated to Paris (1918) and to the United States (1919) and founded the Sikorsky Aero Engineering Corporation (1923), which later was merged into the United States Aircraft Corporation. He built several flying-boats and the first successful helicopter in the western hemisphere (1939). He was awarded the Presidential Certificate of Merit (1948) and the Silver Medal of the British Royal Aeronautical Society (1949).

SILESIUS. See ANGELUS.

SILHOUETTE, Étienne de, *sil-oo-et* (1709–1767), the parsimonious French minister of finance in 1759 whose name was applied to cheap blacked-in shadow outlines.

SILIUS ITALICUS, Gaius (A.D. 25–101), minor Latin poet, became a prominent forensic orator, was consul in 68, and then proconsul in Asia. Having contracted an incurable disease, he starved himself to death. His epic poem, *Punica* is unoriginal. See study by Nicol (1936).

SILLANPÄÄ, Frans Eemil (1888–1964), Finnish writer, born at Hämeenkyrö, author of short stories and novels, in which realism and idealism are fused with remarkable psychological insight. Two of his masterpieces, *The Maid Silja* (1931) and *Meek Heritage* (1938), have been translated into English. He was awarded the Nobel prize for literature in 1939.

SILLIMAN, (1) Benjamin (1779–1864), American chemist, father of (2), born at Trumbull, Conn., was admitted to the bar in 1802, but became professor of Chemistry at Yale and studied this subject at Philadelphia, Edinburgh and London, specializing in electrolysis. He was founder (1818) and editor of the *American Journal of Science.* See Lives by G. P. Fisher (1866) and E. H. Thomson (1947).

(2) **Benjamin** (1816–85), American chemist, son of (1), born in New York, became professor at Yale, assisted his father in his editorial work and showed that petroleum was a mixture of hydrocarbons, different in character from vegetable and oils, and could be separated by fractional distillation.

SILVA, Antonio José da (1705–39), Portuguese playwright and Offenbachian librettist, who was born at Rio de Janeiro, studied law at Coimbra, and was burnt with wife and mother by the Inquisition at Lisbon as a relapsed Jew.

SILVESTER. See SYLVESTER.

SIMENON, Georges, *see-mė-nŏ* (1903–   ), Belgian-born master of the detective story, born at Liège, in Paris became one of the most prolific authors of his day, writing under a variety of pseudonyms. He revolutionized detective fiction by his tough, morbidly psychological Inspector Maigret series (1930 ff.), in which the ordinary, everyday person assumes importance only as a victim of an exceptionally violent crime. Gide once described him as ' the best novelist in French literature today '.

SIMEON, Charles (1759–1836), English evangelical preacher, born at Reading, fellow of King's College, Cambridge, led the evangelical revival in the Church of England. See *Memoirs* by Carus (1857), and studies by Moule (1892) and C. H. Smyth (1940).

SIMEON OF DURHAM (d. before 1138), monkish chronicler, wrote *Historia Ecclesiae Dunelmensis, Historia Regum Anglorum et Dacorum.* Arnold edited his *Opera* (Rolls Series, 1882–85).

SIMEON STYLITES, St, *stī-lī′teez* (A.D. 387–459), earliest of the Christian ascetic Pillar-saints, after living nine years in his Syrian monastery without leaving his cell, at Telanessa near Antioch established himself on the top of a pillar 72 feet high. Here he spent thirty years, preaching to crowds.

SIMMS, William Gilmore (1806–70), American novelist, born at Charleston, where he edited the *City Gazette* and published *Lyrical and other Poems* (1827), *The Vision of Cortes* (1829), *The Tricolour* (1830), *Atalantis* (1832), *The Yemassee* (1835), *The Partisan* (1835), *Charlemont* (1856), and many other works. He was an apologist for slavery and the South. See Lives by Cable (1888) and Trent (1892).

SIMNEL, Lambert (*c.* 1477–*c.* 1534), English impostor, a baker's son, in 1487 was set up in Ireland as, first, a son of Edward IV, and then as the Duke of Clarence's son, Edward, Earl of Warwick (1475–99), then imprisoned in the Tower, and afterwards beheaded, by Henry VII. Backed by Margaret of Burgundy, his suppositious aunt, Simnel had some success in Ireland and was crowned at Dublin as Edward VI, but, landing in Lancashire with 2000 German mercenaries, he was defeated at Stoke Field, Notts (June 16), and subsequently became a royal scullion and falconer.

SIMON, (1) Sir John (1816–1904), English pathologist, was surgeon at St Thomas's Hospital, London, and first medical officer of health for London. He was responsible for many sanitary reforms. See study by R. Lambert (1963).

(2) **John Allsebrook Simon, 1st Viscount** (1873–1954), English statesman and lawyer, born at Bath, educated at Fettes College, Edinburgh, and Wadham, Oxford, was junior counsel for the British government in the Alaska boundary arbitration. He became Liberal M.P. in 1906, took silk in 1908 and was knighted in 1910 when he became solicitor-general. He was attorney-general (1913–15), home secretary (1915–16), resigned from the Cabinet for his opposition to conscription, served at the front (1917–18) and returned to become one of the wealthiest members of the legal profession. As chairman of the Indian statutory commission (1927–30) he proved in advance of Conservative opinion of the time. Deserting the Liberals, he fully supported MacDonald's coalition governments and became foreign secretary (1931) and leader of the National Liberals. He attempted a middle-of-the-road policy in European affairs but without much success, proposing the ' Eastern Locarno ' pact. He was home secretary again (1935–1937), was chancellor of the Exchequer (1937–40) and lord chancellor in Churchill's wartime coalition government (1940–45). His second wife, **Kathleen Harvey,** was a well-known anti-slavery crusader. He was created viscount in 1940. He wrote a standard legal work on income tax (1956). See his autobiographical *Retrospect* (1952).

(3) **Jules François,** *see-mŏ* (1814–96), French statesman and philosopher, a philosophy lecturer at the Sorbonne in 1839, became a deputy in 1848 and, refusing the oath of allegiance, established himself as a leader of the left-wing republicans in 1873, when he resigned as minister of public instruction because his educational reforms were severely attacked. He directed the *Siècle* newspaper from 1874, became prime minister in 1876, but resigned following a

dispute with President Macmahon. He edited the French rationalists Descartes, Malebranche and Arnauld, and wrote a number of works on political philosophy and biographical studies. See Life by Séché (1878).

(4) **Richard** (1638–1712), French biblical critic, born at Dieppe, entered the Oratory in 1659, lectured on philosophy, and catalogued the oriental MSS. in the library of the order at Paris. His criticisms upon Arnauld caused great displeasure among the Port-Royalists, and the scandal caused by the liberalism of his *Histoire critique du Vieux Testament* (1678) in which he denied that Moses was the author of the Pentateuch, led to his expulsion from the order and retirement to Belleville as *curé*. In 1682 he resigned his parish, and lived thereafter in literary retirement. Few writers of his age played a more prominent part in polemics. His *Histoire critique* (Eng. trans. 1682), suppressed through Bossuet's and the Jansenists' influence, often anticipates the later German rationalists, and is the first work which treats the Bible as a literary product.

SIMONIDES OF AMARGOS, *sī-mon'i-deez* (fl. 660 B.C.), Greek iambic poet, native of Samos, founded a colony on the island of Amargos.

SIMONIDES OF CEOS, *see'os* (556–468 B.C.), Greek lyric poet, born in the island of Ceos, lived many years at Athens. From the Persian invasion of Greece he devoted his powers to celebrating the heroes and the battles of that struggle in elegies, epigrams, odes and dirges. He won fifty-six times in poetical contests, and carried off the prize from Æschylus by an elegy on the heroes who fell at Marathon. He spent his last years at the court of Hiero of Syracuse.

SIMON MAGUS (' Simon the Magician ') appears about A.D. 37 as having become a commanding personality in Samaria through his sorceries. With Peter's reply to his offer to buy the gift of the Holy Ghost, and Simon's submission, the narrative of the Acts (viii. 9–24) leaves him. Later Christian authors bring him to Rome, and make him the author of heresies.

SIMONOV, Konstantin Mikhailovich (1915–), Russian writer, achieved a considerable reputation by his historical poem about Alexander Nevski, his poems of the second World War, *Days and Nights*, a novel about the defence of Stalingrad, and the play *The Russians*. He was awarded the Stalin prize three times.

SIMPSON, (1) **Sir George** (1792–1860), Canadian explorer, born in Scotland, was administrator (1821–56) of the Hudson's Bay Company's territory. In 1828 he made an overland journey round the world. Simpson's Falls and Cape George Simpson are named after him.

(2) **Sir George Clarke** (1878–1965), English meteorologist, was born at Derby and became a lecturer at Manchester University (1905). He was Scott's meteorologist on the Antarctic expedition (1910), investigated the causes of lightning, and was elected president of the Royal Meteorological Society (1940–1942).

(3) **Sir James Young, 1st Bart.** (1811–70), Scottish obstetrician, born at Bathgate,

studied medicine at Edinburgh, where he became professor of Midwifery in 1840. He originated the use of ether as anaesthetic in childbirth, January 19, 1847, and experimenting on himself in the search for a better anaesthetic, discovered the required properties in chloroform, November 4, 1847, and championed its use against medical and religious opposition until its employment at the birth of Prince Leopold (1853) signalized general acceptance. He founded gynaecology by his sound tests, championed hospital reform, and in 1847 became physician to the Queen in Scotland. An enthusiastic archaeologist, he was created a baronet in 1866. See Lives by Duns (1873), H. L. Gordon (1898), and J. D. Comrie, *History of Scottish Medicine* (II, 1932).

(4) **Thomas** (1710–61), English mathematician, ' the oracle of Nuneaton ', where he was born, educated himself, became professor of Mathematics at Woolwich (1743) and was elected F.R.S. in 1746. He published a long series of works (1737–57) on fluxions, chance, annuities, algebra, trigonometry, &c. See Life by Hutton prefixed to Davis's edition of the *Fluxions* (1805).

SIMROCK, Karl Joseph (1802–76), German poet and scholar, born at Bonn, entered the Prussian state service. He translated the *Nibelungenlied* (1827), edited German mediaeval poets and legends, wrote on Shakespeare's sources (1831), &c. He was professor of Old German at Bonn from 1850. See monograph by Hocker (1877).

SIMS, George Robert (1847–1922), English author, born in London, contributed his ' Dagonet ' ballads and other articles to the *Referee*. He wrote plays, including *The Lights o' London* (1881), and novels. He was made a Swedish knight of St Olaf in 1905. See *My Life* (1916).

SIMSON, Robert (1687–1768), Scottish mathematician, became professor of Mathematics at Glasgow (1711). His great work was his restoration of Euclid's lost treatise on *Porisms* (1776). He published *Sectiones Conicae* (1735) and a restoration of Apollonius's *Loci Plani* (1749); his *Elements of Euclid* (1756) was the basis of nearly all editions for over a century. See a volume of *Reliqua* (1776) and Memoir by Trail (1812).

SINATRA, Francis Albert (Frank) (1917–), American singer and film actor, born in New Jersey, started his long and highly-successful career as recording artist singing with bands and on radio, and as one of the most-publicized teenage idols. He made his film début in musicals in 1943, but later successfully switched to dramatic rôles, most notably in *From Here to Eternity* (1953, Oscar as Best Supporting Actor). See study by A. Shaw (1968).

SINCLAIR, or St Clair, the name of the Earls of Orkney (1379–1471) and afterwards of Caithness. They were hereditary grandmaster masons of Scotland 1455–1736. Roslin Castle near Edinburgh was the seat of the St Clairs.

SINCLAIR, (1) **Sir Archibald Henry MacDonald, 1st Viscount Thurso** (1890–1970), Scottish Liberal politician, descendant of (2), educated at Eton and Sandhurst, served in the army (1910–21), entered parliament in

1922, became chief whip (1930–31) and leader of the Liberals (1935–45), and was secretary of state for Air in the Churchill administration (1940–45).

(2) **Sir John, 1st Bart.** (1754–1835), Scottish politician and agriculturalist, born at Thurso Castle, studied at Edinburgh, Glasgow and Oxford, was admitted to both the Scottish and English bars (1775–82), and sat in parliament (1780–1811). In 1784 he published a *History of the Revenue of the British Empire*; and in 1786 was created a baronet. He established the Board of Agriculture in 1793, and compiled a *Statistical Account of Scotland* (1791–99), comprising a description of every parish in Scotland, mainly by help of the parish ministers. See Correspondence (1831) and Life (1837). His daughter, **Catherine** (1800–64), wrote children's books, &c.

(3) **May** (1865?–1946), British novelist, born at Rock Ferry, Cheshire, and educated at Cheltenham, wrote *The Divine Fire* (1904), *The Creators* (1910), *The Dark Night* (1924), *Anne Severn*, &c. She also wrote books on philosophical idealism.

(4) **Upton Beall** (1878–1968), American novelist, born at Baltimore, horrified the world with his exposure of meat-packing conditions in Chicago in his novel *The Jungle* (1906). Later novels such as *Metropolis* (1908), *King Coal* (1917), *Oil* (1927) are more and more moulded by his socialist beliefs. He was for many years prominent in Californian politics and attempted to found a communistic colony at Englewood, New Jersey. His *Dragon's Teeth* (1942) won the Pulitzer prize. See his autobiographical works (1932, 1962) and *A World to Win* (1946).

SINDHIA, the title of the Mahratta princes of Gwalior. Their founder was **Ranaji Sindhia**, who rose to high rank in the bodyguard of the Peshwa, and had a grant of half the province of Mala. His most noteworthy successors in chronological order, were: (1) **Mádhava Ráo Sindhia** (d. 1794), illegitimate son of the above, joined the Mahratta confederation, and was crippled for life at Panipat (1761). In 1770, along with the Peshwa and Holkar, he aided the Moghul to expel the Sikhs and became virtually supreme in Hindustan. He came into collision with the British in 1779, and was thoroughly beaten by Hastings, but by the treaty of Salbai (1783) was confirmed in all his possessions. In 1784 he captured Gwalior, in 1785 marched on Delhi, and subsequently seized Agra, Alighur and nearly the whole of the Doab. He raised and drilled an army in European fashion, neglecting the cavalry, and won Akbar and crushed Jodhpur, Udaipur and Jaipur, three Rajput states, and Holkar remained his ally. He died, or was murdered, at Poona. See Keene's *Mádhava Ráo Sindhia* (1892). (2) **Daulat Rao Sindhia** (1779–1827), grandnephew of (1), ravaged Indore and Poona, but was routed by Holkar (1802), and next year brought upon himself the vengeance of the East India Company. The Mahrattas were routed at Assaye and Argaum by Sir Arthur Wellesley, and were scattered at Laswari by Lord Lake. Thereupon Sindhia ceded all his possessions in the

Doab and along the right bank of the Jumna to the British. Gwalior was restored in 1805. (3) **Baji Rao** (d. 1886), who during the Mutiny took the field against the rebels; but most of his troops deserted him, and he fled to Agra. He was reinstated, and was succeeded by his adopted son.

SINDING, Christian (1856–1941), Norwegian composer, born at Kongsberg, studied in Germany. He wrote two violin and a piano concerto, and three symphonies, as well as chamber music and songs. His brother, **Otto** (1842–1909), was a painter. Another, **Stephan** (1846–1922), a sculptor.

SINGER, Isaac Merritt (1811–75), American inventor and manufacturer of sewing-machines, born at Pittstown, New York, patented a rock drill (1839), a carving machine (1849) and at Boston (1852) an improved single-thread, chain-stitch sewing-machine, and although he had to pay **Elias Howe** (1819–67) compensation for his use of the Howe needle, the success of his Singer Manufacturing Company was assured. He died at Torquay, England.

SIQUEIROS, David Alfaro, *si-kay'ros* (1898–), Mexican mural painter, born at Chihuahua. With Rivera and Orozco, he launched the review *El Machete* in Mexico City in 1922, and in 1930 he was imprisoned for revolutionary activities. He was later expelled from the U.S.A., and during the 'thirties he worked in South America. He is one of the principal figures in 20th-century Mexican mural painting, and notable for his experiments in the use of modern synthetic materials. He exhibited at the Venice Biennale of 1950.

SISLEY, Alfred, *sees-lay* (1839–99), French Impressionist painter and etcher, born in Paris, of English ancestry. He joined Monet and Renoir in Gleyre's studio and was also influenced by Corot. He painted landscapes almost exclusively, particularly in the valleys of the Seine, the Loing and the Thames, and was noted for his subtle treatment of skies.

SISMONDI, Jean Charles Léonard Simonde de, *-mon'-* (1773–1842), Swiss historian and economist of Italian descent, was born at Geneva. The French Revolution drove his family into exile, but in 1800 Sismondi himself went back to Geneva, and obtained a municipal office. His *Histoire des républiques italiennes du moyen âge* (1807–18), a pioneer work, contributed greatly to the Italian Liberal tradition. In 1813 appeared his *Littérature du midi de l'Europe* (Eng. by Roscoe), and in 1819 he began his *Histoire des Français*. His *Richesse commerciale* (1803) is written from the standpoint of the *Wealth of Nations*; but his *Nouveaux Principes d'économie politique* (1819) inclines to socialism. See *Lettres inédites* (1863), and Life by J. R. De Salis (1932).

SITTER, Willem de (1872–1934), Dutch astronomer, became director and professor of Astronomy at Leyden (1908). He computed the size of the universe as two thousand million light years in radius, containing about 80,000 million galaxies. As opposed to Einstein's static conception, he visualized the universe as an expanding space-time continuum with motion and no matter (dynamic).

SITTING BULL (1834–90), American Indian warrior, chief of the Dakota Sioux, was a leader in the Sioux War of 1876–77, after which he escaped to Canada but surrendered in 1881. Still rebellious, he was killed while attempting to evade the police in the ' ghost dance ' uprising of 1890.

SITWELL, (1) **Edith** (1887–1964), English poet, sister of (2) and (3), daughter of Sir George Sitwell of Renishaw, Derbyshire, and Lady Ida Sitwell, daughter of Lord Londesborough, born at Scarborough. In his *The Scarlet Tree* her brother Sir Osbert Sitwell has described the isolation and frustration experienced by the young girl till her governess introduced her to music and literature. She first attracted notice by her editorship of an anthology on new poetry entitled *Wheels* (1916–21). This was the *avant garde* of a poetry which repudiated the flaccid quietism of Georgian verse, but Miss Sitwell's shock tactics were not fully displayed till *Façade* appeared in 1922, when, with William Walton's music, it was given a stormy public reading in London. *Façade* was succeeded by *Bucolic Comedies*, which is for the most part in the same fantastic vein, but the elegiac romantic begins to appear and this vein is fully exploited in *The Sleeping Beauty* (1924), and finally worked out in the amazing *Elegy for Dead Fashion* (1926), with its profusion of riches which perhaps tire the imagination in the end. The short poems of this romantic period, ' Colonel Fantock ', ' Daphne ', ' The Strawberry ' and above all ' The Little Ghost who died for Love ' are probably the tenderest, most beautiful things she ever wrote. At the close of this period Miss Sitwell suddenly flamed into indignation over the evil in society—in *Gold Coast Customs* (1929) the gaiety of *Façade* is replaced by the horror underlying civilization. In the 'thirties she turned to prose work. *Alexander Pope* (1930) rather mothers the poet, but contributed to the modern revival of his fame by close analysis of the beauty of his texture. Perhaps she chose Swift also as the subject of her novel *I Live Under a Black Sun* because of the madness which threatens those too finely constituted to bear the horrors of life in a grim age. During World War II Miss Sitwell denounced with great vehemence the cruelty of man. The brittle artifice of *Façade* would not suit the vatic utterance of *Street Songs* (1942) or *Green Song* (1944), *The Song of the Cold* (1945) and *The Shadow of Cain* (1947). Direct statement does not, however, chill her imagerial faculty though the symbolism is less esoteric. Christian symbolism now triumphs, though mingled with that of the oriental mystics and even the anthropologists. Horror and compassion inspire poems like ' Still falls the Rain ', ' An Old Woman ', and ' Invocation ' (from *Green Song*). Opinions differ as to whether she is a greater poet in her early or her late work. She set out to refresh the exhausted rhythms of traditional poetry by introducing the rhythms of jazz and other dance music and also by free association in expression and the transference of the bodily senses (light ' creaked ' and the rain ' squawks down . . .

grey as a guinea-fowl ')—with the result that sense was sacrificed to the evocation of states of feeling. In her late verse these gay vanities disappear, but one detects a certain lack of control in her poems on the age of the atom bomb—*Dirge for the New Sunrise, The Shadow of Cain* and *The Canticle of the Rose* (1949). Other works include *The English Eccentrics* (1933), *Victoria of England* (1936), *Fanfare for Elizabeth* (1946), *The Outcasts* (verse; 1962), *The Queens and the Hive* (on Elizabeth and Mary; 1962). She was created D.B.E. in 1954. See her autobiography *Taken Care Of*, published posthumously, (1965) and critical studies by R. L. Mégroz, *The Three Sitwells* (1927), D. Powell, C. M. Bowra (1947), also *Celebrations for Edith Sitwell*, ed. J. G. Villa (1948).

(2) **Sir Osbert** (1892–1969), English author, brother of (1), was born in London and educated at Eton. His youth was spent mainly at Renishaw with occasional visits to Scarborough, which figures a good deal in his own satiric work, and in that of Edith Sitwell, as a symbol of Victorian decrepitude. He served in the Brigade of Guards in World War I, and in 1916 was invalided home. This provided him with the leisure to set up as a satirist of war and the types which ingloriously prosper at home. Many of his satirical poems were published in the *Nation* and collected in *Argonaut and Juggernaut* (1919) and *Out of the Flame* (1923). After the war he narrowed his literary acquaintance to the *habitués*, i.e., his sister and brother, Ezra Pound, T. S. Eliot and Wyndham Lewis. The object of the group was the regeneration of arts and letters, and in this pursuit the Sitwells acquired notoriety, Sir Osbert not least by his novel *Before the Bombardment* (1927), which anatomized the grandees of Scarborough and by implication the social orders in general. Neither this nor his other novel, *Miracle on Sinai* (1933), was successful, and he has always done better in the short story, especially in those, like the collection *Dumb Animal* (1930), where his delicacy of observation and natural compassion are more in evidence than is satire. The paternalism of the aristocracy is expressed in *England Reclaimed, a Book of Eclogues* (1927). When he came to collect his short stories and his verse, the same volume offers this contrast between mordant satire and human kindliness—the satiric sharpness of *Triple Fugue* (1924) with the humanity of the stories in *Dumb Animal* parallels the resentment of the early verse with the acceptance of rural manners in the *Eclogues*. His aristocratic bent took the form of travel in the grand manner in the 'thirties. He had published *Discursions on Travel, Art and Life* in 1925, but now *Winters of Content* (1932) displayed mature descriptive powers. *Brighton* (1935, in collaboration with Miss Margaret Barton) anticipated the vogue of 18th- and early 19th-century architecture and at the close of the 'thirties *Escape with Me*, describing a journey to China, proved his most charming book of travel. All these elements enter into the great autobiography he was planning. The first volume of *Left Hand: Right Hand*

appeared in 1944, to be followed by *The Scarlet Tree* (1946), *Great Morning* (1947) and *Laughter in the Next Room* (1948). *Noble Essences* (1950) completed this great work, which must rank with the finest of its kind in any language. Other collections of essays and stories include *Penny Foolish* (1935), *Sing High, Sing Low* (1944), *Alive-Alive Oh* (1947) and *Pound Wise* (1963). He succeeded to the baronetcy in 1942. See study by Fulford (1951), Mégroz, *Five Novelists of Today* (1933), Joyce, *Triad of Genius* (1943).

(3) **Sacheverell** (1897–   ), English poet and art critic, younger brother of (2), went through the same preparatory stages as Sir Osbert—the same private school, Eton, officer in a Guards regiment and unlimited travel abroad. After the war of 1914 the brothers toured Spain and Italy. Italy became their second country, the fruit of which is Sacheverell's case was *Southern Baroque Art*, a remarkable achievement for a man in his twenties. *The Gothick North* followed in 1929, and this with his *German Baroque Art* completed his study of European art. The popularity of the baroque today owes much to his persistent praise of this mode. Poetry went hand in hand with the sister muse. The critics so far have not accepted Dame Edith's assurance that he is one of the greatest poets of the last one hundred and fifty years. His verse is much more traditional than his sister's, indeed at his best, and it can be very good, he is an imitator of past modes, playing quite lovely variations on the Pope and others in which the note is a sumptuous melancholy. His descriptions of paintings in *Canons of Giant Art* are interesting, but his ambitious study of good and evil, *Dr Donne and Gargantua*, seems to get bogged down in philosophical subtleties. His poems include, beside the works mentioned, *Hortus Conclusus, The People's Palace, The Hundred and One Harlequins, The Thirteenth Caesar* and *The Cyder Feast*. The life can best be disengaged from the various volumes of Sir Osbert's *Left Hand: Right Hand*, but see also Mégroz, *The Three Sitwells* (1927) and Sacheverell's *Journey to the Ends of Time* (Vol. I, 1959).

SIVERTSEN. See ADELAER.

SIXTUS, the name of five popes.—The first was beheaded *c.* A.D. 125; the second was martyred in 258; the third was pope (432–440) when St Patrick began his mission in Ireland:

Sixtus IV, or Francesco della Rovere (1414–84), pope from 1471, was a famous Franciscan preacher. His nepotism led to many abuses, and he is said to have connived at the Pazzi conspiracy against the Medici at Florence; it was certainly engineered by his nephew. He fostered learning, built the Sistine chapel and the Sistine bridge, enriched the Vatican library, and was a patron of painters; but he lowered the moral authority of the Papacy. In 1482 he entered into an alliance with the Venetians which led to a general Italian war. His private life seems to have been blameless. See Pastor's *Popes from the Close of the Middle Ages* (trans. 1895).

Sixtus V (Felice Peretti) (1521–90), pope from 1585, was also a great Franciscan preacher and a professor of Theology. Created a cardinal (Montalto) in 1570, his assumed feebleness procured him election to the Papacy in succession to Gregory XIII in 1585. But his rule was marked by vigorous measures of improvement. He repressed licence and disorder, reformed the administration of the law and the disposal of patronage, carried on many public enterprises, and having found an empty treasury, secured a surplus of five million crowns. To the Jews he extended liberty. The great aim of his foreign policy was to combat Protestantism and uphold the balance of the Catholic powers. He fixed the number of cardinals at seventy. Under his authority were published new editions of the Septuagint and Vulgate—the latter very inaccurate.

SKANDERBEG, i.e., **Iskander** or **Alexander Bey**, also known as **George Castriota** (1403–1468), Albanian patriot, was born of Serb descent. Carried away by Turks when seven, brought up a Moslem, he was a favourite commander of Sultan Murad II. In 1443 he changed sides, renounced Islam, and drove the Turks from Albania, where he valiantly defeated every force sent against him. For 20 years he maintained the independence of Albania with only occasional support from Naples, Venice and the pope. After his death Albanian opposition to the Turk collapsed. See Paganel's *Histoire du Scanderbeg* (1855).

SKEAT, Walter William (1835–1912), English philologist, born in London, and educated at King's College School and Christ's College, Cambridge, graduated as fourteenth wrangler in 1858, and became a fellow in 1860, and in 1878 professor of Anglo-Saxon. He was the first director of the Dialect Society (established 1873), and he contributed more than any scholar of his time to a sound knowledge of Middle English and English philology generally. He edited important texts, especially for the Early English Text Society. Other works are *A Moeso-Gothic Glossary* (1868), his admirable *Etymological English Dictionary* (new ed. 1910) and its abridgment (1911); *Principles of English Etymology* (1887–91); his great *Chaucer* (6 vols. 1894–95); the *Student's Chaucer* (1895); *A Student's Pastime* (1896); *Chaucerian and other Pieces* (1897); *The Chaucer Canon* (1900); *Glossary of Tudor and Stuart Words* (1914); and papers on place names.

SKELTON, (1) John (*c.* 1460–1529), English satirical poet, studied at Cambridge, perhaps also at Oxford, was created ' poet laureate ' by both, was tutor to Prince Henry, and became rector of Diss, but seems later to have been suspended for having a concubine or wife. He had produced some translations and elegies in 1489, but began to strike an original vein of satirical vernacular poetry, overflowing with grotesque words and images and unrestrained jocularity, as in *The Bowge of Courte, Colyn Cloute* and *Why come ye nat to Courte*. Of these, the first is an allegorical poem; the second an unsparing attack on the corruptions of the church; and the last a sustained invective against Wolsey for which Skelton had to take sanctuary at Westminster. Other poems include *Garlande of Laurell* and *Magnyfycence*, his one surviving morality. See Dyce's edition (1843), books by Lloyd (1938), Gordon (1943).

(2) **Sir John** (1831–97), Scottish lawyer and writer, born in Edinburgh, wrote a defence of Mary Stuart (1876), sumptuous Lives of her (1893) and Charles I (1898), besides *Maitland of Lethington* (1887), *Table Talk of Shirley* (1895–96), &c.

SKENE, *skeen*, (1) **Sir John, Lord Curriehill** (c. 1543–1617), Scottish advocate, regent of St Mary's College, St Andrews, lived in Scandinavia, was ambassador, lord advocate, lord clerk-register and lord of session. He edited and translated into Scots a collection of old laws, *Regiam Majestatem* (1609).

(2) **William Forbes** (1809–92), Scottish historian, born at Inverie, a close friend of Scott. In 1881 succeeded Hill Burton as Scottish historiographer. Among his works are *The Highlanders of Scotland* (1837), *Celtic Scotland* (1876–80), &c.

SKINNER, (1) **James** (1778–1841), Indian soldier of Eurasian origin, joined the Indian army at fifteen, was promoted to lieutenant for gallantry, but dismissed by General Perron in 1803 because of his mixed origin. Under General Lord Lake, he formed Skinner's Horse, one of the most famous regiments in India. His rank of lieutenant-colonel was not recognized in London until 1827, when he was also made a Companion of the Bath. With these honours, the fabulous wealth of thirty years' looting, and several wives, he settled down to the life of a rich Mogul in his town house at Delhi and his country seat near by. Always inclined to scholarship and philanthropy, he now wrote books in flawless Persian, with decorations and numerous paintings by local artists, on the princes, castes and tribes of Hindustan; and built a mosque, a temple and the Church of St James in Delhi. Of his burial there it has been said that 'None of the Emperors of Hindustan was ever brought into Delhi in such state as Sikander Sahib'—the name associates his military genius with Alexander (Sikander) the Great. See Life by J. B. Fraser (1851).

(2) **John** (1721–1807), Scottish historian and songwriter, born at Birse, Aberdeenshire, became an Episcopalian minister at Longside near Peterhead. Although no Jacobite, his house was pillaged and his chapel burnt in 1746. He wrote *The Ecclesiastical History of Scotland* (1788) and several songs, of which 'The Ewie wi' the crookit horn' and 'Tullochgorum' are the best known. See Life by Walker (1883). His son, **John** (1744–1816), was Bishop of Aberdeen.

SKOBELEFF, Mikhail Dmitrievich, *sko'byi-lyef* (1843–82), Russian soldier, fought against the Polish insurgents (1863), and in 1871–75 was at the conquest of Khiva and Khokand. In the Russo-Turkish war of 1877–78 he bore a conspicuous part at Plevna, in the Shipka pass, and at Adrianople; in 1881 he stormed the Turkoman stronghold Göktepe. He was an ardent Panslavist.

SKORZENY, Otto (1908–), Austrian colonel, born in Vienna, was personally chosen by Hitler to kidnap Mussolini from co-belligerent internment in a mountain hotel on the Gran Sasso range. In September 1943 he succeeded in landing with a detachment of men in gliders on the short inclined slope in front of the hotel and after a short engagement whisking the dictator off in a small aeroplane, and so to Hitler's headquarters in East Prussia. In September 1944 he daringly infiltrated into the Citadel of Budapest and forcibly prevented Horthy from making a separate peace with Stalin, thus endangering German troops, and during the Ardennes offensive in December of that year carried out widespread sabotage behind Allied lines, for which he was tried as a war criminal but acquitted. See his memoirs, *Skorzeny's Special Missions* (trans. 1959).

SKRIABIN. See SCRIABIN.

SLADE, Felix, *slayd* (1790–1868), English antiquary and art collector of Halsteads, Yorkshire, bequeathed to the British Museum his engravings and Venetian glass, and founded art professorships at Oxford, Cambridge, and University College, London.

SLATER, Oscar (1873–1948), supposed murderer. A German Jew, he was convicted of the murder of Marion Gilchrist in Glasgow in 1909. Three witnesses identified him as the man seen leaving the scene of the crime, although their descriptions varied considerably and at least one of them was thought to have seen Slater's photograph before identifying him. After the trial, at which he was not called to give evidence, he was sentenced to death but this was commuted to life imprisonment. Because of protests of injustice by Conan Doyle and others, he was released after nineteen years and received £6000 in compensation.

SLATIN, Baron Rudolf Carl von, *slah'teen* (1857–1932), Austrian-born soldier in the British service, born near Vienna, in 1878 took service under Gordon in the Sudan. Governor of Darfur (1881), on the defeat of Hicks Pasha he surrendered (1883) to the Mahdi, escaped in 1895, and wrote a vivid description of his experiences, *Fire and Sword in the Soudan* (trans. 1896). As colonel he served in the Dongola and Omdurman expeditions (1896–98). He was inspector-general of the Sudan in 1900–14; and in World War II president of the Austrian Red Cross.

SLEIDANUS, properly Philippi, Johannes (1506–56), German historian, born at Schleiden, in 1537 entered the service of Francis I of France; but turning Protestant, was dismissed (1541), and served as ambassador of the Protestant princes of Germany. He wrote a Latin history of Charles V (1555). See Life by Baumgarten (1876).

SLESSOR, (1) **Sir John Cotesworth** (1897–), British air-marshal, born at Rhanikhet, India, educated at Haileybury, served in the Royal Flying Corps in World War I and was awarded the M.C. He was instructor at the R.A.F. Staff College (1924–25) and at Camberley (1931–34). His part in the Waziristan operations (1936–37) earned him the D.S.O. During World War II he was c.-in-c. of Coastal Command (1943) and of the Mediterranean theatre (1944–45). Promoted marshal in 1940, he was chief of the Air Staff (1950–52). His often original, penetrating and unorthodox views on nuclear strategy are expressed in *Strategy for the West* (1954) and *The Great Deterrent* (1957). He was knighted in 1943.

(2) **Mary** (1848–1915), Scottish missionary, born at Dundee, worked in a factory from childhood but, conceiving a burning ambition to become a missionary, got herself accepted by the United Presbyterian Church for teaching in Calabar, Nigeria, where she spent many years of devoted work among the natives. See *Life* by Livingstone (1931).

SLEVOGT, Max, *slay'fōкнт* (1868–1932), German Impressionist painter and engraver, born at Landshut. He studied in Munich and Berlin (where he later taught at the Academy), and worked with the Impressionist Corinth. His works comprise murals of historical scenes and swiftly executed landscapes and portraits.

SLEZER, John (d. 1714), Dutch engraver employed by Charles II and the Duke of York to make engravings of Scottish buildings. His *Theatrum Scotiae* (1693) was reprinted, with memoir, in 1874.

SLIM, William Joseph, 1st Viscount (1891–1970), British field-marshal, educated at King Edward's School, Birmingham. During World War I he served in Gallipoli, France and Mesopotamia. Transferring to the Gurkha Rifles, a succession of command and staff appointments brought him to high command in World War II. His greatest achievement was to restore morale in Burma and lead his reorganized forces, the famous 14th 'forgotten' army to victory over the Japanese. He was chief of the Imperial General Staff 1948–52, and governor-general of Australia 1953–60. He was created K.C.B. in 1944 and viscount in 1960. See his *Defeat into Victory* (1956) and memoirs, *Unofficial History* (1959).

SLOANE, Sir Hans, 1st Bart. (1660–1753), British physician, born at Killyleagh, County Down, the son of an Ulster Scot, studied in London and in France, and settled in London as a physician. Already F.R.S., he spent over a year (1685–86) in Jamaica, collecting a herbarium of 800 species. He was secretary to the Royal Society (1693–1713), president (1727), and, a baronet from 1710, was physician-general to the army (1716) and royal physician. His museum and library of 50,000 volumes and 3560 MSS. formed the nucleus of the British Museum. His great work was the *Natural History of Jamaica* (1707–25). See study by G. de Beer (1953).

SLOCUM, Joshua, *slō'kĕm* (1844–c. 1910), American mariner, born at Wilmot Township, Nova Scotia, went early to sea as a ship's cook and in 1869 captained a trading vessel off the Californian coast. In 1886 he set off with his second wife and two sons on a converted bark, *Aquidneck*, for South America, was wrecked on a Brazilian sandbar, but from the wreckage built a canoe which took them all back to New York. In 1895 he set out from Boston without capital on the sloop *Spray* for the first solo cruise

around the world, arriving back at Newport in 1898, having supported himself by lecturing on the way. In November 1909 he set out once more, but was not heard of again. See his *Sailing Alone Around the World* (1900), and *Life* by W. M. Teller (1959).

SŁOWACKI, Juljusz, *slo-vat'ski* (1809–49), Polish poet, born at Krzemieniec, settled in Paris in 1831. He belonged to the Romantic school, the influence of Byron, among others being perceptible in his work, which includes the historical drama *Marie Stuart* (1830), the dramatized legend *Balladyna* (1834), *Lilla Weneda* (1840), perhaps the most famous Polish tragedy, and *Mazeppa* (1839), which was translated into English.

SLUTER, Claus (c. 1350–1405/6), Flemish sculptor, born probably at Haarlem, went to Dijon under the patronage of Philip the Bold of Burgundy, and died there. His chief works are the porch sculptures of the Carthusian house of Champmol near Dijon, and the tomb of Philip the Bold. See study by Troescher (1932).

SMART, (1) Christopher (1722–71), English poet, born at Shipbourne near Tonbridge, was elected fellow of Pembroke College, Cambridge, in 1745. Improvidence, wit and a secret marriage upset his academic career and he settled to a precarious living in London. He died insane. Samuel Johnson assisted him in his monthly *Universal Visitor*. Smart's works include epigrams, birthday odes and occasional poems; the *Hilliad*, a heavy satire; and several translations from the Bible and the classics. His one real poem, *A Song to David* (first printed 1763; ed. Blunden, 1924), though marred by repetitions and defects of rhythm, shows a genuine spark of inspiration. See Browning's *Parleyings* and Gosse's *Gossip in a Library* (1892), and Lives by Mackenzie (1925) and Ainsworth and Noyes (1943).

(2) **Sir George Thomas** (1776–1867), English musician, uncle of (3), friend of Haydn and Weber, visited Beethoven and promoted Mendelssohn's music in England. He composed anthems, chants and glees.

(3) **Henry Thomas** (1813–79), English composer, nephew of (2), was organist to the Chapel Royal and composed an *Ave Maria* and part-songs, &c. See *Life* by Sparks (1880).

SMEATON, John (1724–94), English engineer, born at Austhorp near Leeds, gave up law and about 1750 removed to London as a mathematical-instrument maker. Elected F.R.S. in 1753, he won the Copley Medal for his mathematical and experimental researches into the mechanics of waterwheels and windmills and established his reputation with his novel design for the third Eddystone lighthouse (1756–59), which remained in use till 1877, and was re-erected on Plymouth Hoe as a memorial. His other chief engineering works include Ramsgate Harbour (1774), the Forth and Clyde Canal, &c. See Smiles's *Lives of the Engineers* (1905).

SMECTYMNUUS, a composite pseudonym used by Stephen Marshal, Edward Calamy, Thomas Young, Matthew Newcomen, and William Spurstow, who published in 1641 a pamphlet attacking Episcopacy which was answered by Hall and defended by Milton.

SMETANA, Bedřich, *smet'-* (1824–84), Czech composer, born in Litomyšl. He studied in Prague, and in 1884 opened a music school with the financial support of Liszt, who recommended his music to the German publisher Kistner. From 1856 to 1859 and again in 1860 he was conductor of the Philharmonic Orchestra in Göteborg, Sweden, but after his return to Prague he opened a new music school, and in 1866 became conductor of the new National Theatre, for which his operas were composed. Overwork destroyed his health, and in 1874 he became totally deaf, though he continued to compose until his mental breakdown in 1883. His compositions, intensely national in character, include nine operas (one unfinished), of which the best known are *The Bartered Bride*, *Dalibor* and *The Kiss*; his many orchestral and chamber works include the series of symphonic poems entitled *Má Vlast* (My Country) and the string quartet *Aus meinem Leben* (From My Life), both composed when he was deaf. See study by Bartoš (trans. 1953).

SMILES, Samuel (1812–1904), Scottish author and social reformer, was born at Haddington, took his Edinburgh M.D. at twenty, and published *Physical Education* (1838). He practised in Haddington, and then settled as a surgeon in Leeds, but became editor of the *Leeds Times*, secretary of the Leeds and Thirsk Railway in 1845, and in 1854 secretary of the Southeastern Railway, retiring in 1866. While at Leeds he met George Stephenson, and undertook a *Life* of him (1857). His famous *Self-Help* (1859; n.e. intro. A. Briggs 1958), with its short *Lives* of great men and the admonition 'Do thou likewise', was the ideal Victorian school-prize. An *Autobiography* (published 1905) completed a long series of works, including *Lives of the Engineers* (3 vols. 1861–62; rev. eds. 1874, 1904, 5 vols.; reprinted 1969), *Character* (1871), *Thrift* (1875), *Duty* (1880), &c. See Life by A. Smiles (1956).

SMILLIE, Robert, *smĭ'li* (1857–1940), Scottish Labour politician, born of Scottish parents in Belfast, was president of the Scottish Miners' Federation 1894–1918, and again from 1921; and from 1912 to 1921 president of the Miners' Federation of Great Britain. He was Labour M.P. for Morpeth (1923–29).

SMIRKE, Sir Robert (1781–1867), English architect, son of Robert Smirke (1752–1845), painter and book-illustrator, was born in London. He became R.A. in 1811, was architect to the Board of Works and was knighted in 1831. Smirke's public buildings are usually classical, his domestic architecture Gothic. Covent Garden Theatre (1809) was his first great undertaking; the British Museum (1823–47) his best known. His brother, **Sydney** (1799–1877), completed the west wing of the museum and the reading room (1854), and rebuilt the Carlton Club (1857). He was elected R.A. in 1859.

SMITH, (1) Adam (1723–90), Scottish economist and philosopher, whose *Wealth of Nations* is the first masterpiece in political economy, born June 5 at Kirkcaldy, the posthumous son of the comptroller of customs, studied at Glasgow and Balliol College, Oxford. From 1748 he became one of the brilliant circle in Edinburgh which included David Hume, John Home, Hugh Blair, Lord Hailes and Principal Robertson. In 1751 he became professor of Logic at Glasgow, but exchanged the professorship for that of Moral Philosophy the following year. In 1759 he published his *Theory of Moral Sentiments*, based on Humeian doctrines. The essence of moral sentiments was sympathy, but a specialized conscience-stricken sympathy which Smith defined as that of an impartial and well-informed spectator. He met Quesnay, Turgot, Necker and others in Paris, when he was travelling tutor to the Duke of Buccleuch. He watched over the illness and death of his illustrious friend Hume, edited his noncontroversial papers and wrote a moving account of the latter's end to a Mr Strahan of London, which became controversial since respectability resented a prominent atheist dying with such dignity. Shortly afterwards (1776) Smith removed himself to London, where he became a member of the club to which Reynolds, Garrick and Johnson belonged. The same year he published a volume in five chapters intended as the first of a complete theory of society in the tradition of Scottish ' Moral Philosophy ', i.e., comprising natural theology, ethics, politics and law. This one volume, entitled *Inquiry into the Nature and Causes of the Wealth of Nations*, his magnum opus, examined in detail the consequences of economic freedom such as division of labour, the function of markets and mediums of exchange and the international implications. He attacked mediaeval mercantile monopolies and the theories of the French physiocrats, who made land the economic basis of wealth. But his doctrines were not yet those of full-blooded *laissez faire* for which the 19th-century utilitarians were responsible, for Smith wanted his economics to implement his earlier work on moral sentiments. Few works have had such influence. At a public dinner at Wimbledon, Pitt asked Smith to be seated first because prophetically in his words 'we are all your scholars '. His appointment as commissioner of customs (1778) brought him back to Edinburgh, where he died July 17, 1790, and was buried in the Canongate churchyard. He was elected F.R.S. (1767) and in 1787 lord rector of Glasgow University. Other works include essays on the formation of languages, the history of astronomy, classical physics and logic and the arts. His works were edited by Dugald Stewart (1811–12), who contributed a biography. Smith's Glasgow *Lectures on Justice, Police, Revenue, Arms* were edited from notes by a student in 1896. See Lives by Haldane (1887), Macpherson (1899), Hirst (1904), Scott (1937) and Fay (1956).

(2) Alexander (1829–67), Scottish poet, born at Kilmarnock, became a pattern-designer in Glasgow, sending occasional poems to the *Glasgow Citizen*. His *Life Drama* (1851) was highly successful at first but was strongly satirized by Aytoun in *Firmilian, a Spasmodic Tragedy*, and the adjective has stuck to Smith's poetry ever since. Immature and extravagant the poem was certainly, and its unconscious echoes of

Keats and Tennyson gave colour to the charge of plagiarism; still, Smith has a richness and originality of imagery that more than atone for all defects of taste and knowledge. In 1854 he was appointed secretary to Edinburgh University, and next year produced *Sonnets on the War* with Sydney Dobell, his brother poet of the ' Spasmodic ' school. *City Poems* (1857) and *Edwin of Deira* (1861) were followed by essays, collected under the title *Dreamthorp* (1863), and novels. See Memoir by P. P. Alexander prefixed to his *Last Leaves* (1869), and Life by T. Brisbane (1869).

(3) **Alfred Emanuel** (1873–1944), American Democrat politician, born in New York, rose from newsboy to be governor of N.Y. State (1919–20, 1923–28). ' Al ' Smith was beaten as Democratic candidate for the U.S. presidentship in 1928.

(4) **Augustus John** (1804–72), English lessee or ' king ' from 1834 of the Scilly Islands, was M.P. for Truro from 1857.

(5) **Bernard** (1630–1708), English organbuilder, called ' Father Smith '. See HARRIS, RENATUS.

(6) **Mrs Burnett.** See SWAN, ANNIE.

(7) **Dodie,** pseud. until 1935 **C. L. Anthony** (   ), English playwright, novelist, and theatre producer, started as an actress but took up a business career. Her first play, *Autumn Crocus* (1930), was an instant success and enabled her to devote all her time to writing. Other plays include *Dear Octopus* (1938), *Letter from Paris* (adapted from *The Reverberator* by Henry James, 1952) and *I Capture the Castle* (adapted from her own novel, 1952). Other works include the children's book *The Hundred and One Dalmations* (1956).

(8) **Lady Eleanor Furneaux** (1902–45), English novelist, born in Birkenhead, a daughter of the 1st Earl of Birkenhead. She possessed a lively imagination and an intimate knowledge of Romany and circus life, and her novels, which include *Red Wagon* (1930), *Flamenco* (1931) and *Man in Grey* (1941), were, if rather sentimental, colourful and romantic. See her autobiographical *Life's a Circus* (1939), and Life by Birkenhead (1953).

(9) **Eli** (1801–57), American Congregational missionary from 1829 in Syria, born at Northford, Conn., died at Beirut, translated the Bible into Arabic. His son, **Benjamin Eli** (1857–1913), edited *The Century Dictionary, Atlas,* &c.

(10) **Sir Francis Pettit** (1808–74), English inventor, born at Hythe, was first with Ericsson in building screw-propelled ships (1834–1836). He also built the first screw steamship, the *Rattler* (1841–43). In 1860 was appointed curator of the Patent Office Museum, South Kensington, and in 1871 was knighted.

(11) **Frederick Edwin.** See BIRKENHEAD.

(12) **George** (1840–76), English Assyriologist, born in London, was a banknote engraver who studied cuneiform inscriptions in the British Museum, and in 1867 became an assistant there. He helped Sir H. Rawlinson with his *Cuneiform Inscriptions* (1870), furnished (1871) the key to the Cypriote character, and deciphered from Layard's tablets in 1872 the Chaldaean account of the

Deluge. In 1873 he was dispatched to Nineveh to find the missing fragment of the tablet. It and other results of his excavations were presented to the British Museum, which itself sent him out again next year. While on a homeward journey from his third expedition, he died at Aleppo. See his *Assyrian Discoveries* (1875), &c.

(13) **George** (1824–1901), English publisher, joined his father's firm of Smith & Elder in 1838, becoming head in 1846. He founded the *Pall Mall Gazette* in 1865, in 1882 began the *Dictionary of National Biography*, and published the works of George Eliot, the Brownings, Mrs Gaskell, Trollope, &c.

(14) **Sir George Adam** (1856–1942) Scottish Biblical scholar, born in Calcutta, was a minister in Aberdeen (1882–92) and at the same time professor of Hebrew at Glasgow, wrote studies on Isaiah and the minor prophets. In 1909 he became principal of Aberdeen University, was knighted in 1916 and made moderator. See Life by L. A. Smith (1943).

(15) **George Joseph** (1872–1915), British murderer, born in London, drowned his three ' brides in the bath ', Beatrice Williams, Alice Burnham and Margaret Lofty, for the total gain of £3500, the first and last in London (1912, 1914), the second in Blackpool (1913). See trial account, ed. Watson (1949).

(16) **Gerrit** (1797–1874), American philanthropist, active in these and and other reform movements such as dress, prison, women's suffrage, &c., aided John Brown (q.v.). See Life by Frothingham (1878).

(17) **Sir Grafton Elliot** (1871–1937), Australian anatomist and ethnologist, authority on brain anatomy and human evolution, born at Grafton, N.S.W., was professor in Cairo School of Medicine, Manchester and London. His books, *Migrations of Early Culture* (1915), *The Evolution of the Dragon* (1919), *The Diffusion of Culture* (1933), &c., explain similarities in culture all over the world by diffusion from Egypt.

(18) **Sir Harry George Wakelyn, 1st Bart.** (1788–1860), English soldier, born at Whittlesey, fought in the Peninsular, Waterloo, Kaffir and Sikh campaigns, by his strategy winning the battle of Aliwal (1846), and, as Cape governor, all but brought the Kaffir war to a successful issue.

(19) **Henry John Stephen** (1826–83), Irish mathematician, born in Dublin, and educated at Rugby and Balliol College, Oxford, of which he was elected a fellow. In 1861 he became Savilian professor of Geometry. He was the greatest authority of his day on the theory of numbers, and also wrote on elliptic functions and modern geometry. See biographical sketches in his *Mathematical Papers* (ed. by Glaisher, 1897).

(20) **Horace** or **Horatio.** See (23).

(21) **Ian Douglas** (1919–), Rhodesian politician, born at Selukwe, educated in Rhodesia and at Rhodes University, S. Africa. He was a fighter pilot in World War II and became an M.P. in 1948. From 1953 he was a member of the United Federal Party, resigning in 1961 to become a founder of the Rhodesian Front, dedicated to immediate independence without African majority rule.

He was minister of the treasury (1962–64), and prime minister from April 1964, and of external affairs (to Aug. 1964), of defence (to May 1965). With an overwhelming majority, despite lengthy talks and strenuous attempts to avert it, he unilaterally declared independence in Nov. 1965. Britain declared his government rebels and, supported by many other countries, applied increasingly severe economic sanctions. His meetings (1966 and 1968) with Harold Wilson, the British prime minister, aboard H.M.S. *Tiger* and H.M.S. *Fearless* off Gibraltar failed to resolve the situation.

(22) **James** (1789–1850), Scottish agricultural engineer, of Deanston, Perthshire, manager of the cotton mills there from 1807, the inventor of 'thorough drainage' by means of a subsoil plough. He was a philanthropist.

(23) **James** (1775–1839) and **Horace** (1779–1849), English authors of *The Rejected Addresses*, were educated at Chigwell, Essex. James succeeded his father as solicitor to the Board of Ordnance; Horace made a fortune as a stockbroker. Both wrote for magazines. When a prize was advertised for an address to be spoken at the opening of the new Drury Lane Theatre in 1812, the brothers produced a series of supposed ' Rejected Addresses ', James furnishing imitations of Wordsworth, Southey and Coleridge; Horace those of Scott, Byron, ' Monk ' Lewis and Moore. James also wrote Charles Mathews' entertainments; and Horace the *Tin Trumpet* (1836) and more than a score of novels. Of Horace's *Poems* (1846) the best known is the ' Ode to an Egyptian Mummy '. See Beavan, *James and Horace Smith* (1899).

(24) **Sir James Edward** (1759–1828), English botanist, born at Norwich, was founder and first president (1788) of the Linnean Society. He compiled *English Botany* (36 vols. 1790–1814).

(25) **John** (1580–1631), English adventurer, born at Willoughby, Lincolnshire, was apprenticed to a Lynn merchant, but went to France, and saw some soldiering under Henry IV. Next he served with distinction against the Turks in Hungary, but was captured and sold as a slave. In 1605 he joined an expedition to colonize Virginia; and he was saved from death by Princess Pocahontas (q.v.). His energy and tact in dealing with the Indians were useful to the colonists and he was elected president of the colony in 1608, but returned to England in 1609. During 1610–17 he was again in North Virginia. His works, reprinted in 1910, include *A Description of New England* (1616) and *History of Virginia* (1624). See Lives by Scheibler (1782), Warner (1881), Bradley (1905), Johnson (1915), Syme (1954), and Barbour (1964).

(26) **John** (1790–1824), British missionary in Demerara, who was sentenced to death by the governor for refusing to help in suppressing a Negro uprising. Public protests at home, led by Wilberforce, caused the government to override the governor, but instructions arrived after Smith had perished in an insanitary jail. His fate hastened the passing of the Emancipation Act (1833). See Life by D. Chamberlin (1823).

(27) **John Raphael** (1750–1812), English miniaturist, portrait painter and especially mezzotinter, son of **Thomas Smith** (c. 1709–1767), Derby landscapist. Many of his plates are from the works of Reynolds, Romney, &c.

(28) **John Stafford** (1750–1836), English composer. The tune of *The Star-spangled Banner* has been attributed to him.

(29) **Joseph** (1805–44), founder of the Mormons, was born at Sharon, Vt., December 23, received his first ' call ' as a prophet at Manchester, N.Y., in 1820. In 1823 an angel told him of a hidden gospel on golden plates, with two stones which should help to translate it from the ' Reformed Egyptian '; and on the night of September 22, 1827, the sacred records were delivered into his hands. The *Book of Mormon* (1830) contained a fanciful history of America from its colonization at the time of the confusion of tongues to the 5th century of the Christian era, and claimed to have been written by a prophet named Mormon. Despite ridicule and hostility, and sometimes open violence, the new ' Church of the Latter-day Saints ' rapidly gained converts. In 1831 it established its headquarters at Kirtland, Ohio, and built Zion in Missouri. Things culminated in 1838 in a general uprising in Missouri against the Mormons; and Smith was often arrested. In Illinois, near Commerce, was founded Nauvoo (1840), and within three years the Mormons in Illinois numbered 20,000, Smith meanwhile starting ' spiritual wives '. But on June 27, 1844, 150 masked men broke into Carthage jail, where Smith and his brother Hyrum were imprisoned, and shot them dead. See YOUNG (BRIGHAM), and Kennedy's *Early Days of Mormonism* (N.Y. 1888).

(30) **Logan Pearsall** (1865–1946), American writer, born at Millville, N.J., took British nationality in 1913. He is remembered for his delightful essays, collected in *All Trivia* (1933), his short stories, critical writings, and works on the English language.

(31) **Madeleine Hamilton** (1835–1928), Scottish defendant in the most baffling murder trial of modern times, the daughter of a Glasgow architect, stood trial in Edinburgh (1857) for the alleged murder by arsenic poisoning of her former lover Pierre Emile L'Angelier, a clerk and native of Jersey. Her uninhibited love letters to him, published during the trial, stirred up much Victorian resentment against her. But although she had sufficient motive for ridding herself of L'Angelier, after her engagement to a more congenial suitor, and although she had purchased arsenic on three occasions, evidence was lacking of any meeting between them on the last days or nights prior to his last violent illness. She was brilliantly defended by John Inglis (q.v.), Dean of Faculty, and the verdict was ' Not Proven '. In 1861 she married a London artist-publisher George Wardle, an associate of William Morris, and after a normal family life in Bloomsbury, separated from her husband and eventually emigrated to America, resisting Hollywood's endeavours to make her take part in a film of her life by threatening to have her deported. She died in 1928, the widow of

her second husband, an American, Sheehy. See account of the trial, ed. F. Tennyson Jesse (1927), and books by G. L. Butler (1935), P. Hunt (1950) and N. Norland (1957).

(32) **Sir Matthew Arnold Bracy** (1879–1959), English artist, born at Halifax, studied at the Slade School, and first went to Paris in 1910, when he met Matisse and the Fauves. In 1915 he exhibited with the London Group and he later painted much in Provence. His flowers, nudes and landscapes are modelled with a full brush in rich glowing colour, e.g., *Gladioli in a Yellow Jug* (1938) in the Tate Gallery, London. See the monograph by P. Hendy (1944).

(33) **Norman Kemp** (1872–1958), Scottish philosopher, born at Dundee, lectured at Glasgow (1879–1906). He was then appointed professor of Psychology (1906) and of Philosophy (1914) at Princeton. After war work in London (1916–18) he became professor of Logic and Metaphysics at Edinburgh (1919–45) and achieved an enduring reputation with his remarkable *Studies* (1902) and *New Studies* (1952) in, and selected translations (1953) of, Descartes' philosophical writings, his book on Hume (1941) and especially with his monumental *Commentary to Kant's Critique of Pure Reason* (1918), in which he advocated the ' patchwork ' theory to solve many problems of interpretation of that difficult work, which he also translated (1929) into such unambiguous English that even German students preferred to tackle Kant via Kemp Smith's translation.

(34) **Robert** (1689–1768), English mathematician, Plumian professor of Astronomy at Cambridge from 1716, and master of Trinity from 1742, published works on optics, sound and hydrostatics and discovered a theorem on the *n*th roots of unity.

(35) **Rodney** (1860–1947), English evangelist, known as ' Gipsy Smith ', born of nomadic gipsy parents near Epping Forest, was converted at a Primitive Methodist meeting in 1876, soon afterwards joined William Booth (q.v.) and became one of the first officers in the newly formed Salvation Army, which he left in 1882 to carry on his evangelism under the auspices of the Free Church, preaching forcefully in America, Australia and elsewhere as well as in Britain. See Murray, *Sixty Years an Evangelist* (1937).

(36) **Sydney** (1771–1845), English journalist, clergyman and wit, born at Woodford, Essex, was educated at Winchester and New College, Oxford, of which he became a fellow. He was ordained (1794) and served at Netheravon near Amesbury, and Edinburgh. There he married, and in 1802, with Jeffrey, Horner and Brougham, started the *Edinburgh Review*. He next lived six years in London, and soon made his mark as a preacher, a lecturer at the Royal Institution on moral philosophy (1804–06), and a brilliant talker; but in 1809 was ' transported ' to the living of Foston in Yorkshire. In 1828 Lord Lyndhurst presented him to a prebend of Bristol, and next year enabled him to exchange Foston for Combe-Florey rectory, Somerset. In 1831 Earl Grey appointed him a canon of St Paul's. His

writings include sixty-five articles, collected in 1839 from the *Edinburgh Review; Peter Plymley's Letters* (1807–08) in favour of Catholic emancipation; *Three Letters on the Ecclesiastical Commission* (1837–39); and other letters and pamphlets on the ballot, American repudiation, the game laws, prison abuses, &c. Their author is chiefly remembered as the creator of ' Mrs Partington ', the kindly, sensible humorist who stands immeasurably above Theodore Hook, if a good way below Charles Lamb. See *Selected Writings*, ed. Auden (1957), Lives by Holland (1855), Russell (1905), Pearson (1934), and study by Chevrilon (1894).

(37) **Sir Sydney Alfred** (1883–1969), New Zealand-born medico-legal expert, father of (38), born at Roxburgh, N.Z., was educated at Victoria College, Wellington, and Edinburgh University, was Medical Officer of Health for New Zealand, professor of Forensic Medicine at Cairo and from 1917 principal medico-legal expert for the Egyptian government, particularly in the case of the assassination of Sir Lee Stack Pasha, the commander-in-chief in 1924. He was regius professor of Forensic Medicine at Edinburgh (1928–53) and dean of the Medical Faculty from 1931 and played a foremost part in the medical and even ballistic aspects of crime detection, not least in the Merrett (1926) and Ruxton (1936) murder cases, often effectively opposing his brilliant English colleague, Spilsbury (q.v.). He wrote a *Text-Book of Forensic Medicine* (1925) and edited Taylor's *Principles and Practices of Medical Jurisprudence*, was knighted (1949) and elected rector of Edinburgh University (1954). See his autobiographical, *Mostly Murder* (1959).

(38) **Sydney Goodsir** (1915–), Scottish poet, born in Wellington, N.Z., son of (37), studied at Oriel College, Oxford, and with such works as *Skail Wind* (1941), *The Deevil's Waltz* (1946), *Under the Eildon Tree* (1948), a great modern love poem, spiced with a satirical sketch of the Edinburgh bohemian, *Orpheus and Eurydice* (1955), *Figs and Thistles* (1959) has established a reputation as the best modern Lallans poet after MacDiarmid. His first play, *The Wallace*, was commissioned for the Edinburgh Festival for 1960.

(39) **Sir Thomas** (1514–77), English statesman and Greek scholar, author of *De Republica Anglorum*, born at Saffron Walden, became a fellow of Queen's College, Cambridge, and was knighted in 1548. He negotiated the peace of Troyes (1564).

(40) **Thomas.** See (27).

(41) **Thomas Southwood** (1788–1861), English sanitary reformer, born at Martock, Somerset, took charge of a Unitarian chapel in Edinburgh in 1812 and at the same time studied medicine. In 1824 he became physician at the London Fever Hospital, publishing in 1830 his *Treatise on Fever*. Bentham left him his body for dissection and Smith kept the skeleton fully clothed until it was transferred to University College, London. He served on the Poor Law and Children's Employment Commissions, &c. See Life by C. L. Lewis (1894).

(42) **Walter Chalmers** (1824–1908), Scottish poet, born in Aberdeen, studied at Aberdeen

and Edinburgh, and from 1876 to 1894 was a Free Church minister in Edinburgh, and was moderator (1893). He wrote *The Bishop's Walk*, by ' Orwell ' (1861); *Olrig Grange*, by ' Hermann Kunst ' (1872); *North-Country Folk* (1883); *Kildrostan, a Dramatic Poem* (1884); *A Heretic* (1890), &c. A collected edition appeared in 1902.

(43) **William** (1769–1839), the father of English geology, was born at Churchill, Oxfordshire, and in 1794, appointed engineer to the Somerset Coal Canal, began his study of the strata of England, introducing the law of strata identified by fossils. His epoch-making Geological Map of England (1815) was followed by twenty-one geologically-coloured maps of English counties (1819–24), in which he was assisted by his nephew, John Phillips (q.v.). He was awarded the first Wollaston medal (1831) and was an expert on irrigation. See study by T. Sheppard (1920).

(44) **Sir William** (1813–93), English lexicographer, born in London, in 1840 edited parts of Plato and Tacitus. His great *Dictionary of Greek and Roman Antiquities* (1840–42; 3rd ed. 1891), was followed by the *Dictionary of Greek and Roman Biography and Mythology* (1843–49) and *Dictionary of Greek and Roman Geography* (1853–57). His Gibbon appeared in 1854. Another famous series comprises the *Dictionary of the Bible* (1860–63; new ed. 1893), *Dictionary of Christian Antiquities* (with Archdeacon Cheetham, 1875–80) and *Dictionary of Christian Biography and Doctrines* (with Dr Wace, 1877–87). Editor of the *Quarterly* from 1867, a D.C.L. of Oxford (1870), &c., Smith was knighted in 1892.

(45) **William Henry** (1792–1865), father of (46) entered the newsagent's business of his father in the Strand, London, in 1812 and aided by his brother, **Henry Edward**, expanded it into the largest in Britain by making extensive use of railways and fast carts for country deliveries.

(46) **William Henry** (1825–91), English newsagent, bookseller and statesman, son of (45), born in London, became his father's partner in 1846 and later assumed full control. The business steadily expanded, and in 1849 secured the privilege of selling books and newspapers at railway stations. Smith entered parliament in 1868, was financial secretary of the Treasury (1874–77), first lord of the Admiralty (1877–80), secretary for War (1885); in the second Salisbury ministry he was first lord of the Treasury and leader of the Commons till his death, October 6, 1891. See Life by Sir Herbert Maxwell (1893).

(47) **William Robertson** (1846–94), Scottish theologian and orientalist, born at Keig, Aberdeenshire, studied at Aberdeen, Edinburgh, Bonn and Göttingen, and in 1870 became professor of Hebrew and Old Testament Exegesis in the Free Church College, Aberdeen. His *Encyclopaedia Britannica* article ' Bible ' (1875) was strongly attacked for heterodoxy, but he was acquitted of heresy (1880). He was deprived of his professorship (1881) for another article on ' Hebrew Language and Literature '. In

1883 he became Lord Almoner's professor of Arabic at Cambridge, in 1886 university librarian and Adams professor of Arabic (1889). In 1887 he became chief editor of the *Encyclopaedia Britannica*. His chief works are: *The Old Testament in the Jewish Church* (1881), *The Religion of the Semites* (1889), &c. See Life by J. S. Black and G. Chrystal (1902).

(48) **Sir William Sidney** (1764–1840), English sailor, born at Westminster, entered the navy, and in 1780 was promoted lieutenant for his bravery at Cape St Vincent. He became captain in 1782, was knighted in 1792, and aided Hood in burning the ships and arsenal at Toulon in 1793. He next watched the Channel for French privateers, but was taken prisoner in 1796, escaped in 1798, and was sent as plenipotentiary to Constantinople, whence he hastened to St Jean d'Acre on hearing of Bonaparte's threatened attack. On March 16, 1709, he captured the enemy's vessels, and held the town heroically until the siege was raised, May 20. For this he received the thanks of parliament and a pension. He aided Abercromby in Egypt, destroyed the Turkish fleet off Abydos (1807), blockaded the Tagus, became vice-admiral of the blue in 1810, a K.C.B. in 1815, and admiral in 1821. He died at Paris, May 26, 1840. See Life by Barrow (1848).

SMITHSON, James Macie (1765–1829), English founder of the Smithsonian Institution, a natural son of the first Duke of Northumberland (see PERCY), devoted himself to chemistry and mineralogy, and died at Genoa. In a fit of pique at the Royal Society's rejection of a paper by him in 1826, bequeathed the reversion of £105,000 to found an institution at Washington ' for the increase and diffusion of knowledge among men '. See two works by W. R. Rhees (1879–80), and *The Smithsonian Institution*, by Goode (1898).

SMOLLETT, Tobias George (1721–71), Scottish novelist, was born in Dunbartonshire, grandson of Sir James Smollett. He was educated at Glasgow University, but leaving without means, sailed as surgeon's mate in the expedition to Carthagena in 1741. Three years later he settled in London, practising as a surgeon, but literature in the form of novel writing was his real interest. His first efforts succeeded—*Roderick Random* (1748) and *Peregrine Pickle* (1751), a picaresque novel—despite the ill-humoured attacks of Fielding in the *Covent Garden Journal*. The former is modelled on Le Sage's *Gil Blas* and besides describing episodes in the life of the unprincipled hero utilizes Smollett's experiences in the Carthagena expedition. *Peregrine Pickle* pursues the hero's amatory and military adventures throughout Europe. There is also the amusing episode of Commodore Trunnion and his man Pipes and the novel closes with much vitriolic satire on English literary and social coteries. *Ferdinand, Count Fathom* (1753) is the story of another heartless villain, whom an easy repentance saves from the gallows. Cervantes now succeeded Le Sage as a model—Smollett's translation of *Don Quixote* (1755) is still current—but his imitation of the master, *Sir Launcelote Greaves*, is crude work. In 1753 he was settled at Chelsea editing the new *Critical Review*—which led to his imprisonment for libel in 1760—and writing his *History of England*, which is not now current. Ordered abroad for his health, he visited France and Italy and saw little to please him there. His ill-natured record, *Travels in France and Italy* (1766), earned for him Sterne's nickname of ' Smelfungus '. His next publication was a coarse satire on public affairs, *The Adventures of an Atom* (1769). Fortunately he was still to write *Humphrey Clinker* (1771), which is much more kindly in tone and is still a favourite. A series of letters from and to members of a party touring round England and ' North Britain ', it amuses us with the humours of various eccentrics, including Lieutenant Lismahago, a needy but proud Scot who wins the heart of the termagant sister of Matthew Bramble, the valetudinarian who arranges the tour. Smollett died at Leghorn in 1771. Saintsbury edited the Works (12 vols. 1925); Noyes the Letters in 1926. See also studies by Buck (1925–27), Martz (1943) and Kahrl (1945).

SMUTS, Jan Christiaan (1870–1950), South African statesman, was born at Malmesbury, Cape Colony, and educated at Christ's College, Cambridge. Late in the Boer War he took the field with de la Rey; entered the House of Assembly in 1907 and held several cabinet offices, subsequently succeeding Botha as the premier of the Union of South Africa (1919). Entrusted during World War I with minor operations in German East Africa, as a political gesture he was made a member of the Imperial War Cabinet. As minister of justice under Hertzog, his coalition with the Nationalists in 1934 produced the United Party, of which he became prime minister. Despite numerous wild utterances—he informed a 1939 Royal Institute of National Affairs audience that ' the expectation of war tomorrow or in the near future is sheer nonsense '—he acquired a reputation as a political oracle, his counsel being freely sought by the War Cabinet during World War II. In the immediate postwar years he proclaimed his readiness to see Russia ' bestride Europe like a colossus '. He was created field-marshal 1941, O.M. 1947. See Armstrong, *Grey Steel* (1937), and Lives by Smuts (1952) and Hancock (2 vols. 1962, 1968).

SMYTH, Dame Ethel (1858–1944), English composer and suffragette, born in London, studied at Leipzig, composed a Mass in D, symphonies, choral works, the operas *Der Wald* (1901), *The Wreckers* (1906), &c., contended for women's suffrage—in 1911 she was imprisoned for 3 months—was created D.B.E. in 1922, and wrote reminiscences. See Life by C. St John (1959).

SMYTHE, (1) Francis Sydney (1900–49), British mountaineer, was born at Maidstone. He was member of three Everest expeditions, 1933, 1936 and 1938, and he shared the world's altitude climbing record with Norton, Harris and Wager. In 1930 he was a member of the Swiss Kanchenjunga expedition and was the first to climb the Himalayan peak Kamet in 1931. During World War II, he commanded the Commando Mountain Warfare School. His many books, beautifully illustrated by his fine mountain photography, include *Kamet Conquered* (1932), *Camp Six* (1937), *Adventures of a Mountaineer* (1940), *Over Welsh Hills* (1941), &c.

(2) **George Augustus**, &c. See STRANGFORD.

SNELL, (1) John (1629–79), Scottish philanthropist, born at Colmonell, Ayrshire, founded the Snell exhibitions at Balliol College, Oxford. See W. J. Addison, *The Snell Exhibitions* (1901).

(2) **Willebrod van Roijen**, Lat. **Snellius** (1591–1626), Dutch mathematician, was professor of Mathematics at Leyden (1613) and discovered the law of refraction known as Snell's law, based on a constant known as the refractive index. He attempted to use triangulation in a survey of the earth (1617).

SNIDER, Jacob (1820–66), American inventor, a Philadelphia wine merchant, who devised *inter alia* a system of converting muzzle-loading rifles into breechloaders.

SNORRI STURLASON (1179–1241), Icelandic historian, in 1215 was elected supreme judge of the island, but, meddling with the domestic troubles of Norway, incurred the ill-will of King Haakon, who had him murdered. Snorri was a poet of no mean order, and composed the Younger or Prose *Edda* (trans. by Brodeur, 1916) and the *Heimskringla*, a series of sagas of the Norwegian kings down to 1177 (trans. and ed. Monsen, 1932). See Lives by W. Morris (1905), E. Monsen (1932), and study by W. P. Ker (1906).

SNOW, Charles Percy, 1st Baron (1905–), English novelist and physicist, born at Leicester, was educated at Leicester and Cambridge and was a fellow of Christ's College (1930–50) and a tutor there (1935–45). During World War II he was chief of scientific personnel for the ministry of labour. He was editor of *Discovery* (1938–40) and the author of a cycle of successful novels portraying English life from 1920 onwards. The continuity is maintained by means of the character Lewis Eliot, through whose eyes the dilemmas of the age are focused, starting with *Strangers and Brothers* (1940), the general title of the series. *Time of Hope* (1949) and *Homecomings* (1956) deal with Eliot's personal life. *The Masters* (1951) stages the conflict aroused by the election of a new master in a Cambridge college. *The New Men* (1954) poses the dilemma of the scientists in the face of the potentials of nuclear fission. Other volumes are *The Light and the Dark* (1947), *The Conscience of the Rich* (1958), *The Affair* (1960), *Corridors of Power* (1964), and *The Sleep of Reason* (1968). Several have been adapted for theatre and TV. Though the chief characters of his cycle are rather supine, being manipulated to exhibit the expressed problems, mostly of power and prestige in all their facets, his work shows a keen appreciation of moral issues in a science-dominated epoch. His controversial *Two Cultures* (Rede lecture, 1959) discussed the dichotomy between science and literature and his belief in closer contact between them. He was made a C.B.E. in

1943, knighted in 1957 and created a life peer in 1964. He was parliamentary secretary at the ministry of technology (1964–66), and lord rector of St Andrews University (1961-64). In 1950 he married another outstanding novelist, **Pamela Hansford Johnson** (1912–), best known for her sensitive portrayal of her native London postwar, stripped of its wartime poise and a prey to the second rate in mind and heart. Her works include *An Avenue of Stone* (1947), its sequel *A Summer to Decide* (1948), the tragi-comical *The Unspeakable Skipton* (1958), her study of I. Compton Burnett (1953), and *Six Proust Reconstructions* (1958).

SNOWDEN, Philip Snowden, 1st Viscount (1864–1937), English Labour statesman, born near Keighley, was crippled in a cycling accident and forced to leave the civil service. He was chairman of the I.L.P. (1903–06), Socialist M.P. from 1906, opposed conscription (1915) and as chancellor of the Exchequer in the Labour governments of 1924 and 1929 maintained orthodox policies and aggravated the financial crises. As a free trader he resigned from the national government in 1932, having been created viscount in 1931. See his *Autobiography* (1934) and Life by Cross (1966).

SNYDERS, Frans (1579–1657), Dutch painter of Antwerp, specialized in still life and animals, often assisting Rubens and other painters in the latter field. He was court painter to the governor of the Low Countries.

SOANE, Sir John (1753–1837), English architect, son of a mason, Swan, near Reading, gained the travelling scholarship of the Royal Academy, and spent 1777–80 in Italy. He designed the Bank of England and held various official appointments. He bequeathed to the nation his house in Lincoln's Inn Fields. See books by Britton (1834) and Birnstingl (1925).

SOBIESKI. See JOHN III (of Poland); and for the 'SOBIESKI-STUARTS', see ALBANIE.

SOBRERO, Ascanio, *sob-ray'rō* (1812–88), Italian chemist, was the discoverer of nitroglycerine (1847).

SOCINUS, *so-sī'noos*, (1) **Faustus** (1539–1604), nephew of (2), one of the founders of the sect of Socinians, was born at Siena, December 5, studied theology at Basel (1575), and in 1579 went to Poland, teaching that Luther and Calvin had not gone far enough, and that human reason was the only solid basis of Protestantism. Driven from Cracow, he combated, at the Synod of Bresz in 1588, all the chief Christian dogmas—the divinity of Christ, propitiatory sacrifice, original sin, human depravity, the doctrine of necessity, and justification by faith. In 1594, on the publication of his *De Jesu Christo Servatore*, he was nearly murdered, and sought refuge in the village of Łucławice, where he died, March 3, 1604. See Life by Wallace (1850), and E. M. Wilbur, *History of Unitarianism* (1945).

(2) **Lælius**, or **Lelio Sozzini** (1525–62), born at Siena, was, with (1), a founder of the sect of Socinians. Driven from Siena he travelled widely in Europe and finally settled at Zürich. See the *Vita* by Illgen (1814).

SOCRATES, *sok'ra-teez* (before 469–399 B.C.), Athenian philosopher, was the son of Sophroniscus, a sculptor, and Phaenaretē, a midwife. He received the usual education of an Athenian youth, and also learned geometry and astronomy. The most important influence on his mental development was his intercourse with the sophists who frequented Athens. He took part in three campaigns at Potidaea (432–29), Delium (424) and Amphipolis (422), and distinguished himself by his bravery, extraordinary physical vigour, and indifference to fatigue or cold or heat. He was a good citizen, but the only political office he ever held was when in 406 he was one of the senate of Five Hundred. He held aloof from politics because of a call to philosophy. The Delphic Oracle declared him the wisest man in the world, but he wrote no books. Out of his wide circles of acquaintances some came to be attached to him more closely by ties of affection and admiration; yet there was no formal bond of discipleship. From two of these friends, Xenophon and Plato, we learn all we can know with certainty about his personality and his way of thinking. Yet, while Plato often makes Socrates the mouthpiece of ideas that in all likelihood were not held by him, Xenophon, a soldier and by no means a philosopher, makes Socrates a very much more commonplace person than he must have been. Despite this, we can accept the picture Plato gives us of the habits and conversation of Socrates. Socrates was ugly, snubnosed, with a paunch. His wife, Xanthippe, was supposed to have had a shrewish temper which Socrates bore patiently. There has been much diversity of opinion about the ' divine sign ', of which Socrates used to speak, a supernatural voice that stopped him doing wrong; certainly to the average Athenian there was something blasphemous in his attitude towards religion and his aristocratic connections did not improve matters when the democracy was restored. He was charged in 399 as ' an evil doer and a curious person, searching into things under the earth and above the heaven; and making the worse appear the better cause, and teaching all this to others '. The substance of Socrates' magnificent defence appears in Plato's *Apology*. He was condemned by only a majority of six in a jury numbering possibly five hundred. His refusal at first even to contemplate the alternative to death, a fine, was interpreted as insolence by the judges, who then voted for the death penalty. Thirty days elapsed because of a sacred mission to Delos. Socrates' friends planned his escape, but he refused to break the law. Having spent his last days conversing with his friends as described in Plato's *Phaedo*, although possibly the views expressed on the immortality of the soul are those of Plato, Socrates drank the hemlock. For Socrates, virtue was knowledge, and knowledge was to be elicited by the dialectical technique which he derived from Zeno. Feigning total ignorance before the opinionated, he would with celebrated Socratic irony pose a simple question such as ' What is courage? ' From the replies given he would construct contradictory consequences and so start again. His aim was to act as a midwife to those in labour for knowledge. He exposed the mere sophist. Apart from his overwhelming influence upon his celebrated pupil, Plato, who made him the chief spokesman in most of his dialogues, his unwritten philosophy was the starting-point of the Megaric, Cynic and Cyrenaic schools. See Xenophon, *Memorabilia* and *Symposium*, Plato, *Apology*, *Crito*, *Phaedo* and *Symposium*, Aristophanes' caricature in *The Clouds*, and studies by E. Zeller (1877), J. Burnet, *Greek Philosophy* (1914), F. Cornford (1932), A. E. Taylor (1933), Sir R. W. Livingstone (1938), W. Jaeger, *Paideia*, vol. 2 (trans. 1944), L. Nelson (trans. 1949) and the critical biographical study by A. J. Chroust (1957).

SODDY, Frederick (1877–1956), British radiochemist, born at Eastbourne, studied at the University College of Wales and Merton College, Oxford, and became professor of Chemistry at Glasgow, Aberdeen and Oxford. He collaborated with Lord Rutherford and in 1904 with Ramsay discovered the transformation of radium emanation into helium. In 1913 he gave the name *isotope* to forms of the same element having identical chemical qualities but different atomic weights; and his discovery of this phenomenon earned him the Nobel prize in 1921 and in 1955 the Albert medal. He was elected F.R.S. in 1910. See Life by M. Howorth (1959).

SÖDERBLOM, Nathan (1866–1931), Swedish theologian, born at Trönö near Söderhamm, studied at Uppsala and was ordained in 1893. He became Archbishop of Uppsala and primate of the Swedish Lutheran Church in 1914, after a period as minister of the Swedish Church in Paris and twelve years as professor of Theology at Uppsala from 1901 to 1914. A leader in the ecumenical movement, author of theological books, and a great worker for peace, he was awarded the Nobel peace prize in 1930. See Lives by Herklots (1948) and Katz (1949).

SODOMA, Il, *sod'-*, the sobriquet of **Giovanni Antonio Bazzi** (1477–1549), Italian religious and historical painter. He was born a Lombard at Vercelli, painted frescoes in Monte Oliveto Maggiore near Siena, before being called to the Vatican in 1508, where he was, however, superseded by Raphael, but where he painted the frescoes of *Alexander and Roxana* in the Villa Farnesina. His masterpieces date from his second Siena period and include *Christ at the Column*, *St Sebastian* (Uffizi, Florence) and *Ecstasy of St Catherine*. The influence of Michelangelo is apparent in his work, which often shows great insight into the portrayal of religious feeling, if sometimes lacking finality. See works by Hobart Cust (1960) and Le Gielly (1911).

SOEKARNO. See SUKARNO.

SOFFICI, Ardengo, *sof'fi-chee* (1878–1964), Italian artist and author, born at Rignano, lived in Paris (1900–08). In his painting early experiments in Futurism were followed by a return to a more representational style founded on a study of the techniques of early Italian masters. Among his writings are *Giornale di bordo* (1915), *Estetica futurista* (1920) and *Diario di Borghi* (1933).

SOLARIO, Antonio, *so-lah'ryō* (*c.* 1382–1455), Neapolitan painter, born at Civita in the Abruzzi, and nicknamed 'Lo Zingaro', originally a blacksmith, painted frescoes in the Benedictine monastery at Naples.

SOLIMAN. See SULAIMAN.

SOLIS, Juan Díaz de, *so-lees'* (*c.* 1470–1516), Spanish navigator, sailed with Pinzón, and, himself sent out to find a passage to the E. Indies via America, discovered the Río de la Plata, but was killed by the natives (1516). See Life by Medina (1897).

SOLIS Y RIBADENEYRA, Antonio de (1610–86), Spanish author, wrote poems and dramas and *Historia de la Conquista de Mexico* (1684), &c.

SOLOGUB, Fedor, pseud. of **Fedor Kuzmich Teternikov** (1863–1927), Russian novelist, wrote *The Little Demon* (trans. 1916), and many short stories, fables, fairy tales and poems.

SOLOMON (*c.* 1015–977 B.C.), king of Israel, was the second son of David and Bathsheba. His reign was outwardly splendid. The kingdom attained its widest limit; the temple and royal palaces were built on a scale of magnificence heretofore unknown. But the taxation entailed by the luxury of the court bred the discontent that led in the next reign to the disruption of the kingdom; and the king's alliance with heathen courts and his idolatrous queens and concubines provoked the discontent of the prophetic party. Solomon was credited with transcendent wisdom; in later Jewish and Mohammedan literature he was believed to control the spirits of the invisible world. There is no reason to suppose that he had anything to do with any of the works to which his name has been attached—Proverbs, Ecclesiastes, Song of Solomon, and, in the Apocrypha, the Wisdom of Solomon. See studies by M. D. Conway (1900) and Thieberger (1947).

SOLOMON, (1) professional name of **Solomon Cutner** (1902–), English pianist, born in London; after appearing with enormous success as a child prodigy, he retired for some years' further study, and has won a high reputation as a performer of the works of Beethoven, Brahms and some of the modern composers, though he has not toured so extensively as most players of his rank.

(2) **Solomon Joseph** (1860–1927), English portrait and mural painter, born in London, served in World War I and initiated the use of camouflage in the British army. He was elected R.A. in 1906, P.R.B.A. in 1918.

SOLON (*c.* 640 or 638–*c.* 559 B.C.), Athenian lawgiver, a merchant and a poet, archon in 594 (or 591), in a time of economic distress, he was appointed to reform the constitution. He set free all people who had been enslaved for debt (Seisachtheia), reformed the currency, and admitted a fourth class (Thetes) to the Ecclesia, so that they elected the magistrates, and to the Heliaea, so that they judged them. Thus he laid the foundations for the Athenian democracy; but he was a moderate and kept many privileges of the wealthy. After ten years' voluntary exile, he returned (580), and, in a poem, stirred up the Athenians to capture 'lovely Salamis' (*c.* 569). He died soon after the usurpation of Pisistratus, the story of his connection with Croesus being legendary. See Lives by K. Freeman (1926) and W. J. Woodhouse (1938).

SOLOVIEV, Vladimir, *sol'ĕ-vyof* (1853–1900), the 'first Russian philosopher', was born at Moscow, son of Sergei Soloviev (1820–79), historian of Russia. He wrote *Justification of Good* (trans. 1918), &c. See studies by Séverac (1912), D'Herbigny (1918) and Muckermann (1946).

SOLVAY, Ernest (1838–1922), Belgian chemist, born at Rebecq, Brussels, devised a process for the production of sodium carbonate (1863). Later this was replaced by the Leblanc process.

SOMBART, Werner (1863–1941), German economist, born at Ermsleben, studied under Schmoller, and became professor at Breslau in 1890 and at Berlin in 1914. One of the founders of modern social science, he reacted against the Marxism which he had early supported, but was not a believer in National Socialism. Among his best works are *Sozialismus und soziale Bewegung* (1911), *Der moderne Kapitalismus* (1902–28), *Die Juden und das Wirtschaftsleben* (1911) and *Deutscher Sozialismus* (1934). Several have been translated, notably *New Social Philosophy* (1937).

SOMERS, sum'-, (1) **Sir George** (1554–1610), whose shipwreck on the Bermudas led to their colonization from Virginia by him in 1610. They were known as the Somers Islands during their early history.

(2) **John, 1st Baron** (1651–1716), English Whig statesman, was born at Worcester, an attorney's son, studied at Trinity College, Oxford, and was called to the bar in 1676. Associated with the 'country party', he was one of the counsel for the Seven Bishops (1688) and presided over the drafting of the Declaration of Rights; and after the Revolution was successively solicitor-general, attorney-general, and lord keeper of the Great Seal, until in 1697 he became lord chancellor and Baron Somers of Evesham. He was William's most trusted minister, and was the object of frequent attacks, one of which in 1700 resulted in his being deprived of the seal, and another in 1701 in an impeachment by the Commons, rejected by the Lords. He was president of the council (1708–10). The *Somers Tracts* (1748), state papers from his library, were re-edited by Sir Walter Scott (1809–15).

SOMERSET, Dukes of. See SEYMOUR.

SOMERSET, (1) Edward. See WORCESTER (1).

(2) **Henry.** See BEAUFORT.

(3) **James.** See SHARP (3).

SOMERVELL, Sir Arthur (1863–1937), English composer, known for the cantata *The Forsaken Merman, Thalassa,* a symphony, children's operettas and for his collection of English folksongs.

SOMERVILLE, (1) Edith Oenone. See MARTIN (9).

(2) **Sir James Fownes** (1882–1949), English sailor, saw service in the Dardanelles (1915), was c.-in-c. in the West Indies (1938–39), and, recalled from retirement as vice-admiral in the Mediterranean, sank the French ships at Oran (1940), shelled Genoa (1941), helped

in the sinking of the *Bismarck* (1941), took part in the Malta convoy battle (1941), and after the entry of the Japanese into the war, became c.-in-c. of the British fleet in the Indian ocean. In 1945 he was promoted admiral of the Fleet.

(3) *née* **Fairfax, Mary** (1780–1872), Scottish mathematician and scientific writer, born at Jedburgh, the daughter of Admiral Sir William Fairfax, wrote *Celestial Mechanism* (1830), a popular version of Laplace's work, &c. Somerville College at Oxford is named after her. See her Autobiography (1873).

(4) **William** (1675–1742), English poet, squire of Edstone, Warwickshire, was born at Wolseley in Staffordshire. He wrote *The Chase* (1735) and other poetry.

SOMMERFELD, Arnold (1868–1951), German physicist, born at Königsberg, professor of Mathematics at Clausthal (1897), of Physics at Aachen (1900) and at Munich (1906), with Klein developed the theory of the gyroscope, researched into wave spreading in wireless telegraphy, applied the quantum theory to spectral lines and the Bohr atomic model and evolved a theory of the electron in the metallic state.

SONNINO, Baron Sidney (1847–1922), Italian statesman, born at Pisa—his mother was English—entered parliament in 1880, was finance minister 1893–96, premier 1906 and 1909–10, and as foreign minister (1914–20) denounced the Triple Alliance and brought Italy into the European war (May 1915).

SOONG, name of an influential Chinese family:

(1) **Charles Jones** (d. 1927), Chinese merchant and Methodist missionary, father of (2), (3) and (4), born on Hainan Island, went to U.S.A., was converted to Christianity and educated at Vanderbilt University. He returned to Shanghai, founded the first Y.M.C.A. there and set up as Bible publisher and salesman.

(2) **Ching Ling.** See SUN YAT-SEN.

(3) **Mayling.** See CHIANG KAI-SHEK.

(4) **Tse-ven,** abbreviated T.V. (1891–1971), Chinese financier, son of (1), studied at Harvard and Columbia, became finance minister of the Nationalist Government, Canton (1925–27), and at Nanking (1928–33), westernizing Chinese finances.

SOPER, Donald Oliver, 1st Baron (1903–), English Methodist minister, born at Wandsworth. Widely-known for his open-air speaking on London's Tower Hill, he became superintendent of the West London Mission in 1936, and has written many books on Christianity and social questions, and particularly on international issues from the pacifist angle. He was president of the Methodist Conference in 1953, and was created a life peer in 1965.

SOPHIA (1630–1714), electress of Hanover, youngest daughter of Elizabeth (q.v.), queen of Bohemia, in 1658 married Ernest Augustus, Duke of Brunswick-Lüneburg, afterwards elector of Hanover, and was the mother of George I. See her Memoirs, and a book by Sir A. W. Ward (2nd ed. 1909). For the wife of George I (q.v.), see KÖNIGSMARK.

SOPHOCLES, *sof'ō-kleez* (c. 496–c. 405 B.C.), Athenian tragedian, one of the great figures of

Greek drama, born at Colonus Hippius, an Athenian suburb, had to forgo his ambitions for the stage on account of a weak voice. He wrote well over a hundred items, most of them conventional satyr plays of which only the *Ichneutae* survives, as well as seven major plays, still extant, all written after his victory over Aeschylus in a dramatic contest in 468. He won first prize at the Great Dionysia 18 times. The problem of burial is prominent in both the *Ajax* and *Antigone* (possibly *c.* 441), in the first an Olympian directive that hatred should not pursue a noble adversary beyond the grave, in the second as a clash between sisterly compassion for a dead traitor brother and the stately proprieties of King Creon. Aeschylus, Euripides and Sophocles each wrote versions of *Electra*, the gruesome matricide by Orestes in revenge for his father's death at the hands of his mother's paramour. The great Sophoclean master-piece, however, is *Oedipus Tyrannus*, on which Aristotle based his aesthetic theory of drama in the *Poetica* and from which Freud derived the name and function of the ' Oedipus complex '. King Oedipus pro-claims sentence on the unknown murderer of his father Laius, whose presence is thought to be the cause of a plague at Thebes. By a gradual unfolding of incidents, he learns that he was the assassin and that Jocasta his wife is also his mother. He blinds himself, goes into exile and Jocasta commits suicide. The dramatic characteristics are the gradual reversal in fortune of an estimable, con-ventionally ' good ' person, through some untoward discovery in personal relationships, but also linked to some seemingly minor defect in character, in Oedipus' case, pride. This combination of a minor defect with the external cruel machinations of *atē*, or personal destiny abetted by the gods, constitutes, according to Aristotle, the famous ' tragic flaw ' which arouses the tragic emotions of pity and fear in the spectator and allows their purgation in a harmless manner. This is in sharp contrast to Aeschylean tragedy, which is essentially static. There is no development in the plot; the hero is doomed from the beginning. The *Trachiniae* explores the ruinous love of Heracles and Deianira. The *Philoctetes* (produced in 409) and *Oedipus Coloneus* would hardly be called tragic, except for the grave circumstances which attend the achievement of glory. See editions and translations by L. Campbell (1871–81), R. C. Jebb (1883–1908), F. Storr (1919) and A. C. Pearson (1924), and studies by Earp (1944), Bowra (1944), Whitman (Harvard 1951), Waldock (1951), Letters (1953), Kitto (1958), and also the latter's studies in Greek drama (1939 and 1956), and Lattimore, *The Poetry of Greek Tragedy* (1958).

SOPHONISBA, *sof-ō-niz'ba* (d. *c.* 204 B.C.), daughter of the Carthaginian general Hasdrubal, was betrothed to the Numidian prince Masinissa but married for reasons of state his rival Syphax, whom the former however defeated in battle, recapturing his one-time betrothed and marrying her. The Romans objected to this marriage and Masinissa gave her up but sent her poison to prevent her falling into Roman hands.

Corneille, Voltaire and Alfieri have written tragedies around this theme.

SOPWITH, Sir Thomas Octave Murdoch (1888–), British aircraft designer and sportsman, won the Baron de Forest prize in 1910 for flying across the English Channel; founded the Sopwith Aviation Company at Kingston-on-Thames (1912), where he de-signed and built many of the aircraft used in World War I. He was chairman of the Hawker Siddeley Group from 1935, president from 1963, and chairman of the Society of British Aircraft Constructors (1925–27). A keen yachtsman, he competed for the America cup in 1934. He was made C.B.E. in 1918 and knighted in 1953.

SORAYA, properly **Princess Soraya Esfandiari Bakhtiari** (1932–), ex-Queen of Persia, born at Isfahan of Persian and German parents. She was educated at Isfahan, and later in England and Switzerland, and became Queen of Persia on her marriage in 1951 to His Majesty Mohammad Reza Shah Pahlavi. The marriage was dissolved in 1958. See *Life* by Krause (trans. 1956).

SORBON, Robert de (1201–74), Louis IX's confessor, founded the college of the Sor-bonne (1253).

SORBY, Henry Clifton (1826–1908), English chemist and geologist, born at Woodbourne, Sheffield; elected F.R.S. in 1857, he devised a method of examining metals by treating polished surfaces with etching materials under the microscope. He wrote on biology, architecture and Egyptian hieroglyphics.

SORDELLO (d. *c.* 1270), Italian troubadour named by Dante, was born at Mantua. His poems (mostly in the ballad form) in the Provençal language alone survive. Palazzi edited his poems (Venice 1887).

SOREL, (1) Agnes (*c.* 1422–50), French-woman, mistress from 1444 of Charles VII of France, was born at Fromenteau, Touraine. Her influence may have been partly beneficial. See study by Champion (1931).

(2) **Albert** (1842–1906), French historian, born at Honfleur, elected to the Academy in 1894, wrote *L'Europe et la révolution française* (8 vols. 1885–1904).

(3) **Georges** (1847–1922), French syndi-calist philosopher, a road engineer who in middle age turned to politics and became the champion of Dreyfus. Influenced by Nietzsche, Marx and Bergson, he formulated a political theory set down in his *Refléxions sur la violence* (1908; trans. T. E. Hulme, 1915) by which he showed that true Socialism could only come by violent revolution at the hands of a disciplined proletariat, educated through trade union organizations. Theoreti-cally extreme, he compromised nevertheless with his political opponents and had little effect on the French trade unions. His emphasis on the ' social myth ' as a means to collective action, however, impressed Musso-lini and foreshadowed the hideous Nazi con-cept of the *Herrenvolk*. See his *Matériaux pour une théorie du prolétariat* (1919), studies by A. Lanzillo (1910) and P. Perrin (1925), and *Lives* by P. Pirou (1927), P. Lasserre (1928) and V. Sartre (1937).

SÖRENSEN, Sören Peter Lauritz (1868–1939), Danish biochemist, director of Chemistry at the Carlsberg Laboratory, did pioneer work on hydrogen-ion concentration, devising the symbol pH for the negative logarithm of the hydrogen-ion concentration.

SORGE, Reinhard Johannes, *zor'gĕ* (1892–1916), German poet, born at Rixdorf, pioneered dramatic expressionism with his play *Der Bettler* (1912). At first a believer in the Nietzschean doctrine, he was converted to Catholicism in 1913, and thereafter his work tended to be tinged with mysticism. His poems include *Mutter der Himmel* (1918). He was killed in the battle of the Somme.

SOROKIN, Pitirim Alexandrovich (1889–1968), Russian sociologist, lived in the United States after 1923, was born in Turia, Russia, became after a varied career as factoryhand, journalist, tutor, cabinet minister (1917), professor of Sociology at Leningrad (1919–1922), specializing in the study of the social structure of rural communities. Banished by the Soviet government in 1922, he became professor at Minnesota and then (1931-64) at Harvard. His works include *Sociology of Revolution* (1925), *Principles of Rural-Urban Sociology* (1929), *Crisis of our Age* (1941), *Russia and the United States* (1944), *Altruistic Love* (1950), *Fads and Foibles of Modern Sociology* (1956), &c.

SOROLLA Y BASTIDA, Joaquín, *so-rol'ya ee bas-tee'*THa (1863–1923), Spanish painter, born at Valencia, became one of the leading Spanish Impressionists, known especially for his sunlight effects, as in *Swimmers, Beaching the Boat* (Metropolitan, New York), &c.

SOTHEBY, John, *suTH'*- (1740–1807), English auctioneer and antiquarian, nephew of **Samuel Baker** (d. 1778) who founded at York Street, Covent Garden, in 1744 the first sale room in Britain exclusively for books, manuscripts and prints. John became a director of the firm (1780–1800) which became known as Leigh and Sotheby. In 1803 it was transferred to the Strand. His nephew, **Samuel** (1771–1842), and grandnephew, **Samuel Leigh** (1806–61), an authority on cataloguing and early printing, continued the business.

SOTHERN, Edward Askew, *suTH'*- (1826–81), English comic actor, born at Liverpool, in 1849 joined a company of players in Jersey, and soon afterwards the stock company at Birmingham. From 1852 he appeared in the United States, with small success, until in 1858 he made his name as Lord Dundreary in Taylor's *Our American Cousin*. See *Memoir* by T. E. Pemberton (1890), and *The Melancholy Tale of Me* (1916) by his son, **Edward Hugh** (1859–1933), also an actor.

SOTO, Ferdinando de. See DE SOTO.

SOUBISE, Charles de Rohan, Prince de, *soo-beez* (1715–87), French general, was defeated by Frederick the Great at Rossbach (1757); next year he gained victories at Sondershausen and Lützelburg.

SOUFFLOT, Jacques Germain, *soof-lō* (1709–1780), French architect, born at Irancy, designed the Panthéon and the École de Droit in Paris.

SOULAGES, Pierre, *soo-lahzh* (1919–), French artist, born at Rodez. He is one of the most original of the established non-figurative painters, and has designed décors for the theatre and ballet. In 1952 he exhibited at the Venice Biennale.

SOULT, Nicolas Jean de Dieu, *soolt* (1769–1851), French marshal, born at Saint-Amans-la-Bastide, Tarn, March 29, enlisted in 1785, and in 1794 became general of brigade. Masséna made him general of division (April 1799), and owed to him much of the glory of his Swiss and Italian campaigns. In 1804 Soult was appointed by Napoleon marshal of France. He led the right wing in the campaign closed at Austerlitz, did good service in the Prussian and Russian campaigns (1806–07), and after the peace of Tilsit was created Duke of Dalmatia. In Spain he pursued the retreating British, and, though repulsed at Coruña, forced them to evacuate the country. He then conquered Portugal, and governed it till the arrival of Wellesley at Coimbra made him retreat to Galicia. In 1809–10, as commander-in-chief in Spain, he gained a brilliant victory at Ocaña and overran Andalusia. In attempting to succour Badajos he was defeated by Beresford at Albuera (1811). After Salamanca and the advance of the British on Madrid, Soult, vexed at the obstinacy of Joseph Bonaparte and the rejection of his plans, demanded his recall; but Napoleon, after Vitoria, sent him back to Spain. By brilliant tactics he neutralized the strategy of Wellington, but was defeated at Orthez and Toulouse. He turned a royalist after Napoleon's abdication, but joined him again on his return from Elba and was made chief of staff. After Waterloo he rallied the wreck of the army at Laon, but agreed with Carnot as to the uselessness of further resistance. He was banished and recalled till 1819, but was gradually restored to all his honours and was minister of war (1830–34). He died at Soultberg, his château near his birthplace, November 26. See Soult's *Mémoires* (1854), and works by Salle (1834) and Clerc (1893).

SOUSA, John Philip, *soo'za* (1854–1932), American composer and bandmaster, born in Washington, D.C. His early training as a conductor was gained with theatre orchestras, and in 1880 he became conductor of the United States Marine Band. His own band, formed twelve years later, won an international reputation. As well as more than a hundred popular marches, Sousa composed ten comic operas, the most successful of which was *El Capitan*. See his *Marching Along* (1928).

SOUTAR, William, *soo'*- (1898–1943), Scottish poet, born at Perth, was educated at Perth Academy and, after active service with the Royal Navy (1916–18), at Edinburgh University. Extreme osteoarthritis (1923) confined him to bed for the last fourteen years of his life, but in the words of his best-loved poem ' Gang doun wi' a sang, gang doun '. The best examples of his output in English were *In the Time of Tyrants* (1939) and the collection *The Expectant Silence* (1944). His *Poems in Scots* (1935), containing the remarkable ' Auld Tree ', and the four last lyrics included in the posthumous collection, ed. MacDiarmid (1948), as well as the earlier collection of bairn-rhymes, *Seeds in the Wind* (1933), give him a permanent place in the Scottish literary revival. See his remarkable *Diaries of a Dying Man*, ed. A. Scott (1954), and the latter's biography, *Still Life* (1958).

SOUTH, (1) **Sir James** (1785–1867), English astronomer, born at Southwark, practised medicine and discovered 160 compound stars. In 1829 he was elected president of the Astronomical Society, and was knighted the following year.

(2) **Robert** (1634–1716), English high-church theologian and preacher, born at Hackney; from Westminster passed as a student to Christ Church in 1651. He was for a time in sympathy with Presbyterianism, but in 1658 he received orders secretly and in 1660 was appointed public orator of Oxford. His vigorous sermons, full of mockery of the Puritans, delighted the restored Royalists. He became domestic chaplain to Clarendon, prebendary of Westminster in 1663, canon of Christ Church in 1670, rector of Islip in 1678, but his outspokenness prevented any further preferment. He ' aquiesced in ' the Revolution, but strongly opposed the scheme of Comprehension. In 1693 began his great controversy with Sherlock, Dean of St Paul's, who had defended the Trinity against the Socinians. South scorned mysticism and extravagance, but was a stern apologist for the Stuart theories of divine right. See his *Sermons on Several Occasions* (new ed. 1878), &c.

SOUTHAMPTON, Earls of, (1) **Sir Thomas Wriothesley, 1st Earl,** *riz'li* (1505–50), English statesman, son of William Wriothesley the York Herald, held various state offices under Thomas Cromwell, with whom he actively participated in the iconoclastic measures associated with the Dissolution, and in 1538 was ambassador to the Netherlands. Having avoided sharing Cromwell's fate only by turning evidence against him and through his own erstwhile opposition to Anne of Cleves as a wife for Henry VIII, he again came into favour, and as the author of the defensive treaty with Spain was created a baron. Lord chancellor in 1544–47, he won an unenviable reputation for brutality, especially towards reformers; he is said to have personally racked Anne Askew (q.v.). He was created an earl on the accession of Edward VI, but soon after was deprived of the Great Seal for dereliction of duty.

(2) **Henry Wriothesley, 2nd Earl** (1545–81), son of the above, turned Catholic and became involved in intrigues for the advancement of Mary, Queen of Scots, for which activity he was imprisoned in the Tower.

(3) **Henry Wriothesley, 3rd Earl** (1573–1624), son of the above, soldier and patron of poets, particularly of Shakespeare, who dedicated to him his *Venus and Adonis* (1593) and *The Rape of Lucrece* (1594), graduated from Cambridge in 1589, accompanied Essex to the Azores (1597), incurred Elizabeth's displeasure by marrying Essex's cousin, took part in Essex's rebellion, reviving *Richard II* in order to arouse antimonarchic feeling, and was sentenced to death (afterwards commuted to life imprisonment) but was released by James I. He helped the expedition to Virginia (1605), was imprisoned

in 1621 on charges of intrigue, and died of fever at Bergen-op-Zoom while in charge of the English volunteer contingent helping the Dutch against Spain. See Life by Stopes (1922).

(4) **Thomas Wriothesley, 4th Earl** (1607–67), son of the above, educated at Eton and Magdalen, sided with the Commons on certain aspects of royal privilege, but became one of Charles I's foremost advisers. Owing perhaps to his moderate views, he was leniently treated by Cromwell, and at the Restoration was made lord high treasurer.

SOUTHCOTT, Joanna (*c.* 1750–1814), English fanatic, a farmer's daughter in Devon, about 1792 declared herself to be the woman of Rev. xii. She came to London on the invitation of William Sharp the engraver, and published *A Warning* (1803), *The Book of Wonders* (1813–14), &c. At length she announced that she was to give birth on October 19, 1814, to a second Prince of Peace. Her followers received this announcement with devout reverence. But she merely fell into a trance, and died December 27. Her followers, who believed that she would rise again, still numbered over 200 in 1851, and were not yet extinct at the beginning of the 20th century. See Life by C. Lane (1912).

SOUTHERNE, Thomas (1660–1746), British dramatist, born at Oxmantown, Co. Dublin, from Trinity College, Dublin, passed to the Middle Temple, London, and in 1682 began his career with a compliment to the Duke of York in *The Loyal Brother*. Dryden wrote the prologue and epilogue, and Southerne finished Dryden's *Cleomenes* (1692). He served a short time under the Duke of Berwick and at his request, wrote the *Spartan Dame*. His best plays were *The Fatal Marriage* (1694) and *Oroonoko* (before 1696), based on Aphra Behn. His comedies are thin, but made him fat. See Life by J. W. Dodds (1933).

SOUTHEY, Robert (1774–1843), English poet and writer, was born at Bristol. His father died early, and an uncle sent him to Westminster, whence he was expelled for applying his Jacobin principles to a school magazine. He was at Balliol in 1793, where he was infected with Coleridge's dream of a 'pantisocracy ', and in 1795 he married Edith Fricker, whose elder sister Sara married Coleridge. He made two trips to Lisbon (1795 and 1800), and then, after studying law, settled at Great Hall, Keswick (where Coleridge and his wife and sister-in-law were already); and there he remained. He had only £160 a year from his school friend Wynn on which to live, until the government gave him a similar amount. By this time his political views had mellowed and Southey had become something of a Tory; and Peel raised the pension by £300 in 1835—he had been poet laureate since 1813. He had joined the *Quarterly Review* in 1809 and remained a contributor under Gifford and Lockhart. Essentially a family man, he sustained a great shock when his wife died insane in 1837; and, though he married Catherine Anne Bowles, the poetess, in 1839, she became little more than a nurse, and on March 21, 1843, he died of softening of the brain. No poet so well known by name is so little known by his poetry, yet some of his ballads—the 'Holly Tree', 'Battle of Blenheim', 'Old Woman of Berkeley'—had an influence at the time; and in them there is evidence that he appreciated the ballad principle of 'anapaestic equivalents' at least as early as Coleridge. His fanciful epics, in which he used a rimeless metre not blank verse, have little appeal, but his prose, written in the middle style, has clearness and ease, and no mannerisms. His *Nelson* belongs to universal literature. Yet even here he wrote too much and his subjects in history are often too large. His works include *Joan of Arc* (1795), *The Curse of Kehama* (1810), *Roderick* (1814), *Lives of Nelson* (1813), *Wesley* (1820) and *Bunyan* (1830), *A Vision of Judgment* (1821), *Book of the Church* (1824), *Colloquies on Society* (1829), *Naval History* (1833–40) and *The Doctor* (1834–47), a miscellany, in which appears the nursery classic, *The Three Bears.* He was a voluminous letter writer, as illustrated in his *Life and Correspondence* (1849–1850), by his younger son, the Rev. **Cuthbert Southey** (1819–89); and there is his *Commonplace Book* (1849–51), his *Correspondence with Caroline Bowles* (1881), and his *Journal of a Tour of Scotland in 1819* (1929). See also books by Dowden (1880), Dennis (new ed. 1895), S. R. Thompson (1888), the *Early Life* by Wm. Hather (1917), J. Simmons (1945) and G. Carnall (1960).

SOUTHWELL, Robert, sUTH'él (1561?–95), English poet and Jesuit martyr, was born at Horsham, Norwich. He was educated at Douai and Rome, being received into the Society of Jesus in 1578. He was appointed prefect of the English College, was ordained priest in 1584, and two years later, arriving in England with Garnet (q.v.), was first sheltered by Lord Vaux, and next became chaplain to the Countess of Arundel, when he wrote his *Consolation for Catholics* and most of his poems. In 1592 he was betrayed, tortured and thrown into the Tower, and on February 21, 1595, he was hanged and quartered at Tyburn for high treason. He was beatified in 1929. His longest poem is *Saint Peter's Complaint*; his most famous, *The Burning Babe,* an exquisite little piece of sanctified fancy. See a book by Mrs Hood (1926) and study by P. Janelle (1935).

SOUTINE, Chaim, *soo-teen'* (1893–1943), Lithuanian artist, born at Smilovich, studied at Vilna and went to Paris in 1911. He is best known for his paintings of carcases, his series of *Choirboys* (1927) and the magnificent psychological study, *The Old Actress* (1924; Moltzau collection, Norway). After his death his vivid colours and passionate handling of paint gained him recognition as one of the foremost Expressionist painters. See *Life* by M. Wheeler (1950).

SOUZA, Madame de (1761–1836), French novelist, born Adélaïde Marie Émilie Filleul at the Norman château of Longpré, married the Comte de Flahaut (1727–93). At the Revolution she found refuge with her only son in Germany and England, and here learned of her husband's execution at Arras. She turned to writing, her first book the delightful *Adèle de Sénange* (1794). In 1802

she married the Marquis de Souza-Botelho (1758–1825), Portuguese minister at Paris. Later novels include *Émilie et Alphonse* (1799) and *Charles et Marie* (1801).

SOWERBY, (1) James (1757–1822), English illustrator, born at Lambeth, commenced as portraitist and miniaturist, but is remembered by his illustrated *English Botany* (1792–1807, the text by Sir J. E. Smith; new ed. 1863–86). Three sons followed in his footsteps: **James de Carle** (1787–1871), **George Brettingham** (1788–1854) and **Charles Edward** (1795–1842); as did a son of the second, **George Brettingham** (1812–84), and of the third, **John Edward** (1825–70).

(2) **Leo** (1895–), American composer and organist, born at Grand Rapids, Mich., studied in Chicago and Rome. His music employs a traditional European style in works often evocative of American scenes, such as *Prairie*, an orchestral tone poem, and the suite *From the Northland.*

SOYER, Alexis, *swa-yay* (1809–58), born at Meaux, was destined for the church, but became the most famous cook of his time. He fled to London in 1830, and was chef in the Reform Club 1837–50. He went to Ireland during the famine (1847), and in 1855 to reform the food system in the Crimea, where he introduced the 'Soyer Stove'. He wrote, amongst other works, *Culinary Campaign in the Crimea* (1857). See Memoirs by Volant and Warren (1858), and H. Morris, *Portrait of a Chef* (1938).

SPAAK, Paul Henri (1899–1972), Belgian statesman, was born in Brussels, where he began to practise law in 1922. A Socialist deputy for Brussels in 1932, he rose to become, in 1938, the first Socialist premier of Belgium, but resigned the following year. He was foreign minister with the government-in-exile in London during World War II, and in 1946 was elected president of the first General Assembly of the United Nations. Prime minister again in 1946 and from 1947 to 1949, as president of the consultative assembly of the Council of Europe (1949–51) he was in the forefront of the movement for European unity. He was again foreign minister 1954–1957, secretary-general of N.A.T.O. 1957–61, and foreign minister from 1961 until his resignation from parliament in 1966.

SPAGNOLETTO. See RIBERA.

SPAHLINGER, Henry (1882–1965), Swiss bacteriologist, was educated at Geneva. In 1912, he discovered a serum for the treatment of tuberculosis, and also did research on endocrine glands and on cancer.

SPALDING, John (*c.* 1609–70), Aberdeen diarist, royalist and commissary clerk, after whom was named a book club (1839–70; revived 1887).

SPALLANZANI, Lazaro, *spal-lan-tsah'nee* (1729–99), Italian biologist, born at Scandiano in Modena, held chairs at Reggio, Modena and Pavia, disposed of the doctrine of spontaneous generation. In 1780 he demonstrated the true nature of digestion and the functions of spermatozoa and ovum and discovered artificial insemination.

SPARK, Muriel (1918–), British novelist and poet, born in Edinburgh, educated at James Gillespie's High School, editor of *Poetry*

Review (1947–49), has published poetry, short stories, and critical biographies. She is best known, however, for her distinctive novels, written in a highly formal and ironic style, witty and fantastic in content. Her works include *The Comforters* (1957), *Memento Mori* (1959), a tragi-comic study of old age, *The Bachelors* (1960), *The Prime of Miss Jean Brodie* (1961) and *The Mandelbaum Gate* (1965). She was made an O.B.E. in 1967. See study by D. Stanford (1963).

SPARKS, Jared (1789–1866), American biographer, was tutor at Harvard and, for a time, a Unitarian minister at Baltimore, and chaplain to congress (1821). He edited the *North American Review* (1824–31) and in 1832 began his *Library of American Biography*. At Harvard, he was McLean professor of History (1839–49) and president (1849–53). He wrote, among other works, Lives of John Ledyard (1828) and Gouverneur Morris (1832), and edited works of Washington and Franklin. See Life by Adams (1892).

SPARTACUS (d. 71 B.C.), Roman rebel, a Thracian shepherd who became a robber and was captured and sold to a trainer of gladiators at Capua. In 73 B.C. he escaped, with about seventy others, to Vesuvius, where he was joined by many runaway slaves. He repulsed C. Claudius Pulcher, defeated several Roman armies and laid waste much of Italy. He was defeated and killed by Crassus near the river Silarus in 71.

SPEAIGHT, Robert William (1904–), English actor and author, son of **Frederick William** (1869–1942) the architect, played most of the major Shakespearean rôles for the Old Vic from 1930, played Becket in Eliot's *Murder in the Cathedral* at the Canterbury Festival (1935), wrote many biographies including *Hilaire Belloc* (1956), edited the latter's correspondence (1958) and published works on drama.

SPEAR, Ruskin (1911–), English artist, born in London, studied at the Royal College of Art, was elected to the London Group in 1942, and was its president in 1949–50. His paintings of London life are in the Sickert tradition and have had considerable influence through his teaching at the Royal College of Art and the St Martin's School of Art.

SPECKBACHER, Joseph, -*ba*KH-*ér* (1767–1820), Tirolese patriot, known as ' Der Mann vom Rinn ', who, like Hofer (q.v.), fought with distinction in 1809 against the French. See Lives by Mayr (1851) and Knauth (1868).

SPEDDING, James (1808–81), English scholar, born at Mirehouse near Bassenthwaite, entered the colonial service, served as secretary to Lord Ashburton's mission to the U.S.A. (1842) and to the newly founded civil service commission (1855), was a fellow of Trinity, Cambridge, and the editor and vindicator of Bacon (q.v.). He published his *Life and Letters* (1861–74) and *Evenings with a Reviewer* (1848), a refutation of Macaulay's *Essay* on Bacon. See brief Memoir by G. S. Venables prefixed to last and also Edward FitzGerald's *Letters* (1889).

SPEE, Count Maximilian von, *shpay* (1861–1914), German admiral, born in Copenhagen, entered the Imperial German Navy in 1878. In 1908 he became chief of staff of the North Sea Command. In late 1914 he was in command of a commerce-raiding force in the Pacific. Off Coronel he encountered a British squadron of inferior speed and gun power, which he punished severely, sinking H.M.S. *Good Hope* and *Monmouth*. A powerful armament was sent out to deal with him, and off the Falkland Islands exacted a grim vengeance, sinking six out of eight enemy vessels. Von Spee went down with his flagship. See Life by Pochhammer (1933).

SPEED, John (1542–1629), English antiquary and cartographer, born in Cheshire, worked most of his days in London as a tailor. His extraordinary historical learning gained him the acquaintance of Sir Fulke Greville and Spelman, and opened up the door for the publication of his fifty-four *Maps of England and Wales* (1608–10; incorporated into *The Theatre of Great Britain*, 1611) and *History of Great Britain* (1611).

SPEIDEL, Hans, *shpī'del* (1897–), German general, born in Metzingen, Württemberg, served in World War I and in 1939 was senior staff officer. From 1940 to 1942 he was chief of staff to the German commander in occupied France. In July 1944, when he was chief of staff to Rommel during the Allied invasion of Europe, he was imprisoned after the anti-Hitler bomb plot. In 1951 he became military adviser to the West German government. His N.A.T.O. appointment as c.-in-c. land forces, Central Europe (1957–63), aroused wide controversy. He became president of the Institution of Science and Politics in 1964. See his *Invasion 1944*, and *The Destiny of Rommel and the Reich* (1949).

SPEKE, John Hanning (1827–64), British explorer, born at Jordans, Ilminster, in the Indian army saw service in the Punjab. In 1854 he joined Burton in a hazardous expedition to Somaliland; in 1857 the Royal Geographical Society sent out the two to search for the equatorial lakes of Africa. Speke, while travelling alone, discovered the Victoria Nyanza, and saw in it the head-waters of the Nile. In 1860 he returned with Captain J. A. Grant, explored the lake, and tracked the Nile flowing out of it. He was about to defend the identification against Burton's doubts at the British Association meeting at Bath, September 15, 1864, when, that very morning, he accidentally shot himself while partridge-shooting. He wrote *Journal of the Discovery of the Source of the Nile* (1863) and *What led to the Discovery of the Source of the Nile* (1864).

SPELMAN, Sir Henry (1562–1641), English antiquary, born at Congham, Lynn, passed from Trinity College, Cambridge, to Lincoln's Inn. He was high sheriff of Norfolk in 1604, was employed in public affairs at home and in Ireland, and was knighted. In 1612 he settled in London to pursue his studies. His ponderous *Glossarium Archaiologicum* (1626–1664) was completed by his son and Dugdale; his *Concilia Ecclesiastica Orbis Britannici* (1639–64) he also left incomplete. *Reliquiae Spelmannianae* was edited, with a Life, by (Bishop) Edmund Gibson (1698). His son, **Sir John** (1594–1643), is remembered for his *Life of King Alfred*.

SPEMANN, Hans (1869–1941), German zoologist, educated in Stuttgart and Heidelberg, was director of the Institute of Biology at Rostock (1914) and professor at Freiburg (1919). He worked on embryonic development, discovering the ' organizer function ' of certain tissues. For this he received a Nobel prize in 1935.

SPENCE, (1) Sir Basil Unwin (1907–), Scottish architect, born in India of Scots parents, educated at George Watson's College, Edinburgh, and London and Edinburgh Schools of Architecture, assisted Lutyens (q.v.) with the drawings of the viceregal buildings at Delhi. He was twice mentioned in dispatches during World War II, and gradually emerged as the leading postwar British architect with his fresh approach to new university buildings and conversions at Queen's College, Cambridge, Southampton, Sussex, &c., Universities; his pavilions for the Festival of Britain (1951); and his prizewinning designs for housing estates at Sunbury-on-Thames (1951) and the fishermen's houses in a traditional setting at Dunbar (1952) and Newhaven, Edinburgh (1960), &c. But best known by far is his prize design for the new Coventry Cathedral (1951) which boldly merged new and traditional structural methods, and the controversial design for Hampstead's new civic centre (1958). He was professor of Architecture at Leeds (1955–56) and at the Royal Academy from 1961, and president of the R.I.B.A. (1958–60). His crusading zeal in the interests of modern architecture have earned him the nickname ' St Basil ' and he was awarded the O.B.E. (1948), a knighthood (1960), and the O.M. (1962). See his *Phoenix at Coventry* (1962).

(2) **(James) Lewis (Thomas Chalmers)** (1874–1955), Scottish anthropologist, author and poet, born at Broughty Ferry, studied at Edinburgh, was subeditor on *The Scotsman* and subsequently edited various magazines. He ranks first as an authority on the mythology and customs of ancient Mexico, South America, the Middle East as well as Celtic Britain, having written numerous books including *Mythologies of Mexico and Peru* (1907), *Dictionary of Mythology* (1913), *Encyclopaedia of Occultism* (1920), &c., and secondly as a poet whose researches into the style and language of the Makars, subtly exploited in such collections as *The Phoenix* (1924) and *Weirds and Vanities* (1927), can be said to have given the cue to the Scottish literary renaissance. He was a fellow of the Royal Anthropological Institute.

(3) **Joseph** (1699–1768), English anecdotist, educated at Winchester and New College, Oxford, where he became professor of Poetry (1727), is remembered for his *Essay on Pope's Odyssey* (1727) and his anecdotes of Pope and other celebrities.

SPENCER, Earls, a family founded by the Hon. John Spencer, youngest son of the 3rd Earl of Sunderland by Anne, daughter of the great Duke of Marlborough; his brother became 3rd duke. His only son, **John** (1734–83), was created Earl Spencer in 1765. Noteworthy members were:

(1) **George John Spencer, 2nd Earl** (1758–1834), son of the above, who, as Pitt's First Lord of the Admiralty (1794–1801), improved naval administration, put down mutinies at the Nore and Spithead, and sent out Nelson to the Eastern Mediterranean. He was a famous collector of books and first president of the Roxburgh Club.

(2) **John Charles Spencer, 3rd Earl** (1782–1845), son of the above, who was educated at Harrow and Trinity College, Cambridge. Known under his courtesy title of Lord Althorp, he became Whig chancellor of the Exchequer and leader of the House of Commons, and was mainly responsible for carrying through the Reform Bill of 1832, and the bill for reforming the Irish Church. He resigned on account of the Irish Coercion Bill, but resumed office in the Melbourne administration. On succeeding as earl in 1834 he passed to the House of Lords. See a memoir by D. Le Marchant (1876); Bagehot, *Biographical Studies* (1881); and Life by Myres (1890).

(3) **John Poyntz Spencer, 5th Earl** (1835–1910), was lord-lieutenant of Ireland in 1868–74 and 1882–85. In 1880 he became lord president of the Council, and again in 1886, having embraced Gladstone's Home Rule policy. He was first lord of the Admiralty in 1892–95.

SPENCER, (1) Gilbert (1892–), English artist, brother of (3), born at Cookham. He has executed many watercolours (e.g., the *Tolpuddle Martyrs* in the Tate Gallery) and murals. From 1932–48 he was professor of Painting at the Royal College of Art, and was head of the department of Painting and Drawing at the Glasgow School of Art from 1948–50, and held a similar post at the Camberwell School of Art 1950–57.

(2) **Herbert** (1820–1903), English evolutionary philosopher, born at Derby, became a railway engineer in 1837 but engaged extensively in journalism. Subeditor of *The Economist* (1848–53), he wrote a defence of *laissez faire* economics in *Social Statics* (1851), later modified in *Man Versus the State* (1884). A firm believer in evolution before Darwin, he propounded evolutionary *Principles of Psychology* (1855), and when *The Origin of Species* appeared four years later, regarded it merely as a special application of his own *a priori* principles. In his *System of Synthetic Philosophy* (1862–93) he argued that the ultimate scientific principles are unknowable and, agnostically, that the Unknowable must be a power, or God. The function of philosophy is as a science of the sciences, unifying their only partial unity. He applied evolution to biology and sociology and worked out evolutionary *Principles of Ethics* (1879–93). Darwin confessed that he could not understand Spencer's philosophy and Bradley pungently said of his agnosticism that he was taking something for God, because he did not know ' what the devil it can be '. Deeply enmeshed in the scientific outlook of his day, his philosophy has dated. See his *Autobiography* (1904), Lives by D. Duncan (1908), W. H. Hudson (1908) and E. Compayré (trans. 1908), and studies by A. D. White (1897), H. Macpherson (1900), J. Royce (1904), J. A. Thomson (1906) and H. S. R. Elliot (1917).

(3) **Sir Stanley** (1891–1959), English artist, brother of (1), born at Cookham, where he mainly lived and worked. He studied at the Slade School. From 1926 to 1933 he executed murals (utilizing his war experiences) in the Oratory of All Souls, Burghclere. He produced many purely realistic landscapes, but his main works interpret the Bible in terms of everyday life (e.g., the *Christ Carrying the Cross* and the two paintings of the *Resurrection* in the Tate Gallery, London), using bold distortion of the figures. During World War II he painted a series of panels depicting *Shipbuilding on the Clyde*. He was elected R.A. in 1950 and knighted in 1959. See monographs by Rothenstein (1945) and Newton (1947), and Lives by (1), and by Collis (1962).

(4) **Sir Walter Baldwin** (1860–1929), British ethnologist, born at Stretford, Lancashire, crossed Australia from south to north with F. J. Gillen, and jointly with him wrote standard works on the aborigines.

SPENDER, (1) Edward Harold (1864–1926), English journalist, biographer and novelist, son of (3) and father of (4), wrote *One Man Returns* (1914), and biographies of Asquith, Botha and Lloyd George. See his autobiographical *Fire of Life* (1926).

(2) **John Alfred** (1862–1942), English journalist and biographer, son of (3), born at Bath, became editor of the Liberal *Westminster Gazette* (1896–1922) and one of the leading journalists of the day. A member of Lord Milner's special mission to Egypt (1919–20), he wrote a number of political books and biographies of Campbell-Bannerman, Asquith, &c. See his *Life* (1926).

(3) **Lilian** (1835–95), English novelist, married John Kent Spender in 1858 and became mother of (1) and (2). Her novels include *Lady Hazleton's Confession* (1890).

(4) **Stephen** (1909–), English poet and critic, son of (1), born in London. Educated at University College, Oxford, he was in the 'thirties one of the ' modern poets ', left-wing in outlook, who set themselves the task of recharging the impulses of poetry both in style and subject matter. In his thought he is essentially a Liberal, despite his earlier flirtings with Communism. He translated Schiller, Toller, Rilke and Lorca, among others, besides writing much penetrating literary criticism. From his beginnings in 1930 with *Twenty Poems* to 1957—*Engaged in Writing* (a nouvelle), he relived his experiences in his work. *Poems from Spain* (1939) link up with his service in the Spanish Civil War. In World War II he served as a fireman in the London blitz, and volumes of poems, *Runes and Visions* (1941), *Poems of Dedication* (1941), *The Edge of Darkness* (1949), carry on his self-analysis. Alongside these are critical evaluations such as *The Destructive Element* (1936), *Life and the Poet* (1942), *The Creative Element* (1944), and his first autobiography, *World within World* (1951). From 1939 to 1941 he was co-editor, with Cyril Connolly, of the brilliant monthly, *Horizon*, and in 1953 was co-editor of *Encounter*.

SPENER, Philipp Jakob, *shpay'ner* (1635–1705), German theologian, ' the Father of Pietism', born in Alsace. At Strasbourg and Frankfurt he tried to reawaken the dormant Christianity of the day. His *Pia Desideria* (1675) spread the movement far beyond the range of his personal influence, but not without enmity. See Lives by Hossbach (1828; 3rd ed. 1861), Wildenhalm (1842–47; trans. 1881) and Grünberg (1893–1906).

SPENGLER, Oswald (1880–1936), German historicist writer, born at Blankenburg, Harz, studied at Halle, Munich and Berlin and taught mathematics (1908) in Hamburg before devoting himself entirely to the compilation of the morbidly prophetic *Untergang des Abendlandes* (Vol. I, 1918; Vol. II, 1922) ' Decline of the West ', trans. C. F. Atkinson (1926–29), in which he argues by analogy, in the historicist manner of Hegel and Marx, that all civilizations or cultures are subject to the same cycle of growth and decay in accordance with predetermined ' historical destiny '. The soul of Western civilization is dead. The age of soulless expansionist Caesarism is upon us. It is better for Western man, therefore, to be engineer rather than poet, soldier rather than artist, politician rather than philosopher. Unlike Toynbee, whom he influenced, he was concerned with the present and future rather than with the origins of civilizations. His verdict, achieved by his specious method, greatly encouraged the Nazis although he never became one himself. Another work attempted the identification of Prussianism with Socialism (1920). See study by M. Schroeter (1922), E. Heller, *The Disinherited Mind* (1952), and K. R. Popper, *The Poverty of Historicism* (1957).

SPENSER, Edmund (1552?–99), English poet, was born in London, the son of a gentleman tradesman who was connected with the Spencers of Althorp. He was educated at Merchant Taylors' School and Pembroke Hall, Cambridge. His juvenilia, partly written at Cambridge, include the *Visions* of Petrarch and some sonnets of Du Bellay translated. Shortly after leaving Cambridge (1576) he obtained a place in Leicester's household and this led to a friendship with Sir Philip Sidney and a circle of wits, called the Areopagus. His first original work, *The Shepheards Calendar* (1579), dedicated to Sydney, was the first clear note of Elizabethan poetry and no doubt assisted in his career as a courtier. In 1580 he was appointed secretary to Lord Grey de Wilton, lord deputy in Ireland, whose assignment was to crush native rebellion, and Spenser was drawn into the tragic business. His reward for his work as one of the ' undertakers ' for the settlement of Munster was Kilcolman Castle in the county of Cork, where he settled in 1586 and where he hoped to have leisure to write his *Faerie Queene* and other courtly works, written with an eye to the court no less than as a brilliant presentation of the art and thought of the Renaissance. In 1589 he visited London in company with Sir Walter Raleigh, who had seen the first three books of *The Faerie Queene* at Kilcolman and now carried him off to lay them at Elizabeth's feet. Published in 1590, they were an immediate success, but a previous misdemeanour, viz., the attack in *Mother*

Hubberd's Tale on the proposed match between Elizabeth and the Duc d'Alençon, was not forgotten and the poet returned to Ireland in 1591 a disappointed man. The charming *Colin Clout's Come Home Again* commemorates the visit. *Complaints*, published the same year, contains, beside his juvenilia, the brilliantly coloured but enigmatic *Muiopotmos*; *Mother Hubberd's Tale*, which is now provided with a bitter satire on Court favour; *The Early Tears of the Muses*, which lamented the lack of patronage; and his pastoral elegy for Sydney which is so frigid as to make us question their intimacy. In 1594 Spenser married again, celebrating his wooing of Elizabeth Boyle in the sonnet sequence *Amoretti* and his wedding in the supreme marriage poem *Epithalamion*. He revisited London in 1596, with three more books of *The Faerie Queene*, which were published along with the *Four Hymns*. These consisted of the early *Hymns in Honour of Love and Beauty* and two new ones of *Heavenly Love and Beauty* in which his early Platonism is overlaid by Christian feeling. This was a year of unwonted activity. Under the roof of Lord Essex he wrote *Prothalamion*, which is sufficiently praised when we say it rivals *Epithalamion*, and his prose *View of the Present State of Ireland*, which, taken with the fifth book of *The Faerie Queene*, is probably the first explicit statement of the imperialism which is now discredited. *The Faerie Queene* is designed to show the ideal gentleman or courtier in action—a favourite Renaissance theme, of which Castiglione's *Il Cortigiano* (from which Spenser drew extensively) is the exemplar. The charming Book I is evangelical and has been transposed as a coloured tract. Book II on the Aristotelian virtue of Temperance (which Spenser misconceived) shows the puritan in him at odds with the artist in the provocative scenes in Acrasia's bower. Book III is a tribute to the Virgin Queen, but also demonstrates that marriage is the end of love, *amour courtois* being a false species. Book IV, of friendship, is a tangle of romantic episodes. Book V treats of England's wars on behalf of Protestantism and dominion. Here Lord Grey, as Sir Arthegal, is the maligned hero pursued by the Blatant Beast, i.e., Scandal, which it is Caledore's assignment to destroy in Book VI. This last book however, of the specific virtue of the gentleman, i.e., courtesy, is largely taken up with devising tests for the hero's courtesy. The Blatant Beast looks in from time to time but Spenser's experience had taught him that scandal can never be destroyed. This summary gives no idea of the qualities which make Spenser the ' poet's poet '—the lulling harmonies of the verse, the brilliant artistry specially in chiaroscuro, the poetic diction which, though avoided today, was probably salutary at that stage of English poetry if ever it was to vie with Continental poetry. Modern editions are by de Selincourt and Smith (1924 and 1952); Renwick's edition (1928–34), discontinued at the fourth volume (*View of the State of Ireland*), probably on the appearance of the sumptuous Columbia edition, ed. Greenlaw and others (10 vols.

1952–57). See also Kate Warren's ed. of *The Faerie Queen* (1913); there are studies by Renwick (a valuable treatment of Spenser as the Renaissance poet), Legouis (1926), Davis (1933) and Atkinson (1937).

SPERANSKI, Mikhail, Count, *spyay-rahns' kyee* (1772–1839), Russian statesman and reformer, became Tsar Alexander I's adviser and in 1809 produced a plan for the reorganization of the Russian structure of government on the Napoleonic model, but was dismissed when Napoleon invaded Russia (1812). Under Nicholas I he was restored to power and was responsible for the trial and conviction of the Decembrist conspirators in 1825. See *Life* by M. Raeff (The Hague 1958), and Tolstoy's *War and Peace*.

SPERRY, Elmer Ambrose (1860–1930), American inventor, born at Cartland, invented a new-type dynamo, arc-light and searchlight, the gyroscopic compass (1911) and stabilizer for ships and devised an electrolytic process for obtaining pure caustic soda from salt. He also founded several companies for the manufacture of these inventions.

SPEUSIPPUS, *spyoo-sip'us* (*c.* 394–336 B.C.), Athenian philosopher, nephew of Plato, accompanied the latter to Sicily and in 361 succeeded him as head of the Academy. Only one fragment, on Pythagorean numbers, of his works is still extant.

SPIELHAGEN, Friedrich, *speel'hah-gén* (1829–1911), German novelist, was born at Magdeburg. His works include (besides poems, plays, books of travel, &c.) *Durch Nacht zum Licht* (1861), *Die von Hohenstein* (1863), *In Reih und Glied* (1866), *Susi* (1895). See his Autobiography (1890), and study by M. Geller (1917).

SPILSBURY, Sir Bernard Henry (1877–1947), British pathologist, born in Leamington, studied physiology at Magdalen College, Oxford, then entered the medical school of St Mary's Hospital, Paddington, and specialized in what was at that time the new science of pathology. He made his name at the trial of Crippen (1910), where his expert evidence was delivered with the imperturbable objectivity and serenity he was invariably to show under cross-examination. Appointed pathologist to the Home Office, his abilities were recognized by a knighthood (1923). As expert witness for the Crown, Sir Bernard was involved in many notable murder trials, such as those of Mahon (1924), Thorne (1925) and Rouse (1931). His last important case was the murder of de Antiquis (1947). By then his strength was failing and on December 17, 1947, he died by his own hand. He has been described as the ideal scientific witness. See study by Browne and Tullett (1951).

SPINELLO ARETINO (*c.* 1330–1410), Italian painter, spent nearly all his life between Arezzo (his birthplace) and Florence. His principal frescoes were done for San Miniato, at Florence, for the *campo santo* of Pisa, and for the municipal buildings of Siena.

SPINOLA, Ambrogio, Marquis of Los Balbases (1569–1630), Italian soldier in Spanish service, was born at Genoa. In 1602 he raised and maintained at his own cost 9000 troops and served under Mendoza in the Netherlands. In 1603 he succeeded to the marquisate on the death of his brother Federigo in a naval battle against the Dutch. Spinola was meanwhile besieging Ostend, which fell in 1604 after a three years' siege. War continued largely as a duel between Spinola and Maurice of Nassau; but the former saw the necessity for peace and was one of the plenipotentiaries at the Hague Conference, which made the twelve-year truce in 1609. Early in the Thirty Years' War, Spinola was in Germany, subduing the Lower Palatinate. But he was recalled to the Netherlands to fight once more against his old opponent. Maurice, however, died of fever while attempting to relieve Breda, which fell to Spinola in 1625. Shortly afterwards, ill-health forced him to resign. His long service found little reward, but in 1629 he was in Italy, acting as governor of Milan; and in the same year, while besieging Casale, he died. See French Life by Siret (1851).

SPINOZA, Baruch, *Lat.* **Benedict, de,** *spi-nō′za* (1632–77), Dutch-Jewish philosopher and theologian, born November 24 at Amsterdam into one of the many Jewish émigré families from Spain and Portugal who had been compelled to profess Christianity but secretly kept loyal to their faith. His deep interest in optics, the new astronomy and Cartesian philosophy made him unpopular at the synagogue, and at the age of twenty-four he was formally excommunicated from the only society to which he naturally belonged. He made a living grinding and polishing lenses from 1656, and became the leader of a small philosophical circle. In 1660 he settled in Rijnsburg near Leyden, and wrote his *Short Treatise on God, Man and his Well-being* and *Tractatus de Intellectus Emendatione* (1677), ' Short Treatise on the Correction of the Understanding '. In the beautiful opening passage he outlines his aim of discovering ' a true good, capable of imparting itself, by which alone the mind could be affected to the exclusion of all else . . . a joy continuous and supreme to all eternity '. He also wrote most of his commentary on Cartesian geometry (1663), the first part of his masterpiece *Ethica*, and carried on a correspondence with Oldenburg, the secretary of the English Royal Society, Huygens and Boyle. In 1663 he moved to Voorburg, near The Hague, and began the *Tractatus Theologica politicus*, published in 1670, which despite its anonymity made him famous. In 1671 he sent to Leibniz a tract on optics and in 1676 the latter stayed at The Hague and they met. The details of their conversations are unfortunately not preserved, possibly because the socially ambitious Leibniz, so utterly opposed in temperament and ambition to the otherworldly Spinoza, did not wish to publicize any debt to a thinker, such as the latter, commonly thought subversive of religion. *Ethica* (posthumously 1677), despite its title, is a thoroughgoing metaphysical system, developed in Euclidean fashion from axioms, theorems and definitions. The basic substance is *deus sive natura*, ' God or nature '. Thought and extension are merely two of the infinite attributes of God, applicable to human beings. Minds and bodies are mere

modes, or aspects, termed *natura naturata* of the divine being, *natura naturans*. This pantheistic activist monism resolves the Cartesian dualism of mind and matter. Finite things are defined by their boundaries, by negation. Only God is infinite. Everything happens according to a ' logical ' necessity. There is nothing which corresponds to ordinary notions of free will. We are limited in so far as our passions make us subject to outside causes, and ' free ' in so far as we act in accordance with God. Wrong action is synonymous with rational error. It is ' logically ' impossible that events should be other than they are. In 1672 Spinoza risked his life protesting against the murder of the de Witt brothers by the mob. In 1673 he refused the professorship of Philosophy at Heidelberg, offered by the Elector Palatine, in order to keep his independence. In the last years of his life he worked on the unfinished *Tractatus Politicus*, a popular exposition of his political philosophy, which derived from Hobbes but differed in Spinoza's advocacy of democracy. He died February 21, 1677, at Amsterdam of phthisis, aggravated by the glass dust in his lungs. Van Vloten and Land edited Spinoza's works (The Hague 1883). See J. A. Froude, *Short Studies* (1867), Matthew Arnold, *Essays in Criticism* (1865), and studies by Sir F. Pollock (1880 and 1935), J. Martineau (1882), J. Caird (1888), H. H. Joachim (1901 and 1940), R. A. Duff (1903), R. McKeon (1928), L. Roth (1929), H. F. Hallett (1930, 1949 and 1957), S. Hampshire (1951), R. L. Saw (1951), G. H. R. Parkinson (1954), and A. G. Wernham, *Political Works* (1958).

SPITTELER, Karl Friedrich Georg (1845–1924), Swiss poet and novelist, born at Liestal (Basel), studied law and theology at Basel, Zürich and Heidelberg, was a tutor in Russia, teacher and journalist in Switzerland, and retired to Lucerne in 1892. *Der Olympische Frühling* (1900–03) is a great mythological epic, but perhaps his most mature work is *Prometheus der Dulder* (1924). Besides poetry he wrote tales (*Konrad der Leutnant*, &c.), essays (*Lachende Wahrheiten*) and reminiscences. He was awarded the Nobel prize in 1919.

SPODE, Josiah (1754–1827), English potter, born at Stoke-on-Trent, learnt his trade in his father's workshops, and in 1800 began to use bone as well as felspar in the paste, which resulted in porcelain of a special transparency and beauty. He did much to popularize the willow pattern and he became the foremost china manufacturer of his time. He was appointed potter to George III in 1806. See W. B. Honey, *English Pottery and Porcelain* (1947).

SPOFFORTH, Frederick Robert (1853–1926), Australian cricketer, known as ' the demon ', the greatest bowler in the history of the game, was born at Balmain, Sydney. On May 27, 1878, he took 11 wickets for 20 runs against the M.C.C., and during 1884 he took 218 wickets in first-class cricket with a bowling average of 12·53.

SPOHR, Ludwig (1784–1859), German composer, violinist and conductor, born at

Brunswick, was *kapellmeister* at the court of Hesse-Kassel in 1822–57. Remembered chiefly as a composer for the violin, for which he wrote 17 concertos, he also composed operas, oratorios, symphonies, &c. See his Autobiography (trans. 1864), Lives by Malibran (1860) and Schletterer (1881), and D. M. Mayer, *The Forgotten Master* (1959).

SPONTINI, Gasparo Luigi Pacifico, *spon-tee' nee* (1774–1851), Italian composer, born near Ancona, went to Paris in 1803. His operas *La Vestale* (1807) and *Ferdinand Cortez* (1809) were greeted with enthusiasm. In Berlin (1820–42) only court influence supported him against the public and the press. *Hohenstaufen* (1829) is his greatest work. Spontini was dismissed by Frederick-William IV in 1842. See Life by Robert (1883).

SPOONER, William Archibald (1844–1930), Anglican clergyman and educationalist, dean (1876–89) and warden (1903–24) of New College, Oxford. As an albino he suffered all his life from weak eyesight, but surmounted his disabilities with heroism and earned a reputation for kindness and hospitality. His life was bound up with his college and his popularity was not lessened by his occasional scathing comments. His name is forever associated with his own nervous tendency to transpose initial letters or syllables—as in the ' spoonerism ' ' a half-warmed fish ' for ' a half-formed wish '.

SPOTTISWOODE, (1) **Alicia Ann, Lady John Scott** (1811–1900), Scottish composer and author of *Annie Laurie* and other songs.

(2) **John** (1565–1639), Scottish churchman, educated at Glasgow University, at first a Presbyterian, he later became Episcopalian. He was Archbishop of Glasgow (1610) and of St Andrews (1615). He promoted Episcopal government, and forced the Perth Assembly (1618) to sanction the Perth Articles. He officiated at the coronation of Charles I at Holyrood in 1633, and in 1635 was appointed chancellor of Scotland. He reluctantly entered into the king's liturgical scheme, and so made himself hateful to the Covenanters. The king compelled him to resign the chancellorship in 1683, and he was deposed and excommunicated. He died in London. His chief work is the *History of the Church of Scotland* (1655).

(3) **William** (1825–83), English mathematician, physicist and publisher, born in London, was educated at Harrow and Balliol, where he lectured in Mathematics. In 1846, he succeeded his father as head of the printing house of Eyre and Spottiswoode and did original work in polarization of light, electrical discharge in rarefied gases and wrote a mathematical treatise on determinants. He was elected F.R.S. in 1853 and was president of the British Association.

SPRENGEL, (1) **Christian Konrad** (1750–1816), German botanist, born at Brandenburg, became rector of Spandau, but neglected his duties for his original observations of pollination in plants and the rôle of insects, which aroused Darwin's interest. His nephew, **Kurt** (1766–1833), wrote histories of medicine (1803) and botany (1818).

(2) **Hermann Johann Philipp** (1834–1906), German-born British chemist, born near Hanover, came from Göttingen and Heidelberg for research in Oxford and London and remained in Britain. He invented a new type of vacuum pump (1865) and devised the U-tube method for comparing liquid densities.

SPRENGER, (1) **Aloys** (1813–93), Austrian orientalist, was born at Nassereut in Tyrol, studied at Vienna, came to London, in 1843 sailed to Calcutta, worked as interpreter, librarian, and translator, and in 1857 became Oriental professor at Bern. In 1881 he settled at Heidelberg. He wrote a great *Leben und Lehre des Mohammed* (1861–65) and books on the ancient geography of Arabia, Babylonia, &c.

(2) **Jacob,** German theologian, Dominican and professor of Theology in Cologne, and **Henricus Institor** (Latinized form of Krämer), compiled the famous *Malleus Maleficarum* (1489), which first formulated the doctrine of witchcraft, and formed a text-book of procedure for witch trials. They were appointed inquisitors by Innocent VIII in 1484.

SPRING, Howard (1889–1965), British novelist, born in Cardiff, from errand boy became newspaper reporter and literary critic and established himself as a writer with his best-selling *Oh Absalom* (1938), renamed *My Son, My Son.* Other novels include *Fame is the Spur* (1940), *Dunkerleys* (1946), *These Lovers Fled Away* (1955), *Time and the Hour* (1957), as well as three autobiographical works (1939, 1942 and 1946).

SPRUNER VON MERTZ, Karl (1803–92), German cartographer and Bavarian general, whose name is associated with a great historical *Handatlas* (1837–52; 3rd ed. by Menko, 1862–79).

SPURGEON, Charles Haddon (1834–92), English Baptist preacher, born at Kelvedon, Essex, became in 1854 pastor of the New Park Street Chapel, London. The Metropolitan Tabernacle, seating 6000, was erected for him in 1859–61 (burnt April 1898). In 1887 he withdrew from the Baptist Union because no action was taken against persons charged with fundamental errors. Apart from sermons, he wrote *John Ploughman's Talk* (1869) and many other works. See *Letters* (ed. by his son, 1924), Lives by Shindler (1892), Fullerton (1920), and the Autobiography, compiled by his wife and J. Harrald (1897–1900).

SPURR, Josiah Edward (1870–1950), American geologist, was mining engineer to the Sultan of Turkey (1901), geologist in the U.S. Geological Survey (1902) and eventually professor of Geology at Rollins College (1930–32). As a result of his work, the age of the Tertiary period has been estimated as 45 to 60 million years. His exploration in Alaska in 1896 and 1898 was commemorated by the name Mt Spurr. Among other works, he wrote *Geology Applied to Mining* (1904).

SPURZHEIM, Johann (Christoph) Caspar, *spoorts'him* (1776–1832), German phrenologist, born near Trier, studied medicine in Vienna and became the disciple of Gall (q.v.) the phrenologist, and, lecturing in Britain, gained a powerful adherent in George Combe (q.v.). See Memoir by Carmichael (1833).

SQUARCIONE, Francesco, *skwahr-chō′nay* (1394–1474), Italian painter, Mantegna's master, founded the Paduan school of painters.

SQUIER, skwīr, (1) Ephraim George (1821–1888), American archaeologist, born at Bethlehem, N.H., in 1841–48 was a newspaper editor, latterly in Ohio. He explored the antiquities of the Mississippi Valley, and then of New York, and in 1849 was appointed *chargé d'affaires* to Central America, in 1863 U.S. commissioner to Peru. Among his works are *Nicaragua* (1852), *Serpent Symbols* (1852), *Waikau* (1855), *Central America* (1857) and *Peru* (1877).

(2) **George Owen** (1865–1934), American military and electrical engineer, chief signals officer in the U.S. army (1917), invented the polarizing chronophotograph sine-wave system of cable telegraphy and multiline radio systems, &c.

SQUIRE, Sir John Collings (1884–1958), English author, born at Plymouth, educated at Blundell's and St John's College, Cambridge, and was literary editor of *The New Statesman* and (1919–34) *The London Mercury*. He leant towards the lighter side of verse and to parody, as in *Steps to Parnassus* (1913) and *Tricks of the Trade* (1917), and in anthologies was a friend to the minor poet. He was knighted in 1933. His writings also include criticisms and short stories. See his autobiographical *Water Music* (1939), &c.

SSU-MA CH'IEN, soo-mah chi-yen (c. 145–87 B.C.), Chinese historian, born at Lungmen, succeeded his father in 110 B.C. as grand astrologer, but incurred the emperor's wrath for taking the part of a friend who, in command of a military expedition, had surrendered to the enemy. Ssu-ma Ch'ien was imprisoned for three years and castrated, but was gradually restored to favour. He is chiefly remembered for the *Shih Chi*, the first history of China compiled as dynastic histories in which annals of the principal events are supplemented by princely and other biographies and notes on economic and institutional history. It had been begun by his father, Ssu-ma T'an. See Life by B. Watson (1958).

SSU-MA HSIANG-JU, -shi-ang-yoo (d. 117 B.C.), Chinese poet, born in Ch'engtu, Sezechwan province, wrote the *Tzu Hsu Fu*, a series of poems describing and denouncing the pleasures of the hunt and which hold an important place in Chinese literary history.

STAAL, Marguerite Jeanne, Baronne de, stahl (1684–1750), French writer of memoirs, born the daughter of a poor Parisian painter, Cordier, whose name she dropped for that of her mother, Delaunay. Her devotion to the interests of her employer, the Duchesse de Maine, brought her two years in the Bastille, where she had a love affair with the Chevalier de Menil. In 1735 she married the Baron de Staal. Her *Mémoires* (1755; trans. 1892) describe the world of the regency with intellect, observation and a subtle irony, and are written in a clear, firm and individual style. Her *Œuvres complètes* appeared in 1821. See study by Frary (1863).

STACPOOLE, Henry de Vere (1863–1951), British physician and writer, born in Kingstown (Dun Laoghaire), Ireland. He was the author of many popular novels, including *The Blue Lagoon* (1909), *The Pearl Fishers* (1915) and *Green Coral* (1935). See his autobiographical *Men and Mice* (1942 and 1945).

STAËL, (1) Anne Louise Germaine Necker, Madame de (Baronne de Staël-Holstein) (1766–1817), the greatest of French women writers, the only child of Necker (q.v.), was born in Paris, April 22. In her girlhood she wrote romantic comedies, tragedies, novels, essays and *Lettres sur Rousseau* (1789). She married in 1786 the Baron de Staël-Holstein (1742–1802), the bankrupt Swedish ambassador. She bore him two sons (1790 and 1792) and a daughter (1797), but to protect her fortune separated formally from him in 1798. Her vast enthusiasms and the passionate intensity of her affections gave force and colour to her rich and versatile character, and combined to form a personality whose influence was irresistible. Her brilliant *salon* became the centre of political discussion, but the Revolution opened up new horizons for France; Necker's fall only hastened the dénouement of the tragedy; and she quitted Paris for Coppet in September 1792. From Coppet she went to England, where at Mickleham in Surrey she was surrounded by Talleyrand and others of the French *émigrés*. She joined her husband at Coppet in May 1793, and published her *Réflexions sur le procès de la reine* in the vain hope of saving Marie Antoinette. In 1795 she returned to Paris, where her husband had re-established himself as ambassador. She prepared for a political rôle by her *Réflexions sur la paix intérieure* (1795), but was advised to return to Coppet. Her *Influence des passions* appeared in 1796. Bonaparte allowed her to return to Paris in 1797, but received her friendly advances with such studied coldness that admiration soon turned to hatred. In 1800 she published her famous *Littérature et ses rapports avec les institutions sociales*. She was again back in Paris in 1802, when her *salon* was more brilliant than ever, and published *Delphine*, a novel. At length the epigrams of Constant, her friendship with disaffected men like Moreau and Bernadotte, and the appearance of Necker's *Dernières vues* exhausted the patience of Napoleon, and in the autumn of 1803 she received orders to keep forty leagues from Paris. Her husband had died, and in December 1803 she set out with her children for Weimar, where she dazzled the whole court, and met Schiller and Goethe. At Berlin she made acquaintance with August Schlegel. She next turned her steps towards Vienna, but learned of her father's death, and returned to Coppet, writing the touching eulogy, *Du caractère de M. Necker*. Then she set out for Italy with Schlegel, Wilhelm von Humboldt, and Bonstetten, but returned to Coppet, where, as usual, a brilliant circle assembled, in June 1805 to write *Corinne* (1807), a romance, which at once brought her European fame. She revisited Germany at the end of 1807, and began to turn for consolation to religion—she was a Protestant. Her famous *De l'Allemagne* was finished in 1810, passed by the censor, and partly printed, when the whole impression was seized and destroyed, and herself ordered from Paris to Coppet. The work was published by John Murray at London in 1813. But her exile had now become a bitter reality; she found herself encompassed with spies. She escaped secretly to Bern, and thence made her way to St Petersburg, Stockholm and (1813) London. In England admiration reached its climax on the publication of *De l'Allemagne*, the most finished of all her works. It revealed Germany to the French and made Romanticism—she was the first to use the word—acceptable to the Latin peoples. Louis XVIII welcomed her to Paris in 1814, and the two millions which Necker had left in the Treasury was honourably paid to her. The return of Napoleon drove her from Paris, and she spent the winter in Italy for the sake of the health of Albert de Rocca, an Italian officer in the French service, whom she had married secretly in 1811. She died in Paris, July 14, 1817. Her surviving son and daughter published her unfinished *Considérations sur la Revolution française* (1818), esteemed by Sainte-Beuve her masterpiece, the *Dix Années d'exil* (1821), and her complete works (1820–21). See Lives by Stevens (1880), Blennerhassett (Berlin 1887–89; trans. 1889), Wilson (1931), studies by Duffy (1887), Sorel (trans. 1892), Cléron (1925), Larg (trans. 1926), de Pange (1938), *Mistress to an Age* by Hérold (1959), and her *Lettres à Ribbing* (ed. by Balayé, 1961).

(2) **Nicolas de** (1914–55), French painter, born in St Petersburg. He studied in Brussels, travelled in Spain and Italy, and worked in Paris. His paintings were mainly abstract, and he made inspired use of rectangular patches of colour; his later pictures were more representational and in subdued colours. See monograph by Duthuit (1950), and study by Cooper (1962).

STAFFORD, William Howard, 1st Viscount **Stafford** (1614–80), English Catholic nobleman, beheaded on Tower Hill as a victim of the perjuries of Oates (q.v.). His attainder was reversed in 1824.

STAHL, (1) **Friedrich Julius** (1802–61), German philosopher and politician, born of Jewish parents at Munich, turned Protestant, studied law, and published *Die Philosophie des Rechts* (1830–37; rev. 1878). In 1840 he became professor of Philosophy of Law at Berlin, and was a leader of the reactionary party in the First Chamber. Among his other works was *Der christliche Staat* (1847), in which he advocated a sovereign despotism based on divine right.

(2) **Georg Ernest** (1660–1734), German chemist, born at Ansbach, became professor of Medicine (1694) at Halle, body physician (1714) to the king of Prussia and expounded the phlogiston theory and animism.

STÅHLBERG, Kaarlo Juho (1865–1952), Finnish lawyer, was professor of Law at Helsingfors and first president (1919–25) of Finland. Kidnapped in 1930, he was narrowly defeated in 1931.

STAINER, (1) **Jakob,** *shtī'nèr* (1621–83), Austrian violinmaker born at Absam near Hall in Tirol, made violins at Innsbruck, and died in a Benedictine monastery. See two works by Ruf (1872–92).

(2) **Sir John,** *stay'-* (1840–1901), English composer, born in London, became organist of Magdalen College, Oxford, in 1860, and of St Paul's (1872), and Oxford professor of Music (1889). He was knighted in 1888. He wrote cantatas and church music, notably *The Crucifixion* (1887), also a *Treatise on Harmony,* a *Dictionary of Musical Terms* (with W. A. Barrett), &c.

STAIR, a Scottish title derived from an Ayrshire village by the Dalrymple family, one of whom was among the Lollards of Kyle summoned before James IV; his great-grandson embraced the Reformed doctrines. See also DALRYMPLE, HAILES, and J. Murray Graham's *Stair Annals* (1875). Its most noteworthy members, in chronological order, were:

(1) **James Dalrymple, 1st Viscount, new line** (1619–95), Scottish jurist, father of (2), studied at Glasgow University, served in the army, acted as Regent in Philosophy at Glasgow, joined the bar (1648), and was recommended by Monk to Cromwell for the office of a lord of session. He advised the former to call a free parliament (1600). He was confirmed in office and created a Nova Scotia baronet in 1664. The luckless marriage in 1669 of his daughter Janet to Baldoon suggested to Scott *The Bride of Lammermoor.* In 1670 Dalrymple was made president of the Court of Session and member of the privy council; but when the Duke of York came to govern at Edinburgh in 1679 he retired to the country, and prepared his famous *Institutes of the Law of Scotland.* His wife and his tenants were devoted to the Covenant, and he was soon involved in a fierce dispute with Claverhouse. He fled in 1682 to Holland, returned with the Prince of Orange, and, restored to the presidency, was created in 1690 Viscount Stair. See Memoir by J. G. Mackay (1873), and study by A. H. Campbell (1954).

(2) **Sir John Dalrymple, 1st Earl of** (1648–1707), Scottish judge and politician, son of (1), studied law, and was knighted in 1667. He came into violent collision with Claverhouse, and was flung into prison in Edinburgh and heavily fined, but early in 1686 became king's advocate, and in 1688 lord justice-clerk. Under William III he was lord advocate, and as secretary of state from 1691 had the chief management of Scottish affairs. On his shoulders, therefore, with Breadalbane and the king, mainly rests the infamy of the massacre of Glencoe. He was accused of exceeding his instructions and resigned (1695). In 1703 he was created an earl. He took an active part in the debates and intrigues that led to the Treaty of Union, and died suddenly, January 8, 1707. See Omond, *Lord Advocates of Scotland* (1883), Sir John Dalrymple, *Memoirs of Great Britain* (1788).

(3) **John Dalrymple, 2nd Earl** (1673–1747), Scottish soldier, was born at Edinburgh. At eight he shot his elder brother dead by accident, so was exiled by his parents to Holland, studied at Leyden, fought under the Prince

of Orange at Steenkerk, and by 1701 was lieutenant-colonel in the Scots Footguards, in 1706 colonel of the Cameronians. He was aide-de-camp to Marlborough in 1703, commanded an infantry brigade at Ramillies, was made colonel of the Scots Greys in 1706 and in 1708 secretly married Viscountess Primrose. He distinguished himself greatly at Oudenarde (1708) and Malplaquet. General in 1712, he retired to Edinburgh to intrigue for the Hanoverian succession. Under George I he was ambassador to Paris, and checkmated the Pretender and Alberoni. Recalled in 1720, he devoted himself to agriculture, growing turnips and cabbages. Made field-marshal (1742), he was governor of Minorca and fought at Dettingen.

STAKHANOV, Aleksei Grigorievich, stě-KHah'nof, Russian coalminer, who started an incentive scheme (1935) for exceptional output and efficiency by individual steel workers, coalminers, &c. Such prize workers were called Stakhanovites.

STALIN, Joseph, properly **Iosif Vissarionovich Dzhugashvili** (1879–1953), Russian leader, born in Georgia, was educated at the Tiflis Theological Seminary, from which he was expelled for ' propagating Marxism '. Joining the Bolshevik ' underground ', he was arrested and transported to Siberia, whence he escaped in 1904. The ensuing years witnessed his closer identification with revolutionary Marxism, his many escapes from captivity, his growing intimacy with Lenin and Bukharin, his early disparagement of Trotsky, and his co-option, in 1912, to the illicit Bolshevik Central Committee. With the 1917 Revolution and the forcible replacement of the feeble Kerensky government by Lenin and his supporters, Stalin was appointed commissar for nationalities and a member of the Politbureau, although his activities throughout the counter-revolution and the war with Poland were confined to organizing a Red ' terror ' in Tsaritsin—subsequently renamed Stalingrad. With his appointment as general secretary to the Central Committee in 1922, Stalin began stealthily to build up the power that would ensure his control of the situation after Lenin's death. When this occurred in 1924, he took over the reins, putting his overriding authority to successful test in 1928 by engineering Trotsky's degradation and banishment. Stalin's reorganization of the Soviets' resources, with its successive Five Year Plans, suffered many industrial setbacks and encountered consistently stubborn resistance in the field of agriculture, where the *kulaks*, or peasant proprietors, steadfastly refused to accept the principle of ' collectivization '. The measures taken by the dictator to ' discipline ' those who opposed his will involved the death by execution or famine of up to 10 million peasantry (1932–33). The blood bath which eliminated the ' Old Bolsheviks ' and the alleged right-wing ' intelligentsia ', and the carefully staged ' engineers' trial ', were followed by a drastic purge of some thousands of the Officer corps, including Marshal Tuchachevsky, Stalin professing to believe them guilty of pro-German sympathies. Red Army forces and

material went to the support of the Spanish Communist government in 1936, although Stalin was careful not to commit himself too deeply. After the Munich crisis Franco-British negotiations for Russian support in the event of war were guilefully protracted until they ended in the *volte face* of a non-aggression pact with Hitler, which gained Stalin the time to prepare for the German invasion he sensed to be inevitable. In 1941 the prosperity of the Nazis' initial thrust into Russia could be accounted for in part by the disposal of the Red Army on the frontiers, ready to invade rather than repel invasion. Thereafter, Stalin's strategy followed the traditional Muscovite pattern of plugging gaps in the defences with more and more bodies and trading space for time in which the attrition begotten of impossible climatic conditions could whittle away the opponents' strength. Sustained by many millions of pounds' worth of war material furnished by Britain and America, the Red Army obediently responded to Stalin's astutely phrased call to defend not the principles of Marx and Engels, but ' Mother Russia '; although the Red dictator lost no time in demanding a ' Second Front ' in Europe to relieve the strain on his unnumbered forces. Quick to exploit the unwarranted Anglo-American fear that Russia might ' go out of the war ', Stalin easily outwitted the allied leaders at the Teheran and Yalta conferences. Seeming to acquiesce in decisions he had no intention of implementing, he never deviated an inch from the path he had marked out for himself. With the Red Army's invasion of German soil, Soviet bayonets were encouraged to penetrate far beyond the point where they had last been employed. Thus Stalin's domination of the Potsdam conference, followed by the premature break-up of the Anglo-American forces, left the Red dictator with actual possessions enlarged by 182,480 square miles which, with ' satellites ' increased the Soviet sphere of influence by 763,940 square miles, bearing alien but submissive populations totalling 134,188,000. While Stalin consolidated his gains an ' iron curtain ' was dropped to cut off Soviet Russia and her satellites from the outside world. At the same time the ' Hozyain ' inaugurated a ' cold war ' against all non-Communist countries—which included the blockade of Berlin—prosecuting it with all the ruthlessness, resource and illimitable Oriental cunning at his command. An entirely unscrupulous *arrivist*, Stalin consistently manipulated Communist imperialism for the greater glory of Soviet Russia and the strengthening of his own autocratic sway as its satrap. He died, in somewhat mysterious circumstances, in 1953. See works by Souvarine (n.d.), Deutscher (1949), Basseches (1952), and E. H. Carr, *Socialism in One Country* (3 vols., 1958–64); Stalin's *Works* (trans. 13 vols., 1953–55); and *Twenty Letters to a Friend* (1967), by his daughter, Svetlana, published after her much-publicized departure from Russia to America in 1967.

STAMBOLOV, Stephan Nikolov (1854–95), Bulgarian statesman, born at Trnova, took part in the rising of 1875–76. Chief of the

Russophobe regency (1886) and premier (1887–94), he ruled with a strong hand. Forced then to retire, he was assassinated (1895). See Life by Beaman (1895).

STAMITZ, (1) **Carl Philipp** (1746–1801), German composer and violinist, son of (2), studied under the latter and became a travelling instrumentalist in Paris, London, St Petersburg, Prague and Nuremberg. He wrote 80 symphonies, one of which was for a double orchestra, and concertos for violin, viola, 'cello, flute, oboe, clarinet and harpsichord. His brother, **Anton Johann Baptista** (1754–?1809), was also a musician.

(2) **Johann** (1717–57), Bohemian violinist and composer, father of (1), founder of the Mannheim school, was born at Havlickuv Brod. He first attracted attention at the coronation celebrations in Prague (1741) and was engaged by the Mannheim court, where he became a highly salaried court musician and concert master. He visited Paris (1754–1755). His compositions include 74 symphonies, concertos for harpsichord, violin, oboe, flute and clarinet (the last possibly the first of its kind), chamber music and a mass. He developed the sonata form, introduced sharp contrasts into symphonic movements and wrote some of the finest concerto music of the 18th century.

STAMP, Josiah Charles, 1st Baron Stamp of Shortlands (1880–1941), British economist, born in London, served on the Dawes Committee on German reparations, was chairman of the L.M.S. railway, director of Nobel Industries, and on the outbreak of World War II was made economic adviser to the government. An expert on taxation, he wrote on this and other financial subjects. He was killed in an air-raid.

STANDISH, Myles (*c*. 1584–1656), English colonist, born probably at Ormskirk, served in the Netherlands, and sailed with the *Mayflower* in 1620. He was military head of Massachusetts (against the Indians), and long its treasurer. Longfellow and Lowell wrote about his exploits against the Indians. See R. G. Usher, *The Pilgrims and their History* (1918), and Life by Porteus (1920).

STANFIELD, Clarkson (1794–1867), Irish marine painter, born of Irish Catholic parentage at Sunderland, left the navy for scene painting. He painted *Market-boats on the Scheldt* (1826), and *The Battle of Trafalgar* (1836).

STANFORD, (1) Sir Charles Villiers (1852–1924), Irish composer, was born at Dublin, studied at Cambridge, Leipzig and Berlin, and became organist at Trinity College (1872–93), professor in the Royal College of Music (1882), and Cambridge professor of Music (1887). He was knighted in 1901. Among his works are choral settings of Tennyson's *Revenge* (1886) and *Voyage of Maeldune* (1889); the oratorios *The Three Holy Children* (1885) and *Eden* (1891); the operas *The Veiled Prophet of Khorassan* (1881), *Savonarola*, *The Canterbury Pilgrims* (1884), *Shamus O'Brien* (1896), *Much Ado About Nothing* (1901), *The Critic* (1916); and he set a high standard in English church music. See his *Pages from an Unwritten Diary* (1914) and Life by Greene (1935).

(2) **Leland** (1824–93), American railway magnate, born at Watervliet, N.Y., in 1856 settled in San Francisco, became president of the Central Pacific Company, superintended the construction of the line, and was governor of California 1861–63, and U.S. senator from 1885. In memory of their only child, he and his wife founded and endowed a university at Palo Alto (1891). See Life by G. T. Clark (1932).

STANHOPE, an English family descended from the first Earl of Chesterfield. Its most noteworthy members, in chronological order, were:

(1) **James, 1st Earl Stanhope** (1675–1721), an eminent soldier and favourite minister of George I. See Life by B. Williams (1932).

(2) **Charles, 3rd Earl Stanhope** (1753–1816), English scientist and politician, father of (3), born in London, educated at Eton and Geneva, became an M.P. and married the sister of the younger Pitt, and his continued enthusiasm for the French Revolution made him the 'minority of one' in advocating non-interference in French affairs (1794) and peace with Napoleon (1800). Neglecting his wives and children, he invented a cylindrical biconvex lens to eliminate spherical aberration, calculating machines, the first iron hand printing press and a method of stereotyping adopted by the Clarendon press (1805). See Life by G. Stanhope and Gooch (1914).

(3) **Lady Hester Lucy** (1776–1839), eldest daughter of (2), went in 1803 to reside with her uncle, William Pitt, and as mistress of his establishment and his most trusted confidante, had full scope for her queenly instincts. On Pitt's death (1806) the king gave her a pension of £1200. The change from the excitements of public life was irksome to her; in 1809 she was grieved by the death at Coruña of her brother Major Stanhope, and of Sir John Moore, whom she had loved; and in 1810 she left England, wandered in the Levant, went to Jerusalem, camped with Bedouins in Palmyra, and in 1814 settled on Mount Lebanon. She adopted Eastern manners, interfered in Eastern politics, and obtained a wonderful ascendency over the tribes around her, who regarded her as a sort of prophetess; her last years were poverty-stricken on account of her reckless liberality. See her *Memoirs* by C. L. Meryon (1845), *Life and Letters* (1913) by the Duchess of Cleveland, books by Hamel (1913), J. Haslip (1934).

(4) **Philip Dormer.** See CHESTERFIELD.

(5) **Philip Henry, 5th Earl Stanhope** (1805–1875), English historian, born at Walmer, studied at Oxford, entered parliament in 1830, was instrumental in passing the Copyright Act (1842), and was foreign under-secretary under Peel (1834–35), and secretary to the Indian Board of Control (1845–46). He edited Peel's memoirs. He was known as Lord Mahon till in 1855 he succeeded to the earldom. His principal work was *A History of England, 1713–83* (1836–54); and his other works include Lives of Belisarius, Condé and Pitt; *War o*, *the Succession in Spain, History of Spain under Charles II, Essays* and *Miscellanies*. He was president of the Society of Antiquaries

(1846) and lord rector of Aberdeen University (1858). He helped to secure the appointment of the Historical MSS. Commission and the foundation of the National Portrait Gallery.

(6) **Edward Stanhope** (1840–93), English politician, second son of (5), became Conservative colonial secretary (1886) and as secretary for War (1887–92) reformed army administration, established the Army Service Corps and adopted the magazine rifle.

(7) **James Richard, 7th Earl Stanhope** (1880–1967), English politician, grandson of (5), served in the Boer War (1902) and in World War I, winning the M.C. (1916) and the D.S.O. (1917), became the first commissioner of works (1936), first lord of the Admiralty (1938–39) and lord president of the Council (1939–40).

STANISLAUS LESZCZYŃSKI, *lesh-chin'y' skee* (1677–1766), born at Lemberg, was elected king of Poland in 1704, but in 1709 was driven out by Peter the Great to make room for Augustus II (q.v.). He formally abdicated in 1736, receiving the duchies of Lorraine and Bar; and he died of a burning accident at Lunéville. See also PONIATOWSKI.

STANISLAVSKY, professional name of **Konstantin Sergeivitch Alexeyev** (1865–1938), Russian actor, producer and teacher, born in Moscow. His first notable production was in 1891, Tolstoi's *Fruits of Enlightenment*, and when he joined the Moscow Arts Theatre in 1898 he was able to develop his theories to the full. These were: to present an illusion of reality by means of a highly stylized combination of acting, setting and production, based on an exhaustive examination of the background and psychology of the characters. His ' method ' was most successful in Chehov, Gorky, Maeterlinck and Andreyev. A superb actor, he gave up acting because of illness, but his influence on the theatre remains enormous. See his autobiographical *My Life in Art* (1924), his posthumous *Stanislavsky rehearses Othello* (1948), study by D. Magarshack (1951), and *Stanislavsky's Legacy*, ed. and trans. E. R. Hapgood (1959).

TANLEY, (1). See DERBY (EARL OF).

(2) **Arthur Penrhyn** (1815–81), English divine, born at Alderley, Cheshire, educated at Rugby under Arnold, whose *Life* he wrote (1844), and at Balliol, won the Ireland and Newdigate prizes, and in 1838 was elected fellow of University College and took orders. He travelled in the East, accompanied the Prince of Wales to the Holy Land, in 1851 became a canon of Canterbury, in 1856 professor of Ecclesiastical History at Oxford and in 1864 Dean of Westminster. For all his large tolerance, charity and sympathy, High Church Anglicans could never forgive him for championing Colenso and for preaching in Scottish Presbyterian pulpits. He was pre-eminently representative of the broadest theology of the Church of England. He cared little for systematic theology and not at all for the pretensions of the priesthood; while he regarded as ' infinitely little ' the controversies about postures, lights, vestments and the like. His works include *Memorials of Canterbury* (1854), *Sinai and Palestine* (1856),

Christian Institutions (1881). See Lives by G. G. Bradley (1883), R. E. Prothero (1893), and *A Victorian Dean*, ed. A. V. Baillie and H· Bolitho (1930).

(3) **Sir Henry Morton** (1841–1904), British explorer and journalist, was born of unmarried parents at Denbigh, Wales, and at first bore the name of John Rowlands. In 1859 he went as cabin boy to New Orleans, where he was adopted by a merchant named Stanley. He served in the Confederate army and U.S. navy, contributed to several journals, and in 1867 joined the *New York Herald*. As its special correspo aent he accompanied Lord Napier's Abyssinian expedition; and the first news of the fall of Magdala was conveyed to Britain by the *New York Herald*. Stanley next went to Spain for his paper, and in October 1869 recieved from Mr Gordon Bennett the laconic instruction, ' Find Livingstone '. But first he visited Egypt for the opening of the Suez Canal, and travelled through Palestine, Turkey, Persia and India. In March 1871, he left Zanzibar for Tanganyika and on November 10 he ' found ' Livingstone at Ujiji. The two explored the north end of Lake Tanganyika, and settled that it had no connection with the Nile basin. In 1872, he returned alone and published *How I found Livingstone*. An expedition under Stanley, who had followed the Ashanti campaign for the *New York Herald*, was fitted out jointly by the *Herald* and the *Daily Telegraph* to complete Livingstone's work, and in August 1874 he left England for Bagamoyo. Thence he made for the Victoria Nyanza, circumnavigated the lake, formed a close friendship with King Mtesa of Uganda, next determined the shape of Lake Tanganyika, passed down the Lualaba to Nyangwé, and traced the Congo to the sea. Having published *Through the Dark Continent* (1878), in 1879 he again went out to found, under the auspices of the king of the Belgians, the Congo Free State, having been refused help in England. He took part in the Congo Congress at Berlin in 1884–85. In March 1886 his expedition for the relief of Emin Pasha (q.v.) landed at the mouth of the Congo. In June he left a part of his 650 men under Major Barttelot on the Aruwimi, and with 388 men marched into the forest. Disaster overtook the rear column but Emin and Stanley met in April 1888 on the shores of Lake Albert. After relieving the rearguard he returned with Emin overland to the east coast, and Bagamoyo was reached in December 1889. He had discovered Lake Edward and Mount Ruwenzori. In 1890 he married the artist, Miss Dorothy Tennant. He was naturalized as a British subject in 1892, and sat as a Unionist for Lambeth (1895–1900). Other works include a novel, *My Kalulu* (1873), *Coomassie and Magdala* (1874), *The Congo* (1885), *My Early Travels in America and Asia* (1895). See his Autobiography (1909), Wassermann, *Bula Mataria* (1932), Life by Anstruther (1956), B. Farwell, *The Man who Presumed* (1958), and T. Sterling, *Stanley's Way* (1960).

(4) **John** (1713–86), English composer, born in London, was blind from the age of two, having fallen on a stone hearth while holding a china bowl, but his musical talent

was such that he became organist at All Hallows, Bread Street, at the age of eleven. Later he held posts at St Andrew's, Holborn, and at the Inner Temple. His compositions, which include oratorios (*Zimri* and *The Fall of Egypt*), cantatas, organ voluntaries, concerti grossi and instrumental sonatas, have won increasing recognition, and Stanley is today regarded as one of the greatest of 18th-century English composers.

(5) **Thomas** (1625–78), English author, born at Cumberlow, Herts, studied at Pembroke Hall, Cambridge, practised law, and published translations from the Greek, Latin, French, Spanish and Italian poets; but his great works were the *History of Philosophy* (1655–62) based on Diogenes Laertius, and an edition of Aeschylus, with Latin translation and commentary (1663–64). See the *Poems*, ed. Brydges (1814–15, with Life); *Original Lyrics*, ed. Guiney (1907).

(6) **Venetia.** See DIGBY (1).

(7) **Wendell Meredith** (1904–), American biochemist, educated at Earlham College and Illinois University, professor of Molecular Biology and of Biochemistry at California University from 1948, did important work on the chemical nature of viruses. He isolated and crystallized the tobacco mosaic virus and worked on sterols and stereo-isomerism. He shared the Nobel prize for chemistry in 1946 with Northrop and Sumner.

(8) **William** (1858–1916), American electrical engineer, after working for Maxim, set up on his own and invented the transformer. His work also included a long-range transmission system for alternating current.

STANSGATE, William Wedgwood Benn, 1st Viscount (1877-1960), English politician, was a Liberal M.P. from 1906 until 1927, when he joined the Labour Party and was next year elected for N. Aberdeen. In 1929–31 he was secretary for India and in 1945–46 secretary for Air. He won the D.S.O. and D.F.C. in World War I, served in the R.A.F. in World War II, and was created a viscount in 1941. His son **Anthony** (b. 1925), a Labour M.P. (1950–60), was debarred from the Commons on succeeding to the title, but was able to renounce it in 1963, and was re-elected to parliament the same year. He was postmaster-general from 1964 to 1966, when he became minister of technology.

STANTON, Edwin McMasters (1814–69), American lawyer and statesman, was born at Steubenville. He rose to legal prominence when he successfully opposed the plan for bridging the Ohio at Wheeling on the grounds of interference with navigation. He was secretary of war under Lincoln, was suspended by Johnson (1867) and reinstated by the Senate. When Johnson's impeachment failed, Stanton resigned (1868).

STAPELDON, Walter de (1261–1326), Bishop of Exeter 1308–26, and founder of Exeter College, Oxford, was born at Annery in Devon, was favoured by Edward II, and for this reason was beheaded by the insurgent Londoners.

STAPLETON, Thomas (1535–98), English controversial theologian, born at Henfield, Sussex, educated at Winchester and New College, Oxford, became prebendary of Chichester, but was deprived of his prebend in 1563, went in 1569 to Douai, became a professor there and in 1590 at Louvain. A learned Catholic controversialist in Latin, he is remembered for his fine Elizabethan English prose translations of Bede (Antwerp 1565; ed. Hereford, 1930), and his careful Latin life of Sir Thomas More (Douai 1588).

STARK, (1) **Johannes** (1874–1957), German physicist, was educated at Munich and became professor at Würzburg. He discovered the Stark effect concerning the splitting of spectrum lines by subjecting the light source to a strong electrostatic field, and also the Doppler effect in canal rays. He was awarded a Nobel prize in 1919.

(2) **John** (1728–1822), American general, saw much service against the Indians, by whom he was captured (1752). He served at Bunker's Hill, and won a victory at Bennington (1777). He was a member of the court martial which condemned André.

STARLEY, James (1831–81), English inventor, born at Albourne, Sussex, worked in Coventry, invented a sewing-machine and the 'Coventry' tricycle and the 'Ariel' geared bicycle and set up as a manufacturer of these.

STARLING, Ernest Henry (1866–1927), English physiologist, born in London, was lecturer in Physiology at Guy's Hospital and later professor at University College. He introduced the term *hormones* for the internal secretions of the ductless glands and, with Bayliss, discovered the intestinal hormone *secretin* (1902). He wrote *Principles of Human Physiology* (1912).

STAS, Jean Servais (1813–91), Belgian chemist, born at Louvain, was professor of Chemistry at Brussels. He developed more up-to-date methods for determination of atomic weights and analysis. He apparently disproved Prout's hypothesis.

STASSEN, Harold Edward (1907–), American politician, born at West St Paul, Minnesota. He studied law at the University of Minnesota, and became at thirty-one the youngest governor in Minnesota history. He served in the navy in World War II, failed in 1948 and 1952 to secure the Republican presidential nomination, and became administrator of foreign aid under Eisenhower. He represented the U.S. at the London disarmament conference in 1957. He resigned in 1958 following disagreements with John Foster Dulles (q.v.). He wrote *Where I Stand* (1947).

STATIUS, Publius Papinius (c. A.D. 45–96), Latin poet, born at Naples, flourished as a court poet and a brilliant improviser in the favour of Domitian till 94, when he retired to Naples. His *Thebaïs*, an epic on the struggle between the brothers Eteocles and Polynices of Thebes, is tedious as a whole, marred by over-alliteration and allusiveness, but redeemed by exquisite passages. Of another epic, the *Achilleïs*, only a fragment remains. His *Silvae*, or occasional verses, have freshness and vigour. Dante (*Purgatorio* xxii, 89) refers to him.

STAUDINGER, Hermann, *shtow'-* (1881–1965), German chemist, born at Worms, was professor of Organic Chemistry at Freiburg (1926–51) and was awarded the Nobel prize for chemistry in 1953 for his research in macro-molecular chemistry.

STAUFFENBURG, Count Berthold von, *shtow'fën-boorg* (1907–44), German soldier, born in Bavaria, was a colonel on the General Staff in 1944. One of the ringleaders, he placed the bomb in the unsuccessful attempt to assassinate Adolf Hitler on July 20, 1944. He was shot next day.

STAUNTON, Howard (1810–74), English Shakespearean scholar and chess player, studied at Oxford, and settled down to journalism in London. His victory in 1843 over M. St Amand made him the champion chess player of his day. He wrote *The Chess-player's Handbook* (1847), &c. His Shakespeare (1858–60) contained excellent textual emendations.

STAVISKY, Serge Alexandre (1886?–1934), French swindler, born in Kiev. He came to Paris in 1900 and became naturalized in 1914. He floated fraudulent companies, liquidating the debts of one by the profits of its successor until, in 1933, he was discovered to be handling bonds to the value of more than five hundred millions francs on behalf of the municipal pawnshop in Bayonne. Stavisky fled to Chamonix and probably committed suicide; but in the meantime the affair had revealed widespread corruption in the government and ultimately caused the downfall of two ministries. Stavisky was found guilty during a trial that ended in 1936 with the conviction of nine other persons.

STEAD, William Thomas (1849–1912), English journalist, born at Embleton, Alnwick, and educated at Wakefield, was a Darlington editor 1871–80, and then on the *Pall Mall* till 1889, from 1883 as editor. He got three months over the 'Maiden Tribute' (1885), founded his *Review of Reviews*, and worked for peace, spiritualism, the 'civic church', and friendship with Russia. Although pro-Boer, admired Cecil Rhodes. He was drowned in the *Titanic* disaster, April 15, 1912. See Lives by his daughter (1913), Whyte (1925).

STEDMAN, (1) **Charles** (1753–1812), American historian, born at Philadelphia, Pa., wrote a standard history (with valuable maps) of the American War of Independence from the British point of view (1794).

(2) **Edmund Clarence** (1833–1908), American poet and critic, born at Hartford, Conn., studied at Yale, was war correspondent of the *New York World* 1861–63, and then became a New York stockbroker and banker. He published *Poems* (1860), *Victorian Poets* (1875), *Edgar Allan Poe* (1880), *Poets of America* (1886), *Nature of Poetry* (1892), *Victorian Anthology* (1896), &c. See Stedman and Gould, *Life and Letters.*

STEED, Henry Wickham (1871–1956), English journalist and author, born in Long Melford. In 1896, as correspondent in Berlin, he began his long association with *The Times,* later becoming correspondent in Rome and Vienna, foreign editor during World War I, when he directed much Allied propaganda, and editor from 1919 until his resignation in 1922. From 1923 to 1930 he was proprietor and editor of *The Review of Reviews.* He wrote many authoritative books on European history and affairs, and lectured on Central

European history at King's College, London, from 1925 to 1938.

STEELE, Sir Richard (1672–1729), English essayist, dramatist and politician, was born in Dublin and educated at Charterhouse, where Addison was a contemporary, and Merton College, Oxford, whence he entered the army as a cadet in the Life Guards. Reacting against the 'irregularity' of military life, he wrote *The Christian Hero* (1701), to show that the gentlemanly virtues can be practised only on a Christian basis. He next wrote three comedies, *The Funeral, or Grief à la mode* (1702), *The Tender Husband* (1703) and *The Lying Lover* (1704). In 1706 he became gentleman waiter to Princ George of Denmark, and in 1707 Harley appointed him gazetteer. Steele's first venture in periodical literature, *The Tatler,* ran from April 1709 to January 1711 and was published on Tuesdays, Thursdays and Saturdays to suit the outgoing post-coaches. It had a predecessor in Defoe's *Review,* and like the *Review* included items of current news, but after No. 83 it concentrated on the social and moral essay, with occasional articles on literature, usually from the pen of Addison who had joined forces with Steele at the eighteenth issue. The chief fare, however, was social comedy, which covered the affectations and vices of society. These were exposed by humorous raillery, with the aim of putting the Christian at ease in society. Christianity was to become fashionable and to this end—for formal preaching was unpalatable—a wealth of concrete social situations and types was created, including coffee-house politicians, 'pretty fellows', pedants and bores at every level of society. The coffee houses and chocolate houses provided most of these types, but society women and the family were the theme of many of the articles, for Steele's plea in *The Christian Hero* for a more chivalrous attitude to women implied the correction of female frivolity in high places and the insistence on the family as the source of genuine happiness. Types which satisfy the moralist's notion of good-breeding allied to virtue—Sophronius, the true gentleman (No. 21), Paulo, the generous merchant (No. 25), Aspasia, the ideal woman, &c.—offset the satirical portraits. Aspasia, identified as Lady Elizabeth Hastings, evoked Steele's famous tribute ' to behold her is an immediate check to loose behaviour; and to love her is a liberal education '. Steele is perhaps at his best in scenes of domestic felicity (cf. Nos. 95, 104 and 150), and here we note the intrusion of bourgeois sentiment and morality which is to be the mark of the age, in contrast to the aristocratic ethos of the Restoration. The beginnings of the domestic novel are here, not only in the relations between the pseudonymous editor, and Isaac Bickerstaff, and his half-sister Jennie, but in numerous conversation pieces and in the social context provided by the Trumpet Club, forerunner of the more famous Spectator Club which Steele first outlined in No. 2 of that periodical, though Addison wrote most of the articles. In 1713 Steele entered parliament, but was expelled the following year on account of a pamphlet, *The Crisis*, written in favour of the house of Hanover, a cause to which his periodical *The Englishman* was also devoted. He was rewarded on the succession of George I with the appointment of supervisor of Drury Lane theatre, and a knighthood followed. In 1718 a difference on constitutional procedure led to an estrangement from Addison, who was in the ministry, and loss of his office. In 1722 financial troubles made him retire to Wales, where he died in 1729. His letters to his wife (' dearest Prue '), whom he married in 1707, attest the sincerity of his preachments on married love. The standard *Life* is by G. A. Aitken (2 vols. 1889), but see also *Sir Richard Steele* by Willard Connely (1934). *The Tatler* was published in full, 4 vols. by G. A. Aitken (1898–99); the Correspondence by R. Blanchard (1941).

STEELL, Sir John (1804–91), Scottish sculptor, born at Aberdeen, was educated as an artist at Edinburgh and Rome. Most of his chief works are in Edinburgh, including the equestrian statue of the Duke of Wellington (1852), and that of Prince Albert (1876), for which Steell was knighted.

STEEN, Jan, *stayn* (1626–79), Dutch painter, born at Leyden, the son of a brewer, joined the Leyden guild of painters in 1648 and next year went to The Hague until 1654, afterwards following his father's trade at Delft. He spent his last years as an innkeeper at Leyden. His best works were genre pictures of social and domestic scenes depicting the everyday life of ordinary folk with rare insight and subtle humour, as in *The Music Lesson* (Nat. Gall.), *The Christening Feast* (Wallace Coll.), *Tavern Company*, *The Doctor's Visit*, &c.

STEENSEN, Niels. See STENSEN.

STEENSTRUP, (1) Johannes (1844–1935), Norwegian antiquarian, son of (2), was professor of Northern Antiquities at Copenhagen (1877) and wrote *Normannerne* (1876–82), a book about Viking times, &c.

(2) **Johannes Iapetus Smith** (1813–97), zoologist, father of (1), born at Vang in Norway, was professor of Zoology at Copenhagen (1845–85). His books treat of hermaphroditism, alternation of generations, flounders' eyes, and Cephalopods; and he explored the kitchen middens of Denmark for prehistoric relics.

STEENWIJK, Hendrik van, *stayn'vīk* (c. 1550–1603), Dutch painter of architectural interiors, settled at Frankfurt in 1579. His son **Hendrik** (1580–1649), also a painter, came to London on Van Dyck's advice in 1629.

STEER, Philip Wilson (1860–1942), English painter, was born at Birkenhead and studied at Paris. He began as an exponent of Impressionism and to this added a traditionally English touch. A founder and faithful member of the New English Art Club, he taught at the Slade. He excelled, too, as a figure painter, as shown in the Pitti *Self-Portrait*, *The Music Room* (Tate), and the *Portrait of Mrs Hammersley*, painted in the style of Gainsborough. He was awarded the O.M. in 1931. See Life by D. S. MacColl (1945) and study by R. Ironside (Phaidon 1943).

STEEVENS, George (1736–1800), English Shakespearean commentator, called by Gifford ' the Puck of commentators ', born at Stepney, was educated at Eton and King's College, Cambridge. His reprint from the original quartos of *Twenty Plays of Shakespeare* (1766) brought him employment as Johnson's collaborator in his edition (1773). Jealous of Malone (q.v.), Steevens issued a doctored text using his own emendations (1793–1803), which held authority till Boswell's publication of Malone's *Variorum Shakespeare* (1821). See I. D'Israeli, ' On Puck the Commentator ' in *Curiosities of Literature* (1817).

STEFAN, Joseph (1835–93), Austrian physicist, born near Klagenfurt, became professor at Vienna in 1863. He proposed Stefan's law (or the Stefan–Boltzmann law), that the amount of energy radiated per second from a black body is proportional to the fourth power of the absolute temperature.

STEFÁNSSON, Vilhjálmur (1879–1962), Canadian Arctic explorer, born of Icelandic parents at Arnes, Manitoba, explored Arctic America and wrote on the Eskimos. See his *Unsolved Mysteries of the Arctic* (1939), *Greenland* (1943), &c.

STEFFANI, Agostino (1654–1728), Italian priest, operatic composer, diplomatist, friend of Handel, born at Castelfranco, in 1688 settled at Hanover court. He wrote a fine *Stabat Mater*, several operas and vocal duets.

STEIN, *stīn*, (1) Sir Aurel (1862–1943), British archaeologist, born at Budapest, held educational and archaeological posts under the Indian government, for which from 1900 he made important explorations in Chinese Turkestan and Central Asia.

(2) **Charlotte von** (1742–1827), the friend of Goethe, married in 1764 the Duke of Saxe-Weimar's Master of the Horse. Her friendship with Goethe was broken suddenly (1788), but renewed before her death. Goethe's Letters to her were published in 1848–51. See works by Düntzer (1874), Bode (1910), Calvert (1877).

(3) **Gertrude** (1874–1946), American writer, born in Allegheny, Pa. She studied psychology under William James, and medicine at Johns Hopkins; but settled in Paris, where she was absorbed into the world of experimental art and letters. She sometimes attempted to apply the theories of abstract painting to her own writing, which led to a magnified reputation for obscurity and meaningless repetition. Her first book, *Three Lives* (1908), reveals a sensitive ear for speech rhythms, and by far the larger part of her work is immediately comprehensible. Her influence on contemporary artists—particularly Picasso—is probably less than she imagined, though her collection of pictures was representative of the best of its era. Her main works include *Tender Buttons* (1914), *The Making of Americans* (1925), *The Autobiography of Alice B. Toklas* (1933), *Four Saints in Three Acts* (1934) and *Everybody's Autobiography* (1937). See Life by E. Sprigge (1957), study by Sutherland (1951), and J. M. Brinnin, *The Third Rose* (1960).

(4) **Heinrich Friedrich Carl, Baron vom**

(1757–1831), Prussian Liberal statesman and German nationalist, born at Nassau, entered the service of Prussia in 1780, and became president of the Westphalian chambers (1796). His tenure as secretary for trade (1804–07) was unfruitful and he resigned, only to be recalled after the treaty of Tilsit, when he abolished the last relics of serfdom, created peasant proprietors, extirpated monopolies and hindrances to free trade, promoted municipal government, and supported Scharnhorst in his schemes of army reform. Napoleon insisted upon his dismissal, and Stein withdrew (1808) to Austria, but not before issuing his *Political Testament*. In 1812 he went to St Petersburg and built up the coalition against Napoleon. From the battle of Leipzig to the Congress of Vienna he was the ruling spirit of the opposition to French imperialism. Stein liberalized the Prussian state, but at the same time fostered the dangerous myth of German destiny and aggressive nationalism, not least by founding the *Monumenta Germaniae Historica* in 1815. See Lives by J. R. Seeley (1878), F. Schnabel (1931) and G. Ritter (Stuttgart 1958).

STEINBECK, John Ernest, *stīn'bek* (1902–68), American novelist, born at Salinas, California. *Tortilla Flat* (1935), his first novel of repute, is a faithful picture of the shifting *paisanos* of California, foreshadowing the solidarity which characterizes his major work, *The Grapes of Wrath* (1939), a study of the poor in the face of disaster and threatened disintegration. His journalistic grasp of significant detail and pictorial essence make this book a powerful plea for consideration of human values and common justice. It led, like *Uncle Tom's Cabin*, to much-needed reform, and won for Steinbeck the 1940 Pulitzer prize. His other works include *Of Mice and Men* (1937), *The Moon is Down* (1942), *East of Eden* (1952), *Winter of our Discontent* (1961), as well as the light-hearted and humorous *Cannery Row* (1945), *The Wayward Bus* (1942) and *The Short Reign of Pippin IV* (1957). He received the Nobel prize for literature in 1962. See *Writers in Crisis*, by M. Geismar (1942).

STEINER, *shtī'nėr*, (1) **Jakob** (1796–1863), German-Swiss geometrician, born at Utzendorf, from 1834 was professor at Berlin, pioneered 'synthetic' geometry, particularly the properties of geometrical constructions, ranges and curves. His collected works were edited by Weierstrass (Berlin 1881–1882).

(2) **Rudolf** (1861–1925), Austrian social philosopher, founder of 'anthroposophy', born at Kraljevec, studied science and mathematics and edited Goethe's scientific papers at Weimar (1890–97) before coming temporarily under the spell of Annie Besant (q.v.) and the Theosophists. In 1912, however, he propounded his own 'science' of spirituality and established the 'Goetheanum', a centre at Dornach near Basel where he applied his theories for research. He claimed that in modern times, the psychologically valuable, play-acting, myth-making and artistic activities had become isolated from the practical activities of life and aimed at reuniting them for therapeutic and especially for educational purposes, advocating the art of eurhythmy. Steiner schools for maladjusted children have since been established in Europe and the U.S.A. See his *Philosophy of Spiritual Activity, Knowledge of the Higher Worlds* and *Outline of Occult Science* (all in trans.), and studies by Weisshaar (1928), Edmunds (1955) and Freeman (1956).

STEINITZ, William, *shtīn'its* (1836–1900), Czech chess champion of the world (1862–1894), was born at Prague.

STEINLEN, Théophile Alexandre, *shtīn'len* (1859–1923), Swiss painter and illustrator, born at Lausanne, settled in Paris, made his name as a poster-designer and by his work in French illustrated papers.

STEINMETZ, *shtīn'mets*, (1) **Carl Friedrich von** (1796–1877), Prussian general, born at Eisenach, fought through the campaign of 1813–14, and in 1866 routed three Austrian corps at Náchod and Skalitz. In 1870 he commanded the right wing of the German advance; but he proved unequal to the task, and after Gravelotte was appointed governor-general of Posen and Silesia.

(2) **Charles Proteus** (1865–1923), American electrical engineer, born in Breslau, educated at the Technical High School, Berlin, emigrated to America, discovered magnetic hysteresis, a simple notation for calculating alternating current circuits, &c.

STEINTHAL, Heymann, *shtīn'tahl* (1823–99), German philologist, born at Gröbzig in Anhalt, in 1850 became lecturer on Philology at Berlin, and in 1863 extra-ordinary professor. He wrote *The Origin of Language* (1851), &c.

STEINWAY, Heinrich Engelhard, *stīn'-*, orig. Steinweg, *-vеKH* (1797–1871), German-born American piano-maker, established a piano factory in Brunswick, but in 1850 transferred the business to New York, leaving his son, Theodor, to carry on the German branch. The latter was eventually handed over to the Grotian family and Theodor joined his father in America.

STENDHAL, pseud. of **Marie Henri Beyle** (1783–1842), French writer, born in Grenoble. He was a soldier under Napoleon and served through the disastrous Russian campaign of 1812. In 1821 he settled in Paris. After the Revolution of 1830 he was appointed consul at Trieste and then at Civitavecchia. He wrote biographies of Haydn (1814), Rossini (1824) and others, a history of Italian painting (1817), and the very popular novels for which he is best known, *Le Rouge et le noir* (1831) and *La Chartreuse de Parme* (1839). Unappreciated in his own time, his works had considerable vogue from 1880 onwards, when his influence on the later realists became felt. See studies by Mélia (1910), Green (1939), Martineau (1945), Bardèche (1947). See the autobiographical *Life of Henry Brulard*, trans. J. Stewart and C. J. G. Knight (1958).

STENSEN, or Steenson or Steno, Niels (1638–1686), Danish anatomist, geologist and theologian, born at Copenhagen. Brought up a strict Lutheran, he settled in Florence, turned Catholic and became bishop and in 1677 vicar-apostolic to North Germany. He was the first to point out the true origin of fossil animals (1669), explain the structure of the earth's crust and differentiate between stratified and volcanic rocks. As a physician to the grand-duke of Florence, he gained a considerable reputation, discovered Steno's duct of the parotid gland and explained the function of the ovaries.

STEPHAN, Heinrich von (1831–97), German administrator, was the chief promoter of the International Postal Union (1874).

STEPHANUS BYZANTIUS, a Greek geographical writer of the 5th century A.D., lived at Constantinople, wrote a geographical dictionary.

STEPHEN, St, one of the seven chosen to manage the finance and alms of the early church. Tried by the Sanhedrin for blasphemy, he was stoned to death—the first Christian martyr.

STEPHEN, the name of ten popes, of whom the following are noteworthy:

Stephen I, saint, martyr and pope (254–257), maintained against Cyprian that heretics baptized by heretics need not be rebaptized.

Stephen II died two days after his election (752), and so is often not reckoned as a pope.

Stephen II or III, pope (752–757), when Rome was threatened by the Lombards, turned to Pepin, King of the Franks, who forced the Lombards to withdraw, and gave the pope the exarchate of Ravenna, the real foundation of the temporal power.

STEPHEN (1097?–1154), king of England, was the third son of Stephen, Count of Blois, by Adela, daughter of William the Conqueror (q.v.). He was sent in 1114 to the court of his uncle, Henry I, received from him the countship of Mortain in Normandy, and acquired that of Boulogne by marriage. When Henry I resolved to settle the crown on his daughter Matilda or Maud, Empress of Germany, and afterwards wife of Geoffrey Plantagenet, Stephen with the rest swore fealty to her, but on Henry's death (December 1, 1135), he hurried over from Normandy, was enthusiastically received, and was crowned on the 22nd. He attempted to strengthen his position with the help of Fleming mercenaries, and he made more enemies than friends by the favours he heaped on some of the great lords. King David of Scotland invaded the north on Matilda's behalf, was defeated near Northallerton (1138), but retained Cumberland. The first powerful enemy that the king made was Robert, Earl of Gloucester, an illegitimate son of Henry I; next he arrayed against himself the clergy, by his quarrel with the justiciar, Bishop Roger of Salisbury. The realm now fell into sheer anarchy; the barons plundered and burned at their pleasure. In 1139 Matilda landed at Arundel, in 1141 took Stephen prisoner at Lincoln, and was acknowledged queen, but her harshness and greed soon disgusted Englishmen. The men of London rose, and she fled to Winchester. In November 1141 Stephen regained his liberty, and 1142 saw him again in the ascendant. In 1148 Matilda finally left England, but her son Henry (see HENRY II) in 1153 crossed over to England, and forced Stephen to acknowledge him as his successor. Stephen died at Dover, October 24, 1154. See study by R. H. C. Davis (1967).

STEPHEN, the name of five kings of Hungary:

Stephen I, Saint (c. 975–1038), first king of Hungary from 997, was baptized about 985, formed Pannonia and Dacia, inhabited by semi-independent Magyar clans, into a regular kingdom, organized Christianity, and laid the foundation of many institutions surviving to this day. He received from Pope Sylvester III the title of 'Apostolic King', and was canonized in 1083. See B. Hóman, *Szent István* (1938).

STEPHEN (1533–86), king of Poland, uncle of Elizabeth Bathori (q.v.), succeeded to the throne in 1576. A born ruler and soldier, he won campaigns against Ivan the Terrible (1579–81), but his plans for Hungary's liberation from Turkish rule were cut short by his early death.

STEPHEN, (1) James (1758–1832), English lawyer, grandfather of (2) and (3), born at Poole, first a parliamentary reporter, then a colonial official at St Kitts in the West Indies, which experience turned him into a slavery abolitionist. He married Wilberforce's sister (1800), entered parliament (1808) and became colonial under-secretary. He was the author of *The Slavery of the British West Indies* (1824–30).

(2) **Sir James Fitzjames, 1st Bart.** (1829–1894), British jurist, grandson of (1), born at Kensington, was a legal member of the Viceregal Council (1869–72), professor of Common Law at the Inns of Court (1875–79) and a judge of the High Court (1879–91). Holding in the main a retributive theory of punishment, he wrote a standard *History of the Criminal Law* (1883) and was responsible for the Indian Evidence Act. See Lives by his brother (3) and L. Radzinowicz (1958).

(3) **Sir Leslie** (1832–1904), English critic, biographer, mountaineer and philosopher, brother of (2), born at Kensington, educated at Eton and King's College, London, and at Trinity Hall, Cambridge, where he became fellow and tutor until reading the works of Mill, Kant and Comte made him openly reject Christianity, and he was (1875) obliged to give up his tutorship (1864) and relinquished his orders. He later became president of Ethical Societies in London, greatly popularized the term 'agnostic', coined by Huxley in 1870, and published his collected addresses to these societies under the title *Essays on Free Thinking and Plain Speaking* (1873) and *An Agnostic's Apology* (1893). A distinguished athlete, he once walked fifty miles to London in twelve hours and was president of the Alpine Club (1865–68). He became editor of the *Cornhill* in 1871 and of the first 26 volumes of the new *Dictionary of National Biography* (1885–91), from 1890, conjointly with Sir Sidney Lee (q.v.). He also wrote studies of Samuel Johnson (1878), Pope (1880), Swift (1882) and George Eliot

(1902). *The Science of Ethics* (1882), which combined utilitarianism with a modified evolutionary ethics, his edition of J. R. Green's *Letters* (1903) and his study on Hobbes (1904) are his principal philosophical works. He died of cancer. In 1905, the Leslie Stephen Lectureship at Cambridge was founded by his friends. His first wife was a daughter of Thackeray. His two daughters were Virginia Woolf (q.v.) and Vanessa (see Clive Bell). See *Lives* by Maitland (1906) and Annan (1951).

STEPHEN DUSHAN, *doo'shan* (*c.* 1308–1355), Serbia's greatest tsar (1336–55), the subjugator of Bulgaria, Macedonia and Albania.

STEPHENS (French **Éstienne** or **Étienne**), a Provençal family renowned as printers. See works by Renouard (1843), Bernard (1856), Clément (1899), and Mark Pattison, *Essays* (1889). Its prominent members were:

(1) **Antoine** (1592–1674), grandson of (4), printed in Paris.

(2) **Charles** (1504–64), son of (3), took charge of his brother's business in Paris when he withdrew to Geneva, and wrote and printed an encyclopaedic work *Dictionarium Historicum ac Poeticum* (1553), *Praedium Rusticum* (1554), &c.

(3) **Henri** (*c.* 1460–1520), established the business in Paris.

(4) **Henri** (1528–98), son of (5), a classical scholar, travelled in Italy, England and the Netherlands, collating MSS. In 1556 he set up a press in Geneva, and issued many ancient Greek authors, including some twenty 'first editions', as also his own Greek dictionary (1572). He wrote also, in French, the semi-satirical *Apologie pour Hérodote* (1566). His son, **Paul** (1566–1627), continued the family printing business in Paris.

(5) **Robert** (1503–59), son of (3), succeeded his father, and was in 1539 and 1540 appointed printer to the king in Latin, Greek and Hebrew. He early became a Protestant, more than once got into difficulties with the University of Paris, and in 1550 retired to Geneva, where he printed several of Calvin's works. A scholar as well as a printer, he published (1532) a famour Latin dictionary (*Thesaurus Linguae Latinae*). His Latin New Testament (1523), Latin Bible (1528) and Greek New Testament (1550) deserve mention. He also printed classic authors and Latin grammars.

STEPHENS, (1) **Alexander Hamilton** (1812–1883). American politician, born near Crawfordsville, Ga., was admitted to the bar in 1834, and sat in congress 1843–59. He advocated the annexation of Texas in 1838, in 1854 defended the Kansas-Nebraska act, at first opposed secession, but in 1861 became Confederate vice-president. He sat in congress again 1874–83, in 1882 was elected governor of Georgia, and wrote *War between the States* (1867–70). See *Life* by R. von Abele (1946).

(2) **George** (1813–95), English archaeologist, born in Liverpool, and educated at University College London, settled at Stockholm in 1833, and became in 1855 professor of English at Copenhagen. His great works are his *Old Northern Runic Monuments* (1866–68–84), &c.

(3) **James** (1824–1901), Fenian agitator, born at Kilkenny, became an active agent of the Young Ireland party. Slightly wounded at Ballingarry (1848), he hid for three months in the mountains, and then escaped to France. In 1853 he journeyed over Ireland, preparing for the Fenian conspiracy; as its 'Head Centre' he exercised an enormous influence. He started the *Irish People* to urge armed rebellion, visited America in 1864, was arrested in Dublin November 11, 1865, but easily escaped. He found his way to New York, was deposed by the Fenians and with the decline in his political importance was allowed to return to Ireland in 1891. See O'Leary's *Recollections of Fenianism* (1896).

(4) **James** (1882–1950), Irish poet, born and died at Dublin, came into notice with *Insurrections* (1909), *The Crock of Gold* (1912, a story), followed by *Songs from the Clay* (1914), *The Demi-Gods* (1914), *Reincarnation* (1917), *Deirdre* (1923), &c.

(5) **John Lloyd** (1805–52), American traveller and archaeologist, born at Shrewsbury, N.J., wrote two books of Levant travel, and on the archaeology of Central America, where he was U.S. minister.

(6) **Joseph Rayner** (1805–79), Scottish social reformer, born in Edinburgh, was expelled from his Methodist ministry in 1834 for supporting church disestablishment. He made himself a name as a factory reformer, opened three independent chapels at Ashton-under-Lyne, and took an active part in the anti-poor-law demonstrations (1836–37) and the Chartist movement, of which, however, he refused actual membership. He was imprisoned for his struggle for the Ten Hours Act (1847). See *Life* by G. J. Holyoake (1881), and G. D. H. Cole, *Chartist Portraits* (1941).

STEPHENSON, (1) **George** (1781–1848), English inventor of the locomotive, son of a colliery enginekeeper, father of (2), was born at Wylam near Newcastle, June 9. He rose to be fireman in a colliery, and contrived meanwhile to pay for a rudimentary education at night school. In 1815 he invented, contemporaneously with Davy, a colliery safety lamp, the 'Geordie', for which he received a public testimonial of £1000. In 1812 he had become enginewright at Killingworth Colliery, and here in 1814 he constructed his first locomotive. 'My Lord', running 6 miles an hour, for the colliery tram roads; his invention next year of the steam-blast made it an ultimate success. In 1821 Stephenson was appointed engineer for the construction of the Stockton and Darlington mineral railway (opened September 27, 1825), and in 1826 for the Liverpool and Manchester Railway, which, after inconceivable difficulties, was opened September 15, 1830. The October before had seen the memorable competition of engines, resulting in the triumph of Stephenson's 'Rocket', running 30 miles an hour. In 1834–37 he was engineer on the North Midland, York and North Midland, Manchester and Leeds, Birmingham and Derby.

and Sheffield and Rotherham Railways; and during the railway mania his offices in London were crowded. In 1845 he visited Belgium and Spain. He died at his country seat of Tapton near Chesterfield, August 12, 1848. See Lives by Smiles (1857; vol. iii of *Lives of the Engineers*), Rowland (1954) and Rolt (1960).

(2) **Robert** (1803–59), English engineer, son of (1), born at Willington Quay, was apprenticed to a coalviewer at Killingworth. In 1822 his father sent him for six months to Edinburgh University. In 1823 he assisted his father in surveying the Stockton and Darlington Railway; and after three years in Colombia, he became manager of his father's locomotive engine-works at Newcastle. He attained independent fame by his Britannia Tubular Bridge (1850), those at Conway (1848) and Montreal (1859), the High Level Bridge at Newcastle (1849), the Border Bridge at Berwick (1850), &c. He was M.P. for many years from 1847 and was buried in Westminster Abbey. See Smiles's *Lives of the Engineers* (vol. iii), and Jeaffreson's Life (1864); also book on George and Robert by L. T. C. Rolt (1960).

STEPINAC, Aloysius (1898–1960), Yugoslav cardinal, Primate of Hungary, born at Krasić near Zagreb, was imprisoned by Tito (1946–1951) for alleged wartime collaboration and with failing health, released, but lived the remainder of his life under house arrest.

STEPNYAK, 'Son of the Steppe', *nom de guerre* of **Sergius Mikhailovich Kravchinsky** (1852–95), Russian revolutionary, was an artillery officer, but becoming obnoxious to government as an apostle of freedom, he was arrested, and subsequently kept under such surveillance that he left Russia and settled (1876) in Geneva, and then (1885) in London. He was, however, held to be the assassin of General Mesentzeff, head of the St Petersburg police (1878). He was run over by a train in a London suburb. Among his works were *La Russia Sotteranea* (Milan 1881; Eng. trans *Underground Russia*, 1883), studies of the Nihilist movement; *Russia under the Tsars* (trans. 1885); *The Career of a Nihilist*, a novel (1889).

STERLING, John (1806–44), British writer, was born at Kames Castle, Bute, where his father, Edward Sterling (1773–1847), an ex-army officer, was farming, but later settled in London, and became a noted contributor to *The Times*. John went to Glasgow University and to Cambridge, where he distinguished himself at the Union; he left without a degree in 1827, and soon was busy on the *Athenaeum*. Influenced by Coleridge, and liberal in sympathies, he nearly sailed on the expedition to Spain which ended in the execution at Málaga of his friend General Torrijos and his own cousin Boyd. He married in November 1830, but soon fell dangerously ill, and spent fifteen months in St Vincent. In 1833 he took orders, and served eight months as Julius Hare's curate at Herstmonceux. His health again giving way, he resigned. He contributed to *Blackwood's* and the *Westminster*. In August 1838 he founded the (later) Sterling Club, among whose members were Carlyle, Allan

Cunningham, G. C. Lewis, Maiden, Mill, Milnes, Spedding, Tennyson, Thirlwall, W. H. Thompson and Venables. See Julius Hare's edition of his *Essays and Tales* (1848) with a memoir, and Carlyle's *Life* (1857).

STERN, (1) Daniel. See AGOULT.

(2) **Otto** (1888–1969), German-American physicist, born at Sohrau, was educated at Breslau and worked at Zürich, Frankfurt, Rostock and Hamburg, before becoming research professor of Physics at the Carnegie Technical Institute (1933–45). He worked on the quantum theory and the kinetic theory of gases; and, for his work on the magnetic moment of the proton and for his development of the molecular-ray method of studying atomic particles, he was awarded a Nobel prize in 1943.

STERNE, Laurence (1713–68), English novelist, was born at Clonmel, November 24, 1713. His father, Roger, was an infantry ensign, and Laurence's early youth was a struggle. In 1724, he was sent to Halifax Grammar School, and, seven years later, to Jesus College, Cambridge. In 1738, he was ordained, and appointed to the living of Sutton-on-the-Forest and made a prebendary of York, where his great-grandfather had been archbishop. In 1741 he made an unsuccessful marriage with Elizabeth Lumley. Of their two daughters, only Lydia survived. In 1759 he wrote the first two volumes of *The Life and Opinions of Tristram Shandy*, first published at York, but published anew at London in 1760. The public welcomed it; and in April Dodsley brought out a second edition. This was followed by *Sermons* of the 'Rev. Mr Yorick'. In January 1761, vols. III and IV of *Tristram* came out, Sterne having meanwhile moved to Coxwold, thenceforward his infrequent home. Between 1761 and 1767 the rest of *Tristram* appeared; Sterne, whose health was now failing, spending much of the time in France and Italy. *A Sentimental Journey through France and Italy* appeared in 1768; and the author, succumbing to pleurisy, died in London on March 18. Few writers of any age or country have displayed such mastery over every form of humour both in situation and in character, a humour at times coming near to that of his acknowledged master Cervantes. Yet it is impossible to overlook the imperfections of his art, alike in conception and in execution. The wild eccentricity of his manner and arrangement—a deliberate and usually successful bid for laughter—was also the convenient cloak for what some, such as Goldsmith, might call a singularly slipshod literary style. His indecencies, less gross than those of Swift or Rabelais, are all too prurient. He was unscrupulous in his borrowings. His pathos too often takes the form of overstrained sentimentalism. Yet this very sentimentalism was also his strength. For Sterne's great contribution to the development of the novel was to widen its scope and loosen its structure; and in his hands it became the channel for the utterance of the writer's own sentiments. See his *Letters from Yorick to Eliza* (1775–79); also Lives by J. Ferriar (1798), P. Stapfer (1870), F. Fitzgerald (1896), H. D. Traill (1882),

Sichel (1910), Lewis Melville (1911), W. L. Cross (1909, rev. ed 1929), editor of the *Works* (12 vols. 1904), who first printed his *Journal to Eliza* (Mrs Draper his ' Bramine ' and inspirer), and his *Letter Book* (1925), and reprinted (1914) his *Political Romance* (1759), and Jefferson (1954); and studies by L. P. Curtis (1929), J. B. Priestley, *English Comic Characters* (1925), P. Quennell, *Four Portraits* (1945) and H. Fluchère (1961).

STERNHOLD, Thomas (1500–49), joint-author of the English version of psalms formerly attached to the Prayer Book, was born near Blakeney in Gloucestershire, or, according to Fuller and Wood, in Hampshire. He was Groom of the Robes to Henry VIII and Edward VI. The first edition (undated) contains only nineteen psalms; the second (1549), thirty-seven. A third edition, by Whitchurch (1551), contains seven more by J. H. (John Hopkins) (d. 1570). The complete book of psalms, which appeared in 1562, formed for nearly two centuries almost the whole hymnody of the Church of England and was known as the ' Old Version ' after the rival version of Tate and Brady appeared (1696). Forty psalms bore the name of Sternhold. See J. Julian's *Dict. of Hymnology* (new ed. 1907).

STESICHORUS, *-sik'-* (*c.* 630–556 B.C.), greatest of the old Dorian lyric poets, was born at Himera in Sicily, and died in Catania. Only some thirty short fragments of his works remain.

STEUBEN, Frederic William Augustus, Baron, *shtoy'ben* (1730–94), German soldier in the American revolutionary army, born at Magdeburg, at fourteen served at the siege of Prague, and in 1762 was on the staff of Frederick the Great. While at Paris in 1777 he was induced to go to America, and his services were joyfully accepted by congress and Washington. He was appointed inspector-general, prepared a manual of tactics for the army, remodelled its organization, and improved its discipline. In 1780 he received a command in Virginia, and took part in the siege of Yorktown. Congress in 1790 voted him an annuity of 2400 dollars and land near Utica, N.Y. See Life by F. Kapp (1860).

STEVENS, (1) Alfred (1818–75), English artist and sculptor, born at Blandford, Dorset, studied in Italy and became assistant to Thorvaldsen (q.v.) in Rome and, returning home, became teacher of architectural design at Somerset House, London (1845–47). During the next ten years he decorated and designed household furniture, fireplaces, porcelain, including plans for the dining-room and salon at Dorchester House, the mantelpiece of the former being preserved in the Tate Gallery. His portrait of Mrs Collman (1854) is in the National Gallery. From 1856 he worked on the Wellington monument (completed after his death by John Tweed) and the mosaics under the dome of St Paul's Cathedral. See study by H. Stannus (1891) and Life by K. R. Towndrow (1939).

(2) **Richard John Samuel** (1757–1837), English organist and composer, born in London, composed harpsichord sonatas and glees, mostly to Shakespeare's songs.

(3) **Thaddeus** (1792–1868), American statesman, born at Danville, Vt., in 1816 settled as a lawyer at Gettysburg, Pa., was member of congress (1849–53), a Republican leader, and chairman at the trial of President Johnson (1868).

(4) **Wallace** (1879–1955), American poet, born in Reading, Pa., educated at Harvard, practised journalism, law and then joined a Hartford insurance company, of which he became vice-president. For many years he wrote impressionist and highly intellectual verse relying for effect upon rhythmic and tonal imagery, but he was over forty when his first volume, *Harmonium* (1923), was published, followed by *Ideas of Order* (1936), *Owl's Clover* (1936), &c. His *Collected Poems* (1954) won him his second National Book Award, and he won the Pultizer prize in 1955. See studies by Pack (1958), Kermode (1960), and *Selected Letters* (ed. Stevens, 1967).

STEVENSON, (1) Adlai Ewing (1900–65), American Democrat politician and lawyer, the grandson of another A. E. Stevenson (1835–1914) who was vice-president under Cleveland (1893–97). He was born in Los Angeles, studied at Princeton, spent two years editing a family newspaper and then took up law practice in Chicago. From 1943 he took part in several European missions for the State Department and from 1945 served on the American delegations to the foundation conferences of the U.N.O. In 1948 he was elected governor of Illinois, where his administration was exceptional for efficiency and lack of corruption. He stood against Eisenhower as Democratic presidential candidate in 1952 and 1956, but each time his urbane ' egg-headed ' campaign speeches, published under the titles *Call to Greatness* (1954) and *What I Think* (1956), had more appeal abroad than at home. See his *Friends and Enemies* (1959), Life by N. F. Busch (1952) and studies by K. S. Davis and J. H. Muller (1968).

(2) **Robert** (1772–1850), Scottish engineer, born at Glasgow, lost his father in infancy; and his mother in 1786 married Thomas Smith, first engineer of the Lighthouse Board. Stevenson then took to engineering, and in 1796 succeeded his stepfather. During his forty-seven years' tenure of office he planned or constructed twenty-three Scottish lighthouses, employing the catoptric system of illumination, and his own invention of ' intermittent ' and ' flashing ' lights. He also acted as a consulting engineer for roads, bridges, harbours, canals and railways. See Life by his son, David Stevenson (1878). Another son, **Alan** (1807–65), built the Skerryvore Lighthouse (1844).

(3) **Robert Louis Balfour** (1850–94), Scottish author, son of Thomas Stevenson, engineer to the Board of Northern Lighthouses, was born in Edinburgh. At the University of Edinburgh he studied engineering for a session (1867) with a view to the family calling, but transferred to law, becoming an advocate in 1875. His true bent, however, was for letters. For the next few years he travelled chiefly in France. His *Inland Voyage* (1878) describes a canoe tour in Belgium and northern France, and his

Travels with a Donkey in the Cevennes a tour undertaken in the same year. In 1876 he was at Fontainebleau (which he made the subject of travel sketches), and it was at the neighbouring Barbizon that he met the divorcée, Fanny Osbourne, whom he followed to America and married in 1880. His return to Europe with his wife and stepson Lloyd Osbourne marked the beginning of a struggle against tuberculosis which his natural gaiety as a writer conceals. His wife and stepson have described the inconvenience and *ennui* experienced at makeshift homes—Davos, Pitlochry and elsewhere—but in those difficult circumstances he was ' making himself ' not only as a writer of travel sketches but of essays and short stories which found their way into the magazines. *Thrawn Janet,* in the vernacular, his first venture in fiction, appeared in *Cornhill Magazine* (1881) and *The Merry Men* serially the following year, in which year also appeared *The New Arabian Nights.* *Treasure Island,* the perfect romantic thriller, brought him fame in 1883 and entered him on a course of romantic fiction which still endears him to young and old alike. *Kidnapped* (1886) is probably the high water mark here if pure adventure is in question, but *Catriona* (1893), introducing the love element, has its passionate adherents. The *Master of Ballantrae* (1889) is a study in evil of a sort not uncommon in Scottish fiction, but here also are the wildest adventures. *Dr Jekyll and Mr Hyde* is not a romance, but it further illustrates Stevenson's metaphysical interest in evil. *The Black Arrow* (1888) shows declining powers, but *Weir of Hermiston,* though unfinished, is acclaimed his masterpiece and it may be, for the canvas is larger, the issues involved more serious and the touch as sure as ever in delineating the types of character he knew at first hand. *St Ives,* which was also left unfinished, was completed by A. Quiller-Couch in 1897. Stevenson's work as an essayist is seen at its best in *Virginibus Puerisque* (1881) and *Familiar Studies of Men and Books* (1882). If in these we sometimes see the ' sedulous ape ' at work —Hazlitt and Montaigne imitation particularly—he is always readable. The verse in those years is another matter. Though *A Child's Garden of Verses* (1885) is not poetry in the adult sense, it is one of the best recollections of childhood in verse. *Underwoods* (1887) illustrates the Scot's predilection for preaching in prose or verse and is the poetry of the good talker rather than the singer and the tone is usually nostalgic. Only occasionally, as in *The Woodman,* does he touch on metaphysical problems, but vernacular poems such as *A Loudon Sabbath Morn* subtly describe the Calvinism whose moorings he had dropped but which intrigued him to the end. In 1888 Stevenson settled in Samoa and there with his devoted wife and stepson he passed the last five years of his life on his estate of Vailima, which gives its name to the incomparable series of letters which he wrote chiefly to friends in Britain. It was in no derogatory sense that Desmond Mac-Carthy called Stevenson ' a little master '. Nobody knew better than MacCarthy how much toil it takes to make a little master and

how much delight he may convey to posterity. See Lives by G. Balfour (1901), S. Colvin (1924) and J. Steuart (1924); also studies by D. Daiches (1947), M. Elwin (1950), and E. N. Caldwell (1960); also Furnas's *Voyage to Windward* (1950).

(4) **William** (d. 1575), English scholar, entered Christ's College, Cambridge, in 1546, and became a fellow. He was probably the author of *Gammer Gurtons Nedle* (1575), sometimes attributed to John Still or John Bridges.

STEVINUS, Simon (1548–1620), Flemish mathematician and physicist, born at Bruges, held offices under Prince Maurice of Orange. He wrote on fortification, book-keeping and decimals; and invented a system of sluices and a carriage propelled by sails.

STEWART, House of, a Scottish family, from whom came the royal line of the Kings of Scotland, and, later, of Great Britain and Ireland, was descended from a Breton, **Alan Fitzflaald** (d. *c.* 1114), who received the lands of Oswestry in Shropshire from Henry I. His elder son, **William Fitzalan** (*c.* 1105–60), was the ancestor of the Earls of Arundel. Members in chronological order were:

(1) **Walter** (d. 1177), second son of the above, coming to Scotland, received from David I large possessions in Renfrewshire, Teviotdale, Lauderdale, &c., along with the hereditary dignity of Steward of Scotland, which gave his descendants the surname of Stewart, by some branches modified to Steuart or the French form Stuart.

(2) **Walter,** grandson of (1), was also justiciary of Scotland.

(3) **Alexander** (1214–83), fourth Steward, was regent of Scotland in Alexander III's minority and commanded at the battle of Largs (1263). From his second son's marriage with the heiress of Bonkyl sprang the Stewarts of Darnley, Lennox and Aubigny.

(4) **James** (1243–1309), fifth Steward, was one of the six regents of Scotland after the death of Alexander III.

(5) **Walter** (1293–1326), sixth Steward, did good service at Bannockburn, and defended Berwick against Edward II. His marriage in 1315 with Marjory, Bruce's daughter, brought the crown of Scotland to his family.

(6) **Robert** (1316–90), seventh Steward, son of (5), on the death of David II in 1371, ascended the throne as Robert II. He was twice married—first (1349) to Elizabeth, daughter of Sir Adam Mure of Rowallan, and secondly (1355) to Euphemia, Countess of Moray, daughter of Hugh, Earl of Ross. Elizabeth Mure was related to him within the prohibited degrees, so in 1347 he obtained a papal dispensation (only discovered in the Vatican in 1789) for the marriage, legitimizing the children already born.

(7) **John, Earl of Carrick** (*c.* 1337–1406), eldest son of (6), succeeded him as Robert III.

(8) **Robert** (*c.* 1339–1420), third son of (6), was in 1398 created Duke of Albany.

(9) **Alexander, Earl of Buchan** (*c.* 1343–*c.* 1405), fourth son of (6), and overlord of Badenoch, received the earldom on his

marriage (1382). His continued attacks on the bishopric of Moray earned him the title of the ' Wolf of Badenoch '.

(10) **John** (c. 1381–1424), nephew of (9), leading a Scottish force, defeated the English at Baugé (1421). He became constable of France but fell fighting at Verneuil. Between 1371 and 1714, fourteen Stewarts sat upon the Scottish, and six of these also on the English, throne, and these, listed below, have separate entries:

ROBERT II (1316–90)
ROBERT III (c. 1340–1406)
JAMES I (1394–1437)
JAMES II (1430–60)
JAMES III (1451–88)
JAMES IV (1473–1513)
JAMES V (1512–42)
MARY (1542–87)
JAMES VI and I (1566–1625)
CHARLES I (1600–49)
CHARLES II (1630–85)
JAMES VII and II (1633–1701)
MARY (1662–94)
ANNE (1665–1714).

(11) **James Francis Edward** (1688–1766), known as the ' Old Pretender ', only son of James VII and II and his second wife, Mary of Modena, and father of (12), was born at St James's Palace, June 10, by many falsely believed to have been introduced in a warming-pan. Six months later, he was conveyed by his fugitive mother to St Germain, where, on his father's death in 1701, he was proclaimed his successor. On an attempt (1708) to make a descent upon Scotland, the young ' Chevalier de St George ' was not allowed to land; after his return he served with the French in the Low Countries, distinguishing himself at Malplaquet. But in Mar's ill-conducted rebellion, he landed at Peterhead (December 1715), only to sneak away six weeks afterwards from Montrose. France was now closed to him by the treaty of Utrecht, and almost all the rest of his life was passed at Rome, where he died, January 1, 1766. In 1719 he had married Princess Clementina Sobieski (1702–35), who bore him two sons. See Lives by M. Haile (1907), Shield and Lang (1907) and A. and H. Tayler (1934).

(12) **Charles Edward Louis Philip Casimir** (1720–88), known variously as the ' Young Pretender ', the ' Young Chevalier ', and ' Bonny Prince Charlie ', elder son of (11), was born in Rome, December 31, and educated there and became the centre of Jacobite hopes. He first saw service at the siege of Gaeta (1734); fought bravely at Dettingen (1743); and next year repaired to France, to head Marshal Saxe's projected invasion of England. But the squadron which was to have convoyed the transports with 15,000 troops to Kent fled before the British fleet; the transports themselves were scattered by a tempest; and for a year and a half Charles was kept hanging on in France, until at last, sailing from Nantes, he landed with seven followers at Eriskay in the Hebrides on July 23, 1745, and on August 19 raised his father's standard in Glenfinnan. The clansmen flocked in; on September 17 Edinburgh surrendered, though the castle held out; and

Charles kept court at Holyrood, the palace of his ancestors. There followed the victory over Sir John Cope at Prestonpans (September 21), and on November 1 he left for London at the head of 6500 men. He took Carlisle and advanced as far as Derby. Londoners became alarmed, especially since the cream of the British army was engaged on the Continent. Eventually the Duke of Cumberland was dispatched against the insurgents. Charles meanwhile had been unwillingly argued into a withdrawal by his commanders and the Highlanders turned back, winning one last victory against the government forces at Falkirk, January 17, 1746, before suffering a crushing defeat at the hands of Cumberland's troops at Culloden Moor, April 16. The rising was ruthlessly suppressed by the duke, who earned the name ' Butcher Cumberland ', and Charles was hunted in the highlands and islands for five months with a price of £30,000 on his head, but no one betrayed him. He was helped by Flora Macdonald (q.v.) when he crossed from Benbecula to Portree in June 1746, disguised as ' Betty Burke ', her maid. He landed in Brittany, September 29, and was given hospitality at the French court until the peace of Aix-la-Chapelle (1748) caused his forcible expulsion from France, although he spent a while at Avignon until the English found out and protested, and afterwards lived secretly in Paris with his mistress, Clementina Walkinshaw. He made two or three secret visits to London between 1750 and 1760, even declaring himself a protestant. He assumed the title of Charles III of Great Britain and retired to Florence, where he married in 1772 the Countess of Albany (q.v.), but the marriage was later dissolved. His natural daughter, Charlotte (1753–89) by his mistress Walkinshaw, he had created Duchess of Albany. He died in Rome, January 31, was buried at Frascati, later at St Peter's. See Lives by A. C. Ewald (1875), A. Lang (1903), W. D. Norrie (1903–04), Wilkinson (1932), Dumont-Wilden (1934), H. Tayler (1945) and under MAC-DONALD, Flora.

(13) **Henry Benedict Maria Clement, Duke of York** (1725–1807), Scottish cardinal, brother of (12), was born in Rome. After the failure of the '45 he became in 1747 a cardinal and priest, and in 1761 Bishop of Frascati. He enjoyed, through the favour of the French court, the revenues of two rich abbeys, as well as a Spanish pension. The French Revolution stripped him of his fortune, and he had to take refuge in Venice for three years. In 1800 George III granted him a pension of £4000; he died, the last of the Stuarts, July 13, 1807. The crown jewels, carried off by James II, were bequeathed by him to George IV, then Prince of Wales, who in 1819 gave fifty guineas towards Canova's monument in St Peter's to ' James III, Charles III, and Henry IX '. See H. M. Vaughan, *Last of the Royal Stuarts* (1906); and Lives by A. Shield (1908) and B. Fothergill (1958).

Next to the exiled Stuarts came the descendants of Henrietta (q.v.), Charles I's youngest daughter, who in 1661 was married to the Duke of Orleans. From this marriage sprang Anne Mary (1669–1728), who married Victor Amadeus, Duke of Savoy and King of Sardinia; their son Charles Emmanuel III (1701–73), King of Sardinia; his son, Victor Amadeus III (1726–96), King of Sardinia; his son, Victor Emmanuel I (1759–1824), King of Sardinia; his daughter, Mary (1792–1840), who married Francis, Duke of Modena; their son, Ferdinand (1821–49), who married Elizabeth of Austria; and their daughter, Maria Teresa (1849–1919), who in 1868 married Prince (from 1913 to 1918 King) Louis of Bavaria, and whom, as ' Mary III and IV ', the ' Legitimist Jacobites ' of 1891 put forward as the ' representative of the Royal House of these realms '. Rupert, her son, was ninth in descent from Charles I; he represented Bavaria at Queen Victoria's Diamond Jubilee, June 1897, and early in World War I took command of a German army group in France. The branch of the family which the Act of Settlement (1701) called to the throne on the death of Anne were the descendants of the Electress Sophia of Hanover, granddaughter of James VI and I by her mother the Princess Elizabeth (q.v.), Electress Palatine and Queen of Bohemia. By that act the above-mentioned descendants of Henrietta of Orleans were excluded, and also the Roman Catholic descendants of the Princess Elizabeth's sons. Queen Elizabeth II is 26th in descent from Walter Fitzalan, 20th from Robert II and 12th from James VI and I.

Arabella (1575–1615), was the daughter of the Earl of Lennox, Darnley's younger brother, and so a great-great-granddaughter of Henry VII, a third cousin to Queen Elizabeth, and a first cousin to James VI and I. At twenty-seven she was suspected of having a lover in the boy William Seymour, who had Tudor blood in his veins; but on James's accession (1603) she was restored to favour, only, however, to contract a secret marriage in 1610 with him. Both were imprisoned, and both escaped—Seymour successfully to Ostend, but she was retaken and died, insane, in the Tower. See Lives by M. E. Bradley (1889), M. Lefuse (1913), B. C. Hardy (1913).

The cadets of the house of Stewart are: (1) descendants of Robert II; (2) descendants of natural sons of his descendants; (3) descendants of natural sons of Stewart kings; and (4) legitimate branches of the Stewarts before their accession to the throne. To the first belong the Stuarts of Castle-Stewart, descended from Robert, Duke of Albany, Robert II's third son, through the Lords Avondale and Ochiltree. They received the titles of Lord Stuart of Castle-Stewart in the peerage of Ireland (1619), Viscount Castle-Stewart (1793), and Earl (1809). To the second class belong the Stuart Earls of Traquair (1633–1861), descended from a natural son of James Stewart, Earl of Buchan. To the third class belong the Regent Moray, the Marquis of Bute, and the Shaw-Stewarts; and to the fourth belong the Earls of Galloway (from a brother of the fifth High

Steward), the Lords Blantyre, the Stewarts of Fort-Stewart, and the Stewarts of Grand-tully (from the fourth High Steward; the last baronet died in 1890).

See, besides works cited in the articles on the several Stewart sovereigns and in Marshall's *Genealogist's Guide* (new ed. 1903), Stewart genealogies, &c., by Symson (1712), Hay of Drumboote (1722), Duncan Stewart (1739), Noble (1795), Andrew Stuart of Castlemilk (1798), A. G. Stuart (Castle-Stewart branch, 1854), Sir W. Fraser (Grand-tully branch, 1868), W. A. Lindsay (1888); William Townend, *Descendants of the Stuarts* (1858); the Marchesa Campana de Cavelli, *Les Derniers Stuarts* (1871); books by Gibb and Skelton (1890), F. W. Head (1901), J. J. Foster (1902), S. Cowan (1908), T. F. Henderson (1914); M. Stewart and J. Balfour, *Scottish Family Histories* (1930), and *Study of the Kings* by J. P. Kenyon (1958).

STEWART, (1) Alexander Turney (1803–76), American merchant, born near Belfast, who acquired great wealth in America in the retail store business. His body was stolen in 1878, and restored to his widow three years after on payment of $20,000 through a lawyer.

(2) **Balfour** (1828–87), Scottish physicist, born at Edinburgh, studied at St Andrews and Edinburgh, and became assistant to Forbes at Edinburgh and afterwards director of Kew Observatory (1859), and professor of Physics at Owens College, Manchester (1870). He made his reputation by his work on radiant heat (1858), was one of the founders of spectrum analysis and wrote papers on terrestrial magnetism and sunspots.

(3) **Sir Charles.** See CASTLEREAGH.

(4) **Dugald** (1753–1828), Scottish philosopher, son of Matthew Stewart the mathematician (1717–85), born November 22 at Edinburgh, studied there and under Reid at Glasgow, became assistant in Mathematics at Edinburgh under his father (1775) and joint-professor in 1775. He succeeded Ferguson to the chair of Moral Philosophy (1785–1810) and in 1806 was awarded a Whig sinecure. A disciple of the ' common sense ' philosophy of Reid, he systematized the doctrines of the Scottish school and allowed psychological considerations their full share in a philosophy of mind. See his *Elements of the Philosophy of the Human Mind* (vol. I, 1792; vols. II and III, 1814–17), *Outlines of Moral Philosophy* (1793), *Philosophical Essays* (1810), *Philosophy of the Active and Moral Powers* (1828) and his Life and edition of Adam Smith's works (1811–12). He died in Edinburgh, June 11, 1828. See Veitch's *Life* in Sir William Hamilton's edition of his works (1954–58), and J. McCosh, *Scottish Philosophy* (1874).

(5) **Frances Teresa, Duchess of Richmond and Lennox** (1647–1702), the granddaughter of Lord Blantyre, was appointed maid of honour to Catherine of Braganza. Described by Pepys as ' the greatest beauty ' he ever saw in his life, her charms made a deep impression on the susceptible Charles II. Despite contemporary whispers to the contrary, she resisted his proposals: although consenting to pose as the effigy of Britannia

on the coinage. In 1667 ' la belle Stewart' married the oafish 3rd Duke of Richmond, and fled the Court. In later years she was restored to the King's favour. See works by Bryant (1931) and Grammont (1903).

(6) **(Robert) Michael (Maitland)** (1906-), British Labour politician, born in London, educated at Christ's Hospital and St John's College, Oxford. A schoolmaster before World War II, he stood unsuccessfully for parliament in 1931 and 1935. M.P. for Fulham since 1945, he has had a varied ministerial career. Secretary of state for war (1947-51), for education and science (1964-65), he came to the fore as foreign minister (1965-66), as minister for economic affairs (1966-67) and as first secretary of state from 1966. He replaced George Brown as foreign minister on the latter's resignation in March 1968.

STEYN, Martinus Theunis, *stayn* (1857-1916), South African statesman, born in Winburg, Orange Free State, of which he was president (from 1896), joined the Transvaal in the war (1899-1902). He promoted the Union of 1910, but later encouraged Boer extremists and their rebellion of 1914. His son, **Colin Fraser** (1887-1959), mediated between Generals Botha and de Wet, and was minister of justice in the Smuts government (1939-45) and of labour (1945-48).

STIFTER, Adalbert (1805-68), Austrian novelist and painter, born at Oberplan, Bohemia, studied at Vienna and as private tutor to various aristocratic families had several unhappy love affairs. Deeply disturbed by the Revolution of 1848, he settled in Linz and became an official in the ministry of education. Unhappiness and illness terminated in suicide. His humanism, his love of traditional values, his belief in the greatness of life pervade the *Bildungroman, Der Nachsommer* (1857), *Witiko* (1865-67), a heroic tale set in 12th-century Bohemia, and the short stories *Der Condor* (1840), &c. He was also a considerable painter of city views. See also *Studien* (1844-50) and *Bunte Steine* (1853), complete works, ed. A. Sauer (1901-1928), study by A. von Grotman (1926), and Lives by Blackall (1948) and Steffen (1955).

STIGAND (d. 1072), English ecclesiastic, was made his chaplain by Edward the Confessor, Bishop of Elmham (1044), Bishop of Winchester (1047), and, uncanonically, Archbishop of Canterbury (1052). On the death of Harold, whom, possibly, he had crowned, Stigand supported Edgar Atheling. Hence he was deprived by William I, whom he had helped to crown, of Canterbury and Winchester (1070), and he died a prisoner at Winchester.

STILICHO, Flavius, *stil'i-kō* (c. A.D. 359-408), Roman general, by blood a Vandal, was sent as ambassador to Persia in 384, and rewarded with the hand of Serena, niece of the Emperor Theodosius. In 394 he departed from Constantinople for Rome in charge of the youthful Honorius, placed him on the throne of the Western empire, and administered in his name the affairs of state. On the death of Theodosius (394) Stilicho's rival, Rufinus, instigated Alaric to invade Greece. Stilicho marched against Alaric, blocked him up in

the Peloponnesus, but permitted him to escape with captives and booty. In 398 his daughter became the wife of Honorius. Alaric invaded Northern Italy, but was signally defeated by Stilicho at Pollentia (403) and Verona. When Radagaisus, at the head of 200,000 to 400,000 Goths, ravaged the country as far as Florence (406), Stilicho routed the invaders and saved the Western empire a second time. Next Vandals, Alans and Suevi invaded Gaul; Stilicho's proposed alliance with Alaric against them was interpreted as treachery and he was credited with aiming at the imperial dignity. A Roman army mutinied, and Stilicho fled to Ravenna, where he was murdered. Three months later Alaric was at the gates of Rome.

STILL, William Grant (1895-   ), American Negro composer, born in Woodville, Mississippi, worked as an arranger of popular music and played in theatre and night-club orchestras while studying under Varèse. His music shows the influence of this work and of racial and European styles. It includes five operas, four symphonies, one of which is a study of the modern American Negro, three ballets, chamber and choral music and orchestral pieces.

STILLING. See JUNG (2).

STILLINGFLEET, (1) **Benjamin** (1702-71), English author and botanist, grandson of (2), born in Norfolk, studied at Trinity College, Cambridge, published essays on music and the art of conversation, but is best known for his preface ' Observation on Grasses ' to his own translation (1759) from the Latin of six of Linnaeus's botanical essays. The term ' blue stocking ' originated from those he habitually wore at the fashionable, mixed ' evening assemblies without card playing ' at Mrs Vesey's of Bath, to which he contributed erudite conversation.

(2) **Edward** (1635-99), English divine, grandfather of (1), born at Cranborne in Dorset, became in 1653 fellow of St John's College, Cambridge, later vicar of Sutton, Bedfordshire. His *Irenicum* (1659) advocated union between the Episcopalians and the Presbyterians. His *Origines Sacrae* (1662) and *Rational Account of the Grounds of the Protestant Religion* (1664), defending the Church of England's breach with Rome, led to preferment. He became chaplain to Charles II, Dean of St Paul's (1678) and after the deposition of James II Bishop of Worcester. In three letters or pamphlets (1696-1697) he defended the doctrine of the Trinity against the consequences of what he understood to be Locke's denial of substance in the latter's *Essay*, but Locke merely denied that one can have a genuine idea of ' pure substance in general ' and give it a significant content. See Life by R. Bentley, prefaced to the Collected Works (1710).

STILWELL, Joseph, nicknamed ' Vinegar Joe ' (1883-1946), American soldier, was born in Florida, graduated at West Point in 1904, and rose to lt.-col. in the first World War. An authority on Chinese life and an expert Chinese speaker, he was military attaché to the U.S. Embassy in Peking from 1932 to 1939. In 1941 he became U.S. military representative in China and in 1942 commander of the 5th and 6th Chinese Armies in Burma. In the Burma counter-offensive in 1943 he was commanding general of the U.S. Forces in China, Burma and India, but was recalled to America following a dispute with Chiang Kai-shek. See *The Stilwell Papers* (posthumous, 1949).

STINFALICO. See MARCELLO.

STIRLING, (1) James Hutchison (1820–1909), Scottish idealist philosopher, born at Glasgow, studied both arts and medicine at Glasgow and philosophy at Heidelberg. His *Secret of Hegel* (1865) introduced that philosopher's system into Britain and was a masterly exposition despite the unkind critic's remark that the secret had been well kept. He also wrote a *Complete Textbook to Kant* (1881) and three attacks, one on *Sir William Hamilton; being the Philosophy of Perception* (1865), another on Huxley's biology, entitled *As Regards Protoplasm* (1869), a third on *Darwinianism* (1894). He delivered the first Gifford lectures at Edinburgh in 1890. See Life by his daughter, A. H. Stirling (1912), and J. H. Muirhead, *The Platonic Tradition in Anglo-Saxon Philosophy* (1931).

(2) **Mary Ann,** *née* **Kehl** (1816–95), English actress, born in Mayfair, London, was educated in France, made her début in 1833, and played till 1886, her finest parts ' Peg Woffington ' and the Nurse in *Romeo and Juliet*. She married early the Drury Lane stage manager, Edward Stirling, and in 1894 Sir Charles Hutton Gregory.

(3) **William Alexander, 1st Earl of** (*c.* 1567–1640), minor Scottish poet, born at Alva. Knighted by 1609, in 1613 he was attached to the household of Prince Charles; in 1614 he published part i of his huge poem *Doomesday* (part ii 1637). He received in 1621 the grant of ' Nova Scotia '—a vast tract in N. America soon rendered valueless by French expansion; in 1631 he was made sole printer of King James's version of the Psalms. From 1626 till his death he was the (unpopular) secretary of state for Scotland. He was created Viscount (1630) and Earl of Stirling (1633), also Earl of Dovan (1639), but he died insolvent in London. His tragedies—*Darius* (1603), *Croesus* (1604), *The Alexandrean Tragedy* (1605), *Julius Caesar* (1607)— are of French Senecan type; their quatrains are graceful. The songs, sonnets, elegies, madrigals of *Aurora* (1604) are marred by conceits, yet show fancy and ingenuity. See Kastner and Charlton's edition of his poems (1921–29); *Memorials* by Rogers (1877).

STIRLING-MAXWELL, Sir William, Bart. (1818–78), Scottish historian and art critic, born in Glasgow, added the name of Maxwell to his own on succeeding to the estates of his uncle, Sir John Maxwell, in 1866. He travelled in Italy and Spain, was the first British collector to buy Spanish paintings of the 16th and 17th centuries, and wrote *Annals of the Artists of Spain* (1848), *Cloister Life of Charles V* (1852), *Velazquez* (1855), &c. His second wife (1877) was the Hon. Mrs Norton (q.v.).

STIRNER, Max, pseud. of **Kaspar Schmidt** (1806–56), German anarchistic writer, who was born at Bayreuth, and taught in a girls' school in Berlin, wrote *Der Einziger und das Eigentum* (1845, trans. 1912). See works by R. Engert (1921) and H. Schultheiss (1932).

STITNY, Thomas (*c.* 1325–1404), a Bohemian philosophical writer, a predecessor of Huss.

STOBAEUS, Johannes (fl. A.D. 500), Greek anthologist, born at Stobi in Macedonia, compiled about A.D. 500 an anthology from 500 Greek poets and prose-writers. It has preserved fragments from many lost works.

STOCKHAUSEN, Karlheinz (1928–), German composer, born at Mödrath, near Cologne, educated at Cologne and Bonn Universities, studied under Frank Martin and Messaien, employed the twelve-tone system, but advanced further, joined the *Musique Concrète* group in Paris and experimented with compositions based on electronic sounds. He has written orchestral, choral and instrumental works, including some which combine electronic and normal sonorities; also some effective piano pieces in an advanced idiom.

STOCKMAR, Christian Friedrich, Baron (1787–1863), German diplomat, born of Swedish descent at Coburg, became physician and adviser to Prince Leopold (q.v.) of Coburg, the husband first of the Princess Charlotte and then king of the Belgians. He was made a baron in 1831. In 1836 he became the mentor of Prince Albert, and was the trusted friend of the young queen of England. See his *Denkwürdigkeiten* (Eng. trans. *Notabilia*, 1872), Juste, *Le Baron Stockmar* (1873), and Sir T. Martin, *Monographs* (1923).

STOCKTON, (1) Francis Richard (1834–1902), American humorist and engraver, born in Philadelphia, became assistant editor of *St Nicholas*. He first attracted notice by his stories for children, but is best known as author of *Rudder Grange* (1879). Later works are *The Lady, or the Tiger?* (1884), *Mrs Cliff's Yacht* (1896), *The Great Stone of Sardis* (1897), *The Girl at Cobhurst* (1898), &c.

(2) **Robert Field** (1795–1866), American naval officer, conquered California with Frémont (1846–47) and organized a government.

STODDARD, Richard Henry (1825–1903), American poet, was born at Hingham, Massachusetts. His poems include *Songs in Summer* (1857), *The King's Bell* (1862), *The Book of the East* (1867), *Lion's Cub* (1891). *Under the Evening Lamp* (1893) and *Recollections* (1903) contain literary studies. His wife, **Elizabeth Drew,** *née* **Barstow** (1823–1902), was also a novelist and poet.

STODDART, Thomas Tod (1810–80), Scottish angler poet, lived at Kelso from 1836. His *Death-Wake, or Lunacy* (1830), was reprinted in 1895, with an introduction by Andrew Lang, and his *Songs of the Seasons* (2nd ed. 1881) contains an autobiography.

STOKER, Bram, properly **Abraham** (1847–1912), Irish writer, born in Dublin, educated at Trinity College there, studied law and science, partnered Henry Irving in running the Lyceum Theatre from 1878 and wrote, among other books, the classic horror tale *Dracula* (1897) and *Personal Reminiscences of Henry Irving* (1906). See study by H. Ludlam (1962).

STOKES, (1) Sir George Gabriel, Bart. (1819–

1903), British mathematician and physicist, born at Skreen, Sligo, graduated in 1841 as senior wrangler from Pembroke College, Cambridge, and in 1849 became Lucasian professor of Mathematics. In 1851 he was made fellow, and in 1854–85 was secretary, of the Royal Society, in 1885–92 president. In 1887–92 he was Conservative M.P. for Cambridge University, in 1889 was created a baronet. He first used spectroscopy as a means of determining the chemical compositions of the sun and stars, published a valuable paper on diffraction (1849), identified X-rays as electromagnetic waves produced by sudden obstruction of cathode rays and formulated the law which bears his name, in terms of a formula for the force opposing a small sphere in its passage through a viscous fluid. See his *Memoir* (1907).

(2) Whitley (1830–1909), Irish jurist, son of William Stokes, regius professor of Medicine at Dublin, studied law at Trinity College, Dublin, went to India in 1862, and was in 1879 president of the Indian law commission and draughtsman of the law and criminal codes. He wrote many legal works and edited Irish and other Celtic texts.

STOKESLEY, John (1475?–1539), English divine, born at Collyweston, Northamptonshire, Bishop of London, was chaplain to Henry VIII and wrote in favour of the divorce (1531). He condemned John Frith (q.v.) and other Protestants, but opposed the translation of the Bible into English and was in opposition to Cromwell.

STOKOWSKI, Leopold, *sto-kof'skĕe* (1882–   ), American conductor of Polish origin, born in London, studied at the Royal College of Music there and built up an international reputation as conductor of the Philadelphia Symphony Orchestra (1912–36), the New York Philharmonic (1946–50) and the Houston Symphony Orchestra (1955–60). He appeared with Deanna Durbin in the film *A Hundred Men and a Girl* (1937) and in Walt Disney's *Fantasia* (1940). In 1962 he founded and has since conducted the American Symphony Orchestra in New York.

STOLBERG, (1) Christian, Count of (1748–1821), German poet, one of the Göttingen poet band, born at Hamburg, was in the public service of Holstein (1777–1800). Besides writing poems, he translated Sophocles.

(2) Friedrich Leopold, Count of (1750–1819), German poet, brother of (1), also of the Göttingen school, was in the Danish service (1789–1800). Then turning Catholic, he published a history of Christianity. He produced poems, dramas, translations from the Greek, &c. See works by Menge (1862), Janssen (3rd ed. 1882) and Keiper (1893).

STONE, (1) Lucy (1818–93), American feminist, born in Massachusetts, became active *c.* 1847 in anti-slavery and suffragist movements, and founded (1855) the *Woman's Journal.* She married Henry Brown Blackwell, the abolitionist, in the same year.

(2) Nicholas, the elder (1586–1647), English mason and architect, carried out designs of Inigo Jones (q.v.) and completed the tombs of Bodley and Donne. His sons, Nicholas, John and Henry, were also sculptors.

STONEY, George Johnstone (1826–1911), Irish mathematical physicist, became professor of Natural Philosophy at Queen's College (1852), and was elected F.R.S. in 1861. He calculated an approximate value for the charge of an electron (1874).

STOPES, Marie Carmichael (1880–1958), English pioneer advocate of birth control, suffragette, and palaeontologist, born near Dorking, Surrey, studied at University College, London, and at Munich and in 1904 became the first female science lecturer at Manchester, specializing in fossil plants and coalmining. In 1907 she lectured at Tokio and with Professor Sakurai wrote a book on the Japanese *No* plays (1913). Alarmed at the unscientific manner in which men and women embark upon married life, after the unhappiness of her first marriage she wrote a number of books on the subject, of which *Married Love* (1918), in which birth control is mentioned, caused a storm of controversy. With her second husband, Humphrey Verdon Roe (1878–1949), the aircraft manufacturer, she founded the first birth control clinic in North London in 1921. Her seventy books also include studies of the sex cycle, a play, *Our Ostriches* (1923), and poetry.

STORACE, *sto-rah'chay*, (1) Anna Selina (1766–1817), English singer and actress of Italian descent, sister of (2), sang at Florence and La Scala, Milan, and in London. She was the original Susanna in Mozart's *Nozze di Figaro*, in Vienna (1786) and partnered John Braham (q.v.) on the continent.

(2) Stephen (1763–96), English composer of *The Haunted Tower* (1789) and other operas, brother of (1), was born in London.

STORM, Theodor Woldsen (1817–88), German poet and storywriter, born at Husum in Schleswig-Holstein, was a magistrate and judge (1864–80), wrote one volume of poems (1857) and a number of tales, characterized by a vivid, often eerie descriptive power. See his correspondence with Keller (1904) and Lives by G. Storm (1912), P Schütze (1925), and study by F. Stuckert (1940).

STÖRMER, Carl Fredrik Mülertz (1874–1957), Norwegian mathematician and geophysicist, was educated at Oslo and became professor there (1903). He carried out research on cosmic rays and discovered the ' forbidden ' directions lying within the Störmer cone. He gave his name to the unit of momentum at which a particle can circle around the equator.

STORR, Paul (1771–1844), English goldsmith, began his career in partnership with William Frisbee in 1792, establishing his firm in Dean Street, Soho, in 1807. He produced much domestic silver and monumental work from the designs of John Flaxman (q.v.) for the royal collection at Windsor Castle. See study by Penzer (1954).

STORY, (1) John (1510?–71), English jurist, first regius professor of Civil Law (1544) at Oxford, opposed the Act of Uniformity (1548) and went into exile at Louvain, whence he returned during Mary's reign to become a persecutor of Protestants and proctor at Cranmer's trial (1555). Pardoned by Elizabeth, he soon fell foul of the authorities again, fled to Spain but was kidnapped and executed at Tyburn.

(2) **Joseph** (1779–1845), American jurist, father of (3), born at Marblehead, Mass., graduated at Harvard in 1798, was admitted to the bar in 1801, elected to the state legislature in 1805, and became a leader of the Republican (Democratic) party. In 1808 he entered congress, in 1811–45 was a justice of the Supreme Court, and also professor of Law at Harvard from 1829. His works include *Commentaries on the Constitution of the U.S.* (1833), *The Conflict of Laws* (1834), and *Equity Jurisprudence* (1835–36). See Life by his son (1851), who also edited his *Miscellaneous Writings* (1851).

(3) **William Wetmore** (1819–95), American poet and sculptor, son of (2), was born at Salem, Mass., and was admitted to the bar, but went to Italy (1848) and became a sculptor as well as a poet. His writings include *Poems* (1847–56–86), *Roba di Roma* (1862), *Castle of St Angelo* (1877), *He and She* (1883), *Fiametta* (1885), *Excursions* (1891) and *A Poet's Portfolio* (1894). See Life by Henry James (1903).

STORY-MASKELYNE. See MASKELYNE (2).

STOSS, or **Stozz**, **Veit**, *shtōs* (1447–1533), German woodcarver and sculptor, born probably in Nuremberg. Except for a period in 1486 when he worked in the church of St Sebald in Nuremberg, he was from 1477 to 1496 in Cracow, where he carved the high altar of the Marienkirche. He returned to Nuremberg, and for the next thirty years worked in various churches there, including St Lorenz's, where is his *Annunciation*. Despite the great size of many of his works, they all show great delicacy of sculpture. See German monographs by H. Wilm (1935) and E. Lutze (1938).

STOTHARD, Thomas (1755–1834), English painter and engraver, born in London, was apprenticed to a pattern-drawer. A series of designs for the *Town and Country Magazine* was followed by illustrations for Bell's *Poets* and the *Novelist's Library*. His earliest pictures exhibited at the Academy were *The Holy Family* and *Ajax defending the Body of Patroclus*. In 1794 he became R.A. and in 1813 Academy librarian. Some 3000 of his designs were engraved, including those to Boydell's *Shakespeare*, *The Pilgrim's Progress*, *Robinson Crusoe* and Rogers's *Poems*. His *Canterbury Pilgrims* and *Flitch of Bacon* are well known by engravings. See Life (1851) by Mrs Bray (q.v.), widow of his son, **Charles Alfred Stothard** (1786–1821), antiquarian draughtsman; and another by A. C. Coxhead (1907).

STOUT, George Frederick (1860–1944), English philosopher and psychologist, born at South Shields, studied at St John's College, Cambridge, was elected fellow (1884) and after lecturing at Cambridge, where his students included Moore and Russell, at Aberdeen and Oxford, was appointed professor of Logic and Metaphysics at St Andrews (1903–36), and was a distinguished editor of the philosophical journal *Mind* (1891–1920). His *Analytic Psychology* (1896) ranks high among the classic contributions to the philosophy of mind. *Manual of Psychology* (1899) was long the English textbook. His Gifford lectures (1919–21)

became the basis of his formidable treatment of the problems of perception, in which psychological considerations weighed heavily and which ultimately tended towards idealistic metaphysics. The first volume, *Mind and Matter*, appeared in 1931 and was somewhat clarified by *God and Nature* (1952). This also contains a memoir by J. A. Passmore. See also his collected *Studies in Philosophy and Psychology* (1930). He was elected F.B.A. in 1903.

STOW, (1) **David** (1793–1864), Scottish pioneer of coeducation, born at Paisley, founder of Glasgow Normal school, advocated the mixing of the sexes and the abolition of prizes and corporal punishment in schools.

(2) **John** (1525–1605), English chronicler, was a tailor in Cornhill, but about his fortieth year devoted himself to antiquarian pursuits. His principal works, which, for his time, are accurate and businesslike, are his *Summary of English Chronicles* (1565); *Annals, or a General Chronicle of England* (1580); and the noted *Survey of London and Westminster* (1598), an account of their history, antiquities, and government for six centuries. Stow also assisted in the continuation of Holinshed's *Chronicle*, Speght's Chaucer, &c. See the *Survey*, ed. Kingsford (1908), and Everyman edition (1955).

STOWE, Harriet Elizabeth Beecher (1811–96), American novelist, daughter of Lyman Beecher (q.v.), born at Litchfield, Connecticut, was brought up with puritanical strictness and joined her sister Catherine (q.v.) at her seminary at Hartford. In 1836 she married the Rev. C. E. Stowe, a theological professor at Lane Seminary, with whom she settled at Brunswick, Maine. She became famous through her *Uncle Tom's Cabin* (1852), which immediately focused anti-slavery sentiment in the North. Her second anti-slavery novel, *Dred* (1856), had a record sale in England, but she lost her English popularity with *Lady Byron Vindicated* (1870), although the charges made therein against Byron were later proven. Her best books deal with New England life, such as *The Minister's Wooing* (1859), *Old Town Folks* (1869), &c. See Life by F. Wilson (1941).

STOWELL, William Scott, 1st Baron (1745–1836), English judge, eldest brother of Lord Eldon (q.v.), born at Heyworth, went up to Corpus, Oxford, in 1761, was a college tutor (1765–77), and in 1780 was called to the bar. In 1788 he was made a judge and privy councillor, and knighted. Both as an ecclesiastical and admiralty judge he won high distinction, and he was the highest English authority on the law of nations. He sat for Oxford 1801–21, when he was made Baron Stowell; in 1828 he retired. See Lives by Surtees (1846), E. S. Roscoe (1916).

STRABO (*c.* 60 B.C.–post A.D. 21), Greek geographer, born at Amasia in Pontus, was of Greek descent on his mother's side. *Strabo* means 'squint-eyed'. He seems to have spent his life in travel and study, was at Corinth in 29 B.C., ascended the Nile in 24, seems to have been settled at Rome after A.D. 14, and died sometime after A.D. 21. Of Strabo's great historical work in forty-seven books—from the fifth a continuation to his own time of Polybius—we have only a few fragments; but his *Geographica* in seventeen books has come down to us almost complete. It is a work of great value in those parts especially which record the results of his own extensive observation. He makes copious use of his predecessors, Eratosthenes, Polybius, Aristotle, Thucydides, and many writers now lost to us, but he depreciates Herodotus and quotes few Roman writers.

STRACHAN, Douglas, *strawn* (1875–1950), Scottish artist, born in Aberdeen, after being political cartoonist for the *Manchester Chronicle* (1895–97) and a portrait painter in London, found his true medium in stained glass work. His first great opportunity was the window group which Britain contributed to the Palace of Peace at The Hague: He designed the windows for the shrine of the Scottish National War Memorial. Other examples of his work may be seen in King's College Chapel, Aberdeen, the University Chapel, Glasgow, and the church of St Thomas, Winchelsea. As an artist Strachan never wholly identified himself with any movement. His work glows with rich colour schemes and his subjects are treated with originality and imagination.

STRACHEY, *stray-chi,* (1) **(Evelyn) John St Loe** (1901–63), English Labour politician, educated at Eton and Magdalen College, Oxford, was Labour M.P. from 1929 until 1931, when he resigned from the Labour Party and gave his support to extremist political organizations. He served in the R.A.F. during World War II and in 1945 became Labour under-secretary for air. His controversial period as minister of food (1946–50) included the food crisis (1947), the unpopular prolongation of rationing, and the abortive Tanganyika ground-nuts and Gambia egg schemes (1947–49). As secretary of state for war (1950–51) he had to contend with the Korean war and the Communist insurrection in Malaya. His numerous books include *The Menace of Fascism* (1933), *The Theory and Practice of Socialism* (1936), *Contemporary Capitalism* (1956), *The Strangled Cry* (1962), &c.

(2) **(Giles) Lytton** (1880–1932), English biographer, was born in London. Educated at Cambridge, he began his writing career as a critic with *Landmarks in French Literature* (1912), which shows clearly his affinities with Sainte-Beuve and his francophile sympathies. *Eminent Victorians* (1918) was a literary bombshell, constituting, as it did, a vigorous, impertinent challenge to Victorian smug self-assurance. The irony, the mordant wit, the ruthless pinpointing of foible that was his method of evoking character, the entire battery of his gifts brought into action to demolish stuffed legendary figures, all combined to make this book a turning-point in the art of biography. After him, pedestrian accumulation of fact (the product of conscientious hacks) could no longer be the accepted thing. Through Strachey, biography had become a literary genre. He followed up his success with *Queen Victoria* (1921), *Books and Characters* (1922), *Elizabeth and Essex* (1928), *Portraits in Miniature* (1931) and *Characters and Commentaries* (1933).

Appreciation of his generosity and catholicity of taste has restored Strachey's reputation, which after his death suffered belittlement. See studies by M. Beerbohm (1943), R. A. Scott-James (1955), C. R. Sanders (1958) and M. Holroyd (2 vols. 1967–68), and J. K. Johnstone, *The Bloomsbury Group* (1954).

STRADELLA, Alessandro (*c.* 1645–81), Italian composer, born in Naples (or Venice). His *San Giovanni Battista* influenced Purcell and Scarlatti. Legend has it that he eloped from Venice to Turin with the mistress of one of the Contarini, who sent assassins to murder him. He was wounded, but recovered. Or, as some say, his would-be murderers found him conducting one of his oratorios, and, touched by the music, allowed him to escape. He was, however, eventually murdered in Genoa. He did not compose *Pietà, Signore.* His legend has furnished the story for operas and Marion Crawford used it for his novel *Stradella* (1909).

STRADIVARI, or Stradivarius, Antonio (*c.* 1644–1737), famous Italian violin maker of Cremona, pupil of Niccolo Amati (q.v.), experimented with the design of string instruments and perfected the Cremona type of violin. His two sons, of two marriages, **Francesco** (1671–1743) and **Omobono** (1679–1742), assisted him. Estimates suggest that he made over a thousand violins, violas and violoncellos in the years 1666–1737. See monographs by H. Petherick (1900) and W. H., A. F. and A. E. Mill (1909).

STRAFFORD, Thomas Wentworth, 1st Earl of (1593–1641), English statesman, was born in London, April 13, of a Yorkshire family with royal connections, studied at St John's College, Cambridge; in 1611 was knighted and married; and having travelled in France and Italy, in 1614 became member for Yorkshire, and succeeded his father in the baronetcy. In 1615 he was appointed *custos rotulorum* for the West Riding, a post from which Buckingham sought two years later to oust him. During James I's reign he was a generally silent member in three brief parliaments, and a frequent attendant at the Court of the Star Chamber. His first wife, a daughter of the Earl of Cumberland, died in 1622, and in 1625 he married a daughter of Lord Clare. Conscious of his own abilities, with no great belief in parliamentary wisdom, loyal in his devotion to crown and church, an eager advocate of domestic reforms, Wentworth in Charles's first parliament (1625) acted with the Opposition; from the second he was excluded by his appointment as sheriff of Yorkshire. In July of that year (1626) he was curtly dismissed from the keepership of the rolls, and for refusing to pay the forced loan was imprisoned. So in the third parliament (1628) he headed the onslaught on the king's ministers. From its meeting in March until May he was the leader of the Lower House; on July 7 the Petition of Right, superseding a similar measure of his own, became law; and on the 22nd he was created Baron Wentworth, in December Viscount Wentworth and President of the North. As such at York he set himself to strengthen government with an efficient militia and ample revenue, and to ' comply with that public and common protection which good kings afford their good people '. Towards these ends he used on occasion high-handed methods, which embroiled him, however, chiefly with the gentry. His second wife died in 1631, leaving a son, William, second Earl of Strafford (1626–95, died *s.p.*), and two daughters; and within a year he married privately the daughter of Sir George Rhodes. In January 1632 he was appointed lord deputy of Ireland, but it was not till July 1633 that he landed at Dublin. He straightway proceeded to coerce Ireland into a state of obedience and well-being, introducing the flax industry, reducing piracy and reconstituting the army. The aim of his policy (he and Laud called it ' Thorough ') was to make his master ' the most absolute prince in Christendom '. Not till 1639 did Wentworth become the king's principal adviser, when he was made Earl of Strafford and lord-lieutenant of Ireland (January 1640). In May 1640 he offered to lead an Irish army against Scotland. It was too late. The rebellion, provoked in Scotland by Charles's unwisdom, was spreading to England; and Pym and his followers judged rightly that Strafford was the one obstacle to their triumph. Strafford was impeached and lodged in the Tower. In the great trial by his peers, which opened in Westminster Hall on March 22, 1641, he defended himself with a fortitude, patience and ability that moved and alarmed his accusers. The twenty-eight charges amounted at most to ' cumulative treason '; the gravest of them, his having counselled the king that ' he had an army in Ireland which he could employ to reduce *this kingdom*' (query England or Scotland), was supported by only one witness, his personal enemy, Vane. Despairing of a conviction by the Lords, the ' inflexibles ' dropped the impeachment for a bill of attainder. It passed a third reading in both Houses; on May 10 it received the royal assent; and Strafford was executed on Tower Hill, May 12, 1641: he is buried at Wentworth-Woodhouse. See Knowler's edition of his *Letters and Correspondence* (1739), with the short Life by Sir George Radcliffe (q.v.); and Lives by W. A. H. C. Gardner (1931), C. V. Wedgwood (1935) and Lord Birkenhead (1938), and study by H. F. Kearney (1959).

STRANG, William (1859–1921), Scottish painter and illustrator, born at Dumbarton, studied at the Slade under Legros and lived all his life in London. His etchings are realistic, but his book illustrations are strongly imaginative. In painting, he was influenced sometimes by the Venetian colourists and sometimes, as in *Bank Holiday* (1912), by Manet. His son Ian (1886–1952) was also a well-known etcher and engraver.

STRANGE, orig. Strang, Sir Robert (1721–92), Scottish line-engraver, was born at Kirkwall, July 14, 1721. He fought on the Stewart side at Prestonpans, Falkirk and Culloden, and in 1747 married a Jacobite, Isabella Lumisden. He studied in Paris and settled in London (1750). He had a European reputation as a historical line-engraver, in opposition to the stippling of his rival, Bartolozzi (q.v.). On a second visit to the Continent (1760–65)

he was made a member of the Academies of Rome, Paris, Florence, Bologna and Parma. He was eventually president of the Academy and was knighted by George III (1787). See his Life by Dennistoun (1855) and that by Woodward prefixed to *Twenty Masterpieces of Strange* (1874).

STRANGFORD, (1) George Augustus Frederick Percy Sydney Smythe, 7th Viscount (1818–57), English author, brother of (3), was one of Disraeli's ' New England ' party. He was member for Canterbury (1841–52), but after 1846 abstained from debate. In 1852, he fought what is said to have been the last duel in England. He wrote articles for the press and *Historic Fancies* (1844).

(2) **Percy Clinton Sydney Smythe, 6th Viscount** (1780–1855), English politician, succeeded in 1801. He was secretary of legation at Lisbon, and ambassador to Portugal, Sweden, Turkey and Russia. He was made Baron Penshurst in 1825. His smooth translation of the *Rimas* of Camoens was published in 1803.

(3) **Percy Ellen Frederick William Smythe, 8th Viscount** (1826–69), English philologist, brother of (1), born at St Petersburg, educated at Harrow and Merton College, Oxford, entered the diplomatic service, early acquired an unexampled command of eastern languages, and was Oriental secretary during the Crimean war. In 1857 he succeeded as eighth and last viscount, thereafter living mostly in London, immersed in philological studies, but wrote little more than a few brilliant *Saturday*, *Pall Mall* and *Quarterly* articles. His *Selected Writings* (1869) and his *Letters and Papers* (1878) were published by his widow. See family history by E. B. de Fonblanque (1877).

STRAPAROLA, Giovan Francesco, -rō'- (d. *c.* 1557), Italian ' novelist ', born at Caravaggio, published in 1550–54 *Piacevoli notti*, a collection of seventy-four stories in the style of the *Decameron*. See Eng. trans. by W. G. Waters (1894).

STRATFORD, John de (d. 1348), English statesman and divine, was Bishop of Winchester (1323). He was closely connected with the deposition of Edward II and was chancellor and principal adviser to Edward III for ten years. He was made Archbishop of Canterbury in 1333.

STRATFORD DE REDCLIFFE, Stratford Canning, 1st Viscount (1786–1880), English diplomat, born in London, was educated at Eton and King's College, Cambridge. In 1807 he became précis writer to his cousin, George Canning, at the Foreign Office; in 1808 first secretary to the Constantinople embassy; and in 1810 minister-plenipotentiary. His duty was to counteract French influence at the Porte, and he negotiated the treaty of Bucharest (1812) between Russia and Turkey. He was minister in Switzerland 1814–17, commissioner at the Vienna Congress of 1815, minister to the United States 1819–23. In 1824 he was sent on a mission to Vienna and St Petersburg, and in 1825 went to Constantinople as ambassador, where he mediated on behalf of Greek independence, but his efforts were frustrated by the battle of Navarino (1827). He resigned in 1828, and was made G.C.B.; in 1831 he was again sent to Constantinople to delimit Greece. When in 1833, after a mission to Portugal, he was gazetted ambassador to St Petersburg the tsar declined to receive him. During the intervals in his diplomatic career he sat in parliament. As ambassador at Constantinople 1842–58 he built up that extraordinary influence which gained him the name of the ' Great Elchi '. He induced the sultan to inaugurate reforms. His peace efforts failed owing to the obstinacy of Nicholas and the weakness of Lord Aberdeen's government. His alleged responsibility for the Crimean war rests on his known determination not to accept Russian protectorate over the Orthodox Christians, and his clear realization that if this could be prevented in no other way, then it was necessary to prepare for war. Created a viscount in 1852, he returned home in 1858, and in 1869 was made K.G. See Lives by S. Lane-Poole (1888), E. F. Malcolm-Smith (1933), and H. W. V. Temperley, *The Crimea* (1936).

STRATHCONA, Donald Alexander Smith, 1st Baron (1820–1914), Canadian statesman, born at Forres, emigrated to Canada and rose from clerk (1838) to governor (1889) of the Hudson's Bay Company. Chief promoter of the Canadian Pacific Railway (completed 1855), he became high commissioner for Canada in London in 1896, and a peer in 1897. See Life by B. Willson (1915), O. D. Stetton, *The Railway Builders* (1916), and J. McAvity, *Lord Strathcona's Horse* (1947).

STRATHNAIRN, Hugh Rose, 1st Baron (1801–85), British soldier, son of the diplomatist Sir George Rose, was born at Berlin. Military attaché to the Turkish army in 1840, he was consul-general for Syria 1841–48, secretary to Lord Stratford de Redcliffe and *chargé d'affaires* at Constantinople in 1852–1854. On the arrival of Menshikoff in 1853, he precipitated a crisis by sending for the British fleet. He was commissioner at French headquarters during the Crimean war. Sent to India in 1857, he virtually reconquered Central India. In 1860 he succeeded Lord Clyde as commander-in-chief in India, held the same post in Ireland 1865–1870, and was made a peer in 1866, a field-marshal in 1877. See Sir O. T. Burne's *Clyde and Strathnairn* (1891).

STRATTON, Charles Sherwood (1838–83), ' General Tom Thumb ', a dwarf 31 inches high, was born at Bridgeport, Conn.

STRATTON-PORTER. See PORTER (7).

STRAUS, Oskar, *shtrows* (1870–1954), Austrian composer, born in Vienna but from 1939 a naturalized French citizen. A pupil of Bruch, he is best known for his many operettas and comic operas, such as *Waltz Dream* (1907) and *The Chocolate Soldier* (1908, from Shaw's *Arms and the Man*). He was the composer of the music for the film *La Ronde*. See Life by Grun (1955).

STRAUSS, *shtrows,* (1) **David Friedrich** (1808–74), German theologian, born at Ludwigsburg in Württemberg, studied for the church at Tübingen, where in 1832 he became *repetent* in the theological seminary, lecturing also on philosophy in the university as a

disciple of Hegel. In his *Leben Jesu* (1835; trans. by George Eliot, 1846) he sought to prove the gospel history to be a collection of myths, and by an analytical dissection of each separate narrative to detect a nucleus of historical truth free from every trace of supernaturalism. The book marks an epoch in New Testament criticism and raised a storm of controversy. Strauss, dismissed from his post at Tübingen, in 1839 was called to be professor of Dogmatics and Church History at Zürich; but the appointment provoked such opposition that it had to be dropped. His second great work followed, *Die christliche Glaubenslehre*, a review of Christian dogma (1840–41). A new *Life of Jesus, composed for the German People* (1864; trans. 1865), attempts to reconstruct a positive life of Christ. In *Der alte und der neue Glaube* (1872) Strauss endeavours to prove that Christianity as a system of religious belief is dead, and that a new faith must be built up out of art and the scientific knowledge of nature. He also wrote several biographies, notably that of Ulrich von Hutten (trans. 1874) and lectures on Voltaire (1870). He separated from his wife, the opera singer Agnese Schebest (1813–70). See Life by Zeller (trans. 1874), and works by Hausrath (1878), Eck, Harräus and Ziegler (1909), and an appreciation of his critical work by A. Schweitzer in *The Quest of the Historical Jesus* (1910).
(2) **Johann, ' the elder '** (1804–49), Viennese violinist and conductor, as were his sons **Eduard** (1835–1916) and **Josef** (1827–70). founded with Lanner (in whose quartet he played for a while) the Viennese Waltz tradition, a development from Schubert. He toured extensively in Europe with his own orchestra, played during Queen Victoria's coronation festivities (1838) in London, composed the *Radetzky March* (1848) in honour of the general, and numerous waltzes including the *Lorelei* and the *Donaulieder*, but was eclipsed by his son (3).
(3) **Johann, ' the younger '** (1825–99), Viennese violinist, conductor and composer, born October 25, son of (2), who made him take up law, began to flout his father's wishes from 1844 when he appeared as a young conductor and composer of promise. He toured with his own orchestra and appeared in London in 1869 and visited the United States in 1872. His waltzes, which number over 400, are more full-blooded, more melodious and tasteful than his father's, and although they often seem to be written purely for the violin, Strauss showed in his introduction to *Wine, Women and Song* (1869) and in *Perpetuum Mobile* that the art of orchestration was not by any means beyond him. The best known include that symbol of romantic Vienna, *The Blue Danube, Artist's Life* (both 1867), *Tales from the Vienna Woods* (1868), *Voices of Spring* (1882) and *The Emperor* (1888). He also wrote a number of operettas, including *Die Fledermaus* (1874) and *A Night in Venice* (1883). He died in Vienna June 3, 1899. See study by H. E. Jacob (1940).
(4) **Richard** (1864–1949), German composer, son of the first horn player in the court

opera in Munich, where he was born. He began to compose at the age of six, and his first publications date from his eleventh year. In 1882 he entered Munich University, but began musical studies in Berlin in the following year, and shortly afterwards became assistant conductor to von Bülow at Meiningen. There he was converted from the school of Brahms, under whose influence his early compositions had been written, to that of Wagner and Liszt, composing his first symphonic poems and succeeding von Bülow in 1885. After a period (1886–89) as assistant conductor at the Munich opera he moved to Weimar, and was invited by Cosima Wagner to conduct at Bayreuth in 1891. His first opera, *Guntram*, was produced at Weimar in 1894 and in the same year Strauss became conductor of the Berlin Philharmonic Orchestra. *Salome*, his opera upon a German translation of Oscar Wilde's play, produced in 1905, led to his concentration upon opera, and *Elektra* (1909) began the collaboration with the dramatic poet Hugo v. Hofmannsthal which produced much of Strauss's best work for the theatre, including the popular *Der Rosenkavalier* (1911) and *Ariadne auf Naxos* (1912). His work with Stefan Zweig upon *Die schweigsame Frau* led him into difficulties with the Nazi government, which had previously appointed him president of the Reichsmusikkammer, a post which he resigned; his commanding position at the head of German musical life protected him from serious political persecution, and, active to the end of his life, he worked on two operas with Josef Gregor. After the completion of *Capriccio*, his final opera, he ended his career with a series of small-scale orchestral works. See Life by W. S. Mann (1954), and studies by Newman (1908), Blom (1930), Armstrong (1931) and Del Mar (1962).

STRAVINSKY, Igor Fedorovich, *-vin'-* (1882–1971), Russian composer, born at Oranienbaum near St Petersburg, June 18, studied law but soon turned to musical composition under Rimsky-Korsakov, whose influence pervades his first symphony in E flat (1907). But it was with the Diaghilev ballet that Stravinsky leapt to fame with the glittering and enchanting music for *The Firebird* (1910). A second ballet, *Petrushka* (1911), consolidated his international reputation. Originally it was intended as a purely orchestral piece, characterized by harmonic warfare between solo pianoforte and the orchestra, but on Diaghilev's suggestion Stravinsky made it into a ballet of puppet drama. His masterful handling of the eternal triangle theme has had a greater influence on modern music than his deliberately violent, chaotic musical protrayal of the primitive *The Rite of Spring* (1913), which infringes every canon of harmony, yet somehow achieves a strange integration. The Hans Andersen opera, *The Nightingale* (1914), was followed by the wartime 'shoe-string' entertainments, *Renard* (1917) and *The Soldier's Tale* (1918), which aptly illustrate Stravinsky's adaptability. Essentially an experimenter, he then plunged headlong into neoclassicism. The ballets *Pulcinella* (1920) based on Pergolesi, *Apollo Musagetes* (1928),

The Card Game (1937), *Orpheus* (1948) and the austere *Agon* (1957), using Schönberg's 12-tone system, exemplify this trend, no less than the opera-oratorio *Oedipus Rex* (1927) based on a Jean Cocteau version but translated into Latin for greater dignity, and the magnificent choral *Symphony of Psalms* (1930) 'composed to the glory of God'. Stravinsky settled in France (1934) and finally in the U.S. (1945). Other characteristic and outstanding works include the *Symphonies of Wind Instruments*, dedicated to Debussy (1921), the *Symphony in C major* (1940), the opera *The Rake's Progress* (1951) for which Auden helped to write the libretto, and the serial-music *In Memoriam Dylan Thomas* (1954), for voice, string quartet and four trombones, *The Flood* (1962), a musical play, *Elegy for J. F. K.* (1964), for voice and clarinets, *Variations* (1965) for orchestra in memory of Aldous Huxley, and *Requiem Canticles* (1966), for voice and orchestra. In 1939, he was Charles Eliot Norton professor of Poetry at Harvard and in 1954 was awarded the gold medal of the Royal Philharmonic Society. See his *Chronicles of My Life* (1936) and *The Poetics of Music*, and studies, ed. M. Armitage (N.Y. 1946), E. W. White (1947), ed. Corle (N.Y. 1949), Lederman (ed.), *Stravinsky in the Theatre* (1951), Life by Vlad (trans. 1960), *Conversations*, I. Stravinsky and R. Craft (3 vols. 1959–62), and White, *The Composer and His Works* (1966). His son, **Sviatoslav Soulima** (1910–), is also pianist, composer and teacher.

STRAWSON, Peter Frederick (1919–), English philosopher, fellow of University College, Oxford (1948–68), and of Magdalen College from 1968. He became Waynflete professor of Metaphysical Philosophy at Oxford in 1968. Strawson applied Wittgensteinian doctrines in his standard work, *Introduction to Logical Theory* (1952), in which he demonstrated the impossibility of justifying induction and in which he ably defended ' informal ' logic against Quine and Russell, whose theory of description he attacked in an article in *Mind* (1950) ' On Referring ', showing that whereas a sentence could be meaningless or significant, only a statement could be classified as true or false. His *Individuals* (1959) tackles the conceptual problems involved in these the fundamentals of human thought. *The Bounds of Sense* appeared in 1966.

STREET, George Edmund (1824–81), British architect, born at Woodford, Essex; an assistant of Sir George Gilbert Scott (q.v.), he restored Christ Church in Dublin, designed the London Law Courts, and wrote *Architecture of N. Italy* (1855) and *Gothic Architecture in Spain* (1865). See Memoirs by his son (1888), by G. G. King (1917).

STREICHER, Julius, *strīkH'ēr* (1885–1946), German journalist and politician, born in Bavaria. He was associated with Hitler in the early days of the National Socialist party, taking part in the 1923 putsch. A ruthless persecutor of the Jews, he incited anti-Semitism through the newspaper *Der Stürmer*, which he founded and edited, and of which copies were widely displayed in prominent red boxes throughout the Reich.

He was hanged at Nuremberg as a war criminal.

STRESEMANN, Gustav, *shtray'zĕ-man* (1878–1929), German statesman, born in Berlin. Entering the Reichstag in 1907 as a National Liberal, he rose to become leader of that party, and after the first World War founded and led its successor, the German People's party. He was chancellor of the new German (Weimar) Republic for a few months in 1923, when, and as minister of foreign affairs (1923–29), he pursued a policy of conciliation, and in 1925 negotiated the Locarno Pact of mutual security with Aristide Briand and Austen Chamberlain. He secured the entry of Germany into the League of Nations in 1926, and shared with Briand the Nobel peace prize for that year. See the biography by A. Vallentin (trans. E. Sutton, 1931) and study by Gatzke (1954).

STREUVELS, Stijn, *stræ'-* (1871–), pen-name of **Frank Lateur,** Flemish writer, until 1905 a baker near Courtrai. His novels of peasant life are masterpieces of Flemish literature. See his *Path of Life* (trans. 1915).

STRIJDOM, Johannes Gerhardus, *strī'dom* (1893–1958), South African statesman, born at Willowmore, Cape Province. He was educated at Stellenbosch and Pretoria, and after a start as a farmer, took up law practice in the Transvaal. Elected M.P. for Waterberg in 1929 he became leader of the extremists in the National party. His two main political ends were native apartheid and the setting up of an Afrikaner Republic outside the Commonwealth. He was prime minister of South Africa from 1954 until shortly before his death.

STRINDBERG, Johan August (1849–1912), Swedish dramatist, born at Stockholm, studied at Uppsala University and settled in Stockholm as a writer. His own unstable personality, three unsuccessful marriages and the critical society around him are reflected in his subjective works against the background of whatever ' ism ' was momentarily holding his attention, for he ranged through realism, naturalism, mysticism, romanticism, and even a hint of expressionism. Novels, plays, critical essays, scientific preoccupations, painting, all laid claim to his time. From his first play, the historical *Mäster Olof* (1872), and in works such as *Hemsöborna* (1887) ' The People of Hemsö ' (trans. 1959), one of the classic novels of Swedish literature, he poured out his views on the social problems of his time. Particularly was he obsessed by a hatred of the idea of emancipation for women and much of his work is vitiated by his misogynist bias, as also by his exasperated sensibilities exploding into violent diatribe or sinking into profoundly mournful brooding. He first achieved fame with his novel *Röda Rummet* (1879), a satire on the art circles of Stockholm, and he followed this up with the plays *Gillets Hemlighet* (1880), *Lycko-Pers Resa* (1882) and *Herr Bengts Hustru* (1882). He sojourned in France, Switzerland and Denmark and published his *Giftas I* and *II* (1884–86), collections of short stories, which led to his recall to Sweden (1884) to stand trial for alleged blasphemy. He next set to work on his autobiography—*Tjänstekvinnans*

son (1886) ' The Son of a Servant ' (trans. 1913), a piece of self-revelation of audacious candour. . He continued to write short stories, but his ideas began to take shape in play form again and *Fadren* (1887) and *Fröken Julie* (1888) brought him to the forefront as the exponent of naturalistic drama. Further reminiscences *Inferno* (1897) and *Legender* (1898), carry on his autobiography. In 1901 appeared *Dödsdansen* ' The Dance of Death ' (trans 1929), followed by historical dramas, miracle plays and ' fairy ' pieces which led him finally to what he called ' chamber plays ' written for his *Intimate Theatre*, which he founded in 1907. His work suffers from his own self-contradictions, which obscured the social problems he was dramatizing. Nevertheless, in terms of imaginative power he ranks high after Ibsen, a major figure in west European literature. See Collected Works (55 vols. 1912–20), and studies by N. Erdmann (Stockholm 1920), K. Jaspers (1922), V. J. McGill (1930), A. Jolivet (Paris 1931), E. M. S. Sprigge (1949) and B. M. E. Mortensen and B. W. Downs (1949).

STRODE, (1) Ralph (fl. 14th cent.), English scholastic philosopher, was fellow of Merton College, Oxford (*c.* 1360), and a colleague of John Wycliffe, whose doctrine of predestination he attacked. Chaucer dedicated to him and to the poet John Gower, his *Troylus and Cryseyde*. Of his works, *Logica* has been lost but *Consequentiae* and *Obligationes* are extant.

(2) **William** (1602–45), English poet and divine, born at Plympton, educated at Westminster and Christ Church College, Oxford, where he became canon and public orator. He is best known for his elegies and lyric verse which were rediscovered by Dobell in 1907 and for his tragi-comedy, *The Floating Island*, acted by the students of Christ Church before Charles I in 1636.

STROHEIM, Erich von, *-hīm* (1886–1957), Austrian film director and actor, born in Vienna, served in the Austrian army and in 1916 appeared in the American film, *Intolerance*. His first success as film director was with *Blind Husbands* (1919), which was followed by the classic film *Greed* (1923), the war film *The Wedding March* (1927), &c. Later he returned to film acting as ' Rommel ' in *Desert Fox*. See monograph by J. M. Finler (1967).

STROMEYER, Friedrich (1776–1835), German chemist, born in Göttingen, and professor of Chemistry there, was the discoverer of cadmium in 1817.

STRONG, Leonard Alfred George (1896–1958), British novelist and poet, of Irish extraction on his mother's side, born at Plymouth, was educated at Brighton College and Wadham College, Oxford, took up school teaching until he established a reputation as a lyric poet and author of *Dewer Rides* (1929), a macabre novel set in Dartmoor. The element of cruelty survived in *The Brothers* (1932). His collected poems appeared under *The Body's Imperfections* (1957). He also wrote a study of James Joyce (1950) and a Life of the singer John McCormack (1949). His collection of short stories, *Travellers*, won the James Tait Black memorial prize (1945). See his autobiographical *Green Memory* (1960).

STRONGBOW, name by which **Richard de Clare, 2nd Earl of Pembroke** (c. 1130–1176), was known. He succeeded to estates in Normandy and Wales and in 1170 crossed to Ireland by permission of Henry II to give military help to Dermot, King of Leinster, whose daughter he married. He offered his Irish conquests to Henry to appease the latter's jealousy of his success.

STROUD, William, *strowd* (1860–1938), English physicist and inventor, born in Bristol. From 1885 to 1909 he was Cavendish professor of Physics at Leeds, where began his long association with Archibald Barr (q.v.).

STROZZI, *strot'see,* a noble Italian family which figured prominently in the Florentine renaissance. Important members include:
(1) **Filippo the Elder** (1428–91), having been deprived by the Medici, was exiled to Sicily but returned in 1466. He began building the famous Palazzo Strozzi in 1489.
(2) **Filippo the Younger** (1489–1538), was prominent in the revolt which overthrew the Medici in 1527, but the republic then established lasted only three years. The restored Medici, Alessandro, having been assassinated in 1537, Filippo judged the time opportune to launch an attack on his successor Cosimo, but was captured and executed.
(3) **Palla** (1372–1462), promoted Greek studies in Florence and founded the first public library there.
(4) **Pietro** (d. 1558), Italian soldier, fought the Medici, escaped to France and was made a marshal of France by Henry II in 1556 after campaigns in Italy. He found out the weaknesses of the defences of Calais before its capture by Guise in 1558, and was killed at the siege of Thionville.

STRUENSEE, Johann Friedrich, Count, *shtrün'zay* (1737–72), German-born Danish statesman, son of a Halle pastor, in 1768 became physician to Christian VII of Denmark. He soon gained the confidence of the weak young king and of his consort, Caroline Matilda (1751–75), George III's sister, and, with her monopolizing all power, sought to free Denmark from Russian influence and to find an ally in Sweden. His reforms and retrenchments were unpopular; but it was solely by a court intrigue that in January 1772 the queen and her new-made count were arrested. From both a confession of criminal intimacy was extorted; and Struensee, found guilty of treason, was beheaded. Queen Caroline's marriage was dissolved; she was conveyed by a British frigate to Hanover, and died at Zell (Celle). See *Memoirs* (1849) of Sir R. M. Keith, British envoy; Wraxall's *Life of Queen Caroline* (1864); and Wilkins, *A Queen of Tears* (1903).

STRUTHER, Jan, pseud. of Mrs Joyce Anstruther Piaczek (1901–53), English writer, born in London. Her most successful creation was Mrs Miniver, whose activities, first narrated in articles to *The Times*, became the subject of one of the best films of World War II. Miss Struther's writings were varied in character and included hymns, verse,

short stories and novels, all exhibiting considerable talent but little originality. Her books of verse include *Betsinda Dances* (1931) and *The Glassblower* (1940).

STRUTT, (1) **Jedediah** (1726–97), English cotton spinner and inventor, born at Blackwell, Derbyshire. With his brother-in-law, William Woollatt, he patented (1758–59) a machine which, fixed to a stocking-frame, made possible the manufacture of ribbed goods. In 1771 he was joined in partnership by Richard Arkwright (q.v.). See R. S. Fitton and A. P. Wadsworth, *The Strutts and the Arkwrights, 1758–1830* (1959).
(2) **John William.** See RAYLEIGH (1).
(3) **Joseph** (1742–1802), English antiquary and engraver, born at Springfield in Essex, at fourteen was apprenticed to an engraver, studied at the Royal Academy, and from 1771 devoted himself to research at the British Museum. He published *Regal and Ecclesiastical Antiquities of England* (1773); *Chronicle of England*, down to the Conquest (1777–78); *Dictionary of Engravers* (1785–1786); *Dresses of the People of England* (1796–99); and, his best-known work, *Sports and Pastimes of the People of England* (1801; enlarged 1903). See Life by Miller-Christy (1898).

STRUVE, *shtroo've*, (1) **Friedrich Georg Wilhelm** (1793–1864), German astronomer, father of (2), grandfather of (3), born at Altona, became director of the Dorpat observatory in 1817, and in 1839 of Pulkova near St Petersburg, which was constructed to his specifications through the patronage of Tsar Nicholas. He made important observations of double stars, carried out one of the first determinations of stellar distance and several geodetic operations.
(2) **Otto Wilhelm** (1819–1905), German astronomer, son of (1), born at Dorpat, succeeded his father at Pulkova, discovered 500 double stars, and in 1847 a satellite of Uranus, and studied the rings of Saturn. His son **Hermann** (1854–1920) was director of the Berlin observatory (1904) and superintended its transfer to Babelsberg. He made micrometric observations of the satellites of Mars, Neptune and Saturn. Another son, **Ludwig** (1858–1920), was professor of Astronomy at Kharkov and investigated the proper motion of the solar system. Ludwig's son **Otto** (1897–1963) became a U.S. citizen and director of the Yerkes and McDonald observatories (1932).
(3) **Peter Berngardovich** (1870–1944), Russian political economist, grandson of (1), born in Perm, as a leading Marxist wrote *Critical Observations on the Problem of Russia's Economic Development* (1894), which Lenin attacked for its 'revisionism'. He edited several political magazines with Liberal tendencies, was professor at the St Petersburg Polytechnic (1907–17), was closely connected with the 'White' movement in South Russia, after the revolution and after 1925 lived in exile in Belgrade and Paris, where he died during the Nazi occupation. Perhaps the greatest Russian economist, his principal work is *Economy and Price* (1913–1916). See S. Hoare, *The Fourth Seal* (1930),

and Bernard Pares, *My Russian Memoirs* (1931).

STRYDOM. See STRIJDOM.

STRYPE, John (1643–1737), English ecclesiastical historian, born in London, was educated at St Paul's School and Cambridge, and became curate of Low Leyton, Essex. His prolix and reliable, if ill-arranged, works (19 vols., Clar. Press edn., 1812–24) include *Memorials of Cranmer* (1694); Lives of Bishop Aylmer (1701), Sir John Cheke (1705), Archbishop Grindal (1710), Archbishop Parker (1711), and Archbishop Whitgift (1718); *Annals of the Reformation* (1709–31); *Ecclesiastical Memorials, 1513–58* (1721). He also completely re-edited and enlarged Stow's *Survey of London* (1720).

STUART (noble family). See STEWART and ALBANIE.

STUART, (1) Gilbert Charles (1755–1828), American painter, born at Narragansett, Rhode Island, in 1772 came to Edinburgh with a Scottish painter, Cosmo Alexander, but on the latter's death worked his passage home, and began to paint portraits at Newport. In 1775 he made his way to London, where he endured much hardship till in 1778 his talent was recognized by West, and he became a fashionable portrait painter in the manner of Reynolds. In 1792 he returned to America, and painted portraits of Washington, Jefferson, Madison and John Adams. He died at Boston. He is well represented in the National Portrait Gallery, London. See Lives by G. C. Mason (1879), L. Park (1926) and J. H. Morgan (1936).

(2) **James** (1713–88), English architect, born in London, known as the 'Athenian Stuart' for his drawings and measurements with Nicholas Revett of the *Antiquities of Athens* (1762–1814). He also rebuilt the interior of the chapel of Greenwich Hospital (1779), &c.

(3) **John McDouall** (1815–66), Scottish-born Australian explorer, born at Dysart, Fife, accompanied Captain Sturt's expedition (1844–45), made six expeditions into the interior (1858–62), and in 1860 traversed Australia from south to north. Mount Stuart is named after him. See Life by M. S. Webster (1959).

(4) **Lady Louisa** (1757–1851), Sir Walter Scott's witty correspondent, the Earl of Bute's youngest daughter. See Life by S. Buchan (1932).

(5) **Marie Pauline Rose.** See BLAZE DE BURY.

(6) **Moses** (1780–1852), American theologian, born at Wilton, Conn., studied at Yale, was professor of Sacred Literature at Andover (1810–48). He published Hebrew grammars, commentaries on the Old Testament, &c.

STUBBES, (1) John (c. 1541–91), English Puritan pamphleteer, kinsman of (2), educated at Cambridge and Lincoln's Inn, wrote an answer to Cardinal Allen's *Defence of the English Catholics* and *The Discoverie of a Gaping Gulf* (1579), against the marriage of Elizabeth with the Duke of Anjou, for which he and his printer had their right hands struck off. He died in France.

(2) **Philip** (d. 1593), English Puritan pamphleteer, kinsman of (1), was author of the *Anatomie of Abuses* (1583), a vehement denunciation of the luxury of the times. The work was reprinted by Turnbull in 1836, and by Furnivall (1879–82).

STUBBS, (1) George (1724–1806), English anatomist, painter of animals, and engraver, born at Liverpool. He studied and taught anatomy at York Hospital, and in 1754 travelled in Italy and Morocco. In 1766 he published his monumental *Anatomy of the Horse*, illustrated by his own engravings. He was best known for his sporting pictures, and excelled in painting horses. One of his noted works is his picture of *The Grosvenor Hunt*. In 1780 he was elected A.R.A., and R.A. in 1781. See Life by Gilbey (1898), and Memoir by Mayer (1876). His son, George Townley (1756–1815), was also an engraver.

(2) **William** (1825–1901), English historian, born at Knaresborough, studied at Ripon and Christ Church, Oxford. He became a fellow of Trinity, vicar of Navestock, Essex (1850), diocesan inspector of schools (1860), Oxford regius professor of Modern History (1866), rector of Cholderton, Wilts (1875), a canon of St Paul's (1879), and Bishop of Chester (1884), of Oxford (1889). His chief works are *Registrum Sacrum Anglicanum*, on the Episcopal succession in England (1858); Mosheim's *Institutes*, revised (1863); *Select Charters*, from the earliest period to the reign of Edward I (1870); the monumental three-volume *Constitutional History of England*, down to 1485 (1874–78), which put the study of English constitutional origins on a firm basis; *The Early Plantagenets* (1876); and a number of volumes for the 'Rolls Series'. With Haddan, he began a collection of *British Councils and Ecclesiastical Documents* (1869–78). See his *Letters* (1904).

STUCKENBERG, Viggo (1863–1905), Danish poet, born at Copenhagen, was an important figure in the lyrical revival of the 1890s. His works include *Fagre Ord* (1895), *Flyvende Sommer* (1898), &c.

STUKELEY, William, the 'Archdruid' (1687–1765), British antiquarian, was born at Holbeach. M.B. and M.D. (Cantab.), in 1729 took orders, and in 1747 became a London rector. His twenty works (1720–26) include records of his valuable and objective fieldwork at Stonehenge and Avebury, but are marred by his later fantastic speculations. He was the dupe of the brilliant 'Richard of Cirencester' forgeries. See his *Diary and Correspondence* (Surtees Soc. 1884–87), and Life by Piggott (1950).

STURDEE, Sir Frederick Charles Doveton, 1st Bart. (1859–1925), British sailor, entered the navy in 1871, commanded the squadron which wiped out the German squadron under von Spee off the Falkland Islands, December 8, 1914, was created baronet, served at the battle of Jutland and was promoted admiral of the fleet (1921).

STURE, stoo´rě, name of a Swedish family which during 1470–1520, when Sweden was nominally united with Denmark, gave it three wise and patriotic regents—Sten Sture the Elder (d. 1503); his nephew, Svante Nilsson

Sture (d. 1512); and his son, Sten Sture the Younger (d. 1520).

STURGE, Joseph (1794–1859), English Quaker philanthropist and Radical, born at Elberton, became a corn merchant in Birmingham and a prominent campaigner against slavery, the Corn Laws, the Crimean war and for Chartism, adult suffrage, &c. See Lives by H. Richard (1864) and S. Hobhouse (1919).

STURGEON, William (1783–1850), English scientist, born at Whittington, North Lancashire, became a shoemaker's apprentice and in 1825 constructed the first practical electromagnet, the first moving-coil galvanometer (1836) and various electromagnetic machines. His *Annals of Electricity* (1836) was the first journal of its kind in Britain.

STURLASON. See SNORRI.

STURM, (1) Jacques Charles François, *stürm* (1803–55), French mathematician, born at Geneva, died, an Academician, in Paris. He discovered the theorem named after him concerning the real roots of an equation. With Colladon, in 1826, he measured the velocity of sound in water by means of a bell submerged in Lake Geneva.

(2) Johannes, *shtoorm* (1507–89), German educationist, born at Schleiden near Aix-la-Chapelle, from the Liège school of the Brethren of the Common Life went to Louvain University, and at Paris in 1530 lectured on Cicero. He favoured the Reformation, and in 1536 was invited by Strasbourg to reorganize the education of the town. Both in religion and politics Sturm took a prominent part, siding with Zwingli against Luther; and he was sent on missions to France, England and Denmark. Through his efforts, Strasbourg became a great educational centre. In 1538 a gymnasium was established, with Sturm as its rector, and in 1564 an academy, the two together supplying a complete course of instruction. In 1581 he was driven from Strasbourg by Lutheran intolerance, but was ultimately permitted to return. See French monograph by Charles Schmidt (Strasbourg 1855), and German works by Laas (1872), Kückelhahn (1872), Heil (1888) and Schnud (1889).

STURT, Charles (1795–1869), British explorer, went as an army captain to Australia, and during 1828–45 headed three important expeditions, discovered the Darling (1828), the lower Murray (1830). Blinded by hardship and exposure, he received in 1851 a pension from the first South Australian parliament. He wrote two narratives of his explorations (1833–48), and died at Cheltenham, England. See Life by N. G. Sturt (1899).

STUYVESANT, Peter, *sti'-* (1592–1672), Dutch administrator, born in Holland, became governor of Curaçao and lost a leg in the attack on St Martin in 1644. As director from 1646 of New Netherland colony (later New York), he proved a vigorous but arbitrary ruler, a rigid sabbatarian, and an opponent of political and religious freedom. Yet he did much for the commercial prosperity of New Amsterdam (later New York city) until his reluctant surrender to the English in 1664. See Life by B. Tuckerman (N.Y. 1893).

STYLITES. See SIMEON STYLITES.

SUAREZ, Francisco de, *swah'reth* (1584–1617), Spanish-Jewish Jesuit theologian and scholastic philosopher, born at Granada, taught theology at Segovia, Valladolid, Rome, Alcala, Salamanca and Coimbra. A Molinist in his views of grace, he foreshadowed in his *Tractatus de Legibus* (1612) the modern doctrine of international law, and wrote the *Defensio Fidei* (1613), a treatise condemning the extravagant divine-right theories of James I of England. See Lives by Deschamps (1671), Werner (1861) and Fichter (1940).

SUCHET, Louis Gabriel, Duc d'Albufera, *sü-shay* (1770–1826), French soldier, born at Lyons, fought in Italy and Egypt and was made a general. He checked an Austrian invasion of the south of France (1800), took part in the campaigns against Austria (1805) and Prussia (1806), and as generalissimo of the French army in Aragon reduced the province to submission, defeating Blake outside Saragossa and again at Belchite, and securing a marshal's baton. He captured Tortosa in 1811, in 1812 destroyed Blake's army at Sagunto, and by his capture of Valencia earned the title of Duc d'Albufera. He was created a peer of France by Louis XVIII, but joined Napoleon on his return from Elba. Deprived of his peerage after Waterloo, he did not return to court till 1819. See his *Mémoires sur les campagnes en Espagne* (1829–34), and Life by Barault-Roullon (1954).

SUCRE, Antonio José de, *soo'kray* (1793–1830), South American soldier-patriot, born in Cumana, Venezuela, was Bolívar's lieutenant and first president (1826) of Bolivia, which he freed. He resigned in 1828, took service with Colombia, winning the battle of Giron (1829) and was assassinated on his way home from the Colombian Congress, of which he had been president. See Life by G. A. Sherwell (1924).

SUDERMANN, Hermann, *soo'-* (1857–1928), German dramatist and novelist, born at Matzicken, East Prussia, wrote a succession of skilful, if superficial, realist plays, *Die Ehre* (1889), *Sodoms Ende* (1891), *Heimat* (1893; English version, *Magda*), &c., and equally successful novels, including *Frau Sorge* (1887), *Der Katzensteg* (1890), *Es war* (1894), &c.

SUE, (Marie Joseph) Eugène, *sü* (1804–57), French novelist, born in Paris, served as surgeon in Spain (1823) and at Navarino Bay (1827) and wrote a vast number of Byronic novels, many of which were dramatized, idealizing the poor to the point of melodramatic absurdity, but nevertheless highly successful at the time and a profound influence upon Victor Hugo, whose *Les Misérables* has much in common with Sue's *Les Mystères de Paris* (1843). Other novels include *Le Juif errant* (1845), *Les Sept Péchés capitaux* (1849) and *Les Mystères du peuple* (1849), the last condemned as immoral and seditious. A republican deputy, he was driven into exile in 1851 and died at Annecy. See Life by E. de Mirecourt (1858), and study by N. Atkinson (1929).

SUESS, Eduard, *züs* (1831–1914), Austrian geologist, founder of the 'new geology', was born in London, became professor of

Geology at Vienna 1857–1901. Of his works, *Das Antlitz der Erde* (1885–1909; trans. as *The Face of the Earth*, 1904–10) was the most important. He was a Radical politician, an economist, an educationist, a geographer, and sat in the Austrian Lower House.

SUETONIUS, Gaius Suetonius Tranquillus (A.D. 75–160), Roman biographer and antiquarian, became Hadrian's secretary, a post he held till about fifty, when, compromised in a court intrigue, he forfeited it. His best-known work is *The Lives of the First Twelve Caesars*, remarkable for terseness, elegance and impartiality. Other works were *De Illustribus Grammaticis* (of which a complete copy existed in the 15th century), *De Claris Rhetoribus*, and fragmentary lives of Terence, Horace, Persius, Lucan, Juvenal and Pliny, a friend of his.

SUETONIUS PAULINUS. See BOADICEA.

SUFFOLK. See BRANDON and POLE (1).

SUFFREN SAINT TROPEZ, Pierre André de, *süf-frã sī trō-pay* (1729–88), French sailor, a younger son of a Provençal noble, entered the French navy, fought in the action with the English off Toulon (1744) and in the vain attempt to retake Cape Breton (1746), was captured by Hawke next year, and served six years in Malta amongst the Knights Hospitallers. He was again captured in Boscawen's destruction of the Toulon fleet (1759), took part in the bombardment of Sallee (1765), was again four years in Malta, and returned to France as captain in 1772. In 1777 he sailed to America, and fought at Grenada in 1779. After an action at the Cape Verde Islands, he fought a series of engagements with the English off Madras and Ceylon, and captured Trincomalee. Returning to Paris in 1784, he was received with great honours. See Laughton's *Naval Studies* (1887).

SUGDEN, Samuel (1892–1950), English chemist, born at Leeds, was professor at Birkbeck College (1932) and University College London (1937). He did original work on molecular volumes and surface tension and introduced the *parachor*.

SUGER, *sü-zhay* (c. 1081–1151), French prelate, abbot of St Denis from 1122, carried out substantial reforms and rebuilt its church in the Gothic style, the first building to be so done. Louis VI and Louis VII employed him on a number of missions, and during the latter's absence on the second crusade, Suger was one of the regents. His Life of Louis VI (ed H. Waquet, 1929) is valuable for the view it affords of the time. See his writings on the church of St Denis and its art treasures, trans. Panofsky (1946).

SUGGIA, Guilhermina, *sood'ja* (1888–1950), Portuguese cellist, born in Oporto. She was a member of the Oporto City Orchestra at the age of twelve, and aided by a royal grant, she subsequently studied at Leipzig and under Casals, whom she married in 1906. After extensive concert tours she settled in England in 1914, last appearing in public at the 1949 Edinburgh Festival.

SUHRAWARDY, Husein Shaheed (1893–1963), Pakistani politician, born in East Bengal and educated at Oxford. In 1921 he became a member of the Bengal Assembly.

He was Pakistan's minister of law (1954–55) and prime minister (1956–57).

SUIDAS, *swee'das*, the reputed author of an encyclopaedic Greek *Lexicon*, about whom nothing is known, although he is placed about A.D. 975.

SUK, Joseph, *sook* (1875–1935), Czech composer and violinist, studied in Prague under Dvořák, whose daughter he married, and carried on the master's romantic tradition by his violin *Fantaisie* (1903), the symphonic poem *Prague* and particularly by his deeply-felt second symphony, *Asrael* (1905), in which he mourned the deaths of his master and of his wife. He was for forty years a member of the Czech Quartet and in 1922 became professor of Composition in the Prague Conservatoire.

SUKARNO, Achmad (1902–70), Indonesian statesman, born in Surabaya, Eastern Java, was early identified with the movement for independence, forming the Partai National Indonesia in 1927. He was freed by the Japanese and became the first president of the Indonesian Republic in 1945. The tremendous popularity of ' Bung Karno ' with the people was gradually eroded as Indonesia suffered increasing internal chaos and poverty, while Sukarno and his government laid themselves open to charges of corruption. His protestations of political ' neutralism ' were offset by his increasingly virulent anti-Western foreign policy. The abortive Communist coup of 1965 led to student riots and Congress criticism of Sukarno's alleged part in it, and the army eventually took over. Sukarno's absolute powers were gradually weakened until finally in 1967 General Suharto took complete control, Sukarno remaining president in name only. See studies by Gerbrandy (1950), Woodman (1955) and Hughes (1968).

SULAIMAN, *sü-lay-man'*, name of three sultans of Turkey:

Sulaiman I (d. 1411), eldest son of Bajazet I, ruled in Adrianople from 1403.

Sulaiman I or II, ' the Magnificent ' (1494–1566), sultan from 1520, son of Sultan Selim I, added to his dominions by conquest Belgrade, Budapest, Rhodes, Tabriz, Baghdad, Aden and Algiers. He fought a war with Venice, and his fleets dominated the Mediterranean, although he failed to capture Malta. He died during the siege of Szigeth in his war with Austria. His system of laws regulating land tenure earned him the name, *Kanuni*, the lawgiver. He was devoted to ' Roxelana ', his Russian consort, was a great patron of arts, wrote poetry and employed Selim Sinan to build such architectural masterpieces as the four mosques to himself and to members of his family in Constantinople. He was the greatest of the sultans. See histories of the Ottoman Empire by H. A. Gibbons (1916), W. Miller (1927).

Sulaiman II or III (1641–91), sultan from 1687, was defeated by the Austrians, but through Mustafa Kuprili introduced many liberal reforms.

SULEIMAN PASHA, *soo-lī'man* (1838–92), Turkish general, entered the army in 1854, fought in Montenegro, Crete and Yemen, and in peace taught in the Military Academy at Constantinople, of which he became director. He distinguished himself against the Serbians in 1876. When the Russians declared war (1877) Suleiman checked them at Eski Zagra, but destroyed his army in heroic attempts to force them from the Shipka Pass. In October he became commander-in-chief of the army of the Danube, but suffered defeat near Philippopolis (January 1878). Court-martialled, he was condemned to fifteen years' imprisonment, but the sultan pardoned him.

SULLA (inaccurately **Sylla**), **Lucius Cornelius,** by himself surnamed **Felix** (138–78 B.C.), Roman general and statesman, was a scion of the illustrious house of the Cornelii. As quaestor in 107 under Marius in Africa he had first secured the line of retreat from Mauretania and then induced the Mauritanian king to surrender Jugurtha (106). The war of the Cimbri and Teutones (104–101) saw Sulla again serving under the jealous Marius. In 93 he was praetor and in 92 propraetor in Cilicia, where, on his own responsibility, he raised an army and restored Ariobarzanes to the throne of Cappadocia, from which Mithradates had expelled him. The private hatred of Marius and Sulla became political, as Sulla took the aristocratic side more strongly; but the breaking out of the Social War put an end to all private quarrels for the time. Marius was aggrieved when the senate bestowed on Sulla, after his consulship in 88, supreme command in the Mithradatic war; and Marius rushed into treason and civil strife. Then followed the expulsion of Sulla, his triumphant return to Rome at the head of six legions, the overthrow of the Marian party, and the first proscription. By the beginning of 87 Sulla was able to embark for the East. During his four years there he won the victories of Chaeronea (86) and Orchomenus. Next he crossed the Hellespont, crushed the army sent out by the Marian party (which, in his absence, had again got the upper hand in Italy), forced Mithradates to sue for peace, then landed in Italy in 83. Marius was dead and had no worthy successors, and the victory over the Samnites and Lucanians at the Colline Gate brought the struggle to a close (82), and left Sulla master of Italy. Then followed his dictatorship, and the proscriptions (81)—a virtual reign of terror. During the next two years he made several important constitutional changes, mostly reactionary, tending to increase the authority of the senate—nearly all were rescinded within ten years—and he effected a permanent reform of the criminal courts. In 79 Sulla rather unexpectedly resigned the dictatorship and retired to his estate at Puteoli, where he ended his life in thorough dissipation. See Life by P. Baker (1927), and French study by J. Carcopina (1931).

SULLIVAN, (1) **Sir Arthur Seymour** (1842–1900), English composer, best known for his partnership with the librettist, Sir William Schwenck Gilbert (q.v.) in the 'Gilbert and Sullivan' light operas; born in London, May 13, studied music under Sterndale Bennett and at the Leipzig *Gewandhaus.* Together with his friend Sir George Grove (q.v.) he discovered the lost *Rosamunde*

music by Schubert. His association with the theatre, begun with his music to Morton's *Box and Cox,* was consolidated by his eighteen years' partnership with Gilbert, which after *Thespis* in 1871 produced thirteen other comic operas; *Trial by Jury* (1875), *The Sorcerer* (1877), *H.M.S. Pinafore* (1878), *The Pirates of Penzance* (1880), *Patience* (1881), *Iolanthe* (1882), *Princess Ida* (1884), *The Mikado* (1885), *Ruddigore* (1887), *The Yeoman of the Guard* (1888), *The Gondoliers* (1889), *Utopia Limited* (1893) and *The Grand Duke* (1896). Sullivan also composed an opera, cantatas, ballads, a *Te Deum,* and hymn-tunes, became first principal of the National Training College (1871), later the Royal College of Music, and was knighted in 1883. He was buried in St Paul's Cathedral. See Life by H. Sullivan and N. Flower (1950), joint Lives by I. Goldberg (1929) and H. Pearson (1935), G. E. Dunn, *Gilbert and Sullivan Dictionary* (1936), and study by G. Hughes (1960).

(2) **John** (1740–95), American general, served in Canada (1776) and at Trenton and Brandywine. He fought against the Six Nations in 1779 and won the battle of Newtown.

(3) **John Lawrence** (1858–1918), American boxer, born in Boston, world heavyweight champion from 1882, when he beat Paddy Ryan. His famous fight with Jake Kilrain in 1889 was the subject of a poem by Vachel Lindsay. See Life by Fleischer.

(4) **Louis Henri** (1856–1924), American architect, born in Boston, studied in Paris and won the New Exposition building contract (1886) with Dankmar Adler. His experimental, functional skeleton constructions of skyscrapers and office blocks, particularly the Gage building and stock exchange, Chicago, earned him the title ' Father of Modernism ' and greatly influenced Frank Lloyd Wright (q.v.) and others.

SULLY, Maximilien de Béthune, Duc de, *sül-lee* (1560–1641), French financier, Henry IV's great minister, the second son of the Huguenot Baron de Rosny, was born at the château of Rosny near Mantes, December 13. He accompanied Henry of Navarre in his flight from the French court (1576), took an active part in the war, and helped materially to decide the victory of Coutras (1587). At Ivry he captured the standard of Mayenne. He approved of the king's politic conversion, but refused himself to become a Roman Catholic, and throughout the reign remained a trusted counsellor. His first task was the restoration of the economy after 30 years of civil war. Before his time the whole administration was an organized system of pillage; but Rosny made a tour through the provinces, examined the accounts, reduced exemptions from taxation and amassed 110 million livres revenue in the Bastille. The arsenals and fleet were put into good order. In 1606 he was created Duc de Sully. After Henry's assassination he had to resign the superintendence of finance, but was presented by Marie de' Médicis with 300,000 livres. He retired to his estates, Rosny and Villebon, and died December 22, 1641. His Memoirs (1634; critical ed. S. R. Lefèvre 1942), if not rigidly historical, are of priceless value for the reign of Henry IV. They contain the famous grouping of Europe, except Russia and Turkey, into a Christian republic of fifteen states, balanced by an international Amphictyonic Assembly. See books by H. Carré (1932) and H. Pourrat (1942).

SULLY-PRUDHOMME, René François Armand, *prü-dom* (1839–1907), French poet, born at Paris, studied science and developed an interest in philosophy which underlies most of his poetical works. His early *Stances et poèmes* (1865) gained the praises of Sainte-Beuve; later volumes, *Les Épreuves, Croquis italiens, Les Solitudes, Impressions de la guerre, Les Destins, Les Vaines Tendresses, La France, La Révolte des fleurs*, extended his fame as a poet. His finest poems are steeped in a serene but penetrating melancholy. Masterpieces of subtlety are his didactic poems *La Justice* (1878) and *Le Bonheur* (1888). Other works are a metrical translation of book i of Lucretius (new ed. 1886); in prose—*L'Expression dans les beaux arts, Réflexions sur l'art des vers* (1892), *Testament poétique* (1901), *La Vraie Religion selon Pascal* (1905). His *Œuvres complètes* appeared in 1883–1908. Elected to the Academy in 1881, he was awarded the Nobel prize in 1901. He died in Paris. See studies by Zyromski and P. Fons (1907), and Life by E. Estève (1925).

SULPICIUS SEVERUS (*c.* 365–425), French monkish historian, born in Aquitania, wrote a *Chronica*, from the Creation to A.D. 403, and a Life of St Martin of Tours. See study by P. Monceaux (trans. 1928).

SUMMERS, Alphonsus Joseph-Mary Augustus Montague (1880–1948), English priest and man of letters. He wrote brilliantly on the theatre and drama of the Restoration and on other literary subjects, but his most important works are two major reference books on witchcraft, *The History of Witchcraft and Demonology* (1926) and *The Geography of Witchcraft* (1927).

SUMNER, (1) Charles (1811–74), American statesman, born in Boston, January 6, graduated at Harvard in 1830, and in 1834 was admitted to the bar and also studied jurisprudence in Europe (1837–40). He took little interest in politics until the threatened extensions of Negro slavery over newly-acquired territory. In 1848 he joined with others to form the Free Soil party. Nominated for congress, he was defeated by the Whig candidate, but in 1851 was elected to the national senate by the combined Free Soil and Democratic votes of the Massachusetts legislature. This post he held for life. At the outset, through abiding by the terms of the Constitution, he stood alone in the senate as the uncompromising opponent of slavery; in 1856, in the senate chamber, he was struck on the head by Preston S. Brooks, a South Carolina member of congress, and incapacitated for public life for nearly four years. In 1860 he delivered a speech on the admission of Kansas as a free state, published as *The Barbarism of Slavery*. The secession of the southern states left the Republican party in full control of both houses of congress, and in 1861 Sumner was elected chairman of the senate committee on foreign affairs. He

supported the impeachment of President Johnson, and opposed President Grant's project for the acquisition of San Domingo. His continuous and acrimonious censures on Grant's administration brought about a rupture with the leading Republican politicians, which was rendered complete by his support of Greeley as candidate for the presidency in 1872.

(2) **James Batcheller** (1887–1955), American biochemist, born at Canton, Mass., was educated at Harvard and became professor of Biochemistry at Cornell in 1929. He is noted for his research on enzymes and proteins and shared the Nobel prize for chemistry in 1946 with Northrop and Stanley.

(3) **John Bird** (1780–1862), English theologian, born at Kenilworth, educated at Eton and King's Coll., Cambridge, became rector of Mapledurham, Oxon. (1818), Bishop of Chester (1828), and Archbishop of Canterbury (1848). An Evangelical but conciliatory and moderate, he wrote *Apostolical Preaching* (1815) and *Evidences of Christianity* (1824).

SUMTER, Thomas (1734–1832), American general in the War of Independence, opposed the British under Tarleton in South Carolina. He was defeated at Fishing Creek but gained a victory at Blackstock Hill (1780).

SUNDERLAND, name of an earldom, granted with that of Spencer (q.v.) and the dukedom of Marlborough (q.v.) to members of the English family of Spencer, originating from Robert Despenser, steward to William the Conqueror, and from the Hugh Despensers, favourites of Edward II. **Henry Spencer, 3rd Baron Spencer** (1620–43), was created 1st Earl of Sunderland (1643) and fell in the Civil War at the first battle of Newbury, fighting for the king. His noteworthy descendants and successors, in chronological order, were:

(1) **Robert Spencer, 2nd Earl of** (1641–1702), English politician, son of the above, father of (2), born in Paris, became in 1679 secretary of state for the Northern Department and united with Essex and Halifax in opposing Shaftesbury, who wished to set Monmouth on the throne. He encouraged Charles II to persevere in the French alliance, and, with the Duchess of Portsmouth, negotiated a treaty by which, for a French pension, Charles agreed to assemble no parliament for three years. Before the year was out a new triumvirate, consisting of himself, Hyde and Godolphin, succeeded to the confidence of Charles. The French treaty was broken off, and Sunderland, now afraid of the Whigs, engaged the king in an alliance with Spain. After the dissolution of the last exclusion parliament he lost his office; but in 1682 he was, 'upon great submission made to the Duke [of York], restored to be secretary'. Under James II his influence grew greater than ever, and in 1685 he became principal secretary of state. He alone was entrusted with a knowledge of the king's intention to establish Catholicism, and he openly professed his own conversion. Yet we find him in correspondence with William of Orange. When William came over, Sunderland went to Amsterdam, but in 1691 he was allowed to return to England, and in 1695 William spent a week at his seat, Althorp, then a

rallying-point for the Whigs. He was made lord chamberlain, allegedly for services to William in James II's reign, but resigned in 1697. See *Life* by J. P. Kenyon (1958).

(2) **Charles Spencer, 3rd Earl of** (1675–1722), English statesman, son of (1), became secretary of state in 1706 and under George I rose to be all-powerful, but was forced to resign in 1721 through public indignation at his part in the South Sea Bubble. His grandson, **John** (1734–83), was created 1st Earl Spencer (q.v.) in 1765.

(3) **Charles Spencer, 3rd Duke of Marlborough, 5th Earl of Sunderland** (1706–58), English soldier, second son of (2), succeeded his brother to the earldom (1729) and in 1733 to the honours of his maternal grandfather, John Churchill, the dukedom of Marlborough. He fought at Dettingen (1743) and in the expedition against St Malo (1758).

SUN YAT-SEN, or **Sun Wen,** *soon* (1866–1925), Chinese revolutionary, born November 12 at Tsuiheng near Canton, brought up by his elder brother in Hawaii, graduated in medicine at Hong Kong in 1892, practising at Macao and Canton. He visited Honolulu in 1894 and founded his first political organization there, the *Hsin Chung Hui* (New China Party). After his first abortive uprising against the Manchus in Canton in 1895, he lived abroad in Japan, America and Britain, studying Western politics and canvassing the support of the Chinese in these countries for his cause. While in London in 1896, he was kidnapped and imprisoned in the Chinese legation and was saved from certain death by the intervention of Sir Edward Cantlie, the surgeon, his former tutor, to whom he smuggled out a letter and who enlisted the help of the British Foreign Office to get him released. After ten unsuccessful uprisings, engineered by Sun from abroad, he was at last victorious in the revolution of 1911. In February 1912 China was proclaimed a republic with Sun as its provisional president. Sun, however, made way for the Northern general, Yüan Shih-kai (q.v.) who had forced the emperor's abdication, but as president (1913–16) sought to make himself dictator. Sun opposing him from the South, was defeated and found himself again in exile. In 1923 he was back in Canton and elected president of the southern republic. With expert help from the Russians, Sun reorganized the Kuomintang and established the Whampoa Military Academy under Chiang Kai-shek (q.v.), who three years after Sun's death achieved the unification of China under a government inspired by Sun's *San Min Chu I* (1927) or *The Three Principles of the People*, in short nationalism, democracy and livelihood. While at a conciliatory conference with other Chinese political leaders he died of cancer in Peking, March 12, 1925. Acknowledged by all political factions as the father of the Chinese Republic, he was reinterred in a mausoleum built in his honour in Nanking in 1928. Sun was essentially empirical in his political teachings and rejected the Communist dogma of the class war. See Lives by J. Cantlie (1912), L. S. Sharman (1934), Buck (1954), and B. Martin, *Strange Vigour* (1944), and studies by F. W.

Price (1929), P. M. A. Linebarger (1937) and N. Gangulee (1945). His second wife, Ching Ling Soong (1890–), one of the Soong family (q.v.), was educated in the United States, became Sun's secretary and in 1916 married him. After his death, she lived in Moscow (1927–31) and became a bitter left-wing opponent of her brother-in-law, Chiang Kai-shek, returning to China from Hong Kong during the Japanese war in 1937. In 1950 she was one of the three non-Communist vice-chairmen of the new Chinese Communist Republic.

SUPERVIELLE, Jules, *sü-per-vyel* (1884–1960), French-Uruguayan writer, born at Montevideo, wrote many volumes of poems (including the notable *Poèmes de la France malheureuse*, 1939–41), novels, tales (*L'Enfant de la haute mer*, 1931; *L'Arche de Noé*, 1938), plays (*La Belle au bois*, 1932; *Shéhérazade*, 1949), and *Bolivar*, an opera with music by Milhaud, 1950. See studies by C. Sénéchal (Paris 1939), L. Specker (Zürich 1942), and D. S. Blair (1960).

SUPPÉ, Franz von, *soop-pay* (1820–95), Viennese composer of operettas, songs, masses, &c., was born at Spalato of Germano-Belgo-Italian origin. His *Light Cavalry* and *Poet and Peasant* overtures are still firm favourites.

SURAJA DOWLAH, Siraj-ud-Dowla, in the *Gentleman's Magazine* of the time **Sir Roger Dowler** (d. 1757), the young Nawab of Bengal, having captured Fort William, the fort of the English factory at Calcutta (1756), confined his 146 prisoners in the military prison, the ' Black Hole ' (300 sq. ft.). In the morning there were twenty-three survivors. Clive (q.v.) at Plassey (*Palási*) on June 23, 1757, inflicted a crushing defeat on Suraja Dowlah, who fled and was slain. See Holwell's *Narrative of the Black Hole* (1758).

SURCOUF, Robert, *sür-koof* (1773–1827), French privateer, was born and died at St Malo. He preyed on the English shipping in the Indian seas during the war, his greatest exploits being the capture of the *Triton* (1785) and *Kent* (1800). See Sir J. K. Laughton's *Studies in Naval History* (1887).

SURREY, Henry Howard, Earl of (*c.* 1517–47), English courtier and poet, was the eldest son of Thomas Howard (q.v.), who in 1524 succeeded as third Duke of Norfolk. In 1532 he accompanied Henry VIII to France; in 1542 he was made a Knight of the Garter, but was sent to the Fleet prison for issuing a challenge; and next year he was again committed for breaking windows in the streets at night. Soon released, he served in the camp near Boulogne, distinguished himself at Montreuil in 1544, and in 1545 held command at Guisnes and Boulogne, but, defeated by a superior French force, was superseded by the Earl of Hertford. For his bitter speeches against Hertford, Surrey was imprisoned at Windsor in July, and in December was, like his father, committed to the Tower on a charge of high treason. His offence was merely that he had assumed the arms of his ancestor Edward the Confessor in conjunction with his own; but he was found guilty, condemned to death, and beheaded, January 21, 1547. He was, almost as much as Sir Philip Sidney, the type of perfect knight and his love poems are a late manifestation of the courtly love of the Middle Ages. He was much under the influence of Petrarch. His poems were first printed, with poems by Wyatt and others, in *Tottel's Miscellany* (1557). They consist of sonnets, lyrics, elegies, translations, paraphrases of the Psalms and Ecclesiastes, besides translations in good blank verse—the first in English—of books ii and iv of Virgil's *Aeneid*. He was among the first in English to employ the sonnet, using not the Petrarchan form but that used by most of the Elizabethans. See Lives by Nott in his edition (1815 and 1866), and Casady (1938); H. W. Chapman, *Two Tudor Portraits* (1960).

SURTEES, (1) **Robert** (1779–1834), English antiquary and topographer, born at Durham, studied at Christ Church, Oxford, and the Middle Temple, and in 1802 inherited Mainsforth near Bishop Auckland. Here he compiled his *History of the County of Durham* (1816–23), to vol. iv of which (ed. by Raine, 1840) a memoir by George Taylor is prefixed. To Scott's *Minstrelsy* Surtees contributed two 'ancient' ballads he himself had made—*Barthram's Dirge* and *The Death of Featherstonhaugh*. The Surtees Society was founded in 1834 to publish unedited MSS. relating chiefly to the northern counties.

(2) **Robert Smith** (1803–64), English sporting writer, of Hamsterley Hall, Durham, wrote anonymously a series of inimitable sporting novels, introducing Mr Jorrocks, grocer and sportsman. Among the best known are *Handley Cross* (1843, 1854) and *Mr Facey Romford's Hounds* (1865)—illustrated by John Leech and 'Phiz'. See memoirs by himself and Cuming (1924), F. Watson (1933), and *Hunting Scenes from Surtees*, ed. Gough (1953).

SUSO, or **Seuse, Heinrich** (c. 1295–1366), German mystic, born at Ueberlingen, Baden, was a Dominican monk and a disciple of Eckhart. His *Das Büchlein der ewigen Weisheit* (1328) achieved great popularity. See his own *Life* (trans. 1952).

SUTHERLAND, Graham Vivian (1903–), English artist, born in London. He studied at Goldsmiths' College of Art, and worked mainly as an etcher till 1930. During the next ten years he made his reputation as a painter of romantic, mainly abstract landscapes, with superb, if arbitrary, colouring. From 1941 to 1945 he was an official war artist. In 1946 he was commissioned to paint a *Crucifixion* for St Matthew's Church, Northampton, and he has since produced several memorable portraits, including *Somerset Maugham* (1949) and *Sir Winston Churchill* (1955). He has also designed ceramics, posters and textiles: his large tapestry, *Christ in Majesty*, was hung in the new Coventry Cathedral in 1962. His work is represented in the Tate Gallery, London, the Musée d'Art Moderne, Paris, and the Museum of Modern Art, New York. He was awarded the O.M. in 1960. See the studies by Sackville-West (1955) and Cooper (1961).

SUTRO, Alfred (1863–1933), English dramatist, born in London, gave up a successful business, translated Maeterlinck, and from

1900 wrote a series of successful plays—*The Foolish Virgins* (1904), *The Walls of Jericho* (1906), *John Glayde's Honour* (1907), *The Perplexed Husband* (1913), *Freedom*, &c. See his autobiographical *Celebrities and Simple Souls* (1933).

SUTTNER, Bertha von, née **Kinsky** (1843–1914), Austrian writer and pacifist, born at Prague, spread anti-war sentiment by her *Die Waffen nieder* ('Lay Down your Arms', 1899), which was translated into many European languages, and other pacifist books. She was awarded the Nobel peace prize in 1905. See her *Memoirs* (1909), and Life by Ellen Key (1919).

SUTTON, Thomas (1552–1611), a London merchant, founder of the Charterhouse, obtained a lease of rich coal lands in Durham and made an enormous fortune.

SUVOROV, or **Suwarrow, Count Aleksandr Vasilyevich** (1729–1800), Russian general, born at Moscow, had won fame in the Seven Years, War, and in Poland and Turkey, when in 1799 he was sent to Italy to assist the Austrians against the French. He defeated Moreau on the Adda, Macdonald at Trebbia, and Joubert at Novi. Then he was directed to join Korsakov to sweep the French out of Switzerland. After a terrible march over the Alps he found that Masséna had defeated Korsakov, and, too weak to attack, he barely escaped over the mountains into Austria. He died at St Petersburg. See Lives by Spalding (1890) and Blease (1920).

SVEDBERG, Theodor, svay-ber'y' (1884–1971), Swedish chemist, born at Valbo, Gävleborg, invented the ultracentrifuge for the study of colloidal particles. He won a Nobel prize in 1926.

SVENDSEN, Johan Severin (1840–1911), Norwegian composer, born at Christiania, after wide travels, became court *kapellmeister* at Copenhagen (1883). He wrote two symphonies and a violin concerto. His best-known work is his *Carnival at Paris*.

SVERDRUP, Otto, svayr-droop (1855–1930), Norwegian explorer, born in Sogndal, led many expeditions to the Arctic.

SVETCHINE. See SWETCHINE.

SVEVO, Italo, pen-name of Ettore Schmitz, zvay'vō (1861–1928), Italian novelist, born at Trieste. A friend of James Joyce, who encouraged his talent, he had a considerable success with *La Coscienza di Zeno* ('The Confessions of Zeno'), a psychological study of the inner tensions and conflicts of an average man. His work is concerned largely with the human unconscious, and shows the influence of Zola. See *A History of Italian Literature* by Ernest Hatch Wilkins (1954).

SWAMMERDAM, Jan (1637–80), Dutch naturalist, born at Amsterdam. His system for classifying insects laid the foundations of entomology. His *Biblia Naturae* (1737–38) are the finest one-man collection of microscopical observations. He first observed red blood corpuscles (1658) and discovered the valves in the lymph vessels and the glands in Amphibia named after him. He finally succumbed to the mystic influences of Bourignon (q.v.) and abandoned science.

SWAN, (1) **Annie S(hepherd)** (1860–1943), Scottish novelist, born near Gorebridge, wife of Dr J. Burnett-Smith, contributed to *The Woman at Home* and the *People's Friend*, and wrote *Aldersyde* (1883) and many other popular stories, and reminiscences. See her autobiography, *My Life* (1934).

(2) **Sir Joseph Wilson** (1828–1914), English physicist and chemist, born at Sunderland, became a manufacturing chemist, patented the carbon process for photographic printing in 1864, invented the dry plate (1871) and bromide paper (1879). In 1860 he invented an electric lamp which anticipated Edison's by twenty years, and in 1897 demonstrated a lamp which improved considerably on Edison's patent model. He first produced practicable artificial silk. He was knighted in 1904.

SWEDENBORG, Emanuel (1688–1772), Swedish mystic, born January 29 in Stockholm, son of Jesper Svedberg, later Bishop of Skara, studied at Uppsala and travelled widely in Europe and on his return was appointed assessor in the college of mines and military engineer. The family was ennobled in 1719 and the name changed to Swedenborg. He wrote books on algebra and the differential calculus, on navigation, astronomy, on docks and sluices and on chemistry considered as atomic geometry. He declined a professorship of Mathematics (1724) because he preferred practical subjects. In 1734 he published at Leipzig, at the expense of the Duke of Brunswick, his monumental *Opera Philosophica et Mineralia* (1734), a mixture of metallurgy and metaphysical speculation on the creation of the world, carried further in *Philosophical Argument on the Infinite* (1734) and concluded by anatomical and physiological studies, *Economy of the Animal Kingdom* (1741) and *Animal Kingdom* (1744–1745). Curious dreams during 1743–44 convinced him that he had direct access to the spiritual world. He resigned his assessorship, communicated his spiritual explorations in *Heavenly Arcana* (1749–56) and spent the rest of his life in Amsterdam, Stockholm and London, expounding his mystical doctrines, based on the law of correspondences, which reveals that there are three heavens and three hells, that creation is dead, except through the intervention of God, who invests man with apparent life, but only himself really lives. He has been regarded, falsely, as a spiritualist 'medium', but he denied that spirits can enter the material world, and his works are too reasoned and matter-of-fact to be called mystical. His other works (all first published in Latin) are *Heaven and Hell*, *The New Jerusalem*, *Divine Love and the Divine Wisdom*, *Divine Providence*, *The Apocalypse Revealed* and *Conjugal Love*. His translated theological works number forty volumes. He died in London, March 29, 1772, was buried first in St George's of the East in London and in 1908 reinterred at Stockholm. He made no attempt to establish a sect; his followers, who call themselves 'the New Church signified by the New Jerusalem in the Revelation', were organized as a distinct denomination in 1787 by some Wesleyan preachers; there are branches throughout the world. Kant, who somewhat admired Swedenborg the mystic, demolished Sweden-

borg the metaphysician in *Dreams of a Ghost Seer* (1776). See Lives by J. G. Wilkinson (1849), W. White (1867), G. Trobridge (1907), S. Toksvig (1949), and studies by S.M. Warren (1885) and E. A. G. Kleen (1917–20).

SWEELINCK, Jan Pieterszoon, *sway'-* (1562–1611), Dutch composer, organist and harpsichordist, born at Deventer or Amsterdam, studied in Venice and composed mainly church music and organ works, and developed the fugue. He founded the distinctive North German school which later included Buxtehude and the young Johann Sebastian Bach.

SWEET, Henry (1845–1912), English philologist, pioneer of Anglo-Saxon philological studies, born in London, became reader in Phonetics at Oxford. His works include Old and Middle English texts, primers, and dictionaries, a historical English grammar, *A History of English Sounds* (1874), and *A History of Language* (1900). He constructed a 'Romaic' phonetic alphabet. Professor Higgins of Bernard Shaw's *Pygmalion* was based on him.

SWETCHINE, Madame, *née* **Anne Sophie Soymanov** (1782–1857), Russian author, born at Moscow, married in 1799 General Swetchine, joined the Roman Catholic communion in 1815, and settled finally in Paris in 1818, where she maintained a famous salon. See Life by de Falloux (1858); his edition of her Letters (1861); and work by Naville (1863).

SWETTENHAM, *swet'nĕm,* (1) **Sir Alexander** (1846–1933), Colonial administrator. He began his career in 1868 as a clerk in the Ceylon civil service, and rose through various posts in Cyprus, Singapore, British Guiana, and the Straits Settlement to become captain-general and governor-in-chief in Jamaica from 1904 to 1907. He was created K.C.M.G. in 1898.

(2) **Sir Frank Athelstane** (1850–1946), brother of (1). He was British resident in Selangor (1882) and Perak (1889–95), and later resident-general in the Federated Malay States (1896–1901). He was governor and commander-in-chief of the Straits Settlement from 1901 to 1904 and became an authority on Malay language and history, writing a number of books on the subject. He was created K.C.M.G. in 1897. Port Swettenham, Selangor, is named after him.

SWEYN, *svay'in,* name of three kings of Denmark:

Sweyn I, known as **Sweyn Forkbeard** (d. 1014), was father of Canute (q.v.) and son of Harold Blaatand, whom he defeated and killed, making himself king (986). He led many plundering expeditions to Britain and defeated and killed the Norwegian Olaf, the Victorious. He died at Gainsborough.

Sweyn II (d. 1075), born in England, became king in 1047, carried on a war with Harold III of Norway until 1064, attempted twice to conquer England, but was driven away by Canute. Five of his sons were kings of Denmark.

Sweyn III (d. 1157), was king of part of Denmark from 1147 and waged civil war against Canute V, whom he killed. He was himself assassinated by Waldemar I.

SWIFT, Jonathan (1667–1745), English satirist,

was born in Dublin, the son of English parents. He was educated at Kilkenny Grammar School and Trinity College, Dublin, where he obtained his degree only by 'special grace' in 1685. Family connections helped him to embark on a career as secretary to the renowned diplomat, Sir William Temple, then resident at Moor Park, Farnham. Here Swift obtained his first acquaintance with the great world, but his relations with Temple were sometimes strained. However, he supported his patron on the side of the Ancients in the 'Querelle des Anciens et des Modernes' which had spread here from France. Swift's contribution was the mock-epic *Battle of the Books* which was published along with the much more powerful satire on religious dissension, *A Tale of a Tub*, in 1704. At Moor Park he first met Esther Johnson, then a child of eight, who henceforward as pupil and lover or friend was to be intertwined with his life and to survive for posterity in Swift's verse tributes and the *Journal to Stella*. When Swift was presented to the living of Laracor near Dublin, Stella accompanied him, but the precautions he took precluded scandal. It is uncertain if he ever married her. In 1708 during one of his numerous visits to London he met Esther Vanhomrigh, who insisted on being near him in Ireland with fatal consequences to herself. She is the Vanessa of Swift's too clever poem *Cadenus and Vanessa*, a tribute to the lady but also a manœuvre of disengagement. His visits to London were largely political, but friendship with the great, literary and aristocratic, bulked largely in them. For the first time the literary world met on equal terms with statesmen. Having been introduced to the political world by Temple, he supported the Whigs, but, his first care being the English Church, he gradually veered to the Tory party. The friendship of Harley, later Earl of Oxford, assisted the change which was decisively made in 1710 when Harley returned to power. His *Four Last Years of the Queen* described the ferment of intrigue and pamphleteering during that period. The chief aims of the Tory party were to make the Establishment secure and to bring the war with France to a close. The latter object was powerfully aided by his *On the Conduct of the Allies* (1713), one of the greatest pieces of pamphleteering. The death of the Queen disappointed all the hopes of Swift and his friends of the 'Scriblerus Club', founded in 1713. Swift accepted his 'exile' to the Deanery of St Patrick's, Dublin, and henceforth, except for two visits in 1726 and 1727, correspondence alone kept him in touch with London. Despite his loathing for Ireland he threw himself into a strenuous campaign for Irish liberties, denied by the Whig government. The *Drapier's Letters* is only the most famous of these activities which were concerned with England's restrictions on Irish trade, particularly the exclusion of Irish wool and cattle. This campaign and his charitable efforts for Dublin's poor greatly retrieved his name. On his first visit to London after the Tory debacle of 1714 he published the world-famous satire *Gulliver's Travels* (1726). The

completion of this work seems to have released the talent for light verse which he had displayed so happily for the amusement of the ladies of the viceregal Lodge in earlier days. His poems of this sort now range from the diverting *The Grand Question Debated* (1729) to the *Verses on His Own Death*, which, with its mingling of pathos and humour, ranks with the great satirical poems in the lighter manner. He himself considered his *On Poetry; a Rhapsody* his best verse satire. An attack on Grub Street, it corresponds in some way to Pope's *Dunciad*. There is also of this period a group of odious satires on women which in a writer of his cloth almost hint at derangement. As a relief we note his constant preoccupation with the speech and manners of the servant class and equally with the banality of fashionable society. The ironical *Directions to Servants* and *A Complete Collection of Genteel and Ingenious Conversation* (in hand in 1731) are examples of both. The satire in the first part of *Gulliver's Travels* is directed at political parties and religious dissension. The second part can be equally enjoyed for the ingenious adventures and the detailed verisimilitude which, as in Defoe, is part of the manner. But there is deepening misanthropy culminating in the King's description of mankind as 'the most pernicious race of little odious vermin that Nature ever suffered to crawl upon the surface of the earth'. The third part, a satire on inventors, is good fun though less plausible. The last part, in the country of the Houyhnhnms, a race of horses governed only by reason, is a savage attack on man which points to the author's final mental collapse. Politics apart, Swift's influence, like that of the 'Scriblerus Club' generally and Pope in particular, was directed powerfully against the vogue of deistic science and modern invention and in favour of orthodoxy and good manners. His religion, as we see from his sermons, was apparently sincere, but as he exalted reason above emotion, there is little Christian warmth in it. The Temple Scott edition of the works (1897–1910) replaced the old edition by Sir Walter Scott (1814). H. Davis edited the *Prose Works* (1939 *et seq.*); Birkbeck Hill, *Unpublished Letters* (1899); and F. E. Ball the *Correspondence* (1910–14). Important studies are by Churton Collins (1893); Stephen Gwynn (1933); R. Quintana (1936); Life by B. Acworth (1948), and I. Ehrenpreis, *The Personality of Jonathan Swift* (1958), and study by K. Williams (1959).

SWINBURNE, (1) **Algernon Charles** (1837–1909), English poet and critic, was born in London, the eldest son of Admiral and Lady Jane Swinburne. He was educated partly in France, passed from Eton to Balliol, left without taking a degree, travelled on the Continent, where he came under the spell of Victor Hugo. He visited Landor in Florence (1864), and on his return became associated with D. G. Rossetti and William Morris. After a breakdown due to intemperate living, he submitted to the care of his friend Watts-Dunton, in whose house, No. 2, The Pines, he continued to live in semiseclusion for the rest of his life. His first publication, the two plays *The Queen Mother* and *Rosamond* (1860), attracted little attention, but *Atalanta in Calydon* (1865), a drama in the Greek form but modern in its spirit of revolt against religious acquiescence in the will of Heaven, proved that a new artist with an exquisite lyrical gift had arisen. He returned to Greek myth with his noble lyric drama *Erectheus* (1876). It was, however, the first of the series of *Poems and Ballads* (1865) which took the public by storm. The exciting or languorous rhythms of *Hesperia, Itylus, The Garden of Proserpine, The Triumph of Time* were intoxicating to English ears, but the uninhibited tone of certain passages affronted English puritanism. The second series of *Poems and Ballads* hardly maintained the excitement and the third series (1889) witnessed his waning vogue in this kind. Meanwhile he found scope for his detestation of kings and priests in the struggle for Italian liberty. *Songs before Sunrise* (1871) best expresses his fervent republicanism. He had been working at a trilogy of Mary, Queen of Scots, since before 1865 when his *Chastelard* appeared. The second play of the series, *Bothwell, a Tragedy*, appeared in 1874 and *Mary Stuart* completed the trilogy in 1881. The year following, *Tristram of Lyonesse*, an Arthurian romance in rhymed couplets, achieved a real success and must be considered among the best of Victorian dealings with the mediaeval cycle. He had resented Tennyson's moralistic treatment of the theme in *The Idylls of the King*. *Tristram* is intense and passionate and has some great descriptive passages. When he returned to mediaeval romance in *A Tale of Balen* (1896), there was obvious lack of power. His dramas are all closet-plays and except for some high passages in the *Mary Stuart* trilogy are forgotten. Swinburne represented the last phase of the Romantic movement—with a little posthumous life in the early Yeats. His absorption in romantic themes which he treated with a wealth of rhetoric hardly experienced in previous poetry and an excess of neologisms and archaisms has caused his reputation to diminish, but this fact cannot entirely negate his genuine and lasting contribution to the poetic scene. His novel, *Love's Cross Currents* (1877), is a curiosity, but his critical works, above all his work on Shakespeare and his contemporaries, are stimulating. His *Essays and Studies* (1875) and *Studies in Prose and Poetry* (1894) are his chief contribution to criticism. Five volumes of the *Collected Poems* appeared in 1917 and twenty volumes of the *Complete Works* from 1926 onwards. A new edition of his *Correspondence*, ed C. Y. Lang, appeared in 1960. Gosse wrote the standard Life in 1917. Studies by Mackail (1909), Nicholson (1926) and Lafourcade (1932) are important. Max Beerbohm's essay *No. 2, the Pines* is a masterly ironic picture of Swinburne's life with Watts-Dunton.

(2) **Sir James, 9th Baronet** (1858-1958), British scientist, ' the father of British plastics ', was a pioneer in that industry and the founder of Bakelite, Ltd. His research on phenolic resins resulted in a process for producing synthetic resin, but his patent for this was anticipated by one day, by the Belgian chemist Baekeland. He lived to be a centenarian.

SWINTON, Sir Ernest Dunlop (1868-1951), British soldier, writer and inventor, born in Bangalore, India. One of the originators of the tank, Swinton was responsible for the use of the word ' tank ' to describe armoured fighting vehicles. Under his pseudonym Ole Luk-Oie he wrote *The Green Curve* (1909), *A Year Ago* (1916), and translations. He was professor of Military History at Oxford (1925-39).

SWITHIN, or Swithun (d. 862), English saint and divine, was adviser to Egbert (q.v.) and was made Bishop of Winchester (852) by Ethelwulf. When in 971 the monks exhumed his body to bury it in the rebuilt cathedral, the removal, which was to have taken place on July 15, is said to have been delayed by violent rains. Hence the current belief that if it rains on July 15 it will rain for forty days more.

SYBEL, Heinrich von, *zee'běl* (1817-95), German historian, born at Düsseldorf, studied at Berlin under Ranke; became professor of History at Bonn (1844), Marburg (1845), Munich (1856) and Bonn again (1861); and in 1875 was made director of the state archives at Berlin. He published the political correspondence of Frederick the Great, shared in issuing the *Monumenta Germaniae Historica*, and founded and edited the *Historische Zeitschrift*. His history of the First Crusade (1841) often ran counter to the accepted opinions of centuries; his next work was on the title ' German king ' (1844). Then came his masterpiece, *Geschichte der Revolutionszeit, 1789-95* (1853-58; 4th ed. to 1800, 1882), a history of the French Revolution based upon official documentary evidence. He also wrote a history of the founding of the German empire (1889-94; trans. 1891-92), marred by its Prussian bias. He was a member of the Prussian Diet.

SYDENHAM, (1) Floyer (1710-87), English scholar, educated at Wadham College, Oxford, in his fiftieth year began the publication of an excellent translation of Plato's *Dialogues* (1759-80). It had no market, neither had his dissertation on Heraclitus (1775) or his *Onomasticon Theologicum* (1784). Arrested for unpaid meals, he died in prison. The Literary Fund was founded as a consequence of his death to help deserving authors.

(2) **Thomas** (1624-89), English physician, ' the English Hippocrates ', born September 10 at Wynford Eagle, Dorset, left Magdalene Hall, Oxford, to fight as captain of horse for the Parliamentarians. He returned to Oxford in 1647, read medicine at Wadham College and was awarded the degree of M.B. (1648) without any previous examinations and was elected fellow of All Souls. In 1651 he was severely wounded at Worcester. From 1655 he practised in London, but although he became a licentiate of the Royal College of Physicians and took an Oxford M.D. (1676) he was never elected a fellow of the Royal College. A great friend of such empiricists as Boyle and Locke, he stressed the importance of observation in clinical medicine. He wrote a masterly account of

gout (1683), a disease from which he himself suffered, distinguished the symptoms of venereal disease (1675), recognized hysteria as a distinct disease and gave his name to the mild convulsions of children, ' Sydenham's chorea ', and to the use of liquid opium, ' Sydenham's laudanum '. He remained in London except when the plague was at its peak (1665). Some of his epidemiological theories on the fevers of London are supported today, although he failed to stress the rôles of contagion and infection. One of his quainter ' remedies ' for senile decrepitude was to put the patient to bed with a young vital person. In England he suffered professional opposition, but on the Continent his fame was immediate. Boerhaave (q.v.) is said never to have referred to him without raising his hat. See W. A. Greenhill's edition (1844; trans. R. G. Latham 1848) for the Sydenham Society of *Opera Omnia* (1705); *Selections*, ed. J. D. Comrie (1922); Life by J. F. Payne (1900); and C. E. A. Winslow, *The Conquest of Epidemic Disease* (1944).

SYDNEY, Algernon. See SIDNEY (1).

SYLLA. See SULLA.

SYLVESTER, the name of three popes:

Sylvester I (pope 314-335), is falsely claimed to have baptized and cured of leprosy Constantine the Great, and to have received from him the famous Donation, now considered apocryphal. Under him the Council of Nicaea (325) defined the articles of the Christian faith. He was canonized.

Sylvester II (c. 940-1003), pope from 999, was born Gerbert at Aurillac in Auvergne, and from his attainments in chemistry, mathematics and philosophy acquired the reputation of being in league with the Devil. He made a large collection of classical manuscripts and is said to have introduced Arabic numerals and to have invented clocks. He became Abbot of Bobbio (982) and Archbishop of Ravenna (988). He upheld the primacy of Rome against the separatist tendencies of the French church. See French works by Olleris (1876), and German by Werner (1878) and Schultess (1891-93).

Sylvester III, was antipope 1044-46 to Benedict IX and was Bishop of Sabina.

SYLVESTER, (1) James Joseph (1814-97), English mathematician, born in London, studied at St John's College, Cambridge (where, as a Jew, though he was second wrangler (1837), he was disqualified from a degree), and was professor at University College, London, at the University of Virginia, at Woolwich, at the Johns Hopkins University in Baltimore, and at Oxford (1883-94). He made important contributions to the theories of invariants, numbers and equations, and took up and graduated in Law. See his *Collected Mathematical Papers* (4 vols. 1904-12).

(2) Joshua (1563-1618), English translator, achieved success neither as merchant nor as poet. His own works are forgotten; his chief literary work was his translation of *Divine Weeks and Works* of Du Bartas (q.v.). Grosart reprinted his *Works* (1878).

SYLVIUS, (1) Franciscus, or Franz de la Boë (1614-72), German physician, born at Hanau, Prussia, became professor of Medicine at Leyden (1658). He first treated the pancreatic, saliva and other body juices chemically, described the relationship between the tubercle and phthisis and founded the iatro-chemical school. He died in Leyden.

(2) properly **Jacques Dubois** (1478-1555), French physician, born at Amiens, became professor of Medicine at the Collège de France. He discovered the fissure in the brain, described many anatomical structures and systematized anatomical terms. He wrote commentaries on Galen and Hippocrates. See C. Singer, *Evolution of Anatomy* (1925).

SYME, James, *sīm* (1799-1870), Scottish surgeon, born in Edinburgh, studied under Robert Liston (q.v.) at the university there and at Paris and in Germany. In 1818, he announced a method of waterproofing afterwards patented by Macintosh (q.v.). In 1823-33 he lectured on Clinical Surgery. In 1831 appeared his treatise on *The Excision of Diseased Joints*; in 1832 his *Principles of Surgery*. In 1833 he became professor of Clinical Surgery. His life abounded in controversies. Syme, who had no superior either as operator or as teacher, wrote further on pathology, stricture, fistula, incised wounds, &c. See *Memoir* by Paterson (1874).

SYMEON OF DURHAM. See SIMEON OF DURHAM.

SYMINGTON, William (1763-1831), Scottish engineer and inventor, born at Leadhills, became a mechanic at the Wanlockhead mines. In 1787 he patented an engine for road locomotion and, in 1788, he constructed for Patrick Miller (q.v.) a similar engine on a boat 25 feet long, having twin hulls with paddle-wheels between, which was launched on Dalswinton Loch. In 1802 he completed at Grangemouth the *Charlotte Dundas*, the first workable steamboat ever built. It was intended as a tug, but vested interests prevented its use, asserting that the wash would injure the sides of the Forth and Clyde Canal. Symington died in London, in poverty.

SYMMACHUS, (1) Coelius, pope 498-514.

(2) **Quintus Aurelius** (c. A.D. 345-410), Roman orator, became prefect of Rome in 384 and consul in 391 under Theodosius. He was devoted to the old religion, and showed the highest nobility of character. His extant writings, edited by Kroll in 1893, consist of letters, three panegyrics on Valentinian I and Gratian, and fragments of six orations. See Morin's *Étude* (1847) and Kroll's *De Symmacho* (1891).

SYMONDS, John Addington, *sim'-* (1840-93), English author, born at Bristol, was educated at Harrow and Balliol, won the Newdigate, and was elected a fellow of Magdalen in 1862. His *Introduction to the Study of Dante* (1872) was followed by *Studies of the Greek Poets* (1873-76), his great *Renaissance in Italy* (6 vols. 1875-86), and *Shakespeare's Predecessors in the English Drama* (1884). He wrote also sketches of travel in Italy and elsewhere; monographs on *Shelley, Sidney,* and *Ben Jonson*; fine translations of the *Sonnets of Michelangelo and Campanella* (1878), of Benvenuto Cellini's autobiography, and of 12th-century students' Latin songs (1884); a *Life of Michelangelo* (1892); some verse; and an account of his residence (for health) at Davos (1892). See *Life* (1895) by H. F. Brown, who edited his *Letters and Papers* (1923); and biographical studies by Brooks (1914) and Grosskurth (1964).

SYMONS, *sim'-*, (1) **Arthur** (1865–1945), British critic and poet, born of Cornish stock in Wales, did much to familiarize the British with the literature of France and Italy—he translated d'Annunzio (1902) and Baudelaire (1925). He also wrote on *The Symbolist Movement in Literature* (1899) and *The Romantic Movement in English Poetry* (1909).

(2) **George James** (1838–1900), English meteorologist, born in London, served as clerk in the meteorological department of the Board of Trade, founded the British Rainfall Organization for collecting rainfall data with the cooperation of the general public. The Royal Society appointed him to investigate the Krakatoa eruption (1883). Fellow of the Royal Society, he was secretary and twice president of the Royal Meteorological Society, the highest award of which, the Symons Memorial Gold Medal, bears his name.

SYNESIUS (*c.* A.D. 375–413), Greek philosopher and poet, Bishop of Ptolemais, born at Cyrene, studied at Alexandria under Hypatia (q.v.) and at Athens, and then returned to the Pentapolis, resolved to spend his life in study and in the pursuits of a country gentleman. About 399 he was appointed a delegate from Cyrene to the emperor at Constantinople, where he remained three years, and wrote an allegory *Concerning Providence*. After his return, he married and wrote *Concerning Dreams, The Praise of Baldness, Dion or Self-discipline,* and *Hymns.* When Libyan nomads made raids upon the fertile Pentapolis, Synesius organized the defence of Cyrene. About 401 he turned Christian; and *c.* 410 the people of Ptolemais begged him to become their bishop. Finally he yielded, and was consecrated at

Alexandria. His 156 letters reveal a man of high spirit, passionately fond of intellectual pursuits and of sport. His *Hymns* show him as the poet of Neoplatonism. See books by Druon (1859), Volkmann (1869), Gardner (1886), Crawford (1901), Grützmacher (1913); Fitzgerald's translation (1926–30).

SYNGE, **John Millington**, *sing* (1871–1909), Irish dramatist, born near Dublin, studied at Trinity College, Dublin, and then spent several years in Paris until, on the advice of Yeats, he settled among the people of the Aran Islands who provided the material for his plays, *In the Shadow of the Glen* (1903), *Riders to the Sea* (1904), *The Well of the Saints* (1905), and his humorous masterpiece *The Playboy of the Western World* (1907) followed by *The Tinker's Wedding* (1909). He had a profound influence on the next generation of Irish playwrights and was a director of the Abbey Theatre from 1904. See biographical study by D. H. Greene and E. M. Stephens (1959).

SZENT-GYÖRGYI, **Albert von Nagyrapolt**, *sent-dyur'dyi*(1893–),Hungarian biochemist, born at Budapest, lectured at Groningen, Cambridge, &c., was professor at Szeged (1931–45) and at Budapest (1945–47), then became director of the Institute of Muscle Research in Massachusetts, U.S. He isolated Vitamin C and was awarded the Nobel prize in 1937. He made important studies of biological combustion, muscular contraction and cellular oxidation.

SZÖNYI, **Stephen** (1894–1960), Hungarian artist, born at Ujpest. He studied at Budapest, and his paintings, particularly those of nudes, gained him a large following among the younger Hungarian artists.

SZYMANOWSKI, **Karol**, *shim-an-of'skee* (1883–1937), Polish composer, born at Tymoszowska, in the Ukraine, eventually became director of the State Conservatoire in Warsaw. Reckoned by many to be the greatest Polish composer since Chopin, he wrote operas, incidental music, symphonies, concertos, chamber music and many songs.

T

TAAFFE, **Eduard Franz Josef, Graf von**, *tah'fè* (1833–95), 11th Viscount Taaffe and Baron of Ballymote in the Irish peerage, Austrian statesman, was born in Vienna, and became minister of the interior (1867) and chief minister (1869–70, 1879–93). He showed great tact in an attempt to unite the various nationalities of the Empire into a consolidated whole. See *Memoirs of the Family of Taaffe* (1856).

TÁBARI, **Abu Jafar Mohammed Ben Jariral-** (839–923), Arab historian, born in Persia, travelled in Syria, Egypt, &c., wrote in Arabic invaluable Moslem annals (ed. De Goeje and others, 1878–91), and died at Baghdad.

TABLEY, **John Byrne Leicester Warren**, **3rd Baron de** (1835–95), English poet, educated at Eton and Christ Church, Oxford, was called to the bar at Lincoln's Inn in 1859, and

succeeded his father as third baron in 1887. He was author of nine volumes of poetry, mostly written anonymously or under a pseudonym, some plays and novels, and a *Guide to Book Plates* (1880). See Memoir by Sir M. Grant Duff prefixed to his *Flora of Cheshire* (1899) and *Selected Poems*, ed. J. Drinkwater (1924).

TACITUS, **Publius** or **Gaius Cornelius**, *tas'i-toos* (*c.* 55–120), Roman historian, was born perhaps at Rome, where he studied rhetoric, rose to eminence as a pleader at the Roman bar, and in 77 married the daughter of Agricola, the conqueror of Britain. By 88 he was already praetor and a member of one of the priestly colleges. Next year he left Rome for Germany; and he did not return till 93. He was an eye witness to Domitian's reign of terror, and we have his own testimony as to the relief wrought by the accession of Nerva and Trajan. Under Nerva he became consul suffrectus, succeeding Virginius Rufus. We may assume that he saw the close of Trajan's reign, if not the opening of Hadrian's. The high reputation he enjoyed is attested by the eulogistic mention of him in Pliny's letters of which there are eleven addressed to him. The earliest work generally attributed to him, the *Dialogus de Oratoribus*, treats of the decline of eloquence under the empire. It is doubtful whether the *Agricola* is a funeral *éloge* or a panegyric for political ends. As biography it has grave defects, partly due to his admiration for his father-in-law; but it will always be read for its elevation of style, its dramatic force, invective and pathos. The third work, the *Germania*, is a monograph of great value on the ethnography of Germany. Fourth in order comes the *Historiae*, or the history of the empire from the accession of Galba in A.D. 68 to the assassination of Domitian in 96. Of the twelve books originally composing it only the first four and a fragment of the fifth are extant. Tacitus is at his strongest here, and his material was drawn from contemporary experience. His last work, the so-called *Annales*, is a history of the Julian line from Tiberius to Nero (A.D. 14 to 68); of probably eighteen books only eight have come down to us entire, four are fragmentary, and the others lost. His statuesque style is often obscure from condensation. He copied much from earlier historians and was biased in his republican ideals and hatreds. See studies by G. Boissier (1908), R. V. Pöhlmann (1913), R. Syme (1958) and C. W. Mendell (1958).

TADEMA. See ALMA-TADEMA.

TAFT, (1) **Robert Alfonso** (1889–1953), American Republican senator and lawyer, son of (2), born at Cincinnati, Ohio, studied law at Yale and Harvard and in 1917 became counsellor to the American Food Administration in Europe under Hoover. Elected Senator in 1938, he co-sponsored the Taft-Hartley act (1947) directed against the power of the trade unions and the 'closed shop'. A prominent isolationist, Taft failed three times (1940, 1948, 1952) to secure Republican nomination for the presidency. He died of cancer.

(2) **William Howard** (1857–1930), 27th president of the United States, rather of (1), was born at Cincinnati, the son of President Grant's secretary of war and attorney-general; and having studied at Yale and qualified as a barrister at Cincinnati, held numerous appointments in Ohio, and in 1890 became solicitor-general for the United States. In 1900 he was made president of the Philippine Commission, and in 1901 first civil governor of the islands. In 1904–08 he was secretary of war for the United States, in 1906 provisional governor of Cuba, in 1909–1913 Republican president of the United States. He secured an agreement with Canada that meant relatively free trade. From 1913 he was professor of Law at Yale and from 1921 chief justice of the United States. See Lives by Duffy (1930), H. F. Pringle (1939) and Hicks (1945).

TAGLIACOZZI, Gasparo, *tahl-yah-kot'see* (1546–99), Italian surgeon, born at Bologna, was professor there of Surgery and of Anatomy, famous for repairing injured noses by transplanting skin from the arm.

TAGLIONI, Maria, *tahl-yō'nee* (1804–84), Italian *danseuse*, born at Stockholm of an Italian ballet master and a Swedish mother. Badly formed and plain, she danced with astonishing grace and after some initial setbacks triumphed with her creation of *La Sylphide* in 1832 which marked the great romantic era in ballet. She may have introduced *sur les pointes* dancing in ballet. She married Count de Voisins in 1832 and ended her career teaching deportment to the British royal children. She died in poverty. Her brother Paul (1808–84) and his daughter were also famous dancers.

TAGORE, Sir Rabindranath (1861–1941), Indian poet and philosopher, born in Calcutta. He studied in England and, for seventeen years, managed his family estates at Shileida, where he collected the legends and tales he afterwards used in his work. His first book was a novel, *Karuna*, followed by a drama, *The Tragedy of Rudachandra*. In 1901 he founded near Bolpur the Santiniketan, a communal school to blend Eastern and Western philosophical and educational systems. He received the Nobel prize for literature in 1913, the first Asiatic to do so, and was knighted in 1915—an honour which he resigned in 1919 as a protest against British policy in the Punjab. He was openly critical of Gandhi's noncooperation as well as of the Government attitude in Bengal. His work includes *Gitanjali* (1913), *Chitra* (1914) his finest play, and *The Religion of Man* (1931). See *My Reminiscences* (1917) and *My Boyhood Days*; also Lives by Rhys (1915), Thompson (1928), and studies by the latter (1926), Sen (1929), H. l'A. Fausset, *Poets and Pundits* (1947), and A. Bose (1958).

TAILLEFER, *tah-y'-fer* (d. 1066), Norman minstrel, sang war songs at the battle of Hastings, in which he was killed.

TAILLEFERRE, Germaine (1892-   ), French pianist and composer, one of 'les Six'. Her works include chamber music, a ballet, *Le Marchand d'oiseaux*, a piano concerto and songs.

TAINE, Hippolyte Adolphe, *ten* (1828–93), French critic, historian and philosopher, born at Vouziers in Ardennes, April 21, studied a year at Paris before turning author. He made a reputation by his critical analysis of La Fontaine's *Fables* (1853), followed by the *Voyage aux eaux des Pyrénées* (1855). His positivism was forcefully expressed in his critical *Les Philosophes français du dix-neuvième siècle* (1857) and also coloured his *Philosophie de l'art* (1881) and *De l'intelligence* (1870), in which moral qualities and artistic excellence are explained in purely descriptive, quasi-scientific terms. Taine's greatest work, *Les Origines de la France contemporaine* (1875-94) constitutes the strongest attack yet made on the men and the motives of the Revolution. Taine died March 5. *Derniers Essais* appeared in 1895, and *Carnets de voyage* in 1897. His *Notes sur l'Angleterre* (1871) are too ambitious in scope on the basis of only ten weeks' stay in England. See his *Life and Letters* (trans. 1902–08) and French studies by V. Giraud (1901) and A. Chevrillon (1932).

TAIT, (1) **Archibald Campbell** (1811–82), Scottish Anglican divine, born at Edinburgh, December 22, was educated at the Edinburgh Academy, Glasgow University and Balliol College, Oxford. A fellow and tutor, he was one of the four who in 1841 protested against Newman's Tract 90; in 1842 he became headmaster of Rugby, in 1849 Dean of Carlisle, and in 1856 Bishop of London. He showed firmness and broad-mindedness, as well as tact in dealing with controversies over church ritual; he condemned the *Essays and Reviews* and Colenso's teaching, but intervened to secure fair play. As Archbishop of Canterbury (1869), he helped to compose the strifes raised by Irish disestablishment, but was less successful with the Public Worship Regulation Act and the Burials Bill. He did much to extend and improve the organization of the church in the colonies; and the Lambeth Conference of 1878 met under his auspices. See Life by Davidson and Benham (1891).

(2) **Peter Guthrie** (1831–1901), Scottish mathematician and golf enthusiast, born at Dalkeith, was educated at the Edinburgh Academy and University and at Cambridge, where he graduated senior wrangler. Professor of Mathematics at Belfast (1854), of Natural Philosophy at Edinburgh (1860–1900) and secretary of the Royal Society of Edinburgh from 1879, he wrote on quaternions, experimented in thermoelectricity and collaborated with Kelvin in a *Treatise on Natural Philosophy*. He played on one occasion a round of golf with phosphorescent balls after nightfall. His mathematical theory of golfing dynamics led to the conclusion (which did not account for spin) that it was impossible to drive a ball more than 190 yards on a calm day. His son, **Freddie** (1870–1900), who lowered the St Andrews record to 72, and twice won the Amateur championship (1896 and 1898), appeared to falsify this result by a tremendous carry of 250 yards at St Andrews in 1893. Freddie was killed in action near Koodoosberg during the Boer war. See Life by C. G. Knott (1911).

(3) **William** (1792–1864), Scottish publisher, was the founder of *Tait's Edinburgh Magazine* (1832–64), a literary and radical political monthly to which De Quincey, John Stuart Mill, Cobden and Bright contributed.

TALBOT, name of an English family, descended from **Richard de Talbot**, named in the *Domesday* book, and from **Gilbert** (d. 1346), the first baron. The Earl of Shrewsbury and Talbot is the premier earl on the Rolls of England and Ireland and hereditary lord high steward of Ireland. The Lords Talbot de Malahide represent a family in Ireland which settled there in 1167. The former's most noteworthy members, in chronological order, were:

(1) **Sir John, 4th Baron**, and **1st Earl of Shrewsbury** (*c.* 1390–1453), twice lord-lieutenant of Ireland (1414 and 1445), was

the famous champion of English arms in France in Henry VI's reign. Successful in many engagements, he was finally checked at Orleans by Joan of Arc (1429), and taken prisoner at Patay (1429), remaining a captive till 1431. Created Earl of Salop (1422), Earl of Shrewsbury (1442) and Earl of Waterford (1455), he fell at Castillon, after taking Bordeaux.

(2) **John, 2nd Earl of Shrewsbury** (*c.* 1413–1460), son of (1), fell at Northampton, fighting for the Lancastrians.

(3) **George, 4th Earl of Shrewsbury** (*c.* 1528–1590), fourth husband of Elizabeth (' Bess of Hardwick ') (1518–1608), long held Mary of Scotland a prisoner at Tutbury, Chatsworth and Sheffield Castle (1569–84).

(4) **Charles, 12th Earl** and only **Duke of Shrewsbury** (1660–1718), though serving under Charles II and James II, gave money to William of Orange and did much to bring about the Revolution of 1688. Twice secretary of state (1689 and 1694), he withdrew from public affairs in 1700, and went to Rome. In 1710 he helped to bring about the fall of the Whigs and was made lord chamberlain. In 1712 he was ambassador to France, and then lord-lieutenant ot Ireland. At the crisis on the death of Anne (1714), as treasurer and lord justice, he acted with courage and decision and did much to secure the peaceful succession of the Hanoverians. He was created Duke of Shrewsbury in 1694, but the dukedom died with him. See Life by Nicholson and Turberville (1930).

(5) **Bertram Arthur, 17th Earl** (1832–56), died without issue, when the title passed to **John Chetwynd, 3rd Earl Talbot** (1803–68), of a 15th-century branch.

TALBOT, (1) **Mary Anne** (1778–1808), the ' British Amazon ', served as a drummer boy in Flanders (1792) and as a cabin boy at the battle of June 1, 1794.

(2) **William Henry Fox** (1800–77), English pioneer of photography, born at Melbury House, Evershot, educated at Harrow and Trinity, Cambridge, sat in the reformed parliament (1833–34) and in 1838 succeeded in making photographic prints on silver chloride paper, for which he was awarded the Royal Society medal (1838) and the Rumford medal (1842). He published works on astronomy and mathematics, and helped to decipher the Ninevite cuneiform inscriptions. His *Pencil of Nature* (1844) was the first photographically illustrated book.

TALFOURD, **Sir Thomas Noon** (1795–1854) English lawyer and author, born at Reading, which he represented in parliament, had his tragedy *Ion* (1835) produced by Macready at Covent Garden, wrote on Charles Lamb and is best known for his Copyright Act (1842). See his *Letters* (1837).

TALIACOTIUS. See TAGLIACOZZI.

TALIESIN, *tal-i-ay'sin* (fl. *c.* 550), Welsh bard, possibly mythical, to whom are ascribed many admirable poems, not older in language than the 12th century, however. See book by D. W. Nash (1858).

TALLARD, **Comte Camille de, Duc d' Hostun,** *tah-lahr* (1652–1728), French soldier, created marshal of France, was defeated and taken prisoner by Marlborough at Blenheim (1704).

TALLEMANT DES RÉAUX, Gédéon, *tal-mã day ray-ō* (*c.* 1619–1700), French man of letters, born at La Rochelle, married his cousin Élisabeth Rambouillet, whose fortune enabled him to· give himself to letters and society. His famous *Historiettes* (written 1657–59; published 1834–40), 376 in number, are illustrative anecdotes rather than biographies. The most finished group is that of the famous circle of the Hôtel de Rambouillet. He was admitted to the Academy in 1666. See studies by E. Magne (1921 and 1922) ând E. Gosse (1925).

TALLEYRAND - PÉRIGORD, Charles Maurice de, Prince of Benevento, *tal-ay-rã* (1754–1838), French statesman, was born at Paris, February 13, son of the Comte Talleyrand de Périgord (1734–88) who fought in the Seven Years' War. He was educated for the church, made himself a fair scholar, and cultivated the character of a rake and a cynical wit. Abbot of St Denis (1775) and *agent-général* to the French clergy (1780), he was by Louis XVI nominated Bishop of Autun in 1788. Next year the clergy of his diocese elected him to the States General, and he was one of the members of the Assembly selected to draw up the Declaration of Rights. He took a cynical delight in attacking the calling to which he still nominally belonged, and proposed the measure confiscating the landed property of the church. In February 1790 he was elected president of the Assembly. In 1791 he consecrated two new bishops, declaring at the same time his attachment to the Holy See, but, excommunicated by the pope, he gave up his clerical career. Early in 1792 Talleyrand was sent to London, but failed to conciliate Pitt; in December he was placed on the list of *émigrés*. He was again in London, an exile, till January 1794, when the Alien Act drove him to the United States. After the fall of Robespierre he returned to Paris (1796), attached himself to Barras, and in 1797 was made foreign minister under the Directory; he was for a time the first man in France. He had already recognized the genius of Bonaparte and established intimate relations with him. For a time he was in disgrace for his willingness to sell his services towards a treaty between Great Britain and the United States. But under the Consulate he was restored to his post, and was privy to the kidnapping and murder (March 1804) of the Duc d'Enghien. He was greatly instrumental in consolidating the power of Napoleon as consul for life (1802) and as emperor (1804). When in 1805 Great Britain formed a European coalition against France, it was partially broken up by Talleyrand. To him as much as to Napoleon was owing the organization (1806) of the Confederation of the Rhine. After being created Prince de Bénévent, he withdrew from the ministry. His voice was on the whole for a policy of wisdom during the later years of the first empire. He was opposed to the invasion of Russia; and this gives some justification for his desertion of Napoleon in 1814. As far back as Tilsit (1807) he seems to have been in communication with Britain; at Erfurt

(1808), he had revealed state secrets to Russia; and he had mortally offended Napoleon, after the disasters in Spain, by making, with Fouché (q.v.), tentative arrangements for the succession. Now, he became the leader of the anti-Napoleonic faction; and through him communications were opened with the allies and the Bourbons. He dictated to the Senate the terms of Napoleon's deposition, and he became minister of foreign affairs under Louis XVIII. He negotiated the treaties by which the allies left France in possession of the boundaries of 1792, and at the Congress of Vienna he established her right to be heard. He had not calculated on the Hundred Days, and offered no help to Louis; being taken back after the second restoration, he became, through pressure of the allies, prime minister for a· short time, but he was not *persona grata* with the king, and was disliked by all parties in France. Under Louis XVIII and Charles X he was little better than a discontented senator; but he was Louis-Philippe's chief adviser at the July revolution, for which he was partly responsible, went to London as ambassador and reconciled the British ministry and court to France. He retired into private life in 1834, and died May 17, 1838. See his *Mémoires*, edited by the Duc de Broglie (1891; Eng. trans. 1891–92), his *Correspondance*, ed. Pallain (1887–91), and Lives by G. Lacour-Gayet (1930–31), A. Duff Cooper (1932) and J. Vivent (1940).

TALLIEN, Jean Lambert, *tal-yi* (1769–1820), French revolutionary, born in Paris, made himself famous in 1791 by his Jacobin broadsheets, *L'Ami des citoyens*. He was conspicuous in the attack on the Tuileries, and in the September massacres, was elected to the Convention (1792), voted for the death of the king, was elected to the Committee of General Safety, and played a part in the downfall of the Girondists. On his mission to Bordeaux he quenched all opposition with the guillotine. Comtesse Thérèse de Fontenay, born Jeanne Marie Ignace Thérésa Cabarrus (1773–1835), whom he married in 1794 after saving her from death on the guillotine, also became famous for her harsh and dissolute conduct. He was recalled to Paris, and in March 1794 was chosen president of the Convention. But Robespierre hated him, and Tallien, recognizing his danger, led the successful attack of 9th Thermidor. He helped to suppress the Revolutionary Tribunal and the Jacobin Club, and drew up the accusations against Carrier, Le Bon and other Terrorists; but his importance ended with the Convention, though he accompanied Napoleon to Egypt and edited the *Décade égyptienne* at Cairo. On the voyage home he was captured by an English cruiser, and in England was made a hero by the Whigs (1801). Consul at Alicante (1805), he lost an eye there by yellow fever, and died in Paris in poverty.

TALLIS, Thomas (*c.* 1505–85), English musician, ' the father of English cathedral music ', was organist of Waltham Abbey at the dissolution in 1540, when it is conjectured he became ' a gentleman of the Chapel Royal '. Elizabeth gave him, with Byrd (q.v.), a monopoly of music printing. In Day's Psalter (1560) there are eight tunes by him, one of which, known as Tallis's Canon, is now used for Ken's Evening Hymn. The *Cantiones* (1575) contained eighteen motets by Byrd and sixteen by Tallis. He was one of the greatest contrapuntists of the English School; an adaptation of his plainsong responses, and his setting of the Canticles in D Minor, are still in use. He wrote much church music, among it a motet in forty parts.

TALMA, François Joseph (1763–1826), French tragedian, was born and died in Paris, and made his début in 1787. Hitherto actors had worn the garb of their own time and country; Talma made a point of accuracy in costume. He achieved his greatest success in 1789 as Charles IX in Chénier's play. See his *Mémoires* (ed. by A. Dumas, 1849–50).

TAMAYO, Rufino (1899–), Mexican artist whose style combines the ancient art of his own country with the art of modern Europe. Among his works are frescoes in the National Conservatory of Music and in Smith College Library.

TAMERLANE (i.e., **Timur-i-Leng**, ' Lame Timur ') (1336–1405), Tatar conqueror, was born at Kesh, S. of Samarkand, his father being a Mongol chief. In 1369 he ascended the throne of Samarkand. He subdued nearly all Persia, Georgia and the Tatar empire, conquered (1398) all the states between the Indus and the lower Ganges, and returned to Samarkand with a fabulous booty. Having set out against the Turks of Asia Minor, he turned aside to win Damascus and Syria from the Mameluke sovereigns of Egypt. At length on the plains of Angora the Mongol and Turkish hosts met, and Sultan Bajazet was routed and taken prisoner. The conqueror died on the march towards China. See Marlowe's tragedy (1590), Howorth's *History of the Mongols* (1876–88), and Life by H. Hookham (1962).

TANCRED (1078–1112), Norman crusader, son of the Palgrave Otho the Good, joined his cousin, Bohemund of Tarentum, Guiscard's son, in the first Crusade, and distinguished himself in the sieges of Nicaea, Tarsus, Antioch, Jerusalem, and at Ascalon. His reward was the principality of Tiberias. For some time he ruled Bohemund's state of Antioch, and shortly before his death was invested with the principality of Edessa. He is the hero of Tasso's *Gerusalemme Liberata*.

TANDY, James Napper (1740–1803), Irish agitator, born in Dublin, became a prosperous merchant there. A Presbyterian, he took an active part in corporation politics, and was the first secretary to the Dublin United Irishmen. In 1792 he challenged the solicitor-general for his abusive language, and was arrested. In 1793 he was to have stood trial on the minor charge of distributing a ' seditious ' pamphlet against the Beresfords, when the government learned that he had taken the oath of the Defenders, a treasonable offence. He fled to America, crossed to France in 1798, shared in the ill-fated invasion of Ireland, by landing on Rutland Island, and at Hamburg was handed over to

the English government. In February 1800 he was acquitted at Dublin. Again put on trial (April 1801) at Lifford for the treasonable landing on Rutland Island, he was sentenced to death, but permitted to escape to France, and died at Bordeaux. See Madden's *United Irishmen* (1846).

TANEY, Roger Brooke, *taw'ni* (1777–1864), American jurist, born in Calvert County, Md., and admitted to the bar in 1799, was elected to the Maryland senate in 1816. In 1824 he passed from the Federal to the Democratic party, and supported Andrew Jackson, who in 1831 made him attorney-general, and in 1833 secretary of the Treasury. The senate, after rejecting his appointment as chief justice in 1835, confirmed it in 1836. His early decisions were strongly in favour of state sovereignty, but his most famous decision was in the Dred Scott case, when he ruled that the Missouri compromise over the colour question was unconstitutional and that no Negro could claim state citizenship for legal purposes. Although an early opponent of slavery, Taney wished to put an end to anti-slavery agitation. See Life by C. B. Swisher (1938).

TANEYEV, Sergei Ivanovich, *tan-yay-ye,* (1856–1915), Russian composer and pianist, was born in Vladimir, studied at the Conservatory, Moscow, and was professor there. A pupil of Tchaikovsky, he wrote music of all kinds, including two cantatas, *John of Damascus* and *After the Reading of a Psalm*, and six symphonies. Well known as a teacher, among his pupils were Scriabin and Rachmaninov.

TANFUCIO, Neri. See FUCINI.

TANGUY, Yves, *tã-gee* (1900–55), American artist, born in Paris. He was mainly self-taught, and began to paint in 1922, joining the surrealists in 1926. In 1930 he travelled in Africa, and went to the U.S.A. in 1939, becoming an American citizen in 1948. All his pictures are at the same time surrealist and nonfigurative, being peopled with numerous small objects or organisms, whose meaning and identity, as in the landscape of another planet, is unknown. See Life by J. T. Soby (1955).

TANNAHILL, Robert (1774–1810), Scottish poet, was born at Paisley, the son of a hand-loom weaver, and composed many of his best songs to the music of his shuttle. His *Poems and Songs* (1807) proved popular, the best-known being *Gloomy Winter's noo awa, Jessie the Flower o' Dunblane, The Braes o' Gleniffer, Loudon's Bonnie Woods and Braes* and *The Wood o' Craigielea*. But after a publisher declined a revised edition his body was found in a canal near Paisley. See Life in Semple's edition of his poems (1876) and Brown's *Paisley Poets* (vol. i 1889).

TANNER, Thomas (1674–1735), English antiquary, born at Market Lavington vicarage, Wiltshire, became a fellow of All Souls (1696), archdeacon of Norwich (1710), canon of Christ Church, Oxford (1724), and Bishop of St Asaph (1732). An enlarged edition of his *Notitia Monastica* (1695) appeared in 1744. Not less valuable is his biographical and bibliographical *Bibliotheca Britannico-Hibernica* (1748).

TANSLEY, Sir Arthur George (1871–1955), British botanist, born in London, Sherardian professor at Oxford (1927–37), founded the precursor (1904) of the Ecological Society (1914), the *New Phytologist* (1902) which he edited for 30 years, published textbooks on botany and contributed to anatomical and morphological botany and to psychology. He was elected F.R.S. in 1915 and received the Linnean Society gold medal in 1921.

TANTIA TOPEE (d. 1859), Brahman soldier from Gwalior, was Nana Sahib's lieutenant in the Indian Mutiny. With the Rani of Jhansi he occupied Gwalior and then held the field after his chief had fled. He was captured April 7, 1859, and executed.

TARKINGTON, (Newton) Booth (1869–1946), American author, born in Indianapolis. Many of his novels have an Indiana setting, including *The Gentleman from Indiana*, which is concerned with political corruption; but he is best known to English readers as the author of *Monsieur Beaucaire* (1900) and his ' Penrod ' books—*Penrod* (1914) and *Seventeen* (1916). His other works include a trilogy, *Growth* (1927), including *The Magnificent Ambersons* (1918), which won the Pulitzer prize, *Alice Adams* (1921, Pulitzer prize), and a book of reminiscences, *The World does Move* (1928).

TARLETON, Sir Banastre, 1st Bart. (1754–1833), English soldier, born in Liverpool, educated at Oxford, served under Clinton and Cornwallis in America. He held Gloucester till it capitulated (1782), and then returned to England. Member for Liverpool (1790–1806; 1807–12), he was created baronet in 1815. See his *History of the Campaigns of 1780 and 1781* (1781).

TARLTON, Richard (d. 1588), English comedian, a man of ' happy unhappy answers ', was introduced to Elizabeth through the Earl of Leicester and became one of the Queen's players (1583). He died in poverty, and on him was fathered *Tarlton's Jests* (1592?–1611?), in three parts.

TARQUINIUS, an Etruscan family, named after the city of Tarquinii, to which two of the kings of Rome belonged:

(1) **Lucius Tarquinius Priscus**, originally Lucumo, arrived a stranger in Rome with a favourable omen, and is said to have reigned 616–578 B.C., to have modified the constitution, and to have begun the Servian agger and the Circus Maximus. He was murdered.

(2) **Lucius Tarquinius Superbus**, king (534–510 B.C.), seventh and last King of Rome, extended his dominion more than any of his predecessors, and by establishing colonies founded Rome's greatness. But his tyranny, especially in the matter of Lucretia (q.v.), excited the discontent of both patricians and plebeians, and in consequence of a rising under his nephew, Brutus, he and all his family were banished. He took refuge with Lars Porsena at Clusium and, with him, levied successful war against Rome. He was later defeated at Lake Regillus (498 B.C.) and died a fugitive.

TARSKI, Alfred (1902–), Polish logician, born in Warsaw, was professor there (1925–1939), at Harvard, New York and Princeton,

and since 1942 at Berkeley, California. He modified Carnap's extreme positivism, pioneered semantics, but for English tastes took too lightly the distinction between questions of logic and questions of fact. Quine (q.v.) is his prominent disciple. His chief works are *Introduction to Logic and the Methodology of Deductive Sciences* (1936; trans. 1941), *Undecidable Theories* with Mostowski and Robinson (1953), *Logic, Semantics and Metamathematics* (1956) and *Logic, Methodology and Philosophy of Science* (ed. with Nagel and Suppers, 1962).

TARTINI, Giuseppe, *tar-tee'nee* (1692–1770), Italian composer, born at Pirano in Istria, gave up the church and the law for music and fencing. Having secretly married the niece of the Archbishop of Padua, he fled to Assisi, but, after living in Venice, Ancona and Prague, returned before 1728 to Padua. Tartini ' was one of the greatest violinists of all time, an eminent composer, and a scientific writer on musical physics '. His best-known work is the *Trillo del Diavolo.*

TASMAN, Abel Janszoon (1603–c. 1659), Dutch navigator, was born in Lutjegast near Groningen. In 1642 he discovered Tasmania —named Van Diemen's Land—and New Zealand, in 1643 Tonga and Fiji, having been dispatched in quest of the ' Great South Land ' by Antony Van Diemen (1593–1645), governor-general of Batavia. He made a second voyage (1644) to the Gulf of Carpentaria and the N.W. coast of Australia. See *Journal*, with trans. and Life by Heeres (Amsterdam 1898).

TASSIE, James (1735–99), Scottish modeller, born at Pollokshaws, Glasgow, in 1766 settled in London, and used a ' white enamel composition ' in his well-known reproductions of the most famous gems. He also executed many cameo portraits of his contemporaries, and the plaster reproductions of the Portland Vase. His nephew, William Tassie (1777–1860), succeeded him. See Life by J. M. Gray (1895).

TASSO, (1) Bernardo (1493–1569), Italian poet, father of (2), was born at Venice of an illustrious family of Bergamo. After suffering poverty and exile owing to the outlawry by Charles V (1547) of his patron, the Duke of Salerno, he took service with the Duke of Mantua. His *Amadigi*, an epic on Amadis of Gaul, is a melodious imitation of Ariosto's manner, but exaggerated in sentiment. He began another epic, *Floridante* (1587), finished by his son, and wrote numerous lyrics (1749). See *Lettere di Bernardo Tasso* (ed. Campori, 1869) and his *Lettere inedite* (ed. Portioli, 1871).

(2) **Torquato** (1544–95), Italian poet, son of (1), was born at Sorrento, March 11, and shared his exiled father's wandering life, but in 1560 he was sent to study law and philosophy at Padua, where he published his first work, a romantic poem, *Rinaldo*. In the service of Cardinal Luigi d'Este he was introduced to the court of the Duke of Ferrara; and there, encouraged by the sisters of the duke, he began his great epic poem and masterpiece, *Gerusalemme Liberata*. In 1571 he accompanied Cardinal d'Este to France, and on his return to Italy

in 1572 became attached to the service of Duke Alfonso at Ferrara. For the court theatre he wrote his beautiful pastoral play, *Aminta* (1581). Tasso completed his great epic in 1575, and submitted it before publication to the critics of the day. Their fault-finding and Tasso's replies are recorded in his correspondence and in his *Apologia*. In 1576 he showed the first signs of mental disorder; he became suspicious and melancholy, and obsessed with fears of assassination. He was confined at Ferrara, but escaped, and eventually made his way to Naples, Rome and Turin, where he was welcomed by the Duke of Savoy. Returning to Ferrara in 1579, he met with a cold reception, and wounded by some real or imagined slight, broke into furious invectives against the duke, his courtiers, all the world. He was confined at Ferrara by order of the duke as insane (not, as is often alleged, for his love for the Princess Leonora, a story on which Byron based his *Lament of Tasso*); and in his seven years' confinement wrote many noble verses and philosophical dialogues and a vigorous defence of his *Jerusalem*, published without his leave and with many errors. The cruel contrast between his fate and the daily growing fame of his great poem had excited popular interest, and in July 1586 he was liberated on the intercession of Prince Vincenzo Gonzaga. He followed his new patron to Mantua, where he wrote his only tragedy, *Torrismondo*. Broken in health and spirits, he began again his restless wanderings, spending, however, most of these later years in Rome and Naples, helped and protected by many kind friends and patrons. He busied himself in rewriting his great epic, according to the modifications proposed by his numerous critics. The result, a poor simulacrum of his masterpiece, was published under the name *Gerusalemme Conquistata* (1593). Summoned to Rome by Pope Clement VIII to be crowned on the Capitol as poet laureate, he took ill on arrival and died in the monastery of Sant' Onofrio on the Janiculum, April 25. His *Jerusalem*, an idealized story of the first Crusade, is a typical product of his time, its blind idolatry of classic forms conflicting with newly-revived religious superstition. See his letters and prose writings (ed. Guasti, 1853–75), and Lives by W. Boulting (1907), E. Donadoni (1921), L. Tonelli (1935) and C. Previtera (1936).

TATA, Jamsetji Nasarwanji (1839–1904), Indian industrialist, born in Gujerat, built cotton mills at Nagpur (1877) and at Cooria near Bombay. He did much to promote scientific education in Indian schools. See Life by F. R. Harris (1958). His son, **Sir Dorabji** (1859–1932), developed the Indian iron-ore industry, applied hydroelectricity to the Cooria cotton mills and founded a commercial airline.

TATE, (1) Sir Henry, 1st Bart. (1819–99), English sugar magnate, art patron and philanthropist, born at Chorley, Lancashire, patented a method for cutting sugar cubes in 1872 and attained great wealth as a Liverpool sugar refiner. He founded the University Library at Liverpool and gave the nation the 'Tate Gallery', Millbank, London, which was opened in 1897, and contained his own valuable private collection. He was made a baronet in 1898.

(2) **Nahum** (1652–1715), Irish poet and dramatist, born in Dublin, studied at Trinity College there and saw his first play staged in London in 1678. With Johnson's approval, he wrote a number of ' improved ' versions of Shakespeare's tragedies, substituting happy endings to suit the popular taste. With Dryden's help he wrote a second part to the poet's *Absalom and Achitophel* (1682) and with Brady compiled a metrical version of the psalms. ' While Shepherds watched their Flocks by Night ' is attributed to him, and he wrote the libretto of Purcell's *Dido and Aeneas* (1689). He became poet laureate in 1692. His best-known work is *Panacea or a Poem on Tea* (1700). See E. K. Broadus, *The Laureateship* (1921).

TATI, Jacques, *tah-tee*, pseud. of **Jacques Tatischeff** (1908–), French actor, author and film producer, born in Pecq (S. et O.). His first appearance before English audiences was as the ghost in *Sylvie et le Fantôme*, but it was not until he appeared in *Jour de Fête* (1951), directed and written by himself, that he made his reputation as the greatest film comedian of the postwar period. This was enhanced by *M. Hulot's Holiday* (1954) and *Mon Oncle* (1958), satirizing the tyranny of luxurious, labour-saving gadgetry, which won a Cannes Festival prize (1958) and the American ' Oscar ' and was hailed as a worthy successor to Chaplin's *Modern Times*.

TATIAN (2nd cent.), Christian apologist, born in Assyria, studied Greek philosophy, but was converted to Christianity by the martyr Justin at Rome in whose lifetime he wrote his *Oratio ad Graecos* (ed. by Schwartz, 1888), a glowing exposure of heathenism as compared with the new ' barbarian philosophy '. After Justin's death (166) Tatian fell into evil repute for heresies, and he retired to Mesopotamia, probably Edessa, writing treatise after treatise, all of which have perished. The notions of his which gave most offence were his excessive asceticism, his rejection of marriage and animal food, and certain Gnostic doctrines about a demiurge and the aeons. He was assailed in turn by Irenaeus, Tertullian, Hippolytus, Clement of Alexandria and Origen. He died, perhaps at Edessa, about 180. Of his writings one maintained a place of importance in the Syrian Church for two centuries. This was the *Diatessaron*, a kind of patchwork gospel freely constructed out of our four gospels. See German works by Zahn, Sellin, Gebhardt and Harnack; English ones by Hemphill (1888), R. Harris (1890), and J. H. Hill (1893).

TATIUS, Achilles (fl. *c.* A.D. 500), Greek romancer, was a rhetorician at Alexandria. He wrote *Leucippe and Cleitophon*.

TATTERSALL, Richard (1724–95), English auctioneer, born at Hurstwood, Lancashire, came early to London. He entered the Duke of Kingston's service, became an auctioneer, and in 1776 set up auction rooms at Hyde Park Corner, which became a celebrated mart of thoroughbred horses and a great racing centre. They were transferred to Knightsbridge in 1867. See *Memories of Hurstwood* by Tattersall Wilkinson and J. F. Tattersall (1889).

TAUBER, Richard, tow'bĕr (1891–1948), Austrian-born British tenor, born at Linz, established himself as one of Germany's leading tenors, particularly in Mozartian opera, until 1925 when he increasingly appeared in light opera, notably Lehár's *Land of Smiles*, which he brought to London in 1931. This won him great popularity, repeated by his part in his own *Old Chelsea* (1943), but at the expense of the finer qualities of his voice. He appeared at Covent Garden in 1938, became a British subject and died in Sydney, Australia. See Life by his wife (1959).

TAUBMAN-GOLDIE, Sir George Dashwood (1846–1925), Manx traveller and administrator, son of Colonel Goldie Taubman, speaker of the House of Keys, was born in the Isle of Man, travelled in Africa, and as founder and governor of the Royal Niger Company greatly extended English commerce and influence.

TAUCHNITZ, Karl Christoph Traugott, towKH'nits (1761–1836), German publisher, born near Grimma, set up in 1796 a small printing business in Leipzig, to which he added publishing and typefounding. In 1809 he began to issue his cheap editions of the classics. He introduced stereotyping into Germany (1816). His nephew, **Christian Bernhard, Baron von Tauchnitz** (1816–95), also founded in 1837 a printing and publishing house in Leipzig famous for its collection of 'British and American Authors', begun in 1841.

TAULER, Johann, tow'ler (c. 1300–61), German mystic, was born at Strasbourg, and became a Dominican (c. 1318). Driven from Strasbourg by a feud between the city and his order, he settled at twenty-four at Basel, and associated with the devout 'Friends of God', having before then been a disciple of Meister Eckhart (q.v.). His fame as a preacher spread far and wide, and he became the centre of the quickened religious life in the middle Rhine valley. He died at Strasbourg. See English Life by S. Winkworth (1857), and German books by Karl Schmidt (1841–75) and Siedl (1911).

TAUNTON, Lord. See LABOUCHÈRE (1).

TAUSSIG, Frank William, tow'sig (1859–1940), American economist, born at St Louis, Mo., became professor at Harvard (1892–1935) and was best known for his *Principles of Economics* (1911).

TAVERNER, (1) John (c. 1495–1545), English musician, organist at Boston and Christ Church, Oxford, composed notable motets and masses. Accused of heresy, he was imprisoned by Wolsey, but released, 'being but a musitian'. He died at Boston.

(2) **Richard** (c. 1505–75), English author, was patronized by Wolsey and Cromwell, for whom he compiled Taverner's Bible (1539), which was really a revision of Matthew's Bible (1537). On the fall of Cromwell, he was imprisoned but soon released and was M.P. for Liverpool (1545).

TAVERNIER, Jean Baptiste, Baron d'Aubonne, ta-ver'nyay (1605–89), French traveller, was born at Paris, the son of a Protestant engraver from Antwerp. His first journey to the East (1631–33) was by way of Constantinople to Persia, thence by Aleppo and Malta to Italy. The second journey (1638–43) was across Syria to Ispahan, Agra and Golconda; the third (1643–49), through Ispahan, much of Hindustan, Batavia and Bantam, thence to Holland by the Cape; and the fourth (1651–55), fifth (1657–62) and sixth (1663–68) to many districts of Persia and India. Tavernier travelled as a dealer in precious stones. Louis XIV, gave him 'letters of nobility' in 1669, and next year he bought the barony of Aubonne near Geneva. In 1684 he started for Berlin to advise the Elector of Brandenburg in his projects for eastern trade. In 1689 he went to Russia, and died at Moscow. His famous *Six Voyages* was published in 1676; the complementary *Recueil* in 1679. See *Travels in India*, trans. by Dr V. Ball (1890), and a French work by Joret (1886).

TAWNEY, Richard Henry (1880–1962), English economic historian, born in Calcutta, was educated at Rugby and Balliol College, Oxford, of which he was elected fellow in 1918. After a spell of social work at Toynbee Hall in the East End of London, he became tutor, executive (1905–47) and president (1928–44) of the Workers' Educational Association. As a sergeant in the Manchester Regiment, he was severely wounded during the battle of the Somme (1916). A socialist in the non-Marxist Keir Hardie tradition and a Christian, he wrote a number of studies in English economic history, particularly of the Tudor and Stuart periods, of which the best known are *The Acquisitive Society* (1926), *Religion and the Rise of Capitalism* (1926), *Equality* (1931) and *Business and Politics under James I* (1958). He was professor of Economic History at London (1931–49) and was elected F.B.A. in 1935. He married a sister, Annette Jeanie (d. 1958), of Lord Beveridge in 1909.

TAYLOR, (1) Alfred Edward (1869–1945), English scholar and philosopher, born at Oundle, Northamptonshire, became professor of Logic at McGill University (1903–08) and of Moral Philosophy at St Andrews (1908–24) and Edinburgh (1924–41). An authority on Plato, he wrote *Plato, The Man and his Work* (1926), *A Commentary on Plato's Timaeus* (1928), and translated his *Laws* (1934). Other notable works are *The Problem of Conduct* (1901), *Elements of Metaphysics* (1903), the Gifford lectures which he gave at St Andrews on *The Faith of a Moralist*, and studies of St Thomas Aquinas (1924) and Socrates (1932).

(2) **Alfred Swaine** (1806–80), English medical jurist, born at Northfleet, for forty-six years was professor of Medical Jurisprudence at Guy's Hospital. Elected F.R.S. (1845), he wrote two standard works on medical jurisprudence (1844 and 1865) and one on poisons (1848).

(3) **Bayard** (1825–78), American traveller and author, was born in Chester county, Penn., and apprenticed to a printer, wrote a volume of poems (1844), visited Europe, published *Views Afoot* (1846), and obtained

a post on the *New York Tribune*. As its correspondent he made extensive travels in California and Mexico, up the Nile, in Asia Minor and Syria, across Asia to India, China and Japan—recorded in a great number of travel books which he published. In 1862–63 he was secretary of legation at St Petersburg; in 1878 became ambassador at Berlin, where he died. His poetical works include *Rhymes of Travel* (1848), *Poems of the Orient* (1854), *Poems of Home and Travel* (1855), *Prince Deukalion* (1878), a play, but he was best known for his translation of Goethe's *Faust* (1870–71). Among his novels is *Hannah Thurston* (1863). See his *Life and Letters* (1884) by M. Hansen-Taylor and H. E. Scudder.

(4) **Brook** (1685–1731), English mathematician, born at Edmonton, studied at St John's College, Cambridge, and in 1715 published his *Methodus*, the foundation of the Calculus of Finite Differences, containing ' Taylor's Theorem '. In 1714–18 he was secretary to the Royal Society. His *Contemplatio Philosophica* (1719) was edited with a Life by Sir W. Young (1793).

(5) **Sir Henry** (1800–86), English poet, was born, the son of a gentleman farmer, at Bishop-Middleham, in Durham, and was a clerk in the colonial office (1824–72). D.C.L. (1862) and K.C.M.G. (1869), he died at Bournemouth. He wrote four tragedies, *Isaac Comnenus* (1827), a remarkable study in character, *Philip van Artefelde* (1834), *Edwin the Fair* (1842) and *St Clement's Eve* (1862). A romantic comedy, *The Virgin Widow* (1850), was afterwards entitled *A Sicilian Summer*. In 1845 he published a volume of lyrical poetry, and in 1847 *The Eve of the Conquest*. His prose included *The Statesman* (1836) and *Autobiography* (1885).

(6) **Isaac** (1787–1865), Anglo-Jewish author, was born at Lavenham, son of the London engraver **Isaac** (1759–1829) and father of (7). After a course of study he settled down to a literary life at Ongar, and among his chief books were *Natural History of Enthusiasm* (1829), *Natural History of Fanaticism* (1833), *Spiritual Despotism* (1835), *Physical Theory of Another Life* (1836), and *Ultimate Civilisation* (1860).

(7) **Isaac** (1829–1901), English philologist, son of (6), born at Stanford Rivers, studied at Trinity College, Cambridge, and became in 1875 rector of Settrington and canon of York in 1885. His *Words and Places* (1864) made him known, while *The Alphabet* (1883) brought him a wide reputation. Other publications include *Etruscan Researches* (1874), *The Origin of the Aryans* (1890) and *Names and their Histories* (1896). See his family history of the Taylors (1867).

(8) **Jeremy** (1613–67), English divine, the third son of a Cambridge barber, entered Caius College, and became a fellow of All Souls, Oxford (1636), chaplain to Archbishop Laud, and in 1638 rector of Uppingham. *The Sacred Order and Offices of Episcopacy* (1642) gained him his D.D. During the Civil War he is said to have accompanied the royal army as a chaplain and was taken prisoner at Cardigan Castle (1645). After the downfall of the cause he sought shelter in Wales,

kept a school, and found a patron in the Earl of Carbery, then living at Golden Grove, Llandilo, immortalized in the title of Taylor's still popular manual of devotion (1655). During the last thirteen years (1647–60) of Taylor's enforced seclusion appeared all his great works, some of them the most enduring monuments of sacred eloquence in the English language. The first was *The Liberty of Prophesying* (1646), a noble and comprehensive plea for toleration and freedom of opinion. *The Life of Christ, or the Great Exemplar* (1649) is an arrangement of the facts in historical order, interspersed with prayers and discourses. *The Rule and Exercises of Holy Living* (1650) and *The Rule and Exercises of Holy Dying* (1651) together form the choicest classic of English devotion. The fifty-two *Sermons* (1651–53), with the discourses in the *Life of Christ* and many passages in the *Holy Living* and *Dying*, contain the richest examples of their author's characteristically gorgeous eloquence. The more formal treatises were *An Apology for Authorised and Set Forms of Liturgy* (1646); *Clerus Dominio* (on the ministerial office, 1651); *The Real Presence in the Blessed Sacrament* (1654); *Unum Necessarium* (on repentance, 1655), which brought on him the charge of Pelagianism; *The Worthy Communicant* (1660); *The Rite of Confirmation* (1663); *The Dissuasive from Popery* (1664); and the famous *Ductor Dubitantium* (1660), the most learned and subtle of all his works, intended as a handbook of Christian casuistry and ethics. During the Civil War Taylor was thrice imprisoned, once for the preface to the *Golden Grove*; the last time in the Tower for an ' idolatrous ' print of Christ in the attitude of prayer in his *Collection of Offices* (1658). In 1658 he got a lectureship at Lisburn, at the Restoration the bishopric of Down and Connor, with next year the administration of Dromore; and became vice-chancellor of Dublin University and a member of the Irish privy council. In his first visitation (in spite of his *Liberty of Prophesying*) he ejected thirty-six Presbyterian ministers, but neither severity nor gentleness could prevail to force a form of religion upon an unwilling people. He died at Lisburn, August 13, and was buried in the cathedral of Dromore. See Heber's edition of his works, with Life (1820–22; revised 1847–54), and Lives by E. Gosse (1904), W. J. Brown (1925) and Stranks (1952).

(9) **John** (1580–1653), English poet, the ' Water-poet ', born at Gloucester, became a Thames waterman, but, pressed into the navy, served at the siege of Cadiz. At the outbreak of the Civil War (1642) he kept a public house in Oxford, gave it up for another in London, and there hawked his own doggerel poems, which yet are not destitute of natural humour and low, jingling wit. The chief event of his life was his journey afoot from London to Edinburgh (1618), described in his *Penniless Pilgrimage* (1618); similar books were his *Travels in Germanie* (1617) and *The Praise of Hempseed*, a story of a voyage in a brown paper boat from London to Queenborough (1618).

(10) **John Edward** (1791–1844), English

journalist, born at Ilminster, son of a Unitarian minister, was the founder in 1821 of the liberal *Manchester Guardian*.

(11) **John Henry** (1871–1963), English golfer, born at Northam in Devon, was the winner of the British Open Championship in 1894. This triumph was repeated in 1895, 1900, 1909 and 1913. Twice he won the French Open Championship, in 1908 and 1909, and once the German Open Championship, in 1912. A brilliant player, he was specially known for his skill with the mashie. He wrote the very popular *Taylor on Golf* (1902).

(12) **Nathaniel William** (1786–1858), American theologian, born at New Milford, Conn., became in 1822 professor of Theology at Yale. His ' New Haven theology ', long assailed as heretical, was a softening of the traditional Calvinism of New England, maintained the doctrine of natural ability, and denied total depravity; sin is a voluntary action of the sinner, but there is, derived from Adam, a bias to sin, which is not itself sinful. Porter edited his works in 1858–59.

(13) **Rowland** (d. 1555), English Protestant martyr, born at Rothbury, became rector of Hadleigh (1544), Archdeacon of Exeter (1551), and a canon of Rochester. Under Mary he was imprisoned as a heretic, and on February 8, 1555, was burned near Hadleigh.

(14) **Thomas** (1758–1835), English scholar, ' the Platonist ', a Londoner educated at St Paul's School, entered Lubbock's bank as a clerk. His fifty works include translations of the Orphic Hymns, parts of Plotinus, Proclus, Pausanias, Apuleius, Iamblichus, Porphyry, &c., Plato (nine of the Dialogues by Floyer Sydenham, 1804), and Aristotle (1806–12). *The Spirit of All Religions* (1790) expresses his strange polytheistic creed. See sketch by Axon (1890).

(15) **Tom** (1817–80), Scottish dramatist and editor, born at Sunderland, studied at Glasgow and Trinity College, Cambridge, and was elected a fellow. Professor for two years of English at University College, London, and called to the bar in 1845, he was secretary to the Board of Health 1850–72, and then to the Local Government Act Office. From 1846 he wrote or adapted over a hundred pieces for the stage, among them *Our American Cousin*, *Still Waters Run Deep* (1855), *The Ticket of Leave Man* (1863), and *'Twixt Axe and Crown*. He edited the autobiographies of Haydon and Leslie, completed the latter's *Life and Times of Reynolds*, translated *Ballads and Songs of Brittany* (1865), and in 1874 became editor of *Punch*. *The Times* art critic, he appeared as a witness for Ruskin in the libel action brought against him by Whistler in 1878.

(16) **William** (1765–1836), English author, ' of Norwich ', son of a Unitarian merchant, entered his father's counting-house in 1779 and, travelling extensively on the Continent introduced the works of Lessing, Goethe &c., to English readers, mainly through, criticisms and translations, collected in his *Historic Survey of German Poetry* (1828–30). Borrow's *Lavengro* describes his scepticism and inveterate smoking. See Life by Robberds (1843).

(17) **Zachary** (1784–1850), American soldier and 12th president of the United States, born in Orange County, Va., entered the army in 1808. In 1812 he held Fort Harrison on the Wabash against Indians, and in 1832 fought with Black Hawk. In 1836, now colonel, he was ordered to Florida, and in 1837 defeated the Seminoles at Okeechobee Swamp, and won the brevet of brigadier-general. In 1840 he was placed in command of the army in the southwest. When Texas was annexed in 1845 he gathered 4000 regulars at Corpus Christi in March 1846, marched to the Rio Grande, and erected Fort Brown opposite Matamoros. The Mexicans crossed the Rio Grande to drive him out. But the battles of Palo Alto and Resaca de la Palma on May 8 and 9 repulsed them, and Taylor seized Matamoros. In September he captured Monterey. After seven weeks' vain waiting for reinforcements the march was resumed. Victoria was occupied, but the line of communication was too long for the meagre force, while Polk's Democratic administration, fearing the rising fame of Taylor, who was a Whig, crippled him by withholding reinforcements. Taylor was falling back to Monterey when his regulars were taken from him to form part of a new expedition under General Scott. Santa Ana, the Mexican general, overtook his 5000 volunteers near the pass of Buena Vista; but Taylor, on February 22, 1847, repulsed the 21,000 Mexicans with a loss thrice as great as his own. In 1848 the Whigs selected Taylor as their candidate for the presidency. He was elected in November and inaugurated next March. The struggle over the extension of slavery had begun. The Democratic congress opposed the admission of California as a free state, while the president favoured it. To avert the threatened danger to the Union Henry Clay introduced his famous compromise. Taylor remained firm and impartial though his son-in-law, Jefferson Davis, headed the extreme proslavery faction. Before a decision was reached President Taylor died, July 9, 1850. See Life by Gen. O. O. Howard (1892).

TCHAIKOVSKY, Piotr Ilyich, *chī-kof'skee* (1840–93), Russian composer, was born May 7 at Kamsko-Votinsk, where his father was inspector of government mines. His early musical talents were encouraged, but on the family's moving to St Petersburg he entered the school of jurisprudence and started his life as a minor civil servant. In 1862 he enrolled at the recently opened conservatoire, but after three years he was engaged by his previous orchestration teacher, Nicholas Rubinstein, to teach harmony at the latter's own conservatoire at Moscow. His operas and 2nd symphony brought him into the public eye, and in 1875 his piano concerto in B flat minor had its première in Moscow. Temperamentally unsuited to marriage, he left his bride Antonina Ivanovna Miliukova a month after the wedding (1877) in a state of nervous collapse. After recuperation abroad he resigned from the conservatoire and retired to the country to devote himself entirely to composition. He made occasional trips abroad and in 1893 was made an honorary Mus.D. of Cambridge University. Soon after his return to Russia from England and after the first performance of his 6th ('Pathétique') symphony, he took cholera and died at St Petersburg. Three years earlier his correspondence, dating back to 1876, with Nadezhda von Meck, widow of a wealthy engineer, had come to a stop. Though they never met, her artistic, moral and financial support played a very important part in his career. Though acquainted with Balakirev, Rimsky-Korsakov and other members of the group of late 19th-century composers known as the 'Five', he was not in sympathy with their avowedly nationalistic aspirations and their use of folk material, and was himself regarded by them as something of a renegade cosmopolitan. The melodiousness, colourful orchestration, and deeply expressive content of his music brought him and still brings him an enthusiastic following exceeding that of any other Russian composer. His introspective and melancholy nature is reflected in some of his symphonies and orchestral pieces, but not in his ballet music—*Swan Lake*, *The Sleeping Beauty* and *Nutcracker*—which are by common consent masterpieces of their kind. In such cases his weakness in large-scale structural organization was concealed. His works include 6 symphonies, of which the last three are best known, 2 piano concertos (a third was left uncompleted), a violin concerto, a number of tone poems, including *Romeo and Juliet* and *Italian Capriccio*, songs and piano pieces. Of his 11 operas, *Eugene Onegin* and *The Queen of Spades* have successfully survived. See studies by E. Blom (1927), E. Evans (1935), Weinstock (1943) and G. Abraham (1946); also *Life and Letters* (1906), ed. M. Tschaikovsky, and his *Diaries* (1945).

TCHEKHOV. See CHEHOV.

TCHEREPNIN, Nikolai Nikolaievich, *che-rep-neen'* (1873–1945), Russian composer, born in St Petersburg. He was trained as a lawyer, but abandoned this profession to study under Rimsky-Korsakov, and first appeared as a pianist. In 1901 he became conductor of the Belaiev Concerts and took charge of opera at the Maryinsky Theatre. From 1908 to 1914 Tcherepnin worked with Diaghilev, conducting ballet and opera throughout Europe. In 1914 he went to Petrograd, leaving there four years later to become director of the Tiflis Conservatory. He settled in Paris in 1921. Works include two operas, a number of ballets, much orchestral music, and piano pieces.

TEBALDI, Renata, *-bal'-* (1922–), Italian operatic soprano, born in Pesaro. She studied at Parma Conservatory, made her début at Rovigo in 1944, and was invited by Toscanini to appear at the re-opening of La Scala, Milan, in 1946. She has appeared in England, France, Spain, South America and at the Metropolitan, New York, and San Francisco.

TECUMSEH (*c.* 1768–1813), American Indian chief of the Shawnees, joined his brother, 'The Prophet', in a rising against the whites suppressed at Tippecanoe by Harrison in 1811, and passing into the English service,

commanded the Indian allies in the war of 1812–13 as brigadier-general. He fell fighting at the Thames in Canada (1813). See Lives by Eggleston (1878) and Raymond (1915).

TEDDER, Arthur William, 1st Baron Tedder of Glenguin (1890–1967), marshal of the R.A.F., born at Glenguin, Stirlingshire, was in the Colonial Service when war broke out in 1914. By 1916 he had transferred to the R.F.C. Remaining in the service, at the outbreak of World War II he was director-general of research and development, Air Ministry. From 1940 he organized the Middle East Air Force with great success, moving on to the Mediterranean theatre and later becoming deputy supreme commander under Eisenhower. His services were recognized in his appointment as marshal of the R.A.F. (1945). Created a baron in 1946, in 1950 he became chancellor of the University of Cambridge and also a governor of the B.B.C. See his *Air Power in the War* (1948) and autobiography, *With Prejudice* (1966).

TEGETMEIER, William Bernhard, *teg'et-mī-ér* (1816–1912), Anglo-German ornithologist, was born at Colnbrook, S. Bucks. He assisted Darwin in his work and for many years edited *The Field.*

TEGETTHOFF, Baron Wilhelm von (1827–1871), Austrian admiral, born at Marburg, defeated the Danes off Heligoland (1864) and an Italian fleet under Persano near Lissa (1866), the first battle between ironclads.

TEGNÉR, Esaias, *teng-nayr* (1782–1846), Swedish poet, born at Krykerud in Värmland, the son of a pastor, graduated in 1802 at Lund University, and was appointed a lecturer in 1803. His stirring *War-song for the Militia of Scania* (1808) made his name known, and *Svea* (1811) made it famous. In 1812 he became professor of Greek. His best poems all belong to eight years—*Song to the Sun* (1817); *Degree Day at Lund* (1820); *Axel*, a romance of the days of Charles XII (1821); and his masterpiece, *Frithiof's Saga* (1825). He became Bishop of Vexiö (1824). See Life by Böttiger prefixed to his collected works (1847–51); also works by Brandes (Stockholm 1878), Kippenberg (Leipzig 1884), and Christensen (3rd ed. Leipzig 1890).

TEILHARD DE CHARDIN, Pierre, *tay-yahr dĕ shahr-dĭ* (1881–1955), French geologist, palaeontologist, Jesuit priest and philosopher, the son of an Auvergne landowner, was educated at a Jesuit school, lectured in pure science at the Jesuit College in Cairo and in 1918 became professor of Geology at the Institut Catholique in Paris. In 1923 he undertook palaeontological expeditions in China, and later in central Asia, but increasingly his researches did not conform to Jesuit orthodoxy and he was forbidden by his religious superiors to teach and publish, and in 1948 was not allowed to stand for a professorship at the Sorbonne in succession to the Abbé Breuil (q.v.). Nevertheless, his work in Cenozoic geology and palaeontology became known and he was awarded academic distinctions, including the Legion of Honour (1946). From 1951 he lived in America. Posthumously published, his philosophical speculations, based on his scientific work, trace the evolution of animate matter to two basic principles: nonfinality and complexification. By the concept of *involution* he explains why *homo sapiens* is the only species which in spreading over the globe has resisted intense division into further species. This leads on to transcendental speculations, which allow him original, if theologically unorthodox, proofs for the existence of God. This work, *The Phenomenon of Man* (trans. 1959; intro. Sir Julian Huxley), is complementary to *Le Milieu divin* (trans. 1960). See Lives by N. Corte (trans. 1960) and C. Cuénot (1965).

TEISSERENC DE BORT, Léon Philippe, *tes-rã dè bor* (1855–1913), French meteorologist, born in Paris, became chief meteorologist at the Bureau Central Météorologique in Paris. He discovered and named the stratosphere as distinct from the troposphere, in the upper atmosphere. He was awarded the Symons Gold Medal by the Royal Meteorological Society in 1908.

TEIXEIRA, Pedro, *tay-shay'ra* (*c.* 1575–1640), Portuguese soldier, in 1614 fought against the French in Brazil. He helped to found Pará in 1615, of which he was governor (1620 and 1640). He led an important expedition up the Amazon (1637–39) and across the mountains to Quito, returning by the same route.

TELEKI, Count Paul, *tel'e-kee* (1879–1941), Hungarian statesman, born in Budapest, where he became professor of Geography at the university in 1919. Combining politics with an academic career, he was also in that year appointed foreign minister and, from 1920 to 1921, premier. Founder of the Christian National League and chief of Hungary's boy scouts, he was minister of education in 1938 and again premier in 1939. He was fully aware of the German threat to his country, but all measures to avert it, including a pact with Yugoslavia, were unavailing through lack of support. When Germany marched against Yugoslavia through Hungary, he took his own life.

TELEMANN, Georg Philipp, *tay'lė-mahn* (1681–1767), German composer, born in Magdeburg, the son of a clergyman, was largely self-taught. He gained his musical knowledge by learning to play a host of instruments (including the violin, recorder and zither, and later the shawm, oboe, flute and bass trombone) and by studying the scores of the masters. In 1700 he was a student of languages and science at Leipzig University and in 1704 was appointed organist of the New Church and *kapellmeister* to Prince Promnitz at Sorau. In 1709 he was *kapellmeister* at Eisenach, from 1712 to 1721 *kapellmeister* to the Prince of Bayreuth and in 1721 was appointed music director of the Johanneum at Hamburg, a post which he held until his death. One of the most prolific composers, Telemann's works include church music, forty-four passions, forty operas, oratorios, including *Der Tag des Gerichts* and *Die Tageszeiten*, countless songs and a large body of instrumental music. In his lifetime ranked above his friend J. S. Bach and admired by Handel, who borrowed from his music, he lost popularity after his death and not until the 1930s

were his musical gifts rediscovered. Though his masterly grasp of the techniques of all forms of musical composition was always recognized, especially his skill as a contrapuntist, critics regarded him as unoriginal and condemned his easily turned out works as lacking in depth and sincerity. But through his study of and admiration for the French composers, notably Lully, a new grace and richness was introduced into German music. Much of the liveliness and gaiety in his work sprang from his sense of humour and also from an interest in folk music aroused at Sorau where he heard the tunes of the Polish and Moravian dances. He wrote three autobiographies, the last of which was published in 1739. See works by H. Hörner (1931), K. Schäfer (1931), and a Life by E. Valentin (1931).

TELFORD, Thomas (1757–1834), Scottish engineer, was born, a shepherd's son, at Westerkirk, Langholm, August 9, 1757, at fourteen was apprenticed to a stonemason, in 1780 went to Edinburgh, and in 1782 to London. In 1784 he got work at Portsmouth dockyard; in 1787 became surveyor of public works for Shropshire; and his two bridges over the Severn at Montford and Buildwas gained him the planning of the Ellesmere Canal (1793–1805). In 1801 he was commissioned by government to report on the public works required for Scotland; and he constructed the Caledonian Canal (1803–23), more than 1000 miles of road, and 1200 bridges, besides churches, manses, harbours, &c. Other works by him were the road from London to Holyhead, with the Menai Suspension Bridge (1825), the Dean Bridge, Edinburgh (1832), and the St Katharine's Docks (1826–28) in London; he was also responsible for draining large tracts of the Fen country. He was elected F.R.S. in 1827 and was the first president of the Institution of Civil Engineers. He was buried in Westminster Abbey. See Lives by himself (1838), Sir Alexander Gibb (1935) and L. T. C. Rolt (1958).

TELL, William, Swiss patriot of Bürglen in Uri, reputed the saviour of his native district from the tyranny of Austria. Johannes von Müller tells at length, in his History of Switzerland (1786), how Albert II of Austria strove to annex the Forest Cantons; how in 1307 his tyrannical steward Gessler compelled the Swiss to do reverence to the ducal hat erected on a pole in Altorf; how Tell, a famous marksman, for noncompliance condemned to shoot an apple off his own son's head; and how afterwards Tell slew the tyrant, and so initiated the movement which secured the independence of Switzerland. Von Müller had no doubt of the truth of the story; but the tale of the 'master shot ' is found in Aryan, Samoyede and Turkish folklore. Tell's very existence is disputed; his name first occurs in a ballad of 1470, and the full story in Tschudi's *Swiss Chronicle* (1572). Albert II was a just, if severe, ruler; and Gessler's name is never once mentioned till 1513. See French studies by Albert Rilliot (1868) and H. Naef (1942) and German ones by Kopp (1851) and K. Meyer, *Der Ursprung der Eidgenossenschaft* (1941).

TELLER, Edward (1908–), Hungarian-born American nuclear physicist, born at Budapest, graduated in chemical engineering at Karlsruhe, studied theoretical physics at Munich, Göttingen and under Niels Bohr at Copenhagen. He left Germany in 1933, lectured in London and Washington (1935) and contributed profoundly to the modern explanation of solar energy, anticipating thereby the theory behind thermonuclear explosions. He worked on the atomic bomb project (1941–46), joined Oppenheimer's theoretical study group at Berkeley, California, where, after his appointment to a professorship at Chicago (1946), he was (1952–53) consultant at and (1958–60) director of the new nuclear laboratories at Livermore. From 1953 he was professor of Physics at California University, and chairman of the department of Applied Science there from 1963. He repudiated as scientist any moral implications of his work, stating that, but for Oppenheimer's moral qualms, the U.S. might have had hydrogen bombs in 1947. After Russia's first atomic test (1949) he was one of the architects of Truman's crash programme to build and test (1952) the world's first hydrogen bomb. See his *Our Nuclear Future* (1958; with A. Latter).

TÉLLEZ. See TIRSO DE MOLINA.

TEMPLE, (1) Frederick (1821–1902), English divine, father of (4), born at Santa Maura in the Ionian islands, educated at Blundell's School and Balliol College, Oxford, of which he became a Mathematics lecturer and fellow. He was principal of Kneller Hall Training College (1858–69), inspector of schools and headmaster of Rugby (1857–69), wrote the first of the allegedly heterodox *Essays and Reviews* (1860) which almost prevented his appointment to the bishopric of Exeter in 1869, and supported the disestablishment of the Irish Church. In 1885 he became Bishop of London and in 1897 Archbishop of Canterbury. He was responsible with Archbishop MacLagen of York for the 'Lambeth Opinions' (1889) which attempted to solve some ritual controversies.

(2) **Richard Grenville, 1st Earl** (1711–79), English statesman, elder brother of George Grenville (q.v.), in 1756–61 held office as first lord of the admiralty and lord privy seal under the elder Pitt, who had married his sister. He bitterly opposed Bute and broke with Pitt (Chatham) on the Stamp Act in 1766.

(3) **Sir William** (1628–99), English diplomatist and essay writer, born in London, studied at Emmanuel College, Cambridge, but at nineteen went abroad, after falling in love with Dorothy Osborne (1627–95). Their seven years of separation gave opportunity for Dorothy's delightful letters and they were married in 1655. His diplomatic career, begun in 1655, was crowned by his part in the Triple Alliance (1668) of England, Holland and Sweden against France. Temple also took part in the Congress of Aix-la-Chapelle (1668), and was ambassador at The Hague—a post to which he returned (1674) after the war between England and Holland. In 1677 he helped to bring about the marriage of the Prince of Orange with the Princess

Mary. He suggested the scheme of a reformed privy council of thirty, and for a short while formed with Halifax, Essex and Sunderland an inner council of four. After the revolution he declined a secretaryship of state to devote himself to literature in retirement at Moor Park in Surrey, where Swift was his secretary. An outstanding essayist, he was one of the reformers of English style, showing a development in rhythmical finish and avoiding unnecessary quotations and long parentheses. See his *Miscellanea* (1679, 1692), a collection of essays, including the famous essay 'Upon the Ancient and Modern Learning', his *Correspondence*, ed. Moore-Smith (1928), study by Marburg (1932), and Life by Woodbridge (1940); for Dorothy Osborne see Cecil's *Two Quiet Lives* (1948).

(4) **William** (1881–1944), English ecclesiastic, son of (1), born at Exeter, was educated at Rugby and Oxford, where he was a fellow of Queen's College (1904–10). He took orders in 1908, was headmaster of Repton School (1910–14) and became a canon of Westminster in 1919. In 1921 he became Bishop of Manchester, in 1929 Archbishop of York and in 1942 Archbishop of Canterbury. With interests as broad as his humanity, he united solid learning and great administrative ability. As Primate, he was one of the greatest moral forces of his time. An outspoken advocate of social reform, he made as his main task the application to current problems of his conception of the Christian philosophy of life, crusading against usury, slums, dishonesty, and the aberrations of the profit motive. Temple's leadership was also seen in his chairmanship of the Doctrinal Commission of the Church of England and in his work for the Ecumenical Movement of Christian Union. His publications include *Church and Nation* (1915), *Christianity and the State* (1928) and *Christianity and the Social Order* (1942). See the study by F. A. Iremonger (1948) and essays, ed. Baker (1958).

TEMPLER, Sir Gerald (1898–), British general, was educated at Wellington College and the R.M.C., Sandhurst. Commissioned in the Royal Irish Fusiliers, he served with them in World War I, becoming a brevet lieut.-col. World War II eventually brought him command of the 6th Armoured Division. He was vice-chief of the Imperial General Staff (1948–50), and C.I.G.S. (1955–58). As high commissioner and c.-in-c. Malaya (1952–54) his military firmness and resourceful support for the loyal elements of the population went far to frustrate the Communist guerillas' offensive. He was created K.B.E. in 1949, G.C.M.G. in 1953, G.C.B. in 1955, and K.G. in 1963.

TEMPLEWOOD, Sir Samuel John Gurney Hoare, 1st Viscount (1880–1959), British Conservative politician, was educated at Harrow and Oxford. He entered politics in 1905 as assistant private secretary to the colonial secretary and in 1910 became M.P. for Chelsea, a seat he held till he received a peerage in 1944. He was secretary of state for Air (1922–29), and as secretary of state for India (1931–35) he piloted the India Act through the Commons against the opposition of Winston Churchill. In 1935, as foreign secretary, he was criticized for his part in the discussions which led to the abortive Hoare-Laval pact over the Italian invasion of Ethiopia. He resigned, and in 1936 was appointed first lord of the Admiralty. Home secretary (1937–39), he was a strong advocate of penal reform. His Criminal Justice Bill (1938) never became law because of the outbreak of war, but much of it was embodied in the Act of 1948. From 1940 to 1944 he was ambassador on special mission to Madrid. In his later years he continued as an apologist for the National Government, whose ' appeasement ' policy towards the dictators he helped to direct, and as a determined opponent of capital punishment. His publications include *The Shadow of the Gallows* (1951) and *Nine Troubled Years* (1954).

TEN BRINK. See BRINK.

TENCIN, Claudine Alexandrine Guérin de, *tã-sĩ* (1681–1749), French beauty and writer, born at Grenoble, entered the religious life, but in 1714 came to Paris, where her wit and beauty attracted a crowd of lovers, among them the Regent and Cardinal Dubois. She had much political influence, enriched herself, and helped the fortunes of her brother, Cardinal Pierre Guérin de Tencin (1680–1758). But her importance died with the regent and the cardinal in 1723. In 1726 she lay a short time in the Bastille, after one of her lovers had shot himself in her house. Her later life was more decorous, and her *salon* one of the most popular in Paris. Fontenelle was one of her oldest lovers; D'Alembert one of her children. Her romances include *Mémoires du Comte de Comminges* (1735), *Le Siège de Calais* (1739) and *Les Malheurs de l'amour* (1747). See her letters to her brother (1790) and the Duc de Richelieu (1806), and books by Nicolaus (1908), Masson (1909) and de Coynart (1910).

TENIERS, *ten-eers'*, (1) **David, the elder** (1582–1649), Flemish genre painter, father of (2), born and died at Antwerp. His subjects are generally homely tavern scenes, rustic games, weddings, &c. His *Temptation of St Anthony* is well known.

(2) **David, the younger** (1610–90), Flemish genre painter, son of (1), quickly gained distinction, enjoying the favour and friendship of the Austrian archduke, the Prince of Orange, and the Bishop of Ghent. In 1647 he took up his abode at Brussels. His seven hundred pictures possess, in superlative degree, the qualities that mark his father's work. None has realized more richly the charm of joyous open-air life. His scriptural subjects alone are unsatisfactory. See Life by G. Eekhoud (1926).

TENISON, Thomas (1636–1715), English divine, born at Cottenham in Cambridgeshire, studied at Corpus Christi, Cambridge, and was made Bishop of Lincoln by William III in 1691, and Archbishop of Canterbury in 1694. He was a favourite at court, crowned Queen Anne and George I, and strongly supported the Hanoverian succession. His works comprise antipapal tracts, sermons, and a criticism of Hobbes. See Life by E. Carpenter (1948).

TENNANT, (1) **Smithson** (1761–1815), English chemist, born at Selby, was educated at Edinburgh and Cambridge. He discovered osmium and iridium (1804) and proved that diamond is pure carbon. Professor of Chemistry at Cambridge (1814), he was killed in a riding accident.

(2) **William** (1784–1848), Scottish poet, born at Anstruther, studied at St Andrews, and, a lifelong cripple, became in 1813 schoolmaster of Dunino. His mock-heroic poem *Anster Fair* (1812) was the first attempt to naturalize the Italian *ottava rima*—soon after adopted with splendid success by Hookham Frere and by Byron. He was teacher from 1816 at Lasswade, from 1819 at Dollar Academy, and from 1835 professor of Oriental Languages at St Andrews. Other poems were the *Thane of Fife* (1822) and *Papistry Stormed* (1827); dramas were *Cardinal Beaton* (1823) and *John Baliol* (1825). See memoir by M. F. Conolly (1861).

TENNIEL, Sir John, *ten'yel* (1820–1914), English caricaturist, born in London, son of a celebrated dancing-master. A self-trained artist, he was selected in 1845 to paint one of the frescoes—Dryden's ' St Cecilia '—in the Houses of Parliament. He is better known as a book illustrator, and best as the cartoonist of *Punch*, the staff of which he joined in 1851, his best-known cartoon being *Dropping the Pilot* (1890). His illustrations to *Alice in Wonderland* and *Through the Looking-glass* (see DODGSON) are remarkable for their delicacy and finish; earlier book illustrations were to *Aesop's Fables*, Moore's *Lalla Rookh*, the *Ingoldsby Legends*, *Once a Week*, &c. He was knighted in 1893. See Life by F. Sarjano (1948).

TENNYSON, Alfred, 1st Baron Tennyson (1809–92), English poet, was born at Somersby rectory, Lincolnshire, the fourth son of the rector. His elder brothers, Frederick and Charles, were both poets and were the subject of a memoir by H. Nicolson (*Tennyson's Two Brothers*, 1947). The father died young, but the family was allowed to stay on at the rectory and Tennyson was somehow enabled to go to Trinity College, Cambridge, where he became a member of an ardent group of young men, including Arthur Hallam, whose early death was to be mourned in that great elegiac poem *In Memoriam*. His early ventures in verse, viz., *Poems Chiefly Lyrical* (1830) and *Poems* (1833) were slighted by the critics as being namby-pamby, and this we can understand for the first volume is largely ' album verse ' and the second is not free from an enervating sentimentality. But the critics ought to have detected the great poet in the first version of ' The Lady of Shalott ', ' Oenone ', ' The Lotus-eaters ' and other poems in the 1833 volume. Nine years of revising these poems and adding fresh material resulted in the volume of 1842, which established his fame. He had been engaged since 1833 in writing the series of loosely connected lyrics or elegies which as *In Memoriam* crowned his fame in 1850, the year he succeeded Wordsworth as poet laureate and the year of his marriage to Emily Sarah Sellwood, a lady from his own county. The long Victorian afternoon followed with shifts of residence to Farringdon in the Isle of Wight and Aldworth in Sussex and sunned by the homage of the entire nation from the Queen downward, so truly and flatteringly did his poetry reflect that world. With his wife he made short tours but rarely left his Victorian England behind him. His poetry has declined in popularity as that insular England has receded, but there should be no doubt that the volume of 1842 and *In Memoriam* contain some of the most finished artistry in English poetry, in which the mood of the poem is perfectly reflected in rhythm and language. After 1850 he devoted himself to the fashionable verse novelette—*Maud; a Monodrama* (1855), *Enoch Arden* (1864), *Locksley Hall Sixty Years After* (1886). Incredibly, for we are inclined to think that *Maud*, apart from the lyrics, verges on the vulgar, Tennyson regarded it as his best poem. The public, however, was waiting for what was to be the crowning triumph. The first instalment of *Idylls of the King* (1859), seemed to the Victorians to be just that, but here again, in *Geraint and Enid* and *Lancelote and Elaine* we are in the domain of the verse novelette and throughout the whole series (completed in 1885) Victorian morality imposed on the old chivalric matter stifles the poetry save in the descriptive passages where Tennyson's hand is as sure as ever. In the 1870s he tried his hand at drama. Irving gave *Becket* a considerable run, but *Harold*, *Queen Mary*, &c., are dead matter. He had a late flowering in his seventies when he wrote the perfect poem *To Virgil, Tiresias,* and the powerful *Rizpah*, but the conflict between science and the Faith, discoursed optimistically in *In Memoriam*, now becomes an obsession—hence the 'double shadow', viz., 'Astronomy and Geology, terrible muses'. He retained to the end the gift of felicitous occasional verse of which the verse letter to F. D. Maurice and *To Virgil* are examples. Perhaps his own estimate of his powers, in a remark to Carlyle, is not far out—'I don't think that since Shakespeare there has been such a master of the English language as I—to be sure, I have nothing to say'. Contemporaries thought he had plenty to say, but it was all occasioned by the topics of the day. *The Princess*, for example (1847), gave him a chance to 'say something', but the subject of woman's education is treated in serio-comic fashion, which we find trying and the image of John Bull he projects in the poem is offensive to modern taste. To be sure there are the lovely lyrics and none disputes his eminence in the lyric any more than in the wonderful pre-Raphaelite and classical poetry in the volume of 1842, the sustained elegiac note of *In Memoriam*, and his felicity in occasional verse. These after all make a considerable body of work. The peerage bestowed on him in 1884 probably was intended to honour the author of *Idylls of the King* (completed in that year), the perfect mirror of the Victorian era. His son Hallam, 2nd Lord Tennyson, issued the authoritative Life in 1897. This was preceded by several studies, the best of

which are those by Churton Collins (1891), and Van Dyke (1896). Since then there have been studies by A. C. Benson (1904), Fausset (1922), Harold Nicolson (1923) and ed. J. Killham (1960). See also T. J. Wise's Bibliography (1897), with a supplement by F. L. Lucas (1957).

TENTERDEN, Charles Abbott, 1st Baron (1762–1832), English lawyer, born a barber's son at Canterbury, became a fellow and tutor of Corpus Christi, Oxford, was called to the bar and in 1801 became recorder of Oxford. Lacking in eloquence, he made his reputation by his revision and novel treatment in terms of principle rather than precedent of the *Law relative to Merchant Ships and Seamen* (1802). In 1816 he became puisne judge in the Court of Common Pleas, in 1818 he was knighted and became chief justice of the King's Bench, and, raised to the peerage in 1827, strongly opposed the Catholic Relief and Reform Bills.

TENZING NORGAY (1914–), Nepalese mountaineer, born at Tsa-chu near Makalu, made his first climb as a porter with a British expedition to Everest in 1935. In the years following he climbed many of the Himalayan peaks and on two later attempts on the ascent of Everest he reached 23,000 ft. in 1938 and 28,215 ft. in 1952. In 1953 on Col. John Hunt's expedition, he, with Edmund Hillary (q.v.), succeeded in reaching the summit of Everest and for this triumph he was awarded the George Medal. In 1954 he studied at a mountaineering school in Switzerland, and on his return to Darjeeling, was appointed head of the Institute of Mountaineering. He also became president of the Sherpa Association. See Sir John Hunt's *Ascent of Everest* (1953), Y. Malartie's *Tenzing of Everest* (1954), and his autobiography, *Man of Everest*, written for him by J. R. Ullman (1955).

TERBORCH, or Terburg, Gerard, *ter-bor*KH (c. 1617–81), Dutch painter, born at Zwolle, studied under Pieter Molijn at Haarlem and visited England, Italy, Germany, painting the conference of 'The Peace of Munster' (1648; National Gallery, London), and Velásquez in Spain. From 1654 to his death he lived at Deventer, where he became burgomaster. He worked mostly on a small scale, producing genre pictures and fashionable portraits characterized by an almost incredible skill in the rendering of textures.

TERBRUGGHEN, Hendrik (1588–1629), Dutch painter, born at Deventer, studied under Bloemaert, was until 1616 in Italy and came under the influence of Caravaggio. Like the latter he excelled in chiaroscuro effects and in the faithful representation of physiognomical details and drapery. His *Jacob and Laban* (1627) is in the National Gallery, London. His works are represented in Edinburgh, Amsterdam, Metropolitan, New York, Ashmolean, Oxford, &c. See study by B. Nicolson (1958).

TERENCE (Publius Terentius Afer) (c. 190–159 B.C.), Roman comic poet, born at Carthage, became the slave of the Roman senator P. Terentius Lucanus, who brought him to Rome, educated him, and manumitted him. His first play was the *Andria* (166); its success introduced Terence to the most refined society of Rome. His chief patrons were Laelius and the younger Scipio. After spending some years in Rome he went to Greece, and died there. We have six of his comedies—*Andria, Eunuchus, Heauton Timoroumenos, Phormio, Hecyra* and *Adelphi.* Terence has no claim to creative originality, his plays, Greek in origin and Greek in scene, being directly based on Menander. But he wrote in singularly pure and perfect Latin. Many of his conventions and plot constructions were later used by Sheridan, Molière, &c. See study by G. Norwood (1923),

TERESA, or **Theresa, Saint** (1515–82), Spanish saint and mystic, born of a noble family at Ávila in Old Castile, March 28, 1515, in 1533 entered a Carmelite convent there. About 1555 her religious exercises reached an extraordinary height of asceticism, she was favoured with ecstasies, and the fame of her sanctity spread far and wide. She obtained permission from the Holy See to remove to a humble house in Ávila, where she re-established (1562) the ancient Carmelite rule, with additional observances. In 1567 the general of the Carmelite order urged on her the duty of extending her reforms; in 1579 the Carmelites of the stricter observance were united into a distinct association; and within her own lifetime seventeen convents of women and sixteen of men accepted her reforms. She died October 4, 1582, and was canonized in 1622. The most famous of her many works are her autobiography, *The Way of Perfection, The Book of the Foundations* (trans. by Dalton, 1853), which describes the journeys she made and the convents she founded or reformed, and *The Interior Castle* (trans. by Dalton, 1852). English Lives are by Dalton (1851), Cardinal Manning (1864), Father Coleridge (3 vols. 1881–88), G. Cunninghame-Graham (1894), A. Whyte (1897), E. A. Peers (1954), E. Hamilton (1960).

TERMAN, Lewis Madison (1877–1956), American psychologist, born at Johnson County, Indiana, became professor at Stanford in 1916 and introduced the Binet-Simon and Terman Group Intelligence Tests into the U.S. army in 1920.

TERNAUX-COMPANS, Henri, *ter-nō-kō-pã* (1807–64), French bibliographer and historian, born in Paris, collected books on America, compiled *Bibliothèque américaine* (1836), and a French translation of voyages of American discovery (1836–40).

TERRY, (1) Daniel (*c.* 1780–1829), English actor and playwright, born in Bath, after an architectural apprenticeship joined a theatrical company under the elder Macready at Sheffield probably in 1805, making his London début in 1812. He played in many dramatizations of Sir Walter Scott's novels, became an intimate friend of the latter, copying him even to the point of calligraphy. He also played the major Shakespearean rôles, and in Sheridan, &c., at Covent Garden and Drury Lane, London.

(2) **Edward O'Connor** (1844–1912), English comedian, born in London, made his début at Christchurch in 1863, and, after four years

in the provinces, played in London 1867. He opened Terry's Theatre in 1887.

(3) **Dame Ellen Alice** (1848–1928), English actress, sister of (4), born at Coventry, the daughter of a provincial actor, was apprenticed to the stage from infancy, and at eight appeared as Mammilius in *The Winter's Tale* at the Prince's Theatre, London. From 1862 she played in Bristol and after a short-lived marriage with the painter, Watts (1864), and a second retirement from the stage (1868–74) during which her two children, Edith and Edward Gordon Craig (q.v.), were born, she established herself as the leading Shakespearean actress in London and from 1878 to 1902 dominated in partnership with Henry Irving (q.v.) the English and American theatre. Her natural gentleness and vivacity made her excel, particularly as Portia and Ophelia, and she would have made an ideal Rosalind, but Irving's professional jealousy withheld such an opportunity at the Lyceum. In 1903 she went herself into theatre management and engaged her son to produce Ibsen's *Vikings.* Barrie and Shaw wrote parts especially for her, e.g., Lady Cicely Waynflete in the latter's *Captain Brassbound's Conversion* (1905). She married Charles Kelly (Wardell) in 1876 and in 1907 the American actor, James Carew. She received the G.B.E. in 1925. See her correspondence with Shaw (1929), her *Memoirs* ed. by Craig and St John (1932), Steen's *A Pride of Terrys* (1962), and Life by R. Manvell (1968).

(4) **Fred** (1863–1933), English actor, brother of (3), born in London, played in the companies of Tree, Forbes Robertson and Irving and established a reputation as a romantic actor as Sir Percy Blakeney in *The Scarlet Pimpernel* (1905). His sisters, **Kate** (1844–1924), **Marion** and **Florence** were also actresses, as was his wife Julia Neilson (q.v.).

TERTULLIAN, properly **Quintus Septimius Florens Tertullianus** (*c.* A.D. 160–220), Carthaginian theologian, one of the fathers of the Latin Church, was born at Carthage. He lived for some time at Rome, was converted (*c.* 196) and then returned to Carthage. That he was married is shown by his two books *Ad Uxorem,* in which he argues against second marriages. His opposition to worldliness in the church culminated in his becoming a leader of the Montanist sect about 207. He had the heart of a Christian with the intellect of an advocate. His style is most vivid, vigorous and concise, abounding in harsh and obscure expressions, abrupt turns and impetuous transitions, with here and there bursts of glowing eloquence. He was the creator of ecclesiastical Latinity, and many of his sentences have become proverbial, e.g., ' The blood of the martyrs is the seed of the church ' and ' The unity of heretics is schism '. His works are divided into three classes: (1) controversial writings against heathens and Jews, as in *Apologeticum, Ad Nationes, Adversus Judaeos*; (2) against heretics, as in *De Praescriptione Haereticorum, Adversus Valentinianos, De Anima, De Carne Christi* (against Docetism), *De Resurrectione Carnis, Adversus Marcionem, Adversus Praxean*; (3) practical and ascetic treatises, in which we can trace his increasing hostility to the church and his adoption of Montanist views. Hence the division of these treatises into Pre-Montanist and Montanist, of which *De Virginibus Velandis* marks the transitional stage. Tertullian had a greater influence on the Latin Church than any theologian between Paul and Augustine. His Montanism, indeed, prevented its direct exercise, but Cyprian was the interpreter who gave currency to his views. See translations of his works in Ante-Nicene Library (1868–70), German study by H. Hoppe (1903) and French study by A. d'Alès (1905).

TESLA, Nikola (1856–1943), Yugoslav-born American inventor, born at Smiljan, Croatia, studied at Graz, Prague and Paris, emigrating to the United States in 1884. He left the Edison Works at Menlo Park to concentrate on his own inventions, which include improved dynamos, transformers and electric bulbs and the high-frequency coil which bears his name.

TETRAZZINI, Luisa, *tet-ra-tzee'nee* (1871–1940), Italian coloratura soprano singer, born at Florence, made her début in 1895 in Meyerbeer's *L'Africaine*. She appeared mostly in Italian opera of the older school, one of her most notable successes being in *Lucia di Lammermoor*. She sang in London and in America and was in 1913–14 a member of the Chicago Opera Company. See *My Life of Song* (1921).

TETZEL, Johann (*c.* 1465–1519), German monk, born at Leipzig, entered the Dominican order in 1489. A famous preacher, he was appointed in 1516 to preach an indulgence in favour of contributors to the building fund of St Peter's at Rome. This he did with great ostentation, thereby provoking the Wittenberg theses of Luther (q.v.). In reply, he published counter-theses, written for him by Conrad Wimpina, but was rebuked by the papal delegate for his literary extravagance.

TEWFIK PASHA, Mohammed, *too-feek'* (1852–92), khedive of Egypt, eldest son of Ismail Pasha (q.v.), succeeded on his abdication in 1879. The chief events of his reign were Arabi's insurrection (1882), the British intervention, the war with the Mahdi (1884–1885), the pacification of the Sudan frontiers, and the improvement of Egypt under British administration. He was succeeded by his son Abbas Hilmi (q.v.).

TEY, Josephine. See MacKintosh (2).

THACKERAY, William Makepeace (1811–63), English novelist, was born at Calcutta, where his father was in the service of the East India Company. The father having died in 1816 and his mother marrying again, the boy was sent home. He went to Charterhouse (1822) and Trinity Hall, Cambridge (1829), but left without taking a degree. His first venture in print was a parody of Tennyson's prize poem *Timbuctoo*. After dissipating much of his patrimony in travel abroad, he decided to repair his fortunes by journalism, though art equally attracted him. A short stay in Paris as an art student came to a close through lack of funds and it was then '(1835) he made his application to illustrate *Pickwick*. He had now married (1836), but financial worry,

due to the bankruptcy of his stepfather, finally determined him to earn a living in London journalism. We find him contributing regularly to *The Times*, the *New Monthly* and *Fraser's Magazine*. Domestic trouble now engulfed him. The birth of his third daughter affected Mrs Thackeray's mind, the home was broken up and the children sent to their grandmother in Paris. His first publications, starting with *The Paris Sketch-book* (1840), and written under various pseudonyms (Wagstaff, Titmarsh, Fitz-Boodle, Yellowplush, Snob, &c.) were a comparative failure although they included *The Yellowplush Papers*, *The Great Hoggarty Diamond* and *The Luck of Barry Lyndon*, all contributed to *Fraser's* (1841–44). It was his work on *Punch* from 1842 onwards which attracted attention by exploiting the view of society as seen by the butler ('Jeames's Diary') and the great theme of English snobbery. The great novels that were to follow—*Vanity Fair* (1847–48), *Pendennis* (1848), *Henry Esmond* (1852) and *The Newcomes* (1853–55), all monthly serials, established his fame. *Vanity Fair* is the first novel to give a conspectus of London society with its mingling of rich parvenus and decadent upper class through both of which the social climber, Becky Sharp, threads her way. The novel is a little marred by the sentimentality of Amelia Sedley and Captain Dobbin, but Thackeray's art moves between the extremes of sentimentality and cynicism. The great historical novel, *Esmond*, shows Thackeray's consuming love of the 18th century. Its sequel, *The Virginians* (1857–59), is not reckoned a success. *The Newcomes* shows young love at the mercy of scheming relatives and mean-spirited rival suitors. Colonel Newcome's portrait has been taken as that of the ideal gentleman, but is also marred by the author's sentimentality. Thackeray retired from *Punch* in 1854 and became the editor of the *Cornhill*, where much of his later work appeared—ballads, novels, &c., now largely unreadable. Mention should be made of the lecturing tours which he undertook in this country and America, the fruit of which, apart from *The Virginians*, was *The English Humorists of the 18th century* (1853) and *The Four Georges* (1860). Trollope's Life is readable but needs to be supplemented by Lewis Melville's 2-vol. Life (1910), and the studies by Whibley (1903) and Ray (1955–58). Best of all perhaps is Saintsbury's Thackeray (1909), and his prefaces to the novels. Thackeray's daughter, Anne Isabella, Lady Ritchie (q.v.), contributed valuable introductions to an edition (1898–99) of his novels.

THAIS, *thay'is* (fl. *c.* 330 B.C.), an Athenian courtesan, famous for wit and beauty, who, according to a doubtful legend, induced Alexander the Great to fire Persepolis. She had several children by Ptolemy Lagus. See opera by Massenet.

THALBERG, Sigismond, *tahl'berg* (1812–71), Swiss-German pianist, was born at Geneva, the natural son of a prince, studied music at Vienna under Hummel and from 1830 made extensive tours in Europe and North America, settling near Naples in 1858. His compositions comprise fantasias and variations, a piano concerto and operas.

THALES, *thay'leez* (fl. 580 B.C.), Greek natural philosopher, one of the Ionian school, the earliest known in Greek philosophy, was born at Miletus. His mercantile journeys took him to Egypt and Babylon, where he acquired land-surveying and astronomical techniques, but is said to have invented geometry by refining these by deductive reasoning. He is supposed to have predicted the solar eclipse in 585 B.C. Aristotle attributes to him the doctrine that water is the original substance and all things derive from and resolve into water. See B. Farrington, *Greek Science* (1949), and J. Burnet, *Greek Philosophy, Thales to Plato* (new ed. 1955).

THANT, U (1909–), Burmese diplomat, born at Pantanaw, became a schoolmaster under Thakin Nu, the future prime minister, whom he later succeeded as headmaster of Pantanaw National High School. When Burma became independent in 1948 he took up government work and after holding several appointments he became permanent U.N. representative for Burma in 1957. In 1961 he was elected acting secretary-general of the U.N. after the death of Hammarskjöld (q.v.), and became permanent secretary-general in 1962. He played a major diplomatic rôle during the Cuban crisis and headed a mission to the Cuban leader (1962). He formulated a plan for the ending of the Congolese civil war (1962) which ended the Katanga secession (1963) and mobilized a U.N. peace-keeping force containing British troops for Cyprus in 1964. He resigned 1971.

THEBAW, *thee'-* (1858–1916), last king of Burma from 1878, in 1885 was deposed by the British, and sent as a prisoner to India.

THEED, William (1804–91), English sculptor, born at Trentham, the son of the sculptor **William Theed** (1764–1817), studied under Thorvaldsen and executed the Africa group on the Albert Memorial.

THEILER, Max, *tī'ler* (1899–1972), South African bacteriologist, born at Pretoria, settled in the U.S.A. in 1922, was awarded the Nobel prize for medicine in 1951 for his work in connection with yellow fever, for which he discovered the vaccine 17D in 1939.

THELLUSSON, Peter (1737–97), a naturalized British merchant, born in Paris, the Genevan ambassador's son, became a London merchant in 1762. After bequeathing fortunes to his family, he left the residue to trustees, to accumulate for his great-grandsons. The will was held valid by Lord Loughborough (1799) and affirmed in the House of Lords in 1805; though the Thellusson Act (1800) thenceforth restrained testators from devising their property for accumulation for more than twenty-one years.

THELWALL, John (1764–1834), English reformer and elocutionist, born in London, was a tailor's apprentice and studied law. He supported Horne Tooke (q.v.), with whom he was arrested (1794) for his revolutionary views. He wrote poems (1787 and 1795) and *Treatment of Cases of Defective Utterance* (1814). See Life by C. Cestre (1906), and Hobhouse's *Liberalism* (1911).

THEMISTOCLES, *the-mis'to-kleez* (c. 523–

c. 458 B.C.), Athenian general and statesman, as archon in 493 convinced his countrymen that a powerful fleet was necessary for their welfare. Against the Persians he commanded the Athenian squadron (200 of the 324 Greek vessels), but agreed to serve under the Spartan Eurybiades; on the eve of Salamis (480) it required all his energy to induce his timid superior to await the attack of the enemy. In his eagerness to precipitate a collision he sent a messenger to urge the Persian generals to make an immediate attack, as the Greeks had resolved on retreat. A great victory was won and Themistocles became a national hero. The rebuilding of the walls of Athens by his advice on a vastly larger scale aroused uneasiness at Sparta, but Themistocles cajoled the ephors till the walls were high. So the Spartan faction in Athens plotted his ruin, and in 470 he was ostracized. Argos was his first retreat, but the Spartans secured his expulsion (467), and he fled to Corcyra and thence to Asia; Artaxerxes received him with great favour, and listened to his schemes for the subjugation of Greece; and at Magnesia he lived securely till his death. His patriotism seems at times to have been merely a larger kind of selfishness, but he was convinced that only he could realize the dream of a great Athenian empire. See Life by Bauer (1881).

THÉNARD, Louis Jacques, *tay-nahr* (1777–1857), French chemist, born at Louptière, a peasant's son, studied pharmacy at Paris and became professor at the Collège de France and was made a baron in 1825 and chancellor of the University of Paris. He discovered sodium and potassium peroxides, Thénard's blue, which is used for colouring porcelain, and which made him wealthy, and proved that caustic soda and potash contain hydrogen. He was closely associated with Gay-Lussac (q.v.) and wrote a once-standard work on chemistry.

THEOBALD, *thee'o-bawld* or *tib'ĕld,* (1) or Tebaldus (d. 1161), English ecclesiastic, was a monk at Bec, abbot (1137) and in 1138 became Archbishop of Canterbury. He crowned Stephen in Canterbury, and after the latter's death refused to regard Stephen's son as his successor and eventually crowned Henry II (1154). He advanced his archdeacon, Thomas à Becket, to the chancellorship, introduced the study of civil law into England and resisted all attempts by the monasteries to throw off episcopal jurisdiction. See Life by Saltman (1956).

(2) **Lewis,** *tib-bold* (1688–1744), English Shakespearean critic, born at Sittingbourne, studied law but took to literature. He published translations of the Greek classics, thirty papers in *Mist's Journal* (1715), and started the *Censor,* a tri-weekly paper. His pamphlet *Shakespeare Restored* (1726) was directed against Pope's edition, and Pope took revenge by making him, unfairly, the hero of the *Dunciad,* though he incorporated many of his corrections in the second edition. Theobald's edition of Shakespeare (1734), however, surpassed that of his rival. See study by R. F. Jones (1919).

THEOCRITUS, *thee-ok'-* (c. 310–250 B.C.), the pastoral poet of Greece, was born probably at Syracuse, was brought up in Cos where he came under the influence of Philetas, lived for a time at the court of Ptolemy Philadelphus in Alexandria, returning later to Cos. In his pastoral poems he struck out an entirely new form of literature, which is for ever fresh. The authenticity of some of the thirty poems of his which we have has been disputed. They fall into three classes—half-epic, mimic and idyllic. Probably the half-epic poems were the earliest. He wrote a series of poems dealing with heroic legend, especially that of Heracles. Theocritus's famous 15th Idyll, *The Ladies of Syracuse*, said to be copied from Sophron, describes delightfully the visit of a Syracusan lady and her friend, both living in Alexandria, to the festival of Adonis. Theocritus raised the rude pastoral poetry of the Doric race in Sicily into a new and perfect form of literature. His short poems dealing with pastoral subjects, and representing a single scene, came to be called Idylls (*eidullia*). His countrymen are genuine, typical of peasants everywhere. He combined realism with romanticism, and every touch is natural. Virgil imitates him closely in his *Eclogues*; Tennyson was deeply influenced by him, as were the pastoral poets of the Renaissance.

THEODORA (*c.* 500–547), Byzantine empress, consort of Justinian I, the daughter of Aracius the Cypriot, had, according to Procopius, already been actress, dancer and courtesan when she won the heart of the austere and ambitious Justinian, to become in succession his mistress, his wife and the sharer of his throne (527). As Justinian's trustiest counsellor she bore a chief share in the work of government, and saved the throne by her high courage at the crisis of the Nika riots (532). She lavished her bounty on the poor, especially the unfortunate of her own sex. Her character descended to history unspotted until the appearance (1623) of the *Secret History* of Procopius (q.v.), who in the full favour of the court had in his other writings extolled Justinian and Theodora. There is not a word of her profligacy in Evagrius or Zonaras. See works by Débidour (1885), Houssaye (1890) and Holmes (1905–1907), Mallet in *Eng. Hist. Rev.* (1887), Diehl, *Byzantine Portraits* (trans. 1927).

THEODORE, (1) or Kassai (1816–68), King of Abyssinia, nephew of the governor of Kuara, in 1853 crushed the vice-regent Ras Ali, and, in 1855 overthrowing the prince of Tigré, had himself crowned negus of Abyssinia as Theodore II. At first he was guided by two Englishmen, Plowden and Bell; but after they were killed in a rebellion (1860) his rule became tyrannical. He had made several vain attempts to procure the alliance of England and France against his Mohammedan neighbours, and he now began to entertain hatred towards Europeans. A letter sent to Queen Victoria in 1862 went somehow unnoticed, and a fancied slight was also received from Napoleon III. Thereupon Theodore imprisoned the consuls along with other Europeans. Negotiations failed, and a British military expedition under General Napier landed in Abyssinia in the spring of 1868, and on April 9 reached Magdala. On the 10th an Abyssinian attack was repulsed. Theodore sued for peace and released the prisoners, but, as he declined to surrender, the fort was stormed on the 13th. Theodore shot himself.

(2) ' King of Corsica ', otherwise Baron von Neuhoff (1686–1756), German adventurer, son of a Westphalian noble, was born at Metz, served in the French army, the Swedish diplomatic service, became chargé d'affaires to the Emperor Charles VI and, in 1736, led a Corsican rising against the Genoese, supported by the Turks and the Bey of Tunis. He was elected king, solemnly crowned and raised money by selling knighthoods. He left after seven months to procure foreign aid, but his attempts to return in 1738 and in 1743 were frustrated. He settled in London in 1749, was imprisoned for debt but was set free by a subscription raised by Horace Walpole. In Spain he had married an Irish lady, daughter of the Earl of Kilmallock. His only son by her, known as Colonel Frederick (*c.* 1725–97), wrote a book on Corsica, and shot himself in the porch of Westminster Abbey. See V. Pirie, *His Majesty of Corsica* (1939).

THEODORE OF MOPSUESTIA (*c.* 350–428), Greek theologian, born at Antioch, became first a monk, then a deacon there, and in 392 Bishop of Mopsuestia in Cilicia. The teacher of Nestorius, he was, perhaps, the real founder of Nestorianism. He wrote commentaries on almost all the books of Scripture, of which remain, in the Greek, only that on the Minor Prophets; in Latin translations, those on the Epistles of Paul (ed. by Swete, Camb. 1880–82), besides many fragments. As an exegete he eschews the allegorical method, adopts the literal meaning, considers the historical and literary circumstances, and assumes varying degrees of inspiration. Already suspected, as he was, of leaning towards the ' Pelagians ', when the Nestorian controversy broke out, he was attacked in his polemical writings, which were condemned by Justinian (544). The fifth ecumenical council (553) confirmed the condemnation. See a book by L. Patterson (1927), Sellers, *Two Ancient Christologies* (1940) and study by Norris (1963).

THEODORE OF TARSUS, St (*c.* 602–690), Archbishop of Canterbury, born at Tarsus and educated at Athens, was sent in 668 by Pope Vitalian to Canterbury, where he established a Greek school. Stubbs described him as the ' real organizer of the administrative system of the English Church '. See study by Reany (1944).

THEODORET, *thee-od'-* (*c.* 393–458), Greek theologian and Church historian, born at Antioch, entered a monastery, and in 423 became Bishop of Cyrrhus, a city of Syria. As a foremost representative of the school of Antioch he became deeply involved in the Nestorian and Eutychian controversies, and was deposed, in his absence, by the ' Robber Council ' of Ephesus in 449. He was restored by the general Council of Chalcedon in 451. His works (edited by Schulze and Nösselt, 1769–74) consist of commentaries on Canticles, the Prophets, Psalms and St Paul's Epistles; a *History of the Church*, from A.D. 325 to 429; *Religious History*, being the lives of the so-called Fathers of the Desert; the *Eranistes*, a dialogue against Eutychianism; *A Concise History of Heresies*, together with orations and nearly 200 letters. See works by Roos (Latin, 1883), Bertram (Latin, 1883), Güldenpenning (German, 1889) and Räder (Latin, 1900).

THEODORIC, the name of two kings of the Visigoths:

Theodoric I (d. 451), was chosen king by the Visigoths in 418. Alternately an ally and an enemy of Rome, in 421 (or 422) he treacherously joined the Vandals and attacked the Roman troops from behind. In 435, he attacked the Romans in Gaul and besieged Narbonne. Forced to retreat to Toulouse, he there defeated a Roman army (439). On the invasion of Attila (q.v.) in 451, he joined the Romans, under Aetius, and at Troyes commanded the right wing. He drove back the Huns under Attila but was killed.

Theodoric II (d. 466), son of the first Theodoric, rebelled against Thorismund, had him assassinated and ascended the throne in 453. His policy at first was to spread Gothic dominion in Spain and Gaul through the Roman alliance. On the murder of the Emperor Maximus, he supported Avitus in his bid for the Empire, and marched with him into Italy, where he was proclaimed emperor. On his abdication in 456, Theodoric broke the friendship with Rome and besieged Arles, but was forced by Majorian to make peace. In 462, he made another attempt in Gaul, but was defeated near Orléans (464). He was murdered in 466 by his brother Euric, who succeeded him.

THEODORIC, or **Theoderic**, surnamed the **Great** (A.D. 455–526), king of the Ostrogoths and founder of the Ostrogothic monarchy. Shortly before he became king (475) the Ostrogoths had overrun Macedonia. After fourteen years of petty warfare, sometimes as the ally, sometimes as the enemy, of the Romans. Theodoric obtained from the Emperor Zeno permission to wrest Italy from Odoacer (q.v.). With 250,000 Ostrogoths he completed the conquest after a five years' war, and Odoacer was soon after murdered by Theodoric's own hand. His thirty-three years' reign secured for Italy tranquillity and prosperity. The Goths and the Romans continued distinct nations, each with its own tribunals and laws. Catholics and Jews enjoyed full liberty of worship, and protection from all encroachment on their civil rights (Theodoric was an Arian). His official letters show his unwearied energy and enlightened zeal for his subjects' welfare. His last three years are tarnished by the judicial murders of Boethius and Symmachus, and by acts of oppression against the Catholic church. To the Germans he is Dietrich von Bern, and one of the great heroes of legend, figuring in the *Nibelungenlied*. See Hodgkin, *Theodoric the Goth* (1891; new ed. 1923), and R. Latouche, *Les Grandes Invasions* (1946).

THEODORUS OF SAMOS, *-do'-* (c. 550 B.C.), Greek artist, worked in metal, inventing several kinds of tools for use in casting. He is said to have made, with Telecles, the Pythian Apollo at Samos.

THEODOSIUS, (1) surnamed **the Elder** (d. 376), Roman general, father of Theodosius the Great, by birth a Spaniard, campaigned in Britain against the Caledonians, naming a reconquered district *Valentia* after the emperors. After a victorious campaign on the Upper Danube he quelled a revolt in Africa, but was executed at Carthage on some trumped-up charge.

(2) **Theodosius I**, surnamed **the Great** (c. 346–395), Roman emperor, son of Theodosius the Elder (q.v.), was born at Cauca in northwest Spain, won fame by his exploits in Moesia and Thrace, but retiring, on his father's death, to his native farm, was summoned thence by Gratian to become his colleague and emperior in the East (379). It was a critical time. The Goths, flushed with victory, were roaming the country at will. Theodosius made Thessalonica his headquarters, and within four years broke up the vast Gothic army, attached many of its members as allies, and restored tranquillity south of the Danube. A serious illness in 380 led to his baptism as a Trinitarian and to edicts against Arianism. He summoned the second general council (at Constantinople, 381). The murder of Gratian at Lyons, the advance towards Italy of Maximus, proclaimed emperor in Britain, and the arrival of Valentinian II begging for help led to Theodosius's victory at Aquileia (388) and to the restoration of his youthful colleague. For some years Theodosius lived at Milan in friendship with St Ambrose. He had cancelled the severe measures meted out to Antioch after a riot (387); but in 390, when the governor of Thessalonica was lynched by a circus mob, Theodosius invited the citizens into the circus, and had 7000 of them massacred. Ambrose wrote upbraiding them with the deed, and even withstood his attempt to enter the church at Milan until after eight months' retirement and public penance. In 392 Valentinian II was murdered, and in 394 Theodosius marched against the Franks and their puppet emperor Eugenius. After a stubborn fight he gained a complete victory, and for four months ruled as sole Roman emperor. He died in Ambrose's arms. See *German Life* by Güldenpenning and Ifland (1878). His grandson, **Theodosius II** (401–450), succeeded his father Arcadius in 408 as Eastern emperor. He allowed affairs to be managed by his sister Pulcheria and his empress Eudocia.

(3) **of Tripolis**, a Greek mathematician and astronomer, born in Bithynia in the 1st or 2nd century B.C., wrote a book on spherical geometry.

THEOGNIS, *-og'-* (fl. 544–541 B.C.), Greek elegiac poet, was a Dorian noble of Megara. During the confusion which followed the overthrow of the tyrant Theagenes, he was driven from Megara, and visited Euboea and Sicily. Under his name survive 1389 elegiac verses, social, political and gnomic, showing shrewd sense and oligarchical principles—perhaps only partly his. See E. Harrison's *Studies in Theognis* (1903), works by T. Hudson Williams (1910) and F. Jacoby (1931).

THEON. See HYPATIA.

THEOPHILUS, *-of'-,* (1) patriarch of Alexandria from 385 till his death in 412, destroyed the pagan temple of Serapis, drove out the Originist monks of Nitria and defended his actions before a synod at Constantinople called by the emperor Arcadius and St John Chrysostom (q.v.). He made peace with the monks but used his influence with the empress to have St John banished to Armenia.

(2) (fl. 2nd cent.), Bishop of Antioch (169 177), wrote an important Apology of Christiantity (*c.* 180).

THEOPHRASTUS, *-fras'-* (*c.* 372–286 B.C.), Greek philosopher, born at Eresus in Lesbos, repaired to Athens, where he heard Plato and Aristotle; of the latter he became the intimate friend and successor. He inherited the whole Aristotelian library, including the philosopher's manuscripts. As head of the peripatetic school he displayed great versatility, was the reputed author of 227 works, and was long a paramount authority. His writings are in great part lost; but we still possess his books on plants (important in botanical history), on stones, on fire, on winds and weather signs, and on the senses. His *Characters,* a masterly delineation of moral types, which, however, some scholars deem a later compilation from a more discursive original of Theophrastus, has had much influence in modern literature.

THEOPHYLACT (*c.* 1078–*c.* 1107), Greek ecclesiastic, born at Euripus in Euboea, became Archbishop of Achrida in Bulgaria in 1078. He wrote Bible commentaries, printed in Venice (1754–58), and *The Education of a Prince* for the son of the emperior Michael VII, to whom he had been tutor.

THEOPOMPUS OF CHIOS, *kīos* (*c.* 378–*c.* 300 B.C.), Greek historian and rhetorician, studied under Isocrates (q.v.). He was twice exiled from Chios and wrote a history of Greece (411–394), &c. Only fragments remain.

THEORELL, Axel Hugo Theodor (1903–), Swedish biochemist, born at Linköping, was assistant professor at Uppsala (1930) and then director of the Nobel Institute of Biochemistry at Stockholm (1937). He worked on myoglobin and was (1955) awarded a Nobel prize for his work on oxidation enzymes.

THEOTOCOPULI. See GRECO (EL).

THERAMENES, *the-ram'i-neez* (fl. 411–403 B.C.), Athenian statesman, made himself unpopular by a policy of compromise between oligarchy and democracy, and while a member of the government of the Thirty Tyrants, incurred the hatred of the most notorious of them all, Critias (q.v.), whose health he drank in the hemlock cup.

THERESA, St. See TERESA.

THESIGER. See CHELMSFORD.

THESEUS, *thee'si-oos,* semi-legendary hero of Athens, the son of Aegeus, king of Athens, by Aethra, daughter of Pittheus, King of Troezen, at whose court he grew up. His perilous journey back to Athens, to succeed his father, according to legend, was a succession of Herculean feats against powerful adversaries, including Procrustes, who fitted everyone he caught into his bed, either by stretching the victim or cutting him down to

size, the grey sow of Crommyon and the rebellious Pallantidae, his uncles, at Athens. He was then sent as part of the annual human tribute of six youths and six maidens exacted by Minos of Crete, who had defeated the Athenians, to the Minotaur's labyrinth on Crete, but was saved by the help of Minos's daughter, Ariadne, who provided him with a sword to slay the Minotaur and a thread to find his way out of the labyrinth. He forgot to change the black sails of his boat to white ones, signalizing success, on his return to Athens, and Aegeus, expecting the worst, drowned himself. Theseus as ruler continued his legendary exploits, such as his defeat of the Amazons, but his unification of the various Attican communities into one state, his exile and death on the island of Scyros are historical facts. His supposed remains were later reinterred in Athens. See Life in Plutarch and novels by Renault, *The King must Die* (1958) and *The Bull from the Sea* (1962).

THESPIS (fl. 534 B.C.), Greek poet, reputed founder at Athens of drama.

THEURIET, André, *tær-yay* (1833–1907), French poet and novelist, born at Marly-le-Roi, Seine-et-Oise, received in 1857 a post under the finance minister. His collections of verse include *Le Chemin des bois* (1867), the so-called epic *Les Paysans de l'Argonne, 1792* (1871) and *Le Bleu et le Noir* (1872). But he is best known by his novels *Le Mariage de Gérard* (1875), *Raymonde* (1877), *Sauvageonne* (1880), &c. In 1897 he became an Academician. See study by Besson (1890).

THÉVENOT, Jean de, *tay-vë-nŏ* (1633–77), French traveller, born in Paris, travelled over Europe, the Levant, Mesopotamia and India, and died on his way to Tabriz. See *Collected Voyages* (1689).

THIARD, Pontus de. See TYARD.

THIBAUD, Jacques, *tee-bō* (1880–1953), French violinist, born at Bordeaux in 1880, studied with Marsick and played with Cortot and Casals. He died in an air crash.

THIBAULT, Jacques. See FRANCE (ANATOLE).

THIERRY, Augustin, *tyer-ree* (1795–1856), French historian, born at Blois, joined the Paris Liberals in 1814, and published *De la réorganisation de la société européenne,* inspired by Saint-Simon, whose secretary Thierry became. In 1817, however, they disagreed, and Thierry attached himself to Comte. In 1825 he published his masterpiece, the *Norman Conquest of England,* followed in 1827 by *Lettres sur l'histoire de France.* In 1835 he became librarian at the Palais Royal, and published his *Dix Ans d'études historiques.* His last work was on the *Tiers État* (1853). He resurrected historical studies, used original documents, where possible, but overdramatized. See monograph by Aubineau (1879) and study by A. A. Thierry (1922). His brother, **Amédée Simon Dominique** (1797–1873), was also a historian.

THIERS, Louis Adolphe, *tyer* (1797–1877), French statesman and historian, born at Marseilles, April 16, was sent in 1815 to study law at Aix, where he made the acquaintance of Mignet, and cultivated literature rather than the law. At twenty-three he was called to the bar; and his articles in the Liberal *Constitutionnel* gained him the entry to the most influential *salons* of the Opposition. Meanwhile he was rapidly preparing his *Histoire de la révolution française* (10 vols. 1823–27), which though untrustworthy and inaccurate gave him a prominent place among politicians and men of letters. In January 1830, along with Carrel and Mignet, he started the *National*, and waged relentless war on the Polignac administration. Its attempted suppression brought about the July Revolution; and Thiers entered on an active career as a politician. He was elected deputy for Aix, was appointed secretary-general to the minister of finance, and became one of the most formidable of parliamentary speakers. Radical though he was as compared with Guizot, he in 1832 became minister of the interior, and of commerce and public affairs, and then foreign minister; his 'spirited foreign policy' is now seen to have been a great mistake. In 1836 he was appointed president of the council, but in August he resigned, and led the Opposition. Again president of the council and foreign minister (1840), he for six months was a terror to the peace of Europe. He refused Palmerston's invitation to enter into an alliance with Britain, Austria and Prussia for the preservation of the integrity of the Ottoman Empire, aiming like Napoleon at French supremacy in the Levant. Irritation at the isolation of France led to his resignation. *L'Histoire du consulat et de l'empire* (20 vols. 1845–62), the most ambitious of all Thiers's literary enterprises, is a large rather than a great work; that it is inaccurate and unfair has been admitted even by French critics. Thiers would have hindered the revolution of 1848, and, though he accepted the Republic, was arrested and banished at the *coup d'état* of 1851, being allowed, however, to return the next year. He re-entered the Chamber in 1863, and his speeches were filled with taunts at the second Empire on account of its loss of prestige. After the collapse of the Empire Thiers declined to become a member of the Government of National Defence, but voluntarily undertook (unsuccessful) diplomatic journeys to Great Britain, Russia, Austria and Italy. Twenty constituencies elected him to the National Assembly, and he became head of the provisional government. With great difficulty he persuaded the Assembly to agree to peace on terms practically dictated by Germany (1871). The Commune he suppressed with characteristic energy. In August he was elected president of the Republic. He was mainly instrumental in securing the withdrawal of the Germans, in paying the war indemnity and in placing the army and the civil service on a more satisfactory footing. He was detested by the extreme Left, and, Reactionaries and Radicals combining to harass him, in 1872 he tendered his resignation. It was not accepted. What he interpreted as a vote of no confidence was carried May 24, 1873, and he resigned. In 1877 he took an active part in bringing about the fall of the de Broglie ministry. He died of apoplexy at St Germain-en-Laye, September 3,

1877. Thiers was not a great statesman or a great historian. But he was a man of indomitable courage, and his patriotism, if narrow and chauvinistic, was deep and genuine. He became a member of the Academy in 1834. His *Discours parlementaires* fill 16 vols. (1879–89). See works by Jules Simon (1878–85), Mazade (1884), Rémusat (1889; trans. 1892), Poincaré (1913), Reclus (1929), Allison (1932) and H. Malo (1932).

THIRKELL, Angela. See MACKAIL.

THIRLWALL, Connop (1797–1875), English divine and historian, born at Stepney, from Charterhouse passed in 1814 to Trinity College, Cambridge, and was elected a fellow. He was called to the bar in 1825, but in 1827 took orders, having two years before translated Schleiermacher's *Essay on St Luke*. Returning to Cambridge, he translated Niebuhr's *Rome* (1828) with Julius Hare; and their *Philological Museum* (1831–33) contained some remarkable papers, among them Thirlwall's ' On the Irony of Sophocles '. He petitioned and wrote (1834) in favour of the admission of Dissenters to degrees and was forced to resign his university appointments. Almost immediately he was presented by Brougham to the Yorkshire living of Kirby-Underdale. Here he wrote for *Lardner's Cyclopaedia* his *History of Greece* (1835–44; improved ed. 1847–52). In 1840 Lord Melbourne raised him to the see of St David's. For thirty-four years he laboured with the utmost diligence in his diocese, building churches, parsonages and schools, and augmenting poor livings. His eleven Charges remain an enduring monument of breadth of view—the first a catholic apology for the Tractarians. He joined in censuring *Essays and Reviews*, but was one of the four bishops who refused to inhibit Colenso. He supported the Maynooth grant, the admission of Jews to parliament, and alone amongst the bishops the disestablishment of the Irish Church. He resigned his see in May 1874, died at Bath, July 27, 1875, and was buried in Westminster Abbey, in the same grave as Grote. Perowne edited his *Remains, Literary and Theological* (1877–78); Perowne and Stokes his *Letters, Literary and Theological* (1881); and Dean Stanley the series of *Letters to a Friend* (1881). See Life by J. C. Thirlwall (1936).

THISTLEWOOD, Arthur (1770–1820), English conspirator, born near Lincoln, served in the army, but having imbibed revolutionary ideas in America and France, organized a mutiny at Spa Fields (1816) and in 1820 the Cato Street Conspiracy to murder Castlereagh and other ministers at Lord Harrowby's. The conspirators were arrested in a stable in Cato (Homer) Street, Edgware Road, and Thistlewood with four others was convicted of high treason and hanged.

THOM, (1) John Nichols. See COURTENAY.

(2) William (1799–1848), Scottish minor poet, author of *The Mitherless Bairn* and other poems, was born at Aberdeen, worked as a handloom weaver there and at Inverurie, and died at Hawkhill, Dundee.

THOMA, tō-mah, (1) Hans (1839–1924), German painter and lithographer, born in Bernau in the Black Forest, was a leader of the modern German school, known especially for his landscapes, genre scenes and religious and allegorical works. His early style was influenced by Courbet. His paintings include *At Lake of Garda*, *Solitude* and *Scenes from the Life of Christ*.

(2) **Wilhelm von** (1891-1948), German general, served in World War I, commanded the German tank forces in the Spanish Civil War, served under Guderian in France at the beginning of World War II, and was captured in Tunisia with remnants of the Afrika Korps in November 1942.

THOMAS, St, called **Didymus,** one of the Twelve Apostles, who according to John xx, 24-29, doubted until he had seen proof of Jesus's resurrection. One tradition has it that he founded the church in Parthia and was buried in Edessa. Another, that he preached in India. The Christians of St Thomas claim him as their founder. He is patron saint of Portugal and his feast day is on December 21.

THOMAS, (1) *tom'as,* Fr. *tō-mah* (fl. 12th cent.), Anglo-Norman poet, author of the earliest extant text (*c.* 1155-70) of the legend of Tristan and Iseult, a fragment of 3144 lines covering the final episodes including the death of the lovers. Though he has greater pretensions to a literary style, Thomas lacks the impressive primitive simplicity of Béroul, author of the slightly later and fuller of the two early versions, both of which appear to be based on an earlier poem now lost. Thomas is sometimes confused with Thomas the Rhymer (q.v.).

(2) **Albert** (1878-1932), French politician, born at Champigny-sur-Marne, was a Socialist member of the Chamber from 1910 to 1921, when he became director of the International Labour Office of the League of Nations.

(3) **(Charles Louis) Ambroise** (1811-96), French composer, born at Metz, studied at the Paris Conservatoire (1828-32). He wrote many light operas, of which *Mignon* (1866) is the best known, for the Opéra Comique and the Grand Opéra, and innumerable cantatas, part-songs and choral pieces. He became a member of the Institute (1851), professor of Composition (1852), director of the Conservatoire (1871).

(4) **Arthur Goring** (1850-92), English composer, born near Eastbourne, wrote the operas *Esmeralda* (1883) and *Nadeshda* (1885), the cantata *Sun-worshippers* (1881), and many songs. He died insane.

(5) **Brandon** (1849-1914), English actor and playwright, born in Liverpool. He first appeared as a comedy actor in 1879, and wrote a number of successful light plays, one of which, *Charley's Aunt* (1892), has retained enormous popularity.

(6) **Dylan Marlais** (1914-53), Welsh poet, born in Swansea. The son of a schoolmaster, he worked for a time as a reporter on the *South Wales Evening Post* and established himself with the publication of *Eighteen Poems* in 1934. He married Caitlin Macnamara in 1936 and published *Twenty-Five Poems* the same year. His other works include *The Map of Love* (1939), *Portrait of the Artist as a Young Dog* (1940), *The World*

I Breathe (1940), *Deaths and Entrances* (1946) and a scenario, *The Doctor and the Devils*. His *Collected Poems, 1934-1952,* were published in 1952 and he then turned to larger dramatic works. From 1944 he worked intermittently on a radio script about a Welsh seaside village and in its first form it was called *Quite Early One Morning.* Thomas expanded it into *Under Milk Wood* (published 1954). Until the appearance of this work, he had enjoyed a *succès d'estime.* Edith Sitwell had eulogized his poetry and other critics had praised his striking rhythms, his original imagery and his technical ingenuities—such as the seventy-two variations of line endings in *I in My Intricate Image*—but he could in no sense be called a popular writer. *Under Milk Wood* was immediately comprehensible, Rabelaisianly funny, had moments of lyric tenderness, fresh yet recognizable similes, and it presented most of the non-intellectual English concepts of Welsh thought and behaviour. It had a second success as a stage play. In 1955 *Adventures in the Skin Trade* was published, an unfinished novel described by the author as 'a mixture of Oliver Twist, Little Dorrit, Kafka, Beachcomber and good old three-adjectives-a-penny, belly-churning Thomas, the Rimbaud of Cwmdonkin Drive'. This description might apply to all his prose works, including *A Prospect by the Sea*, ed. D. Jones (1955). See studies by D. Stanford (1953), E. Olson (1954), H. Treece (1956), J. Brinnin (1956), Caitlin Thomas, *Leftover Life to Kill* (1957), Heppenstall, *Four Absentees* (1960), and his *Selected Letters* (ed. by Fitzgibbon, 1966).

(7) **Edward.** See (13).

(8) **Freeman Freeman-.** See WILLINGDON.

(9) **George Henry** (1816-70), American soldier, born in Virginia, graduated at West Point, entered the artillery in 1840, gained three brevets for gallantry and in the Civil War, in 1861, was appointed brigadier-general of volunteers, and in January 1862 won the battle of Mill Springs. Major-general in command of the centre of Rosencrans's army, he saved the battle of Stone River; and at Chickamauga again rendered the victory a barren one for the Confederates. In October 1863 he was given the command of the Army of the Cumberland, and in November captured Mission Ridge. In 1864 he commanded the centre in Sherman's advance on Atlanta, was sent to oppose Hood in Tennessee in December and won the battle of Nashville. He afterwards commanded the military division of the Pacific. See Lives by Van Horne (1882), Coppée (1893) and Piatt (1893).

(10) **George John** (*c.* 1756-1802), Irish adventurer, born at Tipperary, deserted in India from the navy in 1781, and as general to the Begum Somru performed feats of arms against the Sikhs, and became the independent ruler of extensive Sikh territories, until driven out in 1802. See Compton's *European Adventurers of Hindustan* (1892).

(11) **Hugh Owen** (1833-91), Welsh orthopaedic surgeon, born in Anglesey, studied medicine at University College, London, Edinburgh University and in Paris, and

practised surgery at Liverpool. He pioneered orthopaedic surgery, constructing many appliances which are still used, especially Thomas's splints for the hip and the knee. See Lives by Watson (1935) and Vay (1956).

(12) **James Henry** (1874–1949), British Labour politician, born at Newport, Mon.; an enthusiastic trade unionist, he was elected M.P. for Derby in 1910. As assistant secretary of the Amalgamated Society of Railway Servants he helped to organize the strike of 1911 and the merger of smaller unions in 1913 which formed the National Union of Railwaymen, of which he ultimately became general secretary (1917). He led the successful railway strike of 1919. When Labour came to power in 1924 he was appointed colonial secretary, and in Ramsay MacDonald's 1929 Cabinet he was lord privy seal, subsequently becoming dominions secretary (1930–35). His adherence to the 1931 National Government aroused the hostility of his former Labour colleagues; and the ensuing bitterness clouded the last few years of his political career, which came to an untimely end when, as colonial secretary (1935–36), he was found guilty by a judicial tribunal of divulging budget secrets. See his *My Story* (1937) and Life by Blaxland (1964).

(13) **Philip Edward** (1878–1917), English critic and poet, born in London, educated at St Paul's school and Lincoln College, Oxford, became a hack writer of reviews, critical studies and topographical works. Not until 1914, encouraged by Robert Frost, did he realize his potential as a poet, writing most of his poetry during active service between 1915 and his death at Arras in 1917. His impressive poetry, though rooted in the English tradition of nature poetry, broke with the Georgian tradition in its lack of rhetoric and formality and in its emphasis on the austerity of Nature and solitariness of man. See his *Collected Poems* (1920), some of which appeared under the pseudonym of Edward Eastaway, and study by Farjeon (1958).

(14) **Ronald Stuart** (1913–   ), Welsh priest and poet, educated at the University of Wales and St Michael's College, Llandaff, was ordained in 1937 and has been vicar at Eglwysfach since 1954. His deceptively simple poetry, published in collections such as *Song at the Year's Turning* (1955), *Poetry for Supper* (1958) and *The Bread of Truth* (1963), conveys his love of Wales and its people, particularly evoked by his use of nature imagery.

(15) **Sidney Gilchrist** (1850–85), English metallurgist, born in London; a police-court clerk, he studied at Birkbeck College and discovered a method of separating the phosphorus impurities from iron in the Bessemer converter.

THOMAS THE RHYMER, or Thomas Rymour of Erceldoune (*c.* 1220–*c.* 1297), Scottish seer and poet, lived at Erceldoune (now Earlston, Berwickshire), and in 1286 is said to have predicted the death of Alexander III and the battle of Bannockburn, becoming known as 'True Thomas'; Boece calls him Thomas Learmont. Legend relates that he was carried off to Elfland, and after three years allowed to revisit the earth, but ultimately returned to his mistress, the fairy queen. In a charter of Petrus de Haga of Bemersyde *c.* 1260–70 the Rhymer appears as a witness; and in another of 1294 Thomas of Erceldoune, ' son and heir of Thomas Rymour of Erceldoune ', conveys lands to the hospice of Soutra. The Rhymer's ' prophecies ' were collected and published in 1603. Sir Walter Scott believed him to be the author of the poem of *Sir Tristrem* (as did McNeill), which was founded on a 12th-century French poem by another Thomas, a poet of genius, almost certainly an Englishman. See *The Romances and Prophecies of Thomas of Erceldoune*, edited by Sir J. A. H. Murray (Early English Text Soc. 1875); Brandl's *Thomas of Erceldoune* (Berlin 1880); *Sir Tristrem*, edited by Scott (1804), by Kölbing (1882), and by McNeill (Scot. Text Soc. 1886); Child's *Popular Ballads* (part ii, 1884); and Burnham's study (1908).

THOMAS À BECKET. See BECKET.
THOMAS À KEMPIS. See KEMPIS.
THOMAS AQUINAS. See AQUINAS.
THOMAS OF CELANO. See CELANO.
THOMAS OF HEREFORD, St. See CANTELUPE.
THOMAS OF WOODSTOCK (1355–97), youngest son of Edward III, born at Woodstock, was created Duke of Gloucester in 1385. He led the opposition of the lords appellant to Richard II, was arrested in 1397 and imprisoned at Calais, where he died.

THOMASIUS, Christian (1655–1728), German rationalist, philosopher and international jurist, born at Leipzig, lectured on law there and at Berlin, and at Halle became professor of Jurisprudence. He was the first to lecture not in Latin but German, broke away from pedantry and mediaeval terminology, and was a courageous opponent of trial for witchcraft and torture. See his *Gedanken und Erinnerungen* (1723–26), and works by Landsberg (1894), Fleischmann (1931).

THOMASON, (1) George (d. 1666), English bookseller and publisher who made a complete and valuable collection of tracts and pamphlets printed in England during the years of the Civil War and the Restoration. These were given to the British Museum by George III in 1762. See *Thomason Collection, Catalogue, 1640–1661*, ed. Fortescue (1908).

(2) **James** (1804–53), English administrator in India, as lieutenant-governor of the Northwest Provinces (1843–53) did admirable work in land settlement, education, &c.

THOMPSON, (1) Benjamin. See RUMFORD.

(2) **Sir D'Arcy Wentworth** (1860–1948), Scottish zoologist, born in Edinburgh and educated at Edinburgh Academy and Trinity College, Cambridge, in 1897 became professor of Biology at Dundee and later at St Andrews. His study *On Growth and Form* (1917) has literary as well as scientific merit. Other works include papers on fishery and oceanography, *Glossary of Greek Birds* (1895) and *Glossary of Greek Fishes* (1945). See Life by his daughter (1958).

(3) **David** (1770–1857), Canadian explorer, born in Westminster, went to Canada in 1784, and explored much of the west, including the Columbia River (1807–11).

(4) **Edith** (d. 1923), English murderess, with her accomplice Frederick Bywaters was tried in December 1922 for stabbing her husband two months previously on the way home from a London theatre. The trial at the Old Bailey provided much sensation; the couple were found guilty, and in spite of many petitions for reprieve were executed. See F. Young's study (1951).

(5) **Elizabeth Southerden.** See BUTLER (16).

(6) **Francis** (1859–1907), English poet, born at Preston, Lancs, was brought up in the Catholic faith and studied for the priesthood. By temperament unsuited for this, he turned to medicine at Owens College, Manchester, but failed to graduate. He moved to London, where extreme poverty and ill-health drove him to become an opium addict. From this he was rescued by Wilfrid and Alice Meynell, to whom he had sent some poems for Meynell's magazine *Merry England*. His health was restored at a monastery in Sussex, where he wrote several poems, including the well-known *Hound of Heaven*. Thereafter he was succoured by the Meynells until his death from tuberculosis. His works include *Poems* (1893), *Sister Songs* (1895, written for the Meynell girls) and *New Poems* (1897). His notable *Essay on Shelley* (1909) appeared posthumously, as did his *Life of St Ignatius Loyola* (1909). His poems, mainly religious in theme, are rich in imagery and poetic vision. See the *Works* (1913, ed. E. Meynell), *Poems of Francis Thompson* (1946), studies by Delattre (1909), Mégroz (1927), Olivers (Eng. trans. 1938) and Lives by Meynell (1913), Reid (1959) and Thomson (1961).

(7) **Sir Henry** (1820–1904), English surgeon, born at Framlingham, studied medicine at University College, London, and became professor of Surgery there and at the Royal College of Surgeons. Knighted (1867) and made a baronet (1899), he wrote on the urethra, lithotomy and calculus, and advocated cremation. A collector of Nankin china, and an astronomer, he exhibited at the Royal Academy.

(8) **Sir John Sparrow David** (1844–94), Canadian statesman, born at Halifax, entered the Nova Scotia Legislature in 1877, became premier of Nova Scotia (1881) and of Canada in 1892. He was knighted in 1888 and died at Windsor, on a visit to England.

(9) **John Taliaferro** (1860–1940), American soldier and inventor, was born in Newport, Kentucky, and graduated in 1882 at the Military Academy. In 1920 he invented the submachine gun known as the 'Tommy' gun, which was a ·45 calibre gun weighing 10 lb. It was first used for military purposes by the U.S. Marines in Nicaragua in 1925. A modification was adopted for use by the Allies in World War II. He retired in 1914, but was recalled during World War I as Chief of the Small Arms Division of the U.S. Ordnance Department.

(10) **John Vaughan** (1779–1847), English zoologist, after seeing service as an army surgeon studied marine zoology, distinguishing himself by his publications on barnacles and the common crab.

(11) **Randall** (1899–), American composer, born in New York, studied under Ernest Bloch, and from 1922 to 1925 was a fellow of the American Academy at Rome, subsequently teaching at Harvard, Princeton and California. His music assimilates romantic and popular American idioms, and includes three symphonies, an oratorio *The Peaceable Kingdom*, *The Testament of Freedom*, a setting of passages from the writings of Thomas Jefferson, chamber, piano, orchestral and theatre music.

(12) **Silvanus Phillips** (1851–1916), English physicist, born at York, professor of Physics and principal of the City and Guilds Technical College, Finsbury, wrote on electricity, light and magnetism and a witty, effective little book called *Calculus made Easy* (1910).

(13) **William** (*c.* 1785–1833), Irish landowner and writer on economics, was a follower of Bentham. One of the early socialists, his works include *An Inquiry into the Principles of the Distribution of Wealth most Conducive to Human Happiness* (1824), *An Appeal of one half of the Human Race* (1825), and *Practical Directions for the Speedy and Economical Establishment of Communities on the Principle of Mutual Co-operation* (1830).

(14) **William Hepworth** (1810–86), English Greek scholar, born at York, studied at Trinity College, Cambridge, became regius professor of Greek in 1853, and in 1866 master of Trinity. He edited Plato's *Phaedrus* and *Gorgias*, and is chiefly remembered by a few incomparable sarcasms.

THOMS, William John (1803–85), English antiquary and bibliographer, born in Westminster, after twenty years as a clerk in Chelsea Hospital became a clerk to the House of Lords, and its deputy librarian (1863–82). He founded (1849) and edited (till 1872) *Notes and Queries*, devised the word 'folklore', and edited *Early Prose Romances* (1828).

THOMSEN, Vilhelm (1842–1927), Danish philologist, born at Copenhagen, professor there from 1875, wrote *The Relations between Ancient Russia and Scandinavia* (1878) and deciphered the Orkhon inscriptions (1893).

THOMSON, (1) **Sir Charles Wyville** (1830–1882), Scottish zoologist, born at Bonsyde, Linlithgow, studied at Edinburgh and held professorships in Natural History at Cork, Belfast and Edinburgh. He was famous for his deep-sea researches, described in *The Depths of the Oceans* (1872), and in 1872 was appointed scientific head of the *Challenger* Expedition (1872–76). He was elected F.R.S. in 1869. See his *The Voyage of the Challenger* (1877), and Sir W. A. Herdman, *Founders of Oceanography* (1923).

(2) **Elihu** (1853–1937), English-born American inventor, born in Manchester, emigrated to the United States and was educated in Philadelphia, becoming a chemistry teacher. He cooperated in his 700 patented electrical inventions, which include the three-phase alternating-current generator and arc lighting, with Edward James Houston (q.v.), founding the Thomson-Houston Electric Company (1883), which merged with Edison's in 1892 to form the General Electric Company.

(3) **George** (1757–1851), collector of Scottish music, friend of Burns, born at

Limekilns, was clerk to the Board of Trustees in Edinburgh for sixty years. Burns, Scott and Campbell contributed to his *Collection of Scottish Songs and Airs* (5 vols. 1799–1818). See his Correspondence (ed. Hadden, 1898).

(4) **Sir George Paget** (1892–), English physicist, son of (10), born and educated at Cambridge, where he became a fellow of Trinity College, served in the Royal Flying Corps in World War I, was professor of Physics at Aberdeen (1922), Imperial College, London (1930), and master of Corpus Christi (1952–62). He was elected F.R.S. (1930), and awarded its Hughes (1939) and Royal (1949) medals. In 1937 he shared the Nobel prize with Davisson for their discovery, separately and by different methods, of electron diffraction by crystals. He was knighted (1943), and scientific adviser to the U.N. Security Council (1946–47). In 1960 for his contributions to electrical science he was awarded the Faraday medal by the Institution of Electrical Engineers. See his *The Atom* (1937) and *Theory and Practice of Electron Diffraction* (1939).

(5) **James** (1700–48), Scottish poet, born at Ednam manse, Kelso, educated at Jedburgh School and Edinburgh University for the ministry, abandoned his studies and went to seek his fortune as a writer in London. He published *Winter* (1726), a short poem in blank verse, *Summer* (1727), *Spring* (1728), and *Autumn* appeared with the other three under the collective title *The Seasons* (1730). In 1729 his *Sophonisba* was produced. One luckless line, ' O Sophonisba, Sophonisba O ', is still remembered for the parody, ' O Jemmy Thomson, Jemmy Thomson O ', which killed what little life the piece possessed. His other tragedies were *Agamemnon* (1738), *Edward and Eleonora* (1739), *Tancred and Sigismunda* (1745) and *Coriolanus* (1748). The poem *Liberty* (1735–1736) was inspired by the Grand Tour which he undertook as tutor to Lord Chancellor Talbot's son in 1731, and was dedicated to the Prince of Wales, who awarded him a pension. 'A Poem sacred to the Memory of Isaac Newton ' (1727) and ' Britannia ' (1729), which criticized Walpole's foreign policy, secured him further patronage and the sinecure of surveyor-general of the Leeward Isles (1744). *Alfred, a Masque* (1740) contains the song ' Rule Britannia ', also claimed for Mallet (q.v.). The Spenserian *The Castle of Indolence* (1748) is considered his masterpiece. Thomson stood on the threshold of the Romantic Age. The proper study of mankind was to be no longer man but nature, with science unravelling ever greater harmonies. Despite the pleasing melody of much of his verse, he often substitutes verbosity for feeling. See Lives by L. Morel (1896), W. Bayne (1898) and G. C. Macaulay (1908), and studies by A. D. McKillop (1942) and D. Grant (1951).

(6) **James** (1822–92), Scottish engineer, elder brother of Lord Kelvin (q.v.), born at Belfast, was professor of Engineering at Belfast (1851) and Glasgow (1873–89). He was an authority on hydraulics, invented a turbine, discovered the effect of pressure upon the freezing-point of water, and wrote papers on elastic fatigue, under-currents and trade winds.

(7) **James** (1834–82), British poet, was born, a sailor's son, at Port Glasgow, and educated in an orphan asylum. He was trained as an army schoolmaster, but through his friend Bradlaugh contributed (1860–75) to the *National Reformer*, in which appeared many of his sombre, sonorous poems, including *The City of Dreadful Night* (1874), his greatest work. He became a lawyer's clerk in 1862, went to America as a mining agent (1872), was war correspondent with the Carlists (1873), and from 1875 onwards depended largely on contributions to a tobacconists' trade monthly. Ill-health and melancholia drove him to narcotics and stimulants, and he died in University College Hospital. *The City of Dreadful Night and other Poems* (1880; ed. E. Blunden, 1932) was followed by *Vane's Story* (1881), *Essays and Phantasies* (1881), *A Voice from the Nile* (1884, with memoir by Bertram Dobell), *Shelley, a Poem* (1885), and *Biographical and Critical Studies* (1896). His pseudonym B.V., Bysshe Vanolis, was partly from Shelley's second name, partly from an anagram of Novalis. See Salt's *Life of James Thomson*, ' B.V.' (1889; revised ed. 1914).

(8) **John** (1778–1840), Scottish painter, born at Dailly manse, Ayrshire, was from 1800 the minister of Dailly and from 1805 of Duddingston. He was one of the first landscape painters of Scotland. See Lives by Baird (1895), Napier (1919).

(9) **Joseph** (1858–95), Scottish explorer, born at Penpont, Dumfriesshire, studied at Edinburgh, went (1878–79) to Lake Tanganyika, and in 1883–84 passed through the Masai country. For the Niger Company he visited Sokoto (1885), and for the Geographical Society he explored southern Morocco (1888). He wrote *To the Central African Lakes and Back* (1881), *Through Masai Land* (1885), *Travels in the Atlas* (1889), a Life of Mungo Park (1890), &c. See Life by his brother, J. B. Thomson (1896).

(10) **Sir Joseph John** (1856–1940), British mathematical physicist, one of the outstanding pioneers of nuclear physics, father of (4), was born at Cheetham Hill near Manchester, December 18, the son of a Scottish bookseller. He entered Owen's College, Manchester, at fourteen with the intention of becoming a railway engineer, but a scholarship took him to Trinity College, Cambridge, where he graduated second wrangler. In 1884 at the age of twenty-seven he succeeded Lord Rayleigh as Cavendish professor of Experimental Physics, and in 1919 was himself succeeded by his great student, later Lord Rutherford (q.v.). Thomson's early theoretical work was concerned with the extension of Clerk-Maxwell's electromagnetic theories. This led on to the study of gaseous conductors of electricity and in particular the nature of cathode rays. Using Röntgen's discovery of X-rays (1895), he showed that cathode rays were rapidly-moving particles and by measuring their speed and specific charge, the latter by two independent methods, he deduced that these ' corpuscles ' (electrons) must be nearly

two thousand times smaller in mass than the lightest known atomic particle, the hydrogen ion. This, the greatest revolution in physics since Newton, was inaugurated by his lecture to the Royal Institution, April 30, 1897, and published in October in the *Philosophical Magazine*. Before the outbreak of World War I, Thomson had successfully studied the nature of positive rays (1911), and this work was crowned by the discovery of the isotope. He also formulated a theory for the calculations on the scattering of X-rays by electrons in atoms. During the war he was engaged in admiralty research and helped to found the Department of Scientific and Industrial Research. ' J. J.' made the Cavendish Laboratory the greatest research institution in the world. Although simplicity of apparatus was carried to ' string and sealing wax ' extremes, seven of his research assistants subsequently won the Nobel prize. He was the first man of science to become master of Trinity College (1918–1940). Thomson was awarded the Nobel prize (1906), knighted (1908), O.M. (1912), was president of the British Association (1909) and of the Royal Society (1915–20). He was buried near Newton in the nave of Westminster Abbey. See his *Recollections and Reflections* (1936), Lives by Lord Rayleigh (1942) and his son G. P. Thomson (1964), and *History of the Cavendish Laboratory* (1910).

(11) **Roy Herbert, 1st Baron Thomson of Fleet** (1894–), Canadian-born British newspaper and television magnate, son of a Scottish barber, was born at Toronto. Successively clerk, salesman, farmer, stenographer and book-keeper, he gained a commission in the Canadian militia during World War I. He became prosperous when, as a radio salesman, he set up his own commercial transmitter at North Bay (1931) in an area of poor reception, thus boosting sales and founding what later became the N.B.C. network. He started more radio stations and acquired 28 Canadian and 6 American newspapers, which he turned over to his son in 1953. In that year he settled in Edinburgh on acquiring his first British paper, *The Scotsman*, and associated publications. In 1957 he obtained a licence for commercial television in Scotland and in 1959 he became one of Britain's leading newspaper proprietors with the acquisition of the Kemsley newspapers. Unlike his predecessors, he did not impose a policy on his editors. In 1966 he took over *The Times*. He was created a peer in 1964.

(12) **Virgil** (1896–), American composer and critic, was born at Kansas City and educated at Harvard and Paris. He set some of the writings of Gertrude Stein (q.v.) to music, and wrote operas, *Four Saints in Three Acts* (1934), first performed by a cast of Negroes, and *The Mother of Us All* (1947), besides symphonies, ballets, choral, chamber and film music. His work is notable for its simplicity of style. He was music critic of the *New York Herald Tribune* (1940–54). See study by Hoover and Cage (1959).

(13) **Sir William**. See KELVIN (LORD).

THOREAU, Henry David, *thor'ō* (1817–62), American essayist and poet, the ' hermit of Walden ', born of Jersey stock at Concord, Mass., July 12, 1817, graduated at Harvard in 1837, became a teacher at Concord, and lectured. He soon gave up teaching, and joined his father in making lead pencils, but about 1839 began his walks and studies of nature as the serious occupation of his life. In 1839 he made the voyage described in his *Week on the Concord and Merrimack Rivers* (1849). Thoreau early made the acquaintance of Emerson, and in 1841–43 in 1847 was a member of his household. In 1845 he built himself a shanty in the woods by Walden Pond, where he wrote much of the *Week*, his essay on Carlyle, and the American classic, *Walden, or Life in the Woods* (1854). After the Walden episode he supported himself by whitewashing, gardening, fence building and land surveying. He also lectured now and then, and wrote for magazines. He made three trips to the Maine woods in 1846, 1853 and 1857, described in papers collected after his death (1864). In 1850 he made a trip to Canada, which produced *A Yankee in Canada* (1866). Thoreau began in 1835 to keep a daily journal of his walks and observations, from whose thirty volumes were published *Early Spring in Massachusetts* (1881), *Summer* (1884) and *Winter* (1887). Other publications are *Excursions in Field and Forest*, with memoir by Emerson (1863), *Cape Cod* (1865), *Letters to Various Persons*, with nine poems (1865), *Familiar Letters* (1894) and *Poems of Nature* (1896). See *Collected Poems* (ed. by Bode, 1943, rev. ed. 1964), Correspondence, ed. Harding and Bode (1959), Lives by W. E. Channing (1873), H. S. Salt (1890–96), H. S. Canby (1939), and E. Seybold (1951), and studies by M. van Doren (1916), Krutch (1949) and Keyes (1955).

THORNDIKE, (1) Edward Lee (1874–1949), American psychologist, born at Williamsburg, Mass., studied at Wesleyan University and afterwards, under William James (q.v.), at Harvard. As professor at Columbia (1904–1940), he formulated important theories of educational psychology. He devised intelligence tests and stressed the effect of chance associations in educational processes. His works include *The Principles of Teaching* (1905), *Psychology of Learning* (1914), *Psychology of Arithmetic* (1922) and *of Algebra* (1923), and *The Measurement of Intelligence* (1926).

(2) **Dame Sybil** (1882–), English actress, born in Gainsborough, trained as a pianist but turned, despite considerable discouragement, to the stage. She made her first stage appearance with Greet's Pastoral Players in *The Merry Wives of Windsor* in 1904. After four years spent touring the United States in Shakespearean repertory, she became a prominent member of Miss Horniman's Repertory Company in Manchester, and worked from 1914 to 1919 at the Old Vic, subsequently collaborating with her husband, **Sir Lewis Casson**, whom she married in 1908, in a biography of Lilian Baylis. In 1924 she played the title rôle in the first English performance of Shaw's *Saint Joan*, and, during World War II, was a notable member of the Old Vic Company,

playing at the New Theatre, London. She was created D.B.E. in 1931. See Life by Trewin (1955).

THORNEYCROFT, (George Edward) Peter, Baron (1909–), English politician, educated at Eton and the R.M.A. Woolwich, served as a regular artillery officer (1930–33), left the army to become a barrister, and entered parliament in 1938. President of the Board of Trade in 1951–57, he was appointed chancellor of the Exchequer in 1957, but, disagreeing with government financial policy, resigned after a year in office. Minister of aviation (1960–62), of defence (1962–64), and secretary of state for defence (1964), he lost his parliamentary seat in the 1966 election. In 1967 he was created a life peer.

THORNHILL, Sir James (1675–1734), English painter, born at Melcombe Regis, Dorset, executed paintings for the dome of St Paul's, Blenheim, Hampton Court and Greenwich Hospital. He painted some portraits, including those of Codrington, the criminal Jack Sheppard and a self-portrait; and of his easel paintings the best known is that of the House of Commons (1730). He founded a drawing school and Hogarth (q.v.), who became his son-in-law, was one of his pupils. He was knighted by George I in 1720 and was appointed serjeant-painter, becoming in 1728 history painter to the king. From 1722 he was M.P. for Melcombe Regis.

THORNTON, Henry (1760–1815), English banker and economist, born in London, became in 1782 a member of parliament and gave considerable support to the aims and schemes of his friend Wilberforce. He became known in the government as an astute financier, this reputation being confirmed by his excellent *An Enquiry into the Nature and Effects of the Paper Credit of Great Britain* (1802). He was a member of the bullion committee (1810), a director and governor of the Bank of England, and a great part of his personal fortune he gave to charitable causes.

THORNYCROFT, Sir William Hamo (1850–1925), English sculptor, was born in London. *Artemis* (1880), his first success, was followed by *The Mower* (1884), and statues of General Gordon in Trafalgar Square (1885), John Bright at Rochdale (1892), and Cromwell at Westminster (1899). He was elected R.A. (1888), and was knighted (1917). His grandfather, **John Francis** (1780–1861); his mother, **Mary** (1814–95); and his father, **Thomas** (1815–85), were all sculptors. His brother, **Sir John Isaac** (1843–1928), knighted in 1902, was a naval architect, engineer, and F.R.S.

THORPE, Benjamin (1782–1870), English philologist, edited numerous Anglo-Saxon texts, and wrote *Northern Mythology* (1852).

THORVALDSEN, Bertel (1770–1844), Danish sculptor, born probably at Copenhagen, was the son of an Icelandic woodcarver. He studied at Copenhagen, and from 1797 at Rome, where his model for a 'Jason' was highly admired by Canova, but remained unsold till in 1803 he received from 'Anastasius' Hope a commission for its production in marble. Now famous, he in 1819 made a triumphal return to Denmark. He again

lived in Rome 1820–38 and 1841–44. In the latter year, having revisited Copenhagen to complete some of his works, he died suddenly in the theatre, March 24. All the works in his possession he bequeathed, with the bulk of his fortune, to his country. Among his works are *Christ and the Twelve Apostles*, the reliefs *Night* and *Morning*, the *Dying Lion* at Lucerne and the Cambridge statue of Byron. See Danish Lives by Thiele (1831–50; Eng. abridgment by Barnard, 1865) and Sigurd Müller (1893), French Life by E. Plon (1830; trans. C. Hoey 1874), and Life by S. Trier (1903).

THOTHMES, or Thutmose, the name of four Egyptian pharaohs of the 18th Dynasty:
(1) **Thothmes I and II.** See HATSHEPSUT.
(2) **Thothmes III** (pharaoh 1479–47 B.C.), one of the greatest of Egyptian rulers, son of Thothmes I and father of Amenhotep II, reigned jointly at first with his wife and half-sister, Queen Hatshepsut (q.v.), from c. 1501. He invaded Syria, extended his territories to Carchemish on the Euphrates and made several invasions into Asia. He built the great temple of Amen at Karnak, restored those at Memphis, Heliopolis and Abydos, and erected obelisks, including 'Cleopatra's Needle', now in London.
(3) **Thothmes IV** (pharaoh c. 1420–11 B.C.), son of Amenhotep II and father of Amenhotep III (qq.v.), fought campaigns in Syria and Nubia.

THOU, Jacques Auguste de (Latinized **Thuanus**), *too* (1553–1617), French historian and statesman, born at Paris of a great legal family, was intended for the church, but turned to law, became president of the *parlement* of Paris, and was a distinguished diplomat under Henry III and Henry IV. His great Latin history of his own time (5 vols. 1604–20; ed. by S. Buckley, London 1733) was placed on the Index. At his death, he left also commentaries on his own life and some Latin verse. See Collinson's *Life of Thuanus* (1807), monographs by P. Chasles (1824) and H. Harrisse (1905), and Stirling-Maxwell's *Miscellaneous Essays* (1891).

THRALE. See PIOZZI.

THRASYBULUS, -si-boo'- (d. 388 B.C.), Athenian general, was a strenuous supporter of the democracy. In 411 B.C. he helped to overthrow the Four Hundred, and was responsible for the recall of Alcibiades (q.v.). He was banished by the Thirty Tyrants, but restored the democracy in 403. He conquered Lesbos and defended Rhodes, but was slain in 388 at Aspendus. Nepos has a Life of him.

THRING, Edward (1821–87), English schoolmaster, born at Alford House, Somerset, from Eton passed to King's College, Cambridge, and was elected a fellow. He was curate at Gloucester and elsewhere, but in 1853 found the work of his life as headmaster of Uppingham, which he made one of the best public schools of England, raising its numbers from 25 to 330. His works include volumes of school songs, an English grammar, *Theory and Practice of Teaching* (1883), and *Uppingham Sermons* (1886). See Life by Dr G. R. Parkin (2 vols. 1898), and study by Hoyland (1946).

THROCKMORTON, or Throgmorton, name

of an English family of the 15th and 16th centuries. Its important members were:

(1) **Francis** (1554–84), English conspirator, son of (3), was apprehended in the act of writing in cipher to Mary, Queen of Scots, confessed under torture and was executed at Tyburn.

(2) **Sir John** (d. 1445), was a clerk in the treasury who became chamberlain of the exchequer and under-treasurer to Henry VI.

(3) **Sir John** (d. 1580), English judge, father of (1) and brother of (4), with whom he was involved in Wyatt's rebellion (1554), but was acquitted and made chief justice of Chester.

(4) **Sir Nicholas** (1515–71), English diplomatist, fought bravely at Pinkie (1547), was ambassador to France, where he was imprisoned for siding with the Huguenots, and was repeatedly ambassador to Scotland during 1561–67. In 1569 he was sent to the Tower for promoting the scheme for marrying Mary, Queen of Scots, to the Duke of Norfolk. His daughter, **Elizabeth**, married Sir Walter Raleigh.

THUANUS. See THOU.

THUCYDIDES, *thoo-sid'i-deez* (c. 460–c. 400 B.C.), Greek historian of the Peloponnesian war, son of Olorus, was born near Athens. He suffered in the Athenian plague (430) but recovered. He commanded an Athenian squadron of seven ships at Thasos (424), when he failed to relieve Amphipolis; and, condemned therefore to death as a traitor, took refuge in exile, and retired to his Thracian estates. He lived in exile twenty years (possibly visiting Sicily), and probably returned to Athens in 404. He did not live long enough to revise book viii or to bring his history down to the end of the war. Thucydides wrote in a difficult style, his matter often based on speeches made by prominent politicians and analysed according to his own rationalist principles of historical criticism, which aimed at impartiality. He admired Pericles and clearly understood the causes of Greece's future decline. See studies by G. B. Grundy (1911 and 1948), J. H. Finley (1942) and A. W. Gomme (1945).

THUMB, Tom. See STRATTON.

THURBER, James Grover (1894–1961), American journalist, writer and playwright, born in Ohio. He was a member of the staff of *The New Yorker* from 1927, where his reputation was made. See his *Years with Ross* (1959). His drawings first appeared in his book *Is Sex Necessary?* (1929). They have been described as being 'like what everyone thinks he can do himself', but their crazy yet conventionalized inconsequence has a markedly individual technique. His comic and satirical books, illustrated by himself, include *The Seal in the Bedroom* (1931), *The Owl in the Attic* (1932), *My Life and Hard Times* (1933), with Elliott Nugent, *The Male Animal* (1940), a play, *Fables for Our Times* (1941 and 1951). There are also several anthologies of his work, such as *The Thurber Album* (1952), *Thurber's Dogs* (1955) and the posthumous *Vintage Thurber* (1963).

THURLOE, John (1616–68), English parliamentarian politician, was secretary of the council of state (1652), a member of Oliver Cromwell's second council (1657) and supported Richard Cromwell. He was accused of high treason at the Restoration, but was eventually set free. His correspondence (1742) is an important source for the history of the Protectorate. See *Cromwell's Master Spy* by D. L. Hobman (1961).

THURLOW, Edward, 1st Baron (1731–1806), English politician, born at Bracon-Ash, Norfolk, was as insolent and insubordinate at Caius College, Cambridge, as at King's School, Canterbury, and was sent down. He was called to the bar in 1754 and as King's Counsel in the Douglas peerage case (1769) made his reputation, entered parliament as a loyal supporter of Lord North, became solicitor-general (1770) and attorney-general (1771) and won George III's favour by upholding the latter's American policy. In 1778 he became lord chancellor and while retaining office under the Rockingham administration, opposed all its measures. Under Fox and North he was compelled to retire (1783), but was restored by Pitt and presided at the trial of Warren Hastings (1788). He was finally removed by Pitt in 1792 with the King's approval. He was vulgar, arrogant, profane and immoral, but 'No man' said Fox, ' was so wise as Thurlow looked '. See Life by R. G. Brown (1953).

THUROT, François, *tü-rō* (1726–60), French privateer, born at Nuits in Côte-d'Or, served first on a privateer. Captured and imprisoned for a year at Dover, he escaped by seizing a small boat and crossed the Channel. By 1748 he was able to fit out a merchant ship. He spent a few years in England, dividing his time between music, mathematics and dissipation, varied by smuggling and possibly piracy. At the outbreak of war (1755) he was given the command of a squadron with which he scoured the east coast of Britain, and engaged two frigates off the Forth. In October 1759 he sailed for Lough Foyle with a squadron carrying 1200 soldiers. High gales made it impossible to enter; and three British frigates appearing, Thurot fought till he was struck down.

THURSTAN (d. 1140), English divine, was a native of Bayeux and made Archbishop of York 1114. As archbishop, he struggled for primacy with Canterbury. On the invasion of David of Scotland (1137), he first persuaded him to accept a truce, and then collected forces at York and beat him at the Battle of the Standard (1138). He did much to help the growth of monasticism in the North and was concerned in the foundation of Fountains Abbey (1132). He entered the Cluniac order and died at Pontefract Priory.

THURSTON, (1) **Ernest Charles Temple** (1879–1933), English novelist and playwright, first wrote a volume of poems when he was sixteen. His sentimental novels were popular in his lifetime and include *The Apple of Eden* (1904), *The City of Beautiful Nonsense* (1909), *The Passionate Crime* (1920) and *A Hank of Hair* (1932). Of his plays, *The Wandering Jew* (1920) was the best known.

(2) **Katherine Cecil** (1875–1911), novelist, wife of (1), whom she divorced in 1910, was born in Cork. Her first book, *The Circle* (1903), was followed by several popular novels, the best of which was *John Chilcote*

M.P. (1904), with its theme of impersonation. This was dramatized by her husband as *The Masquerader* (1905).

THURTELL, John (1794–1824), English murderer, son of a Norwich alderman, was hanged at Hertford for the brutal murder, in Gill's Hill Lane, of a fellow-swindler, Weare. He appears in Borrow's *Lavengro.*

THUTMOSE. See THOTHMES.

TIBERIANUS, a 4th-century Latin poet of the African school, author of *Amnis ibat inter arva.*

TIBERIUS (Tiberius Claudius Nero) (42 B.C.–A.D. 37), second emperor of Rome, son of Ti. Claudius Nero and of Livia, was born November 16, three years before her complaisant husband yielded Livia to the triumvir Octavianus. He was nine when his father's death transferred him to the tutelage of his stepfather. Almost the whole of his first twenty years of manhood were spent in the camp—in Spain, Armenia, Gaul, Pannonia and Germany. He brought back the standards lost with Crassus; in 15 B.C. he cooperated with his brother Drusus in subduing the Rhaeti and Vindelici; warred with the Pannonians (12–9), and traversed Germany. Tiberius was compelled (12 B.C.) by Augustus to divorce his wife, Vipsania Agrippina, daughter of Agrippa by his former wife Pomponia, in order to marry Agrippa's widow Julia, the profligate daughter of Augustus. He was then sent to crush a revolt in Dalmatia and Pannonia; and for his wars in Germany received a full triumph (9 B.C.). But he retired to Rhodes (6 B.C.) where he gave himself to study and to astrology. Before his return (A.D. 2) the infamous Julia was banished to Pandataria (2 B.C.), and the deaths of the young princes Lucius and Gaius led Augustus to adopt Tiberius (A.D. 4) as heir to the imperial dignity. He spent the next seven years in active service in north Germany, in quelling insurrections in Pannonia and Dalmatia, and in taking vengeance upon the enemy who had annihilated the army of Varus in A.D. 9. Along with Germanicus he made two marches into the heart of Germany (9–10), returning to enjoy a splendid triumph (12). Tiberius succeeded Augustus in 14. According to Tacitus, the first eight years of his reign were marked by just government, frugality and care for the interests of the provincials. During this period only twelve state trials for high treason are recorded; during 23–28 the number rose to twenty. His minister Sejanus secured vast influence by playing on the morbid suspicions of his master; and in a six years' reign of terror 100 people perished, mostly by direct mandate of the prince who though not vindictive himself lived in terror of assassination. In 26 Tiberius left Rome for Campania, and the year after took up his abode in Capreae, where according to Suetonius he wallowed in brutish sensualities. He had left the whole control of government to Sejanus, but, awakened at length to his ambitious designs, struck him down without hesitation (31). Macro, the successor of Sejanus, had all his vices without his talents. The murder of Agrippa Postumus in 14, the mysterious death of Germanicus in the East

(19), the poisoning of Tiberius's own son Drusus by Sejanus (23), the banishment of Agrippina and the death of her young sons Nero and Drusus (31 and 33) were some of the dark tragedies that befell the house of Augustus. In his last years, the emperor's mind was darkened by gloom, superstition, perhaps insanity. On March 16, 37, he died at Misenum. Tacitus (Annals, Bks 1–6) is factually accurate but is hardly fair to Tiberius. More charitable are the modern studies by F. B. Marsh (1931), R. S. Rogers (1937), D. M. Pippede (1944) and Maranon (trans. Wells, 1956). See also *Claudius* novels by Robert Graves.

TIBULLUS, Albius (*c.* 54–19 B.C.), Roman poet, was born, it is believed, at Gabii. He acquired the friendship of the poet-statesman, M. Valerius Messala, and went on his staff, when Augustus commissioned him (30 B.C.) to crush a revolt in Aquitania. But though he distinguished himself in the campaign, he disliked a soldier's life as much as he enjoyed Roman society; and though again he started with Messala on a mission to Asia, he sickened on the voyage, and turned back at Corcyra. His tender, elegiac love poems to living inamoratas, by their limpid clearness and unaffected finish, still justify Quintilian in placing Tibullus at the head of Roman elegiac poets. The heroine of his first book was the wife of an officer absent on service in Cilicia; of his second, a fashionable courtesan. The third book can hardly be his, while the fourth is also by another hand. See studies by M. Schuster (1930) and N. Salanitro (1938).

TICHBORNE, a pre-Conquest Catholic family of Hampshire, who received a baronetcy in 1626. After the death of Sir Alfred Joseph Tichborne (1839–66), eleventh baronet, a butcher from Wagga-Wagga in New South Wales, Thomas Castro, otherwise Arthur Orton of Wapping, came forward to personate an elder brother, Roger Charles Tichborne (1829–54), who had been lost at sea off America. His case collapsed on March 6, 1872, the 103rd day of a trial to assert his claims. The ' Claimant ', committed for perjury, on February 28, 1874, the 188th day of his new trial, the cost of which was £55,315, got fourteen years' hard labour. Released 1884, in 1895 he confessed the imposture, and died April 1, 1898. See Sir Alex. Cockburn's *Charge* (2 vols. 1875), and studies by J. B. Atlay (1916) and D. Woodruff (1957).

TICKELL, Thomas (1686–1740), English poet, born at Bridekirk, Carlisle, was a fellow of Queen's, Oxford (1710–26). His complimentary verses on *Rosamond* (1709) gained him the favour, and his own virtues the friendship, of Addison, who, on becoming in 1717 secretary of state, made him his undersecretary; from 1725 he was secretary to the lords justices of Ireland. He was skilful in occasional poetry, and was favourably reviewed in the *Spectator*. His translation of book i of the *Iliad* appeared in 1715, about the same time as Pope's. Pope professed to believe it the work of Addison himself, designed to eclipse his version, and wrote the famous satire on Atticus. But though

Addison corrected it, the translation was doubtless by Tickell. His longest poem is *Kensington Gardens*; his most popular, *Colin and Lucy*; his finest, the exquisite elegy prefixed to his edition of Addison's Works (1721). See R. E. Tickell's study (1931).

TICKNOR, (1) **George** (1791–1871), American author, born in Boston, Mass., gave up his legal practice in order to study and travel in Europe, recounted in his interesting *Letters and Journals* (1876). He was professor of French and Spanish and Belles Lettres at Harvard (1819–35) and then spent three more years in Europe, collecting materials for his great *History of Spanish Literature* (1849). See Life by G. W. H. Milburn (1893).

(2) **William Davis** (1810–64), American publisher, born in Lebanon, N.H., became a publisher in Boston in 1832, at first with John Allen, and then with James T. Fields. As Ticknor & Fields they published the *Atlantic Monthly* and the *North American Review*, and their office was the resort of Emerson, Longfellow, Hawthorne, Holmes, Lowell and Whittier. Ticknor was one of the first Americans to remunerate foreign authors. See C. Ticknor, *Hawthorne and his Publisher* (1913).

TIECK, Johann Ludwig, *teek* (1773–1853), German critic and poet of the Romantic school, born in Berlin, lived the life of a man of letters, at Berlin, Dresden and near Frankfurt an der Oder. After two or three immature romances, he struck out a new line in clever dramatized versions of Puss in Boots, Blue Beard, &c. He followed up this first success (1797) by a tragedy, a comedy (1804) and *Phantasus* (1812–17), a collection of traditional lore in story and drama. Besides superintending the completion of A. W. Schlegel's translation of Shakespeare, he edited the doubtful plays and wrote a series of essays (*Shakespeares Vorschule*, 1823–29). *Don Quixote* he himself translated in 1799–1804. He holds an honourable place among Germany's dramatic and literary critics, in virtue of his *Dramaturgische Blätter* (2nd ed. 1852) and *Kritische Schriften* (1848). Some of his fairy tales and novels were translated into English by Carlyle and Thirlwall. See Lives by Köpke (1855), Friesen (1871) and Klee (1894); Carlyle's *Essays*, vol. i, and studies by H. Lüdeke (1922) and R. Minder (1935).

TIEPOLO, Giovanni Battista, *tyay'pō-lō* (1696–1770), Italian artist, the last of the great Venetian painters, was a productive artist, elegant, rich in colour, though inaccurate in representation, as for example his *The Finding of Moses* (in 17th-century costume) in the National Gallery, Edinburgh. In his ceiling paintings in the Würzburg and Madrid palaces he spreads imaginary skies filled with floating, gesticulating baroque figures, apparently unbounded by the structure of the buildings. See monograph by A. Morassi (1955).

TIERNEY, George (1761–1830), a sarcastic Whig politician, born at Gibraltar, fought a bloodless duel with Pitt (1798), and held office under Addington, Grenville, Canning and Goderich. See Life by Olphin (1934).

TIETJENS. See TITIENS.

TIGHE, Mary, *née* **Blachford,** *tī* (1772–1810), Irish poetess of Wicklow, whose Spenserian *Cupid and Psyche* (1805) influenced Keats.

TIGLATH-PILESER, name of three kings of Assyria, of whom the most noteworthy were:

(1) **Tiglath-Pileser I,** king (*c.* 1115–*c.* 1093 B.C.), extended his dominions to the upper Euphrates, and defeated the king of Babylonia.

(2) **Tiglath-Pileser III,** known also as **Pulu,** king (745–727 B.C.), a great empire-builder, conquered the cities of north Syria and Phoenicia, including Damascus and Babylon.

TIGRANES I, the Great (d. after 56 B.C.), king of Armenia, was set on the throne by Parthian troops (*c.* 94 B.C.). In alliance with Mithridates, he was a threat to Rome, to remove which Sulla (q.v.) was sent to the East (92). Left undisturbed owing to a Roman agreement with the Parthians, he made many conquests and founded Tigranocerta. In 69, Lucullus was sent out from Rome, and captured the new capital; and eventually Tigranes surrendered to Pompey (q.v.) (66), ruling henceforward over Armenia only.

TILDEN, (1) **Samuel Jones** (1814–86), American statesman, born, a farmer's son, at New Lebanon, N.Y., was admitted to the bar, and secured a large railway practice. By 1868 he had become leader of the Democrats in the state, and he attacked and destroyed Tweed and Tammany. In 1874 he became governor of New York; in 1876 he was the unsuccessful Democratic candidate for the presidency, after a special tribunal controlled by his opponents had vetted the votes cast. He left much of his fortune to found a free library in New York City. See Life by T. P. Cook (1876), and his Writings and Speeches, edited by John Bigelow (1835).

(2) **Sir William Augustus** (1842–1926), English chemist, born at St Pancras, London, professor at the Royal College of Science, London, made possible the manufacture of artificial rubber by his synthetic preparation of isoprene.

(3) **William Tatem** (1893–1953), American lawn-tennis player and writer, was born in Germantown, Pa. Seven times American champion and three times world champion, he was one of the greatest tennis players of the United States. He was for a time a journalist, a film actor, the publisher and editor of *Racquet Magazine* as well as the author of many books on tennis, including *The Art of Lawn Tennis* (1920), *The Phantom Drive* (1924) and a novel, *Glory's Net*.

TILLEMONT, Louis Sébastien le Nain de, *tee-y'-mõ* (1637–98), French ecclesiastical historian, was born in Paris, and educated by the Port Royalists. He entered the priesthood in 1676, and after the dispersion of the Solitaires in 1679 lived mostly on his estate at Tillemont near Paris. His chief works are the laborious and solid *Histoire ecclésiastique des six premiers siècles* (1693–1712) and *Histoire des empereurs* (1691–1738).

TILLETT, Benjamin (1860–1943), English trade-union leader, born at Bristol, worked as brickmaker, bootmaker, sailor, and Labour M.P. (1917–24, 1929–31). He was notable as organizer of the Dockers' Union in London and leader of the great dockers' strike in 1889, and of the London transport workers' strike, 1911. He was expelled from Hamburg and from Antwerp (1896) for supporting dock strikes.

TILLEY, Vesta, professional name of **Lady de Frece,** *née* **Matilda Alice Powles** (1864–1952), English comedienne, born in Worcester. She first appeared as The Great Little Tilley, aged four, in Nottingham, and did her first male impersonation the following year. She soon adopted the name of Vesta Tilley and became, through her charm, vivacity and attention to sartorial detail, the most celebrated of all male impersonators. Of the many popular songs ' made ' by her, *Burlington Bertie, Following in Father's Footsteps, Sweetheart May* and *Jolly Good Luck to the Girl who loves a Soldier* are still familiar. See her *Recollections of Vesta Tilley* (1934).

TILLICH, Paul Johannes (1886–1965), German Protestant theologian, born at Starzeddel, Prussia, was a Lutheran pastor (1912) and served as chaplain in the German army during World War I. He lectured at Berlin and subsequently held professorships in Theology at Marburg, Dresden, Leipzig, in Philosophy at Frankfurt, and, having been dismissed from this post by the Nazis in 1933, in Philosophy and Theology at the Union Theological Seminary, New York (1933–55), at Harvard Divinity School (1955–1962), and at Chicago Divinity School from 1962. His theology allowed for scientific method, philosophical scepticism and psychoanalysis, and was characterized by a realistic concern for the problems of contemporary society. God is the unconditional fulfilment intended in every ambiguous fulfilment in history. His works include *The Interpretation of History* (1936), *The Protestant Era* (1948), *The Courage to Be* (1952), his *magnum opus, Systematic Theology* (3 vols., 1953–63), essays, *Theology of Culture* (1959), &c. He took American nationality (1940) and was Gifford lecturer at Edinburgh (1953). See theological essays contributed by Marcel, Bultmann, Barth and others in his honour, *Religion and Culture* (1959).

TILLOTSON, John (1630–94), Archbishop of Canterbury, born at Sowerby, Yorkshire, studied at Clare Hall, Cambridge, becoming a fellow in 1651. Although with the Presbyterians at the Savoy conference, he submitted to the Act of Uniformity (1662) and henceforth received preferment, becoming dean of Canterbury in 1672 and archbishop, in place of the deposed nonjuror Sancroft, in 1691. He advocated the Zwinglian doctrine of the eucharist. According to Burnet ' he was not only the best preacher of the age, but seemed to have brought preaching to perfection '. In 1664 he married a niece of Oliver Cromwell. See his complete works, with a Life by Birch (1707–12).

TILLY, (1) Comte Alexandre de (1761–1816), French courtier and libertine, wrote his *Mémoires* in exile. See translation by Mme Delisle (1933).

(2) **Jan Tserklaes, Count of** (1559–1632), Flemish soldier, born at the castle of Tilly in Brabant, and brought up by the Jesuits,

learned the art of war under Parma, fought in Hungary against the Turks, and was appointed in 1610 by Duke Maximilian of Bavaria to reorganize his army. He was given the command of the Catholic army at the oubreak of the Thirty Years' War, and by his decisive victories at Weisser Berg and Prague (both 1620) dissipated the dreams of the Elector Palatine. He separated the armies of Mansfeld and of the Margrave of Baden, beat the latter at Wimpfen (1622), and expelled Christian of Brunswick from the Palatinate, defeating him in two battles. Created a count of the empire, he defeated the king of Denmark at Lutter (1626), and with Wallenstein compelled him to sign the Treaty of Lübeck (1629). Next year he succeeded Wallenstein as commander-in-chief of the imperial forces, and stormed Magdeburg (May 20, 1631), when the atrocities he allowed his Croats and Walloons to perpetrate cast a foul stain upon his reputation. Gustavus Adolphus at Breitenfeld (September 17) drove him to retreat behind the Lech, and forced the passage of the river (April 5, 1632), after a desperate conflict in which Tilly received his death-wound.

TIMBS, John (1801–75), English antiquarian and miscellanist, born in London, wrote over 150 volumes on interesting facts gathered on a varied number of subjects and places, often antiquarian, such as *Curiosities of London* (1855), *Romance of London* (1865), *Abbeys, Castles, and Ancient Halls of England and Wales* (1869), &c. He was elected a fellow of the Society of Antiquaries (1854) and died in poverty.

TIMOLEON, *ti-mō'lee-on* (d. *c.* 337 B.C.), Greek statesman and general of Corinth, overthrew the tyranny of his brother and retired from public life. But when Dionysius II and others tried to establish themselves in Syracuse, he was prevailed upon to return to public life. He manœuvred Dionysius II into abdication and fought the Carthaginians, who were supporting the other tyrants, defeating them at the Crimessus in 341. He then promptly retired again, having taken measures to stabilize the economy of Greek Sicily. See Lives by Plutarch and Diodorus Siculus, and study by Westlake (1952).

TIMON, (1) the Misanthrope of Athens, a contemporary of Socrates. According to the comic writers who attacked him, he was disgusted with mankind on account of the ingratitude of his early friends, and lived a life of almost total seclusion. Lucian made him the subject of a dialogue; Shakespeare's play is based on the story as told in Painter's *Palace of Pleasure*.

(2) the **Sillographer** (*c.* 320–*c.* 230 B.C.), Greek poet and philosopher, lectured at Chalcedon and spent his last years at Athens. He wrote *Silloi,* sarcastic hexameters upon Greek philosophers.

TIMOSHENKO, Semyon Konstantinovich (1895–1970), Russian general, born in Bessarabia of peasant stock, in 1915 was conscripted into the tsarist army. In the revolution he took part in the defence of Tsaritsin. In 1940 he headed 27 divisions to smash the resistance of 3½ Finnish divisions—a Naysmith hammer to crack a walnut. With the German blitz of 1941 Timoshenko replaced Budenny in the Ukraine, ' Russia's breadbasket '; but his attempt to stem the 1942 Nazi drive on the Crimea resulted in no more than a Pyrrhic victory. From 1940–41 he served as People's Commissar of Defence, and commanded the Byelo-Russian district from 1956 to his retiral in 1960. See *Behind the Steel Wall*, Fredborg (1944).

TIMUR. See TAMERLANE.

TINDAL, Matthew (1655–1733), English deistical writer, born at Beer-Ferris rectory, S. Devon, was elected a fellow of All Souls College, Oxford. A Roman Catholic under James II, he reverted to Protestantism of a somewhat freethinking type, and wrote *An Essay of Obedience to the Supreme Powers* (1693), and *Rights of the Christian Church asserted against the Romish and all other Priests* (1706). The latter raised a storm of opposition; but even a prosecution failed to prevent a fourth edition in 1709. In 1730 Tindal published his *Christianity as old as the Creation*, which was soon known as ' the Deist's Bible '; its aim is to eliminate the supernatural element from religion, and to prove that its morality is its only claim to the reverence of mankind. Answers were issued by Waterland, Foster, Conybeare, Leland, &c.

TINDALE, William. See TYNDALE.

TINTORETTO, properly **Jacopo Robusti** (1518–94), the greatest of the late Venetian painters, was born probably in Venice, the son of a dyer or *tintore*. Little is known of his life. He is supposed to have studied under Titian, but only for a short time as the master was jealous of the boy's genius. Tintoretto claims to have set up independently, practically untaught, by 1539, but it is likely that he had some supervision, possibly from Bonifazio. He married (1550), and three of his seven children also became painters. Except for visits to Mantua (1580, 1590–93), he lived all his life in Venice. With an insatiable appetite for creative opportunities rather than for wealth, he often contented himself with little more than the cost price of a painting and went to any length to undercut his fellow-painters. When a work was to be entrusted to Veronese, for example, he undertook to paint it, and actually did, in the style of that artist for a smaller fee. Tintoretto pioneered the way from the classical to the baroque. Already, in his early work, *The Miracle of the Slave* (1548; Accademia, Venice), in which he consciously set out to combine Titian's colours with Michelangelo's sculptural draughtsmanship, there is a tendency towards a dynamic interrelationship of the groups of figures in respect of the central character depicted, rather than the individual self-sufficiency of every detail as in classical composition. His early work, however, is still undecided and experimental, e.g., *The Miracle of St Agnes* (1550; Madonna dell' Orto) and the two votive pictures, *St Louis and St George with the Princess* (1552) and *SS. Andrew and Jerome* (1552; both in the Accademia, Venice). His mastery in depicting the female nude is apparent in the three *Susanna* paintings (*c.* 1555, Louvre, particularly 1556–60, Vienna, and 1560, Prado, Madrid) and there are a number of significant

portraits of this period, e.g., *Portrait of a Venetian* (National Gallery, Edinburgh). After 1556 Tintoretto seems to have found himself. *The Last Judgment*, *The Golden Calf* (both *c.* 1560, Madonna dell' Orto, Venice) and *The Marriage of Cana* (1561, Santa Maria della Salute, Venice) were followed by two masterpieces of perspective and lighting effects, both *c.* 1562, *The Finding* (Brera, Milan) and *The Removal of the Body of St Mark* (Accademia, Venice). From 1564 Tintoretto was employed in decorating the Albergo, and the Halls of the Scuola of San Rocco and its church. The Scuola contains probably the largest collection of works by one artist in a single building, prearranged in a vast iconographical scheme from the Old and New Testaments. These include the dynamic rendering of the *Crucifixion* (1565), teeming with incident, *The Annunciation* and *Massacre of the Innocents* (both 1583–87). Other notable late works are *The Origin of the Milky Way* (after 1570; Nat. Gall., London), the *Paradiso*, famous for its colossal size (1588; Ducal Palace, Venice), his last version of *The Last Supper* (1592–94), no longer an exclusive gathering but set among maids and attendants and fully expressing the religious fervour of the counter-Reformation, and *Entombment* (1594; both San Giorgio Maggiore, Venice). The ' painter of dark turbulence ' left an unrivalled number of paintings. See the contemporary account of his life and work in C. Ridolf's *Le Maraviglie dell' Arte*, vol. ii, ed. D. F. von Hadeln (1924), J. Ruskin, *Stones of Venice* (1863), B. Berenson, *Italian Pictures of the Renaissance* (1932), and monographs by E. M. Phillipps (1911), F. P. B. Osmaston (1915; on the *Paradiso*, 1910), E. von der Bercken (Munich 1942), H. Tietze (1948) and E. Newton (1952).

TINWORTH, George (1843–1913), English artist in terracotta, born in London, the son of a poor wheelwright, in 1864 entered the Royal Academy schools, and in 1867 obtained an appointment in the Doulton art pottery. The works which made him famous were mainly terracotta panels with groups of figures in high relief illustrating scenes from sacred history.

TIPPETT, Sir Michael (1905–   ), English composer, born in London. He studied at the Royal College of Music and became conductor of educational organizations under the London County Council and 1940–51 director of Music at Morley College. He first attracted attention with his chamber music and Concerto for Double String Orchestra (1939), but his oratorio, *A Child of our Time* (1941), reflecting the political and spiritual problems of the 1930s and 1940s, won him wide recognition. A convinced pacifist, Tippett went to prison for three months as a conscientious objector during World War II. He scored a considerable success with the operas, *The Midsummer Marriage* (1952) and *King Priam* (1961). His other works include three symphonies (1934, later withdrawn, 1945, 1958) and a piano concerto (1957). He was created C.B.E. in 1959, and was knighted in 1966.

TIPPOO SAHIB, or **Tipú Sultán** (1749–99),

sultan of Mysore, son of Haidar Ali (q.v.), during his father's wars with the British completely routed Bailey(1780 and 1782) and Braithwaite (1782). In 1782 he succeeded his father as sultan of Mysore. In 1783 he captured and put to death most of the garrison of Bednur, but after the conclusion of peace between France and Britain he agreed to a treaty (1784) stipulating for the *status quo* before the war. He sent ambassadors in 1787 to France to stir up a war with Britain, and, failing in this, invaded (1789) the protected state of Travancore. In the ensuing war (1790–92) the British, under Stuart and Cornwallis, were aided by the Mahrattas and the Nizam, and Tippoo was compelled (1792) to resign one-half of his dominions, pay an indemnity of 3030 lakhs of rupees, restore all prisoners, and give his two sons as hostages. Resuming his intrigues, he sent another embassy to the French. Hostilities began in March 1799, and Tippoo was driven from the open field, attacked in Seringapatam, and after a month's siege slain at the storming, by General Harris, of the fort (May 4). See L. B. Bowring's *Haidar Ali and Tipú Sultán* (1893) and *Select Letters of Tipú Sultán* (ed. Kirkpatrick, 1881).

TIRABOSCHI, Girolamo, *teer-a-bos'kee* (1731–94), Italian scholar, born at Bergamo, became professor of Rhetoric at Milan, and in 1770 librarian to the Duke of Modena. His *Storia della Letteratura Italiana* (1772–81) is an accurate survey down to 1700.

TIRPITZ, Alfred P. Friedrich von (1849–1930), Prussian sailor, born at Küstrin, entered the Prussian navy in 1865, was ennobled in 1900, and rose to be lord high admiral (1911). As secretary of state for the Imperial Navy (1897–1916), he piloted the German navy laws (1900, &c.) and raised a fleet to challenge British supremacy of the seas. An upholder of unrestricted submarine warfare, he commanded the German navy from August 1914 to March 1916 and wrote *Memoirs* (1919).

TIRSO DE MOLINA, pseud. of **Gabriel Téllez** (*c.* 1571–1648), Spanish playwright, born at Madrid, was prior of the monastery of Soria. Lacking his great contemporary Lope's lyrical gifts, he wrote *Comedias*, partly Interludes, and *Autos Sacramentales* (originally about 300), excelling in the portrayal of character, particularly of spirited women, and in his treatment of the Don Juan legend in his masterpiece *Burlador de Sevilla*. See Rios de Lampérez, *Enigma Biográfico* (1929).

TISCHENDORF, Lobegott Friedrich Konstantin von, *tish'en-dorf* (1815–74), German biblical scholar, born at Lengenfeld in Saxony, in 1839 became a lecturer, in 1845 a professor, at Leipzig. His search for MSS. of the New Testament resulted in the discovery of the 4th-century Sinaitic Codex in the monastery on Mount Sinai; he described his journeys in *Reise in den Orient* (1846; trans. 1847) and *Aus dem Heiligen Lande* (1862). Among his works are the editions of the Sinaitic (1862; in facsimile, 1863) and many other MSS., the *Editio VIII* of the New Testament (1864–72), an edition of the Septuagint, and the *Monumenta Sacra Inedita* (1846–71). *When were our Gospels Written?* was translated in 1866.

TISELIUS, Arne Wilhelm Kaurin (1902–), Swedish chemist, born at Stockholm, became professor of Biochemistry at Uppsala (1938), investigated serum proteins by electrophoretic analysis, and in chromatography evolved new methods for the analysis of colourless substances. He won the Nobel prize in 1948, and was president of the Nobel Foundation (1960–64).

TISSANDIER, Gaston, *tee-sã-dyay* (1835–1899), French aeronaut, invented (1883) a navigable balloon.

TISSAPHERNES, *tis-a-fer'neez* (d. 395 B.C.), Persian satrap from 413, notorious for his duplicity in the conflicts between Athens and Sparta. Deprived of a province in favour of Cyrus, he denounced him to King Artaxerxes, for whom he fought and won the battle of Cunaxa (401 B.C.), after which he murdered the leaders of the Greeks, including Cyrus, leaving the ten thousand Greek mercenaries to find their way back. But he was himself defeated in the war with Sparta and executed for the murder of Cyrus.

TISSOT, James Joseph Jacques, *tee-sō* (1836–1902), French painter, was born in Nantes and settled in London. He travelled to Palestine in 1886 and as a result produced his best-known work, a series of the life of Christ in watercolour. Other examples of his work are paintings of life in Victorian times, now in the Tate gallery.

TISZA, *ti'so,* (1) **Kalman** (1830–1902), Hungarian statesman, father of (2), was premier and virtually dictator from 1875 to 1890.

(2) **Count Stephen** (1861–1918), son of (1), also Liberal leader, a chauvinistic Magyar, premier of Hungary 1903–05, 1913–17, supported Germany, and was assassinated on October 31, the first day of the Hungarian Revolution.

TITCHENER, Edward Bradford (1867–1927), English psychologist, born at Chichester, studied at Oxford and Leipzig before going to America to Cornell University. A follower of Wundt (q.v.), under whose influence he had come in Leipzig, he became the great exponent of experimental psychology in America, founding the ' experimental psychologists ' group. He wrote many scholarly works on this subject, including *Psychology of Feeling and Attention* (1908) and *Experimental Psychology of the Thought Processes* (1909).

TITE, Sir William (1798–1873), English architect, born in London, rebuilt the Royal Exchange (1844), was knighted in 1869 and was elected F.R.S. in 1835. He opposed the neo-Gothic revival.

TITIAN, *ti'shèn,* properly **Tiziano Vecelli** (d. 1576), one of the greatest of the Venetian painters, was born at Pieve di Cadore in the Friulian Alps. His year of birth is a matter of controversy, but *c.* 1490 is more probable than *c.* 1477 as indicated by Titian's own statements. He lived from the age of ten with an uncle in Venice and studied under Zuccato, a mosaicist, Gentile and Giovanni Bellini (q.v.) and assisted Giorgione (q.v.). Giovanni's influence is apparent in such early works as *Bishop Pesaro before St Peter* (*c.* 1506; Antwerp). Titian assisted Giorgione with the paintings for the Fondaco dei Tedeschi (1508) and completed many of the latter's works, e.g., *Noli me tangere* (c. 1510; National Gallery, London) and the *Sleeping Venus* (c. 1510; Dresden), which was to serve as a model for Titian's more naturalistic *Venus of Urbino* (1538; Uffizi, Florence). The first works definitely attributable to Titian alone are the three frescoes of scenes in the life of St Anthony at Padua (1511), but Giorgione's influence predominates in these, the pastoral setting of *The Three Ages of Man* (c. 1515; National Gallery Edinburgh) and the masterly fusion of romantic realism and classical idealism achieved in the *poesa, Sacred and Profane Love* (c. 1515; Borghese, Rome), a masterpiece of Renaissance art. After 1516 restrained postures and colouring give way to dynamic compositions in which bright colours are contrasted and the classical intellectual approach gives way to sensuous, full-blooded treatment. *Assumption of the Virgin* (1516-18), *Madonna of the Pesaro Family* (1519-26), both in the Frari, Venice, and *St Peter Martyr* (destroyed 1867) exemplify the beginnings of Titian's own revolutionary style. For the Duke of Ferrara he painted three great mythological subjects, *Feast of Venus* (c. 1515-18), *Bacchanal* (c. 1518; both in the Prado, Madrid) and the richly coloured. exuberant masterpiece *Bacchus and Ariadne* (1523; Nat. Gallery, London). In sharp contrast is the finely-modelled historical picture, *Presentation of the Virgin* (1534-38; Accademia, Venice). In 1530 he met the Emperor Charles V, of whom he painted many portraits, including the striking equestrian *Charles V at the Battle of Mühlberg* (1548; Prado, Madrid), also the portraits of many notables assembled for the Augsburg peace conference, and was ennobled. To this period also belongs *Ecce Homo* (1543; Vienna), portraits of the Farnese family including *Pope Paul III and his nephews* (1545-46; Naples) painted on Titian's first visit to Rome. The impact of the art collections there is reflected in a new sculptural treatment of the *Danae* (1545; Naples, also 1554; Prado, Madrid). For King Philip of Spain, he executed a remarkable series of *poesies* on mythological scenes, to which belong *Diana and Actaeon* (1559) and *Diana and Callistro* (1559; both National Gallery, Edinburgh) and *Perseus and Andromeda* (c. 1556; Wallace, London). To the poignant religious and mythological subjects of his last years belong *The Fall of Man* (c. 1570), *The Entombment* (1565; both Prado, Madrid), *Christ Crowned with Thorns* (c. 1570; Munich), *Madonna Suckling the Child* (1570-1576; Nat. Gallery, London), *Lucrezia and Tarquinius* (c. 1570; Fitzwilliam, Cambridge) and the unfinished *Pietà* (1573-76; Accademia, Venice). Titian was fortunate in his patrons, despite his negligence and delays and a polished courtier's love of pensions, privileges and sinecures. He died August 27 during a plague epidemic, but not of the plague, and was ceremoniously buried in the church of S. Maria dei Frari, Venice. Colour rather than imaginative conception is the touchstone of his art, which greatly influenced Tintoretto, Rubens, Velasquez, Poussin, Van

Dyck and Watteau. See books by G. Gronau (1904), Sir C. Phillips (1906), O. Fischel (1911), especially H. Tietze (1937 and 1950), E. K. Waterhouse, *Titian's Diana and Actaeon* (1952), and F. Fosca (1955).

TITIENS, or **Tietjens**, Teresa (1831-77), Hungarian soprano, born at Hamburg, achieved an international reputation in operatic rôles. During a performance of Weber's *Oberon* in Dublin in 1868, she replied to the tumultuous applause which greeted the *Ocean* song with *The Last Rose of Summer*, before the opera was resumed.

TITO, Marshal, the name adopted by **Josip Broz** (1892-), Yugoslav leader, born near Klanjec. In World War I he served with the Austro-Hungarian Army, and, taken prisoner by the Russians, he adopted Communism and took part in the 1917 Revolution. In 1928 he was imprisoned in Yugoslavia for conspiring against the régime. In mid-1941 he organized partisan forces to harry the Axis conquerors of his country and his efforts were sufficiently effective to pin down about thirty enemy divisions, and to have the price of 100,000 gold marks set on his head. With exceptional guile he contrived to discredit utterly the rival partisan leader Mihailovich in Anglo-American eyes and win support, in arms and material, solely for himself. Following the Axis defeat, and with a ' popular ' franchise constituted to elect the future government, Tito's list of candidates was the only one published, although a small dummy opposition was erected by way of a democratic façade. Established in 1945 as Yugoslavia's first Communist prime minister, in 1953 Tito consolidated his position of supreme power by assuming the office of president. His breach with the Cominform in 1948, however, served notice on the Kremlin of his intention to emulate Kipling's cat and ' walk by himself '. Since then he has successfully ' played the middle against both ends ', alternating his profitable coquetting with those Western powers that can bolster up his shaky economy, with conciliatory gestures to Moscow. Yugoslavia's strategic geographical position, plus Tito's possession of a standing army of 300,000, with ample reserves, encourages the Marshal to exploit his canny sense of opportunism, reinforced by a resolute spirit of independence. See Maclean, *Eastern Approaches* (1949), Clissold, *Whirlwind* (1949), Halperin, *The Triumphant Heretic* (1958), Djilas, *Land without Justice* (1958), and study by Neal (1958).

TITUS, a companion of the apostle Paul, was a Greek, and remained uncircumcised. Ecclesiastical tradition makes Titus ' bishop ' of Crete.

TITUS, Flavius Sabinus Vespasianus (A.D. 39-81), eleventh of the twelve Caesars, was eldest son of Vespasian. He early served with credit in Germany and Britain, and in Judaea under his father. On Vespasian's elevation to the throne Titus brought the Jewish war to a close by the capture of Jerusalem (70). For a time he gave himself up to pleasure, conducting a liaison with Berenice, sister of Herod Agrippa. But when he assumed undivided power (79) his character changed. He put a stop to prosecutions for *laesa majestas*, and decreed heavy punishments against informers. He completed the Colosseum, built the baths which bear his name, and lavished his beneficence upon the sufferers from the eruption of Vesuvius (79), the three days' fire at Rome, and the pestilence. He was now the idol of his subjects, but he died suddenly, not without suspicion of his having been poisoned by his brother Domitian.

TIZARD, Sir Henry Thomas (1885–1959), English scientific administrator, educated at Westminster school and Magdalen College, Oxford, of which he was elected president in 1942, the first scientist to hold such an office in an Oxford College. He served in the R.A.F. during World War I and was assistant comptroller of aeronautical research (1918–1919). He was secretary to the D.S.I.R. (1927–29), chairman of the Aeronautical Research Committee (1933–43), from 1947 chairman of the Defence Research Policy Committee and president of the British Association in 1948. He was elected F.R.S. in 1926 and knighted in 1937.

TOCQUEVILLE, Alexis Charles Henri Clérel de, *tok-veel* (1805–59), French historian, born at Verneuil of an aristocratic Norman family, was called to the bar in 1825 and became assistant-magistrate at Versailles. Sent in 1831 to the United States to report on the prison system, he returned to publish a penetrating political study, *De la démocratie en Amerique* (1835), which gave him a European reputation and in which he came to certain general conclusions, for example, that greater equality requires greater centralization and therefore diminishes liberty. Before publication, then still relatively unknown, he paid, in 1833, his first visit to England, married a Miss Mottley and kept an extensive diary of his *Journeys to England and Ireland* (ed. J. P. Mayer and trans. 1958), in which his abiding impression, confirmed by a later visit in 1857, of the English was of underlying national solidarity, despite political dissensions. In 1839 he was returned to the Chamber of Deputies by the Norman farmers. After 1848 he was the most formidable opponent of the Socialists and extreme Republicans, and as strenuously opposed Louis Napoleon; but he became in 1849 vice-president of the Assembly, and from June to October was minister of foreign affairs. After the *coup d'état* he retired to his Norman estate, Tocqueville, and agricultural pursuits, and there wrote the first volume of *L'Ancien Régime et la Révolution* (1856), in which he argued with masterful objectivity that the Revolution did not constitute a break with, but merely accelerated a trend of, the past, namely centralization of government. See studies by Marcel (1910), Mayer (1939), and introduction to *Democracy in America* by Commager (1947).

TODD, (1) Alexander Robertus, 1st Baron of Trumpington, (1907–), Scottish chemist, born in Glasgow, professor at Manchester (1938) and Cambridge (1944), fellow and master since 1963 of Christ's College, Cambridge, and first chancellor of the new University of Strathclyde. He was awarded the Nobel prize in 1957 for his researches on

vitamins B₁ and E, was elected F.R.S. in 1942, knighted in 1954 and made a life peer in 1962.

(2) **Mike** (1909–58), American showman, born Avrom Hirsch Goldbogen, the son of a poor rabbi in Minneapolis, started life as a fairground attendant at nine, but was already making his first fortune at fourteen in sales promotion. In 1927 he went to Hollywood as a soundproofing expert, staged a real 'Flame Dance' spectacle at the Chicago World Fair in 1933, followed through the years by plays, musical comedies and films, including a jazz version of Gilbert and Sullivan, *The Hot Mikado* (1939), and an up-to-date *Hamlet* (1945). He perfected with Lowell Thomas the three-dimensional film and sponsored 'TODD-AO' wide-screen process, by which his greatest film, Jules Verne's *Around the World in Eighty Days*, which won him the Academy Award (1956), was made and presented. He married his third wife, the film actress Elizabeth Taylor, in 1957 and was killed in an aircrash over New Mexico. See Life by A. Cohn (1959).

TODHUNTER, Isaac (1820–84), English mathematician, born at Rye, studied at University College, London, and St John's, Cambridge, where in 1848 he graduated senior wrangler and Smith's prizeman. Elected fellow of St John's, he became its mathematical lecturer, and wrote textbooks. See Memoir by Mayer (1884).

TODI, Jacopone da (*c.* 1230–1306), Italian religious poet, born at Todi in the duchy of Spoleto, practised as an advocate, was converted in 1268 and became a Franciscan in 1278, and was imprisoned (1298–1303) for satirizing Boniface VIII. To him is ascribed the authorship of the *Stabat Mater*, and other Latin hymns; and he wrote *laude*, which became important in the development of Italian drama. See works by D'Acona (1884 ed.) and Underhill (1928).

TODLEBEN, or Totleben, Eduard Ivanovitch, *tōt-lay'ben* (1818–84), Russian soldier and military engineer, was born of German descent at Mitau in Courland. He served in the Caucasus, and in the Danubian Principalities in 1853. Till he was severely wounded (June 1855) he conducted with skill and energy the defence of Sevastopol; thereafter he completed the fortification of Nikolaieff and Cronstadt. During the Turkish war of 1877–78 he was called to besiege Plevna, which he took after a brilliant defence. See Life by Brialmont (1884).

TODT, Fritz, *tōt* (1891–1942), German engineer, born at Pforzheim, as Hitler's inspector of German roads (1933) was responsible for the construction of the *Reichsautobahnen*. The 'Todt Organization' was also responsible for the construction of the Siegfried Line (1937). Nazi minister for armaments (1940), fuel and power (1941), he was killed in an aircraft.

TOGO, Count Heihachiro (1847–1934), Japanese admiral, was born at Kagoshima and trained at Greenwich. He served against China (1894) and was commander-in-chief during the Russian war (1904–05). He bombarded Port Arthur, and defeated the Russian fleet at Tsushima on May 29, 1905.

He was awarded the English O.M. (1906) and created count (1907).

TOJO, Hideki, *tō-jō* (1885–1948), Japanese soldier, born in Tokyo, attended military college and in 1919 was appointed military attaché in Germany. He served with the Kwantung army in Manchuria as chief of the secret police and chief of staff from 1937 to 1940. He became minister of war (1940–41) and from 1941 he was premier and dictator of Japan, resigning in 1944. Arrested, he attempted and failed to commit suicide. He was sentenced to death in 1948.

TOLAND, John (1670–1722), Irish deistical writer, born of Catholic parents near Redcastle, Londonderry, entered Glasgow University in 1687, took his M.A. at Edinburgh in 1690, and studied theology at Leyden and Oxford. In *Christianity not Mysterious* (1696) he adopted a rationalistic attitude, and his work was burnt by the hangman in Ireland. In *Amyntor* (1699) and other works he debated the comparative evidence for the canonical and apocryphal scriptures. He took refuge in England and his Hanoverian pamphlet *Anglia Libera* secured him the favour of the Princess Sophia when he accompanied the ambassador to Hanover. His later life as literary adventurer is set forth in D'Israeli's *Calamities of Authors*. He also wrote a Life of Milton (1698). See Life by Des Maizeaux prefixed to his miscellaneous works (1747).

TOLKIEN, John Ronald (1892–1973), English philologist and author, born in Bloemfontein, educated at King Edward VII School, Birmingham, and Oxford, where he became professor of Anglo-Saxon (1925–45) and of English Language and Literature (1945–59). His scholarly publications include an edition of Sir Gawain and the Green Knight (1925), and studies on Chaucer (1934) and Beowulf (1936). His interest in language and saga and his fascination for the land of Faerie prompted him to write tales of a world of his own invention peopled by strange beings with their own carefully constructed language and mythology. These include *The Hobbit* (1937), a fascinating tale of the perilous journey of Bilbo Baggins and the dwarfs to recover treasure from Smaug, the dragon, and the more complex sequel, *The Lord of the Rings* (3 vols., 1954–55) in which Bilbo's nephew, Frodo, sets out to destroy a powerful but dangerous ring in Mordor, the land of darkness and evil. Later works include *The Adventures of Tom Bombadil* (1962) and *Smith of Wootton Major* (1967).

TOLLENS, (1) **Bernhard Christian Gottfried** (1841–1918), German chemist, with Fittig, synthesized toluene in 1864.

(2) **Hendrik** (1780–1856), Dutch poet, born at Rotterdam, was the author of the Dutch national hymn, *Wien Neerlandsch Bloed*. He also wrote comedies and a tragedy, romances and ballads.

TOLLER, Ernst (1893–1939), German-Jewish poet and playwright, born at Samotschin, was imprisoned (1919–24) in Germany as a revolutionary. He was elected to the Bavarian diet 1924, escaped from Nazi rule, and committed suicide in New York in 1939. His expressionist plays include *Masse*

Mensch (trans. 1923), *Die Maschinenstürmer* (trans. 1923), &c.; he also wrote poetry and the autobiographical *Eine Jugend in Deutschland* (1933).

TOLSTOY, or Tolstoi, name of a family of Russian nobles. **Count Peter** (1645–1729) was a trusted agent of Peter the Great. **Count Peter Alexandrovich** (1761–1844) was one of Suvorov's generals and under Nicholas I head of a government department. **Count Dmitri Andreievich** (1823–89) was a reactionary minister of Education, champion of Russian orthodoxy and a 'russifier' of the Poles. His *Romanism in Russia* was translated in 1874. The most noteworthy members of the family were:

(1) **Count Alexey Konstantinovich** (1817–1875), Russian dramatist, lyrical poet and novelist, born at St Petersburg, wrote a historical trilogy in verse, *The Death of Ivan the Terrible* (1867), *Tsar Fyodor Ioannovich* (1868) and *Tsar Boris* (1870), nonsense verse and the historical novel, *Prince Serebrenni* (trans. 1874).

(2) **Count Alexey Nikolayevich** (1882–1945), Russian writer, joined the White Army after the 1917 Revolution which he portrayed vividly in *The Road to Calvary* (trans. 1945), emigrated but returned to Russia in 1922. Other novels include *The Lame Squire*, &c.

(3) **Count Leo Nikolayevich** (1828–1910), Russian writer, aesthetic philosopher, moralist and mystic, one of the greatest of European novelists, was born on August 28 on the family estate of Yasnaya Polyana in Tula province. He was educated privately and at Kazan University, where he read law and oriental languages but did not graduate. He led a gay and dissolute life in town, played the gentleman farmer, and finally, in 1851 accompanied his elder brother Nicholay to the Caucasus, where he joined an artillery regiment and there began his literary career. *An Account of Yesterday* (1851) was followed by the autobiographical trilogy, *Childhood* (1852), *Boyhood* (1854) and *Youth* (1856). Commissioned at the outbreak of the Crimean War (1854), he commanded a battery during the defence of Sevastopol (1854–55). After the war, the horrors of which inspired *Tales of Army Life* and the *Sketches of Sevastopol*, he left the army, was lionized by the St Petersburg *literati* (1856), travelled abroad, visiting Britain, and in 1862 married Sophie Andreyevna Behrs, who bore him 13 children. He settled on his Volga estate and combined the duties of a progressive landlord, with the six years' literary toil which produced *War and Peace* (1863–69), by many considered the greatest novel ever written. This is at once a domestic tale, depicting the fortunes of two notable families, the Rostovs and the Bolkonskis, and a national epic of Russia's struggle, defeat and victory over Napoleon. The whole gamut of experience, finds expression somewhere in its pages. The characters grow up naturally with time, and the Bohemian exuberance of youth is superbly recorded. The proud, shy duty-conscious Prince Andrew and the direct, friendly, pleasure-loving but introspective, morally questing Pierre reflect the dualism in Tolstoy's own character. On his vivid description of

military life Tolstoy mounts his conception of history, which demotes 'great men' to mere creatures of circumstance and ascribes victory in battle to the confused, chance events which make up the unpredictable fortunes of war. In Pierre's association with freemasonry, Tolstoy expressed his criticism of the established autocratic order. His second great work, *Anna Karenina* (1874–76), carries with it the seeds of Tolstoy's personal crisis between the claims of the creative novelist and the moralizing, 'committed' propagator of his own ethical code, which culminated in *A Confession* (1879–82) and the dialectical pamphlets and stories such as *The Death of Ivan Ilyitch* (1886), *The Kreutzer Sonata* (1889), *What I Believe*, &c., in which Christianity is purged of its mysticism and transformed into a severe asceticism based on the doctrine of nonresistance to evil. *The Kingdom of God is within You* (1893), *Master and Man* (1894), the play *The Fruits of Enlightenment* (1891) and *Resurrection* (1899–1900) strayed so far from orthodoxy that the Holy Synod excommunicated him (1901) and he denounced the worship of Jesus as blasphemy. In *What is Art?* he argued that only simple works, such as the parables of the Bible, constitute great art. Everything sophisticated, stylized and detailed, such as his own great novels, he condemned as worthless. He made over his fortune to his wife and lived poorly as a peasant under her roof. Domestic quarrels made him leave home clandestinely one October night, accompanied only by a daughter and his personal physician. He caught a chill and died November 7 in a siding of Astapovo railway station, refusing to see his waiting wife to the last. His doctrines founded a sect and Yasnaya Polyana became a place of pilgrimage. Gandhi, who had corresponded with him, adopted the doctrine of nonresistance. But to posterity he is best known as the consummate master of the 'psychological' novel, a blend of Dickens and Stendhal. Boris Pasternak's father, **Leonid**, illustrated Tolstoy's works. See his *Diaries and Journals* (trans. 1917, 1927), his son's *Reminiscences* (trans. 1917), his wife's diary (trans. 1928) and autobiography (trans. 1933), his love letters (trans. 1923), the personal recollections of M. Gorky (trans. 1923) and T. Kuzminskaya (1948), Lives by his friend and translator, Aylmer Maude (1930), E. J. Simmons (1949), and biographical studies by Rolland (trans. 1911), Noyes (1919), Nazarov (1930), Abraham (1935), Leon (1944), Lavrin (rev. 1945), Redpath (1960) and Troyat (1968).

TOMBAUGH, Clyde William (1906–), American astronomer, was born at Streator, Ill., and educated at Kansas. He worked at the Lowell Observatory, Arizona State College and then at California as professor. He is the discoverer (1930) of Pluto, the existence of which had been predicted by Lowell, and of galactic star clusters. In 1946 he became astronomer at the Aberdeen Ballistics Laboratories in New Mexico, and was astronomer (1955–59), associate professor (1961–65) and professor from 1965, at N.M. State University.

TOMKINS, Thomas (1572–1656), English composer and organist, born in St David's where his father was organist, one of five brothers who were all accomplished musicians. Tomkins studied under Byrd, and in his early twenties, became organist of Worcester Cathedral, where most of his life was spent. In 1621 he became one of the organists of the Chapel Royal, and composed music for the coronation of Charles I five years later. His compositions include a vast amount of church music, madrigals, part-songs and instrumental works. See *Life* by Denis Stevens (1957).

TOMLINSON, Henry Major (1873–1958), English author, born in London, wrote *The Sea and the Jungle* (1912), *Tidemarks* (1924) and other travel books as well as novels such as *Gallions Reach* (1927) and a Life of Norman Douglas (1931).

TOMONAGA, Shinichiro (1906–), Japanese scientist, born and educated at Kyoto, professor of Physics at Tokyo University. He was awarded the Nobel prize for physics in 1965 together with Feynman and Schwinger for work in quantum electrodynamics.

TONE, Theobald Wolfe (1763–98), Irish nationalist, was born a coachmaker's son in Dublin, studied at Trinity College, was called to the bar in 1789, acted as secretary of the Catholic Committee, helped to organize the United Irishmen, and had to flee to America and to France (1795). He laboured incessantly to induce the Republican government to invade Ireland, and held a command in Hoche's expedition. In 1798 he again embarked in a small French squadron, which after a fierce fight was captured. Tone was taken to Dublin, tried, and condemned to be hanged as a traitor, but cut his throat in prison. See his *Autobiography* (1826) and Life by F. MacDermot (1939).

TONKS, Henry (1862–1937), English artist, born at Solihull. After becoming a fellow of the Royal College of Surgeons, he gave up medicine for art, joined the New English Art Club, and was associated with Sickert and Steer. From 1917 to 1930 he was Slade Professor of Fine Art in the University of London, where he taught many artists who were later to become famous.

TONSON, Jacob (1656–1736), London bookseller, published for Otway, Dryden and Pope, Addison and Steele. He was one of the founders of the Kit Cat club.

TONTI, Lorenzo (fl. *c.* 1653), a Paris banker, born at Naples, who proposed the tontine or latest-survivor system of life insurance.

TOOKE, John Horne (1736–1812), English politician, born June 25, in Westminster, the son of John Horne, a poulterer, studied at Eton and St John's, Cambridge. He entered the Middle Temple, but in 1760, to please his father, accepted the living of New Brentford. Travelling as a tutor (1763–65), he met John Wilkes at Paris, and conceived the strongest admiration for him, defending him, on his return, in *The Petition of an Englishman* (1765); they afterwards fell out, and in 1771 had a rasping epistolary controversy. Horne, who in 1770 had composed the famous (unspoken) speech of Lord Mayor Beckford to the king, encountered, not without success, the formidable 'Junius'. In 1773 he resigned his living, and resumed the study of law. About this time his spirited opposition to an enclosure bill procured him the favour (plus £8000) of the rich Mr Tooke of Purley in Surrey. To this were due both his assumption in 1782 of the surname Tooke and the subtitle of his *Epea Pteroenta, or the Diversions of Purley* (1786–1805), that witty medley of etymology, grammar, metaphysics and politics which he began writing in prison for promoting a subscription for the Americans 'barbarously murdered at Lexington in 1775'. In 1779 he was refused admission to the bar as a clergyman. He supported Pitt against Fox in *Two Pair of Portraits* (1790). In 1790 and 1797 he stood unsuccessfully for Westminster; in 1794 was tried for high treason, but acquitted; and in 1801 obtained a seat for Old Sarum, but was excluded by special act from the next Parliament. See Lives by A. Stephens (1813), M. C. Yarborough (1927).

TOOLE, John Lawrence (1832–1906), English comedian, born in London, went to the City of London School, and in 1853 gave up his desk in a wine merchant's to become an actor. He first played at Ipswich and in London at the St James's Theatre in 1854. In 1874–75 he played in the United States, and in 1890 in Australia. In 1879 he became lessee of the Folly Theatre, which he enlarged, changing the name to 'Toole's Theatre'. See his *Reminiscences*, chronicled by Joseph Hatton (1888).

TOPELIUS, Zachris (1818–98), Swedish poet and novelist, was born at Nykarleby, Finland, and studied at Helsinki, where he edited the *Helsingfors Tidningar* (1842–61). He was professor of Finnish History at Helsinki (1854–78), in the last three years being rector of the university. He wrote four collections of lyrics and several plays. His six novels, describing life in Sweden and Finland in the 17th and 18th centuries, were published as *The Surgeon's Stories* (1872–74).

TÖPFFER, Rodolphe (1799–1846), Swiss artist and novelist, born at Geneva, founded a boarding-school in 1825, which he conducted till his death, and in 1832 became professor of Rhetoric at Geneva Academy. He wrote the humorous *La Bibliothèque de mon oncle* (1832), *Nouvelles genevoises* (1841), *Rosa et Gertrude* (1846), &c. His own drawings in his *Voyages en zig-zag* (1843–53) are almost better than the text. See Lives by Relave (1886), Blondel Mirabaud (1887), Glöckner (1891) and P. Chaponnière (Lausanne 1930).

TOPINARD, Paul, *top-ee-nahr* (1830–1911), French anthropologist, born at Isle-Adam (Seine-et-Loire), took a degree in medicine in Paris and urged by his master Broca (q.v.) he devoted himself after 1870 to anthropology, becoming assistant director and conservator of the anthropological laboratory. His works include *L'Anthropologie* (1876), *Éléments d'anthropologie générale* (1885) and *L'Homme dans la nature* (1891).

TOPLADY, Augustus Montague (1740–78), English hymnwriter, born at Farnham, and educated at Westminster and Trinity College, Dublin, in 1768 became vicar of Broad Hembury, Devon, and in 1775 preacher in a chapel near Leicester Fields, London. A strenuous defender of Calvinism, he was a bitter controversialist. His *Church of England vindicated from Arminianism* (1769) is forgotten; but no hymn is better known than 'Rock of Ages'. In 1759 he published *Poems on Sacred Subjects*; his *Psalms and Hymns* (1776) was a collection with but few of his own. See Life by T. Wright (1912).

TOPOLSKI, Feliks (1907–), British painter, draughtsman and illustrator, born in Poland. He studied at Warsaw, and in Italy and Paris, and came to England in 1935. From 1940 to 1945 he was an official war artist, and he was naturalized in 1947. Lively and sensitive drawings by him, depicting everyday life, have appeared in many periodicals, and he has also designed for the theatre. His works are represented in the British Museum and the Tate Gallery, London, and his publications include *Britain in Peace and War* (1941), *88 Pictures* (1951) and *Topolski's Chronicle* (1953–).

TORQUEMADA, Tomas de, *tor-kay-mah'da* (1420–98), first inquisitor-general of Spain, born at Valladolid, entered the Dominican order and became prior at Segovia. He persuaded Ferdinand and Isabella to ask the pope to sanction the institution of the 'Holy Office' of the Inquisition, with himself as inquisitor-general from 1483. In this office he displayed pitiless cruelty.

TORRICELLI, Evangelista, *tor-ree-chel'lee* (1608–47), Italian physicist and mathematician, born probably at Faenza, went in 1627 to Rome, where he devoted himself to mathematical studies. His *Trattato del Moto* (1641) led to his being invited by Galileo to become his amanuensis; on Galileo's death he was appointed mathematician to the grand-duke and professor to the Florentine Academy. He discovered that, because of atmospheric pressure, water will not rise above 33 feet in a suction pump. To him we owe the fundamental principles of hydromechanics, and in a letter to Ricci (1644) the first description of a barometer or 'torricellian tube'. He greatly improved both telescopes and microscopes, and made several mathematical discoveries.

TORRIGIANO, Pietro, *tor-ree-jah'no* (c. 1472–1522), Florentine sculptor, was forced to leave his native city after he had broken the nose of his fellow-pupil Michelangelo in a quarrel. After working in Bologna, Siena, Rome and in the Netherlands, he came to England, where he introduced Italian Renaissance art. He executed the tombs of Margaret Beaufort in Westminster Abbey, of Henry VII and his queen and of Dr Young (now in the Record Office) in 1516. The unfinished sarcophagus for Henry VIII's tomb was later used for that of Nelson. He settled in Spain and died in the prisons of the Inquisition.

TORRINGTON, Viscount. See BYNG.

TORSTENSSON, Lennard, Count of Ortala (1603–51), Swedish general, born at Torstena, accompanied Gustavus Adolphus to Germany in 1630, and in 1641 was appointed to the command of the Swedish army in Germany. He invaded Silesia, and, when driven back by the imperialists, turned and defeated them at Breitenfeld (November 2, 1641). Next winter he swept the Danes out of Holstein, and then drove the Austrians back into Bohemia. In 1645 he advanced to the walls of Vienna; in 1646 he returned in ill-health to Sweden.

TORU DUTT (1856–77), Indian authoress, a precocious Christian Hindu girl, born at Calcutta, spent 1869–73 in England and France, published a critical essay on Leconte de Lisle, and translated portions of the *Vishnupurana* into English blank verse. In 1876 appeared her *Sheaf gleaned in French Fields*; in 1879 a romance, *Le Journal de Mdlle d'Arvers*. See Gosse's Memoir in her *Ancient Ballads of Hindustan* (1882) and Life by Das (1921).

TOSCANINI, Arturo, *tos-kah-nee'nee* (1867–1957), Italian conductor, born at Parma, the son of a tailor, won a scholarship at the Parma conservatory at the age of nine and studied the 'cello and composition. While on tour with an Italian opera company, presenting *Aïda* in Rio de Janeiro in 1886, the audience hooted at the conductor and in the crisis the orchestra prevailed upon Toscanini to take the rostrum. His impeccable musical memory made it a triumphant performance. In 1891 he opened the season at the Carlo Felice in Genoa and by 1898 he had reached La Scala, Milan, where he remained until 1908, returning (1920–29). He conducted at the Metropolitan Opera House, New York (1908–15), the New York Philharmonic (1926–36), at Bayreuth (1930–31) and Salzburg (1934–37) festivals, and brought into being the National Broadcasting Orchestra of America (1937–53). As late as 1952 he conducted at the Festival Hall, London. Toscanini was scornful of any need for 'interpreting' a work. His fanatical concern for musical values made him the enemy of exhibitionism, the unremitting slave of every detail of the musical score and possibly the most tyrannical, yet self-effacing, and certainly the greatest conductor of his time. See books by Chotzinoff (1956) and R. C. March (1956).

TOSTI, Sir Francesco Paolo (1846–1916), Italian composer, born at Ortona (Abruzzi), became a naturalized British subject, taught the British royal family and was knighted in 1908. He was the composer of many popular drawing-room songs, including *Good-bye* and *Mattinata*.

TOSTIG. See HAROLD II.

TOTLEBEN. See TODLEBEN.

TOTNES, Earl of. See CAREW (2).

TOTTEL, Richard (d. 1594), London printer, an original member of the Stationers' Company, founded 1557, published from his shop at the Star in Hand in Fleet Street a notable anthology of Elizabethan poetry (1557), including Surrey's and Wyatt's. See *Tottel's Miscellany*, ed. H. E. Rollins (1928–1930).

TOULOUSE-LAUTREC (-MONFA), Henri (Marie Raymond) de, *too-looz-lō-trek* (1864–1901), French painter and lithographer, was born November 24 into a wealthy aristocratic family at Albi. Physically frail, he was encouraged to engage in the traditional field sports, but at the age of fourteen broke both his legs, which then ceased to grow. From 1882 he studied under Bonnat and Cormon in Paris and in 1884 settled in Montmartre, which his paintings and posters were to make famous. Degas was the decisive influence upon him, but whereas Degas painted the world of ballet from a ballet-lover's theatrical point of view, Lautrec's studies of the cabaret stars, the prostitutes, the barmaids, the clowns and actors of Montmartre betrayed an unfailing if detached interest in the individuality of the human being behind the purely professional function. Hence his dislike of models, his concentration on the human form caught in a characteristic posture which his superb draughtsmanship facilitated to the neglect of chiaroscuro and background effects. Often his studies verge on caricature as in *Dolly the English Barmaid* (1899), which recalls Hogarth's *Shrimp Girl*, and more tellingly in the haunting study of a tired, lifeless cabaret star, *Jane Avril Leaving the Moulin Rouge* (c. 1892; Courtauld Institute, London), after a performance. His revolutionary poster designs influenced by Japanese woodcuts which flatten and simplify the subject matter also served to sharpen his gifts for caricature, as in the posters of the music-hall star Aristide Bruant (1892) and Yvette Guilbert (1894). No one has portrayed so effectively the clientèle of these establishments as Lautrec in *Monsieur Boileau at the Café* (1892; Cleveland), *The Bar* (1898; Zürich) and the *Moulin Rouge* paintings (1894; Chicago, Prague, &c.). In 1895 he visited London, in 1896 Spain and in 1897 Holland. His alcoholism brought on a complete breakdown, forcing him to go into a sanatorium; he recovered to resume his hectic life until his death on September 9, 1901, from a paralytic stroke brought on by venereal disease. His works also depict fashionable society, *At the Races* (1899), &c., and he executed remarkable portraits of his mother (1887), of Van Gogh in pastel (1887; Amsterdam) and of Oscar Wilde, a drawing (1899). His life has been the subject of many novels and a film, *Moulin Rouge*. Over 600 of his works are in the Musée Lautrec at Albi, including the above-mentioned works, if not otherwise stated. See works by M. Joyant (Paris 1926–27), G. Mack (1938), J. Lassaigne (1939), D. Cooper (1955), P. H. Wilenski (1955), L. and E. M. Hanson (1956), H. Landholt (N.Y. 1956) and H. Tietze (1958).

TOURGUENIEFF. See TURGENEV.

TOURNEFORT, Joseph Pitton de, *toorn-for* (1656–1708), French botanist, born in Aix, travelled in Greece, &c., and died professor in the Collège de France. His system of grouping plants maintained its ground till the time of Linnaeus.

TOURNEUR, Cyril, *toor-nœr* (c. 1575–1626), English dramatist, served in the Low Countries, and died in Ireland. In 1600 he published his *Transformed Metamorphosis* (discovered in 1872), a satirical poem, marred by pedantic affectations; in 1609 a *Funeral Poem* on Sir Francis Vere; in 1613 an *Elegy* on Prince Henry. His fame rests on two plays, *The Revenger's Tragedy* (assigned by some critics to Webster or Middleton), printed in

1607, and the poorer *The Atheist's Tragedy*, printed in 1611. *The Revenger's Tragedy*, a tangled web of lust and blood, shows tragic intensity, extreme bitterness of mood and fiery strength of phrase. See edition of his works by Allardyce Nicoll (1930), and T. S. Eliot, *Selected Essays* (1932).

TOURVILLE, Anne Hilarion de Cotentin, Comte de, *toor-veel* (1642–1701), French sailor, born at the Château Tourville, near Coutances. In the year 1690 he inflicted a disastrous defeat on the English and Dutch off Beachy Head, and cast anchor in Torbay. In 1692, Louis XIV having resolved to invade England on behalf of James II, Tourville sailed from Brest with forty-two ships of the line. The English and Dutch, eighty-two ships strong, under Admiral Russell, completely defeated him off Cape La Hogue (May 19). In 1693, he defeated an Anglo-Dutch fleet off Cape St Vincent, and a month later (June 27), he defeated Rooke in the Bay of Lagos, capturing or destroying a large part of the Smyrna fleet. Tourville, made a marshal of France, inflicted enormous damage on English shipping (1694). See E. de Broglie's *Tourville* (1908).

TOUSSAINT L'OUVERTURE, Pierre Dominique, *too-sī loo-ver-tür* (1746–1803), Negro revolutionary leader (the surname from his bravery in once making a *breach* in the ranks of the enemy), was born a slave in Haiti. In 1791, he joined the Negro insurgents and in 1797 was made by the French Convention commander-in-chief in the island. He drove out British and Spaniards, restored order and prosperity, and about 1800 began to aim at independence. Bonaparte proclaimed the re-establishment of slavery, but Toussaint declined to obey. He was eventually arrested and died in a prison in France. See his *Mémoires* (1853), James, *The Black Jacobins* (1938), and Leyburn, *The Haitian People* (1941).

TOUT, Thomas Frederick (1855–1929), English historian, born in London, was educated at St Olave's School, Southwark, and Balliol College, Oxford. Professor at Manchester (1890–1925), he wrote *Chapters in the Administrative History of Mediaeval England* (1920–33), in which he first used household and wardrobe accounts in the public record office, so becoming the leading authority on English mediaeval history. See his *Collected Papers* (1932 *et seq.*).

TOVEY, (1) Sir Donald Francis (1873–1940), English pianist, composer and writer on music, was born at Eton. He studied under Parratt at Windsor and Parry at Balliol; and he was influenced by Joachim and by a schoolmistress to whom Tovey owed his musical education until he was nineteen. He made his professional début as a pianist in 1900, but his reputation stood higher on the Continent than in England, where his musical erudition annoyed the critics. In 1914 he became professor of Music at Edinburgh, where he built up the Reid Symphony Orchestra. He was knighted in 1935. He composed an opera, *The Bride of Dionysus*, in 1907–08, a symphony, a piano concerto (1903), a 'cello concerto (for Casals; 1937), and chamber music. But his fame rests largely on his writings, remarkable for great musical perception and learning: *Companion to the Art of Fugue* (1931), *Essays on Musical Analysis* (1935–39), and his articles on music in the *Encyclopaedia Britannica*. He edited Beethoven's sonatas and edited and completed J. S. Bach's *Art of Fugue*. See Life by Mary Grierson (1952).

(2) **John Cronyn, 1st Baron Tovey** (1885–1971), British admiral, a destroyer captain in the First World War, as c.-in-c. of the Home Fleet (1941–43) was responsible for the operations leading to the sinking of the German battleship *Bismarck*. He became admiral of the fleet and G.C.B. in 1943, and was created baron in 1946.

TOWNE, Francis (*c.* 1739–1816), English painter, born probably in London, a landscapist little known until the 20th century, when his gift for painting simple but graphic watercolours was recognized. Works done in Italy, which he visited in 1780, are now in the British Museum.

TOWNES, Charles Hard (1915–), American physicist, professor of Physics at Massachusetts Institute of Technology (1961–67), then professor-at-large at California University. He was joint winner of the Nobel prize for physics with Basov and Prokhorov in 1964 for his work on the development of laser beams.

TOWNSEND, Sir John Sealy Edward (1868–1957), Irish physicist, born at Galway, became a demonstrator at the Cavendish Laboratory, Cambridge, under Sir J. J. Thomson (q.v.) before becoming professor of Physics at Oxford (1900). He was elected F.R.S. in 1903, contributed to the theory of ionization of gases by collision and calculated in 1897 the charge on a single gaseous ion.

TOWNSHEND, (1) Charles, 2nd Viscount Townshend (1674–1738), English statesman, born at Raynham Hall, Norfolk, was educated at Eton and King's College, Cambridge. In 1687, he succeeded his father, Sir Horatio, who, though a Presbyterian, had zealously supported the Restoration and been made baron (1661) and viscount (1682). Charles entered public life as a Tory, but soon, as a disciple of Lord Somers (q.v.), cooperated with the Whigs. He was one of the commissioners for the Union with Scotland (1707), was joint-plenipotentiary with Marlborough at The Hague, and negotiated the Barrier Treaty with the States-General. Dismissed in 1712 on the formation of the Harley ministry, Townshend obtained the confidence of the Elector of Hanover, who, on his succession as George I, made him secretary of state. With Stanhope, he formed a Whig ministry, which had Walpole, his brother-in-law, for chancellor of the Exchequer and which passed the Septennial Act (1716). He was lord-lieutenant of Ireland (1717) and became president of the Council and secretary for the Northern Department. His reputation unsullied by the South Sea scandal, he became secretary of state in 1721, but retired in 1730 to Raynham, to grow turnips and improve the rotation of crops.

(2) **Charles** (1725–67), English statesman, grandson of (1), entered the House of Commons in 1747. Bute gained him over from

Pitt by the offer of the post of secretary at war; but on Bute's resignation in 1763 he was appointed first lord of trade and the plantations. In the Chatham ministry of 1766 he became chancellor of the Exchequer and leader of the Lower House. Chatham relaxing his grip of affairs, Townshend carried those taxation measures that led to the separation of the American colonies. He was about to form a ministry when he died. A brilliant speaker, by his witty irrelevancies he was able to intoxicate the House of Commons, as in his famous ' champagne speech ' (1767). He was, according to Earl Russell, ' a man utterly without principle, whose brilliant talents only made more prominent his want of truth, honour and consistency '. See Life by Fitzgerald (1886).

(3) **Sir Charles Vere Ferrers** (1861–1924), British soldier, great-great-grandson of (4), whose *Military Life* (1901) he wrote, joined the Indian army and held Chitral Fort for 46 days (1895). As major-general in 1915, in conjunction with naval forces up the Tigris, he took Amara. Defeated at Ctesiphon, he fell back upon Kut, where he held out for a month before surrendering. He was M.P. from 1920. See his *My Campaign in Mesopotamia* (1920).

(4) **George, 4th Viscount and 1st Marquess** (1724–1807), English soldier, brother of (2), was educated at St John's College, Cambridge. He fought at Culloden, but retired owing to a difference with the Duke of Cumberland (q.v.). He was brigadier-general under Wolfe at Quebec, and, after Wolfe's death, assumed the command. As lord-lieutenant of Ireland (1767–72), he tried to break down the government by ' undertakers ', but his habits became dissipated and he was recalled. He was created marquess (1786). See *Military Life* by (3) (1901).

TOYNBEE, (1) **Arnold** (1852–83), English economic historian and social reformer, uncle of (2), born in London, lectured in Economic History at Balliol College, Oxford, and to numerous workers' adult education classes, and undertook social work in the East End of London with Samuel Barnett (q.v.). He is best known as the coiner of the phrase and author of *The Industrial Revolution in England* (1884). Toynbee Hall, a university settlement in Whitechapel, London, was founded in his memory in 1885. See Lives by F. C. Montague (1889) and Viscount Milner (1895). His brother, **Paget** (1855–1932), was a biographer and authority on the works of Dante.

(2) **Arnold Joseph** (1889–), English historian, nephew of (1), born in London, educated at Winchester and Balliol College, Oxford, of which he became a fellow, married in 1913 a daughter of Gilbert Murray (divorced 1946), served in the Foreign Office in both World Wars and attended the Paris peace conferences (1919 and 1946). He was Koraes professor of Modern Greek and Byzantine History at London (1919–24) and director and research professor of the Royal Institute of International Affairs, London (1925–55). Profound scholarship in the histories of world civilizations com-

bined with the wide sweep of a near metaphysical turn of mind produced the brilliant, if later unfashionable, historical writing and synthesis on the grand scale, the monumental, ten-volume *History of the World* (1934–54), echoes of which reverberated through his stimulating and controversial B.B.C. Reith Lectures, *The World and the West* (1952). His numerous works include *Greek Historical Thought* (1924), *War and Civilization* (1951), &c. He was made a C.H. in 1956. One of his sons, **(Theodore) Philip** (1916–), is a well-known novelist and journalist (with *The Observer* since 1950). His works include *The Savage Days* (1937), *Comparing Notes* (with his father, 1963) and *Two Brothers* (1964).

TRADESCANT, John (1608–62), English naturalist, born at Meopham, Kent, the son of Charles I's Dutch gardener, whom he succeeded, gave his collection of specimens from Virginia to Elias Ashmole (q.v.). See *The Tradescants* by M. Allen (1964).

TRAHERNE, Thomas, *tré-hærn' (c.* 1636–74), English poet, a Hereford shoemaker's son, studied at Brasenose College, Oxford, became rector of Credenhill and in 1667 chaplain to the lord keeper of the great seal, Sir Orlando Bridgeman. He wrote *Centuries* of religious meditations in prose, as well as poetry, full of the strikingly original imagery of the mystic, yet a mystic who as a ' Christian Epicurean ' was prepared to give *Thanksgiving for the Body.* See critical biography by G. I. Wade (1944), study by G. E. Willet and a complete collection of his works, ed. H. M. Margoliouth (1958).

TRAILL, Henry Duff (1842–1900), English journalist and man of letters, was born at Blackheath and educated at St John's College, Cambridge. He wrote *The New Lucian* (1884, 1899) and several biographies. He was editor of *The Observer* (1889–91) and of *Social England* (1893–97).

TRAJAN, Marcus Ulpius Trajanus, *tray'jén (c.* 53–117), Roman emperor, was born near Seville. Gaining distinction in the Parthian and German campaigns, he was made praetor and consul (91), was adopted (97) by Nerva as his colleague and successor, and became sole ruler in 98. In 101 Trajan set out on his campaign against the Dacians. The struggle was long and fierce; but the Romans at last gained a decisive superiority, and in a second campaign (105) completely subdued their opponents, whose country became the Roman province of Dacia. In 113 the emperor left Italy for his great expedition into the East, directed mainly against the Parthians. He made Armenia and Mesopotamia into Roman provinces, but met with some defeats, as at Ctesiphon which he captured (115). Meanwhile the Jews rose in Cyprus and Cyrene; other enemies took advantage of the emperor's absence; and Trajan, already in failing health, set sail for Italy, but died at Selinus in Cilicia, August 117. Though most of Trajan's reign was spent in the field, the internal administration was excellent. Informers were severely punished and peculating governors of provinces prosecuted. The empire was traversed in all directions by new military routes; canals, bridges, and harbours were constructed, new towns built, the Pontine Marshes partially drained, and the magnificent ' Forum Trajani ' erected. Trajan's mildness and moderation were proverbial, though he persecuted Christianity as subversive of the state. See works by Francke (2nd ed. 1840), Dierauer (1868), de la Berge (1877), and chaps. 8–12 of B. W. Henderson's *Five Roman Emperors* (1927).

TRAPASSI, Pietro. See METASTASIO.

TRAUBE, *trow'bĕ,* (1) **Ludwig** (1818–76), German pathologist, brother of (2), born at Ratibor, became professor at the Friedrich-Wilhelm Institute (1853) and at the university (1872), both at Berlin. He pioneered the study of experimental pathology in Germany.

(2) **Moritz** (1826–94), German chemist, brother of (1), born at Ratibor, at Breslau made artificial semipermeable membranes and so made possible the determination of osmotic pressures.

TRAVERS, (1) **Ben** (1886–), English dramatist and novelist, born at Hendon, educated at Charterhouse, served in the R.A.F. in both world wars and was awarded the Air Force Cross (1920). A master of light farce, he wrote to suit the highly individual comic talents of Ralph Lynn, Robertson Hare and Tom Walls in such pieces as *A Cuckoo in the Nest* (1925), *Rookery Nook* (1926), *Thark* (1927), *Plunder* (1928), &c., which played in the Aldwych Theatre, London, for many years.

(2) **Morris William** (1872–1961), English chemist, born at London and educated at Blundells, London, and Nancy, was an authority on glass technology. Professor at Bristol (1904–37), he was technical consultant to the Ministry of Supply (1940–45). He discovered, with Ramsay, the inert gases krypton, xenon and neon (1894–1908), and investigated the phenomena of low temperatures. He wrote *The Discovery of the Rare Gases* (1928) and a *Life of Sir William Ramsay* (1956).

TREDGOLD, Thomas (1788–1829), English engineer and cabinetmaker, born at Brandon (Durham), became a carpenter and studied building construction and science in London. His *Elementary Principles of Carpentry* (1820) was the first serious manual on the subject. He also wrote manuals on cast iron (1821), *The Steam Engine* (1827), &c.

TREE, Sir Herbert Beerbohm (1853–1917), English actor-manager, half-brother of Sir Max Beerbohm (q.v.), born in London. After a commercial education in Germany, he took to the stage and scored his first success as Spalding in *The Private Secretary.* In 1887 he took over the Haymarket theatre until in 1897, with the box-office success of *Trilby,* he built His Majesty's theatre, where he rivalled, by his mastery of stagecraft, the Shakespearean productions of Irving at the Lyceum. A great character actor, Svengali, Falstaff, Hamlet, Fagin, Shylock, Malvolio, Micawber were all grist to his mill. He scored a tremendous success when he first produced Shaw's *Pygmalion* in 1914. See his *Memoirs,* ed. Sir Max Beerbohm (1920), and Life by Hesketh Pearson (1956). His wife **Helen Maud** (1864–1937), whom he

married in 1883, excelled in such comic rôles as Mrs Quickly, Mrs Malaprop and Lady Teazle. She directed Wyndham's theatre from 1902 and made her last professional appearance in the film *The Private Life of Henry VIII* (1936).

TREGELLES, Samuel Prideaux, *-gel'is* (1813–1875), English biblical scholar, born of Quaker parentage at Falmouth, wrote a critical edition of the Greek New Testament (1857–72).

TREITSCHKE, Heinrich von, *trītsh'kĕ* (1834–1896), German historian, born at Dresden, studied at Bonn, Leipzig, Tübingen and Heidelberg, and became a professor at Freiburg-im-Breisgau (1863), Kiel (1866), Heidelberg (1867) and Berlin (1874). He succeeded Ranke in 1886 as Prussian historiographer. A member of the Reichstag 1871–1888, he died at Berlin. His chief work *History of Germany in the Nineteenth Century* (1879–94; trans. 1915–18), though written from the dogmatic Prussian viewpoint, is of great literary and historical value, and his method, scope and treatment of the subject have been compared to those of Macaulay in his *History of England.* An ardent believer in a powerful Germany with a powerful empire, and in the necessity of war to achieve and maintain this, his writings had a strong influence before World War I. See his *Politics* (trans. 1916); Adolf Hausrath *Treitschke: his Life and Work* (trans. 1914); and H. W. C. Davies on his *Political Thought* (1914).

TRELAWNY, (1) **Edward John** (1792–1881), English author and adventurer, born of a famous Cornish family, entered the navy at eleven but deserted, and lived a life of desperate enterprise in Eastern seas. In 1821 he made the acquaintance of Shelley at Pisa, and helped to burn the drowned poet's body. Next year he accompanied Byron to Greece, and remained there some time after Byron's death. He travelled in America, lived a while in Italy, eloped about 1841 with Lady Goring, and spent his last years in Monmouthshire or Sussex. His *Adventures of a Younger Son* (1830; new ed. 1890) was based on his own youth; his *Recollections of Shelley and Byron* (1858) was recast in 1878. See his *Letters* (1911), and Life by H. J. Massingham (1930).

(2) **Sir Jonathan, 3rd Baronet** (1650–1721), English divine, became bishop in turn of Bristol (1685), Exeter (1688) and Winchester (1707). Though intensely loyal to the crown, he was one of the seven bishops tried under James II, and is the hero of R. S. Hawker's ballad, ' And shall Trelawny die? '

TRENCH, (1) **Frederick Herbert** (1865–1923), Irish poet, dramatist and producer, born at Avoncore, County Cork, educated at Haileybury and Keble College, Oxford, wrote volumes of verse, *Deirdre Wed* (1900) and *New Poems* (1907), &c., was artistic director of the Haymarket theatre (1909–11). See French study by A. Chevalley (1925).

(2) **Richard Chenevix** (1807–86), Irish divine, philologist and poet, was born at Dublin. Educated at Harrow and Trinity College, Cambridge, he became curate in 1841 to Samuel Wilberforce. During 1835–1846 he published six volumes of poetry,

reissued in 1865. In 1845 he became rector of Itchenstoke; in 1847 professor of Theology in King's College, London; in 1856 Dean of Westminster; and from 1864 to 1884 he was Archbishop of Dublin. He was buried in Westminster Abbey. In philology he contrived to fascinate his readers with the ' fossil poetry and fossil history imbedded in language ', and the *Oxford English Dictionary* was begun at his suggestion. His principal works are *Notes on the Parables* (1841), *Notes on the Miracles* (1846), *The Study of Words* (1851), *Lessons in Proverbs* (1853), *New Testament Synonyms* (1854), *Life and Genius of Calderón* (1856), *Select Glossary of English Words* (1859), *Studies on the Gospels* (1867), &c. See his *Letters and Memorials* (1888).

TRENCHARD, Hugh Montague, 1st Viscount Trenchard (1873–1956), British service chief, marshal of the R.A.F., entered the Forces in 1893, serving on the N.W. Frontier, in South Africa, and with the West African Frontier Force. His early interest in aviation led to his appointment as assistant commandant, Central Flying School (1913–14), and to his posting as the first general officer commanding the R.F.C. in the field. Chief of the Air Staff between 1919 and 1929, his subsequent work as commissioner of the metropolitan police did nothing to obscure his fame as the ' Father of the R.A.F. ', though he carried out a number of far-reaching reforms, including the establishment of the Police College at Hendon. He was raised to the peerage in 1930 and awarded the O.M. in 1951.

TRENCK, (1) **Franz, Baron, or Freiherr von der** (1711–49), Austrian adventurer, was born at Reggio in Calabria, where his father was an Austrian general. At sixteen he entered the army, but soon had to leave it, as likewise the service of Russia. In the Austrian War of Succession he raised (1741) at his own cost a body of Pandours, who were even more distinguished for cruelty than for daring. On September 7, 1742, he attacked and destroyed Cham, in the Palatinate, and in 1745 he offered to capture Frederick the Great, and did secure the king's tent and much booty. He was suspected, however, of treachery, and imprisoned, escaped, but was recaptured, and condemned to lifelong imprisonment on the Spielberg at Brünn, where he poisoned himself. See his Autobiography (1748; new ed. 1807), and Life by J. O. Teichman (1927).

(2) **Friedrich, Baron** (1726–94), German adventurer, a cousin of (1), born at Königsberg, the son of a Prussian major-general, in 1742 entered the army, and two years afterwards attempted an intrigue with the Princess Amalie. The discovery of a correspondence with his Austrian cousin led to his imprisonment at Glatz, whence in 1746 he escaped to take service with Russia and Austria. Having returned to Prussia on family business, he was imprisoned at Magdeburg by Frederick the Great (1754), and on his attempting to escape was put in irons. He was released in 1763, and settled at Aix-la-Chapelle as a wine merchant. Having ventured to Paris in 1791, he was guillotined by Robespierre as a political agent. See his autobiography (1787), abridged by Murray (1927).

TRENT. See BOOT.

TREVELYAN, *-vel'-*, (1) **Sir Charles Edward, 1st Bart.** (1807–86), English administrator, father of (4), educated at Charterhouse and Haileybury, became a writer in the Bengal civil service, assistant-secretary to the Treasury (1840–59), governor of Madras (1859–60) and Indian finance minister (1862–1865), when he carried out great social reforms and a public works programme. He had married Hannah Moore, Macaulay's sister, in 1834. He was created a baronet in 1874 and wrote on Indian education (1838), &c.

(2) **Sir Charles Philips, 3rd Bart.** (1870–1958), English politician, son of (4) and brother of (3) and (5), was educated at Harrow and Trinity College, Cambridge, entered Parliament in 1899 and in 1908 became Liberal parliamentary secretary to the Board of Education. He resigned in 1914, disapproving of war with Germany. From 1922 he sat as a Labour M.P. and became president of the Board of Education (1924, 1929–31), but resigned when his School Attendance Bill was rejected. He was lord lieutenant of Northumberland (1930–49).

(3) **George Macaulay** (1876–1962), English historian, son of (4), born at Stratford-on-Avon, was educated at Harrow and Trinity College, Cambridge, of which he was elected master (1940–51). He served in the First World War and was regius professor of Modern History at Cambridge (1927–40). He is probably best known for his *English Social History* (1944), in which his considerable literary gifts find full expression; it is a companion volume to his *History of England* (1926). Other works include studies of Garibaldi (1907, 1909, 1911), Lives of John Bright (1913) and his father, G. O. Trevelyan (1932), *British History in the Nineteenth Century* (1922), &c., and several volumes of lectures and essays, including an autobiography (1949). He was awarded the O.M. in 1930 and elected F.R.S. in 1950. See study by Plumb (1951).

(4) **Sir George Otto, 2nd Bart.** (1838–1928), English statesman, son of (1) and father of (2), (3) and (5), born at Rothley Temple, Leicestershire, and educated at Harrow and Trinity College, Cambridge. He entered parliament in 1865 as a Liberal and became a lord of the Admiralty (1868–70), parliamentary secretary to the same (1880–82), chief secretary for Ireland (1882–84) and a secretary for Scotland (1886, 1892–95). He wrote a number of historical works, among them a Life of his uncle, Macaulay (1876–1908), a Life of Fox (1880), and the *American Revolution* (1909), &c. He was awarded the O.M. in 1911. See Life by his son (3) (1932).

(5) **Robert Calverley** (1872–1951), English poet and playwright, son of (4), educated at Harrow and Trinity College, Cambridge, wrote volumes of verse, *Mallow and Asphodel* (1898), *The Bride of Dionysus* (1912), set to music by Tovey (q.v.), &c., translations from Leopardi and *Windfalls* (1944) a collection of essays.

TREVES, **Sir Frederick,** *treevz* (1853–1923)

English surgeon, born at Dorchester, was educated in London, became professor at the Royal College of Surgeons. He was a founder of the British Red Cross Society and made improvements in operations for appendicitis.

TREVIRANUS, -*rah'*-, (1) Gottfried Reinhold (1776–1837), German biologist and anatomist, brother of (2), born at Bremen, wrote an important work on biology (1802–22) and made histological and anatomical studies of Vertebrates.

(2) Ludolf Christian (1779–1864), German naturalist, brother of (1), was born at Bremen and was professor at Bremen, Rostock, Breslau and Bonn. He is known for his discovery of intercellular spaces.

TREVISA. See JOHN OF TREVISA.

TREVITHICK, Richard (1771–1833), English engineer and inventor, born at Illogan, Redruth, became a mining engineer at Penzance, and in 1796–1801 invented a steam carriage, which ran between Camborne and Tuckingmill at from four to nine miles an hour, and which in 1803 was run from Leather Lane to Paddington by Oxford Street. He was in Peru and Costa Rica 1816–27, where his engines were introduced into the silver mines. The development of the high-pressure engine was largely due to him. See *Life* by his son (1872), study by Dickinson and Titley (1934).

TREVOR, Sir John (*c.* 1637–1717), English politician, was in 1685 elected Speaker, and made master of the Rolls. Though a minion of Judge Jeffreys, he was again Speaker (1690–95). For accepting a bribe as first commissioner of the court of Chancery, he was expelled from parliament in 1695; he still, however, retained the mastership of the Rolls.

TRIBONIANUS (d. *c.* A.D. 544), Roman jurist, born, probably, in Pamphylia, held various offices under the Emperor Justinian, and is famous through his labours on Justinian's Code and the Pandects.

TRICOUPIS, Spyridon, *tri-koo'pees* (1788–1873), Greek statesman and writer, born at Missolonghi, was private secretary to Lord Guilford in the Ionian Isles, studied in Rome, Paris and London, and joined the patriots on the outbreak of the War of Independence (1821). He was thrice envoy-extraordinary to London, was minister of foreign affairs and of public instruction (1843), vice-president of the Senate (1844–49), and envoy-extraordinary to Paris (1850). His *Speeches* appeared in 1836; his *History of the Greek Revolution* in 1853–57. His son, Charilaos (1832–96), was foreign minister (1866) and premier repeatedly in 1875–95.

TRIDUANA, St (4th c.), is said to have come to Scotland with St Rule (q.v.). Legend relates that, troubled by the attentions of the local king and learning of his admiration for her eyes, she plucked them out and sent them to him. She retired to Restalrig, where there is a well once famous as a cure for eye diseases.

TRILLING, Lionel (1905–), American author and critic, was educated at Columbia University, where he was professor of English from 1948. He wrote literary studies on Matthew Arnold (1939), Forster (1948), *The Liberal Imagination* (1950), *The Opposing Sel* (1955) and *A Gathering of Fugitives* (1957).

TRIVET, or Trevet, Nicholas (fl. 1300), an English Dominican friar, who wrote *Annales Sex Regum Angliae*, covering the period 1136–1307.

TROCHU, Louis Jules, *tro-shü* (1815–96), French soldier, born at Palais (Morbihan), who, after a distinguished military career in the Crimea and elsewhere, entered the ministry of war. But the unpalatable truths contained in his *L'Armée française en 1867* set the court against him. In 1870 he received a command at Toulouse, on August 17 was made governor of Paris, and under the republic became chief of the national defence. Regarded as overcautious and timid, he probably saw only too well the hopelessness of his task. He resigned the governorship in January 1871, but remained president of the national defence until 1872. Works by him in his own defence are *Pour la vérité et pour la justice* (1873) and *La Politique et le siège de Paris* (1874).

TROLLOPE, (1) Anthony (1815–82), English novelist, was born in London. His *Auto-biography* tells the story of family misfortunes through the mismanagement of the father but relieved by the mother's industry as a novelist. His career can be divided into two periods—the year of his admission to the Post Office (1834), which entailed service in Ireland, to the publication of *The Warden*, the first of the Barsetshire series, in 1855; and thenceforward as the novelist and clubman who still retains his enthusiasm for his official work. His devotion to hunting is reflected in many of his novels. He married a Miss Heseltine in 1844 and was eminently happy in his family. His first two novels, *The Macdermots of Ballycloran* (1847) and *The Kellys and the O'Kellys* (1848), were not successful, though in character-drawing and episodes they foreshadow the great series to come. The simple story of Hiram's Hospital in *The Warden* gave Trollope the chance to introduce some of his great fictional characters —Mr Harding, who appears in all the Barchester series; Archdeacon Grantly, a study in ecclesiastical politics; and old Bishop Proudie who appears prominently in *Barchester Towers* with his redoubtable wife and finishes greatly in the superb duel with her in *The Last Chronicle*, though this is as much Mr Crawley's book as Mrs Proudie's or the bishop's. The six novels of the series—*The Warden, Barchester Towers, Framley Parsonage, Doctor Thorne, Last Chronicle of Barchester*—include also *The Small House at Allington* which, however, does not 'breathe Barchester air' but which introduces two characters who are to be very important in the political series which followed. *The Eustace Diamonds* and *Can You Forgive Her?* are usually included in this series, but more generally, it comprises *Phineas Finn, Phineas Redux, The Prime Minister* and *The Duke's Children*. In these fine novels Plantagenet Palliser, heir to the Duke of Omnium, and Lady Glencora emerge as Trollope's finest creations—so he thought himself—and figure much more prominently than in their first minor appearance in *The Small House.* These political novels occupy Trollope's middle period from *Phineas Finn* (1869) to *The Duke's Children* (1880), though we should perhaps date this era from his meeting with Thackeray, which resulted in the serial appearance of *Framley Parsonage* in *Cornhill* in 1864. Trollope employed the political novels to express his views on public questions, and he brilliantly evokes the atmosphere of Westminster and well describes the great political houses and clubs. But the hero of the first two, Phineas Finn, is poor stuff and the questions broached chiefly Church reform, are rather nebulous. It is in *The Prime Minister* and *The Duke's Children* that Palliser and Lady Glencora emerge as finished studies of rectitude in high places. Michael Sadleir has done something to correct the notion that the latest novels are of no account. *The Way We Live Now* (1875), *Dr Wortle's School* (1881), *Mr Scarborough's Family* (1883), his ' troubled ' novels, show new range and new interests, and *Ayala's Angel*, published a year before his death, returns to the charming manner of the Barsetshire series with a wealth of new characterization. Michael Sadleir's *Trollope: a Commentary* (1928, revised 1945) is the definitive work on Trollope. See also *Letters*, ed. Brook-Booth (1951), *Autobiography* (World's Classics, 1936), and studies by Escott (1913), Morgan (1946), Page (1950) and Brown (1950); also studies by two novelists, Hugh Walpole (1928) and Elizabeth Bowen (1946), and by B. A. Booth (1958).

(2) **Frances** (1780–1863), *née* **Milton,** English novelist, mother of (1) and (4), was born at Stapleton near Bristol. In 1809 she married Thomas Anthony Trollope (1774–1835), a barrister and fellow of New College, Oxford. In 1827 he fell into dire financial distress, which was not relieved by a removal to Cincinnati. During her three years in the States, Mrs Trollope amassed the material for her *Domestic Manners of the Americans* (1832), a book much resented in America. Left a widow in 1835, she eventually settled in Florence (1843), where she died. Of her novels, the most successful were *The Vicar of Wrexhill* (1837), *The Widow Barnaby* (1839), with its sequel, *The Widow Married* (1840). In all she wrote 115 volumes, now mostly forgotten.

(3) **Sir Henry** (1756–1839), English sailor, in 1796 with the *Glatton* defeated seven French vessels off Helvoetsluys, and next year brought information to Duncan that led to the victory of Camperdown. Long troubled by gout, he blew out his brains.

(4) **Thomas Adolphus** (1810–92), English author, son of (2) and brother of (1), was educated at Winchester and Oxford. In 1841 he settled at Florence, where his house was a meeting-place for many writers, English and foreign. In 1890 he returned to England, and died at Clifton. He wrote works on Italian subjects, including a *Life of Pius IX,* and many novels, such as *Marietta* and *The Garstangs.*

TROMP, (1) **Cornelis** (1629–91), Dutch sailor, the son of (2), shared the glory of de Ruyter's four days' fight (June 1 to 4, 1666) off the Downs, and won fame in the battles against the combined English and French fleets, June 7 and 14, 1673. On a visit to England in 1675 he was created baron by Charles II and was appointed lieutenant-governor of the United Provinces (1676).

(2) **Maarten Harpertszoon** (1597–1653), Dutch admiral, father of (1), born at Briel, went to sea as a child with his father, was captured by an English cruiser, and compelled to serve two years as a cabin boy. In 1624 he was in command of a frigate; lieutenant-admiral, he defeated a superior Spanish fleet off Gravelines in 1639. The same year he defeated another fleet off the Downs, and captured thirteen richly-laden galleons. On May 19, 1652, he was worsted by an English fleet under Blake. In November he again encountered Blake in the Strait of Dover, this time successfully, but whether Tromp actually sailed up the Channel with a broom at his masthead, to denote that he had swept the enemy from the seas, is uncertain. On February 18, 1653, Blake, with Monk and Deane, defeated Tromp off Portland, after an obstinate three days' contest. On June 2 and 3 another terrific battle between Tromp and Deane took place off the North Foreland, the Dutch being defeated. In the final battle with Monk, July 31, 1653, off the coast of Holland, the Dutch lost thirty men-of-war, but their greatest loss was Tromp, who died in the battle, shot through the heart. See *Tromp's Journal of 1639,* ed. C. R. Boxer (1930).

TROTSKY, Leon, alias of *Lev Davidovich Bronstein* (1879–1940), Russian Jewish revolutionary, born in Yanovka in the Ukraine and educated in Odessa. At the age of nineteen he was arrested as a member of a Marxist group and was sent to Siberia. He escaped in 1902, joined Lenin in London, and in the abortive 1905 revolution became president of the first Soviet in St Petersburg. Escaping from a further exile period in Siberia, he became a revolutionary journalist among Russian émigrés in the West. After the March 1917 revolution he returned to Russia, joined the Bolshevik party and with Lenin was mainly responsible for organizing the November Revolution. As commissar for foreign affairs he conducted negotiations with the Germans for the peace treaty of Brest-Litovsk. In the civil war Trotsky as commissar for war brought the Red Army of 5,000,000 men into being from a nucleus of 7000 men. On Lenin's death in 1924 Trotsky's influence began to decline. Within two years Stalin had ousted him from the Politbureau and in 1927 he was exiled to Central Asia. His repetition of Lenin's warnings against Stalin, and his condemnation of Stalin's autocratic ambitions, led to Trotsky's expulsion from Russia in 1929. He continued to agitate and intrigue as an exile in several countries. In 1937, having been sentenced to death in his absence by a Soviet court, he found asylum in Mexico City. There he was assassinated in 1940 by Ramon del Rio (alias Jacques Mornard). Ruthless, energetic, a superb orator and messianic visionary, Trotsky inspired as much confidence in Lenin as he awakened mistrust in the still wilier Stalin. In his later years he was the focus of those Communists, Russian and otherwise, who opposed the endless opportunism of Stalin. He was the revolutionary ' pur sang '—and a writer of power, wit and venom. His publications include *History of the Russian Revolution* (1932) *The Revolution Betrayed* (1937), *Stalin* (1948) and *Diary in Exile* (trans. 1959). See I. Deutscher, *The Prophet Armed* (1954) and *The Prophet Unarmed* (1959) and also *The Trotsky Papers*, vol. I, 1917–21, ed. J. M. Meijer (1964).

TROTZENDORF. See FRIEDLAND.

TROYON, Constant, *trwah-yŏ* (1810–65), French painter of landscapes and particularly of animals, born at Sèvres. Many of his paintings are in the Louvre and two are in the Wallace Collection, London.

TRÜBNER, Nicholas (1817–88), German publisher, born at Heidelberg, came to London in 1843, started up his business in 1852 and developed a business connection in the United States. An oriental scholar, he published a series of oriental texts as well as works for the Early English Text Society. The business was merged in 1889 to become Kegan Paul, Trench, Trübner & Co.

TRUMAN, Harry S. (1884–1972), 33rd president of the United States, was born at Lamar, Missouri, and was educated at Independence, Mo. After World War I, in which he served as an artillery captain on the Western Front, he returned to his farm and later went into partnership in a men's clothing store in Kansas City which failed. In 1922 he became judge for the Eastern District of Jackson County, Mo., and in 1926 presiding judge, a post he held till 1934 when Missouri elected him to the U.S. senate. He was re-elected in 1940 and was chairman of the special committee investigating defence which was said to have saved the U.S. more than 1,000,000,000 dollars. He was elected vice-president in 1944 and became president in April 1945 on the death of President Franklin D. Roosevelt. He was re-elected in November 1948 in a surprise victory over Thomas E. Dewey, which made nonsense of Dr Gallup's forecasts. As the ' everyday American ' who became president, Truman astonished his earlier critics. Few presidents have had to take so many historically important decisions—dropping the first atom bomb on Japan; pushing through congress a huge postwar loan to Britain; making a major change in U.S. policy towards Russia, signalized by the ' Truman doctrine '; sending U.S. troops on behalf of the U.N. to withstand the Communist invasion of South Korea; dismissing General Douglas Mac-Arthur from all his commands in 1951. For seven crucial years President Truman, who called himself ' the hired man of 150,000,000 people ', held the American people together while new alignments were taking shape. He did not stand for re-election in 1952 and retired to Independence. Later he became a strong critic of the Eisenhower Republican administration. See his autobiography (2 vols. 1955–56), *The Man of Independence* by J. Daniels, *Mr President*, by W. Hillman (1957) and study by C. Phillips (1966).

TRUMBULL, (1) James Hammond (1821–97), American philologist and historian, born at Stonington, Conn., was an authority on the languages of the North American Indians, on which he wrote several works.

(2) **John** (1750–1831), American lawyer and poet, wrote a satire on educational methods, *The Progress of Dullness* (1772–73), and a revolutionary satire, *McFingal* (1775–1782), in imitation of Butler's *Hudibras*. See Life by A. Cowie (1936).

(3) **John** (1756–1843), American historical painter, son of (4), born at Lebanon, Conn., served in the Revolutionary War as colonel and deputy adjutant-general. The war inspired him to paint many historical pieces. See his Autobiography (1841).

(4) **Jonathan** (1710–85), American patriot, father of (3), born at Lebanon, Conn., was judge, deputy-governor, and governor of Connecticut, and took a prominent part in the War of Independence. ' Brother Jonathan ', the personification of the United States, was once thought, but erroneously, to refer to him. See Life by J. Trumbull (1919).

TRYON, Sir George (1832–93), English sailor, born at Bulwick Park, Northants, became an admiral in 1884 and commander-in-chief in the Mediterranean in 1891. By his mistaken order during manœuvres, his ship, the iron-clad *Victoria* was rammed and sunk. He and most of the crew perished. See Life by C. C. P. Fitzgerald (1897), and R. Hough's *Admirals in Collision* (1959).

TSAI LUN, *tsī loon* (? A.D.50–?), Chinese alleged inventor (105) of paper made from tree bark and rags, was a eunuch at the Han court.

TSCHAIKOWSKY. See TCHAIKOVSKY.

TSCHUDI, *choo-dee*, (1) **Aegidius,** or **Gilg** (1505–72), Swiss historian, was born at Glarus and was active on the Catholic side during the Reformation in the Swiss canton of Glarus. His *Schweizerchronik* (1734–36) was long the standard Swiss history.

(2) **Johann Jacob von** (1818–89), Swiss naturalist, born at Glarus, investigated the natural history and ethnography of South America. He was ambassador to Brazil (1860) and Austria (1866–83). He wrote on the batrachians, *Fauna Peruana* (1844–46), the Quichua language, Peruvian antiquities, &c.

TSO CH'IU MING (*c.* 6th cent. B.C.), Chinese author, mentioned by Confucius in his *Analects*, wrote the *Tso Chuan*, a commentary on the *Ch'un Ch'iu*, one of the five classics. Modern scholars also ascribe to him the *Kuo Yü* and these two works comprise the most important historical sources of the period. The simplicity of his style served as a model to later writers.

TSWETT or **Tsvett, Mikhail Semenovich** (1872–1919), Russian botanist, devised a percolation method of separating plant pigments in 1906, thus making the first chromatographic analysis.

TUCKER, (1) Charlotte Marie (1821–93), English author, born at Barnet, under the pseudonym **ALOE** (a Lady of England) wrote many stories from 1854, and died at Amritsar, in India, where she was a missionary.

(2) **Josiah** (1712–99), English economist

and divine, became Dean of Gloucester (1758). He wrote on economics, as well as on politics and religion, and anticipated some of Adam Smith's arguments against monopolies.

TUDOR, Owen. See HENRY VII.

TU FU, *doo foo* (712–770), Chinese lyric poet of the T'ang dynasty, born in Shensi province.

TUKE, (1) **Henry Scott** (1858–1929), English painter, great-grandson of (2), studied at the Slade and painted chiefly nudes against sea backgrounds. His *August Blue* (1894; Tate) caused considerable controversy.

(2) **William** (1732–1822), English Quaker philanthropist, founded a home for the mentally sick, and contemporaneously with Pinel in France pioneered new methods of treatment and care of the insane.

TULASNE, Louis René, *tü-lahn* (1815–85), and his brother **Charles** (1816–84), French mycologists, made important researches in the structure and development of fungi. See their *Selecta Fungorum Carpologia* (3 vols. 1861–65; Eng. trans. with intro. 1931).

TULL, Jethro (1674–1741), English agriculturist, born at Basildon in Berkshire, and educated at St John's College, Oxford, invented a drill, introduced new farming methods in his native county, his chief innovation being the planting of seeds in rows. He wrote *The Horse-Hoing Husbandry* (1733; suppl. 1740).

TULLOCH, John (1823–86), Scottish theologian, born at Bridge of Earn, after holding charges in Forfarshire was in 1854 appointed principal and professor of Divinity in St Mary's College, St Andrews. He was a founder of the Scottish liberal church party (1878) and wrote many religious and philosophical works and an address to young men, *Beginning Life* (1862). See Memoir by Mrs Oliphant (1888).

TULLY. See CICERO.

TULSI DAS, *tool-see dahs* (1532–1623), Indian poet, born a Brahman, possibly at Rajpur in Sarwariya, dedicated himself, at the instigation of his wife, to Rama. Inspired to write as well as preach, his great *Rāmāyan, Rām-Charit-Mānas* (The Lake of Rama's Deeds), composed in the language of ordinary people, is one of the masterpieces of Hindu poetry. Venerated still, it is the Bible of the Hindus of northern India. He wrote several lesser works to the glory of Rama before retiring to Benares, where he died aged 91.

TUNSTALL, Cuthbert (1474–1559), English divine, born at Hackforth, Yorkshire, brother of Sir Brian Tunstall who fell at Flodden, became rector of Stanhope, archdeacon of Chester, rector of Harrow-on-the-Hill, master of the Rolls, dean of Salisbury (1519), bishop of London (1522) and of Durham (1530). In 1516–30 he went repeatedly on embassies to the emperor (making friends with Erasmus) and to France. He accepted the royal supremacy, but took alarm at the sweeping reforms under Edward VI, and was in 1552 deprived. The accession of Mary restored him. Under his mild rule not a single victim died for heresy throughout the diocese. On Elizabeth's accession he refused to take the oath of supremacy and

was again deprived. See memoir by G. H. Ross-Lewin (1909).

TUPPER, Martin Farquhar (1810–89), English poet and inventor, born at Marylebone, studied at Charterhouse and at Christ Church, Oxford. He was called to the bar (1835), but soon turned to writing. Of his works, forty in number, only *Proverbial Philosophy* (1838–67), brought him and his publisher considerable profit. His inventions, safety horseshoes, steam vessels with the paddles inside, &c., were less successful. See *My Life as Author* (1886) and Life by D. Hudson (1949).

TURA, Cosimo, *too'ra* (*c.* 1430–95), Italian artist, was born at Ferrara. The leader, with Cossa (q.v.), of the Ferrarese school, he studied under Squarcione at Padua, and his metallic, tortured forms and unusual colours give a strange power to his pictures, e.g., the *Pietà* in the Louvre and the *S. Jerome* in the National Gallery, London. See study by Eberhard Ruhmer (1958) and B. Nicolson, *The Painters of Ferrara* (1950).

TURBERVILE, George (*c.* 1540–*c.* 1610), English poet, and secretary to Sir Thomas Randolph, born at Whitchurch, Dorset, was educated at Winchester and New College, Oxford. He wrote epigrams, songs, sonnets, *The Booke of Falconrie* (1575), *The Noble Art of Venerie* (1576), and translated Ovid (ed. Boas, 1928), the Italian poets and others. He was a pioneer in the use of blank verse.

TURENNE, Henri de la Tour d'Auvergne, Vicomte de (1611–75), French soldier, the second son of the Duke of Bouillon and Elizabeth of Nassau, William the Silent's daughter, was born at Sedan, September 11. Brought up in the Reformed faith, he learned the art of war under his uncle, Prince Maurice, and in 1630 received a commission from Richelieu. During the alliance of France with the Protestants in the Thirty Years' War he fought with distinction, and in 1641 was entrusted with the supreme command. For the conquest of Roussillon from the Spaniards in 1642 he was in 1644 made marshal of France, and received the chief command on the Rhine. For a time he was superseded by Condé; and his restoration to supreme command was followed by his rout by the Imperialists at Marienthal (May 5, 1645). But on August 3 this disgrace was avenged by Condé at Nördlingen; and Turenne concluded France's share in the war by the conquest of Trèves electorate and of Bavaria (with the Swedes, 1646–47), and by a successful campaign in Flanders. In the civil wars of the Fronde, Turenne joined the *frondeurs*, and after being defeated at Rethel (1650) he withdrew to Flanders. On Mazarin's return Turenne joined his party, while Condé deserted to the *frondeurs*. Turenne twice triumphed over his former chief (1652), and forced him to retire from France; afterwards he subdued the disaffected cities, conquered much of the Spanish Netherlands, and defeated Condé at the Dunes (1658). In 1660 he was created marshal-general of France, and in 1668 turned Catholic. His next campaign in Holland was triumphant (1672), and in 1673 he held his ground against both the Imperialist Montecuculi and the Elector of Brandenburg. In 1674 he crossed the Rhine, mercilessly ravaged the Palatinate, crushed Brandenburg at Colmar, laid waste Alsace, and then advanced into Germany again to meet Montecuculi. Here he was killed reconnoitring at Sasbach, July 27, 1675. See Turenne's *Mémoires* (new ed. 1909–14; Lives by Ramsay (1733), Raguenet (1738), Duruy (5th ed. 1889), T. Longueville (London 1907), Weygand (trans. 1930); works by Neuber (1869), Roy (1884), Choppin (1875–1888), Legrand-Girarde (1910).

TURGENEV, Ivan Sergeevich, *toor-gyay' nyef* (1818–83), Russian novelist, born in the province of Orel. Child of landed gentry, he had an unsatisfactory childhood through the cruelty of his mother, whose great inherited wealth made her a petty tyrant in the home. After graduating from St Petersburg University he broke away by going to study philosophy in Berlin and there mingled with the radical thinkers of the day. With Alexander Herzen, in particular, he became firm friends. He returned to Russia in 1841 to enter the civil service, but in 1843 abandoned this to take up literature. His mother strongly disapproved and his infatuation for a singer, Pauline Garcia (Mme Viardot), also displeased her. She stopped his allowance and until her death in 1850, when he came into his inheritance, he had to support himself by his pen. He began with verse, *Parasha* (1843) showing strong Pushkin influence, but Turgenev early recognized prose as his medium and in 1847 produced *Khor and Khalynich*, his first sketch of peasant life, which appeared in *Sportsman's Sketches* (1852). This book, sympathetic studies of the peasantry, made his reputation, but earned governmental ill-favour, as it was interpreted as an attack on serfdom. A laudatory notice of Gogol, on his death in 1852, exacerbated the ill-feeling and resulted in a two years' banishment to his country estates. After his exile he spent much time in Europe, writing nostalgically of life in Russia. *Rudkin* appeared in 1856, *The Nest of Gentlefolk* in 1859, *On the Eve* in 1860, all faithful delineations of Russian liberalism, with its attendant weaknesses and limitations. In his greatest novel, *Fathers and Children* (1862), he portrayed the new generation with its reliance on the practical and materialistic, its faith in science and lack of respect for tradition and authority, in short the Nihilists. But the hero, Bazarov, pleased nobody in Russia. The revolutionaries thought the portrait a libel and the reactionaries thought it a glorification of iconoclasm. Turgenev's popularity slumped in Russia but rose abroad, particularly in England, where the book was recognized as a major contribution to literature. Successive novels, *Smoke* (1867) and *Virgin Soil* (1877), dealt respectively with the Slavophile-Western controversy (he dismisses as nebulous Russian intellectual life) and the underground revolutionary movement. Turgenev returned to the short story, producing powerful pieces like *A Lear of the Steppes*, and tales of the supernatural to which his increasing melancholy of spirit drew him. A passive resignation,

lyrically expressed, is his abiding quality. His style, graceful and controlled in emotion, lacks colour and pulsating life. But he is a balanced and objective commentator, sensitive, intelligent, and dedicated to the highest claims of art. His work lives for its universal qualities of understanding and devotion to aesthetic standards. See studies by E. Garnett (1917), A. Yarmolinsky (1926), J. A. T. Lloyd (1943), R. Freeborn (1960), and *Literary Reminiscences and Autobiographical Fragments*, trans. D. Magarshack (1959).

TURGOT, (1) (d. 1115), a Saxon monk of Durham, where he became an archdeacon, and helped to found the new cathedral, was Bishop of St Andrews 1109–15, and confessor to St Margaret (q.v.) of whose *Life* he was the probable author.

(2) **Anne Robert Jacques,** *tür-gō'* (1727–81), French economist and statesman, born of old Norman stock in Paris, May 10, was destined for the church, but adopted the legal profession, and joined the *Philosophes*. Appointed intendant of Limoges in 1761, he found the people poor, degraded, immoral and superstitious. He introduced a better administration of imposts, and abolished compulsory labour on roads and bridges, securing the support of the central government and of the rural priests. Soon after the accession of Louis XVI (1774) he was appointed comptroller-general of finance, and at once entered upon a comprehensive scheme of reform, reducing the expenditure and augmenting the public revenue without imposing new taxes. He sought to break down the immunity from taxation enjoyed by the privileged classes. He established free trade in grain throughout the interior of France, and removed the fiscal barriers which prevented free intercourse between the provinces. He abolished the exclusive privileges of trade corporations. But these efforts towards a more economical, efficient and equitable administration moved the privileged orders to combine for his overthrow. Louis XVI was too weak to resist such pressure, Turgot was dismissed after holding office for twenty months, and France drifted rapidly into the great catastrophe of 1789. The fallen minister occupied himself with literature and science till his death in Paris, March 8, 1781. His chief work, *Réflexions sur la formation et la distribution des richesses* (1766), was the best outcome of the Physiocratic school, and largely anticipated Adam Smith. See Lives by Condorcet (1786), L. Say (trans. 1888), Stephens (1895) and F. Alengry (1942), and studies by D. Dakin (1939) and F. Alengry (1942).

TURINA, Joaquín, *too-ree'na* (1882–1949), Spanish composer and pianist, born in Seville. His early promise was guided by the organist of Seville Cathedral, and at the age of fifteen he made his first appearance as a pianist. By the time he went to Madrid, in 1902, and came under the influence of de Falla and the Spanish Nationalist composers, he had a large number of compositions, including his first opera, to his credit. In 1905 he went to Paris to study at the Schola Cantorum, and became an important figure, both as a pianist and as a composer, in French musical life. Returning to Madrid in 1914, Turina became immensely active as composer, pianist and critic until the Spanish Civil War, in which he was an ardent supporter of General Franco, curtailed his activities. When peace was restored, Turina found himself regarded as the leader of Spanish music, but he is best known for those of his works, which include four operas, orchestral and chamber works as well as piano pieces, that like *Canto a Sevilla*, the orchestral *La Procesión del Rocio* and the string quartet *La Oración del Torero* combine strong local colour and idiom with traditional forms.

TURLE, James (1800–82), English composer of church music and organist of Westminster Abbey for over fifty years. His son, **Henry Frederick** (1835–83), was editor of *Notes and Queries* from 1878.

TURNEBUS (1512–65), the latinized surname of **Adrien Turnèbe**, French classical scholar, born at Rouen, who attained a European reputation as professor of Greek and Philosophy in the Collège Royal in Paris.

TURNER, (1) **Charles** (1773–1857), English engraver, mezzotinter after Turner, Reynolds, Raeburn, &c., was born at Woodstock, and died in London. He did the engravings for J. M. W. Turner's *Liber Studiorum*.

(2) **Charles Tennyson** (1808–79), English poet, born at Somersby, an elder brother of Alfred Tennyson (q.v.), graduated from Trinity, Cambridge, in 1832, and was for many years vicar of Grasby, Lincolnshire. He took the name Turner under the will of a relation. Besides collaborating with his brother in *Poems by Two Brothers* (1827), he wrote 341 sonnets (collected, with introductory essay by Spedding, 1880).

(3) **Joseph Mallord William** (1775–1851), English painter, one of the greatest masters of landscape art and of watercolour, was born April 23 at 26 Maiden Lane, Covent Garden, London, a barber's son. He was brought up by an uncle at Brentford and had some schooling, but throughout his life he remained almost illiterate. However, at fourteen he entered the Royal Academy and in the following year was already exhibiting. His early work was mostly adaptations of engravings. He also worked for architects, coloured prints for engravers, gave lessons and made sketches for sale in his father's shop. At eighteen he began wandering about England and Wales in search of material and made architectural drawings in the cathedral cities. For three years in the mid-nineties, he joined forces with Thomas Girtin (q.v.), the latter drawing the outlines and Turner washing in the colour. Between them they raised the art of watercolour to new heights of delicacy and charm. Turner remarked after his colleague's death, ' If Tom Girtin had lived, I should have starved '. From 1796 he gradually abandoned his niche as a topographical watercolourist and, strongly influenced by Wilson and Claude, took to oils in *Millbank Moonlight* (1797; Tate). In 1802 he visited the Louvre collections, swollen with Napoleon's loot, and was greatly attracted by Titian and Poussin, although he himself struck out for romanticism in *Calais Pier* (1803). His work led to a battle royal among the critics. More and more he became preoccupied with the delicate rendering of shifting gradations of light on such diverse forms as waves, shipwrecks, fantastic architecture and towering mountain ranges, conveying a generalized mood or impression of a scene, sometimes accentuated by a theatrically arbitrary choice of vivid colour. *Frosty Morning* (1813), *The Shipwreck* and *Crossing the Brook* (1815) embody Turner's trend. For one who defined painting as ' a rum thing ', he found it easier to defend himself against the critics by producing a collection of engravings, *Liber Studiorum* (1807–19), which remained uncompleted and failed because he underpaid the engravers. In 1819 he paid his first visit to Italy and at first his inspiration gave way to literary influences, although *Ulysses deriding Polyphemus* (1829) is generally regarded as one of his masterpieces. His illustrations, however, for T. D. Whitaker's *History of Richmondshire* (1823), the *Rivers of England* (1824), *The Provincial Antiquities of Scotland* (1827–38) and *The Rivers of France* (1834) contain his best achievements in watercolour. His second visit to Italy (1829) marked his last great artistic period, which included the famous pictures of Venice, *The Fighting Téméraire* (1839) and *Rain, Steam and Speed* (1844). The above-mentioned pictures, unless otherwise stated, are in the National Gallery, London. Turner led a secretive private life. He never married and when not staying with his patron Lord Egremont at Petworth, he lived in London taverns such as the ' Ship and Bladebone ' at Limehouse Reach. He died December 19, 1851, in a temporary lodging at Chelsea under the assumed name of Booth. His will was subjected to litigation, and a relation whom Turner had left out benefited at the expense of the hostelry for impoverished artists which Turner had envisaged. But 300 of his paintings and 20,000 watercolours and drawings were bequeathed to the nation. Turner's revolution in art foreshadowed Impressionism and found a timely champion in John Ruskin, whose *Modern Painters* (Vol. I 1843) helped to turn the critical tide in Turner's favour. Turner was elected R.A. at twenty-eight and professor of Perspective (1808). See biographical studies by Thornbury (1862, 1897), Monkhouse (1879), Swinburne (1902), Armstrong (1903), Finberg (1939, 1963) and Clare (1951).

(4) **Sir Tomkyns Hilgrove** (c. 1766–1843), English soldier, fought at Aboukir Bay and Alexandria, whence he brought to Britain from French custody the Rosetta stone (1801–02).

(5) **Walter James Redfern** (1889–1946), Australian poet, novelist and critic, was born in Melbourne and educated there and at Munich and Vienna. He published *The Dark Fire* (1918), *The Landscape of Cytherea* (1923) and other volumes of poetry. His other writings include studies of Beethoven, Mozart and Wagner, a play *The Man Who Ate the Popomack* (1922), and novels such as *The Aesthetes* (1927) and *The Duchess of Popocatepetl* (1939).

(6) **William** (c. 1520–68), English physician,

botanist and dean of Wells, born at Morpeth, fellow of Pembroke Hall, Cambridge, travelled extensively abroad and under the influence of Gesner (q.v.) introduced scientific botany into Britain, through his *New Herball* (1551). He named many plants, including *goatsbeard, hawkweed,* &c.

TURPIN, (1) or **Tilpinus** (d. *c.* 794), French ecclesiastic, became archbishop of Reims (*c.* 753), and was the supposititious author of the *Historia Karoli Magni et Rotholandi,* really written after 1131 by a French monk of Compostela, and continued about 1220.

(2) **Dick** (1705–39), English robber, born at Hempstead, Essex, was, successively or simultaneously, butcher's apprentice, cattle-lifter, smuggler, housebreaker, highwayman and horse-thief. He entered into partnership with Tom King and, going north, was hanged at York, April 10, 1739, for the murder of an Epping keeper. His ride to York belongs, if to any one, to 'Swift John Nevison', who in 1676 is said to have robbed a sailor at Gadshill at 4 a.m., and to have established an 'alibi' by reaching York at 7.45 p.m. See account of his trial by T. Kylls (1739).

TURRETIN, *tür-tī,* (1) **François** (1623–87) Swiss theologian, father of (2), was pastor to the Italian congregation at Geneva, and from 1653 professor of Theology. He took a principal part in originating the Helvetic Consensus, and wrote an *Institutio Theologiae Elencticae* (1679–85; Edinburgh 1847–48). See Life by E. de Budé (1880).

(2) **Jean Alphonse** (1671–1737), Swiss theologian, son of (1), became pastor of the Italian congregation, in 1697 professor of Church History, in 1705 of Theology. He laboured to promote a union of the Reformed and Lutheran Churches, and succeeded in abolishing the Helvetic Consensus in 1725. His famous *Discourse concerning the Fundamental Articles in Religion* was translated in 1720. His *Cogitationes et Dissertationes Theologicae* appeared in 1737. See Life by E. de Budé (1880).

TUSSAUD, Marie, *née* **Grosholtz,** *tü-sō* (1760–1850), Swiss modeller in wax, born in Berne, was early apprenticed to her uncle, Dr Curtius, in Paris and inherited his wax museums after his death. After the revolution, she had to attend the guillotine to take death masks from the severed heads. After a short imprisonment, she married a French soldier, Tussaud, but separated from him in 1800 and came over to England with her two children. She toured Britain with her life-size portrait waxworks, a gallery of heroes and rogues, and in 1835 set up a permanent exhibition in Baker Street, London, which was burnt down in 1925 and re-opened in Marylebone Road in 1928. The exhibition still contains Madame Tussaud's own handi-work, notably of Marie Antoinette, Napoleon, Sir Walter Scott, and Burke and Hare in the Chamber of Horrors, the last two having been joined by a succession of notable murderers, including Christie and his kitchen sink. See Life by L. Cottrell (1951).

TUSSER, Thomas (*c.* 1520–*c.* 1580), English writer on agriculture, in Fuller's phrase

'successively a musician, schoolmaster, serving-man, husbandman, grazier, poet, more skilful in all than thriving in any vocation', was born at Rivenhall, Essex. For a time a chorister at St Paul's, he was educated at Eton and Trinity Hall, Cambridge; and after a residence at court as musician to Lord Paget he married and settled as a farmer at Cattawade in Suffolk, where he compiled his famous work, *A Hundreth Good Pointes of Husbandrie* (1557). Tottel published (1573) an enlarged edition, *Five Hundreth Pointes of Good Husbandrie,* with a curious metrical autobiography. Editions are by Mavor (1812), Arber (1873), and the English Dialect Society (1879; reprod. 1931).

TUT-ANKH-AMEN, *toot-ahnk-ah'men,* Egyptian pharaoh of 18th dynasty, the son-in-law of Akhnaton (q.v.), became king at the age of twelve and died at eighteen in *c.* 1340 B.C. His magnificent tomb at Thebes was discovered in 1922 by Lord Carnarvon and Howard Carter. See archaeological studies by the latter and A. C. Mace (1923–33), T. E. Peet, C. L. Woolley, &c. (1923–39) and P. Fox (1951).

TWAIN, Mark, pseud. of **Samuel Langhorne Clemens** (1835–1910), American writer, born at Florida, Mo. A printer first, and afterwards a Mississippi pilot, he adopted his pen-name from a well-known call of the man sounding the river in shallow places ('mark twain' meaning 'by the mark two fathoms'). In 1861 he went to Nevada as secretary to his brother, who was in the service of the governor, and while there tried goldmining without success. He next edited for two years the Virginia City *Enterprise*; in 1864 he moved to San Francisco, and in 1867 he visited France, Italy and Palestine, gathering material for his *Innocents Abroad* (1869), which established his reputation as a humorist. He was afterwards editor of a newspaper at Buffalo, where he married the wealthy Olivia Langdon. Later he moved to Hartford, Conn., and joined a publishing firm which failed, but largely recouped his losses by lecturing and writing. *Roughing It* (1872) is a humorous account of his Nevada experiences, while *The Gilded Age* (1873), a novel which was later dramatized, takes the lid off the readjustment period after the Civil War. His two greatest masterpieces, *Tom Sawyer* (1876) and *Huckleberry Finn* (1884), drawn from his own boyhood experiences, are firmly established among the world's classics; other favourites are *A Tramp Abroad* (1880) and *A Connecticut Yankee in King Arthur's Court* (1889). Mark Twain pokes fun at entrenched institutions and traditions, but his 'debunking' is mostly without malice and his satire is free from bitterness, except in his later work, when fate had been unkind to him. In places his subject-matter is inclined to date, but his best work is not only classic humorous writing but a graphic picture of the 19th-century American scene. See his autobiography (ed. Neider, 1960), and Lives by Paine (1912) and Grant (1962).

TWEED, (1) **John** (1869–1933), Scottish sculptor, was born at Glasgow. Among his principal works are the Cecil Rhodes memorial at Bulawayo, the completion of Stevens's *Duke of Wellington* at St Paul's and *Clive* in Whitehall. See Life by his daughter Lendal Tweed and F. Watson (1936).

(2) **William Marcy** (1823–78), American criminal and politician, one of the most notorious ' bosses ' of the Tammany Society, born in New York, trained as a chairmaker. He became an alderman (1852–53), sat in congress (1853–55), and was repeatedly in the state senate. In 1870 he was made commissioner of public works for the city; and, as head of the ' Tweed Ring ', he controlled its finances. His gigantic frauds exposed in 1871, he was convicted, and, after escaping to Cuba and Spain (1875–76), died in New York jail while suits were pending against him for recovery of $6,000,000. See Life by Lynch (1927).

TWEEDMOUTH, Edward Marjoribanks, 2nd Baron (1849–1909), English Liberal politician, who as first lord of the Admiralty, speeded up British naval construction to keep pace with rival German increases, but was censured for an alleged disclosure of British naval estimates (1908) and resigned.

TWEEDSMUIR. See BUCHAN.

TWISS, Sir Travers (1809–97), English jurist, born in Westminster, became professor of International Law at King's College, London (1852–55), and then of Civil Law at Oxford. In 1867 he became Queen's advocate-general and was knighted. He resigned all his offices in 1872. In 1884 he drew up a constitution for the Congo Free State and in 1885 was legal adviser to the African Conference at Berlin. His *Law of Nations* (1861–63) was long a standard work.

TWORT, Frederick William (1877–1950), English bacteriologist, born at Camberley, Surrey, became professor of Bacteriology in the University of London. He studied Jöhne's disease and methods for the culture of acid-fast leprosy; and in 1915 he discovered the bacteriophage, a virus for attacking certain bacteria.

TWYSDEN, Sir Roger, 2nd Bart. (1597–1672), English antiquary, represented Kent in the Short Parliament but was imprisoned (1643–50) as a royalist, though, having refused to pay ship money, he was not *persona grata* with the court. He wrote the pioneering *Historia Anglicanae Scriptores Decem* (1652).

TYANA, Apollonius of. See APOLLONIUS.

TYARD, or Thiard, Pontus de, *tyahr* (1521–1605), French poet, born at Bissy-sur-Fleys (Saône-et-Loire), belonged to the group of Lyons poets who took Petrarch for their master. Influenced, however, by the work of Ronsard (q.v.), his verse bridges the gap between the Petrarchan style and that of the Pléiade poets. Volumes of poetry include *Erreurs amoureuses* (1549–55), *Le Livre des vers lyriques* (1555) and *Oeuvres poétiques* (1573). He was bishop of Chalon-sur-Saône and wrote also theological and philosophical works, including *Discours philosophiques* (1587).

TYCHO. See BRAHE.

TYE, Christopher (*c.* 1500–73), English musician, musical instructor to Edward VI,

received his Mus.D. from Cambridge and Oxford in 1545–48. Under Elizabeth he was organist to the Chapel Royal, and wrote some notable church music.

TYLER, (1) John (1790–1862), tenth president of the United States, was born in Charles City Co., Virginia, and in 1809 was admitted to the bar. Having sat in the state legislature 1811–16, he entered congress. In 1825 he was elected governor of Virginia, and in December 1826 U.S. senator. In the case of the United States Bank he resented the despotic methods by which Jackson overthrew it, supported Clay's motion to censure the president, and, declining to vote for expunging this motion from the minutes, in 1836 resigned his seat. In 1840 he was elected vice-president. President Harrison died in 1841, a month after his inauguration, and Tyler became president. The Whig majority, headed by Clay, regarded his election as a victory for them and for the project of a re-established national bank, but the president's firmness destroyed the project. The Ashburton Treaty and the annexation of Texas in 1845 marked his administration. Adhering to the Confederate cause, he was a member of the Confederate congress until his death, January 18, 1862. See Life by O. P. Chitwood (1939).

(2) **Wat** (d. 1381), English leader of the Peasants' Revolt of 1381. According to the most probable account, the commons of Kent after taking Rochester Castle, chose Wat Tyler of Maidstone as their captain. Under him they moved to Canterbury, Blackheath and London. At the Smithfield conference with Richard II (q.v.) blows were exchanged; William Walworth, mayor of London, wounded Wat, and finding he had been removed to St Bartholomew's Hospital, had him dragged out and beheaded (June 15).

TYLOR, Sir Edward Burnet (1832–1917), English anthropologist, born at Camberwell, travelled with Henry Christy to Mexico. Keeper of the University Museum, Oxford, and reader in Anthropology, he was first professor (1895–1909) of Anthropology. He was knighted in 1912. His chief works are *Primitive Culture* (1871) and *Anthropology* (1881). See Life by R. R. Marett (1936).

TYNAN, Katherine (1861–1931), Irish poet and novelist, born at Clondalkin, County Dublin, friend of Parnell, the Meynells and the Rossettis and a leading author of the Celtic literary revival. She married in 1893 H. A. Hinkson, and wrote volumes of tender, gentle verse, over a hundred novels and five autobiographical works, the last of which was *Memories* (1924). See also Yeats' *Letters* to her, ed. McHugh (1955).

TYNDALE, Tindale, or Hutchins, William (d. 1536), English translator of the Bible, born probably at Slymbridge in Gloucestershire, was educated at Magdalen Hall, Oxford (1510–15). After a spell at Cambridge he became chaplain and tutor in a household at Little Sodbury in Gloucestershire. His sympathy with the New Learning aroused suspicion and, already a competent Greek scholar, in 1523 he went up to London. Bishop Tunstall having refused support for his translation of the Bible, he went in 1524 to Hamburg, to Wittenberg, where he visited Luther, and in 1525 to Cologne, where he began that year with Quentel the printing of his English New Testament. This had not proceeded beyond the gospels of Matthew and Mark when the intrigues of Cochlaeus forced Tyndale to flee to Worms, where Peter Schoeffer printed for him 3000 New Testaments in small octavo. The translation owed much to Luther and Erasmus, much to his own scholarship and literary skill. Tunstall and Warham denounced the book; hundreds of copies were burned; but it made its way. In 1527 he removed to Marburg to the protection of Philip the Magnanimous; in 1529 he was shipwrecked on the way to Hamburg, where he met Coverdale; in 1531 he went to Antwerp. There probably (ostensibly at Marburg) was published his Pentateuch (1530–31; reprinted 1885), where the marginal glosses, almost all original, contain violent attacks on the pope and the bishops. Here he leans heavily on Luther. In 1531 appeared his version of Jonah, with a prologue (facsimile, 1863). An unauthorized revision of Tyndale's New Testament was made at Antwerp in August 1534, and in November Tyndale himself issued there a revised version. One copy of this work was struck off on vellum for presentation to Anne Boleyn, under whose favour apparently was printed in 1536 by T. Godfray a reprint of Tyndale's revised New Testament—the first volume of Holy Scripture printed in England. Tyndale revised his Testament in 1535, this time without the marginal notes. The emissaries of Henry VIII had often tried to get hold of him, when in 1535 he was seized at Antwerp through the treachery of Henry Philips, a Roman Catholic zealot, imprisoned in the Castle of Vilvorde, tried (1536), and on October 6 was first strangled, then burned. His chief original works were *A Parable of the Wicked Mammon* (1528); *Obedience of a Christian Man*, his most elaborate book (1528); and *Practyse of Prelates* (1530), a pungent polemic. His *Works* were published, with those of Frith and Barnes, in 1573. See Lives by Demaus (revised ed. by Richard Lovett, 1886), J. F. Mozley (1937), and studies by Bone and Greenslade (1938) and W. E. Campbell (1949).

TYNDALL, John (1820–93), Irish physicist, born at Leighlin-Bridge, County Carlow, and largely self-educated, he was employed on the ordnance survey and as a railway engineer, before studying physics in England and in Germany under Bunsen. Elected F.R.S. in 1852, he became professor at the Royal Institution in 1854. In 1856 he and T. H. Huxley (q.v.) visited the Alps and collaborated in *The Glaciers of the Alps* (1860), when he made the first ascent of the Weisshorn. In 1859 he began his researches on heat radiation, followed by the acoustic properties of the atmosphere and the blue colour of the sky, which he suggested was due to the scattering of light by small particles of water. His presidential address to the British Association in 1874 in Belfast was denounced as materialistic. He was a prolific writer on scientific subjects. He died

from accidental poisoning with chloral. See Life by Eve and Creasy (1945).

TYRCONNEL, Richard Talbot, 1st Earl of (1630–91), Irish Jacobite leader, came at the Restoration to London, and soon gained the favour of the royal family by a readiness for dirty work. James II created him Earl of Tyrconnel, with command of the troops in Ireland, and in 1687 appointed him lord-deputy of Ireland. He strove to undo the Protestant ascendency, but the Revolution brought his schemes to nought; and he tried in vain to intrigue with William. After the Battle of the Boyne Tyrconnel retired to France till 1691, when he returned as lord-lieutenant, dying of apoplexy soon after the Battle of Aughim. He was created earl (1685) and made titular duke (1689) by the deposed James II.

TYRONE. See O'NEILL (2).

TYRRELL, (1) George (1861–1909), Irish theologian, born in Dublin, became a Roman Catholic in 1879, and a Jesuit in 1880. His 'modernism' led to his expulsion from the Society (1906) and the minor excommunication. His works include *Christianity at the Crossroads* (1909) and *Essays on Faith and Immortality* (1914). See his *Autobiography* (1912) and *Letters* (1920).
(2) **Sir Walter.** See WILLIAM II.

TYRTAEUS, tær-tee'us (fl. c. 685–668 B.C.), Greek elegiac poet, probably born in Sparta, whose warsongs inspired the Spartans during the second Messenian War. See C. M. Bowra's *Early Greek Elegists* (1938).

TYRWHITT, Thomas, tir'it (1730–86), English classical commentator, born in London, was educated at Eton and Queen's College, Oxford, and in 1762 became clerk of the House of Commons, resigning in 1768. He published an edition of the *Canterbury Tales* (2 vols. 1775) and commentaries on classical texts, notably Aristotle's *Poetics* (1794).

TYSON, Edward (1651–1708), English physician, born at Bristol, studied at Magdalen Hall, Oxford, and set up practice in London, lectured in anatomy and was a physician to Bridewell and Bethlehem Hospitals. His papers on comparative anatomy, on the porpoise which he classified as both fish and mammal, on the respiratory and genital organs of the rattlesnake and, with William Cowper, on the female and male opossum, as well as his work on the classification of the male pygmy (1699), marked important advances. See Life by M. F. Ashley Montagu (1943) and F. J. Cole, *History of Comparative Anatomy* (1944).

TYTLER, (1) **Alexander Fraser** (1747–1813), Scottish historian, son of (3), became in 1780 professor of Universal History at Edinburgh. He was judge advocate of Scotland (1790) and a judge of session (1802) as Lord Woodhouselee.
(2) **Patrick Fraser** (1791–1849), Scottish historian, son of (1), published a critical *History of Scotland 1249–1603* (1828–43), still valuable. See Life by Dean Burgon (1859).
(3) **William,** of Woodhouselee (1711–92), Scottish historian, father of (1), an Edinburgh Writer to the Signet, published an exculpatory *Inquiry into the Evidence against Mary, Queen*

of Scots (1759; 4th ed. 1790), and edited the *Poetical Remains of James I of Scotland* (1783).

TYUCHEV, Fyodor Ivanovich (1803–73), Russian lyric poet, of a noble landowning family, spent 20 years abroad in the diplomatic service and then worked in the censorship department. His first collection of poems appeared in 1854 and was hailed with enthusiasm. A metaphysical romantic, he reached full recognition with the advent of symbolism. The tragic love poems of his later period are outstanding in Russian literature. See D. S. Mirsky, *History of Russian Literature* (1927) and D. Stremooukhov, *La Poésie et l'idéologie de Tiouttchev* (1937).

TZETZES, Johannes, *tset'seez* (*c.* 1120–83), Byzantine author, wrote *Iliaca*; *Biblos Istorike,* or *Chiliades,* a review of Greek literature and learning, a collection (in worthless verse) of over 600 stories; and commentaries.

TZU-HSI, *tsoo-shee'* (1834–1908), empress-dowager of China, became regent for her nephew Kwang-sü in 1875, and was largely responsible for the antiforeign agitation which culminated in the Boxer rising of 1900.

U

UBALDINI, Petruccio, *oo-bal-dee'nee* (*c.* 1524–88), Florentine illuminator on vellum, came to England in 1549, and wrote an Italian version of Boece's Description of Scotland (1588), Lives of English and Scottish Ladies (1591), &c.

UCCELLO, Paolo, *oo-chel'lō* (1397–1475), the name given to the Florentine painter, di Dono, who trained as a goldsmith, applied the principles of perspective to his paintings, sometimes pedantically insisting on vanishing points. In his best-known work, the *Deluge,* his use of perspective and foreshortening gives a sternly realistic effect which becomes modified and more decoratively imaginative in later works such as the three battle paintings in the Uffizi, Florence, the National Gallery and the Louvre. See studies by J. Pope-Hennessy (1950) and P. D'Ancona (1960).

UDALL or **Uvedale,** *yoo'dèl, oov'dayl,* (1) **John** (1560–92), English Puritan divine, educated at Cambridge, was one of the authors of the Martin Marprelate tracts, was arrested in 1590 and sentenced to death, but pardoned. He was author of a well-known Hebrew grammar (1593) and several volumes of sermons.

(2) **Nicholas** (1504–56), English dramatist, born in Hampshire and educated at Winchester and Corpus Christi College, Oxford, became (*c.* 1534) headmaster of Eton. He published a selection from Terence, *Flowers of Latin Speaking,* for his pupils, who soon learnt of his predilection for corporal punishment. His dismissal in 1541 for indecent offences did not affect his standing at the court. Edward VI appointed him prebendary of Windsor, and despite his great enthusiasm for the Reformation, he survived the reign of Queen Mary without disfavour. He translated Erasmus, selections from the Great Bible and Latin commentaries on the latter, but is chiefly remembered as the author of the rollicking comedy, *Ralph Roister Doister,* written *c.* 1553 but not published until 1567, which, inspired by his favourite classical writers, Plautus and Terence, was to influence later English writers of comedies.

UDET, Ernst, *oo'det* (1896–1941), German airman, born at Frankfurt-am-Main, was a leading German air ace in World War I, and from 1935 worked in the German air ministry. A *Luftwaffe* quartermaster-general in World War II, he committed suicide by an air crash, having fallen foul of the Gestapo. The authorities described his death as an accident while testing a new air weapon. Zuckmayer's play, *The Devil's General,* is based on his life.

UEXKÜLL, Jakob Johann von, *üks'kül* (1864–1944), German biologist, born at Gut Keblas in Estonia in 1864, studied at Dorpat, and became in 1905 professor at Hamburg. From physiological research he developed a vitalistic philosophy in *Theoretische Biologie* (rev. 1928) and other books.

UGOLINO, Count, *oo-gō-lee'nō* (d. 1289), Pisan partisan leader, member of the great Ghibelline house of Gherardesca, with Giovanni Visconti, head of the Guelphic party, laid a plot to secure arbitrary power. The plot was discovered, and they were banished; but Ugolino, allying himself with the Florentines and Lucchese, forced the Pisans in 1276 to restore to him his territories. During the war with the Genoese, in the battle at Malora (1284), Ugolino, by treacherously abandoning the Pisans, occasioned the annihilation of their fleet, with a loss of 11,000 prisoners; but when Florentines and other enemies of the republic gathered together to destroy it, the Pisans had no resource but to throw themselves into his arms. Ugolino now gave free scope to his despotic nature, persecuting and banishing all who were obnoxious to him, till at length a conspiracy was formed against him. Dragged from his palace, July 1, 1288, he was starved to death in the tower of Gualandi, with his two sons and two grandsons. His fate is treated by Dante (*Inferno,* xxxiii).

UHLAND, Johann Ludwig, *oo'lant* (1787–1862), German lyric poet, the leader of the 'Swabian School', was born at Tübingen, where he studied law. He published poems from an early age and gradually added to his *Gedichte* (1815), which contain such popular songs as 'Der gute Kamerad'. He also wrote a number of admirable literary essays. He was a Liberal deputy for Tübingen at the assemblies of Württemberg (1819) and Frankfurt (1848). See Lives by his widow (1874) and H. Schneider (1920).

ULANOVA, Galina, *oo-lahn'ō-va* (1910–), Russian ballerina, studied at the Maryinski Theatre School, and made her début in *Les Sylphides* at the Kirov Theatre in Leningrad in 1928. She became the leading ballerina of the Soviet Union and was four times a Stalin prizewinner. She visited London in 1956 with the Bolshoi Ballet, when she gave a memorable performance in *Giselle*. She has appeared in several films made by the Moscow State Ballet Company and in 1957 was awarded the Lenin prize. See study by Beresovsky, trans. S. Garry and J. Lawson (1952).

ULBRICHT, Walter, *ool'briкнт* (1893–1973), East German Communist politician, born in Leipzig. In 1928, after some years in Russia, he became Communist deputy for Potsdam. He left Germany on Hitler's advent in 1933. He went first to Paris and was in Spain during the civil war, but spent the greater part of his exile in Russia. As Marshal Zhukov's political adviser and head of the German Communist party, he came back in 1945, and by 1950 had become deputy premier of the German Democratic Republic. The same year he was made secretary-general of the Party, and was largely responsible for the ' sovietization ' of E. Germany. He survived a workers' uprising in 1953 and went on to establish his position. He will be remembered chiefly for building the Berlin wall in 1961. He retired in 1971.

ULFILAS, or Wulfila, *ool'fee-las* (*c.* 311–383), Gothic translator of the Bible, was born among the Goths north of the Danube. Consecrated a missionary bishop to his fellow-countrymen by Eusebius of Nicomedia in 341, after seven years' labour he was forced to migrate with his converts across the Danube. For over thirty years he laboured in Lower Moesia, visiting Constantinople in 360 in the interest of the Arian party, and again in 383, only to die a few days after his arrival. See Lives by Waitz (1840), Bessel (1860) and Balg (N.Y. 1891).

ULIANOV. See LENIN.

ULLOA, Antonio de, *ool-yō'a* (1716–95), Spanish statesman and mathematician, born at Seville, twice visited America, and in 1746, having been brought a prisoner to England, was elected F.R.S.

ULPIANUS, Domitius (*c.* A.D. 170–228), Roman jurist, born at Tyre, held judicial offices under Septimius Severus and Caracalla, and, on the accession of Alexander Severus (222), became his principal adviser and *praefectus praetorio*. He was murdered by his own soldiery. He was a voluminous writer. In Justinian's *Digest* there are 2462 excerpts from Ulpian; the originals are almost wholly lost. See Abdy and Walker, *The Commentaries of Gaius and the Rules of Ulpian* (3rd ed. 1885).

ULUGH-BEG, *oo'loog-* (fl. *c.* 1430), grandson of Tamerlane, succeeded in 1447 to the throne. He was a successful warrior, but was defeated and slain (1449) by his rebellious son. He founded the observatory at Samar-

kand, and was a diligent observer. His astronomical works were partly translated into Latin by Greaves (1650) and Hyde (1665).

ULYANOV. See LENIN.

UMBERTO. See HUMBERT.

UNAMUNO, Miguel de, *oo-na-moo'nō* (1864–1936), Spanish philosopher and author, born at Bilbao, of Basque parentage, was professor of Greek at Salamanca from 1892. He wrote mystic philosophy, historical studies, brilliant essays, books on travel, and austere poetry. Among his most important works are *Vida de Don Quijote y Sancho* (1905), his novel *Niebla* (1914), *Del sentimiento trágico de la vida* (1913) and a volume of religious poetry, *El Cristo de Velázquez* (1920). From 1924 to 1930 he was exiled as a republican to the island of Fuerteventura, reinstated at Salamanca on the founding of the republic in 1931. But always a rebel and an individualist though with the deepest faith in and interest of his country at heart, he was soon at variance with the Socialist régime. The Civil War for him was a nationalist struggle and he denounced foreign interference. See study by Barea (1952).

UNDERHILL, Evelyn (1875–1941), English poet and mystic, was born in Wolverhampton, educated at King's College, London, married in 1907 Herbert Stuart Moore, a barrister, and became in 1921 lecturer on the Philosophy of Religion at Manchester College, Oxford. A friend and disciple of Hügel (q.v.), she found her way intellectually from agnosticism to Christianity, wrote numerous books on mysticism, including *The Life of the Spirit* (1922), volumes of verse and four novels. Her *Mysticism* (1911) became a standard work. See Life by M. Cropper (1958).

UNDSET, Sigrid, *oon'set* (1882–1949), Norwegian novelist, born in Kalundborg, Denmark. She was the daughter of a noted Norwegian archaeologist, **Ingvald Undset,** from whom she inherited much of her interest in the Middle Ages in Norway. From 1899 she worked in an office, where her experiences and her concern for the problem of young middle-class women were the basis of her early novels, including *Jenny* (1911). Between 1920 and 1922 she produced her masterpiece *Kristin Lavransdatter*, a 14th-century trilogy, which gives a graphic and authentic picture of the period, followed by the series *Olav Audunssön* (four vols. 1925–27). She became a Roman Catholic in 1924, a circumstance that influenced her subsequent work. Most of this had contemporary settings. She was awarded the Nobel prize for literature in 1928. See study by H. A. Larsen, and Life by Winsnes, trans. Foole (1958).

UNGARETTI, Giuseppe, *oong-gar-ret'ti* (1888–1970), Italian poet, born at Alexandria, studied at Paris, was professor of Italian Literature at São Paulo, Brazil (1936–42) and at Rome (1942–58). He is the author of ' hermetic ' poems characterized by their symbolism, compressed imagery and modern verse structure.

UNRUH, Fritz von, *oon'roo* (1885–1970), German playwright and novelist, born at Koblenz, served in World War I as a cavalry officer. An ardent pacifist, the ideal of a new humanity underlies all his Expressionist works, particularly the novel *Opfergang* (1916), and the two parts of an unfinished dramatic trilogy, *Ein Geschlecht* (1916) and *Platz* (1920). He left Germany in 1932 and went to the U.S., where he wrote *The End is not Yet* (1947) and *The Saint* (1950). He returned to Germany in 1952.

U NU, *oo-noo* (1907–), Burmese politician and writer, born at Wakema, studied at Rangoon, became a schoolmaster although his real ambition was to be a dramatist. He joined the Thakin Party and founded the Red Dragon Book Society. Imprisoned by the British (1940), he was released by the Japanese and served in Ba Maw's puppet administration but retained the confidence of the anti-Japanese resistance. In 1946 he was elected president of the Burmese Constituent Assembly. After the assassination of the cabinet in July 1947, U Nu became the first prime minister of the now independent Burmese Republic. Splits in his own party, the Anti-Fascist People's Freedom League, were followed by his resignation (1956), re-election (1957), defeat at the polls by General Ne Win, who set up a military government (1958), and victory of his rightwing faction and his return to the premiership (1960). He was overthrown by a military *coup* in 1962, declared a rebel and imprisoned but released in 1966. See autobiographical introduction to his novel, *Man, the Wolf of Man*.

UNVERDORBEN, **Otto**, *oon-fer-dor'ben* (1806–73), German chemist, born at Dahme, prepared aniline by the distillation of indigo (1826).

UNWIN, (1) Mary. See COWPER, WILLIAM.

(2) **Sir Stanley** (1884–1968), English publisher, chairman of the firm of George Allen and Unwin, founded in 1914, studied the book-trade in Germany. An international figure in publishing, he was president of the Publishers Association of Great Britain (1933–35) and president of the International Publishers Association (1936–1938, 1946–54). His books include *The Truth about Publishing* (1926; rev. ed. 1960), *Publishing in Peace and War* (1944) and *The Truth about a Publisher* (autobiography; 1960).

URBAIN, Georges, *ür-bī* (1872–1938), French chemist, born in Paris, became professor of Inorganic Chemistry at the Sorbonne (1908), discovered the rare earth lutecium (1907), the law of optimum phosphorescence of binary systems, and showed that several elements which were hitherto considered pure were in fact mixtures.

URBAN, the name of eight popes; the most noteworthy are:

Urban I, bishop of Rome (222–230), said to have been a martyr.

Urban II (1042–99), pope from 1088, born at Châtillon-sur-Marne, France, became cardinal-bishop of Ostia (1078), was elected pope during the schismatical pontificate of Guibert, styled Clement III. He laid Henry IV of Germany under the ban and drove him out of Italy, triumphed by the same means over Philip I of France, and aroused the crusading spirit by his eloquence at the council he held at Piacenza and Clermont (1095).

Urban IV (d. 1264), pope from 1261, born

Jacques Pantaléon, the son of a cobbler of Troyes, was bishop of Verdun and patriarch of Jerusalem. He instituted the feast of Corpus Christi (1264).

Urban V (1309–70), pope from 1362, born Guillaume de Grimoard at Grisac, France. He was abbot of St Victor at Marseilles, was elected at Avignon, but set out for Rome in 1367, only to return a few months before his death.

Urban VI (1318–89), pope from 1378, born Bartolomeo Prignano at Naples, became Archbishop of Bari (1377). The French cardinals set up against him the Bishop of Cambray as the antipope Clement VII, beginning the Great Schism in the West.

Urban VIII (1568–1644), pope from 1623, born Maffeo Barberini, in Florence, supported Richelieu's policy against the Hapsburgs, condemned Galileo, canonized Loyola and Philip Neri, and wrote sacred poetry. He carried out much ecclesiastical reform and established his own family in the Roman aristocracy.

URE, Andrew, *yoor* (1778–1857), Scottish chemist, born at Glasgow, studied at the university, became professor of Chemistry and Natural Philosophy in Anderson's College, astronomer in the city observatory, and in 1834 analytical chemist to the Board of Customs in London. F.R.S. in 1822, he produced a *Dictionary of Chemistry* (1821), and other works.

UREY, Harold Clayton (1893–), American chemist, born at Walkerton, Indiana, educated at Montana, California, and Copenhagen, became professor of Chemistry at Columbia (1934) and at Chicago (1945–52). He was director of war research, Atomic Bomb Project, Columbia (1940–45). In 1932 he isolated heavy water and discovered the heavy hydrogen isotope, deuterium, which was of great importance in the development of nuclear fission. He also investigated entropy of gases, absorption spectra and isotopes. He was awarded the Nobel prize in 1934 and the Davy medal of the Royal Society (1940), of which he was elected foreign member (1947).

URFÉ, Honoré d', *ür-fay* (1568–1625), French writer, born at Marseilles, fought in the religious wars of France and later settled in Savoy. He was the author of the pastoral romance, *Astrée* (1610–27), which is regarded as the first French novel. He was killed at Villefranche-sur-mer during the war between Savoy and Genoa.

URQUHART, *er'kèrt*, (1) **David** (1805–77), Scottish diplomatist, born in Cromarty, served in the Greek navy during the Greek War of Independence and received his first diplomatic appointment in 1831, when he went to Constantinople with Sir Stratford Canning. His anti-Russian policy caused his recall from Turkey in 1837 and he was member of parliament for Stafford from 1847 to 1852. A strong opponent of Palmerston's policy, he believed Turkey was capable of dealing with Russia without European intervention. He founded the *Free Press*, afterwards called the *Diplomatic Review*, in which these views were expressed. He retired in 1864. Among his many writings were *The*

Pillars of Hercules (1850), in which he suggested the introduction of Turkish baths into Britain, and *The Lebanon* (1860).

(2) **Sir Thomas** (*c.* 1611–60), Scottish author, born in Cromarty, studied at King's College, Aberdeen, and travelled in France, Spain and Italy. On his return he took up arms against the Covenanting party in the north but was worsted and forced to flee to England. Becoming attached to the court, he was knighted in 1641. The same year he published his *Epigrams Divine and Moral.* On succeeding his father he went abroad. At Cromarty, though much troubled by his creditors, he produced his *Trissotetras; or a most exquisite Table for resolving Triangles,* &c. (1645). In 1649 his library was seized and sold. He again took up arms in the royal cause, and was present at Worcester, where he lost most of his MSS. At London, through Cromwell's influence, he was allowed considerable liberty, and in 1652 published *The Pedigree* and *The Jewel.* The first was an exact account of the Urquhart family, in which they are traced back to Adam; the second is chiefly a panegyric on the Scots nation. In 1653 he issued his *Introduction to the Universal Language* and the first two books of that English classic, his brilliant translation of *Rabelais* (q.v.). The third was not issued till after his death, which is said to have occurred abroad, in a fit of mirth on hearing of the Restoration. His learning was vast, his scholarship defective. Crazy with conceit, he yet evinces a true appreciation of all that is noble, and has many passages of great power. See his *Works* in the Maitland Club series (1834); Willcock's *Sir Thomas Urquhart* (1899); Whibley's Introduction to the *Rabelais* (' Tudor Trans.' 1900); and study by H. Brown (1933).

URSULA, St, a legendary saint and martyr, especially honoured at Cologne, where she is said to have been slain with her 11,000 virgins by a horde of Huns on her journey home from a pilgrimage to Rome. She became the patron saint of many educational institutes, particularly the teaching order of the Ursulines. Her feast day is October 21.

USHER, or Ussher, James (1581–1656), Irish divine, was born in Dublin, son of a gentleman of good estate; his uncle, **Henry Usher** (*c.* 1550–1631), was his predecessor as archbishop of Armagh. He was a scholar (1594) and fellow (1599–1605) of Trinity College, Dublin. About 1606 he became chancellor of St Patrick's, in 1607 professor of Divinity, in 1620 Bishop of Meath, in 1623 privy councillor for Ireland, and in 1625 Archbishop of Armagh. He left Ireland for England in 1640, continued to live in England, declined to sit in the Westminster Assembly, and for about eight years was preacher at Lincoln's Inn. He was constant in his loyalty

to the throne, yet was treated with favour by Cromwell, and was buried in Westminster Abbey. He was distinguished not only by his learning but also by his charity and sweetness of temper. He was Calvinistic in theology and moderate in his ideas of church government. Of his numerous writings, the greatest is the *Annales Veteris et Novi Testamenti* (1650–54), which gave us the long-accepted chronology of Scripture, the Creation being fixed at 4004 B.C. Amongst his other works, the *De Graeca Septuaginta Interpretum Versione Syntagma* (1655) was the first attempt at a real examination of the Septuagint. His complete writings were edited by Elrington and Todd (17 vols. 1841–64). See the Life prefixed thereto by Carr (1895), and W. Ball Wright's *The Ussher Memoirs* (1889).

USPENSKI, Gleb Ivanovich, *oo-spyen'skee* (*c.* 1840–1902), Russian author of novels of peasant life, such as *Power of the Soil* (1882), notable for their realism as opposed to the prevalent romantic conception of the agricultural worker. He died insane. See D. S. Mirsky, *History of Soviet Literature* (1927).

USTINOV, Peter Alexander, *yoo'stin-of* (1921–), English actor and dramatist, born in London. The son of White Russian parents, Ustinov first appeared on the stage in 1938, and had established himself as an accomplished artist both in revues and legitimate drama by 1942, when four years' army service interrupted his career. His subsequent work for films as actor, writer and producer, and in broadcasting as a satirical comedian, has enhanced his reputation. A prolific playwright, his works—most successful amongst which are *The Love of Four Colonels* (1951) and *Romanoff and Juliet* (1956)—are marked by a serious approach to human problems often presented with an acute sense of comedy and a mastery of unconventional stagecraft.

UTRILLO, Maurice, *oo-tree'lo* (1883–1955), French painter, born in Montmartre, Paris, the son of the painter Suzanne Valadon (q.v.), was adopted by the Spanish writer Miguel Utrillo. He began to paint at Montmagny in 1902, but it was the streets of Paris, particularly old Montmartre, and village scenes which were to provide him with most of his subjects. Despite acute alcoholism, and consequent sojourns in various nursing-homes, his productivity was astonishing, and by 1925 he was famous. His ' White Period ' paintings of about 1908–14 are much sought after, for their subtle colouring and sensitive feeling for atmosphere. He signed his work ' Maurice Utrillo V ', incorporating the initial of his mother's family name. See studies by G. Charenson (1929), F. Jourdan (1948), G. Ribemont-Dessaignes (1948) and W. George (1960).

V

VACHELL, Horace Annesley, *vay'chĕl* (1861–1955), English novelist, great-grandson of the first Lord Lyttelton (q.v.), born at Sydenham, was educated at Harrow and Sandhurst and from 1883 until the death of his American wife in 1899 lived in the United States. He is best known for his school story about Harrow, *The Hill* (1905), and *Quinneys* (1914). He also wrote plays, three autobiographical works, of which the last was his *Methuselah* memoirs (1951) and a volume of essays, *Quests* (1945).

VACHEROT, Étienne, *vash-rō* (1809–97), French philosopher, born at Langres, was appointed professor of Philosophy at the Sorbonne in 1839, but was dismissed in 1852 when he refused to sign the oath of allegiance to the Empire. His anti-clericalism and the publication of his book, *La Démocratie,* caused his imprisonment in 1859. In 1871 he was elected to the Assembly. Other writings include *La Métaphysique et la Science* (1858) and *La Religion* (1868).

VAIHINGER, Hans, *fī'-* (1852–1933), German philosopher, born in Württemberg, professor at Halle (1884–1906), wrote a remarkable commentary to Kant's *Critique of Pure Reason* (1881–92) and developed the idealist positivism of Lange in *The Philosophy of 'As If'* (1911; trans. C. K. Ogden, 1924). See his autobiography in *Philosophie in Selbstdarstellungen,* Vol. 2 (1921).

VALADON, Suzanne, *va-la-dõ* (1869–1938), French painter, mother of Utrillo (q.v.), became an artist's model after an accident ended her career as an acrobat, modelling for Renoir and others. With the encouragement of Toulouse-Lautrec, Degas and Cézanne, she took up painting herself and excelled in her realistic treatment of nudes, portraits and figure studies, her work having some affinity with that of Degas. Two of her flower pieces are in the Luxembourg. See Life by J. Storm (1959).

VALBERT, G. See CHERBULIEZ.

VALDÉS, *vahl'days,* (1) **Armando Palacio** (1853–1938), Spanish novelist, born at Entralgo in Asturias. Some of his novels were translated as *The Marquis of Peñalba, Maximina, Sister Saint Sulpice, Froth* and *The Grandee.*

(2) **Juan de** (1500–41), Spanish religious reformer, born in Cuenca, became an object of suspicion to the Inquisition, and lived in Naples from 1534. But he sought the regeneration of the Church from within, and never inclined to Lutheranism. Among his works are *The Christian Alphabet* (1536) and Commentaries, some of them translated into English (1865–83). See monographs by Stern (1869) and Carrasco (1880), and Life by Wiffen- prefixed to his translation of Valdés' *CX Considerations* (1865).

VALDIVIA, Pedro de, *vahl-dee'vya* (c. 1510–1559), Spanish soldier, born near La Serena, Estremadura, went to Venezuela (c. 1534) and then to Peru, where he became Pizarro's

(q.v.) lieutenant. He won renown at Las Salinas (1538), and was in real command of the expedition to Chile. He founded Santiago (1541) and other cities. In 1559, attempting, with a small force, to relieve Tucapel, which was besieged by the Araucanians, he was captured and killed by the Indians. See study by R. B. Cunninghame Graham (1926).

VALENTINIAN, the name of three Roman Emperors:

Valentinian I (321–375), born at Cibalis in Pannonia, rose rapidly in rank under Constantius and Julian, and on the death of Jovian was chosen as his successor (364). He resigned the East to his brother Valens, and himself governed the West with watchful care until his death.

Valentinian II, his second son (372–392), received from his elder brother, Gratianus (q.v.), the provinces of Italy, Illyricum and Africa. During his minority the Empress Justina administered the government; about three years after her death Valentinian was murdered, probably by Arbogastes, commander-in-chief of his army.

Valentinian III (c. 419–455), grand-nephew of II, the son of Constantius III, was given the Western empire by Theodosius II, emperor of the East, in 425. A weak and contemptible prince, he never really ruled during his thirty years' reign; his mother, Placidia, governed till her death (450), and then the eunuch, Heraclius. Valentinian's treatment of Bonifacius made him throw himself into the arms of the Vandal, Genseric (q.v.), and thus lost Africa to the empire. He stabbed Aetius (q.v.) to death (454), but next year was himself slain by Maximus, whose wife he had ravished.

VALENTINO, Rudolph, *-tee'-* (1895–1926), Italian-born American film actor, born Rodolpho Alphonso Guglielmi di Valentina d'Antonguolla at Castellaneta, studied agriculture but emigrated to the United States and first appeared on the stage as a dancer. In 1919 he made his screen début as Julio in *The Four Horsemen of the Apocalypse,* and his subsequent performances in *The Sheikh* (1921), *Blood and Sand* (1922), *The Young Rajah* (1922), *Monsieur Beaucaire* (1924), *The Eagle* (1925) and *The Son of the Sheikh* (1926) established him as the leading ' screen lover ' of the 'twenties. He died suddenly at the height of his adoration in New York and his funeral resembled that of a popular ruler. Besides good looks and athletic bearing he had considerable dramatic gifts. He wrote *Daydreams* (1923), a book of poems. See Lives by his second wife, N. Rambova (1927), and S. G. Ullman (1927).

VALERA, (1). See DE VALERA.

(2) **Don Juan,** *vah-lay'ra* (1824–1905), Spanish novelist and critic, born at Cabra in Córdoba, held diplomatic posts in Europe and U.S.A., and was a deputy, minister of commerce, minister of public instruction, councillor of state, senator, and member of

the Spanish Academy. His literary studies (1864) and essays (1882) brought him reputation; but his fame depends on his romances, *Pepita Jiménez* (1874; trans. 1891), *Las ilusiones del Doctor Faustino* (1876), *El comendador Mendoza* (1877; trans. 1893), *Doña Luz* (1878; trans. 1892) and *La buena fama* (1895).

VALERIANUS, Publius Licinius (*c.* 193–260), was proclaimed Roman emperor by the legions in Rhaetia after the murder of Gallus (253), and assumed as colleague his eldest son, Gallienus. Throughout his reign trouble hovered on every frontier of the empire; and marching against the Persians, he was completely defeated at Edessa (260). He was seized by King Sapor, and, imprisoned until his death, suffered every oriental cruelty.

VALERIUS FLACCUS. See FLACCUS.

VALERIUS MAXIMUS (fl. A.D. 14–30), Roman historian, wrote *c.* A.D. 29 historical anecdotes, biased in favour of the emperor Tiberius.

VALÉRY, Paul Ambroise, *va-lay-ree* (1871–1945), French poet and writer, born at Cette, settled in Paris in 1892 and after publishing some remarkable Mallarméesque verse, he relapsed into a twenty years' silence, taken up with mathematics and philosophical speculations. He emerged in 1917 with a new poetic outlook and technique in *La Jeune Parque* (1917), a poem full of difficult symbolism, because of the dualism it enveloped—emotion against reason, life against death, being against doing, consciousness against the world of facts and things. This was followed by a remarkable collection, *Charmes* (1922), containing *Le Cimetière marin*, recalling in treatment and metre Gray's *Elegy*, *L'Ébauche d'un serpent*, *Au platane*, &c., remarkable for the poetic shorthand, the compression and conciseness of his imagery and ideas. His prose works comprise *Soirée avec M. Teste* (1895), in which intelligence personified by M. Teste watches itself at work, records its ' inner ' experience and several aesthetic studies, as the dialogue *Eupalinos* (1924), in which architecture and music are compared, and *L'Âme et la danse* (1924). A late, short play, *Le Solitaire*, foreshadows Samuel Beckett. See studies by A. R. Chisholm (1938), Sewell (1952), Suckling (1954), H. Mondor (Paris 1957), and introduction by T. S. Eliot to Vol. VII of the *Collected Works*, trans. by D. Folliot (1959).

VALETTE, Jean Parisot de la (1494–1568), French knight of St John, nobly born at Toulouse, became Grand Master in 1557. His exploits against the Turks culminated in his successful defence of Malta, from May 18 till September 8, 1565. He founded the city of Valetta.

VALLA, Laurentius (*c.* 1405–57), Italian humanist, born at Rome, taught the classics at Pavia, Milan and Naples, incurred many enmities, but in 1435 found a protector in Naples in Alfonso V. He was expelled from Rome for attacking the temporal power in his *De Donatione Constantini Magni*, was prosecuted by the Inquisition in Naples, but in 1448 was again in Rome as apostolic

secretary to Nicholas V. His Latin versions of Xenophon, Herodotus and Thucydides were admirable; and he greatly advanced New Testament criticism by his comparison of the Vulgate with the Greek original. His *De Elegantia Latinae Linguae* was long a textbook. See works by Mancini (1891), Wolff (1893) and Schwabe (1896).

VALLE-INCLÁN, Ramón María del, *val'yay-eeng-klahn* (1869–1936), Spanish novelist, dramatist and poet, was born at Puebla de Caramiñal. Among his works are four *Sonatas* on the seasons (1902–07), written in fine prose in the form of novels, a graphic but erroneous history *La guerra carlista* and the masterly *Águila de blasón* (1907) and *Romance de Lobos* (1908), set in a vivid mediaeval background. Many of his novels and plays are collected in *Esperpentos* and among several volumes of fine verse is his *Cara de Plata* (1923).

VALLIÈRE. See LA VALLIÈRE.

VALLISNIERI, Antonio, *val-lees-nyay'ree* (1661–1730), Italian naturalist, born at Modena, became professor of Medicine at Padua, made important studies of the reproductive systems of insects, and wrote treatises on the ostrich (1712) and the chameleon (1715). The waterweed *Vallisneria spiralis* is named after him.

VALLOTTON, Felix, *va-lō-tō* (1865–1925), Swiss painter, born at Lausanne, studied the graphic arts in Paris and excelled in the woodcut, but later took to painting. At first a member of the ' Nabis ', the symbolist movement, he later pioneered an extreme expressionist realism, inspired by his woodcuts and transferred to his oil painting.

VALOIS, Dame Ninette de, *val-wah*, stage-name of Edris Stannus (1898–   ), British ballerina, born in Ireland. She studied under Cecchetti, and first appeared, in 1914, in the pantomime at the Lyceum Theatre; she subsequently appeared with the Beecham Opera Company and at Covent Garden. After a European tour with Diaghilev (1923–1925) she partnered Anton Dolin in England, and became director of Ballet at the Abbey Theatre, Dublin. In 1931 she founded the Sadler's Wells Ballet School and became artistic director of the company. In 1935 she married Dr A. B. Connell. She organized the National Ballet school of Turkey (1947) and was created D.B.E. in 1951. She wrote *Invitation to the Ballet* (1937) and her autobiography, *Come Dance with Me* (1957). Her choreographic works include *The Rake's Progress*, *Checkmate* and *Don Quixote*.

VÁMBÉRY, Arminius, *vam'bay-ree* (1832–1913), Hungarian traveller and philologist, born at Duna-Szerdahely, Hungary, at twelve was apprenticed to a ladies' dressmaker, but afterwards took to teaching, and struggled to support himself. A desire for Eastern travel led him to Constantinople, where he taught French in the house of a minister, and in 1858 issued a German-Turkish dictionary. Having travelled in 1862–64 in the disguise of a dervish through the deserts of the Oxus to Khiva and Samarkand, he wrote *Travels and Adventures in Central Asia* (1864). In his writings and lectures Vámbéry supported the claim that

Britain's rule in the East was most beneficent. Professor of Oriental Languages in Budapest till 1905, he published works on the Eastern Turkish and Tatar languages, the ethnography of the Turks, the origin of the Magyars, and on many other oriental subjects. See his autobiography (1883) and *Story of My Struggles* (1904).

VANBRUGH, *van'brœ,* (1) **Dame Irene** (1872–1949), English actress, sister of (3), born in Exeter, was trained by Sarah Thorne and made her first appearance at Margate as Phoebe in *As You Like It* (1888). She married Dion Boucicault the younger, in 1901, and acted with Tree, Alexander, Hare and Frohman, winning a reputation as an interpreter of Pinero and Barrie heroines. She was created D.B.E. in 1941. She shared with her sister the family height, dark expressive eyes, magnificent presence and tremendous charm.

(2) **Sir John** (1664–1726), English playwright and baroque architect, the grandson of a Protestant refugee from Ghent, was educated in France, commissioned into Lord Huntingdon's regiment and suffered imprisonment in the Bastille (1690–92). A staunch Whig, he became a leading spirit in society life and scored a success with his first comedy, *The Relapse* (1696), followed, again with applause, by *The Provok'd Wife* (1697). *The Confederacy* (1705) was put on in the Haymarket, where Congreve and Vanbrugh joined together as theatre managers. A natural playwright of the uninhibited Restoration comedy of manners period, Vanbrugh also achieved success as architect of Castle Howard (1702) and in 1705 was commissioned to design Blenheim Palace at Woodstock. The immense baroque structure aroused the ridicule of Swift and Pope, and the Duchess of Marlborough disliked the plans and especially its enormous cost so much that she long refused to pay Vanbrugh. He was made comptroller of royal works in 1714, was knighted and was Clarencieux king-of-arms (1705–25). See *Complete Works*, ed. B. Dobrée and C. Webb (1928), and study by L. Whistler (1938).

(3) **Violet Augusta Mary** (1867–1942), English actress, sister of (1), born in Exeter. She first appeared in burlesque in 1886 and two years later played Ophelia at Margate, where she had been trained by Sarah Thorne. She then joined the Kendals for their American tour and on her return played Ann Boleyn in Irving's production of *Henry VIII,* also understudying Ellen Terry. She married Arthur Bourchier in 1894 and enhanced many of his successes with her elegance and ability.

VAN—those not listed below may be found under their respective surnames.

VAN BUREN, Martin (1782–1862), eighth president of the United States, born at Kinderhook, N.Y., was called to the bar in 1803. In 1812 and 1816 he was elected to the state senate, and in 1816–19 was state attorney-general. In 1821 he entered the U.S. senate as a Republican and was elected governor of New York in 1828. He supported Jackson for the presidency, and in 1829 became secretary of state. In 1832 he was elected vice-president, and in 1836

president, but by a popular majority of less than 25,000, largely owing to his opposition to the 'slightest interference' with slavery. His four years of office were darkened by financial panic; but he did what he could to lighten it by forcing a measure for a treasury independent of private banks. He was strictly neutral during the Canadian rebellion of 1837. In 1840 his party were overwhelmingly defeated by the Whigs. See Lives by W. L. Mackenzie (1846), E. M. Shepard (1888), G. Bancroft (1889), D. T. Lynch (1929).

VANCOUVER, George (*c.* 1758–98), English navigator and explorer, sailed with Cook (q.v.) on his second and third voyages and, promoted captain (1794), did survey work in Australia, New Zealand and the West coast of N. America, sailing round Vancouver Island (1795). See his *Voyage* (1798), and Life by G. Godwin (1930).

VANDAMME, Dominique Joseph, *-dahm* (1770–1830), French soldier, born at Cassel in Nord, in 1799 fought at Austerlitz, in 1806–07 reduced Silesia, but was defeated and taken prisoner at Kulm in 1813. He held a command during the Hundred Days, after the second Restoration was exiled, but returned from America in 1824. See Life by Du Casse (1870).

VANDENBERG, Arthur Hendrick (1884–1951), United States Republican senator, born in Grand Rapids, Michigan, studied at the university there and was elected to the senate (1928). An isolationist before World War II, he strongly supported the formation of U.N.O., was delegate to the San Francisco conference and to the U.N. Assembly from 1946.

VANDERBILT, Cornelius (1794–1877), American financier, born on Staten Island, New York, at sixteen bought a boat and ferried passengers and goods. By forty he had become the owner of steamers running to Boston and up the Hudson; in 1849, during the gold rush, he established a route by Lake Nicaragua to California, and during the Crimean war a line of steamships to Havre. At seventy he entered on a great career of railroad financing, gradually obtaining a controlling interest in a large number of roads. He gave $1,000,000 to found Vanderbilt University at Nashville. **William Henry** (1821–85), his eldest son, greatly extended the Vanderbilt system of railways. **Cornelius** (1843–99), left some £25,000,000. See Croffut, *The Vanderbilts* (1886), and Life by A. D. Howden Smith (1928).

VAN DER GOES, Hugo, ĸʜoos (*c.* 1440–82), Flemish painter, born probably at Ghent, was dean of the painters' guild at Ghent (1473–75) and died insane in a Soignies monastery. His large and dramatic *Portinari Altarpiece* is in the Uffizi and the Stuart triptych has been ascribed to him.

VAN DE VELDE, *-vel'dĕ,* (1) **Henri** (1863–1957), Belgian architect, born at Antwerp, began as a painter before pioneering the modern functional style of architecture. He established the famous Weimar School of Arts and Crafts (1906) from which the *Bauhaus* sprang. Gropius (q.v.) was his pupil. See his *Vom Neuen Stil* (1907) and *Le Nouveau* (1929).

(2) **Willem, the Elder** (*c.* 1611–93), Dutch marine painter, father of (3), born at Leyden, came in 1657 to England and painted large pictures of sea battles in indian ink and black paint for Charles II and James II.

(3) **Willem, the Younger** (1633–1707), the greatest of Dutch marine painters, son of (2), born at Leyden, followed his father to England and became court painter to Charles II in 1674. Smith catalogues 330 of his paintings. His brother, **Adriaen** (1636–1672), was a landscape painter. See E. Michel's family study (1892) and introduction to a catalogue of their drawings compiled by M. S. Robinson (1958).

VAN DIEMEN. See TASMAN.

VAN DOREN, (1) **Carl Clinton** (1885–1950), American critic and biographer, brother of (2), born at Hope, Illinois, studied at the state university and at Columbia, where he lectured in English Literature (1911–30). He was literary editor of the *Nation* (1919–22), of the *Century Magazine* (1922–25) and of the *Cambridge History of American Literature* (1917–21). He was also a distinguished biographer of Thomas Love Peacock (1911), Cabell (1925), Swift (1930), Sinclair Lewis (1933) and Benjamin Franklin (1938), which last work won the Pulitzer prize (1939). He edited Franklin's *Letters and Papers* (1947), and critical studies include *The American Novel* (1921) and with (2), *American and British Literature since 1890* (1925). He also wrote *The Ninth Wave* (1926), a novel, and his autobiography, *Three Worlds* (1936). His first wife (divorced), **Irita Bradford** (1891–1967), was also an editor.

(2) **Mark Albert** (1894–   ), American poet and critic, brother of (1), was born at Hope, Illinois, studied at the state university and at Columbia, where he became professor of English. He served in the army during World War I, succeeded (1) to the editorship of the *Nation* (1924–28) and was awarded the Pulitzer prize (1940) for his *Collected Poems* (1939) chosen from such volumes of verse as *Spring Thunder* (1924), *Now the Sky* (1928), &c. Later volumes include *The Mayfield Deer* (1941), *The Country Year* (1946), *New Poems* (1948) and *Spring Birth* (1953). He collaborated with (1) in *American and British Literature Since 1890* (1925), edited the *Oxford Book of American Prose*, wrote critical studies of Thoreau (1916), Dryden (1920), Shakespeare (1939) and Hawthorne (1949), and the novels *Transients* (1935) and *Windless Cabins* (1940). His wife, **Dorothy Graffe** (1896–   ), was also novelist and editor.

VAN DYCK, Sir Anthony, -*dīk* (1599–1641), Flemish painter, one of the great masters of portraiture of the 17th century, was born March 22 at Antwerp, the son of a cloth manufacturer. He studied painting under H. van Balen and Rubens, and many of his early paintings have been attributed to the latter, who greatly influenced his style. In 1618 he was admitted a master of the Guild of St Luke at Antwerp and in 1620 commissioned to paint the Lady Arundel (Pinakothek, Munich). He visited England, and records show that he also executed a full-length portrait of James I at Windsor. From 1621 he was in Italy. At Genoa he painted a

number of portraits, two of which, that of the *Lomellini* family and the *Knight in Black Armour*, are in the National Gallery, Edinburgh. In Rome, he painted religious subjects including an *Ascension* and an *Adoration of the Magi* for the pope, but in this field he did not rival his Italian contemporaries. By 1627 he was back in Antwerp, where he painted the *Ecstasy of St Augustine* for the monastery there, *Christ Crucified between Thieves* for the church of the Récollets at Mechlin, later transferred to the cathedral, and the portraits of Philippe Le Roy and his wife (Wallace, London). His fine draughtsmanship is apparent in the heads he etched for his *Iconographia* (1641; British Museum). At The Hague he painted the Prince of Orange and his family. In 1632 he came to London, was knighted by Charles I, who made him a painter-in-ordinary with a pension of £200 to induce him to stay. Back in Holland on leave (1634–35), he painted Ferdinand of Austria (Madrid) and *The Deposition* (Antwerp). His flair for, and psychological accuracy in, rendering the character of his sitters, always with a hint of flattery and in the most favourable settings, greatly influenced the great British school of portraiture in the next century and imparted to posterity a thoroughly romantic glimpse of the Stuart monarchy. Among the best of these portraits are the large group of Charles I, Queen Henrietta Maria and the two royal children, the equestrian portrait of the king, the three aspects of the king (1637) to serve as a model for Bernini's sculpture (all at Windsor) and the magnificent *Le Roi à la chasse* (Louvre). There is a remarkable self-portrait in the Uffizi, Florence, a full-length of Henrietta Maria (Hermitage, Stalingrad) and portraits of most of the notables of the time, including Strafford and Archbishop Laud. In 1639 he married Mary Ruthven, a granddaughter of the Earl of Gowrie. His scheme for decorating the banqueting hall in Whitehall with scenes from the history of the Order of the Garter was turned down and he failed to obtain the commission for the decoration of the gallery of the Louvre, which went to Poussin. An amorous, extravagant courtier, he died in his studio at Blackfriars, December 9, 1641, and was buried in Old St Paul's. See studies by L. Cust (1900 and 1902), on the etchings F. Newbolt (1906), E. Schaeffer (1909), A. M. Hind (1923), H. Knackfuss (1923), A. L. Mayer (1923) and G. Glück (1931).

VAN DYKE, Henry (1852–1933), American clergyman and writer, born at Germantown, Pa., studied theology at Princeton and Berlin and was a prominent pastor of the Brick Presbyterian Church, New York (1883–1890). He was professor of English Literature at Princeton (1900–23), and under Woodrow Wilson, American minister to the Netherlands (1913–16). He was awarded the Legion of Honour for his services as naval chaplain in World War I. His many writings include poems, essays and short stories, mostly on religious themes, such as the Christmas tale *The Story of the other Wise Man, The Ruling Passion* (1901), *The Blue Flower* (1902), *The Unknown Quantity* (1912) and *Collected Poems* (1911). His brother Paul (1859–1933) was professor of History at Princeton (1898–1928).

VANE, Sir Henry (1613–62), English statesman, was born at Hadlow, Kent. His father ' Old Sir Henry ' (1589–1654), was a bustling and time-serving statesman, who rose to be principal secretary of state, but who, having, with his son, been a chief agent in Strafford's destruction, was deprived of his offices, and sided thereafter with the triumphant party. Passing in 1628 from Westminster to Magdalen Hall, Oxford, ' Young Sir Henry ' seems there to have embraced those republican principles for which he afterwards became so famous. His travels to Vienna and Geneva (1631) confirmed his aversion to the Church of England, and in 1635 he sailed for New England. He was chosen governor of Massachusetts; but his advocacy of toleration, and bias to the Antinomian views of Anne Hutchinson (q.v.), soon robbed him of his popularity, and in 1637 he returned to England. In 1640 he entered parliament for Hull, was made joint treasurer of the navy, and was knighted (1640). When the Civil War broke out no man was more conspicuous in military and theological politics than Vane, the close friend of Pym and Hampden. He relinquished the profits of his office (equivalent now to £30,000 per annum); he carried to the Upper House the articles of impeachment against Laud; he was a ' great promoter of the Solemn League and Covenant ' (though in his heart he abhorred both it and presbytery, and used them solely to attain his ends); with Cromwell he engineered the Self-denying Ordinance and the New Model (1644–45); and through the ten years 1643–53 he was unmistakably the civil leader—' that in the state ', said his enemy Baxter, ' which Cromwell was in the field '. But he had no share in the execution of the king, and, though a close friend of Cromwell, he did not view with satisfaction the growing power of Cromwell and the army. On the establishment of the Commonwealth he was appointed one of the Council of State; but it was largely Cromwell's dislike of his redistribution bill (1653) that prompted the dissolution of the ' Rump '. Retiring to his Durham seat, Raby Castle, he wrote his *Healing Question* (1656), whose hostility to the protectorate brought him four months' imprisonment in Carisbrooke Castle. On Cromwell's death he returned to public life, but in the July following the Restoration was arrested and sent to the Tower. Thence he was taken to the Scilly Islands, brought back to be tried for high treason, and on June 14, 1662, beheaded upon Tower Hill. His youngest son was raised to the peerage by William III. Vane was a singular compound of high-minded, far-seeing statesman and fanatical Fifth Monarchist. See Lives by Sikes (1662), Upham (1835), Forster (1840), Hosmer, Ireland (1907), Willcock (1913).

VAN GOGH, Vincent Willem (1853–1890), Dutch post-Impressionist painter, goꜱʜ born March 30 at Groot-Zundert, the son of a Lutheran pastor. At sixteen he became an assistant (1869–76) with Goupil and Co., the international firm of art-dealers in their shops in The Hague, London and Paris. An unrequited love affair with an English schoolmistress accentuated his inferiority complex and religious passion. He became an assistant master at Ramsgate and Isleworth (1876) and there trained unsuccessfully to become a Methodist preacher. His family rescued him from despair as a bookshop assistant at Dortrecht and provided him with tuition for the university entrance examination (1877–78), which he finally never sat. He became instead an evangelist for a religious society requiring no academic qualifications at the Belgian coalmining centre of Le Borinage (1878–80), where, first as a resident, later as an itinerant preacher, he practised the Christian virtues with such zeal, sleeping on the floor of a derelict hut and giving away his possessions, that his society became alarmed at his lack of dignity, the mine-owners at his support for strikers, and the miners mocked him for his confessions in public. In April 1881 he at last set off for Brussels to study art, but another unfortunate love affair, this time with a cousin, threw him off balance and he eventually settled at The Hague, where he lived with his model Christien or ' Sien ', a prostitute, whom he chivalrously insisted on marrying when he found her to be pregnant by another man. She appears in the drawing *Sorrow* (1882; Stedelijk, Amsterdam) and *Sien Posing* (1883; Kröller-Müller, Otterlo), but proved a worthless wife. Convalescing at Drenthe from malnutrition and general neglect, Van Gogh became the object of love of another woman, whom he rejected and who tried to commit suicide. In his father's new parish at Nuenen he painted that dark, haunting, domestic scene of peasant poverty, *The Potato Eaters* (1885), his first masterpiece, and *Boots*, both in the Stedelijk, Amsterdam. His devoted brother, Théo, now an art dealer, made it possible to continue his studies in Paris (1886–88) under Cormon, and there he met Gauguin, Toulouse-Lautrec, Seurat and the famous art-collector Tanguy, who is the subject, surrounded by Japanese woodcuts, of one of Van Gogh's remarkable portraits (1887–88; Rodin, Paris). These new influences brightened his palette and on Lautrec's advice he left Paris in February 1888 to seek the intense colours of the Provençal landscape at Arles, the subject of many of his best works. There also he painted *Sunflowers* (1888; Tate, London), *The Bridge* (1888; Cologne), *The Chair and the Pipe* (1888; Tate, London) and invited Gauguin to found a community of artists. Gauguin's stay ended in a tragic quarrel in which Van Gogh in remorse for having threatened the other with a razor, cut off his own ear and was placed in an asylum at St Rémy (1889–90). There he painted the grounds, the *Ravine* (1889; Kröller-Müller Hoenderlo) with increasingly frantic brushstrokes, the keeper and the physician. In May 1890 he went to live at Auvers-sur-Oise near Paris, under the supervision of a physician, *Dr Paul Gachet* (1890; N.Y.), himself an amateur painter and engraver. That year an exhaustive article appeared by A. Aurier which at last brought Van Gogh some recognition. But on July 27, 1890, Van Gogh shot himself at the scene of his last painting, the foreboding *Cornfields with Flight of Birds* (Stedelijk, Amsterdam), and died two days later. Théo, deeply shocked at the news, followed his brother to the grave within six months. Van Gogh was one of the pioneers of Expressionism. He used colour primarily for its emotive appeal and profoundly influenced the Fauves and other experimenters of 20th-century art. See his *Complete Letters* (1958), E. du Q. Van Gogh, *Personal Recollections* (trans. 1913), Lives by J. Meier-Graefe (trans. 1927), P. Burra (trans. 1934), C. Nordenfalk (1953), L. and E. Hanson (1955), studies by J. de Laprade (1953), D. Cooper (1955), F. Elgar (1958), and I. Stone, *Lust for Life*, the popular novel (1935) and film (1957).

VAN GOYEN, Jan Josephszoon (1596–1656), Dutch painter, was born at Leyden. He produced many sea and river pieces in soft browns and greys, and, unusually for his time, omitted small details and developed a broad atmospheric effect. Jan Steen, who became his son-in-law, was one of his pupils. His *River Scene* (c. 1645) is in the National Gallery, London.

VANHOMRIGH, Esther. See SWIFT.

VANINI, Lucilio, *van-ee'nee* (1585–1619), Italian freethinker, born at Taurisano, studied the new learning and science at Naples and Padua, and took orders, but his ' Naturalist ' views soon brought him into collision with the church. Having taught in France, Switzerland and the Low Countries, he had to flee in 1614 to England, where he was again imprisoned. Finally, at Toulouse, having first had his tongue cut out, he was strangled and burned. From his *Amphitheatrum Aeternae Providentiae* (1615) and his *De Admirandis Naturae Arcanis* (1616) it is plain that, if not an atheist, he taught pantheism of an extreme type. He was more notable for vanity and audacity than for learning or originality. See monographs by Fuhrmann (Leipzig 1800), Vaisse (Paris 1871), and Palumbo (Naples 1878), and John Owen, *Skeptics of the Italian Renaissance* (1893).

VANLOO, -lō', (1) **Jean Baptiste** (1684–1745), French painter, brother of (2), born at Aix-en-Provence of Flemish parentage, studied in Rome and became a fashionable portrait painter in Paris, being admitted a member of the Academy (1731) and appointed professor of Painting (1735). In 1737 he visited England, where he painted the actor Colley Cibber, the Prince and Princess of Wales and Sir Robert Walpole.

(2) **Charles André** (1705–65), French painter, brother of (1), born at Nice, likewise studied at Rome and settled as portrait painter in Paris but executed also some sculpture. He became chief painter to Louis XV and member of the Academy (1735). His vigorous, colourful majestic style gave rise to a new French verb ' vanlooter '. He painted Diderot, Helvétius and most of the celebrities of his day.

VAN LOON, Hendrik Willem, *lōn* (1882–1944), Dutch-born American popular historian, born in Rotterdam, emigrated to the United States in 1903 as a journalist and history teacher and in 1922 published the best selling, illustrated *Story of Mankind*, and from then onwards produced a number of popular histories.

VAN MEEGEREN, Han or Henricus, *may'gér-èn* (1889–1947), Dutch artist and forger, was born at Deventer. In 1945 he was accused of selling art treasures to the Germans. To clear himself, he confessed to having forged the pictures, and also the famous *Supper at Emmaus*, ' discovered ' in 1937, and accepted by the majority of experts as by Vermeer. His fakes were subjected to a detailed scientific examination, and in 1947 their maker was sentenced to twelve months' imprisonment for forgery. He died a few weeks later. He was an extremely skilful craftsman, and was reputed to have made about £600,000 by the sale of his fakes. See studies by Coremans (1949) and Lord Kilbracken (1968), Decoen's *Back to the Truth* (1951), and *Vermeer Forgeries* by Baesjou (1956).

VANNUCCI. See PERUGINO.

VAN RENSSELAER, Stephen, *ren'sel-ler* (1765–1839), American statesman, eighth ' patroon ' of the vast estate near Albany, born in New York, was a leader of the Federalists in his state, and served in congress (1823–29). In the war of 1812 he held command on the northern frontier, and captured Queenston Heights; but the refusal of his militia to cross the Niagara enabled the British to recover the place, and he resigned. He promoted the construction of the Erie and Champlain canals and founded the Rensselaer Technical Institute (1826).

VANSITTART, -sit'-, (1) **Nicholas, 1st Baron Bexley** (1766–1851), English statesman, son of Henry (1732–70), a governor of Bengal of Dutch extraction, became a Tory chancellor of the Exchequer (1812–23) and in 1823 was raised to the peerage.

(2) **Robert Gilbert, 1st Baron Vansittart of Denham** (1881–1957), British diplomat, descended from Henry (see (1)), educated at Eton, joined the diplomatic service in 1902 and served successively in Paris, Teheran, Cairo and Stockholm with intervals at the Foreign Office. From 1920 to 1924 he was private secretary to Lord Curzon and in 1930 became permanent under-secretary for foreign affairs. He visited Germany in 1936, talked with Hitler and his henchmen and became the uncompromising opponent of Nazi Germany. His warnings of coming catastrophe unless Britain armed to meet the German menace—warnings expressed with undiplomatic pungency—put him at variance in 1937 with Neville Chamberlain. On January 1, 1938, he was steered into a backwater as ' chief diplomatic adviser to the Government '. He retired in 1941, and was raised to the peerage. He threw himself into parliamentary work, authorship and journalism, fiercely denouncing Nazidom and ridiculing the ' myth ' of the ' two Germanys ' (good and bad). After the war he was no less active in exposing Communist methods, lashing out at injustice and illuminating the shortcomings of statesmen. See his *The Singing Caravan* (poems, 1933); *Black*

Record (1941); *Lessons of My Life* (1943); and his autobiography, *The Mist Procession* (1958).

VAN'T HOFF. See HOFF.

VAN TIEGHEM, Philippe, *tyay-gem'* (1839–1914), French botanist and biologist, well known for his studies of myxomycetes, bacteria, &c., and a new classification of plants.

VAN VEEN, Otto, *vayn* (*c.* 1556–1634), Dutch painter, born at Leyden, settled first at Brussels, later at Antwerp, where Rubens was his pupil. The name Van Veen is also sometimes given to the Haarlem painter, **Martin van Heemskerk** (1498–1574), whose *Ecce Homo* and *Holy Family* are at Haarlem. Hampton Court Palace also has examples of his work.

VANZETTI. See SACCO.

VARDON, Harry (1870–1937), British golfer, born at Grouville in Jersey, first won the British Open Championship in 1896, a success which was repeated five times in 1898, 1899, 1903, 1911 and 1914. Winner of the American championship in 1900, he became a professional in 1903, and other triumphs included the winning of the German Open in 1911 and the *News of the World* Tournament in 1912. His graceful style had a lasting influence and he is remembered also for the grip, which though not original, was popularized by him and is still known as the ' Vardon grip '. He was the author of *The Complete Golfer* (1905), *How to Play Golf* (1912) and *My Golfing Life* (1933).

VARÈSE, Edgar (1885–1965), American composer of Italo-French parentage, born in Paris, studied under Roussel, D'Indy and Widor in Paris, and later under Busoni. Until World War I, Varèse was active in movements to bring music to the French people, and after two years' service in the French Army, he settled in New York, where in 1919 he founded the New Symphony Orchestra to further the cause of modern music, and in 1921 organized the International Composers' Guild, which has become the leading organ of progressive musicians. Varèse's work is almost entirely orchestral, often using unconventional percussion instruments, and its abstract nature is demonstrated by such titles as *Metal, Ionisation* and *Hyperprism.*

VARGAS, Getulio Dornelles (1883–1954), president of Brazil, born at São Borja in southern Brazil, was elected Federal deputy for his native province in 1923. In 1930 he seized power by revolution. From 1937, when he dissolved congress and suppressed all political parties and trade unions, he governed as dictator. In 1945 he was ousted by popular clamour for a new and democratic constitution, but under this in 1950 was voted back to office. Four years later, believed to be planning a new *coup d'état*, he was compelled to resign. He then shot himself. See K. Loewenstein, *Brazil under Vargas.*

VARLEY, a versatile English family of engineers and artists. Of this family:

(1) **Cornelius** (1781–1873), watercolour painter, invented the graphic telescope, experimented in electricity, and exhibited at the Academy and Watercolour Society.

(2) **Cromwell Fleetwood** (1828–83), the son of (1), was an electrical engineer, who invented a double-current key and relay used in telegraphy, and helped to renew the transatlantic cable (1858).

(3) **John** (1778–1842), a watercolourist, the brother of (1) and (4), was born at Hackney. He was a highly successful teacher, exhibited at the R.A., and was a founder member of the Watercolour Society. A friend of William Blake, he was also interested in astrology and wrote on perspective. See *Life* by Bury (1946).

(4) **William Fleetwood** (1785–1856), younger brother of (1) and (3), was also a watercolourist, and wrote on *Colouring* (1820).

VARNHAGEN, Francisco Adolpho de, Viscount de Porto Seguro, *farn'hah-gèn* (1816–1878), Brazilian historian, born at São João de Ypanema, São Paulo, spent his youth in Portugal but took Brazilian nationality in 1841, afterwards holding several diplomatic posts. Amongst his works are a *History of Brazil* (1854–57) and monographs on Amerigo Vespucci.

VARNHAGEN VON ENSE, Karl August, *en'zè* (1785–1858), German writer, born at Düsseldorf, in 1809 joined the Austrian army and was wounded at Wagram. In 1813, he passed over to the Russian service, and went to Paris as adjutant. Here he was called to the Prussian diplomatic service, and accompanied Hardenberg to the Congress of Vienna (1814) and to Paris, becoming next resident minister at Karlsruhe (till 1819). He had married in 1814 the Jewess Rahel (q.v.). He wrote Lives of Goethe (1823), Marshal Keith (1844), Gen. von Bülow (1853), &c.; *Biographische Denkmäler* (1824–1830), and *Denkwürdigkeiten* (1843–59). His Correspondence and Diaries fill 22 vols. (1860–70). See *Life* by Misch (1926), and letters to him by Humboldt (1860) and Carlyle (1892).

VARRO, (1) Marcus Terentius (116–27 B.C.), Roman scholar and author, born at Reate, studied at Athens, saw service under Pompey, and in the Civil War was legate in Spain. He awaited the result of Pharsalia with Cicero and Cato at Dyrrachium, and was kindly treated by the conqueror, who appointed him librarian. Under the second triumvirate Antony plundered his villa, burned his books, and placed his name on the list of the proscribed. But he was soon exempted, and Augustus restored his property. A man of upright and honourable character, he survived till 27 B.C. His total works amounted to 620 books. Of the poems we know nothing but the names. But of the 150 books of the *Saturae Menippeae,* a medley of prose and verse, fragments (ed. Bücheler, 1882) remain. His prose writings embraced oratory, history, jurisprudence, grammar, philosophy, geography and husbandry. The chief were *Antiquitates Rerum Humanarum et Divinarum*; *De Lingua Latina,* of whose twenty-five books only v–x are extant (ed. Goetz and Schoell, Leipzig 1910); and *Rerum Rusticarum Libri III,* almost entire (ed. Goetz, 1912). His *Disciplinarum Libri IX* was an encyclopaedia of the liberal arts; his *Imagines,* or *Hebdomades,* a series of 700

Greek and Roman biographies. His works are translated in the Loeb edition (1912).

(2) Publius Terentius (c. 82–37 B.C.), Roman author, called Atacinus from his birth at Atax in Narbonensian Gaul, wrote satires and an epic on Caesar's Gallic wars. His *Argonautica* was an adaptation of Apollonius Rhodius; his erotic elegies pleased Propertius.

VARUS, Publius Quintilius (d. A.D. 9), Roman official, consul in 13 B.C., as governor of Syria suppressed the revolt of Judaea, and in A.D. 9 was sent by Augustus to command in Germany. Utterly routed by Arminius (q.v.), he killed himself.

VASA. See GUSTAVUS I.

VASARI, Giorgio, *va-zah'ree* (1511–74), Italian art historian, born at Arezzo, studied under Michelangelo, and lived mostly at Florence and Rome. He was a greater architect than painter; but today his fame rests on his *Vite de' più eccellenti Pittori, Scultori, e Architettori* (1550; Eng. trans. by G. de Vere, 10 vols. 1912–15). In spite of inaccuracies in the earlier biographies, it remains a model of art criticism and biography. See Life by Carden (1910).

VASCO DA GAMA. See GAMA.

VASCONCELOS, Caroline Michaelis De, *vash-kōn-se'loosh* (1851–1925), Portuguese scholar and writer, born in Berlin, studied and wrote on romance, philology and literature. An honorary professor of Hamburg University, she lived, after her marriage, in 1876, in Oporto, where she did much scholarly research on the Portuguese language, its literature, and especially its folk literature. Most noteworthy is her edition of the late 13th or early 14th century *Cancioneiro da Ajuda*. Other writings include *Notas Vicentinas* (1912), an edition of the poetry of Sá de Miranda, and essays, studies and correspondence with other Portuguese scholars.

VATTEL, Emmerich de, *fah'tèl* (1714–67), Swiss jurist, born at Couret in Neuchâtel, entered the diplomatic service of Saxony, and was Saxon representative at Bern (1746–64). His *Droits des gens* (1758; trans. 1834) systematized the doctrines of Grotius, Puffendorf and Wolf.

VAUBAN, Sébastien le Prestre de, *vō-bā* (1633–1707), French military engineer, born at Saint Léger near Avallon, May 1, enlisted under Condé, and followed him into the service of Spain. Taken prisoner in 1653, he was persuaded by Mazarin to enter the French king's service; by 1658 he was chief engineer under Turenne; and eight years of peace he devoted to works at Dunkirk and elsewhere. In 1667 he helped to reduce Lille; in 1672–78 in the Netherlands he took part in seventeen sieges and one defence. He introduced the method of approach by parallels at the siege of Maestricht (1673) with great effect; notable also were his defence of Oudenarde and the sieges of Valenciennes and Cambrai. During 1678–88 he surrounded the kingdom with a cordon of fortresses; and he planned the magnificent aqueduct of Maintenon. He invented the socket bayonet (1687). In 1703 he became marshal of France. He conducted the sieges of Philippsburg (1688)—introduc-

ing here his invention of ricochet-batteries— Mannheim, Mons (1691), Namur (1692), Charleroi (1693), Ath (1697) and Breisach (1704), and constructed the entrenched camp near Dunkirk (1706). After the peace of Ryswick in 1697 he had applied himself to study the faults in the government of France. His *Dîme royale* (1707), in which he discussed the question of taxation and anticipated the doctrines which eighty years later overthrew the French monarchy, was condemned and prohibited. He died March 30, 1707. See *Lettres intimes inédites* (1924), and Lives by G. Michel (1879) and R. Blomfield (1938).

VAUGELAS, Claude Favre de, *vōzh-la* (1585–1650), French grammarian, author of *Remarques sur la langue française* (1647), was a founder of the French Academy.

VAUGHAN, yawn, (1) Benjamin (1751–1835), British diplomat, born in Jamaica, promoted unofficially the Anglo-American peace negotiations (1782), settled in Maine, carried out agricultural research and corresponded with the first six presidents. Parts of his library he left to Harvard and Bowdoin.

(2) Charles John (1816–97), English divine, born in Leicester, elected fellow of Trinity College, Cambridge, he was vicar of St Martin's Leicester (1841–44); headmaster of Harrow (1844–59); vicar of Doncaster (1860–1869); master of the Temple (1869–94); and Dean of Llandaff from 1879. An eloquent preacher of the Liberal evangelical school, he prepared in his home a large number of men for ordination, popularly known as 'Vaughan's Doves'.

(3) Henry (1622–95), Welsh religious poet, the self styled 'Silurist' as a native of South Wales, the land of the old Silures, was born at Newton-by-Usk, Llansaintfraed, Breconshire, twin-brother of the alchemist Thomas Vaughan (1622–66). He entered Jesus College, Oxford, in 1638, and in 1646 published *Poems, with the tenth Satyre of Juvenal Englished*. He took his M.D., and practised first at, then near, Brecon. The collection of poems entitled *Olor Iscanus* was published by his brother without authority in 1651. In 1650–55 he printed his *Silex Scintillans*, pious meditations, and in 1652 *The Mount of Olives*, devotions in prose, and the *Flores Solitudinis*, also in prose. *Thalia Rediviva: the Pastimes and Diversions of a Country Muse*, a collection of elegies, translations, religious pieces, &c., was also published without authority (1678) by a friend. He died at his birthplace, April 23, 1695. Vaughan's poetry is very unequal; at his best he reaches an exquisite fantasy of expression beyond the reach of George Herbert. See Life by F. E. Hutchinson (1947) and studies by E. Blunden (1927), E. Holmes (1932), R. Garner (1960), and H. R. Ashton, *The Swan of Usk* (1940).

(4) Herbert (1832–1903), English Roman Catholic divine, born at Gloucester, was educated at Stonyhurst and at Rome, entered the priesthood in 1854, and in 1872 was consecrated Bishop of Salford. In 1892 he succeeded Manning as Archbishop of Westminster, next year was raised to the cardinalate, and died June 19, 1903. He was founder of St Joseph's College for foreign missions at Mill Hill, was responsible for the building of Westminster Cathedral, and proprietor of the *Tablet* and the *Dublin Review*. See Life by J. G. Snead-Cox (1910). His brother, **Roger William Bede** (1834–83), Archbishop of Sydney from 1877, wrote a Life of Aquinas (1871–72). Another brother, **Bernard** (1847–1922), was a notable preacher.

(5) **Keith** (1912–   ), English artist, was born at Selsey Bill. He was associated with the younger Romantic artists influenced by Graham Sutherland. In 1951 he executed a large mural in the Festival of Britain Dome of Discovery, and he illustrated several books. His works (mainly of figures and landscape) are represented in the Tate Gallery, London, and the Museum of Modern Art, New York.

(6) **Robert** (1795–1868), British divine and historian, born in Wales, was Independent minister at Worcester and Kensington, professor of History in London University (1830–43), and president of the Independent College at Manchester (1843–57). He founded the *British Quarterly* in 1845, and edited it till 1867. Among his books are *Life of Wycliffe* (1828), *History of England under the Stuarts* (1840) and *Revolutions in History* (1859–63).

(7) **William** (1577–1641), British poet and colonizer, born in S. Wales, graduated at Jesus College, Oxford (1597), and bought an interest in Newfoundland, where he sent out settlers in 1617. He wrote an allegory *The Golden Fleece* (1626) and other works.

VAUGHAN WILLIAMS, Ralph (1872–1958), English composer, was born October 12 at Down Ampney, Gloucestershire. His early aptitude for music was encouraged by his parents and at Charterhouse School. He subsequently worked under Stanford at the Royal College of Music, under Max Bruch in Berlin and under Ravel in Paris. The essentially English character of all Vaughan Williams' music, unaffected by the European influence which still clung to the work of Stanford and Parry, makes him the first fundamentally national composer since the 16th century. In touch from the start with the English choral tradition, his first success was the choral *Sea Symphony* (1910), set to words of Walt Whitman, in which traditional choral styles were married to a vigorously contemporary outlook. Under the influence of Gustav Holst, Vaughan Williams became an enthusiastic leader in the English folksong movement, adding this tradition to the number of influences—Tudor church music, the choral and orchestral styles of Parry and the refinement gained from Ravel's teaching—that were assimilated in his own work. Of his early orchestral music his *Fantasia on a Theme of Tallis* (1909) for strings is noteworthy and is the work performed most regularly by orchestras outside Britain. Between the *London Symphony* (1914) and the *Pastoral Symphony* (1922), came a large number of works in all forms, vigorous and exploratory in style and including the ballad opera *Hugh the Drover* (1911–14). The ballet *Job* (1930) opened a new chapter in the composer's career, notable for its obvious concern with the moral issues of contemporary life, and it was followed by seven further symphonies (with their varied interests ranging from prophecy in the *Fourth, Fifth and Sixth*, to sheer delight in experimental sonorities in the *Eighth* and *Ninth*), the opera *The Pilgrim's Progress* (1948–49) and numerous choral works. The wide range, exploratory vigour and innate honesty of Vaughan Williams' work was illustrated by his ability to provide music of equal excellence for hymns, for the stage (as for Aristophanes' *The Wasps* (1909), and for films such as *49th Parallel* and *Scott of the Antarctic*. During World War I he served with the R.A.M.C. and with the Artillery; from 1905 onwards he was director of the Leith Hill Festival and in 1935 he was awarded the O.M. His artistic credo is contained in his books *National Music* (1934) and *Beethoven's Choral Symphony and Other Papers*. See studies by H. J. Foss (1950), F. Howes (1954) and S. Pakenham (1957) and Life by his wife, with study (1964).

VAUQUELIN, Louis Nicolas, *vōk-lĭ* (1763–1829), French chemist, was born and died at St André d'Hébertot, rose from laboratory assistant to be professor of Chemistry at Paris (1809). In 1798 he discovered chromium and its compounds, later beryllium compounds and asparagine.

VAUVENARGUES, Luc de Clapiers, Marquis de, *vōv-narg* (1715–47), French moralist, born at Aix, entered the army in 1733, fought at Dettingen, but retired in impaired health in 1743 to settle at Paris. In 1746 he published, anonymously, his *Introduction à la connaissance de l'esprit humain,* with *Réflexions et maximes* appended. In these he singles out the love of fame, courage and energy as noble virtues, tempered by humane sympathies for one's fellow men. To scientific and social progress, he remained curiously indifferent. See Lives by M. Wallas (1928), G. Lanson (1930) and F. Vial (1938).

VAVILOV, (1) Nikolai Ivanovich (1887–1943), Russian plant geneticist, brother of (2), was appointed to direct Soviet agricultural research by Lenin in 1930. He established 400 research institutes and built up a collection of 26,000 species and varieties of wheat. This enabled him to formulate the principle of diversity, which postulates that, geographically, the centre of greatest diversity represents the origin of a plant. Vavilov's international reputation was challenged by the politico-scientific 'theories' of Lysenko (q.v.), who denounced him at a Genetics Conference (1937) and gradually usurped Vavilov's position. The latter died in disgrace, allegedly in a Siberian concentration camp. He was made a foreign member of the Royal Society (1942).

(2) **Sergei** (1891–1951), Russian physicist, brother of (1), was born in Moscow, studied physics at the University there and researched into luminescent materials. He was president of the Soviet Academy of Sciences from 1945, chief editor of the Soviet Encyclopaedia and was twice awarded the Stalin prize.

VAZOV, Ivan (1850–1921), Bulgarian national poet, born at Sopot, wrote a collection of poems and songs under the title *Sorrows of Bulgaria* and *Under the Yoke* and other novels. He was twice exiled from his native land for his nationalist sympathies, but became minister of education in 1897.

VEBLEN, Thorsten (1857–1929), American sociologist, born at Cato, Wis., lectured in Economics in Chicago, Stanford, Missouri and New York and is best known for his *The Theory of the Leisure Class* (1899), *The Theory of Business Enterprise* (1904), *Engineers and the Price System* (1921), &c. See Life by J. A. Hobson (1936).

VECELLIO. See TITIAN.

VEDDER, (1) **David** (1790–1854), Scottish poet, sailor and custom-house officer, was born at Deerness, Orkney, and died in Edinburgh.

(2) **Elihu** (1836–1923), American painter, born at New York, studied at Paris and in Italy, settling in Rome. He executed *Minerva* and other murals in the Library of Congress, Washington, and illustrated the Rubáiyát of Omar Khayyám.

VEEN. See VAN VEEN.

VEGA. See GARCILASO DE LA VEGA.

VEGA CARPIO, Lope Félix de, *vay'gah kahr'pyō* (1562–1635), Spanish dramatist and poet, born at Madrid, November 25, lost his parents early; was a student and graduate of Alcalá; served in the Portuguese campaign of 1580 and in the Armada; was secretary to the Duke of Alva, Marquis of Malpica, and Marquis of Sarria; had many amours, was twice married, and begot at least six children, three of them illegitimate; was banished from Madrid because of a quarrel, and lived two years at Valencia; took orders, became an officer of the Inquisition; and died August 27, 1635, a victim to hypochondria. He died poor, for his large income from his dramas and other sources was all but wholly devoted to charity and church purposes. The mere list of Lope's works presents a picture of unparalleled mental activity. His first work of any length was a poem, the *Angelica*, written at sea in 1588, but not printed till 1602. The *Arcadia*, the story, in a pompous, pastoral setting, of the prenuptial vagaries of the Duke of Alva, was written before the duke's marriage, July 1590, but it was kept back till 1598. The *Dragontea*, a shout of exultation in ten cantos over the death of the Dragon (Drake) appeared the same year, and was Lope's first publication under his name. But it was as a ballad-writer that he first made his mark. The more notable of his miscellaneous works are the *Rimas* (1602); *Peregrino en su Patria* (1604), a romance; *Jerusalén Conquistada* (1609), an epic in competition with Tasso; *Pastores de Belén* (1612), a religious pastoral; *Filomena* and *Circe* (1621–24), miscellanies in emulation of Cervantes; *Corona Trágica* (1627), an epic on Mary Stuart; *Laurel de Apolo* (1630); *Rimas de Tomé de Burguillos* (1634), a collection of lighter verse, with the *Gatomaquia*, a mock-heroic. *Dorotea* (1632), in form a prose drama, is obviously the story of his own early love adventures. All these works show the hand, not of a great artist, but of a consummate artificer. Lope was a master of easy, flowing, musical, graceful verse; but he rarely passes the frontier line into true poetry. Though he had written plays, he did not become a writer for the stage

until after 1588. He gave the public what it wanted—excitement pure and simple; with a boundless invention, he could string striking situations and ingenious complications one after another without stop or stay, and keep the audience breathless and the stage in a bustle for three long acts, all without sign of effort. Imagination and creative power were not among his gifts; his *dramatis personae* have seldom more individuality than a batch of puppets. Lope's plays may be roughly divided into the historical or quasi-historical and those that deal with everyday life. Of the latter the most characteristic are the ' cloak and sword plays '. The *Noche de San Juan*, one of his very last plays; the *Maestro de Danzar*, one of his first; and the *Azero de Madrid*, the source clearly of Molière's *Médecin malgré lui*, are excellent specimens. His peculiarities and excellences may be studied with advantage in such plays as the *Perro del hortelano*, *Desprecio agradecido*, *Esclava de su Galán*, *Premio del bien hablar*; and no student of Calderón should overlook the *Alcalde de Zalamea*, a bold vigorous outline which was filled in in Calderón's famous play. The number of Lope's plays seems to have been 1500, exclusive of 400 *autos*. Of these the very names of all but between 600 and 700 have been lost, and often nothing but the name survives. We have about 440 plays and 40 *autos* in print or MS. See Life by H. A. Rennert (1904), studies by K. Vossler (1933) and M. Romera-Navarro (1935), and chronology of his works, ed. Morley and Bruerton (1940).

VEGETIUS (Flavius Vegetius Renatus), *ve-jee'shus*, Latin writer, produced after A.D. 375 the *Epitome Institutionum Rei Militaris*, mainly extracted from other authors, which during the Middle Ages was a supreme authority on warfare.

VEIT, Philipp, *fīt* (1793–1877), German painter, was born at Berlin. His mother, daughter of Moses Mendelssohn, had for her second husband Friedrich Schlegel, and Veit embraced the ideas of his stepfather. Like him he turned Catholic, and, settling at Rome in 1815, became conspicuous among the young German painters who sought to infuse into modern art the earnestness of mediaeval times. His first famous work was the *Seven Years of Plenty* for the Villa Bartholdy. In 1830 he became director of the Art Institute at Frankfurt-am-Main. Here he painted the large fresco, *Christianity bringing the Fine Arts to Germany*. See Life by M. Spahn (1901).

VEITCH, *veech,* (1) **John** (1829–94), Scottish author, born at Peebles, studied at Edinburgh, and became professor of Logic and Rhetoric at St Andrews (1860), and then at Glasgow (1864). His works include Lives of Dugald Stewart (1857) and Sir W. Hamilton (1869), *Tweed and other Poems* (1875), *History and Poetry of the Scottish Border* (1877; new ed. 1893), *Feeling for Nature in Scottish Poetry* (1887), *Merlin and other Poems* (1889), *Dualism and Monism* (1895) and *Border Essays* (1896). See his Life by Mary Bryce (1896).

(2) **William** (1794–1885), Scottish classical

scholar, born at Spittal near Jedburgh, qualified for the Scottish ministry, but devoted himself to a life of scholarship at Edinburgh, his chief work the invaluable *Greek Verbs Irregular and Defective* (1848; 4th ed. 1878). He revised Liddell and Scott's *Greek Lexicon*, Smith's *Latin Dictionary*, &c.

VELASQUEZ, Diego de Silva y, *vay-las'keth* (1599–1660), one of the great Spanish masters, was born at Seville. He may have studied under Herrera, but in 1613 he did become the pupil of Francisco Pacheco, an indifferent painter but considerable art historian, whose daughter he married in 1618 and who in his *Art of Painting* provides an account of the young Velasquez. In 1618 Velasquez set up his own studio. His early works were *bodegónes*, characteristically Spanish domestic genre pieces, of which *Old Woman Cooking Eggs* (1618; National Gallery, Edinburgh) is a typical example. In 1622 he tried his luck at court in Madrid and persuaded Góngora (Boston) the poet to sit for him. The following year he achieved lifelong court patronage with his equestrian portrait, since lost, of Philip IV, who had all other portraits of himself withdrawn. The other court artists accused Velasquez of being incapable of painting anything but heads. The king ordered a competition on an historical subject, which Velasquez won with his *Expulsion of the Moriscos by Philip III*, now lost. In 1628 Rubens visited Madrid and befriended him. His advice and the palace collection of Italian art encouraged Velasquez's visit to Italy (1629–31). His sombre, austere, naturalistic style was transformed into the lightly modelled, more colourful styles of Titian and Tintoretto, as is apparent in his *Forge of Vulcan* (*c.* 1630) and *Joseph's Coat* (1630; Escorial, Madrid) and in the new type of portrait which Velasquez improvised, of the king (*c.* 1634) or his brother, or son in hunting costume with dog and landscape. One of the most striking of his many portraits of his royal master is full-length (*c.* 1632; National Gallery, London). The only surviving historical painting is his baroque *Surrender of Breda* (*c.* 1634). There are also many portraits of the royal children, particularly *Infante Baltasar Carlos on Horseback* (1635–36), the *Infanta Margarita* (1653–54, 1656, 1659; Vienna) and the *Infanta Maria Theresa* (1652–53; Vienna), and of the court dwarfs (1644, 1655) and jester, nicknamed *Don Juan de Austria* (1652–59). In 1650 he was again in Rome to obtain art treasures for the king and there painted the portrait of *Pope Innocent X* (Doria, Rome) and the two impressionistic *Views from Villa Medici*. On his return he captured the pathetic facial expression of the new queen, the young Maria Anne of Austria, in his best feminine full-length portrait (1552). But he is best remembered for his three late masterpieces, *Las Meniñas*, 'Maids of Honour' (1656), in which the Infanta Margarita, her dwarf and attendants and the artist himself with easel are grouped around a canvas in a large palace room, hung with paintings, *Las Hilanderas*, 'The Tapestry Weavers' (*c.* 1657), and the famous *Venus and Cupid*,

known as the 'Rokeby Venus' (*c.* 1658; National Gallery, London), one of the few nudes in Spanish painting. Velasquez was appointed usher to the king's chamber (1627), superintendent of works (1643), palace chamberlain (1652) and was made a knight of the Order of Santiago (1658), the highest court award. His painting is distinguished for its unflattering realism, which nothing is imaginatively embellished or otherwise falsified, a remarkable achievement for a court painter. Goya carried on his tradition a century later and Whistler, Manet and the French Impressionists acknowledged his influence. All his above-mentioned works, unless otherwise indicated, are in the Prado, Madrid. See studies by J. Justi (trans. 1889), R. A. M. Stevenson (1895, ed. Crombie 1962), A. de Beruete (trans. 1906), J. Allende-Salazar (trans. 1925), A. L. Mayer (trans. 1936), E. Lafuente-Ferrari (1960) and J. López-Rey (1963).

VELLEIUS PATERCULUS. See PATER-CULUS.

VENANTIUS FORTUNATUS, Honorius Clementainus, St (d. *c.* 600), Latin poet, born at Ceneda, Italy, became Bishop of Poitiers and wrote *Pange lingua, Vexilla regis prodeunt,* and many other hymns. Feast day, December 14.

VENDÔME, Louis Joseph, Duc de, *vä-dōm* (1654–1712), French soldier, born at Paris, saw his first service in the Dutch campaign of 1672. He next served with distinction under Turenne in Germany and Alsace, again in the Low Countries under Luxembourg, and in Italy under Catinat; in 1695 he received the command of the army in Catalonia. He crowned a series of brilliant successes by the capture of Barcelona (1697). After five years of sloth and sensuality he superseded Villeroi in Italy. He fought an undecided battle with Prince Eugene at Luzzara (August 15), then burst into Tirol, returning to Italy to check the united Savoyards and Austrians. On August 16, 1705, he fought a second indecisive battle with Prince Eugene at Cassano, and at Calcinato he crushed the Austrians (April 19, 1706). That summer he was recalled to supersede Villeroi in the Low Countries. The defeat at Oudenarde (July 11, 1708) cost him his command, but in 1710 he was sent to Spain to aid Philip V. His appearance turned the tide of disaster; he brought the king back to Madrid, and defeated the English at Brihuega, and next day the Austrians at Villaviciosa. After a month of gluttony beyond even his wont, he died at Vinaroz in Castellón de la Plana, June 11, 1712.

VENIZELOS, Eleutherios, *vay-nyee-zay'los* (1864–1936), Greek statesman, born near Canea, Crete, studied law in Athens, led the Liberal party in the Cretan chamber of deputies and took a prominent part in the Cretan rising against the Turks in 1896. When Prince George became governor of Crete, Venizelos first served under him as minister of justice, then opposed him from the mountains at Therisso with guerilla warfare. In 1909 he was invited to Athens, became prime minister (1910–15), restored law and order but excluded the Cretan deputies from the new parliament and promoted the Balkan League, against Turkey (1912) and Bulgaria (1913) and so extended the Greek kingdom. His sympathies with France and Britain at the outbreak of World War I clashed with those of King Constantine and caused Venizelos to establish a provisional rival government at Salonika and in 1917 forced the king's abdication. He secured further territories from Turkey at the Versailles Peace Conference, but his prestige began to wane with his failure to colonize Turkish Asia Minor and he was heavily defeated in the general elections (1920) which brought the royalists and King Constantine back to power. He was prime minister again (1924, 1928–32 and 1933) and regained his ascendancy by his public works programmes and treaties with Italy and Yugoslavia. His friend General Plastiras tried unsuccessfully to establish a dictatorship during the general elections (1933) in which the Venizelists were doing badly, but Venizelos gained public sympathy once again after an unsuccessful attempt on his life, in which his wife was wounded. In 1935 he came out of retirement to support another Cretan revolt staged by his sympathizers, but it failed and he fled eventually to Paris, where he died. See his *Vindication of Greek National Policy* (1910), Lives by C. Kerofilas (1915), E. B. Chester (1921) and study by W. H. C. Price (1917).

VENN, (1) **Henry** (1725–97), English divine, father of (2), born at Barnes, vicar of Huddersfield (1759), took a prominent part with Lady Huntingdon and Whitefield in the Evangelical revival. He wrote *The Compleat Duty of Man* (1763) and other sermons.

(2) **John** (1759–1813), English divine, son of (1), born in Clapham, in 1792 became vicar there and a prominent member of the wealthy group of families with their distinctive religious and social ideals, known as the Clapham sect. In 1799 he founded the Church Missionary Society, of which his son, Henry (1796–1873), was secretary from 1841 until his death. See Life of John by M. Hennell (1958).

(3) **John** (1834–1923), English logician, developed Bode's symbolic logic and in his *Logic of Chance* (1866) the 'frequency' theory of probability.

VERBOECKHOVEN, Eugen Joseph, *ver'book-hō-ven* (1798–1881), Brussels animal-painter and etcher, noted for landscapes with sheep.

VERCINGETORIX. See CAESAR.

VERDAGUER, Mosen Jacinto, *ver'THah-ger* (1845–1902), Catalan poet, born at Folgarolas, became a priest with a vast popular following. He wrote *L'Atlántida*, and *Lo Canigó*, two epic poems of great beauty, and on the first of these Manuel de Falla based his choral work *Atlántida*. His *Idilis y Cants Místichs* (1870), also set to music, have been embodied in the music of the Catalan church.

VERDI, Giuseppe (Fortunino Francesco), *ver'dee* (1813–1901), Italian composer. Of humble rural origin—his father kept an inn and grocer's store at Le Roncole near Busseto —much of his early musical education came from Provesi, organist of Busseto cathedral.

Subsidized by local admirers of his talent, he was sent to Milan, but was rejected by the conservatoire as over age. Instead he studied profitably under Lavigna, *maestro al cembalo* at La Scala. On returning home he failed in his ambition of succeeding Provesi as cathedral organist, but was given a grant by the Philharmonic Society. Three years later he married the daughter of his friend and patron Barezzi, but wife and both children died in 1839–40. By this time his first opera, *Oberto*, had already been produced at La Scala, but it was with *Nabucco* (1842) that he achieved his first major success. Thereafter his career was one of almost continuous triumph. Although few of his pre-1850 operas apart from *Macbeth* and *Luisa Miller* remain in the normal repertory, *Rigoletto* (1851), *Il Trovatore* (1853) and *La Traviata* (1853) established unshakably his position as the leading Italian operatic composer of the day. These three works and their successors like *Un Ballo in Maschera* (1859) and *La Forza del Destino* (1862) were products of his maturity. This phase came to an end with the spectacular *Aïda*, commissioned for the new opera house in Cairo, built in celebration of the Suez Canal. Its première was in fact delayed until 1871 because of the Franco-Prussian war. Apart from the *Requiem* (1873) written in commemoration of Manzoni, there was then a lull in output until, in his old age, goaded and inspired by his brilliant literary collaborator Boito, he produced two masterpieces, *Otello* (1887) and *Falstaff* (1893). Both had their premières at La Scala, so ending nearly twenty years of feud with that theatre. Apart from some sacred choral pieces, Verdi wrote no more before his death. Though his reputation was worldwide, he stayed at heart a countryman, preferring above all to cultivate his property at Busseto in the intervals of composition. His long association with the former operatic soprano Giuseppina Strepponi, who became his wife in 1859, ensured a happy domestic context for his work. In his young days he had been an enthusiastic nationalist; some of his choruses were freely construed by patriots as being anti-Austrian, and were liable to lead to demonstrations. However, active participation in politics was not to his taste, and he soon resigned his deputyship in the first Italian parliament (1860). Later in life he became a senator. Though rich and greatly esteemed, Verdi led a simple life, and took almost as much pride in his estate management and in the founding of a home for aged musicians in Milan as in his creative work. Verdi dominated Italian opera between the Bellini-Donizetti era and that of Puccini. Over the years his methods changed from the robust melodramatic effectiveness of his youthful production to the extraordinary subtlety and sophistication of his last two operas. But at the root of his genius was his superb sense of theatre and his reservoir of unforgettable tunes. See studies by Bonavia (1934), Hussey (1940), Werfel (1942), Sheean (1959) and Life by Walker (1962).

VERE, Aubrey Thomas de. See DE VERE.

VERE, (1) **Edward de, 17th Earl of Oxford**

(1550–1604), English court poet, was a cousin of (2), (3) and (4). He was an Italianate Englishman, violent and a spendthrift, but one of the best of the Elizabethan courtier-poets. Of his lyrics, published in various collections, *What cunning can expresse* is perhaps the best.

(2) **Sir Francis** (*c*. 1560–1609), English soldier, grandson of the 15th Earl of Oxford, obtained a company in the Bergen-op-Zoom garrison in 1586, and won his first laurels in the defence of Sluys, being knighted by Lord Willoughby, whom he succeeded in 1589 in the chief command in the Netherlands. His skill and energy at Breda, Deventer and a hundred fights carried his fame far beyond the Netherlands. He shared the glory of the Cadiz expedition (1596), and next year the failure of the Island Voyage. Again in Holland, he governed Brill, and helped Maurice to victory at Turnhout (1597) and Nieuwpoort (1600), as well as in the heroic defence of Ostend. He wrote commentaries on his campaigns (1657).

(3) **Sir Horace, 1st Baron** (1565–1635), brother of (2), took a hero's share in all his brother's battles. Knighted for his courage at Cadiz, he succeeded his brother as governor of Brill, and, sent in the Thirty Years' War to defend the Palatinate, was shut in at Mannheim and forced to surrender to Tilly (1623). He was created baron in 1625.

(4) **Robert** (d. 1595), another brother, died in the Netherlands on the battlefield. See Sir Clements R. Markham, *The Fighting Veres* (1888).

VERENDRYE, Pierre Gaultier de Varennes, Sieur de la, *vay-rā-dree* (1685–1749), French explorer, born at Three Rivers, Quebec, served with the French army, and being wounded at Malplaquet, returned to Canada to become a trader with his base at Nipigon on Lake Superior. Fired by Indian tales, he and his three sons travelled over much of unexplored Canada, discovering Rainy Lake, the Lake of the Woods, and Lake Winnipeg. On later expeditions he and hi remaining two sons (the eldest having been killed by the Sioux) reached the Mandan country south of the Assiniboine river, upper Missouri, Manitoba and Dakota. Finally, before his death one of his sons traced the Saskatchewan river to its junction. See his journals and letters, edited by L. J. Burpee (1927).

VERESHCHAGIN, Vasili, *vye-ryesh-chah'-gyin* (1842–1904), Russian painter of battles and executions, born at Tcherepovets in Novgorod, entered the navy in 1859, but studied art under Gérôme at Paris. He was with Kauffmann in the Turkoman campaigns (1867), visited India (1874), saw the Russo-Turkish war (1877), and in 1884 went to India, Syria and Palestine and portrayed what he saw in gruesomely realistic pictures of plunder, mutilated corpses and executions of mutinous sepoys, with Tolstoy's aim of fostering revulsion against war. He was blown up with Admiral Makarov's flagship off Port Arthur on April 13, 1904. His travel sketches (trans. 1887) and study by Zabel (1900).

VERGA, Giovanni, *vayr'gah* (1840–1922), Italian novelist, born at Catania in Sicily, wrote numerous violent short stories describing the hopeless, miserable life of Sicilian peasantry, including *La vita de' campi* (1880) and *Cavalleria rusticana* (1884), which was made into an opera by Mascagni. The same Zolaesque theme prevails in his novels, *I Malavoglia* (1881) and *Mastro Don Gesualdo* (1888), &c. D. H. Lawrence translated some of his works. See Life by L. Russo (Bari 1941) and study by E. De Michelis (Florence 1941).

VERGENNES, Charles Gravier, *ver-zhen* (1717–87), French statesman, Louis XVI's foreign minister, sought to humble England by promoting the independence of the United States. He negotiated the Peace of Paris (1783) and Pitt's commercial treaty (1786). See Life by C. de Chambrun (1944).

VERGIL. See VIRGIL.

VERGIL, Polydore (*c*. 1470–*c*. 1555), Italian historian, otherwise named De Castello, was born at Urbino, and educated at Bologna and Padua. His first work was *Proverbiorum Libellus* (1498); his second, *De Inventoribus Rerum* (1499), also the earliest book of its kind, was translated into English, Spanish and Italian. He was sent by the pope to England in 1501 as deputy-collector of Peter's pence, and was presented to the Leicestershire living of Church Langton in 1503. In 1507 he became a prebendary of Lincoln, in 1508 archdeacon of Wells, and in 1513 a prebendary of St Paul's, having been naturalized in 1510. In 1515 he was imprisoned for slandering Wolsey. In 1525 he published the first genuine edition of Gildas, in 1526 the treatise *De Prodigiis*. His great *Historiae Anglicae Libri XXVI* appeared at Basel in 1534; a 27th book (to 1538) was added in the third edition (1555). About 1550 he returned to Italy. See Camden Soc. works by Sir H. Ellis (1844–46), and study by Hay (1952).

VERGNIAUD, Pierre Victurnien, *vern-yō* (1753–93), French politician, born at Limoges, settled as an advocate at Bordeaux in 1781, and was sent to the National Assembly in 1791. His eloquence made him the leader of the Girondists. In the Convention he voted for the king's death, and as president announced the result. When the Girondists clashed with the rival revolutionary faction, known as the Mountain, composed mainly of Parisians who had borne the brunt of the revolution and wanted to retain power by dictatorial means, Vergniaud and his party were arrested and guillotined on October 31. See Life by Bowers (N.Y. 1950).

VERHAEREN, Emile, *-hahr'-* (1855–1916), Belgian poet, born at St Amand near Termonde, studied law, but took to literature. His poetry hovers between powerful sensuality as in *Les Flamandes* (1883) and the harrowing despair of *Les Débâcles* (1888); the affirmation of the life force and the revulsion against modern industrial conditions. His best work is possibly *La Multiple Splendeur* (1906). He died in a train accident at Rouen. See study by S. Zweig (trans. 1914) and P. M. Jones (1926).

VERHEIDEN, Jakob, *-hī'-*, Dutch publisher at The Hague in 1602 of the *Effigies et Elogia* of the leading Reformers, the portraits (including the well-known one of John Knox based on that in Beza's *Icones*) being engraved by Hondius.

VERLAINE, Paul, *-layn* (1844–96), French poet, born at Metz on March 30, was educated at the Lycée Condorcet and entered the civil service. Already an aspiring poet, he mixed with the leading Parnassian poets and writers in the cafés, and especially at the salon of Nina de Callias and under their romantic battle cry ' Art for art's sake ', against the formless sentimentalizing of the romantic school, gained some recognition by his contribution of articles and poems to their *avant garde* literary magazines, especially the short-lived *Le Parnasse contemporain.* The youthful morbidity of his first volume of poems, *Poèmes saturniens* (1867), was criticized by Sainte-Beuve as trying vainly to outdo Baudelaire. The evocation of a past age, the 18th century of the paintings of Watteau, provided the theme of his second beginning, *Fêtes galantes* (1869), by many considered his finest poetical achievement. His love for the sixteen-year-old Mathilde Mauté during an engagement prolonged by the doubts of the girl's father was sublimated in *La Bonne Chanson* (1870). During the Franco-Prussian war Verlaine did guard duty in Paris and then served as press-officer for the Communards. The birth of a son did nothing to heal the incompatibilities of his married life, from which he escaped (1872) on travels in Flanders, Belgium and England in Bohemian intimacy with the fledgling poe Rimbaud (q.v.), ten years his junior. Their friendship ended in Brussels (1873), when Verlaine, drunk and desolate at Rimbaud's intention to leave him, shot him in the wrist. Verlaine's overpowering remorse made it psychologically impossible for Rimbaud to leave, so he staged an incident in the street and had Verlaine arrested. He did not foresee that the police would in searching for a motive suspect immorality. Verlaine was convicted and sentenced to two years' hard labour and his past associations with the Communards disqualified him from any intercession by the French ambassador. *Romances sans paroles* (1874) were written in Mons prison, where he studied Shakespeare in the original, and after his wife had left him, he turned Catholic (1874). He unsuccessfully attempted to enter a monastery on release, taught French at Stickney, Lincolnshire, and St Aloysius' College, Bournemouth (1875), where he completed his second masterpiece *Sagesse* (1881), full of the spirit of penitence and self-confession that appeared again in *Parallèlement* (1889). In 1877 he returned to France to teach English at the Collège of Notre Dame at Rethel, adopted a favourite pupil, Lucien Létinois, for whom he acquired a farm at Coulommes and whose death of typhus (1883) occasioned *Amour* (1888). *Poètes maudits* (1884), comprising critical studies, were followed by short stories *Louis Leclerc* and *Le Poteau* (1886), sacred and profane verse *Liturgies intimes* (1892) and *Élégies* (1893). The consummate master of a poetry which sacrificed all for sound, in which the commonplace expressions take on a magic freshness, he lived during his last years in Parisian garret poverty, relieved by frequent spells in hospitals and finally by a grand lecture tour in Belgium, Holland and England (1893), the last sponsored in part by William Rothenstein (q.v.), who drew several portraits of him. He died in Paris, January 8, 1896. See the autobiographical *Mes hôpitaux* (1892), *Mes prisons* (1893) and *Confessions* (1895), *Œuvres poétiques complètes*, ed. Y. G. Le Dantec (1938), and books by E. Lepelletier (1907), E. Delahaye (1919), H. Nicolson (1921), P. Martino (1924), M. Coulson (1929), A. Adam (1936), P. Valéry (1937), C. E. B. Roberts (1937), F. Porché (1937), A. Fontaine (1937), V. P. Underwood (Paris 1958) and L. and E. Hanson (1958).

VERMEER, *ver-mayr,* (1) **Jan,** of Haarlem (1628–91), was a notable Dutch landscape painter. His son, **Jan** the Younger (1656–1705), was also a painter.

(2) **Jan** (1632–75), Dutch painter, born in Delft, the son of an art dealer, inherited his father's business and painted purely for pleasure. His life was obscure, possibly because he was a Catholic in a Protestant country. He may have studied under Carel Fabritius. His work shows some Neapolitan influence as well as that of the genre painting of Pieter de Hooch. In 1653 he married Caterina Bolones, who was to bear him eleven children, and the same year he was admitted master painter to the guild of St Luke, which he served as headman (1662–63; 1670–71). He gained some recognition in his lifetime in Holland and his work was sought by collectors, but he made little effort to sell. After his death his baker held two pictures for outstanding bills, and Vermeer's wife, declared a bankrupt, could not retrieve them. His art was forgotten until the researches of Thoré (1866) and Havard (1883) re-established and enhanced his reputation. Apart from a few portraits, *The Allegory of Faith* (Metropolitan, N.Y.), *The Procuress* (1656; Dresden), *Christ in the House of Martha and Mary* (National Gallery, Edinburgh) and two views of Delft (one in The Hague), he confined himself to the domestic interiors of his own house, spiced with an art dealer's furnishings and trappings, every scene perfectly arranged so that everything, material or human, should obtain equal prominence and meticulous attention. His detachment, acute appreciation of perspective, unrivalled paintwork, which shows no trace of the brush and effects a translucent purity and richness of colour (particularly his blues and yellows), and above all his masterly treatment of the manifold tones of daylight, impart to each painting the quality of a still-life. A trivial subject becomes a work of art. Forty of his paintings are known. These include three music-making scenes (two, National Gallery, London; one, Royal Collection, Windsor), the *Allegory of Painting* (Vienna), two *Woman reading a Letter* (Amsterdam and Dresden) and other domestic scenes. During World War II, forged Vermeers were produced by Van Meegeren (q.v.) who for some time deceived the experts. See monograph by J. Chantavoine (1936) and studies by T. Bodkin (1939), de Vries (1961), L.

Gowing (1952), of the Van Meegeren forgeries, J. Baesjou (1956) and L. Goldschneider (1958).

VERMIGLI. See PETER MARTYR.

VERMUYDEN, Sir Cornelius, *-mi'-* (*c.* 1595–*c.* 1683), Dutch drainage engineer, born on the island of Tholen, Zeeland, in 1621 was commissioned to repair the breach of the Thames at Dagenham and drained the Bedford Level (1634–52). See Life by J. K. Altes (1925) and study by L. E. Harris (1953).

VERNE, Jules (1828–1905), French novelist, born at Nantes, studied law, from 1848 wrote opera libretti until in 1863, with the publication of *Cinq Semaines en ballon*, he struck a new vein in fiction—exaggerating and often anticipating the possibilities of science and giving ingenious verisimilitude to adventures carried out by means of scientific inventions in exotic places. He greatly influenced the early science fiction of H. G. Wells. His best-known books, all of which have been translated, are *Voyage au centre de la terre* (1864), *Vingt mille lieues sous les mers* (1870) and *Le Tour du monde en quatre-vingts jours* (1873). Film versions of the last two achieved an astonishing popularity as late as the nineteen-fifties. See Lives by M. A. de la Füye (1928), K. Allott (1940), G. H. Waltz (1943) and I. O. Evans (1956).

VERNET, *ver-nay,* name of a notable family of French painters, of whom the most important members were:

(1) **Antoine Charles Horace** (1758–1835), known as ' Carle ', son of (2) and father of (3), born at Bordeaux, showed early promise and went to Italy, where he decided to become a monk. Back in Paris, however, he took to painting horses again and the vast battle pieces of Marengo and Austerlitz (now at Versailles) for which Napoleon awarded him the Légion d'honneur, and *The Race* (Louvre), which earned him the order of St Michael from Louis XVIII.

(2) **Claude Joseph** (1714–89), landscape and marine painter, father of (1), was born at Avignon. His voyage to Rome gave him a fascination for the sea and he became primarily known for his seascapes and the paintings in the Louvre of France's 16 chief seaports, commissioned by the king.

(3) **Emile Jean Horace** (1789–1863), known as ' Horace ', son of (1), born in Paris, became one of the great French military painters. He decorated the vast Constantine room at Versailles with battle scenes from Valmy, Wagram, Bouvines and *Napoleon at Friedland*. His *Painter's Studio* depicts him as he loved to be, surrounded by groups of people, boxing, playing instruments and leading horses. His paintings lack composition, but are treated vigorously and with an impromptu brilliance. There are five paintings in the National Gallery, London. See study by Rees (1880).

VERNEY, the name of an English family in Buckinghamshire, among whose members was Ralph Verney, lord mayor of London in 1465. Other important members in chronological order were:

(1) **Sir Edmund** (1590–1642), a royalist standard-bearer, who fell at Edgehill.

(2) **Sir Ralph** (1613–96), son of (1), fought for the parliament, but refused the covenant, and in exile at Blois was created a baronet in 1661. His descendants held the titles of Baron Verney, Viscount Fermanagh and Earl Verney, the second and last earl dying in 1791.

(3) **Sir Edmund** (1616–49), son of (1), fought for the king in the Civil War, but did not survive the massacre of Drogheda.

(4) **Frances, Parthenope** (d. 1890), elder sister of Florence Nightingale, married in 1858 **Sir Harry** (1801–94). She wrote novels and the first half of *Memoirs of the Verney Family* (4 vols. 1892–99).

VERNIER, Pierre, *vern-yay* (*c.* 1580–1637), French mathematician, born at Ornans near Besançon, spent most of his life serving the king of Spain in the Low Countries and in 1631 invented the famous auxiliary scale to facilitate an accurate reading of a subdivision of an ordinary scale.

VERNON, (1) **Edward** (1684–1757), British admiral, entered the Royal Navy in 1700. He was present at the capture of Gibraltar in 1704, and fought in the great battle off Málaga. A captain at twenty-one and a rear-admiral at twenty-four, he sat in parliament as M.P. for Penrhyn and then Portsmouth, from 1727 to 1741. In 1739 he was sent to harry the Spaniards in the Antilles, and his capture of Portobello transformed him into a national hero. Against his urgent and reasoned advice, he was sent to reduce Cartagena; but the failure of the attempt owed much to the ineptitude of his military coadjutor. Recalled by the Government, at the time of the '45 Jacobite rebellion his masterly dispositions in the Channel successfully pinned the standby Gallic reinforcements to their ports. But Vernon was too cantankerous, too outspoken, and also too often right in his judgments, for the Cabinet to stomach, and he was jockeyed into resigning his command. He continued to be a thorn in the administration's side until his death in 1757. He was nicknamed ' Old Grog ', from his grogram coat, and in 1740 ordered the dilution of navy rum with water, the mixture being thenceforward known as ' grog '. See Lives by Ford (1907) and Hughes Hartmann (1953), and Beatson's *Naval and Military Memoirs* (1804).

(2) **Robert** (1774–1849), English breeder of horses, in 1847 gave to the nation the Vernon Gallery.

VERNON-HARCOURT, Augustus George (1834–1919), English chemist, born in London, graduated at Oxford, where he became reader in Chemistry. He invented a standard lamp of ten candle power, using pentane as fuel.

VERONESE, Paolo, *vay-ro-nay'zay* (1525–88), the name by which Paolo Cagliari, the greatest of the Venetian decorative painters, is known. He was born a sculptor's son, at Verona, and after some work there and in Mantua, in 1555 settled in Venice, where he soon made both wealth and fame, ranking with Titian and Tintoretto. The church of San Sebastiano in Venice contains many pictures of the period before his visit to Rome (1560). The influence of the Roman school on his style was marked. new dignity, grace of pose, and ease of movement being added to his rich Venetian colouring. In 1563 he painted the *Marriage Feast at Cana* (Louvre), possibly the greatest of his works. Other subjects include *The Family of Darius before Alexander* (c. 1570), *The Adoration of the Magi* (1573), both in the London National Gallery, and *Feast in the House of the Levi* (1753) in the Venice Academy. This last-mentioned painting brought him before the Inquisition for trivializing religious subjects by the introduction of nonhistorical accessories such as dwarfs, jesters and the like. Veronese was incapable of deep emotion, but was an exquisite colourist stamped in the aristocratic milieu of his time. He used architectural detail to heighten the sense of occasion and the rhetorical nature of his work is especially evident in such decorative pieces as the ceiling of the council chamber of the ducal palace at Venice, the *Apotheosis of Venice* (1585). See books by G. Fiocco (1928) and P. H. Osmond (1928).

VERONICA, saint, according to legend, met Christ and offered him her veil to wipe the sweat from his brow, when the divine features were miraculously imprinted upon the cloth. This veil is said to have been preserved in Rome from about 700, and was exhibited in St Peter's in 1933. Possibly *Veronica* is merely a corruption of *vera icon*, ' the true image ' (i.e., of Christ). See Karl Pearson's German monograph (1887).

VERRES, Gaius (d. 43 B.C.), Roman official, was quaestor in 84, and then attached himself to Sulla. He went to Cilicia in 80 under Dolabella, and after helping to plunder the provincials, gave evidence against his chief in 78. He was praetor in 74, owing to bribery, and governor of Sicily (73–70), where he trampled on the rights of Roman and provincial alike. On his return, he was summoned before a senatorial court, and Cicero, for the prosecution, amassed such strong evidence that Verres fled before the trial. He seemed to have lived at Massilia, but perished under Antony's proscription.

VERRIO, Antonio (c. 1640–1707), Italian decorative painter, born in Lecce, Southern Italy, was brought to London by Charles II and decorated Windsor Castle, Hampton Court, &c., and executed an equestrian portrait of the king, now in Chelsea Hospital.

VERROCCHIO, Andrea del, *ver-rok'kee-ō* (1435–88), the name by which Cione, Florentine sculptor, painter and goldsmith is known. Of the paintings ascribed to him only the *Baptism* in the Uffizi can be so with certainty, and this was completed by Leonardo da Vinci. He executed several bronze figures for the Medici tombs in San Lorenzo and is best known for his magnificent equestrian statue of Colleoni at Venice. See monographs by M. Cruttwell (1904) and M. Reymond (1906).

VERTUE, George (1684–1756), English engraver and antiquary, born in London, made his name with a fine line-engraving of Lord Somers. Horace Walpole made use of his MSS. (valuable to the art historian) in *Anecdotes of Painting.*

VERWOERD, Hendrik Freusch, *fer-vœrt'* (1901–66), South African politician, born in

Amsterdam, was a professor at Stellenbosch (1927–37). He edited the nationalist *Die Transvaler* (1938–48) and opposed South Africa's entry into World War II. Exponent of the strict racial segregation policy of apartheid, Verwoerd became vice-chairman of the National Party of the Transvaal in 1946, was elected senator in 1948 and minister of native affairs in 1950. In 1958 he was elected national leader by the Nationalist party parliamentary caucus and as 6th prime minister of South Africa he dedicated himself to the founding of a South African republic. After strong opposition to his policy of apartheid and an attempt on his life in 1960, South Africa broke from the commonwealth on becoming a republic in 1962, after which Verwoerd pursued a strict apartheid policy. He was assassinated in 1966.

VERY, *veer'i*, (1) Edward Wilson (1847–1910). American ordnance expert and inventor. He served in the American Navy from 1867 to 1885, became an admiral, and in 1877 invented chemical flares (' Very Lights ') for signalling at night.

  (2) **Frank Washington** (1852–1927), American astronomer, born at Salem, Mass., estimated lunar temperatures, designed a method for measuring the Fraunhofer lines, proved that white nebulae are galaxies and that the Martian atmosphere contains oxygen and water vapour. He became director of the Westwood Astrophysical observatory in 1906.

  (3) **Jones** (1813–80), American mystic, was born and died at Salem, Mass. He wrote sonnets of mystical inspiration contained in *Essays and Poems* (1839). See Life by W. I. Bartlett (1942).

VESALIUS, Andreas, *ve-zay'lyus* (1514–1564), Belgian anatomist, born in Brussels, became professor at Padua, Bologna and Basle. In 1538 he published his six anatomical tables, still largely Galenian, and in 1541 edited Galen's works. His own great work, however, the celebrated *De Humani Corporis Fabrica* (1543), greatly advanced the science of biology with its excellent description of bones and the nervous system, supplemented by the magnificent drawings of muscle dissections by Jan Stephen van Calcar, a pupil of Titian. It was condemned by the Galenists and he was sentenced to death by the Inquisition for ' body snatching ' and for dissecting the human body. The sentence however was commuted to a pilgrimage to Jerusalem, which he undertook, but died on the return journey on the island of Zante. He was court physician to Charles V and Philip II. He was the first to challenge the Aristotelian doctrine that the heart was the physical correlative of personality, in favour of the brain and the nervous system. See Life by M. Roth (1892), H. Cushing, *Bio-bibliography* (1943), and C. Singer, *A Prelude to Modern Science* (1946).

VESPASIAN, Titus Flavius Vespasianus, *-spay'zhèn* (A.D. 9–79), Roman emperor, born near Reate, served as tribune in Thrace, and as quaestor in Crete and Cyrene. In the reign of Claudius he commanded a legion in Germany and in Britain; was consul in 51, and next proconsul of Africa; and in

67 was sent by Nero to reduce the Jews to subjection. When the struggle began between Otho and Vitellius he was proclaimed imperator by the legions in the East and on the death of Vitellius was appointed emperor. Leaving the war in Judaea to his son Titus, he reached Rome in 70, and soon restored the government and finances to order, besides showing an admirable example to a corrupt age by the simplicity of his life. He embarked however on an ambitious building programme in Rome, began the Colosseum, and extended and consolidated Roman conquests in Britain and Germany. See study by Langford (1928).

VESPUCCI, Amerigo, *ves-poot'chee* (1451–1512), Florentine explorer, born at Florence, was a provision contractor at Seville in 1495–1498. He contracted for one (or two) of the expeditions of Columbus. He had some knowledge of cosmography, but was not a practical navigator (still less a pilot) when, at fifty, he promoted a voyage to the New World in the track of Columbus, sailed with its commander Hojeda (1499), and explored the coast of Venezuela. In 1505 he was naturalized in Spain, and from 1508 till his death was pilot-major of the kingdom. His name was absurdly given to two continents (America) through an inaccurate account of his travels published at St Dié in Lorraine in 1507, in which he is represented as having discovered and reached the mainland in 1497. This account was based on Vespucci's own letters, in which he claims to have made four voyages. Sir Clements Markham in his introduction to a translation of the letters (Hakluyt Society, 1894) proved one of these to be a pure fabrication, the others quite unsupported. But see also books by Coote (1894), H. Vignaud (1918), Pohl (1945), and the Princeton Vespucci Texts and Studies (1916).

VESTRIS, Lucia Elizabeth (1797–1856), English actress, *née* **Bartolozzi**, a granddaughter of the engraver, was born in London. At sixteen she married the dancer Armand Vestris (1787–1825), member of an originally Florentine family that gave to France a series of distinguished chefs, actors and ballet-dancers. In 1815 they separated and she went on the stage in Paris. She appeared at Drury Lane in 1820, became famous in *The Haunted Tower*, was even more popular as Phoebe in *Paul Pry*, and in light comedy and burlesque was equally successful. She had been nine years lessee of the Olympic when in 1838 she married Charles James Mathews (q.v.). She afterwards undertook the management of Covent Garden and the Lyceum. See Life by C. E. Pearce (1923).

VEUILLOT, Louis François, *væ-yō* (1813–1883), French Ultramontane editor of the Paris *L'Univers*, was born at Boynes, Loiret. He wrote novels, poems, polemical essays, &c. See Lives by E. Veuillot (1883), Tavernier (1913) and E. J. M. Gauthier (1939).

VEZIN, Hermann (1829–1910), American actor, born at Philadelphia, made his début at York in 1850 and acted in London from 1852. Among his leading rôles were Hamlet, Jacques and Ford.

VIAN, Sir Philip, *vi'ėn* (1894–1968), British

sailor, educated at Dartmouth. In 1940, in command of the destroyer *Cossack*, Captain Vian penetrated Norwegian territorial waters to rescue 300 British prisoners from the German supply ship *Altmark*; subsequently being sunk in the *Afridi* while covering the withdrawal from Namsos. In 1942 his skill and courage in beating off enemy interception enabled a vital convoy to reach Malta. Subsequently, he was deeply engaged in the Normandy invasion. Service as fifth sea lord was followed by the command of the Home Fleet. He was created K.B.E. in 1944.

VIARDOT-GARCÍA. See GARCÍA (4).

VIAU, Théophile de, *vee-ō* (1590–1626), French poet, born at Clairac, wrote the tragedy *Pyramé et Thisbé* (1621) and much love poetry distinguished by its naturalness. He was condemned to the stake (1623) for the impiety and obscenity of his poems contributed to *Le Parnasse satyrique* but his sentence was commuted to exile for life.

VIAUD, Louis Marie Julien, *vee-ō* (1850–1923), French novelist who wrote under the pseudonym of 'Pierre Loti', was born at Rochefort. His voyages as a sailor and as a traveller provide the scenes for most of his writings, and from the native women of the South Sea Islands he gained his pseudonym Loti, Flower of the Pacific. *Aziyadé* (1879), his first novel, was a series of pictures of life on the Bosporus and it was followed by the very successful *Rarahu* (1880), published in 1882 as *Le Mariage de Loti*. Semi-autobiographical, this story set among the coral seas, of the love of an Englishman for a Tahiti girl, immediately captured the imagination. Of his novels, the best known is *Pêcheur d'Islande* (1886), a descriptive study of Breton fisher life. All his writing is subjective; there is a simplicity yet an intensity of sensuous impressions, a sympathy with nature and a deeply felt melancholy at the transitoriness of human life. Other works include *Le Roman d'un Spahi* (1881), *Mon Frère Yves* (1883), *Madame Chrysanthème* (1887), and *Vers Ispahan* (1904).

VICENTE, Gil, *vee-sen'tay* (c. 1470–c. 1537), the father of Portuguese drama. His *Belém monstrance* is in the Lisbon museum. He wrote 44 plays, 16 in Portuguese, 11 in Spanish and 17 using both languages. His early plays were religious, but gradually social criticism was added. His farces *Inês Pereira, Juiz da Beira* and the three *autos das barcas* (*Inferno, Purgatório and Glória*) are his best. He displays great psychological insight, superb lyricism and a predominantly comical spirit. See Lives by Freire and Pratt (1931).

VICKY (1913–66), professional name of Victor Weisz, British political cartoonist of Hungarian-Jewish extraction, born in Berlin. He emigrated to Britain in 1935, worked with the *News Chronicle*, the *Daily Mirror*, the *New Statesman* and the *Evening Standard*, establishing himself as the most outstanding left-wing political cartoonist of the period. He published collections of his work, including *Vicky's World* (1959), *Home and Abroad* (1964).

VICO, Giovanni Battista, *vee-kō* (1668–1744), Italian philosopher, born at Naples, studied law, but devoted himself to literature, history and philosophy and became in 1697 professor of Rhetoric at Naples. In his *Scienza Nuova* (1725; recast 1730) he argued that the historical method is no less exact than the scientific, and postulated evolutionary cycles in civilizations, corresponding to mental development. His historicism influenced the German Romantics. See his *Autobiography*, intro. Fisch and Bergin (1944), and works by Flint (1884), Croce, trans. R. G. Collingwood (1913), Gentile (1927) and Adams (1935).

VICTOR, Claude Perrin, Duc de Belluno (1764–1841), French soldier, born at La Marche. Napoleon made him marshal on the field of Friedland (1807), and later Duke of Belluno. In 1808–12 he commanded in Spain, and, after initial successes, lost the battles of Talavera and Barrosa; in the Russian campaign he covered the crossing of the Berezina. He fought at Dresden and Leipzig, lost the emperor's favour by neglecting to occupy the bridge of Montereau-sur-Yonne, and was wounded at Craonne. Louis XVIII gave him high command and the presidency of the commission for trying his old companions who had deserted to Napoleon during the 'Hundred Days'. He was minister of war (1821–23). See his *Mémoires* (1846).

VICTOR AMADEUS II (1666–1732), succeeded his father as Duke of Savoy in 1675, and was saved from the clutches of France by the military genius of Price Eugene (q.v.), a distant cousin, who routed the French before Turin in 1706. By the Treaty of Utrecht (1713) he gained the principality of Montferrat and the kingdom of Sicily. Seven years later the Emperor of Austria forced him to exchange the crown of Sicily for that of Sardinia. He abdicated in 1730.

VICTOR EMMANUEL, the name of three kings of Sardinia, of whom two were also kings of Italy:

Victor Emmanuel I (1759–1824), was king of Sardinia (1802–21). His oppression of liberalism led to a rising in 1821, when he abdicated in favour of his brother Charles Felix.

Victor Emmanuel II (1820–78), first king of Italy, son of Charles Albert (q.v.) of Sardinia, was born March 14, in 1848–49 displayed great gallantry at Goito and Novara. Charles Albert abdicating in his favour, he ascended the throne of Sardinia, March 23, 1849; and in August peace was concluded between Sardinia and Austria. Perhaps the most important act of his rule was the appointment (1852) of Cavour (q.v.) as his chief minister. In January 1855 Sardinia joined the allies against Russia, and a contingent of 10,000 men landed in the Crimea. At the Congress of Paris (March 1856) the Sardinian envoys urged upon the attention of France and England the oppressive government of the states of Italy. In 1857 diplomatic relations were broken off with Austria. In 1859 Austria demanded the disarmament of Sardinia; this was refused, and next day the Austrians crossed the Ticino. A French army advanced to aid the Sardinians, and the Austrians were defeated at Montebello (May 20), Magenta (June 4)

and Solferino (June 24). By the Treaty of Villafranca, Lombardy was ceded to Sardinia. In 1860 Modena, Parma, the Romagna and Tuscany were peacefully annexed to Sardinia. Sicily and Naples were added by Garibaldi, while Savoy and Nice were ceded to France. The papal territories were saved from annexation only by the presence of a French force of occupation. In February 1861 Victor Emmanuel was proclaimed king of Italy at Turin, whence the capital of Italy was transferred to Florence. In 1866 the Austro-Prussian war, in which Italy took part as the ally of Prussia, added Venetia to the Italian kingdom. In the same year the French withdrew from Rome, but owing to an incursion by Garibaldi they returned. After the fall of the Empire in 1870 the French occupation of Rome was at an end, the king entered Rome, and the province was added to his kingdom. The 'honest king' reigned as a strictly constitutional monarch. He was succeeded by his eldest son, Humbert I. See Life by C. S. Forester (1927).

Victor Emmanuel III (1869–1947), king of Italy (1900–46), son of Humbert I (q.v.), was born at Naples. He generally ruled as a constitutional monarch with Giolitti as premier but defied parliamentary majorities in bringing Italy into World War I on the side of the Allies in 1915 and in 1922 when he offered Mussolini the premiership. The latter reduced the king to a constitutional façade, conferring on him in May 1936 the title of emperor of Abyssinia. The king, however, supported the dictator until the latter's fall in June 1944. Victor Emmanuel then retired from public life, leaving his son Humbert as lieutenant-general of the realm, and abdicated in May 1946. See HUMBERT II.

VICTORIA, in full **Alexandrina Victoria** (1819–1901), Queen of the United Kingdom of Great Britain and Ireland, and (in 1876) Empress of India, only child of George III's fourth son, Edward, Duke of Kent, and Victoria Maria Louisa of Saxe-Coburg, sister of Leopold, king of the Belgians, was born at Kensington Palace on May 24, 1819. Called to the British throne on the death of her uncle, William IV, June 20, 1837, the provisions of Salic Law excluded her from dominion over Hanover, which passed to another uncle, Ernest, Duke of Cumberland. Crowned at Westminster, June 28, 1838, she speedily demonstrated that clear grasp of constitutional principles and the scope of her own prerogative in which she had been so painstakingly instructed in the many tutelary letters from her uncle, Leopold of Belgium, who remained her constant correspondent. Companioned in girlhood almost exclusively by older folk, her precocious maturity and surprising firmness of will were speedily demonstrated. For with the fall of Melbourne's government in 1839 she resolutely exercised her prerogative by setting aside the precedent which decreed dismissal of the current ladies of the bedchamber. Peel thereupon resigned, and the Melbourne administration, which she personally preferred, was prolonged till 1841. Throughout the early formative years of her reign Melbourne was both her prime minister and her trusted friend and mentor. His ripe experience and thoroughly English outlook served as a useful counter-balance to that more ' Continental ' line of policy of which ' Uncle Leopold ' was the untiring and far from unprejudiced advocate. On reaching marriageable age the Queen became deeply enamoured of Prince Albert of Saxe-Coburg and Gotha, to whom she was wed on February 10, 1840. Four sons and five daughters were born: Victoria, the Princess Royal, who married Frederick III (q.v.) of Germany; Albert Edward, afterwards Edward VII (q.v.); Alice (q.v.), who married the Duke of Hesse; Alfred, Duke of Edinburgh and of Saxe-Coburg-Gotha (q.v.); Helena, who married Prince Christian of Schleswig-Holstein (see MARIE LOUISE); Louise, who married the Marquis of Lorne (see ARGYLL); Arthur, Duke of Connaught (q.v.); Leopold, Duke of Albany (q.v.), and Beatrice, who married Prince Henry of Battenberg. Strongly influenced by her husband with whom she worked in closest harmony, after his death the stricken queen went into lengthy seclusion, which brought her temporary unpopularity. But with the adventurous Disraeli administration vindicated by the queen's recognition as Empress of India, Victoria rose high in her subjects' favour. Her experience, shrewdness and innate political flair brought powerful influence to bear on the conduct of foreign affairs, as did the response to the country's policy made by her innumerable relatives amongst the European Royal Houses. Unswerving in her preference for ministers of conservative principles, such as Melbourne and Disraeli, rather than for counsellors of more radical persuasion, such as Palmerston and Gladstone, in the long run the Queen's judgment of men and events was rarely to be faulted; although her partiality for all things German had the effect of throwing her heir almost too eagerly into the arms of France. Her *Letters* (ed. Benson, 1908, re-issued ed. Buckle, 1926–32), although prolix and pedestrian in style, bear witness to her unwearying industry, her remarkable practicality, and her high sense of mission. See also her *Leaves from the Journal of our Life in the Highlands* (1869), *More Leaves* (1884), and books by Duke of Argyll (1901), Sir Sidney Lee (1902), Sir Theodor Martin (1908), J. Holland Rose (1909), Mrs Jerrold (1912–16), Visc. Esher (1912–14), Lytton Strachey (1921), H. Bolitho (1949), R. Fulford (1951) and E. Longford (1964).

VICTORIA, Tomás Luis De, or Vittoria, Tommaso Ludovico da (c. 1535–1611), Spanish composer, born at Avila, was sent as a priest to Rome by Philip II, to study music. At Loyola's Collegium Germanicum he was appointed chaplain in 1566 and in 1571 choirmaster. In 1576 he became chaplain to the widowed Empress Maria, sister of Philip, returning with her to Madrid in 1583 to the convent of the Descalzas Reales, where he remained as choirmaster until his death. Deeply devout, Victoria wrote only religious music and **all** of equal excellence. Often compared **with** his contemporary Palestrina (**q.v.**), **his** music,

though similar, is more individualistic. Often flavoured with Spanish melody, it is passionate but restrained, exalted but serene. Among his 180 works are the *Officium Hebdonadae Sanctae* (1585), books of motets and masses and his last work, the masterly *Requiem Mass*, composed at the death of the Empress Maria in 1603 and published in 1605. See studies by H. Collet (1914) and F. Pedrell (1918).

VIDA, Marco Girolamo, ' the Christian Virgil ' (c. 1480–1566), Italian Latin poet, born at Cremona, was made Bishop of Alba in 1532. He wrote Latin orations and dialogues, a religious epic, *Christias* (1535), *De Arte Poetica* (1537), and poems on silk-culture and chess (1527).

VIDAL, Pierre, vee-dahl (fl. c. 1200), Provençal troubadour, was a professional court minstrel who accompanied Richard Cœur de Lion to Cyprus (1190).

VIDOCQ, Eugène François, vee-dok (1775–1857), French criminal, ' the detective ', was the son of an Arras baker, whose till he often robbed. After a spell in prison, he was an acrobat, then served in the army till disabled by a wound, and in 1796 was sentenced for forgery to eight years in the galleys. Escaping, he joined a band of highwaymen, whom he betrayed to the authorities. In 1808 he offered his services as a spy on the criminal classes. In 1812 a ' Brigade de Sûreté ' was organized, with Vidocq as chief; its efficiency was marvellous, but suspicions grew rife that Vidocq himself originated many of the burglaries that he showed such skill in detecting, and in 1825 he was superseded. His *Mémoires* (1828) are untrustworthy. See Life by Hodgetts (1929).

VIEBIG, Clara, vee'- (1860–1952), German novelist, born at Trier, married F. Cohn in 1896 and wrote Zolaesque novels and short stories, including *Kinder der Eifel* (1897), *Das Weiberdorf* (1900), *Das schlafende Heer* (1904), &c. See German study by G. Scheuffler (1927).

VIEIRA, Antonio, vyay-ee-ra (1608–97), Portuguese ecclesiastic and missionary, born in Lisbon, was chaplain to John IV and from 1653 to 1661 was in Brazil, where he converted and emancipated the Indians. Unpopular with the colonists, who forced him to return to Portugal, he was imprisoned for two years (1665–67) by the Inquisition. In 1681, with the support of Pope Clement X, he returned to Brazil, became superior in Bahia, where he remained until his death. Of his writings, his *Sermons* are noteworthy and his *Letters* give a clear picture of his time.

VIELÉ-GRIFFIN, Francis, vee-lay-gri-fi (1864–1937), French symbolist poet, the son of the American general Egbert Louis Vielé (1825–1902), born at Norfolk, Virginia, made his home in Touraine, France, and became a leading exponent of *vers libre*. His poems collected under the titles *Cueille d'avril* (1886), *Poèmes et Poésies* (1895), *Sapho* (1911), *La Sagesse d' Ulysse* (1925), &c., are of high lyrical quality, tending towards musical impressionism and embody a serene outlook on life. He was elected to the Belgian academy. His American brother,

Herman Knickerbocker Vielé (1856–1908), was a painter and novelist.

VIERGE, Daniel, *vee-er'hay* (1851–1904), Spanish artist, born at Madrid, worked largely in black-and-white. At Paris, he was employed on *Le Monde Illustré* and *La Vie Moderne*, and he illustrated Hugo (1874–82). His pen-and-ink work shows perfect modelling of figures and artistic rendering of architecture, as in Quevedo's *Don Pablo de Segovia* (1882). See work by Marthold (1905).

VIETA, Franciscus, *vyay-tah,* or **François Viète** (1540–1603), French mathematician, born at Fontenay-le-Comte, became a privy councillor to Henry VI and solved an important Spanish cypher. His *Artem Analyticam Isagoge* (1591) is probably the earliest work on symbolic algebra, and he devised methods for solving algebraic equations to the fourth degree. He also wrote on trigonometry and geometry and obtained the value of π as an infinite product. Descartes expressly denied having borrowed from Vieta's work.

VIEUXTEMPS, Henri, *vyœ-tã* (1820–81), Belgian violinist and composer of six violin concertos, born at Verviers, in 1870 became a teacher in the Brussels conservatoire. See Life by Radoux (1893).

VIGÉE LEBRUN. See LE BRUN (2).

VIGFÚSSON, Guðbrandur, *veeg'foos-son* (1827–89), Scandinavian scholar, born at Breidafjord, Iceland, studied and lived at Copenhagen (1849–64). He edited a long series of sagas, completed the *Icelandic Dictionary* (1873) undertaken by Cleasby (q.v.), and, with York Powell, compiled the magnificent *Corpus poeticum boreale* (1883). He went to London in 1864 and thence to Oxford, where in 1884 he was appointed lector in Icelandic.

VIGNEAUD, Vincent du, *veen-yō* (1901–), American biochemist, born in Chicago, professor at Cornell from 1938, synthesized penicillin and oxytocin, discovered the structure of biotin, and won the 1955 Nobel prize for work on hormone synthesis.

VIGNOLA, Giacomo Barozzi da, *vee-nyo'lah* (1507–73), Italian architect, born at Vignola, studied at Bologna. He designed the Villa di Papa Giulio for Pope Julius III and the church of the Gesù, which with its cruciform plan, side chapels, &c., had a great influence on French and Italian church architecture.

VIGNY, Alfred Victor, Comte de, *veen-yee* (1797–1863), French romantic writer, born at Loches, Indre-et-Loire, March 27, served in the Royal Guards (1814–28), retiring with a captaincy. His experiences provided the material for *Servitude et grandeur militaires* (1835), a candid commentary on the boredom and irresponsibility, yet desire for devotion and self-sacrifice induced by peacetime soldiering. He married an Englishwoman, Lydia Bunbury (1828). He had already published anonymously a volume of verse (1822) followed by *Eloa* (1824), the fallen angel condemned for self-pity, and *Poèmes antiques et modernes* (1826; expanded 1829), which includes his grand poetic conception of Moses, as the hopelessly overburdened servant of God. Vigny's life,

marred by domestic unhappiness, his failure to enter parliament (1848–49), was that of a congenital misfit who bears his loneliness with dignity. This is reflected in his work, especially in that masterpiece of romantic drama, *Chatterton* (1835), written for his love, the actress Marie Dorval, as well as the volume of exhortatory tales, *Stello,* describing the tragic fates of the young poets, Chatterton, Gilbert and Chénier, concluded in the posthumous sequel *Daphné* (1912). These exemplify Vigny's pessimism, his exaltation of the poet as a godlike outsider, whose knowledge is yet necessary for society, his aristocratic stoicism alleviated unexpectedly by a tinge of Saint-Simonism. Other notable works include the historical novel *Cinq Mars* (1826), the plays *Othello* (1829) and *La Maréchale d'Ancre* (1831), the philosophical poems glorifying social order and discipline, *Les Destinées* (posthumous, 1864), and the biographical notes, *Journal* (1867). He was elected to the Academy (1845) and died in Paris, September 17, 1863. See *Oeuvres complètes* (1921–25), Lives by A. France (1868), E. Dupuy (1910–12), F. Baldensperger (1933), A. Whitridge (1933), A. Pravial (1934) and E. Lauvrière (Paris 1948).

VILLA-LOBOS, Heitor, *vee'la-lō'boosh* (1887–1959), Brazilian composer and conductor, born in Rio de Janeiro. His first published composition was *Salon Waltz* (1908), and a set of *Country Songs* (1910) show his interest in Brazilian folk music and folklore. After taking part in a scientific expedition up the Amazon studying folk music in 1915, he composed five symphonies, five operas and a number of large-scale symphonic poems on Brazilian subjects. He was also responsible for several ballets. A meeting with Milhaud in 1918 aroused his interest in modern music and led him to spend several years in Paris, where his music was first heard in 1923. Abandoning symphonic forms, he composed several *Chôros*, in popular Brazilian styles, and he followed these works with the four suites *Bachianas Brasileiras,* in which he treats Brazilian-style melodies in the manner of Bach. In 1932 Villa-Lobos became director of Musical Education for Brazil.

VILLANI, Giovanni (*c.* 1275–1348), Florentine historian, wrote the *Cronica Universale* (1559), valuable for its vivid portrayal of Florence at the beginning of its prosperity. The chronicle was continued by his brother Matteo and his nephew Filippo. See *Selections,* ed. by Selfe and Wicksteed (1906).

VILLARI, Pasquale, *veel'lah-ree* (1827–1917), Italian historian, born at Naples, took part in the Neapolitan revolution of 1848 and was professor of History at Florence (1866–1909). He was made a senator in 1884 and was minister of Education (1891–92). His works, of which *Machiavelli* (1877–82; trans. 1888) was the best, were all translated by his English wife, Linda White.

VILLARS, Claude Louis Hector, Duc de, *vee-lahr* (1653–1734), French soldier, was born at Moulins. He distinguished himself in the wars of the Low Countries, on the Rhine, and in Hungary, fighting against the Turks. From 1699 till 1701 he represented France at Vienna. In 1702, sent to succour the Elector of Bavaria, he crossed the Rhine defeated the Markgraf of Baden at Friedlingen, and was made a Marshal of France; next year he again crossed the Rhine, but his scheme for advancing upon Vienna was defeated by the obstinacy of the Elector. He was next commissioned to put down the Camisards. He defended the northeastern frontier against Marlborough; in 1708 he defeated the attempts of Prince Eugene to penetrate into France. In 1709 he was sent to oppose Marlborough in the north, but at Malplaquet was severely wounded. In 1711 he headed the last army France could raise, and with it fell upon the British and Dutch under Albemarle, who were entrenched at Denain (July 24, 1712), carried their entrenchments, and turning upon Prince Eugene, drove him under the walls of Brussels; then as plenipotentiary he signed the peace of Rastatt (1714). He became the principal adviser on military affairs and on foreign policy, was a strong opponent of Law's financial measures, and for a time lost favour at court. But the war of 1732-34 in Italy showed that the weight of years had left his military genius untouched. He died at Turin, June 17, 1734. See his *Mémoires* (ed. by De Vogüé, 1884–1904), and Lives by Anquetil (1784), Giraud (1881) and De Vogüé (1888).

VILLEHARDOUIN, Geoffroi de, *veel-ahr-dwĭ* (*c*. 1160–1213), first of the French historians, was born at the castle of Villehardouin in Aube, took part in the Fourth Crusade, and became marshal of ' Romania '. His *Conqueste de Constantinople*—he was present at the capture—describing the events from 1198 to 1207, is of even greater value as literature than as history.

VILLEMAIN, Abel François, *veel-mĭ* (1790–1870), French author and politician, born at Paris, became professor of Rhetoric at the Lycée Charlemagne, the École Normale, and the Sorbonne (1816–26), was made a peer in 1831, and was minister of Public Instruction under Guizot. He was long perpetual secretary of the French Academy. He wrote on the history of French literature, studies of Pindar and Chateaubriand, *Histoire de Cromwell* (1819), *Lascaris, ou les Grecs du XVème siècle* (1825), &c. See study by E. G. Atkin (Wisconsin 1924).

VILLENEUVE, Pierre Charles Jean Baptiste Sylvestre de, *veel-nœv* (1763–1806), French sailor, was born at Valensoles (Basses Alpes), December 31. As rear-admiral, he commanded the rear division of the French navy at the battle of the Nile, and saved his vessel and four others. In 1805 he took command of the Toulon squadron. At Cadiz he was joined by the Spanish fleet, and in order to lure the British fleet from the coasts of Europe bore away to the West Indies. A month later he sailed back, still pursued by Nelson. Off Finisterre he fought an undecided battle with Sir Robert Calder, and, returning to Cadiz, was there blockaded by Nelson. This ruined Napoleon's scheme for the invasion of England, and Villeneuve, about to be superseded, determined to fight before his successor could reach Cadiz. In the battle of Trafalgar (October 21) Villeneuve's flagship, the

Bucentaure, was dismasted and forced to strike. The admiral lay a prisoner in England till April 1806. On the journey to Paris he stopped at Rennes to learn how the emperor would receive him; and on April 22 he was found in bed, having stabbed himself to death.

VILLEROI, François de Neuville, Duc de, *veel-rwah* (1644–1730), French soldier, was educated with Louis XIV at court, where he was the glass of fashion, but was banished on account of a love affair. In 1680 he returned to court, and in 1693 became a marshal, having distinguished himself at Neerwinden. As commander in the Netherlands (1695–96) he showed great incapacity; and in Italy in 1701 he was defeated and taken prisoner by Prince Eugene at Cremona (1702). Again in command in the Netherlands, he was defeated by Marlborough at Ramillies (1706). Madame de Maintenon had him made guardian to Louis XV. Orleans sent him to live on his estate in 1722 because of his intrigues; but he was subsequently governor of Lyons.

VILLIERS, (1). See BUCKINGHAM, CLARENDON (2) and CLEVELAND (1).

(2) **Charles Pelham** (1802–98), English statesman and Corn-Law reformer, a younger brother of the fourth Earl of Clarendon. He was educated at Haileybury and St John's College, Cambridge, and was called to the bar in 1827. He was returned for Wolverhampton as a Free Trader in 1835, and continued its member for upwards of sixty years, latterly as a Liberal Unionist, becoming the ' Father of the House of Commons '. He made his first motion in favour of Free Trade in 1838, moving a resolution against the Corn Laws each year till they were repealed in 1846. In 1859–66 he sat with Cabinet rank as president of the Poor-Law Board.

VILLIERS DE L'ISLE ADAM, Auguste, Comte de, *veel-yay dĕ leel a-dä* (1838–89), French writer, pioneer of the symbolist movement, a Breton count who claimed descent from the Knights of Malta, was born at St Brieuc. He dedicated his *Premières Poésies* (1856–58) to de Vigny, but developed into a considerable stylist in prose. His famous short stories, *Contes cruels* (1883) and *Nouveaux Contes cruels* (1888), are in the manner of Poe. Hegelian idealism and Wagnerian romanticism inform his highly didactic novels and plays. The former include *Isis* (1862) on the Ideal and *L'Ève future* (1886) a satire on the materialism of modern science. The latter include his masterpiece, *Axel* (1885). A pronounced Catholic aristocrat, he lived for a while with the monks of Solesmes and died of cancer in a Paris hospital. See Lives by R. de Heussey (1893; trans 1904) and de Rougemont (1910), P. Quennell, *Baudelaire and the Symbolists* (1929), and E. Wilson, *Axel's Castle* (1931).

VILLON, *vee-yŏ*, (1) **François** (1431–?), one of France's greatest poets, was born in Paris. His name was de Montcorbier or de Logos, but took that of his guardian, Guillaume de Villon, a priest and a close relative. The latter enabled François to study at university, to graduate (1449) and to become

M.A. (1452). While a student, he fell into bad company and in 1455 had to flee from Paris after fatally wounding a priest in a street brawl. He joined a criminal organization, the 'Brotherhood of the Coquille', which had its own secret jargon in which Villon was to write some of his ballades. Pardoned in 1456, he returned to Paris and there wrote the *Petit Testament*, took part in the organized robbery of the funds of the Collège of Navarre, and fled to the court of the duke of Orleans at Blois. There he was sentenced to death for another unknown crime, but released as an act of grace on a public holiday. The same happened again at Meung-sur-Loire (1461), the year of the *Grand Testament*. In 1462–63 he was in trouble again for theft and brawling. Sentence of death was commuted to banishment in January 1463. He left Paris and nothing further is known of him. The first printed edition of his works was published in 1489. The *Petit Testament* comprises 40 octosyllabic octaves, the *Grand*, 172 bridged by sixteen ballades and other verse forms. Six of the Coquille jargon ballades have been definitely attributed to him. Villon's artistry is in the vitality with which he imbued the outworn mediaeval verse forms such as the ballade and the rondeau and the stark realism with which he dispassionately observes himself and life around him, whether the subject is the fat old courtesan Margot or the grim 'Ballade of the Hanged' or even the 'Ballade made by Villon at his mother's request as a Prayer to Our Lady', one of the masterpieces of religious poetry. With Chaucer he shares a flair for penetrating, unsentimental, often ironic comment, with Verlaine a longing for forgiveness. See biographical and literary studies by Longnon (1877), G. Paris (1901), M. Schwob (1912), P. Champion (1913), H. de Vere Stacpoole (1916), D. B. Wyndham Lewis (1928) and C. Mackworth (1948).

(2) **Jacques**, pseud. of **Gaston Duchamp** (1875–1963), French artist and engraver, born at Damville. From 1891 to 1930 he drew for various periodicals, and made many etchings and lithographs. In 1912 he organized the Section d'Or exhibition in Paris with Léger, Juan Gris, &c. His paintings, many of which are abstract, transmute nature into crystalline forms reminiscent of Cézanne, using clear, bright colour. In 1950 he exhibited at the Venice Biennale and also won the first prize at the Pittsburgh International with his painting *The Thresher*. See study by P. Eluard and René-Jean (1948).

VINCENT, St (d. 304), Spanish protomartyr, born at Saragossa and according to St Augustine became a deacon. Under Diocletian's persecutions, he was imprisoned and tortured at Valencia, where he died. His feast is on January 22.

VINCENT, (1) Sir Charles Edward Howard (1849–1908), English politician, born at Slinfold, in Sussex, was first director of C.I.D., Scotland Yard. He wrote on criminal law and police code (1882), the law of Extradition (1881), and was knighted (1896). See Life by Jeyes and How (1912).

(2) **William** (1739–1815), English scholar,

born in Westminster, was headmaster of Westminster (1788–1802), canon (1801) and then Dean of Westminster (1802). He wrote on education (1801) and ancient geography (1807). See Life by Nares (1817).

VINCENT DE BEAUVAIS (Latinized *Vincentius Bellovacensius*), *vī-sã* (*c.* 1190–1264), French Dominican and encyclopaedist, gathered together, under the patronage of Loius IX, the entire knowledge of the middle ages in his *Speculum Majus*, in three parts, *Naturale*, *Doctrinale et Historiale* (1473) to which *Speculum Morale* was added anonymously. See Life by Bourgeat (1856).

VINCENT DE PAUL, St (*c.* 1580–1660), French priest and philanthropist, born at Pouy in Gascony, April 24, and admitted to priest's orders in 1600. On a voyage from Marseilles to Narbonne in 1605 he was captured by corsairs and was sold into slavery at Tunis. His master, a renegade Savoyard, was persuaded by Vincent to return to the Christian faith; so, escaping, they landed in France in 1607. Having gone to Rome, he was entrusted with a mission to the French court in 1608, and became almoner of Henry IV's queen. He formed assocations for helping the sick, and in 1619 was appointed almoner-general of the galleys. Meanwhile he had laid the foundation of the Congregation of Priests of the Missions, sanctioned by Urban VIII in 1632, and called Lazarists from their priory of St Lazare in Paris. The Paris Foundling Hospital, the Sisterhood of Charity (1634) and associated lay nursing organizations were of his founding. He died September 27, 1660, and was canonized 1737. His feast day is on July 19. See Lives by E. K. Sanders (1913), P. Coste (1932; trans. 1935) and Giraud (trans. 1955). See OZANAM.

VINCENTIUS LERINENSIS (d. *c.* 450), was a monk of the island of Lerna (Lérins), who defined the three marks of Catholicity—'Quod ubique, quod semper, quod ab omnibus'. Canon Heurtley translated his *Commonitorium* (1895).

VINCI. See LEONARDO DA VINCI.

VINET, Alexandre Rodolphe, *vee-nay* (1797–1847), Swiss Protestant theologian and critic, born at Ouchy near Lausanne, was ordained in 1819, became in 1835 professor of French Language and Literature at Basel and in 1837 of Practical Theology at Lausanne. He was forced to resign when he led a secession from the Swiss church in 1845. He published studies of French literature of the 16th-19th centuries, defended freedom of conscience and the disestablishment of the church. See Lives by Lane (1890) and studies by Rambert (1875) and Molines (1890).

VINJE, Aasmund Olavson, *vin'yě* (1816–70), Norwegian poet and critic, born at Vinje, was in turn teacher, journalist, student and employed in a lawyer's office, before gaining recognition. Intermittently between 1858 and 1866, he brought out a weekly journal *Dölen*, written entirely by himself. He visited England in 1862 and wrote his critical *A Norseman's View of Britain and the British* (in English) (1863). Back in Norway, he indulged in adverse political criticism which led to his dismissal from an official post at Christiania. Best known for his poetry, Vinje was one of the leading writers in the *landsmål* (the language of the people) movement which was rapidly gaining ground. His works include *En Ballade om Kongen* (1853), *Storegut* (1866) and *Blandkorn* (1867).

VINOGRADOFF, Sir Paul, *vee-nō-grah'doff* (1854–1925), Russian social historian, born at Kostroma, studied at Moscow, became professor of History there. He settled in England and in 1903 he was appointed professor of Jurisprudence at Oxford. Knighted in 1917, he was an authority on mediaeval England, and among his writings are *Villeinage in England* (1892), *Growth of the Manor* (1905) and *English Society in the Eleventh Century* (1908).

VIOLLET-LE-DUC, Eugène, *vyō-lay-lė-dük* (1814–79), French architect and archaeologist, born in Paris, in 1840 became director of the restoration of the Sainte Chapelle, and from this time on was the great restorer of ancient buildings in France including the cathedrals of Notre Dame at Paris, Amiens, Laon, and the Château de Pierrefonds. He served as engineer in the defence of Paris, and was an advanced republican politician. His best-known work was his great dictionary of French Architecture (1853–69). See Lives by Sauvageot (1880), Saint-Paul (2nd ed. 1881), Gout (1914).

VIOTTI, Giovanni Battista, *vyot'tee* (1753–1824), Italian violinist and composer of a number of violin and piano concertos, born at Fontanetto, lived mostly in Paris, where he was director of the Italian Opera and from 1792 was a wine merchant in London. He was one of the leading violinists of his day.

VIRCHOW, Rudolf, *feer-*KHō (1821–1902), German pathologist, born at Schivelbein, Pomerania, became professor of Pathological Anatomy at Würzburg (1849) and at Berlin (1856). His *Cellularpathologie* (1858) established that every morbid structure contained cells derived from previous cells. He contributed to the study of tumours, leukaemia, hygiene and sanitation, and as a Liberal member of the *Reichstag* (1880–93) strenuously opposed Bismarck. See studies by Becher (1891) and Pagel (1906).

VIRET, Pierre, *vee-ray* (1511–71), Swiss reformer, born at Orbe in Vaud, converted Lausanne to the Protestant faith (1536). See monograph by Godet (1893).

VIRGIL, (Publius Vergilius Maro) (70–19 B.C.), greatest of Latin poets, was born at Andes near Mantua, October 15. His father owned a small property; the boy was sent to school at Cremona and Milan, and at sixteen went to Rome and studied rhetoric and philosophy. In 41 B.C. the victorious triumvirs were settling disbanded soldiers on confiscated lands throughout Italy. Virgil's farm was part of the confiscated territory; but by advice of the governor of the district, Asinius Pollio, he went to Rome, with special recommendations to Octavianus; and though his own property was not restored to him, he obtained ample compensation from the government, and became one of the endowed court poets who gathered round the prime minister Maecenas. In 37 B.C. his *Eclogues*, ten pastorals modelled on those of Theocritus, were received with unexampled enthusiasm.

Soon afterwards Virgil withdrew from Rome to Campania. The munificence of Maecenas had placed him in affluent circumstances. He had a villa at Naples and a country-house near Nola. The *Georgics*, or *Art of Husbandry*, in four books, dealing with tillage and pasturage, the vine and olive, horses, cattle, and bees appeared in 30 B.C., and confirmed Virgil's position as the foremost poet of the age. The remaining eleven years of his life were devoted to a larger task, undertaken at the urgent request of the emperor, the composition of a great national epic on the story of Aeneas the Trojan, legendary founder of the Roman nation and of the Julian family, from the fall of Troy to his arrival in Italy, his wars and alliances with the native Italian races, and his final establishment in his new kingdom. By 19 B.C. the *Aeneid* was practically completed, and in that year Virgil left Italy to travel in Greece and Asia; but at Athens he fell ill, and returned only to die at Brundisium, September 21. At his own wish he was buried at Naples, on the road to Pozzuoli, his tomb, for many hundreds of years after, being worshipped as a sacred place. His sincerity and sweetness of temper won the warm praise of Horace, and the fastidious purity of his life in an age of very lax morality gained him the same name of 'the lady' by which Milton was known at Cambridge. A few juvenile pieces of more or less probable authenticity are extant under his name. These are the *Culex* and the *Moretum*, both in hexameter verse; the *Copa*, a short elegiac piece; and fourteen little poems in various metres, some serious, others trivial. The *Ciris* is now agreed to be by a contemporary imitator. The supremacy of Virgil in Latin poetry was immediate and almost unquestioned; in the *Eclogues* the Latin tongue assumed a richness, harmony, and sweetness till then unknown. The promise shown in the *Eclogues* was more than fulfilled in the *Georgics*. The workmanship of the *Aeneid* is more unequal; but in its great passages there is the same beauty, with an even fuller strength and range. Virgil's works were established classics even in his lifetime, and soon after his death had become, as they still remain, the textbooks of western Europe. By the 3rd century his poems ranked as sacred books, and were regularly used for purposes of divination. In the Dark Ages his fabled powers as a magician almost eclipsed his real fame as a poet; but with the revival of learning he resumed his old place. Dante chose him as his guide in the *Divine Comedy*. The standard English edition is still that of Conington and Nettleship (4th ed. 1881–83). See works on the poet by W. Y. Sellar (1897), T. R. Glover (1915), T. Frank (1922), E. K. Rand (1931), W. F. J. Knight (1944) and Haarhoff (1949), on the *Aeneid* by M. M. Crump (1920) and D. L. Drew (1924), on the *Eclogues* by R. S. Conway (1907) and H. J. Rose (1942) and C. M. Bowra, *From Virgil to Milton* (1945).

VIRGIL, Polydore. See VERGIL.

VIRGINIA. See CLAUDIUS (APPIUS).

VIRIATHUS, *-ah'toos* (d. 139), a Lusitanian herdsman, headed a rising against the

Romans, and from 151 to 141 B.C. repeatedly defeated Roman armies. He was murdered by the Romans.

VIRTANEN, Artturi Ilmari (1895–), Finnish biochemist, born at Helsinki, became professor of Biochemistry there in 1939. He elucidated the processes by which plants obtain nitrogen and complex organic substances from the soil. He showed that silage can be preserved by dilute hydrochloric acid, and studied nutrition and the development of food resources, for which he was awarded the Nobel prize for chemistry (1945).

VISCHER, Peter, *fish'ér* (1455–1529), German sculptor in bronze, was born and died at Nürnberg. He was responsible for the *King Arthur* statue at Innsbruck, the tomb of Archbishop Ernst at Magdeburg and the basic structure of that of St Sebald at Nürnberg. His sons **Hans** (1489–1550), **Hermann** (1486–1517) and **Peter,** the younger (1487–1528), were also distinguished sculptors. See monograph by C. Headlam (1901).

VISCONTI, the name, taken from the hereditary office of viscount, of a Milanese family of Ghibelline nobility which rose to prominence when **Ottone Visconti** (d. 1295) became archbishop of Milan in 1262 and his nephew **Matteo** (1255–1322) captain of the people. Its most important members in chronological order, were:

(1) **Giovanni** (d. 1354) archbishop and lord of Milan from 1349, brought Genoa and Bologna under his jurisdiction.

(2) **Gian Galeazzo** (1351–1402), Milanese statesman, grandnephew of (1), succeeded his father, Galeazzo II, as joint ruler (1378–85) with his uncle Bernabo, whom he had executed (1385). As duke (1385) he made himself master of the northern half of Italy, bringing many independent cities into one state, arranged marriage alliances with England, France, Austria and Bavaria, and was a great patron of the arts. See Life by D. M. Bueno de Mesquita (1941).

(3) **Filippo Maria** (1392–1447), Milanese statesman, son of (2), restored the unity of his father's dominions, but died without issue. The duchy passed to the Sforza family (q.v.). See D. Muir, *A History of Milan under the Visconti* (1924).

VISCONTI, name of an Italian family of archaeologists and architects:

(1) **Ennio Quirino** (1751–1818), son of (2), father of (3), was keeper of the Capitoline Museum from 1787. During the Roman Republic of 1798 he was one of the five consuls, then fled to Paris, where he became curator at the Louvre and professor of Archaeology. In 1817 he came to England to examine the Elgin marbles. He wrote *Iconographie grecque* (1801) and *romaine* (1817).

(2) **Giovanni Battista Antonio** (1722–84), father of (1), succeeded Winckelmann as prefect of antiquities at Rome (1768), reorganized the Museo Pio-Clementino in the Vatican and with his son edited the catalogue of the museum's engravings. He supervised the excavations which led to the discovery of Scipio's tomb.

(3) **Lodovico Tullio Gioacchino** (1791–1853), son of (1), was a Parisian architect (from 1799). He built Napoleon's mausoleum and was responsible for the scheme joining the Louvre and the Tuileries. His nephew, **Pietro Ercole** (1802–80), was commissioner of antiquities at Rome and curator of the Vatican art collections.

VISSCHER, Cornelis, *vis'ér* (*c.* 1629–58), a Dutch copperplate engraver, famous for his portraits and for engravings after Guido Reni, Brouwer and Ostade.—His brother, **Jan** (1634–92), was similarly distinguished.

VIT, Vincenzo de (1811–91), Italian scholar, born in Padua, was editor of Forcellini's *Lexicon Totius Latinitatis* (1858–79). A canon of Rovigo and town librarian, in 1850 he joined the brotherhood of Rosmini (q.v.). His unfinished *Onomasticon* was to contain all proper names down to the 5th century.

VITELLIUS, Aulus, *-tel'-* (A.D. 15–69), Roman emperor, was a favourite of Tiberius, Caligula, Claudius and Nero. Appointed by Galba to the command of the legions on the Lower Rhine, he was proclaimed emperor at Colonia Agrippinensis (Cologne) at the beginning of 69; and his generals put an end to the reign of Otho by the victory of Bedriacum. Vitellius, during his brief reign, gave himself up to pleasure and debauchery. Many of his soldiers deserted when Vespasian was proclaimed emperor in Alexandria. Vitellius was defeated in two battles by his rival, dragged through the streets of Rome and murdered, December 21.

VITORIA. See ESPARTERO.

VITRUVIUS POLLIO, Marcus, *-troo'vee-oos* (1st cent. A.D.), Roman architect and military engineer, a North Italian in the service of Augustus, wrote *De Architectura* (before A.D. 27), which is the only Roman treatise on architecture still extant. See edition by F. Granger (1931).

VITRY, Jacques de, *vee-tree* (d. 1240), a French cardinal legate, who died at Rome, is known by his *Historia Orientalis*, a valuable source book, letters and sermons.

VITTORINO DA FELTRE, *veet-to-ree'nō da fel-trê* (*c.* 1378–1446), Italian educationist, was summoned to Mantua as tutor to the children of the Marchese Gonzaga (1423) and founded a school for both rich and poor children (1425), in which he applied his own methods of instruction. See study by W. H. Woodward (1897).

VITUS, St, *vī-* (early 4th cent.), is said to have been the son of a Sicilian pagan and converted by his nurse Crescentia and her husband Modestus, with whom he suffered martyrdom under Diocletian. He was invoked against sudden death, hydrophobia and chorea or St Vitus' Dance, and is sometimes regarded as the patron of comedians and actors. His feast day is June 15.

VIVALDI, Antonio, *-vahl'-* (1678–1741), Venetian violinist and composer, known as ' the Red Priest ', on account of his red hair, born at Venice, took orders (1703), but gave up officiating and was attached to the hospital of the Pietà at Venice (1703–40), dying at Vienna. The twelve concertos of *L'Estro Armonico* (1712) gave him a European reputation; *The Seasons* (1725), an early example of programme music, proved highly popular; and he wrote many operas and some sacred music. Though he really consolidated and developed the solo concerto, he was forgotten after his death. Bach transcribed many of his concertos for the keyboard and from the 19th century they were increasingly played. See Life by Mario Rinaldi (Milan 1943) and Italian study by M. Pincherle (1948; abridged and trans. 1958).

VIVARINI, *vee-vah-ree'-nee,* name of a family of Venetian painters of the 15th century, including:

(1) **Antonio** (active *c.* 1440–*c.* 1476/84), first worked in partnership with his brother-in-law Giovanni d'Alemagna and later with his brother (2). His paintings, often of Madonnas and saints, are modelled first on Gentile da Fabriano and then on Mantegna and Giovanni Bellini (q.v.).

(2) **Bartolommeo** (active 1450–99), brother of (1), worked under the same influences, but his painting shows a step forward towards the renaissance style.

(3) **Luigi or Alvise** (active 1457–*c.* 1503/5), son of (1), was possibly a pupil of both his father and uncle. Influenced by Antonello da Messina and Bellini, his works include portrait busts and altarpieces, especially a *Madonna and six Saints* (1480) in the Academy, Venice.

VIVES, Juan Luis, generally known as **Ludovicus Vives,** *vee-vays* (1492–1540), Spanish philosopher and humanist, born at Valencia, studied philosophy at Paris, but, disgusted with the empty quibblings of scholasticism there, went to Louvain in 1519, where, as professor of Humanities, he edited St Augustine's *Civitas Dei.* He dedicated it to Henry VIII, who summoned him to England in 1523 as tutor to Princess Mary. He also taught at Oxford and became a fellow of Corpus Christi. He was imprisoned in 1527 for opposing Henry VIII's divorce from Catharine of Aragon and after 1528 lived mostly at Bruges. His commentary on Aristotle's *De Anima* foreshadowed Bacon in his emphasis on inductive methods. He also wrote a remarkable treatise on education, *De Disciplinis* (1531).

VIVIANI, René, *vee-vyah'nee* (1862–1925), French statesman, born at Sidi-bel-Abbès, Algeria, was prime minister at the outbreak of World War I and in order to demonstrate France's peaceful intentions withdrew French forces from the German frontier. He was minister of justice (1915) and French representative at the League of Nations (1920).

VIVIN, Louis, *vee-vi* (1861–1936), French primitive painter, born at Hadol, was a Post Office employee until he retired in 1922. He painted mainly still-lifes and views of Paris and its parks. His naïve and charmingly coloured pictures are meticulous in every detail.

VIZETELLY, Henry Richard, *viz-è-tel'i* (1820–1894), English publisher of Italian descent, was born in London. As an engraver he early contributed to the newly founded *Illustrated London News* and in 1843 set up in competition his own *Pictorial Times.* He became a foreign correspondent to the

Illustrated London News in Paris (1865–72) and in Berlin (1872). He witnessed the siege of Paris and with his son, Ernest, wrote *Paris in Peril* (1867). As a publisher in later life, he produced translations of French and Russian authors, notably of the works of Zola, which involved him in two legal actions for obscene libel. In 1893 his memoirs were published as *Glances Back Through Seventy Years.* His brother, **Frank** (1830–83), also a foreign correspondent for the *Illustrated London News,* was killed in the Sudan. His sons, **Edward Henry** (1847–1903) and **Ernest Alfred** (1853–1922), were also journalists, while **Frank Horace** (1864–1938) was a notable lexicographer on the staff of the Funk and Wagnall Company in New York.

VLADIMIR, *vla-dee'-meer,* the name of two notable Russian rulers:

Vladimir I, known as Saint Vladimir, or 'the Great' (*c.* 956–1015), ruled from 980 as the first Christian sovereign of Russia, extending its dominions into Lithuania, Galicia and Livonia, with Kiev as his capital.

Vladimir II, surnamed **Monomachus** (1053–1125), became by popular demand Grand Prince of Kiev in 1113 instead of the prior claimants of the Sviatoslav and Iziaslav families, thus founding the Monomakhovichi dynasty. A popular, powerful, enlightened and peaceful ruler, he colonized, built new towns, dethroned unruly princes and introduced laws against usury. He left careful instructions to his son and cousin in the manuals *Puchenie* and *Poslanie.*

VLAMINCK, Maurice de, *vla-mik* (1876–1958), French artist, born in Paris. He was largely self-taught, and for a time was a racing cyclist. About 1900 he began to work with Derain. At this time he was much influenced by Van Gogh, and by 1905 he was one of the leaders of the Fauves, using typically brilliant colour. From 1908 to 1914, however, he painted more realistic landscapes under the influence of Cézanne. After 1915 his palette was more sombre, and his style more romantic than Cézannesque, though still with an expressionist zest. He mainly lived in the country as a farmer, and this may have given him his consistent sensitivity to the nuances of landscape and atmosphere. Also a talented violinist, he wrote several books, including *Communications* (1921). See Lives by K. G. Perls (1941) and R. Queneau (1949).

VODNIK, Valentin (1758–1819), Slovene poet and teacher, born at Zgornja Šiška near Ljubljana, who by his writings helped to revive Slovene nationalism. He wrote poetry, educational and school books in the language of the peasantry and this became established as the literary language of Yugoslavia.

VOELCKER, Augustus, *fœl'kèr* (1822–84), German agricultural chemist and writer, was born at Frankfurt-am-Main. After studying at Göttingen and Utrecht, he worked in Edinburgh under the auspices of the Highland and Agricultural Society of Scotland, was appointed professor of Agriculture at the Royal Agricultural College, Cirencester, in 1849, and in 1857 was attached to the Royal Agricultural Society of England as consulting chemist.

Agricultural chemistry was greatly advanced by Voelcker's work and writings on farm feeding stuffs, on soil research and on artificial manures. In 1870 he was elected a fellow of the Royal Society and in 1875 chairman of the Farmers' Club.

VOGEL, (1) **Hermann Carl** (1841–1907), German astronomer, born at Leipzig, became assistant and later director of the observatory at Potsdam (1882). He discovered spectroscopic binaries.

(2) **Hermann Wilhelm** (1834–98), German chemist, born at Dobrilugk, Brandenburg, taught at Berlin, and invented the orthochromatic photographic plate (1873), studied spectroscopic photography and designed a photometer.

(3) **Sir Julius** (1835–99), New Zealand statesman, born in London, edited and founded newspapers in Australia and New Zealand, where he was elected colonial treasurer in 1869. He established a government public trust office (1872), improved immigration facilities and planned the introduction of trunk railways, borrowing £10,000,000 for his public works programme. He formed a government in 1872 and was premier (1873–75). His resolution (1874) foreshadowed the abolition of the provinces. He resigned in 1875 to devote himself to business, but was again treasurer during the economic crisis in 1884.

(4) **Vladimir** (1896–   ), Russian composer, born at Moscow, studied in Moscow and under Busoni in Berlin. He composed orchestral works and chamber music and secular oratorios, including *Wagadu Destroyed* (1935) with saxophone accompaniment.

VOGLER, **Georg Joseph**, *fōg'lĕr* (1749–1814), German composer, styled Abt Vogler, was born at Würzburg, the son of a violin maker, was ordained priest at Rome in 1773, and made Knight of the Golden Spur and chamberlain to the pope. At Mannheim he established his first school of music; his second was at Stockholm. After years of wandering and brilliant successes in London and Europe as a player on his ' orchestrion ' (a modified organ), he settled as *kapellmeister* at Darmstadt, and opened his third school, having as pupils Weber and Meyerbeer. His compositions and his theories of music are now forgotten; but his name survives in Robert Browning's poem. See study by Schafhäutl (1887).

VOGÜÉ, -*gü-ay*, (1) **Charles Jean Melchior, Marquis de** (1829–1916), French archaeologist and diplomatist, born in Paris, travelled in Syria (1853–54 and 1861), was ambassador at Constantinople (1871–75) and at Vienna (1875–79). Elected to the Académie (1901), he wrote on the churches of Palestine (1860 and 1865).

(2) **Eugène Marie Melchior, Vicomte de** (1848–1910), French historian, cousin of (1), was born at Nice. He was secretary at St Petersburg (1876–82) and was admitted to the Académie (1888). He wrote *Le Roman russe* (1886), a valuable study of the Russian novels of Tolstoy and Dostoevsky, *Les*

Morts qui parlent (1899) and works on Syria and Egypt.

VOITURE, **Vincent**, *vwah-tür* (1598–1648), French poet and letter-writer, born at Amiens, was an original member of the Académie, and enjoyed the favour of Gaston d'Orléans, Richelieu, Mazarin and Louis XIII. His brilliant sonnets and *vers de société* were the delight of the Hôtel Rambouillet, but were not published till 1650. See Sainte-Beuve's *Causeries* and study by E. Magne (1911).

VOLNEY, **Constantin François Chassebœuf, Comte de** (1757–1820), French scholar and author, born at Craon in Mayenne, studied at Paris medicine, history and the Oriental languages, adopted the name of Volney, and travelled in Egypt and Syria (1783–87), publishing his valuable *Voyage* (1787). A zealous reformer, he was elected to the Constituent Assembly in 1789, but later was thrown into prison till the downfall of Robespierre. His reputation chiefly rests on his famous work *Les Ruines, ou Méditations sur les révolutions des empires* (1791). Professor of History at the short-lived École Normale, he collected in the United States (1795–98) materials for his *Tableau du climat et du sol* (1803), and was admitted to the Academy. Napoleon made him senator, count and commander of the Légion d'honneur; Louis XVIII made him a peer. See Life by L. Séché (1899) and Sainte-Beuve's *Causeries*.

VOLSTEAD, **Andrew J.** (1860–1947), American politician, born in Goodhue Co., Minnesota, practised law and entered congress as a Republican in 1903. He was the author of the Farmers' Cooperative Marketing Act, but is best known for the Prohibition Act of 1919, named after him, which forbade the manufacture and sale of intoxicant liquors. This act, passed over President Wilson's veto, was in force until 1933.

VOLTA, **Alessandro, Count**, *vol'tah* (1745–1827), Italian physicist, born at Como, in 1774–1804 was professor of Natural Philosophy at Pavia. He retired to his native town, but was summoned to show his discoveries to Napoleon, and received medals and titles at home and abroad, including the Copley medal (1791). He developed the theory of current electricity, discovered the electric decomposition of water; invented an electric battery, the electrophorus, and an electroscope and made investigations on heat and gases. His name is given to the unit of electric pressure, the volt. See monographs by Bianchi and Mochetti (1829–32), and by Volta (1875).

VOLTAIRE, **François Marie Arouet de**, *voltayr* (1694–1778), French author, the embodiment of the 18th-century ' enlightenment ', was born November 24 in Paris, where his father, François Arouet, held a post in the Chambre des comptes. In his ninth year he entered the Collège Louis-le-Grand, the chief French seminary of the Jesuits. Leaving college at seventeen, he was destined for the bar, but law disgusted him. Alarmed by the dissipated life which he was leading, his father gladly saw him admitted into the suite of his godfather's brother, the Marquis de Châteauneuf, French ambassador to Holland; but in consequence of an undiplomatic love affair with a French Protestant *émigrée* at The Hague, he was sent home. He again entered an attorney's office, but his stay in it was short, and he soon obtained notoriety as the author of a satire on his successful rival in the poetic competition for an Academy prize. In 1716, on suspicion of lampooning the regent, the Duc d'Orléans, he was banished for several months from Paris; and in 1717–18, a savage lampoon, accusing the regent of all manner of crimes, resulted in his eleven months' imprisonment in the Bastille, where he rewrote his tragedy *Œdipe*, began a poem on Henry IV and assumed the name Voltaire, supposed to be an anagram of Arouet l(e) j(eune). *Œdipe* was performed in 1718, and was triumphantly successful. His next dramatic attempts were almost failures, and he devoted himself to his poem on Henry IV. But the authorities refusing to sanction its publication on account of its championship of Protestantism and of religious toleration, Voltaire had the epic poem surreptitiously printed at Rouen (1723) and smuggled into Paris, as *La Ligue ou Henri le grand*. Famous and a favourite at court, he was denounced by the Chevalier de Rohan-Chabot as a parvenu. Voltaire retorted with spirit, and circulated caustic epigrams on the Chevalier, whose revenge was to have Voltaire beaten by his hirelings. Voltaire challenged the author of the outrage, and was once more thrown into the Bastille, and liberated only on the condition that he would proceed at once to England, where he landed in May 1726. Here Bolingbroke made him known to Pope and his circle. He made the acquaintance of Peterborough, Chesterfield, the Herveys and the Duchess of Marlborough, and became intimate with Young, Thomson and Gay. He acquired some knowledge of Shakespeare and Milton, Dryden and Butler, Pope's works, Addison's *Cato*, and the Restoration dramatists. He was strongly attracted to Locke's philosophy, and he mastered the elements of Newton's astronomical physics. The English Deists furnished weapons or at least a stalking-horse (Bolingbroke). Queen Caroline accepted his dedication to her of the *Henriade*, the new form of *La Ligue*; and when permitted to return to France in 1729 he took with him his *History of Charles XII* and the materials for his *Letters on the English*. He laid the foundation of his great wealth by purchasing shares in a government lottery and by speculations in the corn trade, ultimately increased by the profits from large army contracts. He formed an intimacy with Madame du Châtelet (q.v.), and made her husband's château of Cirey in Champagne their headquarters (1734). Here he wrote dramas (*Mahomet* (1741) and *Mérope* (1743) among them), poetry, his *Treatise on Metaphysics*, much of his *Siècle de Louis Quatorze* (1751) and *Les Mœurs et l'esprit des nations*, with his *Elements of the Philosophy of Newton* (1738). Apart from Madame du Châtelet, his correspondence (1640–50) testifies to a

love affair with his niece, the widowed Madame Denis. Since the appearance of his *Letters on the English* he had been out of favour at court. But his *Princesse de Navarre*, performed on the occasion of the Dauphin's marriage (February 1745), pleased Louis XV by its adroit adulation. This and the patronage of Madame de Pompadour procured him the appointments of royal historiographer and of gentleman-in-ordinary to the king, as well as his election to the French Academy. In 1747 an imprudent speech at a court card-party drove him to take refuge with the Duchesse de Maine, for whose amusement he now wrote *Zadig* and others of the Oriental tales. When he was allowed to reappear at court, some injudicious flattery of Madame de Pompadour excited the indignation of the queen, and Voltaire had again to migrate. The death (September 1749) of Madame du Châtelet allowed him at last to accept the repeated invitation of Frederick the Great. In July 1750 Voltaire found himself at Berlin as king's chamberlain, with a pension of 20,000 francs and board in one of the royal palaces. But he entered into some questionable financial operations with a Berlin Jew; Frederick was still more gravely offended by his satirical criticisms on Maupertuis; and in March 1753 Frederick and Voltaire parted, never to meet again. In Prussia Voltaire had published his *Siècle de Louis Quatorze* (1751). On his way home he was arrested at Frankfurt, through Frederick's representative there, instructed to recover from Voltaire a volume of the king's poems. Voltaire avenged himself by writing a malicious sketch of Frederick's character and account of his habits, first printed after the writer's death. Voltaire settled in 1755 near Geneva—after 1758 at Ferney, four miles from Geneva. In 1756–59 appeared his *Mœurs et l'Esprit des nations*, his pessimistic poem on the earthquake of Lisbon and that satirical masterpiece, the short story, *Candide* which attacked what Voltaire understood by the Leibnizian optimistic theology that ' all is for the best in this best of all possible worlds '. The suspension of the *Encyclopédie* by the French government, and the condemnation by the parliament of Paris of a harmless poem of his own on natural religion, impelled Voltaire to declare war by word and deed against the bigoted, ' L'Infâme '. In 1762 appeared the first of his antireligious writings which were to include didactic tragedies, biased histories, pamphlets and the *Dictionnaire philosophique* (1764). The judicial murder (1762) of Jean Calas (q.v.), falsely accused of having, from Protestant zeal, killed one of his sons to keep him from turning a Catholic, aroused Voltaire to exert himself successfully to get his innocence established and to rescue members of the Calas family from punishment. This and similar efforts on behalf of victims of French fanaticism, for whom he provided a refuge at Ferney, won widespread admiration. The Genevan government prevented Voltaire from staging plays and from establishing a theatre at Geneva. Rousseau's support for the Swiss government terminated Voltaire's friendship with the philosopher (1758). In 1778, in his eighty-fourth year, he was given a ' royal ' welcome in Paris, when he arrived to put on his last tragedy, *Irène*. The excitement brought on illness and death on May 30, 1778. After the Revolution, which his works and ideas helped to foster, his remains were fitly reinterred in the Panthéon, Paris. See his *Correspondence with Frederick the Great* (trans. 1927), his *Love Letters to His Niece* (ed. and trans. T. Besterman, 1958); Lives by G. Desnoiresterres (1867–76), Viscount Morley (1872), L. Crouslé (1899), C. E. Vulliamy (1930), H. N. Brailsford (1935), A. Noyes (1936), R. Naves (1942), A. Maurois (1952); and political and philosophical studies by G. Pellissier (1908), A. Bellescort (1925), C. Rowe (1955) and P. Gay (1959).

VOLTERRA, (1) **Daniele da** (*c.* 1509–66), Italian artist, born at Volterra, was Michelangelo's assistant. He painted the *Descent from the Cross* in the Trinità dei Monti at Rome.

(2) **Vito** (1860–1940), Italian mathematician, born at Ancona, professor at Pisa, Turin and Rome, contributed to modern mathematical analysis and theory of equations. He became a foreign member of the Royal Society in 1902.

VOLUSENUS, Florentius-Florence Wilson, or **Wolsey,** *vol-oo-say'noos* (1504–46), Scottish humanist, born near Elgin, went to the University of Paris, and attained a mastery of Latin which ranks him with the first scholars of his time. After acting as tutor to a reputed son of Cardinal Wolsey, he became principal of a school at Carpentras near Avignon; and died at Vienne in Dauphiné. His chief work is his *De Animi Tranquillitate*. See Hume Brown, *Surveys of Scottish History* (1919).

VONDEL, Joost van den (1587–1679), the greatest of the Dutch poets, born at Cologne of Dutch immigrant parents, became a prosperous hosier in Amsterdam and devoted his leisure to the penning of satirical verse, himself turning from Anabaptism through Armenianism to Roman Catholicism. Having acquired a wide knowledge of the classics, Vondel turned to Sophoclean drama and produced *Jephtha* (1659) and *Lucifer* (1654), a masterpiece of lyrical religious drama, which brings to mind Milton's *Paradise Lost* (*c.* 1660–63) and greatly influenced the German poetical revival after the Thirty Years' War. See his complete *Werken*, ed. with Life by J. F. M. Sterck (1927–40) and study by A. J. Barnouw (1926).

VON WRIGHT, Georg Hendrik (1916–), Finnish logician and philosopher, born in Helsinki, took part in the discussions of the Vienna Circle of logical positivists and studied under and succeeded Wittgenstein (q.v.) at Cambridge (1948–51). He was professor of Philosophy at Helsinki (1946–61), visiting professor at Cornell (1954, 1958), California (1963) and Pittsburgh (1966) universities, and professor at large at Cornell since 1965. He was Gifford Lecturer (1959–1960) on *Norms and Values* at St Andrews. Von Wright formalized the traditional, vain attempts at justifying induction in *The Logical Problem of Induction* (1941; rev. ed. 1957) and

A Treatise on Induction and Probability (1951), and has greatly contributed to metalogic with *Form and Content in Logic* (1941), *An Essay in Modal Logic* (1951), *Logical Studies* (1957), and in 1963 *The Varieties of Goodness, The Logic of Preference* and *Norm and Action.* He wrote a memorable introduction to *Ludwig Wittgenstein—A Memoir* by N. Malcolm (1958).

VON DER DECKEN. See DECKEN.

VORAGINE, Jacobus de, *vo-raj'ee-nay* (1230–98), Italian hagiologist, a Dominican, born at Viareggio near Genoa, became Archbishop of Genoa. He wrote the *Golden Legend,* a famous collection of lives of the saints, translated by Caxton in 1483. He is also said to have produced the first Italian translation of the Bible.

VORONOFF, Serge (1866–1951), Russian physiologist, born at Voronezh and educated in Paris, became director of experimental surgery at the Collège de France. He specialized in grafting animal glands into the human body and wrote on his theory connecting gland secretions with senility.

VOROSHILOV, Klimenti Efremovich, *vor-è-shee'léf* (1881–1969), president of the Soviet Union from Stalin's death (1953) to 1960, was born near Dniepropetrovsk in the Ukraine. He joined the Communist Party in 1903 and political agitation soon brought about his exile to Siberia. He remained a fugitive right up to 1914, and took a military rather than a political rôle in the 1917 Revolution. From 1925 to 1940 he was commissar for defence and so mainly responsible for the modernization of the Red Army and its success in defeating Hitler's invasion of 1941. His long friendship with Stalin, dating from 1906, possibly excused some of his later mistakes.

VÖRÖSMARTY, Michael, *vœ'ræsh-mort-y'* (1800–55), Hungarian poet, born at Szekesfehervar, was an advocate and in 1848 a member of the National Assembly. He wrote the national song, *Szozat* (1840), lyric and epic poetry and eleven plays, of which *Csongor es Tünde* (1831) is his masterpiece. He also translated Shakespearean tragedies.

VORTIGERN (fl. 450), the prince of southeast Britain, reported by Bede, Nennius and Geoffrey of Monmouth to have invited the Saxons into Britain to help him against the Picts, and to have married Rowena, daughter of Hengist.

VOS, Cornelis de (1585–1651), Antwerp painter of portraits and religious and mythological pieces, worked occasionally for Rubens. His brother, **Paul** (1590–1678), painted animals and hunting scenes.

VOSS, fos, (1) **Johann Heinrich** (1751–1826), German poet and translator, born at Sommersdorf in Mecklenburg, studied at Göttingen, and in 1778 went from editing the *Musenalmanach* at Wandsbeck to be schoolmaster at Otterndorf. Here he translated the *Odyssey*. In 1782 he became rector of a school at Eutin, whence in 1789 he issued his translation of Virgil's *Georgics*. In 1802 he settled in Jena, in 1805 was appointed professor at Heidelberg, where he translated Horace, Hesiod, Theocritus, Bion, Moschus, Tibullus and Propertius; other translations were of Aristophanes and (with the aid of his two sons) Shakespeare—a work far inferior to Schlegel's. *Luise* (1795), an idyll, is his best original poem. See Lives by Paulus (1826) and by Herbst (1876).

(2) **Richard** (1851–1918), German writer, born at Neugrape in Pomerania, published a long series of poems, dramas and romances.

VOSSIUS, (1) Gerard Jan (1577–1649), Dutch scholar, father of (2), born near Heidelberg, studied at Leyden, and became in 1600 rector of the school at Dort and in 1615 of the theological college of Leyden. His *Historia Pelagiana* (1618), with its Arminian leanings, brought down upon him the wrath of the orthodox. Laud made him a prebend in Canterbury. In his *De Historicis Latinis* (1627) he made a prudent recantation. In 1632 he became professor of History in the Athenaeum at Amsterdam. His chief works are *Commentaria Rhetorica* (1606), *De Historicis Graecis* (1624) and *Aristarchus* (1635).

(2) **Isaak** (1618–88), Dutch scholar, son of (1), born in Leyden, travelled in England, France and Italy, collecting many valuable manuscripts, and was at the court of Queen Christina of Sweden, but returned to Holland in 1658. In 1670 he settled in England, and, although a libertine, was appointed by Charles II a canon of Windsor. He edited the epistles of Ignatius (1646), Justin, Pomponius Mela and Catullus, and wrote on chronology.

VOUET, Simon, *voo-ay* (1590–1649), French painter, born in Paris, after fourteen years in Italy, returned to France, where his religious and allegorical paintings and decorations in the baroque style became very popular. A contemporary of Poussin, who criticized him but was not a serious rival during his lifetime, his pupils included Lebrun and Le Sueur. There are paintings by him in galleries throughout Europe, including the Louvre, the Uffizi and the National Gallery, London.

VOWELL, John. See HOOKER (4).

VOYNICH, E. L. See BOOLE.

VOYSEY, Charles (1828–1912), English theist, born in London, studied at St Edmund's Hall, Oxford, was transferred from his curacy at St Mark's, Whitechapel, in 1863, to the living of Healaugh near Tadcaster, for preaching against the doctrine of perpetual punishment. His sermons and writings on inspiration led to the deprivation of his living in 1871. He then became founder and pastor of a Theistic church in London, and wrote on *The Mystery of Pain, Death and Sin* and on *Theism*.

VRCHLICKÝ, Jaroslav, *værKH'lits-ki* (1853–1912), pseud. of Emil Frída, Czech lyric and epic poet and translator of the classics of European poetry, born at Laun, was a pupil of Victor Hugo who inspired the *Fragments of the Epic of Humanity*. His best ballads, *Legend of St Procopius* (1879), *Peasant Ballads* (1886), are on nationalistic and patriotic themes. His early lyric poetry on love and the pleasures of life gave way to reflections upon suffering and misfortune. In 1893, at the height of his reputation, he was appointed professor of European literature at Prague.

VRIES. See DE VRIES.

VUILLARD, Jean Edouard, *vwee-yahr'* (1868–1940), French artist, born at Cuiseaux, died at La Baule. One of the later Impressionists, he shared a studio with Bonnard, and was strongly influenced by Gauguin and by the vogue for Japanese painting. Although his outlook was limited and mainly devoted to flower pieces and to simple and intimate interiors, these are painted with an exquisite sense of light and colour. See Life by C. Roger-Marx (1948), and studies by same (Paris 1945) and Jacques Mercanton (Paris 1948).

VULPIUS, Christiane. See GOETHE.

VYSHINSKY, Andrei, *vee-shins'kee* (1883–1954), Soviet jurist and politician, born of Polish origin in Odessa, studied law at Moscow University but was debarred from a lecturership on account of his Menshevik revolutionary activities until 1921, when he left the Red Army. He became professor of Criminal Law and simultaneously attorney-general (1923–25) and was rector of Moscow University (1925–28). He was notoriously the public prosecutor at the Metropolitan-Vickers trial (1933) and the subsequent state trials (1936–38) which removed Stalin's rivals, Bukharin, Radek, Zinoviev, Kamenev and Sokolnikov. He was promoted deputy foreign minister under Molotov (1940) and was permanent Soviet delegate to the United Nations (1945–49, 1953–54), succeeding Molotov as foreign minister in 1949 until the death of Stalin (1953). He was the cynically brilliant advocate of the disruptive and negative Stalin-Molotov foreign policies, the author of many textbooks on Soviet Law and the recipient of the Order of Lenin and Stalin prize in 1947.

W

WAAGE, Peter, *vaw'gé* (1833–1900), Norwegian chemist, became (1862) professor in Christiania, and established (1864) with Guldberg (q.v.) the law of mass action.

WAAGEN, Gustav Friedrich, *vah'gen* (1794–1868), German art critic, appointed (1844) Art History professor at Berlin university. One of his best-known books is *The Treasures of Art in Great Britain* (3 vols. 1854).

WAALS, Johannes Diderik van der, *vals* (1837–1923), Dutch physicist, professor at Amsterdam University (1877–1908), famed for the discovery (1873) of van der Waals' equation, defining the physical state of a gas or liquid, and investigator of the weak attractive forces (van der Waals' forces) between molecules. He was awarded a Nobel prize in 1910.

WACE, Robert (?), *ways* (*c.* 1115–*c.* 1183), Anglo-Norman poet, born in Jersey, studied in Paris, and was a canon of Bayeux between 1160 and 1170. He wrote several verse lives of the saints, a free Norman-French version of Geoffrey of Monmouth's *Historia Regum Britanniae* entitled *Roman de Brut* (1155), used by Layamon and Brunne (qq.v.), also the *Roman de Rou*, an epic of the exploits of the Dukes of Normandy. See studies by Payne-Payne (1916) and Philpot (1926).

WACKENRODER, Wilhelm Heinrich, *vak'en-rō-dėr* (1773–98), German writer, an early exponent of Romanticism and a close friend of Tieck (q.v.), with whom he collaborated in *Herzensergiessungen eines kunstliebenden Klosterbruders* (1797) and *Phantasien über die Kunst* (1799).

WADDELL, Helen (1889–1965), English mediaevalist and writer, born in Tokyo, published *Lyrics from the Chinese* (1913), *Mediaeval Latin Lyrics* (1929), *The Wandering Scholars* (1927), *Peter Abelard* (1933), *The Desert Fathers* (1936), &c.

WADDING, Luke (1588–1657), Irish theologian, born at Waterford, in 1607 entered the Franciscan order, in 1617 became president of an Irish college in Salamanca, was founder in 1625 of another college in Rome, famed for his *Annales Ordinis Minorum* (1625–54; the history of the Franciscans), *Scriptores Ordinis Minorum* (1650), and his edition (1639) of Duns Scotus. See Life by J. A. O'Shea (1885) and study by G. Cleary (1925).

WADDINGTON, William Henry, Fr. *vad-ī-tō* (1826–94), French statesman and archaeologist, born in Paris, the son of an Englishman, who became a French subject. He was educated chiefly in England, devoted himself to study and travel in Asia Minor, Syria and Cyprus, and was ambassador at London from 1883 till 1892.

WADE, (1) George (1673–1748), British field-marshal, born probably in Westmeath, entered the army in 1690, after the Jacobite rebellion of 1715 judiciously pacifying and disarming the clans in the Scottish highlands, where he constructed (1726–37) a system of metalled military roads, with forty stone (' Wade ') bridges. Wade became a privy councillor and a lieutenant-general in 1742, and a field-marshal in 1743. Unsuccessful in engagements in the Netherlands in 1744, he was evaded, as commander-in-chief of George II's forces in England, by Prince Charles Edward's army, both on the latter's advance into, and on its retreat from, that country in 1745.

(2) Sir Thomas Francis (1818–95), British diplomatist and scholar, ambassador at Peking (1871–83), professor of Chinese at Cambridge University (1889–95), inventor of the Wade system of transliterating Chinese.

WADSWORTH, Edward (1889–1949), English artist, born in Yorkshire. He studied engineering in Munich, attended the Slade School in 1910, and was associated with Wyndham Lewis, Roger Fry, Unit One, and the London Group. His still-lifes and seascapes with marine objects, painted in tempera with dreamlike clarity and precision, made him internationally known.

WAGNER, *vahg'ner*, (1) **Adolph** (1835–1917), German economist, son of (2), born at Erlangen, was professor at Vienna, Hamburg, Dorpat, Freiburg and Berlin. In his numerous works he represented the historical school and supported state socialism.

(2) **Rudolf** (1805–64), German anatomist and physiologist, father of (1), born at Bayreuth, professor (1832–40) at Erlangen and (1840–64) Göttingen, from whose works were translated (1839) *System of Physiology* and (1844) *Comparative Anatomy*.

(3) (**Wilhelm**) **Richard** (1813–83), German composer, father of (4), born at Leipzig, was educated chiefly at Dresden. His musical training was perfunctory until he was accepted as a pupil by Weinlig of the Thomasschule in 1830 after notice had been taken of a formidable but abortive concert overture which Dorn (q.v.), a friend of the family and conductor at the new Leipzig Court Theatre, had been cajoled into performing. Some immature efforts were followed by his first opera *Die Feen* (1833), adapted from Gozzi's *Donna Serpente* and owing much to Weber's *Oberon*. It was not performed during the composer's lifetime. His next effort, *Das Liebesverbot* (1834), flopped deservedly after one performance at Magdeburg, where he had obtained the post of conductor at the opera house, and where he met Minna Planer, a member of the company, who was to become his wife in 1836. The Magdeburg opera soon went bankrupt, as did the theatre at Königsberg, where Wagner found his next post. Riga, where Dorn was now teaching, seemed more promising, but Wagner resolved to try his luck in Paris with his new partially-finished opera based on Bulwer-Lytton's romance *Rienzi*. There, in spite of Meyerbeer's help, he barely made a living by journalism and doing hack operatic arrangements. He left Paris in 1842 with *Rienzi*, which he had finished in a debtors' prison, still unperformed but now accepted for presentation at Dresden, where it scored a resounding success. *Der fliegende Holländer* (1843) was not so well received, but Wagner was shortly appointed *kapellmeister* at Dresden. *Tannhäuser* (1845) also failed through too stringent economies in production and poor interpretation by the cast; when restaged at a later date it succeeded. *Lohengrin* was finished in 1848, but by this time Wagner was deeply implicated in the revolutionary movement and barely escaped arrest by fleeing from Saxony. Declining an offer of asylum by Liszt at Weimar, he went first to Paris and later to Zürich. *Lohengrin* was eventually produced at Weimar by Liszt in 1850. During his exile he again had to make a living by writing, among other things, *Art of the Future* (1849), the anti-Semitic *Judaism in Music* (1850), *Opera and Drama* (1851), and the autobiographical *Communication to my Friends* (1851–52). The poem of the *Ring* cycle was finished in 1852, and in 1853 he began the music of *Das Rheingold*, followed by *Die Walküre* (1856) and Part I of *Siegfried* (1857). In 1857–59 he was at work on *Tristan und Isolde*, based on the old German version of the legend by Gottfried von Strassburg, and the opera is often claimed

to have been inspired by his current love affair with Mathilde, wife of his friend and patron Otto Wesendonck. Once again he sought to gain favour in Paris, and eventually Napoleon called for a command performance of *Tannhäuser*, but the opera failed. In 1861 he was allowed to return to Germany, but he still had a hard battle for recognition. *Tristan* was accepted at Vienna but abandoned as impracticable before it could be performed, and, now aged fifty, pursued by creditors and vilified by critics, the composer was on the point of giving up in despair when the tide turned with dramatic suddenness. The eccentric young king of Bavaria, Ludwig II, impressed by the pageantry of *Lohengrin*, read Wagner's *Ring* poem with its pessimistic preface. At once he summoned the composer to his court, where every facility was offered and no expense spared. *Tristan* was staged with brilliant success at Munich in 1865, but Wagner's extravagance, political meddling, and preferential treatment aroused so much hostility that he was obliged to withdraw temporarily to Switzerland. Cosima, wife of the musical director, von Bülow, and daughter of Liszt, left her husband and joined him, eventually marrying him in 1868 after being divorced, Minna having died in 1866. In Switzerland he finished *Die Meistersinger*, his only nontragic piece, which scored a success in 1868. But his greatest ambition, a complete performance of the *Ring*, was as yet unfulfilled. A tentative production of *Das Rheingold* in 1869 was a fiasco, the reception of *Die Walküre* in 1870 was lukewarm, and Ludwig had given up his project for a special Wagnerian opera house in Munich. Determined to fulfil his wish, Wagner set about raising funds himself, and on a fraction of the required total plus a large amount of credit he started the now famous theatre at Bayreuth, which opened in 1876 with a first complete programme of the *Ring* cycle. *Parsifal*, his last and perhaps greatest opera, was staged in 1882, a year before his sudden death from a heart attack. Wagner reformed the whole structure of opera. The one canon was to be dramatic fitness, and to this end he abandoned the classical tradition of recitative and aria, replacing it with an ever-changing dramatic line linked with the emotional colour of the story and accentuated skilfully by use of the *leitmotiv*, which he was the first to adopt with a definite purpose. His works show a progressive development. *Rienzi* is in the grand opera style of Meyerbeer and Spontini; *Der fliegende Holländer* strikes out in a new style, followed up in *Tannhäuser* and reaching perfection in *Lohengrin*. From this time dates the music drama, of which *Tristan* is the most uncompromising type. The *Ring* (*Walküre, Siegfried, Gotterdämmerung*, with the *Rheingold* as introduction) is full of Wagner's most characteristic writing and orchestration. It is loosely based on the old Teutonic legend of the Nibelungen, but the symbolism and the purport of the story is purely Wagnerian, while the ideology stems largely from Nietzsche and Schopenhauer. *Parsifal*, from Wolfram von Eschenbach's version of the Grail legend with its mysticism,

stands by itself. Wagner's music, life and writings are apt to arouse either blind adulation or violent antipathy, but seldom indifference. Supremely egotistical and unable to sense when he was wrong, he was capable of somersaults of opinion and conduct which mystified and sometimes antagonized his friends, as with Meyerbeer, his erstwhile Good Samaritan, whom he mercilessly insulted in *Judaism in Music*, and his one-time admirer Nietzsche, for whom *Siegfried* had once appeared as the prototype of his Superman, but who later came to see in the composer the embodiment of decadence. In his own time Wagner was set up with Liszt as the deity of the Romantic faction in opposition to the followers of Brahms and Schumann, and for many years clashes between the rival partisans were the bane of concert-promoters and conductors all over Europe. The bibliography of Wagner is very much split up into ' pro ' and ' anti ', the most objective Life being perhaps Ernest Newman's great work (1933–47). See also Lives by C. F. Glasenapp (6 vols. 1894–1911, trans. Ellis, 1901 *et seq.*), Hadow (1934), Jacobs (1935); also F. Praeger, *Wagner as I Knew Him* (1892), Shaw, *The Perfect Wagnerite* (1898).

(4) **Siegfried** (1869–1930), son of (3), born near Lucerne, was trained as an architect but later turned to music. He was director of the Bayreuth Festspielhaus from 1909 and died at Bayreuth.

(5) **Wieland** (1917–66), son of (4), born at Bayreuth, took over the directorship of the Festspielhaus at his father's death and revolutionized the production of the operas, stressing their universality as opposed to their purely German significance. He died at Munich.

WAGNER-JAUREGG, or **Wagner von Jauregg, Julius**, *yow′rek* (1857–1940), Austrian neurologist and psychiatrist, born in Wels, won the Nobel prize (1927) for his discovery in 1917 of a treatment for general paralysis by infection with malaria.

WAIN, John Barrington (1925–), English critic and novelist, born at Stoke-on-Trent, studied at and was elected fellow of St John's College, Oxford, and lectured in English Literature at Reading University (1947–55) before turning freelance author. His first four novels, *Hurry on Down* (1953), *Living in the Present* (1955), *The Contenders* (1958) and *Travelling Woman* (1959), tilt at postwar British, particularly London, social values as viewed by a provincial. His debunking vigour and humour has affinities with that of Kingsley Amis (q.v.). He has also written poetry such as *Weep Before God* (1961), edited literary magazines and produced a notable collection of *Preliminary Essays* (1957) in literary criticism. See his auto-biographical *Sprightly Running* (1962).

WAINEWRIGHT, Thomas Griffiths (1794–1847), English art critic, painter, forger and probably poisoner, was born at Chiswick. He took to writing (as ' Janus Weathercock ', &c.) art criticisms and miscellaneous articles for the periodicals. He married and, soon outrunning his means, committed forgery (1822, 1824), and almost certainly poisoned with strychnine his half-sister-in-law (1830), probably also his uncle (1828), mother-in-law (1830) and possibly others. The sister-in-law had been fraudulently insured for £16,000, but two actions to enforce payment failed; and Wainewright, venturing back from France in 1837, was sentenced to life transportation for his old forgery. In Van Diemen's Land (Tasmania) he painted portraits, ate opium, and died in Hobart hospital. He is the 'Varney' of Lytton's *Lucretia* (1846) and the 'Slinkton' of Dickens's *Hunted Down* (1860). See his *Essays and Criticisms*, edited, with a memoir, by W. C. Hazlitt (1880); B. W. Procter's *Autobiography* (1877), Oscar Wilde's *Intentions* (1891), J. Curling, *Janus Weathercock* (1938), and R. Crossland, *Wainewright in Tasmania* (1954).

WAINWRIGHT, Jonathan Mayhew (1883–1953), American general, born at Walla-Walla, commanded the epic retreat in the Bataan peninsula after MacArthur's departure during the Philippines campaign in 1942. Taken prisoner, he was released in 1945 and awarded the Congressional Medal of Honour.

WAITZ, vīts, (1) **Georg** (1813–86), German historian, born at Flensburg, professor from 1849 till 1875 at Göttingen, where he formed the Göttingen historical school, editor of (1875–86) and contributor to the *Monumenta Germaniae Historica*, he wrote the great *Deutsche Verfassungsgeschichte* (1844–78) and works on Schleswig-Holstein and Ulfilas. See books by Steindorff (1886) and E. Waitz (1913), his son.

(2) **Theodor** (1821–64), German anthropological psychologist, born at Gotha, professor of Philosophy at Marburg from 1848, author of *Anthropologie der Naturvölker* (1859–71) and works on psychology and pedagogics.

WAKE, William (1657–1737), English churchman, born at Blandford, became Bishop of Lincoln (1705), Archbishop of Canterbury (1716). His writings include *State of the Church and Clergy of England* (1703), &c. He worked for union between the Anglican and Nonconformist churches.

WAKEFIELD, (1) **Edward Gibbon** (1796–1862), British colonial statesman, born in London, sentenced for abduction in 1827, wrote in prison *A Letter from Sydney* (1829), which outlined his theory of colonization, expanded in *England and America* (anon. 1833) and *A View of the Art of Colonization* (1849). He influenced the South Australian Association (which founded South Australia in 1836) and, as a secretary (1838) to Lord Durham (q.v.), the Durham Report, formed (1837) the New Zealand Association and forced the British government to annex (1839) New Zealand. With Lyttelton and Godley he founded (1850) the Anglican colony of Canterbury. See Lives by R. Garnett (1898), A. J. Harrop (1928), I. O'Connor (1929).

(2) **Gilbert** (1756–1801), English scholar and controversialist, born at Nottingham, became fellow of Jesus College, Cambridge, renounced his Anglican orders and became classical tutor in dissenting colleges at Warrington and Hackney. He was opposed to slave trade, field sports, war and public worship, and was a critic of civil and ecclesiastical government and of Pitt, Richard Watson's defence of the latter evoking Wakefield's libellous 'Reply', for which he was imprisoned for two years (1799–1801) in Dorchester. His works include editions of Greek and Roman poets, notably Lucretius (1796–99), and *Silva Critica* (1789–95), illustrating the Scriptures from profane learning. See his *Memoirs* (2nd ed. 1804) and his *Correspondence with Fox* (1813).

WAKLEY, Thomas, wak'li (1795–1862), English surgeon, born at Membury, Devonshire, founder (1823) and first editor of the *Lancet*, through which he denounced abuses in medical practice and made exposures which led to the Adulteration of Food and Drink Act (1860). He was M.P. for Finsbury from 1835 till 1852, and coroner from 1839, procuring reforms for coroners' courts. See Life by Sprigge (1897).

WAKSMAN, Selman Abraham (1888–), American biologist, born at Priluka in the Ukraine, took U.S. nationality in 1915, graduating the same year at Rutgers university, where he ultimately became professor of Microbiology in 1930. His researches into the breaking down of organic substances by micro-organisms and into antibiotics led to his discovery of streptomycin, for which he was awarded the Nobel prize for medicine in 1952. He wrote *Enzymes* (1926), *Principles of Soil Microbiology* (1938), &c., and the autobiographical *My Life with the Microbes* (1954).

WALBURG, Walburga. See WALPURGA.

WALDEN, Paul, val'den (1863–1957), Russian chemist, born at Wenden, Latvia, discovered, and gave his name to, a type of optical isomerism (Walden inversion).

WALDO, or Valdes, Peter (fl. 1175), French merchant, born in Lyons, became a preacher, founded, and gave name to, the Waldenses.

WALDORF. See ASTOR.

WALDSEEMÜLLER, Martin, valt'zay-mül-ér (c. 1480–c. 1521), German cartographer, born at Radolfzell, at St Dié made use of an account of the travels of Vespucci (q.v.) to publish (1507) the map and globe on which the new world was said to have first been called America.

WALDTEUFEL, Émile, valt'toy-fèl or -tœ- (1837–1915), French composer, born in Strasbourg. He studied at the Paris Conservatory and joined a piano manufacturer's until he was appointed pianist to the Empress Eugénie. A prolific composer of dance music, several of his waltzes, notably *The Skaters* and *Estudiantina*, remain popular.

WALEWSKA, Marie, va-lef'- (1789–1817), Polish countess, Bonaparte's mistress, whose son by him became Count Walewski.

WALEWSKI, Alexandre Florian Joseph Colonna, Count (1810–68), French diplomat, natural son of Napoleon I, held various appointments, including that of ambassador to Britain (1851), and was foreign minister (1855–60) and minister of state (1860–63).

WALKER, waw'kèr, (1) **Frederick** (1840–75), English artist, born in London, designed for wood-engravers, his illustrations appearing in *Once a Week*, *Cornhill*, and other periodicals. His works, once popular, include watercolours and oils. He was made an A.R.A. in 1871. See Lives by J. G. Marks (1896) and C. Phillips (1897).

(2) **George** (1618–90), hero of the siege of Londonderry, born of English parents, allegedly in Tyrone, attended Glasgow University, and became rector of Donaghmore, helped to garrison Londonderry for its successful resistance to the siege in 1689 by James II's forces, during which, as joint-governor, he led sallies against the enemy and exhorted the citizens by rousing sermons. For this he received the thanks of king and commons, degrees from Oxford and Cambridge, and was nominated Bishop of Derry. He fell at the Battle of the Boyne and is commemorated by the Walker Monument (1828) in Londonderry. He wrote *A True Account of the Siege of Londonderry* (1689), reprinted in P. Dwyer's *Siege of Derry* (1893).

(3) **Sir James** (1863–1935), Scottish chemist, born in Dundee, professor there (1894–1908) and (1908–28) in Edinburgh. Known for his work on hydrolysis, ionization, and amphoteric electrolytes, he was elected F.R.S. in 1900 and knighted in 1921.

(4) **John** (1674–1747), English ecclesiastical historian, born in Exeter, noted for his account (1714), called forth by the writings of Calamy (q.v.) on the ejected Nonconformists, of the sufferings of the clergy in the Revolution (1689). See C. G. B. Tatham, *Dr John Walker and the Sufferings of the Clergy* (1910).

(5) **John** (1732–1807), English dictionary-maker, born at Colney Hatch, was by turns actor, schoolmaster and peripatetic teacher of elocution. His dictionary for rhyming (1775) has run to many editions (*Rhyming Dictionary of the English Language*, 1957), as did his *Critical Pronouncing Dictionary* (1791).

(6) **John** (1770–1831), English antiquary, born in London, whose works included *Curia Oxoniensis*, *Oxoniana*, *Curious Articles from the Gentleman's Magazine* (all 1809), *Letters Written by Eminent Persons* (1813).

(7) **John** (c. 1781–1859), English inventor, born at Stockton-on-Tees, where, in 1827, as a chemist, he made the first friction matches, called by him 'Congreves' (alluding to Congreve's rocket), later named lucifers and matches by others.

(8) **Thomas** (1784–1836), English author, born at Chorlton-cum-Hardy near Manchester. He was an authority on pauperism, and from May till December 1835, published weekly *The Original*, a general magazine containing well-known articles on gastronomy, and since reappearing in editions and selections under other titles (e.g., *The Art of Dining*, 1928).

(9) **William** (1824–60), American filibuster, born at Nashville, Tennessee, studied medicine at Edinburgh and Heidelberg, which he practised in U.S., as well as law and journalism. He landed (1853) with a force in the Mexican state of Lower California, declaring (1854) it, with the neighbouring Sonora, an independent republic, but was soon forced to withdraw to U.S. territory. He next invaded (1855) Nicaragua, took Granada, and was elected president; his government, recognized (1856) by U.S., restored slavery. He published *The War in Nicaragua* (1860). Twice expelled (1857) from Nicaragua, he entered (1860) Honduras, taking Trujillo, but was apprehended by the captain of a British sloop-of-war and given up to the Honduran authorities, who had him shot. See C. W. Doubleday, *Reminiscences* (1886) and W. O. Scroggs, *Filibusters and Financiers* (1916).

(10) **William Sidney** (1795–1846), English critic, born at Pembroke, of whose invaluable studies some appeared posthumously as *Shakespeare's Versification* (1854), *A Critical Examination of the Text of Shakespeare* (1859) and *Poetical Remains* (1852).

WALKINSHAW, Clementina. See STEWART, HOUSE OF (12).

WALKLEY, Arthur Bingham, *wawk'li* (1855–1926), English dramatic critic, born at Bristol, contributed to the *Star*, *The Times* and other newspapers and periodicals. See his *Dramatic Criticism* (1903).

WALLACE, *wol'is*, (1) **Alfred Russel** (1823–1913), British naturalist, born at Usk, in Monmouthshire, travelled and collected (1848–52) in the Amazon basin, for a time with H. W. Bates, and, (1854–1862) in the Malay Archipelago. His memoir, sent to C. R. Darwin (q.v.) in 1858 from the Moluccas, formed an important part of the Linnaean Society paper which first promulgated the theory of natural selection, modifying the nature, and hastening the publication, of Darwin's *The Origin of Species*, a work amplified by Wallace's *Contributions to the Theory of Natural Selection* (1870) and *Darwinism* (1889). Excluding man from the unaided operation of natural selection, he wrote *On Miracles and Modern Spiritualism* (1881). In his great *Geographical Distribution of Animals* (1876), *Island Life* (1880), and earlier work, Wallace contributed much (including 'Wallace's Line' between faunas) to the scientific foundations of zoogeography. Other works include *Travels on the Amazon and Rio Negro* (1853), *Palm Trees of the Amazon* (1853), *The Malay Archipelago* (1869), *Tropical Nature* (1878), *Australasia* (1879), *Land Nationalization* (an advocation, 1882), *Vaccination, a Delusion* (1898), *The Wonderful Century* (1898), *Man's Place in the Universe* (1903), *My Life, an Autobiography* (1905), *The World of Life* (1910). He was elected F.R.S. in 1893 and awarded the O.M. in 1910. See J. Marchant, *Alfred Russel Wallace* (1916), Life by L. T. Hogben (1918), and B. Petronijevic, *Charles Darwin and A. R. Wallace* (1925).

(2) **Sir Donald Mackenzie** (1841–1919), Scottish author and journalist, born in Dunbartonshire, became foreign correspondent of *The Times*, and after spending six years in Russia wrote his highly successful *Russia* (1877). He was private secretary to two viceroys of India.

(3) **Edgar** (1875–1932), English writer, was found abandoned in Greenwich when nine days' old and brought up by a Billingsgate fish-porter. He served in the army in South Africa, where he later (1899) became a journalist, and in 1905 he published his first success, the adventure story *The Four Just*

Men. Another early series in a different vein was set in West Africa and included *Sanders of the River* (1911), *Bones* (1915), &c. From then on he wrote prolifically—his output numbering over 170 novels and plays—being best remembered for his crime novels, such as *The Clue of the Twisted Candle* and *The Melody of Death*, and plays, including *The Ringer* and *The Squeaker.* See his autobiography, *People* (1926) and Life by M. Lane (1938; rev. 1964).

(4) **Henry** (1836–1916), American agricultural leader, father of (6), born in Pennsylvania, trained for the church but turned to farming and agricultural journalism, founding in 1895 the successful periodical *Wallace's Farmer.*

(5) **Henry Agard** (1888–1965), American agriculturalist and statesman, son of (6), born in Adair County, Iowa, edited *Wallace's Farmer* from 1933 until 1940, when he was nominated vice-president to Roosevelt, whose ' new deal ' policy he supported. He was chairman of the Board of Economic Warfare (1941–45) and secretary of commerce (1945–46). He failed to obtain renomination as vice-president in 1944, and unsuccessfully stood for president in 1948.

(6) **Henry Cantwell** (1866–1924), American agriculturist, son of (4), helped his father to found *Wallace's Farmer*, which he edited from 1916. Long secretary of the Corn Belt Meat Producers' Association, he was appointed secretary of agriculture in 1921.

(7) **Lewis, pop. Lew** (1827–1905), American author and soldier, born at Brookville, Ind., was governor of Utah (1878–81) and minister to Turkey (1881). He was author of the remarkably successful religious novel *Ben Hur* (1880), which has twice formed the subject of a spectacular film. See his *Autobiography* (1906).

(8) **Sir Richard, Bart.** (1818–90), English art collector and philanthropist, born in London, inherited from his putative father, the marquis of Hertford, the paintings and objets d'art later bequeathed (1897) by his widow to the nation. These now comprise the Wallace Collection, housed in Hertford House, London, once his residence. During the siege of Paris (1870–71) Wallace equipped ambulances and founded a British hospital there.

(9) also **Walays or Wallensis** (' Welshman ') **Sir William** (*c.* 1274–1305), Scottish patriot, chief champion of Scotland's independence, was reputedly the second of the three sons of Sir Malcolm Wallace of Elderslie, near Paisley. According to Fordun, he got his early education from an uncle, the priest of Dunipace, and Blind Harry (see HARRY) associates the hero's boyhood with Dundee and his youthful manhood with Ayrshire. Wallace's presence at the burning of the English garrison in the ' Barns of Ayr ', the date of that event, and its being the start of the War of Independence, are matters for conjecture. In 1297 Wallace, at the head of a small band, burnt Lanark, slew Hazelrig, the English sheriff, to avenge, asserts Wyntoun, the murder of the young wife of the patriot, who later retired with a large company into the forest of Selkirk. On

September 11 of the same year Wallace, fighting Edward I's army under Warenne, Earl of Surrey, won the great battle of Stirling Bridge. From positions at the base of the Abbey Craig, on which now stands his national monument, he routed that part of the English army which had crossed the narrow wooden bridge over the Forth to the northeast of Stirling, the remainder fleeing before the Scots. In consequence of this and other actions, the English were expelled from Scotland and a devastating raid was carried out on the north of England; on his return Wallace was elected governor of Scotland. In 1298 Edward invaded Scotland with 88,000 men. Wallace was forced to give battle at Falkirk on July 22, where, deserted by the cavalry, his infantry were shot down by the English archers and routed. Wallace visited France (*c.* 1299), possibly to seek aid, his whereabouts thereafter being unknown until his arrest, allegedly near Glasgow, by Menteith, sheriff of Dumbarton, about August 3, 1305. He was taken to London, tried in Westminster Hall, condemned, and hanged, drawn, beheaded, and quartered, the quarters being sent to Newcastle, Berwick, Stirling and Perth. See J. Stevenson, *Documents illustrative of Sir William Wallace* (Maitland Club, 1841), the Marquis of Bute, *Early Days of Sir William Wallace* (1876) and *Burning of the Barns of Ayr* (1878), A. Brunton, *Sir William Wallace* (1881), H. Gough, *Scotland in 1298* (1888), J. Moir, *Wallace* (1888), A. F. Murison, *Sir William Wallace* (1898), J. Fergusson, *Wallace* (1938), with bibliography and play by Sydney Goodsir Smith (1960).

(10) **William** (1844–97), Scottish philosopher, born in Cupar, wrote works on Hegel, a life of Schopenhauer, *Epicureanism* (1880), &c.

(11) **William** (1860–1940), Scottish composer, born in Greenock, wrote a symphony, symphonic poems, songs, and works on music.

(12) **(William) Vincent** (1813–65), Irish operatic composer, born at Waterford, emigrated to Australia, well-known for the first of his operas, *Maritana* (1845), and, formerly, for *Lurline* (1860).

WALLACH, Otto, *val'*aкн (1847–1931), German organic chemist, born at Königsberg, a Nobel prizewinner in 1910 for his work on the essential oils and terpenes.

WALLAS, Graham (1858–1932), English socialist political psychologist, born at Monkwearmouth, Sunderland, was educated at Shrewsbury and Corpus Christi College, Oxford, and after a spell of schoolmastering and university extension lecturing, became a lecturer in the London School of Economics, which he, a Fabian, had helped to found, and was professor of Political Science there (1914–23). His influential teaching and writings in social psychology, *Human Nature in Politics* (1908), *The Great Society* (1914), &c., emphasized the rôle of irrational forces which determine public opinion and political attitudes.

WALLENSTEIN, or Waldstein, Albrecht Wenzel Eusebius von, *wol'en-stīn,* Ger. *val'en-shtīn, valt'shtīn* (1583–1634), duke of

Friedland and of Mecklenburg, prince of Sagan, born near Jaroměř, in Bohemia. When his father, a Czech Protestant noble, died, a Catholic uncle entrusted the boy's education to the Jesuits. He married a Bohemian widow, whose vast estates he inherited in 1614. In 1617 he personally commanded a force, chiefly of cavalry, which he supplied to Archduke Ferdinand (later Ferdinand II, q.v.) for use against Venice. At the outset of the Thirty Years' War he assisted in the crushing of the Bohemian revolt (1618–20) under Frederick V (q.v.), thereafter acquiring numerous confiscated estates, and consolidating them into Friedland, of which he became (1623) duke. In 1625, for raising an army for Ferdinand II, he was appointed commander-in-chief of all the Imperial forces, and at Dessau bridge defeated the army of Mansfeld (q.v.). Establishing peace in Hungary by a truce imposed on the combined forces of Mansfeld and Bethlen Gabor (q.v.), he subdued (1627) Silesia, acquiring the dukedom of Sagan, joined Tilly against Christian IV, was invested (1628) with the duchies of Mecklenburg, which he had overrun, but encountered resistance in garrisoning the Hanse towns, notably at his unsuccessful siege (1628) of Stralsund, consequently failing to remove the threat of Protestant invasion by sea. This materialized in 1630, following Ferdinand II's Edict of Restitution, when Gustavus Adolphus and his forces invaded northern Germany. Enmity of the Catholic princes, aroused by Wallenstein's ambition, forced Ferdinand to dismiss him (1630) and appoint Tilly commander-in-chief. After Tilly's defeat at Breitenfeld and death on the Lech, Wallenstein was reinstated. His new army, in repulsing the attempt by Gustavus Adolphus's forces to storm his entrenched camp near Nuremberg, prevented the Swedish king from advancing on Ferdinand in Vienna. Wallenstein was defeated (1632) by Gustavus Adolphus at Lützen, where, however, the latter fell. In the interests of a united Germany with himself as its supreme authority, Wallenstein now intrigued with Protestants and Catholics. At length his enemies persuaded the emperor to depose him again and denounce him. Threatened in Pilsen by Piccolomini (q.v.) and others, he went to Eger, hoping for support from Bernhard, Duke of Weimar; there traitors in his train, notably the Irishman, Butler, and the Scotsmen, Gordon and Leslie, killed his faithful adherents, while the first's compatriot, Devereux, slew Wallenstein on the evening of February 25, 1634. He had been throughout a firm believer in astrology. The Wallenstein trilogy by Schiller (q.v.) is based on Wallenstein's career. See Lives by Ranke (5th ed. 1895), Förster (1834), Aretin (1846), Hunter (1855); monographs by Irmer (1888–89), Hildebrand (1885), Huch (1919), Wiegler (1920) and Tritsch (1936); Schmid's *Wallenstein—Litteratur* (1878).

WALLER, wol'ér, (1) **Augustus Volney** (1816–1870), English physiologist, born near Faversham, discovered and gave name to Wallerian degeneration of, and the related Wallerian method of tracing, nerve fibres.

(2) **Edmund** (1606–87), English poet, born at Coleshill near Amersham, Herts (now Bucks), was educated at Eton and King's College, Cambridge. Thought to have represented Amersham in 1621, he was returned for Ilchester in 1624, Chipping Wycombe in 1625 and Amersham in 1627. In 1631 he married a London heiress, who died in 1634, and from about 1635 to 1638 he unsuccessfully courted Lady Dorothy Sidney, eldest daughter of the Earl of Leicester, whom he commemorated in verse as ' Sacharissa '. Returned to the Long Parliament in 1640, he opened the proceedings in 1641 against Crawley, impeached for his judgments in the king's favour. In 1643 Waller plunged into a conspiracy (' Waller's plot ') against Parliament, was arrested, and expelled from the House. He avoided execution, unlike his fellow conspirators, by abject confession and the payment of a £10,000 fine, and was banished the realm. He lived mostly in France, entertaining impoverished exiles in Paris, his own banishment being revoked in 1651, after which he returned to England. His collected poems, reviving the heroic couplet and including ' Go, lovely Rose ', had been published in 1645 and were followed by *A Panegyric to my Lord Protector* (1655) and *To the King upon his Majesty's Happy Return* (1660) addressed to Cromwell and Charles II respectively. See his *Poems* (critical ed. by G. Thorn-Drury, 1893), also *Sacharissa* (1892) by Julia Cartwright.

(3) **Sir William** (c. 1597–1668), English parliamentary general, a member of the Long Parliament, fought in 1643 in the west country, at Oxford and Newbury in 1644, and at Taunton in February 1645. He suggested reforms on which the New Model Army was to be based, but in April 1645 was removed from command by the Self-denying Ordinance. By June 1647 he was levying troops against the army, from 1648 to 1651 he was imprisoned for royalist sympathies, and in 1659 he plotted for a royalist rising and was again imprisoned. In 1660 he became a member of the Convention Parliament, but was unrewarded at the Restoration.

WALLIS, John (1616–1703), English mathematician, born at Ashford, Kent, was trained at Cambridge, and took orders, but in 1649 became Savilian professor of Geometry at Oxford. He sided with the parliament, was secretary in 1644 to the Westminster Assembly, but favoured the Restoration. Besides the *Arithmetica Infinitorum*, in which was presaged the calculus and the binomial theorem and a value given for π, he wrote on proportion, mechanics, the quadrature of the circle (against Hobbes), grammar, logic, theology, and the teaching of the deaf and dumb, was an expert on deciphering, and edited some of the Greek mathematicians. He was a founder of the Royal Society. His collected works appeared in 1791. See J. F. Scott, *The Mathematical Work of John Wallis*.

WALPOLE, (1) **Horace, 4th Earl of Orford** (1717–97), youngest son of (3), was born September 24 in London. At Eton and at King's College, Cambrigge, he had Gray the poet as a friend; and while still at the university was appointed by his father to lucrative government sinecures. Gray and he started on the Grand Tour, but quarrelled and separated at Reggio, where Walpole fell ill. He returned to England (1741) to take his seat for Callington in Cornwall. Although he interested himself in cases like the Byng trial of 1757, his function in politics was that of the chronicling spectator rather than the earnest actor. He exchanged his Cornish seat in 1754 for the family borough of Castle Rising, which he vacated in 1757 for the other family borough of King's Lynn. In 1745 his father died, leaving him with ample means. In 1747 he purchased, near Twickenham, the former coachman's cottage which he gradually ' gothicized ' (1753–76) into the stuccoed and battlemented pseudo-castle of Strawberry Hill, which, mildly ridiculous though it may seem, helped in its way to reverse the fashion for classical and Italianate design. This transformation, correspondence and authorship, visits to Paris, and the establishment of a private press on which some of his own works as well as Lucan's *Pharsalia* with Bentley's notes, and Gray's *Progress of Poesy* and *The Bard*, were printed, constituted the occupations of his life. He inherited his brother's title in 1791 and died March 2, 1797. His essays in Moore's *World* exhibit a light hand, and he had gifts as a verse-writer. In such squibs as the *Letter from Xo Ho to his friend Lien Chi at Pekin* (1757) he is at his best. His *Castle of Otranto* (1764) set the fashion of supernatural romance. His tragedy of *The Mysterious Mother* (1768) is strong but gruesome. Other works are *Catalogue of Royal and Noble Authors* (1758), *Fugitive Pieces in Verse and Prose* (1758), *Anecdotes of Painting in England* (1761–71), *Catalogue of Engravers* (1763), *Historic Doubts on Richard III* (1768), *Essay on Modern Gardening* (1785), &c. Walpole's literary reputation rests chiefly upon his letters, which deal, in the most vivacious way, with party politics, foreign affairs, literature, art and gossip. His firsthand accounts in them of such events as the Jacobite trials after the '45, and the Gordon Riots, are invaluable. Two of his chief correspondents were Sir Horace Mann and Madame du Deffand; with the latter he exchanged more than 1600 letters. See also the *Memoirs* edited by Eliot Warburton (1852), and Life by Austin Dobson (1890; rev. P. Toynbee, 1927), books by Yvon (1924), D. M. Stuart (1927), Gwynn (1932), Cremer (1946), and bibliography by Hazen (1948).

(2) **Sir Hugh Seymour** (1884–1941), English novelist, born in Auckland, N.Z., son of the Rev. G. H. S. Walpole who subsequently became Bishop of Edinburgh, was educated in England and graduated from Emmanuel College, Cambridge, in 1906. He was intended for the church but turned first schoolmaster and then author. Widely read in English literature, he wrote prolifically and was said to have the knack of making the most of a moderate talent; nevertheless his books, which were enormously popular during his lifetime, display a straightforward, easy-flowing style, great descriptive power,

and a genius for evoking atmosphere which he unfortunately overworked at times, as for example in *The Cathedral*, whose down-town scenes with their unnatural aura of malevolence have been a target for the parodist. Many authors have paid tribute to Walpole's kindness and integrity, and he was knighted for his services to literature in 1937. His novels include *Mr Perrin and Mr Traill* (1911), *Fortitude* (1913), *The Dark Forest* (1916), *The Secret City* (1919, Tait Black Memorial Prize), *The Cathedral* (1922), which owes much to Trollope, one of Walpole's favourite authors, and *The Herries Chronicle* (1930–33). See Life by R. Hart-Davis (1952).

(3) **Sir Robert, Earl of Orford** (1676–1745), English statesman, born at Houghton in Norfolk. Educated at Eton and King's College, Cambridge, he was returned to parliament in 1701 for Castle Rising, in 1702 for King's Lynn, quickly winning a high position in the Whig Party. In 1708 he became secretary-at-war and in 1710 treasurer of the navy. Following upon his support of Godolphin in the impeachment of Sacheverell, Walpole was expelled the House and sent to the Tower (1712) for alleged corruption. Restored to fortune on the accession of George I, he was made a privy councillor. He conducted the impeachment of Bolingbroke and others, and became in 1715 chancellor of the Exchequer and first lord of the Treasury. In 1717 he resigned, after introducing the first general sinking fund. Out of office he has been charged with somewhat unscrupulous opposition. He brought about the rejection of the peerage bill (1718) and was given (1720) the post of paymaster-general by Sunderland. After the collapse of the South Sea Scheme, the public looked to Walpole to restore order in their affairs; in 1721 he again became first lord of the Treasury and chancellor of the Exchequer and from this time was responsible for the country's government. Under him there was a transfer of power to the House of Commons and Walpole was involved in the rôle of Britain's first prime minister. By bribery he secured a Whig House of Commons. His first successful trial of strength (1724) was with Carteret (q.v.); later he held his own against Bolingbroke (q.v.) and Pulteney (q.v.); forced on the breach with Townshend (q.v.), who retired (1730); and quarrelled with Chesterfield (q.v.). His failure to secure the passage of an excise bill (1733) against smuggling and fraud weakened his position, which deteriorated further as a result of his unpopular foreign policy. He resigned on February 2, 1742, and was created Earl of Orford, with a pension of £4000 a year. A committee appointed by the House of Commons gave a report against him on the charge of bribery, unsupported by evidence, and proceedings were ultimately dropped. He withdrew to Houghton, and died at Arlington St, London, on March 18. See W. Coxe, *Memoirs of Sir Robert Walpole* (1798), monographs by A. C. Ewald (1877) and J. Morley (1889), F. S. Oliver, *The Endless Adventure* (1930–35), some of the works cited at (1), and a Life by J. H. Plumb 1956–61).

(4) **Sir Spencer** (1839–1907), British historian, born in London, educated at Eton. In the course of his civil service, he was (1882–93) lieutenant-governor of the Isle of Man. His principal work is the *History of England from 1815* (1878–86) continued in his *History of Twenty-Five Years* (1904–08). He wrote Lives of Perceval (1874; his grandfather) and Lord John Russell (1889).

WALPURGA, Walpurgis or Walburga, St, *val-poor'ga* (*c.* 710–*c.* 777), with her brother Willibald, companion of St Boniface (q.v.), went from England to Germany, and was abbess of Heidenheim, where she died, her bones being translated (*c.* 870) to Eichstatt. Walpurgis night (April 30) is so called from a confusion of the saint's day, May 1, and the popular superstitions regarding the flight of witches on that night.

WALSINGHAM, *wawl'sing-am,* (1) **Sir Francis** (*c.* 1530–90), English statesman, born at Chislehurst, Kent, studied at King's College, Cambridge. Burghley sent him on an embassy to France in 1570–73; and having discharged his diplomatic duties with consummate skill, he was appointed one of the principal secretaries of state to Elizabeth, sworn of the privy council, and knighted. In 1578 he was sent on an embassy to the Netherlands, in 1581 to France, and in 1583 to Scotland. He contrived a most corrupt system of espionage at home and abroad, enabling him to reveal the Babington (q.v.) plot, which implicated Mary, Queen of Scots (q.v.) in treason, and to obtain in 1587 details of some plans for the Spanish armada. He was one of the commissioners to try Mary at Fotheringhay. His personal integrity and disinterested patriotism are undoubted. He favoured the Puritan party, and in his later days gave himself up to religious meditation. Elizabeth acknowledged his genius and important services, yet she kept him poor and without honours; and he died in poverty and debt. His daughter Frances became successively the wife of Sir Philip Sidney, of the Earl of Essex, and of Richard de Burgh, fourth Earl of Clanricarde. See Stählin, *Walsingham und seine Zeit* (1908); Conyers Read, *Mr Secretary Walsingham* (1925).

(2) **Thomas** (d. *c.* 1422), English chronicler, associated chiefly with St Albans abbey but for a time prior of Wymondham, an authority for English history from 1377 until 1422, noted for his *Historia Anglicana, 1272–1422* (1863–64) and other works.

WALTER, *val'ter,* (1) properly **Schlesinger, Bruno** (1876–1962), German-American conductor, born in Berlin. He first conducted at Cologne while still in his teens, and work with Mahler in Hamburg and Vienna followed, profoundly influencing his musical outlook. He was in charge of Munich Opera 1913–22, and from 1919 was chief conductor of the Berlin Philharmonic. International tours won him a great British and American reputation, and driven from both Germany and Austria by the Nazis, he settled in the U.S.A., where he became chief conductor of the New York Philharmonic in 1951. Perhaps the last great exponent of the German romantic tradition,

he was most famous for his performances of Haydn, Mozart and Mahler.

(2) **Hubert** (d. 1205), English statesman and prelate, became a judge in 1185, Dean of York in 1189 and Bishop of Salisbury in the same year. He went crusading with Richard I, after whose capture by the Saracens he negotiated the ransom, and on whose recommendation he was made Archbishop of Canterbury (1193). As chief justiciar he played a major part in the suppression of John's rebellion, and during Richard's absence was virtual ruler of England until the pope made him resign political office. On the accession of John (1199) he became chancellor, and was instrumental in avoiding war with France.

(3) **John** (1739–1812), English printer and newspaper publisher, born in London, initially an unsuccessful underwriter at Lloyds, in 1784 acquired a printing office in Blackfriars, London, nucleus of the later Printing House Square buildings, in 1785 founded *The Daily Universal Register* newspaper. which in 1788 was renamed *The Times.*

(4) **John** (1776–1847), son of (3), became manager and editor of *The Times* in 1803; under him the newspaper attained its great status. He obtained news, especially from abroad, often more rapidly transmitted than official reports and from sources independent of them. In 1814 Walter adopted, for the printing of *The Times*, the double-cylinder steam-driven press invented by Friedrich König (q.v.).

(5) **John** (1818–94), son of (4), proprietor of *The Times*, under whom was introduced (1869) the important cylindrical Walter press, in which, for the first time, curved stereotyped plates and reels of newsprint were used. Of the other members of the family, **Arthur Fraser** (1846–1910), under whom the fortunes of *The Times* were impaired by the publication (1887) of articles on C. S. Parnell (q.v.) by R. Pigott (q.v.), was proprietor until 1908, when the controlling interest was acquired by A. Harmsworth (q.v.). A. F. Walter's son, **John** (1873–1968), was chairman from 1910 till 1923, sharing control (after Harmsworth's death in 1922) with J. J. Astor (q.v.). See *The History of 'The Times'* (4 vols. 1935–52).

(6) **Lucy** (1630–58), born probably in Pembrokeshire, was the ' brown, beautiful, bold but insipid ' mistress of Charles II, to whom she bore James, Duke of Monmouth.

WALTHER VON DER VOGELWEIDE, *vahl'ter fon der fōg'el-vī-dė* (*c.* 1170–1230), greatest of the German minnesingers, was born probably in Tirol. In 1180–98 he was in high favour at the court of Austria; later he was at Mainz and Magdeburg; in 1204 he outshone his rivals in the great contest at the Wartburg. He first sided with the Guelphs, but made friends with the victorious Hohenstaufen, Frederick II, who gave him a small estate. See monographs by Uhland (1822), Wustmann (1913), Schönbach (1923), and Halbach (1927).

WALTON, (1) **Brian** (*c.* 1600–61), English divine, editor of the *London Polyglott Bible*, was born at Seymour, Yorkshire, studied at

Cambridge, and held cures in London and Essex. Sequestered in 1641, he found refuge in Oxford, and then in London devoted himself to his great bible (6v ols. 1653–57), in which he had aid from Usher, Lightfoot, Pocock and other scholars. He was consecrated Bishop of Chester in 1660. Nine languages are used in the Polyglott—Hebrew, Chaldee, Samaritan, Syriac, Arabic, Persian, Ethiopic, Greek and Latin. Other works were an *Introductio* to Oriental languages (1654) and *Considerator Considered* (1659), a defence of the *Polyglott*. See Life by H. J. Todd (1821).

(2) **Ernest Thomas Sinton** (1903–   ), Irish physicist, born in Dungarvan, Waterford, became professor of Natural and Experimental Philosophy at Trinity College, Dublin, in 1946. With (Sir) John Cockcroft (q.v.) in 1932 he disintegrated lithium by proton bombardment, for which work they were jointly awarded the 1951 Nobel prize for physics.

(3) **Izaak** (1593–1683), English writer, was born at Stafford, August 9. In 1621 he was settled in London as an ironmonger or a linen-draper, and about 1644 he retired with a modest competence. In 1626 he married a great-grandniece of Cranmer, and in 1647 Ann Ken, a half-sister of Thomas Ken (q.v.). He spent most of his time ' in the families of the eminent clergymen of England '; lived latterly much at Winchester; and died there, December 15, 1683. The first edition of *The Compleat Angler, or the Contemplative Man's Recreation*, appeared in 1653; the fifth, grown from thirteen chapters to twenty-one, in 1676. The latter contained also a treatise by Charles Cotton (q.v.). The discourse of fishes, of English rivers, of fishponds, and of rods and lines is interspersed with scraps of dialogue, moral reflections, quaint old verses, songs, and sayings, and idyllic glimpses of country life and is a book of perennial charm. The anonymous *Arte of Angling* (1577), discovered in 1957, has been found to be one of his chief sources. Not less exquisite are his *Lives*—of Donne (1640), Wotton (1651), Hooker (1665), Herbert (1670) and Sanderson (1678). Editions include those by (Sir) John Hawkins (1760), Major (1824, &c.), Sir Harris Nicolas (1836), Bethune (New York 1847), Jesse and Bohn (1856), Dowling (1857) and A. Lang (1897). See S. Martin, *Walton and his Friends* (1903).

(4) **Sir William Turner** (1902–   ), English composer, born at Oldham, received his earliest musical training as a cathedral chorister at Christ Church, Oxford, whence he passed to university as a student in 1918 and in the same year wrote his first major work, a piano quartet, which was performed at the Salzburg festival of contemporary music in 1923. His *Façade* (1923), originally an extravaganza accompanying declamatory verses by Edith Sitwell (q.v.), created quite a sensation and subsequently reappeared *sans* orator as a pair of suites and as ballet music. Scored for an unusual instrumental combination containing saxophone, glockenspiel and varied percussion, it caricatures in lively manner conventional

song and dance forms. The *Sinfonia Concertante* (1927) for piano and orchestra, and the viola concerto (1929) are more serious efforts; *Belshazzar's Feast* (1931), a biblical cantata with libretto by Osbert Sitwell, is a powerful and vital work in which exciting instrumentation for an augmented orchestra is contrasted with moving unaccompanied choral passages. The *Symphony* (1932–35) is characterized by use of the pedal-point bass to preserve orientation in the midst of advanced harmonies and cross-rhythms. Some of Walton's subsequent compositions make more concessions to melody and his ballet music for *The Wise Virgins* (1940), based on pieces by Bach, contains a concert favourite in his orchestral arrangement of the aria *Sheep May Safely Graze*. During World War II he began composing incidental music for films and emerged as the supreme exponent of this art, with a masterly flair for building up tension and atmosphere, as in Shakespeare's *Henry V*, *Hamlet* and *Richard III*. Later works include the opera *Troilus and Cressida* (1954), a 'cello concerto (1956), a second symphony (1960) and a comic opera, *The Bear* (1967). He was knighted in 1951, and awarded the O.M. in 1967.

WANG WEI, *way* (699–759), Chinese poet and painter of the T'ang dynasty, an ardent Buddhist, founded a monochrome school of painting.

WARBECK, Perkin (*c.* 1474–99), Flemish impostor, pretender to the English throne, born in Tournai, appeared in 1490 at the court of the Duchess of Burgundy, sister of Edward IV of England, and professed to be Richard, Duke of York, younger of the two sons of Edward IV murdered in the Tower. In 1491 he was welcomed at Cork, in 1492 at the court of Charles VIII of France; and from Burgundy he made an ineffectual landing in Kent (July 1495). In Scotland, James IV gave him his kinswoman, Catherine Gordon, a daughter of the Earl of Huntly, in marriage. In 1498 he attempted to besiege Exeter, then went on to Taunton, but ran away to the sanctuary at Beaulieu in Hampshire, surrendered on promise of pardon, and was imprisoned. On a charge of endeavouring to escape, he was thrown into the Tower, and executed in November 1499. See J. Gairdner, *Richard the Third, and the Story of Perkin Warbeck* (1898).

WARBURG, Otto Heinrich, *vahr'boorg* (1883–1970), German physiological chemist, born at Freiburg Baden, was educated at Berlin and Heidelberg, won the *Pour le Mérite*, the German V.C., during World War I and became director of the physiological department of the Max Planck Institute, Berlin. Engaged on cancer research, he won the Nobel prize (1931) for medicine for his work on enzymes and was elected a foreign member of the Royal Society (1934).

WARBURTON, (1) Eliot, fully **Bartholomew Elliott George** (1810–52), Irish novelist, was born at Tullamore, Co. Offaly. He was called to the bar, but soon devoted himself to literature. His eight works include *The Crescent and the Cross* (1844), *Memoirs of Prince Rupert* (1849) and *Darien* (1851).

Sailing to Panamá, he was lost in the *Amazon* off Land's End.

(2) **William** (1698–1779), English divine, born at Newark, the town clerk's son, practised as attorney until he took deacon's orders in 1723. He was ordained priest in 1727 and became rector of Brant Broughton in Lincolnshire in 1728, and for eighteen years immersed himself in study. His *Alliance between Church and State* (1736) first called attention to his powers, but *The Divine Legation of Moses* (1737–41; and some posthumously in Hurd's edition of his works) formed the sure foundation of his fame. The work displays no profundity of thought, but vigour in verbal logic, much, if inaccurate, reading, dogmatism, and extreme arrogance. In 1739 he defended the orthodoxy of Pope's *Essay on Man*, became his friend and literary executor, and secured influential patrons. Successively preacher of Lincoln's Inn (1746), prebendary of Gloucester (1753), king's chaplain (1754), prebendary of Durham (1755), Dean of Bristol (1757) and Bishop of Gloucester (1759), he wore out his days in endless warfare with Hume, Jortin, the Deists, Voltaire, Lowth and Wesley. In his early years he had aided Theobald in his Shakespeare, and in 1747 he himself issued an edition which brought him no credit. Other works were *Julian* (1750) and *The Principles of Natural and Revealed Religion* (1753–67). A sumptuous edition of his works was published in 1788 by Bishop Hurd; another in 1811. See Lives by F. Kilvert (1860), J. S. Watson (1863), and a book by A. W. Evans (1932).

WARD, (1) Sir Adolphus William (1837–1924), English historian, born at Hampstead, became in 1860 a fellow of Peterhouse, Cambridge. In 1866 he was appointed professor of History and English Literature at Owens College, Manchester, of which he was principal in 1890, and he played a major part in the establishment of the independent University of Manchester. In 1900 he became master of Peterhouse, and was knighted in 1913. Notable is his translation (1868–73) of Curtius's *History of Greece*, and he also wrote *Great Britain and Hanover* (1899), *The Electress Sophia* (1903), *Germany 1815–1890* (1916 *et seq.*), an invaluable *History of English Dramatic Literature* (1875), &c. See A. T. Bartholomew's *Bibliography* (1926), with a Memoir by T. F. Tout.

(2) **Artemus.** See BROWNE (1).

(3) **Arthur Sarsfield.** See ROHMER, SAX.

(4) **Edward,** called **Ned** (1667–1731), English ' Grubstreet ' writer, born in Oxfordshire, became a London innkeeper, wrote coarse satirical and humorous verse, and was pilloried for attacking the Whigs in his *Hudibras Redivivus* (1705). His chief work was the *London Spy*, published in monthly parts from 1698. See study by H. W. Troyer (1947).

(5) **Edward Matthew** (1816–79), English painter, father of (12), born in London, studied at the Royal Academy, and in Rome and Munich, becoming R.A. in 1855. He is noted for his historical paintings of 17th- and 18th-century scenes, including *The Escape of Charles II with Jane Lane, Charlotte Corday, The Last Sleep of Argyll* and *A Scene in Lord Chesterfield's Ante-room.* See

Life by Dafforne (1879) and his widow's *Reminiscences* (1911).

(6) **F. Kingdon-.** See KINGDON-WARD.

(7) **Dame Geneviève** (1837–1922), American prima donna and actress, born in New York, a great singer in youth, a great tragedienne in maturity, still acted at 83. She was created D.B.E. in 1921. See *Both Sides of the Curtain* (1918) by herself and Richard Whiteing.

(8) **Harry Marshall.** See KINGDON-WARD.

(9) **Mrs Humphry,** *née* **Mary Augusta Arnold** (1851–1920), English novelist, born in Hobart, Tasmania, a granddaughter of Dr Arnold of Rugby. The family returned to Britain in 1856 and, after attendance at boarding schools, Mary joined them in Oxford in 1867. In 1872 she married **Thomas Humphry Ward** (1845–1926), born in Hull, fellow and tutor of Brasenose College, member of the staff of *The Times*, and editor of *The English Poets* (5 vols., 1880–1918). Mrs Ward contributed to *Macmillan's*, and, a student of Spanish literature, lives of early Spanish ecclesiastics to Smith's *Dictionary of Christian Biography*. A child's story, *Milly and Olly* (1881), *Miss Bretherton* (1884), a slight novel, and a translation (1885) of Amiel's *Journal intime* preceded her greatest success, the spiritual romance *Robert Elsmere* (1888) which inspired the philanthropist Passmore Edwards to found a settlement for the London poor in 1897 in Tavistock Square, now known by her name. Of the many novels which followed, most notable is *The Case of Richard Meynell* (1911). Mrs Ward was also an enthusiastic social worker and anti-suffragette. See her *A Writer's Recollections* (1918), and the Life by her daughter, J. P. Trevelyan, wife of G. M. Trevelyan (1923).

(10) **James** (1843–1925), English psychologist and philosopher, born at Hull, was a Congregational minister until he entered Cambridge in 1872, becoming a fellow of Trinity in 1875. He first made his name as a psychologist, particularly by his articles in the *Encyclopaedia Britannica*, in which he severely criticized the British associationist tradition and put forward his own theory of experience. These articles represented Ward's psychological standpoint until the publication in 1918 of his *Psychological Principles*. In 1897 he was appointed professor of Mental Philosophy at Cambridge, and propounded his philosophy in two sets of Gifford lectures, published as *Naturalism and Agnosticism* (1899), a refutation of naturalism, and *The Realm of Ends* (1911), an exposition of pluralism. His *Study of Kant* appeared in 1922. See O. W. Campbell's *Memoir* in Ward's *Essays in Philosophy* (1927).

(11) **Sir Joseph George** (1856–1930), New Zealand statesman, born in Melbourne, entered parliament in 1887 and was Liberal prime minister in 1906–12, 1928–30.

(12) **Sir Leslie** (1851–1922), English caricaturist, son of (5), was ' Spy ' of *Vanity Fair* (1873–1909). He was knighted in 1918. See his *Forty Years of ' Spy '* (1915).

(13) **Mary** (1585–1645), English founder in 1609 of a Catholic society for women, modelled on the Society of Jesus. She and her devotees founded schools and taught in

them, gave up the cloistered existence and the habit of nuns. Although their work was not questioned, these innovations were and Pope Urban VIII at last called her to Rome and suppressed her society in 1630. She was allowed to return to England in 1639. Her institute was fully restored, with papal permission, in 1877 and became the model for modern Catholic women's institutes. See Life by M. Oliver (1960).

(14) **Mary Augusta.** See (9).

(15) **Nathaniel** (1578–1652), English divine, born at Haverhill, Suffolk, studied at Emmanuel College, Cambridge, was pastor of Agawam, now Ipswich, in Massachusetts till 1645, when he returned to England. He helped to frame the first legal code in New England (enacted 1641), and wrote the controversial *The Simple Cobbler of Agawam* (1647).

(16) **Nathaniel Bagshaw** (1791–1868), English botanist, born in London, invented the Wardian case for the transport of plants.

(17) **Seth** (1617–89), English astronomer and divine, was born in Hertfordshire. He was educated at Sidney Sussex College, Cambridge, was Savilian professor of Astronomy at Oxford from 1649 to 1660, propounded (1653) a theory of planetary motion, and took part with John Wallis (q.v.) in the latter's controversy with Hobbes. He was Bishop of Exeter from 1662 to 1667, when he became Bishop of Salisbury.

(18) **William George** (1812–82), English theologian, born in London, was educated at Winchester and Christ Church, Oxford, and became fellow and tutor of Balliol. A strong Tractarian, he published in 1844 *The Ideal of a Christian Church*, for which he was deprived of his degree and had to leave the university. He joined the Roman Catholic church and became editor of the *Dublin Review*. See studies (1889; 1893) by his son **Wilfrid** (1856–1916), Catholic apologist and biographer.

WARDLAW, (1) Elizabeth, Lady (1677–1727), Scottish poetess, daughter of Sir Charles Halket of Pitfirrane, Fife, married in 1696 Sir Henry Wardlaw, is the reputed author of the ballad *Hardyknute* (1719; see Percy's *Reliques*, 1767 ed.), and, doubtfully, of *Sir Patrick Spens*, which she more probably amended, along with other ballads.

(2) **Henry** (fl. 1378, d. 1440), Scottish divine, studied and lived for some years in France, in 1403 became bishop of St Andrews, and played a prominent part in the foundation (1411) of St Andrews University.

WARHAM, William, *waw′rĕm* (c. 1450–1532), English prelate, born near Basingstoke, took orders, but practised law, and became advocate in the Court of Arches. His diplomatic services to Henry VII obtained for him rapid preferment—master of the Rolls (1494), lord chancellor (1503), Bishop of London (1503) and Archbishop of Canterbury (1503). In 1515 he had to resign the great seal to Wolsey. He was a close friend of the New Learning and its apostles, but had no stomach for fundamental reform, though he agreed to recognize the king's supremacy. See vol. vi of Hook's *Lives of the Archbishops* (1868).

WARLOCK, Peter, pseud. of **Philip Arnold**

Heseltine (1894–1930), English musicologist and composer, born in London. In 1910 he met Delius and in 1916 Bernard van Dieren, both of whom had a profound musical influence on him, and his friendship with D. H. Lawrence is also reflected in his music. In 1920 he founded *The Sackbut*, a spirited musical periodical, and his works include the song cycle *The Curlew* (1920–22), *Serenade* (1923) to Delius, the orchestral suite *Capriol* (1926), many songs, often in the Elizabethan manner, and choral works. He edited much Elizabethan and Jacobean music, wrote *Frederick Delius* (1923; under his own name) and *The English Ayre* (1926). See a Memoir (1934) by Cecil Gray.

WARMING, Johannes Eugenius Bülow, *var′ ming* (1841–1924), Danish botanist, born in the North Frisian island of Manö, was professor at Stockholm (1882–85) and Copenhagen (1885–1911). He wrote important works on systematic botany (1879) and ecology (1895), being regarded as a founder of the latter.

WARNER, (1) Charles Dudley (1829–1900), American writer, born at Plainfield, Mass., practised law in Chicago till 1860, then settled as an editor at Hartford. In 1884 he became co-editor of *Harper's Magazine*, in which his papers on the South, Mexico and the Great West appeared. In 1873 he wrote with Mark Twain *The Gilded Age*. Other works are *My Summer in a Garden* (1871), *Back-log Studies* (1873), *Being a Boy* (1878), *Washington Irving* (1881), *Captain John Smith* (1881), books of travel, such as *In the Levant* (1876), &c.

(2) **Sir Pelham,** nicknamed ' **Plum** ' (1873–1963), English cricketer, born in Trinidad, educated at Rugby and Oriel College, Oxford, won his cricket blue, played for Middlesex, and captained the victorious English team in the Australian tour of 1903. He also led the team in South Africa in 1905 and again in Australia in 1911. He was secretary of the M.C.C. in 1939–45, president in 1950, and was knighted in 1937. Editor of the periodical *Cricket*, his many books on the game include *The Fight for the Ashes*, and *Lord's 1787–1945*. See his *My Cricketing Life* (1921) and *Long Innings* (1951).

(3) **Rex** (1905–), English author, born in Birmingham. A specialist in classical literature, he was a teacher before turning to writing. Pre-eminently a novelist of ideas, his distinction lies in the original, imaginative handling of conflicting ideologies. *The Wild Goose Chase* (1937), *The Professor* (1938) and *The Aerodrome* (1941) established his reputation as a writer concerned with the problems of the individual involved with authority. *Men of Stones* (1949) explores the nature of totalitarianism, but it and *Why was I Killed?* (1944), are less successful than his other works. He is perhaps best known for his later historical novels such as *The Young Caesar* (1958), *Imperial Caesar* (1960) and *Pericles the Athenian* (1963). He is a poet of sensuous quality (*Poems*, 1931, and *Poems and Contradictions*, 1945), and also a translator of Greek classics.

(4) **Susan Bogert** (1819–85), American novelist, born at New York, published under

the pen-name of **Elizabeth Wetherell** *The Wide, Wide World* (1851), next to *Uncle Tom's Cabin* the most succesful American story of its day. There followed *Queechy* (1852), and other sentimental and emotional tales. See *Life* (1910) by her sister and collaborator, **Anna Bartlett** (1827–1915), who, as Amy Lothrop, wrote popular stories, and the study by O. E. P. Stokes (1926).

(5) **William** (c. 1558–1609), English poet, born in London, practised as an attorney, wrote *Pan his Syrinx* (1585), translated Plautus (*Menœchmi*, 1595), and gained a high contemporary reputation with his *Albion's England* (1586-1606), a long metrical history in fourteen-syllable verse.

WARREN, (1) Sir Charles (1840–1927), British general and archaeologist, born at Bangor, Wales, entered the Royal Engineers in 1857. He played a conspicuous part during the last quarter of the 19th century as a commander of British forces in South Africa, where he helped to delimit Griqualand West, and served also elsewhere. He is, however, chiefly remembered for his work in connection with the archaeological exploration of Palestine, especially Jerusalem, and for his writings arising from it: *Underground Jerusalem* (1876), *Temple and Tomb* (1880), *Jerusalem* (with Conder, 1884). He also wrote on ancient weights and measures. See *Life* by W. W. Williams (1941).

(2) **John Byrne Leicester.** See TABLEY.

(3) **Robert Penn** (1905–), American novelist and poet, born at Guthrie, Kentucky, was educated at Vanderbilt, Berkeley and Yale universities, and was a Rhodes scholar at Oxford. Professor of English at Louisiana (1934–42), at Minnesota (1942–50), he was professor of Drama (1951–56), and of English from 1961 at Yale. Recipient of two Pulitzer prizes (Fiction, 1947; Poetry, 1958), he established an international reputation by his novel, *All the King's Men* (1943; filmed 1949), in which the demagogue Willie Stark closely resembles Governor Huey Long (q.v.). Other works include *John Brown* (1929), *Night Rider* (1939), *The Cave* (1959), *Wilderness* (1961) and some volumes of short stories and verse, including *Selected Poems, Old and New, 1923–66* (1966).

(4) **Samuel** (1807–77), British novelist, born near Wrexham, studied medicine and law, was called to the bar, and made a Q.C. (1851). He is chiefly remembered by his *Passages from the Diary of a Late Physician* (1838) and *Ten Thousand a Year* (1841). Other works were *Now and Then* (1847), *The Lily and the Bee* (1851), and several lawbooks.

WARTON, (1) Joseph (1722–1800), English critic, born at Dunsfold, Surrey, was the son of the Rev. Thomas Warton (1688–1745), vicar of Basingstoke and Oxford professor of Poetry. In 1740 he passed from Winchester to Oriel, and, rector of Winslade from 1748, returned to Winchester in 1755, and was its head 1766–93. His preferments were a prebend of St Paul's, the living of Thorley, a prebend of Winchester, and the rectories of Wickham, Easton and Upham. His *Odes* (1746) marked a reaction from Pope. An edition of Virgil (1753), with translation of the *Eclogues* and *Georgics* gained him a

high reputation. He and his brother Thomas associated with Johnson in the Literary club. In 1757 appeared vol. i of his *Essay on Pope* (vol. ii in 1782), with its distinction between the poetry of reason and the poetry of fancy. Later works were editions of Pope (1797) and Dryden (completed by his son, 1811). See the panegyrical *Memoirs* by J. Wooll (1806).

(2) **Thomas** (1728–90), brother of (1), born at Basingstoke, became in 1751 a fellow of Trinity, Oxford, and in 1757 professor of Poetry. He also held two livings. His *Observations on the Faerie Queene* (1754) established his reputation; but he is remembered by his *History of English Poetry* (1774–1781; ed. by W. C. Hazlitt, 1871). In 1785 he became poet laureate and Camden professor of History. His miscellaneous writings included burlesque poetry and prose, genial satires on Oxford, an edition of Theocritus (1770), *Inquiry into the Authenticity of the Rowley Poems*, &c. See *Life* by Clarissa Rinaker (Illinois, 1916), and Dennis's *Studies in English Literature* (1876).

WARWICK, Richard Neville, Earl of, *wor'ik* (1428–71), ' the Kingmaker ', English soldier and statesman, eldest son of Richard, Earl of Salisbury, married as a boy the daughter of the Earl of Warwick, and so at twenty-one got the earldom. The Wars of the Roses began with the battle of St Albans (1455), gained for the Yorkists chiefly by Warwick's help. He was rewarded with the captaincy of Calais, and scoured the Channel at his pleasure. In the campaign of 1459 the Yorkists failed owing to their inactivity. The leaders, including Warwick, fled to the coast of Devon, and thence to Calais. Warwick was in England again in 1460, and in July at Northampton the Yorkists gained a complete victory, taking Henry VI prisoner. Up to this time Warwick's conception of the war was merely the natural struggle of the one party with the other for power; and when the Duke of York made his claim to the throne, Warwick prevailed upon him to waive it till the death of the king. In December 1460 the duke was defeated and slain at Wakefield, and early in 1461 Warwick himself was defeated in the second battle of St Albans. But, with Edward, the Duke of York's son, he marched on London, and proclaimed him as Edward IV. Soon after, the Yorkists gained a complete victory at Towton (1461), the Lancastrian cause was lost, and Henry was captured by Warwick and lodged in the Tower. But now Edward, jealous of Warwick, drove him into open revolt, but was himself compelled to flee to Holland, while the Kingmaker placed Henry once more upon the throne. But soon Edward returned, and at Barnet routed Warwick, who was surrounded and slain, April 14, 1471. See C. W. C. Oman's study (1891), J. Gairdner, *The Houses of Lancaster and York* (1874), Sir J. Ramsay, *Lancaster and York* (1892), and Life by P. M. Kendall (1957).

WASHINGTON, (1) Booker Taliaferro (1856–1915), American educationist, born a Mulatto slave at Hales Ford, Va., educated at Hampton Institute, became a teacher, writer and speaker on Negro problems, and in 1881 principal of the Tuskegee Institute for coloured persons, Alabama. See his *Up from Slavery* (1901), and a study by Stowe and Scott (1916).

(2) **George** (1732–99), commander of American forces and first president of the U.S., born February 22, at Bridges Creek, Westmoreland county, Virginia, of English stock from Northamptonshire. In 1658 his great-grandfather, John Washington, appeared in Virginia, and soon acquired wealth and position. His grandson, Augustine, died while his son George was still a boy, leaving a large family and inadequate means. George seems to have been a good, healthy boy, with a sober-mindedness beyond his years, although the incident of cherry tree and hatchet is probably the invention of his biographer, Mason Weems. In 1747 he went to Mount Vernon, the residence of his eldest half-brother, Lawrence, who had received the better part of the Washington property. Here the boy had access to books, and came to know the Fairfaxes, the family of his brother's wife; in 1748 Lord Fairfax employed him to survey his property. Surveying alternated for a while with hunting; he learned, too, the use of arms, and studied the art of war. In 1751 he accompanied his half-brother, who was dying of consumption, to the Barbados, and at his death next year was left guardian of his only daughter and heir to his estates in the event of her death without issue. The French were at this time connecting their settlements on the Great Lakes with those on the Mississippi by a chain of posts on the Ohio, within the sphere of English influence. Governor Dinwiddie of Virginia determined to warn the intruders off, and his second messenger was Washington. The French, however, paid no attention to these warnings; and an expedition was sent against them, of which Washington was (by the death of his superior early in the campaign) in command. Washington was driven back, shut up in a little fort, and forced to surrender. He served on the personal staff of Braddock (q.v.), and saved the remnant of the van of Braddock's army in 1755. He was then placed at the head of the Virginia forces (1756). In 1759 he married a rich young widow, Martha Custis (1732–1802). His niece was now dead, and the conjoint estates of Mount Vernon and of the widow Custis made him one of the richest men in the land. He kept open house, entertained liberally, led the hunting, and farmed successfully. He represented his county in the House of Burgesses. On the quarrel with the mother country (1765–70) he favoured peaceful measures first, and was thus one of the leaders in the anti-importation movements; but he soon became convinced that nothing save force would secure to his countrymen their rights. He represented Virginia in the first (1744) and second (1775) Continental Congresses, and at once took a leading part. He was neither orator nor writer, but in rude common sense and in the management of affairs he excelled. He was the one American soldier of national reputation, and was the inevitable commander-in-chief. He had remarkable powers as a

strategist and tactician, but was pre-eminent as a leader of men. It was this dignified, well-dressed gentleman who took command of the New England farmers and mechanics assembled at Cambridge in the summer of 1775. It seems scarcely credible that these half-disciplined, half-armed men should have held cooped up in Boston a thoroughly-disciplined and well-equipped British army and forced their evacuation (1776); the retreat from Concord and the slaughter at Bunker Hill were largely due to the incompetence of the English commander. The only really able English commander was Cornwallis, and he was hampered by the stupidity of his superior. Following reverses in the New York area, Washington made a remarkable retreat through New Jersey, inflicting notable defeats on the enemy at Trenton and Princeton (1777). He suffered defeats at Brandywine and Germantown but held his army together through the winter of 1777–78 at Valley Forge. After the alliance with France (1778) and with the assistance of Rochambeau, Washington forced the defeat and surrender of Cornwallis (q.v.), at Yorktown in 1781, which virtually ended the War of Independence. Washington retired to Mount Vernon, and sought to secure a strong government by constitutional means. In 1787 he presided over the convention of delegates from twelve states at Philadelphia which formulated the constitution; and the government under this constitution began in 1789 with Washington as first chief-magistrate or president. Unlike the old, the new administration was a strong consolidated government. Parties were formed, led by Washington's two most trusted advisers, Jefferson and Hamilton. At the outset Washington sought to enlist on the side of the new government the ablest men in the country, whether they had approved or disapproved that precise form of the constitution. As time went on, however, it became evident that those desiring greater liberty for the individual would no longer be content with passive opposition. A strong party sprang into life, and began a campaign which has never been surpassed for personal abuse and virulence. Stung by their taunts, Washington lost his faith in American institutions, went over heart and soul to the Federalist party, and even doubted whether Republicans should be admitted into the army. He retired from the presidency in 1797 and died (childless) at Mount Vernon on the Potomac, December 14, 1799. The federal capital of the U.S., in the planning of which he associated, bears his name. See books by J. Marshall (1804–07), Washington Irving (1855–59), A. Bancroft (new ed. 1851), H. C. Lodge (1889), Woodrow Wilson (1897; new ed. 1927), Frederic Harrison (1901), N. Hapgood (1902), J. A. Harrison (1906), F. T. Hill (1914), J. O'Boyle (1915), Rupert Hughes (1926–30), N. W. Stephenson and W. H. Dunn (1940), D. S. Freeman (1949–55), and its continuation by J. A. Carroll and H. W. Ashworth (1958), M. Cunliffe (1959) and B. Knollenberg (1965); and his *Writings*, ed. W. C. Ford (14 vols. 1889–93), ed. Fitzpatrick (26 vols. 1931–38).

WASSERMANN, *vas'ėr-man*, (1) **August von** (1866–1925), German bacteriologist, born at Bamberg, worked at bacteriology and chemotherapy in Berlin, discovered (1906), and gave his name to, a blood-serum test for syphilis.

(2) **Jakob** (1873–1933), German novelist, born a Jew, at Fürth in Bavaria, lived at Vienna and in Styria. His impressive novel *Die Juden von Zirndorf* (1897) was followed by a succession culminating in the trilogy completed just before his death: *Der Fall Maurizius* (1928), *Etzel Andergast* (1931), *Joseph Kerkhovens dritte Existenz* (1934). He wrote also short stories, lives of Columbus and H. M. Stanley, and an autobiography (1921).

WATERHOUSE, (1) **Alfred** (1830–1905), English architect, was born at Liverpool, and became R.A. in 1885, designed Manchester town hall and assize courts, Owens College, Manchester, Girton College, Cambridge, St Paul's School, Hammersmith, &c.

(2) **John William** (1847–1917), English painter, born in Rome, became R.A. in 1895. Among his pictures are *Ulysses and the Sirens* (1892) and *The Lady of Shalott* (1894).

WATERLAND, **Daniel** (1683–1740), English theologian, born at Walesby, Lincolnshire, a fellow of Magdalene, Cambridge (1704), canon of Windsor (1727), archdeacon of Middlesex and vicar of Twickenham (1730), controversially opposed the views of Samuel Clarke and Daniel Whitby (qq.v.). Van Mildert edited his works, with Memoir (11 vols. 1823–28).

WATERTON, **Charles** (1782–1865), British naturalist, born at Walton Hall near Wakefield, and educated at Stonyhurst, was much in America (South and North) in 1804–24. Besides his *Wanderings in South America* (1825; 6th ed. 1866) he published *Essays on Natural History* (1838–57; with Life by Moore, 1879). See P. Gosse, *The Squire of Walton Hall* (1940).

WATSON, (1) **James Dewey** (1928–), U.S. scientist, born in Chicago, where he graduated at the university. He came to England and worked with Crick and Wilkins (3) on the structure of DNA before becoming professor of Biology at Harvard (1961). He was awarded the Nobel prize for medicine and physiology with Crick and Wilkins in 1962. See his *The Double Helix* (1968).

(2) **John**. See MACLAREN (2).

(3) **John Broadus** (1878–1958), American psychologist, born in Greenville, S.C., a leading exponent of behaviourism. His most important work is *Behavior—An Introduction to Comparative Psychology* (1914).

(4) **Richard** (1737–1816), English divine, born at Heversham, educated at Trinity College, Cambridge, where he later became professor of Chemistry (1764) and regius professor of Divinity (1771), and Bishop of Llandaff (1782), published a famous *Apology for Christianity* (1776) in reply to Gibbon, and an *Apology for the Bible* (1796) in reply to Paine. He gave much time to agriculture at his estate on Windermere, and introduced the larch to that district. See his egotistical *Anecdotes of the Life of R. W.* (1817).

(5) **Robert** (1746–1838), Scottish adventurer, born at Elgin, fought for American independence, took his M.D. in Scotland, and was Lord George Gordon's secretary, president of the revolutionary Corresponding Society, state prisoner for two years in Newgate, Napoleon's tutor in English, and president of the Scots College at Paris. He unearthed the Stuart papers at Rome, and ended by strangling himself in London.

(6) **Thomas** (*c*. 1557–92), English lyric poet, was a Londoner who studied at Oxford. Coming to Marlowe's help in a street fight, he killed a man in 1589. He excelled in Latin verse, but he is best known for his English 'sonnets' in *Hecatompathia* (1582) and *Tears of Fancie* (1593).

(7) **Sir William** (1715–87), English scientist, born in London, was one of the earliest experimenters on electricity, being first to investigate the passage of electricity through a rarefied gas. He did much to introduce the Linnaean system to Britain.

(8) **Sir William** (1858–1935), English poet, born at Burley-in-Wharfedale, Yorks, first attracted notice with *Wordsworth's Grave* (1890). *Odes and other Poems* followed in 1894, *The Father of the Forest* in 1895, *For England* (1903), *Sable and Purple* (1910), *Heralds of the Dawn* (1912), *The Man who Saw* (1917), *The Superhuman Antagonists* (1919), *Poems, Brief and New* (1925), &c. He was knighted in 1917.

WATSON-WATT, **Sir Robert Alexander** (1892–1973), Scottish physicist, born at Brechin, educated at Dundee and St Andrews, worked in the Meteorological Office, the D.S.I.R., and the National Physical Laboratory before becoming scientific adviser to the Air Ministry in 1940. He played a major rôle in the development and introduction of radar, for which he was knighted in 1942. See his *Three Steps to Victory* (1958).

WATT, (1) **James** (1736–1819), Scottish inventor, born at Greenock, January 19, son of a merchant and town councillor, went to Glasgow in 1754 to learn the trade of a mathematical-instrument maker, and there, after a year in London, he set up in business. The hammermen's guild put difficulties in his way, but the university made him its mathematical-instrument maker (1757–63). He was employed on surveys for the Forth and Clyde canal (1767), the Caledonian and other canals; in the improvement of the harbours of Ayr, Port Glasgow and Greenock; and in the deepening of the Forth, Clyde and other rivers. As early as 1759 his attention had been directed to steam as a motive force. In 1763–64 a working model of the Newcomen engine from a college classroom was sent for repair. He easily put it into order, and, seeing the defects of the machine, hit upon the expedient of the separate condenser. Other improvements were the air pump, steam jacket for cylinder, double-acting engine, &c. He entered into a partnership with Matthew Boulton of Soho near Birmingham in 1774, when (under a patent of 1769) the manufacture of the new engine was commenced at the Soho Engineering Works. Watt's soon superseded Newcomen's machine as a pumping-engine; and between 1781 and 1785 he obtained patents for the sun and planet motion, the expansion principle, the double engine, the parallel motion, a smokeless furnace, and the governor. He described a steam locomotive in one of his patents (1784). He also invented a letter-copying press, a machine for copying sculpture, &c. The composition of water was discovered, not by Watt, but by Henry Cavendish (q.v.). The watt, a unit of power, is named after him, and the term horsepower, another unit, was first used by him. He retired in 1800, and died at Heathfield Hall, his seat near Birmingham, August 19. See Lives by Jacks (1901), Dickinson and Jenkins (1927), and study by I. B. Hart (1958).

(2) **Robert** (1774–1819), Scottish bibliographer, born near Stewarton in Ayrshire, became a distinguished physician, known for his great *Bibliotheca Britannica* (1819–24).

WATTEAU, Jean Antoine, *va-tō* (1684–1721), French painter, born at Valenciennes, studied under the local artist Gérin, but in 1702 ran away to Paris and worked as a scene painter at the Opera, as a copyist, and as assistant to Claude Gillot and Claude Audran. The latter was keeper of the Luxembourg, and it was here that Watteau found the opportunity to study the work of Rubens, which influenced him considerably, and to paint from nature the palace-garden landscapes which form the typical backcloth to many of his pictures. After 1712 he enjoyed the patronage of the collector Crozat, who introduced him to the paintings of Veronese, an influence visible in the colouring and style of his later work. His early canvases were mostly military scenes, but it was the mythological *Embarquement pour Cythère* which won him membership of the Academy in 1717. While staying at the castle of Montmorency with Crozat he painted his *Fêtes galantes*, quasi-pastoral idylls in court dress which became fashionable in high society. A lifelong sufferer from tuberculosis, he visited London in 1720 to consult the celebrated Dr Mead (q.v.), but his health was rapidly deteriorating, and on his return he painted his last great work, depicting the interior of the shop of his art-dealer friend Gersaint, drawn from nature and intended as a signboard, but in fact the most classical and most perfectly composed of his paintings, rivalled only by the *Embarquement*. Essentially aristocratic in conception, Watteau's paintings fell into disfavour at the Revolution, and it was not until the end of the 19th century that, aided by de Goncourt's *Catalogue raisonnée* (1875), they regained popularity. Watteau is now regarded as one of the leading French masters, a pioneer in the study of nature, and a forerunner of the Impressionists in his handling of colour. He influenced and was imitated by many later artists, notably Fragonard and Boucher (qq.v.). See studies by Cellier (1867), Mollet (1883), Sir C. Phillips (1902), C. Mauclair (trans. 1906), S. Sitwell (1925) and K. T. Parker (1931).

WATTS, (1) Alaric Alexander (1797–1864), English journalist and poet, born in London, founded the *United Services Gazette* (1833) and the annual *Literary Souvenir* (1824–37), and published two volumes of poetry, but is now remembered chiefly for his alliterative alphabetical *jeu d'esprit* ' An Austrian army

awfully arrayed '. See *Life* by his son A. A. Watts (1884).

(2) **George Frederick** (1817–1904), English painter, born in London, formed his style after the Venetian masters and first attracted notice by his cartoon of *Caractacus* (1843) in the competition for murals for the new Houses of Parliament. He became known for his penetrating portraits of notabilities, 150 of which he presented to the National Portrait Gallery in 1904, and in these his best work is to be seen; but in his lifetime his somewhat sickly subject pieces enjoyed enormous popularity, and monochrome reproductions of *Paolo and Francesca, Sir Galahad, Love Triumphant,* &c., adorned the walls of countless late Victorian middle-class homes. He also executed some sculpture, including *Physical Energy* (Kensington Gardens). In 1864 he married Ellen Terry (q.v.), but parted from her within a year. He declined a baronetcy in 1885 and was awarded the O.M. in 1902. See books by H. Macmillan (1903), Pantini (1904), G. K. Chesterton (1904), Mrs R. Barrington (1905), Mrs M. Watts, his widow (1912), E. H. Short (1925) and R. Chapman (1945).

(3) **Henry** (1815–84), English chemist, born in London, best known by his *Dictionary of Chemistry* (1863–75; supplements, 1872–75–1881; revised by Muir and Morley, 1889–94), based on Ure's.

(4) **Isaac** (1674–1748), English hymnwriter, born at Southampton, in 1702 succeeded an Independent minister in Mark Lane, London, becoming eminent as a preacher. His hymns and psalms are contained in *Horae Lyricae* (1706), *Hymns and Spiritual Songs* (1707–09) and *Psalms of David Imitated* (1719), and include ' Jesus shall reign where'er the sun ', ' When I survey the wondrous cross ', and ' O God, our help in ages past '. See Lives by Dr Gibbons, Dr Johnson, Southey, T. Milner (1834), T. Hood (1875), E. P. Wright (1914) and H. Escott (1962).

(5) **James Winston** (1904–), American neurosurgeon, born at Lynchburg, Va., famous for his brain surgery, with W. Freeman (q.v.) developed the operation known as prefrontal lobotomy.

WATTS-DUNTON, Walter Theodore (1832–1914), English poet and critic, was born at St Ives, Huntingdonshire. To the name Watts he added his mother's name, Dunton, in 1896. In London he became the centre of a very remarkable literary and artistic company, and the intimate friend of Rossetti, William Morris, Swinburne, and afterwards Tennyson. He wrote enough to fill many volumes—in the *Athenaeum* (1876–98) and elsewhere. In *The Coming of Love* (1897) he gave a selection of his poems. In 1898 appeared *Aylwin. Old Familiar Faces* (1915) contains recollections of Borrow, Rossetti, Morris, &c., from the *Athenaeum*. See works cited at ROSSETTI, and Life and Letters by T. Hake and A. Compton-Rickett (2 vols. 1916).

WAUGH, *woКH,* (1) **Alec,** in full **Alexander Raban** (1898–), English novelist and traveller, elder brother of (3), was born in London and educated at Sherborne and Sandhurst. His first novel, a classic of school life, was *The Loom of Youth* (1917), and there followed other novels, including *Wheels within Wheels* (1933), *Where the Clock Chimes Twice* (1952), *Island in the Sun* (1956; filmed 1957), travel books, such as *The Sunlit Caribbean* (1948), and short stories. See his *The Early Years of Alec Waugh* (1962) and *My Brother Evelyn and Other Profiles* (1967).

(2) **Edwin** (1817–90), English dialect writer, the 'Lancashire poet', was born at Rochdale. Among his numerous prose writings are the *Besom Ben Stories* (1892), and the admirable descriptions of natural scenery in *Tufts of Heather* and *Rambles in the Lake Country* (1862). His songs in periodicals were published as *Poems and Lancashire Songs* (1860). There is an edition of his works, with memoir, by G. Milner (8 vols. 1892–93).

(3) **Evelyn Arthur St John** (1903–66), English author, was born in London. Son of the critic and publisher, Arthur Waugh (1866–1943), and younger brother of (1), he turned naturally to writing when he left Oxford. Novels such as *Decline and Fall* (1928), *Vile Bodies* (1930), *Black Mischief* (1932) and *Scoop* (1938) found an eager public, compounded as they are of light-hearted banter and witty conversation pieces at the expense of the follies of social life in the 1920s and onwards. His later books, on the whole, exhibit a more serious attitude and the bantering tone is replaced by a sardonic wit, with occasional rasping undertones. Notable titles are *Put Out More Flags* (1942), *Brideshead Revisited* (1945), *Scott-King's Modern Europe* (1946), *The Loved One* (1948), *Men at Arms* (1952), *Love Among the Ruins* (1953), *Officers and Gentlemen* (1955), *Unconditional Surrender* (1961), and a self-portrait, *Gilbert Pinfold* (1957). *Men at Arms* won the James Tait Black prize, and a Life of Edmund Campion the Hawthornden prize in 1936. See his autobiography *A Little Learning* (1964) and study by F. J. Stopp (1958).

WAUTERS, Emile, *wow'ters* (1846–1933), Belgian historical and portrait painter, born at Brussels. His well-known *Mary of Burgundy before the Magistrates* is in Liège museum.

WAVELL, Archibald Percival Wavell, 1st Earl (1883–1950), British field-marshal, born at Winchester, educated at Winchester and R.M.C. Sandhurst, was commissioned in the Black Watch 1901, and served in South Africa and India. Wounded in 1916, he lost the sight of one eye. Posted to the General Staff, his admiration for Allenby's methods of command and his high commissionership in Egypt was reflected in two books which are models of succinct prose. Between the wars he was entrusted with command and staff appointments of steadily rising importance. In 1939 he was given the Middle East Command. With dangerously slender resources he speedily found himself fighting eight separate campaigns, five of them simultaneously; a task which made heavy demands on his outstanding quality of 'robustness'. His defeat of a numerically superior Italian army, with the capture of 130,000 prisoners, was as notable as his adroit conquest of Abyssinia. Thereafter, lacking

means, his military fortunes declined. Widely read, his love of verse was reflected in his anthology *Other Men's Flowers* (1944). His own masterly little work *Generals and Generalship* (1941), was invariably included in the field kit of his most formidable enemy, Erwin Rommel. From 1943 to 1947, during the difficult years which preceded the transfer of power, he was viceroy of India. He became field-marshal and viscount (1943), earl (1947), constable of the Tower (1948), lord-lieutenant of London (1949). See works by Rowan-Robinson and R. J. Collins (1948) and Life by J. Connell (1964).

WAVERLEY, John Anderson, 1st Viscount (1882–1958), British administrator and politician, was born at Eskbank, Midlothian. Educated at Edinburgh and Leipzig, he entered the Colonial Office in 1905, was chairman of the Board of Inland Revenue (1919–22), and permanent under-secretary at the Home Office from 1922 until his appointment as governor of Bengal in 1932. He was home secretary and minister of Home Security from 1939 to 1940—the Anderson air-raid shelter being named after him—became in 1940 lord president of the Council, and chancellor of the Exchequer in 1943, when he introduced the pay-as-you-earn system of income-tax collection devised by his predecessor Sir Kinglsey Wood. He was created viscount in 1952 and awarded the O.M. (1958). See Life by J. Wheeler-Bennett (1962).

WAYNE, Anthony (1745–96), 'mad Anthony', American soldier, born at Easttown (now Waynesboro), Pa., raised in 1776 a volunteer regiment, and in Canada covered the retreat of the provincial forces at Three Rivers. He commanded at Ticonderoga until 1777, when he joined Washington in New Jersey. He fought bravely at Brandywine; led the attack at Germantown; captured supplies for the army at Valley Forge; carried Stony Point; and saved Lafayette in Virginia (1781). In 1793 he led an expedition against the Indians. See Life by J. R. Spears (1903).

WAYNFLETE. See WILLIAM OF WAYNFLETE.

WEBB, (1) **Sir Aston** (1849–1930), English architect, born in London, R.A. 1903, P.R.A. 1919–24, designed the new front of Buckingham Palace, the Admiralty Arch, Imperial College of Science, and many other London buildings.

(2) **Beatrice.** See (6).

(3) **Daniel** (c. 1719–98), Irish critic of poetry, painting and music, a precursor of the romantics, born at Maidstown (Limerick), lived at Bath. See Life by H. Hecht (1920).

(4) **Mary Gladys,** *née* **Meredith** (1881–1927), English writer, born at Leighton, near the Wrekin, married (1912) H. B. L. Webb, lived mostly in Shropshire, market-gardening and novel-writing, and latterly in London. *Precious Bane* (1924) won her a belated fame as a writer of English and a novelist of Shropshire soil, Shropshire dialect, Shropshire superstition, and 'the continuity of country life'. Her other works are *The Golden Arrow* (1916), *Gone to Earth* (1917), *The House in Dormer Forest* (1920), *Seven for a Secret* (1922) and the unfinished *Armour*

Wherein he Trusted (1929)—novels; *The Spring of Joy* (1917)—nature essays; and poems. See studies by W. R. Chappell (1930), H. Addison (1931), T. Moult (1935) and W. B. Jones (1948).

(5) **Matthew** (1848-83), English swimmer, born at Dawley, Salop, was the first man to swim the English Channel. Starting from Dover, August 25, 1875, he reached Calais in 21¾ hours. He was drowned attempting to swim the Niagara rapids.

(6) **Sidney James, Baron Passfield** (1859–1947) and **(Martha) Beatrice**, *née* **Potter** (1858-1943), English social reformers, social historians and economists, married in 1892. Sidney was born in London, the son of an accountant, and in 1885 graduated LL.B. at London University. In the same year he was introduced by Bernard Shaw to the newly-founded Fabian Society, of which he became one of the most powerful members, writing the tracts *Facts for Socialists* (1887), *Facts for Londoners* (1889) and contributing to *Fabian Essays* (1889). He became a Progressive member of the L.C.C. in 1892. Beatrice was born near Gloucester, the daughter of an industrial magnate. Through her friendship with Herbert Spencer (q.v.) and through rent-collecting she became interested in the social problems of the time, and assisted Charles Booth (q.v.) in research for the survey *Life and Labour of the People in London*. In 1891 she published *The Co-operative Movement in Great Britain*. After their marriage the Webbs began a joint life of service to socialism and trade unionism, publishing in 1894 their classic *History of Trade Unionism* based on a sound personal knowledge of the movement. They also collaborated in *Industrial Democracy* (1897), the invaluable *English Local Government* (9 vols. 1906-29), *The Truth about Russia* (1942), &c. They started the *New Statesman* (1913), and participated in establishing the London School of Economics (1895). Labour M.P. for Seaham (1922–29), Sidney Webb was made president of the Board of Trade in 1924, and in 1929 was raised, much against his inclination, to the peerage, becoming dominions and colonial secretary (1929-30) and colonial secretary (1930-31). In 1931 the Webbs visited Russia, where they accumulated material for several books on Soviet Communism. See Beatrice's *My Apprenticeship* (1926), and *Our Partnership* (1948); also Lives by M. A. Hamilton (1933) and K. Muggeridge and R. Adam (1967).

WEBER, *vay'ber*, (1) **Carl Maria Friedrich Ernst von** (1786-1826), German composer and pianist, was born of a noble but impoverished Austrian family, at Eutin near Lübeck. Soon after, his father with his wife (a singer) and boy began to wander from town to town at the head of a small dramatic company. As soon as he could sit at the piano the boy was plied with music lessons; but his serious training began in 1796. His second opera, *Das Waldmädchen* (1800), produced at Freiberg before he was fourteen, he afterwards remodelled in *Silvana*. At Vienna in 1803 he was warmly welcomed as a pupil by Abt Vogler (q.v.), who obtained for him the conductorship of the opera at Breslau, where he gave evidence of rare talent for organization. In 1806 he became secretary to a brother of the king of Württemberg, ran into debt and dissipation, was through his thriftless old father's fault charged with embezzlement, and with his father ordered to quit the country (1810). The next twelve months he spent at Mannheim and Darmstadt, composing the operetta *Abu Hassan*; at Munich in 1811 he was writing concertos. In 1813 he settled at Prague as opera *kapellmeister*, and about this time composed ten patriotic songs and the cantata *Kampf und Sieg*. In 1816 he was invited by the king of Saxony to direct the German opera at Dresden, superseding Italian opera. In 1817 he married Carolina Brandt, the famous singer. In 1818 he wrote his Mass in E flat and the Jubel cantata and overture, in 1819 the Mass in G for the royal golden wedding. *Der Freischütz* was completed in May 1820, and produced with great success at Berlin (1821). His next opera, *Euryanthe*, was produced at Vienna in 1823. His final masterpiece, *Oberon*, was undertaken at the request of Charles Kemble for Covent Garden Theatre. March 1826 saw Weber in London, and the first performance of *Oberon* was the crowning triumph of his life. During the next few weeks he conducted frequently at the theatre and played at many concerts. Such labour proved too much for his exhausted body. He died June 4, and was buried at St Mary's, Moorfields, whence in 1844 his remains were removed to Dresden. As founder of German romantic opera, Weber was the forerunner of Wagner. Other works include the music to *Preciosa*, the overture, *Der Beherrscher der Geister*, two symphonies, three concertos, sonatas, &c., as well as scenas, cantatas and songs. See Spitta in Grove's *Dictionary*, J. Benedict (1881), and German works by F. W. Jähns (1871–73), J. Kapp (1922), K. Tetzel (1926) and W. Saunders (1939).

(2) **Ernst Heinrich** (1795–1878), German scientist, born in Wittenberg, from 1818 professor of Anatomy, and from 1840 of Physiology at Leipzig, devised a method of determining the sensitivity of the skin, enunciated in 1834, and gave name to the Weber-Fechner Law of the increase of stimuli.

(3) **Max** (1864–1920), German economist, born at Erfurt, professor at Berlin (1893), Freiburg (1894), Heidelberg (1897) and Munich (1919), noted for his work on the relation between the spirit of capitalism and protestant ethics. See studies by H. Robertson (1935) and R. Bendix (1961).

(4) **Max** (1881–1961), Russian-born American painter, studied under Matisse in Paris and was one of the pioneer abstractionist painters in New York. He later abandoned this extreme form for a distorted naturalism. His works include *The Two Musicians* (1917; Modern Art, N.Y.), *Tranquillity* (1928), *Latest News* (c. 1940), *Three Literary Gentlemen* (1945).

(5) **Wilhelm Eduard** (1804-91), German scientist, brother of (2), from 1831 professor of Physics at Göttingen, deposed in 1837; from 1843 professor at Leipzig, associated

with Gauss in his researches on electricity and magnetism, inventor of the electro-dynamometer, first to apply the mirror and scale method of reading deflections, and author, with (2), of a notable treatise on waves.

WEBERN, Anton von (1883–1945), Austrian composer, born in Vienna, studied under Schönberg and became one of his first musical disciples, even surpassing his master in the extreme application of the latter's twelve-tone techniques. Fragmentation of melody to achieve fleeting, impressionistic effects (*Klangfarbenmelodien*) make the maximum demands on the listener, and performances of his works at first always invited hostile demonstrations. For a while he conducted the Vienna Workers' Symphony Orchestra, founded a choir called the *Kunstelle*, but lived most of his life in retirement at Mödling. The Nazis banned his music and he worked as a proofreader during World War II. He was accidentally shot dead by a U.S. soldier near Salzburg, September 15, 1945. His works include a symphony, three cantatas, *Four Pieces for Violin and Pianoforte* (1910), *Five Pieces for Orchestra* (1911–13), a concerto for nine instruments and songs, including several settings of Stefan George's poems (1908–1909).

WEBSTER, (1) Daniel (1782–1852), American orator, lawyer and statesman, born at Salisbury, N.H., studied at Dartmouth, Salisbury and Boston, was admitted to the bar in 1805, and was sent to congress in 1813. Settling in Boston as an advocate in 1816, he distinguished himself in the Dartmouth College case, and as an orator became famous by his oration on the bicentenary of the landing of the Pilgrim Fathers. Returning to congress in December 1823 as a Massachusetts representative he found new rivals there; in 1827 he was transferred to the senate. He had favoured free trade, but in 1828 defended the new protective tariff. His whole career was marked by a deep reverence for established institutions and accomplished facts, and for the principle of nationality. His ' Bunker Hill ' oration was made in 1825 and another, on the supremacy of the Union, in 1830. The Whig party triumphed in 1840, and Webster was called into Harrison's Cabinet as secretary of state; under Tyler he negotiated the Ashburton treaty with Great Britain, but resigned in May 1843. In 1844 he refused his party's nomination for president and supported Clay. He opposed the war with Mexico. In 1850 he said that he abhorred slavery, but was unwilling to break up the Union to abolish it. Under Fillmore he was called to his former post as secretary of state to settle differences with England. On October 24 he died at Marshfield, his Massachusetts home. Daniel Webster was unquestionably the greatest of American orators. His speeches were published in 1851; his *Private Correspondence* in 1857. See Lives by G. T. Curtis (1870), H. C. Lodge (1883), Brooks (1893) J. B. McMaster (1902) and C. M. Fuess (1930), and Fisher's *True Daniel Webster* (1912).

(2) **John** (*c.* 1580–*c.* 1625), English dramatist, supposed to have been at one time clerk of St Andrews, Holborn. In *Lady Jane* and *The Two Harpies* (both lost) he was the collaborator of Dekker, Drayton, Chettle and others. In 1604 he made some additions to *The Malcontent* of Marston. In 1607 were printed the *Famous History of Sir Thomas Wyat*, a tragedy, and two comedies, *Westward Hoe* and *Northward Hoe*, all three the joint work of Webster and Dekker. The *White Divil* (1612) first revealed his powers. The *Dutchesse of Malfi* (1623) is a yet greater achievement. *Appius and Virginia* (first published 1654) may be Heywood's (or partly); *The Devil's Law Case* (1623) is largely disagreeable and sordid. A poem on the death of Prince Henry, and other fragments of verse, survive, with some doubtful works. The tragedy, *A Late Murder of the Son upon the Mother* (1624), unpublished and lost, although licensed, was written by Ford and Webster. Not popular in his own day, Webster was first recognized by Charles Lamb. Webster's works were edited by A. Dyce (1830), W. C. Hazlitt (1857–58), F. L. Lucas (1927). See Rupert Brooke's monograph (1916), and E. E. Stoll, *John Webster* (1905).

(3) **Noah** (1758–1843), American lexicographer, born in Hartford, Conn., graduated at Yale in 1778, and, after a spell as teacher, was admitted to the bar in 1781. But he soon resumed teaching, and made a great hit with the first part (1783; later known as ' Webster's Spelling Book ') of *A Grammatical Institute of the English Language*. Political articles and pamphlets, lecturing, a few years of law and journalism occupied him till 1798, when he retired to a life of literary labour at New Haven. He published an English grammar (1807) and the famous *American Dictionary of the English Language* (1828; latest ed. *Webster's New International Dictionary of the English Language*). See Life by E. Scudder (1882).

WEDDELL, James (1787–1834), English navigator, born at Ostend. In his principal voyage (1822–24) he penetrated to the point $74°\,15'$ S. by $34°\,17'$ W. in that part of Antarctica which later took his name (Weddell Sea; Weddell Quadrant), as did a type of seal taken by him in the area.

WEDDERBURN, Alexander, 1st Baron (1780) **Loughborough, 1st Earl** (1801) **of Rosslyn** (1733–1805), Lord Chancellor, born in Edinburgh, son of a Scottish judge, in 1757 abruptly left the Scottish bar for the English, entered parliament in 1762, and distinguished himself in the Douglas cause (1771).

WEDEKIND, Frank, *vay'dĕ-kint* (1864–1918), German dramatist, born in Hanover, won fame with *Erdgeist* (1895), *Frühlings Erwachen* (1891; first performed 1906), *Die Büchse der Pandora* (1903; first performed 1918), and other unconventional tragedies. See studies by P. Fechter (1920) and A. Kutscher (1922–31).

WEDGWOOD, (1) Dame Cicely Veronica (1910–), English historian, born at Stocksfield, Northumberland, and studied at Lady Margaret Hall, Oxford. A specialist in 17th-century history, her publications include biographies of *Strafford* (1935), *Oliver Cromwell* (1939), *William the Silent* (James Tait Black Memorial prize, 1944) and *Montrose* (1955), *The Thirty Years' War* (1938); also *The King's Peace* (1955), *The King's War* (1958) and *The Trial of Charles I* (1964). She was created D.B.E. in 1968 and awarded the O.M. in 1969.

(2) **Josiah** (1730–95), English potter, born at Burslem of a family notable in the industry, patented (1763) a beautiful cream-coloured ware (Queen's Ware). He emulated antique models, producing the unglazed blue Jasper ware, with its raised designs in white, the black basalt ware, and, in 1769, named his new works, near Hanley, ' Etruria '. His products, and their imitations, were named after him (Wedgwood ware). He associated with the potters T. Whieldon and T. Bentley, and employed J. Flaxman (q.v.), from 1775, to furnish designs. See Life by A. Kelly (1963) and books on the family by L. Jewitt (1865), J. C. Wedgwood (1908); on Josiah by E. Meteyard (1865–66), J. Wedgwood (1915), W. Burton (1922) and C. V. Wedgwood (1951); his *Correspondence* (1903–06), and W. Mankowitz, *Wedgwood* (1953).

WEED, Thurlow (1797–1882), American journalist, born at Cairo, N.Y., in 1830 founded the Albany *Evening Journal*, which he controlled for thirty-five years; in 1867–68 he edited the New York *Commercial Advertiser*. See his *Autobiography* (1884).

WEELKES, Thomas (*c*. 1575–1623), one of the greatest of English madrigal composers, was organist at Winchester College (1597) and Chichester Cathedral (1602). He graduated B.Mus. at New College, Oxford, in 1602. A friend of Thomas Morley (q.v.), he contributed to the *Triumphes of Oriana*.

WEENIX, vay'-, (1) **Jan** (1640–1719), Dutch painter, born at Amsterdam, son of (2), known for hunting scenes, animal subjects and still-life paintings featuring dead game-birds, hares, &c.

(2) **Jan Baptist** (1621–60), Dutch painter, father of (1), specialized in landscapes and seaport subjects.

WEEVER, John (1576–1632), English poet and antiquary, born in Lancashire; his works include *Epigrammes in the Oldest Cut and Newest Fashion* (1599; ed. R. B. McKerrow, 1922), and *Ancient Funerall Monuments* (1621; 3rd ed. by Tooke, 1767).

WEGENER, Alfred Lothar, *vay'gĕ-ner* (1880–1930), German explorer and geophysicist, born in Berlin, professor of Meteorology at Hamburg (1919), of Geophysics and Meteorology at Graz (1924). His theory of continental drift is named after him (Wegener Hypothesis), and is the subject of his chief work (1915; trans. 1924 as *Origin of Continents and Oceans*). He died in Greenland on his fourth expedition there.

WEIERSTRASS, Karl, *vī'ĕr-shtras* (1815–97), German mathematician, born at Ostenfelde, became professor of Mathematics at Berlin, noted for his work on the theory of functions. He proposed coordinates, and devised a curve, with related function, all of which are named from him.

WEIGEL. See BRECHT.

WEIL, vīl, (1) **Gustav** (1808–89), German

orientalist, professor of Oriental Languages at Heidelberg, wrote on Mohammedan history, and translated the *Arabian Nights* (1837–41).

(2) **Simone** (1903–43), French philosophical writer, born in Paris, taught philosophy in schools at Le Puy, Bourges and St Quentin, but interspersed this with periods of hard manual labour on farms and at the Renault works in order to experience the working-class life. In 1936 she served in the Republican forces in the Spanish Civil War. In 1941 she settled in Marseilles, where she befriended the Dominican, Father Perrin, who introduced her to Gustave Thibon and their joint influence was the crucial experience of her short life. A deep mystical feeling for the Catholic faith, yet a profound reluctance to join an organized religion is at the heart of most of her writing which, posthumously published, includes *La Pesanteur et la Grâce* (1947; trans. 1952), *Attente de Dieu* (1950; trans. 1951), *The Notebooks* (1952–55; trans. 1956), and *Oppression and Liberty* (trans. 1959). She escaped to the United States in 1942 and worked for the Free French in London, before her death at Ashford, Kent. See Memoir by J. M. Perrin and G. Thibon (1952; trans. 1953), and studies by Davy (trans. 1951), Tomlin (1954), Rees (1958), and Cabaud (1967).

WEILL, Kurt, *vīl* (1900–50), German composer, born in Dessau. He studied under Humperdinck and Busoni, worked with Brecht, achieved fame with *Die Dreigroschenoper*, a modernization of Gay's *Beggar's Opera*, in 1928. A refugee from the Nazis, he settled in the U.S.A. in 1934. In all his works, Weill was influenced by the idioms of jazz, but his later operas and musical comedies, all of which contain an element of social criticism, did not repeat the success of the first.

WEIMAR, Marguerite Josephine. See GEORGE, MLLE.

WEINBERGER, Jaromir, *vīn'ber-gĕr* (1896–1967), Czech composer, born in Prague, studied under Reger, was professor of Composition at Ithaca Conservatory, New York (1922–26), settling in the U.S.A. in 1939. He wrote theatre music, orchestral works, and four operas, the most famous of which is *Schwanda the Bagpiper* (1927).

WEINGARTNER, (Paul) Felix (1863–1942), Austrian conductor and composer, born in Zara, Dalmatia, studied under Liszt, succeeded Mahler (1908) as conductor of the Vienna Court Opera, and later toured extensively in Britain and America. His works include operas, symphonies, and *Über das Dirigieren* (1895). See his autobiographical *Lebenserinnerungen* (trans. 1937 'Buffets and Rewards').

WEISMANN, August, *vīs'man* (1834–1914), German biologist, born at Frankfurt-am-Main, in 1867 became professor of Zoology at Freiburg. One of his first works was on the development of the Diptera. In 1868–76 appeared a series of papers, translated in 1882 as *Studies in the Theory of Descent*. His theory of germ-plasm (Weismannism—a form of neo-Darwinism), expressed in a series of essays (trans. as *Essays upon Heredity and*

Kindred Biological Problems, 1889–92), raised opposition in Britain. He wrote other works on evolution.

WEISZ, Victor. See VICKY.

WEIZMANN, Chaim, *vīts'man* (1874–1952), Jewish statesman, born near Pinsk, studied in Germany and lectured on Chemistry at Geneva and Manchester. His complete and articulate faith in Zionism played a large part in securing the Balfour Declaration of 1917, by which the Jews were promised a national home in Palestine. He was president of the Zionist Organization (1920–30, 1935–1946), and of the Jewish Agency (from 1929). When the state of Israel came into being in 1948, he became its first president. See *Life* by Berlin (1958), and *A Biography by Several Hands* (ed. Weisgal and Carmichael, 1962).

WEIZSÄCKER, *vīts'ek-êr,* (1) **Julius** (1828–1889), German historian, born at Oehringen near Heilbronn, professor at Tübingen, Strasbourg, Göttingen and Berlin, edited vols. 1–6 of the *Deutsche Reichstagsakten.*

(2) **Karl Heinrich** (1822–99), German Protestant theologian, brother of (1), born at Oehringen, became professor at Tübingen. His most notable work was translated as *The Apostolic Age* (1894–95).

WELCH, John. See WELSH (2).

WELCKER, *vel'ker,* (1) **Friedrich Gottlieb** (1784–1868), German philologist and archaeologist, born at Grünberg (Hessen), professor at Giessen, Göttingen and Bonn, was notable for his works on Greek history and literature. See *Life* (1880) by Kekule.

(2) **Karl Theodor** (1790–1869), German publicist and politician, brother of (1), born at Öberofleiden (Hessen), was professor at Kiel, Heidelberg, Bonn and Freiburg.

WELENSKY, Sir Roy (1907–), Rhodesian politician, born at Salisbury, S. Rhodesia, the son of a Lithuanian-Jew. He was elected to the Legislative Council of N. Rhodesia in 1938, in 1940 became a member of the Executive Council, was knighted in 1953, and from 1956 to its break-up in 1963 was prime minister of the Federation of Rhodesia and Nyasaland, of which he was a most energetic advocate and architect. His handling of the constitutional crisis in 1959 aroused much controversy. See D. Taylor, *The Rhodesian.*

WELLES, (George) Orson (1915–), American director and actor, born in Kenosha, Wisconsin. He appeared at the Gate Theatre, Dublin, in 1931, returned to America, became a radio producer in 1934, and founded the Mercury Theatre in 1937. In 1938 his radio production of Wells's *War of the Worlds* was so realistic that it caused panic in the U.S. In 1941, he wrote, produced, directed and acted in the film *Citizen Kane*, a revolutionary landmark in cinema technique, and in 1942 produced and directed a screen version of Booth Tarkington's *The Magnificent Ambersons*, a masterly evocation of a vanished way of American life. His later work, giving ample rein to his varied and unpredictable talents, although never equalling his two masterpieces, includes his individual film versions of *Macbeth* (1948), *Othello* (1951), Kafka's *The Trial* (1962) and *Chimes at Midnight* (based on Shakespeare's Falstaff character, 1965);

and a variety of memorable stage and film rôles, the most celebrated being that of ' Harry Lime ' in *The Third Man* (1949). See studies by P. Noble (1956) and P. Cowie (1965).

WELLESLEY, *welz'li,* (1) **Arthur.** See WELLINGTON.

(2) **Richard Colley Wellesley, 1st Marquis** (1760–1842), British administrator, brother of (1), born in Co. Meath, became (1781) Earl of Mornington on the death of his father, and was returned to parliament in Westminster in 1784. He supported Pitt's foreign policy and Wilberforce's efforts to abolish the slave trade, and in 1786 became a lord of the treasury. In 1797 he was raised to the English peerage as Baron Wellesley and made governor-general of India. Under his outstanding administration (1797–1805) British rule became supreme in India; the influence of France there was extinguished with the disarming of its forces in Hyderabad, the power of the princes much reduced by the crushing (1799) of Tippoo Sahib at Seringapatam by General Harris, and (1803) of the Marathas, with the help of (1), and the revenue of the East India Company was more than doubled. In 1799 he was given the rank of marquis in the Irish peerage. In 1805 he returned to England and in 1809 went as ambassador to Madrid. On his return he was made foreign minister (1809–12), and later (in 1821 and 1833) lord-lieutenant of Ireland. See M. Martin, *Despatches of the Marquess Wellesley* (1840); *Wellesley Papers: Life and Correspondence* (1914); and a Life by G. B. Malleson (1889).

WELLESZ, Egon Joseph, *vel'es* (1885–), Austrian composer and musicologist, born in Vienna, studied under Schoenberg and subsequently became professor of Musical History at Vienna, specializing in Byzantine, Renaissance and modern music. Exiled from Austria by the Nazis, he became a research fellow at Oxford in 1938, and was lecturer in Music there from 1944 to 1948. His works include five operas and a quantity of choral and chamber music.

WELLHAUSEN, Julius, *vel'how-zēn* (1844–1918), biblical scholar, born at Hameln, professor at Greifswald (1872), Halle (1882), Marburg (1885) and Göttingen (1892), known for his investigations into Old Testament history and source criticism of the Pentateuch, was the author of several works, notably the *Prolegomena zur Geschichte Israels* (1883; trans. as *History of Israel*, 1885).

WELLINGTON, Arthur Wellesley, 1st Duke of (1769–1852), third of the four surviving sons of the 1st Earl of Mornington, was born in Ireland on April 29, 1769. Desultory study at Chelsea, Eton, Brussels and a military school at Angers led, in 1787, to an ensign's Commission in the 73rd Foot. Something of a dilettante, he transferred to the 76th Foot, thence to the 41st, 12th Light Dragoons and then to the 58th Foot, which brought him to Captain's rank. As A.D.C. to two lords-lieutenant of Ireland and member for Trim in the Irish Parliament, his lack of means forbade immediate marriage with Lady Katherine Pakenham. Securing a majority in the 33rd Foot, Wellesley set himself seriously ' to learn the business of a regimental officer ', in his retrospective view the foundation of all successful soldiering. His brother's generosity purchased him command of the 33rd; and in the 1794 retreat of the British forces on the Ems he displayed great coolness and capacity when his regiment formed part of the rearguard. He had ' learned how things should not be done ', and he carefully took note of the lesson. His disillusioned resolve to seek civil employment was reversed by his regiment's dispatch to India in 1797, where his brother arrived as governor-general within a year. With Napoleon gaining victories in Egypt, Wellesley was dispatched to deal with Tippoo Sahib of Mysore, who was speedily cured of giving aid to the French. As brigade commander under General Harris Wellesley did admirable work throughout the Seringa-patam expedition and as subsequent admini-strator of the conquered territory. His campaigns against Holkar and Scindhia saw the enemy capital of Poona subjected in 1803, Mahratta power broken at Ahmednagar and hard-fought Assaye, and final victory achieved at Argaum. Created K.B. for his services, Sir Arthur's Indian fighting had taught him caution and the paramount importance of sound ' logistics '—lessons that were to prove advantageous to him. Returning home in 1805, in 1806 he married ' Kitty ' Pakenham—who bore him three sons and three daughters—and was returned M.P. for Rye; becoming Irish Secretary in 1807. The same year he accompanied the Copenhagen expedition, defeating the Danes at Sjaelland. In 1808 the ' Sepoy General ', as his detractors termed him, was sent to the aid of the Portuguese against the French. Defeating Junot at Roliça his victory at Vimeiro was stultified by his last-minute supersession by General Burrard; at the latter's behest he consented to the Conven-tion of Cintra which spared the French unconditional surrender. Wellesley resumed his secretaryship; but Moore's retreat on Coruña sent him back, in 1809, to assume chief command in the Peninsula. His aim was to maintain a tactical defensive within a strategical offensive until his opponents, uncooperative and ill-nourished over long and vulnerable supply lines, would be so disrupted and worn down that they could be assailed in detail with complete confidence. Talavera (July 1809) was nearly a blunder, but it was speedily retrieved and the overall plan tenaciously pursued. Salamanca (July 1812) unequivocally demonstrated the supe-rior fighting qualities of the British and their Portuguese and German allies; and although there were minor setbacks, ultimately the French were driven out of Spain and brought to submission at Toulouse in 1814. Wellesley was created G.C.B., and by 1814 had become Field-Marshal the Duke of Wellington, K.G., Duke of Ciudad Rodrigo, Magnate of Portugal, Spanish Grandee of the First Class, and the recipient of the most distinguished foreign orders, including the Golden Fleece. A committee of the assembly presented the thanks of the House of Commons which awarded him £400,000. With Napoleon's

escape from Elba Wellington hastened from the Congress of Vienna to take command of the scratch force—' an infamous army ', he termed it—mustered to oppose the Corsican. Blücher's supporting forces having been defeated at Ligny, Wellington took up posi-tion on the well-reconnoitred field of Water-loo, where the French were totally routed on June 18, 1815. Rewarded with the Hampshire estate of Strathfieldsaye, in 1818 the Duke joined the Liverpool administration as master-general of the Ordnance. In 1826 he was made constable of the Tower, and in 1827 commander-in-chief, an office in which he was confirmed for life in 1842. In 1829 he materially assisted in Peel's reorganization of the Metropolitan Police. In general, Wellington's political policy was to refrain from weakening established authority and to avoid foreign entanglements, since Britain never possessed a sufficient army to enforce her will. When Canning intervened to bind Britain, France and Russia to impose recog-nition of Greek autonomy on Turkey, he resigned; but with Canning's death in 1827 and the collapse of the nebulous Goderich administration, the Duke became prime minister. His reluctance to oppose the Test and Corporation Acts cost him the allegiance of Huskisson and the Liberals; while his support of Catholic emancipation culminated in a bloodless duel with the Earl of Winchil-sea. His non-intervention in the East after Navarino offended the majority of his party; while his opposition to the indiscriminate enlargement of the franchise brought wide-spread unpopularity—and broken windows at Apsley House on the anniversary of Waterloo. In the political crisis of 1834 Wellington again formed a government; in Peel's temporary absence abroad he acted for all the secretaries of state. Chosen chan-cellor of the University of Oxford in 1834, with Peel's return to power in 1841 Wellington joined his cabinet, but without portfolio. He retired from public life in 1846. Made lord high constable of England, in 1848 he organized the military in London against the Chartists. He was in the procession for the opening of the Great Exhibition of 1851; retiring thereafter, as lord warden of the Cinque Ports, to Walmer Castle, where he passed peacefully away on September 14, 1852. He was buried in St Paul's Cathedral with the ceremony befitting a brilliant soldier and a great servant of the state. See Lives by Gleig, Stocqueler, Brialmont, W. H. Fitchett (1911), Sir H. Maxwell (1899, new ed. 1914), Fortescue (1925), Guedalla (1931), M. Wellesley (1937), R. Aldington (1946); his dispatches (ed. Gurwood and by his son, 1852–67), Greville's, Stanhope's, Croker's, Creevy's and Mrs Arbuthnot's Memoirs, and works cited at NAPOLEON.

WELLS, (1) Charles Jeremiah (c. 1800–79), English poet, was born in London, and educated at Edmonton. His Stories after Nature (1822) were followed in 1824 by the biblical drama, Joseph and his Brethren, which remained unknown until Swinburne praised it in the Fortnightly (1875).

(2) Herbert George (1866–1946), English author, born in London of lower middle-class

extraction, was initially apprenticed to a draper, but quickly abandoned this for teaching and very shortly made his mark in journalism and thereafter in literature. As biologist, journalist, writer and prophet, he played a vital part in disseminating the ideas which characterized the first quarter of the 20th century. He had a Dickensian exuberance which spilled over into all sorts of activities, and, though much of his writing is dated now, there can be no doubt that as a generative force in literature he pushed back the frontiers of ignorance for a large proportion of his readers. His scientific romances are immensely readable and some of his short stories have real impact and lasting beauty. *Country of the Blind* (1911) and *Collected Short Stories* (1927) contain some of his best writing; while *The Time Machine* (1895), *War of the Worlds* (1898) and *The Shape of Things to Come* (1933) show his fecund imagination at full strength. In his early novels, Wells, as spokesman for the urban worker, creates such unforgettable characters as Kipps, Mr Polly and Bert Smallways, types of the eternal ' little man ', pathetic, sturdy, comic and heroic. Other novels deal with social questions and *Ann Veronica* (1909), *Tono-Bungay* (1909), and *Marriage* (1912) affected the public opinion of his day as radically as did the plays of Bernard Shaw. Wells's preoccupation with Utopian ideals—a belief that the millennium was coincident with the onward march of science—led to scintillating dissertations such as *The Work, Wealth and Happiness of Mankind* (1932), but as he began to see that science could work for evil as well as for good, his faith deserted him, and he declined into pessimism. His compendiums of knowledge, *The Outline of History* (1920) and *Science of Life* (1929–30), written in collaboration with his son and Julian Huxley, are immense achievements. See his *Autobiography* (1934), and studies by Nicholson (1950), Brome (1951) and Meyer (1956).

(3) **Horace** (1815–48), American dentist, born at Hartford, Vt., foresaw the value of nitrous oxide as an anaesthetic but his attempt to demonstrate it at Harvard in 1845 was a failure and he later committed suicide.

(4) **Sir Thomas Spencer** (1818–97), English surgeon, born in St Albans, the first to practise ovariotomy successfully, author of *Diseases of the Ovaries* (1865).

WELSH, (1) **Jane.** See CARLYLE (3).

(2) **John** (c. 1568–1622), Presbyterian divine born at Colliston, Dumfriesshire, imprisoned and banished by James VI, and ancestor of (1). See *Life* by J. Young (1866).

WELTE, Benedikt. See WETZER.

WEMYSS, Francis Wemyss Charteris Douglas, Earl of, *weemz* (1818–1914), British politician, born in Edinburgh, promoter of the volunteer movement (1859 onwards), and of the National Rifle Association.

WENCESLAUS, St (c. 903–935), duke and patron of Bohemia, ' good king Wenceslas ', received a Christian education and after the death of his father encouraged Christianity in Bohemia, against the wishes of his mother. Probably at her instigation, and because of the fact that he had put his duchy under the

protection of Germany, he was murdered by his brother Boleslaw.

WENCESLAUS (1361–1419), son of Charles IV, was crowned king of Bohemia 1363, king of the Romans 1376 (deposed 1400).

WENTWORTH, (1) **Charles Watson.** See ROCKINGHAM.

(2) **Thomas.** See STRAFFORD.

(3) **William Charles** (1793–1872), Australian statesman, born on Norfolk Island, took part in the expedition which explored the Blue Mountains in 1813 before he went to England to study at Cambridge. When called to the bar in 1822 he had already published his classic *Statistical Account of the British Settlements in Australasia* (1819). A staunch protagonist of self-government, which he made the policy of his newspaper *The Australian* (established 1824), he founded Sydney University in 1852.

WERFEL, Franz, *ver'fel* (1890–1945), Austrian-Jewish author, born at Prague, lived in Vienna until 1938, when he moved to France, whence he fled from the Nazi occupation in 1940 to the U.S.A. His early poems and plays were expressionistic; he is best known for his novels, including *The Song of Bernadette* (1941).

WERGELAND, Henrik Arnold, *ver'ge-lan* (1808–45), Norwegian poet, dramatist and patriot, now remembered more for his lyrics than for his efforts in the cause of Norwegian nationalism.

WERNER, (1) **Abraham Gottlob** (1750–1817), German geologist, born at Wehrau in Silesia, teacher at Freiburg in Saxony from 1775, one of the first to frame a classification of rocks, gave his name to the Wernerian or Neptunian theory of deposition, which he advocated in controversy with J. Hutton (q.v.).

(2) **Alfred** (1866–1919), Swiss chemist, born at Mülhausen, Alsace, professor in Zürich from 1893, was notable for his researches on isomerism and the complex salts, and was awarded a Nobel prize in 1913.

(3) **(Friedrich Ludwig) Zacharias** (1768–1823), German romantic dramatist, born at Königsberg. His chief works are *Die Söhne des Thals* (1803), *Das Kreuz an der Ostsee* (1804) and *Martin Luther* (1806). A convert to Catholicism, he died a priest at Vienna. See Carlyle's *Miscellanies*; also studies by Hankamer (1926), Carow (1933), and his diaries, ed. Floeck (1939–40).

WESKER, Arnold (1932–), British dramatist, born in London's East End, of Russian-Jewish parentage, he left school at fourteen. His intimate Jewish family background and his varied attempts at earning a living are important ingredients of his plays. The Kahn family trilogy, *Chicken Soup with Barley, Roots* and *I'm talking about Jerusalem* (1959–60), echo the march of events, pre- and post-World War II, in the aspirations and disappointments of the members of a left-wing family. *Roots* is an eloquent manifesto of Wesker's socialism: an aesthetic recipe for all which he attempted to put into practice by taking art to the workers through his Centre–42 (1961). Other plays are *The Kitchen* (1959), *Chips With Everything* (1962), *The Four Seasons* (1966), &c.

WESLEY, (1) **Charles** (1707–88), English hymnwriter and evangelist, brother of (2), born at Epworth, Lincs, studied at Christ Church, Oxford, where he formed (1729) a small group known as the Oxford Methodists, later joined by (2). Ordained in 1735, he accompanied (2) to Georgia as secretary to Oglethorpe, returning to England in 1736. He was the indefatigable lieutenant of his more famous brother; after his conversion on May 21, 1738, he wrote over 5500 hymns, including ' Jesu, Lover of my soul ' and ' Love divine, all loves excelling '. He married Sarah Gwynne in 1749. See *Representative Verse* (ed. F. Baker, 1962); and Lives by T. Jackson (1841–49), J. Telford (1886) and F. L. Wiseman (1933).

(2) **John** (1703–91), English evangelist and founder of Methodism, was born June 17, son of the rector of Epworth. In 1720 he passed from the Charterhouse to Christ Church, Oxford. He was ordained deacon in 1725, priest in 1728, and in 1726 became a fellow of Lincoln and Greek lecturer. In 1727 he left Oxford to assist his father, but returned as tutor in 1729. At this time he was much influenced by the spiritual writings of William Law (q.v.). He became leader of a small dedicated group which had gathered round his brother Charles (q.v.), called derisively the Holy Club or Methodists, a name later adopted by John for the adherents of the great evangelical movement which was its outgrowth. The members of the Club, who in 1730 were joined by James Hervey and George Whitefield (q.v.), practised their religion with a then extraordinary degree of devotion, in strict accordance with the rubrics. On his father's death (1735), accompanied by Charles, John went as a missionary to Georgia, where his lack of experience led him to make many mistakes and aroused the hostility of the colonists. After an unfortunate love-affair with a Miss Hopkey, he returned to England (1738). He had been influenced by Moravians on the voyage out, and now he met Peter Böhler, and attended society meetings, at one of which, held in Aldersgate Street (May 24), during the reading of Luther's preface to the Epistle to the Romans, he experienced an assurance of salvation which convinced him that he must bring the same assurance to others. But his unwonted zeal alarmed and angered most of the parish clergy, who closed their pulpits against him; this intolerance, Whitefield's example, and the needs of the masses drove him into the open air at Bristol (1739). There he founded the first Methodist chapel. He preached in, and bought, the ruinous Foundry in Moor-fields, London, Methodist anniversaries sometimes being reckoned from this event; the Foundry was for long the headquarters of Methodism in the capital. During his itinerary of half a century, 10,000 to 30,000 people would wait patiently for hours to hear him. He gave his strength to working-class neighbourhoods; hence the mass of his converts were colliers, miners, foundrymen, weavers, and day-labourers in towns. His life was frequently in danger, but he outlived all persecution, and the itineraries of his old age were triumphal processions from one end of

the country to the other. During his unparalleled apostolate he travelled 250,000 miles and preached 40,000 sermons. Yet he managed to do a prodigious amount of literary work, and produced grammars, extracts from the classics, histories, abridged biographies, collections of psalms, hymns and tunes, his own sermons and journals, and a magazine. His works were so popular that he made £30,000 which he distributed in charity during his life. He founded charitable institutions at Newcastle and London and Kingswood School in Bristol. Wesley broke with the Moravians in 1745, and his acceptance of what was then known as an Arminian theology led to divergences with Whitefield in 1741, a separate organization of Calvinistic methodists under the Countess of Huntingdon (q.v.), and to an acute controversy (1769–78) with Toplady. Wesley was determined to remain loyal to the Church of England and urged his followers to do the same; but increasing pressures were brought to bear on him and in 1784 he himself ordained one of his assistants for work in America (much to his brother's distress), a practice which he later extended. However, he always regarded Methodism as a movement within the Church and it remained so during his lifetime. In 1751 he married the widow Mary Vazeille, who deserted him in 1776. He died March 2, 1791. His *Journal* was edited (8 vols. 1909–1916) by N. Curnock. See Lives by R. Southey (1820), J. Wedgwood (1870), J. Telford (1886; new ed. 1953), L. Tyerman (6th ed. 1890), J. H. Overton (1891), W. H. Fitchett (1906), C. T. Winchester (1906), J. S. Simon (1921–34), V. H. H. Green (1964); his *Letters* (1931); and a book on the family by G. J. Stevenson (1876).

(3) **Samuel** (1766–1837), English organist and composer, born in Bristol, son of (1). One of the most famous organists of his day, he was an early and ardent enthusiast of J. S. Bach. Though a Roman Catholic (to the displeasure of his father and uncle), he wrote also for the Anglican liturgy, leaving a number of fine motets and anthems, including *In Exitu Israel*. His natural son **Samuel Sebastian** (1810–76), born in London, was a brilliant cathedral organist.

WESSEL, *vesʹel,* (1) **Horst** (1907–30), German national socialist, born at Bielefeld, composer of the Nazi anthem ' Die Fahne Hoch ', known as the Horst Wessel song.

(2) **Johan,** or **Wessel Harmens Gansfort** (1420–89), Dutch pre-Reformation reformer and theologian, born at Groningen.

WESSON, Daniel Baird (1825–1906), American gunsmith, devised a new type of repeating mechanism for small-arms in 1854 and founded the firm of Smith and Wesson at Springfield, Mass., in 1857.

WEST, (1) **Benjamin** (1738–1820), English painter, born in America at Springfield, Pa., showed early promise, was sent on a sponsored visit to Italy, and on his return journey was induced to settle in London (1763). George III was his patron for 40 years. The representation of modern instead of classical costume in his best-known picture *The Death of General Wolfe* was an innovation in

English historical painting. See *Life* by H. E. Jackson (Philadelphia 1900).

(2) **Mae** (1892–), American film actress, born in Brooklyn, specialized in flamboyant rôles, and gave her name to an airman's pneumatic life-jacket which, when inflated, was considered to give the wearer the generous bosom for which she herself was noted.

(3) **Dame Rebecca**, pen-name (from Ibsen's *Rosmersholm*) of **Mrs H. M. Andrews**, *née* **Cicily Isabel Fairfield** (1892–), British novelist and critic. Born in Kerry, educated in Edinburgh, she was for a short time on the stage but turned to journalism. Her alert observation, style and wit made her work notable, as in *Black Lamb and Grey Falcon* (1942), an account of Yugoslavia in 1937. Novels include *The Judge* (1922), *The Thinking Reed* (1936), *The Fountain Overflows* (1957) and *The Birds Fall Down* (1966). Studies arising from the Nuremberg war trials were *The Meaning of Treason* (1947) and *A Train of Powder* (1955). She was created D.B.E. in 1959.

WESTBURY, Richard Bethell, Baron (1800–1873), English judge, was born at Bradford-on-Avon. In 1823 called to the bar, he became solicitor-general in 1852, attorney-general in 1856, and in 1861 lord chancellor, with the title of Baron Westbury. He promoted measures of law reform, but failed to carry his schemes for codifying the statutes and for combining law and equity. He was noted for his sarcastic wit. See *Lives* by Nash (1888) and by his son Arthur (1903).

WESTCOTT, Brooke Foss (1825–1901), English scholar, born near Birmingham, was a canon of Peterborough, regius professor of Divinity at Cambridge in 1870, Canon of Westminster in 1883, and in 1890 Bishop of Durham. He helped to prepare the revised version (1881) of the New Testament and, with F. J. A. Hort, *The New Testament in the Original Greek* (1881). See *Lives* by A. Westcott (1903) and J. Clayton (1906).

WESTERMARCK, Edvard Alexander, *ves'tèr-mark* (1862–1939), Finnish social philosopher, born at Helsinki, was lecturer on Sociology there, professor of Sociology in London, wrote a *History of Human Marriage* (5th ed. 1925), *The Origin and Development of the Moral Ideas* (1906–08), *Christianity and Morals* (1939), books on Morocco, and an Autobiography (trans. from Swedish 1929).

WESTINGHOUSE, George (1846–1914), American engineer, born at Central Bridge, N.Y., gave name to an air-brake for railways, which he invented (1868), and a company (now a corporation), which he founded for the manufacture of this, and other appliances. He was a pioneer in the use of alternating current for distributing electric power. See *Life* by H. G. Prout (1922).

WESTMACOTT, (1) Sir Richard (1775–1856), English sculptor and sculptor's son, born in London, studied at Rome, in 1816 was elected R.A., and was knighted in 1837. In 1827 he became professor of Sculpture at the Royal Academy.

(2) **Richard** (1799–1872), son of (1), also a sculptor, studied in Italy 1820–26, became F.R.S. and R.A., and succeeded his father as professor of Sculpture. He wrote a *Handbook of Ancient and Modern Sculpture* (1864).

WETHERELL, Elizabeth. See WARNER (4).

WETSTEIN, or Wettstein, Johann Jakob, *vet'shtīn* (1693–1754), Swiss scholar, was born in Basel. Charged with heresy in the preparation of his famous text, *Novum Testamentum Graecum* (1751–52), and his *Prolegomena* (1730) he left Basel, and was appointed (1733) to the chair of Church History in the Remonstrants' College at Amsterdam. See *Life* by C. L. Hulbert-Powell (1938).

WETTACH, Adrien. See GROCK.

WETTE. See DE WETTE.

WETZER, Heinrich Josef, *vets'èr* (1801–53), German scholar, born at Anzefahr, Hesse, editor with Benedikt Welte of the great Roman Catholic theological encyclopaedia (12 vols. 1846–60; revised ed. 1882–1903), became professor of Oriental Philology at Tübingen in 1830.

WEYDEN, Rogier van der, *vī'den* (1400–64), Flemish religious painter, was born at Tournai, and by 1436 was official painter to the city of Brussels. Influenced, and possibly taught, by the Van Eycks, he himself was the teacher of Hans Memling. See studies by Friedlander (1924) and Destrée (Paris 1930).

WEYER. See WIER.

WEYGAND, Maxime, *vay-gã* (1867–1965), French soldier, born in Brussels, trained at St Cyr and became a cavalry officer and instructor. As chief of staff to Foch (1914–1923), he rendered admirable service, but as chief of staff of the army (1931–35) he was gravely handicapped by his lack of experience as a field commander. In 1940 his employment of an outmoded linear defence to hold a penetration in depth completed the rout of the French army. A prisoner of the Germans, and later of the French provisional government, he was allowed to retire into obscurity. See his memoirs, *Recalled to Service* (1952).

WEYL, Hermann, *vīl* (1885–), German-born mathematician, born at Elmshorn, Schleswig-Holstein, was professor of Mathematics at Zürich (1913), Göttingen (1930–33) and from 1933 at Princeton, N.J. He made important mathematical contributions to relativity physics and the philosophy of mathematics.

WEYMAN, Stanley John, *wī'mèn* (1855–1928), English novelist, born at Ludlow, studied at Oxford, and became a barrister. He made himself popular with *A Gentleman of France* (1893), *Under the Red Robe* (1894) and other historical romances.

WHALLEY, Edward (d. 1675?), English regicide, fought at Marston Moor and Naseby, a member of the court which tried Charles I, was a signatory of the death warrant. In 1660 he fled to New England with his son-in-law William Goffe (q.v.) and remained in hiding till his death.

WHARNCLIFFE, James Archibald Stuart Wortley Mackenzie, 1st Baron (1776–1845), British statesman, grandson of the 3rd Earl of Bute, served in the army, entered parliament in 1797, and was made a peer in 1826. A Tory, he opposed Catholic emancipation, but helped to pass the Reform Bill; he opposed Peel's free-trade policy. In 1841 he was president of the council.

WHARTON, (1) Edith, *née* Jones (1861?-1937), American analytical novelist, born in New York, married in 1885 and was divorced in 1912. She published her first stories, *The Greater Inclination*, in 1899. Of her novels, *The House of Mirth* (1905), *Ethan Frome* (1911) and *The Custom of the Country* (1913) are regarded as her greatest. *The Age of Innocence* (1920) and *Old New York* (1924) were each awarded the Pulitzer prize. See her *A Backward Glance* (1934), and Lives by M. J. Lyde (1960), G. Kellogg (1966) and M. Bell (1966).

Philip, Duke of Wharton (1698-1731), son of (2), was given an Irish dukedom in 1718 for his support of the government in the Irish House of Peers, but in England set up an opposition political paper, the *True Briton* (1723-24). While travelling in Europe he accepted the Garter from the Pretender at Rome, assumed the title of Duke of Northumberland, and fought for Spain, for which he was convicted of high treason in his absence and deprived of his estates. See Life by L. Melville (1913).

(3) **Thomas, 1st Marquis of Wharton** (1648-1714), father of (2), Whig statesman, lord-lieutenant of Ireland (1708-10), was created earl in 1706 and marquis in 1714. He is remembered as author of the satirical anti-Catholic ballad *Lilliburlero*.

WHATELY, **Richard** (1787-1863), English Archbishop of Dublin, born in London, in 1805 entered Oriel College, Oxford, and in 1811 was elected a fellow. He became a college tutor and rector of Halesworth, and for the *Encylopaedia Metropolitana* wrote what he afterwards expanded into treatises on Logic (1826) and Rhetoric (1828). In 1825 he was appointed principal of St Alban's Hall, in 1829 professor of Political Economy and in 1831 Archbishop of Dublin. A founder of the Broad Church party, he opposed the Tractarian movement, supported Catholic emancipation, and worked for unsectarian religious instruction. His caustic wit and outspokenness made him unpopular. See the rambling *Memoirs* by Fitzpatrick (1864) and the Life by Whately (1866).

WHEATLEY, **Henry Benjamin** (1838-1917), English bibliographer and scholar, born at Chelsea, became clerk to the Royal Society (1861-79) and assistant secretary (1879-1908) to the Society of Arts. He was one of the founders of the Early English Text Society.

WHEATON, **Henry** (1785-1848), American jurist, born at Providence, R.I., in 1812-15 edited the *National Advocate* in New York, where for four years he was a justice of the Marine Court, and from 1816 to 1827 reporter for the Supreme Court. In 1827-35 he was *chargé d'affaires* at Copenhagen, and in 1835-46 minister at Berlin. His most important work was *Elements of International Law* (1836, with many later editions).

WHEATSTONE, **Sir Charles** (1802-75), English physicist, born in Gloucester, first became known as a result of experiments on sound. He invented the concertina (1829). He became professor of Experimental Philosophy at King's College, London (1834), and F.R.S. (1836). In 1837 he and W. F. Cooke took out a patent for an electric telegraph. In 1838, in a paper to the Royal Society, he explained the principle of the stereoscope (see BREWSTER). He invented a sound magnifier for which he introduced the term *microphone*. Wheatstone's Bridge, a device for the comparison of electrical resistances, was brought to notice (though not invented) by him. He was knighted in 1868.

WHEELER, (1) **Sir Charles** (1892-), English sculptor, born at Codsall, Staffordshire, studied at the Wolverhampton Art School and the Royal College of Art, and is noted for his portrait sculpture and his decorative sculptures on monuments and buildings, e.g., South Africa House and the Jellicoe Memorial Fountain in Trafalgar Square, London. Elected R.A. in 1940, he was created C.B.E. in 1948, knighted in 1958, K.B.E. in 1966, and from 1956 to 1966 was president of the Royal Academy. See the autobiographical *High Relief* (1968).

(2) **Sir Robert Eric Mortimer** (1890-), British archaeologist, was born in Glasgow. In 1924 he became director of the National Museum of Wales. In 1926 he was appointed keeper and secretary of the London Museum where he remained until 1944. In 1945 he led the Government mission from India to Iran and Afghanistan. On his return he became professor of the Archaeology of the Roman Provinces at the University of London, and secretary of the British Academy. He was made C.H. in 1967. His works include *Archaeology from the Earth* (1954), and the autobiographical *Still Digging* (1955).

WHEWELL, **William** (1794-1866), English scholar, born, a joiner's son, at Lancaster, became a fellow and tutor of Trinity. In 1820 he was elected F.R.S., in 1828-32 was professor of Mineralogy, and in 1838-55 professor of Moral Theology. In 1841 he became master of Trinity, and in 1855 vice-chancellor. His works include *History of the Inductive Sciences* (1837), *Elements of Morality* (1855), and other writings on the tides, electricity and magnetism, besides translations of Goethe's *Hermann and Dorothea*, Grotius's *Rights of Peace and War* and Plato. See Life by Todhunter (1876); Life and Correspondence by Stair Douglas (1881).

WHICHCOTE, **Benjamin** (1609-83), English philosopher and theologian, a Cambridge Platonist, born at Stoke in Shropshire, became in 1644 provost of King's, but lost this office at the Restoration. He wrote *Discourses* (1701-07) and *Moral and Religious Aphorisms*, collected from his MSS. (1703).

WHIPPLE, **George Hoyt** (1878-), American pathologist, a graduate of Yale and Johns Hopkins, in 1921 became professor of Pathology at Rochester. In 1934 he shared with Minot and Murphy the Nobel prize for medicine, as a result of their researches on the liver treatment of anaemia.

WHISTLER, (1) **James Abbott McNeill** (1834-1903), American artist, born at Lowell, Mass., spent five years of his boyhood in St Petersburg, where his father, an engineer, was engaged on a railway project for the tsar. Returning home, he studied first for the army at West Point but failed his exams, and after a fruitless year with the Coast Survey he left

America, never to return, and went to study art in Paris. His teacher, Gleyre, had little influence on his subsequent work, but he was deeply impressed by Courbet and later by the newly-discovered Hokusai (q.v.), and he exhibited at the *Salon des réfusés*. He began spending more and more time in London; when his mother came over from the U.S.A. in 1863 it became the centre of his activities, and he became celebrated as a portraitist. Ruskin's vitriolic criticism of his contributions to the Grosvenor Gallery exhibition of 1877, accusing him of ' flinging a pot of paint in the public's face ', provoked the famous lawsuit in which Whistler was awarded a farthing damages. His feelings on the subject are embodied in his *Gentle Art of Making Enemies* (1890), a witty and diverting piece of prose writing. A recalcitrant rebel at a time when the sentimental Victorian subject picture was still *de rigueur*, Whistler conceived his paintings, even the portraits, as experiments in colour harmony and tonal effect; the famous portrait of his mother, now in the Louvre, was originally exhibited at the Royal Academy as *An Arrangement in Grey and Black*, and evening scenes such as the well-known impression of Battersea Bridge (Tate Gallery) were called ' nocturnes '. If there was little emphasis on draughtsmanship in his painting technique, the reverse is true of his etchings, especially his ' Thames ' set, which succeed in imparting beauty to some unpromising parts of the London riverside. Witty, argumentative, quick to take offence, and theatrical in his manner, he often dressed like the cartoonist's stock artist-type. His individual style of painting did not evoke wide imitation and cannot be said to have initiated or belonged to any particular school, but his etchings were emulated by a host of followers, none of whom succeeded in capturing his spontaneity and charm. See studies by Laver (1938), Lane (N.Y. 1942) and Pearson (1952).

(2) **Rex** (1905–44), English artist. He studied at the Slade School, and excelled in the rendering of eighteenth-century life, ornament and architecture, particularly in book illustration (e.g., a fine edition of *Gulliver's Travels* in 1930), murals (e.g., in the Tate Gallery) and designs for the theatre and ballet. See the Life (1948) by his brother Laurence, the poet and designer; also study by L. Whistler and R. Fuller (1960)

WHISTON, William (1667–1752), English clergyman and mathematician, born at Norton rectory in Leicestershire, became in 1693 a fellow of Clare College, Cambridge, chaplain to the Bishop of Norwich in 1696, and in 1698 rector of Lowestoft. His *Theory of the Earth* (1696) attracted attention, and in 1703 he became Lucasian professor at Cambridge. For Arianism he was in 1710 expelled from the university and in 1747 joined the Baptists. He spent the remainder of his life in London, engaged in one controversy after another. His translation of Josephus was his best-known work. See his whimsical Memoirs (1749–50).

WHITAKER, Joseph (1820–95), English bookseller and publisher, was born in London, the son of a silversmith. He started the *Educational Register, Whitaker's Clergyman's Diary, The Bookseller* in 1858, and in 1868 *Whitaker's Almanac.*

WHITBREAD, Samuel (1758–1815), English politician, son of **Samuel** (1720–96), founder of the famous brewing firm, from Eton passed to Oxford, and in 1790 entered parliament. The intimate friend of Fox, under Pitt he was leader of the Opposition, and in 1805 headed the attack on Melville.

WHITBY, Daniel (1638–1726), English divine, born at Rushden near Higham Ferrers, became in 1664 a fellow of Trinity College, Oxford, prebendary of Salisbury in 1668, and rector of St Edmund's here in 1669. After attacking popery he tried from 1682 to find a basis of union with the Dissenters; his *Protestant Reconciler* (1682) was publicly burned at Oxford. His *Last Thoughts* appeared in 1727.

WHITE, (1) Ethelbert (1891–1972), English artist, born at Isleworth, painted many watercolours of the English scene, and also engraved for book illustration.

(2) **Sir George Stuart** (1835–1912), British soldier, field-marshal (1903), O.M. (1905), received the Victoria Cross in the Afghan campaign of 1879–80. Commander-in-chief in India in 1893–98, he defended Ladysmith in 1899–1900, and was governor of Gibraltar (1900–04). See Life by Durand (1915).

(3) **Gilbert** (1720–93), English clergyman and naturalist, born at Selborne in Hampshire, in 1744 obtained a fellowship at Oriel College, Oxford, in 1747 took orders, in 1752 became junior proctor, and in 1758 obtained the sinecure college living of Moreton Pinkney, Northants. From 1755 he lived uneventfully at Selborne as curate of that or a neighbouring parish. His charming *Natural History and Antiquities of Selborne* (1789) has become an English classic. Among its countless editions are those by Jesse (1851), Buckland (1875), Bell (1877), Jefferies (1887), Burroughs (1895), Bowdler Sharpe (1901). See his *Life and Letters* (1901) by R. Holt-White, *Journals* ed. Johnson (1931), and Life by W. S. Scott (1950).

(4) **Henry Kirke** (1785–1806), English poet, born in Nottingham, in 1803 published *Clifton Grove*, which brought him the friendship of Southey and the Rev. Charles Simeon, through whom he became a sizar of St John's College, Cambridge. Southey edited his *Remains* (1807).

(5) **Joseph Blanco** (1775–1841), theological writer, was born at Seville of an Irish Catholic family. Ordained a priest in 1800, he lost his faith, and, coming in 1810 to London, edited a monthly Spanish paper 1810–14, then received an English pension of £250, was tutor to Lord Holland's son 1815–16, and was admitted to Anglican orders. He was tutor in Whately's (q.v.) family at Dublin (1832–35), but fled to Liverpool on adopting Unitarian views. He contributed to the *Quarterly* and *Westminster*, edited the short-lived *London Review*, wrote *Letters from Spain* (1822), *Evidence against Catholicism* (1825), &c., and one notable sonnet, ' Night and Death '. See his Autobiography (1845).

(6) **Patrick** (1912–), London-born Australian author, educated at Cheltenham

College and King's College, Cambridge. He wrote *Happy Valley* (1939), *The Living and the Dead* (1941), *The Aunt's Story* (1946), before achieving international success with *The Tree of Man* (1954). In this symbolic novel about a small community in the Australian Bush, he attempts to portray every aspect of human life and to find the secret that makes it bearable. As the Parker family gradually fail to understand each other we are impressed by the terrible isolation of man, which White stresses even in his early novels. In 1957 appeared *Voss*, an allegorical account, in religious terms, of a gruelling attempt to cross the Australian continent. This was followed by *Riders in the Chariot* (1961) and *The Solid Mandala* (1966). He has also published *The Burnt Ones* (1964) and *Four Plays* (1965). See study by B. Argyle (1968).

(7) **Pearl** (1892–1938), American cinema actress, born in Glen Ridge, Mo., began her film career in 1910, and as the heroine of *The Perils of Pauline* (1914), *The Exploits of Elaine*, &c., made an enormous reputation as the exponent *par excellence* of the type of serial film popularly called ' cliff-hanger '.

(8) **Richard Grant** (1821–85), American Shakespearean scholar, born in New York, after studying medicine and law, became a journalist. His Shakespearean studies include criticisms on J. Payne Collier's folio MS. emendations (1852) and two editions (1857–1865, 1883) of the works. Other works are *Words and their Uses* (1870), *Everyday English* (1881), and *England Without and Within* (1881). His son, **Stanford** (1853–1906), was an eminent architect who designed a number of public buildings in New York.

(9) **William Hale**, pseud. **Mark Rutherford** (1831–1913), English writer, was born at Bedford, the son of William White (1797–1882), bookseller, and doorkeeper (1850–80) to the House of Commons (see his *Inner Life of the House of Commons*, 1897). In 1848–51 Hale White qualified at Cheshunt and New College for the Congregational ministry, but, expelled for his views on inspiration, became a journalist and miscellaneous writer. His translation of Spinoza's *Ethica* (1883; new ed. 1894) was published under his own name but he owed his literary eminence to the series of novels, *The Autobiography of Mark Rutherford* (1881), *Mark Rutherford's Deliverance* (1885), and *The Revolution in Tanner's Lane* (1887), ' edited by Reuben Shapcott '. See studies by Maclean (1955), Stock (1956).

WHITEFIELD, George (1714–70), English evangelist, one of the founders of Methodism, was born in the Bell Inn, Gloucester. At eighteen he entered as servitor Pembroke College, Oxford. The Wesleys had already laid the foundations of Methodism at Oxford, and Whitefield became an enthusiastic evangelist. He took deacon's orders in 1736, and preached his first sermon in the Crypt Church, Gloucester. In 1738 he followed Wesley to Georgia, returning to be admitted to priest's orders, and to collect funds for an orphanage. The religious level of the age was low, and Whitefield was actively opposed by his fellow churchmen. But when the parish pulpits were denied him he preached in the open air, the first time with great effect, on Kingswood Hill near Bristol. His life was then spent in constant travel and preaching. About 1741 differences on predestination led to his separation as a rigid Calvinist from John Wesley as an Arminian. His supporters now built him a chapel in Bristol and a 'Tabernacle' in London; and his preaching gathered immense audiences. But he founded no distinct sect, many of his adherents following the Countess of Huntingdon (q.v.) in Wales, and ultimately helping to form the Calvinistic Methodists. The Countess appointed him her chaplain, and built and endowed many chapels for him. He made seven evangelistic visits to America, and spent the rest of his life in preaching tours through England, Scotland and Wales. One of the most famous of these missionary journeys was that which he made to Scotland in 1741. In that year he married a Welsh widow, Mrs James. He set out for America for the last time in 1769, and died near Boston. His writings (sermons, journals, and letters), with the *Memoirs* by Dr Gillies, fill 7 vols. (1771–72). See Lives by J. P. Gledstone (1871 and 1900), Tyerman (1876) and Belden (1955).

WHITEHEAD, (1) Alfred North (1861–1947), English mathematician and Idealist philosopher, born in London, was educated at Sherborne and Trinity College, Cambridge, where he was senior lecturer in Mathematics until 1911. He became professor of Applied Mathematics at Imperial College, London (1914–24), and of Philosophy at Harvard (1924–37). Extending the Booleian symbolic logic in a highly original *Treatise on Universal Algebra* (1898), he contributed a remarkable memoir to the Royal Society, ' Mathematical Concepts of the Material World ' (1905). Profoundly influenced by Peano (q.v.), he collaborated with his former pupil at Trinity, Bertrand Russell (q.v.), in the *Principia Mathematica* (1910–13), the greatest single contribution to logic since Aristotle. In his Edinburgh Gifford Lectures, *Process and Reality* (1929), he attempted a metaphysics comprising psychological as well as physical experience, with events as the ultimate components of reality. Other more popular works include *Adventures of Ideas* (1933) and *Modes of Thought* (1938). He was elected F.R.S. (1903), was awarded the first James Scott prize (1922) of the Royal Society of Edinburgh, and in 1947 the O.M. See an anthology of his works by F. S. C. Northrop and M. W. Gross (1953), B. Russell, ' Whitehead and Principia Mathematica ' (*Mind* 1948) and studies by D. Emmet (1932), ed., P. A. Schilpp (1941), A. H. Johnston (1950, 1952), I. Leclerc (1958), W. Mays (1959).

(2) **Charles** (1804–62), English poet and novelist, was born in London, the son of a wine merchant. He devoted himself to letters after publishing *The Solitary* (1831), a poem of reflection. His *Autobiography of Jack Ketch* (1834) showed humour, but when Chapman & Hall asked him for a popular book in instalments he declined, recommending young Dickens, who thus began the *Pickwick Papers*. His novel, *Richard Savage*

(1842), earned the praises of Dickens and Rossetti. Whitehead went out to Melbourne in 1857, but died miserably, leaving unfinished the *Spanish Marriage*, a drama. See *A Forgotten Genius*, Mackenzie Bell (1884).

(3) **Paul** (1710–74), English satirist, ' a small poet ' in Johnson's phrase, was born, a tailor's son, in Holborn, was apprenticed to a mercer, married a short-lived imbecile with a fortune of £10,000, lay some years in the Fleet for the nonpayment of a sum for which he had stood security, became active in politics, was one of the infamous ' monks ' of Medmenham Abbey, and became deputy treasurer of the Chamber. Among his satires are *State Dunces* (1733), inscribed to Pope, and *Manners* (1739), for which Dodsley the publisher was brought before the House of Lords. His *Collected Works*, edited by E. Thompson, appeared in 1777.

(4) **Robert** (1823–1905), English inventor, born at Bolton-le-Moors, trained as an engineer in Manchester, settled (1856) at Fiume where he invented the first self-propelling torpedo (1866).

(5) **William** (1715–85), English poet, a Cambridge baker's son, educated at Winchester and Clare Hall, a fellow in 1742, travelled as tutor to Lord Jersey's son, became in 1755 secretary of the Order of the Bath, and in 1757 poet laureate. He wrote tragedies (*The Romén Father*, in imitation of Corneille's *Horace*, 1750; *Creusa*, 1754), farces (*School for Lovers*, 1762), epistles, &c.

WHITELEY, William (1831–1907), English merchant, born at Wakefield, opened in 1863 what became London's first department store, applied to himself the name of ' Universal Provider ', and was murdered. See Lambert, *The Universal Provider* (1938).

WHITELOCKE, Bulstrode (1605–76), English lawyer and statesman, born in London, the son of a judge, studied law, sat in the Long Parliament for Great Marlow, and took a half-hearted part on the popular side in the Civil War. He was appointed a commissioner of the Great Seal (1648), but would not act in the king's trial, and was sent as ambassador to Sweden (1653). Although nominated by Richard Cromwell keeper of the Great Seal he was later included in the Act of Oblivion. He died at Chilton in Wiltshire. Whitelocke's *Memorials* was first published in 1682 in a falsified form; better in 1732. His *Journal of the Embassy to Sweden* was edited by Reeve (1855). See *Memoirs* by Whitelocke (1860).

WHITEMAN, Paul (1891–1967), American bandleader, born in Denver, Colorado. He became famous in the 1920s as a pioneer of ' sweet style ', as opposed to the traditional ' classical ' style jazz. His band employed such brilliant exponents of true jazz as Bix Beiderbecke, the trumpeter, and Whiteman became popularly regarded as the ' inventor ' of jazz itself rather than of a deviation from true jazz style. He was responsible for Gershwin's experiments in ' symphonic ' jazz, commissioning the *Rhapsody in Blue* for a concert in New York in 1924. See *Jazz*, by Paul Whiteman and Mary McBride.

WHITGIFT, John (c. 1530–1604), English prelate, Archbishop of Canterbury, born at Grimsby, in 1555 was elected fellow of Peterhouse, Cambridge, took orders in 1560, and rose to be Dean of Lincoln (1571), Bishop of Worcester (1577), Archbishop of Canterbury (1583), and privy councillor (1586). He was a great pluralist. He attended Queen Elizabeth in her last moments, and crowned James I. With a Calvinistic bias, Whitgift yet was a champion of conformity, and vindicated the Anglican position against the Puritans. His ninety-four writings were edited for the Parker Society (1851–53). See vol. v of Hook's *Archbishops of Canterbury* (1875), and Clayton's *Whitgift and his Times* (1911).

WHITING, John (1917–63), English playwright, educated at Taunton School, studied at the Royal Academy of Dramatic Art (1935–37). After serving in the Royal Artillery in World War II he resumed his acting career before emerging as a dramatist. *Saint's Day* (1951), depicting the sense of hopelessness, failure and self-destruction of the Southman ménage, gained recognition for his talent although it was not a popular success. It was followed by *A Penny for a Song* (1951), a gay comedy, and *Marching Song* (1954), a play of ideas with little action or dramatic situation whose plot deals with the decision facing General Rupert Forster: to stand trial as a scapegoat for his country's failure or to commit suicide. After *Gates of Summer* (1956) he was commissioned by the Royal Shakespeare Company to dramatize Huxley's *The Devils of Loudon*, as *The Devils* (1961), which achieved great success, despite harrowing scenes such as the torture of Grandier.

WHITLEY, John Henry (1866–1935), English politician, born at Halifax, educated at Clifton and London University, was Liberal M.P. for Halifax 1900–28, speaker 1921–28 during the difficult period which culminated in the general strike, and presided over the committee that proposed (1917) Whitley Councils for joint consultation between employers and employees.

WHITMAN, Walt (1819–91), American poet, born at West Hills, Long Island, N.Y., served first in a lawyer's and then in a doctor's office, and finally in a printer's. He next became an itinerant teacher in country schools. He returned shortly to printing, and in 1846 became editor of the *Brooklyn Eagle*. This and his other numerous press engagements were only of short duration. He seemed unable to find free expression for his emotions until he hit upon the curious, irregular, recitative measures of *Leaves of Grass* (1855), originally a small folio of 95 pages, which grew in the eight succeeding editions to nearly 440 pages. This, with his prose book, *Specimen Days and Collect*, constitutes his main life-work as a writer. Summoned to tend his brother, wounded in the war against the South, he became a volunteer nurse in the hospitals of the Northern army. The exertion, exposure, and strain of those few years left Whitman a shattered and almost aged man. About the close of the war he received a government clerkship; was dismissed by Secretary Harlan as the author of ' an indecent book '; but almost immediately obtained a similar post.

In 1873 he left Washington for Camden, N.J., where he spent the remainder of his life. Partially paralysed, he would have fallen into absolute poverty but for the help of trans-Atlantic admirers. Later on several wealthy American citizens liberally provided for his simple wants. Whitman set himself the task of uplifting into the sphere of poetry the whole of modern life and man. Hence the inclusion of subjects at that time tabooed. He was in fact an idealist who bound himself to be a thoroughgoing realist. A selection from Whitman by W. M. Rossetti appeared in 1868 (new ed. 1910), his *Complete Writings* in 1902, *Uncollected Poetry and Prose* (2 vols.), ed. Holloway, in 1922. See books by J. A. Symonds (1893), John Burroughs, Kennedy (1896), Binns (1905), B. de Selincourt (1914), Fausset (1941), Canby (1943), R. V. Chase (1956) and R. Asselineau (1961).

WHITNEY, (1) **Eli** (1765–1825), American inventor, born at Westborough, Mass., was educated at Yale, went to Georgia as a teacher, but finding a patron in the widow of General Greene, resided on her estate, read law and set to work to make a cotton-gin. Reports of his success prompted rogues to break into his workshop and steal and copy his machine; he went to Connecticut to carry out his invention; but lawsuits in defence of his rights carried off all his profits and $50,000 voted him by the state of South Carolina. In 1798 he got a government contract for the manufacture of firearms, and made a fortune in this business.

(2) **Josiah Dwight** (1819–96), American geologist, born at Northampton, Mass., graduated at Yale, and in 1840 joined the New Hampshire survey. He explored the geology of the Lake Superior region, Iowa, the upper Missouri, and California, and in 1855 was made professor at Iowa University, in 1860 state geologist of California, and in 1865 professor at Harvard. Mount Whitney, S. Cal., the highest mountain in the U.S., is named after him

(3) **William Dwight** (1827–94), American philologist, brother of (2), studied at Williams and Yale, and in Germany with Roth prepared an edition of the *Atharva Veda Sanhita* (1856). In 1854 he became professor of Sanskrit at Yale, in 1870 also of Comparative Philology. He was an office-bearer of the American Oriental Society, edited numerous Sanskrit texts, and contributed to the great Sanskrit dictionary of Böhtlingk and Roth (1853–67). He waged war with Max-Müller on fundamental questions of the science of language. Among his works were *Material and Form in Language* (1872), *Life and Growth of Language* (1876), *Essentials of English Grammar* (1877) and *Mixture in Language* (1881). He was editor of the 1864 edition of Webster's Dictionary and editor-in-chief of the *Century Dictionary* (1889–91).

WHITTIER, John Greenleaf (1807–92), American Quaker poet and abolitionist, was born near Haverhill, Mass., the son of a poor farmer, and obtained education with difficulty. In 1829 he embarked on an editorial career; in 1831 appeared *Legends of New England*, a collection of poems and stories. In 1840, he settled at Amesbury, a village

near his birthplace. He devoted himself to the cause of emancipation, but his anti-slavery poems have, like his prose writings, mostly served their purpose. His collection *In War Time* (1864) contains the well-known ballad *Barbara Frietchie*. A final edition of Whittier's poems revised by himself appeared in 1888–89. *At Sundown* was published in 1892. In his day he was considered second only to Longfellow. See monographs by G. K. Lewis (1913), A. Mordell (1933).

WHITTINGTON, Richard (c. 1358–1423), English merchant, is supposed to have been the youngest son of Sir William Whittington of Pauntley in Gloucestershire, on whose death he set out at thirteen for London, and apprenticed himself to Sir John Fitz-Warren, a prosperous mercer, whose daughter he afterwards married. We find him a member of the Mercers' Company in 1392, in 1393 an alderman and sheriff, in 1397 (on the mayor's death), 1398, 1406, 1419 mayor of London, in 1416 member of parliament. Childless, he left all his great wealth to charity. The legend of his cat is an accepted part of English folklore. See Lyson's *Model Merchant of the Middle Ages* (1860) and Besant and Rice's *Sir Richard Whittington* (1881).

WHITTLE, Sir Frank (1907–), English inventor, from Cambridge joined the R.A.F. and began research on the problems of jet propulsion. He successfully developed the jet engine for aircraft (1941) and became government technical adviser on engine design (1946–48). His many honours include F.R.S. (1947) and K.B.E. (1948). See his *Jet* (1953).

WHITWORTH, Sir Joseph (1803–87), English engineer and inventor, born at Stockport, at the Exhibition in 1851 exhibited many tools and machines. In 1859 he invented a gun of compressed steel, with spiral polygonal bore. Created a baronet in 1869, he founded Whitworth scholarships for encouraging engineering science. He was responsible for the standard screw-thread named after him.

WHYMPER, Edward (1840–1911), English wood-engraver and mountaineer, born in London, was trained as an artist on wood, but became even more famous for his mountaineering than for his book illustrations. In 1860–69 he conquered several hitherto unscaled peaks of the Alps, including the Matterhorn. In 1867 and 1872 he made many geological discoveries in N. Greenland. His travels in the Andes (including ascents of Chimborazo) took place in 1879–80. See his own *Scrambles amongst the Alps* (1871, 1893), *Zermatt and the Matterhorn* (1897) and F. S. Smythe, *Edward Whymper* (1940).

WHYTE-MELVILLE, George John (1821–1878), British writer and authority on field sports, born at Mount-Melville, St Andrews, served in the Crimean war, and wrote novels on fox-hunting, steeplechasing, &c.

WICLIFFE. See WYCLIFFE.

WIDOR, Charles Marie (1845–1937), French composer, born at Lyons, organist of St Sulpice, Paris, was professor of Organ and Composition at the Paris Conservatoire (1891) and secretary of the Académie des Beaux-Arts from 1914 until his death. He composed ten symphonies for the organ, as well as a ballet, chamber music and other orchestral works. See his *La Technique de l'orchestre moderne* (1904).

WIECHERT, Ernst, *vee′*KHért (1887–1950), German writer, born at Kleinort in East Prussia, published novels dealing with psychological problems such as postwar readjustment, among them *Der Wald* (1922), *Der Totenwolf* (1924), *Der silberne Wagen* (1928), *Die Majorin* (1934) and *Das einfache Leben* (1939), the last-named probably his masterpiece. *Wälder und Menschen* (1936) is autobiographical, as is *Der Totenwald* (1946), which describes his six months confinement in Buchenwald concentration camp.

WIECK, Clara. See SCHUMANN.

WIELAND, *vee′lant,* (1) **Christoph Martin** (1733–1813), German writer, born near Biberach, the son of a pietist pastor, in 1760 became an official there. Bodmer invited him (1752) to Zürich, and inspired him to write *Der geprüfte Abraham* and other books full of sentimentality and religious mysticism. But Wieland's bent was in the opposite direction, and in 1760–70, besides making the first German translation of Shakespeare (1762–66), he wrote the romances *Agathon* and *Don Silvio von Rosalva, Die Grazien* and other tales, the didactic poem *Musarion*, &c. Their elegance, grace and lightness made Wieland popular with fashionable society. After holding for three years a professorship at Erfurt, he was called to Weimar to train the grand-duchess's sons, and there he spent most of the rest of his life, the friend of Goethe and Herder. The Weimar period produced his heroic poem *Oberon*, by which he is best remembered, and various other works; he also edited several magazines. See Lives by Gruber (1827–28) and Loebel (1858); books about him by Funck (1882), Keil (1885), Hirzel (1891), Michel (1938); Wieland's Correspondence (1815–20); and Stadler, *Wieland's Shakespeare* (1910).

(2) **Heinrich Otto** (1877–1957), German organic chemist, born at Pforzheim, studied at Munich, Berlin and Stuttgart before returning to Munich as professor of Organic Chemistry at the Technische Hochschule (1917). In 1921 he went to Freiburg and in 1925 again became a professor at Munich. In 1927 he was awarded the Nobel prize for chemistry, in recognition of his research on the bile acids, organic radicals, nitrogen compounds, &c.

WIEN, *veen,* (1) **Max Carl** (1866–1938), German physicist, cousin of (2), born at Königsberg, Röntgen's assistant (1892–95) and professor at Jena (1911–35), carried out research on high-frequency waves and discovered a method of measuring alternating current.

(2) **Wilhelm** (1864–1928), German physicist, cousin of (1), born at Gaffken in East Prussia, became professor at Aachen, Giessen, Würzburg and finally Munich (1920). In 1911 he was awarded the Nobel prize for physics, for his work on the radiation of energy from black bodies. His researches also covered X-rays, hydrodynamics, &c.

WIENER, Norbert, *wee′-* (1894–1964), American mathematical logician, founder of cybernetics, born in Columbia, pursued

postgraduate studies at Harvard, Cornell, under Bertrand Russell at Cambridge and at Göttingen, and in 1932 became professor of Mathematics at the Massachusetts Institute of Technology, where he had lectured from 1919. During World War II he worked on predictors and guided missiles and his study of the handling of information by electronic devices, based on the feedback principle, encouraged comparison between these and analogous mental processes in *Cybernetics* (1948) and other works. He won the American Design Award (1933) and was vice-president of the American Mathematical Society (1935–37). See *I am a Mathematician* (1956).

WIENIAWSKI, Henri, *vye-nyaf′skee* (1835–1880), Polish composer of concertos, études, &c., for the violin, born at Lublin, was for twelve years solo violinist to the tsar, and taught at the Brussels Conservatoire. His brother, **Joseph** (1837–1912), pianist, taught in the Moscow Conservatoire, and was a conductor at Warsaw 1871–77.

WIER, or Weyer, Johann, *vī′ér* (1516–88), Belgian physician, one of the first opponents of the witchcraft superstition, born at Grave in North Brabant, studied medicine at Paris and Orleans, and settled about 1545 as a physician at Arnheim, whence he was called to Düsseldorf to be physician to the Duke of Jülich. To him he dedicated his famous *De Praestigiis Daemonum et Incantationibus ac Veneficiis* (1563), a plea against the folly and cruelty of the witchcraft trials. The book roused the fury of the clergy; but the duke protected Wier till his death. His great treatise was followed by other works. See study by Binz (1885).

WIERTZ, Anton Joseph, *veerts* (1806–65), Belgian painter, born at Dinant, in 1836 settled in Liège, and in 1848 at Brussels. His original aim was to combine the excellences of Michelangelo and Rubens; but about 1848–50 he began to paint speculative and mystical pieces, dreams, visions, and the products of a morbid imagination. In 1850 the state built him a studio which became the Musée Wiertz.

WIGGIN, Kate Douglas, *née* Smith (1856–1953), American novelist, born in Philadelphia, wrote novels for both adults and children, but was more successful with the latter. *Rebecca of Sunnybrook Farm* (1903) is probably her best-known book, although the *Penelope* exploits, *The Birds' Christmas Carol* (1888) and *Mother Carey's Chickens* (1911) were all firm favourites. See *My garden of memory* (1923), and the biography by her sister, N. Smith.

WIGNER, Eugene Paul (1902–), Hungarian-born physicist, a native of Budapest, educated at Berlin Technische Hochschule, professor of Mathematical Physics at Princeton from 1938, known for his many contributions to the theory of nuclear physics, especially the Breit-Wigner formula for resonant nuclear reactions and the Wigner theorem concerning the conservation of the angular momentum of electron spin. His name is also given to the most important class of mirror nuclides (Wigner nuclides), and to a number of other physical phenomena. His calculations were used by Fermi (q.v.) in building the first reactor in Chicago. He received the Fermi award in 1958, the Atom for Peace award in 1959, and the Nobel physics prize for 1963.

WILAMOWITZ-MOELLENDORFF, Ulrich von, *vil-a-mō'vits mœ'lén-dorf* (1848–1931), German classical scholar, born at Markowitz, Posen, studied at Bonn and Berlin, and became professor at Greifswald (1876), Göttingen (1883), and Berlin (1897–1922). He was Mommsen's son-in-law. His works on Greek literature and editions of Greek classics were numerous and valuable. See his *Erinnerungen* (1928; trans. 1930).

WILBERFORCE, (1) Henry William (1807–1873), youngest son of (4), educated at Oriel College, Oxford, took Anglican orders in 1834, but joined the Church of Rome in 1850. He then became a journalist as proprietor and editor of *The Catholic Standard* (1854–63).

(2) **Robert Isaac** (1802–57), second son of (4), a fellow of Oriel and prebendary of York, joined the Catholic church in 1854 and died on his way to become a priest at Rome. He collaborated with (3) in writing a Life of his father.

(3) **Samuel** (1805–73), English prelate, third son of (4), was born at Clapham, September 7. In 1826 he graduated from Oriel, Oxford, and was ordained in 1828. In 1830 he became rector of Brightstone, I.O.W., in 1840 rector of Alverstoke, canon of Winchester and chaplain to the Prince Consort, in 1845 Dean of Westminster and Bishop of Oxford. He took part in the controversies of the Hampden, Gorham, *Essays and Reviews*, and Colenso cases. Instrumental in reviving Convocation (1852), he instituted Cuddesdon theological college (1854). The charm of his many-sided personality, his administrative capacity, his social and oratorical gifts, were apt to be forgotten in the versatile ecclesiastic, nicknamed ' Soapy Sam '. He edited *Letters and Journals of Henry Martyn* (1837), wrote along with (2) the Life of his father (1838), and himself wrote *Agathos* (1839), *Rocky Island* (1840) and *History of the American Church* (1844). Bishop of Winchester from 1869, he was killed by a fall from his horse. See Life by his eldest son R. G. Wilberforce (1905). Of his two younger sons, **Ernest Roland** (1840–1908) became first Bishop of Newcastle (1882) and Bishop of Chichester (1895); **Albert Basil Orme** (1841–1916) became Archdeacon of Westminster (1900), chaplain to the Speaker, and an eloquent advocate of temperance.

(4) **William** (1759–1833), English philanthropist, born at Hull, son of a wealthy merchant, father of (1), (2) and (3). Educated at St John's, Cambridge, in 1780 he was returned for Hull, in 1784 for Yorkshire, and was a close friend of Pitt, though he remained independent of party. In 1784–85, during a tour on the Continent with Dean Milner, he came under the latter's strong evangelical influence; and in 1787 he founded an association for the reformation of manners. In 1788, supported by Clarkson and the Quakers, he entered on his nineteen years' struggle for the abolition of the slave trade, crowned with victory in 1807. He next

sought to secure the abolition of the slave trade abroad and the total abolition of slavery itself; but declining health compelled him in 1825 to retire from parliament. He was for long a central figure in the ' Clapham sect ' of Evangelicals. He was buried in Westminster Abbey. He wrote a *Practical View of Christianity* (1797), helped to found the *Christian Observer* (1801), and promoted many schemes for the welfare of the community. See the Life by his sons (1838), his *Private Papers*, edited by Mrs A. M. Wilberforce (1898), and study by R. Coupland (1923).

WILBYE, John (1574–1638), one of the greatest of English madrigal composers, was born at Diss in Norfolk, was a household musician at Hengrave Hall, 1593–1628, and after that at Colchester. His madrigals are marked by sensitive beauty and excellent workmanship.

WILCOX, Ella, *née* **Wheeler** (1850–1919), American writer, prolific producer of verse, born at Johnstown Center, Wis., had completed a novel before she was ten, and later wrote at least two poems a day. The first of her many volumes of verse was *Drops of Water* (1872); the most successful was *Poems of Passion* (1883). Her *Story of a Literary Career* (1905) and *The Worlds and I* (1918) were autobiographical.

WILD, Jonathan (c. 1682–1725), English criminal, born at Wolverhampton, served an apprenticeship to a Birmingham bucklemaker. About 1706 he deserted his wife, came up to London, was imprisoned for debt, consorted with criminals, turned a receiver of stolen goods and a betrayer of such thieves as would not share with him, until for theft and receiving he was hanged at Tyburn. His story suggested the theme of Fielding's satire *Jonathan Wild*.

WILDE, (1) Jane Francisca Speranza, Lady (1826–96), daughter of Archdeacon Elgee, in 1851 married Sir W. R. W. Wilde (1799–1869), a distinguished surgeon, antiquarian, and president of the Irish Academy. As ' Speranza ' she published *Poems* (1864), and in her own name many other works. For years her *salon* was the most famous in Dublin.

(2) **Oscar Fingall O'Flahertie Wills** (1854–1900), Irish poet, wit and dramatist, son of (1), studied at Magdalen College, Oxford, and in 1878 won the Newdigate prize for his *Ravenna*. In 1881 he published *Poems*; in 1891 a novel, *Dorian Gray*; in 1893 the plays *Lady Windermere's Fan*, and (in French) *Salomé*; in 1894 *A Woman of No Importance*; in 1895 *An Ideal Husband*; in 1899 *The Importance of being Earnest*. *The Ballad of Reading Gaol* (1898) and *De Profundis* (1905) bear the impress of two years' hard labour for homosexual practices revealed during his abortive libel action (1895) against the Marquis of Queensberry, who had objected to Wilde's association with his son Lord Alfred Douglas (q.v.). He died an exile in Paris, having adopted the name of **Sebastian Melmoth**. While alive his controversial ' art for art's sake ' personality and the notoriety of his trial made difficult an impartial assessment of his work. He was strongest as a dramatist, his brilliant epigrams lending distinction to his writing and making

a penetrating commentary on the society of his time. See *Complete Works* (4 vols. 1936), studies by Symons (1930), Renier (1933), Woodcock (1949), and H. Pearson, *The Life of Oscar Wilde* (1946); trial proceedings ed. Hyde (1948); *Letters* ed. R. Hart-Davis (1962).

WILDENBRUCH, Ernst von, *vil'dĕn-brook*H (1845–1909), German romantic novelist, poet and dramatist, born at Beirut, served in the army and Foreign Office. His strongly-expressed patriotism made him the national dramatist of Prussia during the empire of the Hohenzollerns, to whom he was related.

WILDER, Thornton Niven (1897–), American author and playwright, born in Madison, Wisconsin. He was educated at Yale and served in both wars, becoming a lieutenant-colonel in 1944. His first novel, *The Cabala,* appeared in 1926. Set in contemporary Rome, it established the cool atmosphere of sophistication and detached irony that was to permeate all his books. These include *The Bridge of San Luis Rey* (1927), a bestseller and winner of the Pulitzer prize, *The Woman of Andros* (1930), *Heaven's My Destination* (1935) and *The Ides of March* (1948). His first plays—*The Trumpet Shall Sound* (1926), *The Angel That Troubled the Waters* (1928) and *The Long Christmas Dinner* (1931)—were literary rather than dramatic; but in 1938 he produced *Our Town,* a successful play that evokes without scenery or costumes a universal flavour of provincial life. This was followed in 1942 by *The Skin of Our Teeth,* an amusing yet profound fable of humanity's struggle to survive. Both these plays were awarded the Pulitzer prize. His later plays include *The Matchmaker* (1954) and *A Life in the Sun* (1955). See Bibliography by J. M. Edelstein (1959).

WILDGANS, Anton, *vilt'-* (1881–1932), Austrian poet and dramatist, born in Vienna. His plays include *Dies Irae* (1918) and the biblical tragedy *Kain* (1920). The epic poem *Kirbisch* appeared in 1927. From 1921 to 1923 he was director of the Vienna Burgtheater.

WILENSKI, Reginald Howard (1887–), English art critic and art historian, born in London. In 1929 and 1930 he was special lecturer in Art at Bristol University, and from 1933 to 1946 at Manchester University. His analysis of the aims and achievements of modern artists, *The Modern Movement in Art* (1927 and later editions), has had considerable influence. His other publications include *English Painting* (1933) and *Modern French Painters* (1940).

WILFRID, or Wilfrith, St (634–709), Bishop of York, born in Northumbria, and trained at Lindisfarne, upheld the Roman views which triumphed at the Synod of Whitby (664). Bishop of York (*c.* 665), he improved the minster of York, built a splendid church at Hexham, and raised a new minster at Ripon. Theodore divided Northumbria into four sees, and Wilfrid appealed to Rome. On the journey he was driven by a storm to the coast of Friesland, where he baptized thousands of pagans. Pope Agatho decided in his favour, but King Ecgfrid flung him into prison. He escaped to Sussex, was allowed to return by the new king, Alfdrid, in 686, and was finally allowed to keep the sees of Ripon and Hexham, but not York. See Eddius's *Vita Wilfridi,* edited by Raine (1879); Browne, *Theodore and Wilfrith* (1897), and historical works by Poole (1934) and Levison (1946).

WILHELMINA (Helena Pauline Maria of Orange-Nassau) (1880–1962), Queen of the Netherlands (1890–1948), succeeded her father William III at a very early age and until 1898 her mother Queen Emma acted as regent. Queen Wilhelmina fully upheld the principles of constitutional monarchy, especially winning the admiration of her people during World War II. Though compelled to seek refuge in Britain, she steadfastly encouraged Dutch resistance to the German occupation. In 1948, in view of the length of her reign, she abdicated in favour of her daughter **Juliana** (q.v.) and assumed the title of Princess of the Netherlands. See her *Lonely but not Alone* (1960).

WILHELMINE, Princess. See ANSPACH.

WILKES, (1) Captain Charles (1798–1877), American naval officer, in 1839–40 explored various Pacific island groups and sailed along the coast of what is now known as Wilkes Land; in 1861 intercepted at sea the British mail-steamer *Trent,* and took off two Confederate commissioners accredited to France, thereby raising a risk of war with Britain.

(2) **John** (1727–97), English politician, born at Clerkenwell, the son of a distiller, studied at Leyden, and became a man of fashion and profligate. To please his parents, he married at twenty-two the daughter of the eminent and wealthy physician, Dr Mead. She was ten years his senior, and after a daughter had been born to them the ill-matched pair separated. One of the infamous ' Monks of Medmenham ', Wilkes took up politics as a supporter of Pitt, was returned for Aylesbury in 1757, and was also high-sheriff for Bucks and colonel of the Bucks Militia. Lord Bute having declined to appoint him ambassador to Constantinople or governor of Quebec, he attacked the ministry in the *North Briton* (1762–63), a weekly journal he had founded. Before the twenty-seventh number appeared he was threatened with prosecution, and had to fight a duel with Lord Talbot. In the forty-fifth number some strong comments were made upon the king's speech on opening parliament. Lord Halifax as secretary of state issued a general warrant for the apprehension of all concerned in the article. Wilkes was seized and committed to the Tower. Lord chief justice Pratt ordered his release on the ground of privilege as M.P.; and it was then determined that general warrants were unconstitutional. He obtained large damages at law, and became the hero of the hour. The Earl of Sandwich read extracts in the House of Lords from the purloined copy of Wilkes's verse ' Essay on Woman ', printed at his private press, which was declared to be an ' obscene libel '; and the House of Commons expelled him on January 19, 1764, as author of *No.* 45 of the *North Briton.* Before this he was wounded in a duel with Mr Martin. He was tried and found guilty during his absence from England for publishing the ' Essay on Woman ' (1763) and was outlawed for non-appearance

Returning to England in 1768, he stood unsuccessfully for the City of London, but was triumphantly returned for Middlesex. His outlawry was reversed on a purely technical point, and he was sentenced to twenty-two months' imprisonment and a fine of £1000. In prison he penned a charge against the secretary of state of instigating the massacre in St George's Fields, and this was made the pretext for his expulsion from parliament. He had been four times re-elected, when the house declared him ineligible. In 1771 he was elected sheriff for London and Middlesex; in 1774 he became lord mayor, and re-entered parliament as M.P. for Middlesex. In 1780 he lost some popularity by his part in suppressing the Gordon riots. In 1782 the resolutions invalidating his previous elections were expunged. He became chamberlain of the City in 1779, and retired from parliament in 1790. The present liberty of the press owes much to his efforts. See J. S. Watson, *Biographies of John Wilkes and William Cobbett* (1870); Thorold Rogers, *Historical Gleanings* (1870); Daly, *Dawn of Radicalism* (1886); Fraser Rae, *Wilkes, Sheridan, Fox* (1873); Nobbe, *The North Briton* (1939); Lives by Percy Fitzgerald (1888), Bleackley (1917), Sherrard (1930), Postgate (1930).

WILKIE, Sir David (1785–1841), Scottish painter, born at Cults manse in Fife, in 1799 was sent to study in the Trustees' Academy at Edinburgh, and returning home in 1804, painted his *Pitlessie Fair*. The great success of *The Village Politicians* (1806) caused him to settle in London. In 1809 he was elected A.R.A., and in 1811 R.A. In 1817 he visited Scott at Abbotsford, and painted the family group now in the Scottish National Gallery. His fame mainly rests on such genre pictures as the *Card Players, Village Festival, Reading the Will*, &c. Later he changed his style, sought to emulate the depth and richness of colouring of the old masters, and chose more elevated subjects, to the height of which he could never raise himself. He also painted portraits, and was successful as an etcher. In 1830 he was made painter-in-ordinary to the king, and in 1836 knighted. In 1840, for his health, he visited Syria, Palestine and Egypt, but died on his voyage home. See books on him by Allan Cunningham (1843), J. W. Mollett (1881) and Lord R. Sutherland-Gower (1902).

WILKINS, (1) Sir George Hubert (1888–1958), Australian polar explorer, born at Mt Bryan East, first went to the Arctic in 1913. In 1919 he flew from England to Australia, 1920–22 he spent in the Antarctic, and after that collected material in Central Australia on behalf of the British Museum. In 1926 he returned to the Arctic, and in 1928 was knighted for a pioneer flight from Alaska to Spitsbergen, over polar ice. In 1931 he was again exploring in the Arctic, this time with the submarine *Nautilus*, but an attempt to reach the North pole under the ice was unsuccessful. After his death his ashes were conveyed to the pole, where they were scattered into the wind. See his books *Flying the Arctic* (1928), *Undiscovered Australia* (1928), *Under the North Pole* (1931).

(2) **John** (1614–72), English churchman and scientist, Bishop of Chester, born near Daventry, graduated B.A. from Magdalen Hall in 1631. As domestic chaplain he studied mathematics and mechanics, and was one of the founders of the Royal Society. In the Civil War he sided with parliament, and was appointed warden of Wadham. In 1656 he married a widowed sister of Oliver Cromwell, and in 1659 was appointed by Richard Cromwell master of Trinity College, Cambridge. Dispossessed at the Restoration, he soon recovered court favour, and became preacher at Gray's Inn, rector of St Lawrence Jewry, Dean of Ripon and Bishop of Chester (1668). In his *Discovery of a World in the Moon* (1628) he discusses the possibility of communication by a flying-machine with the moon and its supposed inhabitants; the *Discourse concerning a New Planet* (1640) argues that the earth is one of the planets; *Mercury, or the Secret and Swift Messenger*, shows how a man may communicate with a friend at any distance; *Mathematical Magic* dates from 1648; the *Essay towards a Real Character and a Philosophical Language* (1668) is founded on Dalgarno's treatise.

(3) **Maurice Hugh Frederick** (1916–), British chemist, born in New Zealand, educated at King Edward's School, Birmingham, and St John's College, Cambridge, did research on uranium isotope separation at the University of California in 1944. He joined the Medical Research Council's Biophysics Research Unit at King's College, London, in 1946, becoming deputy-director in 1955. With Crick and Watson (1) he was awarded the Nobel prize for medicine and physiology in 1962 for work on the structure of DNA.

WILKINSON, (1) Ellen Cicely (1891–1947), English feminist and Labour politician, born in Manchester, was an early member of the Independent Labour Party and an active campaigner for women's suffrage. In 1920 she joined the Communist party, but left it by 1924, when she became M.P. for Middlesbrough East. Losing this seat in 1931, she re-entered parliament in 1935 as member for Jarrow. In 1940 she became parliamentary secretary to the ministry of home security, in 1945 minister of education, the first woman to hold such an appointment.

(2) **Sir John Gardner** (1797–1875), English traveller and Egyptologist, born at Hardendale in Westmorland, and educated at Harrow and Exeter College, Oxford, in 1821–1833 made a complete survey of Egypt, publishing *Materia Hieroglyphica* (1828), *Survey of Thebes* (1830), *Topography of Thebes* (1835), and his famous *Manners and Customs of the Ancient Egyptians* (1837–41). Knighted in 1839, he visited Egypt again several times. He presented his antiquities to Harrow.

WILLARD, Frances Elizabeth (1839–98), American worker for temperance and the enfranchisement of women, was born at Churchville, New York. She studied at the Northwestern University, Evanston, Ill., was professor of Aesthetics there, in 1874 became secretary of the Women's Christian Temperance Union, and edited the Chicago

Daily Post. She helped to found the International Council of Women. Her books include many on temperance, &c., and *My Happy Half-Century* (autobiographical, 1894). She died at New York. See *Lives* by Florence White (1899), Strachey (1912).

WILLCOCKS, Sir William (1852–1932), British engineer, born in India, planned and carried out great irrigation works for Egypt (Aswan), South Africa and Mesopotamia (Hindiya).

WILLETT, William (1856–1915), English builder, born at Farnham, is chiefly remembered for his campaign for ' daylight saving '. A Bill was promoted in parliament in 1908, but opposition was strong and the measure was not adopted until a year after his death.

WILLIAM, name of four kings of England:

William I (1027–87), ' the Conqueror ', was born at Falaise, the bastard son of Robert III, Duke of Normandy, by Arlette, a tanner's daughter. On his father's death in 1035, the nobles accepted him as duke; but his youth was passed in difficulty and danger. In 1047 the lords of the western part of the duchy rebelled, but Henry I of France came to his help, and the rebels were defeated at Val-ès-dunes. In 1051 he visited his cousin, Edward the Confessor, and received the promise of the English succession. He married Matilda, daughter of Baldwin V, Count of Flanders, in 1053. In the next ten years William repulsed two French invasions, and in 1063 conquered Maine. Probably in 1064 Harold (q.v.) was at his court, and swore to help him to gain the English crown on Edward's death. When, however, Edward died, in 1066, Harold became king. William laid his claim before the pope and Western Christendom. The pope approved his claim, and on October 14 William defeated Harold at the battle of Hastings or Senlac. Harold was slain, and William was crowned on December 25. The west and north of England were subdued in 1068; but next year the north revolted, and William devastated the country between York and Durham. The constitution under William assumed a feudal aspect, the old national assembly becoming a council of the king's tenants-in-chief, and all title to land being derived from his grant. Domesday Book contains the land settlement. He brought the English Church into closer relations with Rome. The Conqueror's rule was stern and orderly. In 1070 there was a rebellion in the Fen Country, and under the leadership of Hereward the rebels for some time held out in the Isle of Ely. English exiles were sheltered by the Scottish king, Malcolm, who plundered the northern shires; but William in 1072 compelled Malcolm to do him homage at Abernethy. In 1073 he reconquered Maine. He made a successful expedition into South Wales. His eldest son, Robert, rebelled against him in Normandy in 1079; and, having entered on a war with Philip I of France in 1087, William burned Mantes. As he rode through the burning town his horse stumbled, and he received an injury, of which he died at Rouen on September 9. He left Normandy to his son Robert, and England to William. See Freeman's *Norman*

Conquest, ii, iii, iv, and his *William the Conqueror*; studies by F. M. Stenton (1908), P. Russell (1934), G. Slocombe (1959) and D. C. Douglas (1964); the histories of Palgrave, iii, Stubbs, i, Gneist, i.

William II (reigned 1087–1100), called **Rufus,** third, and second surviving, son of William the Conqueror, was born before 1066. On his father's death in 1087 he was crowned king. The next year many of the Norman nobles in England rebelled against him in favour of his eldest brother Robert, Duke of Normandy. Rufus appealed to the English people for help, promising them good government and a relaxation of the forest laws and of fiscal burdens. The rebellion was suppressed, but he did not keep his promises. Treating ecclesiastical benefices like lay fiefs, Rufus sold them, and kept them vacant, seizing their revenues during vacancy. The see of Canterbury had been vacant four years when, in 1093, he fell sick, repented, and appointed Anselm as archbishop. When he recovered he quarrelled with Anselm for maintaining the liberties of the church. Rufus warred with Robert in Normandy, but peace was made in 1091; and in 1096 the duchy was mortgaged to him. In 1098 he reconquered Maine, but failed to hold the whole of it. Malcolm, king of Scotland, invaded Northumberland in 1093, and was slain at Alnwick. Rufus thrice invaded Wales, twice with little success. As he was hunting in the New Forest on August 2, 1100, he was killed by an arrow, probably shot by Walter Tirel although this was never established. He was buried in Winchester Cathedral. See Freeman's *Reign of William Rufus* (2 vols. 1882) and G. Slocombe, *Sons of the Conqueror* (1960).

William III (1650–1702), posthumous son of William II of Orange (1626–50) by Mary (1631–60), eldest daughter of Charles I of England, was born at The Hague. On the murder of De Witt in 1672 he was chosen Stadthouder of the United Provinces. The republic was at this time carrying on an apparently hopeless contest with Louis XIV of France; but by the valour and wisdom of William the war was in 1678 terminated by the advantageous treaty of Nimeguen (Nijmegen). In 1677 William had married his cousin, the Princess Mary (born April 30, 1662), daughter of James II by Anne Hyde. When James's tyranny had estranged the affections of his subjects, eyes were turned towards the Stadthouder as their only hope; and on the day that the Seven Bishops were acquitted William was invited to come over and redress grievances. On November 5, 1688, he landed at Torbay with an English and Dutch army of 15,000. Men of all parties quickly came over to him; James fled; the Convention Parliament declared the throne vacant; and on February 13, 1689, William and Mary were proclaimed king and queen. The Scottish Convention did the same, April 4 to 11. James's adherents held out in Scotland and Ireland, but the fall of Dundee at Killiecrankie (July 1689) and the surrender of Limerick (October 1691) virtually ended resistance. William thus was left free for his Continental campaigns, in which he was outmatched by the Duke of Luxembourg. The latter's death in 1695 was a turning-point in the war, which was ended by the peace of Ryswick (1697). In spite of his sterling qualities, and of the debt that they owed him, he and his subjects were never in sympathy; his foreign birth, his reserve, his ill-health, were against him. The death (December 28, 1694) of his wife materially injured his position. His schemes were thwarted by parliament; continual plots for his assassination were hatched by James's adherents; and the death in 1700 of Charles II of Spain, and the succession of Philip of Anjou, was another blow to his policy. He pursued it, however, with unflagging vigour till his death, caused by the stumbling of his horse over a molehill. He left no children, and the crown passed to Anne, Mary's sister. During his reign the National Debt was commenced, the Bank of England established, the modern system of finance introduced, ministerial responsibility recognized, the standing army transferred to the control of parliament, the liberty of the press secured, and the British constitution established on a firm basis. See Histories of Burnet, Macaulay and Lodge; the *Memoirs* of Queen Mary, ed. by Doebner (1885); Traill's *William III* (1888); *Mary II*, by M. F. Sandars (1913), by H. Chapman (1953); and studies of William by Trevelyan (1930) and Renier (1939).

William IV (1765–1837), the 'sailor king', third son of George III, was born at Buckingham Palace. He entered the navy in 1779, and saw some service in America and the West Indies. In 1789 he was created Duke of Clarence and St Andrews and Earl of Munster, with an allowance of £12,000 a year. He was formally promoted through the successive ranks to that of admiral of the Fleet (1811), and in 1827–28 he held the revived office of lord high admiral. From 1790 to 1811 he lived with the actress Mrs Jordan (q.v.), who bore him ten children; on July 13, 1818, he married Adelaide (1792–1849), eldest daughter of the Duke of Saxe-Meiningen. The two daughters born (1819 and 1820) of this marriage died in infancy. By the Duke of York's death in 1827 the Duke of Clarence became heir-presumptive to the throne, to which he succeeded at the death of his eldest brother, George IV, June 26, 1830. A Whig up to his accession, he then turned Tory, and did much to obstruct the passing of the first Reform Act (1832). The abolition of colonial slavery (1833), the reform of the poor laws (1834), and the Municipal Reform Act (1835) were results of that great constitutional change. William died June 20, 1837, and was succeeded by his niece, Victoria. See, besides the articles on his premiers, GREY, MELBOURNE and PEEL, the Duke of Buckingham's *Courts and Cabinets of William IV and Victoria* (1861), the *Greville Memoirs*, Percy Fitzgerald's *Life and Times of William IV* (1884), J. F. Molloy's *The Sailor King* (1903), and study by W. G. Allen (1960).

WILLIAM, German **Wilhelm**, name of two German emperors:

William I (1797–1888), seventh king of Prussia and first German emperor, second son of Frederick-William III, was born at Berlin, March 22. In 1814 he received his 'baptism of fire' on French territory at Bar-sur-Aube, and entered Paris with the allies. During the king's absence in Russia he directed Prussian military affairs. In 1829 he married Princess Augusta of Saxe-Weimar (1811–90). On the accession of his brother, Frederick-William IV, in 1840, he became heir-presumptive. In 1844 he visited England and formed a friendship with Queen Victoria and the Prince Consort. During the revolution of 1848 his attitude towards the people made him very unpopular. He was obliged to quit Prussia, and took up his quarters at the Prussian Legation in London. In two months, however, he received his recall. In 1849 he subdued the disaffection in Baden. He was appointed regent (1858) in consequence of the prolonged ill-health of the king, on whose death, January 2, 1861, he succeeded as William I. He soon made plain his intention of consolidating the throne and strengthening the army. A few months after his accession he narrowly escaped assassination. Prince Bismarck was placed at the head of the ministry, with Roon, the author of the new army system, as war minister. The scheme was very unpalatable to the parliament, but the minister-president forced it upon the nation, with the necessary increased expenditure, by overriding the constitution. In 1864 the Schleswig-Holstein difficulty led to a war with Denmark, in which the Prussian and Austrian troops were victorious; but in 1866 the allies quarrelled over the spoils, and struggled for the supremacy over the German states. Austria was crushed at Sadowa, and Prussia gained in territory and prestige. The affair of the Duchy of Luxemburg nearly led to a war between France and Prussia in 1867, but the difficulty was adjusted by the treaty of London. In 1870 the inevitable struggle between France and Prussia was precipitated. The Spanish throne having become vacant, Prince Leopold, son of the Prince of Hohenzollern-Sigmaringen, was put forward as a candidate. As King William was the head of the House of Hohenzollern, this gave great umbrage to France. Although the candidature was withdrawn, Napoleon III forced a quarrel on Prussia, by making impossible demands. William took the field on July 31, and in the deadly struggle which ensued, the French forces were defeated almost everywhere; Napoleon capitulated at Sedan; and by the end of September Paris was invested. At Versailles on January 18, 1871, William was proclaimed German emperor. Peace was signed on February 26. An Austro-German alliance of 1871 was strengthened in 1873 by the adhesion of the tsar. The rapid rise of Socialism in Germany led to severe repressive measures, and in 1878 the emperor's life was twice attempted by Socialists, as again in 1883. William I, though holding tenaciously to the prerogatives of his kingly office, was of a simple and unassuming personal character. See Lives by A. Forbes (1889) and Barnett Smith (1887); Simon (trans. from French, 1886); German Lives by Schmidt and Otto, and

Oncken; Whitman's *Imperial Germany* (1892); and books cited at BISMARCK.

William II (1859–1941), third German emperor (1888–1918), and ninth king of Prussia, the eldest son of Prince Frederick, later Frederick III (q.v.) and of Victoria, the daughter of Britain's Queen Victoria, was born at Potsdam, Berlin, January 27. He received a strict military and academic education at the Kassel gymnasium and the University of Bonn, taking part in military exercises despite a deformed left arm. Early estranged from his mother, he put her under arrest after his accession (1888). A passion for military splendour, a deep conviction of the divine right of the Hohenzollerns, a quick intelligence but an uncertain temperament characterized the young ruler. He quarrelled with and dismissed (1890) the elder statesman Bismarck, who disapproved of William's projected overtures to capture working-class support and who had forbidden any minister to see the emperor except in his, Bismarck's, presence. A long spell of personal rule followed, helped out by political favourites such as Holstein and Von Bülow. William's speeches had as their constant theme German imperialism. In 1896 he sent a telegram to President Kruger of South Africa congratulating him on the suppression of the Jameson raid. He paid state visits to the Arab countries of the Middle East (1898), adopted an anti-British attitude at the start of the Boer war, but after several visits to Queen Victoria at Windsor was for a while seriously, if clumsily, concerned with Anglo-German reconciliation. But despite such temporary goodwill, he backed von Tirpitz's plans for a large German navy to match the British and in 1911 without provocation dispatched the warship *Panther* to the closed Moroccan port of Agadir, but withdrew it after Lloyd George's instant reaction. He supported immoderate demands on Serbia after the assassination of the Archduke Franz Ferdinand at Sarajevo (1914), but made strenuous efforts to preserve the peace once he realized that a world war was imminent. But political power passed from him to the generals and during the war he became a mere figurehead far removed from the great warlord of popular imagination. With the collapse of the German armies and a revolution in progress, William was forced to abdicate, November 9, 1918, and flee the country. He and his family settled first at Amerongen, then at Doorn near Arnheim, where he wrote his *Memoirs 1878–1918* (trans. 1922), felled trees and ignored the Nazi 'Liberation' (1940) of Holland. He married Princess Augusta Victoria of Schleswig-Holstein in 1881, by whom he had six sons and one daughter, and after her death in 1921, Princess Hermine of Reuss. See also *My Early Life* (1926), Speeches, *Reden Kaiser Wilhelms (1888–1912)*, and biographical studies by E. Ludwig (1926), D. V. Beseler (1932), E. Eyck (1948) and J. von Kürenberg (trans. 1954).

WILLIAM OF CHAMPEAUX (1070–1121), French scholastic philosopher, the head of a famous school of logic in Paris, was the founder of scholastic Realism. He was a teacher and rival of Abelard.

WILLIAM OF JUMIÈGES (d. *c.* 1090), Norman Benedictine monk who compiled a history of the Dukes of Normandy from Rollo to 1071, of value for the story of the Conquest.

WILLIAM OF MALMESBURY (*c.* 1090–1143), English chronicler, became a monk in the monastery at Malmesbury, and in due time librarian and precentor. He took part in the council at Winchester against Stephen in 1141. His *Gesta Regum Anglorum* gives the history of the kings of England from the Saxon invasion to 1126; the *Historia Novella* brings down the narrative to 1142. The *Gesta Pontificum* gives an account of the bishops and chief monasteries of England to 1123. Other works are an account of the church at Glastonbury and Lives of St Dunstan and St Wulfstan.

WILLIAM OF NEWBURGH (*c.*1135–*c.*1200), English chronicler, was perhaps a native of Bridlington, a monk of Newburgh Priory (Coxwold). His *Historia Rerum Anglicarum* (ed. Hamilton, 1856; Howlett, 1884–85), is one of the chief authorities for the reign of Henry II.

WILLIAM OF NORWICH, St (1132?–44), English martyr, apparently the prototype of the Christian boys reported to have been crucified by Jews (see HUGH OF LINCOLN). *The Life and Miracles of St William of Norwich*, edited in 1897 by Jessopp and James, is a story from a 12th-century MS. of a boy said to have been martyred March 22, 1144 or 1145.

WILLIAM OF TYRE (*c.* 1130–85), churchman and historian, probably of Italian birth, became Archdeacon of Tyre in 1167, and Archbishop in 1175. He was tutor to Baldwin, son of King Amalric, and one of the six bishops representing the Latin Church of the East at the Lateran Council (1179). His *Historia Rerum in Partibus Transmarinis Gestarum* deals with the affairs of the East in 1095–1184; a 13th-century French translation was edited by P. Paris (1880). English ones were made by William Caxton (ed. Colvin for the Early English Text Society, 1893); and by Krey and Babington (1942). Another work was *Historia de Orientalibus Principibus*, a history of the successors of Mohammed, now lost.

WILLIAM OF WAYNFLETE (1395–1486), English prelate, educated probably at New College, Oxford, became provost of Eton in 1443, Bishop of Winchester in 1447, and in 1448 founded Magdalen College, Oxford. He was involved in the negotiations which ended Jack Cade's rebellion in 1450, and as a Lancastrian played an important rôle as adviser to Henry VI in the Wars of the Roses. He was lord chancellor (1456–60).

WILLIAM OF WYKEHAM (1324–1404), English churchman and statesman, born at Wickham, near Fareham, was sent to school at Winchester, and by Edward III appointed surveyor of Windsor and other royal castles in 1356–59. He built Queensborough Castle in 1361, was keeper of the privy seal and secretary to the king in 1364, became Bishop of Winchester 1367 and chancellor of England 1367–71 and 1389–91. In 1379 he founded New College, Oxford, and in 1382

Winchester School. In 1394 he undertook the transformation of the nave of Winchester Cathedral, and personally supervised the work. The money he laid out on building would represent half a million. In 1404 he endowed a magnificent chantry at Winchester and, dying the same year, was buried in it. Wykeham was not an ardent theologian; he founded his colleges ' first for the glory of God and the promotion of divine service, and secondarily for scholarship '. He has been called the ' father of the public school system '; and he established (though he did not invent) the Perpendicular architecture. See Lives by Lowth (new ed. 1777), Chandler (1842), Moberly (new ed. 1893); *Winchester College 1393–1893* by Old Wykehamists (1894); and *Winchester College* by A. F. Leach (1899).

WILLIAM THE LYON (1143–1214), King of Scotland, was the grandson of David I, and brother of Malcolm IV, whom he succeeded in 1165. Whence he derived his designation is one of the mysteries of history. His predecessors had long contested with England the sovereignty of Northumberland; but under Malcolm these claims were virtually abandoned, and the king of Scots received, as an equivalent, the earldom of Huntingdon and other estates, holding from the English crown. William attended Henry of England in his Continental wars, and is supposed to have pressed for a portion of the old disputed districts. In his disappointment he invaded them, and on July 13, 1174, fell into the hands of an English party near Alnwick Castle. He was conveyed to Normandy, and there, by the treaty of Falaise, consented, as the price of his liberation, to perform homage for his kingdom. The treaty was revoked in 1189 by Richard I of England in consideration of a payment of 10,000 marks. William had disputes with the church, but founded in 1178 the Abbey of Arbroath, where later he was buried.

WILLIAM THE SILENT (1533–84), Prince of Orange, was born, the Count of Nassau's son, at the castle of Dillenburg in Nassau. He inherited from his cousin René the independent principality of Orange (near Avignon) and the family estates in Holland; and by Charles V before his abdication he was made commander-in-chief in the Netherlands and Stadthouder of Holland, Zeeland and Utrecht, though only twenty-two years of age. He opposed the oppressive policy of Philip II, and resigned his offices (1567). Proclaimed a traitor by Alva and put under the ban by Philip, he professed Protestantism, was chosen by the Netherlanders commander by sea and land, and was the soul of the successful rising against Spanish tyranny. Till the capture of Briel by the Gueux (1572), the Spaniards were absolute masters of the Netherlands; the union of the northern provinces was accomplished in 1579; and in 1584 the free Netherlands had renounced for ever their allegiance to Philip or to Spain. But on July 10, 1584, William was shot at Delft by Balthasar Gérard. He was called ' the Silent ' because of his ability to keep a state secret (specifically, Henry II's scheme to massacre all the Protestants of France and

the Netherlands, confided to him when he was a hostage in France in 1559), not for lack of affability. See Motley's Histories; Lives by Barrett (1883), Putnam (1895), F. Harrison (1897), J. C. Squire (1912), C. V. Wedgwood (1944); in French by Juste (1883), in German by Klose (1864), Kolligs (1885), Rachfahl (1906–24).

WILLIAMS, (1) **Emlyn** (1905–), Welsh playwright and actor, born in Flintshire. The son of an ironmonger, he won a scholarship to Oxford, where he entered Christ Church College. In 1927, attracted by the stage, he joined J. B. Fagan's repertory company. His first real success as a dramatist was with *A Murder has been Arranged* (1930). He then adapted a French play by René Fauchois—*The Late Christopher Bean* (1933)—and continued his success with the terrifying psychological thriller *Night Must Fall* (1935). He was not limited to light entertainment, and a seriousness of purpose characterizes most of his other work. Other successes have been *The Corn is Green* (1938), *The Light of Heart* (1940), *The Wind of Heaven* (1945), *Trespass* (1947), *Accolade* (1951). He has generally played the lead in his own and has acted in other dramatists' plays, besides appearing at the Old Vic and at Stratford, and featuring in films. His solo performance as Charles Dickens giving his celebrated readings from his works was a *tour de force*, but a like endeavour as Dylan Thomas did not meet with such success. See his autobiographical *George* (1961).

(2) **Sir George** (1821–1905), English social reformer, born at Dulverton, became a partner in the London drapery firm of Hitchcock, Williams & Co., made a hobby of temperance work, lay preaching, and teaching in ragged schools, and founded in 1844 the Y.M.C.A. He was knighted in 1894, the jubilee year of the association. See Life by J. E. Hodder Williams (1906).

(3) **Isaac** (1802–65), Welsh clergyman and tractarian, born near Aberystwyth, ordained in 1831, wrote religious poetry, but is best remembered as the author of Tract 80, on ' Reserve in Religious Teaching '. See *Autobiography* (1892).

(4) **John** (1796–1839), English missionary the martyr of Erromango, was born at Tottenham, and, sent by the London Missionary Society in 1817 to the Society Islands, laboured in Raïatéa with marvellous success. Going in 1823 to Raratonga, he christianized the whole Hervey group, and during the next four years visited many of the South Sea Islands, including Samoa. In 1834 he returned to England, superintended the printing of his Raratongan New Testament, and raised £4000 to equip a missionary-ship. In 1838 he visited many of his stations, and sailed for the New Hebrides, where he was killed and eaten by the natives of Erromango. He published his *Narrative of Missionary Enterprises* in 1837. See Lives by B. Mathews (1915) and Prater (1947).

(5) **Sir Monier Monier-** (1819–99), English Sanskrit scholar, was born at Bombay, took his B.A. at Oxford in 1844, and was professor of Sanskrit at Haileybury 1844–58, master at Cheltenham 1858–60, and then Boden

professor of Sanskrit at Oxford. He was knighted in 1886 at the opening of the Indian Institute, established mainly through his energy, and completed in 1896. His books include Sanskrit grammars (1846 and 1860) and dictionaries (1854 and 1872), editions of the *Sákuntalá* (1853) and other Sanskrit texts, books on India, and *Reminiscences of Old Haileybury* (1894). He died at Cannes.

(6) **Roger** (*c.* 1604–83), apostle of toleration and founder of Rhode Island, was originally thought to have been born in Wales, but later research makes this London. Educated at the Charterhouse and Pembroke College, Cambridge, he took Anglican orders, became an extreme Puritan, and emigrated to New England in 1630. He refused to join the congregation at Boston because it would not make public repentance for having been in communion with the Church of England; he therefore went to Salem, but was soon in trouble for denying the right of magistrates to punish Sabbath-breaking. For his opposition to the New England theocracy he was driven from Salem, and took refuge at Plymouth. Two years later he returned to Salem, only to meet renewed persecution and banishment (1635). He escaped to the shores of Narragansett Bay, where he purchased lands of the Indians, founded the city of Providence (1636), and established a pure democracy. Having adopted the tenet of adult baptism, he established (1639) the first Baptist church in America. In 1643 and 1651 he came to England to procure a charter for his colony, and published a *Key into the Language of America* (1643), *The Bloudy Tenent of Persecution for Cause of Conscience* (1644), *The Bloudy Tenent yet more bloudy by Mr Cotton's Endeavour to wash it White in the Blood of the Lamb* (1652), &c. He returned to Rhode Island in 1654, and was president of the colony till 1658. He refused to persecute the Quakers, but had a famous controversy with them—recorded in *George Fox digged out of his Burrowes* (1676). See Memoirs by Elton (1853), Dexter (1876), Straus (1894), Easton (1930), Ernst (1932), E. Winslow (1958); his Letters ed. Bartlett (1882); his Works (Narragansett Club, 1866–74).

(7) **Rowland** (1817–70), English scholar and Liberal theologian, born at Halkyn in Flintshire, and educated at Eton, became fellow and tutor of King's College, Cambridge, in 1850 vice-principal and Hebrew professor at Lampeter College, and in 1859 vicar of Broad-Chalke near Salisbury; hither he retired in 1862 after the storm caused by his contribution, ' Bunsen's Biblical Researches ', to *Essays and Reviews*. His chief books are *Christianity and Hinduism* (1856), *The Hebrew Prophets* (1868–71), *Psalms and Litanies* (1872). See Life by his widow (1874).

(8) **Tennessee**, pseud. of **Thomas Lanier Williams** (1912–), American playwright, born at Columbus, Miss., educated at Missouri, Iowa and Washington universities. His work is characterized by fluent dialogue and searching analysis of the psychological deficiencies of his characters. His plays, almost all set in the Deep South against a background of decadence and degradation, include *The Glass Menagerie* (1944), *A Streetcar Named Desire* (1947), awarded the 1948 Pulitzer prize, *Cat on a Hot Tin Roof* (1955), awarded the 1955 Pulitzer prize, *Orpheus Descending* (1957), *Suddenly Last Summer* (1958), and *Night of the Iguana* (1961).

(9) **Sir William Fenwick** (1800–83), British army officer, born at Halifax, Nova Scotia, the hero of Kars, had, as colonel of engineers, been engaged in defining the Turco-Persian boundary when in 1854, during the Crimean war, he was appointed British Military Commissioner with the Turkish army in Asia. He reached Kars in September, and found the Turks utterly demoralized; but with indomitable energy he corrected abuses, got rid of corrupt officials, and became idolized by the Turkish army. In June 1855 the Russians appeared before Kars. After a most heroic defence, Williams had to surrender on November 25. He was detained prisoner in Russia till the peace, when he was given a baronetcy and an annuity of £1000. See works on the siege by Sandwith (1856) and Oliphant (1856).

WILLIAMSON, (1) **Alexander William** (1824–1904), English chemist, studied medicine at Heidelberg and chemistry at Giessen. From 1849 to 1887 he was professor of Chemistry at University College, London. F.R.S. in 1855, he was president of the British Association in 1873. His researches on etherification had great importance. He published a *Chemistry for Students*.

(2) **Henry** (1895–), English author, born in Bedfordshire, after service in World War I became a journalist, but turned to farming in Norfolk. He wrote several novels, semi-autobiographical, including his long series *A Chronicle of Ancient Sunlight* on the life story of his hero Phillip Maddison. He is best known, however, for his classic nature stories *Tarka the Otter* (1927, Hawthornden prize), and *Salar the Salmon* (1935).

(3) **William Crawford** (1816–95), English botanist, born in Scarborough, trained in medicine and became professor of Natural History and later of Botany at Owens College, Manchester (1851–92). He was the first to point out the importance of the plant life forms in coal. At the time, however, the full significance of his work in fossil botany was not appreciated. See his *Reminiscences of a Yorkshire Naturalist* (1896).

WILLIBALD (700–786), a Northumbrian, and brother of St Walpurga (q.v.), made the pilgrimage to Palestine, settled as monk at Monte Cassino, became the companion of St Boniface, and died Bishop of Eichstätt.

WILLIBROD, or **Wilbrord, St** (*c.* 658–739), English missionary, born in Northumbria, became a Benedictine, and, sent about 690 as missionary to Friesland, was made Bishop of Utrecht, and laboured with the utmost zeal and success. See Lives by Thijm (1863), Verbist (1939), and W. Levison's *England and the Continent in the 8th Century* (1946).

WILLINGDON, Freeman Freeman-Thomas, 1st Marquis of (1866–1941), British administrator. Educated at Eton and Cambridge, he was Liberal M.P. for Hastings (1900–06) and for Bodmin (1906–10), governor of Bombay (1913–19) and of Madras (1919–24).

From 1926 to 1931 he was governor-general of Canada. As viceroy of India (1931–36) he persuaded Gandhi to come to London to the second Round Table Conference, helped to shape the Government of India Bill, and started the new machine of government in India. An administrator of great tact and brilliance, he was one of the few commoners to be rewarded with a marquisate (1936).

WILLIS, (1) Nathaniel Parker (1806–67), American editor and writer, born at Portland, Me., issued several volumes of poetry, established the *American Monthly Magazine*, in 1831 visited Europe, and contributed to the *New York Mirror* his *Pencillings by the Way*. Appointed *attaché* to the American legation at Paris, he visited Greece and Turkey, and returned to England in 1837. He contributed to the London *New Monthly* his *Inklings of Adventure* (collected 1836), and published *Letters from under a Bridge* (1840). In 1844 he engaged in editing the *Daily Mirror*, revisited Europe, and published *Dashes at Life with a Free Pencil* (1845). He returned to New York in 1846, and established the *Home Journal*, in which much of his work first appeared. See Life (1885) by H. A. Beers. His sister, **Sara Payson Willis**, ' Fanny Fern ' (1811–72), was a popular writer. See her Life (1873) by her husband, James Parton (q.v.).

(2) **Thomas** (1621–73), English physician, was for a time Sedleian professor of Natural Philosophy at Oxford, but became famous as a physician in Westminster. He was one of the first fellows of the Royal Society, and was a pioneer in the anatomy of the brain. He wrote on the plague.

WILLKIE, Wendell (1892–1944), American politician, born at Elwood, Ind., became first a lawyer, later an industrialist. Having removed his support from the Democrat to the Republican cause in 1940, he was nominated as presidential candidate by the party and narrowly defeated in the election of that year. In 1941–42 he travelled the world representing the president. An opponent of Isolationism, he was leader of the left-wing element in his party.

WILLOUGHBY, Sir Hugh (d. 1554), English explorer, of whom little is known save his unfortunate fate. In 1553 an expedition was fitted out by the merchants of London ' for the discovery of regions, dominions, islands, and places unknown ', and Willoughby was appointed its commander. On May 10 he sailed from Deptford with three vessels, one commanded by Richard Chancellor (q.v.). They crossed the North Sea in company, and sighted the coast of Norway. In September Chancellor's ship parted company in a storm with the two others, which reached Russian Lapland. Here Sir Hugh determined to pass the winter, but here with his sixty-two companions he perished of scurvy. Next year Russian fishermen found the ships with the dead bodies and the commander's journal (published in Hakluyt; new edition by Hakluyt Society, 1903).

WILLS, (1) William Gorman (1828–91), Irish playwright and poet, born in Kilkenny Co., studied at Trinity College, Dublin, and started as an artist. His *Man o' Airlie* (1866)

was followed by *Charles I* (1872), *Jane Shore* (1876), *Olivia*, *Claudian* (1885), &c. He also wrote novels. His ballads include *I'll sing thee Songs of Araby*. See Life by F. Wills (1898).

(2) **William John** (1834–61), Australian explorer, studied medicine, became a surveyor of crown lands in Victoria and was third in command of R. O. Burke's (q.v.) ill-fated expedition to the north, on which he perished.

WILLSTÄTTER, Richard, *vil'shtet-èr* (1872–1942), German chemist, born at Karlsruhe, studied at Munich and became professor at Zürich, Berlin, and finally Munich in 1917. His researches included alkaloids and their derivatives, and the work on plant pigments for which in 1915 he was awarded the Nobel prize for chemistry. In 1925 he resigned his professorship at Munich, and in 1939 left Germany for Switzerland, where he died.

WILLUGHBY, Francis (1635–72), English naturalist, born at Middleton, Warwickshire, the son of Sir Francis Willughby, studied at Cambridge and Oxford, and then started on a Continental tour (1663–64) with John Ray (q.v.), collecting zoological specimens. Ray edited and translated his *Ornithologia* (1676–1678) and edited his *Historia Piscium* (1686).

WILLUMSEN, Jens Ferdinand, *vil'oom-sen* (1863–1958), Danish painter and sculptor, born at Copenhagen. His best-known painting, *After the Storm* (1905), is in the Oslo National Gallery. As a sculptor his masterpiece is the *Great Relief*, in coloured marbles and bronze. He bequeathed his works and his art collection to form a Willumsen museum in Frederikssund.

WILMOT. See ROCHESTER (EARL OF).

WILSON, (1) Alexander (1766–1813), Scottish ornithologist of N. America, born at Paisley, travelled as a pedlar, and published poems (1790) and *Watty and Meg* (1792). Prosecuted for a lampoon, he sailed for America in 1794. He got work in Philadelphia, travelled as a pedlar in New Jersey, and was a schoolteacher in Pennsylvania. His skill in drawing birds led him to make a collection of all the birds of America. In October 1804 he set out on his first excursion, and wrote *The Foresters, a Poem*. In 1806 he was employed on the American edition of *Rees's Cyclopaedia*. He soon prevailed upon the publisher to undertake an American Ornithology, and in 1808–13 he brought out seven volumes. In 1811 he made a canoe voyage down the Ohio, and travelled overland through the Lower Mississippi Valley from Nashville to New Orleans. Vols. viii and ix of the Ornithology were completed after his death by Ord, his assistant. The work was continued by C. L. Bonaparte (1828–33).

(2) **Angus Frank Johnstone** (1913–), British writer, educated at Westminster and Merton College, Oxford, began writing in 1946 and rapidly established a reputation with his brilliant collection of short stories, *The Wrong Set* (1949), satirizing the more aimless sections of pre-war middle-class society. *Such Darling Dodos* (1950), *For Whom the Cloche Tolls* (1953) and *A Bit off the Map* (1957) added to his prestige, and in 1955 he gave up his office of deputy-superintendent of the British Museum reading room to

devote himself solely to writing. The novels *Hemlock and After* (1952), *Anglo-Saxon Attitudes* (1956), &c., and the play *The Mulberry Bush* (1955) were still good but perhaps less successful than his short stories, but *No Laughing Matter* (1967), an ambitious family chronicle of the egocentric Matthews family spanning the 20th century, was hailed as an outstanding work.

(3) Sir **Arthur Knyvet** (1842–1921), G.C.B., G.C.V.O., O.M. (1912), British admiral, served in the Crimea (1854), China (1865), Egypt (1882) and Sudan (1884), where he won the V.C., and was commander-in-chief of the Home and Channel Fleets 1903–07, admiral of the Fleet 1907, and first sea lord 1909–12.

(4) **Charles Thomson Rees** (1869–1959), Scottish pioneer of atomic and nuclear physics, born at Glencorse near Edinburgh, was educated at Manchester and at Cambridge, where later he became professor of Natural Philosophy (1925–34). He was noted for his study of atmospheric electricity, one by-product of which was the successful protection from lightning of Britain's wartime barrage balloons. His greatest achievement was to devise the cloud chamber method of marking the track of alpha-particles and electrons. The movement and interaction of atoms could thus be followed and photographed. In 1927 he shared with Compton the Nobel prize for physics, and in 1937 received the Copley medal.

(5) **Sir Daniel** (1816–92), Scottish archaeologist, born in Edinburgh, educated at the university there, had been secretary to the Scottish Society of Antiquaries when in 1853 he became professor of History and English Literature at Toronto. President of the university from 1881, he was knighted in 1888. His numerous works include *Edinburgh in the Olden Time* (1847; new ed. 1892), *Prehistoric Annals of Scotland* (1851; 2nd ed. 1863), *Chatterton* (1869), *Left-handedness* (1891) and *The Lost Atlantis* (1892).

(6) **Edmund** (1895–1972), American literary and social critic, born at Red Bank, New Jersey, studied at Princeton and became journalist, associate editor of the *New Republic* (1926–31) and book critic of the *New Yorker*. His outstanding critical works include *Axel's Castle* (1931) on the symbolist movement, *The Wound and the Bow* (1941) and on social questions, *The American Earthquake* (1958), &c. He also wrote verse, a number of plays including *This Room and This Gin and These Sandwiches* (1937), historical works such as *The Scrolls of the Dead Sea* (1955) and books on travel. He was married four times, his third wife being Mary McCarthy (q.v.).

(7) **Edmund Beecher** (1856–1939), American zoologist, born at Geneva, Illinois, studied at Yale and Johns Hopkins universities, and after several teaching posts became Da Costa professor of Zoology at Columbia University, New York. He contributed greatly to cytology and embryology. See his *The Cell in Development and Heredity* (1925).

(8) **Edward Adrian** (1872–1912), British physician, naturalist and explorer, born at Cheltenham, in 1901 went to the Antarctic with Scott in the *Discovery*. Back in England he did research on grouse diseases and made use of his skill as a watercolourist in preparing illustrations for books on birds and mammals. In 1910 he returned to the Antarctic with Scott in the *Terra Nova*, acting as chief of the expedition's scientific staff. One of the ill-fated polar party, he perished with his companions on the return journey from the pole in 1912. See G. Seaver, *Edward Wilson of the Antarctic* (1933).

(9) **Sir Erasmus** (1809–84), British surgeon, born in London, was a skilful dissector at the College of Surgeons in London, but was best known as a specialist on skin diseases. He published *Anatomist's Vademecum, Book of Diseases of the Skin, Report on Leprosy*, and *Egypt of the Past*. The great wealth he acquired by his practice he bestowed largely in benefactions to the poor and to science, and in promoting Egyptian research. He brought Cleopatra's Needle to London in 1878 at a cost of £10,000. President of the College of Surgeons, he was knighted in 1881.

(10) **Florence.** See VOLUSENUS.

(11) **(James) Harold** (1916–), British Labour politician, was born in Huddersfield and educated there, in Cheshire and at Oxford, where he became a lecturer in Economics in 1937. From 1943 to 1944 he was director of economics and statistics at the ministry of fuel and power. Becoming M.P. for Ormskirk in 1945, he was appointed parliamentary secretary to the ministry of works. In 1947 he became successively secretary for overseas trade and president of the Board of Trade till his resignation on the tide of Bevanism in April 1951. In 1951 and 1955 he was re-elected M.P. for Huyton, the division he had represented since 1950. The youngest Cabinet minister since Pitt, after 1956, when he headed the voting for the Labour 'shadow' Cabinet, he became the principal Opposition spokesman on economic affairs. An able and hard-hitting debater, in 1963 he succeeded Gaitskell as leader of the Labour party, becoming prime minister in October 1964 with a precariously small majority and being re-elected in April 1966 with comfortably large support. His government's economic plans were badly affected by the balance of payments crisis, leading to severe restrictive measures; while abroad he was faced with the Rhodesian problem (increasingly severe economic sanctions being applied), continued intransigence from de Gaulle over Britain's proposed entry into the Common Market, and the important question of Britain's new status in world politics as a lesser power. His party lost power in the 1970 general election and he became leader of the opposition. See Life by Smith (1967).

(12) **Harriette**, *née* **Dubochet** (1786–1855), English demi-mondaine, was born in Mayfair, London, of French descent. Her long career as a genteel courtesan began at the age of fifteen with the Earl of Craven; subsequent paramours included the Duke of Argyll, the Duke of Wellington, the Marquis of Worcester and a host of others. All these figured in her lively but libellous *Memoirs*, brought out in parts from 1825 to the accompaniment of a barrage of suggestive advance publicity aimed

at blackmail of the victims, most of whom echoed the celebrated outburst of Wellington on the occasion—' Publish and be damned! ' See Life by A. Thirkell (1936), and L. Blanch, *The Game of Hearts* (1957).

(13) **Henry** (1812–73), American politician, vice-president of the United States, was the son of a farm-labourer at Farmington, N.H. Born Jeremiah Jones Colbath, he changed his name when he came of age, worked as a shoemaker, became prominent as an Abolitionist in the 'thirties, and was elected to the Massachusetts legislature and state senate. He was an active leader of the Free-soilers, assisted in forming the new Republican party, sat in the U.S. senate 1855–73, and then became vice-president of the United States. In the Civil War he was chairman of the military committee. He wrote *Rise and Fall of the Slave Power in America* (1872–1875). See Life by Russell and Nason (1872).

(14) **Sir Henry Hughes** (1864–1922), G.C.B., D.S.O., British field-marshal (1919), born at Edgeworthstown, Ireland, served in Burma, S. Africa, &c., and won fame in World War I, starting (1914) as director of Military Operations, and ending (1918) as chief of the Imperial General Staff. He received a baronetcy and a £10,000 grant in 1919. He was shot in London by two Irishmen on June 22, 1922, for having assisted the government of Northern Ireland. See Life by B. Collier (1961).

(15) **Henry Maitland, 1st Baron Wilson** (1881–1964), British field-marshal, was educated at Eton and commissioned in the ' Greenjackets '. He fought in South Africa and in World War I, and by 1937 was G.O.C. 2nd Division, Aldershot. On the outbreak of World War II he was appointed G.O.C.-in-C., Egypt, and after leading successfully the initial British advance in Libya and capturing Bardia, Tobruk and Benghazi, he was given command of the short and ill-fated Greek campaign. In 1943 he was appointed c.-in-c. Middle East, and in 1944 he became Supreme Allied Commander in what had become the relatively subordinate Mediterranean theatre. He headed the British Joint Staff Mission in Washington (1945–47) and in 1955 became constable of the Tower. He was raised to the peerage in 1946.

(16) **Horace Hayman** (1786–1860), English Orientalist, born in London, in 1808 went to India as assistant surgeon, and in the Calcutta mint became Leyden's assistant. In 1833 he became Boden professor of Sanskrit in Oxford, and soon after librarian at the East India House. His dictionary (1819) and grammar (1841) of Sanskrit, together with his other works, helped to lay the foundations of Indian philology in Europe.

(17) **James** (1805–60), British economist, born at Hawick, settled in business in London, and became an authority on the Corn Laws and the currency, founded the *Economist*, entered parliament as a Liberal in 1847, and was financial secretary to the Treasury, vice-president of the Board of Trade, and member of the council of India. See the *Economist* centenary volume (1943).

(18) **John,** pseud. **Christopher North** (1785–1854), Scottish journalist, was born at Paisley,

attended Glasgow and Oxford Universities, becoming famous for his intellectual gifts and as an athlete. In 1807 he settled in Westmorland, where he purchased Elleray, overlooking Windermere, and associated with Wordsworth, Southey, Coleridge, De Quincey and their friends. In May 1811 he married and devoted himself to poetry, in 1812 publishing his *Isle of Palms*, and in 1816 *The City of Plague*. In 1815 the loss of his patrimony through an uncle's unjust stewardship obliged him to give up living constantly at Elleray and settle at his mother's house in Edinburgh. He was called to the Scottish bar, but on the starting in 1817 of *Blackwood's Magazine* he proffered his services; and he and Lockhart were the soul of ' Maga's ' success. Lockhart was withdrawn in 1826 to London; and Wilson was, not formally but practically, editor. In 1820 he was elected to the Edinburgh chair of Moral Philosophy. His works (ed. his nephew and son-in-law, Ferrier, 1855-58), include *Lights and Shadows of Scottish Life* (1822), *The Trials of Margaret Lyndsay* (1823) and *The Foresters* (1825), as well as thirty-nine out of seventy of the ' Noctes Ambrosianae ', which appeared in *Blackwood* (1822–35), and enjoyed an amazing vogue. See the Memoir by his daughter, Mrs Gordon (1862); a study by E. Swann (1934); Watts-Dunton's article in the *Athenaeum* (July 8, 1876); Saintsbury's *Essays* (1891); Mrs Oliphant's work on the Blackwoods (1897); and Sir G. Douglas's *Blackwood Group* (1897).

(19) **John** (1800–49), Scottish singer, born in Edinburgh, was first a compositor, then a precentor, and for years a favourite operatic tenor in London; and finally gave entertainments in Britain and America as an unsurpassed singer of Scots songs.

(20) **John Dover** (1881–1969), English Shakespearean scholar, was born in London and educated at Cambridge. After some years as teacher, lecturer and H.M. Inspector of adult education, he became professor first of Education at King's College, London (1924–35), then of Rhetoric and English Literature at the University of Edinburgh (1935–45). Made C.H. in 1936, he is best known for his Shakespearean studies, the result of penetrating and impartial research over many years, particularly on the problems in *Hamlet*. From 1921 till 1966 he was editor of the New Shakespeare series. Works include *Life in Shakespeare's England* (1911), *The Essential Shakespeare* (1932), *The Fortunes of Falstaff* (1943), *What Happens in Hamlet* (1935) and *Shakespeare's Sonnets—An Introduction for Historians and Others* (1963).

(21) **John** (1804–75), Scottish missionary, born, a farmer's son, near Lauder, and educated at Edinburgh University, ministered in Bombay from 1828 until his death, and was much consulted by government, especially during the crisis of 1857. He was twice president of the Bombay branch of the Asiatic Society, and was vice-chancellor of Bombay University. His chief writings were *The Parsi Religion* (1843) and *Lands of the Bible* (1847). See Life by Dr George Smith (1878). His son, **Andrew** (1830–81), edited

the *China Mail* and later the *Bombay Gazette*, but is best known for his account of Gordon's *Ever-Victorious Army* (1868) and his book on the Himalayas, *The Abode of Snow* (1875).

(22) **John Mackay** (1804–35), Scottish writer and editor, born in Tweedmouth, known for his *Tales of the Borders* (6 vols. 1834–40), originally issued in weekly numbers, and continued after his death for his widow with Alexander Leighton (1800–74) as editor.

(23) **Richard** (1714–82), British landscape-painter, born at Penegoes rectory, Montgomeryshire, after a visit to Italy (1749–56), gave up portrait-painting for landscape and anticipated Gainsborough and Constable in forsaking strait-laced classicism for a lyrical freedom of style. In London in 1760 he exhibited his *Niobe*, and became one of the leading painters of his time. Famous also was his *View of Rome from the Villa Madama*. In 1776 he became librarian to the Royal Academy. Works may be seen in the National Gallery and in the National Museum of Wales. See study by W. G. Constable (1953).

(24) **Sir Robert Thomas** (1777–1849), British soldier, born in London, having served in Belgium, against the Irish rebels (1798), and in the campaign of the Helder, commanded Abercromby's cavalry in Egypt, helped to conquer the Cape of Good Hope in 1806, and went with a mission to Prussia. In the Peninsula he helped to train the Portuguese army, and commanded a Spanish brigade at Talavera. He was attached in 1812 to the Russian army, in Germany and France was in the camp of the allies, and at Lützen commanded the Prussian reserve. Involved in Queen Caroline's affairs, he was dismissed from the army, but reinstated. In 1841 he became general, in 1842–49 was governor of Gibraltar, and in 1818–31 sat as a Liberal for Southwark. He wrote several works on military history. See his *Private Diary* (1861) and the Life by Randolph (1863).

(25) **Thomas** (1663–1755), English churchman, born at Burton in Cheshire, became Bishop of Sodor and Man in 1698. His *Principles of Christianity*, or ' the Manx Catechism ' (1707), and *Instruction for the Indians* were combined to form *The Knowledge of Christianity made Easy* (1755). Better known are *Short Instructions for the Lord's Supper* (1733) and *Sacra Privata* (1781).

(26) **Thomas Woodrow** (1856–1924), American statesman, twenty-eighth president of the United States, born at Staunton, Virginia, studied at Princeton and Johns Hopkins, practised law at Atlanta, lectured at Bryn Mawr and Princeton, became president of Princeton in 1902, and governor of New Jersey in 1911, and in 1912 and 1916, as Democratic candidate, was elected president of the United States. Wilson's administration, ending in tragic failure and physical breakdown, is memorable for the prohibition and women's suffrage amendments of the constitution, trouble with Mexico, America's participation in the Great War, his part in the peace conference, his ' fourteen points ' and championship of the League of Nations, and the Senate's rejection of the Treaty of

Versailles. He wrote a *History of the American People* (1902), &c. See Life by R. S. Baker (1928–39), studies by Link (1947), Hugh-Jones (1947), H. Hoover (1958) and Latham (1959).

WILTON, Marie. See BANCROFT (4).

WINCHILSEA, Anne Finch, Countess of (1661–1720), English poetess, born at Sidmonton, was daughter of Sir William Kingsmill, and wife of Heneage Finch, 4th Earl of Winchilsea. Her longest poem, *The Spleen*, in Cowley's manner, was printed in 1701; her *Miscellany Poems* in 1713. She was a friend of Pope. See *Select Poems*, ed. J. M. Murry (1928), and E. Gosse, *Gossip in a Library* (1891).

WINCKELMANN, Johann Joachim (1717–1768), German archaeologist, was born at Stendal in Prussian Saxony. He studied the history of art, published a treatise on the imitation of the antique (1754), and was librarian to a cardinal at Rome (1755). In 1758 he examined the remains of Herculaneum, Pompeii, and Paestum, and went to Florence. He wrote a treatise on ancient architecture (1762), the epoch-making *Geschichte der Kunst des Alterthums* (1764), and *Monumenti Antichi Inediti* (1766). In 1763 he was made superintendent of Roman antiquities. He was murdered at Trieste. See Life by Justi (new ed. 1923) and study by Curtius (1941).

WINDAUS, Adolf, *vind'ows* (1876–1959), German chemist, educated at Freiburg and Berlin, was professor of Applied Medical Chemistry at Innsbruck and Göttingen. In 1928 he was awarded the Nobel prize for chemistry for his work on sterols, in particular for his discovery that ultraviolet light activates ergosterol and gives vitamin D_2. He was also an authority on cardiac poisons.

WINDHAM, William (1750–1810), English statesman, born at London, studied at Eton, Glasgow and Oxford, opposed Lord North (1778), and in 1784 was returned for Norwich. In 1783 he was principal secretary to Lord Northington, lord-lieutenant of Ireland. He followed Burke in his view of the French Revolution, and in 1794 became secretary-at-war under Pitt. He went out with Pitt in 1801, and eloquently denounced Addington's peace of Amiens (1801). This lost him his seat for Norwich, but he was elected for St Mawes in Cornwall, and on the return of the Grenville party to power (January 1806) became war and colonial secretary. He helped Cobbett to start his *Political Register* (1802), carried a scheme for limited service in the army (1806), and in 1806 was returned by New Romney, and in 1807 by Higham Ferrers. He went out when the Portland administration was formed. Windham was a member of the famous Literary Club, and stood by Johnson's deathbed. His brilliant talents were neutralized by an intellectual timidity, a morbid self-consciousness, and a fondness for paradox. See his speeches (1806, with Life by Amyot); his *Diary 1784–1810*, ed. Mrs Baring (1866); and the *Windham Papers* (1913).

WINDISCHGRÄTZ, Prince Alfred, *vind'ish-grets* (1787–1862), Austrian field-marshal, suppressed the revolution of 1848–49 at

Prague and Vienna, and defeated the Hungarians repeatedly, but was superseded after his defeat by them at Gödöllö.

WINDSOR, Duke and Duchess of. See EDWARD VIII.

WINDTHORST, Ludwig (1812–91), German Catholic politician, was born near Osnabrück, and became distinguished as advocate and politician in Hanover. After the absorption of Hanover by Prussia, he became leader of the Ultramontanes in the German parliament and chief opponent of Bismarck during the Kulturkampf.

WINER, Johann Georg Benedikt, *vee'ner* (1789–1858), German New Testament scholar, born at Leipzig, became a professor of Theology there, at Erlangen in 1823, and at Leipzig again in 1832. The most important of his many works is his *Grammar of New Testament Greek* (1822, trans. Moulton 1882).

WINFRIED. See BONIFACE.

WINGATE, (1) Orde Charles (1903–44), British general, was educated at Charterhouse and R.M.A., joining the R.A. in 1922. With the Sudan Defence Force from 1928 to 1933, he later saw service in Palestine and Transjordan. In the Burma theatre in 1942, realizing that the only answer to penetration is counter-penetration, he obtained sanction to organize the Chindits—specially trained jungle-fighters. Supplied by air, they thrust far behind the enemy lines, gravely disrupting the entire supply system. Wingate was killed in a plane crash in Burma, in March 1944. See Halley, *With Wingate in Burma* (1946), Mosley, *Gideon Goes to War* (1955), and Life by C. Sykes (1959).

(2) Sir Reginald, Bart. (1861–1953), British general, entered the R.A. in 1880. Duty in India and Aden preceded his posting to the Egyptian Army. Service in Evelyn Wood's Nile Expedition and the Dongola campaign lead to his appointment as Sirdar. As governor-general of the Sudan from 1899 to 1916 he left his mark on a territory that owed its security and increasing prosperity to his lifelong devotion to its interests. He retired in 1922 after service as High Commissioner of Egypt. G.C.B. 1914, G.C.V.O. 1912, G.B.E. 1918, K.C.M.G. 1898. See his memoirs, *Wingate of the Sudan* (1955).

WINIFRED, St, legendary 7th-century Welsh saint, a noble British maiden, beheaded by Prince Caradog for repelling his unholy proposals. The legend relates that her head rolled down a hill, and where it stopped a spring gushed forth—famous still as a place of pilgrimage, Holywell in Flintshire. Her head was replaced by St Beuno.

WINKELRIED, Arnold von, *vin'kel-reet* (d. 1386), Swiss patriot, knight of Unterwalden, at the battle of Sempach (July 9, 1386), when the Swiss failed to break the compact line of Austrian spears, is said to have grasped as many pikes as he could reach, buried them in his bosom, and borne them by his weight to the earth. His comrades rushed into the breach, slaughtered the Austrians like sheep, and gained a decisive victory.

WINKLER, Clemens Alexander, *vink'ler* (1838–1904), German chemist, born and educated at Freiberg, where he became professor of Chemistry, in 1886 discovered the element germanium. He also made important contributions to the study of the analysis of gases. He died at Dresden.

WINSLOW, (1) Edward (1595–1655), one of the Pilgrim Fathers, born at Droitwich, sailed in the *Mayflower*, and from 1624 was assistant governor or governor of the Plymouth colony, which he described and defended in *Good Newes from New England* (1624), *Hypocrisie Unmasked* (1646) and *New England's Salamander* (1647). Sent by Cromwell against the West Indies, he died at sea. His son, **Josiah** (1629–80), was assistant governor 1657–73, and then governor. In 1675 he was chosen general-in-chief of the United Colonies. His grandson, **John** (1702–1774), carried out the removal of the Acadians and **John Ancrum** (1811–73), descendant of one of Edward Winslow's brothers, commanded the *Kearsarge* in her action with the *Alabama*.

(2) Forbes Benignus (1810–74), London physician and specialist in mental illnesses, was a pioneer in the humane treatment of the insane. He was instrumental in gaining acceptance for the plea of insanity in criminal cases.

WINSOR, Justin (1831–97), American librarian and historian, born at Boston, Mass., studied at Harvard and Heidelberg; was librarian at Boston 1868–77, and then at Harvard; and published bibliographical works, *Memorial History of Boston* (1880–81), *Narrative History of America* (1884–90) and a Life of Columbus (1891).

WINSTANLEY, Henry (d. 1703), English architect and engraver, perished with his (the first) Eddystone Lighthouse in 1703, when it was swept away in a gale.

WINT, Peter de (1784–1849), English watercolourist, was born, of Dutch descent, at Stone, Staffordshire. His fame rests on his watercolour illustrations of English landscape, English architecture, and English country life. Among them are *The Cricketers*, *The Hay Harvest*, *Nottingham*, *Richmond Hill* and *Cows in Water*. Many of his works are in Lincoln Art Gallery. His watercolours are well represented in the Victoria and Albert Museum, which also owns the oils *A Cornfield* and *A Woody Landscape*. See Memoir by Armstrong (1888) and Redgrave's *David Cox and Peter de Wint* (1891).

WINTER, Jan Willem de (1750–1812), Dutch admiral from 1795, born on the island of Texel, was defeated by Duncan at Camperdown in 1797. He was ambassador to France 1798–1802.

WINTERHALTER, Franz Xaver (1805–73), German painter, made a successful portrait of Grand Duke Leopold of Baden and was appointed his court painter. In 1834 he went to Paris, with Queen Marie Amélie as his patron. One of his many royal sitters was Queen Victoria, and Winterhalter became the fashionable artist of the day. Some of his works are at Versailles, and he is represented in the British royal collection.

WINTHROP, (1) John (1588–1649), English colonist, father of (2), born at Groton in Suffolk, was bred to the law, and in 1629 was appointed governor of Massachusetts colony. He was re-elected governor, with brief intervals, during his life, and had more influence probably than any other man in forming the political institutions of the northern states of America. The first part of his *Journal* was published in 1790, and the whole in 1825–26 (later ed. with additions, 1853). See *Life and Letters*, by R. C. Winthrop (1864–67).

(2) **John** (1606–76), son of (1), governor of Connecticut, went to America in 1631, became a magistrate in Massachusetts, in 1635 went to Connecticut, and founded New London in 1646. In 1657 he was elected governor, and, except for one year, held that post till his death. He obtained from Charles II a charter uniting the colonies of Connecticut and New Haven, and was named first governor under it; and was the father of paper currency in America.

(3) **John**, known as **Fitz-John** (1639–1707), son of (2), served under Monk and in the Indian wars, was agent in London for Connecticut (1693–97), and governor of the colony from 1698. See *Winthrop Papers* (Mass. Hist. Soc. 1889).

(4) **John** (1714–79), physicist, descendant of (1), was born at Boston, and in 1738 became professor of Mathematics and Natural Philosophy at Harvard. In 1740 he observed the transit of Mercury. He published papers on earthquakes, comets, &c.

(5) **Robert Charles** (1809–94), orator descendant of (1), was admitted to the bar in 1831, and was in the state legislature 1834–40, then in congress, and in 1847–49 its speaker. In 1850–51 he was senator from Massachusetts. He published *Addresses and Speeches* (1852–86); a Life of the first John Winthrop; and *Washington, Bowdoin, and Franklin* (1876). See Memoir by son (1897).

(6) **Theodore** (1828–61), descendant of (1), born at New Haven, studied at Yale, was admitted to the bar (1855), but, volunteering in the Civil War, fell in battle at Great Bethel. His novels include *Cecil Dreeme* (1861), *John Brent* (1861) and *Edwin Brothertoft* (1862).

WINTON, Will McClain (1884–), American geologist from Florida, in 1930 became professor of Geology at Texas. He evolved a method of deciding the age of layers of sediments by studying the annual growth rings of bivalve shells buried in them.

WINZET, Ninian, *win'yet* (1518–92), Scottish churchman, born at Renfrew, and ordained priest in 1540, about 1552 became schoolmaster at Linlithgow, then provost of the collegiate church there. At the Reformation (1561) he was deprived of his office, came to Edinburgh, and as a Catholic wrote his *Tractatis* (1562). Forced to quit Scotland in 1563, he held office in the University of Paris. In 1574 he removed to the English College of Douai, and in 1577 became abbot at Ratisbon. See Hewison's edition of his works (Scottish Text Soc. 1891).

WISDOM, Arthur John Terence Dibber (1904–), English philosopher, professor of Philosophy at Cambridge from 1952, was profoundly influenced by Wittgenstein, but worked out his own characteristic, if elusive methods of dealing with philosophical paradoxes, which he showed need not always be written off as mere linguistic confusion,

but may be invoked to point out unexpected similarities and dissimilarities in the use of sentences. See his collected philosophical papers, *Other Minds* (1952), *Philosophy and Psychoanalysis* (1953) and *Paradox and Discovery* (1965). He was president of the Aristotelian Society (1950–51). His cousin, **John Oulton Wisdom,** is professor of Philosophy at the London School of Economics.

WISE, Thomas James (1859–1937), English bibliophile and literary forger, born at Gravesend, began collecting books in his youth and built up a library of rare editions of the English poets and other works, including a collection of pamphlets and MSS., especially of the 19th-century romantics and the literary wing of the pre-Raphaelite movement. In 1934 certain pamphlets which he had sold to dealers and others for high prices were alleged to be faked and a sensational literary scandal ensued which was only checked by his death. His collection (the Ashley Library) was sold to the British Museum. See his *Letters to J. H. Wrenn* (1944); Carter and Pollard, *An Enquiry into the Nature of Certain 19th Century Pamphlets* (1934); W. Partington, *Forging Ahead* (1939); D. F. Foxon, *T. J. W. and the Pre-Restoration Drama* (1959), and studies ed. W. B. Todd (1960).

WISEMAN, (1) **Nicholas Patrick Stephen** (1802–65), cardinal, was born at Seville, of an Irish family settled in Spain. He was brought up at Waterford and Ushaw, entered the English College at Rome, received holy orders in 1825, and became rector of the college (1828). He established the *Dublin Review* (1836), and in 1840 was named Coadjutor Vicar-apostolic and president of St Mary's College at Oscott. In 1847 he was transferred to the London district. His appointment by the pope to be Roman Catholic Archbishop of Westminster and Cardinal in 1850 called forth a storm of religious excitement, which led to the passing of the Ecclesiastical Titles Assumption Act, when he published his conciliatory *Appeal on the Catholic Hierarchy*. One of his best known works was *Fabiola* (1854). See Memoir by G. White (1865), Lives by D. Gwynn (1929) and B. Fothergill (1963), J. J. O'Connor, *The Catholic Revival* (1942), and I. F. Reynolds, *Three Cardinals* (1958).

(2) **Richard** (d. 1679), surgeon to Charles II, was called ' the father of English surgery ', and wrote *Seven Chirurgical Treatises*. See monograph by Sir T. Longmore (1892).

WISHART, George (c. 1513–46), Scottish reformer and martyr, belonged to a Kincardineshire family, his eldest brother King's Advocate. In 1538 he was schoolmaster in Montrose, where he incurred a charge of heresy for teaching the Greek New Testament. In 1539 he was in Bristol, and had to abjure heresy again. The next few years he spent on the Continent, and translated the Swiss *Confession of Faith*. In 1543 he accompanied a commission sent to Scotland by Henry VII in connection with the marriage of his son Edward and Mary Stuart; and he preached the Lutheran doctrine of justification by faith at Dundee and Montrose, in

Ayrshire and East Lothian. At Cardinal Beaton's instance he was arrested on January 16, 1546, and burned at St Andrews on March 1. Knox was first inspired by Wishart. It is doubtful whether he was or was not a Scotsman of the name who was concerned in a proposal made to Henry VIII for the assassination of Beaton. See David Laing, *Works of John Knox* (vols. i and vi); Lorimer's *Precursors of the Reformation*; C. Rogers's *Life of Wishart* (1876); and Maxwell's *Old Dundee* (1891).

WISLICENUS, Johannes Adolf (1835–1902), German chemist, born near Querfurt in Prussian Saxony, went to America as a young man, taught chemistry at Cambridge (U.S.), New York, Zürich and Würzburg, and in 1885 became professor at Leipzig. He had done important work, particularly on the lactic acids, and had edited a handbook of chemistry (1874–77).

WISTER, Owen (1860–1938), American author, born in Philadelphia, took a music degree at Harvard and intended to be a composer but won fame with his novel of cowboy life in Wyoming, *The Virginian* (1902). He wrote several less successful stories and a life of Theodore Roosevelt (1930).

WITHER, George (1588–1667), English poet, born at Bentworth, Hampshire, studied at Magdalen, Oxford (1604–06), and entered Lincoln's Inn in 1615. For his *Abuses Stript and Whipt* (1613) he was imprisoned. It is supposed that his satire addressed to the king (1614), together with the Earl of Pembroke's intercession, procured his release. In 1618 appeared *The Motto*, a curious piece of self-confession. His finest poem, *Fair Virtue, or the Mistress of Philarete* (1622), though often uneven, shows exquisite fancy. There followed his *Hymns and Songs of the Church* (1623), *Psalms of David translated* (1631), *Emblems* (1634), and *Hallelujah* (1641). Now a fiery Puritan, in 1642 he sold his estate to raise a troop of horse for parliament, but was taken prisoner. Later Cromwell made him major-general in Surrey and Master of the Statute Office. At the Restoration he lost his position and property, and, on suspicion of having written the *Vox Vulgi*, a satire on the parliament of 1661, was imprisoned. He was released in 1663. His poetry fell into almost complete oblivion, but the praises of Southey, Sir Egerton Brydges, Hallam, and especially Charles Lamb revived interest in his work. His *Juvenilia* (1622) were reprinted by the Spenser Society (1870–72). See Massingham, *Seventeenth Century English Verse* (1919).

WITHERING, William (1741–99), English physician, born at Wellington in Shropshire and educated at Edinburgh, wrote a *British Flora* and *An Account of the Foxglove* (1785), introducing digitalis as a drug for cardiac disease. He was the first to see the connection between dropsy and heart disease.

WITHERSPOON, John (1723–94), Scottish theologian, born at Yester near Haddington, was minister at Beith and Paisley, and in 1768 emigrated to America and became president of the college and pastor at Princeton. He was a representative of New Jersey to the Continental Congress, and was one of the signatories to the Declaration of Independ-

ence. His writings include *Ecclesiastic Characteristics* (1753), against the Moderates; *Serious Enquiry into the Nature and Effects of the Stage* (1757); and two on *Justification* (1756) and *Regeneration* (1764).

WITSIUS, Hermann (1636–1708), Dutch Calvinist theologian, became in 1675 a professor at Franeker, in 1680 at Utrecht, and in 1698 at Leyden. His great work is *De Oeconomia Foederum Dei cum hominibus* (trans. 1763). Other writings translated are *Antinomians and Neonomians* (1807), *The Creed* (1823), and *The Lord's Prayer* (1839).

WITT, De. See DE WITT, GUIZOT.

WITTGENSTEIN, Ludwig Josef Johann, *vit'gen-shtīn* (1889–1951), Austrian philosopher, was born April 26 in Vienna, the son of a wealthy Jewish engineer, and was baptized a Roman Catholic. Educated privately until fourteen, he studied engineering at Berlin and Manchester (1908–11), where he designed a jet reaction propeller, became seriously interested in mathematics and finally mathematical logic, which he studied, on Frege's advice, under Russell at Cambridge (1912–13). Moore and Russell soon regarded Wittgenstein as a friend and colleague rather than as a student. Wittgenstein extended Russell's doctrines into a full-blown scheme for a logically perfect language, a perfect instrument for assertion and foolproof against philosophical nonsense. Inheriting considerable wealth, he gave it away to support the poets Trakl and Rilke. He served as an Austrian artillery officer during World War I, was captured by the Italians and ended the war in a P.O.W. camp near Monte Cassino, where he completed the *Tractatus Logico-philosophicus* (1921, Leipzig) which was published as a parallel English-German text (1922, London) with a masterly introduction by Russell, of which, however, Wittgenstein strongly disapproved. According to the *Tractatus*, all significant assertion can be analysed into compound propositions containing logical constants and are ' truth functions ' of ' elementary propositions ' which do not. An ' elementary proposition ' (one kind of fact) symbolizes a real or ' atomic fact ' or possibility (*Sachverhalt*). But how can one kind of fact symbolize another, how does language symbolize the world? Wittgenstein's fundamental thesis is that this correspondence can only be shown or ' pictured ' in language, but not stated, for this would require an extra-linguistic medium for expression and extra-worldly medium for expression and ' whereof one cannot speak, thereof one must be silent '. All speculative philosophy, ethics and aesthetics as well as the *Tractatus* (in showing this fallacy by the use of language) attempt to utter the unspeakable. The last, a merely elucidatory aid to seeing the world rightly, must also be discarded. Philosophy becomes merely a corrective activity. Wittgenstein, true to his doctrines, gave up philosophy, became an elementary village schoolmaster in Austria (1920–26), served for a time as a monastery gardener's assistant, designed on the functional lines of Loos a mansion for his sister (1926–28), turned to sculpture and was only reluctantly induced to return to philosophy at Cambridge by his English friends, having for some time corresponded with the ' Vienna Circle ' of logical positivists. He was a fellow of Trinity College, Cambridge (1930–36), and professor (1939–47), interrupting his duties to become a wartime porter in Guy's Hospital and in a laboratory at Newcastle. *The Blue and Brown Books* (posthumously, 1958) are notes taken by his pupils (1933–35) and form the beginnings of the *Philosophical Investigations* (posthumously, English-German parallel text, 1953), an album of arguments compiled in a solitary hut on the Galway coast in Ireland in 1948. These repudiate some of the characteristic *Tractatus* doctrines, particularly the reduction of ordinary language to a logically perfect instrument of assertion. By means of ' language games ', he examined the varieties of linguistic usage of certain philosophically important expressions, as a means of curing philosophically perplexity. He found that the varieties of linguistic usages of a word in many cases pointed to a ' family resemblance ' between them rather than to one single essential meaning. Philosophy was for him still a therapeutic activity, even if the methods had changed. He became a naturalized British subject in 1938. His austere mode of living, his distaste for any form of pretence, made him an exacting companion, even for his friends. In the first half of the 20th century he was the dominating philosophical figure of the English-speaking world. He died of cancer in Cambridge, April 29, 1951. See also *Philosophical Remarks on the Foundations of Mathematics* (1956), memoir by N. Malcolm and G. H. von Wright (1958), studies on the *Tractatus* by E. Stenius (1959) and G. E. M. Anscombe (1959), the later philosophy by D. Pole (1958) and polemically critical works by G. R. G. Mure, *Retreat from Truth* (1958), and E. Gellner, *Words and Things* (1959).

WODEHOUSE, Pelham Grenville (1881–), novelist, English by birth, since 1955 an American citizen, started work in a London bank but gave this up in favour of free-lancing. To begin with he wrote school stories, in one of which the popular Psmith made his first appearance (see the later *Psmith in the City, Leave it to Psmith*, &c.). In 1918 the novel *Piccadilly Jim* was a great success, and Wodehouse was established as a humorous writer. With the creation of Bertie Wooster and his ' gentleman's gentleman ' Jeeves (*The Inimitable Jeeves*, 1924, &c.), his position was assured as the greatest humorous novelist of his time. A prolific writer, he produced a succession of sparkling novels, short stories, sketches and librettos (with Guy Bolton he collaborated in many musical comedies). In 1939 he was living in France, where he was overtaken by the Germans. During the war years he incurred criticism for his Nazi-controlled broadcasts. Subsequently he has lived in the U.S.A., of which he is now a citizen. See the autobiographical *Performing Flea* (1953) and *Over Seventy* (1957). See study by R. Usborne (1961).

WODROW, Robert (1679–1734), Scottish church historian, born at Glasgow, studied theology under his father, who was professor of Divinity there; in 1703 he became minister of Eastwood. His *History of the Sufferings of the Church of Scotland 1660–88* (1721–22) was dedicated to George I. Posthumous works include *Lives of the Scottish Reformers* (1834–45), *Analecta, or a History of Remarkable Providences* (1842–43), &c.

WOFFINGTON, Margaret (' Peg ') (1720–1760), Irish actress, was a Dublin bricklayer's daughter. From seventeen to twenty she played on the Dublin stage, and in 1740 appeared at Covent Garden as Sylvia in *The Recruiting Officer*. Her beauty and vivacity carried all hearts by storm. David Garrick was one of her admirers. On May 3, 1757, she broke down, and left the stage never to return. Her last days were given to charity and good works. See Lives by Daly (1888) and Molloy (1884), and the novel *Peg Woffington* by Charles Reade (1853).

WÖHLER, Friedrich, *væl'ėr* (1800–82), German chemist, born near Frankfurt, educated at Heidelberg, became professor at Göttingen in 1836. He isolated aluminium (1827) and beryllium (1828), and discovered calcium carbide, from which he obtained acetylene. His synthesis of urea from ammonium cyanate in 1828 revolutionized organic chemistry.

WOHLGEMUTH. See WOLGEMUT.

WOLCOT, John, pseud. **Peter Pindar** (1738–1819), English satirist, born at Dodbrooke, Devon, studied medicine for seven years, took his M.D. at Aberdeen (1767), and, going to Jamaica, became physician-general of the island. He returned to England to take orders, but soon started medical practice at Truro. Here he discovered the talents of young Opie, and with him in 1780 removed to London, to devote himself to writing audacious squibs and satires in verse. His sixty or seventy poetical pamphlets (1778–1818) include *The Lousiad, The Apple-dumplings and a King, Whitbread's Brewery visited by their Majesties, Bozzy and Piozzi*, and *Lyrical Odes* on the Royal Academy Exhibitions. Although witty and fluent, his works were coarse and ephemeral. See *Blackwood's Magazine* for July 1868, and H. Walker, *English Satire and Satirists* (1925).

WOLF, (1) Friedrich August (1759–1824), German classical scholar, born at Hagewrode, went to Göttingen in 1777. In 1779, while teacher at Ilfeld, he established his fame by an edition of Plato's *Symposium*, and in 1783 he became professor at Halle. He edited Demosthenes' *Oratio adversus Leptinem* (1789), and in his *Prolegomena ad Homerum* (1795) he unfolded his bold theory that the *Odyssey* and *Iliad* are composed of ballads by different minstrels, strung together by later editors—a view defended in his spirited *Briefe an Heyne* (1797). In 1801 Wolf cast doubts upon the genuineness of some orations of Cicero. After 1806 he became a member of the Academy of Sciences at Berlin, helped to re-organize the university, and became a professor. The *Darstellung der Alterthumswissenschaft* (1807) is his most finished work. See Mark Pattison's *Essays* (i 1889), and Sandys's *Classical Scholarship* (iii 1908).

(2) **Hugo** (1860–1903), Austrian composer, chiefly of songs, born at Windischgraz in Styria, was destined for the family leather business, but early turned to music. For a time he studied without satisfaction at the Vienna Conservatoire, then earned a meagre living by teaching and conducting. From 1884 to 1888 he was music critic of the *Wiener Salonblatt*, violently attacking Brahms and extolling Wagner. All this time he was composing, but his best work came from 1888 onwards. It includes the Mörike set of 53 songs (1888), settings of poems by Goethe (1888–89), the *Italienisches Leiderbuch* of Heyse and Geibel (1889–90), and three sonnets of Michelangelo (1897). He also wrote an opera, *Der Corregidor* (1895), and other works. He was at his best in his treatment of short lyrical poems, to many of which he gave new significance by means of the sensitive commentary of his settings. For the most part he lived in poverty. In 1897 he became insane. After a brief period of recovery he was confined from 1898 onwards in the asylum at Steinhof near Vienna, where he died. See books by Decsey (1919), Newman (1907) and F. Walker (1951).

(3) or **Wolff, Johann Christian von** (1679–1754), German philosopher, born at Breslau, studied at Jena, lectured at Leipzig, and became professor at Halle. His system of philosophy quickly spread; but attacked by pietistic colleagues and ordered in 1723 to quit Prussia, he got a chair at Marburg. Frederick the Great recalled him (1740) to be professor of the Law of Nations, and he became in 1743 chancellor of the university, and was made Baron of the Empire by the Elector of Bavaria. Wolf systematized and popularized the philosophy of Leibniz. His *Theologia Naturalis* (1737) gave a great impulse to rationalism. See his Autobiography, ed. Wuttke (1841), and German works by Frauendienst (1927) and Joesten (1931).

(4) **Maximilian Franz Joseph Cornelius** (1863–1932), German astronomer, educated at Heidelberg, where he was born, and Stockholm, became professor of Astronomy at Heidelberg (1896) and director of the Königstuhl astrophysical observatory there. He invented the photographic method of discovering asteroids, and with Barnard was the first to appreciate ' dark ' nebulae in the sky.

WOLFE, (1) **Charles** (1791–1823), Irish poet, born at Dublin, went to Winchester, and in 1814 took his B.A. at Dublin. He is remembered for his poem *The Burial of Sir John Moore*, which appeared anonymously in 1817 and at once caught the admiration of the public. Wolfe in 1817 became curate of Ballyclog in Tyrone, and then rector of Donoughmore. His *Remains* were published in 1825 by Russell, and his poems by Litton Falkiner in 1903 (each with a memoir).

(2) **Humbert** (1885–1940), English poet and critic, born in Milan, was educated at Bradford and at Wadham College, Oxford. In 1908 he entered the Civil Service, becoming in 1938 deputy secretary to the Ministry of Labour. He was created C.B.E. in 1918 and C.B. in 1925. He published *London Sonnets* (1919), *Lampoons* (1925), *Requiem* (1927), and several other collections of verse, all marked by deep feeling and meticulous craftsmanship. His critical writings include *Notes on English Verse Satire* (1929) and studies of Tennyson, Herrick, Shelley and George Moore. See his autobiographical *Now A Stranger* (1933) and *The Upward Anguish* (1938).

(3) **James** (1727–59), British soldier, was born at Westerham vicarage, Kent, the eldest son of General Edward Wolfe (1685–1759). In 1742 he received an ensign's commission, in 1743 fought at Dettingen, in 1745–46 served against the Scottish Jacobites at Falkirk and Culloden, and in 1747 was wounded at Lawfeldt. In 1749–57 he was engaged in garrison duty in Scotland and England. In the mismanaged expedition against Rochefort (1757) he was quartermaster-general; in 1758, with the rank of colonel, he received from Pitt the command of a brigade in the expedition against Cape Breton under General Amherst; and to him was mainly due the capture of Louisburg. Pitt was now organizing his grand scheme for expelling the French from Canada, and the expedition for the capture of Quebec he entrusted to Wolfe's command. As major-general, and commanding 9000 men, Wolfe sailed from England in February 1759, and on June 26 landed below Quebec. The attack on Montcalm's strong position proved one of stupendous difficulty, and Wolfe was completely foiled. But at last, scaling the cliffs at a point insufficiently guarded, at dawn on September 13 he found himself on the Plains of Abraham. After a short struggle the French were routed; Montcalm (q.v.) was killed; Quebec capitulated; and its fall decided the fate of Canada. Wolfe died in the hour of victory. His body was buried in Greenwich church. See *Lives* by Wright (1864), Bradley (1895), Willson (1909), Waugh (1929), Grinell-Milne (1963), and studies by Parkman (1884), Findlay (1928).

(4) **Thomas Clayton** (1900–38), American novelist, born at Asheville, N.C., studied in the ' 47 workshop ' at Harvard. His *Look Homeward, Angel* (1929) and *Of Time and the River* (1935), first of a projected series of six related novels, enjoyed a great success. *The Web and the Rock* (1939) and *You Can't Go Home Again* (1941) were brought out after his early death from pneumonia. See study by P. H. Johnson (1947).

WOLFENDEN, Sir John Frederick (1906–), British governmental adviser on social questions, born at Halifax, was fellow and tutor in Philosophy at Magdalen College, Oxford (1929–34), headmaster of Uppingham School (1934–44) and Shrewsbury (1944–50), and vice-chancellor of Reading University from 1950. He is best known as the chairman of the Royal Commission on homosexuality and prostitution, the report of which (1957) is known by his name. He was also chairman of another royal commission (1960) on sport.

WOLFF, (1) **G. W.** See HARLAND.

(2) **Sir Henry Drummond** (1830–1908), son of (3), English diplomat, was educated at Rugby, and after holding several Foreign Office appointments, entered parliament in 1874, becoming one of the ' Fourth Party '. In 1892 he was made ambassador to Spain.

(3) Joseph (1795–1862), father of (2), a German Jew who turned Roman Catholic in 1812, but came to England and entered the Anglican Church in 1819, becoming a missionary to the Jews in the East. His adventurous journey to Bokhara (1843), to inquire into the fate of Conolly and Stoddart, is described in *Mission to Bokhara* (1845) and *Travels and Adventures* (1860). He died vicar of Ile-Brewers, Somerset.

(4) Kaspar Friedrich (1733–94), German anatomist and physiologist, founder of embryology, was born at Berlin, was a surgeon in the Seven Years' War, and died a member of the Academy at St Petersburg.

WOLF-FERRARI, Ermanno, *volf-fer-ahr'ee* (1876–1948), Italo-German composer, born in Venice. Sent to Rome to study painting, he turned to music and became a pupil of Rheinberger, in Munich. In 1899 he returned to Venice, where his first opera was unsuccessfully produced in the following year. His later operas were equally successful in both Italy and Germany. From 1902 to 1912 he was director of the Liceo Benedetto Marcello, in Venice. Wolf-Ferrari composed choral and chamber works, and music for organ and piano as well as the operas, notably *Susanna's Secret* (1909), *The Jewels of the Madonna* (1911) and *School for Fathers* (1906).

WOLFIT, Sir Donald (1902–68), English actor-manager, born in Newark-on-Trent. He began his stage career in 1920, and made his first London appearance in 1924 in *The Wandering Jew*. With his own company, formed in 1937, he played Shakespeare in the provinces, and during World War II he instituted the first London season of ' lunchtime Shakespeare ' during the Battle of Britain. Known especially for his portrayal of Shakespearean heroes and of Jonson's Volpone, he was created C.B.E. in 1950 and knighted in 1957. He also appeared in several films and on television. His autobiography, *First Interval*, appeared in 1954.

WOLFRAM VON ESCHENBACH (fl. beginning of 13th cent.), German poet, born near Anspach in Bavaria, lived some time in the Wartburg near Eisenach, at the court of the Count of Thuringia, where he met Walther von der Vogelweide. Besides *Parzival* he left seven *Love Songs*, a short epic, *Willehalm*, and two fragments called *Titurel*. The *Parzival* is an epic, having for its main theme the history of the Grail, and is one of the most notable poems of the Middle Ages. From it Wagner derived the libretto of his *Parsifal*. See study by Richey (1958).

WOLGEMUT, Michael, *võl'ge-moot* (1435–1519), German painter and engraver, born at Nuremberg, the son of Valentin Wolgemut, also an engraver, was the master of Albrecht Dürer (q.v.), who did a portrait of him. His altarpieces show some Flemish influence. See study by Stadler (1913).

WOLLASTON, *wool'-*, **(1) William** (1659–1724), English philosophical writer, author of the *Religion of Nature*, born at Coton near Stafford, studied at Sidney Sussex, Cambridge, took orders in 1681, and in 1682 became assistant master at Birmingham, but in 1688 inherited an ample estate. His one notable work was printed in 1722 for private circula-

tion, but soon reached an issue of over 10,000 copies. See Life prefixed to 6th ed. (1738).

(2) William Hyde (1766–1828), English chemist and natural philosopher, was born at East Dereham, Norfolk, the second son of the Rev. Francis Wollaston (1731–1815), who was the grandson of (1), rector of Chiselhurst, and an astronomer. He went to Caius College, Cambridge, took his M.D. in 1793, and gained a fellowship. Starting practice as a physician at Bury St Edmunds in 1789, he soon removed to London; but being beaten in a competition for the post of physician to St George's Hospital in 1800, he vowed to devote himself to scientific research. His researches were extremely fruitful both in chemistry and in optics. He discovered new compounds connected with the production of gouty and urinary concretions; and in the ore of platinum distinguished two new metals, palladium (1804) and rhodium (1805). By his method of rendering platinum ductile he made £30,000; and other practical discoveries were also highly lucrative. Among his contributions to optics were the reflecting goniometer, the camera lucida, the discovery of the dark lines in the solar spectrum and of the invisible rays beyond the violet. He did much to establish the theory of definite proportions, and demonstrated the identity of galvanism and electricity. He was elected F.R.S. (1793), its second secretary (1806), and F.R.A.S. (1828). See his thirty-nine memoirs in the *Philosophical Trans.* for 1809–29, and George Wilson's *Religio Chemici* (1862).

WOLLSTONECRAFT, Mary. See GODWIN.

WOLSELEY, Garnet Joseph, Viscount, *woolz'li* (1833–1913), British soldier, was born of an old Staffordshire line at Golden Bridge House, County Dublin, June 4, and entered the army in 1852. He served in the Burmese war of 1852–53, and was dangerously wounded; in the Crimea he lost the use of one eye, and received the cross of the *Légion d'honneur*. He was in India during the Mutiny, and in the Chinese war of 1860. Next year he went to Canada, and in 1870 put down the Red River rebellion under Riel without losing a man. On the outbreak of the Ashanti war Wolseley, now K.C.M.G., was appointed to the command, and on his return received the thanks of parliament and a grant of £25,000. In 1875, now a major-general, he was dispatched to Natal; in 1876 he was nominated a member of the Indian Council. In 1878 he was made high commissioner in Cyprus, and in 1879 held supreme civil and military command in Natal and the Transvaal. He was commander-in-chief of the expedition to Egypt in 1882, received the thanks of parliament, was gazetted Baron Wolseley of Cairo and of Wolseley in Stafford and received a large money grant. He was made general in the same year, viscount after the Sudan campaigns of 1884–85, and field-marshal in 1894. In 1890–95 he was commander-in-chief in Ireland, and in 1895–1900 commander-in-chief of the entire army. Besides his *Story of a Soldier's Life* (1903–04), he wrote *Narrative of the War with China in 1860* (1862), the *Soldier's Pocket Book*, *Field Manœuvres* (1872), a novel (*Marley Castle*, 1877), a Life of Marlborough (2 vols. 1894),

The Decline and Fall of Napoleon (1895), and several essays. See his *Story of a Soldier's Life* (1903) and the Lives by Maurice and Arthur (1934) and J. H. Lehmann (1964).

WOLSEY, Thomas (*c.* 1475–1530), English cardinal, was born at Ipswich, the son of a prosperous butcher and grazier. He took early and fruitful advantage of the educational facilities offered by Magdalen College, Oxford, succeeding to a fellowship and obtaining a post as master in the seminary attached to the foundation. After nineteen years at Oxford, the powerful Dorset interest secured him the living at Lymington in Somerset. Influence also brought him the post of secretary and domestic chaplain to the Archbishop of Canterbury. With the primate's death in 1502 Wolsey was endowed with the chaplaincy of Calais, where the ability with which he discharged his duties brought him to the notice of Henry VII. Appointed a chaplain to the king (1507), he was careful to cultivate the favour of Bishop Fox, the lord privy seal, and that of the treasurer of the royal household, Sir Thomas Lovel. Entrusted with the transaction of much of the sovereign's private business, the skill in negotiation he exhibited in his embassies to Scotland and the Low Countries brought him the lucrative deanery of Lincoln. With the accession of Henry VIII, Wolsey sedulously strove to render himself indispensable. From almoner to royal councillor, from the registrarship of the Order of the Garter to a Windsor canonry, his progress to the deanery of York was steady and encouraging for a pluralist whose growing need for money was only matched by his increasing arrogance. In 1513 Wolsey accompanied the king to the seat of war in France; and with the English monarch ready to come to terms with Francis I, Wolsey's conduct of the negotiations brought him the bishopric of Lincoln, the archbishopric of York (1514) and a cardinate (1515), and the promise of Gallic support for further claims to preferment. In the same year, he was made lord chancellor and his very considerable estates were augmented by Henry's award of the administration of the see of Bath and Wells and the temporalities of the wealthy abbey of St Alban's. Wolsey even hazarded a breach of the Statute of Praemunire by accepting the appointment of papal legate from Leo X. Deep in the King's confidence, the Cardinal had attained a position more powerful than that enjoyed by any minister of the Crown since Becket. As the controller of England's foreign policy he lent support to France and Germany alternately, serving his own interests, but also seeking a powerful position for England in Europe. His aim in England was absolute monarchy with himself behind the throne. He established Cardinal (Christ Church) College at Oxford and a grammar school at Ipswich. Wolsey's downfall originated in his prevarication and evasiveness over the question of Henry's divorce from Catherine of Aragon. This not only provoked the king's angry impatience but aroused the bitter enmity of the Boleyn faction and of many other enemies, outraged by the Cardinal's haughtiness, his parvenu display, and his punishing fiscal exactions. In effect, Wolsey's outmoded assertion of the ecclesiastical right to dominate secular policy had proved entirely unacceptable to the upstart but powerful aristocracy of the counting-house bred by the new spirit of mercantilism. Prosecuted under the Statute of Praemunire in 1529, the Cardinal had to surrender the Great Seal and retire to Winchester. Impeachment by the House of Lords was followed by the forfeiture of all his property to the Crown. Arrested again on a charge of high treason, he died—on November 29, 1530—while journeying from his York diocese to London. See works by Brewer (1884), Froude (1891), Innes (1905), Pollard (1929), Belloc (1930), C. Ferguson, *Naked to Mine Enemies* (1958), and the earliest Life of Wolsey, by George Cavendish, his gentleman usher. ed. R. S. Sylvester (1959)

WOLVERHAMPTON, Henry Hartley Fowler, 1st Viscount (1830–1911), English Liberal politician, born at Sunderland, mayor of Wolverhampton 1863, its M.P. 1880, was under-secretary in the Home Office (1884), financial secretary to the Treasury (1886), president of the Local Government Board (1892), secretary for India (1894), and chancellor of the Duchy of Lancaster (1895), and lord president of the Council (1908–10). He was created viscount in 1908.

WOMBWELL, George (1788–1850), a London bootmaker, became a noted menagerie proprietor.

WOOD, (1) Sir Andrew (*c.* 1455–1539), Scottish naval commander, belonged to Largo and was associated with James IV in his efforts to build up a Scottish navy. He was specially successful against English vessels raiding in the Firth of Forth.

(2) or **A Wood, Anthony** (1632–95), English antiquary, born at Oxford, studied at Merton College 1647–52, and being of independent means, devoted himself to heraldry and antiquarian studies. The delegates of the university press had translated his History of Oxford into Latin as *Historia et Antiquitates Universitatis Oxoniensis* (1674). Wood was ill-satisfied with the translation, and made a new copy of his English MS., which was not published until 1786–96. His great *Athenae Oxonienses; an Exact history of all the Writers and Bishops who had their Education in Oxford from 1500 to 1690, to which are added the Fasti or Annals for the said time* was published in 1691–92. Other works were *The Ancient and Present State of the City of Oxford* (1773) and the ill-natured *Modius Salium, a Collection of Pieces of Humour* (1751). A third volume of the *Athenae* is included in the second edition (1721). The *Autobiography* (1848) is included in *The Life and Times of Wood* (Oxford Hist. Soc., 5 vols., 1891–1900), ed. by Andrew Clark, and abridged by L. Powys (1932).

(3) **Sir Charles.** See HALIFAX (2).

(4) **Christopher** (1901–30), English artist, born at Knowsley. Between 1920 and 1924 he wandered over most of Europe, and painted in various styles, but it was in his landscapes of Cornwall and Brittany that

he found himself as an artist. They are simple and apparently childlike in conception, but they show a fine sensitivity to colour, light, and atmosphere. See monograph by Eric Newton (1959).

(5) **Edward Frederick Lindley.** See HALIFAX (3).

(6) **Haydn** (1882–1959), English composer and violinist, was born in Slaithwaite, Yorkshire. He studied at the Royal College of Music and was selected to play at the opening of the College's Concert Hall. He worked for a time in music halls with his wife, Dorothy Court, for whom he wrote a large number of ballads, but withdrew from these activities as his serious compositions attracted attention after his Fantasy String Quartet won the second prize in the first Cobbett Chamber Music Competition. Wood composed very prolifically for orchestra, brass band, chamber music groups and voices. Of his ballads, the best known is ' Roses of Picardy '.

(7) **Mrs Henry,** *née* **Ellen Price** (1814–87), English novelist, born at Worcester, married Henry Wood, a ship agent living in France, and after his death settled in London, and wrote for magazines. *East Lynne* (1861) had an almost unexampled success. She never rose above the commonplace in her many novels, but showed some power in the analysis of character in her anonymous *Johnny Ludlow* stories (1874–80). In 1867 she acquired the monthly *Argosy*, and her novels went on appearing in it long after her death. See *Memorials* of her by her son (1895).

(8) **Sir Henry Evelyn** (1838–1919), British soldier, born at Cressing vicarage, Braintree, entered the navy in 1852, and served in the Crimea in the Naval Brigade. As cavalry officer and brigade-major he fought in the Indian Mutiny, receiving the Victoria Cross and the thanks of the Indian government. As lieutenant-colonel he was with Wolseley during the Ashanti war. He was called to the bar in 1874, but commanded a column through the Zulu war. Created K.C.B. in 1879, he had a share in the Transvaal war (1880–81). As G.C.M.G. he received the thanks of parliament for his services in Egypt in 1882, and in the same year became commander-in-chief of the Egyptian army. From 1886 onwards he held home appointments. In 1897 he was made adjutant-general of the army, in 1903 field-marshal. He wrote *The Crimea in 1854–94*, on Cavalry, *From Midshipman to Field-marshal* (1906), and *Winnowed Memories* (1917).

(9) **Sir Henry Joseph** (1869–1944), English conductor, born in London, with Robert Newman founded the Promenade Concerts which he conducted annually from 1895 until his death. As ' Paul Klenovsky ' he arranged Bach's Organ Toccata and Fugue in D minor as an orchestral work. He composed operettas and an oratorio, *Saint Dorothea* (1889), but his international reputation was gained as conductor of the Queen's Hall symphony and promenade concerts. He was knighted in 1911. See *My Life of Music* (1938), and book by J. Wood (1954).

(10) **John** (*c.* 1705–54), English architect, ' of Bath ', was responsible for many of the best-known streets and buildings of Bath, such as the North and South Parades, Prior Park and other houses. His son **John** (d.1782) designed the Crescent, the Assembly Rooms, &c.

(11) **Sir Kingsley** (1881–1943), English statesman, born in London, was trained as a solicitor, entered parliament in 1918 as Conservative member for Woolwich West, was knighted in 1919, and after holding several junior ministerial offices became postmaster-general (1931–35), minister of health (1935–38), secretary of state for air (1938–40), and chancellor of the exchequer (1940–43), in which capacity he devised the pay-as-you-earn income-tax system.

(12) **Robert Williams** (1868–1955), American physicist, born at Concord, Mass., educated at Harvard, Chicago and Berlin, was professor of Experimental Physics at the Johns Hopkins University (1901–38). He carried out researches on optics, atomic and molecular radiation, sound waves, &c.; wrote *Physical Optics* (1905), some fiction, and illustrated nonsense verse, *How to Tell the Birds from the Flowers* (1907).

(13) **William** (1671–1744), a London ironfounder, to whom was granted a share of the profits from coining ' Wood's Halfpence ' for Ireland. Swift's *Drapier's Letters* (1724) denounced the job with such effect that the patent was cancelled and Wood was compensated with a pension.

WOODFALL, Henry Sampson (1739–1805), English printer and journalist, published the anonymous letters of ' Junius ' in the *Public Advertiser* (1769–72) and in book form (1772 and later editions). Associated with him were his brother, **William** (1746–1803), and his son and successor, **George** (1767–1844).

WOODS, Margaret Louisa (1856–1945), English writer, daughter of Dr Bradley, dean of Westminster, was born at Rugby, and in 1879 was married to the Rev. Henry George Woods, from 1887 till his resignation in 1897 president of Trinity College, Oxford. She published novels such as *A Village Tragedy* (1887), *The Invader* (1907, rev. 1922), *A Poet's Youth* (1924), and verse such as *Lyrics and Ballads* (1889), *Collected Poems* (1913).

WOODVILLE, (1) **Elizabeth** (*c.* 1437–92), eldest of the thirteen children of Sir Richard Woodville (afterwards Lord and Earl Rivers) and the Dowager Duchess of Bedford, married first Sir John Grey, who fell at St Albans (1461), and next, in 1464, Edward IV. She died in the abbey of Bermondsey. Her eldest daughter, **Elizabeth** (1465–1503), in 1486 married Henry VII.

(2) **Richard.** See RIVERS.

WOODWARD, (1) **Sir Arthur Smith** (1864–1944), British geologist, born at Macclesfield, was keeper of geology at the British Museum (1901–24) when he was knighted. He did notable work on fossil fishes, but is chiefly remembered for his part in the controversy over the Piltdown Man. He was the one to whom Charles Dawson (q.v.) gave the skull for identification, and his firm conviction that the remains were human was a main reason for the success of the hoax. See his *Outlines of Vertebrate Palaeontology* (1898).

(2) **Robert Burns** (1917–), U.S. chemist,

born at Boston, Mass., professor of Science at Harvard University since 1950 and director of the Woodward Research Institute at Basel since 1963. He was awarded the Nobel prize for chemistry in 1965 for work on organic synthesis, including his synthesis of chlorophyll in 1961.

WOOLF, (1) **Leonard Sidney** (1880–1969), English publicist, born in London, educated at St Paul's and Cambridge, was in the Ceylon Civil Service (1904–11), and his early writings, *The Village and the Jungle* (1913), &c., have Ceylon as a background. In 1912 he married Virginia Stephen (see below). In 1916 he joined the Fabian Society and in 1917 along with his wife he founded the Hogarth Press. His works include *Socialism and Co-operation* (1921), *After the Deluge* (1931, 1939) and *Principia Politica* (1953). See his autobiography in 4 vols. (1960–67).

(2) **Virginia** (1882–1941), English novelist, born in London, daughter of Sir Leslie Stephen, married (1) in 1912, and from 1915 published novels (*The Voyage Out*, *Mrs Dalloway*, *To the Lighthouse*, *Orlando*, *The Waves*, &c.) and essays (*A Room of One's Own*, *The Common Reader*, &c.). Her style is evasive and impressionistic, a development of the stream-of-consciousness technique, which, allied to psychological penetration, gives her prose a quality more usually found in poetry. Under the strain of World War II she ended her life by drowning. *A Writer's Diary* (1953) contains extracts from her journal, and two vols. of her *Collected Essays* (ed. by (1)) appeared in 1966. See studies by Holtby (1932), Forster (1942), Daiches (1945), Chambers (1948) and Bibliography (1957) by Kirkpatrick.

WOOLLETT, William (1735–85), English line-engraver, born at Maidstone, was one of the greatest of his kind. His first important plate, from Richard Wilson's *Niobe*, was published by Boydell in 1761. In 1775 he was appointed engraver to George III. See L. Fagan's *Catalogue Raisonné* of his 123 engraved works (1885).

WOOLLEY, Sir (Charles) Leonard (1880–1960), English archaeologist, born in London, was educated at St John's School, Leatherhead, and New College, Oxford. He was assistant keeper of the Ashmolean Museum, Oxford, from 1905 to 1907. He carried out excavations at Carchemish (1912–14) and in Sinai, and directed the important excavations (1922–34) at Ur in Mesopotamia, which included the royal cemetery discoveries. He was knighted in 1935, and from 1943 to 1946 was archaeological adviser to the War Office. His publications include *Digging up the Past* (1930), *Ur Excavations* (1934), works on Carchemish, and *Alalakh* (1955).

WOOLMAN, John (1720–72), American Quaker preacher, was born at Northampton, N.J., a farmer's son, and was for some time a tailor. He spoke and wrote against slavery, and published several religious works. His *Journal* (1774, often reprinted) was a favourite book with Lamb. He died at York on a visit to England. See Life by Shore (1913), and study by J. Whitney (1943).

WOOLNER, Thomas (1826–92), English poet-sculptor, was born at Hadleigh, and studied at the Royal Academy from 1842. In 1843 his first major work, *Eleanor sucking the Poison from Prince Edward's Wound*, attracted much attention. As a conspicuous member of the pre-Raphaelite Brotherhood (see ROSSETTI) he contributed poems to *The Germ*, which with others were published in a volume as *My Beautiful Lady* (1863). In 1852–54 he was in Australia. He executed statues or portrait busts of most of his famous contemporaries (his bust of Tennyson is in Westminster Abbey). Made A.R.A. in 1871 and R.A. in 1874, he was professor of Sculpture to the Academy 1877–79. See Life by his daughter, Amy Woolner (1917).

WOOLSEY, (1) **Sarah Chauncey**. See COOLIDGE, SUSAN.

(2) **Theodore Dwight** (1801–89), American scholar, born at New York, was professor of Greek at Yale 1831–46, and then its president till 1871. He was president of the American New Testament revisers. Besides editions of Greek plays, &c., he wrote an *Introduction to International Law* (1860), *Divorce Legislation* (1869) and *Political Science* (1877).

WOOLSTON, Thomas (1670–1731), English Deist, born at Northampton, became a fellow of Sidney Sussex, Cambridge, and took orders. In 1705 he published the *Old Apology for the Truth of the Christian Religion Revived*, affirming that the Old Testament was allegorical only. In 1721 his college deprived him of his fellowship. He joined the Deist controversy with *The Moderator between an Infidel and an Apostate* (1725). In his famous six *Discourses on the Miracles of Our Saviour* (1727–29, with two *Defences*) he maintained that the gospel narratives, taken literally, were a tissue of absurdities. Sixty answers were made to the *Discourses*; and an indictment for blasphemy was brought against him. Fined and sent to prison, he died there. His works were collected in 1733 with a Life.

WOOLTON, Frederick James Marquis, 1st Baron (1883–1964), Conservative politician and businessman, was born in Liverpool. He attended Manchester Grammar School and Manchester University, and then taught mathematics at Burnley Grammar School. During a spell as warden of Liverpool University Settlement, in the dock area, he ran the David Lewis Club and this brought him to the attention of Lewis, the managing director of the Manchester store, who took him into the business. He rose rapidly in Lewis's, where he revolutionized the merchandising side, and became chairman in 1935. He was made a baron in 1939. At the beginning of the war, he went to the Ministry of Supply, but made his name at the Ministry of Food, where from 1940 he had the responsibility of seeing that the entire nation was well-nourished. In 1946 he became chairman of the Conservative party, and is credited with much of the success in rebuilding the party's organization which led it to victory in 1951. Woolton was lord president of the Council, but ill-health later led him to take on the less onerous office of chancellor of the Duchy of Lancaster. See his *Memoirs* (1959).

WOOLWORTH, Frank Winfield (1852–1919),

American merchant, was born in Rodman, Jefferson County, N.Y. He attended country schools, and was a farm worker until becoming a shop-assistant in 1873. His employers backed Woolworth's scheme to open in 1879 in Utica a store for five-cent goods only; this failed, but later the same year a second store, in Lancaster, Pennsylvania, selling also ten-cent goods, was successful. In partnership with his employers, his brother, and cousin, Woolworth began building a large chain of similar stores, and at the time of his death the F. W. Woolworth company controlled over a thousand stores from their headquarters in the Woolworth Building, N.Y., for a time the world's tallest building (792 feet). Woolworth's stores came to Britain in 1910, but their main development outside America was after the death of the founder.

WOOTTON, Barbara Frances, Baroness Wootton of Abinger (1897–), English social scientist, born at Cambridge, the daughter of a don, studied and lectured (1920–22) at Girton College in Economics. She was a research worker for the Labour Party (1922–25), principal of Morley College, London (1926–1927), director of studies (1927–44) and professor in Social Studies (1948–52) at London. A frequent royal commissioner and London magistrate, she is best known for her work, *Testament for Social Science* (1950), in which she attempted to assimilate social to the natural sciences. Another work was *Social Science and Pathology* (1959). She was created a life peeress in 1958.

WORCESTER, *woos'tėr,* **(1) Edward Somerset, Marquis of** (*c.* 1601–67), inventor of a steam engine, was probably born in London, About 1628 we find him engaged in mechanical pursuits with Caspar Kaltoff, his lifelong assistant. At the Rebellion he sided with the king, in 1642 was made General of South Wales, in 1644 was created Earl of Glamorgan, and in 1645 was sent to Ireland to raise troops for the king. His mission failed. Charles disowned him, and he was imprisoned for a short time. In 1646 he succeeded his father, and in 1648 went into exile in France. In 1652, venturing back to England, he was sent to the Tower, but in 1654 was let out on bail, and at the Restoration recovered a portion of his vast estates—he claimed to have disbursed £918,000 'for king and country'. His *Century of Inventions* (written 1655; printed 1663) gives a brief account of a hundred inventions—ciphers, signals, automata, mechanical appliances, &c. No. 68 deals with a steam apparatus which could raise a column of water 40 feet, and which seems to have been at work at Vauxhall (1663–70)—probably an improved form (with two chambers) of Della Porta's contrivance, forcing steam into a chamber containing water, with an opening below the water. See *Life* by Dircks prefixed to his reprint of the *Century* (1863).

(2) **Joseph Emerson** (1784–1865), American lexicographer, born at Bedford, N.H., taught at Salem, Mass., and then turned author. All his works were laborious—gazetteers, manuals of geography and history, &c. He edited Chalmers's abridgment of Todd's Johnson's Dictionary, with Walker's Pronouncing Dictionary (1828), abridged Webster (1829), and printed his own *English Dictionary* (1830; enlarged ed. 1855), *Critical Dictionary* (1846), and great quarto *Dictionary of the English Language* (1860).

(3) **Sir Thomas Percy, Earl of** (1344–1403), English soldier, son of Sir Henry, 3rd Baron Percy, fought in France, accompanied Chaucer on a diplomatic mission to Flanders in 1377, was made an admiral by Richard II and commanded in several expeditions, notably those of John of Gaunt to Spain (1386) and of the Earl of Arundel to La Rochelle (1388). He was created an earl in 1397. Having joined Northumberland's rebellion in 1403 he was captured at Shrewsbury and executed.

WORDE, Wynkyn de (d. 1535?), printer, born in Holland or in Alsace, was a pupil of Caxton, and in 1491 succeeded to his stock-in-trade. He made great improvements in printing and typecutting, printed many books, and was still living in 1535. See study by H. R. Plomer (1925).

WORDSWORTH, (1) Charles (1806–92), English Episcopal clergyman in Scotland, second son of (2), educated at Christ Church, Oxford, became a tutor, Manning and Gladstone being among his pupils. After being a master at Winchester he became the first Warden of Glenalmond School in Perthshire (1846) and thereafter Bishop of St Andrews, in which capacity he ardently sought the reunion of the churches. His *Annals of my Life* (1891–93) is curious reading on that and kindred topics of the day.

(2) **Christopher** (1774–1846), English clergyman, youngest brother of (7), was elected a fellow of Trinity College, Cambridge, in 1798 and after occupying various livings became master of Trinity (1820–21). His *Ecclesiastical Biography* (1809) is a good selection of lives, and his *Christian Institutes* (1836) of the writings of the great English divines. He engaged in the *Eikon Basilike* controversy without much success.

(3) **Christopher** (1807–85), youngest son of (2), had an unsuccessful career as headmaster of Harrow (1836–44), and became Bishop of Lincoln (1869). In 1851 he produced a memoir of his uncle the poet, to whom he was literary executor. His edition of the correspondence of Bentley is a sound work as also is his *Theocritus* (1884). See *Life* by his daughter **Elizabeth** (1840–1932), who became first principal of Lady Margaret Hall, Oxford (1868–1908).

(4) **Dorothy** (1771–1855), only sister of (7), was his companion through life, both before and after his marriage, and on tours to Scotland, the Isle of Man and abroad, the records of which are to be found in her *Journals*. The *Journals* show that Dorothy's keen observation and sensibility provided a good deal of poetical imagery for both her brother and his friend Coleridge—more than that, they regarded her as the embodiment of that joy in Nature which it was their object to depict. In 1829 she suffered a breakdown from which she never fully recovered. Her *Tour made in Scotland* (1874) is a classic. See also *Letters of William and Dorothy*

Wordsworth (ed. De Selincourt, 1935–39), and by De Selincourt (1933).

(5) **John** (1805–39), eldest son of (2), became a fellow of Trinity in 1830, took orders in 1837, and at his death was preparing an edition of Aeschylus and a classical dictionary.

(6) **John** (1843–1911), eldest son of (3), a graduate of New College, Oxford, proceeded in the family path through college preferment and various lectureships (Grinfield, 1876; Bampton, 1881) to the Oriel professorship of Interpretation of the Scriptures (1883) and the see of Salisbury (1885). His studies in the Latin biblical texts, particularly his critical edition of the Vulgate New Testament (1889 *et seq.*) form a landmark in scriptural scholarship.

(7) **William** (1770–1850), English poet, was born at Cockermouth, where his father was an attorney. Having lost both parents at an early age he was sent to Hawkshead in the Lake District for board and education. This, as we learn from *The Prelude*, was one of the formative periods of his life. His guardian sent him to Cambridge (1787–91), where he was troubled in mind by the agnostic and revolutionary ideas he had already picked up. A walking tour through France and Switzerland in his second long vacation (1790) showed him France *en fête* for the earlier stage of the Revolution before disillusionment had set in. Two immature poems belong to this period—*An Evening Walk* and *Descriptive Sketches*, both published in 1793. Leaving Cambridge without a profession, he stayed for a little over a year at Blois, and there, as Legouis and Harper first disclosed, had an affair with Annette Vallon, the result of which was an illegitimate daughter, Ann Caroline. The incident is reflected in *Vaudracour and Julia*. Pitt's declaration of war with France (January 1793) drove the poet back to England, but the depressing poem *Guilt and Sorrow*, which dates from this period, shows that he was not yet cured of his passion for social justice. For a time he fell under the spell of Godwin's philosophic anarchism, but the unreadable *Borderers* shows that by 1795 he was turning his back both on the Revolution and on Godwinism, and with the help of his sister Dorothy, with whom he set up house at Racedown in Dorset, and of Coleridge, who had renounced his revolutionary ardour somewhat earlier, he discovered his true vocation, that of the poet exploring the lives of humble folk living in contact with Divine Nature and untouched by the rebellious spirit of the times. When the Wordsworths settled at Alfoxden in Somerset with Coleridge three miles away at Nether Stowey (1797), there began a close association which resulted in *Lyrical Ballads* (1798), the first manifesto of the new poetry, which opened with Coleridge's *Ancient Mariner* and concluded with Wordsworth's *Tintern Abbey*. The poems between, mostly Wordsworth's, were not all silly sooth, but enough of them were such as to make them the object of parody, a weapon to which Wordsworth, except in his exalted mood, was peculiarly vulnerable. The removal of the Wordsworths to Gras-

mere after a visit to Germany in Coleridge's company, and the marriage of the poet to Mary Hutchinson (1802) closes this first stormy period with Wordsworth set on his proper task and modestly provided for by a legacy of £900. Now followed a long spell of routine work and relative happiness broken only by family misfortunes—the death of his sailor brother John (1805), which may have inspired the *Ode to Duty*, and Dorothy's mental breakdown (1832). Meanwhile Napoleon's ambitions had completely weaned the poet from revolutionary sympathies, as the patriotic sonnets sent to the *Morning Post* at about the time of the Peace of Amiens (1802–03) and after bear witness. Apart from the sonnets, this was his most inspired period. The additions to the third edition of *Lyrical Ballads* (1801) contained the grave pastoral *Michael*, *Ruth* and four of the exquisite *Lucy* poems, while the first of his tours in Scotland (1803), of which Dorothy wrote the perfect tour journal, yielded some fine poems, including *The Solitary Reaper*. The great poem he was now contemplating—*The Recluse*—was never finished, but *The Prelude*, the record of the poet's mind, was read to Coleridge in 1805. It remained unpublished till after his death, when it appeared with all the tamperings of a lifetime but substantially in its form of 1805, which fortunately has survived. Two volumes of poems appeared in 1807, the fruit of five years of intense activity. The ode *Intimations of Immortality* is only the loftiest of a number of masterpieces, including the patriotic sonnets, the *Affliction of Margaret*, the *Memorials of a Tour in Scotland*, the *Ode to Duty*, &c. Critics are inclined to mark the decline of his powers after this remarkable outpouring. Jeffrey was not altogether wrong in saying of *The Excursion* (1814) ' This will never do ', and the ' Memorials ' of various tours he now undertook and the *Ecclesiastical Sonnets* are decidedly below form. Only in two directions does he recall the poet he had been—the classical vein shown in *Laodamia* and *Dion* is impressive, and in the *Duddon* series the lifelong lover of nature reappears, although shorn of the mysticism. Wordsworth resented being called a pantheist, but pantheist he was until the horror of the times drove him to seek the comfort of revealed religion. In his *Ode to Dejection* Coleridge effectively disposed of Wordsworth's nature worship and in his *Biographia Literaria* (1819) he indicated the limitations of his theory about poetic diction, which now seems to be only a protest against the inflated idiom of descriptive poetry. None of these factors, however, detract from Wordsworth's greatness as a poet. Wordsworth succeeded Southey as poet laureate in 1843. He died at Rydal Mount (his home since 1813), April 23, 1850, and was buried at Grasmere. See Works, together with Dorothy's *Journals*, ed. W. Knight (1896), Works, ed. De Selincourt (1940 *et seq.*), *Letters*, ed. De Selincourt (1935–39); Lives by C. Wordsworth (1851), W. Knight (1889) and G. M. Harper (1916); Legouis, *La Jeunesse de Wordsworth* (new ed. 1921) and *Annette Vallon* (1922); also studies by

Coleridge (*Biographia Literaria*), Matthew Arnold, W. Pater, Raleigh (1908), Garrod (1924), Fausset (1923), Smith (1944), Bateson (1954) and Clarke (1962).

(8) **William Brocklesby** (1908–), English composer, a descendant of (2), was born in London. He studied under Sir Donald Tovey, and achieved prominence when his second symphony won the first award in the Edinburgh International Festival Competition in 1950. He has composed four symphonies, a piano concerto, songs and a quantity of chamber music.

WORK, Henry Clay (1832–84), American songwriter, born at Middletown, Conn., a printer by trade, attracted notice during the Civil War by his 'Marching through Georgia'.

WORNUM, Ralph Nicholson (1812–77), English art critic, was born at Thornton, Northumberland, and was from 1853 keeper and secretary of the National Gallery. The first effective holder of this post, he rearranged and catalogued the collections, and vigorously campaigned for better accommodation for the art treasures of the nation.

WORSAAE, Jens Jacob Asmussen, *vor'saw-ė* (1821–85), Danish archaeologist, in 1838–43 was assistant in the Copenhagen Museum of Northern Antiquities. Between 1842 and 1854 he made repeated visits to other Scandinavian lands, to Great Britain, Germany and France, which bore fruit in numerous works, two of which have been translated as *Primeval Antiquities of England and Denmark* (1849) and *The Danes and Norwegians in England* (1852). He opposed the spread of German tendencies in the duchies, as in *Jylland's Danskhed* (1850). He was minister of education 1874–75.

WORTH, Charles Frederick (1825–95), Anglo-French costumier, born at Bourn in Lincolnshire, went to Paris in 1846, and achieved such success as a fashion designer that he gained the patronage of the empress Eugénie, and his establishment in the Rue de la Paix became the centre of the fashion world.

WOTTON, Sir Henry (1568–1639), English traveller, diplomatist, scholar and poet, was born of ancient family at Boughton Malherbe in Kent. He was educated at Winchester and Oxford, then set out for a seven years' sojourn in Bavaria, Austria, Italy, Switzerland and France. On his return he became the confidant of the Earl of Essex. On his friend's downfall he betook himself to France, then to Italy, and was sent by Ferdinand, Duke of Florence, on a secret mission to James VI of Scotland. James on his succession to the throne of England knighted him and sent him as ambassador to Venice (1604), where he was intermittently employed for nearly twenty years, being next sent to the German princes and the Emperor Ferdinand II, returning to England a poor man in 1624. He was made provost of Eton, and took orders. His tracts, letters, &c., were collected as *Reliquiae Wottonianae* (1651), prefaced by Izaak Walton's exquisite little Life. One of his few poems is 'The Character of a Happy Life'. It was Wotton who described an ambassador as an honest man sent abroad to lie for the good of his

country. See Lives by A. W. Ward (1898) and L. P. Smith (1907).

WOUTERS, Rik, *vow'-* (1882–1916), Belgian painter, born at Mechlin, came under the influence of Cézanne and was the leading exponent of Fauvism in Belgium.

WOUWERMAN, Philip, *vow'vėr-man* (1619–1668), Dutch painter of battle and hunting pieces, born at Haarlem, passed his entire life there in the assiduous practice of his art. His pictures are mostly small landscapes, with plenty of figures in energetic action. His cavalry skirmishes, with a white horse generally in the foreground, were specially characteristic and popular. He had two brothers, also painters, **Peter** (1623–82) and **Jan** (1629–66), who chose similar subjects.

WRANGEL, *vrang'gėl*, (1) **Ferdinand Petrovitch, Baron von** (1794–1870), Russian vice-admiral and explorer, was born in Livonia, voyaged much in Arctic waters and on Siberian coasts, and made valuable surveys and observations. The island he nearly reached in 1821 was sighted by Sir H. Kellett in 1849, and named after Wrangel by Long in 1867. See his *Polar Expedition* (trans. 1840).

(2) **Friedrich Heinrich Ernst** (1784–1877), Prussian field-marshal and count, born at Stettin, distinguished himself in the campaigns of 1807, 1813, and 1814, and in 1848 commanded the Federal troops in Schleswig-Holstein. He crushed the insurrection in Berlin (1848); in 1856 became field-marshal; in 1864 had supreme command over Prussian and Austrian troops in the Danish war; and, ennobled in 1866, served that year against the Austrians. See Lives by Brunckow (1876), Meerheimb (1877) and Maltitz (1884).

WRAXALL, Sir Nathanael William (1751–1831), English writer of memoirs, born at Bristol, was for three years in the East India Company's service, travelled over Europe (1772–79), and had a confidential mission from Queen Caroline-Matilda of Denmark to her brother George III. He published his *Cursory Remarks made in a Tour* in 1775, his *Memoirs of the Valois Kings* in 1777, entered parliament in 1780 as a follower of Lord North, but went over to Pitt, and was made a baronet in 1813. His next books were the *History of France from Henry III to Louis XIV* (1795); *Memoirs of the Courts of Berlin, Dresden, Warsaw, and Vienna* (1799); and the famous *Historical Memoirs of my own Time, 1772–84* (1815). For a libel here on Count Woronzov, Russian envoy to England, he was fined £500 and sentenced to six months' imprisonment. Violent attacks on his veracity were made by the reviews, but Wraxall's *Answers* were accounted on the whole satisfactory. A continuation of *Memoirs* (1784–90) was published in 1836. See Wheatley's edition of the whole work (5 vols. 1884).

WREDE, Karl Philipp, *vray'dė* (1767–1838), Bavarian soldier, born at Heidelberg, shared in the campaigns of 1799 and 1800, as commander of the Bavarians invaded Tyrol, fought at Wagram along with the French, and was made a count by Napoleon. He led the Bavarians under Napoleon to Russia in 1812; then commanded a united Bavarian and Austrian army against the French, by whom he was defeated at Hanau. He was, however, victorious in several battles in France in 1814, and was made field-marshal and prince. He represented Bavaria at the Vienna Congress (1814).

WREN, Sir Christopher (1632–1723), English architect, born at East Knoyle in Wiltshire, October 20, was the son of Dr Christopher Wren, dean of Windsor, and the nephew of Dr Matthew Wren (1585–1667), the High Church bishop successively of Hereford, Norwich and Ely. He passed from Westminster to Wadham College, Oxford, became a fellow of All Souls, distinguished himself in mathematics and physics, and helped to perfect the barometer. In 1657 he became professor of Astronomy at Gresham College in London, but in 1661 returned to Oxford as Savilian professor of Astronomy. Before leaving London, Wren had, with Boyle, Wilkins and others, laid the foundation of the Royal Society. In 1663 he was engaged by the Dean and Chapter of St Paul's to make a survey of the cathedral, with a view to repairs. The first work built from a design by Wren was the chapel at Pembroke College, Cambridge, in 1663; and in 1663–66 he designed the Sheldonian Theatre at Oxford and the Library, &c., of Trinity College, Cambridge. In 1665 Wren visited Paris. The Great Fire of London (1666) opened a wide field for his genius. He drew designs for the rebuilding of the whole city, embracing wide streets and magnificent quays but, thwarted by vested interests, the scheme was never implemented. In 1669 he was appointed surveyor-general and was chosen architect for the new St Paul's (1675–1710) and for more than fifty other churches in place of those destroyed by the Great Fire. Other works by him were the Royal Exchange, Custom House, Temple Bar, the College of Physicians, Greenwich Observatory, Chelsea Hospital, the Ashmolean Museum at Oxford, Hampton Court, Greenwich Hospital, Buckingham House, Marlborough House, and the western towers and north transept of Westminster Abbey. In 1672 Wren was knighted, in 1680 made president of the Royal Society, in 1684 comptroller of the works at Windsor Castle, and in 1698 surveyor-general of Westminster Abbey. He was returned for Windsor in 1689, but unseated on petition. Wren was buried in St Paul's. See Lives by Elmes (1852), Weaver (1923), Webb (1937), Briggs (1953), Summerson (1953), Bolton (1956), and the Wren Society publications.

WRIGHT, (1) Sir Almroth Edward (1861–1947), English bacteriologist, born in Yorkshire, educated at Dublin, Leipzig, Strasbourg and Marburg, became professor of Experimental Pathology in the University of London. He was known specially for his work on the parasitic diseases, and for his research on the protective power of blood against bacteria. He introduced a system of antityphoid inoculation.

(2) **Fanny.** See DARUSMONT.

(3) **Frank Lloyd** (1869–1959), American architect, born in Richland Center, Wis., studied civil engineering at the University of Wisconsin, where the collapse of a newly-built wing led to his determination to apply engineering principles to architecture. Having set up in practice, he became known for his low-built prairie-style residences, but soon launched out into more daring and controversial designs, and is regarded as the outstanding designer of modern private dwellings, planned in conformity with the natural features of the land. Among his larger works are the earthquake-proof Imperial Hotel at Tokyo and the Guggenheim Museum of Art in New York, in which the exhibits line the walls of a continuous spiral ramp. He was an innovator in the field of open planning. See his Autobiography (N.Y. 1932) and study by Gutheim (N.Y. 1941).

(4) **Georg von.** See VON WRIGHT.

(5) **Joseph** (1734–97), English genre and portrait painter, called ' Wright of Derby ', passed his whole life in his native town, save a few years spent in London, in Italy and at Bath. His portrait groups often show odd light effects. See Bemrose's folio (1886).

(6) **Joseph** (1855–1930), English philologist, D.C.L., professor of Comparative Philology at Oxford, editor of the *Dialect Dictionary*, and author of many philological works, was born at Bradford and as a boy worked in a wool mill. See Life by his widow and collaborator (1932).

(7) **Orville** (1871–1948), born at Dayton, Ohio, and his brother **Wilbur** (1867–1912), born near Millville, Ind., American airplane pioneers, were the first to fly in a heavier-than-air machine, December 17, 1903, at Kitty Hawk, N.C. Encouraged by this, they abandoned their cycle business and formed an aircraft production company (1909), of which Wilbur was president until his death. In 1915 Orville sold his interests in it in order to devote himself to research.

(8) **Thomas** (1810–87), English antiquary, born of Quaker parentage near Ludlow, graduated from Trinity, Cambridge, was elected F.S.A. in 1837, and helped to found the Camden Society, Archaeological Association, and Percy and Shakespeare Societies. From 1836 he published eighty-four works, including *Biographia Britannica Literaria* (1842–46); *England in the Middle Ages* (1846); *Dictionary of Obsolete and Provincial English* (1857); *Political Poems, 1327–1485* (1859–61); and *Anglo-Latin Twelfth Century Satirical Poets* (1877).

(9) **William Aldis** (1836–1914), English man of letters, born at Beccles, became librarian, and in 1888 vice-master, of Trinity College, Cambridge. He edited the Cambridge and Globe Shakespeares (with W. G. Clark), *Generydes*, Robert of Gloucester, Edward FitzGerald's Letters, &c., and was well known by his *Bible Word-Book* (1866).

WRÓBLEWSKI, Zygmunt Florenty von, *vroo-blef'ski* (1845–88), Polish physicist, born at Grodno, was professor of Physics at Cracow University and noted for his work on the liquefaction of gases. He was the first to liquefy air on a large scale. Working with Olszewski at Cracow he liquefied oxygen, nitrogen and carbon monoxide. He died at Cracow.

WU CHENG-EN, *woo chung-un* (fl. 16th cent.

A.D.), Chinese author of *Monkey* (trans. A. Waley, 1942), based on the pilgrimage of Hsuang Chuang (q.v.).

WULSTAN, or **Wulfstan,** name of several churchmen in Anglo-Saxon England, notably:

(1) (fl. c. 1000), a monk of Winchester, author of a *Life of Bishop Ethelwold* and a poem on St Swithin's Miracles.

(2) (d. 1023), Archbishop of York from *c.* 1002, author of Anglo-Saxon homilies (see Napier's German monograph, 1882).

(3) (*c.* 1009–95), Bishop of Worcester and saint, reputed author of part of the Anglo-Saxon Chronicle, submitted to William the Conqueror and supported William Rufus. By his preaching at Bristol he is understood to have put an end to the slave trade practised there. He was canonized in 1203. See his *Life*, Latin trans. by William of Malmesbury, ed. Darlington (1929), English trans. by Peile (1934).

WUNDERLICH, Carl August, *voon'dèr-leeKH* (1815–77), German physician, born at Sulz-on-Neckar, professor of Medicine at Leipzig, was the first to introduce temperature charts into hospitals, in accordance with his contention that fever is a symptom and not a disease. The clinical thermometer used by him was a foot long and took twenty minutes to register the temperature. He died at Leipzig.

WUNDT, Wilhelm Max, *voont* (1832–1920), German physiologist and psychologist, born at Neckarau, Baden, in 1875 became professor of Physiology at Leipzig. A distinguished experimental psychologist, he wrote on the nerves and the senses, the relations of physiology and psychology, logic, &c. His *Human and Animal Psychology* and *Outlines of Psychology* were translated in 1896, *Ethics* in 1901, *Folk Psychology* in 1916.

WURTZ, Charles Adolphe, *vürts* (1817–84), French chemist, born at Strasbourg, wrote numerous works, of which *The Atomic Theory* (1880), *Modern Chemistry* (4th ed. 1885), &c., have been translated. From 1875 he was professor of Chemistry at the Sorbonne. He was the discoverer of glycol (1856). See *Life* by Gautier (1884).

WYATT, (1) **James** (1746–1813), English architect, born in Staffordshire, succeeded Sir W. Chambers in 1796 as surveyor to the Board of Works. He built Fonthill Abbey for Beckford, and was killed in a carriage accident. See study by Dale (1956). His son, **Matthew Cotes** (1777–1862), was a sculptor.

(2) **Sir Mathew Digby** (1820–77), English architect, was born at Rowde near Devizes, the son of a London police magistrate, a member of a family that produced many architects and sculptors, including (1) and (3). He was secretary to the royal commissioners for the 1851 exhibition, and in 1869 was knighted and made Slade professor of Fine Arts at Cambridge. He wrote *Metal Work and its Artistic Design* (1852), *Industrial Arts of the Nineteenth Century* (1853), *Art Treasures of the United Kingdom* (1857), *Fine Art* (1870), and *Architect's Handbook in Spain* (1872). See study by Pevsner (1950).

(3) **Richard** (1795–1850), English classical and poetical sculptor, of the same family as

(1) and (2), born in London, studied at Paris and Rome, where he died.

(4) **Sir Thomas** (1503–42), English courtier and poet, was born at Allington Castle in Kent, son of Sir Henry Wyatt, and studied at St John's College, Cambridge. He was warmly received at court, in 1536 knighted, and in 1537 made high sheriff of Kent. He contrived to retain the king's favour, and was employed on missions to Spain and the imperial court. In 1541 he got a grant of lands at Lambeth, and in 1542 was named high steward of the king's manor at Maidstone. In 1557 his poems, with Surrey's, were published in *Tottel's Miscellany* (ed. Rollins 1928 *et seq.*). Some of the shorter pieces are models of grace, and the satires possess merit. His poems were edited by Dr Nott (1815–16), Prof. Simonds (1889), and Miss Foxwell (complete variorum edit., 1913). Simonds seeks to show that Anne Boleyn was the object of Wyatt's love. See studies by Alscher (Vienna 1886), Tillyard (1929), E. K. Chambers (1933).

(5) **Sir Thomas, the Younger** (1520?–54), son of (4), fought bravely at the siege of Landrecies (1544), and continued in service on the Continent till 1550. In 1554, with Lady Jane Grey's father, he led the Kentish men to Southwark; and failing to capture Ludgate, was taken prisoner, and executed.

WYCHERLEY, William, *wich'-* (*c.* 1640–1716), English dramatist, born at Clive near Shrewsbury, in early youth was sent to France, left Queen's College, Oxford, without a degree, and entered the Middle Temple. For some years he lived as a man about town and a courtier, but took early to work as a dramatist. *Love in a Wood, or St James's Park*, a brisk comedy founded on Sedley's *Mulberry Garden*, was acted with much applause in 1671. Buckingham gave him a commission in a regiment, and King Charles made him a present of £500. He served for a short time in the fleet, and was present at a sea fight—probably one of the drawn battles fought between Rupert and De Ruyter in 1673. *The Gentleman Dancing-master* (1672) was a clever farcical comedy of intrigue. *The Country Wife* (1675), Wycherley's coarsest but strongest play, partly founded on Molière's *École des Femmes*, was followed in 1677 by *The Plain Dealer*, founded partly on Molière's *Misanthrope*. A little after 1679 Wycherley married the young widowed Countess of Drogheda, with whom he lived unhappily. At her death a few years later she left him all her fortune, a bequest which involved him in a lawsuit whereby he was reduced to poverty and cast into the Fleet prison for some years. At last James II, having seen a representation of *The Plain Dealer*, paid his debts and gave him a pension of £200 a year. At sixty-four Wycherley made the acquaintance of Pope, then a youth of sixteen, to whom he entrusted the revision of a number of his verses, the result being a quarrel. Wycherley's money troubles continued to the end of his days. At seventy-five he married a young woman in order to balk the hopes of his nephew; and he died eleven days after his marriage; according to Pope, in the Roman Catholic faith. In literary brilliance Congreve infinitely outshines him, but Wycherley is a far more dexterous playwright. See Ward's *Wycherley* (' Mermaid ', 1893); Churchill's edition of *The Country Wife* and *The Plain Dealer* (1924); Summers's edition of the *Complete Works* (4 vols. 1924); Nicoll's *Restoration Comedy* (1923); a French study by Perromat (1921); Dobrée's *Restoration Comedy* (1924); and Wilcox, *The Relation of Molière to Restoration Comedy* (1938).

WYCLIFFE, John, *wik'lif* (c. 1329–84), English reformer, is believed to have sprung from a family which held the manor of Wycliffe on Tees, and to have been born at Hipswell near Richmond in Yorkshire. He distinguished himself at Oxford, where he was a popular teacher. In 1360 he was master of Balliol College, but resigned soon afterwards on taking the college living of Fillingham, which he exchanged in 1368 for Ludgershall, Buckinghamshire. He was possibly warden for a time of Canterbury Hall. He also held some office at court, where he was consulted by government and employed as a pamphleteer. In 1374 he became rector of Lutterworth, and the same year was sent (doubtless as a recognized opponent of papal intrusion) to Bruges to treat with ambassadors from the pope concerning ecclesiastical abuses. His strenuous activity gained him support among the nobles and the London citizens. But his maintenance of a right in the secular power to control the clergy was offensive to the bishops, who summoned him before the archbishop in St Paul's in 1377; but the council was broken up by an unseemly quarrel between the Bishop of London and the Duke of Lancaster. The pope now addressed bulls to the king, bishops and University of Oxford, bidding them to imprison Wycliffe and make him answer before the archbishop and the pope. When at last proceedings were undertaken, the prosecution had little effect upon Wycliffe's position. The whole fabric of the church was now (1378) shaken by the election of an antipope. Hitherto Wycliffe had attacked the manifest abuses in the church, but now he began to strike at its constitution, and declared it would be better without pope or prelates. He denied the priestly power of absolution, and the whole system of enforced confession, of penances, and indulgence. Up to this time his works had been written in Latin; he now appealed to the people in their own language, and by issuing popular tracts became a leading English prose writer. He organized a body of itinerant preachers, his ' poor priests ', who spread his doctrines widely through the country, and began his translation of the Bible, of which as yet there was no complete English version. The work was carried through rapidly, and widely circulated. He entered upon more dangerous ground when in 1380 he assailed the central dogma of transubstantiation. A convocation of doctors at Oxford condemned his theses; he appealed without success to the king. In 1382 Archbishop Courtenay convoked a council and condemned Wycliffite opinions. Wycliffe's followers were arrested, and all compelled to recant; but for some unknown

reason he himself was not judged. He withdrew from Oxford to Lutterworth, where he continued his incessant literary activity. His work in the next two years, uncompromising in tone, is astonishing in quantity, and shows no falling off in power. The characteristic of his teaching was its insistence on inward religion in opposition to the formalism of the time; as a rule he attacked the established practices of the church only so far as he thought they had degenerated into mere mechanical uses. The influence of his teaching was widespread in England, and, though persecution suppressed it, continued to work up to the Reformation. Huss (q.v.) was avowedly his disciple; and there were ' Lollards ' or Wycliffites in Ayrshire down to the Reformation. Thirty years after Wycliffe's death forty-five articles extracted from his writings were condemned as heretical by the Council of Constance, which ordered his bones to be dug up and burned and cast into the Swift— a sentence executed in 1428. See Lives by Lewis (1723) and Vaughan (1828); Lechler, *Wycliffe and his English Precursors* (trans. 1884); Poole, *Wycliffe* (1889); Loserth, *Wyclif and Hus* (1884); studies by Workman (1926) and MacFarlane (1953); Trevelyan, *Age of Wycliffe* (1899).

WYKEHAM, WILLIAM OF. See WILLIAM OF WYKEHAM.

WYLIE, Elinor Hoyt (1885–1928?), American authoress, was born at Somerville, N.J. Her first volume of poetry, *Nets to Catch the Wind*, which won the Julia Ellsworth Ford prize in 1921, was followed by several more collections and by four highly individual novels, *Jennifer Lorn* (1923), *The Venetian Glass Nephew* (1925), *The Orphan Angel* (1927) and *Mr Hodge and Mr Hazard* (1928). See studies by H. W. Benét (1932), and N. Hoyt (1934).

WYNANTS, or Wijnants, Jan, *wī'*- (c. 1620–1679), Amsterdam landscape painter, was born at Haarlem.

WYNDHAM, Sir Charles (1837–1919), British actor-manager, born at Liverpool, and trained as a doctor, first appeared on the stage at New York in 1861, and made his début in London in 1866. Among the parts he played were those of Charles Surface and David Garrick. In 1899 he opened Wyndham's Theatre. He was knighted in 1902.

WYNKYN DE WORDE. See WORDE.

WYNTOUN, Andrew of (1350?–1420?), a Scottish rhyming chronicler, was a canon regular of St Andrews, who about 1395 became prior of the monastery of St Serf on Loch Leven, and wrote *The Orygynale Cronykil of Scotland*, specially valuable as a specimen of old Scots. It is brought down to 1406, and of its nine books the first five give a fragmentary outline of the histor and geography of the ancient world.

WYON, a family of noteworthy English medallists and seal-engravers:

(1) **Benjamin** (1802–58), son of (4), was chief engraver of seals to William IV, for whom he designed the great seal and a number of medals.

(2) **Joseph Shepherd** (1836–73), son of (1), succeeded his father as chief engraver of

seals and designed many medals and the great seal of Canada.

(3) **Leonard Charles** (1826–91), eldest son of (6), designed contemporary coinage and military medals, including the South African, Indian, and Albert medals.

(4) **Thomas** (1767–1830), father of (1) and (5), was chief engraver of the seals from 1816.

(5) **Thomas** (1792–1817), son of (4), became chief engraver at the mint at the age of 23. He designed the new silver coinage in 1816 and the Waterloo medal.

(6) **William** (1795–1851), father of (3), born in Birmingham, became chief engraver to the mint in 1828. He designed much of the new British and colonial coinage of George III and IV, and was in 1838 the first medallist to be elected R.A.

WYSPIANSKI, Stanislaw, *vis-pyan'skee* (1869–1907), Polish poet and painter, born at Cracow, was a leader of the Polish neo-Romantics. Besides portraits and genre pictures he executed window designs for the cathedral and the Franciscan church at Cracow before the loss of an arm obliged him to abandon art for poetry and drama, some of which is based on Greek mythology.

WYSS, Johann Rudolf, *vees* (1781–1830), Swiss writer, born at Bern, famous for his connection with *The Swiss Family Robinson.* He completed and edited the MS. originally written by his father, **Johann David Wyss.** He was professor of Philosophy at Bern from 1806. His lectures on the supreme good (1811) and Swiss tales (1815–30) would hardly have preserved his name; but *Der Schweizerische Robinson* (1812–13) has been frequently translated—into English in 1820.

WYSZYNSKI, Stepan, *vi-shin'ski* (1901–), Polish cardinal, was born at Zuzela, near Warsaw, and educated at Włocławek seminary and Lublin Catholic university. During the second World War he was associated with the resistance movement. In 1945 he became rector of Włocławek seminary, in 1946 Bishop of Lublin and in 1948 Archbishop of Warsaw and Gniezno and primate of Poland. In October 1953, following his indictment of the Communist campaign against the Church, he was suspended from his ecclesiastical functions and arrested. He was freed after the ' bloodless revolution ' of October 1956 and agreed to a reconciliation between Church and State under the ' liberalizing ' Gomulka régime.

WYTHER, George. See WITHER.

WYTTENBACH, Daniel (1746–1820), Swiss scholar, born at Bern, became professor of Greek at Amsterdam in 1771, of Philosophy in 1779, and in 1799 of Rhetoric. He retired in 1816. He edited Plutarch's *Moralia* (1795–1830), and wrote on logic, a Life of Ruhnken, &c. See Latin Life by Mahne (1823). His wife, **Johanna Gallien** (d. 1830), whom he married at seventy-two, lived after his death at Paris, was given the doctorate of philosophy by Marburg in 1827, and wrote *Théagène* (1815), *Das Gastmahl des Leomis* (1821) and *Alexis* (1823).

X

XANTHIPPE. See SOCRATES.

XAVIER, Saint Francis. See FRANCIS (SAINTS, 4).

XENOCRATES, *zen-ok'ra-teez* (396–314 B.C.), Greek philosopher, born at Chalcedon, from 339 presided over the Platonic Academy as successor to Speusippus, himself the successor of Plato. He wrote numerous treatises, of which only the titles have been preserved; and he introduced into the Academy the mystic Pythagorean doctrine of numbers.

XENOPHANES, *zen-of'an-eez* (fl. 540–500 B.C.), Greek philosopher, founder of the Eleatic School, emigrated from Colophon to Elea in southern Italy about 536 B.C. He held that a supreme intelligence or deity was identical with the world.

XENOPHON, *zen'o-fon* (*c.* 435–354 B.C.), Greek historian, essayist, and military commander, the son of Gryllus, an Athenian knight, came under Socrates' influence during the thirty-five years he spent at Athens. In 401 he accepted the invitation of Proxenus of Boeotia, a commander of Greek mercenaries, to join him at Sardis and take service under the Persian prince, Cyrus, ostensibly against the Pisidians, but really against that Cyrus's own brother, King Artaxerxes Mnemon. After the failure of this bold scheme, and the death of the rebel prince at Cunaxa (401), Xenophon succeeded Proxenus in the command of the Ten Thousand Greeks. He became the life and soul of the army in its march of 1500 miles, as they fought their way against the ferocious mountain tribes through the highlands of Armenia and the ice and snow of an inclement winter; and with such skill did he lead them that in five months they reached Trapezus (Trebizond), a Greek colony on the Black Sea, and ultimately Chrysopolis (Scutari), opposite Byzantium (399). After serving a while under a Thracian chief, he got his soldiers permanent service in the Lacedaemonian army engaged to fight against the Persians. Sentence of banishment from Athens for thus taking service with Sparta was passed against him. Forming in 396 the closest friendship with the Spartan king, Agesilaus, he accompanied him in his eastern campaign; was in his suite when he returned to Greece to conduct the war against the anti-Spartan league of Athens, Corinth, and Thebes (394); and witnessed the battle of Coronea. He went back with the king to Sparta, where he resided on and off until the Spartans presented him with an estate at Scillus, a town taken from Elis. Hither in 387 he went with his wife Philesia and his two sons, Gryllus and Diodorus; and here he spent some twenty years of his life, indulging his taste for literary work and the pursuits of a country gentleman. But the break-up of Spartan ascendency after the battle of Leuctra (371) drove him from his retreat. The Athenians, who had now joined the Spartans against Thebes, repealed the sentence of banishment against him. But he settled and died at Corinth. His writings give us the idea of having been written with great singleness of purpose, modesty, and love of truth. They may be distributed into four groups: (1) historical—the *Hellenics* (the history of Greece for forty-nine years), *Anabasis* (the story of the expedition with Cyrus) and *Encomium of Agesilaus*; (2) technical and didactic—on *Horsemanship*, the *Hipparchicus* (' guide for a cavalry commander ') and the *Cynegeticus* (' guide to hunting '); (3) politico-philosophical— *The Lacedaemonian Polity*, *The Cyropaedeia* (' the education of Cyrus ', rather a historical romance) and *Athenian Finance*; (4) ethico-philosophical—*Memorials of Socrates* (sketches and dialogues illustrating the life and character of his master), *Symposion*, *Oeconomicus*, *Hieron* and *Apology of Socrates*. The *Polity of Athens* is probably an anonymous work written about 415 B.C. Xenophon's style and language are unaffected, simple and clear, without any attempt at ornamentation. The *editio princeps* of the Greek text was that of Boninus (1516), followed by the Aldine in 1525. Later editions of the whole or part of his works are by Hutchinson, Weiske, Fischer, Schneider, Bornemann, Breitenbach, Krüger, Kühner, Sauppe, Dindorf, Schenkl, Hertlein, Cobet, O. Keller, Hug and Holden. See books by Roquette (1884), Croiset (1873), Lange (1900); Bury's *Greek Historians* (1909), and the *Penguin Classics* (in translation).

XERXES I, *zerks'eez* (519?–465 B.C.), king of Persia in 485–465 B.C., succeeded when his father, Darius, died preparing for a third expedition against Greece. He first subdued the rebellious Egyptians, then started with a vast army drawn from all parts of the empire, and an enormous fleet furnished by the Phoenicians. A bridge, consisting of a double line of boats, was built across the Hellespont, and a canal cut through Mount Athos. In the autumn of 481 B.C. Xerxes arrived at Sardis. Next year the army began its march towards the Hellespont; it took seven days and nights to pass the bridge of boats. Herodotus puts the number of fighting men at 2,641,610, and the ships-of-war at 1207, besides 3000 smaller vessels. When this immense force reached Thermopylae, it was brought to a stand by Leonidas and his 300

Spartans. After these had been slain Xerxes marched on to Athens (480), and, finding it deserted, destroyed temples and houses alike. Meantime the fleet had sailed round from Euboea. Xerxes witnessed the fight in the strait between Salamis and Attica. Confounded at the result, he fled to the Hellespont; and his hopes of conquest died with the fall of his general, Mardonius, on the fatal field of Plataea (479 B.C.). Xerxes, possibly the Ahasuerus of Ezra iv. 6 and Esther i.–x., was later murdered by Artabanus.

XIMENES, Cardinal, in full **Francisco Jiménez de Cisneros,** *hee-may'neth* (1436–1517), Spanish churchman and statesman, was born of an ancient family, at Torrelaguna in Castile, and was educated at Alcalá, Salamanca and Rome, where he obtained from the pope a nomination to the archpriestship of Uzeda in 1473. The archbishop refused to admit him, and for six years imprisoned him. On his release in 1479 he was named vicar-general of Cardinal Mendoza, but gave this up to enter a Franciscan monastery at Toledo (1482). Queen Isabella chose him for her confessor in 1492, and in 1495 made him Archbishop of Toledo. As archbishop he maintained the austerity of the monk and carried out extensive reforms in several monastic orders. As the queen's spiritual counsellor he was the guiding spirit of Spanish affairs; and on her death in 1504 he held the balance between the parties of Ferdinand and Philip of Burgundy, husband of Joanna, the mad heiress to the crown. Appointed regent in 1506, he conducted the affairs of the kingdom through a critical time with consummate skill. In 1507 he was created cardinal, and next year organized at his own expense and commanded the expedition for the conquest of Oran and extirpation of piracy. Ferdinand on his deathbed (1516) named Ximenes regent of Spain till the arrival of his grandson Charles; and the aged cardinal quickly overawed the hostile grandees into submission, and quelled a revolt in Navarre. He died, possibly of poison, at Roa on his way to greet Charles, just arriving in Spain. Ximenes was fanatical in his hatred of heresy, and as grand inquisitor caused the death of 2500 persons. The revolution he effected in breaking down the feudal power of the nobles has often been compared with the change wrought in France by Richelieu. He was a munificent patron of religion and learning and founded out of his private income the University of Alcalá de Henares. He also published the famous Complutensian Polyglot Bible. See Latin Life by Gómez de Castro (1569), English Life by Lyell (1917), and Merton, *Ximenes and the Making of Spain* (1934).

Y

YALE, (1) Elihu (1649-1721), English official in India and benefactor to America, born at Boston, Mass., of British parents. They returned to Britain in 1652, and he was educated in London; in 1672 he went out to India in the service of the East India Company, becoming governor of Madras in 1687. He was resident in England from 1699, and, through the sale in America of some of his effects, donated money to the collegiate school established (1701) at Saybrook, Connecticut, which afterwards moved to New Haven. There in 1718 it took the name of Yale College in honour of its benefactor, and in 1887 the much-expanded institution become Yale University, the third oldest in the United States.

(2) Linus (1821-68), American inventor and manufacturer, born at Salisbury, N.Y. He invented various types of locks, including the small cylinder locks by which his name is known.

YAMAGATA, Prince Aritomo (1838-1922), Japanese general and politician, born at Hagi, became adviser to the emperor, and was appointed war minister (1873) and chief of staff (1878), in which capacity his modernization of the military system led to the emergence of Japan as a significant force in world politics. He was twice prime minister (1889-93, 1898), chief of staff in the Russo-Japanese war (1904), and president of the privy council (1905). See J. Morris, *Makers of Modern Japan* (1906).

YAMASHITA, Tomoyuki (1885-1946), Japanese general, commanded the forces which overran Singapore in 1942 and then took over the Philippines campaign, capturing Bataan and Corregidor. Still in charge when MacArthur turned the tables in 1944-45, he was captured and hanged at Manila for atrocities perpetrated by his troops.

YANG, Chen Ning (1922-), Chinese physicist, born in Hofei, the son of a professor of Mathematics, gained a scholarship to Chicago in 1945, was professor at the Institute for Advanced Studies, Princeton (1955-65), and from 1965 was professor of Science at New York State University Centre. With Tsung-Dao Lee, who had been his fellow-student at Chicago, he disproved the established physical principle known as the parity law, and for this the two were awarded the Nobel prize for 1957.

YARMOUTH, Sophia von Walmoden, Countess of (d. 1765), already known to George II in Hanover, on Queen Caroline's death (1737) was brought to England as the king's mistress, and created a countess.

YATES, (1) Dornford, pseud. of Cecil William Mercer (1885-1960), English novelist, born in London, educated at Harrow and Oxford, achieved great popularity with an entertaining series of fanciful escapist adventure fiction— *Berry and Co* (1921), *Jonah and Co* (1922), &c.

(2) Edmund (1831-94), British journalist and novelist, born at Edinburgh, the son of the actor-manager Frederick Henry Yates (1797-1842). From 1854 he published over a score of novels and other works; was editor of *Temple Bar, Tinsley's* and other periodicals; and in 1874 founded, with Grenville Murray, a successful 'society' weekly, *The World,* which, for a libel on Lord Lonsdale, involved him in 1884 in two months' imprisonment. See his *Recollections* (1884).

YEAMES, William Frederick (1835-1918). British historical and subject painter, born at Taganrog, studied in London, Florence and Rome, and became A.R.A. in 1866, R.A. in 1878. His best-known work is *When did you last see your Father?*

YEATS, *yayts,* (1) Jack Butler (1871-1957), Irish artist and writer, born in London, the brother of (2). Both in his painting and his writing he portrayed life in Ireland with romantic bravura. His publications include *The Amaranthers* (1936) and several plays, and he is represented in many art galleries.

(2) William Butler (1865-1939), Irish poet and dramatist, born near Dublin, son of the distinguished artist, John Butler Yeats (1839-1922). He was educated in London and Dublin and became an art student. He developed an interest in occultism and theosophy, and in his early twenties turned from painting to writing. His first publication was a play, *Mosada* (1886), and two years later he began, with *The Wanderings of Oisin,* a series of ballads and poems that established his reputation. *The Celtic Twilight,* a book of peasant legends, appeared in 1893. Its title was used to label a school of writing that attempted a renaissance of ancient Irish culture. With the help of Lady Gregory Yeats he turned to the formation of an Irish National Theatre. His three most popular plays, *The Countess Kathleen, The Land of Heart's Desire* and *Kathleen ni Houlihan,* appeared respectively in 1892, 1894 and 1903. For the Abbey Theatre he wrote *Shadowy Waters, The King's Threshold, Deirdre* and *The Golden Helmet.* Later, in addition to several volumes of fine poetry, he wrote *Four Plays for Dancers, Resurrection* and *A Vision* (a philosophical treatise); and, in 1938, two plays, *The Herne's Egg* and *Purgatory.* His autobiography is contained in three volumes: *Reveries over Childhood, The Trembling of the Veil* (both 1926) and *Dramatis Personae* (1936). He was awarded the Nobel prize in 1923, and his collected poems appeared in 1933. Yeats died near Roquebrune in the south of France, and in 1948 was re-interred near Sligo, Ireland. See the Lives by Hone (1942) and Jeffares (1949), studies by MacNeice (1941) and Rajan (1965), F. A. C. Wilson, *W. B. Yeats and Tradition* (1957), Stallworthy, *Between the Lines* (1963), and Bibliography by Wade (1951).

YENDYS, Sydney. See DOBELL (2).

YERKES, Charles Tyson (1837-1905), American railway financier, endowed in 1892 the

Yerkes Observatory in connection with the University of Chicago, but 45 miles N.W. of the city.

YERSIN, Alexandre Émile John, *yer-si* (1863–1943), Swiss-French bacteriologist, born at Rougemont and educated at Lausanne, Marburg and Paris, did research at the Pasteur Institute in Paris, working along with Roux on diphtheria antitoxin. In Hong Kong in 1894 he discovered the plague bacillus at the same time as Kitasato. He developed a serum against it, and founded two Pasteur Institutes in China. He introduced the rubber tree into Indo-China.

YONGE, Charlotte Mary, *yung* (1823–1901), English novelist, only daughter of W. C. Yonge of Otterbourne, Hants, achieved great popular success with her *Heir of Redclyffe* (1853) and its successors, publishing some 120 volumes of fiction, High Church in tone. Part of the profits of the *Heir of Redclyffe* was devoted to fitting out the missionary schooner *Southern Cross* for Bishop Selwyn; and those of the *Daisy Chain* (£2000) she gave to build a missionary college in New Zealand. She also published historical works, a book on *Christian Names* (1863), a *Life of Bishop Patteson* (1873), and a sketch of *Hannah More* (1888), besides translating much and editing the *Monthly Packet*. See *Life* by Georgina Battiscombe (1943), and *Victorian Best-seller* by Mare and Percival (1948).

YORCK VON WARTENBURG, Hans David Ludwig (1759–1830), Prussian soldier, was the son of a Pomeranian captain, Von Yorck, York or Jarck, claiming English descent. He entered the army in 1772, was cashiered for insubordination, and served in the Dutch East Indies, but rejoining the Prussian service, gained glory in the wars of 1794, 1806, 1812 and 1813–14. Ennobled in 1814, he was made a field-marshal in 1821.

YORK, Cardinal. See STEWART Family (13).

YORK, Duke of: the title normally reserved for the second son of the English monarch. Edward III's son, **Edmund of Langley,** founded that House of York that fought the Wars of the Roses. Charles II's brother **James** bore the title until his accession in 1685; George I conferred it on his brother **Ernest Augustus; Frederick** (1763–1827), George III's second son, was trained for a military career in Germany; marrying Fredericka, the Princess Royal of Prussia, in 1791. In 1793 he commanded the small British contingent in the Coalition armies confronting the French revolutionary forces in the Netherlands. His personal success at the siege of Valenciennes and Beaumont was not properly exploited, and the campaign collapsed. No better fortune attended the expedition to the Helder of 1799. The duke had been appointed commander-in-chief in Great Britain in 1798, and his steady, knowledgeable and thoroughgoing reform of the army was of lasting benefit, and gave Wellington (q.v.) the first-class fighting material with which he defeated the French. Although exonerated from complicity in the traffic in Commissions carried on by his mistress, Mary Anne Clarke (q.v.), he resigned his office. Reinstated in 1811, he

continued to justify his honourable sobriquet of ' the soldier's friend ' until his death, still in harness, in 1827. **George V** (q.v.) bore the title until created Prince of Wales in 1901; as did **George VI** (q.v.) prior to his accession on the abdication of **Edward VIII.**

YORKE, Philip, Earl of Hardwicke (1690–1764), English judge, a Dover attorney's son, in 1737 became lord chancellor, supported Walpole, and held office under the Duke of Newcastle. He presided at the trial of the rebel lords in 1745, and promoted the laws that proscribed tartan and abolished heritable jurisdiction in Scotland. His Marriage Act of 1754 abolished Fleet marriages. His son, **Philip,** second Earl (1720–90), held public offices, wrote *Athenian Letters* and edited *Walpoliana.*

YOSHIDA, Shigeru (1878–1967), Japanese politician, was born in Tokyo and educated at Tokyo Imperial University. He entered diplomacy in 1906 and after service in several capitals was vice-minister for foreign affairs. From 1930 to 1932 he was ambassador to Italy and from 1936 to 1938 ambassador in London. In October 1945 he became foreign minister and in May 1946, as first chairman of the Liberal party, he formed the Government which inaugurated the new constitution. He was re-elected in 1950 and resigned in 1954. See his *Memoirs* (1961).

YOUNG, (1) **Andrew** (1807–89), Scottish minor poet, an Edinburgh and St Andrews schoolmaster, wrote ' There is a happy Land '.

(2) **Andrew John** (1885–1971), British clergyman and poet, born in Elgin, canon of Chichester Cathedral since 1948, has written nature poems (*Winter Harvest*, 1933, *The White Blackbird*, 1935, &c.), a verse play (*Nicodemus*, 1937), and botanical essays (*A Prospect of Flowers*, 1945, and *A Retrospect of Flowers*, 1950). In 1952 he was awarded the Queen's Medal for Poetry.

(3) **Arthur** (1741–1820), English writer on agriculture, was born at Whitehall, but spent his boyhood, as indeed most of his life, at Bradfield near Bury St Edmunds, his father being rector and a prebendary of Canterbury. In 1763 he rented a small farm of his mother's, on which he made 3000 unsuccessful experiments; during 1766–71 held a good-sized farm in Essex (ruin the result); from 1776 to 1778 was in Ireland; resumed farming at Bradfield; and in 1793 was appointed secretary to the Board of Agriculture, with a salary of £400. Blind from 1811, he died in London, and was buried at Bradfield. Young, in his writings, was one of the first to elevate agriculture to a science. They include *A Tour through the Southern Counties* (1768), *A Tour through the North of England* (1771), *The Farmer's Tour through the East of England* (1770–71), *Tour in Ireland* (1780), *Travels in France during 1787-88-89-90* (a valuable account of the state of France just before the Revolution, 1792–94), *The Farmer's Kalendar* (215th ed. 1862), and ' Agricultural Surveys ' of eight English counties, besides many papers in *The Annals of Agriculture*, which he edited. See A. W. Hutton's edition of the *Tour in Ireland*, with bibliography (1892), and C. Maxwell's (1925); M. Betham-

Edwards's edition of the *Travels in France* (1890) and her edition of his Autobiography (1898); and Life by Defries (1938).

(4) **Brigham** (1801–77), American Mormon leader, born at Whitingham, Vt., was a carpenter, painter, and glazier in Mendon, N.Y. He first saw the ' Book of Mormon ' in 1830, and in 1832, converted by a brother of Joseph Smith (q.v.), was baptized and began to preach near Mendon. Next he went to Kirtland, Ohio, was made an elder, and preached in Canada 1832–33. In 1835 he was appointed one of the twelve apostles of the church, in 1844 president; and the Mormons, when driven from Nauvoo, were led by him to Utah in 1847. In 1840 he visited England and made 2000 proselytes. In 1847 the great body of Mormons arrived at Utah, and founded Salt Lake City; and in 1850 President Fillmore appointed Brigham Young governor. In 1858 a new governor, Cumming, was sent with a force of United States troops. The determination of the United States to abolish polygamy, and the appointment in 1869 of another ' Gentile ' governor, reduced Young's authority. Practical and far-seeing (though a fanatic), he encouraged agriculture and manufactures, made roads and bridges, and carried through a contract for 100 miles of the Union Pacific Railroad. He died leaving $2,500,000 to seventeen wives and fifty-six children.

(5) **Charles Mayne** (1777–1856), English tragedian, son of a rascally London surgeon, was driven from home with his mother and two brothers, and had for a while been a clerk in a West India house, when in 1798 he made his début at Liverpool; in 1807 he appeared in London as ' Hamlet '. He was a really original actor, second only, in some parts superior, to Kean himself. In 1832 he retired with a fortune of £60,000. In 1805 he had married a brilliant young actress, Julia Anne Grimani (1785–1806). Their son, **Julian Charles Young** (1806–73), was rector of Southwick in Sussex (1844–50), and then of Ilmington, Worcestershire; he published a most amusing *Memoir of Charles Mayne Young* (1871), four-fifths of it his own Journal, and supplemented in 1875 by *Last Leaves* from that same Journal.

(6) **Douglas** (1913–), Scottish poet and scholar, born at Tayport, Fife, was educated at Merchiston Castle, St Andrews and Oxford, and became a lecturer in Classics at Aberdeen and St Andrews. His collections of verse include *Auntran Blads* (1943) and *A Braird o' Thristles* (1947). He is best known for *The Puddocks* (1958) and *The Burdies* (1959), translations into Lallans of Aristophanes' plays. He was gaoled for refusing war service except in an independent Scotland's army and his attitude split the Scottish National Party, of which he was controversially elected chairman (1942). After the war he became a Labour parliamentary candidate.

(7) **Edward** (1683–1765), English poet, author of *Night Thoughts*, was born at Upham rectory near Bishop's Waltham, the son of a future dean of Salisbury, and in 1708 received a law fellowship of All Souls, Oxford. He came before the world as a poet in 1712 with an *Epistle* to George Granville on being created Lord Lansdowne. In 1719 he produced a tragedy, *Busiris*, at Drury Lane; in 1716 he was in Ireland in attendance on the dissolute young Marquis (afterwards Duke) of Wharton; and he was tutor in the family of the Marquis of Exeter. His second tragedy, *The Revenge*, was produced in 1721; his third and last, *The Brothers*, in 1753. His satires, *The Love of Fame*, the *Universal Passion* (1725–28), brought money as well as fame; and for *The Instalment* (1726), a poem addressed to Sir Robert Walpole, he got a pension of £200. In 1724 Young took orders; in 1727 he was appointed a royal chaplain; in 1730 he became rector of Welwyn. Next year he married Lady Elizabeth Lee, daughter of the Earl of Lichfield and widow of Colonel Lee. The *Night Thoughts* (1742–44) occasioned by her death and other sorrows, has much fustian sublimity and artificial melancholy, but many of its sententious lines have passed into proverbial use; some parts are real poetry. See his *Life and Letters* by H. C. Shelley (1914); Life by Croft in Johnson's *Poets* (1782); George Eliot's *Essays*; Thomas's *Le Poète E. Young* (1901), J. W. Mackail's *Studies of English Poets* (1926).

(8) **Emily Hilda** (Mrs Daniell) (1880–1949), English writer, born in Northumberland, wrote *Miss Mole* (1930, Tait Black Memorial prize) and other novels of the school of Jane Austen.

(9) **Francis Brett** (1884–1954), English novelist, born at Halesowen, Worcs. Established first as a physician, with a period as ship's doctor, he achieved celebrity as a writer with *Portrait of Clare* (1927), which won the Tait Black Memorial prize. From then on he wrote a succession of acceptable novels of leisurely charm, characterized by a deep love of his native country. Noteworthy titles are *My Brother Jonathan* (1928), *Far Forest* (1936), *Dr. Bradley Remembers* (1935), *A Man about the House* (1942) and *Portrait of a Village* (1951). In 1944 he essayed a long epic poem, *The Island*, cast in lyric, ballad, elegiac and narrative forms, as well as in dialogue. An ambitious undertaking, it remains, however, a storyteller's poem rather than the great work of a poet. *In South Africa* (1952) was his last book, and he died in Cape Town.

(10) **James** (1811–83), Scottish industrial chemist, born in Glasgow, was a joiner, and studied chemistry, &c., at Anderson's College. He became Thomas Graham's assistant there (1832) and (1837) in University College, London. As manager of chemical works near Liverpool (1839) and near Manchester (1843), he discovered cheaper methods of producing sodium stannate and potassium chlorate; and it was his experiments (1847–1850) that led to the manufacture of paraffin oil and solid paraffin on a large scale.

(11) **Thomas** (1587–1655), Scottish Puritan divine, born in Perthshire, studied at St Andrews, was Milton's tutor till 1622, and afterwards held charges at Hamburg and in Essex. He was the chief author in 1641 of an *Answer* to Bishop Hall by ' Smectymnuus ', a name compounded of the initials of Stephen

Marshall, Edmund Calamy, Thomas Young, Matthew Newcomen and William Spurstow.

(12) **Thomas** (1773–1829), English physicist, physician and Egyptologist, born at Milverton, Somerset, studied medicine at London, Edinburgh, Göttingen and Cambridge, and started as doctor in London in 1800, but devoted himself to scientific research, and in 1801 became professor of Natural Philosophy to the Royal Institution. His *Lectures* (1807) expounded the doctrine of interference, which established the undulatory theory of light. He did valuable work in insurance, haemodynamics and Egyptology, and made a fundamental contribution to the deciphering of the inscriptions on the Rosetta Stone. See Life by Peacock (1855) and Prof. Tyndall's *New Fragments* (1892).

YOUNGHUSBAND, Sir Francis (1863–1942), British explorer, born at Murree in India, explored Manchuria in 1886 and on the way back discovered the route from Kashgar into India via the Mustagh Pass. In 1902 he went on the expedition which opened up Tibet to the Western world. British resident in Kashmir (1906–09), he wrote much on India and Central Asia. Deeply religious, he founded the World Congress of Faiths in 1936.

YOURIEFFSKAIA, Princess. See DOLGORUKOVA.

YOUSEF, Sidi Mohammed ben. See SIDI MOHAMMED.

YPRES, Earl of. See FRENCH.

YPSILANTI, *ip-si-lan'tee*, distinguished Greek Phanariot family, claiming descent from the Comneni:

(1) **Alexander** (1725–1805), father of (3), became hospodar of Wallachia, but was put to death on suspicion of fostering Greek ambitions.

(2) **Alexander** (1783–1828), eldest son of (3), served with distinction in the Russian army in 1812–13, and was chosen by the Greek 'Hetairists' as their chief in 1820. He headed a Rouman movement, but, defeated by the Turks, took refuge in Austria, where he died.

(3) **Constantine** (d. 1816), son of (1), became also hospodar of Moldavia and Wallachia. Deposed in 1805, he came back with some thousands of Russian soldiers, stirred up the Serbs to rebellion, and made another plan for restoring Greece, but had to flee to Russia.

(4) **Demetrius** (1793–1832), younger son of (3), also served in the Russian army, and aided his brother's schemes for emancipating the Christian population of Turkey. In Greece he took part in the capture of Tripolita (October 1820). His gallant defence of Argos stopped the victorious march of the Turks, and in 1828–30 he was Greek commander-in-chief. He died in Vienna.

YRIARTE, Charles, *ee-ri-art* (1832–98), French man of letters, born in Paris, of Spanish ancestry, studied architecture but from 1861 devoted himself to literature. He was editor-in-chief of *Le Monde Illustré*. Specially interested in the Italian Renaissance period, he wrote histories of Venice (1877) and Florence (1880), as well as biographies of Francesca da Rimini (1882) and Caesar Borgia (1889).

YSAŸE, Eugène (1858–1931), Belgian violinist, one of the greatest of his time, born at Brussels, made many tours in Europe and America. First teacher of the violin at the Brussels Conservatoire (1886–98), he composed violin concertos, sonatas, &c.

YUAN SHIH-KAI, *-shee-kī* (1859–1916), Chinese dictator, born in Honan province, served in the army and became imperial adviser, minister in Korea (1885–94), governor of Shantung (1900), but was banished after the death of Emperor Kuang Hsü (1908). He participated in the revolution of 1911 and became first president of China (1912–16), Sun Yat-Sen (q.v.) standing down for him, but was opposed by the latter from the south when he tried to make himself emperor. His manner of death is unknown.

YUKAWA, Hideki (1907–), Japanese physicist, predicted (1935) the existence of the meson, a particle hundreds of times heavier than the electron. For his work on quantum-theory and nuclear physics he was awarded the Nobel prize for physics in 1949, the first Japanese so honoured. Professor of Physics at Kyoto University (1939–50) and director of Kyoto Research Institute from 1953, he was visiting professor at Princeton and Columbia Universities (1948–53).

YULE, Sir Henry (1820–89), British orientalist, born at Inveresk, served in the Bengal Engineers (1840–62), sat on the Indian Council (1875–89), and wrote *Cathay and the Way Thither* (1866) and *The Book of Ser Marco Polo* (1871). He was created K.C.S.I. in 1889.

Z

ZACCARIA, Antonio (1502–39), Italian religious, founded the Barnabite preaching order (1530), and was canonized in 1897.

ZACHARIAS, Saint (d. 752), a Greek by descent, born in Calabria, was pope from 741 to 752, and recognized Pepin the Short as king of France (752).

ZADKIEL, pseud. of **Richard James Morrison** (1794–1874), who in 1830 started a best selling astrological almanac.

ZADKINE, Ossip (1890–), Russian sculptor, born at Sindensk, developed an individual style, making effective use of the play of light on concave surfaces, as in *The Three Musicians* (1926), *Orpheus* (1940), and *Destroyed City* (1952). See monograph by Jianou (1965).

ZAHAROFF, Sir Basil, orig. **Basileios Zacharias** (1850–1936), armaments magnate and financier, born in Anatolia, Turkey, of Greek parents, entered the munitions industry and became a shadowy but immensely influential figure in international politics and finance, amassing a huge fortune in arms deals, oil, shipping and banking. Knighted (1918) for his services to the allies in World War I, he donated large sums of money to universities and other institutions, but was suspected by many of using his influence to intrigue for his own profit. See study by Lewinsohn (1934).

ZAHN, Theodor von (1838–1933), German Biblical scholar, born at Mörs, professor in several universities, including Göttingen and Leipzig, known for his series on the New Testament Canon (1881–93), including *Tatian's Diatessaron* and an introduction to the New Testament (1897). With Gebhardt and Harnack he edited the *Patres Apostoli* (1876–78).

ZAMENHOF, Lazarus Ludwig (1859–1917), a Jewish Warsaw oculist, born at Bialystok, invented Esperanto. See Life by M. Boulton (1960).

ZANGWILL, Israel (1864-1926), Jewish writer, born in London, went to school at Plymouth and Bristol, but was mainly self-taught, graduated with honours at London University, and, after teaching, became a journalist. A leading Zionist, he wrote poems, plays, novels, and essays, and became widely known by his Jewish tales— *Children of the Ghetto* (1892), *Ghetto Tragedies* (1894), &c. Other works are *The Master*, *Without Prejudice* (essays), *A Revolted Daughter*, *The Melting Pot* (1908), *We Moderns* (1925).

ZANUCK, Darryl Francis, za'nuk (1902–), American film producer, born in Wahoo, Neb. He worked with Joseph Schenck, Warner Brothers and Twentieth-Century Pictures, becoming vice-president of that company and, after its merger with Fox Films in 1935, of Twentieth-Century Fox Films Corporation. Among his many successful films are *Little Caesar*, *The Jazz Singer*, *How Green was My Valley*, *The Grapes of Wrath*, *The Snake Pit* and *All About Eve*.

ZAPOLYA, a powerful Hungarian family which included:

(1) **John** (1487–1540), prince of Transylvania, who was proclaimed king of Hungary in 1526, despite the superior claim of Ferdinand of Hapsburg, who drove him out in 1527 but was defeated by Suleiman the Magnificent, who reinstated John as puppet ruler.

(2) **John Sigismund** (1540–71), son of (1), succeeded his father, but, Suleiman having made Hungary a Turkish province, he had to content himself with the voivodship of Transylvania.

(3) **Stephen** (d. 1499), father of (1), gained renown as a military leader under Matthias Corvinus (q.v.) by his defeat of the Turks and his conquest of Austria, of which he was made governor (1485).

ZATOPEK, Emil, zat'- (1922–), Czech athlete, born in Moravia. After many successes in Czechoslovak track events, he won the 10,000 metres title at the Olympic Games in London in 1948. In the succeeding four years he showed himself to be the greatest long-distance runner of his time by breaking thirteen world records, and by further successes, including the 5000 metres and the Marathon, at the 1952 Olympics.

ZECHARIAH, minor prophet, born in Babylonia during the captivity, went back with the first band of exiles to Judaea. Of the Book of Zechariah only the first eight chapters are by him.

ZEEMAN, Pieter (1865–1943), Dutch physicist, born at Zonnemaire, Zeeland, lecturer at Leyden (1897), professor at Amsterdam (1900), was an authority on magneto-optics. While at Leyden he discovered the *Zeeman effect*, i.e., when a ray of light from a source placed in a magnetic field is examined spectroscopically the spectral line is widened or occasionally doubled. In 1902 he shared with Lorentz the Nobel prize for physics. In 1922 he was awarded the Rumford medal of the Royal Society.

ZEFFIRELLI, Franco (1923–), Italian stage, opera and film director, born and educated in Florence, began his career as actor and theatre-set and costume designer (1945–51). His first opera production, *La Cenerentola* (1953) at La Scala, was followed by a brilliant series of productions in Italy and abroad, culminating in *Lucia di Lammermoor*, *Cavelleria Rusticana* and *I Pagliacci* at Covent Garden in 1959 and an outstanding *Falstaff* at the New York Metropolitan Opera House in 1964. His stage productions include *Romeo and Juliet* at the Old Vic (1960), almost universally acclaimed for its originality, modern relevance and realistic setting in a recognizable Verona, and *Who's Afraid of Virginia Woolf* (Paris 1964, Milan 1965). He has also filmed zestful and spectacular versions of *The Taming of the Shrew* (1966) and *Romeo and Juliet* (1968).

ZEISS, Carl, tsis (1816-88), German optician, established at Jena (1846) the factory which became noted for the production of lenses, microscopes, field glasses, &c. His business was organized on a system whereby the workers had a share in the profits.

ZELLER, Eduard (1814–1908), German philosopher and theologian, born at Kleinbottwar in Württemberg, studied at Tübingen and Berlin, and settled at Tübingen in 1840 as *privatdozent* in Theology. In 1847 he became professor of Theology at Bern, and in 1849 at Marburg, whence he was called to the chair of Philosophy at Heidelberg in 1862, at Berlin in 1872. He forsook theology and his early Hegelianism for historical work, carried on in an impartial and eclectic spirit. He published Platonic studies in 1839, a trenchant work on the Acts of the Apostles (on Baur's lines, 1854; trans. 1876), books on Zwingli (1853), D. F. Strauss (1874), and Frederick the Great (1886); a history of German philosophy since Leibniz (1872), and a manual of Greek philosophy (1883; trans. 1886); and his masterly work, *Die Geschichte der Griechischen Philosophie* (1844–52).

ZENO (426–491), emperor of the East (474–491), was a weak ruler, and during his reign internal distractions and foreign troubles greatly increased. His *Henoticon* (482), designed to bring about union in the Church only occasioned a new schism.

ZENO OF CITIUM (342–270 B.C.), founder of the Stoic philosophy, a native of Citium, Cyprus, possibly a Phoenician, in 320 went to Athens, where he did the rounds of the philosophical schools, and finally opened his own at the ' Painted Porch ' (*Stoa Poikilē*). He taught that virtue is necessarily good, that most things in life are morally indifferent, e.g., most objects of desire such as goods, honours, children, wife, and that these are at best only relatively good. He wrote eighteen books, including the anarchical *Republic*. In extreme old age he committed suicide. See works on Stoicism by E. Zeller (1870), R. D. Hicks (1911), E. V. Arnold (1911; new ed. 1958), M. Pohlenz (1948–49), and S. Sambursky on the Physics (1959).

ZENO OF ELEA (fl. 5th cent. B.C.), Greek philosopher, a native of Elea, a Greek colony in Lucana, Italy. A favourite disciple of Parmenides (q.v.), he went with him to Athens and on his return to Elea joined an unsuccessful conspiracy against the tyrant Nearchus. He defended Parmenidian monism against Pythagorean pluralism, by taking a Pythagorean postulate such as ' things are a many ' and working out from it a pair of contradictory conclusions. Best known of all are his four arguments against motion, which is a necessary consequence of pluralism. They are ' Achilles and the Tortoise ', ' The Flying Arrow ', ' The Stadium ' and ' The Row of Solids '. They were refuted by Aristotle, but reinstated by Lewis Carroll, Bergson and Bertrand Russell in their different ways. Only fragments of his works remain. He appears in Plato's dialogue, *Parmenides*, as instructor to Socrates. See E. Zeller, *Presocratic Philosophy* (trans. 1881), B. Russell, *Mysticism and Logic* (1918), J. Burnet, *Early Greek Philosophy* (4th ed. 1930), G. S. Kirk and J. E. Raven, *The Presocratic Philosophers* (1957).

ZENO OF SIDON (1st cent. B.C.), Epicurean philosopher, taught at Athens to 78 B.C.

ZENO OF TARSUS (3rd cent. B.C.), succeeded Chrysippus as head of the Stoic school.

ZENOBIA, *-nō'-* (3rd cent. A.D.), queen of Palmyra, born there probably of Arab descent, became the wife of the Bedouin Odenathus, lord of the city, who in A.D. 264 was recognized by Gallienus as governor of the East. On her husband's murder (*c.* 271) nearly the whole of the eastern provinces submitted to her sway. When Aurelian assumed the purple, he marched against her, defeated her in several battles, besieged her in Palmyra, and ultimately captured her as she was attempting flight (272). She saved her life by imputing the blame of the war to her secretary, Longinus (q.v.); he was beheaded and Palmyra destroyed. Zenobia, decked with jewels, was led in triumphal procession at Rome, and presented by her conqueror with large possessions near Tivoli, where, with her two sons, she passed the rest of her life in comfort and even splendour. Strikingly beautiful and of high spirit, she governed with prudence, justice, and liberality. See W. Wright, *Palmyra and Zenobia* (1895).

ZEPHANIAH, *zef-ė-nī'a* (fl. 7th cent. B.C.), Hebrew prophet of the Old Testament whose account of a coming Day of Wrath inspired the mediaeval Latin hymn *Dies Irae*.

ZEPPELIN, Count Ferdinand von (1838–1917),

German army officer, born at Constance, Baden, served in the Franco-German war, and in 1897–1900 constructed his first airship or dirigible balloon of rigid type, named a *zeppelin*, after its inventor, who set up a works for their construction at Friedrichshafen.

ZERNIKE, Frits (1888–1966), Dutch physicist, born at Amsterdam, professor of Physics at Groningen (1910–58), developed the phase-contrast principle used in microscopy. He was awarded the Nobel physics prize in 1953.

ZEROMSKI, Stefan, *zhe-rom'ski* (1864–1925), Polish novelist, born at Strawczyn, wrote *The Homeless* (1900), *The Ashes* (1904, English edition 1928), *The Fight with Satan* (trilogy, 1916–18), &c., pessimistic, patriotic, lyrical in tone.

ZEUSS, Johann Kaspar, *tsoys* (1806–56), German founder of Celtic philology, became professor in the Lyceum at Bamberg in 1847. He edited *Grammatica Celtica* (1853).

ZEUXIS, *zook'sis* (fl. late 5th cent. B.C.), Greek painter, born at Heraclea, excelled in the representation of natural objects. According to legend, his painting of a bunch of grapes was so realistic that birds tried to eat the fruit.

ZHUKOV, Georgi Konstantinovich (1896–), Russian soldier, was born of peasant parents at Strelkovka, Kaluga region, worked in Moscow as an apprentice furrier, was conscripted into the Tsarist Army, and in 1918 joined the Red Army. In 1939 he commanded the Soviet tanks in Outer Mongolia, and in 1941, as general, became Army chief of staff. In December 1941 he lifted the siege of Moscow, and in February 1943 his counter-offensive was successful at Stalingrad. In command of the First Byelo-Russian Army in 1944–45, he captured Warsaw and conquered Berlin. On May 8, 1945, on behalf of the Soviet High Command, he accepted the German surrender. After the war he became c.-in-c. of the Russian zone of Germany, in 1955 becoming minister of defence, and in 1957 supported Khrushchev against the Malenkov-Molotov faction. He was later dismissed by Khrushchev, and in 1958 was attacked for his ' revisionist ' policy and for his alleged ' political mistakes ' in the administration of the forces. He published several war studies and holds the Lenin prize for journalism, being foreign editor of *Pravda* 1952–57, &c.

ZHUKOVSKY, Vasily Andreyevich (1783–1852), Russian poet, born in the government of Tula, known chiefly for his translations into Russian of English, French and German poetry.

ZIEGFELD, Florenz, *zig'feld* (1869–1932), American theatre manager, born in Chicago, the son of the president of Chicago Musical College. He was the deviser and perfector of the American revue spectacle, based on the *Folies Bergères*, and his *Follies of 1907* was the first of an annual series that continued until 1931 and made his name synonymous with extravagant theatrical production. He produced other musical shows, such as *The Red Feather*, *Kid Boots*, *Sally*, *Show Boat*, and the American production of *Bitter Sweet*.

ZIEGLER, Karl (1898–1973), German chemist, born at Helsa (Oberhessen), taught at

Marburg from 1920, at Heidelberg from 1936, and in 1943 was appointed director of the Max Planck Carbon Research Institute at Mulheim. With Giulio Natta he was awarded the Nobel prize in 1963 for researches on long-chain polymers leading to new developments in industrial materials.

ZIETEN, or **Ziethen, Hans Joachim von,** *tzee'tĕn* (1699–1786), Prussian cavalry general, born at Wustrau (Brandenburg), was dismissed from the Prussian cavalry for insubordination in 1727, but in 1730 rehabilitated. As colonel of hussars (1741) he increased the efficiency of the Prussian light cavalry. In 1744 he burst into Bohemia, then executed a dexterous retreat; in the Seven Years' War he covered himself with glory at Prague, Collin, Leuthen, Liegnitz and Torgau. ' Old Father Zieten ' thereafter lived in retirement at Berlin, in high favour with Frederick the Great. See Life by Winter (1886).

ZIMBALIST, Efrem (1889–), violinist and composer, was born in Rostov, Russia, and later took American nationality, becoming director of the Curtis Institute of Music in Philadelphia. He has composed for both violin and orchestra.

ZIMISCES, John, *zi-mis'eez* (925–76), Byzantine emperor in 969–976, fought stoutly against Saracens, Bulgars and Russians. See study of his time by Schlumberger (*L'Épopée Byzantine*, 1897).

ZIMMERMANN, *tzim'-*, (1) **Arthur** (1864–1940), German politician, was born in East Prussia. After diplomatic service in China he directed from 1904 the Eastern Division of the German Foreign Office and was foreign secretary (November 1916–August 1917). In January 1917 he sent the famous ' Zimmermann telegram ' to the German minister in Mexico with the terms of an alliance between Mexico and Germany, by which Mexico was to attack the United States with German and Japanese assistance in return for the American states of New Mexico, Texas and Arizona. This telegram finally brought the hesitant U.S. government into the war against Germany. See Tuchman, *The Zimmermann Telegram* (1959).

(2) **Dominikus** (1685–1766), German architect, born at Wessobrunn, a leading exponent of the Rococo style in southern Germany, as seen in his churches at Wies, Buxheim, Gunzberg, &c.

(3) **Johann Georg, Ritter von** (1728–95), Swiss doctor and writer, born at Brugg, studied medicine at Göttingen, and became town physician at Brugg, where he published his sentimental book *On Solitude* (1755; rewritten 1785), which was translated from the German into almost every European language. He also wrote on ' national pride ' and on medical subjects. In 1768 he went to Hanover with the title of physician to George III, and was summoned to Berlin to the last illness of Frederick the Great. See books by Bodemann (1878) and Ischer (1893).

(4) **Robert** (1824–98), Austrian Herbartian philosopher and writer on aesthetics, an opponent of Hegel.

ZINOVIEV, Grigoriy, *zin-ov'yef* (1883–1936), Russian politician, born at Elisavetgrad, Ukraine, was in 1917–26 a leading member

of the Soviet government, but then suffered expulsion, in 1936 death. The so-called ' Zinoviev Letter ' influenced the British general election of 1924.

ZINSSER, Hans (1878–1940), American bacteriologist, born in New York, professor at Columbia (1913–23), then at Harvard Medical School. In 1915 he was one of the Red Cross Commission to Serbia for the purpose of investigating typhus. In 1923 he was a League of Nations commissioner in Russia, studying cholera. With others he developed immunization methods against typhus (1930).

ZINZENDORF, Nicolaus Ludwig, Graf von (1700–60), German religious leader, refounder of the Moravian Brethren, was born at Dresden, studied at Wittenburg, and held a government post at Dresden. He invited the persecuted Moravians to his Lusatian estates, and there founded for them the colony of Herrnhut (' the Lord's keeping '). His zeal led to troubles with the government, and in 1736–48 he was exiled. He visited England, and in 1741 went to America. During his exile from Saxony he was ordained at Tübingen, and became Bishop of the Moravian Brethren. He died at Herrnhut, having written over a hundred books. His emphasis on feeling in religion influenced German theology. See Life by Weinlick (1956).

ZISKA, or **Žižka, John,** *zhish'ka* (c. 1370–1424), Bohemian Hussite leader, nobly born at Trocznov, was brought up as page to King Wenceslas. He fought for the Teutonic Knights against the Poles, for the Austrians against the Turks, and for the English at Agincourt (1415). In Bohemia soon after the murder of Huss he became chamberlain to King Wenceslas, joined the extremist party of hatred against Rome and lost an eye in the civil wars. After the outbreak at Prague (July 30, 1419), Ziska was chosen leader of the popular party, with 4000 men defeated the Emperor Sigismund's 40,000, captured Prague (1421), and erected the fortress of Tabor, whence his party were called Taborites. In 1421 he lost his remaining eye at the siege of Raby, but continued to lead on his troops to a succession of twelve unexampled victories, with but one defeat, compelling Sigismund to offer the Hussites religious liberty. But he died of plague at the siege of Przibislav before the war was over, and was buried ultimately at Caslav. See study by Heymann (1955).

ZITTEL, Karl Alfred von (1839–1904), German geologist and palaeontologist, born at Bahlingen, Baden, a distinguished authority on his subjects and their history, taught at Vienna, Karlsruhe and Munich, and were president of the Bavarian Academy. His *Textbook of Palaeontology* appeared in English translation 1900–02 (ed. Eastman). It was later revised by Woodward (1925).

ZOË (980–1050), daughter of the Byzantine emperor Constantine VIII, caused the murder of her husband, Romanus III, made her paramour emperor as Michael IV (1034), and after his exile (1042) married Constantine IX.

ZOFFANY, John (1733–1810), R.A. (1769), a London portrait painter, of German origin. After studying art in Rome, in 1758 he settled in London. Securing royal patronage, he painted many portraits and conversation pieces. 1772–79 he spent in Florence; 1783–90 in India. See study by Manners and Williamson (1920).

ZOG I, orig. **Ahmed Bey Zogu,** zŏg (1895–1961), king of Albania, was born the son of a highland tribal chieftain, and was educated in Istanbul. He became head of the clan at the age of twelve, growing up in an atmosphere of tribal feuds, and in 1912, when Albania declared her independence, Zog took a blood oath to defend it. As the outstanding nationalist leader, in 1922 he formed a republican government and was its premier, president and commander-in-chief; in 1928 he proclaimed himself king. After Albania was overrun by the Italians Zog came to Britain, and in 1946 took up residence in Egypt, in 1955 on the French Riviera.

ZOILUS (fl. 3rd cent. B.C.), Greek rhetorician, born at Amphipolis, became known as *Homeromastix* (scourge of Homer), from the bitterness with which he attacked Homer. His name became proverbial for a malignant critic.

ZOLA, Émile (1840–1902), French novelist, was born in Paris, the son of an Italian engineer. He entered the publishing house of Hachette as a clerk, but soon became an active journalist. His work in criticism, politics and drama was almost uniformly unfortunate. His true forte for short stories showed itself in the charming *Contes à Ninon* (1864), *Nouveaux Contes à Ninon* (1874), the collections entitled *Le Capitaine Burle* and *Naïs Micoulin,* and the splendid *Attaque du Moulin* (1880). In the later years of the Empire he had formed with Flaubert, Daudet, the Goncourts, and Turgenev a sort of informal society, out of which grew the 'Naturalist school'. In this direction *Thérèse Raquin* (1867) is a very powerful picture of remorse. But it was not until after the war that he began the great series of novels with a purpose called *Les Rougon-Macquart*; it comprises a score of volumes, all connected by the appearance of the same or different members of the family. The two 'mother ideas' of Zola's naturalism were heredity and a certain cerebral infirmity; and in order to apply his theory to the study of *le document humain,* he mastered the technical details of most professions, occupations and crafts, as well as the history of recent events in France. He began with a sort of general sketch called *La Fortune des Rougon. La Curée* and *Son Excellence Eugène Rougon* deal with the society of the later days of the Second Empire. *La Faute de l'Abbé Mouret* is an attack upon celibacy, and is, like *La Conquête de Plassans,* a vivid study of provincial life. *Le Ventre de Paris* deals with the lowest strata of the Parisian population. *L'Assommoir* depicts drunkenness; *Pot-Bouille* the lower *bourgeoisie* and their servants; *Au Bonheur des dames* 'universal providers'. *Une Page d'amour* and *La Joie de vivre* are more generally human. *Nana* is devoted to the cult of the goddess Lubricity. *L'Oeuvre* deals with art and literature. *La Terre* is an appallingly repulsive study of the French peasant, and *Germinal* of the miner; *La Bête humaine* contains minute information as to the working of railways; *Le Rêve* displays a remarkable acquaintance with the details of church ritual; *L'Argent* exploits financial crashes; and *La Débâcle* recounts the great disaster of 1870. *Dr Pascal* (1893) is a sort of feeble summing-up. *Lourdes* (1894), dealing with faith-healing, is hardly a novel, any more than is *Rome* (1896), a critical study of the Papal Curia, or *Paris* (1898). *Fécondité* (1899), *Travail* (1901), and *Vérité* (1903) form part of 'Les Quatre Évangiles'. Zola espoused the cause of Dreyfus (q.v.), impeached the military authorities, and was sentenced to imprisonment (1898), but escaped for a year to England. He died in Paris, accidentally suffocated by charcoal fumes. See his *Correspondance* (1907–08), works by Sherard (1893), Vizetelly (1904), Josephson (1928), Barbusse (trans. 1932), and (in French) Lepelletier (1908), Seillière (1923), D. Le Blond-Zola (his daughter; 1931), Hemmings (1953) and Laroux (1955).

ZORN, Anders Leonhard (1860–1920), Swedish etcher, sculptor and painter, born at Utmeland, near Mora. His bronze statue of Gustavus Vasa is in his native town of Mora. His paintings deal mainly with Swedish peasant life. He achieved European fame as an etcher, with studies of Verlaine, Proust, Rodin, &c., and a series of nudes executed with unique skill. See a monograph by E. M. Lang (1924).

ZOROASTER, Grecized form of **Zarathushtra,** mod. **Zaradusht,** Iranian prophet, the founder or reformer of the ancient Parsee religion, appears as an historical person only in the earliest portion of the Avesta. His family name was Spitama. As the centre of a group of chieftains, one of whom was King Vîshtâspa, he carried on a political, military, and theological struggle for the defence or wider establishment of a holy agricultural state against Turanian and Vedic aggressors. He lived in N.W. Persia perhaps in the 6th century B.C. Some put him as early as c. 1000 B.C. The keynote of his system is that the world and history exhibit the struggle between Ormuzd and Ahriman (the creator or good spirit, and the evil principle, the devil), in which at the end evil will be banished and the good reign supreme. See studies by Jackson (1898), Dhalla (1938), Herzfeld (1947) and Guillemin (1949).

ZORRILLA Y MORAL, José (1817–93), a fluent Spanish poet, born at Valladolid, wrote many plays based on national legend. He died poor in Madrid, but his play *Don Juan Tenorio* (1844) is performed annually on All Saints' Day in Spanish-speaking countries.

ZOSIMUS, (1) (5th cent. A.D.), a pagan Greek historian, who held office at Constantinople under Theodosius II (408–450). His *Historia Nova* deals with the Roman emperors to A.D. 410.

(2) Pope (417–418), involved in the Pelagian controversy. See PELAGIUS.

ZSCHOKKE, Johann Heinrich Daniel, chŏk'e (1771–1848), German writer, born at Magdeburg, was a strolling playwright, then a student at Frankfurt, lectured there and adapted plays, and finally opened a boarding-school at Reichenau in the Grisons. In 1799 he settled at Aarau, where he became a member of the Great Council. His books include histories of Bavaria and Switzerland, and a long series of tales—*Der Creole, Jonathan Frock, Clementine, Oswald, Meister Jordan*, &c. The most popular of all was the *Stunden der Andacht* (1809–16; trans. as *Hours of Meditation*, 1843)—a Sunday periodical, expounding rationalism with eloquence and zeal. His collected writings fill 35 vols. (1851–54). See his autobiographical *Selbstschau* (trans. 1847).

ZSIGMONDY, Richard Adolf, *zhig'mon-di* (1865–1929), Austrian chemist, born in Vienna, from 1907 a professor at Göttingen, was a pioneer of colloid chemistry, gaining the Nobel prize for 1925. In 1903 he introduced the ultramicroscope.

ZUCCARO, Taddeo, *tsook'ka-rō* (1529–66), Italian painter in Rome, born at S. Angelo in Vado, near Urbino, left some pretentious but not valuable frescoes and easel pieces of no especial merit. He did much work for the Farnese family, and examples may be seen in the Palazzo Farnese, Rome and Caparola. His brother, **Federigo** (1543–1609), during his travels painted portraits (Queen Elizabeth, Mary Stuart, &c.), but devoted most of his time to unsatisfactory frescoes at Florence, Venice, the Escorial, &c. He founded at Rome the Academy of St Luke (1595).

ZUCCHI, Antonio Pietro, *tsook'kee* (1726–95), Italian painter, was brought to England in about 1766 by the Adam brothers (q.v.), for whom he executed many excellent ceiling medallions and wall paintings (Kenwood, Harewood House, Osterley Park, &c.). Also working for the brothers was Angelica Kauffmann (q.v.), whom he married in 1781. He was elected an A.R.A. in 1770.

ZUCKMAYER, Carl (1896–   ), German dramatist, born at Nackenheim, Rhineland, lived in Austria, but after that country's annexation, emigrated to the U.S.A. His best-known plays are *Der Hauptmann von Köpenick* (1931) and *Des Teufels General* (1942–45), both filmed.

ZUKERTORT, Johann Hermann (1842–88), Polish chess master, born at Lublin, studied medicine at Breslau, but from 1867 devoted himself to chess. Settling in England in 1872, he founded and edited the *Chess Monthly*, won tournaments in Paris and London, was defeated by Steinitz in America in 1885, and died in London. He published two German chess manuals (1869–73).

ZULOAGA, Ignacio, *thoo-lo-ah'ga* (1870–1945), Spanish painter, born, the son of a metalworker, at Eibar in the Basque country, studied painting at Rome and Paris, and won recognition abroad and then at home as the reviver of the national tradition in Spanish painting. Works may be seen in the Luxembourg, Paris, and in galleries at Ghent and Leipzig.

ZUMALACÁRREGUY, Tomás, *thoo-mah-la-kar'ray-gee* (1788–1835), greatest of Spanish Carlist generals, was born at Ormáiztegui in the Basque province of Guipúzcoa. He fought against Napoleon, on the re-establish-ment of absolutism was made governor of Ferrol, but in 1832, with other Carlists, was dismissed the army. Head of the Basque Carlist insurrection (1833), he kept his opponents at bay, and gained a series of victories over the Cristino generals. This turned the weak head of Don Carlos, and led him to interfere with the plans of his general, who was anxious to strike for Madrid, but who, ordered to lay siege to Bilbao, was mortally wounded by a musketball. See Henningsen's *Twelve Months' Campaign* (1836) and *Cornhill* for January 1871.

ZÚÑIGA. See ERCILLA Y ZÚÑIGA.

ŽUPANČIČ, Oton, *zhoo'pan-chit-y'* (1878–1949), Slovene poet, the translator of Shakespeare into Slovene.

ZURBARÁN, Francisco, *thoor-ba-rahn'* (1598–1662), Spanish religious painter, born at Fuente de Cantos in Andalusia, the son of a labourer, spent most of his laborious life at Seville. His masterpiece, an altarpiece, is in the museum there. Apart from a few portraits and still-life studies, his main subjects were monastic and historical, and he came to be called the ' Spanish Caravaggio '.

ZWEIG, *tsvig*, (1) **Arnold** (1887–1968), German-Jewish author, was born at Glogau. His writing is socialistic in outlook and is also coloured by the interest in Zionism which led him to seek refuge in Palestine when exiled by the Nazis in 1934. His works include the novels *Claudia* (1912), *Der Streit um den Sergeanten Grischa* (1928), *Junge Frau von 1914* (1931) and *De Vriendt kehrt heim* (1932), all of which have appeared in English translation; also the play *Die Umkehr* (1927) and some penetrating essays.

(2) **Stefan** (1881–1942), Austrian writer, born in Vienna of Jewish parentage, was first known as poet and translator (of Ben Jonson, &c.), then as biographer (Balzac, Dickens, Marie Antoinette, &c.), short-story writer (e.g., *Kaleidoscope*, 1934) and novelist (*Beware of Pity*, 1939, &c.). A feature of all his work is its deep psychological insight. From 1934 to 1940 he lived in London, and acquired British nationality. He later went to U.S.A. and Brazil. It was in Petropolis, Brazil, that he died by his own hand in 1942. See his autobiographical *The World of Yesterday* (published posthumously, 1943).

ZWICKY, Fritz (1898–   ), American physicist, born in Bulgaria, educated at Zürich, joined the staff of the California Institute of Technology in 1927, becoming professor of Astrophysics there in 1942. He is known for his research on novae, cosmic rays and slow electrons.

ZWINGLI, Huldreich, *tsving'lee*, Lat. **Ulricus Zuinglius** (1484–1531), Swiss reformer, was born at Wildhaus in St Gall, studied at Bern, Vienna and Basel, and became priest at Glarus in 1506. Here he taught himself Greek, and twice (1513, 1515) as field-chaplain accompanied the Glarus mercenaries. Transferred in 1516 to Einsiedeln, whose Black Virgin was a great resort of pilgrims, he made no secret of his contempt for such superstition. In 1518 elected preacher in the Zürich minster, he roused the council not to admit within the city gates Bernhardin Samson, a seller of indulgences.

He preached the gospel boldly, and in 1521 succeeded in keeping Zürich from joining the other cantons in their alliance with France. The Bishop of Constance sent his vicar-general, who was quickly silenced in debate with Zwingli (1523), in presence of the council and six hundred; whereupon the city adopted the Reformed doctrines as set forth in Zwingli's sixty-seven theses. A second disputation followed (1523), with the result that images and the mass were swept away. Zwingli married Anna Meyer (*née* Reinhard), a widow of forty-three, in 1524; on Easter Sunday 1525 he dispensed the sacrament in both kinds; and the Reformation spread widely over Switzerland. Zwingli first made public his views on the Lord's Supper in 1524; and the first stage of the controversy with Luther, destined to rend the Protestant Church, closed with the fruitless conference at Marburg (1529). He rejected every form of local or corporeal presence, whether by transubstantiation or consubstantiation. Meantime the progress of the Reformation had aroused bitter hatred in the Forest Cantons. Five of them formed in 1528 an alliance, to which the Archduke Ferdinand of Austria was admitted. Zürich declared war in 1529 on account of the burning alive of a Protestant pastor seized on neutral territory, but bloodshed was averted for a time by the first treaty of Cappel (1529). But the Forest Cantons made a sudden dash on Zürich with 8000 men, and were met at Cappel by 2000, including Zwingli. The men of Zürich made a desperate resistance, but were completely defeated, and Zwingli was among the dead. Zwingli preached sub-stantially the Reformed doctrines as early as 1516, the year before the appearance of Luther's theses. Original sin he regarded as a moral disease rather than as punishable sin or guilt. He maintained the salvation of unbaptized infants, and he believed in the salvation of such virtuous heathens as Socrates, Plato, Pindar, Numa, Scipio and Seneca. On predestination he was as Calvinistic as Calvin or Augustine. With less of fire and power than Luther, he was the most open-minded and liberal of the Reformers. Zwingli's *Opera* fill four folios (1545); later editions are by Schuler and Schulthess (1828–42; supp. 1861); Egli and others (1905 *et seq.*). The chief is the *Commentarius de vera et falsa religione* (1525); the rest are mainly occupied with the exposition of Scripture and controversies on the Eucharist, &c. There are old Lives by Myconius and Bullinger; later studies by Finsler (1897; a bibliography), and Farner (1952). See also numerous works by Köhler, and publications of the Zwingli Society.

ZWORYKIN, Vladimir Kosma (1889–   ), Russian-born physicist, educated at Petrograd Technical Institute and the University of Pittsburgh, took U.S. nationality in 1924, joined the Radio Corporation in 1929, in 1934 was appointed director of electronic research, and in 1947 vice-president and technical consultant. Known for his work in the fields of photoelectricity and tele-vision, he invented the iconoscope and was a pioneer in the development of the electron microscope.

SUBJECT INDEX

Entries refer to the relevant articles. Self-explanatory and relatively obscure or insignificant titles and subjects have not been included.

ART AND ARCHITECTURE

CINEMA

GAY DIVORCE, THE → Astaire
GENTLEMAN'S AGREEMENT → Kazan
GHOST GOES WEST, THE → Clair
GOLD RUSH, THE → Chaplin (1)
GOLDEN COACH, THE → Renoir (1)
GONE WITH THE WIND → See under Olivier (1)
GRANDE ILLUSION, LA → Renoir (1)
GREAT DICTATOR, THE → Chaplin (1)
GREED → Stroheim

HAMLET → Olivier (1)
HENRY V → Olivier (1)
HIROSHIMA MON AMOUR → Resnais

INTOLERANCE → Griffith (2)
IVAN THE TERRIBLE → Eisenstein

KINETOSCOPE → Edison
KING IN NEW YORK, A → Chaplin (1)
KNOCK ON WOOD → Kaye (1)

LADY AND THE TRAMP, THE → Disney
LADY BE GOOD → Astaire
LADY VANISHES, THE → Hitchcock (1)
LITTLE WORLD OF DON CAMILLO, THE → Fernandel
LIVING DESERT, THE → Disney

MILLION, LE → Clair
MODERN TIMES → Chaplin (1)
MON ONCLE → Tati
MORNING GLORY → Hepburn (2)
MOTION PICTURES IN BRITAIN → Friese-Greene
M. HULOT'S HOLIDAY → Tati
MUTINY ON THE BOUNTY → Brando, Laughton

NANA → Renoir (1)
NATURE FILMS → Sielmann
NEWSREELS → Pathé
NIGHT AT THE OPERA, A → Marx (1)
NIGHT TRAIN TO MUNICH → Reed (1)
NINOTCHKA → Garbo

ON THE WATERFRONT → Brando, Kazan
ORPHÉE → Cocteau
OTHELLO → Welles

OTTO E MEZZO → Fellini
OUR MAN IN HAVANA → Reed (1)

PINOCCHIO → Disney
PLAINSMAN, THE → De Mille
PRISONER OF ZENDA → Fairbanks
PRIVATE LIFE OF HENRY VIII → Korda, Laughton

RASHOMON → Kurosawa
RASPUTIN AND THE EMPRESS → Barrymore
REAR WINDOW → Hitchcock (1)
REBECCA → Hitchcock (1)
RED SHOES, THE → Helpmann, Korda
REMBRANDT → Korda
RICHARD III → Olivier (1)

SECRET LIFE OF WALTER MITTY, THE → Kaye (1)
SEVEN SAMURAI, THE → Kurosawa
SEVENTH SEAL → Bergman (3)
SHEEP HAS FIVE LEGS, THE → Fernandel
SHEIK, THE → Valentino
SIN OF MADELON CLAUDET, THE → Hayes (2)
SNOW WHITE AND THE SEVEN DWARFS → Disney
SOUS LES TOITS DE PARIS → Clair
STRADA, LA → Fellini
STREETCAR NAMED DESIRE, A → Brando, Kazan,
  see under Olivier (1)
SUMMER WITH MONIKA → Bergman (3)

TEN COMMANDMENTS, THE → De Mille
THIRD MAN, THE → Reed (1), Welles
THIRTY-NINE STEPS, THE → Hitchcock (1)
THREE-DIMENSIONAL FILM → Todd (2)
THREE MUSKETEERS, THE → Fairbanks
TOP HAT → Astaire
TREASURE ISLAND → Disney

WAY AHEAD, THE → Reed (1)
WEDDING MARCH, THE → Stroheim
WIDE SCREEN → Todd (2)
WILD STRAWBERRIES → Bergman (3)
WONDER MAN → Kaye (1)

YOUNG MR PITT, THE → Reed (1)

EXPLORATION AND GEOGRAPHY

ABYSSINIA → Beke, Bruce (3), Markham
AFGHANISTAN → Burnes
AFRICA → Andersson, Brazza, Caillié, Cameron (8),
  Denham, Galton, Johnston (5), Livingstone,
  Park, Selous, Speke, Stanley (3)
AFRICA, CENTRAL → Barth (1), Livingstone, Thomson
  (9)
AFRICA, EAST → Burton (4), Decken, Elton (3),
  Johnston (3), Schweinfurth
AFRICA, NORTH → Rohlfs
AFRICA, WEST → Du Chaillu, Hanno, Kingsley (4)
AFRICAN COAST → Diaz
ALASKA → Andrews (1), Spurr
AMAZON → Bates (1), Lacondamine, Orellana,
  Teixeira
AMERICA → Cabot (1), Cárdenas (1), Cartier (2), De
  Soto, La Salle (3)
AMERICA, WESTERN → Belcher (1), Frémont
AMERICAS → Hettner (1)
ANNAPURNA, FIRST TO CLIMB, → Herzog (2)
ANTARCTIC → Amundsen, Bellingshausen, Borch-
  grevink, Bruce (10), Byrd (1), Charcot (1),
  Cherry-Garrard, Cook (4), Drygalski, Dumont
  D'Urville, Enderby, Fuchs (3), Hillary, Mawson,
  Mountevans, Nordenskjöld (2), Ross (2), Scott
  (23), Shackleton, Weddell, Wilkins (1), Wilson (8)
ARCTIC → Back, Barrow (2), Bellot, Byrd (1), De
  Long, Ellsworth, Franklin (2), Greely, Hall (4),
  Hayes (2), Heilprin, Kane (1), McClure, Mac-
  Millan, Nansen, Nares, Nordenskjöld (1), Parry
  (3), Peary, Rae, Ross (3), Schwatka, Scoresby,
  Sverdrup, Wilkins (1), Wrangel (1)

ASIA → Hettner (1), La Pérouse, Polo
ASIA, CENTRAL → Bonvalot, Hedin, Humboldt,
  Huntington (3), Stein (1)
ATHENS, FOUNDER OF → Cecrops
AUSTRALASIA (COAST) → Dumont D'Urville
AUSTRALIA → Burke (4), Cadell (1), Cook (4), Eyre,
  Flinders, Forrest (2), Grey (3), Hume (1),
  Jukes, Leichhardt, Mitchell (7), Spencer (4),
  Stuart (3), Sturt, Vancouver
AUSTRALIA, CENTRAL → Wilkins (1)
AUSTRALIA, FIRST TO LOCATE GOLD IN → Hargraves
AUSTRALIAN WATERS → Tasman
AZORES → Henry the Navigator

BAHAMAS → Columbus
BOLIVIA → Bolívar
BOOTHIA FELIX → Ross (3)
BORNEO → Harrisson
BRAZIL → Cabot (2), Cabral, Cousin (2), Fawcett (3),
  Pinzón, Roosevelt (3)
BRITISH GUIANA → Schomburgk

CALCUTTA, FOUNDER OF → Charnock (1)
CANADA → Champlain, Mackenzie (1), Simpson (1),
  Thompson (3), Verendrye
CANARIES → Cadamosto
CAPE OF GOOD HOPE → Diaz
CAPE VERDE → Henry the Navigator
CHINA → Garnier (1)
CHINESE TURKESTAN → Stein (1)
CIRCUMNAVIGATION → Bougainville, Cano (2), Cav-
  endish (3), Drake (2), Magellan

HISTORY

BOSWORTH → Richard III
BOUNTY, THE → Adams (5), Bligh, Christian (1)
BRANDYWINE → Howe (7)
BREITENFELD → Gustavus II, Tilly (2)
BROAD-BOTTOM ADMINISTRATION → Pelham (3)
BRUNANBURH → Athelstan
BULL RUN → Beauregard

CABAL → Arlington, Buckingham (2), Clifford, Lauderdale, Shaftesbury (1)
CAMISARDS → Cavalier, Villars
CAMPERDOWN → Duncan (1)
CANNAE → Scipio
CAPE MATAPAN → Cunningham (3)
CAPE ST VINCENT → Duncan (1), St Vincent
CASKET LETTERS → Morton, 4th Earl of
CATILINE CONSPIRACY → Caesar (1), Catilina, Cato (3)
CATO STREET CONSPIRACY → Thistlewood
CHAERONEA → Archelaus (3)
' CHAMPAGNE ' SPEECH → Townshend (2)
CHANCELLORSVILLE → Jackson (8)
CHARTISM → Duncombe
CHATTANOOGA → Grant (10), Sherman (4)
CHILLIANWALLA → Gough (1)
CHINDITS → Wingate (1)
CLONTARF → Brian
COMMUNIST MANIFESTO → Engels, Marx (2)
CONGRESS OF VIENNA → Alexander I of Russia, Castlereagh, Frederick-William III, Talleyrand-Périgord, Wellington
CONSTITUTIONS OF CLARENDON → Becket (2), Henry II
CONTINENTAL SYSTEM → Napoleon I
COPENHAGEN → Nelson (1)
CORDELIERS → Danton, Desmoulins, Marat
CORN LAWS, REPEAL OF → Bright (3), Cobden
CORONEA → Agesilaus
CORUÑA → Moore (11)
COUNCIL OF NICAEA → Constantine I, Sylvester I
COUNCIL OF TRENT → Paul III
CRÉCY → Edward III, Edward the Black Prince
CRUSADE, THIRD → Frederick I, Richard I
CUBAN REVOLUTION → Castro (3)
CULLODEN → Cumberland, Duke of (3)

DAMBUSTERS → Gibson (4)
DANEGELD → Canute
DARIEN SCHEME → Paterson (4)
DECLINE AND FALL OF THE ROMAN EMPIRE → Gibbon (1)
DETTINGEN → George II
DUNBAR → Cromwell (1)

EDGEHILL → Charles II, Essex (3)
EYLAU → Bennigsen, Napoleon I

FALKLAND ISLANDS → Sturdee
FIVE MEMBERS → Hampden (1), Pym
FLEURUS → Jourdan
FLODDEN → James IV
FONTENOY → Cumberland (3)
FORT SUMTER → Beauregard
FOURTH PARTY → Churchill (3)
FREDERICKSBURG → Burnside
FRIEDLAND → Napoleon I
FRONDE → Condé (2), Longueville, Turenne

GERRYMANDER → Gerry
GETTYSBURG ADDRESS → Lincoln (1)
GIRONDINS → Vergniaud
GLORIOUS FIRST OF JUNE → Howe (5)
GLORIOUS REVOLUTION → William III
GOWRIE CONSPIRACY → James VI, Ruthven (1)
GRAND REMONSTRANCE → Charles I, Pym
GREGORIAN CALENDAR → Gregory XIII
GUNPOWDER PLOT → Catesby (2), Fawkes (2)

HABEAS CORPUS → Charles II
HALIDON HILL → Edward III
HARPERS FERRY → Lee (8)
HASTINGS, BATTLE OF → William I
HEGIRA → Mohammed
HEIGHTS OF ABRAHAM → Wolfe (3)
HOLY ALLIANCE → Alexander I of Russia
HOMILDON HILL → Douglas

ICH DIEN → John (OF BOHEMIA)
INDIAN LAND REFORM → Bhave
INDIAN NATIONALISM → Banerjea, Bose (2), Gandhi, Gokhale
INDULGENCES → Leo X
INDUSTRIAL REVOLUTION → Toynbee (1)
INQUISITION → Torquemada
IRISH LAND LEAGUE → Davitt
IRONSIDES → Cromwell (1)
ITALIAN INDEPENDENCE → Garibaldi, Mazzini

JACOBINS → Hébert, Robespierre
JACOBITE REBELLION → Cadogan (3)
JALALABAD → Sale (2)
JUTLAND → Beatty, Jellicoe

KAPITAL, DAS → Marx (2)
KHARTOUM, SIEGE OF → Gordon (2)
KILLIECRANKIE → Dundee
KULTURKAMPF → Bismarck

LAFFELD → Saxe (2)
LEPANTO → John of Austria
LETTRES DE CACHET → Argenson
LEUCTRA → Epaminondas
LEVELLERS → Lilburne
LEWES → Montfort (2)
LIGNY → Napoleon I
LONG PARLIAMENT → Cromwell (1)
LUCKNOW, RELIEF OF → Campbell (2)
LÜTZEN → Napoleon I

MAFEKING → Plumer
MAGNA CARTA → John
MAJUBA HILL → Colley
MALPLAQUET → Marlborough
MANTINEA → Epaminondas
MARENGO → Napoleon I
MARNE → Foch
MARSTON MOOR → Cromwell (1)
MASSACRE OF GLENCOE → Stair (2)
MASSACRE OF ST BARTHOLOMEW → Catharine Medici, Coligny, Henry III (France)
MATAPAN, CAPE → Cunningham (3)
MEAL-TUB PLOT → Dangerfield
MEIN KAMPF → Hitler
MERXEM → Lynedoch
METAURUS → Hasdrubal
MILAN, EDICT OF → Constantine I
MINORCA → Byng (2)
MODEL PARLIAMENT → Montfort (2)
MONS GRAUPIUS → Agricola (2)

NANTES, EDICT OF → Henry IV (France)
NASEBY → Charles I, Cromwell (1)
NAVARINO → Codrington
NEERWINDEN → Luxembourg
NETHERLANDS → Alva
NEVILLE'S CROSS → David II, Percy (1)
NEW DEAL → Roosevelt (2)
NILE, BATTLE OF → Nelson (1), Villeneuve
NORTHAMPTON, TREATY OF → Bruce (7)
NOYADES → Carrier
NUREMBERG TRIALS → Birkett

OCEANA → Harrington (1)
OMDURMAN → Kitchener
ORDER OF THE GARTER → George, St
ORLEANS, SIEGE OF → Joan of Arc
OTTERBURN → Douglas (1), Percy (1)
OUDENARDE → Marlborough
OXFORD, PROVISIONS OF → Henry III

PATAY → Fastolf
PAVIA → Frundsberg
PEASANTS REVOLT → Ball (1), Tyler (2)
PHARSALIA → Caesar (1)
PILGRIMAGE OF GRACE → Aske
PILGRIM FATHERS → Bradford (1), Carver (2), Robinson (9), Standish, Winslow (1)
PLASSEY → Clive (2)
POITIERS → Edward III, Edward the Black Prince
POLAND, NAZI OCCUPATION → Kluge
POLICE FORCE → Peel
POLYCHRONICON → Higden

LITERATURE AND DRAMA

MUSIC

SWAN OF TUONELA → Sibelius
SWANEE RIVER → Foster (5)
SYMPHONIE CÉVENOLE → Indy
SYMPHONIE FANTASTIQUE → Berlioz
SYMPHONY OF PSALMS → Stravinsky
TALES FROM THE VIENNA WOODS → Strauss (3)
TALES OF HOFFMANN → Barbier (2), Offenbach
TANCREDI → Rossini
TANNHÄUSER → Wagner (3)
TESTAMENT OF FREEDOM → Thompson (11)
THAÏS → Massenet
THESE THINGS SHALL BE → Ireland (2)
THIEVING MAGPIE, THE (La Gazza Ladra) → Rossini
THREE BEARS → Coates (1)
THREE-CORNERED HAT → Falla
THREE ELIZABETHS, THE → Coates (1)
THREEPENNY OPERA → Weill
THUNDERBOLT P. 47 → Martinu
TINTAGEL → Bax
TOM BOWLING → Dibdin (1)
TOM JONES → German
TOMBEAU DE COUPERIN → Ravel
TONIC SOLFA → Curwen, Guido d'Arezzo
TOSCA → Giacosa, Puccini, Sardou
TOWER OF VOIVOD, THE → Dohnanyi
TRAGIC OVERTURE → Brahms
TRAVIATA, LA → Verdi
TRIAL BY JURY → Sullivan (1)
TRISTAN UND ISOLDE → Wagner (3)
TRIUMPHES OF ORIANA, THE → Morley (5)
TROUT QUINTET → Schubert (2)
TROVATORE, IL → Verdi
TROYENS, LES → Berlioz
TRUMPET VOLUNTARY → Clarke (9)
TURANDOT → Puccini
TURN OF THE SCREW, THE → Britten
TWELVE-TONE SYSTEM → Schönberg, Searle (1), Webern

ULYSSES → Seiber
UNDER THE GREENWOOD TREE → Arne

UNFINISHED SYMPHONY → Schubert (2)
VARIATIONS ON A NURSERY THEME → Dohnanyi
VARIATIONS ON A THEME OF HAYDN → Brahms
VENUS AND ADONIS → Blow
VERKLÄRTE NACHT → Schönberg
VESTALE, LA → Spontini
VIDA BREVE, LA → Falla
VILLAGE ROMEO AND JULIET, A → Delius (1)
VINGT REGARDS SUR L'ENFANT JÉSUS → Messiaen
VOICES BY NIGHT → Reizenstein
VOICES OF SPRING → Strauss (3)

WAE'S ME FOR PRINCE CHARLIE → Glen
WALKÜRE, DIE → Wagner (3)
WALTZ DREAM → Straus
WALTZING MATILDA → Paterson (1)
WANDERER FANTASY → Schubert (2)
WANDERN DAS → Schubert (2)
WAT TYLER → Bush
WATER-CARRIER, THE → Cherubini
WATER MUSIC → Handel
WELL-TEMPERED CLAVIER, THE → Bach (4)
WELSH RHAPSODY → German
WERTHER → Massenet
WEST SIDE STORY → Bernstein (3)
WHEN I SURVEY THE WONDROUS CROSS → Watts (4)
WHO IS SYLVIA? → Schubert (2)
WIEN NEERLANDSCH BLOED → Tollens
WINTERREISE → Schubert (2)
WOODLAND SKETCHES → Macdowell
WOZZECK → Berg, Büchner (1)
WRECKERS, THE → Smyth

YATTENDON HYMNAL → Bridges
YE MARINERS OF ENGLAND → Campbell (15)
YEOMAN OF THE GUARD, THE → Sullivan (1)
YOUNG PERSON'S GUIDE TO THE ORCHESTRA, THE → Britten

ZAMPA → Hérold
ZIGEUNERLIEDER → Brahms

NICKNAMES AND PERSONALITIES

ABYSSINIAN, THE → Bruce (3)
ALDIBORONTIPHOSCOPHORNIO → Ballantyne (1)
AMERICAN HOGARTH → Shahn
ANGELIC DOCTOR → Aquinas
APE → Pellegrini
APOSTATE, THE → Julian
APOSTLE OF FREE TRADE → Cobden
APOSTLE OF GERMANY → Boniface, St
APOSTLE OF GREENLAND → Egede
APOSTLE OF IRELAND → Patrick, St
APOSTLE OF THE ALPS → Bernard of Menthon, St
APOSTLE OF THE FRANKS → Remy, St
APOSTLE OF THE GENTILES → Paul
APOSTLE OF THE INDIANS → Las Casas
APOSTLE OF THE INDIES → Francis (4)
ARCHDRUID → Stukeley
ATTICUS → Addison (2)

BAB → Gilbert (10)
BABY-FACED BRETON → Portsmouth
BALAFRÉ, LE → Guise (4)
BASTARD OF ORLEANS → Dunois
BEAUCLERC → Henry I of England
BEAUTY OF HOLINESS → Hurd
BELLE CORDIÈRE, LA → Labé
BELL-THE-CAT → Douglas, 5th Ea of Angus
BELOVED PHYSICIAN → Luke (1)
BLIND JACK OF KNARESBOROUGH → Metcalf
BLIND TRAVELLER → Holman
BLOODY MARY → Mary I
BOBBING JOAN/JOHN → Mar
BOMBA → Ferdinand II
BONNY PRINCE CHARLIE → Stewart, House of (12)
BOSSU D'ARRAS, LE → Halle
BRITISH AMAZON → Talbot (1)
BROWN BOMBER → Louis

CAMBRIDGE PLATONIST → More (2)
CARO SASSONE → Handel

CHAGARLAB → Háfiz
CHRISTIAN VIRGIL → Vida
CITIZEN KING → Louis-Philippe
CLARINDA → Maclehose
COCHER DE L'EUROPE, LE → Choiseul-Amboise
COPERNICUS OF THE MIND → Freud (3)
CORN LAW RHYMER → Elliott (1)
CORNISH METAPHYSICIAN → Drew (2)

DEFENDER OF THE FAITH → Henry VIII
DIGHENIS → Grivas
DOCKERS' K.C. → Bevin
DOCTOR CHRISTIANISSIMUS → Gerson
DOCTOR PROFUNDUS → Bradwardine
DOCTOR RESOLUTISSIMUS → Durandus (2)
DOCTOR SERAPHICUS → Bonaventura, St
DOCTOR SUBTILIS → Duns Scotus
DOCTOR UNIVERSALIS → Albertus Magnus

ÉGALITÉ → Orléans (4)
ÉMINENCE GRISE → Joseph
ENGLISH HIPPOCRATES → Sydenham (2)
ENGLISH HOBBEMA → Nasmyth (3)
ENLIGHTENED DOCTOR → Lully (2)
ETTRICK SHEPHERD → Hogg (1)
EUPHUIST → Lyly
EVER-MEMORABLE → Hales (2)

FA PRESTO → Giordano
FAIR MAID OF KENT → Edward the Black Prince
FATHER PROUT → Mahony
FIRST GENTLEMAN IN EUROPE → George IV
FIRST GRENADIER OF FRANCE → La Tour D'Auvergne
FORMOSAN, THE → Psalmanazar
FRENCH FENIMORE COOPER → Aimard
FULMEN GALLIAE → Biron (3)

GANDHI OF SICILY → Dolci (2)

PHILOSOPHY AND THEOLOGY

SCIENCE AND INDUSTRY

PLANTS, BREEDING OF → Burbank, Johannsen, Lysenko
——, DISTRIBUTION → Schimper
——, SENSITIVITY → Bose (1)
——, SEX OF → Pringsheim (2), Sprengel (1)
PLASTIC SURGERY → Gillies (1), MacIndoe, Tagliacozzi
PLASTICS → Carothers, Kipping, Parkes (1)
PLATINUM → Callendar, Chabaneau, Sainte-Claire Deville, Döbereiner, Macquer, Wollaston (2)
PLESIOSAURUS → Anning
PLUTO → Forbes (5), Lowell (3), Tombaugh
PLUTONIUM → Compton (1), Seaborg
PNEUMATIC CHEMISTRY → Cavendish (2)
PNEUMATIC TYRE → Dunlop (1)
POLARIZATION → Biot, Brewster, Faraday, Fresnel, Huygens, Land, Malus, Röntgen, Savart, Spottiswoode (3)
POLARIZING CHRONOPHOTOGRAPH → Squier (2)
POLAROGRAPHIC ANALYSIS → Heyrovsky
POLIOMYELITIS → Kenney, Salk
POLLINATION → Pringsheim (2), Sprengel (1)
POLYMERS → Natta, Ziegler
PORPHYRINS → Fischer (3)
POSITRON → Anderson (1), Blackett
POTASH → Davy (1), Thénard
POTASSIUM → Davy (1)
—— ARSENATE → Macquer
—— FERRICYANIDE → Gmelin (3)
—— PEROXIDE → Thénard
POTENTIAL → Green (2)
POWER LOOM → Cartwright (1)
PRECESSION OF THE EQUINOXES → Cidenas, Hipparchus
PREFRONTAL LOBOTOMY → Freeman (3), Moniz
PREHISTORIC LIFE → Cuvier, Marsh (3), Owen (3)
PRINTING → Bramah (2), Gutenberg, Lanston, Mergenthaler, Stanhope (2)
——, STEAM → Clowes (2), Cotta, König
—— TELEGRAPH → Edison
PROBABILITY, THEORY OF → Bernoulli (2), Fermat, Keynes, Quételet
PROTACTINIUM → Grosse, Hahn, Meitner
PROTEIN → Kossel (1), Sumner (2), Tiselius
PROTON → Cockcroft, Stern (2), Walton (2)
PROTOPLASM → Mohl (1)
PRUSSIAN BLUE → Dippel
PRUSSIC ACID → Scheele
PSYCHOANALYSIS → Freud (3)
PTERODACTYL → Anning
PUDDLING PROCESSES → Cort
PUERPERAL FEVER → Holmes (2)
PULSE → Galen, Sanctorius
PUMP, DOUBLE FORCING → Hero of Alexandria
——, WATER → Gordon (9)
PUMPING-ENGINE → Watt (1)
PURE-LINE THEORY → Johannsen
PURINES → Fischer (1)
PYRIDINE → Anderson (12)
PYROMETER → Bogardus, Chatelier, Daniell, Musschenbroek, Siemens (2)

QUADRANT → Gunter, Hooke
——, REFLECTING → Hadley (1)
—— ELECTROMETER → Kelvin
QUANTUM MECHANICS → Dirac, Heisenberg
—— PHYSICS → Born (2)
—— THEORY → Bohr, Einstein (1), Franck (2), Landau, Planck
QUATERNIONS → Hamilton (18), Tait (2)
QUININE → Caventou, Pelletier

RADAR → Appleton (2), Randall (2), Sayers (2), Watson-Watt
RADICALS (CHEM.) → Gomberg, Laurent, Wieland (2)
RADIOACTIVITY → Becquerel (3), Boltwood, Curie, Elster, Fajans, Fermi, Geiger (2), Hahn, Joliot-Curie (1) and (2), Rutherford (3), Soddy
——, ARTIFICIAL → Joliot-Curie
RADIO-ASTRONOMY → Lovell, Ryle (4)
RADIOMETER → Crookes
RADIO-MICROMETER → Boys
RADIUM → Curie, Demarçay, Hess (4), Lind (3)
—— EMANATION → Soddy
RADON → Dorn (2)

RAIN GAUGE → Palmieri
REACTION VELOCITY → Bodenstein, Guldberg, Hoff, Polanyi
REFLECTION → Alhazen, Bacon (9), Hero of Alexandria, Malus
REFLEX ACTIONS → Hall (16), Pavlov, Sherrington
REFRACTION → Alhazen, Bradley (6), Gladstone (2). Hamilton (18), Newton (4), Snell (2)
RELATIVITY → Einstein (1), Lemaître (3)
REMONTOIR ESCAPEMENT → Harrison (4)
REPEATER, AUTOMATIC → Edison
REVOLVER → Colt
RHENIUM → Briscoe, Noddack
RHESUS FACTOR → Landsteiner
RHODIUM → Wollaston (2)
RIFLE, MAGAZINE → Hotchkiss, Mauser
ROCKETS → Braun (4), Congreve (3)
ROCKS, AGE FROM RADIOACTIVITY → Fajans, Henderson (3), Holmes (1), Joly Spurr
——, CLASSIFICATION OF → Brongniart, Lapworth, Lonsdale (3), Murchison, Smith (43)
——, FORMATION OF → Hutton (2)
ROLLER-SPINNING MACHINE → Paul (3)
ROSANILINE → Fischer (1)
RUBBER → Goodyear, Lacondamine, Nieuwland, Tilden (2)
—— GLOVES IN SURGERY, FIRST USE → Halsted
——, SYNTHETIC → Nieuwland
RULE OF EIGHT → Abegg

SACCHARIN → Fahlberg
SAFETY LAMP → Davy (1), Stephenson (1
—— RAZOR → Gillette
—— VALVE → Papin
SALVARSAN → Ehrlich
SAMARIUM → Boisbaudran
SAPPHIRE, ARTIFICIAL → Sainte-Claire Deville
SATURN → Herschel (2), Huygens, Keeler, Pickering (3)
SCARLET FEVER → Ingrassia
SCIENCE FOR THE CITIZEN → Hogben
SCOTCH PLOUGH → Anderson (4)
SCREW → Archimedes, Whitworth
SCREW-PROPELLER → Bramah (2), Ericsson
SCREW STEAMSHIP → Brunel (1), Smith (10)
—— TOURNIQUET → Petit (2)
SEARCHLIGHT → Sperry
SECANT → Finck (2), Girard (1)
SECRETIN → Starling
SEISMOLOGY → Michell
SELENIUM → Berzelius
SERUM, DIPHTHERIA → Behring, Roux, Yersin
——, PLAGUE → Yersin
——, POLIO → Landsteiner, Salk
——, TETANUS → Behring
——, TUBERCULOSIS → Spahlinger
——, YELLOW FEVER → Noguchi
SEWING MACHINE → Howe (1), Singer, Starley
SEX HORMONES → Ružička
SILICON → Berzelius, Kipping
SIREN → Cagniard de la Tour
SLEEPING SICKNESS → Bruce (2)
SLIDE-RULE → Oughtred
SMALLPOX, INOCULATION → Jenner (1), Montagu (3)
SNAKE-BITE SERUM → Calmette
SOAP → Chevreul, Hargreaves (2), Lever (2)
SODA → Hargreaves (2), Solvay
SODIUM → Castner, Davy (1)
—— SULPHATE → Glauber
SOUND, VELOCITY OF → Sturm (1)
SOUNDING APPARATUS → Kelvin
SPACE TRAVEL → Gagarin, Glenn
SPECIFIC GRAVITY → Boyle (4)
SPECTROHELIOGRAPH → Hale (2)
SPECTROSCOPIC BINARIES → Vogel (1)
SPECTROSCOPY → Alter, Boisbaudran, Bunsen (2), Kirchhoff, Ritter (1), Seecchi, Stark (1), Stokes (1)
SPECTRUM ANALYSIS → Bunsen (2), Kirchhoff, Plucker, Secchi
SPINNING FRAME → Arkwright
SPINNING-JENNY → Hargreaves (1)
SPINNING-MULE → Crompton
SPINTHARISCOPE → Crookes
SPIROCHAETA PALLIDA → Schaudinn
STABILIZER FOR SHIPS → Sperry

STAR CLUSTERS → Herschel (2)
STATIC ELECTRICITY → Gray (5)
STEAMBOAT → Bell (9), Fitch (1), Fulton, Miller (5), Rumsey, Symington
——, TURBINE → Parsons (2)
STEAM-CARRIAGE → Cugnot, Trevithick
STEAM DIGESTER → Papin
STEAM-ENGINE → Newcomen, Watt (1), Worcester (1)
——, HIGH PRESSURE → Evans (8)
STEAM HAMMER → Nasmyth (2)
STEAM-JET → Gurney (1)
STEAM LOCOMOTIVE → Stephenson (1), Trevithick
—— PILE-DRIVER → Nasmyth (2)
STEAM-PLOUGH → Fowler (4)
STEAM TURBINE → Laval (1), Parsons (2)
STEARIN → Chevreul
STEEL, MANGANESE → Hadfield
——, RAILS → Brown (15)
——, SILICON → Hadfield
——, SMELTING → Bessemer, Siemens
——, STAINLESS → Hadfield, Haynes
STEREO-CAMERA, SINGLE LENS → Clark (4)
STEREOPHONIC SOUND → Baird (2)
STEREOSCOPE → Brewster, Lyons (2), Wheatstone
STEREOTYPING → Ged, Stanhope (2)
STEROLS → Windaus
STETHOSCOPE → Laënnec
STRATOSPHERE → Piccard (2), Teisserenc de Bort
——, IONIZED LAYER → Heaviside
STREPTOMYCIN → Waksman
STRONTIUM → Davy (1)
STRYCHNINE → Caventou, Pelletier
SUBMACHINE GUN → Thompson (9)
SUBMARINE TELEGRAPHY → Crampton, Gooch (1)
SUEZ CANAL → Lesseps
SUGAR, BEET → Achard, Marggraf
——, SYNTHETIC → Fischer (1)
SULFAPYRIDINE → Ewins
SULPHANILAMIDE → Domagk
SULPHURETTED HYDROGEN → Scheele
SUN-AND PLANET WHEELS → Watt (1)
SUN, DARK SPECTRUM LINES → Fraunhofer
SUNSPOTS → Fabricius (3), Galilei, Schwabe
SURVEYING CHAIN → Gunter
SUTURE, SURGICAL → Carrel

TABLES, MATHEMATICAL → Briggs, Napier (3), Regiomontanus, Rheticus
TANGENTS → Finck (2), Girard (1), Roberval
TANTALUM → Ekeberg
TARTARIC ACID → Scheele
TAY BRIDGE → Bouch
TELEGONY → Ewart (1)
TELEGRAPH KEY, DOUBLE-CURRENT → Varley (2)
TELEGRAPH TYPEWRITER → Hughes (2)
TELEGRAPHY → Edison, Gray (3), Morse, Ronalds, Siemans (2), Wheatstone
TELEPATHY → Barrett (1), Rhine
TELEPHONE → Bell (1)
TELEPHOTOGRAPHY → Fournier D'Albe
TELESCOPE, ACHROMATIC → Dollond, Hall (6)
——, REFLECTING → Amici, Foucault, Gregory (3), Herschel (2), Hooke
——, REFRACTING → Galilei, Jansen (2)
TELEVISION → Baird, De Forest
TELLURIUM → Kitaibel, Klaproth (2), Müller (2)
TERPENES → Ružička
TESLA TRANSFORMER → Elster, Geitel
TETANUS → Behring, Kitasato
THALLIUM → Crookes
THAMES TUNNEL → Brunel (1) and (2)
THERMITE PROCESS → Goldschmidt (1)
THERMODYNAMICS → Bridgman (3), Clausius, Hoff, Kelvin, Mayer, Nernst
THERMOMETER → Allbutt, Boulliau, Fahrenheit, Galilei, Réaumur
——, CENTIGRADE → Celsius
——, CLINICAL → Sanctorius
——, DIFFERENTIAL → Leslie (5)
THERMOPILE → Nobili
THERMOS FLASK → Dewar
THIOPHENE → Meyer (4)
THORIUM → Berzelius
THYROXINE → Harington (1), Kendall

TITANIUM IN ILMENITE → Gregor
TOBACCO MOSAIC VIRUS → Stanley (7)
TOLUENE → Fahlberg
TORPEDO → Whitehead (4)
TORSION BALANCE → Boys, Coulomb, Michell
TOURNIQUET → Petit (2)
TRANSFORMER → Elster, Geitel, Stanley (8)
TRANSIT INSTRUMENT → Roemer
TREADMILL → Cubitt (2)
TRIGONOMETRY → Albuzjani, Fourier (2), Girard (1), Gunter, Hipparchus, Vieta
TROPISM → Sachs (2)
TSETSE FLY → Bruce (2)
TUBE, RADIO → De Forest, Fleming (3)
TUBERCULOSIS → Calmette, Spahlinger
TUNGSTEN → Scheele
TUNING FORK → Koenig
TURBINE → Thomson (6)
TYPHUS → Fleming (1), Jenner (2), Leishman, Nicolle
TYROTHRICIN → Du Bos (2)

ULTRACENTRIFUGE → Svedberg
ULTRAMICROSCOPE → Zsigmondy
ULTRAVIOLET RAYS → Ritter
URANIUM → Klaproth (2), Rutherford (3)
URANUS → Herschel (2), Struve (2)
UREA, SYNTHETIC → Wöhler
U-TUBE → Sprengel (2)

VACCINATION → Jenner (1)
VACUUM FLASK → Dewar
VACUUM PUMP → Sprengel (2)
VACUUM TUBE → Crookes
VALVE, RADAR → Randall (2), Sayers (2)
——, RADIO → De Forest, Fleming (3)
VANADIUM → Del Rio, Roscoe (1), Sefström
VARIABLE STARS → Goodricke
VELOCIPEDE → Edgeworth (4)
VENUS → Fontana (3)
VERONAL → Fischer (1)
VETERINARY SCHOOL, FIRST IN EUROPE → Bourgelat
VIRTUAL VELOCITIES → Galilei
VITAMINS → Eijkman, Funk (1), Hopkins (2), Kuhn (2), Sherman (1)
——, A → Heilbron, Karrer, Mendel (2)
——, B → Karrer, Lipmann, Todd (1)
——, C → Haworth, Mendel (2), Szent-Györgyi
——, D → Heilbron, Windaus
——, E → Karrer, Todd (1)
——, H (biotin) → Vigeaud
——, K → Dam, Karrer
VOLKSWAGEN → Porsche
VULCANIZED RUBBER → Goodyear

WATER BRAKE → Chatelier
WATER-METER → Siemens (2)
WAVE THEORY → Huygens, Schrödinger
WEATHER FORECASTING → Bjerknes, Henry (1)
WELDER, ELECTRIC → Thomson (2)
WELDING → Goldschmidt (1)
WHEAT → Biffen
WHOOPING COUGH → Bordet
WINDS → Halley
WIRELESS TELEGRAPHY → Appleton (2), De Forest, Duddell, Heaviside, Lodge (3), Marconi, Popov, Rutherford (3)
WOLFRAMITE → Elhuyar

X-RAYS → Barkla, Compton (1), Moseley, Röntgen, Siegbahn, Stokes (1)
XENON → Ramsay (8), Travers (2)
XYLONITE → Parkes (1)

YEAST → Buchner (1)
YELLOW FEVER → Carroll (1), Gorgas

ZINC AND COPPER ALLOY → Pinchbeck (1)
ZIRCONIUM → Klaproth (2)
ZODIACAL LIGHT → Cassini (3)

ABERDEEN UNIVERSITY → Elphinstone (3)
ALL SOULS, OXFORD → Chichele
ANNUAL REGISTER → Dodsley
ARAB LEGION → Glubb
ATLANTIC, FIRST FLIGHT BY A WOMAN → Earhart
ATLANTIC, FIRST FLIGHT OVER → Alcock (1)
AUTOBAHN → Todt
AUTOSUGGESTION → Coué

BALLOON POST → Anderson (6)
BANK OF ENGLAND → Paterson (4)
BERNERS STREET HOAX → Hook (3)
BIG BEN → Grimthorpe
BLITZKREIG → Guderian, Hitler
BLUE STOCKING → Stillingfleet (1)
BONE CHINA → Spode
BORSTAL → Ruggles-Brise
BOY SCOUT MOVEMENT → Baden-Powell
BRIDES-IN-THE-BATH MURDERS → Smith (15)

CHARTERHOUSE → Sutton
CHEROKEE SYLLABARY → Sequoyah
CHILDREN'S AID SOCIETY → Brace
CHINESE, TRANSLITERATION → Wade (2)
CORPUS CHRISTI, OXFORD → Foxe (2)
'COVENTRY' TRICYCLE → Starley
CRIMINAL IDENTIFICATION → Bertillon
CRIMINOLOGY → Lombroso
CUNEIFORM ALPHABET → Grotefend

DAYLIGHT SAVING → Willett
DETECTIVE AGENCY, FIRST IN U.S.A. → Pinkerton (1)

EDUCATION ACT 1944 → Butler (12)
EIRE, FIRST PRESIDENT → Hyde (1)
ELEVEN-PLUS EXAMINATION → Butler (12)
ELIXIR OF YOUTH → Cagliostro
ENGLISH CHANNEL, FIRST FLIGHT ACROSS → Blériot
——, FIRST BALLOON CROSSING → Blanchard
——, FIRST SWIM → Webb (5)
ESPERANTO → Zamenhof
ETON → Henry VI
EURHYTHMICS → Jaques-Dalcroze

FINGERPRINTS → Galton
FOLK HIGH SCHOOLS → Grundtvig
FOUR-MINUTE MILE → Bannister
FREE LIBRARIES BILL → Ewart (2)

GARDEN CITY MOVEMENT → Howard (1)
GIRL GUIDE MOVEMENT → Baden-Powell
GIRTON COLLEGE → Davies (7)
GROG → Vernon (1)

HARROW → Lyon
HIEROGLYPHICS → Chabas, Champollion (1)
HITTITE LANGUAGE → Hrozny

ITMA → Handley

KAFFIR BOOM → Barnato
KINDERGARTEN SCHOOLS → Froebel
KING'S COLLEGE, CAMBRIDGE → Henry VI
KOH-I-NOOR DIAMOND → Ranjit Singh

LAND SPEED RECORD → Campbell (11), Segrave

LONDON SCHOOL OF JOURNALISM → Pemberton

MADRAS SYSTEM → Bell (3)
MASS-OBSERVATION → Harrisson
MECHANICS' INSTITUTES → Birkbeck
MEISSEN PORCELAIN → Böttger
MIME → Deburau
MONKS OF MEDMENHAM → Dashwood (2), White-
head (3), Wilkes (2)

NATIONAL THEATRE → Olivier
NATIONAL TRUST → Hill (6)
NEW COLLEGE, OXFORD → William of Wykeham
NIAGARA FALLS, TIGHTROPE CROSSING → Blondin
NOVIAL → Jespersen
NUTCRACKER MAN → Leakey

OLD VIC → Baylis, Cons

PAPER PATTERNS → Butterick
PARCEL POST → Fawcett (1)
PARLIAMENTARY REPORTS → Hansard
P.A.Y.E. → Waverley, Wood (11)
PENNY POST → Hill (9)
PEOPLE'S BANK → Schulze-Delitzsch
PHOENIX PARK MURDERS → Burke (6), Carey (3),
Cavendish (6)
PILTDOWN MAN → Dawson (1), Woodward (1)
POSTAL ORDERS → Fawcett (1)
POTATO, INTRODUCTION TO BRITAIN → Raleigh (1)
PUBLIC OPINION POLLS → Gallup
PUPIL-TEACHER SYSTEM → Kay-Shuttleworth

RAGGED SCHOOLS → Pounds
RAILWAY GUIDES → Bradshaw (1)
RED CROSS → Dunant, Treves
ROTARY INTERNATIONAL → Harris (8)
ROYAL EXCHANGE → Gresham
RUGBY SCHOOL → Arnold (9), Sheriff

SADLER'S WELLS BALLET SCHOOL → Valois
ST ANDREWS UNIVERSITY → Wardlaw (2)
ST DUNSTAN'S HOME → Pearson (1)
ST PAUL'S SCHOOL → Colet
SAVINGS BANK → Duncan (2)
SEVERN WILD FOWL TRUST → Scott (21)
SHORTHAND → Bright (5), Gabelsberger, Gregg,
Pitman
SIEGFRIED LINE → Todt
SIGN LANGUAGE FOR DEAF MUTES → Epée, Pereire
SORBONNE, FOUNDER → Sorbon
STAMPS, ADHESIVE → Chalmers (4)

TAMMANY SOCIETY → Tweed (2)
TEMPERATURE CHARTS → Wunderlich
TOBACCO, INTRODUCTION TO BRITAIN → Raleigh (1)

WATER SPEED RECORD → Campbell (11), Segrave
WAXWORKS → Tussaud
WILLOW PATTERN → Minton (2), Spode
WINCHESTER SCHOOL → William of Wykeham
WOMEN, DEGREES FOR → Davies (7)
WORKERS EDUCATIONAL ASSOCIATION → Mansbridge

Y.M.C.A. → Williams (2)